SWEDEN
18

FINLAND
18

BALTIC
STATES
53

EUROPEAN U.S.S.R.
52

UNION   OF   SOVIET   SOCIALIST   REPUBLICS
48

POLAND
47

41

41

ROM.
45

YUGO.
45

34

45

GREECE

TURKEY
62

CYPRUS
62

SYR.
62

IRAQ
66

IRAN
66

AFGHAN.
68

68

MONGOLIA
77

CHINA
77

N. KOREA
60

S. KOREA
60

81

JAPAN

LIBYA
110

EGYPT
110

SAUDI
ARABIA
58

BAH.
58

QATAR
58

U.A.E.
58

KUWAIT 58

OMAN
58

PAKISTAN

NEPAL
68

BH.

BANG.
68

INDIA
68

BURMA
72

LAOS

TAIWAN
77

HONG KONG
78

PACIFIC OCEAN
Page 87

CHAD
110

SUDAN
110

YEMEN
58

P.D.R. YEMEN
58

THAILAND
72

VIETNAM
72

CAMB.
72

PHILIPPINES
82

GUAM
86

C. AFR. REP.
110

DJIB.
110

ETHIOPIA
110

SRI
LANKA
68

14

CONGO
114

UGANDA
114

KENYA
114

SOMALIA
115

BRUNEI

MALAYSIA
72

SING.
72

ZAIRE
114

RWA.
114

BUR.
114

TANZANIA
114

ASIA
Page 54

SEYCHELLES
119

INDONESIA
85

PAPUA
NEW
GUINEA
84

SOLOMAN IS.
86

SAMOA
86

ANGOLA
114

MAL.
114

ZAMBIA
114

MAURITIUS
119

FIJI
86

NAMIBIA
118

ZIMBABWE
119

MOZAMBIQUE
119

MADAGASCAR
119

RÉUNION
119

BOTSWANA
119

SWAZILAND 119

NORTHERN
TERRITORY
93

QUEENSLAND
95

NEW
CALEDONIA
86

SOUTH
AFRICA
119

LESOTHO
119

WESTERN
AUSTRALIA
92

SOUTH
AUSTRALIA
94

NEW SOUTH WALES
96

NEW
ZEALAND
100

VICTORIA
96

TASMANIA
99

AUSTRALIA
Page 88

NORWAY
18

SWEDEN
18

FINLAND
18

UNITED KINGDOM
10

SCOTLAND
15

DENMARK 21

BALTIC
STATES
53

EUROPEAN
U.S.S.R.
52

IRELAND
17

ENGLAND
13

WALES

NETH.
27

EAST
GER.
22

POLAND
47

BELG.

LUX.

WEST
GERMANY

CZECH.
41

FRANCE
28

SWITZ.
39

AUST.
41

HUN. 41

ROMANIA
45

ITALY

AND.

MON.

YUGOSLAVIA
45

BULGARIA
45

34

ALB.
45

GREECE
45

TURKEY
62

PORTUGAL
32

SPAIN
33

MEDITERRANEAN
36

CYPRUS
62

SYRIA
62

IRAN
66

LEBANON
65

ISRAEL
65

IRAQ
66

MOROCCO
106

TUNISIA
106

ALGERIA
106

MALTA
34

LIBYA
110

EGYPT
110

JORDAN

SAUDI ARABIA 58

THE VOLUME LIBRARY

A Modern, Authoritative Reference for Home and School Use

Clear and Complete • Colorfully Illustrated • Totally Indexed

THE SOUTHWESTERN COMPANY

Nashville, Tennessee

THE
VOLUME
LIBRARY

INCLUDING A MAJOR WORLD ATLAS AND COMPREHENSIVE INDEX FROM THE WORLD RENOWNED PUBLISHER, HAMMOND INCORPORATED.

Hammond Publications Advisory Board

Contents

The current edition of the Hammond World Atlas features an outstanding new section devoted to THE PHYSICAL WORLD — a series of terrain maps of land forms and ocean floors. These physical maps were originally produced as sculptured terrain models, thus simulating the earth's surface in a highly realistic manner. The three-dimensional effect is both instructive and pleasing to the eye.

As in previous editions, the atlas is organized to make the retrieval of information as simple and quick as possible. The guiding principle in organizing the atlas material has been to present separate subjects on *separate* maps. In this way, each individual map topic is shown with the greatest degree of clarity, unencumbered with extraneous information that is best revealed on separate maps. Of equal importance from the standpoint of good atlas design is the treatment of all current information on a given country or state as a single atlas unit. Thus, the basic reference map of an area is accompanied on adjacent pages by all supplementary information pertaining to that area. For example, the detailed index for a given map always appears on the same page as, or on the pages immediately following, the reference map. This same map index provides population data for the many cities, towns and villages shown on the map. Highlight information on the area, i.e., the total population and area, the capital, the highest point, is listed in the summary fact listings accompanying each unit. An adjacent locator map relates the subject area to the larger world beyond. A three-dimensional picture of the area is exhibited by means of the accompanying full-color topographic map. A separate economic map defines the vital agricultural, industrial and mineral resources of the area. In the case of the foreign maps, the flag of each independent nation appears on the appropriate page. Finally, certain country units contain special subject maps dealing with the history, climate, demography and vegetation of the area.

An important feature of the atlas is the addition of ZIP codes to the index entries for each of the legion of communities shown on the state maps. With the exception of the U.S. Postal Service directories of limited availability, the ZIP code listings herein are the most extensive published.

The back of the book contains a second type of index. This is a multi-paged "A-to-Z" index of all the world's places that appear on the maps. The use of this map index is essential when the name of a place is known but its country, state, or province is unknown.

Of course, the maps have been thoroughly updated. These revisions echo the new nations, shifting boundaries and the fluid internal divisions of many countries. New communities generated by the opening up of resources in the developing nations are also noted. Up-to-date geographical information, both foreign and domestic, is received daily by the atlas editors. A worldwide correspondence and thorough research brings to the atlas user the latest geographical and demographic information obtainable.

In closing it may be said that the atlas has truly been designed for contemporary use. Just as the information presented on the following pages is as current and up to date as the editors and cartographers could issue it, so the design and organization has been as well planned as possible to create a work useful to present generations.

President
HAMMOND INCORPORATED

Introduction to the Maps and Indexes

The following notes have been added to aid the reader in making the best use of this atlas. Though he may be familiar with maps and map indexes, the publisher believes that a quick review of the material below will add to his enjoyment of this reference work.

Arrangement — *The Plan of the Atlas.* The atlas has been designed with maximum convenience for the user as its obejective. Part I of the atlas is devoted to the physical world — terrain maps of land forms and the sea floor. Part II contains the general political reference maps, area by area. All geographically related information pertaining to a country or region appears on adjacent pages, eliminating the task of searching throughout the entire volume for data on a given area. Thus, the reader will find, conveniently assembled, political, topographic, economic and special maps of a political area or region, accompanied by detailed map indexes, statistical data, and illustrations of the national flags of the area.

The sequence of country units in this American-designed atlas is international in arrangement. Units on the world as a whole are followed by a section on the polar regions which, in turn, is followed by pages devoted to Europe and its countries. Every continent map is accompanied by special population distribution, climatic and vegetation maps of that continent. Following the maps of the European continent and its countries, the geographic sequence plan proceeds as follows: Asia, the Pacific and Australia, Africa, South America, North America, and ends with detailed coverage on the United States.

Political Maps — *The Primary Reference Tool.* The most detailed maps in each country unit are the *political maps.* It is our feeling that the reader is likely to refer to these maps more often than to any other in the book when confronted by such questions as — Where? How big? What is it near? Answering these common queries is the function of the political maps. Each political map stresses *political* phenomena — countries, internal political divisions, boundaries, cities and towns. The major political unit or units, shown on the map, are banded in distinctive colors for easy identification and delineation. First-order political subdivisions (states, provinces, counties on the state maps) are shown, scale permitting.

The reader is advised to make use of the *legend* appearing under the title on each political map. Map *symbols*, the special "language" of maps, are explained in the legend. Each variety of dot, circle, star or interrupted line has a special meaning which should be clearly understood by the user so that he may interpret the map data correctly.

Each country has been portrayed at a *scale* commensurate with its political, areal, economic or tourist importance. In certain cases, a whole map unit may be devoted to a single nation if that nation is considered to be of prime interest to most atlas users. In other cases, several nations will be shown on a single map if, as separate entities, they are of lesser relative importance. Areas of dense settlement and important significance within a country have been enlarged and portrayed in inset maps inserted on the margins of the main map. The scale of each map is indicated as a fractional representation (1:1,000,000). The reader is advised to refer to the linear or "bar" scale appearing on each map or map inset in order to determine the distance between points.

The *projection* system used for each map is noted near the title of the map. Map projections are the special graphic systems used by cartographers to render the curved three-dimensional surface of the globe on a flat surface. Optimum map projections determined by the attributes of the area have been used by the publishers for each map in the atlas.

A word here as to the choice of place names on the maps. Throughout the atlas names appear, with a few exceptions, in their local official spellings. However, conventional Anglicized spellings are used for major geographical divisions and for towns and topographic features for which English forms exist; i.e., "Spain" instead of "España" or "Munich" instead of "München." Names of this type are normally followed by the local official spelling in parentheses. As an aid to the user the indexes are cross-referenced for all current and most former spellings of such names.

Names of cities and towns in the United States follow the forms listed in the *Post Office Directory* of the United States Postal Service. Domestic physical names follow the decisions of the Board on Geographic Names, U.S. Department of the Interior, and of various state geographic name boards.

It is the belief of the publishers that the boundaries shown in a general reference atlas should reflect current geographic and political realities. This policy has been followed consistently in the atlas. The presentation of *de facto* boundaries in cases of territorial dispute between various nations does not imply the political endorsement of such boundaries by the publisher, but simply the honest representation of boundaries as they exist at the time of the printing of the atlas maps.

Indexes — *Pinpointing a Location.* Each political map is accompanied by a comprehensive index of the place names appearing on the map. If you are unfamiliar with the location of a particular geographical place and wish to find its position within the confines of the subject area of the map, consult the map index as your first step. The name of the feature sought will be found in its proper alphabetical sequence with a key reference letter-number combination corresponding to its location on the map. After noting the key reference letter-number combination for the place name, turn to the map. The place name will be found within the square formed by the two lines of latitude and the two lines of longitude which enclose the co-ordinates — i.e., the marginal letters and numbers. The diagram below illustrates the system of indexing.

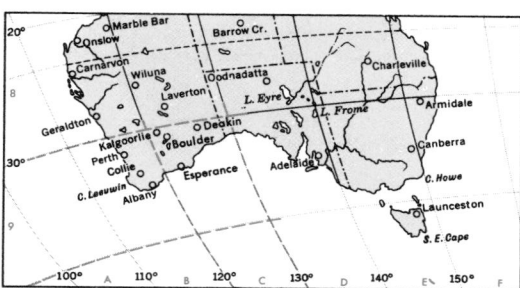

In the case of maps consisting entirely of insets, the place name is found near the intersection point of the imaginary lines connecting the co-ordinates at right angles. See below.

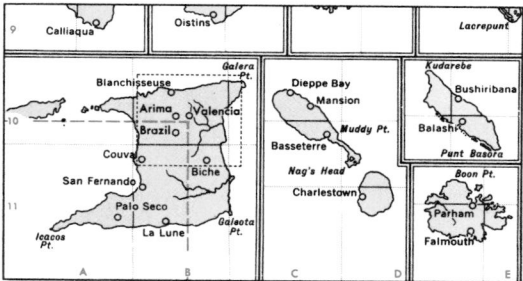

Where space on the map has not permitted giving the complete form of the place name, the complete form is shown in the index. Where a place is known by more than one name or by various spellings of the same name, the different forms have been included in the index. Physical features are listed under their proper names and not according to their generic terms; that is to say, Rio Negro will be found under Negro and not under Rio Negro. On the other hand, Rio Grande will be found under Rio Grande. Accompanying most index entries for cities and towns, and for other political units, are *population figures* for the particular entries. The large number of population figures in the atlas makes this work one of the most comprehensive statistical sources available to the public today. The population figures have been taken from the latest official censuses and estimates of the various nations. Dates and sources for the population figures are listed in the Gazetteer-Index of the World preceding this section.

Population and area figures for countries and major political units are listed in bold type *fact lists* on the margins of the indexes. In addition, the capital, largest city, highest point, monetary unit, principal languages and the prevailing religions of the country concerned are also listed. The Gazetteer-Index of the World on the preceding pages provides a quick reference index for countries and other important areas. Though population and area figures for each major unit area also found in the map section, the Gazetteer-Index provides a conveniently arranged statistical comparison contained in five pages. As mentioned, dates and sources of the population figures appearing in the country indexes are also listed in this section.

All index entries for cities and towns in the indexes accompanying individual state maps for the United States are preceded by a five-digit postal ZIP code number applying to the community. A dagger (†) designates those places that do not possess a post office. The ZIP code number listed in such cases refers to that of the nearest post office. An asterisk (*) marks those larger cities which are divided into multiple ZIP code areas. Using the single ZIP code number listed in such cases will direct your letter to the proper city with dispatch. However, if the precise ZIP code number of the address within the city is needed, it is suggested that the reader refer to the latest National ZIP Code Directory at his local post office. This detailed guide lists every street in a multiple ZIP code city with the proper ZIP code for the street.

Relief Maps. Accompanying each political map is a relief map of the area. These are in addition to the terrain maps of land forms in Part I of the atlas. The purpose of the relief map is to illustrate the surface configuration (TOPOGRAPHY) of the region. A shading technique in color simulates the relative ruggedness of the terrain — plains, plateaus, valleys, hills and mountains. Graded colors, ranging from greens for lowlands, yellows for intermediate elevations to browns in the highlands, indicate the height above sea level of each part of the land. A vertical scale at the margin of the map shows the approximate height in meters and feet represented by each color.

Economic Maps — Agriculture, Industry and Resources. One of the most interesting features that will be found in each country unit is the economic map. From this map one can determine the basic activities of a nation as expressed through its economy. A perusal of the map yields a full understanding of the area's economic geography and natural resources.

The agricultural economy is manifested in two ways: color bands and commodity names. The color bands express broad categories of *dominant land use*, such as, cereal belts, forest lands, livestock range lands, nonagricultural wastes. The red commodity names, on the other hand, pinpoint the areas of production of *specific* crops; i.e., wheat, cotton, sugar beets, etc.

Major mineral occurrences are denoted by standard letter symbols appearing in blue. The relative size of the letter symbols signifies the relative importance of the deposit.

The manufacturing sector of the economy is presented by means of diagonal line patterns expressing the various *industrial areas* of consequence within a country.

The fishing industry is represented by names of commercial fish species appearing offshore in blue letters. Major waterpower sites are designated by blue symbols.

The publishers have tried to make this work the most comprehensive and useful atlas available, and it is hoped that it will prove a valuable reference work. Any constructive suggestions from the reader will be welcomed.

Sources and Acknowledgments

A multitude of sources goes into the making of a large-scale reference work such as this. To list them all would take many pages and would consume space better devoted to the maps and reference materials themselves. However, certain general sources were very useful in preparing this work and are listed below.

STATISTICAL OFFICE OF THE UNITED NATIONS.
Demographic Yearbook. New York. Issued annually.

STATISTICAL OFFICE OF THE UNITED NATIONS.
Statistical Yearbook. New York. Issued annually.

THE GEOGRAPHER, U.S. DEPARTMENT OF STATE.
International Boundary Study papers. Washington. Various dates.

THE GEOGRAPHER, U.S. DEPARTMENT OF STATE.
Geographic Notes. Washington. Various dates.

UNITED STATES BOARD ON GEOGRAPHIC NAMES.
Decisions on Geographic Names in the United States. Washington. Various dates.

UNITED STATES BOARD ON GEOGRAPHIC NAMES.
Official Standard Names Gazetteers. Washington. Various dates.

CANADIAN PERMANENT COMMITTEE ON GEOGRAPHICAL NAMES.
Gazetteer of Canada series. Ottawa. Various dates.

UNITED STATES POSTAL SERVICE.
National Five Digit ZIP Code and Post Office Directory. Washington. Issued annually.

UNITED STATES POSTAL SERVICE.
Postal Bulletin. Washington. Issued weekly.

UNITED STATES DEPARTMENT OF THE INTERIOR. BUREAU OF MINES.
Minerals Yearbook. 4 vols. Washington. Various dates.

UNITED STATES GEOLOGICAL SURVEY.
Elevations and distances in the United States. Reston, Va. 1980.

CARTACTUAL.
Cartactual — Topical Map Service. Budapest. Issued bimonthly.

AMERICAN GEOGRAPHICAL SOCIETY.
Focus. New York. Issued ten times a year.

THE AMERICAN UNIVERSITY.
Foreign Area Studies. Washington. Various dates.

CENTRAL INTELLIGENCE AGENCY.
General reference maps. Washington. Various dates.

A sample list of sources used for specific countries follows:

Afghanistan
CENTRAL STATISTICS OFFICE.
Preliminary Results of the First Afghan Population Census 1979. Kabul.

Albania
DREJTORIA E STATISTIKES.
1979 Census. Tiranë.

Argentina
INSTITUTO NACIONAL DE ESTADISTICA Y CENSOS.
Censo Nacional de Población y Vivienda 1980. Buenos Aires.

Australia
AUSTRALIAN BUREAU OF STATISTICS.
Census of Population and Housing 1981. Canberra.

Brazil
FUNDACAO INSTITUTO BRASILEIRO DE GEOGRAFIA E ESTATISTICA.
IX Recenseamento Geral do Brasil 1980. Rio de Janeiro.

Canada
STATISTICS CANADA.
1981 Census of Canada. Ottawa.

Cuba
COMITE ESTATAL DE ESTADISTICAS.
Censo de Población y Viviendas 1981. Havana.

Hungary
HUNGARIAN CENTRAL STATISTICAL OFFICE.
1980 Census. Budapest.

Indonesia
BIRO PUSAT STATISTIK.
Sensus Penduduk 1980. Jakarta.

Kuwait
CENTRAL OFFICE OF STATISTICS.
1980 Census. Al Kuwait.

New Zealand
DEPARTMENT OF STATISTICS.
New Zealand Census of Population and Dwellings 1981. Wellington.

Panama
DIRECCIÓN DE ESTADISTICA Y CENSO.
Censos Nacionales de 1980. Panamá.

Papua New Guinea
BUREAU OF STATISTICS.
National Population Census 1980. Port Moresby.

Philippines
NATIONAL CENSUS AND STATISTICS OFFICE.
1980 Census of Population. Manila.

Saint Lucia
CENSUS OFFICE.
1980 Population Census. Castries

Singapore
DEPARTMENT OF STATISTICS
Census of Population 1980. Singapore.

U.S.S.R.
CENTRAL STATISTICAL ADMINISTRATION.
1979 Census. Moscow.

United States
BUREAU OF THE CENSUS.
1980 Census of Population. Washington.

Vanuatu
CENSUS OFFICE.
1979 Population Census. Port Vila.

Zambia
CENTRAL STATISTICAL OFFICE.
1980 Census of Population and Housing. Lusaka.

Gazetteer-Index of the World

This alphabetical list of continents, countries, states, colonial possessions and other major geographical areas provides a quick reference to their area in square miles and square kilometers, population, capital or chief town, map page number and index key thereon. The last name indicates the square on the respective page in which the name may be found. An indication of the population sources used is also included, and refers both to the total figures given in this Gazetteer-Index and to the populations appearing in greater detail with the maps throughout the atlas. The population figures used in each case are the latest reliable figures obtainable. A glance at the sources will show that the dates vary considerably throughout the world. In certain areas where no census has ever been taken, we must rely on official estimates. In other areas where censuses have been taken at infrequent intervals, we again rely on estimates. The key to the abbreviations used in the Gazetteer-Index follows:

aut = autonomous	est = estimates	reg = regions
boro = boroughs	excl = excluding	rep = republics
cap = capital	FC = final census	S.S.R. = Soviet Socialist Republic
CE = census (undetermined)	gov = governorates	terr = territories; territory
CIA = U.S. Central Intelligence Agency	incl = including	TP = total population
	isl = islands	U.K. = United Kingdom
cit = cities	met = metropolitan	UN = United Nations
co = counties	OE = official estimate	U.S.A. = United States of America
com = communes	oth = other populations	U.S.S.R. = Union of Soviet
dept = departments	par = parishes	Socialist Republics
dist = districts	PC = preliminary census	ws = with suburbs
div = divisions	prov = provinces; provincial	

Country	Area Square Miles	Area Square Kilometers	Population	Capital or Chief Town	Page and Index Ref.	Sources of Population Data
*Afghanistan	250,775	649,507	15,540,000	Kabul	68/A 2	79 PC
Africa	11,707,000	30,321,130	469,000,000		102/......	80 UN est
Alabama, U.S.A.	51,705	133,916	3,893,888	Montgomery	195/......	80 FC & OE
Alaska, U.S.A.	591,004	1,530,700	401,851	Juneau	196/......	80 FC & OE
*Albania	11,100	28,749	2,590,600	Tiranë	45/E 5	TP—79 PC; cit over 6,000—70 OE; oth—63 OE
Alberta, Canada	255,285	661,185	2,237,724	Edmonton	182/......	81 FC
*Algeria	919,591	2,381,740	17,422,000	Algiers	106/D 3	77 PC
American Samoa	77	199	32,297	Pago Pago	87/J 7; 86/....	80 FC
Andorra	188	487	31,000	Andorra la Vella	33/G 1	TP—79 OE; cap—75 OE
*Angola	481,351	1,246,700	7,078,000	Luanda	114/C 6	TP—80 UN est; oth—70 FC
Anguilla	35	91	6,519	The Valley	156/F 3	74 FC
Antarctica	5,500,000	14,245,000	....		5/......	
*Antigua and Barbuda	171	443	75,000	St. John's	161/E11; 156/G 3	
*Argentina	1,072,070	2,776,661	28,438,000	Buenos Aires	143/......	TP—82 OE; oth—80 PC
Arizona, U.S.A.	114,000	295,260	2,718,425	Phoenix	198/......	80 FC & OE
Arkansas, U.S.A.	53,187	137,754	2,286,435	Little Rock	202/......	80 FC & OE
Armenian S.S.R., U.S.S.R.	11,506	29,800	3,031,000	Erivan	52/F 6	TP, cit over 50,000—79 PC; oth—70 FC
Aruba	75	193	66,790	Oranjestad	161/E 9	TP—86 OE; cap—72 est
Ascension Island, St. Helena	34	88	719	Georgetown	102/A 5	76 FC
Ashmore & Cartier Islands, Australia	61	159		(Canberra, Austr.)	88/C 2	
Asia	17,128,500	44,362,815	2,633,000,000		54/......	80 est
*Australia	2,966,136	7,682,300	14,576,330	Canberra	88/......	81 FC
Australian Capital Territory	927	2,400	221,609	Canberra	96/E 4	81 FC
*Austria	32,375	83,851	7,507,000	Vienna	40/B 3	TP—80 OE; cap, cit over 100,000—73 OE; oth—71 FC
Azerbaidzhan S.S.R., U.S.S.R.	33,436	86,600	6,028,000	Baku	52/G 6	TP, cit over 50,000—79 PC; oth—70 FC
Azores Islands, Portugal	902	2,335	264,400	Ponta Delgada; Angra do Heroísmo; Horta	32/......	TP—77 OE; oth—70 FC & PC
*Bahamas	5,382	13,939	209,505	Nassau	156/C 1	80 PC
*Bahrain	240	622	358,857	Manama	58/F 4	TP—81 PC; oth—71 FC
Baker Island, U.S.A.	1	2.6			87/J 5	
Balearic Islands, Spain	1,936	5,014	558,287	Palma	33/H 3	70 FC
*Bangladesh	55,126	142,776	87,052,024	Dhaka	68/G 4	TP—81 PC; oth—74 FC
*Barbados	166	430	248,983	Bridgetown	161/B 8	80 PC
Belau (Palau)	188	487	12,116	Koror	86/D 5	80 FC
*Belgium	11,781	30,513	9,855,110	Brussels	27/E 7	TP—80 OE; oth—70 FC (com)
*Belize	8,867	22,966	144,857	Belmopan	154/C 2	TP, cap, cit over 1,000—80 PC; oth—70 PC
*Benin	43,483	112,620	3,338,240	Porto-Novo	106/E 6	TP—79 PC; cap, Cotonou—75 OE; oth—73 OE
Bermuda	21	54	67,761	Hamilton	156/H 3	80 PC
*Bhutan	18,147	47,000	1,298,000	Thimphu	68/G 3	TP—80 UN est; oth—70 OE
*Bolivia	424,163	1,098,582	5,600,000	La Paz; Sucre	136/......	TP—80 OE; cap, dept, dept cap—76 FC; oth—50 FC
Bonaire, Neth. Antilles	112	291	8,087	Kralendijk	161/E 9	TP—71 FC; cap—72 est
Bophuthatswana (rep.), South Africa	15,570	40,326	1,200,000	Mmabatho	119/D 5	TP—78 est; oth—70 FC
*Botswana	224,764	582,139	819,000	Gaborone	119/C 4	TP—80 OE; cap, Francistown—74 OE; Selebi-Pikwe—75 FC; oth—71 FC
Bouvet Island	22	57			5/D 1	
*Brazil	3,284,426	8,506,663	119,098,992	Brasília	132/......	80 PC
British Columbia, Canada	366,253	948,596	2,744,467	Victoria	184/......	81 FC
British Indian Ocean Terr.	29	75	2,000	(London, U.K.)	54/L10	78 est
British Virgin Islands	59	153	11,006	Road Town	157/H 1	TP—80 FC; oth—70 FC
Brunei	2,226	5,765	192,832	Bandar Seri Begawan	85/E 4	81 PC
*Bulgaria	42,823	110,912	8,862,000	Sofia	45/F 4	TP—80 OE; oth—75 PC
*Burkina Faso	105,869	274,200	6,908,000	Ouagadougou	106/D 6	TP—80 UN est; oth—75 FC, 73 OE
*Burma	261,789	678,034	32,913,000	Rangoon	72/B 2	TP—79 OE; states, div. cit over 100,000—73 PC; oth—53 FC
*Burundi	10,747	27,835	4,021,910	Bujumbura	114/E 4	79 PC
*Byelorussian S.S.R. (White Russian S.S.R.), U.S.S.R.	80,154	207,600	9,560,000	Minsk	52/C 4	TP, cit over 50,000—79 PC; oth—70 FC
California, U.S.A.	158,706	411,049	23,667,565	Sacramento	204/......	80 FC & OE
*Cambodia (Kampuchea)	69,898	181,036	5,200,000	Phnom Penh	72/E 4	TP—79 CIA est; cap—80 est
*Cameroon	183,568	475,441	8,503,000	Yaoundé	114/B 2	TP—80 OE; cit over 21,000—76 FC; Ebolowa, oth—70 OE
*Canada	3,851,787	9,976,139	24,343,181	Ottawa	162/......	81 FC
Canary Islands, Spain	2,808	7,273	1,170,224	Las Palmas; Santa Cruz	32/B 4	70 FC
Cape Province, South Africa	261,705	677,816	5,543,506	Cape Town	118/C 6	TP—80 PC; oth—70 FC
*Cape Verde	1,557	4,033	324,000	Praia	106/B 8	TP—80 UN est; oth—70 PC
Cayman Islands	100	259	18,000	Georgetown	156/B 3	TP—81 OE; oth—79 FC

*Member of the United Nations.

Gazetteer-Index of the World

Country	Area Square Miles	Area Square Kilometers	Population	Capital or Chief Town	Page and Index Ref.	Sources of Population Data
Celebes, Indonesia	72,986	189,034	7,732,383	Ujung Pandang	85/G 6	71 PC
*Central African Republic	242,000	626,780	2,284,000	Bangui	114/C 2	TP—79 est; oth—75 FC
Central America	197,480	511,475	21,000,000		154/......	79 OE
Ceylon, see Sri Lanka						
*Chad	495,752	1,283,998	4,309,000	N'Djamena	111/C 4	TP—78 OE; oth—72 OE
Channel Islands	75	194	133,000	St. Helier; St. Peter Port	13/E 8	TP—81 OE; oth—71 FC
*Chile	292,257	756,946	11,275,440	Santiago	138/......	TP—82 PC; cit (part)—79 OE; oth—70 FC & PC
*China, People's Rep. of	3,691,000	9,559,690	958,090,000	Beijing	77/......	TP, prov, Peking, Shanghai, Tianjin—78 OE; oth—70 est
China, Republic of (Taiwan)	13,971	36,185	16,609,961	Taipei	77/K 7	TP, cap, Penghu Isl., cit over 300,000—77 OE; oth—70 OE
Christmas Island, Australia	52	135	3,184	Flying Fish Cove	54/M11	80 OE
Ciskei (rep.), S. Africa	2,988	7,740	635,631	Bisho	119/D 6	80 PC
Clipperton Island	2	5.2	....	....	146/H 8	....
Cocos (Keeling) Islands, Australia	5.4	14	555	West Island	54/N11	81 PC
*Colombia	439,513	1,138,339	27,520,000	Bogotá	126/......	TP—80 OE; oth—73 PC
Colorado, U.S.A.	104,091	269,596	2,889,735	Denver	208/......	80 FC & OE
*Comoros	719	1,862	290,000	Moroni	119/G 2	TP—78 est; cap—75 OE; oth—66 FC
*Congo, Republic of	132,046	342,000	1,537,000	Brazzaville	114/B 4	TP—80 UN est; cap—74 FC; oth—74 PC
Connecticut, U.S.A.	5,018	12,997	3,107,576	Hartford	210/......	80 FC & OE
Cook Islands	91	236	17,695	Avarua	87/K 7	81 PC
Coral Sea Islands, Australia	8.5	22	....		88/J 3	75 FC
Corsica, France	3,352	8,682	289,842	Ajaccio; Bastia	28/B 6	TP—80 OE; oth—73 FC
*Costa Rica	19,575	50,700	2,245,000	San José	154/E 5	TP—81 PC; prov, cap—81 PC; oth—81 & 70 PC
*Cuba	44,206	114,494	9,706,369	Havana	158/......	TP—71 FC; cap—75 OE
Curaçao, Neth. Antilles	178	462	145,430	Willemstad	161/G 7	TP—80 OE; oth—73 FC, 72 OE
*Cyprus	3,473	8,995	629,000	Nicosia	62/E 5	TP—80 PC; cap, cit over 100,000—75 OE; rep, reg—74 OE
*Czechoslovakia	49,373	127,876	15,276,799	Prague	41/C 2	TP—75 OE, 70 FC
Delaware, U.S.A.	2,044	5,294	594,317	Dover	245/R 3	80 FC & OE
*Denmark	16,629	43,069	5,124,000	Copenhagen	21/......	TP—80 OE; oth—75 OE, 71 OE, 70 FC
District of Columbia, U.S.A.	69	179	638,432	Washington	244/F 5	80 FC
*Djibouti	8,880	23,000	386,000	Djibouti	111/H 5	TP—79 est; cap—73 OE
*Dominica	290	751	74,089	Roseau	161/E 7	TP—80 PC; oth—70 FC
*Dominican Republic	18,704	48,443	5,647,977	Santo Domingo	158/D 6	81 PC
*East Germany (German Democratic Republic)	41,768	108,179	16,737,000	Berlin (East)	22/......	TP—80 OE; oth—75 OE
*Ecuador	109,483	283,561	8,644,000	Quito	128/C 3	TP—81 OE; oth—74 FC
*Egypt	386,659	1,001,447	41,572,000	Cairo	110/E 2	TP—79 OE; oth—76 PC
*El Salvador	8,260	21,393	4,813,000	San Salvador	154/C 4	TP—80 OE; oth—71 FC
England, U.K.	50,516	130,836	46,220,955	London	13/......	TP—81 PC; co, cap (boro & ws)—76 OE; cit—76 & 73 OE; oth—71 FC
*Equatorial Guinea	10,831	28,052	244,000	Malabo	114/A 3	TP—79 est; terr—68 OE; oth—60 FC
Estonian S.S.R., U.S.S.R.	17,413	45,100	1,466,000	Tallinn	52/C 3; 53/......	TP, cit over 50,000—79 PC; oth—70 FC
*Ethiopia	471,776	1,221,900	31,065,000	Addis Ababa	110/G 5	TP—80 OE; cap, Asmara—78 OE; prov—72 OE; oth—72 & 71 OE
Europe	4,057,000	10,507,630	676,000,000		7/......	80 est
Faeroe Islands, Denmark	540	1,399	41,969	Tórshavn	21/B 2	77 FC
Falkland Islands & Dependencies	6,198	16,053	1,813	Stanley	120/E 8; 143/D 7	76 FC
*Fiji	7,055	18,272	588,068	Suva	87/H 8; 86/......	80 FC
*Finland	130,128	337,032	4,788,000	Helsinki	18/O 6	TP—80 OE; prov—75 OE; oth—75 OE, 70 FC
Florida, U.S.A.	58,664	151,940	9,746,342	Tallahassee	212/......	80 FC & OE
*France	210,038	543,998	53,788,000	Paris	28/......	TP—80 OE; oth—75 OE
French Guiana	35,135	91,000	73,022	Cayenne	131/E 3	82 FC
French Polynesia	1,544	4,000	137,382	Papeete	87/L 8	77 FC
*Gabon	103,346	267,666	551,000	Libreville	114/B 4	TP—80 UN est; oth—70 FC
*Gambia	4,127	10,689	601,000	Banjul	106/A 6	TP—80 OE; oth—73 FC
Gaza Strip	139	360	400,000	Gaza	65/A 4	TP—76 OE; oth—67 CE
Georgia, U.S.A.	58,910	152,577	5,463,105	Atlanta	217/......	80 FC & OE
Georgian S.S.R., U.S.S.R.	26,911	69,700	5,015,000	Tbilisi	52/F 6	TP, cit over 50,000—79 PC; oth—70 FC
*Germany, East (German Democratic Republic)	41,768	108,179	16,737,000	Berlin (East)	22/......	TP—80 OE; oth—75 OE
*Germany, West (Federal Republic)	95,985	248,601	61,658,000	Bonn	22/......	TP—80 OE; states, cap—76 OE; oth—76 OE, 70 FC
*Ghana	92,099	238,536	11,450,000	Accra	106/D 7	TP—80 OE; oth—70 FC
Gibraltar	2.28	5.91	29,760	Gibraltar	33/D 4	79 OE
*Great Britain & Northern Ireland (United Kingdom)	94,399	244,493	55,672,000	London	10/......	TP—81 OE (see England, Wales, Scotland, Northern Ireland)
*Greece	50,944	131,945	9,599,000	Athens	45/F 6	TP—80 OE; oth—71 FC
Greenland	840,000	2,175,600	49,773	Nuuk (Godthåb)	4/B12	TP—80 OE
*Grenada	133	344	103,103	St. George's	161/D 9; 156/G 4	TP, cap—81 OE; oth—70 FC
Guadeloupe & Dependencies	687	1,779	328,400	Basse-Terre	161/A 5; 156/F 4	82 FC
Guam	209	541	105,979	Agaña	87/E 4; 86/......	80 FC
*Guatemala	42,042	108,889	7,262,419	Guatemala	154/B 3	TP—80 OE; oth—73 FC
*Guinea	94,925	245,856	5,143,284	Conakry	106/B 6	TP, cap (ws), Kankan, Kindia, Labé—72 FC; oth—67 OE
*Guinea-Bissau	13,948	36,125	777,214	Bissau	106/A 6	79 PC
*Guyana	83,000	214,970	793,000	Georgetown	131/B 3	TP—80 OE; cap, cit over 10,000—70 FC; oth—60 FC
*Haiti	10,694	27,697	5,053,792	Port-au-Prince	158/C 5	82 PC
Hawaii, U.S.A.	6,471	16,760	964,691	Honolulu	218/......	80 FC & OE
Heard & McDonald Islands, Australia	113	293	....	....	2/N 8	....
Holland, see Netherlands						
*Honduras	43,277	112,087	3,691,000	Tegucigalpa	154/D 3	TP—80 OE; oth—74 FC
Hong Kong	403	1,044	5,022,000	Victoria	77/H 7; 78/......	TP—81 PC; oth—76 FC
Howland Island, U.S.A.	1	2.6	....	....	87/J 5	....
*Hungary	35,919	93,030	10,709,536	Budapest	41/D 3	TP, cap, co—80 PC; oth—80 PC, 70 FC
*Iceland	39,768	103,000	228,785	Reykjavík	21/B 1	TP—80 PC; oth—70 FC
Idaho, U.S.A.	83,564	216,431	944,038	Boise	220/......	80 FC & OE

Gazetteer-Index of the World

Country	Area Square Miles	Area Square Kilometers	Population	Capital or Chief Town	Page and Index Ref.	Sources of Population Data
Illinois, U.S.A.	56,345	145,934	11,426,596	Springfield	222/......	80 FC & OE
*India	1,269,339	3,287,588	683,810,051	New Delhi	68/D 4	TP & states—81 PC; oth—71 FC
Indiana, U.S.A.	36,185	93,719	5,490,260	Indianapolis	227/......	80 FC & OE
*Indonesia	788,430	2,042,034	147,490,298	Jakarta	85/D 7	TP—80 PC; cit—80 PC & 71 PC; isls.—71 PC
Iowa, U.S.A.	56,275	145,752	2,913,808	Des Moines	229/......	80 FC & OE
*Iran	636,293	1,648,000	37,447,000	Tehran	66/F 4	TP—80 PC; div, cit over 50,000—76 PC; oth—66 FC & PC, 56 FC
*Iraq	172,476	446,713	12,767,000	Baghdad	66/C 4	TP—79 OE; oth—65 & 57 FC
*Ireland	27,136	70,282	3,440,427	Dublin	17/......	TP—81 PC; oth—71 FC
Ireland, Northern, U.K.	5,452	14,121	1,543,000	Belfast	17/F 2	TP—81 OE; dist—76 OE; cap, Londonderry—73 OE; oth—71 FC
Isle of Man	227	588	64,000	Douglas	13/C 3	TP—80 OE; oth—71 FC
*Israel	7,847	20,324	3,878,000	Jerusalem	65/B 4	TP—80 OE; cap, cit over 100,000—77 OE; dist, cit over 5,000—72 PC; oth—61 FC
*Italy	116,303	301,225	57,140,000	Rome	34/......	TP—80 OE; oth—71 FC
*Ivory Coast	124,504	322,465	7,920,000	Yamoussoukro	106/C 7	TP—79 OE; oth—75 PC
*Jamaica	4,411	11,424	2,184,000	Kingston	158/......	TP—80 OE; oth—70 & 60 FC
Jan Mayen	144	373	....		6/D 1	
*Japan	145,730	377,441	117,057,485	Tokyo	81/......	TP—80 PC; oth—75 FC
Jarvis Island, U.S.A.	1	2.6	....		87/K 6	
Java, Indonesia	48,842	126,500	73,712,411	Jakarta	85/J 2	71 PC
Johnston Atoll	.91	2.4	327		87/K 4	80 FC
*Jordan	35,000	90,650	2,152,273	Amman	65/D 3	TP—79 PC; cap, cit over 100,000—77 OE; gov, cit 9,000-100,000—73 OE; oth—61 FC
*Kampuchea (Cambodia)	69,898	181,036	5,200,000	Phnom Penh	72/E 4	TP—79 CIA est; cap—80 est
Kansas, U.S.A.	82,277	213,097	2,364,236	Topeka	232/......	80 FC & OE
Kazakh S.S.R., U.S.S.R.	1,048,300	2,715,100	14,684,000	Alma-Ata	48/G 5	TP, cit over 50,000—79 PC; oth—70 FC
Kentucky, U.S.A.	40,409	104,659	3,660,257	Frankfort	237/......	80 FC & OE
*Kenya	224,960	582,646	15,327,061	Nairobi	115/G 3	TP—79 PC; oth—69 FC
Kermadec Islands	13	33	5	....	87/J 9	81 FC
Kingman Reef	0.1	0.26	....		87/K 5	
Kirgiz S.S.R., U.S.S.R.	76,641	198,500	3,529,000	Frunze	48/H 5	TP, cit over 50,000—79 PC; oth—70 FC
Kiribati	291	754	56,213	Bairiki	87/J 6	TP—78 FC; oth—73 FC
Korea, North	46,540	120,539	17,914,000	P'yŏngyang	80/D 3	TP—80 UN est; cap—76 OE; Hamhŭng—72 OE; oth—70 OE
Korea, South	38,175	98,873	37,448,836	Seoul	80/D 5	TP—80 PC; oth—75 FC & PC
*Kuwait	6,532	16,918	1,355,827	Al Kuwait	58/E 4	80 PC
*Laos	91,428	236,800	3,721,000	Vientiane	72/D 3	TP—80 UN est; cap—66 FC; oth—58 OE
Latvian S.S.R., U.S.S.R.	24,595	63,700	2,521,000	**Riga**	52/B 3; 53/......	TP, cit over 50,000—79 PC; oth—70 FC
*Lebanon	4,015	10,399	3,161,000	Beirut	62/F 6	TP—80 UN est; cap—70 FC; Tarabulus—64 OE; oth—61 OE
*Lesotho	11,720	30,355	1,339,000	Maseru	119/D 5	TP—80 OE; oth—80 est
*Liberia	43,000	111,370	1,873,000	Monrovia	106/C 7	TP—80 OE; oth—74 FC
*Libya	679,358	1,759,537	2,856,000	Tripoli	110/B 2	TP—79 OE; oth—73 FC & PC
Liechtenstein	61	158	25,220	Vaduz	39/J 2	80 PC
Lithuanian S.S.R., U.S.S.R.	25,174	65,200	3,398,000	**Vilna**	52/B 3; 53/......	TP, cit over 50,000—79 PC; oth—70 FC
Louisiana, U.S.A.	47,752	123,678	4,206,312	Baton Rouge	238/......	80 FC & OE
*Luxembourg	999	2,587	364,000	Luxembourg	27/J 9	TP—79 OE; cap—74 OE; oth—70 OE
Macau	6	16	271,000	Macau	77/H 7	TP—78 OE; cap—70 FC
*Madagascar	226,657	587,041	8,742,000	**Antananarivo**	119/H 3	TP—80 UN est; prov, cap, cit over 40,000—75 PC; oth—71 OE
Madeira Islands, Portugal	307	796	262,800	Funchal	32/A 2	TP—77 OE; oth—70 FC & PC
Maine, U.S.A.	33,265	86,156	1,125,027	Augusta	243/......	80 FC & OE
*Malawi	45,747	118,485	5,968,000	Lilongwe	114/F 6	TP—80 OE; oth—77 PC
Malaya, Malaysia	50,806	131,588	11,138,227	Kuala Lumpur	72/D 6	TP, states, Kuala Lumpur—80 PC; cit over 100,000—70 FC; oth—70 PC
*Malaysia	128,308	332,318	13,435,588	**Kuala Lumpur**	72/D 6; 85/E 4	TP, states, Kuala Lumpur—80 PC; Kuching, Kota Kinabalu, cit over 100,000—70 FC; oth—70 PC
*Maldives	115	298	143,046	Male	54/L 9	78 FC
*Mali	464,873	1,204,021	6,906,000	Bamako	106/C 6	TP—80 OE; oth—76 PC
*Malta	122	316	343,970	Valletta	34/E 7	TP, cit—79 OE; oth—73 OE
Man, Isle of	227	588	64,000	Douglas	13/C 3	TP—80 OE; oth—71 FC
Manitoba, Canada	250,999	650,087	1,026,241	Winnipeg	179/......	81 FC
Marquesas Islands, French Polynesia	492	1,274	5,419	Atuona	87/N 6	77 FC
Marshall Islands	70	181	30,873	Majuro	87/G 4	80 FC
Martinique	425	1,101	328,566	Fort-de-France	161/D 5	82 FC
Maryland, U.S.A.	10,460	27,091	4,216,975	Annapolis	245/......	80 FC & OE
Massachusetts, U.S.A.	8,284	21,456	5,737,037	Boston	249/......	80 FC & OE
*Mauritania	419,229	1,085,803	1,634,000	Nouakchott	106/B 5	TP—80 UN est; oth—76 PC
*Mauritius	790	2,046	959,000	Port Louis	119/G 5	TP—80 OE; cap—77 OE; Curepipe, Quatre Bornes—74 OE; oth—72 PC
Mayotte	144	373	47,300	Dzaoudzi	119/G 2	TP—78 CE; cap—66 PC
*Mexico	761,601	1,972,546	67,395,826	Mexico City	150/......	TP, states, cap—80 PC; cap (ws), Guadalajara (ws), Monterrey (ws)—78 OE; oth—70 PC
Michigan, U.S.A.	58,527	151,585	9,262,078	Lansing	250/......	80 FC & OE
Micronesia, Federated States of	....	....	73,160	Kolonia	87/E 5	TP—80 FC
Midway Islands	1.9	4.9	453	....	87/J 3	80 FC
Minnesota, U.S.A.	84,402	218,601	4,075,970	St. Paul	255/......	80 FC & OE
Mississippi, U.S.A.	47,689	123,515	2,520,638	Jackson	256/......	80 FC & OE
Missouri, U.S.A.	69,697	180,515	4,916,759	Jefferson City	261/......	80 FC & OE
Moldavian S.S.R., U.S.S.R.	13,012	33,700	3,947,000	Kishinev	52/C 5	TP, cit over 50,000—79 PC; oth—70 FC
Monaco	368 acres	149 hectares	25,029	Monaco	28/G 6	75 FC
*Mongolia	606,163	1,569,962	1,594,800	Ulaanbaatar	77/E 2	TP—79 PC; prov, cap, Darhan—77 OE; oth—69 FC
Montana, U.S.A.	147,046	380,849	786,690	Helena	262/......	80 FC & OE
Montserrat	40	104	12,073	Plymouth	157/G 3	80 PC
*Morocco	172,414	446,550	20,242,000	Rabat	106/C 2	TP—80 OE; oth—71 FC
*Mozambique	303,769	786,762	12,130,000	Maputo	119/E 4	TP, prov, cap—80 PC; oth—70 FC
Namibia (South-West Africa)	317,827	823,172	1,200,000	Windhoek	118/B 3	TP—74 est; oth—70 PC
Natal, South Africa	33,578	86,967	5,722,215	Pietermaritzburg	119/E 5	TP—80 PC; oth—70 PC
Nauru	7.7	20	7,254	Yaren (district)	87/G 6	77 PC
Navassa Island	2	5	....		156/C 3	
Nebraska, U.S.A.	77,355	200,349	1,569,825	Lincoln	264/......	80 FC & OE
*Nepal	54,663	141,577	14,179,301	Kathmandu	68/E 3	TP—81 PC; oth—71 FC
*Netherlands	15,892	41,160	14,227,000	The Hague; Amsterdam	27/F 5	TP—81 OE; oth—76 OE (com)

Gazetteer-Index of the World

Country	Area Square Miles	Square Kilometers	Population	Capital or Chief Town	Page and Index Ref.	Sources of Population Data
Netherlands Antilles	390	1,010	246,000	Willemstad	156/E 4	TP—78 OE; Willemsted—75 OE; oth—72 est.
Nevada, U.S.A.	110,561	286,353	800,493	Carson City	266/......	80 FC & OE
New Brunswick, Canada	28,354	73,437	696,403	Fredericton	170/......	81 FC
New Caledonia & Dependencies	7,335	18,998	133,233	Nouméa	87/G 8	76 FC
Newfoundland, Canada	156,184	404,517	567,681	St. John's	166/......	81 FC
New Hampshire, U.S.A.	9,279	24,033	920,610	Concord	268/......	80 FC & OE
New Hebrides, see Vanuatu						
New Jersey, U.S.A.	7,787	20,168	7,364,823	Trenton	273/......	80 FC & OE
New Mexico, U.S.A.	121,593	314,926	1,302,981	Santa Fe	274/......	80 FC & OE
New South Wales, Australia	309,498	801,600	5,126,217	Sydney	96/B 2	81 FC
New York, U.S.A.	49,108	127,190	17,558,072	Albany	276/......	80 FC & OE
*New Zealand	103,736	268,676	3,175,737	Wellington	100/......	TP, inc. places, isls.—81 FC; oth—76 FC
*Nicaragua	45,698	118,358	2,703,000	Managua	154/D 4	TP—80 OE; oth—71 PC
*Niger	489,189	1,267,000	5,098,427	Niamey	106/F 5	TP, cap, Maradi, Tahoua, Zinder—77 PC; oth—72 OE
*Nigeria	357,000	924,630	82,643,000	Lagos	106/F 6	TP—79 OE; prov—63 FC; oth—75 & 71 OE
Niue	100	259	3,578	Alofi	87/K 7	79 OE
Norfolk Island, Australia	13.4	34.6	2,175	Kingston	88/L 5	81 FC
North America	9,363,000	24,250,170	370,000,000	....	146/......	80 UN est
North Carolina, U.S.A.	52,669	136,413	5,881,813	Raleigh	281/......	80 FC & OE
North Dakota, U.S.A.	70,702	183,118	652,717	Bismarck	282/......	80 FC & OE
Northern Ireland, U.K.	5,452	14,121	1,543,000	Belfast	17/F 2	TP—81 OE; dist—76 OE; cap, Londonderry—73 OE; oth—71 FC
Northern Marianas	184	477	16,780	Capitol Hill	87/E 4	80 FC
Northern Territory, Australia	519,768	1,346,200	123,324	Darwin	93/......	81 FC
North Korea	46,540	120,539	17,914,000	P'yŏngyang	80/D 3	TP—80 UN est; cap—76 OE; Hamhŭng—72 OE; oth—70 OE
Northwest Territories, Canada	1,304,896	3,379,683	45,741	Yellowknife	187/G 3	81 FC
*Norway	125,053	323,887	4,092,000	Oslo	18/F 7	TP—80 OE; co, Svalbard—76 OE; oth—76 OE, 70 FC
Nova Scotia, Canada	21,425	55,491	847,442	Halifax	168/......	81 FC
Oceania	3,292,000	8,526,280	23,000,000		87/......	80 UN est
Ohio, U.S.A.	41,330	107,045	10,797,624	Columbus	284/......	80 FC & OE
Oklahoma, U.S.A.	69,956	181,186	3,025,290	Oklahoma City	288/......	80 FC & OE
*Oman	120,000	310,800	891,000	Muscat	58/G 6	TP—80 UN est; cap, Matrah—66 OE; Salala—68 OE
Ontario, Canada	412,580	1,068,582	8,625,107	Toronto	175, 177/......	81 FC
Orange Free State, South Africa	49,866	129,153	1,833,216	Bloemfontein	119/D 5	TP—80 PC; oth—70 FC
Oregon, U.S.A.	97,073	251,419	2,633,149	Salem	291/......	80 FC & OE
Orkney Islands, Scotland	376	974	17,675	Kirkwall	15/E 1	TP—76 OE; oth—71 FC
*Pakistan	310,403	803,944	83,782,000	Islamabad	68/B 3	TP—81 PC; Abbottabad, Bannu, cit over 50,000—72 PC; oth—61 FC
Palau (Belau)	188	487	12,116	Koror	86/D 5	80 FC
Palmyra Atoll	3.85	1	....	....	87/K 5	
*Panama	29,761	77,082	1,830,175	Panamá	154/G 6	TP, cit over 1,600—80 PC; oth—70 FC
*Papua New Guinea	183,540	475,369	3,010,727	Port Moresby	85/B 7; 87/E 6; 85/E 2	80 PC
Paracel Islands	....	....	....	....	....	
*Paraguay	157,047	406,752	2,973,000	Asunción	144/......	TP—79 OE; oth—72 PC
Pennsylvania, U.S.A.	45,308	117,348	11,863,895	Harrisburg	294/......	80 FC & OE
Persia, see Iran						
*Peru	496,222	1,285,215	17,031,221	Lima	128/......	81 PC
*Philippines	115,707	299,681	48,098,460	Manila	82/......	80 FC
Pitcairn Islands	18	47	54	Adamstown	87/O 8	81 FC
*Poland	120,725	312,678	35,815,000	Warsaw	47/......	TP—81 OE; prov, cap, Cracow, Łódź—75 OE; oth—70 FC
*Portugal	35,549	92,072	9,933,000	Lisbon	32/B 3	TP—80 OE; cap (ws)—76 OE; oth—70 FC & PC
Prince Edward Island, Canada	2,184	5,657	122,506	Charlottetown	168/E 2	81 FC
Puerto Rico	3,515	9,104	3,196,520	San Juan	161/......	80 FC
*Qatar	4,247	11,000	220,000	Doha	58/F 4	TP—80 UN est; cap—79 OE
Québec, Canada	594,857	1,540,680	6,438,403	Québec	172, 174/......	81 FC
Queensland, Australia	666,872	1,727,200	2,295,123	Brisbane	95/......	81 FC
Réunion	969	2,510	491,000	St-Denis	119/F 5	TP—80 OE; oth—74 FC
Rhode Island, U.S.A.	1,212	3,139	947,154	Providence	249/H 5	80 FC & OE
Rhodesia, see Zimbabwe						
*Romania	91,699	237,500	22,048,305	Bucharest	45/F 3	79 OE
Russian S.F.S.R., U.S.S.R.	6,592,812	17,075,400	137,551,000	Moscow	48/D 4	TP, cit over 50,000—79 PC; oth—70 FC
*Rwanda	10,169	26,337	4,819,317	Kigali	114/E 4	78 FC
Sabah, Malaysia	29,300	75,887	1,002,608	Kota Kinabalu	85/F 4	TP—80 PC; Kota Kinabalu—70 FC; oth—70 PC
Saint Helena & Dependencies	162	420	5,147	Jamestown	102/B 6	76 FC
*Saint Kitts and Nevis	104	269	44,404	Basseterre	156/F 3; 161/C 11	TP, isl, cap—80 PC; oth—70 FC
*Saint Lucia	238	616	115,783	Castries	161/G 6	80 PC
Saint Pierre & Miquelon	93.5	242	6,034	Saint-Pierre	166/C 4	82 FC
*Saint Vincent & the Grenadines	150	388	124,000	Kingstown	161/A 8; 157/G 4	TP—80 OE; oth—70 FC
Sakhalin, U.S.S.R.	29,500	76,405	655,000	Yuzhno-Sakhalinsk	48/P 4	TP, cit over 50,000—79 PC; oth—70 FC
*Salvador, El	8,260	21,393	4,813,000	San Salvador	154/C 4	TP—80 OE; oth—71 FC
San Marino	23.4	60.6	19,149	San Marino	34/D 3	TP—76 FC; oth—77 OE
*São Tomé e Príncipe	372	963	85,000	São Tomé	106/F 8	TP—80 UN est; oth—70 PC
Sarawak, Malaysia	48,202	124,843	1,294,753	Kuching	85/E 5	TP—80 PC; Kuching—70 FC; oth—70 PC
Sardinia, Italy	9,301	24,090	1,450,483	Cagliari	34/B 4	71 FC
Saskatchewan, Canada	251,699	651,900	968,313	Regina	181/......	81 FC
*Saudi Arabia	829,995	2,149,687	8,367,000	Riyadh	58/D 4	TP—80 UN est; oth—74 PC
Scotland, U.K.	30,414	78,772	5,117,146	Edinburgh	15/......	TP—81 OE; reg—75 OE; cit—75 & 73 OE, 71 FC; oth—71 FC
*Senegal	75,954	196,720	5,508,000	Dakar	106/A 5	TP—79 OE; oth—76 PC
*Seychelles	145	375	63,000	Victoria	119/H 5	TP—80 OE; oth—77 FC
Shetland Islands, Scotland	552	1,430	18,494	Lerwick	15/G 2	TP—76 OE; oth—73 OE & 71 FC
Siam, see Thailand						
Sicily, Italy	9,926	25,708	4,628,918	Palermo	34/D 6	71 FC
*Sierra Leone	27,925	72,325	3,470,000	Freetown	106/B 7	TP—80 UN est; cap, Bo, Kenema, Makeni—74 PC; oth—63 FC
*Singapore	226	585	2,413,945	Singapore	72/F 6	80 FC
Society Islands, French Polynesia	677	1,753	117,703	Papeete	87/L 7	77 FC
*Solomon Islands	11,500	29,785	221,000	Honiara	87/G 6; 86/......	TP—79 OE; oth—76 FC
*Somalia	246,200	637,658	3,645,000	Mogadishu	115/H 3	TP—80 UN est; prov, cap—75 PC; oth—69, 68, 67, 63 & 62 OE

Gazetteer-Index of the World

Country	Area Square Miles	Area Square Kilometers	Population	Capital or Chief Town	Page and Index Ref.	Sources of Population Data
*South Africa	455,318	1,179,274	23,771,970	Cape Town; Pretoria	118/C 5	TP (excl Transkei, Bophuthatswana, Venda), prov—80 PC; Transkei, Bophuthatswana—78 est; Venda—79 est; oth—70 FC
South America	6,875,000	17,806,250	245,000,000	....	120/......	80 UN est
South Australia, Australia	379,922	984,000	1,285,033	Adelaide	94/......	81 FC
South Carolina, U.S.A.	31,113	80,583	3,121,833	Columbia	296/......	80 FC & OE
South Dakota, U.S.A.	77,116	199,730	690,768	Pierre	298/......	80 FC & OE
South Korea	38,175	98,873	37,448,836	Seoul	80/D 5	TP—80 PC; oth—75 FC & PC
South-West Africa (Namibia)	317,827	823,172	1,200,000	Windhoek	118/B 3	TP—74 est; oth—70 PC
*Spain	194,881	504,742	37,430,000	Madrid	33/......	TP—80 OE; met areas—75 OE; oth—70 FC
Spratly Island	....	....	....		85/E 4	....
*Sri Lanka	25,332	65,610	14,850,001	Colombo	68/E 7	TP—81 PC; cap, Jaffna—73 OE; oth—71 FC
*Sudan	967,494	2,505,809	18,691,000	Khartoum	110/E 4	TP—80 PC; cap, prov, prov cap—73 PC; oth—73 PC, 72 OE
Sumatra, Indonesia	164,000	424,760	19,360,400	Medan	84/B 5	71 PC
*Suriname	55,144	142,823	354,860	Paramaribo	131/C 3	TP, cap—80 PC; dist—71 PC; oth—64 FC
Svalbard, Norway	23,957	62,049	3,431	Longyearbyen	18/C 2	76 OE
*Swaziland	6,705	17,366	547,000	Mbabane	119/E 5	TP—80 OE; oth—76 FC
*Sweden	173,665	449,792	8,320,000	Stockholm	18/J 8	TP—81 OE; oth—75 FC
Switzerland	15,943	41,292	6,365,960	Bern	39/......	TP—80 FC; cantons—78 OE; cap, cit over 100,000 (& ws)—74 OE; cit (com) over 30,000 (& ws)—73 OE; oth—70 FC
*Syria	71,498	185,180	8,979,000	Damascus	62/G 5	TP—80 OE; oth—70 FC
Tadzhik S.S.R., U.S.S.R.	55,251	143,100	3,801,000	Dushanbe	48/G 6	TP, cit over 50,000—79 PC; oth—70 FC
Tahiti, French Polynesia	402	1,041	95,604	Papeete	87/L 7	77 FC
Taiwan	13,971	36,185	16,609,961	Taipei	77/K 7	TP, cap, Penghu Isl., cit over 300,000—77 OE; oth—70 OE
*Tanzania	363,708	942,003	17,527,560	Dar es Salaam	114/F 5	TP—78 OE; div, cap, cit over 17,000—78 PC; oth—67 FC
Tasmania, Australia	26,178	67,800	418,957	Hobart	99/......	81 FC
Tennessee, U.S.A.	42,144	109,153	4,591,120	Nashville	237/......	80 FC & OE
Texas, U.S.A.	266,807	691,030	14,229,288	Austin	303/......	80 FC & OE
*Thailand	198,455	513,990	46,455,000	Bangkok	72/D 3	TP—80 OE; oth—70 FC
Tibet, China	463,320	1,200,000	1,790,000	Lhasa	76/C 5	TP—78 OE; oth—70 est
*Togo	21,622	56,000	2,472,000	Lomé	106/E 7	TP—79 OE; oth—70 FC
Tokelau	3.9	10	1,575	Fakaofo	87/J 6	TP—76 FC; oth—72 OE
Tonga	270	699	90,128	Nuku'alofa	87/J 8	76 PC
Transkei (rep.), South Africa	16,910	43,797	2,000,000	Umtata	119/D 6	TP—80 est; oth—70 FC
Transvaal, South Africa	109,621	283,918	10,673,033	Pretoria	119/D 4	TP—80 PC; oth—70 FC
*Trinidad and Tobago	1,980	5,128	1,067,108	Port-of-Spain	157/G 5; 161/A10	80 PC
Tristan da Cunha, St. Helena	38	98	251	Edinburgh	2/J 7	79 OE
Tuamotu Archipelago, French Polynesia	341	883	9,052	Apataki	87/M 7	77 FC
*Tunisia	63,378	164,149	6,367,000	Tunis	106/F 1	TP—79 OE; oth—75 FC
*Turkey	300,946	779,450	45,217,556	Ankara	62/D 3	TP—80 PC; oth—75.FC
Turkmen S.S.R., U.S.S.R.	188,455	488,100	2,759,000	Ashkhabad	48/F 6	TP, cit over 50,000—79 PC; oth—7C FC
Turks and Caicos Islands	166	430	7,436	Cockburn Town, Grand Turk	156/D 2	80 PC
Tuvalu	9.78	25.33	7,349	Fongafale, Funafuti	87/H 6	79 FC
*Uganda	91,076	235,887	12,630,076	Kampala	114/F 3	TP, cap—80 PC; oth—69 FC
*Ukrainian S.S.R., U.S.S.R.	233,089	603,700	49,755,000	Kiev	52/D 5	TP, cit over 50,000—79 PC; oth—70 FC
*Union of Soviet Socialist Republics	8,649,490	22,402,179	262,436,227	Moscow	48/......	TP, S.S.R., cit over 50,000—79 PC; oth—70 FC
*United Arab Emirates	32,278	83,600	1,040,275	Abu Dhabi	58/F 5	TP—80 PC; oth—79 OE
*United Kingdom	94,399	244,493	55,672,000	London	10/......	TP—81 OE (see England, Wales, Scotland, Northern Ireland)
*United States of America	3,623,420	9,384,658	226,504,825	Washington	188/......	80 FC & OE
*Upper Volta (Burkina Faso)	105,869	274,200	6,908,000	Ouagadougou	106/D 6	TP—80 UN est; oth—75 FC, 73 OE
*Uruguay	72,172	186,925	2,899,000	Montevideo	145/......	TP—80 OE; oth—75 PC
Utah, U.S.A.	84,899	219,888	1,461,037	Salt Lake City	304/......	80 FC & OE
Uzbek S.S.R., U.S.S.R.	173,591	449,600	15,391,000	Tashkent	48/G 5	TP, cit over 50,000—79 PC; oth—70 FC
*Vanuatu	5,700	14,763	112,596	Vila	87/G 7	79 FC
Vatican City	108.7 acres	44 hectares	728		34/B 6	78 OE
Venda (rep.), South Africa	2,510	6,501	450,000	Thohoyandou	119/E 4	79 est
*Venezuela	352,143	912,050	14,313,000	Caracas	124/......	TP—81 OE; oth—71 FC
Vermont, U.S.A.	9,614	24,900	511,456	Montpelier	268/......	80 FC & OE
Victoria, Australia	87,876	227,600	3,832,443	Melbourne	96/B 5	81 FC
*Vietnam	128,405	332,569	52,741,766	Hanoi	72/E 3	TP—79 FC; cap, Haiphong, Ho Chi Minh City—79 PC; oth cit over 100,000 (north)—70 est, (south)—73 & 71 OE; oth—69 OE, 60 OE
Virginia, U.S.A.	40,767	105,587	5,346,818	Richmond	307/......	80 FC & OE
Virgin Islands, British	59	153	11,006	Road Town	157/H 1	TP—80 FC; oth—70 FC
Virgin Islands, U.S.A.	132	342	96,569	Charlotte Amalie	161/A 4	80 FC
Wake Island	2.5	6.5	302	Wake Islet	87/G 4	80 FC
Wales, U.K.	8,017	20,764	2,790,462	Cardiff	13/D 5	TP—81 PC; co—76 OE; cit—76 & 73 OE; par—71 FC
Wallis and Futuna	106	275	9,192	Mata Utu	87/J 7	76 FC
Washington, U.S.A.	68,139	176,480	4,132,180	Olympia	310/......	80 FC & OE
West Bank	2,100	5,439	c. 800,000	....	65/C 3	TP—81 est; oth—67 CE & 61 FC
Western Australia, Australia	975,096	2,525,500	1,273,624	Perth	92/......	81 FC
Western Sahara	102,703	266,000	76,425	....	106/B 3	70 FC
*Western Samoa	1,133	2,934	158,130	Apia	87/J 7	81 PC
*West Germany (Federal Republic)	95,985	248,601	61,658,000	Bonn	22/......	TP—80 OE; states, cap—76 OE; oth—76 OE, 70 FC
West Virginia, U.S.A.	24,231	62,758	1,950,279	Charleston	312/......	80 FC & OE
*White Russian S.S.R. (Byelorussian S.S.R.), U.S.S.R.	80,154	207,600	9,560,000	Minsk	52/C 4	TP, cit over 50,000—79 PC; oth—70 FC
Wisconsin, U.S.A.	56,153	145,436	4,705,521	Madison	317/......	80 FC & OE
World	(land) 57,970,000	150,142,300	4,415,000,000	....	1, 2/......	80 UN est
Wyoming, U.S.A.	97,809	253,325	469,557	Cheyenne	319/......	80 FC & OE
*Yemen, People's Democratic Republic of	111,101	287,752	1,969,000	Aden	58/E 7	TP—81 PC; oth—75 FC
*Yemen Arab Republic	77,220	200,000	6,456,189	San a	58/D 6	TP—80 OE; Mukalla, Seiyun—76 OE; cap—73 OE; Saihut—60 OE
*Yugoslavia	98,766	255,804	22,471,000	Belgrade	45/C 3	TP—81 OE; oth—71 FC
Yukon Territory, Canada	207,075	536,324	23,153	Whitehorse	186/E 3	81 FC
*Zaire	905,063	2,344,113	28,291,000	Kinshasa	114/D 4	TP—80 OE; prov, cap—70 FC; oth—70 FC & PC
*Zambia	290,586	752,618	5,679,808	Lusaka	114/E 7	80 PC
*Zimbabwe	150,803	390,580	7,360,000	Harare	119/D 3	TP—80 OE; cap, cit over 12,000—77 OE; oth—69 FC

Glossary of Abbreviations

A

A. A. F. — Army Air Field
Acad. — Academy
A. C. T. — Australian Capital Territory
adm. — administration; administrative
A. F. B. — Air Force Base
Afgh., Afghan. — Afghanistan
Afr. — Africa
Ala. — Alabama
Alb. — Albania
Alg. — Algeria
Alta. — Alberta
Amer. — American
Amer. Samoa — American Samoa
And. — Andorra
Ant., Antarc. — Antarctica
Ant. & Bar. — Antigua and Barbuda
Ar. — Arabia
arch. — archipelago
Arg. — Argentina
Ariz. — Arizona
Ark. — Arkansas
A. S. S. R. — Autonomous Soviet Socialist Republic
Aust. — Austria
Aust. Cap. Terr. — Australian Capital Territory
Austr., Austral. — Australian, Australia
aut. — autonomous
Aut. Obl. — Autonomous Oblast

B

B. — bay
Bah. — Bahamas
Barb. — Barbados
Battlef. — Battlefield
Bch. — Beach
Belg. — Belgium
Berm. — Bermuda
Bol. — Bolivia
Bots. — Botswana
Br. — Branch
Br. — British
Braz. — Brazil
Br. Col. — British Columbia
Br. Ind. Oc. Terr. — British Indian Ocean Territory
Bulg. — Bulgaria

C

C. — cape
Calif. — California
Can. — Canada
can. — canal
cap. — capital
Cent. Afr. Rep. — Central African Republic
Cent. Amer. — Central America
C. G. Sta. — Coast Guard Station
C. H. — Court House
chan. — channel
Chan. Is. — Channel Islands
Chem. Ctr. — Chemical Center
co. — county
C. of G. H. — Cape of Good Hope
Col. — Colombia
Colo. — Colorado
comm. — commissary
Conn. — Connecticut
cont. — continent
cord. — cordillera (mountain range)
C. Rica — Costa Rica
C. S. — County Seat
C. Verde — Cape Verde
Czech. — Czechoslovakia

D

D. C. — District of Columbia
Del. — Delaware
Dem. — Democratic
Den. — Denmark
depr. — depression
dept. — department
des. — desert
dist., dist's — district, districts
div. — division
Dom. Rep. — Dominican Republic

E

E. — East
Ec., Ecua. — Ecuador
E. Ger. — East Germany
elec. div. — electoral division
El Salv. — El Salvador
Eng. — England
Equat. Guinea, Eq. Guin — Equatorial Guinea

escarp. — escarpment
est. — estuary
Eth. — Ethiopia

F

Falk. Is. — Falkland Islands
Fin. — Finland
Fk., Fks. — Fork, Forks
Fla. — Florida
for. — forest
Fr. — France, French
Fr. Gui. — French Guiana
Fr. Poly. — French Polynesia
Ft. — Fort

G

G. — gulf
Ga. — Georgia
Game Res. — Game Reserve
Ger. — Germany
geys. — geyser
Gibr. — Gibraltar
glac. — glacier
gov. — governorate
Gr. — Group
Greenl. — Greenland
Gren. — Grenada
Gt. Brit. — Great Britain
Guad. — Guadeloupe
Guat. — Guatemala
Guinea-Biss. — Guinea-Bissau
Guy. — Guyana

H

har., harb., hbr. — harbor
hd. — head
highl. — highland, highlands
Hist. — Historic, Historical
Hond. — Honduras
Hts. — Heights
Hung. — Hungary

I

i., isl. — island, isle
I. C. — independent city
Ice., Icel. — Iceland
Ida. — Idaho
Ill. — Illinois
Ind. — Indiana
ind. city — independent city
Indon. — Indonesia
Ind. Res. — Indian Reservation
int. div. — internal division
inten. — intendency
Int'l — International
Ire. — Ireland
is., isls. — islands
Isr. — Israel
isth. — isthmus
Iv. Coast — Ivory Coast

J

Jam. — Jamaica
Jct. — Junction

K

Kans. — Kansas
Ky. — Kentucky

L

L. — Lake, Loch, Lough
La. — Louisiana
Lab. — Laboratory
lag. — lagoon
Ld. — Land
Leb. — Lebanon
Les. — Lesotho
Liecht. — Liechtenstein
Lux. — Luxembourg

M

Mad., Madag. — Madagascar
Man. — Manitoba
Mart. — Martinique
Mass. — Massachusetts
Maur. — Mauritania
Md. — Maryland
met. area — metropolitan area
Mex. — Mexico
Mich. — Michigan
Minn. — Minnesota
Miss. — Mississippi
Mo. — Missouri
Mon. — Monument
Mong. — Mongolia
Mont. — Montana
Mor. — Morocco

Moz., Mozamb. — Mozambique
mt. — mount
mtn. — mountain

N

N., No., North. — North, Northern
N. Amer. — North America
Nam., Namib. — Namibia
N. A. S. — Naval Air Station
Nat'l — National
Nat'l Cem. — National Cemetery
Nat'l Mem. Park — National Memorial Park
Nat'l Mil. Park — National Military Park
Nat'l Pkwy. — National Parkway
Nav. Base — Naval Base
Nav. Sta. — Naval Station
N. B., N. Br. — New Brunswick
N. C. — North Carolina
N. Dak. — North Dakota
Nebr. — Nebraska
Neth. — Netherlands
Neth. Ant. — Netherlands Antilles
Nev. — Nevada
New Bruns. — New Brunswick
New Cal., New Caled. — New Caledonia
Newf. — Newfoundland
New Hebr. — New Hebrides
N. H. — New Hampshire
Nic. — Nicaragua
N. Ire. — Northern Ireland
N. J. — New Jersey
N. Mex. — New Mexico
Nor. — Norway, Norwegian
North. — Northern
North. Terr., No. Terr. — Northern Territory (Australia)
N. S. — Nova Scotia
N. S. W., N.S. Wales — New South Wales
N. W. T., N. W. Terrs. — Northwest Territories (Canada)
N. Y. — New York
N. Z., N. Zealand — New Zealand

O

Obl. — Oblast
O. F. S. — Orange Free State
Okla. — Oklahoma
Okr. — Okrug
Ont. — Ontario
Ord. Depot — Ordnance Depot
Oreg. — Oregon

P

Pa. — Pennsylvania
Pac. Is. — Pacific Islands, Territory of the
Pak. — Pakistan
Pan. — Panama
Papua N. G. — Pàpua New Guinea
Par. — Paraguay
par. — parish
passg. — passage
P.D.R. Yemen — People's Democratic Republic of Yemen
P. E. I. — Prince Edward Island
pen. — peninsula
Phil., Phil. Is. — Philippines
Pk. — Park
pk. — peak
plat. — plateau
P. N. G. — Papua New Guinea
Pol. — Poland
Port. — Portugal, Portuguese
Pr. Edward I. — Prince Edward Island
pref. — prefecture
P. Rico — Puerto Rico
prom. — promontory
prov. — province, provincial
pt. — point

Q

Que. — Québec
Queens. — Queensland

R

R. — River
ra. — range
Rec., Recr. — Recreation, Recreational
reg. — region
Rep. — Republic
res. — reservoir
Res. — Reservation, Reserve
R. I. — Rhode Island

riv. — river
Rom. — Romania

S

S. — South
Sa. — Sierra, Serra
S. Afr., S. Africa — South Africa
salt dep. — salt deposit
salt des. — salt desert
S. Amer. — South America
São T. & Pr. — São Tomé and Príncipe
Sask. — Saskatchewan
Saudi Ar. — Saudi Arabia
S. Aust., S. Austral. — South Australia
S. C. — South Carolina
Scot. — Scotland
Sd. — Sound
S. Dak. — South Dakota
Sen. — Senegal
sen. dist. — senatorial district
Seych. — Seychelles
S. F. S. R. — Soviet Federated Socialist Republic
Sing. — Singapore
S. Leone — Sierra Leone
S. Marino — San Marino
Sol. Is. — Solomon Islands
Sp. — Spanish
Spr., Sprs. — Spring, Springs
S. S. R. — Soviet Socialist Republic
St., Ste. — Saint, Sainte
Sta. — Station
St. Chris.-Nevis — Saint Christopher-Nevis
St. P. & M. — Saint Pierre and Miquelon
St. Vin. & Grens. — St. Vincent & The Grenadines
str., strs. — strait, straits
Sur. — Suriname
S. W. Afr. — South-West Africa
Swaz. — Swaziland
Switz. — Switzerland

T

Tanz. — Tanzania
Tas. — Tasmania
Tenn. — Tennessee
terr., terrs. — territory, territories
Tex. — Texas
Thai. — Thailand
trad. — traditional
Trin. & Tob. — Trinidad and Tobago
Tun. — Tunisia
twp. — township

U

U. A. E. — United Arab Emirates
U. K. — United Kingdom
Upp. Volta — Upper Volta
urb. area — urban area
Urug. — Uruguay
U. S. — United States
U. S. S. R. — Union of Soviet Socialist Republics

V

Va. — Virginia
Ven., Venez. — Venezuela
V. I. (Br.) — Virgin Islands (British)
V. I. (U. S.) — Virgin Islands (U. S.)
Vic. — Victoria
Viet. — Vietnam
Vill. — Village
vol. — volcano
Vt. — Vermont

W

W. — West, Western
Wash. — Washington
W. Aust., W. Austral. — Western Australia
W. Ger. — West Germany
W. Indies — West Indies
Wis. — Wisconsin
W. Samoa — Western Samoa
W. Va. — West Virginia
Wyo. — Wyoming

Y

Yugo. — Yugoslavia
Yukon — Yukon Territory

Z

Zim. — Zimbabwe

Index to Terrain Maps

on pages X through XXXII

This index contains only names of land and ocean physical features. Names of towns, internal divisions and countries are not included. The entry name is followed by a letter-number combination which refers to the area on the map in which the name will be found. The number following the map reference for the entry refers, not to the page on which the entry will be found, but to the map plate number.

Index Continued

HAMMOND®
THE PHYSICAL WORLD
Terrain Maps of Land Forms and Ocean Floors

CONTENTS

RELIEF MODELS BY ERNST G. HOFMANN, ASSISTED BY RAFAEL MARTINEZ

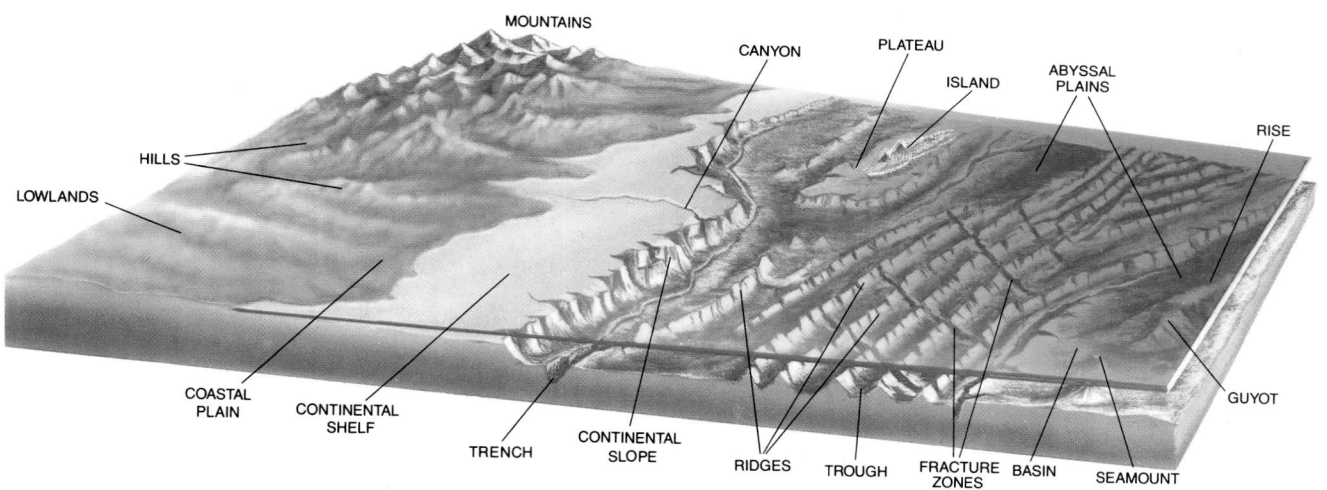

The oblique view diagram above is designed to provide a detailed view of the ocean floor as if seen through the depth of the sea. Graduating blue tones are used to contrast ocean floor depths: from light blue to represent shallow continental shelves to dark blues in the greater depths. Land relief is shown in conventional hypsometric tints.

In this dramatic collection of topographic maps of continents, oceans and major regions of the world, Hammond introduces a revolutionary new technique in cartography.

While most maps depicting terrain are created from painted artwork that is then photographed, Hammond now premiers the use of a remarkable sculptured model mapping technique created by one of our master cartographers.

The process begins with the sculpting of large scale three-dimensional models. Once physical details have been etched on the models and refinements completed, relief work is checked for accurate elevation based on a vertical scale exaggerated for visual effect.

Finished models are airbrushed and painted, then photographed using a single northwesterly light source to achieve a striking three-dimensional effect. The result is the dynamic presentation of mountain ranges and peaks on land, and canyons, trenches and seamounts on the ocean floor. Never before have maps conveyed such rich beauty while providing a realistic representation of the world as we know it.

ARCTIC OCEAN

QUEEN ELIZABETH
ISLANDS

CANADA
BASIN

Ellesmere
I.

GREENLAND

Greenla

Devon I.

Baffin

Greenla
Sea

Wrangel
I.

Beaufort Sea

Banks
I.

Victoria
I.

Baffin
Island

Bay

Arctic Circle

NC
BA

Chukchi
Sea

Pt. Barrow

Yukon

Mackenzie

Great Bear
L.

Labrador
Basin

Norwegian

Iceland

IRMINGER BASIN

Denmark

Bering Sea

Mt. McKinley

Great Slave
L.

ROCKY

NORTH

Hudson
Bay

Great
Britain

ALEUTIAN
BASIN

Gulf of Alaska

Peace

AMERICA

CHARLIE GIBBS
FRACTURE ZONE

ICELAND BASIN

Ireland

Nort
Se

ALEUTIAN ISLANDS

ALEUTIAN TRENCH

Great
Lakes

Newfoundland

Great
Plains

Missouri

C. Race

Appalachian Mts.

MENDOCINO FRACTURE ZONE

C. Mendocino

Mountains

Colorado

Ohio

Mississippi

ATLANTIC

At

M

C. Hatteras

HAWAIIAN

HAWAIIAN RIDGE

MOLOKAI FRACTURE ZONE

Lower

Rio Grande

California

Tropic of Cancer

ISLANDS

Gulf of
Mexico

WEST

Cuba

S

Caribbean
Sea

INDIES

C. Verde

CENTRAL

PACIFIC

CLIPPERTON FRACTURE ZONE

PACIFIC

GUATEMALA
BASIN

Orinoco

A

BASIN

Equator

Negro

Amazon

RIDGE

ROMANCHE FRACTURE ZONE

Madeira

OCEAN

PERU CHILE TRENCH

PERU
BASIN

Andes

SOUTH

AMERICA

BRAZIL

Niger

São Francisco

C. de São Roque

Paraná

BASIN

MID-ATLANTIC

NAZCA RIDGE

Mountains

TONGA
TRENCH

Tropic of Capricorn

CHILE
BASIN

Cerro
Aconcagua

KERMADEC
TRENCH

SOUTHWEST

PACIFIC

ARGENTINE
BASIN

BASIN

Falkland I.

Tierra del Fuego

PACIFIC-ANTARCTIC RIDGE

C. Horn

Drake Passage

SOUTH
SANDWICH
TRENCH

AMUNDSEN ABYSSAL PLAIN

Antarctic
Peninsula

WEDDELL

Antarctic Circle

Bellingshausen
Sea

ABYSSAL PLAIN

Weddell

Sea

ANTARCTICA

0   500   1000   1500   2000   2500   3000 MILES at Equator

0   500   1000   1500   2000   2500   3000 KILOMETERS at Equator

LEGEND FOR TERRAIN MAPS

International Boundaries	—..—	Mountain Peaks	▲
State and Provincial Boundaries	—.—	National Capitals	⊛
Other Boundaries	---	Other Capitals	⊙
Boundaries Along Rivers	⁀⁀	Canals	

© Copyright 1987 by HAMMOND INCORPORATED, Maplewood, N.J.

World | Plate 1

Plate 2 | Europe

500 MILES

500 KILOMETERS

GREENLAND STRAIT
ICELAND-FAEROE RIDGE
KOLBEINSEY RIDGE
Jan Mayen (Nor.)
Nordkapp
Hammerfest
Nordkyn
Murmansk
Kola Peninsula
ICELANDIC PLATEAU
Vesterålen
Inari
WHITE SEA
Muonio
Lofoten
Kiruna
Torne
JAN MAYEN RIDGE
Horn
Fontur
Kemi
ReykJavik
ICELAND
Thjórsá
NORWEGIAN BASIN
Ii
Oulu
AEGIR RIDGE
NORWEGIAN SEA
Arctic Circle
R.
NORWAY
ICELAND BASIN
VORING PLATEAU
FINLAND
ICELAND-FAEROE RISE
Angerman
Lake Onega
ATLANTIC
Faeroe Is. (Den.)
FAEROE SHELF
Trondheim
SWEDEN
Sundsvall
Gulf of Bothnia
Tampere
Saimaa
Lake Ladoga
FAEROE-SHETLAND CHANNEL
Glittertinden 8,110 ft. (2472 m)
Glomma
Dal
Kamo
Helsinki
ROCKALL PLATEAU
Shetland Is.
NORWEGIAN DEEP
Bergen
Klar
Åland Is.
Gulf of Finland
Leningrad
S.
Rockall
HEBRIDEAN SHELF
Orkney Is.
Oslo
Stockholm
Hiiuma
Talinn
L. Peipus
ROCKALL BANK
Hebrides
Lindesnes
Vänern
Vättern
Gotland
Saaremaa
G. of Riga
Riga
S.
FENI RIDGE
NORTH SEA
Skagerrak
Kattegat
Öland
W. Dvina
ROCKALL TROUGH
Ben Nevis 4,406 ft. (1343 m)
Aberdeen
SCOTLAND
Glasgow
DENMARK Jutland
Fyn
Sjaelland
Copenhagen
BALTIC SEA
Niemen
Vilna
Minsk
PORCUPINE BANK
N. IRE.
Belfast
Isle of Man
Pennine Chain
UNITED
Bornholm
Rügen
Kaliningrad
Gdańsk
U.
OCEAN
IRELAND
Shannon
Dublin
IRISH SEA
Liverpool
KINGDOM
Hamburg
Bremen
EAST
Berlin
Szczecin
POLAND
Warsaw
Warta
Łódź
Bug
PORCUPINE ABYSSAL PLAIN
St. George's Channel
Birmingham
WALES
ENGLAND
London
Thames
NETHERLANDS
Amsterdam
Rotterdam
Ems
Weser
GERMANY
Leipzig
Elbe
Dresden
Wrocław
Oder
Vistula
Cracow
L'vov
Dniester
CELTIC SHELF
Land's End
English Channel
BELGIUM
Antwerp
Brussels
Bonn
Cologne
WEST
Frankfurt
Main
Prague
CZECHOSLOVAKIA
Brno
Carpathian Mts.
Channel Is. (U.K.)
Le Havre
Seine
LUX.
Ardennes
Meuse
Moselle
GERMANY
Rhine
Danube
Prut
Siret
Brest
Paris
Jura
Stuttgart
Munich
Linz
Vienna
AUSTRIA
Budapest
Tisza
Cluj-Napoca
ROMANIA
BISCAY ABYSSAL PLAIN
Nantes
Loire
FRANCE
Vienne
Saône
Graz
HUNGARY
L. Balaton
Olt
Bern
Zürich
LIECHT.
SWITZ.
A
L
P
S
Bucharest
Geneva
Lyon
Mt. Blanc 15,771 ft. (4807 m)
Milan
Venice
Zagreb
Sava
Dinaric Alps
YUGOSLAVIA
Danube
Bordeaux
Dordogne
Massif Central
Rhône
Turin
Genoa
Trieste
Belgrade
Sofia
BULGARIA
C. Finisterre
Garonne
Toulouse
Pyrenees
Cantabrian Mts.
Miño
Bilbao
ANDORRA
Nice
MONACO
LIGURIAN SEA
Po
Bologna
SAN MARINO
Arno
ADRIATIC SEA
Vardar
Thessaloniki
PORTUGAL
Porto
Douro
Ebro
Saragossa
Barcelona
Gulf of Lions
Marseille
Corsica
Elba
ITALY
Apennines
VATICAN CITY
Rome
ADRIATIC BASIN
ALBANIA
Tiranë
GREECE
Lisbon
SPAIN
Madrid
Tagus
Júcar
Valencia
Balearic Is.
Minorca
Majorca
Sardinia
Naples
AEGEAN SEA
Évvoia
Guadiana
Iberian Peninsula
Sierra Morena
Guadalquivir
Córdoba
Ibiza
TYRRHENIAN SEA
G. of Taranto
Ionian Is.
Ionian
Athens
Peloponnisos
C. de São Vicente
Seville
Mulhacén 11,411 ft. (3478 m)
Cádiz
Málaga
GIBRALTAR (U.K.)
Str. of Gibraltar
ALGERIAN PLAIN
C. Teulada
TYRRHENIAN BASIN
Palermo
Etna 11,053 ft. (3369 m)
IONIAN SEA
Tangier
Algiers
MEDITERRANEAN
C. Bon
Sicily
C. Passero
IONIAN BASIN
C. Tainaron
Crete
MOROCCO
Oran
AFRICA
ALGERIA
TUNISIA
Tunis
MALTA
Valleta
SEA

Western Europe | Plate 3

0 100 200 300 400 500 MILES
0 100 200 300 400 500 KILOMETERS

Plate 4 | **Asia**

	300	600	900	1200	1500 MILES
0					

	300	600	900	1200	1500 KILOMETERS
0					

XV

Southwest Asia | Plate 5

500 MILES

500 KILOMETERS

© Copyright 1987 by HAMMOND INCORPORATED, Maplewood, N.J.

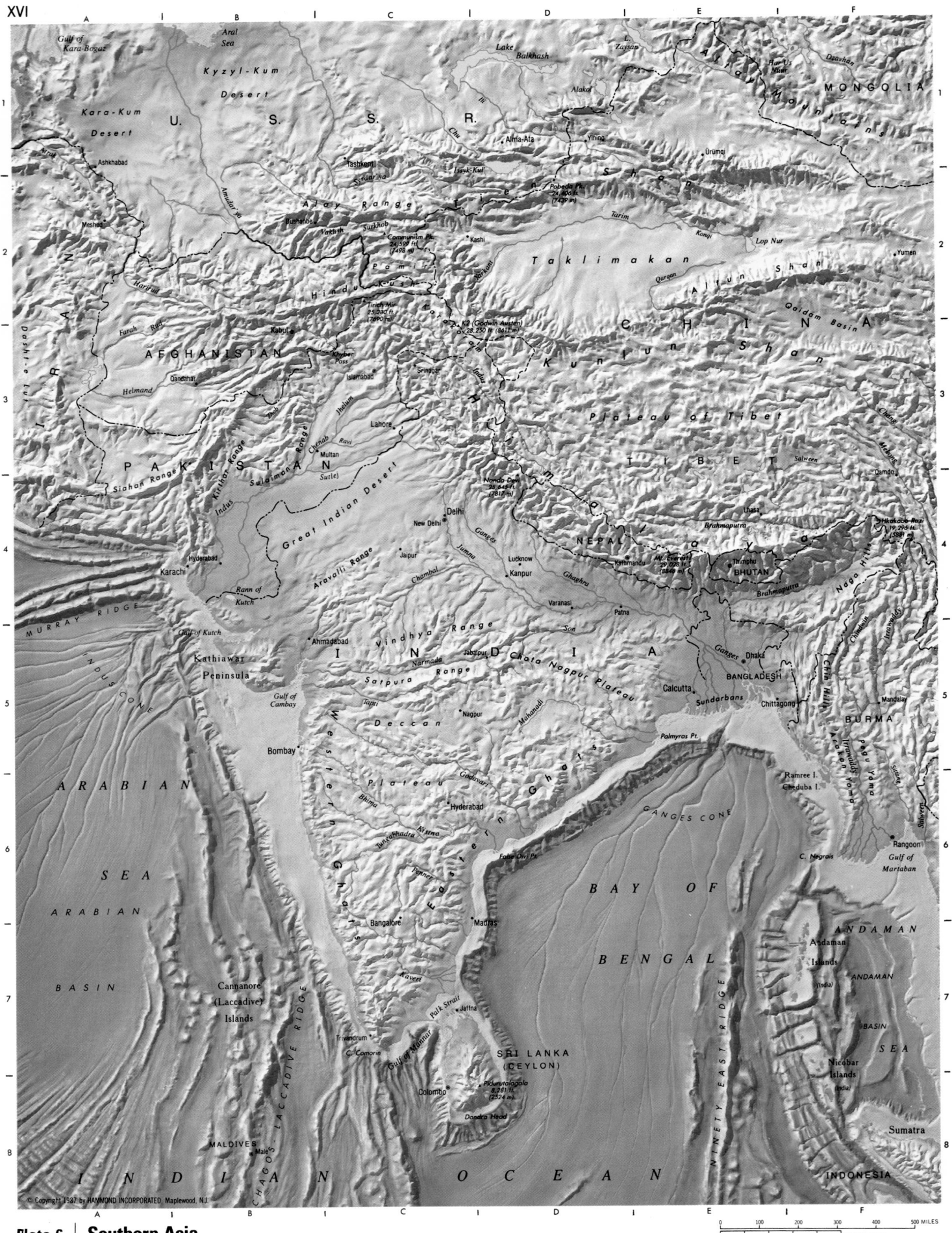

Plate 6 | **Southern Asia**

© Copyright 1987 by HAMMOND INCORPORATED, Maplewood, N.J.

XVII

East Asia | Plate 7

0 100 200 300 400 500 600 MILES
0 100 200 300 400 500 600 KILOMETERS

Plate 8 | **Southeast Asia**

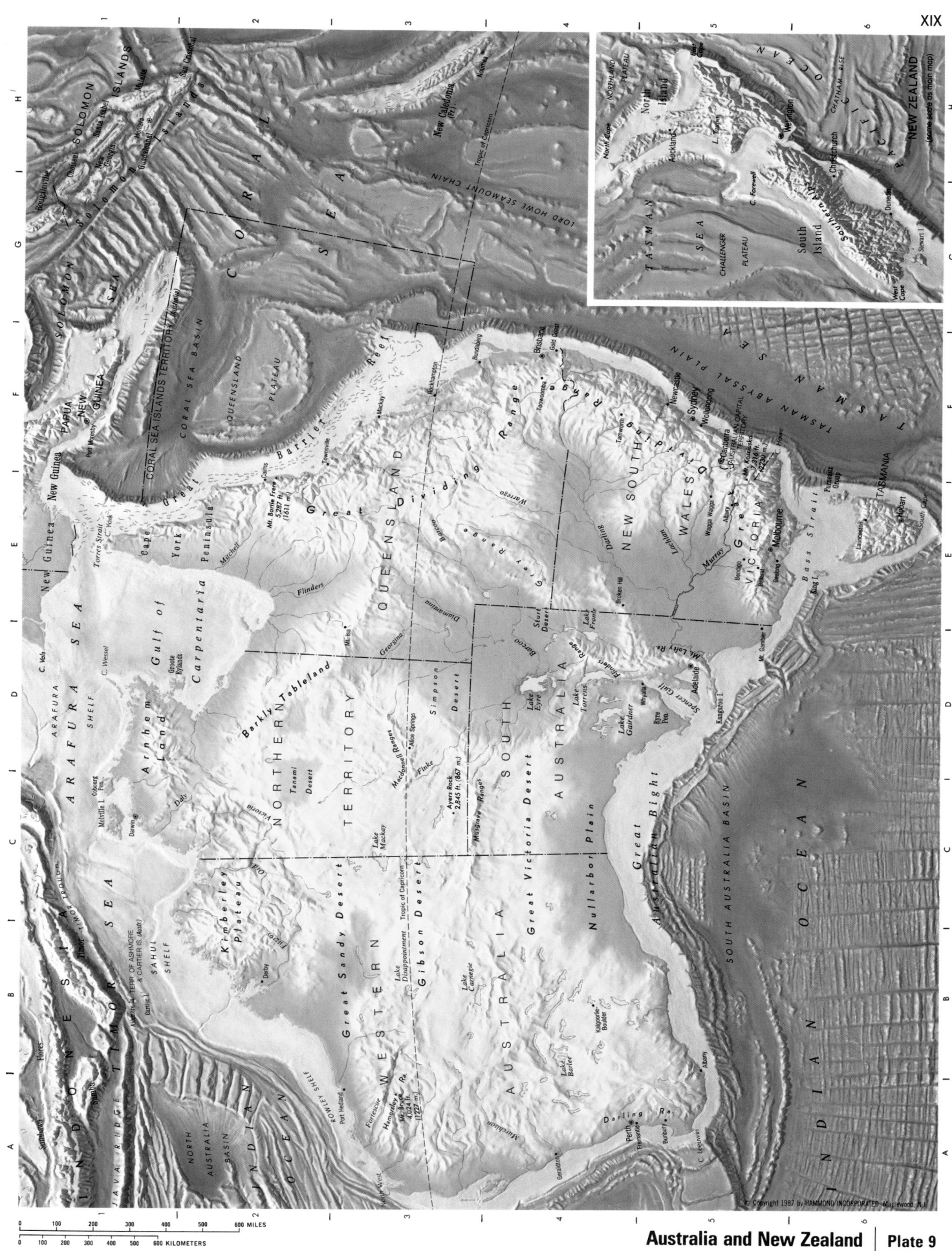

NEW ZEALAND
(same scale as main map)

NORTHLAND PLATEAU

North Cape

North Island

East Cape

Auckland

CHATHAM RISE

L. Taupo

Wellington

C. Farewell

Christchurch

TASMAN SEA

CHALLENGER PLATEAU

South Island

Dunedin

West Cape

Stewart I.

PACIFIC OCEAN

SOLOMON ISLANDS

Bougainville

Choiseul

New Georgia

Santa Isabel

Malaita

Guadalcanal

Kieta

SOLOMON SEA

San Cristobal

New Caledonia (Fr.)

Noumea

Tropic of Capricorn

LORD HOWE SEAMOUNT CHAIN

CORAL SEA

PAPUA NEW GUINEA

New Guinea

New Guinea

Port Moresby

Torres Strait

C. York

Cape York Peninsula

ARAFURA SEA

C. Vols

C. Wessel

Gove

Gulf of Carpentaria

Groote Eylandt

Arnhem Land

Cobourg Pen.

Melville I.

Darwin

Daly

Victoria

Mitchell

Flinders

CORAL SEA ISLANDS TERRITORY (Austl.)

CORAL SEA BASIN

QUEENSLAND PLATEAU

Great Barrier Reef

Cairns

Townsville

Mackay

Rockhampton

Bundaberg

Brisbane

Gold Coast

Toowoomba

QUEENSLAND

Great Dividing Range

Mt. Bartle Frere 5,287 ft. (1611 m.)

Warrego

Condamine

Barcoo

Balonne

Diamantina

Georgina

Mt. Isa

Flinders

NORTHERN TERRITORY

Barkly Tableland

Tanami Desert

Simpson Desert

Macdonnell Ranges

Alice Springs

Finke

Ayers Rock 2,845 ft. (867 m.)

Musgrave Ranges

Tropic of Capricorn

Lake Mackay

Lake Disappointment

Great Sandy Desert

Gibson Desert

Lake Carnegie

WESTERN AUSTRALIA

Kimberley Plateau

Derby

Fitzroy

Ord

SAHUL SHELF

ROWLEY SHELF

Port Hedland

Fortescue

Hamersley Ra.

Mt. Bruce 4,024 ft. (1227 m.)

Murchison

Darling Ra.

Geraldton

Kalbarri

Perth

Fremantle

Bunbury

C. Leeuwin

Albany

Lake Barlee

Kalgoorlie–Boulder

Great Victoria Desert

Nullarbor Plain

SOUTH AUSTRALIA

Lake Eyre

Lake Torrens

Lake Gairdner

Eyre Pen.

Lake Frome

Flinders Range

Mt. Lofty Ra.

Whyalla

Spencer Gulf

Kangaroo I.

Adelaide

Great Australian Bight

Great Bight

SOUTH AUSTRALIA BASIN

INDIAN OCEAN

Sturt Desert

Broken Hill

Darling

Lachlan

Murrumbidgee

Murray

NEW SOUTH WALES

Wagga Wagga

Albury

Newcastle

Sydney

Wollongong

Tamworth

AUSTRALIAN CAPITAL TERRITORY

Canberra

Mt. Kosciusko 7,316 ft. (2230 m.)

VICTORIA

Great Dividing Range

Bendigo

Ballarat

Geelong

Melbourne

Mt. Gambier

Bass Strait

King I.

Furneaux Group

TASMANIA

Launceston

Hobart

South Cape

TASMAN SEA

TASMAN ABYSSAL PLAIN

INDONESIA

Sumba

Flores

Timor

TIMOR SEA

JAVA RIDGE

Ashmore

TERR. OF ASHMORE & CARTIER IS. (Austl.)

Cartier I.

NORTH AUSTRALIA BASIN

INDIAN OCEAN

© Copyright 1987 by HAMMOND INCORPORATED Maplewood, N.J.

0   100   200   300   400   500   600 MILES

0   100   200   300   400   500   600 KILOMETERS

Australia and New Zealand | Plate 9

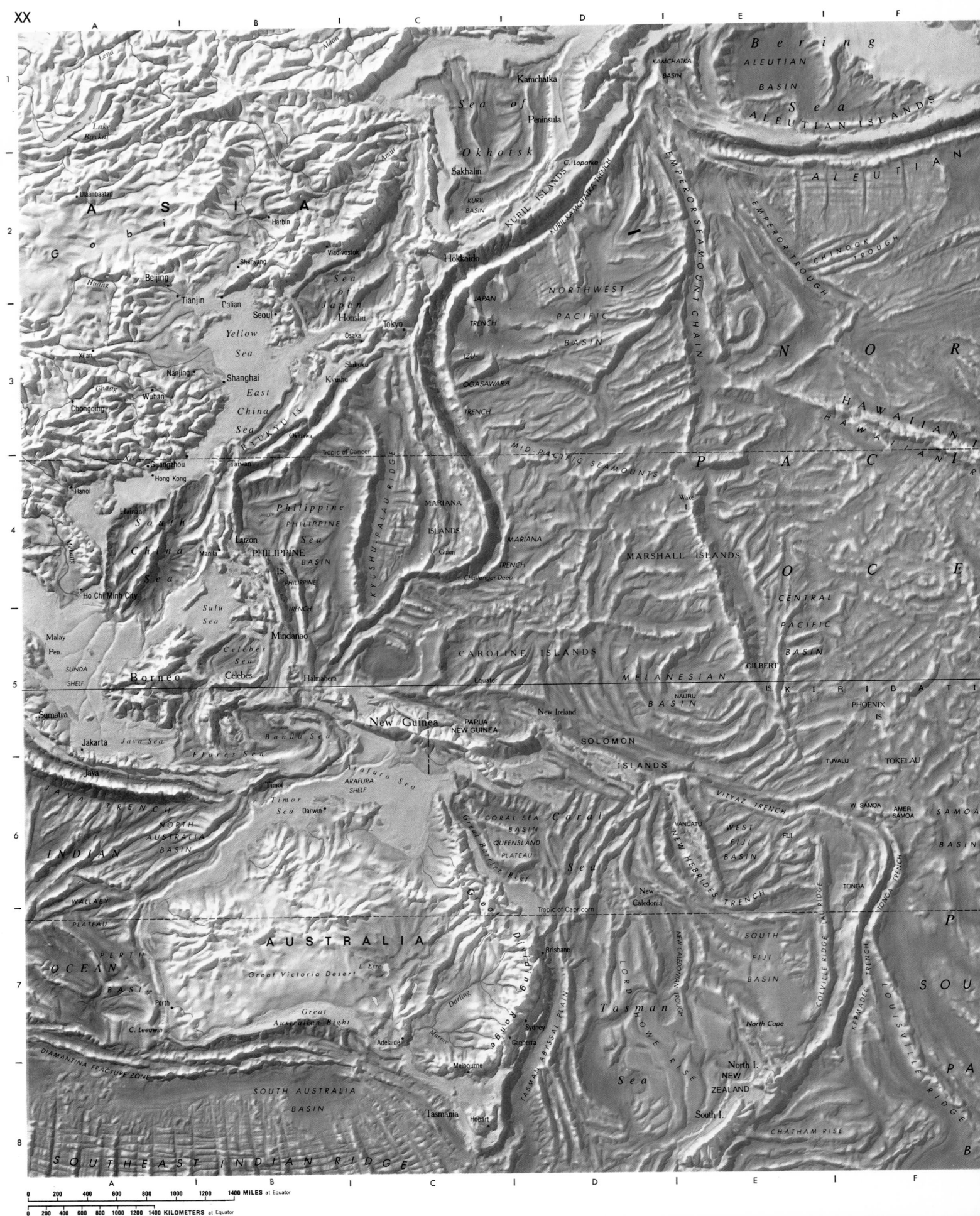

A | I | B | I | C | I | D | I | E | I | F

1

Lena

Lake Baykal

ASIA

Ulaanbaatar

G o b i

Huang

Beijing
Tianjin
Dalian
Shenyang
Harbin

Amur

Vladivostok

Seoul
Osaka

Sea of Japan

Honshu
Tokyo
Shikoku
Kyushu

Sakhalin

KURIL BASIN

KURIL ISLANDS

Sea of Okhotsk

Kamchatka
Peninsula

C. Lopatka

KAMCHATKA BASIN

Bering Sea

ALEUTIAN BASIN

ALEUTIAN ISLANDS

A L E U T I A N

EMPEROR SEAMOUNT CHAIN

EMPEROR TROUGH

CHINOOK TROUGH

N O R

2

Hokkaido

JAPAN TRENCH

IZU

OGASAWARA TRENCH

KURIL-KAMCHATKA TRENCH

NORTHWEST PACIFIC BASIN

3

Xi'an

Chang

Wuhan
Chongqing

Nanjing

Shanghai

Yellow Sea

East China Sea

RYUKYU IS.

Guangzhou
Hong Kong

Hainan

Hanoi

Tropic of Cancer

Taiwan
Okinawa

MID-PACIFIC SEAMOUNTS

P A C I F I

HAWAIIAN

HAWAIIAN

4

M e k o n g

South China Sea

Ho Chi Minh City

Manila
Luzon
PHILIPPINE IS.

PHILIPPINE SEA

PHILIPPINE BASIN

PHILIPPINE TRENCH

KYUSHU-PALAU RIDGE

MARIANA ISLANDS

Guam

MARIANA TRENCH

Challenger Deep

Wake I.

MARSHALL ISLANDS

O C E

CENTRAL PACIFIC BASIN

Malay Pen.

SUNDA SHELF

Borneo

Sulu Sea

Celebes Sea

Celebes
Halmahera

CAROLINE ISLANDS

GILBERT

MELANESIAN

KIRIBATI

5

Equator

Mindanao

Sumatra

Jakarta

Java

Java Sea

Flores Sea

Banda Sea

New Guinea

PAPUA NEW GUINEA

New Ireland

SOLOMON ISLANDS

BASIN

NAURU BASIN

PHOENIX IS.

TUVALU

TOKELAU

6

JAVA TRENCH

INDIAN

NORTH AUSTRALIA BASIN

Timor

Timor Sea

Darwin

Arafura Sea

ARAFURA SHELF

Great Barrier Reef

CORAL SEA BASIN

QUEENSLAND PLATEAU

C o r a l

Coral Sea

VANUATU

NEW HEBRIDES TRENCH

VITYAZ TRENCH

WEST FIJI BASIN

Fiji

TONGA

W. SAMOA

AMER. SAMOA

SAMOA BASIN

7

WALLABY PLATEAU

PERTH BASIN

OCEAN

AUSTRALIA

Great Victoria Desert

L. Eyre

Great Australian Bight

Perth

C. Leeuwin

Darling

Murray

Adelaide

Brisbane

Dividing Range

Sydney
Canberra

Melbourne

New Caledonia

Tropic of Capricorn

LORD HOWE RISE

NEW CALEDONIAN TROUGH

COLVILLE RIDGE

KERMADEC TRENCH

SOUTH FIJI BASIN

North Cape

SOU

PA

LOUISVILLE RIDGE

8

DIAMANTINA FRACTURE ZONE

SOUTH AUSTRALIA BASIN

Tasmania
Hobart

TASMAN ABYSSAL PLAIN

Tasman Sea

North I.
NEW ZEALAND

South I.

CHATHAM RISE

P

B

S O U T H E A S T   I N D I A N   R I D G E

A | I | B | I | C | I | D | I | E | I | F

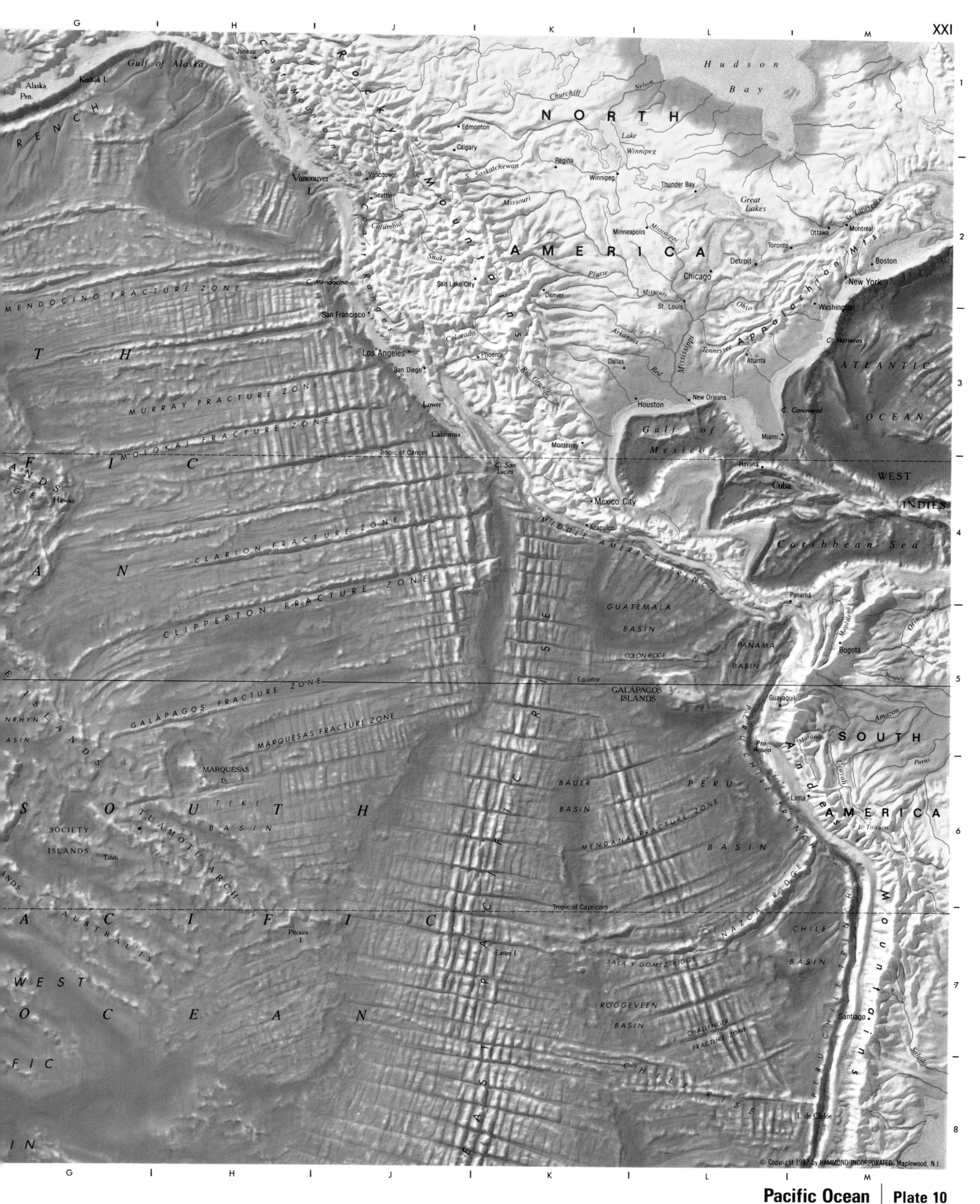

Pacific Ocean | Plate 10

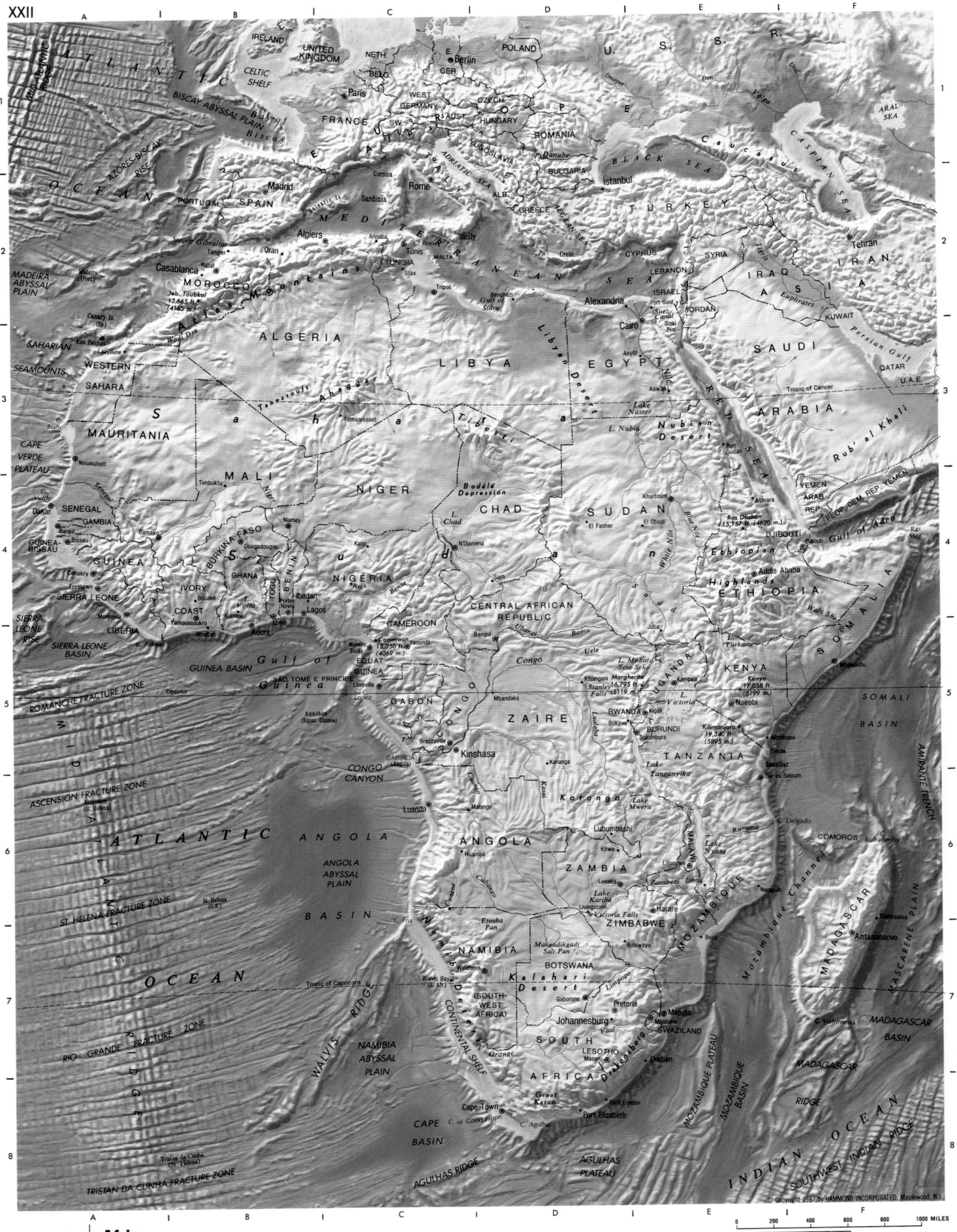

Plate 11 | **Africa**

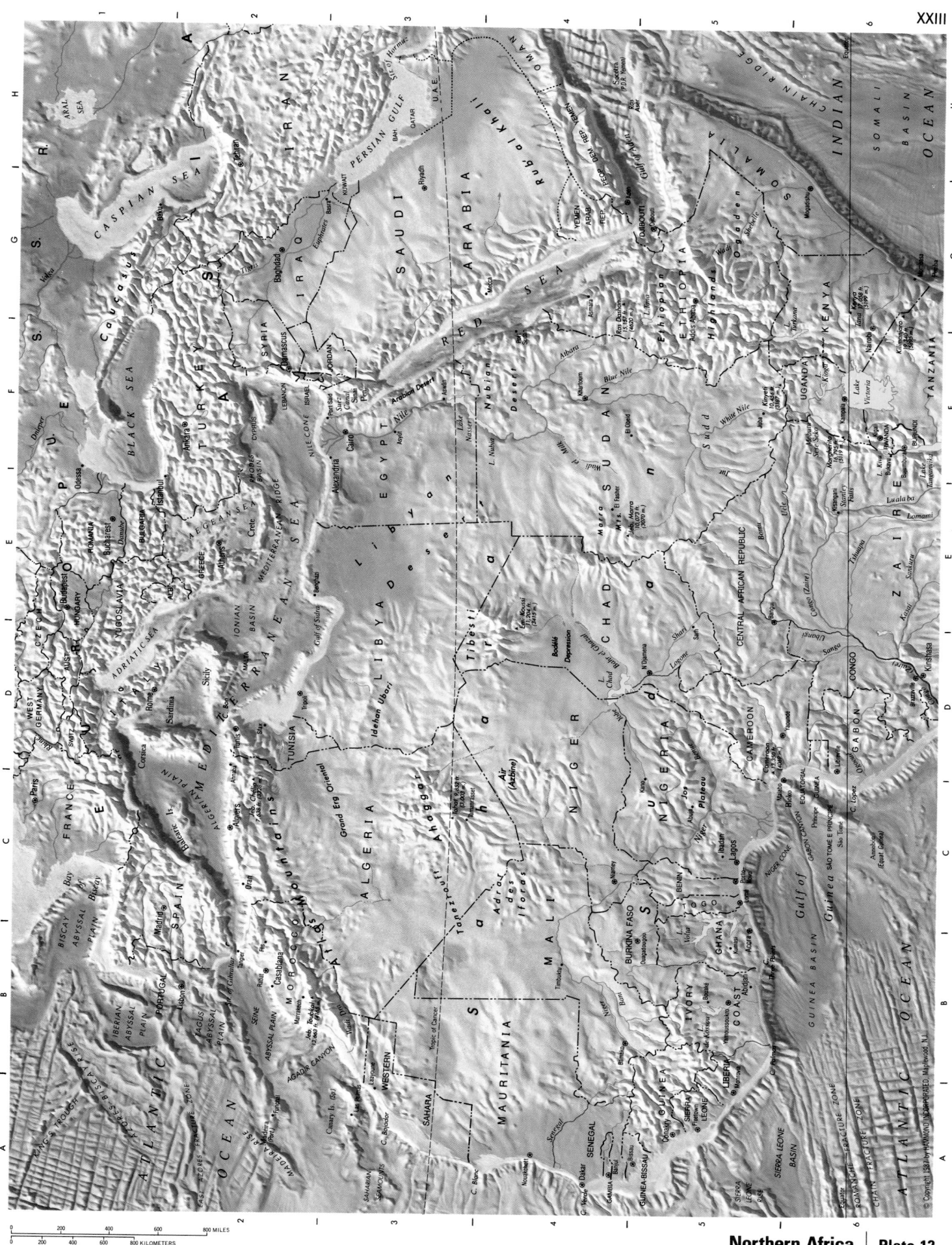

0   200   400   600   800 MILES
0   200   400   600   800 KILOMETERS

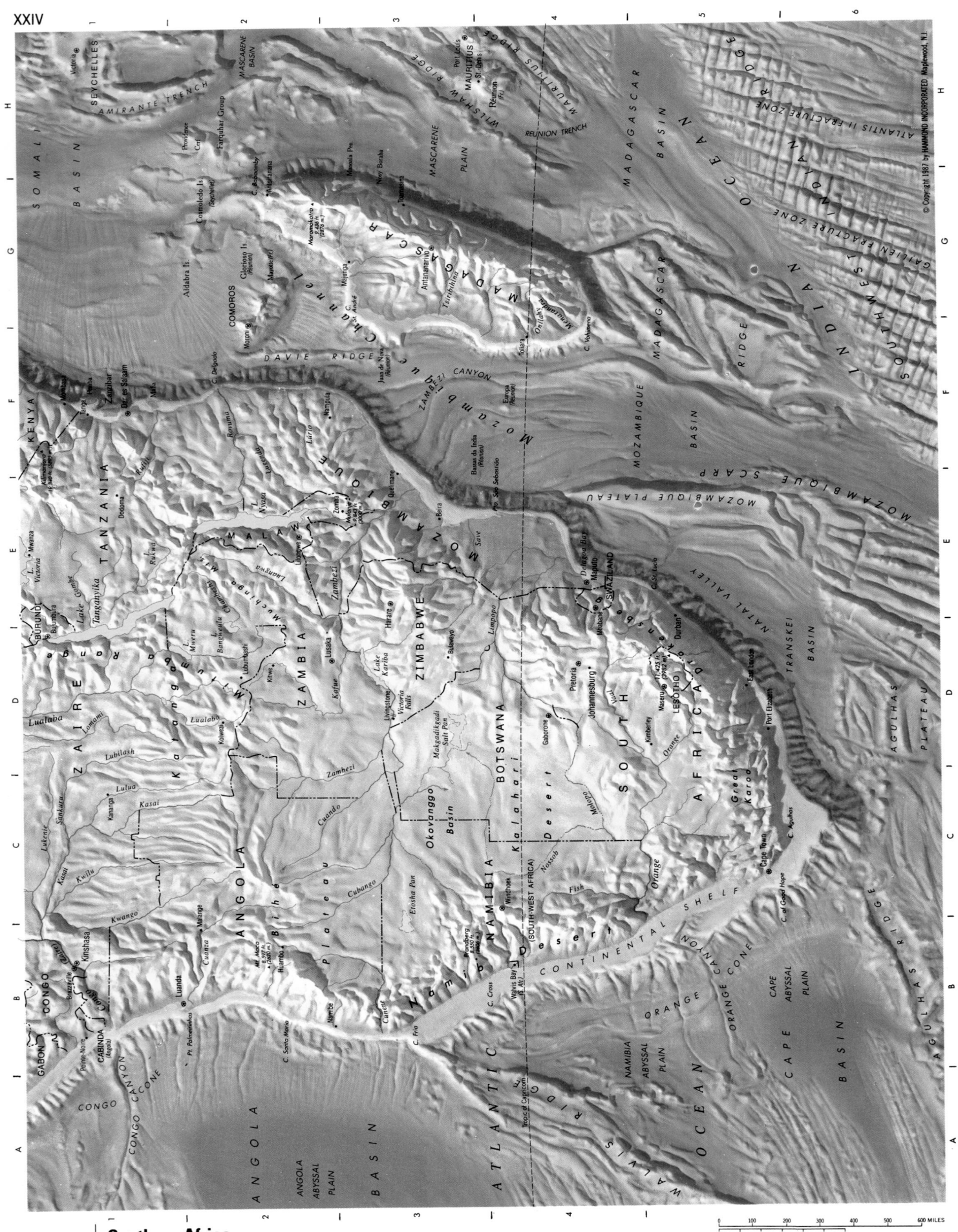

© Copyright 1987 by HAMMOND INCORPORATED, Maplewood, N.J.

Plate 13 | **Southern Africa**

0   100   200   300   400   500   600 MILES

0   100   200   300   400   500   600 KILOMETERS

© Copyright 1987 by HAMMOND INCORPORATED, Maplewood, N.J.

South America | Plate 14

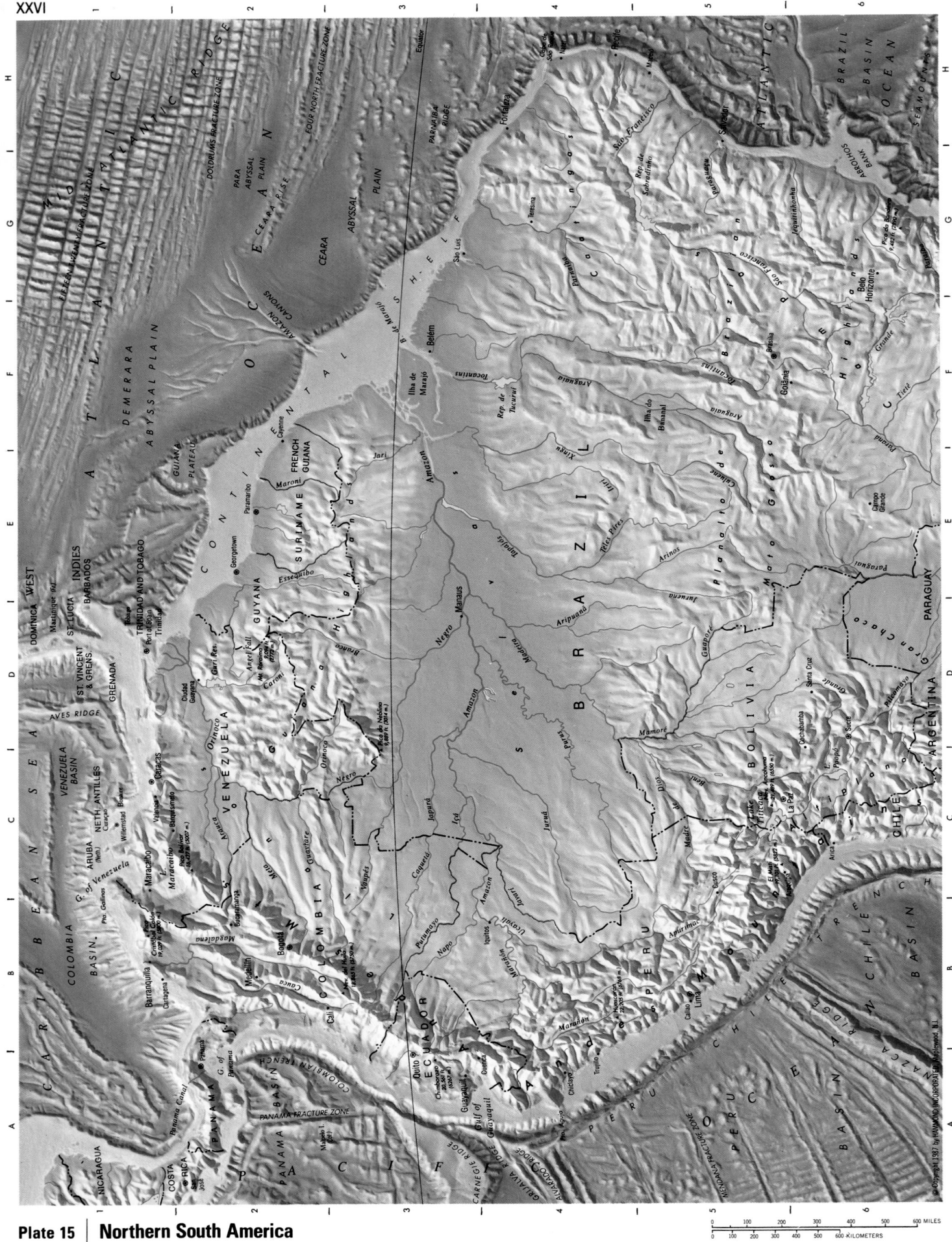

Plate 15 | **Northern South America**

PERU

BOLIVIA

La Paz

BRAZIL

Brazilian

Highlands

Brasília

Goiânia

Belo
Horizonte

Mato Grosso

Planalto de

Cusco

El Misti
19,101 ft.
(5822 m.)

Arequipa

Lake
Titicaca

Cochabamba

Santa
Cruz

Sucre

Campo Grande

Pico
da Bandeira
9,482 ft. (7890 m.)

C. de São Tomé

PARAGUAY

São Paulo

Rio de Janeiro

Tropic of Capricorn

Santos

CHILE

Antofagasta

Vol. Llullaillaco
22,057 ft.
(6723 m.)

Nev. Ojos del Salado
22,572 ft. (6880 m.)

San Miguel
de Tucumán

Asunción

Itaipu
Res.

Iguazú
Falls

Curitiba

I. de Santa
Catarina

SANTOS
PLATEAU

ARGENTINA

Corrientes

Posadas

Porto Alegre

RIO GRANDE
PLATEAU

La Serena

Córdoba

Santa Fe

Salto

Lagoa dos Patos

Cerro
Aconcagua
22,831 ft.
(6959 m.)

Valparaíso

Santiago

Mendoza

Rosario

Negro

URUGUAY

Lagoa
Mirim

ATLANTIC

CHILE

Buenos Aires

La Plata

Río de la Plata

Montevideo

Concepción

C.
San Antonio

OCEAN

Temuco

Colorado

Mar del
Plata

ARGENTINE

Puerto
Montt

Negro

Bahía
Blanca

BASIN

Isla de
Chiloé

Golfo San Matías

Pen. Valdés

ARGENTINE RISE

Archipiélago
de los
Chonos

Chubut

Commodoro
Rivadavia

Golfo San Jorge

ZAPIOLA RIDGE

Pen.
Taitao

Deseado

C. Tres Puntas

ARGENTINE ABYSSAL PLAIN

G. de Penas

FALKLAND ESCARPMENT

Archipiélago
Reina Adelaida

Bahía Grande

Falkland
Islands
(U.K.)

Stanley

FALKLAND
PLATEAU

MAURICE
EWING
BANK

FALKLAND RIDGE

GEORGIA
BASIN

MORNINGTON
ABYSSAL
PLAIN

Str. of Magellan

Punta Arenas

Tierra del Fuego

BURWOOD
BANK

NORTH SCOTIA RIDGE

NORTHWEST
GEORGIA RISE

South
Georgia
(U.K.)

Cape Horn

YAGHAN
BASIN

SCOTIA SEA

DRAKE

PASSAGE

FRACTURE ZONES

ONA BASIN

Southern South America | **Plate 16**

0   100   200   300   400   500   600 MILES

0   100   200   300   400   500   600 KILOMETERS

Plate 17 | North America

Canada | **Plate 18**

© Copyright 1987 by HAMMOND INCORPORATED Maplewood, N.J.

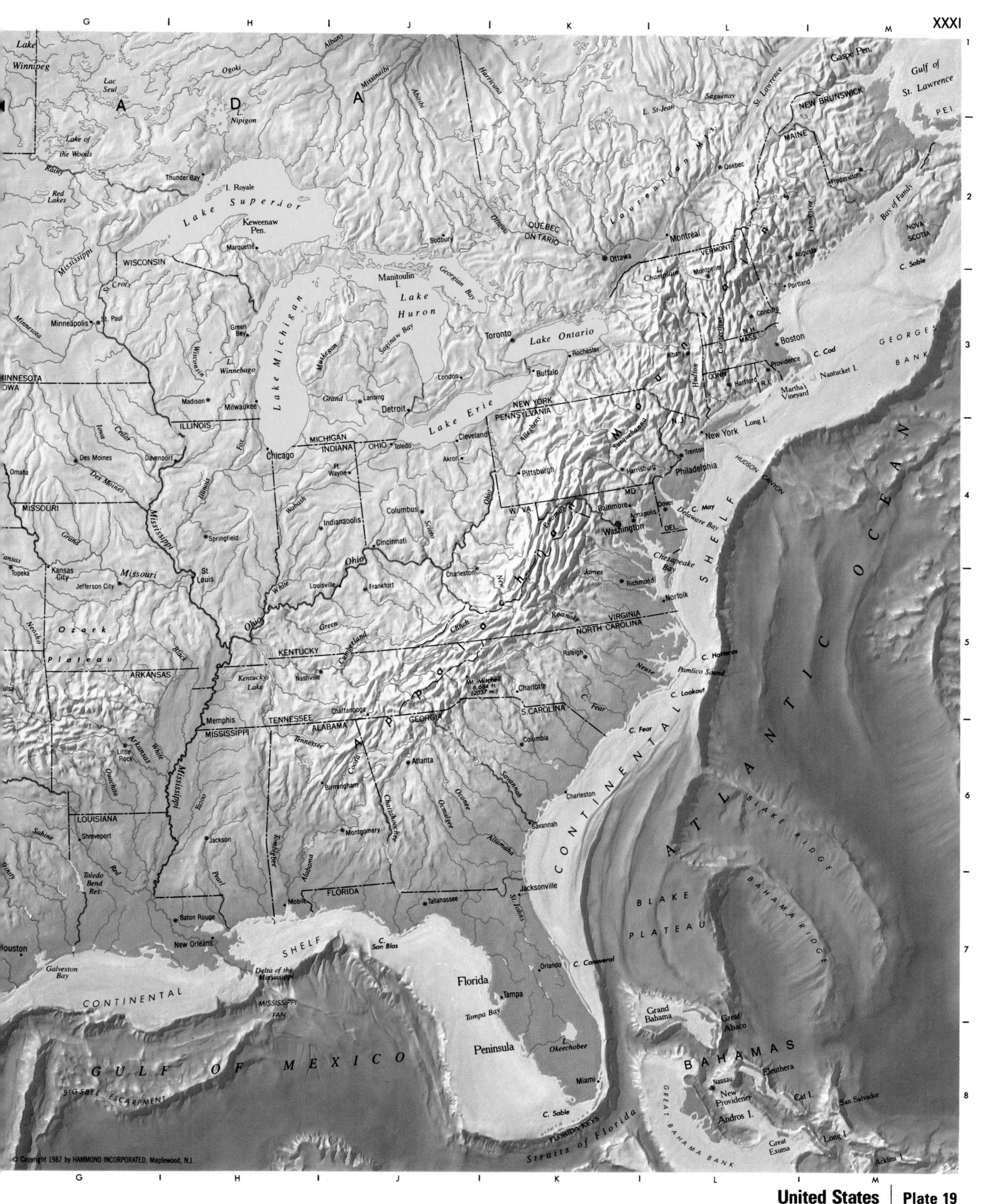

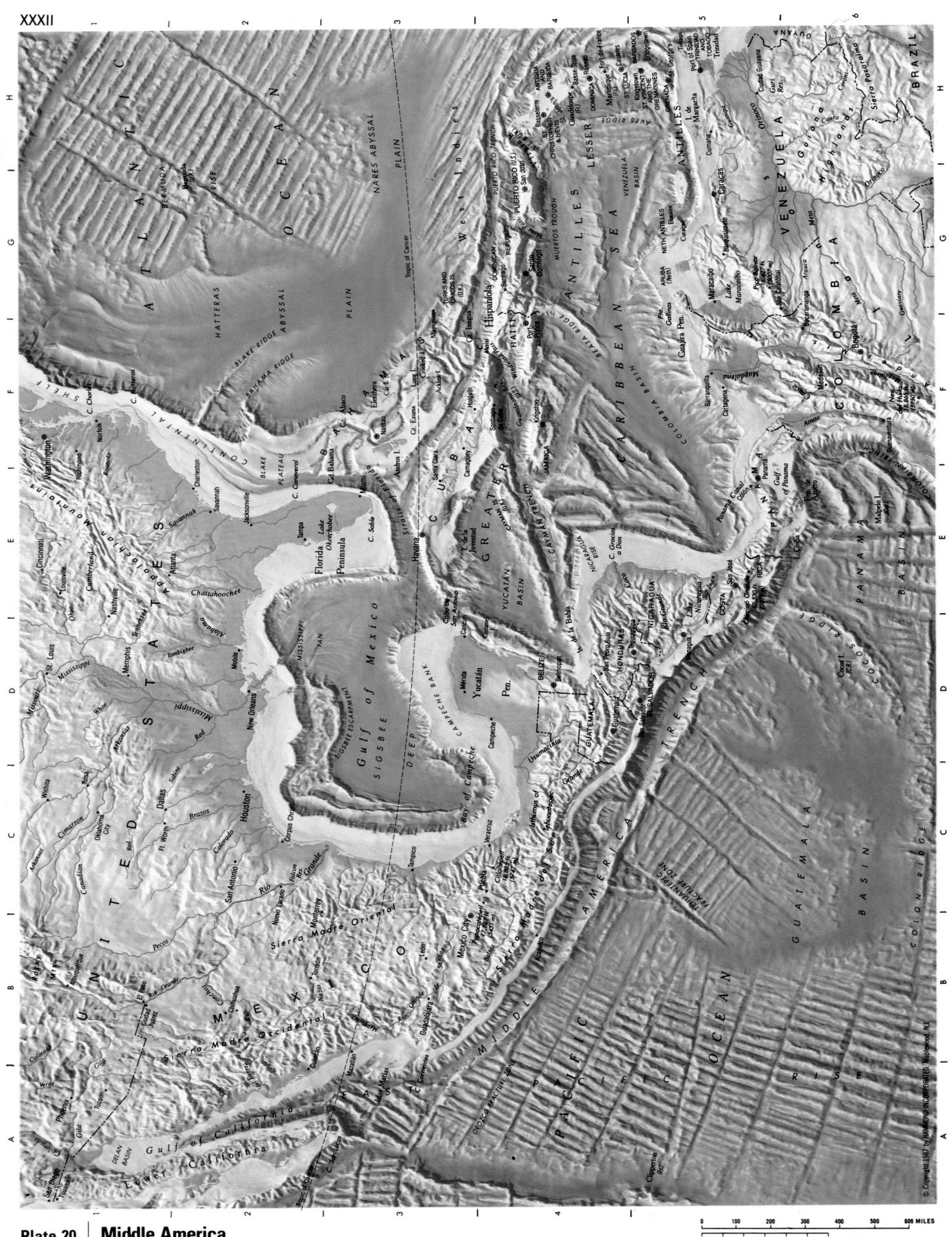

ATLANTIC OCEAN

BERMUDA RISE

Bermuda (U.K.)

C. Hatteras

C. Charles

HATTERAS ABYSSAL PLAIN

NARES ABYSSAL PLAIN

BLAKE RIDGE ABYSSAL PLAIN

BAHAMA RIDGE

Tropic of Cancer

Washington
Richmond
Norfolk
Roanoke
Charleston
Savannah
Jacksonville

CONTINENTAL SHELF

CONTINENTAL RISE

BLAKE PLATEAU

C. Canaveral

WEST INDIES

PUERTO RICO TRENCH

San Juan

PUERTO RICO (U.S.)

DOMINICAN REPUBLIC

MUERTOS TROUGH

LESSER ANTILLES

ANTIGUA AND BARBUDA
ST. CHRISTOPHER & NEVIS
DOMINICA (Fr.)
Basse-Terre
Pointe-à-Pitre
GUADELOUPE (Fr.)
MARTINIQUE (Fr.)
Fort-de-France
ST. LUCIA
ST. VINCENT AND THE GRENADINES
GRENADA
St. George's

BARBADOS
Bridgetown

Kingstown

I. de Margarita

AVES RIDGE

VENEZUELA BASIN

NETH. ANTILLES
Bonaire
Curaçao
ARUBA (Neth.)

Trinidad
Port of Spain
TRINIDAD AND TOBAGO

Cumaná

Caracas

VENEZUELA

GUAYANA

Cd. Guayana
Guri Res.
Orinoco

Guiana Highlands

Sierra Pacaraima

BRAZIL

Orinoco

Meta

Barquisimeto
Pico Bolívar
(16,411 ft.)
(5,002 m.)
San Cristóbal

Bucaramanga

COLOMBIA

Bogotá

Medellín

Magdalena

Barranquilla
Cartagena
Atrato
Buenaventura

HONDURAS TRENCH

COLOMBIA BASIN

CARIBBEAN SEA

BEATA RIDGE

GREATER ANTILLES

Havana
T. de la Juventud
Cd. Cárdenas
San Antonio
Matanzas
Camagüey
Santa Clara

CUBA

JAMAICA
Kingston

CAYMAN TRENCH

Santiago de Cuba
Guantánamo (U.S.)
Holguín

Hispaniola

HAITI
Port-au-Prince

DOMINICAN REPUBLIC
Santo Domingo
Santiago

TURKS AND CAICOS IS. (U.K.)

BAHAMAS

Great Inagua
Acklin I.
Crooked I.
Long I.
Cat I.
Eleuthera
Gt. Exuma

Mayaguana

Nassau
Gd. Bahama
Gt. Abaco

Andros I.

Miami

Tampa
Lake Okeechober
C. Sable

Florida Peninsula

Gulf of Mexico

Straits of Florida

YUCATÁN BASIN

NICARAGUA RISE

C. Gracias a Dios

C. Catoche
Cancún
Mérida

Yucatán Pen.

Cozumel

BELIZE
Belmopan

CAMPECHE BANK

SIGSBEE DEEP

SIGSBEE ESCARPMENT

Campeche

Bay of Campeche

Veracruz

Coatzacoalcos

Isthmus of Tehuantepec

Villahermosa

Usumacinta

GUATEMALA
Guatemala

EL SALVADOR
San Salvador

HONDURAS
Tegucigalpa
San Pedro Sula

NICARAGUA
Managua
Lake Nicaragua

COSTA RICA
San José

Lake Managua

Coco

Cordillera Oriental

PANAMA

Panamá
Panama Canal
Colón
Gulf of Panamá

Pen. de Azuero

COSTA RICA (C.R.)

Cocos I. (C.R.)

Golfito

MIDDLE AMERICA TRENCH

PACIFIC OCEAN

GUATEMALA BASIN

TEHUANTEPEC FRACTURE ZONE

COCOS RIDGE

PANAMA BASIN

COLÓN RIDGE

MALPELO FRACTURE ZONE

Malpelo I. (Col.)

EAST PACIFIC RISE

Clipperton (Fr.)

Clarion Fracture Zone

 UNITED STATES

Cincinnati
Louisville
Ohio
Nashville
Memphis
St. Louis
Missouri
Mississippi
Cumberland
Tennessee
Chattahoochee
Alabama
Tombigbee
Mobile
Atlanta
Savannah

APPALACHIAN MTS.

New Orleans

Red
Arkansas
White
Sabine
Brazos
Houston
Corpus Christi
Dallas
Ft. Worth
San Antonio
Oklahoma City
Wichita
Tulsa
Canadian
Cimarron
Arkansas

Rio Grande

ROCKY MTS.

Albuquerque
El Paso
Ciudad Juárez
Chihuahua
Pecos
Colorado
Gila
Phoenix
Tucson
Verde
San Diego
Tijuana
Colorado

Gulf of California

Lower California

C. San Lucas

La Paz
Mazatlán
Culiacán
Tepic
Guadalajara
Aguascalientes
León
Torreón
Saltillo
Monterrey
Nuevo Laredo
Tampico

MEXICO

Sierra Madre Occidental
Sierra Madre Oriental
Sierra Madre del Sur

Mexico City
Puebla
Popocatépetl
(17,887 ft.)
(5,452 m.)
Orizaba
(18,855 ft.)
(5,747 m.)

Rio Grande

DELTA BASIN

Plate 20 | Middle America

© Copyright 1987 by HAMMOND INCORPORATED, Maplewood, N.J.

0 100 200 300 400 500 600 MILES
0 100 200 300 400 500 600 KILOMETERS

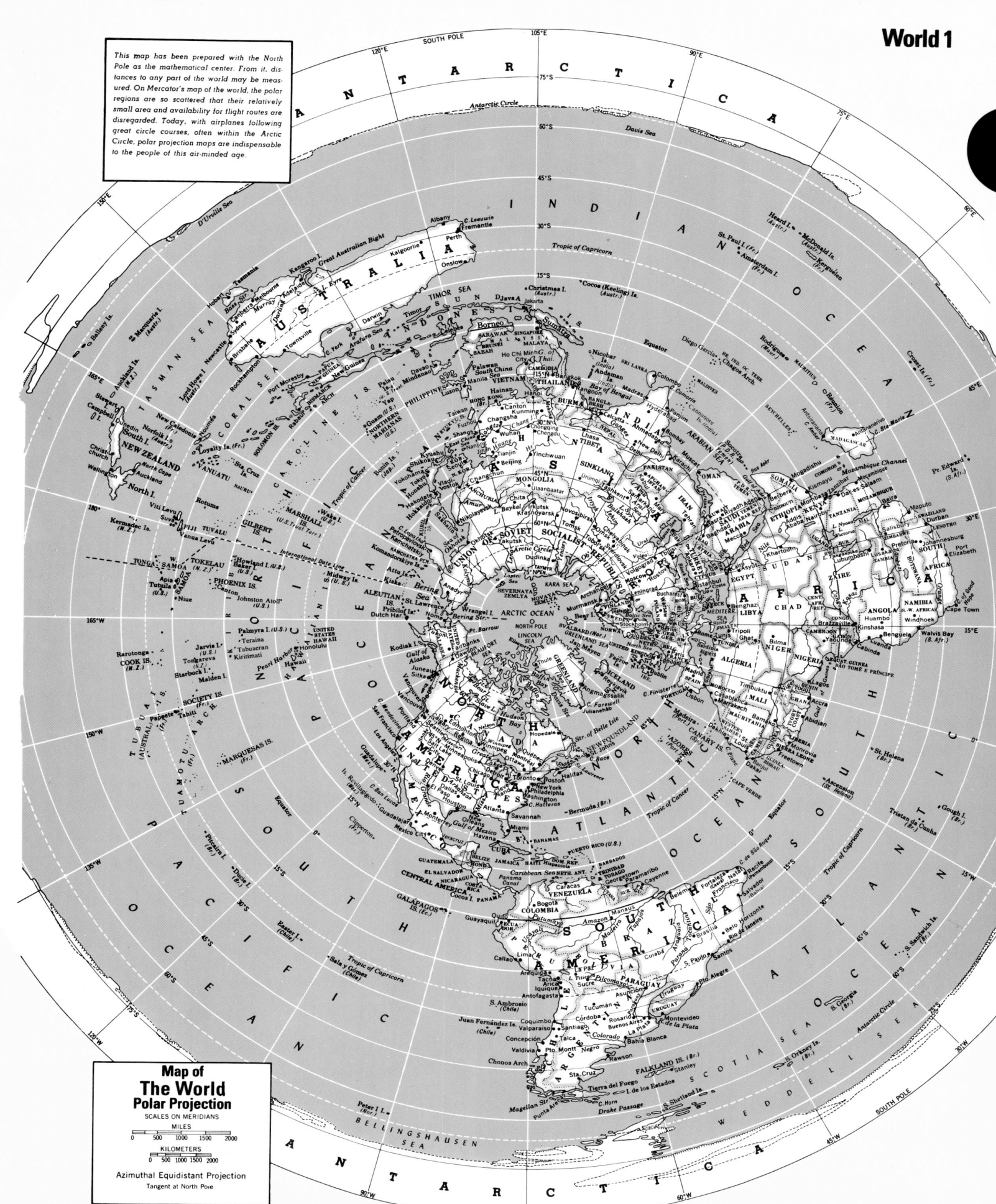

World 1

This map has been prepared with the North Pole as the mathematical center. From it, distances to any part of the world may be measured. On Mercator's map of the world, the polar regions are so scattered that their relatively small area and availability for flight routes are disregarded. Today, with airplanes following great circle courses, often within the Arctic Circle, polar projection maps are indispensable to the people of this air-minded age.

Map of
The World
Polar Projection
SCALES ON MERIDIANS

MILES

| 0 | 500 | 1000 | 1500 | 2000 |

KILOMETERS

| 0 | 500 | 1000 | 1500 | 2000 |

Azimuthal Equidistant Projection
Tangent at North Pole

© Copyright HAMMOND INCORPORATED

The World

BRIESEMEISTER ELLIPTICAL
EQUAL-AREA PROJECTION

Capitals of Countries ....⊗
Other Capitals...........................◉
International Boundaries.... – – –

Time Zones

STANDARD		Areas using half hour deviations.
TIME		
ZONES		Areas not using zone system.

NOTE: Standard time zones in the U.S.S.R. are always advanced one hour.

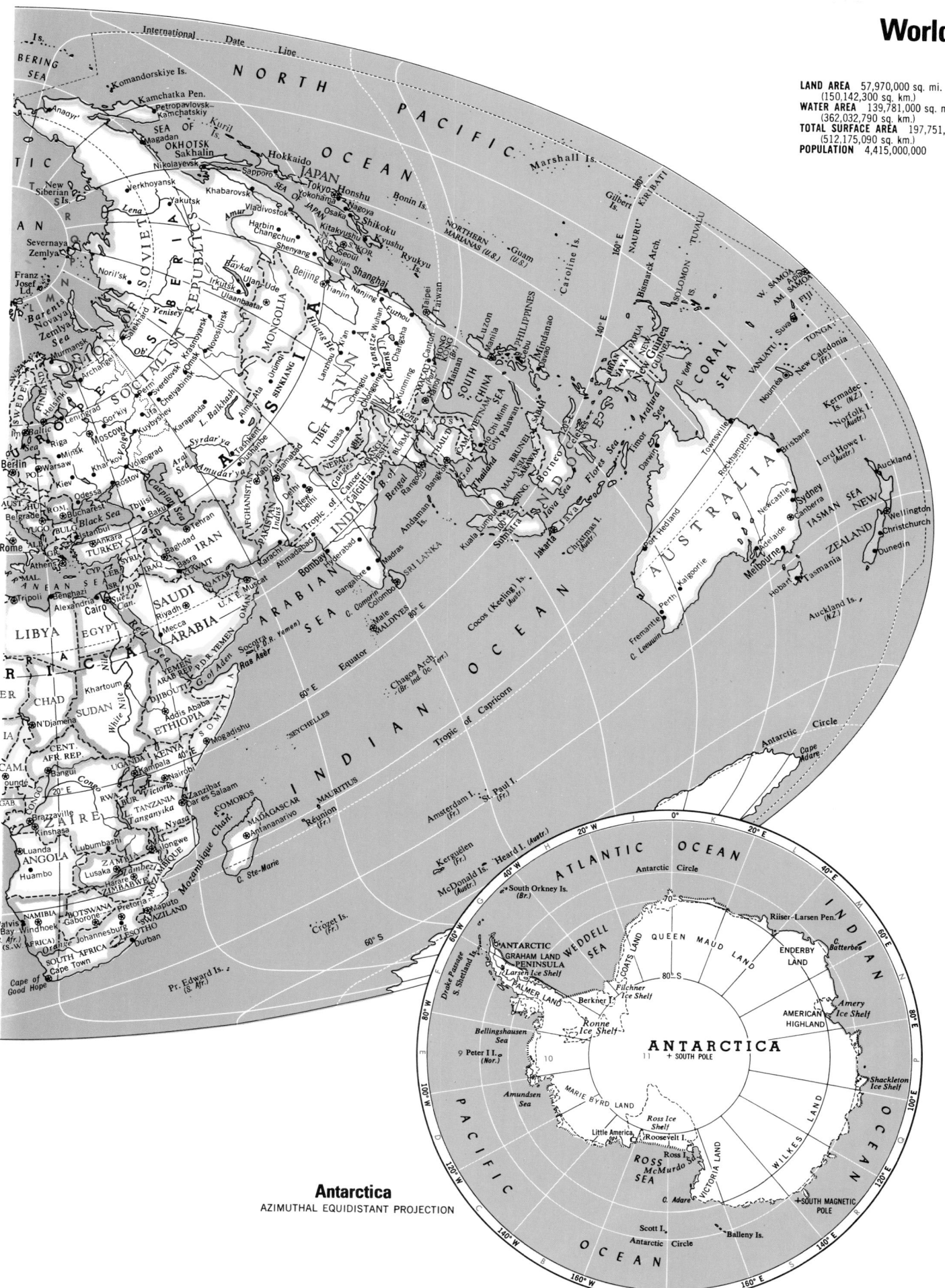

LAND AREA 57,970,000 sq. mi.
(150,142,300 sq. km.)
WATER AREA 139,781,000 sq. mi.
(362,032,790 sq. km.)
TOTAL SURFACE AREA 197,751,000 sq.mi.
(512,175,090 sq. km.)
POPULATION 4,415,000,000

NORTH PACIFIC OCEAN

BERING SEA

International Date Line

Is.

Komandorskiye Is.

Kamchatka Pen.
Petropavlovsk-Kamchatskiy
Anadyr'
Magadan
Kuril Is.
SEA OF OKHOTSK
Nikolayevsk
Sakhalin
Hokkaido
Marshall Is.
Bonin Is.
Sapporo
Verkhoyansk
JAPAN
Tokyo
Honshu
Yokohama
Nagoya
Osaka
Kyushu
Shikoku
Khabarovsk
Vladivostok
Harbin
Changchun
Shenyang
KOR.
Seoul
Ryukyu Is.
Dalian
Beijing
Tianjin
Nanjing
Shanghai

Gilbert Is.
KIRIBATI
NAURU
TUVALU

NORTHERN MARIANAS (U.S.)
Guam (U.S.)
Caroline Is.

Lena
Yakutsk
Amur
Verkhoyansk
Severnaya Zemlya
Noril'sk
Yenisey
SOVIET SOCIALIST REPUBLICS
SIBERIA
MONGOLIA
Ulaanbaatar
Irkutsk
Ulan-Ude
Baykal
Krasnoyarsk
Novosibirsk
Omsk
CHINA
Huang He
Lanzhou
Xi'an
Chengdu
Wuhan
Changsha
Fuzhou
Taipei
Taiwan
HONG KONG
MACAO Canton
Hainan

PHILIPPINES
Luzon
Manila
Cebu
Mindanao
Davao

Bismarck Arch.
SOLOMON IS.
W. SAMOA
AM. SAMOA
FIJI

Bairtic Sea
SWEDEN
FINLAND
Helsinki
Leningrad
Gorkiy
Moscow
Kuybyshev
UNION
Riga
Minsk
EUROPE
Berlin
Warsaw
POL.
Kiev
Kharkov
Volgograd
Rostov
Sverdlovsk
Chelyabinsk
Ufa
Karaganda
L. Balkhash
Alma-Ata
Tashkent
Frunze
Syrdar'ya
Amudar'ya
SINKIANG
Urumqi
TIBET
Lhasa
BURMA
LAOS
VIETNAM
THAILAND
Bangkok
KAMPUCHEA
Ho Chi Minh City
SOUTH CHINA SEA
Palawan
SABAH
BRUNEI
SARAWAK
MALAYSIA
Kuala Lumpur
SINGAPORE
Borneo
Celebes Sea
Celebes
INDONESIA
Sumatra
Java
Jakarta
Java Sea
Flores Sea
Timor
Timor Sea
Arafura Sea

PAPUA NEW GUINEA
New Guinea

VANUATU
New Caledonia (Fr.)
Noumea
TONGA
Suva

CORAL SEA
Townsville
Rockhampton
Brisbane

Kermadec Is. (N.Z.)
Norfolk I. (Austr.)
Lord Howe I. (Austr.)
Auckland

Caspian Sea
Baku
Tbilisi
Tehran
IRAN
AFGHANISTAN
Kabul
Islamabad
PAKISTAN
Karachi
NEPAL
Ganges
BANGLADESH
Calcutta
BHUTAN
B. of Bengal
Rangoon
Andaman Is.
Delhi
New Delhi
Tropic of Cancer
INDIA
Ahmadabad
Bombay
Hyderabad
Madras
Bangalore
C. Comorin
Colombo
SRI LANKA
MALDIVES
Male

Christmas I. (Austr.)

AUSTRALIA
Port Hedland
Darwin
Alice Springs
Kalgoorlie
Perth
Fremantle
C. Leeuwin
Adelaide
Melbourne
Canberra
Sydney
Newcastle
Hobart
Tasmania

TASMAN SEA
NEW ZEALAND
Auckland
Wellington
Christchurch
Dunedin

Rome
Athens
MAL.
MEDITERRANEAN SEA
Tripoli
Benghazi
Alexandria
Cairo
LIBYA
EGYPT
Nile
Istanbul
Ankara
TURKEY
CYP.
LEB.
SYRIA
IRAQ
Baghdad
Basra
KUWAIT
ISR.
JOR.
Suez Can.
Mecca
SAUDI ARABIA
Riyadh
QATAR
U.A.E.
Muscat
OMAN
YEMEN ARAB REP.
P.D.R. YEMEN
G. of Aden
Socotra (P.D.R. Yemen)
Ras Asir
Aden

ARABIAN SEA

Cocos (Keeling) Is. (Austr.)

Equator

INDIAN OCEAN

SEYCHELLES

Chagos Arch. (Br. Ind. Oc. Terr.)

Tropic of Capricorn

Antarctic Circle

Cape Adare

Amsterdam I. (Fr.)
St. Paul I. (Fr.)

Kerguelen (Fr.)
McDonald Is. (Austr.)
Heard I. (Austr.)

MAURITIUS
Réunion (Fr.)

Crozet Is. (Fr.)

60° S

Pr. Edward Is. (S. Afr.)

ER
CHAD
N'Djamena
SUDAN
Khartoum
White Nile
DJIBOUTI
ETHIOPIA
Addis Ababa
SOMALIA
Mogadishu
IA
CENT. AFR. REP.
Bangui
CAM.
Yaoundé
GAB.
UGANDA
Kampala
KENYA
Nairobi
RW.
BUR.
TANZANIA
Tanganyika
Zanzibar
Dar es Salaam
COMOROS
CONGO
Brazzaville
Kinshasa
ZAIRE
Lubumbashi
ANGOLA
Luanda
Huambo
ZAMBIA
Lusaka
Zambezi
Lilongwe
L. Victoria
Nyasa
MOZAMBIQUE
Mozambique Chan.
MADAGASCAR
Antananarivo
C. Ste-Marie
Réunion

40° E

20° E

60° E

NAMIBIA
Walvis Bay (S. Afr.)
Windhoek
BOTSWANA
Gaborone
SOUTH AFRICA (S.-W. AFRICA)
Orange
Johannesburg
Pretoria
ZIMBABWE
Harare
Maputo
SWAZILAND
LESOTHO
Durban
Cape Town
Cape of Good Hope

Antarctica
AZIMUTHAL EQUIDISTANT PROJECTION

ATLANTIC OCEAN
Antarctic Circle

40° W
20° W
0°
20° E
40° E

South Orkney Is. (Br.)
Riiser-Larsen Pen.
Drake Passage
S. Shetland Is.
ANTARCTIC
GRAHAM LAND
PENINSULA
Larsen Ice Shelf
PALMER LAND
COATS LAND
WEDDELL SEA
QUEEN MAUD LAND
ENDERBY LAND
Batterbee
60° E
Filchner Ice Shelf
Berkner I.
Ronne Ice Shelf
AMERICAN HIGHLAND
Amery Ice Shelf
Bellingshausen Sea
80° S
Peter I I. (Nor.)
10
ANTARCTICA
+ SOUTH POLE
11
80° E
Shackleton Ice Shelf
Amundsen Sea
MARIE BYRD LAND
Ross Ice Shelf
WILKES LAND
Little America
Roosevelt I.
Ross I.
VICTORIA LAND
ROSS McMurdo SEA
C. Adare
+SOUTH MAGNETIC POLE
100° W
120° W
140° W
160° W
120° E
140° E
160° E

Scott I.
Balleny Is.
Antarctic Circle
PACIFIC OCEAN
INDIAN OCEAN
180°

© Copyright HAMMOND INCORPORATED Maplewood, N.J.

Arctic Ice

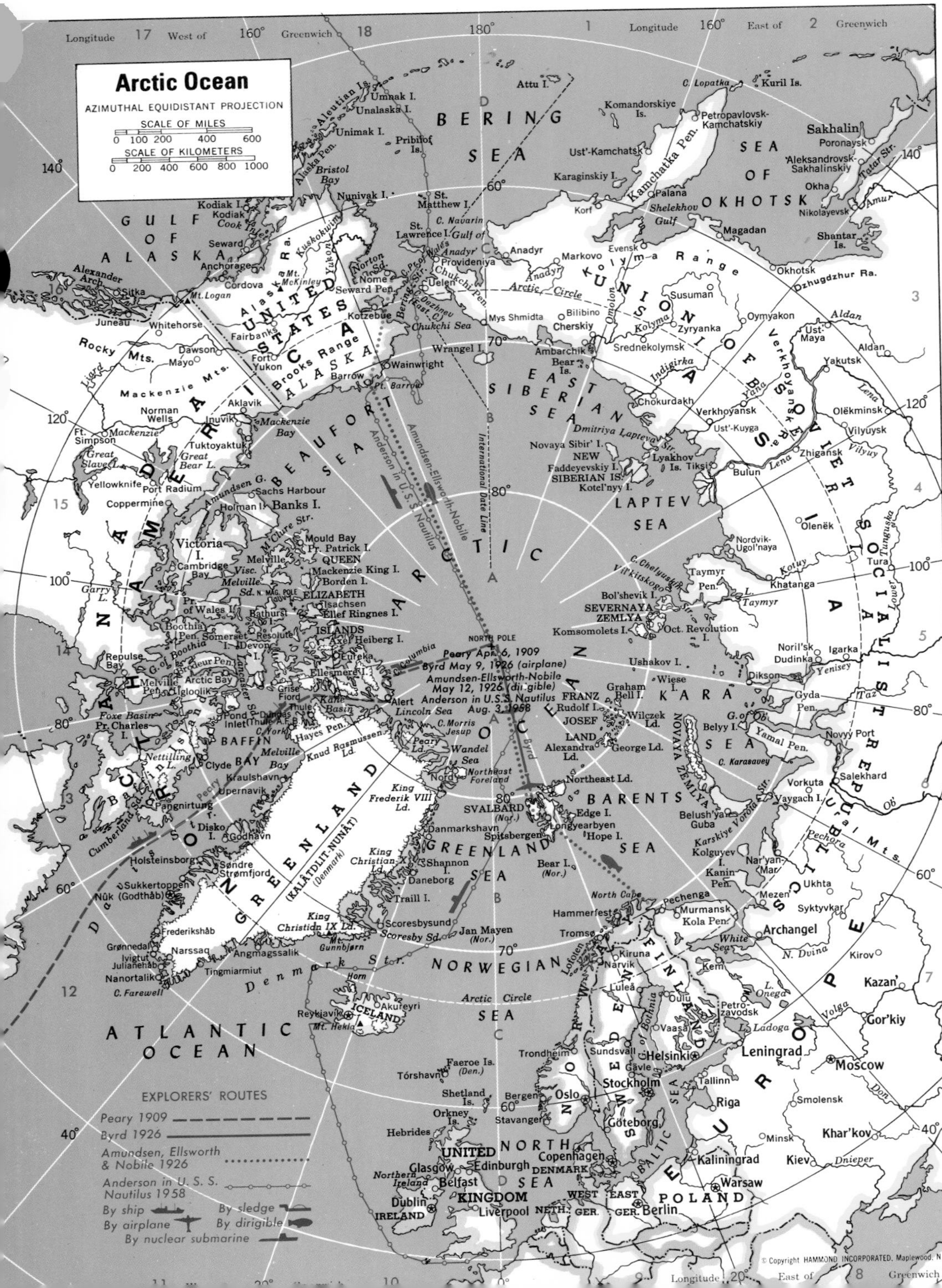

Arctic Ocean

AZIMUTHAL EQUIDISTANT PROJECTION

SCALE OF MILES
0 100 200 400 600

SCALE OF KILOMETERS
0 200 400 600 800 1000

EXPLORERS' ROUTES

Peary 1909
Byrd 1926
Amundsen, Ellsworth & Nobile 1926
Anderson in U.S.S. Nautilus 1958

By ship — By sledge
By airplane — By dirigible
By nuclear submarine

Antarctica
AZIMUTHAL EQUIDISTANT PROJECTION

SCALE OF MILES
0 200 400 600 800

KILOMETERS
0 200 400 600 800 1000

© Copyright HAMMOND INCORPORATED, Maplewood, N.J.

Adare (cape)	B9	Larsen Ice Shelf	C16
Adelaide (isl.)	C15	Lazarev Station	C1
Adélie Coast (reg.)	C7	Levick (mt.)	B8
Alexander (isl.)	B15	Lister (mt.)	B8
American Highland	B4	Little America	B10
Amery Ice Shelf	C4	Luitpold Coast (reg.)	B17
Amundsen (bay)	C3	Lützow-Holm (bay)	C3
Amundsen (sea)	B13	Mackenzie (bay)	C4
Amundsen-Scott Station	A14	Mac-Robertson Land (reg.)	B4
Antarctic (pen.)	C15	Marguerite (bay)	C15
Balleny (isls.)	C9	Marie Byrd Land (reg.)	B13
Banzare Coast (reg.)	C7	Markham (mt.)	A8
Barr Smith (mt.)	C5	Mawson	C4
Batterbee (cape)	C3	McMurdo (sound)	B9
Beardmore (glac.)	A8	Mertz Glacier Tongue	C8
Bellingshausen (sea)	C14	Mirnyy	C5
Berkner (isl.)	B16	New Schwabenland (reg.)	B1
Biscoe (isls.)	C15	Ninnis Glacier Tongue	C8
Bouvet (isl.)	D1	Norvegia (cape)	B18
Bouvetøya (Bouvet) (isl.)	D1	Oates Coast (reg.)	B8
Bransfield (str.)	C16	Palmer (arch.)	C15
Budd Coast (reg.)	C6	Palmer Land (reg.)	B15
Byrd Station	A12	Palmer Station	C15
Caird Coast (reg.)	B17	Peter I (isl.)	B14
Charcot (isl.)	C15	Prince Edward (isls.)	E2
Clarie Coast (reg.)	C7	Prince Olav Coast (reg.)	C3
Coats Land (reg.)	B17	Princess Astrid Coast (reg.)	B1
Colbeck (cape)	B10	Princess Martha Coast (reg.)	B18
Coronation (isl.)	C16	Princess Ragnhild Coast (reg.)	B2
Daly (cape)	C4	Prydz (bay)	C4
Darnley (cape)	C4	Queen Mary Coast (reg.)	C5
Dart (cape)	B12	Queen Maud (mts.)	A12
Davis (sea)	C4	Queen Maud Land (reg.)	B1
Davis Station	C4	Riiser-Larsen (pen.)	C2
Drake (passage)	C15	Ronne Entrance (inlet)	B15
Dumont d'Urville Station	C7	Ronne Ice Shelf	B16
Edward VII (pen.)	B11	Roosevelt (isl.)	A10
Edward VIII (bay)	C4	Ross (isl.)	B9
Eights Coast (reg.)	B14	Ross (sea)	B10
Elephant (isl.)	D16	Ross Ice Shelf	A10
Ellsworth Land (reg.)	B14	Sabine (mt.)	B14
Enderby Land (reg.)	B3	Sabrina Coast (reg.)	C6
English Coast (reg.)	B15	Sanae Station	B18
Executive Committee (range)	B12	Scotia (sea)	D16
Farr (bay)	C5	Scott (isl.)	C10
Filchner Ice Shelf	B16	Scott Station	B9
Ford Ranges (mts.)	B11	Shackleton Ice Shelf	C5
Gaussberg (mt.)	C5	Sidley (mt.)	B12
George V Coast (reg.)	C8	Siple (mt.)	B12
Getz Ice Shelf	B12	South Georgia (isl.)	D17
Goodenough (cape)	C7	South Magnetic Pole	C8
Graham Land (reg.)	C15	South Orkney (isls.)	C16
Grytviken	D17	South Polar (plat.)	A1
Hearst (isl.)	B16	South Pole	A4
Hilton (inlet)	B16	South Sandwich (isls.)	D17
Hobbs Coast (reg.)	B12	South Shetland (isls.)	C15
Hollick-Kenyon (plat.)	B13	Sulzberger (bay)	B11
Hope (bay)	C16	Thurston (isl.)	C14
Indian Ocean	C3	Transantarctic (mts.)	B17
James Ross (isl.)	C16	Victoria Land (reg.)	B8
Joinville (isl.)	C16	Vincennes (bay)	C6
Kainan (bay)	B10	Vinson Massif (mt.)	B14
Keltie (cape)	C7	Walgreen Coast (reg.)	B13
Kemp Coast (reg.)	C3	Weddell (sea)	C16
King George (isl.)	C16	West Ice Shelf	C5
Kirkpatrick (mt.)	A8	Wilhelm II Coast (reg.)	C5
Knox Coast (reg.)	C6	Wilkes Land (reg.)	B7

EXPLORERS' ROUTES

Palmer 1820
Amundsen 1910-12
Scott 1910-13
Byrd 1928-30
Fuchs 1957-58

By ship · By sledge · By airplane
By snow tractor

Amundsen Dec. 14, 1911
Scott Jan. 18, 1912
Byrd Nov. 29, 1929 (airplane)
Fuchs Jan. 19, 1958

AREA OF POLE OF INACCESSIBILITY

Weddell Sea

Traverse of Cross Section Shown Below

+ SOUTH POLE

ANTARCTICA

Ross Sea

Antarctic Cross Section: Weddell Sea to Ross Sea

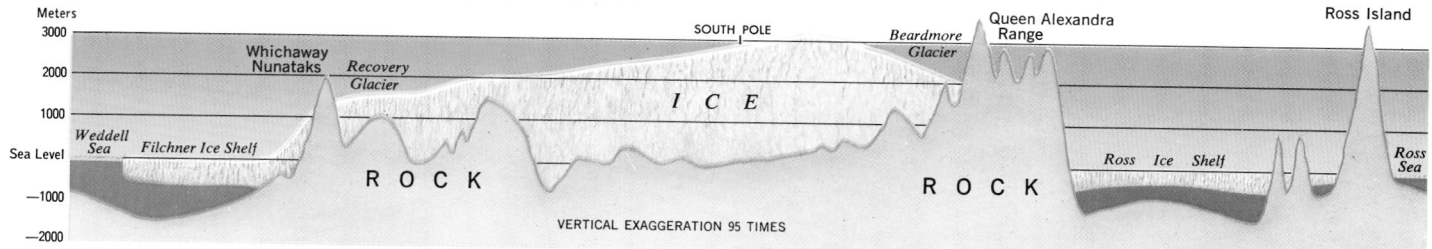

VERTICAL EXAGGERATION 95 TIMES

Information Based on American Geographical Society's "Antarctic Map Folio Series"

Europe

POLYCONIC PROJECTION

SCALE OF MILES
0 100 200 300 400

KILOMETERS
0 100 200 300 400

Capitals of Countries .... ⊛
Other Capitals .... ⊛
International Boundaries ....
Internal Boundaries ....
Canals ....

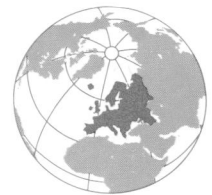

AREA   4,057,000 sq. mi.
(10,507,630 sq. km.)
POPULATION   676,000,000
LARGEST CITY   Paris
HIGHEST POINT   El'brus 18,510 ft.
(5,642 m.)
LOWEST POINT   Caspian Sea -92 ft.
(-28 m.)

Population Distribution

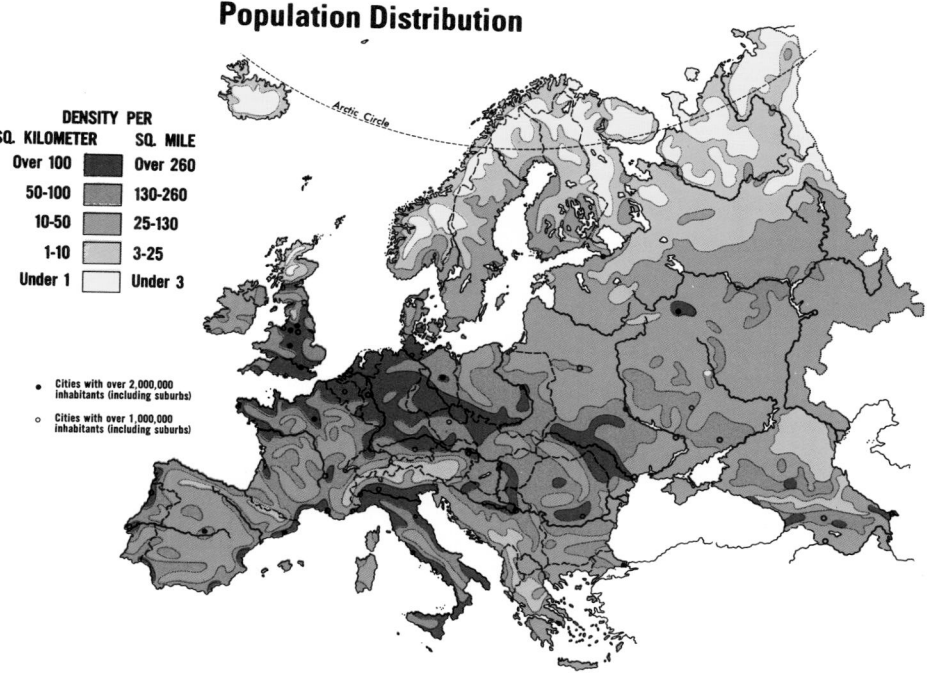

DENSITY PER

SQ. KILOMETER	SQ. MILE
Over 100	Over 260
50-100	130-260
10-50	25-130
1-10	3-25
Under 1	Under 3

● Cities with over 2,000,000
inhabitants (including suburbs)

○ Cities with over 1,000,000
inhabitants (including suburbs)

Vegetation

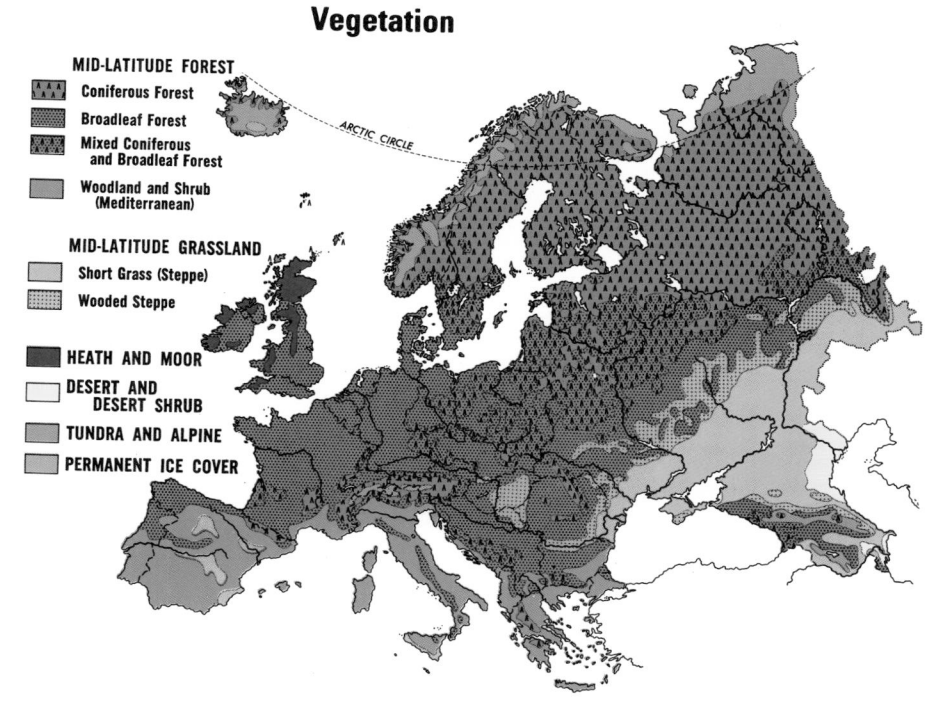

MID-LATITUDE FOREST

- Coniferous Forest
- Broadleaf Forest
- Mixed Coniferous and Broadleaf Forest
- Woodland and Shrub (Mediterranean)

MID-LATITUDE GRASSLAND

- Short Grass (Steppe)
- Wooded Steppe

HEATH AND MOOR

DESERT AND DESERT SHRUB

TUNDRA AND ALPINE

PERMANENT ICE COVER

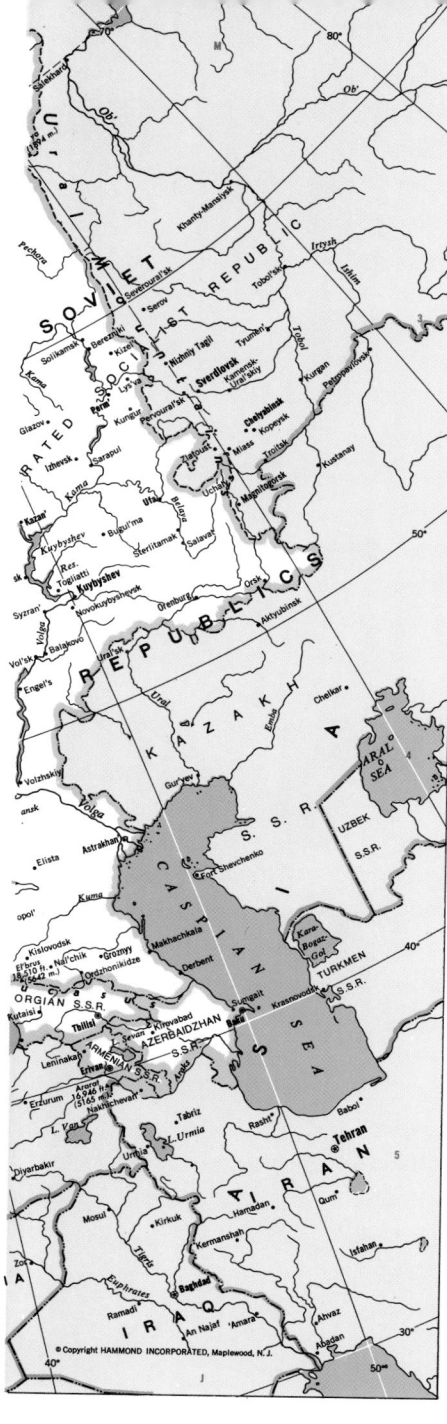

© Copyright HAMMOND INCORPORATED, Maplewood, N.J.

ICELAND

NORWEGIAN

SEA

Arctic Circle

BARENTS
SEA

Kolguyev I.

Cheshkskaya Bay

Pechora

Faeroe Is.
(Den.)

Nordkapp

Vesterålen
Lofoten

Vestfjord

Kola
Pen.

White
Sea

Archangel

Northern Dvina

Shetland
Is.

Hebrides

Orkney
Is.

Moray Firth

FINLAND

Oulu

Lake
Onega

Ben Nevis

Aberdeen

Trondheim

Galdhøpiggen
8100 ft.
(2470 m.)

Sundsvall

Tampere

Lake
Ladoga

U N I O N   O F

NORTH

SEA

UNITED

KINGDOM

Glasgow

Belfast

U.K.

IRELAND

IRISH SEA

Dublin

Liverpool

Birmingham

St. Georges Chan.

C. Clear

Skagerrak

Kattegat

Helsinki

Leningrad

Volga

Gorky

Kuy

Helsinki

Moscow

S O C I A L

ATLANTIC

OCEAN

Land's End

Lindesnes

Oslo

Göteborg

Vänern

Stockholm

Västerås

Åland
Is.

Hiiumaa

Saaremaa

Gotland

Riga

Western Dvina

English Channel

Channel Is.
(U.K.)

London

Frisian Is.

Amsterdam

NETHERLANDS

Hamburg

Elbe

Copenhagen

DENMARK

Bornholm

Rügen

Gdańsk

BALTIC SEA

POLAND

Vistula

Warsaw

Kiev

Khar'kov

Don

Dnieper

Donetsk

Bay of

Biscay

Le Havre

Seine

Paris

Brussels

BELGIUM

Cologne

Bonn

LUX.

WEST
GERMANY

EAST
GERMANY

Berlin

Leipzig

Oder

Łódź

Bug

Cracow

L'vov

Odessa

SEA OF
AZOV

FRANCE

Nantes

Loire

Stuttgart

Prague

CZECHOSLOVAKIA

Brno

Krasnodar

Crimea

Finisterre

Bordeaux

Dordogne

Lyon

Garonne

Bern

Munich

Vienna

Budapest

AUSTRIA

SWITZ.

Mont Blanc
(4810 m.)

Milan

Turin

Zagreb

Drava

Sava

HUNGARY

Cluj-Napoca

ROMANIA

Bucharest

BLACK SEA

PORTUGAL

Porto

Douro

Tagus

Lisbon

SPAIN

Ebro

Zaragoza

Madrid

Tagus

Guadiana

Pyrenees

Genoa

Genoa

MONACO

SAN MARINO

Venice

Po

APENNINES

ADRIATIC SEA

Belgrade

YUGOSLAVIA

Danube

Balkan Mts.

Sofia

BULGARIA

Istanbul

Bosporus

Sea of
Marmara

Dardanelles

Ankara

C. de São
Vicente

Cádiz

Seville

Guadalquivir

Barcelona

Balearic Is.

Ibiza

Minorca

Majorca

Valencia

Corsica

Sardinia

Rome

Naples

VATICAN CITY

TYRRHENIAN
SEA

Tirane

Skopje

Thessaloniki

Lésvos

GREECE

Athens

IONIAN
SEA

C. Tainaron

AEGEAN SEA

Rhodes

TURKEY

SY

Str. of Gibraltar

Tangier

GIBRALTAR
(U.K.)

Rabat

Casablanca

MOROCCO

Oran

Algiers

Constantine

C. Bon

ALGERIA

Tunis

TUNISIA

AFRICA

MEDITERRANEAN

Palermo

Sicily

Etna
11,053 ft.
(3369 m.)

C. Passero

MALTA

Valletta

SEA

Crete

CYPRUS

Nicosia

LEBANON

Beirut

Damascus

Vegetation/Relief

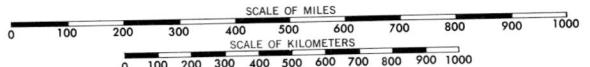

SCALE OF MILES
0 100 200 300 400 500 600 700 800 900 1000

SCALE OF KILOMETERS
0 100 200 300 400 500 600 700 800 900 1000

Capitals of Countries .... ⊛
International Boundaries ....
Canals ....

Elevations in Feet   Depths in Fathoms

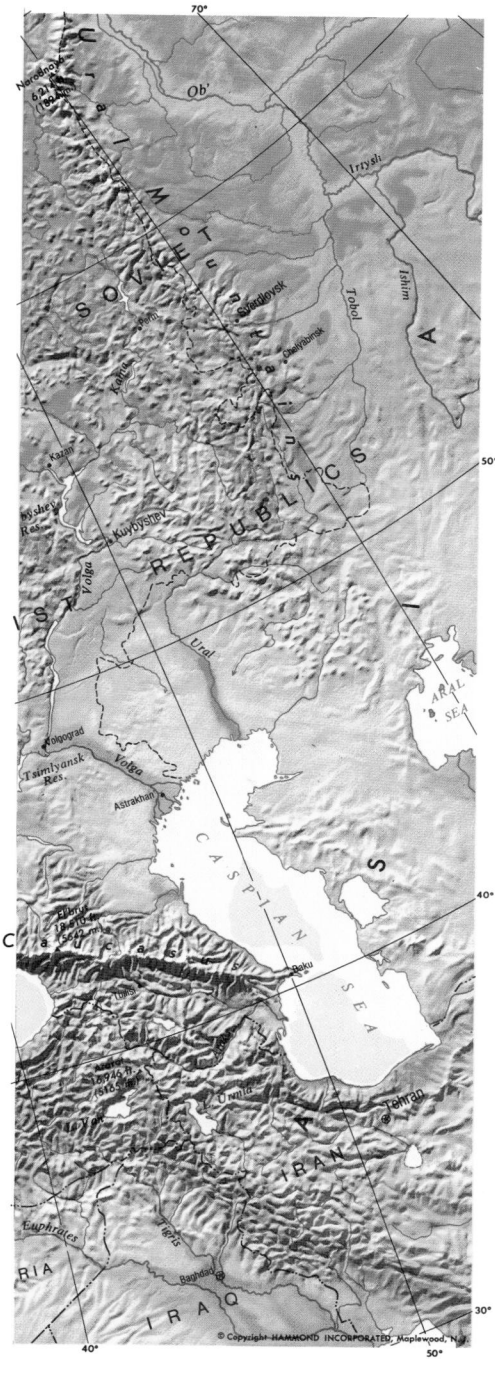

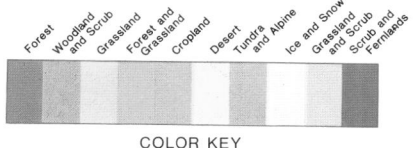

Forest | Woodland and Scrub | Grassland | Forest and Grassland | Cropland | Desert | Tundra and Alpine | Ice and Snow | Grassland and Scrub | Scrub and Fernlands

COLOR KEY

Rainfall

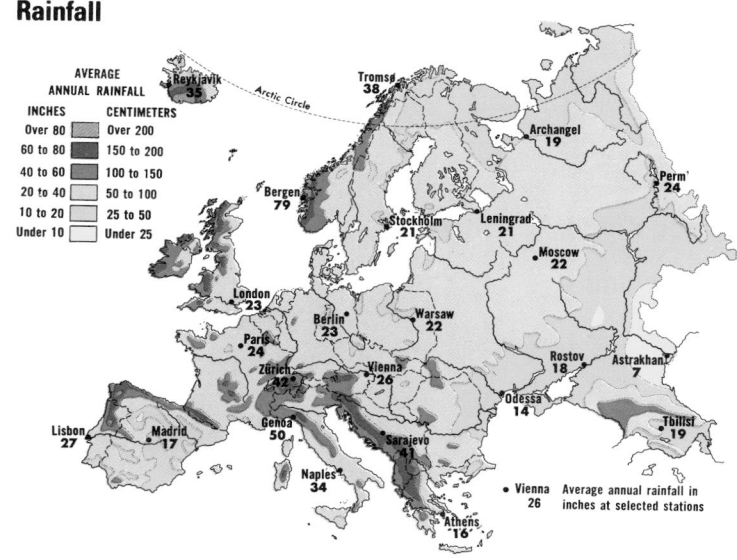

AVERAGE ANNUAL RAINFALL

INCHES	CENTIMETERS
Over 80	Over 200
60 to 80	150 to 200
40 to 60	100 to 150
20 to 40	50 to 100
10 to 20	25 to 50
Under 10	Under 25

Reykjavik 35
Tromsø 38
Archangel 19
Perm' 24
Bergen 79
Stockholm 21
Leningrad 21
Moscow 22
London 23
Berlin 23
Warsaw 22
Paris 24
Zürich 42
Vienna 26
Rostov 18
Astrakhan 7
Odessa 14
Lisbon 27
Madrid 17
Genoa 50
Sarajevo 41
Tbilisi 19
Naples 34
Athens 16

• Vienna 26 Average annual rainfall in inches at selected stations

Average January Temperature

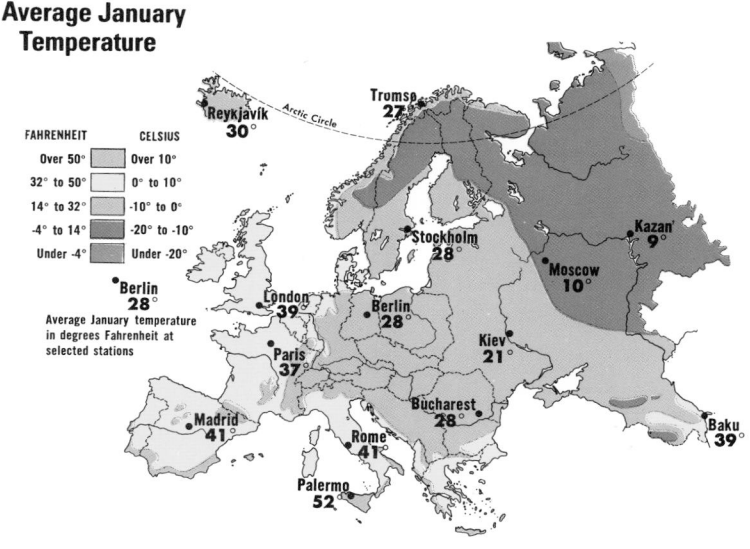

FAHRENHEIT	CELSIUS
Over 50°	Over 10°
32° to 50°	0° to 10°
14° to 32°	-10° to 0°
-4° to 14°	-20° to -10°
Under -4°	Under -20°

Reykjavík 30
Tromsø 27
Stockholm 28
Kazan' 9
Moscow 10
Berlin 28

Average January temperature in degrees Fahrenheit at selected stations

London 39
Berlin 28
Kiev 21
Paris 37
Madrid 41
Rome 41
Bucharest 28
Baku 39
Palermo 52

Average July Temperature

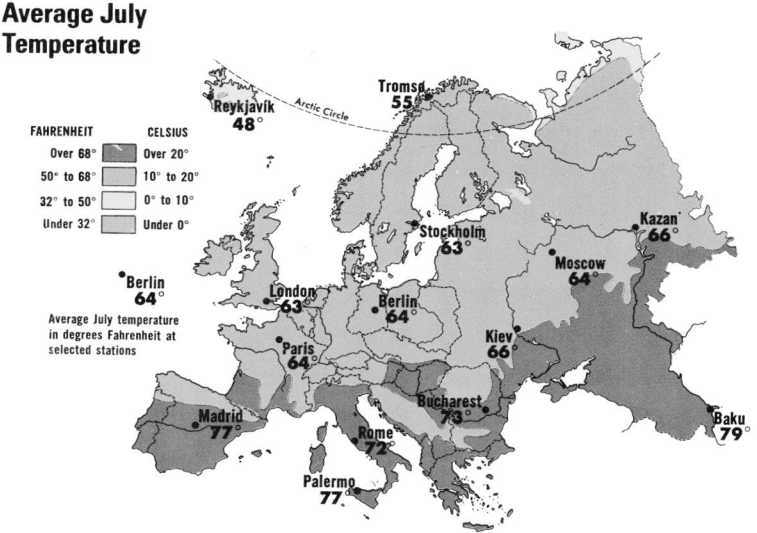

FAHRENHEIT	CELSIUS
Over 68°	Over 20°
50° to 68°	10° to 20°
32° to 50°	0° to 10°
Under 32°	Under 0°

Reykjavík 48
Tromsø 55
Stockholm 63
Kazan' 66
Moscow 64
Berlin 64

Average July temperature in degrees Fahrenheit at selected stations

London 63
Berlin 64
Kiev 66
Paris 64
Madrid 77
Rome 72
Bucharest 73
Baku 79
Palermo 77

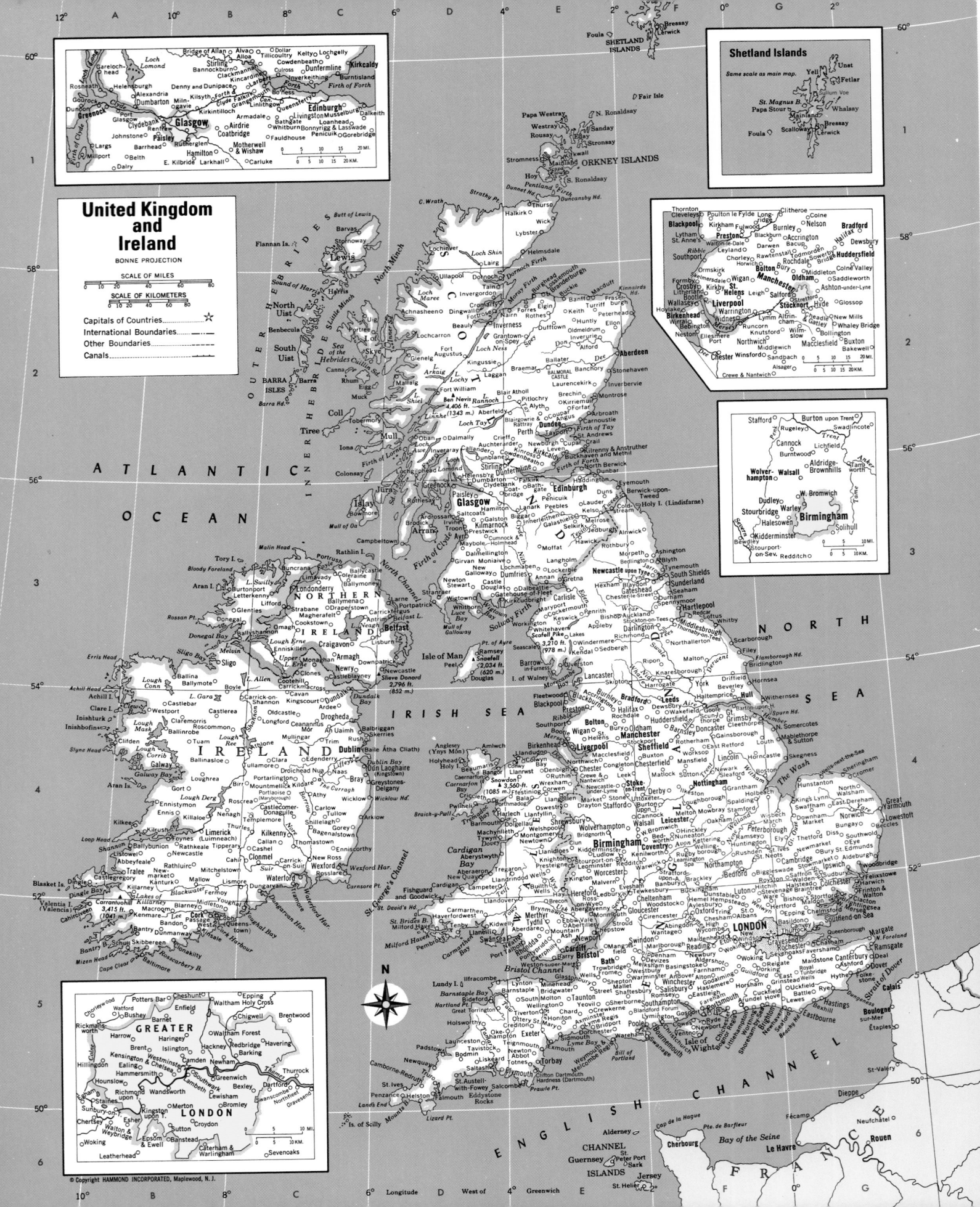

United Kingdom and Ireland

BONNE PROJECTION

SCALE OF MILES

SCALE OF KILOMETERS

Capitals of Countries............☆
International Boundaries..........
Other Boundaries.................
Canals...........................

Shetland Islands

Same scale as main map.

UNITED KINGDOM

AREA 94,399 sq. mi. (244,493 sq. km.)
POPULATION 55,672,000
CAPITAL London
LARGEST CITY London
HIGHEST POINT Ben Nevis 4,406 ft. (1,343 m.)
MONETARY UNIT pound sterling
MAJOR LANGUAGES English, Gaelic, Welsh
MAJOR RELIGIONS Protestantism, Roman Catholicism

IRELAND

AREA 27,136 sq. mi. (70,282 sq. km.)
POPULATION 3,440,427
CAPITAL Dublin
LARGEST CITY Dublin
HIGHEST POINT Carrantuohill 3,415 ft. (1,041 m.)
MONETARY UNIT Irish pound
MAJOR LANGUAGES English, Gaelic (Irish)
MAJOR RELIGION Roman Catholicism

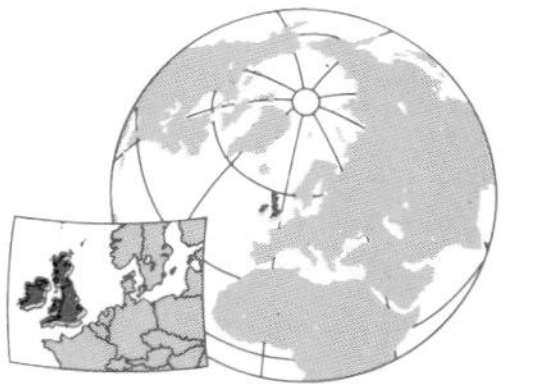

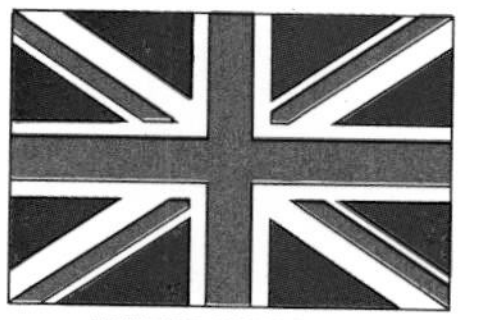

UNITED KINGDOM

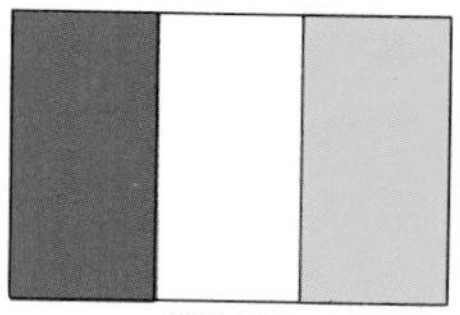

IRELAND

ENGLAND

AREA 50,516 sq. mi. (130,836 sq. km.)
POPULATION 46,220,955
CAPITAL London
LARGEST CITY London
HIGHEST POINT Scafell Pike 3,210 ft. (978 m.)

WALES

AREA 8,017 sq. mi. (20,764 sq. km.)
POPULATION 2,790,462
CAPITAL Cardiff
LARGEST CITY Cardiff
HIGHEST POINT Snowdon 3,560 ft. (1,085 m.)

SCOTLAND

AREA 30,414 sq. mi. (78,772 sq. km.)
POPULATION 5,117,146
CAPITAL Edinburgh
LARGEST CITY Glasgow
HIGHEST POINT Ben Nevis 4,406 ft. (1,343 m.)

NORTHERN IRELAND

AREA 5,452 sq. mi. (14,121 sq. km.)
POPULATION 1,543,000
CAPITAL Belfast
LARGEST CITY Belfast
HIGHEST POINT Slieve Donard 2,796 ft. (852 m.)

ENGLAND

COUNTIES

Avon, 920,200 E 6
Bedfordshire, 491,700 G 5
Berkshire, 659,000 F 6
Buckinghamshire, 512,000 G 6
Cambridgeshire, 563,000 G 5
Cheshire, 916,400 E 4
Cleveland, 567,900 F 3
Cornwall, 405,200 C 7
Cumbria, 473,600 D 3
Derbyshire, 887,600 F 5
Devon, 942,100 D 7
Dorset, 575,800 E 7
Durham, 610,400 F 3
East Sussex, 655,600 H 7
Essex, 1,426,200 H 6
Gloucestershire, 491,500 E 6
Greater London, 7,028,200 H 8
Greater Manchester, 2,684,100 H 2
Hampshire, 1,456,100 F 6
Hereford and Worcester, 594,200 E 5
Hertfordshire, 937,300 G 6
Humberside, 848,600 G 4
Isle of Wight, 111,300 F 7
Isles of Scilly, 1,900 A 7
Kent, 1,448,100 H 6
Lancashire, 1,375,500 E 4
Leicestershire, 837,900 F 5
Lincolnshire, 524,500 G 4
London, Greater, 7,028,200 H 8
Manchester, Greater, 2,684,100 H 2
Merseyside, 1,578,000 G 2
Norfolk, 662,500 H 5
Northamptonshire, 505,900 G 5
Northumberland, 287,300 E 2
North Yorkshire, 653,000 F 3
Nottinghamshire, 977,500 F 4
Oxfordshire 541,800 F6
Shropshire (Salop) 359,000 E5
Somerset 404,400 E6
South Yorkshire 1,318,300 F4
Staffordshire 997,600 E5
Suffolk 577,600 H5
Surrey 1,002,900 G6
Sussex, East 655,600 H7
Sussex, West 623,400 G7
Tyne and Wear 1,182,900 H3
Warwickshire 471,000 F5
West Midlands 2,743,300 F5
West Sussex 623,400 G7
West Yorkshire 2,072,500 J1
Wiltshire 512,800 E6
Yorkshire, North 653,000 F3
Yorkshire, South 1,318,300 F4
Yorkshire, West 2,072,500 J1

CITIES and TOWNS

Abingdon, 20,130 F 6
Accrington, 36,470 H 1
Adwick le Street, 17,650 K 2
Aldeburgh, 2,750 J 5
Aldershot, 33,750 G 8
Aldridge Brownhills, 89,370 E 5
Alfreton, 21,560 F 4
Alnwick, 7,300 F 2
Altrincham, 40,800 H 2
Amersham, ⊙17,254 G 7
Andover, 27,620 F 6
Appleby, 2,240 E 3
Arnold, 35,090 F 4
Arundel, 2,390 G 7
Ashford, 36,380 H 6
Ashington, 24,720 F 2
Ashton-under-Lyne, 48,500 H 2
Axminster, ⊙4,515 D 7
Aycliffe, ⊙20,203 F 3
Aylesbury, 41,420 G 7
Bacup, 14,990 H 1
Bakewell, 4,100 J 2
Banbury, 31,060 F 5
Banstead, 44,100 H 8
Barking, 153,800 H 8
Barnet, 305,200 H 7
Barnsley, 74,730 J 2
Barnstaple, 17,820 D 6
Barrow-in-Furness, 73,400 D 3
Barton-upon-Humber, 7,750 G 4
Basildon, 135,720 J 8
Basingstoke, 60,910 F 6
Bath, 83,100 E 6
Batley, 41,630 J 1
Battle, ⊙4,987 H 7
Bebington, 62,500 G 2
Bedford, 74,390 G 5
Bedlington, 27,200 F 2
Bedworth, 41,600 F 5
Beeston and Stapleford, 65,360 F 5
Benfleet, 49,180 J 8
Bentley with Arksey, 22,320 F 4
Berkhamsted, 15,920 G 7
Beverley, 16,920 G 4
Bexhill, 34,680 H 7
Bexley, 213,500 H 8
Biddulph, 18,720 H 2
Birkenhead, 135,750 G 2
Birmingham, 1,058,800 F 5
Bishop Auckland, 32,940 E 3
Bishop's Stortford, 21,720 H 6
Blackburn, 101,670 H 1
Blackpool, 149,000 G 1
Blaydon, 31,940 H 3
Blyth, 35,390 F 2
Bodmin, 10,430 C 7
Bognor Regis, 34,620 G 7
Boldon, 24,430 J 3
Bolton, 154,480 H 2
Bootle 71,160 G2
Boston 26,700 G5
Bournemouth 144,100 F7
Bracknell† 34,067 G8
Bradford 458,900 J1
Braintree and Bocking 26,300 H6
Brent 256,500 H8
Brentwood 58,690 J8
Bridgwater 26,700 E6
Bridlington 26,920 G3
Bridport 6,660 E7
Brigg 4,870 G4
Brighouse 35,320 J1
Brightlingsea 7,170 J6
Brighton 156,500 G7
Bristol 416,300 E6
Broadstairs and Saint Peter's 21,670 J6
Bromley 299,100 H8
Bromsgrove 41,430 E5
Buckfastleigh 2,870 C7
Buckingham 5,290 G6
Bude-Stratton 5,750 C7
Bungay 4,120 J5
Burgess Hill 20,030 G7
Burnham-on-Crouch 4,920 H6
Burnley 74,300 H1
Burntwood† 23,088 F5
Burton upon Trent 49,480 F5
Bury 69,550 H2
Bury Saint Edmunds 26,800 H5
Bushey 24,500 H7
Buxton 20,050 J2
Caister-on-Sea† 6,287 J5
Camborne-Redruth 43,970 B7
Cambridge 106,400 G5
Camden 185,800 H8
Cannock 56,440 E5
Canterbury 115,600 H6
Canvey Island 29,550 J8
Carlisle, 99,600 D 3
Carlton, 46,690 F 5
Caterham and Warlingham, 35,840 H 8
Chatham, 59,550 J 8
Cheadle and Gatley, 62,460 H 2
Chelmsford, 58,320 J 7
Cheltenham, 75,910 E 6
Chertsey, 45,070 G 8
Chesham, 20,830 G 7
Cheshunt, 45,750 H 7
Chester, 117,200 G 2
Chesterfield, 69,480 J 2
Chester-le-Street, 20,720 J 3
Chichester, 20,940 G 7
Chigwell, 54,220 H 8
Chippenham, 18,550 E 6
Chorley, 31,800 G 2
Christchurch, 31,610 F 7
Cirencester, 14,500 E 6
Clacton, 39,380 J 6
Clay Cross, 9,630 J 2
Cleator Moor, ⊙7,686 D 3
Cleethorpes, 37,200 H 4
Clevedon, 15,140 D 6
Clun, ⊙1,261 D 6
Coalville, 28,740 F 5
Cockermouth, 6,480 D 3
Colchester, 79,600 H 6
Colne, 19,030 H 1
Colne Valley, 21,190 J 2
Congleton, 21,500 H 2
Consett, 35,080 H 3
Corby, 48,850 G 5
Coventry, 336,800 F 5
Cowes, 19,190 F 7
Crawley, 72,600 G 6
Crewe and Nantwich, 98,100 E 4
Cromer, 5,720 J 5
Crook and Willington, 21,120 E 3
Crosby, 56,750 G 2
Croydon, 330,600 H 8
Cuckfield, 26,500 G 6
Darlington, 85,120 F 3
Dartford, 44,130 J 8
Darton, 15,710 J 2
Darwen, 29,290 H 1
Deal, 26,840 J 6
Dearne, 24,780 K 2
Denton, 38,110 H 2
Derby, 213,700 F 5
Dewsbury, 50,560 J 1
Didcot, ⊙14,277 F 6
Doncaster, 81,530 F 4
Dorking, 22,410 G 8
Dover, 34,160 J 6
Downham Market, 4,120 H 5
Droitwich, 13,950 E 5
Dronfield, 20,000 J 2
Dudley, 187,110 E 5
Dunstable, 32,090 G 6
Durham, 88,800 J 3
Ealing, 293,800 H 8
Eastbourne, 73,200 H 7
East Grinstead, 19,420 G 6
Eastleigh, 46,340 F 7
East Retford, 18,260 G 4
Egham, 30,320 G 8
Egremont, ⊙7,253 D 3
Eling, ⊙20,006 F 7
Ellesmere, ⊙2,630 E 5
Ellesmere Port, 63,870 G 2
Enfield, 260,900 H 7
Epsom and Ewell, 70,700 G 8
Esher, 63,970 H 8
Eston, ⊙46,219 F 3
Eton, 4,950 G 8
Evesham, 14,090 F 5
Exeter, 93,300 D 7
Exminster, ⊙3,181 D 7
Exmouth, 26,840 D 7
Falmouth, 17,530 B 7
Fareham, 86,300 F 7
Farnborough, 43,520 G 8
Farnham, 33,140 G 8
Farnworth, 26,110 H 2
Faversham, 15,010 H 6
Felixstowe, 19,460 J 6
Felling, 38,990 J 3
Filey, 5,660 G 3
Fleet, 22,930 G 8
Fleetwood, 30,070 D 4
Folkestone, 45,610 J 6
Formby, 24,850 G 2
Framlingham, ⊙2,258 J 5
Frimley and Camberley, 47,390 G 8
Fulwood, 22,910 G 1
Gainsborough, 17,440 G 4
Gateshead, 91,230 J 3
Gillingham, Dorset, ⊙4,050 E 6
Gillingham, Kent, 93,900 J 8
Glastonbury, 6,580 E 6
Glossop, 24,820 J 2
Gloucester, 91,600 E 6
Godalming, 18,840 G 8
Golborne, 28,720 G 2
Goole, 17,920 G 4
Gosport, 82,300 F 7
Grange, 3,520 E 3
Grantham 27,830 G5
Gravesend 53,500 J8
Great Grimsby 93,800 G4
Great Torrington 3,430 C7
Great Yarmouth 49,410 J5
Greenwich 207,200 H8
Guildford 58,470 G8
Guisborough 14,860 F3
Hackney 192,500 H8
Hale 17,080 H2
Halesowen 54,120 E5
Halifax 88,580 J1
Haltemprice 54,850 G4
Haltwhistle† 3,511 E2
Hammersmith 170,000 H8
Haringey 228,200 H8
Harlow 79,160 H7
Harrogate 64,620 F4
Harrow 200,200 B5
Hartlepool 97,100 F3
Harwich 15,280 J6
Haslingden 15,140 H1
Hastings 74,600 H7
Hatfield† 25,359 H7
Havant and Waterloo 112,430 G7
Haverhill 14,550 H5
Havering 239,200 J8
Hayle† 5,378 B7
Hazel Grove and Bramhall 40,400 H2
Heanor 24,590 F4
Hebburn 23,150 J3
Hedon 3,010 G4
Hemel Hempstead 71,150 G7
Hereford 47,800 E5
Hertford 20,760 H7
Hetton 16,810 J3
Hexham 9,820 E3
Heywood 31,720 H2
High Wycombe 61,190 G8
Hillingdon 230,800 G8
Hinckley 49,310 F5
Hinderwell† 2,551 G3
Hitchin 29,190 G6
Hoddesdon 27,510 H7
Holmfirth 19,790 J2
Horley† 18,593 H8
Hornsea 7,280 G4
Horsham 26,770 G6
Horwich 16,670 G2
Houghton-le-Spring 33,150 J3
Hounslow, 199,100 G 8
Hove, 72,000 G 7
Hoylake, 32,000 G 2
Hoyland Nether, 15,500 J 2
Hucknall, 27,110 F 4
Huddersfield, 130,060 J 2
Hugh Town, ⊙1,958 A 8
Hull, 276,600 G 4
Hunstanton, 4,140 H 5
Huntingdon and Godmanchester, 17,200 G 5
Huyton-with-Roby, 65,950 G 2
Hyde, 37,040 H 2
Ilfracombe, 9,350 C 6
Ilkeston, 33,690 F 5
Immingham, ⊙10,259 G 4
Ipswich, 121,500 J 5
Islington, 171,600 H 8
Jarrow, 28,510 J 3
Kendal, 22,440 E 3
Kenilworth, 19,730 F 5
Kensington and Chelsea, 161,400 G 8
Keswick, 4,790 D 3
Kettering, 44,480 G 5
Keynsham, 18,970 E 6
Kidderminster, 49,960 E 5
Kidsgrove, 22,690 E 4
King's Lynn, 29,990 H 5
Kingston upon Thames, 135,600 H 8
Kingswood, 30,450 E 6
Kirkburton, 20,320 J 2
Kirkby, 59,100 G 2
Kirkby Lonsdale, ⊙1,506 E 3
Kirkby Stephen, ⊙1,539 E 3
Knutsford, 14,840 H 2
Lambeth, 290,300 H 8
Lancaster, 126,300 E 3
Leatherhead, 40,830 G 8
Leeds, 744,500 J 1
Leek, 19,460 H 2
Leicester, 289,400 F 5
Leigh, 46,390 H 2
Leighton-Linslade, 22,590 F 7
Letchworth, 31,520 G 6
Lewes, 14,170 H 7
Lewisham, 237,300 H 8
Leyland, 23,690 G 1
Lichfield, 23,690 F 5
Lincoln, 73,700 G 4
Liskeard, 5,360 C 7
Litherland, 23,530 G 2
Littlehampton, 20,320 G 7

(continued on following page)

Topography

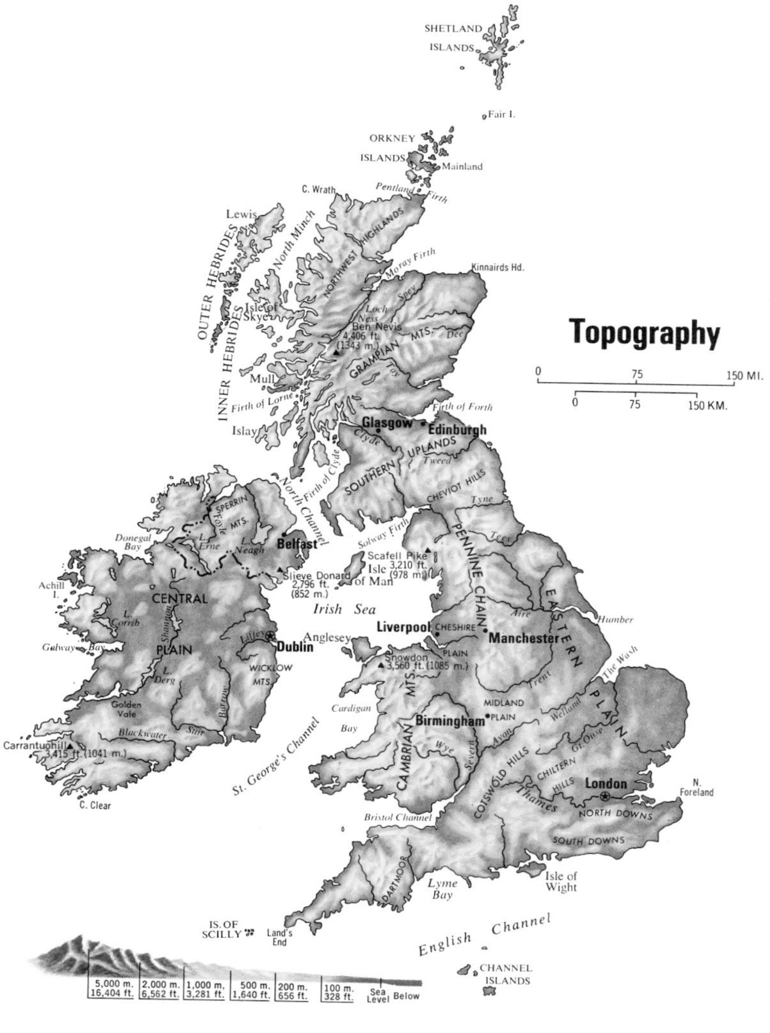
SHETLAND ISLANDS
Fair I.
ORKNEY ISLANDS
Mainland
C. Wrath
Pentland Firth
Lewis
OUTER HEBRIDES
North Minch
Moray Firth
Kinnairds Hd.
INNER HEBRIDES
Isle of Skye
Ben Nevis 4,406 ft. (1343 m.)
GRAMPIAN MTS.
Mull
Firth of Lorne
Islay
Glasgow
Edinburgh
Firth of Forth
SOUTHERN UPLANDS
Tweed
CHEVIOT HILLS
Tyne
North Channel
Donegal Bay
L. Erne
Neagh
Belfast
Slieve Donard 2,796 ft. (852 m.)
Solway Firth
Scafell Pike 3,210 ft. (978 m.)
Isle of Man
Tees
PENNINE CHAIN
Irish Sea
Achill I.
CENTRAL PLAIN
L. Corrib
Galway Bay
Dublin
Anglesey
Liverpool
CHESHIRE PLAIN
Manchester
EASTERN PLAIN
Humber
The Wash
WICKLOW MTS.
Snowdon 3,560 ft. (1085 m.)
CAMBRIAN MTS.
Cardigan Bay
Birmingham
MIDLAND PLAIN
Trent
Golden Vale
Blackwater
Carrantuohill 3,415 ft. (1041 m.)
C. Clear
St. George's Channel
COTSWOLD HILLS
CHILTERN HILLS
London
Thames
N. Foreland
NORTH DOWNS
SOUTH DOWNS
Bristol Channel
DARTMOOR
Lyme Bay
Isle of Wight
IS. OF SCILLY
Land's End
English Channel
CHANNEL ISLANDS
0 75 150 MI.
0 75 150 KM.
5,000 m. 16,404 ft.
2,000 m. 6,562 ft.
1,000 m. 3,281 ft.
500 m. 1,640 ft.
200 m. 656 ft.
100 m. 328 ft.
Sea Level
Below

Liverpool, 539,700 G 2
Loftus, 7,850 G 3
London (cap.), 7,028,200 H 8
London, ★12,332,900 H 8
Long Eaton, 33,560 F 5
Longbenton, 50,120 J 3
Looe, 4,060 C 7
Loughborough, 49,010 F 5
Lowestoft, 53,260 J 5
Ludlow, ⊙7,466 E 5
Luton, 164,500 G 6
Lydd, 4,670 H 7
Lyme Regis, 3,460 E 7
Lymington, 36,780 F 7
Lynton, 1,770 D 6
Lytham Saint Anne's, 42,120 G 1
Mablethorpe and Sutton, 6,750 H 4
Macclesfield, 45,420 H 2
Maidenhead, 48,210 G 8
Maidstone, 72,110 J 8
Maldon, 14,350 H 6
Malmesbury, 2,550 E 6
Malton, 4,010 G 3
Malvern, 30,420 E 5
Manchester, 490,000 H 2
Mangotsfield, 23,000 E 6
Mansfield, 58,450 K 2
Mansfield Woodhouse, 25,400 F 4
March, 14,560 H 5
Margate, 50,290 J 6
Market Harborough, 15,230 G 5
Marlborough, 6,370 F 6
Matlock, 20,300 J 2
Melton Mowbray, 20,680 G 5
Merton, 169,400 H 8
Middlesbrough, 153,900 F 3
Middleton, 53,340 H 2
Middlewich, 7,600 H 2
Mildenhall, ⊙9,269 H 5
Millom, ⊙7,101 D 3
Milton Keynes, 89,900 F 5
Minehead, 8,230 D 6
Moretonhampstead, ⊙1,440 C 7
Morpeth, 14,450 F 2
Mundesley, ⊙1,536 J 5
Nelson, 31,220 H 1
Neston, 18,210 G 2
Newark, 24,760 G 4
Newbury, 24,850 F 6
Newcastle upon Tyne, 295,800 H 3
Newcastle-under-Lyme, 75,940 E 4
Newham, 228,900 H 8
Newhaven, 9,970 H 7
Newport, 22,430 F 7
New Romney, 3,830 J 7
Newton Abbot, 19,940 D 7
Newton-le-Willows, 21,780 H 2
New Windsor, 29,660 G 8
Northallerton F 3
Northam, 8,310 C 6
Northampton, 128,290 F 5
Northfleet, 27,150 J 8
North Sunderland, ⊙1,725 F 2
Northwich, 17,710 H 2
Norton, 5,580 G 3
Norton-Radstock, 15,900 E 6
Norwich, 119,200 J 5
Nottingham, 280,300 F 5
Nuneaton, 69,210 F 5
Oadby, 20,700 F 5
Oakham, 7,280 G 5
Okehampton, 4,000 D 7
Oldham, 103,690 H 2
Ormskirk, 28,860 G 2
Oswaldtwistle, 14,270 H 1
Oxford, 117,400 F 6
Padstow, ⊙2,802 B 7
Penryn, 5,660 B 7
Penzance, 19,360 B 7
Peterborough, 118,900 G 5
Peterlee, ⊙21,846 J 3
Plymouth, 259,100 C 7
Polperro, ⊙1,491 C 7
Poole, 110,600 E 7
Porlock, ⊙1,290 D 6
Portishead, 9,680 E 6
Portland, 14,860 E 7
Portslade-by-Sea, 18,040 G 7
Portsmouth, 198,500 F 7
Potters Bar, 24,670 H 7
Poulton-le-Fylde, 16,340 G 1
Preston, 94,760 G 1
Prestwich, 32,850 H 2
Queenborough, 31,550 H 6
Radcliffe, 29,630 H 2
Ramsbottom, 16,710 H 2
Ramsgate, 40,090 J 6
Rawtenstall, 20,950 H 1
Rayleigh, 26,740 J 8
Reading, 131,200 G 8
Redbridge, 231,600 H 8
Redcar, ⊙46,325 F 3
Redditch, 44,750 E 5
Reigate, 55,600 H 8
Richmond upon Thames, 166,800 H 8
Rickmansworth, 29,030 G 8
Ripley, 18,060 F 4
Rochdale, 93,780 H 2
Rochester, 56,030 J 8
Rothbury, ⊙1,818 E 2
Rotherham, 84,770 K 2
Royal Leamington Spa, 44,950 F 5
Royal Tunbridge Wells, 44,800 H 6
Rugby, 60,380 F 5
Rugeley, 24,440 E 5
Runcorn, 42,730 G 2
Rushden, 21,840 G 5
Ryde, 23,170 F 7
Rye, 4,530 H 7
Ryton, 15,170 H 3
Saddleworth, 21,340 J 2
Saint Agnes, ⊙4,747 B 7
Saint Albans, 123,800 H 7
Saint Austell-with-Fowey, 32,710 C 7
Saint Columb Major, ⊙3,953 B 7
Saint Helens, 104,890 G 2
Saint Ives, Cornwall, 9,760 B 7
Saint Neots, 17,940 G 5
Salcombe, 2,370 D 7
Sale, 59,060 H 2
Salford, 261,100 H 2
Salisbury, 35,460 F 6
Saltburn and Marske-by-the-Sea, 21,170 G 3
Sandbach, 14,280 H 2
Sandown-Shanklin, 14,800 F 7
Sandwich, 4,420 J 6
Saxmundham, 1,820 J 5
Scarborough, 43,300 G 3
Scunthorpe, 68,100 G 4
Seaford, 18,020 H 7
Seaham, 22,470 J 3
Seascale, ⊙2,106 D 3
Seaton, 4,500 D 7
Seaton Valley, 35,880 J 3
Sedbergh, ⊙2,741 E 3
Selsey, ⊙6,491 G 7
Sevenoaks, 18,160 J 8
Shaftesbury, 4,180 E 7
Sheffield, 558,000 J 2
Sherborne, 9,230 E 7
Sheringham, 4,940 J 5
Shildon, 15,360 F 3
Shoreham-by-Sea, 19,620 G 7
Shrewsbury, 56,120 E 5
Silloth, ⊙2,662 D 3
Sittingbourne and Milton, 32,830 H 6
Skelmersdale, 35,850 G 2
Skelton and Brotton, 15,930 G 3
Sleaford, 8,050 G 5
Slough, 89,060 G 8
Solihull, 108,230 F 5
Southampton, 213,700 F 7
Southend-on-Sea, 159,300 H 6
Southport, 86,030 G 1
South Shields, 96,900 J 3
Southwark, 224,900 H 8
Southwold, 1,960 J 5
Sowerby Bridge, 15,700 H 1
Spalding, 17,040 G 5
Spenborough, 41,460 J 1
Spennymoor, 19,050 F 3
Stafford, 54,860 E 5
Staines, 56,380 G 8
Stamford, 14,980 G 5
Stanley, 42,280 H 3
Staveley, 17,620 K 2
Stevenage, 72,600 G 6
Stockport, 138,350 H 2
Stockton-on-Tees, 165,400 F 3
Stoke-on-Trent, 256,200 E 4
Stourbridge, 56,530 E 5
Stourport-on-Severn, 19,430 E 5
Stowmarket, 9,020 J 5
Stratford-upon-Avon, 20,080 F 5
Stretford, 52,450 H 2
Stroud, 19,600 E 6
Sudbury, 8,860 H 5
Sunbury-on-Thames, 40,070 G 8
Sunderland, 214,820 J 3
Sutton, 166,700 H 8
Sutton Bridge, ⊙3,113 H 5
Sutton in Ashfield, 40,330 K 2
Swadlincote, 21,060 F 5
Swanage, 8,000 E 7
Swindon, 90,680 F 6
Tamworth, 46,960 F 5
Taunton, 37,570 D 6
Tavistock, ⊙7,620 C 7
Telford, ⊙79,451 E 5
Tenbury, ⊙2,151 E 5
Tewkesbury, 9,210 E 6
Thetford, 15,690 H 5
Thirsk, ⊙2,884 F 3
Thornaby-on-Tees, ⊙42,385 F 3
Thorne, ⊙16,694 F 4
Thornton Cleveleys, 27,090 G 1
Thurrock, 127,700 J 8
Tiverton, 16,190 D 7
Todmorden, 14,540 H 1
Tonbridge, 31,410 H 8
Torbay, 109,900 D 7
Torpoint, 6,840 C 7
Tower Hamlets, 146,100 H 8
Tow Law, 2,460 H 4
Trowbridge, 20,120 E 6
Truro, 15,690 B 7
Turton, 22,800 H 2
Tynemouth, 67,090 J 3
Upton upon Severn, ⊙2,048 E 5
Urmston, 44,130 H 2
Uttoxeter, 9,100 E 5
Ventnor, 6,980 F 7
Wainfleet All Saints, ⊙1,116 H 4
Wakefield, 306,500 J 2
Wallasey, 94,520 G 2
Wallsend, 45,490 J 3
Walsall, 182,430 E 5
Waltham Forest, 223,700 H 8
Waltham Holy Cross, 14,810 H 7
Walton and Weybridge, 51,270 G 8
Walton-le-Dale, 27,660 G 1
Wandsworth, 284,600 H 8
Wantage, 8,490 F 6
Ware, 14,900 H 7
Wareham, 4,630 E 7
Warley, 161,260 E 5
Warminster, 14,440 E 6
Warrington, 65,320 G 2
Warwick, 17,870 F 5
Washington, 27,720 J 3
Watchet, 2,980 D 6
Watford, 77,000 H 7
Wellingborough, 39,570 G 5
Wells, 8,960 E 6
Wells-next-the-Sea, 2,450 H 5
Welwyn, 39,900 H 7
Wem, ⊙3,411 E 5
West Bridgford, 28,340 F 5
West Bromwich, 162,740 F 5
West Mersea, 4,730 H 6
Westminster, 216,100 H 8
Weston-super-Mare, 51,960 D 6
Weymouth and Melcombe Regis, 41,080 E 7
Whickham, 29,710 J 3
Whitchurch, ⊙7,142 E 5
Whitehaven, 26,260 D 3
Whitley Bay, 37,010 J 3
Widnes, 58,330 G 2
Wigan, 80,920 G 2
Wigston, 31,650 F 5
Wilmslow, 31,250 H 2
Wilton, 4,090 F 6
Winchester, 88,900 F 6
Windermere, 7,860 E 3
Winsford, 26,920 G 2
Wirral, 27,510 G 2
Wisbech, 16,990 H 5
Witham, 19,730 H 6
Withernsea, 6,300 H 4
Wivenhoe, 5,630 J 6
Woking, 79,300 G 8
Wokingham, 22,390 G 8
Wolverhampton, 266,400 E 5
Wombwell, 17,850 K 2
Woodhall Spa, 2,420 G 4
Woodley and Sandford, ⊙24,581 G 8
Woodstock, 2,070 F 6
Wooler, ⊙1,833 F 2
Worcester, 73,900 E 5
Workington, 28,260 D 3
Worksop, 36,590 F 4
Worsbrough, 15,180 J 2
Worsley, 49,530 H 2
Worthing, 89,100 G 7
Wymondham, 9,390 J 5
Yateley, ⊙16,505 G 8
Yeovil, 26,180 E 7
York, 101,900 F 4

OTHER FEATURES

Aire (riv.) F 4
Atlantic Ocean A 7
Avon (riv.) F 5
Avon (riv.) F 7
Axe Edge (mt.) H 2
Barnstaple (bay) C 6
Beachy (head) H 7
Bigbury (bay) C 7
Blackwater (riv.) H 6
Bristol (chan.) C 6
Brown Willy (mt.) C 7
Cheviot (hills) E 2
Cheviot, The (mt.) E 2
Chiltern (hills) G 6
Cleveland (hills) F 3
Colne (riv.) G 8
Cornwall (cape) B 7
Cotswold (hills) E 6
Cross Fell (mt.) E 3
Cumbrian (mts.) D 3
Dart (riv.) D 7
Dartmoor National Park C 7
Dee (riv.) D 4
Derwent (riv.) G 3
Derwent (riv.) H 3
Don (riv.) F 4
Dorset Heights (hills) E 7
Dove (riv.) J 2
Dover (str.) J 7
Dungeness (prom.) J 7
Dunkery (hill) D 6
Eddystone (rocks) C 7
Eden (riv.) E 3
English (chan.) D 8
Esk (riv.) D 2
Exe (riv.) D 7
Exmoor National Park D 6
Fens, The (reg.) G 5
Flamborough (head) G 3
Formby (head) G 2
Foulness Island (pen.) J 6
Gibraltar (pt.) H 4
Great Ouse (riv.) H 5
Hartland (pt.) C 6
High Willhays (mt.) C 7
Hodder (riv.) H 1
Holderness (pen.), 43,900 G 4
Holy (isl.), 189 F 2
Humber (riv.) G 4
Irish (sea) B 4
Kennet (riv.) F 6
Lake District National Park D 3
Land's End (prom.) B 7
Lea (riv.) G 6
Lincoln Wolds (hills) G 4
Lindisfarne (Holy) (isl.), 189 F 2
Liverpool (bay) D 4
Lizard, The (pen.), 7,371 B 8
Lundy (isl.), 49 C 6
Lune (riv.) E 3
Lyme (bay) D 7
Manacle (pt.) C 7
Medway (riv.) H 6
Mendip (hills) E 6
Mersea (isl.), 4,423 J 6
Mersey (riv.) G 2
Morecambe (bay) D 3
Mounts (bay) B 7
Naze, The (prom.) J 6
Nene (riv.) H 5
New (for.) F 6
North (sea) J 4
North Downs (hills) G 6
North Foreland (prom.) J 6
Northumberland National Park E 2
North York Moors National Park G 3
Orford Ness (prom.) J 5
Ouse (riv.) G 4
Ouse (riv.) G 6
Parrett (riv.) E 6
Peak District National Park F 4
Peak, The (mt.) J 2
Peel Fell (mt.) E 2
Pennine Chain (range) E 3
Plymouth (sound) C 7
Portland, Bill of (pt.) E 7
Prawle (pt.) D 7
Purbeck, Isle of (pen.), 39,500 F 7
Ribble (riv.) E 4
Saint Alban's (head) F 7
Saint Bees (head) D 3
Saint Martin's (isl.), 106 A 8
Saint Mary's (isl.), 1,958 A 8
Scafell Pike (mt.) D 3
Scilly (isls.), 1,900 A 7
Selsey Bill (prom.) G 7
Severn (riv.) E 6
Sheppey (isl.), 31,550 J 6
Sherwood (for.) F 4
Skiddaw (mt.) D 3
Solent (chan.) F 7
Solway (firth) D 3
South Downs (hills) G 7
Spithead (chan.) F 7
Spurn (head) H 4
Stonehenge (ruins) F 6
Stour (riv.) E 7
Stour (riv.) H 6
Stour (riv.) J 6
Swale (riv.) F 3
Tamar (riv.) C 7
Taw (riv.) D 7
Tees (riv.) F 3
Test (riv.) F 6
Thames (riv.) H 6
Tintagel (head) C 7
Torridge (riv.) C 7
Trent (riv.) G 4
Tresco (isl.), 246 A 8
Tweed (riv.) E 2
Tyne (riv.) F 3
Ure (riv.) F 3
Ver (riv.) H 7
Walney, Isle of (isl.), 11,241 D 3
Wash, The (bay) H 5
Weald, The (reg.) H 6
Wear (riv.) F 3
Weaver (riv.) G 2
Welland (riv.) G 5
Wey (riv.) G 6
Wharfe (riv.) E 3
Wirral (pen.), 432,900 G 2
Witham (riv.) G 4
Wolds, The (hills) G 4
Wye (riv.) D 5
Wyre (riv.) G 1
Yare (riv.) J 5
Yorkshire Dales National Park E 3

CHANNEL ISLANDS

CITIES and TOWNS

Saint Anne E 8
Saint Helier (cap.), Jersey, ⊙28,135 E 8
Saint Peter Port (cap.), Guernsey, ⊙16,303 E 8
Saint Sampson's, ⊙6,534 E 8

OTHER FEATURES

Alderney (isl.), 1,686 E 8
Guernsey (isl.), 51,351 E 8
Herm (isl.), 96 E 8
Jersey (isl.), 72,629 E 8
Sark (isl.), 590 E 8

ISLE of MAN

CITIES and TOWNS

Castletown, 2,820 C 3
Douglas (cap.), 20,389 C 3
Laxey, 1,170 C 3
Michael, 408 C 3
Onchan, 4,807 C 3
Peel, 3,081 C 3
Port Erin, 1,714 C 3
Port Saint Mary, 1,508 C 3
Ramsey, 5,048 C 3

OTHER FEATURES

Ayre (pt.) C 3
Calf of Man (isl.) C 3
Langness (prom.) C 3
Snaefell (mt.) C 3
Spanish (head) C 3

WALES

COUNTIES

Clwyd, 376,000 D 4
Dyfed, 323,100 C 6
Gwent, 439,600 D 6
Gwynedd, 225,100 C 4
Mid Glamorgan, 540,400 D 6
Powys, 101,500 D 5
South Glamorgan, 389,200 A 7
West Glamorgan, 371,900 D 6

CITIES and TOWNS

Aberaeron, 1,340 C 5
Abercarn, 18,370 B 6
Aberdare, 38,030 A 6
Abertillery, 20,550 B 6
Amlwch, 3,630 C 4
Bala, 1,650 D 5
Bangor, 16,030 C 4
Barmouth, 2,070 C 5
Barry, 42,780 B 7
Beaumaris, 2,090 C 4
Bedwellty, 25,460 B 6
Bethesda, 4,180 D 4
Betws-y-Coed, 720 D 4
Brecknock (Brecon), 6,460 D 6
Brecon, 6,460 D 6
Bridgend, 14,690 A 7
Brynmawr, 5,970 B 6
Builth Wells, 1,480 D 5
Burry Port, 5,990 C 6
Caernarfon, 8,840 C 4
Caerphilly, 42,190 B 6
Cardiff, 281,500 B 7
Cardigan, 3,830 C 5
Chepstow, 8,260 E 6
Chirk, ⊙3,564 D 5
Colwyn Bay, 25,370 D 4
Criccieth, 1,590 C 5
Cwmamman, 3,950 D 6
Cwmbran, 32,980 B 6
Denbigh, 8,420 D 4
Dolgellau, 2,430 D 5
Ebbw Vale, 25,670 B 6
Ffestiniog, 5,510 D 5
Fishguard and Goodwick, 5,020 B 5
Flint, 15,070 G 2
Gelligaer, 33,820 A 6
Harlech, ⊙332 C 5
Haverfordwest, 8,930 B 6
Hawarden, ⊙20,389 G 2
Hay, 1,200 D 5
Holywell, 8,570 G 2
Kidwelly, 3,090 C 6
Knighton, 2,190 D 5
Llandeilo, 1,780 C 6
Llandovery, 2,040 D 5
Llandrindod Wells, 3,460 D 5
Llandudno, 17,700 D 4
Llanelli, 25,870 C 6
Llanfairfechan, 3,800 D 4
Llangefni, 4,070 C 4
Llangollen, 3,050 D 5
Llanguicke, ⊙15,029 D 6
Llanidloes, 2,390 D 5
Llantrisant, ⊙27,490 A 7
Llanwrtyd Wells, 460 D 5
Llwchwr, 27,530 D 6
Machynlleth, 1,830 D 5
Maesteg, 21,100 D 6
Menai Bridge, 2,730 C 4
Merthyr Tydfil, 61,500 A 6
Milford Haven, 13,960 B 6
Mold, 8,700 G 2
Montgomery, 1,000 D 5
Mountain Ash, 27,710 A 6
Mynyddislwyn, 15,590 B 6
Narberth, 970 C 6
Neath, 27,280 D 6
Nefyn, ⊙2,086 C 5
Newcastle Emlyn, 690 C 5
Newport, Dyfed, ⊙1,062 C 5
Newport, Gwent, 110,090 B 6
New Quay, 760 C 5
Newtown, 6,400 D 5
Neyland, 2,690 B 6
Ogmore and Garw, 19,680 A 6
Pembroke, 14,570 C 6
Penarth, 24,180 B 7
Penmaenmawr, 4,050 C 4
Pontypool, 36,710 B 6
Pontypridd, 34,180 A 6
Porthcawl, 14,980 D 6
Porthmadog, 3,900 C 5
Port Talbot, 58,200 D 6
Prestatyn, 15,480 D 4
Presteigne, 1,330 D 5
Pwllheli, 4,020 C 5
Rhondda, 85,400 A 6
Rhyl, 22,150 D 4
Risca, 15,780 B 6
Ruthin, 4,780 D 4
Saint David's, ⊙1,638 B 6
Swansea, 190,800 C 6
Tenby, 4,930 C 6
Tredegar, 17,450 B 6
Tywyn, 3,850 C 5
Welshpool, 7,370 D 5
Wrexham, 39,530 E 4

OTHER FEATURES

Anglesey (isl.), 64,500 C 4
Aran Fawddwy (mt.) C 5
Bardsey (isl.), 9 C 5
Berwyn (mts.) D 5
Black (mts.) D 6
Braich-y-Pwll (prom.) C 5
Brecon Beacons (mt.) D 6
Brecon Beacons National Park D 6
Caldy (isl.), 70 C 6
Cambrian (mts.) D 5
Cardigan (bay) C 5
Carmarthen (bay) C 6
Cemmaes (head) C 5
Dee (riv.) D 4
Dovey (riv.) D 5
Ely (riv.) B 7
Gower (pen.), 17,220 C 6
Great Ormes (head) C 4
Holy (isl.), 13,715 C 4
Lleyn (pen.), 25,800 C 5
Menai (str.) C 4
Milford Haven (inlet) B 6
Pembrokeshire Coast National Park C 6
Plynlimon (mt.) D 5
Preseli (mts.) C 6
Radnor (for.) D 5
Rhymney (riv.) B 6
Saint Brides (bay) B 6
Saint David's (head) B 6
Saint George's (chan.) B 5
Saint Gowans (head) C 6
Severn (riv.) E 5
Snowdon (mt.) D 4
Snowdonia National Park D 4
Taff (riv.) B 7
Teifi (riv.) C 5
Towy (riv.) D 6
Tremadoc (bay) C 5
Usk (riv.) B 6
Wye (riv.) D 5
Ynys Môn (Anglesey) (isl.), 64,500 C 4

★Population of met. area.
⊙Population of parish.

SCOTLAND
(map on page 15)

REGIONS

Borders, 99,409 E 5
Central, 269,281 D 4
Dumfries and Galloway, 143,667 E 5
Fife, 336,339 E 4
Grampian, 448,772 F 3
Highland, 182,044 D 3
Lothian, 754,008 E 5
Orkney (islands area), 17,675 E 1
Shetland (islands area), 18,494 F 2
Strathclyde, 2,504,909 C 4
Tayside, 401,987 E 4
Western Isles (islands area), 29,615 A 3

CITIES and TOWNS

Aberchirder, 877 F 3
Aberdeen, 210,362 F 3
Aberdour, 1,576 D 1
Aberfeldy, 1,552 E 4
Aberfoyle, 793 D 4
Aberlady, 737 F 4
Aberlour, 842 E 3
Abernethy, 776 E 4
Aboyne, 1,040 F 3
Acharacle, ⊙764 C 4
Achiltibuie, ⊙1,564 C 3
Achnasheen, ⊙1,078 C 3
Ae, 239 E 5
Airdrie, 38,491 C 2
Alexandria, 9,758 A 1
Alford, 764 F 3
Alloa, 13,558 C 1
Alness, 2,560 D 3
Altnaharra, ⊙1,227 D 2
Alva, 4,593 C 1
Alyth, 1,738 E 4
Ancrum, 266 F 5
Annan, 6,250 E 6
Annat, ⊙550 C 3
Annbank Station, 2,530 D 5
Applecross, ⊙550 C 3
Arbroath, 22,706 F 4
Ardavasar, ⊙449 B 3
Ardersier, 942 E 3
Ardgay, 193 D 3
Ardrishaig, 946 C 4
Ardrossan, 11,072 D 5
Armadale, 7,200 C 2
Arrochar, 543 D 4
Ascog, 230 A 2
Auchenblae, 339 F 4
Auchencairn, 215 E 6
Auchinleck, 4,883 D 5
Auchterarder, 1,738 E 4
Auchtermuchty, 1,426 E 4
Auldearn, 405 E 3
Aviemore, 1,224 E 3
Avoch, 776 D 3
Ayr, 47,990 D 5
Ayton, 410 F 5
Bailivanish, 347 A 3
Baillieston, 7,671 B 2
Balallan, 283 B 2
Balerno, 3,576 D 2
Balfron, 1,149 B 1
Ballantrae, 262 C 5
Ballater, 981 F 3
Ballingry, 4,332 D 1
Ballinluig, 188 E 4
Balloch, Highland, 572 D 3
Balloch, Strathclyde, 1,484 B 1
Baltasound, 246 G 2
Banchory, 2,435 F 3
Banff, 3,832 F 3
Bankfoot, 868 E 4
Bankhead, 1,492 F 3
Bannockburn, 5,889 C 1
Barrhead, 18,736 B 2
Barrhill, 236 D 5
Barvas, 279 B 2
Bathgate, 14,038 C 2
Bayble, 543 B 2
Bearsden, 25,128 B 2
Beattock, 309 E 5
Beauly, 1,141 D 3
Beith, 5,859 D 5
Bellsbank, 3,066 D 5
Bellshill, 18,166 C 2
Berriedale, ⊙1,927 E 2
Bieldside, 1,137 F 3
Biggar, 1,718 E 5
Birnam, 659 E 4
Bishopbriggs, 21,570 B 2
Bishopton, 2,931 B 2
Blackburn, 7,636 C 2
Blackford, 529 E 4
Blair Atholl, 437 E 4
Blairgowrie and Rattray, 5,681 E 4
Blanefield, 835 B 1
Blantyre, 13,992 B 2
Blyth Bridge, ⊙441 E 5
Bo'ness, 12,959 C 1
Boat of Garten, 406 E 3
Boddam, 1,429 G 3
Bonar Bridge, 519 D 3
Bonhill, 4,385 B 1
Bonnybridge, 5,701 C 1
Bonnyrigg and Lasswade, 7,429 D 2
Bowmore, 947 B 5
Braemar, 394 E 3
Breasclete, 234 B 2
Brechin, 6,759 F 4
Bridge of Allan, 4,638 C 1
Bridge of Don, 4,086 F 3
Bridge of Weir, 4,724 A 2
Brightons, 3,106 C 1
Broadford, 310 B 3
Brodick, 630 C 5
Brora, 1,436 E 2
Broxburn, 7,776 D 1
Buchlyvie, 412 B 1
Buckhaven and Methil, 17,930 F 4
Buckie, 8,145 E 3
Bucksburn, 6,567 F 3
Bunessan, ⊙585 B 4
Burghead, 1,321 E 3
Burnmouth, 300 F 5
Burntisland, 5,626 D 1
Cairndow, ⊙874 D 4
Cairnryan, 199 D 6
Callander, 1,805 D 4
Cambuslang, 14,607 B 2
Campbeltown, 6,428 C 5
Cannich, 203 D 3
Canonbie, 234 F 5
Caol, 3,719 C 4
Carbost, ⊙772 B 3
Cardenden, 6,802 D 1
Carloway, 178 B 2
Carluke, 8,864 E 5
Carnoustie, 6,838 F 4
Carnwath, 1,246 E 5
Carradale, 262 C 5
Carrbridge, 416 E 3
Carron, 2,626 C 1
Carsphairn, 186 D 5
Castlebay, 284 A 4
Castle Douglas, 3,384 E 6
Castle Kennedy, 307 D 6
Castletown, 902 E 2
Catrine, 2,681 D 5
Cawdor, 111 E 3
Chirnside, 888 F 5
Chryston, 8,322 C 2
Clackmannan, 3,248 C 1
Clarkston, 8,404 B 2
Closeburn, 225 E 5
Clovulin, ⊙315 C 4
Clydebank, 47,538 B 2
Coalburn, 1,460 E 5
Coatbridge, 50,806 C 2
Cockburnspath, 233 F 5
Cockenzie and Port Seton, 3,539 D 1
Coldingham, 423 F 5
Coldstream, 1,393 F 5
Coll, 305 B 2
Colmonell, 218 D 5
Comrie, 1,119 E 4
Connel, 300 C 4
Cononbridge, 914 D 3
Corpach, 1,296 C 4
Coupar Angus, 2,010 E 4
Cove and Kilcreggan, 1,402 A 1
Cove Bay, 765 F 3
Cowdenbeath, 10,215 D 1
Cowie, 2,751 C 1
Craigellachie, 382 E 3
Craignure, ⊙544 C 4
Crail, 1,033 F 4
Crawford, 384 E 5
Creetown, 769 D 6
Crieff, 5,718 E 4
Crimond, 313 G 3
Crinan, ⊙462 C 4
Cromarty, 492 E 3
Crosshill, 535 D 5
Crossmichael, 317 D 6
Cruden Bay, 528 G 3
Cullen, 1,199 F 3
Culross, 504 C 1
Cults, 3,336 F 3
Cumbernauld, 41,200 C 1
Cumnock and Holmhead, 6,298 D 5
Cupar, 6,607 E 4
Currie, 6,764 D 2
Dailly, 1,258 D 5
Dalbeattie, 3,659 E 6
Daliburgh, 261 A 3
Dalkeith, 9,713 D 2
Dalmally, 283 D 4
Dalmellington, 1,949 D 5
Dalry, 5,833 D 5
Dalrymple, 1,336 D 5
Darvel, 3,177 D 5
Daviot, ⊙513 D 3
Denholm, 581 F 5
Denny and Dunipace, 10,424 C 1
Dervaig, ⊙1,081 B 4
Dingwall, 4,275 D 3
Dollar, 2,573 E 4
Dornoch, 880 D 3
Douglas, 1,843 E 5
Doune, 859 D 4
Drongan, 3,609 D 5
Drumbeg, ⊙833 C 2
Drummore, 336 D 6
Drumnadrochit, 359 D 3
Drymen, 659 B 1
Dufftown, 1,481 E 3
Dumbarton, 25,469 B 1
Dumfries, 29,259 E 5
Dunbar, 4,609 F 4
Dunbeath, 161 E 2
Dunbeg, 939 C 4
Dunblane, 5,222 E 4
Dundee, 194,732 F 4
Dundonald, 2,256 D 5
Dunfermline, 52,098 D 1
Dunkeld, 273 E 4
Dunning, 564 E 4
Dunoon, 8,759 A 2
Dunragit, 323 D 6
Duns, 1,812 F 5
Duntochter, 3,532 B 2
Dunure, 452 D 5
Dunvegan, 301 B 3
Dyce, 2,733 F 3
Eaglesfield, 581 E 5
Eaglesham, 2,788 D 5
Earlston, 1,415 F 5
East Calder, 2,690 D 2
East Kilbride, 71,200 B 2
East Linton, 882 F 5
Eastriggs, 1,455 E 5
Ecclefechan, 844 E 5
Edinburgh (cap.), 470,085 D 1
Edzell, 658 F 4
Elderslie, 5,204 B 2
Elgin, 17,042 E 3
Elie and Earlsferry, 807 F 4
Ellon, 2,855 F 3
Embo, 260 E 3
Errol, 762 E 4
Evanton, 562 D 3
Eyemouth, 2,704 F 5
Fairlie, 1,029 D 5
Falkirk, 36,901 C 1
Falkland, 998 E 4
Fallin, 3,159 C 1
Fauldhouse, 5,247 C 2
Ferness, ⊙287 E 3
Ferryden, 740 F 4
Findhorn, 664 E 3
Findochty, 1,229 E 3
Fintry, 296 B 1
Fochabers, 1,238 E 3
Forfar, 11,179 F 4
Forres, 5,317 E 3
Fort Augustus, 670 D 3
Forth, 2,929 C 2
Fortrose, 1,150 D 3
Fort William, 4,370 C 4
Foyers, 276 D 3
Fraserburgh, 10,930 G 3
Friockheim, 807 F 4
Furnace, 220 C 4
Fyvie, 405 F 3
Gairloch, 125 C 3
Galashiels, 12,808 F 5
Galston, 4,256 D 5
Gardenstown, 892 F 3
Garelochhead, 1,552 A 1
Gargunnock, 457 B 1
Garlieston, 385 D 6
Garmouth, 352 E 3
Garrabost, 307 B 2
Gartmore, 253 B 1
Gatehouse-of-Fleet, 835 D 6
Giffnock, 10,987 B 2
Gifford, 575 F 5
Girvan, 7,597 D 5
Glamis, 190 F 4
Glasgow, 880,617 B 2
Glasgow, ★1,674,789 B 2
Glenbarr, ⊙691 C 5
Glencaple, 275 E 5
Glencoe, 195 C 4
Glenelg, ⊙1,468 C 3
Glenluce, 725 D 6
Glenrothes, 31,400 E 4
Golspie, 1,374 E 3
Gordon, 320 F 5
Gorebridge, 3,426 D 2
Gourock, 11,192 A 1
Grangemouth, 24,430 C 1
Grantown-on-Spey, 1,578 E 3
Greenlaw, 574 F 5
Greenock, 67,275 A 2
Gretna, 1,907 E 5
Gullane, 1,701 F 4
Haddington, 6,767 F 5
Halkirk, 679 E 2
Hamilton, 45,495 C 2
Hamnavoe, 307 G 2
Harthill, 4,712 C 2
Hatton, 315 G 3
Hawick, 16,484 F 5
Heathhall, 1,365 E 5
Helensburgh, 13,327 A 1
Helmsdale, 727 E 2
Hill of Fearn, 233 D 3
Hillside, 692 F 4
Hillswick, ⊙696 G 2
Hopeman, 1,248 E 3
Huntly, 4,078 F 3
Hurlford, 4,294 D 5
Inchnadamph, ⊙833 D 2
Innellan, 922 A 2
Innerleithen, 2,293 E 5
Insch, 881 F 3
Inveraray, 473 C 4
Inverbervie, 853 F 4
Invercassley, ⊙1,067 D 3
Invergordon, 2,385 D 3
Invergowrie, 1,389 E 4
Inverie, ⊙1,468 C 3
Inverkeithing, 6,102 D 1
Inverness, 35,801 D 3
Inverurie, 5,534 F 3
Irvine, 48,500 D 5
Isle of Whithorn, 222 D 6
Jedburgh, 3,953 F 5
John O'Groats, 195 E 2
Johnshaven, 544 F 4
Johnstone, 23,251 B 2
Kames, 230 C 5
Keiss, 344 E 2
Keith, 4,192 F 3
Kelso, 4,934 F 5
Kelty, 6,573 D 1
Kemnay, 1,042 F 3
Kenmore, 211 E 4
Kilbarchan, 2,669 A 2
Kilbirnie, 8,259 A 2
Kilchoan, ⊙764 B 4
Kildonan, ⊙1,105 E 2
Killearn, 1,086 B 1
Killin, 600 D 4
Kilmacolm, 3,348 A 2
Kilmarnock, 50,175 D 5
Kilmaurs, 2,518 D 5
Kilninver, ⊙247 C 4
Kilrenny and Anstruther, 2,951 F 4
Kilsyth, 10,210 B 1
Kilwinning, 8,460 D 5
Kinbrace, ⊙1,105 E 2
Kincardine, 3,278 C 1
Kinghorn, 2,163 D 1
Kingussie, 1,036 D 3
Kinlochewe, ⊙1,794 C 3
Kinlochleven, 1,243 D 4
Kinloch Rannoch, 241 D 4
Kinloss, 2,378 E 3
Kinross, 2,829 E 4
Kintore, 970 F 3
Kippen, 529 B 1
Kirkcaldy, 50,207 D 1
Kirkcolm, 346 C 6
Kirkconnel, 3,318 E 5
Kirkcowan, 354 D 6
Kirkcudbright, 2,690 E 6
Kirkhill, 210 D 3
Kirkintilloch, 26,664 B 2
Kirkmuirhill, 2,575 E 5
Kirkton of Glenisla, ⊙331 E 4
Kirkwall, 4,777 E 2
Kirriemuir, 4,295 E 4
Kyleakin, 268 C 3
Kyle of Lochalsh, 687 C 3
Kylestrome, ⊙745 D 2
Ladybank, 1,216 E 4
Laggan, 393 D 3
Lairg, 572 D 2
Lamlash, 613 C 5
Lanark, 8,842 E 5
Langholm, 2,509 E 5
Larbert, 4,922 C 1
Largs, 9,461 A 2
Larkhall, 15,926 E 5
Lauder, 639 F 5
Laurencekirk, 1,416 F 4

(continued)

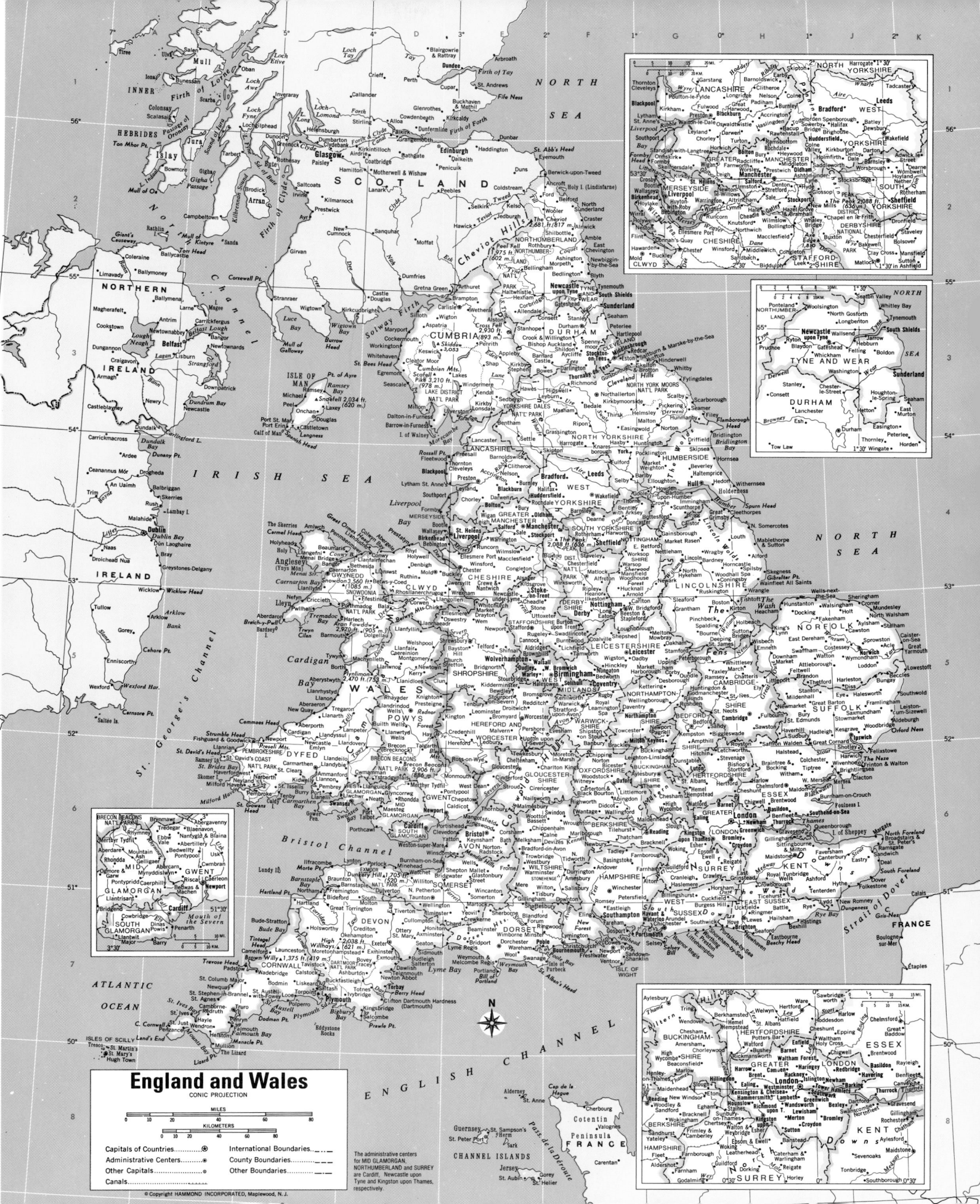

England and Wales

CONIC PROJECTION

MILES

KILOMETERS

Capitals of Countries............⊛
Administrative Centers..........◉
Other Capitals...................◉
Canals...........................

International Boundaries....._ . _
County Boundaries.............. _ _ _
Other Boundaries.............. . . . .

The administrative centers
for MID GLAMORGAN,
NORTHUMBERLAND and SURREY
are Cardiff, Newcastle upon
Tyne and Kingston upon Thames,
respectively.

© Copyright HAMMOND INCORPORATED, Maplewood, N.J.

14 United Kingdom and Ireland

(continued)

Lennoxtown, 3,070 B 1
Lerwick, 6,195 G 2
Leslie, 3,303 E 4
Lesmahagow, 3,906 E 5
Leswalt, 237 C 6
Letham, 804 F 4
Leuchars, 2,482 F 4
Leurbost, 461 B 2
Leven, 9,507 F 4
Leverburgh, 223 B 3
Lhanbryde, 1,184 E 3
Lilliesleaf, 212 F 5
Limekilns, 812 D 1
Linlithgow, 6,098 C 1
Linwood, 10,510 B 2
Lionel, 187 B 2
Livingston, 21,900 C 2
Loanhead, 5,971 D 2
Lochailort, ⊙673 C 4
Lochaline, 213 C 4
Lochans, 355 D 6
Locharbriggs, 2,561 E 5
Lochawe, 200 C 4
Lochboisdale, 382 A 3
Lochcarron, 204 C 3
Lochgelly, 7,754 D 1
Lochgilphead, 1,217 C 4
Lochgoilhead, 216 D 4
Lochinver, 283 C 2
Lochmaben, 1,304 E 5
Lochmaddy, 307 A 3
Lochore, 2,994 D 1
Lochwinnoch, 2,064 A 2
Lockerbie, 3,135 E 5
Lossiemouth and Branderburgh, 5,817 E 3
Lumsden, 248 F 3
Luncarty, 584 E 4
Lybster, 554 E 2
Lyness, ⊙454 E 2
Macduff, 3,682 F 3
Machrihanish, 212 C 5
Maidens, 536 D 5
Mallaig, 903 C 4
Markinch, 2,366 E 4
Mauchline, 3,612 D 5
Maud, 634 F 3
Maybole, 4,703 D 5
Mayfield, 8,232 D 2
Meigle, 357 E 4
Melrose, 2,197 F 5
Melvaig, ⊙1,794 C 3
Methlick, 315 F 3
Methven, 806 E 4
Mid Yell, 220 G 2
Millport, 1,161 A 2
Milnathort, 1,099 E 4
Milngavie, 10,846 B 1
Minnigaff, 658 D 6
Mintlaw, 657 F 3
Moffat, 2,041 E 5
Moniaive, 342 E 5
Monifieth, 7,100 F 4
Montrose, 4,704 F 4
Morar, 184 C 4
Motherwell and Wishaw, 72,991 C 2
Muirkirk, 2,607 E 5
Muir of Ord, 1,339 D 3
Musselburgh, 17,045 D 2
Muthill, 672 E 4
Nairn, 5,821 E 3
Neilston, 4,358 B 2
Nethy Bridge, 431 E 3
New Abbey, 339 E 6
Newarthill, 7,003 C 2
Newburgh, Fife, 2,124 E 4
Newburgh, Grampian, 447 G 3
Newcastleton, 903 F 5
New Cumnock, 5,077 D 5
New Deer, 601 F 3
New Galloway, 337 D 5
Newmains, 6,847 C 2
Newmarket, 613 B 2
Newmill, 449 E 3
Newmilns and Greenholm, 3,509 D 5
New Pitsligo, 1,125 F 3
Newport-on-Tay, 3,762 F 4
New Scone, 3,830 E 4
Newtongrange, 4,555 D 2
Newton Mearns, 6,901 B 2
Newtonmore, 894 D 3
Newton Stewart, 1,983 D 6
Newtown Saint Boswells, 1,101 F 5
Newtyle, 664 E 4
North Berwick, 4,317 F 4
North Tolsta, 527 B 2
Oakley, 3,499 C 1
Oban, 6,515 C 4
Old Kilpatrick, 3,256 B 2
Oldmeldrum, 1,103 F 3
Oykel Bridge, ⊙742 D 3
Paisley, 94,833 B 2
Palnackie, 225 E 6
Patna, 2,867 D 5
Peebles, 6,049 E 5
Penicuik, 10,476 D 2
Penpont, 364 E 5
Perth, 43,098 E 4
Peterculter, 3,226 F 3
Peterhead, 14,846 G 3
Pierowall, ⊙735 E 1
Pitlochry, 2,468 E 4
Pitmedden, 313 F 3
Pittenweem, 1,548 F 4
Plockton, 288 C 3
Poolewe, ⊙1,794 C 3
Port Appin, ⊙2,172 C 4
Port Askaig, ⊙1,795 B 5
Port Bannatyne, 730 A 2
Port Charlotte, 240 B 5
Port Ellen, 932 B 5
Port Glasgow, 22,189 A 2
Portgordon, 814 F 3
Portknockie, 1,217 F 3
Portmahomack, 226 E 3
Portpatrick, 643 C 6
Portree, 1,374 B 3
Portsoy, 1,717 F 3
Port William, 517 D 6
Prestonpans, 3,272 D 1
Prestwick, 13,218 D 5
Queensferry, 5,339 D 1
Reay, 283 E 2
Renfrew, 18,880 B 2
Renton, 3,443 A 1
Rhu, 1,540 A 1
Rhynie, 333 F 3
Rigside, 1,195 E 5
Rosehearty, 1,220 F 3
Rosneath, 946 A 1
Rothes, 1,240 E 3
Rothesay, 6,285 A 2
Rutherglen, 24,091 B 2
Saint Abbs, 203 F 5
Saint Andrews, 12,837 F 4
Saint Combs, 738 G 3
Saint Cyrus, 340 F 4
Saint Margaret's Hope, 210 F 2
Saint Monance, 1,205 F 4
Saline, 831 C 1
Saltcoats, 14,861 D 5
Sandbank, 850 A 1
Sandhead, 248 D 6
Sandwick, 603 B 2
Sanquhar, 2,030 D 5
Sauchie, 6,082 C 1
Scalasaig, ⊙137 B 4
Scalloway, 896 G 2
Scarinish, ⊙875 B 4
Scourie, ⊙745 C 2
Scrabster, 273 E 2
Selkirk, 5,635 F 5
Shader, 258 B 2
Shawbost, 458 B 2
Shieldaig, ⊙550 C 3
Shotts, 9,512 C 2
Skateraw, 674 F 3
Skelmorlie, 1,535 A 2
Skipness, ⊙765 C 5
Slamannan, 1,584 C 2
Spean Bridge, 235 D 4
Springholm, 340 E 5
Stanley, 1,385 E 4
Stenhousemuir, 8,203 C 1
Stevenston, 11,786 D 5
Stewarton, 5,165 D 5
Stirling, 29,799 C 1
Stonehaven, 4,837 F 4
Stonehouse, 7,900 D 5
Stornoway, 5,371 B 2
Stow, 485 F 5
Strachan, ⊙390 F 3
Strachur Bay, ⊙678 C 4
Stranraer, 10,174 C 6
Strathaven, 5,464 D 5
Strathpeffer, 874 D 3
Strichen, 962 F 3
Stromeferry, ⊙1,724 C 3
Stromness, 1,680 E 2
Strontian, ⊙764 C 4
Struan, ⊙772 B 3
Swinton, 235 F 5
Tain, 2,057 D 3
Tarbert, Strathclyde, 1,391 C 5
Tarbert, W. Isles, 479 B 3
Tarbolton, 2,224 D 5
Tarland, 452 F 3
Tayport, 2,848 F 4
Thornhill, Central, 443 D 4
Thornhill, Dumf. & Gall., 1,510 E 5
Thurso, 9,113 E 2
Tillicoultry, 4,320 C 1
Tobermory, 652 B 4
Tolob, ⊙2,033 G 2
Tomatin, 214 D 3
Tomintoul, 306 E 3
Torphins, 499 F 3
Tradespark, 425 E 3
Tranent, 7,212 F 5
Troon, 11,656 D 5
Tullibody, 6,082 C 1
Turriff, 3,051 F 3
Tweedsmuir, ⊙105 E 5
Twynholm, 274 D 6
Tyndrum, ⊙1,153 D 4
Uddingston, 5,278 B 2
Uig, Highland, 103 B 3
Uig, W. Isles, ⊙1,948 A 2
Ullapool, 807 C 3
Uphall, 3,035 C 1
Viewpark, 9,812 C 2
Walkerburn, 842 F 5
Watten, 347 E 2
Wemyss Bay, 323 A 2
West Barns, 659 F 5
West Calder, 2,005 C 2
West Kilbride, 3,883 D 5
West Linton, 705 D 2
Whitburn, 11,647 C 2
Whitehills, 875 F 3
Whithorn, 990 D 6
Whiting Bay, 352 C 5
Wick, 7,804 E 2
Wigtown, 1,118 D 6
Winchburgh, 2,409 D 1
Yetholm, 435 F 5

OTHER FEATURES

A'Chralaig (mt.) C 3
Ailsa Craig (isl.), 3 C 5
Almond (riv.) E 4
Annan (riv.) E 5
Appin (dist.), 2,006 C 4
Ardgour (dist.), 315 C 4
Ardle (riv.) E 4
Ardnamurchan (pen.), 764 B 4
Argyll (dist.), 4,940 C 4
Arkaig, Loch (lake) C 4
Arran (isl.), 3,564 C 5
Askival (mt.) B 4
Assynt (dist.), 833 C 2
Athol (dist.), 1,082 D 4
Atlantic Ocean B 2
Avon (riv.) C 1
Avon (riv.) E 3
Awe, Loch (lake) C 4
Ayr (riv.) D 5
Ayr, Heads of (cape) D 5
Badenoch (dist.), 2,717 D 4
Baleshare (isl.), 64 A 3
Balmoral Castle E 3
Barra (sound) A 3
Barra (isl.), 1,005 A 4
Barra (head) A 4
Barra Isles (isls.), 1,092 A 4
Battock (mt.) F 4
Beauly (riv.) D 3
Beinn Dearg (mt.) D 3
Beinn a Ghlo (mt.) E 4
Bell Rock (isl.), 3 F 4
Ben Alder (mt.) D 4
Ben Avon (mt.) E 3
Benbecula (isl.), 1,355 A 3
Ben Cruachan (mt.) C 4
Ben Lawers (mt.) D 4
Ben Lui (mt.) D 4
Ben Macdhui (mt.) E 3
Ben Mhor (mt.) A 3
Ben More (mt.) B 4
Ben More (mt.) D 4
Ben More Assynt (mt.) D 2
Ben Nevis (mt.) D 4
Bernera (isl.), 276 B 2
Berneray (isl.), 131 A 3
Berneray (isl.), 6 A 4
Bidean nam Bian (mt.) D 4
Black Isle (pen.), 7,209 D 3
Blackwater (res.) D 4
Boisdale, Loch (inlet) A 3
Bracadale, Loch (inlet) B 3
Braemar (dist.), 7,624 E 3
Breadalbane (dist.), 3,649 D 4
Bressay (isl.), 248 G 2
Broad (bay) B 2
Broad Law (mt.) E 5
Broom, Loch (inlet) C 3
Brough Ness (prom.) F 2
Buchan (dist.), 40,089 F 3
Buddon Ness (prom.) F 4
Burray (isl.), 209 F 2
Burrow (head) D 6
Bute (isl.), 8,423 C 5
Bute (sound) C 5
Butt of Lewis (prom.) B 2
Cairn Gorm (mt.) E 3
Cairngorm (mts.) E 3
Cairn Toul (mt.) E 3
Caledonian (canal) D 3
Canna (isl.), 22 B 3
Carn Ban (mt.) D 3
Carn Eige (mt.) C 3
Carrick (dist.), 21,425 D 5
Carron (riv.) C 1
Carron (riv.) C 3
Cheviot (hills) F 5
Cheviot, The (mt.) F 5
Clisham (mt.) B 3
Clyde (riv.) D 5
Clyde (firth) D 5
Coll (isl.), 144 B 4
Colonsay (isl.), 137 B 4
Copinsay (isl.), 3 F 2
Cowal (dist.), 15,548 C 4
Creag Meagaidh (mt.) D 4
Cromarty (firth) D 3
Cuillin (hills) B 3
Cuillin (sound) B 3
Dee (riv.) D 5
Dee (riv.) F 3
Dennis (head) F 1
Deveron (riv.) F 3
Don (riv.) F 3
Doon (riv.) D 5
Dornoch (firth) E 3
Duirinish (dist.), 1,085 B 3
Duncansby (head) F 2
Dunnet (head) E 2
Earn (riv.) E 4
Earn, Loch (lake) D 4
Eday (isl.), 179 F 1
Eddrachillis (bay) C 2
Eden (riv.) F 4
Egilsay (isl.), 39 F 1
Eigg (isl.), 69 B 4
Eil, Loch (lake) C 4
Eishort, Loch (inlet) B 3
Enard (bay) C 2
Eriboll, Loch (inlet) D 2
Ericht, Loch (lake) D 4
Eriskay (isl.), 219 A 3
Erisort, Loch (inlet) B 2
Esk (riv.) F 5
Etive, Loch (inlet) C 4
Ewe, Loch (inlet) C 3
Eye (pen.), 850 B 2
Fair Isle (isl.), 65 F 3
Fetlar (isl.), 88 G 2
Fife Ness (prom.) F 4
Findhorn (riv.) E 3
Flannan (isls.), 3 A 2
Formartine (dist.), 10,768 F 3
Forth (riv.) B 1
Forth (firth) F 4
Forth and Clyde (canal) B 2
Foula (isl.), 33 F 2
Fyne, Loch (inlet) C 5
Galloway (dist.), 54,972 D 5
Galloway, Mull of (prom.) D 6
Gare Loch (inlet) A 1
Garioch (dist.), 6,863 F 3
Garry, Loch (lake) D 3
Gigha (isl.), 174 C 5
Girdle Ness (prom.) G 3
Glass (riv.) D 3
Glen More (dist.), 55,035 D 3
Goat Fell (mt.) C 5
Gometra (isl.), 10 B 4
Grampian (mts.) D 4
Great Cumbrae (isl.), 1,296 A 2
Gruinard (bay) C 3
Hallandale (riv.) E 2
Harris (sound) A 3
Harris (dist.), 2,175 B 3
Hebrides (sea) B 3
Hebrides, Inner (isls.), 14,881 B 4
Hebrides, Outer (isls.), 29,615 A 3
Helmsdale (riv.) E 2
Herma Ness (prom.) G 2
Holy (isl.), 10 C 5
Holy Loch (inlet) A 1
Hoy (isl.), 419 E 2
Inchcape (Bell Rock) (isl.), 3 F 4
Inchkeith (isl.), 3 D 1
Indaal, Loch (inlet) B 5
Inner (sound) C 3
Inner Hebrides (isls.), 14,881 B 4
Iona (isl.), 145 B 4
Isla (riv.) E 4
Islay (isl.), 3,816 B 5
Jura (isl.), 210 C 5
Jura (sound) C 5
Katrine, Loch (lake) D 4
Kerrera (isl.), 27 C 4
Kilbrannan (sound) C 5
Kinnairds (head) G 3
Kintyre (pen.), 10,077 C 5
Kintyre, Mull of (prom.) C 5
Knapdale (dist.), 4,082 C 5
Kyle of Tongue (inlet) D 2
Laggan (bay) B 5
Lammermuir (hills) F 5
Lennox (hills) B 1
Leven (lake) E 4
Leven, Loch (inlet) D 4
Lewis (dist.), 20,047 B 2
Liddel Water (riv.) F 5
Linnhe, Loch (inlet) C 4
Lismore (isl.), 166 C 4
Little Minch (sound) B 3
Lochaber (dist.), 13,813 D 4
Lochnagar (mt.) E 4
Lochy, Loch (lake) D 3
Lomond, Loch (lake) D 4
Long, Loch (inlet) D 4
Lorne (dist.), 12,162 C 4
Lorne (firth) C 4
Loyal, Loch (lake) D 2
Luce (bay) D 6
Luing (isl.), 151 C 4
Lyon (riv.) D 4
Machers, The (pen.), 6,192 D 6
Mainland (isl.), 12,747 E 1
Mainland (isl.), 12,944 G 2
Mar (dist.), 23,931 F 3
Maree, Loch (lake) C 3
May, Isle of (isl.), 10 F 4
Merrick (mt.) D 5
Minginish (dist.), 772 B 3
Moidart (dist.), 155 C 4
Monach (sound) A 3
Monadhliath (mts.) D 3
Moorfoot (hills) E 5
Moray (firth) E 3
Moriston (riv.) D 3
Morven (dist.), 398 C 4
Morven (mt.) E 2
Muck (isl.), 24 B 4
Muckle Flugga (isl.), 3 G 2
Mull (isl.), 2,024 C 4
Mull (head) F 1
Mull (sound) C 4
Nairn (riv.) D 3
na Keal, Loch (inlet) B 4
Naver (riv.) D 2
Ness, Loch (lake) D 3
Nevis, Loch (inlet) C 3
Nith (riv.) E 5
North (chan.) C 5
North (sound) F 1
North (sound) G 4
North Esk (riv.) F 4
North Minch (sound) B 3
North Ronaldsay (isl.), 134 F 1
North Uist (isl.), 1,469 A 3
Oa, Mull of (prom.) B 5
Ochil (hills) E 4
Oich (riv.) D 3
Orchy (riv.) D 4
Orkney (isls.), 17,675 F 1
Oronsay (isl.), 2 B 4
Outer Hebrides (isls.), 29,615 A 3
Oykel (riv.) D 3
Pabbay (isl.), 4 A 3
Papa Stour (isl.), 24 F 2
Papa Westray (isl.), 106 F 1
Paps of Jura (mt.) C 5
Park (dist.), 210 B 2
Peel Fell (mt.) F 5
Pentland (hills) D 2
Pentland (firth) E 2
Pladda (isl.), 2 C 5
Quoich, Loch (lake) C 3
Raasay (isl.), 163 C 3
Rannoch (dist.), 1,177 D 4
Rannoch, Loch (lake) D 4
Rhinns, The (pen.), 8,295 C 6
Roag, Loch (inlet) B 2
Rona (isl.), 3 B 3
Ross of Mull (pen.), 585 B 4
Rousay (isl.), 181 E 1
Rudha Hunish (cape) B 3
Rudh Re (cape) C 3
Rum (isl.), 40 B 3
Ryan, Loch (inlet) C 5
Saint Kilda (isl.), 65 A 2
Saint Magnus (bay) F 2
Sanda (isl.), 9 C 5
Sanday (isl.), 11 B 3
Sanday (isl.), 592 F 1
Scalpay (isl.), 483 B 3
Scalpay (isl.), 5 C 3
Scapa Flow (chan.) E 2
Scarp (isl.), 12 A 2
Scridain, Loch (inlet) B 4
Scurdie Ness (prom.) F 4
Seaforth, Loch (inlet) B 3
Seil (isl.), 326 C 4
Sgurr a Choire Ghlais (mt.) D 3
Sgurr Alasdair (mt.) B 3
Sgurr Mor (mt.) C 3
Sgurr na Lapaich (mt.) C 3
Shapinsay (isl.), 346 F 1
Shetland (isls.), 18,494 G 2
Shiant (sound) B 3
Shiel, Loch (lake) C 4
Shin (falls) D 3
Shin, Loch (lake) D 2
Shona (isl.), 17 C 4
Sidlaw (hills) E 4
Sinclair's (bay) E 2
Skye, Isle of (isl.), 7,183 B 3
Sleat (pt.) B 4
Sleat (dist.), 449 C 3
Small Isles (isls.), 171 B 4
Snizort, Loch (inlet) B 3
Soay (isl.), 5 B 3
Solway (firth) E 6
South Esk (riv.) F 4
South Ronaldsay (isl.), 776 F 2
South Uist (isl.), 2,281 A 3
Spean (riv.) D 4
Spey (riv.) E 3
Start (pt.) F 1
Stinchar (riv.) D 5
Strathbogie (dist.), 7,959 F 3
Strathmore (valley) E 4
Strathspey (dist.), 6,668 E 3
Strathy (pt.) E 2
Stroma (isl.), 8 E 2
Stronsay (isl.), 436 F 1
Sumburgh (head) G 2
Sunart, Loch (inlet) C 4
Swona (isl.), 3 E 2
Taransay (isl.), 5 A 3
Tarbat Ness (prom.) E 3
Tarbert, East Loch (inlet) B 3
Tarbert, Loch (inlet) B 5
Tarbert, West Loch (inlet) A 3
Tay (riv.) E 4
Tay (firth) F 4
Tay, Loch (lake) D 4
Teith (riv.) D 4
Teviot (riv.) F 5
Thurso (riv.) E 2
Tiree (isl.), 875 B 4
Tolsta (head) B 2
Tor Ness (prom.) E 2
Torridon, Loch (inlet) C 3
Trossachs, The (valley) D 4
Trotternish (dist.), 1,948 B 3
Tweed (riv.) F 5
Tyne (riv.) F 5
Ulva (isl.), 23 B 4
Unst (isl.), 1,124 G 2
Vaternish (dist.), 162 B 3
Vatersay (isl.), 77 A 4
West Burra (isl.), 501 G 2
Westray (firth) E 1
Westray (isl.), 735 E 1
Whalsay (isl.), 870 G 2
White Coomb (mt.) E 5
Wigtown (bay) D 6
Wrath (cape) C 2
Wyre (isl.), 36 F 1
Yarrow (riv.) E 5
Yell (isl.), 1,143 G 2
Ythan (riv.) F 3

★Population of met. area
⊙Population of parish.

Agriculture, Industry and Resources

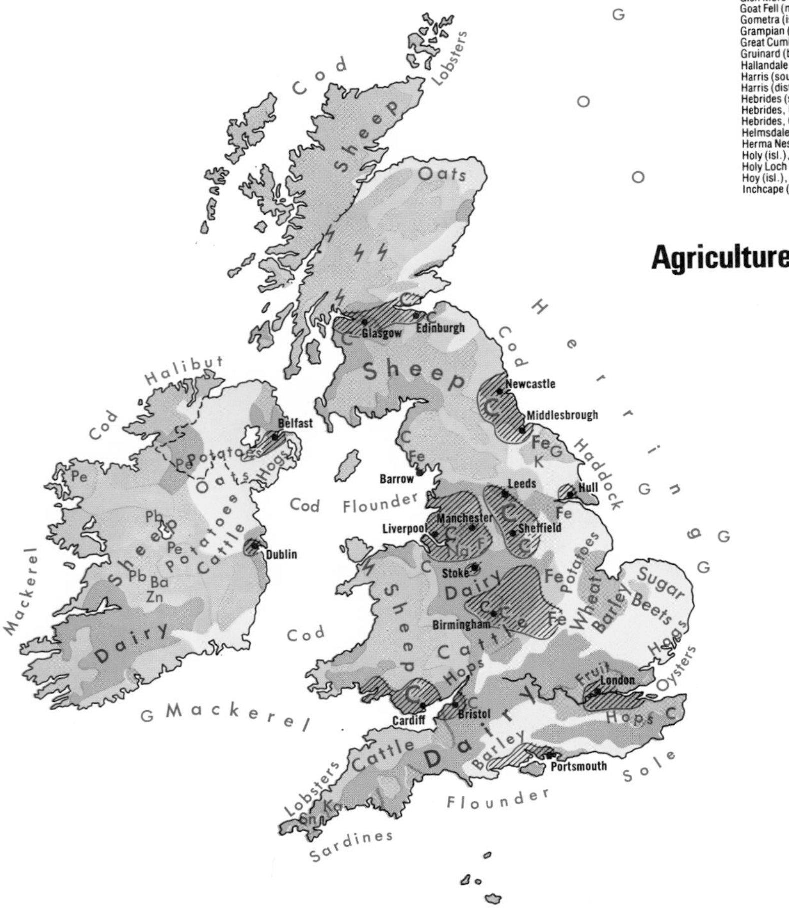

DOMINANT LAND USE

- Cereals (chiefly oats, barley)
- Truck Farming, Horticulture
- Dairy, Mixed Farming
- Livestock, Mixed Farming
- Pasture Livestock

MAJOR MINERAL OCCURRENCES

Ba	Barite	Na	Salt
C	Coal	O	Petroleum
F	Fluorspar	Pb	Lead
Fe	Iron Ore	Pe	Peat
G	Natural Gas	Sn	Tin
K	Potash	Zn	Zinc
Ka	Kaolin (china clay)		

Water Power

Major Industrial Areas

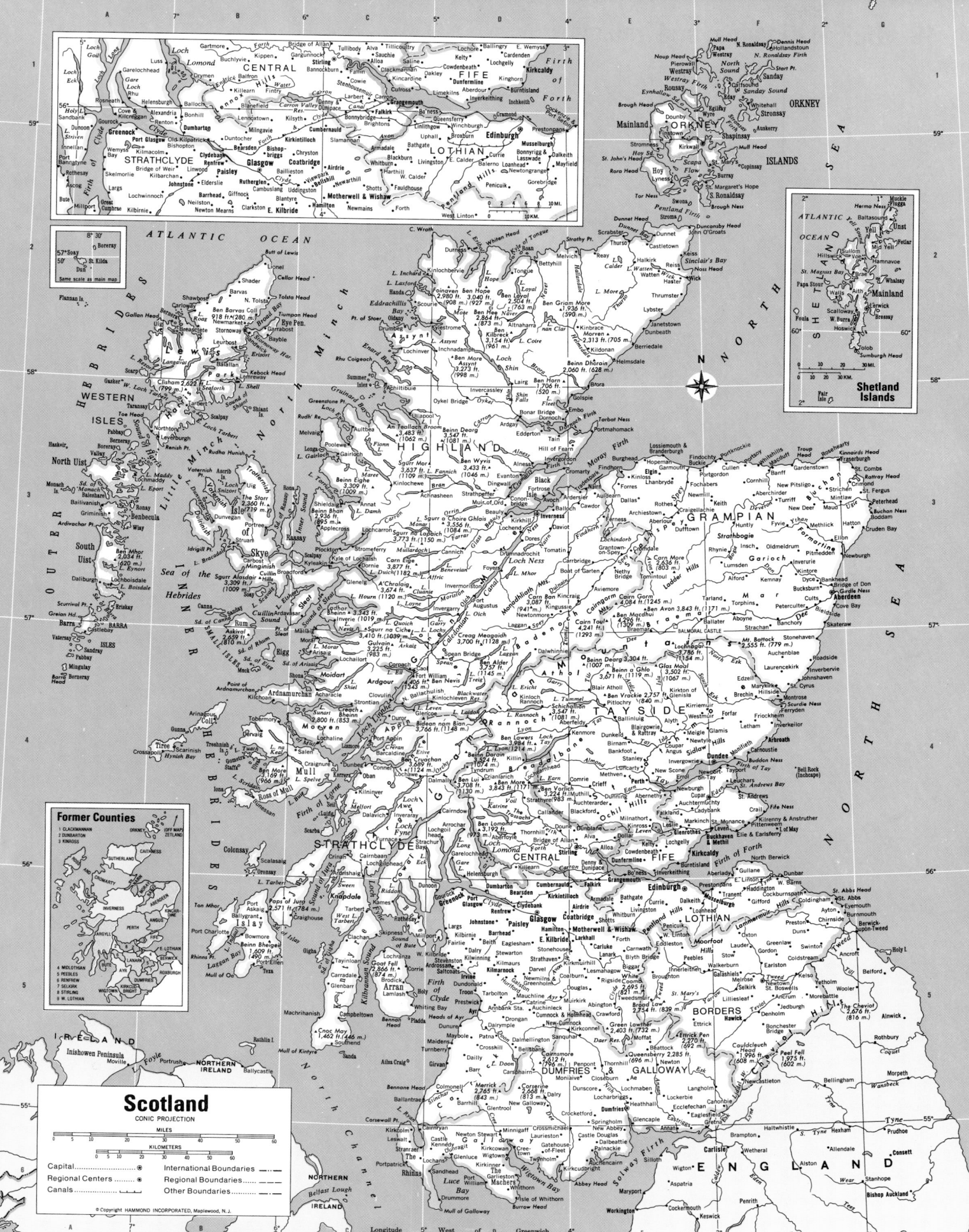

Scotland
CONIC PROJECTION

IRELAND

Carlow 34,237 H6
Cavan 52,618 G4
Clare 75,008 D6
Cork 352,883 D7
Donegal 108,344 K2
Dublin 852,219 J5
Galway 149,223 D5
Kerry 112,772 B7
Kildare 71,977 H5
Kilkenny 61,473 G6
Laois 45,259 G6
Leitrim 28,360 E3
Leix (Laois) 45,259 G6
Limerick 140,459 D7
Longford 28,250 F4
Louth 74,951 J4
Mayo 109,525 C4
Meath 71,729 H4
Monaghan 46,242 H3
Offaly 51,829 F5
Roscommon 53,519 E4
Sligo 50,275 D3
Tipperary 123,565 F6
Waterford 77,315 F7
Westmeath 53,570 G5
Wexford 86,351 H7
Wicklow 66,295 J5

CITIES and TOWNS

Abbeydorney, 188 B 7
Abbeyfeale, 1,337 C 7
Abbeylara, ‡290 F 4
Abbeyleix, 1,033 G 6
Achill Sound, ‡1,163 B 4
Aclare, ‡336 D 3
Adare, 545 D 6
Aghada-Farsid-Rostellan, 461 E 8
Aghadoe, ‡497 B 7
Aghagower, ‡693 C 4
Ahascragh, 221 E 5
Annagry, 201 E 1
Annascaul, 236 B 7
An Uaimh, 4,605 H 4
An Uaimh, *6,665 H 4
Ardagh, Limerick, 213 C 7
Ardagh, Longford, ‡974 F 4
Ardara, 683 E 2
Ardee, *3,183 H 4
Ardee, 3,096 H 4
Ardfert, 286 B 7
Ardfinnan, 510 F 7
Ardmore, 233 F 8
Ardrahan, ‡239 D 5
Arklow, 6,948 J 6
Arthurstown, 1,188 H 7
Arva, 370 F 4
Ashford, 341 J 5
Askeaton, 844 D 6
Athboy, 705 H 4
Athea, 328 C 7
Athenry, 1,240 D 5
Athleague, ‡955 E 4
Athlone, 9,825 F 5
Athlone, *11,611 F 5
Athy, 4,270 H 6
Athy, *4,654 H 6
Aughrim, 451 J 6
Avoca, ‡620 J 6
Bagenalstown (Muinebeag), 2,321 H 6
Baile Átha Cliath (Dublin) (cap.), 567,866 K 5
Bailieborough, 1,293 G 4
Balbriggan, 3,741 J 4
Balla, 293 C 4
Ballaghaderreen, 1,121 E 4
Ballina, Mayo, 6,063 C 3
Ballina, *6,369 C 3
Ballina, Tipperary, 336 E 6
Ballinagh, 459 G 4
Ballinakill, 300 G 6
Ballineen D 8
Ballinamore, 808 F 3
Ballinasloe, 5,969 E 5
Ballincollig-Carrigrohane, 2,110 D 8
Ballindine, 232 C 4
Ballingarry, Limerick, 422 D 7
Ballingarry, Tipperary, ‡574 F 6
Ballinlough, 242 D 4
Ballinrobe, 1,272 C 4
Ballintober, ‡867 E 4
Ballintra, 197 E 2
Ballisodare, 486 E 3
Ballivor, 287 H 4
Ballybay, 754 G 3
Ballybay, *1,159 G 3
Ballybofey-Stranorlar, 2,214 F 2
Ballybunion, 1,287 B 7
Ballycanew, ‡460 J 6
Ballycarney, ‡294 J 6
Ballycastle, ‡724 C 3
Ballyconnell, 421 F 3
Ballycotton, 389 F 8
Ballydehob, 253 C 8
Ballyduff, 406 B 7
Ballygar, 359 E 4
Ballygeary, 725 J 7
Ballyhaise, 274 G 3
Ballyhaunis, 1,093 D 4
Ballyheigue, 450 B 7
Ballyjamesduff, 673 G 4
Ballylanders, 266 E 7
Ballylongford, 504 B 6
Ballymahon, 707 F 4
Ballymakeery, 272 C 8
Ballymore, ‡447 F 5
Ballymore Eustace, 433 J 5
Ballymote, 952 D 3
Ballyporeen, ‡810 E 7
Ballyragget, 519 G 6
Ballyroan, ‡478 G 6
Ballyshannon, 2,325 E 3
Ballytore, ‡580 H 5
Baltimore, 200 C 9
Baltinglass, 909 H 6
Baltray, 236 J 4
Banagher, 1,052 F 5
Bandon, 2,257 D 8
Bandon, *4,071 D 8
Bannow, ‡798 H 7
Bansha, 184 E 7
Bantry, 2,579 C 8
Barna, ‡1,734 C 5
Belmullet, 744 B 3
Belturbet, 1,092 G 3
Bennettsbridge, 367 G 6
Birr, 3,319 F 5
Birr, *3,881 F 5
Blanchardstown, 3,279 H 5
Blarney, 1,128 D 8
Blessington, 637 J 5
Boherbue, 372 C 7
Borris, 430 H 6
Borris-in-Ossory, 276 F 6
Borrisokane, 769 E 6
Borrisoleigh, 471 E 6
Boyle, 1,727 E 4
Boyle, *1,939 E 4
Bray, 14,467 K 5
Bray, *15,841 K 5
Bri Chualann (Bray), 14,467 K 5
Broadford, 226 C 7
Brosna, 250 C 7
Bruff, 547 D 7
Bruree, 243 D 7
Bunbeg-Derrybeg, 878 E 1
Bunclody-Carrickduff, 929 H 6
Buncrana, 2,955 G 1
Buncrana, *3,334 G 1
Bundoran, 1,337 E 3
Burtonport, ‡1,288 E 2
Buttevant, 1,045 D 7
Cahir, 1,747 F 7
Cahirciveen, 1,547 A 8
Callan, 1,283 G 7
Camolin, 306 J 6
Campile, 231 H 7
Cappamore, 567 E 6
Cappawhite, 305 E 6
Cappoquin, 872 F 7
Carbury, ‡894 H 5
Carlingford, 559 J 3
Carlow, 9,588 H 6
Carlow, *10,399 H 6
Carndonagh, 1,146 G 1
Carnew, 570 H 6
Carrickmacross, 2,100 H 4
Carrickmacross, *2,475 H 4
Carrick-on-Shannon, 1,854 F 4
Carrick-on-Suir, 5,006 F 7
Carrigaholt, ‡493 B 6
Carrigaline, 951 E 8
Carrigallen, 230 F 4
Carrigart, ‡753 F 1
Carrigtwohill, 622 E 8
Carrowkeel, ‡326 G 1
Cashel, 2,692 F 7
Castlebar, 5,979 C 4
Castlebar, *6,476 C 4
Castlebellingham, 407 J 4
Castleblayney, 2,118 H 3
Castleblayney, *2,395 H 3
Castlecomer-Donaguile, 1,244 G 6
Castledermot, 583 H 6
Castlefin, 610 F 2
Castlegregory, 216 A 7
Castleisland, 1,929 B 7
Castlemartyr, 491 E 8
Castlepollard, 693 G 4
Castlerea, 1,752 D 4
Castletown, ‡504 F 6
Castletownbere, 812 B 8
Castletownroche, 399 D 7
Castletownshend, 170 C 9
Causeway, 215 B 7
Cavan, 3,273 G 3
Cavan, *4,312 G 3
Ceanannus Mór, 2,391 G 4
Ceanannus Mór, *2,653 G 4
Celbridge, 1,568 H 5
Charlestown-Bellahy, 677 D 4
Charleville (Rathluirc), 2,232 D 7
Clara, 2,156 F 5
Claregalway, ‡594 D 5
Claremorris, 1,718 C 4
Clashmore, ‡379 F 8
Clifden, 790 B 5
Cloghan, 404 F 5
Clogh-Chatsworth, 324 G 6
Clogheen, 530 F 7
Clogherhead, 649 J 4
Clonakilty, 2,430 D 8
Clonaslee, 285 F 5
Clondalkin, 7,009 J 5
Clonegal, 202 H 6
Clones, 2,164 G 3
Clonfert, ‡430 E 5
Clonmany, ‡936 G 1
Clonmel, 11,622 F 7
Clonmel, *12,291 F 7
Clonmellon, 328 H 4
Clonroche, 222 H 7
Clontuskert, 351 E 4
Cloone, ‡460 F 4
Cloughjordan, 480 E 6
Cloyne, 654 E 8
Coachford, 290 D 8
Cóbh, 6,076 E 8
Cóbh, *7,141 E 8
Coill Dubh, 920 H 5
Collon, 262 J 4
Collooney, 546 E 3
Cong, 233 C 4
Convoy, 654 F 2
Coolaney, ‡352 D 3
Coolgreany, ‡603 J 6
Cootehill, 1,415 G 3
Cootehill, *1,542 G 3
Cork, 128,645 E 8
Cork, *134,430 E 8
Corofin, 342 C 6
Courtmacsherry, 210 D 8
Courtown Harbour, 291 J 6
Creeslough, 269 F 1
Crookhaven, ‡400 B 9
Croom, 756 D 6
Crosshaven, 1,222 E 8
Crossmolina, 1,077 C 3
Crusheen, ‡405 D 6
Culdaff, ‡621 G 1
Daingean, 492 G 5
Delvin, 223 G 4
Dingle, 1,401 A 7
Doaghbeg, ‡701 F 1
Donabate, 426 J 5
Donegal, 1,725 F 2
Doneraile, 799 D 7
Dooagh-Keel, 649 A 4
Doon, 387 E 6
Douglas, ‡4,448 D 8
Drimoleague, 415 C 8
Drishane, ‡1,548 C 7
Drogheda, 19,762 J 4
Drogheda, *20,095 J 4
Droichead Nua, 5,053 H 5
Droichead Nua, *6,444 H 5
Dromahair, 177 E 3
Drumcar, ‡1,215 J 4
Drumconrath, ‡1,044 H 4
Drumkeerin, ‡467 E 3
Drumlish, 205 F 4
Drumshanbo, 576 E 3
Dublin (cap.), 567,866 K 5
Dublin, *679,748 K 5
Duleek, 658 J 4
Duncannon, 228 H 7
Dundalk, 21,672 H 3
Dundalk, *23,816 H 3
Dunfanaghy, 303 F 1
Dungarvan, 5,583 F 7
Dungloe, 940 E 2
Dunkineely, 288 E 2
Dún Laoghaire, 53,171 K 5
Dún Laoghaire, *98,379 K 5
Dunlavin, 423 H 5
Dunleer 855 J4
Dunmanway 1,392 C8
Dunmore 522 D4
Dunmore East 656 G7
Dunshaughlin⊙ 283 H5
Durrow, Laois 596 G6
Durrow, Offaly⊙ 441 F5
Easky 184 D3
Edenderry 2,953 G5
Edenderry* 3,116 G5
Elphin 489 E4
Emyvale 281 G3
Ennis 5,972 D6
Ennis* 10,840 D6
Enniscorthy 5,704 J7
Enniscorthy* 6,642 J7
Enniskerry 772 J5
Ennistymon 1,013 C6
Eyrecourt 314 E5
Fahan⊙ 1,023 G1
Falcarragh 506 E1
Feakle⊙ 398 D6
Fenit 360 B7
Ferbane 1,064 F5
Fermoy 3,237 E7
Fermoy* 4,033 E7
Ferns 712 J6
Fethard, Tipperary 1,064 F7
Fethard, Wexford⊙ 637 H7
Foxford 868 C4
Foynes 624 C6
Frankford (Kilcormac) 1,089 F5
Frenchpark⊙ 693 E4
Freshford 585 G6
Galbally 258 E7
Galway 27,726 C5
Galway* 29,375 C5
Geashill⊙ 751 G5
Glandore⊙ 695 C8
Glanmire-Riverstown 1,113 E8
Glanworth 335 E7
Glenamaddy 315 D4
Glenbeigh 266 B7
Glencolumbkille⊙ 787 D2
Glengarriff 244 C8
Glenties 734 E2
Glenville⊙ 264 D7
Glin 623 C6
Golden⊙ 640 F7
Gorey 2,946 J6
Gorey* 3,024 J6
Gormanston⊙ 1,384 J4
Gort 975 D5
Gowran 402 G6
Graiguenamanagh-Tinnahinch 1,303 H6
Granard 1,054 F4
Greencastle 322 H1
Greenore 882 J4
Greystones-Delgany 4,517 K5
Gurteen 165 D3
Hacketstown 574 H6
Headford 673 C5
Holycross⊙ 902 F6
Hospital 525 E7
Inchigeelagh⊙ 516 C8
Inishannon 190 D8
Inistioge 179 G7
Inniscrone 582 C3
Johnstown 303 G6
Kanturk 2,063 D7
Keel-Dooagh 649 A4
Kells⊙ 423 G6
Kells (Ceanannus Mór) 2,391 G4
Kenmare 903 B8
Kilbaha⊙ 471 B6
Kilbeggan 635 G5
Kilcar 273 D2
Kilcock 827 H5
Kilconnell⊙ 629 E5
Kilcoole 679 K5
Kilcormac 1,089 F5
Kilcullen 880 H5
Kildare 3,137 H5
Kildysart 239 C6
Kilfenora⊙ 441 C6
Kilfinane 561 D7
Kilgarvan 228 B8
Kilkee 1,287 B6
Kilkelly 225 D4
Kilkenny 9,838 G6
Kilkenny* 13,306 G6
Killala 368 C3
Killaloe 871 D6
Killarney 7,184 C7
Killarney* 7,541 C7
Killavullen 221 D7
Killenaule 592 F6
Killeshandra 432 F3
Killimor 221 E5
Killinaboy⊙ 297 C6
Killorglin 1,150 B7
Killucan-Rathwire 290 G4
Killybegs 1,094 E2
Kilmacrennan 274 F1
Kilmacthomas 396 G7
Kilmallock 1,170 D7
Kilmeadan⊙ 262 G7
Kilmihill 284 C6
Kilmoganny 181 G7
Kilmore Quay 273 H7
Kilmurry⊙ 387 C6
Kilnaleck 273 G4
Kilronan 243 B5
Kilrush 2,671 C6
Kilsheelan⊙ 665 F7
Kiltimagh 978 C4
Kilworth 360 E7
Kingscourt 1,016 H4
Kingstown (Dún Laoghaire) 53,171 K5
Kinlough 160 E3
Kinnegad 362 G5
Kinnitty⊙ 420 F5
Kinsale 1,622 D8
Kinsale* 1,989 D8
Kinvara 293 D5
Knightstown 236 A8
Knock⊙ 1,202 D4
Knocklong 248 D7
Knocknagashel 168 C7
Labasheeda⊙ 468 C6
Laghy⊙ 625 E2
Lahinch 455 C6
Lanesborough-Ballyleague 906 E4
Laracor⊙ 404 H4
Laytown-Bettystown-Mornington 1,882 J4
Leenane⊙ 271 B4
Leighlindridge 379 H6
Leitrim⊙ 544 F3
Leixlip 2,402 H5
Letterkenny 4,930 F2
Letterkenny* 5,207 F2
Lifford 1,121 F2
Limerick 57,161 D6
Limerick* 63,002 D6
Liscarroll 231 D7
Lisdoonvarna 459 C5
Lismore 884 F7
Lismore⊙ 1,041 F7
Listowel 3,021 C7
Littleton 322 F6
Longford 3,876 F4
Longford* 4,791 F4
Lorrha⊙ 685 E5
Loughrea 3,075 E5
Louisburgh 310 B4
Louth 208 J4
Lucan-Doddsborough 4,245 J5
Luimneach (Limerick) 57,161 D6
Lusk 553 J4
Macroom 2,256 C8
Malahide 3,834 J5
Malin⊙ 552 G1
Mallow 5,901 D7
Mallow* 6,506 D7
Manorhamilton 858 E3
Manulla⊙ 660 C4
Maryborough (Portlaoise) 3,902 G5
Maynooth 1,296 H5
Meathas Truim 546 G4
Midleton 3,075 E8
Midleton* 4,666 E8
Milford 763 F1
Millstreet 1,319 D7
Milltown 260 A7
Miltown-Malbay 677 C6
Minard⊙ 397 A7
Mitchelstown 2,783 E7
Moate 1,378 F5
Mohill 868 F4
Monaghan 5,256 G3
Monasterevan 1,619 H5
Moneygall 282 F6
Monivea⊙ 405 D5
Mooncoin 413 G7
Mount Bellew 275 D5
Mountcharles 445 E2
Mountmellick 2,595 G5
Mountmellick* 2,864 G5
Mountrath 1,098 F5
Moville 1,089 G1
Moycullen⊙ 498 C5
Moynalty⊙ 583 H4
Muff 240 G1
Muinebeag 2,321 H6
Mullagh 293 H4
Mullaghmore⊙ 629 D3
Mullinahone 262 F7
Mullinavat 343 G7
Mullingar 6,790 G4
Mullingar* 9,245 G4
Naas 5,078 H5
Navan (An Uaimh) 4,605 H4
Nenagh 5,085 E6
Nenagh* 5,174 E6
Newbliss⊙ 547 G3
Newbridge (Droichead Nua) 5,053 H5
Newcastle 2,549 D7
Newcastle* 2,680 D7
Newmarket 886 C7
Newmarket-on-Fergus 1,052 D6
New Pallas⊙ 1,271 E6
Newport, Mayo 420 C4
Newport, Tipperary 582 E6
New Ross 4,775 H7
New Ross* 5,153 H7
Newtown Forbes⊙ 495 F4
Newtownmountkennedy 882 J5
Newtownsandes 268 C6
O'Briensbridge-Montpelier 237 D6
Oldcastle 759 G4
Old Leighlin⊙ 309 G6
Oola 348 E6
Oranmore 440 D5
Oughterard 628 C5
Passage East 408 G7
Passage West 2,709 E8
Patrickswell 415 D6
Pettigo 332 F2
Piltown 456 G7
Portarlington 3,117 G5
Portlaoise 3,902 G5
Portlaoise* 6,470 G5
Portlaw 1,166 G7
Portmarnock 1,726 J5
Portumna 913 E5
Queenstown (Cóbh) 6,076 E8
Rahan⊙ 531 F5
Ramelton 807 F1
Raphoe 945 F2
Rathangan 868 G5
Rathcoole 1,740 J5
Rathcormac 191 E7
Rathdowney 892 F6
Rathdrum 1,141 J6
Rathgormuck⊙ 231 F7
Rathkeale 1,543 D7
Rathluirc 2,232 D7
Rathmore 437 J5
Rathmullen 486 F1
Rathnew-Merrymeeting 954 J6
Rathowen⊙ 294 F4
Rathvilly 230 H6
Ratoath 300 J5
Riverstown 236 E3
Rockcorry 233 H3
Rosapenna⊙ 822 F1
Roscommon 1,556 E4
Roscommon* 2,821 E4
Roscrea 3,855 F6
Rosscarbery 309 C8
Rosses Point 464 D3
Rosslare 588 J7
Rosslare Harbour (Ballygeary) 725 J7
Roundstone 204 A5
Roundwood 260 J5
Rush 2,633 J4
Saint Johnston 463 F2
Scarriff 619 E6
Schull 457 B8
Scotstown 264 H3
Shanagolden 231 C6
Shannon Airport 3,657 D6
Shannon Bridge 188 F5
Shercock 313 G4
Shillelagh 246 J6
Shinrone 365 F5
Shrule 288 C4
Sixmilebridge 567 D6
Skerries 3,044 J4
Skibbereen 2,104 C8
Slane 483 H4
Sligo 14,080 E3
Sligo* 14,456 E3
Sneem 285 B8
Spiddal⊙ 819 C5
Stepaside 748 J5
Stradbally, Laois 891 G5
Stradbally, Waterford 158 F7
Strokestown 563 E4
Swanlinbar 257 F3
Swinford 1,105 C4
Swords 4,133 J5
Taghmon 369 H7
Tallaght 6,174 J5
Tallow, 883 F 7
Tarbert, 485 C 6
Teltown, ‡739 H 4
Templemore, 2,174 F 6
Templetuohy, 197 F 6
Termonfeckin, 328 J 4
Thomastown, 1,270 G 7
Thurles, 6,840 F 6
Thurles, *7,087 F 6
Timoleague, 257 D 8
Tinahely, 450 H 6
Tipperary, 4,631 E 7
Tipperary, *4,717 E 7
Toomevara, 272 E 6
Tralee, 12,287 B 7
Tralee, *13,263 B 7
Tramore, 3,792 G 7
Trim, 1,700 H 4
Trim, *2,255 H 4
Tuam, 3,808 D 4
Tuam, *4,952 D 4
Tubbercurry, 959 D 3
Tulla, 415 D 6
Tullamore, 6,809 G 5
Tullamore, *7,474 G 5
Tullaroan, ‡301 G 6
Tullow, 1,838 H 6
Tullow, *1,945 H 6
Tynagh, ‡452 E 5
Tyrrellspass, 289 G 5
Urlingford, 652 F 6
Virginia, 583 G 4
Waterford, 31,968 G 7
Waterford, *33,676 G 7
Waterville, 547 A 8
Westport, 3,023 C 4
Wexford, 11,849 H 7
Wexford, *13,293 H 7
Whitegate, 370 E 8
Wicklow, 3,786 K 6
Wicklow, *3,915 K 6
Woodenbridge, ‡620 J 6
Woodford, 198 E 5
Youghal, 5,445 F 8
Youghal, *5,626 F 8

OTHER FEATURES

Achill (isl.), 3,129 A 4
Allen (lake) E 3
Allen, Bog of (marsh) H 5
Aran (isl.), 773 D 2
Aran (isls.), 1,499 B 5
Arklow (bank) K 6
Arrow (lake) E 3
Awbeg (riv.) D 7
Ballinskelligs (bay) A 8
Ballycotton (bay) F 8
Ballyheige (bay) B 7
Ballyhoura (hills) E 7
Ballyteige (bay) H 7
Bandon (riv.) D 8
Bann (riv.) J 6
Bantry (bay) B 8
Barrow (riv.) H 7
Baurtregaum (mt.) A 7
Bear (isl.), 288 B 8
Blacksod (bay) A 3
Blackstairs (mt.) H 6
Blackwater (riv.) D 7
Blackwater (riv.) H 4
Blasket (isls.) A 7
Bloody Foreland (prom.) E 1
Blue Stack (mts.) E 2
Boderg (lake) E 4
Boggeragh (mts.) D 7
Boyne (riv.) J 4
Brandon (head) A 7
Bride (riv.) E 7
Broad Haven (harb.) B 3
Brosna (riv.) F 5
Bull, The (isl.), 5 A 8
Caha (mts.) B 8
Carlingford (inlet) J 3
Carnsore (pt.) J 7
Carrantuohill (mt.) B 7
Clare (riv.) D 5
Clare (isls.), 168 A 4
Clear (cape) B 9
Clear (isl.), 192 C 9
Clew (bay) B 4
Comeragh (mts.) F 7
Conn (lake) C 3
Connacht (prov.), 390,902 C 4
Connemara (dist.), 7,599 B 5
Cork (harb.) E 8
Corrib (lake) C 5
Courtmacsherry (bay) D 8
Curragh, The H 5
Dee (riv.) H 4
Deel (riv.) D 7
Deele (riv.) F 2
Derg (lake) E 6
Derravaragh (lake) G 4
Derryveagh (mts.) E 2
Dingle (bay) A 7
Donegal (bay) D 3
Drum (hills) F 7
Dublin (bay) J 5
Dundalk (bay) J 4
Dunmanus (bay) B 8
Dursey (isl.), 38 A 8
Ennell (lake) G 5
Erne (riv.) E 3
Errigal (mt.) E 1
Erris (head) A 3
Fanad (head) F 1
Fastnet Rock (isl.), 3 B 9
Feale (riv.) C 7
Fergus (riv.) D 6
Finn (riv.) F 2
Finn (riv.) G 3
Flesk (riv.) C 7
Foyle (inlet) G 1
Foyle (riv.) G 2
Galley (head) D 9
Galtee (mts.) E 7
Galtymore (mt.) E 7
Galway (bay) C 5
Gara (lake) D 4
Garadice (lake) F 3
Gill (lake) E 3
Glyde (riv.) H 4
Golden Vale (plain) E 7
Gorumna (isl.), 1,108 B 5
Gowna (lake) G 4
Grand (canal) G 5
Greenore (pt.) J 7
Gweebarra (bay) D 2
Hags (head) B 6
Helvick (head) G 7
Hook (head) H 7
Horn (head) E 1
Iar Connacht (dist.), 10,774 C 5
Inishbofin (isl.), 236 A 4
Inishbofin (isl.), 103 E 1
Inisheer (isl.), 313 B 5
Inishmaan (isl.), 319 C 5
Inishmore (isl.), 864 B 5
Inishowen (head) H 1
Inishowen (pen.), 24,109 G 1
Inishtrahull (isl.), 3 G 1
Inishturk (isls.), 83 A 4
Inny (riv.) A 8
Inny (riv.) F 4
Inver (bay) E 2
Ireland's Eye (isl.) K 5
Irish (sea) K 4
Joyce's Country (dist.), 2,021 B 4
Kenmare (riv.) A 8
Kerry (head) A 7
Key (lake) E 3
Kilkieran (bay) B 5
Killala (bay) C 3
Killary (harb.) A 4
Kinsale (harb.) E 8
Kippure (mt.) J 5
Knockboy (mt.) B 8
Knockmealdown (mts.) F 7
Lady's Island Lake (inlet) J 7
Lambay (isl.), 24 K 4
Laune (riv.) B 7
Leane (lake) B 7
Leane (lake) G 4
Lee (riv.) D 8
Leinster (mt.) H 6
Leinster (prov.), 1,498,140 G 5
Lettermullan (isl.), 221 B 5
Liffey (riv.) H 5
Liscannor (bay) B 6
Long Island (bay) B 9
Loop (head) A 6
Lugnaquillia (mt.) J 5
Macgillicuddy's Reeks (mts.) B 7
Macnean (lake) F 3
Maigue (riv.) D 6
Maine (riv.) C 7
Malin (head) F 1
Mask (lake) C 4
Maumturk (mts.) B 5
Melvin (lake) E 3
Mizen (head) B 9
Moher (cliffs) B 6
Monavullagh (mts.) F 7
Moy (riv.) C 3
Mulkear (riv.) E 6
Mullaghareirk (mts.) C 7
Mulroy (bay) F 1
Munster (prov.), 882,002 D 7
Mweelrea (mt.) B 4
Mweenish (isl.), 198 B 5
Nagles (mts.) E 7
Nenagh (riv.) E 6
Nephin (mt.) C 3
Nore (riv.) G 7
North (sound) B 5
Omey (isl.), 34 A 5
Oughter (lake) G 3
Ovoca (riv.) J 6
Owenmore (riv.) D 3
Owey (isl.), 51 D 1
Paps, The (mt.) C 7
Partry (mts.) C 4
Pollaphuca (res.) J 5
Punchestown H 5
Rathlin O'Birne (isl.), 3 C 2
Ree (lake) F 5
Roaringwater (bay) B 9
Rosses (bay) D 1
Rosskeeragh (pt.) D 3
Royal (canal) G 4
Saint Finan's (bay) A 8
Saint George's (chan.) K 7
Saint John's (pt.) D 2
Saltee (isls.) H 7
Seven (heads) D 8
Seven Hogs, The (isls.) A 7
Shannon (riv.) E 6
Sheeffry (hills) B 4
Sheelin (lake) G 4
Sheep Haven (harb.) F 1
Sheeps (head) B 8
Sherkin (isl.), 82 C 9
Silvermine (mts.) E 6
Slaney (riv.) H 7
Slieve Aughty (mts.) D 5
Slieve Bloom (mts.) F 5
Slieve Gamph (mts.) D 3
Slievenaman (mt.) F 7
Sligo (bay) D 3
Slyne (head) A 5
South (sound) C 5
Stacks (mts.) B 7
Suck (riv.) E 5
Suir (riv.) G 7
Swilly (inlet) F 1
Tara (hill) H 4
Tory (isl.), 273 E 1
Tory (sound) E 1
Tralee (bay) B 7
Trawbreaga (bay) F 1
Ulster (part) (prov.), 207,204 G 2
Valencia (Valentia) (isl.), 770 A 8
Valentia (isl.), 770 A 8
Waterford (harb.) G 7
Wexford (bay) J 7
Wicklow (head) K 6
Wicklow (mts.) J 6
Youghal (bay) F 8

NORTHERN IRELAND

DISTRICTS

Antrim, 37,600 J 2
Ards, 52,100 K 2
Armagh, 47,500 H 3
Ballymena, 52,200 J 2
Ballymoney, 22,700 J 1
Bainbridge, 28,800 J 3
Belfast, 368,200 J 2
Carrickfergus, 27,500 K 2
Castlereagh, 63,600 K 2
Coleraine, 44,900 H 1
Cookstown, 27,500 H 2
Craigavon, 71,200 J 3
Down, 48,800 K 3
Dungannon, 43,000 H 3
Fermanagh, 50,900 F 3
Larne, 29,000 K 2
Limavady, 25,000 H 1
Lisburn, 80,800 J 2
Londonderry, 86,600 G 2
Magherafelt, 32,200 H 2
Mourne (Newry and Mourne), 75,300 J 3
Moyle, 13,400 J 1
Newtownabbey, 71,500 J 2
North Down, 59,600 K 2
Omagh, 41,800 G 2
Strabane, 35,500 G 2

CITIES and TOWNS

Ahoghill, ‡1,929 J 2
Annalong, 1,001 K 3
Antrim, 8,351 J 2
Ardglass, 1,052 K 3
Armagh, 13,606 H 3
Armoy, ‡1,051 J 1
Augher, ‡1,986 G 3
Aughnacloy, ‡1,885 H 3
Ballycastle, 2,899 J 1
Ballyclare, 5,155 J 2
Ballygawley, ‡2,165 G 3
Ballykelly, 1,116 G 1
Ballymena, 23,386 J 2
Ballymoney, 5,697 J 1
Ballynahinch, 3,485 J 3
Banbridge, 7,968 J 3
Bangor, 35,260 K 2
Belfast (cap.), 353,700 J 2
Belfast, *551,940 J 2
Bellaghy, ‡2,265 H 2
Belleek, ‡2,487 E 3
Beragh, ‡2,137 G 2
Bessbrook, 2,619 J 3
Brookeborough, ‡2,534 G 3
Broughshane, 1,288 J 2
Bushmills, 1,288 J 1
Caledon, ‡1,828 H 3
Carnlough, 1,416 J 2
Carrickfergus, 16,603 K 2
Carrowdore, 2,548 K 2
Castledawson, 1,162 H 2
Castlederg, 1,766 F 2
Castlewellan, 1,488 K 3
Claudy, ‡2,507 G 2
Clogher, ‡1,888 G 3
Coalisland, 3,614 H 2
Coleraine, 16,354 H 1
Comber, 5,575 K 2
Cookstown, 6,965 H 2
Craigavon, 12,740 J 3
Crossgar, 1,098 K 3
Crossmaglen, 1,085 H 3
Crumlin, 1,450 J 2
Cullybackey, 1,649 J 2
Derrygonnelly, ‡2,539 F 3
Dervock, ‡1,191 J 1
Donaghadee, 4,008 K 2
Downpatrick, 7,918 K 3
Draperstown, ‡2,247 H 2
Dromore, Bainbridge, 2,848 J 3
Dromore, Omagh, ‡2,224 G 3
Drumquin, ‡1,982 F 2
Dundrum, ‡2,245 K 3
Dungannon, 8,190 H 3
Dungiven, 1,536 H 2
Dunnamanagh, ‡2,242 G 2
Ederny and Kesh, ‡2,497 F 2
Enniskillen, 9,679 F 3
Feeny, ‡1,459 H 2
Fintona, 1,190 G 3
Fivemiletown, ‡1,649 G 3
Garvagh, ‡2,363 H 2
Gilford, 1,592 J 3
Glenarm, ‡1,728 J 2
Glenavy, ‡2,360 J 2
Glynn, ‡1,872 K 2
Gortin, ‡2,033 G 2
Greyabbey, ‡2,646 K 2
Hillsborough, 1,021 J 3
Holywood, 9,892 K 2
Irvinestown, 1,457 F 3
Keady, 2,145 H 3
Kells, ‡2,560 J 2
Kesh, ‡2,497 F 3
Kilkeel, 4,090 K 3
Killough, ‡3,295 K 3
Killyleagh, 2,359 K 3
Kilrea, 1,196 H 2
Kircubbin, 1,075 K 3
Larne, 18,482 K 2
Limavady, 6,004 H 1
Lisburn, 31,836 J 2
Lisnaskea, 1,443 G 3
Londonderry, 51,200 G 2
Loughbrickland, ‡2,056 J 3
Maghera, 2,085 H 2
Magherafelt, 4,704 H 2
Markethill, ‡2,352 H 3
Millisle, 1,172 K 2
Moneymore, 1,178 H 2
Moy, ‡2,349 H 3
Moygashel, 1,086 H 3
Newcastle, 4,647 J 3
Newry, 20,279 J 3
Newtownabbey, 58,114 K 2
Newtownards, 15,484 K 2
Newtownbutler, ‡2,663 G 3
Newtownhamilton, ‡1,936 H 3
Newtownstewart, 1,433 G 2
Omagh, 14,594 G 2
Pomeroy, ‡1,786 H 2
Portaferry, 1,730 K 3
Portavogie, 1,310 K 3
Portglenone, ‡2,061 H 2
Portrush, 5,376 H 1
Portstewart, 5,085 H 1
Randalstown, 2,799 J 2
Rathfriland, 1,886 J 3
Rostrevor, 1,617 J 3
Saintfield, ‡2,198 K 3
Sion Mills, 1,588 G 2
Sixmilecross, ‡1,980 G 2
Stewartstown, ‡1,759 H 2
Strabane, 9,413 G 2
Strangford, ‡1,987 K 3
Tandragee, 1,725 J 3
Tempo, ‡2,282 G 3
Trillick, ‡2,167 G 3
Warrenpoint, 4,291 J 3
Whitehead, 2,642 K 2

OTHER FEATURES

Bann (riv.) H 2
Belfast (inlet) K 2
Blackwater (riv.) H 3
Bush (riv.) H 1
Derg (riv.) F 2
Divis (mt.) J 2
Dundrum (bay) K 3
Erne (lake) F 3
Foyle (inlet) G 1
Foyle (riv.) G 2
Giant's Causeway H 1
Lagan (riv.) K 2
Larne (inlet) K 2
Magee, Island (pen.), 1,581 K 2
Magilligan (pt.) H 1
Main (riv.) J 2
Mourne (mts.) J 3
Mourne (riv.) G 2
Neagh (lake) J 2
North (chan.) K 1
Rathlin (isl.), 109 J 1
Red (bay) K 1
Roe (riv.) H 1
Saint John's (pt.) K 3
Slieve Donard (mt.) K 3
Sperrin (mts.) G 2
Strangford (inlet) K 3
Torr (head) K 1
Ulster (part) (prov.), 1,537,200 G 2
Upper Lough Erne (lake) F 3

*City and suburbs.
‡Population of district.

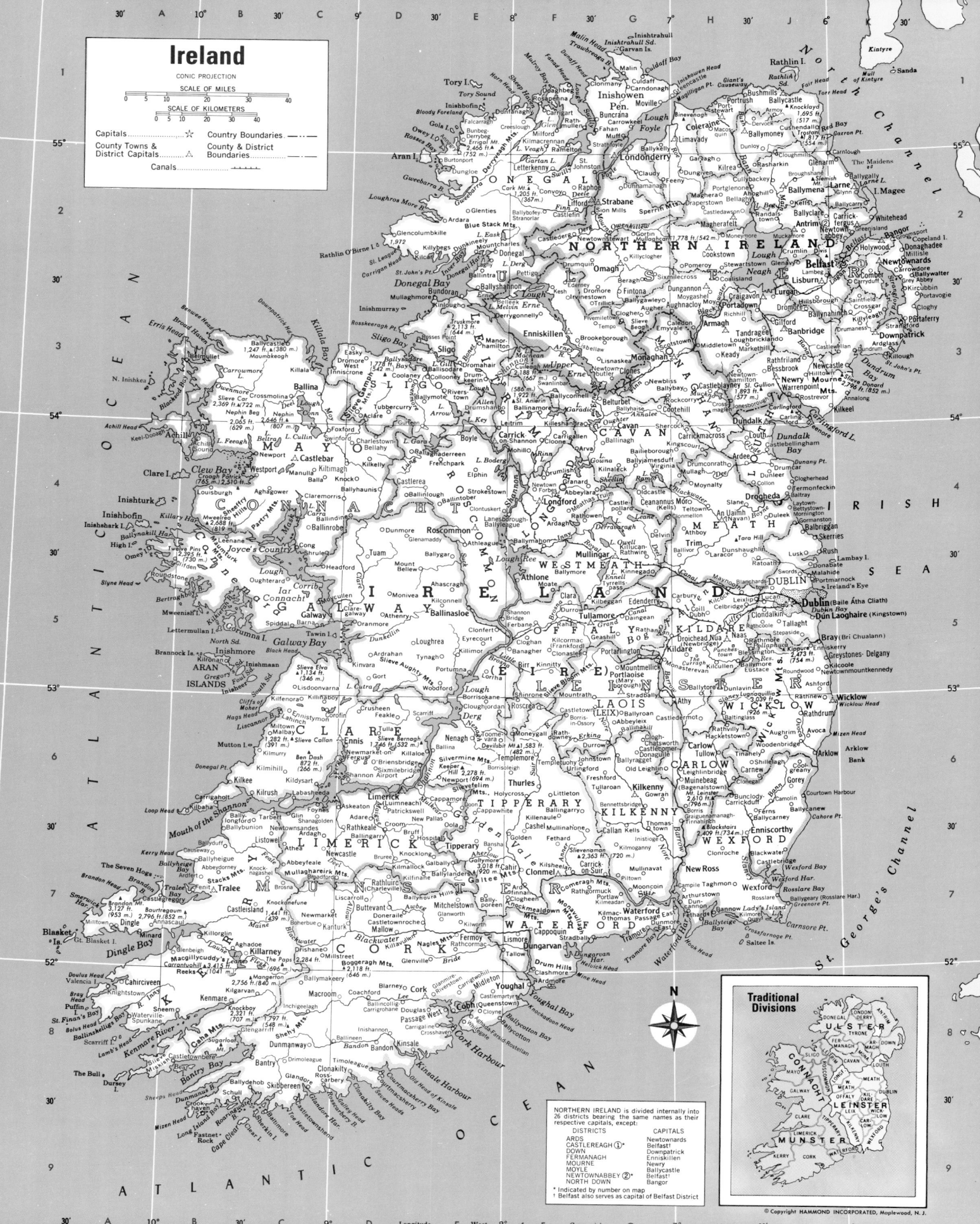

Ireland

CONIC PROJECTION

SCALE OF MILES

SCALE OF KILOMETERS

Capitals .... ☆ Country Boundaries _____

County Towns & County & District

District Capitals .... △ Boundaries ....

Canals .... +++++

Traditional Divisions

ULSTER

CONNACHT

LEINSTER

MUNSTER

NORTHERN IRELAND is divided internally into
26 districts bearing the same names as their
respective capitals, except:

DISTRICTS	CAPITALS
ARDS	Newtownards
CASTLEREAGH ①	Belfast†
DOWN	Downpatrick
FERMANAGH	Enniskillen
MOURNE	Newry
MOYLE	Ballycastle
NEWTOWNABBEY ②	Belfast†
NORTH DOWN	Bangor

* Indicated by number on map
† Belfast also serves as capital of Belfast District

© Copyright HAMMOND INCORPORATED, Maplewood, N.J.

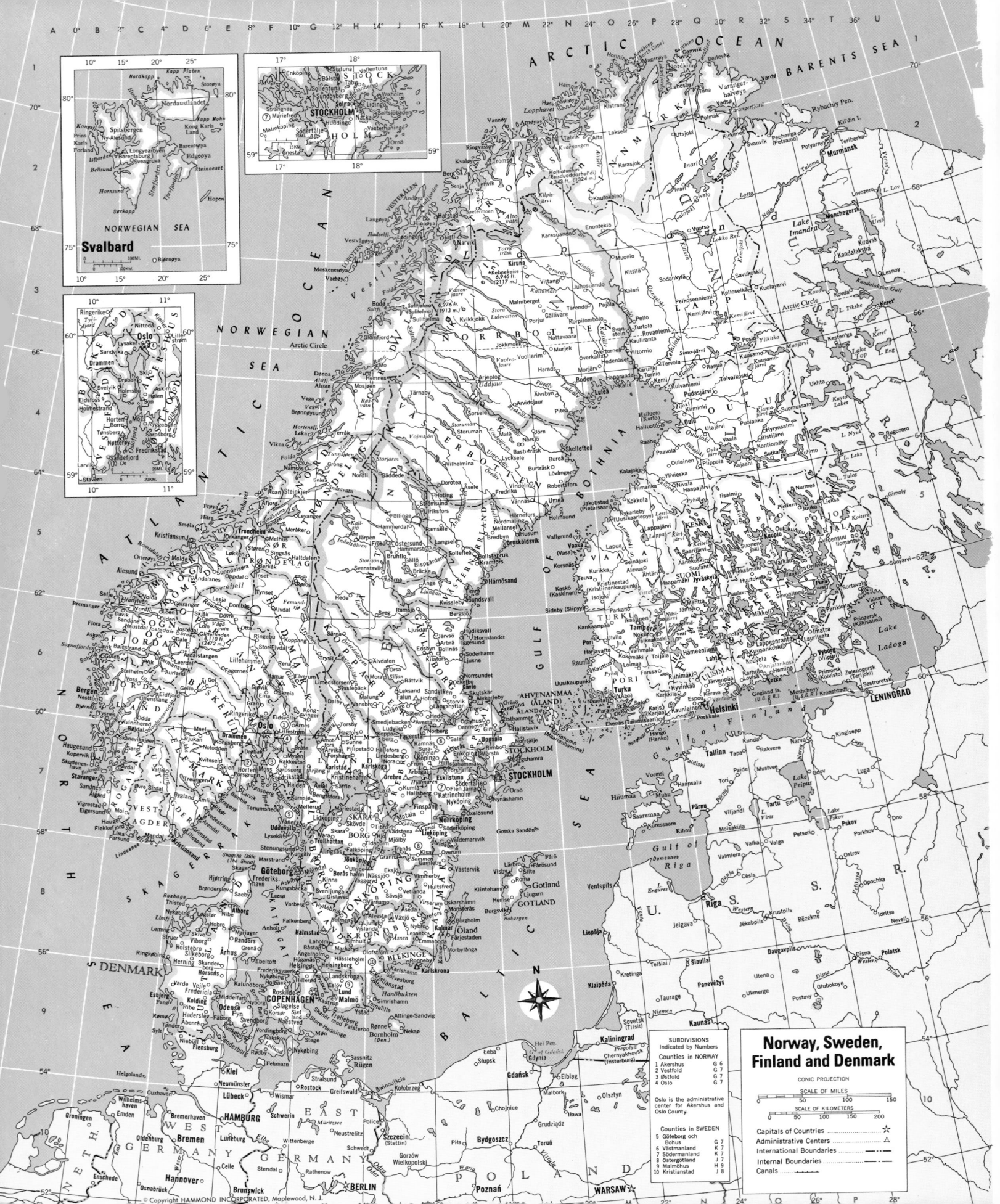

Svalbard

NORWEGIAN SEA

Oslo

STOCKHOLM

Norway, Sweden, Finland and Denmark

CONIC PROJECTION

SCALE OF MILES

0   50   100   150

SCALE OF KILOMETERS

0   50   100   150   200

Capitals of Countries .... ☆
Administrative Centers .... △
International Boundaries .... —·—
Internal Boundaries .... —··—
Canals ....

SUBDIVISIONS
Indicated by Numbers

Counties in NORWAY

1 Akershus   G 6
2 Vestfold   G 7
3 Østfold   G 7
4 Oslo   G 7

Oslo is the administrative
center for Akershus and
Oslo County.

Counties in SWEDEN

5 Göteborg och
  Bohus   G 7
6 Västmanland   K 7
7 Södermanland   K 7
8 Östergötland   J 7
9 Malmöhus   H 9
10 Kristianstad   J 9

© Copyright HAMMOND INCORPORATED, Maplewood, N.J.

AREA 125,053 sq. mi. (323,887 sq. km.)
POPULATION 4,092,000
CAPITAL Oslo
LARGEST CITY Oslo
HIGHEST POINT Glittertinden 8,110 ft. (2,472 m.)
MONETARY UNIT krone
MAJOR LANGUAGE Norwegian
MAJOR RELIGION Protestantism

AREA 173,665 sq. mi. (449,792 sq. km.)
POPULATION 8,320,000
CAPITAL Stockholm
LARGEST CITY Stockholm
HIGHEST POINT Kebnekaise 6,946 ft. (2,117 m.)
MONETARY UNIT krona
MAJOR LANGUAGE Swedish
MAJOR RELIGION Protestantism

AREA 130,128 sq. mi. (337,032 sq. km.)
POPULATION 4,788,000
CAPITAL Helsinki
LARGEST CITY Helsinki
HIGHEST POINT Haltiatunturi 4,343 ft. (1,324 m.)
MONETARY UNIT markka
MAJOR LANGUAGES Finnish, Swedish
MAJOR RELIGION Protestantism

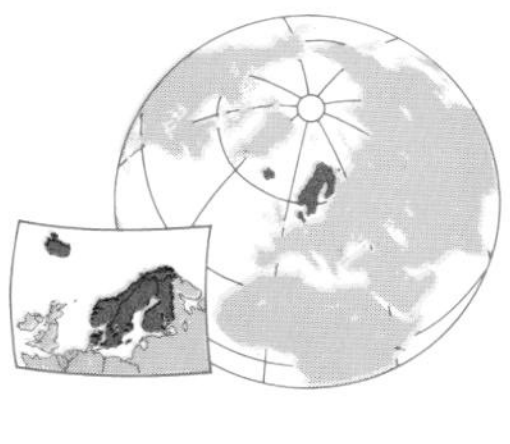

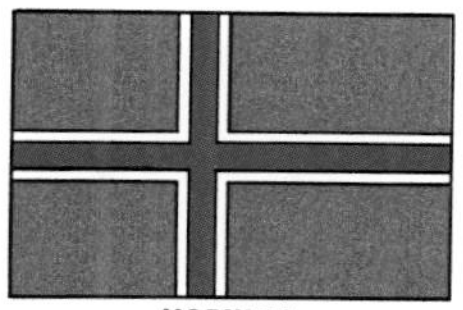
NORWAY

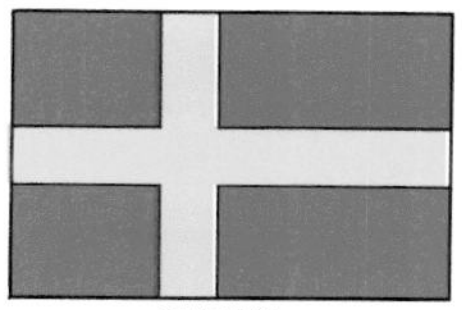
SWEDEN

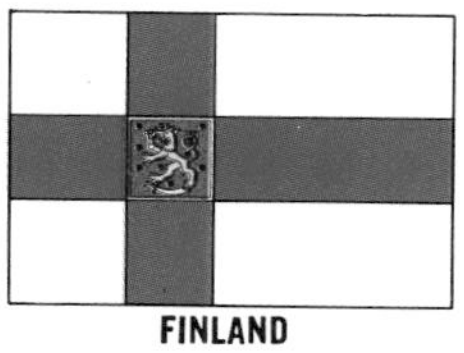
FINLAND

FINLAND

PROVINCES

Ahvenanmaa 22,380 L6
Åland (Ahvenanmaa) 22,380 L6
Häme 662,500 O6
Keski-Suomi 241,770 O5
Kuopio 252,023 P5
Kymi 346,478 Q6
Lappi 196,792 P3
Mikkeli 211,453 P6
Oulu 406,309 P4
Pohjois-Karjala 179,065 Q5
Turku ja Pori 697,988 N6
Uusimaa 1,085,625 O6
Vaasa 425,283 N5

CITIES and TOWNS

Äänekoski 10,725 O5
Åbo (Turku) 164,857 N6
Alavus 10,285 N5
Borgaå 18,740 O6
Ekenäs 7,391 N6
Espoo 117,090 O6
Forssa 18,442 N6
Haapajärvi 7,791 O5
Hämeenlinna 40,761 O6
Hamina 11,055 P6
Hangö 10,374 N7
Hanko (Hangö) 10,374 N7
Harjavalta 8,445 M6
Heinola 15,350 P6
Helsinki (cap.) 502,961 O6
Helsinki* 794,746 O6
Huutokoski† 6,458 P5
Hyvinkää 35,865 O6
Iisalmi 21,159 P5
Ikaalinen 8,364 N6
Imatra 35,590 Q6
Ivalo 2,661 P2
Jakobstad 20,397 N5
Jämsä 12,526 O6
Järvenpää 16,259 O6
Joensuu 41,429 R5
Jyväskylä 61,209 O5
Jyväskylä* 84,185 O5
Kajaani 20,583 P4
Kalajoki 3,624 N4
Kankaanpää 12,564 M6
Karhula 21,834 P6
Karis 8,152 N6
Karjaa (Karis) 8,152 N6
Karkkila 8,678 N6
Kauniainien 6,219 O6
Kauttua 3,297 M6
Kelloselkä† 8,200 Q3
Kemi 27,893 O4
Kemijärvi 12,951 P3
Kerava 19,966 O6
Kokemäki 10,188 N6
Kokkola 22,096 N5
Kotka 34,026 P6
Kotka* 60,235 P6
Kouvola 29,383 P6
Kouvola* 59,507 P6
Kristiinankaupunki (Kristinestad) 9,331 N5
Kristinestad 9,331 N5
Kuhmo 4,150 Q4
Kuopio 71,684 Q5
Kurikka 11,177 M5
Kuusamo 4,449 Q4
Kuusankoski 22,342 P6
Lahti 94,864 O6
Lahti* 112,129 O6
Lappeenranta 52,682 P6
Lapua 15,189 N5
Lieksa 20,274 R5
Loimaa 6,575 N6
Lovisa 8,674 P6
Maarianhamina (Mariehamn) 9,574 M7
Mänttä 7,910 O6
Mariehamn 9,574 M7
Mikkeli 27,112 P6
Naantali 7,814 M6
Nokia 22,308 N6
Nurmes 11,721 Q5
Nykarleby 7,408 N5
Oulainen 7,322 O4
Oulu 93,707 O4
Oulu* 103,044 O4
Outokumpu 10,736 Q5
Parainen 10,170 M6
Parkano 8,518 N6
Pieksämäki 12,923 P5
Pietarsaari (Jakobstad) 20,397 N5
Pori 80,343 M6
Pori* 86,635 M6
Posio† 6,205 Q3
Pudasjärvi† 12,594 P4
Raahe 15,379 O4
Raisio 14,271 M6
Rauma 29,081 M6
Riihimäki 24,106 O6
Rovaniemi 28,411 O3
Saarijärvi 2,714 O5
Salo 19,176 N6
Savonlinna 28,336 Q6
Seinäjoki 22,123 N5
Sodankylä 3,304 P3
Sotkamo 2,316 Q4
Suolahti 5,936 O5
Suonenjoki 9,286 P5
Tammisaari (Ekenäs) 7,391 N6
Tampere 168,118 N6
Tampere* 220,920 N6
Toijala 8,080 N6
Tornio 19,971 O4
Turku 164,857 N6
Turku* 217,423 N6
Turtola† 5,852 O3
Ulvila† 8,040 N6
Uusikaarlepyy (Nykarleby) 7,408 N5
Uusikaupunki 11,915 M6
Vaasa 54,402 M5
Vaasa* 58,224 M5
Valkeakoski 22,588 N6
Vammala 16,363 N6
Varkaus 24,450 Q5
Vasa (Vaasa) 54,402 M5
Vuotso† 10,186 P2
Ylivieska 10,827 O4

OTHER FEATURES

Åland (isls.) L6
Baltic (sea) K9
Bothnia (gulf) M5
Finland (gulf) P7
Hailuoto (isl.) O4
Haltiatunturi (mt.) M2
Hangöudd (prom.) N7
Haukivesi (lake) Q5
Iijoki (riv.) O4
Inari (lake) P2
Ivalojoki (riv.) P2
Juojärvi (lake) Q5
Kalajoki (riv.) O4
Kallavesi (lake) P5
Karlö (Hailuoto) (isl.) O4
Keitele (lake) O5
Kemijärvi (lake) Q3
Kemijoki (riv.) O3
Kiantajärvi (lake) Q4
Kilpisjärvi (lake) M2
Kitinen (riv.) P3
Kivijärvi (lake) O5
Koitere (lake) R5
Kuusamojärvi (lake) Q4
Längelmävesi (lake) O6
Lapland (reg.) O2
Lappajärvi (lake) O5
Lapuanjoki (riv.) N5
Lestijärvi (lake) O5
Lokka (res.) Q3
Muojärvi (lake) R4
Muonio (riv.) M2
Näsijärvi (lake) O6
Onkivesi (lake) P5
Orihvesi (lake) Q5
Oulujärvi (lake) P4
Oulujoki (riv.) O4
Ounasjoki (riv.) O3
Päijänne (lake) O6
Pielinen (lake) Q5
Puruvesi (lake) Q6
Puulavesi (lake) P5
Pyhäjärvi (lake) O5
Pyhäjärvi (lake) M6
Saimaa (lake) Q6
Siikajoki (riv.) O4
Simojärvi (lake) P3
Simojoki (riv.) O4
Tana (riv.) P2
Tornio (riv.) O3
Vallgrund (isl.) M5
Ylikitka (lake) Q3

NORWAY

COUNTIES

Akershus 355,196 G6
Aust-Agder 86,216 E7
Buskerud 209,684 F6
Finnmark 79,373 O2
Hedmark 183,465 G6
Hordaland 386,492 E6
Møre og Romsdal 231,944 E5
Nordland 243,233 J3
Nord-Trøndelag 122,886 H4
Oppland 178,259 F6
Oslo (city) 462,732 D3
Østfold 228,546 G7
Rogaland 287,653 E7
Sogn og Fjordane 103,135 E6
Sør-Trøndelag 241,361 G5
Telemark 158,853 F7
Troms 144,111 L2
Vest-Agder 131,659 E7
Vestfold 182,433 G7

CITIES and TOWNS

Ålesund 40,868 D5
Ålgård 2,322 D7
Alta 5,582 N2
Åndalsnes 2,574 F5
Årdalstangen 2,360 F6
Arendal 11,701 F7
Arendal* 21,228 F7
Årnes 2,267 G6
Askim 8,413 E4
Bamble† 7,031 F7
Barentsburg C2
Bergen 213,434 D6
Bodø 31,077 J3
Borge† 3,294 H2
Brønnøysund 3,130 G4
Dombås 1,114 F5
Drammen 50,777 C4
Drammen* 56,521 C4
Drøbak 4,538 D4
Eidsvoll 2,906 G6
Eigersund 11,379 D7
Elverum 7,391 G6
Farsund 8,908 E7
Flekkefjord 8,750 E7
Flora 8,822 D6
Fredrikstad 29,024 D4
Fredrikstad* 51,141 D4
Gjøvik 25,963 G6
Grimstad 13,091 F7
Halden 27,087 G7
Hamar 16,418 G6
Hamar* 25,138 G6
Hammerfest 7,610 N1
Hammerfest* 8,005 N1
Harstad 21,125 K2
Haugesund 27,386 D7
Haugesund* 29,277 D7
Hermansverk 706 E6
Holmestrand 8,246 C4
Holmsbu 273 D4
Honningsvag 3,780 O1
Horten 13,746 D4
Horten* 17,246 D4
Kirkenes 4,466 Q2
Kongsberg 19,854 F7
Kongsvinger 16,146 H6
Kopervik 4,221 D7
Kornsjø† 6,079 G7
Kragerø 5,249 F7
Kristiansand 59,488 F8
Kristiansund 18,847 E5
Kvinnherad† 2,898 E6
Larvik 9,097 C4
Larvik* 19,202 C4
Lenvik† 11,098 L2
Levanger 5,066 G5
Lillehammer 21,248 F6
Lillesand 3,028 F7
Lillestrøm† 11,550 E3
Longyearbyen D2
Lysaker† 81,612 D3
Mandal 11,579 E7
Meråker† 2,907 G5
Mo 21,033 J3
Molde 20,334 E5
Mosjøen 9,341 H4
Moss 25,786 D4
Moss* 27,430 D4
Mysen 3,760 G7
Namsos 11,452 G4
Narvik 19,582 K2
Nesttun† 11,519 D6
Nittedal† 8,889 D3
Notodden 12,970 F7
Nøtterøy 11,944 D4
Ny-Ålesund C2
Odda 7,401 E6
Oppdal 2,173 F5
Orkanger 3,685 F5
Oslo (cap.) 462,732 D3
Oslo* 645,413 D3
Porsgrunn 31,709 G7
Rakkestad 2,392 G7
Ringerike 30,156 C3
Risør 6,560 F7
Rjukan 5,334 F7
Røros 3,041 G5
Sandefjord 33,350 C4
Sandnes 33,934 D7
Sandvika† 34,337 C3
Sarpsborg 12,889 D4
Sarpsborg* 36,449 D4
Selje† 3,386 D5
Ski 9,081 D4
Skien 47,105 F7
Stavanger 86,639 D7
Stavern 2,604 D4
Steinkjer 20,553 G4
Stor-Elvdal† 2,993 G6
Sunndalsøra 5,114 F5
Sveagruva D2
Svolvaer 3,942 J2
Tønsberg 9,964 D4
Tønsberg* 36,374 D4
Tromsø 43,830 L2
Trondheim 134,910 F5
Ullensvang† 2,326 E6
Vadsø 6,019 Q1
Vardø 3,875 R1
Vik 1,019 E6
Volda 3,511 E5
Voss 5,944 E6

OTHER FEATURES

Alsten (isl.) H4
Andøya (isl.) J2
Barduelv (riv.) L2
Bellsund C2
Bjørnafjorden (fjord) D6
Bjornøya (isl.) D3
Boknafjord (fjord) D7
Bremanger (isl.) D6
Dønna (isl.) H3
Dovrefjell (hills) F5
Edgeøya (isl.) E2
Femundsjø (lake) G5
Folda (fjord) G4
Folda (fjord) J3
Frohavet (bay) F5
Frøya (isl.) F5
Glittertinden (mt.) F6
Hardangervidda (plat.) E6
Hardangerfjord (fjord) D7
Hinlopenstreten (str.) C1
Hinnøya (isl.) K2
Hitra (isl.) F5
Hopen (isl.) E2
Isfjorden (fjord) C2
Jostedalsbreen (glac.) E6
Kjölen (mts.) K3
Kongsfjorden (fjord) B2
Kvaløya (isl.) O1
Lågen (riv.) G6
Laksefjorden (fjord) P1
Langøy (isl.) J2
Lapland (reg.) K2
Leka (isl.) G4
Lindesnes (cape) E8
Lista (pen.) E7
Lofoten (isls.) H2
Lopphavet (bay) M1
Magerøya (isl.) P1
Moskenesøya (isl.) H3
Namsen (riv.) H4
Nordaustlandet (isl.) D1
Nordfjord (fjord) E6
Nordkapp (pt.) C1
Nordkinn (headland) Q1
Nordkinn (pen.) P1
North Cape (Nordkapp) (pt.) P1
Norwegian (sea) F3
Ofotfjorden (fjord) K2
Oslofjord (fjord) D4
Otra (riv.) E7
Otterøya (isl.) E5
Pasvikelv (riv.) Q2
Platen, Kapp (pt.) D1
Porsangen (fjord) O1
Rana (fjord) H3
Rauma (riv.) F5
Ringvassøy (isl.) L2
Romsdalsfjorden (fjord) E5
Saltfjorden (fjord) J3
Seiland (isl.) N1
Senja (isl.) K2
Skagerrak (str.) F8
Smøla (isl.) E5
Sognafjorden (fjord) D6
Sørkapp (pt.) C2
Sorøya (isl.) N1
Spitsbergen (isl.) C2
Storfjorden (fjord) D2
Sulitjelma (mt.) J3
Svalbard (isls.) C3
Tana (riv.) P1
Tanafjord (fjord) Q1
Tokke (riv.) F7
Trondheimsfjorden (fjord) G5
Tyrifjord (lake) C3
Vaerøy (isl.) H3
Vagåvatn (lake) F6
Vannøy (isl.) L1
Varangerhalvøya (pen.) Q1
Varangerfjord (fjord) Q2
Vega (isl.) G4
Vesterålen (isls.) J2
Vestfjord (fjord) H3
Vestvågøya (isl.) H3
Vikna (isls.) G4

SWEDEN

COUNTIES

Älvsborg 418,150 H7
Blekinge 155,391 J8
Gävleborg 294,595 K6
Göteborg och Bohus 714,660 G7
Gotland 54,447 L8
Halland 219,767 H8
Jämtland 133,559 J5
Jönköping 301,905 H8
Kalmar 240,768 K8
Kopparberg 281,082 J6
Kristianstad 272,090 J8

(continued on following page)

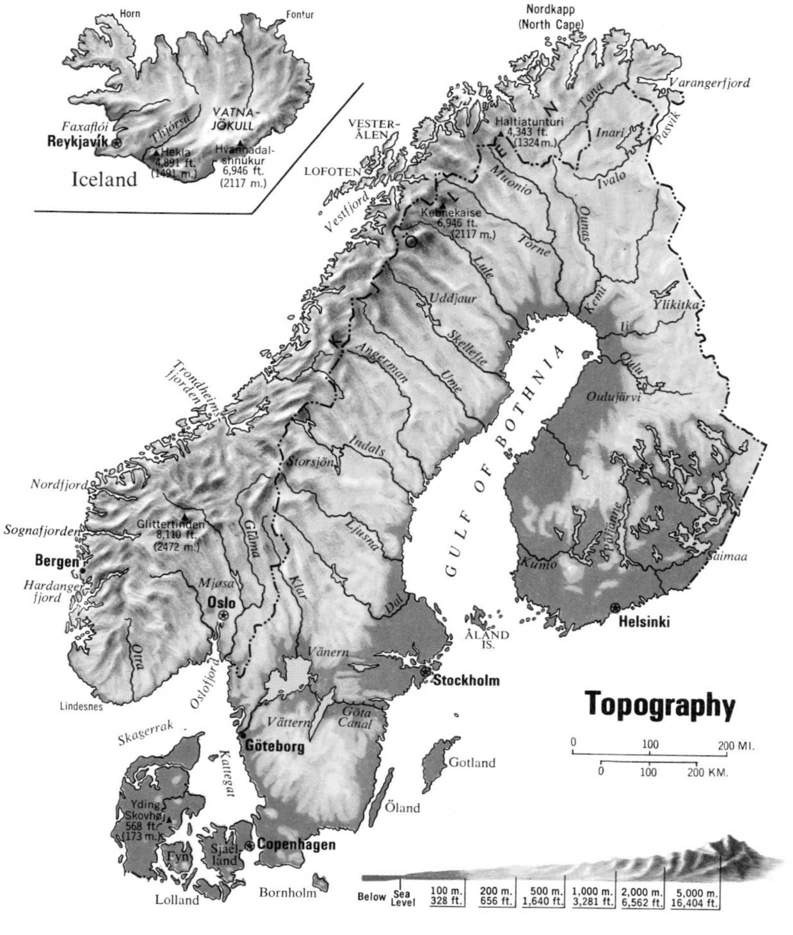
Horn
Fontur
Faxaflói
Reykjavík
VATNA-JÖKULL
Hekla 4,891 ft. (1491 m.)
Hvannadal-shnúkur 6,946 ft. (2117 m.)
Iceland
Nordkapp (North Cape)
Varangerfjord
VESTER-ÅLEN
LOFOTEN
Haltiatunturi 4,343 ft. (1324 m.)
Kebnekaise 6,946 ft. (2117 m.)
Inari
Tana
Pasvik
Ivalo
Muonio
Torne
Ounas
Lule
Uddjaur
Kemi
Ylikitka
Ii
Oulu
Oulujärvi
Skellefte
Ume
Ångerman
GULF OF BOTHNIA
Trondheimsfjorden
Indals
Storsjön
Ljusna
Nordfjord
Sognafjorden
Glittertinden 8,110 ft. (2472 m.)
Bergen
Hardangerfjord
Glåma
Mjøsa
Oslo
Klar
Dal
Kumo
Päijänne
Saimaa
Helsinki
ÅLAND IS.
Vänern
Stockholm
Otra
Oslofjord
Lindesnes
Skagerrak
Vättern
Göta Canal
Göteborg
Kattegat
Gotland
Öland
Yding Skovhøj 568 ft. (173 m.)
Fyn
Sjælland
Copenhagen
Lolland
Bornholm
Topography
0 100 200 MI.
0 100 200 KM.
Below Sea Level
100 m. 328 ft.
200 m. 656 ft.
500 m. 1,640 ft.
1,000 m. 3,281 ft.
2,000 m. 6,562 ft.
5,000 m. 16,404 ft.

Kronoberg 169.454 J8
Malmöhus 740.137 H9
Norrbotten 264.215 L3
Örebro 273.994 J7
Östergötland 387.104 J7
Skaraborg 263.382 J7
Södermanland 252.030 K7
Stockholm 1.493.052 L7
Uppsala 229.879 K7
Värmland 284.442 H7
Västerbotten 236.367 K4
Västernorrland 268.202 K5
Västmanland 259.872 K7

CITIES and TOWNS

Åhus 6.125 J9
Alingsås 18.892 H8
Almhult 7.390 J8
Alvesta 7.261 J8
Älvsbyn 4.707 M4
Åmål 9.556 H7
Ånge 3.760 J5
Angelholm 16.016 H8
Arboga 11.819 J7
Arbrå 2.734 K6
Årjängt 2.596 H7
Arvidsjaur 4.194 H7
Arvika 13.934 H7
Åseda 2.465 J8
Askim 17.609 G8
Åtvidaberg 8.436 K7
Avesta 19.095 J6
Bålsta 8.243 G1
Båstad 2.452 H8
Bengtsfors 3.535 H7
Boden 19.590 M4
Bollnäs 13.305 K6
Bollstabruk 3.548 L5
Borås 6.537 H8
Borås* 187.710 K8
Borgholm 2.789 J8
Borlänge 40.158 J6
Brunflo 3.460 J5
Dalbyt 4.013 H1
Danderydt 36.596 H1
Dannemora 291 J8
Edsbyn 4.388 J8
Eksjö 9.686 J8
Emmaboda 5.652 J8
Enköping 18.541 G1
Eskilstuna 66.409 K7
Eslöv 13.629 H9
Fagersta* 14.148 J7
Falkenberg 15.126 H7
Falun 30.073 J6
Färjestaden 2.995 J8
Filipstad 7.835 H7
Finspång 16.346 J7
Flen 6.770 K7
Forshaga 6.000 H7
Fröso 10.274 J5
Frövi 2.583 J7
Gällivare 8.669 M3
Gamleby 3.666 J8
Gävle 67.454 K6

Gimo 3.154 K6
Gislaved 8.564 H8
Gnesta 3.835 G2
Göteborg 444.540 G8
Göteborg* 690.767 G8
Hagfors 8.060 J7
Hallefors 7.862 J7
Hallsberg 6.799 J7
Hallstahammar 13.583 K7
Hallstavik 5.162 L6
Halmstad 49.558 H8
Haparanda 5.031 N4
Härnösand 18.971 L5
Hässleholm 16.813 H8
Hedemora 7.039 J6
Helsingborg 80.986 H8
Helsingborg* 215.894 H8
Hjo 4.615 J7
Hofors 11.459 J6
Höganäs 10.866 H8
Holmsund 5.467 M5
Hornefors 2.441 L5
Huddinge 48.339 H1
Hudiksvall 15.004 K6
Hultsfred 5.763 J8
Husum 2.517 L5
Hyltebruk 3.469 H8
Iggesund 4.448 K6
Järna 6.237 G2
Jokkmokk 3.186 L3
Jönköping 78.650 H8
Jönköping* 131.499 H8
Kalix 7.668 N4
Kalmar 32.049 K8
Karlshamn 17.447 J8
Karlskogat 35.425 J7
Karlskrona 33.414 J8
Karlstad 51.243 H7
Katrineholm 22.884 K7
Kinna 13.676 H8
Kiruna 25.410 L3
Kisa 4.323 J7
Köping 20.059 J7
Kopparberg 3.942 J7
Kramfors 7.719 L5
Kristianstad 30.780 J9
Kristinehamn 21.146 H7
Kumla 11.451 J7
Kungälv 12.764 G8
Kungsbackat 11.986 G8
Kvissleby 3.413 K5
Laholm 3.898 H8
Landskrona 29.486 H9
Långshyttan 2.744 J6
Laxå 5.166 J7
Leksand 4.410 J6
Lessebo 2.991 J8
Lidingö 30.098 H1
Lidköping 21.001 H7
Lindesberg 8.247 J7
Linköping 80.274 K7
Linköping* 132.839 K7
Ljungby 12.969 J8
Ljusdal 7.075 J6
Ljusne 3.578 K6
Ludvika 18.217 J6
Luleå 42.139 N4
Lund 55.047 H9

Lycksele 8.586 L4
Lysekil 7.815 G7
Malmberget 10.239 M3
Malmö 241.191 H9
Malmö* 453.339 H9
Malung 6.211 H6
Mariefred 2.553 F1
Mariestad 16.454 H7
Markaryd 4.266 H8
Märsta 17.066 K7
Marstrand 1.168 G8
Mellerud 3.579 H7
Mjölby 12.488 J7
Mölndalt 47.248 H8
Mönsterås 5.005 K8
Mora 8.772 J6
Motala 29.454 J7
Nacka 19.708 H1
Nässjö 18.634 J8
Nora 5.515 J7
Norberg 5.438 K6
Norrköping 85.244 K7
Norrköping* 163.206 K7
Norrtälje 12.784 L7
Nybro 13.010 J8
Nyköping 30.352 L7
Nynäshamn 11.070 L6
Ockelbo 2.810 K6
Olofström 10.096 J8
Örebro 117.877 J7
Örebro* 171.440 J7
Örnsköldsvik 29.514 L5
Oxelösund 13.862 K7
Piteå 16.169 M4
Rättvik 4.087 J6
Rimbo 3.404 L7
Ronneby 12.086 J8
Säffle 11.428 H7
Sala 11.216 J7
Saltsjöbaden 8.113 J1
Sandviken 27.994 K6
Säter 4.297 J6
Sävsjö 4.913 J8
Sigtuna 4.780 K7
Simrishamn 5.834 J9
Skanör med Falsterbo 4.909 H9
Skara 10.138 H7
Skellefteå 29.353 M4
Skövde 29.945 H7
Skutskär 7.174 K6
Smedjebacken 8.418 J6
Söderhamn 14.673 K6
Söderköping 5.310 K7
Södertälje 58.408 H1
Sollefteå 8.923 L5
Sollentunat 40.905 H1
Solnat 53.992 H1
Sölvesborg 7.292 J9
Stenungsund 8.361 G8
Stockholm (cap.) 665.550 L7
Stockholm* 1.357.183 L7
Storuman 2.587 K4
Storvik 2.748 K6

Strängnäs 10.255 F1
Strömstad 4.735 G7
Strömsund 4.119 K5
Sundbyberg† 27.058 H1
Sundsvall 52.268 K5
Sunne 4.273 H7
Surahammar 6.509 J7
Sveg 2.608 J5
Svenljunga 3.189 H8
Tåby† 41.285 H1
Tibro 8.476 H7
Tidaholm 8.039 H7
Tierp 5.005 K6
Timrå 11.416 K5
Tomelilla 5.371 H9
Torsby 3.632 H6
Torshälla 8.231 K7
Tranås 14.854 J7
Trelleborg 22.559 H9
Trollhättan 42.499 H7
Trosa 3.128 K7
Uddevalla 32.700 G7
Ulricehamn 7.827 H8
Umeå 49.715 M5
Uppsala 101.850 K7
Uppsala* 157.202 K7
Vadstena 5.294 J7
Vaggeryd 3.974 H8
Valdemarsvik 3.558 K7
Vallentuna 10.477 H1
Vänersborg 20.510 H7
Vännäs 3.876 L5
Vansbro 2.708 H6
Vara 3.049 H7
Varberg 19.467 H8
Värnamo 15.726 J8
Västerås 98.858 J7
Västerås* 147.508 J7
Västerhaninge 14.125 H1
Västervik 21.239 K8
Vaxholm† 3.744 J1
Växjö 40.328 J8
Vetlanda 12.358 J8
Vilhelmina 4.060 K4
Vimmerby 7.405 J8
Virserum 2.495 J8
Visby 19.886 L8
Ystad 14.286 H9

OTHER FEATURES

Ångermanälven (riv.) K5
Åsnen (lake) J8
Baltic (sea) K9
Bolmen (lake) H8
Bothnia (gulf) N4
Dalälven (riv.) J6
Fårö (isl.) L8
Göta (canal) K7
Göta (riv.) H7
Gotland (isl.) L8
Graso (isl.) L6
Hanöbukten (bay) J9
Hjälmaren (lake) J7
Hoburgen (cliff) L8
Hornslandet (pen.) K6
Indalsälven (riv.) H5
Kalixälv (riv.) N3

Kalmarsund (sound) K8
Kattegat (str.) G8
Kebnekaise (mt.) L3
Kölen (mts.) K3
Klarälv (riv.) H6
Lapland (reg.) M2
Ljusnan (riv.) H5
Luleälv (riv.) M4
Mälaren (lake) G1
Muonioälv (riv.) M2
Öland (isl.) J8
Öresund (sound) H9
Orno (isl.) J2
Österdalälven (riv.) H6
Piteälv (riv.) M4
Siljan (lake) J6
Skagerrak (str.) F8
Sommen (lake) J8
Stora Lulevatten (lake) L3
Storsjön (lake) J5
Suiitelma (mt.) K3
Tornealv (riv.) M3
Uddjaur (lake) L4
Umeälv (riv.) L4
Vanern (lake) H7
Vasterdalalven (riv.) J6
Vättern (lake) J7

*City and suburbs
†Population of commune
‡Population of parish

DENMARK

COUNTIES

Århus 534.333 D5
Bornholm 47.241 F9
Copenhagen (commune) 622.612 F6
Faeroe Islands 41.969 B2
Frederiksborg (commune) 101.874 F6
Frederiksborg 260.825 E5
Fyn 433.765 D7
København (Copenhagen) (commune) 622.612 F6
Københaven 616.571 F6
Nordjylland 457.165 D4
Ribe 198.153 B7
Ringkøbing 242.006 B5
Roskilde 154.314 F6
Sønderjylland 238.502 C7
Storstrøm 252.780 E7
Vejle 306.809 C6
Vestsjaelland 259.484 E6
Viborg 221.002 C4

CITIES and TOWNS

Åbenrå 15.196 C7
Åbybro 2.897 C3
Akirkeby 2.001 F9
Ålborg 154.582 D4
Ålestrup 1.926 C4

Haderslev 20.042 C7
Hadsten 3.914 C5
Hadsund 3.652 D4
Hals 1.654 D3
Hammel 3.247 C5
Hammerum 3.227 C5
Hanstholm 1.716 B3
Harboør 1.359 B4
Hårlev 1.228 F7
Hasle 18
Haslev 6.925 E7
Havdrup 1.833 F6
Hedensted 2.659 C6
Hellebaek 2.911 F5
Helsinge 3.613 F6
Helsingør 42.425 F5
Herning 32.973 B5
Hillerød 23.963 F6
Hinnerup 2.061 D5
Hirtshals 6.861 C2
Hjallerup 1.573 D3
Hjerm 647 B5
Hjørring 19.692 C3
Hobro 8.737 C4
Højer 1.416 B8
Højslev 1.641 C4
Holbaek 19.485 E6
Holeby 1.434 E8
Holstebro 25.006 B5
Holsted 1.390 B6
Høng 2.488 E7
Hornslet 2.561 D5
Horsens 44.120 C6
Hørsholm 19.346 F6
Hørve 1.139 D6
Hov 635 D6
Humlum 546 B4
Hundested 5.443 E6
Hurup 2.287 B4
Hvidbjerg 994 B4
Hvide Sande 2.129 A6
Ikast 9.222 C5
Jelling 1.540 C6
Jerslev 798 C3
Juelsminde 1.991 D6
Jyderup 2.901 E6
Kalundborg 12.248 D6
Karise 1.184 F7
Karup 1.694 C5
Kastrupt 17.391 F6
Kerteminde 5.007 D7
Kibaek 1.279 B5
Kjellerup 3.245 C5
Klitmøller 542 B3
København (Copenhagen) (cap.) 603.368 F6
Køge 18.608 F7
Kolding 41.602 C7
Kolind 1.036 D5
Korsør 15.502 E7
Kvaerndrup 891 D7
Langaa 2.320 C5
Lem 1.026 B5
Lemvig 6.448 B4
Løgstør 3.633 C4
Løgumkloster 2.091 B7
Lohals 580 D7
Løjt Kirkeby 1.203 C7
Løkken 1.345 C3
Løsning 1.967 C6
Lundby 747 E7
Lunderskov 1.494 C7
Lyngby 61.516 F6
Malling 1.584 D5
Mariager 1.692 D4
Maribo 5.287 E8
Marstal 4.124 D7
Middelfart 13.315 C7

 Års 4.266 D7
Årup 1.675 D7
Ærøskøbing 1.223 D8
Agerbaek 935 B6
Allingåbro 1.385 D5
Allinge-Sandvig 1.991 F8
Ansager 1.157 B6
Arden 1.303 D4
Asaå 1.344 D3
Askov 904 B6
Asnaes 1.413 E6
Assens* Århus 1.341 D4
Assens, Fyn 5.139 C7
Augustenborg 2.628 D8
Auning 1.516 D5
Avlum 1.729 B5
Baelum 1.169 C3
Bagenkop 776 D8
Ballerup 50.673 F6
Bandholm 693 E8
Bedsted 965 B4
Birkerød 13.663 F6
Bjerringbro 4.761 C5
Bogense 2.861 D6
Bolderslev 774 C7
Børkop 1.410 C6
Borup 1.591 E7
Braedstrup 2.163 C6
Bramming 3.678 B7
Brande 4.784 C6
Bredebro 1.173 B7
Broager 2.143 C8
Brønderslev 10.247 C3
Brørup 2.584 C7
Brovst 4.200 C3
Bryrup 579 C6
Christiansfeld 1.994 C7
Copenhagen (cap.) 603.368 F6
Copenhagen* 1.327.940 F6
Dronninglund 4.661 D3
Dybvad 805 D3
Ebeltoft 3.017 D5
Egernsund 1.347 C8
Egtved 1.311 C6
Ejby 1.372 C7
Esbjerg 68.097 B7
Faåborg 6.495 D7
Fakse 2.720 F7
Fakse Ladeplads 1.799 F7
Farsø 2.821 C4
Farum 9.936 F6
Fjerritslev 2.134 C3
Fredensborg 4.709 F6
Fredericia 36.157 C6
Frederikberg 101.874 F6
Frederikshavn 24.846 D3
Frederikssund 11.272 E6
Frederiksvaerk 8.903 E6
Fugleberg 1.094 E7
Gedser 1.200 E8
Gedsted 1.006 C4
Gelsted 1.307 C7
Gentofte 77.744 F6
Gilleleje 2.943 F5
Give 2.366 C6
Glamsbjerg 2.226 D7
Glostrup 28.326 F6
Glumsø 1.027 E7
Glyngøre 1.071 C4
Gørding 1.261 B7
Gørlev 1.542 E7
Graested 1.654 F6
Gram 2.061 C7
Gråsten 2.947 C8
Grenaa 12.569 D5
Grindsted 7.558 B6
Hårby 1.506 D7

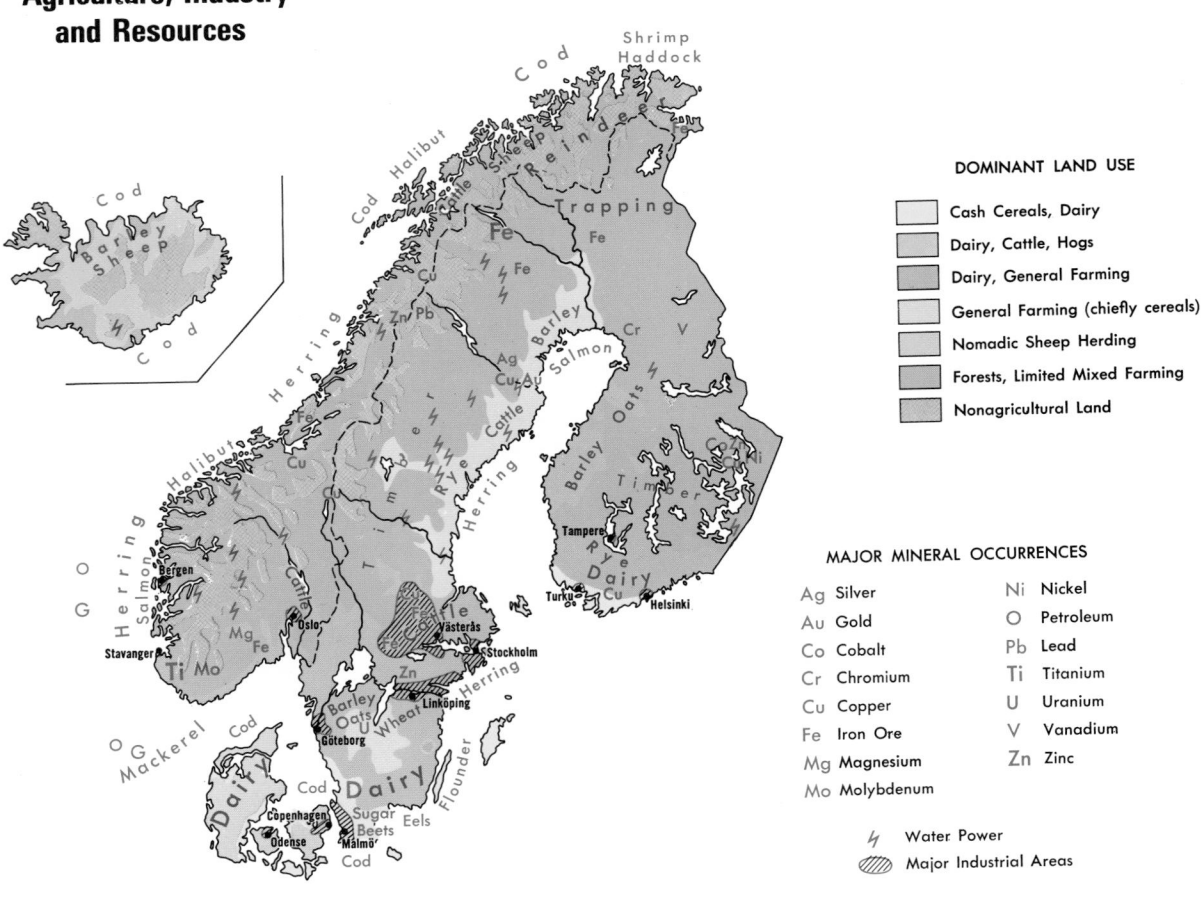

Agriculture, Industry and Resources

DOMINANT LAND USE

- Cash Cereals, Dairy
- Dairy, Cattle, Hogs
- Dairy, General Farming
- General Farming (chiefly cereals)
- Nomadic Sheep Herding
- Forests, Limited Mixed Farming
- Nonagricultural Land

MAJOR MINERAL OCCURRENCES

Ag Silver
Au Gold
Co Cobalt
Cr Chromium
Cu Copper
Fe Iron Ore
Mg Magnesium
Mo Molybdenum

Ni Nickel
O Petroleum
Pb Lead
Ti Titanium
U Uranium
V Vanadium
Zn Zinc

⚡ Water Power
▨ Major Industrial Areas

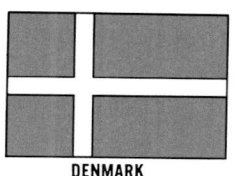

DENMARK

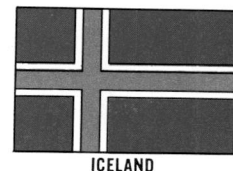

ICELAND

DENMARK

AREA 16,629 sq. mi. (43,069 sq. km.)
POPULATION 5,124,000
CAPITAL Copenhagen
LARGEST CITY Copenhagen
HIGHEST POINT Yding Skovhøj
568 ft. (173 m.)
MONETARY UNIT krone
MAJOR LANGUAGE Danish
MAJOR RELIGION Protestantism

ICELAND

AREA 39,768 sq. mi. (103,000 sq. km.)
POPULATION 228,785
CAPITAL Reykjavík
LARGEST CITY Reykjavík
HIGHEST POINT Hvannadalshnúkur
6,952 ft. (2,119 m.)
MONETARY UNIT króna
MAJOR LANGUAGE Icelandic
MAJOR RELIGION Protestantism

Denmark and Iceland

CONIC PROJECTION

SCALE OF MILES
0   10   20   30   40   50

SCALE OF KILOMETERS
0   10   20   30   40   50

Capitals of Countries _____ ☆
Capitals of Counties (amter) _____ ▲
International Boundaries _____
Internal Boundaries _____

Denmark is divided into fourteen Counties plus Copenhagen and Frederiksberg communes.

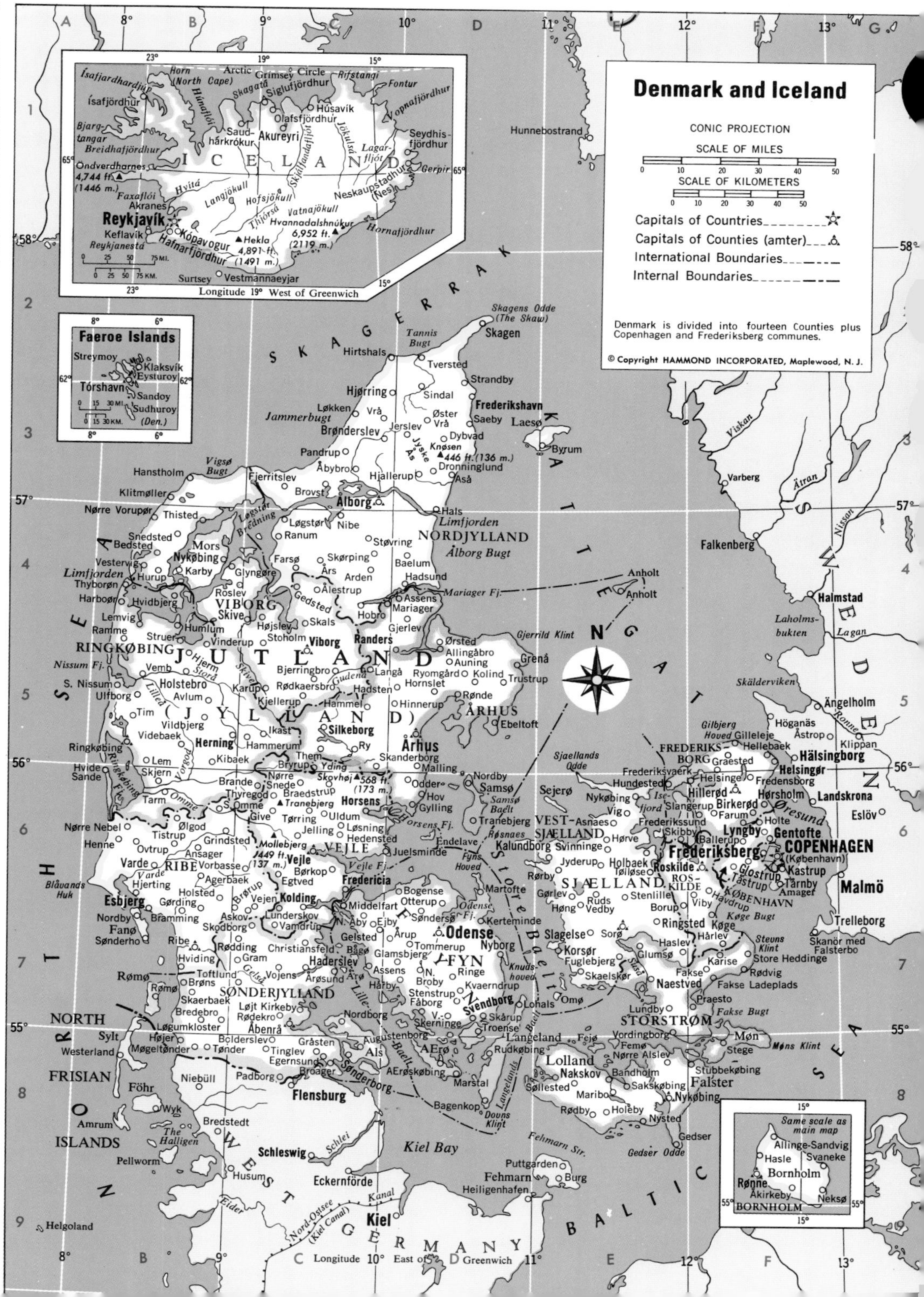

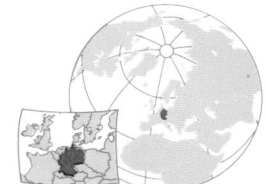

AREA 95,985 sq. mi. (248,601 sq. km.)
POPULATION 61,658,000
CAPITAL Bonn
LARGEST CITY Berlin (West)
HIGHEST POINT Zugspitze 9,718 ft. (2,962 m.)
MONETARY UNIT Deutsche mark
MAJOR LANGUAGE German
MAJOR RELIGIONS Protestantism, Roman
Catholicism

AREA 41,768 sq. mi. (108,179 sq. km.)
POPULATION 16,737,000
CAPITAL Berlin (East)
LARGEST CITY Berlin (East)
HIGHEST POINT Fichtelberg 3,983 ft. (1,214 m.)
MONETARY UNIT East German mark
MAJOR LANGUAGE German
MAJOR RELIGIONS Protestantism, Roman
Catholicism

WEST GERMANY

EAST GERMANY

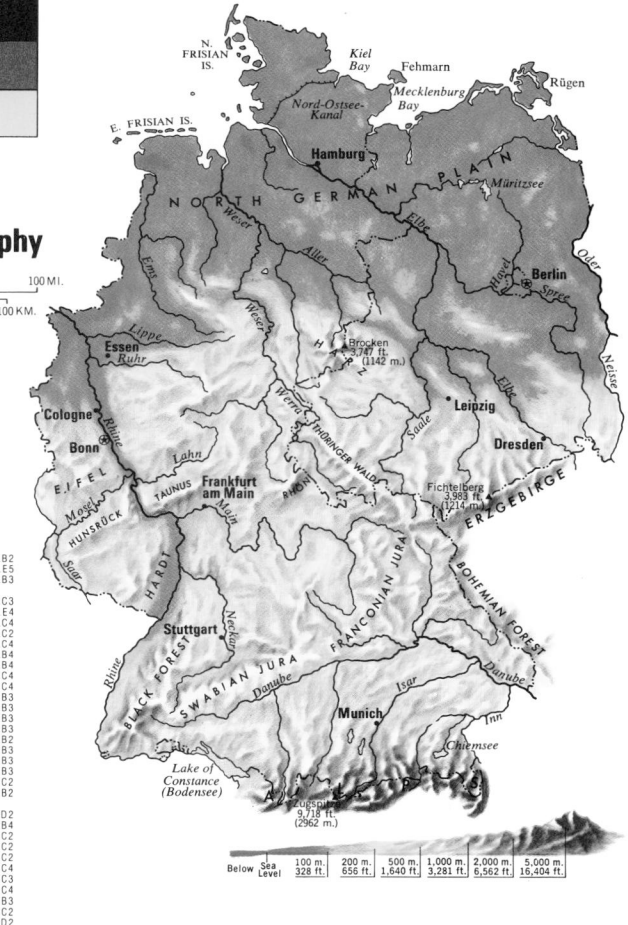

Topography

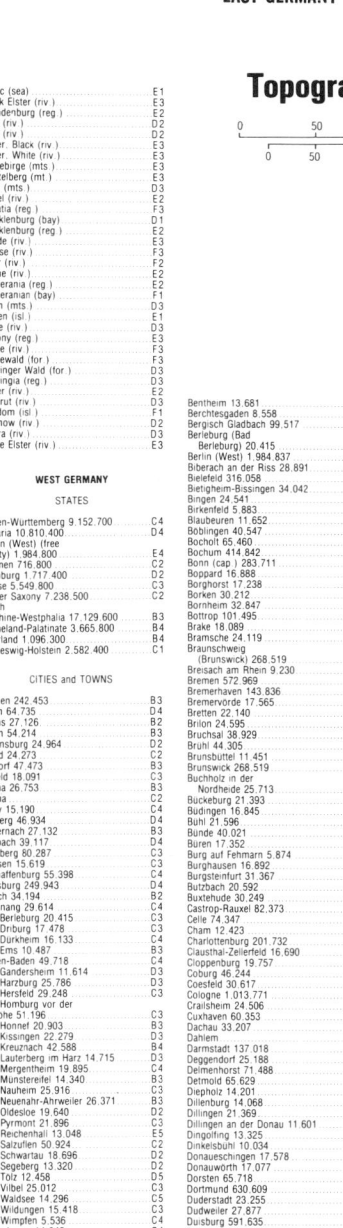

EAST GERMANY

DISTRICTS

Berlin 1,094,147	F4
Cottbus 872,242	F3
Dresden 1,845,459	E3
Erfurt 1,247,213	D3
Frankfurt 688,637	F2
Gera 738,847	D3
Halle 1,890,187	E3
Karl-Marx-Stadt 1,994,115	E3
Leipzig 1,457,817	E3
Magdeburg 1,297,881	D2
Neubrandenburg 628,686	E2
Potsdam 1,124,892	E2
Rostock 867,806	E1
Schwerin 592,334	D2
Suhl 550,497	D3

CITIES and TOWNS

Aken 11,742	D3
Altenburg 51,193	E3
Angermünde 11,786	E2
Anklam 19,099	E2
Annaberg-Buchholz 26,561	E3
Apolda 28,649	D3
Arnstadt 29,462	D3
Aschersleben 36,674	D3
Aue 32,622	E3
Auerbach 18,168	E3
Bad Doberan 12,541	D1
Bad Dürrenberg 15,192	D3
Bad Langensalza 166,282	D3
Bad Salzungen 17,277	D3
Barth 12,069	E1
Bautzen 45,851	F3
Bergen 13,244	E1
Berlin, East (cap.) 1,094,147	F4
Bernau bei Berlin 15,749	E2
Bernburg 44,428	D3
Bischofswerda 11,540	F3
Bitterfeld 27,062	E3
Blankenburg am Harz 18,784	D3
Boizenburg an der Elbe 12,428	D2
Borna 21,807	E3
Brandenburg 94,071	E2
Burg bei Magdeburg 29,027	D2
Calbe 15,976	D3
Chemnitz (Karl-Marx-Stadt) 303,811	E3
Coswig, Dresden 22,149	E3
Coswig, Halle 12,473	E3
Cottbus 94,293	F3
Crimmitschau 28,845	E3
Delitzsch 24,076	E3
Demmin 17,270	E2
Dessau 100,820	D3
Döbeln 27,624	E3
Dresden 507,692	E3
Ebersbach 12,694	F3
Eberswalde-Finow 47,141	E2
Eilenburg 22,245	E3
Eisenach 49,954	D3
Eisenberg 13,450	E3
Eisenhüttenstadt 46,455	F2
Eisleben 29,297	D3
Erfurt 202,979	D3
Falkensee 25,295	E3
Falkenstein 14,367	E3
Finsterwalde 22,466	E3
Forst 28,084	F3
Frankfurt an der Oder 70,817	F2
Freiberg 50,815	E3
Freital 46,061	E3
Friedland	F2
Fürstenwalde 31,065	F2
Gardelegen 12,987	D2
Genthin 15,916	E2
Gera 113,108	E3
Glauchau 30,927	E3
Görlitz 86,658	F3
Gotha 59,243	D3
Greifswald 55,940	E1
Greiz 37,612	E3
Grevesmühlen 12,005	D2
Grimma 17,100	E3
Grimmen 14,571	E1
Grossenhain 18,712	E3
Grossräschen 12,889	E3
Guben (Wilhelm-Pieck-Stadt) 32,731	F3
Güstrow 36,824	E2
Hagenow 46,669	D2
Haldensleben 19,194	D2
Halle 241,425	D3
Halle-Neustadt 67,956	D3
Havelberg	D2
Heidenau 21,315	E3
Heiligenstadt 13,931	D3
Hennigsdorf bei Berlin 24,853	E3
Hettstedt 20,291	D3
Hildburghausen 11,372	D3
Hoyerswerda 64,904	F3
Ilmenau 22,021	D3
Jena 99,431	E3
Johanngeorgenstadt 10,328	E3
Jüterbog 13,871	E3
Kamenz 18,221	F3
Karl-Marx-Stadt 303,811	E3
Kleinmachnow 14,059	E3
Klingenthal 13,614	E3
Königs Wusterhausen 11,825	E2

Köpenick 130,987	F4
Köthen 35,451	E3
Kühlungsborn	D1
Lauchhammer 26,939	E3
Leipzig 570,972	E3
Lichtenberg 192,063	F4
Limbach-Oberfrohna 25,706	E3
Löbau 18,077	F3
Lübben 14,224	F3
Lübbenau 22,350	F3
Luckenwalde 28,544	E2
Ludwigslust 13,280	D2
Magdeburg 276,089	D2
Markkleeberg 22,380	E3
Meerane 25,037	E3
Meiningen 26,134	D3
Meissen 43,561	E3
Merseburg 54,269	D3
Meuselwitz 13,585	E3
Mittweida 19,259	E3
Mühlhausen (Thomas-Müntzer-Stadt) 44,106	D3
Nauen 11,940	E2
Naumburg 36,358	E3
Neubrandenburg 59,971	E2
Neuenhagen bei Berlin 12,603	F4
Neuruppin 24,888	E2
Neustrelitz 27,074	E2
Nordhausen 44,442	D3
Oelsnitz 15,084	E3
Oelsnitz im Erzgebirge 16,063	E3
Olbernhau 13,479	E3
Oranienburg 24,452	E2
Oschatz 18,974	E3
Oschersleben 17,377	D2
Pankow 136,527	F4
Parchim 22,927	D2
Pasewalk 15,099	F2
Peenemünde	E1
Perleberg 15,029	D2
Pirna 41,771	E3
Plauen 80,353	E3
Pössneck 18,648	D3
Potsdam 117,236	E2
Prenzlau 22,738	E2
Pritzwalk 11,887	D2
Quedlinburg 29,796	D3
Radeberg 18,528	E3
Radebeul 34,383	E3
Rathenow 32,011	E2
Reichenbach 27,440	E3
Ribnitz-Damgarten 17,254	E1
Riesa 49,989	E3
Rosslau 16,520	E3
Rostock 210,167	E1
Rudolstadt 31,348	D3
Saalfeld 33,648	D3
Salzwedel 21,741	D2
Sangerhausen 32,721	D3
Sassnitz 13,857	E1
Schkeuditz 15,585	E3
Schmalkalden 15,017	D3
Schmölln 13,406	E3
Schneeberg 20,376	E3
Schönebeck 45,197	D2
Schwedt 45,729	F2
Schwerin 104,984	D2
Sebnitz 13,470	F3
Senftenberg 29,953	F3
Sömmerda 20,712	D3
Sonneberg 23,383	D3
Sonneberg 29,933	D3
Spremberg 22,862	F3
Stassfurt 26,225	D3
Stendal 39,647	D2
Stralsund 72,167	E1
Strausberg 21,334	F2
Suhl 36,642	D3
Tangermünde 12,898	D2
Teltow 16,171	E4
Templin 11,718	E2
Thale 17,248	D3
Thomas-Müntzer-Stadt 44,106	D3
Torgau 21,613	E3
Torgelow 14,320	E2
Treptow 127,448	F4
Ueckermünde 11,423	F2
Waldheim 11,925	E3
Waltershausen 13,893	D3
Waren 22,921	E2
Weida 11,816	E3
Weimar 63,144	D3
Weisswasser 43,191	F3
Weissenfels 78,451	F3
Weisswasser 35,910	F3
Werdau 22,249	E3
Wernigerode 34,658	D3
Wilhelm-Pieck-Stadt 32,731	F3
Wismar 56,765	D2
Wittenberg 51,364	E3
Wittenberge 32,907	D2
Wolfen 21,570	E3
Wolgast 16,384	E1
Wurzen 20,501	E3
Zehdenick 12,651	E2
Zeitz 44,582	E3
Zella-Mehlis 16,301	D3
Zerbst 19,356	E3
Zeulenroda 13,452	E3
Zittau 42,298	F3
Zwickau 123,069	E3

OTHER FEATURES

Altmark (reg.)	D2
Arkona (cape)	E1

Baltic (sea)	E1
Black Elster (riv.)	E3
Brandenburg (reg.)	E2
Elbe (riv.)	D2
Eide (riv.)	D2
Elster, Black (riv.)	E3
Elster, White (riv.)	E3
Erzgebirge (mts.)	E3
Fichtelberg (mt.)	E3
Harz (mts.)	D3
Havel (riv.)	E2
Lusatia (reg.)	F3
Mecklenburg (bay)	D1
Mecklenburg (reg.)	E2
Mulde (riv.)	E3
Neisse (riv.)	F3
Oder (riv.)	F2
Peene (riv.)	E2
Pomerania (reg.)	E2
Pomeranian (bay)	F1
Rhön (mts.)	D3
Rügen (isl.)	E1
Saale (riv.)	E3
Saxony (reg.)	E3
Spree (riv.)	F3
Spreewald (for.)	F3
Thüringer Wald (for.)	D3
Thuringia (reg.)	D3
Ucker (riv.)	E2
Unstrut (riv.)	D3
Usedom (isl.)	F1
Warnow (riv.)	D2
Werra (riv.)	D3
White Elster (riv.)	E3

WEST GERMANY

STATES

Baden-Württemberg 9,152,700	C4
Bavaria 10,810,400	D4
Berlin (West) (free city) 1,984,800	E4
Bremen 716,800	C2
Hamburg 1,717,400	D2
Hesse 5,549,800	C3
Lower Saxony 7,238,500	C2
North Rhine-Westphalia 17,129,600	B3
Rhineland-Palatinate 3,665,800	B4
Saarland 1,096,300	B4
Schleswig-Holstein 2,582,400	C1

CITIES and TOWNS

Aachen 242,453	B3
Aalen 64,735	D4
Ahaus 27,126	B2
Ahlen 54,214	B3
Ahrensburg 24,964	D2
Alfeld 24,273	C2
Alsdorf 47,473	B3
Alsfeld 18,091	C3
Altena 26,753	B3
Altona	D2
Alzey 15,190	C4
Amberg 46,934	D4
Andernach 27,132	B3
Ansbach 39,117	D4
Arnsberg 80,287	C3
Arolsen 15,619	C3
Aschaffenburg 55,398	C4
Augsburg 249,943	D4
Aurich 34,194	B2
Backnang 29,614	C4
Bebra 15,740	C3
Baden-Baden 49,718	C4
Bad Gandersheim 11,614	C3
Bad Harzburg 25,786	D3
Bad Hersfeld 29,248	C3
Bad Homburg vor der Höhe 51,196	C3
Bad Honnef 20,903	B3
Bad Kissingen 22,279	D3
Bad Kreuznach 42,588	B4
Bad Lauterberg im Harz 14,715	D3
Bad Mergentheim 19,895	C4
Bad Münstereifel 14,340	B3
Bad Nauheim 25,916	C3
Bad Neuenahr-Ahrweiler 26,371	B3
Bad Oldesloe 19,640	D2
Bad Pyrmont 21,896	C3
Bad Reichenhall 13,048	E5
Bad Salzuflen 50,924	C2
Bad Segeberg 13,320	D2
Bad Tölz 12,458	D5
Bad Vilbel 25,012	C3
Bad Waldsee 14,296	C5
Baiersbronn 14,845	C4
Balingen 29,310	C4
Bamberg 74,236	D4
Barsinghausen 32,873	C2
Bassum 14,113	C2
Bayreuth 67,035	D4
Bayrischzell 1,639	D5
Bebra 15,740	C3
Bendorf 15,943	B3
Bensheim 32,653	C4

Bentheim 13,681	B2
Berchtesgaden 8,558	E5
Bergisch Gladbach 99,517	B3
Berleburg (Bad Berleburg) 20,415	C3
Berlin (West) 1,984,837	E4
Biberach an der Riss 28,891	C4
Bielefeld 316,058	C2
Bietigheim-Bissingen 34,042	C4
Bingen 24,541	B4
Birkenfeld 5,883	B4
Blaubeuren 11,652	C4
Böblingen 40,547	C4
Bocholt 65,460	B3
Bochum 414,842	B3
Bonn (cap.) 283,711	B3
Boppard 16,888	B3
Borghorst 17,238	B2
Borken 30,212	B3
Bornheim 32,847	B3
Bottrop 101,495	B3
Brake 18,089	C2
Bramsche 24,119	B2
Braunschweig (Brunswick) 268,519	D2
Breisach am Rhein 9,230	B4
Bremen 572,969	C2
Bremerhaven 143,836	C2
Bremervörde 17,565	C2
Bretten 22,140	C4
Brilon 24,595	C3
Bruchsal 38,929	C4
Brühl 44,305	B3
Brunsbüttel 11,451	C2
Brunswick 268,519	D2
Buchholz in der Nordheide 25,713	C2
Bückeburg 21,393	C2
Büdingen 16,845	C3
Bühl 21,596	C4
Bünde 40,021	C2
Büren 17,352	C3
Burg auf Fehmarn 5,874	C1
Burghausen 16,892	E4
Burgsteinfurt 31,367	B2
Butzbach 20,592	C3
Buxtehude 30,249	C2
Castrop-Rauxel 82,373	B3
Celle 74,347	D2
Cham 12,423	E4
Charlottenburg 201,732	E4
Clausthal-Zellerfeld 16,690	D3
Cloppenburg 19,757	B2
Coburg 46,244	D3
Coesfeld 30,617	B3
Cologne 1,013,771	B3
Crailsheim 24,506	D4
Cuxhaven 60,353	C2
Dachau 33,207	D4
Dahlem	E4
Darmstadt 137,018	C4
Deggendorf 25,188	E4
Delmenhorst 71,488	C2
Detmold 65,629	C3
Diepholz 14,201	C2
Dillenburg 14,068	C3
Dillingen 21,369	B4
Dillingen an der Donau 11,601	D4
Dingolfing 13,325	E4
Dinkelsbühl 10,034	D4
Donaueschingen 17,578	C5
Donauwörth 17,077	D4
Dorsten 65,718	B3
Dortmund 630,609	B3
Duderstadt 23,255	D3
Dudweiler 27,877	B4
Duisburg 591,635	B3
Dülmen 37,013	B3
Düren 87,777	B3
Düsseldorf 664,336	B3
Eberbach 15,834	C4
Ebingen 22,594	C4
Eckernförde 22,938	D1
Ehingen 21,600	C4
Eichstätt 13,080	D4
Einbeck 29,821	C3
Eiserfeld 22,346	C3

Eliwangen 21,994	D4
Elmshorn 41,355	C2
Emden 53,509	B2
Emmendingen 24,722	B4
Emmerich 29,113	B3
Emsdetten 30,195	B2
Erlangen 100,671	D4
Eschwege 24,882	C3
Eschweiler 53,603	B3
Espelkamp 22,670	C2
Essen 677,568	B3
Esslingen am Neckar 95,298	C4
Ettlingen 35,159	C4
Euskirchen 43,558	B3
Eutin 17,701	D1
Fellbach 42,501	C4
Felsberg 93,213	C1
Forchheim 23,430	D4
Frankenberg-Eder 15,337	C3
Frankenthal 43,684	C4
Frankfurt am Main 636,157	C3
Frechen 41,453	B3
Freiburg im Breisgau 175,371	B5
Freising 31,524	D4
Friedberg 24,762	C3
Friedrichshafen 51,544	C5
Fritzlar 15,079	C3
Fulda 58,976	C3
Fürstenfeldbruck 27,194	D4
Fürth 101,639	D4
Füssen 10,506	D5
Gaggenau 28,846	C4
Garbsen 56,337	C2
Garmisch-Partenkirchen 26,831	D5
Gatow	E4
Geesthacht 24,745	D2
Geislingen an der Steige 28,693	D4
Geldern 24,082	B3
Gelnhausen 17,889	C3
Gelsenkirchen 322,584	B3
Georgsmarienhütte 30,259	B2
Geretsried 17,330	D5
Germersheim 12,041	C4
Gernsbach 6,857	B3
Gifhorn 31,635	D2
Glückstadt 12,159	C2
Goch 28,213	B3

Goggingen 15,980	D4
Göppingen 54,365	C4
Goslar 53,957	D3
Göttingen 123,797	C3
Greven 27,479	B2
Grevenbroich 56,392	B3
Griesheim 18,548	C4
Gronau 40,527	B2
Gummersbach 49,316	B3
Günzburg 13,528	D4
Gunzenhausen 13,565	D4
Gütersloh 77,128	C3
Haan 18,824	B3
Hagen 229,224	B3
Haltern 29,095	B3
Hamburg 1,717,383	D2
Hameln 61,066	C2
Hamm 172,210	B3
Hammelburg 12,350	C3
Hanau 86,676	C3
Hannover 552,955	C2
Harburg-Wilhelmsburg	C2
Haselünne 11,752	C2
Haunstetten 21,810	D4
Hechingen 15,926	C4
Heide 21,919	C1
Heidelberg 129,368	C4
Heidenheim an der Brenz 49,943	D4
Heilbronn 113,177	C4
Helmstedt 28,095	D2
Hennef 27,815	B3
Herford 64,385	C2
Herne 190,561	B3
Herten 36,657	B3
Hildesheim 105,290	C2
Hockenheim 18,695	C4
Hof 54,357	D3
Hofgeismar 13,380	C3
Holzminden 23,650	C3
Homburg 41,861	B4
Horn-Bad Meinberg 16,927	C3
Höxter 32,759	C3
Huckelhoven 34,865	B3
Hünfeld 13,873	C3
Hürth 51,692	B3
Husum 24,984	C1
Hüttental 39,561	C3
Ibbenbüren 42,202	B2
Idar-Oberstein 37,179	B4
Immenstadt im Allgäu 13,720	C5

Ingolstadt 88,500	D4
Iserlohn 96,174	B3
Isny im Allgäu 12,367	D5
Itzehoe 35,077	C2
Jever 12,090	B2
Jülich 31,564	B3
Kaiserslautern 100,886	B4
Karlsruhe 280,448	C4
Kassel 205,534	C3
Kaufbeuren 42,224	D5
Kehl 29,861	B4
Kelheim 11,996	D4
Kempten 56,944	D5
Kevelaer 20,971	B3
Kiel 262,164	D1
Kirchheim unter Teck 31,666	C4
Kitzingen 19,116	D4
Kleve 44,043	B3
Koblenz 118,394	B3
Köln (Cologne) 1,013,771	B3
Königswinter 34,586	B3
Konstanz 70,152	C5
Korbach 22,998	C3
Kornwestheim 27,771	C4
Krefeld 228,463	B3
Kreuztal 30,473	C3
Kronach 11,538	D3
Kulmbach 25,711	D3
Lage 31,724	C3
Lahnstein 19,725	B3
Lahr 35,570	B4
Lampertheim 31,993	C4
Landau in der Pfalz 37,661	C4
Landsberg am Lech 15,862	D4
Landshut 55,858	E4
Langen 30,227	C4
Langenhagen 47,092	C2
Lauenburg an der Elbe 11,077	D2
Lauf an der Pegnitz 19,443	D4
Lauingen 8,778	D4
Lauterbach 15,007	C3
Leer 32,785	B2
Lehrte 38,272	C2
Lemgo 39,664	C2
Lengerich 20,836	B2
Leverkusen 165,947	B3
Lichtenfels 13,719	D3
Limburg an der Lahn 28,606	C3
Lindau 23,930	C5

(continued on following page)

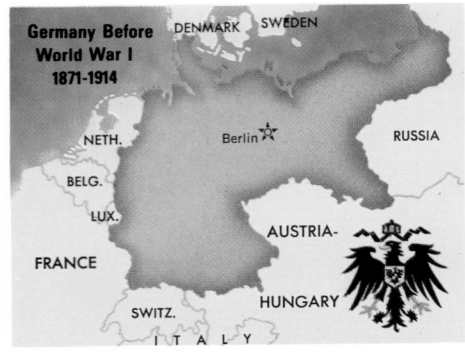

Germany Before World War I 1871-1914

SWEDEN · DENMARK · NETH. · BELG. · LUX. · FRANCE · SWITZ. · ITALY · Berlin · RUSSIA · AUSTRIA-HUNGARY

Germany Between Wars 1919-1937

SWEDEN · DENMARK · LITH. · DANZIG · NETH. · BELG. · LUX. · SAAR (To Germany 1935) · FRANCE · SWITZ. · ITALY · Berlin · POLAND · CZECHOSLOVAKIA · AUSTRIA · YUGO. · HUNG.

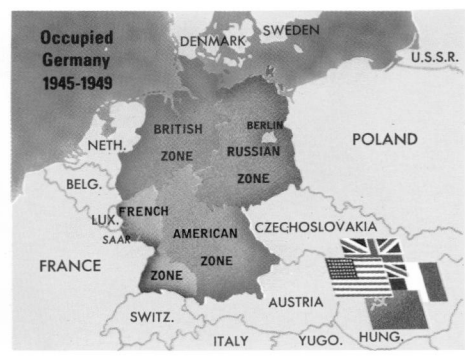

Occupied Germany 1945-1949

SWEDEN · DENMARK · U.S.S.R. · NETH. · BRITISH ZONE · BERLIN · RUSSIAN ZONE · BELG. · LUX. · FRENCH ZONE · SAAR · AMERICAN ZONE · POLAND · CZECHOSLOVAKIA · FRANCE · SWITZ. · ITALY · AUSTRIA · YUGO. · HUNG.

Lingen 43.785	B2	Oberpfalz 29.713	D4	Rastatt 38.030	C4
Lippstadt 63.040	C3	Neumünster 84.777	C1	Rastede 16.905	B2
Löhne 17.859	C2	Neunkirchen 54.992	B4	Ratingen 86.028	B3
Lohr am Main 16.435	C4	Neuss 148.198	B3	Ratzeburg 12.189	D2
Lörrach 44.179	B5	Neustadt an der		Ravensburg 42.725	C5
Lübeck 232.270	D2	Weinstrasse 51.011	B4	Recklinghausen 122.437	B3
Ludenscheid 76.213	B3	Neustadt bei Coburg 12.665	D3	Regensburg 131.886	D4
Ludwigsburg 83.622	C4	Neustadt in Holstein 15.333	D1	Remagen 14.627	B3
Ludwigshafen am Rhein 170.374	C4	Neu-Ulm 31.660	D4	Remscheid 133.145	B3
Lüneburg 64.586	D2	Neuwied 62.029	B3	Rendsburg 34.407	C1
Lünen 85.685	B3	Nienburg 30.978	C2	Reutlingen 95.289	C4
Mainz 183.880	C4	Norden 24.207	B2	Rheda-Wiedenbrück 37.371	C3
Mannheim 314.086	C4	Nordenham 31.457	C2	Rheine 71.539	B3
Marbach am Neckar 12.131	C4	Norderstedt 61.553	D2	Rheinfelden 27.500	B5
Marburg an der Lahn 72.458	C3	Nordhorn 49.598	B2	Rheydt 100.077	B3
Marktredwitz 16.404	E4	Nördlingen 16.480	D4	Rietberg 22.421	C3
Marl 91.930	B3	Northeim 32.665	C3	Rinteln 25.595	C2
Mayen 21.018	B3	Nuremberg 499.060	D4	Rosenheim 38.419	D5
Mechernich 21.498	B3	Nürnberg (Nuremberg) 499.060	D4	Rotenburg 19.155	C2
Meckenheim 13.591	B3	Nürtingen 34.333	C4	Rotenburg an der Fulda 14.438	C3
Melle 41.339	C2	Oberammergau 4.704	D5	Roth bei Nürnberg 17.782	D4
Melsungen 13.444	C3	Oberhausen 237.147	B3	Rothenburg ob der	
Memmingen 34.612	D5	Oberstdorf 11.687	D5	Tauber 11.609	D4
Meppen 27.308	B2	Oberursel 39.802	C4	Rottenburg am Neckar 30.583	C4
Merzig 30.197	B4	Offenbach am Main 115.251	C3	Rottweil 24.534	C4
Meschede 32.472	C3	Offenburg 51.553	B4	Russelsheim 62.067	C4
Metzingen 19.224	C4	Oldenburg 134.706	C2	Sackingen 33.956	B5
Michelstadt 13.591	C4	Oldenburg in Holstein 9.201	D1	Salzgitter 117.341	D2
Minden 78.887	C2	Opladen 42.789	B3	Sankt Goar 3.511	B3
Mittenwald 8.831	D5	Osnabrück 161.671	C2	Sankt Ingbert 43.263	B4
Mölln 15.780	D2	Osterholz-Scharmbeck 22.734	C2	Sankt Wendel 27.558	B4
Monchengladbach 261.367	B3	Osterode am Harz 29.668	D3	Saulgau 15.403	C4
Moosburg an der Isar 12.196	D4	Paderborn 103.705	C3	Schleswig 30.974	C1
Mosbach 23.663	C4	Papenburg 27.039	B2	Schlüchtern 13.801	C3
Muhldorf am Inn 12.638	E4	Passau 50.920	E4	Schoneberg 169.835	E4
Mülheim an der Ruhr 189.259	B3	Peine 49.450	D2	Schoningen 16.348	C2
Mühlheim 12.183	C4	Pfaffenhofen an der Ilm 13.684	D4	Schramberg 19.677	C4
München (Munich) 1.314.865	D4	Pforzheim 108.635	C4	Schwabach 33.136	D4
Münden 27.018	C3	Pfullingen 16.195	C4	Schwäbisch Gmünd 56.422	C4
Munich 1.314.865	D4	Pinneberg 36.844	C2	Schwäbisch Hall 32.129	C4
Munster 264.546	C2	Pirmasens 53.651	B4	Schwalmstadt 17.800	C3
Nagold 19.047	C4	Plettenberg 29.273	B3	Schwandorf im Bayern 22.547	D4
Neckarsulm 20.112	C4	Porz am Rhein 74.915	B3	Schwenfurt 56.164	D3
Neheim-Husten 36.373	C3	Preetz 15.305	D1	Schwelm 31.850	B3
Neuburg an der Donau 19.400	D4	Puttgarden	D1		
Neu-Isenburg 35.631	C4	Radolfzell 23.274	C5		
Neumarkt in der					

Schwetzingen 18.286	C4	Völkingen 47.271	B4	Ammersee (lake)	D4
Seesen 23.577	C2	Waldkirch 19.009	B4	Amrum (isl)	C1
Selb 16.723	E3	Waldkraiburg 20.140	E4	Baltrum (isl)	B2
Sennestadt 20.187	C3	Waldshut-Tiengen 22.046	C5	Bavarian (for)	E4
Siegburg 34.943	B3	Walsrode 23.423	C2	Bavarian Alps (range)	D5
Siegen 116.552	C3	Wangen im Allgau 23.127	C5	Black (for)	C4
Sigmaringen 15.437	C4	Wanne-Eickel 99.156	B3	Bodensee (Constance) (lake)	C5
Sindelfingen 54.134	C4	Warburg 22.150	C3	Bohemian (for)	E4
Singen 45.566	C5	Warendorf 32.273	B3	Borkum (isl)	B2
Soest 40.308	C3	Wedel 30.045	C2	Breisgau (reg)	B4
Solingen 171.810	B3	Weiden in der Oberpfalz 42.697	D4	Chiemsee (lake)	E5
Soltau 19.949	C2	Weilburg 12.652	C3	Constance (lake)	C5
Sonthofen 17.821	D5	Weilheim im Oberbayern 15.347	D5	Danube (riv)	D5
Spandau 197.687	E3	Weingarten 21.143	C4	Donau (Danube) (riv)	D4
Speyer 44.471	C4	Weinheim 41.005	C4	East Friesland (reg)	B2
Springe 30.968	C2	Weissenburg im Bayern 16.083	D4	East Frisian (isls)	B2
Stade 42.097	C2	Wertheim 20.942	C4	Eder (res)	C3
Stadthagen 23.003	C2	Wesel 56.584	B3	Elbe (riv)	C2
Starnberg 57.379	D4	Westerland 9.652	B1	Ems (riv)	B2
Straubing 43.774	E4	Westerstede 16.977	B2	Fehmarn (isl)	D1
Stuttgart 600.421	C4	Wiehl 19.004	B3	Feldberg (mt)	B5
Sulzbach 22.133	B4	Wiesbaden 250.592	C4	Fichtelgebirge (range)	D3
Sulzbach-Rosenberg 18.596	D4	Wildbad im Schwarzwald 11.611	C4	Föhr (isl)	C1
Taiflingen 17.278	C4	Wildeshausen 12.055	C2	Franconian Jura (range)	D4
Tegel	E3	Wilhelmshaven 103.417	B2	Frisian, East (isls)	B2
Teigte 15.165	B3	Witten 108.771	B3	Frisian, North (isls)	B1
Tempelhof 159.730	F4	Wittingen 12.189	D2	Grosser Arber (mt)	E4
Timmendorfer Strand 10.690	E1	Wittlich 15.321	B4	Halligen (isl)	C1
Traunstein 14.088	E5	Witzenhausen 16.877	C3	Hardt (mts)	B4
Trier 100.338	B4	Wolfenbüttel 51.386	D2	Harz (mts)	D3
Troisdorf 56.402	B3	Wolfsburg 126.298	D2	Hase (riv)	B2
Tübingen 56.341	C4	Worms 75.732	C4	Hegau (reg)	C4
Tuttlingen 32.342	C4	Wunstorf 36.795	C2	Helgoland (bay)	C1
Ubach-Palenberg 22.403	B3	Wuppertal 405.369	B3	Helgoland (isl)	B1
Überlingen 17.735	C5	Wurzburg 112.584	C4	Hunsruck (mts)	B4
Uelzen 37.550	D2	Xanten 15.688	B3	Hunte (riv)	C2
Uetersen 16.330	C2	Zirndorf 13.661	D4	Iller (riv)	C5
Ulm 98.237	D4	Zülpich 16.171	B3	Inn (riv)	E4
Uslar 17.251	C3	Zweibrücken 35.978	B4	Isar (riv)	D4
Varel 24.435	C2	Zwischenahn 22.581	B2	Juist (isl)	B2
Vechta 21.786	C2			Kaisersturl (mt)	B4
Verden 24.247	C2	**OTHER FEATURES**		Kiel (bay)	D1
Viersen 84.220	B3			Kiel (Nord-Ostsee) (canal)	C1
Villingen-Schwenningen 80.646	C4	Aller (riv)	C2	Königssee (lake)	E5
		Allgau (reg)	D5	Lahn (riv)	C3
		Altmuhl (riv)	D4	Langeoog (isl)	B2

Lech (riv)	D4
Leine (riv)	C2
Lippe (riv)	B3
Luneburger Heide (dist)	C2
Main (riv)	D4
Mecklenburg (bay)	D1
Mosel (riv)	B3
Naab (riv)	D4
Neckar (riv)	C4
Norderney (isl)	B2
Nord-Ostsee (canal)	C1
Nordstrand (isl)	C1
North (sea)	B2
North Friesland (reg)	C1
North Frisian (isls)	B1
Odenwald (for)	C4
Oker (riv)	D2
Pellworm (isl)	C1
Regen (riv)	E4
Regnitz (riv)	D4
Rhine (riv)	B3
Rhon (riv)	D3
Ruhr (riv)	B3
Saar (riv)	B4
Sauer (riv)	B4
Sauerland (reg)	B3
Schneeberg (mt)	D3
Schwarzwald (Black) (for)	C4
Spessart (mts)	C4
Spiekeroog (isl)	B2
Swabian Jura (range)	C4
Sylt (isl)	B1
Tauber (riv)	C4
Taunus (range)	C3
Tegernsee (lake)	D5
Teutoburger Wald (for)	C2
Vogelsberg (mts)	C3
Walchensee (lake)	D5
Wangerooge (isl)	B2
Watzmann (mt)	E5
Weser (riv)	C2
Westerwald (for)	B3
Wurmsee (Starnbergersee) (lake)	D5
Zugspitze (mt)	D5

Agriculture, Industry and Resources

DOMINANT LAND USE

- Wheat, Sugar Beets
- Cereals (chiefly rye, oats, barley)
- Potatoes, Rye
- Dairy, Livestock
- Mixed Cereals, Dairy
- Truck Farming
- Grapes, Fruit
- Forests

MAJOR MINERAL OCCURRENCES

Ag	Silver	K	Potash
Ba	Barite	Lg	Lignite
C	Coal	Na	Salt
Cu	Copper	O	Petroleum
Fe	Iron Ore	Pb	Lead
G	Natural Gas	U	Uranium
Gr	Graphite	Zn	Zinc

 Water Power
Major Industrial Areas

AREA 15,892 sq. mi. (41,160 sq. km.)
POPULATION 14,227,000
CAPITALS The Hague, Amsterdam
LARGEST CITY Amsterdam
HIGHEST POINT Vaalserberg 1,056 ft. (322 m.)
MONETARY UNIT guilder (florin)
MAJOR LANGUAGE Dutch
MAJOR RELIGIONS Protestantism, Roman Catholicism

AREA 11,781 sq. mi. (30,513 sq. km.)
POPULATION 9,855,110
CAPITAL Brussels
LARGEST CITY Brussels (greater)
HIGHEST POINT Botrange 2,277 ft. (694 m.)
MONETARY UNIT Belgian franc
MAJOR LANGUAGES French (Walloon), Flemish
MAJOR RELIGION Roman Catholicism

AREA 999 sq. mi. (2,587 sq. km.)
POPULATION 364,000
CAPITAL Luxembourg
LARGEST CITY Luxembourg
HIGHEST POINT Ardennes Plateau 1,825 ft. (556 m.)
MONETARY UNIT Luxembourg franc
MAJOR LANGUAGES Luxembourgeois (Letzeburgisch), French, German
MAJOR RELIGION Roman Catholicism

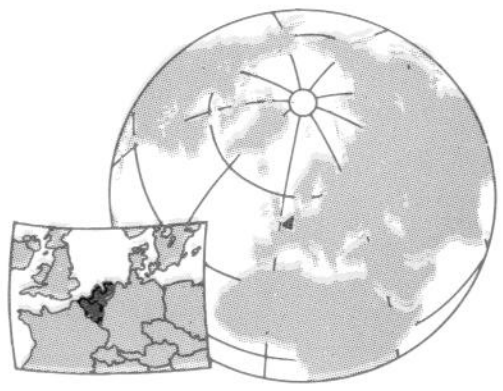

NETHERLANDS

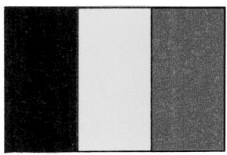

BELGIUM

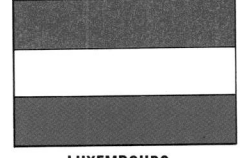

LUXEMBOURG

BELGIUM

PROVINCES

Antwerp 1,533,249 .... F6
Brabant 2,176,373 .... F7
East Flanders 1,310,117 .... D7
Hainaut 1,317,453 .... D7
Liège 1,008,905 .... H7
Limburg 652,547 .... G7
Luxembourg 217,310 .... G9
Namur 380,561 .... F8
West Flanders 1,054,429 .... B7

CITIES and TOWNS†

Aalst 46,659 .... D7
Aalter 9,173 .... C6
Aarlen (Arlon) 13,745 .... H9
Aarschot 12,474 .... F7
Aat (Ath) 11,842 .... D7
Alken 8,677 .... G7
Alost (Aalst) 46,659 .... D7
Amay 7,617 .... G7
Andenne 8,091 .... G8
Anderlecht 103,796 .... B9
Anderlues 12,176 .... E8
Ans H7
Antoing 3,426 .... C7
Antwerp 224,543 .... E6
Antwerp* 928,000 .... E6
Antwerpen (Antwerp) 224,543 .... E6
Ardooie 7,081 .... C7
Arendonk 9,919 .... G6
Arlon 13,745 .... H9
As 5,496 .... H6
Asse 6,583 .... E7
Ath 11,842 .... D7
Attert H9
Aubange 3,761 .... H9
Audenarde (Oudenaarde) 26,615 .... D7
Auderghem 34,546 .... C9
Auvelais 8,287 .... F8
Aywaille 3,850 .... H8
Baerle-Hertog F6
Balen 15,110 .... G6
Basse-Sambre F8
Bastenaken (Bastogne) 6,816 .... H9
Bastogne 6,816 .... H9
Beernem C6
Beloeil D7
Berchem 50,241 .... F6
Berchem-Sainte-Agathe 19,087 .... B9
Bergen (Mons) 59,362 .... E8
Beringen G6
Bertogne H8
Bertrix 4,562 .... G9
Beveren 15,913 .... E6
Bilzen 7,178 .... G7
Binche 10,098 .... E8
Blankenberge 13,969 .... C6
Bocholt 6,497 .... H6
Boom 16,584 .... E6
Borgerhout 49,002 .... E6
Borgloon 3,412 .... G7
Borgworm (Waremme) 10,956 .... G7
Bourg-Léopold (Leopoldsburg) 9,593 .... G6
Boussu 11,474 .... D8
Braine-l'Alleud 18,531 .... E7
Braine-le-Comte 11,957 .... D7
Brecht F6
Bredene 9,244 .... B6
Bree 10,389 .... H6
Bruges 117,220 .... C6
Brugge (Bruges) 117,220 .... C6
Brussels (cap.)* 1,054,970 .... C9
Bruxelles (Brussels) (cap.)* 1,054,970 .... C9
Cerfontaine E8
Charleroi 23,689 .... E8
Charleroi* 458,000 .... E8
Chastre F7
Châtelet 14,752 .... F8
Chièvres 3,283 .... D7
Chimay 3,288 .... E8
Chiny G9
Ciney 7,536 .... G8
Comblain-au-Pont 3,582 .... G8
Comines 8,192 .... B7
Courcelles 17,015 .... E8
Courtrai (Kortrijk) 44,961 .... C7
Couvin 4,234 .... F8
Damme C6
De Haan C6
Deinze 16,711 .... C7
Denderleeuw 9,925 .... E7
Dendermonde 22,119 .... E6
De Panne 6,985 .... B6
Dessel 7,505 .... G6
Destelbergen D6
Deurne 80,766 .... F6
Diest 10,799 .... F7
Diksmuide 6,669 .... B6
Dilbeek 15,108 .... B9
Dilsen H6
Dinant 9,747 .... G8
Dison 8,466 .... H7
Dixmude (Diksmuide) 6,669 .... B6
Doische F8
Doornik (Tournai) 32,794 .... C7
Dour 10,059 .... D8
Drogenbos 4,840 .... B10
Duffel 13,802 .... F6
Durbuy H8
Ecaussinnes 6,630 .... E7
Edingen (Enghien) 4,115 .... D7
Eeklo 19,144 .... D6
Éghezée F7
Eigenbrakel (Braine-l'Alleud) 18,531 .... E7
Ekeren 27,648 .... E6
Ellezelles 3,556 .... D7
Enghien 4,115 .... D7
Érezée G8
Erquelinnes 4,471 .... E8
Esneux 6,183 .... H7
Essen 10,795 .... F6
Estampuis C7
Etterbeek 51,030 .... B9
Eupen 14,879 .... J7
Evere 26,957 .... C9
Evergem 12,886 .... D6
Farciennes E8
Fernelmont F7
Ferrières H8
Flémalle 8,135 .... G7
Fleurus 8,523 .... E8
Florennes 4,107 .... F8
Forest 55,135 .... B9
Fosses-La-Ville 3,972 .... F8
Frameries 11,224 .... D8
Froidchapelle E8
Furnes (Veurne) 9,496 .... B6
Ganshoren 21,147 .... B9
Geel 29,346 .... F6
Geldenaken (Jodoigne) 4,132 .... F7
Gembloux-sur-Orneau 11,249 .... F7
Genk 57,913 .... H7
Gent (Ghent) 148,860 .... D6
Geraardsbergen 17,533 .... D7
Gerpinnes F8
Ghent 148,860 .... D6
Ghent* 477,000 .... D6
Gistel B6
Gooik E7
Gouvy H8
Grammont (Geraardsbergen) 17,533 .... D7
Grez-Doiceau F7
Grimbergen E7
Haacht 4,436 .... F7
Habay H9
Hal (Halle) 20,017 .... E7
Halen 5,322 .... G7
Halle 20,017 .... E7
Hamme 17,559 .... E6
Hamois G8
Hamont-Achel 6,893 .... H6
Hannuit (Hannut) 7,232 .... G7
Hannut 7,232 .... G7
Harelbeke 18,498 .... C7
Hasselt 39,663 .... G7
Hastière F8
Heist-Knokke 27,582 .... C6
Heist-op-den-Berg 13,472 .... F6
Hensies D8
Herentals 18,639 .... F6
Herne E7
Herselt 7,412 .... F6
Herstal 29,600 .... H7
Herve 4,118 .... H7
Heuvelland B7
Hoboken 33,693 .... E6
Hoei (Huy) 12,736 .... G8
Hoeselt 6,884 .... G7
Honnelles D8
Hoogstraten 4,381 .... F6
Hotton G8
Huy 12,736 .... G8
Ichtegem B6
Ieper 20,825 .... B7
Ingelmunster 10,245 .... C7
Ittre E7
Ixelles 86,450 .... C9
Izegem 22,928 .... C7
Jabbeke C6
Jemappes 18,632 .... D8
Jette 40,013 .... B9
Jodoigne 4,132 .... F7
Kalmthout 12,724 .... F6
Kapellen 13,352 .... E6
Kasterlee F6
Kinrooi H6
Knokke-Heist 27,582 .... C6
Koekelare 7,807 .... B6
Koekelberg 17,570 .... B9
Koksijde B6
Kontich 14,432 .... E6
Kortemark 5,904 .... C6
Kortrijk 44,961 .... C7
Kraainem 11,390 .... C9
La Louvière 23,310 .... E8
La Louvière* 113,259 .... E8
Lanaken 8,659 .... H7
Landen 5,740 .... G7
Langemark-Poelkapelle 5,457 .... B7
Lasne F7
Lede 10,316 .... D7
Léglise H9
Leopoldsburg 9,593 .... G6
Le Roeulx E8
Lessen (Lessines) 8,906 .... D7
Lessines 8,906 .... D7
Leuven 30,623 .... F7
Leuze-en-Hainaut 7,185 .... D7
Libin G9
Libramont-Chevigny 2,975 .... G9
Lichtervelde 7,459 .... C6
Liedekerke 10,482 .... D7
Liège 145,573 .... H7
Liège* 622,000 .... H7
Lier 28,416 .... F6
Lierre (Lier) 28,416 .... F6
Limbourg 3,762 .... J7
Limburg (Limbourg) 3,762 .... J7
Linkebeek 4,265 .... C10
Linter G7
Lochristi D6
Lokeren 26,740 .... D6
Lommel 21,984 .... G6
Lontzen H9
Looz (Borgloon) 3,412 .... G7
Lo-Reninge B7
Louvain (Leuven) 30,623 .... F7
Luik (Liège) 145,573 .... H7
Lummen G7
Maaseik 8,622 .... H6
Maasmechelen H7
Machelen 7,057 .... C9
Maldegem 14,474 .... C6
Malines (Mechelen) 65,466 .... F6
Malmédy 6,464 .... J8
Manage E7
Manhay H8
Marche-en-Famenne 4,567 .... G8
Marchin 4,206 .... G8
Mechelen 65,466 .... F6
Meerhout 8,567 .... G6
Meise E7
Menen 22,037 .... C7
Menin (Menen) 22,037 .... C7
Merchtem 8,998 .... E7
Merelbeke 13,837 .... D7
Merksem 39,768 .... E6
Merksplas 5,065 .... F6
Messancy 3,150 .... H9
Mettet 3,372 .... F8
Meulebeke 10,458 .... C7
Middelkerke B6
Moeskroen (Mouscron) 37,311 .... C7
Mol 28,823 .... G6
Molenbeek-Saint-Jean 68,411 .... B9
Momignies E8
Mons 59,362 .... E8
Montigny-le-Tilleul E8
Moorslede B7
Mortsel 28,012 .... E6
Mouscron 37,311 .... C7
Namen (Namur) 32,269 .... F8
Namur 32,269 .... F8
Nassogne G8
Nazareth D7
Neerpelt 8,771 .... G6
Neufchâteau 2.670 .... G9
Nevele D6
Nieuport (Nieuwpoort) 8,273 .... B6
Nieuwpoort 8,273 .... B6
Nijvel (Nivelles) 16,126 .... E7
Ninove 12,428 .... D7
Nivelles 16,126 .... E7
Ohey G8
Onhaye F8
Oostende (Ostend) 71,227 .... B6
Oostkamp 8,999 .... C6
Opwijk 9,699 .... E7
Ostend 71,227 .... B6
Oudenaarde 26,615 .... D7
Oudenburg B6
Oud-Turnhout 9,245 .... F6
Oupeye H7
Overijse 16,181 .... F7
Overpelt 10,470 .... G6
Paliseul G9
Peer 7,201 .... G6
Péruwelz 7,878 .... D8
Philippeville 2,076 .... E8
Plombières F7
Pont-à-Celles E8
Poperinge 12,671 .... B7
Profondeville F8
Putte 6,953 .... F6
Quaregnon 17,688 .... D8
Quévy D8
Quiévrain 5,510 .... D8
Raeren 3,655 .... J7
Ravels G6
Rebecq 3,744 .... E7
Renaix (Ronse) 25,056 .... D7
Rendeux H8
Retie 6,619 .... G6
Rochefort 4,357 .... G8
Roeselare 40,428 .... C7
Ronse 25,056 .... D7
Roulers (Roeselare) 40,428 .... C7
Rouvroy G9
Ruislede C6
Sainte-Ode H8
Saint-Georges-sur-Meuse 6,003 .... G7
Saint-Gilles 55,055 .... B9
Saint-Hubert 3,091 .... G8
Saint-Josse-ten-Noode 23,633 .... C9
Saint-Nicolas G7
Saint-Trond (Sint-Truiden) 21,473 .... G7
Saint-Vith (Sankt Vith) 3,001 .... J8
Sankt Vith 3,001 .... J8
Schaerbeek 118,950 .... C9
Schoten 29,914 .... F6
Seraing 40,545 .... G7
's-Gravenbrakel (Braine-le-Comte) 11,957 .... D7
Sint-Laureins D6
Sint-Niklaas 49,214 .... E6

(continued on following page)

Agriculture, Industry and Resources

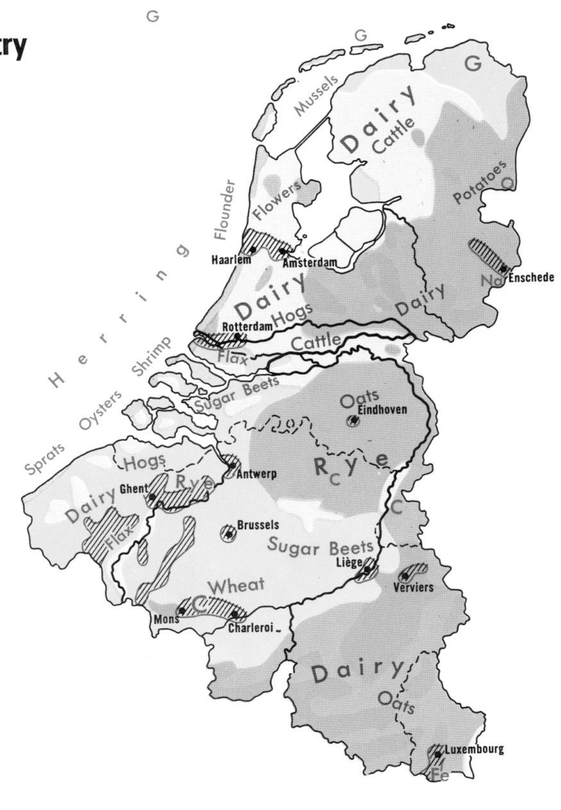

G
Mussels
Dairy
Cattle
Potatoes
O
Flounder
Flowers
Haarlem
Amsterdam
Na
Enschede
Herring
Dairy
Hogs
Rotterdam
Cattle
Dairy
Shrimp
Flax
Oysters
Sugar Beets
Sprats
Oats
Eindhoven
Hogs
Antwerp
Rye
Ghent
Rye
C
Dairy
Flax
Brussels
Sugar Beets
Liège
Verviers
Wheat
Mons
Charleroi
Dairy
Oats
Luxembourg
Fe

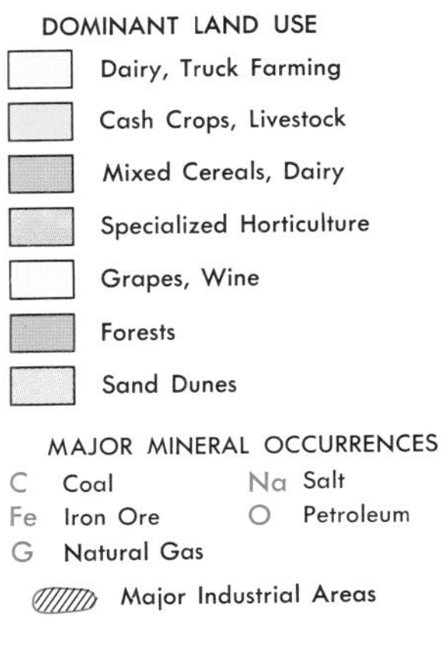

DOMINANT LAND USE
Dairy, Truck Farming
Cash Crops, Livestock
Mixed Cereals, Dairy
Specialized Horticulture
Grapes, Wine
Forests
Sand Dunes
MAJOR MINERAL OCCURRENCES
C Coal
Na Salt
Fe Iron Ore
O Petroleum
G Natural Gas
Major Industrial Areas

(continued)

Sint-Pieters-Leeuw 16,856 B9
Sint-Truiden 21,473 G7
Soignies 12,006 D7
Somme-Leuze G8
Spa 9,504 H8
Sprimont H8
Staden 5,499 B7
Stavelot 4,723 H8
Steenokkerzeel 4,037 C9
Stekene E6
Stoumont H8
Tamise (Temse) 14,950 E6
Tellin G8
Temse 14,950 E6
Tenneville H8
Termonde (Dendermonde) 22,119 E6
Tessenderlo 11,778 G6
Theux 5,316 H8
Thuin 5,777 E8
Tielt 14,077 C7
Tielt-Winge 3,743 F7
Tienen 24,134 F7
Tintigny G9
Tirlemont (Tienen) 24,134 F7
Tongeren 20,136 G7
Tongres (Tongeren) 20,136 G7
Torhout 15,156 C6
Tournai 32,794 C7
Trois-Ponts H8
Tubeke (Tubize) 11,507 E7
Tubize 11,507 E7
Turnhout 38,007 F6
Uccle 78,909 B9
Ukkel (Uccle) 78,909 B9
Vaux-sur-S0re H9
Verviers 33,587 H7
Veurne 9,496 B6
Vielsalm 3,587 H8
Vilvoorde 34,633 F7
Vilvorde (Vilvoorde) 34,633 F7
Viroinval F8
Virton 3,558 H9
Visé 6,880 H7
Vleteren B7
Vorst (Forest) 55,135 B9
Vresse-sur-Semois F9
Waarschoot 7,905 D6
Wachtebeke D6
Waregem 17,725 C7
Waremme 10,956 G7
Waterloo 17,764 E7
Watermaal-Bosvoorde
(Watermael-Boitsfort C9
Watermael-Boitsfort 25,123 C9
Waver (Wavre) 11,767 F7
Wavre 11,767 F7
Wellin G8
Wemmel 12,631 B9
Wervik 12,672 B7
Westerlo 14,173 F6
Westmalle F6
Wetteren 20,816 D7
Wezembeek-Oppem 10,899 D9
Wezet (Visé) 6,880 H7
Willebroek 15,726 E6
Wilrijk 43,485 E6
Wingene 7,140 C6
Woluwe-Saint-Lambert 47,360 C9
Woluwe-Saint-Pierre 40,884 C9
Ypres (Ieper) 20,825 B7
Zaventem 10,625 C9
Zedelgem C6
Zeebrugge C6
Zele 18,585 E6
Zelzate 12,785 D6
Zemst E7
Zinnik (Soignies) 12,006 D7
Zonhoven 13,484 G6
Zottegem 21,461 D7
Zuienkerke C6

OTHER FEATURES

Albert, (canal) F6
Ardennes, (for.) F9
Botrange, (mt.) J8
Dender, (riv.) D7
De0le, (riv.) B7
Dyle, (riv.) F7
Hohe Venn, (plat.) H8
Lesse, (riv.) F8
Lys, (riv.) B7
Mark, (riv.) F6
Meuse, (riv.) F8
Nethe, (riv.) F6
North, (sea) D4
Ourthe, (riv.) G8
Rupel, (riv.) F7
Sambre, (riv.) D8
Schelde (Scheldt), (riv.) C7
Scheldt, (riv.) C7
Schnee Eifel, (plat.) J8
Semois, (riv.) G9
Senne, (riv.) E7
Vaalserberg, (mt.) J7
Vesdre, (riv.) H7
Weisserstein, (mt.) J8
Yser, (riv.) B7
Zitterwald, (plat.) J8

LUXEMBOURG

CITIES and TOWNS

Clervaux 916 J8
Diekirch† 5,059 J9
Differdange 9,287 H9
Dudelange† 14,615 J10
Echternach† 3,792 J9
Esch-sur-Alzette† 27,574 J9
Ettelbruck† 5,990 J9
Grevenmacher† 2,918 J9
Luxembourg (cap.) 78,272 J9
Mamer 3,123 H9
Mersch 1,869 J9
Pétange 6,234 H9
Remich† 12,138 J9
Vianden† 1,520 J9
Wiltz 1,601 H9

OTHER FEATURES

Alzette, (riv.) J9
Clerf, (riv.) J8
Eisling, (mts.) H9
Mosel, (riv.) J9
Our, (riv.) J9
Sauer, (riv.) J9

NETHERLANDS

PROVINCES

Drenthe 405,924 K3
Flevoland G4
Friesland 560,614 H2
Gelderland 1,639,997 H4
Groningen 540,062 K2
Limburg 1,051,620 H6
North Brabant 1,967,261 F5
North Holland 2,295,875 F3
Overijssel 985,569 J4
South Holland 3,048,648 E5
Utrecht 867,909 G4
Zeeland 332,286 D6

CITIES and TOWNS†

Aalsmeer 20,779 F4
Aalten 17,486 K5
Aardenburg 3,869 C6
Akkrum 5,044 H2
Alkmaar 65,199 F3
Almelo 62,634 K4
Alphen aan de Rijn 46,065 F4
Amersfoort 87,784 G4
Amstelveen 71,803 B5
Amsterdam (cap.) 751,156 B4
Amsterdam* 987,205 B4
Andijk 5,301 G3
Apeldoorn 134,055 H4
Apeldoorn* 237,231 H4
Appingedam 13,295 K2
Arnhem 126,051 H4
Arnhem* 281,126 H4
Assen 43,783 K3
Asten 12,295 H6
Axel 12,072 D6
Baarle-Nassau 5,583 F6
Baarn 25,045 G4
Barneveld 34,189 H4
Bath E6
Beilen 12,948 K3
Bemmel 14,218 H5
Bergeijk 9,009 G6
Bergen 14,306 F3
Bergen op Zoom 40,770 E5
Bergum 28,047 H2
Berkel 9,367 F5
Berkhout 5,167 F3
Beverwijk 37,551 F4
Blerick J6
Bloemendaal 17,940 E4
Blokzijl H3
Bodegraven 15,848 F4
Bolsward 9,934 H2
Borculo 9,859 J4
Borger 12,017 K3
Borne 18,216 K4
Boskoop 12,985 F4
Boxmeer 12,662 H5
Boxtel 22,465 G5
Breda 118,086 F5
Breda* 151,182 F5
Breezand F3
Breskens C6
Brielle 10,620 E5
Brouwershaven 3,263 D5
Brummen 20,460 J4
Brunssum 26,116 J7
Buiksloot C4
Bussum 37,848 G4
Capelle 35,696 F5
Coevorden 13,089 K3
Colijnsplaat D5
Culemborg 17,682 G5
Cuyk 15,366 H5
Dalen 5,084 K3
De Bilt 32,588 G4
Dedemsvaart 12,975 J3
De Koog F2
Delft 86,103 E4
Delfzijl 23,316 K2
Den Burg 12,132 F2
Denekamp 11,533 L4
Den Helder 60,421 F3
Deurne 26,539 H6
Deventer 65,557 J4
Didam 14,263 J5
De Wijk 4,631 J3
Diemen 13,704 C5
Dieren J4
Diever 3,162 J3
Dinxperlo 7,296 K5
Dirksland 6,495 E5
Doesburg 9,759 J4
Doetinchem 34,915 J5
Dokkum 11,203 H2
Domburg 3,874 C5
Dongen 19,219 F5
Doorn 11,966 G4
Dordrecht 101,840 F5
Dordrecht* 186,793 F5
Drachten 45,390 J2
Driebergen 17,022 G4
Dronten 16,544 H3
Druten 11,113 H5
Echt 17,035 H6
Edam-Volendam 21,507 G4
Ede 79,897 H4
Egmond aan Zee 5,734 E3
Eindhoven 192,562 G6
Eindhoven* 358,234 G6
Elburg 18,082 H4
Elst 16,686 H5
Emmeloord 34,467 H3
Emmen 86,700 K3
Enkhuizen 13,430 G3
Enschede 141,597 K4
Enschede* 239,015 K4
Epe 32,267 H4
Erica K3
Ermelo 23,835 H4
Etten-Leur 26,167 F5
Europoort E5
Flushing 43,806 C6
Franeker 11,415 H2
Geertruidenberg 6,185 F5
Geldermalsen 8,952 G5
Geldrop 25,879 H6
Geleen 35,910 H7
Gemert 15,267 H5
Gendringen 19,086 J5
Genemuiden 6,058 H3
Gennep 14,773 H5
Giessendam-Hardinxveld 15,523 F5
Giethoorn J3
Gilze 19,603 F5
Goes 28,505 D6
Goirle 13,447 G5
Goor 11,435 K4
Gorinchem 28,337 G5
Gorredijk J2
Gouda 56,403 F4
Graauw E6
Gramsbergen 5,866 K3
Grave 9,492 H5
Groenlo 8,693 K4
Groesbeek 18,094 H5
Groningen 163,357 K2
Groningen* 201,662 K2
Grouw 8,567 H2
Haamstede 4,575 D5
Haarlem 164,672 F4
Haarlem* 232,048 F4
Haarlemmermeer
(Hoofddorp) 72,046 F4
Hague, The (cap.) 479,369 E4
Hague, The* 682,452 E4
Halfweg 4,456 B4
Hallum H2
Hardenberg 28,489 J3
Harderwijk 28,508 H4
Hardinxveld-Giessendam 15,523 G5
Harlingen 14,533 G2
Hasselt 5,817 J3
Hattem 11,074 H4
Heemskert 31,728 F3
Heemstede 27,376 F4
Heer H7
Heerde 16,833 H4
Heerenveen 34,948 H3
Heerhugowaard 26,019 F3
Heerlen 71,500 J7
Heesch 8,659 G5
Heiloo 20,524 F3
Hellendoorn 32,068 J4
Hellevoetsluis 14,186 E5
Helmond 59,249 H6
Hengelo, Gelderland 8,015 J4
Hengelo, Overijssel 72,281 K4
Heusden 5,542 G5
Hillegom 17,489 E4
Hilvarenbeek 8,408 G6
Hilversum 94,041 G4
Hilversum* 110,498 G4
Hippolytushoef 7,847 G3
Hoek D6
Hoek van Holland (Hook of
Holland) D4
Hoensbroek 22,441 H7
Holijsloot C4
Hollum H2
Holwerd H2
Hoofddorp
(Haarlemmermeer) 72,046 F4
Hoogeveen 42,673 J3
Hoogezand-Sappemeer 33,860 K2
Hoogkarspel 5,112 G3
Hook of Holland D4
Hoorn 24,609 G3
Horst 16,242 H6
Huissen 11,049 H5
Huizen 25,603 G4
Hulst 17,283 E6
IJmuiden 6,633 E4
IJsselstein 15,450 F4
Ilpendam 3,310 C4
Joure 14,329 H3
Kampen 29,488 H3
Katwijk aan Zee 37,437 E4
Kerkdriel 7,584 G5
Kerkrade 46,609 J7
Kesteren 8,257 G5
Klazienaveen 9,520 L3
Kollum 11,887 J2
Krimpen aan den IJssel 26,396 F5
Landsmeer 8,082 C4
Laren 13,615 G4
Leek 15,713 J2
Leerdam 15,030 F5
Leeuwarden 85,074 H2
Leiden 99,891 E4
Leiden* 167,554 E4
Lelystad H3
Lemmer 10,013 H3
Lisse 19,182 F4
Lith 5,088 G5
Lochem 17,274 J4
Lonneker K4
Loon op Zand 18,000 G5
Losser 20,688 L4
Maarssen 18,346 F4
Maasbree 9,462 H6
Maassluis 28,170 E5
Maastricht 111,044 H7
Maastricht* 145,862 H7
Margraten 3,318 H7
Medemblik 6,432 G3
Meerssen 8,414 H7
Meppel 21,057 J3
Middelburg 36,372 C6
Middelharnis 14,245 E5
Middenmeer F3
Millingen aan den Rijn 5,035 J5
Moerdijk F5
Monnickendam 8,127 C4
Montfoort 3,442 G4
Muiden 6,567 G4
Muntendam 4,147 K2
Naaldwijk 24,117 E4
Naarden 17,319 G4
Nagele H3
Neede 10,842 K4
Nes 3,012 H2
Nieuwegein 22,648 G4
Nieuwe-Pekela 5,086 L2
Nieuwkoop 8,923 F4
Nieuw-Schoonebeek 7,556 L3
Nijkerk 21,615 H4
Nijmegen 148,493 H5
Nijmegen* 213,981 H5
Noordwijk 22,386 E4
Norg 6,041 J2
Numansdorp 7,072 E5
Nunspeet 21,340 H4
Odoorn 11,973 K3
Oisterwijk 16,263 G5
Oldenzaal 26,624 K4
Olst 8,480 J4
Ommen 16,136 J3
Onstwedde K2
Oostburg 18,461 C6
Oosterhout 40,077 F5
Ooosterwolde 5,845 J2
Oostmahorn J2
Oostzaan 6,336 C4
Ootmarsum 3,901 K4
Oss 45,643 H5
Otterlo H4
Oud-Beijerland 14,251 E5
Ouddorp 9,091 D5
Oudenbosch 11,061 E5
Oude-Pekela 8,067 K2
Oudewater 6,870 F4
Purmerend 32,614 F4
Putten 18,243 H4
Raalte 23,598 J4
Renkum 34,547 H5
Reusel 6,901 G6
Rheden 49,755 J4
Rhenen 16,893 H5
Ridderkerk 45,069 F5
Rijnsburg 10,698 F4
Rijssen 20,008 J4
Rijswijk 54,123 E4
Roden 16,437 J2
Roermond 36,695 J6
Roosendaal 51,685 F5
Rotterdam 614,767 E5
Rotterdam* 1,016,505 E5
Rutten H3
Ruurlo 7,557 J4
Sappemeer-Hoogezand 33,860 K2
Schagen 13,929 F3
Scheveningen E4
Schiedam 78,068 E5
Schijndel 18,658 G5
Schiphol B5
Schoonhoven 10,753 F5
's Gravendeel 7,242 E5
's Gravenhage (The Hague)
(cap.) 479,369 E4
's Gravenhage* 682,452 E4
's Gravenzande 15,833 E4
's Heerenberg 18,326 J5
's Hertogenbosch 86,184 G5
Simpelveld 6,783 H7
Sint Annaland E5
Sint Jacobiparochie H2
Sittard 34,278 H6
Sliedrecht 21,839 F5
Slochteren 13,447 K2
Sloten, North Holland B5
Sloterdijk B4
Sluis 3,140 C6
Smilde 8,247 K3
Sneek 28,123 H2
Soest 40,165 G4
Soesterberg G4
Stadskanaal 13,946 L3
Staphorst 11,608 J3
Steenbergen 12,930 E5
Steenwijk 20,721 J3
Stiens 7,711 H2
Swifterbant H3
Tegelen 18,386 J6
Ter Apel L3
Termunten 4,803 K2
Terneuzen 33,731 D6
Tholen 17,213 E5
Tiel 24,974 G5
Tilburg 151,513 G5
Tilburg* 212,510 G5
Twello 22,542 J4
Uden 28,946 H5
Uithoorn 22,812 F4
Uithuizen 5,194 K2
Ulrum 3,665 J2
Urk 9,397 H3
Utrecht 250,887 G4
Utrecht* 464,357 G4
Vaals 11,057 H7
Vaassen 7,225 H4
Valkenswaard 27,121 H6
Veendam 26,168 K2
Veenendaal 35,845 G4
Veenhuizen J2
Veere 4,252 D5
Veghel 22,308 H5
Veldhoven 30,030 G6
Velp J5
Velsen 64,035 F4
Venlo 61,659 J6
Venraij 31,526 H6
Vianen 12,821 G5
Vlaardingen 78,311 E5
Vlagtwedde 16,719 L3
Vlijmen 13,515 G5
Vlissingen (Flushing) 43,806 C6
Volendam-Edam 21,507 G4
Voorburg 45,209 E4
Voorst 22,542 J4
Vorden 7,276 J4
Vriezenveen 16,025 K4
Vught 23,261 G5
Waalre 13,219 G6
Waalwijk 25,977 F5
Wageningen 28,659 H5
Wamel 8,979 H5
Warmenhuizen 3,818 F3
Weert 36,850 H6
Weesp 17,037 C5
West-Terschelling 4,542 G2
Wierden 20,618 K4
Wijhe 6,888 J4
Wijk bij Duurstede 7,927 G5
Wijk en Aalburg 9,266 F5
Winschoten 19,760 L2
Winsum 5,007 K2
Winterswijk 27,413 K5
Woensdrecht 9,101 E6
Woerden 22,064 F4
Wolvega 22,812 J3
Workum 4,135 G3
Zaandam (Zaanstad) 124,795 B4
Zaandam (Zaanstad)* 137,371 B4
Zaltbommel 8,010 G5
Zandvoort 16,289 E4
Zeist 58,630 G4
Zevenaar 26,560 J5
Zevenbergen 13,307 E5
Zierikzee 8,816 D5
Zundert 12,444 F6
Zutphen 29,188 J4
Zwartsluis 4,391 H3
Zwijndrecht 38,271 E5
Zwolle 77,826 J3

OTHER FEATURES

Alkmaardermeer (lake) F3
Ameland (isl.) H2
Bergumermeer (lake) J2
Beulaker Wijde (lake) H3
Borndiep (chan.) H2
De Fluessen (lake) G3
De Honte (bay) D6
De Peel (reg.) H6
De Twente (reg.) K4
De Zaan (riv.) B4
Dollard (bay) L2
Dommel (riv.) H6
Duiveland (isl.) D5
Eastern Scheldt (est.) D5
Eems (riv.) K2
Eijerlandsche Gat (str.) F2
Flevoland Polders 35,618 G4
Friesche Gat (chan.) J2
Frisian, West (isls.) G2
Galgenberg (hill) H4
Goeree (isl.) D5
Grevelingen (str.) E5
Griend (isl.) G2
Groninger Wad (sound) J2
Groote IJ Polder B4
Haarlemmermeer Polder 72,046 B5
Haringvliet (str.) E5
Het IJ (est.) C4
Hoek van Holland (cape) D5
Hondsrug (hills) K3
Houtrak Polder A4
Hunse (riv.) K3
IJmeer (bay) C4
IJssel (riv.) J4
IJsselmeer (lake) G3
Lauwers (chan.) J1
Lauwers Zee (bay) J2
Lek (riv.) F5
Lemelerberg (hill) J4
Lower Rhine (riv.) H5
Maas (riv.) G5
Mark (riv.) F6
Marken (isl.) G4
Markerwaard Polder G3
Marsdiep (chan.) F3
North (sea) E3
North Beveland (isl.) D5
North East Polder 34,467 H3
North Holland (canal) C4
North Sea (canal) F4
Old Rhine (riv.) E4
Oostzaan Polder 6,336 B4
Orange (canal) K3
Overflakkee (isl.) E5
Pinke Gat (chan.) H2
Regge (riv.) K4
Rhine (riv.) J5
Roer (riv.) J6
Rottumeplaat (isl.) J1
Rottumeroog (isl.) J1
Schiermonnikoog (isl.) J1
Schouwen (isl.) D5
Slotermeer (lake) H3
Sneekermeer (lake) H2
South Beveland (isl.) D6
Terschelling (isl.) G2
Texel (isl.) F2
Tjeukemeer (lake) H3
Tjonger (riv.) J3
Vaalserberg (mt.) J7
Vecht (riv.) F4
Vechte (riv.) J3
Veersche Meer (lake) D5
Veluwe (reg.) H4
Vlieland (isl.) F2
Vliestroom (str.) G2
Voorne (isl.) D5
Waal (riv.) G5
Waddenzee (sound) G2
Walcheren (isl.) C5
Wester Eems (chan.) K1
Western Scheldt (De Honte)
(bay) D6
West Frisian (isls.) F2
Westgat (chan.) F3
Wieringermeer Polder 11,870 G3
Wilhelmina (canal) G6
Willems (canal) G5

*City and suburbs.
†Population of cities in Belgium & Netherlands are communes

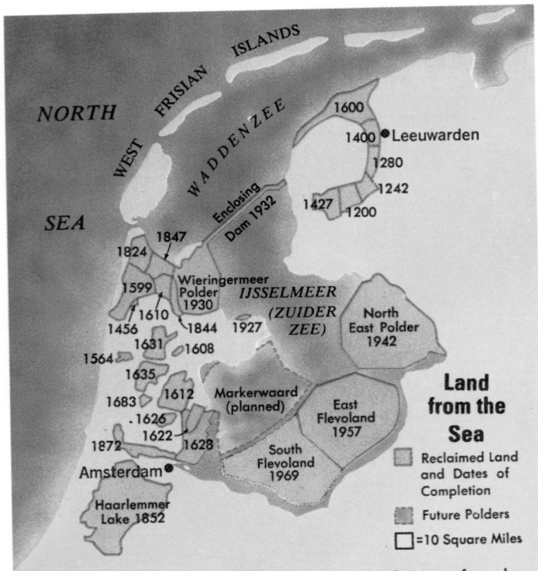

NORTH
SEA
WEST FRISIAN ISLANDS
WADDENZEE
Enclosing Dam 1932
Leeuwarden
Wieringermeer Polder 1930
IJSSELMEER (ZUIDER ZEE)
North East Polder 1942
Markerwaard (planned)
East Flevoland 1957
South Flevoland 1969
Amsterdam
Haarlemmer Lake 1852
Land from the Sea
Reclaimed Land and Dates of Completion
Future Polders
=10 Square Miles

For centuries the Dutch have been renowned for the drainage of marshes and the construction of polders, i.e., arable land reclaimed from the sea. Future projects will convert much of the present IJsselmeer to agricultural land.

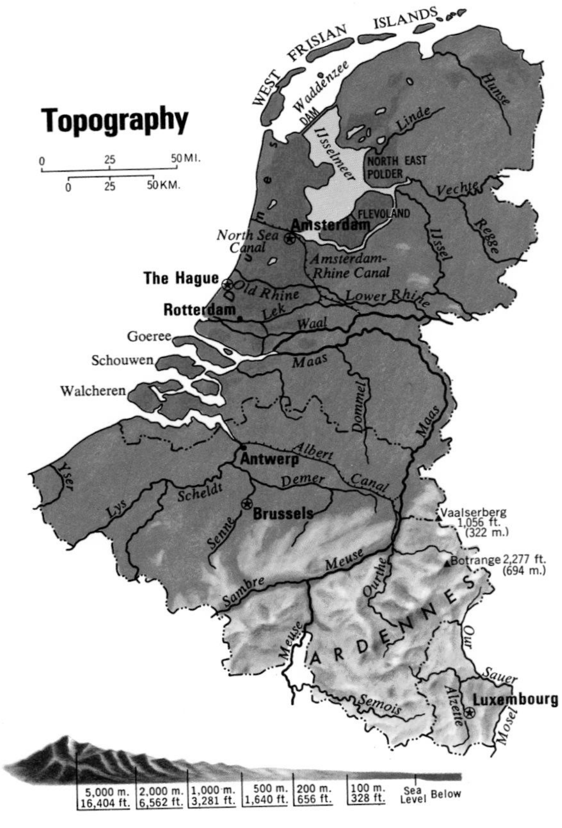

Topography
0 25 50 MI.
0 25 50 KM.
WEST FRISIAN ISLANDS
Waddenzee
DAM
IJsselmeer
NORTH EAST POLDER
FLEVOLAND
Hunse
Linde
Vechte
Regge
IJssel
Amsterdam
North Sea Canal
Amsterdam-Rhine Canal
The Hague
Old Rhine
Lower Rhine
Rotterdam
Lek
Waal
Goeree
Schouwen
Walcheren
Maas
Dommel
Antwerp
Albert
Canal
Scheldt
Demer
Brussels
Lys
Yser
Senne
Vaalserberg 1,056 ft. (322 m.)
Botrange 2,277 ft. (694 m.)
Meuse
Sambre
Ourthe
ARDENNES
Our
Sauer
Semois
Alzette
Mosel
Luxembourg
5,000 m. 16,404 ft.
2,000 m. 6,562 ft.
1,000 m. 3,281 ft.
500 m. 1,640 ft.
200 m. 656 ft.
100 m. 328 ft.
Sea Level
Below

Netherlands, Belgium and Luxembourg

CONIC PROJECTION

SCALE OF MILES

0 5 10 20 30 40

SCALE OF KILOMETRES

0 10 20 30 40 50

Capitals of Countries .... ☆
Provincial Capitals .... △
International Boundaries ....
Provincial Boundaries ....
Canals ....

© Copyright HAMMOND INCORPORATED, Maplewood, N. J.

AMSTERDAM

Westzaan Zaandijk Ilpendam
Koog aan de Zaan Oostzaan Polder Monnickendam
Zaandam Oostzaan Landsmeer
North Broek in
Sea Canal Waterland
Houtrak Polder Nieuwendam
Groote IJ Polder Durgerdam
Halfweg Sloterdijk
Zwanenburg Sloten Diemen
Badhoevedorp Bijl H.
Haarlemmermeer Polder Amstelveen Duivendrecht
Schiphol Amsterdam Weesp
0 1 2 3 4 5 MI.
0 1 2 3 4 5 KM.

BRUSSELS

Wemmel Machelen
Jette Steenokkerzeel
Berchem- Ganshoren Evere Zaventem
Ste.-Agathe Koekelberg Schaerbeek Kraainem
Molenbeek-St.-Jean St.-Josse-ten-Noode
Dilbeek Wezembeek-
Anderlecht Etterbeek Oppem
St.- Ixelles Woluwe-St.-Pierre
Gilles Woluwe-St.-Lambert
Forest (Vorst) Bruxelles
Auderghem
Watermael-Boitsfort
(Watermaal-Bosvoorde)
Sint-Pieters- Uccle (Ukkel)
Leeuw
Drogenbos Linkebeek
0 1 2 3 4 5 MI.
0 1 2 3 4 5 KM.

© Copyright HAMMOND INCORPORATED, Maplewood, N. J.

Longitude 5° East of Greenwich

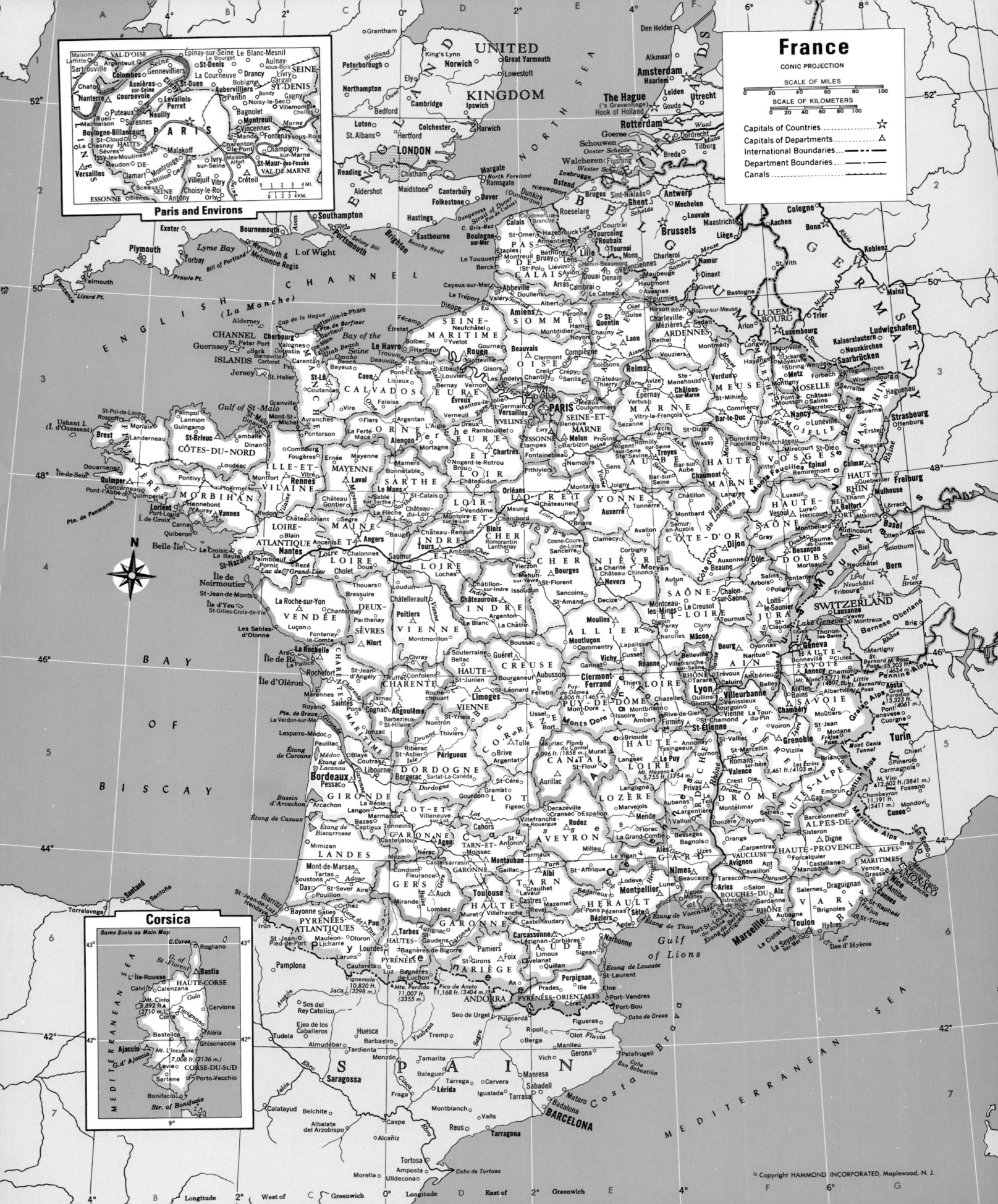

Paris and Environs

France
CONIC PROJECTION
SCALE OF MILES
SCALE OF KILOMETERS

Capitals of Countries ....☆
Capitals of Departments ....△
International Boundaries ....━ ━ ━
Department Boundaries ....━━━
Canals ....

Corsica
Same Scale as Main Map

© Copyright HAMMOND INCORPORATED, Maplewood, N.J.

DEPARTMENTS

Ain 418,516 F 4
Aisne 533,970 E 3
Allier 369,580 E 4
Alpes-de-Haute-Provence 119,068 G 5
Alpes-Maritimes 881,198 G 6
Ardèche 267,970 F 5
Ardennes 302,338 F 3
Ariège 135,725 D 6
Aube 289,300 E 3
Aude 280,686 E 6
Aveyron 278,654 E 5
Bas-Rhin 915,676 G 3
Belfort 131,999 G 4
Bouches-du-Rhône 1,724,199 F 6
Calvados 589,559 C 3
Cantal 162,838 E 5
Charente 340,770 D 5
Charente-Maritime 513,220 C 5
Cher 320,174 E 4
Corrèze 241,448 D 5
Corse du Sud 108,604 B 6
Côte-d'Or 473,548 F 4
Côtes-du-Nord 538,869 B 3
Creuse 139,968 D 4
Deux-Sèvres 342,812 C 4
Dordogne 377,356 D 5
Doubs 477,163 G 4
Drôme 389,781 F 5
Essonne 988,000 E 3
Eure 462,323 D 3
Eure-et-Loir 362,813 D 3
Finistère 828,364 A 3
Gard 530,478 F 6
Gers 174,154 D 6
Gironde 1,127,546 C 5
Haute-Corse 131,574 B 6
Haute-Garonne 824,501 D 6
Haute-Loire 205,895 E 5
Haute-Marne 210,670 F 3
Hautes-Alpes 105,070 G 5
Haute-Saône 231,962 G 4
Haute-Savoie 494,505 G 5
Hautes-Pyrénées 227,922 D 6
Haute-Vienne 355,737 D 5
Haut-Rhin 650,372 G 4
Hauts-de-Seine 1,387,039 A 2
Hérault 706,499 E 6
Ille-et-Vilaine 749,764 C 3
Indre 243,191 D 4
Indre-et-Loire 506,097 D 4
Isère 936,771 F 5
Jura 242,925 F 4
Landes 297,424 C 5
Loire 739,521 F 5
Loire-Atlantique 995,498 C 4
Loiret 535,669 E 4
Loir-et-Cher 296,220 D 4
Lot 154,533 D 5
Lot-et-Garonne 298,522 D 5
Lozère 74,294 E 5
Maine-et-Loire 675,321 C 4
Manche 465,948 C 3
Marne 543,627 F 3
Mayenne 271,784 C 3
Meurthe-et-Moselle 716,846 G 3
Meuse 200,101 F 3
Morbihan 590,889 B 4
Moselle 1,007,189 G 3
Nièvre 239,635 E 4
Nord 2,520,526 E 2
Oise 661,781 E 3
Orne 295,472 C 3
Paris 2,188,918 B 2
Pas-de-Calais 1,412,413 E 2
Puy-de-Dôme 594,365 E 5
Pyrénées-Atlantiques 555,696 C 6
Pyrénées-Orientales 334,557 E 6
Rhône 1,445,208 F 5
Saône-et-Loire 571,852 F 4
Sarthe 504,768 D 3
Savoie 323,675 G 5
Seine-et-Marne 887,112 E 3
Seine-Maritime 1,324,301 D 3
Seine-Saint-Denis 1,324,301 C 1
Somme 544,570 E 3
Tarn 339,345 E 6
Tarn-et-Garonne 190,485 D 5
Val-de-Marne 1,193,655 C 1
Val-d'Oise 920,598 E 3
Var 708,331 G 6
Vaucluse 427,343 F 6
Vendée 483,027 C 4
Vienne 371,428 D 4
Vosges 395,769 G 3
Yonne 311,019 E 4
Yvelines 1,196,111 D 3

CITIES and TOWNS

Aigues-Mortes 4,106 F 6
Aix-en-Provence 100,221 F 6
Aix-les-Bains 22,331 G 5
Ajaccio 48,324 B 7
Alençon 30,952 D 3
Amboise 10,823 D 4
Amiens 130,302 E 3
Angers 135,293 C 4
Angoulême 45,495 D 5
Annecy 49,753 G 5
Antibes 62,427 G 6
Argenteuil 94,826 A 1
Arles 37,554 F 6
Armentières 22,849 E 2
Arras 41,376 E 2
Asnières-sur-Seine 71,058 A 1
Aubervilliers 67,684 B 1
Aubusson 5,326 E 4
Aulnay-sous-Bois 75,543 B 1
Aurignac 772 D 6
Avignon 75,178 F 6
Ax-les-Thermes 1,283 D 6
Bagnolet 32,556 B 2
Barbizon 478 E 3
Barcelonnette 2,674 G 5
Barfleur 617 C 3
Bastia 43,502 B 6
Bayeux 14,568 C 3
Bayonne 40,088 C 6
Beaucaire 10,622 F 6
Beaune 19,110 F 4
Beauvais 51,542 E 3
Belfort 51,034 G 4
Bergerac 24,604 D 5
Besançon 112,023 G 4
Bessèges 4,352 F 5
Béziers 74,114 E 6
Biarritz 26,579 C 6
Blois 46,925 D 4
Bobigny 42,630 B 1
Bonifacio 1,727 B 7
Bordeaux 201,965 C 5
Boulogne-Billancourt 102,582 A 2
Boulogne-sur-Mer 47,482 D 2
Bourg-en-Bresse 37,582 F 4
Bourges 74,622 E 4
Brest 154,110 A 3
Brignoles 8,529 G 6
Brive-la-Gaillarde 50,898 D 5
Bruay-en-Artois 22,502 E 2
Caen 112,332 C 3
Calais 76,206 D 2
Caluire-et-Cuire 41,864 F 5
Cambrai 35,070 E 2
Cannes 71,888 G 6
Carcassonne 38,379 E 6
Castres 39,216 E 6
Châlons-sur-Marne 49,941 F 3

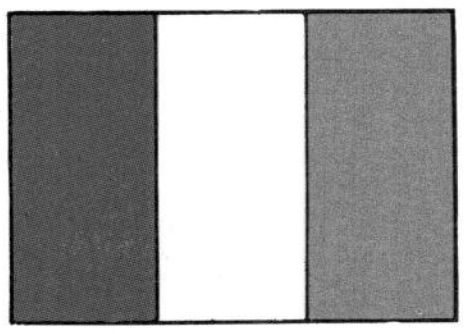

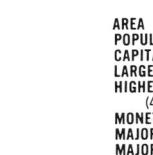

AREA 210,038 sq. mi. (543,998 sq. km.)
POPULATION 53,788,000
CAPITAL Paris
LARGEST CITY Paris
HIGHEST POINT Mont Blanc 15,771 ft. (4,807 m.)
MONETARY UNIT franc
MAJOR LANGUAGE French
MAJOR RELIGION Roman Catholicism

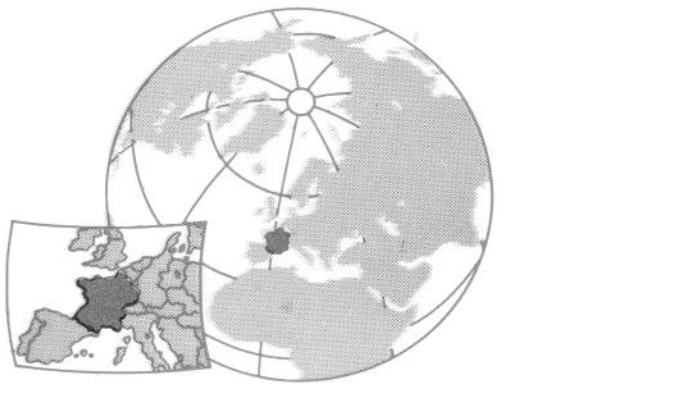

Topography

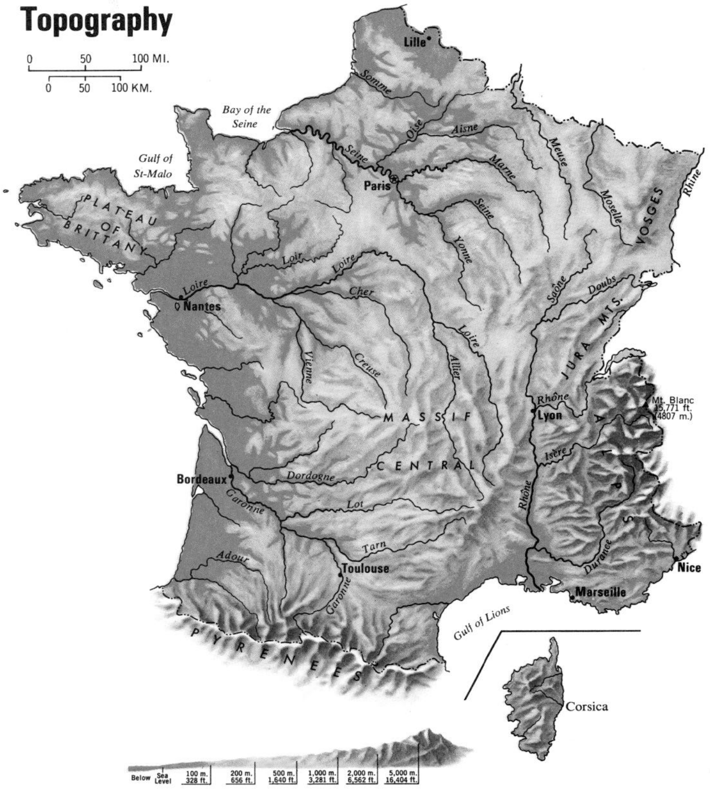

Historic Provinces

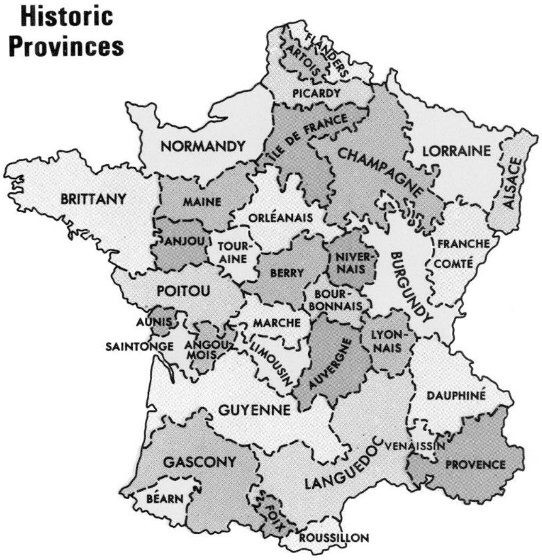

A resident of the city of Caen thinks of himself as a Norman rather than as a citizen of the modern department of Calvados. In spite of the passing of nearly two centuries, the historic provinces which existed before 1790 command the local patriotism of most Frenchmen.

Chalon-sur-Saône 53,893 F 4
Chambéry 49,465 F 5
Chambord 159 D 4
Chamonix-Mont-Blanc 7,406 G 5
Champigny-sur-Marne 76,039 C 2
Chantilly 10,065 E 3
Charleville-Mézières 7,814 F 3
Chartres 36,706 D 3
Chateaudun 15,905 D 3
Chateauneuf-sur-Loire 5,630 E 4
Chateauroux 51,744 D 4
Chateau-Thierry 14,427 E 3
Chatou 28,435 A 1
Cherbourg 28,324 C 3
Chinon 6,030 D 4
Choisy-le-Roi 35,443 B 2
Cholet 51,620 C 4
Clamart 48,210 A 2
Clermont-Ferrand 145,901 E 5
Clichy 46,830 B 1
Cluny 4,133 F 4
Cognac 20,247 C 5
Colmar 61,560 G 3
Colombes 78,485 A 1
Compiègne 39,909 E 3
Courbevoie 59,821 A 1
Creil 34,332 E 3
Créteil 71,559 B 2
Deauville 4,682 C 3
Dieppe 35,659 D 3
Digne 12,540 G 5
Dijon 139,188 F 4
Dinard 9,562 B 3
Domrémy-la-Pucelle 162 F 3
Douai 41,576 E 2
Drancy 60,122 B 1
Dunkirk 71,756 E 2
Ernée 5,253 C 3
Évreux 45,215 D 3
Falaise 8,424 C 3
Fécamp 21,212 D 3
Foix 9,212 D 6
Fontainebleau 14,687 E 3
Fontenay-sous-Bois 52,397 C 2
Gex 4,776 G 4
Grasse 24,257 G 6
Grenoble 156,437 F 5
Guise 6,179 E 3
Harfleur 9,470 D 3
Hazebrouck 19,266 E 2
Hendaye 10,492 C 6
Héricourt 9,239 G 4
Honfleur 8,125 D 3
Issy-les-Moulineaux 45,702 A 2
Istres 21,286 F 6
Ivry-sur-Seine 55,682 B 2
La Baule-Escoublac 13,151 B 4
La Courneuve 33,525 B 1
Langres 9,718 F 4
Lapalisse 3,173 E 4
La Rochelle 74,728 C 4
La Roche-sur-Yon 42,026 C 4
Laval 53,582 C 3
Le Bourget 11,020 B 1
Le Creusot 32,013 F 4
Le Havre 198,700 C 3
Le Mans 145,976 C 3
Le Puy 22,806 F 5
Le Tréport 6,330 D 2
Levallois-Perret 53,485 B 1
Lille 167,791 E 2
Limoges 137,809 D 5
Lisieux 24,454 D 3
Lorient 62,207 B 4
Lourdes 17,252 C 6
Lunéville 21,200 G 3
Lyon 410,455 F 5
Mâcon 36,517 F 4
Maisons-Alfort 51,041 B 2
Maisons-Laffitte 22,565 A 1
Mantes-la-Jolie 43,551 D 3
Marmande 14,264 C 5
Marseille 868,435 F 6
Maubeuge 35,424 F 2
Mayenne 12,156 C 3
Meaux 44,386 E 3
Melun 34,379 E 3
Mende 10,520 E 5
Menton 22,234 G 6
Metz 113,236 G 3
Meudon 29,356 A 2
Montauban 36,122 D 5
Montbéliard 31,174 G 4
Montceau-les-Mines 26,877 F 4
Mont-de-Marsan 25,896 C 6
Mont-Dore 2,091 E 5
Montfort 4,029 C 3
Montluçon 49,737 E 4
Montmédy 1,880 F 3
Montpellier 190,423 E 6
Montreuil 96,441 B 2
Mont-Saint-Michel 65 C 3
Mulhouse 111,742 G 4
Nancy 95,654 G 3
Nanterre 88,567 A 1
Nantes 237,789 C 4
Narbonne 38,222 E 6
Nemours 11,624 E 3
Neufchatel-en-Bray 5,452 D 3
Neuilly-sur-Seine 64,093 A 1
Nice 331,165 G 6
Nîmes 120,515 F 6
Niort 56,256 C 4
Nogent-le-Rotrou 11,963 D 3
Noisy-le-Sec 36,821 B 1
Nontron 3,407 D 5
Noyon 13,949 E 3
Nyons 5,219 F 5
Orléans 81,615 D 3
Orly 23,729 B 2
Oyonnax 22,516 F 4
Paris (cap.) 2,165,892 B 2
Paris *10,073,059 B 2
Pau 82,186 C 6
Périgueux 32,632 D 5
Perpignan 107,812 E 6
Pessac 49,019 C 5
Poitiers 76,793 D 4
Pontoise 27,885 E 3
Port-Vendres 4,871 E 6
Privas 9,253 F 5
Quimper 52,335 A 4
Rambouillet 21,136 D 3
Redon 9,071 C 4
Reims 176,419 E 3
Rennes 190,861 C 3
Roanne 48,574 E 4
Rochefort 25,392 C 4
Roubaix 101,488 E 2
Rouen 100,696 D 3
Rueil-Malmaison 63,310 A 2
Saint-Brieuc 48,259 B 3
Saint-Cloud 28,561 A 2
Saint-Denis 90,686 B 1
Saint-Dizier 34,074 F 3
Sainte-Mère-Église 1,205 C 3
Saint-Étienne 193,938 F 5
Saint-Germain-en-Laye 36,585 D 3
Saint-Jean-d'Angély 8,268 C 4

(continued on following page)

Saint-Jean-de-Luz
12,124. . . . . .C 6
Saint-Lô 21,790. . . . . . .C 3
Saint-Malo 44,030. . . . . .B 3
Saint-Maur-des-Fossés
80,686. . . . . .B 2
Saint-Nazaire 68,040. . . .B 4
Saint-Ouen 43,589. . . . .B 1
Saint-Quentin
63,010. . . . . .E 3
Saint-Raphaël
22,221. . . . . .G 6
Saint-Tropez 4,956. . . . .G 6
Salon-de-Provence
31,185. . . . . .F 6
Sarreguemines
23,699. . . . . .G 3
Sartrouville 46,018. . . . .A 1
Saumur 30,037. . . . . . .C 4
Sedan 23,357. . . . . . . .F 3
Senlis 14,345. . . . . . . .E 3
Sens 25,793. . . . . .E 3
Sète 39,258. . . . . .E 6
Sèvres 20,184. . . . . . . .A 2
Soissons 29,871. . . . . . .E 3
Sotteville-les-Rouen
29,335. . . . . .D 3
Stiring-Wendel
13,563. . . . . .G 3
Strasbourg 247,068. . . . .H 3
Tarascon 8,968. . . . . . .F 6
Tarbes 50,306. . . . . . . .D 6
Thiers 13,492. . . . . . . .E 5
Thionville 34,758. . . . . .G 3
Thiviers 3,047. . . . . . . .D 5
Thonon-les-Bains
26,421. . . . . .G 4
Tonneins 7,162. . . . . . .D 5
Tonnerre 5,744. . . . . . .E 4
Toulon 177,443. . . . . . .F 6
Toulouse 344,917. . . . . .D 6
Tourcoing 96,536. . . . . .E 2
Tours 131,265. . . . . . . .D 3
Trouville. . . . . .F 3
Troyes 62,946. . . . . . . .E 3
Uckange 9,524. . . . . . .G 3
Uzès 5,975. . . . . .F 5
Valence 66,143. . . . . . .F 5
Valenciennes 39,979. . . . .E 2
Vannes 39,214. . . . . . . .B 4
Vendôme 16,949. . . . . . .D 4
Vénissieux 64,621. . . . . .F 5

Verdun-sur-Meuse
21,170. . . . . .F 3
Vernon 21,271. . . . . . .D 3
Versailles 91,014. . . . . .A 2
Vesoul 18,257. . . . . . . .F 4
Vichy 30,522. . . . . . . .E 4
Vienne 25,414. . . . . . . .F 5
Villefranche 6,627. . . . . .G 6
Villefranche-sur-Saône
28,858. . . . . .F 4
Villejuif 50,970. . . . . . .B 2
Villeneuve-Saint-
Georges 27,839. . . . .E 3
Villeurbanne
115,378. . . . . .F 5
Vincennes 42,852. . . . . .B 2
Vitry-sur-Seine
84,956. . . . . .B 2
Voiron 16,383. . . . . . . .F 5
Yssingeaux 4,393. . . . . .F 5
Yvetot 10,574. . . . . . . .D 3

OTHER FEATURES

Adour (riv.). . . . . .C 6
Ain (riv.). . . . . .F 4
Aisne (riv.). . . . . .E 3
Ajaccio (gulf). . . . . . . .B 7
Allier (riv.). . . . . .E 5
Aube (riv.). . . . . .E 5
Auvergne (mt.). . . . . . .E 5
Belle-Île (isl.). . . . . . . .B 4
Biscay (bay). . . . . .B 5
Blanc (mt.). . . . . .G 5
Bonifacio (strait). . . . . .B 7
Calais, Pas de (Dover)
(strait). . . . . .D 2
Causses (reg.). . . . . . . .D 5
Cévennes (mt.). . . . . . .E 5
Charente (riv.). . . . . . . .C 5
Cher (riv.). . . . . .D 4
Corse (cape). . . . . .B 6
Corsica (isl.) 240,178. . . .B 6
Côte-d'Or (mt.). . . . . . .F 4
Cotentin (pen.). . . . . . .C 3
Cottian Alps (range). . . .G 5
Creuse (riv.). . . . . .D 4
Dordogne (riv.). . . . . . .D 5
Dore Alps (mt.). . . . . . .E 5
Doubs (riv.). . . . . .G 4
Dover (strait). . . . . . . .D 2
Drôme (riv.). . . . . .F 5

Dronne (riv.). . . . . .D 5
Durance (riv.). . . . . . . .F 6
English (chan.). . . . . . . .B 3
Eure (riv.). . . . . .D 3
Faucilles (mt.). . . . . . . .G 3
Forez (mt.). . . . . .E 5
Fréjus (pass). . . . . .G 5
Gard (riv.). . . . . .F 5
Garonne (riv.). . . . . . . .C 5
Gave de Pau (riv.). . . . .C 6
Geneva (lake). . . . . . . .G 4
Gers (riv.). . . . . .D 6
Gironde (riv.). . . . . . . .C 5
Graian Alps (range). . . . .G 5
Groix (isl.) 2,605. . . . . . .B 4
Hague (cape). . . . . . . .C 3
Hérault (riv.). . . . . .E 6
Hyères (isl.). . . . . .G 6
Indre (riv.). . . . . .D 4
Isère (riv.). . . . . .F 5
Isle (riv.). . . . . .D 5
Jura (mt.). . . . . .G 4
Langres (plat.). . . . . . . .F 4
Limousin (reg.). . . . . . .D 5
Lions (gulf). . . . . .F 6
Little Saint Bernard
(pass). . . . . .G 5
Loir (riv.). . . . . .D 4
Loire (riv.). . . . . .C 4
Lot (riv.). . . . . .D 5
Maritime Alps
(range). . . . . .G 5
Marne (riv.). . . . . .C 2
Mayenne (riv.). . . . . . . .C 4
Mediterranean (sea). . . . .E 7
Médoc (reg.). . . . . .C 5
Meuse (riv.). . . . . .F 3
Mézenc (mt.). . . . . . . .E 5
Mont Cenis (tunnel). . . . .G 5
Morvan (plat.). . . . . . . .E 4
Moselle (riv.). . . . . .G 3
Noirmoutier (isl.). . . . . .B 4
North (sea). . . . . .E 1
Oise (riv.). . . . . .E 3
Oléron (isl.). . . . . .C 5
Omaha (beach). . . . . . . .C 3
Orb (riv.). . . . . .E 6
Orne (riv.). . . . . .C 3
Penmarch (pt.). . . . . . . .A 4
Perche (reg.). . . . . .D 3
Puy-de-Dôme (mt.). . . . .E 5
Pyrenees (range). . . . . . .C 6

Ré (isl.). . . . . .C 4
Rhine (riv.). . . . . .G 3
Rhône (riv.). . . . . .F 5
Risle (riv.). . . . . .D 3
Riviera (reg.). . . . . .G 6
Saar (riv.). . . . . .G 3
Saint-Florent (gulf). . . . .B 6
Saint-Malo (gulf). . . . . . .B 3
Saône (riv.). . . . . .F 4
Sarthe (riv.). . . . . .D 4
Sein (isl.) 504. . . . . . . .A 3
Seine (bay). . . . . .C 3
Seine (riv.). . . . . .D 3
Sologne (reg.). . . . . . . .D 4
Somme (riv.). . . . . .E 6
Tarn (riv.). . . . . .D 5
Ushant (isl.) 1,255. . . . . .A 3
Utah (beach). . . . . .C 3
Vaccarès (lag.). . . . . . . .F 6
Vienne (riv.). . . . . .D 4
Vilaine (riv.). . . . . .C 4
Vosges (mt.). . . . . .G 3
Yonne (riv.). . . . . .E 3

Monaco

CITIES and TOWNS

Monte Carlo (cap.)
11,599. . . . . .G 6

* City and Suburbs.

MONACO

AREA 368 acres
(149 hectares)
POPULATION 25,029

Wine Regions

Climate, soil and variety of grape planted determine the quality of wine. Long, hot and fairly dry summers with cool, humid nights constitute an ideal climate. The nature of the soil is such a determining influence that identical grapes planted in Bordeaux, Burgundy and Champagne, will yield wines of widely different types.

Agriculture, Industry and Resources

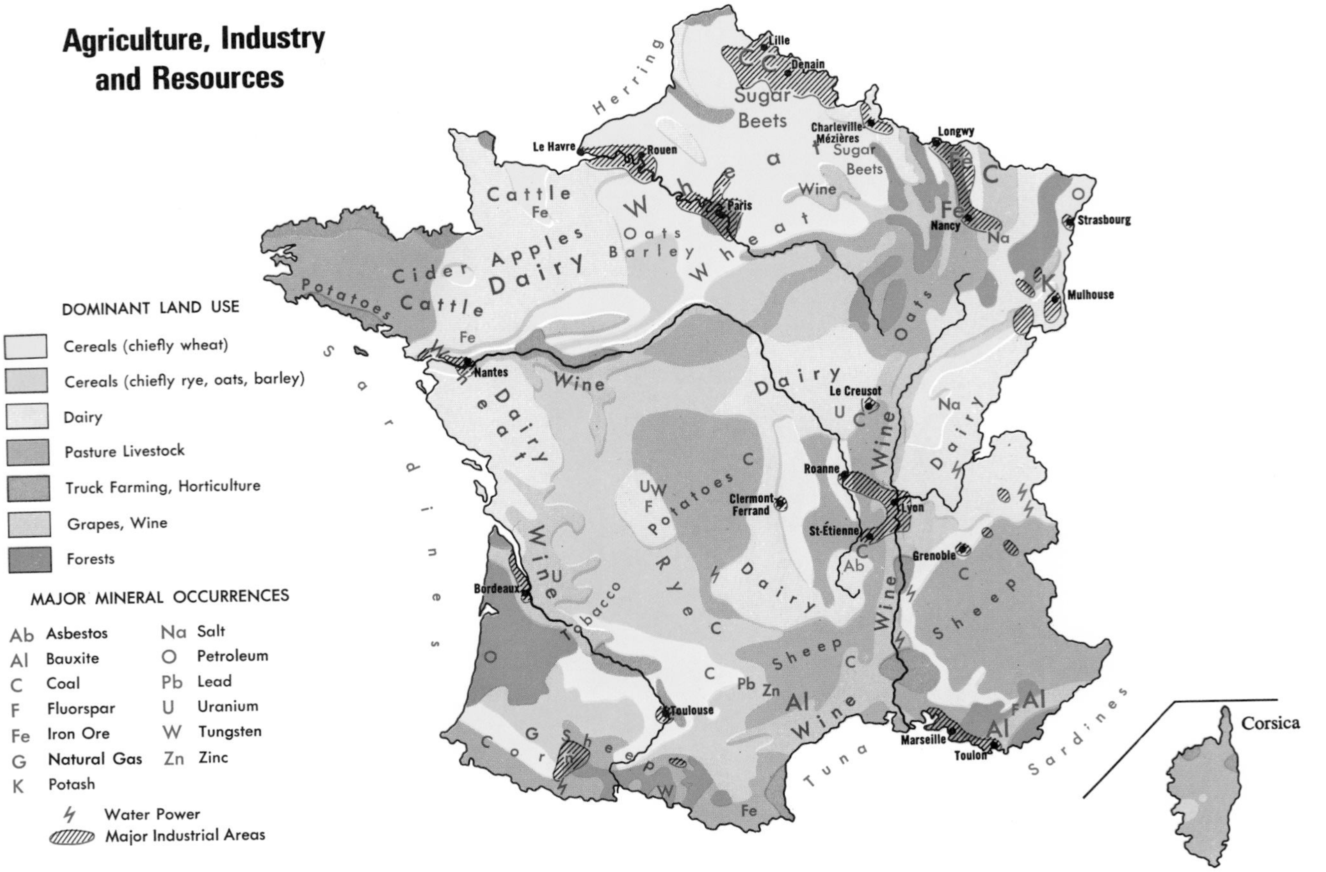

DOMINANT LAND USE

Cereals (chiefly wheat)

Cereals (chiefly rye, oats, barley)

Dairy

Pasture Livestock

Truck Farming, Horticulture

Grapes, Wine

Forests

MAJOR MINERAL OCCURRENCES

Ab	Asbestos	Na	Salt
Al	Bauxite	O	Petroleum
C	Coal	Pb	Lead
F	Fluorspar	U	Uranium
Fe	Iron Ore	W	Tungsten
G	Natural Gas	Zn	Zinc
K	Potash		

⚡ Water Power
▨ Major Industrial Areas

Corsica

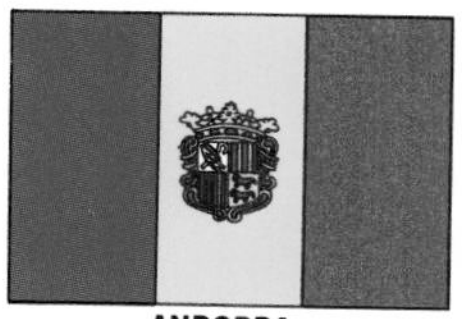

ANDORRA

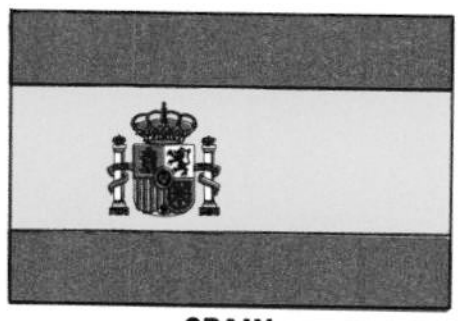

SPAIN

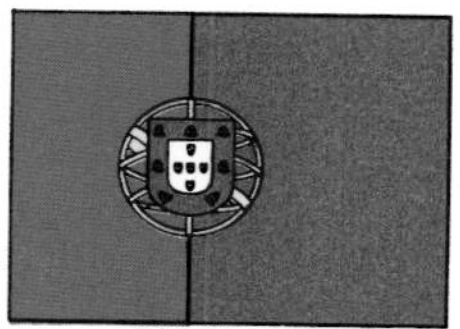

PORTUGAL

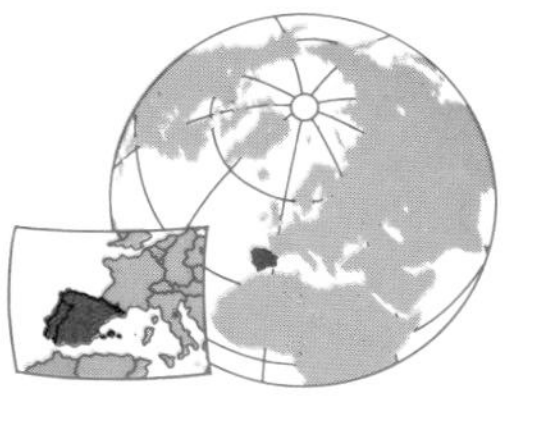

SPAIN

AREA 194,881 sq. mi. (504,742 sq. km.)
POPULATION 37,430,000
CAPITAL Madrid
LARGEST CITY Madrid
HIGHEST POINT Pico de Teide 12,172 ft. (3,710 m.) (Canary Is.); Mulhacén 11,411 ft. (3,478 m.) (mainland)
MONETARY UNIT peseta
MAJOR LANGUAGES Spanish, Catalan, Basque, Galician, Valencian
MAJOR RELIGION Roman Catholicism

ANDORRA

AREA 188 sq. mi. (487 sq. km.)
POPULATION 31,000
CAPITAL Andorra la Vella
MONETARY UNITS French franc, Spanish peseta
MAJOR LANGUAGE Catalan
MAJOR RELIGION Roman Catholicism

PORTUGAL

AREA 35,549 sq. mi. (92,072 sq. km.)
POPULATION 9,933,000
CAPITAL Lisbon
LARGEST CITY Lisbon
HIGHEST POINT Malhão da Estrela 6,532 ft. (1,991 m.)
MONETARY UNIT escudo
MAJOR LANGUAGE Portuguese
MAJOR RELIGION Roman Catholicism

GIBRALTAR

AREA 2.28 sq. mi. (5.91 sq. km.)
POPULATION 29,760
CAPITAL Gibraltar
MONETARY UNIT pound sterling
MAJOR LANGUAGES English, Spanish
MAJOR RELIGION Roman Catholicism

SPAIN

PROVINCES

Álava 204,323 E1
Albacete 335,026 E3
Alicante 920,105 F3
Almería 375,004 E4
Ávila 203,798 D2
Badajoz 687,599 C3
Baleares 558,287 H3
Barcelona 3,929,194 G2
Burgos 358,075 E1
Cáceres 457,777 C3
Cádiz 885,433 D4
Castellón 385,823 G2
Ciudad Real 507,650 D3
Córdoba 724,116 D3
Cuenca 247,158 E2
Gerona 414,397 H1
Granada 733,375 E4
Guadalajara 147,732 E2
Guipúzcoa 631,003 E1
Huelva 397,683 C4
Huesca 222,238 F1
Jaén 661,146 E4
La Coruña 1,004,188 B1
Las Palmas 579,710 C4
León 548,721 C1
Lérida 347,015 G2
Logroño 235,713 E1
Lugo 415,052 C1
Madrid 3,792,561 E2
Málaga 867,330 D4
Murcia 832,313 F4
Navarra 464,867 F1
Orense 413,733 C1
Oviedo 1,045,635 C1
Palencia 198,763 D1
Pontevedra 750,701 B1
Salamanca 371,607 C2
Santa Cruz de Tenerife 590,514 B5
Santander 467,138 D1
Segovia 162,770 D2
Sevilla 1,327,190 D4
Soria 114,956 E2
Tarragona 431,961 G2
Teruel 170,284 F2
Toledo 468,925 D3
Valencia 1,767,327 F3
Valladolid 412,572 D2
Vizcaya 1,043,310 E1
Zamora 251,934 D2
Zaragoza 760,186 F2

CITIES and TOWNS

Adra 10,851 E4
Aguilar 12,893 D4
Aguilas 15,525 F4
Alagón 5,114 F2
Alayor 5,124 J3
Albacete 82,607 F3
Albox 5,072 E4
Alburquerque 7,530 C3
Alcalá de Guadaira 28,781 D4
Alcalá de Henares 59,783 G4
Alcalá de los Gazules 5,262 D4
Alcalá la Real 9,849 E4
Alcanar 5,961 G2
Alcañiz 10,229 F2
Alcantarilla 19,895 F4
Alcaudete 8,557 E4
Alcázar de San Juan 24,620 E3
Alcira 30,493 F3
Alcora 6,711 F2
Alcoy 61,371 F3
Alfaro 8,766 F1
Algeciras 74,754 D4
Algemesí 21,158 F3
Alhama de Granada 6,148 E4
Alhama de Murcia 9,274 F4
Alicante 177,918 F3
Almadén 10,713 D3
Almagro 9,066 E3
Almansa 16,965 F3
Almendralejo 21,929 C3
Almería 104,008 E4
Almodóvar del Campo 7,310 D3
Almonte 9,960 C4
Almuñécar 7,812 E4
Álora 8,209 D4
Altea 7,262 G3
Amposta 11,767 G2
Andorra 6,485 F2
Andújar 25,962 D3
Antequera 28,039 D4
Aracena 5,390 C4
Aranda de Duero 18,183 E2
Aranjuez 28,559 E2
Archena 7,118 F3
Archidona 6,084 D4
Arcos de la Frontera 16,217 D4
Arenas de San Pedro 5,225 D2
Arenys de Mar 8,325 H2
Arévalo 5,807 D2
Argamasilla de Alba 6,192 E3
Arganda 11,876 G4
Arnedo 9,809 E1
Arrecife 21,310 C4
Arroyo de la Luz 8,130 C3
Artá 5,284 H3
Arucas 9,095 B5
Aspe 13,229 F3
Astorga 11,794 C1
Ávila de los Caballeros 30,958 D2
Avilés 67,186 C1
Ayamonte 9,897 C4
Ayora 5,249 F3
Azpeitia 7,835 E1
Azuaga 10,719 D3
Badajoz 80,793 C3
Badalona 162,888 H2
Baena 16,496 D4
Baeza 12,607 E4
Bailén 13,207 E3
Balaguer 11,676 G2
Bañolas 9,807 H1
Baracaldo 108,757 E1
Barbastro 13,243 F1
Barcarrota 5,012 C3
Barcelona 1,741,144 H2
Barcelona‡ 2,000,000 H2
Baza 14,290 E4
Beas de Segura 6,592 E3
Béjar 16,804 D2
Bélmez 5,161 D3
Benavente 11,779 D1
Benicarló 12,831 G2
Berga 11,163 G1
Berja 7,081 E4
Bermeo 16,714 E1
Betanzos 7,283 B1
Bilbao 393,179 E1
Bilbao‡ 450,000 E1
Binéfar 6,821 G2
Blanes 15,810 H2
Borjas Blancas 4,991 G2
Bujalance 8,236 D4
Bullas 8,131 F4
Burgos 118,366 E1
Burriana 21,298 G3
Cabeza del Buey 8,704 D3
Cabra 16,177 D4
Cáceres 53,108 C3
Cádiz 135,743 C4
Calahorra 16,315 E1
Calasparra 7,238 F3
Calatayud 16,524 F2
Calella 9,696 H2
Callosa de Ensarriá 5,701 G3
Calzada de Calatrava 5,751 E3
Campanario 7,722 D3
Campillos 7,014 D4
Campo de Criptana 12,604 E3
Candás 5,517 D1
Candeleda 5,153 D2
Cangas de Narcea 4,826 C1
Caniles 5,099 E4
Caravaca de le Cruz 10,411 E3
Carballo 5,542 B1
Carcagente 18,223 F3
Carmona 22,832 D4
Cartagena 52,312 F4
Caspe 8,766 G2
Cassá de la Selva 5,248 H2
Castellón de la Plana 79,773 G2
Castro del Río 10,087 D4
Castro-Urdiales 8,369 E1
Castuera 8,060 D3
Caudete 7,332 F3
Cazalla de la Sierra 5,382 D4
Cazorla 6,938 E4
Cehegín 9,661 F3
Cervera 5,693 G2
Ceuta 60,639 D5
Chiclana de la Frontera 22,986 C4
Chiva 5,394 F3
Ciempozuelos 9,185 F5
Cieza 22,929 F3
Ciudadela 13,701 H2
Ciudad Real 39,931 D3
Ciudad-Rodrigo 11,694 C2
Cocentaina 8,375 F3
Coín 14,190 D4
Colmenar de Oreja 4,930 G5
Colmenar Viejo 12,886 F4
Constantina 10,227 D4
Consuegra 10,026 E3
Córdoba 216,049 D4
Corella 5,850 F1
Coria 8,083 C3
Coria del Río 18,085 C4
Corral de Almaguer 8,006 E3
Crevillente 15,749 F3
Cuéllar 6,118 D2
Cuenca 33,980 E2
Cullera 15,128 F3
Daimiel 17,710 E3
Denia 14,514 G3
Dolores 5,420 F3
Don Benito 21,351 C3
Dos Hermanas 36,921 D4
Durango 20,403 E1
Écija 27,295 D4
Eibar 36,729 E1
Ejea de los Caballeros 9,766 F1
El Arahal 14,703 D4
Elche 101,271 F3
Elda 41,404 F3
Elizondo 2,516 F1
El Puerto de Santa María 36,451 C4
Espejo 5,925 D4
Estella 10,371 E1
Estepa 9,376 D4
Estepona 18,560 D4
Felanitx 9,100 H3
Ferrol del Caudillo 75,464 B1
Figueras 22,087 H1
Fraga 9,665 G2
Fregenal de la Sierra 6,826 C3
Fuengirola 20,597 D4
Fuente de Cantos 5,967 C3
Fuenterrabiá 2,350 E1
Fuentes de Andalucía 8,257 D4
Gandía 30,702 F3
Gerona 37,095 H2
Getafe 68,680 F4
Gijón 159,806 D1
Granada 185,799 E4
Granollers 30,066 H2
Guadalajara 30,924 E2
Guadix 15,311 E4
Guareña 7,706 C3
Guernica y Luno 12,046 E1
Haro 8,393 E1
Hellín 15,934 F3
Herencia 8,212 E3
Hinojosa del Duque 9,873 D3
Hortaleza G4
Hospitalet 241,978 H2
Huelma 5,260 E4
Huelva 96,689 C4
Huercal-Overa 5,158 F4
Huesca 33,076 F1
Huéscar 6,384 E4
Ibiza 16,943 G3
Igualada 27,941 G2
Inca 16,930 H3
Irún 38,014 F1
Iscar 5,192 D2
Isla Cristina 11,402 C4
Iznalloz 4,814 E4
Jaca 9,936 F1
Jaén 71,145 E4
Jaraíz de la Vera 6,379 D2
Játiva 20,934 F3
Jávea 6,228 G3
Jerez de la Frontera 112,411 C4
Jerez de los Caballeros 8,607 C3
Jijona 8,117 F3
Jódar 11,973 E4
Jumilla 16,407 F3
La Almunia de Doña Godina 4,835 F2
La Bañeza 8,480 C1
La Bisbal 6,374 H1
La Carolina 13,138 E3
La Coruña 184,372 B1
La Granja (San Ildefonso) 3,198 E2
La Guardia 4,967 B2
La Línea de la Concepción 51,021 D4
La Orotava 8,246 B4
La Palma del Condado 9,256 C4
La Puebla 9,923 H3
La Puebla de Montalbán 6,629 D3
La Rambla 6,525 D4
Laredo 9,114 E1
La Roda 11,460 E3
La Solana 13,894 E3
Las Palmas de Gran Canaria 260,368 B4
Las Pedroñeras 5,846 E3
La Unión 9,998 F4
Lebrija 15,081 D4
Leganés 57,537 F4
León 99,702 D1
Lérida 73,148 G2
Linares 45,330 E3
Liria 11,323 F3
Llerena 5,728 C3
Llivia 801 G1
Llodio 15,587 E1
Lluctmayor 9,630 H3
Logroño 83,117 E1
Loja 11,549 D4
Lora del Río 15,741 D4
Lorca 25,208 F4
Los Santos de Maimona 7,899 C3
Los Yébenes 5,477 E3
Lucena 21,527 D4
Lugo 53,504 C1
Madrid (cap.) 3,146,071 F4
Madrid‡ 3,500,000 F4
Madridejos 9,948 E3
Madroñera 5,397 D3
Mahón 17,802 J3
Málaga 334,988 D4
Málaga‡ 400,000 D4
Malagón 7,732 E3
Malpartida de Cáceres 5,054 C3
Manacor 20,266 H3
Mancha Real 7,547 E4
Manlleu 13,169 H1
Manresa 52,526 G2
Manzanares 15,024 E3
Marbella 19,648 D4
Marchena 16,227 D4
Marín 10,948 B1
Martos 16,395 E4
Mataró 73,129 H2
Medina del Campo 16,345 D2
Medina de Rioseco 4,874 D2
Medina-Sidonia 7,523 D4
Mérida 36,916 C3
Miajadas 8,042 D3
Mieres 22,790 D1
Minas de Ríotinto 3,939 C4
Miranda de Ebro 29,355 E1
Moguér 7,629 C4
Mollerusa 6,685 G2
Monesterio 5,923 C3
Monforte 14,002 C1
Monóvar 9,071 F3
Montehermoso 5,952 C2
Montellano 6,658 D4
Montijo 11,931 C3
Montilla 18,670 D4
Montoro 9,295 D3
Monzón 14,089 G2
Mora 10,523 E3
Moratalla 5,101 E3
Morón de la Frontera 25,662 D4
Mota del Cuervo 5,130 E3
Motril 25,121 E4
Mula 9,168 F3
Munera 5,003 E3
Murcia 102,242 F4
Navalcarnero 6,212 F4
Navalmoral de la Mata 9,650 D3
Nerja 7,413 E4
Nerva 10,830 C4
Novelda 16,867 F3
Nules 9,027 F3
Ocaña 5,603 E3
Oliva 16,717 F3
Oliva de la Frontera 8,560 C3
Olivenza 7,616 C3
Olot 18,062 H1
Olvera 9,825 D4
Onda 13,012 F3
Onteniente 23,685 F3
Orense 63,542 C1
Orihuela 17,610 F3
Osuna 17,384 D4
Oviedo 130,021 C1
Padul 6,377 E4
Palafrugell 10,421 H2
Palamós 7,679 H2
Palencia 58,327 D2
Palma 191,416 H3
Palma del Río 15,075 D4
Pamplona 142,686 F1
Pego 8,861 F3
Peñafiel 4,794 E2
Peñaranda de Bracamonte 6,094 D2
Peñarroya-Pueblonuevo 15,649 D3
Pinos-Puente 7,634 E4
Plasencia 26,897 C2
Pola de Lena 5,760 D1
Pollensa 7,625 H3
Ponferrada 22,838 C1
Pontevedra 27,118 B1
Porcuna 8,169 D4
Port-Bou 2,230 H1
Portugalete 45,589 E1
Posadas 7,245 D4
Pozoblanco 13,280 D3
Pozuelo de Alarcón 14,041 D2
Priego de Córdoba 12,676 D4
Puente-Genil 22,888 D4
Puertollano 50,609 D3
Puerto Real 13,993 D4
Puigcerdá 4,418 G1
Quesada 6,965 E4
Quintana de la Serena 5,171 D3
Quintanar de la Orden 7,764 E3
Reinosa 10,863 D1
Requena 9,836 F3
Reus 47,240 G2
Ripoll 9,283 H1
Ronda 22,094 D4
Roquetas 5,617 G2
Rosas 5,448 H1
Rota 20,021 C4
Rute 8,294 D4
Sabadell 148,223 H2
Sagunto 17,052 F3
Salamanca 125,132 D2
Sallent 7,118 H2
Salobreña 5,961 E4
Salt 5,572 H1
Sama 9,863 D1
San Carlos de la Rápita 8,946 G2
San Clemente 6,016 E3
San Feliu de Guíxols 12,006 H2
San Fernando 59,309 C4
San Ildefonso 3,198 E2

Agriculture, Industry and Resources

DOMINANT LAND USE

- Cereals (chiefly wheat)
- Livestock (chiefly sheep goats)
- Mixed Cereals, Livestock
- Olives, Fruit
- Grapes, Fruit, Nuts, Mixed Cereals
- Forests
- Nonagricultural Land

MAJOR MINERAL OCCURRENCES

Ag	Silver	Na	Salt
C	Coal	O	Petroleum
Cu	Copper	Pb	Lead
Fe	Iron Ore	Py	Pyrites
G	Natural Gas	Sb	Antimony
Hg	Mercury	Sn	Tin
K	Potash	U	Uranium
Lg	Lignite	W	Tungsten
Mg	Magnesium	Zn	Zinc

Water Power

Major Industrial Areas

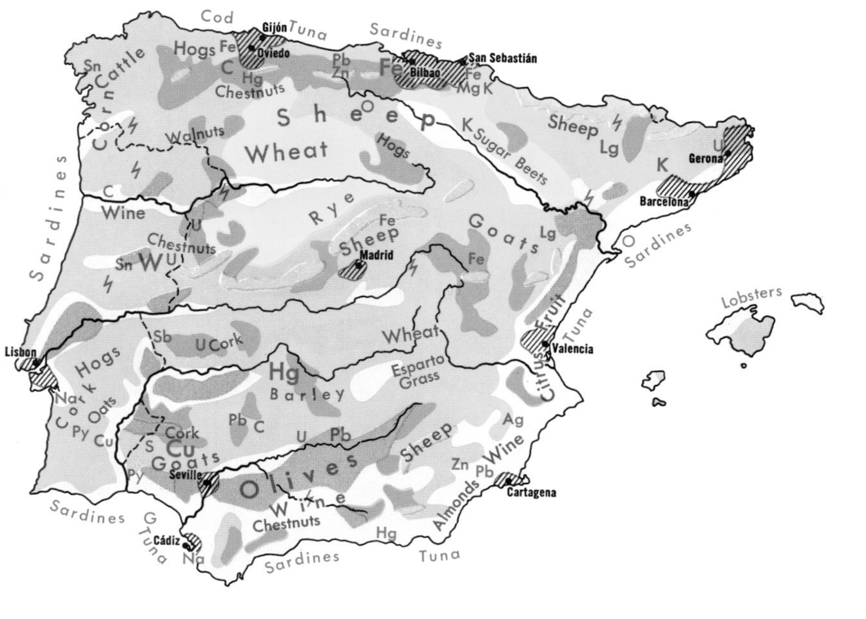

(continued on following page)

Topography

0   50   100 MI.

0   50   100 KM.

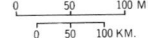

Below Sea Level	100 m. 328 ft.	200 m. 656 ft.	500 m. 1,640 ft.	1,000 m. 3,281 ft.	2,000 m. 6,562 ft.	5,000 m. 16,404 ft.

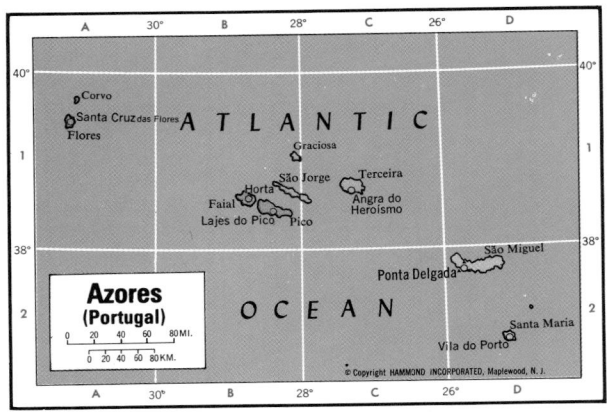

Azores (Portugal)

0 20 40 60 80MI.

0 20 40 60 80KM.

© Copyright HAMMOND INCORPORATED, Maplewood, N.J.

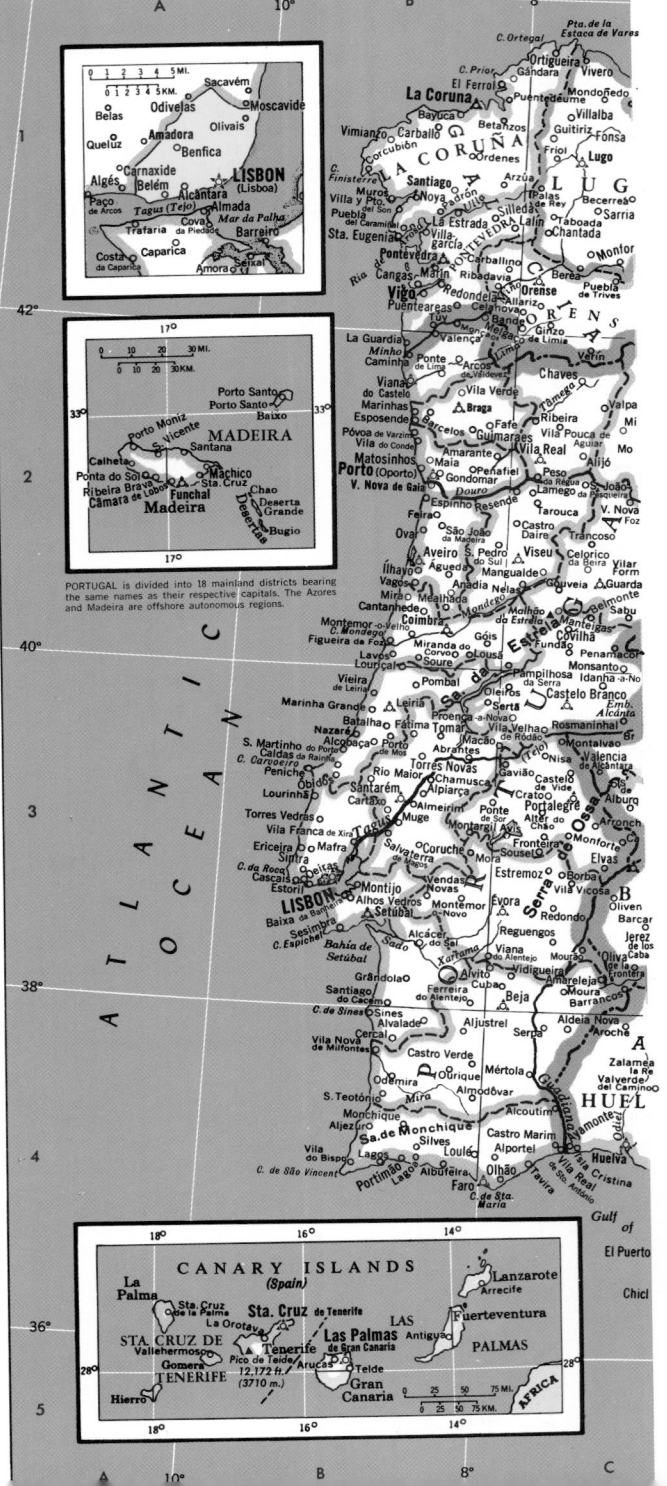

PORTUGAL is divided into 18 mainland districts bearing the same names as their respective capitals. The Azores and Madeira are offshore autonomous regions.

Spain and Portugal

CONIC PROJECTION

SCALE OF MILES
0 20 40 60 80 100

KILOMETERS
0 20 40 60 80 100

Capitals of Countries .... ☆
Provincial and District Capitals .... △
International Boundaries ....
Provincial & District Boundaries ....

SPAIN is divided into 17 autonomous communities consisting of one or more provinces. They are as follows: ANDALUSIA (Almería, Cádiz, Córdoba, Granada, Huelva, Jaén, Málaga, Sevilla); ARAGÓN (Huesca, Teruel, Zaragoza); ASTURIAS (Oviedo); BALEARIC ISLANDS (Balearic Islands); BASQUE COUNTRY (Álava, Guipúzcoa, Vizcaya); CANARY ISLANDS (Las Palmas, Sta. Cruz de Tenerife); CANTABRIA (Santander); CASTILE-LA MANCHA (Albacete, Ciudad Real, Cuenca, Guadalajara, Toledo); CASTILE AND LEON (Ávila, Burgos, León, Palencia, Salamanca, Segovia, Soria, Valladolid, Zamor); CATALONIA (Barcelona, Gerona, Lérida, Tarragona); ESTREMADURA (Badajoz, Cáceres); GALICIA (La Coruña, Lugo, Orense, Pontevedra); LA RIOJA (Logroño); MADRID (Madrid); MURCIA (Murcia); NAVARRA (Navarra); VALENCIA (Alicante, Castellón, Valencia).

© Copyright HAMMOND INCORPORATED, Maplewood, N.J.

Italy

CONIC PROJECTION

SCALE OF MILES

SCALE OF KILOMETERS

Capitals of Countries ☆
Regional Capitals
Provincial Capitals
International Boundaries
Regional Boundaries

The regions are subdivided into provinces bearing the same names as their respective capitals, except:

PROVINCE	CAPITAL
MASSA-CARRARA	Massa
PESARO-URBINO	Pesaro

Vatican City

SCALE

Rome and Environs

© Copyright HAMMOND INCORPORATED, Maplewood, N.J.

VATICAN CITY

AREA 108.7 acres (44 hectares)
POPULATION 728

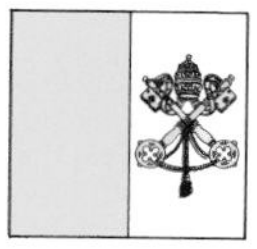

SAN MARINO

AREA 23.4 sq. mi. (60.6 sq. km.)
POPULATION 19,149

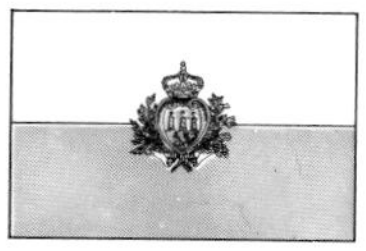

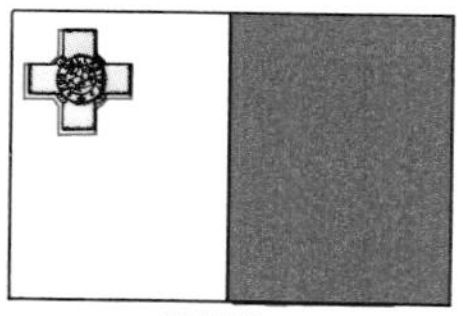

MALTA

AREA 122 sq. mi. (316 sq. km.)
POPULATION 343,970
CAPITAL Valletta
LARGEST CITY Sliema
HIGHEST POINT 787 ft. (240 m.)
MONETARY UNIT Maltese pound
MAJOR LANGUAGES Maltese, English
MAJOR RELIGION Roman Catholicism

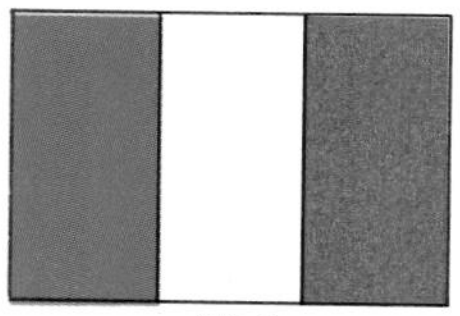

ITALY

AREA 116,303 sq. mi. (301,225 sq. km.)
POPULATION 57,140,000
CAPITAL Rome
LARGEST CITY Rome
HIGHEST POINT Dufourspitze (Mte. Rosa) 15,203 ft. (4,634 m.)
MONETARY UNIT lira
MAJOR LANGUAGE Italian
MAJOR RELIGION Roman Catholicism

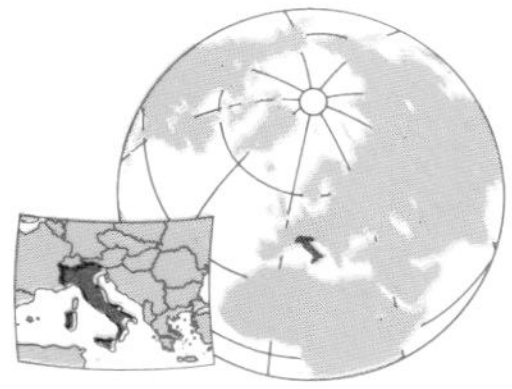

ITALY

REGIONS

Abruzzi 1.166.664	D3
Aosta 109.150	A2
Apulia (Puglia) 3.582.787	F4
Basilicata 603.064	F4
Calabria 1.988.051	F5
Campania 5.059.348	E4
Emilia-Romagna 3.846.755	C2
Friuli-Venezia Giulia 1.213.532	D1
Latium (Lazio) 4.689.482	D3
Liguria 1.853.578	B2
Lombardy 8.543.657	B2
Marche 1.359.907	D3
Molise 319.807	E4
Piedmont 4.432.313	A2
Sardinia 1.473.800	B4
Sicily 4.680.715	D6
Trentino-Alto Adige 841.886	C1
Tuscany 3.473.097	C3
Umbria 775.783	D3
Veneto 2.109.502	D3

PROVINCES

Agrigento 454.045	D6
Alessandria 483.183	B2
Ancona 416.611	D3
Aosta 109.150	A2
Arezzo 306.340	C3
Ascoli Piceno 340.758	D3
Asti 218.547	B2
Avellino 427.509	E4
Bari 1.351.288	F4
Belluno 221.155	D1
Benevento 286.499	E4
Bergamo 829.019	B2
Bologna 918.844	C2
Bolzano-Bozen 414.041	C1
Brescia 957.686	C2
Brindisi 366.027	G4
Cagliari 802.888	B5
Caltanissetta 282.069	D6
Campobasso 227.641	E4
Caserta 677.959	E4
Catania 938.273	E6
Catanzaro 718.069	F5
Chieti 351.567	E3
Como 720.463	B2
Cosenza 691.659	F5
Cremona 334.281	B2
Cuneo 540.504	A2
Enna 202.131	E6
Ferrara 383.639	C2
Florence 1.146.367	C3
Foggia 657.292	E4
Forlì 565.470	D2
Frosinone 422.630	D4
Genoa 1.087.973	B2
Gorizia 142.412	D2
Grosseto 216.315	C3
Imperia 225.127	B3
Isernia 92.166	E4
L'Aquila 293.066	D3
La Spezia 244.435	B2
Latina 376.238	D4
Lecce 696.503	G4
Leghorn 335.265	C3
Lucca 380.356	C3
Macerata 286.155	D3
Mantua 376.892	C2
Massa-Carrara 200.955	C2
Matera 194.629	F4
Messina 654.703	E5
Milan 3.903.685	B2
Modena 553.852	C2
Naples 2.709.929	E4
Novara 496.811	B2
Nuoro 273.021	B4
Padua 762.998	C2
Palermo 1.124.015	D5
Parma 395.497	C2
Pavia 526.389	B2
Perugia 552.936	D3
Pesaro e Urbino 316.383	D3
Pescara 264.981	E3
Piacenza 284.881	B2
Pisa 375.933	C3
Pistoia 254.335	C2
Pordenone 253.906	D2
Potenza 408.435	E4
Ragusa 255.047	E6
Ravenna 351.876	D2
Reggio di Calabria 578.323	E5
Reggio nell'Emilia 392.696	C2
Rieti 143.162	D3
Rome 3.490.377	F6
Rovigo 251.908	C2
Salerno 957.452	E4
Sassari 397.891	B4
Savona 296.043	B2
Siena 257.221	C3
Sondrio 169.149	B1
Syracuse 365.039	E6
Taranto 511.677	F4
Teramo 257.080	D3
Terni 222.847	D3
Trapani 405.393	D5
Trento 427.845	C1
Treviso 668.620	D2
Trieste 300.304	E2
Turin 2.287.016	A2
Udine 516.910	D1
Varese 725.823	B2
Venice 807.251	D2
Vercelli 406.252	B2
Verona 733.595	C2
Vicenza 677.884	C2
Viterbo 257.075	C3

CITIES and TOWNS

Acireale 34.081	E6
Acqui Terme 20.099	B2
Acri 8.150	F5
Adrano 31.988	E6
Adria 11.951	D2
Agira 11.262	E6
Agnone 3.965	E4
Agrigento 40.513	D6
Agropoli 9.413	E4
Alassio 13.512	A2
Alatri 5.710	D4
Alba 23.522	B2
Albano Laziale 15.561	F7
Albenga 13.397	B3
Albino 8.837	B2
Alcamo 41.448	D6
Alessandria 78.644	B2
Alghero 28.454	B4
Altamura 44.879	F4
Amalfi 4.205	E4
Amantea 6.132	E5
Amelia 4.331	D3
Ancona 88.427	D3
Andria 76.405	F4
Anguillara Sabazia 3.241	F6
Anzio 14.966	D4
Aosta 35.053	A2
Aprilia 18.412	D4
Aragona 11.213	D6
Arezzo 56.693	C3
Argenta 6.682	D2
Ariano Irpino 9.796	E4
Ariccia 7.287	F7
Artena 5.034	F7
Ascoli Piceno 43.041	D3
Assisi 4.630	D3
Asti 62.277	B2
Atessa 3.079	E3
Atri 4.686	D3
Augusta 32.501	E6
Avellino 44.750	E4
Aversa 46.536	E4
Avezzano 26.456	D3
Avigliano 5.400	E4
Avola 29.089	E6
Bagheria 32.465	D5
Barcellona Pozzo di Gotto 25.280	E5
Bari 339.110	F4
Barletta 75.116	F4
Bassano del Grappa 33.002	C2
Bellagio 3.258	B2
Belluno 22.180	D1
Benevento 48.523	E4
Bergamo 127.553	B2
Biancavilla 18.743	E6
Biella 46.453	B2
Bisceglie 45.014	F4
Bitonto 39.714	F4
Bitti 4.606	B4
Bologna 493.282	C2
Bolzano (Bolzen) 102.806	C1
Bondeno 7.451	C2
Bonorva 5.232	B4
Bordighera 8.994	A3
Borgo 4.013	C1
Borgomanero 16.655	B2
Bòrgo San Lorenzo 7.699	C2
Bosa 8.045	B4
Boves 3.896	A2
Bra 18.399	A2
Bracciano 7.681	C3
Brescia 189.092	C2
Bressanone 12.261	C1
Brindisi 76.612	G4
Bronte 17.823	E6
Brunico 5.175	D1
Budrio 5.635	C2
Busto Arsizio 72.400	B2
Cagli 4.356	D3
Cagliari 211.015	B5
Caltagirone 34.444	E6
Caltanissetta 52.838	D6
Camaiore 8.578	C3
Camerino 4.644	D3
Campobasso 35.551	E4
Campo Tures 1.325	C1
Canicattì 28.761	E6
Canosa di Puglia 30.263	E4
Cantù 28.617	B2
Capua 13.938	E4
Caravaggio 11.298	B2
Carbonia 23.031	B5
Carini 14.255	D5
Carloforte 6.671	B5
Carmagnola 16.469	A2
Carpi 41.789	C2
Carrara 56.236	C2
Casale Monferrato 35.156	B2
Casalmaggiore 6.374	C2
Cascina-Navacchio 28.263	C3
Caserta 51.621	E4
Cassano allo Ionio 9.661	F5
Cassino 14.747	D4
Castelfranco Veneto 16.042	D2
Castel Gandolfo 2.965	F7
Castellammare del Golfo 13.144	D5
Castellammare di Stabia 64.341	E4
Castel San Pietro Terme 6.985	C2
Castelvetrano 29.167	D6
Castiglion Fiorentino 3.797	C3
Castrovillari 15.207	F5
Catania 403.390	E6
Catanzaro 52.054	F5
Caulonia 3.402	F5
Cava de'Tirreni 33.868	E4
Cavarzere 7.917	D2
Cecina 19.415	C3
Cefalù 11.043	E5
Ceglie Messapico 17.512	F4
Celano 9.531	D3
Cerignola 44.648	E4
Cernobbio 8.026	B2
Cerveteri 5.239	E6
Cesano 2.883	F6
Cesena 49.915	D2
Cesenatico 12.805	D2
Chiari 12.017	C2
Chiavari 29.950	B2
Chieri 27.548	A2
Chieti 31.895	E3
Chioggia 24.044	D2
Chivasso 21.369	A2
Ciampino 36.728	F7
Cittadella 9.321	C2
Città di Castello 18.880	C3
Cittanova 11.045	F5
Cividale del Friuli 8.345	D1
Civitavecchia 41.305	C3
Clusone-Fiorine 6.428	C2
Codroipo 6.117	D2
Colle di Val d'Elsa 8.657	C3
Comacchio 10.437	D2
Comiso 24.508	E6
Como 73.257	B2
Conegliano 28.635	D2
Conversano 16.805	F4
Corato 38.163	F4
Cori 6.829	F7
Corigliano Calabro 14.518	F5
Corleone 11.057	D6
Correggio 11.415	C2
Cortina d'Ampezzo 7.285	D1
Cortona 3.482	C3
Cosenza 94.565	F5
Courmayeur 1.401	A2
Crema 26.061	B2
Cremona 75.988	B2
Crotone 44.081	F5
Cuneo 41.633	A2
Cuorgnè 6.752	A2
Desenzano del Garda 14.624	C2
Diano Marina 6.001	B3
Domodossola 18.562	A1
Dorgali 6.714	B4
Eboli 19.787	E4
Edolo 3.707	C1
Empoli 30.526	C3
Enna 27.351	E6
Este 12.992	C2
Fabriano 18.355	D3
Faenza 36.241	D2
Fano 31.238	D3
Fasano 21.247	F4
Favara 27.940	D6
Feltre 11.806	C1
Fermo 17.521	D3
Ferrandina 8.372	F4
Ferrara 97.507	C2
Fidenza 18.064	B2
Fiesole 3.772	C3
Finale Emilia 7.474	C2
Finale Ligure 11.461	B2
Firenze (Florence) 441.654	C3
Fiumicino 13.180	F7
Florence 441.654	C3
Floridia 16.562	E6
Foggia 136.436	E4
Foligno 26.887	D3
Fondi 16.472	D4
Forlì 83.303	D2
Formia 18.978	D4
Fossano 15.857	A2
Fossombrone 5.882	D3
Francavilla Fontana 30.347	F4
Frascati 14.217	F7
Frosinone 34.066	D4
Gaeta 21.973	D4
Galatina 22.137	G4
Galatone 13.880	F4
Gallarate 43.773	B2
Gallipoli 16.878	F4
Garessio 3.359	A2
Gela 66.845	E6
Gemona 6.863	D1
Genoa 787.011	B2
Genova (Genoa) 787.011	B2
Genzano di Roma 14.147	F7
Giarre 18.233	E6
Gioia del Colle 23.299	F4
Gioiosa Ionica 3.811	F5
Giovinazzo 17.768	F4
Giulianova 17.926	E3
Gorizia 35.912	D2
Gravina in Puglia 32.006	F4
Grosseto 48.309	C3
Grottaferrata 10.639	F7
Grottaglie 23.556	F4
Guardiagrele 4.122	E3
Guastalla 7.639	C2
Gubbio 12.371	D3
Guidonia 8.413	F6
Iglesias 24.472	B5
Imola 42.111	C2
Imperia 37.585	B3
Isernia 12.290	E4
Ivrea 26.530	B2
Jesi 33.011	D3
Ladispoli 6.625	E6
Lagonegro 5.613	E4
La Maddalena 10.405	B4
Lanciano 19.652	E3
Lanusei 5.508	B5
Lanuvio 2.970	F7
L'Aquila 36.233	D3
Larino 5.166	E4
La Spezia 121.254	B2
Latina 53.003	D4
Lauria 4.927	E4
Lavello 11.486	E4
Lecce 80.114	G4
Lecco 53.165	B2
Leghorn 170.369	C3
Legnago 15.534	C2
Lendinara 7.079	C2
Lentini 31.429	E6
Leonforte 16.317	E6
Lerici 5.407	B2
Licata 40.997	D6
Lido di Ostia 61.492	F7
Lido di Venezia 18.794	D2
Lipari 3.886	E5
Livigno 2.135	C1
Livorno (Leghorn) 170.369	C3
Lodi 42.489	B2
Lonigo 6.368	C2
Lucca 54.280	C3
Lucera 29.355	E4
Lugo 19.497	D2
Macerata 33.470	D3
Macomer 9.433	B4
Maglie 13.326	G4
Manduria 25.194	F4
Manfredonia 44.463	F4
Mantua 59.529	C2
Marino 12.135	F7
Marsala 34.150	D6
Marsciano 5.372	D3
Martina Franca 31.811	F4
Massa 56.591	C2
Massafra 22.610	F4
Massa Marittima 6.438	C3
Matera 43.026	F4
Mazara del Vallo 37.441	D6
Mazzarino 14.981	E6
Melfi 13.355	E4
Menfi 12.386	D6
Merano 30.951	C1
Mesagne 26.955	G4
Messina 203.937	E5
Mestre 184.818	D2
Milan 1.724.557	B2
Milazzo 18.576	E5
Minturno 2.428	D4
Mirandola 11.551	C2
Mira Taglio 10.194	D2
Mistretta 6.631	E6
Modena 149.029	C2
Modica 31.074	E6
Mola di Bari 23.778	F4
Molfetta 63.250	F4
Moncalieri 49.953	A2
Mondovì Breo 12.524	A2
Monfalcone 29.589	D2
Monopoli 29.776	F4
Monreale 19.348	D5
Monselice 9.047	C2
Montalto Uffugo 3.173	E5
Montebelluna 9.573	D2
Montefiascone 6.885	D3
Montepulciano 4.069	C3
Monterotondo 15.869	F6
Monte Sant'Angelo 17.756	F4
Montevarchi 16.849	C3
Monza 110.735	B2
Mortara 13.929	B2
Naples 1.214.775	E4
Nardò 24.142	F4
Narni 6.213	D3
Naro 13.171	D6
Nettuno 20.927	D4
Nicastro 27.206	F5
Nicosia 13.982	E6
Niscemi 23.925	E6
Nizza Monferrato 7.532	B2
Nocera Inferiore 44.415	E4
Noto 21.606	E6
Novara 92.634	B2
Novi Ligure 29.944	B2
Nuoro 30.551	B4
Olbia 20.998	B4
Oliena 7.030	B4
Orbetello 6.884	C3
Oristano 20.966	B5
Ortona 11.966	E3
Orvieto 8.813	D3
Osimo 12.034	D3
Ostia Antica 2.583	F7
Ostuni 27.241	F4
Otranto 3.707	G4
Ozieri 9.149	B4
Pachino 20.427	E6
Padua 210.950	C2
Palazzolo Acreide 8.981	E6
Palermo 556.374	D5
Palestrina 9.239	F7
Palma di Montechiaro 22.381	D6
Palmi 14.405	E5
Palombara Sabina 5.292	F6
Pantelleria 3.116	C6
Paola 11.330	E5
Parma 151.967	C2
Partanna 10.303	D6
Partinico 25.447	D6
Paterno 41.504	E6
Patti 7.500	E5
Pavia 80.639	B2
Pavullo nel Frignano 5.026	C2
Penne 5.889	D3
Pergine Valsugana 6.248	C1
Pergola 3.866	D3
Perugia 65.975	D3
Pesaro 72.104	D3
Pescara 125.391	E3
Pescia 9.918	C3
Piacenza 100.001	B2
Piazza Armerina 21.754	E6
Pietrasanta 6.620	B3
Pinerolo 33.935	A2
Piombino 35.641	C3
Piove di Sacco 7.035	C2
Pisa 91.156	C3
Pisticci 11.239	F4
Pistoia 55.403	C2
Poggibonsi 21.271	C3
Pomezia 11.915	F7
Pont Canavese 4.075	A2
Pontecorvo 5.986	D4
Pontinia 3.166	D4
Pontremoli 5.222	B2
Popoli 5.372	E3
Pordenone 43.230	D2
Portocivitanova 25.773	D3
Porto Empedocle 15.986	D6
Portoferraio 7.579	C3
Portofino 720	B2
Portogruaro 12.258	D2
Portomaggiore 6.343	C2
Porto Recanati 5.389	D3
Porto Torres 15.422	B4
Potenza 46.869	E4
Pozzallo 12.199	E6
Pozzuoli 53.546	D4
Prato 108.385	C3
Prima Porta 11.393	F6
Priverno 9.950	D4
Putignano 19.290	F4
Quartu Sant'Elena 29.715	B5
Ragusa 55.751	E6
Rapallo 22.272	B2
Ravenna 75.153	D2
Recanati 10.176	D3
Reggio di Calabria 110.291	E5
Reggio nell'Emilia 102.337	C2
Rho 39.206	B2
Riesi 15.855	E6
Rieti 26.775	D3
Rimini 101.579	D2
Rionero in Vulture 11.230	E4
Riva del Garda 8.513	C2
Roccastrada 2.629	C3
Rome (cap.) 2.535.018	F6
Ronciglione 5.900	C3
Rossano 12.119	F5
Rovereto 26.827	C2
Rovigo 31.124	C2
Ruvo di Puglia 23.133	F4

(continued on following page)

Topography

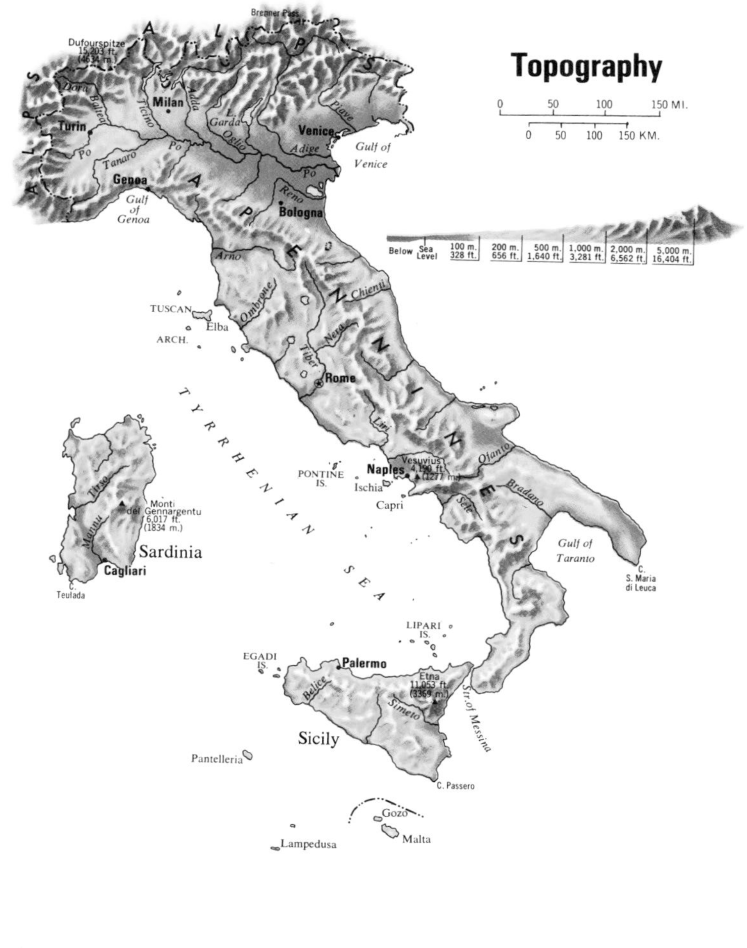
Brenner Pass
Dufourspitze 15,203 ft. (4634 m.)
A L P S
Milan
Turin
Venice
Gulf of Venice
Genoa
Gulf of Genoa
Bologna
A P E N N I N E S
Po
Tanaro
Adige
Piave
Reno
Arno
Tiber
TUSCAN ARCH.
Elba
Rome
T Y R R H E N I A N S E A
PONTINE IS.
Naples
Ischia
Capri
Vesuvius
Sardinia
Cagliari
Teulada
Monti del Gennargentu 6,017 ft. (1834 m.)
Gulf of Taranto
C. S. Maria di Leuca
LIPARI IS.
EGADI IS.
Palermo
Etna 11,053 ft. (3369 m.)
Str. of Messina
Sicily
Pantelleria
C. Passero
Gozo
Malta
Lampedusa
0 50 100 150 MI.
0 50 100 150 KM.
Below Sea Level
100 m. 328 ft.
200 m. 656 ft.
500 m. 1,640 ft.
1,000 m. 3,281 ft.
2,000 m. 6,562 ft.
5,000 m. 16,404 ft.

Agriculture, Industry and Resources

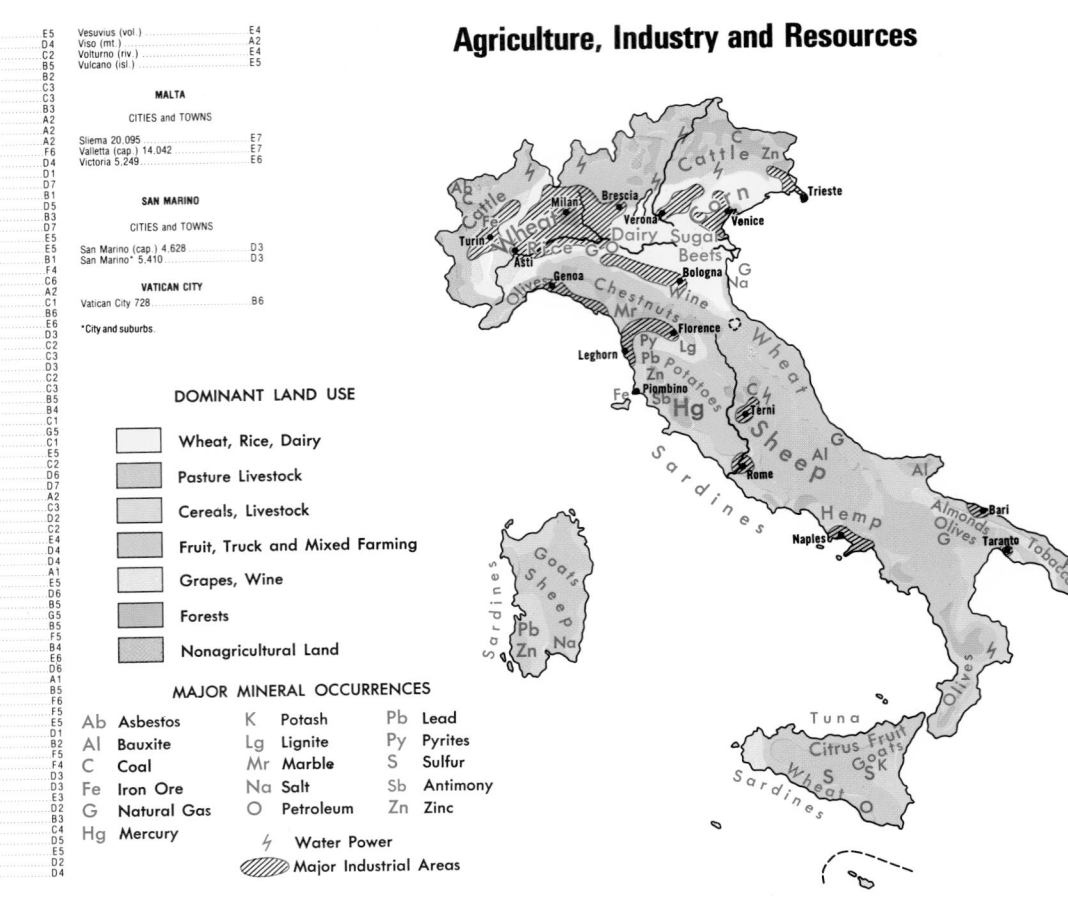

DOMINANT LAND USE

- Wheat, Rice, Dairy
- Pasture Livestock
- Cereals, Livestock
- Fruit, Truck and Mixed Farming
- Grapes, Wine
- Forests
- Nonagricultural Land

MAJOR MINERAL OCCURRENCES

Ab Asbestos
Al Bauxite
C   Coal
Fe Iron Ore
G   Natural Gas
Hg Mercury

K   Potash
Lg Lignite
Mr Marble
Na Salt
O   Petroleum

Pb Lead
Py Pyrites
S   Sulfur
Sb Antimony
Zn Zinc

⚡ Water Power
⫽ Major Industrial Areas

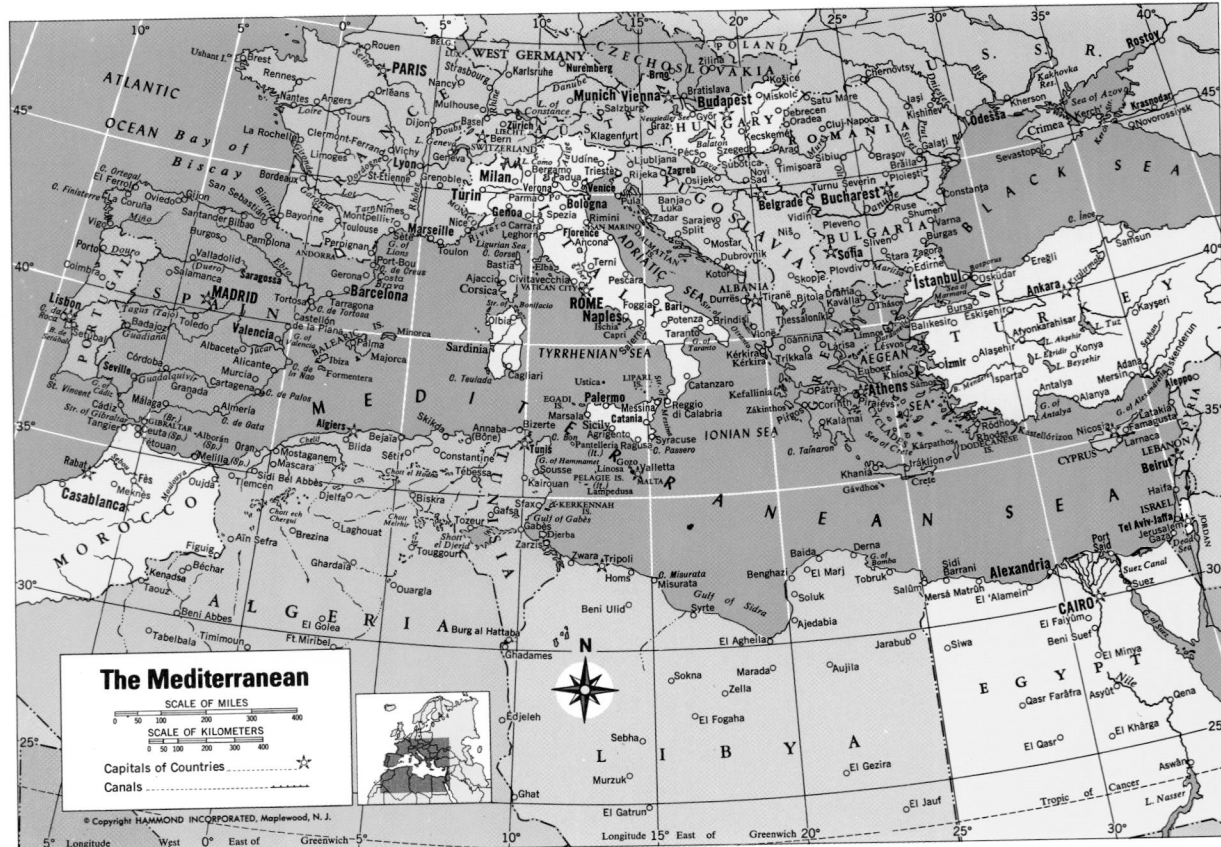

The Mediterranean

SCALE OF MILES
0 50 100   200   300   400

SCALE OF KILOMETERS
0 50 100   200   300   400

Capitals of Countries .... ☆
Canals ....

© Copyright HAMMOND INCORPORATED, Maplewood, N.J.

SWITZERLAND
AREA 15,943 sq. mi. (41,292 sq. km.)
POPULATION 6,365,960
CAPITAL Bern
LARGEST CITY Zürich
HIGHEST POINT Dufourspitze
  (Mte. Rosa) 15,203 ft. (4,634 m.)
MONETARY UNIT Swiss franc
MAJOR LANGUAGES German, French,
  Italian, Romansch
MAJOR RELIGIONS Protestantism,
  Roman Catholicism

LIECHTENSTEIN
AREA 61 sq. mi. (158 sq. km.)
POPULATION 25,220
CAPITAL Vaduz
LARGEST CITY Vaduz
HIGHEST POINT Grauspitze 8,527 ft.
  (2,599 m.)
MONETARY UNIT Swiss franc
MAJOR LANGUAGE German
MAJOR RELIGION Roman Catholicism

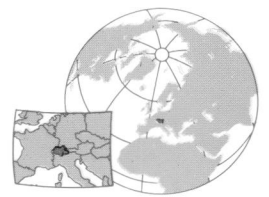

SWITZERLAND

LIECHTENSTEIN

Languages

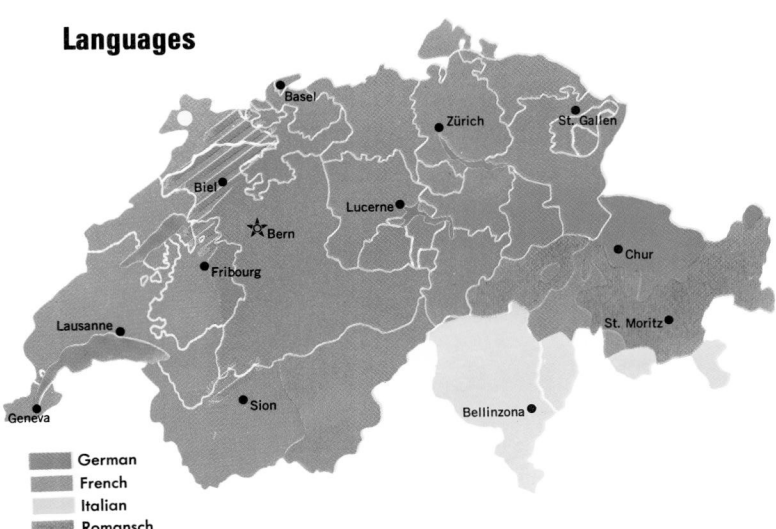

German
French
Italian
Romansch

Switzerland is a multilingual nation with four
official languages. 70% of the people speak
German, 19% French, 10% Italian and 1% Romansch.

Agriculture, Industry and Resources

DOMINANT LAND USE

Cereals, Dairy

Pasture Livestock

General Farming, Livestock

Fruit, Truck, Mixed Farming

Forests

Nonagricultural Land

⚡ Water Power
▨ Major Industrial Areas

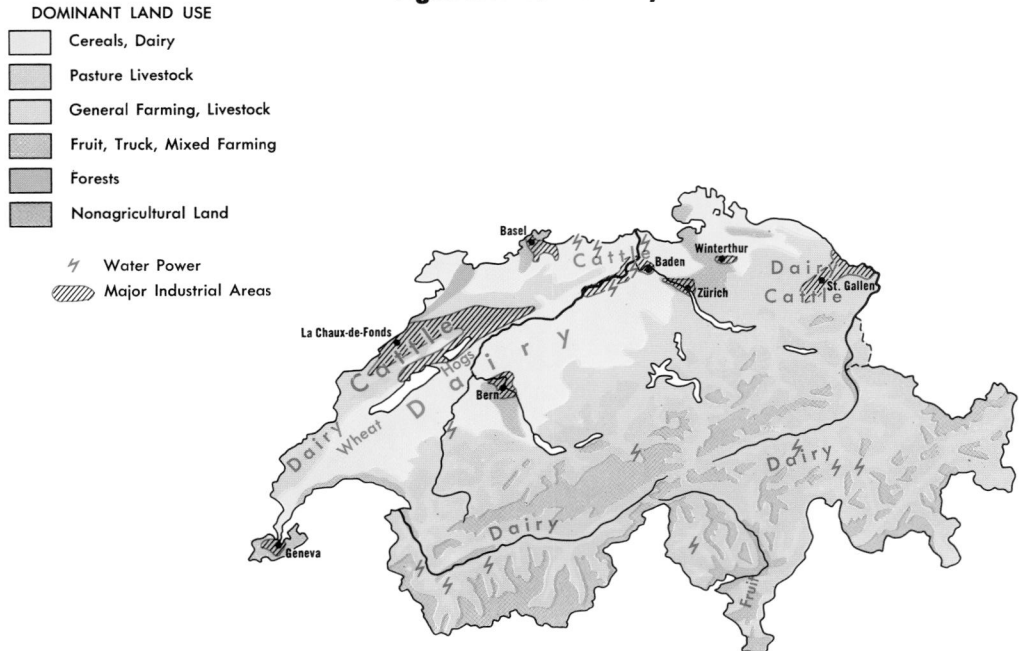

SWITZERLAND

CANTONS

Aargau 442,400	F2
Appenzell, Ausser	
Rhoden 46,700	H2
Appenzell, Inner Rhoden 13,500	H2
Baselland 219,500	E2
Baselstadt 209,700	E1
Bern 920,900	D2
Fribourg 181,600	D3
Geneva (Genève) 338,600	B4
Glarus 35,700	H3
Graubünden (Grisons) 164,300	H3
Grisons (Graubünden) 164,300	H3
Jura 67,200	D2
Lucerne (Luzern) 292,900	F2
Luzern 292,900	F2
Neuchâtel 162,200	C3
Nidwalden 26,900	F3
Obwalden 25,400	F3
Sankt Gallen 385,000	H2
Schaffhausen 69,300	G1
Schwyz 93,100	G2
Soleure (Solothurn) 221,800	E2
Solothurn 221,800	E2
Thurgau 183,500	H1
Ticino 264,400	G4
Uri 34,000	G3
Valais 214,000	D4
Vaud 523,500	B3
Zug 73,600	G2
Zürich 1,117,300	G2

CITIES and TOWNS

Aadorf 3,022	G2
Aarau 16,881	F2
Aarau* 51,800	F2

Aarberg 3,122	D2
Aarburg 5,943	E2
Adelboden 3,326	E3
Adliswil 15,920	G2
Aeschi bei Spiez 1,402	E3
Affoltern am Albis 7,363	G2
Affoltern im Emmental 1,223	E2
Aigle 6,532	C4
Airolo 2,140	G3
Alle 1,615	D2
Allschwil 17,638	D1
Alpnach 3,277	F3
Altdorf 8,647	G3
Altstätten 9,084	J2
Amriswil 7,601	H1
Andelfingen 1,453	G1
Andermatt 1,589	G3
Appenzell 5,217	H2
Arbedo-Castione 2,456	G4
Arbon 12,227	H1
Arbon* 15,400	H1
Ardon 1,498	D4
Arosa 2,717	J3
Arth 7,580	F2
Ascona 4,086	H3
Attalens 1,116	C3
Au 4,944	J2
Aubonne 1,983	B4
Avenches 2,235	D3
Baar 14,074	F2
Baden 14,115	F2
Baden* 66,800	F2
Bad Ragaz 3,713	H2
Balerna 3,885	G5
Balsthal 5,607	E2
Bäretswil 2,733	G2
Basel 199,600	E1
Basel* 379,700	E1
Bassecourt 2,985	D2
Bätterkinden 1,757	E2

Bauma 3,159	G2
Beatenberg 1,263	E3
Beinwil am See 2,520	F2
Belfaux 1,075	D3
Bellinzona 16,979	H4
Bellinzona* 31,000	H4
Belp 6,981	D3
Berg 1,039	H1
Bern (cap.) 154,700	D3
Bern* 285,300	D3
Beromünster 1,552	F2
Bettlach 4,046	D2
Bex 5,069	D4
Biasca 4,696	H4
Biberist 7,769	D2
Biel 63,400	D2
Biel**89,900	D2
Bière 1,252	B3
Binningen 15,344	D1
Bischofszell 4,233	H1
Blumenstein 1,049	E3
Bodio 1,425	G4
Boltigen 26,121	E3
Boltigen 1,519	D3
Bonaduz 1,289	H3
Boncourt 1,528	C2
Bonigen 1,738	E3
Boswil 1,904	F2
Boudry 4,372	C3
Bourg Saint-Pierre 236	D5
Breil-Brigels 1,215	H3
Breitenbach 2,455	E2
Bremgarten 4,873	F2
Brienz 2,796	F3
Brig 5,191	F4
Brissago 2,120	G4
Brittnau 2,888	E2
Broc 1,842	D3
Brugg 8,635	F2
Brusio 1,344	K4
Bubendorf 2,070	E2
Bubikon 3,244	G2
Buchs 8,454	H2
Bülach 11,043	G1
Bulle 7,556	D3
Buochs 3,232	F3
Büren an der Aare 3,085	D2
Burgdorf 15,888	E2
Burgdorf* 18,400	E2
Bürglen, Thurgau 1,920	H1
Bürglen, Uri 3,401	G3
Bussigny-près-Lausanne 4,509	B3
Bütschwil 3,270	H2
Carouge 14,055	B4
Castagnola 4,430	G4
Cazis 1,687	H3
Cernier 1,717	C2
Chalais 1,651	E4
Cham 8,209	F2
Chamoson 2,049	D4
Charmey 1,155	D3
Château-d'Oex 3,203	D4
Châtel-Saint-Denis 2,842	C3
Chêne-Bougeries 8,670	B4
Chavornay 1,521	C3
Chexbres 1,607	C3
Chiasso 8,868	G5
Chippis 1,561	E4
Chur 32,400	J3
Churwalden 1,052	J3
Claro 1,143	G4
Collombey-Muraz 2,279	C4
Collonge-Bellerive 3,541	B4
Conthey 4,259	D4
Coppet 1,097	B4
Corcelles-près-Payerne 1,256	C3
Corgémont 1,645	D2
Cossonay 1,529	B3
Courgenay 1,954	D2
Courrendlin 2,656	D2
Courroux 1,788	D2
Courtelary 1,462	C2
Courtételle 1,864	D2
Couvet 3,481	C3
Cully 1,535	C4
Davos 10,238	J3
Degersheim 3,400	H2
Delémont 11,797	D2
Derendingen 4,917	E2
Dielsdorf 2,691	F1
Diemtigen 1,913	D3
Diepoldsau 3,311	J2
Diessenhofen 2,532	G1
Dietikon 22,705	F2
Disentis-Muster 2,319	G3
Domat-Ems 5,701	H3
Dombresson 1,109	C2
Dornach 5,258	E1
Döttingen 3,380	F1
Dübendorf 19,639	G2
Düdingen 4,932	D3
Dürnten 4,820	G2
Dürrenroth 1,084	E2
Ebnat-Kappel 5,131	H2
Echallens 1,643	C3
Ecublens 6,379	B3
Egg 5,250	G2
Eggiwil 2,391	E3
Eglisau 2,160	G1
Egnach 3,466	H1

(continued on following page)

(continued)

Topography

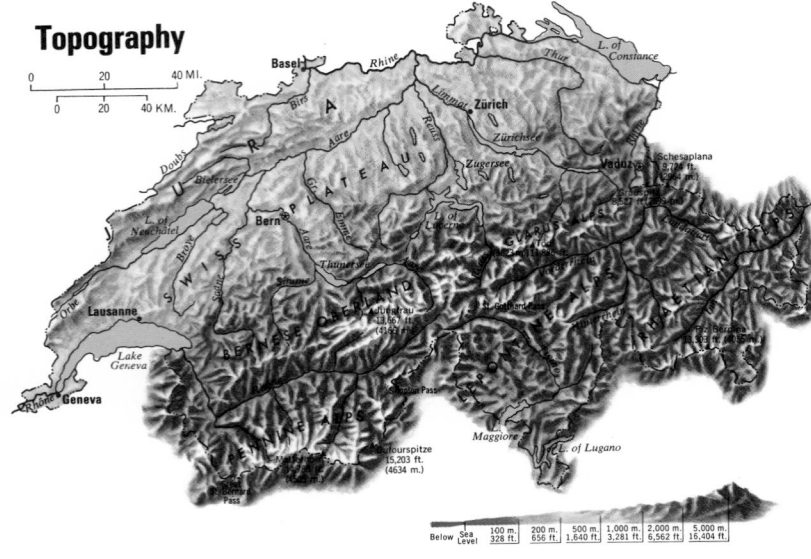

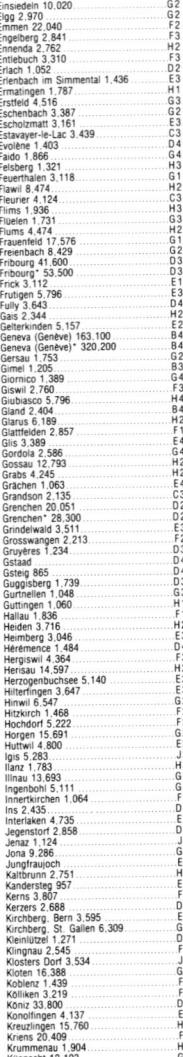

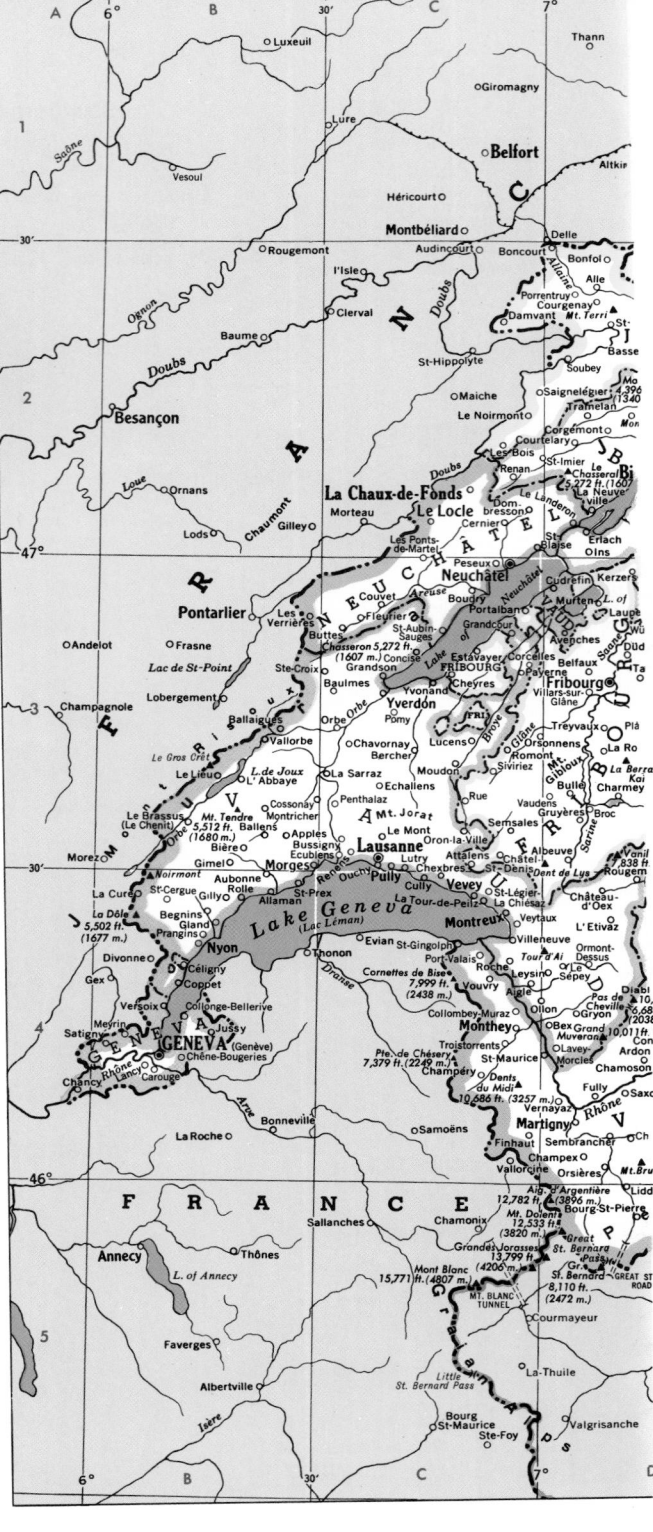

Einsiedeln 10,020 ... G2
Elgg 2,970 ... G2
Emmen 22,040 ... F2
Engelberg 2,841 ... F3
Ennenda 2,762 ... H2
Entlebuch 3,310 ... F3
Erlach 1,052 ... D2
Erlenbach im Simmental 1,436 ... E3
Ermatingen 1,787 ... H1
Erstfeld 4,516 ... G3
Eschenbach 3,387 ... G2
Escholzmatt 3,161 ... E3
Estavayer-le-Lac 3,439 ... C3
Evolène 1,403 ... D4
Faido 1,866 ... G4
Felsberg 1,321 ... H3
Feuerthalen 3,118 ... G1
Flawil 8,474 ... H2
Fleurier 4,124 ... C3
Flims 1,936 ... H3
Flüelen 1,731 ... G3
Flums 4,474 ... H2
Frauenfeld 17,576 ... G1
Freienbach 8,429 ... G2
Fribourg 41,600 ... D3
Fribourg* 53,500 ... D3
Frick 3,112 ... E1
Frutigen 5,796 ... E3
Fully 3,643 ... D4
Gais 2,344 ... H2
Gelterkinden 5,157 ... E2
Geneva (Genève) 163,100 ... B4
Geneva (Genève)* 320,200 ... B4
Gersau 1,753 ... G2
Gimel 1,205 ... B3
Giornico 1,389 ... G4
Giswil 2,760 ... F3
Giubiasco 5,796 ... H4
Gland 2,404 ... B4
Glarus 6,189 ... H2
Glattfelden 2,857 ... F1
Glis 3,389 ... E4
Gordola 2,586 ... G4
Gossau 12,793 ... H2
Grabs 4,245 ... H2
Grächen 1,063 ... E4
Grandson 2,135 ... C3
Grenchen 20,051 ... D2
Grenchen* 28,300 ... D2
Grindelwald 3,511 ... E3
Grosswangen 2,213 ... F2
Gruyères 1,234 ... D3
Gstaad ... D4
Gsteig 865 ... D4
Guggisberg 1,739 ... D3
Gurtnellen 1,048 ... G3
Guttingen 1,060 ... H1
Hallau 1,836 ... F1
Heiden 3,716 ... H2
Heimberg 3,046 ... E3
Hérémence 1,484 ... D4
Hergiswil 4,364 ... F3
Herisau 14,597 ... H2
Herzogenbuchsee 5,140 ... E2
Hilterfingen 3,647 ... E3
Hinwil 6,547 ... G2
Hitzkirch 1,468 ... F2
Hochdorf 5,222 ... F2
Horgen 15,691 ... G2
Huttwil 4,800 ... E2
Igis 5,283 ... J3
Ilanz 1,783 ... H3
Illnau 13,693 ... G2
Ingenbohl 5,111 ... G2
Innertkirchen 1,064 ... F3
Ins 2,435 ... D2
Interlaken 4,735 ... E3
Jegenstorf 2,858 ... D2
Jenaz 1,124 ... J3
Jona 9,286 ... G2
Jungfraujoch ... E3
Kaltbrunn 2,751 ... H2
Kandersteg 957 ... E4
Kerns 3,807 ... F3
Kerzers 2,688 ... D3
Kirchberg, Bern 3,595 ... E2
Kirchberg, St. Gallen 6,309 ... G2
Kleinlützel 1,271 ... D2
Klingnau 2,545 ... F1
Klosters Dorf 3,534 ... J3
Kloten 16,388 ... G2
Koblenz 1,439 ... F1
Kölliken 3,219 ... F2
Köniz 33,800 ... D3
Konolfingen 4,137 ... E3
Kreuzlingen 15,760 ... H1
Kriens 20,409 ... F2
Krummenau 1,904 ... H2
Küsnacht 12,193 ... G2
Küssnacht am Rigi 7,956 ... F2
Küttigen 4,181 ... F2
L'Abbaye 1,319 ... B3
La Chaux-de-Fonds 42,500 ... C2
Lachen 4,914 ... G2
Lancy 20,523 ... B4
La Neuveville 3,917 ... D2
Langenthal 13,077 ... E2
Langenthal* 22,100 ... E2
Langnau am Albis 4,879 ... G2
Langnau in Emmental 8,950 ... E3
La Roche 1,069 ... D3
La Sarraz 1,190 ... C3
La Tour-de-Peilz 8,864 ... C4
Läufelfingen 1,243 ... E2
Laufen 4,723 ... D2
Laufenburg 2,128 ... F1
Laupen 2,139 ... D3
Lauperswil 2,542 ... E3
Lausanne 136,100 ... C3
Lausanne* 228,700 ... C3
Lauterbrunnen 3,431 ... E3
Le Brassus 5,465 ... B3
Le Châble 4,541 ... D4
Le Chenit (Le Brassus) 5,465 ... B3
Le Landeron 2,768 ... C2
Le Locle 14,452 ... C2
Le Mont-sur-Lausanne 2,692 ... C3
Lengau 4,736 ... D2
Lenk 1,876 ... D4
Le Noirmont 1,516 ... C2
Lens 2,052 ... D4
Lenzburg 7,594 ... F2
Les. Bois 1,110 ... C2
Les Ponts-de-Martel 1,327 ... C2
Leuk 2,796 ... E4
Leukerbad 1,056 ... E4
Leysin 2,752 ... C4
Liechtensteig 2,131 ... H2
Liestal 12,500 ... E2
Liestal-Sissach* 40,800 ... E2
Linthal 1,458 ... H3
Littau 13,495 ... F2
Locarno 14,143 ... G4
Locarno* 39,200 ... G4
Lodrino 1,075 ... G4
Lotzwil 2,323 ... E2
Lucens 2,144 ... C3
Lucerne 70,200 ... F2
Lucerne* 158,600 ... F2
Lugano 22,280 ... G4
Lugano* 64,200 ... G4
Lungern 1,813 ... F3
Luthern 1,706 ... E2
Lutry 4,994 ... C3
Lützelflüh 3,842 ... E3
Luzern (Lucerne) 70,200 ... F2
Lyss 8,131 ... D2
Maienfeld 1,542 ... J2
Malans 1,294 ... J3
Malleray 1,969 ... D2
Malters 5,100 ... F2
Malvaglia 1,099 ... H4
Männedorf 7,419 ... G2
Marbach 1,265 ... E3
Martigny 10,478 ... C4
Meilen 9,881 ... G2
Meiringen 3,759 ... F3
Melide 1,315 ... G5
Mellingen 3,211 ... F2
Mels 5,969 ... H2
Mendrisio 6,223 ... G5
Menzingen 3,483 ... G2
Menznau 2,185 ... E2
Mesocco 1,376 ... H4
Meyrin 14,255 ... B4
Minusio 5,027 ... G4
Möhlin 6,003 ... E1
Mollis 2,628 ... H2
Montana 1,725 ... D4
Monthey 10,114 ... C4
Montreux 20,421 ... C4
Morges 11,931 ... B3
Morges* 17,200 ... B3
Moudon 3,773 ... C3
Moutier 8,794 ... D2
Müllheim 1,620 ... G1
Mümliswil-Ramiswil 2,702 ... E2
Münchenbuchsee 6,459 ... E2
Münsingen 8,350 ... E3
Muotathal 2,763 ... G3
Muri 4,853 ... F2
Muri bei Bern 3,057 ... E3
Mürren ... E3
Murten 4,256 ... D3
Muttenz 15,518 ... E1
Näfels 3,739 ... H2
Naters 5,517 ... E4
Nebikon 1,378 ... F2
Nendaz 4,051 ... D4
Nesslau 1,934 ... H2
Netstal 2,771 ... H2
Neuchâtel 38,400 ... C3
Neuchâtel* 61,700 ... C3
Neuenegg 3,452 ... D3
Neuhausen am Rheinfall 12,103 ... G1
Neunkirch 1,239 ... F1
Nidau 7,962 ... D2
Niederbipp 3,293 ... E2
Niederurnen 3,354 ... G2
Nunningen 1,450 ... E2
Nyon 11,424 ... B4
Oberägeri 2,992 ... G2
Oberburg 3,015 ... E2
Oberdiessbach 2,145 ... E3
Oberdorf 1,953 ... E2
Oberriet 6,123 ... J2
Obersiggenthal 6,623 ... F1
Oberzwil 4,659 ... H2
Oensingen 3,387 ... E2
Oftringen 9,189 ... E2
Ollon 4,470 ... D4
Olten 21,209 ... E2
Olten* 49,000 ... E2
Opfikon 11,115 ... G2
Orbe 4,522 ... C3
Orsières 2,470 ... D4
Ouchy ... C4
Paradiso 3,101 ... G5
Payerne 6,899 ... C3
Penthalaz 1,701 ... C3
Péry 1,486 ... D2
Peseux 5,578 ... C3
Pfaffnau 2,584 ... E2
Pieterlen 3,485 ... D2
Plaffeien 1,448 ... D3
Pontresina 1,646 ... J3
Porrentruy 7,827 ... C2
Port-Valais 1,363 ... C4
Poschiavo 3,563 ... J4
Prangins 1,466 ... B4
Pratteln 15,127 ... E1
Pully 15,917 ... C4
Quinto 1,490 ... G3
Rafz 2,215 ... G1
Ramsen 1,217 ... G1
Rapperswil 8,713 ... G2
Raron 1,257 ... E4
Regensdorf 8,566 ... F2
Reichenbach im Kandertal 2,900 ... E3
Reiden 3,275 ... F2
Reinach in Aargau 5,862 ... F2
Reinach in Baselland 13,419 ... E2
Renan 1,094 ... C2
Renens 17,391 ... C3
Rheinau 2,075 ... G1
Rheineck 3,275 ... J2
Rheinfelden 6,866 ... E1
Richterswil 7,380 ... G2
Riehen 21,026 ... E1
Riggisberg 2,193 ... E3
Riva San Vitale 1,607 ... G5
Rivera 1,146 ... G4
Roggwil 3,403 ... E2
Rolle 3,658 ... B4
Romanshorn 8,329 ... H1
Romont 3,276 ... C3
Rorschach 11,963 ... H2
Rorschach* 24,200 ... H2
Rosenlaui ... F3
Rothrist 5,883 ... E2
Roveredo 2,037 ... H4
Rüeggisberg 1,857 ... E3
Rumlang 5,677 ... G2
Rüschegg 1,346 ... D3
Ruswil 4,756 ... F2
Rüthi 1,493 ... J2
Rüti, Zürich 9,546 ... G2
Saanen 5,840 ... D4
Sachseln 3,059 ... F3
Saignelégier 1,745 ... D2
Saint-Aubin-Sauges 2,058 ... C3
Saint-Blaise 2,586 ... D2
Sainte-Croix 6,240 ... B3
Saint-Imier 6,740 ... D2
Saint-Légier-La Chiésaz 2,230 ... C4
Saint-Martin 1,120 ... E4
Saint-Maurice 3,808 ... C4
Saint Moritz 5,699 ... J3
Saint Niklaus 2,043 ... E4
Saint-Prex 2,306 ... B4
Saint Stephan 1,213 ... D3
Saint-Ursanne 1,073 ... D2
Samedan 2,574 ... J3
Sankt Gallen 81,900 ... H2
Sankt Gallen* 90,400 ... H2
Sankt Margrethen 5,101 ... J2
Sargans 4,058 ... H2
Sarnen 6,952 ... F3
Satigny 1,877 ... A4
Savièse 3,585 ... D4
Saxon 2,409 ... D4
Schaffhausen 36,800 ... G1
Schaffhausen* 55,800 ... G1
Schänis 2,355 ... H2
Schattdorf 3,292 ... G3
Scherzingen 1,420 ... H1
Schiers 2,342 ... J3
Schinznach-Dorf 1,154 ... F2
Schleitheim 1,544 ... G1
Schlieren 11,869 ... F2
Schönenwerd 4,793 ... E2
Schübelbach 4,395 ... G2
Schüpfheim 3,773 ... F3
Schwanden 2,823 ... H2
Schwyz 12,194 ... G2
Scuol 1,686 ... K3
Sempach 1,619 ... F2
Seon 3,628 ... F2
Seuzach 3,258 ... G1
Sevelen 2,742 ... H2
Sierre 11,017 ... D4
Signau 2,642 ... E3
Sigriswil 3,540 ... E3
Silenen 2,338 ... G3
Sils im Domleschg 762 ... H3
Silvaplana 714 ... J4
Sins 2,435 ... F2
Sion 21,925 ... D4
Sirnach 3,706 ... G2
Sissach 4,938 ... E2
Solothurn (Soleure) 17,708 ... E2
Solothurn* 35,600 ... E2
Somvix 1,555 ... G3
Sonvico 1,129 ... G4
Spiez 9,911 ... E3
Stäfa 9,937 ... G2
Stalden 1,121 ... E4
Stans 5,180 ... F3
Steckborn 3,752 ... G1
Steffisburg 12,621 ... E3
Stein 1,763 ... E1
Stein am Rhein 2,751 ... G1
Suhr 7,223 ... F2
Sulgen 1,834 ... H1
Sumiswald 5,334 ... E2
Sursee 7,052 ... F2
Tafers 2,021 ... D3
Täuffelen 1,761 ... D2
Tavannes 3,869 ... D2
Tavetsch 1,273 ... G3
Teufen 5,300 ... H2
Thal 4,919 ... J2
Thalwil 13,591 ... G2
Thayngen 3,640 ... G1
Therwil 5,412 ... E1
Thun 37,000 ... E3
Thun* 63,600 ... E3
Thunstetten 2,483 ... E2
Thusis 2,381 ... H3
Trachselwald 1,199 ... E2
Tramelan 5,549 ... D2
Trimmis 1,109 ... J3
Troistorrents 2,208 ... C4
Trub 1,833 ... E3
Trun 1,607 ... G3
Turbenthal 2,939 ... G2
Uetendorf 3,132 ... E3
Unterägeri 4,671 ... G2
Unteriberg 1,344 ... G2
Unterkulm 2,596 ... F2
Unterseen 4,192 ... E3
Untervaz 1,230 ... H3
Urnäsch 2,313 ... H2
Uster 21,819 ... G2
Utzenstorf 3,193 ... E2
Uznach 3,984 ... H2
Uzwil 9,133 ... H2
Vallorbe 4,028 ... B3
Vaz-Obervaz 2,003 ... J3
Vechigen 3,595 ... E3
Vernayaz 1,356 ... D4
Versoix 5,627 ... B4
Vevey 17,957 ... C4
Vevey-Montreux* 62,300 ... C4
Villeneuve 3,705 ... C4
Visp 5,252 ... E4
Vouvry 1,851 ... C4
Vuadens 1,278 ... C3
Wädenswil 15,695 ... G2
Wahlern 4,832 ... D3
Wald 8,185 ... G2
Waldenburg 1,449 ... E2
Waldkirch 2,669 ... H2
Walenstadt 3,446 ... H2
Wallisellen 10,415 ... G2
Walzenhausen 2,082 ... J2
Wangen an der Aare 2,013 ... E2
Wängi 2,730 ... H1
Wartau 3,604 ... H2
Wattwil 8,566 ... H2
Weesen 1,308 ... H2
Weggis 2,517 ... F2
Weinfelden 8,621 ... H1
Wettingen 19,900 ... F2
Wetzikon 13,469 ... G2
Wil 14,646 ... H2
Wil* 20,500 ... H2
Wilchingen 1,066 ... F1
Wilderswil 1,666 ... E3
Wildhaus 1,104 ... H2
Willisau 2,728 ... F2
Wimmis 1,833 ... E3
Windisch 7,444 ... F1
Winterthur 93,500 ... G1
Winterthur* 110,100 ... G1
Wohlen 12,024 ... F2
Wohlen* 16,000 ... F2
Wohlen bei Bern 4,190 ... D3
Wolfenschiessen 1,470 ... F3
Wolhusen 3,556 ... F2
Worb 9,526 ... E3
Wünnewil 3,652 ... D3
Wynigen 1,986 ... E2
Yverdon 20,538 ... C3
Yvonand 1,321 ... C3
Zell, Luzern 1,590 ... E2
Zell, Zürich 4,008 ... G2
Zermatt 3,101 ... E4
Zizers 1,913 ... J3
Zofingen 9,292 ... F2
Zollikofen 9,069 ... E3
Zollikon 12,117 ... G2
Zug 22,972 ... G2
Zug* 51,300 ... G2
Zuoz 1,165 ... J3
Zürich 401,600 ... F2
Zürich* 718,100 ... F2
Zurzach 3,098 ... F1
Zweisimmen 2,738 ... D3

OTHER FEATURES

Aa (riv.) ... F3
Aare (riv.) ... E3
Ägerisee (lake) ... G2
Aiguille d'Argentière (mt.) ... C5
Aletschhorn (mt.) ... F4
Aroser Rothorn (mt.) ... J3
Ault (peak) ... H3
Balmhorn (mt.) ... E4
Bernese Oberland (reg.) ... E3
Bernina (peak) ... J4
Bernina (pass) ... K4
Bielersee (lake) ... D2
Bietschhorn (mt.) ... E4
Birs (riv.) ... D2
Blinnenhorn (mt.) ... F4
Blümlisalp (mt.) ... E3
Bodensee (Constance) (lake) ... H1
Borgne (riv.) ... D4
Breithorn (mt.) ... E5
Breithorn (mt.) ... E4
Brienzer Rothorn (mt.) ... F3
Brienzersee (lake) ... F3
Broye (riv.) ... C3
Buchegg (mts.) ... D2
Buin (peak) ... K3
Campo Tencia (peak) ... G4
Chasseron (mt.) ... C3
Churfirsten (mt.) ... H2
Clariden (mt.) ... G3
Constance (lake) ... H1
Cornettes de Bise (mts.) ... C4
Dammastock (mt.) ... F3
Davos (valley) ... J3
Dent Blanche (mt.) ... E4
Dent de Lys (mt.) ... D4

Switzerland and Liechtenstein

CONIC PROJECTION

SCALE OF MILES

SCALE OF KILOMETERS

Capitals of Countries	☆
Capitals of Cantons	◉
International Boundaries	-·-·-
Canals	

© Copyright HAMMOND INCORPORATED, Maplewood, N.J.

Longitude 8° East of Greenwich

Dent de Ruth (mt.)	D3	Grauehörner (mts.)	H3
Dent d'Hérens (mt.)	E5	Great Saint Bernard (mt.)	C5
Dents du Midi (mt.)	C4	Great Saint Bernard (pass)	C5
Diablerets (mt.)	D4	Greifensee (lake)	G2
Doldenhorn (mt.)	E4	Greina (pass)	G3
Dolent (mt.)	C5	Grimsel (pass)	F3
Dom (mt.)	E4	Gross Emme (riv.)	E3
Doubs (riv.)	C2	Gross Litzner (mt.)	K3
Drance (riv.)	D4	Hinterrhein (riv.)	H3
Dufourspitze (mt.)	E5	Hochwang (mt.)	J3
Emmental (riv.)	E3	Hohenstollen (mt.)	F3
Engadine (valley)	K3	Hörnli (mt.)	H2
Err (peak)	J3	Inn (riv.)	K3
Finsteraarhorn (mt.)	F3	Jorat (mt.)	C4
Finstermünz (pass)	K3	Jungfrau (mt.)	E3
Fletschhorn (mt.)	E4	Jura (mts.)	B3
Fluchthorn (mt.)	K3	Kaiseregg (mt.)	D3
Fluela (pass)	J3	Kesch (peak)	J3
Furka (pass)	F3	La Dôle (mt.)	B4
Generoso (mt.)	H5	Landquart (riv.)	J3
Geneva (lake)	B4	Le Chasseral (mt.)	C3
Glärnisch (mt.)	H2	Le Gros Crêt (mt.)	B3
Glarus Alps (mts.)	H3	Léman (Geneva) (lake)	C4
Grand Combin (mt.)	D5	Leone (mt.)	E4
Grande Dixence (dam)	D4	Lepontine Alps (range)	F4
Grand Muveran (mt.)	D4	Limmat (riv.)	F2

Linard (peak)	K3	Oberalpstock (mt.)	G3
Linden (mt.)	F2	Ochsen (mt.)	D3
Linth (riv.)	G2	Ofen (pass)	K3
Lötschberg (tunnel)	E4	Ofenhorn (mt.)	F4
Lower Engadine (valley)	K3	Orbe (riv.)	C3
Lucerne (lake)	F3	Pennine Alps (range)	D5
Lugano (lake)	G5	Pilatus (mt.)	F3
Maggia (riv.)	G4	Plessur (riv.)	J3
Maggiore (lake)	G5	Poschiavo (valley)	K4
Männliflu (mt.)	E3	Pragel (pass)	G2
Marmontana (mt.)	H4	Quaternals (pass)	J4
Matterhorn (mt.)	E4	Reuss (riv.)	F2
Mauvoisin (dam)	D4	Rhaetian Alps (range)	J3
Moësa (riv.)	H4	Rhine (riv.)	J2
Morat (lake)	D3	Rhône (riv.)	D4
Muota (riv.)	G2	Rigi (mt.)	F3
Murg (riv.)	G1	Ringelspitz (mt.)	H3
Murtaröl (peak)	K3	Risoux (mt.)	B3
Muttler (mt.)	K3	Rosa (mt.)	E5
Naafkopf (mt.)	J2	Rosstock (mt.)	G3
Napf (mt.)	E3	Rothorn (mt.)	D4
National Park	J3	Saane (Sarine) (riv.)	D4
Neuchâtel (lake)	C3	Saint Gotthard (pass)	G3
Noirmont (mt.)	B4	
Oberalp (pass)	G3	

Saint Gotthard (tunnel)	G3	Tamina (riv.)	H3
Ochsen (mt.)	D3	Tendre (peak)	B3
San Bernardino (pass)	H3	Terri (mt.)	H3
Säntis (mt.)	H2	Thunersee (lake)	E3
Sarine (Saane) (riv.)	D3	Thur (riv.)	G1
Sarnen (lake)	F3	Ticino (riv.)	G4
Schesaplana (mt.)	J3	Titlis (mt.)	F3
Scherhorn (mt.)	G3	Tödi (mt.)	G3
Schreckhorn (mt.)	F3	Toggenburg (dist.)	H2
Schwarzhorn (mt.)	E4	Töss (riv.)	G2
Seez (riv.)	H2	Tour d'Aï (mt.)	C4
Sempach (lake)	F2	Umbrail (peak)	K3
Septimer (pass)	J4	Untersee (lake)	H1
Sesvenna (peak)	K3	Unterwalden (reg.)	F3
Sihlsee (lake)	G2	Upper Engadine (valley)	J4
Silvretta (mt.)	K3	Urirotstock (mt.)	G3
Simme (riv.)	D4	Vadret (peak)	J3
Simplon (pass)	E4	Valserrhein (riv.)	H3
Simplon (tunnel)	E4	Vanil Noir (mt.)	D4
Sonnenhorn (mt.)	F4	Vélan (mt.)	D5
Splügen (pass)	H4	Visp (riv.)	E4
Stockhorn (mt.)	E3	Vorab (mt.)	H3
Sulzfluh (mt.)	J3	Vorderrhein (riv.)	G3
Susten (pass)	G3	Wandfluhhorn (mt.)	G4
Sustenhorn (mt.)	F3	Weissenstein (mts.)	D2
Tamaro (mt.)	G4	Weisshorn (mt.)	E4

Weisshorn (mt.)	J3
Weissmies (mt.)	E4
Wetterhorn (mt.)	F3
Wildhorn (mt.)	D4
Wildstrubel (mt.)	E4
Zellersee (lake)	G1
Zugersee (lake)	F2
Zürichsee (lake)	G2

LIECHTENSTEIN

CITIES and TOWNS

Schaan 4,552	H2
Triesen 2,971	H2
Vaduz (cap.) 4,614	H2

OTHER FEATURES

Grauspitz (mt.)	J2
Ochsenkopf (mt.)	J2
Rhätikon (mts.)	J2
Rhine (riv.)	J2

*City and suburbs

AUSTRIA

PROVINCES

Burgenland 272,119 .... D3
Carinthia 525,728 .... C3
Lower Austria 1,414,161 .... B3
Salzburg 401,766 .... B3
Styria 1,192,442 .... C3
Tirol 540,771 .... A3
Upper Austria 1,223,444 .... B2
Vienna (city) 1,614,841 .... D2
Vorarlberg 271,473 .... A3

CITIES and TOWNS†

Admont 3,126 .... C3
Allentsteig 2,783 .... C2
Altheim 4,766 .... B2
Altheim 3,886 .... C2
Amstetten 13,330 .... C2
Andau 3,058 .... D3
Arnoldstein 6,740 .... B3
Aspang Markt 2,316 .... C3
Attnang-Puchheim 7,837 .... B2
Bad Aussee 5,039 .... B3
Baden 22,631 .... D2
Badgastein 5,228 .... B3
Bad Goisern 6,360 .... B3
Bad Hofgastein 5,525 .... B3
Bad Ischl 12,740 .... B3
Bad Leonfelden 2,712 .... C2
Bad Sankt-Leonhard im
  Lavanttal 4,882 .... C3
Berndorf 8,371 .... D3
Bischofshofen 9,417 .... B3
Bludenz 12,050 .... A3
Bramberg am Wildkogel 3,129 .... B3
Braunau am Inn 16,432 .... B2
Bregenz 22,839 .... A3
Bruck an der Leitha 7,506 .... D2
Bruck an der Mur 16,359 .... C3
Deutsch Feistritz 3,820 .... C3
Deutschkreutz 3,673 .... D3
Deutsch Landsberg 6,614 .... C3
Deutsch Wagram 4,481 .... D2
Dornbirn 33,810 .... A3
Ebenfurth 2,272 .... D3
Ebensee 9,413 .... B3
Eferding 3,014 .... C2
Eggenburg 3,730 .... C2
Ehrwald 2,198 .... A3

Eisenerz 11,563 .... C3
Eisenkappel-Vellach 3,761 .... C3
Eisenstadt 10,059 .... D3
Enns 9,622 .... C2
Feldbach 3,887 .... C3
Feldkirch 21,214 .... A3
Feldkirchen in
  Kärnten 11,188 .... B3
Ferlach 7,621 .... C3
Fieberbrunn 3,651 .... B3
Fohnsdorf 11,169 .... C3
Frankenmarkt 2,960 .... B3
Frauenkirchen 2,749 .... D3
Freistadt 5,956 .... C2
Freidberg 2,504 .... D3
Friesach 7,257 .... C3
Frohnleiten 5,081 .... C3
Fulpmes 2,553 .... A3
Fürstenfeld 6,054 .... D3
Gaming 4,181 .... C3
Gänserndorf 4,211 .... D2
Gleisdorf 4,921 .... C3
Gloggnitz 7,078 .... D3
Gmünd, Carinthia 2,267 .... C3
Gmünd, Lower Austria 6,323 .... C2
Gmunden 12,270 .... B3
Golling an der Salzach 3,089 .... B3
Götzis 7,931 .... A3
Gratwein 2,747 .... C3
Graz 251,900 .... C3
Graz* 314,200 .... C3
Grein 2,767 .... C2
f21Grieskirchen 4,519 .... B2
Grosssiegharts 3,288 .... C2
Grünburg 3,775 .... C3
Güssing 3,675 .... D3
Haag 5,060 .... C2
Hainburg an der Donau 6,009 .... D2
Hainfeld 3,897 .... C3
Hallein 14,371 .... B3
Hartberg 5,702 .... C3
Haslach an der Mühl 2,636 .... C2
Heidenreichstein 4,340 .... C2
Heiligenblut 1,324 .... B3
Hermagor-Presseggersee 7,531 .... B3
Herzogenburg 7,293 .... C2
Hohenau an der March 3,591 .... D2
Hohenberg 2,016 .... C3
Hohenems 11,487 .... A3
Hollabrunn 6,563 .... D2
Hopfgarten in Nordtirol 4,784 .... B3

Horn 6,264 .... C2
Hüttenberg 3,251 .... C3
Imst 5,855 .... A3
Innsbruck 115,800 .... A3
Innsbruck* 167,200 .... A3
Jenbach 5,868 .... A3
Jennersdorf 4,210 .... C3
Judenburg 11,346 .... C3
Kapfenberg 26,001 .... C3
Kappl 2,156 .... A3
Kaprun 2,604 .... B3
Kindberg 6,128 .... C3
Kirchdorf an der Krems 3,471 .... C2
Kitzbühel 7,995 .... B3
Klagenfurt 74,326 .... C3
Klagenfurt* 112,600 .... C3
Klosterneuburg 21,912 .... D2
Knittelfeld 14,517 .... C3
Koflach 12,612 .... C3
Königswiesen 2,921 .... C2
Korneuburg 8,892 .... D2
Kössen 2,764 .... B3
Kötschach-Mauthen 3,740 .... B3
Kremsan der Donau 21,733 .... C2
Kufstein 12,766 .... A3
Kundl 3,020 .... A3
Laa an der Thaya 5,455 .... D2
Laakirchen 7,664 .... B3
Lambach 3,301 .... C3
Landeck 7,388 .... A3
Langenfeld 2,838 .... B3
Langenlois 4,957 .... C2
Langenwang 4,071 .... C3
Lavamünd 4,120 .... C3
Leibnitz 6,646 .... C3
Lenzing 5,385 .... B3
Leoben 35,153 .... C3
Lienz 11,696 .... B3
Lilienfeld 3,126 .... C3
Liezen 6,244 .... C3
Linz 205,700 .... C2
Linz* 356,500 .... C2
Lustenau 15,239 .... A3
Mannersdorf am
  Leithagebirge 4,012 .... D2
Marchegg 2,678 .... D2
Mariazell 2,298 .... C3
Matrei in Osttirol 4,003 .... B3
Mattersburg 5,417 .... D3
Mattighofen 4,344 .... B2
Mauerkirchen 2,237 .... B2
Mautern in Steiermark 2,536 .... C3

Mauthausen 4,419 .... C2
Mauthen-Kötschach 3,750 .... B3
Mayrhofen 3,174 .... A3
Melk 5,108 .... C3
Mistelbach an der Zaya 6,306 .... D2
Mittersill 4,361 .... B3
Mödling 18,712 .... D2
Mondsee 2,141 .... B3
Murau 2,710 .... C3
Mürzzuschlag 11,564 .... C3
Neuberg an der Mürz 2,183 .... C3
Neumarkt am Wallersee 3,267 .... B3
Neunkirchen 10,922 .... D3
Neusiedl am See 3,999 .... D3
Neustift im Stubaital 2,789 .... A3
Ober Grafendorf 4,109 .... C2
Oberndorf bei Salzburg 3,293 .... B3
Obervellach 2,420 .... C3
Oberwart 5,661 .... D3
Paternion 5,805 .... C3
Perg 4,872 .... C2
Peuerbach 2,161 .... C2
Pfunds 2,043 .... A3
Pinkafeld 4,610 .... C3
Pochlarn 3,199 .... C2
Pörtschach am
  Wörthersee 2,511 .... C3
Poysdorf 5,774 .... D2
Pregarten 3,249 .... C2
Raabs an der Thaya 4,194 .... C2
Radenthein 6,847 .... C3
Radkersburg 2,000 .... C3
Radstadt 3,585 .... B3
Rankweil 8,440 .... A3
Rechnitz 3,412 .... D3
Reichenau an der Rax 4,053 .... C3
Retz 4,780 .... C2
Ried im Innkreis 10,534 .... B2
Rottenmann 4,781 .... C3
Saalfelden am Steinernen
  Meer 10,172 .... B3
Salzburg 122,100 .... B3
Salzburg* 213,430 .... B3
Sankt Aegyd am Neuwalde 3,165 .... C3
Sankt Anton am Arlberg 2,286 .... A3
Sankt Michael in Tirol 5,942 .... B3
Sankt Michael in Lungau 2,839 .... B3
Sankt Michael i.
  Obersteiermark 3,717 .... C3
Sankt Michael im Lungau 2,839 .... B3
Sankt Paul im Lavanttal 6,721 .... C3
Sankt Pölten 43,300 .... C2

Sankt Valentin 8,715 .... C2
Sankt Veit an der Glan 11,047 .... C3
Sankt Wolfgang im
  Salzkammergut 2,746 .... B3
Schärding 5,874 .... B2
Scheibbs 4,419 .... C3
Schladming 3,460 .... B3
Schrems 3,393 .... C2
Schruns 3,607 .... A3
Schwanenstadt 3,616 .... B3
Schwaz 10,253 .... A3
Schwechat 14,997 .... D2
Schwertberg 3,881 .... C2
Sierning 8,162 .... C2
Sillian 1,988 .... B3
Solbad Hall in Tirol 12,335 .... A3
Spital am Pyhrn 2,315 .... C3
Spittal an der Drau 13,690 .... C3
Steinach 2,698 .... A3
Steyr 40,578 .... C2
Stockerau 12,634 .... D2
Strassburg 2,850 .... C3
Tamsweg 5,060 .... B3
Telfs 5,060 .... A3
Ternitz 10,287 .... D3
Traiskirchen 8,878 .... C2
Traun 20,843 .... C2
Trieben 4,639 .... C3
Trofaiach 8,731 .... C3
Tulln 7,705 .... C2
Velden am Wörthersee 7,306 .... C3
Vienna (cap.) 1,700,000 .... D2
Vienna* 1,858,700 .... D2
Villach 50,979 .... C3
Vöcklabruck 10,627 .... B3
Voitsberg 11,094 .... C3
Völkermarkt 11,262 .... C3
Vordernberg 2,508 .... C3
Waidhofen an der Thaya 4,200 .... C2
Waidhofen an der Ybbs 5,218 .... C3
Weitensfeld-Flattnitz 5,206 .... C3
Weitra 3,250 .... C2
Weiz 8,241 .... C3
Wels 47,279 .... C2
Weyer Markt 2,518 .... C3
Wien (Vienna) (cap.) 1,700,000 .... D2
Wiener Neustadt 34,774 .... D3
Wildon 2,002 .... C3
Wilhelmsburg 6,307 .... C2
Wolfsberg 31,176 .... C3
Wörgl 7,811 .... A3
Ybbs an der Donau 6,422 .... C2

Zams 3,120 .... A3
Zell am See 7,456 .... B3
Zell am Ziller 1,882 .... A3
Zeltweg 8,431 .... C3
Zirl 4,157 .... A3
Zistersdorf 3,412 .... D2
Zwettl-Niederösterreich 11,624 .... C2

OTHER FEATURES

Allgäu Alps (mts.) A3
Bavarian Alps (mts.) A3
Bodensee (Constance) (lake) A3
Brenner (pass) A3
Carnic Alps (mts.) B3
Constance (lake) A3
Danube (riv.) C2
Donau (Danube) (riv.) C2
Drau (riv.) C3
Enns (riv.) B3
Grossglockner (mt.) B3
Hohe Tauern (range) B3
Inn (riv.) B2
Karawanken (range) C3
March (riv.) D2
Mühlviertel (reg.) C2
Mur (riv.) C3
Neusiedler See (lake) D3
Niedere Tauern (range) C3
Ötztal Alps (mts.) A3
Raab (riv.) C3
Rhine (riv.) A3
Salzach (riv.) B3
Salzkammergut (reg.) B3
Semmering (pass) C3
Thaya (riv.) C2
Traun (riv.) C2
Wildspitze (mt.) A3
Zugspitze (mt.) A3

CZECHOSLOVAKIA

REPUBLICS

Czech Socialist Rep. 9,964,338 .... B1
Slovak Socialist Rep. 4,670,409 ...... E2

REGIONS

Bratislava (city) 333,000 .... D2
Jihočesky 662,002 .... C2
Jihomoravsky 1,966,850 .... D2
Praha (city) 1,161,200 .... C1

Severočeský 1,122,035 .... C1
Severomoravsky 1,849,286 .... D2
Středočesky 1,193,041 .... C1
Stredoslovensky 1,436,351 .... E2
Vychodočesky 1,214,581 .... C1
Vychodoslovensky 1,298,481 .... E2
Západočesky 865,094 .... B2
Západoslovensky 1,610,542 .... D2

CITIES and TOWNS

Aš 120,000 .... B1
Austerlitz (Slavkov) D2
Bánovce nad Bebravou 11,400 .... D2
Banská Bystrica 53,000 .... E2
Banská Štiavnica 7,486 .... F2
Bardejov 17,400 .... F2
Benešov 11,100 .... C1
Beroun 17,600 .... D1
Bílina 13,800 .... B1
Blansko 13,800 .... D2
Boskovice 8,531 .... D2
Brandys nad Labem-Stará
  Boleslav 333,000 .... C1
Bratislava 333,000 .... D2
Břeclav 21,100 .... D2
Brezno 14,800 .... E2
Brno 335,700 .... D2
Broumov 7,782 .... D1
Bruntál 12,300 .... D2
Bystrice nad
  Pernstejnem 5,101 .... D2
Bystrice pod
  Hostynem 6,681 .... D2
Bytča 6,922 .... E2

Čadca 16,800 .... E2
Čálovo 6,591 .... D2
Časlav 10,200 .... C1
Česká Lípa 18,600 .... C1
Česká Třebová 14,700 .... D1
České Budějovice 80,800 .... C1
Český Brod 6,640 .... C1
Český Krumlov 12,000 .... C2
Český Tešín 17,200 .... E2
Cheb 27,000 .... B1
Chocen 8,198 .... C1
Chodov 14,400 .... B1
Chomutov 44,200 .... B1
Chotěboř 6,692 .... C1
Chrudim 18,800 .... C1
Cierny Balog 6,435 .... E2
Děčín 46,500 .... C1
Detva 13,100 .... E2
Dobruška 5,779 .... D1
Dolny Kubín 9,900 .... E2
Domažlice 9,100 .... B2
Dubnica nad Vahom 11,300 .... D2
Duchcov 9,712 .... B1
Dunajská Streda 13,000 .... D3
Dvor nad Žitavou 5,847 .... D2
Dvůr Králové nad
  Labem 16,800 .... C1
Falknov (Sokolov) 23,900 .... B1
Fil'akovo 7,822 .... E2
Frenštat pod
  Radhoštem 8,516 .... E2
Frydek-Mistek 43,800 .... E2
Frydlant v.
  Čechách 5,948 .... E2

Frydlant nad
  Ostravicí 6,250 .... E2
Galanta 12,300 .... D2
Gottwaldov 84,300 .... D2
Handlová 16,200 .... E2
Havřov 85,000 .... E2
Havlíčkuv Brod 19,200 .... C1
Hlinsko 8,890 .... C1
Hodonín 15,200 .... D2
Hlučín 15,300 .... E2
Hnušt'a-Likier E2
Holešov 9,091 .... D2
Holič 7,602 .... D2
Holice 6,151 .... C1
Horažd'ovice B2
Hořice v
  Podkrkonoší 7,715 .... C1
Horná Štubna E2
Horní Benešov D2
Horní Libina D1
Hořovice 5,665 .... C1
Horšovsky Tyn B2
Hostinné C1
Hradec Králové 85,600 .... C1
Hranice 13,300 .... D2
Hrinova 7,800 .... E2
Hronov 9,767 .... D1
Hrušovany D2
Humenné 22,200 .... F2
Humpolec 7,810 .... C2
Hurbanovo E3
Hustopeče D2
Ilava E2
Ivančice 7,314 .... D2

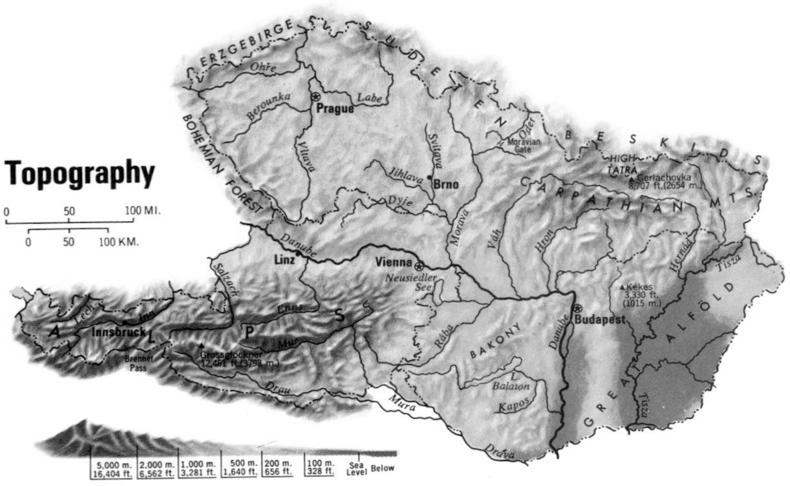

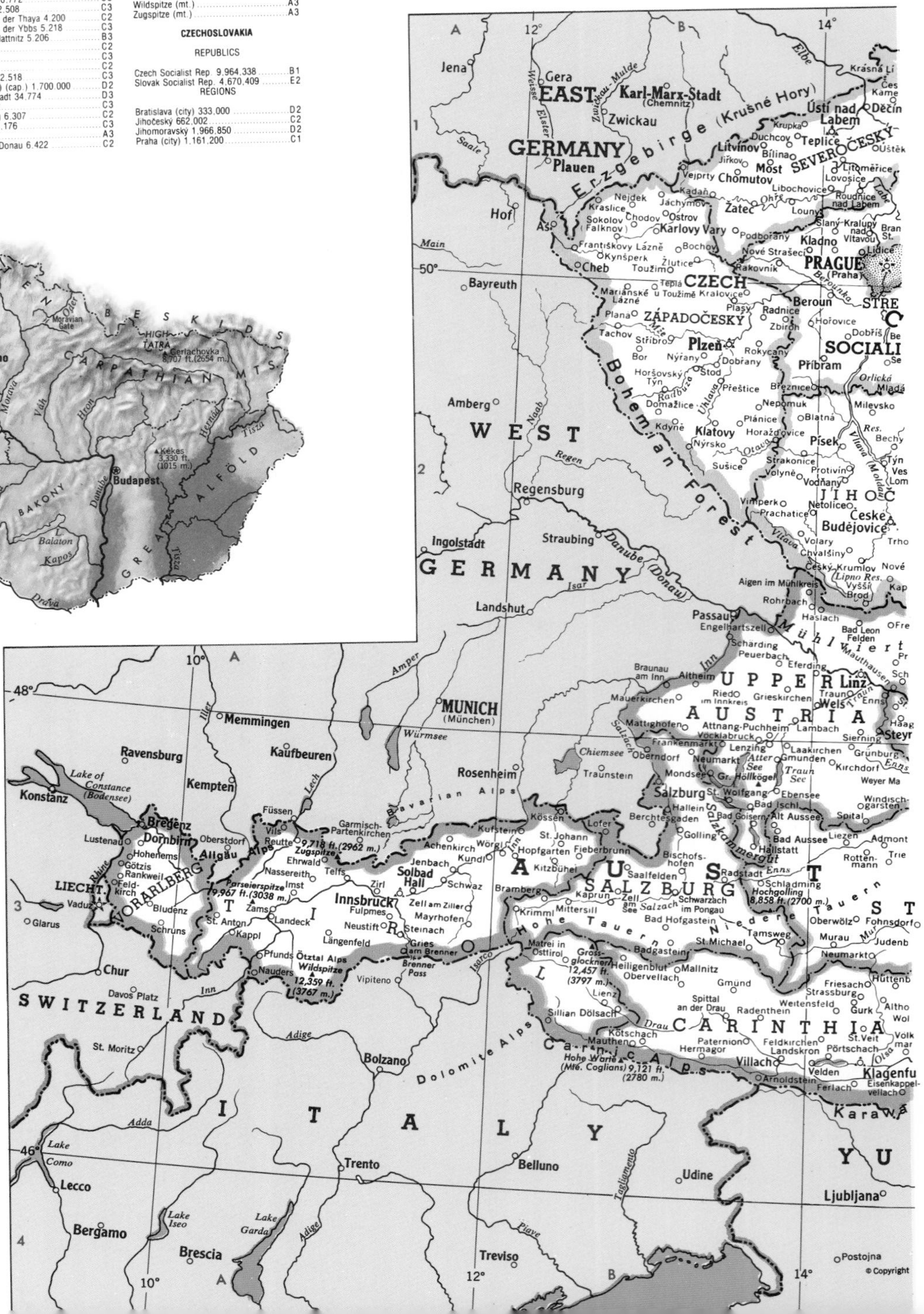

AREA 32,375 sq. mi. (83,851 sq. km.)
POPULATION 7,507,000
CAPITAL Vienna
LARGEST CITY Vienna
HIGHEST POINT Grossglockner
12,457 ft. (3,797 m.)
MONETARY UNIT schilling
MAJOR LANGUAGE German
MAJOR RELIGION Roman Catholicism

AREA 49,373 sq. mi. (127,876 sq. km.)
POPULATION 15,276,799
CAPITAL Prague
LARGEST CITY Prague
HIGHEST POINT Gerlachovka 8,707 ft.
(2,654 m.)
MONETARY UNIT koruna
MAJOR LANGUAGES Czech, Slovak
MAJOR RELIGIONS Roman Catholicism,
Protestantism

AREA 35,919 sq. mi. (93,030 sq. km.)
POPULATION 10,709,536
CAPITAL Budapest
LARGEST CITY Budapest
HIGHEST POINT Kékes 3,330 ft.
(1,015 m.)
MONETARY UNIT forint
MAJOR LANGUAGE Hungarian
MAJOR RELIGIONS Roman Catholicism,
Protestantism

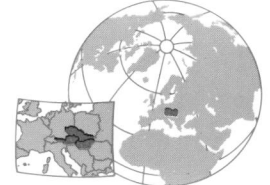

AUSTRIA

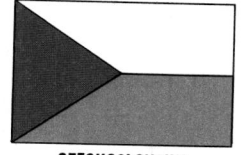

CZECHOSLOVAKIA

HUNGARY

Austria, Czechoslovakia and Hungary

CONIC PROJECTION

SCALE OF MILES
0   10   20   40   60   80

SCALE OF KILOMETERS
0   10   20   40   60   80

Capitals of Countries ☆   International Boundaries
Republic Capital ◉   Internal Boundaries
Administrative Centers △   Canals

Czechoslovakia is divided into two socialist republics, Czech (capital-Prague) and Slovak (capital-Bratislava), ten regions (Kraj) and the independent cities of Prague and Bratislava.

HAMMOND INCORPORATED, Maplewood, N.J.   Longitude East of Greenwich

Jablonec nad Nisou 36,300 C1
Jablonica D2
Jablunkov 9,405 E2
Jáchymov B1
Jakubany F2
Jaroměř 11,600 C1
Jelšava F2
Jemnice C2
Jeseník 10,900 D1
Jesenské F2
Jevíčko D2
Jičín 13,200 C1
Jihlava 44,500 C2
Jilemnice C1
Jindřichův Hradec 15,700 C2
Jiřkov 11,400 B1
Kadaň 18,100 B1
Kamenice C2
Kaplice C2
Karlovy Vary 43,300 B1
Karviná 79,100 E2
Kdyně B2
Kežmarok 11,000 F2
Kladno 61,200 B1
Klatovy 18,500 B2
Kojetín 5,852 D2
Kokava nad Rimavicou 5,391 E2
Kolárovo 10,500 D3
Kolín 29,100 C1
Komárno 28,200 D3
Košice 169,100 F2
Kostelec nad Orlicí 5,575 D1
Kráľovský Chlmec 5,329 G2
Kralupy nad Vltavou 16,900 C1
Kraslice 6,733 B1
Kremnica 5,941 E2
Krnov 25,000 D1
Kroměříž 23,200 D2
Krompachy 6,332 F2
Krupina 6,627 E2
Krupka 8,301 B1
Kutná Hora 19,200 C2
Kyjov 10,700 D2
Kynšperk 5,524 B1
Kysucké Nové Mesto 11,700 E2
Lanškroun 8,683 D2
Levice 19,000 E2
Levoča 10,100 F2
Libáň C1
Liberec 75,600 C1
Lidice C1
Lipník nad Bečvou 7,358 D2
Liptovský Mikuláš 19,400 E2
Litoměřice 19,700 C1
Litomyšl 8,112 D2
Litovel 5,805 D2
Litvínov 23,300 B1
Lomnice C2
Louny 15,200 B1
Lovosice 9,323 C1
L'ubica F2
Lučenec 23,300 E2
Lysá nad Labem 9,920 C1
Malacky 13,200 D2
Mariánské Lázně 14,600 B2
Martin 47,800 E2
Medzilaborce F2
Mělník 17,800 C1
Michalovce 23,600 G2
Mikulov 6,267 D2
Milevsko 7,091 C2
Mimoň 6,773 C1
Mladá Boleslav 36,900 C1
Mladá Vožice C2
Mnichovo Hradiště 5,239 C1
Modra 7,219 D2
Modrý Kameň 6,200 E2
Mohelnice 6,050 D2
Moldava nad Bodvou 5,397 F2
Moravská Třebová 9,052 D2
Moravské Budějovice 5,576 D2
Most 59,400 B1
Myjava 6,657 D2
Náchod 19,300 D1
Námestovo E2
Neded D2
Nejdek 8,187 B1
Nepomuk B2
Nesvady 5,453 E3
Netolice C2
Nitra 50,000 E2
Nová Baňa 6,218 E2
Nová Bystrica E2
Nová Bystřice C2
Nové Hrady C2
Nové Město na Moravě 6,581 D2
Nové Město nad Váhom 15,900 D2
Nové Strašecí B1
Nové Zámky 27,300 D3
Nový Bohumín 16,700 E2
Nový Bor 7,621 C1
Nový Bydžov 6,824 C1
Nový Hrozenkov E2
Nový Jičín 21,400 E2
Nymburk 13,600 C1
Nýřany 6,204 B2
Nýrsko B2
Odry D2
Olomouc 82,800 D2
Opava 53,800 E2
Orlová 25,500 E2
Ostrava 293,500 E2
Ostrov 18,200 B1
Pardubice 78,500 C1
Partizánske 15,100 E2
Pelhřimov 11,900 C2
Pezinok 13,100 D2
Piešťany 25,400 D2
Písek 25,100 C2
Plzeň 155,000 B2
Počátky C2
Podbořany B1
Poděbrady 13,400 C1
Pohořelice D2
Polička 6,529 D2
Polná C2
Polomka E2
Poprad 25,800 F2
Považská Bystrica 19,300 E2
Prachatice 7,900 B2
Prague (Praha) (cap.) 1,161,200 C1
Přelouč 6,251 C1
Přerov 43,500 D2
Prešov 61,000 F2
Přeštice B2
Příbor 7,726 E2
Příbram 31,300 B2
Prievidza 30,900 E2
Prostějov 44,200 D2
Protivín C2
Púchov 9,306 E2
Radnice B2
Rajec E2
Rakovník 14,200 B1
Revúca 5,901 F2
Říčany u Prahy 8,407 C2
Rimavská Sobota 5,800 E2
Rokycany 12,800 B2
Rokytnice nad Jizerou C1
Rosice D2
Roudnice nad Labem 11,800 C1
Rožňava 12,400 F2
Rožnov pod Radhoštěm 11,600 E2
Rumburk C1
Ružomberok 22,600 E2
Rychnov nad Kněžnou 7,500 D1
Rýmařov 7,522 D2
Sabinov 5,473 F2
Šafárikovo F2
Šahy 5,049 E2
Šaľa 15,200 D2
Samorín 8,287 D2
Sečovce 5,744 F2
Sedlčany C2
Semily 8,200 C1
Senec 8,544 D2
Senica 12,300 D2
Sereď 12,500 D2
Skalica 11,100 D2
Skuteč D2
Sládečkovce 5,598 D2
Slaný 13,200 C1
Slavkov D2
Snina 10,900 G2
Soběslav 6,140 C2
Sobotka C1
Sobrance G2
Sokolov 23,900 B1
Spišská Belá F2
Spišská Nová Ves 26,100 F2
Stará L'ubovňa 5,800 F2
Staré Město 6,293 D2
Šternberk 13,700 D2
Stod B2
Strakonice 19,000 B2
Strážnice 5,482 D2
Stříbro B2
Stropkov 5,645 F2
Studénka 9,744 D2
Štúrovo 8,287 E3
Šumperk 25,900 D1
Šurany 6,693 E2
Sušice 10,300 B2
Svárov C1
Svidník 4,600 F2
Svitavy 15,000 D2
Tábor 28,100 C2
Tachov 11,400 B2
Telč 5,285 C2
Teplice 52,300 B1
Tišnov 8,263 D2
Topoľčany 17,500 D2
Třebíč 23,900 C2
Trebišov 13,700 F2
Třeboň 6,068 C2
Trenčín 38,800 E2
Třešť 5,053 C2
Třinec 32,000 E2
Trnava 48,600 D2
Trutnov 24,500 D1
Turnov 13,600 C1
Turzovka 6,107 E2
Uherské Hradiště 32,100 D2
Uherský Brod 12,800 D2
Uničov 10,800 D2
Úpice 6,323 C1
Ústí nad Labem 74,900 C1
Ústí nad Orlicí 13,700 D2
Valašské Meziříčí 19,400 D2
Varnsdorf 14,700 C1
Važec E2
Vejprty B1
Velká Bíteš D2
Velká Bystřice D2
Veľké Kapušany G2
Velké Meziříčí 7,590 D2
Veľké Rovné E2
Veselí nad Lužnicí C2
Veselí nad Moravou 11,500 D2
Vimperk 5,749 B2
Vítkov 5,138 D2
Vizovice D2
Vlašim 8,873 C2
Vodňany 5,620 C2
Vojnice E3
Volary B2
Volyně B2
Votice C2
Vráble E2
Vracov D2
Vranov nad Teplou 14,700 F2
Vrbno pod Pradědem 5,594 D1
Vrbovce D1
Vrbové D2
Vrchlabí 11,700 C1
Vrútky 5,756 E2
Vsetín 24,100 D2
Vyškov 15,100 D2
Vysoké Mýto 8,830 D2
Vysoké Tatry F2
Vyšší Brod C2
Zábřeh 11,300 D2
Žamberk 5,040 D1
Žatec 17,400 B1
Zázrivá E2
Zbiroh B2
Zborov F2
Žďár nad Sázavou 17,800 C2
Želiezovce 5,478 E2
Žiar nad Hronom 14,800 E2
Židlochovice D2
Žilina 56,000 E2
Zlaté Moravce 10,300 E2
Zlín (Gottwaldov) 84,300 D2
Žlutice B1
Znojmo 28,500 D2
Zvolen 29,000 E2

OTHER FEATURES

Berounka (riv.) C2
Beskids, East (mts.) F1
Beskids, West (mts.) E2
Bohemian (for.) B2
Bohemian-Moravian Heights (hills) C2
Danube (riv.) C2
Dunajec (riv.) F2
Dyje (riv.) D2
Erzgebirge (mts.) B1
Gerlachovka (mt.) E2
Hornád (riv.) F2
Hron (riv.) E2
Ipeľ (riv.) E2
Jablunka (pass) E2
Jeseníky (mts.) D1
Jihlava (riv.) D2
Krušné Hory (Erzgebirge) (mts.) B1
Labe (riv.) C1
Lipno (res.) C2
Lužnice (riv.) C2
Moldau (Vltava) (riv.) C2
Morava (riv.) D2
Nitra (riv.) E2
Oder (Odra) (riv.) D2
Ohře (riv.) B1
Ondava (riv.) F2
Orava (riv.) E2
Orlická (res.) C2
Sázava (riv.) C2
Slovenské Rudohorie (mts.) E2
Sudeten (mts.) C1
Svitava (riv.) D2
Svratka (riv.) D2
Tatra, High (mts.) E2
Torysa (riv.) F2
Úhlava (riv.) B2
Váh (riv.) D2
Vltava (riv.) C2
White Carpathians (mts.) E2

HUNGARY

COUNTIES

Bács-Kiskun 568,532 E3
Baranya 434,030 E4
Békés 436,987 F3
Borsod-Abaúj-Zemplén 808,924 F2
Budapest (city) 2,060,170 E3
Csongrád 456,862 F3
Fejér 421,568 E3
Győr-Sopron 428,476 D3
Hajdú-Bihar 552,417 F3
Heves 350,874 F3
Komárom 321,579 E3
Nógrád 239,907 E3
Pest 973,486 E3
Somogy 360,308 D3
Szabolcs-Szatmár 593,746 G3
Szolnok 446,379 F3
Tolna 266,414 E3
Vas 285,527 D3
Veszprém 386,740 D3
Zala 316,610 D3

CITIES and TOWNS

Aba 4,271 E3
Abádszalók 6,386 F3
Abaújszántó 4,209 F2
Abony 15,624 E3
Ács 8,423 E3
Ajka 29,601 D3
Albertirsa 11,252 E3
Alsózsolca 5,045 F2
Arló 4,203 F2
Aszód 6,218 E3
Bácsalmás 9,025 E3
Badacsonytomaj 2,933 D3
Baja 38,456 E3
Baktalórántháza 3,736 G2
Balassagyarmat 18,534 E2
Balatonfüred 12,599 D3
Balkány 7,667 G3
Balmazújváros 17,371 F3
Barcs 11,448 D4
Bátaszék 7,274 E3
Battonya 9,324 F3
Békés 22,287 F3
Békéscsaba 67,266 F3
Berettyóújfalu 16,406 F3
Berzence 3,406 D3
Bicske 10,720 E3
Biharkeresztes 4,788 F3
Biharnagybajom 4,093 F3
Böhönye 3,215 D3
Bonyhád 14,841 E3
Budafok 40,623 E3
Budaörs 13,958 E3
Budakeszi 10,429 E3
Budapest (cap.) 2,060,170 E3
Bugak 4,989 E3
Cegléd 40,567 E3
Celldömölk 12,533 D3
Cigánd 4,767 F2
Csabrendek 3,045 D3
Csákvár 5,238 E3
Csanádpalota 4,642 F3
Csenger 4,792 G3
Csepel 71,693 E3
Csepreg 4,079 D3
Csongrád 22,202 E3
Csorna 12,131 D3
Csorvás 6,826 F3
Csurgó 5,463 D3
Dabas 13,075 E3
Debrecen 192,484 F3
Derecske 9,579 F3
Dévaványa 11,208 F3
Devecser 5,482 D3
Dombóvár 19,917 E3
Dombrád 6,328 F2
Dömsöd 6,545 E3
Dorog 10,754 E3
Dunaföldvár 10,318 E3
Dunaharaszti 15,788 E3
Dunakeszi 25,187 E3
Dunaszekcső 2,999 E3
Dunaújváros 60,694 E3
Dunavecse 4,521 E3
Edelény 9,559 F2
Eger 61,283 F3
Egyek 7,956 F3
Elek 6,032 F3
Enes 2,565 F2
Endrőd 8,136 F3
Enying 7,518 E3
Érd 41,210 E3
Erdőtelek 4,250 F3
Esztergom 30,476 E3
Fadd 4,805 E3
Fegyvernek 8,421 F3
Fehérgyarmat 6,729 G3
Földeák 3,855 F3
Földes 5,293 F2
Fonyód 3,957 D3
Füzesabony 6,965 F3
Füzesgyarmat 7,097 F3
Gödöllő 28,057 E3
Gönc 2,875 F2
Gyoma 10,392 F3
Gyöngyös 36,927 E3
Gyönk 2,507 E3
Győr 123,618 D3
Gyula 34,514 F3
Hajdúböszörmény 32,145 F3
Hajdúdorog 10,118 F3
Hajdúhadház 13,626 F3
Hajdúnánás 18,146 F3
Hajdúsámson 7,492 F3
Hajdúszoboszló 23,374 F3
Hajós 5,113 E3
Hatvan 24,790 E3
Heves 10,943 F3
Hódmezővásárhely 54,481 F3
Hőgyész 3,534 E3
Ibrány 7,037 F2
Izsák 7,686 E3
Izsófalva 6,816 F2
Jánoshalma 12,534 E3
Jánosháza 3,274 D3
Jászapáti 10,424 E3
Jászárokszállás 10,139 E3
Jászberény 31,347 E3
Jászfényszaru 6,869 E3
Jászkarajenő 4,101 E3
Jászkisér 6,816 F3
Jászladány 7,823 F3
Kaba 6,654 F2
Kalocsa 18,613 E3
Kaposvár 72,330 D3
Kapuvár 11,243 D3
Karád 2,754 D3
Karcag 25,264 F3
Kazincbarcika 37,481 F2
Kecel 10,493 E3
Kecskemét 91,929 E3
Kemecse 4,583 F2
Keszthely 21,671 D3
Kétegyháza 4,728 F3
Kisbér 4,562 D3
Kiskőrös 15,499 E3
Kiskunfélegyháza 35,339 E3
Kiskunhalas 30,552 E3
Kiskunmajsa 14,439 E3
Kispest 65,106 E3
Kistelek 8,544 E3
Kisterenye 6,844 E2
Kisújszállás 13,699 F3
Kisvárda 17,828 G2
Komádi 8,765 F3
Komárom 19,955 E3
Komló 30,301 E3
Kondoros 7,319 F3
Körmend 11,787 D3
Körösladány 6,565 F3
Kőszeg 12,705 D3
Kunágota 4,622 F3
Kunhegyes 10,116 F3
Kunmadaras 7,343 F3
Kunszentmárton 11,103 F3
Kunszentmiklós 7,952 E3
Lajosmizse 12,872 E3
Lébénymiklós 6,190 D3
Lengyeltóti 3,389 D3
Leninváros 18,667 F3
Lenti 8,106 D3
Létavértes 9,106 G3
Letenye 4,395 D3
Lökösháza 2,514 F3
Lőrinci 10,679 E3
Madaras 4,519 E3
Makó 29,943 F3
Mándok 5,093 G2
Marcali 12,485 D3
Mátészalka 17,709 G3
Mélykút 7,640 E3
Mérk 3,211 G3
Mezőberény 12,702 F3
Mezőcsát 6,729 F3
Mezőfalva 5,008 E3
Mezőhegyes 8,631 F3
Mezőkovácsháza 7,473 F3
Mezőkövesd 18,435 F3
Mezőszilas 2,792 E3
Mezőtúr 22,018 F3
Mindszent 8,730 F3
Miskolc 206,727 F2
Mohács 21,385 E4
Monor 16,838 E3
Mór 12,066 E3
Mosonmagyaróvár 29,732 D3
Nádudvar 9,447 F3
Nagyatád 12,946 D3
Nagybajom 4,402 D3
Nagyecsed 8,225 G3
Nagyhalász 6,437 F2
Nagykálló 11,282 F3
Nagykanizsa 48,494 D3
Nagykáta 11,922 E3
Nagykőrös 27,900 E3
Nagyszénás 7,124 F3
Nyírábrány 4,509 G3
Nyíradony 7,146 G3
Nyírbátor 13,388 G3
Nyíregyháza 108,156 F3
Nyírmada 4,744 F2
Örkény 5,013 E3
Orosháza 36,243 F3
Oroszlány 20,604 E3
Ózd 48,521 F2
Pacsa 1,984 D3
Paks 19,514 E3
Pannonhalma 3,731 D3
Pápa 32,202 D3
Pásztó 7,962 E3
Pécs 168,788 E3
Pécsvárad 3,672 E3
Pétervására 2,753 F3
Pilis 9,055 E3
Pilisvörösvár 10,217 E3
Polgár 9,429 F3
Polgárdi 5,767 E3
Püspökladány 15,730 F3
Pusztaszabolcs 5,794 E3
Putnok 7,103 F2
Ráckeve 7,534 E3
Rajka 2,448 D3
Rakamaz 5,407 F2
Rákospalota 60,983 E3
Répcelak 1,997 D3
Ricse 2,992 G2
Sajószentpéter 13,992 F2
Salgótarján 49,320 E2
Sándorfalva 5,949 F3
Sárbogárd 11,178 E3
Sarkad 11,937 F3
Sárospatak 15,316 F2
Sárvár 15,126 D3
Sátoraljaújhely 19,252 F2
Sellye 2,804 D4
Siklós 10,567 E4
Simontornya 4,892 E3
Siófok 20,084 E3
Solt 6,911 E3
Soltvadkert 7,934 E3
Sopron 53,930 D3
Sükösd 4,430 E3
Sümeg 6,229 D3
Szabadszállás 8,223 E3
Szarvas 20,598 F3
Szécsény 5,690 E2
Százhalombatta 13,963 E3
Szeged 171,342 E3
Szeghalom 9,736 F3
Szegvár 6,395 F3
Székesfehérvár 103,197 E3
Szekszárd 34,592 E3
Szendrő 4,098 F2
Szentendre 16,844 E3
Szentes 35,326 F3
Szentgotthárd 5,837 D3
Szentlőrinc 3,926 E3
Szerencs 8,612 F2
Szigetvár 12,114 D3
Szikszó 6,419 F2
Szil 2,073 D3
Szolnok 75,203 F3
Szombathely 82,830 D3
Tab 3,922 E3
Tamási 7,602 E3
Tápiószele 5,575 E3
Tapolca 17,161 D3
Tarpa 3,436 G2
Tata 24,114 E3
Tatabánya 75,942 E3
Tét 4,441 D3
Tiszacsege 6,263 F3
Tiszaföldvár 12,560 F3
Tiszafüred 12,259 F3
Tiszakécske 12,378 E3
Tiszalök 6,230 F2
Tiszavasvári 13,292 F3
Tokaj 4,845 F2
Tolna 8,997 E3
Tompa 5,365 E3
Törökszentmiklós 25,551 F3
Tótkomlós 8,803 F3
Tura 8,235 E3
Túrkeve 11,393 F3
Újfehértó 14,412 F3
Újpest 80,384 E3
Újszász 7,098 F2
Vác 34,837 E3
Vál 2,488 E3
Vámospércs 5,213 F3
Várpalota 28,293 E3
Vásárosnamény 8,637 G2
Vasvár 4,275 D3
Vecsés 19,193 E3
Velence 3,463 E3
Véménd 2,293 E3
Verpelét 4,622 F2
Veszprém 54,898 D3
Vésztő 9,815 F3
Villány 2,764 E4
Záhony 3,049 G2
Zalaegerszeg 39,671 D3
Zalaszentgrót 5,346 D3
Zirc 5,980 D3

OTHER FEATURES

Bakony (mts.) D3
Balaton (lake) D3
Berettyó (riv.) F3
Bükk (mts.) F2
Csepelsziget (isl.) E3
Danube (riv.) E3
Dráva (riv.) D3
Duna (Danube) (riv.) E3
Fertő tó (Neusiedler See) (lake) D3
Great Alföld (plain) F3
Hernád (riv.) F2
Kapos (riv.) D3
Kékes (mt.) E3
Körös (riv.) F3
Maros (riv.) F3
Mátra (mts.) E3
Mecsek (mts.) D3
Mura (riv.) D3
Rába (riv.) D3
Sajó (riv.) F2
Sárviz csatorna (canal) E3
Sió csatorna (canal) E3
Szentendreisziget (isl.) E3
Tisza (riv.) F3
Zala (riv.) D3

*City and suburbs.
†Population of Austrian cities are communes.

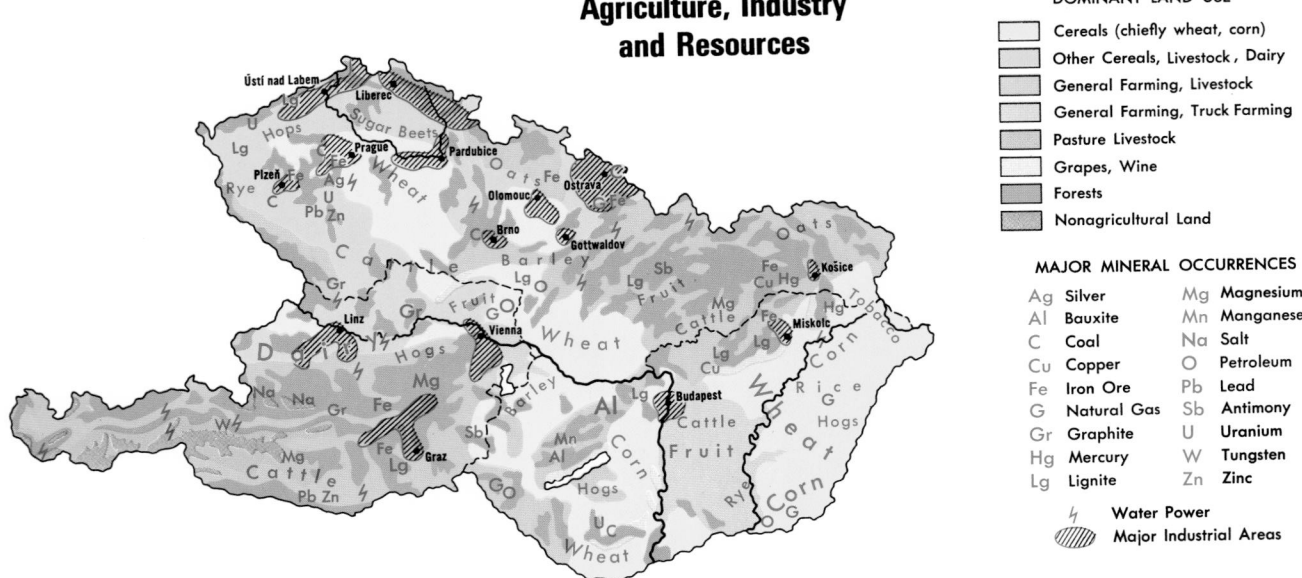

Agriculture, Industry and Resources

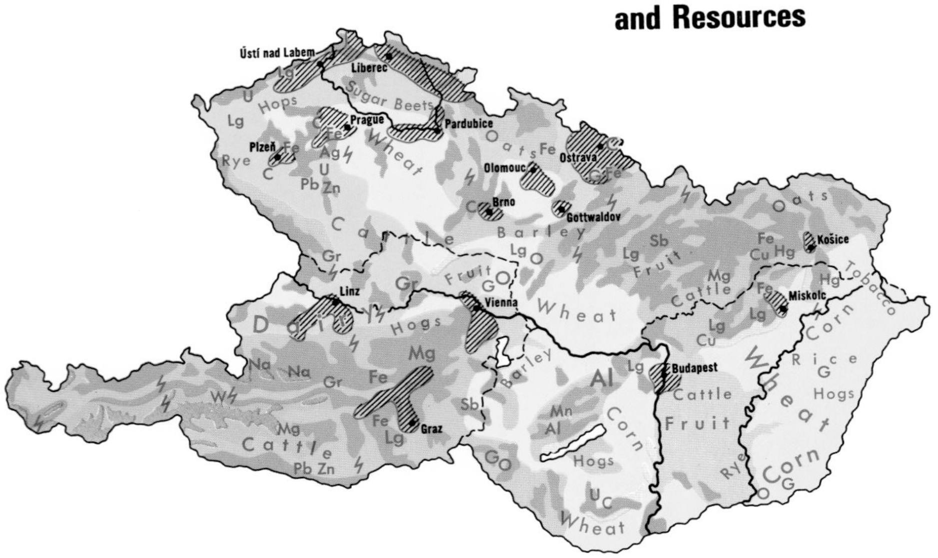

DOMINANT LAND USE

- Cereals (chiefly wheat, corn)
- Other Cereals, Livestock, Dairy
- General Farming, Livestock
- General Farming, Truck Farming
- Pasture Livestock
- Grapes, Wine
- Forests
- Nonagricultural Land

MAJOR MINERAL OCCURRENCES

Ag	Silver	Mg	Magnesium
Al	Bauxite	Mn	Manganese
C	Coal	Na	Salt
Cu	Copper	O	Petroleum
Fe	Iron Ore	Pb	Lead
G	Natural Gas	Sb	Antimony
Gr	Graphite	U	Uranium
Hg	Mercury	W	Tungsten
Lg	Lignite	Zn	Zinc

- Water Power
- Major Industrial Areas

YUGOSLAVIA

AREA 98,766 sq. mi. (255,804 sq. km.)
POPULATION 22,471,000
CAPITAL Belgrade
LARGEST CITY Belgrade
HIGHEST POINT Triglav 9,393 ft. (2,863 m.)
MONETARY UNIT Yugoslav dinar
MAJOR LANGUAGES Serbo-Croatian, Slovenian, Macedonian, Montenegrin, Albanian
MAJOR RELIGIONS Eastern Orthodoxy, Roman Catholicism, Islam

ALBANIA

AREA 11,100 sq. mi. (28,749 sq. km.)
POPULATION 2,590,600
CAPITAL Tiranë
LARGEST CITY Tiranë
HIGHEST POINT Korab 9,026 ft. (2,751 m.)
MONETARY UNIT lek
MAJOR LANGUAGE Albanian
MAJOR RELIGIONS Islam, Eastern Orthodoxy, Roman Catholicism

ROMANIA

AREA 91,699 sq. mi. (237,500 sq. km.)
POPULATION 22,048,305
CAPITAL Bucharest
LARGEST CITY Bucharest
HIGHEST POINT Moldoveanul 8,343 ft. (2,543 m.)
MONETARY UNIT leu
MAJOR LANGUAGES Romanian, Hungarian
MAJOR RELIGION Eastern Orthodox

BULGARIA

AREA 42,823 sq. mi. (110,912 sq. km.)
POPULATION 8,862,000
CAPITAL Sofia
LARGEST CITY Sofia
HIGHEST POINT Musala 9,597 ft. (2,925 m.)
MONETARY UNIT lev
MAJOR LANGUAGE Bulgarian
MAJOR RELIGION Eastern Orthodoxy

GREECE

AREA 50,944 sq. mi. (131,945 sq. km.)
POPULATION 9,599,000
CAPITAL Athens
LARGEST CITY Athens
HIGHEST POINT Olympus 9,570 ft. (2,917 m.)
MONETARY UNIT drachma
MAJOR LANGUAGE Greek
MAJOR RELIGION Eastern (Greek) Orthodoxy

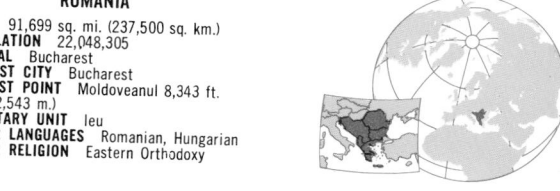

BULGARIA

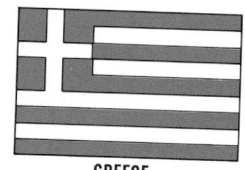

GREECE

YUGOSLAVIA

ALBANIA

ROMANIA

Agriculture, Industry and Resources

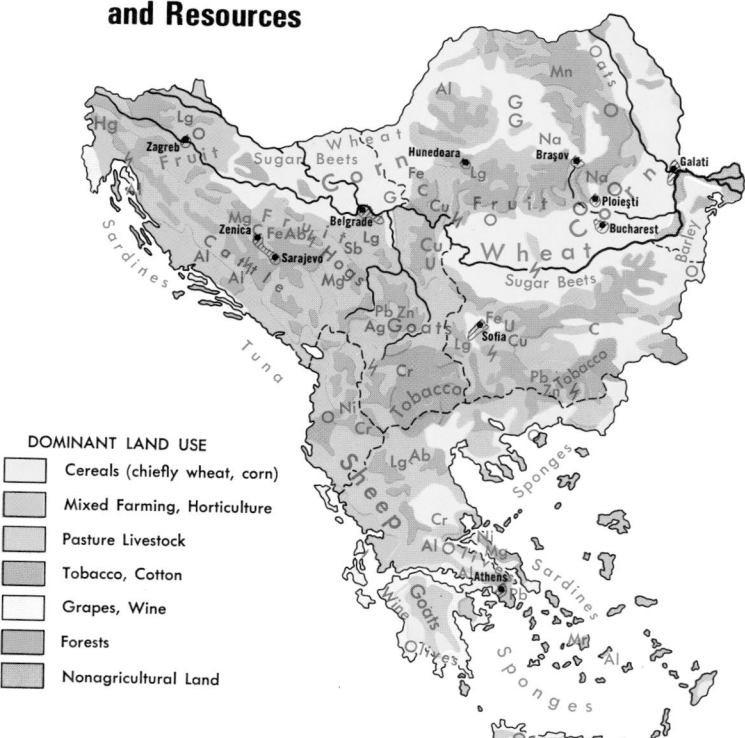

DOMINANT LAND USE

- Cereals (chiefly wheat, corn)
- Mixed Farming, Horticulture
- Pasture Livestock
- Tobacco, Cotton
- Grapes, Wine
- Forests
- Nonagricultural Land

MAJOR MINERAL OCCURRENCES

Ab	Asbestos	Mg	Magnesium
Ag	Silver	Mn	Manganese
Al	Bauxite	Mr	Marble
C	Coal	Na	Salt
Cr	Chromium	Ni	Nickel
Cu	Copper	O	Petroleum
Fe	Iron Ore	Pb	Lead
G	Natural Gas	Sb	Antimony
Hg	Mercury	U	Uranium
Lg	Lignite	Zn	Zinc

⚡ Water Power
▨ Major Industrial Areas

ALBANIA

CITIES and TOWNS

Berat 25,700	D5
Çorovode	E5
Burrel	D5
Delvinë 6,000	D6
Durrës (Durazzo) 53,800	D5
Elbasan 41,700	E5
Ersekë	E5
Fier 23,000	D5
Gjirokastër 17,100	D5
Kavajë 18,700	D5
Korçë 47,300	E5
Krujë 7,900	D5
Kuçovë (Stalin) 14,000	D5
Kukës 6,100	E4
Leskovik	E5
Lezhë	D5
Lushnjë 18,900	D5
Memaliaj	D5
Pegin	D5
Permet	D5
Peshkopi 6,600	E5
Pogradec 10,100	E5
Pukë	E4
Sarandë 8,700	D6
Shëngin	D5
Shijak 6,200	D5
Shkodër 55,300	D5
Stalin 14,000	D5
Tepelenë	D5
Tiranë (Tirana) (cap.) 171,300	E5
Vlorë 50,000	D5

OTHER FEATURES

Adriatic (sea)	B4
Drin (riv.)	E4
Korab (mt.)	E5
Ohrid (lake)	E5
Otranto (str.)	D5
Prespa (lake)	E5
Sazan (isl.)	D5
Scutari (lake)	D4
Vijosë (riv.)	D5

BULGARIA

CITIES and TOWNS

Akhtopol 938	H4
Alfatar 3,249	H4
Ardino 5,080	G5
Asenovgrad 43,049	G5
Aytos 20,967	H4
Balchik 11,070	H4
Bansko 10,011	F5
Belogradchik 6,892	F4
Berkovitsa 16,253	F4
Blagoevgrad 50,043	F5
Botevgrad 17,789	F4
Bregovo 5,567	F3
Breznik 4,699	F4
Burgas 144,449	H4
Byala 10,564	G4
Byala Slatina 15,788	F4
Chirpan 20,595	G4
Devin 7,120	G5
Dimitrovgrad 45,596	G4
Dobrich (Tolbukhin) 86,184	H4
Dryanovo 9,804	G4
Elena 7,008	G4
Elin Pelin 5,499	F4
Elkhovo 12,397	H4
Gabrovo 75,034	G4
General-Toshevo 8,928	H4
Godech 5,225	F4
Gorna Oryakhovitsa 34,157	G4
Gotse Delchev 17,015	F5
Grudovo 9,871	H4
Ikhtiman 11,482	F4
Isperan 10,500	H4
Ivaylovgrad 3,900	H5
Karapelit	H4
Karlovo 25,472	G4
Karnobat 21,480	H4
Kavarna 10,872	J4
Kazanlŭk 53,607	G4
Kharmanli 19,240	H5
Khaskovo 75,031	G5
Kotel 8,229	H4
Krumovgrad 5,211	G5
Kubrat 9,826	H4
Kula 5,667	F4
Kŭrdzhali 47,757	G5
Kyustendil 48,239	F4
Lom 30,538	F4
Lovech 43,858	G4
Lukovit 10,400	G4
Malko Tŭrnovo 4,233	H4
Maritsa 8,664	H4
Michurin 4,434	H4
Mikhaylovgrad 40,064	F4
Momchilgrad 8,185	G5
Nesebŭr 6,768	H4
Nikopol 5,563	G4
Nova Zagora 21,872	H4
Novi Pazar 15,751	H4
Omurtag 9,067	H4
Oryakhovo 14,012	F4
Panagyurishte 20,649	F4
Pazardzhik 65,577	G4
Pernik 87,432	F4
Peshtera 16,882	G4
Petrich 24,381	F5
Pirdop 8,248	G4
Pleven 107,567	G4
Plovdiv 300,242	G4
Pomorie 11,960	H4
Popina	H4
Popovo 19,428	H4
Provadiya 15,143	H4
Radomir 10,436	F4
Razgrad 42,486	H4
Razlog 13,690	F5
Rositsa	H4
Ruse 160,351	H4
Samokov 25,763	F4
Sandanski 19,003	F5
Sevlievo 24,421	G4
Shabla 4,471	J4
Shumen 83,525	H4
Silistra 58,270	H3
Simeonovgrad (Maritsa) 8,664	H4
Sliven 90,137	H4
Smolyan 29,032	G5
Smyadovo 5,020	H4
Sofia (cap.) 965,728	F4
Sozopol 3,877	H4
Stanke Dimitrov 42,034	F4
Stara Zagora 122,200	G4
Svilengrad 15,150	G5
Svishtov 29,412	G4
Teteven 12,555	G4
Tolbukhin 86,184	H4
Topolovgrad 7,230	H4
Troyan 23,692	G4
Trŭn 3,435	F4
Tŭrgovishte 38,796	H4
Tutrakan 11,447	H4
Varna 251,654	J4
Veliko Tŭrnovo 56,497	G4
Vidin 53,030	F4
Vratsa 61,265	F4
Yambol 75,861	H4
Zimnitsa	H4
Zlatograd 7,732	G5

OTHER FEATURES

Balkan (mts.)	G4
Black (sea)	J4
Danube (riv.)	H4
Dunav (Danube) (riv.)	H4
Emine (cape)	J4
Iskŭr (riv.)	G4
Kaliakra (cape)	J4
Maritsa (riv.)	G4
Mesta (riv.)	F5
Midzhur (mt.)	F4
Musala (mt.)	F4
Osŭm (riv.)	G4
Rhodope (mts.)	F5
Rujen (mt.)	F4
Struma (riv.)	F4
Timok (riv.)	F3
Tundzha (riv.)	G4
Vit (riv.)	G4

GREECE

REGIONS

Aegean Islands 417,813	G6
Athens, Greater 2,566,775	F7
Áyion Óros (aut. dist.) 1,732	G5
Central Greece and Euboea 966,543	F6
Crete 456,642	G8
Epirus 310,334	E6
Ionian Islands 184,443	D6
Macedonia 1,888,952	E5
Peloponnisos 986,912	F6
Thessaly 659,913	F6
Thrace 329,582	G5

CITIES and TOWNS

Agrínion 30,973	E6
Alyína 5,704	F7
Aíyion 18,829	F6
Alexandroúpolis 22,995	H5
Alivérion 4,414	G6
Almirós 5,680	F6
Amaliás 14,177	E7
Amfilokhía 4,668	E6
Ámfissa 6,605	F6
Andíssa 1,762	H6
Andravídha 3,046	E6
Ándros 1,827	G7
Ano Viánnos 1,431	G8
Anóyia 2,750	G8
Ardhéa 3,555	F5
Areópolis 674	F7
Argalastí 1,621	F6
Argos 18,890	F7
Argostólion 7,060	E6
Arkhángelos 3,016	J7
Arnaía 2,424	F5
Árta 19,498	E6
Astipálaia 787	H7
Ataláadi 4,581	F6
Athens (cap.) 867,023	F7
Athens* 2,566,775	F7
Ayiá 3,241	F6
Áyios Kírikos 1,083	H7
Áyios Matthaíos 1,596	D6
Áyios Nikólaos 5,002	G8
Candia (Iráklion) 77,506	G8
Canea (Khaniá) 40,564	G8
Corinth 20,773	F7
Delfí 1,185	F6
Delvinákion 1,067	E6
Dhidhimótikhon 8,388	H5
Dhíkaia 1,222	H4
Dhimitsána 996	F7
Dhomokós 1,991	F6
Dráma 29,692	F5
Édhessa 13,967	F5
Elassón 7,200	F6
Elevtheroúpolis 4,888	G5
Ermoúpolis 13,502	G7
Farsala 6,967	F6
Fílates 2,993	E6
Filiátra 5,919	E7
Filippiás 3,248	E6
Flórina 11,164	E5
Gargaliánoi 5,888	E7
Grevená 8,106	E5
Ídhra 2,381	F7
Ierápetra 7,055	G8
Igoumenitsa 4,109	E6
Ioánnina 40,130	E6
Íos 1,270	G7
Iráklion 77,506	G8
Istaía 4,059	F6
Íthaki 2,293	E6
Kalámai 39,133	E7
Kalampáka 5,453	E6
Kalávrita 1,948	F6
Kálimnos 6,492	H7
Kándanos 403	F8
Kardhítsa 25,685	F6
Kariá 1,350	E6
Karial 301	G5
Káristos 3,550	G6
Kárpathos 1,363	H8
Karpenísion 4,414	E6
Kastéllion (Kíssamos) 2,996	F8
Kastéllion 1,152	G8
Kastoría 15,407	E5
Katákolon 690	E7
Kateríni 28,808	F5
Kaválla 46,234	G5
Kéa 693	G7
Kérkira 28,630	D6
Khalkís 36,300	F6
Khaniá 40,564	G8
Khíos 24,084	G6
Khóra Sfakíon 246	G8
Kíaton 7,392	F6
Kilkís 10,538	F5
Kími 2,772	G6
Kipaníssia 3,882	E7
Kíssamos 2,996	G8
Kíthira 349	F7
Komotiní 28,896	G5
Kónitsa 3,150	E5
Koropí 9,367	G7
Kos 7,828	H7
Kozáni 23,240	F5
Kranídhion 3,657	F7
Lagkadiá 1,350	F7
Lamía 37,872	F6
Langadhás 6,707	F5
Langadhía 1,350	F7
Lárisa 72,336	F6
Lávrion 8,283	G7
Leonídhion 3,181	F7
Levádheia 15,445	F6
Levkás 6,818	E6
Limenária 1,507	G5

(continued on following page)

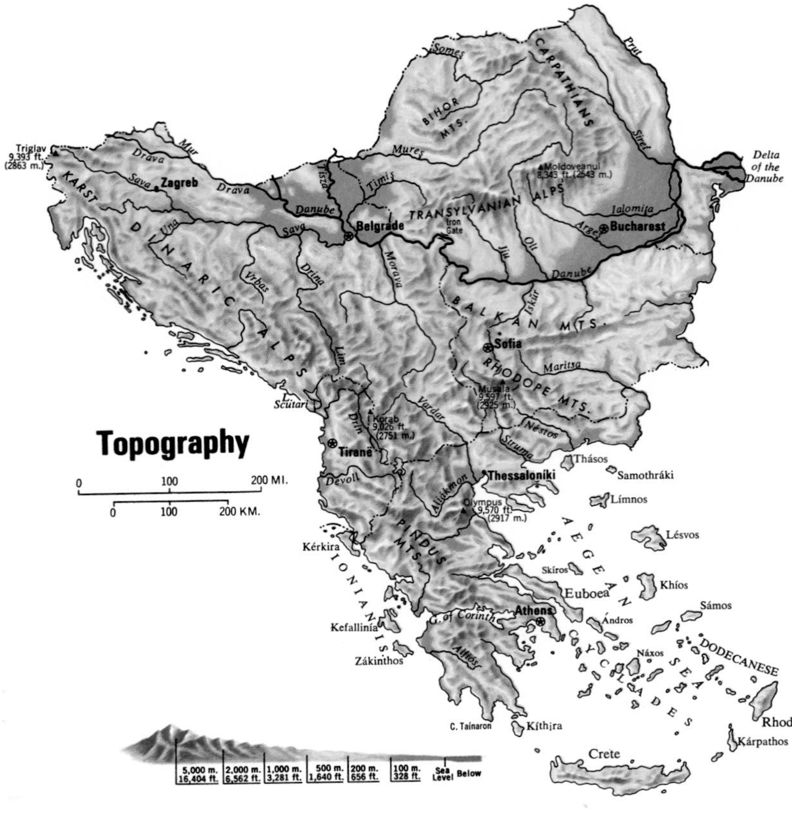

Límni 2,394 F6
Líndos 700 J7
Litókhoron 5,561 F5
Lixoúrion 3,364 E6
Loutrá Aidhipsoú 2,195 F6
Marathón 1,976 G6
Megalópolis 3,357 E7
Mégara 17,294 F6
Meligalá 1,724 F7
Mesolóngion 11,614 E6
Messíni 6,625 E7
Métsovon 2,823 E6
Mikínai 390 F7
Mílos 850 G7
Mírina 3,982 G6
Míthimna 1,414 G6
Mitilíni 23,426 H6
Moírai 2,948 G8
Moláoi 2,484 F7
Monólithos 247 H7
Moúdhros 1,024 G6
Náousa 17,375 F5
Návpaktos 8,170 F6
Návplion 9,281 F7
Náxos 2,892 G7
Neápolis 3,070 F7
Neméa 4,356 F7
Néon Karlóvasi 4,401 H7
Nestórion 1,143 E5
Nigríta 7,301 F5
Oinóï 188 F6
Orestías 10,727 H5
Paramithía 2,747 E6
Pátrai 111,607 E6
Pérdika 1,198 E6
Péta 2,116 E6
Pílos 2,258 E7
Piraiévs (Piraeus) 187,362 F7
Pírgos 20,599 E7
Piryí 1,455 G6
Píthion 1,047 H5
Plomárion 4,353 H6
Políkastron 5,279 F5
Políkhnitos 4,152 G6
Políyiros 3,707 F5
Póros 4,051 F7
Préveza 11,439 E6
Psakhná 4,650 F6
Psári 622 E7
Ptolemaís 16,588 E5
Réthimnon 14,969 G8
Rhodes (Ródhos) 32,092 J7
Salamís 18,256 F6
Salonika
(Thessaloníki) 345,799 F5
Sámi 957 E6
Sámos 5,146 H7
Samothráki 508 G5
Sápai 2,456 G5
Sérrai 39,897 F5
Sérvia 3,834 F5
Siátista 4,852 E5
Sidhirókastron 6,363 F5
Sími 2,344 H7
Sitía 6,167 H8
Skíathos 3,707 F6
Skíros 1,925 G6
Skópelos 2,545 F6
Souflíon 5,637 H5
Sparta 10,549 F7
Spétsai 3,427 F7
Spíli 789 G8
Stavrós 1,700 F5
Stílis 4,427 F6
Thásos 2,052 G5
Thessaloníki 345,799 F5
Thessaloníki* 482,361 F5
Thíra 1,322 G7
Thívai 15,971 F6
Timbákion 3,229 G8
Tínos 3,423 G7
Tírnavos 10,451 F6
Tríkkala 34,794 E6
Trípolis 20,209 F7
Vámos 652 F8
Vartholomión 3,015 E7
Vathí 2,491 H7
Velvendós 4,063 F5
Vérroia 29,528 F5
Vólos 51,290 F6
Vónitsa 3,324 E6
Vrondádhes 4,253 G6
Xánthi 24,867 G5
Yerolimín 73 F7
Yiannitsá 18,151 F5
Yíthion 4,915 F7
Zákinthos 9,339 E7
Zante (Zákinthos) 9,339 E7

OTHER FEATURES

Aegean (sea) G6
Akrítas (cape) E7
Aktí (pen.) G5
Amorgós (isl.) G7
Anáfi (isl.) G7
Andikíthira (isl.) F8
Ándros (isl.) G7
Árda (riv.) G5
Argolís (gulf) F7
Astipálaia (isl.) H7
Áthos (mt.) G5
Áyios Evstrátios
(isl.) G6
Áyios Yeóryios (cape) G5
Cephalonia (Kefallinía)
(isl.) E6
Corfu (Kérkira) (isl.) D6
Corinth (gulf) F6
Crete (isl.) G8
Crete (sea) G7
Cyclades (isls.) G7
Día (isl.) G8
Dodecanese (isls.) H8
Euboea (Évvoia)
(isl.) G6
Évros (riv.) H5
Évvoia (isl.) G6
Gávdhos (isl.) F8
Ídhi (mt.) G8
Ikaría (isl.) G7
Ionian (sea) D7
Íos (isl.) G7
Itháki (Ithaca) (isl.) E6
Kafirévs (cape) G6
Kálimnos (isl.) H7
Kárpathos (isl.) H8
Kásos (isl.) H8
Kassándra (pen.) F6
Kéa (isl.) G7
Kefallinía (isl.) E6
Kérkira (isl.) D6
Khálki (isl.) H7
Khaniá (gulf) G8
Khíos (isl.) G6
Kímolos (isl.) G7
Kiparissía (gulf) E7
Kíthira (isl.) F7
Kíthnos (isl.) G7
Kos (isl.) H7
Kriós (cape) F8
Kríti (Crete) (isl.) G8
Lakonía (gulf) F7
Léros (isl.) H7
Lésvos (isl.) G6
Levítha (isl.) H7
Levkás (isl.) E6
Límnos (isl.) G6
Maléa (cape) F7
Matapan (Taínaron) (cape) F7
Merabéllou (gulf) H8
Mesará (gulf) G8
Messíni (gulf) E7
Míkonos (isl.) G7
Mílos (isl.) G7
Mirtóön (sea) F7
Náxos (isl.) G7
Néstos (riv.) G5
Nísiros (isl.) H7
Northern Sporades (isls.) F6
Olympia (isls.) E7
Olympus (mt.) F5
Parnassus (mt.) F6
Páros (isl.) G7
Pátmos (isl.) H7
Paxoí (isl.) D6
Pindus (mts.) E6
Piniós (riv.) E6
Prespa (lake) E5
Psará (isl.) G6
Psevdhókavos (cape) G6
Rhodes (isl.) H7
Rhodope (mts.) G5
Salonika (Thermaic) (gulf) F6
Sámos (isl.) H7
Samothráki (isl.) G5
Saría (isl.) H8
Saronic (gulf) F7
Sérifos (isl.) G7
Sídheros (cape) H8
Sífnos (isl.) G7
Sími (isl.) H7
Síros (isl.) G7
Sithoniá (pen.) F5
Skíros (isl.) G6
Spátha (cape) F8
Strimón (gulf) G5
Strofádhes (isls.) E7
Taínaron (cape) F7
Thásos (isl.) G5
Thermaic (gulf) F6
Thíra (isl.) G7
Tílos (isl.) H7
Tínos (isl.) G7
Toronaic (gulf) F5
Vardar (riv.) E5
Voïvís (lake) F6
Vólvi (lake) F5
Voúxa (cape) F8
Zákinthos (Zante)
(isl.) E7

ROMANIA

CITIES and TOWNS

Aiud 25,173 F2
Alba Iulia 44,552 F2
Alexandria 38,296 G3
Anina 11,594 E3
Arad 161,568 E2
Babadag 8,423 J3
Bacău 131,413 H2
Baia de Aramă 5,065 F3
Baia Mare 112,893 F2
Băile Herculane 4,606 F3
Băileşti 21,246 F3
Balş 16,091 G3
Beiuş 9,992 F2
Bereşti Tîrg H2
Bicaz 9,490 G2
Bîrlad 59,059 H2
Bistriţa 47,562 G2
Bivolari H2
Blaj 21,678 F2
Borşa 25,287 G2
Botoşani 69,881 H2
Brad 18,391 F2
Brăila 203,983 H3
Braşov 259,108 G3
Bucharest (Bucureşti)
(cap.) 1,832,015 G3
Bucharest* 1,960,097 G3
Buhuşi 20,204 H2
Buzău 106,738 H3
Buziaş 8,310 E3
Calafat 16,421 F3
Călăraşi 58,960 H3
Caracal 31,159 G3
Caransebeş 27,429 F3
Carei 24,496 F2
Cernavodă 14,686 J3
Chişineu Criş 9,344 E2
Cîmpeni 7,722 F2
Cîmpia Turzii 23,745 F2
Cîmpina 33,259 H3
Cîmpulung 33,448 G3
Cîmpulung Moldovenesc 19,270 G2
Cisnădie 21,114 G3
Cluj-Napoca 274,095 F2
Cogealac J3
Comaneşti 18,177 H2
Constanţa 279,308 J3
Corabia 20,454 G4
Costeşti 10,446 G3
Craiova 220,893 F3
Cujmir F3
Curtea de Argeş 23,555 G3
Dăbuleni F4
Dăeni J3
Darabani 12,207 H1
Dej 35,396 F2
Deta 6,956 E3
Deva 68,290 F3
Dorohoi 23,121 H2
Drăgăneşti Olt 11,606 G3
Drăgăşani 16,290 F3
Drobeta-Turnu Severin 80,114 F3
Făgăraş 34,762 G3
Fălçiu J2
Fălticeni 22,463 H2
Făurei 3,620 H3
Feteşti 28,730 H3
Focşani 62,275 H3
Folteşti H3
Găeşti 13,384 G3
Galaţi 252,884 H3
Gheorghe Gheorghiu-Dej 41,297 H2
Gheorghieni 20,592 G2
Gherla 19,303 G2
Giurgiu 53,241 G3
Haţeg 9,706 F3
Hîrlău 8,135 H2
Hîrşova 8,434 J3
Huedin 8,557 F2
Hunedoara 83,159 F3
Huşi 24,329 J2
Iaşi 262,493 H2
Ineu 10,414 E2
Isaccea 5,283 J3
Jibou F2
Jimbolia 15,325 E3
Lipova 12,427 E2
Luduş 15,771 G2
Lugoj 48,558 F3
Lupeni 28,251 F3
Mangalia 27,263 J4
Medgidia 43,691 J3
Mediaş 68,442 G2
Miercurea Ciuc 38,097 G2
Mizil 14,294 H3
Mociu G2
Moineşti 21,015 H2
Moldova Nouă 18,498 E3
Moreni 17,743 G3
Nădlac 8,407 E2
Năsăud 8,646 G2
Negreşti 7,435 H2
Ocna Mureş 16,381 G2
Odobeşti 8,440 H3
Odorheiu Secuiesc 33,392 G2
Olteniţa 25,536 H3
Oradea 175,400 E2
Orăştie 18,769 F3
Oraviţa 13,628 E3
Orşova 14,873 F3
Panciu 7,772 H3
Paşcani 26,937 H2
Pătulele F3
Pechea H3
Pecica E2
Periam E2
Petrila 25,087 F3
Petroşeni 42,316 F3
Piatra Neamţ 84,192 G2
Pincota 7,494 E2
Piteşti 125,029 G3
Pleniţa F3
Ploieşti 207,009 H3
Poenari Burchi G3
Poiana Mare F4
Pucioasa 14,056 G3
Rădăuţi 24,222 G2
Reghin 31,948 G2
Reşiţa 90,698 E3
Rîmnicu Sărat 29,815 H3
Rîmnicu Vîlcea 75,070 G3
Roman 56,466 H2
Roşiori de Vede 28,832 G3
Săcele 29,391 G3
Salonta 19,698 E2
Satu Mare 108,152 F2
Săveni 7,913 H1
Sebeş 27,448 F3
Sebiş 6,401 F2
Segarcea 8,783 F3
Sfîntu Gheorghe 51,210 G3
Sfîntu Gheorghe J3
Sibiu 156,854 G3
Sighetu Marmaţiei 38,879 F2
Sighişoara 32,296 G2
Şimleul Silvaniei 14,780 F2
Sinaia 14,215 G3
Sînnicolaul Mare 13,565 E2
Siret 6,677 G1
Slănic 8,017 G3
Slatina 54,954 G3
Slobozia 35,207 H3
Solca 4,835 G2
Sovata 10,745 G2
Ştefăneşti H2
Strehaia 11,431 F3
Suceava 66,857 G2
Sulina 5,240 J3
Tăşnad 10,441 F2
Techirghiol 11,228 J3
Tecuci 37,928 H3
Timişoara 281,320 E3
Tinca F2
Tîrgovişte 71,533 G3
Tîrgu Cărbuneşti 7,536 F3
Tîrgu Frumos 6,428 H2
Tîrgu Jiu 70,629 F3
Tîrgu Mureş 129,284 G2
Tîrgu Neamţ 15,756 G2
Tîrgu Ocna 12,960 H2
Tîrgu Secuiesc 18,265 H2
Tîrnăveni 27,799 F2
Topliţa 14,347 G2
Tulcea 67,091 J3
Turda 57,972 F2
Turnu Măgurele 30,003 G4
Urlaţa 10,900 H3
Urziceni 13,500 H3
Vasile Roaită J3
Vaslui 44,134 H2
Vatra Dornei 16,748 G2
Videle 11,323 G3
Vişeul de Sus 20,697 F2
Viziru H3
Zalău 36,158 F2
Zărneşti 23,378 G3
Zimnicea 15,111 G4

OTHER FEATURES

Argeş (riv.) G3
Bîrlad (riv.) H2
Black (sea) J4
Brăila (marshes) H3
Buzău (riv.) H3
Carpathian (mts.) G2
Crişul Alb (riv.) F2
Crişul Repede (riv.) F2
Danube (delta) J3
Danube (riv.) H4
Ialomiţa (marshes) J3
Ialomiţa (riv.) H3
Jijia (riv.) H2
Jiu (riv.) F3
Moldoveanul (mt.) G3
Mureş (riv.) E2
Olt (riv.) G3
Peleaga (mt.) F3
Pietrosul (mt.) G2
Prut (riv.) J2
Siret (riv.) H2
Someş (riv.) F2
Timiş (riv.) E3
Tîrnava Mare (riv.) G2
Transylvanian Alps (mts.) G3

YUGOSLAVIA

INTERNAL DIVISIONS

Bosnia and Hercegovina
(rep.) 3,710,965 C3
Croatia (rep.) 4,396,397 C3
Kosovo (aut. reg.) 1,240,919 E4
Macedonia (rep.) 1,623,598 E5
Montenegro (rep.) 527,207 D4
Serbia (rep.) 8,401,673 E3
Slovenia (rep.) 1,697,068 B2
Vojvodina (aut.
prov.) 1,953,980 D3

CITIES and TOWNS

Aleksinac 11,943 E4
Apatin 17,501 D3
Arendjelovac 15,659 E3
Bačka Topola 16,028 D3
Bakar B3
Banja Luka 85,786 C3
Bar 3,594 D4
Bečej 26,616 E3
Bela Crkva 11,137 E3
Belgrade (cap.) 727,945 E3
Beli Manastir 7,325 D3
Beograd (Belgrade)
(cap.) 727,945 E3
Berovo 5,053 F5
Bihać 24,155 B3
Bijeljina 24,888 D3
Bijelo Polje 9,298 D4
Bileća 4,083 D4
Biograd 3,595 B4
Bitola 64,467 E5
Bjelovar 21,019 C3
Blato 5,591 C4
Bled 4,710 A2
Bor 27,520 E3
Bosanska Dubica 9,191 C3
Bosanska Gradiška 9,742 C3
Bosanska Kostajnica 2,535 B3
Bosanska Krupa 8,947 C3
Bosanski Brod 10,113 D3
Bosanski Novi 9,861 C3
Bosanski Petrovac 4,113 C3
Bosanski Šamac 4,949 D3
Brčko 25,575 D3
Brežice 3,271 B3
Budva 2,483 D4
Bugojno 9,079 C3
Čačak 38,890 E4
Čakovec 11,766 C2
Čapljina 4,677 C4
Caribrod (Dimitrovgrad) 5,449 F4
Cazin 1,213 B3
Celje 30,827 B2
Cetinje 12,089 D4
Ćuprija 17,691 E4
Daruvar 8,478 C3
Debar 8,597 E5
Derventa 11,887 C3
Dimitrovgrad 5,449 F4
Djakovica 29,499 E4
Djakovo 15,833 D3
Doboj 18,073 C3
Donji Vakuf 4,928 C3
Drvar 6,237 C3
Dubrovnik 31,213 C4
Fiume (Rijeka) 128,883 B3
Foča 9,370 D4
Gacko 1,641 D4
Gevgelija 9,319 F5
Glamoč 2,627 C3
Gnjilane 21,359 E4
Gornji Milanovac 11,114 D3
Gornji Vakuf 2,429 C4
Gospić 8,238 B3
Gostivar 18,805 E5
Gračac 3,228 B3
Gračanica 9,302 D3
Gradačac 7,571 D3
Grubišno Polje 2,771 C3
Gusinje 2,616 D4
Herceg Novi 6,645 D4
Ivangrad 11,373 E4
Ivanjica 5,719 E4
Jajce 9,221 C3
Jesenice 16,163 A2
Kanjiža 11,348 D2
Karlovac 47,046 B3
Kavadarci 17,974 E5
Kičevo 14,189 E5
Kikinda 37,392 E3
Kladanj 3,255 D3
Ključ 3,466 C3
Knin 7,279 C3
Knjaževac 11,734 F4
Kočani 16,611 F5
Kočevje 7,277 B3
Kolašin 2,111 D4
Konjic 9,161 D4
Koper 16,683 A3
Koprivnica 16,398 C2
Kosovska Mitrovica 42,526 E4
Kostajnica 9,161 C3
Kotor 5,728 D4
Kragujevac 72,080 E3
Kraljevo 28,065 E4
Kranj 26,341 B2
Križevci 8,501 C2
Krk 1,500 B3
Krško 4,451 B3
Kruševac 29,902 E4
Kulen Vakuf 1,078 B3
Kumanovo 44,791 E4
Kutina 10,892 C3
Leskovac 46,050 E4
Livno 7,223 C4
Ljubinje 785 D4
Ljubljana 169,064 B3
Ljubuški 2,891 C4
Loznica 13,513 D3
Maglaj 5,869 D3
Makarska 6,589 C4
Maribor 94,976 B2
Modriča 7,406 D3
Mostar 47,821 D4
Murska Sobota 9,665 C2
Našice 5,836 C3
Negotin 11,325 F3
Nevesinje 3,077 D4
Nikšić 28,940 D4
Nin 1,782 B3
Niš 128,231 F4
Nova Gorizia A2
Nova Gradiška 11,765 C3
Novi 2,682 B3
Novi Pazar 28,696 E4
Novi Sad 143,591 D3
Novo Mesto 9,553 B3
Novska 5,168 C3
Ogulin 9,975 B3
Ohrid 26,352 E5
Omiš 3,515 C4
Opatija 9,238 A3
Osijek 94,989 D3
Pag 2,318 B3
Pančevo 53,979 E3
Paraćin 21,555 E4
Peć 41,783 E4
Petrinja 12,296 B3
Piran 5,485 A3
Pirot 29,658 F4
Plav 3,072 D4
Pljevlja 14,459 D4
Ploče 4,257 C4
Pola (Pula) 47,117 A3
Poreč 4,512 A3
Postojna 6,085 B3
Požarevac 33,336 E3
Preševo 7,634 E4
Priboj 12,556 D4
Prijedor 22,379 C3
Prijepolje 7,960 D4
Prilep 48,045 E5
Priština 71,264 E4
Prizren 41,875 E4
Prokuplje 20,617 E4
Prozor 1,420 C4
Ptuj 9,245 C2
Pula 47,117 A3
Rab 1,675 B3
Radoviš 9,373 F5
Ragusa (Dubrovnik) 31,213 C4
Raška 3,935 E4
Ravne na Koroškem 6,529 B2
Rijeka 128,883 B3
Rogatica 4,801 D4
Rovinj 8,998 A3
Rožaj E4
Ruma 24,180 D3
Šabac 43,539 D3
Samobor 7,821 B3
Sanski Most 8,718 C3
Sarajevo 245,058 D4
Senj 4,927 B3
Senta 24,694 D3
Šibenik 29,619 C4
Šid 11,867 D3
Sinj 4,705 C4
Sisak 37,215 C3
Sjenica 9,118 E4
Škofja Loka 4,971 A2
Skopje 308,117 E5
Skradin 893 B4
Slavonska Požega 18,160 C3
Slavonski Brod 38,829 D3
Smederevo 39,200 E3
Smederevska Palanka 18,837 E3
Sombor 44,210 D3
Split 150,739 C4
Srebrenica 3,101 D3
Sremska Mitrovica 32,569 D3
Štip 27,218 F5
Stolac 3,862 D4
Ston 407 C4
Struga 11,369 E5
Strumica 22,770 F5
Subotica 89,476 D2
Surdulica 7,048 F4
Svetozarevo 27,812 E4
Svilajnac 7,848 E3
Teslić 4,940 C3
Tetovo 35,293 E5
Titograd 54,639 D4
Titovo Užice 35,465 D4
Titov Veles 35,583 E5
Travnik 12,745 C3
Trbovlje 16,393 B2
Trebinje 3,553 D4
Trogir 6,162 C4
Trstenik 7,167 E4
Tržič 4,435 B2
Tuzla 53,836 D3
Ub 3,785 E3
Ulcinj 7,472 D5
Umag 3,228 A3
Uroševac E4
Valjevo 26,655 D3
Varaždin 34,662 B2
Vareš 7,632 D3
Velenje 11,225 B2
Velika Plana E3
Veliki Bečkerek
(Zrenjanin) 60,201 E3
Vinkovci 29,257 D3
Virovitica 16,389 C3
Višegrad 4,753 D4
Visoko 9,365 D4
Vlasenica 4,033 D3
Vranje 25,909 F4
Vrbas 22,502 D3
Vršac 33,573 E3
Vučitrn 11,701 E4
Vukovar 29,500 D3
Žabljak 1,023 D4
Zadar 43,588 B3
Zagreb 561,773 C3
Zaječar 27,724 E4
Zara (Zadar) 43,588 B3
Zenica 49,522 C3
Žepče 3,177 D3
Zrenjanin 60,201 E3
Zvornik 8,498 D3

OTHER FEATURES

Adriatic (sea) B4
Bobotov Kuk (mt.) D4
Bosna (riv.) D3
Brač (isl.) C4
Cazma (riv.) C3
Cres (isl.) B3
Čvrsnica (mt.) C4
Dalmatia (reg.) C4
Danube (riv.) E3
Dinaric Alps (mts.) B3
Drava (riv.) C3
Drina (riv.) D3
Dugi Otok (isl.) B3
Hvar (isl.) C4
Ibar (riv.) E4
Istria (pen.) A3
Kamenjak (cape) A3
Kladovo F3
Korab (mt.) E5
Korčula (isl.) C4
Kornat (isl.) B4
Krk (isl.) B3
Kupa (riv.) B3
Kvarner (gulf) B3
Lastovo (Lagosta) (isl.) C4
Lim (riv.) D4
Lošinj (isl.) B3
Midzhur (mt.) F4
Mljet (isl.) C4
Morava (riv.) E3
Mur (riv.) B2
Neretva (riv.) D4
Ohrid (lake) E5
Pag (isl.) B3
Palagruža (Pelagosa) (isl.) C4
Prespa (lake) E5
Rab (isl.) B3
Rujen (mt.) F4
Sava (riv.) D3
Scutari (lake) D4
Slavonia (reg.) C3
Šolta (isl.) C4
Tara (riv.) D4
Timok (riv.) F3
Tisa (riv.) E3
Triglav (mt.) A2
Una (riv.) C3
Vardar (riv.) E5
Vis (isl.) C4
Vrbas (riv.) C3
Žirje (isl.) B4

*City and suburbs.

The Balkan States

CONIC PROJECTION

SCALE OF MILES

0 25 50 75 100 125 150 175

SCALE OF KILOMETERS

0 25 50 75 100 125 150 175

Capitals of Countries ⎯⎯⎯⎯ ☆
Administrative Centers ⎯⎯⎯ △
International Boundaries ⎯ ⎯ ⎯
Major Internal Boundaries ⎯ · ⎯ ·
Minor Internal Boundaries ⎯ ·· ⎯ ··
Canals ⎯⎯⎯⎯⎯⎯

BULGARIA and GREECE are divided into counties and
departments, respectively. Because of the scale no
attempt has been made to delimit and name these subdivisions; their administrative centers have, however,
been designated.
    The larger divisions named in Greece are well-known
geographical regions, without administrative function.
ROMANIA consists of thirty-nine counties and
three cities of regional status, Bucharest, Constanța
and Petroșeni. Scale does not permit delimiting
these counties.
ALBANIA is divided into twenty-seven districts. Scale
does not permit the delimitation of these divisions.
YUGOSLAVIA is a federation of six republics. The
Serbian republic includes an autonomous province
(Vojvodina), and an autonomous region (Kosovo).

© Copyright HAMMOND INCORPORATED, Maplewood, N.J.

Topography

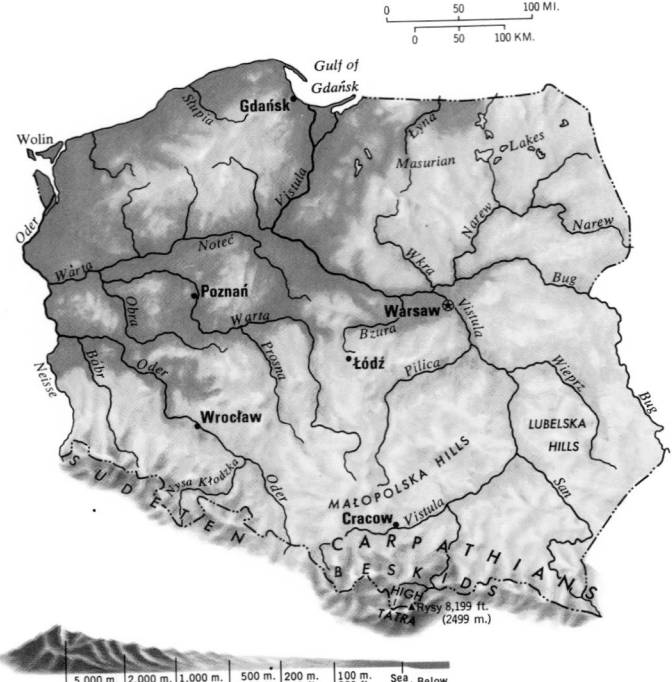

Agriculture, Industry and Resources

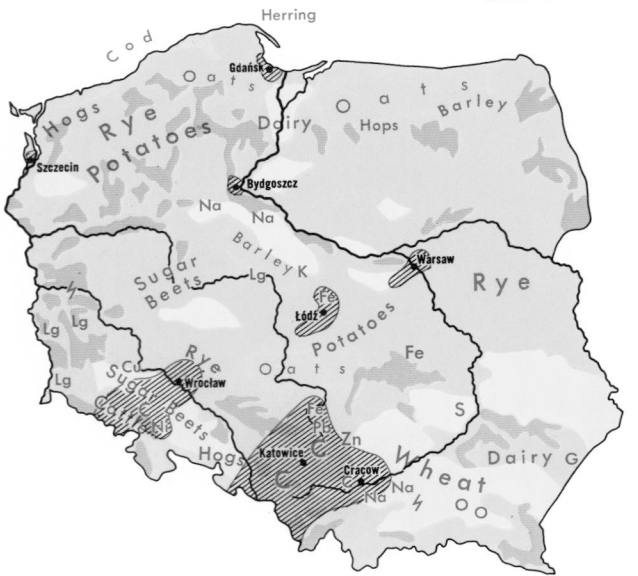

MAJOR MINERAL OCCURRENCES

Ag Silver
C Coal
Cu Copper
Fe Iron Ore
G Natural Gas
K Potash
Lg Lignite

Na Salt
Ni Nickel
O Petroleum
Pb Lead
S Sulfur
Zn Zinc

⚡ Water Power
▨ Major Industrial Areas

DOMINANT LAND USE

☐ Cereals (chiefly wheat)

☐ Rye, Oats, Barley, Potatoes

☐ General Farming, Livestock

☐ Forests

PROVINCES		
Biała Podlaska 283,200	F3	
Białystok 613,800	D4	
Bielsko 765,500	C2	
Bydgoszcz 982,100	F3	
Chełm 221,000	E2	
Ciechanów 398,500	E4	
Cracow (Kraków) 1,097,600	E4	
Cracow (city) 651,300	D3	
Częstochowa 723,200	D1	
Elbląg 419,800	B2	
Gdańsk 1,312,300	B3	
Gorzów 428,700	D3	
Jelenia Góra 483,400	D3	
Kalisz 640,300	E3	
Katowice 3,439,700	D2	
Kielce 1,030,400	C1	
Konin 423,700	E4	
Koszalin 428,500	C4	
Krosno 418,000	C3	
Legnica 405,600	D3	
Leszno 340,600	D3	
Łódź 1,063,700	D3	
Łódź (city) 777,800	F2	
Łomża 320,600	F3	
Lublin 875,300		

Nowy Sącz 600,300	E4	
Olsztyn 654,400	E2	
Opole 961,600	C3	
Ostrołęka 360,700	E2	
Piła 414,000	C2	
Piotrków 581,900	D3	
Płock 479,700	D2	
Poznań 1,156,500	C2	
Przemyśl 373,100	F4	
Radom 674,400	E3	
Rzeszów 602,200	F4	
Siedlce 602,100	F2	
Sieradz 388,000	D3	
Skierniewice 388,300	E3	
Słupsk 352,900	C1	
Suwałki 412,700	F1	
Szczecin 841,400	B2	
Tarnobrzeg 532,200	E3	
Tarnów 573,900	E4	
Toruń 580,500	D2	
Wałbrzych 709,600	C3	
Warsaw 2,117,700	C4	
Warsaw (city) 1,377,100	E2	
Włocławek 402,000	D2	
Wrocław 1,014,600	C3	
Zamość 472,300	B3	
Zielona Góra 575,000	B3	

CITIES and TOWNS		
Aleksandrów Kujawski 9,600	D2	
Aleksandrów		
Łódzki 14,400	D3	
Allenstein (Olsztyn) 94,119	E2	
Andrespol 12,400	D3	
Andrychów 14,300	D4	
Augustów 19,784	F2	
Auschwitz		
(Oświęcim) 39,600	D3	
Bartoszyce 15,500	E1	
Będzin 42,787	B3	
Beuthen (Bytom) 186,993	F3	
Biała Podlaska 26,100	C1	
Białogard 20,500	F2	
Białystok 166,619	C3	
Bielawa 30,900	D4	
Bielsk Podlaski 14,000	F3	
Bielsko-Biała 105,601	E2	
Biłgoraj 12,888	C3	
Błonie 12,500	E4	
Bochnia 14,500	B3	
Bogatynia 11,800	B3	
Boguszów-Gorce 11,900	B3	
Bolesławiec 30,500		

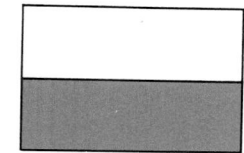

AREA 120,725 sq. mi. (312,678 sq. km.)
POPULATION 35,815,000
CAPITAL Warsaw
LARGEST CITY Warsaw
HIGHEST POINT Rysy 8,199 ft.
    (2,499 m.)
MONETARY UNIT zloty
MAJOR LANGUAGE Polish
MAJOR RELIGION Roman Catholicism

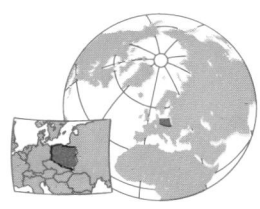

Braniewo 12,100 ....D1
Breslau (Wrocław) 461,900 ....C3
Brieg (Brzeg) 30,780 ....C3
Brodnica 17,300 ....D2
Brzeg 30,780 ....C3
Brzeg Dolny 10,800 ....C3
Brzesko 9,701 ....E3
Busko Zdrój 11,100 ....E3
Bydgoszcz 280,460 ....C2
Bytom 186,993 ....A3
Bytów 10,642 ....C1
Chełm 38,789 ....F3
Chełmno 17,906 ....D2
Chełmża 14,200 ....C2
Chodzież 14,100 ....C2
Chojnice 23,500 ....C2
Chojnów 11,000 ....B3
Chorzów 151,338 ....B3
Choszczno 9,800 ....B2
Chrzanów 29,300 ....B4
Ciechanów 28,500 ....E2
Cieplice
  Śląskie-Zdrój 15,400 ....B3
Cieszyn 25,234 ....D4
Cracow 651,300 ....E4
Czechowice-Dziedzice 25,400 ....D4
Czeladź 31,843 ....B4
Częstochowa 187,613 ....D3
Dąbrowa Górnicza 61,660 ....B3
Danzig (Gdańsk) 364,285 ....D1
Darłowo 11,200 ....C1
Dębica 22,900 ....E3
Dęblin 14,600 ....E3
Działdowo 10,100 ....D2
Dzierżoniów 32,800 ....C3
Elbing (Elbląg) 89,835 ....D1
Ełk 27,188 ....E2
Gdańsk 364,285 ....D1
Gdynia 190,125 ....D1
Giżycko 18,200 ....E1
Gleiwitz (Gliwice) 170,912 ......A4
Głogów 20,226 ....C3
Głowno 12,800 ....D3
Głubczyce 11,300 ....C3
Głuchołazy 13,200 ....C3
Gniezno 50,643 ....C2
Golenów 14,600 ....B2
Gorlice 15,200 ....E4
Gorzów Wielkopolski 74,267 .....B2
Gostyń 13,000 ....C3
Gostynin 12,000 ....D2
Grajewo 11,200 ....E2
Grodzisk Mazowiecki 20,400 ....E2
Grójec 10,300 ....E3
Grudziądz 75,511 ....D2
Grünberg (Zielona
  Góra) 89,835 ....B3
Gryfice 13,200 ....B2
Guben (Gubin) 14,600 ....B3
Hajnówka m4,345 ....F2
Hindenburg (Zabrze) 199,400 ...A4
Hirschberg (Jelenia
  Góra) 55,720 ....B3
Hrubieszów 14,999 ....F3
Iława 16,400 ....D2
Inowrocław 54,817 ....D2

Jarocin 18,100 ....C3
Jarosław 29,000 ....F4
Jasło 17,025 ....E4
Jastrzębie Zdrój 34,400 ....D3
Jaworzno 63,271 ....B4
Jędrzejów 13,264 ....E3
Jelenia Góra 55,720 ....B3
Kalisz 81,227 ....D3
Kamienna Góra 21,000 ....B3
Kartuzy 10,558 ....D1
Katowice 303,264 ....B4
Kędzierzyn-Koźle 45,600 ....C3
Kępno 10,151 ....C3
Kętrzyn 19,300 ....E1
Kielce 125,952 ....E3
Kłobuck 12,600 ....D3
Kłodzko 26,000 ....C3
Kluczbork 18,000 ....D3
Knurów 28,400 ....A4
Koło 13,100 ....D2
Kołobrzeg 25,419 ....B1
Konin 40,600 ....D2
Końskie 13,100 ....E3
Konstantynów
  Łódzki 12,800 ....D3
Kościan 18,700 ....C2
Kościerzyna 18,914 ....D1
Köslin (Koszalin) 64,414 ......C1
Kostrzyn 11,200 ....B2
Koszalin 64,414 ....C1
Kraków (Cracow) 651,300 .....E4
Krapkowice 13,800 ....D3
Kraśnik Fabryczny 14,800 .....E3
Krasnystaw 12,495 ....F3
Krosno 26,500 ....E4
Krotoszyn 21,900 ....C3
Krynica 10,200 ....E4
Kustrin 11,200 ....B2
Kutno 30,800 ....D2
Kwidzin 23,104 ....D2
Łańcut 12,049 ....F3
Landsberg (Gorzów
  Wielkopolski) 74,267 ......B2
Łaziska Górne 10,800 ......A4
Łębork 25,000 ....C1
Łęczyca 13,900 ....D2
Legionowo 20,800 ....E2
Legnica 75,843 ....B3
Leszczyny 12,200 ....A4
Leszno 33,890 ....C3
Libiąż 10,800 ....D3
Lidzbark Warmiński 12,900 ...E1
Liegnitz (Legnica) 75,843 ...B3
Lipno 10,900 ....D2
Łódź 777,800 ....D3
Łomża 25,500 ....E2
Łowicz 20,400 ....D2
Luban 17,200 ....B3
Lubartów 10,000 ....F3
Lublin 28,400 ....F3
Lublin 235,937 ....F3
Lubliniec 19,800 ......D3
Luboń 16,400 ....C2
Lubsko 12,600 ....B3
Łuków 15,500 ....F2
Malbork (Marienburg) 30,900 ...D1

Międzyrzec Podlaski 13,500 ......F2
Międzyrzecz 14,900 ....B2
Mielec 26,800 ....E3
Mików 21,300 ....B4
Mińsk Mazowiecki 24,200 ....F2
Mława 20,007 ....D2
Police 12,700 ....B2
Morąg 9,681 ....D2
Mrągowo 13,400 ....E2
Mysłowice 44,737 ....B4
Myszków 18,000 ....D3
Namysłów 11,076 ....C3
Neisse (Nysa) 31,837 ....C3
Nidzica 9,642 ....E2
Nisko 10,000 ....E3
Nowa Ruda 18,400 ....C3
Nowa Sól 33,300 ....B3
Nowy Dwór Mazowiecki 16,900 ..B3
Nowy Sącz 41,103 ....E4
Nowy Targ 21,900 ....E4
Nysa 31,837 ....C3
Oława 17,746 ....C3
Oleśnica 75,843 ....C3
Olkusz 15,800 ....D3
Olsztyn 94,119 ....D2
Opoczno 12,168 ....D3
Opole 86,510 ....C3
Oppeln 86,510 ....C3
Orzesze 9,600 ....A4
Ostróda 21,300 ....D2
Ostrołęka 21,981 ....E2
Ostrów Mazowiecka 15,000 ..E2
Ostrów Wielkopolski 56,500 ..C3
Ostrowiec
  Świętokrzyski 49,958 ....E3
Oświęcim 39,800 ....D3
Otwock 39,863 ....E2
Ozorków 18,200 ....D3
Pabianice 62,000 ....D3
Piekary Śląskie 36,300 ..B4
Piła 43,778 ....C2

Pionki 13,600 ....E3
Piotrków Trybunalski 59,683 ...D3
Pisz 11,100 ....E2
Pleszew 13,348 ....C3
Płock 71,727 ....D2
Płońsk 11,619 ....D2
Police 12,700 ....B2
Poznań 469,085 ....C2
Prudnik 20,300 ....C3
Pruszcz Gdański 13,000 ...D1
Pruszków 42,961 ....E2
Przasnysz 11,100 ....E2
Przemyśl 53,228 ....F4
Puck 9,500 ....D1
Puławy 34,800 ....F3
Pułtusk 12,600 ......E2
Rabka 10,700 ....D4
Raciborz 40,418 ....C3
Radom 158,640 ....E3
Radomsko 31,179 ..D3
Ratibor (Racibórz) 40,418 ..C3
Rawa Mazowiecka 9,800 ...D3
Rawicz 14,100 ....C3
Ruda Śląska 142,407 ....B4
Rumia 23,300 ....D1
Rybnik 43,415 ....D3
Rypin 10,029 ....D2
Rzeszów 82,192 ....E4
Sandomierz 16,800 ...E3
Sanok 21,600 ....F4
Schneidemühl (Piła) 36,600 ..C2
Schweidnitz
  (Świdnica) 47,542 ....C3
Siedlce 38,983 ....F2
Siemianowice
  Śląskie 67,278 ....B4
Sieradz 38,500 ....D3
Sierpc 12,700 ....D2
Skarżysko-Kamienna 39,194 ..E3
Skawina 15,900 ....D4
Skierniewice 25,590 ...E2
Sławno 10,700 ....C1
Słubice 12,000 ......B2
Słupsk 68,311 ......C1

Sochaczew 20,500 ....E2
Sokółka 10,023 ....F2
Sokołów Podlaski 9,569 ....F2
Sopot 47,573 ....D1
Sosnowiec 144,652 ....B4
Śrem 15,600 ....C2
Środa Śląska 10,259 ....C3
Środa Wielkopolska 14,800 ...C2
Stalowa Wola 29,768 ....F3
Starachowice 42,807 ....E3
Stargard Szczeciński 44,400 ..B2
Stargard Gdański 33,400 .....D2
Stary Sącz 57,400 ....E4
Stettin (Szczecin) 337,294 ..B2
Stolp (Słupsk) 68,311 ....C1
Strzegom 14,000 ....C3
Strzelce Opolskie 14,700 ...D3
Strzelin 9,800 ....C3
Sulechów 10,200 ....B2
Sulejów 10,200 ....B2
Suwałki 25,360 ....F1
Swarzędz 12,100 ......C2
Świdnica 47,542 .....C3
Świdnik 24,300 .....F3
Świdwin 12,500 ....B2
Świebodzice 18,500 ..C3
Świebodzin 14,900 ..B2
Świecie 17,900 ....D2
Świętochłowice 58,311 ..A4
Świnoujście
  (Swinemünde) 27,900 ...B1
Szamotuły 14,600 ....C2
Szczecin 337,204 ......B2
Szczecinek 28,600 ....C2
Szczytno 17,371 .....E2
Szprotawa 11,200 ...B3
Tarnobrzeg 18,800 ..E3
Tarnów 85,514 .....E4
Tarnowskie Góry 34,200 ..B4
Tczew 40,794 .....D1
Tomaszów Lubelski 12,329 ..F4
Tomaszów Mazowiecki 54,911 ..E3
Toruń 129,152 ....D2
Trzcianka 10,900 ..C2
Trzebinia-Siersza C2

Turek 18,500 ....D2
Tychy 71,384 ....B4
Ustka 9,900 ....C1
Wąbrzeźno 11,800 ....D2
Wadowice 11,700 ....D4
Wągrowiec 15,600 ....C2
Wałbrzych 125,048 ....C3
Wałcz 18,900 ....C2
Waldenburg
  (Wałbrzych) 125,048 ....C3
Warsaw (Warszawa)
  (cap.) 1,377,100 ....E2
Wejherowo 33,600 ....D1
Wieliczka 13,600 ....E4
Wieluń 14,300 ....D3
Wisła 9,800 ....D4
Włocławek 77,169 ....D2
Wodzisław Śląski 25,600 ..D4
Wolin 35,458 ....B1
Wołomin 24,000 ....E2
Wołów 10,500 ....C3
Wrocław 523,318 ....C3
Września 17,800 ......C2
Wschowa 10,000 ......C3
Wyszków E2
Ząbki 16,000 ....E2
Zakopane 27,039 ....E4
Zambrów 14,082 ....E2
Zamość 34,734 ....F3
Żary 28,300 ....B3
Zawiercie 39,410 ..D3
Zduńska Wola 29,066 ..D3
Zgierz 42,838 ....D3
Zgorzelec 28,400 ....B3
Ziębice 9,700 ....C3
Zielona Góra 73,156 ..B3
Złocieniec 10,100 ....C2
Złotoryja 12,000 .....B3
Złotów 11,600 ....C2
Żnin 9,600 ....C2
Żyrardów 33,196 ....E2

Żywiec 22,400 ....D4

OTHER FEATURES

Baltic (sea) B1
Beskids (range) D4
Brda (riv.) C2
Brynica (riv.) B3
Bug (riv.) F2
Danzig (Gdańsk) (gulf) D1
Dukla (pass) E4
Dunajec (riv.) E4
Gwda (riv.) C2
Hel (pen.) D1
High Tatra (range) D4
Kłodnica (riv.) A4
Łyna (riv.) E1
Mamry, Jezioro (lake) E1
Masurian (lkes) E2
Narew (riv.) E2
Neisse (riv.) B3
Notec (riv.) B2
Nysa Kłodzka (riv.) C3
Nysa Łużycka (Neisse)
  (riv.) B3
Oder (riv.) B2
Orava (res.) D4
Pilica (riv.) D3
Pomeranian (bay) B1
Prosna (riv.) B4
Przemsza (riv.) B4
Rysy (mt.) D4
Słupia (riv.) C1
Śniardwy, Jezioro (lake) E2
Sudeten (range) B3
Uznam (Usedom) (isl.) B1
Vistula (riv.) D1
Warmia (reg.) D1
Warta (riv.) F3
Wieprz (riv.) F3
Wisła (Vistula) (riv.) D1
Wkra (riv.) E2
Wolin (Wollin) (isl.) B2

© Copyright HAMMOND INCORPORATED, Maplewood, N.J.

UNION REPUBLICS

Armenian S.S.R. 3,031,000	E6
Azerbaidzhan S.S.R. 6,028,000	E6
Estonian S.S.R. 1,466,000	C4
Georgian S.S.R. 5,015,000	D5
Kazakh S.S.R. 14,684,000	G5
Kirgiz S.S.R. 3,529,000	H5
Latvian S.S.R. 2,521,000	C4
Lithuanian S.S.R. 3,398,000	C4
Moldavian S.S.R. 3,947,000	C5
Russian S.F.S.R. 137,551,000	D4
Tadzhik S.S.R. 3,801,000	H6
Turkmen S.S.R. 2,759,000	F6
Ukrainian S.S.R. 49,755,000	C5
Uzbek S.S.R. 15,391,000	G5
White Russian S.S.R. 9,560,000	C4

INTERNAL DIVISIONS

Abkhaz A.S.S.R. 505,000	E5
Adygey Aut. Obl. 405,000	D5
Adzhar A.S.S.R. 354,000	E5
Aginsk Buryat Aut. Okr. 69,000	M4
Bashkir A.S.S.R. 3,849,000	F4
Buryat A.S.S.R. 900,000	M4
Chechen-Ingush A.S.S.R. 1,154,000	E5
Chukchi Aut. Okr. 133,000	R3
Chuvash A.S.S.R. 1,292,000	E4
Dagestan A.S.S.R. 1,628,000	E5
Evenki Aut. Okr. 16,000	K3
Gorno-Altay Aut. Obl. 172,000	J4
Gorno-Badakhshan Aut. Obl. 127,000	H6
Jewish Aut. Obl. 190,000	O5
Kabardin-Balkar	

A.S.S.R. 674,000	E5
Kalmuck A.S.S.R. 294,000	E5
Karachay-Cherkess Aut. Obl. 368,000	E5
Karakalpak A.S.S.R. 904,000	G5
Karelian A.S.S.R. 736,000	D3
Khakass Aut. Obl. 500,000	J4
Khanty-Mansi Aut. Okr. 569,000	H3
Komi A.S.S.R. 1,119,000	F3
Komi-Permyak Aut. Okr. 173,000	F4
Koryak Aut. Okr. 34,000	R3
Mari A.S.S.R. 703,000	E4
Mordvinian A.S.S.R. 991,000	E4
Nagorno-Karabakh Aut. Obl. 161,000	E6
Nakhichevan A.S.S.R. 239,000	E6
Nenets Aut. Okr. 47,000	F3
North Ossetian A.S.S.R. 597,000	E5
South Ossetian Aut. Obl. 98,000	E5
Tatar A.S.S.R. 3,445,000	F4
Taymyr Aut. Okr. 44,000	K2
Tuvinian A.S.S.R. 267,000	K4
Udmurt A.S.S.R. 1,494,000	F4
Ust-Ordynsky Buryat Aut. Okr. 133,000	L4
Yakut A.S.S.R. 839,000	N3
Yamal-Nenets Aut. Okr. 158,000	H3

CITIES and TOWNS

Abakan 128,000	K4
Abay 34,245	H5
Abaza 15,202	J4
Achinsk 117,000	K4
Agata	K3
Aginskoye 7,922	M4
Akmolinsk (Tselinograd) 234,000	H4
Aksay 10,010	F5
Aktas	G5
Aktash	F4
Aktyubinsk 191,000	F4
Aldan 17,689	N4
Aleksandrovsk-Sakhalinskiy 20,342	P5
Alekseyevka 18,041	M4
Aleysk 32,487	J4
Alga 12,000	F5
Aliskerovo	R3
Alma-Ata 910,000	H5
Almazny	N3
Ambarchik	F3
Anderma	J4
Amursk 24,010	O4
Anadyr' 7,703	S3
Andizhan 230,000	H5
Angarsk 239,000	L4
Angren	G5
Anzhero-Sudzhensk 105,000	J4
Aral'sk 37,722	G5
Archangel (Arkhangel'sk) 385,000	E3
Arkalyk 15,108	G4
Armavir 162,000	E5
Arsen'yev 60,000	O5
Artem 69,000	O5
Artemovskiy	M4
Arys' 26,414	G5
Arzamas 93,000	E4
Asbest 79,000	G4

Ashkhabad 312,000	F6
Asino 29,395	J4
Astrakhan' 461,000	E5
Atbasar 37,228	G4
Atka	Q3
Ayaguz 35,827	J5
Ayan	O4
Aykhal	M3
Bagdarin	L4
Baku 1,022,000	F5
Baku* 1,550,000	F5
Balakovo 152,000	E4
Balashov 93,000	E4
Baley 27,215	M4
Balkhash 78,000	H5
Balykshi 22,397	F5
Bam	H4
Barabinsk 37,274	H4
Baranovichi 131,000	C4
Barnaul 533,000	J4
Batagay 10,000	N3
Baykit 123,000	K3
Baykit	K3
Baykonur	G5
Bayram-Ali 31,987	G6
Belgorod 240,000	D4
Belogorsk 63,000	N4
Belomorsk 16,595	D3
Beloretsk 71,000	F4
Belovo 112,000	J4
Berdichev 80,000	C5
Berdsk 67,000	J4
Berezniki 185,000	F4
Berezovo 6,000	G3
Beringovskiy	T3
Bikin 17,473	O5
Bira	O5

Birobidzhan 69,000	O5
Biruni	G5
Biysk 212,000	J4
Blagoveshchensk 172,000	N4
Bodaybo 19,000	M4
Borisoglebsk 68,000	E4
Borzya 27,815	M4
Bratsk 214,000	L4
Brest 177,000	C4
Brindakit	O4
Bryansk 394,000	D4
Bugul'ma 80,000	F4
Bukachacha 10,000	M4
Bukhara 185,000	G5
Bulun	N2
Buzuluk 76,000	F4
Chadan	K4
Chapayevsk 85,000	F4
Chara	G6
Chardzhou 140,000	G6
Charsk 10,100	J5
Cheboksary 308,000	E4
Chegdomyn 16,499	O4
Chelkar 19,377	F5
Chelyabinsk 1,030,000	G4
Cheremkhovo 77,000	L4
Cherepovets 266,000	D4
Cherkessk 91,000	E5
Chernigov 238,000	D4
Chernogorsk 71,000	K4
Chernovtsy 219,000	C5
Chernyshevsk 10,000	M4
Chersky	Q3
Chimbay 18,899	F5
Chimkent 322,000	H5
Chirchik 132,000	H5

Chita 303,000	M4
Chokurdakh	P2
Chumikan	O4
Dal'negorsk 33,506	O5
Dal'nerechensk 28,224	O5
Daugavpils 116,000	C4
Denau	G6
Dikson	J2
Dimitrovgrad 106,000	F4
Dnepropetrovsk 1,066,000	D5
Donetsk 1,021,000	D5
Drogobych 66,000	C5
Druzhba	J5
Druzhina	P3
Dubinka 19,701	E4
Dushanbe 494,000	G6
Dzerzminsk 257,000	E4
Dzhalal-Abad 55,000	H5
Dzhalinda	M5
Dzhambul 264,000	H5
Dzhelinda	M3
Dzhetygara 32,169	G4
Dzhezkazgan 89,000	G5
Dzhusaly 20,658	G5
Egvekinot	T3
Ekibastuz 66,000	H4
Ekimchan	O4
El'dikan	O4
Elista 70,000	E5
Emba 17,820	F5
Engel's 161,000	E4
Erivan 1,019,000	E6
Fergana 176,000	H5
Fort-Shevchenko 12,000	F5
Frolovo 33,398	E4
Frunze 533,000	H5

Gasan-Kuli	F6
Gol'chikha	J2
Gomel 383,000	D4
Gor'kiy 1,344,000	E4
Gorno-Altaysk 34,413	J4
Gornyak 16,643	J4
Grodno 195,000	C4
Groznyy 375,000	E5
Gubakha 33,243	F4
Gulistan 30,879	G5
Gur'yev 131,000	F5
Gusinoozersk 10,000	L4
Gyda	H2
Igarka 15,624	J3
Igrim	G3
Ilanskiy 22,852	K4
Indiga	E3
Inta 51,000	G3
Iolotan' 10,000	G6
Irkutsk 550,000	L4
Ishim 63,000	G4
Isil'kul' 25,958	H4
Ivano-Frankovsk 150,000	C5
Ivanovo 465,000	E4
Ivdel 15,308	G4
Izhevsk (Ustinov) 549,000	F4
Izmail 83,000	C5
Kagan 34,117	G6
Kalachinsk 20,809	H4
Kaluga 265,000	D4
Kalina 412,000	F4
Kaliningrad 355,000	B4
Kalmykovo	F5
Kaluga 265,000	D4
Kamen'-na-Obi 35,604	H4

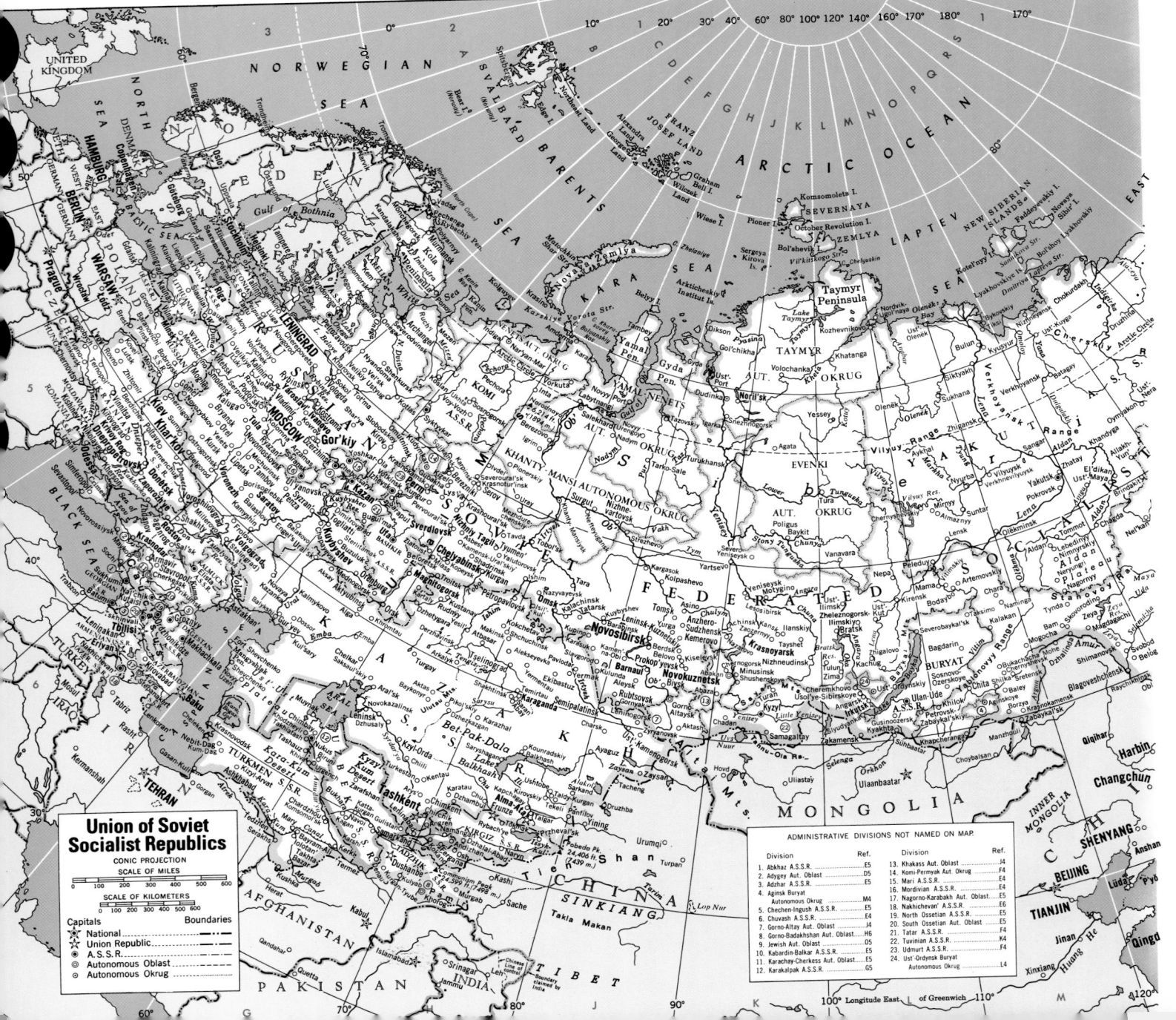

Union of Soviet Socialist Republics

CONIC PROJECTION

SCALE OF MILES

0 100 200 300 400 500 600

SCALE OF KILOMETERS

0 100 200 300 400 500 600

Capitals	Boundaries
★ National	National
☆ Union Republic	Union Republic
◉ A.S.S.R.	A.S.S.R.
◎ Autonomous Oblast	Autonomous Oblast
○ Autonomous Okrug	Autonomous Okrug

ADMINISTRATIVE DIVISIONS NOT NAMED ON MAP

Division	Ref.	Division	Ref.
1. Abkhaz A.S.S.R.	E5	13. Khakass Aut. Oblast	K4
2. Adygey Aut. Oblast	E5	14. Komi-Permyak Aut. Okrug	F4
3. Adzhar A.S.S.R.	E5	15. Mari A.S.S.R.	E4
4. Aginsk Buryat Autonomous Okrug	M4	16. Mordvinian A.S.S.R.	E4
5. Chechen-Ingush A.S.S.R.	E5	17. Nagorno-Karabakh Aut. Oblast	E6
6. Chuvash A.S.S.R.	E4	18. Nakhichevan A.S.S.R.	E6
7. Gorno-Altay Aut. Oblast	J4	19. North Ossetian A.S.S.R.	E5
8. Gorno-Badakhshan Aut. Oblast	H6	20. South Ossetian Aut. Oblast	E5
9. Jewish Aut. Oblast	O5	21. Tatar A.S.S.R.	F4
10. Kabardin-Balkar A.S.S.R.	E5	22. Tuvinian A.S.S.R.	K4
11. Karachay-Cherkess Aut. Oblast	E5	23. Udmurt A.S.S.R.	F4
12. Karakalpak A.S.S.R.	G5	24. Ust-Ordynsk Buryat Autonomous Okrug	L4

AREA 8,649,490 sq. mi. (22,402,179 sq. km.)
POPULATION 262,436,227
CAPITAL Moscow
LARGEST CITY Moscow
HIGHEST POINT Communism Peak 24,599 ft. (7,498 m.)
MONETARY UNIT ruble
MAJOR LANGUAGES Russian, Ukrainian, White Russian, Uzbek, Azerbaidzhani, Tatar, Georgian, Lithuanian, Armenian, Yiddish, Latvian, Mordvinian, Kirgiz, Tadzhik, Estonian, Kazakh, Moldavian (Romanian), German, Chuvash, Turkmenian, Bashkir
MAJOR RELIGIONS Eastern (Russian) Orthodoxy, Islam, Judaism, Protestantism (Baltic States)

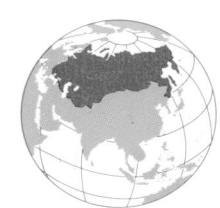

Kamenskoye	R3	Kavalerovo 16,415		O5
Kamensk-Ural'skiy 187,000	G4	Kazan' 993,000		F4
Kamyshin 112,000	E4	Kem' 21,025		D3
Kandalaksha 42,656	C3	Kemerovo 471,000		J4
Kansk 101,000	K4	Kentau 52,000		G5
Kapchagay	H5	Kerki 10,000		G6
Kara	G3	Khabarovsk 528,000		O5
Karaganda 572,000	H5	Khandyga		O3
Karasuk 22,637	H4	Khanty-Mansiysk 24,754		H3
Karatau 26,962	H5	Khar'kov 1,444,000		D4
Karazhal 17,702	H5	Khatanga		L2
Kargasok	J4	Kherson 319,000		D5
Karpinsk	F4	Khilok 17,000		M4
Karshi 108,000	G6	Khiva 24,139		F5
Kartaly 42,801	G4	Khodzheyli 36,435		F5
Katangli	P4	Kholmsk 37,412		P5
Kattakurgan 53,000	G5	Khorog 12,295		H6
Kaunas 370,000	C4	Kiev 2,144,000		D4

UNION REPUBLICS

	AREA (sq. mi.)	AREA (sq. km.)	POPULATION	CAPITAL and LARGEST CITY
RUSSIAN S.F.S.R.	6,592,812	17,075,400	137,551,000	Moscow 7,831,000
KAZAKH S.S.R.	1,048,300	2,715,100	14,684,000	Alma-Ata 910,000
UKRAINIAN S.S.R.	233,089	603,700	49,755,000	Kiev 2,144,000
TURKMEN S.S.R.	188,455	488,100	2,759,000	Ashkhabad 312,000
UZBEK S.S.R.	173,591	449,600	15,391,000	Tashkent 1,780,000
WHITE RUSSIAN S.S.R.	80,154	207,600	9,560,000	Minsk 1,262,000
KIRGIZ S.S.R.	76,641	198,500	3,529,000	Frunze 533,000
TADZHIK S.S.R.	55,251	143,100	3,801,000	Dushanbe 494,000
AZERBAIDZHAN S.S.R.	33,436	86,600	6,028,000	Baku 1,022,000
GEORGIAN S.S.R.	26,911	69,700	5,015,000	Tbilisi 1,066,000
LITHUANIAN S.S.R.	25,174	65,200	3,398,000	Vilna 481,000
LATVIAN S.S.R.	24,595	63,700	2,521,000	Riga 835,000
ESTONIAN S.S.R.	17,413	45,100	1,466,000	Tallinn 430,000
MOLDAVIAN S.S.R.	13,012	33,700	3,947,000	Kishinev 503,000
ARMENIAN S.S.R.	11,506	29,800	3,031,000	Erivan 1,019,000

Kirensk 10,000	L4	Krasnokamsk 56,000	F4	Leninakan 207,000	E5	Miass 150,000	G4	Nazarovo 54,000	K4
Kirov 390,000	E4	Krasnotur'insk 61,000	G3	Leningrad 4,073,000	D4	Michurinsk 101,000	E4	Nazyvayevsk 15,792	H4
Kirovabad 232,000	E5	Krasnoural'sk 39,743	G4	Leningrad* 4,588,000	D4	Millerovo 34,627	E5	Nebit-Dag 71,000	F6
Kirovograd 237,000	D5	Krasnovodsk 53,000	F5	Leninogorsk 54,000	J5	Minsk 1,262,000	C4	Nefteyugansk 52,000	H3
Kirovskiy	H5	Krasnoyarsk 796,000	K4	Leninsk	G5	Minsk* 1,276,000	C4	Nel'kan	O4
Kiselevsk 122,000	J4	Kremenchug 210,000	D5	Leninsk-Kuznetskiy 132,000	J4	Minusinsk 56,000	K4	Nepa	L4
Kishinev 503,000	C5	Krivoy Rog 650,000	D5	Leninskoye	O5	Mirnyy 23,826	M3	Neryungri	N4
Kizel 46,264	F4	Kudymkar 26,350	F4	Lenkoran' 35,505	E6	Mogilev 290,000	D4	Nevel'sk 20,726	P5
Kizyl-Arvat 21,671	F6	Kul'sary 16,427	F5	Lensk 16,758	M3	Mogocha 17,884	N4	Nikolayev 440,000	D5
Klaipeda 176,000	B4	Kulunda 15,264	H4	Lesosibirsk	K4	Molodechno 73,000	C4	Nikolayevsk-na-Amure 30,082	P4
Kokand 153,000	H5	Kulyab 55,000	H6	Lesozavodsk 34,957	O5	Monchegorsk 51,000	D3	Nikol'skoye	R4
Kokchetav 103,000	H4	Kum-Dag 10,000	F6	Liepāja 108,000	B4	Moscow (cap.) 7,831,000	D4	Nizhneudinsk 39,743	K4
Kolomna 147,000	D4	Kungur 80,000	F4	Lipetsk 396,000	E4	Moscow* 8,011,000	D4	Nizhnevartovsk 109,000	H3
Kolpashevo 24,911	J4	Kupino 20,799	H4	Lutsk 137,000	C4	Motygino 10,000	K4	Nizhneyansk	O3
Komsomol'sk 15,385	G4	Kurgan 310,000	G4	L'vov 667,000	C4	Mozyr' 73,000	C4	Nizhniy Tagil 398,000	G4
Komsomol'sk-na-Amure 264,000	O4	Kurgan-Tyube 34,620	G6	Lys'va 75,000	F4	Murgab	H6	Nordvik-Ugol'naya	M2
Kondopoga 27,908	D3	Kursk 375,000	D4	Magadan 121,000	P4	Murmansk 381,000	D3	Noril'sk 180,000	J3
Kopeysk 146,000	G4	Kushka	G6	Magdagachi 15,059	N4	Muynak 12,000	F5	Novaya Kazanka	F5
Korf	R3	Kustanay 165,000	G4	Magnitogorsk 406,000	G4	Mys Shmidta	U3	Novgorod 186,000	D4
Korsakov 38,210	P5	Kutaisi 194,000	E5	Makhachkala 251,000	E5	Nadym	H3	Novokazalinsk 34,815	G5
Koslan	E3	Kuybyshev 1,216,000	F4	Makinsk 22,810	H4	Nagornyy	N4	Novokuznetsk 541,000	J4
Kostroma 255,000	E4	Kuybyshev 40,166	H4	Makinsk 22,810	H4	Nakhichevan' 33,279	E6	Novomoskovsk 147,000	E4
Kotlas 61,000	E3	Kyakhta 15,316	L4	Mama	M4	Nakhodka 133,000	O5	Novorossiysk 159,000	D5
Kovel' 33,351	C4	Kyusyur	N2	Markovo	S3	Nal'chik 207,000	E5	Novosibirsk 1,312,000	J4
Kovrov 143,000	E4	Kyzyl 66,000	K4	Mary (Merv) 74,000	G6	Namangan 227,000	H5	Novosybkov 34,433	D4
Kozhevnikovo	L2	Kyzyl-Orda 156,000	G5	Maykop 128,000	D5	Naminga	M4	Novyy Port	G3
Krasino	F2	Labytnangi	G3	Mednogorsk 38,024	F4	Nar yan-Mar 16,864	F3	Novyy Uzen' 18,073	F5
Krasnodar 560,000	E5	Lebedinyy	N4	Medvezh'yegorsk 17,465	D3	Naryn 21,098	H5	Novyy Urengoy	H3
Krasnokamensk 51,000	M4	Leninabad 130,000	G5	Mezen'	E3	Navoi 84,000	G6	Nukus 109,000	G5

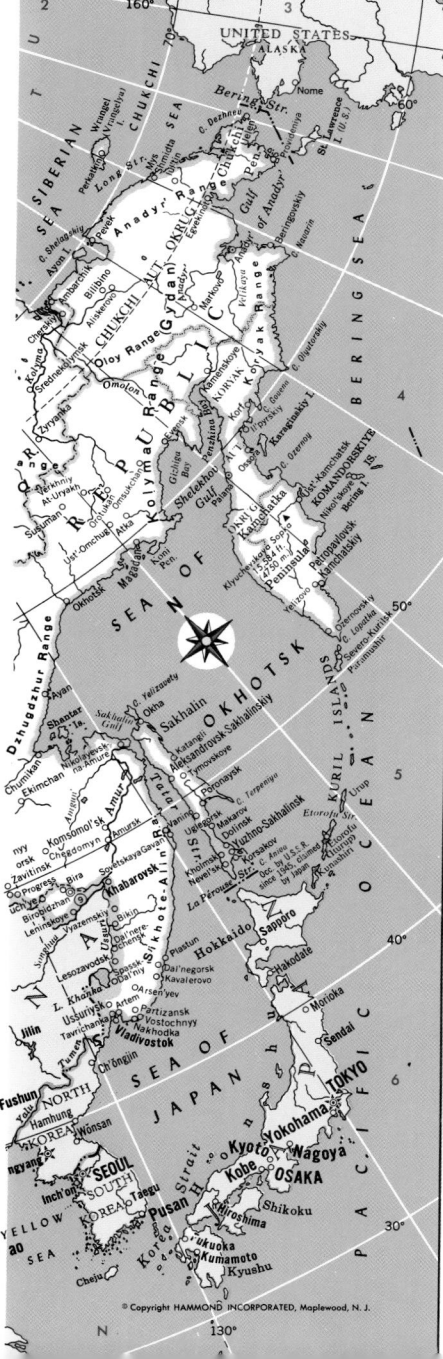

Topography

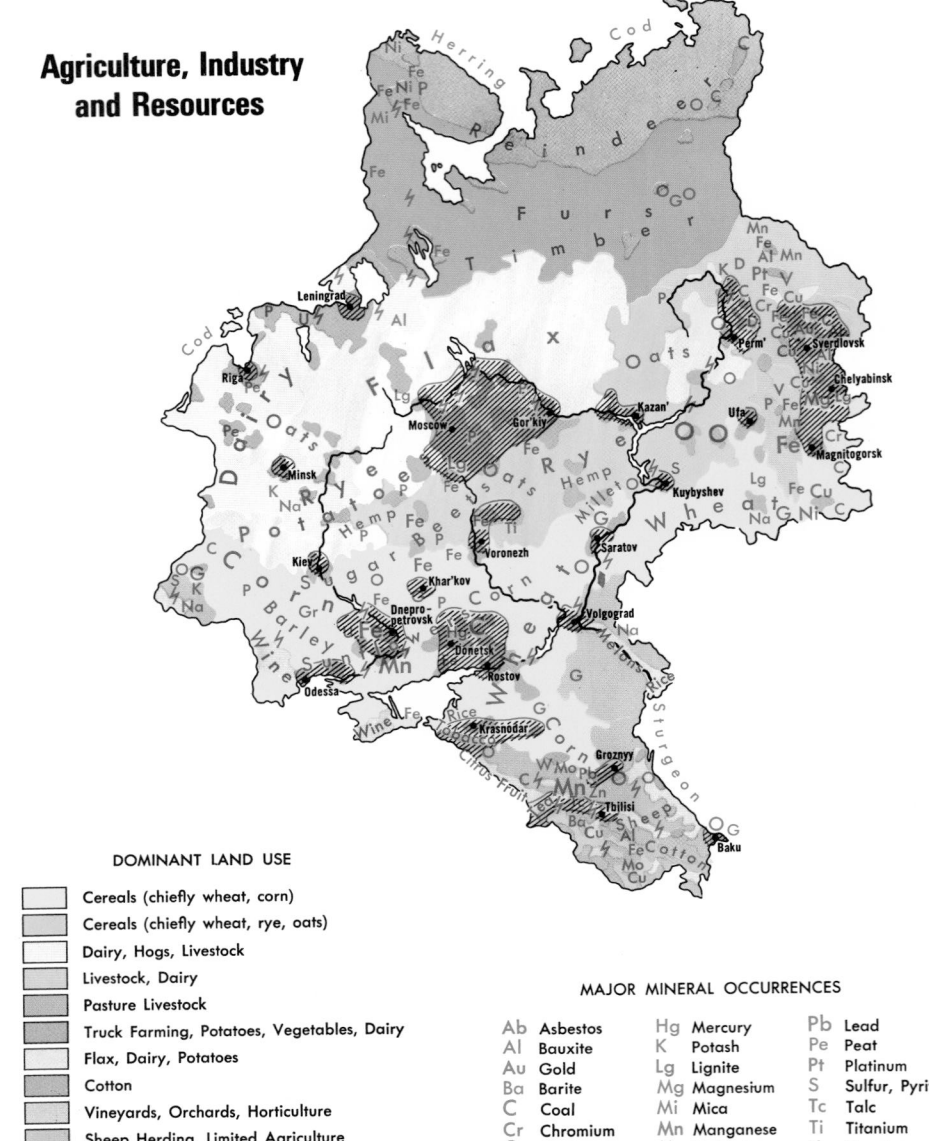

Agriculture, Industry and Resources

DOMINANT LAND USE

- Cereals (chiefly wheat, corn)
- Cereals (chiefly wheat, rye, oats)
- Dairy, Hogs, Livestock
- Livestock, Dairy
- Pasture Livestock
- Truck Farming, Potatoes, Vegetables, Dairy
- Flax, Dairy, Potatoes
- Cotton
- Vineyards, Orchards, Horticulture
- Sheep Herding, Limited Agriculture
- Forests
- Nonagricultural Land

MAJOR MINERAL OCCURRENCES

Ab	Asbestos	Hg	Mercury	Pb	Lead
Al	Bauxite	K	Potash	Pe	Peat
Au	Gold	Lg	Lignite	Pt	Platinum
Ba	Barite	Mg	Magnesium	S	Sulfur, Pyrites
C	Coal	Mi	Mica	Tc	Talc
Cr	Chromium	Mn	Manganese	Ti	Titanium
Cu	Copper	Mo	Molybdenum	U	Uranium
D	Diamonds	Na	Salt	V	Vanadium
Fe	Iron Ore	Ni	Nickel	W	Tungsten
G	Natural Gas	O	Petroleum	Zn	Zinc
Gr	Graphite	P	Phosphates		

⚡ Water Power   ▨ Major Industrial Areas

Agriculture, Industry and Resources

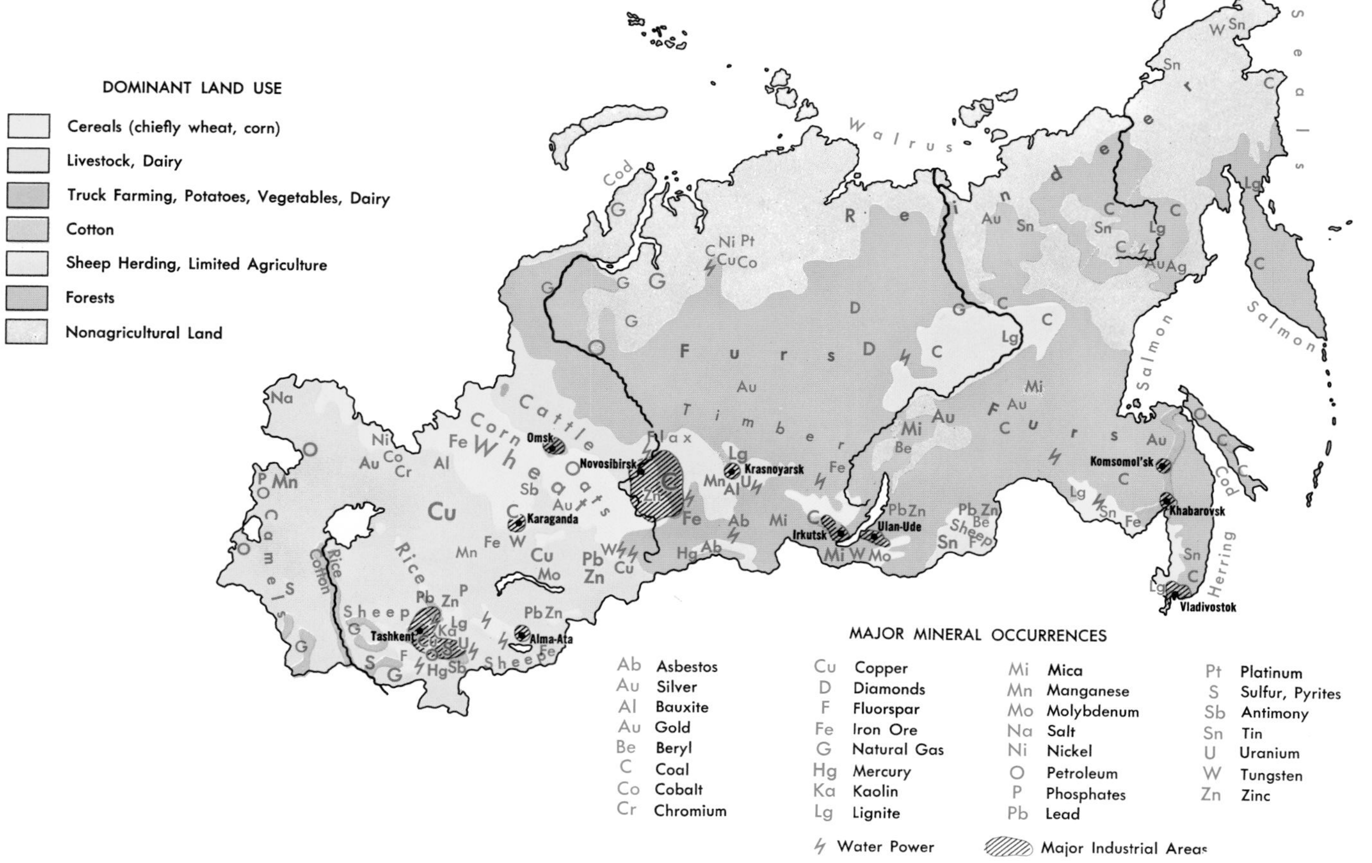

DOMINANT LAND USE

- Cereals (chiefly wheat, corn)
- Livestock, Dairy
- Truck Farming, Potatoes, Vegetables, Dairy
- Cotton
- Sheep Herding, Limited Agriculture
- Forests
- Nonagricultural Land

MAJOR MINERAL OCCURRENCES

Ab Asbestos	Cu Copper	Mi Mica	Pt Platinum
Au Silver	D Diamonds	Mn Manganese	S Sulfur, Pyrites
Al Bauxite	F Fluorspar	Mo Molybdenum	Sb Antimony
Au Gold	Fe Iron Ore	Na Salt	Sn Tin
Be Beryl	G Natural Gas	Ni Nickel	U Uranium
C Coal	Hg Mercury	O Petroleum	W Tungsten
Co Cobalt	Ka Kaolin	P Phosphates	Zn Zinc
Cr Chromium	Lg Lignite	Pb Lead	

⚡ Water Power   ▨ Major Industrial Areas

U.S.S.R.—Railroads and Navigation

Principal Railroads
Navigable Rivers
Canals
Main Sea Routes
Major Russian Ports ⚓

SCALE OF MILES
0   500   1000

SCALE OF KILOMETERS
0   500   1000

® Copyright HAMMOND INCORPORATED, Maplewood, N.J.

U.S.S.R. — EUROPEAN

UNION REPUBLICS

Armenian S.S.R. 3,031,000 F6
Azerbaidzhan S.S.R. 6,028,000 G6
Estonian S.S.R 1,466,000 C3
Georgian S.S.R. 5,015,000 F6
Latvian S.S.R 2,521,000 B3
Lithuanian S.S.R. 3,398,000 B3
Moldavian S.S.R. 3,947,000 C5
Russian S.F.S.R. 137,551,000 F3
Ukrainian S.S.R. 49,755,000 D5
White Russian S.S.R. 9,560,000 C4

INTERNAL DIVISIONS

Abkhaz A.S.S.R. 505,000 F6
Adygey Aut. Obl. 405,000 F6
Adzhar A.S.S.R. 354,000 F6
Bashkir A.S.S.R. 3,849,000 J4
Chechen-Ingush A.S.S.R. 1,154,000 G6
Chuvash A.S.S.R. 1,292,000 G3
Crimean Oblast 2,183,000 D6
Dagestan A.S.S.R. 1,628,000 G6
Kabardin-Balkar A.S.S.R. 674,000 F6
Kalmuck A.S.S.R. 294,000 F5
Karachay-Cherkess Aut. Obl. 368,000 F6
Karelian A.S.S.R. 736,000 D2
Komi A.S.S.R. 1,119,000 H2
Komi-Permyak Aut. Okr. 173,000 H3
Mari A.S.S.R. 703,000 G3
Mordvinian A.S.S.R. 991,000 G4
Nagorno-Karabakh Aut. Obl. 161,000 G7
Nakhichevan' A.S.S.R. 239,000 F7
Nenets Aut. Okr. 47,000 H1
North Ossetian A.S.S.R. 597,000 F6
South Ossetian Aut. Obl. 98,000 F6
Tatar A.S.S.R. 3,436,000 G3
Trans-Carpathian Oblast 1,155,000 B5
Udmurt A.S.S.R. 1,494,000 H3
Volyn Oblast 1,015,000 C4

CITIES and TOWNS

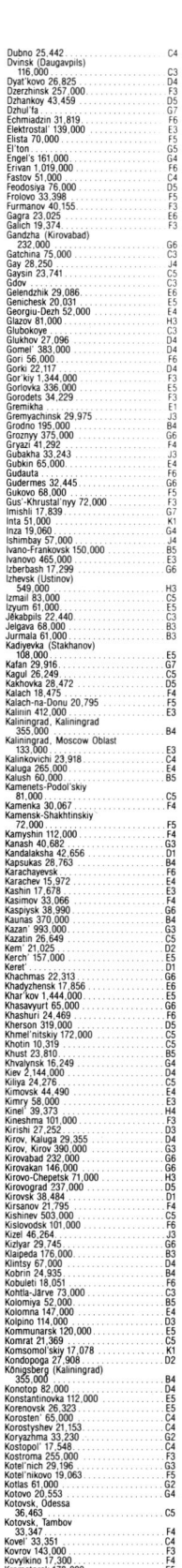

Abdulino 26,010 H4
Agdam 21,277 G6
Agryz 19,267 H3
Akhaltsikhe 18,972 F6
Akhtubinsk 43,466 G5
Akhty G6
Akhtyrka 41,354 E4
Akkerman (Belgorod-Dnestrovskiy) 32,928 D5
Alagir 18,161 F6
Alatyr' 43,499 G4
Alaverdi 21,311 F6
Aleksandriya 82,000 D5
Aleksandrovsk 18,286 J3
Alekseyevka 25,562 E4
Aleksin 67,000 E4
Ali-Bayramly 33,828 G7
Al'met'yevsk 110,000 H3
Alushta 22,016 D6
Amderma K1
Anapa 29,900 E6
Andropov 239,000 E3
Apatity 62,000 D1
Apsheronsk 32,867 F6
Archangel (Arkhangel'sk) 385,000 F2
Armavir 162,000 F5
Arzamas 93,000 F3
Astara G7
Astrakhan' 461,000 G5
Atkarsk 28,881 G4
Azov 75,000 E5
Bakhchisaray 15,912 D6
Baku 1,022,000 H6
Balakhna 36,542 F3
Balaklava D6
Balakovo 152,000 G4
Balashov 93,000 F4
Baltiysk 20,300 A4
Baranovichi 131,000 C4
Barysh 20,792 G4
Bataysk 90,000 E5
Batumi 123,000 F6
Belaya Tserkov' 151,000 C5
Belebey 32,460 H4
Belev 17,733 E4
Belgorod 240,000 E4
Belgorod-Dnestrovskiy 32,928 D5
Belomorsk 16,595 D2
Belorechensk 35,970 E6
Beloretsk 71,000 J4
Belozersk E3
Bel'tsy 125,000 C5
Belush'ya Guba H1
Bendery 101,000 C5
Berdichev 80,000 C5
Berdyansk 122,000 E5
Beregovo 27,308 B5
Berezniki 185,000 J3
Beslan 26,893 F6
Bezhetsk 30,030 E3
Birsk 29,607 J3
Bobrov 17,977 F4
Bobruysk 192,000 C4
Bologoye 33,949 D3
Bor 63,000 F3
Borislav 33,800 B5
Borisoglebsk 68,000 F4
Borisov 112,000 C4
Borovichi 60,000 D3
Brest 177,000 B4
Brezhnev 301,000 H3
Bryansk 394,000 D4
Bugul'ma 80,000 H4
Buguruslan 54,000 H4
Buturlinovka 21,643 F4
Buy 29,946 F3
Buynaksk 37,946 G6
Buzuluk 76,000 H4
Bykhov 17,371 C4
Cēsis 17,696 C3
Chadyr-Lunga 20,474 C5
Chapayevsk 85,000 G4
Chaykovskiy 48,034 H3
Cheboksary 308,000 G3
Cherepovets 266,000 E3
Cherkassy 228,000 D5
Cherkessk 91,000 F6
Chernigov 238,000 D4
Chernovtsy 219,000 C5
Chernushka 21,106 J3
Chervonograd 55,000 B4
Chiatura 25,474 F6
Chistopol' 64,000 H3
Chortkov 19,183 B5
Chudovo D3
Chusovoy 56,000 J3
Danilov 17,500 E3
Dankov 20,030 E4
Daugavpils 116,000 C3
Davlekanovo 20,123 H4
Derbent 70,000 G6
Dimitrovgrad 106,000 G4
Dneprodzerzhinsk 250,000 D5
Dnepropetrovsk 1,066,000 D5
Dobrush 16,809 D4
Dobryanka 18,349 J3
Donetsk 1,021,000 E5
Drogobych 66,000 B5
Dubna 55,000 E3
Dubna E4
Dubno 25,442 C4
Dvinsk (Daugavpils) 116,000 C3
Dyat'kovo 26,825 D4
Dzerzhinsk 257,000 F3
Dzhankoy 43,459 D5
Dzhul'fa G7
Echmiadzin 31,819 F6
Elektrostal' 139,000 E3
Elista 70,000 F5
El'ton G5
Engel's 161,000 G4
Erivan 1,019,000 F6
Fastov 51,000 C4
Feodosiya 76,000 D5
Frolovo 33,398 F5
Furmanov 40,155 F3
Gagra 23,025 E6
Galich 19,374 F3
Gandzha (Kirovabad) 232,000 G6
Gatchina 75,000 C3
Gay 28,250 J4
Gaysin 23,741 C5
Gdov C3
Gelendzhik 29,086 E6
Genichesk 20,031 E5
Georgiu-Dezh 52,000 E4
Glazov 81,000 H3
Glubokoye C3
Glukhov 27,096 D4
Gomel' 383,000 D4
Gori 56,000 F6
Gorki 22,117 D4
Gor'kiy 1,344,000 F3
Gorlovka 336,000 E5
Gorodets 34,229 F3
Gremikha E1
Gremyachinsk 29,975 J3
Grodno 195,000 B4
Groznyy 375,000 G6
Gryazi 41,292 F4
Gubakha 33,243 J3
Gubkin 65,000 E4
Gudauta F6
Gudermes 32,445 G6
Gukovo 68,000 F5
Gus'-Khrustal'nyy 72,000 F3
Imishli 17,839 G7
Inta 51,000 K1
Inza 19,060 G4
Ishimbay 57,000 J4
Ivano-Frankovsk 150,000 B5
Ivanovo 465,000 E3
Izberbash 17,299 G6
Izhevsk (Ustinov) 549,000 H3
Izmail 83,000 C5
Izyum 61,000 E5
Jēkabpils 22,440 C3
Jelgava 68,000 B3
Jurmala 61,000 B3
Kadiyevka (Stakhanov) 108,000 E5
Kafan 29,916 G7
Kagul 26,249 C5
Kakhovka 28,472 D5
Kalach 18,475 F4
Kalach-na-Donu 20,795 F5
Kalinin 412,000 E3
Kaliningrad, Kaliningrad 355,000 B4
Kaliningrad, Moscow Oblast 133,000 E3
Kalinkovichi 23,918 C4
Kaluga 265,000 E4
Kalush 60,000 B5
Kamenets-Podol'skiy 81,000 C5
Kamenka 30,067 F4
Kamensk-Shakhtinskiy 72,000 F5
Kamyshin 112,000 F4
Kanash 40,682 G3
Kandalaksha 42,656 D1
Kapsukas 28,763 B4
Karachayevsk F6
Karachev 15,972 E4
Kashin 17,678 E3
Kasimov 33,066 F4
Kaspiysk 38,990 G6
Kaunas 370,000 B4
Kazan' 993,000 G3
Kazatin 26,649 C5
Kem' 21,025 D2
Kerch' 157,000 E5
Keret' D1
Khachmas 22,313 G6
Khadyzhensk 17,856 E6
Khar'kov 1,444,000 E5
Khasavyurt 65,000 G6
Khashuri 24,469 F6
Kherson 319,000 D5
Khmel'nitskiy 172,000 C5
Khotin 10,319 C5
Khust 23,810 B5
Khvalynsk 16,249 G4
Kiev 2,144,000 D4
Kiliya 24,276 C5
Kimovsk 44,490 E4
Kimry 58,000 E3
Kinel' 39,373 H4
Kineshma 101,000 F3
Kirishi 27,252 D3
Kirov, Kaluga 29,355 D4
Kirov, Kirov 390,000 G3
Kirovabad 232,000 G6
Kirovakan 146,000 G6
Kirovo-Chepetsk 71,000 H3
Kirovograd 237,000 D5
Kirovsk 38,484 D1
Kirsanov 21,795 F4
Kishinev 503,000 C5
Kislovodsk 101,000 F6
Kizel 46,264 J3
Kizlyar 29,745 G6
Klaipeda 176,000 B3
Klintsy 67,000 D4
Kobrin 24,935 B4
Kobuleti 18,051 F6
Kohtla-Järve 73,000 C3
Kolomiya 52,000 B5
Kolomna 147,000 E4
Kolpino 114,000 D3
Kommunarsk 120,000 E5
Komrat 21,369 C5
Komsomol'skiy 17,078 K1
Kondopoga 27,908 D2
Königsberg (Kaliningrad) 355,000 B4
Konotop 82,000 D4
Konstantinovka 112,000 E5
Korenovsk 26,323 E5
Korosten' 65,000 C4
Korostyshev 21,153 C4
Koryazhma 33,230 G2
Kostopol' 17,548 C4
Kostroma 255,000 F3
Kotel'nich 29,196 G3
Kotel'nikovo 19,063 F5
Kotlas 61,000 G2
Kotovo 20,553 G4
Kotovsk, Odessa 36,463 C5
Kotovsk, Tambov 33,347 F4
Kovel' 33,351 C4
Kovrov 143,000 F3
Kovylkino 17,300 F4
Kramatorsk 178,000 E5
Krasnoarmeysk 60,000 G4
Krasnodar 560,000 E6
Krasnograd 18,386 E5
Krasnokamsk 56,000 H3
Krasnoslobodsk 17,749 G5
Krasnovishersk J2
Krasnyy Kut 17,087 G4

The government of the United States has not recognized the incorporation of Estonia, Latvia and Lithuania into the Soviet Union, nor does it recognize other post-war territorial changes shown on this map. The flags shown here were the official flags of the independent Baltic States prior to 1939.

© Copyright by HAMMOND INCORPORATED, Maplewood, N.J.

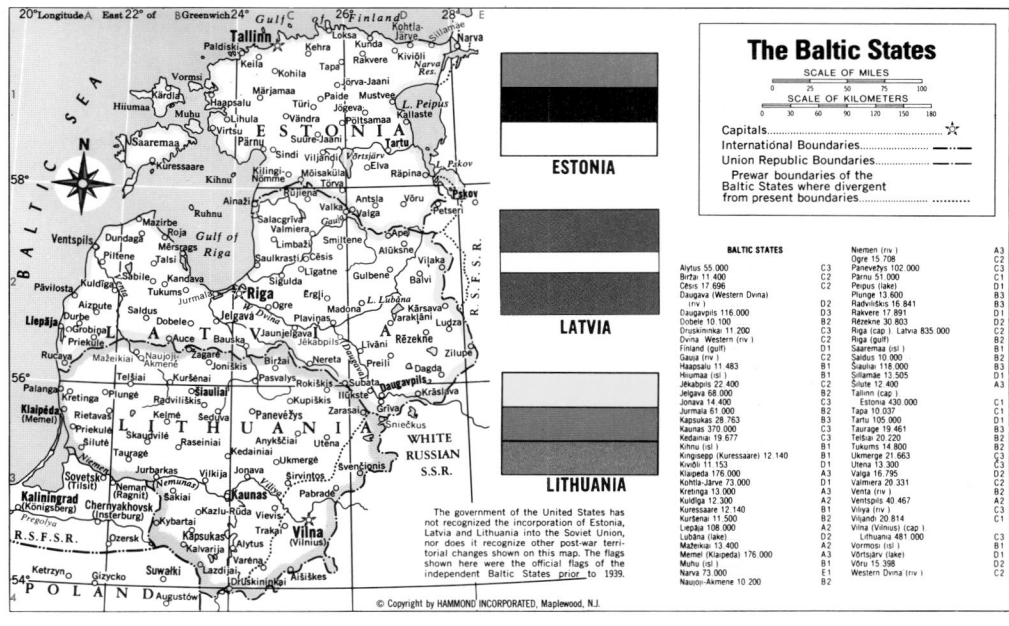

The Baltic States

SCALE OF MILES 0 25 50 75 100
SCALE OF KILOMETERS 0 30 60 90 120 150 180

Capitals ☆
International Boundaries
Union Republic Boundaries
Prewar boundaries of the Baltic States where divergent from present boundaries

BALTIC STATES

Alytus 55.000 C3
Biržai 11.400 C2
Cēsis 17.696 C2
Daugava (Western Dvina) (riv.) D2
Daugavpils 116.000 D3
Dobele 10.100 B2
Druskininkai 11.200 C3
Dvina, Western (riv.) C2
Finland (gulf) D1
Gauja (riv.) C2
Haapsalu 11.483 B1
Hiiumaa (isl.) B1
Jēkabpils 22.400 C2
Jelgava 68.000 B2
Jonava 14.400 C3
Jurmala 61.000 B2
Kapsukas 28.763 B3
Kaunas 370.000 C3
Kedainiai 19.677 C3
Kihnu (isl.) B1
Kingisepp (Kuressaare) 12.140 B1
Kiviõli 11.153 D1
Klaipeda 176.000 A3
Kohtla-Järve 73.000 D1
Kretinga 13.000 A3
Kuldīga 12.300 A2
Kuressaare 12.140 B1
Kuršenai 11.500 B2
Liepāja 108.000 A2
Lubāna (lake) D2
Mažeikiai 13.400 A2
Memel (Klaipeda) 176.000 A3
Muhu (isl.) B1
Narva 73.000 E1
Naujoji-Akmene 10.200 B2
Niemen (riv.) A3
Ogre 15.708 C2
Panevežys 102.000 C3
Pärnu 51.000 C1
Peipus (lake) D1
Plunge 13.600 B3
Radviliškis 16.841 B3
Rakvere 17.891 D1
Rēzekne 30.803 D2
Riga (cap.), Latvia 835.000 C2
Riga (gulf) B2
Saaremaa (isl.) B1
Saldus 10.000 B2
Šiauliai 118.000 B3
Sillamäe 13.505 D1
Šilute 12.400 A3
Tallinn (cap.), Estonia 430.000 C1
Tapa 10.037 C1
Tartu 105.000 D1
Taurage 19.461 B3
Telšiai 20.220 B2
Tukums 14.800 B2
Ukmerge 21.663 C3
Utena 13.300 C3
Valga 16.795 D2
Valmiera 20.331 C2
Venta (riv.) B2
Ventspils 40.467 A2
Viliya (riv.) C3
Viljandi 20.814 C1
Vilna (Vilnius) (cap.), Lithuania 481.000 C3
Vormosi (isl.) B1
Võrtsjärv (lake) D1
Võru 15.398 D2
Western Dvina (riv.) C2

Krasnyy Luch 106,000 E5
Krasnyy Sulin 41,684 F5
Kremenchug 210,000 D5
Krichev 25,682 D4
Krivoy Rog 650,000 D5
Krolevets 18,307 D4
Kronshtadt 39,477 C3
Kropotkin 70,000 F5
Krymsk 41,430 E5
Kuba 18,871 G6
Kudymkar 26,350 H3
Kulebaki 46,252 F3
Kumertau 52,000 J4
Kunda C3
Kungur 80,000 J3
Kupyansk 30,055 E5
Kuressaare 12,140 B3
Kursk 375,000 E4
Kutaisi 194,000 F6
Kuvandyk 22,914 J4
Kuybyshev 1,216,000 H4
Kuznetsk 94,000 G4
Kuzomen' E1
Labinsk 54,000 F6
Lakhdenpokh'ya C2
Lebedin 29,240 D4
Leninakan 207,000 F6
Leningrad 4,073,000 C3
Leningrad* 4,588,000 C3
Leninogorsk 54,000 H4
Lenkoran' 35,505 G7
L'gov 25,110 E4
Lida 66,000 C4
Liepāja 108,000 B3
Likhoslavl' E3
Lipetsk 396,000 E4
Lisichansk 119,000 E5
Livny 37,290 E4
Lodeynoye Pole 19,632 D2
Lozovaya 53,000 E5
Lubny 54,000 D4
Luga 31,905 C3
Lutsk 137,000 B4
L'vov (Lwów) 667,000 B5
Lys'va 75,000 J3
Lyubertsy 160,000 E3
Lyubotin 33,324 E4
Lyudinovo 33,871 D4
Makeyevka 436,000 E5
Makhachkala 251,000 G6
Makharadze 21,679 F6
Malaya Vishera 15,381 D3
Malgobek 20,548 F6
Manturovo 21,510 F3
Marganets 50,000 E5
Mariupol' (Zhdanov) 503,000 E5
Marks 17,132 G4
Maykop 128,000 F6
Mednogorsk 38,024 J4
Medvezh'yegorsk 17,465 D2
Melenki 18,545 F3
Meleuz 24,851 J4
Melitopol' 161,000 D5
Memel (Klaipeda) 176,000 B3
Merefa 29,985 E5
Mezen' F1
Michurinsk 101,000 F4
Mikhaylovka 58,000 F4
Millerovo 34,627 F5
Mineral'nye Vody 67,000 F6
Mingechaur 60,000 G6
Minsk 1,262,000 C4
Minsk* 1,276,000 C4
Mirgorod 28,407 D5
Mogilev 290,000 C4
Mogilev-Podol'skiy 26,051 C5
Molodechno 73,000 C4
Molotov (Perm') 999,000 J3
Monchegorsk 51,000 D1
Morshansk 44,245 F4
Moscow (Moskva) (cap.) 7,831,000 E3
Moscow* 8,011,000 E3
Mozhaysk 20,321 E3
Mozhga 38,930 H3
Mozyr' 73,000 C4
Mtsensk 27,833 E4
Mukachevo 72,000 B5
Murmansk 381,000 D1
Murom 114,000 F3
Mytishchi 141,000 E3
Nakhichevan' 33,279 F7
Nal'chik 207,000 F6
Narva 73,000 C3
Nar'yan-Mar 16,864 H1
Neftekamsk 70,000 J3
Nelidovo 29,813 D3
Nerekhta 25,722 F3
Nevel' 17,804 D3
Nevinnomyssk 104,000 F6
Nezhin 70,000 D4
Nikel' 21,299 C1
Nikolayev 440,000 D5
Nikol'sk 20,740 G4
Nikopol' 146,000 D5
Nizhnekamsk 134,000 H3
Nizhniy Lomov 17,460 F4
Nizhniy Novgorod (Gor'kiy) 1,344,000 F3
Nosovka 19,430 D4
Novaya Kakhovka 52,000 D5
Novgorod 186,000 D3
Novgorod-Severskiy D4
Novoanninskiy 20,461 F4
Novocherkassk 183,000 F5
Novograd-Volynskiy 41,194 C4
Novogrudok 19,374 C4
Novokuybyshevsk 109,000 G4
Novomoskovsk 147,000 E4
Novopolotsk 67,000 C3
Novorossiysk 159,000 E6
Novoshakhtinsk 104,000 E5
Novotroitsk 95,000 J4
Novoukrainka 19,554 D5
Novouzensk G4
Novovolynsk 41,187 B4
Novovyatsk 26,408 G3
Novozybkov 34,433 D4
Nurlat 17,533 H4
Nyandoma 23,366 F2
Nytva 17,491 H3
Nyuvchim H2
Obninsk 73,000 E3
Ochamchira 18,718 F6
Odessa 1,046,000 D5
Oktyabr'sk 33,981 G4
Oktyabr'skiy 88,000 H4
Okulovka 19,194 D3
Olenegorsk 21,485 D1
Olonets D2
Omutninsk 28,777 H3
Onega 25,047 E2
Ordzhonikidze 279,000 F6
Orel 305,000 E4
Orenburg 459,000 J4
Orgeyev 25,798 C5
Orsha 112,000 C4
Orsk 247,000 J4
Osa 15,038 J3
Osipenko (Berdyansk) 122,000 E5
Osipovichi 19,705 C4
Ostashkov 23,419 D3
Ostrogozhsk 29,921 E4
Ostrov 22,369 C3
Otradnyy 44,426 H4
Panevežys 102,000 B3
Pärnu 51,000 C3
Pavlograd 107,000 E5
Pavlovo 68,000 F3
Pechenga D1
Pechora 56,000 J1
Penza 483,000 G4
Perm' 999,000 J3
Pervomaysk 72,000 D5
Petrokrepost' D3
Petrovsk 30,953 G4
Petrozavodsk 234,000 D2
Petsamo (Pechenga) D1
Pinsk 90,000 C4
Podol'sk 202,000 E3
Podporozh'ye 21,545 D2
Pokhvistnevo 26,125 H4
Polonnoye 22,484 C4
Polotsk 71,000 C3
Poltava 279,000 D5
Polyarnyy 15,321 D1
Ponoy F1
Poti 45,979 F6
Povenets E2
Povorino 20,591 F4
Prikumsk 35,768 F6
Priluki 65,000 D4
Primorsk C2
Primorsko-Akhtarsk 25,981 E5
Priozersk 16,652 D2
Privolzhskiy 23,041 G4
Priyutovo 21,051 H4
Prokhladnyy 40,074 F6
Pskov 176,000 C3
Pugachev 33,963 G4
Pushkin 90,000 C3
Pyatigorsk 110,000 F6
Rabocheostrovsk D1
Rakhov B5
Rakvere 17,891 C3
Rasskazovo 40,038 F4
Razdan 26,833 G6
Rechitsa 60,000 C4
Reni 19,625 C5
Revel (Tallinn) 430,000 B3
Rēzekne 30,803 C3
Riga 835,000 B3
Romny 53,000 D4
Roslavl' 56,000 D4
Rossosh' 36,438 E4
Rostov 30,815 E3
Rostov-na-Donu 934,000 F5
Rovno 179,000 C4
Rtishchevo 37,146 F4
Rubezhnoye 66,000 E5
Rustavi 129,000 G6
Ruzayevka 41,084 F4
Ryazan' 453,000 E4
Ryazhsk 25,425 F4
Rybinsk (Andropov) 239,000 E3
Rybnitsa 32,266 C5
Rzhev 69,000 D3
Safonovo 53,000 D3
Saki 24,208 D5
Salavat 137,000 H4
Sal'sk 57,000 F5
Sal'yany 24,228 G7
Samara (Kuybyshev) 1,216,000 H4
Sambor 29,253 B5
Saransk 263,000 G4
Sarapul 107,000 H3
Saratov 856,000 G4
Sasovo 27,228 F4
Segezha 28,810 D2
Semenov 23,633 F3
Semiluki 18,221 E4
Sengiley G4
Serdobol (Sortavala) 22,188 D2
Serdobsk 33,783 F4
Sergach 22,509 F3
Serpukhov 140,000 E4
Sevastopol' 301,000 D6
Severodonetsk 113,000 E5
Severodvinsk 197,000 E2
Severomorsk 50,000 D1
Shakhty 209,000 F5
Shakhun'ya 20,009 G3
Shar'ya 25,788 G3
Shchekino 70,000 E4
Shchigry 17,133 E4
Sheki 43,158 G6
Shemakha 17,986 G6
Shepetovka 38,707 C4
Shostka 82,000 D4
Shpola 19,806 D5
Shumerlya 33,816 G3
Shuya 72,000 F3
Šiauliai 118,000 B3
Sibay 37,656 J4
Simferopol' 302,000 D6
Skadovsk D5
Skopin 24,429 F4
Slantsy 41,146 C3
Slavuta 25,573 C4
Slavyansk 140,000 E5
Slavyansk-na-Kubani 54,000 E5
Slobodskoy 34,374 H3
Slonim 30,279 B4
Slutsk 35,609 C4
Smela 62,000 D5
Smolensk 276,000 D4
Sochi 287,000 E6
Sokol 48,243 F3
Soligorsk 65,000 C4
Solikamsk 101,000 J3
Sol'-Iletsk 22,227 J4
Sorochinsk 23,235 H4
Soroki 21,924 C5
Sortavala 22,188 D2
Sosnogorsk 24,688 H2
Sovetsk (Tilsit) 38,456 B4
Sovetsk 17,027 G3
Stakhanov 108,000 E5
Stalingrad (Volgograd) 929,000 F5
Staraya Russa 34,577 D3
Staryy Oskol 115,000 E4
Stavropol' 258,000 F5
Stepanakert 30,293 G7
Sterlitamak 220,000 J4
Stupino 70,000 E4
Sudak E6
Sukhumi 114,000 F6
Sumgait 190,000 G6
Sumy 228,000 E4
Svetlogorsk 55,000 C4
Svetlograd 40,265 F5
Syktyvkar 171,000 H2
Syzran' 178,000 G4
Taganrog 276,000 E5
Tallinn 430,000 B3
Tambov 270,000 F4
Tartu 105,000 C3
Taurage 19,461 B3
Tbilisi 1,066,000 F6
Telavi 21,179 G6
Telšiai 20,220 B3
Temryuk 23,172 E5
Ternopol' 144,000 C5
Teykovo 41,607 E3
Tiflis (Tbilisi) 1,066,000 F6
Tighina (Bendery) 101,000 C5
Tikhoretsk 64,000 F5
Tikhvin 59,000 D3
Tilsit (Sovetsk) 38,456 B4
Timashevsk 29,055 E5
Tiraspol' 139,000 D5
Togliatti (Tol'yatti) 502,000 G4
Tokmak 59,000 E5
Toropets 16,863 D3
Torzhok 45,443 D3
Troitsko-Pechorsk J2
Tskhinvali 30,311 F6
Tuapse 60,000 E6
Tula 514,000 E4
Tutayev 16,839 E3
Tuymazy 37,021 H4
Tver (Kalinin) 412,000 E3
Tyrnyauz 18,253 F6
Uchaly 21,808 J4
Ufa 969,000 J4
Uglich 35,463 E3
Ukmerge 21,663 C3
Ul'yanovsk 464,000 G4
Uman' 79,000 D5
Unecha 21,749 D4
Ungeny 17,228 C5
Uryupinsk 38,192 F4
Usinsk J1
Usman' 20,150 E4
Ustinov 549,000 H3
Uvarovo 24,946 F4
Uzhgorod 91,000 B5
Uzlovaya 65,000 E4
Valga 16,795 C3
Valmiera 20,331 C3
Valuyki 29,093 E4
Vasil'kov 26,741 D4
Velikiye Luki 102,000 D3
Velikiy Ustyug 36,737 F2
Vel'sk 21,899 F2
Ventspils 40,467 B3
Vereshchagino 23,585 H3
Vichuga 52,000 F3
Viipuri (Vyborg) 76,000 C2
Vileyka C4
Vilna (Vilnius) 481,000 C4
Vinnitsa 314,000 C5
Vinogradov 20,580 B5
Vitebsk 297,000 C3
Vladimir 296,000 F3
Vladimir-Volynskiy 28,412 B4
Volgodonsk 91,000 F5
Volgograd 929,000 F5
Volkhov 47,025 D3
Volkovysk 28,266 B4
Vologda 237,000 F3
Vol'sk 66,000 G4
Volzhsk 52,000 G3
Volzhskiy 209,000 G5
Vorkuta 100,000 K1
Voronezh 783,000 E4
Voroshilovgrad 463,000 E5
Voskresensk 76,000 E3
Votkinsk 90,000 H3
Voznesensk 36,457 D5
Vyatskiye Polyany 32,729 H3
Vyaz'ma 52,000 D3
Vyborg 76,000 C2
Vyksa 54,000 F3
Vyshniy Volochek 72,000 D3
Yalta 80,000 D6
Yanaul 20,115 J3
Yaroslavl' 597,000 E3
Yartsevo 36,662 D3
Yefremov 53,000 E4
Yelabuga 31,728 H3
Yelets 112,000 E4
Yenakiyevo 114,000 E5
Yershov 21,731 G4
Yessentuki 78,000 F6
Yevlakh 29,462 G6
Yevpatoria 93,000 D5
Yeysk 71,000 E5
Yoshkar-Ola 201,000 G3
Yur'yevets 20,144 F3
Zagorsk 107,000 E3
Zapolyarnyy 22,084 D1
Zaporozh'ye 781,000 E5
Zelenodol'sk 85,000 G3
Zelenokumsk 29,691 F6
Zernograd 20,324 F5
Zhdanov 503,000 E5
Zheleznodorozhnyy 76,000 H2
Zheleznogorsk 65,000 E4
Zhigulevsk 52,130 G4
Zhitomir 244,000 C4
Zhlobin 25,359 D4
Zhmerinka 36,195 C5
Zhodino 22,083 C4
Zhovtnevoye 31,102 D5
Znamenka 27,393 D5
Zolotonosha 27,639 D5
Zugdidi 39,896 F6
Zuyevka 17,001 H3

OTHER FEATURES

Apsheron (pen.) H6
Araks (riv.) G7
Azov (sea) E5
Baltic (sea) B3
Barents (sea) E1
Belaya (riv.) H3
Beloye (lake) E2
Black (sea) D6
Bug (riv.) B4
Bug (riv.) D5
Caspian (sea) G6
Caucasus (mts.) F6
Crimea (pen.) D5
Desna (riv.) D4
Dnieper (riv.) D5
Dniester (riv.) C5
Don (riv.) F5
Donets (riv.) E5
Dvina (bay) E2
Dvina, Northern (riv.) F2
Dvina, Western (riv.) C3
Dykh-Tau (mt.) F6
El'brus (mt.) F6
Finland (gulf) C3
Hiiumaa (isl.) B3
Il'men' (lake) D3
Imandra (lake) D1
Kakhovka (res.) D5
Kama (riv.) H2
Kandalaksha (gulf) D1
Kanin (pen.) G1
Kara (sea) K1
Karskiye Vorota (str.) J1
Kazbek (mt.) F6
Khoper (riv.) F4
Kola (pen.) E1
Kolguyev (isl.) G1
Kuban' (riv.) E5
Kura (riv.) G6
Kuybyshev (res.) G4
Ladoga (lake) D2
Lapland (reg.) D1
Mezen' (riv.) G1
Moksha (riv.) F4
Narodnaya (mt.) J1
Niemen (riv.) B4
Novaya Zemlya (isls.) H1
Oka (riv.) F4
Onega (bay) E2
Onega (lake) E2
Onega (riv.) E2
Pechora (riv.) H1
Peipus (lake) C3
Pripet (marshes) C4
Pripyat' (riv.) C4
Prut (riv.) C5
Riga (gulf) B3
Rybachiy (pen.) D1
Rybinsk (res.) E3
Saaremaa (isl.) B3
Samara (riv.) H4
Sevan (lake) G6
Seym (riv.) D4
Sura (riv.) G4
Svir' (riv.) D2
Timan (ridge) G1
Tsil'ma (riv.) H1
Tsimlyansk (res.) F5
Tuloma (riv.) D1
Ural (mts.) J2
Ural (riv.) J4
Usa (riv.) K1
Valday (hills) D3
Vaygach (isl.) K1
Velikaya (riv.) C3
Volga (riv.) G5
Volga-Don (canal) F5
Volgograd (res.) G5
Volkhov (riv.) D3
Vorskla (riv.) E4
Vyatka (riv.) H3
Vychegda (riv.) G2
Vyg (lake) E2
White (sea) E1
Yamantau (mt.) J4
Yugorskiy (pen.) K1

*City and suburbs.

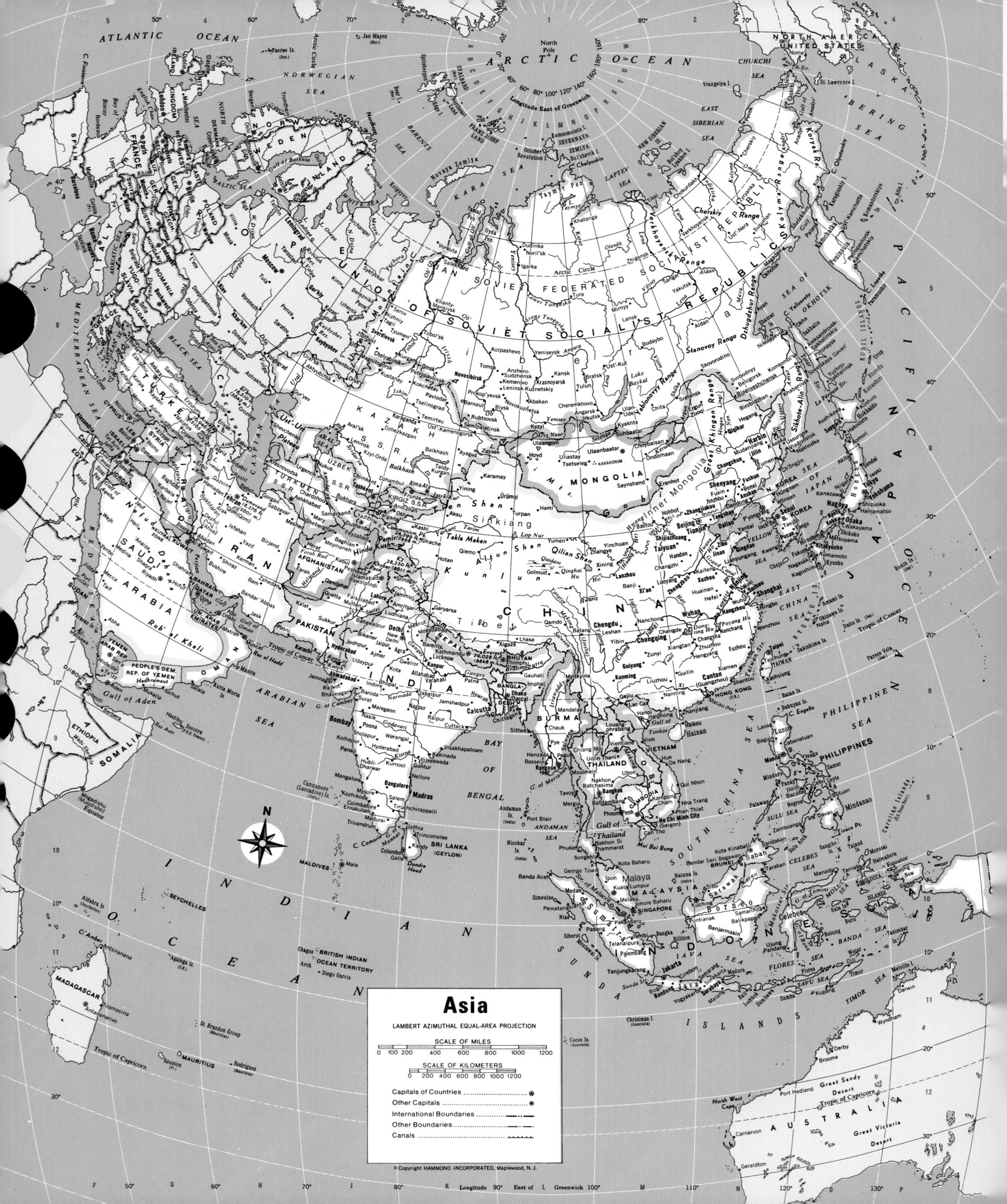

Asia

LAMBERT AZIMUTHAL EQUAL-AREA PROJECTION

SCALE OF MILES

0 100 200   400   600   800   1000   1200

SCALE OF KILOMETERS

0 200 400 600 800 1000 1200

Capitals of Countries ....⊛

Other Capitals ....⊕

International Boundaries ...._ _ _

Other Boundaries...................._ ...._ ...._

Canals ....

© Copyright HAMMOND INCORPORATED, Maplewood, N.J.

Population Distribution

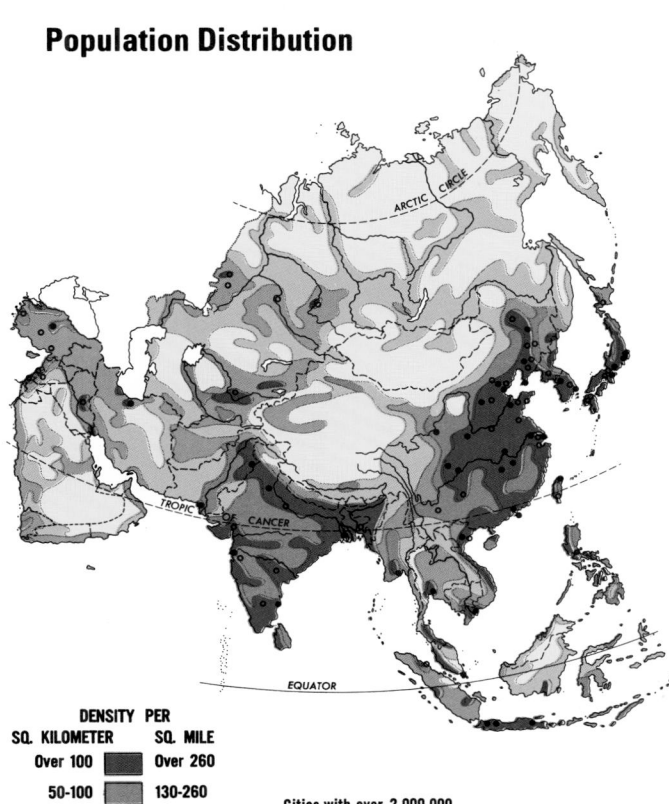

AREA 17,128,500 sq. mi.
(44,362,815 sq. km.)
POPULATION 2,633,000,000
LARGEST CITY Tokyo
HIGHEST POINT Mt. Everest 29,028 ft.
(8,848 m.)
LOWEST POINT Dead Sea -1,296 ft.
(-395 m.)

ASIA

Vegetation

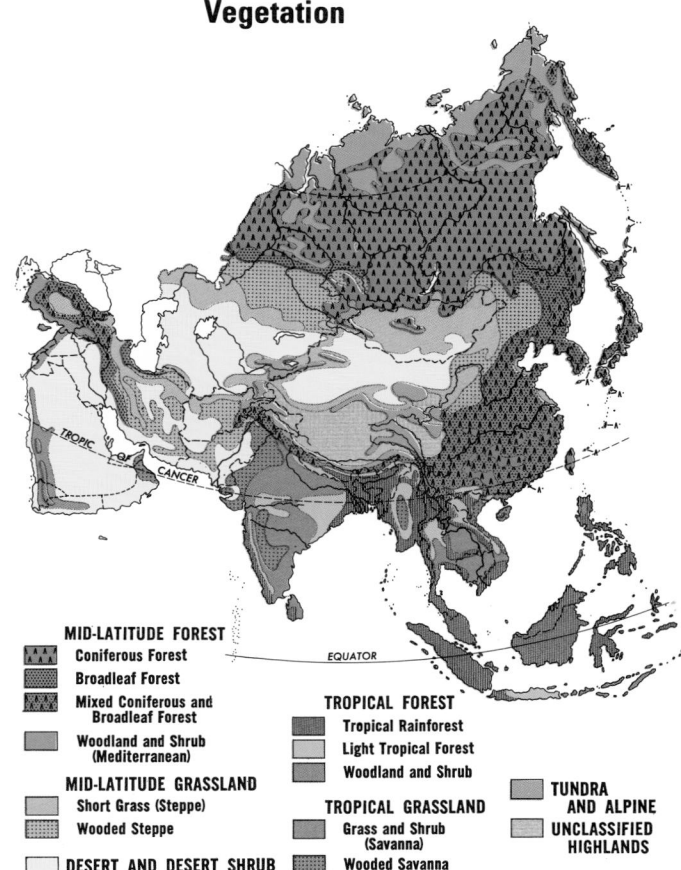

DENSITY PER
SQ. KILOMETER	SQ. MILE
Over 100	Over 260
50-100	130-260
10-50	25-130
1-10	3-25
Under 1	Under 3

• Cities with over 2,000,000 inhabitants (including suburbs)

○ Cities with over 1,000,000 inhabitants (including suburbs)

MID-LATITUDE FOREST
Coniferous Forest
Broadleaf Forest
Mixed Coniferous and Broadleaf Forest
Woodland and Shrub (Mediterranean)

MID-LATITUDE GRASSLAND
Short Grass (Steppe)
Wooded Steppe

DESERT AND DESERT SHRUB

TROPICAL FOREST
Tropical Rainforest
Light Tropical Forest
Woodland and Shrub

TROPICAL GRASSLAND
Grass and Shrub (Savanna)
Wooded Savanna

TUNDRA AND ALPINE
UNCLASSIFIED HIGHLANDS

Average January Temperature

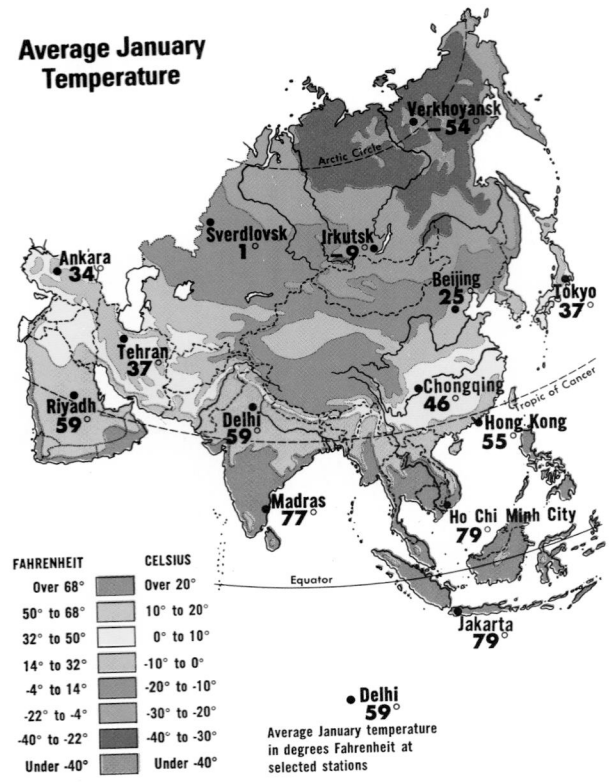

Verkhoyansk -54°
Sverdlovsk 1°
Irkutsk -9°
Ankara 34°
Beijing 25°
Tokyo 37°
Tehran 37°
Chongqing 46°
Riyadh 59°
Delhi 59°
Hong Kong 55°
Madras 77°
Ho Chi Minh City 79°
Jakarta 79°

Arctic Circle
Tropic of Cancer
Equator

FAHRENHEIT	CELSIUS
Over 68°	Over 20°
50° to 68°	10° to 20°
32° to 50°	0° to 10°
14° to 32°	-10° to 0°
-4° to 14°	-20° to -10°
-22° to -4°	-30° to -20°
-40° to -22°	-40° to -30°
Under -40°	Under -40°

• Delhi
59°
Average January temperature
in degrees Fahrenheit at
selected stations

Average July Temperature

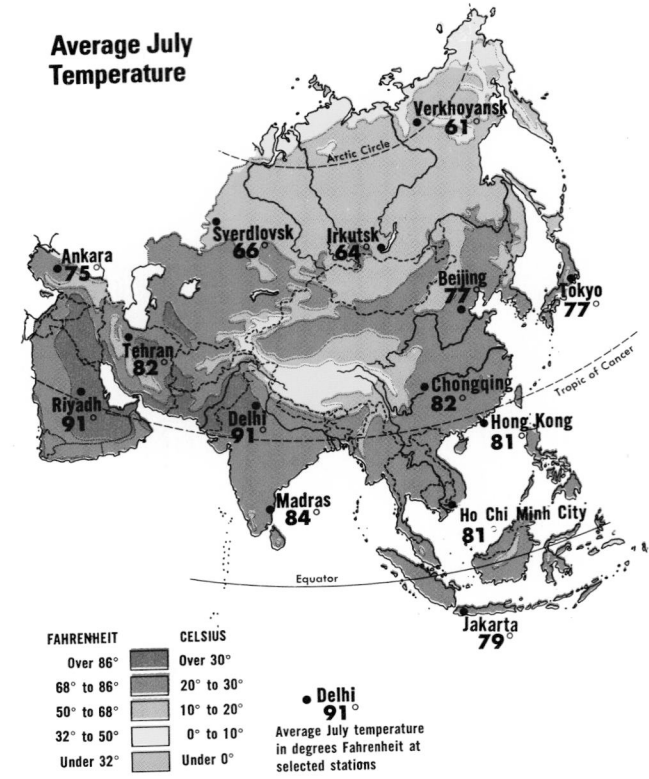

Verkhoyansk 61°
Sverdlovsk 66°
Irkutsk 64°
Ankara 75°
Beijing 77°
Tokyo 77°
Tehran 82°
Chongqing 82°
Riyadh 91°
Delhi 91°
Hong Kong 81°
Madras 84°
Ho Chi Minh City 81°
Jakarta 79°

Arctic Circle
Tropic of Cancer
Equator

FAHRENHEIT	CELSIUS
Over 86°	Over 30°
68° to 86°	20° to 30°
50° to 68°	10° to 20°
32° to 50°	0° to 10°
Under 32°	Under 0°

• Delhi
91°
Average July temperature
in degrees Fahrenheit at
selected stations

Rainfall

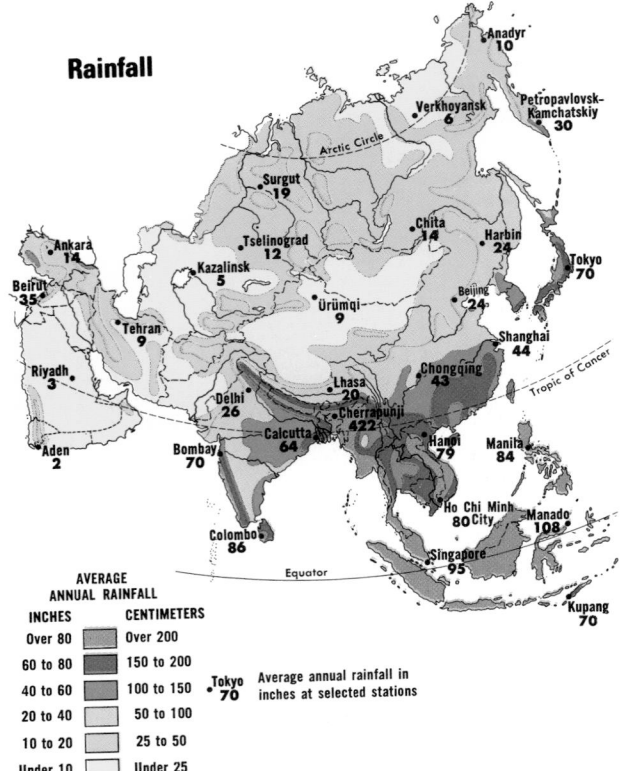

Anadyr 10
Petropavlovsk-Kamchatskiy 30
Verkhoyansk 6
Surgut 19
Chita 14
Harbin 24
Tokyo 70
Tselinograd 12
Ankara 14
Beirut 35
Kazalinsk 5
Ürümqi 9
Beijing 24
Tehran 9
Shanghai 44
Riyadh 3
Lhasa 20
Chongqing 43
Delhi 26
Cherrapunji 422
Calcutta 64
Hanoi 79
Manila 84
Aden 2
Bombay 70
Ho Chi Minh City 80
Manado 108
Colombo 86
Singapore 95
Kupang 70

Arctic Circle
Tropic of Cancer
Equator

AVERAGE
ANNUAL RAINFALL

INCHES	CENTIMETERS
Over 80	Over 200
60 to 80	150 to 200
40 to 60	100 to 150
20 to 40	50 to 100
10 to 20	25 to 50
Under 10	Under 25

• Tokyo
70
Average annual rainfall in
inches at selected stations

Vegetation/Relief

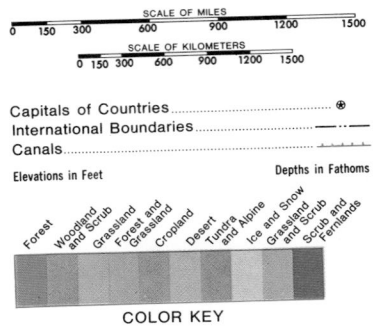

SCALE OF MILES
0 150 300 600 900 1200 1500

SCALE OF KILOMETERS
0 150 300 600 900 1200 1500

Capitals of Countries..................................⊛
International Boundaries..............................
Canals...

Elevations in Feet   Depths in Fathoms

Forest
Woodland and Scrub
Grassland
Forest and Grassland
Cropland
Desert
Tundra and Alpine
Ice and Snow
Grassland and Scrub
Scrub and Farmlands

COLOR KEY

ATLANTIC OCEAN

ICELAND

GREENLAND

Alaska
UNITED STATES

North Pole

Arctic Circle

NORWEGIAN SEA

BARENTS SEA

KARA SEA

EAST SIBERIAN SEA

LAPTEV SEA

BERING SEA

Aleutian Islands

Kamchatka Peninsula

IRELAND
UNITED KINGDOM
London

NORTH SEA

BALTIC SEA

FINLAND

POLAND

Moscow

UNION OF SOVIET SOCIALIST REPUBLICS

Severnaya Zemlya

Novaya Zemlya

Yenisey

Norilsk

Chelyuskin

New Siberian Is.

Dezhnev

BERING Str.

SEA OF OKHOTSK

Sakhalin

Kuril Is.

PACIFIC

PORTUGAL
SPAIN
Bay of Biscay

MEDITERRANEAN SEA

Rome

BLACK SEA

Volga

Svetlovsk

Chelyabinsk

Ural

Tobol

Omsk

Irtysh

Ob

Novosibirsk

Krasnoyarsk

Angara

Lena

Lake Baykal

Yakutsk

Vilyuy

Verkhoyansk

Kolyma

Honshu

SEA OF JAPAN

Vladivostok

Hokkaido

L. Lopatka

CYPRUS
LEBANON
ISRAEL
JORDAN

Cairo

SAUDI ARABIA

Riyadh

Baghdad

IRAN

Tehran

CASPIAN SEA

ARAL SEA

Syrdarya

Amudarya

Tashkent

Alma-Ata

Karaganda

L. Balkhash

Ürümqi

Tien Shan

Tarim

Takla Makan

MONGOLIA

Ulaanbaatar

Gobi Desert

Harbin

Shenyang

N. KOREA
Seoul
S. KOREA

Beijing

Tianjin

Luda

Nagoya

Tokyo

Shikoku

Kyushu

YEMEN ARAB REP.
PEOP. DEM. REP. YEMEN

RED SEA

Aden

Gulf of Aden

SOMALIA

Ras Asér

ETHIOPIA

EQUAT.

Nile

KUWAIT

BAHRAIN
QATAR
U.A.E.

Persian Gulf

OMAN

Gulf of Oman

Muscat

AFGHANISTAN

Kabul

Hindu Kush

Helmand

Indus

PAKISTAN

Karachi

Godwin Austen 28,250 (8611 m)

K2

Kunlun

Tibet

CHINA

Lanzhou

Xian

Chengdu

Chongqing

Wuhan

Nanjing

Shanghai

EAST CHINA SEA

Taipei

Taiwan

Ryukyu Is.

Tropic of Cancer

C. Engaño

Luzon

PHILIPPINES

Manila

Rub' al Khali

INDIA

Ahmadabad

Narbada

Bombay

Godavari

Hyderabad

Krishna

Bangalore

Madras

ARABIAN SEA

Socotra

1000

100

Delhi

New Delhi

Jumna

Kanpur

Ganges

Everest 29,028 (8848 m)

Brahmaputra

BANGLADESH

Dhaka

Calcutta

BURMA

BAY OF BENGAL

Rangoon

Hwang (Yellow R.)

Taiyuan

Huang He

Yangtze

Yunnan

Hanoi

Canton (Guangzhou)

HONG KONG (U.K.)

Hainan

SOUTH CHINA SEA

SEYCHELLES

C. Comorin

SRI LANKA (CEYLON)

Colombo

Dondra Head

MALDIVES

Nicobar Is.

ANDAMAN SEA

Andaman Is.

THAILAND

Bangkok

Gulf of Siam

CAMBODIA

VIETNAM

Ho Chi Minh City

Palawan

SULU SEA

Mindanao

COMOROS

BRITISH INDIAN OCEAN TERR.

INDIAN OCEAN

Equator

MALAYSIA

Kuala Lumpur

Singapore

BRUNEI

Borneo

CELEBES SEA

Celebes

New Guinea

MADAGASCAR

Réunion (Fr.)
MAURITIUS

Sumatra

Sunda Islands

INDONESIA

Jakarta

Java

Surabaya

JAVA SEA

FLORES SEA

BANDA SEA

Timor

TIMOR SEA

Tropic of Capricorn

AUSTRALIA

© Copyright HAMMOND INCORPORATED, Maplewood, N. J.

Longitude 70° East of Greenwich

SAUDI ARABIA   KUWAIT   YEMEN ARAB REPUBLIC   BAHRAIN   QATAR   OMAN   PEOPLE'S DEM. REP. OF YEMEN

AFGHANISTAN

CITIES and TOWNS

Anar Darreh	H3	Balkh	J2
Andkhvoy	H2	Bamian 7.355	J3
Aqcheh	J2	Baraki Barak	J3
Aybak 33.016	J2	Belcheragh	J2
Baghlan 75.130	J2	Chahar Borjak	H3
		Charikan 25.093	J2
		Dowlat Yar	J3
		Dowlatabad	J2
		Dowshi	J2
		Farah 18.797	H3

Farsi	H3	Jorm	K2
Feyzabad 10.142	K2	Kabul (cap.) 1.905.108	J3
Gardez 11.415	J3	Kalat (Qalat) 5.946	J3
Gereshk	H3	Kandahar (Qandahar) 178.409	J3
Ghazni 30.425	J3	Khanabad	J2
Ghurian	H3	Khugiani	H3
Gizab	J3	Kowst	J3
Hazar Qadam	J3	Kuhestan	H2
Herat 163.960	H3	Landay	H3
Jalalabad 56.384	K3	Lash-e Joveyn	H3

Lashkar Gah 26.646	H3	Qalat 5.946	H3
Mar uf	J3	Qale h-ye Now 5.340	H2
Mazar-e Sharif 122.567	J2	Qale h-ye Panjeh	K2
Meymaneh 54.954	H2	Qandahar 178.409	J3
Mirabad	H3	Qonduz 107.191	J2
Moqor	H3	Rostaq	J2
Now Zad	H3	Rudbar	H3
Owbeh	H3	Sakhar	J3
Panjab	J3	Sar-e Pol	J2
Pol-e Khomri	H3	Shah Juy	J3

Sheberghan 54.870	H2	Teyvareh	H3
Shindand	J3	Tulak	H3
Spin Buldak	J3	Zarani 6.477	H3
Tagab	J3	Zibak	K2
Taloqan 46.202	J2		

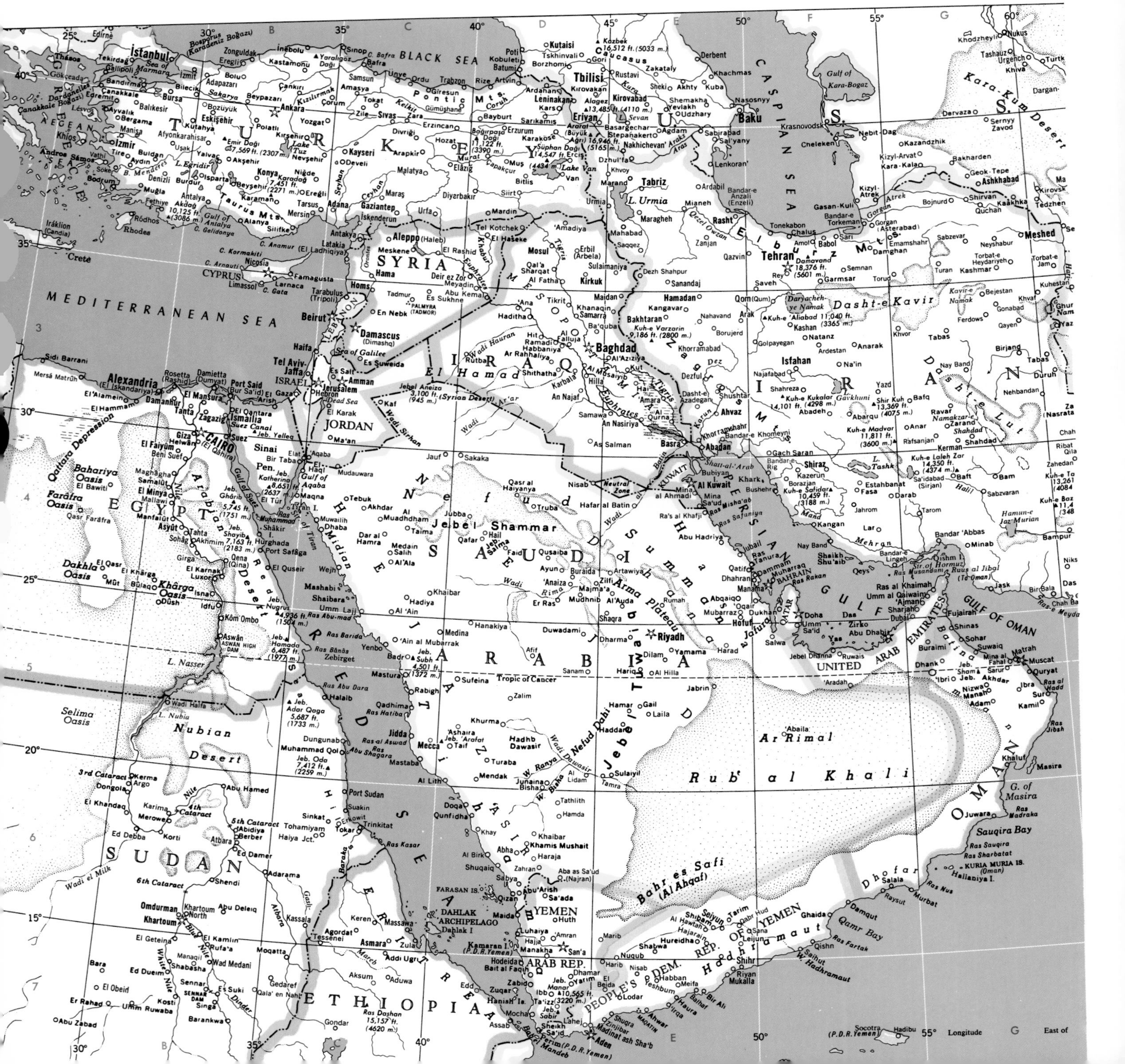

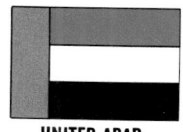

UNITED ARAB EMIRATES

OTHER FEATURES

Farah Rud (riv.) H3
Gowd-e Zerreh (depr.) H4
Harirud (riv.) H3
Helmand (riv.) J3
Hindu Kush (mts.) J2
Kabul (riv.) K3
Konar (riv.) K2
Lurah (riv.) J3

Margow, Dasht-e (des.) H3
Murghab (riv.) H2
Namaksar (salt lake) H3
Paropamisus (mts.) H3
Rigestan (reg.) H3

BAHRAIN

CITIES and TOWNS

Manama (cap.) 88,785 ....F4
Muharraq 37,732 ....F4

GAZA STRIP

CITIES and TOWNS

Gaza* 118,272 ....B3

IRAN

CITIES and TOWNS

Abadan 296,081 ....E3
Abadeh 16,000 ....F3
Abarqu 8,000 ....F3
Ahvaz 329,006 ....E3

Amol 68,782 ....F2
Anar 463 ....G3
Anarak 2,038 ....F3
Arak 114,507 ....E3
Ardabil 147,404 ....E2
Ardestan 5,868 ....F3
Asterabad (Gorgan) 88,348 ....F2
Babol 67,790 ....F2
Bafq 5,000 ....G3
Baft 6,000 ....G4

(continued on following page)

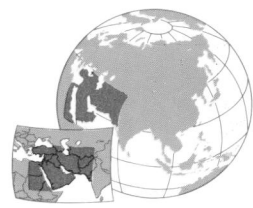

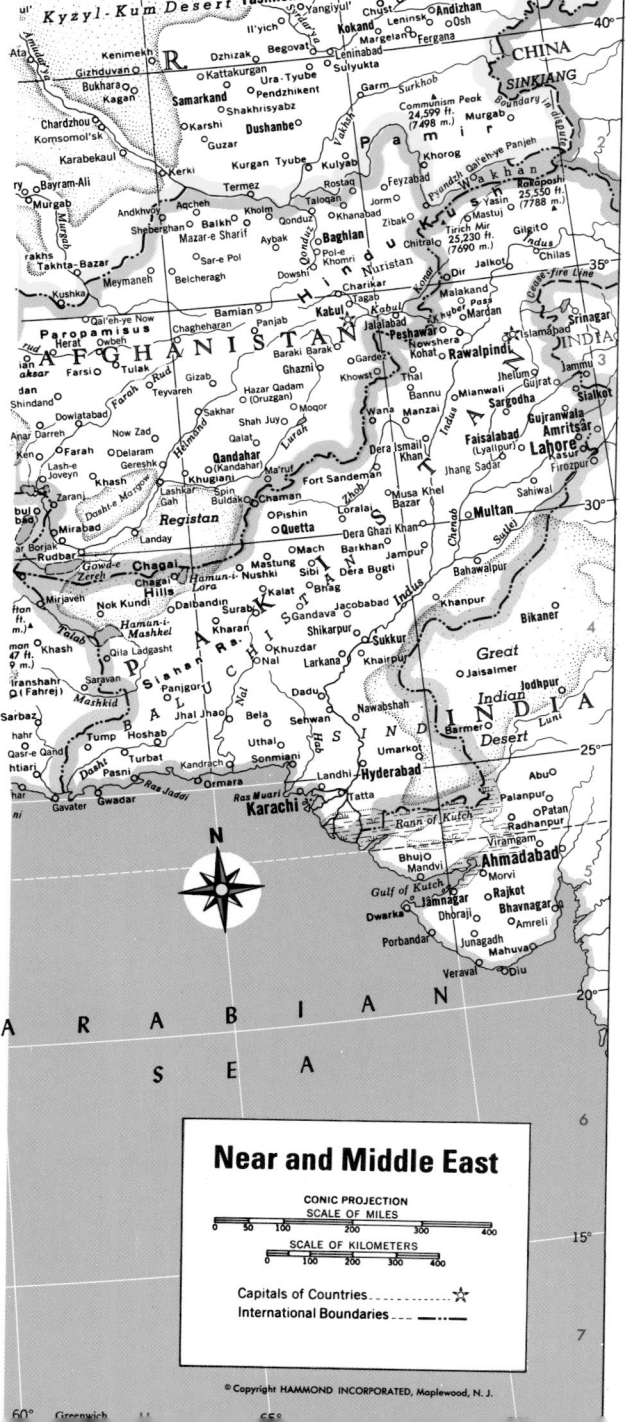

Near and Middle East

CONIC PROJECTION
SCALE OF MILES

SCALE OF KILOMETERS

Capitals of Countries .... ☆
International Boundaries ____ ___

© Copyright HAMMOND INCORPORATED, Maplewood, N.J.

SAUDI ARABIA

AREA 829,995 sq. mi.
(2,149,687 sq. km.)
POPULATION 8,367,000
CAPITAL Riyadh
MONETARY UNIT Saudi riyal
MAJOR LANGUAGE Arabic
MAJOR RELIGION Islam

YEMEN ARAB REPUBLIC

AREA 77,220 sq. mi. (200,000 sq. km.)
POPULATION 6,456,189
CAPITAL San'a
MONETARY UNIT Yemeni rial
MAJOR LANGUAGE Arabic
MAJOR RELIGION Islam

QATAR

AREA 4,247 sq. mi. (11,000 sq. km.)
POPULATION 220,000
CAPITAL Doha
MONETARY UNIT Qatari riyal
MAJOR LANGUAGE Arabic
MAJOR RELIGION Islam

PEOPLE'S DEM. REP. OF YEMEN

AREA 111,101 sq. mi. (287,752 sq. km.)
POPULATION 1,969,000
CAPITAL Aden
MONETARY UNIT Yemeni dinar
MAJOR LANGUAGE Arabic
MAJOR RELIGION Islam

KUWAIT

AREA 6,532 sq. mi. (16,918 sq. km.)
POPULATION 1,355,827
CAPITAL Al Kuwait
MONETARY UNIT Kuwaiti dinar
MAJOR LANGUAGE Arabic
MAJOR RELIGION Islam

BAHRAIN

AREA 240 sq. mi. (622 sq. km.)
POPULATION 358,857
CAPITAL Manama
MONETARY UNIT Bahraini dinar
MAJOR LANGUAGE Arabic
MAJOR RELIGION Islam

OMAN

AREA 120,000 sq. mi. (310,800 sq. km.)
POPULATION 891,000
CAPITAL Muscat
MONETARY UNIT Omani rial
MAJOR LANGUAGE Arabic
MAJOR RELIGION Islam

UNITED ARAB EMIRATES

AREA 32,278 sq. mi. (83,600 sq. km.)
POPULATION 1,040,275
CAPITAL Abu Dhabi
MONETARY UNIT dirham
MAJOR LANGUAGE Arabic
MAJOR RELIGION Islam

Topography

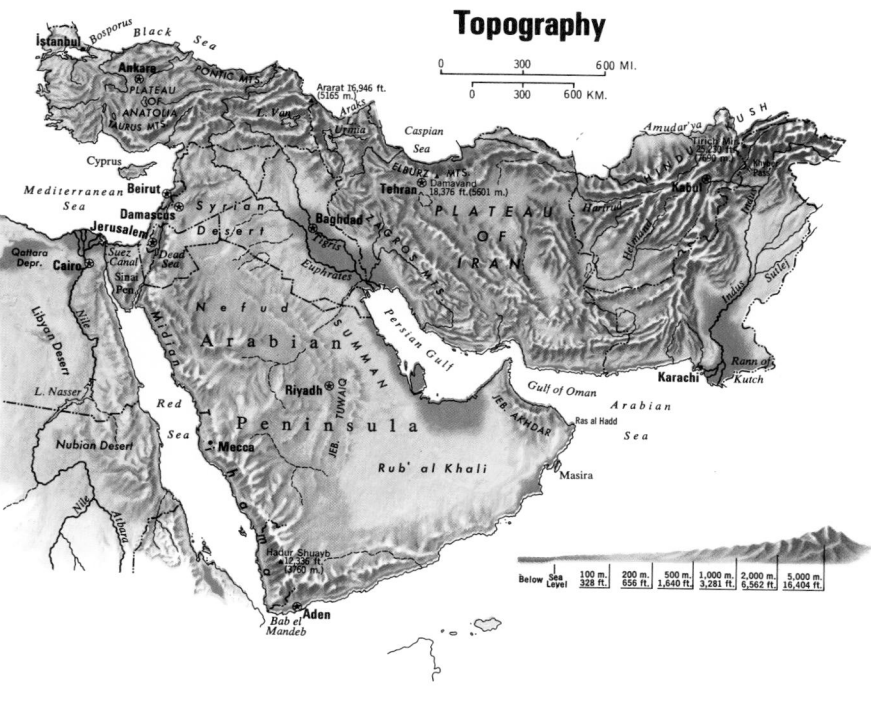

0   300   600 MI.
0   300   600 KM.

Below Sea Level | 100 m. 328 ft. | 200 m. 656 ft. | 500 m. 1,640 ft. | 1,000 m. 3,281 ft. | 2,000 m. 6,562 ft. | 5,000 m. 16,404 ft.

Bakhtaran 290,861 ... E3
Bam 22,000 ... G4
Bampur 1,585 ... G4
Bandar 'Abbas 89,103 ... G4
Bandar-e Anzali (Enzeli) 55,978 ... E2
Bandar-e Khomeyni 6,000 ... E3
Bandar-e Lengeh 4,920 ... F4
Bandar-e Rig 1,889 ... F2
Bandar-e Torkeman 13,000 ... F2
Bejestan 3,823 ... G3
Birjand 25,854 ... G3
Bojnurd 31,248 ... G2
Borazjan 20,000 ... F4
Borujerd 100,103 ... E3
Bushehr 57,681 ... F4
Chah Bahar 1,800 ... H4
Chalus 15,000 ... F2
Damghan 13,000 ... F2
Darab 13,000 ... G4
Dasht-e Azadegan 21,000 ... H4
Dashtiari ... H4
Dezful 110,287 ... E3
Dezh Shahpur 1,384 ... E2
Emamshahr 30,767 ... G2
Enzeli 55,978 ... E2
Estahbanat 18,187 ... F4
Fahrej (Iranshahr)5,000 ... H4
Fasa 19,000 ... F4
Ferdows 11,000 ... G3
Gach Saran ... F4
Garmsar 4,723 ... F2
Golpayegan 20,515 ... F3
Gonabad 8,000 ... G3
Gorgan 88,348 ... F2
Hamadan 155,846 ... E3
Iranshahr 5,000 ... H4
Isfahan 671,825 ... F3
Jahrom 38,236 ... F4
Kangan 2,682 ... F4
Kangavar 9,414 ... E3
Kashan 84,545 ... F3
Kashmar 17,000 ... G3
Kazerun 51,309 ... F4
Kerman 140,309 ... H4
Khash 7,439 ... H4
Khorramabad 104,928 ... E3
Khorramshahr 146,709 ... E3
Khvoy 70,040 ... E2
Lar 22,000 ... F4
Mahabad 28,610 ... E2
Maragheh 60,820 ... E2
Marand 24,000 ... E2
Meshed 670,180 ... H2
Mianeh 28,447 ... E2
Minab 4,228 ... G4
Mirjaveh 11,000 ... H4
Nahavand 24,000 ... E3
Na'in 5,925 ... F3
Najafabad 76,236 ... F3
Nasratabad (Zaboli) 20,000 ... H3
Nehbandan 2,130 ... G3
Neyshabur 59,101 ... G2
Nikshahr ... H4
Pahlevi (Enzeli) 55,978 ... E2
Qasr-e Qand 1,879 ... H4
Qayen 6,000 ... G3
Qazvin 138,527 ... E2
Qom 246,831 ... F3
Quchan 29,133 ... G2
Qum (Qom) 246,831 ... F3
Rafsanjan 21,000 ... G3
Rasht 187,203 ... E2
Ravar 5,074 ... G3
Rey 102,825 ... F2
Reza'iyeh (Urmia) 163,991 ... D2

Sabzevar 69,174 ... G2
Sabzvaran 7,000 ... G4
Sa'idabad 20,000 ... G4
Sanandaj 95,834 ... E2
Saqqez 17,000 ... E2
Saravan ... H4
Sari 70,936 ... F2
Saveh 17,565 ... F2
Semnan 31,058 ... F2
Shahdad 2,777 ... G3
Shahreza 34,220 ... F4
Shiraz 416,408 ... F4
Shirvan 11,000 ... G2
Shustar 24,000 ... E3
Sirjan (Sa'idabad) 20,000 ... G4
Tabas 10,000 ... G3
Tabas-Masina (Tabas) 466 ... H3
Tabriz 598,576 ... E2
Tarom 394 ... F2
Tehran (cap.) 4,496,159 ... F2
Tonekabon 12,000 ... F2
Torbat-e Heydariyeh 30,106 ... G2
Torbat-e Jam 13,000 ... H2
Torud 721 ... G2
Turbat-i-Shaikh Jam 13,000 ... H2
Urmia 163,991 ... D2
Yazd 135,978 ... F3
Yazdan ... H3
Zabol 20,000 ... H3
Zahedan 92,628 ... H4
Zanjan 99,967 ... E2
Zarand 5,000 ... G3

OTHER FEATURES

Araks (riv.) ... E2
Atrek (riv.) ... F2
Bazman, Kuh-e (mt.) ... H4
Damavand (mt.) ... F2
Dez (riv.) ... E3
Elburz (mts.) ... F2
Gavkhuni (lake) ... F3
Gorgan (riv.) ... G2
Halil (riv.) ... G4
Jaz Murian, Hamun-e (marsh) ... G4
Karun (riv.) ... E3
Kavir, Dasht-e (salt des.) ... G3
Kavir-e Namak (salt des.) ... G3
Lut, Dasht-e (des.) ... G3
Maidani, Ras (cape) ... F4
Mand Rud (riv.) ... F4
Mashkid (riv.) ... H4
Namak, Daryacheh-ye (salt lake) ... F3
Namaksar (salt lake) ... H3
Namakzar-e Shahdad (salt lake) ... G3
Oman (gulf) ... G5
Persian (gulf) ... F4
Qeys (isl.) ... F4
Qezel Owzan (riv.) ... E2
Qeshm (isl.) ... G4
Safidar, Kuh-e (mt.) ... F4
Shaikh Shua'ib (isl.) ... F4
Shir Kuh (mt.) ... F3
Taftan, Kuh-e (mt.) ... H4
Talab (riv.) ... H4
Tashk (lake) ... F4
Urmia (lake) ... E2
Zagros (mts.) ... E3

IRAQ
CITIES and TOWNS

Al 'Aziziya 7,450 ... E3
Al Falluja 38,072 ... D3
Al Fathat 15,329 ... D2
Al Musaiyib 15,955 ... D3
Al Qurna 5,638 ... E3
'Amadiya 2,578 ... D2
'Ana 15,729 ... D2
An Najaf 128,096 ... D3
An Nasiriya 60,405 ... E3
Arbela (Erbil) 90,320 ... D2
Ar Rahhaliya 1,579 ... D3
As Salman 3,584 ... D3
Baghdad (cap.) 502,503 ... D3
Baghdad * 1,745,328 ... D3
Baq'uba 34,575 ... D3
Basra 313,327 ... E3
Erbil 90,320 ... D2
Habbaniya 14,405 ... D3
Halabja 6,870 ... E3
Hilla 84,717 ... D3
Hit 9,131 ... D3
Karbal'a 83,301 ... D3
Khanaqin 23,522 ... E3
Kirkuk 167,413 ... D2
Kirkuk* 176,794 ... D2
Kut 42,116 ... E3
Maidan 354 ... E3
Mosul 315,157 ... D2
Qala' Sharqat 2,434 ... D2
Ramadi 28,723 ... D3
Rutba 5,091 ... D3
Samarra 24,746 ... D3
Samawa 33,473 ... D3
Shithatha 2,326 ... D3
Sulaimaniya 86,822 ... E2
Tikrit 9,921 ... D3

OTHER FEATURES

'Aneiza, Jebel (mt.) ... C3
'Ara'r, Wadi (dry riv.) ... D3
Batin, Wadi al (dry riv.) ... E4
Euphrates (riv.) ... D3
Hauran, Wadi (dry riv.) ... D3
Mesopotamia (reg.) ... D3
Syrian (El Hamad) (des.) ... D3
Tigris (riv.) ... D3

KUWAIT
CITIES and TOWNS

Al Kuwait (cap.) 181,774 ... E4
Mina al Ahmadi ... E4
Mina Saud ... E4

OTHER FEATURES

Bubiyan (isl.) ... E4
Persian (gulf) ... F4

OMAN
CITIES and TOWNS

Adam ... G5
Buraimi ... G5
Dhank ... G5
Ibra ... G5
I'bri ... G5
Juwara ... G6
Kamil ... G5
Khaluf ... G5
Khasab ... G4
Manah ... G5
Masqat (Muscat) (cap.) 7,500 ... G5
Matrah 15,000 ... G5
Mina al Fahal ... G5

Murbat ... G6
Muscat (cap.) 7,500 ... G6
Nizwa ... G5
Quryat ... G5
Raysut (Risut) ... F6
Salala 4,000 ... F6
Sarur ... G5
Shinas ... G5
Sohar ... G5
Sur ... G5
Suwaiq ... G5

OTHER FEATURES

Akhdar, Jebel (range) ... G5
Batina (reg.) ... G5
Dhofar (reg.) ... F6
Hadd, Ras al (cape) ... G5
Jibsh, Ras (cape) ... G5
Kuria Muria (isls.) ... G6
Madraka, Ras (cape) ... G6
Masira (gulf) ... G5
Masira (isl.) ... G5
Musandam, Ras (cape) ... G4
Nus, Ras (cape) ... G6
Oman (gulf) ... G5
Oman (reg.) ... G5
Ruus al Jibal (dist.) ... G4
Saugira (bay) ... G6
Saugira, Ras (cape) ... G6
Sham, Jebel (mt.) ... G5
Sharbatat, Ras (cape) ... G6

QATAR
CITIES and TOWNS

Doha (cap.) 150,000 ... F4
Dukhan ... F4
Umm Sa'id ... F5

OTHER FEATURES

Persian (gulf) ... F4
Rakan, Ras (cape) ... F4

SAUDI ARABIA
CITIES and TOWNS

Aba as Sau'd 47,501 ... D6
'Abaila ... D5
Abha 30,150 ... D6
Abqaiq ... E4
Abu 'Arish ... D6
Abu Hadriya ... E4
'Ain al Mubarrak ... C4
Al 'Ain ... E4
Al 'Ala ... C4
Al 'Auda ... E4
Al Birk ... D6
Al Hilla ... D5
Al Lidam ... E5
Al Lith ... D5
Al Muadhdham ... D4
'Anaiza ... D4
Artawiya ... E4
'Ashaira ... D5
Ayun ... D4
Badr ... C5
Buraida 69,940 ... D4
Dam ... E4
Dammam 127,844 ... F4
Dar al Hamra ... D4
Dhaba ... C4
Dhahran ... E4
Dharma ... D5
Dilam ... E5

Doqa ... D6
Duwadami ... D4
Er Ras ... E5
Faid ... D4
Gail ... E5
Haddar ... D5
Hadiya ... C5
Hafar al Batin ... E4
Hail 40,502 ... D4
Hamar ... D6
Hanakiya ... D5
Haql ... C4
Harad ... E5
Haraja ... E5
Hariq ... E5
Hatiba, Ras (cape) ... C5
Hofuf 101,271 ... E5
Jabrin ... E5
Jauf ... C4
Jidda 561,104 ... C5
Jizan (Qizan) 32,812 ... D6
Jubail ... E4
Jubba ... D4
Junaina ... C3
Kaf ... C4
Khaibar, 'Asir ... D6
Khaibar, Hejaz ... C4
Khamis Mushait 49,581 ... D6
Khay ... E5
Khurma ... D5
Laila ... E5
Majmaa' ... D4
Marib ... E6
Mastura ... C5
Mecca 366,801 ... C5
Medain Salih ... C4
Medina 198,186 ... C5
Mendak ... D5
Mina Sau'd ... E4
Mubarraz 54,325 ... E4
Mudhnib ... D4
Muwailih ... C4
Najran (Aba as Sau'd) 47,501 ... D6
Nisab ... D4
O'qair ... E4
Qadhima ... C5
Qafar ... D4
Qasr al Haiyanya ... E4
Qatif ... E4
Qizan 32,812 ... D6
Qunfidha ... D6
Qusaiba ... D4
Rabigh ... C5
Ra's al Khafji ... F4
Ras Tanura ... F4
Riyadh (cap.) 666,840 ... E5
Rumah ... E4
Sabya ... D6
Sakaka ... D4
Salwa ... E5
Shaqra ... D5
Shuqaiq ... D6
Sufeina ... D5
Sulaiyil ... E5
Taif 204,857 ... D5
Taima ... C4
Tamra ... E5
Tathlith ... D6
Tebuk (Tabuk) 74,825 ... C4
Turaba ... D5
Umm Lajj ... C5
Wejh ... C5
Yamama ... E5
Yenbo ... C5
Zahran ... D6
Zalim ... D5
Zilfi ... D5

OTHER FEATURES

Abu-Mad, Ras (cape) ... C5
'Aneiza, Jebel (mt.) ... C4
'Aqaba (gulf) ... C4
Arafat (plat.) ... D6
'Ara'r, Wadi (dry riv.) ... D4
Arma (plat.) ... E4
Aswad, Ras al (cape) ... C5
Bahr es Safi (des.) ... E6
Barida, Ras (cape) ... C5
Bisha, Wadi (dry riv.) ... D5
Dahana (des.) ... E4
Dawasir, Wadi (dry riv.) ... E5
Dawasir, Hadhb (range) ... E5
Farasan (isls.) ... D6
Hatiba, Ras (cape) ... C5
Jafura (des.) ... F5
Jauf (dist.) ... C4
Jizan (Qizan) 32,812 ... D6
Jubba (des.) ... D5
Khaibar (dist.) ... C4
Nefud (des.) ... D4
Nefud Dahi (des.) ... D5
Persian (gulf) ... E4
Ranya, Wadi (dry riv.) ... D5
Red (sea) ... C5
Rima', Wadi (dry riv.) ... D4
Rimal, Ar (des.) ... F5
Rub al Khali (des.) ... E5
Safaniya, Ras (cape) ... E4
Salma, Jebel (mts.) ... D4
Shaibara (isl.) ... C5
Shammar, Jebel (plat.) ... D4
Sirhan, Wadi (dry riv.) ... C4
Subh, Jebel (mt.) ... C5
Summan (plat.) ... E4
Tihama (reg.) ... C5
Tiran (isl.) ... C4
Tiran (str.) ... C4
Tuwaiq, Jebel (range) ... D5

UNITED ARAB EMIRATES
CITIES and TOWNS

Abu Dhabi (cap.) 347,000 ... F5
'Ajman ... F5
'Aradah ... F5
Buraimi ... G5
Dubai ... G4
Fujairah ... G4
Jebel Dhanna ... F5
Ras al Khaimah ... G4
Ruwais ... F4
Sharjah ... G4
Umm al Qaiwain ... G4

OTHER FEATURES

Das (isl.) ... F4
Oman (gulf) ... G5
Yas (isl.) ... F5
Zirko (isl.) ... F5

WEST BANK
CITIES and TOWNS

Hebron 38,309 ... C3

OTHER FEATURES

Dead (sea) ... C3

YEMEN ARAB REP.
CITIES and TOWNS

'Amran ... D6
Bait al Faqih ... D7
Dhamar 19,467 ... D7
El Beida 5,975 ... D6
Hajja 5,814 ... D6
Harib ... E7
Hodeida 80,314 ... D7
Huth ... D6
Ibb 19,066 ... D7
Luhaiya ... D6
Marib 292 ... D6
Mocha ... D7
Sa'da 4,252 ... D6
Sana' 134,588 ... D7
Sheikh Sa'id ... D7
Ta'izz 78,642 ... D7
Yarim ... D7
Zabid ... D7

OTHER FEATURES

Hanish (isls.) ... D7
Manar, Jebel (mt.) ... D7
Mandeb, Bab el (str.) ... D7
Red (sea) ... C5
Sabir, Jebel (mt.) ... D7
Tihama (reg.) ... D7
Zuqar (isl.) ... D7

YEMEN, PEOPLE'S DEM. REPUBLIC OF
CITIES and TOWNS

Aden (cap.) 240,370 ... E7
Ahwar ... E7
Balhaf ... F7
Bir 'Ali ... F7
Damqut ... G6
Ghaida ... F6
Habban ... E7
Hadibu ... G7
Hajarain ... E7
Haura ... E7
Hureidha ... E7
I'rqa ... E7
Lahej ... E7
Lejjun ... E7
Lodar ... E7
Madinat ash Shab' ... E7
Meifa ... E7
Mukalla 45,000 ... E7
Nisab ... E6
Nuqub ... E6
Qishn ... F6
Raydat ... E7
Saihut ... F6
Seiyun 20,000 ... E7
Shabwa ... E6
Shihr ... F6
Shuqra ... E7
Tarim ... E7
Yeshbum ... E7
Zinjibar ... E7

OTHER FEATURES

Fartak, Ras (cape) ... F6
Hadhramaut (dist.) ... E7
Hadhramaut, Wadi (dry riv.) ... E7
Kamaran (isl.) ... D6
Perim (isl.) ... D7
Socotra (isl.) ... F7

*City and suburbs.

Agriculture, Industry and Resources

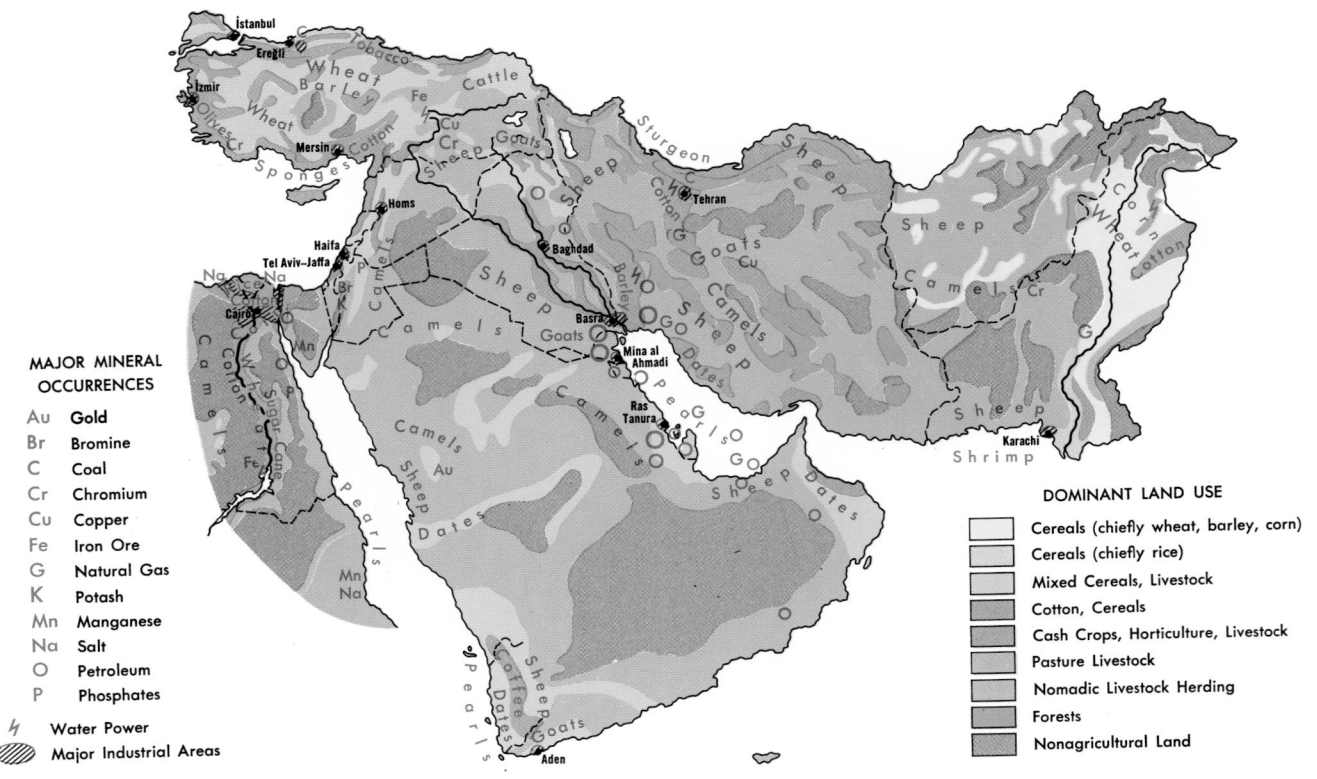

MAJOR MINERAL OCCURRENCES

Au Gold
Br Bromine
C   Coal
Cr Chromium
Cu Copper
Fe Iron Ore
G   Natural Gas
K   Potash
Mn Manganese
Na Salt
O   Petroleum
P   Phosphates

⚡ Water Power
▨ Major Industrial Areas

DOMINANT LAND USE

Cereals (chiefly wheat, barley, corn)
Cereals (chiefly rice)
Mixed Cereals, Livestock
Cotton, Cereals
Cash Crops, Horticulture, Livestock
Pasture Livestock
Nomadic Livestock Herding
Forests
Nonagricultural Land

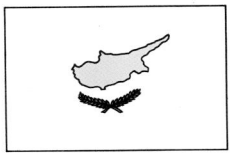
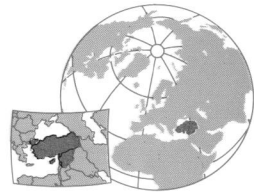

TURKEY **SYRIA** **LEBANON** **CYPRUS**

AREA 300,946 sq. mi. (779,450 sq. km.)
POPULATION 45,217,556
CAPITAL Ankara
LARGEST CITY Istanbul
HIGHEST POINT Ararat 16,946 ft. (5,165 m.)
MONETARY UNIT Turkish lira
MAJOR LANGUAGE Turkish
MAJOR RELIGION Islam

AREA 71,498 sq. mi. (185,180 sq. km.)
POPULATION 8,979,000
CAPITAL Damascus
LARGEST CITY Damascus
HIGHEST POINT Hermon 9,232 ft. (2,814 m.)
MONETARY UNIT Syrian pound
MAJOR LANGUAGES Arabic, French, Kurdish, Armenian
MAJOR RELIGIONS Islam, Christianity

AREA 4,015 sq. mi. (10,399 sq. km.)
POPULATION 3,161,000
CAPITAL Beirut
LARGEST CITY Beirut
HIGHEST POINT Qurnet es Sauda 10,131 ft. (3,088 m.)
MONETARY UNIT Lebanese pound
MAJOR LANGUAGES Arabic, French
MAJOR RELIGIONS Christianity, Islam

AREA 3,473 sq. mi. (8,995 sq. km.)
POPULATION 629,000
CAPITAL Nicosia
LARGEST CITY Nicosia
HIGHEST POINT Troödos 6,406 ft. (1,953 m.)
MONETARY UNIT Cypriot pound
MAJOR LANGUAGES Greek, Turkish, English
MAJOR RELIGIONS Eastern (Greek) Orthodoxy,

CYPRUS

CITIES and TOWNS

Dhali 2,970 ...... E5
Episkopi 2,150 ...... F5
Famagusta 38,960 ...... E5
Ktima E5
Kyrenia 3,892 ...... E5
Kythrea 3,400 ...... E5
Lapithos 3,600 ...... E5
Larnaca 19,608 ...... E5
Lefka 3,650 ...... E5
Limassol 79,641 ...... E5
Morphou 9,040 ...... E5
Nicosia (cap.) 115,718 ...... E5
Paphos 8,984 ...... E5
Polis 2,200 ...... F5
Rizokarpasso 3,600 ...... F5
Yialousa 2,750 ...... E5

OTHER FEATURES

Andreas (cape) F5
Arnauti (cape) E5
Gata (cape) F5
Greco (cape) F5
Kormakiti (cape) E5
Troodos (mt.) E5

LEBANON

CITIES and TOWNS

A'leih 18,630 ...... F6
Amyun 7,926 ...... F5
Baa'lbek 15,560 ...... G5
Batrun 5,976 ...... F5
Beirut (cap.) 474,870 ...... F6
Beirut* 938,940 ...... F6
Hermil 2,652 ...... G5
Merj U'yun 9,318 ...... F6
Rasheiya 6,731 ...... F6
Rayak 1,480 ...... G6
Saida 32,200 ...... F6
Sidon (Saida) 32,200 ...... F6
Sur 16,483 ...... F6
Tripoli (Tarabulus) 127,611 ...... F5
Tyre (Sur) 16,483 ...... F6
Zahle 53,121 ...... F6
Zegharta 18,210 ...... G5

OTHER FEATURES

Lebanon (mts.) F6
Leontes (Litani) (riv.) F6
Litani (riv.) F6
Sauda, Qurnet es (mt.) G5

SYRIA

PROVINCES

Aleppo 1,316,872 ...... G4
Damascus 1,457,934 ...... G6
Deir ez Zor 292,780 ...... H5
Dera' 230,481 ...... F6
El Quneitra 16,490 ...... F6
Es Suweida 139,650 ...... G6
Hama 514,748 ...... G5
Haseke 468,506 ...... J4
Homs 546,176 ...... G5
Idlib 383,695 ...... G5
Latakia 389,552 ...... G5
Rashid 243,736 ...... H5
Tartus 302,065 ...... G5

CITIES and TOWNS

Abu Kemal 6,907 ...... J5
A'in el A'rab 4,529 ...... H4
Aleppo 639,428 ...... G4
Azaz 13,923 ...... G4
Baniyas 8,537 ...... F5
Busra G6
Damascus (cap.) 836,668 ...... G6
Damascus* 923,253 ...... G6
Deir ez Zor 66,164 ...... H5
Dera' 27,651 ...... G6
Dimashq (Damascus) (cap.) 836,668 ...... G6
Duma 30,050 ...... G6
El Bab 27,366 ...... G4
El Haseke 32,746 ...... J4
El Ladhiqiya (Latakia) 125,716 ...... F5
El Quryatein G5
El Quneitra 17,752 ...... F6
El Rashid 37,151 ...... H4
En Nebk 16,334 ...... G5
Es Suweide 29,524 ...... G6
Et Tell el Abyad H4
Haffe 4,656 ...... G5
Haleb (Aleppo) 639,428 ...... G4
Hama 137,421 ...... G5
Harim 6,837 ...... G4
Homs 215,423 ...... G5
Idlib 34,515 ...... G5
Izra 3,226 ...... G6
Jeble 15,715 ...... F5
Jerablus 8,610 ...... H4
Jisr esh Shughur 13,131 ...... G5
Khan Sheikhun G5
Masyaf 7,058 ...... G5
Membij 13,796 ...... G4
Meskene H5
Meyadin 12,515 ...... H5
Qala't es Salihiye J5
Qamishliye 31,448 ...... J4
Quteife 4,993 ...... G6
Raqqa (El Rashid) 37,151 ...... H5
Sabkha 3,375 ...... H5
Safita 9,650 ...... G5
Selemiya 21,677 ...... G5
Tadmur 10,670 ...... H5
Tartus 29,842 ...... F5
Telkalakh 6,242 ...... G5
Zebdani 10,010 ...... G6

OTHER FEATURES

A'mrit (ruins) F5
Arwad (Ruad) (isl.) F5
A'si (Orontes) (riv.) G5
Druz, Jebel ed (mts.) G6
El Furat (riv.) H4
Euphrates (El Furat) (riv.) H4
Hermon (mt.) F6
Khabur (riv.) J5
Orontes (riv.) G5
Palmyra (Tadmor) (ruins) H5
Ruwaq, Jebel er (mts.) G5

TURKEY

PROVINCES

Adana 1,240,475 ...... F4
Adiyaman 346,892 ...... H4
Afyonkarahisar 579,171 ...... D3
Ağri 330,201 ...... K3
Amasya 322,806 ...... F2
Ankara 2,585,293 ...... D4
Antalya 669,357 ...... D4
Artvin 228,026 ...... J2
Aydin 609,869 ...... B4
Balikesir 789,255 ...... B3
Bilecik 137,120 ...... D2
Bingöl 210,804 ...... J3
Bitlis 218,305 ...... J3
Bolu 428,704 ...... D4
Burdur 222,896 ...... D4
Bursa 961,639 ...... C2
Çanakkale 369,385 ...... B2
Çankiri 265,468 ...... E2
Çorum 547,580 ...... F2
Denizli 560,916 ...... C4
Diyarbakir 651,233 ...... H4
Edirne 340,732 ...... B2
Elâziğ 417,924 ...... H3
Erzincan 283,683 ...... H3
Erzurum 746,666 ...... J3
Eskişehir 495,097 ...... D3
Gaziantep 715,939 ...... H4
Giresun 463,587 ...... H2
Gümüşhane 293,673 ...... H2
Hakkâri 126,036 ...... K4
Hatay 744,113 ...... F4
Içel 714,817 ...... E4
Isparta 322,685 ...... D4
Istanbul 3,904,588 ...... C2
Izmir 1,673,966 ...... B3
Kahramanmaraş 641,480 ...... G4
Kars 707,398 ...... K2
Kastamonu 438,243 ...... E2
Kayseri 676,809 ...... F3
Kirklareli 268,399 ...... B2
Kirşehir 232,853 ...... F3
Kocaeli 477,736 ...... C2
Konya 1,422,461 ...... E4
Kütahya 470,423 ...... C3
Malatya 574,558 ...... H3
Manisa 872,375 ...... B3
Mardin 519,687 ...... J4
Muğla 400,796 ...... C4
Muş 267,203 ...... J3
Nevşehir 249,308 ...... F3
Niğde 463,121 ...... F4
Ordu 664,290 ...... G2
Rize 336,278 ...... J2
Sakarya 495,649 ...... D2
Samsun 906,381 ...... F2
Siirt 381,503 ...... J4
Sinop 267,605 ...... F2
Sivas 741,713 ...... G3
Tekirdağ 319,987 ...... B2
Tokat 599,166 ...... G2
Trabzon 719,008 ...... H2
Tunceli 164,591 ...... H3
Urfa 597,277 ...... H4
Uşak 229,679 ...... C3
Van 386,314 ...... K3
Yozgat 500,371 ...... F3
Zonguldak 836,156 ...... D2

CITIES and TOWNS

Acigöl 3,934 ...... F3
Acipayam 5,046 ...... C4
Adalia (Antalya) 130,774 ...... D4
Adana 475,384 ...... F4
Adapazari 114,130 ...... D2
Adilcevaz 9,022 ...... K3
Adiyaman 43,782 ...... H4
Afşin 18,231 ...... G3
Afyonkarahisar 60,150 ...... D3
Aglasun 4,288 ...... D4
Ağli 3,399 ...... E2
Ağri (Karaköse) 35,284 ...... K3
Ahlat 7,366 ...... J3
Akçaabat 10,756 ...... H2
Akçadağ 9,579 ...... G3
Akçakoca 9,066 ...... D2
Akdağmadeni 7,909 ...... F3
Akhisar 53,357 ...... B3
Aksaray 45,564 ...... E3
Akşehir 35,544 ...... D3
Akşin 5,141 ...... D4
Akviran 3,799 ...... E4
Alaca 12,438 ...... F2
Alaca 12,552 ...... F2
Alaçam 2,321 ...... G3
Alaçam 10,013 ...... F2
Alanya 18,520 ...... D4
Alaşehir 23,243 ...... C3
Alexandretta (Iskenderun) 107,437 ...... H3
Aliağa 5,727 ...... B3
Alibeyköyü 33,387 ...... D6
Almus 4,225 ...... G2
Alpu 3,718 ...... D3
Altindağ 512,392 ...... E2
Altinova 6,980 ...... B3
Altintaş 3,986 ...... C3
Altinözü 5,158 ...... G4
Alucra 7,070 ...... H2
Amasra 4,369 ...... E2
Amasya 41,496 ...... G2
Anamur 21,475 ...... E4
Andirin 5,018 ...... G4
Ankara (cap.) 1,701,004 ...... E3
Antakya 77,518 ...... G4
Antalya 130,774 ...... D4
Antioch (Antakya) 77,518 ...... G4
Araç 3,594 ...... E2
Aralik 4,155 ...... L3
Arapkir 8,436 ...... H3
Ardahan 16,285 ...... K2
Ardeşen 7,980 ...... J2
Ardanuç 2,942 ...... K2
Arguvan 2,461 ...... H3
Arhavi 6,311 ...... J2
Arpaçay 2,651 ...... K2
Arsin 6,557 ...... H2
Bolu 32,812 ...... D2
Artova 2,813 ...... G2
Artvin 13,390 ...... J2
Aşkale 10,017 ...... J3
Avanos 8,635 ...... F3
Ayancik 7,202 ...... F1
Ayaş 4,575 ...... E2
Aybasti 13,180 ...... G2
Aydin 59,579 ...... B4
Aydincik 6,739 ...... E4
Ayrancı 2,664 ...... E4
Ayvacik 3,120 ...... B3
Ayvalik 18,041 ...... B3
Babadağ 5,890 ...... C4
Babaeski 17,090 ...... B2
Bafra 34,288 ...... F2
Bahçe 10,212 ...... G4
Baikirköy 200,942 ...... D6
Baklan 3,327 ...... C4
Balâ 4,107 ...... E3
Balikeşir 99,443 ...... B3
Balya 2,362 ...... B3
Banaz 6,264 ...... C3
Bandirma 45,752 ...... C2
Bartin 18,409 ...... E2
Başkale 8,558 ...... K3
Başmakçi 5,925 ...... C4
Batman 64,384 ...... J4
Bayat 4,671 ...... F2
Bayburt 20,156 ...... J2
Bayindir 14,078 ...... B3
Baykan 2,690 ...... J4
Bayramiç 6,385 ...... B3
Bergama 29,749 ...... B3
Beşiktaş 174,931 ...... D6
Beşiri 4,165 ...... J4
Besni 16,613 ...... G4
Beykoz 76,804 ...... D5
Beyoğlu 230,532 ...... D6
Beypazari 14,963 ...... D2
Beyşehir 15,060 ...... D4
Beytüşşebap 2,766 ...... K4
Biga 15,188 ...... B2
Bigadiç 7,535 ...... C3
Bingöl (Çapakçur) 22,047 ...... J3
Birecik 20,104 ...... H4
Bismil 12,775 ...... J4
Bitlis 25,054 ...... J3
Bodrum 7,858 ...... B4
Boğazliyan 10,329 ...... F3
Bolu 32,812 ...... D2
Bolvadin 29,218 ...... D3
Bor 16,560 ...... F4
Borçka 4,636 ...... J2
Bornova 45,096 ...... B3
Boyabat 13,139 ...... F2
Bozdoğan 7,218 ...... C4
Bozkir 5,294 ...... E4
Bozkurt 2,948 ...... F2
Bozova 5,462 ...... H4
Bozüyük 15,197 ...... C3
Bucak 15,090 ...... D4
Bulancak 14,153 ...... H2
Bulanik 8,296 ...... K3
Buldan 11,115 ...... C3
Bünyan 12,277 ...... G3
Burdur 36,633 ...... D4
Burhaniye 12,800 ...... B3
Bursa 346,103 ...... C2
Büyükada D6
Büyükdere D5
Çal 3,274 ...... C3
Çala 2,450 ...... K2
Çaldiran 3,366 ...... K3

(continued on following page)

Agriculture, Industry and Resources

DOMINANT LAND USE

- Cereals (chiefly wheat, barley), Livestock
- Cash Crops, Horticulture, Livestock
- Pasture Livestock
- Nomadic Livestock Herding
- Forests
- Nonagricultural Land

MAJOR MINERAL OCCURRENCES

Ab	Asbestos	Na	Salt
Al	Bauxite	O	Petroleum
C	Coal	P	Phosphates
Cr	Chromium	Pb	Lead
Cu	Copper	Py	Pyrites
Fe	Iron Ore	Sb	Antimony
Hg	Mercury	Zn	Zinc
Mg	Magnesium		

⚡ Water Power
▨ Major Industrial Areas

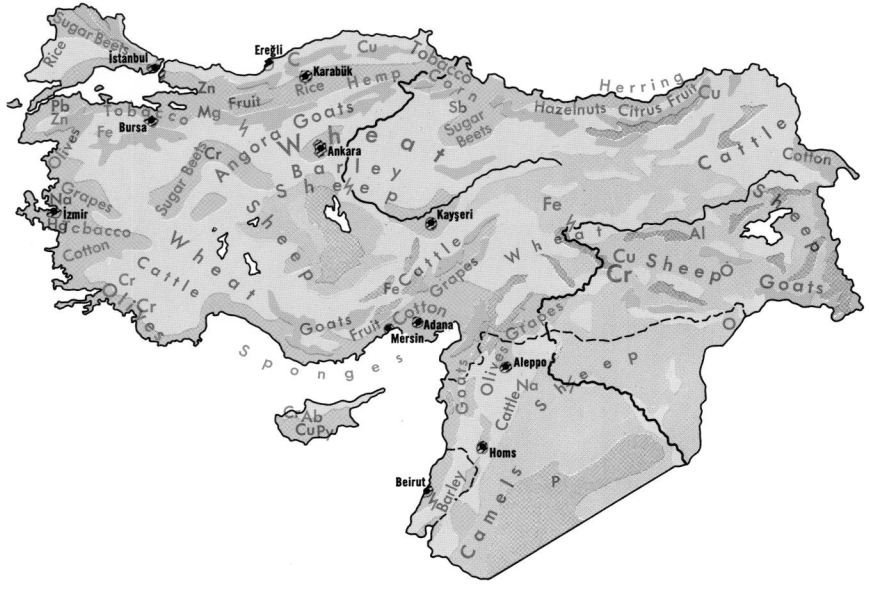

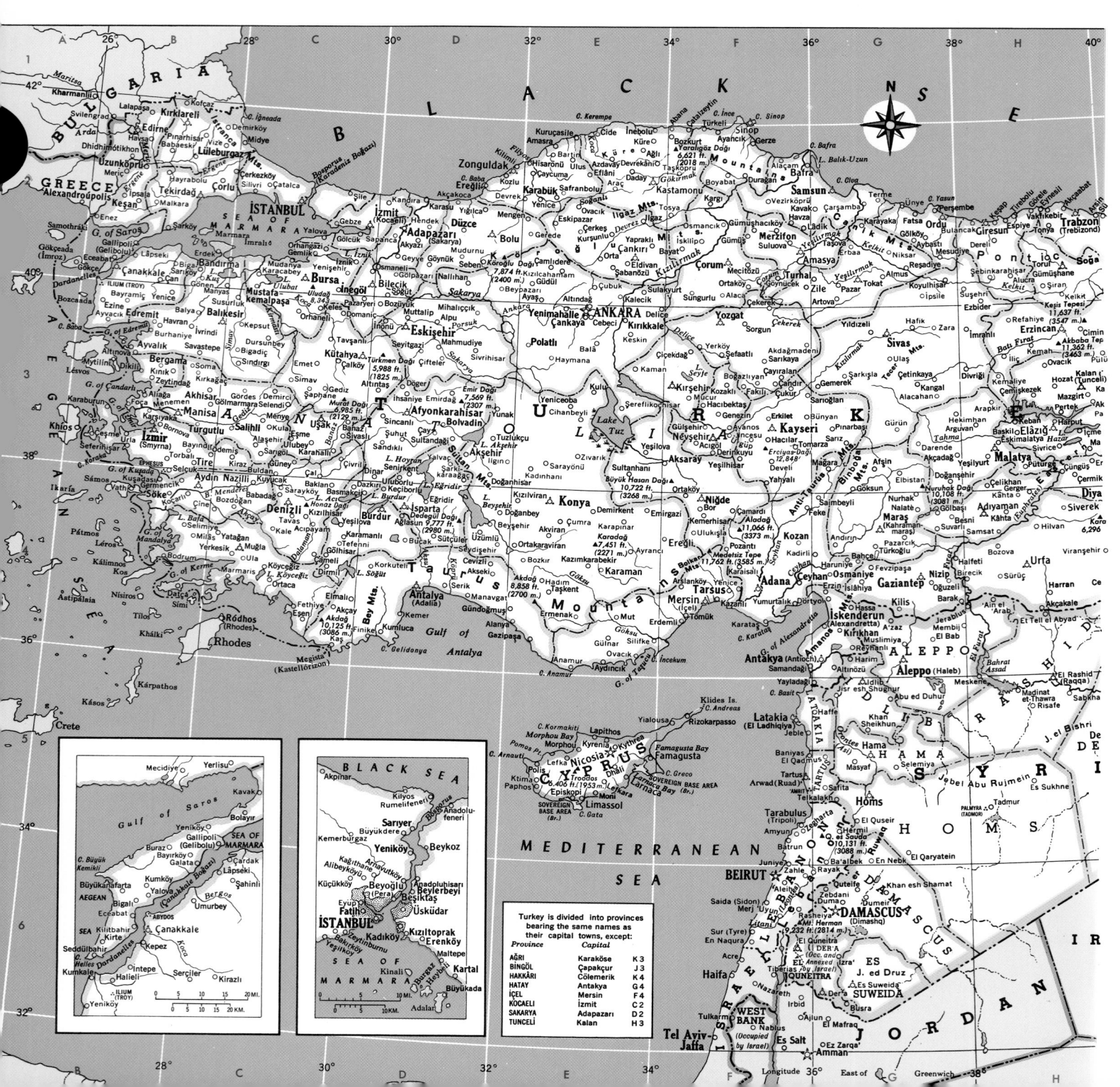

Turkey is divided into provinces bearing the same names as their capital towns, except:

Province	Capital
AĞRI	Karaköse ... K3
BİNGÖL	Çapakçur ... J3
HAKKÂRİ	Çölemerik ... K4
HATAY	Antakya ... G4
İÇEL	Mersin ... F4
KOCAELİ	İzmit ... C2
SAKARYA	Adapazarı ... D2
TUNCELİ	Kalan ... H3

Turkey, Syria, Lebanon and Cyprus 63

Hayrabolu 12,331 B2
Hazro 4,896 J3
Hekimhan 11,818 G3
Hendek 15,291 D2
Hilvan 6,473 H4
Hinis 10,226 J3
Hisarönü 4,485 E2
Hizan 2,545 K3
Hopa 9,089 J2
Horasan 7,724 K2
Hozat 5,796 H3
Içel (Mersin) 152,236 F4
Idil 4,862 J4
Iğdir 29,542 K3
Ilgaz 6 624 E2
Ilgin 11,830 D3
Ilica 8,947 J3
Imranli 5,667 H2
Incesu 7,089 F3
Inebolu 6,824 E2
Inegöl 37,805 C2
Inönü 4,152 D3
Ipsala 6,829 B2
Ipsile 2,328 G2
Iskenderun 107,437 G4
Iskilip 16,588 F2
Islâhiye 20,683 G4
Isparta 62,870 D4
Ispir 3,929 J2
Istanbul 2,547,364 D6
Ivrindi 3,730 B3
Izmir 636,834 B3
Izmit 165,483 D2
Iznik 11,614 C2
Kadiköy 354,957 D6
Kadinhani 11,802 E3
Kadirli 34,779 F4
Kağithane 164,448 D6
Kağizman 11,517 K2
Kâhta 15,602 H4
Kalan 11,637 H3
Kale 3,399 C4
Kalecik 4,707 E2
Kaman 16,516 E3
Kandira 10,187 D2
Kangal 5,937 G3
Karabük 69,182 E2
Karacabey 21,648 C2
Karahalli 5,539 C3
Karaisali 2,316 F4
Karakoçan 5,604 H3
Karaköse (Ağri) 35,284 K3

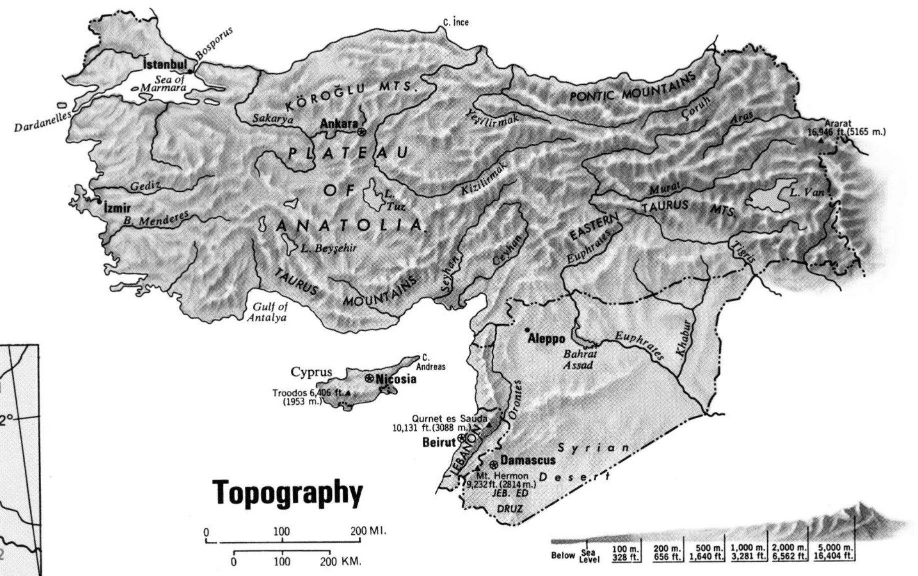
Istanbul
Bosporus
Sea of Marmara
Dardanelles
C. İnce
KÖROĞLU MTS.
PONTIC MOUNTAINS
Sakarya
Ankara
Yeşilirmak
Çoruh
Aras
Ararat 16,946 ft.(5165 m.)
PLATEAU OF ANATOLIA
Gediz
İzmir
B. Menderes
L. Tuz
Kizilirmak
Murat
TAURUS MTS.
L. Van
EASTERN
Euphrates
L. Beyşehir
Tigris
TAURUS MOUNTAINS
Seyhan
Ceyhan
Gulf of Antalya
Aleppo
Bahrat Assad
Euphrates
Khabur
Cyprus
C. Andreas
Nicosia
Troodos 6,406 ft.(1953 m.)
Orontes
Qurnet es Sauda 10,131 ft.(3088 m.)
Beirut
LEBANON
Damascus
Syrian Desert
Mt. Hermon 9,232 ft.(2814 m.)
JEB. ED DRUZ
0 100 200 MI.
0 100 200 KM.
Below Sea Level
100 m. 328 ft.
200 m. 656 ft.
500 m. 1,640 ft.
1,000 m. 3,281 ft.
2,000 m. 6,562 ft.
5,000 m. 16,404 ft.

Topography

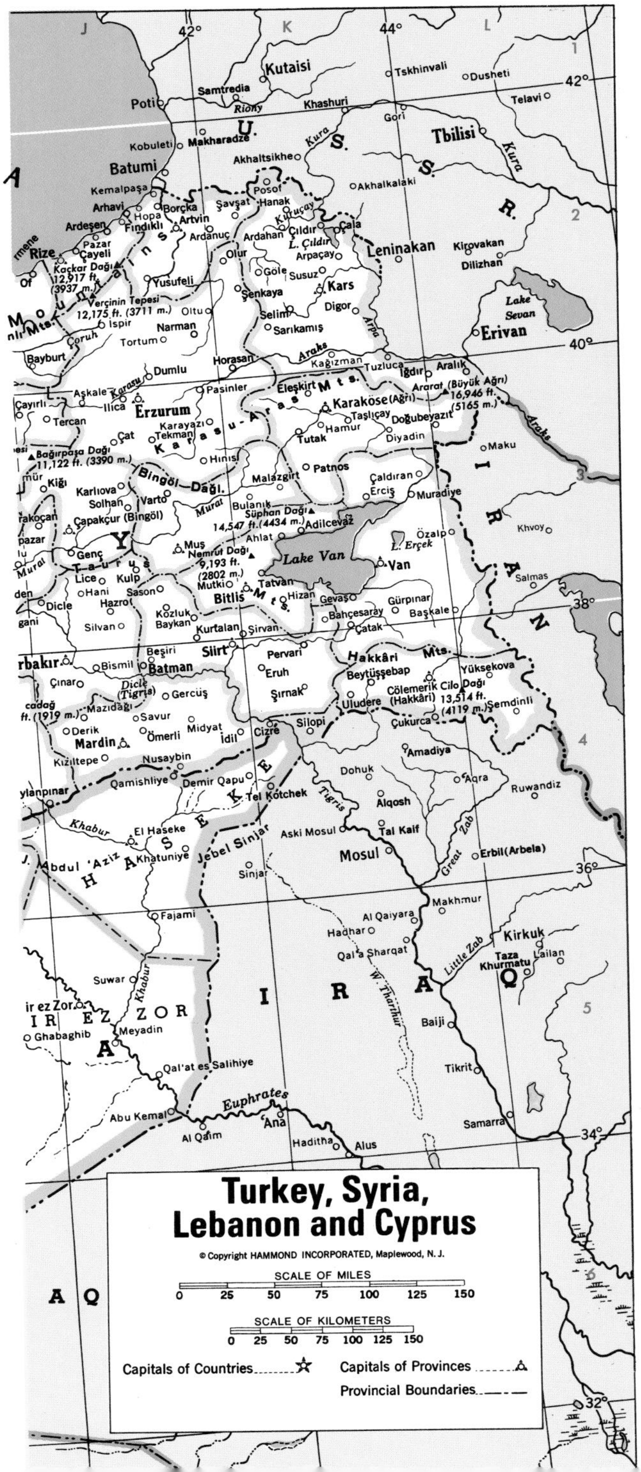
Kutaisi
Tskhinvali
Dusheti
Samtredia
Poti
Riony
Khashuri
Telavi
Gori
Tbilisi
Kobuleti
Makharadze
U. S. S. R.
Batumi
Akhaltsikhe
Kura
Kemalpaşa
Akhalkalaki
Hopa
Arhavi
Borçka
Şavşat
Posof
Artvin
Ardeşen
Rize
Çayeli
Ardanuç
Ardahan
Çildir
Çala
Leninakan
Kirovakan
Dilizhan
Kaçkar Dağı 12,917 ft. (3937 m.)
Of
Olur
Arpaçay
Susuz
Yusufeli
Şenkaya
Kars
Lake Sevan
Verçinin Tepesi 12,175 ft. (3711 m.)
Oltu
Ispir
Narman
Selim
Digor
Sarıkamış
Erivan
Çoruh
Tortum
Bayburt
Horasan
Araks
Kağızman
Tuzluca
Iğdır
Aralık
Dumlu
Aşkale
Pasinler
Eleşkirt
Ararat (Büyük Ağrı) 16,946 ft. (5165 m.)
Ilica
Erzurum
Karaköse (Ağrı)
Taşlıçay
Doğubeyazıt
Tercan
Çat
Karayazı
Tekman
Hamur
Tutak
Diyadin
Maku
Bağırpaşa Dağı 11,122 ft. (3390 m.)
Hınıs
Bingöl Dağl.
Malazgirt
Patnos
Çaldıran
Kiğı
Karlıova
Varto
Erciş
Muradiye
Solhan
Çapakçur (Bingöl)
Bulanık
Süphan Dağı 14,547 ft.(4434 m.)
Adilcevaz
Ahlat
Khvoy
Genç
Muş
Nemrut Dağı 9,193 ft. (2802 m.)
Lake Van
L. Erçek
Özalp
Van
Lice
Kulp
Mutki
Salmas
Hani
Sason
Bitlis
Tatvan
Hizan
Gevaş
Gürpınar
Dicle
Hazro
Kozluk
Baykan
Bahçesaray
Başkale
Silvan
Kurtalan
Şirvan
Çatak
Beşiri
Siirt
Pervari
Hakkâri
Batman
Bismil
Eruh
Beytüşşebap
Yüksekova
Çınar
Dicle (Tigris)
Gercüş
Şırnak
Cilo Dağı 13,514 ft. (4119 m.)
Çölemerik (Hakkâri)
Uludere
Şemdinli
Mazıdağı
Savur
Midyat
İdil
Cizre
Silopi
Çukurca
Derik
Mardin
Ömerli
Kızıltepe
Nusaybin
Amadiya
Dohuk
Qamishliye
Demir Qapu
Aqra
Rawandiz
Tel Kotchek
Alqosh
Khabur
El Haseke
Aski Mosul
Tal Kaif
Jebel Sinjar
Erbil (Arbela)
Mosul
Khatuniye
Sinjar
Great Zab
Fajami
Makhmur
Al Qaiyara
Hadhar
Qal'a Sharqat
Kirkuk
Little Zab
Taza Khurmatu
Lailan
Suwar
Khabur
I R A Q
ZOR
Baiji
Meyadin
Tikrit
Qal'at es Salihiye
Euphrates
Abu Kemal
'Ana
Samarra
Al Qaim
Haditha
Alus
Turkey, Syria, Lebanon and Cyprus
© Copyright HAMMOND INCORPORATED, Maplewood, N. J.
SCALE OF MILES
0 25 50 75 100 125 150
SCALE OF KILOMETERS
0 25 50 75 100 125 150
Capitals of Countries
Capitals of Provinces
Provincial Boundaries

Karaman 43,759 E4
Karamanli 5,904 C4
Karapinar 19,589 E4
Karasu 11,600 D2
Karataş 5,598 F4
Karayaka 4,242 G2
Karayazi 3,595 J3
Kargi 5,021 F2
Karliova 3,631 J3
Kars 54,892 K2
Karşiyaka 171,600 B3
Kartal 53,073 D6
Kaş 2,493 C4
Kastamonu 29,993 F2
Kavak, Çanakkale 3,932 C5
Kavak, Samsun 3,964 F2
Kayseri 207,037 F3
Kazanli 4,461 F4
Kazimkarabekir 4,086 E4
Keban 5,800 H3
Keçiborlu 7,096 D4
Keles 2,423 C3
Kelkit 6,928 H2
Kemah 3,038 H3
Kemaliye 3,014 H3
Kemalpaşa 7,572 J2
Kemerburgaz 7,234 D5
Kemirhisar 6,205 F4
Kepsut 4,704 C3
Keşan 27,088 B2
Keşap 5,264 H2
Keskin 10,540 E3
Kiği 5,598 J3
Kilimli 26,649 D2
Kilis 54,055 G4
Kinik 11,785 B3
Kiraz 5,284 C3
Kirikhan 38,118 G4
Kirikkale 137,874 E3
Kirkağaç 15,078 B3
Kirklareli 33,265 B2
Kirşehir 41,415 F3
Kizilcahamam 7,050 E2
Kizilhisar 11,119 C4
Kiziltepe 21,531 J4
Kizilviran 3,260 E4
Kocaeli (Izmit) 165,483 D2
Koçarli 5,182 B4
Konya 246,727 E4
Korkuteli 10,334 D4
Köyceğiz 4,612 C4
Koyulhisar 3,861 G2
Kozakli 6,200 F3
Kozan 32,045 F4
Kozlu 27,322 D2
Kozluk 6,197 J3
Küçükköy 56,411 C6
Kula 10,807 C3
Kulp 4,474 J3
Kulu 11,707 E3
Kumkale 1,752 B6
Kumluca 7,704 D4
Küre 2,378 E2
Kurşunlu 6,562 E2
Kurtalan 7,001 J3
Kuşadasi 10,269 B4
Kütahya 82,442 C3
Kuyucak 6,039 C4
Lâdik 6,785 G2
Lâpseki 3,727 C6
Lice 8,625 J3
Lüleburgaz 32,401 B2
Maden 15,151 H3
Mağara 4,314 G3
Mahmudiye 5,240 D3
Malatya 154,505 H3
Malazgirt 13,094 K3
Malkara 14,399 B2
Maltepe 66,343 D6
Manavgat 10,804 D4
Manisa 78,114 B3
Manyas 4,410 B3
Maraş
(Kahramanmaraş) 135,782 G4
Mardin 36,629 J4
Marmaris 5,596 C4
Mazgirt 3,141 H3
Mazidaği 4,842 J4
Mecitözü 6,066 F2
Menemen 18,464 B3
Mengen 2,459 D2
Meriç 3,922 B2
Mersin 152,236 F4
Merzifon 30,801 F2
Mesudiye 4,294 F4
Midyat 16,905 J4
Midye 2,003 C2
Mihaliççik 4,004 D3
Milâs 17,929 B4
Mucur 9,398 F3
Mudanya 8,399 C2
Mudurnu 3,905 D2
Muğla 24,178 C4
Muradiye 6,334 K3
Muş 27,761 J3
Mustafakemalpaşa 27,706 C3
Mut 11,466 E4
Mutki 2,815 J3
Muttalip 3,917 D3
Nallihan 7,883 D2
Narman 4,607 J2
Nazilli 52,176 C4
Nevşehir 30,203 F3
Niğde 31,844 F4
Niksar 19,156 G2
Nizip 36,190 G4
Nurhak 5,330 G4
Nusaybin 23,684 J4
Ödemiş 37,364 C3
Of 10,376 J2
Oğuzeli 7,194 G4
Oltu 10,093 J2
Ömerli 4,738 J4
Ordu 47,481 G2
Orhaneli 3,335 C3
Orhangazi 12,181 C2
Orta 3,596 E2
Ortaca 8,604 C4
Ortakaraviran 3,856 E4
Ortaköy, Çorum 2,657 F2
Ortaköy, Niğde 6,371 F3
Osmancik 11,921 F2
Osmaneli 4,789 D2
Osmaniye 61,581 G4
Ovacik, Tunceli 2,248 H3
Özalp 4,188 K3
Palu 5,489 H3
Pasinler 14,267 J3
Patnos 15,918 K3
Pazar, Rize 8,856 J2
Pazar, Tokat 4,337 G2
Pazarcik 15,943 G4
Pazaryeri 5,633 C3
Pera (Beyoğlu) 230,532 D6
Perşembe 6,701 G2
Pertek 4,176 H3
Pervari 4,126 K4
Pinarbaşi 9,503 G3
Pinarhisar 10,523 B2
Polatli 35,267 E3
Posof 2,209 K2
Pozanti 5,408 F4
Pülümür 3,442 H3
Pütürge 4,878 H3
Refahiye 6,570 H3
Reşadiye 9,022 G2
Reyhanli 25,749 G4
Rize 36,044 J2
Şabanözü 3,442 E2
Safranbolu 14,793 E2
Saimbeyli 3,622 G4
Sakarya (Adapazari) 114,130 D2
Salihli 45,514 C3
Samandaği 22,540 F4
Samsat 2,083 H4
Samsun 168,478 F2
Sandikli 13,181 D3
Sapanca 9,040 D2
Şaphane 3,919 C3
Sarayköy 10,513 C4
Sarayönü 8,946 E3
Sarigöl 6,979 C3
Sarikamiş 21,262 K2
Sarikaya 5,160 F3
Sariköy 4,695 B2
Sarioğlan 3,245 G3
Sariyer 79,329 D5
Sariz 3,591 G3
Şarkikaraağaç 4,772 D3
Şarkişla 12,763 G3
Şarköy 5,396 B2
Sason 3,211 J3
Savaştepe 7,179 B3
Şavşat 3,078 K2
Savur 4,983 J4
Seben 2,471 D2
Şebinkarahisar 10,214 H2
Şefaatli 6,769 F3
Seferihisar 6,484 B3
Selçuk 12,251 B3
Selendi 4,457 C3
Selim 3,569 K2
Selimiye 2,989 B4
Senirkent 8,247 D3
Şenkaya 3,190 K2
Şereflikoçhisar 20,523 E3
Serik 14,161 D4
Seydişehir 25,651 D4
Seyitgazi 2,819 D3
Siirt 35,654 J4
Şile 4,062 C2
Silifke 19,257 E4
Silivri 8,525 C2
Silopi 4,460 K4
Silvan 29,599 J3
Simav 11,601 C3
Sincanli 3,847 D3
Sindirgi 7,818 C3
Sinop 16,098 F2
Şiran 5,048 H2
Şirnak 10,587 K4
Şirvan 5,166 K3
Sivas 149,201 G3
Sivasli 4,394 C3
Siverek 40,990 H4
Sivrihisar 8,713 D3
Smyrna (Izmir) 636,834 B3
Söğüt 5,329 D3
Söke 35,407 B4
Solhan 7,014 J3
Soma 23,713 B3
Sorgun 14,081 F3
Şuhut 8,154 D3
Sulakyurt 4,311 E2
Sultandaği 4,017 D3
Sultanhani 5,112 E3
Suluova 21,278 F2
Sungurlu 21,641 F2
Sürmene 8,096 J2
Sürüç 20,395 H4
Suşehri 10,863 H2
Susurluk 14,000 C3
Susuz 5,006 K2
Sütçüler 2,721 D4
Tarsus 102,186 F4
Taşkent 7,098 E4
Taşköprü 8,146 F2
Taşliçay 3,684 K3
Taşova 6,516 F4
Tatvan 29,271 K3
Tavas 9,728 C4
Tavşanli 19,575 C3
Tefenni 4,280 C4
Tekirdağ 41,257 B2
Tercan 6,068 J3
Terme 15,660 G2
Tire 30,694 B3
Tirebolu 7,385 H2
Tokat 48,588 G2
Tomarza 6,548 F3
Tömük 7,660 F4
Tonya 10,544 H2
Torbali 17,237 B3
Tortum 4,110 J2
Torul 3,221 H2
Tosya 17,515 F2
Trabzon 97,210 H2
Trebizond (Trabzon) 97,210 H2
Tunceli (Kalan) 11,637 H3
Turgutlu 47,009 B3
Turhal 39,170 F2
Türkeli 2,194 F2
Türkoğlu 9,207 G4
Tutak 4,325 K3
Tuzluca 5,209 K3
Tuzlukçu 4,613 D3
Ula 5,117 C4
Ulaş 2,469 G3
Ulubey 4,214 C3
Uluborlu 10,016 D3
Uludere 4,050 K4
Ulukişla 6,336 F4
Umurbey 2,754 C6
Ünye 23,366 G2
Urfa 132,934 H4
Ürgüp 6,758 F3
Urla 13,903 B3
Uşak 58,578 C3
Üsküdar 202,957 D6
Üzümlü 4,365 D4
Uzunköprü 27,005 B2
Vakfikebir 12,556 H2
Van 63,663 K3
Varto 5,572 J3
Vezirköprü 11,705 F2
Viranşehir 26,244 H4
Vize 8,203 B2
Yahyali 13,738 F3
Yalova, Istanbul 27,289 C2
Yalvaç 18,305 D3
Yaprakli 3,020 E2
Yatağan 4,903 C4
Yayladaği 4,471 F5
Yenice, Çanakkale 4,004 B3
Yenice, Içel 4,106 F4
Yenice, Zonguldak 5,791 E2
Yeniceoba 5,740 E3
Yeniköy, Istanbul D6
Yenimahalle 198,643 E3
Yenişehir 15,188 C2
Yerkesik 2,381 C4
Yerköy 19,927 F3
Yeşilhisar 10,409 F3
Yeşilköy D6
Yeşilova, Burdur 3,685 C4
Yeşilova, Niğde 5,237 E3
Yeşilyurt 7,451 H3
Yildizeli 7,043 G3
Yozgat 32,501 F3
Yüksekova 7,329 L4
Yumurtalik 2,442 F4
Yunak 6,187 D3
Yusufeli 3,050 J2
Zara 10,376 G3
Zeytinburnu 123,548 D6
Zeytindağ 3,517 B3
Zile 32,157 G2
Zivarik 2,703 E3
Zonguldak 90,221 D2

OTHER FEATURES

Abydos (ruins) B6
Aci (lake) C4
Adalar (isl.) D6
Aegean (sea) A3
Ağri, Büyük (Ararat)
(mt.) L3
Akdağ (mt.) C4
Aladağ (mt.) F4
Alexandretta (gulf) F4
Amanos (mts.) G4
Anamur (cape) E5
Anatolia (reg.) D3
Ankara (riv.) D3
Antalya (gulf) D4
Anti-Taurus (mts.) G3
Araks (riv.) K2
Ararat (mt.) L3
Arpa (riv.) K2
Baba (cape) A3
Bati Firat (riv.) H3
Beyşehir (lake) D4
Black (sea) E1
Bosporus (str.) C2
Bozcaada (isl.) A3
Burgaz (isl.) D6
Büyük Ağri (Ararat)
(mt.) L3
Çanakkaie Boğazi (Dardanelles) (str.) B6
Çandarli (gulf) B3
Canik (mts.) G2
Ceyhan (riv.) F4
Cilo Daği (mt.) K4
Çoruh (riv.) J2
Dardanelles (str.) B6
Dicle (riv.) J4
Eastern Taurus (mts.) J3
Ephesus (ruins) B3
Erciyas Daği (mt.) F3
Ergene (riv.) B2
Euphrates (Firat) (riv.) G4
Firat (riv.) G4
Gediz (riv.) C3
Gelidonya (cape) D4
Gökçeada (isl.) A2
Göksu (riv.) E4
Helles (cape) B6
Heybeli (isl.) D6
Ilium (ruins) B6
Imroz (Gökçeada)
(isl.) A2
Ince (cape) F1
Istranca (mts.) B2
Kaçkar Daği (mt.) J2
Karadeniz Boğazi (Bosporus)
(str.) C2
Karasu-Aras (mts.) J3
Kelkit (riv.) G2
Kerme (gulf) B4
Keşiş Tepesi (mt.) H3
Kizilirmak (riv.) F2
Koca (riv.) C3
Köroğlu (mts.) E2
Küre (mts.) E2
Mandalya (gulf) B4
Marmara (isl.) B2
Marmara (sea) C2
Menderes, Büyük (riv.) C4
Meriç (riv.) B2
Murat (riv.) H3
Pontic (mts.) H2
Porsuk (riv.) D3
Prinkipo (Adalar) (isl.) D6
Sakarya (riv.) D2
Saros (gulf) B2
Seyhan (riv.) F4
Simav (riv.) C3
Sinop (cape) F1
Sultan (mts.) D3
Süphan Daği (mt.) K3
Taurus (mts.) D4
Tigris (Dicle) J4
Troy (Ilium) (ruins) B6
Tuz (lake) E3
Van (lake) K3
Yeşilirmak (riv.) G2

* City and suburbs

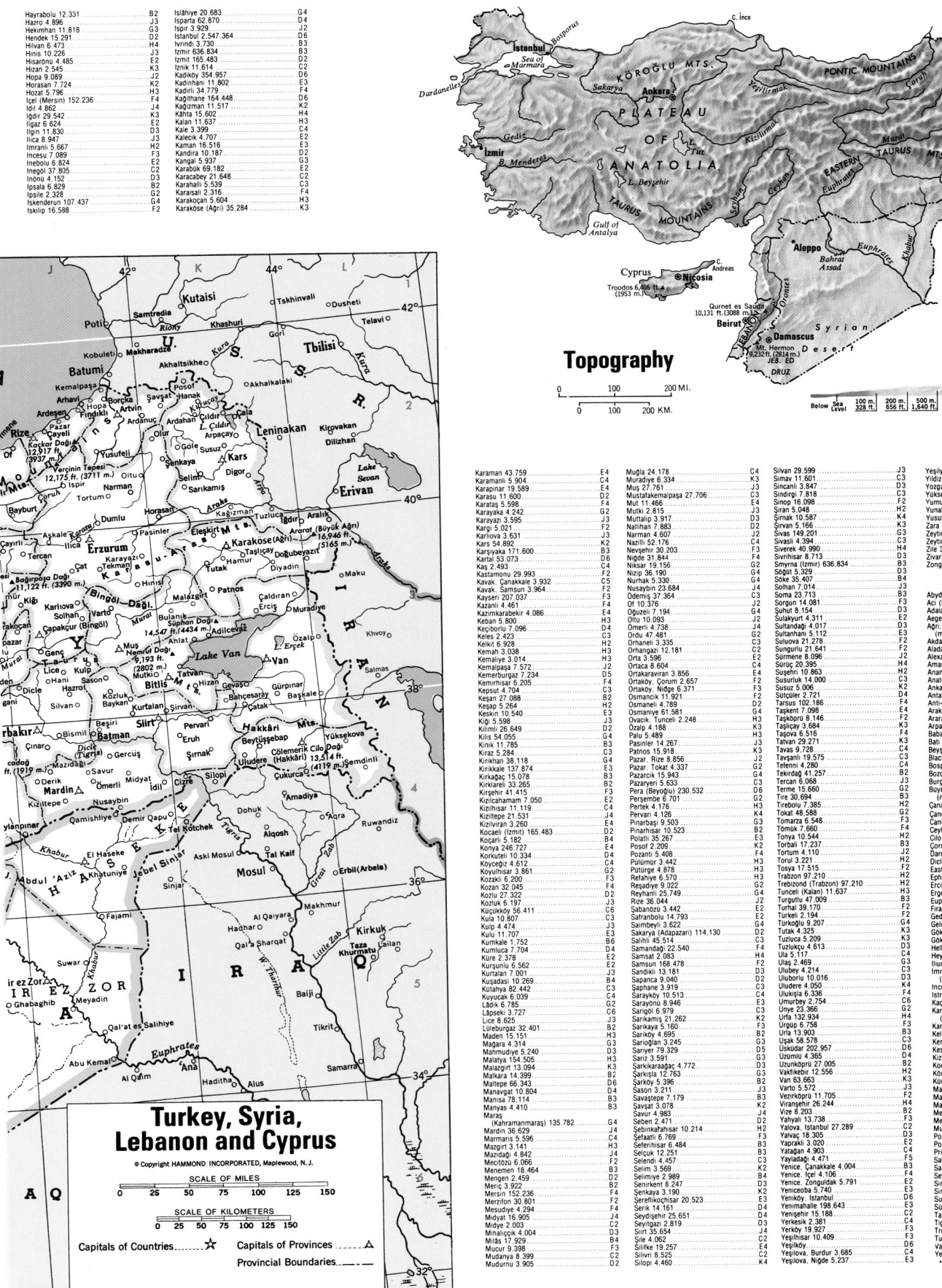

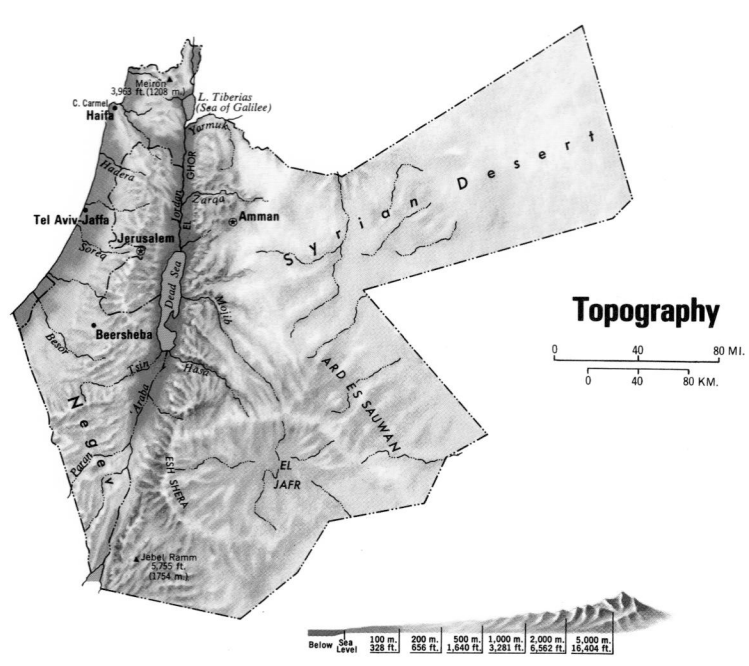

Topography

```
Below Sea    100 m.   200 m.   500 m.  1,000 m.  2,000 m.  5,000 m.
Level        328 ft.  656 ft. 1,640 ft. 3,281 ft. 6,562 ft. 16,404 ft.
```

0   40   80 MI.
0   40   80 KM.

ISRAEL

DISTRICTS

Central 572,300	B3
Haifa 480,800	B2
Jerusalem 338,600	B4
Northern 473,700	C2
Southern 351,300	B5
Tel Aviv 905,100	B3

CITIES and TOWNS

Acre 34,400	C2
Afiqim 1,243	D2
'Afula 17,400	C2
Ahuzzam 407	B4
Akko (Acre) 34,400	C2
Arad 5,400	C5
'Arrabe 6,000	C2
Ashdod 40,500	B4
Ashdot Yaa'qov 1,197	D2
Ashqelon 43,100	A4
Atlit 1,516	B2
Avihayil 579	B3
Bat Shelomo 218	B2
Be'eri 390	A5
Be'er Menuha	D5
Beersheba (Be'er Sheva) 101,000	B5
Be'er Tuveya 602	B4
Beit Guvrin	B4
Bene Beraq 74,100	B3
Bet Qama 228	B5
Bet She'an 11,300	C2
Bet Shemesh 10,100	B4
Binyamina 2,701	B2
Carmiel	C2
Dafna 577	D1
Dalyat al-Karmel 6,200	C2
Dan 498	D1
Dimona 23,700	D4
Dor 195	B2
E'in Gedi	C5
E'in Harod 1,372	C2
Elat	D6
Elath (Elat) 12,800	D6
El 'Auja	D5
Elyakim 568	C2
Elyashiv 435	B3
Even Yehuda 3,464	B3
Gat 430	B4
Gat'on 356	B4
Gedera 5,400	B4
Gerofit	D5
Gesher 360	C2
Gesher Haziv 238	C1
Gevara'm 283	B4
Gilat 561	B5
Ginnosar 473	D2
Giv'atayim 48,500	B3
Giva't Brenner 1,505	B4
Giv'at Hayyim 1,360	B3
Haboninim 189	B2
Hadera 31,900	B3
Haifa 227,800	B2
Haifa* 367,400	B2
Hatseva	D5
Hazerim 127	B5
Hazor Hageliit	D2
Helez 466	B4
Herzeliyya 41,200	B3
Hod Hasharon 13,500	B3
Hodiyya 400	B4
Holon 121,200	B3
Iksal 2,156	C2
Jerusalem (cap.) 376,000	C4
Jish 1,498	C1
Kafar Kanna 5,200	C2
Kafr Yasif 2,975	C2
Karkur-Pardes Hanna 13,600	C3
Kefar Blum 565	D1
Kefar Gila'di 701	C1
Kefar Ruppin 306	D3
Kefar Sava 26,500	B3
Kefar Vitkin 808	B3
Kefar Zekhariya 420	B4
Kinneret 909	D2
Lod (Lydda) 30,500	B4
Lydda 30,500	B4
Magen 149	A5
Maa'lot-Tarshiha	C1
Malkiya	D1
Mash 'Abbe Sade 238	B6
Mavqii'm 177	B4
Megiddo	C2
Metula 261	D1
Migdal 688	C2
Migdal Ha E'meq	C2
Mikhmoret 608	B3
Mishmar Hanegev 336	B5
Mishmar Hayarden	D1
Mivtahim 398	A5
Mizpe Ramon 331	D5
Moza Illit 219	C4
Mugeible 459	C2
Mughar 4,010	C2
Naharriyya 24,000	C1
Nazareth 33,300	C2
Nazerat I'lit	C2
Negba 453	B4
Nes Ziyyona 11,700	B4
Netanya 70,700	B3
Netivot	B5
Nevatim 436	B5
Newe Yam 211	B2
Newe Zohar	C5
Nir Yitzhaq 209	A5
Nizzanim 479	B4
Ofaqim	B5
O'mer	B5
Oron	C6
Or Yehuda	B4
Pardes Hanna-Karkur 13,600	B2
Peduyim 361	B5
Petah Tiqwa 112,000	B3
Qadima 2,937	B3
Qalansuwa	B3
Qedma 157	B4
Qiryat 473	D2
Qiryat Bialik 18,000	C2
Qiryat Gat 19,200	B4
Qiryat Mal'akhi	B4
Qiryat Motzkin 17,600	C2
Qiryat Shemona 15,200	C1
Qiryat Tivo'n 9,800	C2
Qiryat Yam 19,800	C2
Raa'nana 14,900	B3
Ramat Gan 120,900	B3
Ramat Hasharon 20,100	B3
Rame 2,986	C2
Ramla 34,100	B4
Rehovot 39,200	B4
Rei'm 155	A5
Revadim 175	B4
Revivim 258	D5
Rishon Le Ziyyon 51,900	B4
Rosh Ha 'Ayin	B3
Rosh Pinna 700	D2
Ruhama 497	B4
Saa'd 418	B5
Safad (Zefat) 13,600	C1
Sakhnin 8,400	C2
Sede Boqer	D5
Sederot	B4
Sedom	D5
Sedot Yam 511	B3
Shave Ziyyon 269	B2
Shefaram 11,800	C2
Shefayim 614	B3
Shoval 393	B5
Tayibe 11,700	C3
Tel Aviv-Jaffa 343,300	B3
Tel Aviv-Jaffa* 1,219,900	B3
Tiberias 23,800	C2
Tirat Hakarmel 14,400	B2
Tirat Zevi 353	D3
Tur'an 2,304	C2
Umm el Fahm 13,300	C2
Urim 203	B5
Uzza 487	B4
Yad Mordekhai 416	A4
Yagur 1,266	C2
Yahav	D5
Yavne 10,100	B4
Yavne'el 1,580	C2
Yehud 8,900	B3
Yeroham 5,800	B6
Yesodot 293	B4
Yesud Hamaa'la 428	D1
Yiftah	D1
Yirka 2,715	C2
Yotvata	D6
Zavdi'el 396	B4
Ze'elim 148	A5
Zefat 13,600	C1
Zikhron Yaa'qov 6,500	B2
Zippori 241	C2

OTHER FEATURES

Aqaba (gulf)	D6
'Araba, Wadi (valley)	D5
Beer Sheva (dry riv.)	B5
Besor (riv.)	B5
Carmel (cape)	B2
Carmel (mt.)	C2
Dead (sea)	C4
Galilee, Sea of (Tiberias) (lake)	D2
Galilee (reg.)	C2
Gerar (dry riv.)	B5
Hadera (dry riv.)	B3
Haniqra, Rosh (cape)	C1
Jordan (riv.)	D3
Judaea (reg.)	B5
Lakhish (dry riv.)	B4
Meiron (mt.)	C1
Negev (reg.)	D5

Archaeological Sites in Palestine

■ Major Excavations

Miles
0   10   20   30

Agriculture, Industry and Resources

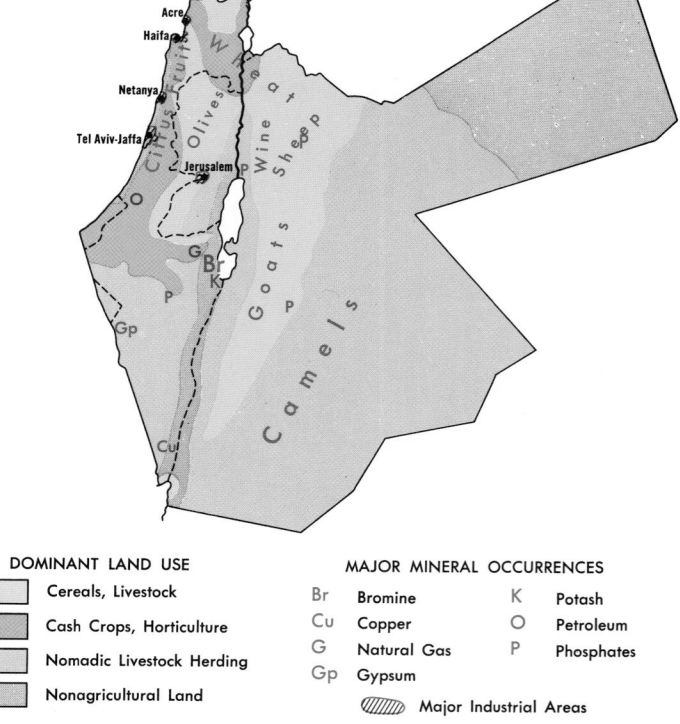

DOMINANT LAND USE

- Cereals, Livestock
- Cash Crops, Horticulture
- Nomadic Livestock Herding
- Nonagricultural Land

MAJOR MINERAL OCCURRENCES

- Br Bromine
- Cu Copper
- G Natural Gas
- Gp Gypsum
- K Potash
- O Petroleum
- P Phosphates
- ▨ Major Industrial Areas

© Copyright HAMMOND INCORPORATED

ISRAEL

JORDAN

ISRAEL

AREA 7,847 sq. mi. (20,324 sq. km.)
POPULATION 3,878,000
CAPITAL Jerusalem
LARGEST CITY Tel Aviv-Jaffa
HIGHEST POINT Meiran 3,963 ft. (1,208 m.)
MONETARY UNIT shekel
MAJOR LANGUAGES Hebrew, Arabic
MAJOR RELIGIONS Judaism, Islam, Christianity

JORDAN

AREA 35,000 sq. mi. (90,650 sq. km.)
POPULATION 2,152,273
CAPITAL Amman
LARGEST CITY Amman
HIGHEST POINT Jeb. Ramm 5,755 ft. (1,754 m.)
MONETARY UNIT Jordanian dinar
MAJOR LANGUAGE Arabic
MAJOR RELIGION Islam

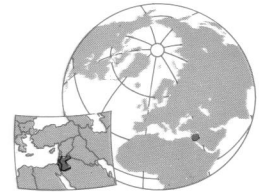

GAZA STRIP

CITIES and TOWNS

'Abasan 1,481 .... A5
Bani Suheila 7,561 .... A5
Beit Hanun 4,756 .... A4
Deir el Balah 10,854 .... A5
Deir el Balah* 18,118 .... A5
Gaza 87,793 .... A5
Gaza* 118,272 .... A5
Jabaliya 10,508 .... A4
Jabaliya* 43,604 .... A4
Khan Yunis 29,522 .... A5
Khan Yunis* 52,997 .... A5
Rafah 10,812 .... A5
Rafah* 49,812 .... A5

WEST BANK

CITIES AND TOWNS

'Ajja 1,322 .... C3
'Anabta 3,426 .... C2
Anin 914 .... C2
'Anza 807 .... C3
'Aqqaba 1,127 .... C3
'Aqraba 2,501 .... C3
Ariha (Jericho) 5,312 ...... C4
'Araba 4,231 .... C3
'Arura 849 .... C3
'Attil 3,806 .... C3
Beit Fajjar 2,474 .... C4
Beit Hanina 1,177 .... C4
Beit Jala 6,041 .... C4
Beit Lahm (Bethlehem) 14,439 ... C4
Beit Nuba 1,350 .... C4
Beit Sahur 5,380 .... C4
Bethlehem 14,439 .... C4
Biddu 1,239 .... C4
Birqin 2,036 .... C3
Bir Zeit 2,311 .... C4
Burqa 2,477 .... C3
Deir Ballut 1,058 .... C3
Deir Sharaf 973 .... C3
Dhahiriya 4,875 .... B5
Duma 524 .... C3
Dura 4,954 .... C4
El Bira 9,674 .... C4
El Bira* 13,037 .... C4
El Khalil (Hebron) 38,309 ... C4
Er Rihiya 679 .... C4
Ez Zababida 1,474 .... C3
Falama 162 .... C3
Halhul 6,041 .... C4
Haris 641 .... C3
Hebron 38,309 .... C4
Idna 3,713 .... C4
I'mwas 1,955 .... B4
Jaba 2,817 .... C3
Jalama 784 .... C3
'Jalbun 914 .... C3
Jalud 227 .... C3
Jenin 8,346 .... C3
Jenin* 13,365 .... C3
Jericho 5,312 .... C4
Jericho* 6,931 .... C4
Jifna 655 .... C4
Kharas 1,364 .... C4
Nablus (Nabulus) 41,799 ... C3
Nahhalin 1,109 .... C4
Nil'in 1,227 .... C4
Qabalan 1,970 .... C3
Qabatiya 6,005 .... C3
Qaffin 2,480 .... C3
Qalqiliya 8,926 ...... C3
Qibya 926 .... C4
Rafidiya 1,123 .... C3
Ramallah 12,134 ..... C4
Rammun 1,198 .... C3
Rantis 897 .... C3
Salfit 3,201 .... C3
Samu 3,261 .... C4
Shuf'at 14,000 ...... C4
Shuweika 2,332 ...... C3
Silat Dhahr 2,104 ... C3
Sinjil 1,823 .... C3
Siris 1,285 .... C3
Tammun 2,952 .... C3
Tarqumiya 2,412 ..... C4
Tubas 5,262 .... C3
Tulkarm 10,255 ...... C3
Tulkarm* 15,275 ..... C3
Tur 12,200 .... C4
Yab'ad 4,857 .... C3
Yabrud 277 .... C4
Yamun 4,384 .... C3
Yatta 7,281 .... C5
Zububa 633 .... C2

OTHER FEATURES

Qishon (riv.) C2
Ramon (mt.) D5
Rubin (dry riv.) B4
Tabor (mt.) C2
Tiberias (lake) D2
Yarmuk (riv.) D2
Yarqon (riv.) B3

JORDAN

GOVERNORATES

El Asima 1,000,000 ... D4
El Balqa 113,000 ..... D4
El Karak 93,000 ...... E5
Irbid 506,000 .... D3
Ma'an 62,000 .... D5

CITIES and TOWNS

'Ajlun⊙ 42,000 .... D3
Amman (cap.) 711,850 ... D4
'Anjara 3,163 .... D6
Aqaba 15,000 .... D6
Bala'ma 769 .... E3
Baqura 3,042 .... D2
Damiya 483 .... D3
Dana 844 .... E5
Deir Abu Sa'id 1,927 ... D3
Dhira D5
El 'Al 492 .... D4
El Husn 3,728 .... D3
El Karak 10,000 ..... E4
El Kitta 987 .... D3
El Madwar 164 ...... E3
El Mafraq 15,500 .... E3
El Majdal 259 ...... D3
El Quweira 268 ..... E5
El Yaduda 251 ...... D4
Er Ramtha 19,000 ... D3
Er Rumman 293 .... D3
Er Ruseifa 6,200 ... E3
Esh Shaubak 01 .... D5
Ghor es Safi 2,580 ... D4
Es Salt 24,000 ..... D3
Es Sukhna 649 ..... D3
Et Tafila⊙ 17,000 ... E5
Et Taiyiba 2,600 ... D2
Faraz 263,400 ..... D3
Harima 635 .... D4
Hawara 2,342 ..... D3
Hisban 718 .... D4
Ibbin 1,364 ...... D3
Irbid 136,770 ..... D3
Jabir 132 .... E2
Jarash⊙ 29,000 .... D3
Kitim 1,026 ...... D3
Kufrinja 3,922 .... D3
Kuraiyima D3
Ma'd 125 .... D2
Ma'n 9,500 ...... E5
Ma'daba 22,600 ... D4
Ma'in 1,271 ...... D4
Manja 353 .... D4
Mazra' C5
Nau'r 2,382 ..... D4
Nitil 348 .... D4
Qumeim 955 ..... D2
Ra's en Naqb 225 ... E5
Safi D4
Salut 4,210 ..... D3
Samar 716 ...... D2
Sarih 3,390 ..... D2
Shunat Nimrin 109 ... D4
Suf D3
Suweilih 3,457 .... D3
Suweima 315 ..... D4
Um Jauza 582 .... D4
Wadi es Sir 4,455 ... D4
Waqqas 2,321 .... D2
Zuweiza 126 ..... D4

OTHER FEATURES

'Ajlun (range) D3
Aqaba (gulf) D6
Araba, Wadi (valley) ... D5
Dead (sea) C4
Ebal (mt.) C3
El Ghor (reg.) C3
El Lisan (pen.) D5
Hasa, Wadi el (dry riv.) ... E5
Jordan (riv.) D3
Judaea (reg.) C4
Khirbet Qumran (site) ... D4
Mashash, Wadi (dry riv.) ... D4
Nebo (mt.) D4
Petra (ruins) D5
Ramm, Jebel (mt.) ... D6
Samaria (reg.) C3
Shallala, Wadi esh (dry riv.) ... D2
Shu'eib, Wadi (dry riv.) ... D4
Tell 'Asur (mt.) C4
Yabis, Wadi el (dry riv.) ... D3

*City and suburbs.
⊙Population of subdivision.

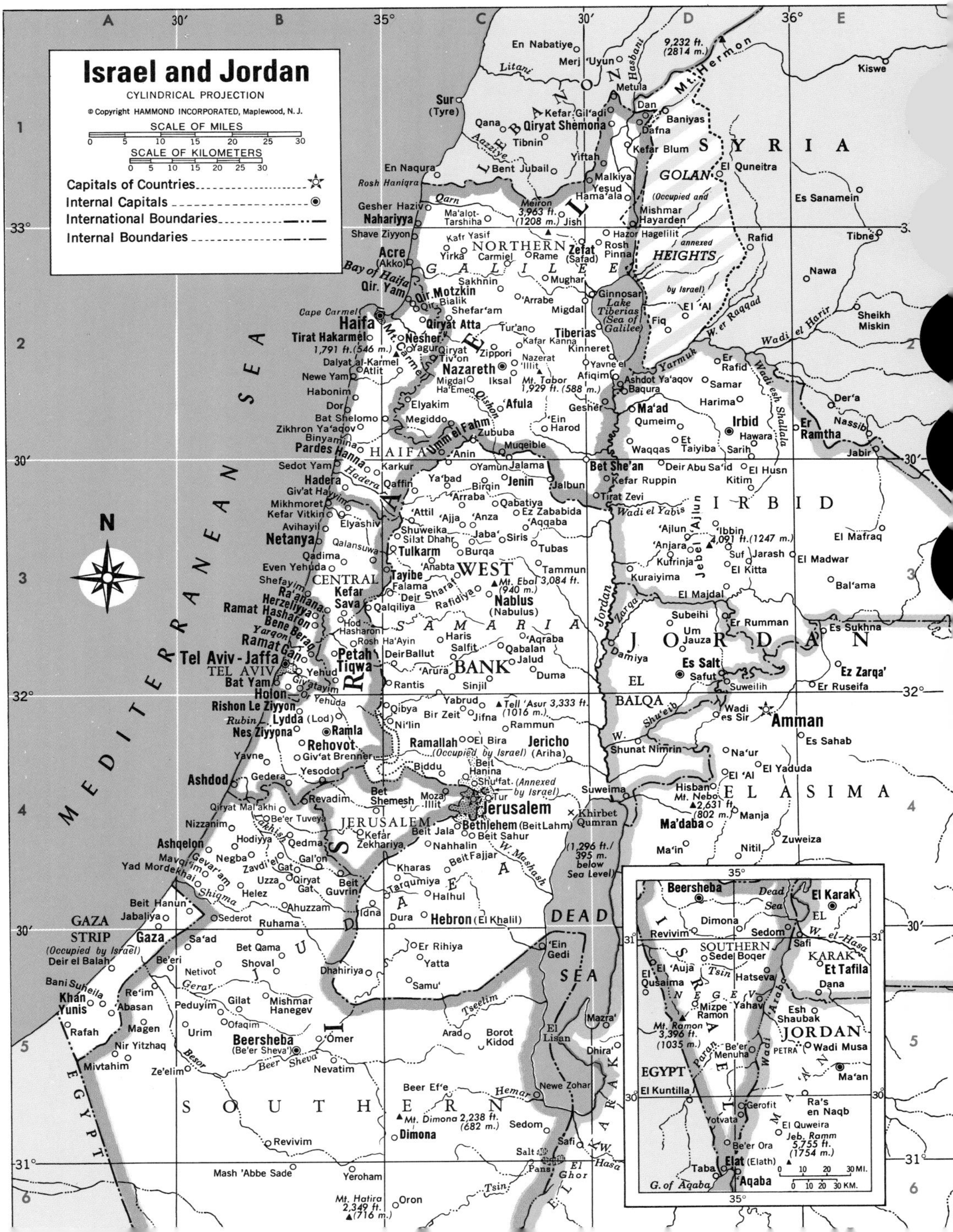

Israel and Jordan
CYLINDRICAL PROJECTION
® Copyright HAMMOND INCORPORATED, Maplewood, N.J.

SCALE OF MILES
0 5 10 15 20 25 30
SCALE OF KILOMETERS

Capitals of Countries .... ☆
Internal Capitals .... ◉
International Boundaries .... ———
Internal Boundaries .... ----

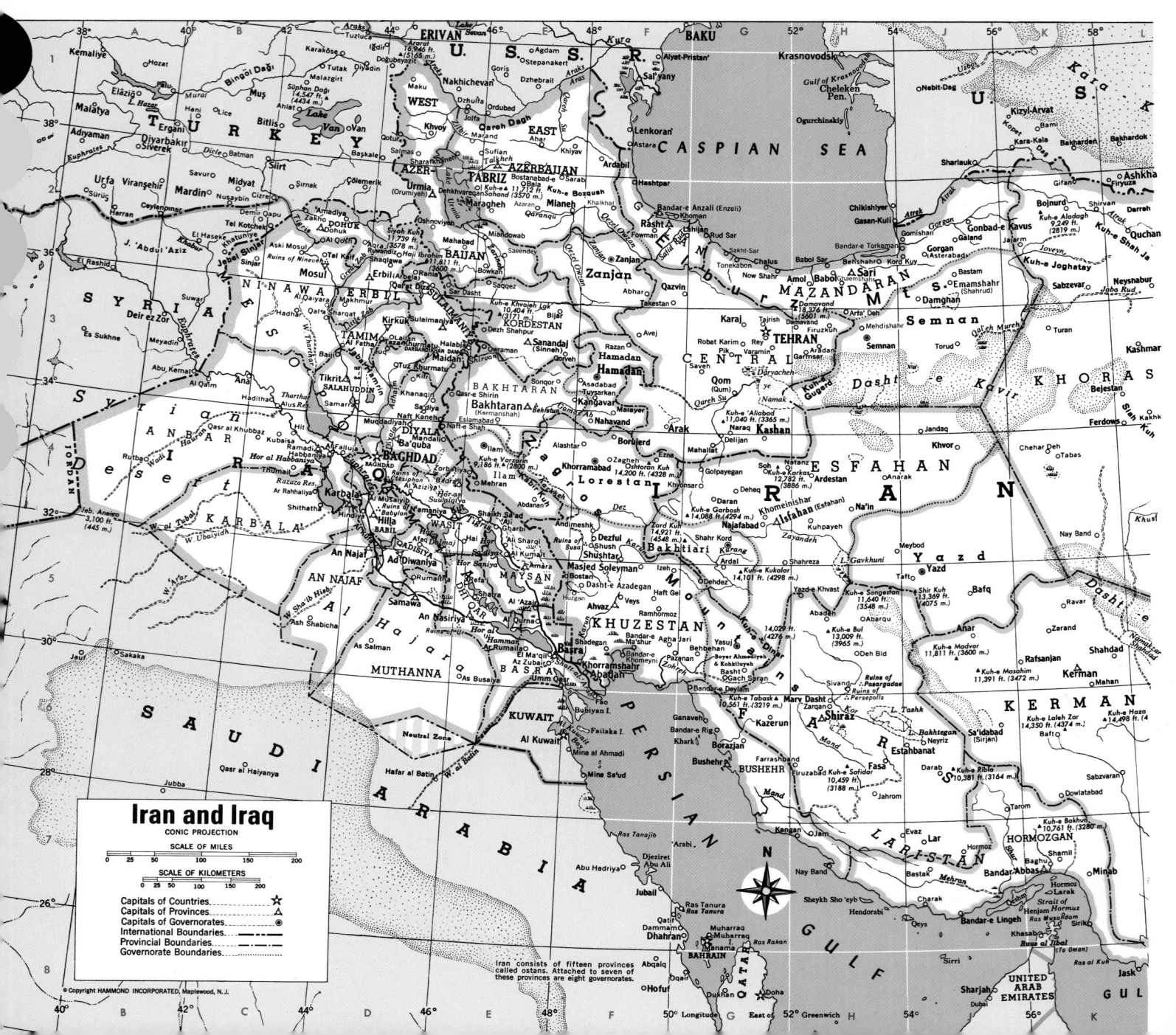

66 Iran and Iraq

IRAN

INTERNAL DIVISIONS

Azerbaijan, East (prov.) 3,194,543 .... E1
Azerbaijan, West (prov.) 1,404,875 .... D1
Bakhtaran (prov.) 1,016,199 .... E3
Bakhtari F4
Boyer Ahmediyeh and Kohkiluyeh (governorate) 244,750 .... G5
Bushehr (prov.) 345,427 .... G6
Central (Markazi) (prov.) 6,921,283 .... G3
Esfahan (Isfahan) (prov.) 1,974,938 .... H4
Fars (prov.) 2,020,947 .... H6
Hamadan (governorate) 1,086,512 .... F3
Hormozgan (prov.) 463,419 .... J7
Ilam (governorate) 244,222 .... E4
Isfahan (prov.) 1,974,938 .... H4
Kerman (prov.) 1,088,045 .... K6
Khorasan (prov.) 3,266,650 .... K3
Khuzestan (prov.) 2,176,612 .... F5
Kordestan (Kurdistan) (prov.) 781,889 .... E3
Lorestan (Luristan) (prov.) 924,848 .... F4
Mazandaran (prov.) 2,384,226 .... H2
Semnan (governorate) 485,875 .... J3
Sistan and Baluchestan (prov.) 659,297 .... M6
Yazd (governorate) 356,218 .... J5
Zanjan (governorate) 579,000 .... F2

CITIES and TOWNS

Abadan 296,081 .... F5
Abadeh 16,000 .... H5
Abarqu 8,000 .... H5
Abhar 6,000 .... F2
Agha Jari 24,195 .... F5
Ahar 24,000 .... E1
Ahvaz (Ahwaz) 329,006 .... F5
Amol 68,782 .... H2
Anarak 2,038 .... J4
Andimeshk 16,000 .... F4
Aradan 8,978 .... H3
Arak 114,507 .... G3
Ardabil 147,404 .... F1
Ardestan 5,868 .... H3
Asadabad 7,000 .... F3
Asterabad (Gorgan) 88,348 .... J2
Babol 67,790 .... H2
Babol Sar 7,237 .... H2
Baft 6,000 .... J7
Bakhtaran 290,861 .... E3
Bam 22,000 .... K6
Bandar-e Anzali (Enzeli) 55,978 .... F2
Bandar-e Deylam 3,691 .... G5
Bandar-e Khomeyni 6,000 .... F5
Bandar-e Lengeh 4,920 .... J7
Bandar-e Mas hur 17,000 .... F5
Bandar-e Rig 1,889 .... G5
Bandar-e Torkeman 13,000 .... H2
Bandar Shahpur 6,000 .... F5
Bastak 2,473 .... J7
Bastam 3,296 .... J2
Behbehan 39,874 .... G5
Behshahr 26,032 .... H2

Bejestan 3,823 .... K3
Bijar 12,000 .... E3
Bojnurd 31,248 .... K2
Borazjan 20,515 .... G6
Borujerd 100,103 .... F4
Bostan 4,619 .... F5
Bowkan 9,000 .... E2
Bushehr (Bushire) 57,681 .... G6
Chalus 15,000 .... G2
Damavand 5,319 .... H3
Damghan 13,000 .... J2
Darab 13,000 .... J6
Darreh 4,609 .... G4
Darreh Gaz 11,000 .... L2
Dasht-e Azadegan 21,000 .... F5
Dehkhvaregan 6,000 .... D2
Delijan 6,000 .... G3
Dezful 110,287 .... F4
Dizful (Dezful) 110,287 .... F4
Duzdab (Zahedan) 92,628 .... M6
Emamshahr 30,767 .... J2
Eslamabad 12,000 .... E3
Estahanat 18,187 .... J6
Evaz 6,064 .... J7
Ezna 5,000 .... F4
Fahrej (Iranshahr) 5,000 .... M7
Fariman 8,000 .... L3
Farrashband 3,532 .... G6
Fasa 19,000 .... H6
Ferdows 11,000 .... K3
Firuzabad 8,718 .... H6
Firuzkuh 4,000 .... H3
Fowman 9,000 .... F2
Gach Saran G5

Ganaveh 9,000 .... G6
Garmsar 4,723 .... H3
Gavater M8
Ghaemshahr 63,289 .... H2
Golpaygan 20,515 .... G4
Golshan (Tabas) 10,000 .... K4
Gomishan 6,000 .... J2
Gonabad 8,000 .... L3
Gonbad-e Kavus 59,868 .... J2
Gonbadli 531 .... M2
Gorgan (Gurgan) 88,348 .... J2
Haft Gel 10,000 .... F5
Hamadan 155,846 .... F3
Hashtpar 5,000 .... F2
Hormoz 2,569 .... J7
Huzgan 4,722 .... F5
Ilam 15,000 .... E4
Iranshahr 55,978 .... M7
Isfahan (Isfahan) 671,825 .... G4
Jahrom 38,236 .... H6
Jajarm 3,641 .... J2
Jask 1,078 .... K8
Kakhk 4,043 .... L3
Kangan 2,682 .... G6
Kangavar 9,414 .... F3
Karaj 138,774 .... G3
Kashan 84,545 .... G3
Kashmar 17,000 .... L3
Kazerun 51,309 .... G6
Kazvin (Qazvin) 138,527 .... F2
Kerman 140,309 .... K5
Khaf 5,000 .... L3
Khalkhal 5,422 .... F2
Khash 7,439 .... M6
Khiyav 9,000 .... E1
Khoman 3,054 .... F2
Khomeinishar 46,836 .... G4

Khorramabad 104,928 .... F4
Khorramshahr 146,709 .... F5
Khvaf 5,000 .... L3
Khvor 2,912 .... J4
Khvoy (Khoi) 70,040 .... D1
Kord Kuy 9,855 .... J2
Lahijan 25,725 .... G2
Lar 22,000 .... J7
Mahabad 28,610 .... D2
Mahallat 12,000 .... G4
Mahan 8,000 .... K5
Maku 7,000 .... D1
Malamir (Izeh) 1,983 .... F5
Malayer 28,434 .... F3
Marand 24,000 .... D1
Marv Dasht 25,498 .... H6
Mashhad (Meshed) 670,180 .... L2
Masjed Soleyman 77,161 .... F5
Medishahr 9,000 .... H3
Mehran 664 .... E4
Meshed 670,180 .... L2
Meshed-i-Sar (Babol Sar) 12,000 .... H2
Meybod 15,000 .... J4
Miandowab 19,000 .... D2
Mianeh 28,447 .... E2
Minab 4,287 .... K7
Mirjaveh 17,000 .... M6
Najafabad 76,236 .... H4
Nahavand 24,000 .... F3
Na'in 5,925 .... H4
Nasratabad (Zabol) 20,000 .... M5
Natanz 4,370 .... H4
Neyriz 16,114 .... J6
Neyshabur 59,101 .... L2

Nishapur (Neyshabur) 59,101 .... L2
Nosratabad 20,000 .... L6
Now Shahr 8,000 .... G2
Orumiyeh (Urmia) 163,991 .... D2
Oshnoviyeh 5,000 .... D2
Pahlevi (Enzeli) 55,978 .... F2
Pazanan 81 .... F5
Qayen 6,000 .... L3
Qazvin 138,527 .... F2
Qom 246,831 .... G4
Qorveh 2,929 .... E3
Qum (Qom) 246,831 .... G4
Rafsanjan 21,000 .... K5
Ramhormoz 9,000 .... F5
Rasht 187,203 .... F2
Ravar 5,074 .... K5
Reza'iyeh (Urmia) 163,991 .... D2
Rey 102,825 .... G3
Rigan 8,251 .... L6
Rud Sar 7,460 .... G2
Sabzevar 69,174 .... K2
Sabzvaran 7,000 .... K6
Saeendey 4,195 .... E2
Sai abad 20,000 .... J6
Sakht-Sar 12,000 .... G2
Salmas 13,161 .... D1
Sanandaj 95,834 .... E2
Sarakhs 3,461 .... M2
Sari 70,936 .... H2
Sarvan 4,012 .... N7
Semnan 31,058 .... H3

Shadegan 6,000 .... F5
Shahdad 2,777 .... K5
Shahistan (Saravan) 4,012 .... N7
Shahreza 34,220 .... H4
Shahr Kord 24,000 .... H4
Sharafkhaneh 1,260 .... D1
Shiraz 416,408 .... H6
Shush 1,433 .... F4
Shushtar 24,000 .... F5
Sinneh (Sanandaj) 95,834 .... E3
Sirjan (Sa'idabad) 20,000 .... J6
Sivand 1,811 .... H5
Songor 10,433 .... F3
Sufian 2,914 .... D1
Sultanabad (Kashmar) 17,000 .... L3
Tabas 10,000 .... K4
Tabriz 598,576 .... D2
Takestan 13,485 .... F2
Tehran (cap.) 4,496,159 .... G3
Tonekabon 12,000 .... G2
Torbat-e Heydariyeh 30,106 .... L3
Torbat-e Jam 13,000 .... M3
Tun (Ferdows) 11,000 .... K3
Turbat-i-Shaikh Jam 13,000 .... M3
Urmia 163,991 .... D2
Varamin 11,183 .... G3
Yazd (Yezd) 135,978 .... J5
Yezd J5
Zabol 20,000 .... M5
Zahedan 92,628 .... M6
Zanjan 99,967 .... F2
Zanjan (Zanjan) 99,967 .... F2
Zarand 5,000 .... K5
Zarqam 7,000 .... H6

Iran and Iraq

CONIC PROJECTION

SCALE OF MILES
0 25 50 100 150 200

SCALE OF KILOMETERS
0 25 50 100 150 200

Capitals of Countries ....☆
Capitals of Provinces ....△
Capitals of Governorates ....◉
International Boundaries ....
Provincial Boundaries ....
Governorate Boundaries ....

Iran consists of fifteen provinces called ostans. Attached to seven of these provinces are eight governorates.

© Copyright HAMMOND INCORPORATED, Maplewood, N.J.

OTHER FEATURES

Aji Chai (riv.) E1
A'rabi (isl.) G7
Araks (Aras) (riv.) E1
Atrak (Atrek) (riv.) J2
Bakhtegan (lake) J6
Baluchistan (reg.) M7
Bampur (riv.) M7
Behistun (ruins) E3
Caspian (sea) G1
Damavand (Demavend) (mt.) .. H3
Dez (riv.) F4
Elburz (mts.) G2
Farsi (isl.) J7
Gorgan (riv.) J2
Hari Rud (riv.) M3
Karkheh (riv.) E4
Karun (riv.) F5
Kashaf Rud (riv.) M2
Khark (Kharg) (isl.) G6
Kuh (cape) K8
Kurang (riv.) G4
Laristan (reg.) H7
Makran (reg.) M8
Mand Rud (riv.) G6
Mehran (riv.) J7
Namaksar (lake) M4
Nezwar (mt.) H3
Oman (gulf) M8
Pasargadae (ruins) H5
Persepolis (ruins) H6
Persian (gulf) H7
Qareh Su (riv.) E1
Qareh Su (riv.) G3
Qeshm (isl.) J7
Qezel Owzam (riv.) F2
Safid Rud (riv.) F2

Shaikh Shua'ib (isl.) H7
Shelagh (riv.) M5
Shirvan (riv.) E3
Shur (riv.) J7
Siah Kuh (mt.) L3
Silup (riv.) M8
Susa (ruins) F4
Talab (riv.) N6
Tashk (lake) J6
Urmia (lake) D2
Zagros (mts.) E4
Zarineh (riv.) E2
Zilbir (riv.) D1
Zohreh (riv.) F5

IRAQ
GOVERNORATES

Anbar B4
An Najaf C5
Babil D4
Baghdad D4
Basra E5
Dhi Qar E5
Diyala D4
Dohuk C2
Erbil C2
Karbala B4
Maysan E4
Muthanna D5
Ninawa B3
Qadisiya D4
Salahuddin C3
Sulaimaniya D3
Tamin D3
Wasit D4

CITIES and TOWNS

Ad Diwaniya 60,553 .... D5
A'faq 5,390 .... D4
Al A'ziziya 7,450 .... D4
Al Falluja 38,072 .... C4
Al Fathal 15,329 .... C3
Al Gharbi 15,456 .... E4
A'li Sharqi 8,398 .... E4
Al Kufa 30,862 .... D4
Al Musaylib 15,955 .... D4
Al Q'aim 3,372 .... B3
Al Qaiyara 3,060 .... C3
Al Qosh 3,863 .... C2
Al Qurna 5,638 .... E5
A'madiya 2,578 .... C2
A'mara 64,847 .... E5
A'na 15,276 .... B3
An Najaf 128,096 .... D5
An Nasiriya 60,405 .... D5
A'qra 8,659 .... D2
Arbela (Erbil) 90,320 .... D2
Aski Mosul 643 .... C2
As Salman 1,789 .... D5
Az Zubair 41,408 .... E5
Badra 3,564 .... D4
Baghdad (cap.) 502,503 ..... D4
Baghdad* 1,745,328 .... D4
Baiji 6,785 .... C3
Baq'uba 34,575 .... D4
Basra 313,327 .... E5
Dohuk 16,998 .... C2
Erbil 90,320 .... D2
Fao 19,000 .... F6
Habbaniya 14,405 .... C4
Haditha 6,870 .... C3
Hai 15,988 .... E4
Halabja 11,206 .... D3
Hilla 84,717 .... D4
Hindiya 16,436 .... C4
Hit 9,131 .... C4
Karbal'a 83,301 .... C4
Khanaqin 23,522 .... D3
Kifri 8,500 .... D3
Kirkuk 167,413 .... D3
Kirkuk* 176,794 .... D3
Kubaisa 4,023 .... C4
Kut 42,116 .... D4
Makhmur 2,556 .... C3
Mandali 11,262 .... D4
Mosul 315,157 .... C2
Muqdadiyah 12,181 .... D4
Naft Kaneh D3
Na'maniya 11,943 .... D4
Qal'at Diza 6,250 .... D2
Ramadi 28,723 .... C4
Rania 4,090 .... D2
Refai' 7,681 .... E5
Rumaitha 10,222 .... D5
Rutba 5,091 .... B4
Ruwandiz 5,801 .... D2
Sad'iya 5,285 .... D3
Samarra 24,746 .... D3
Samawa 33,473 .... D5
Shaikh Saa'd 2,958 .... E4
Shaqlawa 6,814 .... D2
Shatra 18,822 .... E5
Sinjar 7,942 .... B2
Sulaimaniya 86,822 .... D3
Tal Kaif 7,482 .... C2
Taza Khurmatu 2,681 ...... D3
Tikrit 9,921 .... D3
Tuz Khurmatu 13,860 ...... D3
Zakho 14,790 .... C2

OTHER FEATURES

Adhaim (riv.) D3
Anjeza, Jebel (mt.) A4
A'rab, Shatt al- (riv.) F5
A'ra'r, Wadi (dry riv.) B5
Babylon (ruins) D4
Batin, Wadi al (dry riv.) E6
Ctesiphon (ruins) D3
Darbandikhan (dam) D3
Euphrates (riv.) D4
Great Zab (riv.) C2
Hauran, Wadi (dry riv.) B4
Little Zab (riv.) C3
Mesopotamia (reg.) B3
Nineveh (ruins) C2
Sad'iya, Hor (lake) E4
Saniya, Hor (lake) E5
Shai'b Hisb, Wadi (dry riv.) .. C5
Sinjar, Jebel (mts.) B2
Siyah Kuh (mt.) D2
Syrian (des.) B4
Tigris (riv.) E4
Ubaiyidh, Wadi (dry riv.) ... B5
Ur (ruins) E5

*City and suburbs.
†Population of commune.

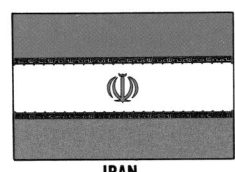

IRAN

IRAQ

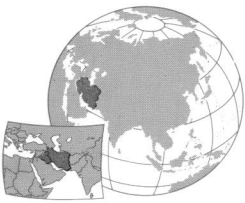

AREA 636,293 sq. mi. (1,648,000 sq. km.)
POPULATION 37,447,000
CAPITAL Tehran
LARGEST CITY Tehran
HIGHEST POINT Damavand 18,376 ft. (5,601 m.)
MONETARY UNIT Iranian rial
MAJOR LANGUAGES Persian, Azerbaijani, Kurdish
MAJOR RELIGION Islam

AREA 172,476 sq. mi. (446,713 sq. km.)
POPULATION 12,767,000
CAPITAL Baghdad
LARGEST CITY Baghdad
HIGHEST POINT Haji Ibrahim 11,811 ft. (3,600 m.)
MONETARY UNIT Iraqi dinar
MAJOR LANGUAGES Arabic, Kurdish
MAJOR RELIGION Islam

Topography

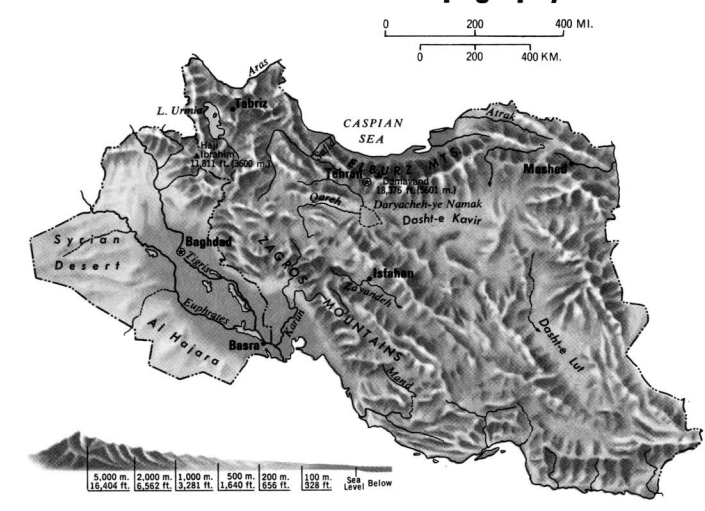

Agriculture, Industry and Resources

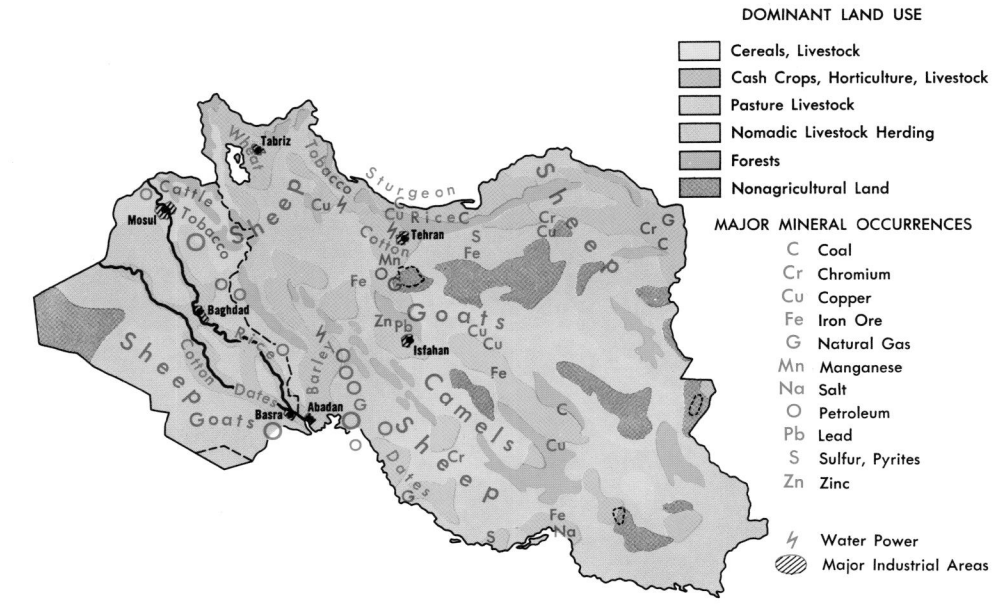

DOMINANT LAND USE

Cereals, Livestock
Cash Crops, Horticulture, Livestock
Pasture Livestock
Nomadic Livestock Herding
Forests
Nonagricultural Land

MAJOR MINERAL OCCURRENCES

C Coal
Cr Chromium
Cu Copper
Fe Iron Ore
G Natural Gas
Mn Manganese
Na Salt
O Petroleum
Pb Lead
S Sulfur, Pyrites
Zn Zinc

⚡ Water Power
◎ Major Industrial Areas

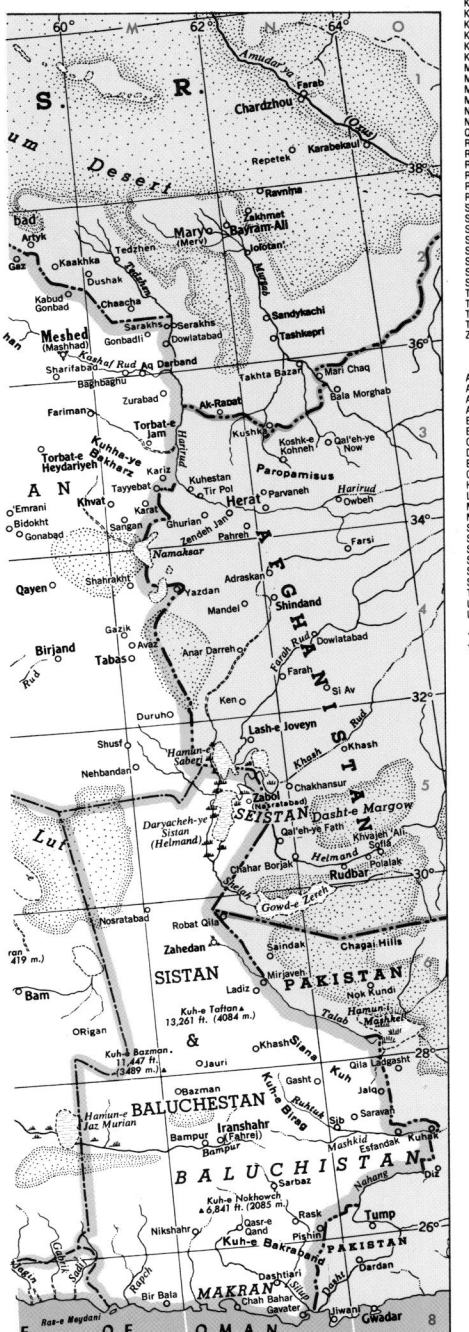

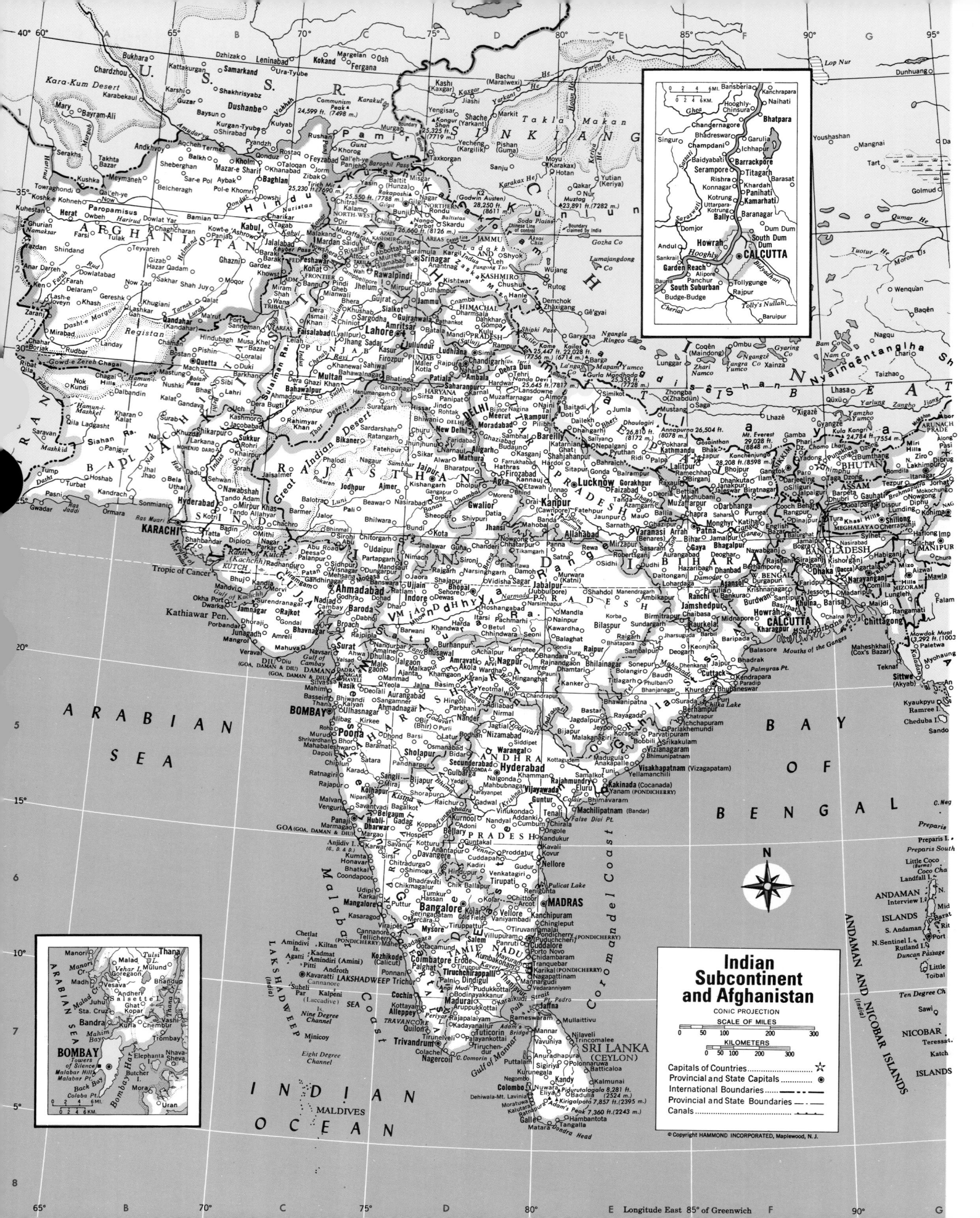

Indian Subcontinent and Afghanistan

CONIC PROJECTION

SCALE OF MILES
0   50   100   200   300

KILOMETERS
0 50 100   200   300

Capitals of Countries .... ☆
Provincial and State Capitals .... ◉
International Boundaries .... —·—
Provincial and State Boundaries .... —··—
Canals .... —·—·—

© Copyright HAMMOND INCORPORATED, Maplewood, N.J.

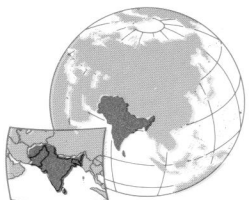

INDIA

AREA 1,269,339 sq. mi. (3,287,588 sq. km.)
POPULATION 683,810,051
CAPITAL New Delhi
LARGEST CITY Calcutta (greater)
HIGHEST POINT Nanda Devi 25,645 ft. (7,817 m.)
MONETARY UNIT Indian rupee
MAJOR LANGUAGES Hindi, English, Bihari, Telugu, Marathi, Bengali, Tamil, Gujarati, Rajasthani, Kanarese, Malayalam, Oriya, Punjabi, Assamese, Kashmiri, Urdu
MAJOR RELIGIONS Hinduism, Islam, Christianity, Sikhism, Buddhism, Jainism, Zoroastrianism, Animism

PAKISTAN

AREA 310,403 sq. mi. (803,944 sq. km.)
POPULATION 83,782,000
CAPITAL Islamabad
LARGEST CITY Karachi
HIGHEST POINT K2 (Godwin Austen) 28,250 ft. (8,611 m.)
MONETARY UNIT Pakistani rupee
MAJOR LANGUAGES Urdu, English, Punjabi, Pushtu, Sindhi, Baluchi, Brahui
MAJOR RELIGIONS Islam, Hinduism, Sikhism, Christianity, Buddhism

SRI LANKA (CEYLON)

AREA 25,332 sq. mi. (65,610 sq. km.)
POPULATION 14,850,001
CAPITAL Colombo
LARGEST CITY Colombo
HIGHEST POINT Pidurutalagala 8,281 ft. (2,524 m.)
MONETARY UNIT Sri Lanka rupee
MAJOR LANGUAGES Sinhala, Tamil, English
MAJOR RELIGIONS Buddhism, Hinduism, Christianity, Islam

AFGHANISTAN

AREA 250,775 sq. mi. (649,507 sq. km.)
POPULATION 15,540,000
CAPITAL Kabul
LARGEST CITY Kabul
HIGHEST POINT Nowshak 24,557 ft. (7,485 m.)
MONETARY UNIT afghani
MAJOR LANGUAGES Pushtu, Dari, Uzbek
MAJOR RELIGION Islam

NEPAL

AREA 54,663 sq. mi. (141,577 sq. km.)
POPULATION 14,179,301
CAPITAL Kathmandu
LARGEST CITY Kathmandu
HIGHEST POINT Mt. Everest 29,028 ft. (8,848 m.)
MONETARY UNIT Nepalese rupee
MAJOR LANGUAGES Nepali, Maithili, Tamang, Newari, Tharu
MAJOR RELIGIONS Hinduism, Buddhism

MALDIVES

AREA 115 sq. mi. (298 sq. km.)
POPULATION 143,046
CAPITAL Male
LARGEST CITY Male
HIGHEST POINT 20 ft. (6 m.)
MONETARY UNIT Maldivian rupee
MAJOR LANGUAGE Divehi
MAJOR RELIGION Islam

BHUTAN

AREA 18,147 sq. mi. (47,000 sq. km.)
POPULATION 1,298,000
CAPITAL Thimphu
LARGEST CITY Thimphu
HIGHEST POINT Kula Kangri 24,784 ft. (7,554 m.)
MONETARY UNIT ngultrum
MAJOR LANGUAGES Dzongka, Nepali
MAJOR RELIGIONS Buddhism, Hinduism

BANGLADESH

AREA 55,126 sq. mi. (142,776 sq. km.)
POPULATION 87,052,024
CAPITAL Dhaka
LARGEST CITY Dhaka
HIGHEST POINT Keokradong 4,034 ft. (1,230 m.)
MONETARY UNIT taka
MAJOR LANGUAGES Bengali, English
MAJOR RELIGIONS Islam, Hinduism Christianity

INDIA   **PAKISTAN**   **SRI LANKA (CEYLON)**   **BHUTAN**

AFGHANISTAN   **MALDIVES**   **BANGLADESH**   **NEPAL**

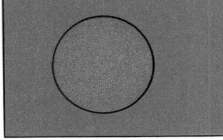

AFGHANISTAN

CITIES and TOWNS

Andkhvoy	A1
Aqcheh	B1
Aybak 33,016	B1
Baghlan 75,130	B1
Balkh	B1
Bamian 7,355	B2
Belcheragh	B1
Chaghcharan 2,974	B2
Chahar Borjak	A2
Charikar 25,093	B1
Delaram	A2
Dowlatabad	A1
Dowlat Yar	B2
Dowshi	B1
Farah 18,797	A2
Farsi	A2
Feyzabad 10,142	C1
Gardez 11,415	B2
Gereshk	A2
Ghazni 30,425	B2
Ghurian	A2
Gizab	B2
Hazar Qadam	B2
Herat 163,960	A2
Jalalabad 56,384	C2
Jorm	C1
Kabul (cap.) 905,108	B2
Kalat (Qalat) 5,946	B2
Kandahar (Qandahar) 178,409	A2
Ken	B1
Khanabad	B1
Khash	A2
Kholm	B1
Khowst	B2
Khugiani	A2
Koshke-e Kohneh	A2
Kowt-e 'Ashrow	B2
Kuhestan	A2
Landay	A2
Lash-e Joveyn	A2
Lashkar Gah 26,646	A2
Mar'uf	B2
Mazar-e Sharif 122,567	B1
Meymaneh 54,954	A1
Mirabad	A2
Moqor	B2
Now Zad	A2
Oruzgan (Hazar Qadam)	B2
Owbeh	A2
Panjab	B2
Pol-e Khomri	B1
Qalat 5,946	B2
Qale'h-ye Now 5,340	A1
Qale'h-ye Panjeh	C1
Qandahar 178,409	B2
Qonduz 107,191	B1
Rostaq	B1
Rudbar	A2
Sakhar	B1
Sar-e Pol	B1
Shay Juy	B2
Sheberghan 54,870	B1
Shindand	A2
Spin Buldak	B2
Tagab	B2
Taloqan 46,202	B1
Teyvareh	A2
Towraghondi	A1
Tulak	A2
Zaranj 6,477	A2
Zibak	C1

OTHER FEATURES

Farah Rud (riv.)	A2

Harirud (riv.)	A1
Helmand (riv.)	B2
Hindu Kush (mts.)	B1
Kabul (riv.)	C2
Konar (riv.)	C1
Lurah (riv.)	B2
Margow, Dasht-e (des.)	A2
Namaksar (salt lake)	A2
Paropamisus (range)	A2
Tarnak (riv.)	B2

BANGLADESH

CITIES and TOWNS

Barisal 98,127	G4
Bogra 47,154	F3
Chalna Port 14,590	F4
Chittagong 889,760	G4
Comilla 86,446	G4
Cox's Bazar (Maheshkhali) 15,720	G4
Dhaka (Dacca) (cap.) 1,679,572	G4
Dinajpur 61,866	F3
Faridpur 46,232	F4
Habiganj 16,281	G4
Jamalpur 60,261	F4
Jessore 76,168	F4
Khulna 437,304	F4
Kishorganj 35,605	G4
Madaripur 32,488	G4
Maheshkhali 15,720	G4
Mymensingh (Nasirabad) 182,153	G4
Narayanganj 270,680	G4
Nasirabad 182,153	G4
Nawabganj 46,059	F4
Noakhali 32,490	G4
Pabna 62,254	F4
Rajshahi 132,909	F4
Rangamati 20,473	G4
Rangpur 72,829	F3
Saidpur 74,457	F4
Sylhet 59,546	G4
Teknaf	G4

OTHER FEATURES

Bengal, Bay of (sea)	F5
Brahmaputra (riv.)	G3
Ganges (riv.)	F3
Sundarbans (reg.)	F4

BHUTAN

CITIES and TOWNS

Bumthang 10,000	G3
Paro 35,000	F3
Punakha 12,000	G3
Taga Dzong 18,000	G3
Thimphu (cap.) 50,000	G3
Tongsa Dzong 2,500	G3

OTHER FEATURES

Chomo Lhari (mt.)	F3
Himalaya (mts.)	E2
Kula Kangri (mt.)	G3

INDIA

INTERNAL DIVISIONS

Andaman and Nicobar Isls. (terr.) 188,254	G6
Andhra Pradesh (state) 53,403,619	D5
Arunachal Pradesh (terr.) 628,050	G3

(continued on following page)

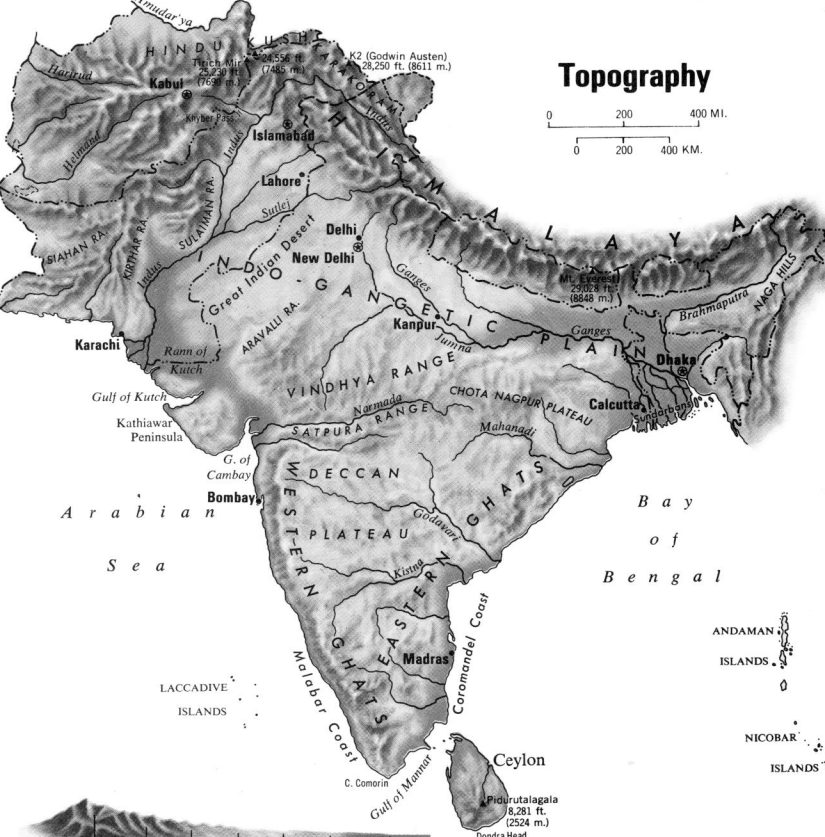

Topography

0   200   400 MI.
0   200   400 KM.

| 5,000 m. 16,404 ft. | 2,000 m. 6,562 ft. | 1,000 m. 3,281 ft. | 500 m. 1,640 ft. | 200 m. 656 ft. | 100 m. 328 ft. | Sea Level | Below |

70 Indian Subcontinent and Afghanistan

(continued)

Assam (state) 19.902.826 ..... G3
Bihar (state) 69.823.154 ..... F4
Chandigarh (terr.) 450.061 ..... D2
Dadra and Nagar Haveli
(terr.) 103.677 ..... C4
Delhi (terr.) 6.196.414 ..... D3
Goa, Daman and Diu
(terr.) 1.082.117 ..... C4
Gujarat (state) 33.960.905 ..... C4
Haryana (state) 12.850.902 ..... D3
Himachal Pradesh
(state) 4.237.569 ..... D2
Jammu and Kashmir
(state) 5.981.600 ..... D2
Karnataka (state) 37.043.451 ..... D6
Kerala (state) 25.403.217 ..... D6
Lakshadweep (terr.) 40.237 ..... C6
Madhya Pradesh
(state) 52.131.717 ..... D4
Maharashtra (state) 62.693.898 ..... C5
Manipur (state) 1.433.691 ..... G4
Meghalaya (state) 1.327.874 ..... G3
Mizoram (terr.) 487.774 ..... G4
Nagaland (state) 773.281 ..... G3
Orissa (state) 26.272.054 ..... E5
Pondicherry (terr.) 604.136 ..... E6
Punjab (state) 16.669.755 ..... D2
Rajasthan (state) 34.102.912 ..... C3
Sikkim (state) 315.682 ..... F3
Tamil Nadu (state) 48.297.456 ..... D6
Tripura (state) 2.060.189 ..... G4
Uttar Pradesh
(state) 110.858.019 ..... D3
West Bengal (state) 54.485.560 ..... F4

CITIES and TOWNS

Abu 9.840 ..... C4
Abu Road 25.331 ..... C4
Achalpur 42.326 ..... D4
Addanki 10.223 ..... D5
Adilabad 30.368 ..... D5
Adoni 85.311 ..... D5
Agartala 59.625 ..... G4
Agartala□ 100.264 ..... G4
Agra 591.917 ..... D3
Agra□ 634.622 ..... D3
Ahmadabad 1.591.832 ..... C4
Ahmadabad□ 1.741.522 ..... C4
Ahmadnagar 118.236 ..... C5
Ahmadnagar□ 148.405 ..... C5
Aizwal 31.740 ..... G4
Ajanta D4
Ajmer 262.851 ..... C3
Akola 168.438 ..... D4
Alibag 11.913 ..... C5
Aligarh 252.314 ..... D3
Alipore F2
Allahabad 490.622 ..... E3
Allahabad□ 513.036 ..... E3
Alleppey-Cochin 160.166 ..... D7
Almora 19.671 ..... D3
Along 3.524 ..... G3
Alwar 100.378 ..... D3
Amalner 55.544 ..... C4
Ambala 83.633 ..... D2
Ambala□ 186.168 ..... D2
Ambikapur 23.087 ..... E4
Amravati 193.800 ..... D4
Amreli 39.520 ..... C4
Amritsar 407.628 ..... C2
Amritsar□ 458.029 ..... C2
Anakapalle 57.273 ..... E5
Anantapur 80.069 ..... D6
Anantnag 27.643 ..... D2
Andheri B7
Andul 3.602 ..... F2
Arcot 30.230 ..... D6
Arrah 92.919 ..... E3
Aruppukkottai 62.223 ..... D7
Arvi 26.494 ..... D4
Asansol 155.968 ..... F4
Asansol□ 241.792 ..... F4
Aurangabad, Bihar 18.714 ..... E4
Aurangabad,
Maharashtra 150.483 ..... D5
Aurangabad□ 165.253 ..... D5
Azamgarh 40.963 ..... E3
Badagara 53.938 ..... D6
Bagalkot 51.746 ..... D5
Bahraich 73.931 ..... E3
Baidyabati 54.130 ..... F1
Balaghat 27.872 ..... E4
Balasore 46.239 ..... F4
Ballia 47.101 ..... E3
Bally 38.892 ..... F1
Balotra 17.595 ..... C3
Balrampur 36.191 ..... E3
Balurghat 67.088 ..... F3
Banda 50.575 ..... D3
Bandar (Machilipatnam) 112.612 ..... E5
Bandra B7
Bangalore 1.540.741 ..... D6
Bangalore□ 1.653.779 ..... D6
Bankura 79.129 ..... F4
Bansberia 61.748 ..... F1
Banswara 27.363 ..... C4
Baramati 27.912 ..... C5
Baramula 26.334 ..... C2
Baranagar 136.842 ..... F1
Barasat 42.642 ..... F1
Barbil 24.342 ..... F4
Bareilly 296.248 ..... D3
Bareilly□ 326.106 ..... D3
Baripada 28.725 ..... F4
Barmer 38.630 ..... C3
Baroda (Vadodara) 466.696 ..... C4
Barpeta 26.479 ..... G3
Barrackpore 96.889 ..... F1
Barrackpore□ 198.255 ..... F1
Barsi 62.374 ..... D5
Baruipur 20.501 ..... F2
Barwani 22.099 ..... D4
Basim 32.496 ..... D4
Basirhat 63.816 ..... F4
Bassein 30.594 ..... C5
Bastar E5
Batala 58.200 ..... D2
Baudh 8.891 ..... E4
Bauria 10.610 ..... E2
Beawar 66.114 ..... C3
Belgaum 192.427 ..... C5
Belgaum□ 213.872 ..... C5
Bellary 125.183 ..... D5
Benares (Varanasi) 583.856 ..... E3
Berhampore 72.605 ..... F4
Berhampur 117.662 ..... F5
Bettiah 51.018 ..... E3
Betul 30.862 ..... D4
Bhadrak 40.487 ..... F4
Bhadravati 40.203 ..... D6
Bhadravati□ 101.358 ..... D6
Bhadreswar 45.586 ..... F1
Bhagalpur 172.202 ..... F4
Bhandara 39.423 ..... E4
Bhandup B7
Bhanjanagar 12.353 ..... E4
Bharatpur 68.036 ..... D3
Bharuch 91.589 ..... C4
Bhatapara 20.980 ..... E4
Bhatinda 53.684 ..... C2
Bhatkal 18.732 ..... C6
Bhatpara 204.750 ..... F1
Bhavnagar 225.358 ..... C4
Bhavnagar□ 225.974 ..... C4
Bhawanipatna 22.808 ..... E5
Bhilai 157.173 ..... E4
Bhilwara 82.155 ..... C3
Bhimavaram 63.762 ..... E5
Bhimunipatnam 14.291 ..... E5
Bhind 42.371 ..... D3
Bhinmal 14.050 ..... C3
Bhir (Bir) 49.965 ..... D5
Bhiwandi 79.576 ..... C5
Bhiwani 73.086 ..... D3
Bhopal 298.022 ..... D4
Bhor 10.708 ..... C5
Bhubaneswar 105.491 ..... F4
Bhuj 52.177 ..... B4
Bhusawal 96.800 ..... D4
Bhusawal□ 104.708 ..... D4
Bidar 50.670 ..... D5
Bihar 100.046 ..... F3
Bijapur, Karnataka 103.931 ..... D5
Bijapur, Madhya Pradesh 5.289 ..... E5
Bijnor 43.290 ..... D3
Bikaner 188.518 ..... C3
Bikaner□ 208.894 ..... C3
Bilaspur 98.410 ..... E4
Bina-Itawa 33.106 ..... D4
Bir 49.965 ..... D5
Birmitrapur 28.063 ..... E4
Bobbili 30.649 ..... E5
Bodhan 37.589 ..... D5
Bodinayakkanur 54.176 ..... D6
Bolangir 35.748 ..... E4
Bombay (Greater)* 5.970.575 ..... B7
Bomdila 2.264 ..... G3
Broach (Bharuch) 91,589 ..... C4
Budaun 72.204 ..... D3
Budge-Budge 51.039 ..... F2
Bundi 34.279 ..... D3
Burdwan 143.318 ..... F4
Burhanpur 105.246 ..... D4
Calcutta 3.148.746 ..... F2
Calcutta□ 7.031.382 ..... F2
Calicut (Kozhikode) 333.979 ..... D6
Cambay 62.097 ..... C4
Cannanore 55.162 ..... C6
Cawnpore (Kanpur) 1.154.388 ..... E3
Chaibasa 35.386 ..... F4
Chamba 11.814 ..... D2
Champdani 58.596 ..... F1
Chanderi 10.294 ..... D4
Chandernagore 75.238 ..... F1
Chandigarh 218.743 ..... D2
Chandigarh□ 232.940 ..... D2
Chandrapur 75.134 ..... D5
Chapra 83.101 ..... F3
Chatrapur 10.835 ..... F5
Chembur B7
Cherrapunji⊙ 83.987 ..... G3
Chhatarpur 32.271 ..... D4
Chhindwara 53.492 ..... D4
Chidambaram 48.811 ..... E6
Chik Ballapur 29.227 ..... D6
Chikmagalur 41.639 ..... D6
Chingleput 38.419 ..... E6
Chiplun 20.942 ..... C5
Chirala 54.487 ..... E5
Chitorgarh 25.917 ..... C4
Chitradurga 50.254 ..... D6
Chittoor 63.035 ..... D6
Churachandpur 8.706 ..... G4
Churu 52.502 ..... D3
Chushul D2
Cocanada (Kakinada) 164.200 ..... E5
Cochin-Alleppey 439.066 ..... D6
Coimbatore 356.368 ..... D6
Coimbatore□ 736.203 ..... D6
Colachel 18.819 ..... D7
Cooch Behar 53.684 ..... F3
Coondapoor 23.831 ..... C6
Cuddalore 101.335 ..... E6
Cuddapah 66.195 ..... D6
Cumbum 9.745 ..... D5
Cuttack 194.068 ..... F4
Cuttack□ 205.759 ..... F4
Dabhoi 37.892 ..... C4
Daltonganj 32.367 ..... E4
Damoh 59.489 ..... D4
Dapoli 6.296 ..... C5
Darbhanga 132.059 ..... F3
Darjeeling 42.873 ..... F3
Datia 36.439 ..... D3
Davangere 121.110 ..... D6
Deesa 28.324 ..... C4
Dehra Dun 166.073 ..... D2
Dehra Dun□ 203.464 ..... D2
Delhi 3.287.883 ..... D3
Delhi□ 3.647.023 ..... D3
Demchok D2
Deogarh, Orissa 8.906 ..... E4
Deoghar, Bihar 40.356 ..... F4
Deolali 55.436 ..... C5
Deoria 38.161 ..... E3
Dewas 51.545 ..... D4
Dhamtari 34.546 ..... E4
Dhanbad 79.838 ..... F4
Dhanbad□ 434.031 ..... F4
Dhar 36.172 ..... C4
Dharmsala 10.939 ..... D2
Dharwar-Hubli 379.166 ..... C5
Dhenkanal 19.615 ..... E4
Dholpur 31.865 ..... D3
Dhond 16.583 ..... C5
Dhoraji 59.773 ..... C4
Dhubri 36.503 ..... G3
Dhulia 137.129 ..... C4
Dibrugarh 80.348 ..... G3
Digboi 16.538 ..... H3
Dindigul 128.429 ..... D6
Diphu 10.200 ..... G3
Dispur 1.725 ..... G3
Diu 6.214 ..... C4
Dohad 44.506 ..... C4
Domjor 10.896 ..... F1
Dudhi 5.084 ..... E4
Dum Dum 31.363 ..... F1
Dum Dum□ 273.812 ..... F1
Dungarpur 19.773 ..... C4
Durg 67.892 ..... E4
Durgapur 206.638 ..... F4
Dwarka 17.801 ..... B4
Eluru 127.023 ..... E5
English Bazar 61.335 ..... F3
Erode 105.111 ..... D6
Etawah 85.894 ..... D3
Faizabad-cum-Ayodhya 102.835 ..... E3
Faridabad 85.762 ..... D3
Farrukhabad-cum-Fatehgarh 102.768 ..... D3
Farrukhabad-cum-Fatehgarh□ 110.835 D3
Fatehpur, Rajasthan 34.929 ..... C3
Fatehpur, Uttar Pradesh 54.665 ..... E3
Firozabad 133.863 ..... D3
Firozpur 49.545 ..... C2
Gadag-Betgeri 95.426 ..... D5
Gadwal 21.828 ..... D5
Gandhinagar 24.055 ..... C4
Ganganagar 90.042 ..... C3
Gangapur 27.453 ..... D3
Gangtok 12.000 ..... F3
Garden Reach 154.913 ..... F2
Garulia 44.271 ..... F1
Gauhati 123.783 ..... G3
Gauhati□ 200.377 ..... G3
Gaya 179.884 ..... F4
Ghat Kopar 34.256 ..... B7
Ghaziabad 118.836 ..... D3
Ghaziabad□ 127.700 ..... D3
Ghazipur 45.635 ..... E3
Goalpara 16.703 ..... G3
Godhra 66.403 ..... C4
Gonda 52.662 ..... E3
Gondal 54.928 ..... C4
Gondia 77.992 ..... E4
Gorakhpur 230.911 ..... E3
Goregaon B7
Gudur 33.778 ..... D6
Gulbarga 145.588 ..... D5
Guna 40.006 ..... D4
Guntakal 66.320 ..... D5
Guntur 269.991 ..... D5
Gurais D2
Gwalior 384.772 ..... D3
Gwalior□ 406.140 ..... D3
Haflong 5.197 ..... G3
Hanle D2
Hanumangarh 30.017 ..... C3
Harda 28.504 ..... D4
Hardoi 46.639 ..... E3
Hardwar 77.864 ..... D2
Hassan 51.325 ..... D6
Hathras 74.349 ..... D3
Hazaribagh 54.818 ..... F4
Hindupur 42.959 ..... D6
Hinganghat 44.349 ..... D4
Hingoli 31.948 ..... D5
Hissar 89.437 ..... D3
Honavar 12.444 ..... C6
Hooghly-Chinsura 105.241 ..... F1
Hoshangabad 27.011 ..... D4
Hospet 65.196 ..... D5
Howrah 737.877 ..... F2
Hubli-Dharwar 379.166 ..... C5
Hyderabad 1.607.396 ..... D5
Hyderabad□ 1.796.339 ..... D5
Ichchapuram 15.850 ..... F5
Ichhapur 11.975 ..... F1
Imphal 100.366 ..... G4
Indore 543.381 ..... D4
Indore□ 560.936 ..... D4
Itanagar⊙ 18.787 ..... G3
Itarsi 44.191 ..... D4
Jabalpur 426.224 ..... D4
Jabalpur□ 534.845 ..... D4
Jagdalpur 31.344 ..... E5
Jagtial 30.900 ..... D5
Jaipur 615.258 ..... D3
Jaipur□ 636.768 ..... D3
Jaisalmer 16.578 ..... C3
Jajpur 16.707 ..... F4
Jalgaon 106.711 ..... D4
Jalna 91.099 ..... D4
Jalor 15.478 ..... C3
Jalpaiguri 55.159 ..... F3
Jamalpur 61.731 ..... F3
Jammu 155.338 ..... D2
Jammu□ 164.207 ..... D2
Jamnagar 214.816 ..... B4
Jamnagar□ 227.640 ..... B4
Jamshedpur 341.576 ..... F4
Jamshedpur□ 456.146 ..... F4
Jaora 37.235 ..... D4
Jaunpur 80.737 ..... E3
Jeypore 34.319 ..... E5
Jhalawar 20.035 ..... D4
Jhansi 173.292 ..... D3
Jhansi□ 198.135 ..... D3
Jharsuguda 24.727 ..... E4
Jhunjhunu 32.024 ..... D3
Jind 38.161 ..... D3
Jodhpur 317.612 ..... C3
Jorhat 30.247 ..... G3
Jubbulpore (Jabalpur) 426.224 ..... D4
Juhu B7
Jullundur 296.106 ..... D2
Jullundur□ 329.830 ..... D2
Junagadh 95.485 ..... B4
Kadayanallur 50.295 ..... D7
Kadiri 33.810 ..... D6
Kakinada 164.200 ..... E5
Kalyan 99.547 ..... C5
Kamarhati 169.404 ..... F1
Kamptee 53.412 ..... D4
Kanchipuram 110.657 ..... E6
Kanchrapara 78.768 ..... F1
Kandla 17.995 ..... C4
Kandukur 16.654 ..... E5
Kanker 9.278 ..... E4
Kannauj 28.187 ..... D3
Kanpur 1.154.388 ..... E3
Kanpur□ 1.275.242 ..... E3
Karad 42.329 ..... C5
Karaikudi 55.449 ..... D7
Karanja 31.150 ..... D4
Kargil 2.390 ..... D2
Karikal 26.080 ..... E6
Karkal 18.593 ..... C6
Karnal 92.784 ..... D3
Karwar 27.770 ..... C6
Kasaragod 34.984 ..... C6
Kasganj 46.467 ..... D3
Katarnian Ghat E3
Katihar 67.014 ..... F3
Katni (Murwara) 54.864 ..... E4
Kavali 29.616 ..... E6
Kavaratti 4.420 ..... C6
Kawardha 11.226 ..... E4
Kendrapara 20.079 ..... F4
Keonjhar 19.340 ..... F4
Khamgaon 53.692 ..... D4
Khamman 56.919 ..... D5
Khandwa 84.517 ..... D4
Kharagpur 61.783 ..... F4
Khardah 32.302 ..... F1
Khurda 15.879 ..... F4
Kirkee 65.497 ..... C5
Kishangarh 37.405 ..... D3
Kishtwar 5.276 ..... D2
Kohima 21.545 ..... G3
Kolar 43.418 ..... D6
Kolar Gold Fields 76.112 ..... D6
Kolhapur 259.050 ..... C5
Konnagar 34.424 ..... F1
Koppal 27.277 ..... D5
Koraput 21.505 ..... E5
Korba 30.963 ..... E4
Kota 212.991 ..... D3
Kottaguden 75.542 ..... E5
Kottayam 59.714 ..... D7
Kotturu 12.873 ..... D6
Kovur 16.846 ..... E6
Kozhikode 333.979 ..... D6
Krishnanagar 85.923 ..... F4
Kulu 8.958 ..... D2
Kumbakonam 113.130 ..... D6
Kumta 19.112 ..... C6
Kurla B7
Kurnool 136.710 ..... D5
Laful⊙ 8.161 ..... G7
Lansdowne 6.670 ..... D3
Latur 70.156 ..... D5
Leh 5.519 ..... D2
Lohardaga 17.087 ..... E4
Lucknow 749.239 ..... E3
Lucknow□ 813.982 ..... E3
Ludhiana 397.850 ..... D2
Ludhiana□ 401.176 ..... D2
Lumding 29.253 ..... G3
Lungleh 6.019 ..... G4
Machilipatnam 112.612 ..... E5
Madh B7
Madhubani 32.919 ..... F3
Madras 2.469.449 ..... E6
Madras□ 3.169.930 ..... E6
Madugula 8.376 ..... E5
Madurai 549.114 ..... D7
Madurai□ 711.501 ..... D7
Mahabaleshwar 7.318 ..... C5
Mahbubnagar 51.756 ..... D5
Mahe 8.972 ..... D6
Mahim 11.344 ..... C5
Mahoba 29.707 ..... D3
Mahuva 39.497 ..... C4
Malad B6
Malakanagiri 7.494 ..... E5
Malegaon 191.847 ..... C4
Maler Kotla 48.536 ..... D2
Malkapur 35.476 ..... D4
Malvan 17.579 ..... C5
Mandi 16.849 ..... D2
Mandla 24.406 ..... E4
Mandsaur 52.347 ..... C4
Mandvi 27.849 ..... B4
Manendragarh 11.936 ..... E4
Mangalore 165.174 ..... C6
Mangrol 27.183 ..... B4
Manmad 29.571 ..... C4
Mannargudi 42.783 ..... E6
Manori B6
Margao 41.655 ..... C5
Marmagao 44.065 ..... C5
Mathura 132.028 ..... D3
Mau 64.058 ..... E3
Mayuram 60.195 ..... D6
Meerut 270.993 ..... D3
Mehsana 51.598 ..... C4
Mercara 19.357 ..... D6
Mhow 59.037 ..... D4
Midnapore 71.326 ..... F4
Miraj 77.606 ..... D5
Mirzapur-cum-Vindhyachal 105.939 ..... E4
Modasa 22.483 ..... C4
Mokokchung 17.423 ..... G3
Monghyr 102.474 ..... F3
Mora B7
Moradabad 258.590 ..... D3
Morena 44.901 ..... D3
Morvi 60.976 ..... C4
Mulund B6
Murud 11.210 ..... C5
Murwara 54.864 ..... E4
Muzaffarnagar 114.783 ..... D3
Muzaffarpur 126.379 ..... E3
Mysore 355.685 ..... D6
Nadiad 108.269 ..... C4
Nagapattinam 68.026 ..... E6
Nagaur 36.448 ..... C3
Nagercoil 141.288 ..... D7
Nagina 37.066 ..... D3
Nagpur 866.076 ..... D4
Nagpur□ 930.459 ..... D4
Nahan 16.017 ..... D2
Naihati 82.080 ..... F1
Naini Tal 23.986 ..... D3
Nainpur 14.683 ..... E4
Nalgonda 33.126 ..... D5
Nander 126.538 ..... D5
Nandurbar 54.070 ..... C4
Nandyal 63.193 ..... D5
Narayanpet 21.744 ..... D5
Narnaul 31.875 ..... D3
Narsimhapur 25.552 ..... D4
Narsinghgarh 13.814 ..... D4
Nasik 176.091 ..... C5
Nasirabad 25.732 ..... C3
Navsari 72.979 ..... C4
Nellore 133.590 ..... E6
New Delhi (cap.) 301.801 ..... D3
Nhava-Sheva B7
Nimach 47.113 ..... D4
Nipani 35.116 ..... C5
Nirmal 28.529 ..... D5
Nizamabad 115.640 ..... D5
North Lakhimpur 20.094 ..... G3
Nova Goa (Panaji) 34.953 ..... C5
Nowgong, Assam 56.537 ..... G3
Nowgong, Madhya Pradesh 10.248 ..... D3
Okha Port 10.687 ..... B4
Ongole 53.330 ..... E5
Ootacamund 63.310 ..... D6
Orai 42.513 ..... D3
Osmanabad 27.279 ..... D5
Pachmarhi 1.212 ..... D4
Palanpur 42.114 ..... C4
Palayankottai 70.070 ..... D7
Palghat 95.788 ..... D6
Pali 49.834 ..... C3
Palni 49.575 ..... D6
Panaji 34.953 ..... C5
Panchur 59.021 ..... F2
Pandharpur 53.638 ..... D5
Panihati 148.046 ..... F1
Panipat 87.981 ..... D3
Panna 22.316 ..... E4
Panruti 34.065 ..... D6
Paradip F4
Parbhani 61.570 ..... D5
Parlakhemundi 26.917 ..... E5
Partapgarh 17.402 ..... C4
Parvatipuram 30.025 ..... E5
Pasighat 5.116 ..... G3
Patan 64.519 ..... C4
Pathankot 76.355 ..... D2
Patiala 148.686 ..... D2
Patiala□ D2
Patna 473.001 ..... F3
Patna□ F3
Pauni 17.781 ..... E4
Phalodi 17.379 ..... C3
Phulbani 10.677 ..... E4
Pilibhit 68.273 ..... D3
Pokaran 7.769 ..... C3
Pondicherry 90.537 ..... E6
Ponnani 35.723 ..... D6
Poona (Pune)□ C5
Porbandar 96.881 ..... B4
Porbandar□ B4
Port Blair 26.218 ..... G6
Porto Novo 17.412 ..... E6
Proddatur 70.822 ..... D6
Puduchcheri
(Pondicherry) 90.537 ..... E6
Pudukkottai 66.384 ..... D6
Pune 856.105 ..... C5
Puri 72.674 ..... F5
Purli 31.078 ..... D5
Purnea 56.484 ..... F3
Purulia 57.708 ..... F4
Puttur 17.483 ..... D6
Quilon 124.208 ..... D7
Radhanpur 18.360 ..... C4
Raichur 79.831 ..... D5
Raigarh 46.745 ..... E4
Raipur 174.518 ..... E4
Raipur□ E4
Rajahmundry 165.912 ..... E5
Rajahmundry□ E5
Rajapalaiyam 86.952 ..... D7
Rajapur 9.017 ..... C5
Rajgarh 11.475 ..... D4
Rajkot 300.612 ..... C4
Rajnandgaon 41.183 ..... E4
Rajpipla 25.769 ..... C4
Rajpur 34.393 ..... F2
Rajpura 14.840 ..... D2
Rameswarem 16.755 ..... D7
Rampur, Him. Pradesh 2.623 ..... D2
Rampur, Uttar Pradesh 161.417 ..... D3
Ranchi 175.934 ..... F4
Ratangarh 31.506 ..... C3
Ratlam 106.666 ..... C4
Ratnagiri 37.551 ..... C5
Raurkela 47.076 ..... F4
Raxaul 12.064 ..... E3
Rayagada 25.064 ..... E5
Renigunta 8.567 ..... E6
Rewa 69.182 ..... E4
Rishra 63.486 ..... F1
Robertsganj 7.093 ..... E4
Roha 8.631 ..... C5
Rohtak 124.783 ..... C5
Sadiya⊙ 64.252 ..... H3

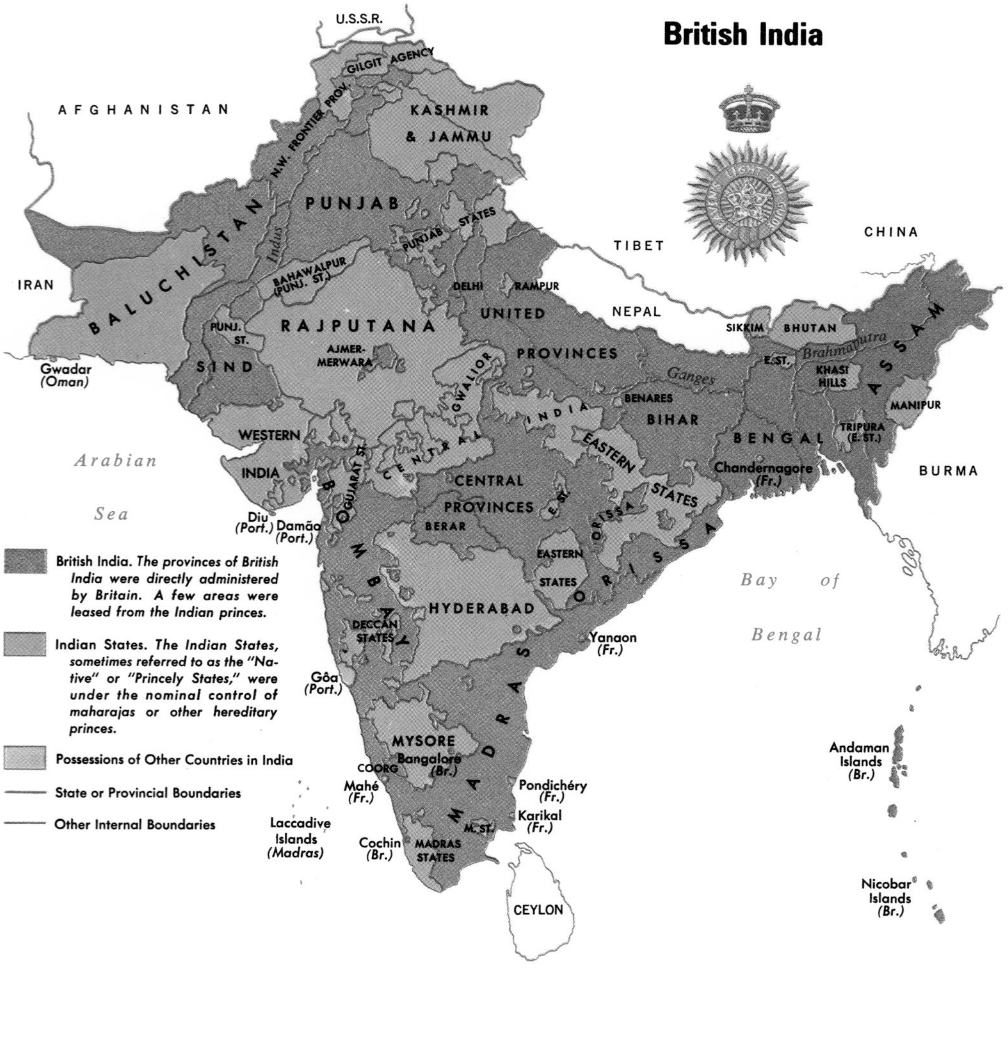

British India
U.S.S.R.
GILGIT AGENCY
AFGHANISTAN
KASHMIR & JAMMU
N.W. FRONTIER PROV.
PUNJAB
Indus
BALUCHISTAN
PUNJAB STATES
IRAN
BAHAWALPUR (PUNJ. ST.)
DELHI
RAMPUR
TIBET
CHINA
NEPAL
RAJPUTANA
UNITED PROVINCES
PUNJ. ST.
SIND
AJMER-MERWARA
SIKKIM
BHUTAN
E. ST.
Brahmaputra
KHASI HILLS
ASSAM
Gwadar (Oman)
Ganges
GWALIOR
CENTRAL INDIA
BENARES
BIHAR
MANIPUR
WESTERN INDIA
EASTERN STATES
BENGAL
TRIPURA (E. ST.)
Arabian Sea
GUJARAT ST.
CENTRAL PROVINCES
Chandernagore (Fr.)
BURMA
Diu (Port.)
Damão (Port.)
BERAR
E. ST.
ORISSA ST.
BOMBAY
ORISSA
HYDERABAD
Bay of Bengal
DECCAN STATES
Yanaon (Fr.)
Gôa (Port.)
MADRAS
MYSORE
Bangalore (Br.)
COORG
Mahé (Fr.)
Pondichéry (Fr.)
Karikal (Fr.)
M. ST.
Laccadive Islands (Madras)
Cochin (Br.)
MADRAS STATES
CEYLON
Andaman Islands (Br.)
Nicobar Islands (Br.)
British India. The provinces of British India were directly administered by Britain. A few areas were leased from the Indian princes.
Indian States. The Indian States, sometimes referred to as the "Native" or "Princely States," were under the nominal control of maharajas or other hereditary princes.
Possessions of Other Countries in India
State or Provincial Boundaries
Other Internal Boundaries

Indian Subcontinent and Afghanistan 71

Sagar 118,574 D4
Saharanpur 225,396 D3
Saharsa 23,217 F3
Salem 308,716 D6
Salem□ 416,440 D6
Samalkot 34,607 E5
Sambalpur 64,675 E4
Sambhal 86,323 D3
Sangamner 28,594 C5
Sangli 115,138 C5
Sankrail 11,300 E2
Santa Cruz B7
Santipur 61,166 F4
Sardarshahr 37,703 C3
Sarnath E3
Sasaram 48,282 E4
Satara 66,433 C5
Satna 57,531 E4
Savantvadi 16,873 C5
Savanur 18,302 D6
Sawi⊙ 13,504 G7
Secunderabad 250,636 D5
Secunderabad□ 345,052 D5
Sehore 35,657 D4
Seoni 38,396 D4
Serampore 102,023 F1
Seringapatam 14,100 D6
Shahdol 28,490 E4
Shahjahanpur 135,604 E3
Shajapur 25,189 D4
Sheopur 16,418 D3
Shillong 87,659 G3
Shimoga 102,709 D6
Shivpuri 42,120 D3
Sholapur 398,361 D5
Shorapur 21,056 D5
Shyok D2
Sibsagar 27,426 H3
Siddipet 26,296 D5
Sidhi 8,341 E4
Sidhpur 40,521 C4
Sikar 70,987 D3
Silchar 52,596 G4
Siliguri 97,484 F3
Silvassa C4
Simla 55,368 D2
Singur 10,957 F1
Sirohi 18,774 C4
Sironj 22,413 D4
Sirsa 48,808 D3
Sirsi 28,576 D6
Sitapur 66,715 E3
Sonepur 8,084 E4
South Dum Dum 174,538 F2
South Suburban 272,600 F2
Srikakulam 45,179 E5
Srinagar 403,413 D2
Srinagar□ 423,253 D2
Srivardhan 12,342 C5
Sundargarh 17,244 E4
Surada 9,833 E5
Surat 471,656 C4
Surat□ 493,001 C4
Suratgarh 14,491 C3
Surendranagar 66,667 C4
Tanda 41,611 E3
Tehri 5,480 D2
Tellicherry 68,759 C6
Tenali 102,937 E5
Tezpur 39,870 G3
Tezu 3,055 H3
Thana 170,675 B6
Thanjavur 140,547 D6
Tikamgarh 27,007 D4
Tinsukia 54,911 H3
Tiruchchirappalli 307,400 D6
Tiruchchirappalli□ 464,624 D6
Tiruchendur 18,126 D7
Tirunelveli 108,498 D7
Tirupati 65,843 D6
Tiruppattur 40,357 D6
Tiruppur 113,302 D6
Tiruvannamalai 61,370 D6
Titagarh 88,218 F1
Titlagarh 14,504 E4
Toibalawe G6
Tollygunge F2
Tonk 55,866 D3
Tranquebar 17,318 E6
Trichur 76,241 D6
Trivandrum 409,627 D7
Trombay B7
Tumkur 70,476 D6
Tuni 28,344 E5
Tura 15,489 G3
Tuticorin 155,310 D7
Udaipur 161,278 C4
Udhampur 16,392 D2
Udipi 29,753 C6
Ujjain 203,278 D4
Ulhasnagar 168,462 C5
Umrer 27,092 D4
Unnao 38,195 E3
Uran 12,616 B7
Uttarpara-Kotrung 67,568 F1
Vadodara 466,696 C4
Vadodara□ 467,487 C4
Valsad 43,254 C4
Vaniyambadi 51,810 D6
Varanasi 583,856 E3
Varanasi□ 606,721 E3
Vashi B7
Vedaranniyam 21,471 E6
Vellore 139,082 D6
Vellore□ 178,554 D6
Vengurla 11,805 C5
Venkatagiri 17,546 D6
Veraval 58,771 C4
Vesava B7
Vidisha 43,212 D4
Vijayawada 317,258 D5
Villupuram 60,242 D6
Vinukonda 16,259 D5
Virajpet 9,782 D6
Viramgam 43,790 C4
Visakhapatnam 352,504 E5
Visnagar 34,863 C4
Vizagapatam
(Visakhapatnam) 352,504 E5
Vizianagaram 86,608 E5
Warangal 207,520 D5
Wardha 69,037 D4
Wun 24,455 D5
Yadgir 32,756 D5
Yanam 8,291 E5
Yellamanchili 15,318 E5
Yeola 24,533 C4
Yeotmal 64,836 D4

OTHER FEATURES

Abor (hills) G3
Adam's Bridge (sound) D7
Agatti (isl.) C6
Amindiri (isl.) C6
Amindivi (isls.) C6
Amini (Amindiri) (isl.) C6
Andaman (isls.) G6
Andaman (sea) G6
Androth (isl.) C6
Anjidiv (Angedeva) (isl.) C6
Arabian (sea) B5
Back (bay) B7
Bengal, Bay of (sea) F5
Berar (reg.) D4
Brahmaputra (riv.) G3
Butcher (isl.) B7
Cambay (gulf) C4
Cannanore (isls.) C6
Car Nicobar (isl.) G7
Chambal (riv.) D3
Chenab (riv.) C2
Chetlat (isl.) C6
Chilka (lake) F5
Coco (chan.) G6
Colaba (pt.) B7
Colair (lake) E5
Comorin (cape) D7
Coromandel Coast (reg.) E6
Daman (dist.) C4
Damodar (riv.) F4
Deccan (plat.) D6
Diu (dist.) C4
Eastern Ghats (mts.) D6
Elephanta (isl.) B7
Ganga (Ganges) (riv.) F3
Ganges, Mouths of the
(delta) F4
Ganges (riv.) F3
Ghaghra (riv.) E3
Goa (dist.) C5
Godavari (riv.) D5
Golconda (ruins) D5
Great (chan.) G7
Great Indian (des.) C3
Great Nicobar (isl.) G7
Himalaya (mts.) D2
Hindu Kush (mts.) C1
Hooghly (riv.) F2
Indus (riv.) B3
Jhelum (riv.) C2
Jumna (riv.) E3
Kadmat (isl.) C6
Kalpeni (isl.) C7
Kamet (mt.) D2
Kanchenjunga (mt.) F3
Karakoram (mts.) D1
Kaveri (riv.) D6
Khakchh (Kutch) (gulf) B4
Khasi (hills) G3
Kiltan (isl.) C6
Kistna (Krishna) (riv.) D5
Kunlun (range) D1
Kutch, Rann of
(salt marsh) B4
Laccadive (Cannanore)
(isls.) C6
Ladakh (reg.) D2
Little Andaman (isl.) G6
Little Nicobar (isl.) G7
Mahanadi (riv.) E4
Malabar (hill) B7
Malabar Coast (reg.) C6
Mannar (gulf) D7
Middle Andaman (isl.) G6
Minicoy (isl.) C7
Miri (hills) G3
Mishmi (hills) H3
Nancowry⊙ (isl.) G7
Nanda Devi (mt.) D2
Narmada (riv.) D4
North Andaman⊙ (isl.) G6
Palk (str.) D7
Penganga (riv.) D5
Periyar (lake) D7
Pitti (isl.) C6
Pulicat (lake) E6
Salsette (isl.) B7
Sambhar (lake) C3
Satpura (range) D4
Shipki (pass) D2
South Andaman (isl.) G6
Sundarbans (reg.) F4
Sutlej (riv.) C3
Ten Degree (chan.) G7
Towers of Silence B7
Travancore (reg.) D7
Tungabhadra (riv.) D5
Vindhya (range) D4
Western Ghats (mts.) C5
Zaskar (mts.) D2

MALDIVES

Maldives 143,046 C7

NEPAL

CITIES and TOWNS

Bhaktapur 40,112 F3
Bhaktapur⊙ 110,157 F3
Biratnagar 45,100 F3
Birganj 12,999 F3
Dhangarhi E3
Ilam 7,299 F3
Jaleswar F3
Janakpur 14,294 F3
Jumla⊙ 122,753 E3
Kathmandu (cap.) 150,402 E3
Kathmandu⊙ 353,752 E3
Lalitpur 59,049 E3
Lalitpur⊙ 154,998 E3
Mustang⊙ 26,944 E3
Nepalganj 23,523 E3
Pokhara 20,611 E3
Pyuthan⊙ 137,338 E3
Ridi E3
Sallyan⊙ 141,457 E3
Simikot E3

OTHER FEATURES

Annapurna (mt.) E3
Bheri (riv.) E3
Dhaulagiri (mt.) E3
Everest (mt.) F3
Himalaya (mts.) D2
Kanchenjunga (mt.) F3

PAKISTAN

PROVINCES

Azad Kashmir C2
Baluchistan 2,409,000 B3
Federal Administrated Tribal Areas C2
Islamabad District 235,000 C2
Northern Areas D1
North-West Frontier 10,909,000 C2
Punjab 37,374,000 C2
Sind 13,965,000 B3

CITIES and TOWNS

Abbottabad 47,011 C2
Ahmadpur East 32,423 C3
Attock C2
Badin 6,387 B4
Bahawalnagar 36,290 C2
Bahawalpur 133,956 C3
Baltit C1
Bannu 43,795 C2
Barkhan 930 B3
Bhag 4,316 B3
Bhera 17,992 C2
Bostan B2
Bunji C1
Campbellpore 19,041 C2
Chachro C3
Chagai⊙ 41,263 A3
Chaman 12,208 B2
Chilas C1
Chiniot 69,124 C2
Chitral C1
Dadu 19,142 B3
Dalbandin 1,724 A3
Dera Ghazi Khan 71,429 C3
Dera Ismail Khan 59,892 C2
Diplo B4
Dir C1
Duki 464 B2
Faisalabad 822,263 C2
Fort Sandeman 8,058 B2
Ghizar C1
Gilgit C1
Gujranwala 360,419 C2
Gujrat 100,581 C2
Gwadar 8,146 A4
Hindubagh 2,217 B2
Hoshab A3
Hunza (Baltit) C1
Hyderabad 628,310 B3
Islamabad (cap.) 77,318 C2
Jacobabad 57,292 B3
Jhal Jhao B3
Jhang Sadar 135,722 C2
Jhelum 63,653 C2
Jhudo 6,950 B3
Kalam C1
Kalat 5,321 B3
Kandrach A3
Karachi 3,498,634 B4
Karachi* 3,650,000 B4
Kashmor C3
Kasur 102,531 C2
Khairpur 34,144 B3
Khanewal 67,617 C2
Khanpur 31,465 C3
Kharan Kalat 2,692 A3
Khushab 24,851 C2
Kohat 64,634 C2
Kotri 20,262 B3
Ladgasht (Qila Ladgasht) A3
Lahore 2,165,372 C2
Lahri B3
Larkana 71,943 B3
Leiah 19,608 C2
Loralai 5,519 B2
Lyallpur (Faisalabad) 822,263 C2
Mach 4,921 B3
Malakand C2
Mardan 115,218 C2
Mastung 5,962 B3
Mianwali 31,398 C2
Miram Shah C2
Mirpur C2
Mirpur Khas 81,617 B3
Misgar C1
Mithi C4
Multan 542,195 C2
Multan* 723,000 C2
Murree 13,486 C2
Musa Khel Bazar 429 B2
Muzaffarabad C2
Nagar D1
Nagar Parkar C4
Nal B3
Nawabshah 80,779 B3
Nok Kundi 861 A3
Nowshera 56,117 C2
Nushki 3,153 B3
Ormara A3
Panjgur 2,032 A3
Pasni 7,483 A3
Peshawar 268,366 C2
Pindi Gheb 12,416 C2
Pishin 2,906 B2
Qila Ladgasht A3
Quetta 156,000 B2
Rahimyar Khan 74,407 C3
Rawalpindi 615,392 C2
Ribat Qila A3
Risalpur Cantonment 11,291 C2
Rohri 19,072 B3
Rondu D1
Sahiwal 106,213 C2
Saidu 15,920 C2
Sargodha 201,407 C2
Sehwan 4,169 B3
Shahbandar B4
Shikarpur 70,301 B3
Sialkot 203,779 C2
Sibi 13,327 B3
Skardu D1
Sonmiani B3
Sorah B3
Sui 1,082 B3
Sukkur 158,876 B3
Surab B3
Tando Adam 31,246 B3
Tando Allahyar B3
Tatta 12,786 B4
Tump A3
Turbat 4,578 A3
Uch 5,483 B3
Uthal B3
Wah 107,671 C2
Wana C2
Yasin C1

OTHER FEATURES

Arabian (sea) B5
Bolan (pass) B3
Chagai (hills) A3
Chenab (riv.) C2
Hindu Kush (mts.) B1
Indus (riv.) B3
Jhelum (riv.) C2
K2 (mt.) D1
Konar (riv.) C1
Kutch, Rann of (salt marsh) B4
Mohenjo Daro (ruins) B3
Muari, Ras (cape) B4
Ravi (riv.) C2
Siahan (range) A3
Sulaiman (range) C3
Sutlej (riv.) C3
Talab (riv.) A3
Taxila (ruins) C2
Tirich Mir (mt.) C1
Zhob (riv.) B2

SRI LANKA (CEYLON)

CITIES and TOWNS

Anuradhapura 34,836 E7
Badulla 34,658 E7
Batticaloa 36,761 E7
Colombo (cap.) 618,000 D7
Colombo* 852,098 D7
Dehiwala-Mt. Lavinia 154,785 D7
Galle 72,720 D7
Hambantota 6,908 E7
Jaffna 112,000 E7
Kalmunai 19,176 E7
Kalutara 28,748 D7
Kandy 93,602 E7
Kurunegala 25,189 E7
Mannar 11,157 E7
Matara 36,641 E7
Moratuwa 96,489 D7
Mullaittivu 4,930 E7
Negombo 57,115 D7
Nilaveli 4,556 E7
Nuwara Eliya 16,347 E7
Polonnaruwa 9,551 E7
Puttalam 17,982 D7
Ratnapura 29,116 D7
Sigiriya 1,446 E7
Tangalla 8,748 E7
Trincomalee 41,780 E7
Vavuniya 15,639 E7

OTHER FEATURES

Adam's (peak) E7
Adam's Bridge (shoals) D7
Dondra (head) E7
Kirigalpota (mt.) E7
Mannar (gulf) D7
Palk (str.) D7
Pedro (pt.) E6
Pidurutalagala (mt.) E7

*City and suburbs.
⊙Population of district.
□Population of urban areas.

Agriculture, Industry and Resources

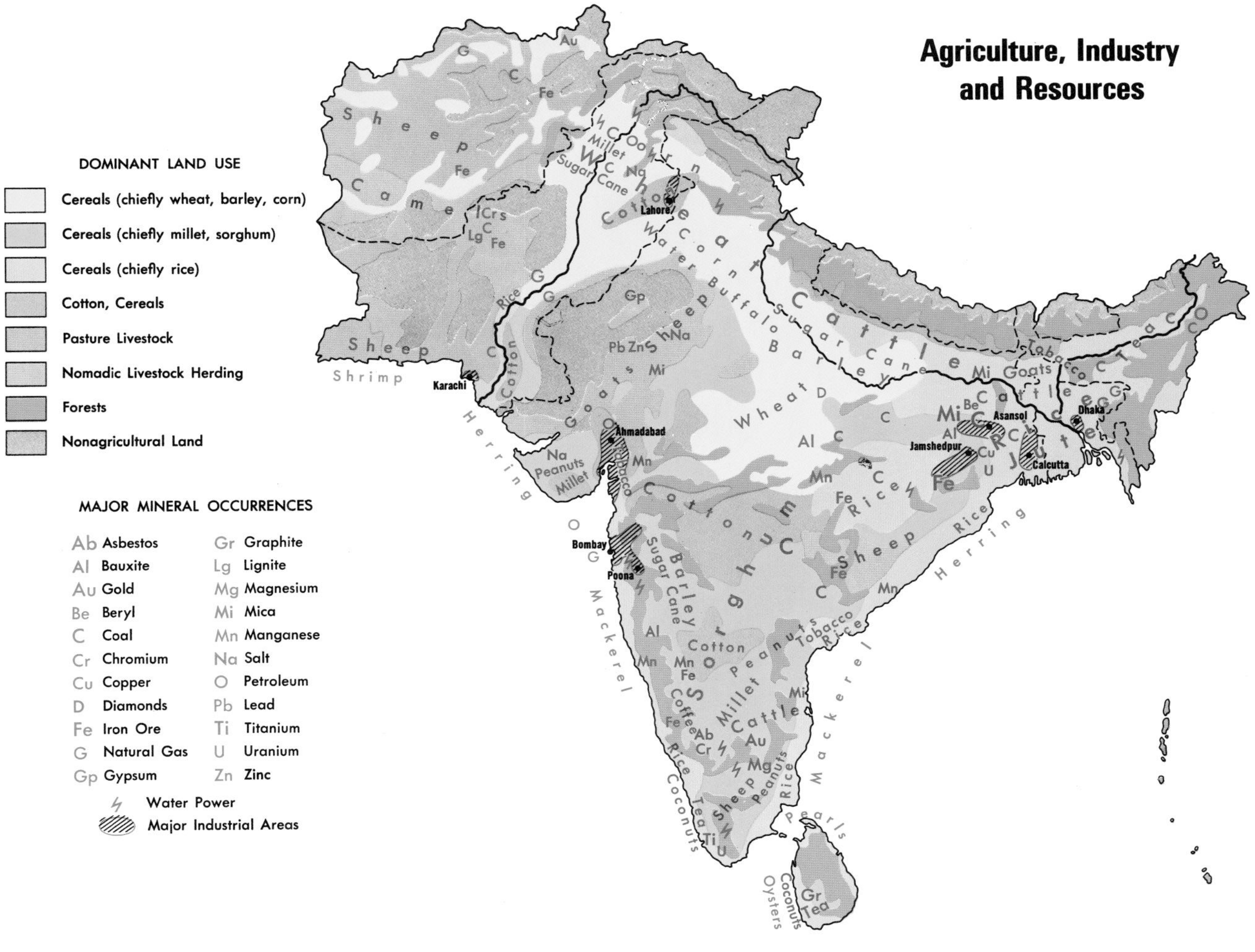

DOMINANT LAND USE
Cereals (chiefly wheat, barley, corn)
Cereals (chiefly millet, sorghum)
Cereals (chiefly rice)
Cotton, Cereals
Pasture Livestock
Nomadic Livestock Herding
Forests
Nonagricultural Land
MAJOR MINERAL OCCURRENCES
Ab Asbestos
Al Bauxite
Au Gold
Be Beryl
C Coal
Cr Chromium
Cu Copper
D Diamonds
Fe Iron Ore
G Natural Gas
Gp Gypsum
Gr Graphite
Lg Lignite
Mg Magnesium
Mi Mica
Mn Manganese
Na Salt
O Petroleum
Pb Lead
Ti Titanium
U Uranium
Zn Zinc
Water Power
Major Industrial Areas
Sheep
Camels
Millet
Sugar Cane
Cotton
Lahore
Corn
Water Buffalo
Sugar Cane
Barley
Cattle
Wheat
Goats
Tobacco
Tea
Rice
Shrimp
Karachi
Herring
Ahmadabad
Peanuts
Millet
Tobacco
Asansol
Jamshedpur
Calcutta
Dhaka
Bombay
Poona
Barley
Sorghum
Mackerel
Peanuts
Coffee
Coconuts
Pearls
Oysters
Tea

Burma, Thailand, Indochina and Malaya

CONIC PROJECTION

SCALE OF MILES

SCALE OF KILOMETERS

International Boundaries ——————————
Division and State Boundaries ——·—·—·—
Capitals of Countries ————————☆
Division and State Capitals ————————⊛

© Copyright HAMMOND INCORPORATED, Maplewood, N.J.

Longitude East 96° of Greenwich

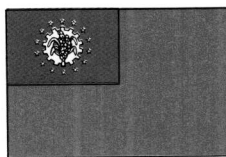

BURMA

THAILAND

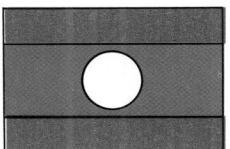

LAOS

CAMBODIA

VIETNAM

MALAYSIA

SINGAPORE

BURMA

AREA 261,789 sq. mi. (678,034 sq. km.)
POPULATION 32,913,000
CAPITAL Rangoon
LARGEST CITY Rangoon
HIGHEST POINT Hkakabo Razi 19,296 ft. (5,881 m.)
MONETARY UNIT kyat
MAJOR LANGUAGES Burmese, Karen, Shan, Kachin, Chin, Kayah, English
MAJOR RELIGIONS Buddhism, tribal religions

LAOS

AREA 91,428 sq. mi. (236,800 sq. km.)
POPULATION 3,721,000
CAPITAL Vientiane
LARGEST CITY Vientiane
HIGHEST POINT Phou Bia 9,252 ft. (2,820 m.)
MONETARY UNIT kip
MAJOR LANGUAGE Lao
MAJOR RELIGIONS Buddhism, tribal religions

VIETNAM

AREA 128,405 sq. mi. (332,569 sq. km.)
POPULATION 52,741,766
CAPITAL Hanoi
LARGEST CITY Ho Chi Minh City (Saigon)
HIGHEST POINT Fan Si Pan 10,308 ft. (3,142 m.)
MONETARY UNIT dong
MAJOR LANGUAGES Vietnamese, Thai, Muong, Meo, Yao, Khmer, French, Chinese, Cham
MAJOR RELIGIONS Buddhism, Taoism, Confucianism, Roman Catholicism, Cao-Dai

THAILAND

AREA 198,455 sq. mi. (513,998 sq. km.)
POPULATION 46,455,000
CAPITAL Bangkok
LARGEST CITY Bangkok
HIGHEST POINT Doi Inthanon 8,452 ft. (2,576 m.)
MONETARY UNIT baht
MAJOR LANGUAGES Thai, Lao, Chinese, Khmer, Malay
MAJOR RELIGIONS Buddhism, tribal religions

CAMBODIA

AREA 69,898 sq. mi. (181,036 sq. km.)
POPULATION 5,200,000
CAPITAL Phnom Penh
LARGEST CITY Phnom Penh
HIGHEST POINT 5,948 ft. (1,813 m.)
MONETARY UNIT riel
MAJOR LANGUAGE Khmer (Cambodian)
MAJOR RELIGION Buddhism

MALAYSIA

AREA 128,308 sq. mi. (332,318 sq. km.)
POPULATION 13,435,588
CAPITAL Kuala Lumpur
LARGEST CITY Kuala Lumpur
HIGHEST POINT Mt. Kinabalu 13,455 ft. (4,101 m.)
MONETARY UNIT ringgit
MAJOR LANGUAGES Malay, Chinese, English, Tamil, Dayak, Kadazan
MAJOR RELIGIONS Islam, Confucianism, Buddhism, tribal religions, Hinduism, Taoism, Christianity, Sikhism

SINGAPORE

AREA 226 sq. mi. (585 sq. km.)
POPULATION 2,413,945
CAPITAL Singapore
LARGEST CITY Singapore
HIGHEST POINT Bukit Timah 581 ft. (177 m.)
MONETARY UNIT Singapore dollar
MAJOR LANGUAGES Chinese, Malay, Tamil, English, Hindi
MAJOR RELIGIONS Confucianism, Buddhism, Taoism, Hinduism, Islam, Christianity

Topography

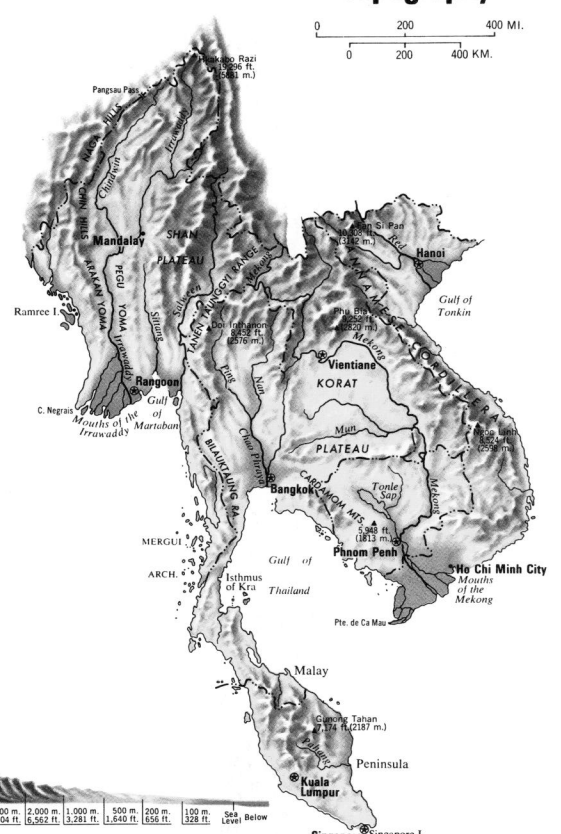

0 200 400 MI.	
0 200 400 KM.	

5,000 m. / 16,404 ft. — 2,000 m. / 6,562 ft. — 1,000 m. / 3,281 ft. — 500 m. / 1,640 ft. — 200 m. / 656 ft. — 100 m. / 328 ft. — Sea Level — Below

BURMA

INTERNAL DIVISIONS

Arakan (state) 1,710,913	B3
Chin (state) 323,094	B2
Irrawaddy (div.) 4,152,521	B3
Kachin (state) 735,144	C1
Karen (state) 865,218	C3
Kayah (state) 126,492	C3
Magwe (div.) 2,632,144	B2
Mandalay (div.) 3,662,312	B2
Mon (state) 1,313,111	C3
Pegu (div.) 3,174,109	C3
Rangoon (div.) 3,186,886	C3
Sagaing (div.) 3,115,502	B1
Shan (state) 3,178,214	C2
Tenasserim (div.) 717,607	C4

CITIES and TOWNS

Akyab (Sittwe) 42,329	B2
Allanmyo 15,580	B3
Amarapura 11,268	B2
Amherst 6,000	C3
An	B3
Anin	C4
Bassein 126,045	B3
Bhamo 9,821	C1
Chauk 24,466	B2
Danubyu	B3
Falam	B2
Fort Hertz (Putao)	C1
Gawai	C1
Gokteik	C2
Gwa	B3
Gyobingauk 9,922	C3
Haka	B2
Henzada 61,972	B3
Hmawbi 23,032	C3
Homalin	B1
Hsenwi	C2
Hsipaw	C2
Htawgaw	C1
Insein 143,625	C3
Kamaing	C1
Karathuri	C5
Katha 7,648	C1
Kawludo	C3
Kawthaung 1,520	C5
Keng Hkam	C2
Keng Tung	C2
Koma	C4
Kunlong	C2
Kyaikto 13,154	C3
Kya-in Seikkyi	C3
Kyangin 6,073	B3
Kyaukme	C2
Kyaukpadaung 5,480	B2
Kyaukpyu 7,335	B3
Kyaukse 8,659	C2
Labutta 12,982	B3
Lai-hka	C2
Lamu	B3
Lashio	C2
Lenya	C5
Letpadan 15,896	C3
Lewe	B3
Loi-kaw	C3
Lonton	B1
Magwe 13,270	B2
Maingkwan	C1
Maliwun	C5
Mandalay 418,008	C2
Man Hpang	C2
Martaban 5,661	C3
Ma-ubin 23,362	B3
Mawkmai	C2
Mawlaik 2,993	B2
Mawlu	C1
Maymyo 22,287	C2
Meiktila 19,474	B2
Mergui 33,697	C4
Minbu 9,096	B2

Minhla 6,470	B3
Mogaung 2,920	C1
Mogok 8,334	C2
Mohnyin	C1
Möng Hsat	C3
Möng Mau	C3
Möng Mit	C2
Möng Pan	C2
Möng Si	C2
Möng Ton	C2
Möng Tung	C2
Monywa 26,279	B2
Moulmein 171,977	C3
Mudon 20,136	C3
Myanaung 11,155	B3
Myaungmya 24,532	B3
Myingyan 36,439	B2
Myitkyina 12,382	C1
Myohaung 6,534	B2
Naba	B1
Namhkam	C2
Namlan	C2
Namtu	C2
Natmauk	B2
Okkan 14,443	C3
Okpo 12,155	C3
Pakokku 30,943	B2
Palaw 5,596	C4
Paletwa	B2
Pantha	B2
Papun	C3
Pasawng	C3
Paungde 17,286	B3
Pegu 47,378	C3
Prome (Pye) 36,997	B3
Putao	C1
Pyapon 19,174	B3
Pye 36,997	B3
Pyinmana 22,025	C2
Pyu 10,443	C3
Rangoon (cap.) 1,586,422	C3
Rangoon* 2,055,365	C3
Rathedaung 2,969	B2
Sadon	C1
Sagaing 15,382	B2
Samka	C2
Sandoway 5,172	B3
Shingbwiyang	B1
Shwebo 17,827	B2
Shwenyaung	C2
Singkaling Hkamti	B1
Singu 4,027	C2
Siniumkaba	C1
Sittwe 42,329	B2
Sumprabum	C1
Syriam 15,296	C3
Taungdwingyi 16,233	B2
Taunggyi	C2
Tavoy 40,312	C4
Tharrawaddy 8,977	C3
Thaton 38,047	C3
Thaungdut	B1
Thayetmyo 11,649	B3
Thazi 7,531	C2
Thongwa 10,829	C3
Toungoo 31,589	C3
Wakema 20,716	B3
Yamethin 11,167	C2
Yandoon 15,245	B3
Ye 12,852	C4
Yenangyaung 24,416	B2
Yesagyo 7,880	B2
Ye-u 5,307	B2
Ywathit	C3
Zadi	C4
Zalun 899	B3

OTHER FEATURES

Amya (pass)	C4
Andaman (sea)	B4
Arakan Yoma (mts.)	B3
Ataran (riv.)	C3
Bengal, Bay of (sea)	B3
Bentinck (isl.)	C5

(continued on following page)

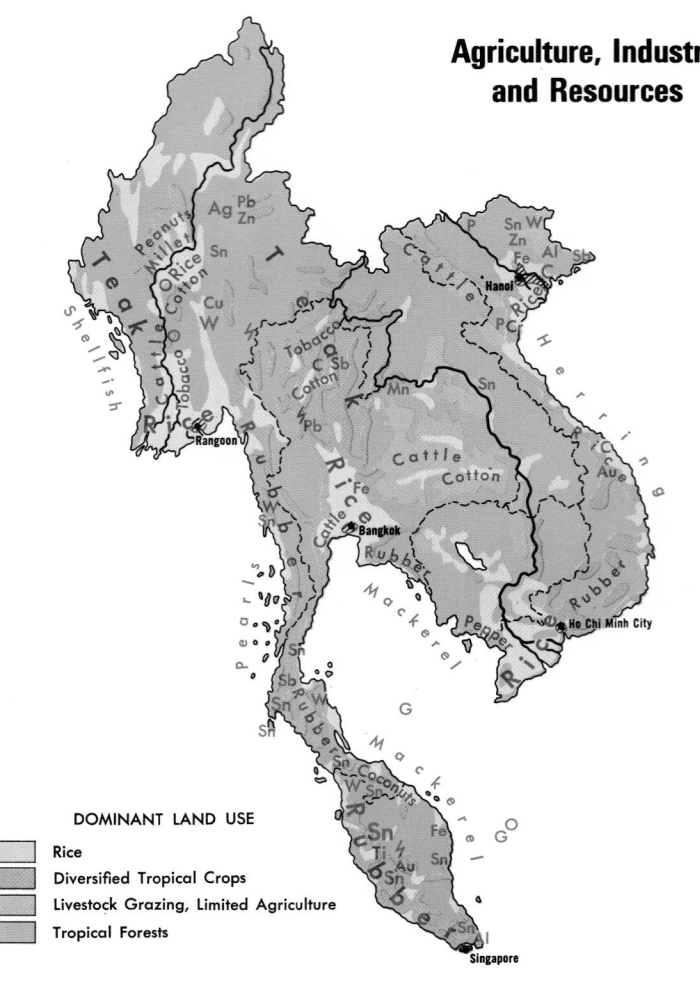

Agriculture, Industry and Resources

DOMINANT LAND USE

- Rice
- Diversified Tropical Crops
- Livestock Grazing, Limited Agriculture
- Tropical Forests

MAJOR MINERAL OCCURRENCES

Ag Silver	Cu Copper	O Petroleum	Sn Tin
Al Bauxite	Fe Iron Ore	P Phosphates	Ti Titanium
Au Gold	G Natural Gas	Pb Lead	W Tungsten
C Coal	Mn Manganese	Sb Antimony	Zn Zinc
Cr Chromium			

⚡ Water Power   ▨ Major Industrial Areas

CHINA (MAINLAND)

AREA 3,691,000 sq. mi. (9,559,690 sq. km.)
POPULATION 958,090,000
CAPITAL Beijing
LARGEST CITY Shanghai
HIGHEST POINT Mt. Everest 29,028 ft.
(8,848 m.)
MONETARY UNIT yuan
MAJOR LANGUAGES Chinese, Chuang, Uigur,
Yi, Tibetan, Miao, Mongol, Kazakh
MAJOR RELIGIONS Confucianism, Buddhism,
Taoism, Islam

CHINA (TAIWAN)

AREA 13,971 sq. mi. (36,185 sq. km.)
POPULATION 16,609,961
CAPITAL Taipei
LARGEST CITY Taipei
HIGHEST POINT Yü Shan 13,113 ft. (3,997 m.)
MONETARY UNIT new Taiwan yüan (dollar)
MAJOR LANGUAGES Chinese, Formosan
MAJOR RELIGIONS Confucianism, Buddhism,
Taoism, Christianity, tribal religions

MONGOLIA

AREA 606,163 sq. mi. (1,569,962 sq. km.)
POPULATION 1,594,800
CAPITAL Ulaanbaatar
LARGEST CITY Ulaanbaatar
HIGHEST POINT Tabun Bogdo 14,288 ft.
(4,355 m.)
MONETARY UNIT tughrik
MAJOR LANGUAGES Khalkha Mongolian,
Kazakh (Turkic)
MAJOR RELIGION Buddhism

HONG KONG

AREA 403 sq. mi. (1,044 sq. km.)
POPULATION 5,022,000
CAPITAL Victoria
MONETARY UNIT Hong Kong dollar
MAJOR LANGUAGES Chinese, English
MAJOR RELIGIONS Confucianism, Buddhism,
Christianity

MACAU

AREA 6 sq. mi. (16 sq. km.)
POPULATION 271,000
CAPITAL Macau
MONETARY UNIT pataca
MAJOR LANGUAGES Chinese, Portuguese
MAJOR RELIGIONS Confucianism, Buddhism,
Taoism, Christianity

CHINA (MAINLAND)

CHINA (TAIWAN)

MONGOLIA

CHINA

PROVINCES

Anhui (Anhwei) 47,130,000 ....J5
Chekiang (Zhejiang) 37,510,000 ...K6
Fujian (Fukien) 24,500,000 ....J6
Gansu (Kansu) 18,730,000 ....E3
Guangdong
  (Kwangtung) 55,930,000 ....H7
Guangxi Zhuangzu (Kwangsi Chuang Aut.
  Reg. 34,020,000 ....G7
Guizhou (Kweichow) 26,860,000 ...G6
Heilongjiang
  (Heilungkiang) 33,760,000 ......K2
Hebei (Hopei) 50,570,000 ....J4
Henan (Honan) 70,660,000 ....H5
Hubei (Hupei) 45,750,000 ....H5
Hunan 51,660,000 ....H6
Inner Mongolian Aut. Reg. (Nei
  Monggol) 8,900,000 ....H3
Jiangxi (Kiangsi) 31,830,000 .....J6
Jiangsu (Kiangsu) 58,340,000 ....K5
Jilin (Kirin) 24,740,000 ....L3
Kansu (Gansu) 18,730,000 ....E3
Kiangsi (Jiangxi) 31,830,000 .....J6
Kiangsu (Jiangsu) 58,340,000 ....K5
Kirin (Jilin) 24,740,000 ....L3
Kwangsi Chuang Aut. Reg. (Guangxi
  Zhuang 34,020,000 ....G7
Kwangtung
  (Guangdong) 55,930,000 ....H7
Kweichow (Guizhou) 26,860,000 ..G6
Liaoning 37,430,000 ....L3
Nei Monggol (Inner Mongolian Aut.
  Reg.) 8,900,000 ....H3
Ningxia Huizu (Ningsia Hui Aut.
  Reg.) 3,660,000 ....F3
Qinghai (Tsinghai) 3,650,000 .....E4
Shaanxi (Shensi) 27,790,000 .....G5
Shanxi (Shansi) 24,340,000 ......H4
Shandong (Shantung) 71,660,000 .J4
Sichuan (Szechwan) 97,070,000 ..F5
Sinkiang-Uigur Aut. Reg. (Xinjiang
  Uygur 12,330,000 ....B3
Taiwan 16,609,961 ....K7
Tibet Aut. Reg.
  (Xizang) 1,790,000 ....B5
Tsinghai (Qinghai) 3,650,000 .....E4
Xinjiang Uygur (Sinkiang-Uigur Aut.
  Reg. 12,330,000 ....B3
Xizang (Tibet Aut.
  Reg.) 1,790,000 ....B5
Yunnan 30,920,000 ....F7
Zhejiang (Chekiang) 37,510,000 ..K6

CITIES AND TOWNS†

Aba F5
Abagnar (Siilinhot) J3
Aihui (Aigun) (Heihe) L1
Aksu (Aqsu) B3
Altay C2
Alxa Youqi F4
Alxa Zuoqi F4
Amoy (Xiamen) 400,000 ....J7
Anda (Anta) L2
Ankang G5
Anqing (Anking) 160,000 ....J5
Anshan 1,500,000 ....L3
Anshun G6
Antu L3
Anxi E3
Anyang 225,000 ....H4
Aqsu (Aksu) B3
Aratürük (Yiwu) D3
Ar Horqin K3
Arixang (Wenquan) A4
Artux (Atushi) A4
Bachu (Maralwexi) A4
Baicheng, Jilin K2
Baicheng (Bay), Xinjiang
  Uygur B3
Bairin Zuoqi J3
Baoding (Paoting) 350,000 .....J4
Baoji (Paoki) 275,000 ....G5
Baoshan E7
Baoting G8
Baotou (Pactow) 800,000 ....G3
Bargrax (Bohu) C3
Batang E7
Bay (Baicheng) B3
Bayan Obo G3
Ba Xian J4
Bei'an (Pehan) 130,000 ....L2
Beihai (Pakhoi) 175,000 ....G7
Beijing (Peking)
  (cap.)● 8,500,000 ....J3
Bengbu (Pengpu) 400,000 ......J5
Benxi (Penki) 750,000 ....K3
Bohu (Bagrax) C3
Bole B3
Bortala (Bole) B3
Bosban J4
Bo Xian (Pohsien) J5
Butha K2
Cangzhou (Tsangchow) J4
Canton (Guangzhou) 2,300,000 ..H7
Chamdo (Qamdo) E5
Changchih (Changzhi) H4
Changchow (Changzhou) 400,000 .J5
Changchow (Changzhou) J5
Changchun 1,500,000 ....K3
Changde (Changteh) 225,000 ....H6
Changhua 137,236 ....K7
Changji C3
Changjiang G8
Changsha 850,000 ....H6
Changteh (Changde) 225,000 ....H6
Changyeh (Zhangye) H4
Changzhi (Changchih) H4
Changzhou (Changchow) 400,000 .K5
Chankiang (Zhanjiang) 220,000 ..H7
Chao'an (Chaochow) J7
Chaotung (Zhaotong) F6
Chaoyang, Liaoning J3
Chaoyang, Guangdong J7
Charkhlia (Ruoqiang) C4
Chefoo (Yantai) 180,000 ....K4
Chengchow (Zhengzhou) 1,500,000 .H5
Chengde (Chengteh) 200,000 ....J3
Chengdu (Chengtu) 2,000,000 ...F5
Chen Xian (Diemo) C4
Cherchen (Qiemo) C4
Chiai 238,713 ....K7
Chifeng J3
Chinchow (Jinzhou) 750,000 ....K3
Chindu E5
Chinkiang (Zhenjiang) 250,000 ..J5
Chinsi (Jinxi) K3
Chinwangtao
  (Qinhuangdao) 400,000 ....K4
Chishui G6
Chongqing (Chungking) 3,500,000 .G6
Chüanchow (Quanzhou) 130,000 .J7
Chuchow (Zhuzhou) 350,000 .....H6
Chuguchak (Tacheng) B2
Chumatien (Zhumadian) H5
Chungking (Chongqing) 3,500,000 .G6
Chungshan (Zhongshan) 135,000 .H7
Da'an (Talai) K2
Danba F5
Dandong (Tantung) 450,000 .....K3
Dali E6
Da Xian G8
Da Qaidam E4
Datong (Tatung),
  Shanxi 300,000 ....H3
Datong, Qinghai F4
Da Xian G8
Dazhai H4
Dengkou G3
Deyang F5
Dezhou (Tehchow) J4
Dingxing H4
Dongchuan F6
Dongfang G8
Dongsheng G3
Dongtai K5
Dorbiljin (Emin) B2
Dukou F6
Dulan E4
Dunhua (Tunhwa) L3
Dunhuang E3
Duolun J3
Dushan G6
Duyun (Tuyün) G6
Ejin F3
Emin (Dorbiljin) B2
Erenhot H3
Ergun Youqi K1
Ergun Zuoqi K1
Ertai D3
Fatshan (Foshan) H7

(continued on following page)

China and Mongolia Transportation

Railroads
Under Construction
Connecting Roads
Navigable Rivers
Canals
Major Seaports ⚓

© Copyright HAMMOND INCORPORATED, Maplewood, N.J.

Foochow (Fuzhou) 900,000 ....J6
Foshan (Fatshan) H7
Fowyang (Fuyang) J5
Fushun 1,700,000 ....K3
Fusingchen (Simao) F7
Fu Xian, Shaanxi G4
Fuxin, Liaoning K4
Fuyang (Fowyang) J5
Fuyu, Heilongjiang K2
Fuyu, Jilin L2
Fuyuan, Heilongjiang M2
Fuyuan, Yunnan F6
Fuyun C2
Fuzhou (Foochow) J6
Fuzhou, Jiangxi J6
Ganzhou (Kanchow) 135,000 ....H6
Garyarsa (Gartok) B5
Geju (Koku) 250,000 ....F7
Gonghe E4
Guangyuan G5
Guan Xian F5
Guangzhou (Canton) 2,300,000 ....H7
Guilin (Kweilin) 225,000 ....G6
Guiyang (Kweiyang) G6
Guizhou 1,500,000 ....G6
Guiyang, Hunan H6
Gulja (Yining) 160,000 ....B3
Guma (Pishan) A4
Guyang G3
Guyuan F4
Gyaca D6
Gyangzê C6
Habahe C2
Haikou (Hoihow) 500,000 ....H7
Hailar J2
Hami (Kumul) D3
Hancheng H4
Hanchung (Hanzhong) 120,000 ....H4
Handan (Hantan) 500,000 ....H4
Hangzhou (Hangchow) 1,100,000 ....K5
Hantan (Handan) 500,000 ....H4
Hanzhong (Hanchung) 120,000 ....G5
Harbin 2,750,000 ....K3
Hebi H4
Hechuan (Hochwan) G5
Hefei (Hofei) 400,000 ....J5
Hegang (Hokang) 350,000 ....L1
Heihe (Aihui) (Aigun) L1
Hekou F7
Hengchun K7
Hengyang 310,000 ....H6
Hepu (Hoppo) G7
Hexigten J3
Hezuo F4
Hezuan (Hechuan) G5
Hofei (Hefei) 400,000 ....J5
Hohhot (Huhehot) 700,000 ....H3
Hoihow (Haikou) 500,000 ....H7
Hokang (Hegang) 350,000 ....L2
Hoppo (Hepu) G7
Horqin Youyi Qianqi
  (Ulanhot) 100,000 ....K2
Houma H4
Hsüchang (Xuchang) H5

Huadian L3
Huaibei J5
Huaide (Hwaiteh) K3
Huainan 350,000 ....J5
Hualien K7
Huangling G4
Huangshi 200,000 ....J5
Huangzhong F4
Huhehot (Hohhot) 700,000 ....H3
Huizhou H7
Hulin M2
Hunchun M3
Hunjiang L3
Hwainan (Huainan) 350,000 ....J5
Hwaiteh (Huaide) K3
Hwangshih (Huangshi) 200,000 ....J5
Ichang (Yichang) 150,000 ....H5
Ichun (Yichun) 200,000 ....L2
Ilan K7
Ipin (Yibin) 275,000 ....F6
Jeminay C2
Jiamusi (Kiamusze) 275,000 ....M2
Ji'an (Kian) 100,000 ....J6
Jiangmen (Kongmoon) 150,000 ....H7
Jian'ou J6
Jiaozuo (Tsiaotso) 300,000 ....H4
Jiaxing (Kashing) K5
Jiayuguan E4
Jieyang J6
Jilin (Kirin) 1,200,000 ....L3
Jinan (Tsinan) 1,500,000 ....J4
Jingdezhen
  (Kingtehchen) 300,000 ....J6
Jinghong F7
Jingxi G7
Jing Xian, Anhui J5
Jing Xian, Hunan H6
Jingyuan F4
Jinhua (Kinhwa) J6
Jining (Tsining), Nei
  Monggol 160,000 ....H3
Jining (Tsining), Shandong J4
Jinshi (Tsingshih) 100,000 ....H6
Jinxi (Chinsi) K3
Jinzhou (Chinchow) 750,000 ....K3
Jiujiang (Kiukiang) 120,000 ....J6
Jiuquan (Kiuchüan) E4
Jixi (Kisi) 350,000 ....M2
Juichin (Ruijin) J6
Kaba (Habahe) C2
Kaifeng 330,000 ....H4
Kailu K3
Kaiyuan, Liaoning K3
Kaiyuan, Yunnan F7
Kalgan (Zhangjiakou) 1,000,000 ....J3
Kanchow (Ganzhou) 135,000 ....H6
Kangding F5
Kaohsiung 1,028,334 ....K7
Karakax (Kara Kash) (Moyu) A4
Karamay B2
Karghalik (Yecheng) A4
Kashi (Kashgar) 175,000 ....A4
Kashing (Jiaxing) K5
Kaxgar (Kashi) 175,000 ....A4
Keelung 342,604 ....K7
Kenli J4
Keriya (Yutian) B4
Khotan (Hotan) B4

Kiamusze (Jiamusi)
  275,000 ....M2
Kian (Ji'an) 100,000 ....J6
Kienyang (Qianyang) H6
Kingtehchen (Jingdezhen)
  300,000 ....J6
Kinhwa (Jinhua) J6
Kirin (Jilin) 1,200,000 ....L3
Kisi (Jixi) 350,000 ....M2
Kiuchüan (Jiuquan) E4
Kiukiang (Jiujiang) 120,000 ....J6
Kongmoon (Jiangmen)
  150,000 ....H7
Korla C3
Kuldja (Yining) 160,000 ....B3
Kumul (Hami) D3
Künes (Xinyuan) B3
Kunming 1,700,000 ....F6
Kuqa B3
Kuytun C3
Kwangchow (Canton)
  2,300,000 ....H7
Kweichu (Baicheng) G6
Kweilin (Guilin) 225,000 ....G6
Kweisui (Hohhot) 700,000 ....H3
Kweiyang (Guiyang)
  1,500,000 ....G6
Lanzhou (Lanchow) i,500,000 ....G4
Lenghu D4
Lengshuijiang H6
Leshan (Loshan) 250,000 ....F6
Lhasa 175,000 ....D6
Lhazê (Lhatse) C6
Lienyungang (Lienyünkang) J5
Liaoyang 250,000 ....K3
Liaoyuan 300,000 ....K3
Lijiang F6
Linfen H4
Lingling H6
Linhe G3
Linqing (Lintsing) J4
Linxi J3
Linxia (Linsia) F4
Liuzhou (Liuchow) 250,000 ....G7
Loho (Luohe) H5
Longjiang K2
Lopnur (Yuli) C3
Loshan (Leshan) 250,000 ....F6
Loyang (Luoyang) 750,000 ....H5
Lu'an J5
Luchow (Luzhou) 225,000 ....G6
Lüda (Dalian) 1,480,240 ....K4
Luohe H5
Luoyang (Loyang) 750,000 ....H5
Luxi K4
Luzhou (Luchow) 225,000 ....G6
Ma'anshan J5
Manas C3
Manzhouli (Manzhouli) J2
Maoming (Mowming) H7
Maralwexi (Bachu) A4
Mengcheng J5
Mengzi F7
Mianyang, Hubei H5
Mianyang, Sichuan F5
Minfeng (Niya) B4
Mingshui, Gansu E3
Mingshui, Heilongjiang L2
Minle F4
Mowming (Maoming) H7
Moyu (Karakax) A4

Mudanjiang (Mutankiang) 400,000 ....M3
Mukden (Shenyang) 3,750,000 ....K3
Muli F6
Nagqu D5
Nanchang 900,000 ....J6
Nanchong (Nanchung) 275,000 ....G5
Nanjing (Nanking) 2,000,000 ....J5
Nanning 375,000 ....G7
Nantong 300,000 ....K5
Nanyang H5
Neijiang (Neikiang) 240,000 ....G6
Nenjiang K2
Ningbo (Ningpo) 350,000 ....K6
Ningpo (Ningbo) 350,000 ....K6
Ningsia (Yinchuan) G4
Niya (Minfeng) B4
Orogen K1
Ongniud J3
Oroqen E5
Paicheng (Baicheng) K2
Pakhoi (Beihai) 175,000 ....G7
Paoki (Baoji) 275,000 ....G5
Paoting (Baoding) 350,000 ....J4
Paotow (Baotou) 800,000 ....G3
Pehan (Bei'an) 130,000 ....L2
Peking (Beijing)
  (cap.) ●8,500,000 ....J4
Pengpu (Bengbu) 400,000 ....J5
Penki (Benxi) 750,000 ....K3
Pingdingshan H5
Pingjiang H6
Pingliang G4
Pingtung 165,360 ....K7
Pingxiang, Guangxi Zhuangzu G7
Pingxiang, Jiangxi H6
Piqan (Shanshan) D3
Pishan (Guma) A4
Pohsien (Bo Xian) J5
Qamdo E5
Qarkilik (Ruoqiang) C4
Qargan (Qiemo) C4
Qiamyang (Kienyang) H6
Qiemo (Qarqan) C4
Qingdao (Tsingtao) 1,900,000 ....K4
Qingjiang J6
Qingjiang 110,000 ....J6
Qinhuangdao
  (Chinwangtao) 400,000 ....K4
Qionghai H8
Qiqihar (Tsitsihar) 1,500,000 ....K2
Qitai C3
Qog G3
Qoqek (Tacheng) B2
Quanzhou (Chüanchow) 130,000 ....J7
Qu Xian, Sichuan G5
Qu Xian, Zhejiang J6
Qüxü D6
Ruijin (Juichin) J6
Ruoqiang (Qarkilik) C4
Rutog A6
Sanmenxia H5
Sanming J6
Sêrxü E5
Shache (Yarkand) A4
Shandan F4
Shanghai ●10,980,000 ....K5
Shangqiu (Shangkiu) 250,000 ....J5

Shangrao (Shangjao) 100,000 ....J6
Shangshui 100,000 ....J5
Shanshan (Piqan) D3
Shantou (Swatow) 400,000 ....J7
Shaoguan (Shiukwan) 125,000 ....H7
Shaoxing (Shaohing) 225,000 ....K5
Shaoyang 275,000 ....H6
Shashi 125,000 ....H5
Shenyang (Mukden) 3,750,000 ....K3
Shigatse (Xigazê) C6
Shihezi (Shihhotzu) C3
Shijiazhuang
  (Shihkiachwang) 1,500,000 ....J4
Shiquanhe A5
Shiukwan (Shaoguan) 125,000 ....H7
Shiyan H5
Shizuishan (Shihsuishan) G4
Shuangcheng L2
Shuangyashan 150,000 ....M2
Shuo Xian H4
Sikwan (Xiaguan) E6
Sian (Xi'an) 1,900,000 ....G5
Siangfan (Xiangfan) 150,000 ....H5
Siangtan (Xiangtan) 300,000 ....H6
Sienyang (Xianyang) 125,000 ....G5
Siinhot (Abnagar) J3
Simao (Fusingchen) F7
Sinchu 208,038 ....K7
Singtai (Xingtai) H4
Sining (Xining) 250,000 ....F4

Sinsiang (Xinxiang) 300,000 ....H4
Sinyang (Xinyang) 125,000 ....H5
Siping (Szeping) 180,000 ....K3
Sitzien (Shache) A4
Soochow (Suzhou) 1,300,000 ....K5
Suao K7
Süchow (Xuzhou) 1,500,000 ....J5
Suifenhe M3
Suihua L2
Suining G5
Suzhou (Soochow) 1,300,000 ....K5
Swatow (Shantou) 400,000 ....J7
Szeping (Siping) 180,000 ....K3
Tacheng (Qoqek) B2
Tai'an J4
Taibus J3
Taichow (Taizhou) 275,000 ....K5
Taichung 565,255 ....K7
Taigu H4
Tainan 541,390 ....K7
Taipei 2,108,193 ....K7
Taitung K7
Taiyuan 2,725,000 ....H4
Taizhou (Taichow) 275,000 ....K5
Tal (Da'an, Dalai) K2
Tali (Dali) E6
Tangshan 1,200,000 ....J4
Tantung (Dandong) 450,000 ....K3
Tao'an K2
Taoyuan 105,841 ....K6

Tart D4
Tatung (Datong) 300,000 ....H3
Taxkorgan A4
Tehchow (Dezhou) J4
Techong E6
Tianjin (Tientsin) ●7,210,000 ....J4
Tianjun E4
Tianshui 100,000 ....F5
Tianshui (Tianshui) 100,000 ....F5
Tieling K3
Tientsin (Tianjin) ●7,210,000 ....J4
Tingri C6
Togton D5
Toksu (Xinhe) B3
Toksun C3
Tongchuan (Tungchwan) G4
Tonghua (Tunghua) 275,000 ....L3
Tongjiang (Tungkiang) M2
Tongliao K3
Tongling J5
Tongren G6
Tsangchow (Cangzhou) J4
Tsiaotso (Jiaozuo) 300,000 ....H4
Tsinan (Jinan) 1,500,000 ....J4
Tsingkiang (Qingjiang) 110,000 ....J5
Tsingshih (Jinshi) 100,000 ....H6
Tsingtao (Qingdao) 1,900,000 ....K4
Tsining (Jining), Nei H3
Monggol 160,000 ....H3

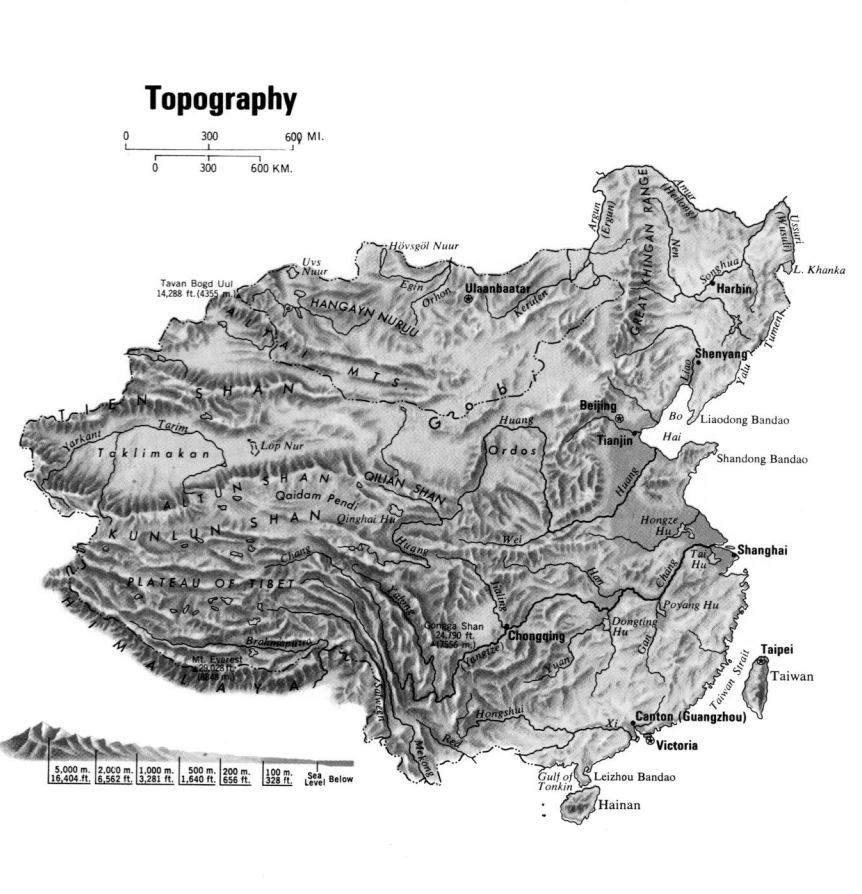

Topography

On this map Chinese place-names have been rendered according to the
Pinyin spelling system within the area controlled by the People's Republic of
China. Alphabetically listed below are selected Chinese place-names
spelled in the traditional manner, followed by the equivalent Pinyin form.

Amoy (Hsiamen)	Xiamen	Kirin	Jilin	Sian	Xi'an
Anhwei	Anhui	Kiukiang	Jiujiang	Siangtan	Xiangtan
Canton		Kwangsi	Guangxi	Sining	Xining
(Kwangchow)	Guangzhou	Chuang	Zhuangzu	Sinkiang-	
Chefoo (Yentai)	Yantai	Kwangtung	Guangdong	Uighur	Xinjiang Uygur
Chekiang	Zhejiang	Kweichow	Guizhou	Soochow	Suzhou
Chengchow	Zhengzhou	Kweilin	Guilin	Süchow	Xuzhou
Chengtu	Chengdu	Kweiyang	Guiyang	Swatow	Shantou
Chinchow	Jinzhou	Lanchow	Lanzhou	Szechwan	Sichuan
Chungking	Chongqing	Liuchow	Liuzhou	Tachai	Dazhai
Foochow	Fuzhou	Loyang	Luoyang	Tatung	Datong
Fukien	Fujian	Lüta	Dalian	Tibet	Xizang
Hangchow	Hangzhou	Mutankiang	Mudanjiang	Tientsin	Tianjin
Heilungkiang	Heilongjiang	Nanking	Nanjing	Tsinan	Jinan
Honan	Henan	Ningpo	Ningbo	Tsingtao	Qingdao
Hopei	Hebei	Ningsia Hui	Ningxia Huizu	Tsining	Jining
Huhehot	Hohhot	Paoting	Baoding	Tsitsihar	Qiqihar
Hupeh	Hubei	Paotow	Baotou	Tsunyi	Zunyi
Hwainan	Huainan	Penki	Benxi	Tzepo	Zibo
Inner Mongolia	Nei Monggol	Peking	Beijing	Urumchi	Urumqi
Kansu	Gansu	Pengpu	Bengbu	Wusih	Wuxi
Kiangsi	Jiangxi	Shansi	Shanxi	Yenan	Yan'an
Kiangsu	Jiangsu	Shantung	Shandong	Yungpingchuan	Tongchuan
Kingtehchen	Jingdezhen	Shensi	Shaanxi	Yunnan	Yunnan
		Shihkiachwang	Shijiazhuang	Yinchwan	Yinchuan

(continued on following page)

China and Mongolia

SCALE OF MILES
0   100   200   300   400   500

SCALE OF KILOMETERS
0   100   200   300   400   500

Capitals of Countries.....★   International Boundaries _____
Provincial Capitals.........●   Provincial Boundaries..........
Canals..................   Walls.................. ∿∿∿∿∿

† Populations of mainland cities, excluding Peking (Beijing), Shanghai and Tianjin (Tientsin), courtesy of Kingsley Davis, Office of Int'l Pop. and Research, Inst. of Int'l Studies Univ. of California.

● Population of municipality
*City and suburbs

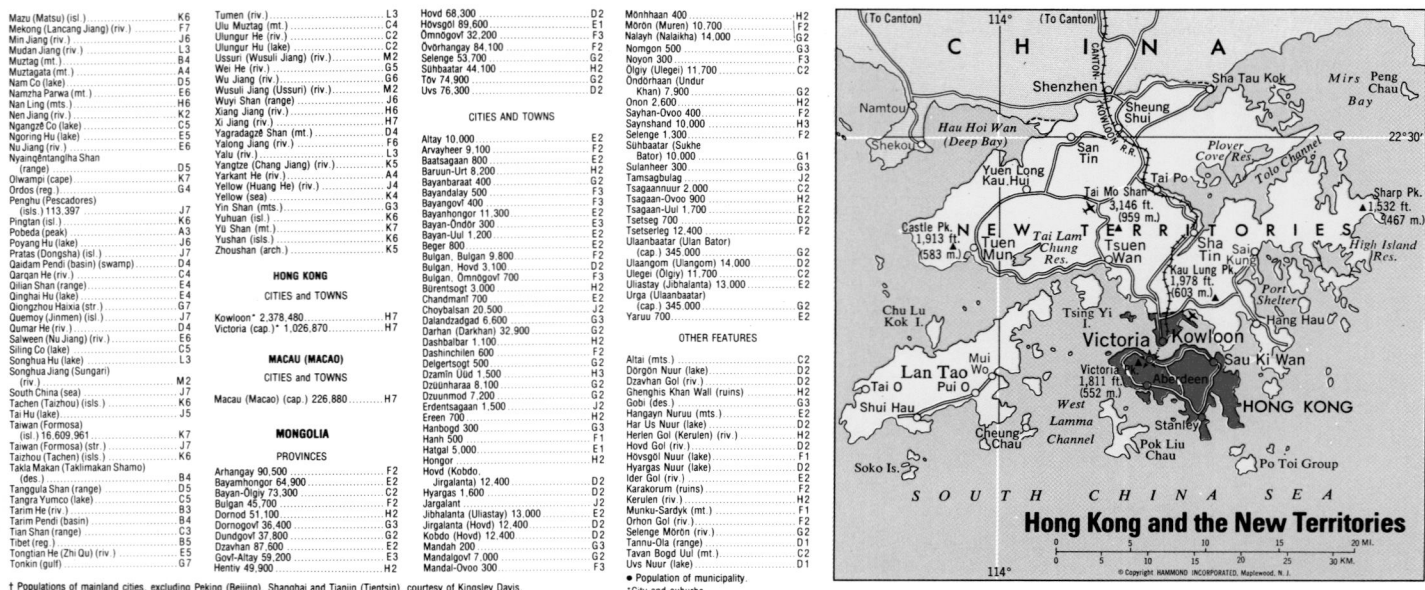

Hong Kong and the New Territories

© Copyright HAMMOND INCORPORATED, Maplewood, N.J.

Agriculture, Industry and Resources

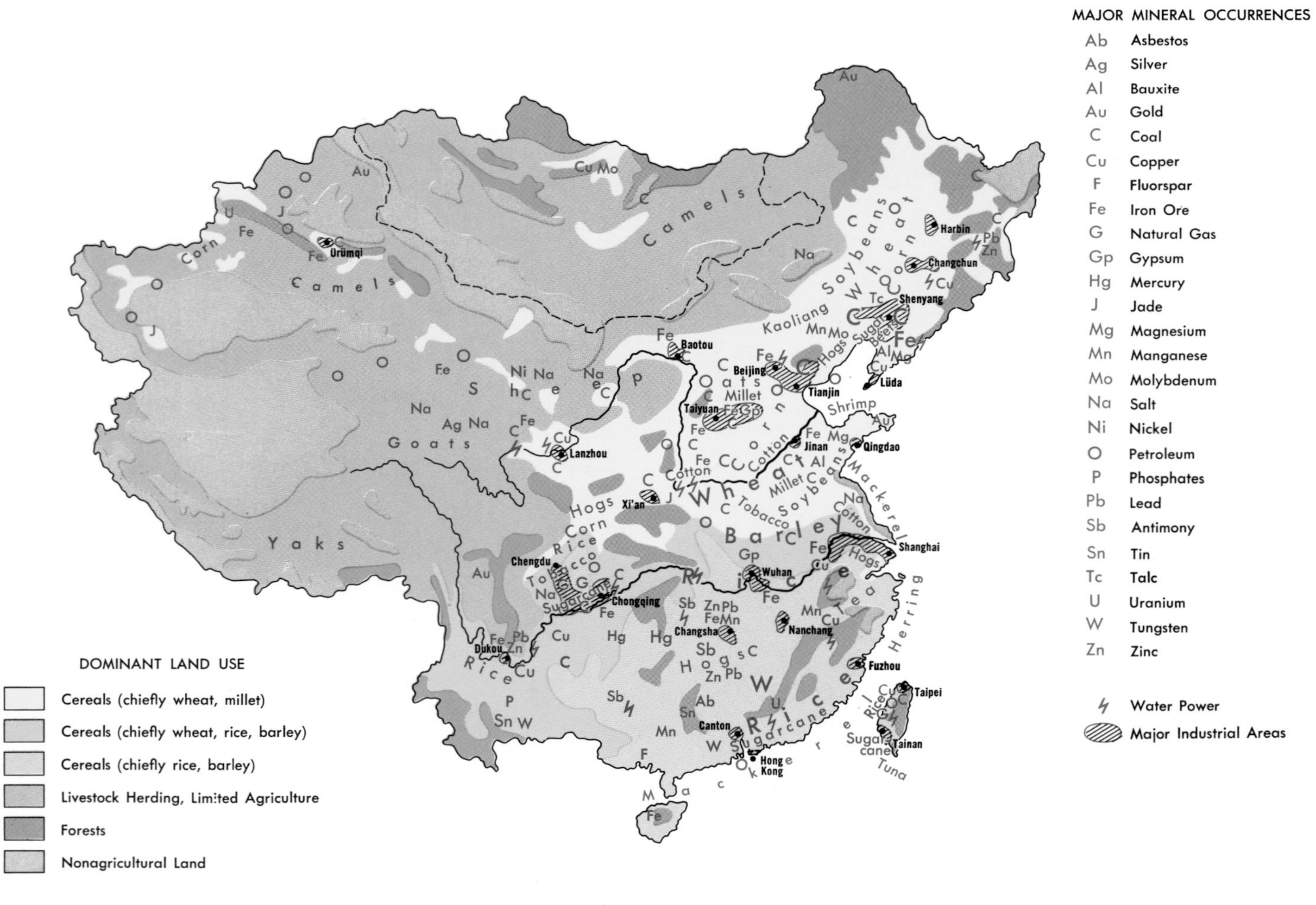

MAJOR MINERAL OCCURRENCES

Ab	Asbestos	
Ag	Silver	
Al	Bauxite	
Au	Gold	
C	Coal	
Cu	Copper	
F	Fluorspar	
Fe	Iron Ore	
G	Natural Gas	
Gp	Gypsum	
Hg	Mercury	
J	Jade	
Mg	Magnesium	
Mn	Manganese	
Mo	Molybdenum	
Na	Salt	
Ni	Nickel	
O	Petroleum	
P	Phosphates	
Pb	Lead	
Sb	Antimony	
Sn	Tin	
Tc	Talc	
U	Uranium	
W	Tungsten	
Zn	Zinc	

⚡ Water Power

▨ Major Industrial Areas

DOMINANT LAND USE

- Cereals (chiefly wheat, millet)
- Cereals (chiefly wheat, rice, barley)
- Cereals (chiefly rice, barley)
- Livestock Herding, Limited Agriculture
- Forests
- Nonagricultural Land

AREA 145,730 sq. mi. (377,441 sq. km.)
POPULATION 117,057,485
CAPITAL Tokyo
LARGEST CITY Tokyo
HIGHEST POINT Fuji 12,389 ft. (3,776 m.)
MONETARY UNIT yen
MAJOR LANGUAGE Japanese
MAJOR RELIGIONS Buddhism, Shintoism

AREA 46,540 sq. mi. (120,539 sq. km.)
POPULATION 17,914,000
CAPITAL P'yŏngyang
LARGEST CITY P'yŏngyang
HIGHEST POINT Paektu 9,003 ft. (2,744 m.)
MONETARY UNIT won
MAJOR LANGUAGE Korean
MAJOR RELIGIONS Confucianism, Buddhism, Ch'ondogyo

AREA 38,175 sq. mi. (98,873 sq. km.)
POPULATION 37,448,836
CAPITAL Seoul
LARGEST CITY Seoul
HIGHEST POINT Halla 6,398 ft. (1,950 m.)
MONETARY UNIT won
MAJOR LANGUAGE Korean
MAJOR RELIGIONS Confucianism, Buddhism, Ch'ondogyo, Christianity

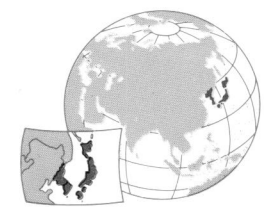

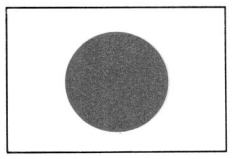

JAPAN

NORTH KOREA

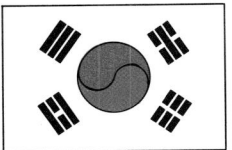

SOUTH KOREA

JAPAN

PREFECTURES

Aichi 5,923,569 ......H6
Akita 1,232,481 ......J4
Aomori 1,468,646 ......K3
Chiba 4,149,147 ......P2
Ehime 1,465,215 ......F7
Fukui 773,599 ......G5
Fukuoka 4,292,963 ......D7
Fukushima 1,970,616 ......K5
Gifu 1,867,978 ......H6
Gumma 1,756,480 ......J5
Hiroshima 2,646,324 ......E6
Hokkaido 5,338,206 ......K2
Hyogo 4,992,140 ......H7
Ibaraki 2,342,198 ......K5
Ishikawa 1,069,872 ......H5
Iwate 1,385,563 ......K4
Kagawa 961,292 ......G6
Kagoshima 1,723,902 ......E8
Kanagawa 6,397,748 ......O2
Kochi 808,397 ......F7
Kumamoto 1,715,273 ......E7
Kyoto 2,424,856 ......J7
Mie 1,626,002 ......H6
Miyagi 1,955,267 ......K4
Miyazaki 1,085,055 ......E8
Nagano 2,017,564 ......J5
Nagasaki 1,571,912 ......D7
Nara 1,077,491 ......J8
Niigata 2,391,938 ......J5
Oita 1,190,314 ......E7
Okayama 1,814,305 ......F6
Okinawa 1,042,572 ......N6
Osaka 8,278,925 ......J8
Saga 837,674 ......E7

Saitama 4,821,340 ......O2
Shiga 985,621 ......J7
Shimane 768,886 ......F6
Shizuoka 3,308,799 ......H6
Tochigi 1,698,003 ......K5
Tokushima 805,166 ......G7
Tokyo 11,673,554 ......O2
Tottori 581,311 ......F6
Toyama 1,070,791 ......H5
Wakayama 1,072,118 ......G6
Yamagata 1,220,302 ......K4
Yamaguchi 1,555,218 ......E6
Yamanashi 783,050 ......J6

CITIES and TOWNS

Abashiri 43,825 ......M1
Ageo 146,358 ......O2
Aikawa 13,546 ......H4
Aizuwakamatsu 108,650 ......J5
Aiigasawa 18,086 ......J3
Akashi 234,905 ......H8
Aki 24,480 ......F7
Akita 261,246 ......K4
Akkeshi 16,778 ......M2
Akune 30,295 ......D7
Amagasaki 545,783 ......H8
Amagi 42,725 ......E7
Anan 60,439 ......G7
Aomori 264,222 ......K3
Asahi 34,028 ......K6
Asahikawa 320,526 ......L2
Ashibetsu 36,520 ......L2
Ashikaga 162,359 ......J5
Ashiya 76,211 ......H8
Atami 51,437 ......J6
Atsugi 108,955 ......O2
Awaji 9,623 ......H8

Ayabe 43,490 ......G6
Beppu 133,894 ......E7
Bibai 38,416 ......L2
Biratori 9,331 ......E6
Chiba 659,356 ......P2
Chichibu 61,798 ......J5
Chigasaki 152,023 ......O3
Chitose 61,031 ......K2
Chofu 175,924 ......K4
Choshi 90,358 ......K6
Daito 110,829 ......J8
Ebetsu 77,624 ......K2
Eniwa 39,884 ......K2
Esashi, Hokkaido 10,172 ......L1
Esashi, Hokkaido 14,409 ......J3
Esashi, Iwate 36,336 ......K4
Fuchu, Hiroshima 50,217 ......F6
Fuchu, Tokyo 182,474 ......O2
Fuji 199,195 ......J7
Fujieda 90,358 ......H6
Fujisawa 265,975 ......O3
Fukagawa 36,000 ......L2
Fukuchiyama 60,003 ......G6
Fukue 32,018 ......D7
Fukui 231,364 ......G5
Fukuoka 1,002,201 ......D7
Fukushima 246,531 ......K5
Fukuyama 329,714 ......E6
Funabashi 423,101 ......P2
Furukawa 54,356 ......K4
Gifu 408,707 ......H6
Gobo 30,272 ......G7
Gose 37,554 ......J8
Gosen 39,376 ......J5
Goshogawara 49,040 ......J3
Gotsu 27,992 ......F6
Habikino 94,160 ......J8
Haboro 13,624 ......K1

Hachinohe 224,366 ......K3
Hachioji 322,580 ......O2
Hadano 103,663 ......O3
Hagi 52,724 ......E6
Hakodate 307,453 ......K3
Hakui 28,726 ......H5
Hamada 50,316 ......E6
Hamamatsu 468,884 ......H6
Hanamaki 65,826 ......K4
Hanno 55,926 ......O2
Haramachi 43,483 ......K5
Hayama 24,026 ......O3
Higashiosaka 524,750 ......J8
Hikone 85,066 ......H6
Himeji 436,086 ......G6
Himi 61,789 ......H5
Hino 126,847 ......O2
Hirakata 297,618 ......J7
Hirata 29,301 ......L7
Hirata 30,942 ......F6
Hiratsuka 195,635 ......O3
Hiroo 11,399 ......L2
Hirosaki 164,911 ......K4
Hiroshima 852,611 ......E6
Hitachi 202,383 ......K5
Hitachiota 35,322 ......K5
Hitoyoshi 41,118 ......E7
Hofu 105,540 ......E6
Hondo 40,437 ......E7
Honjo 40,488 ......J4
Hyuga 53,448 ......E7
Ibaraki 210,286 ......J7
Ibusuki 32,339 ......E8
Ichihara 194,068 ......P3
Ichikawa 319,291 ......P2
Ichinomiya 238,463 ......H6
Ichinoseki 59,122 ......K4

Ide 9,112 ......J7
Iida 77,112 ......H6
Iizuka 75,417 ......E7
Ikeda, Hokkaido 12,306 ......L2
Ikeda, Osaka 100,268 ......H7
Ikoma 48,848 ......J8
Ikuno 6,658 ......G6
Imabari 119,726 ......F6
Imari 60,913 ......D7
Imazu 11,519 ......G6
Ina 54,468 ......H6
Isahaya 73,341 ......D7
Ise 104,957 ......H6
Ishigaki 34,657 ......L7
Ishige 19,220 ......P2
Ishinomaki 115,085 ......K4
Ishioka 43,679 ......K5
Itami 171,978 ......H8
Ito 68,072 ......J7
Itoigawa 36,646 ......H5
Itoman 39,363 ......N7
Iwaizumi 20,219 ......K4
Iwaki 330,213 ......K5
Iwakuni 111,069 ......E6
Iwami 16,063 ......G6
Iwamizawa 72,305 ......L2
Iwanai 25,823 ......K2
Iwasaki 4,437 ......J3
Iwata 67,665 ......H6
Iwatsuki 83,825 ......O2
Iyo 27,805 ......F7
Izuhara 18,460 ......D6
Izumi 118,237 ......J8
Izumiotsu 66,252 ......J8
Izumisano 86,139 ......J8
Izumo 71,568 ......F6
Joetsu 123,418 ......H5
Joyo 58,923 ......J7

Kadoma 143,238 ......J7
Kaga 61,599 ......H5
Kagoshima 456,827 ......E8
Kaizuka 79,506 ......J8
Kakogawa 169,293 ......G6
Kamaishi 68,981 ......L4
Kamakura 165,552 ......O3
Kameoka 58,184 ......J7
Kamisco 27,229 ......K5
Kaminoyama 37,858 ......J4
Kamiyaku 8,668 ......E8
Kamo 8,953 ......J5
Kanazawa 395,263 ......H5
Kanonji 44,131 ......F6
Kanoya 67,951 ......E8
Kanuma 81,799 ......J5
Karatsu 75,224 ......D7
Kaseda 24,969 ......D8
Kashihara 95,701 ......J8
Kashiwa 203,065 ......P2
Kashiwara 63,586 ......J8
Kashiwazaki 80,351 ......J5
Kasugai 213,857 ......H6
Kasukabe 121,639 ......O2
Katsuta 79,996 ......K5
Katsuura 26,755 ......K6
Kawachinagano 66,936 ......J8
Kawagoe 225,465 ......O2
Kawaguchi 345,538 ......O2
Kawanishi 115,773 ......H7
Kawasaki 1,014,951 ......O2
Kesennuma 66,616 ......K4
Kikonai 10,034 ......K3
Kimitsu 76,016 ......O3
Kiryu 134,239 ......J5
Kisarazu 96,840 ......P3
Kishiwada 174,952 ......J8
Kitaibaraki 44,332 ......K5

Kitakami 48,759 ......K4
Kitakata 37,471 ......J5
Kitakyushu 1,058,058 ......E6
Kitami 91,519 ......L2
Kizu 11,890 ......J7
Kobayashi 38,325 ......E8
Kobe 1,360,605 ......H7
Kochi 280,962 ......F7
Kodaira 156,181 ......O2
Kofu 193,879 ......J6
Koga 55,973 ......J5
Koganei 102,714 ......O2
Kokubu 31,660 ......E8
Komagane 30,318 ......H6
Komatsu 100,273 ......H5
Koriyama 264,628 ......K5
Koshigaya 195,917 ......P2
Koyama 16,394 ......E8
Kubohama 17,817 ......F6
Kuji 38,122 ......K3
Kuki 45,797 ......O2
Kumagaya 131,485 ......O2
Kumamoto 488,166 ......E7
Kumano 27,026 ......G7
Kumiyama 11,540 ......J7
Kurashiki 392,755 ......F6
Kurayoshi 50,785 ......F6
Kure 242,655 ......E6
Kuroiso 42,349 ......K5
Kurume 204,474 ......E7
Kushikino 30,456 ......E8
Kushiro 30,038 ......M2
Kushimoto 18,997 ......G7
Kushiro 206,840 ......M2
Kyonan 13,067 ......O3
Kyoto 1,461,059 ......J7
Machida 255,305 ......O2
Maebashi 250,241 ......J5
Maihara 12,845 ......G6
Maizuru 97,780 ......G6
Makubetsu 18,444 ......L2
Makurazaki 29,685 ......D3
Mashike 9,312 ......K2
Masuda 50,734 ......E6
Matsubara 132,662 ......H8
Matsue 127,440 ......F6
Matsumae 18,307 ......J3
Matsumoto 185,595 ......H5
Matsusaka 108,893 ......H6
Matsuto 36,170 ......H5
Matsuyama 367,323 ......F7
Mihara 83,679 ......F6
Miki 53,731 ......H7
Mikuni 21,602 ......G5
Minamata 36,782 ......E7
Minobu 10,345 ......J7
Minoo 79,621 ......J7
Misawa 37,437 ......K3
Mitaka 164,950 ......O2
Mito 197,953 ......K5
Mitsukaido 38,820 ......O2
Miura 47,888 ......O3
Miyako 61,912 ......L4
Miyakonojo 118,289 ......E8
Miyazaki 234,347 ......E8
Miyazu 30,194 ......G6
Miyoshi 37,193 ......F6
Mizusawa 52,266 ......K4
Mobara 64,942 ......K6
Mombetsu 52,825 ......L1
Monbetsu 15,029 ......L2
Mooka 47,345 ......K5
Mori 17,030 ......K2
Moriguchi 178,383 ......J7
Morioka 216,223 ......K4
Motobu 17,823 ......N6
Muko 45,886 ......J7
Murakami 32,939 ......J4
Muroran 158,715 ......K2
Muroto 26,660 ......G7
Musashino 139,508 ......O2
Mutsu 44,646 ......K3
Nachikatsuura 23,596 ......H7
Nagahama, Ehime 13,144 ......F7
Nagahama, Shiga 54,064 ......H6
Nagano 306,637 ......J5
Nagaoka, Kyoto 65,557 ......J7
Nagaoka, Niigata 171,742 ......J5
Nagaokakyo 65,557 ......J7
Nagasaki 450,194 ......D7
Nago 27,327 ......N6
Nago 45,210 ......N6
Nagoya 2,079,740 ......H6
Naha 295,006 ......N6
Nakaminato 33,147 ......K5
Nakamura 34,437 ......F7
Nakasato 14,248 ......K3
Nakatsu 59,111 ......E7
Nanao 49,493 ......H5
Nankoku 42,832 ......F7
Nara 257,538 ......J8
Narashino 117,852 ......P2
Nayoro 35,145 ......L1
Naze 46,359 ......O5
Nemuro 45,817 ......M2
Neyagawa 254,311 ......J7
Nichinan 52,171 ......E8
Niigata 423,188 ......J5
Niihama 131,712 ......F6
Niimi 30,014 ......F6
Niitsu 58,970 ......J5
Nishinomiya 400,622 ......H8

(continued on following page)

Agriculture, Industry and Resources

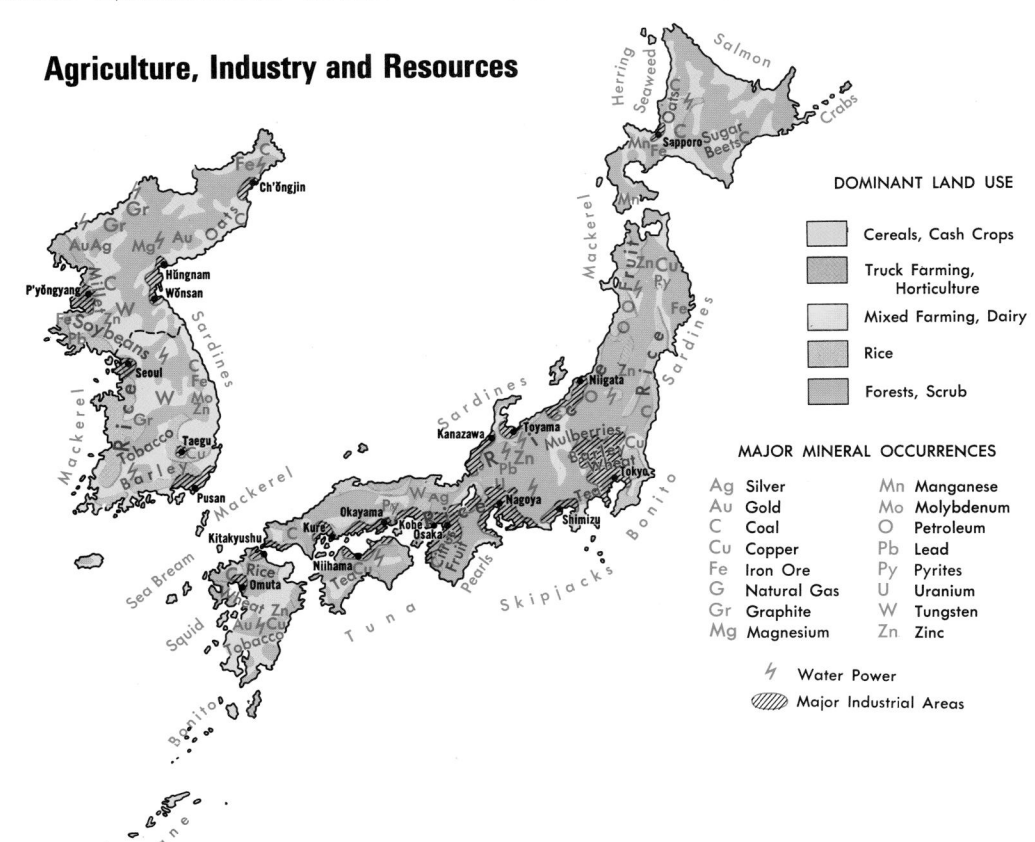

DOMINANT LAND USE

- Cereals, Cash Crops
- Truck Farming, Horticulture
- Mixed Farming, Dairy
- Rice
- Forests, Scrub

MAJOR MINERAL OCCURRENCES

Ag	Silver	Mn	Manganese
Au	Gold	Mo	Molybdenum
C	Coal	O	Petroleum
Cu	Copper	Pb	Lead
Fe	Iron Ore	Py	Pyrites
G	Natural Gas	U	Uranium
Gr	Graphite	W	Tungsten
Mg	Magnesium	Zn	Zinc

⚡ Water Power

▨ Major Industrial Areas

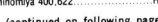

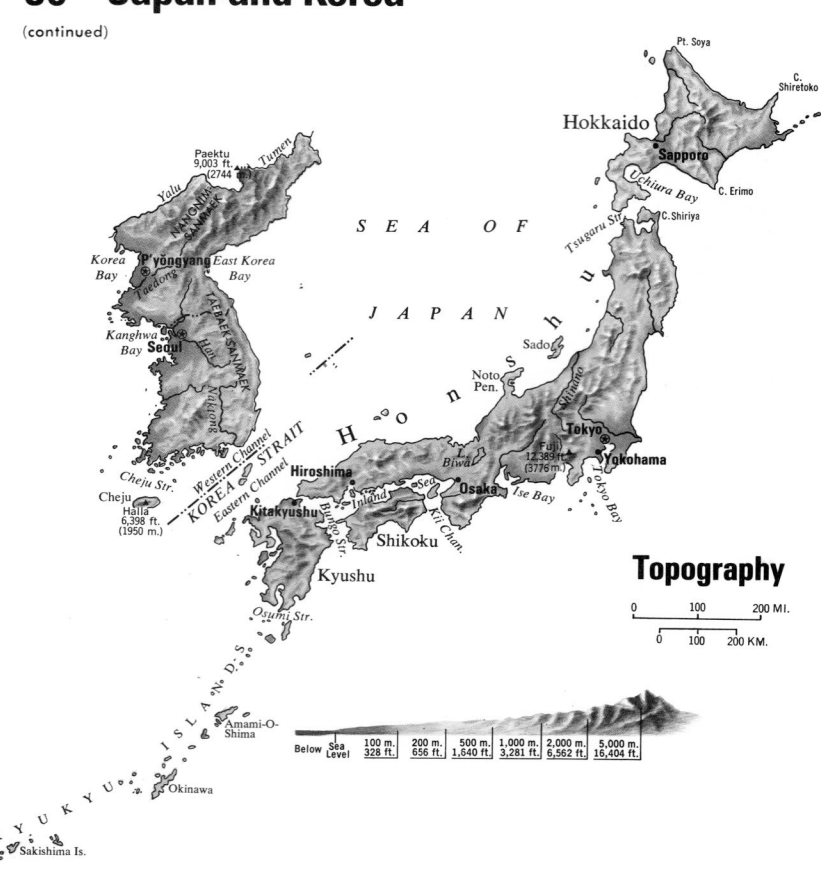

Hokkaido

Sapporo

SEA OF JAPAN

Honshu

Tokyo
Yokohama
Fuji 12,389 ft. (3776 m.)

Hiroshima
Osaka
Shikoku
Kyushu

Yongyang
Seoul

Korea Bay
East Korea Bay

Cheju
Halla 6,398 ft. (1950 m.)

KOREA STRAIT

RYUKYU ISLANDS

Amami-O-Shima

Okinawa

Sakishima Is.

Topography

| Below Sea Level | 100 m. 328 ft. | 200 m. 656 ft. | 500 m. 1,640 ft. | 1,000 m. 3,281 ft. | 2,000 m. 6,562 ft. | 5,000 m. 16,404 ft. |

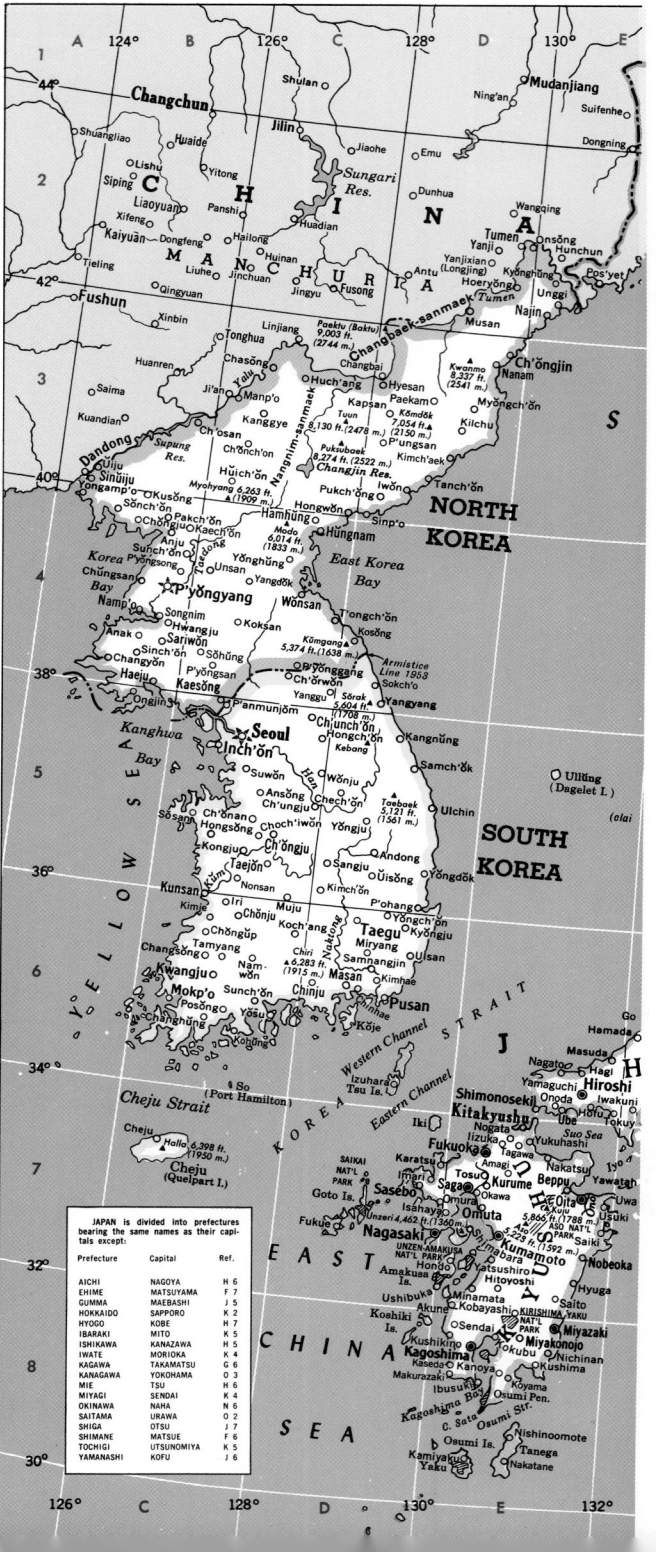

JAPAN is divided into prefectures bearing the same names as their capitals except:

Tarama (isl.) L7
Tazawa (lake) K4
Teshio (mt.) L1
Teshio (riv.) L1
Tobi (isl.) J4
Tokachi (mt.) L2
Tokachi (riv.) L2
Tokara (isls.) O5
Tokuno (isl.) O5
Tokyo (bay) O2
Tone (riv.) K6
Tosa (bay) F7
Towada (lake) K3
Towada-Hachimantai National Park K3
Toya (lake) K2
Toyama (bay) H5
Tsu (isls.) D6
Tsugaru (str.) K3
Tsurugi (mt.) G7
Uchiura (bay) K2
Unzen (mt.) D7
Unzen-Amakusa National Park D7
Volcano (isls.) M4
Wakasa (bay) G6

Yaeyama (isls.) K7
Yaku (isl.) E8
Yodo (riv.) J7
Yonaguni (isl.) K7
Yoron (isl.) N6
Yoshino (riv.) G6
Yoshino-Kumano National Park H7
Zao (mt.) K5

KOREA (NORTH)

CITIES and TOWNS

Ch'ŏngjin 306.000 E3
Chŏngju B4
Haeju 140.000 B4
Hamhŭng 484.000 C4
Hŭngnam C4
Hyesan D3
Hŭich'ŏn C3
Iwŏn D3

Kaech'ŏn B4
Kaesŏng 175.000 C5
Kanggye C3
Kapsan D3
Kilchu D3
Kimch'aek 100.000 D3
Najin E2
Namp'o 140.000 B4
Onsŏng E2
P'anmunjŏm C5
P'yŏngyang (cap.) 1.250.000 C4
Sariwŏn C4
Sinŭiju 300.000 B3
Songnim B4
Wŏnsan 275.000 C4

OTHER FEATURES

Baktu (Paektu) (mt.) C3
Changjin (res.) C3
East Korea (bay) D4
Japan (sea) D4
Kanghwa (bay) B5
Kŏmdŏk (mt.) D3
Kŭmgang (mt.) D4

Kwanmo (mt.) D3
Myohyang (mt.) C4
Nangnim-sanmaek (range) C3
Paektu (mt.) C3
Puksubaek (mt.) C3
Sasu (mt.) B3
Supung (res.) B3
Taedong (riv.) C4
Tumen (riv.) D2
Tuun (mt.) D2
Yalu (riv.) C3
Yellow (sea) B6

KOREA (SOUTH)

CITIES and TOWNS

Andong 95.364 D5
Ansŏng 27.723 C5
Changhŭng 22.227 C6
Changsŏng 26.266 C6
Chech'ŏn 74.239 D5
Cheju 135.081 C7
Chinhae 103.640 D6

Chinju 154.646 D6
Choch'iwŏn 29.198 C5
Chŏngju 46.766 C5
Ch'ŏngju 192.707 C5
Chŏngŭp 54.864 C6
Chŏnju 311.393 C6
Ch'ŏrwŏn 8.180 C4
Ch'unch'ŏn 140.530 D5
Ch'ungju 105.274 C5
Hongch'ŏn 29.499 D5
Hongsŏng 26.995 C5
Inch'ŏn 800.007 C5
Iri 117.155 C6
Kangnŭng 84.981 D5
Kimch'ŏn 67.078 D5
Kimje 221.414 C6
Kimhae 203.428 D6
Koch'ang 23.721 C6
Kohŭng 217.446 C6
Kongju 39.756 C5
Kunsan 154.780 C6
Kwangju 607.011 C6
Kyŏngju 108.431 D6
Masan 371.917 D6
Miryang 42.951 D6

Mokp'o 192.958 C6
Muju 18.130 C6
Namwŏn 50.857 C6
Nonsan 226.429 C5
P'anmunjŏm C5
P'ohang 134.418 D5
Posŏng 20.256 C6
Pusan 2.453.173 D6
Samch'ŏk 42.526 D5
Samnangjin 19.374 D6
Sangju 52.839 D5
Seoul (cap.) 6.889.502 C5
Sŏch'ŏn 71.387 C6
Sŏsan 38.081 C6
Sunch'ŏn 108.063 C6
Suwŏn 224.145 C5
Taegu 1.310.768 D6
Taejŏn 506.708 C5
Tamyang 15.494 C6
Uichŏn 27.607 D5
Ulsan 252.570 D6
Wŏnju 120.276 D5
Yanggu 277.986 C4
Yangyang 10.819 D4

Yŏngch'ŏn 50.765 D6
Yŏngdŏk 18.671 D5
Yŏngju 70.793 D5
Yŏsu 130.623 D6

OTHER FEATURES

Cheju (isl.) C7
Cheju (str.) C7
Chiri (mt.) C6
Dagelet (Ullŏng) (isl.) E5
East China (sea) C8
Halla (mt.) C7
Han (riv.) C5
Japan (sea) G4
Kanghwa (bay) B5
Kebang (mt.) D5
Kŏje (isl.) D6
Korea (str.) D6
Kŭm (riv.) C5
Naktong (riv.) D6
Port Hamilton (So) (isl.) C7
Quelpart (Cheju) (isl.) C7
So (isl.) D6

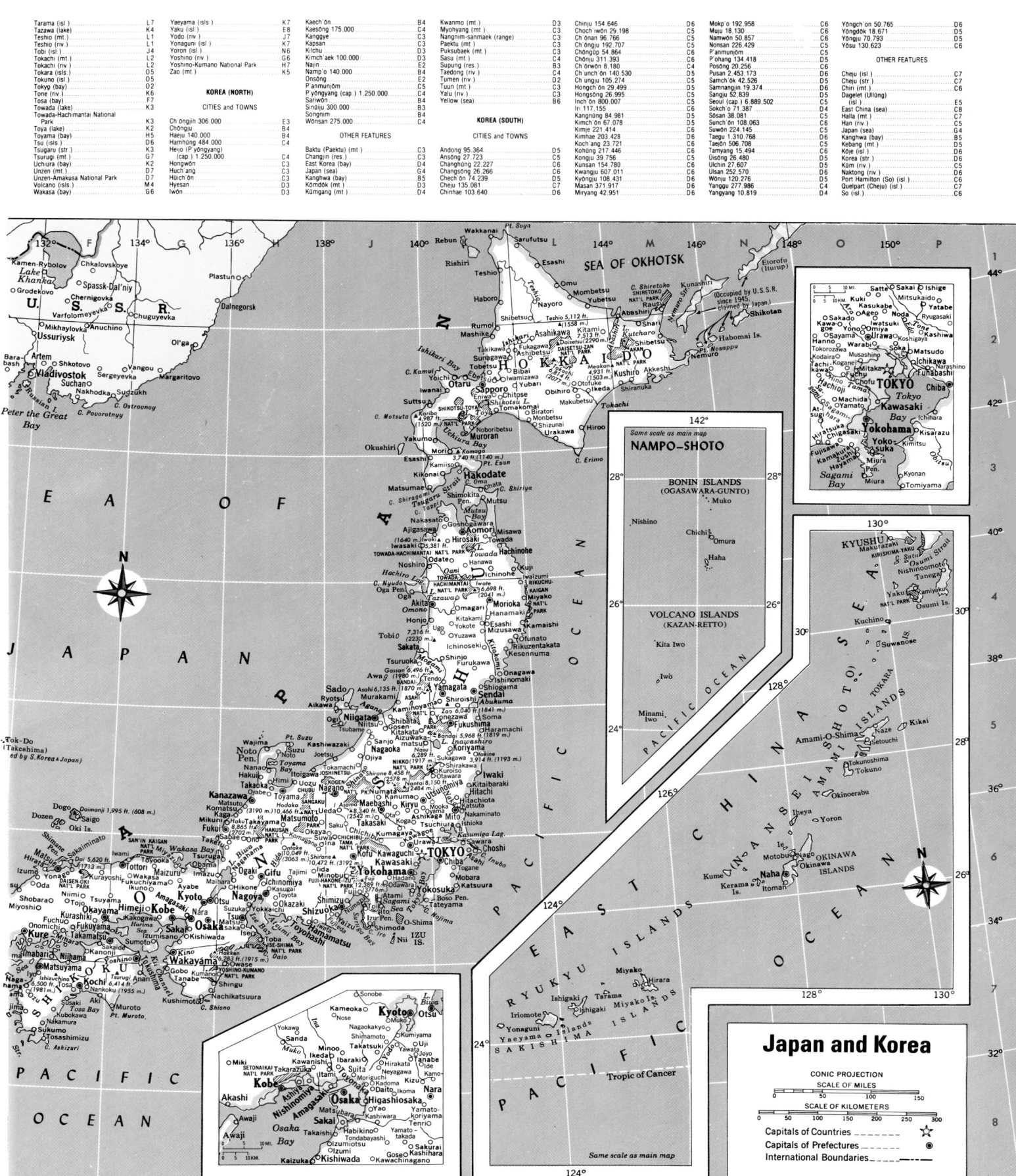

Japan and Korea

CONIC PROJECTION

SCALE OF MILES
0 50 100 150

SCALE OF KILOMETERS
0 50 100 150 200 250 300

Capitals of Countries _____ ☆
Capitals of Prefectures _____ ◉
International Boundaries _____

© Copyright HAMMOND INCORPORATED, Maplewood, N. J.

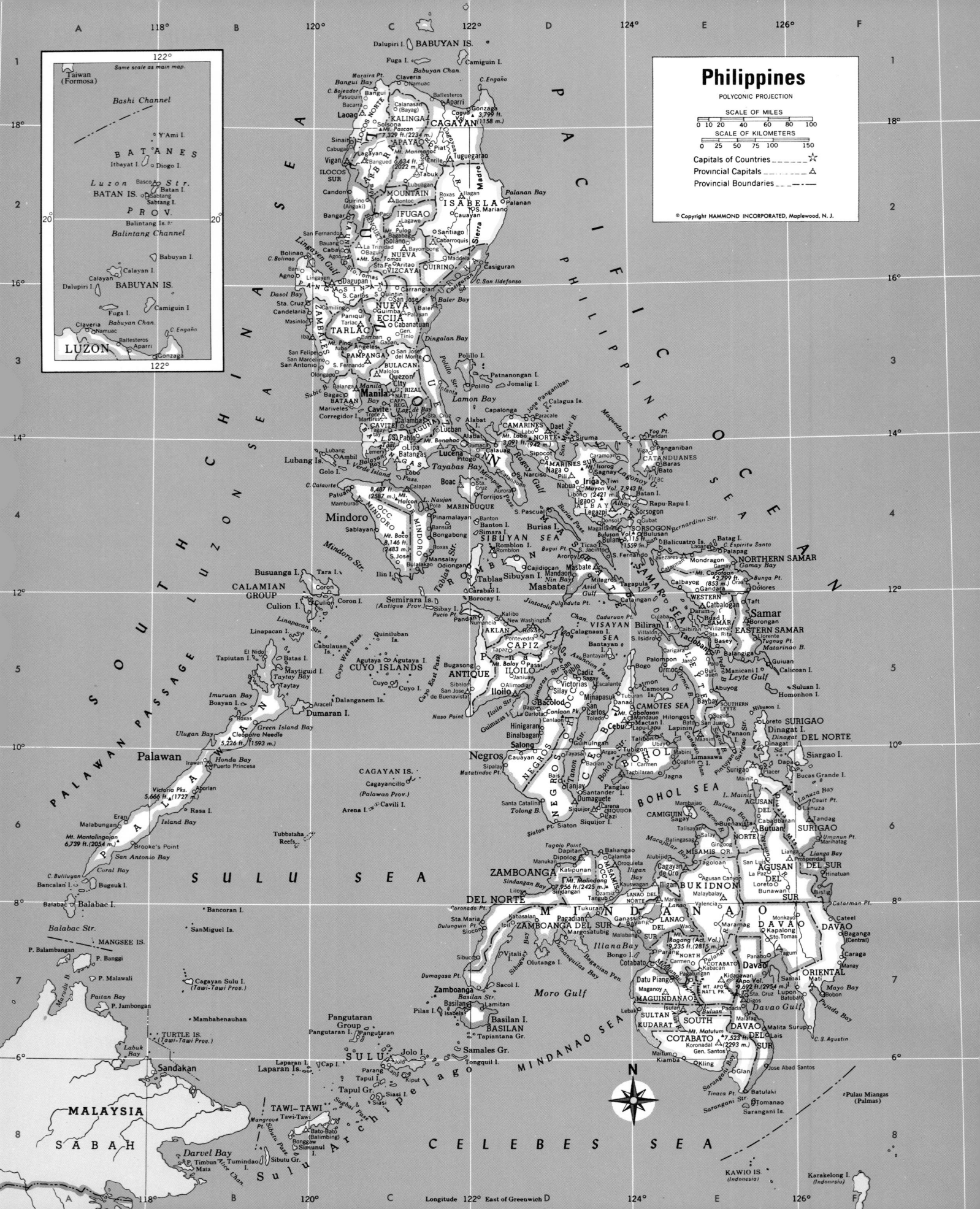

Philippines

POLYCONIC PROJECTION

SCALE OF MILES

0 10 20 40   60   80   100

SCALE OF KILOMETERS

0 25 50 75 100   150

Capitals of Countries _____ ☆
Provincial Capitals _____ △
Provincial Boundaries ____ - ___

© Copyright HAMMOND INCORPORATED, Maplewood, N.J.

Philippines 83

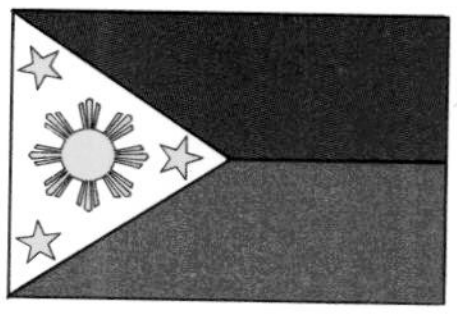

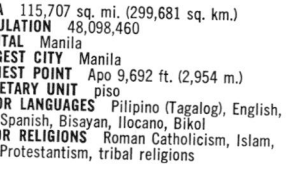

AREA 115,707 sq. mi. (299,681 sq. km.)
POPULATION 48,098,460
CAPITAL Manila
LARGEST CITY Manila
HIGHEST POINT Apo 9,692 ft. (2,954 m.)
MONETARY UNIT piso
MAJOR LANGUAGES Pilipino (Tagalog), English, Spanish, Bisayan, Ilocano, Bikol
MAJOR RELIGIONS Roman Catholicism, Islam, Protestantism, tribal religions

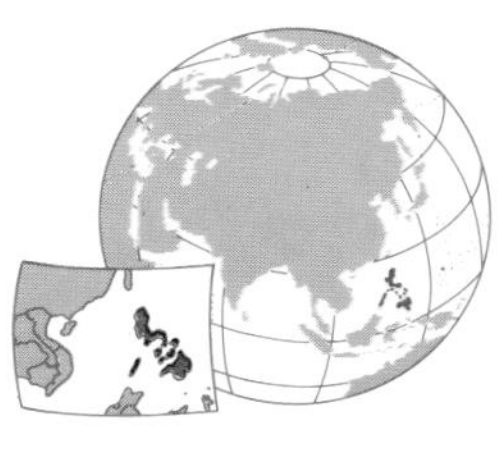

PROVINCES

Abra 160,198 .... C2
Agusan del Norte 365,421 .. E6
Agusan del Sur 631,634 .... E6
Aklan 324,563 .... D5
Albay 809,177 .... D4
Antique 344,879 .... D5
Aurora 107,145 .... C3
Basilan 201,407 .... D7
Bataan 323,254 .... C3
Batanes 12,091 .... A2
Batangas 1,174,201 .... C4
Benguet 354,751 .... C2
Bohol 806,031 .... E6
Bukidnon 631,634 .... E6
Bulacan 1,098,046 .... C3
Cagayan 711,476 .... C1
Camarines Norte 368,007 ... D3
Camarines Sur 1,099,346 .. D4
Camiguin 57,126 .... E6
Capiz 492,231 .... D5
Catanduanes 175,247 ...... E4
Cavite 771,320 .... C3
Cebu 2,091,602 .... D5
Davao 725,153 .... E7
Davao del Sur 1,133,599 ... E7
Davao Oriental 339,931 ..... F7
Eastern Samar 320,637 ..... E5
Ifugao 111,368 .... C2
Ilocos Norte 390,666 .... C1
Ilocos Sur 443,591 .... C2
Iloilo 1,433,641 .... D5
Isabela 870,604 .... C2
Kalinga-Apayao 185,063 .... C1
Laguna 973,104 .... C3
Lanao del Norte 461,049 ... E6
Lanao del Sur 404,971 ..... E7
La Union 452,578 .... C2
Leyte 1,302,648 .... E5
Maguindanao 536,546 ...... E7
Manila 5,925,884 .... C3
Marinduque 173,715 .... C4
Masbate 584,526 .... D4
Misamis Occidental 386,328 D6
Misamis Oriental 690,032 ... E6
Mountain 103,052 .... C2
National Capital Region (Manila) 5,925,884 ...... C3
Negros Occidental 1,930,301 .... D6
Negros Oriental 819,399 ... D6
North Cotabato 564,599 .... E7
Northern Samar 378,516 .... E4
Nueva Ecija 1,069,409 ..... C3
Nueva Vizcaya 241,690 ..... C2
Occidental Mindoro 222,431 C4
Oriental Mindoro 448,938 ... C4
Palawan 371,782 .... B6
Pampanga 1,181,590 ...... C3
Pangasinan 1,636,057 ..... C3
Quezon 1,129,277 .... C3
Quirino 83,230 .... C2
Rizal 555,533 .... C3
Romblon 193,174 .... D4
Siquijor 70,300 .... D6
Sorsogon 500,685 .... E4
South Cotabato 770,473 .... E7
Southern Leyte 298,294 .... E5
Sultan Kudarat 303,784 .... E7
Sulu 360,588 .... C7
Surigao del Norte 363,414 .. F5
Surigao del Sur 377,647 .... F6
Tarlac 638,457 .... C3
Tawi-Tawi 194,651 .... B8
Western Samar 501,439 .... E5
Zambales 444,037 .... C3
Zamboanga del Norte 588,015 .... D6
Zamboanga del Sur 1,183,845 .... D7

CITIES and TOWNS

Angeles 188,834 .... C3
Aparri 45,070 .... C1
Bacolod 262,415 .... D5
Bagac 13,109 .... C3
Bago 99,631 .... D5
Baguio 119,009 .... C2
Balanga 39,132 .... C3
Baler 18,349 .... C3
Balimbing (Bato-Bato) 22,189 .... C8
Bamban 26,072 .... C3
Basco 4,341 .... A2
Batangas 143,570 .... C4
Bato-Bato 22,189 .... C8
Baybay 74,640 .... E5
Bislig 81,615 .... F6
Boac 37,005 .... C4
Bontoc 17,091 .... C2
Burauen 48,058 .... E5
Butuan 172,489 .... E6
Cabanatuan 138,298 .... C3
Cabarroquis 17,450 .... C2
Cadiz 129,632 .... D5
Cagayan de Oro 227,312 ... E6
Calamba 121,175 .... C3
Calbayog 106,719 .... E4
Carigara 34,377 .... E5
Cauayan 70,017 .... D6
Cavite 87,666 .... C3
Cebu 490,281 .... D5
Cotabato 83,871 .... D7
Dagupan 98,344 .... C2
Davao 610,375 .... E7
Digos 70,065 .... E7
Escalante 71,293 .... D5
General Santos 149,396 .... E7
Gingoog 79,937 .... E6
Guihulngan 84,156 .... D5
Guimba 58,847 .... C3
Iba 22,791 .... B3
Ilagan 79,336 .... C2
Iligan 167,358 .... E6
Iloilo 244,827 .... D5
Infanta 27,914 .... C3
Jaro 29,739 .... E5
Jolo 52,429 .... C8
Koronadal 80,566 .... E7
Lagawe 15,075 .... C2
Lapu-Lapu 98,723 .... E5
Legazpi 99,766 .... D4
Ligao 69,860 .... D4
Lingayen 65,187 .... C2
Lipa 121,166 .... C4
Lucena 107,880 .... C4
Maganoy 45,845 .... E7
Mainit 18,078 .... E6
Malabang 18,955 .... D7
Malolos 95,699 .... C3
Mandaue 110,590 .... E5
Manila (cap.) 1,630,485 .... C3
Mariveles 48,594 .... C3
Mati 78,178 .... F7
Naga 90,712 .... D4
Olongapo 156,430 .... C3
Ormoc 104,978 .... E5
Ozamiz 77,832 .... D6
Pagadian 80,861 .... D7
Palo 31,124 .... E5
Palompon 40,242 .... E5
Panabo 71,098 .... E7
Prosperidad 33,824 .... F6
Puerto Princesa 60,234 .... B6
Quezon City 1,165,865 ..... C3
Romblon 24,251 .... D4
Roxas 81,183 .... D5
Sagay 99,118 .... D5
San Antonio 42,969 .... B3
San Carlos, Negros Occ. 91,627 .... D5
San Carlos, Pangasinan 101,243 .... C3
San Fernando, La Union 68,410 .... C2
San Fernando, Pampanga 110,891 .... C3
San Jose 64,254 .... C3
San Jose del Monte 90,732 . C3
San Pablo 131,655 .... C3
Santa Fe 6,338 .... C2
Santiago 69,877 .... C2
Silay 111,131 .... D5
Siquijor 17,533 .... D6
Surigao 79,745 .... E6
Tacloban 102,523 .... E5
Tagaytay 16,322 .... C3
Tagum 86,201 .... E7
Tarlac 175,691 .... C3
Toledo 91,668 .... D5
Tuguegarao 73,507 .... C2
Zamboanga 343,722 .... C7

OTHER FEATURES

Agusan (riv.) E6
Alabat (isl.) D3
Apo (vol.) E7
Babuyan (isl.) B2
Balabac (isl.) A7
Balayan (bay) C4
Balintang (chan.) A2
Baloy (mt.) D5
Bantayan (isl.) D5
Banton (isl.) D4
Bashi (chan.) A1
Basilan (isl.) D7
Batan, Albay (isl.) E4
Batan, Batanes (isl.) B2
Batan (isls.) A2
Bay, Laguna de (lake) C3
Biliran (isl.) E5
Bohol (isl.) E6
Bojeador (cape) C1
Borocay (isl.) D5
Bucas Grande (isl.) F6
Bugsuk (isl.) A6
Buliluyan (cape) A6
Bunga (pt.) E4
Burias (isl.) D4
Busuanga (isl.) B4
Cabalasan (mt.) E5
Cabulauan (isls.) C5
Cagayan (isls.) C6
Cagayan (riv.) C2
Cagayan Sulu (isl.) B7
Cagua (vol.) D1
Calagua (isls.) D3
Calamian Group (isls.) B4
Calayan (isl.) A2
Calicoan (isl.) E5
Camiguin, Cagayan (isl.) ... B3
Camiguin, Camiguin (isl.) ... E6
Camotes (isls.) E5
Camotes (sea) E5
Canigao (chan.) E5
Canlaon (peak) D5
Capotoan (mt.) E4
Carabao (isl.) D4
Catanduanes (isl.) E4
Cebu (isl.) D5
Celebes (sea) D8
Cleopatra Needle (mt.) B5
Coron (isl.) C5
Corregidor (isl.) C3
Culion (isl.) B5
Cuyo (isl.) C5
Cuyo (isls.) C5
Daram (isl.) E5
Davao (gulf) E7
Dinagat (isl.) E5
Diuata (mts.) E6
Dumanquilas (bay) D7
Dumaran (isl.) C5
Engaño (cape) D1
Espiritu Santo (cape) E4
Fuga (isl.) A3
Guimaras (isl.) D5
Halcon (mt.) C4
Hibuson (isl.) E5
Homonhon (isl.) E5
Honda (bay) B6
Iligan (bay) E6
Ilin (isl.) C4
Illana (bay) D7
Imuruan (bay) B5
Island (bay) B6
Itbayat (isl.) A2
Jintotolo (chan.) D5
Jolo (isl.) C7
Jomalig (isl.) D3
Lagonoy (gulf) E4
Lamon (bay) C3
Lanao (lake) E7
Laparan (isls.) B8
Lapinin (isl.) E5
Leyte (gulf) E5
Leyte (isl.) E5
Limasawa (isl.) E6
Linapacan (isl.) B5
Lingayen (gulf) C2
Lubang (isls.) B4
Luzon (isl.) C3
Luzon (str.) A2
Macajalar (bay) E6
Malindang (mt.) D6
Mangsee (isls.) A7
Manila (bay) C3
Mantalingajan (mt.) A6
Maqueda (chan.) D3
Maraira (pt.) C1
Marinduque (isl.) C4
Masbate (isl.) D4
Mayon (vol.) D4
Maytiguid (isl.) B5
Mindanao (isl.) D7
Mindanao (riv.) E7
Mindoro (isl.) C4
Mindoro (str.) C4
Mompog (passg.) D4
Moro (gulf) D7
Mount Apo National Park ... E7
Naso (pt.) C5
Negros (isl.) D6
Olutanga (isl.) D7
Pacsan (mt.) C2
Palawan (isl.) B6
Palawan (passg.) A6
Panaon (isl.) E5
Panay (isl.) D5
Panglao (isl.) D6
Pangutaran (isl.) C7
Pangutaran Group (isls.) ... C7
Patnanongan (isl.) D3
Philippine (sea) D3
Pilas (isl.) C7
Pinatubo (mt.) C3
Polillo (isl.) C3
Pujada (bay) F7
Pulangi (riv.) E7
Ragang (vol.) E7
Ragay (gulf) D4
Rapu-Rapu (isl.) E4
Romblon (isl.) D4
Sabtang (isl.) B2
Sacol (isl.) D7
Samal (isl.) E7
Samales Group (isls.) D7
Samar (isl.) E5
Samar (sea) E4
San Agustin (cape) F7
San Bernardino (str.) E4
San Miguel (bay) D3
San Pedro (bay) E5
Santo Tomas (mt.) C2
Semirara (isls.) C5
Siargao (isl.) F6
Sibay (isl.) C5
Sibuguey (bay) D7
Sibutu Group (isls.) B8
Sibuyan (isl.) D4
Sibuyan (sea) D4
Sierra Madre (mt.) D2
Simunul (isl.) B8
Siquijor (isl.) D6
South China (sea) B3
Subic (bay) C3
Sulu (arch.) B8
Sulu (sea) B6
Suluan (isl.) F5
Surigao (str.) E6
Taal (lake) C4
Tablas (isl.) D4
Tablas (str.) C4
Tagapula (isl.) E4
Tagolo (pt.) D6
Tanon (str.) D6
Tapul (isl.) C8
Tapul Group (isls.) C8
Tara (isl.) C4
Tawi-Tawi (isl.) B8
Tayabas (bay) C4
Ticao (isl.) D4
Tinaca (pt.) E8
Tongquil (isl.) D8
Tumindao (isl.) B8
Turtle (isls.) B7
Verde Island (passg.) C4
Victoria (peaks) B6
Visayan (sea) D5

Topography

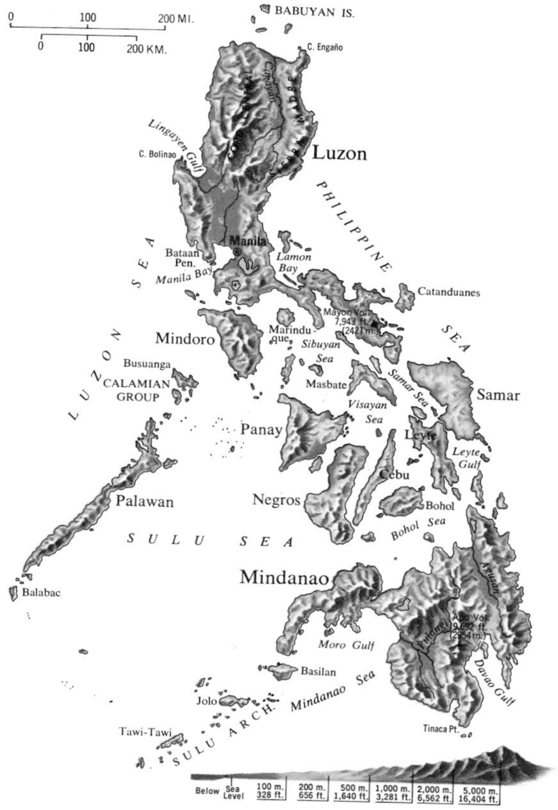

0 100 200 MI.
0 100 200 KM.
BABUYAN IS.
C. Engaño
Lingayen Gulf
C. Bolinao
Luzon
PHILIPPINE
Manila
Bataan Pen.
Manila Bay
Lamon Bay
Catanduanes
Mayon Vol.
Mindoro
Marinduque
Sibuyan Sea
Busuanga
CALAMIAN GROUP
Masbate
Samar Sea
Samar
SEA
LUZON SEA
Visayan Sea
Panay
Leyte
Leyte Gulf
Cebu
Palawan
Negros
Bohol
Bohol Sea
SULU SEA
Mindanao
Balabac
Moro Gulf
Basilan
Jolo
Mindanao Sea
Davao Gulf
Tawi-Tawi
SULU ARCH.
Tinaca Pt.
Below Sea Level
100 m. 328 ft.
200 m. 656 ft.
500 m. 1,640 ft.
1,000 m. 3,281 ft.
2,000 m. 6,562 ft.
5,000 m. 16,404 ft.

Agriculture, Industry and Resources

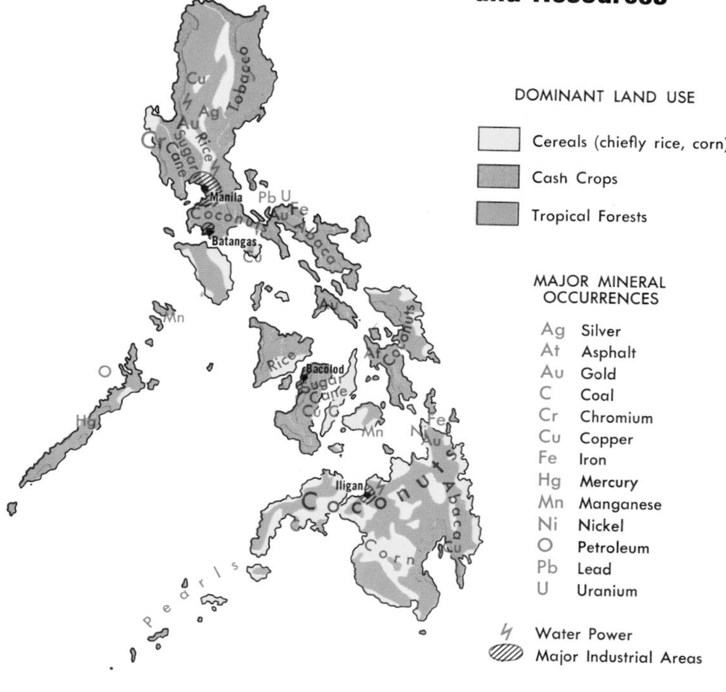

Tobacco
Cu
Ag
Au
Cr
Sugar Cane
Rice
Manila
Pb U
Coconuts
Fe
Batangas
Mn
Rice
Bacolod
Sugar Cane
Cu
Mn
Ni
Fe
Iligan
Coconuts
Abaca
Corn
Hg
Pearls
DOMINANT LAND USE
Cereals (chiefly rice, corn)
Cash Crops
Tropical Forests
MAJOR MINERAL OCCURRENCES
Ag Silver
At Asphalt
Au Gold
C Coal
Cr Chromium
Cu Copper
Fe Iron
Hg Mercury
Mn Manganese
Ni Nickel
O Petroleum
Pb Lead
U Uranium
Water Power
Major Industrial Areas

BRUNEI

CITIES and TOWNS

Bandar Seri Begawan 63,868 .....E4
Seria 23,511 ....E5

INDONESIA

CITIES and TOWNS

Adaut J7
Agats K7
Ambon (Amboina) 208,898 ..H6
Amuntai F6
Amurang G5
Atambua H7
Aubâ H7
Baa G8
Bagansiapiapi C5
Balikpapan 280,675 ....F6
Banda Aceh 72,090 ....A4
Bandanaira H6
Bandung 1,462,637 ....H2
Banggai G6
Banjarmasin 381,286 ......F6
Banyumas J2
Batang J2
Batavia (Jakarta) (cap.)
  6,503,449 ....H1
Baukau H7
Bekasi H2
Belawan B5
Bengkulu 64,783 ....C6
Beo H5
Biak K6
Binjai 76,464 ....B5
Bintuhan C6
Blitar 78,503 ....K2
Bogor 247,409 ....H2
Bojonegoro J2
Bukittinggi 70,771 ....B6
Bula J6
Bulukumba G7
Buntok E6
Cianjur H2
Cimahi H2
Cirebon 223,776 ....H2
Demta L6
Denpasar E7
Dili H7
Djambi (Jambi) 230,373 ....C6
Djokjakarta (Yogyakarta)
  398,727 ....J2
Dobo J7
Donggala F6
Enarotoli K6
Ende G7
Fakfak J6
Garut H2

Gorontalo 97,628 ....G5
Hollandia (Jayapura) K6
Indramayu H2
Jailolo H5
Jakarta (cap.) 6,503,449 ..H1
Jambi 230,373 ....C6
Jayapura (Hollandia) K6
Jogjakarta (Yogyakarta)
  398,727 ....J2
Jombang K2
Kaimana J6
Kampung Baru (Tolitoli) ...G5
Kediri 221,820 ....K2
Kendari G6
Kepi K7
Ketapang E6
Kokonau K6
Kolonodale G6
Kotabaru F6
Kotabaru E6
Kotawaringin E6
Kragen K2
Kupang G8
Kutaraja (Banda Aceh)
  72,090 ....A4
Labuha H6
Labuhan G2
Laiwui H6
Larantuka G7
Lekitobi G6
Longiram F5
Madiun 150,562 ....K2
Magelang 123,484 ....J2
Majalengka H2
Makassar (Ujung Pandang)
  709,038 ....F7
Malang 511,780 ....G6
Malili G6
Manado 217,159 ....G5
Manokwari J6
Maumere G7
Medan 1,378,955 ....B5
Menggala D6
Merauke K7
Mindiptana L7
Mojokerto 68,849 ....K2
Muarasiberut B6
Nangatayap E6
Pacitan J2
Padang 480,922 ....B6
Padangpanjang 34,517 .....B6
Padangsidempuan B5
Pakanbaru 186,262 ....C5
Palangkaraya 60,447 ......E6
Palembang 787,187 ....D6
Pangkalanbuun E6
Pangkalpinang 90,096 .....D6
Parepare 86,450 ....F7
Pasangkayu F6
Pasuruan 95,864 ....K2

Payakumbuh 78,836 ....C6
Pekalongan 132,558 ....J2
Pemalang J2
Pematangsiantar 150,376 ..B5
Pinrang F6
Plaju D6
Pontianak 304,778 ....D6
Probolinggo 100,296 ......K2
Purbolinggo J2
Raha G6
Rantauprapat C5
Rembang K2
Sabang, Celebes F5
Sabang, Weh 23,821 ....B4
Salatiga 85,849 ....J2
Samarinda 264,718 ....F6
Sampit E6
Sarmi K6
Sawahlunto 13,561 ....C6
Seba G8
Semarang 1,026,671 ....J2
Semitau E5
Serui K6
Sibolga 59,897 ....B5
Sigli B4
Singaraja F7
Solo (Surakarta) 469,888 ..J2
Solok 31,724 ....C6
Sorong J6
Sragen J2
Subang H2
Sukabumi 109,994 ....H2
Sumbawa Besar F7
Sumedang H2
Surabaya 2,027,913 ....K2
Surakarta 469,888 ....J2
Tanahmerah K7
Tanjungbalai 41,894 ......C5
Tanjungkarang 284,275 .....D7
Tanjungpinang C5
Tanjungselor F5
Tarakan F5
Tebingtinggi 92,087 ......B5
Tegal 131,728 ....J2
Telukbayur C6
Tepa H7
Terempa D5
Tjilatjap (Cilacap) J2
Tjirebon (Cirebon) 223,776 .H2
Tolitoli G5
Tuban K2
Ujung Pandang 709,038 ....F7
Vikeke H7
Wahai H6
Waigama H6
Wajabula H5
Waren K6
Weda H5
Wonreli H7

Yogyakarta 398,727 ....J2

OTHER FEATURES

Anambas (isls.) 29,572· ...C6
Arafura (sea) J8
Aru (isls.) 34,195 ....K7
Babar (isl.) H7
Bali (isl.) 2,074,438 .....F7
Banda (sea) H7
Banggai (arch.) 169,025 ...G6
Bangka (isl.) 298,017 .....D6
Banyak (isl.) 1,980 ......B5
Barisan (mts.) B6
Barito (riv.) E6
Batu (isls.) 16,390 ......B6
Bawean (isl.) 64,551 .....K1
Belitung (Billiton) (isl.)
  128,694 ....D6
Berau (bay) J6
Biak (isl.) K6
Billiton (isl.) 128,694 ...D6
Binongko (isl.) 11,549 ....G7
Bone (gulf) F6
Borneo (isl.) E5
Bosch, van den (cape) J6
Bunguran (Great Natuna)
  (isl.) D5
Buru (isl.) 23,034 ....H6
Butung (isl.) 188,173 .....G6
Celebes (Sulawesi) (isl.)
  7,732,383 ....G6
Celebes (sea) G5
Cenderawasih (bay) J6
Dampier (str.) J6
Digul (riv.) L7
Doberai (pen.) J6
Enggano (isl.) 1,082 ......C7
Ewab (Kai) (isls.) 108,328 .J7
Flores (isl.) 860,328 .....G7
Flores (sea) F7
Frederik Hendrik (Kolepom)
  (isl.) K7
Geelvink (Cenderawasih)
  (bay) K6
Great Kai (isl.) 38,748 ...J7
Halmahera (isl.) 122,521 ..H5
Irian Jaya (reg.) 923,440 ..J6
Jambuair (cape) B4
Jamursba (cape) J5
Java (head) C7
Java (isl.) 73,712,411 ....J2
Java (sea) D6
Jaya, Puncak (mt.) J6
Jayawijaya (range) K7
Jemaja (isl.) 5,628 ......D5
Kabaena (isl.) G7
Kai (isls.) 108,328 ......J7
Kalao (isl.) G7
Kalaotoa (isl.) G5

Kalimantan (reg.) 4,956,865 .E5
Kangean (isl.) F7
Kapuas (riv.) D6
Karakelong (isl.) H5
Karimata (arch.) 9,398 ....D6
Karimunjawa (isls.) 5,025 ..J1
Kerinci (mt.) C6
Kisar (isl.) H7
Komodo (isl.) 30,407 .....F7
Krakatau (Rakata) (isl.) ..C7
Laut (isl.) 55,711 ....F6
Leuser (mt.) B5
Lingga (arch.) 46,658 .....D5
Lingga (isl.) 18,027 .....D6
Lombok (isl.) 1,581,193 ...F7
Madura (isl.) 1,509,774 ...K2
Mahakam (riv.) F6
Makassar (str.) F6
Malacca (str.) B5
Mamberamo (riv.) K6
Maoke (mts.) K6
Mapia (isls.) J5
Mentawai (isls.) 30,107 ...B6
Misool (isl.) J6
Molucca (sea) H6
Moluccas (isls.) 944,240 ..H6
Morotai (isl.) 27,333 .....H5
Muli (str.) K7
Müller (mts.) E5
Muna (isl.) 156,186 ......G7
Musi (riv.) C6
Natuna (isls.) 23,893 .....D5
Ngunju (cape) F8
Nias (isl.) 356,093 ......B5
Numfoor (isl.) J6
Obi (isls.) 12,437 ....H6
Ombai (str.) H7
Pantar (isl.) 28,259 .....G7
Perkam (cape) K6
Puting, Borneo (cape) E6
Puting, Sumatra (cape) C7
Raja Ampat Group (isls.) ..H6
Rakata (isl.) C7
Rantekombola (mt.) F6
Raya (mt.) E6
Riau (arch.) 483,230 ......C5
Rokan (riv.) C5
Roti (isl.) 76,270 ....G8
Salawati (isl.) J6
Sangihe (isl.) H5
Sangihe (isls.) 183,000 ...G5
Sawu (isl.) 51,002 ....G8
Sawu (sea) G7
Schouten (isls.) 110,148 ..K6
Schwaner (mts.) E6
Sebuku (bay) F5
Selatan (cape) E6
Selayar (isl.) 92,342 .....G7
Semeru (mt.) K2
Siau (isl.) 46,801 ....H5

Siberut (str.) B6
Simeulue (isl.) 29,147 ....A5
Singkep (isl.) 28,631 .....D6
Sipura (isl.) 6,051 ......B6
Slamet (mt.) J2
Sorikmerapi (mt.) B5
South Natuna (isls.) D5
Sudirman (range) K6
Sula (isls.) 36,922 ......H6
Sulawesi (isl.) 7,732,383 ..G6
Sumatra (isl.) 19,360,400 ..B5
Sumba (isl.) 291,190 ......F7
Sumba (str.) F7
Sumbawa (isl.) 621,140 ....F7
Sunda (str.) C7
Tahulandang (isl.) 21,493 ..H5
Talaud (isl.) 46,395 .....H5
Taliabu (isl.) 18,303 ....G6
Tambelan (isls.) 4,032 ....D5
Tanimbar (isls.) 55,405 ...J7
Tariku (riv.) K6
Tidore (isl.) 28,655 .....H5
Timor (reg.) 1,435,527 ....H7
Timor (sea) H8
Toba (lake) B5
Tolo (gulf) G6
Tomini (gulf) G6
Tukangbesi (isls.) 73,106 ..G7
Vals (cape) K7
Vogelkop (Doberai) (pen.) ..J6
Waigeo (isl.) J5

Wakde (isl.) K6
Wangiwangi (isl.) 28,469 ..G7
We (isl.) B4
Wetar (isl.) H7
Yapen (isl.) 50,888 ......K6

MALAYSIA

STATES

North Borneo (Sabah)
  1,002,608 ....F3
Sarawak 1,294,753 ....E5

CITIES and TOWNS

Beaufort 2,709 ....F4
Bintulu 4,424 ....E5
Kabong E5
Kampong Sibuti E5
Kapit 1,929 ....E5
Keningau 2,037 ....F4
Kota Kinabalu 40,939 .....F4
Kuching 63,535 ....E5
Kudat 5,089 ....F4
Labuan 7,216 ....F4
Lahad Datu 5,169 ....F5
Lamag F4
Marudi 4,700 ....E5
Miri 35,702 ....E5
Mukah 1,717 ....E5

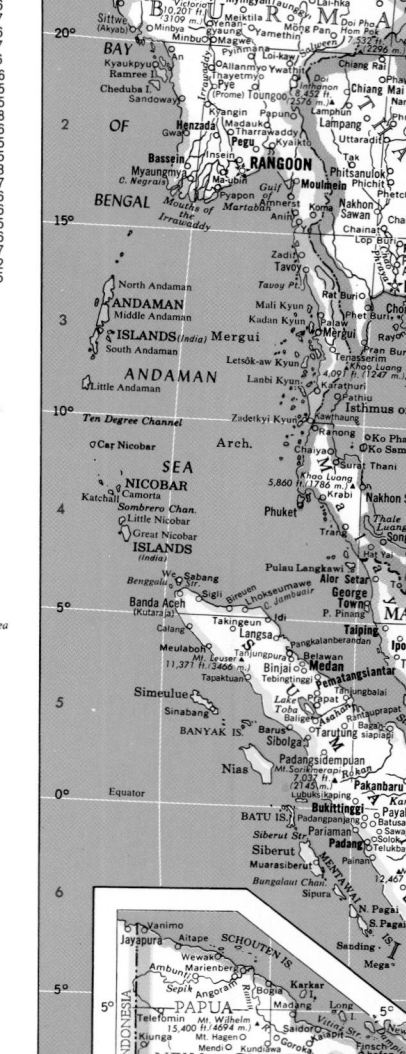

Topography

0   300   600 MI.

0   300   600 KM.

Agriculture, Industry and Resources

DOMINANT LAND USE

Cereals (chiefly rice, corn)

Diversified Tropical Crops

Forests

MAJOR MINERAL OCCURRENCES

Al Bauxite   Cu Copper   Mn Manganese   O Petroleum
Au Gold   Fe Iron Ore   Ni Nickel   Sn Tin
C   Coal   G   Natural Gas

Major Industrial Areas

INDONESIA

AREA 788,430 sq. mi. (2,042,034 sq. km.)
POPULATION 147,490,298
CAPITAL Jakarta
LARGEST CITY Jakarta
HIGHEST POINT Puncak Jaya 16,503 ft. (5,030 m.)
MONETARY UNIT rupiah
MAJOR LANGUAGES Bahasa Indonesia, Indonesian and Papuan languages, English
MAJOR RELIGIONS Islam, tribal religions, Christianity, Hinduism

PAPUA NEW GUINEA

AREA 183,540 sq. mi. (475,369 sq. km.)
POPULATION 3,010,727
CAPITAL Port Moresby
LARGEST CITY Port Moresby
HIGHEST POINT Mt. Wilhelm 15,400 ft. (4,694 m.)
MONETARY UNIT kina
MAJOR LANGUAGES pidgin English, Hiri Motu, English
MAJOR RELIGIONS Tribal religions, Christianity

BRUNEI

AREA 2,226 sq. mi. (5,765 sq. km.)
POPULATION 192,832
CAPITAL Bandar Seri Begawan
LARGEST CITY Bandar Seri Begawan
HIGHEST POINT Pagon 6,070 ft. (1,850 m.)
MONETARY UNIT Brunei Dollar
MAJOR LANGUAGES Malay, English, Chinese
MAJOR RELIGIONS Islam, Buddhism, Christianity, tribal religions

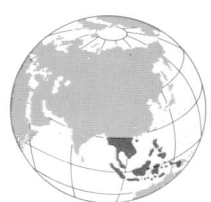

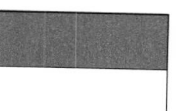

INDONESIA

PAPUA NEW GUINEA

BRUNEI

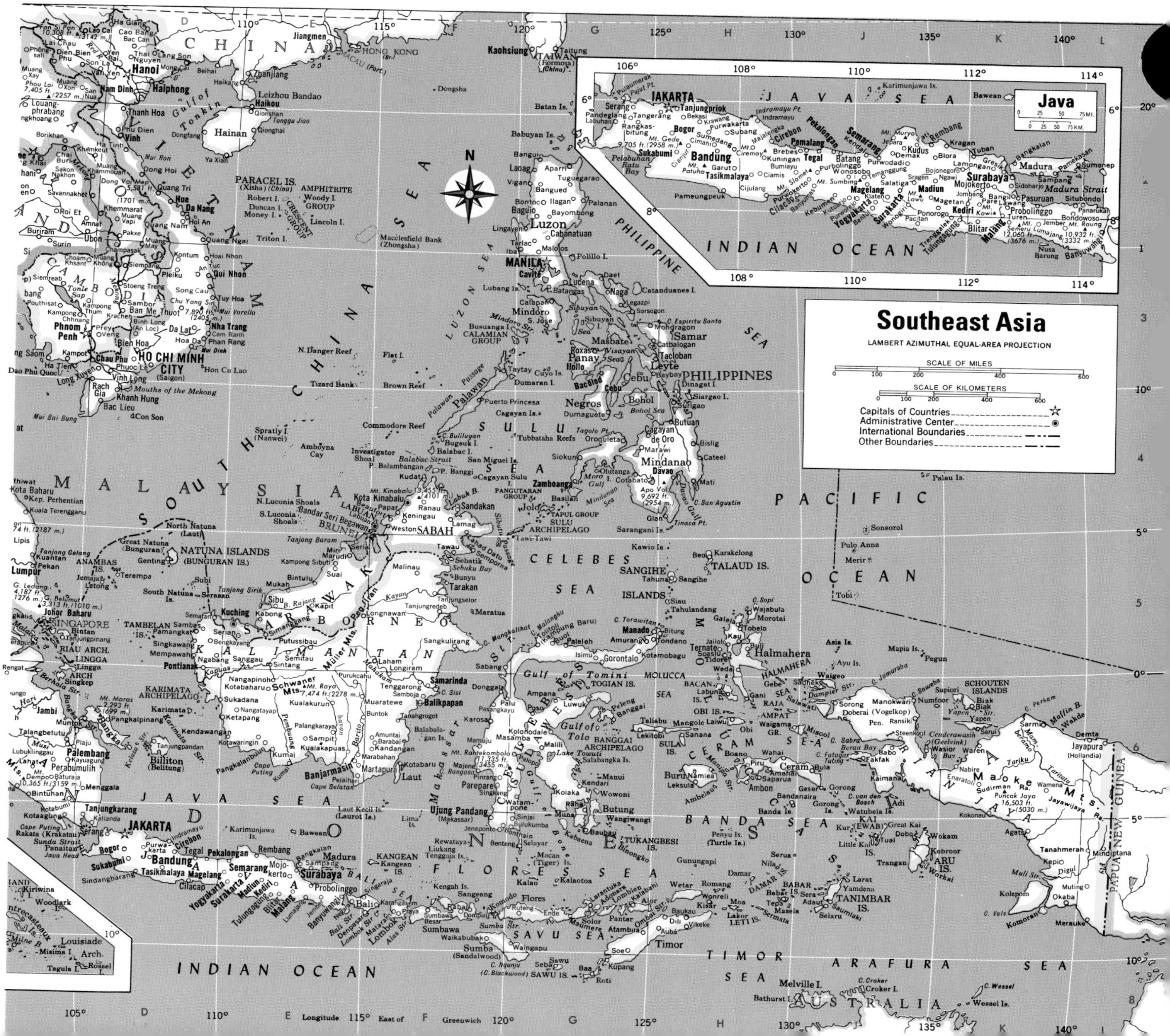

Java

Southeast Asia

LAMBERT AZIMUTHAL EQUAL-AREA PROJECTION

SCALE OF MILES
0   100   200   300   400   500

SCALE OF KILOMETERS
0   100   200   300   400   500   600

Capitals of Countries _____ ☆
Administrative Center _____ ◉
International Boundaries _____ ▬ ▬ ▬
Other Boundaries _____ ▬ ▬ ▬

FIJI

AREA 7,055 sq. mi. (18,272 sq. km.)
POPULATION 588,068
CAPITAL Suva
LARGEST CITY Suva
HIGHEST POINT Tomaniivi 4,341 ft.
(1,323 m.)
MONETARY UNIT Fijian dollar
MAJOR LANGUAGES Fijian, Hindi, English
MAJOR RELIGIONS Protestantism, Hinduism

KIRIBATI

AREA 291 sq. mi. (754 sq. km.)
POPULATION 56,213
CAPITAL Bairiki (Tarawa)
HIGHEST POINT (on Banaba I.) 285 ft. (87 m.)
MONETARY UNIT Australian dollar
MAJOR LANGUAGES I-Kiribati, English
MAJOR RELIGIONS Protestantism, Roman
Catholicism

NAURU

AREA 7.7 sq. mi. (20 sq. km.)
POPULATION 7,254
CAPITAL Yaren (district)
MONETARY UNIT Australian dollar
MAJOR LANGUAGES Nauruan, English
MAJOR RELIGION Protestantism

SOLOMON ISLANDS

AREA 11,500 sq. mi. (29,785 sq. km.)
POPULATION 221,000
CAPITAL Honiara
HIGHEST POINT Mount Popomanatseu
7,647 ft. (2,331 m.)
MONETARY UNIT Solomon Islands dollar
MAJOR LANGUAGES English, pidgin English,
Melanesian dialects
MAJOR RELIGIONS Tribal religions,
Protestantism, Roman Catholicism

TONGA

AREA 270 sq. mi. (699 sq. km.)
POPULATION 90,128
CAPITAL Nuku'alofa
LARGEST CITY Nuku'alofa
HIGHEST POINT 3,389 ft. (1,033 m.)
MONETARY UNIT pa'anga
MAJOR LANGUAGES Tongan, English
MAJOR RELIGION Protestantism

TUVALU

AREA 9.78 sq. mi. (25.33 sq. km.)
POPULATION 7,349
CAPITAL Fongafale (Funafuti)
HIGHEST POINT 15 ft. (4.6 m.)
MONETARY UNIT Australian dollar
MAJOR LANGUAGES English, Tuvaluan
MAJOR RELIGION Protestantism

Abaiang (atoll) 3,296 .... H 5
Abemama 2,300 .... H 5
Adamstown (cap.), Pitcairn Is.
54 .... N 8
Admiralty (isls.) .... E 6
Agaña (cap.), Guam 896 .. E 4
Agrihan (isl.) .... G 5
Ailinglapalap (atoll) 1,385 .. L 3
Ailuk 413 .... K 7
Aitutaki (atoll) 2,348 ..... K 7
Alofi (cap.), Niue 960 ..... E 7
Alotau 4,310 .... G 7
Ambrym (isl.) 6,324 .... J 7
American Samoa 32,297 ... M 7
Anaa (atoll) 444 .... D 5
Angaur (isl.) 243 .... M 7
Apataki (atoll) .... M 7
Apia (cap.), W. Samoa 33,100 .. J 7
Arno (atoll) 1,487 .... H 5
Arorae (atoll) 1,626 ...... H 6
Atafu (atoll) .... J 6
Atiu (isl.) 1,225 .... L 8
Austral (isls.) 5,208 ...... L 8
Avarua (cap.), Cook Is. .. L 8
Babelthuap (isl.) 10,391 .. D 5
Bairiki (cap.), Kiribati 1,777 .. H 5
Baker (isl.) .... J 5
Banaba (isl.) 2,314 ...... G 6
Banks (isls.) 3,158 ...... G 7
Belau (Palau) 12,116 ..... D 5
Belep (isls.) 624 .... G 7
Bellona (reefs) .... G 8
Beru (atoll) 2,318 .... H 6
Bikini (atoll) .... G 4
Bismarck (arch.) 218,339 .. E 6
Bonin (isls.) 1,879 ...... E 3
Bora-Bora (isl.) 2,572 .... L 7
Bougainville (isl.) 71,761 .. F 6
Bounty (isls.) .... H 10
Bourail 3,149 .... G 8
Butaritari (atoll) 2,971 ... H 5
Canton (isl.) .... J 6
Capitol Hill (cap.), No.
Marianas 592 .... E 4
Caroline (isl.) .... E 5
Caroline (isl.) .... E 3
Chichi (isl.) 1,879 .... E 3
Choiseul (isl.) 10,349 .... F 6
Christmas (Kiritimati) (isl.) 674 .. L 5
Cook (isls.) 17,695 ...... K 7
Coral (sea) .... F 7
Danger (Pukapuka) (atoll)
797 .... K 7
Daru 7,127 .... E 6
Disappointment (isls.) 373 .. N 7
Ducie (isl.) .... O 8
Easter (isl.) 1,598 ...... Q 8
Ebon (atoll) 887 .... G 5
Efate (isl.) 18,038 ...... G 7
Enderbury (isl.) .... J 6
Enewetak (Eniwetok) (atoll)
542 .... G 4
Erromanga (isl.) 945 ..... H 7
Espiritu Santo (isl.) 16,220 .. G 7
Fais (isl.) 207 .... E 5
Fakaofo (atoll) 654 ...... J 6
Fanning (Tabuaeran) (isl.) 340 .. L 5
Faraulep (atoll) 132 ..... E 5
Fatuhiva (isl.) 386 ...... N 7
Fiji 588,068 .... H 8
Flint (isl.) .... L 7
Fly (riv.) .... E 6
Fongafale (cap.), Tuvalu .. H 6
French Polynesia 137,382 .. L 8
Funafuti (atoll) 2,120 .... H 6
Futuna (Hoorn) (isls.) 3,173 .. J 7
Gambier (isls.) 556 ...... N 8
Gardner (isl.) .... J 6
Gilbert (isls.) 47,711 .... H 6
Greenwich (Kapingamarangi)
(atoll) 508 .... F 5
Guadalcanal (isl.) 46,619 .. F 7
Guam 105,979 .... E 4
Hall (isls.) 647 .... F 5
Hawaiian (isls.) 964,691 .. J 3
Henderson (isl.) .... O 8
Hivaoa (isl.) 1,159 ...... N 6
Honiara (cap.), Solomon Is.
14,942 .... F 6
Hoorn (isls.) 3,173 ...... J 7
Howland (isl.) .... J 5
Huahine (isl.) 3,140 ..... L 7
Hull (isl.) .... J 6
Huon (gulf) .... E 6
Ifalik (atoll) 389 .... E 5
Iwo (isl.) .... E 3
Jaluit (atoll) 1,450 ..... G 5
Jarvis (isl.) .... K 6
Johnston (atoll) 327 ..... K 4
Kadavu (Kandavu) (isl.) 8,699 .. H 7
Kapingamarangi (atoll) 508 .. F 5
Kavieng 4,633 .... E 6
Kermadec (isls.) 5 ...... J 9
Kieta 3,491 .... F 6
Kimbe 4,662 .... F 6
Kingman (reef) .... K 5
Kiritimati (isl.) 674 ..... L 5
Kolonia (cap.), Micronesia
5,549 .... F 5
Koror (cap.), Belau 6,222 .. D 5
Kosrae (isl.) 5,491 ...... G 5
Kwajalein (atoll) 6,624 ... G 5
Lae 61,617 .... E 6
Lau Group (isls.) 14,452 .. J 7
Lavongai (isl.) .... F 6
Lifu (isl.) 7,585 .... G 8
Line (isls.) .... K 5
Little Makin (atoll) 1,445 .. H 5
Lord Howe (Ontong Java) (isl.)
1,082 .... G 6
Lord Howe (isl.) 287 ..... G 9
Lorengau 3,986 .... E 6
Louisiade (arch.) .... F 7
Loyalty (isls.) 14,518 .... G 8
Luganville 4,935 .... G 7
Madang 21,335 .... E 6

Majuro (atoll) (cap.), Marshall
Is. 8,583 .... H 5
Makin (Butaritari) (atoll) 2,971 H 5
Malaita (isl.) 50,912 ..... G 6
Malden (isl.) .... L 6
Malekula (isl.) 15,931 .... G 7
Maloelap (atoll) 763 ..... H 4
Mangaia (isl.) 1,364 ..... L 8
Mangareva (isl.) 556 ..... N 8
Manihiki (atoll) 405 ..... K 7
Manua (isls.) 1,459 ...... K 7
Manus (isl.) 25,844 ...... E 6
Marcus (isl.) .... F 3
Maré (isl.) 4,156 .... G 8
Marianas, Northern 16,780 .. E 4
Mariana Trench .... E 4
Marquesas (isls.) 5,419 ... N 6
Marshall Islands 30,873 ... G 4
Marutea (atoll) .... H 5
Mata Utu (cap.), Wallis and
Futuna 558 .... J 7
Mauke (isl.) 684 .... L 8
Melanesia (reg.) .... E 6
Micronesia (reg.) .... E 4
Micronesia, Federated States
of 73,160 .... F 5
Midway (isls.) 453 ...... J 3
Mili (atoll) 763 .... H 5
Moen (isl.) 10,351 ...... F 5
Moorea (isl.) 5,788 ..... L 7

Mururoa (isl.) .... M 8
Nadi 6,938 .... H 7
Namonuito (atoll) 783 .... E 5
Namorik (atoll) 617 ..... G 5
Nanumea (atoll) 844 ..... H 6
Nauru 7,254 .... G 6
Ndeni (isl.) 4,854 ...... G 7
New Britain (isl.) 148,773 .. F 6
New Caledonia 133,233 ... G 8
New Caledonia (isl.) 118,715 .. G 8
New Georgia (isl.) 16,472 .. F 6
New Guinea .... E 6
New Ireland (isl.) 65,657 .. F 6
Ngatik (atoll) 560 .... F 5
Ngulu (atoll) 21 .... D 5
Niuatoputapu (isl.) 1,650 .. J 7
Niue (isl.) 3,578 .... K 7
Niutao (atoll) 866 ...... H 6
Nomoi (isls.) 1,879 ..... F 5
Nonouti (atoll) 2,223 .... H 6
Norfolk Island (terr.) 2,175 .. G 8
Northern Marianas 16,780 .. E 4
Nouméa (cap.), New Caled.
56,078 .... G 8
Nui (atoll) '74,335 ...... H 6
Nuku'alofa (cap.), Tonga
18,356 .... J 8
Nukuhiva (isl.) 1,484 .... M 6
Ocean (Banaba) (isl.) 2,314 .. G 6

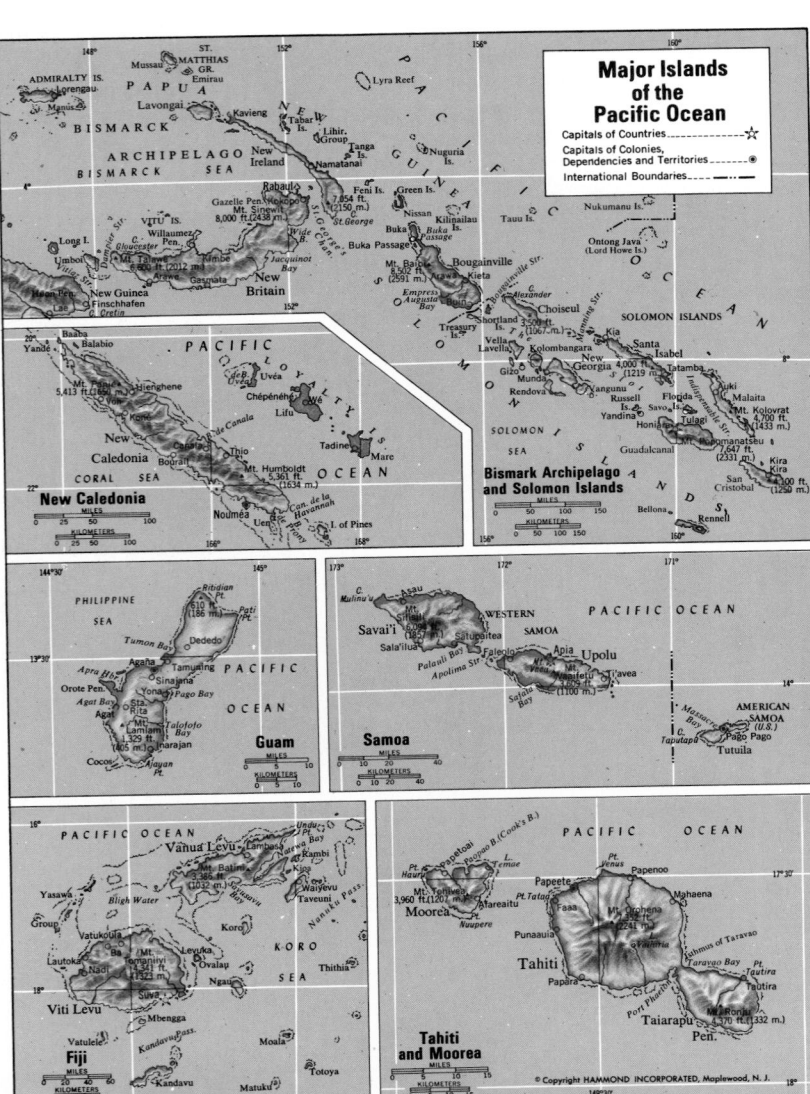

Major Islands of the Pacific Ocean
Capitals of Countries .... ☆
Capitals of Colonies,
Dependencies and Territories ..... ◉
International Boundaries ....

New Caledonia

Bismark Archipelago and Solomon Islands

Guam

Samoa

Fiji

Tahiti and Moorea

© Copyright HAMMOND INCORPORATED, Maplewood, N.J.

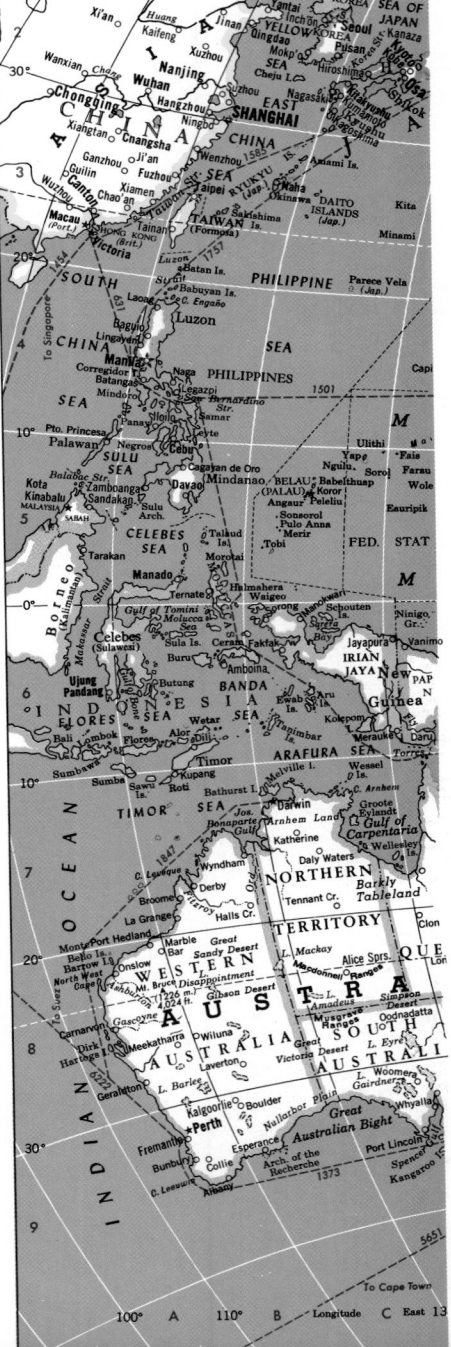

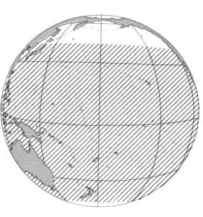

VANUATU

AREA 5,700 sq. mi. (14,763 sq. km.)
POPULATION 112,596
CAPITAL Vila
HIGHEST POINT Mt. Tabwemasana
6,165 ft. (1,879 m.)
MONETARY UNIT vatu
MAJOR LANGUAGES Bislama, English,
French
MAJOR RELIGIONS Christian, animist

WESTERN SAMOA

AREA 1,133 sq. mi. (2,934 sq. km.)
POPULATION 158,130
CAPITAL Apia
LARGEST CITY Apia
HIGHEST POINT Mt. Silisili 6,094 ft.
(1,857 m.)
MONETARY UNIT tala
MAJOR LANGUAGES Samoan, English
MAJOR RELIGIONS Protestantism,
Roman Catholicism

The map (Pacific Ocean, Lambert Azimuthal Equal-Area Projection) and flag insets (FIJI, TONGA, KIRIBATI, TUVALU, NAURU, VANUATU, SOLOMON ISLANDS, WESTERN SAMOA) are shown.

Australia

CONIC PROJECTION

MILES

0 50 100   200   300   400   500

KILOMETERS

0 50 100   200   300   400   500

Capital of Country ....⊛   State & Territorial Capitals ....⊛
International Boundaries ....–··–··–   State & Territorial Boundaries ....—— ——

© Copyright HAMMOND INCORPORATED, Maplewood, N.J.

AREA 2,966,136 sq. mi. (7,682,300 sq. km.)
POPULATION 14,576,330
CAPITAL Canberra
LARGEST CITY Sydney
HIGHEST POINT Mt. Kosciusko 7,310 ft.
(2,228 m.)
LOWEST POINT Lake Eyre -39 ft. (-12 m.)
MONETARY UNIT Australian dollar
MAJOR LANGUAGE English
MAJOR RELIGIONS Protestantism,
Roman Catholicism

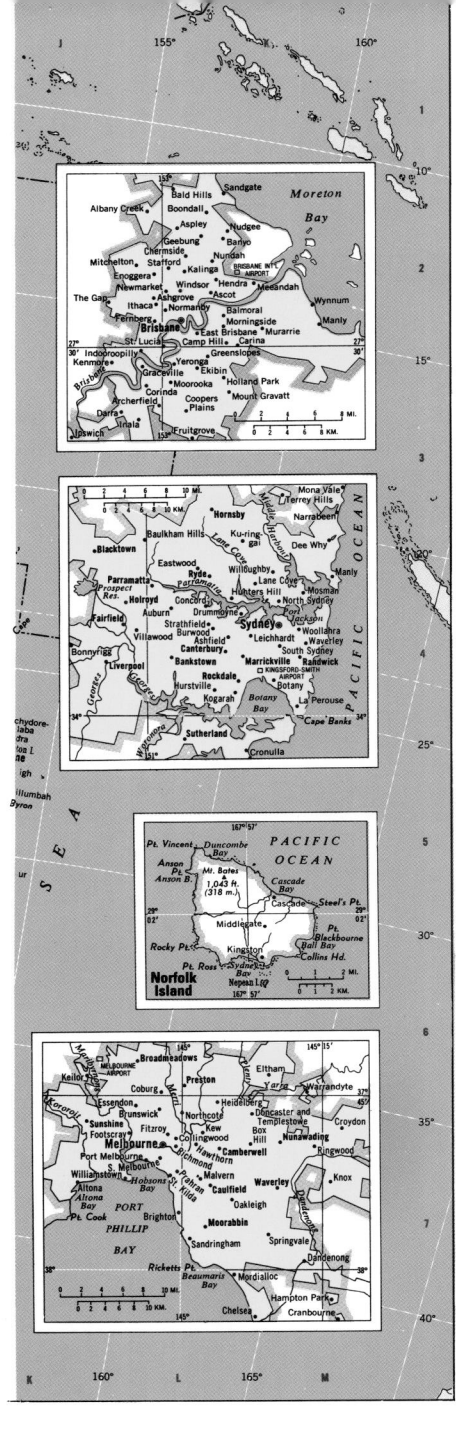

Population Distribution

● Cities with over
1,000,000 inhabitants
(including suburbs)

○ Cities with over
100,000 inhabitants
(including suburbs)

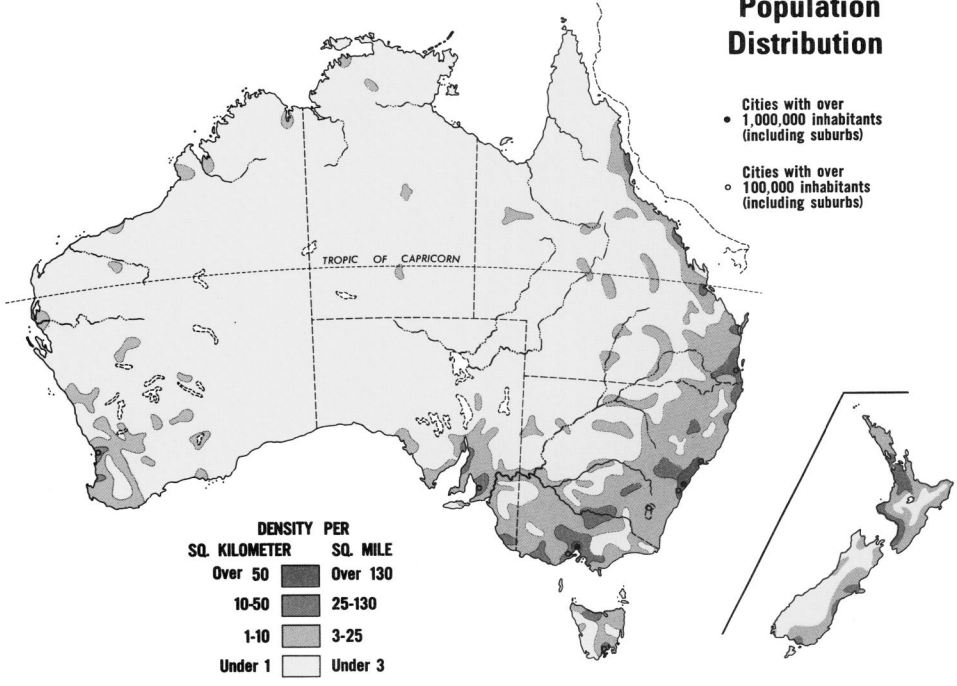

DENSITY PER

SQ. KILOMETER	SQ. MILE
Over 50	Over 130
10-50	25-130
1-10	3-25
Under 1	Under 3

Vegetation

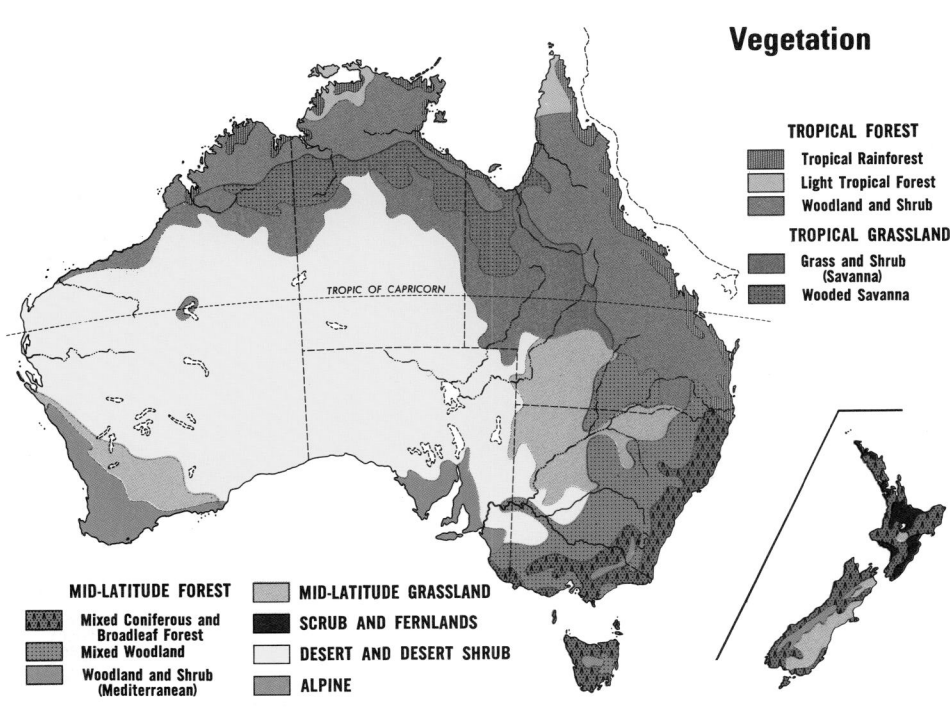

TROPICAL FOREST
Tropical Rainforest
Light Tropical Forest
Woodland and Shrub

TROPICAL GRASSLAND
Grass and Shrub (Savanna)
Wooded Savanna

MID-LATITUDE FOREST
Mixed Coniferous and Broadleaf Forest
Mixed Woodland
Woodland and Shrub (Mediterranean)

MID-LATITUDE GRASSLAND
SCRUB AND FERNLANDS
DESERT AND DESERT SHRUB
ALPINE

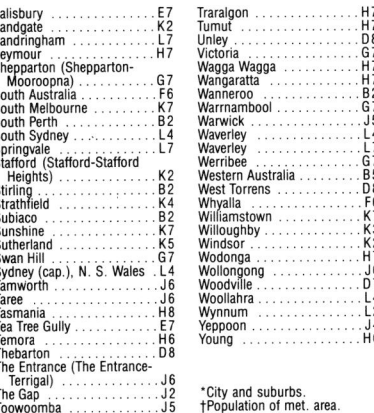

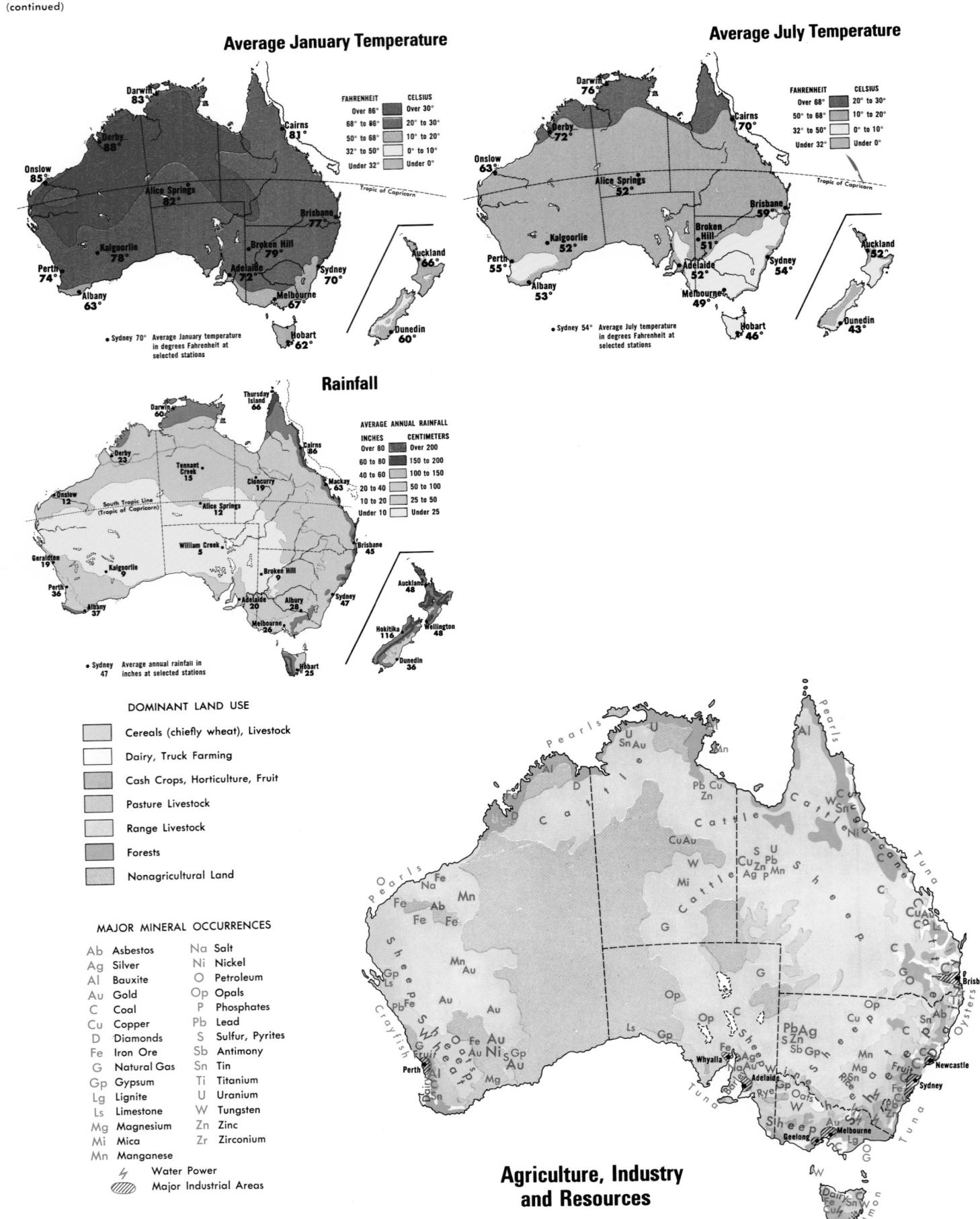

Average January Temperature

Average July Temperature

Rainfall

DOMINANT LAND USE

- Cereals (chiefly wheat), Livestock
- Dairy, Truck Farming
- Cash Crops, Horticulture, Fruit
- Pasture Livestock
- Range Livestock
- Forests
- Nonagricultural Land

MAJOR MINERAL OCCURRENCES

Ab	Asbestos	Na	Salt
Ag	Silver	Ni	Nickel
Al	Bauxite	O	Petroleum
Au	Gold	Op	Opals
C	Coal	P	Phosphates
Cu	Copper	Pb	Lead
D	Diamonds	S	Sulfur, Pyrites
Fe	Iron Ore	Sb	Antimony
G	Natural Gas	Sn	Tin
Gp	Gypsum	Ti	Titanium
Lg	Lignite	U	Uranium
Ls	Limestone	W	Tungsten
Mg	Magnesium	Zn	Zinc
Mi	Mica	Zr	Zirconium
Mn	Manganese		

Water Power
Major Industrial Areas

Agriculture, Industry and Resources

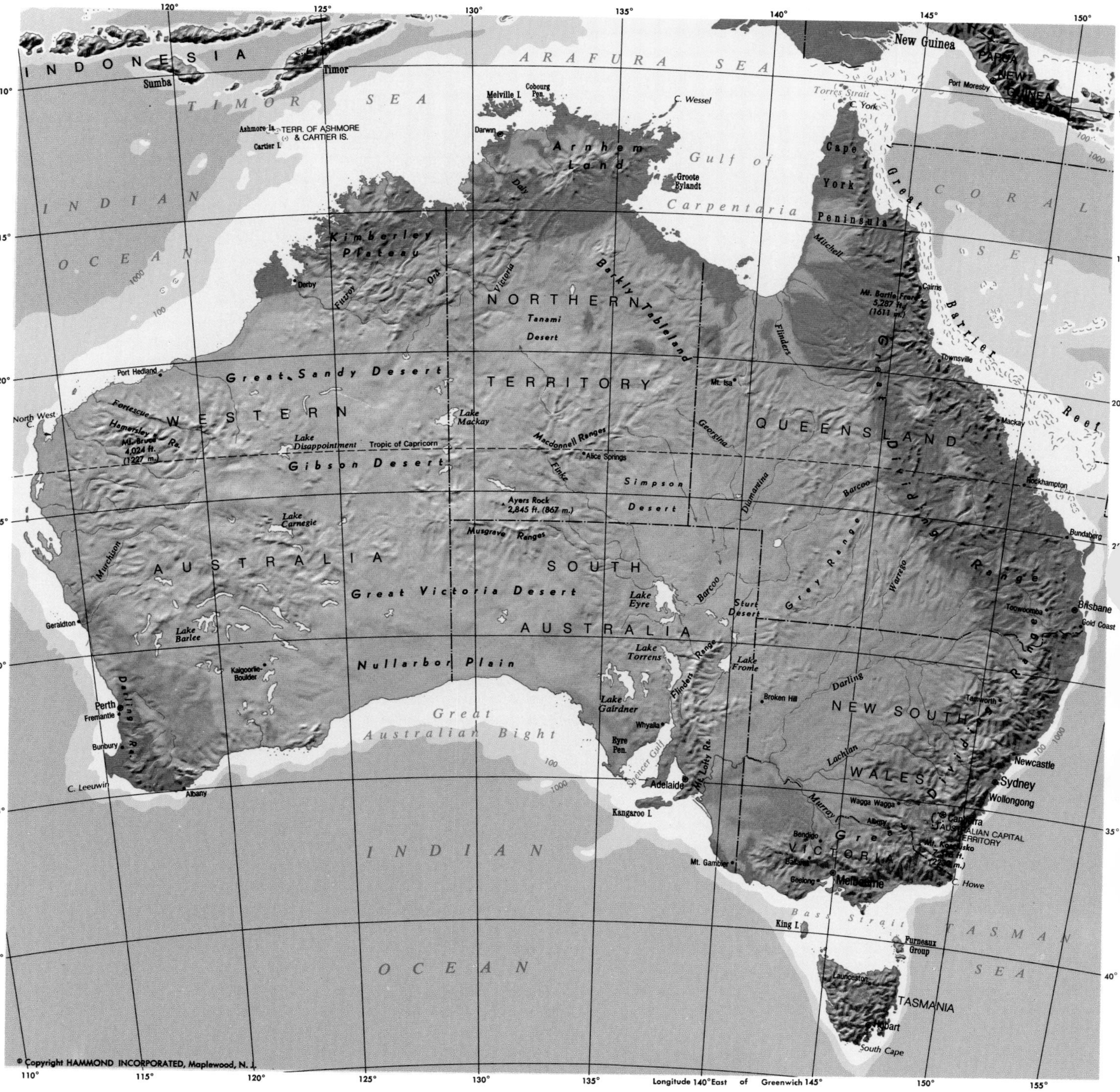

Vegetation/Relief

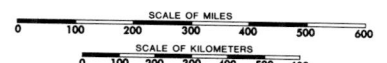

SCALE OF MILES
0   100   200   300   400   500   600

SCALE OF KILOMETERS
0   100   200   300   400   500   600

Capital of Country.....................⊛
State and Territorial Capitals...........⊙
International Boundaries...................━ ‧ ━ ‧ ━
State and Territorial Boundaries...........━ ━ ━

Elevations in Feet   Depths in Fathoms

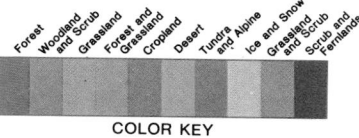

Forest
Woodland and Scrub
Grassland
Forest and Grassland
Cropland
Desert
Tundra and Alpine
Ice and Snow
Grassland and Scrub
Scrub and Fernlands

COLOR KEY

Manjimup 4,150 . . . . B6
Marble Bar 357 . . . . C3
Margaret River 798 . . . . . . A6
Meekatharra 989 . . . . B4
Melville 61,211 . . . . A1
Menzies 232 . . . . C5
Merredin 3,520 . . . . B5
Mingenew 368 . . . . A5
Moora 1,677 . . . . B5
Morawa 694 . . . . B5
Mount Barker 1,519 . . . . . . B6
Mount Magnet 618 . . . . . . B4
Mukinbudin 370 . . . . B5
Mullewa 918 . . . . A5
Mundijong 356 . . . . A2
Nannup 552 . . . . B6
Narrogin 4,969 . . . . B5
Nedlands 20,257 . . . . A1
Newman 5,466 . . . . B3
New Norcia A5
New Norcia A5
Norseman 1,895 . . . . C6
Northam 6,791 . . . . B1
Northampton 750 . . . . A5
Northcliffe B6
Nungarin ○332 . . . . B5
Onslow 594 . . . . A3
Pannawonica 1,170 . . . . . . B3
Paraburdoo 2,357 . . . . B3
Pardoo B3
Pemberton 871 . . . . A6
Perenjori 257 . . . . B5
Perth (cap.) 809,035 . . . . . A1
Perth *898,918 . . . . A1
Pingelly 937 . . . . B2
Pinjarra 1,336 . . . . A2
Port Denison-Dongara 1,155 A5
Port Hedland 12,948 . . . . . B3
Quairading 741 . . . . B1
Ravensthorpe 327 . . . . B6
Rockingham 24,932 . . . . . . A2
Roebourne 1,688 . . . . B3

AREA 975,096 sq. mi.
(2,525,500 sq. km.)
POPULATION 1,273,624
CAPITAL Perth
LARGEST CITY Perth
HIGHEST POINT Mt. Bruce 4,024 ft.
(1,227 m.)

CITIES and TOWNS

Albany 15,222 . . . . B6
Augusta 588 . . . . A2
Australind 1,681 . . . . D6
Balladonia B1
Beverley 756 . . . . B2
Boddington 367 . . . . B2
Boulder-Kalgoorlie 19,848 . . C5
Boyanup 365 . . . . A2
Bridgetown 1,521 . . . . B2
Brookton 595 . . . . B2
Broome 3,666 . . . . C2
Bruce Rock 565 . . . . B5
Brunswick Junction 889 . . . A2
Bunbury 21,749 . . . . A2
Busselton 6,463 . . . . A2
Canning 52,816 . . . . A1
Capel 680 . . . . A2
Carnamah 422 . . . . A5
Carnarvon 5,053 . . . . A4
Collie 7,667 . . . . B2
Coolgardie 891 . . . . C5

Coorow 226 . . . . B5
Corrigin 841 . . . . B6
Cranbrook 316 . . . . B6
Cuballing ○647 . . . . B2
Cue 320 . . . . B4
Cunderdin 731 . . . . B5
Dalwallinu 639 . . . . B5
Dampier 2,471 . . . . B3
Dandaragan ○1,748 . . . . . A2
Darkan 242 . . . . B2
Denham 402 . . . . A4
Denmark 985 . . . . B6
Derby 2,933 . . . . C2
Dongara-Port Denison 1,155 A5
Donnybrook 1,197 . . . . A2
Dwellingup 453 . . . . B2
Esperance 6,375 . . . . C6
Eucla E5
Exmouth 2,583 . . . . A3
Fitzroy Crossing D2
Fremantle 22,484 . . . . A1
Geraldton 20,895 . . . . A5
Gingin 382 . . . . A1
Gnowangerup 872 . . . . B6

Goldsworthy 923 . . . . B3
Goomalling 600 . . . . B1
Halls Creek 966 . . . . D2
Harvey 2,479 . . . . A2
Hopetoun C6
Hyden B6
Jarrahdale 315 . . . . B2
Kalbarri 820 . . . . A4
Kalgoorlie 9,145 . . . . C5
Kalgoorlie-Boulder 19,848 . . C5
Kambalda 4,463 . . . . C5
Karratha 8,341 . . . . B3
Katanning 4,413 . . . . B6
Kellerberrin 1,091 . . . . B5
Kojonup 544 . . . . B6
Koolyanobbing 277 . . . . . . B5
Kununurra 2,081 . . . . E2
Kwinana New Town 12,355 . A1
Lake Grace 575 . . . . B6
Laverton 872 . . . . C5
Learmonth A3
Leonora 524 . . . . C5
Madura D5
Mandurah 10,978 . . . . A2

Topography

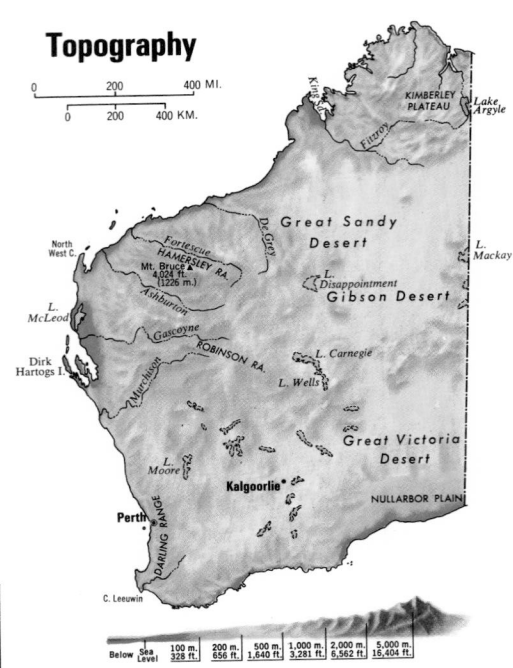

Great Sandy Desert
Gibson Desert
Great Victoria Desert
KIMBERLEY PLATEAU
L. Argyle
L. Mackay
L. Disappointment
L. Carnegie
L. Wells
L. McLeod
L. Moore
HAMERSLEY RA.
Mt. Bruce 4,024 ft. (1226 m.)
ROBINSON RA.
DARLING RANGE
NULLARBOR PLAIN
Kalgoorlie
Perth
North West C.
Dirk Hartogs I.
C. Leeuwin
King Sd.
Fitzroy
De Grey
Fortescue
Ashburton
Gascoyne
Murchison

Below Sea Level	100 m. 328 ft.	200 m. 656 ft.	500 m. 1,640 ft.	1,000 m. 3,281 ft.	2,000 m. 6,562 ft.	5,000 m. 16,404 ft.

Sandstone ○133 . . . . B4
Shay Gap 853 . . . . C3
Southern Cross 798 . . . . . . B5
South Perth 31,524 . . . . . . A1
Stirling 161,858 . . . . A1
Three Springs 638 . . . . . . A5
Tom Price 3,540 . . . . B3
Toodyay 560 . . . . B1
Turkey Creek 212 . . . . E2
Wagin 1,488 . . . . B6
Walpole 291 . . . . B6
Wandering ○470 . . . . A1
Wanneroo 6,745 . . . . A2
Waroona 1,462 . . . . B2
Wickepin 267 . . . . B3
Wickham 2,387 . . . . B3
Williams 453 . . . . B2
Wiluna 221 . . . . C4
Wittenoom 247 . . . . B3
Wongan Hills 947 . . . . B5
Wundowie 720 . . . . B1
Wyalkatchem 453 . . . . B5
Wyndham 1,509 . . . . E1
Yalgoo ○315 . . . . B5
Yampi Sound C2
York 1,136 . . . . B1

OTHER FEATURES

Adele (isl.) C1
Admiralty (gulf) D1
Aloysius (mt.) E4
Argyle (lake) E2
Arid (cape) C6
Ashburton (riv.) A3
Augustus (mt.) B4
Austin (lake) B4
Australia Aboriginal Res. . . B6
Bald (head) B6
Balwina Aboriginal Res. . . . E3
Barlee (lake) B5
Barrow (isl.) A3
Beaglebay Aboriginal Res. . C2
Bluff Knoll (mt.) B6
Bonaparte (arch.) D1
Bougainville (cape) D1
Brassey (range) C4
Bruce (mt.) B3
Brunswick (bay) D1
Buccaneer (arch.) C2
Carey (lake) C5
Carnegie (lake) C4
Central Aboriginal Res. . . . E3
Churchman (mt.) C1
Collier (bay) C1
Cosmo Newbery Aboriginal
Res. C5
Cowan (lake) C5
Cundeelee Aboriginal Res. . C5
Dale (mt.) B1
Dampier (arch.) B3
Dampier Land (reg.) C2
Darling (range) A1
De Grey (riv.) B3
D'Entrecasteaux (pt.) A6
Dirk Hartogs (isl.) A4
Disappointment (lake) C3
Drysdale (riv.) D1
Dundas (lake) C6
Egerton (mt.) B4
Eighty Mile (beach) C2
Enid (mt.) B3
Esperance (bay) C6

Exmouth (gulf) A3
Fitzroy (riv.) D2
Flinders (bay) A6
Forrest River Aboriginal Res. D1
Fortescue (riv.) B3
Garden (isl.) B4
Gascoyne (riv.) A4
Geelvink (chan.) A5
Geographe (bay) A6
Geographe (chan.) A4
Gibson (des.) D3
Great Australian (bight) . . . E6
Great Sandy (des.) C3
Great Victoria (des.) D5
Hamersley (range) B3
Hann (mt.) D1
Hopkins (lake) E4
Houtman Abrolhos (isls.) . . A5
Indian Ocean A5
Johnston, The (lakes) C6
Joseph Bonaparte (gulf) . . . E1
Kimberley (plat.) D2
King (sound) C2
King Leopold (range) D2
Koolan (isl.) C1
Leeuwin (cape) A6
Le Grand (cape) C6
Lévêque (cape) D1
Londonderry (cape) D1
Lyons (riv.) A4
Macdonald (lake) E3
Mackay (lake) E3
McLeod (lake) A4
Minigwal (lake) C5
Monte Bello (isls.) A3
Moore (lake) B5
Murchison (riv.) B4
Murray (riv.) A2
Naturaliste (cape) A6
Naturaliste (chan.) A4
North West (cape) A3
North-West Aboriginal Res. . E4
Nullarbor (plain) D5
Oakover (riv.) C3
Ord (mt.) D2
Ord (riv.) E2
Percival (lakes) D3
Peron (cape) A4
Petermann (ranges) E4
Rason (lake) D5
Rebecca (lake) C5
Recherche (arch.) C6
Robinson (ranges) B4
Roebuck (bay) C2
Rottnest (isl.) A1
Saint George (ranges) D2
Shark (bay) A4
Southese Tablelands D3
Sturt (creek) D2
Swan (riv.) A1
Timor (sea) D1
Tomkinson (ranges) E4
Wanna (lakes) E5
Warburton Aboriginal Res. . D4
Way (lake) C4
Weld (range) B4
Wells (lake) C4
Whaleback (mt.) B3
Wooramel (riv.) A4
York (sound) D1

○ Population of district.
*Population of met. area.

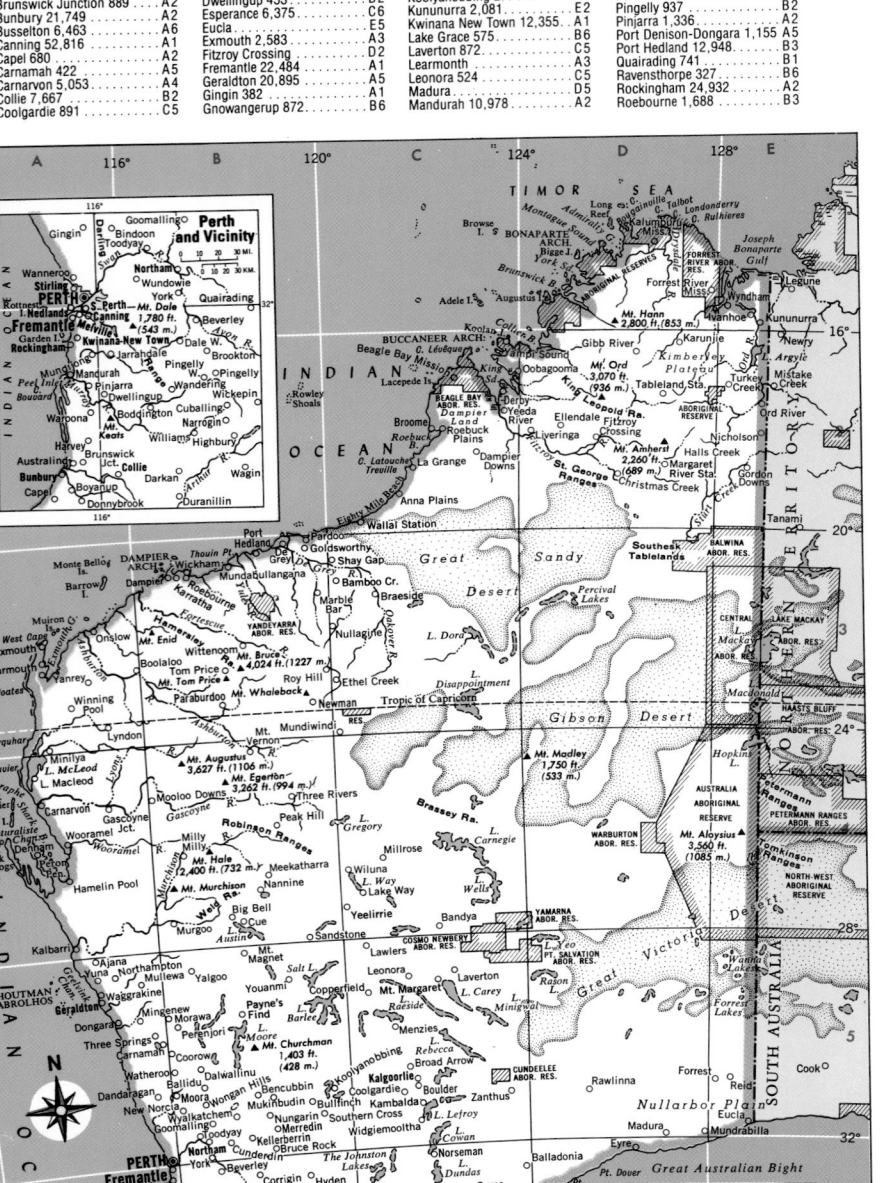

Perth and Vicinity

Western Australia

SCALE OF MILES

KILOMETERS

State Capital . . . . ◉
State and Territorial Boundaries . . . . . ─·─·─

© Copyright HAMMOND INCORPORATED, Maplewood, N.J.

Longitude 120° East of Greenwich 124°

CITIES and TOWNS

Adelaide River B2
Aileron C7
Alice Springs 18,395 . . . . . D7
Alyangula 1,181 . . . . E2
Angurugu 597 . . . . E3
Anthony Lagoon D4
Areyonga C8
Arltunga D7
Avon Downs E5
Bamyili-Beswick 685 . . . . . C3
Banka Banka C5
Barrow Creek D6
Batchelor B2
Bathurst Island 1,032 . . . . . B1
Birdum C3
Birrimbah C3
Birrindudu A5
Borroloola 420 . . . . E4
Bundooma D8
Burramurra E6
Charlotte Waters D8
Claravale B3
Coniston C7
Coolibah B3
Creswell Downs E4
Croker Island Mission C1
Daly River B2
Daly Waters C4
Darwin (cap.) 56,482 . . . . . B2
Docker River 217 . . . . A8
Elliott C4
Epenarra D6
Erldunda C8
Eva Downs D5

Ewaninga D7
Goulburn Island 277 . . . . . C1
Gove (Nhulunbuy) 3,879 . . . E2
Harts Range D7
Hatches Creek D6
Helen Springs C5
Henbury C8
Hermannsburg 541 . . . . . . C7
Hooker Creek 671 . . . . B5
Humpty Doo B2
Katherine 3,737 . . . . B3
Kildurk A4
Koolpinyah B2
Kulgera C8
Kurundi D6
Lake Nash E6
Larrimah C3
Limbunya B4
Lucy Creek E7
Mainoru C3
Maningrida 702 . . . . C2
Mataranka C3
Milingimbi 564 . . . . D2
Mistake Creek A4
Montejinnie C4
Mount Cavenagh C8
Mount Doreen B7
Murray Downs D6
Napperby C7
Newcastle Waters C4
Nhulunbuy 3,879 . . . . E2
Numbulwar 422 . . . . D3
Oenpelli 452 . . . . C2
O. T. Downs D4
Papunya 635 . . . . B7
Pine Creek 214 . . . . C2

Plenty River Mine D7
Port Keats 819 . . . . A3
Powell Creek C5
Rankine Store E5
Robinson River E4
Rockhampton Downs D5
Rodinga D8
Rum Jungle B2
Santa Teresa 479 . . . . D8
Soudan E6
Stirling Station C6
Tanami A5
Tarlton Downs E7
Tea Tree Well C7
Tempe Downs C8
Tennant Creek 3,118 . . . . . C5
The Granites B6
Top Springs C4
Ucharonidge C4
Umbakumba 247 . . . . E3
Umbeara C8
Urapunga D3
Utopia D7
Victoria River Downs B4
Warrabri 459 . . . . D6
Warrego 991 . . . . C5
Wave Hill B4
White Quartz Hill D7
Willeroo B3
Willowra C6
Wollogorang F4
Yambah C7
Yirrkala 543 . . . . E2
Yuendumu 687 . . . . B7

OTHER FEATURES

Amadeus (lake) B8

Arafura (sea) D1
Arnhem (cape) E2
Arnhem Land (reg.) D2
Arnhem Land Aboriginal
  Res. C2
Arnold (riv.) D3
Ayers Rock Nat'l Park B8
Barkly Tableland D4
Beagle (gulf) A1
Beatrice (cape) A2
Bennett (lake) E3
Beswick Aboriginal Res. . . . C3
Bickerton (isl.) E2
Blaze (pt.) A2
Carpentaria (gulf) E3
Central Wedge (mt.) C7
Clarence (str.) B2
Cobourg (pen.) C1
Conner (mt.) C8
Croker (cape) C1
Daly (riv.) B2
Daly River Aboriginal Res. . . A2
Davenport (mt.) A3
Dundas (str.) B1
East Alligator (riv.) C2
Ehrenberg (range) A7
Elcho (isl.) D1
Finke (riv.) C8
Fitzmaurice (riv.) A3
Ford (cape) A2
Georgina (riv.) E6
Goulburn (isls.) C1
Goyder (riv.) D2
Groote Eylandt (isl.) 2,230 . . E3
Haasts Bluff Aboriginal Res. . B7
Hale (riv.) D8

Hanson (riv.) C6
Hay (dry riv.) E7
Hogarth (mt.) E6
Hopkins (mt.) A8
Joseph Bonaparte (gulf) . . . A3
Katherine (riv.) C3
Lake MacKay Aboriginal
  Res. A6
Lander (riv.) C6
Leisler (mt.) A7
Limmen (bight) D3
Limmen Bight (riv.) D4
Macdonald (lake) B7
Macdonnell (ranges) C7
MacKay (lake) A7
Mann (riv.) D2
Marshall (riv.) D7
Melville (bay) E2
Melville (isl.) B1
Mount Olga Nat'l Park B8

Murchison (range) D6
Napier (mt.) A4
Neale (lake) A8
Newcastle (creek) C4
Nicholson (riv.) E5
Olga (mt.) B8
Peron (isls.) A2
Petermann (ranges) A8
Petermann Ranges
  Aboriginal Res. A8
Port Darwin (inlet) B2
Ranken (riv.) E6
Robinson (riv.) E4
Roper (riv.) C3
Sandover (riv.) D6
Simpson (des.) E8
Singleton (mt.) B6
Sir Edward Pellew Group
  (isls.) E3
South Alligator (riv.) C2

Stanley (mt.) B7
Stewart (cape) D1
Stirling (creek) A4
Sturt (plain) C4
Tanami (des.) C5
Timor (sea) A2
Todd (riv.) D8
Vanderlin (isl.) E3
Van Diemen (cape) A1
Van Diemen (gulf) B1
Victoria (riv.) B3
Wagait Aboriginal Res. B2
Warwick (chan.) E3
Wessel (cape) E1
Wessel (isls.) E1
West Baines (riv.) A4
White (riv.) A6
Woods (lake) C4
Young (mt.) D3
Ziel (mt.) C7

AREA 519,768 sq. mi.
  (1,346,200 sq. km.)
POPULATION 123,324
CAPITAL Darwin
LARGEST CITY Darwin
HIGHEST POINT Mt. Ziel 4,955 ft.
  (1,510 m.)

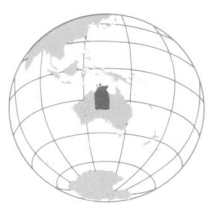

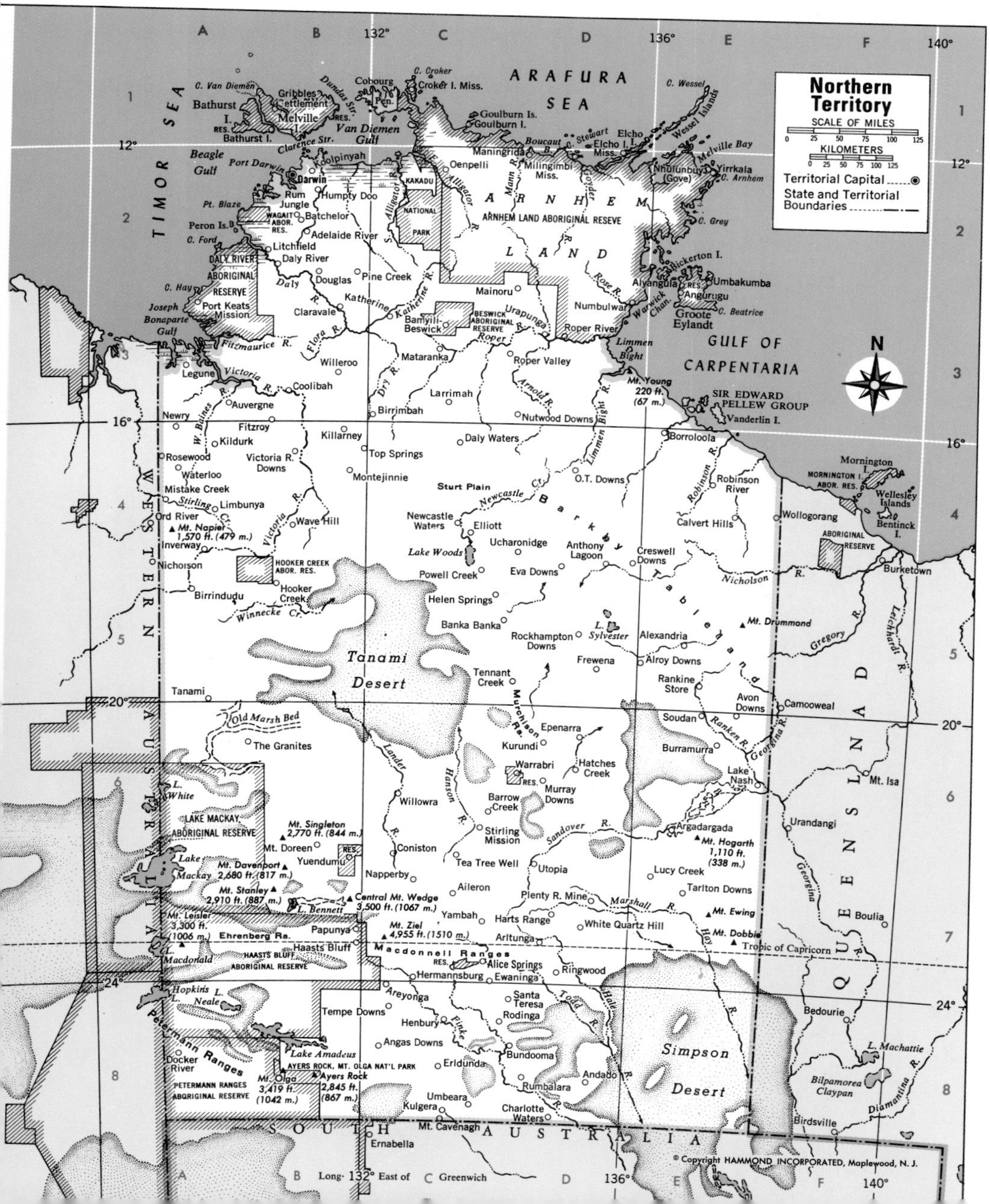

Topography

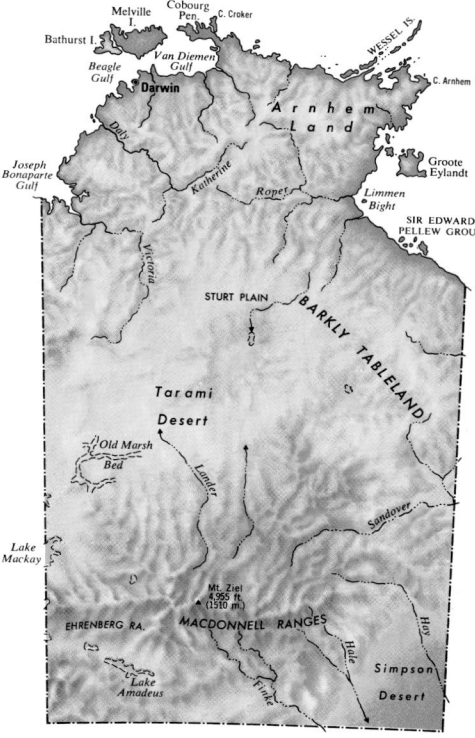

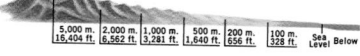

5,000 m.	2,000 m.	1,000 m.	500 m.	200 m.	100 m.	Sea
16,404 ft.	6,562 ft.	3,281 ft.	1,640 ft.	656 ft.	328 ft.	Level Below

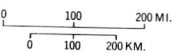

© Copyright HAMMOND INCORPORATED, Maplewood, N.J.

AREA 379,922 sq. mi. (984,000 sq. km.)
POPULATION 1,285,033
CAPITAL Adelaide
LARGEST CITY Adelaide
HIGHEST POINT Mt. Woodroffe 4,970 ft.
(1,515 m.)

CITIES and TOWNS

Adelaide (cap.) 882,520 . . . . B6
Adelaide *931,886 . . . . E4
Andamooka 402 . . . . F6
Angaston 1,753 . . . . F6
Balaklava 1,306 . . . . G6
Barmera 2,014 . . . . F7
Beachport 357 . . . . F7
Berri 3,419 . . . . G6
Birdwood 397 . . . . C7
Blinman F4
Bordertown 2,138 . . . . G7
Brighton 19,441 . . . . A8
Burnside 37,593 . . . . B8
Burra 1,222 . . . . F5
Campbelltown 43,084 . . . . B6
Ceduna 2,794 . . . . D5
Clare 2,381 . . . . F5
Cleve 827 . . . . E5
Coober Pedy 2,078 . . . . D3
Cowell 626 . . . . E5

Crafters-Bridgewater 9,764 . . B8
Crystal Brook 1,240 . . . . E5
Cummins 767 . . . . D6
Edithburgh 359 . . . . E6
Elizabeth 32,608 . . . . B7
Elliston ○1,345 . . . . D5
Enfield 66,797 . . . . B7
Gawler 9,433 . . . . B6
Gladstone 680 . . . . F5
Glenelg 13,306 . . . . A8
Gumeracha 387 . . . . C7
Hahndorf 1,274 . . . . C8
Hawker 351 . . . . F4
Hindmarsh 7,593 . . . . A7
Iron Knob 398 . . . . E5
Jamestown 1,384 . . . . F5
Kadina 2,943 . . . . F5
Kapunda 1,340 . . . . F6
Keith 1,147 . . . . G7
Kensington and Norwood
8,950 . . . . B8
Kimba 862 . . . . E5
Kingscote 1,236 . . . . E6

Kingston 1,325 . . . . G7
Lameroo 599 . . . . G6
Laura 504 . . . . F5
Leigh Creek 1,635 . . . . F4
Lobethal 1,522 . . . . C7
Lock 213 . . . . D5
Loxton 3,100 . . . . G6
Lyndoch 539 . . . . C6
Maitland 1,085 . . . . E6
Mannum 1,984 . . . . F6
Marion 66,580 . . . . A8
Marree E3
Meadows 388 . . . . B8
Meningie 807 . . . . F6
Millicent 5,255 . . . . F7
Minlaton 865 . . . . E6
Mitcham 60,309 . . . . B8
Moonta 1,751 . . . . E5
Mount Barker 4,190 . . . . C8
Mount Gambier 18,193 . . . . G7
Murray Bridge 8,664 . . . . F6
Nairne 706 . . . . C8
Nangwarry 758 . . . . G7

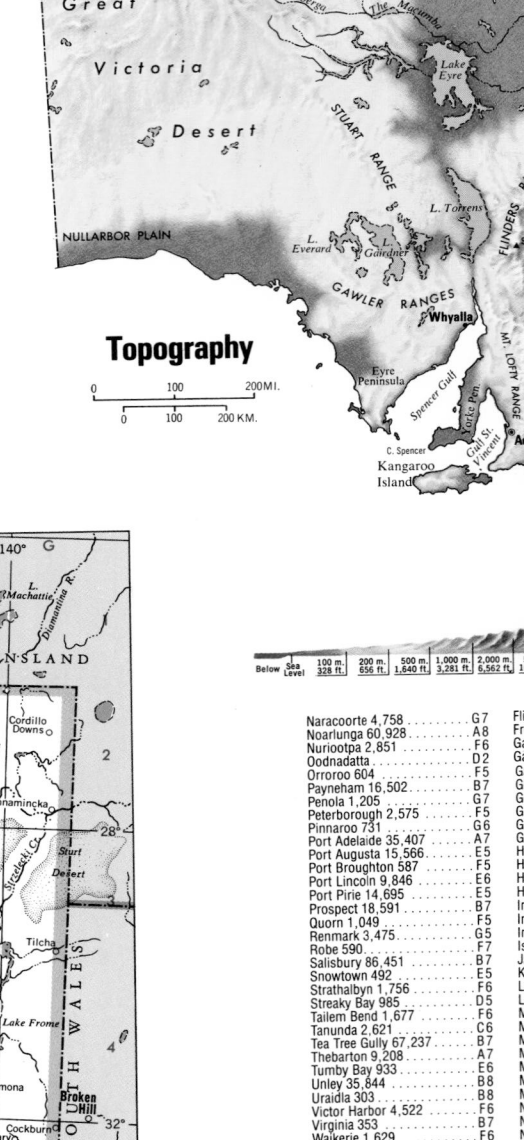

Topography

0   100   200MI.
0   100   200 KM.

Below Sea Level | 100 m. 328 ft. | 200 m. 656 ft. | 500 m. 1,640 ft. | 1,000 m. 3,281 ft. | 2,000 m. 6,562 ft. | 5,000 m. 16,404 ft.

Naracoorte 4,758 . . . . G7
Noarlunga 60,928 . . . . A8
Nuriootpa 2,851 . . . . F6
Oodnadatta D2
Orroroo 604 . . . . F5
Payneham 16,502 . . . . B7
Penola 1,205 . . . . G7
Peterborough 2,575 . . . . F5
Pinnaroo 731 . . . . G6
Port Adelaide 35,407 . . . . A7
Port Augusta 15,566 . . . . E5
Port Broughton 587 . . . . E5
Port Lincoln 9,846 . . . . E6
Port Pirie 14,695 . . . . E5
Prospect 18,591 . . . . B7
Quorn 1,049 . . . . F5
Renmark 3,475 . . . . G5
Robe 590 . . . . F7
Salisbury 86,451 . . . . B7
Snowtown 492 . . . . E5
Strathalbyn 1,756 . . . . D5
Streaky Bay 985 . . . . F6
Tailem Bend 1,677 . . . . C6
Tanunda 2,621 . . . . F6
Tea Tree Gully 67,237 . . . . B7
Thebarton 9,208 . . . . A7
Tumby Bay 933 . . . . E6
Unley 35,844 . . . . B8
Uraidla 303 . . . . B8
Victor Harbor 4,522 . . . . F6
Virginia 353 . . . . B7
Waikerie 1,629 . . . . F6
Wallaroo 2,043 . . . . E5
West Torrens 45,099 . . . . A8
Whyalla 30,518 . . . . E5
Williamstown 495 . . . . C7
Willunga 667 . . . . F6
Wilmington 227 . . . . F5
Woodside 724 . . . . C8
Woodville 77,634 . . . . A7
Woomera 1,658 . . . . E4
Wudinna 572 . . . . D5
Yorketown 713 . . . . E6

OTHER FEATURES

Acraman (lake) D5
Alberga, The (riv.) D2
Alexandrina (lake) F6
Anxious (bay) D5
Arckaringa (creek) D2
Barcoo (creek) G1
Birksgate (range) A2
Blanche (lake) F3
Brady (mt.) D3
Cadibarrawirracanna (lake) D3
Callabonna (lake) F3
Catastrophe (cape) D6
Coffin (bay) D6
Coffin Bay (pen.) D6
Coopers (Barcoo) (creek) F3
Coorong, The (lag.) F6
Dey Dey (lake) C3
Encounter (bay) F6
Everard (lake) D4
Everard (ranges) C2
Eyre (pen.) D5
Eyre North (lake) E3
Eyre South (lake) E3
Finke (riv.) C1

Flinders (range) F4
Frome (lake) G4
Gairdner (lake) D4
Gawler (ranges) E5
Gawler (riv.) B6
Gilles (lake) E5
Goyders (lag.) F2
Great Australian (bight) A5
Great Victoria (des.) B3
Gregory (lake) F3
Hack (mt.) F4
Hamilton, The (riv.) D2
Harris (lake) D4
Head of Bight (bay) B4
Indian Ocean E7
Investigator (str.) E6
Investigator Group (isls.) D5
Island (lag.) E4
Jaffa (cape) F7
Kangaroo (isl.) 3,515 . . . . E7
Lacepede (bay) F7
Lofty (mt.) B8
Macfarlane (lake) E5
Macumba, The (riv.) E2
Maurice (lake) B3
Meramangye (lake) C3
Morris (mt.) B2
Murray (res.) F6
Musgrave (ranges) B2
Neales, The (riv.) E3
Northumberland (cape) F8
Nukey Bluff (mt.) D5
Nullarbor (plain) A4
Nuyts (arch.) C5
Nuyts (cape) C5
Peera Peera Poolanna (lake) . F2
Saint Mary (peak) F4
Saint Vincent (gulf) F6
Serpentine (lakes) A3
Simpson (des.) E1
Sir Joseph Banks Group
(isls.) E6
Spencer (cape) E6
Spencer (gulf) E6
Stevenson, The (riv.) D2
Streaky (bay) C5
Strzelecki (creek) G3
Stuart (range) D3
Sturt (des.) G3
The Alberga (riv.) D2
The Coorong (lag.) F6
The Hamilton (riv.) D2
The Macumba (riv.) E2
The Neales (riv.) E3
The Stevenson (riv.) D2
The Warburton (riv.) F2
Thistle (isl.) E6
Torrens (lake) E4
Torrens (riv.) C7
Warburton, The (riv.) F2
Wilkinson (lakes) C3
Woodroffe (mt.) B2
Yalata Aboriginal Res. B4
Yarle (lakes) B4
Yorke (pen.) E6

○ Population of district.
*Population of met. area.

South Australia

SCALE OF MILES
0 25 50 75 100 125 150
KILOMETERS
0 25 50 75 100 125 150

State Capital . . . . ⊙
State and Territorial
Boundaries . . . .

Adelaide and Vicinity

0 12MI.
0 12 KM.

© Copyright HAMMOND INCORPORATED, Maplewood, N. J.

CITIES and TOWNS

Aramac 428	C4
Archerfield 785	D3
Ascot 4,298	E2
Atherton 4,196	C3
Ayr 8,787	C3
Balmoral 2,915	E2
Barcaldine 1,432	C4
Beaudesert 3,780	E6
Biloela 4,643	D5
Birdsville	A5
Blackall 1,609	C5
Blackwater 5,434	D4
Boulia 292	A4
Bowen 7,663	D3
Brisbane (cap.) 689,378	D2
Brisbane *1,028,527	D2
Bucasia 1,356	D4
Bundaberg 32,560	D5
Burketown 210	A3
Cairns 48,557	C3
Caloundra 16,758	E5
Camooweal 251	A3
Camp Hill 8,999	E3
Capella 660	C4
Cardwell 1,249	C3
Charleville 3,523	C5
Charters Towers 6,823	C4
Cherbourg 963	D5
Chermside 6,892	C2
Clermont 1,659	C4
Cloncurry 1,961	B4
Collinsville 2,756	C4
Cooktown 913	C2
Coopers Plains 4,492	C4
Corinda 4,894	D3
Croydon ○255	B3
Cunnamulla 1,627	C5
Dalby 8,784	D5
Dirranbandi 480	D6
East Brisbane 4,853	E3
Eidsvold 613	D5
Emerald 4,628	C4
Esk 676	E5
Gatton 4,190	E5
Gayndah 1,708	D5
Geebung 4,850	E2
Georgetown 319	B3
Gladstone 22,083	D4
Gold Coast 135,437	E6
Goondiwindi 3,576	D6
Gordonvale 2,375	C3
Greenslopes 7,219	E3
Gympie 10,768	E5

Hervey Bay 13,569	E5
Holland Park 7,363	E3
Home Hill 3,138	C3
Hughenden 1,657	B4
Inala 17,383	D3
Indooroopilly 7,959	D3
Ingham 5,598	C3
Injune 407	D5
Innisfail 7,933	C3
Ipswich 68,297	E5
Isisford ○605	C5
Jandowae 781	D5
Jericho ○1,177	C4
Julia Creek 602	B4
Karumba 670	B3
Kilcoy 1,257	D5
Kingaroy 5,134	D5
Longreach 2,971	B4
Mackay 35,361	D4
Mareeba 6,309	C3
Marian 796	D4
Maroochydore-Mooloolaba 17,460	E5
Maryborough 20,111	E5
Mary Kathleen 830	A4
McKinlay ○1,477	B4
Millmerran 1,107	D5
Mitchell 1,171	C5
Mitchelton 5,810	D2
Monto 1,397	D5
Moorooka 8,740	D3
Moranbah 4,362	C9
Mossman 1,614	C3
Moura 2,871	D5
Mount Isa 23,679	A4
Murgon 2,327	D5
Nambour 7,965	E5
Newmarket 3,520	D2
Normanton 926	B3
Nundah 7,358	E2
Proserpine 3,058	D4
Quilpie 694	C5
Ravenshoe 915	C3
Redcliffe 42,223	E5
Richmond 784	B4
Rockhampton 50,146	D4
Roma 5,706	D5
Saint George 2,204	D5
Saint Lucia 6,075	D3
Sandgate 6,776	D2
Sarina 2,815	D4
Springsure 774	C5
Stafford (Stafford Heights) 13,731	D2
Stanthorpe 3,966	D6
Tara 864	D5

Taroom 688	D5
Tewantin-Noosa 9,965	E5
Theodore 643	D5
Thursday Island 2,283	B1
Toowoomba 63,401	D5
Townsville 86,112	C3
Tully 2,728	C3
Walkerston 1,277	D4
Warwick 8,853	D6
Weipa 2,433	B2
Windsor 6,119	D2
Winton 1,259	B4
Wynnum 10,794	E5

Yeppoon 6,447	D4
Yeronga 4,579	D3

OTHER FEATURES

Albatross (bay)	B2
Archer (riv.)	B2
Balonne (riv.)	D6
Banks (isl.)	B1
Barcoo (creek)	B5
Barkly Tableland	A4
Bartle Frere (mt.)	C3
Beal (range)	B5

AREA 666,872 sq. mi. (1,727,200 sq. km.)
POPULATION 2,295,123
CAPITAL Brisbane
LARGEST CITY Brisbane
HIGHEST POINT Mt. Bartle Frere 5,287 ft. (1,611 m.)

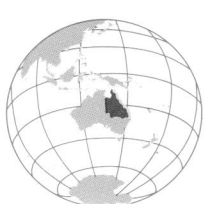

Topography

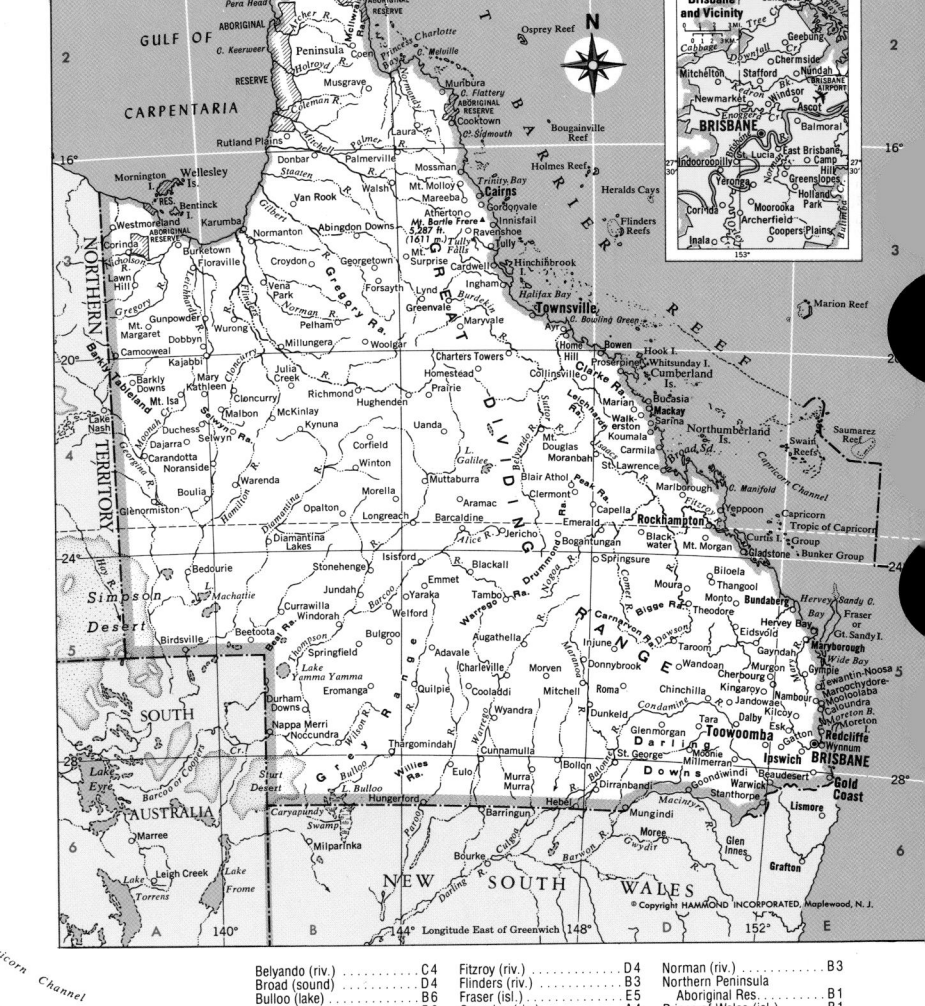

Belyando (riv.)	C4	Fitzroy (riv.)	D4
Broad (sound)	D4	Flinders (riv.)	B3
Bulloo (lake)	B6	Fraser (isl.)	E5
Bulloo (riv.)	B6	Georgina (riv.)	A4
Bunker Group (isls.)	E4	Gilbert (riv.)	B3
Burdekin (riv.)	C3	Great Dividing (range)	B3
Cape York (pen.)	B2	Gregory (range)	B3
Capricorn (chan.)	E4	Gregory (riv.)	A3
Capricorn Group (isls.)	E4	Grey (range)	B5
Carnarvon (range)	D5	Hamilton (riv.)	B4
Carpentaria (gulf)	A2	Hervey (bay)	E5
Cloncurry (riv.)	B4	Hinchinbrook (isl.)	C3
Coopers (Barcoo) (creek)	B5	Hook (isl.)	D4
Coral (sea)	C6	Leichhardt (riv.)	A3
Culgoa (riv.)	C6	Machattie (lake)	B5
Cumberland (isls.)	D4	Macintyre (riv.)	D6
Curtis (isl.)	D4	Maranoa (riv.)	C5
Darling Downs	D5	Mary (riv.)	E5
Dawson (riv.)	D5	Melville (cape)	C2
Diamantina (riv.)	B4	Mitchell (riv.)	B2
Drummond (range)	C4	Moreton (bay)	E5
Duifken (pt.)	B2	Moreton (isl.)	E5
Endeavour (str.)	B1	Mornington (isl.)	A3

Norman (riv.)	B3
Northern Peninsula Aboriginal Res.	B1
Prince of Wales (isl.)	B1
Princess Charlotte (bay)	C2
Sandy (cape)	E5
Selwyn (range)	B4
Simpson (des.)	A5
Sturt (des.)	B3
Suttor (riv.)	C4
Swain (reefs)	E4
Thompson (riv.)	B5
Torres (str.)	B1
Warrego (range)	C5
Warrego (riv.)	C5
Wellesley (isls.)	A3
Whitsunday (isl.)	D4
Willies (range)	C6
Yamma Yamma (lake)	B5
York (cape)	B1

○ Population of district.
*Population of met. area.

Cobbadah F2
Coffs Harbour 16,020 G2
Collarenebri 602 E1
Collie E2
Comboyne G2
Concord 23,926 J3
Condobolin 3,355 D3
Conoble C3
Coogee K3
Coolah 878 E2
Coolamon 1,088 D4
Cooma 7,978 E5
Coonabarabran 3,001 E2
Coonamble 3,090 E2
Cootamundra 6,540 D4
Copmanhurst ◯2,857 G1
Coraki 895 G1
Coramba 202 G2
Corowa-Wahgunyah 3,390 D4
Cowra 7,900 E3
Crescent Head 944 G2
Cronulla J4
Crookwell 2,063 E4
Cudal 400 E3
Cullburra-Orient Point 2,068 F4
Culcairn 1,027 D4
Cullen Bullen 231 F3
Cumnock 252 E3
Curlewis 487 F2
Dareton 612 B4
Darlington Point 599 C4
Deepwater 260 F1
Dee Why K3
Delegate 347 E5
Delungra 332 F1
Deniliquin 7,354 C4
Denman 1,122 F3
Dorrigo 1,192 G2
Drummoyne 30,961 J3
Dubbo 23,986 E3
Dunedoo 836 E3
Dungalear Station D1
Dungog 2,126 F3
Eden 3,107 E5
Emmaville 503 F1
Ermeran Station D3
Eugowra 577 E3
Evans Head 1,802 G1

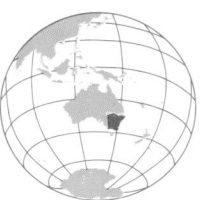

NEW SOUTH WALES

AREA 309,498 sq. mi. (801,600 sq. km.)
POPULATION 5,126,217
CAPITAL Sydney
LARGEST CITY Sydney
HIGHEST POINT Mt. Kosciusko 7,310 ft. (2,228 m.)

VICTORIA

AREA 87,876 sq. mi. (227,600 sq. km.)
POPULATION 3,832,443
CAPITAL Melbourne
LARGEST CITY Melbourne
HIGHEST POINT Mt. Bogong 6,508 ft. (1,984 m.)

Topography

Fairfield 129,557 H3
Finley 2,193 C4
Forbes 8,029 E3
Forest Hill 1,977 D4
Forster-Tuncurry 9,261 G3
Frederickton 616 G2
Ganmain 650 D4
Gerringong 1,775 F4
Geurie 290 E3
Gilgai 257 F1
Gilgandra 2,700 E2
Gilgunnia C3
Glen Innes 6,052 F1
Glenreagh 233 G2
Gloucester 2,488 F2
Goodooga 248 D1
Goolgowi 245 C3
Gooloogong 221 E3
Goombalie C1
Goulburn 21,755 E4
Grafton 17,005 G1
Grenfell 2,070 E3
Greta-Branxton 2,849 F3
Greta East 398 F3
Griffith 13,187 C4
Gulargambone 457 E2
Gulgong 1,740 E3
Gundagai 2,308 D4
Gunnedah 8,909 F2
Gunning 438 E4
Guyra 1,840 F2
Hanwood 306 C4
Harrington 1,183 G2
Hay 2,958 C4
Henty 883 D4
Hillston 999 C3
Holbrook 1,276 D4
Holroyd 80,116 H3
Hornsby 111,081 J3
Howlong 1,072 D4
Hunters Hill 12,537 J3
Hurstville 64,910 J4
Huskisson 2,296 F4
Iluka 1,362 G1
Inverell 9,734 F1
Ivanhoe 517 C3
Jerilderie 1,075 C4
Jindabyne 1,602 E5
Junee 3,993 D4
Kandos 1,626 F3
Karpakora B3
Katoomba-Wentworth Falls 13,942 F3
Keewong C3
Kempsey 9,037 G2
Kendall 522 G2
Khancoban 515 E5
Kiama 7,717 F4
Kinalung B3
Kogarah 46,322 J4
Koorawatha 262 E4
Kootingal 731 F2
Ku-ring-gai 101,501 J3
Kurri Kurri-Weston 12,795 F3
Kyogle 3,070 G1
Lake Cargellico 1,240 D3
Lane Cove 29,113 J3
Leeton 6,498 D4
Leichhardt 57,332 J3
Lette B4
Lidcombe J3
Lightning Ridge 1,112 E1
Lismore 24,033 G1
Lithgow 12,793 F3
Liverpool 92,715 H4
Lockhart 923 D4
Macksville 2,352 G2
Maclean 2,593 G1
Maitland 38,865 F3
Manildra 520 E3
Manilla 1,884 F2
Manly 37,080 K3
Maroubra K3
Marrickville 83,448 J3
Marsden D3
Marsden Park 518 H3
Marulan 330 E4
Mathoura 582 C4
Melrose D3
Mendooran 325 E2
Menindee 455 B3
Merimbula 2,899 F5
Merriwa 943 F3
Millthorpe 607 E5
Milpa B2
Milperra H4
Milton 740 F4
Mittagong 4,266 F4
Moama C5
Mogil Mogil E1
Molong 1,374 E3
Mona Vale K2
Moree 10,459 E1
Morisset 1,593 F3
Moruya 2,003 F4
Mosman 26,200 J3
Moss Vale 4,415 F4
Mossgiel C4
Moulamein 396 C4
Mount Arrowsmith A2
Mount Drysdale C2
Mount Hope C3
Mudgee 6,015 E3
Mullumbimby 2,234 G1
Mungindi 707 E1
Murrumburrah 2,070 E4
Murrurundi 861 F2
Murwillumbah 7,807 G1
Muswellbrook 8,548 F3
Nabiac 363 G3
Nambucca Heads 4,053 G2
Narellan 2,104 F3
Narooma 2,758 F5
Narrabeen K3
Narrabri 7,296 E2
Narrandera 5,013 D4
Narromine 2,994 E3
New Angledool E1
Newcastle 135,207 F3
Newcastle †389,237 F3
Nimmitabel 257 E5
North Sydney 48,500 J3
Nowra-Bomaderry 17,887 F4
Nundle 235 F2
Nymboida ◯2,044 G1
Nyngan 2,485 D2
Oaklands 283 D4
Oberon 1,937 E3
Old Bar 970 G2
Orange 27,626 E3
Pallamallawa 340 F1
Pambula 604 E5
Parkes 9,047 E3
Parramatta 130,943 H3
Peak Hill 1,037 E3
Penrith 108,720 F3
Perthville 639 E3
Picton 1,817 F4
Pilliga 206 E2
Popiltah A3
Portland 1,980 E3
Port Kembla F4
Port Macquarie 19,581 G2
Queanbeyan 19,383 E4
Quirindi 2,851 F2
Randwick 116,202 J3
Raymond Terrace 7,548 F3
Richmond-Windsor 15,491 F3
Rockdale 83,719 J4

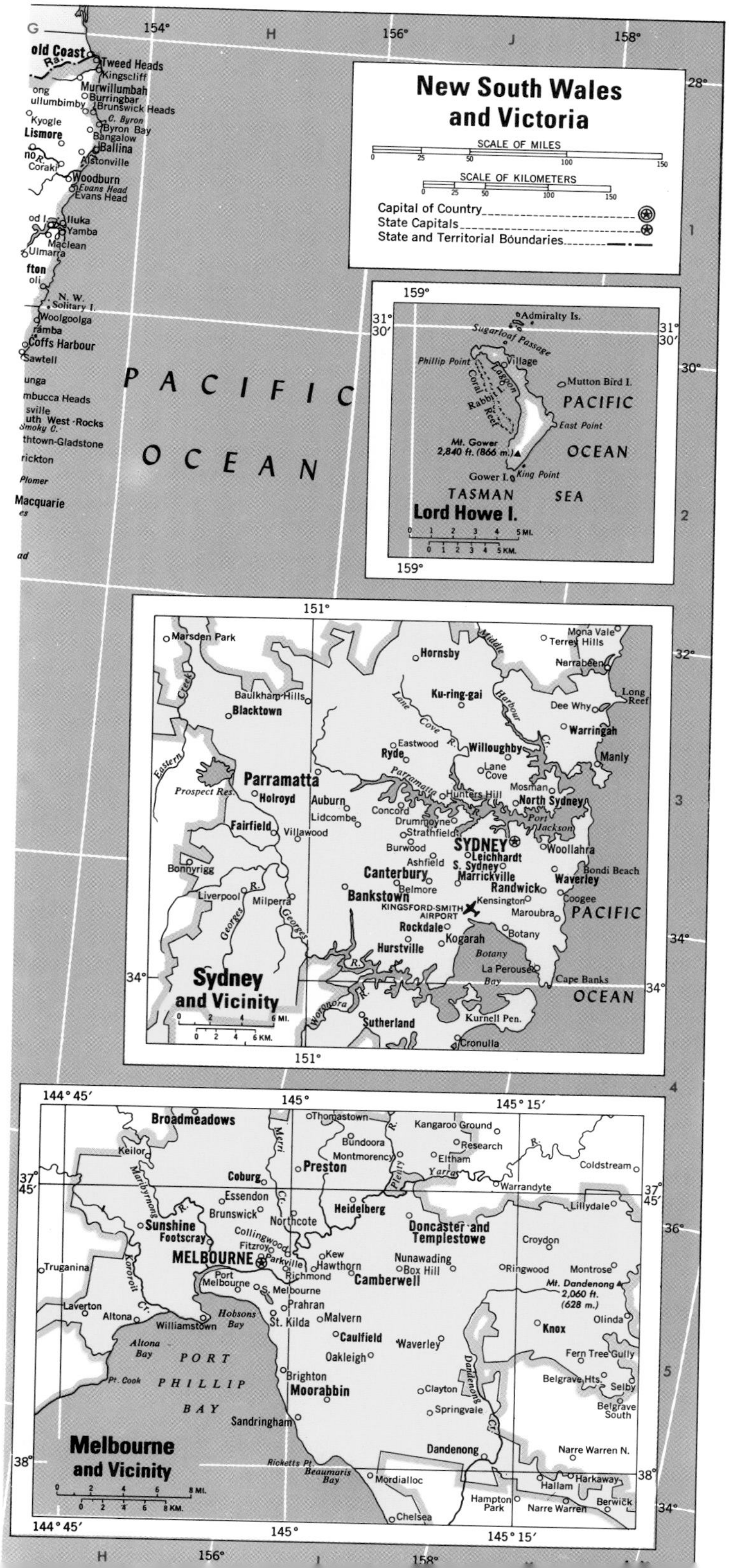

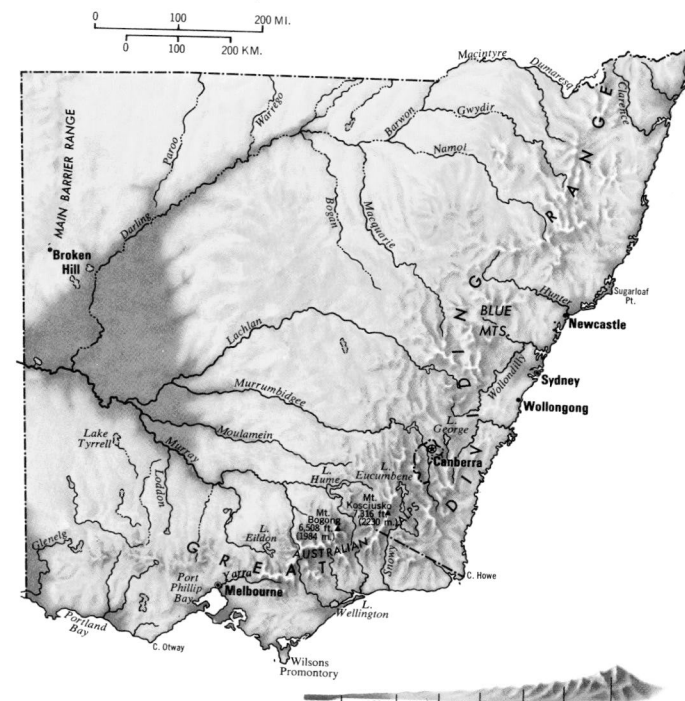

(continued on following page)

(continued)

Ryde 88,948 J3
Rylstone 651 E3
Salisbury Downs B1
Sawtell 5,970 G2
Scone 3,949 F3
Shellharbour 41,790 F4
Singleton 9,572 F3
Smithtown-Gladstone 953 G2
South Sydney 30,776 J3
South West Rocks 1,314 G2
Stephen's Creek A2
Strathfield 25,882 J3
Stroud 522 G3
Sussex Inlet 1,293 F4
Sutherland 165,336 J4
Sydney (cap.) 2,876,508 J3
Sydney †3,204,696 J3
Talbingo 481 E4
Tamworth 29,657 F2
Taralga 272 E4
Tarcutta 263 D4
Taree 14,697 G2
Tathra 1,077 F5
Temora 4,350 D4
Tenterfield 3,402 G1
Terrigal-The Entrance 37,891 F3
The Rock 693 D4
Thurloo Downs B1
Tibbita C4
Tibooburra B1
Tiltagara C2
Tingha 886 F1
Tocumwal 1,174 C4
Tongo B2
Torrowangee A2
Tottenham 366 D3
Trangie 977 D3
Trundle 515 D3
Tullamore 324 D3
Tumbarumba 1,536 D4
Tumut 5,816 E4
Tweed Heads G1
Ulladulla 6,018 F4
Ulmarra 395 G1
Ungarie 428 D3
Uralla 2,090 F2
Urana 419 D4
Urbenville 282 G1
Urunga 2,045 G2
Villawood H3
Wagga Wagga 36,837 D4
Wakool 278 C4
Walcha 1,674 F2
Walgett 2,157 E2
Walla Walla 593 D4
Wallerawang 1,855 F3
Wangi-Rathmines 5,106 F3
Warialda 1,340 F1
Warragamba 1,406 F3
Warren 2,153 D2
Warringah ○172,653 K3
Wauchope 3,645 G2
Waverley 61,575 K3
Waverley Downs B1
Wee Waa 1,904 E2
Wellington 5,280 E3
Wentworth 1,180 B4
Werris Creek 1,924 F2
West Wyalong 3,778 D3
Wetuppa B4
White Cliffs B2
Whitton 344 D4
Whyjonta B1
Wilcannia 982 B2
Willoughby 52,120 J3
Willow Tree 258 F2
Wingham 3,937 G2
Wollongong 169,381 F4
Wollongong †222,539 F4
Woodburn 647 G1
Woodenbong 409 G1
Woodstock 266 E3
Woolgoolga 2,081 G2
Wooli 457 G1
Woollahra 51,659 K3
Wyong 3,902 F3
Yallock C3
Yalpunga A1
Yamba 2,528 G1
Yancannia B2
Yanco 415 D4
Yantara B1
Yass 4,283 E4
Yenda 697 D4
Yeoval 288 E3
Young 6,906 E4

OTHER FEATURES

Ana Branch, Darling (riv.) A3
Australian Alps (mts.) D5
Barrington Tops (mt.) F2
Barwon (riv.) D2
Blue (mts.) F3
Bogan (riv.) D2
Bondi (beach) K3
Botany (bay) J4
Broken (bay) F3
Burrinjuck (res.) E4
Byron (cape) G1
Caryapundy (swamp) B1
Castlereagh (riv.) E2
Cawndilla (lake) A3
Clarence (riv.) G1
Colo (riv.) F3
Cowal (lake) D3
Culgoa (riv.) D1
Cuttaburra (creek) C1
Darling (riv.) B3
Dumaresq (riv.) F1
Eucumbene (lake) E5
George (lake) E4
Georges (riv.) H4
Gower (mt.) J2
Great Dividing (range) E3
Green (cape) F5
Gunderbooka (ranges) C2
Gwydir (riv.) E1
Howe (cape) F5
Hume (res.) D4
Hunter (riv.) F3
Kosciusko (mt.) E5
Kurnell (pen.) J4
Lachlan (range) C3
Lachlan (riv.) C3
Liverpool (range) F2
Lord Howe (isl.) 287 J2
Macintyre (riv.) E1
Macquarie (lake) F3
Macquarie (riv.) D2
Main Barrier (range) A2
Manning (riv.) F2
Marthaguy (creek) D2
McPherson (range) G1
Menindee (lake) B3
Monaro (range) E5
Moonie (riv.) E1
Moulamein (creek) C4
Mount Royal (range) F2
Murray (riv.) A4
Murrumbidgee (riv.) C4
Myall (lake) G3
Namoi (riv.) E2
Narran (lake) D1
New England (range) F1
Paroo (riv.) C1
Parramatta (riv.) J3
Poopeloe (lake) C2
Port Jackson (inlet) J3
Port Stephens (inlet) G3
Richmond (range) G1
Richmond (riv.) G1
Riverina (reg.) C4
Robe (mt.) A2
Round, The (mt.) G2
Salt, The (lake) B2
Shoalhaven (riv.) E4
Smoky (cape) G2
Snowy (mts.) E5
Snowy (riv.) E5
Stony (ranges) B2
Sturt (mt.) A1
Sugarloaf (pt.) G3
Talyawalka (creek) B2
Tandou (lake) A3
Tasman (sea) F5
The Round (mts.) G2
The Salt (lake) B2
Timbarra (riv.) G1
Tuggerah (lake) F3
Victoria (lake) A3
Warrego (riv.) C1
Willandra Billabong (creek) C3
Wollondilly (riv.) F4

VICTORIA

CITIES and TOWNS

Alexandra 1,756 C5
Altona 30,909 H5
Apollo Bay 921 B6
Ararat 8,336 B5
Avoca 1,032 B5
Bacchus Marsh 6,224 C5
Bairnsdale 9,459 D5
Ballarat 35,681 C5
Ballarat †71,930 C5
Balmoral 257 A5
Beaufort 1,214 B5
Beechworth 3,154 D5
Belgrave Heights J5
Belgrave South K5
Benalla 8,151 D5
Bendigo 31,841 C5
Bendigo †58,818 C5
Berwick 36,181 K6
Beulah 290 B4
Birchip 895 B4
Birregurra 416 B6
Boort 863 B5
Box Hill 47,579 J5
Bright 1,545 D5
Brighton 33,697 J5
Broadford 1,580 C5
Broadmeadows 103,540 H4
Brunswick 44,464 H5
Bruthen 449 D5
Bundoora J4
Camberwell 85,883 J5
Camperdown 3,545 C6
Cann River 345 E5
Casterton 1,945 A5
Castlemaine 7,583 C5
Caulfield 69,922 J5
Charlton 1,377 B5
Chelsea 26,034 J6
Churchill 4,796 D6
Clunes 761 B5
Cobden 1,453 B6
Cobram 3,817 C4
Coburg 55,035 H5
Cohuna 2,178 C4
Colac 10,587 B6
Coldstream 1,395 K4
Coleraine 1,232 A5
Collingwood 15,089 J5
Corryong 1,320 D5
Craigieburn 4,296 C5
Cranbourne 9,400 C6
Creswick 2,036 B5
Croydon 36,210 K5
Dandenong 54,962 K5
Darby D6
Dartmoor 349 A5
Daylesford 2,883 C5
Derrinallum 287 B5
Dimboola 1,675 B5
Donald 1,609 B5
Doncaster and Templestowe 90,660 J5
Drouin 3,492 C6
Dunkeld 402 B5
Dunolly 621 B5
Eaglehawk 7,355 C5
Echuca 7,943 C5
Edenhope 827 A5
Eildon 737 C5
Eltham 34,648 J4
Erica 236 D5
Essendon 56,380 H5
Euroa 2,640 C5
Fitzroy 19,112 H5
Footscray 49,756 H5
Geelong 14,471 C6
Geelong †137,173 C6
Geelong West 14,823 C6
Goroke 370 A5
Gunbower 259 C4
Hamilton 9,751 B5
Hawthorn 30,689 J5
Healesville 4,526 C5
Heathcote 1,213 C5
Heidelberg 64,757 J5
Heyfield 1,635 D6
Heywood 1,266 A6
Hopetoun 1,832 B4
Horsham 12,034 B5
Inglewood 674 B5
Inverloch 1,523 C6
Kaniva 956 A5
Keilor 81,762 H5
Kerang 4,049 B4
Kew 28,870 J5
Kilmore 1,728 C5
Knox 88,902 K5
Koroit 1,988 B6
Korumburra 2,798 D6
Kyabram 5,414 C5
Kyneton 3,185 C5
Lake Boga 502 B4
Lake Bolac 211 B5
Lakes Entrance 3,414 E5
Lara 4,231 C6
Leongatha 3,736 C6
Lillydale 62,077 J4
Macarthur 322 A6
Maffra 3,822 D5
Maldon 1,009 C5
Mallacoota 726 E5
Malvern 43,211 J5
Mansfield 1,920 D5
Maryborough 7,858 B5
Melbourne (cap.) 2,578,759 H5
Melbourne †2,722,817 H5
Melton 20,599 C5
Merbein 1,735 A4
Merino 298 A5
Mildura 15,763 A4
Minyip 567 B5
Moe 16,649 D6
Montmorency J4
Montrose K5
Moorabbin 97,810 J5
Mooroopna C5
Mordialloc 27,869 J6
Morea A5
Mornington 23,512 C6
Mortlake 1,056 B6
Morwell 16,491 D5
Mount Beauty 1,509 D5
Murrayville 313 A4
Murtoa 946 B5
Myrtleford 2,815 D5
Nagambie 1,102 C5
Narre Warren North 761 K5
Nathalia 1,222 C5
Natimuk 482 A5
Newtown 10,210 C6
Nhill 1,567 A5
Northcote 51,235 J5
Numurkah 2,713 C5
Nunawading 97,052 J5
Nyah 351 B4
Nyah West 535 B4
Oakleigh 55,612 J5
Omeo 272 D5
Orbost 2,586 E5
Ouyen 1,527 B4
Penshurst 558 B5
Porepunkah 268 D5
Port Albert 267 D6
Port Fairy 2,276 B6
Portland 9,353 A6
Port Melbourne 8,585 H5
Prahran 45,018 J5
Preston 84,519 J4
Quambatook 359 B4
Queenscliff 3,420 C6
Rainbow 700 A4
Red Cliffs 2,409 B4
Richmond 24,506 J5
Ringwood 38,665 K5
Robinvale 1,751 B4
Rochester 2,399 C5
Rushworth 994 C5
Rutherglen 1,454 D5
Saint Arnaud 2,721 B5
Saint Kilda 49,366 J5
Sale 12,968 D6
Sandringham 31,175 J5
Sea Lake 943 B4
Sebastopol 6,462 B5
Seymour 6,494 C5
Shepparton-Mooroopna ‡28,373 C5
South Barwon 35,307 C6
South Melbourne 19,955 J5
Springvale 80,186 J5
Stawell 6,160 B5
Sunbury 11,085 C5
Sunshine 94,419 H5
Swan Hill 8,398 B4
Swifts Creek 288 D5
Tallangatta 950 D5
Tatura 2,697 C5
Templestowe and Doncaster 90,660 J5
Terang 2,111 B6
Tongala 994 C5
Traralgon 18,057 D6
Underbool 274 A4
Wangaratta 16,202 D5
Warburton 2,009 C5
Warracknabeal 2,735 B5
Warragul 7,712 D6
Warrnambool 21,414 B6
Waverley 122,471 J5
Wedderburn 868 B5
Werrimull A4
Whittlesea 65,657 C5
Willaura 377 B5
Williamstown 25,554 H5
Winchelsea 825 B6
Wodonga 19,208 D5
Wonthaggi 4,797 C6
Woodend 1,785 C5
Wycheproof 938 B5
Yallourn 26 D6
Yarram 2,085 D6
Yarrawonga 3,442 C5
Yea 996 C5

OTHER FEATURES

Australian Alps (mts.) D5
Avoca (riv.) B5
Barry (mts.) D5
Bogong (mt.) D5
Bridgewater (cape) A6
Buller (mt.) D5
Campaspe (riv.) C5
Corangamite (lake) B6
Corner (inlet) D6
Dandenong (mt.) K5
Difficult (mt.) B5
Discovery (bay) A6
Eildon (lake) C5
French (isl.) 123 C6
Gippsland (reg.) D6
Glenelg (riv.) A5
Goulburn (riv.) C5
Hindmarsh (lake) A5
Hobsons (bay) H5
Hopkins (riv.) B5
Hume (lake) D4
Indian Ocean B6
Loddon (riv.) B5
Mitchell (riv.) D5
Mitta Mitta (riv.) D5
Mornington (pen.) C6
Mount Emu (creek) B5
Murray (riv.) A4
Nelson (cape) A6
Ninety Mile (beach) D6
Otway (cape) B6
Ovens (riv.) D5
Phillip (isl.) 2,832 C6
Portland (bay) A6
Port Phillip (bay) C6
Rocklands (res.) B5
Snowy (riv.) E5
South East (pt.) D6
Tasman (sea) F5
Tyrrell (lake) B4
Waratah (bay) C6
Wellington (lake) D6
Western Port (inlet) C6
Wilsons (prom.) D6
Wimmera (riv.) A5
Yarra (riv.) C5

*City and suburbs.
○ Population of district.
†Population of met. area.
‡Population of urban area.

Irrigation Areas and Artesian Basins in Australia

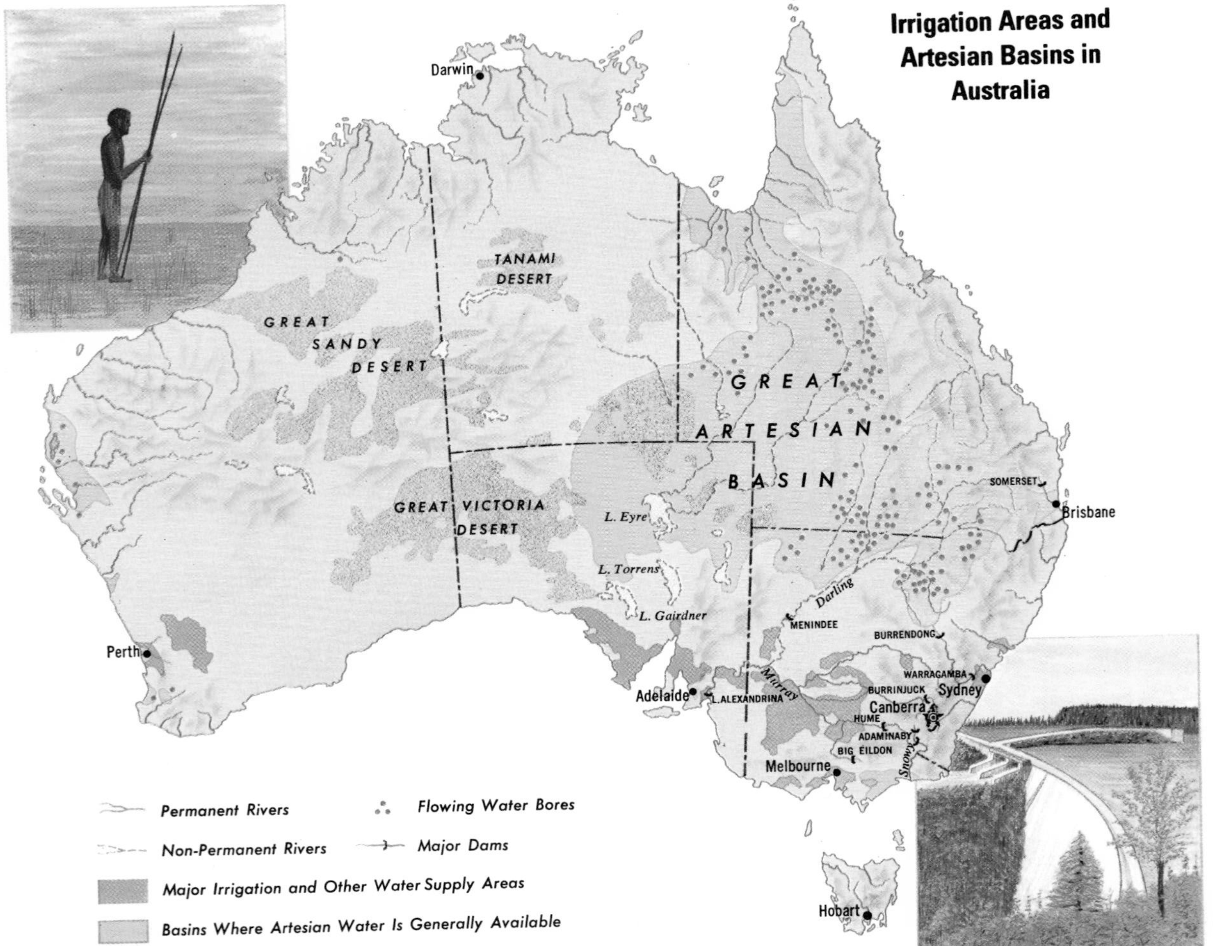
Darwin
TANAMI DESERT
GREAT SANDY DESERT
GREAT ARTESIAN BASIN
GREAT VICTORIA DESERT
L. Eyre
L. Torrens
L. Gairdner
SOMERSET
Brisbane
Darling
MENINDEE
BURRENDONG
Perth
Adelaide
L. ALEXANDRINA
Murray
WARRAGAMBA
BURRINJUCK
Sydney
Canberra
HUME
ADAMINABY
BIG EILDON
Snowy
Melbourne
Hobart
Permanent Rivers
Flowing Water Bores
Non-Permanent Rivers
Major Dams
Major Irrigation and Other Water Supply Areas
Basins Where Artesian Water Is Generally Available

Prepared from Atlas of Australian Resources.

Topography

0   30   60 MI.
0   30   60 KM.

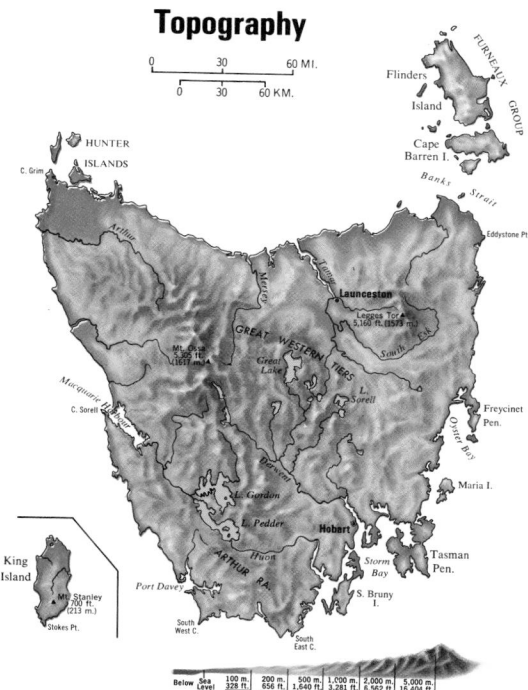

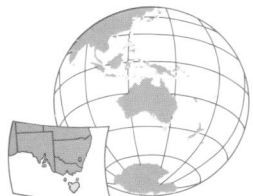

TASMANIA

AREA 26,178 sq. mi. (67,800 sq. km.)
POPULATION 418,957
CAPITAL Hobart
LARGEST CITY Hobart
HIGHEST POINT Mt. Ossa 5,305 ft.
(1,617 m.)

Below Sea Level	100 m. 328 ft.
200 m. 656 ft.	500 m. 1,640 ft.
1,000 m. 3,281 ft.	2,000 m. 6,562 ft.
5,000 m. 16,404 ft.	

Forth (riv.) C3
Frankland (cape) C3
Frankland (range) D1
Franklin (riv.) B4
Frenchmans Cap (mt.) B4
Freycinet (pen.) E4
Furneaux Group (isls.) 1,039 E1
Gordon (lake) C4
Gordon (riv.) B4
Great (lake) C3
Great Western Tiers (mts.) . . C3
Grim (cape) A2
Hartz (mt.) C5
Hibbs (pt.) B4
Hogan Group (isl.) D1
Hummock (isl.) D2
Hunter (isl.) A2
Hunter (isls.) B2
Huon (riv.) C5
Indian Ocean A4
Kent Group (isls.) D1
King (isl.) 2,592 . . . . A1

King (riv.) B4
King William (lake) C4
Lake (riv.) D3
Legges Tor (mt.) D3
Leven (riv.) B3
Lofty (range) B3
Low Rocky (pt.) B4
Lyell (mt.) B4
Maatsuyker (isls.) C5
Macquarie (harb.) B4
Macquarie (riv.) D3
Maria (isl.) E4
Marion (bay) E4
Mersey (riv.) C3
Munro (mt.) E2
Naturaliste (cape) E2
Nive (riv.) C4
Norfolk (bay) D4
North (pt.) E1
North Bruny (isl.) D5
North Esk (riv.) D3
Ossa (mt.) C3

Ouse (riv.) C4
Oyster (bay) E4
Pedder (riv.) B4
Phoques (bay) A1
Picton (mt.) C5
Pieman (riv.) B3
Pillar (cape) E5
Port Davey (inlet) B5
Portland (cape) D2
Ramsey (mt.) B3
Raoul (cape) D5
Reid (rapid) B1
Ringarooma (bay) D2
Robbins (isl.) B2
Saint Clair (lake) C4
Saint Helens (pt.) E3
Saint Vincent (cape) B5
Savage (riv.) B3
Schouten (isl.) E4
Sorell (isl.) E4
Sorell (lake) D4
South (cape) C5

South Bruny (isl.) D5
South East (cape) C5
South Esk (riv.) D3
South West (cape) B5
Stanley (mt.) A1
Stokes (pt.) A1
Storm (bay) D5
Strzelecki (mt.) D5
Tamar (riv.) D3
Tasman (head) D5
Tasman (pen.) E5
Tasman (sea) E4
Three Hummock (isl.) B2
Vansittart (isl.) E2
West (pt.) A2
West Sister (isl.) D1
Wickham (cape) A1

○ Population of district.
*Population of met. area.

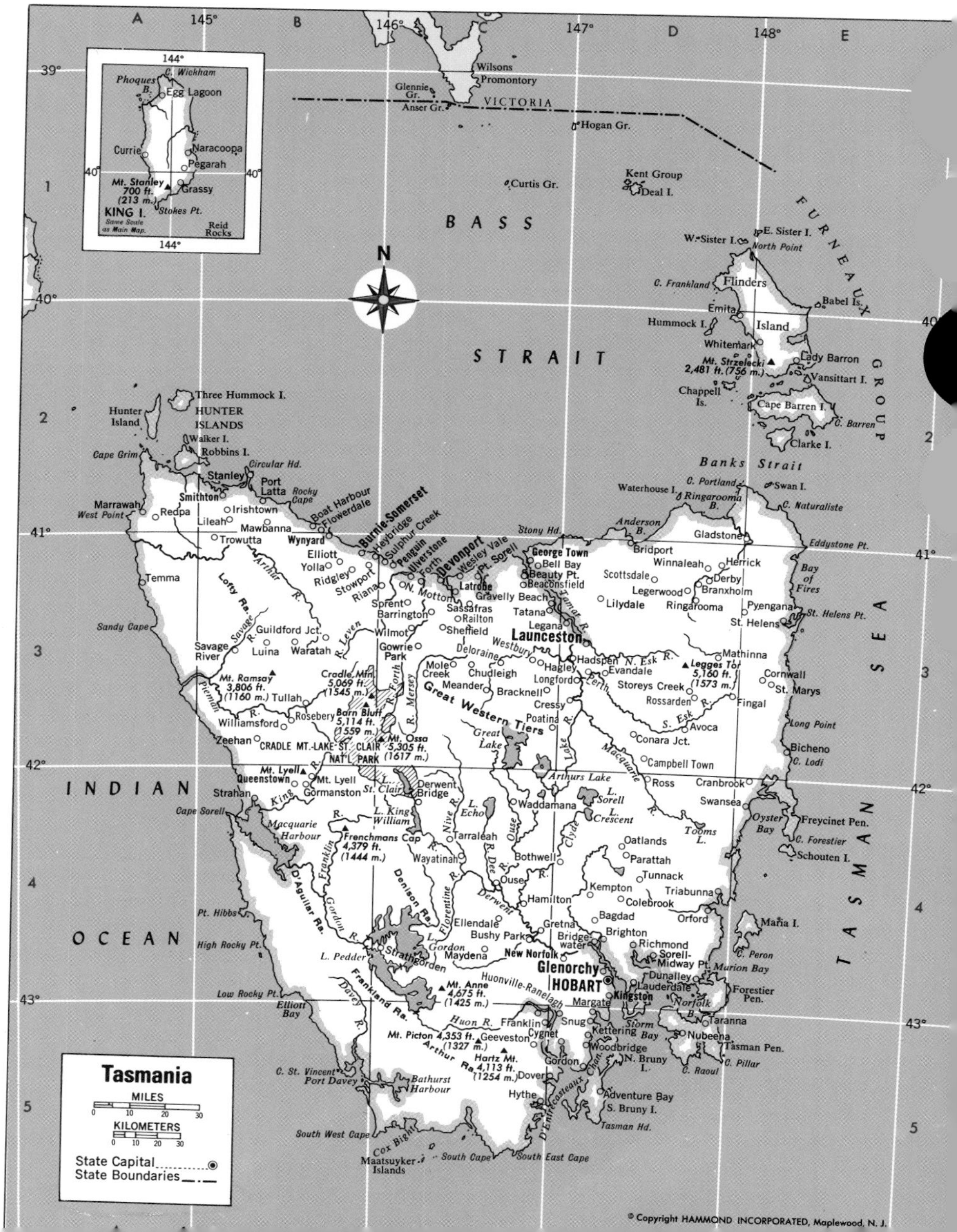

CITIES and TOWNS

Adventure Bay D5
Avoca D3
Bagdad D4
Beaconsfield 898 . . . . C3
Beauty Point 998 . . . . C3
Bell Bay C3
Bicheno 674 . . . . E3
Boat Harbour B2
Bothwell 356 . . . . C4
Bracknell 347 . . . . C3
Branxholm 273 . . . . D3
Bridgewater 6,880 . . . . D4
Bridport 885 . . . . D3
Brighton 9,441 . . . . D4
Burnie 19,994 . . . . B3
Campbell Town 879 . . . . . . D3
Chudleigh C3
Colebrook D4
Cressy 640 . . . . C3
Currie 859 . . . . A1
Cygnet 715 . . . . C5
Deloraine 1,923 . . . . C3
Derwent Bridge C4
Devonport 21,424 . . . . C3
Dover 570 . . . . C5
Dunalley 203 . . . . D4
Evandale 614 . . . . D3
Exeter 353 . . . . C3
Fingal 424 . . . . E3
Forth 273 . . . . C3
Franklin 479 . . . . C5
Geeveston 860 . . . . C5
George Town 5,592 . . . . . . C3
Glenorchy 41,019 . . . . D4
Gormanston 126 . . . . B4
Gowrie Park C3
Grassy 780 . . . . B1
Gravelly Beach 535 . . . . . . C3
Hadspen 908 . . . . D3
Hagley 232 . . . . C3
Hamilton 2,488 . . . . C4
Heybridge 395 . . . . C3
Hobart (cap.) 128,603 . . . . D4
Hobart *168,359 . . . . D4
Huonville-Ranelagh 1,347 . . C5
Kettering 288 . . . . D5
Kingston 8,556 . . . . D4
Latrobe 2,401 . . . . C3
Lauderdale 2,117 . . . . D4
Launceston 31,273 . . . . . . D3
Launceston *64,555 . . . . . . C3
Legana 964 . . . . C3
Lilydale 308 . . . . D3
Longford 2,027 . . . . C3
Luina 522 . . . . B3
Margate 476 . . . . D4
Maydena 461 . . . . C4
Meander C3
Mole Creek 303 . . . . C3
New Norfolk 6,243 . . . . C4
Nubeena 225 . . . . D5
Oatlands 545 . . . . D4
Orford 378 . . . . D4
Penguin 2,616 . . . . C3
Perth 1,229 . . . . D3
Poatina C3
Port Sorell 859 . . . . C3
Queenstown 3,714 . . . . . . B4
Railton 857 . . . . C3
Richmond 587 . . . . D4
Ridgley 452 . . . . B3

Ringarooma 223 . . . . D3
Rosebery 2,675 . . . . B3
Ross 289 . . . . D4
Rossarden 365 . . . . D3
Saint Helens 1,005 . . . . . . E3
Saint Marys 653 . . . . E3
Sassafras C3
Savage River 1,141 . . . . . . B3
Scottsdale 2,002 . . . . D3
Sheffield 945 . . . . C3
Smithton 3,378 . . . . A2
Snug 684 . . . . D5
Sorell-Midway Point 2,544 . . D4
Stanley 603 . . . . B2
Storeys Creek D3
Strahan 402 . . . . B4
Strathgordon C4
Sulphur Creek 367 . . . . C3
Swansea 428 . . . . D4
Tarraleah 498 . . . . C4
Temma A3
Triabunna 924 . . . . D4
Tullah 1,894 . . . . B3
Ulverstone 9,413 . . . . C3
Waratah 342 . . . . B3
Wesley Vale C3
Westbury 1,161 . . . . C3
Whitemark D2
Woodbridge 259 . . . . D5
Wynyard 4,582 . . . . B3
Zeehan 1,750 . . . . B3

OTHER FEATURES

Anderson (bay) D2
Anne (mt.) C4
Anser Group (isls.) C1
Arthur (lake) D4
Arthur (range) C5
Arthur (riv.) B3
Babel (isl.) E1
Banks (str.) D2
Barn Bluff (mt.) B3
Barren (cape) E2
Bass (str.) C1
Bathurst (gulf) C5
Cape Barren (isl.) E2
Chappell (isls.) B2
Circular (gulf) B2
Clarke (isl.) E2
Clyde (riv.) D4
Cox (bight) C5
Cradle (mt.) B3
Cradle Mt. Lake St. Clair
  Nat'l Park B3
Crescent (lake) D4
Curtis Group (isls.) C1
D'Aguilar (range) B4
Davey (riv.) B4
Deal (isl.) D1
Dee (riv.) C4
Denison (range) C4
D'Entrecasteaux (chan.) . . . D5
Derwent (riv.) C4
East Sister (isl.) E1
Echo (lake) C4
Eddystone (pt.) E2
Elliott (bay) B5
Fires (bay) E3
Flinders (isl.) 2,150 . . . . . . D1
Florence (riv.) C4
Forestier (chan.) E4
Forestier (pen.) E4

Tasmania

MILES
0   10   20   30
KILOMETERS
0   10   20   30

State Capital .... ◉
State Boundaries _ . _ . _

© Copyright HAMMOND INCORPORATED, Maplewood, N. J.

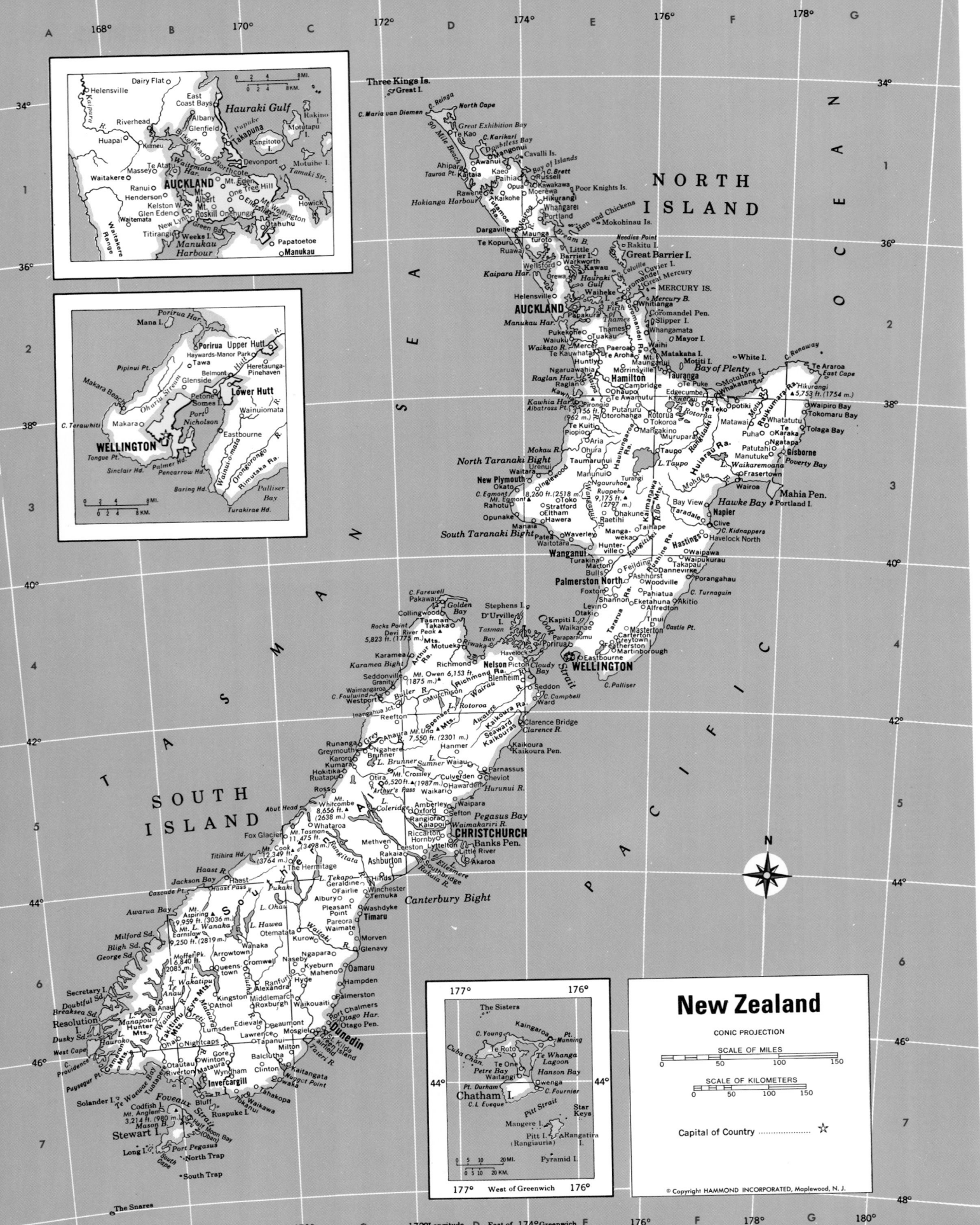

New Zealand

CONIC PROJECTION

SCALE OF MILES
0   50   100   150

SCALE OF KILOMETERS
0   50   100   150

Capital of Country .... ☆

© Copyright HAMMOND INCORPORATED, Maplewood, N.J.

Topography

Three Kings Is.
C. Maria van Diemen
North Cape
Bay of Islands
Great Barrier I.
Kaipara Har.
Coromandel Pen.
Auckland
North Island
Bay of Plenty
East Cape
Lake Taupo
Ruapehu 9,175 ft. (2796 m.)
Hawke Bay
C. Egmont
Mt. Egmont 8,260 ft. (2518 m.)
Mahia Pen.
C. Farewell
Tasman Bay
Cook Strait
Wellington
C. Palliser
C. Foulwind
South Island
SOUTHERN ALPS
Pegasus Bay
Christchurch
Banks Pen.
Mt. Cook (3764 m.)
Canterbury Plains
Canterbury Bight
Cascade Pt.
Otago Pen.
Dunedin
West Cape
Foveaux Str.
Stewart I.

0   75   150 MI.
0   75   150 KM.

Below Sea Level | 100 m. 328 ft. | 200 m. 656 ft. | 500 m. 1,640 ft. | 1,000 m. 3,281 ft. | 2,000 m. 6,562 ft. | 5,000 m. 16,404 ft.

AREA 103,736 sq. mi. (268,676 sq. km.)
POPULATION 3,175,737
CAPITAL Wellington
LARGEST CITY Auckland
HIGHEST POINT Mt. Cook 12,349 ft. (3,764 m.)
MONETARY UNIT New Zealand dollar
MAJOR LANGUAGES English, Maori
MAJOR RELIGIONS Protestantism, Roman Catholicism

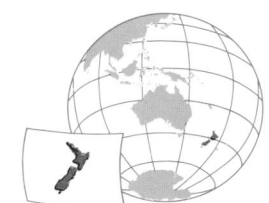

CITIES and TOWNS

Albany 2,001 .... B1
Alexandra 4,348 .... B6
Ashburton 14,151 .... C5
Ashhurst 1,906 .... E4
Auckland 144,963 .... B1
Auckland †769,558 .... B1
Balclutha 4,495 .... B7
Belmont 2,402 .... B2
Birkenhead 21,324 .... B1
Blenheim 17,849 .... D4
Bluff 2,720 .... B7
Bulls 1,839 .... E4
Cambridge 8,514 .... E2
Carterton 3,971 .... E4
Christchurch 164,680 .... D5
Christchurch †289,959 ... D5
Cromwell 2,364 .... B6
Dannevirke 5,663 .... F4
Dargaville 4,747 .... D1
Devonport 10,410 .... C1
Dunedin 77,176 .... C6
Dunedin †107,445 .... C6
Eastbourne 4,561 .... B3
East Coast Bays 28,866 .. B1
Edgecumbe 1,929 .... F2
Ellerslie 5,404 .... C1
Eltham 2,411 .... E3
Fairfield 1,849 .... C6
Featherston 2,458 .... E4
Feilding 11,522 .... E4
Foxton 2,719 .... E4
Geraldine 2,128 .... C6
Gisborne 29,986 .... G3
Gisborne †32,062 .... G3
Glen Eden 9,406 .... B1
Glenfield 3,691 .... B1
Gore 9,185 .... B7
Green Bay 3,035 .... B1
Green Island 6,899 ...... C7
Greymouth 8,103 .... C5
Greytown 1,797 .... E4
Half Moon Bay (Oban) 2,448 B7
Hamilton 91,109 .... E2
Hamilton †97,907 .... E2
Hastings 36,083 .... F3
Hastings †52,563 .... F3
Havelock North 8,507 .... F3
Hawera 8,400 .... E3
Helensville 1,360 .... B1
Henderson 6,645 .... B1
Heretaunga-Pinehaven 6,171 C2
Hokitika 3,414 .... C5
Hornby 8,215 .... D5
Howick 13,866 .... C1
Huntly 6,534 .... E2
Hutt (Upper and Lower) †131,257 .... B2
Inglewood 2,839 .... E3

Invercargill 49,446 ..... B7
Invercargill †53,868 .... B7
Kaiapoi 4,894 .... D5
Kaikohe 3,663 .... D1
Kaikoura 2,180 .... D5
Kaitaia 4,737 .... D1
Kawerau 8,593 .... F3
Kumeu 3,414 .... B1
Levin 14,652 .... E4
Lower Hutt 63,245 .... B2
Lyttelton 3,184 .... D5
Manukau 159,362 .... C1
Marton 4,858 .... E4
Masterton 18,785 .... E4
Mataura 2,345 .... B7
Milton 2,193 .... B7
Morrinsville 5,080 ...... E2
Mosgiel 9,264 .... C6
Motueka 4,693 .... D4
Mount Albert 26,462 ..... B1
Mount Eden 18,305 .... B1
Mount Maunganui 11,391 .. E2
Mount Roskill 33,577 .... B1
Mount Wellington 19,528 . C1
Murupara 2,964 .... F3
Napier 48,314 .... F3
Napier †51,330 .... F3
Nelson 33,304 .... D4
Nelson †43,121 .... D4
New Lynn 10,445 .... B1
New Plymouth 36,048 ..... D3
New Plymouth †44,095 .... D3
Ngaruawahia 4,435 .... E2
Northcote 10,061 .... B1
Oamaru 13,043 .... C6
Oban (Half Moon Bay) 2,448 B7
Onehunga 15,386 .... B1
One Tree Hill 11,078 .... B1
Opotiki 3,388 .... F3
Orewa 5,552 .... E2
Otahuhu 10,298 .... C1
Otaki 4,301 .... E4
Otorohanga 2,574 .... E3
Paeroa 3,702 .... E2
Pahiatua 2,599 .... F4
Paihia 1,740 .... D1
Palmerston North 60,105 . E4
Palmerston North †66,691 E4
Papakura 22,473 .... E2
Papatoetoe 21,700 .... C1
Patea 1,938 .... E3
Petone 8,113 .... B2
Picton 3,220 .... D4
Pinehaven (Heretaunga-Pinehaven) 6,171 .... C2
Porirua 41,104 .... B2
Port Chalmers 2,917 ..... C6
Pukekohe 9,070 .... E2
Putaruru 4,222 .... E2
Queenstown 3,367 .... B6

Raetihi 1,247 .... E3
Raglan 1,414 .... E2
Rangiora 6,385 .... D5
Reefton 1,200 .... C5
Riccarton 6,709 .... D5
Richmond 6,847 .... D4
Riverton 1,479 .... B7
Rotorua 36,157 .... F3
Rotorua †48,314 .... F3
Runanga 1,264 .... C5
Russell 932 .... E1
Saint Kilda 6,147 .... C7
Shannon 1,465 .... E4
Stratford 5,518 .... E3
Taihape 2,586 .... E3
Takapuna 64,844 .... B1
Tapanui 1,042 .... B6
Taradale 4,681 .... F3
Taumarunui 6,541 .... E3
Taupo 13,651 .... F3
Tauranga 37,099 .... F2
Tauranga †53,097 .... F2
Tawa 12,216 .... B2
Te Anau 2,610 .... A6
Te Aroha 3,331 .... E2
Te Atatu 14,713 .... B1
Te Awamutu 7,922 .... E3
Te Kauwhata 842 .... E2
Te Kuiti 4,795 .... E3
Te Puke 4,577 .... F2
Temuka 3,771 .... C6
The Hermitage C5
Timaru 28,412 .... C6
Timaru †29,225 .... C6
Tirangi 8,426 .... B1
Tokoroa 18,713 .... F3
Tuakau 1,982 .... E2
Tuatapere 884 .... A7
Turangi 5,517 .... E3
Upper Hutt 31,405 .... B2
Waihi 3,538 .... E2
Waikanae 4,818 .... E4
Waikouaiti 858 .... C6
Waimate 3,393 .... C6
Wainuiomata 19,192 ...... B3
Waipawa 1,732 .... F3
Waipukurau 3,648 .... F4
Wairoa 5,439 .... F3
Waitangi D7
Waitara 6,012 .... E3
Waitemata 87,452 .... B1
Waiuku 3,654 .... E2
Wanganui 37,012 .... E3
Wanganui †39,595 .... E3
Warkworth 1,734 .... E2
Washdyke 949 .... C6
Waverley 1,239 .... E3
Wellington (cap.) 135,688 A3

Wellington †321,004 ..... A3
Wellsford 1,621 .... E2
Westport 4,686 .... C4
Whakatane 12,286 .... F2
Whangamata 1,566 .... F2
Whangarei 36,550 .... E1
Whangarei †40,212 .... E1
Whitianga 1,960 .... E2
Winton 2,035 .... B7
Woodville 1,647 .... F4

OTHER FEATURES

Arthur's (pass) C5
Aspiring (mt.) B6
Banks (pen.) D5
Bream (bay) E1
Brett (cape) E1
Buller (riv.) D4
Campbell (cape) E4
Canterbury (bight) D6
Cascade (pt.) B6
Chatham (isls.) 751 ..... D7
Cloudy (bay) E4
Clutha (riv.) B6
Coleridge (lake) C5
Colville (cape) E2
Cook (mt.) C5
Cook (str.) E4
Coromandel (pen.) F2
Devil River (peak) D4
D'Urville (isl.) D4
Dusky (sound) A6
East (cape) G2
Egmont (cape) D3
Egmont (mt.) D3
Ellesmere (lake) D5
Farewell (cape) D4
Foulwind (cape) C4
Fournier (peak) E7
Foveaux (str.) A7
Golden (bay) D4
Great Barrier (isl.) 572 E2
Haast (pass) B6
Hauraki (gulf) C1
Hawke (bay) F3
Hikurangi (mt.) G2
Hokianga (harb.) D1
Huiarau (range) F3
Hutt (riv.) C2
Islands (bay) E1
Jackson (bay) B5
Kaikoura (range) D5
Kaimanawa (range) E3
Kaipara (harb.) D2
Karamea (bight) C4
Kawhia (harb.) E3
Kidnappers (cape) F3
Mahia (pen.) G3
Manapouri (lake) A6
Manukau (harb.) B6
Manukau (harb.) B1
Maria van Diemen (cape) . D1
Mataura (riv.) B6
Mercury (isls.) F2
Milford (sound) A6
Needles (pt.) E2
Nicholson, Port (inlet) . B3
Ninety Mile (beach) D1
North (cape) D1
North (isl.) 2,322,989 .. F1
North Taranaki (bight) .. D3
Otago (pen.) C6
Owen (mt.) D4
Palliser (cape) E4
Pegasus (bay) D5
Pitt (isl.) E7
Plenty (bay) F2
Port Nicholson (inlet) .. B3
Port Pegasus (inlet) B7
Pukaki (lake) B6
Puysegur (pt.) A7
Rakaia (riv.) C5
Rangitata (riv.) C5
Rangitikei (riv.) E3
Raukumara (range) F3
Reinga (cape) D1
Resolution (isl.) A6
Richmond (range) D4
Rocks (pt.) C4
Rotorua (lake) F3
Ruahine (range) F4
Ruapehu (mt.) E3
Ruapuke (isl.) B7
South (cape) A7
South (isl.) 852,748 .... B5
Southern Alps (range) ... C5
South Taranaki (bight) .. D3
Spenser (mts.) D5
Stewart (isl.) 600 ...... A7
Tararua (range) E4
Tasman (bay) D4
Tasman (mt.) B5
Tasman (mts.) D4
Tasman (sea) B4
Taupo (lake) E3
Tauroa (pt.) D1

Te Anau (lake) A6
Tekapo (lake) C5
Terawhiti (cape) A3
Thames (firth) E2
Three Kings (isls.) D1
Turakirae (head) B3
Una (mt.) D5
Waiheke (isl.) 3,223 .... E2
Waikato (riv.) E2
Waimakariri (riv.) D5
Waipa (riv.) E2
Wairau (riv.) D4
Waitaki (riv.) C6
Waitemata (harb.) B1
Wakatipu (lake) B6
Wanaka (lake) B6
Wanganui (riv.) E3
West (cape) A6
Whitcombe (mt.) C5

†Population of urban area.

Agriculture, Industry and Resources

Snapper
Fruit
Auckland
Sheep
Dairy
Wellington
Sheep
Wheat
Christchurch
Crayfish
Sheep
Wheat
Soles
Dunedin
Oysters
Crayfish

DOMINANT LAND USE

Mixed Farming, Livestock
Dairy
Truck Farming, Horticulture
Pasture Livestock (chiefly sheep)
Livestock Herding
Forests
Nonagricultural Land

MAJOR MINERAL OCCURRENCES

C Coal
G Natural Gas
J Jade
Ka Kaolin
Lg Lignite
O Petroleum
U Uranium

⚡ Water Power
▨ Major Industrial Areas

Population Distribution

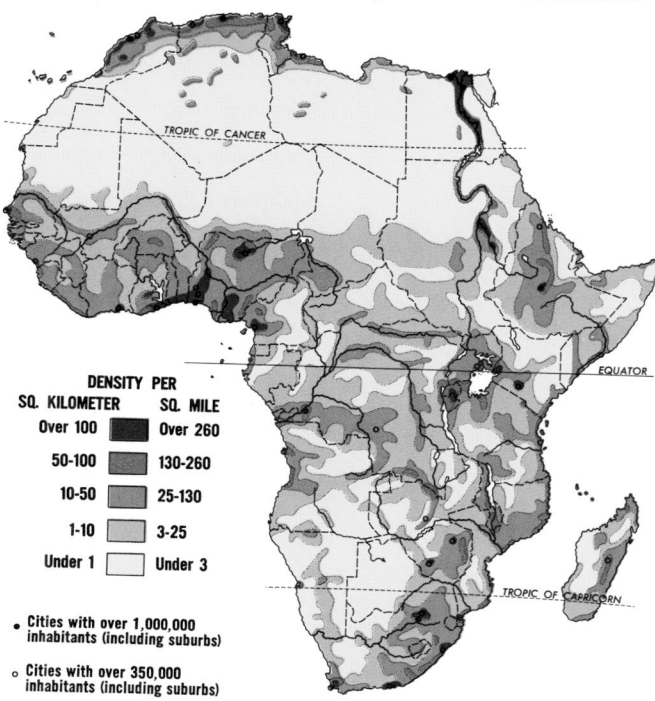

AREA 11,707,000 sq. mi. (30,321,130 sq. km.)
POPULATION 469,000,000
LARGEST CITY Cairo
HIGHEST POINT Kilimanjaro 19,340 ft. (5,895 m.)
LOWEST POINT Lake Assal, Djibouti -512 ft. (-156 m.)

DENSITY PER

SQ. KILOMETER		SQ. MILE
Over 100	■	Over 260
50-100		130-260
10-50		25-130
1-10		3-25
Under 1		Under 3

• Cities with over 1,000,000 inhabitants (including suburbs)

○ Cities with over 350,000 inhabitants (including suburbs)

Vegetation

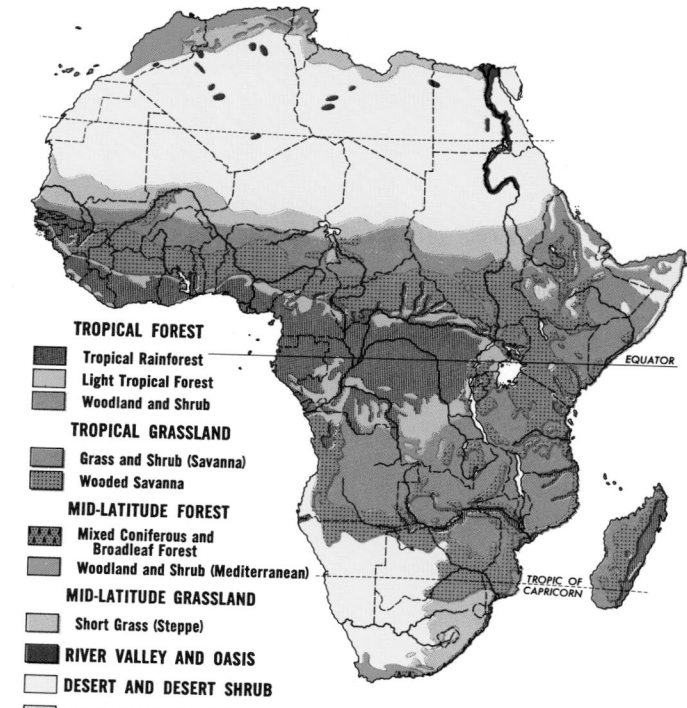

TROPICAL FOREST
Tropical Rainforest
Light Tropical Forest
Woodland and Shrub

TROPICAL GRASSLAND
Grass and Shrub (Savanna)
Wooded Savanna

MID-LATITUDE FOREST
Mixed Coniferous and Broadleaf Forest
Woodland and Shrub (Mediterranean)

MID-LATITUDE GRASSLAND
Short Grass (Steppe)

RIVER VALLEY AND OASIS

DESERT AND DESERT SHRUB

UNCLASSIFIED HIGHLANDS

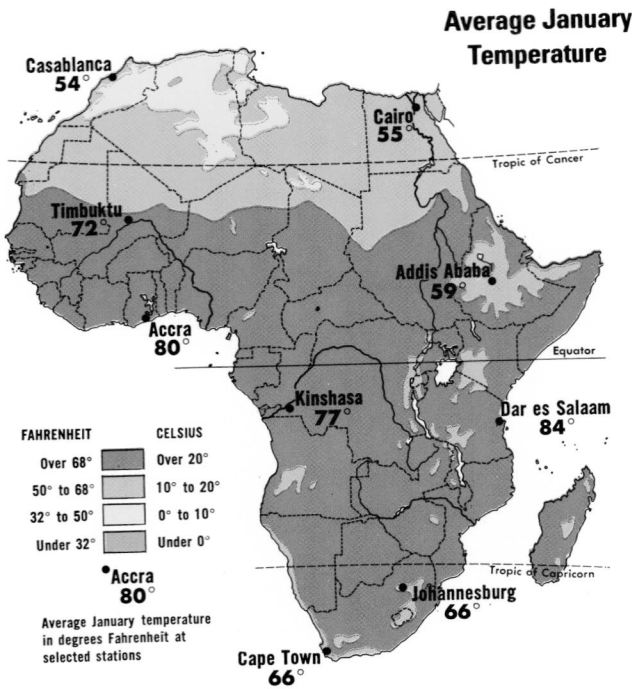

Average January Temperature

Casablanca 54°
Cairo 55°
Timbuktu 72°
Addis Ababa 59°
Accra 80°
Kinshasa 77°
Dar es Salaam 84°
Johannesburg 66°
Cape Town 66°

Tropic of Cancer
Equator
Tropic of Capricorn

FAHRENHEIT	CELSIUS
Over 68°	Over 20°
50° to 68°	10° to 20°
32° to 50°	0° to 10°
Under 32°	Under 0°

● Accra 80°

Average January temperature in degrees Fahrenheit at selected stations

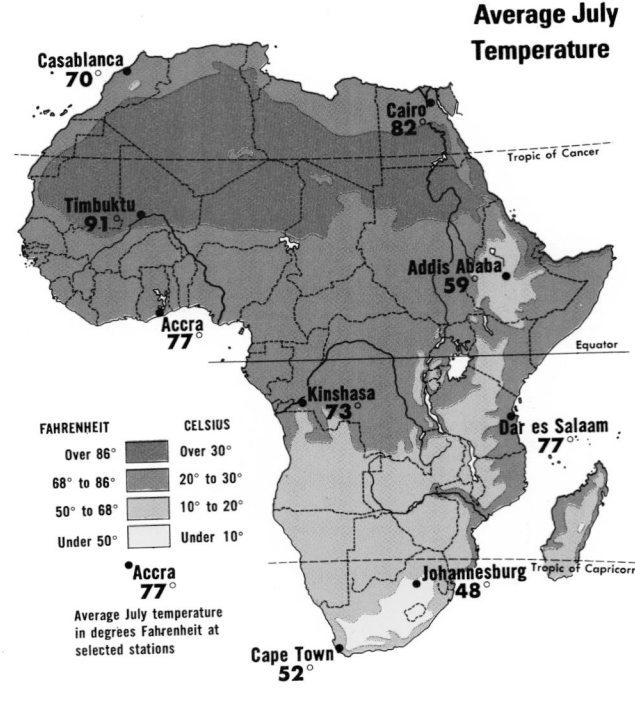

Average July Temperature

Casablanca 70°
Cairo 82°
Timbuktu 91°
Addis Ababa 59°
Accra 77°
Kinshasa 73°
Dar es Salaam 77°
Johannesburg 48°
Cape Town 52°

Tropic of Cancer
Equator
Tropic of Capricorn

FAHRENHEIT	CELSIUS
Over 86°	Over 30°
68° to 86°	20° to 30°
50° to 68°	10° to 20°
Under 50°	Under 10°

● Accra 77°

Average July temperature in degrees Fahrenheit at selected stations

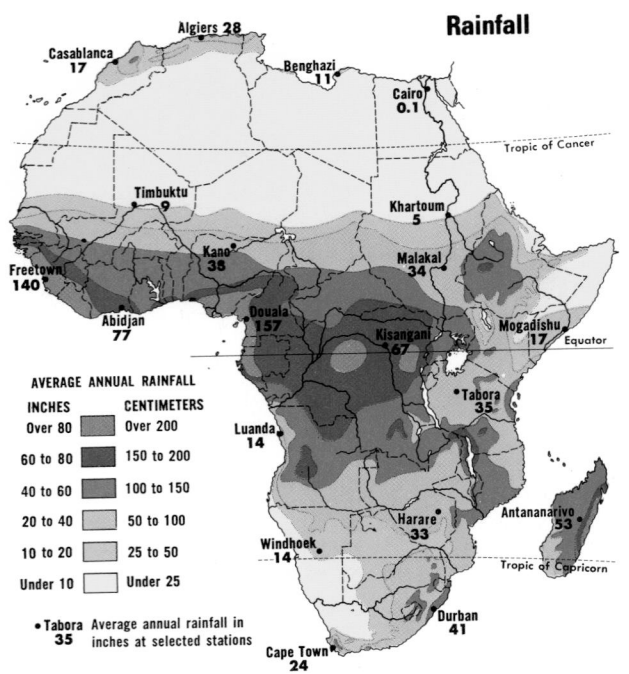

Rainfall

Algiers 28
Casablanca 17
Benghazi 11
Cairo 0.1
Timbuktu 9
Khartoum 5
Kano 35
Malakal 34
Freetown 140
Abidjan 77
Douala 157
Kisangani 67
Mogadishu 17
Tabora 35
Luanda 14
Harare 33
Antananarivo 53
Windhoek 14
Durban 41
Cape Town 24

Tropic of Cancer
Equator
Tropic of Capricorn

AVERAGE ANNUAL RAINFALL

INCHES	CENTIMETERS
Over 80	Over 200
60 to 80	150 to 200
40 to 60	100 to 150
20 to 40	50 to 100
10 to 20	25 to 50
Under 10	Under 25

● Tabora 35 — Average annual rainfall in inches at selected stations

Vegetation/Relief

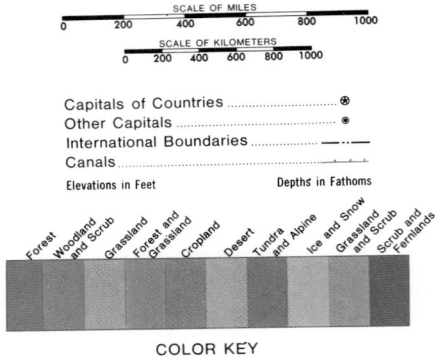

SCALE OF MILES
0 200 400 600 800 1000

SCALE OF KILOMETERS
0 200 400 600 800 1000

Capitals of Countries .... ⊗
Other Capitals .... ⊛
International Boundaries .... —·—·—
Canals ....

Elevations in Feet   Depths in Fathoms

Forest | Woodland and Scrub | Grassland | Forest and Grassland | Cropland | Desert | Tundra and Alpine | Ice and Snow | Grassland and Scrub | Scrub and Fernlands

COLOR KEY

ATLANTIC OCEAN

Paris

FRANCE
WEST GERMANY
SW. CZECH AUST. HUNGARY
YUGOSLAVIA
ROMANIA
BULGARIA
Danube
BLACK SEA
Caucasus
Volga
CASPIAN SEA
U. S. S. R.

Bay of Biscay

PORTUGAL SPAIN
Madrid
Corsica
Rome
Sardinia
ADRIATIC SEA
ALB.
GREECE
Istanbul
TURKEY
SYRIA
IRAQ
Tehran
IRAN

Balearic Is.
MEDITERRANEAN SEA
Sicily
MALTA
Crete
CYPRUS
LEBANON
ISRAEL
JORDAN
KUWAIT

Madeira (Port.)
Str. of Gibraltar
Tangier
Algiers
Annaba
C. Bon
Tunis
TUNISIA
Sfax
Tripoli
Benghazi
Gulf of Sidra
Alexandria
Port Said
Suez Canal
Sinai Pen.
SAUDI
QATAR
U.A.E.

Casablanca
Rabat
Oran
MOROCCO
Jeb. Toubkal 13,665 ft. (4165 m.)
ATLAS Mountains
Wadi Draa
Cairo
Libyan Desert
EGYPT
Nile
Aswan
Lake Nasser
Tropic of Cancer
ARABIA
Rub' al Khali

Canary Is. (Sp.)
Las Palmas
Laayoune
ALGERIA
LIBYA
L. Nubia
Nubian Desert
Port Sudan

WESTERN SAHARA
S a h a r a
Tanezrouft
Ahaggar
Tibesti
a
C. Blanc
Nouakchott
MAURITANIA
Timbuktu
Bodélé Depression
CHAD
Khartoum
SUDAN
El Fasher
El Obeid
Ras Dashan 15,157 ft. (4620 m.)
Asmara
YEMEN
ARAB REP.
DJIBOUTI
Djibouti
Gulf of Aden
Ras Aser

MALI
NIGER
L. Chad
Niger
Senegal
C. Verde
Dakar
SENEGAL
GAMBIA
Banjul
GUINEA-BISSAU
Bissau
Conakry
GUINEA
Bamako
Niamey
Kano
N'Djamena
Sarh
Benue
Abuja
Blue Nile
White Nile
Sudd
PEOP. DEM. REP. YEMEN
Addis Ababa
Ethiopian Highlands
ETHIOPIA
Wabi Shebele

SIERRA LEONE
Freetown
BURKINA FASO
Ouagadougou
GHANA
Kumasi
IVORY COAST
Bouaké
TOGO
BENIN
Porto-Novo
Lomé
NIGERIA
Ibadan
Lagos
CAMEROON
Yaoundé
Bangui
CENTRAL AFRICAN REPUBLIC
Ubangi
Bomu
Uele
Juba
Turkana
SOMALIA
Mogadishu (Muqdisho)

Monrovia
LIBERIA
C. Palmas
Abidjan
Accra
Gulf of Guinea
Malabo Bioko
EQUAT. GUINEA
SÃO TOMÉ E PRÍNCIPE
Libreville
C. Lopez
GABON
Cameroon 13,350 ft. (4069 m.)
Mbandaka
Congo
ZAIRE
L. Mobutu Sese Seko
Kisangani
Margherita
Stanley Falls 16,795 ft. (5119 m.)
RWANDA
Kigali
Bukavu
BURUNDI
Bujumbura
UGANDA
Kampala
L. Victoria
KENYA
Kenya 17,058 ft. (5199 m.)
Nairobi
Mombasa
Pemba

Equator

Ascension (St. Helena)
Annobón (Equat. Guinea)
Brazzaville
Kinshasa
CABINDA (Angola)
Luanda
Malanje
Cuanza
Kasai
Lualaba
Kalanga
Lake Tanganyika
TANZANIA
Dar es Salaam
Zanzibar
Lake Mweru

ATLANTIC OCEAN

St. Helena (U.K.)
C. Fria
ANGOLA
Huambo
Cubango
Cunene
Etosha Pan
Lubumbashi
Kitwe
ZAMBIA
Lusaka
Lake Kariba
Livingstone
Victoria Falls
Zambezi
Zomba
Lilongwe
MALAWI
Lake Nyasa
Ruvuma
C. Delgado
COMOROS
C. Bobaomby
Nampula
Mozambique Channel
Toamasina
MADAGASCAR
Antananarivo

Tropic of Capricorn
Walvis Bay (S. Afr.)
NAMIBIA
(SOUTH-WEST AFRICA)
Windhoek
Makgadikgadi Salt Pan
BOTSWANA
Kalahari Desert
Gaborone
Pretoria
ZIMBABWE
Bulawayo
Harare
Limpopo
Beira
MOZAMBIQUE

OCEAN

C. Fria
Orange
Vaal
Johannesburg
SOUTH AFRICA
LESOTHO
Maseru
SWAZILAND
Mbabane
Maputo
Durban
C. Vohimena

Cape Town
Great Karoo
C. of Good Hope
C. Agulhas
East London
Port Elizabeth
INDIAN OCEAN

Longitude 10° West of Greenwich
Longitude 10° East of Greenwich

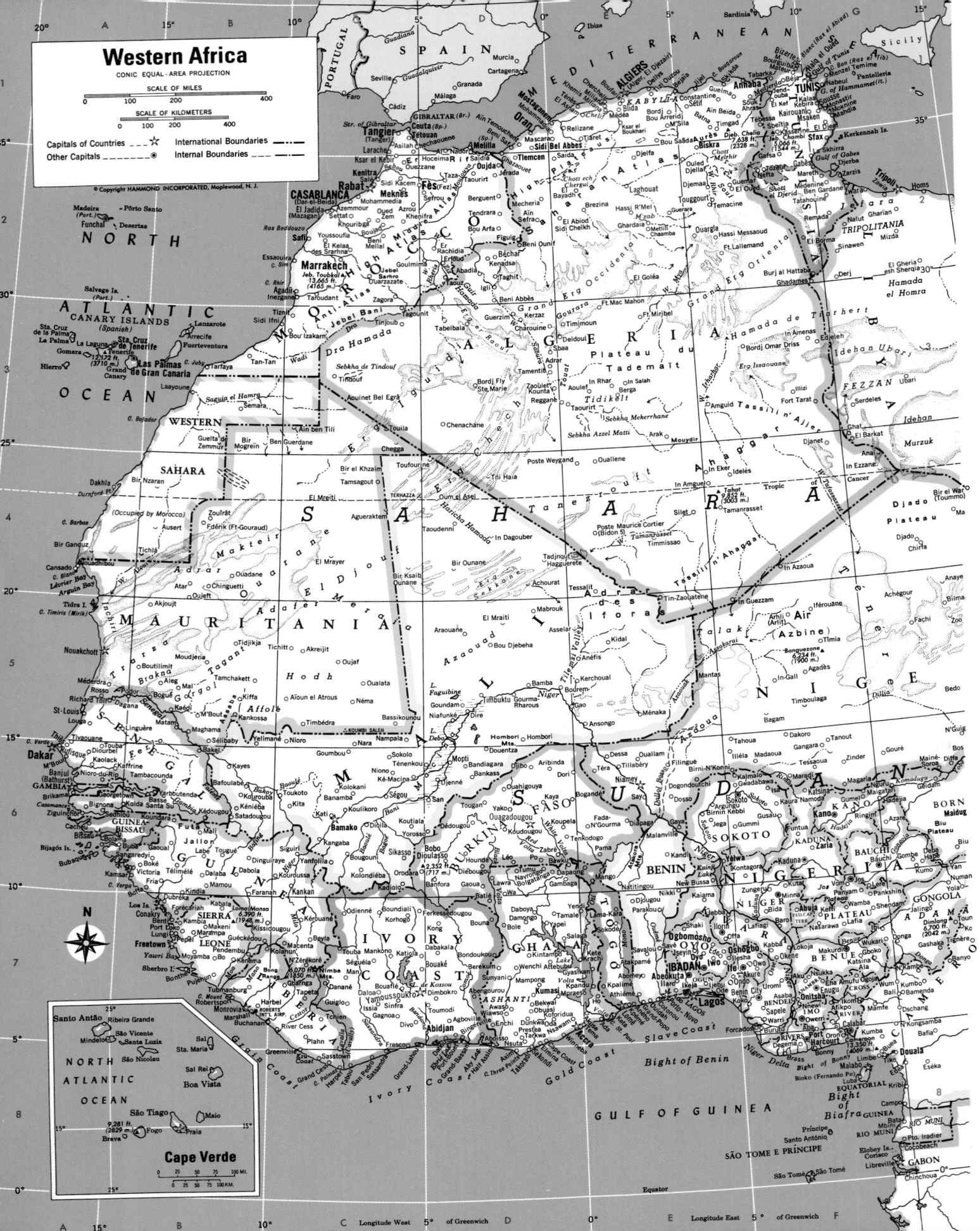

Western Africa

CONIC EQUAL-AREA PROJECTION

SCALE OF MILES

0   100   200   400

SCALE OF KILOMETERS

0   100   200   400

Capitals of Countries ___ ☆   International Boundaries ___
Other Capitals ___ ◉   Internal Boundaries ___

© Copyright HAMMOND INCORPORATED, Maplewood, N.J.

Cape Verde

ALGERIA

AREA 919,591 sq. mi. (2,381,740 sq. km.)
POPULATION 17,422,000
CAPITAL Algiers
LARGEST CITY Algiers
HIGHEST POINT Tahat 9,852 ft. (3,003 m.)
MONETARY UNIT Algerian dinar
MAJOR LANGUAGES Arabic, Berber, French
MAJOR RELIGION Islam

BENIN

AREA 43,483 sq. mi. (112,620 sq. km.)
POPULATION 3,338,240
CAPITAL Porto-Novo
LARGEST CITY Cotonou
HIGHEST POINT Atakora Mts. 2,083 ft. (635 m.)
MONETARY UNIT CFA franc
MAJOR LANGUAGES Fon, Somba, Yoruba, Bariba, French, Mina, Dendi
MAJOR RELIGIONS Tribal religions, Islam, Roman Catholicism

CAPE VERDE

AREA 1,557 sq. mi. (4,033 sq. km.)
POPULATION 324,000
CAPITAL Praia
LARGEST CITY Praia
HIGHEST POINT 9,281 ft. (2,829 m.)
MONETARY UNIT Cape Verde escudo
MAJOR LANGUAGE Portuguese
MAJOR RELIGION Roman Catholicism

GAMBIA

AREA 4,127 sq. mi. (10,689 sq. km.)
POPULATION 601,000
CAPITAL Banjul
LARGEST CITY Banjul
HIGHEST POINT 100 ft. (30 m.)
MONETARY UNIT dalasi
MAJOR LANGUAGES Mandingo, Fulani, Wolof, English, Malinke
MAJOR RELIGIONS Islam, tribal religions, Christianity

GHANA

AREA 92,099 sq. mi. (238,536 sq. km.)
POPULATION 11,450,000
CAPITAL Accra
LARGEST CITY Accra
HIGHEST POINT Togo Hills 2,900 ft. (884 m.)
MONETARY UNIT cedi
MAJOR LANGUAGES Twi, Fante, Dagbani, Ewe, Ga, English, Hausa, Akan
MAJOR RELIGIONS Tribal religions, Christianity, Islam

GUINEA

AREA 94,925 sq. mi. (245,856 sq. km.)
POPULATION 5,143,284
CAPITAL Conakry
LARGEST CITY Conakry
HIGHEST POINT Nimba Mts. 6,070 ft. (1,850 m.)
MONETARY UNIT syli
MAJOR LANGUAGES Fulani, Mandingo, Susu, French
MAJOR RELIGIONS Islam, tribal religions

GUINEA-BISSAU

AREA 13,948 sq. mi. (36,125 sq. km.)
POPULATION 777,214
CAPITAL Bissau
LARGEST CITY Bissau
HIGHEST POINT 689 ft. (210 m.)
MONETARY UNIT Guinea-Bissau escudo
MAJOR LANGUAGES Balante, Fulani, Crioulo, Mandingo, Portuguese
MAJOR RELIGIONS Islam, tribal religions, Roman Catholicism

IVORY COAST

AREA 124,504 sq. mi. (322,465 sq. km.)
POPULATION 7,920,000
CAPITAL Yamoussoukro
LARGEST CITY Abidjan
HIGHEST POINT 5,745 ft. (1,751 m.)
MONETARY UNIT CFA franc
MAJOR LANGUAGES Bale, Bete, Senufu, French, Dioula
MAJOR RELIGIONS Tribal religions, Islam

LIBERIA

AREA 43,000 sq. mi. (111,370 sq. km.)
POPULATION 1,873,000
CAPITAL Monrovia
LARGEST CITY Monrovia
HIGHEST POINT Wutivi 5,584 ft. (1,702 m.)
MONETARY UNIT Liberian dollar
MAJOR LANGUAGES Kru, Kpelle, Bassa, Vai, English
MAJOR RELIGIONS Christianity, tribal religions, Islam

MALI

AREA 464,873 sq. mi. (1,204,021 sq. km.)
POPULATION 6,906,000
CAPITAL Bamako
LARGEST CITY Bamako
HIGHEST POINT Hombori Mts. 3,789 ft. (1,155 m.)
MONETARY UNIT Mali franc
MAJOR LANGUAGES Bambara, Senufu, Fulani, Soninke, French
MAJOR RELIGIONS Islam, tribal religions

MAURITANIA

AREA 419,229 sq. mi. (1,085,803 sq. km.)
POPULATION 1,634,000
CAPITAL Nouakchott
LARGEST CITY Nouakchott
HIGHEST POINT 2,972 ft. (906 m.)
MONETARY UNIT ouguiya
MAJOR LANGUAGES Arabic, Wolof, Tukolor, French
MAJOR RELIGION Islam

MOROCCO

AREA 172,414 sq. mi. (446,550 sq. km.)
POPULATION 20,242,000
CAPITAL Rabat
LARGEST CITY Casablanca
HIGHEST POINT Jeb. Toubkal 13,665 ft. (4,165 m.)
MONETARY UNIT dirham
MAJOR LANGUAGES Arabic, Berber, French
MAJOR RELIGIONS Islam, Judaism, Christianity

NIGER

AREA 489,189 sq. mi. (1,267,000 sq. km.)
POPULATION 5,098,427
CAPITAL Niamey
LARGEST CITY Niamey
HIGHEST POINT Banguezane 6,234 ft. (1,900 m.)
MONETARY UNIT CFA franc
MAJOR LANGUAGES Hausa, Songhai, Fulani, French, Tamashek, Djerma
MAJOR RELIGIONS Islam, tribal religions

NIGERIA

AREA 357,000 sq. mi. (924,630 sq. km.)
POPULATION 82,643,000
CAPITAL Lagos
LARGEST CITY Lagos
HIGHEST POINT Dimlang 6,700 ft. (2,042 m.)
MONETARY UNIT naira
MAJOR LANGUAGES Hausa, Yoruba, Ibo, Ijaw, Fulani, Tiv, Kanuri, Ibibio, English, Edo
MAJOR RELIGIONS Islam, Christianity, tribal religions

SÃO TOMÉ E PRÍNCIPE

AREA 372 sq. mi. (963 sq. km.)
POPULATION 85,000
CAPITAL São Tomé
LARGEST CITY São Tomé
HIGHEST POINT Pico 6,640 ft. (2,024 m.)
MONETARY UNIT dobra
MAJOR LANGUAGES Bantu languages, Portuguese
MAJOR RELIGIONS Tribal religions, Roman Catholicism

SENEGAL

AREA 75,954 sq. mi. (196,720 sq. km.)
POPULATION 5,508,000
CAPITAL Dakar
LARGEST CITY Dakar
HIGHEST POINT Futa Jallon 1,640 ft. (500 m.)
MONETARY UNIT CFA franc
MAJOR LANGUAGES Wolof, Peul (Fulani), French, Mende, Mandingo, Dida
MAJOR RELIGIONS Islam, tribal religions, Roman Catholicism

SIERRA LEONE

AREA 27,925 sq. mi. (72,325 sq. km.)
POPULATION 3,470,000
CAPITAL Freetown
LARGEST CITY Freetown
HIGHEST POINT Loma Mts. 6,390 ft. (1,947 m.)
MONETARY UNIT leone
MAJOR LANGUAGES Mende, Temne, Vai, English, Krio (pidgin)
MAJOR RELIGIONS Tribal religions, Islam, Christianity

TOGO

AREA 21,622 sq. mi. (56,000 sq. km.)
POPULATION 2,472,000
CAPITAL Lomé
LARGEST CITY Lomé
HIGHEST POINT Agou 3,445 ft. (1,050 m.)
MONETARY UNIT CFA franc
MAJOR LANGUAGES Ewe, French, Twi, Hausa
MAJOR RELIGIONS Tribal religions, Roman Catholicism, Islam

TUNISIA

AREA 63,378 sq. mi. (164,149 sq. km.)
POPULATION 6,367,000
CAPITAL Tunis
LARGEST CITY Tunis
HIGHEST POINT Jeb. Chambi 5,066 ft. (1,544 m.)
MONETARY UNIT Tunisian dinar
MAJOR LANGUAGES Arabic, French
MAJOR RELIGION Islam

BURKINA FASO (UPPER VOLTA)

AREA 105,869 sq. mi. (274,200 sq. km.)
POPULATION 6,908,000
CAPITAL Ouagadougou
LARGEST CITY Ouagadougou
HIGHEST POINT 2,352 ft. (717 m.)
MONETARY UNIT CFA franc
MAJOR LANGUAGES Mossi, Lobi, French, Samo, Gourounsi
MAJOR RELIGIONS Islam, tribal religions, Roman Catholicism

WESTERN SAHARA

AREA 102,703 sq. mi. (266,000 sq. km.)
POPULATION 76,425
HIGHEST POINT 2,700 ft. (823 m.)
MAJOR LANGUAGE Arabic
MAJOR RELIGION Islam

Topography

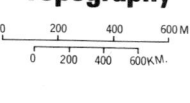

0 200 400 600 MI.

0 200 400 600 KM.

| 5,000 m. 16,404 ft. | 2,000 m. 6,562 ft. | 1,000 m. 3,281 ft. | 500 m. 1,640 ft. | 200 m. 656 ft. | 100 m. 328 ft. | Sea Level | Below |

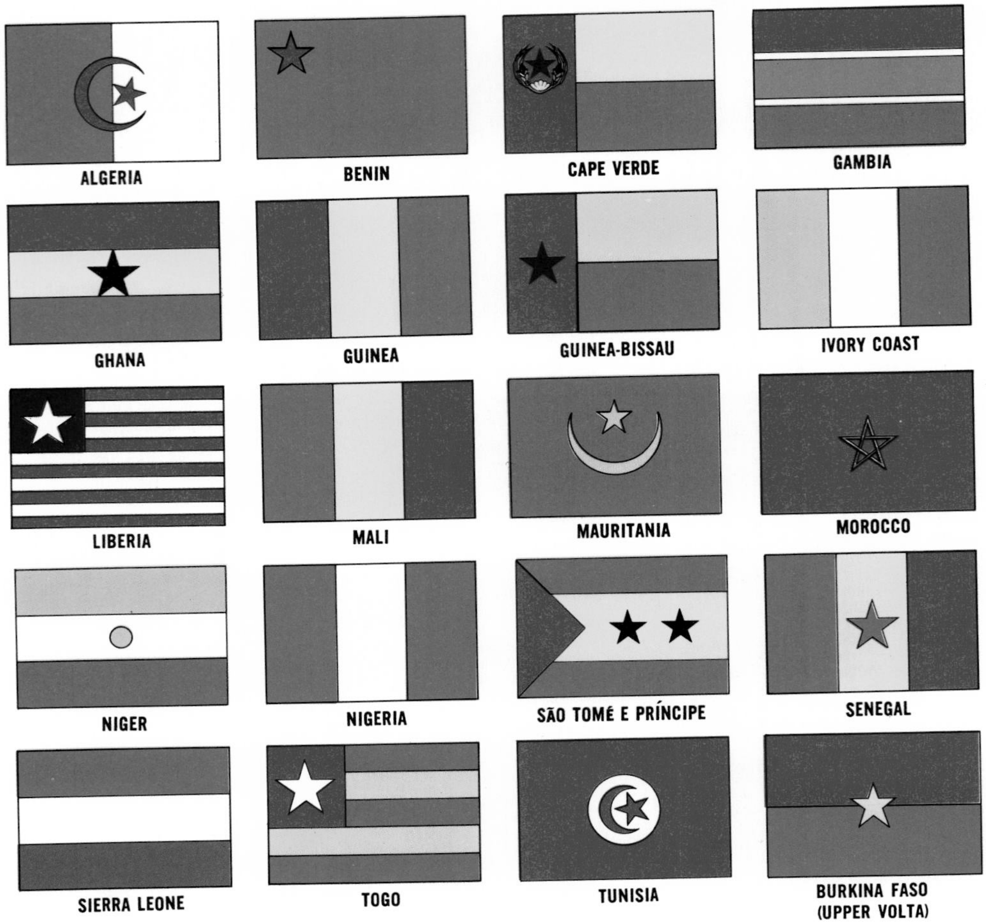

ALGERIA

CITIES and TOWNS

Abadla 12.200 . . . . D2
Adrar 22.800 . . . . D3
Aïn Belda 26.976 . . . . D1
Aïn Sefra 22.400 . . . . E1
Aïn Temouchent 42.000 . . . . D1
Algiers (cap.) 1.365.400 . . . . E1
Amguid F3
Annaba 255.900 . . . . F1
Aoulef 17.200 . . . . E3
Arak E3
Batna 112.100 . . . . F1
Béchar 72.800 . . . . D2
Bejaïa 89.500 . . . . F1
Beni Abbès 5.000 . . . . D2
Beni Ounif 7.500 . . . . D2
Beni Sat 30.700 . . . . D1
Berga E3
Bidon 5 (Poste Maurice
    Cordier) E4
Biskra 90.500 . . . . F1
Blida 160.900 . . . . E1
Bône (Annaba) 255.900 . . . . F1
Bordj Bou Arreridj 65.000 . . . F1
Bordj Fly Sainte Marie D3
Bordj Omar Driss 1.900 . . . . . F3
Boufarik 50.000 . . . . E1
Bougie (Béjaïa) 89.500 . . . . . F1
Bou Saâda 50.000 . . . . E2
Brezina 10.000 . . . . D3
Charouine D3
Chenachane D3
Cherchell 36.800 . . . . E1
Constantine 335.100 . . . . F1
Deldoul E3
Dellys 29.700 . . . . E1
Djanet 5.300 . . . . F4
Djelfa 51.000 . . . . E2
Djemaa 34.600 . . . . F2
Edjeleh F3
El Abiod Sidi Cheikh 15.300 . . E2
El Asnam 106.100 . . . . E1
El Bayadh 38.500 . . . . E2
El Djezair (Algiers)
    (cap.) 1.365.400 . . . . . . E1
El Goléa 24.400 . . . . E2
El Oued 72.100 . . . . F2
Fort Lallemand F2
Fort MacMahon E3
Fort Miribel E3
Fort Tarat F2
Ghardaïa 70.500 . . . . E2
Ghazaouet 25.900 . . . . D1
Guelma 60.100 . . . . F1
Guemar F2
Guerara 22.300 . . . . E2
Guerzim D3
Hassi Messaoud F2
Hassi R'Mel E2
Ideles F4
Igli 3.400 . . . . D2
Illizi 4.600 . . . . F3
In Amenas 4.200 . . . . F3
In Amguel F4
In Eker F4
In Guezzam F5
In Rhar E3
In Salah 18.800 . . . . E3
Jijel 49.800 . . . . F1
Kenadsa 7.600 . . . . D2
Kerzaz 2.900 . . . . D3
Khemis Miliana 57.800 . . . . . E1
Ksar el Boukhari 41.200 . . . . E1
Laghouat 59.200 . . . . E2
Mascara 62.300 . . . . D1
Mecheria 22.600 . . . . D2
Médéa 72.300 . . . . E1
Metlili Chaamba 21.300 . . . . . E2
Miliana 36.400 . . . . E1
Mohammadia 53.700 . . . . D1
Mostaganem 101.600 . . . . . . D1
M'Sila 49.100 . . . . E1
Oran 491.900 . . . . D1
Orléansville (El
    Asnam) 106.100 . . . . E1
Oualène E4
Ouargla 77.400 . . . . F2
Ouled Djellal 22.700 . . . . F2
Philippeville (Skikda) 107.700 . F1
Poste Maurice Cortier D4
Poste Weygand D4
Reggane 11.300 . . . . D3
Relizane 60.000 . . . . E2
Saïda 62.100 . . . . D2
Sbaa D3
Sétif 144.200 . . . . F1
Sidi Bel-Abbès 116.000 . . . . . D1
Silet E4
Skikda 107.700 . . . . F1
Souk Ahras 60.200 . . . . F1
Tabelbala 3.100 . . . . D2
Taghit 3.500 . . . . D2
Tamanrasset 23.200 . . . . F4
Tamentit D3
Taourirt D2
Tébessa 67.200 . . . . F1
Temacine F2
Ténès 30.100 . . . . E1
Tiaret 62.900 . . . . E1
Tiguentourine F3
Timgad 9.800 . . . . F1
Timimoun 20.500 . . . . E3
Tindouf 6.500 . . . . C3
Tinjoub C3
Tin-Zaouatene E5
Tizi Ouzou 73.100 . . . . E1
Tlemcen 109.400 . . . . D2
Touggourt 75.600 . . . . F2
Zaouiet Kounta 13.800 . . . . . D3

OTHER FEATURES

Adrar des Iforas (plat.) E5
Ahaggar (range) F4
Anaf (well) G4
Aouinet Bel Egrâ (well) C3
Atlas (mts.) E2
Aurès (reg.) F1
Azzel Mati, Sebkha (lake) E3
Bougaroun (cape) F1
Chech, Erg (des.) C3
Chelia (mt.) F1
Chélif (riv.) E1
Chergui, Chott Ech
    (salt lake) E2
Gourara (reg.) E3
Grand Erg Occidental (des.) . . E2
Grand Erg Oriental (des.) F2
Guir Hamada (des.) D2
High Plateaus (ranges) C3
Iguidi, Erg (des.) C3
In Ezzane (well) G4
Irharhar, Wadi (dry riv.) F3
Issaouane Erg (des.) F3
Kabylia (reg.) F1
Mediterranean (sea) E1
Medjerda (riv.) F1
Melrhir, Chott (salt lake) F2
Mouydir (mts.) E3
Mya, Wadi (dry riv.) F2
M'zab (reg.) E2
Raoui, Erg er (des.) D3
Rhir, Wadi (dry riv.) F2
Sahara (des.) E3
Saharan Atlas (ranges) E2
Saoura, Wadi (dry riv.) D3

Souf (oasis) F2
Tademaït, Plateau du
    (plat.) E3
Tafassasset, Wadi (dry riv.) . . . F4
Tahat (mt.) F4
Tamanrasset, Wadi (dry riv.) . . E4
Tanezrouft (des.) E4
Tassili N'Ahagger (plat.) F3
Tassili N'Ajjer (plat.) F3
Tidikelt (oasis) E3
Timmissao (well) E4
Tindouf, Sebkha de
    (salt lake) C3
Tinrhert, Hamada de (des.) . . . F3
Tni Hala (well) D4
Touat (oasis) E3
Touila (well) C3

BENIN

CITIES and TOWNS

Abomey 38.000 . . . . E7
Cotonou 178.000 . . . . E7
Djougou E7
Grand-Popo E7
Kandi E6
Lokossa 6.000 . . . . E7
Malanville E6
Natitingou 49.000 . . . . E6
Nikki E7
Ouidah E7
Parakou 21.000 . . . . E7
Porto-Novo (cap.) 104.000 . . . E7
Savalou E7
Savé E7

OTHER FEATURES

Atakora (mts.) E6
Benin (bight) E8
Guinea (gulf) E8
Mono (riv.) E7
Niger (riv.) E6
Ouémé (riv.) E7
Slave Coast (reg.) E7
Sudan (reg.) E6

CAPE VERDE

CITIES and TOWNS

Mindelo 28.797 . . . . A7
Praia (cap.) 21.494 . . . . B8
Ribeira Grande 1.892 . . . . B7
Sal Rei 1.296 . . . . B8
Santa Maria 956 . . . . B8

OTHER FEATURES

Boa Vista (isl.) B8
Brava (isl.) B8
Fogo (isl.) B8
Maio (isl.) B8
Sal (isl.) B7
Santa Luzia (isl.) B7
Santo Antão (isl.) A7
São Nicolau (isl.) B8
São Tiago (isl.) B8
São Vicente (isl.) B7

GAMBIA

CITIES and TOWNS

Banjul (cap.) 39.476 . . . . A6
Basse Santa Su 2.899 . . . . . . B6
Brikama 9.483 . . . . A6
Georgetown 2.510 . . . . A6

GHANA

CITIES and TOWNS

Accra (cap.) 564.194 . . . . D7
Accra* 738.498 . . . . D7
Ada 4.285 . . . . E7
Akuse 3.791 . . . . E7
Attebubu 6.630 . . . . D7
Awaso 5.449 . . . . D7
Axim 8.107 . . . . D8
Bawku 20.567 . . . . D6
Bekwai 11.287 . . . . D7
Berekum 14.296 . . . . D7
Bole 4.772 . . . . D6
Bolgatanga 18.896 . . . . D6
Cape Coast 51.653 . . . . D7
Daboya 1.872 . . . . D6
Damongo 7.760 . . . . D7
Dunkwa 15.437 . . . . D7
Elmina 11.401 . . . . D8
Enchi 4.382 . . . . D7
Gambaga 3.730 . . . . D6
Gyasikan 6.403 . . . . D7
Half Assini 5.429 . . . . D8
Ho 24.199 . . . . E7
Keta 14.446 . . . . E7
Kete Krachi 5.097 . . . . D7
Kintampo 7.149 . . . . D7
Koforidua 46.235 . . . . D7
Kpandu 12.842 . . . . D7
Kumasi 260.286 . . . . D7
Kumasi* 345.117 . . . . D7
Lawra 2.709 . . . . D6
Mampong 13.895 . . . . D7
Mpraeso 5.908 . . . . D7
Navrongo D6
Nsawam 25.518 . . . . D7
Nsuta 3.854 . . . . D7
Obuasi 31.005 . . . . D7
Oda 20.957 . . . . D7
Prestea 15.143 . . . . D7
Salaga 6.413 . . . . D7
Sekondi 33.713 . . . . D8
Sekondi-Takoradi* 160.868 . . . D8
Sunyani 23.780 . . . . D7
Takoradi 58.161 . . . . D8
Tamale 83.653 . . . . D6
Tarkwa 14.702 . . . . D7
Tema 60.767 . . . . E7
Tumu 4.366 . . . . D6
Wa 21.374 . . . . D6
Wenchi 13.836 . . . . D7
Wiawso 5.558 . . . . D7
Winneba 30.778 . . . . D7
Yapei 1.203 . . . . D7
Yendi 22.072 . . . . D7

OTHER FEATURES

Ashanti (reg.) D7
Benin (bight) E8
Black Volta (riv.) D6
Gold Coast (reg.) D8
Guinea (gulf) D8
Oti (riv.) D7
Red Volta (riv.) D6
Saint Paul (cape) E7
Three Points (cape) D8
Volta (lake) D7
Volta (riv.) E7
White Volta (riv.) D6

GUINEA

CITIES and TOWNS

Beyla C7
Boffa B6
Boké B6
Conakry (cap.)* 525.671 . . . . B7
Dabola B6
Dalaba B6
Dinguiraye B6
Dubréka B7
Faranah B6
Forécariah B7
Fria B6
Gaoual B6
Guéckédou C7
Kamsar B6
Kankan 85.310 . . . . C7
Kérouané C7
Kindia 79.861 . . . . B7
Kissidougou C7
Koundara 6.000 . . . . B6
Kouroussa C6
Labé 79.670 . . . . B6
Macenta C7
Mali B6
Mamou B6
N'Zérékoré 23.000 . . . . C7
Sangaredyi B6
Siguiri C6
Télimélé 12.000 . . . . B6
Tougué B6
Victoria B6

OTHER FEATURES

Bafing (riv.) B6
Bagoé (riv.) B6
Bandama (riv.) C6
Baoulé (riv.) C6
Futa Jallon (lag.) B6
Los (isls.) B7
Milo (riv.) C7
Moa (riv.) B7
Niger (riv.) C7
Nimba (lag.) C7
Verga (cape) B6

GUINEA-BISSAU

CITIES and TOWNS

Bissau (cap.) 109.486 . . . . . . A6
Bolama 9.133 . . . . A6
Bubaí 6.706 . . . . B6
Bubaque 8.441 . . . . A6
Cacheu 15.194 . . . . A6

OTHER FEATURES

Bijagós (isls.) A6

IVORY COAST

CITIES and TOWNS

Abengourou 31.239 . . . . D7
Abidjan 685.828 . . . . D7
Aboisso 14.272 . . . . D7
Agboville 27.192 . . . . D7
3ingerville 18.218 . . . . D7
Bondoukou 19.111 . . . . C7
Bouaflé 15.917 . . . . C7
Bouaké 173.248 . . . . C7
Bouna 5.787 . . . . D7
Boundiali 9.869 . . . . C7
Dabakala 3.272 . . . . C7
Dabou 23.870 . . . . D7
Daloa 60.958 . . . . C7
Danané 19.872 . . . . C7
Dimbokro 30.986 . . . . C7
Divo 37.896 . . . . C7
Ferkessédougou 25.307 . . . . . C7
Fresco 1.865 . . . . C7
Gagnoa 42.362 . . . . C7
Grand-Bassam 25.808 . . . . . . D7
Grand-Lahou 4.070 . . . . C8
Guiglo 10.441 . . . . C7
Issia 11.143 . . . . C7
Katiola 21.559 . . . . C7
Kong 2.551 . . . . D7
Korhogo 47.657 . . . . C7
Man 50.315 . . . . C7
Mankono 6.570 . . . . C7
Odienné 13.864 . . . . C7
Port-Bouët 72.616 . . . . D7
San Pedro 27.616 . . . . C8
Sassandra 9.404 . . . . C7
Séguéla 12.587 . . . . C7
Sinfra 16.399 . . . . C7
Tabou 7.255 . . . . C8
Touba 5.256 . . . . C7
Toumodi 12.983 . . . . C7
Yamoussoukro (cap.) 50.000 . . C7

OTHER FEATURES

Aby (lag.) D8
Bagoé (riv.) C6
Bandama (riv.) C7
Baoulé (riv.) C6
Black Volta (riv.) D6
Cavally (riv.) C7
Comoé (riv.) D7
Ebrié (lag.) D8
Guinea (gulf) C8
Ivory Coast (reg.) C7
Kossou, Lac de (lake) C7
Nimba (riv.) C7
Sassandra (riv.) C7

LIBERIA

CITIES and TOWNS

Buchanan 23.999 . . . . B7
Gbarnga 6.896 . . . . C8
Grand Cess C8
Greenville 8.462 . . . . C8
Harbel 11.445 . . . . B7
Harper 10.627 . . . . C8
Kolahun B7
Marshall B7
Monrovia (cap.) 166.507 . . . . . B7
Plahn C7
River Cess 2.041 . . . . C7
Robertsport 2.562 . . . . B7
Sasstown C8

Tapeta 3.927 . . . . C7
Tchien 6.094 . . . . C7
Tubmanburg 14.089 . . . . B7

OTHER FEATURES

Bong (range) B7
Cavalla (riv.) C7
Cestos (riv.) C7
Grain Coast (reg.) B8
Kru Coast (reg.) C8
Mano (riv.) B7
Mount (cape) B7
Nimba (lag.) C7
Palmas (cape) C7
Roberts Field Int'l Airport B7

MALI

CITIES and TOWNS

Anéfis E5
Ansongo 3.485 . . . . E5
Araouane D5
Bafoulabé 2.163 . . . . B6
Bamako (cap.) 404.022 . . . . . C6
Bamba D5
Bananba 6.776 . . . . C6
Bandiagara 8.920 . . . . D6
Bankass 3.229 . . . . D6
Bou Djebeha D5
Bougouni 17.246 . . . . C6
Bourem 4.538 . . . . E5
Dioïla 4.953 . . . . C6
Diré 8.941 . . . . D5
Djenné 10.251 . . . . D6
Douentza 6.746 . . . . D6
Gao 30.714 . . . . E5
Goundam 10.262 . . . . D5
Gourma-Rharous 4.671 . . . . . D5
Hombori D6
Kadiolo 3.991 . . . . C6
Kangaba 3.184 . . . . C6
Kati 24.991 . . . . C6
Kayes 44.736 . . . . B6
Ké-Macina 5.426 . . . . C6
Kéniéba 4.510 . . . . B6
Kerchoual E5
Kidal 3.308 . . . . E5
Kita 17.538 . . . . B6
Kolokani 6.923 . . . . C6
Kolondiéba 5.882 . . . . C6
Koulikoro 16.376 . . . . C6
Kourouba C6
Koutiala 27.497 . . . . C6
Mabrouk D5
Menaka 3.693 . . . . E5
Mopti 53.885 . . . . D6
Nampala C5
Nara 6.091 . . . . C5
Niafunké 6.399 . . . . C5
Nioro 12.290 . . . . C5
Nioro 11.617 . . . . C6
San 22.962 . . . . C6
Satadougou B6
Ségou 64.890 . . . . C6
Sikasso 47.030 . . . . C6
Sokolo C5
Taoudenni D4
Ténénkou 4.708 . . . . C6
Tessalit E4

Timbuktu (Tombouctou) 20.483 . D5
Toukoto C6
Yanfolila 3.809 . . . . C6
Yelimané 1.481 . . . . B5
Yorosso 2.390 . . . . C6

OTHER FEATURES

Achourat (well) D4
Adrar des Iforas (plat.) E5
Asselar (well) D5
Azaouad (reg.) D5
Azaouak (dry riv.) E5
Bafing (riv.) B6
Bagoé (riv.) C6
Bakoy (riv.) B6
Bani (riv.) C6
Baoulé (dry riv.) C5
Baoulé (riv.) C6
Bir Ounane (well) D4
Chech, Erg (des.) D5
Debo (lake) D5
El Mraiti (well) D4
Faguibine (lake) D5
Falémé (riv.) B6
Haricha Hamada (des.) D4
Hombori (mts.) D5
In Dagouber (well) D4
Macina (depr.) D6
Niger (riv.) C6
Oum el Asel (well) C4
Sahara (des.) D4
Sekkane, Erg (des.) D5
Senegal (riv.) B5
Sudan (reg.) C6
Tadjnout Hagguerete (well) . . . C4
Terhazza (ruins) C4
Tilemsi (valley) E5
Toufourine (well) C4

MAURITANIA

CITIES and TOWNS

Aioun el Atrous C5
Akjoujt 8.044 . . . . C5
Akrelijt C5
Aleg 6.415 . . . . B5
Atar 16.326 . . . . B4
Bassikounou D5
Bir Mogrein B3
Boutilimit 7.261 . . . . B5
Bogué 8.056 . . . . B5
Chinguetti B4
Fderik (Fort-Gouraud) 2.160 . . B4
Kaedi 20.848 . . . . B5
Kankossa C5
Kiffa 10.629 . . . . B5
Maghama B5
M'Bout B5
Mederdra A5
Néma 8.232 . . . . C5
Nouakchott (cap.) 134.986 . . . A5
Nouadhibou 21.961 . . . . A4
Ouadane B4
Oualata C5
Oujaf C4
Oujeft B4
Rosso 16.466 . . . . A5
Sélibaby 5.994 . . . . B5
Tamchakett B5

Tamsagout C4
Tazadit B4
Tichitt C5
Tidjikja 7.870 . . . . B5
Timbédra 5.317 . . . . C5
Zouîrât 17.474 . . . . B4

OTHER FEATURES

Adafer (reg.) B4
Adrar (reg.) B4
Aftolé (reg.) B5
Aguerakten (well) C3
Aïn ben Tili (well) C3
Arguin (bay) A4
Assaba (reg.) B5
Atoui, Wadi (dry riv.) B4
Ben Guerdane (well) B3
Bir el Khzaim (well) C4
Blanc (cape) A4
Brakna (reg.) B5
Chegga (well) C4
Djouf, El (des.) C4
El Mrayer (well) C4
El Mrefti (well) B5
Gorgol (reg.) B5
Hodh (reg.) C5
Iguidi, Erg (des.) A5
Inchiri (reg.) B4
Koumbi Saleh (ruins) C5
Lévrier (bay) A4
Maktelér (des.) B4
Meraia (reg.) C4
Mirik (Timiris) (cape) A4
Ouarane (reg.) B4
Sahara (des.) B3
Senegal (riv.) B5
Tagant (reg.) B5
Tidra (isl.) A5
Timiris (cape) A5
Touila (well) A5
Trarza (reg.) A5

MOROCCO

CITIES and TOWNS

Agadir 61.192 . . . . C2
Al Hoceima 18.686 . . . . D1
Asilah 14.074 . . . . C1
Azemmour 17.182 . . . . C2
Azrou 20.756 . . . . C2
Beni Mellal 53.826 . . . . C2
Berguent 3.356 . . . . D2
Bou Arfa D2
Bou Izakarn 2.342 . . . . C3
Boujad 18.838 . . . . C2
Casablanca 1.506.373 . . . . . . C2
Chechaouene 15.362 . . . . D1
Dar-el-Beida
    (Casablanca) 1.506.373 . . . C2
El Jadida 55.501 . . . . C2
El Kelaa des Srarhna 17.163 . . C2
Erfoud 5.400 . . . . D2
Er Rachidia 16.775 . . . . D2
Essaouira 30.061 . . . . B2
Fédala (Mohammedia) 70.392 . C2
Fès (Fez) 325.327 . . . . C2
Figuig 13.660 . . . . D2
Goulmima 4.056 . . . . C2
Inezgane 11.495 . . . . C2

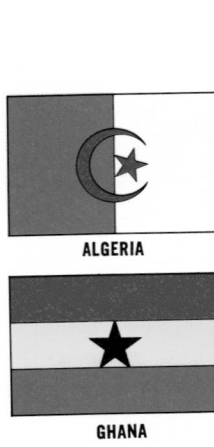

ALGERIA

BENIN

CAPE VERDE

GAMBIA

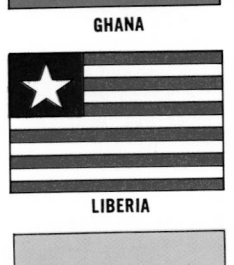

GHANA

GUINEA

GUINEA-BISSAU

IVORY COAST

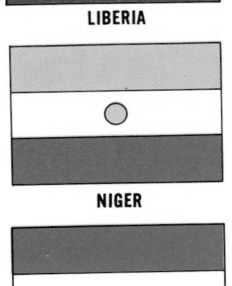

LIBERIA

MALI

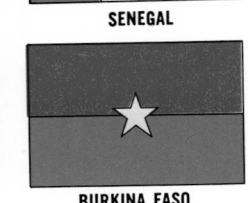

MAURITANIA

MOROCCO

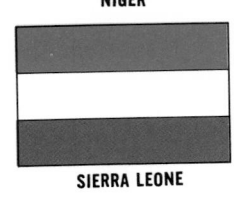

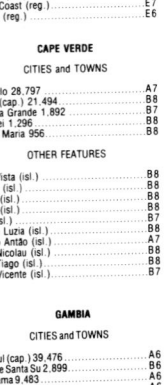

NIGER

NIGERIA

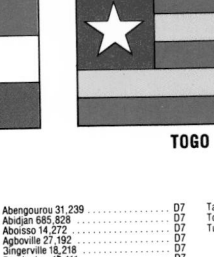

SÃO TOMÉ E PRÍNCIPE

SENEGAL

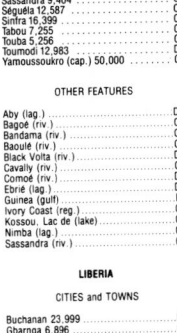

SIERRA LEONE

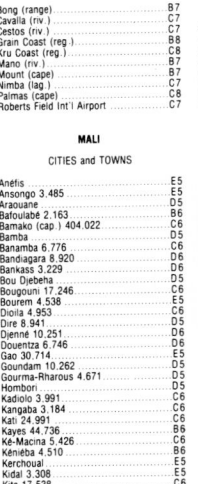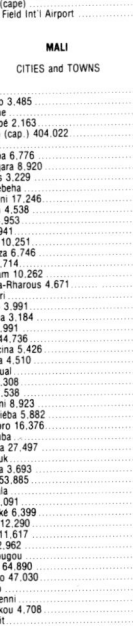

TOGO

TUNISIA

BURKINA FASO (UPPER VOLTA)

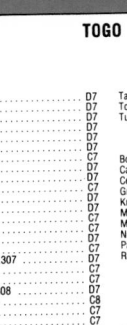

Jerada 30,633 D2
Kenitra 139,206 C2
Khenifra 25,526 C2
Khouribga 73,667 C2
Ksar el Kebir 48,262 C2
Larache 45,710 C1
Marrakech 332,741 C2
Mazagan (El Jadida) 55,501 C2
Meknès 248,369 C2
Mogador (Essaouira) 30,061 B2
Mohammedia 70,392 C2
Nador 32,490 D1
Ouarzazate 11,142 C2
Oued Zem 33,323 C2
Ouezzane 33,267 C2
Oujda 175,532 D2
Petitjean (Sidi Kacem) 26,831 C2
Port-Lyautey (Kénitra) 139,206 C2
Rabat (cap.) 367,620 C2
Safi 129,113 C2
Saïdia D2
Salé 155,557 C2
Sefrou 28,607 D2
Settat 42,325 C2
Sidi Ifni 13,650 B3
Sidi Kacem 26,831 C2
Tagounite C3
Tangier (Tanger) 187,894 C1
Tan-Tan 10,772 B3
Taourirt 15,580 D2
Taouz D2
Tarfaya 1,104 B3
Taroudant 22,272 C2
Taza 55,157 D2
Tendrara D2
Tétouan 139,105 C1
Tiznit 11,391 B3
Youssoufia 22,435 C2
Zagora 5,306 C2

OTHER FEATURES

Anti-Atlas (ranges) C3
Atlas (mts.) C2
Bani, Jebel (mts.) C3
Beddouza, Ras (cape) C2
Dra, Wadi (dry riv.) C3
Er Rif (range) D2
Gibraltar (str.) C1
High Atlas (ranges) C2
Juby (cape) B3
Mediterranean (sea) D1
Middle Atlas (ranges) C2
Moulouya (riv.) D2
Rhéris, Wadi (dry riv.) D2
Rhir (cape) B2
Rif, Er (range) D2
Sarhro, Jebel (mts.) C2
Sebou (riv.) C2
Sim (cape) B2
Toubkal, Jebel (mt.) C2
Ziz, Wadi (dry riv.) D2

NIGER

CITIES and TOWNS

Agadès 11,000 F5
Arhli (Arlit) F4
Bilma G5
Birni-N'Konni 10,000 E6
Bosso G6
Chirfa G4
Dakoro F6
Dessa E6
Diffa G6
Djado G4
Dogondoutchi 9,000 E6
Dosso E6
Fachi G5
Filingué 10,000 E6
Gangara F6
Gaya 5,000 E6
Gouré G6
Iférouane F5
Illéla 9,000 F6
In-Gall F5
Madama G4
Madaoua F6
Magaria F6
Mainé-Soroa G6
Maradi 45,852 F6
N'Guigmi G6
Niamey (cap.) 225,314 E6
Quallam E6
Say E6
Tahoua 31,265 F6
Tanout F6
Téra 8,000 E6
Tessaoua 5,000 F6
Tillabéry E6
Timia F4
Zinder 58,436 F6

OTHER FEATURES

Achégour (well) G5
Agadem (well) G5
Air (mts.) F5
Anaye (well) G5
Assakarai (dry riv.) F5
Azaoua (reg.) E5
Azbine (Air) (mts.) F5
Bagam (well) F5
Banguezane (mt.) F5
Bedouaram (well) G5
Chad (lake) G6
Dallol Bosso (dry riv.) E6
Dillia (dry riv.) G5
Djado (plat.) G4
El War (well) G4
In Azaoua (well) F4
Komadugu Yobe (riv.) G6
Mantas (well) E5
Niger (riv.) E6
Sahara (des.) F4
Sudan (reg.) F6
Tafassasset, Wadi (dry riv.) F4
Talak (reg.) E5
Ténéré (des.) G5
Timboulaga (well) F5
Tummo (El War) (well) G4
Zoo Baba (well) G5

NIGERIA

STATES

Anambra 2,300,000 F7
Bauchi 2,496,329 F6
Bendel 2,336,000 F7
Benue 2,641,496 F7
Borno 2,853,553 G6
Cross River 3,633,582 F7
Gongola 1,585,200 G7
Imo 5,000,000 F7
Kaduna 4,098,303 F6
Kano 5,775,000 F6
Kwara 1,600,600 E7
Lagos 1,100,000 E7
Niger 2,900,000 F7
Ogun 1,448,966 E7
Ondo 2,727,676 F7
Oyo 5,208,884 E7
Plateau 1,367,450 F7
Rivers 1,544,314 F8
Sokoto 1,367,450 F6

CITIES and TOWNS

Aba 177,000 F7
Abeokuta 253,000 E7
Abuja F7
Ado 213,000 E7
Afikpo F7
Aku F7
Akure F7
Argungu E6
Asaba F7
Azare G6
Baga G6
Bama G6
Baro F7
Bauchi F6
Benin City 136,000 F7
Bida F7
Birnin Kebbi E6
Biu G6
Bonny F8
Brass F8
Burutu F7
Calabar 103,000 F7
Deba Habe G6
Degema F8
Dikwa G6
Donga G7
Ede 182,000 E7
Eha Amufu F7
Enugu 187,000 F7
Forcados E7
Funtua F6
Gashaka G7
Gbogo F7
Geidam G6
Gombe G6
Gumel F6
Gummi F6
Gusau F6
Gwadabawa F6
Hadejia G6
Ibadan 847,000 E7
Ibi F7
Ife 176,000 E7
Ijebu-Ode E7
Ikeja E7
Ikom F7
Ilesha 224,000 F7
Ilorin 282,000 E7
Isa F6
Iseyin 115,083 E7
Iwo 214,000 E7
Jalingo G7
Jebba E7
Jega E6
Jos F7
Kabba F7
Kaduna 202,000 F6
Kaiama E7
Kalmalo F6
Kano 399,000 F6
Katsina 109,424 F6
Katsina Ala F7
Kaura Namoda F6
Keffi F7
Koko F7
Kontagora F6
Kukawa G6
Kumo G7
Kuta F7
Lafia F7
Lafiagi F7
Lagos (cap.) 1,060,848 E7
Laro E7
Lere F7
Lokoja F7
Maiduguri 189,000 G6
Maigatari F6
Makurdi F7
Minna F7
Mubi G6
Nasarawa F7
New Bussa E6
Nguru G6
Nnewi F7
Nsukka F7
Offa E7
Ogbomosho 432,000 E7
Ogoja F7
Okene F7
Ondo F7
Onitsha 220,000 F7
Oron F8
Oshogbo 282,000 F7
Owerri F7
Owo F7
Oyo 152,000 E7
Pankshin F7
Panyam F7
Port Harcourt 242,000 F8
Ringim F6
Sapele F7
Shaki E7
Shendam F7
Sokoto F6
Toungo G7
Uromi F7
Vom F7
Wamba F7
Warri F7
Wukari F7
Yan G7
Yelwa F6
Yola G7
Zaria 224,000 F6
Zungeru F7

OTHER FEATURES

Adamawa (reg.) G7
Benin (bight) E8
Benue (riv.) F7
Biafra (bight) F8
Biu (plat.) G6
Bonny (bight) F8
Chad (lake) G6
Cross (riv.) F7
Dimlang (mt.) G7
Donga (riv.) G7
Foge (isl.) E6
Gongola (riv.) G6
Guinea (gulf) E8
Hadejia (riv.) F6
Jos (plat.) F7
Kaduna (riv.) F7
Kainji (res.) E6
Kebbi (riv.) E6
Komadugu Yobe (riv.) G6
Niger (delta) F8
Niger (riv.) F7
Osse (riv.) F7
Slave Coast (reg.) E7
Sokoto (riv.) F6
Sudan (reg.) F6

PORTUGAL-Madeira

CITIES and TOWNS

Funchal (cap.) 38,340 A2

OTHER FEATURES

Desertas (isls.) A2
Madeira (isl.) A2
Pôrto Santo (isl.) A2
Salvage (isls.) A2

SÃO TOMÉ E PRÍNCIPE

CITIES and TOWNS

Santo António 1,618 F8
São Tomé (cap.) 7,681 F8

OTHER FEATURES

Guinea (gulf) E8
Príncipe (isl.) F8
São Tomé (isl.) F8

SENEGAL

CITIES and TOWNS

Bakel 6,339 B6
Bignona 14,537 A6
Dagana 10,506 A5
Dakar (cap.) 798,792 A6
Diourbel 50,618 A6
Kaolack 106,899 A6
Kédougou 7,575 B6
Kaffrine 11,211 A6
Kolda 19,302 B6
Linguère 7,890 B5
Louga 35,063 A5
Matam 10,002 B5
M'Bour 37,663 A6
Nioro-du-Rip 7,824 A6
Podor 6,914 B5
Richard Toll A5
Rufisque A6
Saint-Louis 88,404 A5
Sedhiou 9,421 A6
Tambacounda 25,147 B6
Thiès 117,333 A5
Tivaouane 17,351 A5
Touba A6
Yarboutenda B6
Ziguinchor 72,726 A6

OTHER FEATURES

Casamance (riv.) A6
Falémé (riv.) B6
Ferlo (reg.) B6
Gambia (riv.) B6
Senegal (riv.) B5
Verde (cape) A6

SIERRA LEONE

CITIES and TOWNS

Bo 42,216 B7
Bonthe 6,230 B7
Freetown (cap.) 274,000 B7
Kabala 4,610 B7
Kambia 3,700 B7
Kenema 33,880 B7
Lungi 2,170 B7
Marampa B7
Makeni 28,684 B7
Moyamba 4,564 B7
Pendembu 2,696 B7
Pepel 3,793 B7
Port Loko 5,809 B7
Pujehun 1 B7

OTHER FEATURES

Loma, Mansa (lag.) B7
Mano (riv.) B7
Moa (riv.) B7
Sherbro (isl.) B7
Yawri (bay) B7

SPAIN-Canary Islands. Ceuta and Melilla

CITIES and TOWNS

Arrecife 21,310 B3
Ceuta 60,639 C1
La Laguna A3
Las Palmas de Gran Canaria 260,368 B3
Melilla 64,942 D1
Santa Cruz de la Palma 10,393 A3
Santa Cruz de Tenerife 74,910 A3

OTHER FEATURES

Canary (isls.) A3
Fuerteventura (isl.) B3
Gomera (isl.) A3
Grand Canary (isl.) A3
Hierro (isl.) A3
Lanzarote (isl.) B3
La Palma (isl.) A3
Tenerife (isl.) A3

TOGO

CITIES and TOWNS

Aného (Anécho) 10,889 E7
Atakpamé 17,440 E7
Dapaong 10,100 E6
Kpalimé 19,801 E7
Kpémé 3,600 E7
Lama-Kara 9,400 E7
Lomé (cap.) 148,443 E7
Mango 9,600 E6
Sokodé 29,623 E7

OTHER FEATURES

Benin (bight) E8
Guinea (gulf) E8
Mono (riv.) E7
Oti (riv.) E7
Slave Coast (reg.) E7

TUNISIA

CITIES and TOWNS

Béja 39,226 F1
Ben Gardane 6,593 G2
Bizerte 62,856 F1
Burj al Hattaba F2
El Borma F2
El Djem 10,666 G1
El Kef 27,939 F1
Gabès 40,585 F2
Gafsa 42,225 F2
Halq el Oued 41,912 G1
Jendouba 18,127 F1
Kairouan 54,546 F1
Kalaa-Kebira 23,508 F1
Kasserine 22,594 F1
La Goulette (Halq el Oued) 41,912 G1
La Skhirra 4,565 G2
Le Kef (El Kef) 27,939 F1
Mahdia 25,711 G1
Mareth 2,185 F2
Mateur 19,645 F1
Médenine 15,826 F2
Menzel Bourguiba 42,111 F1
Menzel Temime 18,857 G1
Moknine 26,035 G1
Monastir 26,759 G1
Msaken 33,559 G1
Nabeul 30,476 G1
Nefta 12,476 F2
Remada 6,100 F2
Sbeitla 8,039 F1
Sfax 171,297 G2
Sousse 69,530 G1
Tabarka 3,140 F1
Tatahouine 10,399 G2
Tozeur 16,772 F2
Tunis (cap.) 550,404 G1
Tunis* 873,515 G1
Zarzis 14,420 G2

OTHER FEATURES

Abiad, Ras el (Blanc) (cape) G1
Blanc (cape) G1
Bon (cape) G1
Chambi, Jebel (mt.) F2
Djerba (isl.) G2
Djerid, Shott el (salt lake) F2
Gabès (gulf) G2
Grand Erg Oriental (des.) F2
Hammamet (gulf) G1
Jefara (reg.) G2
Kerkennah (isls.) G2
Mediterranean (sea) F1
Medjerda (riv.) F1
Tib, Ras el (Bon) (cape) G1
Tunis (gulf) G1

BURKINA FASO (UPPER VOLTA)

CITIES and TOWNS

Aribinda D6
Banfora 12,358 D6
Batié D7
Bobo Dioulasso 115,063 D6
Bogandé E6
Dédougou D6
Diapaga E6
Diébougou D6
Djibo D6
Dori D6
Fada-N'Gourma 12,000 E6
Gaoua D6
Houndé D6
Kaya 18,000 D6
Koudougou 36,838 D6
Koupela D6
Léo D6
Ouagadougou (cap.) 172,661 D6
Ouahigouya 25,690 D6
Pama E6
Po D6
Tenkodogo E6
Tougan D6
Yako D6
Zabré D6

OTHER FEATURES

Black Volta (riv.) D6
Comoé (riv.) D7
Oti (riv.) E7
Red Volta (riv.) D6
Sudan (reg.) D6
White Volta (riv.) D6

WESTERN SAHARA

CITIES and TOWNS

Dakhla 6,554 A4
El Aaiún (Laayoune) 24,519 B3
Semara 2,655 B3
Villa Cisneros (Dakhla) 6,554 A4

OTHER FEATURES

Atoui, Wadi (dry riv.) B4
Ausert (well) B4
Barbas (cape) A4
Bir Ganduz (well) A4
Bir Nzaran (well) B4
Blanc (cape) A4
Bojador (cape) B3
Durnford (pt.) A4
Guelta de Zemmur (well) B3
Saguia el Hamra (dry riv.) B3
Tichlá (well) B4

*City and suburbs.
○Population of sub-district or division.

Agriculture, Industry and Resources

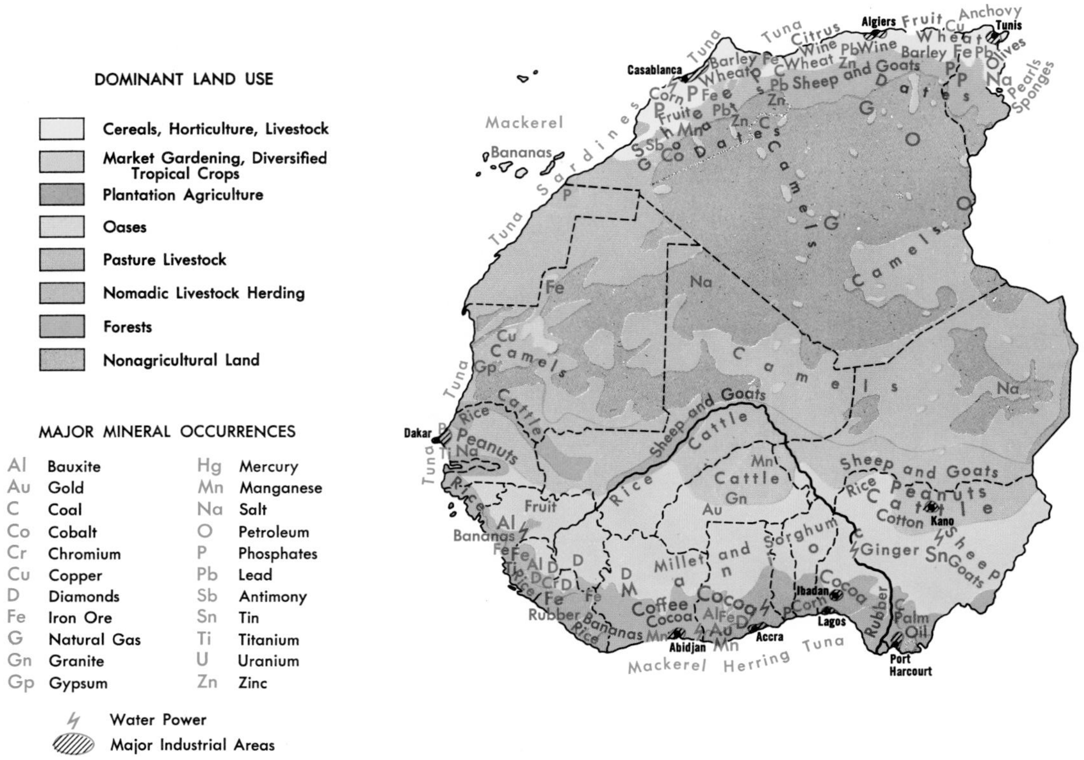
DOMINANT LAND USE
Cereals, Horticulture, Livestock
Market Gardening, Diversified Tropical Crops
Plantation Agriculture
Oases
Pasture Livestock
Nomadic Livestock Herding
Forests
Nonagricultural Land
MAJOR MINERAL OCCURRENCES
Al Bauxite
Au Gold
C Coal
Co Cobalt
Cr Chromium
Cu Copper
D Diamonds
Fe Iron Ore
G Natural Gas
Gn Granite
Gp Gypsum
Hg Mercury
Mn Manganese
Na Salt
O Petroleum
P Phosphates
Pb Lead
Sb Antimony
Sn Tin
Ti Titanium
U Uranium
Zn Zinc
Water Power
Major Industrial Areas
Algiers
Tunis
Casablanca
Dakar
Kano
Ibadan
Lagos
Accra
Abidjan
Port Harcourt
Mackerel
Bananas
Sardines
Tuna
Anchovy
Herring
Sheep and Goats
Camels
Cattle
Peanuts
Rice
Cotton
Ginger
Millet and Sorghum
Coffee
Cocoa
Rubber
Palm Oil
Fruit
Wheat
Barley
Dates
Citrus
Wine
Olives
Corn
Pearls
Sponges

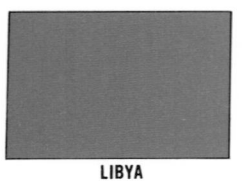
LIBYA

EGYPT

CHAD

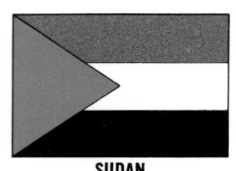
SUDAN

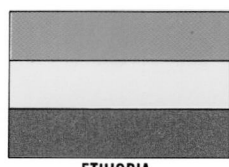
ETHIOPIA

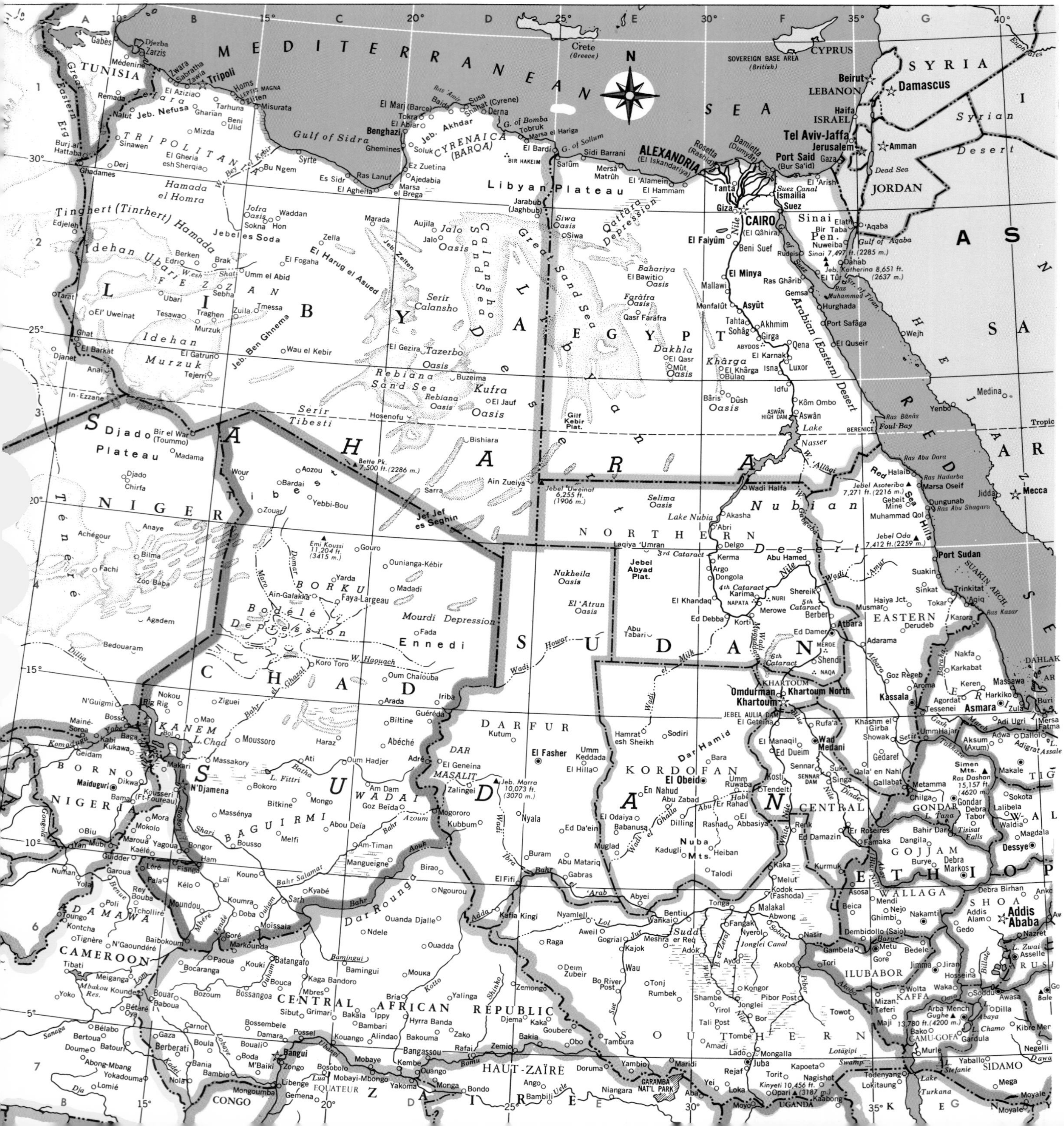

MEDITERRANEAN SEA

TUNISIA · Tripoli · Benghazi · CYRENAICA (BARQA) · Gulf of Sidra

CYPRUS · SYRIA · Damascus · LEBANON · Beirut · ISRAEL · Tel Aviv-Jaffa · Jerusalem · Amman · JORDAN · Syrian Desert · Dead Sea

ALEXANDRIA (El Iskandariya) · Port Said (Bûr Sa'îd) · CAIRO (El Qâhira) · Suez Canal · Ismailia · Suez · Giza · Libyan Plateau · Qattâra Depression · Siwa Oasis

E G Y P T · Sinai Pen. · Gulf of Aqaba · Jeb. Katherina 8,651 ft. (2637 m.)

L I B Y A · Libyan Desert · Great Sand Sea · Calansho Sand Sea · Rebiana Sand Sea · Kufra · Serir Tibesti

Ghadames · Murzuk · Idehan Murzuk · FEZZAN · Sebha · TRIPOLITAN · Hamada el Homra

RED SEA · Aswân · Lake Nasser · Lake Nubia · Luxor · Qena · Aswân High Dam · Port Sudan · Suakin · Jidda · Mecca · Medina

NIGER · Ténéré · Emi Koussi 11,204 ft. (3415 m.) · Bilma · Agadem

CHAD · Tibesti · Faya-Largeau · BORKU · Bodélé Depression · Ennedi · Mourdi Depression · ENNEDI · WADAI · Abéché · Am Timan · L. Chad · N'Djamena · KANEM · BAGUIRMI

SUDAN · Nubian Desert · NORTHERN Desert · Wadi Halfa · Dongola · Karima · Merowe · Berber · Atbara · Khartoum · Omdurman · Khartoum North · DARFUR · El Fasher · MASALIT · Jeb. Marra 10,073 ft. (3070 m.) · Nyala · KORDOFAN · El Obeid · Nuba Mts. · EASTERN · Kassala · Asmara

NIGERIA · Maiduguri · BORNO · CAMEROON · N'Gaoundéré

ETHIOPIA · Addis Ababa · Simen Mts. Ras Dashen 15,157 ft. (4620 m.) · Gondar · L. Tana · Tisisat Falls · GOJJAM · WALLAGA · SHOA · ILUBABOR · KAFFA · WALO · TIGRE · GONDAR · SIDAMO

CENTRAL AFRICAN REPUBLIC · Bangui · Bangassou

HAUT-ZAÏRE · ZAÏRE · CONGO · EQUATOR · UGANDA · Lake Turkana · KENYA

SOUTHERN · Juba · Wau · Malakal · Jonglei Canal · Sudd

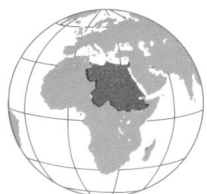

DJIBOUTI

LIBYA
AREA 679,358 sq. mi. (1,759,537 sq. km.)
POPULATION 2,856,000
CAPITAL Tripoli
LARGEST CITY Tripoli
HIGHEST POINT Bette Pk. 7,500 ft. (2,286 m.)
MONETARY UNIT Libyan dinar
MAJOR LANGUAGES Arabic, Berber
MAJOR RELIGION Islam

EGYPT
AREA 386,659 sq. mi. (1,001,447 sq. km.)
POPULATION 41,572,000
CAPITAL Cairo
LARGEST CITY Cairo
HIGHEST POINT Jeb. Katherina 8,651 ft. (2,637 m.)
MONETARY UNIT Egyptian pound
MAJOR LANGUAGE Arabic
MAJOR RELIGIONS Islam, Coptic Christianity

CHAD
AREA 495,752 sq. mi. (1,283,998 sq. km.)
POPULATION 4,309,000
CAPITAL N'Djamena
LARGEST CITY N'Djamena
HIGHEST POINT Emi Koussi 11,204 ft. (3,415 m.)
MONETARY UNIT CFA franc
MAJOR LANGUAGES Arabic, Bagirmi, French, Sara, Massa, Moudang
MAJOR RELIGIONS Islam, tribal religions

SUDAN
AREA 967,494 sq. mi. (2,505,809 sq. km.)
POPULATION 18,691,000
CAPITAL Khartoum
LARGEST CITY Khartoum
HIGHEST POINT Jeb. Marra 10,073 ft. (3,070 m.)
MONETARY UNIT Sudanese pound
MAJOR LANGUAGES Arabic, Dinka, Nubian, Beja, Nuer
MAJOR RELIGIONS Islam, tribal religions

ETHIOPIA
AREA 471,776 sq. mi. (1,221,900 sq. km.)
POPULATION 31,065,000
CAPITAL Addis Ababa
LARGEST CITY Addis Ababa
HIGHEST POINT Ras Dashan 15,157 ft. (4,620 m.)
MONETARY UNIT birr
MAJOR LANGUAGES Amharic, Gallinya, Tigrinya, Somali, Sidamo, Arabic, Ge'ez
MAJOR RELIGIONS Coptic Christianity, Islam

DJIBOUTI
AREA 8,880 sq. mi. (23,000 sq. km.)
POPULATION 386,000
CAPITAL Djibouti
LARGEST CITY Djibouti
HIGHEST POINT Moussa Ali 6,768 ft. (2,063 m.)
MONETARY UNIT Djibouti franc
MAJOR LANGUAGES Arabic, Somali, Afar, French
MAJOR RELIGIONS Islam, Roman Catholicism

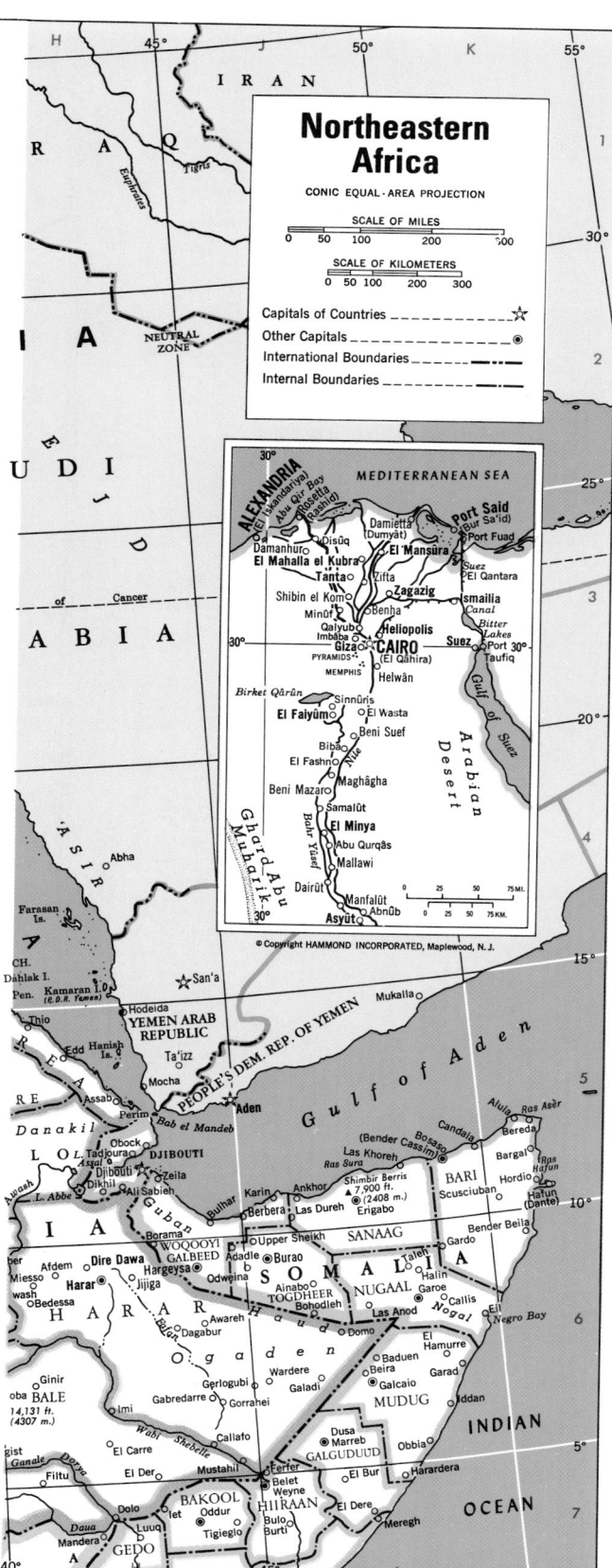

Northeastern Africa
CONIC EQUAL-AREA PROJECTION

SCALE OF MILES
0 50 100   200   300

SCALE OF KILOMETERS
0 50 100   200   300

Capitals of Countries _ _ _ _ _ _ _ ☆
Other Capitals _ _ _ _ _ _ _ _ _ ◉
International Boundaries _ _ _ _ _ _
Internal Boundaries _ _ _ _ _ _ _

© Copyright HAMMOND INCORPORATED, Maplewood, N.J.

CHAD

CITIES and TOWNS

Abéché 28,100	D5
Abou Dela	C5
Adré	D5
Ain-Galakka	C4
Am-Dam	D5
Am-Timan 4,200	D5
Arada	D4
Ati 7,500	C5
Baibokoum 5,500	C6
Bardaï	C3
Biltine 3,900	D5
Bitkine 5,000	C5
Bokoro 6,500	C5
Bol 2,500	B5
Bongor 14,300	C5
Bousso 4,500	C5
Doba 13,300	C6
Fada	D4
Faya-Largeau 6,800	C4
Fianga 10,000	C6
Goré	C6
Gouro	C4
Goz Belda	D5
Guéréda	D5
Ham	C5

Haraz	C5
Iriba	D4
Kélo 16,800	C6
Koro Toro	C4
Koumra 17,000	C6
Kouno	C5
Kyabé 5,000	C6
Lal 10,400	C6
Léré	B6
Madadi	D4
Mangueigne	C6
Mao 4,900	C5
Massakory	C5
Massénya	C5
Melfi	C5
Mogororo	D5
Moïssala 5,100	C6
Mongo 8,300	C5
Moundou 39,600	C6
Moussoro 7,700	C5
N'Djamena (cap.) 179,000	C5
Nokou	B5
Oum Chalouba	D4
Oum Hadjer 5,600	D5
Ounianga-Kébir	D4
Pala 13,200	B6
Rig Rig	B5
Sarh 43,700	C6
Wour	C3
Yarda	C4

Yebbi-Bou	C3
Ziguei	C5
Zouar	C3

OTHER FEATURES

Azoum, Bahr	D5
Baguirmi (reg.)	C5
Bahr el Ghazal (dry riv.)	C5
Batha (riv.)	C5
Bodélé (depr.)	C4
Borku 72	C4
Chad (lake)	B5
Domar (dry riv.)	C4
Emi Koussi (mt.)	C4
Ennedi (plat.)	D4
Fittri (lake)	C5
Haouach, Wadi (dry riv.)	C4
Jef Jef es Seghin (plat.)	D3
Kanem (reg.)	C5
Logone (riv.)	C5
Maro (dry riv.)	C6
Mbéré (riv.)	C6
Mourdi (depr.)	D4
Ouham (riv.)	C6
Pendé (riv.)	C6
Sahara (des.)	C3
Salamat, Bahr (riv.)	C6
Sara (riv.)	C5
Shari (riv.)	C5

Sudan (reg.)	C5
Tibesti (mts.)	C3
Wadai (reg.)	D5

DJIBOUTI

CITIES and TOWNS

Ali Sabieh	H5
Dikhil	H5
Djibouti (cap.) 96,000	H5
Obock	H5
Tadjoura	H5

OTHER FEATURES

Abbe (lake)	H5
Aden (gulf)	J5
Bab el Mandeb (str.)	H5

EGYPT

CITIES and TOWNS

Abnūb 39,343	J4
Abu Qurqâs	J4
Akhmim 53,234	F2
Alexandria 2,318,655	J2

(continued on following page)

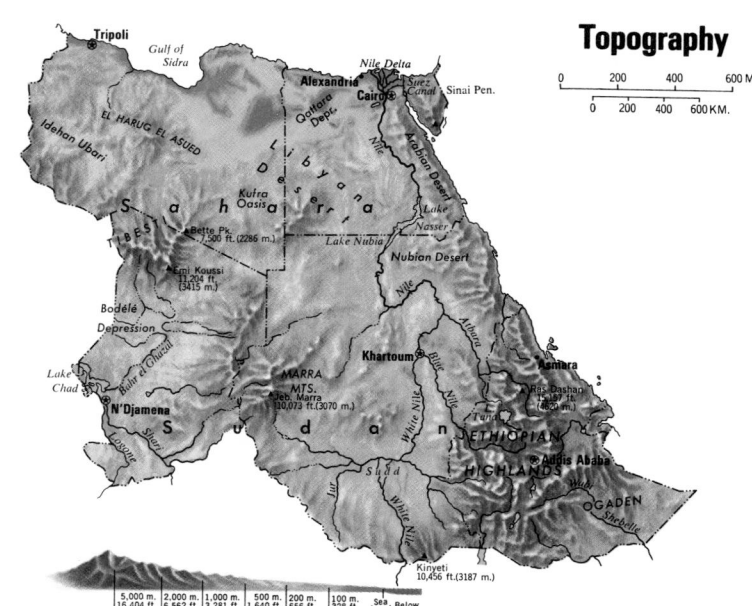

Topography

0   200   400   600 MI.

0   200   400   600 KM.

Tripoli
Gulf of Sidra
Nile Delta
Alexandria
Cairo
Suez Canal
Sinai Pen.
Qattara Depr.
EL HARUG EL ASUED
Idehan Ubari
Kufra Oasis
Libyan Desert
Sahara
Arabian Desert
Nile
Lake Nasser
Lake Nubia
Nubian Desert
Bette Pk. 7,500 ft. (2286 m.)
TIBESTI
Emi Koussi 11,204 ft. (3415 m.)
Bodélé Depression
Lake Chad
N'Djamena
Sudan
Bahr el Ghazal
Jur
Sudd
White Nile
Blue Nile
Atbara
Khartoum
MARRA MTS. Jeb. Marra 10,073 ft. (3070 m.)
Asmara
Ras Dashan
ETHIOPIAN HIGHLANDS
Addis Ababa
Ogaden
Webi Shebelle

Kinyeti 10,456 ft. (3187 m.)

5,000 m.	2,000 m.	1,000 m.	500 m.	200 m.	100 m.	Sea
16,404 ft.	6,562 ft.	3,281 ft.	1,640 ft.	656 ft.	328 ft.	Level / Below

(continued on following page)

(Map — Northeastern Africa)

IRAN
IRAQ
Tigris
Euphrates
NEUTRAL ZONE
SAUDI ARABIA
Tropic of Cancer
'ASIR
Abha
Farasan Is.
CH. I.
Dâhlak I.
Kamaran I. (P.D.R. Yemen)
Pen.
San'a ☆
Hodeida
YEMEN ARAB REPUBLIC
Ta'izz
Mocha
PEOPLE'S DEM. REP. OF YEMEN
Mukalla
Aden
Gulf of Aden
Bab el Mandeb
Perim
ERITREA
Danakil
Assab
Thio
Edd
Hanish Is.
Obock
DJIBOUTI
Tadjoura
Asal
Zeila
Dikhil
Ali Sabieh
L. Abbe
Awash
Bulhar
Karin
Ankhor
Berbera
Las Dureh
Erigabo
Shimbir Berris 7,900 ft. (2408 m.)
Ras Sura
Las Khoreh
Bosaso
(Bender Cassim)
Candala
Bargal
Ras Aser
Alula
Bereda
Ras Hafun
Hordio
Hafun (Dante)
Scusciuban
BARI
SANAAG
Upper Sheikh
WOQOOYI GALBEED
Borama
Adadle
Burao
Galeb
Gardo
Bender Beila
NUGAAL
Garoe
Negro Bay
Domo
El Hamure
Baden
El Der
El Bur
Dusa Mareb
Obbia
Galcaio
Iddan
Harardera
Mustahil
Belet Weyne
Ferfer
MUDUG
GALGUDUUD
HIIRAAN
INDIAN OCEAN
SOMALIA
HARAR
Harar
Dire Dawa
Hargeysa
Jijiga
Odweina
TOGDHEER
Bohodleh
Aïnabo
Las Anod
Ogaden
Awareh
Wardere
Galadi
Beira
Garad
Callis
El Nogal
 Gist
Ganale
Filtu
Daua
Mandera
GEDO
Dolo
Luuq
Tigieglo
Bulo Burti
Mereghe
El Dere
BAKOOL
Oddur
Wabi Shebelle
BALE 14,131 ft. (4307 m.)
Ginir
Imi
Bedessa
Miesso
Afdem
Dagabur
Gabredarre
Gorrahei
Callafo
Beledi
oba
Longitude East of Greenwich

(continued)

Aswân 144,377 F3
Asyût 213,983 J4
Bâris F3
Benha 88,992 J3
Beni Mazar 39,373 J4
Beni Suef 118,148 J3
Biba 33,074 J4
Bûlaq F2
Bur Sai'd (Port Said) 262,620 K2
Cairo (cap.) 5,084,463 J3
Dahab F2
Dairût 31,624 J4
Damanhur 188,927 J3
Damietta 93,546 J3
Disûq 58,650 J3
Dumyât (Damietta) 93,546 J3
Dûsh F3
El A'lamein E1
El A'rish F1
El Bawiti E2
El Faiyûm 167,081 J3
El Fashn 33,506 J4
El Hammam 6,588 E1
El Iskandariya (Alexandria) 2,318,655 J2
El Karnak F2
El Khârga 26,375 F2
El Mahalla el Kubra 292,853 J3
El Mansûra 257,866 K3
El Minya 146,423 J4
El Qâhira (Cairo) (cap.) 5,084,463 J3
El Qantara 919 K3
El Qasr E2
El Quseir 12,297 F2
El Tûr F2
El Wasta 17,659 J3
Gemsa F2
Girga 51,110 F2
Giza 1,246,713 J3
Heliopolis J3
Helwân J3
Hurghada F2
Idfu 34,858 F3
Imbâba J3
Ismailia 145,978 K3
Isna 34,186 F2
Karnak (El Karnak) F2
Kôm Ombo 44,531 F3
Luxor 92,748 F2
Maghâgha 40,802 J4
Mallawi 74,256 J4
Manfalût 41,126 J4
Mersá Matrûh 27,857 E1
Minûf 55,131 J3
Mût 8,032 E2
Nuweiba F2
Port Fuad K3
Port Safâga F2
Port Said 262,620 K2
Port Taufiq K3
Qalyub 62,739 J3
Qasr Farâfra E2
Qena 94,013 F2
Ras Ghârib F2
Rashid (Rosetta) 42,962 J2
Rudeis F2
Salûm 4,161 E1
Samalût 48,146 J4
Shibin el Kom 102,844 J3
Sidi Barrani 1,574 E1
Sinnûris 42,022 J3
Siwa 4,999 E2
Sohâg 101,758 F2
Suez 194,001 K3
Tahta 45,242 F2
Tanta 284,636 J3
Zagazig 202,637 K3
Zifta 50,410 J3

OTHER FEATURES

Abu Qir (bay) J2
Abydos (ruins) F2
A'llaqi, Wadi (dry riv.) F3
A'qaba (gulf) G2
Arabian (des.) F2
Aswân (dam) F3
Aswân High (dam) F3
Bahariya (oasis) E2
Bahr Yusef (stream) J4
Bânâs, Ras (cape) G3
Berenice (ruins) F3
Birket Qârûn (lake) J3
Bir Taba (well) F2
Bitter (lkes) K3
Dakhla (oasis) E2
Eastern (Arabian) (des.) F2
El Sollum (gulf) E1
Farâfra (oasis) E2
Foul (bay) G3
Ghard Abu Muharik (des.) J4
Gilf Kebir (plat.) E3
Great Sand Sea (des.) D2
Katherina, Jebel (mt.) F2
Khârga (oasis) F2
Libyan (des.) E2
Libyan (plat.) E1
Mediterranean (sea) E1
Memphis (ruins) J3
Muhammad, Ras (cape) F2
Nasser (lake) F3
Nile (riv.) F2
Pyramids (ruins) J3
Qattara (depr.) E2
Red (sea) G3
Sahara (des.) E3
Sinai (mt.) F2
Sinai (pen.) F2
Siwa (oasis) E2
Suez (canal) K3
Suez (gulf) F2
Tiran (str.) F2
U'weinat, Jebel (mt.) E3

ETHIOPIA

PROVINCES

Arusi 852,900 G6
Bale 707,800 H6
Eritrea 1,947,600 G4
Gamu-Gofa 698,800 G6
Gojjam 1,750,100 G5
Gondar 1,355,800 G5
Harar 3,359,200 H6
Ilubabor 688,800 F6
Kaffa 1,693,000 G6
Shoa 5,369,500 G6
Sidamo 2,479,800 G7
Tigre 1,828,900 H5
Wallaga 1,269,100 G6
Wallo 2,459,900 H5

CITIES and TOWNS

Addis Ababa (cap.) 1,196,300 G6
Addis Alam 5,500 G6
Adigrat 9,400 G5
Adi Ugri 12,800 G5
Adwa 16,400 G5
Afdem H6
Agordat G4
Aksum 12,800 G5
Ankober H6
Arba Mench 7,660 G6
Asmara 393,800 G4
Asosa F5
Assab 16,000 H5
Asselle 19,390 G6
Awareh H6
Awasa 16,790 G6
Awash H6
Axum (Aksum) 12,800 G5
Bahir Dar 25,100 G5
Burye G5
Callafo H6
Chilga G5
Dagabur H6
Dallol G5
Dangila G5
Debra Birhan 16,700 G6
Debra Markos 30,260 G5
Debra Tabor 8,700 G5
Dembidollo 7,600 F6
Dessye 49,750 G5
Dilla 13,800 G6
Dire Dawa 63,700 H6
Dolo H7
Domo J6
Edd H5
El Carre H6
El Der H6
Filtu H6
Gabredarre H6
Galadi J6
Gambela F6
Gardula 5,800 G6
Gedo G6
Gerlogubi H6
Ghimbi 8,300 G6
Ginir H6
Goba 13,500 H6
Gondar 38,600 G5
Gore 8,500 G6
Gorrahei H6
Harar 48,440 H6
Harkiko G4
Hosseina 8,500 G6
Imi H6
Jijiga 8,000 H6
Jimma 47,360 G6
Jiran G6
Karkabat G4
Keren G4
Kibre Mengist 8,300 G6
Lalibela G5
Magdala G5
Maji G6
Makale 30,780 G5
Massawa 19,800 G4
Mega G7
Mendi G6
Mersa Fatma H5
Metamma G5
Metu G6
Miesso H6
Mizan Teferi G6
Moyale G7
Murle G6
Mustahil H6
Nakamti 18,310 G6
Nakfa G4
Nazret 42,900 G6
Negelli 8,800 G6
Nejo G6
Saio (Dembidollo) 7,600 F6
Soddu 11,900 G6
Sokota G5
Tessenei G4
Thio H5
Tori F6
Umm Hajar G5
Waka G6
Waldia 9,600 G5
Wardere J6
Wolta G6
Yaballo G6
Zula G4

OTHER FEATURES

Abay (riv.) G5
Abaya (lake) G6
Akobo (riv.) F6
Assale (lake) H5
Atbara (riv.) G4
Awash (riv.) H5
Bale (mt.) G6
Baraka (riv.) G4
Baro (riv.) G6
Billate (riv.) G6
Blue Nile (Abay) (riv.) G5
Buri (pen.) H4
Chamo (lake) G6
Dahlak (arch.) H4
Dahlak (isl.) H4
Danakil (reg.) H5
Dawa (riv.) G7
Fafan (riv.) H6
Ganale Dorya (riv.) H6
Gash Mareb (riv.) G5
Gughe (mt.) G6
Haud (reg.) J6
Kasar, Ras (cape) G4
Ogaden (reg.) H6
Omo (riv.) G6
Ras Dashan (mt.) G5
Red (sea) H4
Rudolf (Turkana) (lake) G7
Simen (mts.) G5
Stefanie (lake) G7
Takkaze (riv.) G5
Tana (lake) G5
Tisisat (fall) G5
Turkana (lake) G7
Wabi (riv.) H6
Wabi Shebelle (riv.) H6
Zwai (lake) G6

LIBYA

CITIES and TOWNS

Ajedabia○ 53,170 D1
Aujila○ 6,695 D2
Baida○ 59,765 D1
Barce (El Marj)○ 55,444 D1
Benghazi (cap.)○ 286,943 C1
Beni Ulid○ 19,113 B1
Berken B2
Brak○ 12,507 B2
Bu Ngem C1
Cyrene (Shahat)○ 17,157 D1
Derj○ 2,152 B1
Derna○ 44,145 D1
Edri B2
El Abiar○ 17,685 D1
El Agheila C1
El Azizia○ 34,077 B1
El Bardi○ 4,330 D1
El Barkat○ 2,139 B3
El Fogaha C2
El Gatrun B3
El Gezira D2
El Jauf○ 6,481 D3
El Marj○ 55,444 D1
El' Uweinat B2
Es Sidr○ 706 C1
Ez Zuetina○ 7,256 D1
Ghadames○ 6,172 A2
Gharfan○ 65,224 B1
Ghat○ 6,924 B3
Ghemines○ 4,313 C1
Homs○ 66,890 B1
Hon○ 2,766 C2
Jaghbub (Jarabub)○ 1,436 D2
Jalo D2
Jarabub○ 1,436 D2
Marada○ 3,201 C2
Marsa el Brega○ 2,618 D1
Marsa el Hariga○ 5,043 D1
Mekili D1
Misurata○ 102,439 C1
Mizda○ 11,472 B1
Murzuk○ 22,185 B2
Nalut○ 23,535 B1
Ras Lanuf○ 1,990 C1
Sabrathaa○ 30,836 B1
Sebha○ 35,879 B2
Shahat○ 17,157 D1
Sinawen○ 1,549 B1
Sokna○ 3,757 C2
Soluk○ 6,501 D1
Susa D1
Syrte○ 22,797 C1
Tarhuna○ 52,657 B1
Tejerri B3
Tesawa B2
Tmessa C2
Tobruk○ 58,384 D1
Tokra○ 10,714 D1
Traghen B2
Tripoli (cap.)○ 550,438 B1
Ubari○ 19,132 B2
Umm el Abid C2
Waddan○ 5,347 C2
Wau el Kebir C2
Zawia○ 72,092 B1
Zella○ 4,835 C2
Zliten○ 58,981 C1
Zuila C2
Zwara○ 15,078 B1

OTHER FEATURES

Ain Zueiya (well) D3
Akhdar, Jebel (mts.) D1
A'mir, Ras (cape) D1
Barqa (Cyrenaica) (reg.) D1
Ben Ghnema, Jebel (mts.) C2
Bette (peak) C3
Bey el Kebir, Wadi (dry riv.) B1
Bir Hakeim (ruins) D1
Bishiara (well) D3
Bomba (gulf) D1
Buzeima (well) D3
Calansho Sand Sea (des.) D2
Calansho, Serir (des.) D2
Cyrenaica (reg.) D1
Fezzan (reg.) B2
Great Sand Sea (des.) D2
Harug el Asued, El (mts.) C2
Homra, Hamada el (des.) B2
Hosenofu (well) D3
Idehan Ubari (des.) B2
Idehan Murzuk (des.) B2
Jalo (oasis) D2
Jefara (reg.) B1
Jef Jef es Seghin (plat.) D3
Jofra (oasis) C2
Kufra (oasis) D3
Leptis Magna (ruins) B1
Libyan (des.) D2
Libyan (plat.) D1
Mediterranean (sea) C1
Nefusa, Jebel (mts.) B1
Rebiana○ (oasis) D3
Rebiana Sand Sea (des.) D3
Sahara (des.) C3
Sarra (well) D3
Shati, Wadi esh (dry riv.) B2
Sidra (gulf) C1
Soda, Jebel es (mts.) C2
Tazerbo○ (oasis) D2
Tibesti, Serir (des.) C3
Tinghert Hamada (Tinrhert) (des.) B2
Tripolitania (reg.) B1
U'weinat, Jebel (mt.) E3
Zelten, Jebel (mts.) D2

SUDAN

PROVINCES

Central F5
Darfur D5
Eastern G4
Khartoum F4
Kordofan E5
Northern E3
Southern E6

CITIES and TOWNS

A'bri F3
Abu Hamed F4
Abu Matariq E5
Abu Zabad E5
Abwong F6
Abyei E6
Adarama G4
Adok F6
Akasha F3
Akobo F6
Amadi F6
A'qiq G4
Argo F4
Aroma G4
Atbara 66,000 F4
Aweil E6
Ayod F6
Babanusa E5
Bara F5
Bentiu E6
Berber F4
Bor F6
Bo River Post E6
Buram E5
Damazin (Ed Damazin) 12,000 F5
Deim Zubeir E6
Delgo F3
Derudeb G4
Dilling E5
Dongola 6,000 F4
Dungunab G3
Ed Dae'in E5
Ed Damer 17,000 F4
Ed Damazin 12,000 F5
Ed Debba F4
Ed Dueim 27,000 F5
El Abbasiya F5
El Fasher 52,000 E5
El Fifi D5
El Geneina 33,000 D5
El Geteina F5
El Hilla E5
El Khandaq E4
El Manaqil F5
El Obeid 90,000 E5
El Odaiya E5
En Nahud 23,000 E5
Er Rahad F5
Er Roseires F5
Famaka F5
Fangak F6
Fashoda (Kodok) F6
Gabras E5
Gallabat G5
Gebeit Mine G3
Gedaref 92,000 G5
Gogrial E6
Goz Regeb G4
Haiya Junction G4
Halaib G3
Heiban F5
Jonglei F6
Juba 57,000 F7
Kadugli 18,000 E5
Kafia Kingi D6
Kajok E6
Kaka F5
Kapoeta F7
Karima F4
Karora G4
Kassala 99,000 G4
Kerma F4
Khartoum (cap.) 334,000 F4
Khartoum North 151,000 F4
Khashm el Girba G5
Kodok F6
Kongor F6
Korti F4
Kosti 57,000 F5
Kubbum D5
Kurmuk F5
Kutum D5
Lado F6
Loka F7
Malakal 35,000 F6
Maridi E7
Marsa Oseif G3
Melut F5
Merowe F4
Meshra er Req E6
Mongalla F6
Muglad E5
Muhammad Qol G3
Musmar G4
Nagishot F7
Nasir F6
Nimule F7
Nyala 60,000 E5
Nyamlell E6
Nyerol F6
Omdurman 299,000 F4
Opari F7
Pibor Post F6
Port Sudan 133,000 G4
Qalae'n Nahl F5
Raga E6
Rashad F5
Rejaf F7
Renk F5
Rufaa' F5
Rumbek 17,000 E6
Sennar F5
Shambe F6
Shendi F4
Shereik F4
Showak G5
Singa F5
Sinkat G4
Sodiri E5
Suakin G4
Suki F5
Tali Post F6
Talodi F5
Tambura E6
Tendelti F5
Tokar G4
Tombe F6
Tonga F6
Tonj E6
Torit F7
Towot F6
Trinkitat G4
Umm Keddada E5
Umm Ruwaba F5
Wadi Halfa F3
Wad Medani 107,000 F5
Wankai E6
Wau 53,000 E6
Yambio 7,000 E7
Yei F7
Yirol F6
Zalingei D5

OTHER FEATURES

Abu Dara, Ras (cape) G3
Abu Habl, Wadi (dry riv.) F5
Abu Shagara, Ras (cape) G3
Abu Tabari (well) E4
Adda (riv.) D6
Akobo (riv.) F6
A'mur, Wadi (dry riv.) G4
Asoteriba, Jebel (mt.) G3
Atbara (riv.) G4
Bahr Azoum (riv.) D5
Bahr el A'rab (riv.) E6
Bahr ez Zeraf (riv.) F6
Baraka (riv.) G4
Blue Nile (riv.) F5
Dar Hamid (reg.) F5
Dar Masalit (reg.) D5
Dinder (riv.) F5
El A'trun (oasis) E4
Fifth Cataract F4
Fourth Cataract F4
Gabgaba, Wadi (dry riv.) F3
Gezira, El (reg.) F5
Ghalla, Wadi el (dry riv.) E5
Hadarba, Ras (cape) G3
Howar, Wadi (dry riv.) E4
Ibra, Wadi (dry riv.) D5
Jebel Abyad (plat.) E4
Jebel Aulia (dam) F4
Jur (riv.) E6
Kasar, Ras (cape) G4
Kinyeti (mt.) F7
Laqiya U'mran (well) E3
Libyan (des.) E3
Lol (dry riv.) E6
Lotagipi Swamp (plain) F6
Marra, Jebel (mt.) D5
Meroe (ruins) F4
Milk, Wadi el (dry riv.) E4
Muqaddam, Wadi (dry riv.) F4
Napata (ruins) F4
Naqa (ruins) F4
Nile (riv.) F4
Nuba (mts.) E5
Nubia (lake) F3
Nubian (des.) F3
Nukheila (oasis) E4
Nuri (ruins) F4
Oda, Jebel (mt.) G3
Pibor (riv.) F6
Red (sea) G3
Sahara (des.) E3
Second Cataract F3
Selima (oasis) E3
Sennar (dam) F5
Setit (riv.) G5
Sixth Cataract F4
Sobat (riv.) F6
Suakin (arch.) G4
Sudan (reg.) E5
Sudd (swamp) F6
Sue (riv.) E6
Third Cataract E4
U'weinat, Jebel (mt.) E3
White Nile (riv.) F5

○Population of sub-district or division.

Agriculture, Industry and Resources

DOMINANT LAND USE

- Cereals, Horticulture, Livestock
- Cash Crops, Mixed Cereals
- Cotton, Cereals
- Market Gardening, Diversified Tropical Crops
- Plantation Agriculture
- Oases
- Pasture Livestock
- Nomadic Livestock Herding
- Forests
- Nonagricultural Land

MAJOR MINERAL OCCURRENCES

Ab	Asbestos	Mn	Manganese
Au	Gold	Na	Salt
Cr	Chromium	O	Petroleum
Fe	Iron Ore	P	Phosphates
G	Natural Gas	Pt	Platinum
K	Potash		

ϟ Water Power
Major Industrial Areas

ANGOLA
AREA 481,351 sq. mi. (1,246,700 sq. km.)
POPULATION 7,078,000
CAPITAL Luanda
LARGEST CITY Luanda
HIGHEST POINT Mt. Moco 8,593 ft. (2,620 m.)
MONETARY UNIT kwanza
MAJOR LANGUAGES Mbundu, Kongo, Lunda, Portuguese
MAJOR RELIGIONS Tribal religions, Roman Catholicism

BURUNDI
AREA 10,747 sq. mi. (27,835 sq. km.)
POPULATION 4,021,910
CAPITAL Bujumbura
LARGEST CITY Bujumbura
HIGHEST POINT 8,858 ft. (2,700 m.)
MONETARY UNIT Burundi franc
MAJOR LANGUAGES Kirundi, French, Swahili
MAJOR RELIGIONS Tribal religions, Roman Catholicism, Islam

CAMEROON
AREA 183,568 sq. mi. (475,441 sq. km.)
POPULATION 8,503,000
CAPITAL Yaoundé
LARGEST CITY Douala
HIGHEST POINT Cameroon 13,350 ft. (4,069 m.)
MONETARY UNIT CFA franc
MAJOR LANGUAGES Fang, Bamileke, Fulani, Duala. French, English
MAJOR RELIGIONS Tribal religions, Christianity, Islam

CENTRAL AFRICAN REP.
AREA 242,000 sq. mi. (626,780 sq. km.)
POPULATION 2,284,000
CAPITAL Bangui
LARGEST CITY Bangui
HIGHEST POINT Gao 4,659 ft. (1,420 m.)
MONETARY UNIT CFA franc
MAJOR LANGUAGES Banda, Gbaya, Sangho, French
MAJOR RELIGIONS Tribal religions, Christianity, Islam

CONGO
AREA 132,046 sq. mi. (342,000 sq. km.)
POPULATION 1,537,000
CAPITAL Brazzaville
LARGEST CITY Brazzaville
HIGHEST POINT Leketi Mts. 3,412 ft. (1,040 m.)
MONETARY UNIT CFA franc
MAJOR LANGUAGES Kikongo, Bateke, Lingala, French
MAJOR RELIGIONS Christianity, tribal religions, Islam

EQUATORIAL GUINEA
AREA 10,831 sq. mi. (28,052 sq. km.)
POPULATION 244,000
CAPITAL Malabo
LARGEST CITY Malabo
HIGHEST POINT 9,868 ft. (3,008 m.)
MONETARY UNIT ekuele
MAJOR LANGUAGES Fang, Bubi, Spanish
MAJOR RELIGIONS Tribal religions, Christianity

GABON
AREA 103,346 sq. mi. (267,666 sq. km.)
POPULATION 551,000
CAPITAL Libreville
LARGEST CITY Libreville
HIGHEST POINT Ibounzi 5,165 ft. (1,574 m.)
MONETARY UNIT CFA franc
MAJOR LANGUAGES Fang and other Bantu languages, French
MAJOR RELIGIONS Tribal religions, Christianity, Islam

KENYA
AREA 224,960 sq. mi. (582,646 sq. km.)
POPULATION 15,327,061
CAPITAL Nairobi
LARGEST CITY Nairobi
HIGHEST POINT Kenya 17,058 ft. (5,199 m.)
MONETARY UNIT Kenya shilling
MAJOR LANGUAGES Kikuyu, Luo, Kavirondo, Kamba, Swahili, English
MAJOR RELIGIONS Tribal religions, Christianity, Hinduism, Islam

MALAWI
AREA 45,747 sq. mi. (118,485 sq. km.)
POPULATION 5,968,000
CAPITAL Lilongwe
LARGEST CITY Blantyre
HIGHEST POINT Mulanje 9,843 ft. (3,000 m.)
MONETARY UNIT Malawi kwacha
MAJOR LANGUAGES Chichewa, Yao, English, Nyanja, Tumbuka, Tonga, Ngoni
MAJOR RELIGIONS Tribal religions, Islam, Christianity

RWANDA
AREA 10,169 sq. mi. (26,337 sq. km.)
POPULATION 4,819,317
CAPITAL Kigali
LARGEST CITY Kigali
HIGHEST POINT Karisimbi 14,780 ft. (4,505 m.)
MONETARY UNIT Rwanda franc
MAJOR LANGUAGES Kinyarwanda, French, Swahili
MAJOR RELIGIONS Tribal religions, Roman Catholicism, Islam

SOMALIA
AREA 246,200 sq. mi. (637,658 sq. km.)
POPULATION 3,645,000
CAPITAL Mogadishu
LARGEST CITY Mogadishu
HIGHEST POINT Surud Ad 7,900 ft. (2,408 m.)
MONETARY UNIT Somali shilling
MAJOR LANGUAGES Somali, Arabic, Italian, English
MAJOR RELIGION Islam

TANZANIA
AREA 363,708 sq. mi. (942,003 sq. km.)
POPULATION 17,527,560
CAPITAL Dar es Salaam
LARGEST CITY Dar es Salaam
HIGHEST POINT Kilimanjaro 19,340 ft. (5,895 m.)
MONETARY UNIT Tanzanian shilling
MAJOR LANGUAGES Nyamwezi-Sukuma, Swahili, English
MAJOR RELIGIONS Tribal religions, Christianity, Islam

UGANDA
AREA 91,076 sq. mi. (235,887 sq. km.)
POPULATION 12,630,076
CAPITAL Kampala
LARGEST CITY Kampala
HIGHEST POINT Margherita 16,795 ft. (5,119 m.)
MONETARY UNIT Ugandan shilling
MAJOR LANGUAGES Luganda, Acholi, Teso, Nyoro, Soga, Nkole, English, Swahili
MAJOR RELIGIONS Tribal religions, Christianity, Islam

ZAIRE
AREA 905,063 sq. mi. (2,344,113 sq. km.)
POPULATION 28,291,000
CAPITAL Kinshasa
LARGEST CITY Kinshasa
HIGHEST POINT Margherita 16,795 ft. (5,119 m.)
MONETARY UNIT zaire
MAJOR LANGUAGES Tshiluba, Mongo, Kikongo, Kingwana, Zande, Lingala, Swahili, French
MAJOR RELIGIONS Tribal religions, Christianity

ZAMBIA
AREA 290,586 sq. mi. (752,618 sq. km.)
POPULATION 5,679,808
CAPITAL Lusaka
LARGEST CITY Lusaka
HIGHEST POINT Sunzu 6,782 ft. (2,067 m.)
MONETARY UNIT Zambian kwacha
MAJOR LANGUAGES Bemba, Tonga, Lozi, Luvale, Nyanja, English
MAJOR RELIGIONS Tribal religions

ANGOLA

DISTRICTS

Bengo 68,885	B5
Benguela 474,897	B6
Bié 650,337	C6
Cabinda 80,857	B5
Cuando Cubango 112,073	C7
Cuanza-Norte 209,062	B5
Cuanza-Sul 458,592	C6
Cunene 147,394	C7
Huambo 837,627	C6
Huíla 497,470	B7
Luanda 491,704	B5
Lunda Norte 210,000	C5
Lunda Sul 98,000	D5
Malange 558,630	C5
Moxico 213,119	D6
Namibe 53,058	B7
Uíge 386,037	B5
Zaire 41,766	B5

CITIES and TOWNS

Alto Chicapa	C6
Alto Cuale	C5
Ambriz	B5
Andulo	C6
Bala dos Tigres	B7
Baia Farta	B6
Balombo	B6
Bela Vista	C6
Bembe	B5
Benguela 40,996	B6
Caála 8,894	C6
Cabinda 21,124	B5
Caconda	B6
Cacuso	C5
Caiundo	C7
Calulo	C6
Caluquembe	B6
Camacupa 5,740	C6
Camanongue	D5
Cambulo	C5
Cangamba	C6
Capelongo	C6
Capenda-Camulemba	C5
Cassai	D6
Cassamba	D6
Catete	B5
Catumbela	B6
Caúngula	C5
Caxito	B5
Cazombo	D6
Cela 2,784	B6
Chiange	B7
Chingar	C6
Chipindo	C6
Chitado	B7
Chitembo	C6
Coambo	C5
Cuango	C5
Cuchi	C6
Cuilo	C5
Cuito-Cuanavale	C7
Cuma	B6
Damba	B5
Dirico	D7
Dombe Grande	B6
Dondo	B5
Folgares	C7
Forte República	C5

Foz do Cunene	B7
Gabela 6,930	B6
Gambos	B7
Golungo Alto	B5
Huambo 61,885	C6
Iona	C7
Kalandula	C5
Kassinga	C7
Kuito 18,941	C6
Lobito 59,528	B6
Lóvua	C5
Longa	C6
Luacano	D6
Luachimo	D5
Lucira	B6
Luiana	D7
Lukapa	D5
Macondo	D6

Malange 31,599	C5
Maquela do Zombo	B5
Massango (Forte República)	C5
Mavinga	D7
Mbanza Congo 4,002	B5
Menongue 3,023	C6
Moçâmedes (Namibe) 12,076	B7
Muconda	D6
Mucope	B7
Mucusso	D7
Munhango	C6
Muxima	B5
Namibe 12,076	B7
Nana Candundo	D6
Ndalatando 7,342	B5
N'gage 2,548	C5
Ngiva	C7
Nguuza (Sumbe) 7,911	B6
Nharêa	C6
Noqui	B5

Nova Gaia	C5
Nzeto	B5
Oncócua	B7
Porto Alexandre 8,235	B7
Porto Amboim	B6
Quela	C6
Quibala	C6
Quibaxe	B5
Quinzau	B5
Sanza Pombo	C5
São Nicolau	B7
Saurimo 12,901	D5
Songo	B5
Soyo	B5
Sumbe 7,911	B6
Uíge 11,972	B5
Vila Guilherme Capelo	B5
Xangongo	C7

OTHER FEATURES

Bero (riv.)	B7
Chicapa (riv.)	C5
Chiumbe (riv.)	D5
Congo (riv.)	C4
Coporolo (riv.)	B6
Cuando (riv.)	C6
Cuango (riv.)	C5
Cuanza (riv.)	C5
Cubango (riv.)	C7
Cuito (riv.)	C7
Cunene (riv.)	B7
Cunene (dam)	C7
Cuvo (riv.)	B6
Kasai (riv.)	D5
Kwilu (riv.)	C5
Loange (riv.)	C5
Loge (riv.)	B5
Lungwebungu (riv.)	D6
Matala (dam)	B6

M'Bridge (riv.)	B5
Moco (mt.)	C6
Palmeirinhas (pt.)	B5
Ruacana Falls (dam)	B7
Santa Maria (cape)	B6
Zambezi (riv.)	D6

BURUNDI

CITIES and TOWNS

Bujumbura (cap.) 141,040	E4
Bururi 7,800	F4
Gitega 19,500	F4

OTHER FEATURES

Ruzizi (riv.)	E4

Tanganyika (lake)	E5

CAMEROON

CITIES and TOWNS

Abong-Mbang 6,000	B3
Ambam 4,000	B3
Bafia 12,000	B3
Bafoussam 62,239	B2
Bali	A2
Bamenda 48,111	A2
Banyo	B2
Batouri 7,000	B3
Belabo	B3
Bengbis	B3
Bertoua 10,000	B3
Bétaré-Oya	B2
Bonabéri	A3

ANGOLA

EQUATORIAL GUINEA

SOMALIA

BURUNDI

GABON

TANZANIA

CAMEROON

KENYA

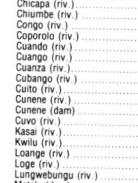
UGANDA

CENTRAL AFRICAN REP.

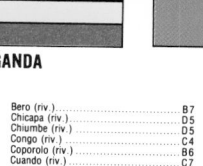
MALAWI

ZAIRE

CONGO

RWANDA

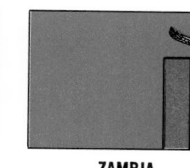
ZAMBIA

(continued on following page)

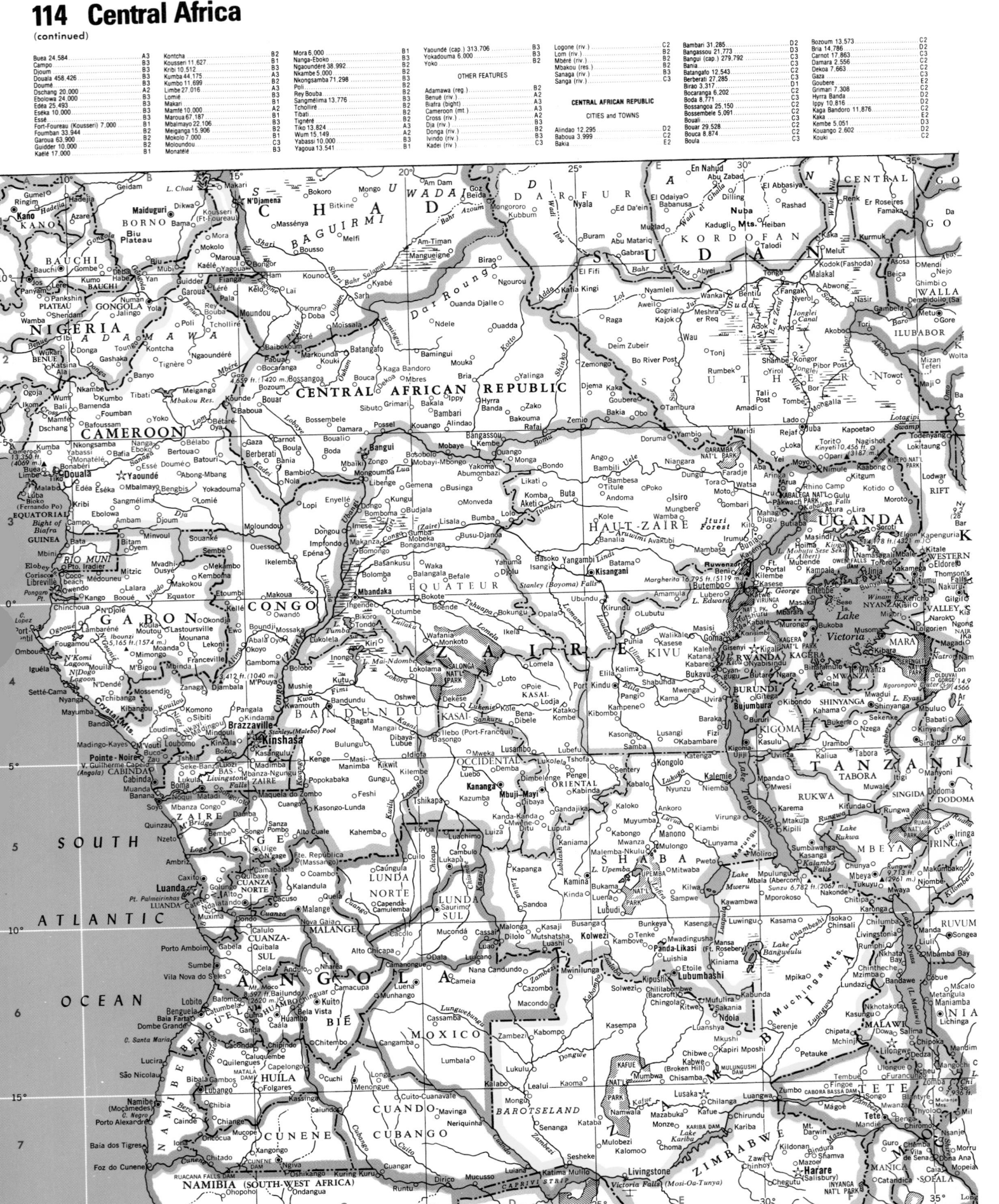

Kounde B2
Mbaiki 12,346 .... D2
Mbres 2,622 .... D2
Mobaye 4,220 .... D3
Mouka D2
Ndele 5,858 .... D2
Ngourou D2
Nola 6,703 .... C2
Obo 3,978 .... E2
Ouadda 3,009 .... D2
Paoua 7,052 .... C2
Possel C2
Sibut 13,341 .... C2
Zako D2
Zemio 3,259 .... D2

Zemongo E2

OTHER FEATURES
Bamingui (riv.) C2
Bomu (riv.) D3
Dar Rounga (reg.) D2
Gao (mt.) D2
Koto (riv.) D2
Lobaye (riv.) C2
Mbéré (riv.) B2
Ouham (riv.) C2
Pende (riv.) C2
Sanga (riv.) C2

Sara (riv.) C2
Shari (riv.) C2
Shinko (riv.) D2
Ubangi (riv.) C3

CONGO
CITIES and TOWNS
Abala C4
Boko B4
Brazzaville (cap.) 298,967 .... C4
Boundji C4
Djambala B4

Dongou C3
Enyellé C3
Epéna C3
Etoumbi B4
Ewo B4
Gamboma C4
Ikelemba C3
Impfondo C3
Kéllé B4
Kibangou A4
Kindama B4
Kinkala B4
Komono B4
Loubomo 29,600 .... B4
Loudima B4

Madingo-Kayes B4
Madingou B4
Makoua C3
Mbinda B4
Mindouli B4
Mossaka C4
Mossendjo B4
M'Pouya C4
M'Vouti B4
Nkayi 30,600 .... B4
Okoyo B4
Ouesso C3
Owando C4
Oyo C4
Pangala B4
Pointe-Noire 141,700 .... B4
Sembé B3
Sibiti B4
Souanké B4
Zanaga B4

Tchibanga 14,001 .... B4

OTHER FEATURES
Crystal (mts.) B4
Ibounzi (riv.) B4
Ivindo (riv.) B3
Dja (riv.) B3
Lopez (cape) A4
N'Dogo (lag.) A4
N'Gounie (riv.) A4
N'Komi (lag.) A4
Ogooué (riv.) A4
Onangué (lake) A4
Pongara (pt.) A3

EQUATORIAL GUINEA
TERRITORIES
Bioko 78,000 .... A3
Río Muni 300,000 .... B3

CITIES and TOWNS
Bata 27,024 .... B3
Luba 19,933 .... A3
Malabo (cap.) 37,237 .... A3
Mbini 14,503 .... A3

OTHER FEATURES
Biafra (bight) A3
Bioko (isl.) A3
Corisco (isl.) A3
Elobey (isls.) A3
Fernando Po (Bioko) (isl.) A3

GABON
CITIES and TOWNS
Banda B4
Bitam 5,936 .... B3
Booué B3
Chinchoua A4
Cocobeach A4
Fougamou A4
Franceville 9,345 .... B4
Iguéla A4
Kango B3
Kemboma B3
Koula-Moutou 8,032 .... B4
Lalara B3
Lambaréné 17,770 .... B4
Lastoursville B4
Lékoni B4
Libreville (cap.) 105,080 .... A3
Makokou 5,005 .... B3
Mayumba A4
M'Bigou B4
Médouneu B3
Mekambo B3
Mimongo B4
Minvoul B3
Moanda 10,709 .... B4
Mouila 15,016 .... B4
Mounana 4,000 .... B4
N'Dendé B4
N'Djolé B4
Nyanga A4
Okondja B4
Omboué A4
Owendo A4
Oyem 12,455 .... B3
Port-Gentil 48,190 .... A4
Setté-Cama A4

KENYA
PROVINCES
Central 1,675,647 .... G4
Coast 944,082 .... G4
Eastern 1,907,301 .... G4
Nairobi 509,286 .... G4
North-Eastern 245,757 .... G3
Nyanza 2,122,045 .... F4
Rift Valley 2,210,289 .... G3
Western 1,328,298 .... G3

CITIES and TOWNS
Buna G3
Bunyala G4
Bura H4
Eldoret 18,196 .... G3
El Wak H3
Embu 3,928 .... G4
Fort Hall 4,750 .... G4
Galole 3,609 .... G4
Garba Tula G3
Garissa G4
Garsen G4
Gilgil 4,178 .... G4
Isiolo 8,201 .... G3
Kakamega 6,244 .... F3
Kaningo G4
Kericho 10,144 .... F4
Kiambu 2,776 .... G4
Kilifi 2,662 .... G4
Kipini H4
Kisii 6,080 .... F4
Kisumu 32,431 .... F3
Kitale 11,573 .... G3
Kitui 3,071 .... G4
Kolbio H4
Konza G4
Laisamis G3
Lamu 7,403 .... H4
Lodwar G3
Lokitaung 4,090 .... G4
Lolgorien F4
Machakos 6,312 .... G4
Magadi G4
Malindi 10,757 .... H4
Mambrui H4
Marsabit 3,878 .... G3
Marsabit 6,635 .... G3
Mombasa 247,073 .... G4
Moyale G3
Nairobi (cap.) 509,286 .... G4
Naivasha 6,920 .... G4
Nakuru 47,151 .... G4
Namanga G4
Nanyuki 11,624 .... G4
Narok 2,608 .... G4
North Horr G3
South Horr G3
Taveta G4
Thika 18,387 .... G4
Thomson's Falls 7,602 .... G4
Todenyang G3
Tsavo G4
Vanga G4
Voi 5,313 .... G4
Wajir H3
Wamba 2,650 .... G3

OTHER FEATURES
Daua (riv.) H3
Elgon (mt.) F3
Formosa (bay) H4
Galana (riv.) G4
Gedi (ruins) G4
Kavirondo (gulf) F4
Kenya (mt.) G4
Lak Dera (dry riv.) H3
Lorian (swamp) H3
Natron (lake) G4
Nyiru (mt.) G3
Patta (isl.) H4

Rudolf (Turkana) (lake) G3
Tana (riv.) G4
Tsavo Nat'l Park G4
Turkana (lake) G3
Victoria (lake) F4
Winam (bay) F4

MALAWI
CITIES and TOWNS
Bandawe F6
Blantyre 222,153 .... F7
Chilumba F6
Chipoka F6
Chiromo F7
Chitipa 3,079 .... F6
Dedza 5,448 .... F6
Karonga 11,873 .... F5
Kasungu F6
Lilongwe (cap.) 102,924 .... F6
Livingstonia F6
Mamgochi 3,341 .... G6
Mzimba 4,962 .... F6
Nkhata Bay 4,024 .... F6
Nkhotakota 10,312 .... F6
Nsanje 6,091 .... G7
Rumphi 3,998 .... F6
Salima 4,646 .... F6
Thyolo 4,186 .... F7
Zomba 21,000 .... G7

OTHER FEATURES
Chilwa (lake) G7
Malawi (Nyasa) (lake) G7
Mulanje (mts.) G7
Nyasa (lake) F6
Shire (riv.) G7

RWANDA
CITIES and TOWNS
Butare 21,691 .... E4
Cyangugu 7,042 .... E4
Gisenyi 12,436 .... E4
Kigali (cap.) 117,749 .... F4
Nyabisindu 8,587 .... F4

OTHER FEATURES
Kagera Nat'l Park F4
Karisimbi (mt.) E4
Kivu (lake) E4
Ruzizi (riv.) E4
Virunga (range) E4

SOMALIA
PROVINCES
Bakool 100,000 .... H3
Bari 155,000 .... J1
Bay 302,000 .... J2
Galguduud 182,000 .... J2
Gedo 212,000 .... H3
Hiiraan 147,000 .... J3
Jubbada Hoose 246,000 .... H3
Mogadiscio 371,000 .... J3
Mudug 215,000 .... J2
Nugaal 85,000 .... J2
Sanaag 146,000 .... J2
Shabeellaha Dhexe 237,000 .... J3
Shabeellaha Hoose 398,000 .... H3
Togdheer 258,000 .... J2
Woqooyi Galbeed 440,000 .... H1

CITIES and TOWNS
Adaale H2
Afgoi J3
Afmadu 2,580 .... H3
Alula K1
Ankhor J1
Audegle J3
Baden J3
Barawa (Brava) H3
Bardera H3
Bargal K1
Baydhabo 14,962 .... J3
Belet Weyne 11,426 .... J3
Bender Beila K2
Bender Cassim (Bosaso) J1
Berbera 12,219 .... J1
Bereda K1
Bircao H4
Bohodieh J1
Borama 3,244 .... H1

(continued on following page)

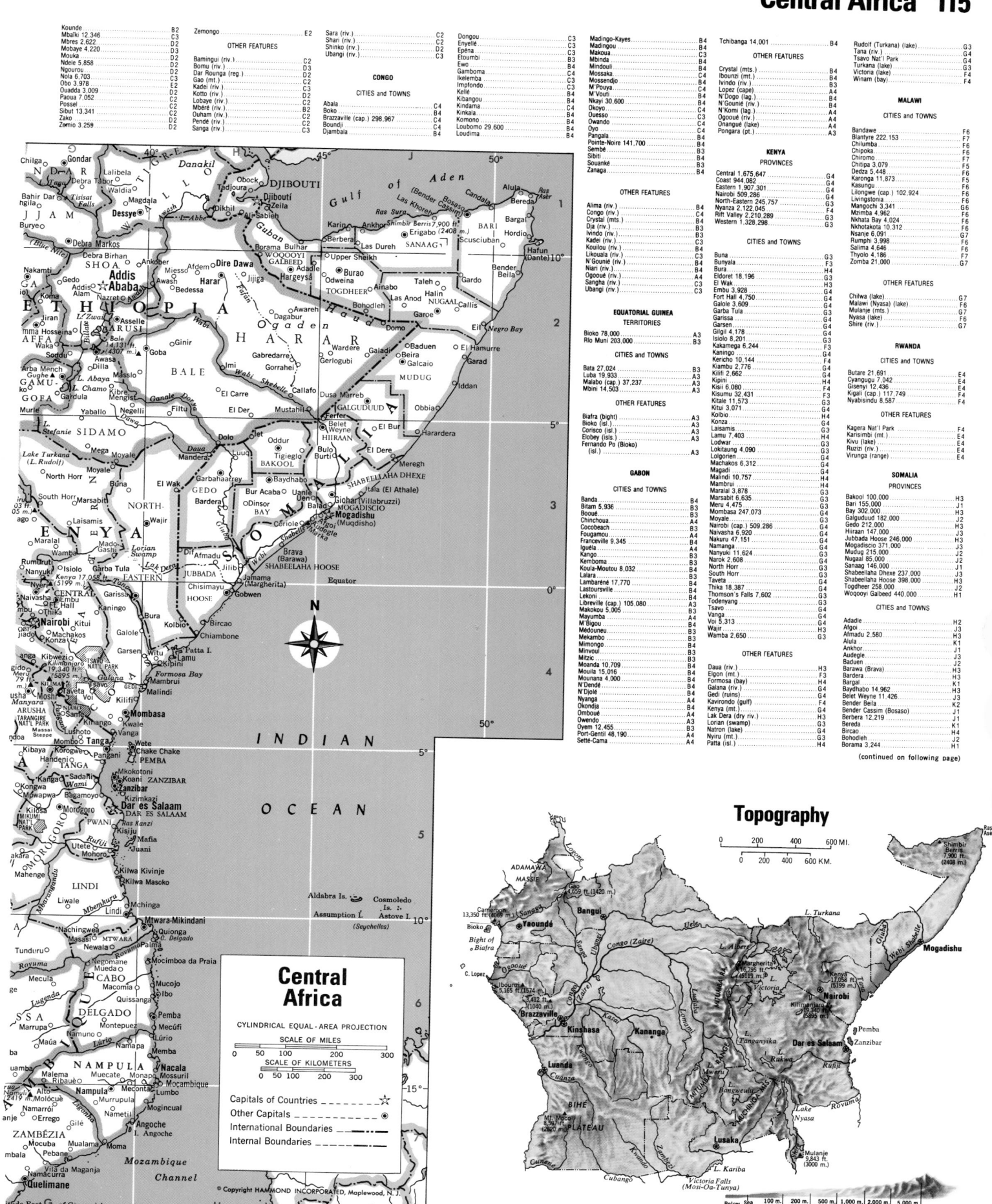

Central Africa

CYLINDRICAL EQUAL-AREA PROJECTION

SCALE OF MILES
0 50 100 200   300

SCALE OF KILOMETERS
0 50 100   200   300

Capitals of Countries .... ☆
Other Capitals .... ⊙
International Boundaries ....
Internal Boundaries ....

© Copyright HAMMOND INCORPORATED, Maplewood, N.J.

Topography

0   200   400   600 MI.
0   200   400   600 KM.

Below Sea Level | 100 m. 328 ft. | 200 m. 656 ft. | 500 m. 1,640 ft. | 1,000 m. 3,281 ft. | 2,000 m. 6,562 ft. | 5,000 m. 16,404 ft.

(continued)

Bosaso J1
Brava 6,167 H3
Bulhar H1
Bulo Burti 5,247 J3
Bur Acaba H3
Burao 12,617 J2
Callis J2
Candala J1
Chisimayu 17,872 H4
Chiambone H4
Coriole 4,341 H3
Dante (Hafun) K1
Dif H3
Dinsor H3
Dusa Marreb J2
Eil J2
El Athale (Itala) J3
El Bur J3
El Dere J3
El Hamurre J2
Erigabo 4,279 J1
Ferfer J2
Galcaio J2
Garad J2
Garbahaarrey H3
Gardo J2
Garoe J2
Giohar 13,156 J3
Gobwen H4
Hafun K1
Halin J2
Harardera J3
Hargeysa 40,254 H2
Hordio K1
Iddan J2
Iet H3
Itala J3
Jamama 5,408 H3
Jilib 3,232 H3
Karin J1
Kismayu (Chisimayu) 17,872 H4
Las Dureh J1
Luuq H3
Margherita (Jamama) H3
Marka (Merka) 17,708 H3
Mogadishu (cap.) 371,000 J3
Muqdisho (Mogadishu)
(cap.) 371,000 J3
Obbia J2
Oddur H3
Taleh J2
Uanle Uen H3
Upper Sheikh J2
Villabruzzi (Johar) J3
Zeila 1,226 H1

OTHER FEATURES

Aden (gulf) J1
Asèr, Ras (cape) K1
Giuba (riv.) H3
Guban (reg.) H1
Hafun, Ras (cape) K1
Haud (plat.) J2
Lak Dera (dry riv.) H3
Negro (bay) J2
Nogal (reg.) J2
Shimbir Berris (mt.) J1
Sura, Ras (cape) J1
Surud Ad (mt.) J1
Webi Shabelle (riv.) H3

TANZANIA

REGIONS

Arusha 928,478 G4
Dar es Salaam 851,222 G5
Dodoma 971,921 G5
Iringa 922,801 G5
Kagera 1,009,379 F4
Kigoma 648,950 F4
Kilimanjaro 902,394 G4
Lindi 527,902 G5
Mara 723,295 F4
Mbeya 1,080,241 F5
Morogoro 939,190 G5
Mtwara 771,726 G5
Mwanza 1,443,418 F4
Pemba 205,870 H5
Pwani (Coast) 516,949 G5
Rukwa 451,897 F5
Ruvuma 564,113 G6
Shinyanga 1,323,482 F4
Singida 614,030 F5
Tabora 818,049 F5
Tanga 1,088,592 G5
Zanzibar Mjini 143,616 G5
Zanzibar Shambani North 77,424 G5
Zanzibar Shambani South 52,325 G5

CITIES and TOWNS

Arusha 55,281 G4
Babati G4
Bagamoyo 5,112 G5
Bukoba 20,430 F4
Chake Chake 4,862 H5
Dar es Salaam (cap.) 757,346 G5
Dodoma 45,703 G5
Geita 3,066 F4
Handeni G5
Ifakara G5
Iringa 57,182 G5
Itigi F5
Kahama 3,211 F4
Kaliua F5
Kanga G5
Karema F5
Kasanga F5
Kasulu F4
Kibara F4
Kibaya G5
Kibondo F4
Kigoma-Ujiji 50,044 E4
Kilosa 4,458 G5
Kilwa Kivinje 2,790 G5
Kilwa Masoko G5
Kinyangiri G4
Kipili F5
Kisiju G5
Kitunda F5
Kizimkazi G5
Kondoa 4,514 G4
Kongwa G5
Korogwe 6,675 G5
Lindi 27,308 G5
Liuli F6
Liwale G5
Longido G4
Mahenge G5
Makumbako G5
Manda F6
Manyoni G5
Masasi G6
Mbamba Bay G6
Mbeya 76,606 F5
Mbulu G4
Mchinga H5
Mohoro G5
Mombo G4
Morogoro 61,890 G5
Moshi 52,223 G4
Mpanda F5
Mtakuja F5
Mtwara-Mikindani 48,510 H6
Murongo F4
Musoma 32,658 F4
Muwale F5
Mwadui 7,383 F4
Mwanza 110,611 F4
Mwaya F5
Mwesi F5
Nachingwea 3,751 G6
Newala G6
Ngara F4
Njombe F5
Pangani 2,955 G5
Rungwa F5
Sadani G5
Same G4
Sekenke F4
Shinyanga 21,703 F4
Singida 29,252 F4
Songea 17,954 G6
Sumbawanga 28,586 F5
Tabora 67,392 F5
Tanga 103,409 G4
Tukuyu 4,089 F5
Tunduru G6
Urambo F4
Utete G5
Uvinza F5
Wete 8,469 G4
Zanzibar 110,669 G5

OTHER FEATURES

Eyasi (lake) F4
Great Ruaha (riv.) G5
Juani (isl.) G5
Kalambo (falls) F5
Kanzi (cape) G5
Kilimanjaro (mt.) G4
Kilombero (riv.) G5
Mafia (isl.) H5
Manyara (lake) G4
Masai (steppe) G4
Mbarangandu (riv.) G5
Mbemkuru (riv.) G5
Meru (mt.) G4
Mikumi Nat'l Park G5
Natron (lake) G4
Ngorongoro (crater) F4
Njombe (riv.) F5
Nyasa (lake) F6
Olduvai Gorge (canyon) G4
Pangani (riv.) G4
Pemba (isl.) H5
Rovuma (riv.) G6
Rufiji (riv.) G5
Ruaha Nat'l Park F5
Rukwa (lake) F5
Rungwa (riv.) F5
Rungwe (mt.) F5
Serengeti Nat'l Park F4
Tanganyika (lake) E5
Tarangire Nat'l Park G4
Victoria (lake) F4
Wami (riv.) G5
Wembere (riv.) F4
Zanzibar (isl.) G5

UGANDA

CITIES and TOWNS

Arua 10,837 F3
Atura F3
Butiaba 261 F3
Entebbe 21,096 F4
Fort Portal 7,947 F3
Gulu 18,170 F3
Hoima 2,339 F3
Jinja 52,509 F3
Kabale 8,234 E4
Kampala (cap.) 478,895 F3
Kasese 7,213 F3
Kilembe F3
Kitgum 3,242 F3
Lira 7,340 F3
Masaka 12,987 F4
Masindi 2,100 F3
Mbale 23,544 F3
Mbarara 16,078 F4
Moroto 5,488 F3
Moyo 2,656 F3
Mubende 6,004 F3
Rhino Camp 198 F3
Soroti 8,130 F3
Tororo 15,977 F3

OTHER FEATURES

Albert (Mobuto Sese Seko)
(lake) F3
Edward (lake) E4
Elgon (mt.) F3
George (lake) F4
Kabalega (falls) F3
Kagalega Nat'l Park F3
Kidepo Nat'l Park F3
Kioga (lake) F3
Margherita (mt.) E3
Mobuto Sese Seko (lake) F3
Owen Falls (dam) F3
Ruwenzori (range) E3
Sese (isls.) F4
Victoria (lake) F4
Virunga (range) E4
Virunga Nat'l Park F4

ZAIRE

PROVINCES

Bandundu 2,600,556 C4
Bas-Zaïre 1,504,361 B4
Equateur 2,431,812 D3
Haut-Zaïre 3,356,419 E3
Kasai-Occidental 2,433,861 D4
Kasai-Oriental 1,872,231 D5
Kinshasa 1,323,039 C4
Kivu 3,361,883 E4
Shaba 2,753,714 E5

CITIES and TOWNS

Aba 7,600 F3
Abumombazi D3
Aketi 17,200 D3
Andoma E3
Ango E3
Ankoro E5
Bagata C4
Balangala D3
Bambesa E3
Bambili E3
Banalia E3
Banana B5
Bandundu 74,467 C4
Baraka E4
Basankusu C3
Basoko 9,100 D3
Basongo D4
Befale D3
Bena-Dibele D4
Beni 22,800 E3
Bikoro C4
Boende 12,800 D4
Bokote D4
Bokungu D4
Bolobo 10,300 C4
Bolomba 7,200 C3
Boma 61,100 B5
Bomboma C3
Bomongo C3
Bondo 10,000 D3
Bongandanga 12,900 D3
Bosobolo 11,100 D3
Budjala C3
Bukama E5
Bukavu 134,861 E4
Bulungu 16,300 C4
Bumba 34,700 D3
Bunia 28,800 E3
Bunkeya 5,100 E6
Businga 11,000 D3
Busu-Djanoa D3
Buta 19,800 D3
Butembo 27,800 E3
Dekese D4
Demba 22,000 D5
Dibaya 11,400 D5
Dibaya-Lubue 7,900 C4
Dilolo 14,000 D6
Dimbelenge D5
Djolu D3
Djugu F3
Dongo C3
Doruma E3
Dungu 9,100 E3
Etoile E6
Faradje 10,400 E3
Feshi C5
Fizi E4
Gandajika 60,100 D5
Gemena 37,300 D3
Goma 48,600 E4
Gungu C5
Idiofa C4
Ikela D4
Ilebo 32,200 D4
Imese C3
Ingende C4
Inongo 14,800 C4
Irumu 9,300 E3
Isangi D3
Isiro 49,300 E3
Kabalo 22,600 E5
Kabambare E4
Kabare 12,600 E4
Kabinda 60,500 D5
Kabongo 6,500 E5
Kahemba C5
Kalehe E4
Kalemie 62,300 E5
Kalima 27,500 E4
Kama 17,700 E4
Kambove 18,900 E6
Kamina 56,300 D5
Kampene 14,600 E4
Kananga 428,960 D5
Kanda-Kanda D5
Kaniama D5
Kapanga D5
Kasaji D6
Kasangulu 11,900 C4
Kasenga E6
Kasenyi E3
Kasese E4
Kasongo 37,800 E4
Kasongo-Lunda C5
Katako-Kombe D4
Katenga E5
Kazumba D5
Kenge 17,500 C4
Kiambi E5
Kibombo E4
Kikwit 111,960 C5
Kilembe C5
Kilwa E5
Kilo E3
Kinda D5
Kiniama E6
Kinshasa (cap.) 1,323,039 C4
Kipushi 32,900 E6
Kiri C4
Kirundu E4
Kisangani 229,596 E3
Kole, Kasai-Oriental D4
Kole, Haut-Zaïre E3
Kolwezi 81,600 E6
Komba D3
Kongolo 14,800 E5
Kungu C3
Kutu 10,000 C4
Kwamouth C4
Libenge 12,500 C3
Likasi, Panda- 146,394 E6
Likati D3
Lisala D3
Lodja 20,300 D4
Lokolama D4
Lomela D4
Loto D4
Luashi D6
Lubefu D4
Lubero E4
Lubudi 6,000 E5
Lubumbashi 318,000 E6
Lubutu E4
Luebo 21,800 D5
Luishia E6
Luiza D5
Lukolela, Equateur C4
Lukolela, Kasai-Oriental D5
Lukula 9,400 B5
Luozi 7,000 B5
Lusambo 13,100 D4
Makanza C3
Malemba-Nkulu E5
Mambasa 7,400 E3
Mangai 15,200 C4
Manono 44,500 E5
Masi-Manimba 6,300 C4
Masisi E4
Matadi 110,436 B5
Mbandaka 107,910 C3
Mbanza-Ngungu 55,800 C5
Mbuji-Mayi 256,154 D5
Mitwaba E5
Moanda 6,400 B5
Mobayi-Mbongo D3
Moliro E5
Monga D3
Monkoto D4
Mulongo E5
Mungbere E3
Mushie 13,700 C4
Mutshatsha D6
Muyumba E5
Mwadingusha E6
Mwanza E5
Mweka 24,900 D4
Mwene-Ditu 71,200 D5
Mwenga E4
Niangara 9,200 E3
Niemba E5
Nyunzu 11,300 E5
Opala D4
Oshwe C4
Panda-Likasi 146,394 E6
Pangi E4
Penge D5
Poko E3
Popokabaka C5
Port Kindu 42,800 E4
Punia E4
Pweto E5
Rutshuru E4
Sakania E6
Sampwe E5
Sandoa D5
Seke-Banza B5
Sentery 24,300 E5
Shabunda 6,900 E4
Songololo 4,600 B5
Tenke E6
Titule E3
Tshela 10,700 B4
Tshikapa 38,900 D5
Tshofa D5
Ubundu 6,300 E4
Uvira 15,900 E4
Virunga 21,900 E5
Waka D3
Walikale E4
Wamba 11,500 E3
Watsa 21,300 E3
Yahuma D3
Yakoma D3
Yangambi 22,600 D3
Zongo C3

OTHER FEATURES

Albert (Mobuto Sese Seko)
(lake) F3
Aruwimi (riv.) E3
Bomu (riv.) D3
Boyoma (Stanley) (falls) D3
Chicapa (riv.) D5
Congo (riv.) C4
Edward (lake) E4
Elila (riv.) E4
Fimi (riv.) C4
Garamba Nat'l Park E3
Giri (riv.) C3
Itimbiri (riv.) D3
Ituri (for.) E3
Karisimbi (mt.) E4
Kasai (riv.) C4
Kivu (lake) E4
Kwa (riv.) C4
Kwango (riv.) C5
Kwilu (riv.) C5
Lindi (riv.) E3
Livingstone (falls) B5
Loange (riv.) C5
Lokoro (riv.) C4
Lomami (riv.) D4
Lomela (riv.) D4
Lowa (riv.) E4
Lua (riv.) C3
Lualaba (riv.) E4
Luapula (riv.) E6
Lubilash (riv.) D5
Lufira (riv.) E5
Luilaka (riv.) C4
Lukenie (riv.) D4
Lukuga (riv.) E5
Lulua (riv.) D5
Luvua (riv.) E5
Mai-Ndombe (lake) C4
Malebo (Stanley Pool) (lake) C4
Margherita (mt.) E3
Marungu (mts.) E5
Mobuto Sese Seko (lake) F3
Mweru (lake) E5
Ruwenzori (range) E3
Ruzizi (riv.) E4
Salonga Nat'l Park D4
Sankuru (riv.) D4
Stanley (falls) D3
Stanley Pool (lake) C4
Tanganyika (lake) E5
Tshuapa (riv.) D4
Tumba (lake) C4
Ubangi (riv.) C3
Uele (riv.) E3
Ulindi (riv.) E4
Upemba (lake) E5
Upemba Nat'l Park E5
Virunga (range) E4
Virunga Nat'l Park E4
Zaire (Congo) (riv.) C4

ZAMBIA

CITIES and TOWNS

Abercorn (Mbala) 11,179 F5
Bancroft
(Chililabombwe) 61,928 E6
Broken Hill (Kabwe) 143,635 E6
Chibwe E6
Chilanga 12,503 E7
Chililabombwe 61,928 E6
Chingola 145,869 E6
Chinsali 4,211 F6
Chipata 32,291 F6
Choma 17,943 E7
Fort Rosebery (Mansa) 34,801 E6
Isoka 6,832 F6
Kabompo 5,357 D6
Kabwe 143,635 E6
Kafue 29,794 E7
Kalabo 7,398 D6
Kalomo 5,878 E7
Kaoma 6,731 D6
Kapiri Mposhi 13,677 E6
Kasama 38,093 F6
Kasempa 3,063 E6
Kataba D7
Kawambwa 7,235 E5
Kitwe 314,794 E6
Lealui D6
Livingstone 71,987 E7
Luanshya 132,164 E6
Lundazi 4,083 F6
Lusaka (cap.) 538,469 E7
Luwingu 3,763 E6
Mansa 34,801 E6
Mazabuka 29,602 E7
Mbala 11,179 F5
Mkushi 4,104 E6
Mongu 24,919 D7
Monze 13,141 E7
Mpika 25,880 F6
Mporokoso 6,008 F5
Mpulungu 6,354 F5
Mufulira 149,778 E6
Mulobezi 2,589 E7
Mumbwa 7,570 E6
Mwinilunga 3,169 D6
Nakonde 4,599 F5
Namwala 3,008 E7
Ndola 282,439 E6
Petauke 7,531 F6
Senanga 7,204 D7
Serenje 6,008 F6
Sesheke 3,500 D7
Solwezi 15,032 E6
Zambezi 8,166 D6

OTHER FEATURES

Bangweulu (lake) F6
Barotseland (reg.) D7
Chambeshi (riv.) F6
Cuando (riv.) D7
Dongwe (riv.) D6
Kabompo (riv.) D6
Kafue (riv.) E7
Kafue Nat'l Park E6
Kalambo (falls) F5
Kariba (dam) E7
Kariba (lake) E7
Luangwa (riv.) F6
Luapula (riv.) E6
Lungwebungu (riv.) D6
Mosi-Oa-Tunya (Victoria)
(falls) E7
Mulungushi (dam) E6
Mweru (lake) E5
Sunzu (mt.) F5
Tanganyika (lake) E5
Victoria (falls) E7
Zambezi (riv.) D7

Agriculture, Industry and Resources

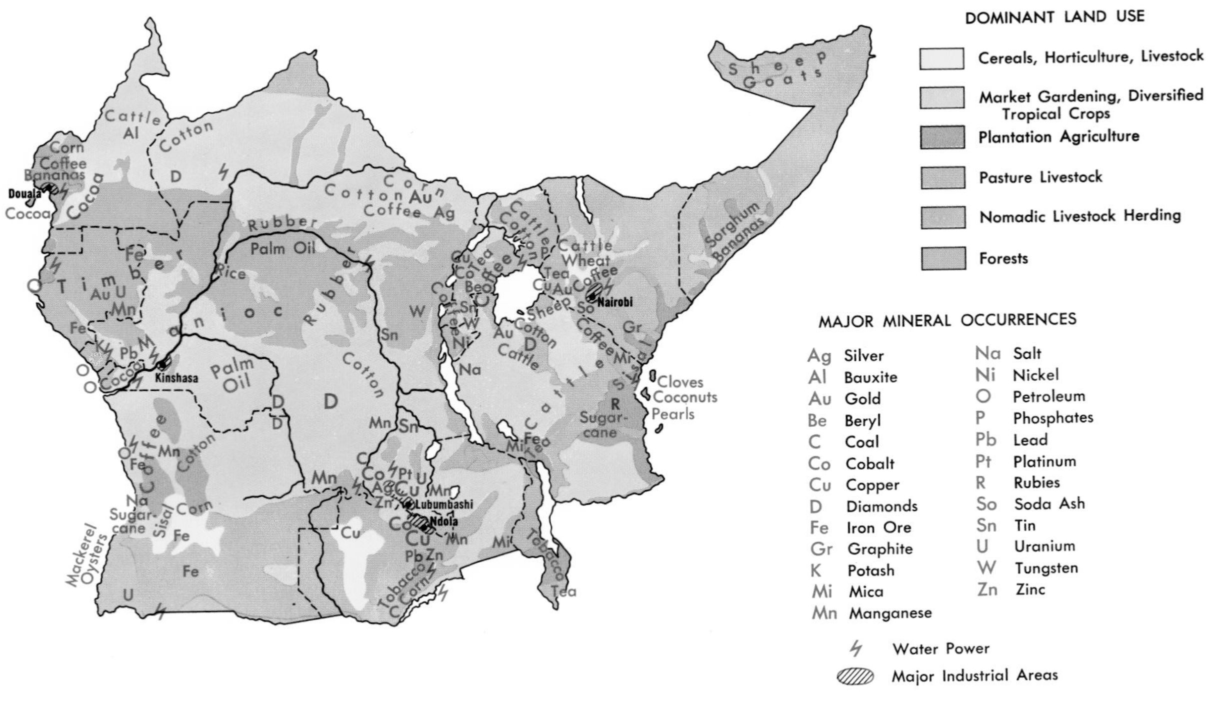

Sheep
Goats
Cattle
Al
Cotton
Corn
Coffee
Bananas
Douala
Cocoa
D
Cotton
Au
Coffee
Ag
Rubber
Palm Oil
Rice
Fe
Timber
Au
U
Mn
Manioc
Rubber
W
Sn
Cattle
Cotton
Wheat
Tea
Coffee
Nairobi
Sheep
Cotton
Cattle
Sorghum
Bananas
Gr
Fe
K
Pb
Mn
Kinshasa
O
Cocoa
Palm Oil
Cotton
D
Na
Cloves
Coconuts
Pearls
R
Sugar-cane
Mn
Sn
Coffee
Mn
Fe
Cotton
Co
Pt
U
Ag
Cu
Zn
Lubumbashi
Ndola
Na
Sugar-cane
Sisal
Corn
Fe
Cu
Mi
Tobacco
Pb
Zn
Tobacco
Corn
Tea
Mackerel
Oysters
U
DOMINANT LAND USE
Cereals, Horticulture, Livestock
Market Gardening, Diversified Tropical Crops
Plantation Agriculture
Pasture Livestock
Nomadic Livestock Herding
Forests
MAJOR MINERAL OCCURRENCES
Ag Silver
Al Bauxite
Au Gold
Be Beryl
C Coal
Co Cobalt
Cu Copper
D Diamonds
Fe Iron Ore
Gr Graphite
K Potash
Mi Mica
Mn Manganese
Na Salt
Ni Nickel
O Petroleum
P Phosphates
Pb Lead
Pt Platinum
R Rubies
So Soda Ash
Sn Tin
U Uranium
W Tungsten
Zn Zinc
Water Power
Major Industrial Areas

NAMIBIA (SOUTH-WEST AFRICA)

AREA 317,827 sq. mi. (823,172 sq. km.)
POPULATION 1,200,000
CAPITAL Windhoek
LARGEST CITY Windhoek
HIGHEST POINT Brandberg 8,550 ft.
(2,606 m.)
MONETARY UNIT rand
MAJOR LANGUAGES Ovambo, Hottentot,
Herero, Afrikaans, English
MAJOR RELIGIONS Tribal religions,
Protestantism

SOUTH AFRICA

AREA 455,318 sq. mi. (1,179,274 sq. km.)
POPULATION 23,771,970
CAPITALS Cape Town, Pretoria
LARGEST CITY Johannesburg
HIGHEST POINT Injasuti 11,182 ft. (3,408 m.)
MONETARY UNIT rand
MAJOR LANGUAGES Afrikaans, English,
Xhosa, Zulu, Sesotho
MAJOR RELIGIONS Protestantism,
Roman Catholicism, Islam, Hinduism,
tribal religions

LESOTHO

AREA 11,720 sq. mi. (30,355 sq. km.)
POPULATION 1,339,000
CAPITAL Maseru
LARGEST CITY Maseru
HIGHEST POINT 11,425 ft. (3,482 m.)
MONETARY UNIT loti
MAJOR LANGUAGES Sesotho, English
MAJOR RELIGIONS Tribal religions,
Christianity

BOTSWANA

AREA 224,764 sq. mi. (582,139 sq. km.)
POPULATION 819,000
CAPITAL Gaborone
LARGEST CITY Francistown
HIGHEST POINT Tsodilo Hill 5,922 ft.
(1,805 m.)
MONETARY UNIT pula
MAJOR LANGUAGES Setswana, Shona,
Bushman, English, Afrikaans
MAJOR RELIGIONS Tribal religions,
Protestantism

MOZAMBIQUE

AREA 303,769 sq. mi. (786,762 sq. km.)
POPULATION 12,130,000
CAPITAL Maputo
LARGEST CITY Maputo
HIGHEST POINT Mt. Binga 7,992 ft.
(2,436 m.)
MONETARY UNIT metical
MAJOR LANGUAGES Makua, Thonga,
Shona, Portuguese
MAJOR RELIGIONS Tribal religions,
Roman Catholicism, Islam

SWAZILAND

AREA 6,705 sq. mi. (17,366 sq. km.)
POPULATION 547,000
CAPITAL Mbabane
LARGEST CITY Manzini
HIGHEST POINT Emlembe 6,109 ft.
(1,862 m.)
MONETARY UNIT lilangeni
MAJOR LANGUAGES siSwati, English
MAJOR RELIGIONS Tribal religions,
Christianity

ZIMBABWE

AREA 150,803 sq. mi. (390,580 sq. km.)
POPULATION 7,360,000
CAPITAL Harare
LARGEST CITY Harare
HIGHEST POINT Mt. Inyangani 8,517 ft.
(2,596 m.)
MONETARY UNIT Zimbabwe dollar
MAJOR LANGUAGES English, Shona,
Ndebele
MAJOR RELIGIONS Tribal religions,
Protestantism

MADAGASCAR

AREA 226,657 sq. mi. (587,041 sq. km.)
POPULATION 8,742,000
CAPITAL Antananarivo
LARGEST CITY Antananarivo
HIGHEST POINT Maromokotro 9,436 ft.
(2,876 m.)
MONETARY UNIT Madagascar franc
MAJOR LANGUAGES Malagasy, French
MAJOR RELIGIONS Tribal religions,
Roman Catholicism, Protestantism

COMOROS

AREA 719 sq. mi. (1,862 sq. km.)
POPULATION 290,000
CAPITAL Moroni
LARGEST CITY Moroni
HIGHEST POINT Karthala 7,746 ft.
(2,361 m.)
MONETARY UNIT CFA franc
MAJOR LANGUAGES Arabic, French,
Swahili
MAJOR RELIGION Islam

MAURITIUS

AREA 790 sq. mi. (2,046 sq. km.)
POPULATION 959,000
CAPITAL Port Louis
LARGEST CITY Port Louis
HIGHEST POINT 2,711 ft. (826 m.)
MONETARY UNIT Mauritian rupee
MAJOR LANGUAGES English, French,
French Creole, Hindi, Urdu
MAJOR RELIGIONS Hinduism, Christianity,
Islam

SEYCHELLES

AREA 145 sq. mi. (375 sq. km.)
POPULATION 63,000
CAPITAL Victoria
LARGEST CITY Victoria
HIGHEST POINT Morne Seychellois
2,993 ft. (912 m.)
MONETARY UNIT Seychellois rupee
MAJOR LANGUAGES English, French,
Creole
MAJOR RELIGION Roman Catholicism

RÉUNION

AREA 969 sq. mi. (2,510 sq. km.)
POPULATION 491,000
CAPITAL St-Denis

MAYOTTE

AREA 144 sq. mi. (373 sq. km.)
POPULATION 47,300
CAPITAL Dzaoudzi

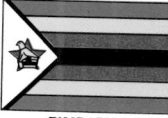
ZIMBABWE

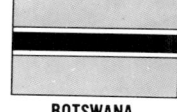
BOTSWANA

SOUTH AFRICA

LESOTHO

SWAZILAND

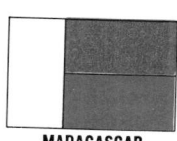
MOZAMBIQUE

COMOROS

MADAGASCAR

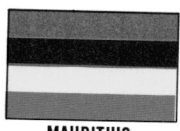
MAURITIUS

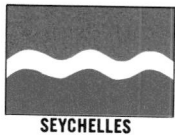
SEYCHELLES

Agriculture, Industry and Resources

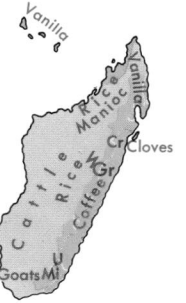
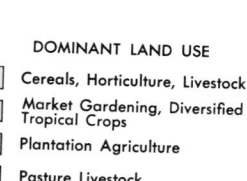

DOMINANT LAND USE

- Cereals, Horticulture, Livestock
- Market Gardening, Diversified Tropical Crops
- Plantation Agriculture
- Pasture Livestock
- Nomadic Livestock Herding
- Forests
- Nonagricultural Land

MAJOR MINERAL OCCURRENCES

Ab	Asbestos	Cu	Copper	Mn	Manganese
Ag	Silver	D	Diamonds	Na	Salt
Al	Bauxite	Fe	Iron Ore	Ni	Nickel
Au	Gold	Gr	Graphite	P	Phosphates
Be	Beryl	Lt	Lithium	Pb	Lead
C	Coal	Mg	Magnesium	Pt	Platinum
Cr	Chromium	Mi	Mica		

Sb	Antimony	
Sn	Tin	
U	Uranium	
V	Vanadium	
W	Tungsten	
Zn	Zinc	

⚡ Water Power
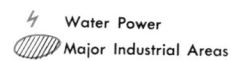 Major Industrial Areas

(continued on following page)

Topography

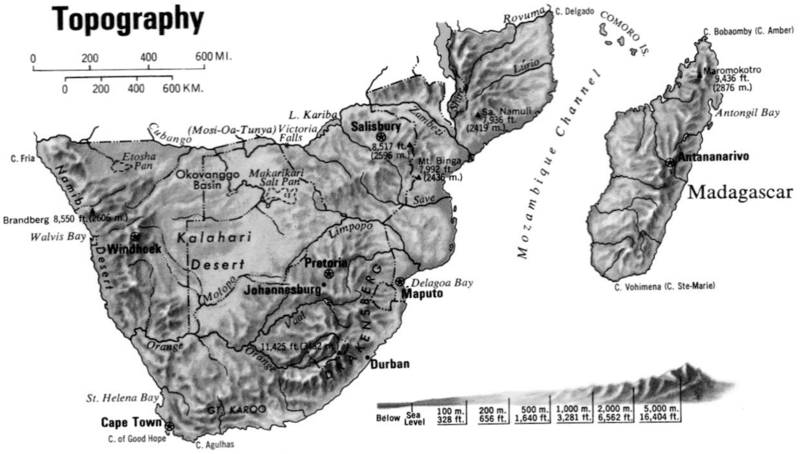
0 200 400 600 MI.
0 200 400 600 KM.
Rovuma
C. Delgado
COMORO IS.
C. Bobaomby (C. Amber)
Maromokotro 9,436 ft. (2876 m.)
Antongil Bay
Antananarivo
Madagascar
Mozambique Channel
L. Kariba
(Mosi-Oa-Tunya) Victoria Falls
Cubango
Salisbury
Zambezi
Sa. Namuli
Mt. Binga
Etosha Pan
Okovango Basin
Makarikari Salt Pan
C. Fria
Namib
Brandberg 8,550 ft. (2606 m.)
Walvis Bay
Windhoek
Kalahari
Desert
Limpopo
Save
Pretoria
Johannesburg
Molopo
Vaal
Orange
Delagoa Bay
Maputo
DRAKENSBERG
Durban
11,425 ft. (3482 m.)
St. Helena Bay
Cape Town
C. of Good Hope
GT. KAROO
C. Agulhas
C. Vohimena (C. Ste-Marie)
Below Sea Level
100 m. 328 ft.
200 m. 656 ft.
500 m. 1,640 ft.
1,000 m. 3,281 ft.
2,000 m. 6,562 ft.
5,000 m. 16,404 ft.

Miandrivazo 2,371 G3
Midongy Atsimo 1,068 H4
Mitsinjo 3,118 H3
Moramanga 10,806 H3
Morombe 6,967 G4
Morondava 19,061 G3
Nosy-Varika 1,252 H4
Port-Bergé 4,734 H3
Sambava 6,215 J2
Soanierana-Ivongo 2,876 H3
Sosumav 10,946 H2
Tamatave (Toamasina) 77,395 H3
Tambohorano 1,383 G3
Tananarive (Antananarivo)
(cap.) 451,808 H3
Tangainony 6,952 H4
Toamasina 77,395 H3
Toliara (Tuléar) 45,676 G4
Tsihombe 1,008 H5
Tsiroanomandidy 11,444 H3
Tsivory 1,036 H4
Vangaindrano 3,249 H4
Vatomandry 4,202 H3
Vohibinany 1,741 H3
Vohimarina (Vohémar) 4,289 J2
Vohipeno 2,736 H4

OTHER FEATURES

Alaotra (lake) H3
Amber (Bobaomby) (cape) H2
Antongil (bay) J3
Betsiboka (riv.) H3
Bobaomby (Amber) (cape) H2
Mangoky (riv.) G4
Mangoro (riv.) H3
Maromokotro (mt.) H2
Masoala (pen.) J3
Mozambique (chan.) G3
Nosy Be (isl.) H2
Nosy Boraha (isl.) J3
Onilahy (riv.) G4
Saint-André (cape) G3
Sainte-Marie (Vohimena)
(cape) G5
Sainte-Marie (Nosy Boraha)
(isl.) J3
Tsiafajavona (mt.) H3
Tsiribihina (riv.) G3
Vohimena (cape) G5

MAURITIUS

CITIES and TOWNS

Curepipe 52,709 G5
Mahébourg 15,463 G5
Port Louis (cap.) 141,022 G5
Poudre d'Or 1,799 G5
Quatre Bornes 51,638 G5
Souillac 3,361 G5

OTHER FEATURES

Mascarene (isls.) F5

MAYOTTE

CITIES and TOWNS

Dzaoudzi (cap.) 196 H2

MOZAMBIQUE

PROVINCES

Cabo Delgado 940,000 F2
Gaza 999,900 E4
Inhambane 977,000 E4
Manica 541,200 E4
Maputo 491,800 E5
Maputo (city) 755,300 E5
Nampula 2,402,700 F2
Niassa 514,100 F2
Sofala 1,055,200 E3
Tete 831,000 E3
Zambézia 2,500,000 F3

CITIES and TOWNS

Alto Molócuè 415 F3
Angoche 1,714 G3
Bartolomeu Dias○ 6,102 F4
Beira 46,293 F3
Beira* 130,398 F3
Bela Vista 851 E5
Benga 1,398 E3
Caia 1,363 E3
Catandica 663 E3
Chemba 588 E3
Chibuto 23,763 E4
Chicualacuala 2,050 E4
Chimoio 4,507 E3
Chinde 742 F3
Cóbuè○ 770 F2
Cuamba 1,416 F2
Dona Ana (Mutarara) 686 F3
Dondo 2,112 F3
Errego 418 F3
Espungabera 405 E4
Fíngoè 1,137 E2
Funhalouro○ 42,366 E4
Gorongoza 435 E3
Guija 530 E4
Homoíne 1,122 E4
Ibo 1,015 G2
Inhambane 4,975 F4
Inhaminga 1,607 F3
Inharrime 856 F4
Lichinga 3,011 F2
Lumbo○ 11,080 G3
Lúrio○ 13,417 G2
Mabalane○ 13,158 E4
Mabote○ 28,970 E4
Machanga○ 15,754 F4
Machaze○ 42,255 E4
Macia 1,203 E4
Macomia 730 F2
Magude 1,502 E5
Malema 430 F2
Mandié○ 24,382 E3
Mandimba○ 7,634 F2
Manhiça 1,680 E5
Maniamba○ 2,045 F2
Manica 1,529 E3
Manjacaze 641 E5
Maputo (cap.) 755,300 E5
Marracuene 1,342 E5
Marromeu 1,330 F3
Marrupa 824 F2
Massangena○ 3,301 E4
Massinga 517 F4
Maxixe 902 F4
Meconta 1,051 F3
Memba 379 G2
Metangula 1,502 F2
Milanje 1,048 F3
Moamba 643 E5
Moçambique 1,730 G3
Mocímboa da Praia 935 G2
Mocuba 2,293 F3
Moma 433 F3
Monapo 902 G2
Montepuez 2,837 F2
Morrumbala 415 F3
Morrumbene 1,121 F4
Mualama○ 34,992 F3
Mucojo○ 15,867 G2
Mueda 1,583 F2
Murrupula 444 F3
Mutarara (Dona Ana) 686 F3
Nacala 4,601 G2
Namacurra 399 F3
Namapa 440 F2
Nametil 453 F3
Nampula 23,072 F3
Negomane○ 656 F2
Nova Lusitânia 1,363 E3
Nova Mambone 883 F4
Nova Sofala 274 F4
Pafúri○ 2,599 E4
Pemba 3,629 G2
Quelimane 10,522 F3
Quionga○ 3,181 G2
Quissico 2,615 F4
Ribáuè 437 F3
Songo 1,350 E3
Tete 4,549 E3
Ulongue 451 E2
Vila de Sena○ 21,074 E3
Vilanculos 887 E4
Xai-Xai 5,234 E5

OTHER FEATURES

Angoche (isl.) G3
Bazaruto, Ilha do (isl.) F4
Binga (mt.) E3
Changane (riv.) E4
Chilwa (lake) F3
Delagoa (bay) E5
Delgado (cape) G2
Ligonha (riv.) F3
Limpopo (riv.) E4
Lugenda (riv.) F2
Lúrio (riv.) F2
Mazoe (riv.) E3
Mozambique (chan.) G3
Namuli, Serra (mt.) F3
Nyasa (lake) E2
Olifants (riv.) D4
Rovuma (riv.) F2
São Sebastião (pt.) F4
Save (riv.) E4
Shire (riv.) E3
Zambezi (riv.) E3

NAMIBIA (SOUTH-WEST AFRICA)

CITIES and TOWNS

Aroab 783 B5
Aus 767 B5
Berseba B5
Bethanie 1,207 B5
Gibeon B5
Gobabis 4,428 B4
Grootfontein 4,627 B3
Kalkfeld 587 B4
Kamanjab 713 A3
Karasburg 2,693 B5
Karibib 1,653 B4
Katima Mulilo C3
Keetmanshoop 10,297 B5
Khorixas 1,299 A4
Koes 514 B5
Lüderitz 6,642 A5
Maltahöhe 1,313 B4
Mariental 4,629 B4
Ohopoho A3
Okahandja 1,688 B4
Omaruru 2,783 B4
Ondangua B3
Ongwediva B3
Oranjemund 2,594 B5
Otavi 1,814 B3
Otjiwarongo 8,018 B4
Outjo 2,545 B4
Rehoboth 5,363 B4
Runtu 521 B3
Stampriet 271 B4
Swakopmund 5,681 A4
Tsumeb 12,338 B3
Usakos 2,334 B4
Warmbad 810 B5
Windhoek (cap.) 61,369 B4
Witvlei 303 B4

OTHER FEATURES

Brandberg (mt.) A4
Caprivi Strip (reg.) C3
Chobe (riv.) C3
Cubango (riv.) B3
Damaraland (reg.) B4
Diamond Coast (reg.) A5
Elephant (riv.) B5
Etosha Pan (salt pan) B3
Fish (riv.) B5
Great Namaland (reg.) B4
Hottentot (bay) A5
Kalahari (des.) C4
Kaokoveld (reg.) A3
Kaukauveld (mts.) C3
Namib (des.) A3
Nossob (riv.) B4
Okovango (riv.) C3
Ovamboland (reg.) B3
Skeleton Coast (reg.) A3
Swakop (riv.) B4
Zambezi (riv.) C3

RÉUNION

CITIES and TOWNS

Le Port 21,564 F5
Saint-André 6,584 G5
Saint-Benoît 7,778 G5
Saint-Denis (cap.) 80,075 F5
Saint-Denis* 104,603 F5
Saint-Joseph 8,928 G6
Saint-Louis 10,252 F5
Saint-Pierre 21,817 F6

OTHER FEATURES

Bassas da India (isl.) F4
Europa (isl.) G4
Glorioso (isls.) H2
Juan de Nova (isl.) G3
Piton des Neiges (mt.) G5

SEYCHELLES

CITIES and TOWNS

Anse Boileau† 3,420 H5
Anse Royale† 3,182 H5
Cascade† 2,600 H5
Victoria (cap.) 15,559 H5
Victoria* 23,012 H5

OTHER FEATURES

Aldabra (isls.) H1
Assumption (isl.) H1
Astove (isl.) H2
Cosmoledo (isls.) H1
Frigate (isl.) J5
La Digue (isl.) J5
Mahé (isl.) H5
North (isl.) H5
Praslin (isl.) H5
Silhouette (isl.) H5

SOUTH AFRICA

PROVINCES

Cape Province 5,543,506 C6
Natal 5,722,215 E5
Orange Free State 1,833,216 D5
Transvaal 10,673,033 D4

AUTONOMOUS REPUBLICS

Bophuthatswana 1,200,000 D5
Ciskei 345,191 D6
Transkei 2,000,000 D6
Venda 450,000 E4

CITIES and TOWNS

Aberdeen 4,968 C6
Adelaide 7,227 D6
Alberton 23,988 H6
Alexandra 57,040 H6
Alexander Bay 2,675 B5
Aliwal North 12,311 D6
Barberton 12,382 E5
Barkly East 4,023 D6
Beaufort West 17,862 C6
Bellville 49,026 F6
Benoni 151,294 J6
Benoni□ 164,543 J6
Bethlehem 29,918 D5
Bethulie 4,918 D6
Bloemfontein 149,836 C5
Bloemfontein□ 182,329 C5
Bloubergstrand 378 E6
Boksburg 106,126 J6
Botrivier 743 F7
Brakpan 73,210 J6
Brandvlei 1,337 B6
Bredasdorp 5,264 B6
Brentwood Park 5,296 J6
Brits 12,182 D5
Britstown 3,039 C6
Burgersdorp 8,340 D6
Butterworth (Gcuwa) 2,769 D6
Caledon 5,406 G7
Calvinia 6,386 B6
Cape Town (cap.) 697,514 E6
Cape Town□ 833,731 E6
Carltonville 40,641 G7
Carnarvon 5,199 C6
Ceres 9,230 B6
Christiana 6,882 D5
Clanwilliam 2,724 B6
Clayville 3,994 H6
Colesberg 7,088 D6
Constantia 7,220 E6
Cradock 20,822 D6
De Aar 18,057 C6
Delmas 6,424 J6
Dibeng 945 C5
Douglas 4,335 C5
Dundee 17,162 E5
Dunnottar 3,089 J6
Durban 736,852 E5
Durban□ 975,494 E5
Durbanville 7,438 F6
East London 119,727 D6
East London□ 126,671 D6
Edenburg 3,710 D5
Edendale 41,194 D5
Edenvale 25,126 H6
Eersterivier 1,459 F6
Elliot 3,739 D6
Eloff 1,134 J6
Elsburg 3,501 H6
Elsiesrivier 63,706 F6
Empangeni 7,532 E5
Ermelo 19,036 E5
Eshowe 4,552 E5
Estcourt 10,922 D5
Ficksburg 9,504 D5
Firgrove 2,551 F6
Fort Beaufort 11,640 D6
Franschhoek 1,216 F6
Garies 1,339 B6
Gcuwa 2,769 D6
George 24,625 C6
Germiston 221,972 H6
Germiston□ 293,257 H6
Glencoe 10,513 E5
Goodwood 31,592 F6
Gordon's Bay 1,112 F7
Graaff-Reinet 22,392 C6
Grabouw 4,286 F7
Grahamstown 41,302 D6
Grassy Park 32,709 E6
Greytown 9,028 E5
Griquatown 2,996 C5
Halfway House 3,639 H6
Harrismith 16,082 D5
Hawston 2,501 G7
Heidelberg 12,521 J7
Heilbron 8,258 D5
Hermanus 4,956 G7
Hopetown 3,273 C5
Houtbaai 5,691 E6
Howick 12,429 E5
Humansdorp 4,215 C6
Ingwavuma 718 E5
Jagersfontein 4,142 D5
Jameson Park 2,280 J7
Johannesburg 654,232 H6
Johannesburg□ 1,417,818 H6
Keimoes 4,534 C5
Kempton Park 37,205 J6
Kenhardt 3,230 C5
Kimberley 105,258 C5
Kimberley□ 108,609 C5
King William's Town 15,798 D6
Kirkwood 5,151 D6
Kleinmond 1,115 F7
Klerksdorp 63,558 D5
Knysna 13,479 C6
Koffiefontein 3,672 D5
Kokstad 10,227 D6
Kraaifontein 10,286 F6
Kroonstad 51,988 D5
Krugersdorp 92,725 H6
Kuilsrivier 8,132 F6
Kuruman 5,758 C5
Ladybrand 8,757 D5
Ladysmith 28,920 D5
Lambert's Bay 3,247 B6
Lombardy 3,395 H6
Louis Trichardt 8,906 E4
Lydenburg 7,427 E4
Macassar 882 F6
Maclear 3,279 D6
Mafikeng (Mafeking) 6,515 C5
Malmesbury 9,314 B6
Margate 4,410 E6
Matatiele 3,853 D6
Melkbosstrand 453 E6
Messina 12,121 D4
Meyerton 8,654 H7
Middelburg, C. of Good
Hope 11,121 D6
Middelburg, Transvaal 26,942 D5
Milnerton 10,893 F6
Modderfontein 8,538 H6
Molteno 5,825 D6
Montagu 5,504 C6
Moorreesburg 4,945 B6
Mossel Bay 17,574 C6
Nababeep 8,293 B5
Nelspruit 25,092 E5
Newcastle 14,407 E5
Nigel 41,179 J7
Noupoort 7,403 C6
Nyanga 15,655 F6
Nylstroom 6,906 D4
Odendaalsrus 15,603 D5
Okiep 4,983 B5
Oudtshoorn 26,907 C6
Paarl 49,244 F6
Parow 60,768 F6
Parys 17,447 D5
Phalaborwa 7,543 E4
Pietermaritzburg 114,822 E5
Pietermaritzburg□ 174,179 E5
Pietersburg 27,174 D4
Piet Retief 10,056 D5
Piketberg 3,638 B6
Pinelands 11,769 F6
Pinetown 22,721 E6
Pniel 1,596 F6
Port Alfred 8,640 D6
Port Elizabeth 392,231 D6
Port Elizabeth□ 413,961 D6
Port Nolloth 2,893 B5
Port Saint Johns
(Umzimbuvu) 1,817 D6
Port Shepstone 5,581 E6
Postmasburg 9,020 C5

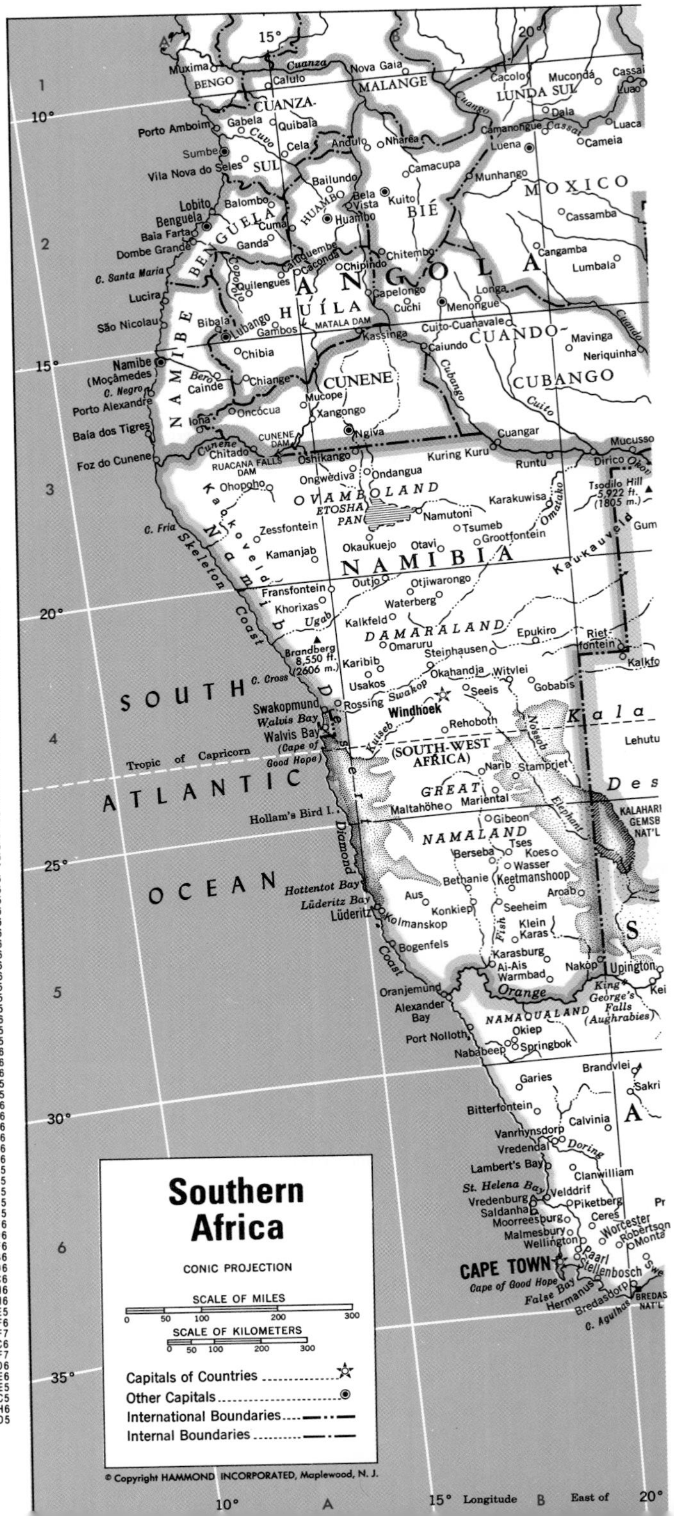
Southern Africa
CONIC PROJECTION
SCALE OF MILES
0 50 100 200 300
SCALE OF KILOMETERS
0 50 100 200 300
Capitals of Countries
Other Capitals
International Boundaries
Internal Boundaries
ANGOLA
NAMIBIA
(SOUTH-WEST AFRICA)
SOUTH ATLANTIC OCEAN
Tropic of Capricorn
OVAMBOLAND
DAMARALAND
GREAT NAMALAND
NAMAQUALAND
Windhoek
CAPE TOWN
Cape of Good Hope
Walvis Bay
Swakopmund
Lüderitz
Keetmanshoop
Skeleton Coast
Diamond Coast
10° 15° 20°
Longitude East of Greenwich

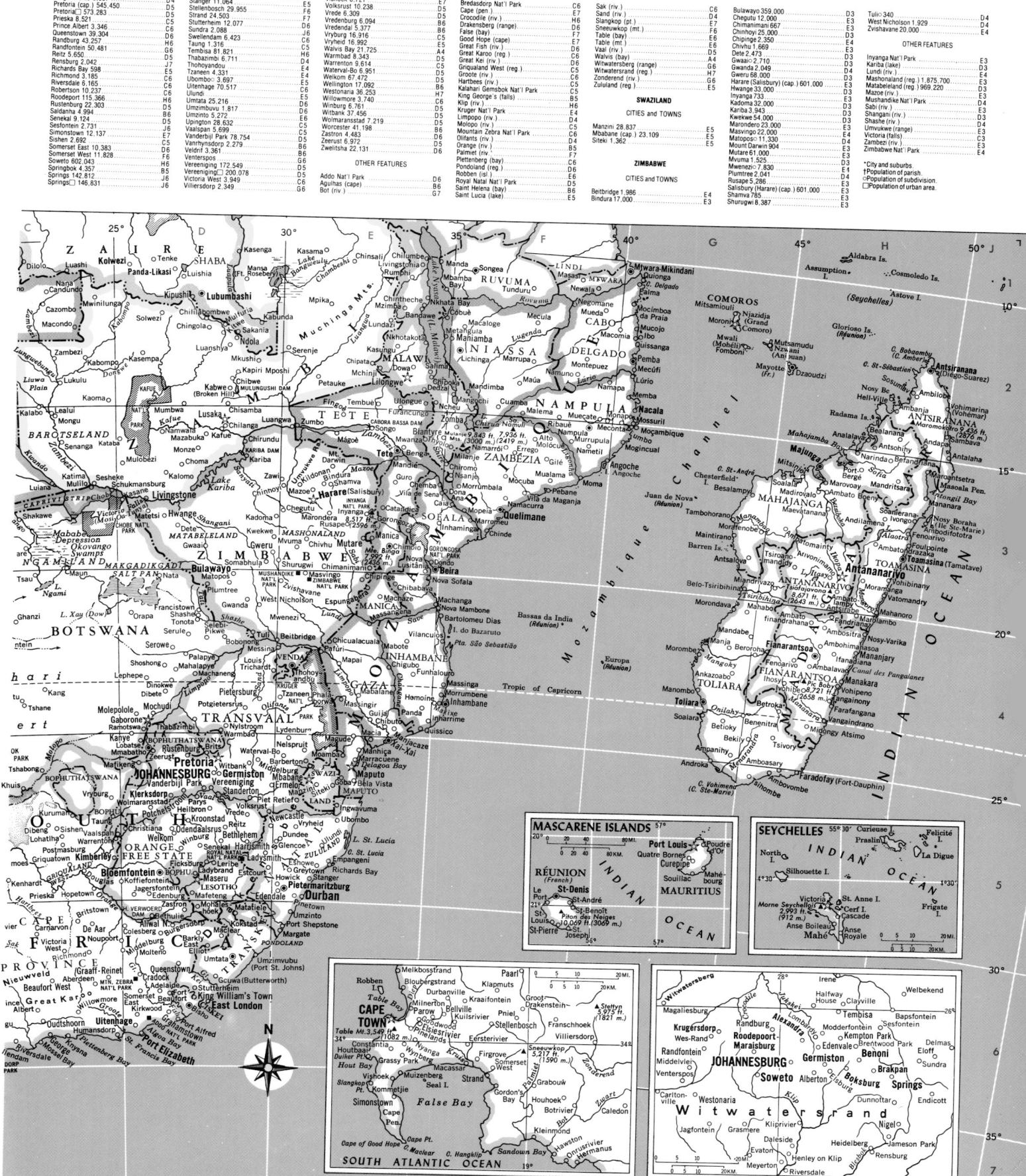

South America

AZIMUTHAL EQUAL-AREA PROJECTION

MILES
0   100   200   400   600

KILOMETERS
0 100 200   400   600

Capitals of Countries .... ⊛
Other Capitals .... ⊙
International Boundaries .... —·—·—·—
Canals ....

© Copyright HAMMOND INCORPORATED, Maplewood, N.J.

Longitude West 50° of Greenwich

Population Distribution

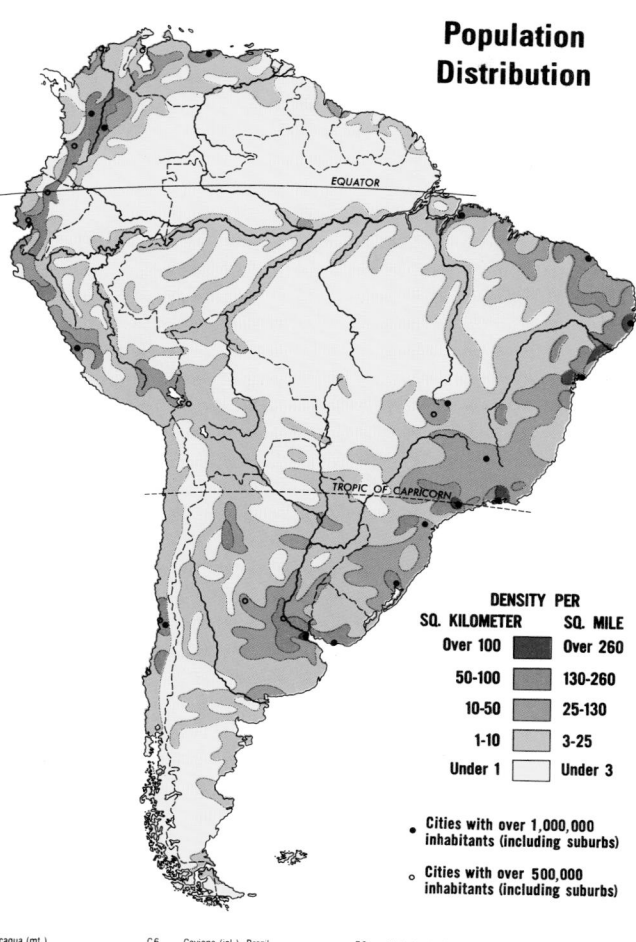

EQUATOR

TROPIC OF CAPRICORN

AREA 6,875,000 sq. mi. (17,806,250 sq. km.)
POPULATION 245,000,000
LARGEST CITY São Paulo
HIGHEST POINT Cerro Aconcagua 22,831 ft.
  (6,959 m.)
LOWEST POINT Salina Grande -131 ft. (-40 m.)

Vegetation

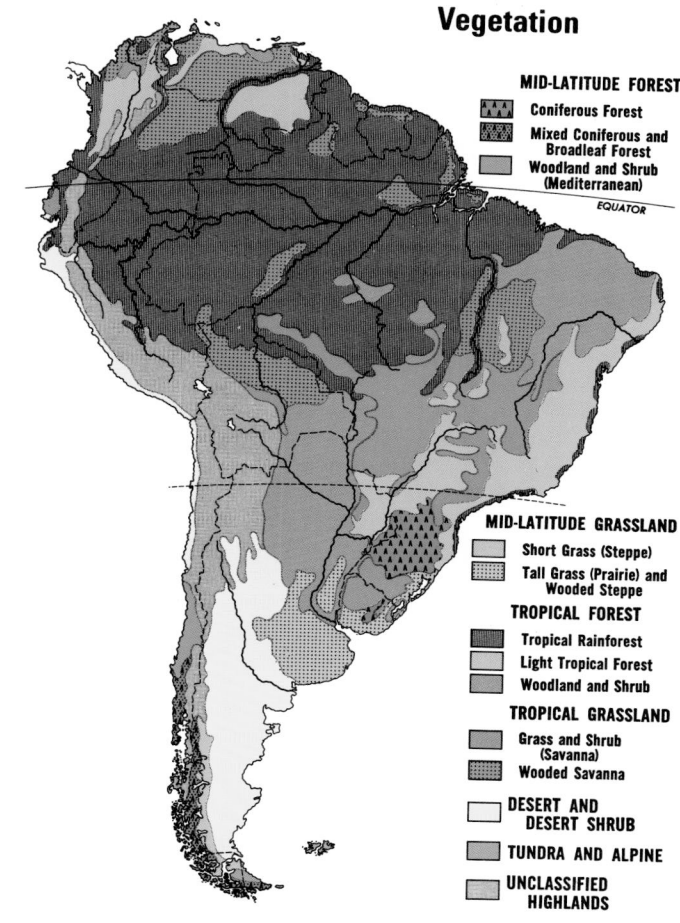

EQUATOR

DENSITY PER

SQ. KILOMETER	SQ. MILE
Over 100	Over 260
50-100	130-260
10-50	25-130
1-10	3-25
Under 1	Under 3

● Cities with over 1,000,000 inhabitants (including suburbs)

○ Cities with over 500,000 inhabitants (including suburbs)

MID-LATITUDE FOREST
- Coniferous Forest
- Mixed Coniferous and Broadleaf Forest
- Woodland and Shrub (Mediterranean)

MID-LATITUDE GRASSLAND
- Short Grass (Steppe)
- Tall Grass (Prairie) and Wooded Steppe

TROPICAL FOREST
- Tropical Rainforest
- Light Tropical Forest
- Woodland and Shrub

TROPICAL GRASSLAND
- Grass and Shrub (Savanna)
- Wooded Savanna

DESERT AND DESERT SHRUB

TUNDRA AND ALPINE

UNCLASSIFIED HIGHLANDS

SOUTH AMERICA

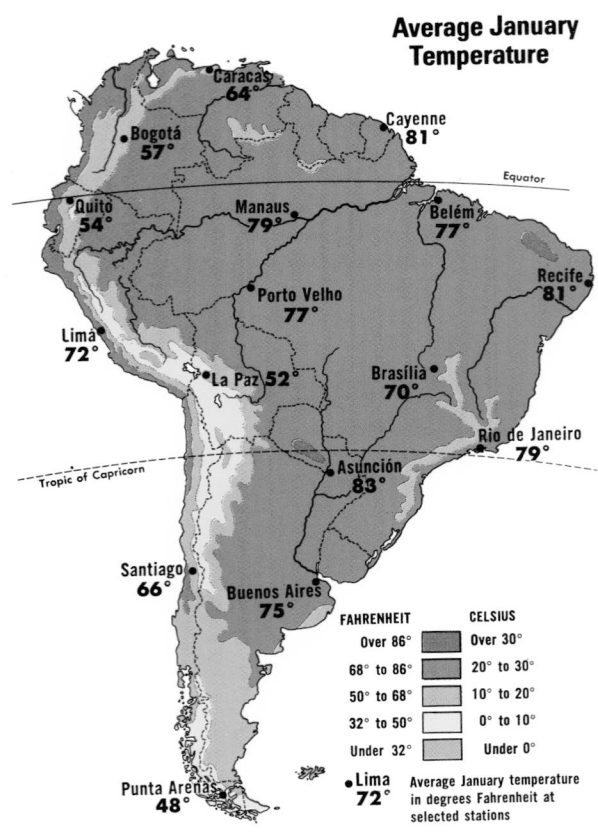

Average January Temperature

Caracas 64°
Bogotá 57°
Cayenne 81°
Quito 54°
Manaus 79°
Belém 77°
Recife 81°
Porto Velho 77°
Lima 72°
La Paz 52°
Brasília 70°
Rio de Janeiro 79°
Asunción 83°
Santiago 66°
Buenos Aires 75°
Punta Arenas 48°

Equator
Tropic of Capricorn

FAHRENHEIT	CELSIUS
Over 86°	Over 30°
68° to 86°	20° to 30°
50° to 68°	10° to 20°
32° to 50°	0° to 10°
Under 32°	Under 0°

•Lima 72° Average January temperature in degrees Fahrenheit at selected stations

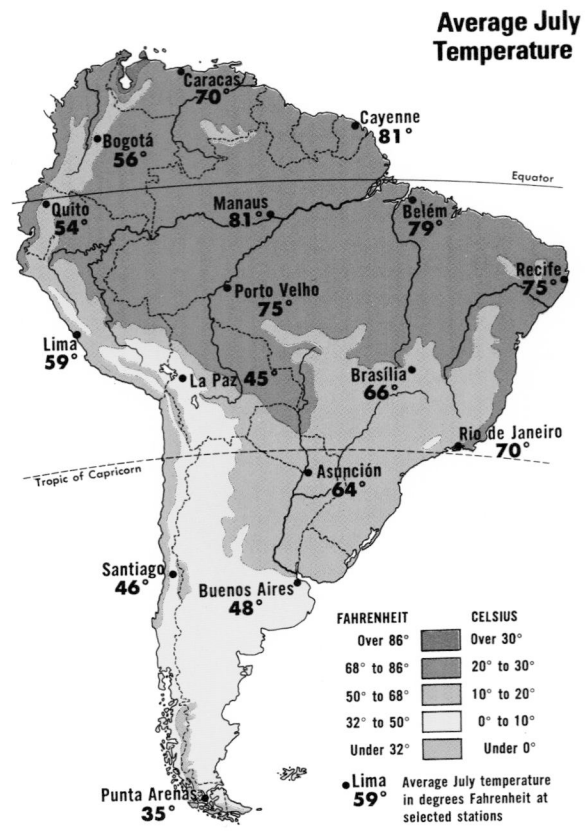

Average July Temperature

Caracas 70°
Bogotá 56°
Cayenne 81°
Quito 54°
Manaus 81°
Belém 79°
Recife 75°
Porto Velho 75°
Lima 59°
La Paz 45°
Brasília 66°
Rio de Janeiro 70°
Asunción 64°
Santiago 46°
Buenos Aires 48°
Punta Arenas 35°

Equator
Tropic of Capricorn

FAHRENHEIT	CELSIUS
Over 86°	Over 30°
68° to 86°	20° to 30°
50° to 68°	10° to 20°
32° to 50°	0° to 10°
Under 32°	Under 0°

•Lima 59° Average July temperature in degrees Fahrenheit at selected stations

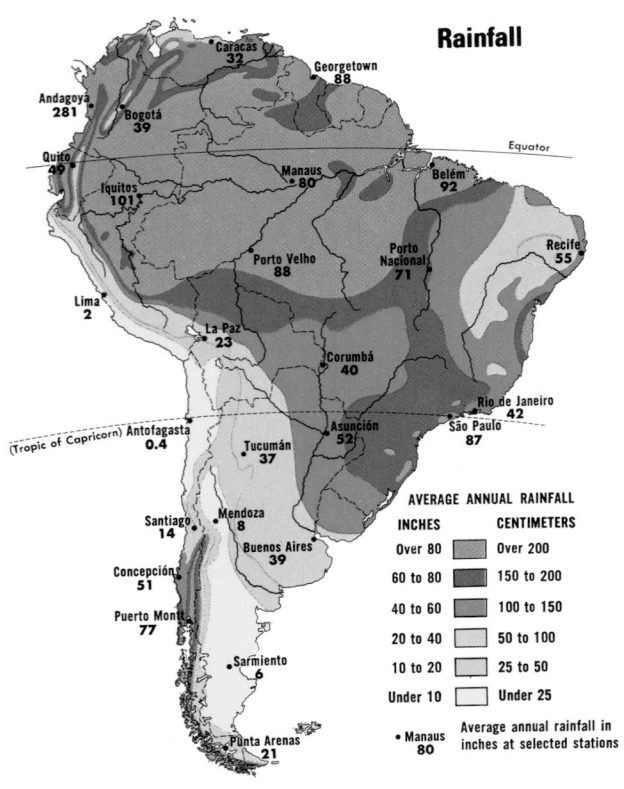

Rainfall

Caracas 32
Georgetown 88
Andagoya 281
Bogotá 39
Quito 49
Iquitos 101
Manaus 80
Belém 92
Porto Velho 88
Porto Nacional 71
Recife 55
Lima 2
La Paz 23
Corumbá 40
Rio de Janeiro 42
Asunción 52
São Paulo 87
(Tropic of Capricorn) Antofagasta 0.4
Tucumán 37
Santiago 14
Mendoza 8
Buenos Aires 39
Concepción 51
Puerto Montt 77
Sarmiento 6
Punta Arenas 21

Equator

AVERAGE ANNUAL RAINFALL
INCHES	CENTIMETERS
Over 80	Over 200
60 to 80	150 to 200
40 to 60	100 to 150
20 to 40	50 to 100
10 to 20	25 to 50
Under 10	Under 25

• Manaus 80 Average annual rainfall in inches at selected stations

Vegetation/Relief

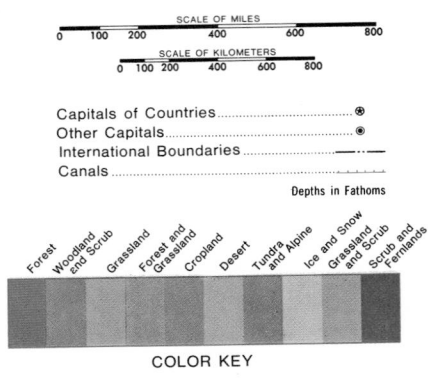

SCALE OF MILES
0 100 200 400 600 800

SCALE OF KILOMETERS
0 100 200 400 600 800

Capitals of Countries..................................⊛
Other Capitals..⊛
International Boundaries...........................
Canals...

Depths in Fathoms

Forest | Woodland and Scrub | Grassland | Forest and Grassland | Cropland | Desert | Tundra and Alpine | Ice and Snow | Grassland and Scrub | Scrub and Fernlands

COLOR KEY

STATES

Amazonas (terr.) 21,696 ... E5
Anzoátegui 506,297 ... F3
Apure 164,705 ... D4
Aragua 543,170 ... E3
Barinas 231,046 ... D3
Bolívar 391,665 ... F7
Carabobo 659,339 ... D2
Cojedes 94,351 ... D3
Delta Amacuro (terr.) 48,139 ... H3
Dependencias Federales ... E2
  (terr.) 463 ... E2
Distrito Federal 1,860,637 ... E2
Falcón 407,957 ... D2
Guárico 318,905 ... E3
Lara 671,410 ... C3
Mérida 347,095 ... C3
Miranda 856,272 ... E2
Monagas 298,239 ... G3
Nueva Esparta 118,830 ... G2
Portuguesa 297,047 ... D3
Sucre 469,004 ... G2
Táchira 511,346 ... C4
Trujillo 381,334 ... C3
Yaracuy 223,545 ... D2
Zulia 1,299,030 ... B2

CITIES and TOWNS

Acarigua 56,743 ... D3
Achaguas 4,633 ... D4

Adícora 707 ... D2
Aguada Grande 2,901 ... D2
Agua Fría ... E5
Agua Linda ... E5
Aguasay 1,752 ... G3
Altagracia 11,116 ... G3
Altagracia de Orituco 18,717 ... E3
Amuay ... C2
Anaco 29,487 ... F3
Aparurén ... G5
Apurito 740 ... D4
Arabopo ... H5
Aragua de Barcelona 9,107 ... F3
Aragua de Maturín 4,051 ... G3
Araure 22,466 ... D3
Aricagua 231 ... C3
Arichuna 1,204 ... E4
Aripao 296 ... F4
Arismendi 1,257 ... D3
Aroa 5,418 ... D2
Atapirire 337 ... F3
Bachaquero ... B2
Baragua 859 ... D2
Barbacoas 2,513 ... E3
Barcelona 78,201 ... F2
Barinas 56,329 ... D3
Barinitas 9,644 ... C3
Barquisimeto 330,815 ... D2
Barrancas, Barinas 4,489 ... C3
Barrancas, Monagas 5,738 ... G3
Betijoque 5,851 ... C3
Biruaca 2,266 ... E4

Biscucuy 6,114 ... D3
Bobare 1,204 ... D3
Bobures 2,468 ... C3
Boca de Aroa 2,756 ... D2
Boca del Mangle ... G3
Boca del Pao 403 ... F3
Bocono 15,915 ... C3
Borbón ... F4
Borojó 423 ... C2
Bruzual 941 ... D4
Buena Vista, Anzoátegui ... F3
Buena Vista, Apure ... D4
Buena Vista, Falcón 944 ... C2
Cabimas 118,037 ... B2
Cabruta 1,927 ... E4
Cabudare 14,593 ... D2
Cabure 1,673 ... G3
Cachipo ... F5
Cacuri ... E5
Cagua 29,601 ... E2
Caicara 6,092 ... D2
Caicara de Orinoco 6,867 ... E3
Calabozo 37,282 ... E3
Calderas 1,195 ... C3
Camaguán 4,143 ... E3
Camatagua 3,335 ... E3
Campo Claro 1,832 ... C3
Candelaria ... F4
Cantaura 15,839 ... F3
Capatárida 1,375 ... C2
Capibara ... E6
Carabobo, Bolívar ... H4
Cojoro ... C2

Carabobo, Carabobo ... D3
Caracas, Carabobo ... D3
Caracas (cap.) 1,035,499 ... E2
Caracas* 2,183,935 ... E2
Carache 3,966 ... C3
Carapa 119 ... G3
Cariaco 6,549 ... G2
Caribén ... E4
Caripe 4,729 ... G2
Caripito 19,053 ... G2
Carirubana 15,701 ... C2
Carmelo 2,556 ... C2
Carora 36,115 ... B2
Carúpano 50,935 ... G2
Carrasquero 2,193 ... G2
Casanay 4,985 ... G2
Casigua, Falcón 460 ... C2
Casigua, Zulia 3,665 ... B3
Caucagua 6,218 ... E2
Cazorla 700 ... E3
Chaguaramas 2,748 ... E3
Chichiriviche 3,236 ... D2
Chivacoa 19,210 ... D2
Choroní 384 ... E2
Churuguara 6,636 ... D2
Ciudad Bolívar 103,728 ... G3
Ciudad Bolivia 4,864 ... C3
Ciudad de Nutrias 769 ... D3
Ciudad Guayana 143,540 ... G3
Ciudad Ojeda 83,083 ... B2
Ciudad Piar 3,965 ... F3
Clarines 2,099 ... F2
Cojoro ... C2

Colón ... E6
Comunidad ... H3
Coporito ... H3
Coro 68,701 ... D2
Corozo Pando ... E3
Cúa 9,953 ... E2
Cubiro 1,988 ... D3
Cubro 1,988 ... D3
Cuchivero ... E3
Cumaná 119,751 ... F2
Cumanacoa 9,179 ... G2
Cunaviche 795 ... E4
Curiapo ... H3
Delicias 1,616 ... B4
Democracia ... E6
Dolores 1,454 ... C3
Duaca 7,519 ... D2
Ejido 11,170 ... C3
El Almacén ... G4
El Amparo de Apure 2,015 ... C4
El Baúl 1,715 ... D3
El Callao 4,270 ... G4
El Calvario 384 ... E3
El Chaparro 3,768 ... F3
El Cristo ... E6
El Dorado 1,888 ... H4
El Empedrado 1,788 ... C3
El Guapo 1,231 ... F2
El Manteco 1,962 ... G4
El Miamo 335 ... H4
Elorza 3,184 ... D4
El Oso ... H5

El Palmar 2,758 ... G4
El Pao, Anzoátegui 761 ... F3
El Pao, Bolívar 1,259 ... G3
El Pao, Cojedes 1,715 ... D3
El Perú ... H4
El Pilar 3,278 ... G2
El Rastro 903 ... D3
El Roque ... E2
El Samán de Apure 1,399 ... D4
El Socorro ... E3
El Sombrero 8,373 ... E3
El Tigre 49,801 ... F3
El Tocuyo 19,351 ... C3
El Toro ... C3
El Vigía 20,970 ... C3
El Vínculo ... D1
El Yagual 699 ... D4
Encontrados 5,607 ... B3
Esperanza ... E6
Garcitas ... C3
Guacara 35,111 ... D2
Guachara 577 ... D2
Guadarrama 334 ... D3
Guaina ... G5
Guana ... G5
Guanare 34,148 ... D3
Guanarito 3,150 ... D3
Guanoco ... G2
Guanta 9,017 ... F2
Guardatinajas 1,206 ... E3
Guarero ... B2

Guárico 3,259 ... D3
Guariquén 619 ... G2
Guasdualito 7,793 ... C4
Guasimal 582 ... D2
Guasipati 4,807 ... H4
Guayabal, Amazonas ... E6
Guayabal, Guárico 1,403 ... E3
Güiri 13,905 ... G4
Guri ... G4
Guzmán Blanco ... E6
Higuerote 4,897 ... E2
Icabarú ... H5
Independencia 4,897 ... D4
Iraja 4,470 ... E2
Juangriego 6,062 ... G2
Judibana ... C2
Juseplín ... G3
Kavanayén ... H5
La Aduana ... D3
La Asunción 6,381 ... G2
La Canoa ... F3
La Ceiba, Apure ... D4
La Ceiba, Trujillo 212 ... C3
La Concepción ... B2
La Concepción 13,885 ... C3
La Esmeralda ... E6
La Esperanza ... H3
La Fría 8,134 ... B3
La Grita 12,934 ... C3
La Guaira 20,344 ... E2
Lagunetas ... C3
Lagunillas ... C3

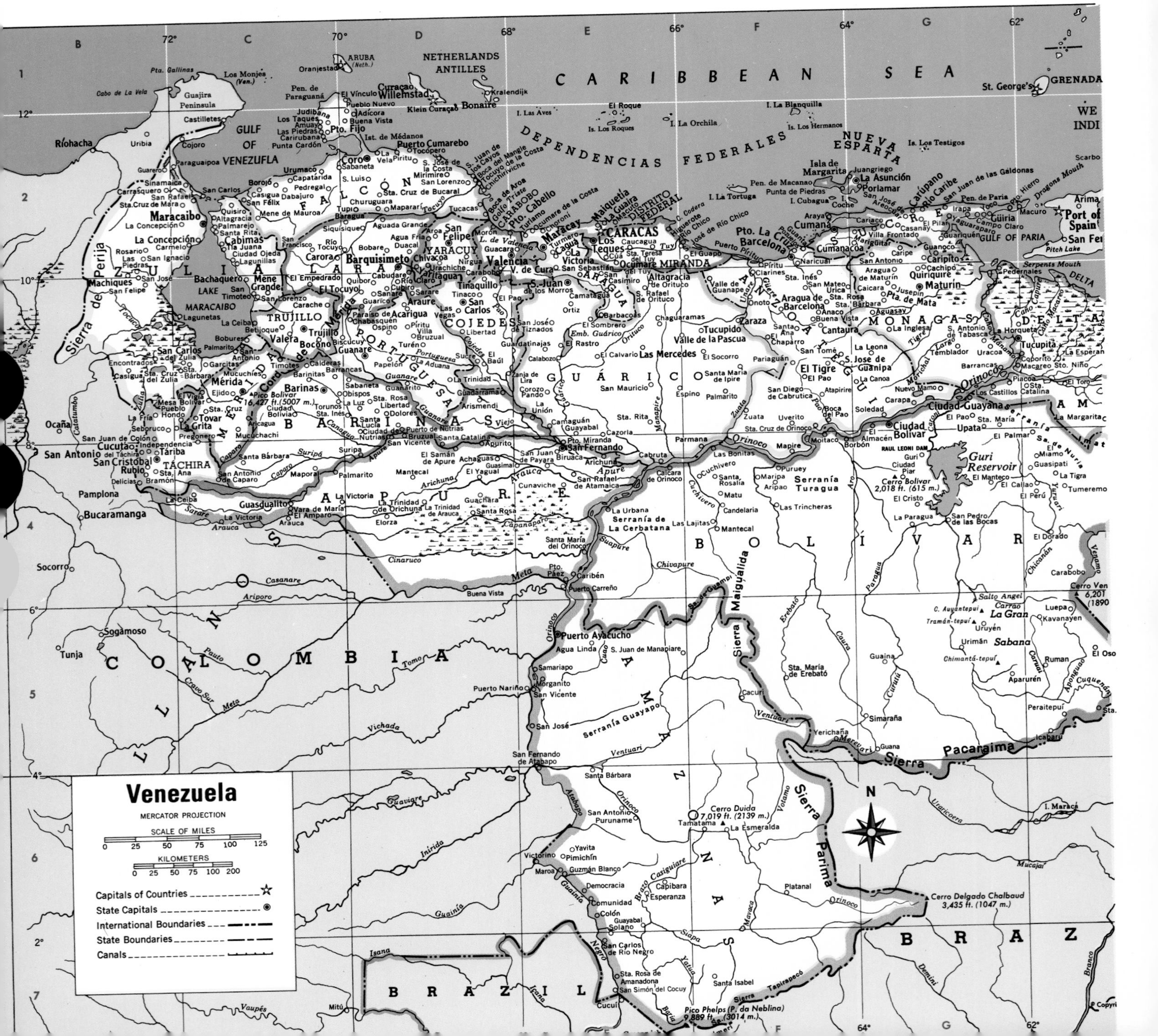

La Horqueta...G3
La Inglesa...G3
La Leona...D3
La Luz 672...F4
La Margarita...D3
La Paragua 1,676...G4
Las Bonitas 343...F4
Las Lajitas...F4
Las Mercedes 6,739...E3
Las Piedras, Falcón...
Las Piedras, Zulia 4,583...B2
Las Trincheras...F4
Las Vegas 3,212...D3
La Tigra...H4
La Trinidad 129...H4
La Trinidad de Arauca...
La Trinidad de Orichuna 665...F3
La Unión 713...D2
La Urbana 661...E4
La Vela de Coro 7,172...D2
La Victoria, Apure 689...D4
La Victoria, Apure...C4
La Victoria, Aragua 40,731...E2
Libertad, Barinas 2,072...D3
Libertad, Cojedes 1,919...D3
Los Castillos...G3
Los Taques 1,160...C2
Los Teques 63,106...E2
Macareo Santo Niño...H3
Machiques 18,898...B3
Macuro 1,122...H2
Macuto 11,704...E2

Maiquetía 59,238...E2
Mantecal, Apure 1,136...D4
Mantecal, Bolívar...F4
Mapararí 1,376...D2
Mapire 1,195...F4
Maporal 249...C4
Maracaibo 651,574...B2
Maracay 255,134...E2
Marigüitar 5,645...G2
Maripa 913...F4
Maroa 408...E6
Matu...F4
Maturín 98,188...G3
Mene de Mauroa 4,336...C2
Mene Grande 11,498...C2
Mérida 74,214...C3
Mesa Bolívar 956...C3
Mirimire 3,424...D2
Moitaco 458...F4
Morganito...E5
Morón 19,451...D2
Mucuchachí 472...C3
Mucuchíes 1,625...C3
Naricual 1,047...F2
Nirgua 11,918...D2
Nuevo Mamo...G3
Obispos 1,140...D3
Ocumare de la Costa 2,840...D2
Ocumare del Tuy 24,229...E2
Onoto 1,991...F3
Ortiz 1,793...E3
Ospino 3,544...D3
Palmarejo...C2
Palmarito, Apure 926...D4
Palmarito, Guárico...F3
Palmarito, Mérida 988...C3
Papelón 774...D3
Paraguaipoa 3,850...B2
Paraíso de Chabasquén 2,094...D3
Pariaguán 8,173...F4
Parmana...F4
Pedernales...G3
Pedregal 1,317...C2
Peraitepuí...H5
Piacoa...H3
Pimichín...E6
Píritu, Anzoátegui 2,479...F2
Píritu, Falcón 1,186...D2
Píritu, Portuguesa 8,128...D3
Platanal...F6
Porlamar 31,985...G2
Pozuelos 45,391...F2
Pregonero 3,598...C3
Pueblo Hondo...B3
Pueblo Nuevo 3,426...D1
Puerto Ayacucho 10,417...E5
Puerto Cabello 72,103...D2
Puerto Cumarebo 10,064...D2
Puerto de Nutrias 675...D3
Puerto Hierro...H2
Puerto La Cruz 63,276...F2
Puerto Miranda...E4
Puerto Páez 954...E4
Puerto Píritu 3,495...F2
Punta Cardón 18,182...C2
Punta de Mata 7,777...G3
Punta de Piedras 2,826...F2
Punto Fijo 5,548...D2
Puruey...F4
Puruname...E6
Quibor 12,216...D2
Quiriquire 7,304...G3
Quisiro 1,383...C2
Río Caribe 8,963...G2
Río Chico 4,491...F2
Río Claro 2,460...D3
Río Tocuyo 916...C2
Rosario...B4
Rubio 19,156...B4
Sabaneta, Barinas 4,680...D3
Sabaneta, Falcón 650...D2
Samariapo...E5
San Antonio, Amazonas...E6
San Antonio, Monagas 4,235...G2
San Antonio, Zulia...C3
San Antonio de Caparo 289...C4
San Antonio del Táchira 20,342...B4
San Antonio de Tabasca...D3
San Carlos 6,717...D3
San Carlos, Cojedes 21,029...D3
San Carlos, Zulia 749...C2

San Carlos del Zulia 26,762...C3
San Carlos de Río Negro 515...E7
San Casimiro 4,843...E3
San Cristóbal 151,717...B4
San Diego de Cabrutica 432...F3
San Felipe, Yaracuy 43,801...D2
San Felipe, Zulia...B3
San Félix 379...C2
San Fernando de Apure 38,960...E4
San Fernando de Atabapo 1,537...E5
San Francisco, Lara 861...C2
San Ignacio...B2
San José, Amazonas...E5
San José, Zulia 4,498...B3
San José de Amacuro...H3
San José de Areocuar 985...G2
San José de Guanipa 22,530...G3
San José de la Costa...D2
San José de Río Chico 3,600...F2
San José de Tiznados 666...E3
San Juan de Colón...B3
San Juan de las Galdonas 1,196...G2
San Juan de los Cayos 1,692...D2
San Juan de los Morros 38,265...E3
San Juan de Manapiare...E5
San Juan de Payara 1,018...E4
San Lorenzo, Falcón 716...D2
San Lorenzo, Zulia...C3
San Luis 1,405...D2
San Mateo 2,424...F3
San Mauricio...E3
San Pedro de las Bocas...G4
San Rafael 10,910...C2
San Rafael de Atamaica 635...E4
San Rafael de Ortuco 1,378...E3
San Sebastián 5,582...E2
San Simón del Cocuy...E3
Santa Ana, Anzoátegui 3,558...F3
Santa Ana, Táchira 5,116...B4
Santa Bárbara, Amazonas...E6
Santa Bárbara, Barinas 6,155...C4
Santa Bárbara, Monagas 2,344...G3
Santa Bárbara, Zulia...B3
Santa Catalina, Barinas 1,077...D4
Santa Catalina, Delta Amacuro...H3
Santa Cruz...H3
Santa Cruz de Bucaral 2,904...D2
Santa Cruz del Zulia 4,221...B3
Santa Cruz de Mara 5,773...C2
Santa Cruz de Orinoco 513...C2
Santa Elena 608...H5
Santa Inés, Anzoátegui 1,049...F4
Santa Inés, Barinas 391...D3
Santa Isabel...F7
Santa Lucía 619...D3
Santa María, Anzoátegui...G3
Santa María de Erebato...F5
Santa María de Ipire 3,307...F3
Santa María del Orinoco...E4
Santa Rita, Guárico...E3
Santa Rita, Zulia 15,668...C2
Santa Rosa, Anzoátegui 954...F3

Santa Rosa, Apure...D4
Santa Rosa, Barinas 1,514...D3
Santa Rosa de Amanadona...E7
Santa Rosalía 513...F4
Santa Teresa 10,220...E2
Santa Timoteo 3,635...C3
San Tomé...F3
San Vicente, Amazonas...E5
San Vicente, Aragua 365...D4
Sarare 4,236...D3
Seboruco 2,616...B3
Simaraña...G5
Sinamaica...B2
Siquisique 3,821...D2
Solano...E6

Soledad 7,108...G3
Sucre 608...D3
Suripa...D3
Tamatama...F6
Táriba 15,683...B4
Temblador 5,380...G3
Turén 88...D2
Turiamo...E2
Turmero 43,832...E2
Tía Juana...C2
Timotes 3,229...C3
Tinaco 7,263...D3
Tinaquillo 12,015...D3
Tocópero 1,033...D2
Tocuyo de la Costa 4,023...D2
Torunos 739...C3
Tovar 12,814...C3
Trujillo 25,921...C3

Tucacas 4,780...D2
Tucupido 9,522...F3
Tucupita 21,417...H3
Tumeremo 5,036...H4
Tupí 88...D2
Turiamo...E2
Upata 22,793...G3
Urachiche 4,759...D2
Uracoa 1,165...G3
Urica 1,881...F3
Uriman...G5
Urumaco 829...C2
Uruyén...G5
Uverito 468...F3
Valencia 367,171...E2
Valera 76,740...C3
Valle de Guanape 3,468...F3
Valle de la Pascua 36,809...F3
Vara de María...
Villa Bruzual 14,003...D3
Villa de Cura 27,832...E2
Villa Frontado 1,600...G2
Yaguaraparo 3,931...G2
Yaritagua 21,363...D2
Yavita...E6
Yericheña...F5
Yoco 2,196...G2
Zanja de Lira...E3
Zaraza 15,480...F3
Zuata 914...F3

OTHER FEATURES

Amacuro (riv.)...H4
Angel (fall)...G5
Aponguao (riv.)...H5
Apure (riv.)...E4
Arichuna (riv.)...E4
Aro (riv.)...F4
Atabapo (riv.)...E6
Auyantepui (mt.)...G5
Baria (riv.)...E7
Bolívar, Cerro (mt.)...
Bolívar, Pico (peak)...C3
Canagua (riv.)...C3
Caño Capure (riv.)...H3
Caño Macareo (riv.)...H3
Caño Mánamo (riv.)...G3
Capanaparo (riv.)...E4
Caparo (riv.)...C4
Caroní (riv.)...G5
Carrao (riv.)...G5
Caruai (riv.)...H5
Casiquiare, Brazo (riv.)...E6
Catatumbo (riv.)...B3
Caura (riv.)...F5
Chicanán (riv.)...H4
Chimanta-tepui (mt.)...G5
Chivapure (riv.)...E4
Cinaruco (riv.)...D4
Coche (isl.)...F2
Codera (cape)...E2
Coiedes (riv.)...D3
Cuao (riv.)...E5
Cubagua (isl.)...F2
Cuchivero (riv.)...F4
Cuquenán (riv.)...H5
Curutú (riv.)...E5
Cuyuni (riv.)...H4
Delgado Chalbaud, Cerro (mt.)...G6
Dragons Mouth (str.)...H2
Duida, Cerro (mt.)...E6
Erebato (riv.)...F5
Gran Sabana, La (plain)...G5
Guainía (riv.)...E6
Guampí, Sierra de (mts.)...F4

Guanare (riv.)...D3
Guanare Viejo (riv.)...D3
Guanipa (riv.)...G3
Guárico (res.)...E3
Guárico (riv.)...E3
Guayapo, Serranía (mts.)...E5
Güere (riv.)...F3
Guri (res.)...G4
Icabarú (riv.)...G5
Imataca, Serranía (mts.)...H4
Imerí, Sierra (mts.)...F7
La Blanquilla (isl.)...F2
La Gran Sabana (plain)...G5
La Orchila (isl.)...F2
Las Aves (isls.)...E2
La Tortuga (isl.)...F2
Los Hermanos (isls.)...F2
Los Monjes (isls.)...C1
Los Roques (isls.)...E2
Los Testigos (isls.)...G2
Macanao (pen.)...F2
Maigualida, Sierra (range)...F4
Manapire (riv.)...E3
Maracaibo (lake)...C2
Margarita (isl.)...F2
Mavaca (riv.)...F6
Médanos (isth.)...D2
Merevari (riv.)...F5
Mérida, Cordillera de (range)...C3
Meta (riv.)...E4
Morichal Largo (riv.)...G3
Neblina (Phelps) (peak)...E7
Negro (riv.)...E7
Nuria, Sierra de (mts.)...H4
Ocamo (riv.)...F6
Orinoco (delta)...H3
Orinoco (riv.)...G3
Orituco (riv.)...E3
Pacaraima, Sierra (mts.)...G5
Pao (riv.)...D3
Pao (riv.)...F3
Paragua (riv.)...G4
Paraguaná (pen.)...C2
Paria (gulf)...H2
Paria (pen.)...G2
Parima, Sierra (mts.)...F6
Perijá, Sierra de (mts.)...B2
Phelps (peak)...E7
Portuguesa (riv.)...D3
Roraima (mt.)...H5
Salto Angel (fall)...G5
Sarare (riv.)...C4
Serpents Mouth (passage)...H3
Siapa (riv.)...E7
Sipapo (riv.)...E5
Suapure (riv.)...E4
Suripa (riv.)...C4
Taparapecó, Sierra (mts.)...F7
Tigre (riv.)...G3
Tocuco (riv.)...B3
Tocuyo (riv.)...D2
Tramán-tepui (mt.)...G5
Triste (gulf)...D2
Turagua, Serranía (mts.)...F4
Tuy (riv.)...E2
Unare (riv.)...F3
Valencia (lake)...E2
Venamo, Cerro (mt.)...H4
Venamo (riv.)...H4
Venezuela (gulf)...C2
Venturi (riv.)...E5
Votamo (riv.)...F6
Yatua (riv.)...E7
Yuruari (riv.)...H4
Zuata (riv.)...F3
Zulia (riv.)...B3

*City and suburbs

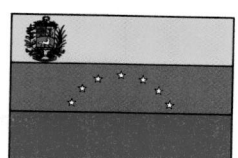

AREA 352,143 sq. mi. (912,050 sq. km.)
POPULATION 14,313,000
CAPITAL Caracas
LARGEST CITY Caracas
HIGHEST POINT Pico Bolívar 16,427 ft. (5,007 m.)
MONETARY UNIT Bolívar
MAJOR LANGUAGE Spanish
MAJOR RELIGION Roman Catholicism

Topography

0   100   200 MI.
0   100   200 KM.

5,000 m. 16,404 ft. | 2,000 m. 6,562 ft. | 1,000 m. 3,281 ft. | 500 m. 1,640 ft. | 200 m. 656 ft. | 100 m. 328 ft. | Sea Level | Below

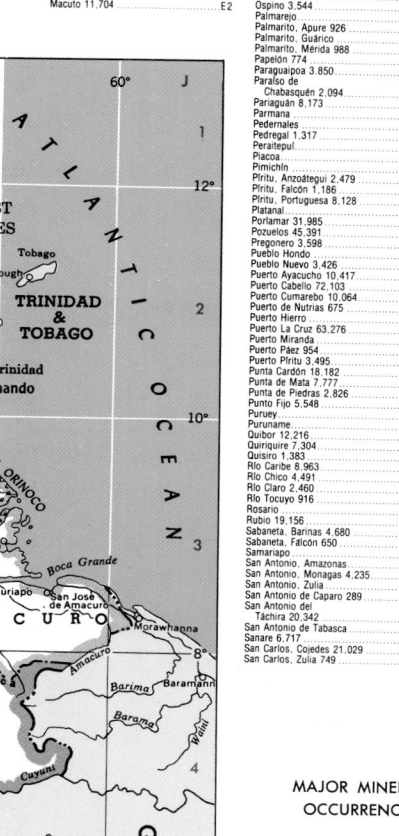

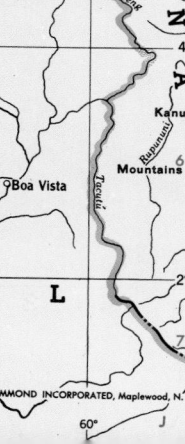

Agriculture, Industry and Resources

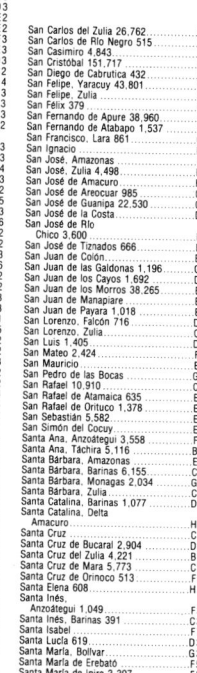

MAJOR MINERAL OCCURRENCES

Al Bauxite
Au Gold
C Coal
D Diamonds
Fe Iron Ore
G Natural Gas
Mn Manganese
Na Salt
O Petroleum
⚡ Water Power
▨ Major Industrial Areas

DOMINANT LAND USE

Diversified Tropical Crops (chiefly plantation agriculture)
Upland Cultivated Areas
Upland Livestock Grazing, Limited Agriculture
Extensive Livestock Ranching
Forests

Colombia

MERCATOR PROJECTION

SCALE OF MILES
0 25 50 75 100 125 150

SCALE OF KILOMETERS
0 25 50 75 100 125 150

Capitals of Countries _____ ★
Other Capitals _____ ●
International Boundaries _____
Other Boundaries _____
Canals _____

CARIBBEAN SEA

PACIFIC OCEAN

PANAMA

VENEZUELA

ECUADOR

PERU

BRAZIL

BOGOTÁ

CARACAS ☆

Quito ☆

INTENDENCIA DE
SAN ANDRÉS Y PROVIDENCIA
Same scale as main map

CARIBBEAN SEA

© Copyright HAMMOND INCORPORATED, Maplewood, N.J.

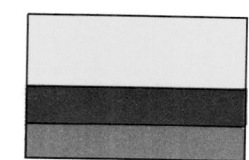

AREA 439,513 sq. mi. (1,138,339 sq. km.)
POPULATION 27,520,000
CAPITAL Bogotá
LARGEST CITY Bogotá
HIGHEST POINT Pico Cristóbal Colón 19,029 ft. (5,800 m.)
MONETARY UNIT Colombian peso
MAJOR LANGUAGE Spanish
MAJOR RELIGION Roman Catholicism

INTERNAL DIVISIONS

Agriculture, Industry and Resources

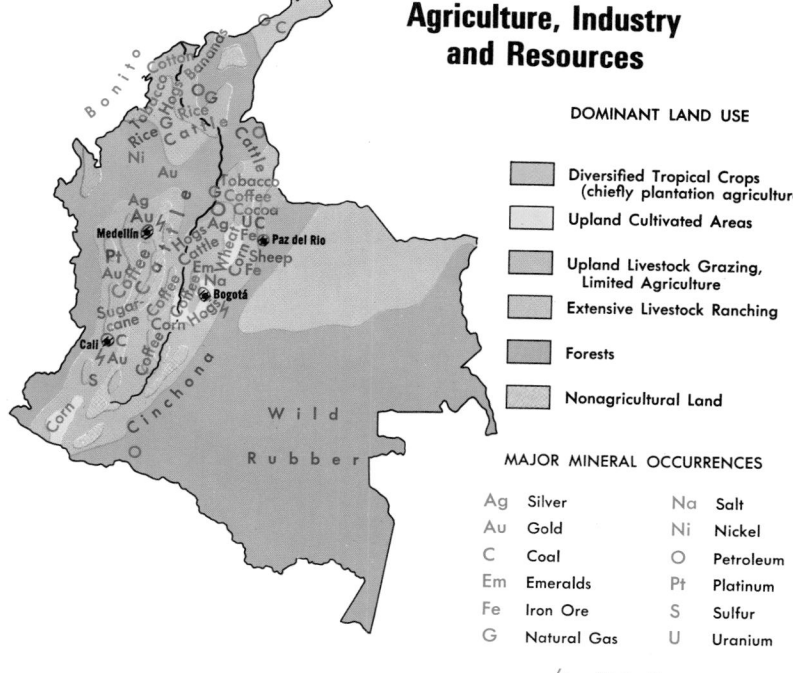

DOMINANT LAND USE

- Diversified Tropical Crops (chiefly plantation agriculture)
- Upland Cultivated Areas
- Upland Livestock Grazing, Limited Agriculture
- Extensive Livestock Ranching
- Forests
- Nonagricultural Land

MAJOR MINERAL OCCURRENCES

Ag	Silver	Na	Salt
Au	Gold	Ni	Nickel
C	Coal	O	Petroleum
Em	Emeralds	Pt	Platinum
Fe	Iron Ore	S	Sulfur
G	Natural Gas	U	Uranium

⚡ Water Power

▨ Major Industrial Areas

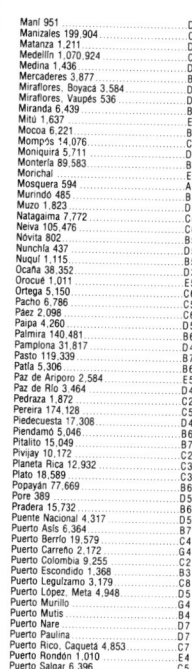

Topography

0   100   200 MI.
0   100   200 KM.

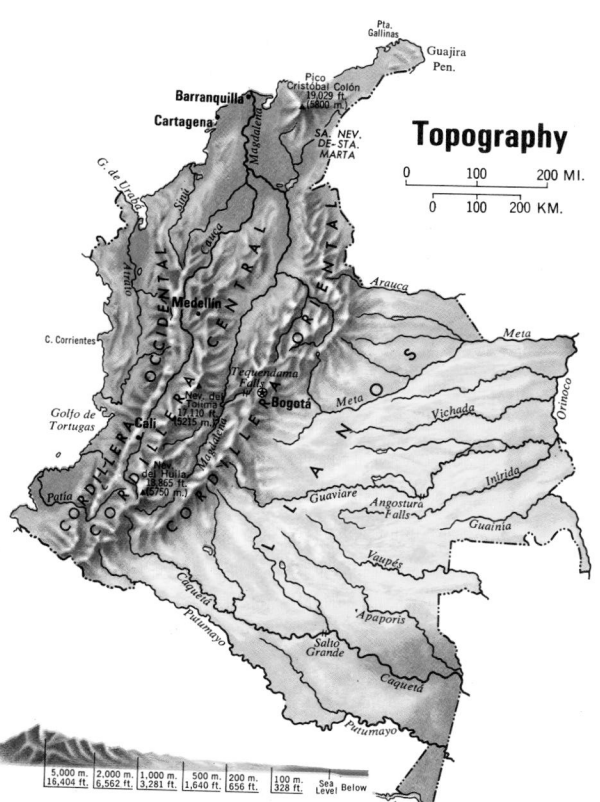

5,000 m. / 16,404 ft. — 2,000 m. / 6,562 ft. — 1,000 m. / 3,281 ft. — 500 m. / 1,640 ft. — 200 m. / 656 ft. — 100 m. / 328 ft. — Sea Level — Below

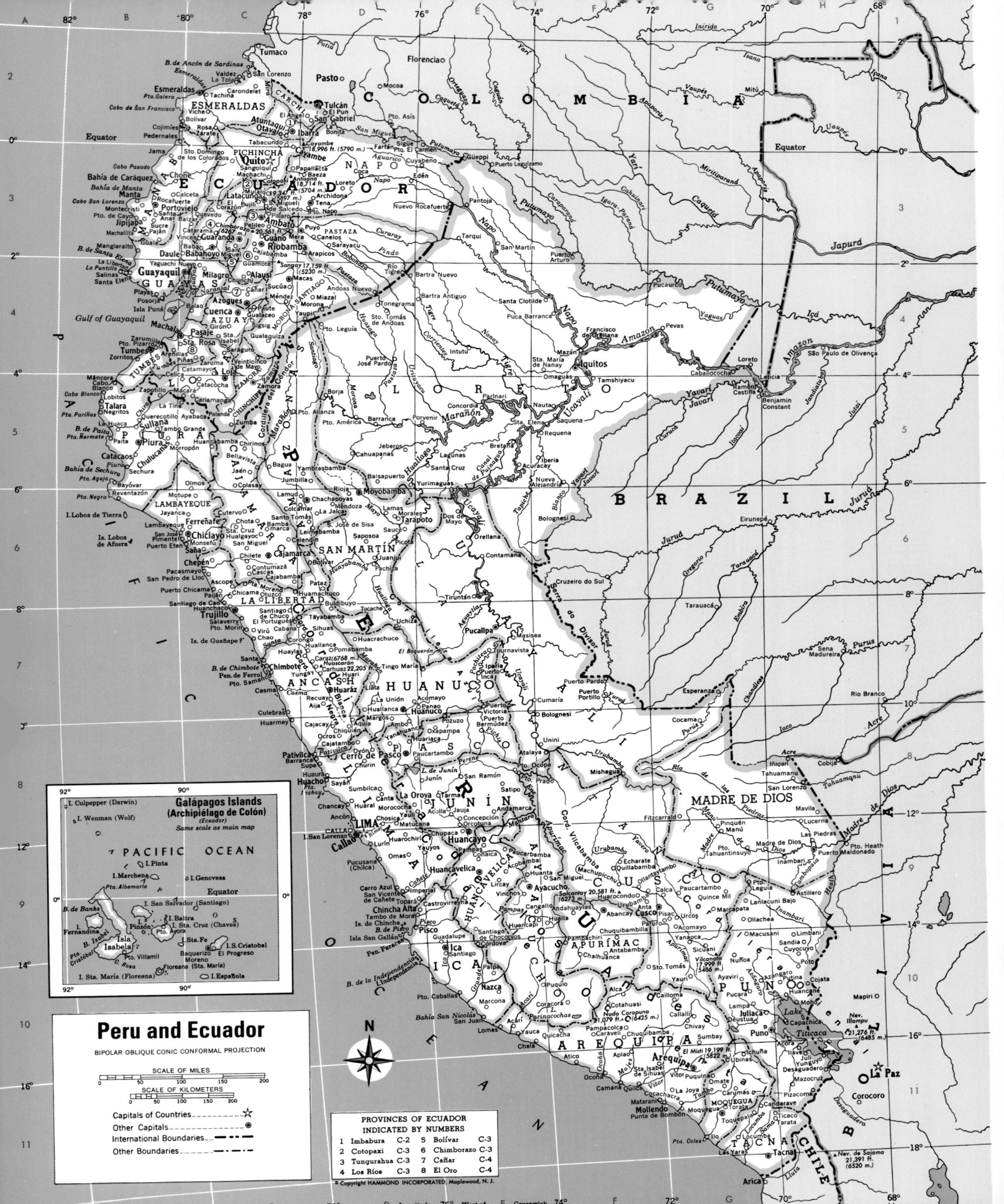

Peru and Ecuador

BIPOLAR OBLIQUE CONIC CONFORMAL PROJECTION

SCALE OF MILES
0   50   100   150   200

SCALE OF KILOMETERS
0   50   100   150   200

Capitals of Countries .... ☆
Other Capitals .... ◉
International Boundaries .... ▬ ▪ ▬ ▪ ▬
Other Boundaries .... ▬ ▪ ▪ ▬ ▪ ▪ ▬

Galápagos Islands
(Archipiélago de Colón)
(Ecuador)
Same scale as main map

PACIFIC OCEAN

PROVINCES OF ECUADOR
INDICATED BY NUMBERS

1	Imbabura	C-2	5 Bolívar C-3
2	Cotopaxi	C-3	6 Chimborazo C-3
3	Tungurahua	C-3	7 Cañar C-4
4	Los Ríos	C-3	8 El Oro C-4

© Copyright HAMMOND INCORPORATED, Maplewood, N. J.

PERU

ECUADOR

PERU

AREA 496,222 sq. mi. (1,285,215 sq. km.)
POPULATION 17,031,221
CAPITAL Lima
LARGEST CITY Lima
HIGHEST POINT Huascarán 22,205 ft. (6,768 m.)
MONETARY UNIT sol
MAJOR LANGUAGES Spanish, Quechua, Aymara
MAJOR RELIGION Roman Catholicism

ECUADOR

AREA 109,483 sq. mi. (283,561 sq. km.)
POPULATION 8,644,000
CAPITAL Quito
LARGEST CITY Guayaquil
HIGHEST POINT Chimborazo 20,561 ft. (6,267 m.)
MONETARY UNIT sucre
MAJOR LANGUAGES Spanish, Quechua
MAJOR RELIGION Roman Catholicism

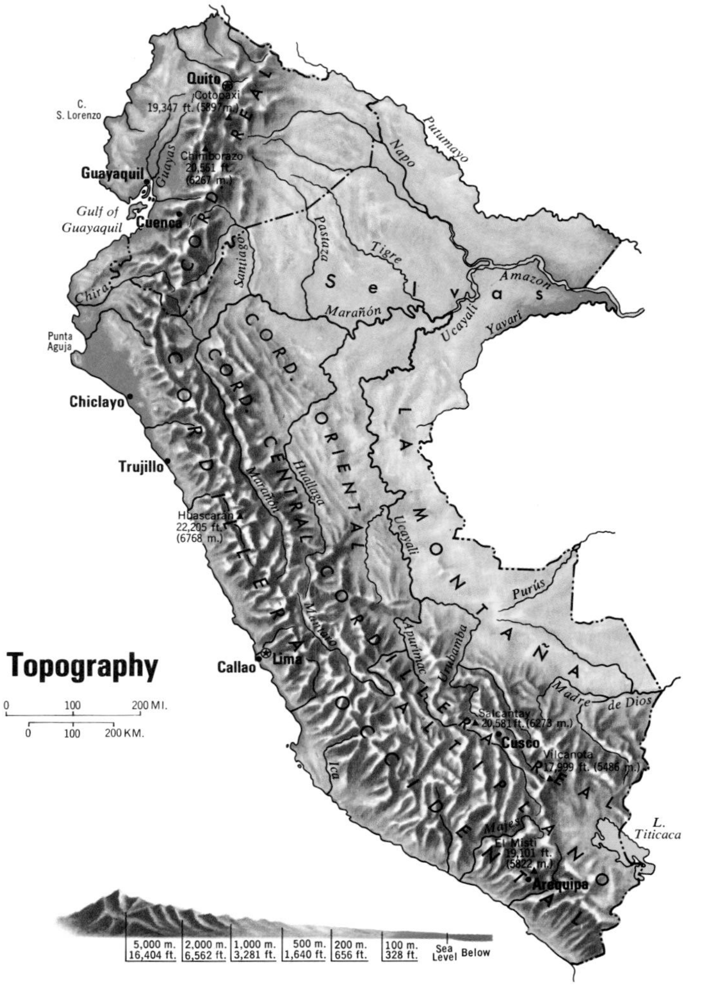

PERU

DEPARTMENTS

Amazonas 256,460	C5
Ancash 815,646	D7
Apurímac 321,936	F10
Arequipa 702,308	F10
Ayacucho 500,732	E9
Cajamarca 1,044,689	C6
Callao (prov.) 446,730	D9
Cusco 829,294	F9
Huancavelica 346,460	E9
Huánuco 481,924	D7
Ica 431,442	E10
Junín 848,993	E8
La Libertad 960,537	C6
Lambayeque 683,425	B6
Lima 4,738,266	D8
Loreto 446,316	E5
Madre de Dios 36,555	G8
Moquegua 99,287	G11
Pasco 221,219	E8
Piura 1,168,442	B5
Puno 893,586	G10
San Martín 319,670	D6
Tacna 133,240	G11
Tumbes 103,979	B4
Ucayali 200,085	E6

CITIES and TOWNS

Abancay 19,807	F9
Acarí 4,907	E10
Acobamba 2,156	E9
Acolla 5,717	E8
Acomayo, Cusco 1,419	G9
Acomayo, Huánuco 2,883	E7
Acora 1,910	H11
Acuracay 1,282	F5
Aija 1,843	D7
Alca 755	F10
Ambo 3,060	D8
Ananea 668	H10
Ancón 8,610	D8
Andahuaylas 7,654	F9
Andamarca 470	E8
Anta 3,703	F9
Antabamba 2,223	F10
Aplao 1,941	F11
Aquia 970	D8
Arequipa 107,858	G11
Arequipa* 447,431	G11
Ascope 12,070	C6
Astillero	H9
Atalaya 2,229	E8
Atico 2,316	F11
Ayabaca 4,543	C5
Ayacucho 68,535	F9
Ayaviri 11,067	G10
Azángaro 7,658	H10
Bagua 9,735	C5
Balsapuerto 164	D5
Bambamarca 6,867	C6
Barranca, Lima 31,312	C8
Barranca, Loreto 1,351	D5
Bartra Antiguo	E4
Bartra Nuevo	E4
Bayóvar	B5
Bellavista 4,906	C5
Bolívar 1,106	D6
Bolognesi	F6
Bolognesi 661	F8
Borja 215	D5
Bretaña 1,035	E5
Buldibuyo 582	D7
Cabana 1,804	C7
Cabo Blanco	B5
Cahuapanas 304	D5
Cailloma 1,187	G10
Cajabamba 7,282	C6
Cajacay 668	D8
Cajamarca 60,280	C6
Cajatambo 1,721	D8
Calca 6,112	G9
Callalli 819	G10
Callao 260,581	D9
Callao* 441,374	D9
Camaná 11,386	F11
Candarave 1,207	G11
Cangallo 1,584	E9
Canta 3,431	D8
Capachica 307	H10
Caraz 6,376	D7
Caravelí 1,827	F10
Carhuás 3,147	D7
Carumás 1,031	G11
Cascas 2,638	C6
Casma 12,725	C7
Castrovirreyna 1,749	E9
Catacaos 30,927	B5
Celendín 8,538	D6
Cerro Azul 2,314	D9
Cerro de Pasco 71,558	D8
Chachapoyas 11,919	D6
Chala 1,646	E10
Chalhuanca 3,071	F10
Chancay 18,993	D8
Chao	C7
Chepén 29,919	C6
Chicama 11,160	C6
Chiclayo 280,244	C6
Chilca (Pucusana) 3,329	D9
Chilete 2,537	C6
Chimbote 216,406	C7
Chincha Alta 237,475	D9
Chiquián 3,521	D8
Chirinos 1,061	C5
Chivay 3,296	G10
Chosica	D8
Chota 8,299	C6
Chulucanas 34,977	B5
Chupaca 5,422	E9
Chuquibamba 2,630	F10
Chuquibambilla 2,147	F9
Churín 1,801	D8
Cocachacra 5,985	G11
Cocama	G8
Cojata 888	H10
Colasay 721	C5
Colcamar 1,216	D6
Conaica 1,154	E9
Concepción 7,129	E8
Concordia 1,372	E5
Contamana 5,718	E6
Contumazá 2,491	C6
Coracora 4,598	F10
Córdova 453	E10
Corongo 1,762	D7
Cotahuasi 1,301	F10
Culebras	C7
Cumaría	F7
Cusco (Cuzco) 85,044	F9
Cusco* 181,604	F9
Cutervo 6,890	C6
Cuyocuyo 1,101	H10
Desaguadero 2,682	H11
Deustua 544	G10
Dos de Mayo 574	E6
Echarate 1,071	F9
El Portugués	C7
Esperanza 375	G7
Espinar 6,381	G10
Ferreñafe 22,200	C6
Francisco de Orellana 445	F4
Guadalupe 7,613	E9
Güeppi	E3
Huacho 43,402	D8
Huacrachuco 1,210	D7
Hualgayoc 1,691	C6
Hualla 4,042	F9
Huallanca, Ancash 930	D7
Huallanca, Huánuco 4,806	D7
Huamachuco 8,273	D6
Huancabamba 4,393	C5
Huancané 5,227	H10
Huancapi 2,539	E9
Huancavelica 20,889	E9
Huancayo 165,132	E9
Huanchaco 6,005	C7
Huanta 11,213	E9
Huánuco 52,628	E7
Huaral 34,235	D8
Huaráz 45,116	D7
Huari 2,344	D7
Huariaca 2,671	E8
Huarmey 11,094	C8
Huarochirí 1,828	D9
Huarocondo 2,498	F9
Huaura 9,338	D8
Huaylas 1,344	C7
Iberia 2,307	F5
Ica 111,087	E10
Ichuña 277	G11
Ilave 9,891	H11
Ilo 31,549	G11
Imperial 20,894	D9
Iñapari 188	H8
Intutu 746	E4
Iparia 278	E7
Iquitos 173,629	F4
Jaén 24,356	C5
Jauja 14,630	E8
Jayanca 6,401	B6
Jeberos 1,493	D5
Juanjuí 9,324	D6
Juli 5,575	H11
Juliaca 77,976	G10
Jumbilla 1,035	C5
Junín 8,988	E8
Lagunas 4,601	E5
La Huaca 5,161	B5
La Jalca 1,769	D6
La Joya 5,000	G11
Lamas 8,937	D6
Lambayeque 23,746	B6
Lampa 4,319	G10
Lamud 2,405	C6
Lanlacuni Bajo 405	G9
La Oroya 33,305	D8
Las Piedras	H9
Las Yaras 759	G11
La Unión 2,828	D7
Leimebamba 1,957	D6
Lima (cap.) 375,957	D8
Lima* 3,968,972	D8
Limbani 728	H10
Lircay 5,213	E9
Llata 2,922	D7
Lobitos 2,975	B5
Locumba 369	G11
Lomas 287	E10
Lucerna	H9
Lurín 14,405	D9
Machupicchu 544	F9
Macusani 3,389	G10
Madre de Dios 660	G9
Máncora 5,358	B5
Manú 234	G9
Marcapata 369	G9
Marcona 25,962	E10
Margos 1,622	D8
Masisea 1,586	E7
Matarani	F11
Matucana 4,196	D8
Mavila	H8
Mazán 281	F4
Mazocruz 1,580	H11
Mendoza 1,902	D6
Mishagua	F8
Moho 2,560	H10
Mollendo 21,206	F11
Monsefú 17,186	C6
Moquegua 21,488	G11
Morales 4,370	D6
Morococha 11,234	D8
Morropón 7,611	C5
Motupe 3,411	C6
Moyobamba 14,319	D6
Nauta 4,083	F5
Nazca 22,756	E10
Negritos 12,476	B5
Nuñoa 3,613	G10
Ocoña 1,062	F11
Ocros 1,037	D8
Ollachea 1,308	G9
Ollantaytambo 1,500	F9
Olmos 7,946	C5
Omaguas	F5
Omas 249	D9
Omate 1,131	G11
Orcotuna 3,359	E8
Orellana 2,886	E6
Otuzco 5,765	C6
Oxapampa 5,233	E8
Oyón 6,279	D8
Pacasmayo 17,588	C6
Pachiza 889	D6
Paiján 12,699	C6
Paita 18,749	B5
Palpa 3,393	E10
Pampachiri 428	F10
Pampacolca 2,010	F10
Pampas 3,850	E9
Panao 1,363	E7
Pantoja 457	E3
Parinari 375	E5
Paruro 1,727	F9
Pataz 759	D6
Paucarbamba 534	E9
Paucartambo, Cusco 1,620	G9
Paucartambo, Pasco 3,497	E8
Pevas 1,325	G4
Picota 2,288	D6
Pimentel 9,129	B6
Pinquén	G9
Pisac 1,566	G9
Pisco 53,414	D9
Piura 186,354	B5
Pizacoma 400	H11
Pomabamba 2,489	D7
Porvenir	E5
Pozuzo 326	E8
Puca Barranca	E4
Pucallpa 91,953	E7
Pucará 2,268	G10
Pucaurco 628	G4
Pucusana 3,329	D9
Puerto Alianza	D5
Puerto América 240	D5
Puerto Arturo	F3
Puerto Bermúdez 1,133	E8
Puerto Caballas	E10
Puerto Chicama 3,136	C6
Puerto Eten 2,575	B6
Puerto Inca 1,286	E7
Puerto José Pardo	D4
Puerto Leguía, Loreto	D4
Puerto Leguía, Puno	G9
Puerto Maldonado 12,609	H9
Puerto Morín	C7
Puerto Ocopa 1,088	E8
Puerto Pardo	F7
Puerto Pizarro	B4
Puerto Portillo 86	F7
Puerto Prado 328	E8
Puerto Samanco 1,435	C7
Puerto Tahuantinsuyo	G9
Puerto Victoria	E7
Puno 66,477	G10
Punta de Bombón 4,647	F11
Punta Moreno	C6
Puquina 1,026	G11
Puquio 8,099	F10
Putina 5,414	H10
Querecotillo 10,637	B5
Quicacha 255	F10
Quilca 235	F11
Quillabamba 16,837	F9
Quince Mil	G9
Ramón Castilla 1,811	G5
Recuay 2,764	D7
Requena 8,270	F5
Reventazón	B6
Rioja 9,876	D6
Salaverry 5,539	C7
Saña 40,144	C6
Sandia 1,682	H10
San José 4,070	B6
San José de Sisa 3,782	D6
San Juan	E10
San Lorenzo 124	H8
San Martín	E3
San Miguel, Ayacucho 1,440	F9
San Miguel, Cajamarca 1,798	C6
San Pedro de Lloc 11,463	C6
San Ramón 7,145	E8
Santa 20,490	C7
Santa Clotilde 1,068	E4
Santa Cruz, Cajamarca 2,739	C6
Santa Cruz, Loreto 449	E5
Santa Elena 368	F5
Santa María de Nanay 294	F4
Santiago 5,092	E10
Santiago de Cao 22,119	C6
Santiago de Chocorvos 525	E9
Santiago de Chuco 5,189	C7
Santo Tomás, Amazonas 1,093	C6
Santo Tomás, Cusco 2,755	G10
Santo Tomás de Andoas 272	D4
San Vicente de Cañete 15,277	D9
Saposoa 4,541	D6
Saquena 2,755	F5
Satipo 9,208	E8
Sauce 2,263	D6
Sayán 5,129	D8
Sechura 11,724	B5
Sicuani 21,176	G10
Sihuas 2,178	D7
Sullana 80,947	B5
Sumbay	G10
Sumbilca 1,155	D8
Supe 10,061	D8
Tacna 92,640	G11
Tahuamanu 2,619	H8
Talara 55,122	B5
Tambo de Mora 2,790	D9
Tambo Grande 10,087	B5
Tamshiyacu 2,040	F5
Tarapoto 33,429	D6
Tarata 2,624	H11
Tarma 34,369	E8
Tarqui	E3
Tayabamba 1,649	D7
Ticaco 781	H11
Tingo María 25,030	D7
Tiruntán 723	E6
Tocache 5,940	D7
Tonegrama	D4
Topará	D9
Toquepala	G11
Torata 6,320	G11
Tournavista	E7
Trujillo 354,557	C7
Tumbes 48,187	B4
Ubinas 422	G11
Uchiza 2,471	D7
Unini	F8
Urcos 4,155	G9
Urubamba 4,686	F9
Vinchos 735	E9
Virú 6,587	C7
Vitor 416	G11
Yambrasbamba 277	D5
Yanahuanca 5,109	D8
Yanaoca 1,152	G10
Yauca 1,805	E10
Yauli 1,020	D8
Yauyos 1,296	E9
Yunguyo 7,253	H11
Yurimaguas 22,858	E5
Zarumilla 9,713	B4
Zorritos 4,497	B4

OTHER FEATURES

Acarí (riv.)	E10
Aguaytía (riv.)	E7
Aguja (pt.)	B5
Amazon (riv.)	F4
Andes, Cordillera de los (mts.)	F10
Apurímac (riv.)	F9
Azángaro (riv.)	G10
Azul, Cordillera (mts.)	E7
Blanca, Cordillera (mts.)	D7
Blanco (cape)	B5
Blanco (riv.)	F6
Boquerón, El (pass)	E7
Cañete (riv.)	D9
Casma (riv.)	C7
Chimbote (bay)	C7
Chincha (isls.)	D9
Coles (pt.)	G11
Cóndor, Cordillera del (range)	C5
Coropuna, Nudo (mt.)	F10
Corrientes (riv.)	E4
El Boquerón (pass)	E7
El Misti (mt.)	G11
Ene (riv.)	E8
Ferrol (pen.)	C7
Grande (riv.)	E10
Guañape (isls.)	C7
Heath (riv.)	H9
Huallaga (riv.)	D5
Huasaga (riv.)	D4
Huascarán (mt.)	D7
Huayabamba (riv.)	D6
Ica (riv.)	E10
Inambari (riv.)	H9
Independencia (bay)	D10
Independencia (isl.)	D10
Junín (lake)	E8
Juruá (riv.)	F7
Lachay (pt.)	D8
Lobos de Afuera (isls.)	B6
Lobos de Tierra (isl.)	B6
Locumba (riv.)	G11
Madre de Dios (riv.)	G9
Majes (riv.)	F11
Mantaro (riv.)	E8
Manú (riv.)	G8
Marañón (riv.)	E5
Mayo (riv.)	D6
Misti, El (mt.)	G11
Montaña, La (reg.)	F8
Morona (riv.)	D5
Nanay (riv.)	E4
Napo (riv.)	F4
Negra, Cordillera (mts.)	D7
Negra (pt.)	B6
Ñermete (pt.)	B5
Occidental, Cordillera (range)	F10
Ocoña (riv.)	F11
Oriental, Cordillera (range)	H10
Pachitea (riv.)	E7
Paita (bay)	B5
Pampas (riv.)	E9
Paracas (pen.)	D9
Parinacochas (lake)	F10
Pariñas (pt.)	B5
Pastaza (riv.)	D5
Pativilca (riv.)	D8
Perené (riv.)	E8
Pichis (riv.)	E8
Piedras, Las (riv.)	G8
Pisco (bay)	D9
Pisco (riv.)	D9
Piura (riv.)	B5
Puinagua, Canal de (riv.)	E5
Purús (riv.)	G8
Putumayo (riv.)	G4
Rímac (riv.)	D9
Salcantay (mt.)	F9
Sama (riv.)	G11
San Gallán (isl.)	D9
San Lorenzo (isl.)	D9
San Nicolás (bay)	E10
Santa (riv.)	C7
Santiago (riv.)	D4
Sechura (bay)	B5
Tahuamanu (riv.)	H8
Tambo (riv.)	G11
Tambopata (riv.)	H9
Tapiche (riv.)	E6
Tigre (riv.)	E4
Titicaca (lake)	H10
Tumbes (riv.)	B4
Ucayali (riv.)	F5

(continued on following page)

Agriculture, Industry and Resources

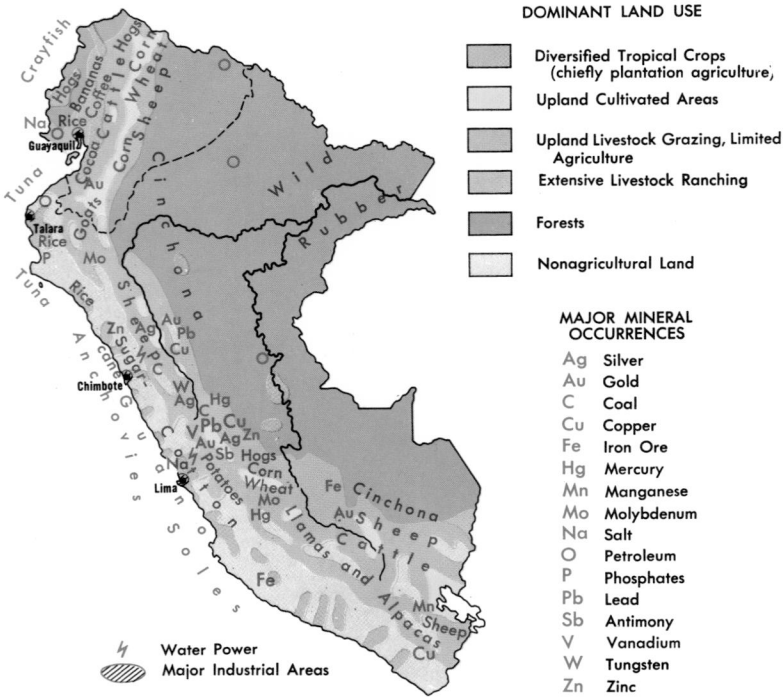

DOMINANT LAND USE

- Diversified Tropical Crops (chiefly plantation agriculture)
- Upland Cultivated Areas
- Upland Livestock Grazing, Limited Agriculture
- Extensive Livestock Ranching
- Forests
- Nonagricultural Land

MAJOR MINERAL OCCURRENCES

Ag Silver
Au Gold
C Coal
Cu Copper
Fe Iron Ore
Hg Mercury
Mn Manganese
Mo Molybdenum
Na Salt
O Petroleum
P Phosphates
Pb Lead
Sb Antimony
V Vanadium
W Tungsten
Zn Zinc

⚡ Water Power
▨ Major Industrial Areas

Agriculture, Industry and Resources

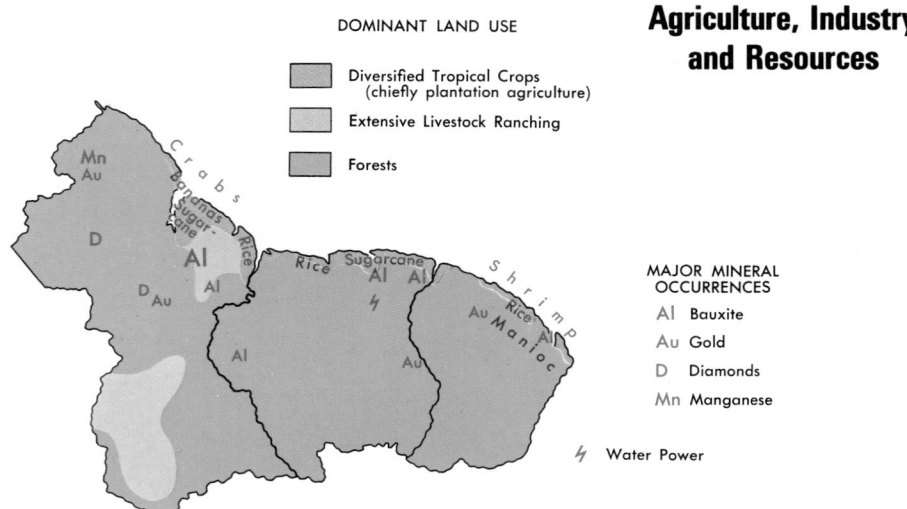

DOMINANT LAND USE

- Diversified Tropical Crops (chiefly plantation agriculture)
- Extensive Livestock Ranching
- Forests

MAJOR MINERAL OCCURRENCES

Al Bauxite
Au Gold
D Diamonds
Mn Manganese

⚡ Water Power

* City and suburbs
○ Population of district.

GUYANA

AREA 83,000 sq. mi. (214,970 sq. km.)
POPULATION 793,000
CAPITAL Georgetown
LARGEST CITY Georgetown
HIGHEST POINT Mt. Roraima 9,094 ft. (2,772 m.)
MONETARY UNIT Guyana dollar
MAJOR LANGUAGES English, Hindi
MAJOR RELIGIONS Christianity, Hinduism, Islam

SURINAME

AREA 55,144 sq. mi. (142,823 sq. km.)
POPULATION 354,860
CAPITAL Paramaribo
LARGEST CITY Paramaribo
HIGHEST POINT Julianatop 4,200 ft. (1,280 m.)
MONETARY UNIT Suriname guilder
MAJOR LANGUAGES Dutch, Hindi, Indonesian
MAJOR RELIGIONS Christianity, Islam, Hinduism

FRENCH GUIANA

AREA 35,135 sq. mi. (91,000 sq. km.)
POPULATION 73,022
CAPITAL Cayenne
LARGEST CITY Cayenne
HIGHEST POINT 2,723 ft. (830 m.)
MONETARY UNIT French franc
MAJOR LANGUAGE French
MAJOR RELIGIONS Roman Catholicism, Protestantism

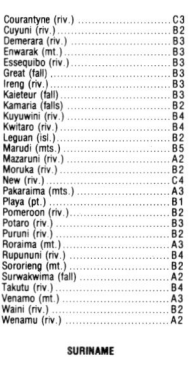

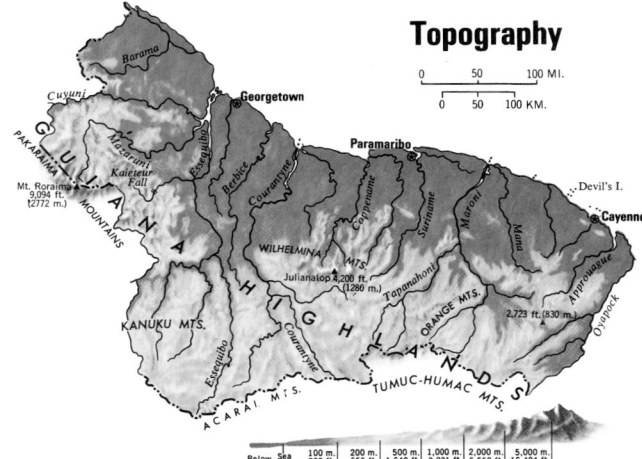

Topography

0   50   100 MI.
0   50   100 KM.

Mt. Roraima 9,094 ft. (2772 m.)

Julianatop 4,200 ft. (1280 m.)

2,723 ft. (830 m.)

Devil's I.

Georgetown
Paramaribo
Cayenne

GUIANA HIGHLANDS
PAKARAIMA MOUNTAINS
Kaieteur Fall
WILHELMINA Mts.
ORANGE MTS.
KANUKU MTS.
ACARAI MTS.
TUMUC-HUMAC MTS.

Below Sea Level | 100 m. 328 ft. | 200 m. 656 ft. | 500 m. 1,640 ft. | 1,000 m. 3,281 ft. | 2,000 m. 6,562 ft. | 5,000 m. 16,404 ft.

GUYANA

SURINAME

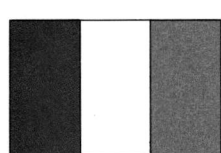

FRENCH GUIANA

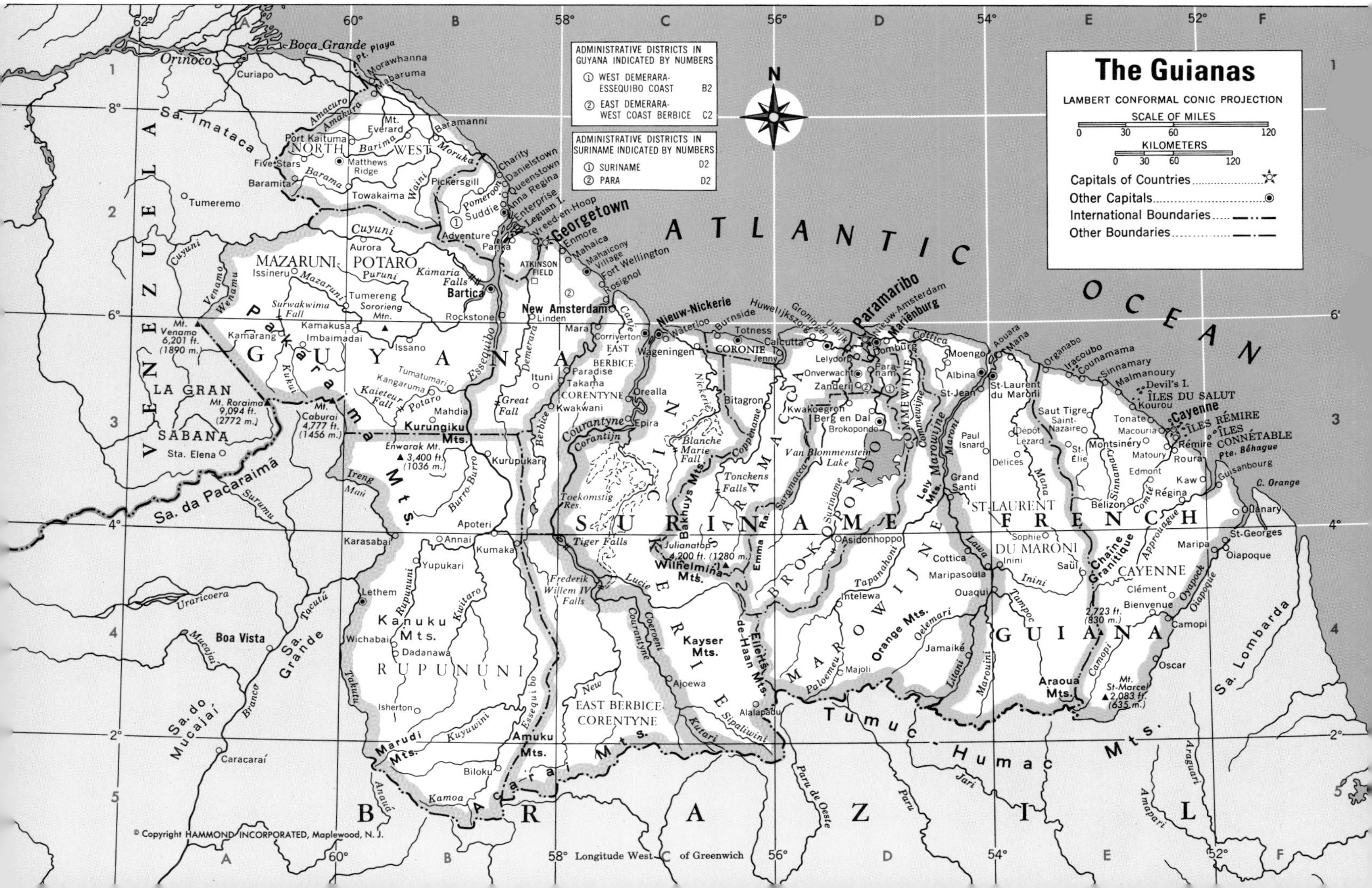

The Guianas

LAMBERT CONFORMAL CONIC PROJECTION

SCALE OF MILES
0   30   60   120
KILOMETERS
0   30   60   120

Capitals of Countries .... ☆
Other Capitals .... ◉
International Boundaries ...... —·—·—
Other Boundaries .... —··—··—

ADMINISTRATIVE DISTRICTS IN GUYANA INDICATED BY NUMBERS
① WEST DEMERARA-ESSEQUIBO COAST ... B2
② EAST DEMERARA-WEST COAST BERBICE ... C2

ADMINISTRATIVE DISTRICTS IN SURINAME INDICATED BY NUMBERS
① SURINAME ... D2
② PARA ... D2

© Copyright HAMMOND INCORPORATED, Maplewood, N.J.

58° Longitude West of Greenwich

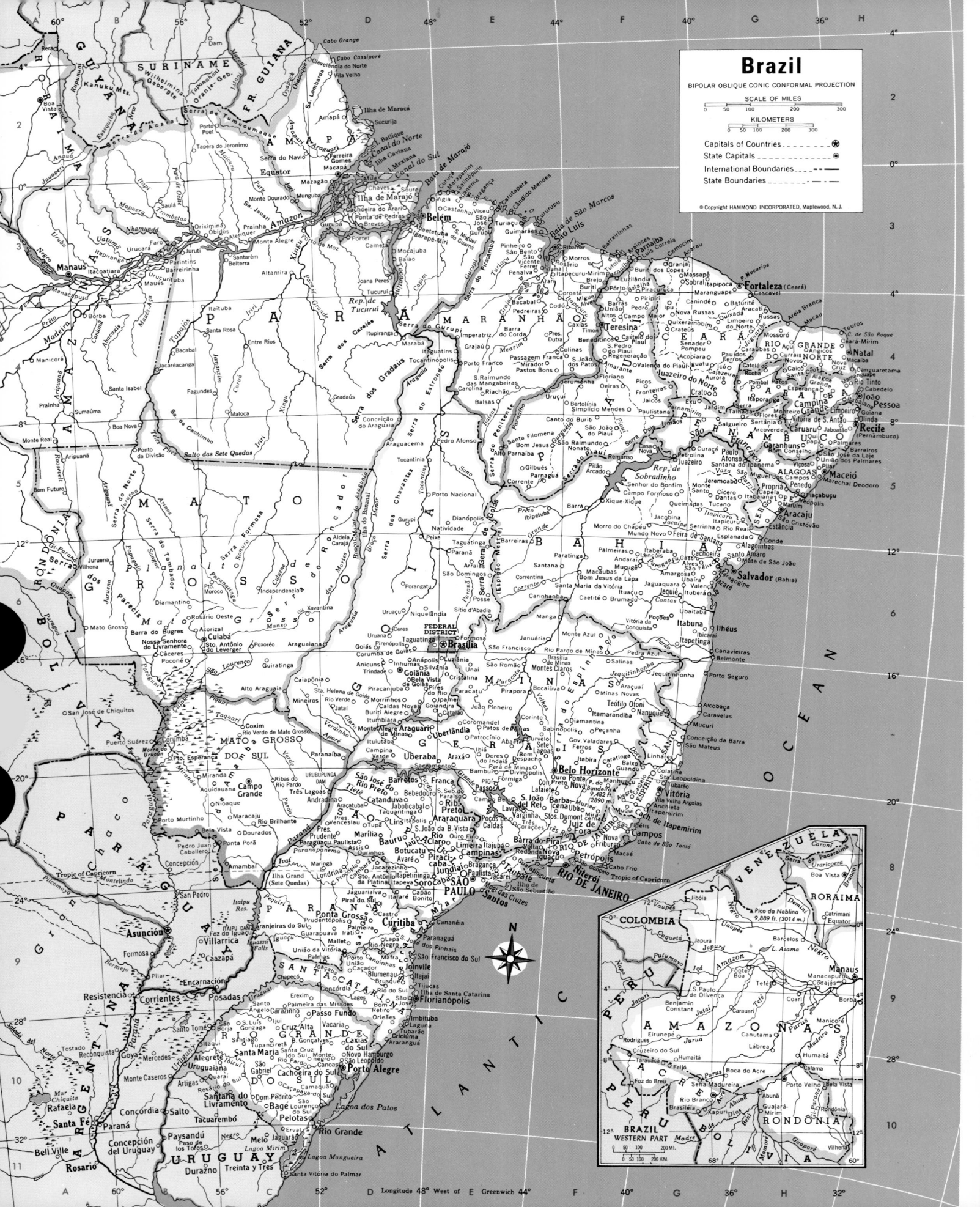

Brazil

BIPOLAR OBLIQUE CONIC CONFORMAL PROJECTION

SCALE OF MILES

0 50 100 200 300

KILOMETERS

0 50 100 200 300

Capitals of Countries .... ⊛
State Capitals .... ◉
International Boundaries ...... _ _ _
State Boundaries .... ___

© Copyright HAMMOND INCORPORATED, Maplewood, N.J.

BRAZIL
WESTERN PART

0 50 100 300 MI.

0 50 100 200 KM.

STATES and TERRITORIES

Acre 301,605 ... G10
Alagoas 1,987,581 ... G5
Amapá (terr.) 175,634 ... D2
Amazonas 1,432,066 ... G9
Bahia 9,474,263 ... F6
Ceará 5,294,876 ... G4
Espírito Santo 2,023,821 ... F7
Federal District 1,177,393 ... E6
Goiás 3,865,482 ... D6
Maranhão 4,002,599 ... E4
Mato Grosso 1,141,661 ... B6
Mato Grosso do Sul 1,370,333 ... C7
Minas Gerais 13,390,805 ... E7
Pará 3,411,868 ... C4
Paraíba 2,772,600 ... G4
Paraná 7,630,466 ... D9
Pernambuco 6,147,102 ... G5
Piauí 2,140,066 ... F4
Rio de Janeiro 11,297,327 ... F8
Rio Grande do Norte 1,899,720 ... G4
Rio Grande do Sul 7,777,212 ... C10
Rondônia (terr.) 492,810 ... H10
Roraima (terr.) 79,153 ... H8
Santa Catarina 3,628,751 ... D9
São Paulo 25,040,698 ... D8
Sergipe 1,141,834 ... G5

CITIES and TOWNS

Abaeté 12,861 ... E7
Abaetetuba 33,031 ... D3
Acaraú 7,144 ... F3
Acopiara 10,747 ... G4
Açu 20,544 ... G4
Agudos 18,790 ... *B3
Alagoa Grande 14,204 ... H4
Alagoinhas 76,377 ... G6
Alcobaça 3,430 ... G7
Alegre 9,441 ... *F2
Alegrete 54,786 ... B10
Além Paraíba 23,028 ... *E2
Alenquer 16,477 ... C3
Alfenas 31,815 ... *D2
Altamira 24,846 ... C3
Altos 13,621 ... F4
Amambaí 12,507 ... C8
Amapá 2,676 ... D2
Amarante 6,848 ... F4
Amargosa 11,118 ... F6
Americana 121,794 ... *C3
Amparo 26,970 ... *C3
Anápolis 160,520 ... D7
Anchieta 5,741 ... F8
Andaraí 2,476 ... F6
Andradina 42,036 ... D8
Andrelândia 8,737 ... *D2
Angra dos Reis 24,894 ... *D3
Antonina 11,950 ... *B4
Aparecida 27,265 ... *D3
Apiaí 7,809 ... *B4
Aquidauana 21,514 ... C8
Aracaju 288,106 ... G5
Aracati 20,282 ... G4
Araçatuba 113,486 ... *A2
Araçuaí 12,292 ... F7
Araguari 73,302 ... D7
Araranguá 22,468 ... D10
Araraquara 77,202 ... *B2
Araras 54,323 ... *C3
Araxá 51,339 ... E7
Arcoverde 40,646 ... G5
Areia Branca 12,979 ... G4
Assis 57,217 ... *A3
Avaré 40,716 ... *B3
Bacabal 43,229 ... E4
Bagé 66,743 ... C10
Bahia (Salvador) 1,496,276 ... G6
Baixo Guandu 13,714 ... F7
Balsas 13,566 ... E4
Bambuí 14,172 ... *C2
Barão de Cocais 11,950 ... *E1
Barbacena 69,675 ... *E2
Barcelos 1,846 ... H9
Bariri 15,372 ... *B3
Barra 10,809 ... F5
Barra do Corda 19,280 ... E4
Barra do Piraí 51,214 ... *E3
Barra Mansa 123,421 ... *D3
Barras 8,904 ... F4
Barreiras 30,355 ... E6
Barreiros 19,419 ... H5
Barretos 65,294 ... *B2
Batatais 30,478 ... *C2
Baturité 12,388 ... G4
Bauru 178,861 ... *B3
Bebedouro 39,070 ... *B2
Bela Vista 11,936 ... C8
Belém 758,117 ... E3
Belém †1,000,349 ... E3
Belo Horizonte 1,442,483 ... *D1
Belo Horizonte †2,541,788 ... *D1
Benjamin Constant 6,563 ... G9
Bento Gonçalves 40,323 ... C10
Betim 71,599 ... *D2
Bicas 8,611 ... *E2
Birigui 45,348 ... *A2
Blumenau 144,819 ... D9
Boa Esperança 17,394 ... *D2
Boa Vista 43,131 ... H8
Bocaiúva 16,616 ... E7
Bom Conselho 13,196 ... G5
Bom Despacho 22,941 ... *D1
Bom Jesus da Lapa 19,978 ... F6
Bom Sucesso 10,331 ... *D2
Borba 5,366 ... H9
Bragança Paulista 61,021 ... *C3
Brasiléia 4,835 ... G10
Brasília (cap.) 411,305 ... E6
Brasília de Minas 10,171 ... F7
Brejo 5,859 ... F3
Breves 31,452 ... D3
Brumado 24,663 ... F6
Brusque 37,898 ... D9
Cabedelo 18,581 ... H4
Cabo Frio 40,668 ... *F3
Caçador 25,287 ... D9
Caçapava 45,258 ... *D3
Caçapava do Sul 15,180 ... C10
Cáceres 33,472 ... B7
Cachoeira 11,520 ... G6
Cachoeira do Sul 59,967 ... C10
Cachoeiro de Itapemirim 84,994 ... G8
Caeté 23,331 ... *E1
Caetité 8,823 ... F6
Caiapônia 9,358 ... C7
Caicó 30,777 ... G4
Cajazeiras 30,834 ... G4
Cajuru 9,670 ... *C2
Camaquã 28,078 ... C10
Cambará 13,218 ... *A3
Cambuí 8,552 ... *C3
Cametá 15,539 ... D3
Camocim 19,921 ... F3
Campina Grande 222,229 ... G4
Campinas 566,517 ... *C3
Campo Belo 30,392 ... *D2
Campo Formoso 10,324 ... F5
Campo Grande 282,844 ... C8
Campo Largo 34,506 ... *B4
Campo Maior 24,009 ... F4
Campos 174,218 ... *F2
Cananéia 5,581 ... *C4
Canavieiras 14,076 ... G6
Canindé 18,573 ... G4
Canoas 214,115 ... D10
Canoinhas 25,880 ... D9
Capanema 28,272 ... E3
Capão Bonito 24,081 ... *B4
Caraguatatuba 22,932 ... *D3
Carangola 15,621 ... *E2
Caratinga 39,621 ... *E1
Caravelas 3,704 ... G7
Carazinho 41,913 ... C10
Carolina 10,136 ... E4
Caruaru 137,636 ... G5
Casa Branca 13,739 ... *C2
Cascavel 16,238 ... G4
Cássia 10,701 ... *C2
Castanhal 51,797 ... E3
Castelo 9,162 ... F8
Castro 21,079 ... *B4
Castro Alves 11,286 ... G6
Cataguases 40,659 ... *E2
Catalão 30,516 ... E7
Catanduva 64,813 ... *B2
Catolé do Rocha 12,165 ... G4
Caxambu 16,221 ... *D2
Caxias 56,755 ... F4
Caxias do Sul 198,824 ... D10
Ceará (Fortaleza) 648,815 ... G3
Ceará-Mirim 17,097 ... H4
Ceres 13,671 ... D6
Chapecó 53,198 ... C9
Coari 14,841 ... H9
Codajás 4,923 ... H9
Codó 11,593 ... E4
Colatina 61,057 ... F7
Conceição do Araguaia 18,143 ... D5
Concórdia 17,973 ... D9
Conselheiro Lafaiete 66,262 ... *E2
Corinto 17,056 ... E7
Cornélio Procópio 31,201 ... D8
Coroatá 16,070 ... F3
Coromandel 11,604 ... E7
Corumbá 66,014 ... B7
Coxim 14,876 ... C7
Crateús 29,905 ... F4
Crato 49,244 ... G4
Criciúma 74,003 ... D10
Cristalina 10,521 ... E7
Cruz Alta 53,315 ... C10
Cruzeiro 55,175 ... *D3
Cruzeiro do Sul 11,189 ... G10
Cubatão 78,327 ... *C3
Cuiabá 167,894 ... C6
Curitiba 843,733 ... *B4
Curitiba †1,441,743 ... *B4
Currais Novos 25,663 ... G4
Cururupu 10,358 ... E3
Curvelo 37,734 ... E7
Diamantina 20,197 ... F7
Divinópolis 108,344 ... *D2
Dois Córregos 11,811 ... *B3
Dom Pedrito 25,773 ... C10
Dores do Indaiá 13,058 ... E7
Dourados 76,838 ... C8
Duque de Caxias 306,057 ... *E3
Erexim 46,927 ... C9
Esperança 12,964 ... G4
Esplanada 9,822 ... G5
Estância 28,250 ... G5
Feira de Santana 225,003 ... G5
Fernandópolis 39,737 ... *A2
Floriano 35,761 ... F4
Florianópolis 153,547 ... E9
Fonte Boa 3,278 ... G9
Formiga 36,681 ... *D2
Formosa 29,304 ... E6
Fortaleza 648,815 ... G3
Fortaleza †1,581,588 ... G3
Foz do Iguaçu 93,619 ... C9
Franca 143,630 ... *C2
Frutal 22,955 ... *B2
Garanhuns 64,854 ... G5
Garça 26,527 ... *B3
Goiana 30,108 ... H4
Goiânia 703,263 ... D7
Goiás 15,768 ... D6
Governador Valadares 173,699 ... F7
Grajaú 11,147 ... E4
Guacuí 12,715 ... *F2
Guajará-Mirim 19,992 ... H10
Guarapuava 17,189 ... C9
Guaratinguetá 68,370 ... *D3
Guarujá 67,730 ... *C4
Guarulhos 395,117 ... *C3
Guaxupé 23,637 ... *C2
Guiratinga 8,981 ... C7
Gurupi 27,319 ... D5
Humaitá 10,004 ... H10
Ibaiti 11,352 ... *A3
Ibiá 11,161 ... E7
Ibicaraí 18,202 ... G6
Ibitinga 23,359 ... *B2
Icó 13,007 ... G4
Igarapava 15,342 ... *C2
Igarapé-Miri 12,172 ... D3
Iguape 16,827 ... *C4
Iguatu 39,611 ... G4
Ijuí 51,925 ... C10
Ilhéus 71,240 ... G6
Imbituba 9,998 ... D10
Imperatriz 111,818 ... E4
Inhumas 23,455 ... D7
Ipameri 14,163 ... E7
Ipu 12,787 ... F4
Irati 21,956 ... *A4
Itabaiana, Paraíba 17,843 ... H4
Itabaiana, Sergipe 26,055 ... G5
Itaberaba 27,590 ... F6
Itabira 57,691 ... F7
Itabirito 22,978 ... *E2
Itabuna 129,938 ... G6
Itacoatiara 26,737 ... B3
Itaituba 19,644 ... C4
Itajaí 78,867 ... D9
Itajubá 53,506 ... *D3
Itanhaem 26,181 ... *C4
Itapecerica 10,234 ... *D2
Itapecuru-Mirim 12,216 ... F3
Itapemirim 16,829 ... F8
Itaperuna 34,644 ... *F2
Itapetinga 36,897 ... G6
Itapetininga 61,344 ... *B3
Itapeva 36,551 ... *B3
Itapipoca 19,463 ... G3
Itapira 36,308 ... *C3
Itápolis 13,750 ... *B2
Itaporanga 8,988 ... G4
Itaqui 23,136 ... B10
Itararé 24,368 ... *B4
Itatiba 35,537 ... *C3
Itaúna 49,372 ... *D2
Itu 62,211 ... *C3
Ituaçu 1,749 ... F6
Ituiutaba 65,178 ... D7
Itumbiara 56,602 ... D7
Iturama 12,363 ... *A1
Ituverava 21,323 ... *C2
Jaboatão 67,120 ... H5
Jaboticabal 40,276 ... *B2
Jacareí 103,652 ... *D3
Jacarezinho 23,684 ... *A3
Jacobina 26,723 ... F5
Jacupiranga 7,044 ... *B4
Jaguaquara 11,336 ... F6
Jaguarão 18,165 ... C11
Jaguariaíva 8,566 ... *B4
Januária 20,484 ... E6
Jataí 40,957 ... D7
Jaú 59,522 ... *B3
Jequié 84,792 ... F6
Jequitinhonha 10,900 ... F7
Ji-Paraná 31,724 ... H10
Joaçaba 16,195 ... D9
João Pessoa 290,424 ... H4
João Pinheiro 17,013 ... E7
Joinvile 217,074 ... D9
Juazeiro 60,940 ... G5
Juazeiro do Norte 125,248 ... F4
Juiz de Fora 299,728 ... *E2
Jundiaí 210,015 ... *C3
Lages 108,768 ... D9
Laguna 27,743 ... D10
Lambari 9,722 ... *D2
Lapa 13,314 ... D9
Laranjeiras do Sul 19,329 ... C9
Lavras 35,345 ... *D2
Leme 40,155 ... *C3
Leopoldina 28,554 ... *E2
Limeira 137,812 ... *C3
Limoeiro 36,088 ... H4
Limoeiro do Norte 13,112 ... G4
Linhares 51,575 ... F7
Lins 44,633 ... *B2
Londrina 258,054 ... D8
Lorena 51,276 ... *D3
Luís Correia 3,576 ... F3
Luz 10,068 ... *D1
Luziânia 67,284 ... E7
Macaé 39,644 ... *F3
Macaíba 17,036 ... H4
Macapá 89,081 ... D2
Macau 17,543 ... G4
Maceió 376,479 ... H5
Machado 16,164 ... *C2
Mafra 26,226 ... D9
Magé 37,597 ... *E3
Mamanguape 16,321 ... H4
Manacapuru 17,016 ... H9
Manaus 613,068 ... H9
Manhuaçu 22,678 ... *E2
Manhumirim 11,085 ... *E2
Manicoré 9,532 ... H9
Marabá 41,564 ... D4
Maracaju 9,699 ... C8
Maragogipe 13,512 ... G6
Maranguape 20,098 ... G3
Marechal Deodoro 9,400 ... H5
Mariana 11,785 ... *E2
Marília 103,904 ... *A3
Maringá 158,047 ... D8
Mata de São João 23,741 ... G6
Mato Grosso (Vila Bela da Santissima Trindade) 1,401 ... B6
Maués 10,846 ... B3
Mazagão 1,824 ... D3
Mineiros 16,844 ... C7
Miracema 15,545 ... *E2
Mirassol 25,173 ... *B2
Mococa 33,682 ... *C2
Mogi das Cruzes 122,265 ... *C3
Mogi-Mirim 41,827 ... *C3
Monte Alegre 10,646 ... C3
Monte Aprazível 9,767 ... *A2
Monteiro 11,051 ... G4
Montenegro 27,246 ... D10
Montes Claros 151,881 ... E7
Morrinhos 20,154 ... D7
Mossoró 118,007 ... G4
Muriaé 50,040 ... *E2
Muzambinho 8,803 ... *C2
Nanuque 34,445 ... F7
Natal 376,552 ... H4
Nazaré 18,068 ... G6
Niquelândia 8,828 ... D6
Niterói 386,185 ... *E3
Nova Cruz 12,824 ... H4
Nova Era 11,126 ... *E1
Nova Friburgo 88,943 ... *E3
Nova Iguaçu 491,802 ... *E3
Nova Lima 35,035 ... *E2
Nova Russas 10,021 ... F4
Novo Hamburgo 132,066 ... D10
Novo Horizonte 18,439 ... *B2
Óbidos 17,143 ... C3
Oeiras 12,406 ... F4
Olímpia 24,376 ... *B2
Olinda 266,392 ... H4
Oliveira 22,642 ... *D2
Oriximiná 12,078 ... C3
Orlândia 22,924 ... *C2
Osasco 376,689 ... *C3
Ourinhos 52,698 ... *B3
Ouro Preto 27,821 ... *E2
Palmares 40,624 ... H5
Palmas 15,823 ... C9
Palmeira 11,521 ... *B4
Palmeira das Missões 23,943 ... C9
Pará (Belém) 758,117 ... E3
Paracatu 29,911 ... E7
Pará de Minas 37,127 ... *D1
Paraguaçu Paulista 17,399 ... D8
Paraíba do Sul 13,510 ... *E3
Paranaíba 21,305 ... D7
Paranaguá 68,366 ... *B4
Parati 8,684 ... *D3
Parintins 29,369 ... B3
Parnaíba 78,718 ... F3
Passo Fundo 103,121 ... D10
Passos 56,998 ... *C2
Patos 58,735 ... G4
Patos de Minas 59,896 ... E7
Patrocínio 29,520 ... E7
Pau dos Ferros 12,985 ... G4
Paulo Afonso 62,066 ... G5
Pederneiras 18,864 ... *B3
Pedra Azul 13,615 ... F6
Pedreiras 30,843 ... E4
Pedro Segundo 9,693 ... F4
Pelotas 197,092 ... C10
Penápolis 32,168 ... *A2
Penedo 27,064 ... G5
Pernambuco (Recife) 1,184,215 ... H5
Petrolina 73,436 ... G5
Petrópolis 149,427 ... *E3
Picos 33,098 ... F4
Piedade 13,054 ... *C3
Pilar 14,778 ... H5
Pindamonhangaba 51,174 ... *D3

(continued on following page)

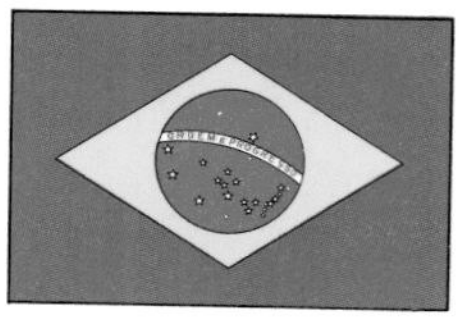

AREA 3,284,426 sq. mi. (8,506,663 sq. km.)
POPULATION 119,098,992
CAPITAL Brasília
LARGEST CITY São Paulo (greater)
HIGHEST POINT Pico da Neblina 9,889 ft. (3,014 m.)
MONETARY UNIT cruzado
MAJOR LANGUAGE Portuguese
MAJOR RELIGION Roman Catholicism

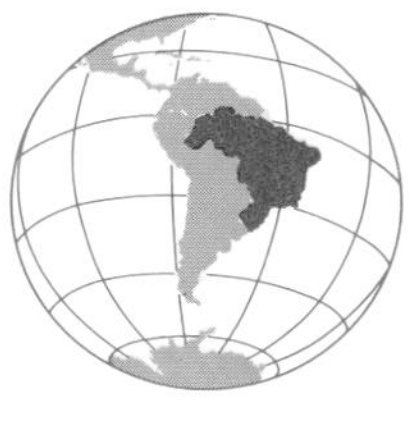

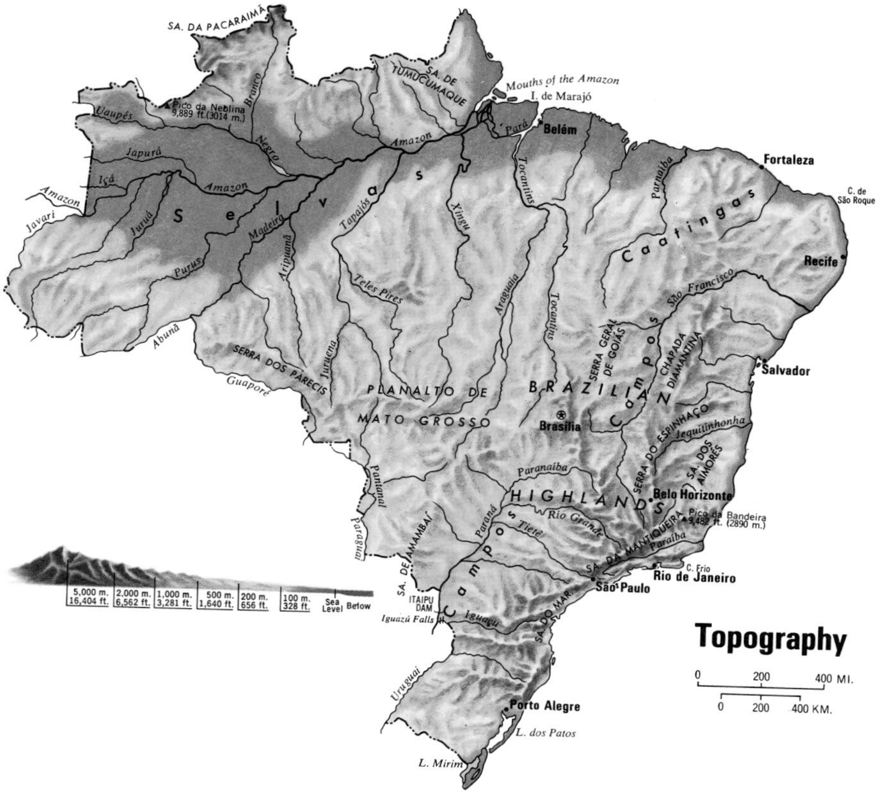
SA. DA PACARAIMÃ
SA. DE TUMUCUMAQUE
Mouths of the Amazon
I. de Marajó
Pico da Neblina 9,889 ft. (3014 m.)
Uaupés
Branco
Negro
Amazon
Pará
Belém
Fortaleza
C. de São Roque
Japurá
Içá
Amazon
Javari
Juruá
Purus
Madeira
Aripuanã
Tapajós
Xingu
Tocantins
Parnaíba
S e l v a s
Caatingas
Recife
Teles Pires
Araguaia
São Francisco
Abunã
SERRA DOS PARECIS
Guaporé
Juruena
SERRA GERAL DE GOIÁS
CHAPADA DIAMANTINA
Campos
Salvador
PLANALTO DE MATO GROSSO
BRAZILIAN HIGHLANDS
Brasília
SERRA DO ESPINHAÇO
Jequitinhonha
SA. DOS AIMORÉS
Paranaíba
Pantanal
Paraguai
Belo Horizonte
SERRA DO
Pico da Bandeira 9,482 ft. (2890 m.)
Rio Grande
Tietê
Paraná
SA. DE AMAMBAÍ
SA. DA MANTIQUEIRA
Paraíba
C. Frio
Rio de Janeiro
São Paulo
ITAIPU DAM
Iguazú Falls
Iguaçu
SA. DO MAR
Campos
Uruguai
Porto Alegre
L. dos Patos
L. Mirim
5,000 m. 16,404 ft.
2,000 m. 6,562 ft.
1,000 m. 3,281 ft.
500 m. 1,640 ft.
200 m. 656 ft.
100 m. 328 ft.
Sea Level
Below
0
200
400 MI.
0
200
400 KM.

Topography

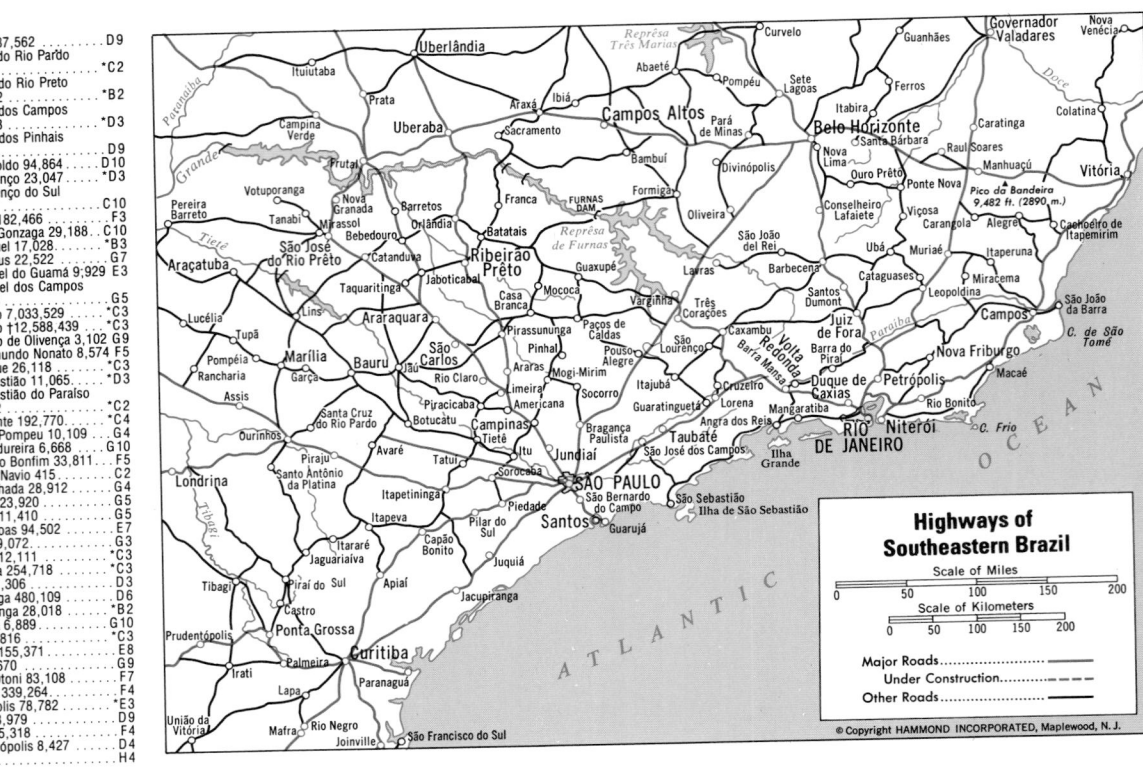

Highways of Southeastern Brazil

Scale of Miles
0   50   100   150   200

Scale of Kilometers
0   50   100   150   200

Major Roads ....
Under Construction ....
Other Roads ....

© Copyright HAMMOND INCORPORATED, Maplewood, N.J.

Agriculture, Industry and Resources

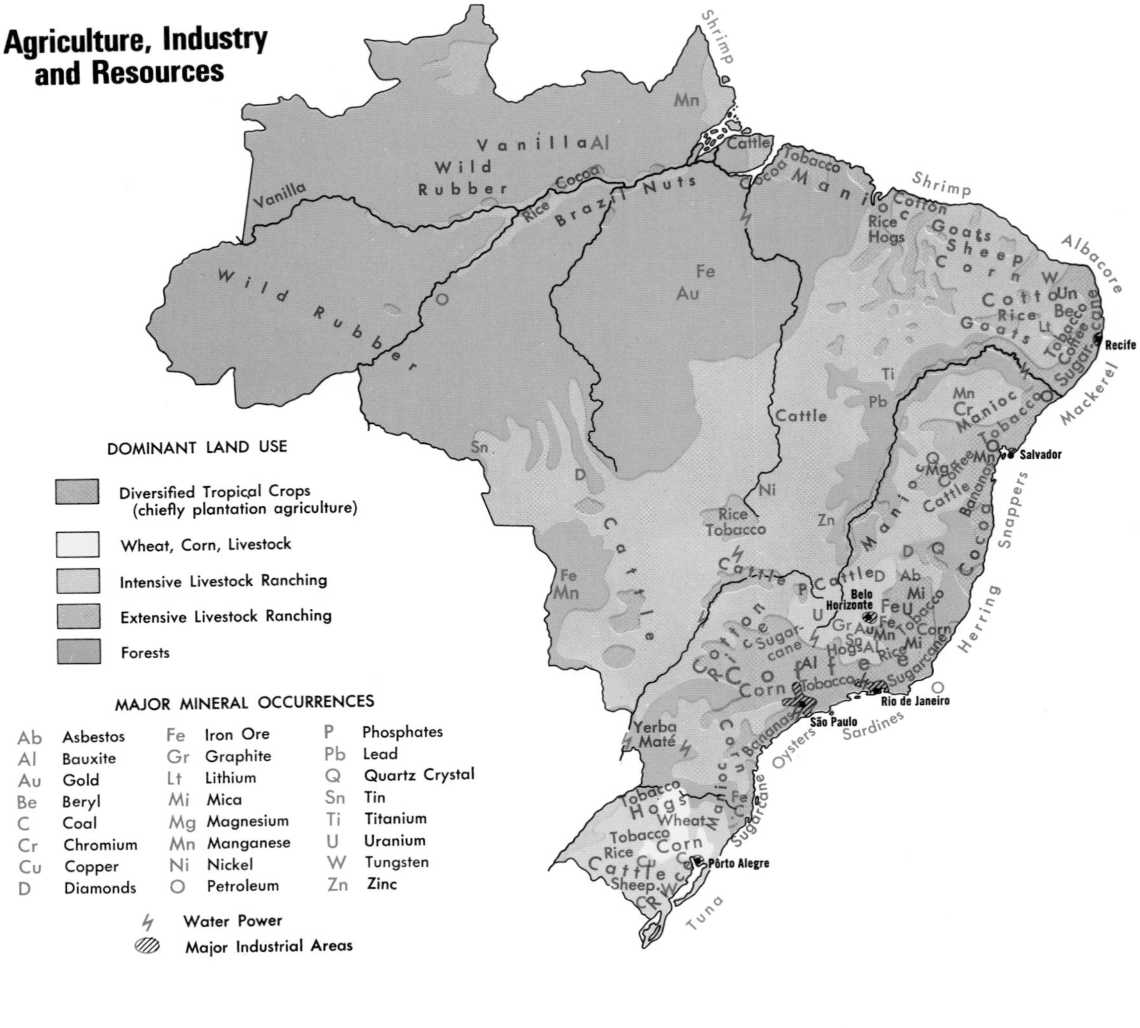

DOMINANT LAND USE

Diversified Tropical Crops (chiefly plantation agriculture)

Wheat, Corn, Livestock

Intensive Livestock Ranching

Extensive Livestock Ranching

Forests

MAJOR MINERAL OCCURRENCES

Ab	Asbestos	Fe	Iron Ore	P	Phosphates
Al	Bauxite	Gr	Graphite	Pb	Lead
Au	Gold	Lt	Lithium	Q	Quartz Crystal
Be	Beryl	Mi	Mica	Sn	Tin
C	Coal	Mg	Magnesium	Ti	Titanium
Cr	Chromium	Mn	Manganese	U	Uranium
Cu	Copper	Ni	Nickel	W	Tungsten
D	Diamonds	O	Petroleum	Zn	Zinc

⚡ Water Power

▨ Major Industrial Areas

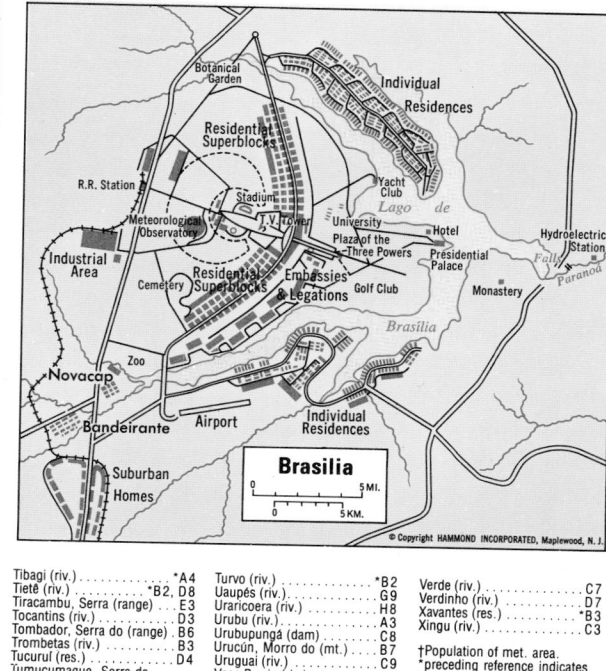

Brasilia

© Copyright HAMMOND INCORPORATED, Maplewood, N.J.

Southeastern Brazil

POLYCONIC PROJECTION

SCALE OF MILES
0 25 50 100 150

SCALE OF KILOMETERS
0 25 50 100 150

State Capitals .... ⊚
State Boundaries ....

© Copyright HAMMOND INCORPORATED, Maplewood, N.J.

Longitude West 46° of Greenwich

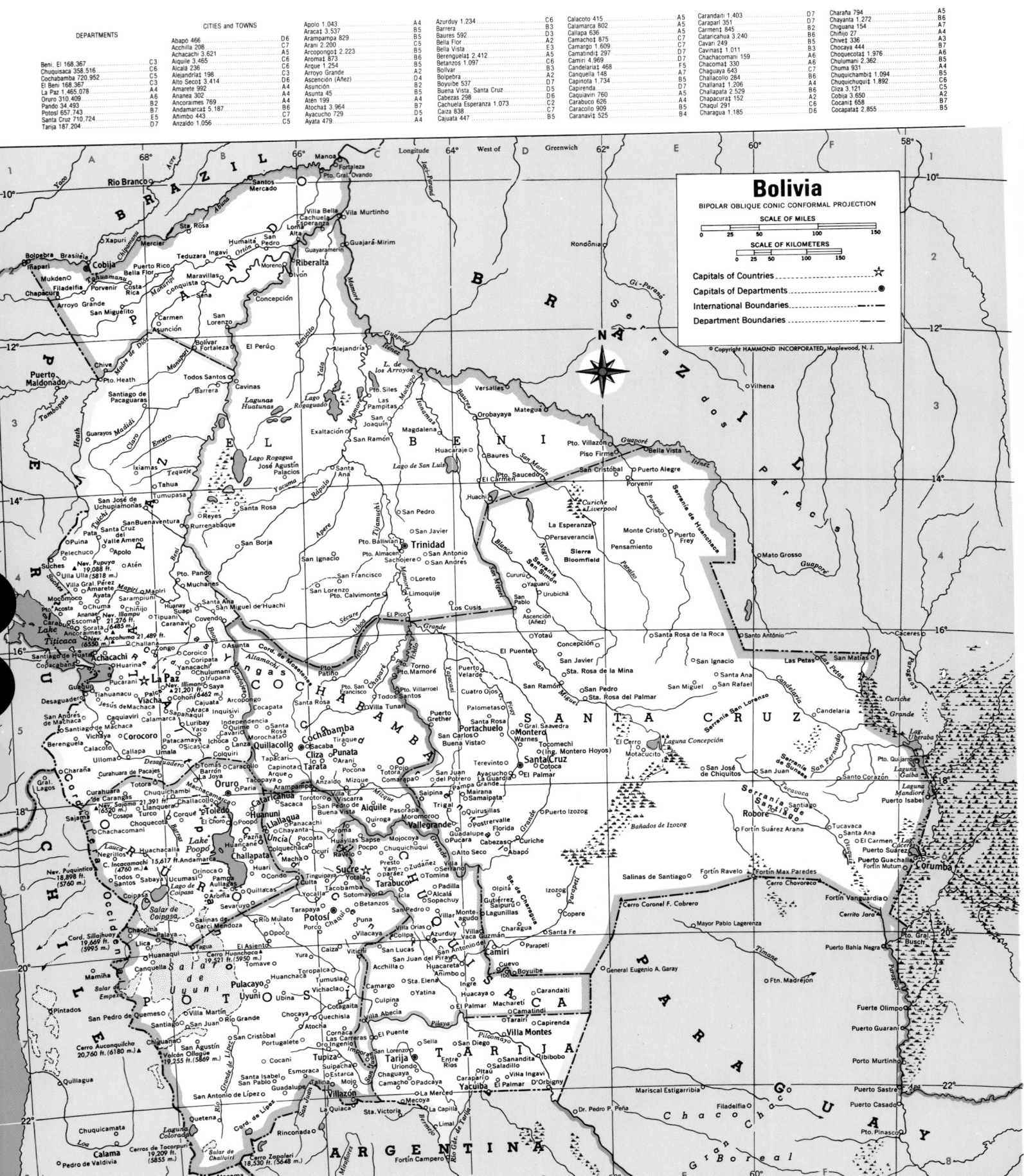

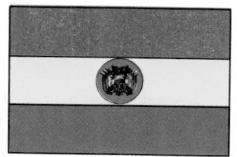

AREA 424,163 sq. mi. (1,098,582 sq. km.)
POPULATION 5,600,000
CAPITALS La Paz, Sucre
LARGEST CITY La Paz
HIGHEST POINT Nevada Ancohuma 21,489 ft. (6,550 m.)
MONETARY UNIT Bolivian peso
MAJOR LANGUAGES Spanish, Quechua, Aymara
MAJOR RELIGION Roman Catholicism

Topography

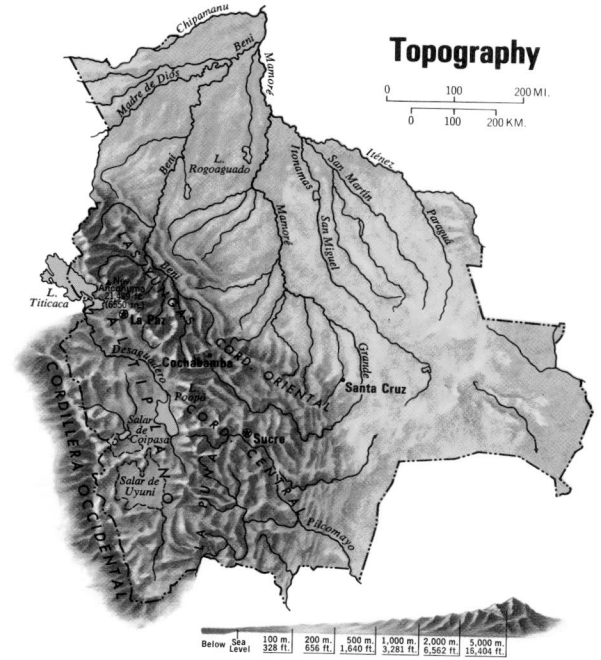

0   100   200 MI.
0   100   200 K.M.

Below Sea Level	100 m. 328 ft.	200 m. 656 ft.	500 m. 1,640 ft.	1,000 m. 3,281 ft.	2,000 m. 6,562 ft.	5,000 m. 16,404 ft.

Agriculture, Industry and Resources

DOMINANT LAND USE

- Diversified Tropical Crops (chiefly plantation agriculture)
- Upland Cultivated Areas
- Upland Livestock Grazing, Limited Agriculture
- Extensive Livestock Ranching
- Forests
- Nonagricultural Land

MAJOR MINERAL OCCURRENCES

Ag Silver
Au Gold
Cu Copper
Fe Iron Ore

G Natural Gas
O Petroleum
Pb Lead
S Sulfur

Sb Antimony
Sn Tin
W Tungsten
Zn Zinc

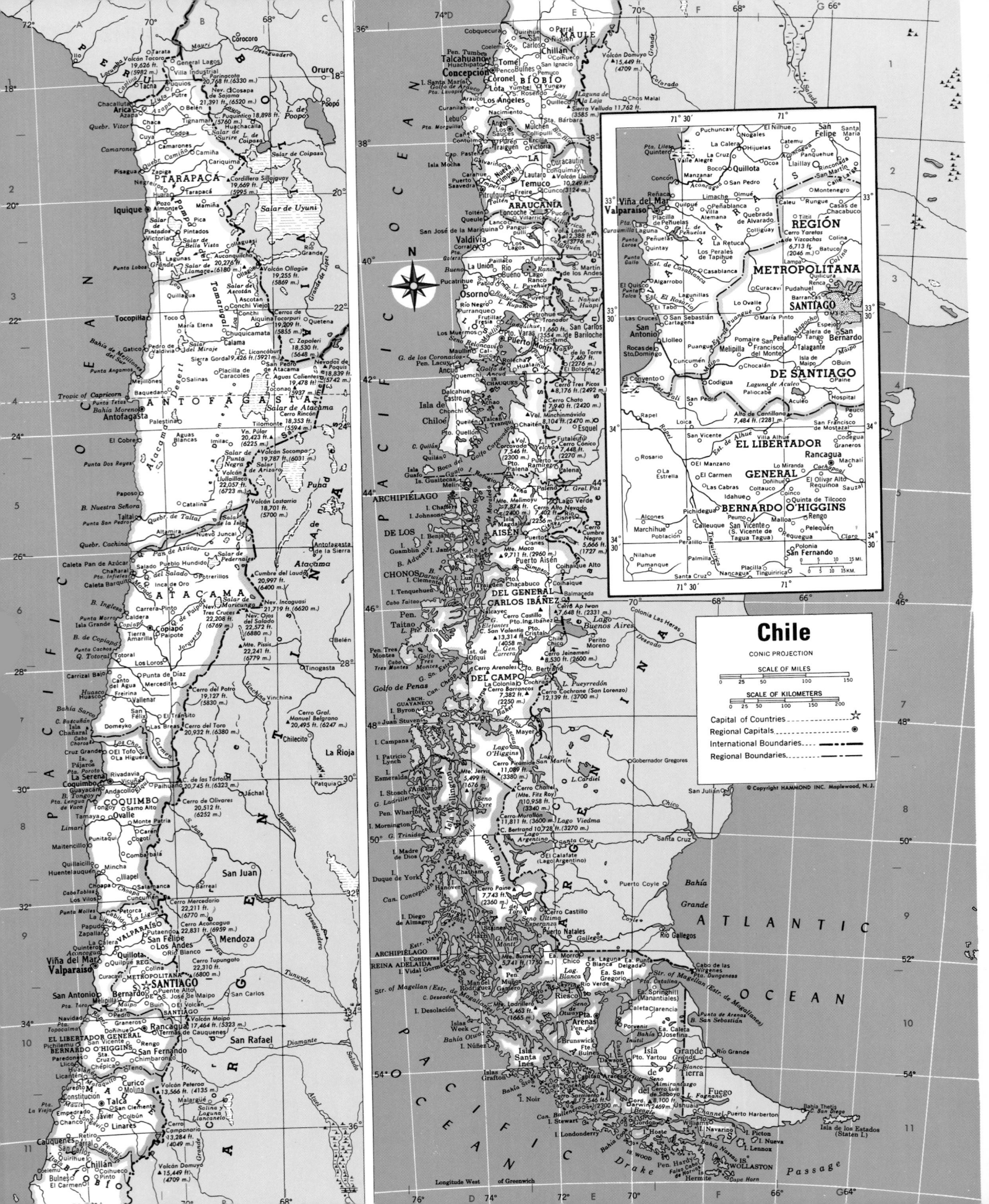

Chile

CONIC PROJECTION

SCALE OF MILES
0 25 50 100 150

SCALE OF KILOMETERS
0 25 50 100 150 200

Capital of Countries --------- ★
Regional Capitals --------- ◉
International Boundaries ----
Regional Boundaries ----

© Copyright HAMMOND INC. Maplewood, N.J.

AREA 292,257 sq. mi. (756,946 sq. km.)
POPULATION 11,275,440
CAPITAL Santiago
LARGEST CITY Santiago
HIGHEST POINT Ojos del Salado 22,572 ft. (6,880 m.)
MONETARY UNIT Chilean escudo
MAJOR LANGUAGE Spanish
MAJOR RELIGION Roman Catholicism

Topography

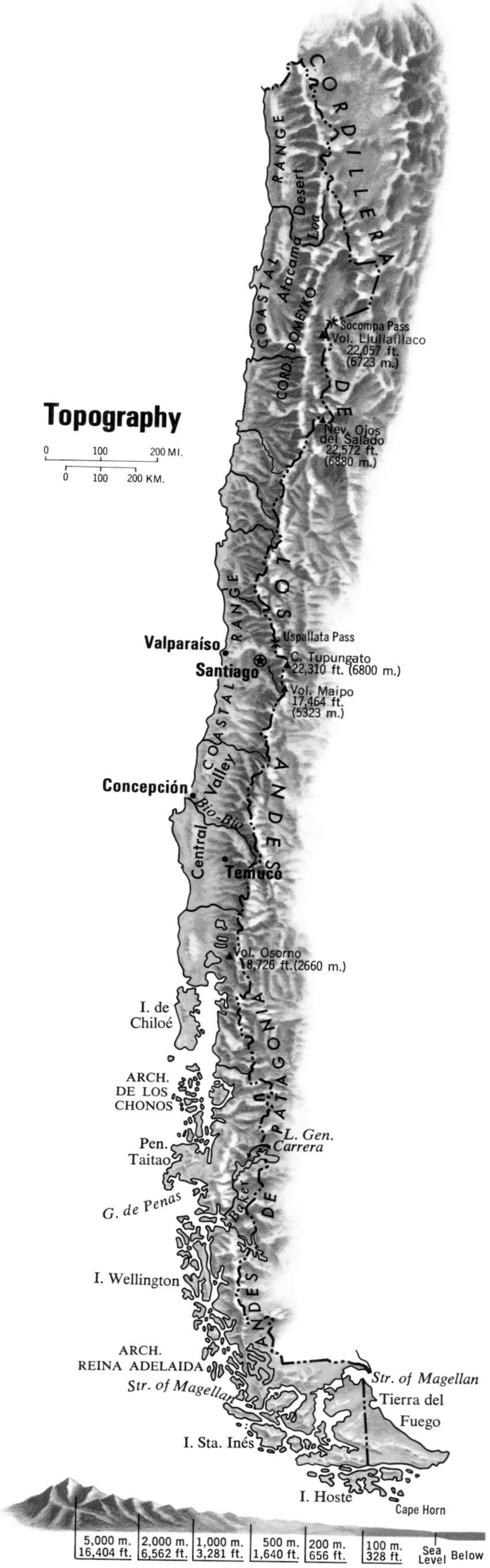

0 100 200 MI.
0 100 200 KM.
CORDILLERA DE LOS ANDES
COASTAL RANGE
Atacama Desert
Loa
CORD. DOMEYKO
Socompa Pass
Vol. Llullaillaco 22,057 ft. (6723 m.)
Nev. Ojos del Salado 22,572 ft. (6880 m.)
Valparaíso
Santiago
Uspallata Pass
C. Tupungato 22,310 ft. (6800 m.)
Vol. Maipo 17,464 ft. (5323 m.)
Concepción
Central Valley
Bío-Bío
Temuco
Vol. Osorno 8,726 ft.(2660 m.)
I. de Chiloé
ARCH. DE LOS CHONOS
Pen. Taitao
L. Gen. Carrera
Baker
G. de Penas
PATAGONIA
ANDES DE PATAGONIA
I. Wellington
ARCH. REINA ADELAIDA
Str. of Magellan
Tierra del Fuego
I. Sta. Inés
I. Hoste
Cape Horn
5,000 m. 16,404 ft.
2,000 m. 6,562 ft.
1,000 m. 3,281 ft.
500 m. 1,640 ft.
200 m. 656 ft.
100 m. 328 ft.
Sea Level
Below

REGIONS

Aisén del General Carlos Ibáñez del Campo 65,478 . . . . E6
Antofagasta 341,203. . . . . . B4
Atacama 183,071 . . . . B6
Bíobío 1,516,552 . . . . E1
Coquimbo 419,178. . . . . A8
El Libertador General Bernardo O'Higgins 584,989 . . . . A10
La Araucanía 692,924. . . . . . E2
Los Lagos 843,430 . . . . D3
Magallanes 132,333 . . . . . . E10
Maule 723,224 . . . . A11
Santiago, Región Metropolitana de (Santiago Metropolitan Region) 4,294,938 . . . . A9
Tarapacá 273,427 . . . . B2
Valparaíso 1,204,693 . . . . . . A9

CITIES and TOWNS

Achao ○11,501 . . . . D4
Aguas Blancas ○203 . . . . . . B4
Algarrobo ○3,941 . . . . F3
Ancud 11,900. . . . . D4
Andacollo 6,000 . . . . A8
Angol 42,670 . . . . D1
Antofagasta 125,100. . . . . . . A4
Arauco 5,400 . . . . D1
Arica 87,700 . . . . A1
Ascotán. B3
Barrancas ○184,241 . . . . . . G3
Belén ○925 . . . . B1
Buin 11,800 . . . . G4
Bulnes 6,900. . . . . E1
Cabildo 5,800 . . . . A9
Calama 45,900 . . . . B3
Calbuco ○21,673. . . . . D4
Caldera ○3,268 . . . . A6
Calera de Tango ○6,198 . . . G4
Calle Larga ○7,172 . . . . . . G2
Cañete 7,900 . . . . D2
Carahue ○12,733 . . . . D2
Cartagena ○7,124 . . . . F3
Casablanca 5,500 . . . . F3
Casas de Chacabuco. G2
Castro 11,200. . . . . D4
Catalina ○1,637 . . . . B5
Catemu ○8,728 . . . . G2
Cauquenes 20,200 . . . . A11
Cerro Castillo ○537 . . . . E9
Cerro Manantiales F10
Chaitén ○4,067 . . . . E4
Chañaral ○36,949 . . . . A6
Chanco ○12,433 . . . . A11
Chépica ○11,199 . . . . A10
Chillán 128,515 . . . . A11
Chimbarongo 5,300 . . . . . . A10
Chonchi ○8,911 . . . . D4
Chuquicamata 22,100. . . . . . B3
Cobquecura ○6,298. . . . . D1
Cochamó ○5,042. . . . . E3
Codegua ○6,757 . . . . G4
Codpa ○950. . . . . B1
Coelemu 5,400 . . . . D1
Coihaique 32,129 . . . . E6
Coihueco ○17,276. . . . . A11
Coinco ○4,942 . . . . G5
Colbún ○12,924 . . . . A11
Colina 7,400. . . . . G3
Collipulli 7,200 . . . . E2
Coltauco ○11,857 . . . . F5
Combarbalá ○17,332. . . . . . A8
Concepción 206,226. . . . . D1
Constitución 11,500 . . . . . . A11
Contulmo ○13,987 . . . . D2
Copiapó 45,200 . . . . B6
Coquimbo 73,953. . . . . A8
Coronel 37,300. . . . . D1
Corral ○5,533 . . . . D3
Cunco ○18,836 . . . . E2
Curacautín 9,800 . . . . E2
Curacaví 5,800 . . . . G3
Curanilahue 13,200 . . . . D1
Curepto ○13,020. . . . . A10
Curicó 41,300. . . . . A10
Dalcahue ○7,084. . . . . D4
Domeiko A7
Doñihue ○8,837 . . . . G5
El Carmen ○13,226 . . . . A11
El Monte 7,000. . . . . G4
El Quisco ○2,152. . . . . E3
El Tabo ○2,180 . . . . F3
El Tofo. A7
Empedrado ○7,887 . . . . . . A11
Ercilla ○8,061 . . . . E2
Estancia Caleta Josefina ○1,042. . . . . . . F10
Estancia Morro Chico ○785 . E9
Estancia San Gregorio ○1,156 . . . . E9
Estancia Springhill (Cerro Manantiales). F10
Freire ○23,313. . . . . E2
Freirina ○5,523 . . . . A7
Fresia ○15,359 . . . . D3
Frutillar ○12,721 . . . . D3
Futaleufú ○2,366 . . . . E4
Futrono ○7,109 . . . . E3
Galvarino ○9,495. . . . . D2
General Lagos ○810 . . . . . . B1
Graneros 8,900 . . . . G5
Guayacán A8
Hijuelas ○7,128 . . . . F2
Hualañé ○6,912. . . . . A10
Huara ○1,934 . . . . B2
Huasco ○4,971 . . . . A7
Illapel 12,200 . . . . A8
Inca de Oro 1,406. . . . . B6
Iquique 64,500 . . . . A2
Isla de Maipo ○12,903 . . . . G4
La Calera 24,600. . . . . F2
La Cruz ○8,907 . . . . F2
La Estrella ○3,707 . . . . F5
Lago Ranco ○12,767. . . . . . . E3
Lagunas ○5,653 . . . . B3
La Higuera ○6,991 . . . . A7
La Ligua 7,500 . . . . A9
Lampa ○10,220. . . . . G3
Lanco 5,200. . . . . D2
Las Cabras ○12,119. . . . . F5
La Serena 99,908 . . . . A8
La Unión 15,200. . . . . D3
Lautaro 11,900 . . . . E2
Lebu 12,500 . . . . D1
Licantén ○6,354 . . . . A10
Limache 15,200 . . . . F2
Linares 37,900 . . . . A11
Llay-Llay 9,700. . . . . G2
Loica F4
Loncoche ○17,539 . . . . D2
Longaví ○15,909 . . . . A11
Lonquimay ○9,524 . . . . E2
Los Andes 23,500 . . . . B9
Los Ángeles 49,500 . . . . D1
Los Lagos ○14,934. . . . . D3
Los Muermos ○9,296 . . . . . . D3
Los Sauces ○7,613. . . . . D2
Los Vilos ○10,453. . . . . A9
Lota 48,100 . . . . D1
Machalí 5,800. . . . . G5
Maipú ○117,872 . . . . G3
Malloa ○9,742. . . . . G5
Marchigüe ○4,451 . . . . F5
María Elena 5,900. . . . . B3
María Pinto ○5,980 . . . . G3
Maullín ○14,544 . . . . D4
Mejillones ○3,333 . . . . A4
Melipilla 23,900 . . . . F4
Mincha ○11,329 . . . . A8
Molina 9,400 . . . . A10
Monte Patria ○18,927 . . . . . A8
Mulchén 13,700 . . . . E1
Nacimiento ○17,651 . . . . D1
Nancagua ○11,076. . . . . F6
Navidad ○6,618 . . . . A10
Negreiros ○1,144 . . . . B2
Ñiquén ○13,640. . . . . E1
Nogales ○18,529 . . . . F2
Nueva Imperial 8,000 . . . . . . D2
Olivar Alto ○5,414. . . . . G5
Ollagüe B3
Olmué ○8,804 . . . . F2
Osorno 68,800 . . . . D3
Ovalle 31,700 . . . . A8
Paihuano ○6,048. . . . . B8
Paillaco 5,200. . . . . D3
Paine ○21,876. . . . . G4
Palena ○2,508 . . . . E5
Palmilla ○7,965 . . . . F6
Panguipulli 5,700 . . . . E2
Panquehue ○4,230 . . . . G2
Papudo ○2,594 . . . . A9
Paredones ○7,404 . . . . A10
Parral 17,000 . . . . A11
Pedro de Valdivia 6,200 . . . . B4
Pemuco ○7,577. . . . . E1
Peñaflor 15,500 . . . . G4
Penco ○33,962 . . . . D1
Peñuelas F3
Petorca ○8,343 . . . . A9
Petrohué E3
Peumo ○11,308. . . . . F5
Pica ○1,487. . . . . B2
Pichidegua ○13,550. . . . . . . F5
Pichilemu ○8,042 . . . . A10
Pinto ○8,687 . . . . A11
Pisagua ○1,880 . . . . A2
Pitrufquén 7,800 . . . . D2
Placilla ○6,441. . . . . F6
Porvenir ○4,000. . . . . E10
Potrerillos 5,800. . . . . B6
Pozo Almonte ○1,798 . . . . . B2
Puchuncaví ○7,542 . . . . F2
Pucón 18,000 . . . . E2
Pudahuel G3
Pueblo Hundido 6,200 . . . . . B6
Puente Alto 65,100 . . . . B10
Puerto Aisén 17,848 . . . . E6
Puerto Cisnes ○2,800 . . . . . E5
Puerto Ingeniero Ibáñez ○1,900 . . . . E6
Puerto Montt 119,059. . . . . . E4
Puerto Natales 17,280 . . . . . . E9
Puerto Quellón ○7,734 . . . . D4
Puerto Varas 10,900 . . . . E3
Puerto Williams ○949 . . . . F11
Pumanque ○3,137 . . . . F6
Punitaqui ○16,167. . . . . A8
Punta Arenas 2,140 . . . . . . E10
Purén ○11,604 . . . . D2
Purranque 5,900. . . . . D3
Putaendo ○12,806. . . . . A9
Putre ○855. . . . . B1
Puyehue E3
Queilén ○6,055 . . . . D4
Quemchi ○6,707 . . . . D4
Quilicura 8,100. . . . . G3
Quillagua B3
Quilleco ○16,043. . . . . E1
Quillota 36,500 . . . . F2
Quilpué 40,600 . . . . F2
Quinta de Tilcoco ○6,513 . . G5
Quintero 9,900 . . . . F2
Quirihue ○11,178 . . . . E1
Rancagua 140,589 . . . . G5
Renca ○67,168 . . . . G3
Rengo 12,400. . . . . G5
Requínoa ○10,730. . . . . G5
Retiro ○15,146 . . . . A11
Rinconada San Martín ○4,118 . . . . G2
Río Blanco B9
Río Bueno 9,600 . . . . D3
Río Negro 5,100. . . . . D3
Río Verde ○554 . . . . E10
Rocas de Santo Domingo ○4,114 . . . . F4
Rosario ○3,383 . . . . F5
Salamanca ○18,741. . . . . A9
Samo Alto ○5,689. . . . . A8
San Antonio 46,700 . . . . F3
San Bernardo ○117,766 . . . G4
San Carlos 17,000 . . . . E1
San Clemente ○23,273 . . . A11
San Felipe 26,100. . . . . G2
San Fernando 23,600 . . . . . . G6
San Francisco de Mostazal ○11,439 . . . . . . G4
San Ignacio ○13,523 . . . . . . E1
San Javier 10,800. . . . . A11
San José de Maipo ○9,601 . . . . B10
San Pablo ○7,978 . . . . D3
San Pedro ○8,255 . . . . F4
San Pedro de Atacama C4
San Rosendo ○14,337. . . . . . E1
Santa Bárbara ○14,345 . . . . E1
Santa Cruz 8,600 . . . . F6
Santa María ○8,162. . . . . . . G2
Santiago (cap.) 3,614,947 . . G3
Santiago *3,672,374 . . . . . . G3
San Vicente F4
San Vicente (San Vicente de Tagua Tagua) ○28,333 F5
Sierra Gorda ○8,805 . . . . . . B4
Talagante 16,500 . . . . G4
Talca 133,160 . . . . A11
Talcahuano 148,300 . . . . D1
Taltal 6,400. . . . . A5
Tamaya A8
Tarapacá B2
Temuco 197,232. . . . . E2
Teno ○17,675 . . . . A10
Termas de Cauquenes. B10
Tierra Amarilla ○7,899. . . . . A6
Tiltil ○9,198. . . . . G2
Toco ○8,734 . . . . B3
Toconao C4
Tocopilla 22,000 . . . . A3
Toltén ○16,265 . . . . D2
Tomé 29,600 . . . . D1
Traiguén 11,400 . . . . D2
Valdivia 115,536. . . . . D3
Vallenar 26,800. . . . . A7
Valparaíso 271,580 . . . . E2
Victoria 16,500. . . . . D2
Vicuña 5,100 . . . . A8
Villa Alemana 29,600 . . . . . . F2
Villa Alhué ○5,078. . . . . G4
Villarrica 25,091 . . . . E2
Viña del Mar 281,361 . . . . . . F2
Yumbel ○21,858 . . . . E1
Yungay ○10,725 . . . . E1
Zapallar ○2,894 . . . . A9
Zapiga B2

OTHER FEATURES

Aconcagua (riv.) F2
Aculeo (lag.). G4
Adventure (bay) D5
Aguas Calientes, Cerro (mt.) C4
Almirantazgo (bay) F11
Almirante Montt (gulf) D9
Ancud (gulf) D4
Angamos (isl.) D8
Angamos (pt.) A4
Ap Iwan, Cerro (mt.). E6
Arauco (gulf) D1
Arenales, Cerro (mt.) D7
Atacama (des.) B4
Atacama, Salar de (salt dep.). C4
Aucanquilcha, Cerro (mt.) . . B3
Azapa, Quebrada (riv.) B1
Baker (riv.) D7
Ballenero (chan.) E11
Bascuñán (cape). A7
Beagle (chan.). E11
Bella Vista, Salar de (salt dep.). B3
Benjamín (isl.) D5
Bío-Bío (riv.) E2
Blanca (lag.) E10
Blanco (lake) F10
Bravo (riv.) D7
Brunswick (pen.) E10
Bueno (riv.) D3
Buenos Aires (lake). E6
Byron (isl.). D7
Cachapoal (riv.) G5
Cachina, Quebrada (riv.). . . . A5
Cachos (pt.) A6
Calafquén (lake) E3
Camarones (riv.). A2
Camiña, Quebrada (riv.) B2
Campana (isl.) D7
Campanario, Cerro (mt.) . . A10
Capitán Aracena (isl.) E10
Carmen (riv.) B7
Castillo, Cerro (mt.) E6
Catalina (pt.). F10
Chaffers (isl.) D5
Chaltel, Cerro (mt.). E8
Chañaral (isl.). A7
Chatham (isl.). D9
Chauques (isls.) D4
Cheap (chan.). D7
Chiloé (isl.) 119,286. . . . . . . D4
Choapa (riv.). A9
Chonos (arch.) D6
Choros (cape) A7
Cisnes (riv.) E5
Clarence (isl.) E10
Clemente (isl.) D6
Cochrane (lake). E7
Cochrane, Cerro (mt.). E7
Cockburn (chan.) E11
Concepción (chan.) D9
Cónico, Cerro (mt.) E4
Contreras (isl.) D9
Cook (bay) E11
Copiapó (bay) A6
Copiapó (riv.) A6
Corcovado (gulf). D4
Corcovado (vol.). D5
Coronados (gulf) D4
Curaumilla (pt.). E2
Darwin (bay). D6
Darwin, Cordillera (mts.) . . . D8
Darwin, Cordillera (mts.) . . E11

(continued on following page)

Agriculture, Industry and Resources

DOMINANT LAND USE

Cereals, Livestock

Mediterranean Agriculture (cereals, fruit, livestock)

Pasture Livestock

Extensive Livestock Ranching

Limited Seasonal Grazing

Forests

Nonagricultural Land

MAJOR MINERAL OCCURRENCES

Ag	Silver	Hg	Mercury
Au	Gold	Id	Iodine
C	Coal	Mn	Manganese
Cu	Copper	Mo	Molybdenum
Fe	Iron Ore	N	Nitrates
G	Natural Gas	Na	Salt
Gp	Gypsum	O	Petroleum
		S	Sulfur

⚡ Water Power   ▨ Major Industrial Areas

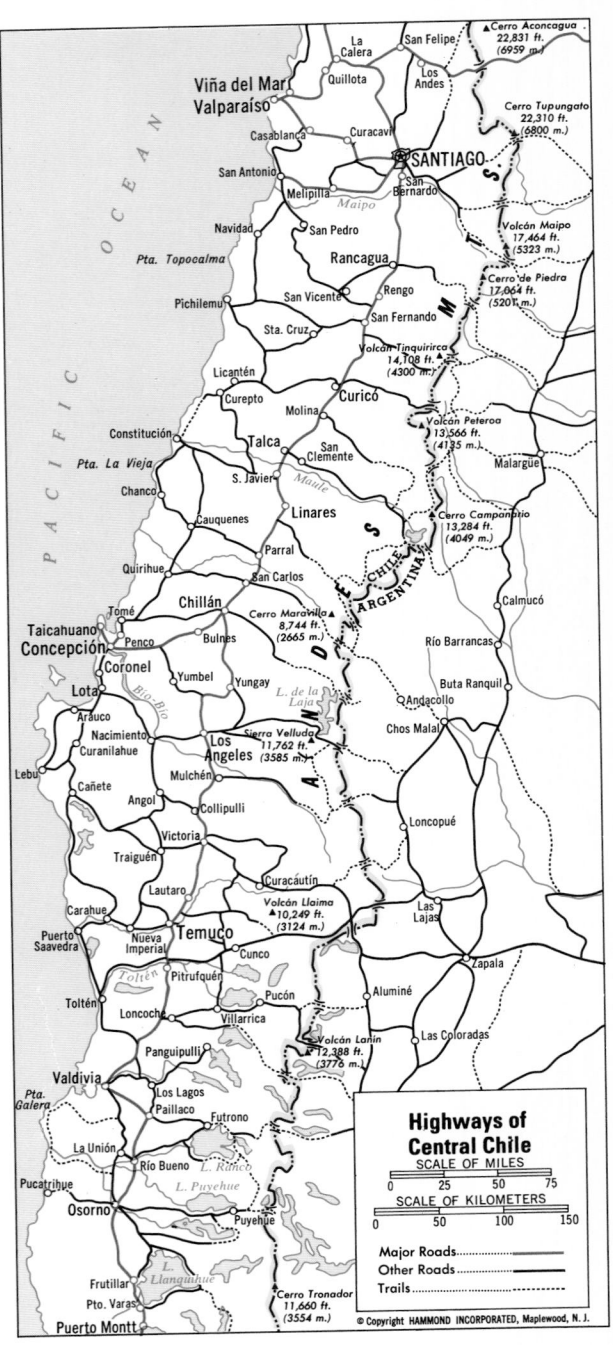

Highways of Central Chile

SCALE OF MILES

0   25   50   75

SCALE OF KILOMETERS

0   50   100   150

Major Roads ....
Other Roads ....
Trails ....

© Copyright HAMMOND INCORPORATED, Maplewood, N.J.

*City and suburbs.
○ Population of commune.

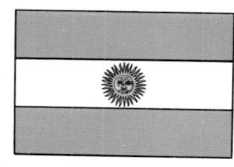

PROVINCES

Buenos Aires 10,796,036 . . . D4
Catamarca 206,204 . . . . . . C2
Chaco 692,410 . . . . D2
Chubut 262,196 . . . . C5
Córdoba 2,407,135 . . . . . . D3
Corrientes 657,716 . . . . . . E2
Distrito Federal 2,908,001 . . H7
Entre Ríos 902,241 . . . . . . E3
Formosa 292,479 . . . . D1
Jujuy 408,514 . . . . C1
La Pampa 207,132 . . . . . . C4
La Rioja 163,342 . . . . C2
Mendoza 1,187,305 . . . . . . C4
Misiones 579,725 . . . . F2
Neuquén 241,904 . . . . C4
Río Negro 383,896 . . . . . . C5
Salta 662,369 . . . . D1
San Juan 469,973 . . . . C3
San Luis 212,837 . . . . C3
Santa Cruz 114,479 . . . . . . C6
Santa Fe 2,457,188 . . . . . . D3
Santiago del Estero 652,318 D2
Tierra del Fuego, Antártida,
  e Islas del Atlántico
  Sur 29,451 . . . . C7
Tucumán 968,066 . . . . C2

CITIES and TOWNS

Abra Pampa 2,929 . . . . C1
Adolfo Alsina 7,707 . . . . . . D4
Aguaray 4,802 . . . . D1
Aguilares 20,286 . . . . C2
Aimogasta 4,640 . . . . C2
Alberti 6,440 . . . . G7
Alcorta 5,818 . . . . F6
Algarrobo del Águila C4
Allen 14,041 . . . . C4
Alpachiri 1,657 . . . . D4
Alta Gracia 30,628 . . . . . . D3
Aluminé 1,560 . . . . B4
Alvear 5,419 . . . . E2
Ameghino 2,775 . . . . D3
Anatuya 15,025 . . . . D2
Andalgalá 6,853 . . . . C2
Antofagasta de la Sierra . . . C2
Apóstoles 11,252 . . . . F2
Arrecifes 17,719 . . . . F7
Arroyo Seco 12,886 . . . . . . F6
Ascensión 3,031 . . . . F7
Avellaneda 330,654 . . . . . . G7
Ayacucho 12,363 . . . . E4
Azul 43,582 . . . . E4
Bahía Blanca 220,765 . . . . D4
Bahía Bustamante C6
Bahía Thetis C7
Balcarce 28,985 . . . . E4
Balnearia 4,531 . . . . D3
Baradero 20,103 . . . . G6
Barrancas 3,602 . . . . F6
Barranqueras E2
Barreal 2,739 . . . . C3
Basavilbaso 7,657 . . . . G6
Belén 7,411 . . . . C2

Bella Vista, Corrientes
  14,229 . . . . E2
Bella Vista, Tucumán 9,177 . D2
Bell Ville 26,559 . . . . D3
Bolívar 16,382 . . . . D4
Bovril 4,735 . . . . G5
Bragado 27,101 . . . . F7
Buenos Aires (cap.)
  2,908,001 . . . . H7
Buenos Aires *9,927,404 . . . H7
Cafayate 5,048 . . . . C2
Calafate B7
Calchaquí 5,958 . . . . F5
Caleta Olivia 20,141 . . . . . . C6
Camarones C5
Campana 51,498 . . . . G6
Cañada de Gómez 24,706 . . F6
Canals 6,627 . . . . D3
Cañuelas 14,831 . . . . G7
Carcarañá 11,121 . . . . F6
Carlos Casares 13,286 . . . . F7
Carlos Tejedor 4,421 . . . . . D4
Carmen de Areco 7,882 . . . F7
Carmen de Patagones
  13,981 . . . . D5
Casilda 23,492 . . . . F6
Castelli 4,507 . . . . H7
Catamarca 88,432 . . . . C2
Caucete 14,512 . . . . C3
Ceres 10,743 . . . . D2
Chabás 5,156 . . . . F6
Chacabuco 26,492 . . . . F7
Chajarí 15,242 . . . . G5

Chamical 6,333 . . . . C3
Charadai 1,078 . . . . D2
Charata 13,070 . . . . D2
Chascomús 21,864 . . . . . . H7
Chepes 4,775 . . . . C3
Chicoana 1,844 . . . . C2
Chilecito 14,010 . . . . C2
Chivilcoy 43,779 . . . . F7
Choele-Choel 6,191 . . . . . . C4
Chos-Malal 4,823 . . . . C4
Cinco Saltos 15,094 . . . . . . C4
Cipolletti 40,123 . . . . C4
Clorinda 21,008 . . . . D1
Colón, Buenos Aires 16,070 . F6
Colón, Entre Ríos 11,648 . . . G6
Colonia Las Heras 3,176 . . . C6
Comandante Fontana 4,468 . D2
Comandante Luis Piedrabuena
  2,492 . . . . C6
Comodoro Rivadavia 96,865 . C6
Concepción 29,359 . . . . . . C2
Concepción de
  la Sierra 4,992 . . . . E2
Concepción del
  Uruguay 46,065 . . . . G6
Concordia 93,618 . . . . G5
Constanza 1,313 . . . . G6
Córdoba 982,018 . . . . D3
Coronda 11,554 . . . . F6
Coronel Brandsen 10,484 . . . H7
Coronel Dorrego 10,661 . . . . D4
Coronel Pringles 16,592 . . . . D4
Coronel Suárez 16,359 . . . . D4

Coronel Vidal 4,774 . . . . . . E4
Corral de Bustos 8,613 . . . . D3
Corrientes 179,590 . . . . . . E2
Cosquín 13,929 . . . . D3
Crespo 10,668 . . . . F6
Cruz del Eje 23,473 . . . . . . C3
Curuzú Cuatiá 24,955 . . . . . G5
Cutral-Có 25,870 . . . . C4
Daireaux 8,150 . . . . D4
Deán Funes 16,306 . . . . . . D3
Diamante 13,464 . . . . F6
Dolavon 1,778 . . . . C5
Dolores 19,307 . . . . E4
Eduardo Castex 5,397 . . . . . D4
El Bolsón 5,001 . . . . B5
Eldorado 22,821 . . . . F2
El Maitén 2,350 . . . . B5
Elortondo 4,939 . . . . F6
El Quebrachal 2,202 . . . . . . D2
Embarcación 9,016 . . . . D1
Empedrado 4,732 . . . . E2
Escobar 70,829 . . . . G7
Esperanza 22,838 . . . . F5
Esquel 17,228 . . . . B5
Esquina 10,380 . . . . G5
Famatina 1,237 . . . . C2
Federación 7,259 . . . . G5
Felipe Yofré 1,140 . . . . G4
Fernández 6,062 . . . . D2
Fiambalá 1,201 . . . . C2
Firmat 13,588 . . . . F6
Formosa 95,067 . . . . E2
Fortín Olmos 1,101 . . . . F4
Frías 20,901 . . . . D2
Gaiman 2,651 . . . . C5
Gálvez 14,711 . . . . F6
General Acha 7,647 . . . . . . C4
General Alvear, Buenos Aires
  5,481 . . . . F7
General Alvear,
  Mendoza 21,250 . . . . C3
General Arenales 3,332 . . . . F7
General Belgrano 10,909 . . . G7
General Conesa 3,566 . . . . . C5
General Galarza 3,057 . . . . . C6
General Güemes 15,534 . . . . D1
General José de
  San Martín 16,296 . . . . . . D2
General Juan Madariaga
  13,409 . . . . E4
General La Madrid 5,154 . . . . D4
General Las Heras 6,005 . . . G7
General Paz 5,127 . . . . H7
General Pico 30,180 . . . . . . D4
General Ramírez 5,393 . . . . . F6
General Roca 38,296 . . . . . . C4
General San Martín, Buenos
  Aires 384,306 . . . . G7
General San Martín,
  La Pampa 2,168 . . . . D4
General Viamonte 10,112 . . . F7
General Villegas 11,307 . . . . D4
Gobernador Crespo 2,972 . . . F5
Godoy Cruz 141,553 . . . . . . C3
Goya 47,357 . . . . G4
Gualeguay 24,883 . . . . G6
Gualeguaychú 51,057 . . . . . G6
Guandacol 1,351 . . . . C2
Hasenkamp 2,804 . . . . F5
Helvecia 3,927 . . . . F5
Hernandarias 3,002 . . . . . . F5
Hernando 8,619 . . . . D3
Huinca Renancó 7,187 . . . . . D3
Humahuaca 3,963 . . . . C1
Humberto (Humberto
  Primo) 4,163 . . . . F5
Ibarreta 5,262 . . . . D2
Ibicuy 3,082 . . . . G6
Ingeniero Huergo 3,385 . . . . C4
Ingeniero Jacobacci 4,045 . . C5
Ingeniero Luiggi 3,002 . . . . . D4
Intendente Alvear 3,640 . . . . D4
Itatí 3,269 . . . . E2

Ituzaingó 8,687 . . . . E2
Jáchal 8,832 . . . . C3
Jesús María 17,594 . . . . . . D3
Joaquín V. González 6,054 . . D2
Juárez 11,798 . . . . E4
Jujuy 124,487 . . . . C1
Junín 62,080 . . . . F7
Junín de los Andes 5,638 . . . B4
La Banda 46,994 . . . . D2
Laboulaye 16,883 . . . . D3
La Carlota 8,614 . . . . D3
La Cruz 4,132 . . . . E2
La Cumbre 6,110 . . . . C3
La Falda 12,502 . . . . D3
Laguna Paiva 11,129 . . . . . . F5
Lanús 465,891 . . . . H7
La Paz, Entre Ríos 14,920 . . G5
La Paz, Mendoza 4,604 . . . . C3
La Plata 560,341 . . . . H7
Laprida 6,495 . . . . D4
La Quiaca 8,289 . . . . C1
La Rioja 66,826 . . . . C2
Larroque 3,147 . . . . F5
Las Flores 18,287 . . . . E4
Las Lomitas 4,047 . . . . D1
Las Palmas 5,061 . . . . E2
Las Parejas 7,430 . . . . F6
Las Rosas 9,725 . . . . F6
Las Varillas 10,605 . . . . D3
La Toma 4,325 . . . . C3
Lincoln 19,009 . . . . F7
Loberia 8,898 . . . . E4
Lobos 20,798 . . . . G7
Lomas de Zamora 508,620 . . G7
Lucas González 3,015 . . . . . G6
Luján 38,919 . . . . G7
Lules 11,391 . . . . C2
Maciel 4,066 . . . . F6
Magdalena 7,135 . . . . H7
Maipú 7,289 . . . . E4
Malabrigo 3,294 . . . . F4
Malargüe 9,496 . . . . C4
Maquinchao 1,299 . . . . C5
Marcos Juárez 19,827 . . . . . D3
Mar del Plata 407,024 . . . . . E4
Máximo Paz 3,216 . . . . F6
Mburucuya 3,044 . . . . E2
Médanos 4,511 . . . . D4
Mendoza 596,796 . . . . C3
Mercedes, Buenos Aires
  46,581 . . . . G7
Mercedes, Corrientes
  20,603 . . . . G4
Mercedes, San Luis 50,856 . . C3
Merlo 293,059 . . . . G7
Metán 18,928 . . . . D2
Miramar 15,473 . . . . E4
Monte Caseros 18,247 . . . . . G5
Monte Quemado 4,707 . . . . . D2
Monteros 15,832 . . . . C2
Morón 596,769 . . . . G7
Morteros 11,456 . . . . D3
Navarro 7,176 . . . . G7
Necochea 50,939 . . . . E4
Neuquén 90,037 . . . . C4
Nogoyá 15,862 . . . . F6
Norquincó B5
Nueve de Julio 26,608 . . . . . F7
Oberá 27,311 . . . . F2
Olavarría 63,686 . . . . D4
Oliva 9,231 . . . . D3
Palo Santo 3,088 . . . . E2
Paraná 159,581 . . . . F5
Paso de Los Libres 24,112 . . E2
Pedro Luro 3,142 . . . . D4
Pehuajó 25,613 . . . . D4
Pellegrini 3,940 . . . . D4
Pergamino 68,989 . . . . F6
Pico Truncado 9,626 . . . . . . C6
Pigüé 10,793 . . . . D4
Pilar 3,805 . . . . F5
Pirané 9,039 . . . . E2
Plaza Huincul 7,988 . . . . . . B4

(continued on following page)

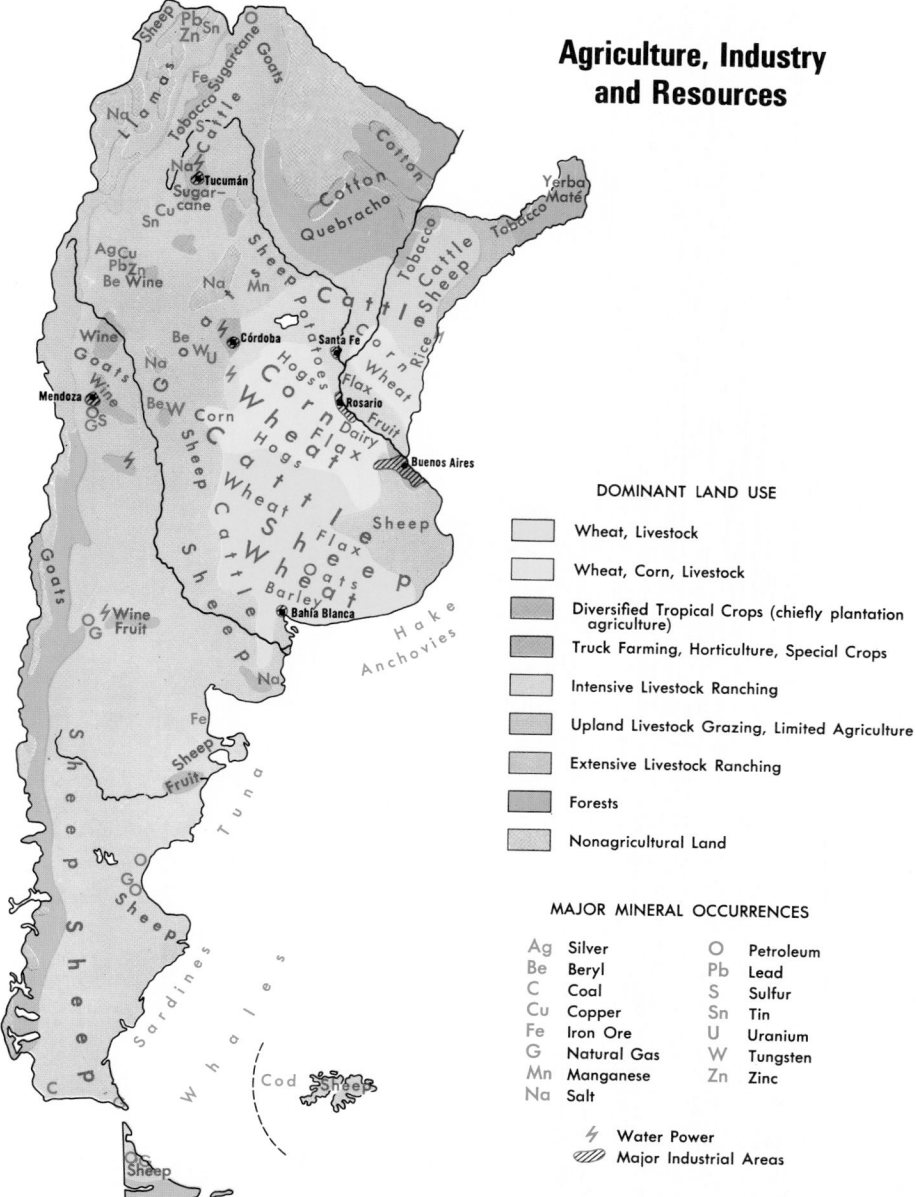

Agriculture, Industry and Resources

AREA 1,072,070 sq. mi. (2,776,661 sq. km.)
POPULATION 28,438,000
CAPITAL Buenos Aires
LARGEST CITY Buenos Aires
HIGHEST POINT Cerro Aconcagua 22,831 ft.
  (6,959 m.)
MONETARY UNIT austral
MAJOR LANGUAGE Spanish
MAJOR RELIGION Roman Catholicism

DOMINANT LAND USE

Wheat, Livestock
Wheat, Corn, Livestock
Diversified Tropical Crops (chiefly plantation agriculture)
Truck Farming, Horticulture, Special Crops
Intensive Livestock Ranching
Upland Livestock Grazing, Limited Agriculture
Extensive Livestock Ranching
Forests
Nonagricultural Land

MAJOR MINERAL OCCURRENCES

Ag	Silver	O	Petroleum
Be	Beryl	Pb	Lead
C	Coal	S	Sulfur
Cu	Copper	Sn	Tin
Fe	Iron Ore	U	Uranium
G	Natural Gas	W	Tungsten
Mn	Manganese	Zn	Zinc
Na	Salt		

⚡ Water Power
▨ Major Industrial Areas

Posadas 139,941 ....E2	San Cristóbal 13,345 ......F5	Tapalqué 5,356 ....E4	Argentino (lake) B7
Presidencia de la Plaza 4,904 ....D2	San Fernando 128,939 ....G7	Tartagal 31,367 ....D1	Arizaro, Salar de (salt dep.) ..C2
Presidencia Roque Sáenz Peña 49,261 ....D2	San Francisco, Córdoba 58,616 ....D3	Tigre 199,366 ....G7	Arrecifes (riv.) G6
Puán 4,148 ....D4	San Francisco, San Luis 2,448 ....C3	Tinogasta 7,829 ....C2	Atacama, Puna de (reg.) C2
Puerto Deseado 4,017 ....D6	San Genaro 2,977 ....F6	Toay 3,617 ....D4	Atuel (riv.) C4
Puerto Harberton C7	San Ignacio 3,437 ....E2	Tornquist 4,696 ....D4	Bermejo (riv.) E2
Puerto Iguazú 10,250 ....F2	San Jaime de la Frontera 2,811 ....G5	Tostado 10,492 ....C5	Blanca (bay) D4
Puerto Madryn 20,709 ....C5	San Javier 7,557 ....F5	Trelew 52,073 ....C5	Brazo Sur, Pilcomayo (riv.) ..E1
Puerto Rico 8,195 ....D1	San José de Feliciano 4,986 ..G5	Trenque Lauquen 22,504 ..D4	Buenos Aires (lake) B6
Punta Alta 54,375 ....D4	San Juan 290,479 ....C3	Tres Arroyos 42,118 ......B5	Campanario, Cerro (mt.) C4
Quequén 11,737 ....D4	San Julián 4,278 ....C6	Trevelín 2,935 ....C3	Chaco Austral (reg.) D2
Quimili 8,972 ....D2	San Justo 14,135 ....F5	Tunuyán 14,665 ....C3	Chaco Central (reg.) D1
Quines 3,352 ....C3	San Luis 70,632 ....C3	Urdinarrain 5,472 ....G6	Chico (riv.) C5
Quitilipi 9,937 ....D2	San Martín 29,746 ....C3	Ushuaia 10,988 ....C7	Chico (riv.) C6
Rafaela 53,132 ....F6	San Martín de los Andes 9,507 ..C5	Valcheta 2,994 ....C5	Chubut (riv.) C5
Ramallo 8,248 ....F6	San Miguel del Monte 8,414 ..G7	Vedia 6,273 ....F7	Colhué Huapi (lake) C6
Rauch 8,348 ....E4	San Miguel de Tucumán 496,914 ....D2	Veinticinco de Mayo 18,936 ..F7	Colorado (riv.) D4
Rawson 12,981 ....D5	San Nicolás 96,313 ....F6	Venado Tuerto 46,775 ......D3	Cónico, Cerro (mt.) B5
Reconquista 32,442 ......E2	San Pedro, Buenos Aires 27,058 ....F6	Vera 13,555 ....F5	Corrientes (riv.) E2
Recreo 3,502 ....C2	San Pedro, Jujuy 36,907 ....D1	Verónica 5,657 ....H7	Coyle (riv.) B7
Resistencia 218,438 ......C1	San Rafael 70,477 ....C3	Viale 5,635 ....F5	Delgada (pt.) C5
Rinconada D4	San Ramón de la Nva. Orán 32,955 ....D1	Vicente López 289,815 ....G7	Desaguadero (riv.) C3
Río Colorado 7,361 ....D4	San Salvador 4,342 ....G5	Victoria 18,883 ....F6	Deseado (riv.) C6
Río Cuarto 110,148 ......D3	San Sebastián C7	Victorica 3,895 ....C4	Diamante (riv.) C3
Río Gallegos 43,479 ......C7	Santa Cruz 2,353 ....C7	Vicuña Mackenna 5,665 ....D3	Domuyo (vol.) B4
Río Grande 13,271 ....C7	Santa Elena 14,655 ....F5	Viedma 24,338 ....D5	Dos Bahías (cape) D5
Río Segundo 12,839 ......D3	Santa Lucía 4,452 ....E2	Villa Ángela 25,586 ....D2	Dulce (riv.) D2
Río Tercero 34,735 ....D3	Santa María 5,380 ....C2	Villa Cañas 7,303 ....F6	Dungeness (pt.) C7
Rivadavia 10,953 ....C7	Santa Rosa, Córdoba 4,306 ..D3	Villa Constitución 36,157 ..F6	El Chocón (res.) C4
Rojas 14,247 ....F7	Santa Rosa, La Pampa 51,689 ....C4	Villa del Rosario 10,133 ....D3	Estados, Los (isl.) D7
Romang 4,017 ....F4	Santa Rosa, San Luis 2,878 ..C3	Villa Dolores 21,508 ....C3	Fagnano (lake) C7
Roque Pérez 5,434 ....G7	Santa Victoria D1	Villa Elisa 4,106 ....G5	Famatina, Sierra de (mts.) ..C2
Rosario 954,606 ....F6	Santiago del Estero 148,357 ..D2	Villa Federal 9,222 ....G5	Feliciano (riv.) G5
Rosario de la Frontera 13,531 ....D2	Santo Tomé, Corrientes 14,352 ....E2	Villaguay 18,699 ....G6	Gallegos (riv.) B7
Rosario de Lerma 9,540 ....C1	Santo Tomé, Santa Fe 35,363 ....F5	Villa Guillermina 2,971 ....D2	General Manuel Belgrano, Cerro (mt.) C2
Rosario del Tala 9,552 ....G6	Sarmiento 6,313 ....B6	Villa Huidobro 4,154 ....D3	Gran Chaco (reg.) D1
Rufino 15,306 ....D3	Sauce 4,677 ....G5	Villa María 67,490 ....D3	Grande (bay) C7
Saladas 7,345 ....E2	Sierra Grande 9,585 ....C5	Villa María Grande 4,517 ..F5	Grande (falls) E3
Saladillo 14,806 ....G7	Suipacha 4,505 ....G7	Villa Nueva 4,604 ....D3	Grande de Tierra del Fuego (isl.) C7
Salliqueló 5,479 ....D4	Sunchales 12,493 ....F5	Villa Ocampo 9,162 ....D2	Gualeguay (riv.) G5
Salta 260,323 ....C1	Suncho Corral 3,837 ....D2	Villa Regina 14,017 ....C4	Guayaquilaró (riv.) G5
Salto 18,462 ....F7	Tafí Viejo 26,625 ....C2	Villa San José 6,800 ....G6	Iguazú (falls) F2
San Antonio de Areco 12,932 ....G7	Tandil 78,821 ....E4	Villa San Martín 6,237 ......D2	Iguazú Nat'l Park E2
San Antonio de los Cobres 2,357 ....C1		Vinchina 1,070 ....C2	Lanín (vol.) B4
San Antonio Oeste 8,690 ..C5		Zapala 18,293 ....B4	Lanín Nat'l Park B4
San Carlos 7,613 ....F6		Zárate 65,504 ....G7	Lechiguanas (isls.) G6
San Carlos de Bariloche 48,222 ....B5		Zavalla 3,800 ....F6	Lennox (isl.) C8
San Cayetano 5,960 ....E4			Limay (riv.) C4
		OTHER FEATURES	Llancanelo, Salina y Laguna (salt lake) C4
		Aconcagua, Cerro (mt.) ..C3	Llullaillaco (vol.) C7
		Andes, Cordillera de los (mts.) C2	Magallenes (Magellan) (str.) ..C7

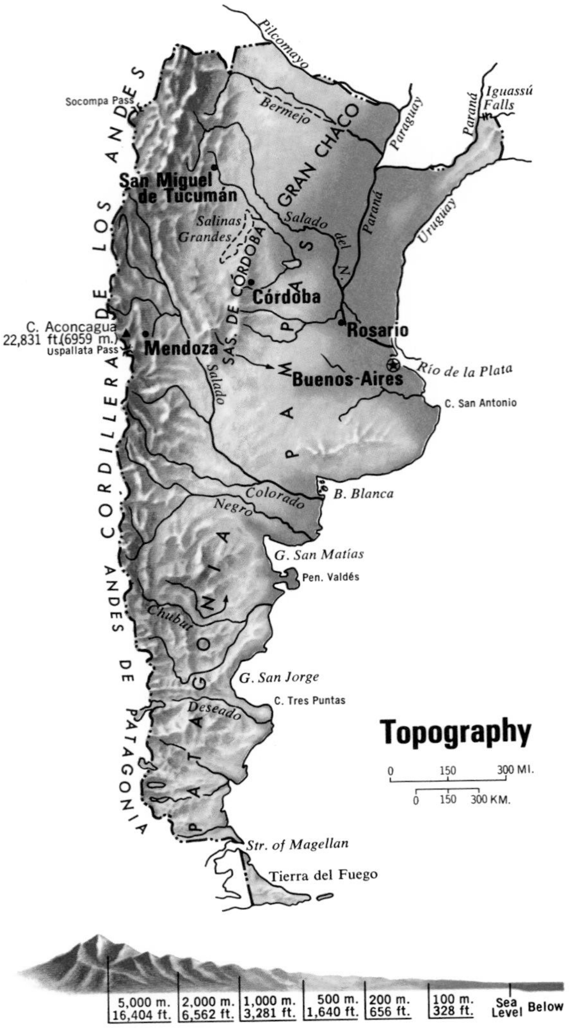

C. Aconcagua
22,831 ft.(6959 m.)
uspallata Pass

Topography

0   150   300 MI.

0   150   300 KM.

| 5,000 m. 16,404 ft. | 2,000 m. 6,562 ft. | 1,000 m. 3,281 ft. | 500 m. 1,640 ft. | 200 m. 656 ft. | 100 m. 328 ft. | Sea Level | Below |

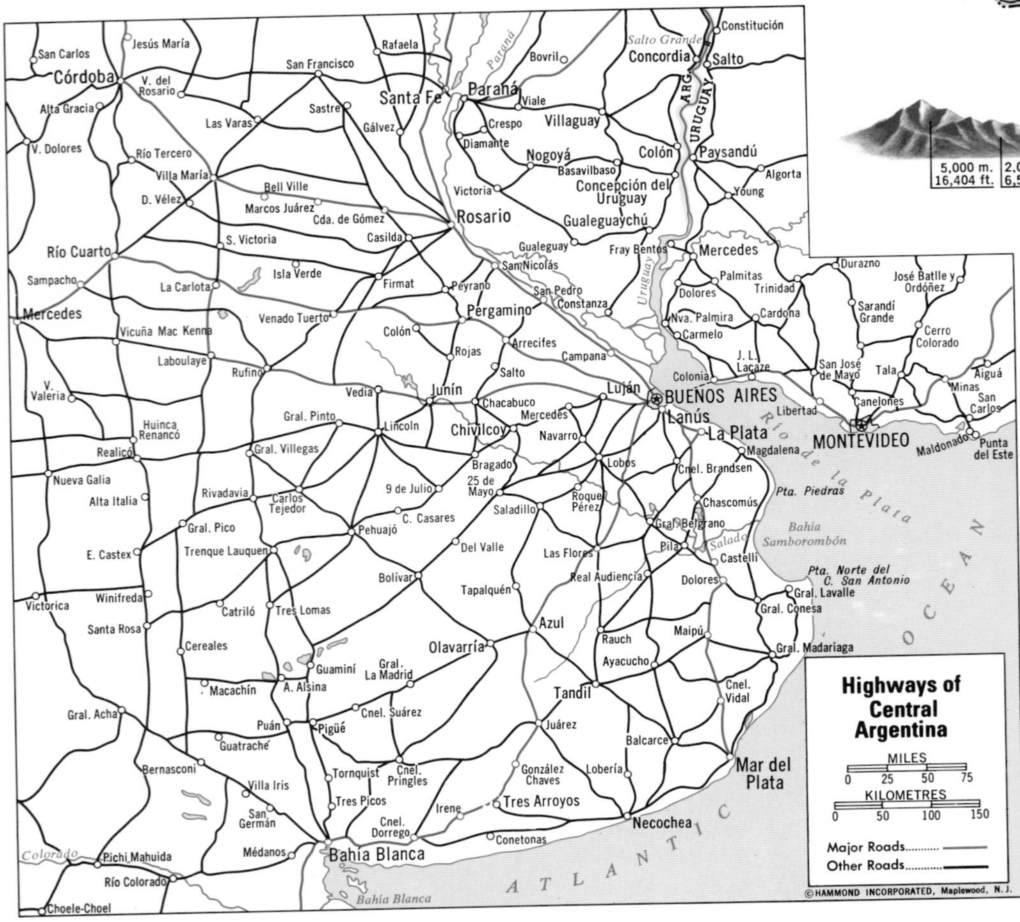

Maipo (vol.) C3		Senguerr (riv.) B6	
Mar Chiquita (lake) D3		Staten (Los Estados) (isl.) ..D7	
Mendoza (riv.) C3		Tarija (riv.) D1	
Mercedario, Cerro (mt.) ..B3		Tercero (riv.) D3	
Mogotes (pt.) E4		Teuco (riv.) D1	
Montemayor (plat.) C5		Tierra del Fuego, Grande de (isl.) C7	
Nahuel Huapi (lake) B5		Toro, Cerro del (mt.) B2	
Nahuel Huapi Nat'l Park ..B5		Tres Puntas (cape) D6	
Negro (riv.) D4		Trinidad (isl.) D4	
Neuquén (riv.) C4		Tronador (mt.) B5	
Ninfas (pt.) D5		Tunuyán (riv.) C3	
Norte (pt.) D5		Tupungato, Cerro (mt.) B3	
Nuevo (gulf) D5		Uruguay (riv.) E3	
Ojos del Salado, Cerro (mt.) ..C2		Valdés (pen.) D5	
Pampa de las Tres Hermanas (plain) C6		Viedma (lake) B6	
Pampas (plain) D4		Zapaleri, Cerro (mt.) C1	
Paraná (riv.) E2			
Patagonia (reg.) C5		**FALKLAND ISLANDS**	
Peteroa (vol.) B4		**CITIES and TOWNS**	
Pilcomayo (riv.) E1		Stanley (cap.) 1,050 ......E7	
Pissis (mt.) C2		**OTHER FEATURES**	
Plata, Río de la (est.) E4		Adventure (sound) E7	
Pueyrredón (lake) B6		Choiseul (sound) D7	
Puna de Atacama (reg.) ..C2		East Falkland (isl.) 1,491 ..E7	
Quinto (riv.) C1		Falkland (sound) D7	
Rincón, Cerro (mt.) D2		Falkland (sound) D7	
Saladillo (riv.) D2		George (isl.) E7	
Salado (riv.) D3		Jason (isls.) D7	
Salado (riv.) H7		Lively (isl.) E7	
Salado del Norte (riv.) D2		Malvinas (Falkland) (isls.) ..D7	
Salí (riv.) C2		Pebble (isl.) E7	
Salto (riv.) F7		Saunders (isl.) D7	
Samborombón (bay) E4		Weddel (isl.) D7	
San Antonio (cape) E4		West Falkland (isl.) 322 ..D7	
San Diego (cape) D7			
San Jorge (gulf) C6		*City and suburbs.	
San Juan (riv.) C3			
San Lorenzo, Cerro (mt.) ..B6			
San Martín (lake) B6			
San Matías (gulf) D5			
Santa Cruz (riv.) B7			

Highways of Central Argentina

MILES
0   25   50   75

KILOMETRES
0   50   100   150

Major Roads ———
Other Roads - - - - -

© HAMMOND INCORPORATED, Maplewood, N.J.

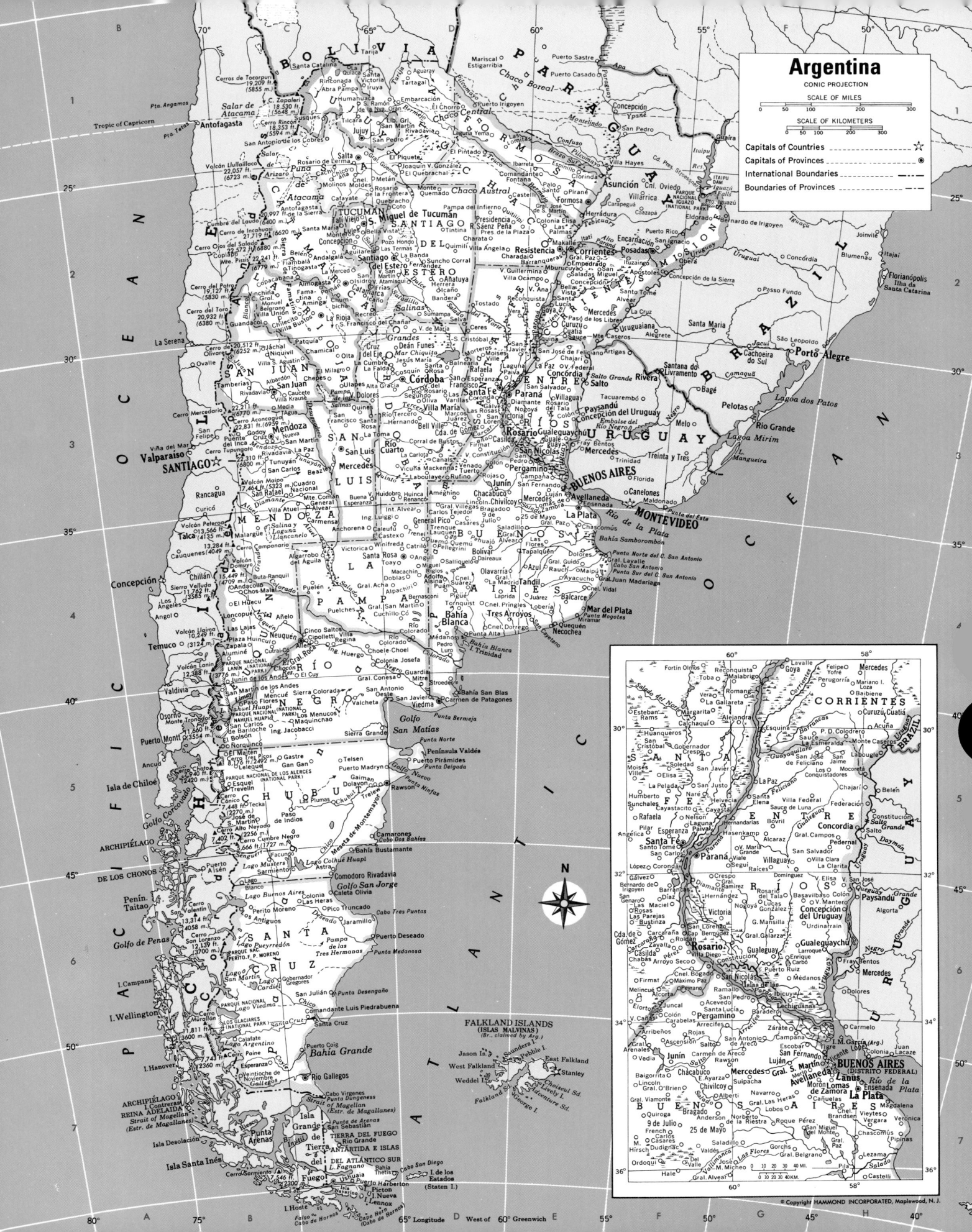

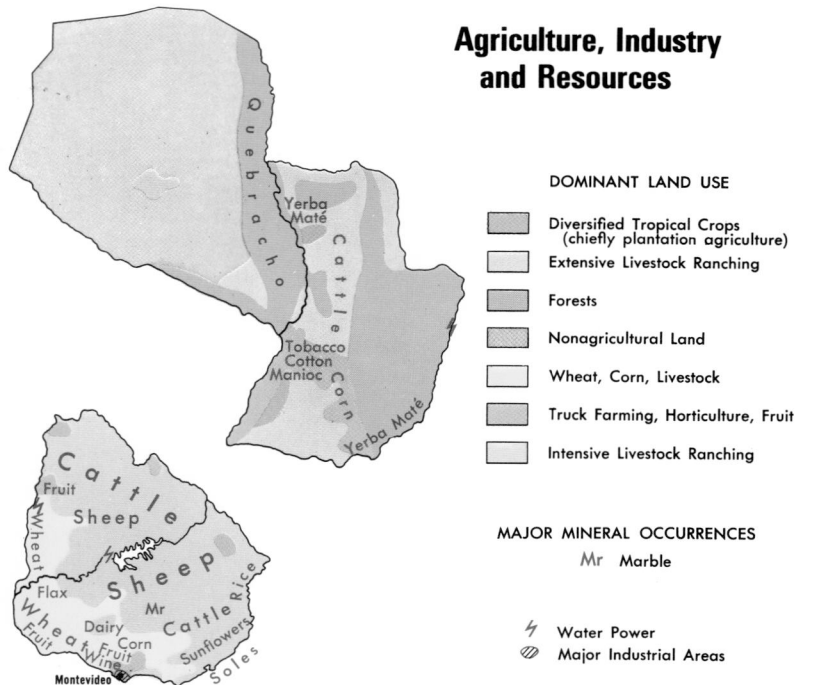

Paraguay
CONIC PROJECTION

SCALE OF MILES
0 20 40 60 80 100 120 140

SCALE OF KILOMETERS
0 20 40 60 80 100 120 140

Capitals of Countries .... ☆
Capitals of Departments .... ◉
International Boundaries .... — — —
Department Boundaries .... —·—·—

© Copyright HAMMOND INCORPORATED, Maplewood, N.J.

PARAGUAY

DEPARTMENTS

Alto Paraguay	C2
Alto Paraná	E4
Amambay	D3
Asunción	A4
Boquerón	B3
Caaguazú	D-E4
Caazapá	D-E5
Canendiyú	E4
Central	A4
Chaco	B-C2
Concepción	D3
Cordillera	D4
Guairá	D4
Itapúa	E5
Misiones	D5
Ñeembucú	C-D5
Nueva Asunción	B2
Paraguarí	D4-5
Presidente Hayes	C3
San Pedro	D4-5

CITIES and TOWNS

Abaí 1,507	E4
Acahay 1,937	D5
Alberdi 2,346	D5
Altos 1,441	B4
Antequera 1,281	D4
Aregua 3,941	B4
Arroyos y Esteros 1,253	B4
Asunción (cap.) 387,676	A4
Atyrá 1,427	B4
Ayolas 309	D5
Belén 1,219	D3
Bella Vista 3,101	D3
Bella Vista 1,421	E5
Benjamín Aceval 2,877	C4
Buena Vista 1,353	D4
Caacupé 7,278	B5
Caaguazú 7,950	D4
Caapucú 1,400	D5
Caazapá 3,132	D5
Caballero 1,225	B5
Capiatá 2,827	B4
Capitán Bado 915	E3
Capitán Meza 375	E5
Caraguatay 1,439	B4
Carapeguá 3,416	B5
Carayaó 1,190	C4
Carmen del Paraná 1,980	D5
Cerrito 958	C5
Ciudad Presidente Stroessner 7,085	E4
Concepción 19,392	D3
Coronel Bogado 3,973	D5
Coronel Martínez 1,598	B5
Coronel Oviedo 13,786	C5
Curuguaty 1,112	E4
Desmochados 551	D5
Doctor Cecilio Báez 1,300	D4
Doctor Juan L. Mallorquín 1,913	E4
Doctor Juan Manuel Frutos 1,494	E4
Doctor M. Irala 468	E4
Emboscada 1,222	B4
Encarnación 23,343	E5
Escobar 548	B5
Eusebio Ayala 4,328	B4
Fernando de la Mora 36,834	B4
Filadelfia 1,438	B3
Fram 1,090	E5
Fuerte Olimpo 3,063	C2
General Artigas 3,542	D5
General Elizardo Aquino 1,304	D4
General Eugenio A. Garay 740	A2
Guarambaré 3,640	B5
Hernandarias 3,898	E4
Hohenau 1,121	E5
Horqueta 4,328	D3
Hugo Stroessner 536	C4
Humaitá 938	C5
Isla Pucú 1,766	B4
Isla Umbú 236	C5
Itá 7,041	B5
Itacurubí 1,997	B5
Itacurubí del Rosario 2,467	D4
Itapé 1,376	C5
Itaquyry	E4
Itauguá 3,767	B5
Iturbe 3,413	C5
Jesús 1,495	E5
Juan de Mena 1,027	D4
La Colmena 1,804	D5
Lambaré 31,656	A4
Laureles 435	D5
Lima 1,098	D3
Limpio 2,219	B4
Loreto 1,258	D3
Luque 13,921	B4
Maciel 376	D5
Mariano Roque Alonso 1,492	A4
Mariscal Estigarribia 3,150	B3
Mayor Martínez 324	C5
Mayor Pablo Lagerenza	B1
Mbocayaty 925	C5
Mbuyapey 1,560	D5
Ñacunday 380	E5
Natalicio Talavera 1,228	D4
Nueva Germania 572	D3
Nueva Italia 1,517	B5
Numí 941	D5
Paraguarí 5,036	B5
Paso de Patria 698	C5
Pedro Juan Caballero 21,033	E3
Pilar 12,506	C5
Pirayú 2,698	B5
Piribebuy 4,497	B5
Primero de Marzo 696	B4
Puerto Casado 4,078	C3
Puerto Guaraní 302	C2
Puerto Pinasco 5,477	C3
Puerto Presidente Franco 4,152	E4
Puerto Sastre 160	C3
Quiindy 2,664	D5
Quyquyhó 928	D5
Roque González de Santa Cruz 1,375	B5
Rosario 4,165	D4
Salto del Guairá	E4
San Antonio 4,906	A5
San Bernardino 949	B5
San Cosme y Damián 602	D5
San Estanislao 4,753	D4
San Ignacio 6,116	D5
San Joaquín 536	C4
San José 3,102	B5
San Juan Bautista 6,457	D5
San Juan Bautista de Ñeembucú 688	C5
San Juan Nepomuceno 2,974	E5
San Lázaro 1,767	D3
San Lorenzo 11,616	B4
San Miguel 1,030	D5
San Patricio 1,130	D5
San Pedro 3,186	D3
San Pedro del Paraná 2,723	D5
San Salvador 1,393	C5
Santa Elena 1,439	B5
Santa María 793	D5
Santa Rosa 3,736	D5
Santiago 1,265	D5
Sapucaí 1,864	B5
Tacuaras 193	C5
Tacuatí 836	D3
Tavaí 472	D5
Tobatí 4,983	B4
Trinidad 837	E5
Unión 1,286	D4
Valenzuela 1,108	B5
Valle Mí 1,318	C2
25 de Diciembre 439	D4
Villa Florida 1,261	D5
Villa Franca 359	C5
Villa Hayes 4,749	A4
Villa Oliva 564	C5
Villarrica 17,687	C5
Villeta 3,156	A5
Yabebyry 797	D5
Yaguarón 3,368	B5
Yataity 1,159	C5
Ybycuí 1,736	B5
Ybytymí 816	B5
Yegros 1,051	D5
Ygatimí 396	E4
Yhú 964	D4
Ypacaraí 5,195	B5
Ygané 1,474	B5
Ypé Jhú 645	E3
Yuty 2,392	D5

OTHER FEATURES

Acaray (riv.)	E4
Alto Paraná (riv.)	D5
Amambay, Cordillera de (mts.)	D-E3
Apa (riv.)	D3
Aquidabán (riv.)	D3
Chaco Boreal (reg.)	B2-3
Chovoreca (mt.)	C1
Confuso (riv.)	C4
Coronel F. Cabrera (mt.)	B1
González, Riacho (riv.)	C3
Gran Chaco (reg.)	B2-3
Iguazú (falls)	E4
Itaipú (res.)	E4
Jara (hill)	C1
Mbaracayú, Cordillera de (mts.)	E4
Monday (riv.)	E4
Montelindo (riv.)	C3
Mosquito, Riacho (riv.)	C3
Negro (riv.)	C4
Paraguay (riv.)	D4
Pilcomayo (riv.)	C4
Tebicuary (riv.)	C5
Tímane (riv.)	B2
Vera (lag.)	D5
Verde (riv.)	C3

Agriculture, Industry and Resources

DOMINANT LAND USE

- Diversified Tropical Crops (chiefly plantation agriculture)
- Extensive Livestock Ranching
- Forests
- Nonagricultural Land
- Wheat, Corn, Livestock
- Truck Farming, Horticulture, Fruit
- Intensive Livestock Ranching

MAJOR MINERAL OCCURRENCES

Mr   Marble

⚡   Water Power

⚙   Major Industrial Areas

Topography

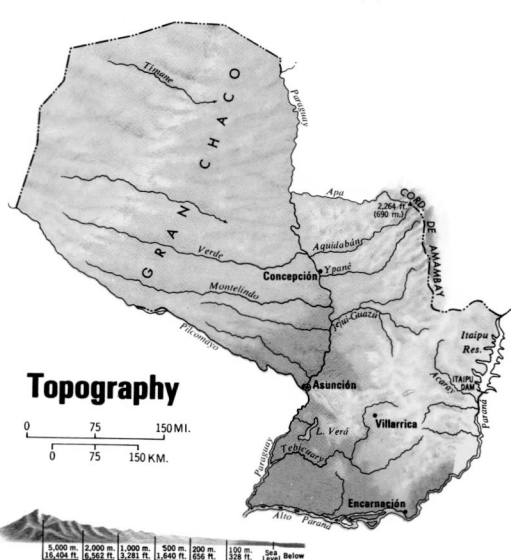

5,000 m. / 16,404 ft. — 2,000 m. / 6,562 ft. — 500 m. / 1,640 ft. — 200 m. / 656 ft. — 100 m. / 328 ft. — Sea Level / Below

0   75   150 MI.
0   75   150 KM.

URUGUAY

DEPARTMENTS

Artigas 52,843 ..... B1
Canelones 258,195 ..... D5
Cerro Largo 71,023 ..... E3
Colonia 105,350 ..... B5
Durazno 53,635 ..... C3
Flores 23,530 ..... C4
Florida 63,987 ..... D4
Lavalleja 65,823 ..... D5
Maldonado 61,259 ..... E5
Montevideo 1,202,757 ..... B7
Paysandú 88,029 ..... B3
Río Negro 46,861 ..... B3
Rivera 77,086 ..... D2
Rocha 55,097 ..... E4
Salto 92,183 ..... B2
San José 79,563 ..... C5
Soriano 77,906 ..... B4
Tacuarembó 76,964 ..... D3
Treinta y Tres 43,419 ..... E4

CITIES and TOWNS

Aceguá 930 ..... E2
Achar 606 ..... C3
Agraciada 638 ..... A4
Aguas Corrientes 992 ..... A6
Aiguá 2,470 ..... E5
Algorta 1,372 ..... B3
Artigas 29,256 ..... C1
Atlántida 2,268 ..... B6
Balneario El Tesoro E5
Balneario La Barra E5
Balneario Solís 288 ..... D5
Baltasar Brum 1,753 ..... B1
Belén 2,129 ..... B1
Bella Unión 7,778 ..... B1
Bernabé Rivera 540 ..... B1
Blanquillo 1,053 ..... D3
Cañada Nieto 503 ..... B4
Canelones 15,938 ..... B6
Cardal 847 ..... C5
Cardona 4,126 ..... B4
Cardozo 143 ..... C3
Carlos Reyles 961 ..... C4
Carmelo 13,631 ..... A4
Carmen 2,318 ..... D4
Carrasco B7
Castillos 6,446 ..... F5
Casupá 2,265 ..... D5
Cebollatí 1,233 ..... F4
Cerrillos 1,690 ..... A6
Cerro Chato, Treinta y Tres 1,850 ..... D4
Chamizo 486 ..... D5
Chuy 4,472 ..... F4
Colón, Lavalleja 367 ..... E4
Colonia 16,895 ..... B5
Colonia Lavalleja C2
Colonia Rossel y Rius 130 ..... D4
Colonia Valdense 2,113 ..... B5
Conchillas 748 ..... B5
Constitución 3,217 ..... A2
Costa Azul 453 ..... E5
Cufré 430 ..... B5
Cuñapirú D2
Curtina 723 ..... C3
Diez y Nueve (19) de Abril 308 ..... E5
Diez y Ocho (18) de Julio 742 ..... F4
Dolores 12,771 ..... A4
Durazno 25,811 ..... C4
Egaña 667 ..... B4
Empalme Olmos 2,084 ..... B6
Estación Atlántida 1,845 ..... B6
Estación Migues 241 ..... C6
Florida 25,030 ..... C5
Fortaleza de Santa Teresa F5
Fraile Muerto 2,468 ..... E3
Fray Bentos 19,569 ..... A4
Fray Marcos 1,573 ..... D5
Garzón 258 ..... E5
General Enrique Martínez 973 ..... F4
Goñi 278 ..... C4
Grecco 447 ..... B3
Guichón 4,720 ..... B3
Ituzaingó 717 ..... A6
Javier de Viana 286 ..... C1
Joanico 692 ..... B6
Joaquín Suárez, Canelones 3,517 ..... B6
José Batlle y Ordóñez 2,044 ..... D4
José Enrique Rodó 1,334 ..... B4
José Pedro Varela 3,541 ..... E4
Juan L. Lacaze 11,133 ..... B5
Julio María Sanz E4
La Bolsa C1
La Coronilla 571 ..... F4
La Cruz 633 ..... C4
La Cuchilla F3
La Floresta C7
La Lata E2
La Paloma 1,558 ..... F5
La Paz, Canelones 14,402 ..... B6
La Paz, Colonia B5
La Pedrera 116 ..... F5
Lascano 6,043 ..... E4
Las Flores 403 ..... D5
La Sierra D5
Las Piedras 53,983 ..... B6
Las Toscas 893 ..... E3
Libertad 6,071 ..... C5
Lorenzo Geyres 474 ..... B3
Mal Abrigo 209 ..... C5
Maldonado 22,159 ..... D6
Mariscala 1,393 ..... E5
Mazangano E3
Melo 38,260 ..... E3
Mercedes 34,667 ..... B4
Merinos 403 ..... C3
Miguelete 533 ..... B5
Migues 2,183 ..... C6
Minas 35,433 ..... D5
Minas de Corrales 2,518 ..... D2
Montes 2,217 ..... D5
Montevideo (cap.) 1,173,254 ..... B7
Nico Pérez D4
Nueva Helvecia 8,598 ..... B5
Nueva Palmira 6,934 ..... A4
Nuevo Berlín 1,970 ..... B3
Ombúes de Lavalle 1,689 ..... B4
Ombúes de Oribe C4
Palmitas 1,332 ..... B4
Pan de Azúcar 4,862 ..... D5
Pando 16,184 ..... B6
Paso de la Laguna, Salto B2
Paso de la Laguna, Tacuarembó D3
Paso de León B1
Paso del Borracho D2
Paso del Cerro 317 ..... C2
Paso de los Toros 13,178 ..... C3
Paso Potrero C2
Paysandú 62,412 ..... A3
Peralta C3
Piedra Sola 233 ..... C3
Piedras Coloradas 487 ..... B3
Piñera 261 ..... C3
Pintado, Artigas C1
Piraraja 774 ..... E4
Piriápolis 5,221 ..... D5
Porvenir 705 ..... B3
Progreso 8,257 ..... B6
Pueblo del Sauce E4
Pueblo Nuevo B2
Punta del Este 6,914 ..... E6
Quebracho 1,514 ..... B2
Reboledo 373 ..... D4
Río Branco 5,697 ..... F3
Rivera 49,013 ..... D1
Rocha 21,612 ..... E5
Rodríguez 1,575 ..... C5
Rosario 8,302 ..... B5
Salto 72,94 ..... B2
San Antonio, Canelones 1,122 ..... B6
San Bautista 1,472 ..... B6
San Carlos 16,883 ..... E5
San Gregorio, San José C4
San Gregorio, Tacuarembó 2,892 ..... D3
San Jacinto 2,292 ..... C6
San Javier 1,583 ..... A3
San José de Mayo 28,427 ..... C5
San Ramón 6,570 ..... D5
San Servando F3
Santa Catalina 885 ..... B4
Santa Clara de Olimar 2,867 ..... D3
Santa Lucía 14,101 ..... B6
Santa Rosa 2,736 ..... B6
Santiago Vázquez 1,323 ..... A7
Sarandí del Yí 6,326 ..... D4
Sarandí de Navarro 259 ..... C3
Sarandí Grande 5,598 ..... C4
Sauce, Canelones 3,942 ..... B6
Sauce del Yí D4
Saucedo B2
Sequeira C1
Solís 356 ..... D5
Solís de Mataojo 1,763 ..... D5
Soriano 1,125 ..... A4
Tacuarembó 34,152 ..... D2
Tala 3,611 ..... D5
Tambores 1,534 ..... C2
Toledo 3,127 ..... B6
Tomás Gomensoro 2,105 ..... B1
Totoral C3
Tranqueras 3,922 ..... D2
Treinta y Tres 25,757 ..... E4
Tres Bocas B2
Tres Islas E3
Trinidad 17,598 ..... B4
Tupambaé 1,039 ..... E3
Unión B7
Valentines 153 ..... E4
Veinticinco (25) de Agosto 1,891 ..... A6
Veinticinco (25) de Mayo 1,744 ..... C5
Velázquez 1,042 ..... E5
Vergara 2,822 ..... E3
Vichadero 1,989 ..... E2
Villa Darwin 507 ..... B4
Villa del Cerro A7
Young 11,080 ..... B3
Zapicán 764 ..... E4
Zapucay D2

OTHER FEATURES

Aiguá (riv.) E4
Alférez (riv.) E5
Arapey Chico (riv.) B1
Arapey Grande (riv.) B2
Belén (range) C1
Bonete (dam) C3
Brava (pt.) B7
Cañas (range) C2
Caraguatá (riv.) D3
Castillos (lag.) F5
Cebollatí (riv.) F4
Cordobés (riv.) D3
Cuareim (riv.) B1
Cuñapirú, Arroyo (riv.) D2
Daymán (range) B2
Daymán (riv.) B2
Durazno, Grande del (range) D4
Espinillo (pt.) A7
Este (pt.) D6
Flores (isl.) D5
Garzón (lag.) E5
Grande (range) D4
Grande, Arroyo (riv.) B4
Grande Inferior (range) C4
Haedo (range) C2
India Muerta (riv.) E4
José Ignacio (lag.) E5
Lobos (isl.) E6
Maciel, Arroyo (riv.) C4
Merín (lag.) F4
Mirador Nacional (mt.) D5
Negra (lag.) F5
Negra (range) D2
Negro (riv.) B4
Negro, Arroyo (riv.) B3
Olimar Grande (riv.) E4
Pando (riv.) B6
Parao (riv.) E3
Plata, La (riv.) B5
Polonio (cape) F5
Quequay Chico (riv.) B3
Quequay Grande (riv.) B3
Río Negro (res.) D3
Rocha (lag.) E5
Salto Grande (falls) A2
San José (riv.) C4
San Miguel (swamp) F4
San Salvador (riv.) B4
Santa Ana (range) D2
Santa Lucía (riv.) D5
Santa Lucía Chico (riv.) D4
Santa María (cape) F5
Sauce (lag.) D5
Sopas, Arroyo (riv.) C2
Tacuarembó (riv.) D2
Tacuarí (riv.) E3
Tigre (isl.) A7
Uruguay (riv.) A3
Yaguarón (riv.) F3
Yí (riv.) B4

PARAGUAY

AREA 157,047 sq. mi. (406,752 sq. km.)
POPULATION 2,973,000
CAPITAL Asunción
LARGEST CITY Asunción
HIGHEST POINT Amambay Range 2,264 ft. (690 m.)
MONETARY UNIT guaraní
MAJOR LANGUAGES Spanish, Guaraní
MAJOR RELIGION Roman Catholicism

URUGUAY

AREA 72,172 sq. mi. (186,925 sq. km.)
POPULATION 2,899,000
CAPITAL Montevideo
LARGEST CITY Montevideo
HIGHEST POINT Mirador Nacional 1,644 ft. (501 m.)
MONETARY UNIT Uruguayan peso
MAJOR LANGUAGE Spanish
MAJOR RELIGION Roman Catholicism

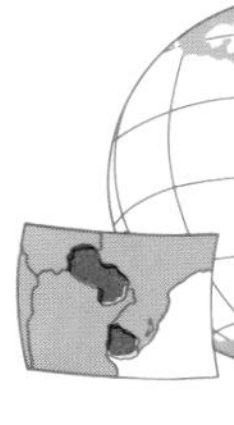

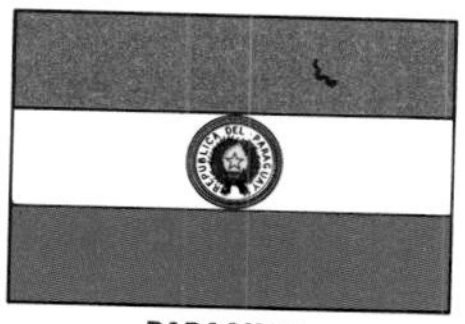

PARAGUAY

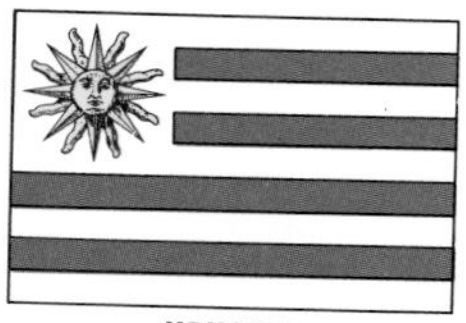

URUGUAY

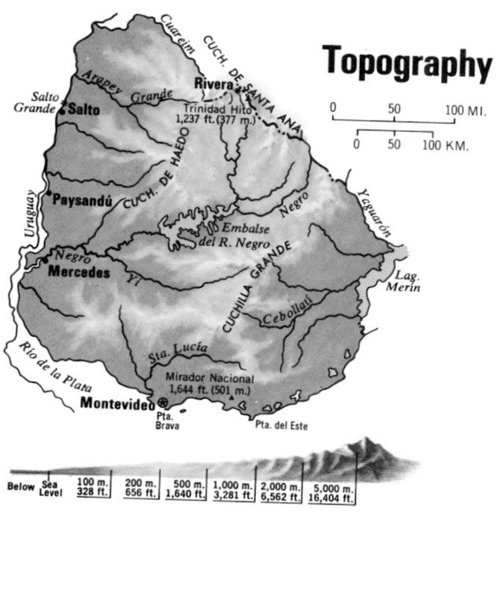
Topography
0 50 100 MI.
0 50 100 KM.
Salto
Rivera
Paysandú
Mercedes
Montevideo
Mirador Nacional 1,644 ft. (501 m.)
Trinidad Hito 1,237 ft. (377 m.)
Below Sea Level
100 m. 328 ft.
200 m. 656 ft.
500 m. 1,640 ft.
1,000 m. 3,281 ft.
2,000 m. 6,562 ft.
5,000 m. 16,404 ft.

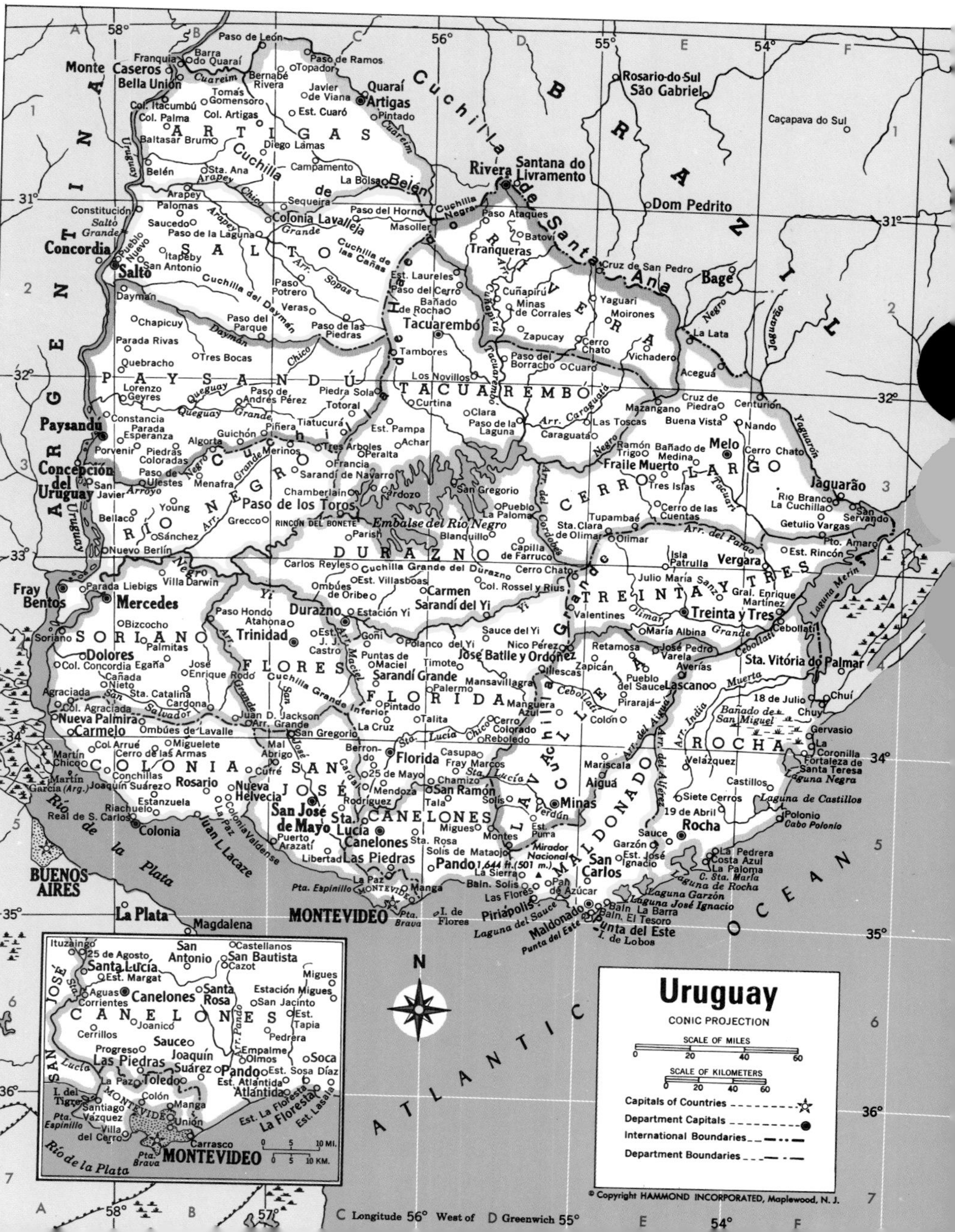
Uruguay
CONIC PROJECTION
SCALE OF MILES
0 20 40 60
SCALE OF KILOMETERS
0 20 40 60
Capitals of Countries
Department Capitals
International Boundaries
Department Boundaries
MONTEVIDEO
BUENOS AIRES
ATLANTIC OCEAN
Longitude 56° West of Greenwich 55°
© Copyright HAMMOND INCORPORATED, Maplewood, N. J.

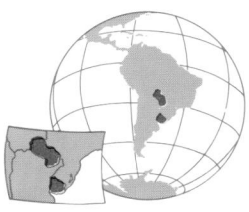

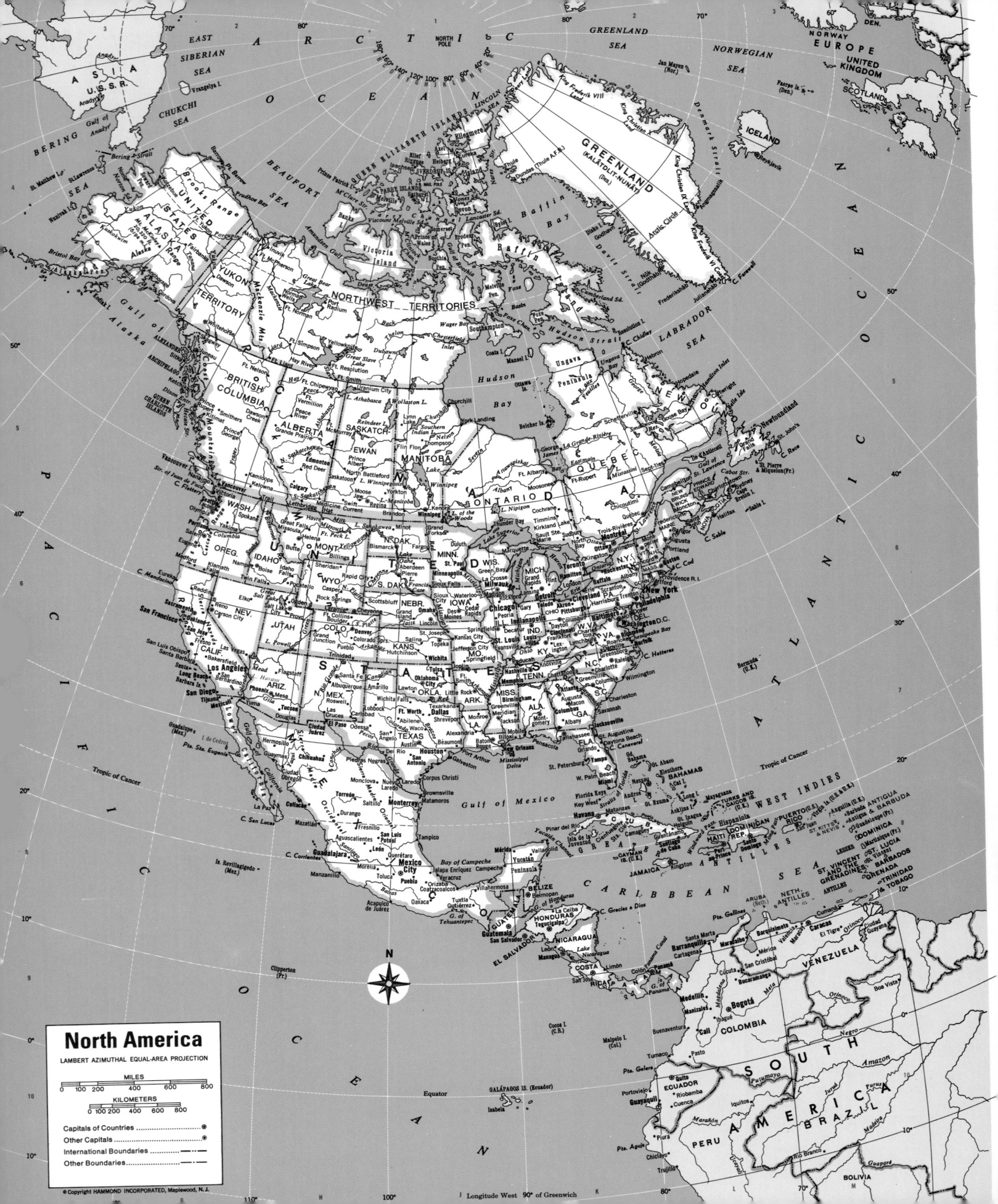

Population Distribution

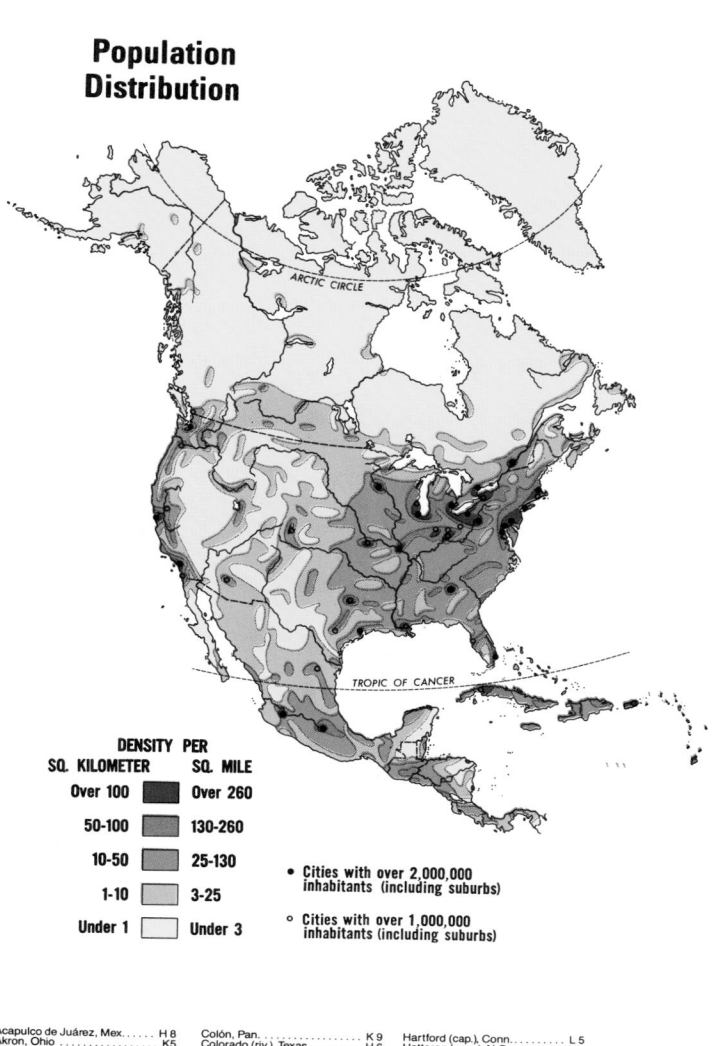

AREA 9,363,000 sq. mi.
(24,250,170 sq. km.)
POPULATION 370,000,000
LARGEST CITY New York
HIGHEST POINT Mt. McKinley 20,320 ft.
(6,194 m.)
LOWEST POINT Death Valley -282 ft.
(-86 m.)

Vegetation

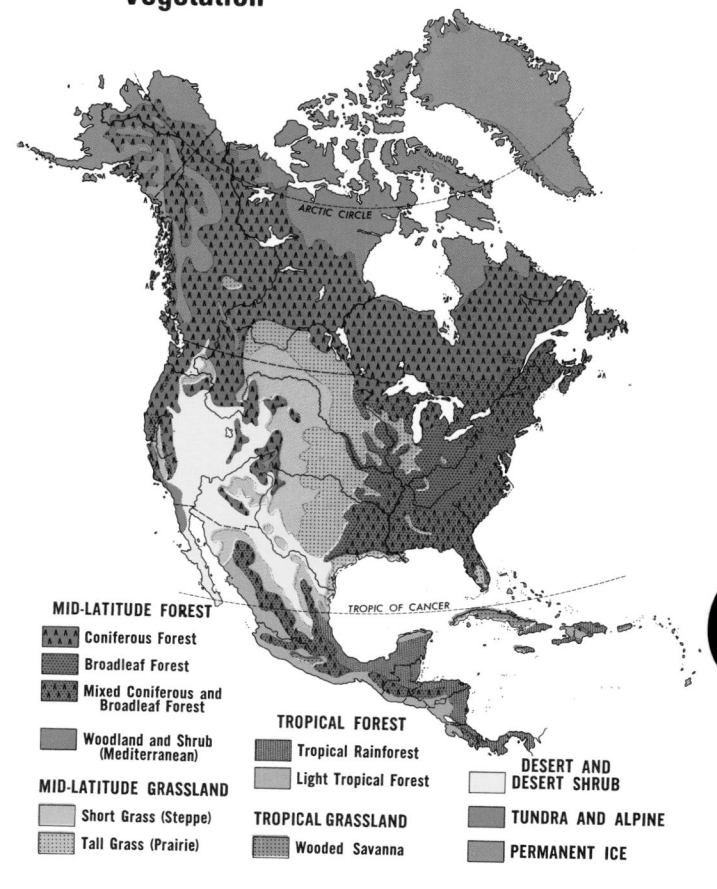

DENSITY PER

SQ. KILOMETER	SQ. MILE
Over 100	Over 260
50-100	130-260
10-50	25-130
1-10	3-25
Under 1	Under 3

• Cities with over 2,000,000 inhabitants (including suburbs)
○ Cities with over 1,000,000 inhabitants (including suburbs)

MID-LATITUDE FOREST
- Coniferous Forest
- Broadleaf Forest
- Mixed Coniferous and Broadleaf Forest
- Woodland and Shrub (Mediterranean)

MID-LATITUDE GRASSLAND
- Short Grass (Steppe)
- Tall Grass (Prairie)

TROPICAL FOREST
- Tropical Rainforest
- Light Tropical Forest

TROPICAL GRASSLAND
- Wooded Savanna

DESERT AND DESERT SHRUB

TUNDRA AND ALPINE

PERMANENT ICE

NORTH AMERICA

Average January Temperature

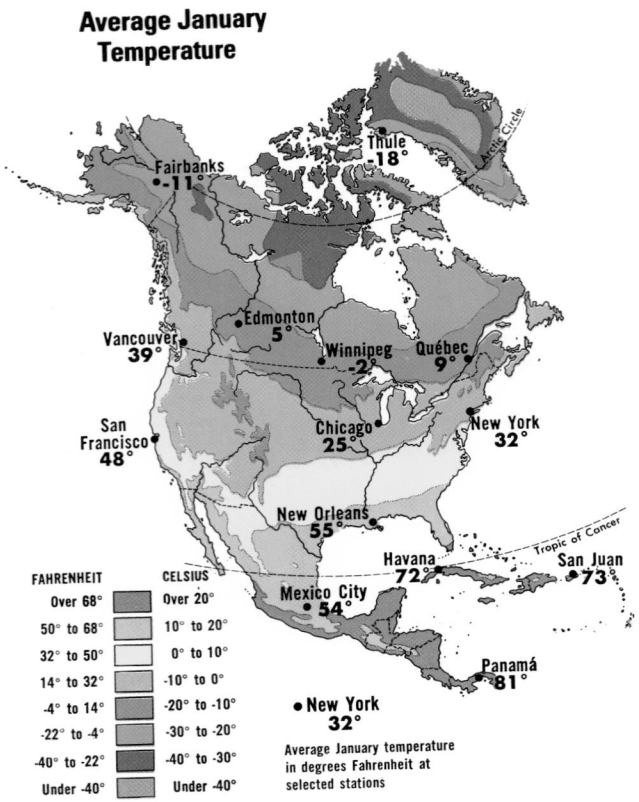

Thule
-18°

Fairbanks
-11°

Edmonton
5°

Vancouver
39°

Winnipeg
-2°

Québec
9°

San Francisco
48°

Chicago
25°

New York
32°

New Orleans
55°

Havana
72°

San Juan
73°

Mexico City
54°

Panamá
81°

FAHRENHEIT	CELSIUS
Over 68°	Over 20°
50° to 68°	10° to 20°
32° to 50°	0° to 10°
14° to 32°	-10° to 0°
-4° to 14°	-20° to -10°
-22° to -4°	-30° to -20°
-40° to -22°	-40° to -30°
Under -40°	Under -40°

● New York
32°

Average January temperature in degrees Fahrenheit at selected stations

Average July Temperature

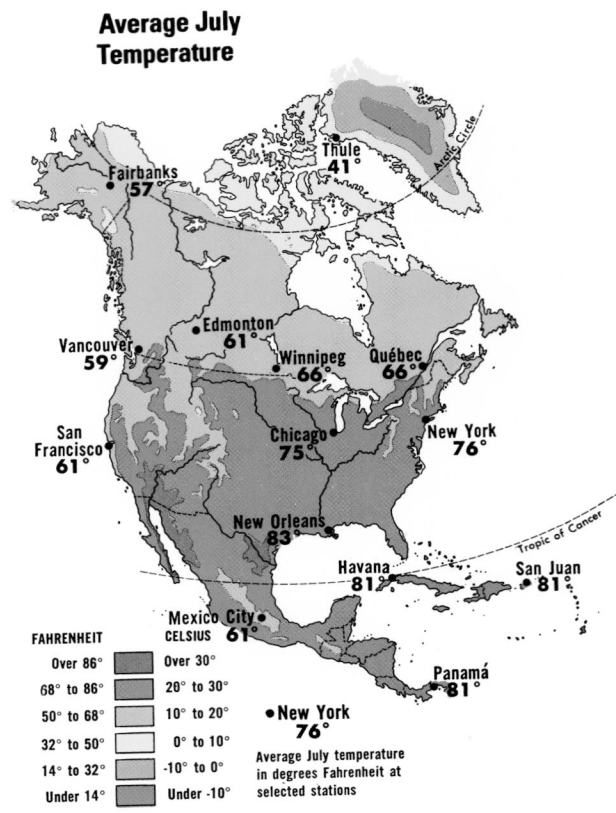

Thule
41°

Fairbanks
57°

Edmonton
61°

Vancouver
59°

Winnipeg
66°

Québec
66°

San Francisco
61°

Chicago
75°

New York
76°

New Orleans
83°

Havana
81°

San Juan
81°

Mexico City
61°

Panamá
81°

FAHRENHEIT	CELSIUS
Over 86°	Over 30°
68° to 86°	20° to 30°
50° to 68°	10° to 20°
32° to 50°	0° to 10°
14° to 32°	-10° to 0°
Under 14°	Under -10°

● New York
76°

Average July temperature in degrees Fahrenheit at selected stations

Rainfall

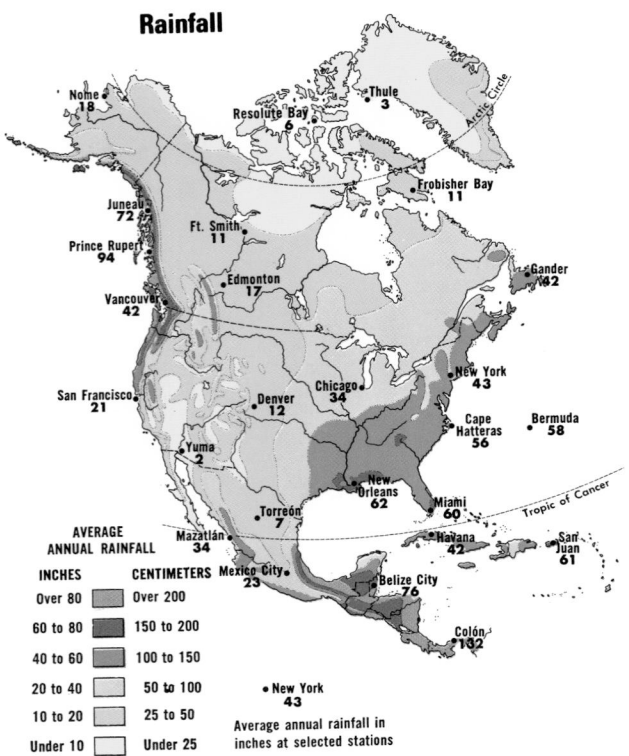

Nome
18

Thule
3

Resolute Bay
5

Frobisher Bay
11

Juneau
72

Ft. Smith
11

Prince Rupert
94

Gander
62

Vancouver
42

Edmonton
17

San Francisco
21

Chicago
34

Denver
12

New York
43

Cape Hatteras
56

Bermuda
58

Yuma
2

Torreón
7

New Orleans
62

Miami
60

Mazatlán
34

Havana
42

San Juan
61

Mexico City
23

Belize City
76

Colón
132

AVERAGE ANNUAL RAINFALL

INCHES	CENTIMETERS
Over 80	Over 200
60 to 80	150 to 200
40 to 60	100 to 150
20 to 40	50 to 100
10 to 20	25 to 50
Under 10	Under 25

● New York
43

Average annual rainfall in inches at selected stations

Vegetation/Relief

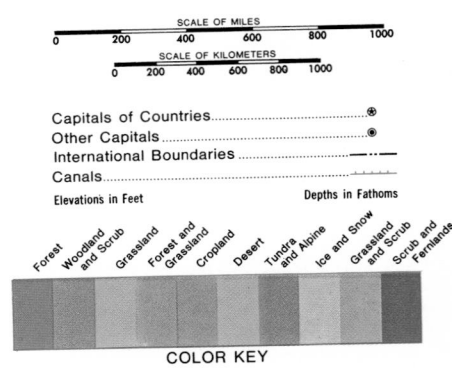

SCALE OF MILES
0 200 400 600 800 1000

SCALE OF KILOMETERS
0 200 400 600 800 1000

Capitals of Countries.............................⊕
Other Capitals..◉
International Boundaries.......................
Canals...

Elevations in Feet   Depths in Fathoms

Forest | Woodland and Scrub | Grassland | Forest and Grassland | Cropland | Desert | Tundra and Alpine | Ice and Snow | Grassland and Scrub | Scrub and Fernlands

COLOR KEY

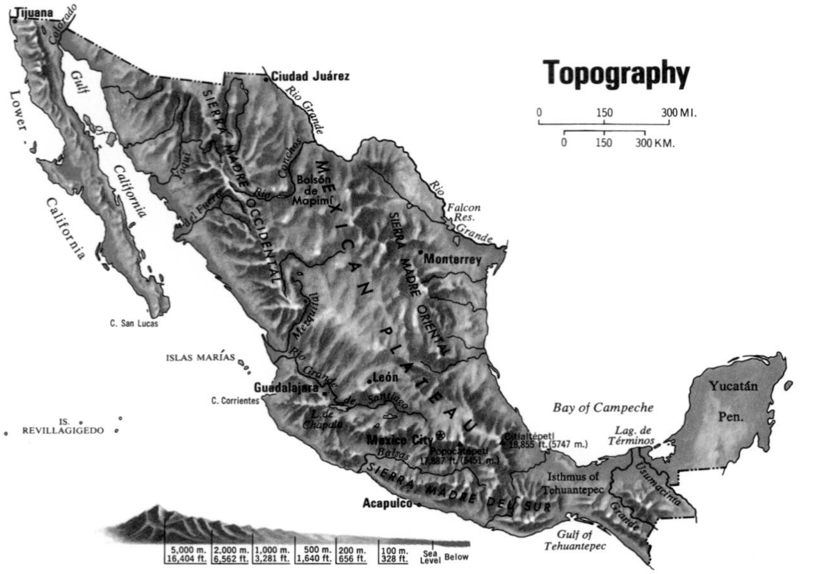

STATES

Aguascalientes 504,300 H6
Baja California 1,227,400 B1
Baja California Sur 221,000 C3
Campeche 371,800 O7
Chiapas 2,097,500 N8
Chihuahua 1,935,100 F2
Coahuila 1,561,000 H3
Colima 339,400 G7
Distrito Federal 9,377,300 L1
Durango 1,160,300 G4
Guanajuato 3,045,600 J6
Guerrero 2,174,200 J8
Hidalgo 1,518,200 K6
Jalisco 4,296,500 H6
México 7,542,300 K7
Michoacán 3,049,400 H7
Morelos 931,400 K7
Nayarit 729,500 G6
Nuevo León 2,463,500 K4
Oaxaca 2,517,500 L8
Puebla 3,285,300 L7
Querétaro 730,900 J6
Quintana Roo 209,900 P7
San Luis Potosí 1,669,900 J5
Sinaloa 1,882,200 F4
Sonora 1,498,100 D2
Tabasco 1,150,000 N7
Tamaulipas 1,924,900 K4
Tlaxcala 548,500 N1
Veracruz 5,263,800 L7
Yucatán 1,034,300 P6
Zacatecas 1,144,700 H5

CITIES and TOWNS

Acala 11,483 N8
Acámbaro 32,257 J7
Acaponeta 11,844 G5
Acapulco de Juárez 309,254 K8
Acatlán de Osorio 7,624 K7
Acatzingo de Hidalgo 6,905 N2
Acayucan 21,173 M8
Aconchi 1,596 D2
Actopan, Hidalgo 11,037 K6
Actopan, Veracruz 2,265 Q1
Agua Dulce 21,060 M7
Agualeguas 2,502 J3
Agua Prieta 20,754 E1
Aguascalientes 181,277 H6
Aguililla 5,715 H7
Ahome 4,182 E4
Ahuacatitlán 6,436 L1
Ahuacatlán 5,350 G6
Ahumada 6,466 F1
Ajalpan 8,238 L7
Alamo 9,954 L6
Álamos 4,269 E3
Aldama, Chihuahua 6,047 G2
Aldama, Tamaulipas 3,033 L5
Aljojuca 3,204 O1
Allende, Coahuila 11,076 J2
Allende, Nuevo León 9,914 J4
Almoloya del Río 3,714 K1
Altamira 6,053 L5
Altar 2,519 D1
Altepexi 6,661 L7
Alto Lucero 3,698 P1
Altotonga 6,754 P1
Alvarado 15,592 M7
Amatlán de los Reyes 3,664 P2
Amealco 2,960 K6
Ameca 21,018 H6
Amecameca de Juárez 16,276 L1
Amozoc de Mota 9,203 N2
Anáhuac, Chihuahua 10,886 F2
Anáhuac, Nuevo León 8,168 J3
Angostura 2,663 E4
Antiguo Morelos 1,569 K5
Apan 13,705 M1
Apatzingán de la Constitución 44,849 H7
Apizaco 21,189 N1
Aquiles Serdán 2,565 G2
Aramberri 1,786 J5
Arandas 18,934 H6
Arcelia 10,024 J7
Ario de Rosales 8,774 J7
Arizpe 1,736 D1
Armería 10,616 G7
Arriaga 13,193 N8
Arteaga 5,324 H7
Ascensión 4,104 E1
Asunción Nochixtlán 3,235 L8
Atlixco 41,967 M2
Atotonilco el Alto 16,271 H6
Atoyac de Álvarez 8,874 J8
Autlán de Navarro 20,398 G7
Axochiapan 8,283 M2
Ayutla de los Libres 3,618 K8
Azcapotzalco 534,554 L1
Azoyú 3,446 K8
Bacadéhuachi 1,514 E2
Bacalar 2,121 P7
Bachíniva 1,809 F2
Bácum 2,668 D3
Bahía Tortugas 1,457 B3
Balancán de Domínguez 3,669 O8
Bamoa 5,866 E4
Banderilla 3,488 P1
Baviácora 2,049 E2
Benjamín Hill 5,366 D1
Bernardino de Sahagún 12,327 M1
Boca del Río 2,354 Q2
Bolonchén de Rejón 2,342 O7
Buenaventura 3,924 F2
Burgos 673 K4
Cabo San Lucas 1,534 E5
Cacahoatán 5,079 N9
Cadereyta Jiménez 13,586 K4
Calkiní 6,870 O6
Calnali 3,318 K6
Calpulálpan 8,659 M1
Calvillo 6,453 H6
Campeche 69,506 O7
Cananea 17,518 D1
Canatlán 5,983 G4
Cancún 326 Q6
Candela 1,689 J3
Candelaria 1,982 O7
Cañitas de Felipe Pescador 4,885 H5
Capulhuac de Mirafuentes 8,289 K1
Carbo 2,804 D2
Cárdenas, San Luis Potosí 12,020 K6
Cárdenas, Tabasco 15,643 N8
Carichic 1,520 F2
Castaños 8,996 J3
Catemaco 11,786 M7
Ceballos 2,937 H3
Cedral 4,057 J5
Celaya 79,977 J6
Celestún 1,490 O6
Cerritos 10,421 J5
Cerro Azul 20,259 L6
Chahuites 5,218 M8
Chalchihuites 1,894 G5
Chalco de Díaz Covarrubias 12,172 M1
Champotón 6,606 O7
Charcas 10,491 J5
Chetumal 23,685 Q7
Chiapa de Corzo 8,571 N8
Chiautempan 12,327 N1
Chietla 4,602 M2
Chignahuapan 3,805 N1
Chihuahua 327,313 F2
Chilapa de Álvarez 9,204 K8
Chilpancingo de los Bravos 36,193 K8
China, Nuevo León 4,958 K4
Chocomán 5,114 P2
Choix 2,503 E3
Cholula de Rivadavia 15,399 M1
Cihuatlán 9,451 G7
Cintalapa de Figueroa 12,036 N8
Ciudad Acuña (Villa Acuña) 30,276 J2
Ciudad Altamirano 8,694 J7
Ciudad Camargo, Chihuahua 24,030 G3
Ciudad Camargo, Tamaulipas 5,953 K3
Ciudad del Carmen 34,656 N7
Ciudad Delicias 52,446 G2
Ciudad del Maíz 5,241 K5
Ciudad de Río Grande 11,651 H5
Ciudad Guerrero 3,110 F2
Ciudad Guzmán 48,166 H7
Ciudad Hidalgo, Chiapas 4,105 N9
Ciudad Hidalgo, Michoacán 24,692 J7
Ciudad Juárez 424,135 F1
Ciudad Lerdo 19,803 H4
Ciudad Madero 115,302 L5
Ciudad Mante 51,247 K5
Ciudad Mendoza 18,696 O2
Ciudad Miguel Alemán 11,259 K3
Ciudad Obregón 144,795 E3
Ciudad Río Bravo 39,018 K4
Ciudad Satélite 35,083 L1
Ciudad Serdán 9,581 O2
Ciudad Valles 47,587 K5
Ciudad Victoria 83,897 K5
Coalcomán de Matamoros 4,875 H7
Coatepec 21,542 P1
Coatetelco 5,268 L2
Coatzacoalcos 69,753 M7
Coatzingo 3,038 N2
Cocorit 4,478 E3
Colima 58,450 H7
Colón 3,346 K6
Colotlán 6,135 H5
Comala 5,592 H7
Comalcalco 14,963 N7
Comitán de Domínguez 21,249 O8
Compostela 9,801 G6
Concepción del Oro 8,144 J4
Concordia 3,947 G5
Contla 7,517 N1
Copala 3,783 K8
Coquimatlán 6,212 G7
Córdoba 78,495 P2
Cosalá 2,279 F4
Cosamaloapan de Carpio 19,766 M7
Cosautlán de Carvajal 2,039 P1
Coscomatepec de Bravo 6,023 P2
Cosío 2,680 H5
Costa Rica 11,795 F4
Cotija de la Paz 9,178 H7
Coyoacán 339,446 L1
Coyotepec 8,888 L1
Coyuca de Benítez 6,328 J8
Coyuca de Catalán 2,926 J7
Coyutla 3,726 L6
Cozumel 5,858 Q6
Creel 2,449 E3
Cuatrociénagas de Carranza 5,523 H3
Cuauhtémoc 26,598 F2
Cuautepec de Hinojosa 5,501 K6
Cuautitlán de Romero Rubio 11,439 L1
Cuautla Morelos 13,946 L2
Cuencamé de Ceniceros 3,774 H4
Cuernavaca 239,813 L2
Cuicatlán 2,733 L8
Cuitlahuac 4,813 P2
Culiacán 228,001 F4
Cumpas 2,395 E1
Cunduacán 4,397 N7
Dimas 2,194 F5
Doctor Arroyo 4,290 K5
Dolores Hidalgo de la Independencia Naci 16,849 J6
Durango 182,633 G1
Dzibalchén 1,917 P7
Dzidzantún 7,064 P6
Dzitbalché 4,393 P6
Ebano 17,489 K5
Ecatepec de Morelos 11,899 L1
Ejutla de Crespo 5,263 L8
Eldorado 8,115 E4
El Fuerte 7,179 E3
El Porvenir 3,030 G1
El Potosí 2,032 J4
El Salto 7,818 G5
El Zacatón 2,686 J5
Empalme 24,927 D2
Encarnación de Díaz 10,474 H6
Ensenada 77,687 A1
Escalón 2,998 G3
Escarcega 7,248 O7
Escuinapa de Hidalgo 16,442 G5
Escuintla 4,111 N9
Esperanza, Puebla 4,258 O2
Esperanza, Sonora 11,762 E3
Espita 5,394 Q6
Esqueda 1,458 E1
Etchojoa 4,398 E3
Ezequiel Montes 3,139 K6
Fortín de las Flores 9,358 P2
Francisco I. Madero 12,613 H4
Fresnillo de González Echererría 44,475 H5
Frontera 10,066 N7
Galeana, Nuevo León 3,429 J4
General Bravo 2,894 K4
General Cepeda 3,486 J4
General Terán 5,354 K4
Gómez Farías 3,030 F2
Gómez Palacio 79,650 G4
González 6,440 K5
Guadalajara 1,478,383 H6
Guadalajara* 2,343,034 H6
Guadalupe, Nuevo León 51,899 K4
Guadalupe, Zacatecas 13,246 H5
Guadalupe Bravo 3,333 F1
Guadalupe Victoria, Durango 7,931 H4
Guadalupe Victoria, Puebla 3,946 O1
Guamúchil 17,151 E4
Guanajuato 36,809 J6
Guasave 26,080 E4
Guaymas 57,492 D3
Gustavo Díaz Ordaz 10,154 K3
Gutiérrez Zamora 9,099 L6
Halachó 4,804 O6
Hecelchakán 4,279 O6
Hermosillo 232,691 D2
Heroica Caborca 20,771 C1
Heroica Nogales 52,108 D1
Hidalgo, Tamaulipas 2,450 K4
Hidalgo del Parral (Parral) 57,619 G3
Hopelchén 3,699 P7
Huajuapan de León 13,822 L8
Huamantla 15,565 N1
Huaquechula 2,294 M2
Huatabampo 18,506 D3
Huatusco de Chicuellar 9,501 P2
Huauchinango 16,826 L6
Huautla de Jiménez 6,132 L7
Huehuetlán el Chico 2,667 M2
Huejotzingo 8,552 M1
Huejutla 6,854 K6
Huetamo 9,333 J7
Hueyotlipan de Hidalgo 2,353 M1
Huimanguillo 7,075 N8
Huitzilán 3,573 O1
Huitzuco de los Figueroa 9,406 K7
Huixcolotla 4,039 N2
Huixtepec 5,927 L8
Huixtla 15,737 N9
Hunucmá 8,020 O6
Ignacio de la Llave 3,962 Q2
Iguala de la Independencia 45,355 K7
Imuris 1,958 D1
Irapuato 135,596 J6
Isla Mujeres 2,663 Q6
Isla, Veracruz 8,075 M7
Ixmiquilpan 6,048 K6
Ixtapa J8
Ixtapalapa 522,095 L1
Ixtenco 5,035 N1
Ixtepec 14,025 M8
Ixtlán del Río 10,986 G6
Izamal 9,749 P6
Izúcar de Matamoros 21,164 M2
Jala 4,535 G6
Jalacingo 3,427 P1
Jalapa Enríquez 161,352 P1
Jalpa 9,904 H6
Jalpa de Méndez 4,785 N7
Jalpan 1,878 K6
Jáltipan de Morelos 15,170 M8
Jantetelco 2,015 L2
Jaumave 3,072 K5
Jerez de García Salinas 20,325 H5
Jico 7,269 P1
Jilotepec de Abasolo 4,252 K7
Jiménez, Chihuahua 18,095 G3
Joachín 3,918 Q2
Jojutla de Juárez 14,438 L2
Jonacatepec 3,868 M2
Jonuta 2,746 N7
José Cardel 5,396 Q1
Juan Aldama 9,667 H4
Juchipila 6,328 H6
Juchitán de Zaragoza 30,218 M8
Kantunilkin 1,970 Q6
La Barca 18,055 H6
La Barra de Navidad 1,829 G7
La Concordia 3,559 N9
La Cruz, Sinaloa 4,218 F5
Lagos de Moreno 33,782 J6
La Huerta 4,328 G7
La Paz, Baja California Sur 46,011 D5
La Paz, San Luis Potosí 3,735 J5
La Piedad Cavadas 34,963 H6
Las Choapas 20,166 M7
Las Hadas G7
Las Nieves 2,262 G3
Las Rosas 7,658 N8
León 468,887 J6
Lerdo de Tejada 11,628 M8
Lerma 4,158 O7
Libres 4,830 O1
Linares 24,456 K4
Llera de Canales 3,564 K5
Loma Bonita 15,804 M7
Loreto, Baja California 2,570 D4
Loreto, Zacatecas 7,132 J5
Los Mochis 67,953 E4
Los Reyes de Salgado 19,452 H7
Macuspana 12,293 N8
Madera 9,759 F2
Magdalena de Kino 10,281 D1
Maltrata 5,457 O2
Manzanillo 20,777 G7
Mapastepec 5,907 N9
Mapimí 2,737 G4
Martínez de la Torre 17,203 L6
Mascota 5,674 G6
Matamoros, Coahuila 15,125 H4
Matamoros, Tamaulipas 165,124 L4
Matehuala 28,799 J5
Matías Romero 13,200 M8
Maxcanú 6,505 O6
Mazatlán 147,010 F5
Melchor Múzquiz 18,868 H3
Melchor Ocampo del Balsas 4,766 H8
Meoquí 12,308 G2
Mérida 233,912 P6
Metepec 4,625 M2
Metlatonoc 1,870 K8
Mexicali 317,228 B1
Mexico City (cap.) 9,377,300 L1
Mexico City* 13,993,866 L1
Miacatlán 3,980 K2
Mier 5,636 K3
Miguel Auza 9,303 H4
Minatitlán 68,397 M8
Mineral del Monte 8,887 K6
Miquihuana 1,971 J5
Misantla 8,799 P1
Miahuatlán de Porfirio Díaz 5,714 L8
Mocorito 3,993 F4
Moctezuma, San Luis Potosí 1,734 J5
Moctezuma, Sonora 2,700 E2
Monclova 78,134 J3
Montemorelos 18,642 K4
Monterrey 1,006,221 J4
Monterrey* 1,923,402 J4
Morelia 199,099 J7
Morelos 4,241 J2
Morelos Cañada 2,288 O2
Moroleón 25,620 J6
Motozintla de Mendoza 4,682 N9
Motul de Felipe Carillo Puerto 12,949 P6
Muna 5,491 P6
Naco 3,580 D1
Nacozari 2,976 E1
Nadadores 2,461 H3
Naica 7,190 G2
Namiquipa 4,875 F2
Nanacamilpa 6,356 M1
Naolinco de Victoria 4,365 P1
Naranjos 14,732 L6
Naucalpan de Juárez 9,425 L1
Nautla 1,935 L6
Nava 4,097 J2
Navojoa 43,817 E3
Navolato 12,799 E4
Nazas 2,881 G4
Netzahualcóyotl 580,436 L1
Nieves 3,966 H5
Nochistlán 8,780 H6
Nogales 14,254 P2
Nombre de Dios 3,188 G5
Nopalucan de la Granja 3,002 O1
Nueva Casas Grandes 20,023 F1
Nueva Ciudad Guerrero 3,300 K3
Nueva Italia de Ruiz 14,718 J7
Nueva Rosita 34,706 J2
Nuevo Ideal 5,252 G4
Nuevo Laredo 184,622 J3
Oaxaca de Juárez 114,948 L8
Ocampo, Coahuila 1,613 H3
Ocampo, Tamaulipas 4,801 K5
Ocosingo 2,946 O8
Ocotlán 35,361 H6
Ocotlán de Morelos 5,882 L8
Ojinaga 12,757 G2
Ojocaliente 7,582 H5
Ometepec 7,342 K8
Oriental 6,009 O1
Orizaba 105,150 P2
Otumba de Gómez Farías 3,198 M1
Oxkutzcab 8,182 P6
Ozuluama 2,851 L6
Ozumba de Alzate 6,876 M1
Pachuca de Soto 83,892 K6
Padilla 4,581 K5
Palenque 2,595 O8
Palizada 2,332 O7
Palomas 2,129 F1

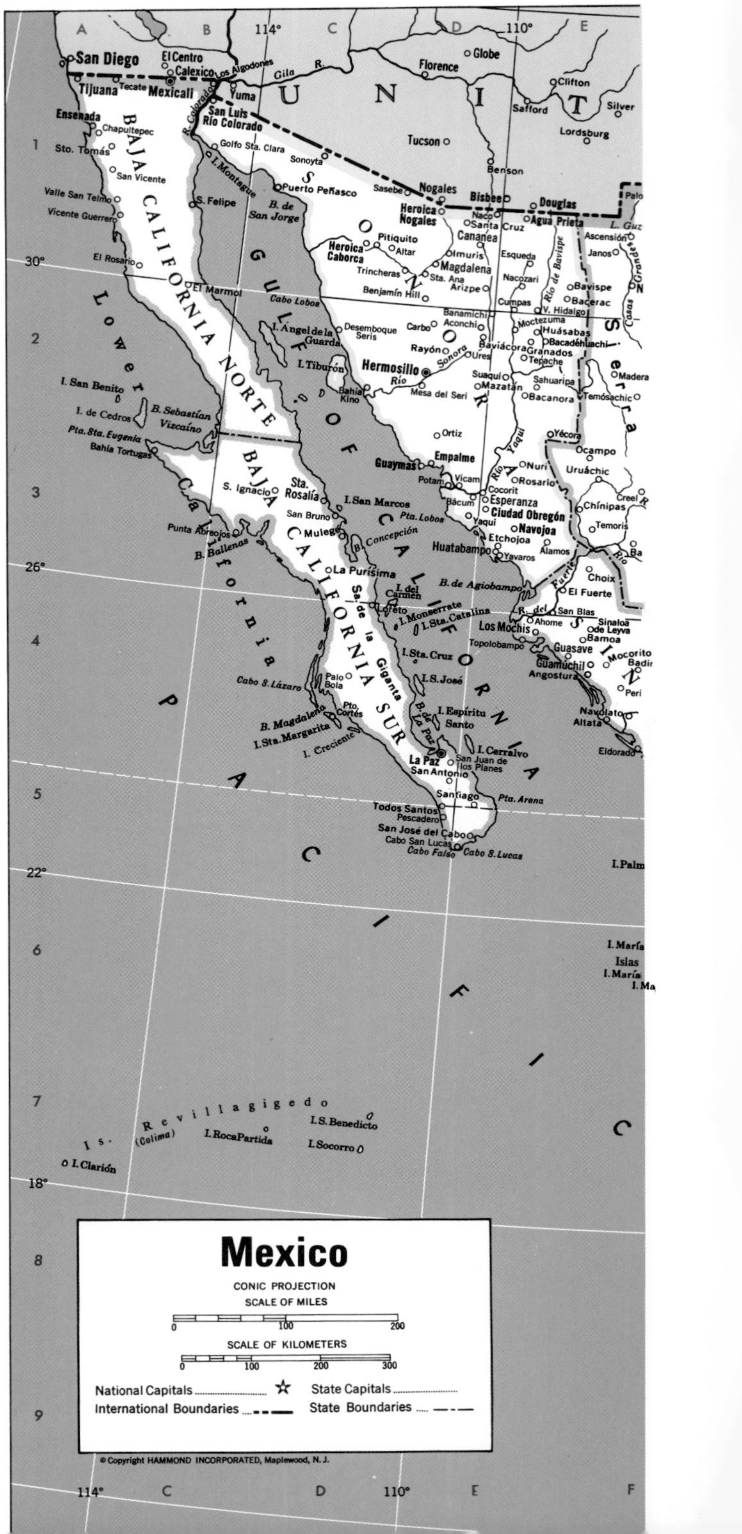

Panabá 3,056	P6	Profesor Rafael	
Pánuco 14,277	K6	Ramírez 5,338	O1
Papanoa 3,033	J8	Progreso 17,518	P6
Papantla de Olarte 26,773	L6	Puebla de Zaragoza 465,985	N2
Paraíso 7,561	N7	Puente de Ixtla 10,435	K2
Parral 57,619	G3	Puerto Ángel 1,489	L9
Parras de la Fuente 18,207	H4	Puerto Escondido 3,845	L9
Paso de Ovejas 4,371	H4	Puerto Juárez 100	Q6
Pátzcuaro 17,299	J7	Puerto Madero 1,908	N9
Pedro Montoya 4,563	K6	Puerto Peñasco 8,452	C1
Pénjamo 9,245	J6	Puerto Vallarta 24,155	G6
Peñón Blanco 2,726	H4	Purificación 3,311	G7
Pericos 4,445	F4	Purundiro 9,956	J7
Perote 12,742	O1	Putla de Guerrero 3,572	L8
Petatlán 9,419	J8	Quecholac 3,374	O2
Peto 8,362	P6	Querétaro 142,448	J6
Pichucalco 4,615	N8	Ramos Arizpe 6,205	J4
Piedras Negras,		Rayón, San Luis	
Coahuila 41,033	J2	Potosí 4,451	K6
Piedras Negras, Veracruz 4,099	Q2	Rayón, Sonora	D2
Pijijiapan 5,053	N9	Reynosa 181,646	K3
Pitiquito 2,268	D1	Rincón de Romos 8,348	H5
Potam 2,825	D3	Ríoverde 16,804	J6
Poza Rica de Hidalgo 152,276	L6	Rodeo 2,584	G4
Praxedis G. Guerrero 2,399	G1	Rosamorada 2,635	G5

(continued on following page)

AREA 761,601 sq. mi. (1,972,546 sq. km.)
POPULATION 67,395,826
CAPITAL Mexico City
LARGEST CITY Mexico City
HIGHEST POINT Citlaltépetl 18,855 ft. (5,747 m.)
MONETARY UNIT Mexican peso
MAJOR LANGUAGE Spanish
MAJOR RELIGION Roman Catholicism

States Indicated by Numbers

1	Tlaxcala	6	Querétaro
2	Morelos	7	Guanajuato
3	Distrito Federal	8	Aguascalientes
4	México	9	Nayarit
5	Hidalgo	10	Colima

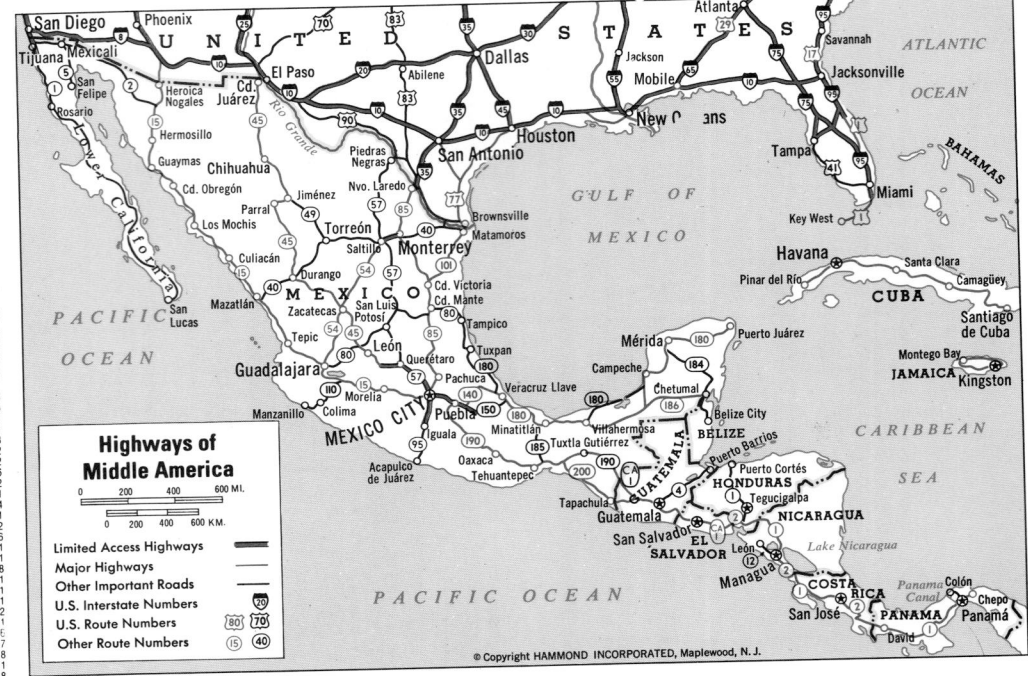

Highways of Middle America

Limited Access Highways
Major Highways
Other Important Roads
U.S. Interstate Numbers
U.S. Route Numbers
Other Route Numbers

© Copyright HAMMOND INCORPORATED, Maplewood, N.J.

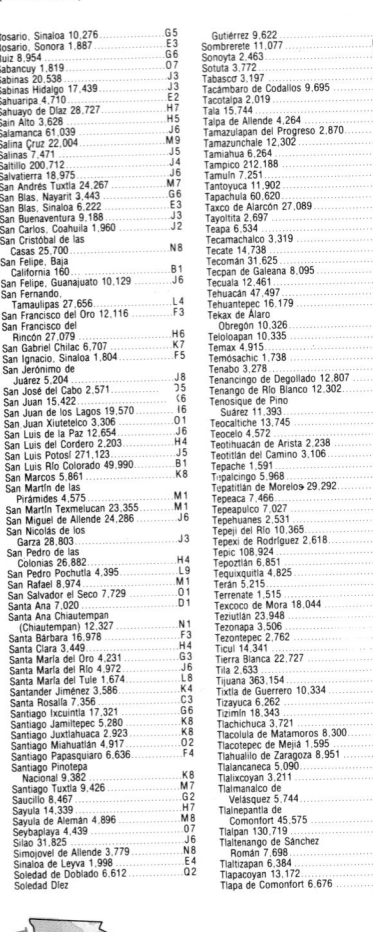

Agriculture, Industry and Resources

DOMINANT LAND USE

Wheat, Livestock
Cereals (chiefly corn), Livestock
Diversified Tropical Cash Crops
Cotton, Mixed Cereals
Livestock, Limited Agriculture
Range Livestock
Forests
Nonagricultural Land

MAJOR MINERAL OCCURRENCES

Ag Silver
Au Gold
C Coal
Cu Copper
F Fluorspar
Fe Iron Ore
G Natural Gas
Gr Graphite
Hg Mercury
Mn Manganese
Mo Molybdenum
Na Salt
O Petroleum
Pb Lead
S Sulfur
Sb Antimony
Sn Tin
W Tungsten
Zn Zinc

Water Power
Major Industrial Areas

*City and suburbs

GUATEMALA
AREA 42,042 sq. mi. (108,889 sq. km.)
POPULATION 7,262,419
CAPITAL Guatemala
LARGEST CITY Guatemala
HIGHEST POINT Tajumulco 13,845 ft. (4,220 m.)
MONETARY UNIT quetzal
MAJOR LANGUAGES Spanish, Quiché
MAJOR RELIGION Roman Catholicism

BELIZE
AREA 8,867 sq. mi. (22,966 sq. km.)
POPULATION 144,857
CAPITAL Belmopan
LARGEST CITY Belize City
HIGHEST POINT Victoria Peak 3,681 ft. (1,122 m.)
MONETARY UNIT Belize dollar
MAJOR LANGUAGES English, Spanish, Mayan
MAJOR RELIGIONS Roman Catholicism, Protestantism

EL SALVADOR
AREA 8,260 sq. mi. (21,393 sq. km.)
POPULATION 4,813,000
CAPITAL San Salvador
LARGEST CITY San Salvador
HIGHEST POINT Santa Ana 7,825 ft. (2,385 m.)
MONETARY UNIT colón
MAJOR LANGUAGE Spanish
MAJOR RELIGION Roman Catholicism

HONDURAS
AREA 43,277 sq. mi. (112,087 sq. km.)
POPULATION 3,691,000
CAPITAL Tegucigalpa
LARGEST CITY Tegucigalpa
HIGHEST POINT Las Minas 9,347 ft. (2,849 m.)
MONETARY UNIT lempira
MAJOR LANGUAGE Spanish
MAJOR RELIGION Roman Catholicism

NICARAGUA
AREA 45,698 sq. mi. (118,358 sq. km.)
POPULATION 2,703,000
CAPITAL Managua
LARGEST CITY Managua
HIGHEST POINT Cerro Mocotón 6,913 ft. (2,107 m.)
MONETARY UNIT córdoba
MAJOR LANGUAGE Spanish
MAJOR RELIGION Roman Catholicism

COSTA RICA
AREA 19,575 sq. mi. (50,700 sq. km.)
POPULATION 2,245,000
CAPITAL San José
LARGEST CITY San José
HIGHEST POINT Chirripó Grande 12,530 ft. (3,819 m.)
MONETARY UNIT colón
MAJOR LANGUAGE Spanish
MAJOR RELIGION Roman Catholicism

PANAMA
AREA 29,761 sq. mi. (77,082 sq. km.)
POPULATION 1,830,175
CAPITAL Panamá
LARGEST CITY Panamá
HIGHEST POINT Vol. Baru 11,401 ft. (3,475 m.)
MONETARY UNIT balboa
MAJOR LANGUAGE Spanish
MAJOR RELIGION Roman Catholicism

Agriculture, Industry and Resources

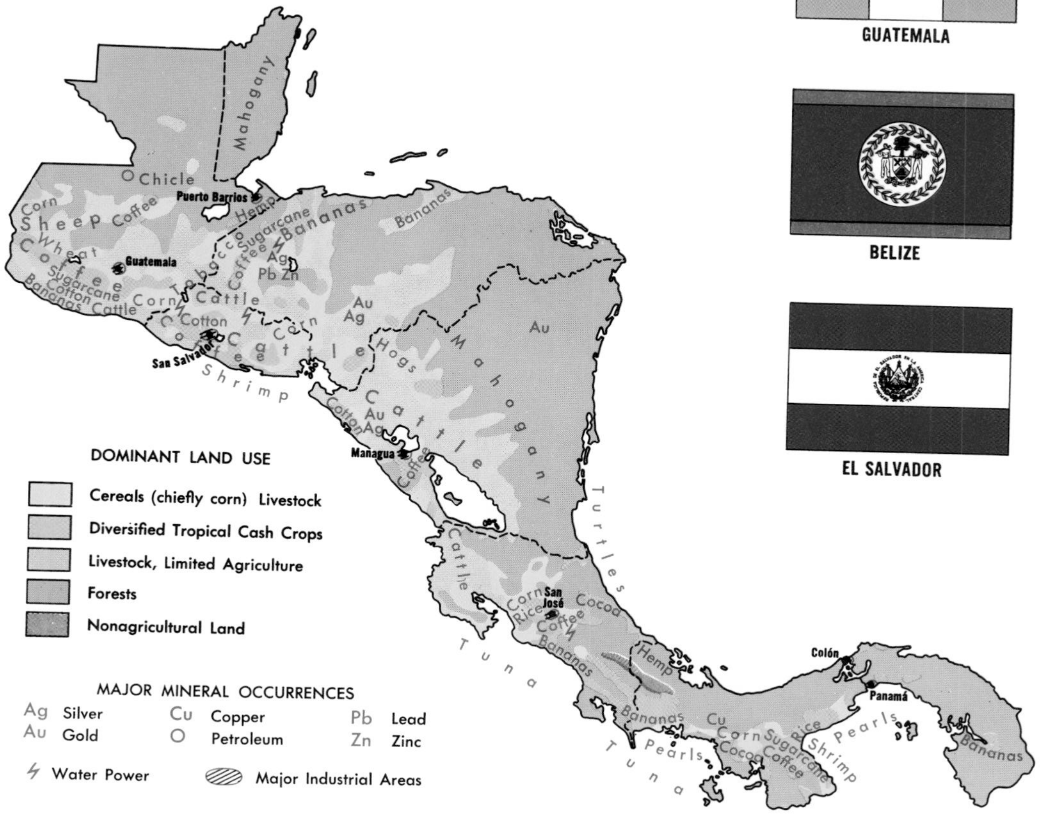

DOMINANT LAND USE
- Cereals (chiefly corn) Livestock
- Diversified Tropical Cash Crops
- Livestock, Limited Agriculture
- Forests
- Nonagricultural Land

MAJOR MINERAL OCCURRENCES
Ag Silver
Au Gold
Cu Copper
O Petroleum
Pb Lead
Zn Zinc

⚡ Water Power
Major Industrial Areas

GUATEMALA
HONDURAS 
BELIZE
NICARAGUA 
EL SALVADOR
COSTA RICA 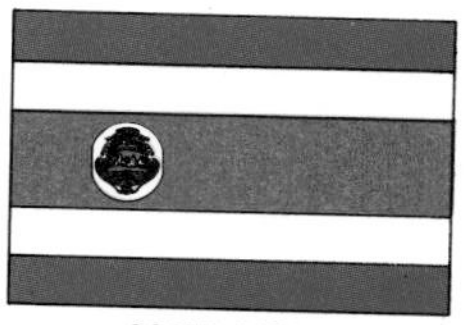
PANAMA 

BELIZE

CITIES and TOWNS

Belize City 39,887 .....C2
Belize City* 50,925 .....C2
Belmopan (cap.) 2,932 .....C2
Corozal Town 6,862 .....C1
Hattieville 904 .....C2

Libertad 856 .....C1
Orange Walk Town 8,441 .....C1
Punta Gorda 2,219 .....C2
San Ignacio 5,606 .....C2
Stann Creek Town 6,627 .....C2

OTHER FEATURES

Ambergris (cay) D1
Belize (riv.) C2

Bokel (cay) D2
Glover (reef) D2
Half Moon (cay) D2
Hondo (riv.) C1
Honduras (gulf) D2
Mauger (cay) C2
New (riv.) C2
Saint Georges (cay) D2
Sarstún (riv.) C3
Turneffe (isls.) D2

COSTA RICA

CITIES and TOWNS

Alajuela 33,122 .....E6
Atenas 1,728 .....E6
Bagaces 2,129 .....E5
Boruca⊙ 1,892 .....F6

Buenos Aires⊙ 302 .....F6
Cañas 6,053 .....E5
Cartago 21,753 .....F6
Ciudad Quesada 9,754 .....E5
Esparta 4,699 .....E5
Filadelfia 2,958 .....E5
Golfito 6,962 .....F6
Grecia 8,355 .....E5
Guácimo 1,168 .....F5
Guápiles 3,524 .....F5

Heredia 22,700 .....E5
Las Juntas 1,129 .....E5
Liberia 10,802 .....E5
Limón 29,621 .....F6
Miramar 1,673 .....E5
Nicoya 7,474 .....E5
Orotina 3,170 .....E6
Palmares 3,083 .....E5
Paraíso 8,446 .....F6
Puerto Cortés 2,070 .....F6

Puntarenas 26,331 .....E6
Quepos 2,155 .....F6
Sán José (cap.) 215,441 .....F5
San José* 391,107 .....F5
San Marcos 917 .....F6
San Ramón 9,245 .....E5
Santa Cruz 5,777 .....E5
Santo Domingo 5,148 .....F5
Siquirres 4,361 .....F5
Turrialba 12,151 .....F6

(continued on following page)

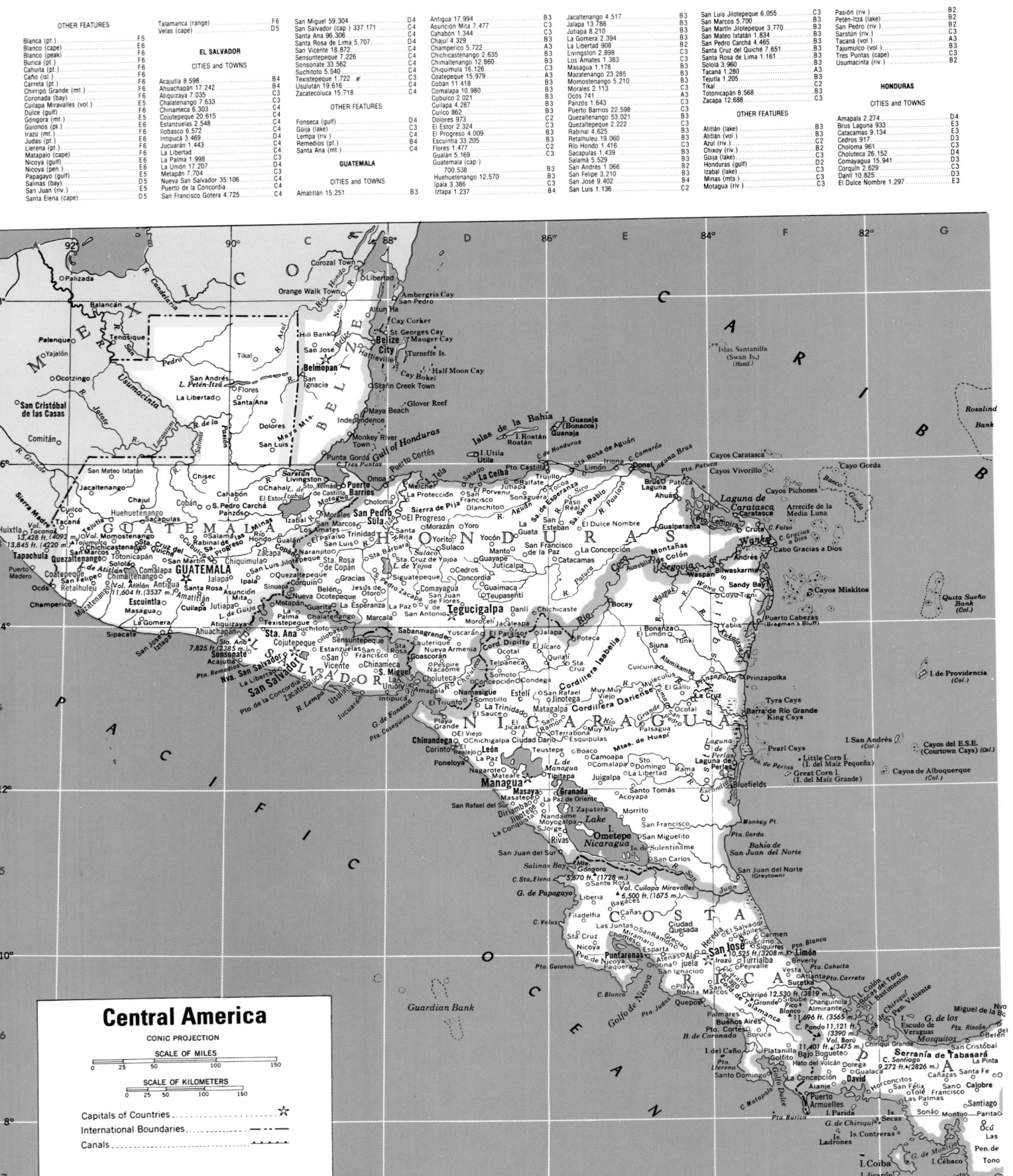

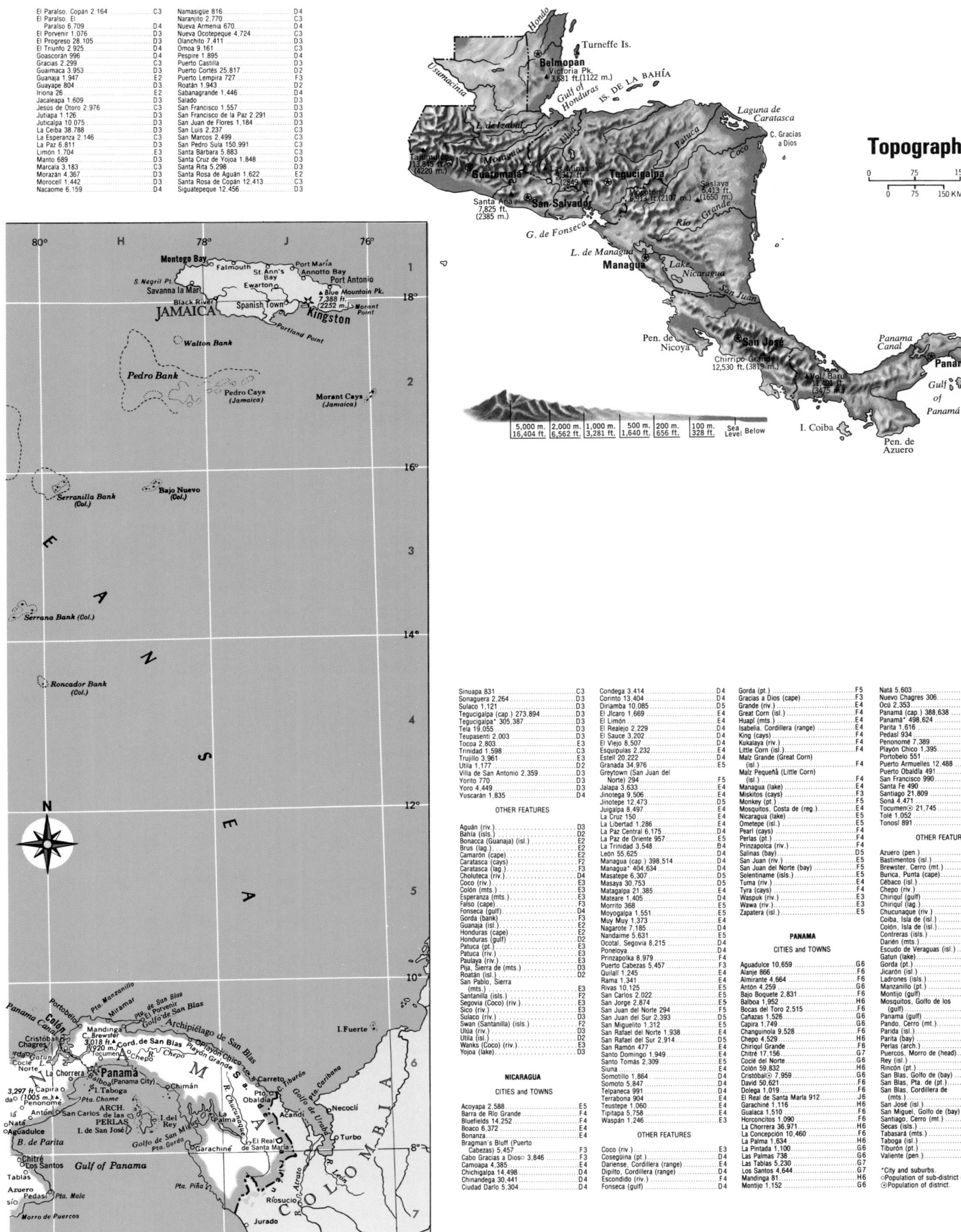

Topography

0   75   150 MI.

0   75   150 KM.

5,000 m. 16,404 ft.	2,000 m. 6,562 ft.	1,000 m. 3,281 ft.	500 m. 1,640 ft.	200 m. 656 ft.	100 m. 328 ft.	Sea Level	Below

CUBA **HAITI** **DOMINICAN REPUBLIC** **JAMAICA** **TRINIDAD AND TOBAGO** **BARBADOS**

 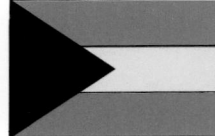   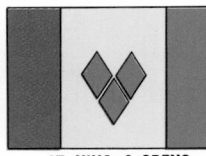 

GRENADA **BAHAMAS** **DOMINICA** **ST. LUCIA** **ST. VINC. & GRENS.** **ANTIGUA AND BARBUDA**

CUBA
AREA 44,206 sq. mi. (114,494 sq. km.)
POPULATION 9,706,369
CAPITAL Havana
LARGEST CITY Havana
HIGHEST POINT Pico Turquino
6,561 ft. (2,000 m.)
MONETARY UNIT Cuban peso
MAJOR LANGUAGE Spanish
MAJOR RELIGION Roman Catholicism

HAITI
AREA 10,694 sq. mi. (27,697 sq. km.)
POPULATION 5,053,792
CAPITAL Port-au-Prince
LARGEST CITY Port-au-Prince
HIGHEST POINT Pic La Selle 8,793 ft. (2,680 m.)
MONETARY UNIT gourde
MAJOR LANGUAGES Creole French, French
MAJOR RELIGION Roman Catholicism

DOMINICAN REPUBLIC
AREA 18,704 sq. mi. (48,443 sq. km.)
POPULATION 5,647,977
CAPITAL Santo Domingo
LARGEST CITY Santo Domingo
HIGHEST POINT Pico Duarte
10,417 ft. (3,175 m.)
MONETARY UNIT Dominican peso
MAJOR LANGUAGE Spanish
MAJOR RELIGION Roman Catholicism

JAMAICA
AREA 4,411 sq. mi. (11,424 sq. km.)
POPULATION 2,184,000
CAPITAL Kingston
LARGEST CITY Kingston
HIGHEST POINT Blue Mountain Peak
7,402 ft. (2,256 m.)
MONETARY UNIT Jamaican dollar
MAJOR LANGUAGE English
MAJOR RELIGIONS Protestantism,
Roman Catholicism

PUERTO RICO
AREA 3,515 sq. mi. (9,104 sq. km.)
POPULATION 3,196,520
CAPITAL San Juan
MONETARY UNIT U.S. dollar
MAJOR LANGUAGES Spanish, English
MAJOR RELIGION Roman Catholicism

NETHERLANDS ANTILLES
AREA 390 sq. mi. (1,010 sq. km.)
POPULATION 246,000
CAPITAL Willemstad
MONETARY UNIT Antilles guilder
MAJOR LANGUAGES Dutch, Papiamento, English
MAJOR RELIGIONS Roman Catholicism,
Protestantism

BERMUDA
AREA 21 sq. mi. (54 sq. km.)
POPULATION 67,761
CAPITAL Hamilton
MONETARY UNIT Bermuda dollar
MAJOR LANGUAGE English
MAJOR RELIGION Protestantism

ARUBA
AREA 75 sq. mi (193 sq. km.)
POPULATION 66,790
CAPITAL Oranjestad
MONETARY UNIT Aruba guilder
MAJOR LANGUAGES Dutch, Papiamento
MAJOR RELIGION Roman Catholic

ANGUILLA

Anguilla (isl.) 6,519 .... F3

ANTIGUA and BARBUDA

Antigua (isl.) 76,213 .... G3
Barbuda (isl.) 1,071 .... G3
Caribbean (sea) B4
Codrington 1,071 .... G3
Falmouth 1,134 .... F3
Redonda (isl.) F3
Saint John's (cap.) 21,814 .... G3

ARUBA

Aruba (isl.) 66,790 .... E4

BAHAMAS

Acklins (isl.) 616 .... C2
Andros (isl.) 8,397 .... B1
Atwood (Samana) (cay) D2
Berry (isls.) 509 .... B1
Biminis, The (isls.) 1,432 .... B1
Caicos (passg.) D2
Cat (isl.) 2,143 .... C1
Cay Sal (bank) B2
Crooked (isl.) 517 .... D2
Eleuthera (isl.) 8,326 .... C1
Exuma (cays) C1
Flamingo (cay) C2
Freeport 22,301 .... B1
Grand Bahama (isl.) 33,102 .... B1
Great Abaco (isl.) 7,324 .... C1
Great Bahama (bank) B1
Great Exuma (isl.) C2
Great Inagua (isl.) 939 .... D2
Great Isaac (isl.) B1

BARBADOS

Bridgetown (cap.) 7,552 .... G4
Speightstown G4

BERMUDA

Bermuda (isl.) H3
Castle (harb.) H2
Great (sound) G3
Hamilton (cap.) 1,617 .... G3
Harrington (sound) H3
Ireland (isl.) G3
North (rapid) H2
Saint Davids (isl.) H2
Saint George 1,647 .... H2
Saint George's (isl.) H2
Somerset (isl.) G3

CAYMAN ISLANDS

Bartlett Deep B3
Cayman Brac (isl.) 1,603 .... B3
George Town (cap.) 7,617 .... B3
Grand Cayman (isl.) 15,000 .... B3
Little Cayman (isl.) 74 .... B3
Misteriosa (bank) A3

CUBA

Bayamo 109,201 .... C2
Camagüey 245,235 .... B2
Cienfuegos 107,396 .... B2
Florida (str.) B1
Guanabacoa 89,741 .... A2
Guantánamo 178,129 .... C2
Havana (cap.) 1,924,886 .... A2
Holguín 190,155 .... C2
Juventud (Pines) (isl.) 57,879 .... A2
Manzanillo 95,420 .... C2
Marianao ○127,563 .... A2
Matanzas 103,302 .... A2
Pinar del Río 104,598 .... A2
San Felipe (cays) A2
Santa Clara 175,113 .... B2
Santiago de Cuba 362,432 .... C3
Windward (passg.) C3

DOMINICA

Portsmouth 2,329 .... G4
Roseau (cap.) 9,968 .... G4

DOMINICAN REPUBLIC

La Romana 91,571 .... E3
San Francisco de Macorís 64,906 ... E3
San Pedro de Macorís 78,562 .... E3
Santiago 278,638 .... E3
Santo Domingo (cap.) 1,313,172 .... E3

GRENADA

Carriacou (isl.) 6,052 .... G4
Gouyave 2,498 .... F4
Grenadines (isls.) G4
Saint George's (cap.) 6,463 .... F5

GUADELOUPE

Basse-Terre (cap.) 13,397 .... F4
Saint-Barthélemy (isl.) 3,059 ..... F3
Saint Martin (isl.) 8,072 .... F3

HAITI

Cap-Haïtien 64,406 .... D3
Gonaïves 34,209 .... D3
Port-au-Prince (cap.) 449,831 ..... D3
Gonâve (isl.) D3
Jamaica (chan.) D3
Tortuga (isl.) D2

JAMAICA

Blue Mountain (peak) C3
Jamaica (chan.) A2
Kingston (cap.) 106,791 .... C3
Montego Bay 43,521 .... B3
Pedro (cays) C3
Savanna-la-Mar 11,759 .... B3

MARTINIQUE

Fort-de-France (cap.) 96,649 ...... G4
Saint-Pierre 4,923 .... G4
Pelée (vol.) G4

MONTSERRAT

Plymouth (cap.) 1,623 .... F3

NETHERLANDS ANTILLES

Bonaire (isl.) E4
Curaçao (isl.) E4
Oranjestad 10,100 .... D4
Saba (isl.) F3
Saint Eustatius (isl.) F3
Saint Martin (Sint Maarten) (isl.) F3
Willemstad (cap.) 95,000 .... E4

PUERTO RICO

Bayamón 185,087 .... G1
Caguas 87,214 .... G1
Culebra (isl.) 1,265 .... G1
Mayagüez 82,968 .... F1
Mona (passg.) E3
Ponce 161,739 .... F1

San Juan (cap.) 424,600 .... G1
Vieques (isl.) 7,662 .... G1

SAINT KITTS and NEVIS

Basseterre 14,725 .... F3
Nevis (isl.) 9,300 .... F3
Saint Christopher (isl.) 35,104 ... F3

SAINT LUCIA

Castries (cap.) ●42,770 .... G4
Vieux Fort ●10,675 .... G4

**SAINT VINCENT and
THE GRENADINES**

Bequia (isl.) G4
Georgetown 1,100 .... G4
Grenadines (isls.) 8,371 .... G4
Kingstown (cap.) 17,117 .... G4

TRINIDAD and TOBAGO

Port-of-Spain (cap.) 67,978 .... G5
Scarborough 6,057 .... G5
Tobago (isl.) 39,695 .... G5
Trinidad (isl.) 1,020,130 .... G5

TURKS and CAICOS ISLANDS

Caicos (isls.) 4,008 .... D2
Cockburn Harbour D2
Grand Caicos (isl.) 371 .... D2
Grand Turk (isl.) 3,146 .... D2
Providenciales (isl.) 979 .... D2
Turks (isl.) 3,348 .... D2

VIRGIN ISLANDS (British)

Anegada (isl.) 89 .... H1
Jost Van Dyke (isl.) 135 .... H1
Road Town (cap.) 2,200 .... H1
Tortola (isl.) 9,257 .... H1
Virgin Gorda (isl.) 1,443 .... H1

VIRGIN ISLANDS (U.S.)

Charlotte Amalie (cap.) 11,842 .... H1
Christiansted 2,914 .... H2
Fredriksted 1,046 .... H2
Saint Croix (isl.) 49,725 .... H2
Saint John (isl.) 2,472 .... H1
Saint Thomas (isl.) 44,372 .... G1

WEST INDIES

Antilles, Greater (isls.) B2
Antilles, Lesser (isls.) E4
Aves (Bird) (isl.) F4
Hispaniola (isl.) D2
Leeward (isls.) F3
Navassa (isl.) C3
Windward (isls.) G4

● Population of district.
○ Population of municipality.

Topography

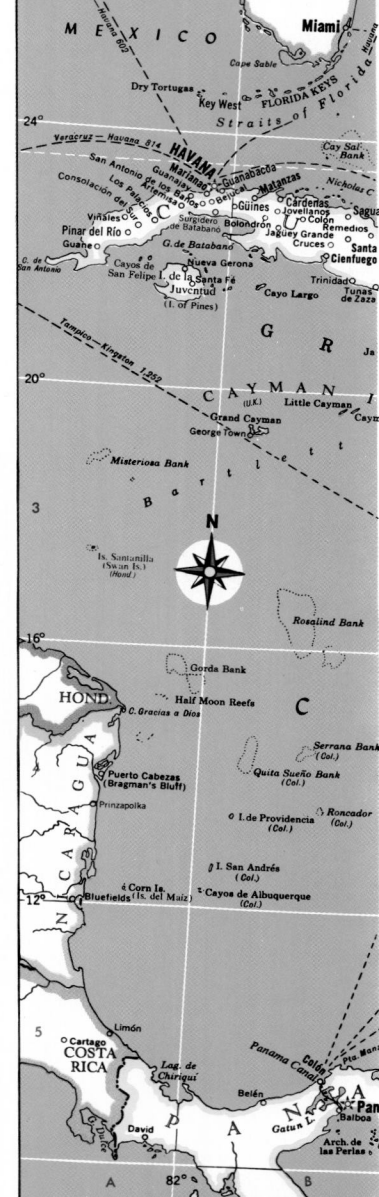

TRINIDAD AND TOBAGO

AREA 1,980 sq. mi. (5,128 sq. km.)
POPULATION 1,067,108
CAPITAL Port of Spain
LARGEST CITY Port of Spain
HIGHEST POINT Mt. Aripo 3,084 ft. (940 m.)
MONETARY UNIT Trinidad and Tobago dollar
MAJOR LANGUAGES English, Hindi
MAJOR RELIGIONS Roman Catholicism,
Protestantism, Hinduism, Islam

BARBADOS

AREA 166 sq. mi. (430 sq. km.)
POPULATION 248,983
CAPITAL Bridgetown
LARGEST CITY Bridgetown
HIGHEST POINT Mt. Hillaby 1,104 ft.
(336 m.)
MONETARY UNIT Barbadian dollar
MAJOR LANGUAGE English
MAJOR RELIGION Protestantism

GRENADA

AREA 133 sq. mi. (344 sq. km.)
POPULATION 103,103
CAPITAL St. George's
LARGEST CITY St. George's
HIGHEST POINT Mt. St. Catherine
2,757 ft. (840 m.)
MONETARY UNIT East Caribbean dollar
MAJOR LANGUAGES English, French patois
MAJOR RELIGIONS Roman Catholicism,
Protestantism

SAINT KITTS AND NEVIS

BAHAMAS

AREA 5,382 sq. mi. (13,939 sq. km.)
POPULATION 209,505
CAPITAL Nassau
LARGEST CITY Nassau
HIGHEST POINT Mt. Alvernia 206 ft. (63 m.)
MONETARY UNIT Bahamian dollar
MAJOR LANGUAGE English
MAJOR RELIGIONS Roman Catholicism,
Protestantism

DOMINICA

AREA 290 sq. mi. (751 sq. km.)
POPULATION 74,089
CAPITAL Roseau
HIGHEST POINT Morne Diablotin
4,747 ft. (1,447 m.)
MONETARY UNIT Dominican dollar
MAJOR LANGUAGES English, French patois
MAJOR RELIGIONS Roman Catholicism,
Protestantism

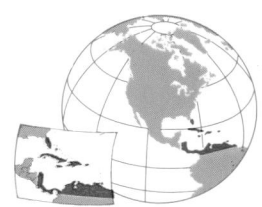

SAINT LUCIA

AREA 238 sq. mi. (616 sq. km.)
POPULATION 115,783
CAPITAL Castries
HIGHEST POINT Mt. Gimie 3,117 ft. (950 m.)
MONETARY UNIT East Caribbean dollar
MAJOR LANGUAGES English, French patois
MAJOR RELIGIONS Roman Catholicism,
Protestantism

SAINT VINCENT AND THE GRENADINES

AREA 150 sq. mi. (388 sq. km.)
POPULATION 124,000
CAPITAL Kingstown
HIGHEST POINT Soufrière 4,000 ft. (1,219 m.)
MONETARY UNIT East Caribbean dollar
MAJOR LANGUAGE English
MAJOR RELIGIONS Protestantism,
Roman Catholicism

ANTIGUA AND BARBUDA

AREA 171 sq. mi. (443 sq. km.)
POPULATION 75,000
CAPITAL St. John's
HIGHEST POINT Boggy Peak 1,319 ft. (402 m.)
MONETARY UNIT East Caribbean dollar
MAJOR LANGUAGE English
MAJOR RELIGION Protestantism

SAINT KITTS & NEVIS

AREA 104 sq. mi. (269 sq. km.)
POPULATION 44,404
CAPITAL Basseterre
HIGHEST POINT Mt. Misery 4,314 ft.
(1,315 m.)
MONETARY UNIT East Caribbean dollar
MAJOR LANGUAGE English
MAJOR RELIGIONS Protestantism,
Roman Catholicism

The West Indies

CONIC PROJECTION

SCALE OF MILES
0   50   100   150   200

SCALE OF KILOMETERS
0 50 100   200   300

Capitals .... ☆

ATLANTIC OCEAN

Puerto Rico

Bermuda Islands

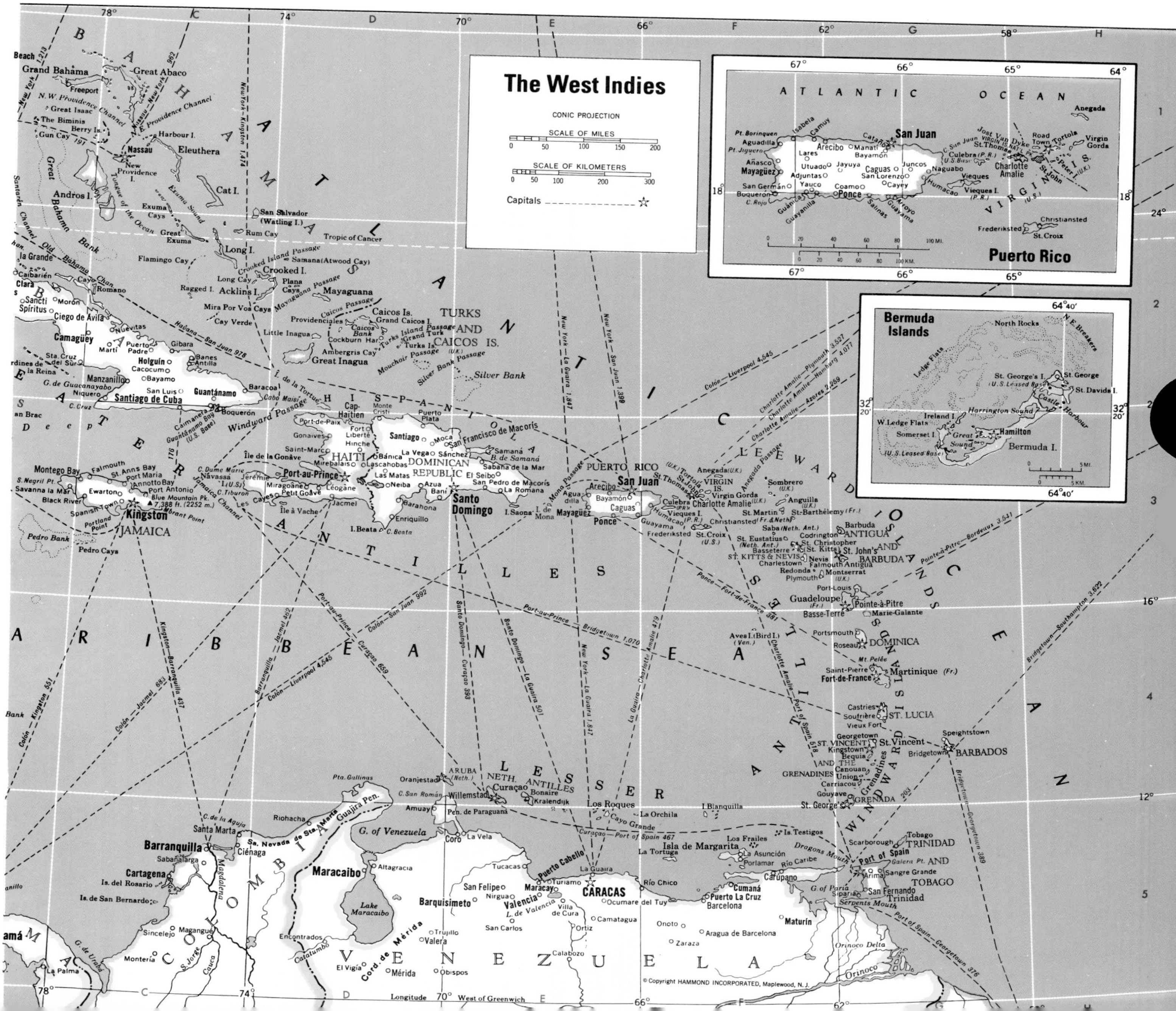

CUBA

PROVINCES

Camagüey 664,566 . . . . G2
Ciego de Avila 320,961 . . . . F2
Cienfuegos 326,412 . . . . . . E2
Granma 739,335 . . . . H4
Guantánamo 466,609 . . . . . K4
Habana 1,924,886 . . . . C1
Habana, La (Havana)
  586,029 . . . . C1
Holguín 911,034 . . . . J3
Juventud (municipio
  especial) 57,879 . . . . . . C2
Las Tunas 436,341 . . . . . . H3
Matanzas 557,628 . . . . . . D1
Pinar del Río 640,740 . . . . A2
Sancti Spíritus 399,700 . . . F2
Santiago de Cuba 909,506 . . H4
Villa Clara 764,743 . . . . . . E1

CITIES and TOWNS

Abreus 14,267 . . . . D2
Agramonte 4,603 . . . . D1
Aguada de Pasajeros 20,219 D2
Alacranes 4,959 . . . . C1
Alonso Rojas 1,427 . . . . . . B2
Alquízar 12,691 . . . . C1
Altagracia 1,722 . . . . G3
Alto Songo-La Maya 25,188 . J4

Amarillas 2,767 . . . . D2
Amazonas 1,066 . . . . F2
Antilla 10,052 . . . . J3
Arroyo Blanco 1,431 . . . . . F2
Artemisa 45,689 . . . . B1
Báez 4,178 . . . . E2
Báguanos 12,678 . . . . J3
Bahía Honda 16,901 . . . . . B1
Baire 4,879 . . . . H4
Banao 803 . . . . F2
Banes 38,905 . . . . J3
Baracoa 36,702 . . . . K4
Baraguá 12,633 . . . . F2
Bauta 26,826 . . . . C1
Bayamo 109,201 . . . . H4
Bejucal 15,649 . . . . C1
Bolondrón 5,840 . . . . D1
Buenaventura 4,711 . . . . . . H3
Buenavista 1,303 . . . . F2
Buey Arriba 8,017 . . . . H4
Cabaiguán 36,544 . . . . F2
Cabañas 4,897 . . . . D1
Cabezas 5,262 . . . . H3
Cacocum 14,145 . . . . J3
Caibarién 32,094 . . . . F2
Caimanera 6,664 . . . . K4
Calabazar de Sagua 9,023 . . E1
Calimete 19,925 . . . . D1
Camagüey 245,235 . . . . . . G3
Camajuaní 26,653 . . . . E1
Campechuela 20,743 . . . . . G4
Canasí 1,637 . . . . C1

Candelaria 10,810 . . . . B1
Cárdenas 65,585 . . . . D1
Cartagena 2,166 . . . . D2
Cascajal 3,530 . . . . D1
Cauto del Embarcadero 949 . H4
Cauto el Cristo 1,626 . . . . . J3
Central Amancio Rodríguez
  22,506 . . . . G3
Central Bolivia 6,301 . . . . . G2
Central Brasil 4,904 . . . . . . G2
Central Cándido González
  3,414 . . . . G3
Central Colombia 16,799 . . . G3
Central Frank País 9,066 . . . K3
Central Guatemala 5,584 . . . J3
Central Haití 3,609 . . . . . . G3
Central Loynaz Echevarría
  3,245 . . . . D1
Central Manuel Tames 7,864 K4
Céspedes 6,634 . . . . G2
Chambas 19,877 . . . . F2
Chaparra 8,428 . . . . H3
Cidra 3,567 . . . . D1
Ciego de Ávila 80,010 . . . . F2
Cienfuegos 107,396 . . . . . . D2
Colón 47,010 . . . . D1
Condado 33,115 . . . . E2
Consolación del Norte 4,681 . B1
Consolación del Sur 34,334 . B1
Contramaestre 44,991 . . . . . H4
Corralillo 15,822 . . . . D1

Cruces 20,324 . . . . E2
Cueto 23,183 . . . . J3
Cumanayagua 25,338 . . . . . J4
Daiquirí . . . .
Delicias 10,562 . . . . H3
Dos Caminos 3,772 . . . . . . J4
Dos Ríos 1,786 . . . . J4
El Caney 3,921 . . . . J4
El Cobre 3,952 . . . . J4
El Santo 2,473 . . . . E1
Encrucijada 23,029 . . . . . . E1
Esmeralda 17,205 . . . . G1
Esperanza 9,241 . . . . E1
Florencia 6,979 . . . . F2
Florida 43,881 . . . . G2
Fomento 17,310 . . . . E2
Gaspar 2,682 . . . . F2
Gibara 23,137 . . . . J3
Güáimaro 29,712 . . . . G3
Guanabacoa 89,741 . . . . . . C1
Guanajay 21,042 . . . . B1
Guane 14,126 . . . . A2
Guantánamo 178,129 . . . . . K4
Guaro 3,086 . . . . J3
Guasimal 3,057 . . . . F2
Guayabal 3,703 . . . . G3
Guayos 6,753 . . . . F2
Güines 51,691 . . . . C1
Güira de Melena 19,851 . . . C1
Guisa 15,182 . . . . H4
Havana (cap.) 1,924,886 . . . B1
Herradura 3,762 . . . . B1

Holguín 190,155 . . . . J3
Ignacio Agramonte 1,487 . . G3
Imías 4,491 . . . . K4
Isabela de Sagua 3,721 . . . E1
Jagüey Grande 30,205 . . . . D2
Jamaica 5,128 . . . . K2
Jaruco 16,844 . . . . C1
Jatibonico 17,047 . . . . F2
Jíbaro 1,263 . . . . F2
Jiguaní 25,069 . . . . H4
Jobabo 14,899 . . . . H3
Jovellanos 35,043 . . . . D1
La Coloma 3,462 . . . . B2
La Maya-Alto Songo 25,188 . J4
Las Martinas 4,511 . . . . . . A2
Limonar 9,629 . . . . D1
Los Arabos 10,664 . . . . . . E1
Los Palacios 21,884 . . . . . . B1
Lugareño 4,396 . . . . G2
Mabay 6,176 . . . . H4
Maceo 2,652 . . . . H3
Majagua 9,110 . . . . F2
Manacas 5,914 . . . . E1
Manatí 11,054 . . . . H3
Manguito 2,739 . . . . D1
Manicaragua 33,900 . . . . . . E2
Mantua 9,165 . . . . A2
Mapos (Amazonas) 1,066 . . F2
Manzanillo 95,420 . . . . H4
Mariano C1
Mariel 24,115 . . . . B1
Martí 11,474 . . . . D1

Matanzas 103,302 . . . . C1
Máximo Gómez, Ciego
  de Avila 5,116 . . . . F2
Máximo Gómez, Matanzas
  4,970 . . . . D1
Mayajigua 4,425 . . . . F2
Mayarí 54,699 . . . . J3
Mayarí Arriba 2,302 . . . . . . J3
Media Luna 13,794 . . . . . . G4
Mendoza 2,914 . . . . A2
Meneses 4,768 . . . . F2
Minas 17,675 . . . . G2
Minas de Matahambre
  14,976 . . . . A1
Moa 28,696 . . . . K3
Morón 40,396 . . . . F2
Nicaro 9,506 . . . . J3
Niquero 15,544 . . . . G4
Nueva Gerona 17,175 . . . . C2
Nuevitas 35,103 . . . . G2
Orozco 4,256 . . . . B1
Palma Soriano 66,222 . . . . J4
Palmira 19,680 . . . . D1
Pedro Betancourt 22,915 . . . D1
Perico 20,633 . . . . D1
Pilón 10,194 . . . . H4
Pinar del Río 104,598 . . . . B2
Placetas 46,038 . . . . E2
Primero Enero 14,807 . . . . . F2
Puerto Esperanza 3,499 . . . A1
Puerto Padre 46,806 . . . . . H3
Quemado de Güines 11,208 . E1

Rancho Veloz 3,966 . . . . . . D1
Ranchuelo 34,255 . . . . E2
Regla 38,491 . . . . C1
Remedios 27,722 . . . . E2
República Dominicana
  2,540 . . . . F2
Río Cauto 19,550 . . . . H4
Rodas 16,350 . . . . D2
Sagua de Tánamo 15,327 . . K3
Sagua la Grande 52,315 . . . E1
San Andrés 2,127 . . . . H3
San Antonio de los Baños
  28,137 . . . . C1
San Cristóbal 30,769 . . . . . B1
Sancti Spíritus 79,542 . . . . E2
San Diego de los Baños
  1,430 . . . . B1
San Germán 12,362 . . . . . . J3
San José de las Lajas
  37,149 . . . . C1
San José de los Ramos . . . .
San Juan y Martínez 13,227 . B2
San Luis, Pinar del Río
  5,677 . . . . B2
San Luis, Santiago de Cuba
  32,826 . . . . J4
San Nicolás 12,368 . . . . . . C1
San Ramón 2,676 . . . . H4
Santa Clara 175,113 . . . . . E2
Santa Cruz del Norte
  15,239 . . . . C1

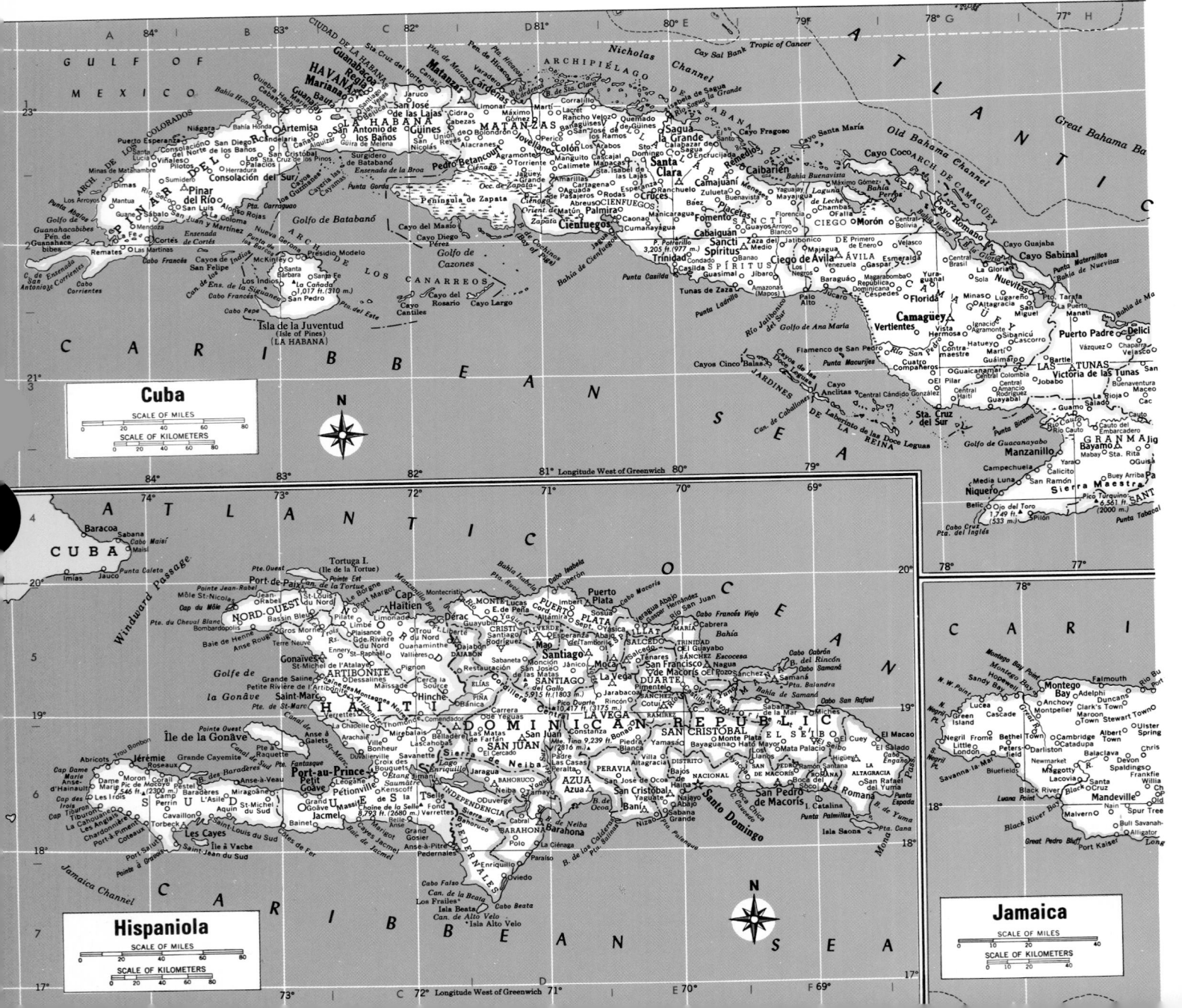

LEGEND
Capitals of Countries .... ☆
Provincial Capitals .... △
International Boundaries .... ___ ___
Provincial Boundaries .... _ _ _

© Copyright HAMMOND INCORPORATED, Maplewood, N.J.

Agriculture, Industry and Resources

DOMINANT LAND USE
Diversified Tropical Cash Crops
Tobacco
Fruit
Livestock, Limited Agriculture
Forests
Nonagricultural Land

MAJOR MINERAL OCCURRENCES
Al Bauxite
At Asphalt
Au Gold
Co Cobalt
Cr Chromium
Cu Copper
Fe Iron Ore
Gp Gypsum
Mn Manganese
Na Salt
Ni Nickel
O Petroleum
P Phosphates

⚡ Water Power
Major Industrial Areas

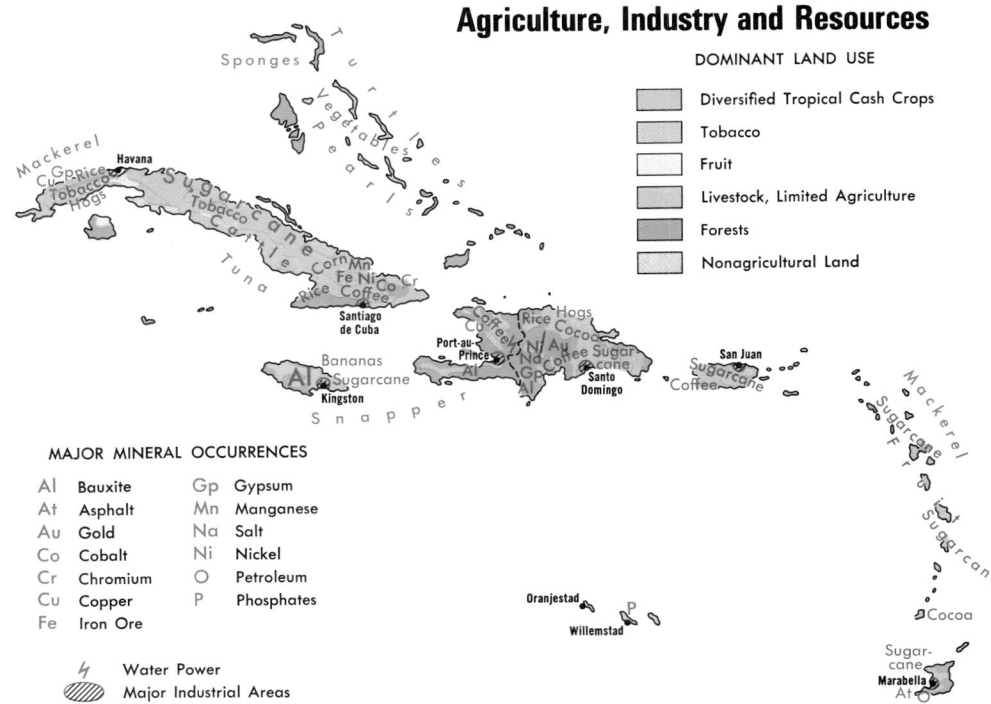

(continued)

PUERTO RICO

DISTRICTS

Aguadilla A1
Arecibo C1
Bayamón D1
Guayama D2
Humacao E2
Mayagüez B2
Ponce C2
San Juan D1

CITIES and TOWNS

Adjuntas 5,239 B2
Aguada 5,025 A1
Aguadilla 22,039 A1
Aguas Buenas 3,766 E2
Aibonito 9,331 D2
Añasco 5,646 A1
Ángeles ○2,817 B2
Arecibo 48,779 B1
Arroyo 8,435 E3
Bahomamey A1
Bajadero 3,678 C1
Barceloneta 4,502 C1
Barranquitas 3,618 D2
Bayamón 185,087 D1
Boquerón ○3,675 A3
Cabo Rojo 10,292 A2
Caguas 87,214 E2
Caguas †156,819 E2
Camuy 3,834 B1
Carolina 147,835 E1
Cataño 26,243 D1
Cayey 23,305 D2
Ceiba 4,973 F2
Central Aguirre 1,049 D3
Ciales 3,582 C1
Cidra 6,069 D2
Coamo 12,851 D2
Comerío 5,736 D2
Coquí 3,018 D3
Corozal 5,889 D1
Coto Laurel ○5,192 C2
Culebra (Dewey) 938 G1
Dorado 10,203 D1
Ensenada B3
Esperanza 1,130 G2
Fajardo 26,928 F1
Florida 3,641 C1
Guánica 9,628 B3
Guayama 21,097 E3
Guayanilla 6,163 B3
Guaynabo 65,075 D1
Gurabo 7,645 E2
Hatillo 5,019 B1
Hato Rey E1
Hormigueros 12,031 A2
Humacao 19,147 E2
Isabela 12,087 A1
Isabel Segunda 2,330 G2
Jayuya 3,588 C2
Jobos 4,194 D3
Juana Díaz 10,469 C2
Juncos 7,851 E2
Lajas 4,275 A2
Lares 5,224 B2
Las Piedras 4,857 E2
Levittown 31,613 D1
Loíza 3,932 E1
Loíza Aldea E1
Luquillo 4,531 F1
Manatí 17,347 C1
Maricao 1,390 B2
Mayagüez 82,968 A2
Mayagüez †98,155 A2
Moca 3,960 A1
Naguabo 4,135 F2
Naranjito 2,849 D1
Palmer 1,566 F1
Palo Seco 1,172 D1
Parguera A3
Patillas 3,172 E2
Peñuelas 4,235 B2
Playa de Fajardo F1
Playa de Humacao ○5,573 F2
Ponce 161,739 C3
Ponce †168,272 C3
Puerto Nuevo D1
Puerto Real 2,390 A2
Puerto Real (Playa de Fajardo) F1
Punta Santiago (Playa de Humacao) ○5,573 F2
Quebradillas 3,770 B1
Río Blanco 1,433 F2
Río Grande 12,047 E1
Río Piedras E1
Rosario A2
Sabana Grande 7,435 B2
Sabana Seca 11,431 D1
Salinas 6,220 D3
San Antonio 2,681 A1
San Germán 13,054 A2
San Juan (cap.) 424,600 E1
San Juan †1,081,193 E1
San Lorenzo 8,880 E2
San Sebastián 10,619 B1
Santa Isabel 6,948 C3
Santurce E1
Tallaboa 1,059 B3
Toa Alta 4,427 D1
Toa Baja 1,992 D1
Trujillo Alto 41,141 E1
Utuado 11,113 B2
Vega Alta 10,582 D1
Vega Baja 18,233 D1
Vieques (Isabel Segunda) 2,330 G2
Villalba 3,469 C2
Yabucoa 6,797 E2
Yauco 14,594 B2

OTHER FEATURES

Aguadilla (bay) A1
Algarrobo (pt.) A2
Añasco (bay) A1
Arenas (pt.) F2
Bauta (riv.) C2
Bayamón (riv.) D1
Boquerón (bay) A3
Borinquen (pt.) A1
Cabullones (pt.) C3
Caja de Muertos (isl.) C3
Camuy (riv.) B1
Canovanas (riv.) E1
Caonillas (lake) C2
Carite (lake) E2
Carraízo (lake) E1
Cayey, Sierra de (mts.) D2
Central, Cordillera (range) C2
Cerro Gordo (pt.) D1
Coamo (res.) D3
Coamo (riv.) D3
Culebra (isl.) 1,265 G1
Culebrinas (riv.) A1
Culebrita (isl.) G2
El Toro (mt.) F2
El Yunque (mt.) F1
Este (pt.) G2
Fajardo (riv.) F1
Figuras (pt.) E3
Fosforescente (bay) A3
Grande de Añasco (riv.) B2
Grande de Arecibo (riv.) C1
Grande de Loíza (riv.) E1
Grande de Manatí (riv.) C1
Guajataca (lake) B1
Guanajibo (pt.) A2
Guanajibo (riv.) A2
Guánica (lake) B3
Guaniquilla (pt.) A2
Guayabal (lake) C2
Guayanés (pt.) F2
Guayanés (riv.) E2
Guayanilla (bay) B3
Guayo (lake) B2
Guilarte (mt.) B2
Honda (bay) F2
Jacaguas (riv.) C2
Jaicoa, Cordillera (mts.) B1
Jiguero (pt.) A1
Jobos (bay) D3
Lima (pt.) F2
Luquillo, Sierra de (mts.) E2
Mangillo (pt.) B3
Mayagüez (bay) A2
Miquillo (pt.) F1
Molinos (pt.) G1
Mona (passg.) A2
Negra (pt.) G2
Nigua (riv.) D2
Ola Grande (pt.) D3
Palmas Altas (pt.) C1
Patillas (lake) E2
Petrona (pt.) D3
Pirata (mt.) F2
Plata (riv.) D2
Puerca (pt.) F2
Puerto Medio Mundo (bay) F2
Punta, Cerro de (mt.) C2
Ramey A.F.B. A1
Rincón (bay) D3
Rojo (cape) A3
Roosevelt Road Naval Res. F2
Salinas (pt.) D1
San José (lag.) E1
San Juan, Cabezas de (prom.) F1
San Juan Nat'l Hist. Site D1
Soldado (pt.) G2
Sucia (bay) A3
Tanamá (riv.) B1
Toro, El (mt.) F2
Torrecilla (lag.) E1
Tortuguero (lag.) D1
Tuna (pt.) E3
Vacía Talega (pt.) E1
Vieques (isl.) 7,662 G2
Vieques (passg.) F2
Vieques (sound) G2
Yagüez (riv.) A2
Yauco (lake) B2
Yeguas ((pt.) F3

ANTIGUA

CITIES and TOWNS

All Saints 1,796 E11
Cedar Grove 1,460 E11
Falmouth 1,134 E11
Freetown 1,250 E11
Jennings 1,370 D11
Liberta 2,394 E11
Old Road 1,244 D11
Parham 1,570 E11
Saint John's (cap.) 21,814 E11
Willikies 1,843 E11

OTHER FEATURES

Antigua (isl.) 76,213 E11
Boggy (peak) D11
Boon (pt.) E11
Green (isl.) E11
Guiana (isl.) E11
Long (isl.) E11
Saint John's (harb.) C11
Standfast (pt.) E11
Willoughby (bay) E11

ARUBA

CITIES and TOWNS

Aresji D9
Balashi E10
Bubali D10
Bushiribana E10
Druif D1
Oranjestad (cap.) Aruba 10,100 D10
Sint Nicolaas E10
Westpunt D10

OTHER FEATURES

Aruba (isl.) 66,790 E9
Basora (pt.) E10
Jamanota (mt.) E10
Paarden (bay) D10
Palm (beach) D10

BARBADOS

CITIES and TOWNS

Bathsheba B8
Belleplaine B8
Bridgetown (cap.) 7,552 B9
Carlton B8
Cave Hill B9
Checker Hall B8
Codrington B8
Crab Hill B8
Crane C9
Drax Hall B8
Ellerton B9
Greenland B8
Holetown B8
Kendal B8
Lodge Hill B8
Marchfield B9
Mount Standfast B8
Oistins B9
Rose Hill B8
Rouen B9
Saint Lawrence B9
Saint Martins C9
Scarboro B9
Seawell B9
Six Mens B8
Speightstown B8
Spring Hall B8
Welchman Hall B8

OTHER FEATURES

Carlisle (bay) B9
Hillaby (mt.) B8
Long (bay) B9
North (pt.) B8
Oistins (bay) B9
Pelican (isl.) B9
Ragged (pt.) C8
Sam Lord's Castle C9
South (pt.) B9

DOMINICA

CITIES and TOWNS

Barroui 1,480 E6
Castle Bruce 1,975 F6
Coulihaut 1,735 E6
Delice F7
Grand Bay 3,152 F7
Hampstead E5
La Plaine F6
Mahout 2,095 F6
Marigot 3,183 F6
Petit Soufrière F6
Portsmouth 2,329 E5
Rosalie F6
Roseau (cap.) 9,968 E7
Roseau *16,035 E7
Saint Joseph 2,643 E6
Salybia F6
Soufrière E7
Vieille Case E5
Wesley 2,002 F5

OTHER FEATURES

Capuchin (cape) E5
Carib Reserve F6
Clyde (riv.) F6
Crumpton (pt.) F5
Diablotin, Morne (mt.) E6
Dominica (passg.) E5
Douglas (bay) E5
Grand (bay) F7
Jaquet (pt.) E5
Layou (riv.) E6
Martinique (passg.) E7
Micotrin (mt.) F6
Pagoua (bay) F6
Prince Rupert (bay) E5
Scotts (head) E7
Soufrière (bay) E7
Trois Pitons, Morne (mt.) E6

GRENADA

CITIES and TOWNS

Gouyave 2,498 C8
Grand Roy C8
Grenville 1,723 D8
Hermitage D8
La Taste D8
Marquis D8
Mount Tivoli D8
Saint George's (cap.) 6,463 C9
Saint George's *34,624 C9
Sauteurs 605 D8
Victoria 1,673 D8
Woodford C8

OTHER FEATURES

Bedford (pt.) D8
David (pt.) D8
Great Bacolet (pt.) D8
Green (isl.) D8
Grenville (bay) D8
Gros (pt.) C8
Halifax (harb.) C8
Irvin's (bay) D8
Les Tantes (isls.) D7
Molinière (pt.) C8
Prickly (pt.) C9
Ronde (isl.) D7
Saint Catherine (mt.) D8
Saline (pt.) C9
Sinai (mt.) D8
Telescope (pt.) D8

GUADELOUPE

Total Population 329,017

CITIES and TOWNS

Anse-Bertrand 1,921 A5
Baie-Mahault 5,874 A6
Baillif 3,844 A7
Bananier A7
Basse-Terre (cap.) 13,397 A7
Bouillante 1,821 A6
Bourg-des-Saintes 907 A7
Capesterre 7,541 A7
Ferry A6
Gosier 13,741 B6
Gourbeyre 5,637 A7
Goyave 1,709 A6
Grand-Bourg 3,249 B7
Lamentin 2,319 A6
Les Abymes 51,837 B6
Morne-à-l'Eau 9,457 A6
Moule 9,800 B6
Petit-Bourg 5,097 A6
Petit-Canal 1,581 A6
Pigeon A6
Pointe-à-Pitre 25,151 B6
Pointe-Noire 2,180 A6
Port-Louis 4,517 B5
Saint-Claude 6,755 A7
Sainte-Anne 11,527 B6
Sainte-Marguerite B6
Sainte-Marie A6
Sainte-Rose 4,805 A6
Saint-François 3,141 B6
Trois-Rivières 7,881 A7
Vieux-Fort 1,073 B7
Vieux-Habitants 4,065 A7

OTHER FEATURES

Allègre (pt.) A6
Antigues (pt.) A5
Basse-Terre (isl.) 138,777 A6
Châteaux (pt.) B6
Constant, Morne (hill) B7
Désirade, La (isl.) 1,602 B6
Fajou (isl.) A6
Grand Cul-de-Sac Marin (bay) A6
Grande-Terre (isl.) B6
Grande Vigie (pt.) B5
Grand-Ilet (isl.) A7
Guadeloupe (isl.) 167,896 B6
Guadeloupe (passg.) A5
Guadeloupe Nat'l Park A6
Kahouanne (isl.) A6
Marie-Galante (isl.) 13,757 B7
Nord (pt.) B7
Nord-Est (bay) B6
Petit Cul-de-Sac Marin (bay) A6
Petite-Terre (isls.) B6
Saintes (chan.) A7
Saintes (isls.) 2,901 A7
Salée (riv.) A6
Sans Toucher (mt.) A6
Soufrière (mt.) A7
Terre-de-Bas (isl.) 1,427 A7
Terre-de-Haut (isl.) 1,453 A7
Vieux-Fort (pt.) A7

MARTINIQUE

Total Population 330,220

CITIES and TOWNS

Ajoupa-Bouillon 1,569 C5
Basse-Pointe 2,163 C5
Bellefontaine 818 C6
Case-Pilote 1,776 C6
Ducos 4,429 D6
Fond-Saint-Denis 962 C6
Fort-de-France (cap.) 96,649 C6
Grand' Rivière 1,053 C5
Gros-Morne 1,976 D6
La Trinité 3,380 D6
Le Carbet 2,321 C6
Le François 2,940 D6
Le Lamentin 6,872 D6
Le Lorrain 2,024 D6
Le Marin 2,651 D7
Le Morne-Rouge 2,650 C5
Le Prêcheur 1,350 C5
Le Robert 3,610 D6
Le Saint-Esprit 3,947 D6
Les Trois-Ilets 1,484 D6
Le Vauclin 3,054 D6
Macouba 1,142 C5
Marigot 1,765 D5
Rivière-Pilote 1,587 D7
Rivière-Salée 1,859 D7
Sainte-Luce 1,502 D7
Sainte-Marie 3,966 D5
Saint-Joseph 2,052 D6
Saint-Pierre 4,923 C6
Schoelcher 16,412 C6

OTHER FEATURES

Cabet, Pitons du (mt.) C6
Cabrits (isl.) D7
Caravelle (pen.) D6
Cul-de-Sac du Marin (bay) D7
Diable (pt.) D7
Ferré (cape) E7
Fort-de-France (bay) C6
Galion (bay) D6
Lézarde (riv.) D6
Long (isl.) D6
Lorrain (riv.) D5
Martinique (passg.) C5
Pelée (vol.) C5
Pilote (riv.) D7
Ramiers (isl.) C6
Ramville (isl.) D6
Robert (harb.) D6
Rose (pt.) D6
Saint-Martin (cape) C5
Saint-Pierre (bay) C6
Salines (pt.) D7
Salomon (pt.) C7
Vauclin (mt.) D6

NETHERLANDS ANTILLES

CITIES and TOWNS

Ascension F8
Bacuna E8
Boven Bolivia E8
Dokterstuin F8
Emmastad F9
Entrejo E8
Fontein E8
Groot Sint Joris G9
Hato G8
Kralendijk (cap.), Bonaire 2,500 E8
Lagoen F8
Montanja di Reij G9
New Port G9
Noord di Salinja E8
Onima E8
Otrabanda F9
Patrick E8
Rincon E8
Rooi E8
Santa Barbara G9
Santa Catharina G9
Savonet F8
Sint Kruis F8
Sint Martha F8
Sint Michiel F9
Sint Willebrordus F8
Terra Corra E8
Westpunt F8
Willemstad (cap.) 95,000 F9
Willemstad *130,000 F9

OTHER FEATURES

Bonaire (isl.) 8,087 E9
Bullen (bay) F8
Caracas (bay) G9
Curaçao (isl.) 145,430 G7
Goto (lake) D8
Kanon (pt.) G9
Klein Bonaire (isl.) E8
Kudarebe (pt.) D9
Lac (bay) D9
Lacre (pt.) E9
Malmok (mt.) E8
Noord (pt.) D8
Noord (pt.) E8
Pekelmeer (lake) E9
Piscadera (bay) F9
Schottegat (bay) G9
Sint Anna (bay) F9
Sint Christoffel (mt.) F8
Sint Joris (bay) G9
Slag (bay) D8
Vierkant (pt.) E8

SAINT KITTS and NEVIS

CITIES and TOWNS

Basseterre (cap.) 14,725 C10
Cayon C10
Charlestown 1,326 C11
Cotton Ground 471 C11
Dieppe Bay C10
Frigate Bay C10
Gingerland D11
Golden Rock C10
Newcastle D11
Old Road Town C10
Sadlers Village C10
Sandy Point 862 C10
Tabernacle C10
Zion Hill D11

OTHER FEATURES

Brimstone (hill) C10
Dogwood (pt.) D11
Fort (pt.) C11
Great Salt (pond) D10
Heldens (pt.) C10
Horse Shoe (pt.) C11
Misery (mt.) C10
Monkey (hill) C10
Narrows, The (str.) D11
Nevis (isl.) 9,300 D11
Nevis (peak) D11
North Friars (bay) D10
Pinney's (beach) D11
Saint Christopher (Saint Kitts) (isl.) 35,104 D10
South Friars (bay) C10

SAINT LUCIA

CITIES and TOWNS

Anse la Raye •5,007 F6
Canaries •2,075 G6
Castries (cap.) •42,770 G6
Choc G5
Choiseul •6,382 F7
Dauphin G5
Dennery •9,654 G6
Gros Islet •10,329 G5
Laborie •6,944 G7
Marigot G6
Marquis G6
Micoud •12,264 G6
Praslin G6
Soufrière •7,456 F6
Vieux Fort •10,675 G7

OTHER FEATURES

Beaumont (pt.) F6
Canaries, Piton (mt.) G6
Cannelles (pt.) G7
Cannelles (riv.) G6
Cap (pt.) G5
Choc (bay) G5
Fond d'Or (bay) G6
Gimie (mt.) G6
Grand Caille (pt.) F6
Grand Cul de Sac (riv.) G6
Gros Islet (bay) G5
Gros Piton (mt.) G6
La Sorcière (mt.) G6
Maria (isls.) G7
Ministre (pt.) G7
Moule-à-Chique (cape) G7
Petit Piton (mt.) G6
Pigeon (isl.) G5
Port Castries (harb.) G6
Port Praslin (bay) G6
Roseau (riv.) G6
Saint Lucia (chan.) G5
Saint Vincent (chan.) G7
Savannes (bay) G7
Sorcière, La (mt.) G6
Soufrière (bay) F6
Vierge (pt.) G6

SAINT VINCENT and THE GRENADINES

CITIES and TOWNS

Barrouallie 1,298 A9
Calliaqua 627 A9
Camden Park A9
Colonarie A9
Georgetown 1,100 A8
Kingstown (cap.) 17,117 A9
Kingstown *23,330 A9
Layou 1,147 A9
Wallibu A8

OTHER FEATURES

Colonarie (pt.) A9
Cumberland (bay) A8
Dark (head) A8
De Volet (pt.) A8
Espagnol (pt.) A8
Greathead (bay) A9
Kingstown (bay) A9
Owia (bay) A8
Porter (pt.) A8
Richmond (peak) A8
Saint Andrew (mt.) A9
Saint Vincent (passg.) A8
Soufrière (mt.) A8
Yambou (head) A9

TRINIDAD and TOBAGO

CITIES and TOWNS

Arima 11,390 B10
Arouca B10
Basse Terre B11
Biche B10
Blanchisseuse B10
California A11
Carapichaima B10
Caroni B10
Cedros A11
Chaguanas 6,122 B10
Chaguaramas A10
Couva 3,635 B10
Cunapo B10
Flanagin Town B10
Fullarton A11
Fyzabad 1,564 A11
Grande Rivière B10
Guaico B10
Guayaguayare B11
La Brea 1,487 A11
Marabella 18,158 A11
Matelot B10
Matura B10
Mayaro 2,638 B11
Moruga B11
Mucurapo A10
Palo Seco A11
Peñal 3,606 B11
Point Fortin 6,538 A11
Port-of-Spain (cap.) 67,978 A10
Princes Town 8,288 B11
Redhead B10
Rio Claro 2,423 B11
Saint Joseph 4,132 B10
Saint Joseph B11
San Fernando 33,490 A11
San Francique A11
Sangre Grande 8,948 B1
San Juan A10
Sans Souci B10
Siparia 5,773 B11
Tabaquite 2,309 B11
Talparo B10
Toco 1,287 B10
Tunapuna 10,251 B10
Upper Manzanilla B1
Valencia B10
Waterloo A10

OTHER FEATURES

Aripo, El Cerro del (mt.) B10
Boca Grande (passg.) A10
Chacachacare (isl.) A10
Chupara (pt.) B10
Cocos (bay) B10
Dragons Mouth (str.) A10
El Tucuche (mt.) B10
Erin (bay) A11
Galeota (pt.) B11
Galera (pt.) C10
Guapo (bay) A11
Guatuaro (pt.) B11
Icacos (pt.) A11
Maracas (bay) C10
Pitch (lake) A11

VIRGIN ISLANDS (Br.)

CITIES and TOWNS

Road Town (cap.) 2,200 D3
West End C4

OTHER FEATURES

Flanagan (passg.) D4
Frenchman (cay) C4
Great Thatch (isl.) C4
Great Tobago (isl.) B3
Jost Van Dyke (isl.) 135 C3
Little Tobago (isl.) B3
Narrows, The (str.) C4
Norman (isl.) D4
Peter (isl.) D4
Road (bay) D3
Sage (mt.) D4
Sir Francis Drake (chan.) D4
Tortola (isl.) 9,257 D3

VIRGIN ISLANDS (U.S.)

CITIES and TOWNS

Bethlehem E4
Canebay E3
Charlotte Amalie (cap.) 11,842 B4
Christiansted 2,914 F4
Cruz Bay 1,928 C4
Diamond F4
Eastend D4
Emmaus C4
Fredensdal F4
Frederiksted 1,046 E4
Grove Place 3,599 E4
Kingshill F4
Longford F4
Negro Bay E4

OTHER FEATURES

Altona (lag.) F4
Annaly (bay) E3
Baron Bluff (prom.) E3
Bordeaux (mt.) C4
Brass (isls.) A4
Buck (isl.) G3
Buck Island (chan.) F3
Buck Island Reef Nat'l Mon. G3
Butler (bay) E4
Caneel (bay) B4
Capella (isls.) B4
Christiansted Nat'l Hist. Site F4
Coral (bay) C4
Crown (mt.) A4
Dutch Cap (cay) A4
Eagle (mt.) E4
East (pt.) G4
Flanagan (passg.) D4
Flat (cays) A4
Grass (pt.) G4
Great (pond) F4
Great Pond (bay) F4
Green (cay) F4
Hams Bluff (prom.) E3
Hans Lollik (isls.) B4
Hassel (isl.) B4
Jersey (bay) B4
Krause Lagoon (chan.) F4
Leeward (passg.) B4
Long (pt.) B4
Long (pt.) E4
Lovango (cay) C4
Magens (bay) B4
Maho (bay) C4
Narrows, The (str.) C4
Nulliberg (mt.) B4
Perseverance (bay) A4
Picara (pt.) B4
Pillsbury (sound) B4
Privateer (pt.) D4
Pull (pt.) F3
Ram (head) C5
Red (pt.) D4
Reef (bay) C4
Saba (isl.) A4
Saint Croix (isl.) 49,725 G4
Saint James (isls.) B4
Saint John (isl.) 2,472 C4
Saint Thomas (harb.) B4
Saint Thomas (isl.) 44,372 A4
Salt (cay) A4
Salt (riv.) F4
Salt River (bay) F3
Sandy (pt.) D4
Savana (isl.) A4
Southwest (cape) E4
Tague (bay) G4
Thatch (cay) B4
Turner Hole (bay) G4
U.S. Nav. Air Sta. A4
Virgin (str.) A4
Virgin Isls. Nat'l Park C4
Water (isl.) A4
Westend Saltpond (lag.) E4

*City and suburbs.
• Population of district.
†Population of met. area.
○ Population of municipality.

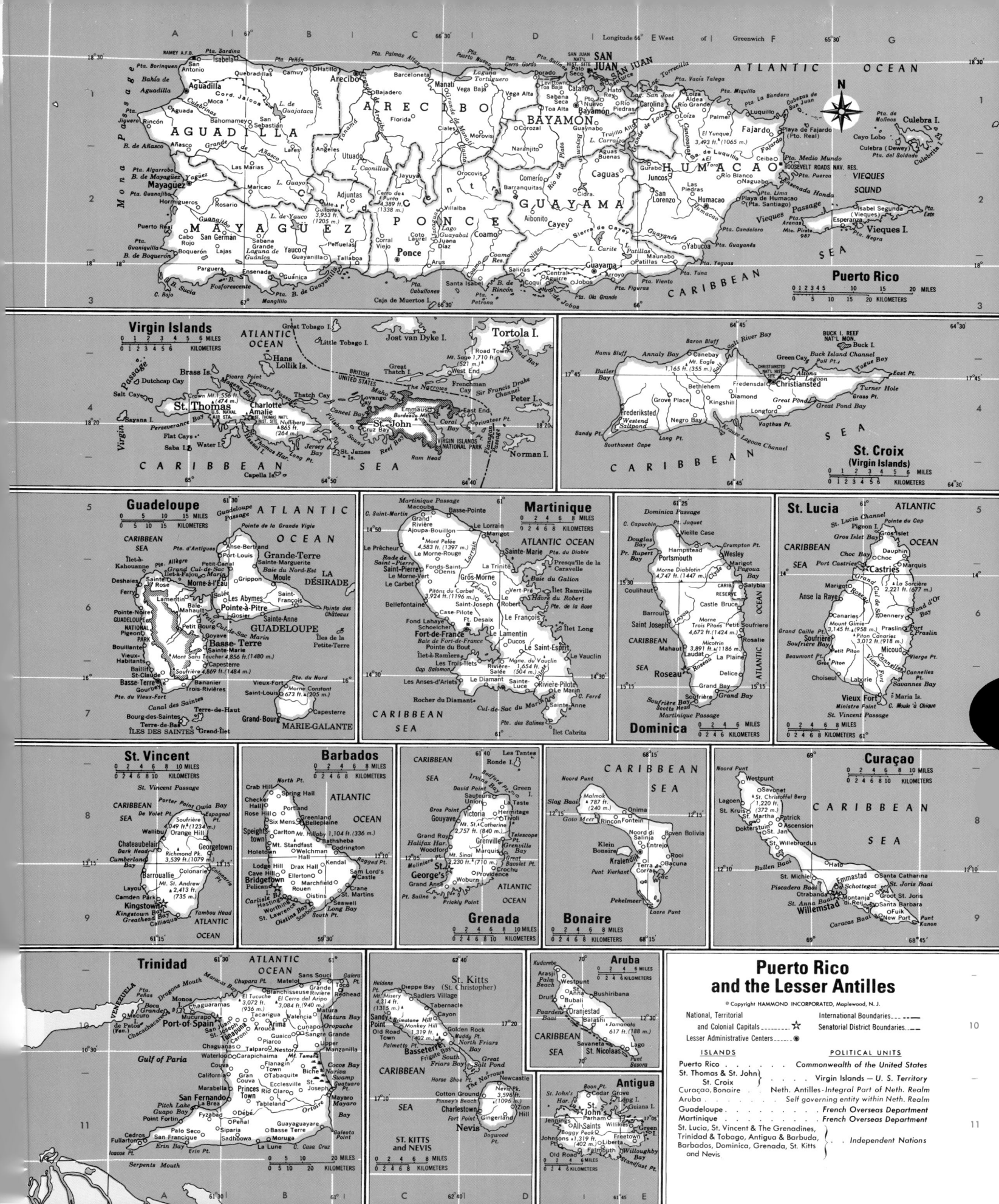

Puerto Rico and the Lesser Antilles

© Copyright HAMMOND INCORPORATED, Maplewood, N.J.

National, Territorial and Colonial Capitals ☆
International Boundaries
Lesser Administrative Centers ◉
Senatorial District Boundaries

ISLANDS	POLITICAL UNITS
Puerto Rico	Commonwealth of the United States
St. Thomas & St. John	Virgin Islands — U.S. Territory
St. Croix	
Curaçao, Bonaire	Neth. Antilles-Integral Part of Neth. Realm
Aruba	Self governing entity within Neth. Realm
Guadeloupe	French Overseas Department
Martinique	French Overseas Department
St. Lucia, St. Vincent & The Grenadines, Trinidad & Tobago, Antigua & Barbuda, Barbados, Dominica, Grenada, St. Kitts and Nevis	Independent Nations

Canada
CONIC PROJECTION

SCALE OF MILES
0 50 100   200   300

SCALE OF KILOMETERS
0 50 100 200   300   400   500

Capitals of Countries .... ☆
Provincial & Territorial Capitals .... ⊕
Administrative Centers .... ○
International Boundaries ....____ —
Provincial Boundaries ...._ _ _
Regional Boundaries ....

© Copyright HAMMOND INCORPORATED, Maplewood, N.J.

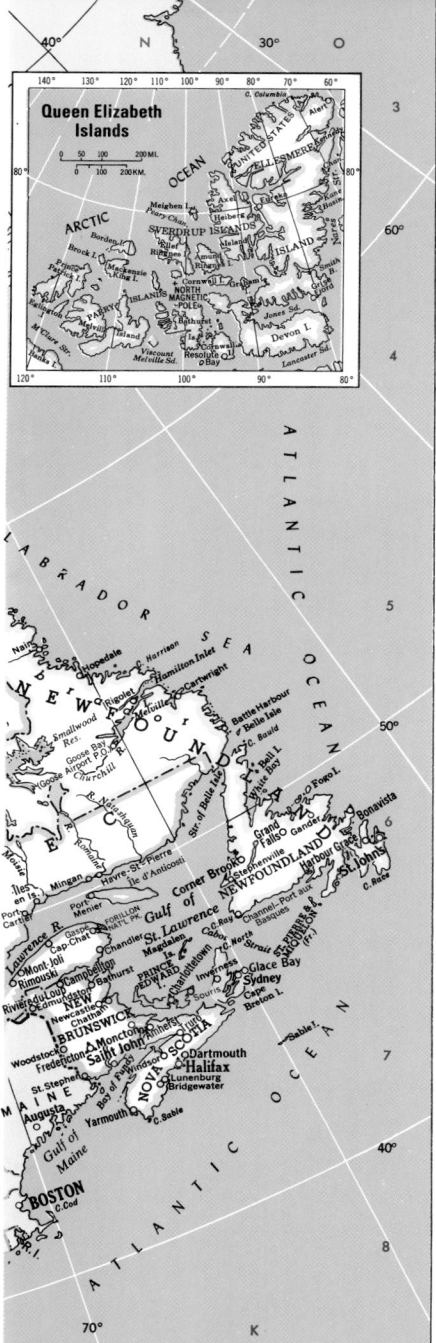

AREA 3,851,787 sq. mi. (9,976,139 sq. km.)
POPULATION 24,343,181
CAPITAL Ottawa
LARGEST CITY Montréal
HIGHEST POINT Mt. Logan 19,524 ft. (5,951 m.)
MONETARY UNIT Canadian dollar
MAJOR LANGUAGES English, French
MAJOR RELIGIONS Protestantism, Roman Catholicism

Population Distribution

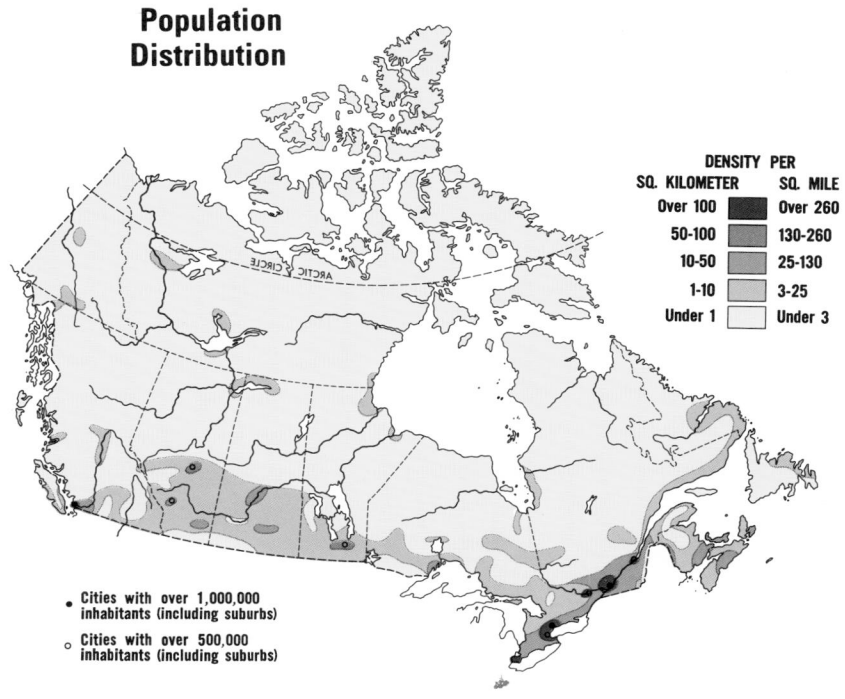

DENSITY PER

SQ. KILOMETER	SQ. MILE
Over 100	Over 260
50-100	130-260
10-50	25-130
1-10	3-25
Under 1	Under 3

● Cities with over 1,000,000 inhabitants (including suburbs)

○ Cities with over 500,000 inhabitants (including suburbs)

Vegetation

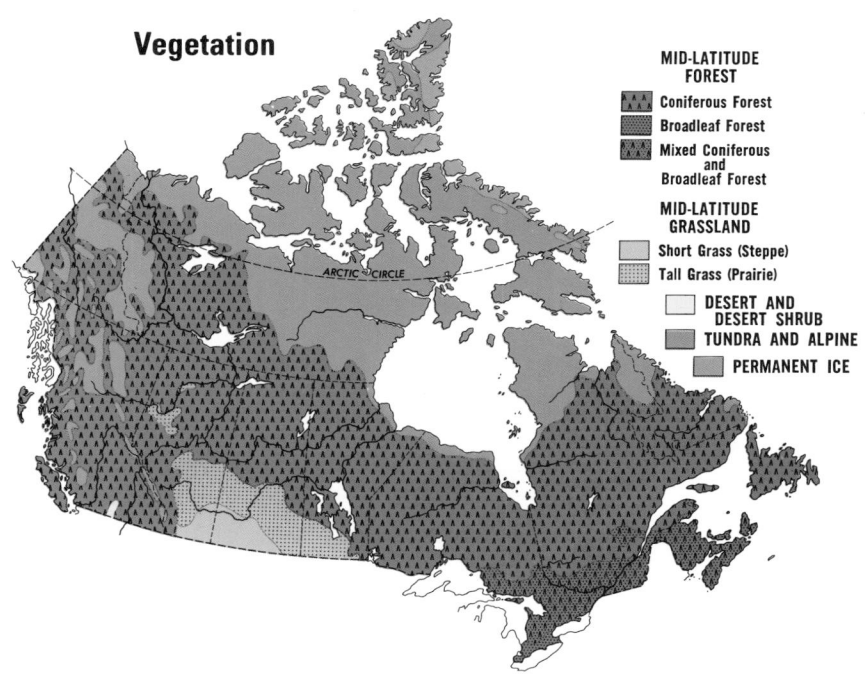

MID-LATITUDE FOREST

Coniferous Forest

Broadleaf Forest

Mixed Coniferous and Broadleaf Forest

MID-LATITUDE GRASSLAND

Short Grass (Steppe)

Tall Grass (Prairie)

DESERT AND DESERT SHRUB

TUNDRA AND ALPINE

PERMANENT ICE

CANADA

Saint Pierre & Miquelon (isls.)
  6,041 . . . . L 6
Sarnia, Ont. 50,892 . . . . H 7
Saskatchewan (prov.) 968,313 F 5
Saskatchewan (riv.) . . . . F 5
Saskatoon, Sask. 154,210 . . . F 5
Sault Sainte Marie, Ont.
  82,697 . . . . H 6
Schefferville, Que. 1,997 . . . . K 5
Selkirk, Man. 10,037 . . . . G 5
Sept-Iles (Seven Is.), Que.
  29,262 . . . . K 5
Shawinigan, Que. 23,011 . . . . J 6
Sherbrooke, Que. 74,075 . . . . J 7
Sioux Lookout, Ont. 3,074 . . . . G 5
Skeena (riv.), Br. Col. . . . . D 5
Slave (riv.) . . . . E 3
Smallwood (res.), Newf. . . . . . K 5
Southampton (isl.), N.W.T. . . . . H 2
Stettler, Alta. 5,136 . . . . E 5
Stewart (riv.), Yukon . . . . C 3
Stikine (riv.), Br. Col. . . . . C 4
Sudbury, Ont. 91,829 . . . . H 6
Swift Current, Sask. 14,747 . . F 5
Sydney, N.S. 29,444 . . . . K 6
Terrace, Br. Col. ○10,914 . . . . D 5
The Pas, Man. 6,390 . . . . F 5
Thompson, Man. 14,288 . . . . . G 4
Thunder Bay, Ont. 112,486 . . . H 6
Timmins, Ont. 46,114 . . . . H 6
Toronto (cap.), Ont. 599,217 . . H 7
Trail, Br. Col. 9,599 . . . . E 6
Trois-Rivières, Que. 50,466 . . J 6
Truro, N.S. 12,552 . . . . K 6
Tuktoyaktuk, N.W.T. 772 . . . . . C 2

Val-d'Or, Que. 21,371 . . . . J 6
Vancouver, Br. Col. 414,281 . . D 6
Vancouver (isl.), Br. Col. . . . . . D 6
Vanderhoof, Br. Col. 2,323 . . . D 5
Vegreville, Alta. 5,251 . . . . E 5
Vernon, Br. Col. 19,987 . . . . . . E 5
Victoria (cap.), Br. Col. 64,379 D 6
Victoria (isl.), N.W.T. . . . . E 1
Wabush, Newf. 3,155 . . . . K 5
Waterton-Glacier International
  Peace Park, Alta. . . . . E 6
Wetaskiwin, Alta. 9,597 . . . . . E 5
Weyburn, Sask. 9,523 . . . . F 6
Whitehorse (cap.), Yukon
  14,814 . . . . C 3
Williams Lake, Br. Col. 8,362 . D 5
Williston (lake), Br. Col. . . . . . D 4
Windsor, N.S. 3,646 . . . . K 7
Windsor, Ont. 192,083 . . . . . . H 7
Winnipeg (cap.), Man.
  564,473 . . . . G 6
Winnipeg (lake), Man. . . . . G 5
Winnipegosis (lake), Man. . . . . F 5
Wood Buffalo Nat'l Park, Alta. . E 4
Woods (lake) . . . . G 6
Wrigley, N.W.T. 137 . . . . D 3
Yarmouth, N.S. 7,475 . . . . K 7
Yellowknife (cap.), N.W.T.
  9,483 . . . . E 3
Yoho Nat'l Park, Br. Col. . . . . . E 5
York Factory, Man. . . . . G 4
Yorkton, Sask. 15,339 . . . . F 5
Yukon Territory 23,153 . . . . C 3

○Population of municipality.

Average January Temperature

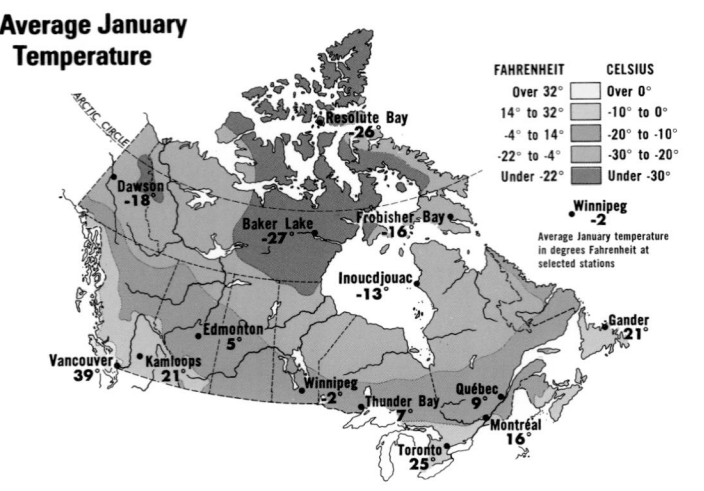

FAHRENHEIT	CELSIUS
Over 32°	Over 0°
14° to 32°	-10° to 0°
-4° to 14°	-20° to -10°
-22° to -4°	-30° to -20°
Under -22°	Under -30°

Winnipeg -2
Average January temperature in degrees Fahrenheit at selected stations

Resolute Bay -26°
Dawson -18°
Baker Lake -27°
Frobisher Bay -16°
Inoucdjouac -13°
Edmonton 5°
Vancouver 39°
Kamloops 21°
Winnipeg -2°
Thunder Bay 7°
Québec 9°
Montréal 16°
Toronto 25°
Gander 21°

Average July Temperature

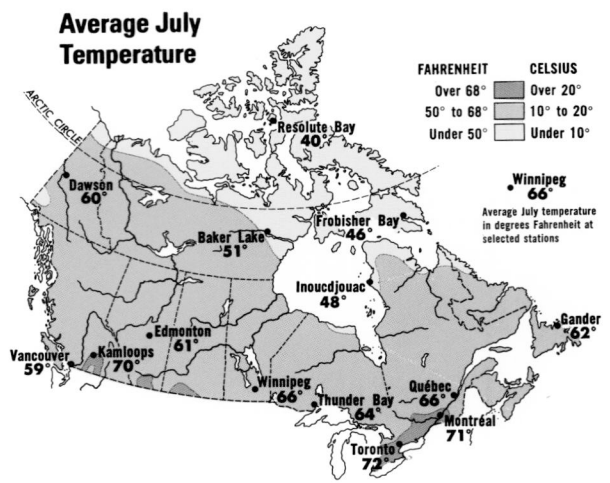

FAHRENHEIT	CELSIUS
Over 68°	Over 20°
50° to 68°	10° to 20°
Under 50°	Under 10°

Winnipeg 66°
Average July temperature in degrees Fahrenheit at selected stations

Resolute Bay 40°
Dawson 60°
Baker Lake 51°
Frobisher Bay 46°
Inoucdjouac 48°
Edmonton 61°
Vancouver 59°
Kamloops 70°
Winnipeg 66°
Thunder Bay 64°
Québec 66°
Montréal 71°
Toronto 72°
Gander 62°

Agriculture, Industry and Resources

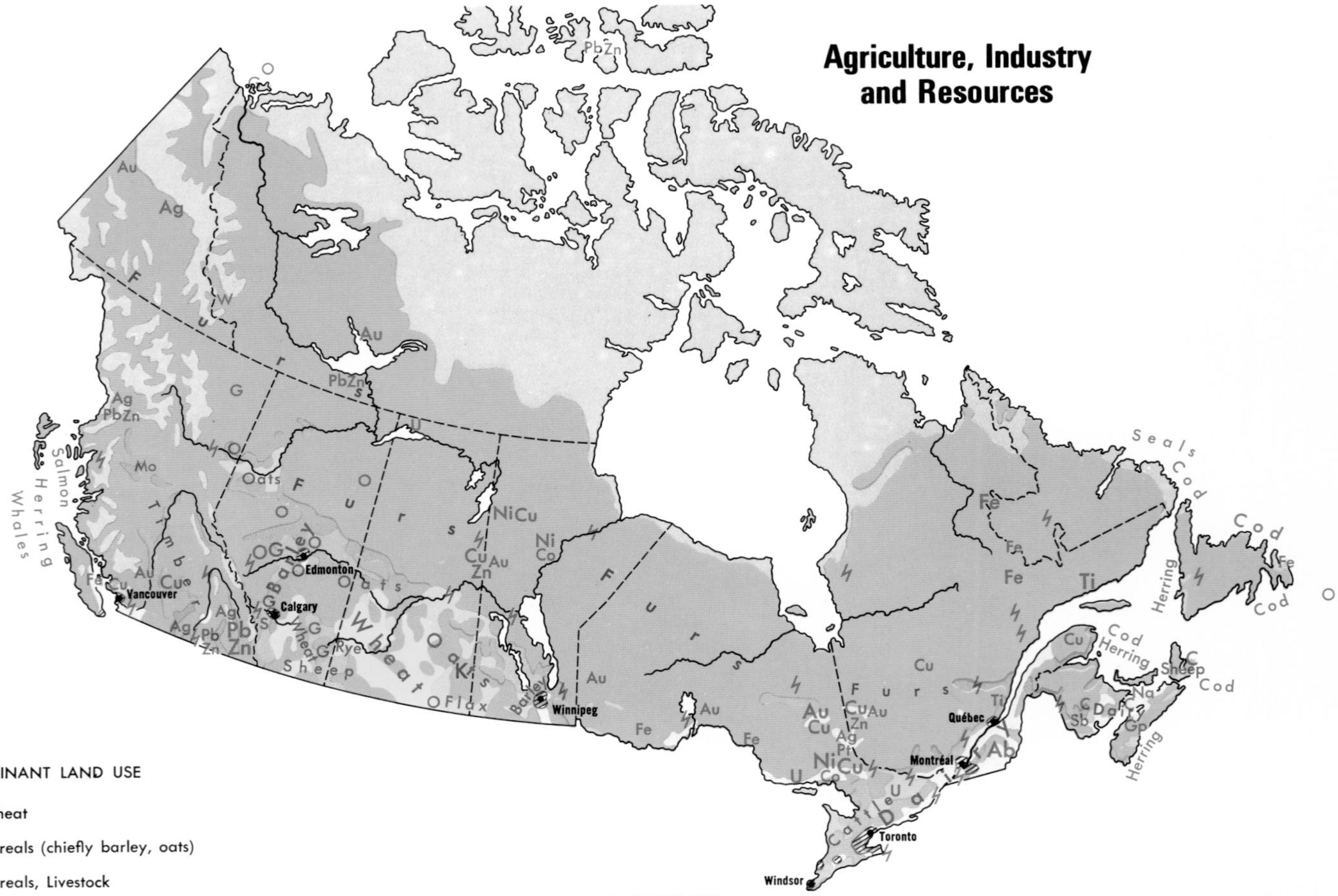

DOMINANT LAND USE

- Wheat
- Cereals (chiefly barley, oats)
- Cereals, Livestock
- General Farming, Livestock
- Dairy
- Fruit, Vegetables
- Pasture Livestock
- Range Livestock
- Forests
- Nonagricultural Land

MAJOR MINERAL OCCURRENCES

Ab	Asbestos	Fe	Iron Ore	Ni	Nickel
Ag	Silver	G	Natural Gas	O	Petroleum
Au	Gold	Gp	Gypsum	Pb	Lead
C	Coal	K	Potash	Pt	Platinum
Co	Cobalt	Mo	Molybdenum	S	Sulfur
Cu	Copper	Na	Salt		

Sb	Antimony
Ti	Titanium
U	Uranium
W	Tungsten
Zn	Zinc

Water Power
Major Industrial Areas

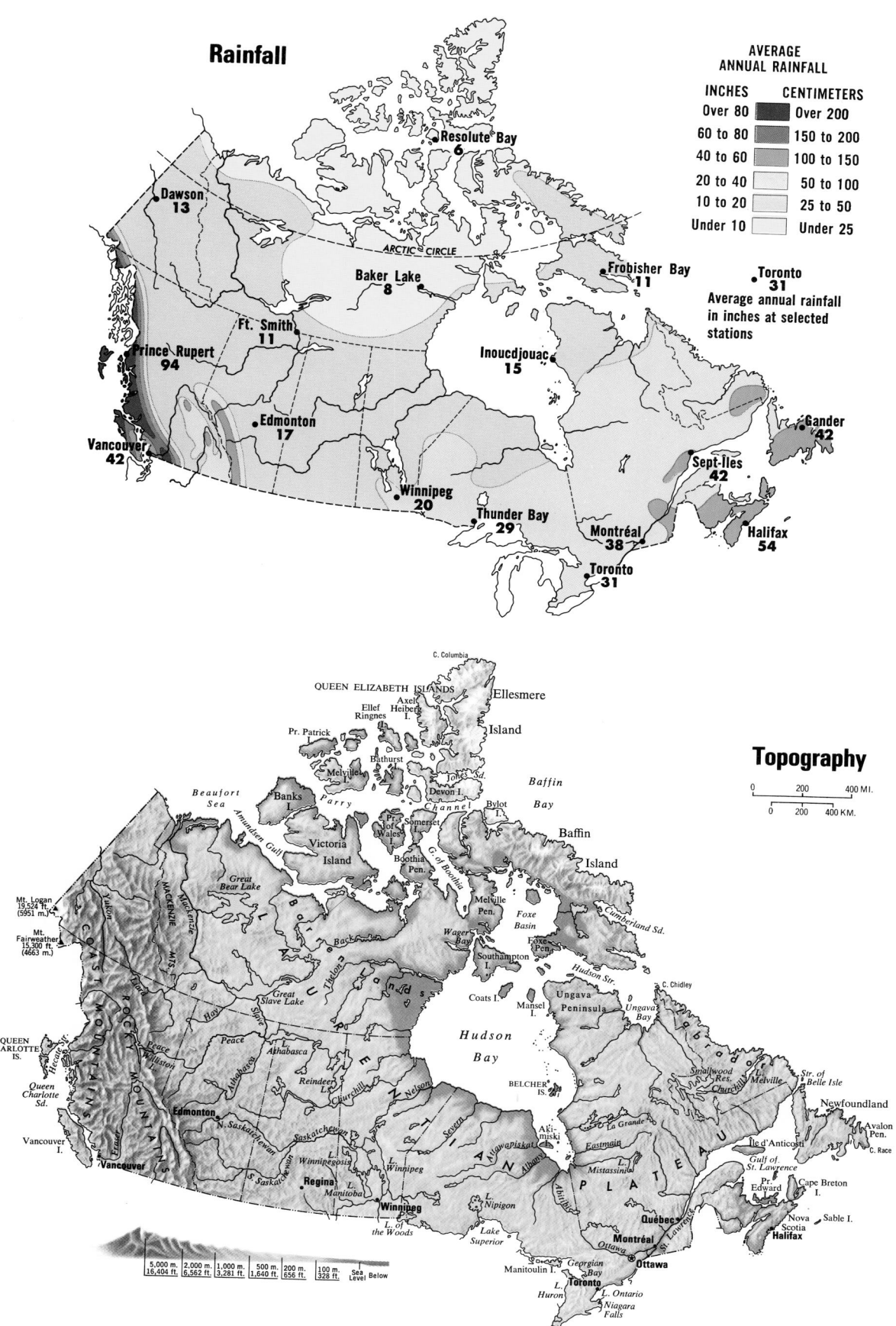

Rainfall

AVERAGE ANNUAL RAINFALL

INCHES	CENTIMETERS
Over 80	Over 200
60 to 80	150 to 200
40 to 60	100 to 150
20 to 40	50 to 100
10 to 20	25 to 50
Under 10	Under 25

Toronto 31
Average annual rainfall in inches at selected stations

Resolute Bay 6
Dawson 13
ARCTIC CIRCLE
Baker Lake 8
Frobisher Bay 11
Ft. Smith 11
Prince Rupert 94
Inoucdjouac 15
Gander 42
Edmonton 17
Vancouver 42
Sept-Îles 42
Winnipeg 20
Thunder Bay 29
Montréal 38
Halifax 54
Toronto 31

Topography

0 200 400 MI.
0 200 400 KM.

C. Columbia
QUEEN ELIZABETH ISLANDS
Ellef Ringnes I.
Axel Heiberg I.
Ellesmere Island
Pr. Patrick I.
Bathurst
Melville I.
Jones Sd.
Devon I.
Baffin Bay
Beaufort Sea
Banks
Parry Channel
Bylot I.
Amundsen Gulf
Pr. of Wales I.
Somerset
Baffin Island
Victoria Island
Boothia Pen.
G. of Boothia
Great Bear Lake
Cumberland Sd.
Mt. Logan 19,524 ft. (5951 m.)
Melville Pen.
Foxe Basin
Mt. Fairweather 15,300 ft. (4663 m.)
Wager Bay
Foxe Pen.
Great Slave Lake
Southampton I.
Hudson Str.
C. Chidley
Coats I.
Mansel I.
Ungava Peninsula
Ungava Bay
QUEEN CHARLOTTE IS.
Peace
Athabasca
Reindeer
Nelson
Hudson Bay
BELCHER IS.
Queen Charlotte Sd.
Churchill
Smallwood Res.
Melville
Str. of Belle Isle
Edmonton
N. Saskatchewan
Saskatchewan
La Grande
Newfoundland
Avalon Pen.
Vancouver I.
Fraser
Winnipegosis
L. Winnipeg
Eastmain
Île d'Anticosti
C. Race
Vancouver
Regina
S. Saskat.
L. Manitoba
Mistassini
Gulf of St. Lawrence
Cape Breton I.
Pr. Edward
Nova Scotia
Sable I.
Winnipeg
L. of the Woods
L. Nipigon
Lake Superior
Québec
St. Lawrence
Halifax
Montréal
Ottawa
Manitoulin I.
Georgian Bay
Toronto
L. Huron
L. Ontario
Niagara Falls

| 5,000 m. 16,404 ft. | 2,000 m. 6,562 ft. | 1,000 m. 3,281 ft. | 500 m. 1,640 ft. | 200 m. 656 ft. | 100 m. 328 ft. | Sea Level | Below |

Newfoundland
including Labrador

SCALE

0   25   50   100   150 MI.

0   25   50   100   150 KM.

Capitals of Provinces .... ⊛

Provincial Boundaries .... —·—·—

Provincial Boundary according to
Imperial Privy Council decision, 1927 .... – – – –

NEWFOUNDLAND

CITIES and TOWNS

Admiral's Beach 362 .... D2
Admiral's Cove 99 .... D2
Anchor Point 368 .... C3
Aquaforte 200 .... D2
Argentia 93 .... C2
Arnold's Cove 1,124 .... C2
Avondale 890 .... D2
Badger 1,090 .... C4
Badger's Quay-Valleyfield-Pool's Island 1,566 .... D4
Baie Verte 2,491 .... C4
Battle Harbour C3
Bauline 423 .... D2
Bay Bulls 1,081 .... D2
Bay de Verde 786 .... D2
Bay L'Argent 483 .... D4
Bay Roberts 4,512 .... D2
Bellburns 147 .... C3
Belleoram 565 .... C4
Bellevue 286 .... D2
Bide Arm 339 .... C3
Big Pond 167 .... D2
Birchy Bay 707 .... D4
Bird Cove 400 .... C3
Bishop's Falls 4,395 .... C4
Black Tickle 194 .... C3
Blackhead Road 1,855 .... D2
Blaketown 617 .... D2
Bloomfield 715 .... D2
Bonavista 4,460 .... D2
Botwood 4,074 .... C4
Branch 462 .... D2
Brigus 898 .... D2
Broad Cove 198 .... D2
Brooklyn 197 .... D2
Brownsdale 199 .... D2
Buchans 1,655 .... C4
Bunyan's Cove 590 .... C2
Burgeo 2,504 .... C4
Burin 2,904 .... C4
Burnt Islands 991 .... C4
Burnt Point 260 .... D2
Calvert 482 .... D2
Campbellton 703 .... D4
Cape Broyle 698 .... D2
Cape Ray 484 .... C4
Caplin Cove 150 .... D2
Carbonear 5,335 .... D2
Carmanville 966 .... D4
Cartwright 658 .... C3
Catalina 1,162 .... D2
Cavendish 343 .... D2
Champney's West 141 .... D2
Chance Cove 498 .... D2
Change Islands 580 .... D4
Channel-Port aux Basques 5,988 .... C4
Chapel Arm 689 .... D2
Charlottetown 330 .... D2
Charlottetown 250 .... C3
Churchill Falls 936 .... B3
Clarenville 2,878 .... C2
Clarke's Beach 1,009 .... D2
Codroy 346 .... C4
Colinet 318 .... D2
Colliers 819 .... D2
Come By Chance 337 .... C2
Conception Harbour 917 .... D2
Conche 464 .... C3
Cook's Harbour 388 .... C3
Corner Brook 24,339 .... C4
Cow Head 695 .... C4
Cox's Cove 980 .... C4
Cupids 706 .... D2
Daniell's Harbour 614 .... C3
Dark Cove 1,344 .... D4
Davis Inlet 240 .... B2
Deep Bight 243 .... C2
Deer Lake 4,348 .... C4
Dildo 877 .... D2
Dunville 1,817 .... D2
Durrell 1,145 .... D4
Eastport 597 .... D1
Elliston 527 .... D2
Embree 846 .... C4
Englee 998 .... C3
English Harbour 118 .... D2
English Harbour West 327 .... C4
Fermeuse 584 .... D2
Ferryland 795 .... D2
Flat Bay 322 .... C4
Flat Rock 808 .... D2
Fleur de Lys 616 .... C3
Flowers Cove 459 .... C3
Fogo 1,105 .... D4
Forteau 520 .... C3
Fortune 2,473 .... C4
Fox Harbour 280 .... C3
Fox Harbour 538 .... D2
François 219 .... C4
Freshwater 1,276 .... C2
Freshwater 209 .... D2
Gambo 2,932 .... D4
Gander 10,404 .... D4
Garnish 761 .... C4
Gaskiers-Point la Haye 505 .... D2
Gaultois 558 .... C4
Georges Brook 356 .... D2
Glenwood 1,129 .... D4
Glovertown 2,165 .... C1
Goobies 185 .... D2
Goose Bay-Happy Valley 7,103 .... B3
Gooseberry Cove 195 .... C2
Goose Cove 134 .... C2
Goose Cove 368 .... C3
Goulds 4,242 .... D2
Grand Bank 3,901 .... C4
Grand Falls 8,765 .... C4
Grates Cove 275 .... D2
Green Island Cove 222 .... C3
Green's Harbour 785 .... D2
Greenspond 423 .... D4
Grey River 234 .... C4
Gull Island 362 .... D2
Hampden 838 .... C4
Hant's Harbour 542 .... D2
Happy Adventure 352 .... D2
Happy Valley-Goose Bay 7,103 .... B3
Harbour Breton 2,464 .... C4
Harbour Deep 278 .... C3
Harbour Grace 2,988 .... D2
Harbour Main-Chapel Cove-Lakeview 1,303 .... D2
Hare Bay 1,520 .... D4
Hawke's Bay 553 .... C3
Head of Bay d'Espoir 586 .... C4
Heart's Content 625 .... D2
Heart's Delight-Islington 899 .... D2
Heart's Desire 416 .... D2
Heatherton 328 .... C4
Hermitage 863 .... C4
Hickman's Harbour 479 .... D2
Hillview 295 .... D2
Hodge's Cove 438 .... D2
Holyrood 1,789 .... D2
Hopedale 425 .... B2
Howley 456 .... C4
Isle aux Morts 1,238 .... C4
Jackson's Arm 623 .... C4
Jeffrey's 276 .... C4
Jerseyside 641 .... B3
Job's Cove 201 .... D2
Joe Batt's Arm-Barr'd Islands 1,155 .... D4
Keels 129 .... D1
Kelligrews (Foxtrap-Greeleytown-Peachtown-Kelligrews) 2,292 .... D2
Kilbride 5,014 .... D2
King's Cove 253 .... D1
King's Point 825 .... C4
Kippens 1,219 .... C4
Labrador City 11,538 .... A3
Lamaline 548 .... C4
L'Anse-au-Clair 267 .... C3
L'Anse-au-Loup 589 .... C3
L'Anse au Meadow 66 .... C3
La Poile 186 .... C4
Lark Harbour 783 .... C4
La Scie 1,422 .... C4
Lawn 999 .... C4
Lethbridge 686 .... D2
Lewisporte 3,963 .... C4
Little Bay Islands 407 .... C4
Little Catalina 750 .... D2
Little Heart's Ease 467 .... D2
Lodge Bay 124 .... C3
Long Harbour-Mount Arlington Heights 660 .... D2
Lourdes 932 .... C4
Lower Island Cove 415 .... D2
Lumsden 645 .... D4
Main Brook 514 .... C3
Makkovik 347 .... C2
Markland 344 .... D2
Mary's Harbour 408 .... C3
Marystown 6,299 .... D4
McCallum 243 .... C4
Melrose 416 .... D2
Middle Arm, Green Bay 575 .... C4
Millertown 228 .... C4
Milltown-Head of Bay d'Espoir 1,376 .... C4
Milton 258 .... C2
Mobile 171 .... D2
Mount Carmel-Mitchell's Brook-St. Catherine's 699 .... D2
Mount Pearl 11,543 .... D2
Musgrave Harbour 1,554 .... D4
Musgravetown 635 .... C2
Nain 938 .... B2
New Bonaventure 106 .... D2
New Chelsea 144 .... D2
New Harbour 777 .... D2
Newmans Cove 231 .... D2
New Perlican 350 .... D2
Newtown 511 .... D4
Nippers Harbour 259 .... C4
Norman's Cove-Long Cove 1,152 .... D2
Norris Arm 1,216 .... C4
Norris Point 1,033 .... C4
North Harbour 151 .... D2
North River 245 .... D2
North West Brook 279 .... C2
North West River 515 .... B3
O'Donnells 280 .... D2
Old Bonaventure 111 .... D2
Old Perlican 709 .... D2
Paradise 2,861 .... D2
Parkers Cove 424 .... D4
Parson's Pond 605 .... C3
Pasadena 2,685 .... C4
Patrick's Cove 155 .... C2
Perry's Cove 141 .... D2
Peterview 1,119 .... C4
Petites 108 .... C4
Petley 147 .... D2
Petty Harbour-Maddox Cove 853 .... D2
Picadilly 524 .... C4
Pinware River 201 .... C3
Placentia 2,204 .... C2
Plate Cove 474 .... D2
Point La Haye 195 .... D2
Point Lance 141 .... C2
Point Leamington 848 .... C4
Point Verde 296 .... C2
Pollards Point 502 .... C4
Port au Bras 366 .... D4
Port au Choix 1,311 .... C3
Port au Port 603 .... C4
Port Blandford 702 .... C2
Port Hope Simpson 581 .... C3
Port Kirwan 164 .... D2
Port Rexton 489 .... D2
Port Saunders 769 .... C3
Portugal Cove 2,361 .... D2
Portugal Cove South 371 .... D2
Port Union 671 .... D2
Postville 223 .... B3
Pouch Cove 1,522 .... D2
Princeton 204 .... D2
Raleigh 373 .... C3
Ramea 1,386 .... C4
Red Bay 316 .... C3
Red Head Cove 225 .... D2
Rencontre East 230 .... C4
Renews-Cappahayden 578 .... D2
Rigolet 271 .... C3
Riverhead 431 .... D2
River of Ponds 304 .... C3
Robert's Arm 1,005 .... C4
Rocky Harbour 1,273 .... C4
Roddickton 1,142 .... C3
Rose Blanche-Harbour le Cou 975 .... C4
Rushoon 520 .... D4
Saint Alban's 1,968 .... C4
Saint Andrew's 262 .... C4
Saint Anthony 3,107 .... C3
Saint Brendan's 468 .... D4
Saint Bride's 599 .... C2
Saint George's 1,756 .... C4
St. John's (cap.) 83,770 .... D2
Saint Joseph's 262 .... D2
Saint Lawrence 2,012 .... C4
Saint Lunaire-Griquet 1,010 .... C3
Saint Mary's 701 .... D2
Saint Paul's 454 .... C4
Saint Phillips 1,365 .... D2
Saint Shotts 239 .... D2
Saint Vincent's-Saint Stephens-Peter's River 796 .... D2
Sally's Cove 100 .... C4
Salmon Cove 786 .... D2
Seal Cove 751 .... C3
Seal Cove-White Bay 498 .... C4
Seldom-Little Seldom 560 .... D4
Ship Harbour 265 .... D2
Shoal Cove 223 .... C3
Shoal Harbour 1,000 .... C2
South Branch 264 .... C4
South Brook, Hall's Bay Dist. 786 .... C4
South Brook, Humber Dist. 477 .... C4
Southern Harbour 772 .... C2
South River 645 .... D2
Spaniard's Bay 2,125 .... D2
Springdale 3,501 .... C4
Stephenville 8,876 .... C4
Stephenville Crossing 2,172 .... C4
Summerford 1,198 .... C4
Summerville 346 .... D2
Sunnyside 703 .... D2
Sweet Bay 204 .... D2
Swift Current 329 .... C2
Terrenceville 796 .... D4
Tilting 427 .... D4
Torbay 3,394 .... D2
Tors Cove 355 .... D2
Traytown 383 .... D1
Trepassey 1,473 .... D2
Trinity 522 .... D2
Trinity 375 .... D4
Trout River 759 .... C4
Twillingate 1,506 .... C4
Upper Island Cove 2,025 .... D2
Victoria 1,870 .... D2
Wabana 4,254 .... D2
Wabush 3,155 .... A3
Wesleyville 1,125 .... D4
Western Bay 463 .... D2
West Saint Modeste 273 .... C3
Whitbourne 1,233 .... D2
Wild Cove 152 .... C3
Windsor 5,747 .... C4
Winterton 753 .... D2
Witless Bay 907 .... D2

OTHER FEATURES

Alexis (riv.) C3
Anguille (cape) C4
Annieopscotch (mts.) C4
Ashuanipi (lake) A3
Ashuanipi (riv.) A3
Atikonak (lake) B3
Attikamagen (lake) A3
Avalon (pen.) D2
Barachois Pond Prov. Park C4
Bauld (cape) C3
Bell (isl.) C3
Bell (isl.) D2
Belle Isle (isl.) C3
Belle Isle (str.) C3
Blackhead (bay) D2
Bonavista (bay) D1
Bonavista (cape) D1
Bonne (bay) C4
Branch (riv.) C2
Broyle (cape) D2
Bull Arm (inlet) D2
Burin (pen.) C4
Butter Pot Prov. Park D2
Cabot (str.) B4
Canada (bay) C3
Chidley (cape) B1
Churchill (falls) B3
Churchill (riv.) B3
Cirque (mt.) B2
Clode (sound) D2
Conception (bay) D2
Deep (inlet) B2
Double Mer (lake) C3
Dyke (lake) A3
Eagle (riv.) C3
Espoir (bay) C4
Exploits (riv.) C4
Fogo (isl.) D4
Fortune (bay) C4
Freels (cape) D3
Gander (lake) D4
Gander (riv.) D4
Glover (isl.) C4
Goose (riv.) B3
Grand (lake) B3
Grand (lake) C4
Grates (pt.) D2
Great Colinet (isl.) D2
Grey (isls.) C3
Groais (isl.) C3
Gros Morne (mt.) C4
Gros Morne Nat'l Park C4
Groswater (bay) C3
Hamilton (inlet) C3
Hamilton (sound) D4
Hare (bay) C3
Hawke (hills) D2
Hebron (fjord) B2
Hermitage (bay) C4
Holyrood (bay) D2
Horse (isls.) C3
Horse Chops (head) D2
Humber (riv.) C4
Ingornachoix (bay) C3
Ireland's Eye (isl.) D2
Islands (bay) C4
Kaipokok (bay) B2
Kanairiktok (riv.) B3
Kaumajet (mts.) B2
Kingurutik (mesa) B2
Labrador (reg.) B2
Labrador (sea) C2
La Manche Valley Prov. Park D2
La Poile (bay) C4
Little Mecatina (riv.) B3
Long (isl.) C2
Long (lake) A3
Long (pt.) C4
Long Range (mts.) C4
Main Topsail (mt.) C4
Makkovik (cape) C2
McLelan (str.) B1
Mealy (lake) C3
Meelpaeg (lake) C4
Melville (lake) C3
Menihek (lakes) A3
Merasheen (isl.) C2
Mistaken (pt.) D2
Mistastin (lake) B2
Nachvak (fjord) B2
Naskaupi (riv.) B3
Newfoundland (isl.) C4
Newman (sound) D2
New World (isl.) C4
Norman (cape) C3
North Aulatsivik (isl.) B2
Notre Dame (bay) C4
Okak (bay) B2
Ossokmanuan (res.) B3
Petitsikapau (lake) A3
Pine (cape) D2
Pinware (riv.) C3
Pistolet (bay) C3
Placentia (bay) C2
Ponds (isl.) C3
Port au Port (bay) C4
Port au Port (pen.) C4
Port Manvers (harb.) B2
Race (cape) D2
Ramah (bay) B2
Ramea (isls.) C4
Random (isl.) D2
Random (sound) D2
Ray (cape) C4
Red (isl.) C2
Red Indian (lake) C4
Red Wine (riv.) B3
Rocky (riv.) D2
Round (pond) C4
Saglek (bay) B2
Saint Francis (cape) D2
Saint George (cape) C4
Saint George's (bay) C4
Saint John (bay) C3
Saint John (cape) C3
Saint Lawrence (gulf) B4
Saint Lewis (cape) C3
Saint Mary's (bay) C2
Saint Mary's (cape) C2
Saint Michaels (bay) C3
Salmonier (riv.) D2
Sandwich (bay) C3
Shabogamo (lake) A3
Shoal (bay) D2
Smallwood (res.) B3
Smith (sound) D2
South Aulatsivik (isl.) B2
Spear (cape) D2
Squires Mem. Park C4
Swale (isl.) D1
Terra Nova (riv.) C2
Terra Nova Nat'l Park D2
Territok (cape) B2
Thoresby (mt.) B2
Torbay (pt.) D2
Torngat (mts.) B2
Trespassey (bay) D2
Trinity (bay) D2
Tunungayualok (isl.) B2
Ukasiksalik (isl.) B2
Victoria (lake) C4
White (bay) C3
White Bear (lake) C4
White Handkerchief (cape) B2

SAINT PIERRE and MIQUELON

CITIES and TOWNS

Saint-Pierre (cap.) 5,415 .... C4

OTHER FEATURES

Miquelon (isl.) 626 .... C4
Saint Pierre (isl.) 5,415 .... C4

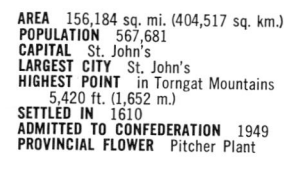

AREA 156,184 sq. mi. (404,517 sq. km.)
POPULATION 567,681
CAPITAL St. John's
LARGEST CITY St. John's
HIGHEST POINT in Torngat Mountains 5,420 ft. (1,652 m.)
SETTLED IN 1610
ADMITTED TO CONFEDERATION 1949
PROVINCIAL FLOWER Pitcher Plant

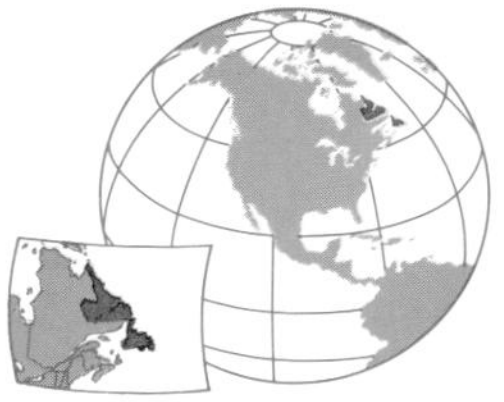

Agriculture, Industry and Resources

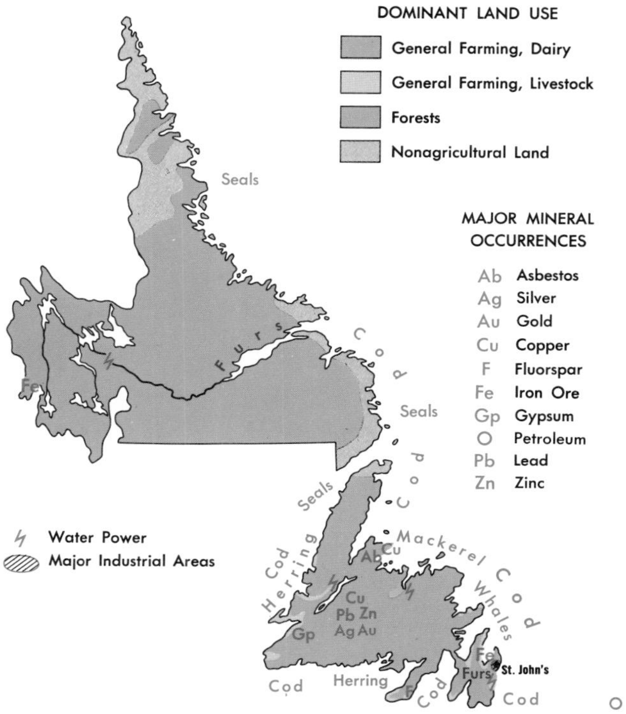

DOMINANT LAND USE
General Farming, Dairy
General Farming, Livestock
Forests
Nonagricultural Land
MAJOR MINERAL OCCURRENCES
Ab Asbestos
Ag Silver
Au Gold
Cu Copper
F Fluorspar
Fe Iron Ore
Gp Gypsum
O Petroleum
Pb Lead
Zn Zinc
Water Power
Major Industrial Areas
Seals
Furs
Cod
Herring
Mackerel
Whales
St. John's

Topography

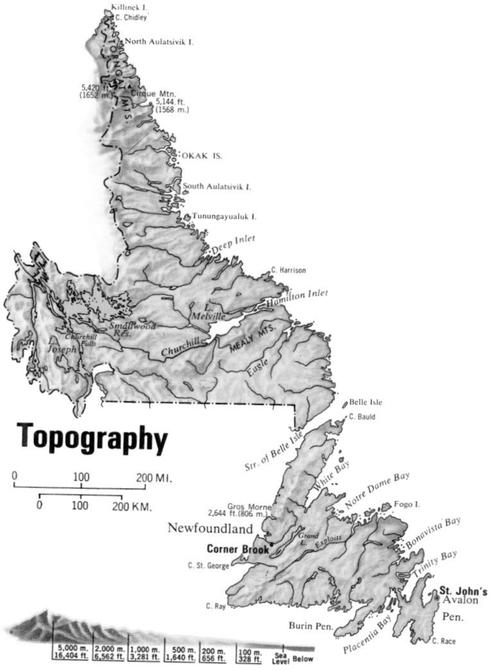

Killinek I.
C. Chidley
North Aulatsivik I.
OKAK IS.
South Aulatsivik I.
Tunungayualuk I.
Deep Inlet
C. Harrison
Hamilton Inlet
Melville
Smallwood Res.
Churchill
MEALY MTS.
Eagle
Belle Isle
C. Bauld
Str. of Belle Isle
White Bay
Notre Dame Bay
Fogo I.
Gros Morne 2,644 ft. (806 m.)
Newfoundland
Corner Brook
C. St. George
Bonavista Bay
Trinity Bay
St. John's
Avalon Pen.
C. Ray
Burin Pen.
Placentia Bay
C. Race
0 100 200 MI.
0 100 200 KM.
5,000 m. 16,404 ft.
2,000 m. 6,562 ft.
1,000 m. 3,281 ft.
500 m. 1,640 ft.
200 m. 656 ft.
100 m. 328 ft.
Sea Level
Below

NOVA SCOTIA

CITIES and TOWNS

COUNTIES

Annapolis 22,522 .... C 4
Antigonish 18,110 .... F 3
Cape Breton 127,035 .... H 2
Colchester 43,224 .... E 3
Cumberland 35,231 .... D 3
Digby 21,689 .... C 4
Guysborough 12,752 .... G 3
Halifax 288,126 .... E 4
Hants 33,121 .... D 4
Inverness 22,337 .... G 2
Kings 49,739 .... D 4
Lunenburg 45,746 .... D 4
Pictou 50,350 .... F 3
Queens 13,126 .... D 4
Richmond 12,284 .... H 3
Shelburne 17,328 .... C 5
Victoria 8,432 .... H 2
Yarmouth 26,290 .... C 5

Alder Point 651 .... H 2
Aldershot .... D 3
Amherst⊙ 9,684 .... D 3
Annapolis Royal⊙ 631 .... C 4
Antigonish⊙ 5,205 .... H 3
Arichat 824 .... H 3
Aylesford 744 .... D 3
Baddeck⊙ 972 .... H 2
Barrington Passage 722 .... C 5
Bear River-Sissiboo 854 .... C 4
Beaverbank 1,322 .... E 4
Berwick 1,699 .... D 4
Bridgetown 1,047 .... C 4
Bridgewater 6,669 .... D 4
Brookfield 619 .... E 3
Brooklyn 1,269 .... D 4
Cambridge Station 799 .... D 3
Canning 763 .... D 3
Canso 1,255 .... H 3
Centreville 765 .... D 3
Chéticamp 1,022 .... G 2

Chester 1,131 .... D 4
Chester Basin 639 .... D 4
Church Point 318 .... B 4
Clark's Harbour 1,059 .... C 5
Coldbrook Station 617 .... D 3
Cow Bay 670 .... E 4
Dartmouth 62,277 .... E 4
Debert 618 .... E 3
Digby⊙ 2,558 .... C 4
Dominion 2,856 .... J 2
Donkin 873 .... J 2
Ellershouse-Hartville 662 .... D 4
Elmsdale 1,172 .... E 4
Enfield 1,510 .... E 4
Fall River 1,897 .... E 4
Falmouth 1,110 .... D 3
Glace Bay 21,466 .... J 2
Guysborough⊙ 496 .... G 3
Halifax (cap.)⊛ 114,594 .... E 4
Halifax *277,727 .... E 4
Hantsport 1,395 .... D 4
Herring Cove 1,323 .... E 3
Hilden 1,262 .... E 3

Ingonish 471 .... H 2
Inverness 2,013 .... G 2
Judique 925 .... G 3
Kentville⊙ 4,974 .... D 3
Kingston 1,612 .... D 4
Lakeside 936 .... E 4
Lantz 1,172 .... E 4
Liverpool⊙ 3,304 .... D 4
Lockeport 929 .... C 5
Louisbourg 1,410 .... J 3
Louisdale 979 .... G 3
Lower West Pubnico 790 .... C 5
Lunenburg⊙ 3,014 .... D 4
Mahone Bay 1,228 .... D 4
Meteghan 890 .... B 4
Middleton 1,834 .... C 4
Milford Station 748 .... D 4
Milton 1,678 .... D 4
Mount Uniacke 1,145 .... D 4
Mulgrave 1,099 .... G 3
Musquodoboit Harbour 936 .... E 4
New Glasgow 10,464 .... F 3
New Victoria 1,374 .... H 2

New Waterford 8,808 .... J 2
North Sydney 7,820 .... J 2
Oxford 1,470 .... E 3
Parrsboro 1,799 .... D 3
Pictou⊙ 4,628 .... F 3
Porters Lake 893 .... E 4
Port Hastings 312 .... G 3
Port Hawkesbury 3,850 .... G 3
Port Hood⊙ 701 .... G 2
Port Morien 717 .... J 2
Port Williams 1,227 .... D 3
Prospect 693 .... E 4
Pugwash 648 .... E 3
Reserve Mines 2,472 .... J 2
River Hébert 835 .... D 3
Saint Peters 669 .... C 5
Sandy Point 691 .... C 5
Scotchtown 2,037 .... J 2
Sheet Harbour 819 .... F 4
Shelburne⊙ 2,303 .... C 5
Shubenacadie 984 .... E 3
Springhill 4,896 .... D 3
Stellarton 5,435 .... F 3

Stewiacke 1,174 .... E 3
Sydney⊙ 29,444 .... J 2
Sydney Mines 8,501 .... H 2
Terence Bay 960 .... E 4
Thorburn 1,014 .... F 3
Three Mile Plains 1,355 .... D 4
Timberlea 1,159 .... E 4
Trenton 3,154 .... F 3
Truro⊙ 12,552 .... E 3
Waterville 687 .... D 3
Waverley 1,699 .... E 4
Wedgeport 827 .... C 5
Western Shore 1,712 .... D 4
Westmount 3,097 .... H 2
Westville 4,522 .... F 3
Wileville 746 .... D 4
Windsor⊙ 3,646 .... D 3
Wolfville 3,235 .... D 3
Yarmouth⊙ 7,475 .... B 5

OTHER FEATURES

Advocate (bay) .... D 3

Ainslie (lake) .... G 2
Amet (sound) .... E 3
Andrew (isl.) .... H 3
Annapolis (basin) .... C 4
Annapolis (riv.) .... C 4
Antigonish (harb.) .... G 3
Argos (cape) .... G 3
Aspy (bay) .... H 2
Avon (riv.) .... D 4
Baccaro (pt.) .... C 5
Baddeck (riv.) .... H 2
Barachois (pt.) .... G 4
Barren (isl.) .... G 4
Barrington (bay) .... C 5
Bedford (basin) .... E 4
Berry (head) .... G 3
Boularderie (isl.) .... H 2
Bras d'Or (lake) .... H 3
Breton (cape) .... J 3
Brier (isl.) .... B 4
Canso (cape) .... H 3
Canso (str.) .... G 3
Cap d'Or (cape) .... D 3

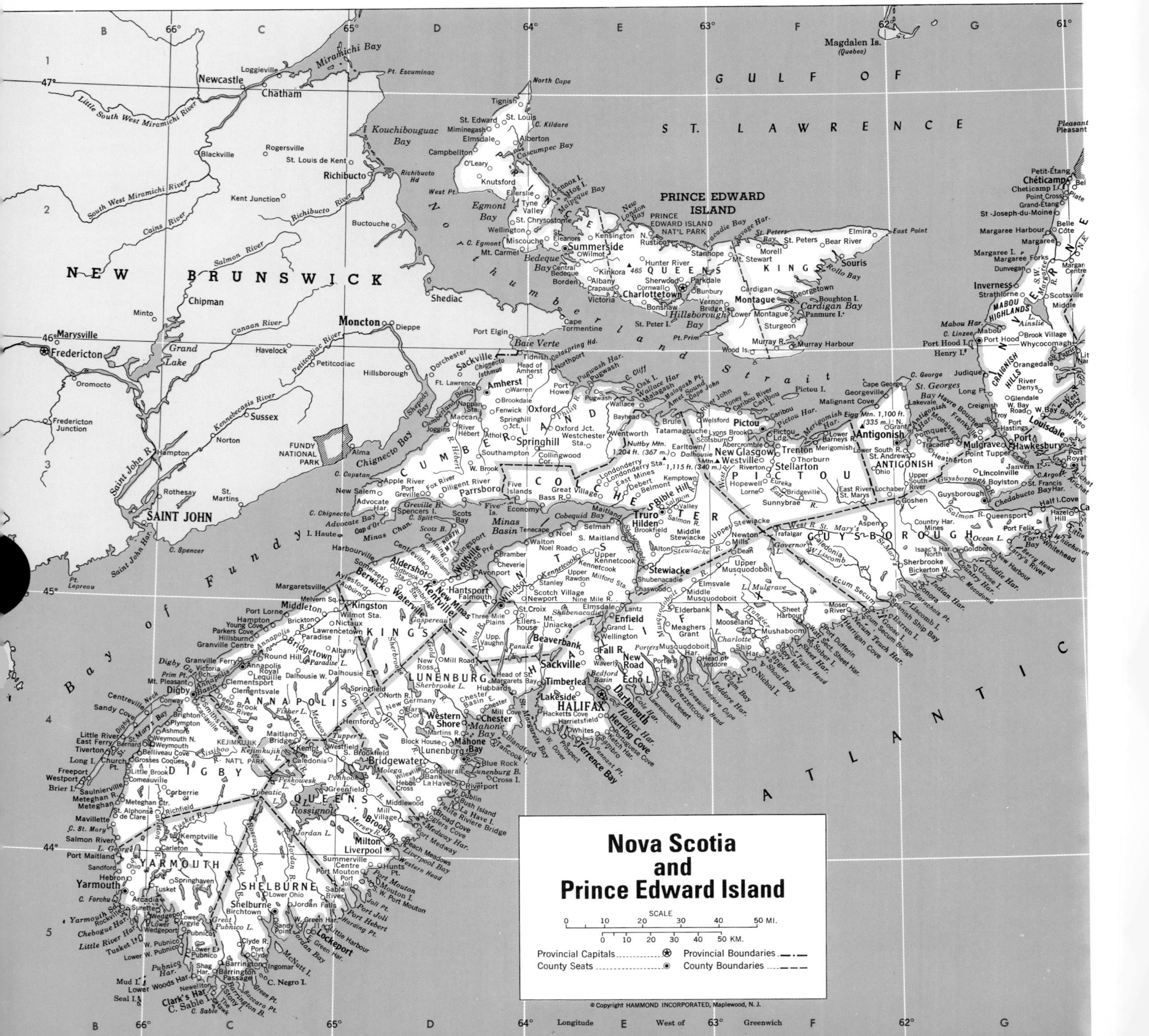

Nova Scotia and Prince Edward Island

© Copyright HAMMOND INCORPORATED, Maplewood, N.J.

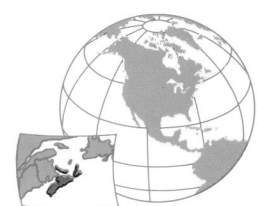

PRINCE EDWARD ISLAND

AREA 2,184 sq. mi. (5,657 sq. km.)
POPULATION 122,506
CAPITAL Charlottetown
LARGEST CITY Charlottetown
HIGHEST POINT 465 ft. (142 m.)
SETTLED IN 1720
ADMITTED TO CONFEDERATION 1873
PROVINCIAL FLOWER Lady's Slipper

NOVA SCOTIA

AREA 21,425 sq. mi. (55,491 sq. km.)
POPULATION 847,442
CAPITAL Halifax
LARGEST CITY Halifax
HIGHEST POINT Cape Breton Highlands
 1,747 ft. (532 m.)
SETTLED IN 1605
ADMITTED TO CONFEDERATION 1867
PROVINCIAL FLOWER Trailing Arbutus or
 Mayflower

Topography

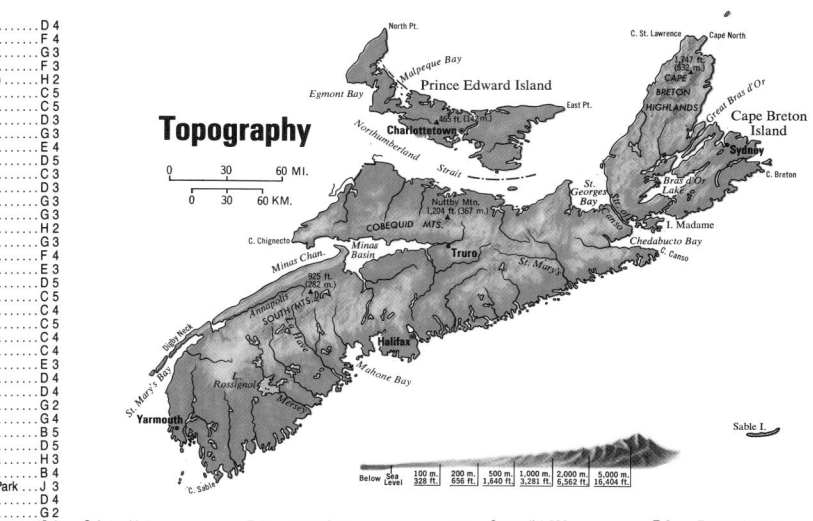

0   30   60 MI.

0   30   60 KM.

Below Sea Level	100 m. 328 ft.	200 m. 656 ft.	500 m. 1,640 ft.	1,000 m. 3,281 ft.	2,000 m. 6,562 ft.	5,000 m. 16,404 ft.

Agriculture, Industry and Resources

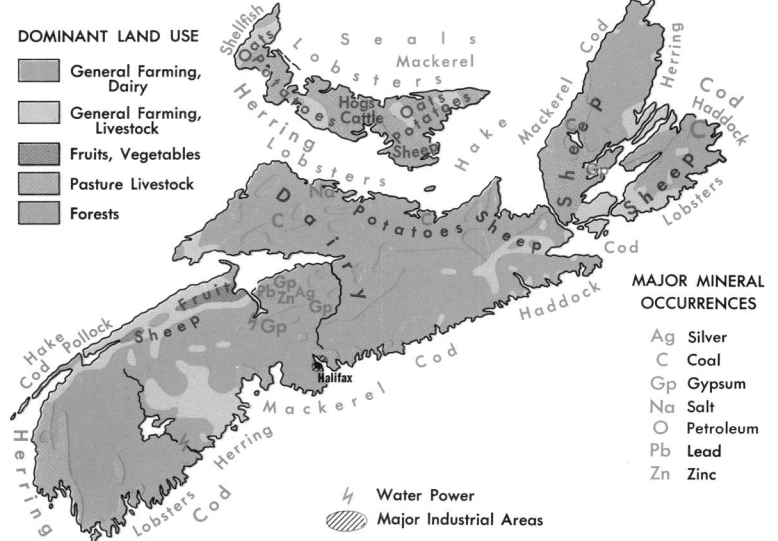

DOMINANT LAND USE

- General Farming, Dairy
- General Farming, Livestock
- Fruits, Vegetables
- Pasture Livestock
- Forests

MAJOR MINERAL OCCURRENCES

Ag Silver
C   Coal
Gp Gypsum
Na Salt
O   Petroleum
Pb Lead
Zn Zinc

⚡ Water Power
▨ Major Industrial Areas

COUNTIES

Albert 23,632	F 3
Carleton 24,659	C 2
Charlotte 26,571	C 3
Gloucester 86,156	E 1
Kent 30,799	E 2
King's 51,114	E 3
Madawaska 34,892	A 1
Northumberland 54,134	D 2
Queen's 12,485	D 3
Restigouche 40,593	C 1
Saint John 86,148	E 3
Sunbury 21,012	D 3
Victoria 20,815	C 2
Westmorland 107,640	F 2
York 74,213	D 3

CITIES and TOWNS

Acadie Siding 64	E 2
Acadieville 176	E 2
Adamsville 94	E 2
Albert Mines 120	F 3
Alcida 174	D 1
Aldouane 64	E 2
Allardville 478	E 1
Alma 329	F 3
Anagance 114	E 3
Anse-Bleue 562	E 1

Apohaqui 341	E 3
Argyle 63	C 2
Armstrong Brook 191	E 1
Aroostook 403	C 2
Arthurette 178	C 2
Astle 201	D 2
Atholville 1,694	D 1
Aulac 113	F 2
Back Bay 455	D 3
Baie-Sainte-Anne 709	E 2
Baie-Verte 175	F 2
Bairdsville 81	C 2
Baker Brook 527	B 1
Balmoral 1,823	D 1
Barachois 686	F 2
Barnaby River 38	E 2
Barnettville 117	D 2
Bartibog Bridge 122	E 1
Bas-Caraquet 1,859	F 1
Bass River 112	E 2
Bath 794	C 2
Bathurst⊙ 15,705	E 1
Bayfield 81	G 2
Bayside	C 3
Beaubois 211	E 1
Beaver Brook Station 95	E 1
Beaver Harbour 316	D 3
Beechwood 111	C 2
Beersville 52	E 2
Belledune 690	E 1

Bellefleur 83	C 1
Bellefond 243	E 1
Belleisle Creek 145	E 3
Benjamin River 171	D 1
Ben Lomond	E 3
Benton 101	C 3
Beresford 3,652	E 1
Berry Mills 238	E 2
Bertrand 1,288	E 1
Berwick 129	E 3
Black Point 131	D 1
Black River 150	E 3
Blacks Harbour 1,356	D 3
Blackville 892	E 2
Blissfield 119	D 2
Bloomfield Ridge 153	D 2
Bloomfield Station 62	E 3
Bocabec 34	C 3
Boiestown 299	D 2
Bonny River 153	D 3
Bosse 193	B 1
Bourgeois 215	F 2
Brantville 1,066	E 1
Breau-Village 293	F 2
Brest 94	E 2
Brewers Mills 199	E 2
Briggs Corner 89	E 2
Bristol 824	C 2
Brockway (Lower Brockway-Brockway) 97	C 3

Browns Flat 295	D 3
Buctouche 2,476	F 2
Burnsville 156	E 1
Burton⊙ 291	D 3
Burtts Corner 484	D 3
Cambridge-Narrows 433	E 3
Campbellton 9,818	D 1
Canaan 115	E 2
Canaan Forks 78	E 2
Canaan Road 86	E 2
Cap-Bateau 417	F 1
Cape Tormentine 229	G 2
Cap Lumière 262	F 2
Cap-Pelé 2,199	F 2
Caraquet 4,315	E 1
Carlingford 229	C 2
Carlisle 75	C 2
Caron Brook 171	B 1
Carrolls Crossing 119	D 2
Castalia 145	D 4
Central Blissville 155	D 3
Centre-Saint-Simon (St. Simon) 991	E 1
Centreville 577	C 2
Chance Harbour 63	D 3
Charlo 1,603	D 1
Chatham 6,779	E 1
Chatham Head	E 1
Chipman 1,829	E 2

Clair 915	B 1
Clarendon 80	D 3
Cliffordvale (Limestone-Cliffordvale) 69	C 2
Clifton 194	E 1
Coal Branch 90	E 2
Coal Creek 61	E 2
Cocagne Cape 278	F 2
Cocagne-Cocagne Sud 600	F 2
Codys 125	E 3
Coldstream 217	C 2
Coles Island 144	E 3
College Bridge 536	F 3
Collette 198	E 2
Connell 58	C 2
Connors 96	B 1
Cork 54	D 3
Cornhill 111	E 3
Coughlan 181	C 1
Cross Creek 192	D 2
Cumberland Bay 231	E 2
Dalhousie⊙ 4,958	D 1
Dalhousie Junction 105	D 1
Darlington 749	D 1
Daulnay 398	E 2
Dawsonville 278	C 1
Debec 200	C 2
Dieppe 8,511	F 2
Dipper Harbour 166	D 3
Doaktown 1,009	D 2

Dorchester⊙ 1,101	F 3
Dorchester Crossing 605	F 2
Douglastown 1,091	E 1
Drummond 398	C 1
Duguayville 337	E 1
Dumfries 150	C 3
Dupuis Corner 303	F 2
Durham Bridge 255	D 2
East Riverside-Kingshurst 989	E 3
Edmundston⊙ 12,044	B 1
Eel River Bridge 377	E 1
Eel River Crossing 1,431	D 1
Elgin 301	E 3
Enniskillen 63	D 3
Escuminac 194	E 2
Evandale 58	E 3
Evangeline 356	E 1
Everett 48	C 1
Fairfield 250	F 3
Fairisle 415	E 1
Fairvale 3,960	E 3
Ferry Road 325	E 1
Fielding 197	C 2
Five Fingers 189	C 1
Flatlands 249	D 1
Florenceville 709	C 2
Forest City 25	C 3
Fosterville 58	C 3

Four Falls 69	C 2
Fredericton (cap.) 43,723	D 3
Fredericton Junction 711	D 3
Gagetown⊙ 618	D 3
Gardner Creek 56	E 3
Geary 654	D 3
Germantown 62	F 3
Gillespie 96	C 2
Glassville 147	C 2
Glencoe 147	D 1
Glenlivet 284	D 1
Gondola Point 3,076	E 3
Grafton 385	C 2
Grand Bay 3,173	D 3
Grande-Anse 817	E 1
Grand Falls 6,203	C 1
Grand Falls Hill 152	C 1
Grand Harbour 614	D 4
Gray Rapids 266	E 2
Hammondvale 72	E 3
Hampstead 87	D 3
Hampton⊙ 3,141	E 3
Harcourt 127	E 2
Hardwicke 114	E 1
Hardwood Ridge 191	E 2
Hartland 846	C 2
Harvey, Albert 58	F 3
Harvey, York 356	D 3
Hatfield Point 176	E 3

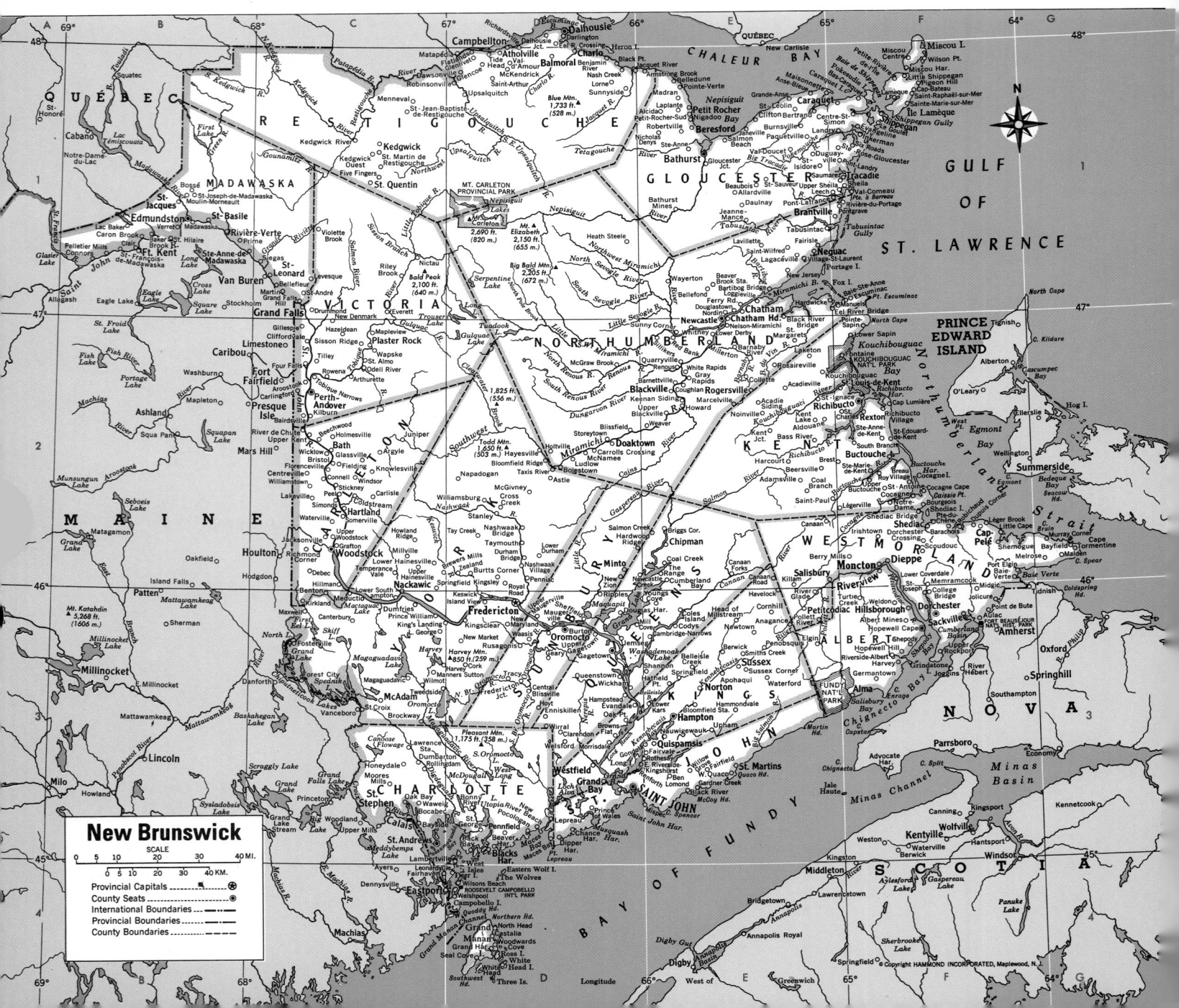

Havelock 439 .... E 3
Hayesville 107 .... D 2
Hazeldean 108 .... C 2
Head of Millstream 61 .... E 3
Hillman 69 .... C 2
Hillsborough 1,239 .... F 3
Holmesville 146 .... C 2
Holtville 222 .... D 2
Honeydale 77 .... C 3
Hopewell Cape⊙ 144 .... F 3
Hopewell Hill 172 .... F 3
Howard 77 .... E 2
Howland Ridge 55 .... C 2
Hoyt 114 .... D 3
Inkerman 396 .... F 1
Irishtown 605 .... F 2
Island View 240 .... D 3
Jacksonville 363 .... C 2
Jacquet River 778 .... E 1
Janeville 204 .... E 1
Jeanne Mance 89 .... E 1
Jemseg 228 .... D 3
Jolicure 96 .... F 3
Juniper 525 .... C 2
Kedgwick 1,222 .... C 1
Keenan Siding 86 .... E 2
Kent Junction 112 .... E 2
Kent Lake 57 .... E 2
Keswick 260 .... D 3
Kilburn 134 .... C 2
Killam 60 .... E 2
Kingsclear 250 .... D 3
Kingsley 145 .... D 2
Kirkland 69 .... C 3
Knowlesville 82 .... C 2
Kouchibouguac 213 .... F 2
Lac Baker 292 .... B 1
Lagacéville 227 .... E 1
Lake George 170 .... C 3
Laketon 81 .... E 2
Lakeville 201 .... C 2
Lambertville 109 .... C 3
Lamèque 1,571 .... F 1
Landry 281 .... E 1
Laplante 197 .... E 1
Lavillette 576 .... E 1
Lawrence Station 229 .... C 3
Leech 584 .... E 1
Léger Brook .... F 2
Légerville 184 .... F 2
Le Goulet 1,173 .... F 1
Leonardville 158 .... C 4
Lepreau 208 .... D 3
Levesque 77 .... C 1
Little Cape 513 .... F 2
Little Shippegan 131 .... F 1
Loggieville 781 .... E 1
Lorne 937 .... D 1
Lower Coverdale 616 .... F 2
Lower Derby 206 .... E 2
Lower Durham 52 .... D 2
Lower Hainesville 66 .... C 2
Lower Kars 30 .... E 3
Lower Millstream 184 .... E 3
Lower Sapin .... F 2
Lower Southampton .... C 3
Ludlow 100 .... D 2
Maces Bay 182 .... D 3
Madran 247 .... E 1
Magaguadavic 126 .... C 3
Maisonnette 757 .... E 1
Malden 93 .... G 2
Manners Sutton 159 .... D 3
Manuels 332 .... F 1
Mapleview 65 .... C 2
Marcelville 61 .... E 2
Martin 104 .... C 1
Maugerville 249 .... D 3
Maxwell 64 .... C 3
McAdam 1,837 .... C 3
McGivney 156 .... D 2
McKendrick 608 .... D 1
McNamee 147 .... D 2
Meductic 234 .... C 3
Melrose 121 .... F 2
Memramcook 276 .... F 2
Menneval 110 .... C 1
Midgic Station 208 .... F 3
Mill Cove 253 .... D 3
Millerton 130 .... E 2
Millville 309 .... C 2
Minto 3,399 .... D 2
Miscou Centre 554 .... F 1
Miscou Harbour 106 .... F 1
Mispec 180 .... E 3
Moncton 54,743 .... F 2
Moores Mills 117 .... C 3
Morrisdale 202 .... D 3
Moulin-Morneault 459 .... B 1
Murray Corner 233 .... G 2
Nackawic 1,357 .... C 2
Napadogan 103 .... D 2
Nash Creek 235 .... D 1
Nashwaak Bridge 142 .... D 2
Nashwaak Village 258 .... D 2
Nauwigewauk 139 .... E 3
Neguac 1,755 .... E 1
Nelson-Miramichi 1,452 .... E 2
Newcastle⊙ 6,284 .... E 2
Newcastle Creek 210 .... D 2
New Denmark 112 .... C 1
New Jersey 65 .... E 1
New Market 143 .... D 3
New Maryland 485 .... D 3
New River Beach 33 .... D 3
Newtown 154 .... E 3
New Zion 171 .... D 2
Nicholas Denys 170 .... D 1
Nictau 30 .... C 1
Nigadoo 1,075 .... E 1
Noinville 50 .... E 2
Nordin 393 .... E 1
North Head 661 .... D 4
Norton 1,372 .... E 3
Notre-Dame 344 .... F 2
Oak Bay 183 .... C 3
Oak Point 83 .... D 3
Oromocto 9,064 .... D 3
Paquetville 626 .... E 1
Peel 117 .... C 2
Pelletier Mills 88 .... B 1
Pennfield .... D 3
Penniac 179 .... D 2
Penobsquis 259 .... E 3
Perth-Andover⊙ 1,872 .... C 2
Petitcodiac 1,401 .... E 3
Petite-Rivière-de-l'Île 549 .... F 1
Petit Rocher 1,860 .... E 1
Petit Rocher Sud .... E 1
Pigeon Hill 595 .... F 1
Plaster Rock 1,222 .... C 2
Pocologan 150 .... D 3
Point de Bute 155 .... F 3
Pointe-du-Chêne 482 .... F 2
Pointe-Sapin 331 .... F 2
Pointe-Verte 1,335 .... E 1
Pollett River 73 .... E 3
Pontgrave 229 .... F 1
Pont-Lafrance 875 .... E 1
Pont-Landry 444 .... F 1
Port Elgin 504 .... F 2
Prime 89 .... B 1
Prince of Wales 138 .... D 3
Prince William 225 .... C 3
Quarryville 205 .... E 2
Queenstown 112 .... D 3
Quispamsis 6,022 .... E 3
Red Bank 141 .... E 2
Renforth 1,490 .... E 3
Renous 192 .... E 2
Rexton 928 .... F 2
Richardsville .... D 1
Richibucto⊙ 1,722 .... E 2
Richibucto Village 442 .... F 2
Richmond Corner 84 .... C 2
Riley Brook 126 .... C 1
Ripples 233 .... D 3
River de Chute 22 .... C 2
River Glade 268 .... E 3
Riverside-Albert 478 .... F 3
Riverview 14,907 .... F 2
Rivière-du-Portage 661 .... F 1
Rivière Verte 1,054 .... B 1
Robertville 733 .... E 1
Robichaud 485 .... F 2
Robinsonville 206 .... C 1
Rogersville 1,237 .... E 2
Rollingdam 65 .... C 3
Rosaireville 86 .... E 2
Rothesay 1,764 .... E 3
Rowena 73 .... C 2
Roy 173 .... F 2
Royal Road 41 .... D 2
Rusagonis 231 .... D 3
Sackville 5,654 .... F 3
Saint Almo 17 .... C 2
Saint-André 385 .... C 1
Saint Andrews⊙ 1,760 .... C 3
Saint-Antoine 1,217 .... F 2
Saint Arthur 369 .... D 1
Saint-Basile 3,214 .... B 1
Saint-Charles 355 .... F 2
Saint Croix 86 .... C 3
Sainte-Anne 329 .... E 1
Sainte-Anne-de-Kent 337 .... F 2
Sainte-Anne-de-Madawaska 1,332 .... B 1
Saint-Édouard-de-Kent 157 .... F 2
Sainte-Marie-de-Kent 283 .... F 2
Sainte-Marie-sur-Mer 539 .... F 1
Sainte-Rose-Gloucester 410 .... F 1
Saint-François-de-Madawaska 753 .... B 1
Saint George 1,163 .... D 3
Saint Hilaire 244 .... B 1
Saint-Ignace 96 .... F 2
Saint-Isidore 794 .... E 1
Saint-Jacques 2,297 .... B 1
Saint-Jean-Baptiste-de-Restigouche 228 .... C 1
Saint John⊙ 80,521 .... E 3
Saint-Joseph 630 .... F 3
Saint-Joseph-de-Madawaska 173 .... B 1
Saint-Léolin 799 .... E 1
Saint Leonard 1,566 .... C 1
Saint-Louis-de-Kent 1,166 .... F 2
Saint Margarets 63 .... E 2
Saint Martin de Restigouche 124 .... C 1
Saint Martins 530 .... E 3
Saint-Paul 365 .... E 2
Saint Quentin 2,334 .... C 1
Saint-Raphaël-sur-Mer 562 .... F 1
Saint Sauveur 252 .... E 1
Saint Stephen 5,120 .... C 3
Saint Wilfred .... E 1
Salisbury 1,672 .... E 2
Salmon Beach 277 .... E 1
Salmon Creek 38 .... E 2
Saumarez 690 .... E 1
Scoudouc 207 .... F 2
Seal Cove 548 .... D 4
Shannon 39 .... E 3
Shediac 4,285 .... F 2
Shediac Bridge 441 .... F 2
Sheffield 112 .... D 3
Sheila 1,172 .... F 1
Shemogue 199 .... F 2
Shepody 86 .... F 3
Shippegan 2,471 .... F 1
Siegas 227 .... C 1
Sillikers 292 .... E 2
Simonds 221 .... C 2
Sisson Ridge 170 .... C 2
Six Roads 239 .... F 1
Smiths Creek 163 .... E 3
Somerville 326 .... C 2
South Branch 86 .... F 2
Springfield, King's 116 .... E 3
Springfield, York 130 .... C 2
Stanley 432 .... D 2
Stickney 232 .... C 2
Storeytown 140 .... D 2
Sunny Corner 405 .... E 2
Sunnyside 87 .... D 1
Sussex 3,972 .... E 3
Sussex Corner 1,023 .... E 3
Tabusintac 231 .... E 1

AREA 28,354 sq. mi. (73,437 sq. km.)
POPULATION 696,403
CAPITAL Fredericton
LARGEST CITY Saint John
HIGHEST POINT Mt. Carleton 2,690 ft. (820 m.)
SETTLED IN 1611
ADMITTED TO CONFEDERATION 1867
PROVINCIAL FLOWER Purple Violet

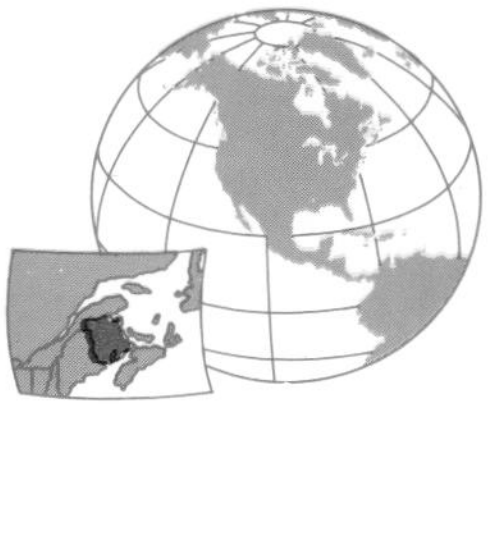

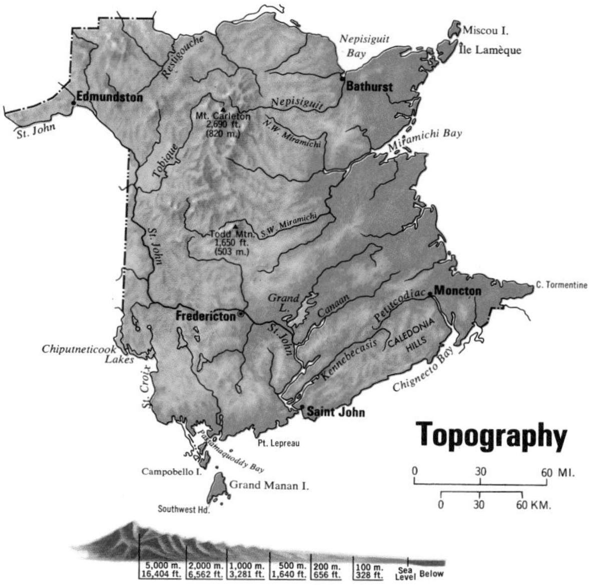
Miscou I.
Île Lamèque
Nepisiguit Bay
Bathurst
Edmundston
Restigouche
St. John
Nepisiguit
Mt. Carleton 2,690 ft. (820 m.)
N.W. Miramichi
Miramichi Bay
Tobique
S.W. Miramichi
Todd Mtn. 1,650 ft. (503 m.)
St. John
C. Tormentine
Moncton
Grand L.
Canaan
Petitcodiac
Fredericton
St. John
Kennebecasis
CALEDONIA HILLS
Shepody Bay
Chignecto Bay
Chiputneticook Lakes
St. Croix
Saint John
Pt. Lepreau
Passamaquoddy Bay
Campobello I.
Grand Manan I.
Southwest Hd.
0 30 60 MI.
0 30 60 KM.
5,000 m. 16,404 ft.
2,000 m. 6,562 ft.
1,000 m. 3,281 ft.
500 m. 1,640 ft.
200 m. 656 ft.
100 m. 328 ft.
Sea Level
Below

Topography

Agriculture, Industry and Resources

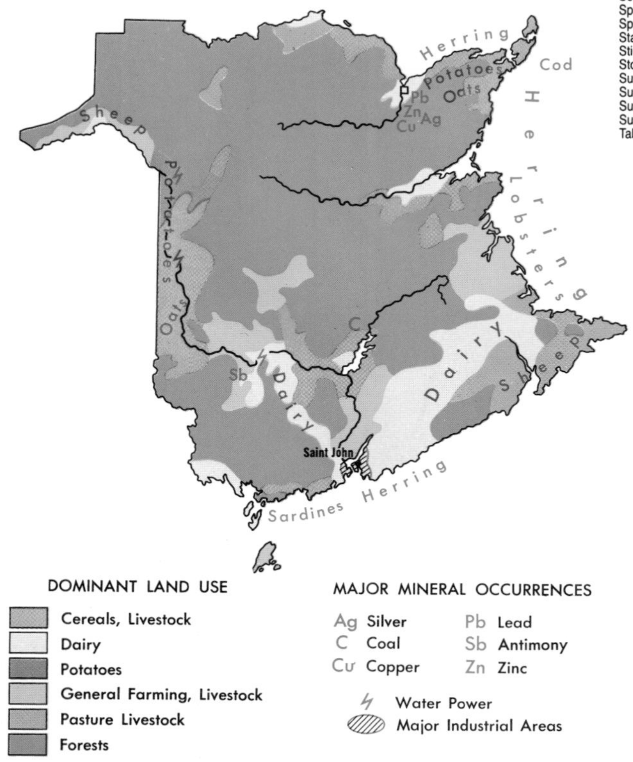
Herring
Cod
Potatoes
Oats
Pb
Zn
Ag
Cu
Sheep
Herring
Lobsters
Potatoes
Oats
C
Dairy
Sheep
Sb
Dairy
Saint John
Herring
Sardines
DOMINANT LAND USE
Cereals, Livestock
Dairy
Potatoes
General Farming, Livestock
Pasture Livestock
Forests
MAJOR MINERAL OCCURRENCES
Ag Silver
C Coal
Cu Copper
Pb Lead
Sb Antimony
Zn Zinc
Water Power
Major Industrial Areas

Taxis River 118 .... D 2
Tay Creek 161 .... D 2
Taymouth 301 .... D 2
Temperance Vale 357 .... C 2
The Range 58 .... E 2
Thibault 306 .... C 1
Tide Head 952 .... D 1
Tilley 95 .... C 2
Tobique Narrows 140 .... C 2
Tracadie 2,452 .... F 1
Tracy 636 .... D 3
Turtle Creek 81 .... F 3
Tweedside 87 .... C 3
Upham 107 .... E 3
Upper Blackville 60 .... E 2
Upper Buctouche 158 .... F 2
Upper Gagetown 236 .... D 3
Upper Hainesville 189 .... C 2
Upper Kent 203 .... C 2
Upper Maugerville 543 .... D 3
Upper Mills 153 .... C 3
Upper Rockport 18 .... F 3
Upper Sheila 706 .... E 1
Upper Woodstock 257 .... C 2
Upsalquitch 112 .... D 1
Val-Comeau 534 .... F 1
Val d'Amour 462 .... D 1
Val Doucet 505 .... E 1
Verret 637 .... B 1
Village-Saint-Laurent 187 .... E 1
Waasis 264 .... D 3
Wapske 195 .... C 2
Waterford 120 .... E 3
Waterville 181 .... C 2
Waweig .... C 3
Wayerton 188 .... E 1
Weaver 86 .... E 2
Weldon 227 .... F 3
Welsford 230 .... D 3
Welshpool 260 .... D 4
Westfield 1,100 .... D 3
West Quaco 48 .... E 3
White Head 185 .... D 4
White Rapids 238 .... E 2
Whitney 216 .... E 2
Wickham 72 .... D 3
Wicklow 143 .... C 2
Williamsburg 258 .... D 2
Williamstown 156 .... C 2
Willow Grove 509 .... E 3
Wilmot 57 .... C 3
Wilson Point 45 .... F 1
Wilsons Beach 844 .... D 4
Windsor 43 .... C 2
Wirral 110 .... D 3
Woodstock⊙ 4,649 .... C 2
Woodwards Cove 146 .... D 4
Youngs Cove 65 .... E 3
Zealand 458 .... D 2

OTHER FEATURES

Bald (mt.) .... C 1
Bartibog (riv.) .... E 1
Bay du Vin (riv.) .... E 2
Big Tracadie (riv.) .... E 1
Buctouche (harb.) .... F 2
Buctouche (riv.) .... F 2
Campobello (isl.) .... D 4
Canaan (riv.) .... E 2
Carleton (mt.) .... D 1
Chaleur (bay) .... E 1
Chignecto (bay) .... F 3
Chiputneticook (lakes) .... C 3
Cocagne (isl.) .... F 2
Cumberland (basin) .... F 3
Deer (isl.) .... D 4
Digdeguash (riv.) .... C 3
Escuminac (bay) .... D 1
Escuminac (pt.) .... F 1
Fundy (bay) .... E 3
Fundy Nat'l Park .... E 3
Gaspereau (riv.) .... D 2
Grand (bay) .... D 3
Grand (lake) .... C 3
Grand (lake) .... D 3
Grand Manan (chan.) .... C 4
Grand Manan (isl.) .... D 4
Grande (riv.) .... C 1
Green (riv.) .... B 1
Hammond (riv.) .... E 3
Harvey (lake) .... C 3
Heron (isl.) .... D 1
Kedgwick (riv.) .... C 1
Kennebecasis (riv.) .... E 3
Keswick (riv.) .... C 2
Kouchibouguac (bay) .... F 2
Kouchibouguacis (riv.) .... E 2
Kouchibouguac Nat'l Park .... F 2
Lamèque (isl.) .... F 1
Lepreau (riv.) .... D 3
Little (riv.) .... D 2
Long (isl.) .... D 3
Long Reach (inlet) .... D 3
Maces (bay) .... D 3
Mactaquac (lake) .... C 3
Madawaska (riv.) .... B 1
Magaguadavic (lake) .... C 3
Magaguadavic (riv.) .... C 3
Miramichi (bay) .... E 1
Miscou (isl.) .... F 1
Miscou (pt.) .... F 1
Mount Carleton Prov. Park .... D 1
Musquash (harb.) .... D 3
Nashwaak (riv.) .... D 2
Nepisiguit (bay) .... E 1
Nepisiguit (riv.) .... D 1
Nerepis (riv.) .... D 3
Northern (head) .... D 4
North Sevogle (riv.) .... D 1
Northumberland (str.) .... F 2
Northwest Miramichi (riv.) .... D 1
Oromocto (lake) .... C 3
Oromocto (riv.) .... D 3
Passamaquoddy (bay) .... C 3
Patapédia (riv.) .... C 1
Petitcodiac (riv.) .... F 3
Pokemouche (riv.) .... E 1
Pokesudie (isl.) .... F 1
Pollett (riv.) .... E 3
Quaco (head) .... E 3
Renous (riv.) .... D 2
Restigouche (riv.) .... C 1
Richibucto (harb.) .... F 2
Richibucto (riv.) .... E 2
Roosevelt Campobello Int'l Park .... D 4
Saint Croix (riv.) .... C 3
Saint Francis (riv.) .... A 1
Saint John (harb.) .... E 3
Saint John (riv.) .... C 2
Saint Lawrence (gulf) .... F 1
Salisbury (bay) .... F 3
Salmon (riv.) .... C 1
Salmon (riv.) .... E 2
Shediac (isl.) .... F 2
Shepody (bay) .... F 3
Shippegan (bay) .... E 1
Shippegan Gully (str.) .... F 1
South Sevogle (riv.) .... D 1
Southwest (head) .... D 4
Southwest Miramichi (riv.) .... D 2
Spear (cape) .... G 2
Spednik (lake) .... C 3
Spencer (cape) .... E 3
Tabusintac (riv.) .... E 1
Tabusintac Gully (str.) .... F 1
Tetagouche (riv.) .... D 1
Tobique (riv.) .... C 2
Upsalquitch (riv.) .... D 1
Utopia (lake) .... D 3
Verte (bay) .... G 2
Washademoak (lake) .... E 3
West (isls.) .... D 4
White Head (isl.) .... D 4

⊙County seat.

Topography

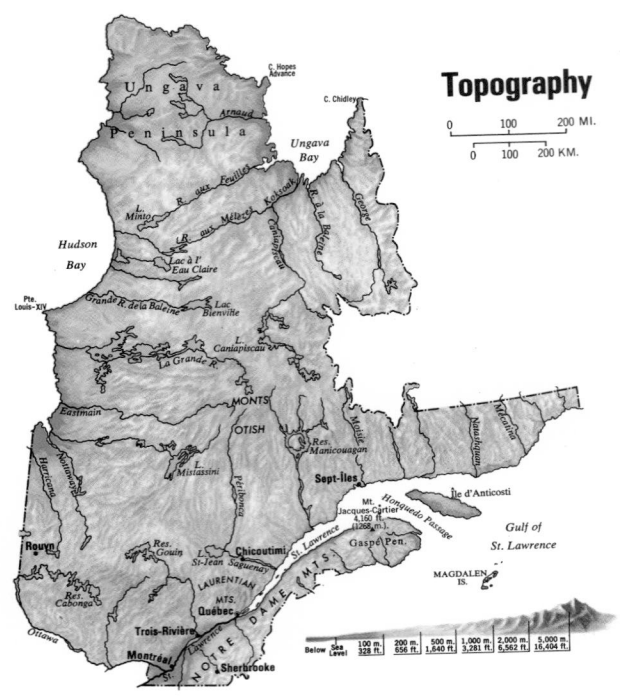

0   100   200 MI.

0   100   200 KM.

Below Sea Level 100 m. 328 ft. | 200 m. 656 ft. | 500 m. 1,640 ft. | 1,000 m. 3,281 ft. | 2,000 m. 6,562 ft. | 5,000 m. 16,404 ft.

COUNTIES

Argenteuil 32,454	C 4
Arthabaska 59,277	E 4
Bagot 26,840	E 4
Beauce 73,427	G 3
Beauharnois 54,034	C 4
Bellechasse 23,559	G 3
Berthier 31,096	C 3
Bonaventure 40,487	C 2
Brome 17,436	E 4
Chambly 307,090	J 4
Champlain 119,595	E 2
Charlevoix-Est 17,448	G 2
Charlevoix-Ouest 14,172	G 2
Châteauguay 59,968	D 4
Chicoutimi 174,441	G 1
Compton 20,536	F 4
Deux-Montagnes 71,252	C 4
Dorchester 33,949	G 3
Drummond 69,770	E 4
Frontenac 26,814	G 4
Gaspé-Est 41,173	D 1
Gaspé-Ouest 18,943	C 1
Hull 131,213	B 4
Huntingdon 16,953	C 4
Iberville 23,180	D 4
Île-de-Montréal 1,760,122	H 4
Île-Jésus 268,335	H 4
Joliette 60,384	C 3
Kamouraska 28,642	H 2
Labelle 34,395	B 3
Lac-Saint-Jean-Est 47,891	F 1
Lac-Saint-Jean-Ouest 62,952	E 1
Laprairie 105,962	H 4
L'Assomption 109,705	J 3
Lévis 94,104	G 2
L'Islet 22,062	F 3
Lotbinière 29,653	D 3
Maskinongé 20,763	D 3
Matane 29,955	B 1
Matapédia 23,715	B 2
Mégantic 57,892	F 3
Missisquoi 36,161	D 4
Montcalm 27,557	C 3
Montmagny 25,622	G 3
Montmorency No. 1 23,048	F 2
Montmorency No. 2 6,436	G 3
Napierville 13,562	D 4
Nicolet 33,513	E 3
Papineau 37,975	B 4
Pontiac 20,283	A 3
Portneuf 58,843	E 3
Québec 458,980	D 4
Richelieu 53,058	D 4
Richmond 40,871	E 4
Rimouski 69,099	J 1
Rivière-du-Loup 41,250	H 1
Rouville 42,391	D 4
Saguenay 115,881	H 1
Saint-Hyacinthe 55,888	D 4
Saint-Jean 55,576	D 4
Saint-Maurice 107,703	D 3
Shefford 70,733	E 4
Sherbrooke 115,983	E 4

CITIES and TOWNS

Acton Vale 4,371	E 4
Albanel 992	E 1
Alma⊚ 26,322	F 1
Amqui⊚ 4,048	B 2
Ancienne-Lorette 12,935	B 4
Angers	B 4
Anjou 37,346	H 4
Annaville 712	E 3
Armagh 878	G 3
Arthabaska⊚ 6,827	F 1
Arvida	G 1
Asbestos 7,967	F 4
Ascot Corner 847	C 4
Audet 760	E 4
Ayer's Cliff⊚ 810	E 4
Aylmer 26,695	A 1
Baie-Comeau 12,866	A 1
Baie-d'Urfé 3,674	G 4
Baie-Saint-Paul⊚ 3,961	G 2
Baie-Trinité 749	B 1
Beaconsfield 19,613	H 4
Beauceville 4,302	G 3
Beauharnois⊚ 7,025	C 4
Beaumont 791	F 3
Beauport 60,447	J 3
Beaupré 2,740	G 2
Bécancour⊚ 10,247	E 3
Bedford 2,832	E 4
Beebe Plain 1,072	E 4
Bélair (Val-Bélair) 12,695	H 3
Beloeil 17,540	H 4
Bernierville 2,120	F 3
Berthier-en-Bas 562	G 3
Berthierville⊚ 4,049	D 3
Bic 2,994	J 1
Biencourt 824	J 2
Black Lake 5,148	F 3
Blainville 14,682	H 4
Boischatel 3,345	H 3
Bois-des-Filion 4,943	H 4
Bolduc 1,565	G 4
Bonaventure 1,371	C 2
Boucherville 29,704	J 4
Bromont 2,731	E 4
Bromptonville 3,035	F 4
Brossard 52,232	H 4
Brownsburg 2,875	C 4
Buckingham 7,992	B 4
Cabano 3,291	J 2
Cacouna 1,160	H 2
Calumet 729	C 4
Candiac 8,502	J 4
Cap-à-l'Aigle 819	G 2
Cap-Chat 3,464	B 1
Cap-de-la-Madeleine 32,626	E 3
Caplan-Rivière Caplan 1,139	C 2
Cap-Saint-Ignace 1,485	G 2
Cap-Santé⊚ 671	F 3
Carignan 4,544	J 4
Carleton 2,710	C 2
Causapscal 2,501	J 4
Chambly 12,190	J 4
Chambord 961	E 1
Chandler 3,946	D 2
Charlemagne 4,827	H 4
Charlesbourg 68,326	J 3
Charny 8,240	J 3
Châteauguay 36,928	H 4
Château-Richer⊚ 3,628	F 3
Chénéville 633	B 4
Chicoutimi⊚ 60,064	G 1
Chicoutimi-Jonquière ⊛135,172	G 1
Chute-aux-Outardes 2,280	A 1
Clermont 3,621	G 2
Coaticook 6,271	F 4
Coleraine 1,660	F 4
Compton 728	F 4
Contrecoeur 5,449	D 4
Cookshire⊚ 1,480	F 4
Coteau-du-Lac 1,247	C 4
Coteau-Landing⊚ 1,386	C 4
Côte-Saint-Luc 27,531	H 4
Courcelles 608	G 4
Courville	J 3
Cowansville 12,240	E 4
Crabtree 1,950	D 4
Danville 2,200	E 4
Daveluyville 1,257	E 3
Deauville 942	H 4
Dégelis 3,477	J 2
Delisle 4,011	F 1
Delson 4,935	H 4
Desbiens 1,541	E 1
Deschaillons-sur-Saint-Laurent	E 3
Deschambault 977	E 3
Deschênes	B 4
Deux-Montagnes 9,944	H 4
Didyme 667	E 1
Disraëli 3,181	F 4
Dolbeau 8,766	E 1
Dollard-des-Ormeaux 39,940	H 4
Donnacona 5,731	F 3
Dorion 5,749	C 4
Dorval 17,727	H 4
Dosquet 703	D 4
Douville	D 4
Drummondville⊚ 27,347	E 4
Drummondville-Sud 9,220	E 4
Durham 2,881	E 4
Durham-Sud 1,045	E 4
East Angus 4,016	F 4
East Broughton 1,397	F 3
East Broughton Station 1,302	F 3
Eastman 612	E 4
Entrelacs 1,735	C 3
Farnham 6,498	E 4
Ferme-Neuve 2,266	B 3
Forestville 4,271	H 1
Frampton 684	G 3
Francoeur 1,422	F 3
Gaspé 17,261	D 2
Gatineau 74,988	B 4
Giffard	J 3
Girardville 1,128	E 1
Gracefield 869	A 3
Granby 38,069	E 4
Grande-Rivière 4,420	D 2
Grandes-Bergeronnes 748	H 1
Grande-Vallée 700	D 1
Greenfield Park 18,527	J 4
Grenville 1,417	C 4
Gros-Morne 672	C 1
Hampstead 7,598	H 4
Ham-Sud⊚ 62	F 4
Hauterive 13,995	A 1
Hébertville 2,515	F 1
Hébertville-Station 1,442	F 1
Hemmingford 737	D 4
Henryville 595	D 4
Howick 639	D 4
Hudson 4,414	C 4
Hull⊚ 56,225	B 4
Huntingdon⊚ 3,018	C 4
Île-Perrot 5,945	G 4
Iberville⊚ 8,587	D 4
Inverness⊚ 329	F 3
Joliette⊚ 16,987	D 3
Jonquière 60,354	F 1
Jonquière-Chicoutimi ⊛135,172	F 1
Kingsey Falls 818	E 4
Kirkland 10,476	H 4
Knowlton (Lac-Brome)⊚ 4,316	E 4
La Baie 20,935	G 1
Labelle 1,534	C 3
Lac-à-la-Croix 1,017	F 1
Lac-Alouette-Lac-Brière 1,356	C 4
Lac-au-Saumon 1,332	B 2
Lac-aux-Sables 838	E 3
Lac-Beaufort	F 3
Lac-Bouchette 1,703	E 1
Lac-Carré 717	C 4
Lac-des-Écorces 766	B 3
Lac-Drolet 1,120	G 4
Lac-Etchemin 2,729	G 3
Lachenaie 8,631	H 4
Lachine 37,521	H 4
Lachute⊚ 11,729	C 4
Lac-Mégantic⊚ 6,119	G 4
Lacolle 1,319	D 4
Lac-Saint-Charles 5,837	H 3
Lafontaine 4,799	C 4
La Guadeloupe 1,692	F 4
La Malbaie⊚ 4,030	G 2
Lambton 1,559	F 4
L'Annonciation 2,384	C 3
Lanoraie (Lanoraie-d'Autry) 1,613	D 4
La Pêche 4,977	B 4
La Pérade 1,039	E 3
La Pocatière 4,560	H 2
La Prairie⊚ 10,627	J 4
La Providence	E 4
Larouche 662	F 1
La Salle 76,299	H 4
L'Ascension 1,287	F 1
L'Assomption⊚ 4,844	D 4
La Station-du-Coteau 892	C 4
Laterrière 788	E 2
La Tuque 11,556	D 4
Laurentides 1,947	F 3
Laurier-Station 1,123	F 3
Laurierville 939	F 3
Lauzon 13,362	H 3
Laval 268,335	H 4
Lavaltrie 2,053	D 4
L'Avenir 1,116	E 4
Lawrenceville 562	E 4
Le Moyne 6,137	J 4
L'Épiphanie 2,971	D 4
Léry 2,239	H 4
Lévis⊚ 17,895	J 3
Lennoxville 3,922	F 4
Les Méchins 803	B 1
Linière 1,168	G 3
L'Islet 1,070	G 2
L'Islet-sur-Mer 774	G 2
L'Isle-Verte 1,142	G 1
Longueuil⊚ 124,320	J 4
Lorettéville 15,060	H 3
Lorraine 6,881	H 4
Louiseville⊚ 3,735	E 3
Luceville 1,524	J 1
Lyster 830	F 3
Magog 13,604	E 4
Maniwaki⊚ 5,424	B 3
Manseau 626	E 3
Maple Grove 2,009	H 4
Maria 1,178	C 2
Marieville⊚ 4,877	D 4
Mascouche 20,345	H 4
Maskinongé 1,005	E 3
Masson 4,264	B 4
Massueville 671	D 4
Matane⊚ 13,612	B 1
Matapédia 586	C 2
Melocheville 1,892	C 4
Mercier 6,352	H 4
Metabetchouan 3,406	F 1
Mirabel⊚ 14,080	H 4
Mistassini 6,682	E 1
Montauban 557	E 3
Mont-Carmel 807	H 2
Montcerf 570	A 3
Montebello 1,229	B 4
Mont-Joli 6,359	J 1
Mont-Laurier⊚ 8,405	B 3
Mont-Louis 756	C 1
Montmagny⊚ 12,405	G 3
Montréal⊚ 980,354	H 4
Montréal ⊛2,828,349	H 4
Montréal-Est 3,778	J 4
Montréal-Nord 94,914	H 4
Mont-Rolland 1,517	C 4
Mont-Royal 19,247	H 4
Mont-Saint-Hilaire 10,066	J 4
Morin Heights 592	C 1
Murdochville 3,396	C 1
Nantes 1,167	F 4

Agriculture, Industry and Resources

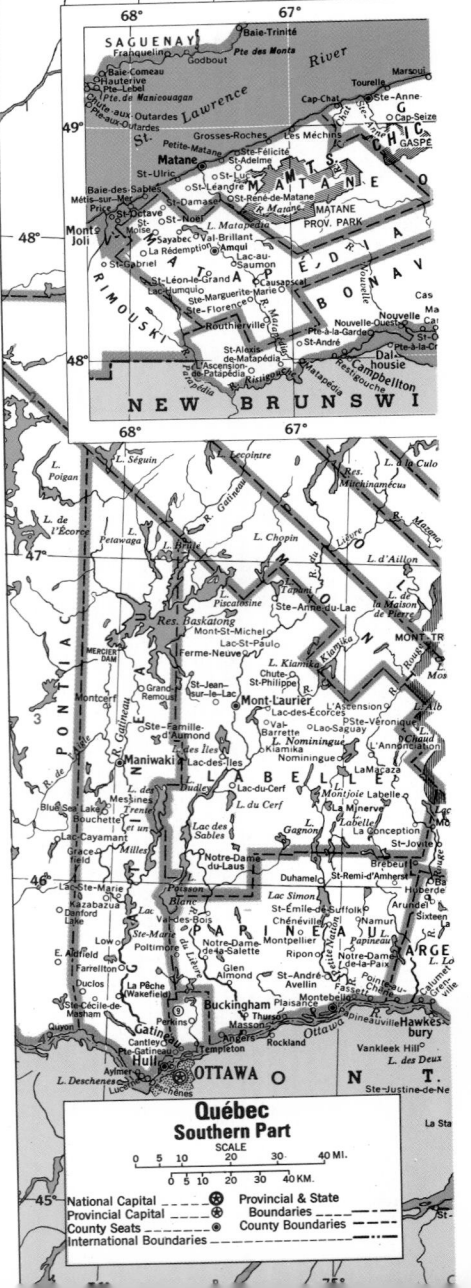

MAJOR MINERAL OCCURRENCES

Ab	Asbestos		Ni	Nickel	
Au	Gold		Pb	Lead	
Cu	Copper		Py	Pyrites	
Fe	Iron Ore		Ti	Titanium	
Mi	Mica		Zn	Zinc	
Mo	Molybdenum				

⚡ Water Power

▨ Major Industrial Areas

DOMINANT LAND USE

▨ Cereals, Livestock	▨ Pasture Livestock, Dairy
▨ Dairy	▨ Forests
▨ Nonagricultural Land	

Québec
Southern Part

SCALE

0 5 10   20   30   40 MI.

0 5 10   20   30   40 KM.

⊛ National Capital	Provincial & State
⊚ Provincial Capital	Boundaries
⊚ County Seats	County Boundaries
International Boundaries	

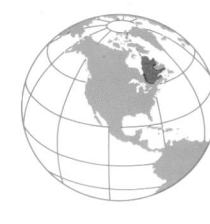

Napierville® 2,343	D 4	Pincourt 8,750	D 4	Rivière-à-Pierre 615	E 3
Neuville 996	F 3	Pintendre 1,849	J 3	Rivière-au-Renard 2,211	D 1
New Carlisle® 1,292	D 2	Plaisance 748	B 4	Rivière-Bleue 1,690	J 2
New Richmond 4,257	C 2	Plessisville 7,249	F 3	Rivière-Bois-Clair 604	F 3
Nicolet 4,880	E 3	Pohénégamook 3,702	H 2	Rivière-du-Loup® 13,459	H 2
Nominingue 881	B 3	Pointe-à-la-Croix 1,481	C 2	Rivière-du-Moulin	G 1
Normandin 4,041	E 1	Pointe-au-Père 796	J 1	Rivière-Eternité 659	G 1
North Hatley 689	F 4	Pointe-au-Pic 1,054	G 2	Rivière-Portneuf-Portneuf-sur-	
Notre-Dame-de-la-Doré 1,064	E 1	Pointe-aux-Outardes 1,056	A 1	Mer 1,255	H 1
Notre-Dame-des-Laurentides	H 3	Pointe-aux-Trembles 36,270	J 4	Robertsonville 1,987	F 3
Notre-Dame-des-Prairies		Pointe-Calumet 2,935	G 4	Roberval® 11,429	E 1
6,150	D 3	Pointe-Claire 24,571	H 4	Rock Island 1,179	F 4
Notre-Dame-du-Bon-Conseil		Pointe-du-Lac 5,359	E 3	Rosemère 7,778	H 4
1,089	E 3	Pointe-Gatineau	B 4	Rougemont 972	D 4
Notre-Dame-du-Lac® 2,258	J 2	Pointe-Lebel 1,573	A 1	Roxboro 6,292	H 4
Nouvelle 669	C 2	Pont-Rouge 3,580	F 3	Roxton Falls 1,245	E 4
Oka 1,538	C 4	Port-Alfred 8,621	G 1	Sacré-Coeur-de-Saguenay	
Omerville 1,398	E 4	Portneuf 1,333	F 3	1,678	H 1
Ormstown 1,659	D 4	Portneuf-sur-Mer (Rivière-		Saint-Adelme 618	B 1
Orsainville	H 3	Portneuf-sur-Mer) 1,255	H 1	Saint-Adelphe 1,159	E 3
Otis 673	G 1	Price 2,273	J 1	Saint-Adolphe-d'Howard	
Otterburn Park 4,268	D 4	Princeville 4,023	F 3	1,686	C 4
Outremont 24,338	H 4	Proulxville 588	E 3	Saint-Adrien 597	F 4
Pabos 1,295	D 2	Québec (cap.) 166,474	H 3	Saint-Aimé-des-Lacs 861	G 2
Pabos-Mills 1,565	D 2	Québec *576,075	H 3	Saint-Alban 673	E 3
Papineauville 1,481	C 4	Quyon 744	A 4	Saint-Alexandre-de-	
Paspébiac 1,914	C 2	Rawdon 2,958	D 3	Kamouraska 1,048	H 2
Percé® 4,839	D 1	Repentigny 34,419	J 4	Saint-Alexis-des-Monts 1,984	D 3
Petit-Cap 1,023	D 1	Richelieu 1,832	D 4	Saint-Amable 2,424	J 4
Petite-Matane 1,065	B 1	Richmond 3,568	E 4	Saint-Ambroise 3,606	F 1
Petit-Saguenay (Saint-		Rigaud 2,268	C 4	Saint-Anaclet 1,377	J 1
François-d'Assise) 804	G 1	Rimouski® 29,120	J 1	Saint-André-Avellin 1,312	B 4
Pierrefonds 38,390	H 4	Rimouski-Est 2,506	J 1	Saint-André-Est 1,293	C 4
Pierreville 1,212	E 3	Ripon 620	B 4		

Saint-Anselme 1,808	F 3	Saint-Dominique 2,068	E 4	Sainte-Catherine 1,474	F 3
Saint-Antoine 7,012	H 4	Saint-Donat-de-Montcalm		Sainte-Claire 1,566	G 3
Saint-Antonin 941	H 2	1,521	C 3	Sainte-Croix® 1,814	F 3
Saint-Aubert 884	G 2	Sainte-Adèle 4,675	C 4	Sainte-Félicité 711	B 1
Saint-Augustin-de-Québec		Sainte-Agathe 709	F 3	Sainte-Foy 68,883	H 3
2,475	E 3	Sainte-Agathe-des-Monts		Sainte-Geneviève 2,573	H 4
Saint-Basile-Sud 1,719	F 3	5,641	C 3	Sainte-Geneviève-de-	
Saint-Basile-le-Grand 7,658	J 4	Sainte-Anne-de-Beaupré		Batiscan® 356	E 3
Saint-Benjamin 1,027	G 3	3,292	F 2	Sainte-Hélène-de-Bagot	
Saint-Bernard 585	F 3	Sainte-Anne-de-Bellevue		1,328	E 4
Saint-Bernard-sur-Mer 711	G 2	3,981	H 4	Sainte-Hénédine® 639	F 3
Saint-Boniface-de-Shawinigan		Sainte-Anne-des-Monts®		Sainte-Julie-de-Verchères	
3,164	D 3	6,062	C 1	14,243	J 4
Saint-Bruno 2,580	F 1	Sainte-Anne-des-Plaines		Sainte-Julienne® 750	D 4
Saint-Bruno-de-Montarville		4,258	H 4	Sainte-Justine 1,080	G 3
22,880	H 4	Sainte-Anne-du-Lac 686	B 3	Sainte-Marie 8,937	G 3
Saint-Camille-de-Bellechasse		Sainte-Aurélie 1,045	G 3		
1,744	G 3	Sainte-Blandine 849	J 1		
Saint-Casimir 1,133	E 3			Sainte-Martine® 2,196	D 4
Saint-Césaire 2,935	D 4			Sainte-Émile 5,216	G 3
Saint-Charles 1,019	F 3			Sainte-Monique 705	F 1
Saint-Charles-de-Mandeville				Sainte-Pétronille 982	J 3
1,392	D 3			Sainte-Perpétue-de-l'Islet	
Saint-Chrysostome 1,018	D 4			1,232	H 2
Saint-Côme 660	D 3			Sainte-Éphrem-de-Tring 973	G 3
Saint-Constant 9,938	H 4			Saint-Épiphane 647	H 2
Saint-Cyprien 860	J 2			Sainte-Pudentienne 866	E 4
Saint-Cyrille 1,041	E 4			Sainte-Rosalie 2,862	E 4
Saint-Damien-de-Buckland				Saint-Esprit 1,068	D 4
1,522	G 3			Sainte-Thérèse 18,750	H 4
Saint-David 5,380	J 3			Sainte-Thérèse-Ouest	
Saint-David-de-Falardeau				(Boisbriand) 13,471	H 4
1,876	F 1			Saint-Thècle 1,703	E 3
Saint-Denis 861	D 4			Saint-Étienne-de-Grès 845	E 3
				Saint-Étienne-de-Lauzon	
				1,218	J 3

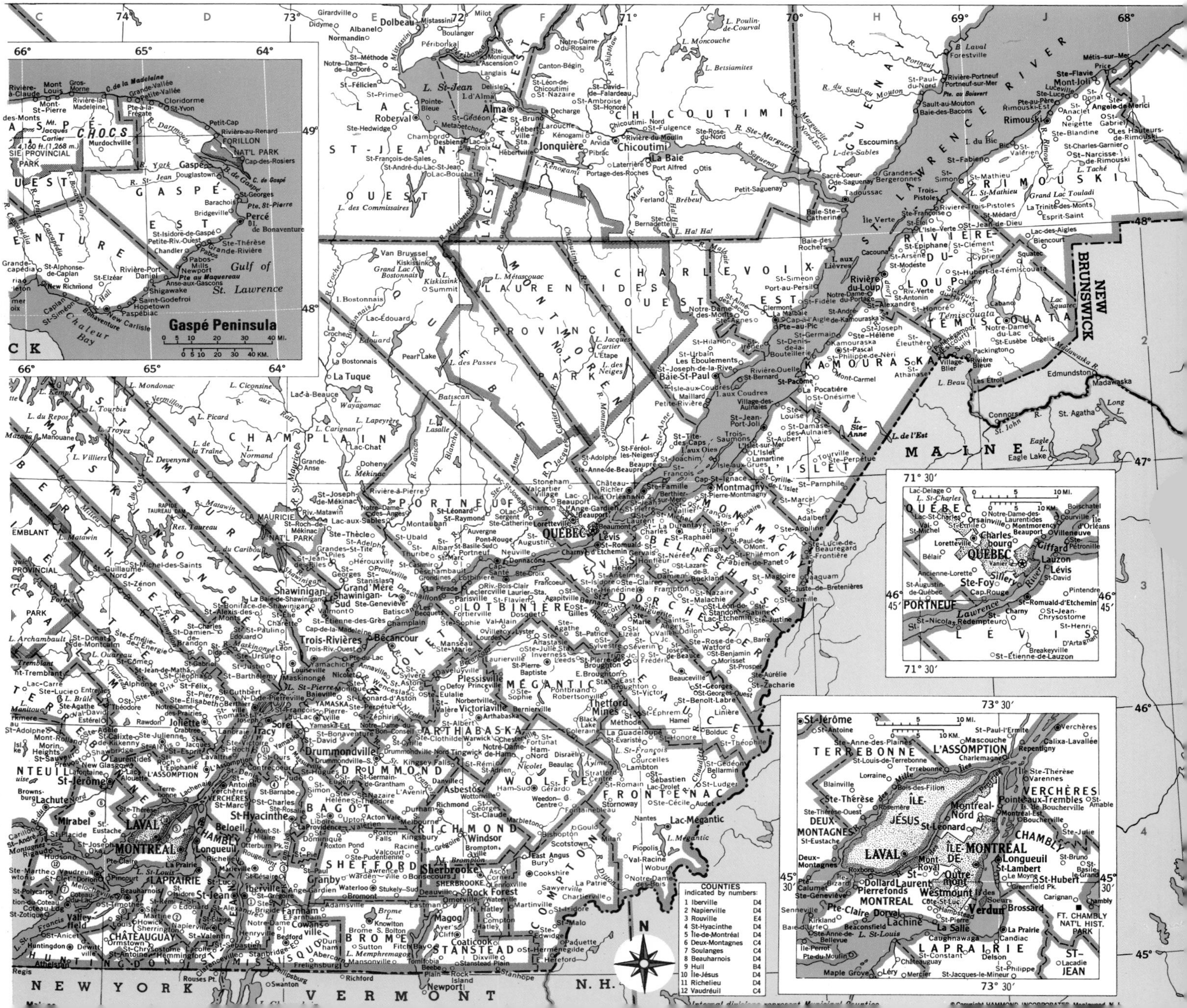

AREA 594,857 sq. mi. (1,540,680 sq. km.)
POPULATION 6,438,403
CAPITAL Québec
LARGEST CITY Montréal
HIGHEST POINT Mont D'Iberville 5,420 ft. (1,652 m.)
SETTLED IN 1608
ADMITTED TO CONFEDERATION 1867
PROVINCIAL FLOWER White Garden Lily

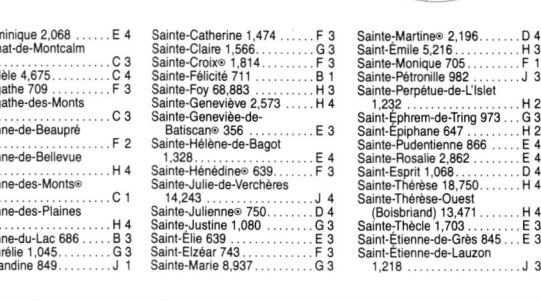

(continued)

Saint-Eustache 29,716 . . . H 4
Saint-Fabien 1,361 . . . J 1
Saint-Félicien 9,058 . . . E 1
Saint-Félix-de-Valois 1,462 . . . D 3
Saint-Ferréol-les-Neiges 1,758 . . . G 2
Saint-Flavien 734 . . . F 3
Saint-François-de-Sales 831 . . . E 1
Saint-François-du-Lac⊙ 942 . . . E 3
Saint-Fulgence 950 . . . G 1
Saint-Gabriel 3,161 . . . D 3
Saint-Gabriel-de-Rimouski 779 . . . J 1
Saint-Gédéon, Frontenac 1,569 . . . G 4
Saint-Gédéon, Lac-St-Jean-E. 1,000 . . . F 1
Saint-Georges, Beauce 10,342 . . . G 3
Saint-Georges, Champlain 3,344 . . . E 3
Saint-Georges-Ouest 6,378 . . . G 3
Saint-Germain-de-Grantham 1,373 . . . E 4
Saint-Gervais 973 . . . G 3
Saint-Gilles 912 . . . F 3
Saint-Grégoire (Mont-St-Grégoire) 740 . . . D 4
Saint-Henri 1,970 . . . J 3
Saint-Honoré, Beauce 1,116 . . . G 4
Saint-Honoré, Chicoutimi 1,790 . . . F 1
Saint-Hubert 60,573 . . . J 4
Saint-Hubert-de-Témiscouata 871 . . . J 2
Saint-Hyacinthe⊙ 38,246 . . . D 4
Saint-Isidore 811 . . . F 3
Saint-Isidore-de-Laprairie 769 D 4
Saint-Jacques 2,152 . . . D 4
Saint-Jacques-le-Mineur 1,203 . . . H 4
Saint-Jean-Chrysostome 6,930 . . . J 3
Saint-Jean-de-Dieu 1,377 . . . J 1
Saint-Jean-de-Matha 931 . . . D 3
Saint-Jean-Port-Joli⊙ 1,813 . . . G 2
Saint-Jean-sur-Richelieu⊙ 35,640 . . . D 4
Saint-Jérôme 25,123 . . . H 4
Saint-Joachim 1,139 . . . G 2
Saint-Joseph-de-Beauce 3,216 . . . G 3
Saint-Joseph-de-Sorel 2,545 . . . D 3
Saint-Jovite 3,841 . . . C 3
Saint-Lambert 20,557 . . . J 4
Saint-Laurent 65,900 . . . H 4
Saint-Lazare 731 . . . G 3
Saint-Léonard 79,429 . . . H 4
Saint-Léonard-d'Aston 992 . . . E 3
Saint-Léon-de-Chicoutimi 749 F 1
Saint-Léon-de-Standon 816 . . . G 3
Saint-Léon-le-Grand 722 . . . B 2
Saint-Liboire⊙ 746 . . . E 4
Saint-Louis-de-Gonzague 615 . . . D 4
Saint-Louis-de-Terrebonne 14,172 . . . H 4
Saint-Louis-du-Ha! Ha! 809 . . . H 2
Saint-Luc 8,815 . . . D 4
Saint-Luc-de-Matane 598 . . . B 1
Saint-Marc-des-Carrières 2,822 . . . E 3
Saint-Méthode-de-Frontenac 925 . . . F 3
Saint-Michel-de-Bellechasse 963 . . . G 3
Saint-Michel-des-Saints 1,584 . . . D 3
Saint-Nazaire-de-Chicoutimi 962 . . . F 1
Saint-Nérée 970 . . . G 3
Saint-Nicolas 5,074 . . . H 3
Saint-Noël 666 . . . B 1
Saint-Odilon 580 . . . G 3
Saint-Omer 718 . . . C 2
Saint-Ours 625 . . . D 4
Saint-Pacôme 1,996 . . . G 2
Saint-Pamphile 3,428 . . . H 3
Saint-Pascal⊙ 2,763 . . . H 2
Saint-Paul-de-Montminy 602 . . . G 3
Saint-Paulin 663 . . . D 3
Saint-Paul-l'Ermite (Le Gardeur) 8,312 . . . J 4
Saint-Philippe-de-Néri 715 . . . H 2
Saint-Pie 1,725 . . . E 4
Saint-Pierre 5,305 . . . H 4
Saint-Pierre-d'Orléans 880 . . . G 3
Saint-Polycarpe 602 . . . C 4
Saint-Prime 2,522 . . . E 1
Saint-Prosper-de-Dorchester 2,150 . . . G 3
Saint-Raphaël⊙ 1,346 . . . G 3
Saint-Raymond 3,605 . . . F 3
Saint-Rédempteur 4,463 . . . J 3
Saint-Régis 1,370 . . . C 4
Saint-Rémi 5,146 . . . D 4
Saint-Roch-de-l'Achigan 1,160 . . . D 4
Saint-Roch-de-Richelieu 1,650 . . . D 4
Saint-Romuald-d'Etchemin⊙ 9,849 . . . J 3
Saint-Sauveur-des-Monts 2,348 . . . C 4
Saint-Siméon 1,152 . . . G 2
Saint-Simon 602 . . . H 1
Saint-Stanislas 1,443 . . . E 3
Saint-Sylvère 1,006 . . . E 3
Saint-Timothée 2,113 . . . D 4
Saint-Tite 3,031 . . . E 3
Saint-Tite-des-Caps 626 . . . G 2
Saint-Ubald 1,605 . . . E 3
Saint-Ulric 792 . . . B 1
Saint-Urbain-de-Charlevoix 1,079 . . . G 2
Saint-Victor 1,104 . . . G 3
Saint-Zacharie 1,284 . . . G 3
Saint-Zotique 1,774 . . . C 4
Sault-au-Mouton 828 . . . H 1
Sawyerville 939 . . . F 4
Sayabec 1,721 . . . B 2
Scotstown 762 . . . F 4
Senneville 1,221 . . . G 4
Shannon 3,488 . . . F 3
Shawbridge 942 . . . C 4
Shawinigan 23,011 . . . E 3
Shawinigan-Sud 11,325 . . . E 3
Shawville 1,608 . . . A 4
Sherbrooke⊙ 74,075 . . . E 4
Sherrington 614 . . . D 4
Sillery 12,825 . . . J 3
Sorel⊙ 20,347 . . . D 4
Squatec 1,000 . . . J 2
Stanstead Plain 1,093 . . . F 4
Sutton 1,599 . . . E 4
Tadoussac⊙ 900 . . . H 1
Templeton . . . B 4
Terrebonne 11,769 . . . H 4
Thetford Mines 19,965 . . . F 3
Thurso 2,780 . . . B 4
Tourelle (Tourelle-Grand-Tourelle) 942 . . . C 1
Tourville 659 . . . H 2
Tracy 12,843 . . . D 3
Tring-Jonction 1,315 . . . F 3
Trois-Pistoles 4,445 . . . H 1
Trois-Rivières 50,466 . . . E 3
Trois-Rivières *111,453 . . . E 3
Trois-Rivières-Ouest 13,107 . . . E 3
Upton 926 . . . E 4
Val-Barrette 609 . . . B 3
Val-Brillant 687 . . . B 1
Valcourt 2,601 . . . E 4
Val-David 2,336 . . . C 3
Vallée-Jonction 1,200 . . . G 3
Valleyfield (Salaberry-de-Valleyfield) 29,574 . . . C 4
Vanier 10,725 . . . J 3
Varennes 8,764 . . . J 4
Vaudreuil⊙ 7,608 . . . C 4
Verchères⊙ 4,473 . . . J 4
Verdun 61,287 . . . H 4
Victoriaville 21,838 . . . F 3
Villeneuve . . . J 3
Warwick 2,847 . . . F 4
Waterloo⊙ 4,664 . . . E 4
Waterville 1,397 . . . F 4
Weedon-Centre 1,263 . . . F 4
Westmount 20,480 . . . H 4
Wickham 2,043 . . . E 4
Windsor 5,233 . . . F 4
Wottonville 673 . . . F 4
Yamachiche⊙ 1,258 . . . E 3

OTHER FEATURES

Alma (isl.) . . . F 1
Aylmer (lake) . . . F 4
Baskatong (res.) . . . B 3
Batiscan (riv.) . . . E 2
Bécancour (riv.) . . . F 3
Bonaventure (isl.) . . . D 1
Bonaventure (riv.) . . . C 1
Brome (lake) . . . E 4
Brompton (lake) . . . E 4
Cascapédia (riv.) . . . C 1
Chaleur (bay) . . . C 2
Champlain (lake) . . . D 4
Chaudière (riv.) . . . G 4
Chic-Chocs (mts.) . . . C 1
Chicoutimi (riv.) . . . F 2
Coudres (isl.) . . . G 2
Deschênes (lake) . . . A 4
Deux Montagnes (lake) . . . C 4
Ditton (riv.) . . . F 4
Forillon Nat'l Park . . . D 1
Fort Chambly Nat'l Hist. Park . . . J 4
Gaspé (bay) . . . D 1
Gaspé (cape) . . . D 1
Gaspé (pen.) . . . D 2
Gaspésie Prov. Park . . . C 1
Gatineau (riv.) . . . B 3
Îles (lake) . . . B 3
Jacques-Cartier (mt.) . . . C 1
Jacques-Cartier (riv.) . . . F 2
Kénogami (lake) . . . F 1
Kiamika (lake) . . . B 3
La Maurice Nat'l Park . . . D 3
Laurentides Prov. Park . . . F 2
Lièvre (riv.) . . . B 4
Lièvres (isl.) . . . H 2
Maskinongé (riv.) . . . D 3
Matane (riv.) . . . B 1
Matane Prov. Park . . . B 1
Matapédia (riv.) . . . B 2
Mégantic (lake) . . . G 4
Memphremagog (lake) . . . E 4
Mercier (dam) . . . A 3
Métabetchouane (riv.) . . . F 1
Mille Îles (riv.) . . . H 4
Montmorency (riv.) . . . F 2
Mont-Tremblant Prov. Park . . . C 3
Nicolet (riv.) . . . E 3
Nominingue (lake) . . . B 3
Nord (riv.) . . . C 4
Orléans (isl.) . . . F 3
Ottawa (riv.) . . . B 4
Ouareau (riv.) . . . D 3
Ouelle (riv.) . . . H 2
Patapédia (riv.) . . . B 2
Péribonca (riv.) . . . F 1
Petite Nation (riv.) . . . B 4
Prairies (riv.) . . . H 4
Rimouski (riv.) . . . J 1
Ristigouche (riv.) . . . B 2
Saguenay (riv.) . . . G 1
Sainte-Anne (riv.) . . . F 3
Sainte-Anne (riv.) . . . G 2
Saint-François (lake) . . . F 4
Saint-François (riv.) . . . E 4
Saint-Jean (lake) . . . E 1
Saint Lawrence (gulf) . . . D 2
Saint Lawrence (riv.) . . . H 1
Saint-Louis (lake) . . . H 4
Saint-Maurice (riv.) . . . E 2
Saint-Pierre (lake) . . . E 3
Shawinigan (riv.) . . . E 3
Shipshaw (riv.) . . . F 1
Soeurs (isl.) . . . H 4
Témiscouata (lake) . . . H 2
Tremblant (lake) . . . C 3
Trente et un Milles (lake) . . . B 3
Verte (isl.) . . . H 1
Yamaska (riv.) . . . E 4
York (riv.) . . . D 1

⊙County seat.
*Population of metropolitan area.

QUÉBEC, NORTHERN

INTERNAL DIVISIONS

Abitibi (county) 93,529 . . . B 2
Abitibi (terr.) . . . B 3
Berthier (county) 31,096 . . . B 3
Bonaventure (county) 40,487 . . . D 3
Champlain (county) 119,595 . . . C 3
Charlevoix-Est (co.) 17,448 . . . C 3
Charlevoix-Ouest (county) 14,172 . . . C 3
Chicoutimi (county) 174,441 . . . C 2
Gaspé-Est (county) 41,173 . . . E 3
Gaspé-Ouest (county) 18,943 D 3
Gatineau (county) 54,229 . . . B 3
Joliette (county) 60,384 . . . B 3
Lac-Saint-Jean-Est (county) 47,891 . . . C 3
Lac-Saint-Jean-Ouest (county) 62,952 . . . C 2
Maskinongé (county) 20,763 . . . C 3
Matane (county) 29,955 . . . D 3
Matapédia (county) 23,715 . . . D 3
Mistassini (terr.) . . . B 2
Montcalm (county) 27,557 . . . B 3
Montmorency No. I (county) 23,048 . . . C 3
Nouveau-Québec (terr.) . . . E 1
Pontiac (county) 20,283 . . . B 3
Portneuf (county) 58,843 . . . C 3
Québec (county) 458,980 . . . C 3
Rimouski (county) 69,099 . . . D 3
Saguenay (county) 115,881 . . . D 2
Saint-Maurice (co.) 107,703 . . . C 3
Témiscamingue (co.) 52,570 . . . B 3

CITIES and TOWNS

Alma⊙ 26,322 . . . C 3
Amos⊙ 9,421 . . . B 3
Baie-Comeau 12,866 . . . D 3
Baie-du-Poste 1,690 . . . C 2
Chicoutimi⊙ 60,064 . . . C 3
Gaspé 17,261 . . . E 3
Hauterive 13,995 . . . D 3
Jonquière 60,354 . . . C 3
Lévis 17,895 . . . C 3
La Tuque 11,556 . . . C 3
Manicouagan . . . D 2
Maniwaki⊙ 5,424 . . . B 3
Matane⊙ 13,612 . . . D 3
Mistassini (Baie-du-Poste) 1,690 . . . C 2
Mont-Laurier⊙ 8,405 . . . B 3
Montmagny⊙ 12,405 . . . C 3
New Carlisle⊙ 781 . . . E 3
Nouveau-Comptoir . . . B 2
Percé⊙ 4,839 . . . E 3
Port-Cartier-Ouest . . . D 3
Port-Menier⊙ 275 . . . E 3
Povungnituk 745 . . . E 1
Québec (cap.)⊙ 166,474 . . . C 3
Rimouski⊙ 29,120 . . . D 3
Rivière-au-Tonnerre 480 . . . D 2
Rivière-du-Loup 13,459 . . . D 3
Rouyn 17,224 . . . B 3
Sept-Îles 29,262 . . . D 2
Seven Islands (Sept-Îles) 29,262 . . . D 2
Shawinigan 23,011 . . . C 3
Tadoussac 900 . . . C 3
Val d'Or 21,371 . . . B 3
Ville-Marie 2,651 . . . B 3

OTHER FEATURES

Allard (lake) . . . E 2
Anticosti (isl.) . . . E 3
Baleine, Grand Rivière de la (riv.) . . . B 1
Bell (riv.) . . . B 3
Betsiamites (riv.) . . . C 2
Bienville (lake) . . . C 2
Broadback (riv.) . . . B 2
Cabonga (res.) . . . B 3
Caniapiscau (riv.) . . . D 1
Eastmain (riv.) . . . B 2
Eau Claire (lake) . . . C 1
Feuilles (riv.) . . . C 1
Gaspésie Prov. Park . . . D 3
George (riv.) . . . F 2
Gouin (res.) . . . C 3
Grande Rivière, La (riv.) . . . B 2
Honguedo (passage) . . . E 3
Hudson (bay) . . . A 1
Hudson (str.) . . . F 1
Jacques-Cartier (passage) . . . E 3
James (bay) . . . A 2
Koksoak (riv.) . . . D 1
Laurentides Prov. Park . . . C 3
Louis-XIV (pt.) . . . B 2
Manicouagan (res.) . . . D 2
Minto (lake) . . . E 2
Mistassibi (riv.) . . . C 3
Mistassini (lake) . . . C 2
Moisie (riv.) . . . D 2
Natashquan (riv.) . . . E 2
Nottaway (riv.) . . . B 2
Nouveau-Québec (crater) . . . F 1
Otish (mts.) . . . C 2
Ottawa (riv.) . . . B 3
Péribonca (riv.) . . . C 3
Plétipi (lake) . . . C 2
Saguenay (riv.) . . . C 3
Saint-Jean (lake) . . . C 3
Saint Lawrence (gulf) . . . E 3
Saint Lawrence (riv.) . . . D 3
Ungava (pen.) . . . E 1

⊙County seat.
*Population of metropolitan area.

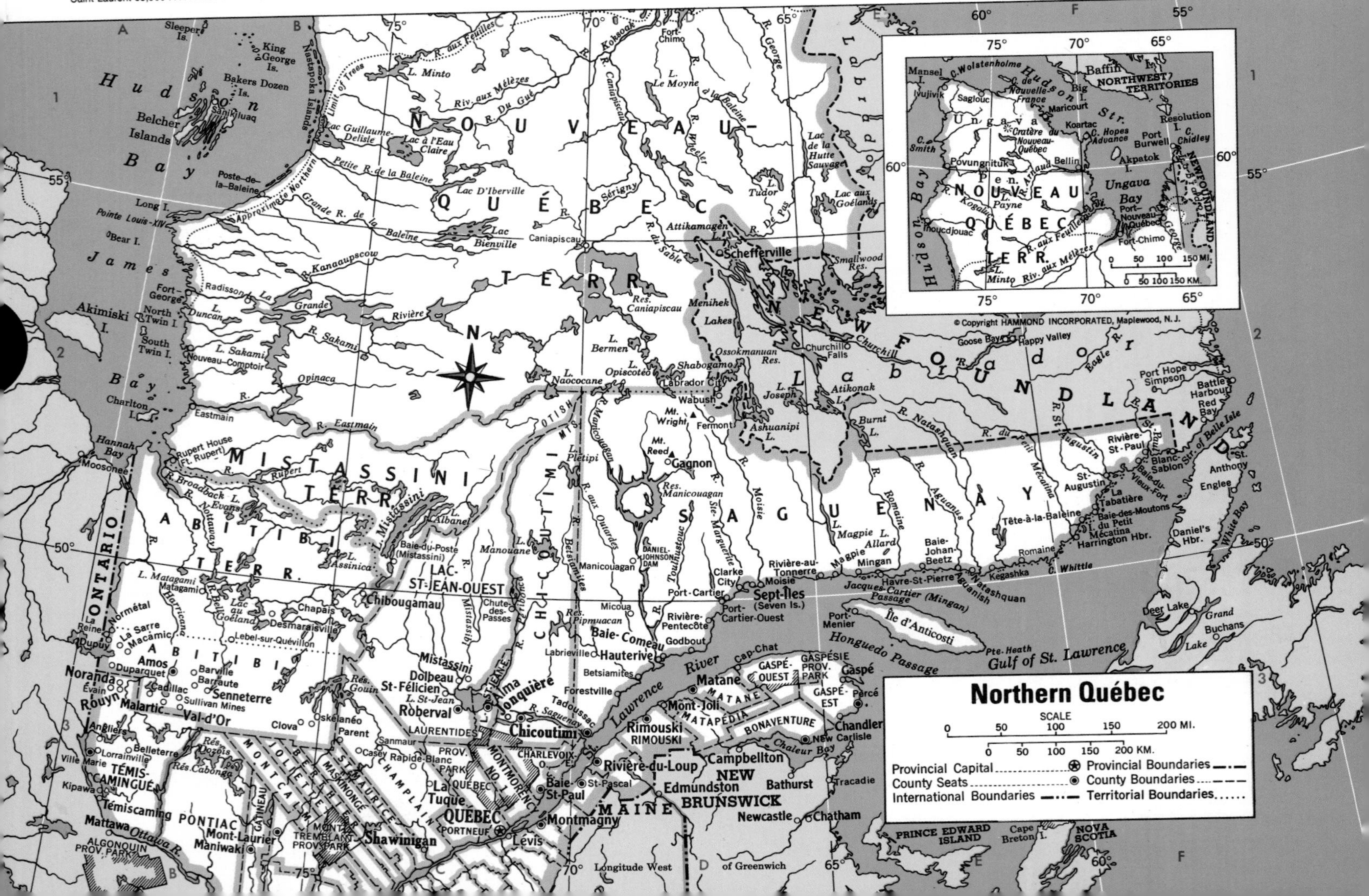

ONTARIO, NORTHERN

INTERNAL DIVISIONS

Algoma (terr. dist.) 133,553 ... D 3
Cochrane (terr. dist.) 96,875 ... D 2
Kenora (terr. dist.) 59,421 ... C 2
Manitoulin (terr. dist.) 11,001 ... D 3
Nipissing (terr. dist.) 80,268 ... E 3
Parry Sound (terr. dist.) 33,528 ... E 3
Rainy River (terr. dist.) 22,798 ... B 3
Renfrew (county) 87,484 ... E 3
Sudbury (reg. munic.) 159,779 ... D 3
Sudbury (terr. dist.) 27,068 ... D 3
Thunder Bay (terr. dist.) 153,997 ... C 3
Timiskaming (terr. dist.) 41,288 ... D 3

CITIES and TOWNS

Chalk River 1,010 ... E 3
Elliot Lake 16,723 ... D 3
Fort Albany 482 ... D 2
Fort Frances◎ 8,906 ... B 3
Kapuskasing 12,014 ... D 3
Kenora◎ 9,817 ... B 3
Kirkland Lake 12,219 ... D 3
Moose Factory 1,452 ... D 2
Moosonee 1,433 ... D 2
Nickel Centre 12,318 ... D 3
North Bay◎ 51,268 ... E 3
Pembroke◎ 14,026 ... E 3
Sault Sainte Marie◎ 82,697 ... D 3
Sudbury 91,829 ... D 3
Thunder Bay◎ 112,486 ... C 3
Timmins 46,114 ... D 3
Valley East 20,433 ... D 3

OTHER FEATURES

Abitibi (lake) ... E 3
Abitibi (riv.) ... D 2
Albany (riv.) ... C 2
Algonquin Prov. Park ... E 3
Asheweig (riv.) ... C 2
Attawapiskat (lake) ... C 2
Attawapiskat (riv.) ... C 2
Basswood (lake) ... B 3
Berens (riv.) ... A 2
Big Trout (lake) ... B 2
Black Duck (riv.) ... C 1
Bloodvein (riv.) ... A 2
Caribou (isl.) ... C 3
Cobham (riv.) ... A 2
Eabamet (lake) ... C 2
Ekwan (riv.) ... C 2
English (riv.) ... B 2
Fawn (riv.) ... C 2
Finger (lake) ... B 2
Georgian (bay) ... D 3
Hannah (bay) ... D 2
Henrietta Maria (cape) ... D 1
Hudson (bay) ... D 1
Huron (lake) ... D 3
James (bay) ... D 2
Kapiskau (riv.) ... D 2
Kapuskasing (riv.) ... D 3
Kenogami (riv.) ... C 2
Kesagami (riv.) ... E 2
Lake of the Woods (lake) ... B 3
Lake Superior Prov. Park ... D 3
Little Current (riv.) ... C 2
Long (lake) ... C 3
Manitoulin (isl.) ... D 3
Mattagami (riv.) ... D 3
Michipicoten (isl.) ... C 3
Mille Lacs (lake) ... B 3
Missinaibi (lake) ... D 3
Missinaibi (riv.) ... D 2
Missisa (lake) ... D 2
Nipigon (lake) ... C 3
Nipissing (lake) ... E 3
North (chan.) ... D 3
North Caribou (lake) ... B 2
Nungesser (lake) ... B 2
Ogidaki (mt.) ... D 3
Ogoki (riv.) ... C 2
Opazatika (riv.) ... D 3
Opinnagau (riv.) ... D 2
Otoskwin (riv.) ... B 2
Ottawa (riv.) ... E 3
Pipestone (riv.) ... B 2
Polar Bear Prov. Park ... D 2
Pukaskwa Prov. Park ... C 3
Quetico Prov. Park ... B 3
Rainy (lake) ... B 3
Red (lake) ... B 2
Sachigo (riv.) ... B 2
Saganaga (lake) ... B 3
Saint Ignace (isl.) ... C 3
Saint Joseph (lake) ... B 2
Sandy (lake) ... B 2
Savant (lake) ... B 2
Seine (riv.) ... B 3
Seul (lake) ... B 2
Severn (lake) ... B 2
Severn (riv.) ... B 2
Shamattawa (riv.) ... C 2
Shibogama (lake) ... C 2
Sibley Prov. Park ... C 3
Slate (isls.) ... C 3
Stout (lake) ... B 2
Superior (lake) ... C 3
Sutton (lake) ... D 2
Sutton (riv.) ... D 2
Timagami (lake) ... D 3
Timiskaming (lake) ... E 3
Trout (lake) ... B 2
Wabuk (pt.) ... D 1
Winisk (lake) ... C 2
Winisk (riv.) ... C 2
Winnipeg (riv.) ... A 2
Woods (lake) ... B 3

ONTARIO

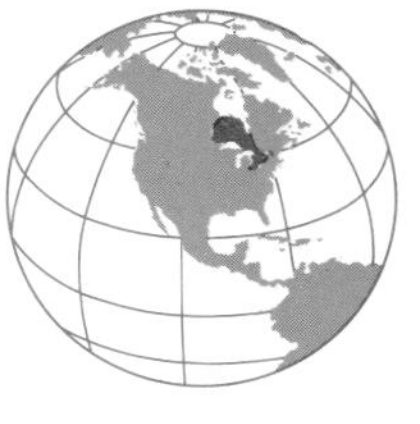

AREA 412,580 sq. mi. (1,068,582 sq. km.)
POPULATION 8,625,107
CAPITAL Toronto
LARGEST CITY Toronto
HIGHEST POINT in Timiskaming Dist. 2,275 ft. (693 m.)
SETTLED IN 1749
ADMITTED TO CONFEDERATION 1867
PROVINCIAL FLOWER White Trillium

INTERNAL DIVISIONS

Algoma (terr. dist.) 133,553 ... J 5
Brant (county) 104,427 ... D 4
Bruce (county) 60,020 ... C 3
Cochrane (terr. dist.) 96,875 ... J 4
Dufferin (county) 31,145 ... D 3
Dundas (county) 18,946 ... J 2
Durham (reg. munic.) 283,639 ... F 3
Elgin (county) 69,707 ... C 5
Essex (county) 312,467 ... B 5
Frontenac (county) 108,133 ... H 3
Glengarry (county) 20,254 ... K 2
Grenville (county) 27,176 ... J 3
Grey (county) 73,824 ... D 3
Haldimand-Norfolk (reg. munic.) 89,456 ... E 5
Haliburton (county) 11,361 ... F 2
Halton (reg. munic.) 253,883 ... E 4
Hamilton-Wentworth (reg. munic.) 411,445 ... D 4
Hastings (county) 106,883 ... G 3
Huron (county) 56,127 ... C 4
Kenora (terr. dist.) 59,421 ... G 5
Kent (county) 107,022 ... B 5
Lambton (county) 123,445 ... B 5
Lanark (county) 45,676 ... H 3
Leeds (county) 53,765 ... H 3
Lennox and Addington (county) 33,040 ... G 3
Manitoulin (terr. dist.) 11,001 ... B 2
Middlesex (county) 318,184 ... C 4
Muskoka (dist. munic.) 38,370 ... E 3
Niagara (reg. munic.) 368,288 ... E 4
Nipissing (terr. dist.) 80,268 ... F 2
Northumberland (county) 64,966 ... G 3
Ottawa-Carleton (reg. munic.) 546,849 ... J 2
Oxford (county) 85,920 ... D 4
Parry Sound (terr. dist.) 33,528 ... D 2
Peel (reg. munic.) 490,731 ... E 4
Perth (county) 66,096 ... C 4
Peterborough (county) 102,452 ... F 3
Prescott (county) 30,365 ... K 2
Prince Edward (county) 22,336 ... G 3
Rainy River (terr. dist.) 22,798 ... G 5
Renfrew (county) 87,484 ... G 2
Russell (county) 22,412 ... J 2
Simcoe (county) 225,071 ... E 3
Stormont (county) 61,927 ... K 2
Sudbury (reg. munic.) 159,779 ... K 6
Sudbury (terr. dist.) 27,068 ... J 5
Thunder Bay (terr. dist.) 153,997 ... H 5
Timiskaming (terr. dist.) 41,288 ... K 5
Toronto (metro. munic.) 2,137,395 ... K 4
Victoria (county) 47,854 ... F 3
Waterloo (reg. munic.) 305,496 ... D 4
Wellington (county) 129,432 ... D 4
York (reg. munic.) 252,053 ... E 4

CITIES and TOWNS

Ailsa Craig 765 ... C 4
Ajax 25,475 ... E 4
Alban 342 ... D 1
Alexandria 3,271 ... K 2
Alfred 1,057 ... K 2
Alliston 4,712 ... E 3
Almonte 3,855 ... H 2
Alvinston 736 ... B 5
Amherstburg 5,685 ... A 5
Amherst View 6,110 ... H 3
Ancaster 14,428 ... D 4
Angus 3,085 ... E 3
Apsley 264 ... F 3
Arkona 473 ... C 4
Armstrong 378 ... H 4
Arnprior 5,828 ... H 2
Aroland 291 ... H 4
Arthur 1,700 ... D 4
Astorville 340 ... E 1
Athens 948 ... J 3
Atherley 366 ... E 3
Atikokan 4,452 ... G 5
Atwood 723 ... D 4
Aurora 16,267 ... J 3
Avonmore 273 ... K 2
Aylmer 5,254 ... C 5
Ayr 1,295 ... D 4
Ayton 424 ... D 3
Baden 945 ... D 4
Bala 577 ... E 2
Bancroft 2,329 ... G 2
Barrie◎ 38,423 ... E 3
Barry's Bay 1,216 ... G 2
Batawa 430 ... G 3
Bath 1,071 ... H 3
Bayfield 649 ... C 4
Beachburg 682 ... H 2
Beachville 917 ... D 4
Beardmore 583 ... H 5
Beaverton 1,952 ... E 3
Beeton 1,989 ... E 3
Belle River 3,568 ... B 5
Belleville◎ 34,881 ... G 3
Belmont 831 ... C 5
Bethany 365 ... F 3
Bewdley 508 ... F 3
Binbrook 306 ... E 4
Blackstock 720 ... F 3
Blenheim 4,044 ... C 5
Blind River 3,444 ... J 5
Bloomfield 718 ... G 4
Blyth 926 ... C 4
Bobcaygeon 1,625 ... F 3
Bonfield 540 ... E 1
Bothwell 915 ... C 5
Bourget 1,057 ... J 2
Bracebridge◎ 9,063 ... E 2
Bradford 7,370 ... E 3
Braeside 492 ... H 2
Brampton◎ 149,030 ... J 4
Brantford◎ 74,315 ... D 4
Bridgenorth 1,633 ... F 3
Brigden 635 ... B 5
Brighton 3,147 ... G 3
Britt 419 ... D 2
Brockville◎ 19,896 ... J 3
Bruce Mines 635 ... J 5
Brussels 962 ... C 4
Burford 1,461 ... D 4
Burgessville 302 ... D 4
Burk's Falls 922 ... E 2
Burlington 114,853 ... E 4
Cache Bay 665 ... D 1
Caesarea 551 ... F 3
Calabogie 256 ... H 2
Caledon 26,645 ... E 4
Callander 1,158 ... E 1
Cambridge 77,183 ... D 4
Campbellford 3,409 ... G 3
Cannington 1,623 ... E 3
Capreol 3,845 ... K 5
Caramat 265 ... H 5
Cardinal 1,753 ... J 3
Carleton Place 5,626 ... H 2
Carlisle 781 ... D 4
Carlsbad Springs 616 ... J 2
Carp 707 ... H 2
Cartier 590 ... J 5
Casselman 1,675 ... J 2
Castleton 346 ... F 3
Chalk River 1,010 ... G 1
Chapleau 3,243 ... J 5
Charing Cross 443 ... B 5
Chatham◎ 40,952 ... B 5
Chatsworth 383 ... D 3
Cherry Valley 289 ... G 4
Chesley 1,840 ... C 3
Chesterville 1,430 ... J 2
Chute-à-Blondeau 365 ... K 2
City View ... J 2
Clarence Creek 796 ... J 2
Clarksburg 508 ... D 3
Clifford 645 ... D 4
Clinton 3,081 ... C 4
Cobalt 1,759 ... K 5
Cobden 997 ... H 2
Coboconk 426 ... F 3
Cobourg◎ 11,385 ... F 4
Cochrane◎ 4,848 ... K 5
Colborne 1,796 ... G 4
Colchester 711 ... B 6
Coldwater 964 ... E 3
Collingwood 12,064 ... D 3
Comber 667 ... B 5
Consecon 295 ... G 3
Cookstown 918 ... E 3
Cornwall◎ 46,144 ... K 2
Cottam 404 ... B 5
Courtland 647 ... D 5
Courtright 1,024 ... B 5
Crediton 370 ... C 4
Creemore 1,182 ... D 3
Crysler 540 ... J 2
Cumberland 518 ... J 2
Cumberland Beach-Bramshot-Buena Vista 679 ... E 3
Dashwood 426 ... C 4
Deep River 5,095 ... G 1
Delaware 481 ... C 5
Delhi 4,043 ... D 5
Delta 360 ... H 3
Deseronto 1,740 ... G 3
Douglas 303 ... H 2
Drayton 809 ... D 4
Dresden 2,550 ... B 5
Drumbo 476 ... D 4
Dryden 6,640 ... G 4
Dublin 295 ... C 4
Dubreuilville △988 ... J 5
Dundalk 1,250 ... D 3
Dundas 19,586 ... D 4
Dungannon 284 ... C 4
Dunnville 11,353 ... E 5
Durham 2,458 ... D 3
Dutton 1,115 ... C 5
Earlton 1,028 ... K 5
East York 101,974 ... J 4
Echo Bay 786 ... J 5
Eden Mills 318 ... D 4
Eganville 1,245 ... G 2
Egmondville 465 ... C 4
Elgin 327 ... H 3
Elk Lake 526 ... K 5
Elliot Lake 16,723 ... B 1
Elmira 7,063 ... D 4
Elmvale 1,183 ... E 3
Elmwood 364 ... C 3
Elora 2,666 ... D 4
Embro 727 ... C 4
Embrun 1,883 ... J 2
Emeryville-Puce 1,611 ... B 5
Emo 762 ... F 5
Englehart 1,689 ... K 5
Enterprise 357 ... H 3
Erieau 430 ... C 5
Erin 2,313 ... D 4
Espanola 5,836 ... J 5
Essex 6,295 ... B 5
Etobicoke 298,713 ... J 4
Everett 570 ... E 3
Exeter 3,732 ... C 4
Fauquier 561 ... J 5
Fenelon Falls 1,701 ... F 3
Fergus 6,064 ... D 4
Field 462 ... E 1
Finch 353 ... J 2
Fingal 380 ... C 5
Fitzroy Harbour 446 ... H 2
Flesherton 565 ... D 3
Foleyet 484 ... J 5
Fordwich 365 ... C 4
Forest 2,671 ... C 4
Formosa 393 ... C 3
Fort Erie 24,096 ... E 5
Fort Frances◎ 8,906 ... F 5
Foxboro 597 ... G 3
Frankford 1,919 ... G 3
Fraserdale 303 ... J 5
Freelton 307 ... D 4
Gananoque 4,863 ... H 3
Garden Village 270 ... E 1
Geraldton 2,956 ... H 5
Glencoe 1,694 ... C 5
Glen Miller 639 ... G 3
Glen Robertson 378 ... K 2
Glen Walter 710 ... K 2
Goderich◎ 7,322 ... C 4
Gogama 652 ... J 5
Goodwood 335 ... E 3
Gore Bay◎ 777 ... B 2
Gorrie 468 ... C 4
Grafton 409 ... G 4
Grand Bend 680 ... C 4
Grand Valley 1,226 ... D 4
Granton 315 ... C 4
Gravenhurst 8,532 ... E 3
Greely 567 ... J 2
Green Valley 459 ... K 2
Grimsby 15,797 ... E 4
Guelph◎ 71,207 ... D 4

(continued on following page)

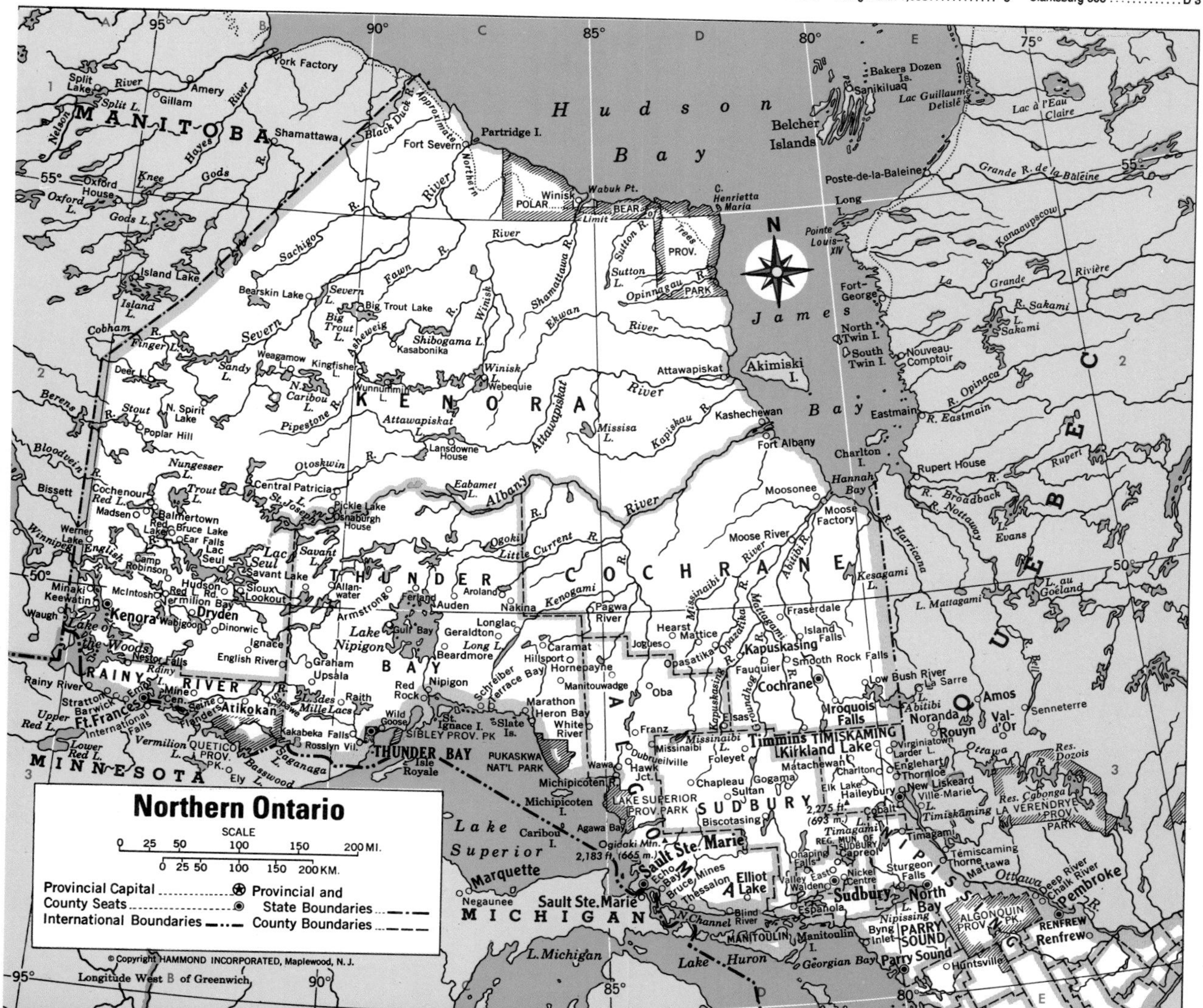

Northern Ontario
SCALE
0 25 50 100 150 200 MI.
0 25 50 100 150 200 KM.
Provincial Capital
County Seats
International Boundaries
Provincial and State Boundaries
County Boundaries
Hudson Bay
James Bay
MANITOBA
KENORA
THUNDER BAY
COCHRANE
SUDBURY
ALGOMA
NIPISSING
TIMISKAMING
QUEBEC
MINNESOTA
MICHIGAN
Lake Superior
Lake Huron
L. Michigan
Georgian Bay
Thunder Bay
Sault Ste. Marie
Sudbury
North Bay
Timmins
Kenora
Dryden
Moosonee
Pembroke
Longitude West of Greenwich
© Copyright HAMMOND INCORPORATED, Maplewood, N. J.

Haileybury® 4,925 . . . . . . K 5
Haldimand 16,866 . . . . . . E 5
Haliburton 1,443 . . . . . . E 4
Halton Hills 35,190 . . . . . E 4
Hamilton 306,434 . . . . . . E 4
Hamilton *542,095 . . . . . E 4
Hanover 6,316 . . . . C 3
Harriston 1,954 . . . . D 4
Harrow 2,274 . . . . B 5
Harrowsmith 599 . . . . . . H 3
Harwood 332 . . . . F 3
Hastings 975 . . . . G 3
Havelock 1,385 . . . . G 3
Hawkesbury 9,877 . . . . . . K 1
Hawkestone 275 . . . . E 3
Hawk Junction 349 . . . . . J 5
Hearst 5,533 . . . . J 5
Hensall 973 . . . . C 4
Hepworth 393 . . . . C 3
Hickson 263 . . . . D 4
Highgate 435 . . . . C 5
Hillsburgh 1,065 . . . . . . E 4
Hillsdale 370 . . . . E 3
Holland Landing 2,771 . . . E 3
Honey Harbour 505 . . . . . E 3
Hornepayne 1,848 . . . . . . J 5
Hudson 515 . . . . G 4
Huntsville 11,467 . . . . . . E 3
Huron Park 1,104 . . . . . . C 4
Ignace 2,499 . . . . G 5
Ilderton 301 . . . . C 4
Ingersoll 8,494 . . . . D 4
Ingleside 1,400 . . . . J 2
Innerkip 751 . . . . D 4
Inverhuron 438 . . . . C 3
Iron Bridge 821 . . . . A 1

Iroquois 1,211 . . . . J 3
Iroquois Falls 6,339 . . . . J 5
Johnstown 789 . . . . J 3
Kakabeka Falls 300 . . . . . G 5
Kanata 19,728 . . . . J 2
Kapuskasing 12,014 . . . . . J 5
Kars 449 . . . . J 2
Kearney 538 . . . . E 3
Keene 353 . . . . F 3
Keewatin 1,863 . . . . F 5
Kemptville 2,362 . . . . . . J 2
Kenora® 9,817 . . . . F 5
Killaloe Station 634 . . . . G 2
Killarney 433 . . . . C 2
Kincardine 5,778 . . . . . . C 3
Kingston 52,616 . . . . . . H 3
Kingsville 5,134 . . . . . . B 6
Kinmount 262 . . . . F 3
Kirkland Lake 12,219 . . . . K 5
Kitchener 139,734 . . . . . D 4
Kitchener *287,801 . . . . . D 4
Komoka 262 . . . . C 4
Lakefield 2,374 . . . . F 3
Lanark 753 . . . . H 2
Lancaster 637 . . . . K 2
Langton 348 . . . . D 5
Lansdowne 540 . . . . H 3
Larder Lake 1,084 . . . . . K 5
Latchford 397 . . . . K 5
Leamington 12,528 . . . . . B 5
Limoges 930 . . . . J 2
Lincoln 14,196 . . . . E 4
Linden Beach 579 . . . . . . B 6
Lindsay 13,596 . . . . F 3
Linwood 450 . . . . D 4
Lion's Head 467 . . . . C 2

Lisle 265 . . . . E 3
Listowel 5,026 . . . . D 4
Little Britain 265 . . . . . . F 3
Little Current 1,507 . . . . B 2
London 254,280 . . . . . . C 5
London *283,668 . . . . . . C 5
Longlac 2,431 . . . . H 5
Long Sault 1,227 . . . . . . K 2
L'Orignal 1,819 . . . . K 1
Lucan 1,616 . . . . C 4
Lucknow 1,088 . . . . C 4
Lyn 518 . . . . J 3
Lynden 451 . . . . D 4
Lynhurst 685 . . . . C 5
MacGregor's Bay 861 . . . . E 2
MacTier 647 . . . . E 2
Madawaska 264 . . . . F 2
Madoc 1,249 . . . . G 3
Maitland 667 . . . . J 3
Mallorytown 368 . . . . . . J 3
Manitouwadge 3,155 . . . . H 5
Manitowaning 518 . . . . . . C 2
Manotick-Hillside Gardens
2,694 . . . . J 2
Marathon 2,271 . . . . H 5
Markdale 1,289 . . . . D 3
Markham 77,037 . . . . . . K 4
Markstay 444 . . . . D 1
Marmora 1,304 . . . . G 3
Martintown 388 . . . . K 2
Massey 1,274 . . . . C 1
Matachewan 444 . . . . . . J 5
Matheson 966 . . . . K 5
Mattawa 2,652 . . . . F 1
Mattice 803 . . . . J 5
Maxville 836 . . . . K 2

Maynooth 277 . . . . G 2
McGregor 1,145 . . . . B 5
McKerrow 260 . . . . C 1
Meaford 4,367 . . . . D 3
Melbourne 346 . . . . C 5
Merlin 745 . . . . B 5
Merrickville 984 . . . . . . J 2
Metcalfe 687 . . . . J 2
Midhurst 1,457 . . . . E 3
Midland 12,132 . . . . D 3
Mildmay 928 . . . . C 3
Milford Bay 401 . . . . E 2
Millbank 337 . . . . D 4
Millbrook 927 . . . . F 3
Milton 28,067 . . . . E 4
Milverton 1,463 . . . . D 4
Minaki 319 . . . . F 5
Mindemoya 376 . . . . B 2
Minden® 838 . . . . F 3
Mississauga 315,056 . . . . J 4
Mitchell 2,777 . . . . C 4
Monkton 520 . . . . C 4
Moonbeam 838 . . . . J 5
Moorefield 308 . . . . D 4
Mooretown 344 . . . . B 5
Moose Creek 393 . . . . . . K 2
Morewood 264 . . . . J 2
Morpeth 284 . . . . C 5
Morrisburg 2,308 . . . . . . J 3
Mount Albert 1,165 . . . . . E 3
Mount Brydges 1,557 . . . . C 5
Mount Forest 3,474 . . . . . D 4
Mount Hope 925 . . . . E 4
Munster 1,531 . . . . H 4
Nakina 936 . . . . H 5
Nanticoke® 19,816 . . . . . E 5

Napanee 4,803 . . . . G 3
Navan 419 . . . . J 2
Neustadt 511 . . . . D 3
Newboro 260 . . . . H 3
Newburgh 617 . . . . H 3
Newbury 441 . . . . C 5
Newcastle 32,229 . . . . . . F 4
New Hamburg 3,923 . . . . D 4
New Liskeard 5,551 . . . . . K 5
Newmarket® 29,753 . . . . E 3
Niagara Falls 70,960 . . . . E 4
Niagara-on-the-Lake 12,186 . E 4
Nickel Centre 12,318 . . . . D 1
Nipigon 2,377 . . . . H 5
Nobel 386 . . . . D 2
Nobleton 1,861 . . . . E 4
Noelville 702 . . . . D 1
North Bay® 51,268 . . . . . E 1
North Gower 818 . . . . . . J 2
North York 559,521 . . . . . J 4
Norwich 2,117 . . . . D 5
Norwood 1,278 . . . . F 3
Nottawa 360 . . . . E 3
Oakville 75,773 . . . . E 4
Oakwood 404 . . . . F 3
Odessa 849 . . . . H 3
Oil City 266 . . . . B 5
Oil Springs 627 . . . . B 5
Omemee 819 . . . . F 3
Onaping Falls 6,198 . . . . J 5
Opasatika 413 . . . . J 5
Orangeville® 13,740 . . . . D 4
Orillia 23,955 . . . . E 3
Osgoode 1,138 . . . . J 2
Oshawa 117,519 . . . . . . F 3
Oshawa *154,217 . . . . . . F 4

Ottawa® (cap.), Canada
295,163 . . . . J 2
Ottawa-Hull ®717,978 . . . J 2
Otterville 776 . . . . D 5
Owen Sound® 19,883 . . . . D 3
Paincourt 414 . . . . B 5
Paisley 1,039 . . . . C 3
Pakenham 367 . . . . H 2
Palmerston 1,989 . . . . . . D 4
Paris 7,485 . . . . D 4
Parkhill 1,358 . . . . C 4
Parry Sound® 6,124 . . . . E 2
Pefferlaw 857 . . . . E 3
Pelham 11,104 . . . . E 4
Pembroke® 14,026 . . . . . G 2
Penetanguishene 5,315 . . . D 3
Perth® 5,655 . . . . H 3
Petawawa 5,520 . . . . . . F 2
Peterborough® 60,620 . . . B 5
Petrolia 4,234 . . . . K 4
Pickering 37,754 . . . . . . F 4
Picton® 4,361 . . . . G 3
Plantagenet 870 . . . . . . K 2
Plattsville 495 . . . . D 4
Point Edward 2,383 . . . . . B 4
Pontypool 759 . . . . F 3
Port Burwell 655 . . . . . . D 5
Port Carling 629 . . . . . . E 2
Port Colborne 19,225 . . . . E 5
Port Elgin 6,131 . . . . . . C 3
Port Franks 547 . . . . C 4
Port Hope 9,992 . . . . . . F 4
Port Lambton 921 . . . . . . B 5
Port McNicoll 1,883 . . . . . E 3
Portland 271 . . . . H 3
Port Perry 4,712 . . . . . . E 3

Port Rowan 811 . . . . D 5
Port Stanley 1,891 . . . . . C 5
Pottageville 286 . . . . . . J 3
Powassan 1,169 . . . . E 1
Prescott® 4,670 . . . . J 3
Princeton 462 . . . . D 4
Puce-Emeryville 1,611 . . . B 5
Rainy River 1,061 . . . . . . F 5
Ramore 382 . . . . K 5
Rayside-Balfour 15,017 . . . H 5
Red Rock 1,260 . . . . H 5
Renfrew 8,283 . . . . G 2
Richards Landing 405 . . . . J 5
Richmond 2,880 . . . . J 2
Richmond Hill 37,778 . . . . J 4
Ridgetown 3,062 . . . . . . C 5
Ripley 591 . . . . C 3
River Valley 275 . . . . . . D 1
Rockcliffe Park 1,869 . . . . J 2
Rockland 3,961 . . . . J 2
Rockwood 1,068 . . . . D 4
Rodney 1,007 . . . . C 5
Rosslyn Village 362 . . . . . G 5
Round Lake Centre 255 . . . G 2
Russell 1,099 . . . . J 2
Ruthven 649 . . . . B 6
Saint Albert 254 . . . . . . J 2
Saint Catharines® 124,018 . . E 4
Saint Catharines-Niagara
*304,353 . . . . E 4
Saint Charles 382 . . . . . . D 1
Saint Clair Beach 2,845 . . . B 5
Saint Clements 890 . . . . . D 4
Saint-Eugène 470 . . . . . . K 2
Saint George 865 . . . . . . D 4
Saint Isidore de Prescott 746 . K 2

Saint Jacobs 1,189 . . . . D 4
Saint Mary's 4,883 . . . . C 4
Saint Thomas◉ 28,165 . . . . C 5
Saint Williams 442 . . . . D 5
Salem 825 . . . . D 4
Sarnia◉ 50,892 . . . . B 5
Sauble Beach 729 . . . . C 3
Sault Sainte Marie◉ 82,697 . . . J 5
Scarborough 443,353 . . . . K 4
Schomberg 923 . . . . J 3
Schreiber 1,968 . . . . H 5
Scotland 600 . . . . D 4
Seaforth 2,114 . . . . C 4
Searchmont 384 . . . . J 5
Sebringville 579 . . . . C 4
Seeleys Bay 503 . . . . H 3
Shakespeare 602 . . . . D 4
Shallow Lake 418 . . . . C 3
Shannonville 314 . . . . G 3
Shanty Bay 358 . . . . E 3
Sharbot Lake 495 . . . . H 3
Shedden 292 . . . . C 5
Shelburne 2,862 . . . . D 3
Simcoe◉ 14,326 . . . . D 5
Sioux Lookout 3,074 . . . . G 4
Sioux Narrows 394 . . . . F 5
Smithfield 349 . . . . G 3
Smiths Falls 8,831 . . . . H 3
Smithville 1,936 . . . . E 4
Smooth Rock Falls 2,352 . . . . . J 5
Sombra 420 . . . . B 5
Southampton 2,830 . . . . C 3
South Mountain 285 . . . . J 3
South River 1,109 . . . . E 2
Spanish 1,063 . . . . J 5
Sparta 283 . . . . C 5

Spencerville 438 . . . . J 3
Springfield 555 . . . . C 5
Springford 309 . . . . D 5
Stayner 2,530 . . . . E 3
Stirling 1,638 . . . . G 3
Stittsville 2,652 . . . . J 2
Stoney Creek 36,762 . . . . E 4
Stoney Point 1,090 . . . . B 5
Stratffordville 752 . . . . D 5
Stratford◉ 26,262 . . . . C 4
Strathroy 8,748 . . . . C 5
Sturgeon Falls 6,045 . . . . E 1
Sudbury◉ 91,829 . . . . K 5
Sudbury *149,923 . . . . K 5
Sunderland 703 . . . . E 3
Sundridge 734 . . . . E 2
Sydenham 595 . . . . H 3
Tamworth 402 . . . . H 3
Tara 687 . . . . C 3
Tavistock 1,885 . . . . D 4
Tecumseh 6,364 . . . . B 5
Teeswater 1,026 . . . . C 3
Terrace Bay 2,639 . . . . H 5
Thamesford 1,920 . . . . C 4
Thamesville 961 . . . . C 5
Thedford 694 . . . . C 4
Thessalon 1,620 . . . . J 5
Thornbury 1,435 . . . . D 3
Thorndale 581 . . . . C 4
Thornton 414 . . . . E 3
Thorold 15,412 . . . . E 4
Thunder Bay◉ 112,486 . . . . H 5
Thunder Bay *121,379 . . . . H 5
Tilbury 4,298 . . . . B 5
Tillsonburg 10,487 . . . . D 5

Tiverton 806 . . . . C 3
Tobermory 282 . . . . C 2
Toronto (cap.)◉ 599,217 . . . . . . K 4
Toronto *2,998,947 . . . . K 4
Tottenham 3,022 . . . . E 3
Trenton 15,085 . . . . G 3
Trout Creek 652 . . . . E 2
Turkey Point 407 . . . . D 5
Tweed 1,574 . . . . G 3
Udora 375 . . . . E 3
Union 485 . . . . C 5
Uxbridge 4,209 . . . . E 3
Valley East 20,433 . . . . J 5
Vanier 18,792 . . . . J 2
Vankleek Hill 1,774 . . . . K 2
Vars 527 . . . . J 2
Vaughan 29,674 . . . . J 4
Vermilion Bay 505 . . . . G 4
Verner 1,076 . . . . D 1
Vernon 303 . . . . J 2
Verona 754 . . . . H 3
Victoria Harbour 1,125 . . . . E 3
Vienna 369 . . . . D 5
Virginiatown 1,010 . . . . K 5
Vittoria 420 . . . . D 5
Wabigoon 268 . . . . G 5
Walden 10,139 . . . . J 5
Walkerton◉ 4,682 . . . . C 3
Wallaceburg 11,506 . . . . B 5
Wardsville 450 . . . . C 5
Warkworth 618 . . . . G 3
Warren 579 . . . . D 1
Warsaw 314 . . . . F 3
Wasaga Beach 4,705 . . . . D 3
Washago 569 . . . . E 3
Waterloo 49,428 . . . . D 4
Watford 1,402 . . . . C 5
Waubaushene 878 . . . . E 3
Wawa 4,206 . . . . J 5
Webbwood 519 . . . . C 1
Welcome 293 . . . . F 4
Welland 454,448 . . . . E 5
Wellesley 997 . . . . D 4
Wellington 1,082 . . . . G 4
Wendover 326 . . . . J 2
West Lorne 1,258 . . . . C 5
Westmeath 262 . . . . H 2
Westport 621 . . . . H 3
Wheatley 1,638 . . . . B 5
Whitby◉ 36,698 . . . . F 4
Whitchurch-Stouffville 13,557 . J 3
White River △1,006 . . . . H 5
Whitney 766 . . . . F 2
Wiarton 2,074 . . . . C 3
Wikwemikong 1,030 . . . . C 2
Williamsburg 407 . . . . J 3
Williamsford 256 . . . . D 3
Williamstown 328 . . . . K 2
Winchester 2,001 . . . . J 3
Windsor◉ 192,083 . . . . B 5
Windsor *246,110 . . . . B 5
Wingham 2,897 . . . . C 4
Wolfe Island 271 . . . . H 3
Woodstock 26,603 . . . . D 4
Woodville 575 . . . . F 3
Wroxeter 350 . . . . C 4
Wyoming 1,682 . . . . B 5
Yarker 319 . . . . H 3
York 134,617 . . . . J 4
Zephyr 330 . . . . E 3
Zurich 795 . . . . C 4

OTHER FEATURES

Abitibi (riv.) . . . . J 5
Algonquin Prov. Park . . . . F 2
Amherst (isl.) . . . . H 3
Balsam (lake) . . . . F 3
Barrie (isl.) . . . . B 1
Bays (lake) . . . . F 2
Big Rideau (lake) . . . . H 3
Black (riv.) . . . . E 3
Bruce (pen.) . . . . C 2
Buckhorn (lake) . . . . F 3
Cabot (head) . . . . C 2
Charleston (lake) . . . . J 3
Christian (isl.) . . . . D 3
Clear (lake) . . . . F 3
Cockburn (isl.) . . . . A 2
Couchiching (lake) . . . . E 3
Croker (cape) . . . . D 3

Don (riv.) . . . . J 4
Doré (lake) . . . . G 2
Douglas (pt.) . . . . C 3
Erie (lake) . . . . E 5
Flowerpot (isl.) . . . . C 2
French (riv.) . . . . D 1
Georgian (bay) . . . . D 2
Georgian Bay Is.
  Nat'l Park . . . . C 2, D 3
Georgina (isl.) . . . . E 3
Grand (riv.) . . . . D 4
Humber (riv.) . . . . J 3
Hurd (cape) . . . . C 2
Huron (lake) . . . . B 3
Ipperwash Prov. Park . . . . C 4
Joseph (lake) . . . . E 2
Killarney Prov. Park . . . . C 1
Killbear Point Prov. Park . . . . . . D 2
Lake of the Woods (lake) . . . . . F 5

Lake Superior Prov. Park . . . . . J 5
Lonely (isl.) . . . . C 2
Long (pt.) . . . . D 5
Long Point (bay) . . . . D 5
Madawaska (riv.) . . . . G 2
Magnetawan (riv.) . . . . D 2
Main (chan.) . . . . C 2
Manitou (lake) . . . . C 2
Manitoulin (isl.) . . . . B 2
Mattagami (riv.) . . . . J 5
Michipicoten (isl.) . . . . H 5
Missinaibi (lake) . . . . J 5
Mississagi (riv.) . . . . A 1
Mississippi (lake) . . . . H 2
Muskoka (lake) . . . . E 2
Niagara (riv.) . . . . E 4
Nipigon (lake) . . . . H 5
Nipissing (lake) . . . . E 1
North (chan.) . . . . A 1
Nottawasaga (bay) . . . . D 3
Ogidaki (mt.) . . . . J 5
Opeongo (lake) . . . . F 2
Ottawa (riv.) . . . . H 2
Owen (sound) . . . . D 3
Panache (lake) . . . . C 1
Parry (isl.) . . . . D 2
Parry (sound) . . . . D 2
Pelee (pt.) . . . . B 6
Petre (pt.) . . . . G 4
Point Pelee Nat'l Park . . . . B 5
Presqu'ile Prov. Park . . . . G 4
Pukaskwa Prov. Park . . . . H 5
Quetico Prov. Park . . . . G 5

Rainy (lake) . . . . G 5
Rice (lake) . . . . F 3
Rideau (lake) . . . . H 3
Rondeau Prov. Park . . . . C 5
Rosseau (lake) . . . . E 2
Saint Clair (lake) . . . . B 5
Saint Clair (riv.) . . . . B 5
Saint Lawrence (lake) . . . . K 3
Saint Lawrence (riv.) . . . . J 3
Saint Lawrence Is. Nat'l Park . . J 3
Saugeen (riv.) . . . . C 3
Scugog (lake) . . . . F 3
Seul (lake) . . . . G 4
Severn (riv.) . . . . E 3
Sibley Prov. Park . . . . H 5
Simcoe (lake) . . . . E 3
South (bay) . . . . C 2
Spanish (riv.) . . . . C 1
Stony (lake) . . . . G 3
Superior (lake) . . . . H 5
Sydenham (riv.) . . . . B 5
Thames (riv.) . . . . B 5
Theano (pt.) . . . . J 5
Thousand (isls.) . . . . H 3
Timagami (lake) . . . . K 5
Trout (lake) . . . . E 1
Vernon (lake) . . . . E 2
Walpole (isl.) . . . . B 5
Welland (canal) . . . . E 5
Woods (lake) . . . . F 5

◉County seat.
*Population of metropolitan area.
△Population of town or township.

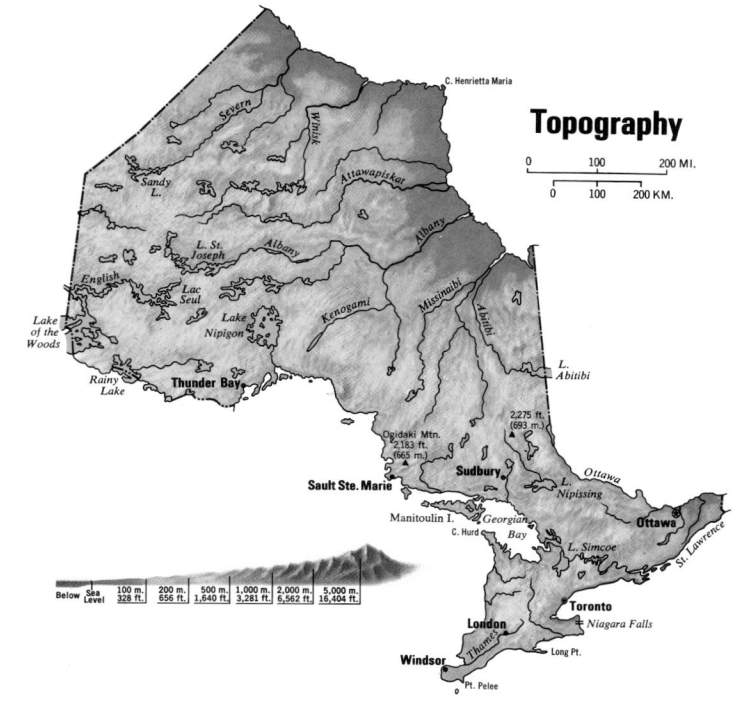

Topography

0   100   200 MI.
0   100   200 KM.

| Below Sea Level | 100 m. 328 ft. | 200 m. 656 ft. | 500 m. 1,640 ft. | 1,000 m. 3,281 ft. | 2,000 m. 6,562 ft. | 5,000 m. 16,404 ft. |

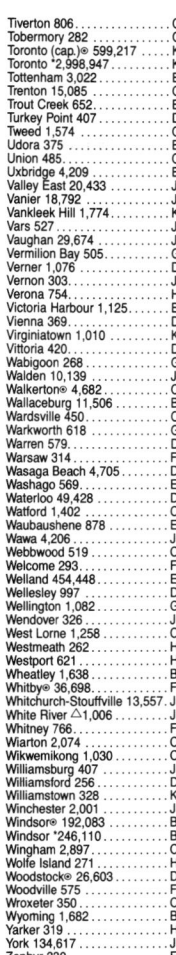

Ontario
Southern Part

SCALE
0 10 20 30 40 50 MI.
0 10 20 30 40 50 KM.

National Capital . . . . ◉
Provincial Capital . . . . ⊛
County Seats . . . . ●
International Boundaries . . . —·—

Provincial & State Boundaries . . . —·—·—
County Boundaries . . . ---
Canals

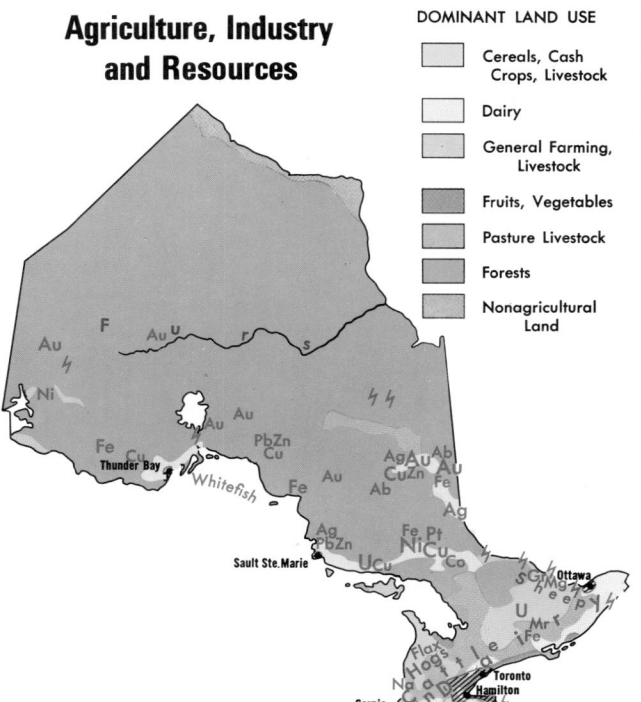

Agriculture, Industry and Resources

DOMINANT LAND USE

Cereals, Cash Crops, Livestock

Dairy

General Farming, Livestock

Fruits, Vegetables

Pasture Livestock

Forests

Nonagricultural Land

MAJOR MINERAL OCCURRENCES

Ab Asbestos   Mg Magnesium
Ag Silver   Mr Marble
Au Gold   Na Salt
Co Cobalt   Ni Nickel
Cu Copper   Pb Lead
Fe Iron Ore   Pt Platinum
G   Natural Gas   U   Uranium
Gr Graphite   Zn Zinc

⚡ Water Power
▨ Major Industrial Areas

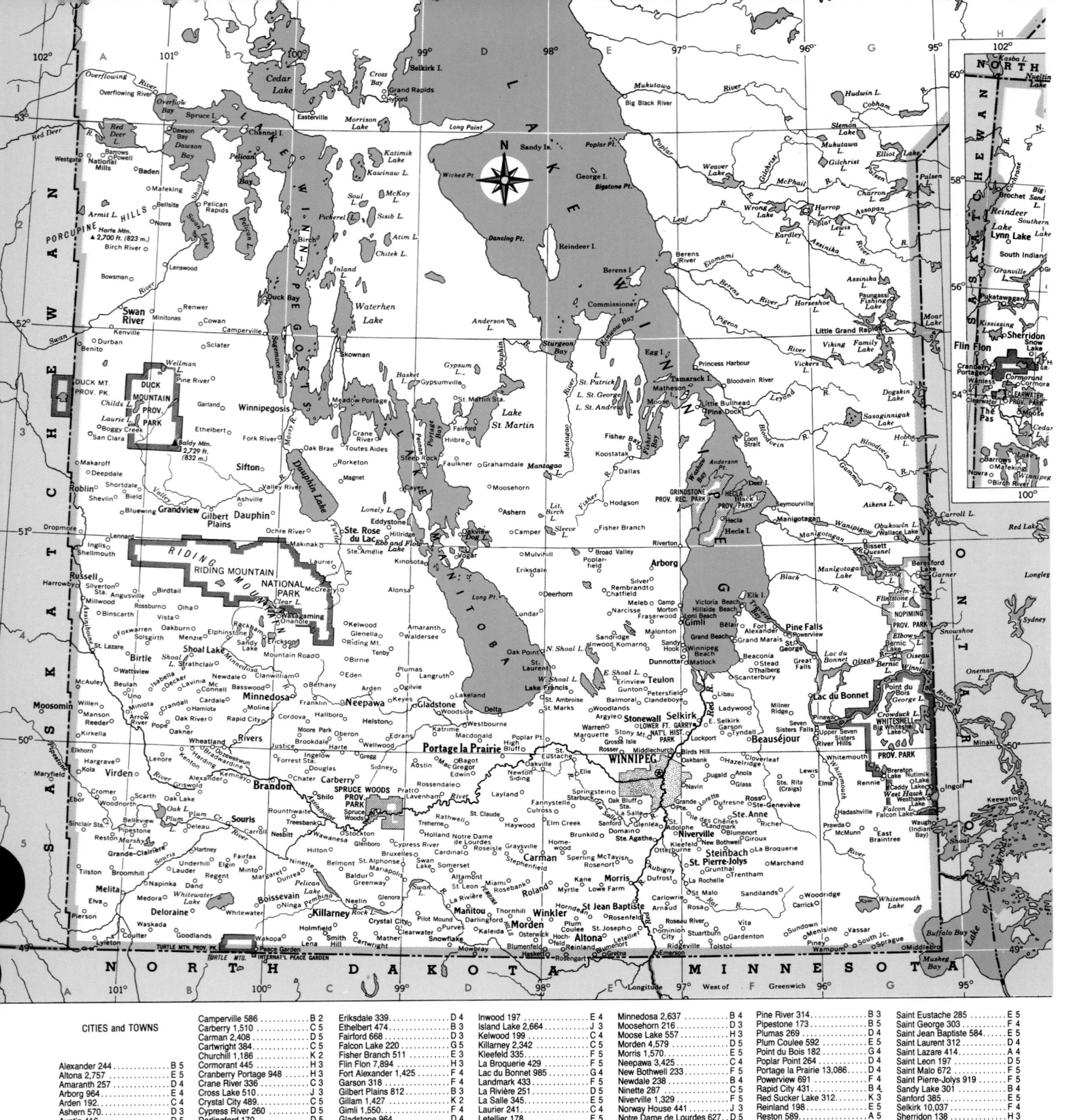

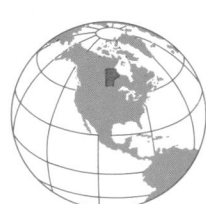

Manitoba Northern Part

40 80 120 MI.
0 40 80 120 KM.

WESTERN TERRS.

HUDSON BAY

ONTARIO

Manitoba
Southern Part

SCALE

0 5 10   20   40   60 MI.
0 5 10   20   40   60 KM.

Provincial Capital ....⊛
International Boundaries ___.___.___
Provincial Boundaries ___..___..___

© Copyright HAMMOND INCORPORATED, Maplewood, N.J.

The Pas 6,390	H 3
Thicket Portage 195	J 3
Thompson 14,288	J 2
Treherne 743	D 5
Tyndall 421	F 4
Virden 2,940	A 5
Vita 364	F 5
Wabowden 655	J 3
Wallace Lake ●2,044	G 3
Wanless 193	H 3
Warren 459	E 4
Waskada 239	B 5
Wawanesa 492	C 5
Whitemouth 320	G 5
Whitewater ●856	B 5
Winkler 5,046	E 5
Winnipeg (cap.) 564,473	E 5
Winnipeg *584,842	E 5
Winnipeg Beach 565	F 4
Winnipegosis 855	B 3
Woodlands 185	E 4
Wooodridge 170	G 5
York Landing 229	J 2

AREA 250,999 sq. mi. (650,087 sq. km.)
POPULATION 1,026,241
CAPITAL Winnipeg
LARGEST CITY Winnipeg
HIGHEST POINT Baldy Mtn. 2,729 ft.
(832 m.)
SETTLED IN 1812
ADMITTED TO CONFEDERATION 1870
PROVINCIAL FLOWER Prairie Crocus

East Shoal (lake)	E 4	Manigotagan (riv.)	G 3	Saint Andrew (lake)	E 3
Ebb and Flow (lake)	C 3	Manitoba (lake)	D 4	Saint George (lake)	E 3
Egg (isl.)	E 3	Mantagao (riv.)	E 3	Saint Martin (lake)	D 3
Elbow (lake)	G 4	Marshy (lake)	B 5	Saint Patrick (lake)	E 3
Elk (isl.)	F 4	McKay (lake)	C 2	Sale (riv.)	E 5
Elliot (lake)	F 4	McPhail (riv.)	F 2	Sandy (isls.)	D 2

OTHER FEATURES

		Etawney (lake)	J 2	Minnedosa (riv.)	B 4
		Etomami (riv.)	F 2	Moar (lake)	G 2
Aikens (lake)	G 3	Falcon (lake)	G 5	Molson (lake)	J 3
Anderson (lake)	D 2	Family (lake)	G 3	Moose (isl.)	E 3
Anderson (pt.)	F 3	Fisher (bay)	E 3	Morrison (lake)	C 1
Armit (lake)	A 2	Fisher (riv.)	E 3	Mossy (riv.)	C 3
Assapan (riv.)	G 2	Fishing (lake)	G 2	Mukutawa (lake)	G 2
Assiniboine (riv.)	C 5	Flintstone (lake)	G 4	Mukutawa (riv.)	G 2
Assinika (lake)	G 2	Fox (isl.)	K 2	Muskeg (bay)	E 1
Assinika (riv.)	G 2	Gammon (riv.)	G 3	Nejanilini (lake)	G 6
Atim (lake)	C 2	Garner (lake)	G 4	Nelson (riv.)	J 1
Baldy (mt.)	B 3	Gem (lake)	G 4	Nopiming Prov. Park	G 4
Basket (lake)	C 3	George (isl.)	E 2	Northern Indian (lake)	J 2
Beaverhill (lake)	J 3	George (lake)	G 4	North Knife (lake)	J 2
Berens (isl.)	E 2	Gilchrist (creek)	F 2	North Seal (riv.)	H 2
Berens (riv.)	F 2	Gilchrist (lake)	G 2	North Shoal (lake)	E 4
Bernic (lake)	G 4	Gods (lake)	K 3	Nueltin (lake)	H 1
Big Sand (lake)	H 2	Gods (riv.)	K 3	Oak (lake)	B 5
Bigstone (lake)	J 3	Granville (lake)	H 2	Obukowin (lake)	G 3
Bigstone (pt.)	E 2	Grass (riv.)	J 3	Oiseau (lake)	G 4
Bigstone (riv.)	J 3	Grass (riv.)	J 3	Oiseau (riv.)	G 4
Birch (isl.)	C 2	Grass River Prov. Park	H 2	Overflow (bay)	A 1
Black (isl.)	F 3	Grindstone Prov. Rec. Park	F 3	Overflowing (riv.)	A 1
Black (riv.)	F 4	Gunisao (lake)	G 3	Owl (riv.)	K 2
Bloodvein (riv.)	F 3	Gypsum (lake)	D 3	Oxford (lake)	J 3
Bonnet (lake)	G 2	Harrop (lake)	C 2	Paint (lake)	J 2
Buffalo (bay)	G 5	Harte (mt.)	A 2	Palsen (riv.)	G 2
Burntwood (riv.)	J 2	Hayes (riv.)	K 3	Pelican (bay)	B 2
Caribou (riv.)	J 1	Hecla (isl.)	F 3	Pelican (lake)	B 2
Carroll (lake)	G 3	Hecla Prov. Park	F 3	Pelican (lake)	C 5
Cedar (lake)	B 1	Hobbs (lake)	G 3	Pembina (hills)	D 5
Channel (isl.)	B 2	Horseshoe (lake)	G 2	Pembina (riv.)	C 5
Charron (lake)	G 2	Hubbart (pt.)	K 2	Peonan (pt.)	D 3
Childs (lake)	A 3	Hudson (bay)	K 2	Pickerel (lake)	C 2
Chitek (lake)	C 2	Hudwin (lake)	G 1	Pigeon (riv.)	F 2
Churchill (cape)	K 2	Inland (lake)	C 2	Pipestone (creek)	A 5
Churchill (riv.)	J 2	International Peace Garden	B 5	Plum (creek)	B 5
Clear (lake)	C 4	Island (lake)	K 3	Plum (lake)	B 5
Clearwater Lake Prov. Park	H 3	Katimik (lake)	C 2	Poplar (riv.)	E 2
Cobham (riv.)	G 1	Kawinaw (lake)	C 2	Porcupine (hills)	A 2
Cochrane (riv.)	H 2	Kinwow (bay)	E 2	Portage (bay)	D 3
Commissioner (isl.)	E 2	Kississing (lake)	H 2	Quesnel (lake)	G 4
Cormorant (lake)	H 3	Knee (lake)	J 3	Rat (riv.)	F 5
Cross (bay)	C 1	Lake of the Woods (lake)	H 5	Red (riv.)	F 4
Cross (lake)	J 3	La Salle (riv.)	E 5	Red Deer (lake)	A 2
Crowduck (lake)	G 4	Laurie (lake)	A 3	Red Deer (riv.)	A 2
Dancing (pt.)	D 2	Leaf (riv.)	F 2	Reindeer (isl.)	E 2
Dauphin (lake)	C 3	Lewis (lake)	G 2	Reindeer (lake)	H 2
Dauphin (riv.)	D 3	Leyond (riv.)	F 3	Riding (mt.)	B 4
Dawson (bay)	B 2	Little Birch (lake)	E 3	Riding Mountain Nat'l Park	B 4
Dog (lake)	D 3	Lonely (lake)	C 3	Rock (lake)	C 5
Dogskin (lake)	G 3	Long (lake)	A 2	Ross (isl.)	J 3
Duck Mountain Prov. Park	B 3	Long (pt.)	D 1	Sagemace (bay)	B 3
Eardley (lake)	F 2	Long (pt.)	D 4		
		Manigotagan (lake)	G 4		

Saint George (lake)	E 3
Sasaginnigak (lake)	G 3
Seal (riv.)	J 2
Selkirk (isl.)	C 1
Setting (lake)	H 3
Shoal (lake)	G 5
Shoal (lake)	B 2
Sipiwesk (lake)	J 3
Sisib (lake)	C 2
Sleeve (lake)	E 3
Siemon (lake)	G 1
Snowshoe (lake)	G 4
Soul (lake)	C 2
Souris (riv.)	B 5
Southern Indian (lake)	H 2
South Knife (riv.)	J 2
South Seal (riv.)	J 2
Split (lake)	J 2
Spruce (isl.)	B 1
Spruce Woods Prov. Park	C 5
Stevenson (lake)	J 3
Sturgeon (bay)	E 3
Swan (lake)	B 2
Swan (lake)	D 5
Swan (riv.)	A 3
Tadoule (lake)	J 1
Tamarack (isl.)	F 3
Tatnam (cape)	K 2
Traverse (bay)	F 4
Turtle (mts.)	B 5
Turtle (riv.)	C 3
Turtle Mountain Prov. Park	B 5
Valley (riv.)	B 3
Vickers (lake)	F 3
Viking (lake)	G 3
Wanipigow (riv.)	G 3
Washow (bay)	F 3
Waterhen (lake)	C 2
Weaver (lake)	F 2
Wellman (lake)	B 3
West Hawk (lake)	G 5
West Shoal (lake)	E 4
Whitemouth (lake)	G 5
Whitemouth (riv.)	G 5
Whiteshell Prov. Park	G 4
Whitewater (lake)	B 5
Wicked (pt.)	D 2
Winnipeg (lake)	E 2
Winnipeg (lake)	G 4
Winnipegosis (lake)	C 2
Woods (lake)	H 5
Wrong (lake)	F 2

*Population of metropolitan area.
●Population of rural municipality.

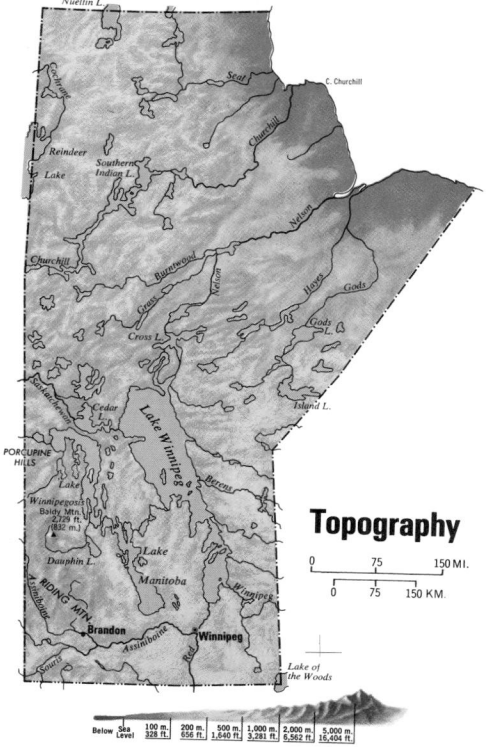

Topography

0   75   150 MI.
0   75   150 KM.

Below Sea Level | 100 m. 328 ft. | 200 m. 656 ft. | 500 m. 1,640 ft. | 1,000 m. 3,281 ft. | 2,000 m. 6,562 ft. | 5,000 m. 16,404 ft.

Agriculture, Industry and Resources

DOMINANT LAND USE

- Cereals (chiefly barley, oats)
- Cereals, Livestock
- Dairy
- Livestock
- Forests
- Nonagricultural Land

MAJOR MINERAL OCCURRENCES

Au	Gold	Ni	Nickel	
Co	Cobalt	O	Petroleum	
Cu	Copper	Pb	Lead	
Na	Salt	Pt	Platinum	
		Zn	Zinc	

⚡ Water Power

▧ Major Industrial Areas

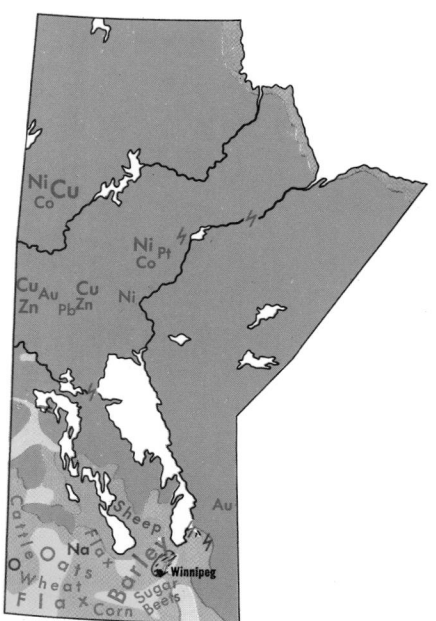

Topography

0   60   120 MI.

0   60   120 KM.

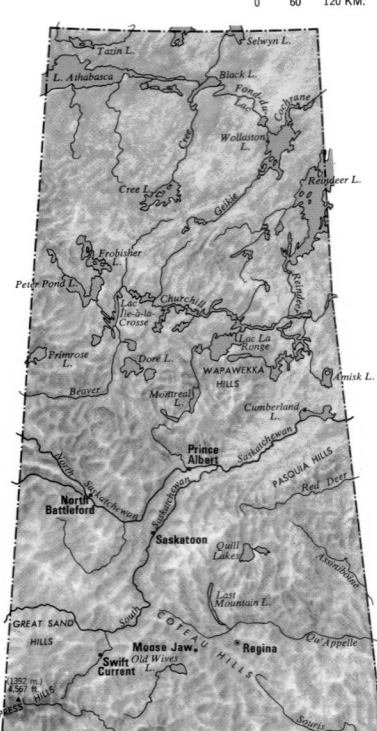

5,000 m. | 2,000 m. | 1,000 m. | 500 m. | 200 m. | 100 m. | Sea
16,404 ft. | 6,562 ft. | 3,281 ft. | 1,640 ft. | 656 ft. | 328 ft. | Level Below

CITIES and TOWNS

Abbey 218	C 5
Aberdeen 496	E 3
Abernethy 300	H 5
Air Ronge 557	M 3
Alameda 318	K 6
Alida 169	K 6
Allan 871	B 4
Alsask 652	A 3
Annaheim 209	C 5
Antelope ●231	H 2
Arborfield 439	H 3
Archerwill 286	H 3
Arcola 493	J 6
Arlington Beach ●432	F 4
Asquith 567	E 3
Assiniboia 2,924	E 6
Avonlea 442	F 5
Baildon ●799	F 5
Balcarres 739	H 5
Balgonie 777	G 5
Batoche	E 3
Battleford 3,565	C 3
Beauval 606	L 3
Beechy 279	D 5
Bengough 536	F 6
Bethune 369	F 5
Bienfait 835	J 6
Biggar 2,561	C 3
Big River 819	D 2
Birch Hills 957	F 3
Bjorkdale 269	H 3
Blaine Lake 653	D 3
Borden 197	D 3
Brabant Lake 245	M 3
Bradwell 168	E 4
Bredenbury 467	K 5
Briercrest 151	F 5
Broadview 840	J 5
Brock 184	C 4
Browning ●687	F 3
Bruno 772	F 3
Buchanan 392	J 4
Buffalo Gap ●598	F 6
Buffalo Narrows 1,088	L 3
Burstall 550	C 5
Cabri 632	D 6
Cadillac 173	D 6
Calder 164	K 4
Candle ●1,238	J 5
Candle Lake 219	F 2
Cando 163	C 3
Canoe Lake 182	L 3
Canora 2,667	J 4
Canwood 340	E 2
Carievale 246	K 6
Carlyle 1,074	J 6
Carnduff 1,043	K 6
Carrot River 1,169	H 2

Central Butte 548	E 5
Ceylon 184	G 6
Chaplin 389	D 2
Chitek Lake 170	G 2
Choiceland 543	F 2
Christopher Lake 227	J 5
Churchbridge 972	J 5
Clavet 234	E 4
Climax 293	C 2
Cochin 221	C 2
Codette 236	G 2
Coleville 383	C 4
Colonsay 594	F 4
Connaught Heights ●982	G 3
Conquest 256	D 4
Consul 153	B 6
Coronach 1,032	F 6
Craik 565	F 4
Craven 206	G 5
Creelman 184	H 6
Creighton 1,636	N 4
Cudworth 947	F 3
Cumberland House 831	J 2
Cupar 669	G 5
Cut Knife 584	B 3
Dalmeny 1,064	E 3
Davidson 1,166	E 4
Debden 403	E 2
Delisle 980	M 4
Denare Beach 592	N 3
Denzil 199	B 3
Deschambault Lake 386	M 3
Dinsmore 398	C 4
Dodsland 272	C 4
Domremy 209	F 3
Drake 211	G 4
Duck Lake 699	E 3
Dundurn 531	E 4
Dysart 275	H 5
Earl Grey 303	G 5
Eastend 723	C 6
Eatonia 583	B 4
Ebenezer 164	J 4
Edam 384	C 2
Edenwold 143	G 5
Elbow 313	E 4
Eldorado 229	L 2
Elfros 199	H 4
Elrose 624	D 4
Elstow 154	E 4
Endeavour 199	J 3
Englefeld 271	G 3
Erwood 149	J 3
Esterhazy 3,065	J 5
Estevan 9,174	J 6
Eston 1,413	C 4
Eyebrow 168	E 5
Fillmore 396	H 6
Fleming 141	K 5
Flin Flon 367	N 4

Foam Lake 1,452	H 4
Fond du Lac 494	L 2
Fort Qu'Appelle 1,827	H 5
Fox Valley 380	B 5
Francis 182	H 5
Frobisher 166	J 6
Frontier 619	C 6
Gainsborough 308	K 6
Gerald 197	K 5
Glaslyn 430	D 2
Glenavon 284	J 5
Glen Ewen 168	J 6
Goodsoil 263	L 4
Govan 394	G 5
Grand Coulee 208	G 5
Gravelbourg 1,338	E 6
Grayson 264	J 5
Green Acres 139	F 2
Green Lake 634	L 4
Grenfell 1,307	J 5
Guernsey 198	F 4
Gull Lake 1,095	D 5
Hafford 557	E 3
Hague 625	E 3
Hanley 484	E 4
Harris 259	E 4
Hawarden 137	E 4
Hearts Hill ●552	E 3
Hepburn 411	D 5
Herbert 1,019	E 5
Hodgeville 329	E 5
Holdfast 297	F 5
Hudson Bay 2,361	J 3
Humboldt 4,705	F 3
Hyas 165	J 4
Ile-à-la-Crosse 1,035	L 3
Imperial 501	F 4
Indian Head 1,889	H 5
Invermay 353	J 4
Ituna 870	H 4
Jansen 223	G 4
Jasmin ●14	H 4
Kamsack 2,688	J 4
Kelliher 397	H 4
Kelvington 1,054	H 3
Kenaston 345	E 4
Kennedy 275	J 5
Kerrobert 1,141	C 3
Kincaid 256	D 6
Kindersley 3,969	B 4
Kinistino 783	F 3
Kipling 1,016	J 5
Kisbey 228	J 6
Kronau 154	G 5
Kyle 516	C 6
Lac Pelletier ●586	E 6
Laflèche 583	E 6
Laird 233	E 3
Lake Lenore 361	G 3
La Loche 1,632	L 3
Lampman 651	J 6
Landis 277	C 3
Lang 219	G 6
Langenburg 1,324	K 5
Langham 1,151	E 3
Lanigan 1,732	F 4
La Ronge 2,579	L 3
Lashburn 813	B 2
Leader 1,108	B 5
Leask 478	E 2
Lebret 411	H 5
Lemberg 414	H 5
Leoville 393	D 2
Leroy 504	G 4
Lestock 402	G 4
Limerick 164	E 6
Lintlaw 234	H 3

Lipton 364	H 5
Lloydminster 6,034	A 2
Loon Lake 369	B 1
Loreburn 201	E 4
Lucky Lake 333	D 5
Lumsden 1,303	G 5
Luseland 704	B 3
Macdowall 171	E 2
Macklin 976	A 3
Macoun 190	H 6
Maidstone 1,001	B 2
Mankota 375	D 6
Manor 368	K 6
Maple Creek 2,470	B 6
Marcelin 238	E 3
Margo 153	H 4
Marriott ●627	D 4
Marsden 229	B 3
Marshall 453	A 2
Martensville 1,966	E 3
Maryfield 431	K 6
Maymont 212	D 3
McLean 189	G 5
Meacham 178	F 3
Meadow Lake 3,857	C 1
Meath Park 262	F 2
Medstead 163	C 2
Melfort 6,010	G 3
Melville 5,092	J 5
Meota 235	C 2
Mervin 155	C 2
Midale 564	H 6
Middle Lake 275	F 3
Milden 251	D 4
Milestone 602	G 5
Montmartre 544	H 5
Montreal Lake 411	F 1
Moose Jaw 33,941	F 5
Moose Range ●679	H 2
Moosomin 2,579	K 5
Morse 416	D 5
Mortlach 293	E 5
Mossbank 464	E 6
Muenster 385	G 3
Naicam 886	G 3
Neilburg 354	B 3
Neuanlage 144	E 3
Neudorf 425	J 5
Neuhorst 146	E 3
Nipawin 4,376	H 2
Nokomis 524	F 4
Norquay 552	J 4
North Battleford 14,030	C 3
North Portal 164	J 6
Odessa 232	H 5
Ogema 441	G 6
Osler 527	E 3
Outlook 1,976	E 4
Oxbow 1,191	J 6
Paddockwood 211	F 2
Pangman 227	G 6
Paradise Hill 421	L 3
Patuanak 173	L 3
Paynton 210	B 2
Pelican Narrows 331	K 4
Pelly 391	J 4
Pennant 202	C 5
Pense 472	G 5
Perdue 407	K 4
Pierceland 425	K 4
Pilger 150	F 3
Pilot Butte 1,255	G 5
Pine House 612	M 3
Plenty 175	C 4
Plunkett 150	F 4
Ponteix 769	D 6
Porcupine Plain 937	H 3
Preeceville 1,243	J 4

Prelate 317	B 5
Prince Albert 31,380	F 2
Prud'homme 222	F 3
Punnichy 394	G 4
Qu'Appelle 653	H 5
Quill Lake 514	G 3
Quinton 169	G 4
Rabbit Lake 159	D 2
Radisson 439	D 3
Radville 1,012	G 6
Rama 133	H 4
Raymore 635	G 4
Redvers 859	K 6
Regina (cap.) 162,613	G 5
Regina *164,313	G 5
Regina Beach 603	F 5
Rhein 271	J 4
Richmound 188	B 5
Riverhurst 193	E 5
Rocanville 934	K 5
Roche Percé 142	J 6
Rockglen 511	F 6
Rosetown 2,664	D 4
Rose Valley 538	H 3
Rosthern 1,609	E 3
Rouleau 443	G 5
Saint Benedict 157	F 3
Saint Brieux 401	G 3
Saint Louis 448	F 3
Saint Philips ●538	K 4
Saint Walburg 802	L 3
Saltcoats 549	J 4
Sandy Bay 756	N 3
Saskatoon 154,210	E 3
Saskatoon 154,210	E 3
Sceptre 271	C 3
Scott 203	C 3
Sedley 373	H 5
Semans 344	G 4
Shaunavon 2,112	C 6
Sheho 285	H 4
Shell Lake 220	E 2
Shellbrook 1,228	E 2
Simpson 231	F 4
Sintaluta 215	H 5
Smeaton 246	G 2
Southey 697	G 5
Spalding 337	G 3
Spiritwood 926	D 2
Springside 533	J 4
Spy Hill 354	K 5
Star City 527	G 3
Stenen 143	J 4
Stockholm 391	J 5
Stonehenge ●701	F 6
Storthoaks 142	K 6
Stoughton 716	J 6
Strasbourg 842	G 4
Sturgis 789	J 4
Swift Current 14,747	D 5
Tantallon 196	K 5
Theodore 473	J 4
Timber Bay 152	F 1
Tisdale 3,107	H 3
Togo 181	K 4
Tompkins 275	C 5
Torch River ●2,440	G 2
Torquay 311	H 6
Tramping Lake 178	B 3
Tugaske 175	E 5
Turnor Lake 166	L 3
Turtleford 505	B 2
Unity 2,408	B 3
Uranium City 2,507	L 2
Val Marie 236	D 6
Vanguard 292	D 6
Vanscoy 298	D 4
Vibank 369	H 5

Viscount 386	F 4
Vonda 313	F 3
Wadena 1,495	H 4
Wakaw 1,030	F 3
Waldeck 292	D 5
Waldheim 758	E 3
Walpole ●711	K 6
Wapella 487	K 5
Warman 2,076	E 3
Waseca 169	B 2
Waskesiu Lake 176	F 1
Watrous 1,830	F 4
Watson 901	G 3
Wawota 622	J 6
Weldon 279	F 3
Welwyn 170	K 5
Weyburn 9,523	H 6
White City 602	G 5
White Fox 394	H 2
Whitewood 1,003	J 5
Wilcox 202	G 5
Wilkie 1,501	C 3
Willow Bunch 494	F 6
Willow Creek ●1,218	B 6
Windthorst 254	J 5
Wiseton 195	D 4
Wishart 231	H 4
Wollaston Lake 248	N 2
Wolseley 904	H 5
Wynyard 1,462	G 4
Wynyard 2,147	G 4
Yarbo 158	K 5

OTHER FEATURES

Allan (hills)	E 4
Amisk (lake)	M 4
Antelope (lake)	C 5
Antler (riv.)	K 5
Arm (riv.)	F 5
Assiniboine (riv.)	J 3
Athabasca (lake)	L 2
Bad (lake)	C 4
Bad (hills)	C 4
Basin (lake)	F 3
Batoche Nat'l Hist. Site	E 3
Battle (creek)	B 6
Battle (riv.)	B 3
Bear (hills)	C 4
Beaver (lake)	H 4
Beaver (riv.)	L 4
Beaverlodge (lake)	L 2
Big Muddy (lake)	G 6
Bigstick (lake)	B 5
Birch (lake)	C 2
Bitter (lake)	B 5
Black (lake)	M 2
Boundary (plat.)	B 6
Brightsand (lake)	B 2
Bronson (lake)	B 2

Agriculture, Industry and Resources

DOMINANT LAND USE

- Wheat
- Cereals (chiefly barley, oats)
- Cereals, Livestock
- Livestock
- Forests

MAJOR MINERAL OCCURRENCES

Au	Gold	Na	Salt
Cu	Copper	O	Petroleum
G	Natural Gas	S	Sulfur
He	Helium	U	Uranium
K	Potash	Zn	Zinc
Lg	Lignite		

⚡ Water Power

▨ Major Industrial Areas

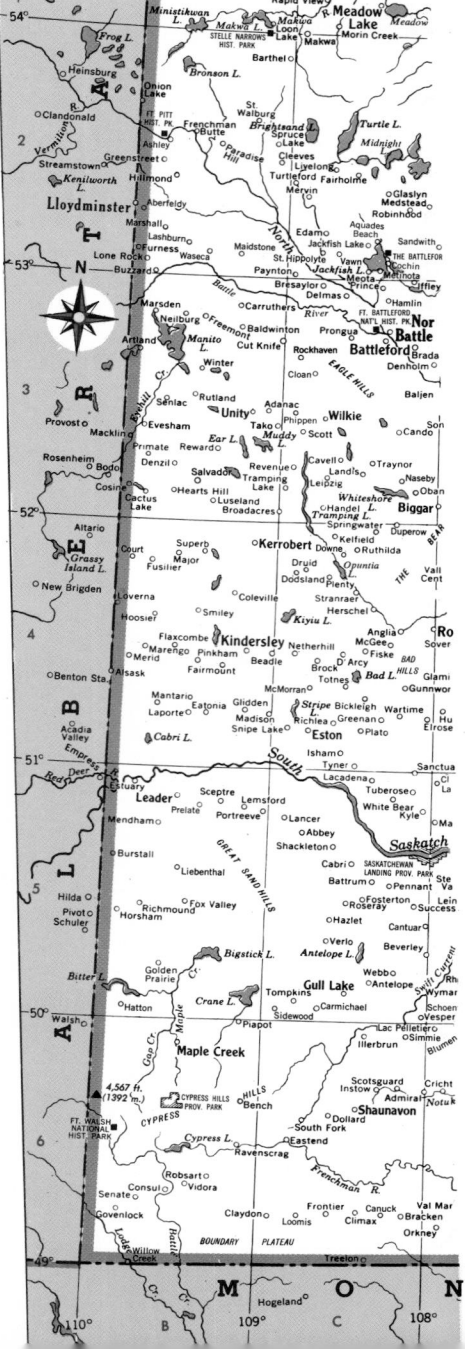

Saskatchewan 181

Buffalo Pound Prov. Park .... F 5
Cabri (lake) .... B 4
Cactus (hills) .... F 5
Candle (lake) .... F 2
Cannington Manon Hist. Park J 6
Canoe (lake) .... L 3
Carrot (riv.) .... J 2
Chaplin (riv.) .... E 5
Chipman (riv.) .... M 2
Chitek (lake) .... D 2
Churchill (riv.) .... M 3
Clearwater (riv.) .... L 3
Cochrane (riv.) .... N 2
Coteau (hills) .... D 4
Cowan (lake) .... D 2
Crane (lake) .... B 5
Crean (lake) .... E 1
Cree (lake) .... L 3
Cree (riv.) .... M 2
Cumberland (lake) .... J 1
Cypress (hills) .... B 6
Cypress (lake) .... B 6
Cypress Hills Prov. Park .... B 6
Danielson Prov. Park .... B 6
Delaronde (lake) .... E 1
Diefenbaker (lake) .... E 4
Doré (lake) .... L 3
Douglas Prov. Park .... E 4
Duck Lake Hist. Park .... E 3
Duck Mountain Prov. Park ... K 4
Eagle (hills) .... C 3
Eaglehill (creek) .... D 4

Ear (lake) .... B 3
Echo Valley Prov. Park ..... G 5
Etomami (riv.) .... J 4
Eyebrow (lake) .... E 5
Eyehill (creek) .... B 3
Fife (lake) .... E 6
File (hills) .... H 5
Fir (riv.) .... J 2
Fond du Lac (riv.) .... L 3
Forrest (lake) .... L 3
Fort Battleford Nat'l Hist. Park C 3
Fort Carlton Hist. Park ..... E 3
Fort Pitt Hist. Park .... C 3
Fort Walsh Nat'l Hist. Park . A 6
Foster (riv.) .... M 3
Frenchman (riv.) .... C 6
Frobisher (lake) .... L 3
Gap (creek) .... B 6
Gardiner (dam) .... D 4
Geikie (riv.) .... M 3
Good Spirit (lake) .... J 4
Goodspirit Lake Prov. Park . J 4
Great Sand (hills) .... B 5
Green (lake) .... D 1
Greenwater Lake Prov. Park H 3
Haultain (riv.) .... L 3
Ile-à-la-Crosse (lake) ...... L 3
Ironspring (creek) .... G 3
Jackfish (lake) .... C 3
Katepwa Prov. Park .... H 5
Kingsmere (lake) .... E 1
Kiyiu (lake) .... C 4

Lac La Ronge Prov. Park .... M 3
Lanigan (creek) .... F 4
Last Mountain (lake) .... F 4
Leaf (lake) .... J 4
Leech (lake) .... J 4
Lenore (lake) .... G 3
Little Manitou (lake) .... F 4
Lodge (creek) .... A 6
Long (creek) .... H 6
Loon (creek) .... G 4
Makwa (lake) .... B 1
Makwa (riv.) .... B 2
Manito (lake) .... B 3
Maple (creek) .... B 3
McFarlane (riv.) .... M 3
Meadow (lake) .... C 1
Meadow Lake Prov. Park ... K 4
Meeting (lake) .... D 2
Midnight (lake) .... C 2
Ministikwan (lake) .... B 1
Missouri Coteau (hills) .... J 4
Montreal (lake) .... F 1
Moose (mt.) .... J 6
Moose Jaw (riv.) .... G 5
Moose Mountain (creek) ... J 6
Moose Mountain Prov. Park J 6
Mossy (riv.) .... H 1
Muddy (lake) .... B 3
Mudjatik (riv.) .... L 3
Nipawin Prov. Park .... G 1
North Saskatchewan (riv.) . D 3
Notukeu (creek) .... D 6

Oldman (riv.) .... L 2
Old Wives (lake) .... E 5
Opuntia (lake) .... C 4
Overflowing (riv.) .... K 2
Pasquia (hills) .... J 2
Pasquia (riv.) .... K 2
Pelican (lake) .... E 5
Peter Pond (lake) .... L 3
Pheasant (hills) .... J 5
Pine Lake Prov. Park ...... E 4
Pinto (creek) .... D 6
Pipestone (creek) .... K 6
Pipestone (riv.) .... L 2
Ponass (lake) .... H 3
Poplar (riv.) .... E 6
Porcupine (hills) .... K 3
Primrose (lake) .... L 3
Primrose Lake Air Weapons
  Range .... L 3
Qu'Appelle (riv.) .... J 5
Quill (lake) .... G 4
Red Deer (lake) .... J 4
Red Deer (riv.) .... A 5
Reindeer (lake) .... K 3
Reindeer (riv.) .... M 3
Riou (lake) .... M 2
Rivers (lake) .... F 6
Ronge, La (lake) .... M 3
Rowans Ravine Prov. Park . F 4
St. Victor Petroglyphs Hist.
  Park .... E 6

Saskatchewan (riv.) .... H 2
Saskatchewan Landing Prov.
  Park .... C 5
Saskeram (lake) .... K 2
Scott (lake) .... M 2
Selwyn (lake) .... M 2
Souris (riv.) .... H 6
South Saskatchewan (riv.) . C 5
Steele Narrows Hist. Park . B 1
Stripe (lake) .... C 4
Sturgeon (riv.) .... E 2
Swan (riv.) .... J 3
Swift Current (creek) ..... D 5
Tazin (lake) .... L 2
The Battlefords Prov. Park . C 2

Thickwood (hills) .... D 2
Thunder (hills) .... L 4
Tobin (lake) .... H 2
Torch (riv.) .... H 2
Touchwood (hills) .... G 4
Tramping (lake) .... C 3
Trout (riv.) .... L 3
Turtle (lake) .... C 2
Twelvemile (lake) .... E 6
Vermilion (riv.) .... E 5
Wapawekka (hills) .... M 4
Waskana (creek) .... G 5
Waskesiu (lake) .... E 2
Wathaman (riv.) .... M 3
Weed (hills) .... J 5

White Fox (riv.) .... G 2
White Gull (creek) .... G 2
Whiteshore (lake) .... C 3
Whiteswan (lakes) .... F 1
Wilam (riv.) .... L 2
Willow Bunch (lake) ..... F 6
Witchekan (lake) .... D 2
Wollaston (lake) .... N 2
Wood (lake) .... E 6
Wood (mt.) .... E 6
Wood Mountain Hist. Park . E 6

AREA 251,699 sq. mi. (651,900 sq. km.)
POPULATION 968,313
CAPITAL Regina
LARGEST CITY Regina
HIGHEST POINT Cypress Hills 4,567 ft.
  (1,392 m.)
SETTLED IN 1774
ADMITTED TO CONFEDERATION 1905
PROVINCIAL FLOWER Prairie Lily

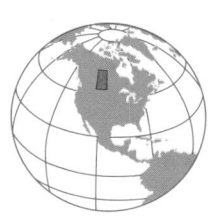

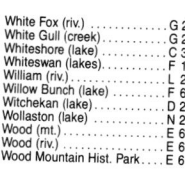

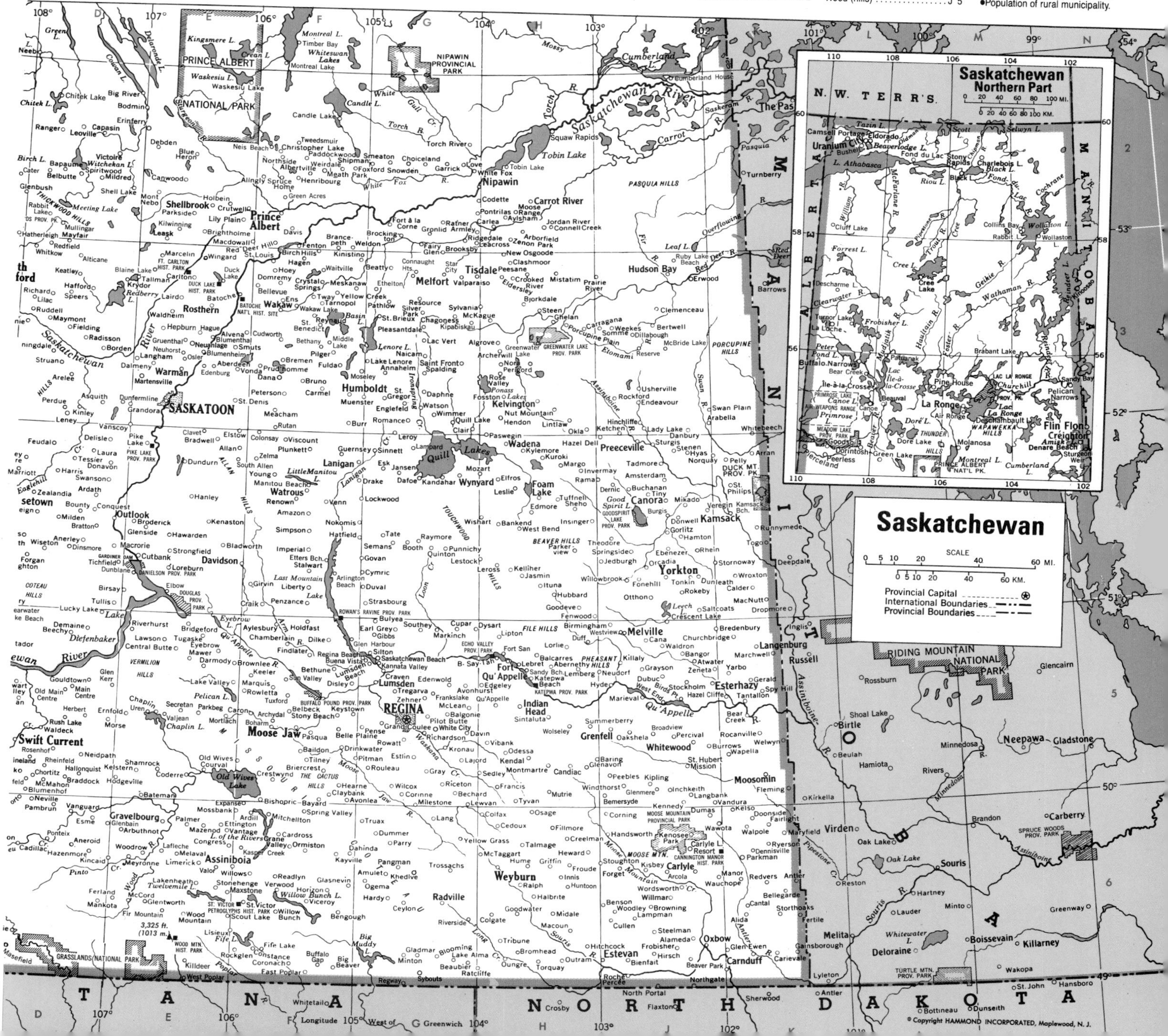

*Population of metropolitan area.
•Population of rural municipality.

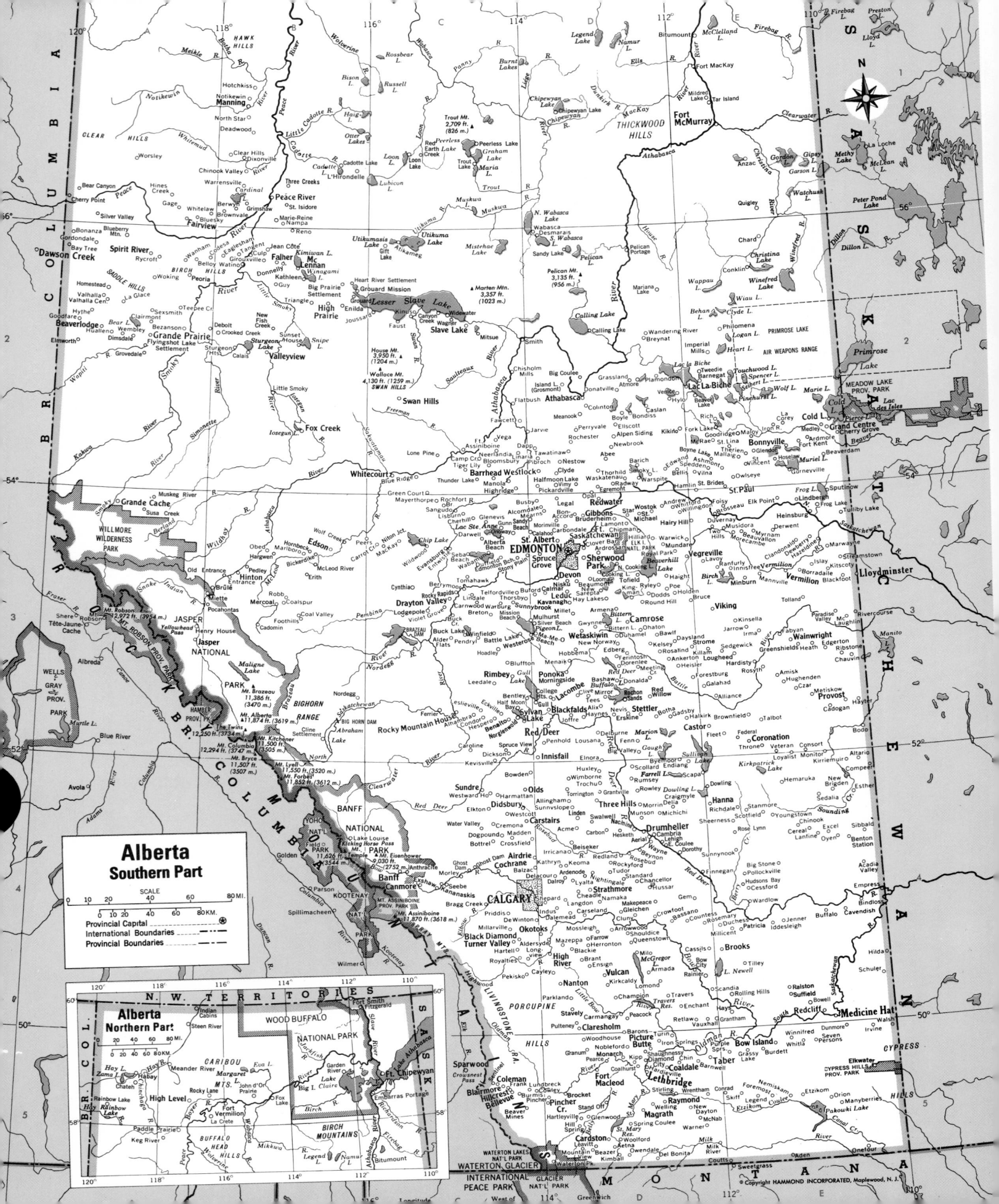

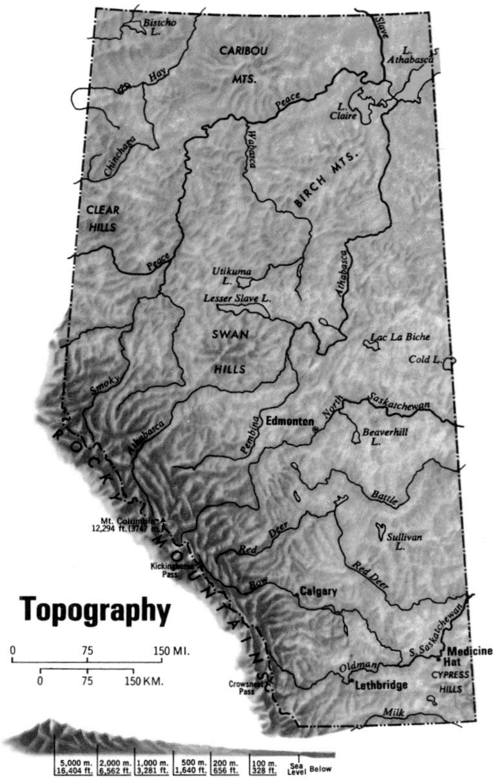
Bistcho L.
CARIBOU MTS.
Hay
Slave
L. Athabasca
Peace
L. Claire
Wabasca
Chinchaga
BIRCH MTS.
CLEAR HILLS
Utikuma L.
Lesser Slave L.
Athabasca
SWAN HILLS
Lac La Biche
Cold L.
Smoky
Edmonton
North Saskatchewan
Pembina
Beaverhill L.
Battle
Mt. Columbia 12,294 ft. (3747 m.)
Sullivan L.
Red Deer
Kicking Horse Pass
ROCKY MOUNTAINS
Bow
Calgary
S. Saskatchewan
Medicine Hat
Oldman
Lethbridge
CYPRESS HILLS
Crowsnest Pass
Milk
Topography
0 75 150 MI.
0 75 150 KM.
5,000 m. 16,404 ft.
2,000 m. 6,562 ft.
1,000 m. 3,281 ft.
500 m. 1,640 ft.
200 m. 656 ft.
100 m. 328 ft.
Sea Level
Below

AREA 255,285 sq. mi. (661,185 sq. km.)
POPULATION 2,237,724
CAPITAL Edmonton
LARGEST CITY Edmonton
HIGHEST POINT Mt. Columbia 12,294 ft. (3,747 m.)
SETTLED IN 1861
ADMITTED TO CONFEDERATION 1905
PROVINCIAL FLOWER Wild Rose

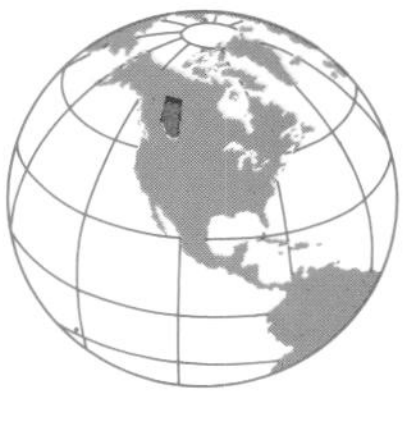

CITIES and TOWNS

Acme 457 . . . D 4
Airdrie 8,414 . . . C 4
Alberta Beach 485 . . . C 3
Alix 837 . . . D 3
Andrew 548 . . . D 3
Antler Lake 334 . . . D 3
Ardmore 224 . . . E 2
Arrowwood 156 . . . D 4
Athabasca 1,731 . . . D 2
Banff 4,208 . . . C 4
Barnwell 359 . . . D 5
Barons 315 . . . D 4
Barrhead 3,736 . . . C 2
Bashaw 875 . . . D 3
Bassano 1,200 . . . D 4
Bawlf 350 . . . D 3
Beaumont 2,638 . . . D 3
Beaverlodge 1,937 . . . A 2
Beiseker 580 . . . D 4
Bentley 823 . . . C 3
Berwyn 557 . . . B 1
Big Valley 360 . . . D 3
Black Diamond 1,444 . . . C 4
Blackfalds 1,488 . . . D 3
Blackfoot 220 . . . E 3
Blackie 298 . . . D 4
Bon Accord 1,376 . . . D 3
Bonnyville 4,454 . . . E 2
Bowden 989 . . . C 4
Bow Island 1,491 . . . E 5
Boyle 638 . . . D 2
Bragg Creek 505 . . . C 4
Breton 552 . . . C 3
Brooks 9,421 . . . E 4
Bruce 88 . . . E 3
Bruderheim 1,136 . . . D 3
Burdett 220 . . . E 5
Calgary 592,743 . . . C 4
Calgary *592,743 . . . C 4
Calmar 1,003 . . . D 3
Camrose 12,570 . . . D 3
Canmore 3,484 . . . C 4
Carbon 434 . . . D 4
Cardston 3,267 . . . D 5
Carmangay 266 . . . D 4
Caroline 436 . . . C 3
Carseland 484 . . . D 4
Carstairs 1,587 . . . D 4
Castor 1,123 . . . D 3
Cereal 249 . . . E 4
Champion 339 . . . D 4
Chauvin 298 . . . E 3
Chipman 266 . . . D 3
Clairmont 469 . . . A 2
Claresholm 3,493 . . . D 4
Clive 364 . . . D 3
Clyde 364 . . . D 2
Coaldale 4,579 . . . D 5
Coalhurst 882 . . . D 5
Cochrane 3,544 . . . C 4
Cold Lake 2,110 . . . E 2
College Heights 267 . . . D 3
Consort 632 . . . E 3
Cooking Lake 218 . . . D 3
Coronation 1,309 . . . E 3
Coutts 400 . . . D 5
Cowley 304 . . . D 5
Cremona 382 . . . C 4
Crossfield 1,217 . . . C 4
Daysland 679 . . . D 3
Delburne 574 . . . D 3
Desmarais 260 . . . D 2
Devon 3,885 . . . D 3
Didsbury 3,095 . . . C 4
Donalda 280 . . . D 3
Donnelly 336 . . . B 2
Drayton Valley 5,042 . . . C 3
Drumheller 6,508 . . . D 4
Duchess 429 . . . E 4
East Coulee 218 . . . D 4
Eckville 870 . . . C 3
Edgerton 387 . . . E 3
Edmonton (cap.) 532,246 . . . D 3
Edmonton *657,057 . . . D 3
Edmonton Beach 280 . . . C 3
Edson 5,835 . . . B 3
Elk Point 1,022 . . . E 3
Elnora 249 . . . D 3
Entwistle 462 . . . C 3
Erskine 259 . . . D 3
Evansburg 779 . . . C 3
Exshaw 353 . . . C 4
Fairview 2,869 . . . A 1
Falher 1,102 . . . B 2
Faust 399 . . . C 2
Foremost 568 . . . E 5
Forestburg 924 . . . E 3
Fort Assiniboine 207 . . . C 2
Fort Chipewyan 944 . . . C 5
Fort Macleod 3,139 . . . D 5
Fort McKay 267 . . . E 1
Fort McMurray 31,000 . . . E 1
Fort Saskatchewan 12,169 . . . D 3
Fort Vermilion 752 . . . B 5
Fox Creek 1,978 . . . B 2
Fox Lake 634 . . . B 5
Gibbons 2,276 . . . D 3
Gift Lake 428 . . . C 2
Girouxville 325 . . . B 2
Gleichen 381 . . . D 4
Glendon 430 . . . E 2
Glenwood 259 . . . D 5
Grand Centre 3,146 . . . E 2
Grande Cache 4,523 . . . A 3
Grande Prairie 24,263 . . . A 2
Granum 399 . . . D 5
Grimshaw 2,316 . . . B 1
Grouard Mission 221 . . . C 2
Hanna 2,806 . . . E 4
Hardisty 641 . . . E 3
Hay Lakes 302 . . . D 3
Heisler 212 . . . D 3
High Level 2,194 . . . A 5
High Prairie 2,506 . . . B 2
High River 4,792 . . . D 4
Hines Creek 575 . . . A 1
Hinton 8,342 . . . B 3
Holden 430 . . . D 3
Hughenden 267 . . . E 3
Hythe 639 . . . A 2
Innisfail 5,247 . . . D 3
Innisfree 255 . . . E 3
Irma 474 . . . E 3
Irricana 558 . . . D 4
Irvine 360 . . . E 5
Jasper 3,269 . . . B 3
John d'Or Prairie 437 . . . B 5
Joussard 330 . . . B 2
Killam 1,005 . . . E 3
Kinuso 285 . . . C 2
Kitscoty 497 . . . E 3
Lac La Biche 2,007 . . . E 2
Lacombe 5,591 . . . D 3
La Crete 479 . . . B 5
Lake Louise 355 . . . B 4
Lamont 1,563 . . . D 3
Leduc 12,471 . . . D 3
Legal 1,022 . . . D 3
Lethbridge 54,072 . . . D 5
Linden 407 . . . D 4
Little Buffalo Lake 253 . . . B 1
Lloydminster 8,997 . . . E 3
Longview 301 . . . C 4
Lougheed 226 . . . E 3
Lundbreck 244 . . . C 5
Magrath 1,576 . . . D 5
Manning 1,173 . . . B 1
Mannville 788 . . . E 3
Marlboro 211 . . . B 3
Marwayne 500 . . . E 3
Mayerthorpe 1,475 . . . C 3
McLennan 1,125 . . . B 2
Medicine Hat 40,380 . . . E 4
Milk River 894 . . . D 5
Millet 1,120 . . . D 3
Mirror 507 . . . D 3
Monarch 212 . . . D 5
Morinville 4,657 . . . D 3
Morrin 244 . . . D 4
Mundare 604 . . . D 3
Myrnam 397 . . . E 3
Nacmine 369 . . . D 4
Nampa 334 . . . B 1
Nanton 1,641 . . . D 4
New Norway 291 . . . D 3
New Sarepta 417 . . . D 3
Nobleford 534 . . . D 5
North Calling Lake 234 . . . D 2
Okotoks 3,847 . . . C 4
Olds 4,813 . . . D 4
Onoway 621 . . . C 3
Oyen 975 . . . E 4
Peace River 5,907 . . . B 1
Penhold 1,531 . . . D 3
Picture Butte 1,404 . . . D 5
Pincher Creek 3,757 . . . D 5
Plamondon 259 . . . D 2
Pollockville 19 . . . E 4
Ponoka 5,221 . . . D 3
Provost 1,645 . . . E 3
Rainbow Lake 504 . . . A 5
Ralston 357 . . . E 4
Raymond 2,837 . . . D 5
Redcliff 3,876 . . . E 4
Red Deer 46,393 . . . D 3
Redwater 1,932 . . . D 3
Rimbey 1,685 . . . C 3
Robb 230 . . . B 3
Rockyford 329 . . . D 4
Rocky Mountain House 4,698 . C 3
Rosemary 328 . . . E 4
Rycroft 649 . . . A 2
Ryley 483 . . . D 3
Saint Albert 31,996 . . . D 3
Saint Paul 4,884 . . . E 3
Sangudo 398 . . . C 3
Sedgewick 879 . . . E 3
Sexsmith 1,180 . . . A 2
Shaughnessy 270 . . . D 5
Sherwood Park 29,285 . . . D 3
Slave Lake 4,506 . . . C 2
Smith 216 . . . D 2
Smoky Lake 1,074 . . . D 2
Spirit River 1,104 . . . A 2
Spruce Grove 10,326 . . . D 3
Standard 379 . . . D 4
Stavely 504 . . . D 4
Stettler 5,136 . . . D 3
Stirling 688 . . . D 5
Stony Plain 4,839 . . . C 3
Strathmore 2,986 . . . D 4
Strome 281 . . . E 3
Sundre 1,742 . . . C 4
Swan Hills 2,497 . . . C 2
Sylvan Lake 3,779 . . . C 3
Taber 5,988 . . . E 5
Thorhild 576 . . . D 2
Thorsby 737 . . . C 3
Three Hills 1,787 . . . D 4
Tilley 345 . . . E 4
Tofield 1,504 . . . D 3
Trochu 880 . . . D 4
Turner Valley 1,311 . . . C 4
Two Hills 1,193 . . . E 3
Valleyview 2,061 . . . B 2
Vauxhall 1,049 . . . D 4
Vegreville 5,251 . . . E 3
Vermilion 3,766 . . . E 3
Veteran 314 . . . E 3
Viking 1,232 . . . E 3
Vilna 345 . . . E 2
Vulcan 1,489 . . . D 4
Wabamun 662 . . . C 3
Wabasca 701 . . . D 2
Wainwright 4,266 . . . E 3
Warburg 501 . . . C 3
Warner 477 . . . D 5
Waskatenau 290 . . . D 2
Wembley 1,169 . . . A 2
Westlock 4,424 . . . C 2
Wetaskiwin 9,597 . . . D 3
Whitecourt 5,585 . . . C 2
Wildwood 441 . . . C 3
Willingdon 366 . . . E 3
Youngstown 297 . . . E 4

OTHER FEATURES

Abraham (lake) . . . B 3
Alberta (mt.) . . . B 3
Assiniboine (mt.) . . . C 4
Athabasca (lake) . . . C 5
Athabasca (riv.) . . . D 1
Banff Nat'l Park . . . B 4
Battle (riv.) . . . D 3
Bear (lake) . . . A 2
Beaver (riv.) . . . E 2
Beaverhill (lake) . . . D 3
Behan (lake) . . . E 2
Belly (riv.) . . . D 5
Berland (riv.) . . . A 3
Berry (creek) . . . E 4
Biche (lake) . . . E 2
Big (isl.) . . . B 5
Big Horn (dam) . . . B 3
Bighorn (range) . . . B 3
Birch (hills) . . . A 2
Birch (lake) . . . E 3
Birch (mts.) . . . B 5
Birch (riv.) . . . B 5
Bison (lake) . . . B 1
Bittern (lake) . . . D 3
Botha (riv.) . . . B 1
Bow (riv.) . . . D 4
Boyer (riv.) . . . A 5
Brazeau (mt.) . . . B 3
Brazeau (riv.) . . . B 3
Buffalo (lake) . . . D 3
Buffalo Head (hills) . . . B 5
Burnt (lakes) . . . C 1
Cadotte (lake) . . . B 1
Cadotte (riv.) . . . B 1
Calling (lake) . . . D 2
Canal (creek) . . . E 5
Cardinal (lake) . . . B 1
Caribou (mts.) . . . B 5
Chinchaga (riv.) . . . A 5
Chip (lake) . . . C 3
Chipewyan (lake) . . . D 1
Chipewyan (riv.) . . . D 1
Christina (lake) . . . E 2
Christina (riv.) . . . E 1
Claire (lake) . . . B 5
Clear (hills) . . . A 1
Clearwater (riv.) . . . C 4
Clearwater (riv.) . . . E 1
Clyde (lake) . . . E 2
Cold (lake) . . . E 2
Columbia (mt.) . . . B 3
Crowsnest (pass) . . . C 5
Cypress (hills) . . . E 5
Cypress Hills Prov. Park . . . E 5
Dillon (riv.) . . . E 2
Dowling (lake) . . . D 4
Dunkirk (riv.) . . . D 1
Eisenhower (mt.) . . . C 4
Elbow (riv.) . . . C 4
Elk Island Nat'l Park . . . D 3
Ells (riv.) . . . D 1
Etzikom Coulee (riv.) . . . E 5
Eva (lake) . . . B 5
Farrell (lake) . . . D 4
Firebag (riv.) . . . E 1
Forbes (mt.) . . . B 4
Freeman (riv.) . . . C 2
Frog (lake) . . . E 3
Garson (lake) . . . E 1
Gipsy (lake) . . . E 1
Gordon (lake) . . . E 1
Gough (lake) . . . D 3
Graham (lake) . . . C 1
Gull (lake) . . . C 3
Haig (lake) . . . B 1
Hawk (hills) . . . B 1
Hay (lake) . . . A 5
Hay (riv.) . . . A 5
Heart (lake) . . . E 2
Highwood (riv.) . . . C 4
House (mt.) . . . C 2
House (riv.) . . . D 2
Iosegun (lake) . . . B 2
Iosegun (riv.) . . . B 2
Jackfish (riv.) . . . B 5
Jasper Nat'l Park . . . A 3
Kakwa (riv.) . . . A 2
Kickinghorse (pass) . . . B 4
Kimiwan (lake) . . . B 2
Kirkpatrick (lake) . . . E 4
Kitchener (mt.) . . . B 3
Legend (lake) . . . D 1
Lesser Slave (lake) . . . C 2
Liége (riv.) . . . D 1
Little Bow (riv.) . . . D 4
Little Cadotte (riv.) . . . B 1
Little Smoky (riv.) . . . B 2
Livingstone (range) . . . C 4
Logan (lake) . . . E 2
Loon (lake) . . . C 1
Loon (riv.) . . . C 1
Lubicon (lake) . . . C 1
Lyell (mt.) . . . B 4
MacKay (riv.) . . . D 1
Maligne (lake) . . . B 3
Margaret (lake) . . . B 5
Marie (lake) . . . E 2
Marion (lake) . . . D 3
Marten (mt.) . . . C 2
McClelland (lake) . . . E 1
McGregor (lake) . . . D 4
McLeod (riv.) . . . B 3
Meikle (riv.) . . . A 1
Mikkwa (riv.) . . . B 5
Milk (riv.) . . . D 5
Mistehae (lake) . . . C 2
Muriel (lake) . . . E 2
Muskwa (lake) . . . C 1
Muskwa (riv.) . . . C 1
Namur (lake) . . . D 1
Newell (lake) . . . E 4
Nordegg (riv.) . . . C 3
North Saskatchewan (riv.) . . . E 3
North Wabasca (lake) . . . D 1
Notikewin (riv.) . . . A 1
Oldman (riv.) . . . D 5
Otter (lakes) . . . B 1
Pakowki (lake) . . . E 5
Panny (riv.) . . . C 1
Peace (riv.) . . . B 1
Peerless (lake) . . . C 1
Pelican (lake) . . . D 2
Pelican (mts.) . . . D 2
Pembina (riv.) . . . C 3
Pigeon (lake) . . . D 3
Pinehurst (lake) . . . E 2
Porcupine (hills) . . . C 4
Primrose (lake) . . . E 2
Rainbow (lake) . . . A 5
Red Deer (lake) . . . D 3
Red Deer (riv.) . . . D 4
Richardson (riv.) . . . C 5
Rocky (mts.) . . . B-C 4
Rosebud (riv.) . . . D 4
Russell (lake) . . . C 1
Saddle (hills) . . . A 2
Sainte Anne (lake) . . . C 3
Saint Mary (res.) . . . D 5
Saint Mary (riv.) . . . D 5
Saulteaux (riv.) . . . C 2
Seibert (lake) . . . E 2
Simonette (riv.) . . . A 2
Slave (riv.) . . . C 5
Smoky (riv.) . . . A 2
Snake Indian (riv.) . . . A 3
Snipe (lake) . . . B 2
Sounding (creek) . . . E 4
South Saskatchewan (riv.) . . . E 4
South Wabasca (lake) . . . D 2
Spencer (lake) . . . E 2
Spray (mts.) . . . C 4
Sturgeon (lake) . . . B 2
Sullivan (lake) . . . D 3
Swan (hills) . . . C 2
Swan (riv.) . . . C 2
Temple (mt.) . . . B 4
The Twins (mt.) . . . B 3
Thickwood (hills) . . . D 1
Touchwood (lake) . . . E 2
Travers (res.) . . . D 4
Trout (mt.) . . . C 1
Trout (riv.) . . . C 1
Utikuma (lake) . . . C 2
Utikuma (riv.) . . . C 1
Utikumasis (lake) . . . C 2
Vermilion (riv.) . . . E 3
Wabasca (riv.) . . . C 1
Wallace (mt.) . . . C 2
Wapiti (riv.) . . . A 2
Wappau (lake) . . . E 2
Watchusk (lake) . . . E 1
Waterton-Glacier Int'l Peace Park . . . C 5
Waterton Lakes Nat'l Park . . . C 5
Whitemud (riv.) . . . A 1
Wildhay (riv.) . . . B 3
Willmore Wilderness Prov. Park . . . A 3
Winagami (lake) . . . B 2
Winefred (lake) . . . E 2
Winefred (riv.) . . . E 2
Wolf (lake) . . . E 2
Wolverine (riv.) . . . B 1
Wood Buffalo Nat'l Park . . . B 5
Yellowhead (pass) . . . A 3
Zama (lake) . . . A 5

*Population of metropolitan area.

Agriculture, Industry and Resources

DOMINANT LAND USE

- Wheat
- Cereals (chiefly barley, oats)
- Cereals, Livestock
- Dairy
- Pasture Livestock
- Range Livestock
- Forests
- Nonagricultural Land

MAJOR MINERAL OCCURRENCES

- C Coal
- G Natural Gas
- Na Salt
- O Petroleum
- S Sulfur
- Water Power
- Major Industrial Areas

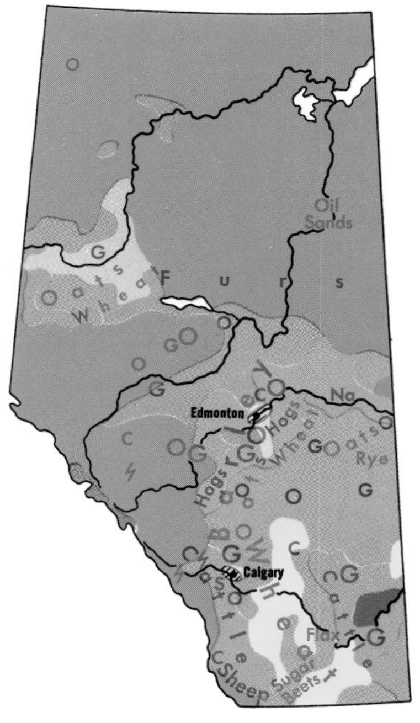
Oil Sands
F u r s
Oats
Wheat
Edmonton
Hogs
Rye
Calgary
Flax
Sugar Beets
Sheep

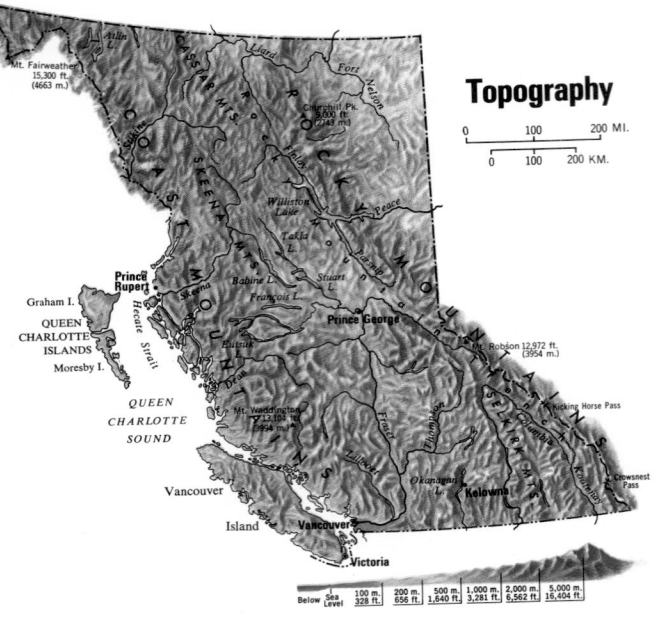

Topography

0   100   200 MI.
0   100   200 KM.

Below Sea Level | 100 m. 328 ft. | 200 m. 656 ft. | 500 m. 1,640 ft. | 1,000 m. 3,281 ft. | 2,000 m. 6,562 ft. | 5,000 m. 16,404 ft.

Agriculture, Industry and Resources

DOMINANT LAND USE

Cereals, Livestock
Dairy
Fruits, Vegetables
Pasture Livestock
Forests
Nonagricultural Land

MAJOR MINERAL OCCURRENCES

Ab Asbestos
Ag Silver
Au Gold
C Coal
Cu Copper
Fe Iron Ore
G Natural Gas
Gp Gypsum
Mo Molybdenum
Ni Nickel
O Petroleum
Pb Lead
S Sulfur
Sn Tin
Zn Zinc

↯ Water Power
⬭ Major Industrial Areas

CITIES and TOWNS

Abbotsford 12,745 .... L 3
Alert Bay 626 .... D 5
Armstrong 2,683 .... H 5
Ashcroft 2,156 .... G 5
Ashton Creek 452 .... H 4
Balfour 472 .... F 3
Barlow 441 .... F 3
Barrière 1,370 .... H 4
Blueberry Creek 635 .... J 5
Blue River 384 .... H 4
Boston Bar 498 .... G 5
Bowen Island 1,125 .... F 5
Brackendale 1,719 .... F 5
Burnaby ○136,494 .... K 3
Burns Lake 1,777 .... D 3
Cache Creek 1,308 .... G 5
Campbell River 15,370 ..... E 5
Canal Flats 919 .... J 5
Canyon 698 .... J 5
Cassiar 1,045 .... K 2
Castlegar 6,902 .... J 5
Cawston 785 .... H 5
Central Saanich ○9,890 .... K 3
Chase 1,777 .... H 5
Chemainus 2,069 .... J 3
Cherry Creek 450 .... G 5
Chetwynd 2,553 .... G 2
Chilliwack ○40,642 .... M 3
Clearwater 1,461 .... G 4
Clinton 804 .... G 4
Coldstream ○6,450 .... H 5
Comox 6,607 .... H 2
Coquitlam ○61,077 .... K 3
Courtenay 8,992 .... E 5
Cranbrook 15,915 .... K 5
Creston 4,190 .... J 5
Crofton 1,303 .... J 3
Cultus Lake 481 .... M 3
Cumberland 1,947 .... E 5
Dawson Creek 11,373 .... G 2
Delta ○74,692 .... K 3
Duncan 4,228 .... J 3
Elkford 3,126 .... K 5
Enderby 1,816 .... H 5
Erickson 972 .... J 5
Errington 609 .... J 3
Esquimalt ○15,870 ...... K 4
Falkland 478 .... H 5
Fernie 5,444 .... K 5
Forest Grove 444 ...... G 4
Fort Fraser 574 .... E 3
Fort Langley 2,326 .... L 3
Fort Nelson 3,724 ..... M 2
Fort Saint James 2,284 .. E 3
Fort Saint John 13,891 .. G 2
Fraser Lake 1,543 ...... H 2
Fruitvale 1,904 .... J 5
Gabriola 1,627 .... J 3
Galiano 669 .... K 3
Ganges 1,118 .... K 3
Gibsons 2,594 .... K 3
Gold River 2,225 ...... D 5
Golden 3,476 .... J 4
Grand Forks 3,486 ..... H 6
Granisle 1,480 .... D 3
Greenwood 856 .... H 5
Hagensborg 350 ...... D 4
Harrison Hot Springs 569 .. M 3
Hatzic 1,055 .... L 3

Hazelton 393 .... D 2
Hedley 426 .... G 5
Holberg 444 .... C 5
Honeymoon Bay 474 ... J 3
Hope 3,205 .... M 3
Hornby Island 474 .... H 2
Horsefly 430 .... G 4
Houston 1,714 .... D 3
Hudson Hope 984 ..... F 2
Invermere 1,969 ...... J 5
Kaleden 998 .... H 5
Kamloops 64,048 ..... G 5
Kaslo 854 .... J 5
Kelowna 59,196 ...... H 5
Kent ○3,394 .... M 3
Keremeos 830 .... G 5
Kimberley 7,375 ..... K 5
Kitimat 12,462 ...... C 3
Kitsault 554 .... C 2
Kitwanga 369 .... D 2
Lac La Hache 647 .... G 4
Ladysmith 4,558 .... J 3
Lake Cowichan 2,391 .. J 3
Langley 15,124 ...... J 3
Lantzville 969 ...... G 4
Likely 425 .... G 5
Lillooet 1,725 ...... G 5
Lion's Bay 1,078 .... K 3
Logan Lake 2,637 .... G 5
Lumby 1,266 .... H 5
Lytton 428 .... G 5
Mackenzie 5,797 .... F 2
Mackenzie ○5,890 ... F 2
Malakwa 392 .... H 5
Maple Bay 393 ..... K 3
Maple Ridge ○32,232 .. L 3
Masset 1,569 .... B 3
Matsqui ○42,001 .... L 3
Mayne 546 .... K 3
McBride 641 .... G 3
Merritt 6,110 ...... H 5
Midway 633 .... H 6
Mill Bay 583 ...... K 3
Mission ○20,056 ... L 3
Mission City 9,948 .. L 3
Montrose 1,229 .... J 5
Nakusp 1,495 ...... J 5
Nanaimo 47,069 .... J 3
Naramata 876 ..... H 5
Nelson 9,143 ...... J 5
New Denver 642 ... J 5
New Hazelton 792 .. K 3
New Westminster 38,550 .. K 3
Nicomen Island 360 .. L 3
Nootka .... D 5
North Cowichan ○18,210 .. J 3
North Pender Island 906 .. K 3
North Saanich ○6,117 .. K 3
North Vancouver 33,952 .. K 3
North Vancouver ○65,367 .. K 3
Oak Bay ○16,990 .... K 4
Okanagan Falls 1,030 .. H 5
Okanagan Landing 834 .. H 5
Okanagan Mission .... H 5
Old Barkerville 11 .... G 3
One Hundred Mile House
    1,925 .... G 4
Osoyoos 2,738 ...... H 5
Oyama 430 .... H 5
Parksville 5,216 .... J 3
Peachland ○2,865 ... G 5

Penticton 23,181 ...... H 5
Pitt Meadows ○6,209 .. L 3
Port Alberni 19,892 ... H 3
Port Alice 1,668 ..... D 5
Port Clements 380 .... B 3
Port Coquitlam 27,535 .. L 3
Port Edward 989 ..... B 3
Port Hardy 3,778 .... D 5
Port McNeill 2,474 ... D 5
Port Moody 14,917 ... K 3
Pouce-Coupé 821 .... G 2
Powell River ○13,423 .. E 5
Prince George 67,559 .. F 3
Prince Rupert 16,197 .. G 5
Princeton 3,051 ..... G 5
Qualicum Beach 2,844 .. A 3
Queen Charlotte 1,070 .. F 4
Quesnel 8,240 ...... G 4
Radium Hot Springs 419 .. J 5
Revelstoke 5,544 .... J 5
Richmond ○96,154 ... K 3
Roberts Creek 926 ... K 3
Robson 1,008 ...... J 5
Rossland 3,967 ..... H 6
Royston 754 ...... H 2
Saanich ○78,710 ... K 3
Salmo 1,169 ...... J 5
Salmon Arm 1,946 ... H 5
Salmon Arm ○10,780 .. H 5
Saltair 1,356 ..... J 3
Sandspit 794 ..... B 3
Sayward 482 ..... D 5
Sechelt 1,096 .... J 2
Shawnigan Lake 419 .. J 3
Shoreacres 555 .... J 5
Sicamous 1,057 ... H 5
Sidney 7,987 ..... K 3
Slocan 351 ...... J 5
Slocan Park 414 .. J 5
Smithers 4,570 ... D 3
Sointula 567 ..... D 5
Sooke 852 .... J 4
Sorrento 659 .... H 5
South Hazelton 500 .. D 2
South Wellington 620 .. J 3
Spallumcheen 4,213 .. H 5
Sparwood 3,267 ... K 5
Sproat Lake 440 ... H 3
Squamish 1,590 ... F 5
Stewart 1,456 .... C 2
Summerland ○7,473 .. G 5
Sidney ○147,138 ... K 3
Tahsis 1,739 ..... D 5
Taylor 966 ...... G 2
Telkwa 840 ..... D 3
Terrace 8,893 ... C 3
Terrace ○10,914 .. C 3
Thornhill 4,281 .. C 3
Thrums 360 ..... J 5
Tofino 705 ..... E 5
Trail 9,599 .... J 6
Ucluelet 1,593 .. E 6
Union Bay 601 .. H 2
Valemount 1,130 .. H 4
Vancouver 414,281 .. K 3
Vancouver (Greater)
    *1,169,831 ...... K 3
Vanderhoof 2,323 ... E 3
Vavenby 479 ...... H 4
Vernon 19,987 .... H 5
Victoria 64,379 .. K 4
Victoria *233,481 .. K 4
Warfield 1,969 ... J 5
Wasa 345 ...... K 5
Wells 417 ..... G 3
Westbank 1,271 .. H 5
West Vancouver ○35,728 .. K 3
Westwold 409 ... G 5
Whistler ○1,365 .. F 5
White Rock 13,550 .. K 3
Williams Lake 8,362 .. F 4
Wilson Creek 611 ... J 2
Windermere 611 .... K 5
Winlaw 435 .... J 5
Woss Lake 395 .... D 5
Wynndel 566 ..... J 5
Yarrow 1,201 ..... M 3
Youbou 965 ...... J 3

OTHER FEATURES

Adams (lake) .... H 4
Adams (riv.) .... H 4
Alberni (inlet) .... H 1
Alsek (riv.) .... A 1
Aristazabal (isl.) ..... C 4
Assiniboine (mt.) ...... K 5
Atlin (lake) .... G 1
Azure (lake) .... E 3
Babine (lake) .... D 2
Babine (riv.) .... B 3
Banks (isl.) .... E 6
Barkley (sound) .... E 6
Beale (cape) .... G 1
Beatton (riv.) .... D 4
Bella Coola (riv.) ..... D 4
Bennett, W.A.C. (dam) .. F 2
Birkenhead Lake Prov. Park .. F 5
Bowron Lake Prov. Park .. G 3
Bowser (lake) .... C 2
Brooks (pen.) .... D 5
Browning Entrance (str.) .. B 3
Bryce (mt.) .... J 4
Bugaboo Glacier Prov. Park .. J 5
Bulkley (riv.) .... D 2
Burke (chan.) .... D 4
Burnaby (isl.) .... B 4
Bute (inlet) .... E 5
Caamaño (sound) ..... C 4
Calvert (isl.) ...... C 4
Canim (lake) .... G 4
Canoe (riv.) .... H 4
Cariboo (mts.) ..... G 3
Carpenter (lake) ... F 5
Carp Lake Prov. Park .. F 3
Cassiar (mts.) ..... K 2
Castle (mt.) .... A 2

Charlotte (lake) .... E 4
Chatham (sound) ...... B 3
Chehalis (lake) .... L 4
Chilcotin (riv.) ...... F 4
Chilko (lake) .... F 4
Chilko (riv.) .... F 4
Chilkoot (pass) ...... J 1
Chuchi (lake) .... E 2
Churchill (peak) ..... L 2
Clayoquot (sound) ... D 5
Clearwater (lake) .... G 4
Coast (mts.) .... D 3
Columbia (lake) ..... J 4
Columbia (mt.) ...... J 4
Columbia (riv.) ..... H 5
Cook (cape) .... C 5
Cowichan (lake) .... J 3
Crowsnest (pass) .... K 5
Cypress Prov. Park .. K 3
Dean (chan.) .... D 4
Dean (riv.) .... D 4
Dease (lake) .... K 2
Dease (riv.) .... K 2
Devils Thumb (mt.) .. A 1
Dixon Entrance (chan.) .. A 3
Douglas (chan.) .... C 3
Duncan (riv.) ...... J 5
Dundas (isl.) ...... B 3
Elk (riv.) .... K 5
Elk Lakes Prov. Park .. K 5
Eutsuk (lake) ...... D 3
Fairweather (mt.) ... H 1
Finlay (riv.) ...... E 1
Fitzhugh (sound) ... D 4
Flathead (riv.) .... K 6
Flores (isl.) ..... D 5
Fontas (riv.) ..... M 2
Forbes (mt.) ..... J 4
Fort Nelson (riv.) .. M 2
François (lake) ... D 3
Fraser (lake) .... E 3
Fraser (riv.) .... F 4
Fraser Reach (chan.) .. C 3
Galiano (isl.) .... K 3
Gardner (canal) .. C 3
Garibaldi Prov. Park .. F 5
Georgia (str.) .... J 3
Germansen (riv.) .. E 2
Gil (isl.) .... C 3
Glacier Nat'l Park .. J 4
Golden Ears Prov. Park .. L 2
Gordon (riv.) .... H 3
Graham (isl.) .... A 3
Graham Reach (chan.) .. C 3
Grenville (chan.) .. B 3
Halfway (riv.) ... F 2
Hamber Prov. Park .. H 4
Harrison (lake) .. L 3
Hawkesbury (isl.) .. C 3
Hazelton (mts.) .. C 2
Hecate (str.) .... B 3
Hobson (lake) ... H 4
Homathko (riv.) .. E 4
Horsefly (lake) .. G 4

© Copyright HAMMOND INCORPORATED, Maplewood, N.J.

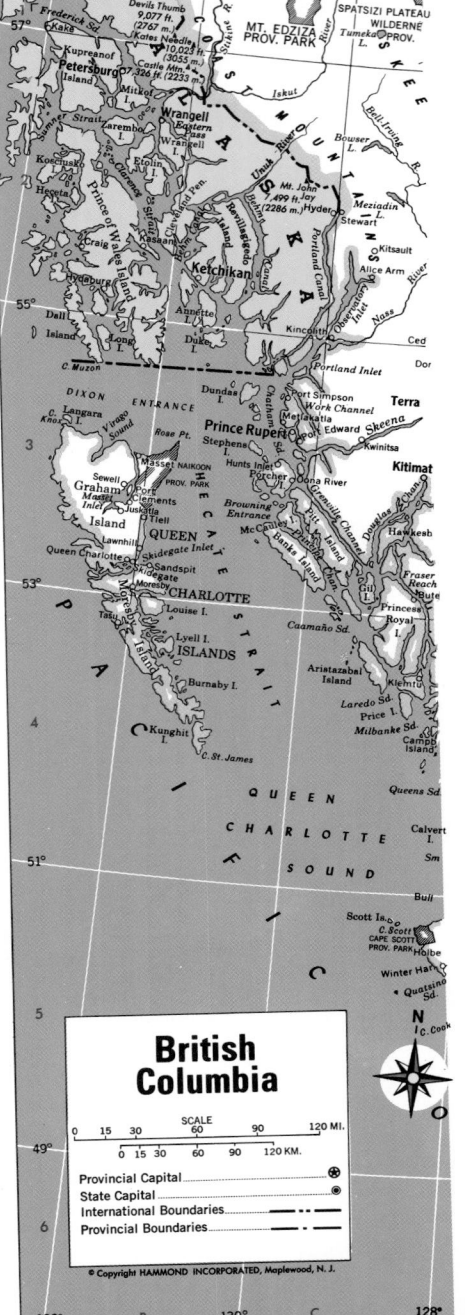

British Columbia

SCALE
0 15 30   60   90   120 MI.
0 15 30   60   90   120 KM.

Provincial Capital .... ⊛
State Capital .... ⊙
International Boundaries .... —··—··—
Provincial Boundaries .... ———

Howe (sound) . . . . K 2
Hunter (isl.) . . . . C 4
Inklin (riv.) . . . . J 2
Inzana (lake) . . . . E 3
Isaac (lake) . . . . G 3
Iskut (riv.) . . . . B 2
Jervis (inlet) . . . . E 5
John Jay (mt.) . . . . B 2
Johnstone (str.) . . . . D 5
Juan de Fuca (str.) . . . . J 4
Kates Needle (mt.) . . . . A 1
Kechika (riv.) . . . . L 2
Kenney (dam) . . . . E 3
Kettle (riv.) . . . . H 5
Kicking Horse (pass) . . . . J 4
King (isl.) . . . . D 4
Klinaklini (riv.) . . . . E 4
Kloch (lake) . . . . E 2
Knight (inlet) . . . . E 5
Knox (cape) . . . . A 3
Kokanee Glacier Prov. Park . . . . J 5
Koocanusa (lake) . . . . K 6
Kootenay (lake) . . . . J 5
Kootenay (riv.) . . . . K 5
Kootenay Nat'l Park . . . . J 4
Kotcho (lake) . . . . M 2
Kotcho (riv.) . . . . M 2
Kunghit (isl.) . . . . B 4
Kyuquot (sound) . . . . D 5
Langara (isl.) . . . . A 3
Laredo (sound) . . . . C 4
Liard (riv.) . . . . L 2
Lillooet (riv.) . . . . F 5
Louise (isl.) . . . . B 4
Lower Arrow (lake) . . . . H 5
Lyell (isl.) . . . . B 4
Lyell (mt.) . . . . J 4
Mabel (lake) . . . . H 5
Mahood (lake) . . . . G 4
Malaspina (str.) . . . . J 2
Manning Prov. Park . . . . G 5
Masset (inlet) . . . . A 3
McCauley (isl.) . . . . B 3
McGregor (riv.) . . . . G 3
Meziadin (lake) . . . . C 2
Milbanke (sound) . . . . C 4
Moberly (lake) . . . . F 2
Monashee (mts.) . . . . H 4
Moresby (isl.) . . . . B 4
Morice (lake) . . . . D 3
Morice (riv.) . . . . D 3
Mount Assiniboine Prov. Park . . . . K 5
Mount Edziza Prov. Park and Rec. Area . . . . B 1
Mount Revelstoke Nat'l Park . . . . H 4
Mount Robson Prov. Park . . . . H 3
Muncho Lake Prov. Park . . . . L 2
Murray (riv.) . . . . G 3
Murtle (lake) . . . . H 4
Muskwa (riv.) . . . . M 2
Nanika (dam) . . . . D 3
Nass (riv.) . . . . C 2
Nation (riv.) . . . . F 2
Nechako (riv.) . . . . E 3
Nitinat (lake) . . . . H 3
Nootka (isl.) . . . . D 5
Nootka (sound) . . . . D 5
North Thompson (riv.) . . . . G 4
Observatory (inlet) . . . . C 2
Okanagan (lake) . . . . H 5
Okanagan Mtn. Prov. Park . . . . G 5
Okanogan (riv.) . . . . H 6
Omineca (mts.) . . . . E 2
Omineca (riv.) . . . . E 2
Ootsa (lake) . . . . D 3
Owikeno (lake) . . . . D 4
Pacific Rim Nat'l Park . . . . E 6
Parsnip (riv.) . . . . F 3
Peace (riv.) . . . . G 2
Pend Oreille (riv.) . . . . J 6
Petitot (riv.) . . . . M 2
Pinchi (lake) . . . . E 3
Pine (riv.) . . . . G 2
Pitt (isl.) . . . . C 3
Pitt (lake) . . . . L 2
Porcher (isl.) . . . . B 3
Portland (canal) . . . . B 2
Portland (inlet) . . . . C 3
Price (isl.) . . . . C 4
Princess Royal (isl.) . . . . C 4
Principe (chan.) . . . . C 3
Prophet (riv.) . . . . M 2
Purcell (mts.) . . . . J 5
Quatsino (sound) . . . . C 5
Queen Charlotte (isls.) . . . . B 3
Queen Charlotte (sound) . . . . C 4
Queen Charlotte (str.) . . . . D 5
Queens (sound) . . . . C 4
Quesnel (lake) . . . . G 4
Quesnel (riv.) . . . . F 4
Rivers (inlet) . . . . D 4
Robson (mt.) . . . . H 3
Rocky (mts.) . . . . F 2
Roderick (isl.) . . . . C 4
Rose (pt.) . . . . B 3
Saint James (cape) . . . . B 4
Salmon (riv.) . . . . F 3
Salmon Arm (inlet) . . . . J 2
San Juan (riv.) . . . . J 3
Schoen Lake Prov. Park . . . . E 5
Scott (cape) . . . . C 5
Scott (isls.) . . . . C 5
Seechelt (inlet) . . . . J 2
Seechelt (pen.) . . . . J 2
Selkirk (mts.) . . . . J 4
Seymour (inlet) . . . . D 4
Sheslay (riv.) . . . . J 2
Shuswap (lake) . . . . H 4
Sikanni Chief (riv.) . . . . F 1
Silver Star Prov. Park . . . . H 5
Sir Sandford (mt.) . . . . H 4
Skagit (riv.) . . . . G 6
Skeena (mts.) . . . . C 2
Skeena (riv.) . . . . C 3
Skidegate (inlet) . . . . B 3
Slocan (lake) . . . . J 5
Smith (sound) . . . . C 4
South Bentinck Arm (inlet) . . . . D 4
Stave (lake) . . . . L 3
Stephens (isl.) . . . . B 3
Stikine (riv.) . . . . B 1
Stone Mountain Prov. Park . . . . L 2

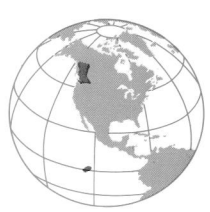

AREA 366,253 sq. mi. (948,596 sq. km.)
POPULATION 2,744,467
CAPITAL Victoria
LARGEST CITY Vancouver
HIGHEST POINT Mt. Fairweather 15,300 ft. (4,663 m.)
SETTLED IN 1806
ADMITTED TO CONFEDERATION 1871
PROVINCIAL FLOWER Dogwood

Strathcona Prov. Park . . . . E 5
Stuart (lake) . . . . E 3
Sustut (riv.) . . . . D 2
Tagish (lake) . . . . J 1
Tahtsa (lake) . . . . D 3
Takla (lake) . . . . D 2
Taku (riv.) . . . . J 2
Tatlatui (lake) . . . . D 2
Tatlayoko (lake) . . . . E 4
Tchentlo (lake) . . . . E 2
Teslin (lake) . . . . K 1
Tetachuck (lake) . . . . E 3
Texada (isl.) . . . . J 2
Tezzeron (lake) . . . . E 3
Thompson (riv.) . . . . G 5
Three Guardsmen (mt.) . . . . H 1
Thutade (lake) . . . . D 2
Tiedemann (mt.) . . . . E 4
Toad (riv.) . . . . L 2
Toba (inlet) . . . . E 5
Tochcha (lake) . . . . E 3
Top Of The World Prov. Park . . . . K 5
Trembleur (lake) . . . . E 3
Troitsa (lake) . . . . D 3
Tumeka (lake) . . . . C 1
Turnagain (riv.) . . . . K 2
Tuya (riv.) . . . . K 2
Tweedsmuir Prov. Park . . . . D 3
Upper Arrow (lake) . . . . H 5
Valdes (isl.) . . . . K 3
Vancouver (isl.) . . . . D 5
Virago (sound) . . . . A 3
Waddington (mt.) . . . . E 4
Wapiti (riv.) . . . . H 3
Wells Gray Prov. Park . . . . H 4
West Road (riv.) . . . . E 3
Whitesail (lake) . . . . D 3
Williston (lake) . . . . F 2
Work (chan.) . . . . C 3
Yellowhead (pass) . . . . H 4
Yoho Nat'l Park . . . . J 4

*Population of metropolitan area.
○Population of municipality.

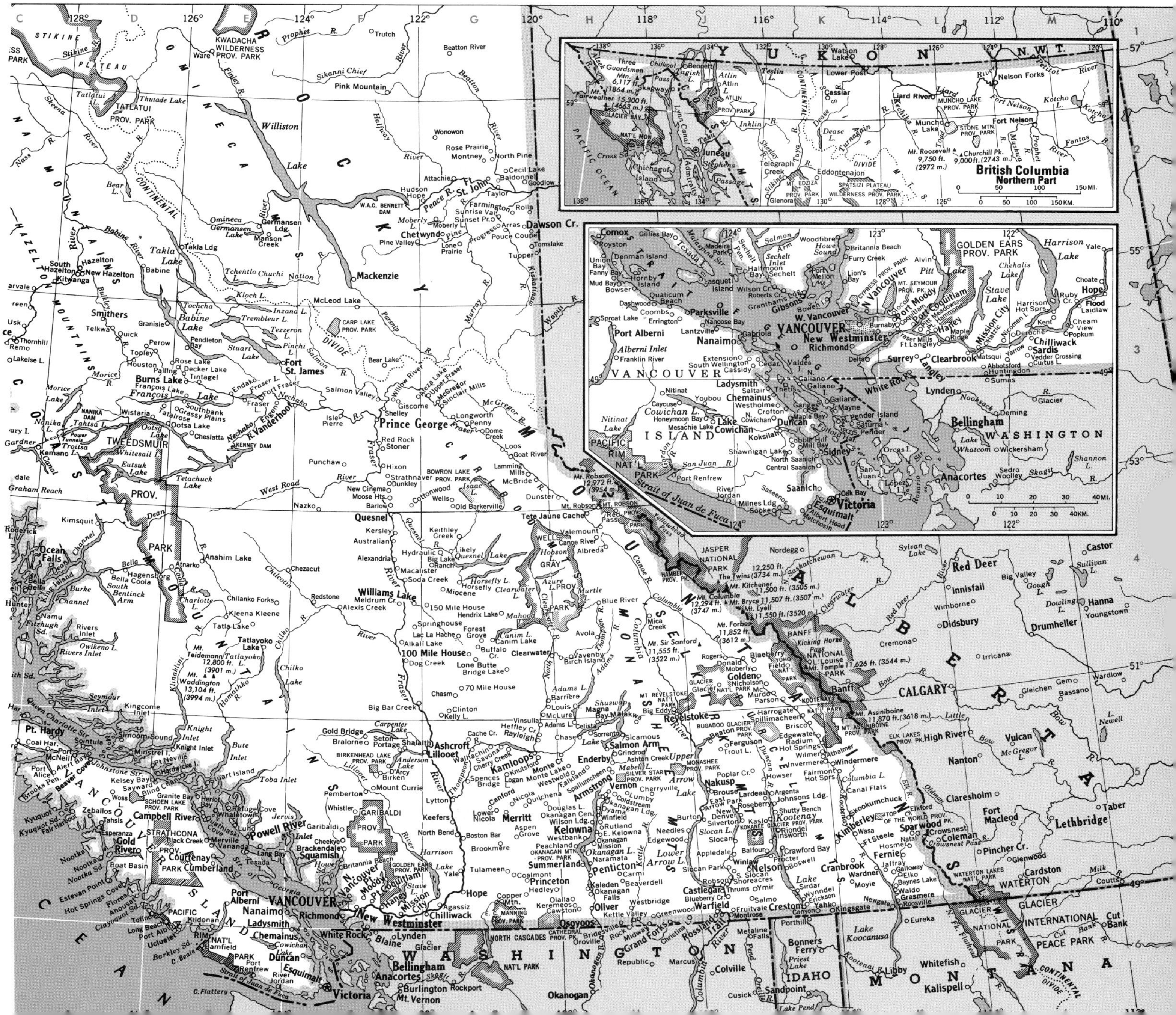

NORTHWEST TERRITORIES

DISTRICTS

Baffin 8,300 ....J2
Fort Smith 22,384 ....G3
Inuvik 7,485 ....F3
Keewatin 4,327 ....J3
Kitikmeot 3,245 ....G2

CITIES and TOWNS

Aklavik 721 ....E3
Alert M1
Amadjuak L3
Arctic Bay 375 ....K2
Arctic Red River 120 ...E3
Baker Lake 954 ....J3
Bathurst Inlet 20 ....H3
Bay Chimo 60 ....H3
Bell Rock G3
Broughton Island 378 ...M3
Buffalo River Junction. .G3
Cambridge Bay 815 .....L3
Cape Dorset 784 ....M3
Cape Dyer L3
Cape Smith K3
Chesterfield Inlet 249 ..K3
Clyde (Clyde River) 443 .F3
Colville Lake 57 ....F3
Coppermine 809 ....G3
Coral Harbour 429 ......K3
Detah 143 ....G3
Dory Point G3
Enterprise 46 ....G3
Eskimo Point 1,022 .....J3
Eureka K2
Fort Franklin 521 ......F3
Fort Good Hope 463 ....F3
Fort Liard 405 ....F3
Fort McPherson 632 ....E3
Fort Norman 286 ....F3
Fort Providence 605 ...G3
Fort Resolution 480 ...G3
Fort Simpson 980 ......F3
Fort Smith 2,298 ......G4
Frobisher Bay 2,333. ..M3
Gjoa Haven 523 ....J3
Grise Fiord 106 ....K2
Hall Beach 349 ....K3
Hay River 2,863 ....G2
Holman Island 300 .....K3
Igloolik 746 ....E3
Inuvik 3,147 ....H2
Isachsen ....
Jean-Marie River 69 ...F3
Kakisa 36 ....M3
Kipisa 43 ....L3
Lac la Martre 268 .....G3
Lake Harbour 252 ......L3
Mould Bay F2
Nahanni Butte 85. .....F3
Nanisivik 261 ....K2
Norman Wells 420. ....F3
Pangnirtung 839 ......M3
Paulatuk 174 ....G3
Pelly Bay 257 ....J3
Pine Point 1,861 ......G3
Pond Inlet 705 ....L2
Port Burwell M3
Port Radium 56 ....G3
Rae-Edzo 1,378 ....G3
Rae Lakes 200 ....G3
Rankin Inlet 1,109 ....G3
Reliance 15. ....H3
Repulse Bay 352 ......K3
Resolute Bay 168 .....J2

Resolution Island M3
Rocher River G3
Sachs Harbour 161 .....F2
Salt River G3
Sawmill Bay G3
Snare Lake 69 ....G3
Snowdrift 253 ....G3
Spence Bay 431 ....J3
Trout Lake 59 ....F3
Tuktoyaktuk 772 ......F3
Tungsten 320 ....F3
Whale Cove 188 ......J3
Wrigley 137 ....F3
Yellowknife (cap.) 9,483 .G3

OTHER FEATURES

Adelaide (pen.) J3
Admiralty (inlet) K2
Air Force (isl.) L3
Akpatok (isl.) M3
Amadjuak (lake) L3
Amund Ringnes (isl.) ..J2
Amundsen (gulf) F2
Anderson (riv.) F3
Arctic Red (riv.) E3
Artillery (lake) H3
Auyuittuq Nat'l Park ..M3
Axel Heiberg (isl.) J2
Aylmer (lake) H3
Back (riv.) J3
Baffin (bay) M2
Baffin (isl.) L2
Baker (lake) J3
Banks (isl.) F2
Barbeau (peak) L1
Barrow (str.) J2
Bathurst (cape) F2
Bathurst (inlet) H3
Bathurst (isl.) H2
Beaufort (sea) D2
Bellot (str.) K3
Boothia (gulf) K2
Boothia (pen.) G2
Borden (isl.) G2
Borden (pen.) K2
Brodeur (pen.) L2
Bruce (mts.) L2
Buchan (gulf) L2
Burnside (riv.) G3
Byam Martin (chan.) ..H2
Byam Martin (isl.) H2
Bylot (isl.) L2
Camsell (riv.) G3
Challenger (mts.) L1
Chantrey (inlet) J3
Chesterfield (inlet) ...J3
Chidley (cape) M3
Clinton-Colden (lake) ..H3
Clyde (inlet) M2
Coats (isl.) K3
Coburg (isl.) L2
Columbia (cape) M1
Colville (lake) F3
Committee (bay) K3
Contwoyto (lake) H3
Coppermine (riv.) G3
Cornwall (isl.) J2
Cornwallis (isl.) J2
Coronation (gulf) G3
Croker (isl.) K2
Crown Prince Frederik .K3
Cumberland (pen.) M3
Cumberland (sound) ..E2
Dalhousie (cape) E2
Davis (str.) M3
Dease (str.) H3

Denmark (bay) H2
Devon (isl.) K2
Dolphin and Union (str.) .G3
Dubawnt (lake) H3
Dubawnt (riv.) H3
Dundas (pen.) M3
Dyer (cape) L2
Eclipse (sound) F2
Eglinton (isl.) F2
Ellef Ringnes (isl.) ...H2
Ellesmere (isl.) K2
Ennadai (lake) H3
Eskimo (lakes) E3
Eureka (sound) K2
Evans (str.) K3
Exeter (sound) M3
Fisher (str.) K3
Fosheim (pen.) K1
Foxe (basin) L3
Foxe (chan.) K3
Foxe (pen.) L3
Franklin (bay) F2
Franklin (mts.) F3
Franklin (str.) J2
Frobisher (bay) M3
Frozen (str.) K3
Fury and Hecla (str.) .K3
Gabriel (str.) M3
Garry (lake) J3
Gods Mercy (bay) K3
Great Bear (lake) F3
Great Bear (riv.) F3
Great Slave (lake) ...G3
Greely (fjord) K1
Grinnell (pen.) H2
Hadley (bay) G3
Hall (basin) M1
Hall (pen.) M3
Hayes (riv.) J3
Hazen (lake) L1
Hazen (str.) G2
Henik (lakes) J3
Henry Kater (cape) ...M3
Home (bay) M3
Hood (riv.) G3
Horn (mts.) G3
Hornaday (riv.) F3
Horton (riv.) F3
Hottah (lake) G3
Hudson (bay) K3
Hudson (str.) L3
Isachsen (cape) H2
James Ross (str.) J3
Jenny Lind (isl.) H3
Jens Munk (isl.) K3
Jones (sound) K2
Kaminuriak (lake) J3
Kane (basin) K3
Kasba (lake) H3
Kazan (riv.) J3
Keele (riv.) F3
Keith Arm (inlet) F2
Kellett (cape) G2
Kellett (str.) M1
Kennedy (chan.) H3
Kent (pen.) H3
King Christian (isl.) ..H2
King William (isl.) ...J3
Lady Ann (str.) K2
La Martre (lake) G3
Lancaster (sound) K2
Lands End (cape) F2
Larsen (sound) J2
Liard (riv.) F4
Lincoln (sea) M1
Liverpool (bay) E2
Lockhart (riv.) H3

Lougheed (isl.) H2
Lyon (inlet) K3
MacKay (lake) G3
Mackenzie (bay) E3
Mackenzie (mts.) F3
Mackenzie (riv.) F3
Mackenzie King (isl.) .F3
Macmillan (pass) F3
Maguse (lake) J3
Makinson (inlet) L2
Mansel (isl.) K3
Marian (lake) G3
Markham (lake) L1
McLeod (bay) H3
M'Clintock (chan.) ...H2
M'Clure (str.) F2
McTavish Arm (inlet) .G3
Meighen (isl.) H1
Melville (isl.) G2
Melville (pen.) K3
Mercy (cape) M3
Mills (lake) G3
Minto (inlet) G2
Mistake (bay) J3
Nahanni Nat'l Park ...F3
Nansen (sound) J1
Nares (str.) K2
Navy Board (inlet) ...K2
Nelson Head (prom.) ..F2
Nettiling (lake) L3

Nonacho (lake) H3
North Arm (inlet) G3
North Magnetic Pole ..H2
Norwegian (bay) J2
Nottingham (isl.) L3
Nueltin (lake) H3
Ommanney (bay) J3
Padloping (isl.) M3
Parry (bay) K3
Parry (chan.) G2
Parry (isls.) G2
Parry (chan.) F2
Peary (chan.) H2
Peel (sound) J2
Pelly (bay) J3
Penny (str.) J2
Point (lake) G3
Pond (inlet) L2
Prince Albert (pen.) ..G2
Prince Albert (sound) .G2
Prince Charles (isl.) ..L3
Prince Gustav Adolf (sea) .H2
Prince of Wales (isl.) .J2
Prince of Wales (str.) .G2
Prince Patrick (isl.) ..F2
Prince Regent (inlet) ..K3
Queen Elizabeth (isls.) .H1
Queen Maud (gulf) ...H3
Queens (chan.) J2
Raanes (pen.) K2

Topography

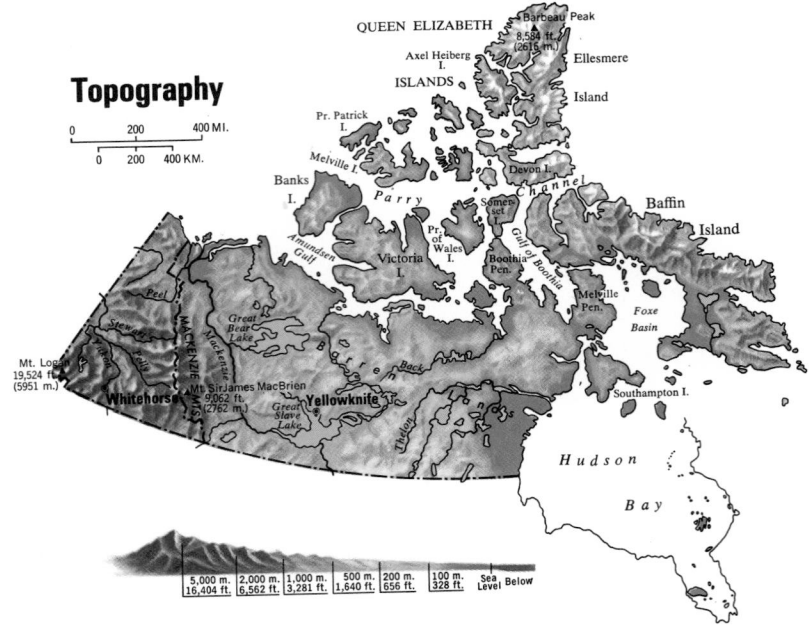

5,000 m. 16,404 ft. | 2,000 m. 6,562 ft. | 1,000 m. 3,281 ft. | 500 m. 1,640 ft. | 200 m. 656 ft. | 100 m. 328 ft. | Sea Level | Below

Agriculture, Industry and Resources

DOMINANT LAND USE

Forests

Nonagricultural Land

MAJOR MINERAL OCCURRENCES

Ab Asbestos   G Natural Gas
Ag Silver   O Petroleum
Au Gold   Pb Lead
C Coal   W Tungsten
Cu Copper   Zn Zinc
Fe Iron Ore

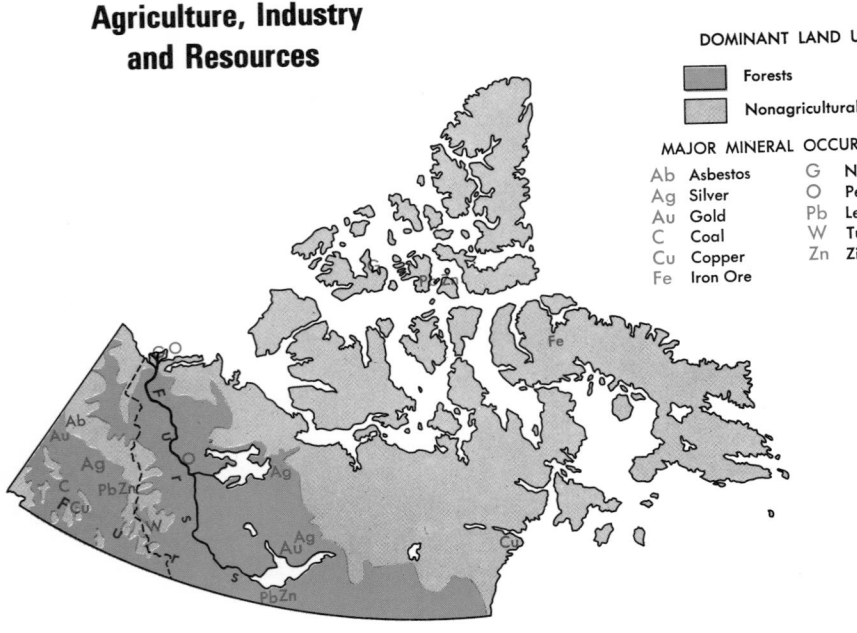

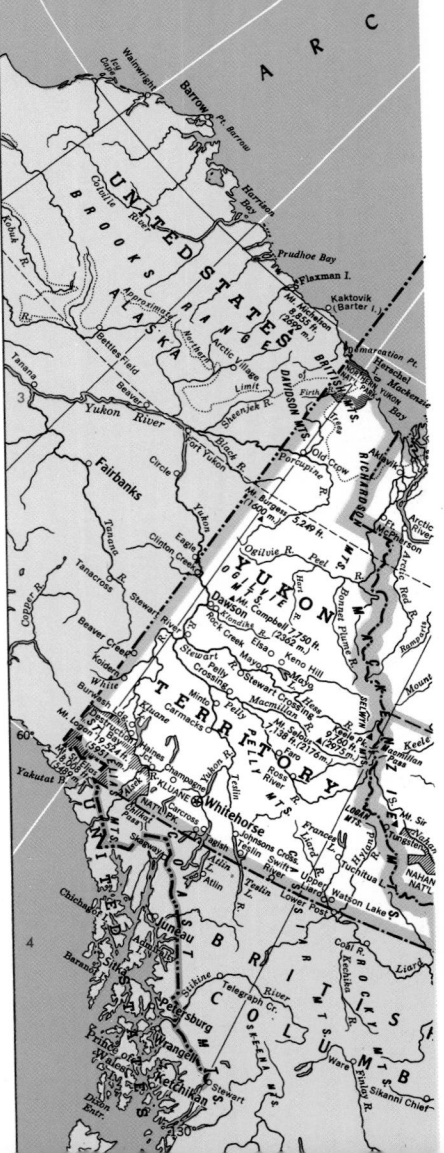

Rae (isth.)	K3
Rae (riv.)	G3
Rae (str.)	J3
Ramparts (riv.)	E3
Resolution (isl.)	M3
Richard Collinson (inlet)	G2
Richards (isl.)	E3
Richardson (mts.)	E3
Robeson (chan.)	M1
Roes Welcome (sound)	K3
Rowley (isl.)	K3
Royal Geographical Society (isls.)	J3
Russell (isl.)	J2
Sabine (pen.)	H2
Salisbury (isl.)	L3
Seahorse (pt.)	L3
Selwyn (lake)	H4
Sherman (inlet)	J3
Simpson (pen.)	K3
Sir James MacBrien (mt.)	F3
Slave (riv.)	G3
Smith (bay)	L2
Smith (cape)	L3
Smith (sound)	L2
Snare (riv.)	G3
Snowbird (lake)	H3
Somerset (isl.)	J2
South (bay)	K3
Southampton (isl.)	K3
South Nahanni (riv.)	F3
Stallworthy (cape)	J1
Steensby (inlet)	L2
Stefansson (isl.)	H2

Sverdrup (chan.)	J1
Sverdrup (isls.)	J2
Talbot (inlet)	L2
Taltson (riv.)	G3
Tathlina (lake)	G3
Tha-anne (riv.)	J3
Thelon (riv.)	H3
Thlewiaza (riv.)	J3
Trout (lake)	F3
Ungava (bay)	M4
Vansittart (isl.)	K3
Victoria (isl.)	G2
Victoria (str.)	H3
Viscount Melville (sound)	G2
Wager (bay)	K3
Wales (isl.)	K3
Walsingham (cape)	M3
Wellington (chan.)	J2
Wholdaia (lake)	H3
Winter (harb.)	H2
Wollaston (pen.)	F3
Wood Buffalo Nat'l Park	G3
Wynniatt (bay)	G2
Yathkyed (lake)	J3
Yellowknife (riv.)	G3

YUKON TERRITORY

CITIES and TOWNS

Beaver Creek 90	D3
Burwash Landing 73	D3
Carcross 216	E3
Carmacks •256	E3

Champagne	E3
Clinton Creek	D3
Cowley	E3
Dawson 697	D3
Destruction Bay 45	E3
Elsa 336	E3
Faro 1,652	E3
Haines Junction •366	E3
Johnson's Crossing 13	E3
Keno Hill 88	E3
Koidern	D3
Mayo 398	E3
Minto	E3

Old Crow 243	E3
Pelly Crossing 182	E3
Rock Creek 59	E3
Ross River 294	E3
Stewart Crossing 20	E3
Stewart River	D3
Swift River 24	E3
Tagish 89	E3
Teslin •310	E3
Tuchitua Lake	F3
Upper Liard 130	F3
Watson Lake •748	E3
Whitehorse (cap.) 14,814	E3

OTHER FEATURES

Alsek (riv.)	E3
Bonnet Plume (riv.)	E3
British (mts.)	D3
Campbell (mt.)	E3
Cassiar (mts.)	E3
Frances (lake)	E3
Herschel (isl.)	E3
Hess (riv.)	E3
Hyland (riv.)	F3
Keele (peak)	E3
Klondike (riv.)	E3
Kluane (lake)	E3

Kluane Nat'l Park	E3
Liard (riv.)	F3
Logan (mt.)	D3
Logan (mts.)	F3
Mackenzie (mts.)	E3
Macmillan (riv.)	E3
Mayo (lake)	E3
Northern Yukon Nat'l Pk.	E3
Ogilvie (mts.)	E3
Ogilvie (riv.)	E3
Peel (riv.)	E3
Pelly (mts.)	E3
Pelly (riv.)	E3

Porcupine (riv.)	E3
Richardson (mts.)	E3
Rocky (mts.)	F4
Saint Elias (mt.)	D3
Saint Elias (mts.)	E3
Selous (mt.)	E3
Selwyn (mts.)	E3
Stewart (riv.)	E3
Teslin (lake)	E4
Teslin (riv.)	E3
White (riv.)	D3
Yukon (riv.)	E3

• Population of district.

YUKON TERRITORY

AREA 207,075 sq. mi.
(536,324 sq. km.)
POPULATION 23,153
CAPITAL Whitehorse
LARGEST CITY Whitehorse
HIGHEST POINT Mt. Logan 19,524 ft.
(5,951 m.)
SETTLED IN 1897
ADMITTED TO CONFEDERATION 1898
PROVINCIAL FLOWER Fireweed

NORTHWEST TERRITORIES

AREA 1,304,896 sq. mi. (3,379,683 sq. km.)
POPULATION 45,741
CAPITAL Yellowknife
LARGEST CITY Yellowknife
HIGHEST POINT Mt. Sir James MacBrien
9,062 ft. (2,762 m.)
SETTLED IN 1800
ADMITTED TO CONFEDERATION 1870
PROVINCIAL FLOWER Mountain Avens

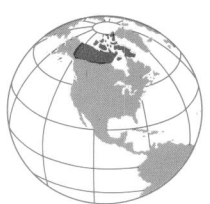

Yukon and Northwest Territories

SCALE
0 50 100 200 300 MI.
0 50 100 200 300 KM.

Territorial Capitals	⊛
Regional Capitals	⊛
International Boundaries	— ·· —
Provincial & Territorial Boundaries	— · —
Regional Boundaries	— — —

All islands in Hudson and James Bay lie within the Northwest Territories

© Copyright HAMMOND INCORPORATED, Maplewood, N.J.

United States

POLYCONIC PROJECTION

SCALE OF MILES

SCALE OF KILOMETERS

Capitals of Countries .... ☆
State Capitals .... △
International Boundaries ....

© Copyright HAMMOND INCORPORATED, Maplewood, N.J.

AREA 3,623,420 sq. mi.
(9,384,658 sq. km.)
POPULATION 226,504,825
CAPITAL Washington
LARGEST CITY New York
HIGHEST POINT Mt. McKinley 20,320 ft.
(6,194 m.)
MONETARY UNIT U.S. dollar
MAJOR LANGUAGE English
MAJOR RELIGIONS Protestantism,
Roman Catholicism, Judaism

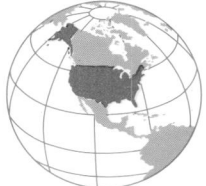

Population Distribution

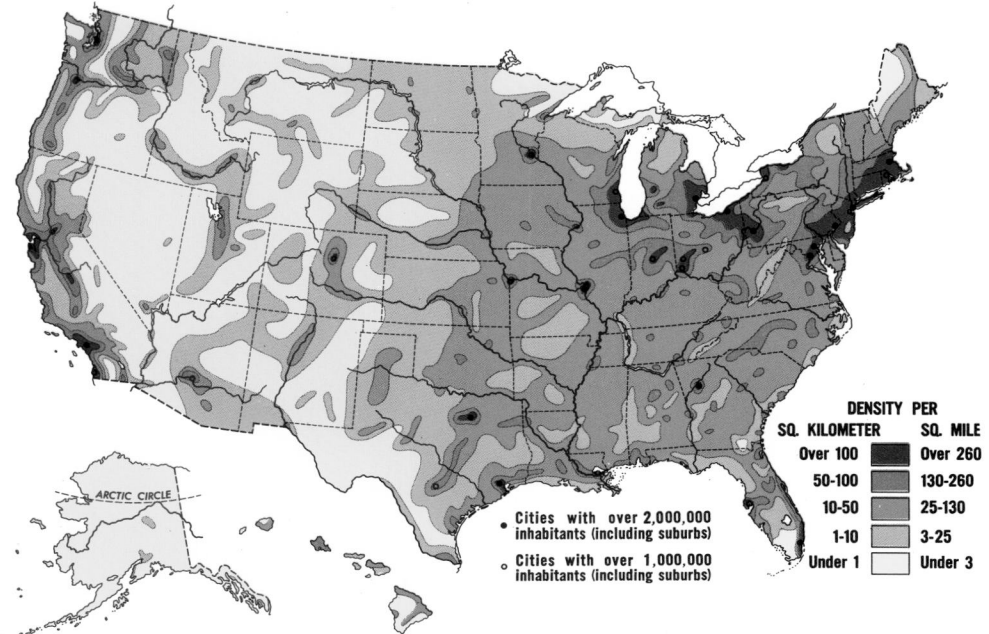

DENSITY PER

SQ. KILOMETER	SQ. MILE
Over 100	Over 260
50-100	130-260
10-50	25-130
1-10	3-25
Under 1	Under 3

• Cities with over 2,000,000 inhabitants (including suburbs)

○ Cities with over 1,000,000 inhabitants (including suburbs)

ARCTIC CIRCLE

Vegetation

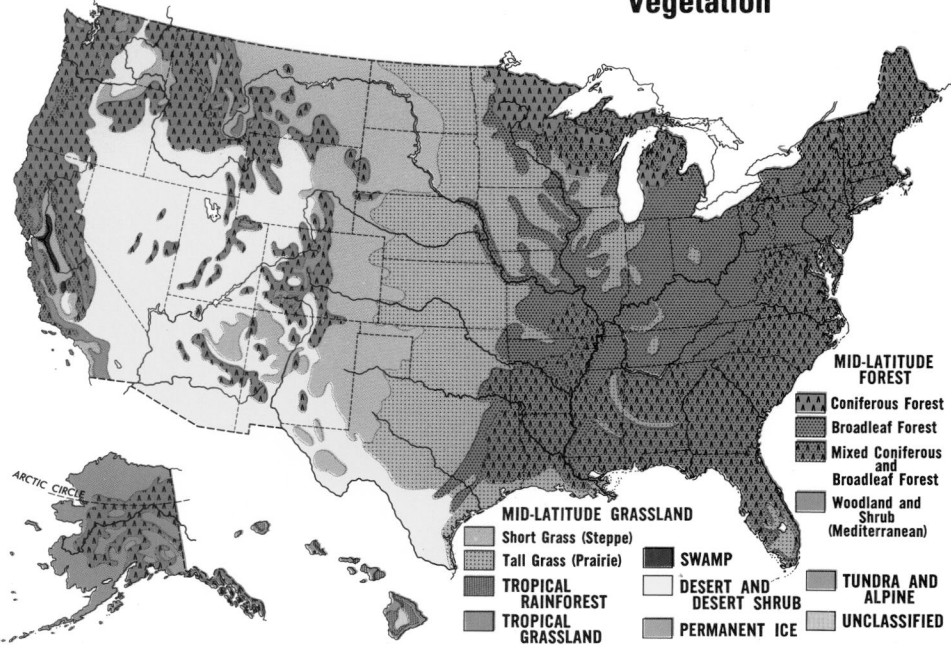

ARCTIC CIRCLE

MID-LATITUDE GRASSLAND

- Short Grass (Steppe)
- Tall Grass (Prairie)

TROPICAL RAINFOREST

TROPICAL GRASSLAND

- SWAMP
- DESERT AND DESERT SHRUB
- PERMANENT ICE

MID-LATITUDE FOREST

- Coniferous Forest
- Broadleaf Forest
- Mixed Coniferous and Broadleaf Forest
- Woodland and Shrub (Mediterranean)

TUNDRA AND ALPINE

UNCLASSIFIED

UNITED STATES

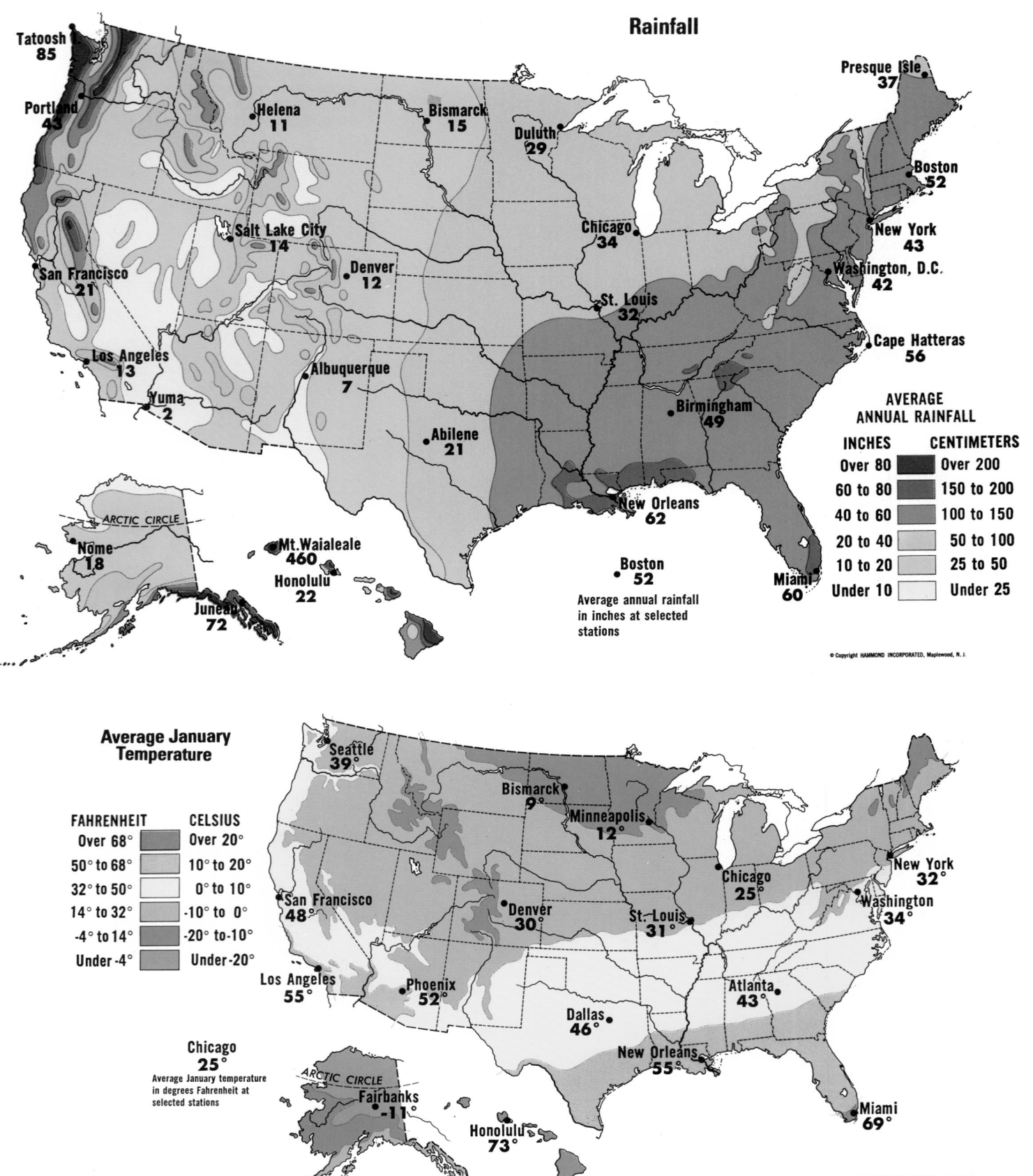

Rainfall

Tatoosh 85
Portland 43
Helena 11
Bismarck 15
Duluth 29
Presque Isle 37
Boston 52
Chicago 34
New York 43
Washington, D.C. 42
Salt Lake City 14
Denver 12
San Francisco 21
St. Louis 32
Cape Hatteras 56
Los Angeles 13
Albuquerque 7
Yuma 2
Birmingham 49
Abilene 21
New Orleans 62
Miami 60
Nome 18
ARCTIC CIRCLE
Mt. Waialeale 460
Honolulu 22
Juneau 72
Boston 52

Average annual rainfall
in inches at selected
stations

**AVERAGE
ANNUAL RAINFALL**

INCHES	CENTIMETERS
Over 80	Over 200
60 to 80	150 to 200
40 to 60	100 to 150
20 to 40	50 to 100
10 to 20	25 to 50
Under 10	Under 25

© Copyright HAMMOND INCORPORATED, Maplewood, N.J.

Average January Temperature

FAHRENHEIT	CELSIUS
Over 68°	Over 20°
50° to 68°	10° to 20°
32° to 50°	0° to 10°
14° to 32°	-10° to 0°
-4° to 14°	-20° to -10°
Under -4°	Under -20°

Seattle 39°
Bismarck 9°
Minneapolis 12°
Chicago 25°
New York 32°
Washington 34°
San Francisco 48°
Denver 30°
St. Louis 31°
Los Angeles 55°
Phoenix 52°
Dallas 46°
Atlanta 43°
New Orleans 55°
Miami 69°

Chicago 25°

Average January temperature
in degrees Fahrenheit at
selected stations

ARCTIC CIRCLE
Fairbanks -11°
Honolulu 73°

© Copyright HAMMOND INCORPORATED, Maplewood, N.J.

Topography

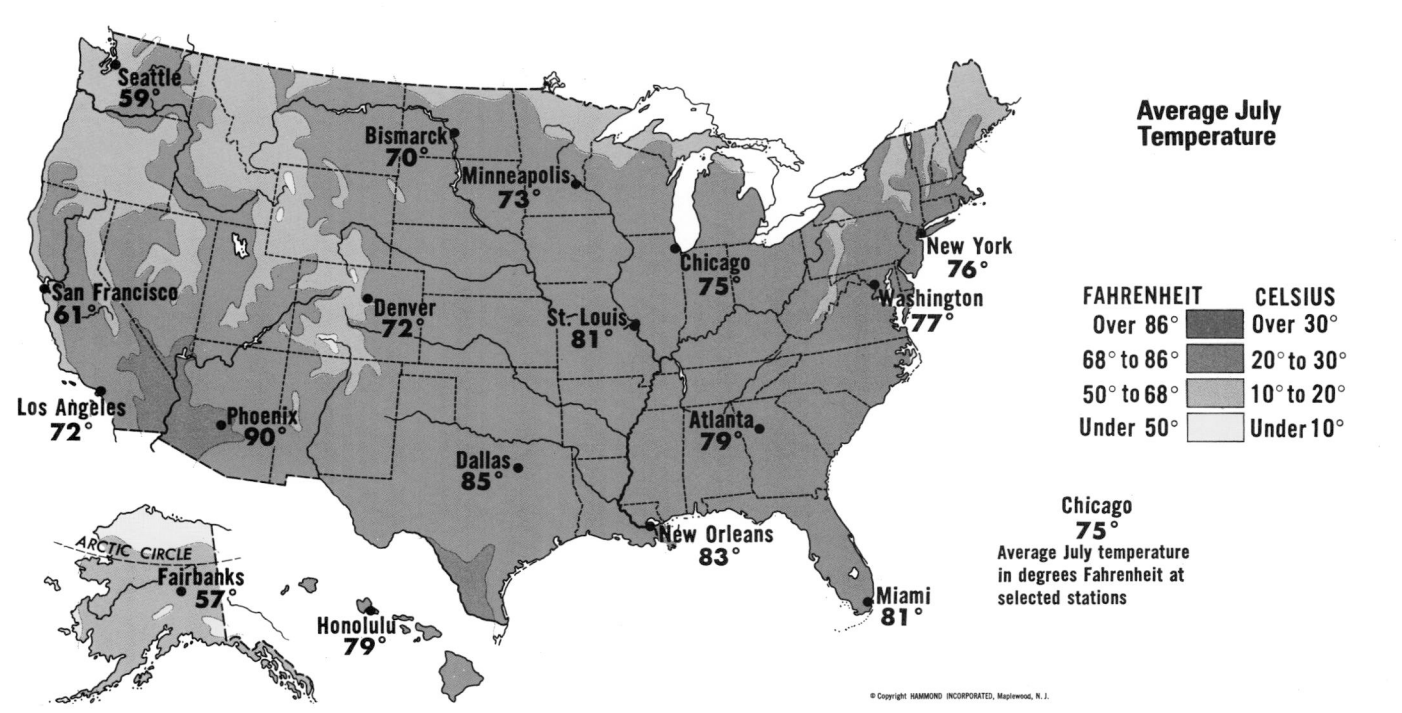

Average July Temperature

FAHRENHEIT	CELSIUS
Over 86°	Over 30°
68° to 86°	20° to 30°
50° to 68°	10° to 20°
Under 50°	Under 10°

Chicago
75°
Average July temperature
in degrees Fahrenheit at
selected stations

© Copyright HAMMOND INCORPORATED, Maplewood, N.J.

United States Standard Time Zones

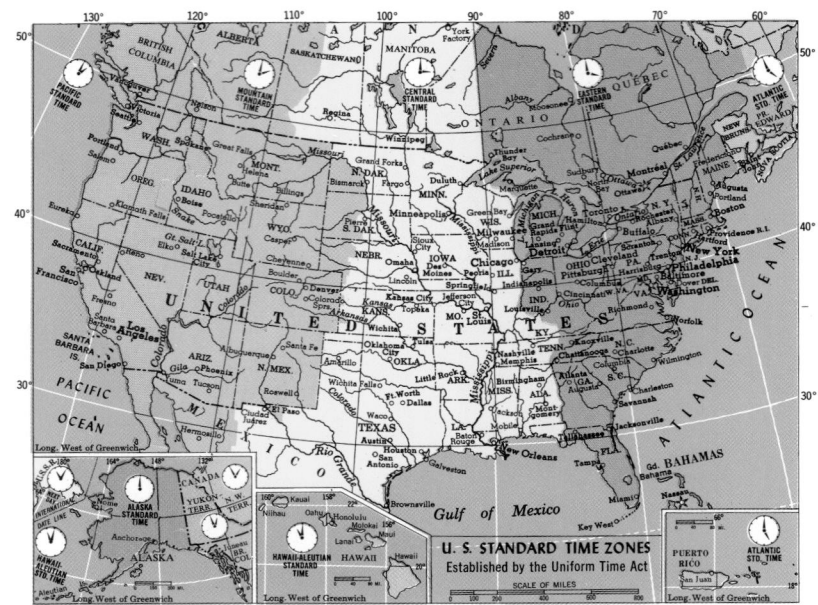

Agriculture, Industry and Resources

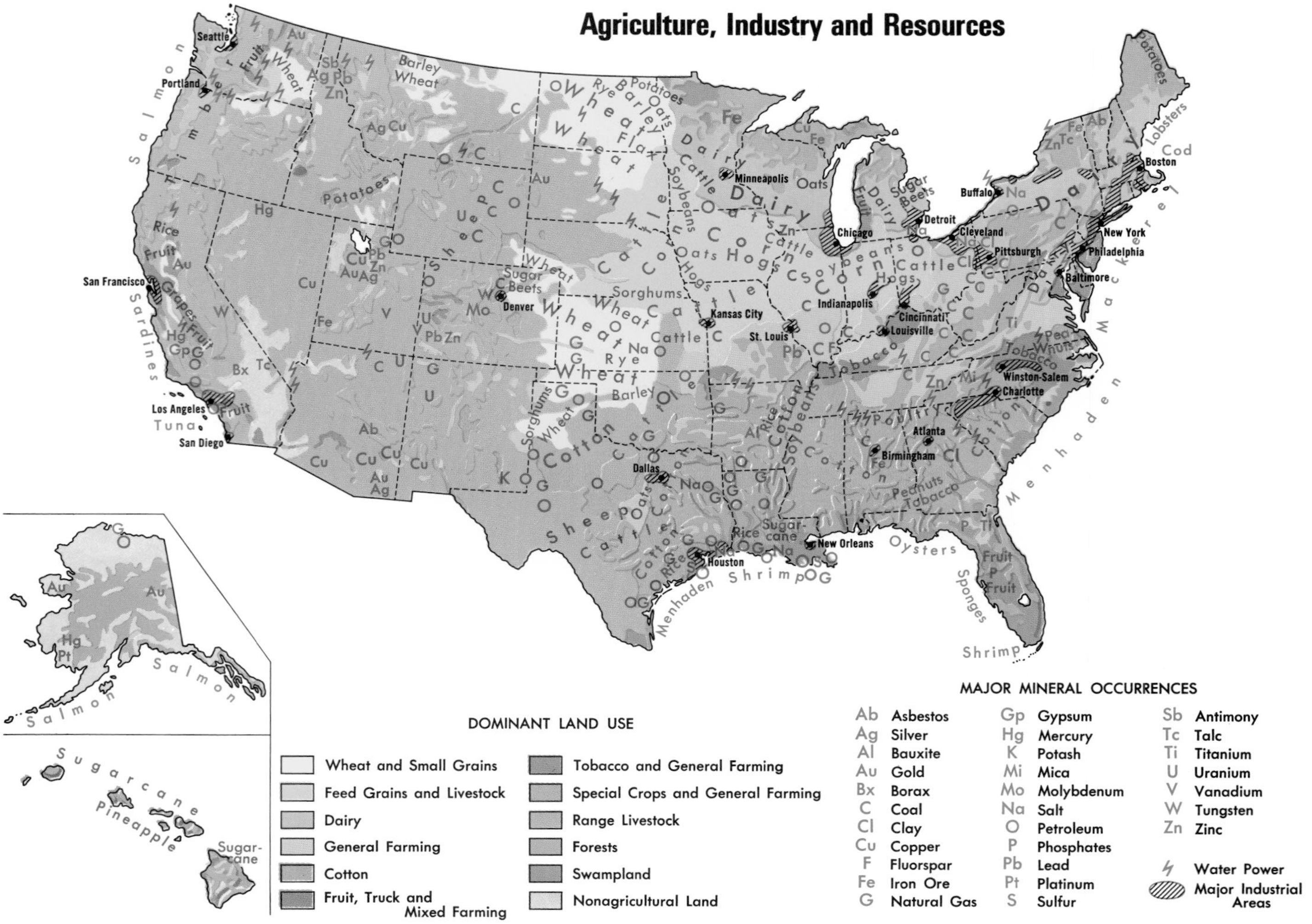

DOMINANT LAND USE

- Wheat and Small Grains
- Feed Grains and Livestock
- Dairy
- General Farming
- Cotton
- Fruit, Truck and Mixed Farming
- Tobacco and General Farming
- Special Crops and General Farming
- Range Livestock
- Forests
- Swampland
- Nonagricultural Land

MAJOR MINERAL OCCURRENCES

Ab	Asbestos	Gp	Gypsum
Ag	Silver	Hg	Mercury
Al	Bauxite	K	Potash
Au	Gold	Mi	Mica
Bx	Borax	Mo	Molybdenum
C	Coal	Na	Salt
Cl	Clay	O	Petroleum
Cu	Copper	P	Phosphates
F	Fluorspar	Pb	Lead
Fe	Iron Ore	Pt	Platinum
G	Natural Gas	S	Sulfur

Sb	Antimony
Tc	Talc
Ti	Titanium
U	Uranium
V	Vanadium
W	Tungsten
Zn	Zinc

⚡ Water Power
▨ Major Industrial Areas

AREA 51,705 sq. mi. (133,916 sq. km.)
POPULATION 3,893,888
CAPITAL Montgomery
LARGEST CITY Birmingham
HIGHEST POINT Cheaha Mtn. 2,407 ft. (734 m.)
SETTLED IN 1702
ADMITTED TO UNION December 14, 1819
POPULAR NAME Heart of Dixie; Cotton State; Yellowhammer State
STATE FLOWER Camellia
STATE BIRD Yellowhammer

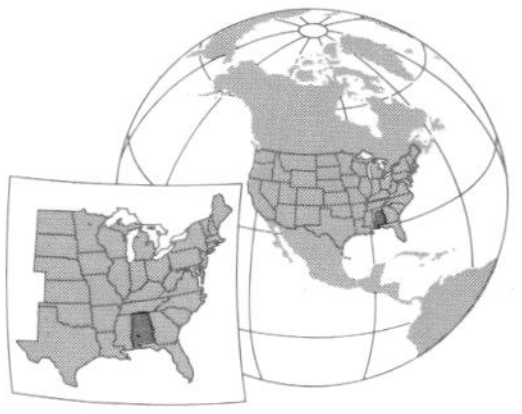

COUNTIES

Autauga 32,259 ..... E5
Baldwin 78,556 ..... C9
Barbour 24,756 ..... H7
Bibb 15,723 ..... D5
Blount 36,459 ..... E2
Bullock 10,596 ..... G6
Butler 21,680 ..... E7
Calhoun 119,761 ..... G3
Chambers 39,191 ..... H5
Cherokee 18,760 ..... G2
Chilton 30,612 ..... E5
Choctaw 16,839 ..... B6
Clarke 27,702 ..... C7
Clay 13,703 ..... G4
Cleburne 12,595 ..... G3
Coffee 38,533 ..... G8
Colbert 54,519 ..... C1
Conecuh 15,884 ..... E8
Coosa 11,377 ..... F5
Covington 36,850 ..... F8
Crenshaw 14,110 ..... F7
Cullman 61,642 ..... E2
Dale 47,821 ..... G8
Dallas 53,981 ..... D6
De Kalb 53,658 ..... G2
Elmore 43,390 ..... F5
Escambia 38,440 ..... D8
Etowah 103,057 ..... F2
Fayette 18,809 ..... C3
Franklin 28,350 ..... C2
Geneva 24,253 ..... G8
Greene 11,021 ..... C5
Hale 15,604 ..... C5
Henry 15,302 ..... H7
Houston 74,632 ..... H8
Jackson 51,407 ..... F1
Jefferson 671,324 ..... E3
Lamar 16,453 ..... B3
Lauderdale 80,546 ..... C1
Lawrence 30,170 ..... D1
Lee 76,283 ..... H5
Limestone 46,005 ..... E1
Lowndes 13,253 ..... E6
Macon 26,829 ..... G6
Madison 196,966 ..... E1
Marengo 25,047 ..... C6
Marion 30,041 ..... C2
Marshall 65,622 ..... F2
Mobile 364,980 ..... B9
Monroe 22,651 ..... D7
Montgomery 197,038 ..... F6
Morgan 90,231 ..... E2
Perry 15,012 ..... D5
Pickens 21,481 ..... B4
Pike 28,050 ..... G7
Randolph 20,075 ..... H4
Russell 47,356 ..... H6
Saint Clair 41,205 ..... F3
Shelby 66,298 ..... E4
Sumter 16,908 ..... B5
Talladega 73,826 ..... F4
Tallapoosa 38,676 ..... G5
Tuscaloosa 137,541 ..... C4
Walker 68,660 ..... D3
Washington 16,821 ..... B8
Wilcox 14,755 ..... D7
Winston 21,953 ..... D2

CITIES and TOWNS

Zip *Name/Pop.* *Key*

36310 Abbeville⊙ 3,155 ..... H7
35440 Abernant 405 ..... D4
35005 Adamsville 2,498 ..... D3
35540 Addison 746 ..... D2
35006 Adger 400 ..... D4
35441 Akron 604 ..... C5
35007 Alabaster 7,079 ..... E4
35950 Albertville 12,039 ..... F2
†35115 Aldrich 500 ..... E4
35010 Alexander City 13,807 ..... G5
36250 Alexandria 600 ..... G3
35442 Aliceville 3,207 ..... B4
35013 Allgood 387 ..... F3
36501 Alma 500 ..... C8
35952 Altoona 928 ..... F2
36420 Andalusia⊙ 10,415 ..... E8
35610 Anderson 405 ..... D1
36201 Anniston⊙ 29,523 ..... G3
Anniston‡ 116,936 ..... G3
35016 Arab 5,967 ..... E2
35805 Ardmore 1,096 ..... E1
†35173 Argo 600 ..... E3
36311 Ariton 844 ..... G7
35033 Arkadelphia 150 ..... E3
35541 Arley 276 ..... D2
†35035 Ashby 500 ..... E4
36312 Ashford 2,165 ..... H8
36251 Ashland⊙ 2,052 ..... G4
35953 Ashville⊙ 1,489 ..... F3
35611 Athens⊙ 14,558 ..... E1
36503 Atmore 8,789 ..... C8
35954 Attalla 7,737 ..... F2
36830 Auburn 28,471 ..... H5
36003 Autaugaville 843 ..... E6
†36312 Avon 433 ..... H8
36505 Axis 500 ..... B9
†36420 Babbie 553 ..... F8
35019 Baileyton 396 ..... E2
36005 Banks 160 ..... G7
†36532 Barnwell 700 ..... C10
36507 Bay Minette⊙ 7,455 ..... C9
36509 Bayou La Batre 2,005 ..... B10
35543 Bear Creek 353 ..... C2
36425 Beatrice 558 ..... D7
35544 Beaverton 360 ..... B3
†35653 Belgreen 500 ..... C2
35545 Belk 308 ..... C3
36901 Bellamy 700 ..... B6
35615 Belle Mina 675 ..... E1
36313 Bellwood 400 ..... G8
36785 Benton 74 ..... E6
35546 Berry 916 ..... C3
35020 Bessemer 31,729 ..... D4
†36872 Beulah 500 ..... H5
36006 Billingsley 106 ..... E5
*35201 Birmingham⊙ 284,413 ..... D3
Birmingham‡ 847,360 ..... D3
36314 Black 156 ..... G8
35031 Blountsville 1,509 ..... E2
36201 Blue Mountain 284 ..... G3
†36017 Blue Springs 112 ..... G7
35957 Boaz 7,151 ..... F2
35443 Boligee 164 ..... C5
35032 Bon Air 118 ..... F4
36511 Bon Secour 850 ..... C10
†35120 Branchville 365 ..... F3
36009 Brantley 1,151 ..... F7
35034 Brent 2,862 ..... D5
36426 Brewton⊙ 6,680 ..... D8
35740 Bridgeport 2,974 ..... G1
35020 Brighton 5,308 ..... D4
35548 Brilliant 871 ..... C2
35036 Brookside 1,409 ..... E3
35444 Brookwood 492 ..... D4
36010 Brundidge 3,213 ..... G7
36725 Burkville 250 ..... E6
36431 Burnt Corn 60 ..... D7
36904 Butler⊙ 1,882 ..... B6
†36767 Cahaba 75 ..... D6
35040 Calera 2,035 ..... E4
†36047 Calhoun 950 ..... F6
36513 Calvert 600 ..... B8
36726 Camden⊙ 2,406 ..... D7
36850 Camp Hill 1,628 ..... G5
†36502 Canoe 560 ..... D8
†36726 Canton Bend 300 ..... D6
35549 Carbon Hill 2,452 ..... D3
35041 Cardiff 140 ..... E3
†36420 Carolina 203 ..... E8
35447 Carrollton⊙ 1,104 ..... B4
†36023 Carrville 820 ..... G5
†36548 Carson 400 ..... C8
36432 Castleberry 847 ..... D8
35959 Cedar Bluff 1,129 ..... G2
35960 Centre⊙ 2,351 ..... G2
35042 Centreville⊙ 2,504 ..... D5
36518 Chatom⊙ 1,122 ..... B8
35043 Chelsea 600 ..... E4
35616 Cherokee 1,589 ..... C1
36611 Chickasaw 7,402 ..... B9
35044 Childersburg 5,084 ..... F4
36254 Choccolocco 500 ..... G3
36905 Choctaw 600 ..... B6
†36550 Chrysler 400 ..... C8
36521 Chunchula 700 ..... B9
36522 Citronelle 2,841 ..... B8
35045 Clanton⊙ 5,832 ..... E5
†36322 Clayhatchee 560 ..... G8
36015 Clayton⊙ 1,589 ..... G7
35049 Cleveland 487 ..... E3
36017 Clio 1,224 ..... G7
35449 Coaling 400 ..... D4
36523 Coden 600 ..... B10
36318 Coffee Springs 339 ..... G8
36524 Coffeeville 448 ..... B7
35452 Coker 800 ..... C4
35961 Collinsville 1,383 ..... G2
36319 Columbia 881 ..... H8
35051 Columbiana⊙ 2,655 ..... E4
36020 Coosada 980 ..... F5
35550 Cordova 3,123 ..... D3
35453 Cottondale 500 ..... D4
36320 Cottonwood 1,352 ..... H8
†35172 County Line 199 ..... E3
†36467 County Line 124 ..... F8
35618 Courtland 456 ..... D1
36321 Cowarts 418 ..... H8
36435 Coy 950 ..... D7
36525 Creola 1,652 ..... B9
36906 Cromwell 650 ..... B6
35962 Crossville 1,222 ..... G2
36907 Cuba 486 ..... B6
35055 Cullman⊙ 13,084 ..... E2
36852 Cusseta 650 ..... H5
36853 Dadeville⊙ 3,263 ..... G5
36322 Daleville 4,250 ..... G8
36526 Daphne 3,406 ..... C9
36528 Dauphin Island 950 ..... B10
36256 Daviston 334 ..... G4
36731 Dayton 113 ..... C6
*35601 Decatur⊙ 42,002 ..... D1
36257 De Armanville 350 ..... G3
36732 Demopolis 7,678 ..... C6
35552 Detroit 326 ..... B2
35062 Dora 2,327 ..... D3
*36303 Dothan⊙ 48,750 ..... H8
35553 Double Springs⊙ 1,057 ..... D2
35964 Douglas 116 ..... F2
36028 Dozier 494 ..... F7
35744 Dutton 276 ..... G1
36426 East Brewton 3,012 ..... E8
36024 Eclectic 1,124 ..... F5
36261 Edwardsville 207 ..... H3
36323 Elba⊙ 4,355 ..... F8
36530 Elberta 491 ..... C10
35554 Eldridge 230 ..... C3
35620 Elkmont 429 ..... E1
36025 Elmore 600 ..... F5
35458 Elrod 746 ..... C4
35063 Empire 600 ..... D3
36330 Enterprise 18,033 ..... G8
35460 Epes 399 ..... B5
35461 Ethelsville 95 ..... B4
36027 Eufaula 12,097 ..... H7
†36340 Eunola 169 ..... G8
35462 Eutaw⊙ 2,444 ..... C5
35621 Eva 185 ..... E2
36401 Evergreen⊙ 4,171 ..... E8
36439 Excel 385 ..... D8
35746 Fackler 250 ..... G1
36854 Fairfax 3,776 ..... H5
35064 Fairfield 13,242 ..... E4
36532 Fairhope 7,286 ..... C10
35208 Fairview 450 ..... E2
35622 Falkville 1,310 ..... E2
36738 Faunsdale 174 ..... C6
35555 Fayette⊙ 5,287 ..... C3
36855 Five Points 197 ..... H4
35966 Flat Rock 750 ..... G1
†35601 Flint City 673 ..... D1
36441 Flomaton 1,882 ..... D8
36442 Florala 2,165 ..... F8
*35630 Florence⊙ 37,029 ..... C1
Florence‡ 135,023 ..... C1
36535 Foley 4,003 ..... C10
35214 Forestdale 10,814 ..... E3
36740 Forkland 429 ..... C5
36031 Fort Davis 500 ..... G6
36032 Fort Deposit 1,519 ..... E7
36856 Fort Mitchell 900 ..... H6
35967 Fort Payne⊙ 11,485 ..... G2
35463 Fosters 400 ..... C4
36444 Franklin 133 ..... G6
36445 Frisco City 1,424 ..... D8
36539 Fruitdale 500 ..... B8
36262 Fruithurst 239 ..... G3
36446 Fulton 606 ..... C7
35068 Fultondale 6,217 ..... E3
35971 Fyffe 1,305 ..... G2
*35901 Gadsden⊙ 47,565 ..... G2
Gadsden‡ 103,057 ..... G2
35464 Gainesville 207 ..... B5
35972 Gallant 475 ..... F2
36038 Gantt 314 ..... E8
35070 Garden City 655 ..... E2
35071 Gardendale 7,928 ..... E3
35973 Gaylesville 192 ..... G2
†35459 Geiger 200 ..... B5
36340 Geneva⊙ 4,866 ..... G8
36033 Georgiana 1,993 ..... E7
35974 Geraldine 911 ..... G2
36908 Gilbertown 218 ..... B7
35559 Glen Allen 312 ..... C3
35905 Glencoe 4,648 ..... G3
36034 Glenwood 341 ..... F7
†35010 Goldville 89 ..... G4
†36024 Good Hope 1,442 ..... E2
35072 Goodwater 1,895 ..... F4
35466 Gordo 2,112 ..... C4
36343 Gordon 362 ..... H8
†35580 Gorgas 500 ..... D3
36035 Goshen 365 ..... F7
†36482 Gosport 500 ..... C7
36541 Grand Bay 3,185 ..... B10
35747 Grant 632 ..... F1
35073 Graysville 2,642 ..... D3
35074 Green Pond 750 ..... D4
36744 Greensboro⊙ 3,248 ..... C5
36037 Greenville⊙ 7,807 ..... E7
†36350 Grimes 298 ..... H8
36451 Grove Hill⊙ 1,912 ..... C7
35563 Guin 2,418 ..... C3
36542 Gulf Shores 1,349 ..... C10
35976 Guntersville⊙ 7,041 ..... F2
35748 Gurley 735 ..... F1
†35563 Gu-Win 266 ..... C3
35564 Hackleburg 883 ..... C2
†36319 Haleburg 106 ..... H8
35565 Haleyville 5,306 ..... C2

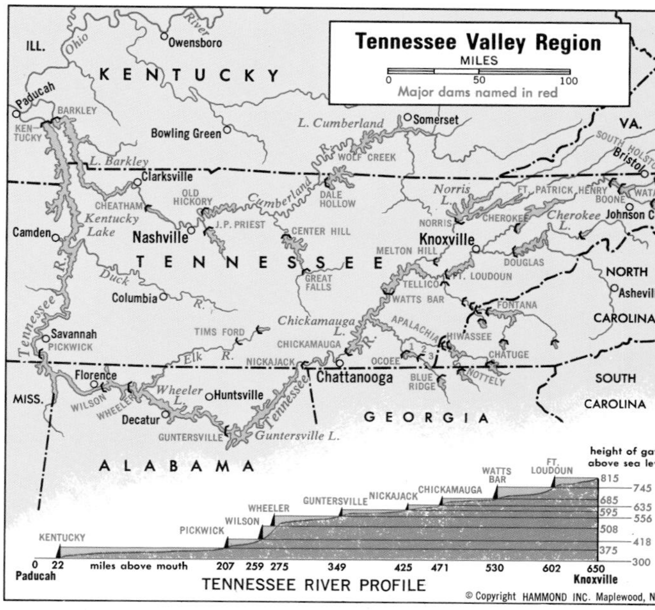
Tennessee Valley Region
MILES
0 50 100
Major dams named in red
ILL.
KENTUCKY
Owensboro
Ohio
Paducah
BARKLEY
KENTUCKY
Bowling Green
L. Cumberland
Somerset
VA.
Bristol
L. Barkley
Clarksville
WOLF CREEK
Norris L.
FT. PATRICK HENRY
BOONE
WATAUGA
Johnson City
CHEATHAM
OLD HICKORY
Cumberland
DALE HOLLOW
NORRIS
CHEROKEE
Cherokee L.
Camden
Kentucky Lake
Nashville
J.P. PRIEST
CENTER HILL
Knoxville
MELTON HILL
TENNESSEE
DOUGLAS
NORTH
Duck
GREAT FALLS
FT. LOUDOUN
Asheville
Columbia
TELLICO
WATTS BAR
FONTANA
CAROLINA
Chickamauga L.
Savannah
PICKWICK
TIMS FORD
CHICKAMAUGA
HIWASSEE
Elk R.
NICKAJACK
OCOEE
CHATUGE
Florence
Wheeler L.
Huntsville
Chattanooga
BLUE RIDGE
NOTTELY
SOUTH
CAROLINA
MISS.
WILSON
WHEELER
Decatur
GUNTERSVILLE
Guntersville L.
GEORGIA
ALABAMA
height of gates above sea level
KENTUCKY
PICKWICK
WILSON
WHEELER
GUNTERSVILLE
NICKAJACK
CHICKAMAUGA
WATTS BAR
FT. LOUDOUN
815
745
685
635
595
556
508
418
375
300
0 22 miles above mouth 207 259 275 349 425 471 530 602 650
Paducah
Knoxville
TENNESSEE RIVER PROFILE

35570 Hamilton⊙ 5,093 ..... C2
†35989 Hammondville 369 ..... G1
35077 Hanceville 2,220 ..... E2
36039 Hardaway 600 ..... G6
35078 Harpersville 934 ..... F4
36344 Hartford 2,647 ..... G8
35640 Hartselle 8,858 ..... E2
36858 Hatchechubbee 840 ..... H6
†35672 Hatton 950 ..... D1
35079 Hayden 268 ..... E3
36040 Hayneville⊙ 592 ..... E6
35750 Hazel Green 1,503 ..... E1
36345 Headland 3,327 ..... H8
†36558 Healing Springs 100 ..... B7
†36420 Heath 354 ..... F8
36264 Heflin⊙ 3,014 ..... G3
35080 Helena 2,130 ..... E4
35978 Henagar 1,188 ..... G1
35979 Higdon 925 ..... G1
†35013 Highland Lake 210 ..... F3
35643 Hillsboro 278 ..... D1
†36201 Hobson City 1,268 ..... G3
35571 Hodges 250 ..... C2
35903 Hokes Bluff 3,216 ..... G3
35082 Hollins 500 ..... F4
35083 Holly Pond 493 ..... E2
35752 Hollywood 1,110 ..... G1
35209 Homewood 21,412 ..... E4
†35216 Hoover 19,792 ..... E4
36043 Hope Hull 975 ..... F6
†36467 Horn Hill 186 ..... F8
35020 Hueytown 13,478 ..... D4
*35801 Huntsville⊙ 142,513 ..... E1
Huntsville‡ 308,593 ..... E1
36860 Hurtsboro 752 ..... H6
35981 Ider 698 ..... G1
35210 Irondale 6,510 ..... E3
36545 Jackson 6,073 ..... C8
36861 Jacksons Gap 800 ..... G5
36265 Jacksonville 9,735 ..... G3
35501 Jasper⊙ 11,894 ..... D3
35085 Jemison 1,828 ..... E5
35573 Kansas 267 ..... C3
35574 Kennedy 604 ..... B3
35645 Killen 747 ..... D1
35091 Kimberly 1,043 ..... E3
†36301 Kinsey 1,239 ..... H8
36453 Kinston 604 ..... F8
36862 Lafayette⊙ 3,647 ..... H5
†35986 Lakeview 441 ..... G2
36863 Lanett 6,897 ..... H5
36864 Langdale 2,034 ..... H5
†35768 Larkinsville 425 ..... F1
36911 Lavaca 500 ..... B6
35094 Leeds 8,638 ..... E3
35983 Leesburg 116 ..... G2
35646 Leighton 1,218 ..... D1
36548 Leroy 699 ..... B8
35647 Lester 117 ..... D1
†36322 Level Plains 867 ..... G8
35648 Lexington 884 ..... D1
†36420 Libertyville 141 ..... F8
35096 Lincoln 2,081 ..... F3
36748 Linden⊙ 2,773 ..... C6
36266 Lineville 2,257 ..... G4
35020 Lipscomb 3,741 ..... E4
36912 Lisman 638 ..... B6
†36876 Little Shawmut 2,793 ..... H5
†35653 Littleville 1,262 ..... C1
35470 Livingston⊙ 3,187 ..... B5
36865 Loachapoka 335 ..... G5
36455 Lockhart 547 ..... F8
35097 Locust Fork 488 ..... E3
†35137 Longview 475 ..... E4
36048 Louisville 791 ..... G7
36751 Lower Peach Tree 926 ..... C7
36752 Lowndesboro 207 ..... E6
36551 Loxley 804 ..... C9
36049 Luverne⊙ 2,639 ..... F7
35575 Lynn 554 ..... C2
35758 Madison 4,057 ..... E1
36348 Madrid 172 ..... H8
36555 Magnolia Springs 800 ..... C10
36349 Malvern 558 ..... G8
36750 Maplesville 754 ..... E5
35112 Margaret 757 ..... F3
36756 Marion⊙ 4,467 ..... D5
35114 Maylene 500 ..... E4
35111 McCalla 657 ..... E4
36552 McCullough 500 ..... D8
36553 McIntosh 319 ..... B8
36456 McKenzie 605 ..... E7
†35442 Memphis 95 ..... B4
35984 Mentone 476 ..... G1
35759 Meridianville 1,403 ..... F1
35228 Midfield 6,203 ..... E4
36350 Midland City 1,903 ..... H8
36053 Midway 593 ..... H6
†35150 Mignon 2,054 ..... F4
36054 Millbrook 3,101 ..... F6
35576 Millport 1,287 ..... B3
36558 Millry 956 ..... B7
36761 Minter 450 ..... D6
*36601 Mobile⊙ 200,452 ..... B9
Mobile‡ 442,819 ..... B9
36460 Monroeville⊙ 5,674 ..... D7
†35804 Monrovia 500 ..... E1
35115 Montevallo 3,965 ..... E4
*36101 Montgomery (cap.)⊙ 178,857 ..... F6
Montgomery‡ 272,687 ..... F3
36559 Montrose 750 ..... C9
†35125 Moody 1,840 ..... F3
35649 Mooresville 58 ..... E1
35116 Morris 623 ..... E3
35650 Moulton⊙ 3,197 ..... D2
35474 Moundville 1,310 ..... C5
†35957 Mountainboro 266 ..... F2
35223 Mountain Brook 19,718 ..... E4
36560 Mount Vernon 1,038 ..... B8
36268 Munford 700 ..... F3
35660 Muscle Shoals 8,911 ..... C1
36763 Myrtlewood 252 ..... C6
36764 Nanafalia 500 ..... B6
36303 Napier Field 493 ..... H8
35578 Nauvoo 259 ..... D3
†35049 Nectar 367 ..... E3
36765 Newbern 307 ..... C5
36351 New Brockton 1,392 ..... G8
35760 New Hope 1,546 ..... F1
35761 New Market 680 ..... F1
†35010 New Site 340 ..... G4
36352 Newton 1,540 ..... G8
36353 Newville 814 ..... H8
35086 North Johns 243 ..... D4
35476 Northport 14,291 ..... C4
36866 Notasulga 876 ..... G5
35006 Oak Grove 638 ..... F4
36766 Oak Hill 63 ..... D7
35579 Oakman 770 ..... D3
35120 Odenville 724 ..... F3
36271 Ohatchee 860 ..... G3
35121 Oneonta⊙ 4,824 ..... E3
†36467 Onycha 147 ..... F8
36801 Opelika⊙ 21,896 ..... H5
36467 Opp 7,204 ..... F8
36561 Orange Beach 600 ..... C10
36767 Orrville 349 ..... D6
35763 Owens Cross Roads 804 ..... E1
36203 Oxford 8,939 ..... G3
36360 Ozark⊙ 13,188 ..... G8
35764 Paint Rock 221 ..... F1
35580 Parrish 1,583 ..... D3
35124 Pelham 6,759 ..... E4
35125 Pell City⊙ 6,616 ..... F3
36916 Pennington 355 ..... B6
36562 Perdido 500 ..... C8
36471 Peterman 600 ..... D7
36062 Petrey 93 ..... F7
36867 Phenix City⊙ 26,928 ..... H6
35581 Phil Campbell 1,549 ..... C2
†35447 Pickensville 132 ..... B4
36272 Piedmont 5,544 ..... G3
36371 Pinckard 771 ..... G8
36768 Pine Apple 298 ..... E7
36769 Pine Hill 510 ..... C7
35765 Pisgah 699 ..... G1
36758 Plantersville 650 ..... E5
35127 Pleasant Grove 7,102 ..... D4
36564 Point Clear 1,812 ..... C10
†36441 Pollard 144 ..... D8

(continued on following page)

Agriculture, Industry and Resources

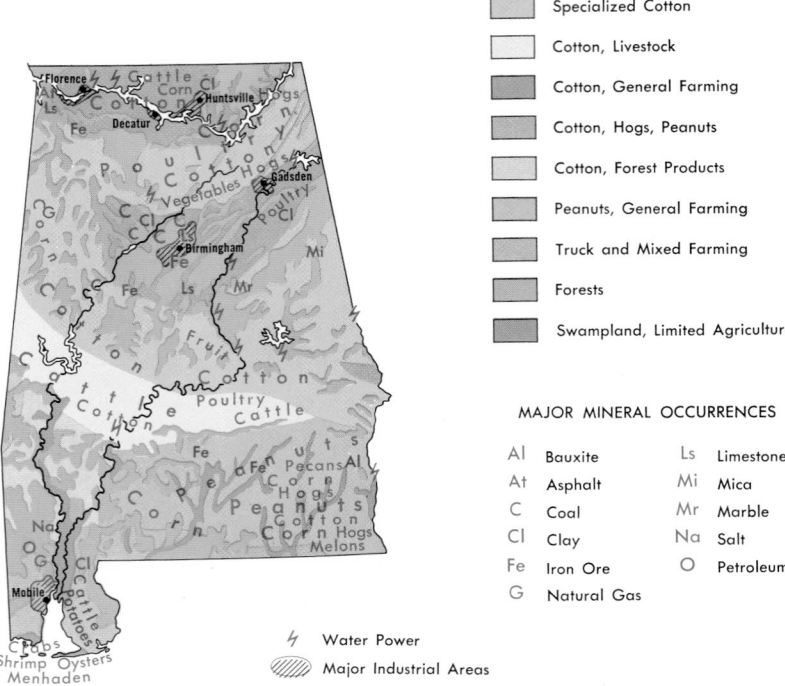

DOMINANT LAND USE

- Specialized Cotton
- Cotton, Livestock
- Cotton, General Farming
- Cotton, Hogs, Peanuts
- Cotton, Forest Products
- Peanuts, General Farming
- Truck and Mixed Farming
- Forests
- Swampland, Limited Agriculture

MAJOR MINERAL OCCURRENCES

Al	Bauxite	Ls	Limestone
At	Asphalt	Mi	Mica
C	Coal	Mr	Marble
Cl	Clay	Na	Salt
Fe	Iron Ore	O	Petroleum
G	Natural Gas		

⚡ Water Power

Major Industrial Areas

Topography

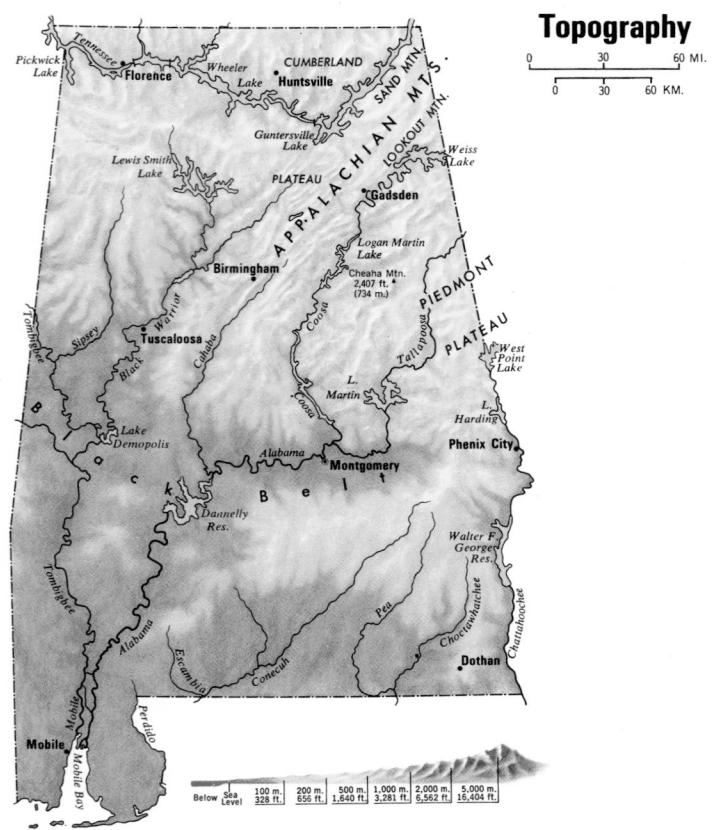

0   30   60 MI.

0   30   60 KM.

Below Sea Level | 100 m. 328 ft. | 200 m. 656 ft. | 500 m. 1,640 ft. | 1,000 m. 3,281 ft. | 2,000 m. 6,562 ft. | 5,000 m. 16,404 ft.

Alabama

SCALE

0 5 10 20 30 40 MI.

0 5 10 20 30 40 KM.

State Capitals ⊛
County Seats ⊛
Major Limited Access Hwys.

© Copyright HAMMOND INCORPORATED, Maplewood, N.J.

GULF OF MEXICO

CITIES and TOWNS

Zip	Name/Pop.	Key
†99609	Akolmiut (Kasigluk) 641	F2
99554	Alakanuk 522	E2
*99501	Anchorage 174,431	B1
	Anchorage‡ 174,431	B1
†99760	Anderson 517	H2
†99723	Barrow 2,207	G1
99559	Bethel 3,576	F2
99704	Clear 504	J2
99701	College 4,043	J1
99574	Cordova 1,879	D1
99921	Craig 527	M2
99737	Delta Junction 945	J2
99576	Dillingham 1,563	G3
†99685	Dutch Harbor 250	E4
99581	Emanguk (Emmonak) 567	E2
99701	Fairbanks 22,645	J2
99740	Fort Yukon 619	J1
99741	Galena 765	G2
99588	Glennallen 511	D1
99827	Haines 993	M1
99603	Homer 2,209	B2
99829	Hoonah 680	M1
99604	Hooper Bay 627	E2
99801	Juneau (cap.) 19,528	M1
99830	Kake 555	M1
99609	Kasigluk 641	F2
99611	Kenai 4,324	B1
99901	Ketchikan 7,198	N2
99615	Kodiak 4,756	H3
99752	Kotzebue 2,054	F1
99926	Metlakatla 1,056	N2
†99901	Mountain Point 396	N2
99632	Mountain Village 583	E2
99762	Nome 2,301	E2
99763	Noorvik 492	F1
99645	Palmer 2,141	C1
99833	Petersburg 2,821	N2
99660	Saint Paul Island 551	D3
99661	Sand Point 625	G3
99664	Seward 1,843	C1
99835	Sitka 7,803	M1
99840	Skagway 768	M1
99669	Soldotna 2,320	B1
99503	Spenard	C1
99672	Sterling 919	B1
99780	Tok 589	K2
99684	Unalakleet 623	F2
99685	Unalaska 1,322	E4
99686	Valdez 3,079	D1
99929	Wrangell 2,184	N2
99689	Yakutat 449	L3

OTHER FEATURES

Name	Key
Adak (isl.)	L4
Admiralty (isl.)	M1
Afognak (isl.)	H3
Agattu (isl.)	J3
Akutan (isl.)	E4
Alaska (gulf)	K3
Alaska (range)	H2
Aleutian (isls.)	J4
Aleutian (range)	G3
Alexander (arch.)	L1
Amchitka (isl.)	K4
Amlia (passage)	L4
Amukta (isl.)	D4
Andreanof (isls.)	L4
Atka (isl.)	L4
Attu (isl.)	J3
Baird (mts.)	F1
Baranof (isl.)	M1
Barrow (pt.)	G1
Bear (mt.)	K2
Becharof (lake)	G3
Beaufort (sea)	K1
Bering (glac.)	K2
Bering (sea)	D2
Bering (str.)	E1
Blackburn (mt.)	K2
Bona (mt.)	K2
Bristol (bay)	F3
British (mts.)	K1
Brooks (range)	H1
Chandalar (riv.)	J1
Chatham (str.)	M1
Chichagof (isl.)	M1
Chignik (bay)	G3
Chilkoot (pass)	M1
Chirikof (isl.)	G3
Chitina (riv.)	K2
Christian (sound)	M2
Chugach (mts.)	C1
Chukchi (sea)	E1
Clarence (str.)	N2
Clark (lake)	H2
Coast (mts.)	N1
Columbia (glac.)	C1
Colville (riv.)	G1
Constantine (cape)	G3
Cook (inlet)	B1
Cook (mt.)	K2
Copper (riv.)	J2
Cordova (bay)	M2
Coronation (isl.)	M2
Cross (sound)	L1
Dease (inlet)	H1
Decision (cape)	M2
Denali Nat'l Park	H2
Devils Paw (mt.)	N1
Dixon Entrance (chan.)	M2
Douglas (mt.)	H3
Dry (bay)	L3
Eielson A.F.B. 5,232	J2
Elmendorf A.F.B.	B1
Endicott (mts.)	H1
Etolin (isl.)	N2
Fairweather (cape)	L1
Fairweather (mt.)	L1
Firth (riv.)	K1
Foraker (mt.)	H2
Fort Davis	E2
Fort Greely 1,635	J2
Fort Richardson	C1
Fort Wainwright	J1
Four Mountains (isls.)	E4
Fox (isls.)	E4
Frederick (sound)	N1
Gates of the Arctic Nat'l Park	H1
Glacier (bay)	M1
Glacier Bay Nat'l Park	M1
Goodhope (bay)	F1
Great Sitkin (isl.)	L4
Guyot (glac.)	K2
Hagemeister (isl.)	F3
Halkett (cape)	H2
Hall (isl.)	D2
Harding Icefield	C2
Harrison (bay)	H1
Hayes (mt.)	J2
Hazen (bay)	E2
Hinchinbrook (isl.)	D1
Hoonah (sound)	M1
Hope (pt.)	E1
Howard (pass)	G1
Icy (bay)	K3
Icy (cape)	F1
Icy (pt.)	L1
Icy (str.)	M1
Iliamna (lake)	G3
Iliamna (vol.)	H2
Innoko (riv.)	G2
Kachemak (bay)	B2
Kanaga (isl.)	L4
Kates Needle (mt.)	N1
Katmai (vol.)	H3
Katmai Nat'l Park	H3
Kayak (isl.)	K3
Kenai (lake)	C1
Kenai (mt.)	C2
Kenai (pen.)	C2
Kenai Fjords Nat'l Park	C2
Kennedy Entrance (str.)	H3
King (isl.)	E1
Kiska (isl.)	J4
Kiska (vol.)	J4
Klondike Gold Rush Nat'l Hist. Park	N1
Knight (isl.)	D1
Knik Arm (inlet)	B1
Kobuk (riv.)	G1
Kobuk Valley Nat'l Park	F1
Kodiak (isl.)	H3
Kotzebue (sound)	F1
Koyukuk (riv.)	G1
Krusenstern (cape)	F1
Kuiu (isl.)	M2
Kuskokwim (bay)	F3
Kuskokwim (mts.)	G2
Kuskokwim (riv.)	G2
Kvichak (riv.)	G3
Kvichak (bay)	G3
Lake Clark Nat'l Park	H2
Little Diomede (isl.)	E1
Little Sitkin (isl.)	K4
Lisburne (cape)	E1
Lynn Canal (inlet)	M1
Makushin (vol.)	E4
Malaspina (glac.)	K3
Marcus Baker (mt.)	C1
Marmot (isl.)	H3
Matanuska (riv.)	C1

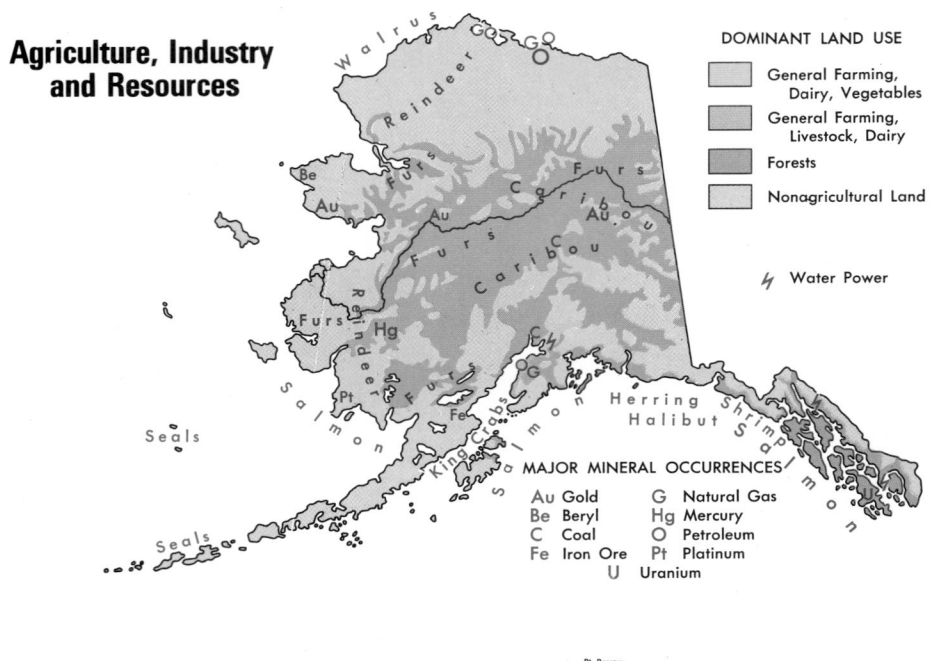

Agriculture, Industry and Resources

DOMINANT LAND USE

- General Farming, Dairy, Vegetables
- General Farming, Livestock, Dairy
- Forests
- Nonagricultural Land

⚡ Water Power

MAJOR MINERAL OCCURRENCES

Au	Gold	G	Natural Gas
Be	Beryl	Hg	Mercury
C	Coal	O	Petroleum
Fe	Iron Ore	Pt	Platinum
		U	Uranium

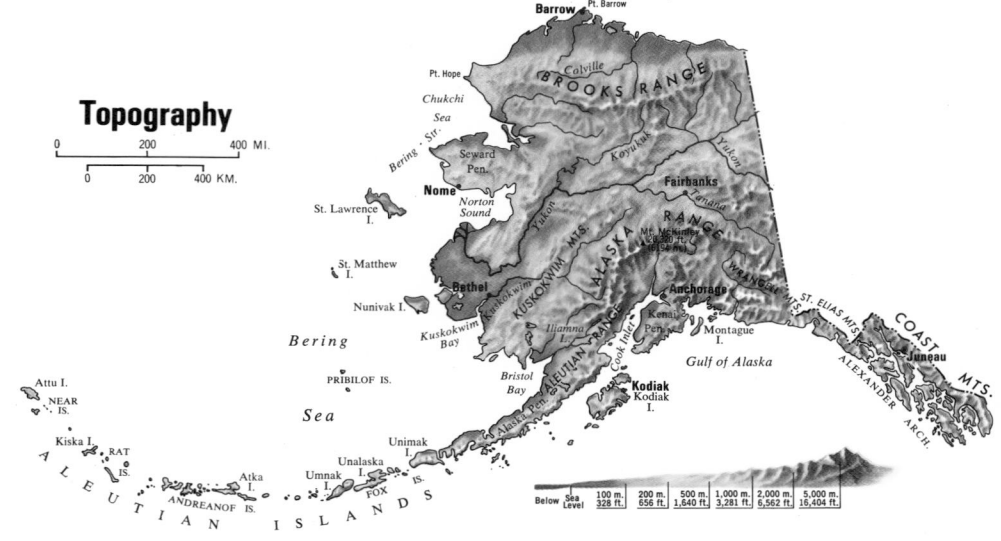

Topography

0 — 200 — 400 MI.

0 — 200 — 400 KM.

| Below Sea Level | 100 m. 328 ft. | 200 m. 656 ft. | 500 m. 1,640 ft. | 1,000 m. 3,281 ft. | 2,000 m. 6,562 ft. | 5,000 m. 16,404 ft. |

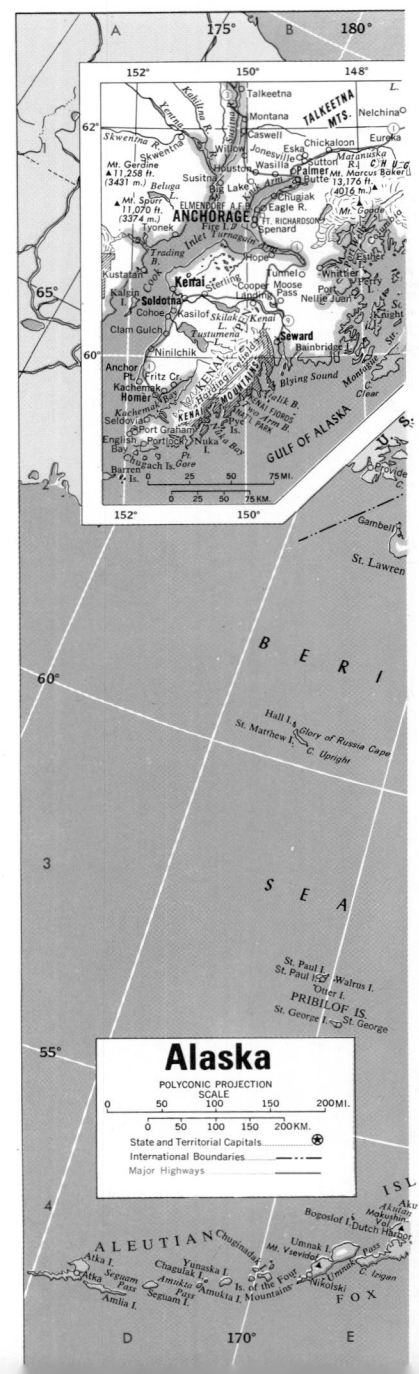

Alaska

POLYCONIC PROJECTION

SCALE

0 — 50 — 100 — 150 — 200 MI.

0 — 50 — 100 — 150 — 200 KM.

State and Territorial Capitals ⊛

International Boundaries

Major Highways

⊙Court House
‡Population of metropolitan area.
† Zip of nearest p.o.
* Multiple zips.

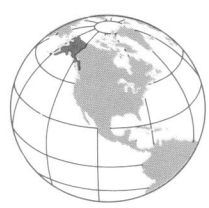

AREA 591,004 sq. mi. (1,530,700 sq. km.)
POPULATION 401,851
CAPITAL Juneau
LARGEST CITY Anchorage
HIGHEST POINT Mt. McKinley 20,320 ft. (6194 m.)
SETTLED IN 1801
ADMITTED TO UNION January 3, 1959
POPULAR NAME Great Land; Last Frontier
STATE FLOWER Forget-me-not
STATE BIRD Willow Ptarmigan

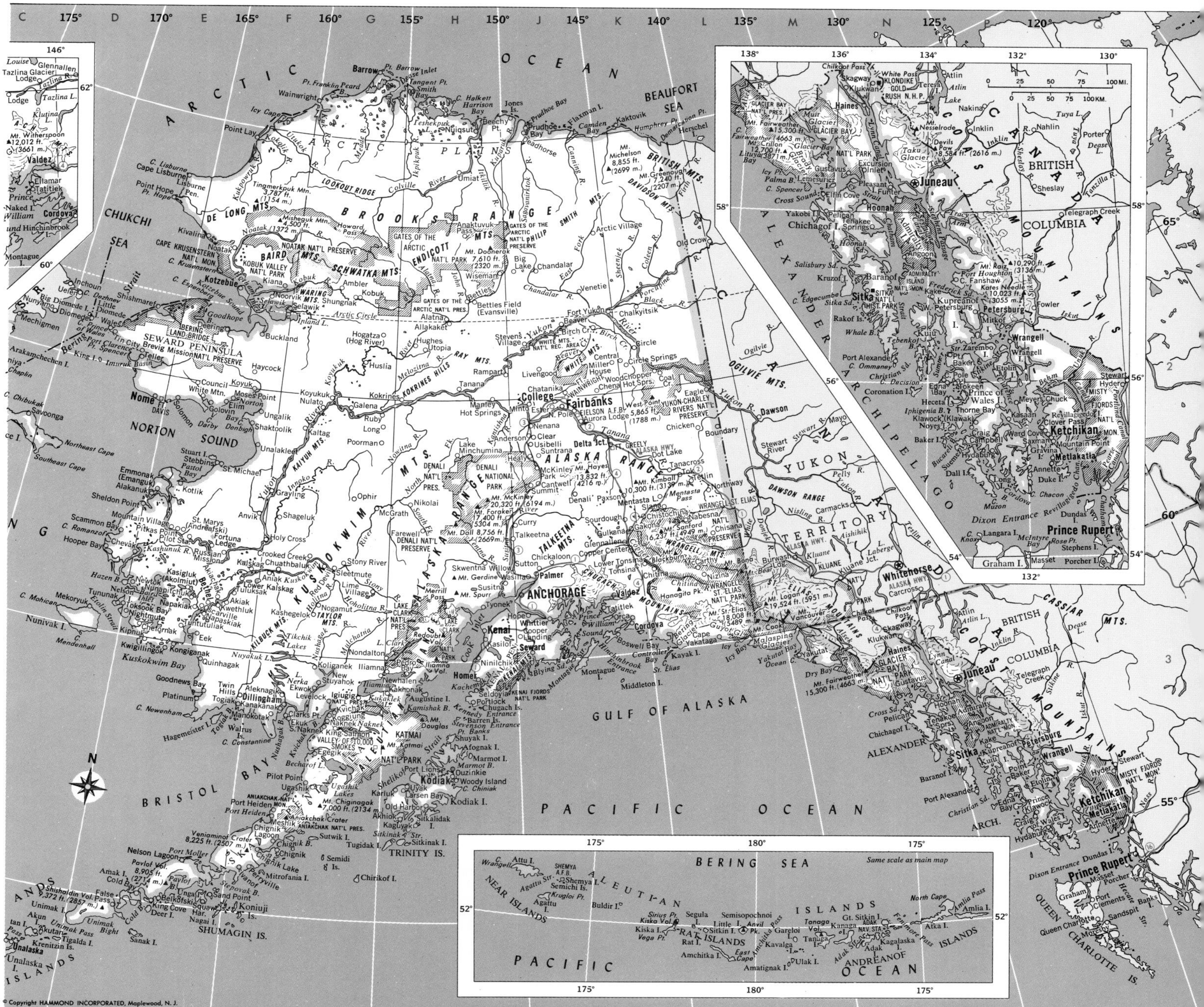

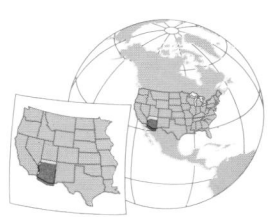

AREA 114,000 sq. mi. (295,260 sq. km.)
POPULATION 2,718,425
CAPITAL Phoenix
LARGEST CITY Phoenix
HIGHEST POINT Humphreys Pk. 12,633 ft.
   (3851 m.)
SETTLED IN 1752
ADMITTED TO UNION February 14, 1912
POPULAR NAME Grand Canyon State
STATE FLOWER Saguaro Cactus Blossom
STATE BIRD Cactus Wren

Agriculture, Industry and Resources

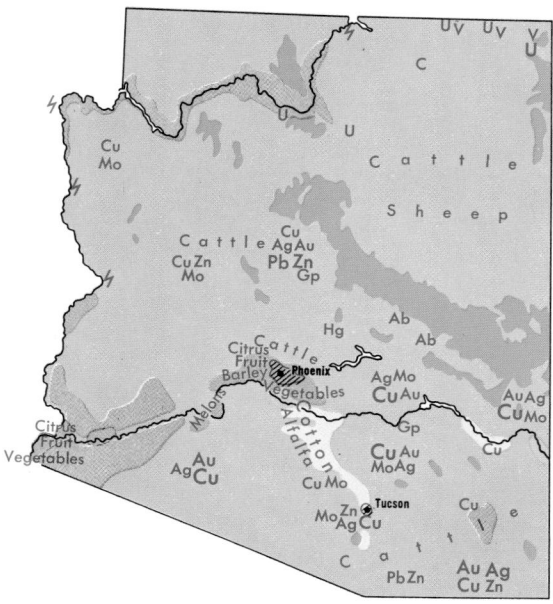

MAJOR MINERAL OCCURRENCES

Ab	Asbestos	Cu	Copper	Pb	Lead
Ag	Silver	Gp	Gypsum	U	Uranium
Au	Gold	Hg	Mercury	V	Vanadium
C	Coal	Mo	Molybdenum	Zn	Zinc

DOMINANT LAND USE

Fruit, Truck and Mixed Farming
Cotton and Alfalfa
General Farming, Livestock, Special Crops
Range Livestock
Forests
Nonagricultural Land

⚡ Water Power
▨ Major Industrial Areas

COUNTIES

Apache 52,108 .... F3
Cochise 85,686 .... F7
Coconino 75,008 .... C3
Gila 37,080 .... E5
Graham 22,862 .... E6
Greenlee 11,406 .... F5
La Paz• 13,100 .... A5
Maricopa 1,509,052 .... C5
Mohave 55,865 .... A3
Navajo 67,629 .... E3
Pima 531,443 .... D6
Pinal 90,918 .... D6
Santa Cruz 20,459 .... E7
Yavapai 68,145 .... C4
Yuma• 81,800 .... A6

•1982 official estimate.

CITIES and TOWNS

Zip	Name/Pop.	Key
†85333	Agua Caliente 60	B6
85320	Aguila 900	B5
85321	Ajo 5,189	C6
85920	Alpine 450	F5
85640	Amado 75	D7
85220	Apache Junction 9,935	D5
†85901	Aripine 25	E4
85601	Arivaca 400	D7
85223	Arizona City 825	D6
85625	Arizona Sunsites 825	F7
85322	Arlington 950	C5
86320	Ash Fork 800	C3
85323	Avondale 8,168	C5
†85333	Aztec 20	B6
86321	Bagdad 2,331	B4
85221	Bapchule 400	D5
86015	Bellemont 210	D3
85602	Benson 4,190	E7
85603	Bisbee⊙ 7,154	F7
85324	Black Canyon City 600	C4
85922	Blue 50	F5
†85643	Bonita 20	E6
85325	Bouse 500	A5
85605	Bowie 600	F6
85326	Buckeye 3,434	C5
86430	Bullhead City-Riviera 10,364	A3
†86301	Bumble Bee 15	C4
85530	Bylas 1,175	E5
†85530	Calva 10	E5
86020	Cameron 600	D3
86322	Camp Verde 1,125	D4
†86022	Cane Beds 30	B2
85331	Carefree 986	C5
†85640	Carmen 200	D7
85222	Casa Grande 14,971	D6
85329	Cashion 3,014	C5
†85342	Castle Hot Springs 50	C5
85331	Cave Creek 1,589	D5
85531	Central 300	F6
†85501	Central Heights-Midland City 2,791	E5
86502	Chambers 500	F3
85224	Chandler 29,673	D5
†86327	Cherry 20	C4
86503	Chinle 2,815	F2
86323	Chino Valley 2,858	C4
86431	Chloride 225	A3
85292	Christmas 201	E5
85911	Cibecue 100	E4
86324	Clarkdale 1,512	C4
85532	Claypool 2,362	E5
†85934	Clay Springs 500	E4
†86326	Clemenceau 300	C4
85533	Clifton⊙ 4,245	F5
85606	Cochise 150	F6
86021	Colorado City 350	B2
85924	Concho 100	F4
85332	Congress 800	C4
†85640	Continental 250	D7
85228	Coolidge 6,851	D6
†85542	Coolidge Dam 42	E5
†86505	Cornfields 200	F3
86325	Cornville 425	D4
85230	Cortaro 375	D6
86326	Cottonwood 4,550	D4
86333	Crown King 100	C4
85333	Dateland 100	B6
†86430	Davis Dam 125	A3
86327	Dewey 100	C4
†86047	Dilkon 90	E3
86441	Dolan Springs 870	A3
†85364	Dome 48	A6
†85643	Dos Cabezas 30	F6
85607	Douglas 13,058	F7
85609	Dragoon 150	F6
85534	Duncan 603	F6
85925	Eagar 2,791	F4
85535	Eden 89	F6
85334	Ehrenburg 93	A5

(continued on following page)

Topography

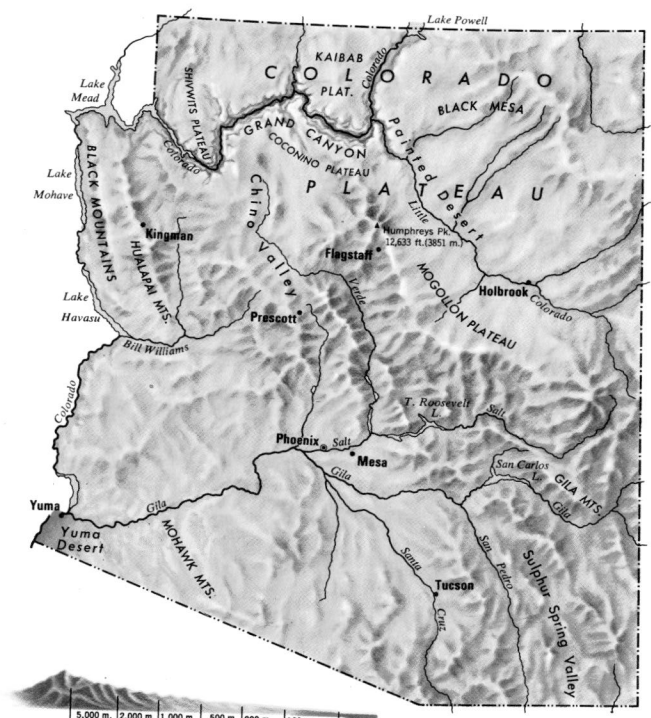

| 5,000 m. 16,404 ft. | 2,000 m. 6,562 ft. | 1,000 m. 3,281 ft. | 500 m. 1,640 ft. | 200 m. 656 ft. | 100 m. 328 ft. | Sea Level | Below |

(continued)

†85617 Elfrida 700 .... F7
†85637 Elgin 525 .... E7
85335 El Mirage 4,307 .... C5
85231 Eloy 6,240 .... D6
85612 Fairbank 100 .... E7
86001 Flagstaff⊙ 34,743 .... D3
85232 Florence⊙ 3,391 .... D5
†85220 Florence Junction 35 .... D5
85926 Fort Apache 500 .... F5
86504 Fort Defiance 3,431 .... F3
85643 Fort Grant 240 .... E6
85536 Fort Thomas 450 .... E5
85534 Franklin 300 .... F6
86022 Fredonia 1,040 .... C2
85336 Gadsden 250 .... A6
86505 Ganado 816 .... F3
†85536 Geronimo 25 .... F5
85337 Gila Bend 1,585 .... C6
85234 Gilbert 5,717 .... D5
†85617 Gleeson 15 .... F7
*85301 Glendale 97,172 .... C5
85501 Globe⊙ 6,886 .... E5
85323 Goodyear 2,747 .... C5
86023 Grand Canyon 1,348 .... C2
†85637 Greaterville 15 .... E7
85614 Green Valley 7,999 .... D7
85927 Greer 385 .... F4
†85634 Gu Achi 339 .... C6
86411 Hackberry 250 .... B3
86024 Happy Jack 50 .... D4
85235 Hayden 1,205 .... E5
85928 Heber 750 .... E4
85615 Hereford 10 .... E7
85236 Higley 500 .... D5
†86301 Hillside 100 .... B4
†85632 Hilltop 9 .... F6
86025 Holbrook⊙ 5,785 .... E4
86030 Hotevilla 3,009 .... E3
86506 Houck 900 .... F3
85616 Huachuca City 1,661 .... E7
86329 Humboldt 787 .... C4
86031 Indian Wells 150 .... E3
85537 Inspiration 500 .... D5
86330 Iron Springs 175 .... C4
86051 Jacob Lake 16 .... C2
†86025 Jeddito 20 .... E3
86331 Jerome 420 .... C4
86032 Joseph City 650 .... E4
86053 Kaibito 275 .... D2
†86430 Katherine 102 .... A3
86033 Kayenta 3,343 .... E2
86034 Keams Canyon 400 .... E3
85237 Kearny 2,646 .... E5
86401 Kingman⊙ 9,257 .... A3
86332 Kirkland 100 .... C4
†86505 Klagetoh 200 .... F3
85643 Klondyke 86 .... E6
85538 Kohls Ranch 100 .... D4
†85339 Komatke 300 .... C5
86403 Lake Havasu City 15,909 .... A4
86342 Lake Montezuma 900 .... D4
85929 Lakeside 1,333 .... E4
85339 Laveen 800 .... C5
†86036 Lees Ferry 10 .... D2
86035 Leupp 150 .... E3
†85326 Liberty 150 .... C5
†85901 Linden 50 .... E4
85340 Litchfield Park 3,657 .... C5
86432 Littlefield 40 .... B2
86507 Lukachukai 1,049 .... F2
85341 Lukeville 50 .... C7
86508 Lupton 250 .... F3
†85637 Madera Canyon 75 .... E7
85618 Mammoth 1,906 .... E6
86538 Many Farms 1,364 .... F2
85238 Marana 1,674 .... D6
86036 Marble Canyon 6 .... D2
85239 Maricopa 750 .... C5

†85920 Maverick 50 .... F5
86333 Mayer 810 .... C4
85930 McNary 1,320 .... F4
85617 McNeal 100 .... F7
*85201 Mesa 152,453 .... D5
85539 Miami 2,716 .... E5
†85239 Mobile 100 .... C5
†86022 Moccasin 150 .... C2
†86045 Moenkopi D2
85540 Morenci 2,736 .... F5
86038 Mormon Lake 20 .... D4
85342 Morristown 400 .... C5
85619 Mount Lemmon 400 .... E6
†84770 Mount Trumbull 14 .... B2
85620 Naco 750 .... E7
86509 Navajo 100 .... F3
†86434 Nelson 39 .... B3
85621 Nogales⊙ 15,683 .... E7
86052 North Rim 50 .... C2
85932 Nutrioso 500 .... F5
86433 Oatman 175 .... A3
†85247 Olberg 65 .... D5
85623 Oracle 2,484 .... E6
86039 Oraibi 600 .... E3
†85704 Oro Valley 1,489 .... E6
85933 Overgaard 750 .... E4
86040 Page 4,907 .... D2
85343 Palo Verde 500 .... C5
†85632 Paradise 15 .... F7
85253 Paradise Valley 11,085 .... D5
85344 Parker⊙ 2,542 .... A4
86018 Parks 175 .... C3
85624 Patagonia 980 .... E7
86334 Paulden 350 .... C4
†85607 Paul Spur 34 .... F7
85541 Payson 5,068 .... D4
86434 Peach Springs 900 .... B3
85625 Pearce 700 .... F7
85345 Peoria 12,307 .... C5
85542 Peridot 950 .... E5
86028 Petrified Forest 80 .... F3
*85001 Phoenix (cap.)⊙ 789,704 .... C5
Phoenix‡ 1,508,030 .... C5
85241 Picacho 850 .... D6
85543 Pima 1,599 .... F6
85544 Pine 800 .... D4
85934 Pinedale 400 .... E4
85935 Pinetop 1,527 .... F4
86510 Pinon 100 .... E2
85634 Pisinimo 187 .... C6
†85540 Plantsite F5
86042 Polacca 500 .... E3
85627 Pomerene 365 .... E6
85632 Portal 72 .... F7
85371 Poston 500 .... A4
86301 Prescott⊙ 20,055 .... C4
†86301 Prescott Valley 2,284 .... C4
85346 Quartzsite 255 .... A5
85242 Queen Creek 600 .... D5
†85634 Quijotoa 200 .... C6
85243 Randolph 350 .... D6
85245 Red Rock 250 .... D6
85246 Rillito 400 .... D6
86335 Rimrock 217 .... D4
85237 Riverside Stage Stop 418 .... D5
86440 Riviera-Bullhead City 10,364 .... A3
85347 Roll 700 .... A6
85545 Roosevelt 125 .... D5
85247 Sacaton 1,951 .... D5
85546 Safford⊙ 7,010 .... F6
85629 Sahuarita 200 .... E7
85630 Saint David 800 .... E7
85936 Saint Johns⊙ 3,368 .... F4
86511 Saint Michaels 250 .... F3
85348 Salome 800 .... B5
85550 San Carlos 2,668 .... E5
86512 Sanders 900 .... F3

85349 San Luis 1,946 .... A6
85631 San Manuel 5,443 .... E6
85632 San Simon 400 .... F6
85633 Sasabe 50 .... D7
*85251 Scottsdale 88,622 .... D5
86043 Second Mesa 450 .... E3
86336 Sedona 5,368 .... D4
86337 Seligman 510 .... B3
85634 Sells 1,864 .... D7
†85333 Sentinel 40 .... B6
86054 Shonto 700 .... E2
85901 Show Low 4,298 .... F4
†86043 Shungopavy (Shongopovi) 570 .... E3
85635 Sierra Vista 24,937 .... E7
85270 Silver Bell 900 .... D6
86338 Skull Valley 250 .... C4
85937 Snowflake 3,510 .... E4
85551 Solomon 700 .... F6
85350 Somerton 5,761 .... A6
85637 Sonoita 220 .... E7
85713 South Tucson 6,554 .... D6
85938 Springerville 1,452 .... F4
85272 Stanfield 150 .... C6
†85540 Stargo 1,038 .... F5
†86505 Steamboat 100 .... F3
*85351 Sun City 40,505 .... C5
86435 Supai 350 .... C2
85273 Superior 4,600 .... D5
85345 Surprise 3,723 .... C5
85352 Tacna 950 .... B6
†85701 Tanque Verde 850 .... E6
85939 Taylor 1,915 .... E4
86514 Teec Nos Pos 550 .... F2
*85282 Tempe 106,743 .... D5
86443 Temple Bar 84 .... A2
85552 Thatcher 3,374 .... F6
85353 Tolleson 4,433 .... C5
85638 Tombstone 1,632 .... F7
86044 Tonalea 125 .... E2
85354 Tonopah 54 .... B5
85553 Tonto Basin 250 .... D5
85639 Topawa 500 .... D7
86436 Topock 325 .... A4
85290 Tortilla Flat 37 .... D5
85640 Tubac 140 .... E7
86045 Tuba City 5,045 .... D2
*85701 Tucson⊙ 330,537 .... D6
Tucson‡ 531,263 .... D6
85640 Tumacacori 100 .... D7
85641 Vail 175 .... E6
86437 Valentine 120 .... B3
85291 Valley Farms 240 .... D6
85940 Vernon 75 .... F4
†85348 Vicksburg 16 .... B5
85355 Waddell 100 .... C5
85356 Wellton 911 .... A6
85357 Wenden 400 .... B5
85941 Whiteriver 2,256 .... E5
85321 Why 65 .... C6
85358 Wickenburg 3,535 .... C5
85360 Wikieup 150 .... B4
85643 Willcox 3,243 .... F6
86046 Williams 2,266 .... C3
86515 Window Rock 2,230 .... F3
85292 Winkelman 1,060 .... E6
†86001 Winona 25 .... D3
86047 Winslow 7,921 .... E3
†85322 Wintersburg 400 .... B5
85361 Wittmann 600 .... C5
85942 Woodruff 280 .... E4
85362 Yarnell 800 .... C4
†86301 Yava 40 .... C4
85554 Young 500 .... D4
85363 Youngtown 2,254 .... C5
86438 Yucca 250 .... A4
85364 Yuma⊙ 42,481 .... A6

OTHER FEATURES

Agassiz (peak) D3
Agua Fria (riv.) C5
Alamo (lake) B4
Apache (lake) D5
Aquarius (range) B4
Aravaipa (creek) E6
Aubrey (cliffs) B3
Baboquivari (mts.) D7
Baker Butte (mt.) D4
Balakai (mesa) F3
Baldy (peak) F5
Bartlett (dam) D5
Bartlett (res.) D5
Big Chino Wash (dry riv.) C3
Big Horn (mts.) B5
Big Sandy (riv.) B4
Bill Williams (riv.) B4
Black (mesa) E2
Black (mts.) A3
Black (riv.) E5
Blue (riv.) F5
Bouse Wash (dry riv.) A4
Buckskin (mts.) B4
Burro (creek) B4
Canyon (lake) D5
Canyon de Chelly Nat'l Mon. F2
Carrizo (creek) E4
Carrizo (mts.) G2
Casa Grande Ruins Nat'l Mon. D6
Castle Dome (mts.) A5
Cataract (creek) C3
Centennial Wash (dry riv.) B5
Cerbat (mts.) A3
Cherry (creek) E4
Chevelon (creek) E4
Chinle (creek) F2
Chinle (valley) F2
Chinle Wash (dry riv.) F2
Chino (valley) C3
Chiricahua (mts.) F6
Chiricahua Nat'l Mon. F6
Chocolate (mts.) A5
Clear (creek) D4
Coconino (plat.) C3
Cocopah Ind. Res. 355 .... A6
Colorado (riv.) A5
Colorado River Ind. Res. 6,640 .... A5
Coolidge (dam) E5
Copper (mts.) B6
Corn (creek) E3
Coronado Nat'l Memorial E7
Cottonwood (cliffs) B3
Cottonwood Wash (dry riv.) E4
Davis (dam) A3
Davis-Monthan A.F.B. 6,279 .... E6
Defiance (plat.) F3
Detrital Wash (dry riv.) A3
Diablo (canyon) D4
Dinnebito Wash (dry riv.) E3
Dot Klish (canyon) E2
Dragoon (mts.) F7
Eagle (creek) F5
East Verde (riv.) D4
Echo (cliffs) D2
Elden (mt.) D3
Fort Apache Ind. Res. 7,774 .... E5
Fort Bowie Nat'l Hist. Site F6
Fort Huachuca E7
Fort McDowell Ind. Res. 349 .... D5
Fort Mohave Ind. Res. 183 .... A4
Fort Pearce Wash (dry riv.) B2
Fossil (creek) D4
Four Peaks (mt.) D5
Galiuro (mts.) E6
Gila (mts.) A6
Gila (mts.) F5

Gila (riv.) B6
Gila Bend (mts.) B5
Gila Bend Ind. Res. 353 .... C6
Gila River Ind. Res. 7,445 .... C5
Glen Canyon (dam) D2
Glen Canyon Nat'l Rec. Area D1
Gothic (mesa) F2
Government (mt.) C3
Graham (mt.) F6
Grand Canyon Nat'l Park C2
Grand Wash (butte) B2
Grand Wash (riv.) B2
Greens (peak) F4
Growler (mts.) B6
Harcuvar (mts.) B5
Harquahala (mts.) B5
Hassayampa (riv.) C5
Havasu (lake) A4
Havasupai Ind. Res. 282 .... C2
Hohokam Pima Nat'l Mon. D5
Hoover (dam) A2
Hopi (buttes) E3
Hopi Ind. Res. 6,896 .... E2
Horseshoe (lake) D5
Huachuca (peak) E7
Hualapai (mts.) B4
Hualapai (peak) B3
Hualapai Ind. Res. 849 .... B3
Hubbell Trading Post Nat'l Hist. Site F3
Humphreys (peak) D3
Hurricane (cliffs) B2
Imperial (res.) A6
Ives (mesa) E3
Juniper (mts.) C3
Kaibab (plat.) C2
Kaibab Ind. Res. 173 .... C2
Kaibito (plat.) D2
Kanab (creek) C2
Kanab (plat.) C2
Kellogg (mt.) E6
Kendrick (peak) D3
Kitt (peak) D7
Kofa (mts.) B5
Laguna (creek) E2
Laguna (res.) A6
Lake Mead Nat'l Rec. Area A2
Lechuguilla (des.) A6
Lemmon (mt.) E6
Little Colorado (riv.) D3
Lukachukai (mts.) F2
Luke A.F.B. 3,515 .... C5
Maple (peak) F5
Marble Canyon Nat'l Mon. D2
Maricopa (mts.) C5
Maricopa Ind. Res. 397 .... C6
Mazatzal (peak) D4
Mead (lake) A2
Meteor (crater) E3
Miller (peak) E7
Moencopi (plat.) D3
Moenkopi Wash (dry riv.) D2
Mogollon (plat.) D4
Mogollon Rim (cliffs) D4
Mohave (lake) A3
Mohave (mts.) A4
Mohawk (mts.) B6
Montezuma Castle Nat'l Mon. D4
Mormon (lake) D4
Mule (mts.) E7
Navajo (creek) D2
Navajo Ind. Res. 76,173 .... D2
Navajo Nat'l Mon. E2
Navajo Ord. Depot D3
O'Leary (peak) D3
Oraibi Wash (dry riv.) E3
Ord (mt.) D5
Organ Pipe Cactus Nat'l Mon. C6

Painted (des.) D2
Painted Desert Section (Petrified Forest F3
Painted Rock (dam) C5
Papago Ind. Res. 7,171 .... C6
Paria (plat.) D2
Paria (riv.) D1
Parker (dam) A4
Pastora (peak) F2
Peloncillo (mts.) F6
Petrified Forest Nat'l Park F4
Pictograph (rocks) B5
Pinal (peak) E5
Pinaleno (mts.) F6
Pink (cliffs) E4
Pipe Spring Nat'l Mon. C2
Pleasant (lake) C5
Plomosa (mts.) A5
Polacca Wash (dry riv.) E3
Powell (lake) E1
Pueblo Colorado Wash (dry riv.) F3
Puerco (riv.) F3
Quajote Wash (dry riv.) D6
Rainbow (plat.) D2
Rincon (peak) E6
Roof Butte (mt.) F2
Rose (peak) F5
Sacramento Wash (dry riv.) A4
Saguaro (lake) D5
Saguaro Nat'l Mon. E6
Salt (riv.) D5
Salt River Ind. Res. 4,089 .... D5
San Carlos (lake) E5
San Carlos (riv.) E5
San Carlos Ind. Res. 6,104 .... E5
Sand Tank (mt.) C6
San Francisco (riv.) F5
San Pedro (riv.) E6
San Simon (riv.) F6
Santa Catalina (mts.) E6
Santa Cruz (riv.) D6
Santa Maria (riv.) B4
Santa Rosa Wash (dry riv.) D6
San Xavier Ind. Res. 875 .... D6
Sauceda (mts.) C6
Shivwits (plat.) B2
Shonto (plat.) E2
Sierra Ancha (mts.) D5
Sierra Apache (mts.) E5
Silver (creek) E4
Slate (mt.) D3
Sulphur Spring (valley) F6
Sunset Crater Nat'l Mon. D3
Superstition (mts.) D5
Theodore Roosevelt (lake) D5
Tonto (creek) D4
Tonto Nat'l Mon. D5
Trout (creek) B3
Trumbull (mt.) B2
Tumacacori Nat'l Mon. E7
Tuzigoot Nat'l Mon. D4
Tyson Wash (dry riv.) A5
Uinkaret (plat.) B2
Union (mt.) C4
Verde (riv.) D5
Vermilion (cliffs) D2
Virgin (mts.) B2
Walker (creek) F2
Walnut Canyon Nat'l Mon. D3
White (riv.) E5
Williams A.F.B. 3,435 .... D5
Woody (mt.) D3
Wupatki Nat'l Mon. D3
Yuma (des.) A6
Yuma Proving Ground 1,098 .... A6
Zuni (riv.) F4

⊙County seat.
‡Population of metropolitan area.
† Zip of nearest p.o. * Multiple zips.

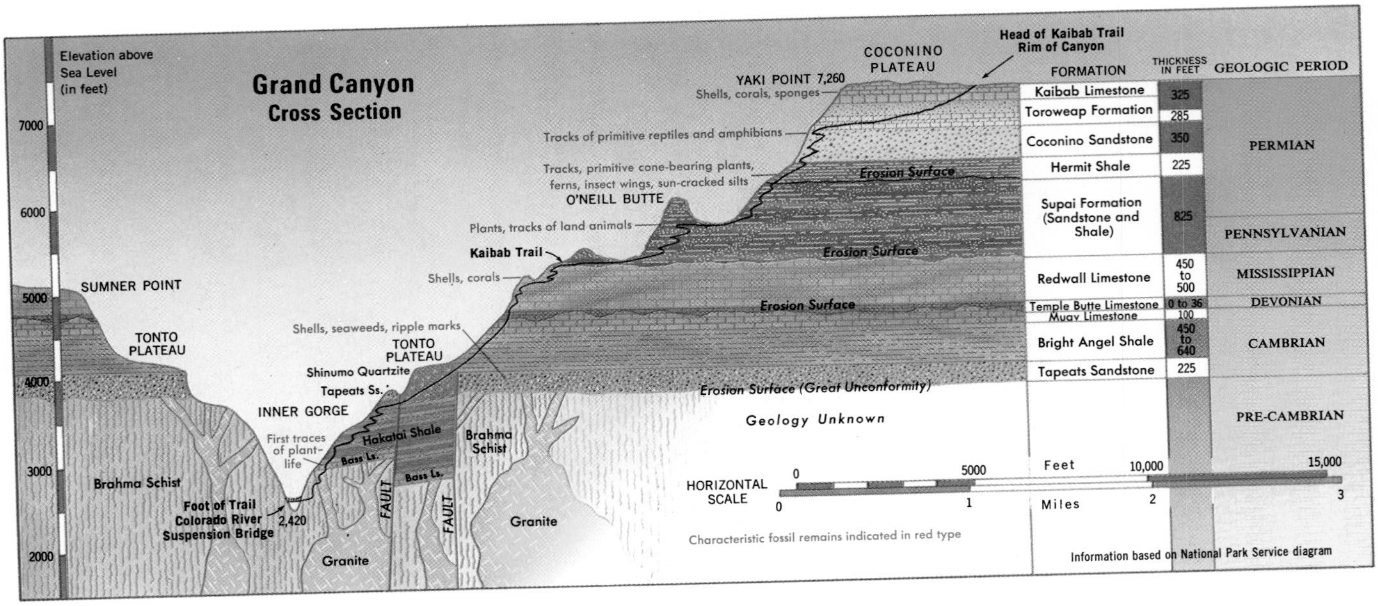

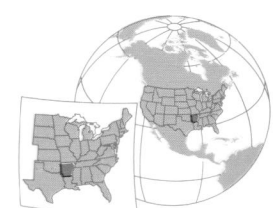

AREA 53,187 sq. mi. (137,754 sq. km.)
POPULATION 2,286,435
CAPITAL Little Rock
LARGEST CITY Little Rock
HIGHEST POINT Magazine Mtn. 2,753 ft. (839 m.)
SETTLED IN 1685
ADMITTED TO UNION June 15, 1836
POPULAR NAME Land of Opportunity
STATE FLOWER Apple Blossom
STATE BIRD Mockingbird

COUNTIES

Arkansas 24,175 .... H5
Ashley 26,538 .... G7
Baxter 27,409 .... F1
Benton 78,115 .... B1
Boone 26,067 .... D1
Bradley 13,803 .... F7
Calhoun 6,079 .... E6
Carroll 16,203 .... C1
Chicot 17,793 .... H7
Clark 23,326 .... D5
Clay 20,616 .... K1
Cleburne 16,909 .... F2
Cleveland 7,868 .... F6
Columbia 26,644 .... D7
Conway 19,505 .... E3
Craighead 63,239 .... J2
Crawford 36,892 .... B2
Crittenden 49,499 .... K3
Cross 20,434 .... J3
Dallas 10,515 .... E6
Desha 19,760 .... H6
Drew 17,910 .... G6
Faulkner 46,192 .... F3
Franklin 14,705 .... C2
Fulton 9,975 .... G1
Garland 70,531 .... D4
Grant 13,008 .... F5
Greene 30,744 .... J1
Hempstead 23,635 .... C6
Hot Spring 26,819 .... E5
Howard 13,459 .... C5
Independence 30,147 .... G2
Izard 10,768 .... G1
Jackson 21,646 .... H2
Jefferson 90,718 .... G5
Johnson 17,423 .... C2
Lafayette 10,213 .... C7
Lawrence 18,447 .... H1
Lee 15,539 .... J4
Lincoln 13,369 .... G6
Little River 13,952 .... B6
Logan 20,144 .... C3
Lonoke 34,518 .... G4
Madison 11,373 ...... C1
Marion 11,334 .... E1
Miller 37,766 .... C7
Mississippi 59,517 .... K2
Monroe 14,052 .... H4
Montgomery 7,771 .... C4
Nevada 11,097 .... D6
Newton 7,756 .... D2
Ouachita 30,541 ...... E6
Perry 7,266 .... E4
Phillips 34,772 ...... J5
Pike 10,373 .... C5
Poinsett 27,032 ...... J2
Polk 17,007 .... B5
Pope 39,021 .... D3
Prairie 10,140 ...... G4
Pulaski 340,613 .... F4
Randolph 16,834 .... H1
Saint Francis 30,858 .. J3
Saline 53,161 .... E4
Scott 9,685 .... B4
Searcy 8,847 .... E2
Sebastian 95,172 .... B3
Sevier 14,060 .... B6
Sharp 14,607 .... G1
Stone 9,022 .... F2
Union 48,573 .... E7
Van Buren 13,357 .... E2
Washington 100,494 .. B2
White 50,835 .... G3
Woodruff 11,222 .... H3
Yell 17,026 .... D3

CITIES and TOWNS

Zip   Name/Pop.   Key

72001 Adona 230 .... E3
72002 Alexander 223 .... F4
72410 Alicia 246 .... H2
72820 Alix 225 .... C3
†72046 Allport 295 .... G4
72921 Alma 3,453 .... B3
72003 Almyra 294 .... H5
72611 Alpena 344 .... D1
72004 Altheimer 1,231 .... G5
72821 Altus 441 .... C3
72005 Amagon 126 .... H2
71921 Amity 859 .... D5
71922 Antoine 194 .... D5
71923 Arkadelphia⊙ 10,005 .... D5
71630 Arkansas City⊙ 668 ...... H6
72310 Armorel 500 .... L2
71822 Ashdown⊙ 4,218 .... B6
72513 Ash Flat‡ 524 .... G1
72823 Atkins 3,002 .... E3
72311 Aubrey 267 .... J4
72006 Augusta⊙ 3,496 .... H3
72007 Austin 269 .... G4
72711 Avoca 256 .... B1
72010 Bald Knob 2,756 .... G3
71631 Banks 216 .... F6

72922 Barber 35 .... B3
72923 Barling 3,761 .... B3
72313 Bassett 243 .... K2
72924 Bates B4
72501 Batesville⊙ 8,263 .... G2
72411 Bay 1,605 .... J2
71720 Bearden 1,191 .... E6
72012 Beebe 3,599 .... G3
72014 Beedeville 183 .... H3
†72712 Bella Vista 2,589 ...... B1
†72601 Bellefonte 393 .... D1
72824 Belleville 571 .... D3
71823 Ben Lomond 155 ...... B6
72015 Benton⊙ 17,717 ...... E4
72712 Bentonville⊙ 8,756 .... B1
72615 Bergman 320 .... E1
72616 Berryville⊙ 2,966 .... C1
72764 Bethel Heights 296 .... B1
72016 Bigelow 373 .... E3
72617 Big Flat 150 .... F1
72413 Biggers 363 .... J1
72017 Biscoe 486 .... H4
72414 Black Oak 309 ...... K2
72415 Black Rock 848 .... H1
†71960 Black Springs 92 .... C5
71825 Blevins 314 .... C6
65611 Blue Eye 43 .... D1
72826 Blue Mountain 112 .. C3
71722 Bluff City 292 ...... D6
72315 Blytheville⊙ 23,844 .. L2
†71858 Bodcaw 197 .... D6
72416 Bono 967 .... J2
†72901 Bonanza 553 ...... B3
72927 Booneville⊙ 3,718 .. C3
72020 Bradford 950 ...... G3
71826 Bradley 790 ...... C7
72928 Branch 353 ...... C3
72021 Brinkley 4,909 .... H4
72417 Brookland 840 .... J2
72022 Bryant 2,682 .... F4
71827 Buckner 436 .... D7
72619 Bull Shoals 1,312 .. E1
72321 Burdette 328 .... L2
72023 Cabot 4,806 .... F4
72322 Caldwell 283 .... J3
71828 Cale 110 .... D6
72519 Calico Rock 1,046 .. F1
71724 Calion 638 ...... E7
71701 Camden⊙ 15,356 .. E6
†72201 Cammack Village 920 .. E4
†72473 Campbell Station 297 .. H2
72419 Caraway 1,165 .... K2
72024 Carlisle 2,567 .... G4
71725 Carthage 568 .... E5
72025 Casa 179 .... D3
72421 Cash 285 .... J2
72026 Casscoe 297 .... H4
†72951 Caulksville 344 .. C3
72521 Cave City 1,634 .. G2
72718 Cave Springs 429 .. B1
72932 Cedarville 375 .... B2
72719 Centerton 425 .... B1
72829 Centerville 300 .... D3
†72923 Central City 339 .... B3
72933 Charleston⊙ 1,748 .. B3
†72525 Cherokee Village-Hidden
     Valley 4,058 .... G1
72324 Cherry Valley 729 .... J3
72934 Chester 139 .... B2
71726 Chidester 342 ...... D6
72029 Clarendon⊙ 2,361 .... H4
72325 Clarkedale 300 ...... K3
72830 Clarksville⊙ 5,237 .... D3
72031 Clinton⊙ 1,284 ...... F2
72326 Colt 378 .... J3
71831 Columbus 265 .... C6
72523 Concord 234 ...... G2
72032 Conway⊙ 20,375 .... F3
72422 Corning⊙ 3,650 .... J1
72626 Cotter 920 .... E1
72036 Cotton Plant 1,323 .. H3
71937 Cove 391 .... B5
72037 Coy 183 .... G4
72327 Crawfordsville 685 .. K3
71635 Crossett 6,706 .... G7
71728 Curtis 300 .... D6
72526 Cushman 556 .... G2
†71950 Daisy 177 .... C5
72039 Damascus 307 .... F3
72833 Danville⊙ 1,698 .... D3
72834 Dardanelle⊙ 3,621 .. D3
72424 Datto 112 .... J1
72722 Decatur 1,013 .... A1
72425 Delaplaine 161 .... J1
71940 Delight 431 ...... C5
72426 Dell 310 .... K2
†72821 Denning 238 ...... C3
71832 De Queen⊙ 4,594 .. B5
71638 Dermott 4,731 .... H7
72040 Des Arc⊙ 2,001 .... G4
72041 De Valls Bluff⊙ 738 .. H4
72042 De Witt⊙ 3,928 .... H5

72644 Diamond City 650 ...... E1
72043 Diaz 1,192 .... H2
71833 Dierks 1,249 .... B5
71941 Donaldson 300 .... E5
72837 Dover 948 .... D3
71639 Dumas 6,091 .... H6
72935 Dyer 608 .... B3
72330 Dyess 446 .... K2
72331 Earle 3,517 .... K3
71701 East Camden 632 .... E6
72332 Edmondson 344 .... K3
72333 Elaine 991 .... J5
71730 El Dorado⊙ 25,270 .. E7
72727 Elkins 579 .... C1
72728 Elm Springs 781 .... B1
71740 Emerson 444 ...... D7
72047 Enola 186 .... F3
71640 Eudora 3,840 ...... H7
72632 Eureka Springs⊙ 1,989 .. C1
72532 Evening Shade 397 .... G1
72633 Everton 134 .... E1
72730 Farmington 1,283 .... B1
72701 Fayetteville⊙ 36,608 .. B1
   Fayetteville-Springdale
     07 .... B1
†71747 Felsenthal 220 ...... F7
72429 Fisher 302 .... J2
72634 Flippin 1,072 ...... E1
71742 Fordyce⊙ 5,175 .... F6
71836 Foreman 1,377 .... B6
72335 Forrest City⊙ 13,803 .. J3
*72901 Fort Smith‡ 71,626 .. B3
   Fort Smith‡ 203,269 .. B3
71837 Fouke 614 .... C7
71642 Fountain Hill 352 .... G7
†72016 Fourche 51 .... E4
72536 Franklin 253 .... G1
72017 Fredonia (Biscoe) 486 .. H4
71942 Friendship 163 .... E5
71838 Fulton 326 .... C6
72732 Garfield 187 ...... C1
71839 Garland 660 ...... C7
72052 Garner 216 ...... G3
72635 Gassville 859 .... F1
72733 Gateway 75 ...... B1
71840 Genoa 350 ...... C7
72734 Gentry 1,468 .... A1
72636 Gilbert 43 ...... E2
72055 Gillett 927 ...... H5
71841 Gillham 252 .... B5
72339 Gilmore 503 .... K3
71943 Glenwood 1,402 .. C5
72340 Goodwin 225 .... J4
†72315 Gosnell 3,215 .... K2
71643 Gould 1,671 ...... G6
71644 Grady 488 .... G5
71944 Grannis 349 ...... B5
72838 Gravelly 300 ...... C4
72736 Gravette 1,218 .... B1
72058 Greenbrier 1,423 .. F3
72638 Green Forest 1,609 .. D1
72737 Greenland 622 .... B1
72430 Greenway 317 .... K1
72936 Greenwood⊙ 3,317 .. B3
†72067 Greers Ferry 558 .... F2
72060 Griffithville 254 .... G3
72431 Grubbs 546 .... H2
72540 Guion 177 .... G2
†71923 Gum Springs 255 .... D5
71743 Gurdon 2,707 ...... D6
72061 Guy 209 .... F3
72937 Hackett 505 ...... B3
†71638 Halley H6
71646 Hamburg⊙ 3,394 .... G7
71744 Hampton⊙ 1,627 .... F6
72542 Hardy 643 .... H1
71745 Harrell 302 .... F7
72432 Harrisburg⊙ 1,921 .. J2
72601 Harrison⊙ 9,567 .... D1
72938 Hartford 613 .... B3
72840 Hartman 517 .... C3
†72015 Haskell 1,074 ...... E4
71945 Hatfield 410 .... B5
72842 Havana 352 .... D3
72341 Haynes 359 .... J4
72064 Hazen 1,636 .... G4
72543 Heber Springs⊙ 4,589 .. G2
72843 Hector 449 .... E3
72342 Helena⊙ 9,598 ...... J4
72065 Hensley 500 .... F4
71647 Hermitage 378 ...... F7
72347 Hickory Ridge 478 .. J3
72067 Higden 45 .... F2
72068 Higginson 333 ...... G3
†72734 Highfill 92 .... B1
72738 Hindsville C1
72069 Holly Grove 754 .... H4
†72958 Hon 250 .... B4
71801 Hope⊙ 10,290 ...... C6
71842 Horatio 989 .... B3
72512 Horseshoe Bend 1,909 .. G1
71901 Hot Springs National
     Park⊙ 35,781 .... D4
72070 Houston 183 .... E3

(continued on following page)

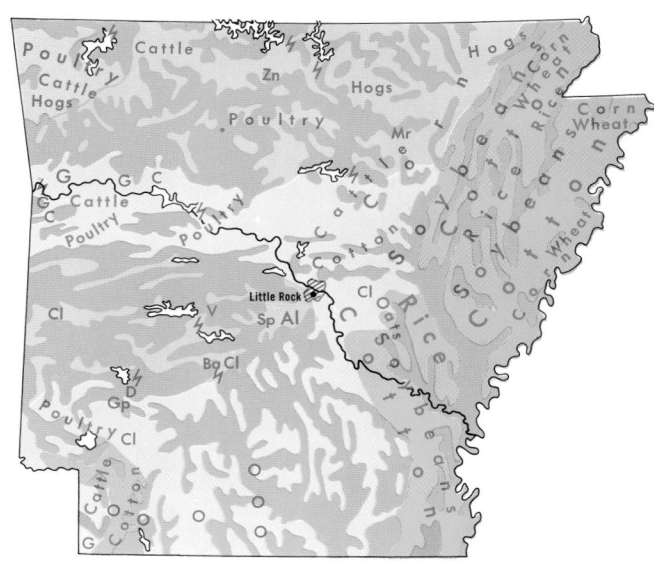

Agriculture, Industry and Resources

DOMINANT LAND USE

    Fruit and Mixed Farming

    Specialized Cotton

    Cotton, General Farming

    Rice, General Farming

    General Farming, Livestock, Truck Farming, Cotton

    Forests

    Swampland, Limited Agriculture

MAJOR MINERAL OCCURRENCES

Al	Bauxite	Gp	Gypsum
Ba	Barite	Mr	Marble
C	Coal	O	Petroleum
Cl	Clay	Sp	Soapstone
D	Diamonds	V	Vanadium
G	Natural Gas	Zn	Zinc

 Water Power   Major Industrial Areas

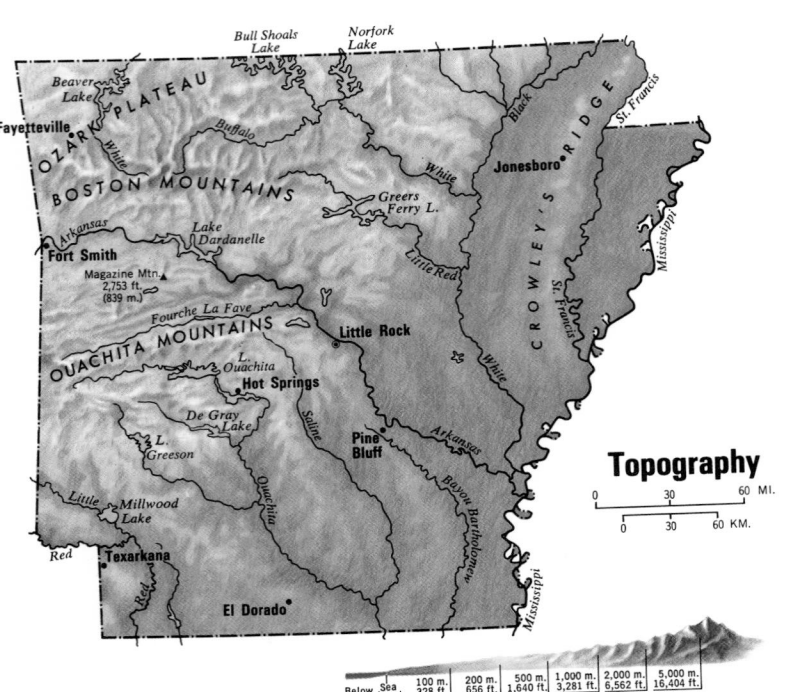

Topography

0   30   60 MI.

0   30   60 KM.

Below | 100 m. | 200 m. | 500 m. | 1,000 m. | 2,000 m. | 5,000 m.
Sea Level | 328 ft. | 656 ft. | 1,640 ft. | 3,281 ft. | 6,562 ft. | 16,404 ft.

71764 Stephens 1,366	E7	72770 Tontitown 615	B1
72159 Steprock 600	H2	72167 Traskwood 459	E5
72469 Strawberry 280	F7	72472 Trumann 6,405	J2
71765 Strong 785	H4	72168 Tucker 375	G5
72160 Stuttgart⊙ 10,941	C3	72473 Tuckerman 2,078	H2
72865 Subiaco 744	J1	†72015 Tull 281	E5
72470 Success 223	H2	72169 Tupelo 248	H3
72579 Sulphur Rock 316	H2	72384 Turrell 1,041	K3
72768 Sulphur Springs 496	B1	72386 Tyronza 777	K3
72677 Summit 506	E1	72170 Ulm 201	H4
72471 Swifton 859	H2	72955 Uniontown 600	B2
71861 Taylor 657	D7	71768 Urbana 500	E7
75502 Texarkana⊙ 21,459	C7	72682 Valley Springs 190	D1
Texarkana‡ 127,019	C7	72956 Van Buren⊙ 12,020	B3
71766 Thornton 711	F6	71972 Vandervoort 98	B5
72166 Tichnor 350	H5	72370 Victoria 175	K2
71670 Tillar 280	H6	72173 Vilonia 736	F3
71767 Tinsman 112	F6	†72002 Vimy Ridge 600	F4
71851 Tollette 407	C6	72583 Viola 362	G1

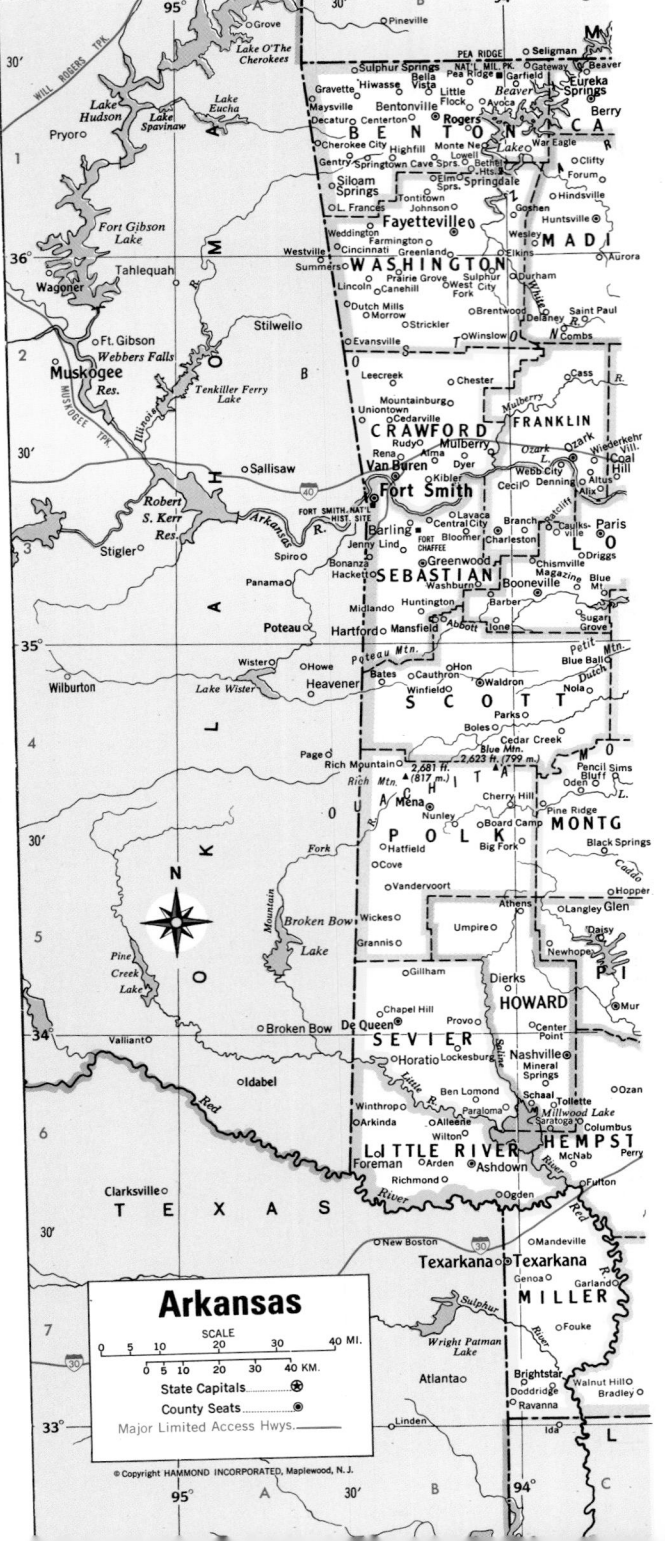

72433 Hoxie 2,961	H1	72365 Marked Tree 3,201	K2	†71801 Patmos 88	C7
72348 Hughes 1,919	J4	72443 Marmaduke 1,168	K1	72123 Patterson 567	H3
72072 Humnoke 442	G4	72650 Marshall⊙ 1,595	E2	72453 Peach Orchard 243	J1
72073 Humphrey 872	G5	72366 Marvell 1,724	J4	71964 Pearcy 400	D5
72074 Hunter 383	H3	72106 Mayflower 1,381	F4	72751 Pea Ridge 1,488	B1
72940 Huntington 662	B3	72444 Maynard 381	J1	72104 Perla 149	E5
72740 Huntsville⊙ 1,394	C1	71847 McCaskill 87	C6	72125 Perry 254	E3
71747 Huttig 976	H1	72101 McCrory 1,942	H3	71801 Perrytown 282	C6
72434 Imboden 661	H2	72441 McDougal 239	K1	72126 Perryville⊙ 1,058	E3
72075 Jacksonport 288	F4	71654 McGehee 5,671	H6	72454 Piggott⊙ 3,762	K1
72076 Jacksonville 27,589	G2	71752 McNeil 725	D7	†71601 Pine Bluff⊙ 56,636	F5
†72501 Jasper⊙ 519	D1	72102 McRae 641	G3	Pine Bluff‡ 90,718	F5
72079 Jefferson 250	F5	72556 Melbourne⊙ 1,619	G1	†72847 Piney 2,283	D3
71650 Jerome 54	G7	72367 Mellwood 250	H5	72857 Plainview 752	D4
72080 Jerusalem 300	E3	71953 Mena⊙ 5,154	B4	72568 Pleasant Plains 267	G2
71949 Jessieville 350	D4	72107 Menifee 368	E3	72127 Plumerville 785	E3
72741 Johnson 519	B1	72945 Midland 286	C6	72455 Pocahontas⊙ 5,995	H1
72350 Joiner 725	K3	71851 Mineral Springs 936	C6	72456 Pollard 298	K1
72401 Jonesboro⊙ 31,530	J2	72445 Minturn 169	H6	72374 Poplar Grove 300	J4
72081 Judsonia 2,025	G3	†71639 Mitchellville 618	K2	72457 Portia 480	H1
71749 Junction City 813	E7	72447 Monette 1,165	H4	71663 Portland 701	H7
72351 Keiser 962	K2	72108 Monroe 250	H3	72858 Pottsville 564	D3
72082 Kensett 1,751	G3	71655 Monticello⊙ 8,259	G6	72458 Powhatan 49	H1
72083 Keo 208	G4	71658 Montrose 541	H7	72128 Poyen 329	E5
†72956 Kibler 798	B3	†72501 Moorefield 129	G2	72753 Prairie Grove 1,708	B2
71652 Kingsland 320	F6	72368 Moro 327	H4	72129 Prattsville 317	F5
71950 Kirby 800	C5	72110 Morrilton⊙ 7,355	E3	71857 Prescott⊙ 4,103	D6
72435 Knobel 503	J1	71659 Moscow 325	G5	72672 Pyatt 217	E1
72845 Knoxville 264	J1	72946 Mountainburg 595	B2	72130 Quitman 556	F3
72436 Lafe 215	K2	72653 Mountain Home⊙ 8,066	F1	72951 Ratcliff 197	C3
72437 Lake City⊙ 1,842	E1	71956 Mountain Pine 1,068	D4	†72333 Ratio 250	J5
72642 Lakeview 512	F1	72560 Mountain View⊙ 2,147	F2	72459 Ravenden 338	H1
†72389 Lake View 609	H7	71758 Mount Holly 250	E7	72460 Ravenden Springs 230	H1
71653 Lake Village⊙ 3,088	D3	71957 Mount Ida⊙ 1,023	C4	71726 Reader 127	D6
72846 Lamar 708	B3	72561 Mount Pleasant 438	G2	72461 Rector 2,336	F5
72941 Lavaca 1,092	F7	72111 Mount Vernon 157	F3	72132 Redfield 745	H6
71750 Lawson 250	J1	72947 Murphy 1,444	B2	71670 Reed 395	H6
72438 Leachville 1,882	K2	71958 Murfreesboro⊙ 1,883	C5	72462 Reyno 521	J1
72644 Lead Hill 247	D1	71852 Nashville⊙ 4,554	C6	71665 Rison⊙ 1,325	F6
72084 Leola 481	E5	72562 Newark 1,128	H2	†72104 Rockport 231	E5
72354 Lepanto 1,964	K2	72851 New Blaine 200	D3	72134 Roe 136	H4
72645 Leslie 501	E2	71959 Newhope 300	C5	72756 Rogers 17,429	B1
72085 Letona 231	G3	72112 Newport⊙ 8,339	H2	†72355 Rondo 330	J4
71845 Lewisville⊙ 1,476	C7	72461 Nimmons 112	K1	72137 Rose Bud 202	F3
72355 Lexa 500	J4	†71601 Noble Lake 250	G5	71858 Rosston 274	D6
72744 Lincoln 1,422	B2	72658 Norfork 399	F1	72952 Rudy 70	B3
†72712 Little Flock 663	B1	71960 Norman 539	C5	72139 Russell 232	G3
†72201 Little Rock		71759 Norphlet 756	E7	72801 Russellville⊙ 14,031	D3
(cap.)⊙ 158,461	F4	†72801 Norristown 825	D3	72140 Saint Charles 199	H5
Little Rock-North Little		†71635 North Crossett 3,513	G7	72464 Saint Francis 266	K1
Rock‡ 393,494	F4	*72114 North Little Rock 64,288	F4	72760 Saint Paul 198	C2
71846 Lockesburg 616	B6	72660 Oak Grove 265	C6	72576 Salem⊙ 1,424	G1
72847 London 859	D3	†71801 Oakhaven 72	C4	72658 Salesville 406	F1
72086 Lonoke⊙ 4,128	G4	71961 Oden 186	B6	72863 Scranton 244	C3
72087 Lonsdale 117	E4	71853 Ogden 334	B2	72143 Searcy⊙ 13,612	G3
71751 Louann 282	E7	72564 Oil Trough 280	G2	72465 Sedgwick 205	J2
72745 Lowell 1,078	B1	72751 O'Kean 291	J1	72103 Shannon Hills 1,656	F4
†72856 Lurton 38	D2	71962 Okolona 200	D5	72150 Sheridan⊙ 3,042	F5
72358 Luxora 1,739	K2	72853 Ola 1,121	D3	72152 Sherrill 161	F5
72440 Lynn 345	H2	72662 Omaha 191	D1	72116 Sherwood 10,406	F4
72359 Madison 1,238	J4	†72110 Oppelo 486	E3	72153 Shirley 354	F2
72943 Magazine 799	C3	72370 Osceola⊙ 8,881	K2	72577 Sidney 270	G1
72553 Magness 196	H2	72565 Oxford 520	G1	72761 Siloam Springs 7,940	B1
71753 Magnolia⊙ 11,909	D7	71855 Ozan 111	C6	71762 Smackover 2,453	E7
72104 Malvern⊙ 10,163	E5	72949 Ozark⊙ 3,597	C3	72466 Smithville 113	H1
72554 Mammoth Spring 1,158	G1	72372 Palestine 976	J4	†71658 Snyder 700	H1
72442 Manila 2,553	K2	72121 Pangburn 673	G3	71763 Sparkman 622	E6
72944 Mansfield 1,000	B3	72450 Paragould⊙ 15,248	J1	72764 Springdale 23,458	B1
72360 Marianna⊙ 6,220	J4	72855 Paris⊙ 3,991	C3	Springdale-Fayetteville‡	
†72395 Marie 287	K3	71661 Parkdale 471	H7	177,850	B1
72364 Marion⊙ 2,996	K3	72373 Parkin 2,035	J3	71860 Stamps 2,859	D7
		72950 Parks 600	B4	71667 Star City⊙ 2,066	G6

72389 Wabash 300	J5
72175 Wabbaseka 428	G5
72475 Waldenburg 124	J2
71770 Waldo 1,685	D7
72958 Waldron⊙ 2,642	B4
72476 Walnut Ridge⊙ 4,152	J1
72176 Ward 981	F3
71671 Warren⊙ 7,646	F6
71862 Washington 265	C6
71674 Watson 433	H6
72479 Weiner 750	J2
72177 Weldon 161	H3
†71635 West Crossett 1,466	F7
72685 Western Grove 378	D1
72774 West Fork 1,526	B2
72390 West Helena 11,367	J4
72301 West Memphis 28,138	K3
72178 West Point 226	G3
72391 West Ridge 300	K2

72392 Wheatley 523	H4
71772 Whelen Springs 156	D6
71602 White Hall 2,214	F5
71973 Wickes 464	B5
72394 Widener 316	J3
72482 Williford 169	H1
71675 Wilmar 747	G6
71676 Wilmot 1,227	G7
72395 Wilson 1,115	K2
71865 Wilton 495	B6
71677 Winchester 279	G6
72959 Winslow 247	B2
71866 Winthrop 238	B6
72587 Wiseman 327	G1
72180 Woodson 450	F4
72181 Wooster 398	F3
72183 Wrightsville-Tafton 1,434	F4
72396 Wynne⊙ 7,805	J3
72687 Yellville⊙ 1,044	E1

†72601 Zinc 113	E1

OTHER FEATURES

Arkansas (riv.)	G5
Arkansas Post Nat'l Mem.	H5
Bartholomew (bayou)	G6
Bayou Bodcau (res.)	C7
Bayou Des Arc (riv.)	G3
Beaver (lake)	C1
Black (riv.)	H2
Blue Mountain (lake)	C3
Blytheville A.F.B.	K2
Boston (mts.)	B2
Buffalo (riv.)	E2
Bull Shoals (lake)	E1
Cache (riv.)	H3
Caddo (riv.)	D5
Catherine (lake)	E5

Chinkapin Knob (mt.)	E2
Conway (lake)	F3
Current (riv.)	J1
Cypress (bayou)	F3
Dardanelle (lake)	C3
De Gray (lake)	D5
Des Arc (bayou)	G3
De View (bayou)	J3
Erling (lake)	C7
Fort Smith Nat'l Hist. Site	B3
Fourche LaFave (riv.)	D4
Greers Ferry (lake)	G2
Greeson (lake)	C5
Hamilton (lake)	D5
Hot Springs Nat'l Park	D4
Illinois (bayou)	D3
L'Anguille (riv.)	J3
La Grue (bayou)	H5
Little (riv.)	B6

Little Missouri (riv.)	D6
Little Red (riv.)	G3
Little Rock A.F.B.	F4
Magazine (mt.)	C3
Meto (bayou)	H5
Millwood (lake)	C6
Mississippi (riv.)	H7
Mountain Fork (riv.)	A5
Mulberry (riv.)	C2
Nebo (mt.)	D3
Nimrod (lake)	D4
Norfork (lake)	F1
Ouachita (lake)	C4
Ouachita (mts.)	B4
Ouachita (riv.)	E7
Ozark (plat.)	C1
Pea Ridge Nat'l Mil. Park	B1
Peckerwood (lake)	G4
Petit Jean (mt.)	C3

Petit Jean (riv.)	D3
Pine Bluff Arsenal	F5
Poteau (mt.)	B4
Red (riv.)	C6
Reeves Knob (mt.)	E2
Saint Francis (riv.)	J4
Saline (riv.)	B6
Saline (riv.)	E5
Seven Devils (res.)	G6
Spring (riv.)	H1
Sulphur (riv.)	B7
Table Rock (riv.)	D1
Tyronza (riv.)	K2
Wattensaw (bayou)	G4
White (riv.)	H5
White Oak (lake)	D6
Winona (lake)	E4

⊙County seat.
‡Population of metropolitan area.
† Zip of nearest p.o.   * Multiple zips.

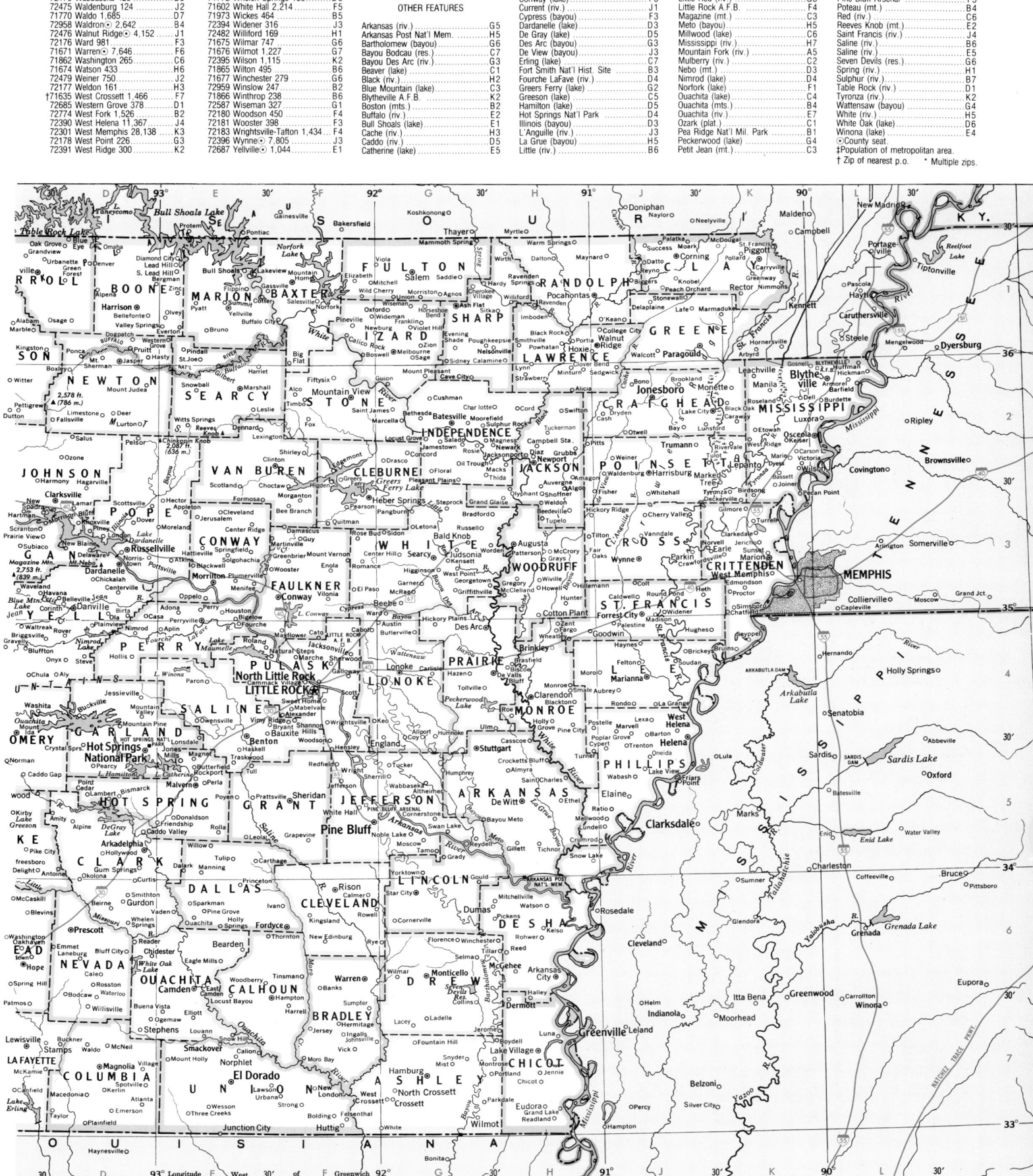

California

SCALE
0 10 20   40   60   80 MI.
0 10 20 40 60 80KM.

State Capitals .... ⊛
County Seats .... ⊙
Canals ....
Major Limited Access Hwys.

San Francisco
and Vicinity

0 5 10 15   20MI.
0 5 10 15 20KM.

Sacramento
and Vicinity

0 5 10 15 20MI.
0 5 10 15 20KM.

Los Angeles
and Vicinity

0 5 10 15 20MI.
0 5 10 15 20KM.

COUNTIES

Alameda 1,105,379 ... D6
Alpine 1,097 ... F5
Amador 19,314 ... E5
Butte 143,851 ... D4
Calaveras 20,710 ... E5
Colusa 12,791 ... C4
Contra Costa 656,380 ... D6
Del Norte 18,217 ... B2
El Dorado 85,812 ... E5
Fresno 514,229 ... E7
Glenn 21,350 ... C4
Humboldt 108,514 ... B3
Imperial 92,110 ... K10
Inyo 17,895 ... H7
Kern 403,089 ... G8
Kings 73,738 ... G8
Lake 36,366 ... C4
Lassen 21,661 ... E3
Los Angeles 7,477,503 ... G9
Madera 63,116 ... F6
Marin 222,592 ... C5
Mariposa 11,108 ... E6
Mendocino 66,738 ... B4
Merced 134,558 ... E6
Modoc 8,610 ... E2
Mono 8,577 ... F5
Monterey 290,444 ... D7
Napa 99,199 ... C5
Nevada 51,645 ... E4
Orange 1,932,709 ... H10
Placer 117,247 ... E4
Plumas 17,340 ... E4
Riverside 663,199 ... J10
Sacramento 783,381 ... D5
San Benito 25,005 ... D7
San Bernardino 895,016 ... J9
San Diego 1,861,846 ... J10
San Francisco (city county) 678,974 ... J2
San Joaquin 347,342 ... D6
San Luis Obispo 155,435 ... E8
San Mateo 587,329 ... J3
Santa Barbara 298,694 ... E9
Santa Clara 1,295,071 ... D6
Santa Cruz 188,141 ... C6
Shasta 115,715 ... C3
Sierra 3,073 ... E4
Siskiyou 39,732 ... C2
Solano 235,203 ... D5
Sonoma 299,681 ... C5
Stanislaus 265,900 ... D6
Sutter 52,246 ... D4
Tehama 38,888 ... C3
Trinity 11,858 ... B3
Tulare 245,738 ... G7
Tuolumne 33,928 ... F5
Ventura 529,174 ... F9
Yolo 113,374 ... D5
Yuba 49,733 ... D4

CITIES and TOWNS

Zip *Name/Pop.* *Key*

94501 Alameda 63,852 ... J2
94507 Alamo 8,505 ... K2
94706 Albany 15,130 ... J2
*91801 Alhambra 64,615 ... C10
92001 Alpine 5,368 ... J11
91001 Altadena 40,983 ... C10
96101 Alturas⊙ 3,025 ... E2
†95116 Alum Rock 16,890 ... L3
*92801 Anaheim 219,494 ... D11
Anaheim-Santa Ana-Garden Grove‡ 1,931,570 ... D11
96007 Anderson 7,381 ... C3
95222 Angels Camp 2,302 ... E5
94508 Angwin 3,526 ... C5
94509 Antioch 42,683 ... L1
92307 Apple Valley 14,305 ... H9
95003 Aptos 7,039 ... K4
91006 Arcadia 45,994 ... C10
95521 Arcata 12,850 ... A3
95825 Arden-Arcade 87,570 ... B8
93420 Arroyo Grande 11,290 ... E8
90701 Artesia 14,301 ... C11
93203 Arvin 6,863 ... G8
†94577 Ashland 13,983 ... K2
95413 Asti 75 ... C5
93422 Atascadero 16,232 ... E8
94025 Atherton 7,797 ... K3
95301 Atwater 17,530 ... E6
95603 Auburn⊙ 7,540 ... C8
90704 Avalon 2,022 ... G10
93204 Avenal 4,137 ... E8
91702 Azusa 29,380 ... D10
*93301 Bakersfield⊙ 105,735 ... G8
Bakersfield‡ 403,089 ... G8
91706 Baldwin Park 50,554 ... D10
92220 Banning 14,020 ... J10
92311 Barstow 17,690 ... H9
†93402 Baywood Park-Los Osos 10,933 ... E8
92223 Beaumont 6,818 ... J10
90201 Bell 25,450 ... C11
90706 Bellflower 53,441 ... C11
90201 Bell Gardens 34,117 ... C11
94002 Belmont 24,505 ... J3
94510 Benicia 15,376 ... K1
95005 Ben Lomond 7,238 ... K4
*94701 Berkeley 103,328 ... J2
*90210 Beverly Hills 32,367 ... B10
92315 Big Bear Lake ... J9
93920 Big Sur 500 ... D7
93514 Bishop 3,333 ... G6
92316 Bloomington 18,888 ... E10
92225 Blythe 6,805 ... L10
94923 Bodega Bay 800 ... B5
93516 Boron 2,040 ... H8
92004 Borrego Springs 1,405 ... J10
95006 Boulder Creek 5,662 ... J4
92227 Brawley 14,946 ... K11
92621 Brea 27,913 ... D11
94513 Brentwood 4,434 ... L2
93517 Bridgeport⊙ 525 ... F5
94005 Brisbane 2,969 ... J2
95605 Broderick-Bryte 10,194 ... B8
*90622 Buena Park 64,165 ... D11
*91501 Burbank 84,625 ... C10
94010 Burlingame 26,173 ... J2
96013 Burney 3,187 ... D3
92231 Calexico 14,412 ... K11
93505 California City 2,743 ... H8
94515 Calistoga 3,879 ... C5
93745 Calwa 6,640 ... F7
93010 Camarillo 37,797 ... F9
95008 Campbell 26,910 ... K3
*91303 Canoga Park ... B10
92624 Capistrano Beach 6,168 ... H10
95010 Capitola 9,095 ... K4
92007 Cardiff-by-the-Sea 10,054 ... H10
92008 Carlsbad 35,490 ... H10
93923 Carmel 4,707 ... D7
93924 Carmel Valley 4,013 ... D7
95608 Carmichael 43,108 ... C8
93013 Carpinteria 10,835 ... F9
90745 Carson 81,221 ... C11
94546 Castro Valley 44,011 ... K2
95012 Castroville 4,396 ... D7
92234 Cathedral City 4,130 ... J10
96019 Central Valley 3,424 ... C3
95307 Ceres 13,281 ... D6
†90701 Cerritos 53,020 ... C11
†94541 Cherryland 9,425 ... K2
95926 Chico 26,603 ... D4
Chico‡ 143,851 ... D4
†93555 China Lake 4,275 ... H8
95309 Chinese Camp 150 ... E6
91710 Chino 40,165 ... D10
93610 Chowchilla 5,122 ... E6
*92010 Chula Vista 83,927 ... J11
95610 Citrus Heights 85,911 ... C8
91711 Claremont 30,950 ... D10
95425 Cloverdale 3,989 ... B5
93612 Clovis 33,021 ... F7
92236 Coachella 9,129 ... J10
93210 Coalinga 6,593 ... E7
95713 Colfax 981 ... E4
92324 Colton 15,201 ... E10
95932 Colusa⊙ 4,075 ... C4
90040 Commerce 10,509 ... C10
*90220 Compton 81,286 ... C11
*94520 Concord 103,255 ... K1
93212 Corcoran 6,454 ... F7
96021 Corning 4,745 ... C4
91720 Corona 37,791 ... E11
92118 Coronado 18,790 ... H11
94925 Corte Madera 8,074 ... J2
*92626 Costa Mesa 82,562 ... D11
94928 Cotati 3,346 ... C5
*91722 Covina 33,751 ... D10
95531 Crescent City⊙ 3,075 ... A2
92325 Crestline 6,715 ... H9
90201 Cudahy 17,984 ... C11
90230 Culver City 38,139 ... B10
95014 Cupertino 34,265 ... K3
93615 Cutler 3,149 ... F7
90630 Cypress 40,391 ... D11
*94014 Daly City 78,519 ... H2
92629 Dana Point 10,602 ... H10
94526 Danville 26,446 ... K2
95616 Davis 36,640 ... B8
93215 Delano 16,491 ... F8
95315 Delhi 2,832 ... E6
92014 Del Mar 5,017 ... H11
92240 Desert Hot Springs 5,941 ... J9
93618 Dinuba 9,907 ... F7
95620 Dixon 7,541 ... B9
93620 Dos Palos 3,121 ... E6
*90240 Downey 82,602 ... C11
95936 Downieville⊙ 500 ... E4
91010 Duarte 16,766 ... D10
94566 Dublin 13,496 ... K2
93219 Earlimart 4,578 ... F8
90022 East Los Angeles 100,017 ... C10
*92020 El Cajon 73,892 ... J11
92243 El Centro⊙ 23,996 ... K11
94530 El Cerrito 22,731 ... J2
95630 El Dorado Hills 3,453 ... C8
94018 El Granada 3,582 ... H3
95624 Elk Grove 10,959 ... B9
*91731 El Monte 79,494 ... D10
†93030 El Rio 5,674 ... F9
90245 El Segundo 13,752 ... B11
92630 El Toro 38,153 ... E11
94608 Emeryville 3,714 ... J2
92024 Encinitas 10,796 ... H10
91316 Encino ... B10
95320 Escalon 3,127 ... E6
*92025 Escondido 64,355 ... J10
95501 Eureka⊙ 24,153 ... A3
93221 Exeter 5,606 ... F7
94930 Fairfax 7,391 ... H1
94533 Fairfield⊙ 58,099 ... K1
95628 Fair Oaks 22,602 ... C8
92028 Fallbrook 14,041 ... H10
93223 Farmersville 5,544 ... F7
95018 Felton 4,564 ... K4
93015 Fillmore 9,602 ... G9
93622 Firebaugh 3,740 ... E7
95828 Florin 16,523 ... B8
95630 Folsom 11,003 ... C8
92335 Fontana 37,107 ... E10
†93268 Ford City 3,392 ... F8
95437 Fort Bragg 5,019 ... B4
†95421 Fort Ross 30 ... B5
95540 Fortuna 7,591 ... A3
94404 Foster City 23,287 ... J2
92708 Fountain Valley 55,080 ... D11
95019 Freedom 6,416 ... L4
*94536 Fremont 131,945 ... K3
*93706 Fresno⊙ 217,289 ... F7
Fresno‡ 515,013 ... F7
*92631 Fullerton 102,034 ... D11
95632 Galt 5,514 ... C9
*90747 Gardena 45,165 ... C11
*92640 Garden Grove 123,307 ... D11
95020 Gilroy 21,641 ... D6
92509 Glen Avon Heights 8,444 ... E10
*91201 Glendale 139,060 ... C10
91740 Glendora 38,500 ... D10
93926 Gonzales 2,891 ... D7
91344 Granada Hills ... B10
92324 Grand Terrace 8,498 ... E10
95945 Grass Valley 6,697 ... D4
93308 Greenacres 5,381 ... F8
93927 Greenfield 4,181 ... D7
95948 Gridley 3,982 ... D4
93433 Grover City 8,827 ... E8
93434 Guadalupe 3,629 ... E9
95322 Gustine 3,142 ... D6
94019 Half Moon Bay 7,282 ... H3
93230 Hanford⊙ 20,958 ... F7
90250 Hawthorne 56,447 ... C11
*94541 Hayward 94,342 ... K2
95448 Healdsburg 7,217 ... B5
92343 Hemet 22,454 ... H10
94547 Hercules 5,963 ... J1
90254 Hermosa Beach 18,070 ... B11
92345 Hesperia 13,540 ... H9
92346 Highland 10,908 ... H9
94010 Hillsborough 10,372 ... J2
95023 Hollister⊙ 11,488 ... D7
90028 Hollywood ... C10
92250 Holtville 4,399 ... K11
†91720 Home Gardens 5,783 ... E11
95326 Hughson 2,943 ... E6
*92646 Huntington Beach 170,505 ... C11
90255 Huntington Park 46,223 ... C11
92251 Imperial 3,451 ... K11
92032 Imperial Beach 22,689 ... H11
93526 Independence⊙ 748 ... H7
92201 Indio 21,611 ... J10
*90301 Inglewood 94,245 ... B11
92713 Irvine 62,134 ... D11
95642 Jackson⊙ 2,331 ... C9
†94701 Kensington 5,342 ... J2
93600 Kerman 4,002 ... E7
93930 King City 5,495 ... D7
93631 Kingsburg 5,115 ... F7
91011 La Canada 20,153 ... C10
91214 La Crescenta-Montrose 16,531 ... C10
94549 Lafayette 20,879 ... K2
*92651 Laguna Beach 17,901 ... G10
92653 Laguna Hills 33,600 ... D11
92677 Laguna Niguel 12,237 ... H10
90631 La Habra 45,232 ... D11
92037 La Jolla ... H11
92352 Lake Arrowhead 6,272 ... H9
92330 Lake Elsinore 5,982 ... F11
93240 Lake Isabella 3,428 ... G8
95453 Lakeport⊙ 3,675 ... C4
*90712 Lakewood 74,654 ... C11
92041 La Mesa 50,308 ... H11
90638 La Mirada 40,986 ... D11
93241 Lamont 9,616 ... G8
93534 Lancaster 48,027 ... G9
*91744 La Puente 30,882 ... D10
94939 Larkspur 11,064 ... H1
95330 Lathrop 3,717 ... D6
91750 La Verne 23,508 ... D10
90260 Lawndale 23,460 ... B11
92045 Lemon Grove 20,780 ... J11
93245 Lemoore 8,832 ... F7
†92311 Lenwood 2,974 ... H9
92024 Leucadia 9,478 ... H10
95648 Lincoln 4,132 ... B8
†95901 Linda 10,225 ... D4
93247 Lindsay 6,924 ... F7
95953 Live Oak 3,103 ... D4
†95073 Live Oak 11,482 ... K4
94550 Livermore 48,349 ... L2
95334 Livingston 5,326 ... E6
95240 Lodi 35,221 ... C9
92354 Loma Linda 10,694 ... F10
90717 Lomita 18,807 ... C11
93436 Lompoc 26,267 ... E9
*90801 Long Beach 361,334 ... C11
90720 Los Alamitos 11,529 ... D11
94022 Los Altos 25,769 ... K3
94022 Los Altos Hills 7,421 ... J3
*90001 Los Angeles⊙ 2,966,850 ... C10
Los Angeles-Long Beach‡ 7,477,657 ... C10
93635 Los Banos 10,341 ... E6
95030 Los Gatos 26,906 ... K4
†93402 Los Osos-Baywood Park 10,933 ... E8
90262 Lynwood 48,548 ... C11
93637 Madera⊙ 21,732 ... E7
90265 Malibu ... B10
93546 Mammoth Lakes 3,929 ... G6
90266 Manhattan Beach 31,542 ... B11
95336 Manteca 24,925 ... D6
93933 Marina 20,647 ... D7
95338 Mariposa⊙ 1,150 ... F6
94553 Martinez⊙ 22,582 ... K1
95901 Marysville⊙ 9,898 ... D4
90201 Maywood 21,810 ... C10
93250 McFarland 5,151 ... F8
93023 Meiners Oaks-Mira Monte 9,512 ... F9
93640 Mendota 5,038 ... E7
94025 Menlo Park 26,369 ... J3
95340 Merced⊙ 36,499 ... E6
94030 Millbrae 20,058 ... J2
94941 Mill Valley 12,967 ... H2
95035 Milpitas 37,820 ... L3
91752 Mira Loma 8,707 ... E10
92691 Mission Viejo 50,666 ... D11
*95350 Modesto⊙ 106,602 ... D6
Modesto‡ 265,902 ... D6
93501 Mojave 2,886 ... G8
91016 Monrovia 30,531 ... D10
91763 Montclair 22,628 ... D10
90640 Montebello 52,929 ... C10
93940 Monterey 27,558 ... D7
91754 Monterey Park 54,338 ... C10
95030 Monte Sereno 3,434 ... K4
91214 Montrose-La Crescenta 16,531 ... C10
93021 Moorpark 4,030 ... G9
94556 Moraga 15,014 ... K2
95037 Morgan Hill 17,060 ... L4
93442 Morro Bay 9,064 ... D8
*94042 Mountain View 58,655 ... K3
96067 Mount Shasta 2,837 ... C5
92405 Muscoy 6,188 ... E10
94558 Napa⊙ 50,879 ... C5
92050 National City 48,772 ... J11
92363 Needles 4,120 ... L9
95959 Nevada City⊙ 2,431 ... D4
94560 Newark 32,126 ... K3
91321 Newhall 12,029 ... G9
95360 Newman 2,785 ... D6
*92660 Newport Beach 62,556 ... D11
93444 Nipomo 5,247 ... E8
91760 Norco 21,126 ... E11
95660 North Highlands 37,825 ... B8
*91601 North Hollywood ... B10
90650 Norwalk 85,286 ... C11
94947 Novato 43,916 ... H1
95361 Oakdale 8,474 ... E6
*94601 Oakland⊙ 339,337 ... J2
93022 Oak View 4,671 ... F9
93445 Oceano 4,478 ... E8
92054 Oceanside 76,698 ... H10
93308 Oildale 23,382 ... F8
93023 Ojai 6,816 ... F9
*91761 Ontario 88,820 ... D10
†95060 Opal Cliffs 5,041 ... K4
*92666 Orange 91,450 ... D11
93646 Orange Cove 4,026 ... F7
94563 Orinda 16,825 ... J2
95963 Orland 4,031 ... C4
93647 Orosi 4,076 ... F7
95965 Oroville⊙ 8,683 ... D4
93030 Oxnard 108,195 ... F9
Oxnard-Simi Valley-Ventura‡ 529,899 ... F9
94553 Pacheco-Vine Hill 6,129 ... K1
94044 Pacifica 36,866 ... H2
93950 Pacific Grove 15,755 ... C7
93550 Palmdale 12,277 ... G9
92260 Palm Desert 11,801 ... J10
92262 Palm Springs 32,366 ... J10
*94301 Palo Alto 55,225 ... K3
90274 Palos Verdes Estates 14,376 ... B11
95969 Paradise 22,571 ... D4
90723 Paramount 36,407 ... C11
93648 Parlier 2,902 ... F7
*91101 Pasadena 118,072 ... C10
93446 Paso Robles 9,163 ... E8
95363 Patterson 3,908 ... D6
93953 Pebble Beach ... C7
92370 Perris 6,827 ... F11
94952 Petaluma 33,834 ... H1
90660 Pico Rivera 53,387 ... C10
94611 Piedmont 10,498 ... J2
94564 Pinole 14,253 ... J1
93449 Pismo Beach 5,364 ... E8
94565 Pittsburg 33,034 ... L1
92670 Placentia 35,041 ... D11
95667 Placerville⊙ 6,739 ... C8
94523 Pleasant Hill 25,124 ... K2
94566 Pleasanton 35,160 ... L2
*91766 Pomona 92,742 ... D10
93257 Porterville 19,707 ... G7
93041 Port Hueneme 17,803 ... F9
94025 Portola Valley 3,939 ... J3
92064 Poway 32,263 ... J11
93534 Quartz Hill 7,421 ... G9
95971 Quincy⊙ 4,451 ... E4
92065 Ramona 8,173 ... J10
95670 Rancho Cordova 42,881 ... C8
91730 Rancho Cucamonga 55,250 ... E10
92270 Rancho Mirage 6,281 ... J10
90274 Rancho Palos Verdes 36,577 ... B11
92067 Rancho Santa Fe 4,014 ... H10
96080 Red Bluff⊙ 9,490 ... C3
96001 Redding⊙ 41,995 ... C3
Redding○ ... 80
92373 Redlands 43,619 ... H9
*90277 Redondo Beach 57,102 ... B11
*94061 Redwood City⊙ 54,951 ... J3
93654 Reedley 11,071 ... F7
92376 Rialto 37,474 ... E10
*94801 Richmond 74,676 ... J1
93555 Ridgecrest 15,929 ... H8
95562 Rio Dell 2,687 ... A3
95673 Rio Linda 7,359 ... B8
94571 Rio Vista 3,142 ... L1
95366 Ripon 3,509 ... D6
95367 Riverbank 5,695 ... E6
*92501 Riverside⊙ 170,591 ... E11
Riverside-San Bernardino-Ontario‡ 1,557,080 ... E11
95677 Rocklin 7,344 ... B8
94572 Rodeo 8,286 ... J1
94928 Rohnert Park 22,965 ... C5
90274 Rolling Hills 2,049 ... B11
90274 Rolling Hills Estates 7,701 ... B11
91770 Rosemead 42,604 ... C10
95678 Roseville 24,347 ... B8
94957 Ross 2,801 ... H1
92509 Rubidoux 17,048 ... E10

(continued on following page)

AREA 158,706 sq. mi. (411,049 sq. km.)
POPULATION 23,667,565
CAPITAL Sacramento
LARGEST CITY Los Angeles
HIGHEST POINT Mt. Whitney 14,494 ft. (4418 m.)
SETTLED IN 1769
ADMITTED TO UNION September 9, 1850
POPULAR NAME Golden State
STATE FLOWER Golden Poppy
STATE BIRD California Valley Quail

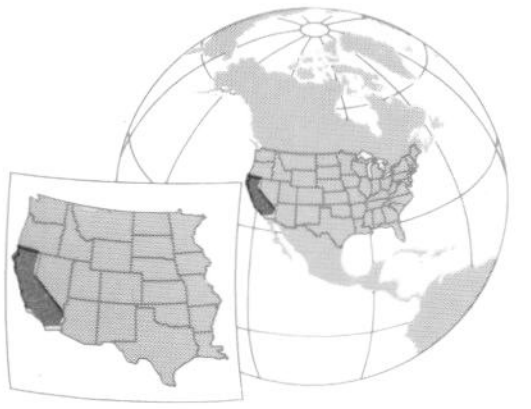

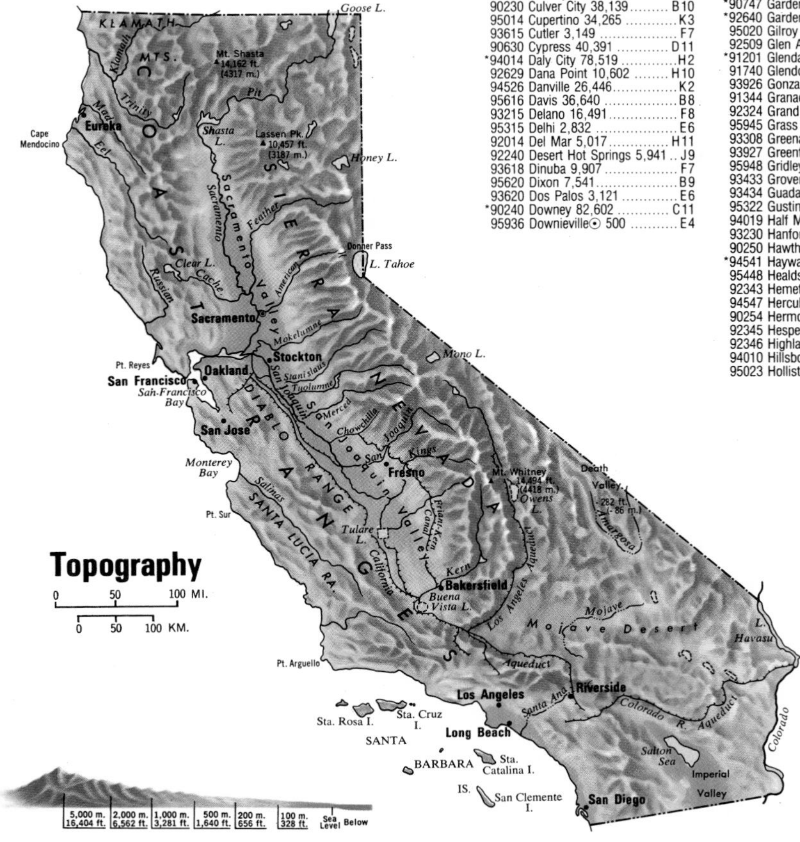

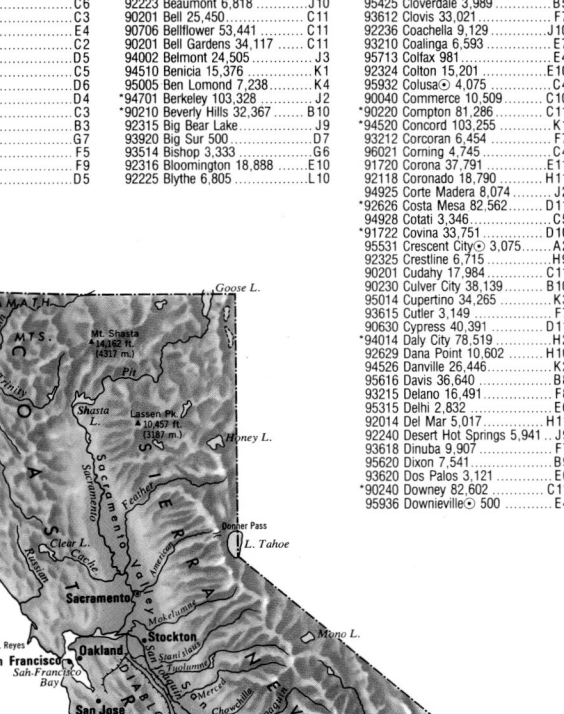

Topography
0 50 100 MI.
0 50 100 KM.
Goose L.
KLAMATH MTS.
Mt. Shasta 14,162 ft. (4317 m.)
Pit
Eureka
Cape Mendocino
Eel
Trinity
Shasta L.
Lassen Pk. 10,457 ft. (3187 m.)
Honey L.
Sacramento
Feather
Donner Pass
L. Tahoe
Clear L.
Russian
American
SIERRA
NEVADA
Sacramento
Mokelumne
Stockton
Mono L.
Pt. Reyes
Oakland
San Francisco
San Francisco Bay
Stanislaus
Tuolumne
Merced
Chowchilla
San Joaquin
DIABLO RANGE
San Jose
Monterey Bay
Kings
Fresno
Mt. Whitney 14,494 ft. (4418 m.)
Death Valley
-282 ft. (-86 m.)
Owens L.
Pt. Sur
Salinas
SANTA LUCIA RA.
Tulare L.
California
Kern
Bakersfield
Buena Vista L.
Mojave
Mojave Desert
L. Havasu
Pt. Arguello
Aqueduct
Los Angeles
Riverside
Colorado R. Aqueduct
Colorado
Sta. Rosa I.
Sta. Cruz I.
SANTA BARBARA IS.
Long Beach
Sta. Catalina I.
San Clemente I.
Salton Sea
Imperial Valley
San Diego
5,000 m. 16,404 ft.
2,000 m. 6,562 ft.
1,000 m. 3,281 ft.
500 m. 1,640 ft.
200 m. 656 ft.
100 m. 328 ft.
Sea Level
Below

*95801 Sacramento (cap.)⊙ 275,741 ... B8
Sacramento‡ 1,014,002 ... B8
94574 Saint Helena 4,898 ... C5
93901 Salinas⊙ 80,479 ... D7
Salinas-Seaside-Monterey‡ 290,444 ... D7
95249 San Andreas⊙ 1,912 ... E5
94960 San Anselmo 12,067 ... H1
*92401 San Bernardino⊙ 118,794 ... E10
94066 San Bruno 35,417 ... J2
94070 San Carlos 24,710 ... J3
92672 San Clemente 27,325 ... H10
*92101 San Diego⊙ 875,538 ... H11
San Diego‡ 1,861,846 ... H11
91773 San Dimas 24,014 ... D10
*91340 San Fernando 17,731 ... C10
*94101 San Francisco⊙ 678,974 ... H2
San Francisco-Oakland‡ 3,252,721 ... H2
*91775 San Gabriel 30,072 ... C10
93657 Sanger 12,542 ... F7
92383 San Jacinto 7,098 ... H10
*95101 San Jose⊙ 629,546 ... L3
San Jose‡ 1,295,071 ... L3
†92691 San Juan Capistrano 18,959 ... H10
*94577 San Leandro 63,952 ... J2
94580 San Lorenzo 20,545 ... K2
93401 San Luis Obispo⊙ 34,252 ... E8
92069 San Marcos 17,479 ... H10
91108 San Marino 13,307 ... D10
*94401 San Mateo 77,640 ... J3
94806 San Pablo 19,750 ... J1
94964 San Quentin 450 ... H1
*94901 San Rafael⊙ 44,700 ... J1
94583 San Ramon 22,356 ... K2
93452 San Simeon 350 ... D8
*92701 Santa Ana⊙ 204,023 ... D11
*93101 Santa Barbara⊙ 74,414 ... F9
Santa Barbara-Santa Maria-Lompoc‡ 298,660 ... F9
*95050 Santa Clara 87,700 ... K3
*95060 Santa Cruz⊙ 41,483 ... K4
Santa Cruz‡ 188,141 ... K4
90670 Santa Fe Springs 14,520 ... C11
93454 Santa Maria 39,685 ... E9
*90401 Santa Monica 88,314 ... B10
93060 Santa Paula 20,552 ... F9
*95401 Santa Rosa⊙ 83,320 ... C5
Santa Rosa‡ 299,827 ... C5
92071 Santee 47,080 ... J11
95070 Saratoga 29,261 ... K4
94965 Sausalito 7,338 ... H2
95060 Scotts Valley 6,891 ... K4
90740 Seal Beach 25,975 ... C11
93955 Seaside 36,567 ... D7
95472 Sebastopol 5,595 ... C5
93662 Selma 10,942 ... F7
93263 Shafter 7,010 ... F8
96125 Sierra City 500 ... E4
91024 Sierra Madre 10,837 ... D10
†90806 Signal Hill 5,734 ... C11
*93065 Simi Valley 77,500 ... G9
92075 Solana Beach 13,047 ... H11
93960 Soledad 5,928 ... D7
93463 Solvang 3,091 ... E9
95476 Sonoma 6,054 ... C5
95370 Sonora⊙ 3,247 ... E6
95073 Soquel 6,212 ... K4
91733 South El Monte 16,623 ... D10
90280 South Gate 66,784 ... C11
95705 South Lake Tahoe 20,681 ... F5
†95965 South Oroville 7,246 ... D4
91030 South Pasadena 22,681 ... C10
94080 South San Francisco 49,393 ... J2
94305 Stanford 11,045 ... J3
90680 Stanton 23,723 ... D11
*95201 Stockton⊙ 149,779 ... D6
Stockton‡ 347,342 ... D6
94585 Suisun City 11,087 ... K1
92381 Sun City 8,460 ... F11
92388 Sunnymead 11,554 ... F11
*94086 Sunnyvale 106,618 ... K3
96130 Susanville⊙ 6,520 ... E3
95685 Sutter Creek 1,705 ... C9
93268 Taft 5,316 ... F8
95730 Tahoe City ... E4
93561 Tehachapi 4,126 ... G8
91780 Temple City 28,972 ... D10
†95965 Thermalito 4,961 ... D4
*91360 Thousand Oaks 77,072 ... G9
92276 Thousand Palms 1,718 ... J10
94920 Tiburon 6,685 ... J2
90290 Topanga ... B10
*90501 Torrance 129,881 ... C11
95376 Tracy 18,428 ... D6
93274 Tulare 22,526 ... F7
95380 Turlock 26,287 ... E6
92680 Tustin 32,317 ... D11
92277 Twentynine Palms 7,465 ... K9
†95060 Twin Lakes 4,502 ... K4
95482 Ukiah⊙ 12,035 ... B4
94587 Union City 39,406 ... K2
91786 Upland 47,647 ... E10
95688 Vacaville 43,367 ... D5
91355 Valencia 12,163 ... G9
94590 Vallejo 80,303 ... J1
Vallejo-Fairfield-Napa‡ 334,402 ... J1
*91401 Van Nuys ... B10
90291 Venice ... B11
*93001 Ventura⊙ 74,393 ... F9
92392 Victorville 14,220 ... H9
92667 Villa Park 7,137 ... D11
93277 Visalia⊙ 49,729 ... F7
Visalia-Tulare-Porterville‡ 245,738 ... F7
92083 Vista 35,834 ... H10
91789 Walnut 12,478 ... D10
*94595 Walnut Creek 53,643 ... K2
93280 Wasco 9,613 ... F8
95386 Waterford 2,683 ... E6
95076 Watsonville 23,663 ... D7
96093 Weaverville⊙ 2,787 ... B3
96094 Weed 2,879 ... C2
*91790 West Covina 80,291 ... D10
†90069 West Hollywood 35,703 ... B10
90025 West Los Angeles ... B10
92683 Westminster 71,133 ... D11
†90047 Westmont 27,916 ... C11
†94565 West Pittsburg 8,773 ... K1
95691 West Sacramento 10,875 ... B8
*90601 Whittier 69,717 ... D11
95490 Willits 4,008 ... B4
95988 Willows⊙ 4,777 ... C4
*90744 Wilmington ... C11
95388 Winton 4,995 ... E6
93286 Woodlake 4,343 ... G7
95695 Woodland⊙ 30,235 ... B8
*91364 Woodland Hills ... B10
94062 Woodside 5,291 ... J3
95697 Yolo 600 ... B8
92686 Yorba Linda 28,254 ... D11
94599 Yountville 2,893 ... C5
96097 Yreka⊙ 5,916 ... C2
95991 Yuba City⊙ 18,736 ... D4
Yuba City‡ 101,979 ... D4
92399 Yucaipa 23,345 ... J9
92284 Yucca Valley 8,294 ... J9

OTHER FEATURES

Agua Caliente Ind. Res. ... J10
Alameda (creek) ... K3
Alamo (riv.) ... K10
Alcatraz (isl.) ... J2
Alkali (lkes) ... E2
All American (canal) ... K11
Almanor (lake) ... D3
Amargosa (range) ... J7
Amargosa (riv.) ... J7
American (riv.) ... C8
Anacapa (isl.) ... F10
Angel (isl.) ... J2
Ano Nuevo (pt.) ... J4
Arena (pt.) ... B5
Arguello (pt.) ... E9
Argus (range) ... H7
Arroyo del Valle (dry riv.) ... L3
Arroyo Hondo (dry riv.) ... L3
Arroyo Mocho (dry riv.) ... L2
Arroyo Seco (dry riv.) ... K10
Beale A.F.B. ... D4
Berryessa (lake) ... D5
Bethany (res.) ... L2
Big Sage (res.) ... E2
Black Butte (lake) ... C4
Bodega (bay) ... B5
Bonita (pt.) ... H2
Bristol (lake) ... K9
Buchon (pt.) ... D8
Buena Vista (lake) ... F8
Cabrillo Nat'l Mon. ... H11
Cachuma (lake) ... F9
Cadiz (lake) ... K9
Cahuilla Ind. Res. ... J10
Calaveras (res.) ... L3
California Aqueduct ... E7
Camanche (res.) ... C9
Camp Pendleton 10,017 ... H10
Campo Ind. Res. ... J11
Capitan Grande Ind. Res. ... J11
Cascade (range) ... D1
Castle A.F.B. ... E6
Channel Islands Nat'l Park ... E11
China Lake Naval Weapons Center ... H8
Chemehuevi Valley Ind. Res. ... L9
Chocolate (mts.) ... K10
Clair Engle (lake) ... C3
Clear (lake) ... C4
Clear Lake (res.) ... D2
Coachella (canal) ... K10
Coast (ranges) ... D7
Colorado (riv.) ... L8
Colorado River Aqueduct ... K10
Colorado River Ind. Res. ... L10
Conception (pt.) ... E9
Cooper (pt.) ... D7
Copco (lake) ... C2
Cosumnes (riv.) ... C9
Cottonwood (creek) ... C3
Coyote (res.) ... L4
Crowley (lake) ... G6
Crystal Springs (res.) ... J3
Cuyama (riv.) ... E8
Cuyapaipe Ind. Res. ... J11
Danby (lake) ... K9
Death (valley) ... H7
Death Valley Nat'l Mon. ... H7
Delgada (pt.) ... A3
Del Valle (lake) ... L3
Devils Postpile Nat'l Mon. ... F6
Donner (pass) ... E4
Dume (pt.) ... G10
Duxbury (pt.) ... H2
Eagle (lake) ... E3
Eagle (peak) ... E2
Eagle Crags (mt.) ... J8
Edison (lake) ... F6
Edwards A.F.B. 8,554 ... H9
Eel (riv.) ... B4
Elsinore (lake) ... E11
El Toro Marine Air Sta. 7,632 ... D11
Estero (bay) ... D8
Estero (pt.) ... D8
Estrella (riv.) ... E8
Eugene O'Neill Nat'l Hist. Site ... K2
Farallon (isls.) ... B6
Farallons, The (gulf) ... H2
Feather (riv.) ... D4
Florence (lake) ... G6
Folsom (lake) ... C8
Fort Bidwell Ind. Res. ... E2
Fort Hunter Liggett ... D8
Fort Independence Ind. Res. ... G7
Fort MacArthur ... C11
Fort Mohave Ind. Res. ... L9
Fort Ord ... D7
Fort Point Nat'l Hist. Site ... J2
Freel (peak) ... F5

Agriculture, Industry and Resources

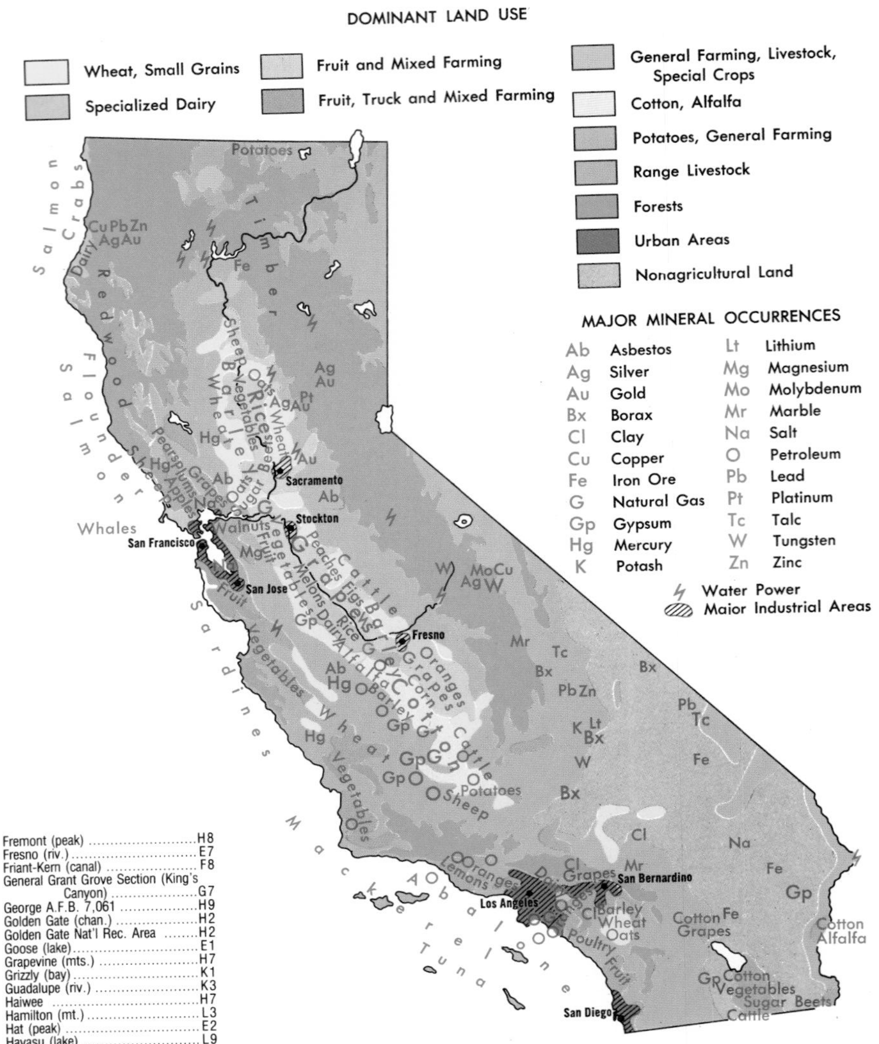
DOMINANT LAND USE
Wheat, Small Grains
Specialized Dairy
Fruit and Mixed Farming
Fruit, Truck and Mixed Farming
General Farming, Livestock, Special Crops
Cotton, Alfalfa
Potatoes, General Farming
Range Livestock
Forests
Urban Areas
Nonagricultural Land
MAJOR MINERAL OCCURRENCES
Ab Asbestos
Ag Silver
Au Gold
Bx Borax
Cl Clay
Cu Copper
Fe Iron Ore
G Natural Gas
Gp Gypsum
Hg Mercury
K Potash
Lt Lithium
Mg Magnesium
Mo Molybdenum
Mr Marble
Na Salt
O Petroleum
Pb Lead
Pt Platinum
Tc Talc
W Tungsten
Zn Zinc
Water Power
Major Industrial Areas
Potatoes
Salmon
Crabs
Timber
Redwood
Flounder
Salmon
Whales
Sardines
Mackerel
Tuna
Sacramento
Stockton
San Francisco
San Jose
Fresno
Los Angeles
San Bernardino
San Diego
Sheep
Rice
Barley
Wheat
Oats
Pears
Plums
Apples
Grapes
Walnuts
Vegetables
Peaches
Figs
Melons
Cattle
Dairy
Oranges
Cotton
Corn
Potatoes
Lemons
Poultry
Fruit
Cotton
Grapes
Cotton
Alfalfa
Vegetables
Sugar Beets
Cattle

Fremont (peak) ... H8
Fresno (riv.) ... E7
Friant-Kern (canal) ... F8
General Grant Grove Section (King's Canyon) ... G7
George A.F.B. 7,061 ... H9
Golden Gate (chan.) ... H2
Golden Gate Nat'l Rec. Area ... H2
Goose (lake) ... E1
Grapevine (mts.) ... H7
Grizzly (bay) ... K1
Guadalupe (riv.) ... K3
Haiwee ... H7
Hamilton (mt.) ... L3
Hat (peak) ... E2
Havasu (lake) ... L9
Hetch Hetchy (res.) ... F6
Hoffman (mt.) ... D2
Honey (lake) ... E3
Hoopa Valley Ind. Res. ... A2
Humboldt (bay) ... A3
Imperial (res.) ... L10
Imperial (valley) ... K10
Ingalls (mt.) ... E3
Inyo (mts.) ... G6
Iron Gate (res.) ... C2
Isabella (lake) ... G8
John Muir Nat'l Hist. Site ... K1
Joshua Tree Nat'l Mon. ... J10
Kern (riv.) ... G8
Kings (riv.) ... F7
Kings Canyon Nat'l Park ... G7
Klamath (riv.) ... B2
Laguna (res.) ... L11
La Jolla Ind. Res. ... J10
Lassen (peak) ... D3
Lassen Volcanic Nat'l Park ... D3
Lava Beds Nat'l Mon. ... D2
Lemoore N.A.S. 5,888 ... F7
Leroy Anderson (res.) ... L4
Lopez (pt.) ... D7
Los Angeles Aqueduct ... G8
Los Coyotes Ind. Res. ... J10
Lost (riv.) ... D1
Lower Alkali (lake) ... E2
Lower Klamath (lake) ... D2
Mad (riv.) ... B3
Manzanita Ind. Res. ... J11
March A.F.B. 3,607 ... E11
Mare Island Navy Yard ... J1
Mather A.F.B. 5,245 ... C8
Mathews (lake) ... E11
McClellan A.F.B. ... B8
McClure (lake) ... E6
Mendocino (cape) ... A3
Merced (riv.) ... E6
Middle Alkali (lake) ... E2
Mill (creek) ... D3
Millerton (lake) ... F6
Moffett Nav. Air Sta. ... K3
Mojave (des.) ... H9
Mojave (riv.) ... J9
Mokelumne (riv.) ... C9
Mono (lake) ... G5
Monterey (bay) ... K4
Moon (lake) ... E2
Morongo Ind. Res. ... J10
Mountain Meadows (res.) ... E3
Muir Woods Nat'l Mon. ... H2
Nacimiento (riv.) ... D8
Navarro (riv.) ... B4
Nevada, Sierra (mts.) ... E4
New (riv.) ... K11
Norton A.F.B. ... F10
Noyo (riv.) ... B4
Oakland Army Base ... J2
Old (riv.) ... L1
Oroville (lake) ... D4
Owens (lake) ... H7
Owens (peak) ... H8
Owens (riv.) ... G6
Oxnard A.F.B. ... F9
Paiute Ind. Res. ... G6
Pala Ind. Res. ... H10
Palomar (mt.) ... J10
Panamint (range) ... H7
Panamint (valley) ... H7
Pescadero (pt.) ... J3
Piedras Blancas (pt.) ... D8
Pillar (pt.) ... H3
Pillsbury (lake) ... C4
Pine (creek) ... D3
Pine Flat (lake) ... F7
Pinnacles Nat'l Mon. ... D7
Pit (riv.) ... D2
Point Mugu Pacific Missile Test Center ... F9
Point Reyes Nat'l Seashore ... H1
Presidio ... J2
Providence (mts.) ... K8
Punta Gorda (pt.) ... A3
Quartz (peak) ... L11
Railroad Canyon (res.) ... E11
Redwood Nat'l Park ... A2
Reyes (pt.) ... B6
Rogers (lake) ... H9
Rosamond (lake) ... G9
Round Valley Ind. Res. ... B4
Russian (riv.) ... B4
Sacramento (riv.) ... D5
Sacramento Army Depot ... B8
Saint George (pt.) ... A2
Salinas (riv.) ... D7
Salmon (riv.) ... B2
Salton Sea (lake) ... K10
San Andreas (lake) ... H2
San Antonio (lake) ... E8
San Benito (riv.) ... D7
San Bernardino (mts.) ... J10
San Clemente (isl.) ... G11
San Diego (bay) ... H11
San Francisco (bay) ... J2
San Gabriel (res.) ... D10
San Joaquin (riv.) ... E6
San Joaquin (valley) ... D6
San Lorenzo (riv.) ... K4
San Luis (res.) ... E7
San Martin (cape) ... D8
San Miguel (isl.) ... E9
San Nicolas (isl.) ... F10
San Pablo (bay) ... J1
San Pedro (bay) ... C11
Santa Ana (riv.) ... E11
Santa Barbara (chan.) ... E9
Santa Barbara (isl.) ... G10
Santa Barbara (isls.) ... F10
Santa Catalina (gulf) ... G11
Santa Catalina (isl.) ... G10
Santa Cruz (chan.) ... F10
Santa Cruz (isl.) ... F10
Santa Maria (riv.) ... E9
Santa Monica (bay) ... B11
Santa Rosa (isl.) ... E10
Santa Rosa Ind. Res. ... J10
Santa Ynez (riv.) ... E9
Santa Ysabel Ind. Res. ... J10
Searles (lake) ... H8
Sequoia Nat'l Park ... G7
Sharpe Army Depot ... D6
Shasta (lake) ... C3
Shasta (mt.) ... C2
Shasta (riv.) ... C2
Sierra Army Depot ... E3
Sierra Nevada (mts.) ... E4
Siskiyou (mts.) ... C2
Smith (riv.) ... A2
Soda (lake) ... K8
South Bay Aqueduct ... L2
South Cow (creek) ... C3
Stony Gorge (res.) ... C4
Suisun (bay) ... K1
Sur (pt.) ... D7
Tahoe (lake) ... F4
Tamalpais (mt.) ... H1
Tehachapi (mts.) ... G9
Telescope (peak) ... H7
Tomales (pt.) ... B5
Torres Martinez Ind. Res. ... J10
Travis A.F.B. ... L1
Trinidad (head) ... A2
Trinity (riv.) ... B3
Truckee (riv.) ... F4
Tulare (lake) ... F7
Tule (lake) ... D2
Tule River Ind. Res. ... G7
Twentynine Palms Marine Base 7,079 ... J9
Twitchell (res.) ... E9
Upper Alkali (lake) ... E2
Vandenberg A.F.B. 8,136 ... E9
Vizcaino (cape) ... B4
Walnut (creek) ... K1
Wheeler (peak) ... F5
Whipple (mts.) ... L9
Whiskeytown-Shasta-Trinity Nat'l Rec. Area ... C3
Whitney (mt.) ... G7
Willow (creek) ... E3
Wilson (mt.) ... D10
Yosemite Nat'l Park ... F6
Yuba (riv.) ... D4
Yuma Ind. Res. ... L11

⊙County seat.
‡Population of metropolitan area.
† Zip of nearest p.o. * Multiple zips.

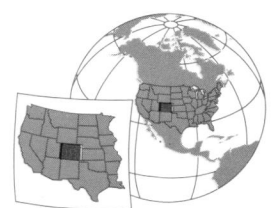

AREA 104,091 sq. mi. (269,596 sq. km.)
POPULATION 2,889,735
CAPITAL Denver
LARGEST CITY Denver
HIGHEST POINT Mt. Elbert 14,433 ft. (4399 m.)
SETTLED IN 1858
ADMITTED TO UNION August 1, 1876
POPULAR NAME Centennial State
STATE FLOWER Rocky Mountain Columbine
STATE BIRD Lark Bunting

COUNTIES

- Adams 245,944 .... L3
- Alamosa 11,799 .... H7
- Arapahoe 293,621 .... L3
- Archuleta 3,664 .... E8
- Baca 5,419 .... O8
- Bent 5,945 .... N7
- Boulder 189,625 .... J2
- Chaffee 13,227 .... G5
- Cheyenne 2,153 .... O5
- Clear Creek 7,308 .... H3
- Conejos 7,794 .... G8
- Costilla 3,071 .... J8
- Crowley 2,988 .... M6
- Custer 1,528 .... J6
- Delta 21,225 .... D5
- Denver 492,365 .... K3
- Dolores 1,658 .... C7
- Douglas 25,153 .... K4
- Eagle 13,320 .... F3
- Elbert 6,850 .... L4
- El Paso 309,424 .... K5
- Fremont 28,676 .... J5
- Garfield 22,514 .... C3
- Gilpin 2,441 .... H3
- Grand 7,475 .... G2
- Gunnison 10,689 .... E5
- Hinsdale 408 .... E7
- Huerfano 6,440 .... K7
- Jackson 1,863 .... G1
- Jefferson 371,741 .... J3
- Kiowa 1,936 .... O6
- Kit Carson 7,599 .... O4
- Lake 8,830 .... G4
- La Plata 27,195 .... D8
- Larimer 149,184 .... H1
- Las Animas 14,897 .... L8
- Lincoln 4,663 .... M5
- Logan 19,800 .... N1
- Mesa 81,530 .... B5
- Mineral 804 .... F7
- Moffat 13,133 .... C1
- Montezuma 16,510 .... B8
- Montrose 24,352 .... C6
- Morgan 22,513 .... M2
- Otero 22,567 .... M7
- Ouray 1,925 .... D6
- Park 5,333 .... H4
- Phillips 4,542 .... P1
- Pitkin 10,338 .... F4
- Prowers 13,070 .... P7
- Pueblo 125,972 .... K6
- Rio Blanco 6,255 .... C3
- Rio Grande 10,511 .... G7
- Routt 13,404 .... E1
- Saguache 3,935 .... G6
- San Juan 833 .... D7
- San Miguel 3,192 .... C6
- Sedgwick 3,266 .... P1
- Summit 8,848 .... G3
- Teller 8,034 .... J5
- Washington 5,304 .... N3
- Weld 123,438 .... L1

- Washington 5,304 .... N3
- Weld 123,438 .... L1

- Yuma 9,682 .... P2

CITIES and TOWNS

Zip *Name/Pop.* *Key*

- 80101 Agate 90 .... M4
- 81020 Aguilar 624 .... K8
- 80720 Akron⊙ 1,716 .... N2
- 81101 Alamosa⊙ 6,830 .... H8
- 80510 Allenspark 200 .... J2
- 80420 Alma 132 .... G4
- 81210 Almont 135 .... F5
- 80721 Amherst 85 .... P1
- 80801 Anton 55 .... N3
- 81120 Antonito 1,103 .... H8
- 80802 Arapahoe 300 .... P5
- 81021 Arlington 37 .... N6
- 80804 Arriba 236 .... N4
- †81323 Arriola 56 .... B8
- *80001 Arvada 84,576 .... J3
- 81611 Aspen⊙ 3,678 .... F4
- 80722 Atwood 100 .... N1
- 80610 Ault 1,056 .... K1
- *80010 Aurora 158,588 .... K3
- 81410 Austin D5
- 81620 Avon 640 .... F3
- 81022 Avondale 750 .... L6
- 80421 Bailey 150 .... H4
- †80624 Barnesville 20 .... L2
- 81621 Basalt 529 .... E4
- 81122 Bayfield 724 .... D8
- 81411 Bedrock 45 .... B6
- †80758 Beecher Island 5 .... P3
- 80512 Bellvue 250 .... J1
- 80102 Bennett 942 .... L3
- 80513 Berthoud 2,362 .... J2
- †80438 Berthoud Pass 40 .... H3
- 80805 Bethune 149 .... P4
- 81023 Beulah 650 .... K6
- 80908 Black Forest 3,372 .... K4
- 80422 Black Hawk 232 .... J3
- 81123 Blanca 252 .... H8
- †80424 Blue River 230 .... G4
- †81155 Bonanza 8 .... G6
- 81024 Boncarbo 200 .... K8
- 80423 Bond 65 .... F3
- 81025 Boone 431 .... L6
- *80301 Boulder⊙ 76,685 .... J2
- †81428 Bowie 18 .... D5
- 80821 Boyero 12 .... N5
- 81026 Brandon 30 .... P6
- 81027 Branson 73 .... M8
- 80424 Breckenridge⊙ 818 .... G4
- 80611 Briggsdale 85 .... L1
- 80601 Brighton⊙ 12,773 .... K3
- 81028 Bristol 200 .... P6
- †81212 Brookside 178 .... J6
- 80020 Broomfield 20,730 .... J3
- 80723 Brush 4,082 .... M2
- †80742 Buckingham 5 .... L1
- 81211 Buena Vista 2,075 .... G5
- 80425 Buffalo Creek 150 .... J4
- 80807 Burlington⊙ 3,107 .... P4
- 80426 Burns 100 .... F3
- 80103 Byers 490 .... L3
- 81320 Cahone 200 .... B7
- 80808 Calhan 541 .... L4
- 81029 Campo 185 .... O8
- 81212 Canon City⊙ 13,037 .... J6
- 81124 Capulin 600 .... G8
- 81623 Carbondale 2,084 .... E4
- 80612 Carr 49 .... K1
- 80909 Cascade 950 .... K5
- 80104 Castle Rock⊙ 3,921 .... K4
- 81413 Cedaredge 1,184 .... D5
- 81125 Center 1,630 .... G7
- 80427 Central City⊙ 329 .... J3
- 81126 Chama 239 .... J8
- 81030 Cheraw 233 .... N6
- 80810 Cheyenne Wells⊙ 950 .... P5
- 81127 Chimney Rock 76 .... E8
- 81031 Chivington 20 .... O6
- 81128 Chromo 115 .... F8
- 81220 Cimarron 50 .... D6
- 80428 Clark 20 .... F1
- 81520 Clifton 5,223 .... C4
- 80429 Climax 975 .... G4
- 81221 Coal Creek 190 .... J6
- 81222 Coaldale 153 .... H6
- 80430 Coalmont 50 .... F1
- 81032 Cokedale 90 .... K8
- 81624 Collbran 344 .... C4
- †81401 Colona 54 .... D6
- 81019 Colorado City 411 .... K6
- *80901 Colorado Springs⊙ 214,821 .... K5
  - Colorado Springs‡ 317,458 K5
- †80428 Columbine 12 .... E1
- 80022 Commerce City 16,234 .... K3
- 80432 Como 30 .... H4
- 81129 Conejos⊙ 200 .... G8
- 80812 Cope 110 .... O3
- †80611 Cornish 15 .... L2
- 81321 Cortez⊙ 7,095 .... B8
- 81223 Cotopaxi 250 .... H6
- 80434 Cowdrey 80 .... G1
- 81625 Craig⊙ 8,133 .... D2
- 81415 Crawford 268 .... D5
- 81130 Creede⊙ 610 .... E7
- 81224 Crested Butte 959 .... E5
- 81131 Crestone 54 .... H7
- 80813 Cripple Creek⊙ 655 .... J5
- 80726 Crook 177 .... O1
- 81033 Crowley 192 .... M6
- 81055 Cuchara 43 .... J8
- 80514 Dacono 2,321 .... K2
- †80728 Dailey 20 .... O1
- 81630 De Beque 279 .... C4
- †80135 Deckers 4 .... J4
- 80105 Deer Trail 463 .... M3
- †81059 Delhi 10 .... M7
- 81132 Del Norte⊙ 1,709 .... G7
- 81416 Delta⊙ 3,931 .... D5
- *80201 Denver (cap.)⊙ 492,365 .... K3
  - Denver‡ 1,619,921 .... K3
- †81054 Deora 2 .... O7
- 80435 Dillon 337 .... H3
- 81610 Dinosaur 313 .... B2
- 80814 Divide 700 .... J5
- 81323 Dolores 802 .... C8
- 81324 Dove Creek⊙ 826 .... A7
- †81239 Doyleville 75 .... F6
- 80515 Drake 300 .... J2
- 81301 Durango⊙ 11,649 .... D8
- 81036 Eads⊙ 878 .... O6
- 81631 Eagle⊙ 950 .... F3
- 80615 Eaton 1,932 .... K1
- 80727 Eckley 262 .... P2
- 80214 Edgewater 4,766 .... J3
- 81632 Edwards 250 .... F3
- 81325 Egnar 50 .... B7
- 80106 Elbert 200 .... L4
- †80466 Eldora 100 .... H3
- 80107 Elizabeth 789 .... K4
- 81633 Elk Springs 18 .... C2
- 80438 Empire 423 .... H3
- †80110 Englewood 30,021 .... K3
- 80516 Erie 1,254 .... K2
- 80517 Estes Park 2,703 .... J2
- †81433 Eureka 25 .... D7
- 80620 Evans 5,063 .... K2
- 80439 Evergreen 6,376 .... J3
- 80440 Fairplay⊙ 421 .... H4
- 81037 Farisita 116 .... J7
- †80221 Federal Heights 7,846 .... J3
- 80520 Firestone 1,204 .... K2
- †80810 Firstview 6 .... O5
- 80815 Flagler 550 .... N4
- 80728 Fleming 388 .... O1
- 81226 Florence 2,987 .... J6
- 80816 Florissant 130 .... J5
- 80521 Fort Collins⊙ 65,092 .... J1
  - Fort Collins‡ 149,184 .... J1
- 81133 Fort Garland 700 .... J8
- 80621 Fort Lupton 4,251 .... K2
- 81038 Fort Lyon 500 .... N6
- 80701 Fort Morgan⊙ 8,768 .... M2
- 80817 Fountain 8,324 .... K5
- 81039 Fowler 1,227 .... L6
- 80441 Foxton 12 .... J4
- 80116 Franktown 200 .... K4
- 80442 Fraser 470 .... H3
- 80530 Frederick 855 .... K2
- 80820 Freshwater (Guffey) 24 .... H5
- 80443 Frisco 1,221 .... G3
- 81521 Fruita 2,810 .... B4
- 80622 Galeton 200 .... K1
- 81134 Garcia 75 .... J8
- 81040 Gardner 100 .... J7
- 81227 Garfield 30 .... G5
- 81522 Gateway 350 .... B5
- 80818 Genoa 165 .... N4
- 80444 Georgetown⊙ 830 .... H3
- 80623 Gilcrest 1,025 .... K2
- 80624 Gill 250 .... L2
- 81634 Gilman 160 .... G3
- 81523 Glade Park 100 .... B5
- †80485 Glendevey 50 .... H1
- 80532 Glen Haven 110 .... H2
- 81601 Glenwood Springs⊙ 4,637 E4
- 80401 Golden⊙ 12,237 .... J3
- †80653 Goodrich 85 .... M2
- †80480 Gould 12 .... G2
- 81041 Granada 557 .... P6
- 80446 Granby 963 .... H2
- 81501 Grand Junction⊙ 27,956 .... B4
- 80447 Grand Lake 382 .... H2
- 81228 Granite 47 .... G4
- 80448 Grant 50 .... H4
- 80631 Greeley⊙ 53,006 .... K2
  - Greeley‡ 123,438 .... K2
- †80118 Greenland 21 .... K4
- 80819 Green Mountain Falls 607 .... K5
- †81640 Greystone 2 .... B1
- 80729 Grover 158 .... L1
- 80820 Guffey 24 .... H5
- 81042 Gulnare 6 .... K8
- 81230 Gunnison⊙ 5,785 .... E5
- 81637 Gypsum 743 .... F3
- 80730 Hale 4 .... P3
- 81638 Hamilton 100 .... D2
- 81043 Hartman 122 .... P6
- 80449 Hartsel 69 .... H4
- 81044 Hasty 150 .... O6
- 81045 Haswell 126 .... N6
- 80731 Haxtun 1,014 .... O1
- 81639 Hayden 1,720 .... E2
- 80732 Hereford 50 .... L1
- 81326 Hesperus 250 .... C8
- 80733 Hillrose 213 .... N2
- 81232 Hillside 79 .... H6
- 81046 Hoehne 400 .... L8
- 81047 Holly 969 .... P6
- 80734 Holyoke⊙ 2,092 .... P1
- 81136 Hooper 71 .... H7
- 81419 Hotchkiss 849 .... D5
- 80451 Hot Sulphur Springs⊙ 405 .... H2
- 81233 Howard 200 .... H6
- 80641 Hoyt 60 .... L2
- 80642 Hudson 698 .... K2
- 80821 Hugo⊙ 776 .... N4
- 80533 Hygiene 450 .... J2
- 80452 Idaho Springs 2,077 .... H3
- 80735 Idalia 125 .... P3
- 81137 Ignacio 667 .... D8
- 80736 Iliff 218 .... N1
- 80455 Jamestown 223 .... J2
- †81082 Jansen 267 .... K8
- 81138 Jaroso 50 .... H8
- 80456 Jefferson 50 .... H4
- 80822 Joes 100 .... O3
- 80534 Johnstown 1,535 .... K2
- 80737 Julesburg⊙ 1,528 .... P1
- 80823 Karval 51 .... N5
- 80643 Keenesburg 541 .... L2
- †80729 Keota 4 .... L1
- 80644 Kersey 913 .... L2
- 81049 Kim 100 .... N8
- 80117 Kiowa⊙ 206 .... L4
- 80824 Kirk 30 .... P3
- 80825 Kit Carson 278 .... O5
- 80459 Kremmling 1,296 .... G2
- †80832 Kutch 2 .... M5
- 80026 Lafayette 8,935 .... K3
- †81132 La Garita 10 .... G7
- 80739 Laird 105 .... P2
- 81140 La Jara 858 .... H8
- 81050 La Junta⊙ 8,388 .... M7
- 81235 Lake City⊙ 206 .... E6
- 80827 Lake George 500 .... J5
- 80215 Lakewood 113,808 .... J3
- 81052 Lamar⊙ 7,713 .... O6
- 80535 Laporte 950 .... J1
- 80118 Larkspur 141 .... K4
- 80645 La Salle 1,929 .... K2
- 81054 Las Animas⊙ 2,818 .... N6
- †81151 Lasauces 150 .... H8
- †81153 Lavalley 237 .... J8
- 81055 La Veta 611 .... J8
- †80452 Lawson 108 .... H3
- †81625 Lay 40 .... D2
- 81420 Lazear 60 .... D5
- 80461 Leadville⊙ 3,879 .... G4
- †81323 Lebanon 50 .... B8
- 81327 Lewis 150 .... B8
- 80828 Limon 1,805 .... M4
- †81212 Lincoln Park 2,984 .... J6
- 80740 Lindon 60 .... N3
- *80120 Littleton⊙ 28,631 .... K3
- 80536 Livermore 150 .... J1
- †80601 Lochbuie 895 .... K2
- †80701 Log Lane Village 709 .... M2
- 81524 Loma 265 .... B4
- 80501 Longmont 42,942 .... J2
- †80135 Longview 10 .... J4
- 80027 Louisville 5,593 .... J3
- 80131 Louviers 300 .... K4
- 80537 Loveland 30,244 .... J2
- 80646 Lucerne 135 .... K2
- †81054 Lycan 4 .... P7
- 80540 Lyons 1,137 .... J2
- 81525 Mack 380 .... B4
- 81421 Maher 75 .... D5
- †80461 Malta 200 .... G4
- 81141 Manassa 945 .... H8
- 81328 Mancos 870 .... C8
- 80829 Manitou Springs 4,475 .... J5
- 81058 Manzanola 459 .... M6
- †81623 Marble 30 .... E4
- 81329 Marvel 176 .... C8
- 80541 Masonville 200 .... J2
- †80649 Masters 50 .... L2
- 80830 Matheson 120 .... M4
- 81640 Maybell 130 .... C2
- 81057 McClave 125 .... O6
- 80463 McCoy 62 .... F3
- 80542 Mead 356 .... K2
- 81641 Meeker⊙ 2,356 .... D2
- 81642 Meredith 47 .... F4
- 80741 Merino 255 .... N2
- 81005 Mesa 120 .... C4
- 81330 Mesa Verde National Park 45 .... C8
- 81142 Mesita 70 .... H8
- 80543 Milliken 1,506 .... K2
- 80477 Milner 196 .... F2
- 81645 Minturn 1,060 .... G3

(continued on following page)

Agriculture, Industry and Resources

DOMINANT LAND USE

- Specialized Wheat
- Wheat, Range Livestock
- Wheat, Grain Sorghums, Range Livestock
- Dry Beans, General Farming
- Sugar Beets, Dry Beans, Livestock, General Farming
- Fruit, Mixed Farming
- General Farming, Livestock, Special Crops
- Range Livestock
- Forests
- Urban Areas
- Nonagricultural Land

MAJOR MINERAL OCCURRENCES

Ag	Silver	Mi	Mica
Au	Gold	Mo	Molybdenum
Be	Beryl	Mr	Marble
C	Coal	O	Petroleum
Cl	Clay	Pb	Lead
Cu	Copper	U	Uranium
F	Fluorspar	V	Vanadium
Fe	Iron Ore	W	Tungsten
G	Natural Gas	Zn	Zinc

ϟ Water Power
▨ Major Industrial Areas

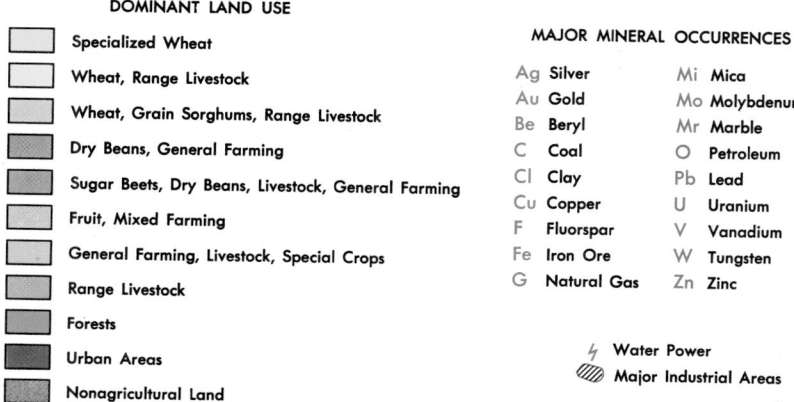

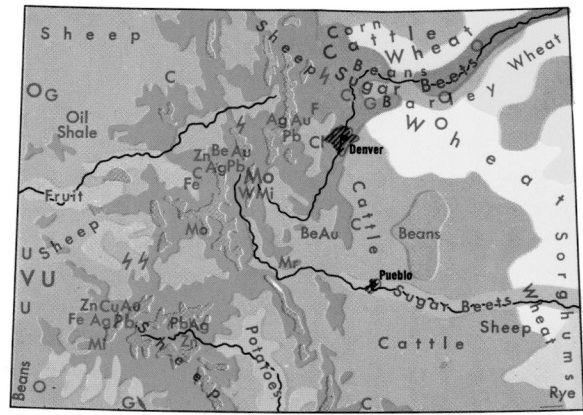

Topography

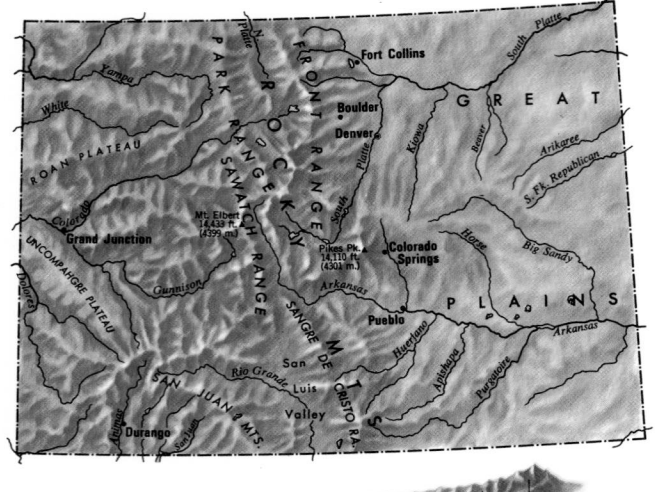

0   50   100 MI.

0   50   100 KM.

Below Sea Level	100 m. 328 ft.	200 m. 656 ft.	500 m. 1,640 ft.	1,000 m. 3,281 ft.	2,000 m. 6,562 ft.	5,000 m. 16,404 ft.

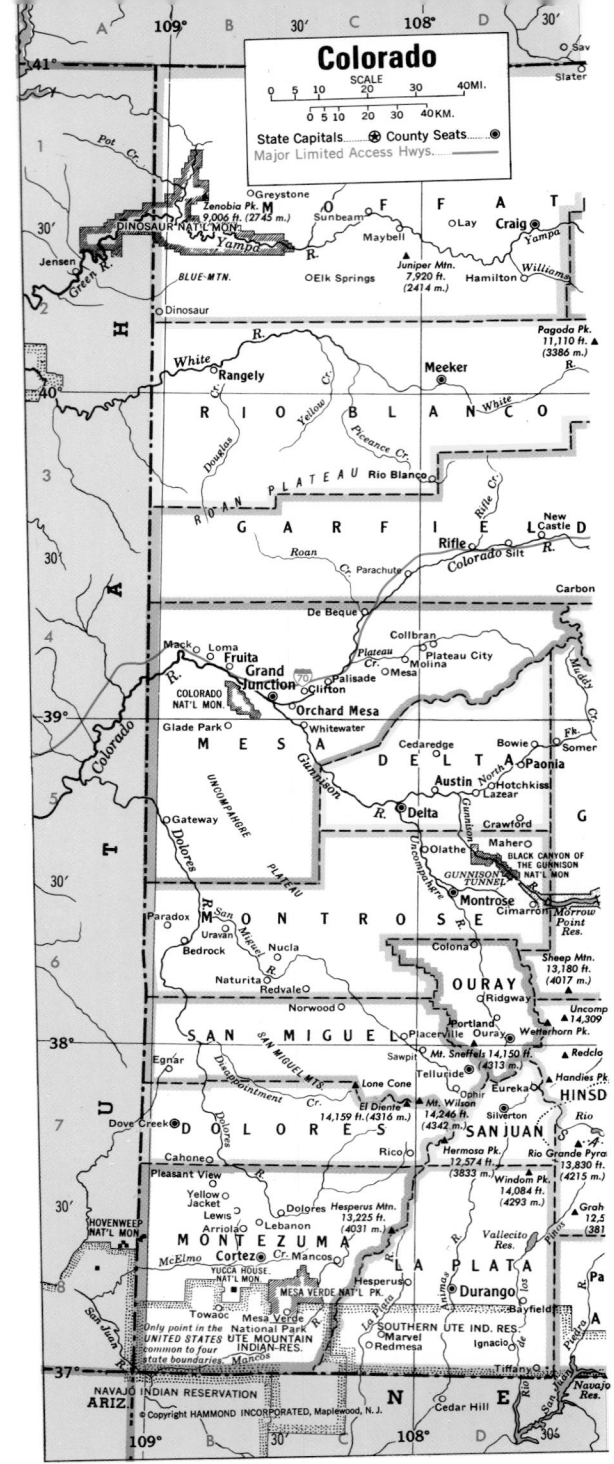

Colorado

SCALE

0 5 10   20   30   40MI.

0 5 10   20   30   40 KM.

State Capitals ⊛   County Seats ◉

Major Limited Access Hwys. ———

© Copyright HAMMOND INCORPORATED, Maplewood, N.J.

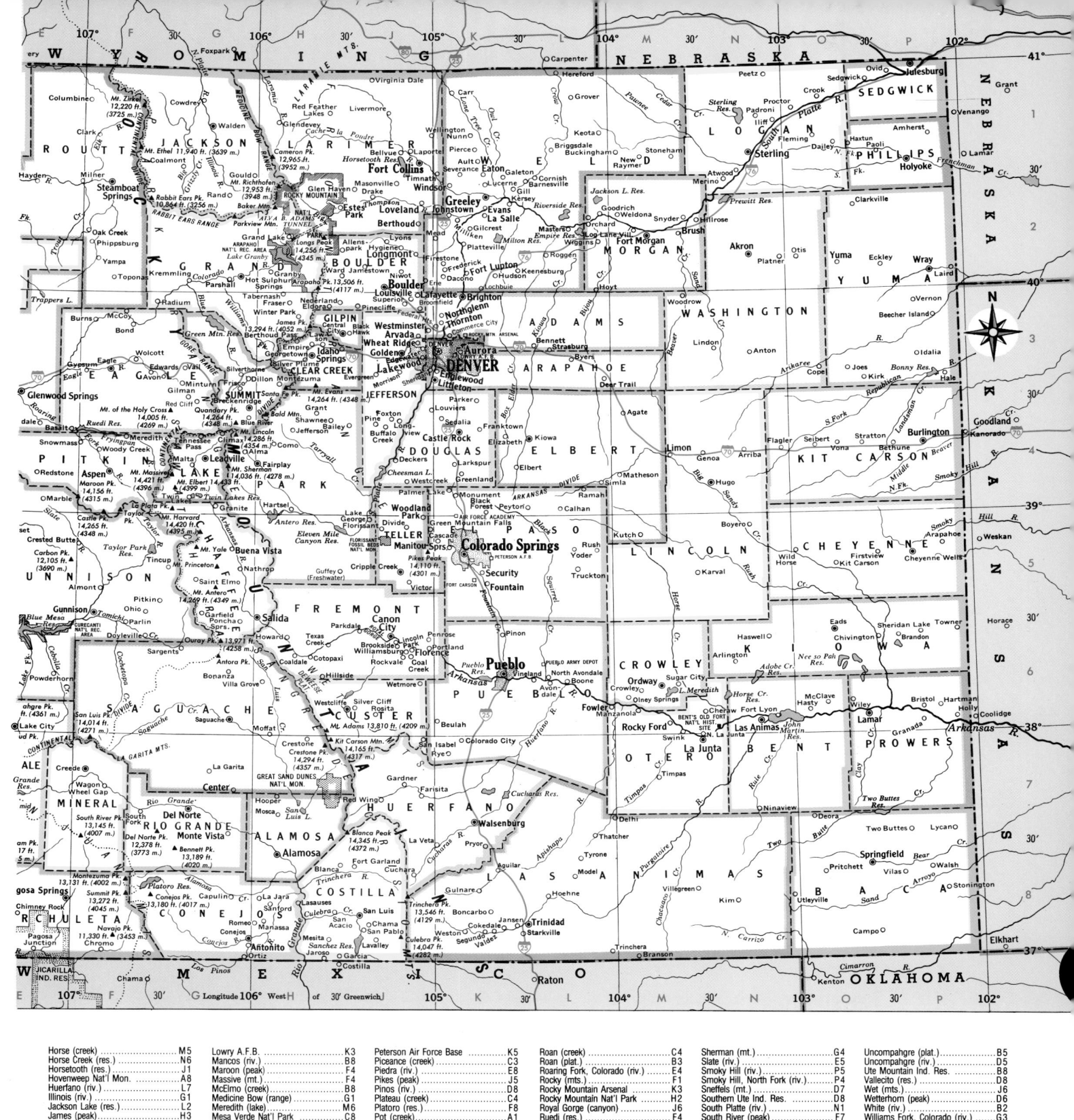

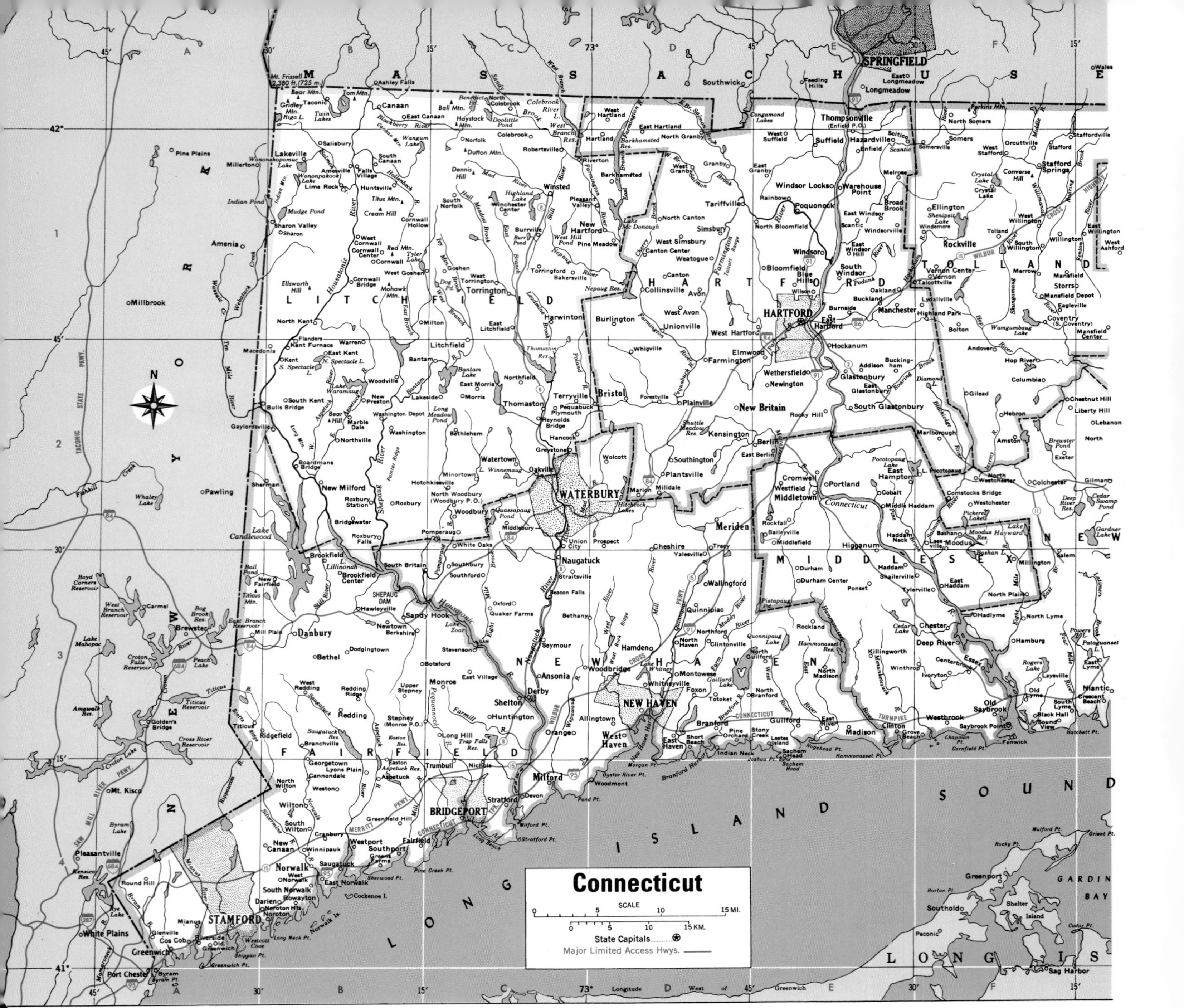

Connecticut
SCALE
0 5 10 15 MI.
0 5 10 15 KM.
State Capitals
Major Limited Access Hwys.
MASSACHUSETTS
NEW YORK
LONG ISLAND SOUND
LITCHFIELD
HARTFORD
TOLLAND
MIDDLESEX
NEW HAVEN
FAIRFIELD
HARTFORD
SPRINGFIELD
WATERBURY
NEW HAVEN
BRIDGEPORT
STAMFORD
Mt. Frissell 2,380 ft. (725 m.)
73° Longitude West of Greenwich

Topography
0 15 30 MI.
0 15 30 KM.
Mt. Frissell 2,380 ft. (725 m.)
Housatonic
Shepaug
Farmington
Hartford
Connecticut
Willimantic
Natchaug
Quinebaug
Shetucket
Waterbury
Naugatuck
Norwich
Thames
Lake Candlewood
Quinnipiac
New Haven
New London
Stamford
Bridgeport
Below
Sea Level
100 m. 328 ft.
200 m. 656 ft.
500 m. 1,640 ft.
1,000 m. 3,281 ft.
2,000 m. 6,562 ft.
5,000 m. 16,404 ft.

COUNTIES

County/Pop.	Key
Fairfield 807,143	B3
Hartford 807,766	D1
Litchfield 156,769	B1
Middlesex 129,017	E3
New Haven 761,337	D3
New London 238,409	G2
Tolland 114,823	F1
Windham 92,312	H1

CITIES and TOWNS

Zip	Name/Pop.	Key
06230	Abington 600	G1
06231	Amston 900	F2
06232	Andover○ 2,144	F2
06401	Ansonia 19,039	C3
06278	Ashford○ 3,221	G1
06278	Ashford P.O. (Warrenville) 500	G1
†06241	Attawaugan 400	H1
06001	Avon○ 11,201	D1
06001	Avon 1,434	D1
06233	Ballouville 800	H1
06330	Baltic	G2
06750	Bantam 860	B2
†06063	Barkhamsted○ 2,935	D1
†06423	Bashan 90	F2
06403	Beacon Falls○ 3,995	C3
06037	Berlin○ 15,121	E2
†06501	Bethany○ 4,330	C3
06801	Bethel○ 16,004	B3
06801	Bethel 8,755	B3
06751	Bethlehem○ 2,573	C2
06751	Bethlehem 1,762	C2
06002	Bloomfield○ 18,608	E1
06112	Blue Hills	E1
06040	Bolton○ 3,951	F1
06404	Botsford 400	C3
†06829	Branchville 600	B3
06405	Branford○ 23,363	D3
06405	Branford 5,438	D3
*06601	Bridgeport 142,546	C4
	Bridgeport‡ 395,455	C4
06752	Bridgewater○ 1,563	B2
06010	Bristol 57,370	D2
	Bristol‡ 73,762	D2
06016	Broad Brook	E1
06804	Brookfield○ 12,872	B3
06234	Brooklyn○ 5,691	H1
06013	Burlington○ 5,660	D1
06830	Byram	A4
06018	Canaan○ 1,002	B1
06018	Canaan 1,160	B1
†06897	Cannondale 400	B4
06331	Canterbury○ 3,426	H2
06019	Canton○ 7,635	D1
06019	Canton 1,680	D1
06409	Centerbrook 800	F3
06332	Central Village 950	H2
06235	Chaplin○ 1,793	G1
06410	Cheshire○ 21,788	D2
06410	Cheshire 5,722	D2
06412	Chester○ 3,068	F3
06412	Chester 1,388	F3
06413	Clinton○ 11,195	E3
06413	Clinton 3,168	E3
06414	Cobalt 700	E2
06415	Colchester○ 7,761	F2
06415	Colchester 3,190	F2
06021	Colebrook○ 1,221	C1
06022	Collinsville 2,555	D1
06237	Columbia○ 3,386	F2
06753	Cornwall○ 1,288	B1
06807	Cos Cob	A4
06238	Coventry○ 8,895	F1
06416	Cromwell○ 10,265	E2
06810	Danbury 60,470	B3
	Danbury‡ 146,405	B3
06239	Danielson 4,553	H1
06820	Darien○ 18,892	B4
06241	Dayville	H1
06417	Deep River○ 3,994	F3
06417	Deep River 2,495	F3
06418	Derby 12,346	C3
06422	Durham○ 5,143	E3
06422	Durham 2,641	E3
06023	East Berlin 950	E2
†06239	East Brooklyn 1,251	H1
06024	East Canaan 800	B1
06242	Eastford○ 1,028	G1
06025	East Glastonbury 300	E2
06026	East Granby○ 4,102	E1
06423	East Haddam○ 5,621	F3
06424	East Hampton○ 8,572	E2

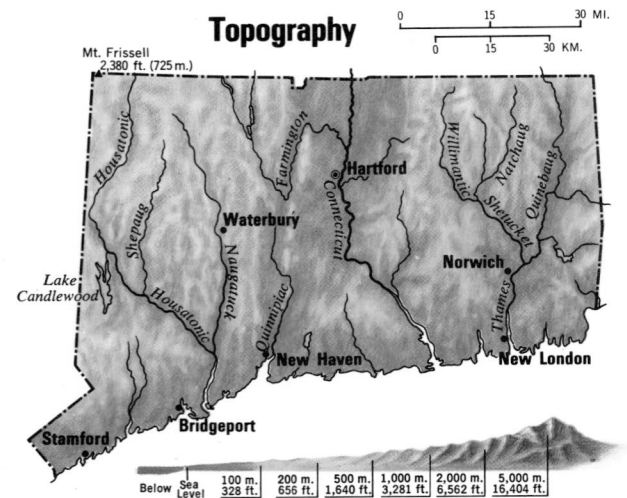

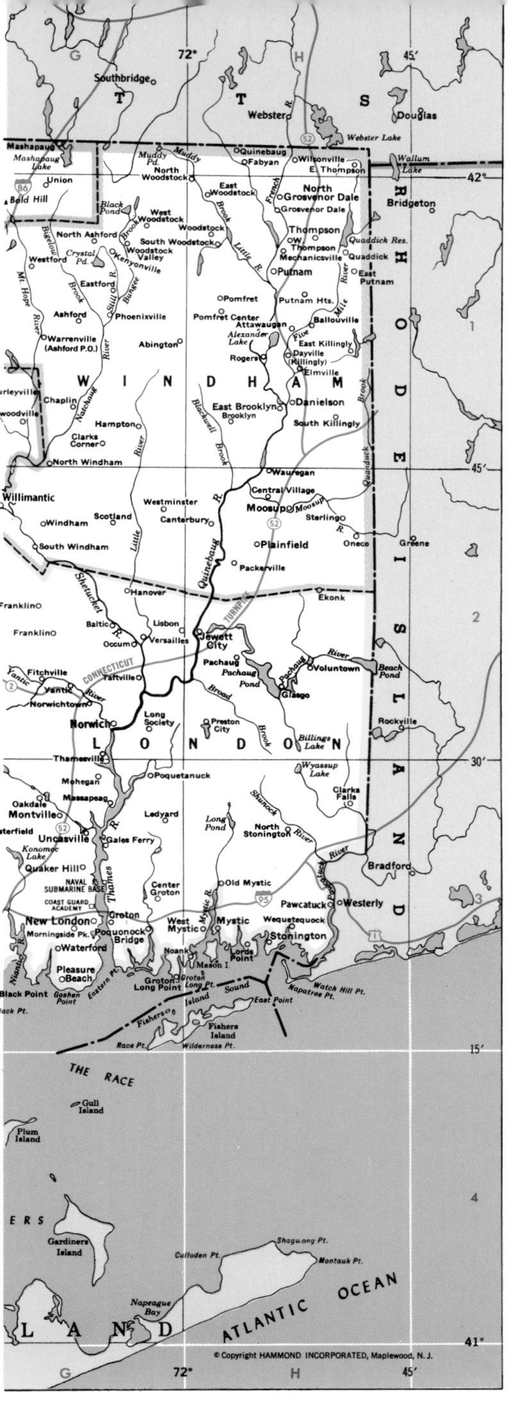

Southbridge
Webster
Douglas
Webster Lake
Mashapaug Lake
Wallum Lake
Union
Bald Hill
North Woodstock
Quinebaug
Fabyan
Wilsonville
E. Thompson
East Woodstock
North Grosvenor Dale
Grosvenor Dale
Bridgeton
West Woodstock
Woodstock
South Woodstock
Woodstock Valley
Kenyonville
Thompson
Quaddick Res.
Mechanicsville
Quaddick
North Ashford
Westford
Crystal Pd.
Eastford
Putnam
East Putnam
Ashford
Phoenixville
Pomfret
Pomfret Center
Putnam Hts.
Abington
Attawaugan
Ballouville
Warrenville (Ashford P.O.)
Alexander Lake
Rogers
East Killingly
Dayville (Killingly)
Elmville
W I N D H A M
Gurleyville
Chaplin
East Brooklyn
Brooklyn
Danielson
Atwoodville
Hampton
South Killingly
Clarks Corner
North Windham
Wauregan
Willimantic
Westminster
Central Village
Windham
Scotland
Canterbury
Moosup
Sterling
South Windham
Plainfield
Oneco
Greene
Packerville
Hanover
Ekonk
Franklin
Baltic
Lisbon
Occum
Versailles
Jewett City
Fitchville
Taftville
Pachaug
Pachaug Pond
Voluntown
Beach Pond
Yantic
Norwichtown
Glasgo
Norwich
Long Society
Preston City
Rockville
Billings Lake
L O N D O N
Thamesville
Wyassup Lake
Mohegan
Poquetanuck
Massapeag
Clarks Falls
Oakdale
Montville
Ledyard
Long Pond
North Stonington
Chesterfield
Uncasville
Gales Ferry
Konomoc Lake
Quaker Hill
Bradford
NAVAL SUBMARINE BASE
COAST GUARD ACADEMY
Center Groton
Old Mystic
Pawcatuck
Westerly
Groton
New London
Morningside Pk.
Poquonock Bridge
West Mystic
Mystic
Wequetequock
Stonington
Waterford
Noank
Lords Point
Mason I.
Pleasant Beach
Black Point
Goshen Point
Eastern Pt.
Groton Long Point
Sound
Watch Hill Pt.
Napatree Pt.
East Point
Black Pt.
Fishers Island
Race Pt.
Wilderness Pt.
THE RACE
Gull Island
Plum Island
Gardiners Island
Culloden Pt.
Shagwong Pt.
Montauk Pt.
Napeague Bay
ATLANTIC OCEAN
RHODE ISLAND
© Copyright HAMMOND INCORPORATED, Maplewood, N. J.
72°
45′
42°
41°
30′
15′

Connecticut

AREA 5,018 sq. mi. (12,997 sq. km.)
POPULATION 3,107,576
CAPITAL Hartford
LARGEST CITY Bridgeport
HIGHEST POINT Mt. Frissell (S. Slope) 2,380 ft. (725 m.)
SETTLED IN 1635
ADMITTED TO UNION January 9, 1788
POPULAR NAME Constitution State; Nutmeg State
STATE FLOWER Mountain Laurel
STATE BIRD Robin

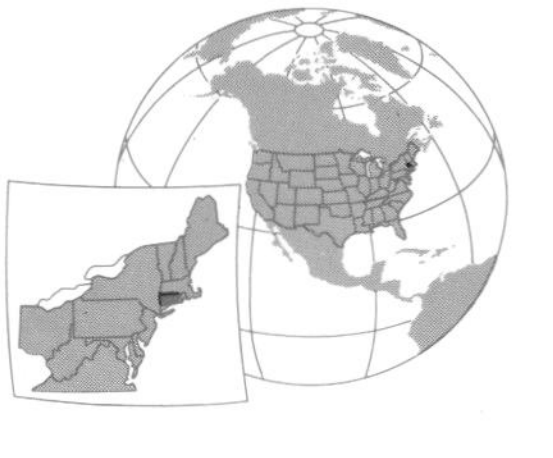

06424 East Hampton 2,152 .... E2
06108 East Hartford○ 52,563 ...... E1
06027 East Hartland 900 .... D1
06512 East Haven○ 25,028 .... D3
06243 East Killingly 900 .... H1
06333 East Lyme○ 13,870 .... G3
†06763 East Morris 800 .... C2
06612 Easton○ 5,962 .... B4
†06088 East Windsor○ 8,925 .... E1
06028 East Windsor Hill 500 .... E1
06244 East Woodstock 400 .... H1
06029 Ellington○ 9,711 .... F1
06082 Enfield○ 42,695 .... E1
06082 Enfield 8,151 .... E1
06426 Essex○ 5,078 .... F3
06426 Essex 2,501 .... F3
06245 Fabyan 600 .... H1
06430 Fairfield○ 54,849 .... B4
06031 Falls Village 600 .... B1
06032 Farmington○ 16,407 .... D2
06334 Fitchville 400 .... G2
†06254 Franklin○ 1,592 .... G2
06335 Gales Ferry 1,191 .... G3
06755 Gaylordsville 960 .... A2
06829 Georgetown 1,834 .... B4
06336 Gilman 350 .... G2
06337 Glasgo 450 .... H2
06033 Glastonbury○ 24,327 .... E2
06033 Glastonbury 7,049 .... E2
06756 Goshen○ 1,706 .... C1
06035 Granby○ 7,956 .... D1
06035 Granby 1,912 .... D1

06830 Greenwich○ 59,578 .... A4
06246 Grosvenor Dale 700 .... H1
06340 Groton○ 41,062 .... G3
06340 Groton 10,086 .... G3
06437 Guilford○ 17,375 .... E3
06437 Guilford 2,555 .... E3
06438 Haddam○ 6,383 .... E3
06439 Hadlyme 450 .... F3
06514 Hamden○ 51,071 .... D3
06247 Hampton○ 1,322 .... G1
06350 Hanover 500 .... G2
*06101 Hartford (cap.) 136,392 .... E1
Hartford‡ 726,114 .... E1
†06091 Hartland○ 1,416 .... D1
06791 Harwinton○ 4,889 .... C1
06791 Harwinton 3,293 .... C1
06440 Hawleyville 600 .... B3
06082 Hazardville 5,436 .... E1
06248 Hebron○ 5,453 .... F2
06441 Higganum 1,660 .... E2
†06040 Highland Park 500 .... F1
06351 Jewett City 3,294 .... H2
06037 Kensington 7,502 .... D2
06757 Kent○ 2,505 .... B2
†06241 Killingly○ 14,519 .... H1
†06413 Killingworth○ 3,976 .... E3
†06424 Lake Pocotopaug 2,137 .... F2
06758 Lakeside 350 .... B2
06249 Lebanon○ 4,762 .... G2
06339 Ledyard○ 13,735 .... G3
†06437 Leetes Island 500 .... E3
†06039 Lime Rock 350 .... B1

06351 Lisbon○ 3,279 .... G2
06759 Litchfield○ 7,605 .... C2
06759 Litchfield 1,489 .... C2
†06378 Lords Point 500 .... H3
06443 Madison○ 14,031 .... E3
06443 Madison 2,069 .... E3
06040 Manchester○ 49,761 .... E1
06040 Manchester 31,058 .... E1
†06250 Mansfield○ 20,634 .... F1
06250 Mansfield Center 1,043 ..... G1
06777 Marble Dale 300 .... B2
06444 Marion 900 .... D2
06447 Marlborough○ 4,746 .... F2
06447 Marlborough 1,039 .... F2
†06382 Massapeag 350 .... G3
06252 Mechanicsville 425 .... H1
06450 Meriden 57,118 .... D2
Meriden‡ 57,118 .... D2
06762 Middlebury○ 5,995 .... C2
06455 Middlefield○ 3,796 .... E2
06456 Middle Haddam 325 .... E2
06457 Middletown 39,040 .... E2
06460 Milford 49,101 .... C4
06467 Milldale 975 .... D2
†06759 Milton 600 .... C1
06468 Monroe○ 14,010 .... C3
06468 Monroe P.O. (Stepney) B3
06353 Montville○ 16,455 .... G3
06353 Montville 1,711 .... G3
06469 Moodus 1,179 .... F2
06354 Moosup 3,308 .... H2
06763 Morris○ 1,899 .... C2
06355 Mystic 2,333 .... H3
06770 Naugatuck 26,456 .... C3
*06050 New Britain 73,840 .... E2
New Britain‡ 142,241 ...... E2
06840 New Canaan○ 17,931 .... B4
06810 New Fairfield○ 11,260 ...... B3
06057 New Hartford○ 4,884 .... C1
06057 New Hartford 1,310 .... C1
*06501 New Haven 126,109 .... D3
New Haven-West
Haven‡ 417,592 .... D3
06111 Newington○ 28,841 .... E2
06320 New London 28,842 .... G3
New London-Norwich‡
248,554 .... G3
06776 New Milford○ 19,420 .... B2
06776 New Milford 5,186 .... B2
06777 New Preston 1,209 .... B2
06470 Newtown○ 19,107 .... B3
06470 Newtown 2,022 .... B3
06357 Niantic 3,151 .... G3
06340 Noank 1,406 .... G3
06058 Norfolk○ 2,156 .... C1
06471 North Branford○ 11,554 .... E3
06778 Northfield 600 .... C2
06254 North Franklin 500 .... G2
06060 North Granby 450 .... D1
06255 North Grosvenor
Dale 1,856 .... H1
†06437 North Guilford E3
06473 North Haven○ 22,080 .... D3
06359 North Stonington○ 4,219 ... H3
06256 North Windham 200 .... G1
*06850 Norwalk 77,767 .... B4
06360 Norwich 38,074 .... G2
06370 Oakdale 608 .... G3
06779 Oakville 8,737 .... C2
06371 Old Lyme○ 6,159 .... F3

06372 Old Mystic 600 .... H3
06475 Old Saybrook○ 9,287 .... F3
06475 Old Saybrook 1,857 .... F3
06373 Oneco 550 .... H2
06477 Orange○ 13,237 .... C3
06483 Oxford○ 6,634 .... C3
06379 Pawcatuck 5,216 .... H3
06781 Pequabuck 642 .... C2
06061 Pine Meadow 400 .... D1
†06405 Pine Orchard 300 .... D3
06374 Plainfield○ 12,774 .... H2
06374 Plainfield 2,799 .... H2
06062 Plainville○ 16,401 .... D2
06063 Pleasant Valley 300 .... C1
†06385 Pleasure Beach 1,356 .... G3
06782 Plymouth○ 10,732 .... C2
06258 Pomfret○ 2,775 .... H1
†06340 Poquonock Bridge 2,549 ... G3
06480 Portland○ 8,383 .... E2
06480 Portland 5,914 .... E2
06712 Prospect○ 6,807 .... D2
06260 Putnam○ 8,580 .... H1
06260 Putnam 6,855 .... H1
06375 Quaker Hill 2,052 .... G3
06262 Quinebaug 1,088 .... H1
06875 Redding○ 7,272 .... B3
06876 Redding Ridge 550 .... B3
06877 Ridgefield○ 20,120 .... B3
06877 Ridgefield 6,066 .... B3
06065 Riverton 250 .... D1
06481 Rockfall 900 .... E2
†06066 Rockville F1
06067 Rocky Hill○ 14,559 .... E2
06263 Rogers 650 .... H1
06783 Roxbury○ 1,468 .... B2
†06415 Salem○ 2,335 .... F3
06068 Salisbury○ 3,896 .... B1
06264 Scotland○ 1,072 .... G2
06483 Seymour○ 13,434 .... C3
06069 Sharon○ 2,623 .... B1
06484 Shelton 31,314 .... C3
06784 Sherman○ 2,281 .... B2
06070 Simsbury○ 21,161 .... D1
06070 Simsbury 5,488 .... D1
06071 Somers○ 8,473 .... F1
06071 Somers 1,643 .... F1
06072 Somersville 750 .... F1
06487 South Britain 390 .... B3
06488 Southbury○ 14,156 .... C3
†06238 South Coventry
(Coventry) 3,769 .... F1
06073 South Glastonbury E2
06489 Southington○ 36,879 .... D2
06785 South Kent 450 .... B2
06265 South Willington 450 .... F1
06266 South Windham 1,399 ...... G2
06074 South Windsor○ 17,198 .... E1
06267 South Woodstock 1,319 .... G1
06075 Stafford○ 9,268 .... F1
06076 Stafford Springs 3,392 ..... F1
06077 Staffordville 500 .... G1
*06901 Stamford 102,453 .... A4
Stamford‡ 198,854 .... A4
†06468 Stepney B3
06377 Sterling○ 1,791 .... H2
06491 Stevenson 300 .... C3
06378 Stonington○ 16,220 .... H3
06378 Stonington 1,228 .... H3
06268 Storrs 11,394 .... F1
06497 Stratford○ 50,541 .... C4

06078 Suffield○ 9,294 .... E1
06078 Suffield 1,122 .... E1
06079 Taconic 400 .... B1
06380 Taftville G2
06081 Tariffville 1,324 .... D1
06786 Terryville 5,234 .... C2
06787 Thomaston○ 6,276 .... C2
06277 Thompson○ 8,141 .... H1
†06082 Thompsonville E1
06084 Tolland○ 9,694 .... F1
06790 Torrington 30,987 .... C1
06611 Trumbull○ 32,989 .... C4
06382 Uncasville 1,597 .... G3
†06076 Union○ 546 .... G1
06066 Vernon○ 27,974 .... F1
06383 Versailles 540 .... G2
06384 Voluntown○ 1,637 .... H2
06492 Wallingford○ 37,274 .... D3
06492 Wallingford 17,821 .... D3
06754 Warren○ 1,027 .... B2
†06278 Warrenville 500 .... G1
06793 Washington○ 3,657 .... B2
06794 Washington Depot 900 ..... B2
*06701 Waterbury 103,266 .... C2
Waterbury‡ 228,178 .... C2
06385 Waterford○ 17,843 .... G3
06385 Waterford 2,736 .... G3
06795 Watertown○ 19,489 .... C2
06089 Weatogue 2,249 .... D1
06498 Westbrook○ 5,216 .... F3
06498 Westbrook 2,035 .... F3
06796 West Cornwall 425 .... B1
06090 West Granby 567 .... D1
06107 West Hartford○ 61,301 ..... D1
06516 West Haven 53,184 .... D3
06388 West Mystic 3,364 .... H3
06883 Weston○ 8,284 .... B4
06880 Westport○ 25,290 .... B4
06896 West Redding 500 .... B3
06092 West Simsbury 2,140 .... D1
06109 Wethersfield○ 26,013 .... E2
06517 Whitneyville D3
06226 Willimantic 14,652 .... G2
†06279 Willington○ 4,694 .... F1
06897 Wilton○ 15,351 .... B4
06094 Winchester○ 10,841 .... C1
06094 Winchester Center 350 ...... C1
06280 Windham○ 21,062 .... G2
06095 Windsor○ 25,204 .... E1
06095 Windsor 17,517 .... E1
06096 Windsor Locks○ 12,190 .... E1
06097 Windsorville 450 .... E1
06098 Winsted 8,092 .... C1
†06417 Winthrop 750 .... E3
06716 Wolcott○ 13,008 .... D2
†06515 Woodbridge○ 7,761 .... D3
06798 Woodbury○ 6,942 .... C2
06798 Woodbury 1,290 .... C2
†06460 Woodmont 1,797 .... D4
06281 Woodstock○ 5,117 .... H1

OTHER FEATURES

Aspetuck (res.) B4
Bantam (lake) C2
Barkhamsted (res.) D1
Bear (mt.) B1
Byram (riv.) A4
Candlewood (lake) A2
Coast Guard Academy G3
Colebrook River (lake) C1
Congamond (lkes) E1
Connecticut (riv.) E2
Dennis (hill) C1
Easton (res.) B3
Eight Mile (riv.) F3
Farmington (riv.) D1
French (riv.) H1
Frissell (mt.) B1
Gaillard (lake) D3
Gardner (lake) G2
Hammonasset (pt.) E3
Hammonasset (res.) E3
Haystack (mt.) C1
Highland (lake) C1
Hockanum (riv.) E1
Hop (riv.) F1
Housatonic (riv.) C3
Lillinonah (lake) B3
Little (riv.) G2
Long Island (sound) C4
Mad (riv.) C1
Mashapaug (lake) G1
Mason (isl.) H3
Mattabesset (riv.) E2
Mianus (riv.) A4
Mohawk (mt.) B1
Moosup (riv.) H2
Mount Hope (riv.) G1
Mudge (pond) B1
Mystic (riv.) H3
Natchaug (riv.) G1
Naugatuck (riv.) C3
Nepaug (res.) D1
Niantic (riv.) G3
Norwalk (riv.) B4
Pachaug (pond) H2
Pawcatuck (riv.) H3
Pequabuck (riv.) D2
Pequonnock (riv.) C3
Pocotopaug (lake) E2
Quaddick (res.) H1
Quinebaug (riv.) H2
Quinnipiac (riv.) D3
Rippowam (riv.) A4
Sachem (head) E4
Salmon (brook) D1
Salmon (riv.) F2
Saugatuck (res.) B3
Scantic (riv.) E1
Shenipsit (lake) F1
Shepaug (riv.) B2
Shetucket (riv.) G2
Silvermine (riv.) B4
Spectacle (lkes) B2
Still (riv.) B3
Still (riv.) C1
Talcott (range) D1
Thames (riv.) G3
Thomaston (res.) C2
Titicus (riv.) A3
Trap Falls (res.) C3
Twin (lkes) B1
Wamgumbaug (lake) F1
Waramaug (lake) B2
West Rock Ridge (hills) D3
Willimantic (riv.) F1
Wononskopomuc (lake) B1
Yantic (riv.) G2

‡Population of metropolitan area.
○Population of town or township.
† Zip of nearest p.o. * Multiple zips.

Agriculture, Industry and Resources

DOMINANT LAND USE

- Specialized Dairy
- Dairy, Poultry, Mixed Farming
- Forests
- Urban Areas

MAJOR MINERAL OCCURRENCES

Cl Clay   Mi Mica

Major Industrial Areas

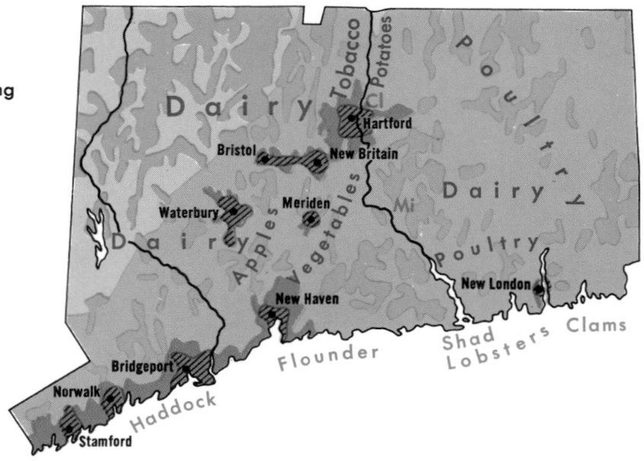

Dairy
Tobacco
Cl
Potatoes
Poultry
Hartford
Bristol
New Britain
Waterbury
Meriden
Mi
Dairy
Apples
Vegetables
Poultry
New London
New Haven
Bridgeport
Norwalk
Stamford
Haddock
Flounder
Shad
Lobsters
Clams

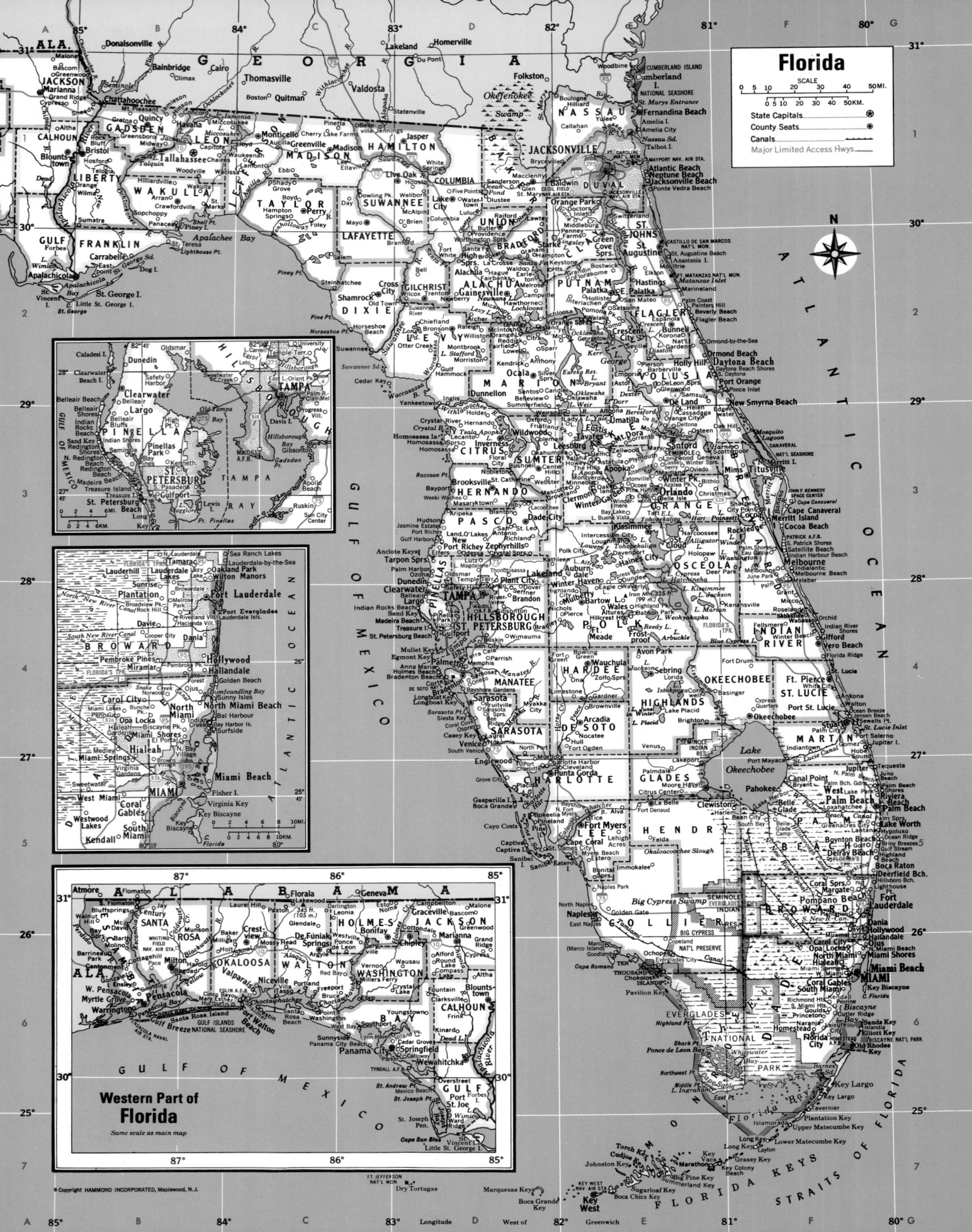

Florida

AREA 58,664 sq. mi. (151,940 sq. km.)
POPULATION 9,746,342
CAPITAL Tallahassee
LARGEST CITY Jacksonville
HIGHEST POINT (Walton County) 345 ft. (105 m.)
SETTLED IN 1565
ADMITTED TO UNION March 3, 1845
POPULAR NAME Sunshine State; Peninsula State
STATE FLOWER Orange Blossom
STATE BIRD Mockingbird

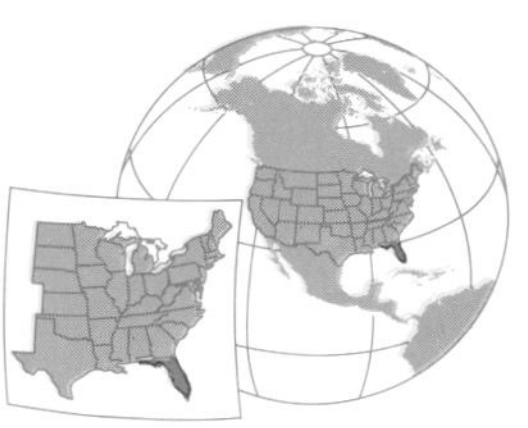

Topography

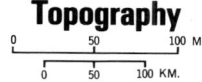

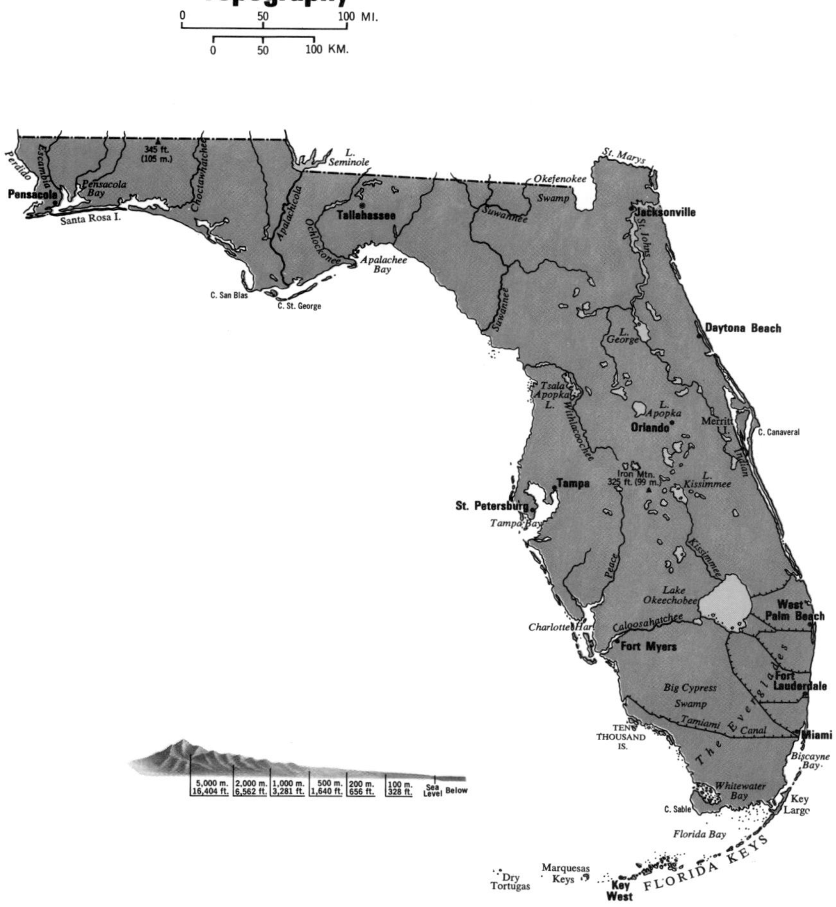
0 50 100 MI.
0 50 100 KM.
Perdido
Escambia
Pensacola
Pensacola Bay
Santa Rosa I.
345 ft. (105 m.)
Choctawhatchee
Apalachicola
L. Seminole
Ochlockonee
Tallahassee
Apalachee Bay
C. San Blas
C. St. George
Suwannee
Okefenokee Swamp
St. Marys
Jacksonville
St. Johns
L. George
Daytona Beach
Tsala Apopka L.
Withlacoochee
L. Apopka
Orlando
Merritt I.
C. Canaveral
Indian
Iron Mtn. 325 ft. (99 m.)
Tampa
St. Petersburg
Tampa Bay
L. Kissimmee
Kissimmee
Peace
Lake Okeechobee
West Palm Beach
Charlotte Har.
Caloosahatchee
Fort Myers
Big Cypress Swamp
The Everglades
Fort Lauderdale
Tamiami Canal
TEN THOUSAND IS.
Miami
Biscayne Bay
Whitewater Bay
C. Sable
Key Largo
Florida Bay
FLORIDA KEYS
Marquesas Keys
Dry Tortugas
Key West
5,000 m. 16,404 ft.
2,000 m. 6,562 ft.
1,000 m. 3,281 ft.
500 m. 1,640 ft.
200 m. 656 ft.
100 m. 328 ft.
Sea Level
Below

COUNTIES

Alachua 151,348 .... D2
Baker 15,289 .... D1
Bay 97,740 .... C6
Bradford 20,023 .... D2
Brevard 272,959 .... F3
Broward 101,820 .... F5
Calhoun 9,294 .... D6
Charlotte 58,460 .... E5
Citrus 54,703 .... D3
Clay 67,052 .... E2
Collier 85,791 .... E5
Columbia 35,399 .... D1
Dade 1,625,781 .... F6
De Soto 19,039 .... E4
Dixie 7,751 .... C2
Duval 571,003 .... E1
Escambia 233,794 .... B6
Flagler 10,913 .... E2
Franklin 7,661 .... B2
Gadsden 41,565 .... B1
Gilchrist 5,767 .... D2
Glades 5,992 .... E5
Gulf 10,658 .... D7
Hamilton 8,761 .... D1
Hardee 19,379 .... E4
Hendry 18,599 .... E5
Hernando 44,4693
Highlands 47,526 .... E4
Hillsborough 646,960 .... D4
Holmes 14,723 .... C5
Indian River 59,896 .... F4
Jackson 39,154 .... D5
Jefferson 10,703 .... C1
Lafayette 4,035 .... C2
Lake 104,870 .... E3
Lee 205,266 .... E5
Leon 148,655 .... B1
Levy 19,870 .... D2
Liberty 4,260 .... B1
Madison 14,894 .... C1
Manatee 148,442 .... D4
Marion 122,488 .... D2
Martin 64,014 .... F4
Monroe 63,188 .... E7
Nassau 32,894 .... E1
Okaloosa 109,920 .... C6
Okeechobee 20,264 .... F4
Orange 471,016 .... E3
Osceola 49,287 .... E3
Palm Beach 576,863 .... F5
Pasco 193,643 .... D3
Pinellas 728,531 .... D4
Polk 321,652 .... E4
Putnam 50,549 .... E2
Saint Johns 51,303 .... E2
Saint Lucie 87,182 .... F4
Santa Rosa 55,988 .... B6
Sarasota 202,251 .... D4
Seminole 179,752 .... E3
Sumter 24,272 .... D3
Suwannee 22,287 .... C1
Taylor 16,532 .... C1
Union 10,166 .... D1
Volusia 258,762 .... E2
Wakulla 10,887 .... B1
Walton 21,300 .... C6
Washington 14,509 .... C6

CITIES and TOWNS

Zip *Name/Pop.* *Key*

32615 Alachua 3,561 .... D2
32420 Alford 548 .... D6
32701 Altamonte Springs 22,028 . E3
32421 Altha 478 .... A1
33820 Alturas 900 .... E4
33501 Anna Maria 1,537 .... D4
32320 Apalachicola⊙ 2,565 .... A2
33570 Apollo Beach 4,014 .... C3
32703 Apopka 6,019 .... E3
33821 Arcadia⊙ 6,002 .... E4
32618 Archer 1,230 .... D2
33502 Aripeka 450 .... D3
32705 Astatula 755 .... E3
32233 Atlantic Beach 7,847 .... E1
33823 Auburndale 6,501 .... E3
33825 Avon Park 8,026 .... E4
32807 Azalea Park 8,301 .... E3
32530 Bagdad 1,479 .... B6
32234 Baldwin 1,526 .... E1
†33101 Bal Harbour 2,973 .... C4
33830 Bartow⊙ 14,780 .... E4
32423 Bascom 134 .... A1
†33101 Bay Harbor Islands 4,869 .. B4
†32786 Bay Lake 74 .... E3
33504 Bay Pines 5,757 .... B3
33507 Bayshore Gardens 14,945 .. D4
†33578 Bee Ridge 3,313 .... D4
32619 Bell 227 .... D2
33540 Belleair 3,673 .... B2
†33540 Belleair Beach 1,643 .... B2
33540 Belleair Bluffs 2,522 .... B3
†33540 Belleair Shores 80 .... B3
33430 Belle Glade 16,535 .... F5
†33430 Belle Glade Camp 1,645 .... F5
†32801 Belle Isle 2,848 .... E3
32620 Belleview 1,913 .... D2
†32036 Beverly Beach 217 .... E2
33152 Biscayne Park 3,088 .... B4
†32801 Bithlo 3,143 .... E3
32424 Blountstown⊙ 2,632 .... A1
33921 Boca Grande 900 .... D5
*33432 Boca Raton 49,505 .... F5
32425 Bonifay⊙ 2,534 .... C5
33923 Bonita Springs 5,435 .... E5
33834 Bowling Green 2,310 .... E4
*33435 Boynton Beach 35,624 .... F5
*33506 Bradenton⊙ 30,170 .... D4
Bradenton‡ 148,442 .... D4
33510 Bradenton Beach 1,595 ..... D4
33835 Bradley 1,108 .... D4
33511 Brandon 41,826 .... D4
32008 Branford 622 .... D2
†33435 Briny Breezes 387 .... G5
32321 Bristol⊙ 1,044 .... B1
†33314 Broadview Park 6,022 .... B4
32621 Bronson⊙ 853 .... D2
32622 Brooker 429 .... D2
33512 Brooksville⊙ 5,582 .... D3
†33311 Browardale 7,409 .... B4
32010 Bunnell⊙ 1,816 .... E2
33513 Bushnell⊙ 983 .... D3
32011 Callahan 869 .... E1
32401 Calloway 7,154 .... D6
32426 Campbellton 336 .... D5
32624 Candler 275 .... E2
32920 Cape Canaveral 5,733 .... F3
33904 Cape Coral 32,103 .... E5
33055 Carol City 47,349 .... B4
Carrabelle 1,304 .... B2
32427 Caryville 633 .... C6
32707 Casselberry 15,247 .... E3
†32401 Cedar Grove 1,104 .... D6
32625 Cedar Key 700 .... C2
33514 Center Hill 751 .... D3
32535 Century 495 .... B5
†33950 Charlotte Harbor 2,084 ..... E5
32324 Chattahoochee 5,332 .... B1
32626 Chiefland 1,986 .... D2
32428 Chipley⊙ 3,330 .... D6
†32548 Cinco Bayou 202 .... B6
*33515 Clearwater⊙ 85,528 .... B2
32711 Clermont 5,461 .... E3
†33950 Cleveland 2,417 .... E5
33440 Clewiston 5,219 .... E5
32922 Cocoa 16,096 .... F3
32931 Cocoa Beach 10,926 .... F3
†33060 Coconut Creek 6,288 .... F5
33521 Coleman 1,022 .... D3
33328 Cooper City 10,140 .... B4
†33559 Coral Cove 2,042 .... D4
33134 Coral Gables 43,241 .... B5
33060 Coral Springs 37,349 .... F5
33522 Cortez 3,821 .... D4
32431 Cottondale 1,056 .... D6
32327 Crawfordville⊙ 1,110 .... B1
32012 Crescent City 1,722 .... E2
32536 Crestview⊙ 7,617 .... C6
32628 Cross City⊙ 2,154 .... C2
32629 Crystal River 2,778 .... D3
33157 Cutler Ridge 20,886 .... F6
33880 Cypress Gardens 8,043 ..... E3
†33472 Cypress Quarters 1,479 .... F4
33525 Dade City⊙ 4,923 .... D3
33004 Dania 11,811.B4
33837 Davenport 1,509 .... E3
33314 Davie 20,877 .... B4
*32014 Daytona Beach 54,176 ...... F2
Daytona Beach‡ 258,762 .. F2
32016 Daytona Beach Shores 1,324 .... F2
32713 De Bary 4,980 .... E3
33441 Deerfield Beach 39,193 ..... F5
32433 De Funiak Springs⊙ 5,563 C6
32720 De Land⊙ 15,354 .... E2
32028 De Leon Springs 1,669 ..... E2
*33444 Delray Beach 34,325 .... F5
32725 Deltona 15,710 .... E3
32541 Destin 3,672 .... C6
33527 Dover 2,354 .... D4
33838 Dundee 2,227 .... E3
33528 Dunedin 30,203 .... B2
32630 Dunnellon 1,427 .... D2
33839 Eagle Lake 1,678 .... E4
†33601 East Lake-Orient Park 5,612 .... C2
†33940 East Naples 12,127 .... E5
32031 East Palatka 1,613 .... E2
32328 Eastpoint 1,246 .... B2
32751 Eatonville 2,185 .... E3
32437 Ebro 233 .... C6
32032 Edgewater 6,726 .... F3
†32801 Edgewood 1,034 .... E3
†33614 Egypt Lake 11,932 .... C2
33531 Elfers 11,396 .... D3
†33101 El Portal 1,819 .... B4
33533 Englewood 9,633 .... D5
32504 Ensley 14,422 .... B6
32425 Esto 304 .... C5
32726 Eustis 9,453 .... E3
33929 Everglades City 524 .... E6
32634 Fairfield 450 .... D2
†32693 Fanning Springs (Suwannee Riv.) 314 .... D2
32948 Fellsmere 1,161 .... F4
32034 Fernandina Beach⊙ 7,224 . E1
32922 Five Points 1,691 .... D1
32036 Flagler Beach 2,208 .... E2
32636 Floral City 1,181 .... D3
33034 Florida City 6,174 .... F6
†32960 Florida Ridge 4,988 .... F4
†33472 Fort Drum 70 .... F4
*33301 Fort Lauderdale⊙ 153,279. C4
Fort Lauderdale-Hollywood‡ 1,014,043 .. C4
33841 Fort Meade 5,546 .... E4
*33901 Fort Myers⊙ 36,638 .... E5
Fort Myers-Cape Coral‡ 205,266 .... E5
33931 Fort Myers Beach 5,753 .... E5
33842 Fort Ogden 900 .... E4
*33450 Fort Pierce⊙ 33,802 .... F4
32548 Fort Walton Beach 20,829 . C6
Fort Walton Beach‡ 109,920 .... C6
32038 Fort White 386 .... D2
32438 Fountain 900 .... D6
32439 Freeport 669 .... C6
33843 Frostproof 2,995 .... E4
32731 Fruitland Park 2,259 .... D3
33578 Fruitville 3,070 .... D4
*32601 Gainesville⊙ 81,371 .... D2
Gainesville‡ 151,348 .... D2
32732 Geneva 1,120 .... E3
33534 Gibsonton 7,219 .... C3
32960 Gifford 6,240 .... F4
32040 Glen Saint Mary 462 .... D1
†33160 Golden Beach 612 .... C4
33999 Golden Gate 4,327 .... E5
†33444 Golf 110 .... F5
32560 Gonzalez 6,084 .... B6
33933 Goodland 600 .... E6
†32502 Goulding 5,352 .... B6
33170 Goulds 7,078 .... F6
32440 Graceville 2,918 .... D5
32442 Grand Ridge 591 .... A1
33463 Greenacres City 8,843 ...... F5
32043 Green Cove Springs⊙ 4,154 .... E2
32330 Greensboro 562 .... B1
32331 Greenville 1,096 .... C1
32443 Greenwood 577 .... A1
32332 Gretna 1,448 .... B1
33533 Grove City 1,932 .... D5
32736 Groveland 1,992 .... E3
32561 Gulf Breeze 5,478 .... B6
33737 Gulfport 11,180 .... B3
†33444 Gulf Stream 475 .... F5
†33301 Hacienda Village 126 .... B4
33844 Haines City 10,799 .... E3
33009 Hallandale 36,517 .... B4
32044 Hampton 466 .... D2
33440 Harlem 2,669 .... F5
32045 Hastings 636 .... E2
32333 Havana 2,782 .... B1
32640 Hawthorne 1,303 .... D2
32642 Hernando 1,653 .... D3
*33010 Hialeah 145,254 .... B4
†33010 Hialeah Gardens 2,700 ...... B4
33431 Highland Beach 2,030 ...... F5
33846 Highland City 1,555 .... E4
32401 Highland Park 184 .... E4
32643 High Springs 2,491 .... D2
32405 Hiland Park 4,763 .... C6
†33827 Hillcrest Heights 177 .... E4
32046 Hilliard 1,869 .... E1
†33060 Hillsboro Beach 1,554 ...... F5
33455 Hobe Sound 6,822 .... F4
32047 Hollister 980 .... E2
32017 Holly Hill 9,953 .... E2
*33020 Hollywood 121,323 .... B4
33509 Holmes Beach 4,023 .... D4
*33030 Homestead 20,668 .... F6
32646 Homosassa 1,426 .... D3
32648 Horseshoe Beach 304 .... C2
32334 Hosford 750 .... B1
32737 Howey In The Hills 626 ..... E3
33568 Hudson 5,799 .... D3
†33460 Hypoluxo 573 .... F5
33934 Immokalee 11,038 .... E5
32903 Indialantic 2,883 .... F3
†33139 Indian Creek 103 .... B4
†32901 Indian Harbour Beach 5,967 .... F3
32960 Indian River Shores 1,254 . F4
33535 Indian Rocks Beach 3,717 . B3
†33535 Indian Shores 984 .... B3
33456 Indiantown 3,383 .... F4
32649 Inglis 1,173 .... D2
32048 Interlachen 848 .... E2
32650 Inverness⊙ 4,095 .... D3
33036 Islamorada 1,441 .... F7
†33101 Islandia 12 .... F6
*32201 Jacksonville⊙ 540,920 ..... E1
Jacksonville‡ 737,519 ...... E1
32250 Jacksonville Beach 15,462 . E1
†33568 Jasmine Estates 11,995 .... D3
32052 Jasper⊙ 2,093 .... D1
32565 Jay 633 .... B5
32053 Jennings 749 .... C1
33457 Jensen Beach 6,639 .... F4
†32901 June Park 4,051 .... F3
†33404 Juno Beach 1,142 .... F5
33458 Jupiter 9,868 .... F5
†33455 Jupiter Island 364 .... F4
33849 Kathleen 1,866 .... D3
33156 Kendall 73,758 .... B5
33709 Kenneth City 4,344 .... B3
33149 Key Biscayne 6,313 .... B5
33051 Key Colony Beach 977 ...... F7
33037 Key Largo 7,447 .... F6
32656 Keystone Heights 1,056 .... E2
33040 Key West⊙ 24,382 .... E7
32741 Kissimmee⊙ 15,487 .... E3
33935 La Belle⊙ 2,287 .... E5
33537 Lacoochee 1,720 .... D3
32658 La Crosse 170 .... D2
32659 Lady Lake 1,193 .... E3
33850 Lake Alfred 3,134 .... E3
†32830 Lake Buena Vista 98 .... E3
32054 Lake Butler⊙ 1,830 .... D1
†33601 Lake Carroll 13,012 .... C2
32055 Lake City⊙ 9,257 .... D1
32744 Lake Helen 2,047 .... E3
*33801 Lakeland 47,406 .... D3
Lakeland-Winter Haven‡ 321,652 .... D3
†33612 Lake Magdalene 13,331 .... D3
32746 Lake Mary 2,853 .... E3
33403 Lake Park 6,909 .... F5
33852 Lake Placid 963 .... E4
33853 Lake Wales 8,466 .... E4
*33460 Lake Worth 27,048 .... G5
33539 Land O'Lakes 4,515 .... D3
33462 Lantana 8,048 .... F5
*33540 Largo 58,977 .... B3
33308 Lauderdale-by-the-Sea 2,639 .... C3
†33313 Lauderdale Lakes 25,426 ... B3
33313 Lauderhill 37,271 .... B3
33545 Laurel 6,368 .... D4
32567 Laurel Hill 610 .... C5
32058 Lawtey 692 .... D1
†33050 Layton 88 .... F7
†33301 Lazy Lake 31 .... B3
32059 Lee 297 .... C1
32748 Leesburg 13,191 .... E3
33936 Lehigh Acres 9,604 .... E5
33033 Leisure City 17,905 .... F6
†33614 Leto 9,003 .... C2
33064 Lighthouse Point 11,488 ... F5
32060 Live Oak⊙ 6,732 .... D1
32662 Lochloosa 450 .... E2
33548 Longboat Key 4,843 .... D4
32750 Longwood 10,029 .... E3
33549 Lutz 5,555 .... D3
32444 Lynn Haven 6,239 .... C6
32063 Macclenny⊙ 3,851 .... D1

(continued on following page)

33738 Madeira Beach 4,520 .... B3
32340 Madison⊙ 3,487 .... C1
32751 Maitland 8,763 .... E3
32950 Malabar 1,118 .... F3
32445 Malone 897 .... A1
33550 Mango 6,493 .... D4
33050 Marathon 7,568 .... E7
33937 Marco (Marco Island) 4,679 .... E6
33063 Margate 35,900 .... F5
32446 Marianna⊙ 7,006 .... A1
†32084 Marineland 31 .... E2
†32569 Mary Esther 3,530 .... B6
32753 Mascotte 1,112 .... E3
32066 Mayo⊙ 891 .... C1
32664 McIntosh 404 .... D2
†33101 Medley 537 .... B4
*32901 Melbourne 46,536 .... F3
Melbourne-Titusville-Cocoa‡ 272,959 .... F3
32951 Melbourne Beach 2,713 .... F3
†33301 Melrose Park 5,672 .... B4
†33561 Memphis 5,501 .... D4
32952 Merritt Island 30,708 .... F3
32410 Mexico Beach 632 .... D6
*33101 Miami⊙ 346,931 .... B5
Miami‡ 1,625,979 .... B5
33139 Miami Beach 96,298 .... C5
†33101 Miami Lakes 9,809 .... B4
33153 Miami Shores 9,244 .... B4
33166 Miami Springs 12,350 .... B5
32667 Micanopy 737 .... D2
†32960 Micco 3,585 .... F4
32343 Midway 950 .... B1
32570 Milton⊙ 7,206 .... B6
32754 Mims 7,583 .... F3
32755 Minneola 851 .... E3
33023 Miramar 32,813 .... B4
32577 Molino 1,456 .... B6
32344 Monticello⊙ 2,994 .... C1
32756 Montverde 397 .... E3
33471 Moore Haven⊙ 1,250 .... E5
32757 Mount Dora 5,883 .... E3
33860 Mulberry 2,932 .... E4
33938 Murdock 272 .... D4
32506 Myrtle Grove 14,238 .... B6
*33940 Naples⊙ 17,581 .... E5
†33940 Naples Park 5,438 .... E5
33032 Naranja 10,381 .... F6
32233 Neptune Beach 5,248 .... E1
32669 Newberry 1,826 .... D2
*33552 New Port Richey 11,196 .... D3
32069 New Smyrna Beach 13,557 F2
32578 Niceville 8,543 .... C6
33555 Nokomis 3,108 .... D4
32452 Noma 113 .... C5
†33169 Norland 19,471 .... B4
33141 North Bay Village 4,920 .... B4
33903 North Fort Myers 22,808 .... E5
†33063 North Lauderdale 18,653 .... B3
33161 North Miami 42,566 .... B4
33161 North Miami Beach 36,481 C4
33940 North Naples 7,950 .... E5
33403 North Palm Beach 11,344 .. F5
33595 North Port 6,205 .... D4
†33708 North Redington Beach 1,156 .... B3
32759 Oak Hill 938 .... F3
32760 Oakland 658 .... E3
33334 Oakland Park 23,035 .... B3
*32670 Ocala⊙ 37,170 .... D2
Ocala‡ 122,488 .... D2
†33457 Ocean Breeze Park 469 .... F4
33444 Ocean Ridge 1,355 .... F5
32761 Ocoee 7,803 .... E3
33163 Ojus 17,344 .... B4
32762 Okahumpka 900 .... D3
33472 Okeechobee⊙ 4,225 .... F4
33557 Oldsmar 2,608 .... B2
33558 Oneco 6,417 .... D4
33054 Opa Locka 14,460 .... B4
32763 Orange City 2,795 .... E3
32073 Orange Park 8,766 .... E1
†32970 Orchid 42 .... F4
*32801 Orlando⊙ 128,291 .... E3
Orlando‡ 700,699 .... E3
32074 Ormond Beach 21,378 .... E2
32074 Ormond-by-the-Sea 7,665 . E2
33559 Osprey 1,660 .... D4
32683 Otter Creek 167 .... D2
32765 Oviedo 3,074 .... E3
32570 Pace 5,006 .... B6
33476 Pahokee 6,346 .... F5
†32036 Painters Hill 40 .... E2
32077 Palatka⊙ 10,175 .... E2
32905 Palm Bay 18,560 .... F3
33480 Palm Beach 9,729 .... G4
†33403 Palm Beach Gardens 14,407 .... F5
†33404 Palm Beach Shores 1,232 . G5
33490 Palm City 2,177 .... F4
32037 Palm Coast 2,837 .... E2
33561 Palmetto 8,637 .... D4
33563 Palm Harbor 5,215 .... D3
33619 Palm River-Clair Mel 14,447 .... C3
†32901 Palm Shores 77 .... F3
33460 Palm Springs 8,166 .... F5
*32401 Panama City⊙ 33,346 .... C6
Panama City‡ 97,740 .... C6
32407 Panama City Beach 2,148 . C6
32401 Parker 4,298 .... C6
†33441 Parkland 545 .... F5
32538 Paxton 659 .... C5
†33023 Pembroke Park 4,783 .... B4
33024 Pembroke Pines 35,776 .... B4
32079 Penney Farms 630 .... E2
†33010 Pennsuco 15 .... B4
*32501 Pensacola⊙ 57,619 .... B6
Pensacola‡ 289,782 .... B6
33157 Perrine 16,129 .... F6
32347 Perry⊙ 8,254 .... C1
32080 Pierson 1,085 .... E2
32808 Pine Hills 35,771 .... E3
33565 Pinellas Park 32,811 .... B3
33317 Plantation 48,653 .... B4
33566 Plant City 17,064 .... D3
33868 Polk City 576 .... E3
32081 Pomona Park 791 .... E2
*33060 Pompano Beach 52,618 .... F5
32455 Ponce de Leon 454 .... C6
†32019 Ponce Inlet 1,003 .... F2
33952 Port Charlotte 25,770 .... D5
32019 Port Orange 18,756 .... F2
33568 Port Richey 2,165 .... D3
32456 Port Saint Joe 4,027 .... D6
33452 Port Saint Lucie 14,690 .... F4
33492 Port Salerno 4,511 .... F4
33032 Princeton 10,381 .... F6
*33950 Punta Gorda⊙ 6,797 .... E5
32351 Quincy⊙ 8,591 .... B1
32083 Raiford 259 .... D1
32686 Reddick 657 .... D2
33708 Redington Beach 1,708 .... B3
†33708 Redington Shores 2,142 .... B3
†33158 Richmond Heights 8,577 .... F6
†33301 Riverland 5,919 .... B4
33404 Riviera Beach 26,489 .... G5
32955 Rockledge 11,877 .... F3
32957 Roseland 1,607 .... F4
33570 Ruskin 5,117 .... C3
33572 Safety Harbor 6,461 .... B2
32084 Saint Augustine⊙ 11,985 .. E2
32084 Saint Augustine Beach 1,289 .... E2
32769 Saint Cloud 7,840 .... E3
33956 Saint James City 1,298 .... D5
33574 Saint Leo 917 .... D3
33452 Saint Lucie 593 .... F4
32355 Saint Marks 286 .... B1
*33701 Saint Petersburg 238,647 .. B3
33736 Saint Petersburg Beach 9,354 .... B3
†33508 Samoset 5,747 .... D4
†32069 Samsula 1,971 .... E2
33576 San Antonio 529 .... D3
32771 Sanford⊙ 23,176 .... E3
33957 Sanibel 3,363 .... D5
*33577 Sarasota⊙ 48,868 .... D4
Sarasota‡ 202,251 .... D4
†33577 Sarasota Springs 13,860 .... D4
32935 Satellite Beach 9,163 .... F3
32775 Scottsmoor 900 .... F3
†33301 Sea Ranch Lakes 584 .... C3
32958 Sebastian 2,831 .... F4
33870 Sebring⊙ 8,736 .... E4
33584 Seffner 6,493 .... D4
33542 Seminole 4,586 .... B3
†33457 Sewalls Point 1,187 .... F4
32579 Shalimar 390 .... C6
32959 Sharpes 4,149 .... F3
32688 Silver Springs 1,082 .... D2
32460 Sneads 1,690 .... B1
32358 Sopchoppy 444 .... B1
33493 South Bay 3,886 .... F5
32021 South Daytona 11,252 .... F2
33143 South Miami 10,944 .... B5
†33157 South Miami Heights 23,559 .... F6
33707 South Pasadena 4,188 .... B3
†32901 South Patrick Shores 9,816 .... F3
†32401 Southport 1,992 .... C6
33452 South Port Saint Lucie (Port Saint Lucie 14,690 .... F4
33595 South Venice 8,075 .... D4
32690 Sparr 902 .... D2
32401 Springfield 7,220 .... D6
32091 Starke⊙ 5,306 .... D2
33494 Stuart⊙ 9,467 .... F4
33586 Sun City D4
†33570 Sun City Center 5,605 .... C3
†33450 Sunland Gardens F4
33160 Sunny Isles 12,564 .... C4
33313 Sunrise 39,681 .... B4
33154 Surfside 3,763 .... B4
32692 Suwannee (Fanning Sprs.) 314 .... C2
†33144 Sweetwater 8,251 .... B5
†32043 Switzerland 3,906 .... E1
32809 Taft 900 .... E3
*32301 Tallahassee (cap.)⊙ 81,548 .... B1
Tallahassee‡ 159,542 .... B1
†33321 Tamarac 29,376 .... B3
*33601 Tampa⊙ 271,523 .... C2
Tampa-Saint Petersburg‡ 1,569,492 .. C2
*33589 Tarpon Springs 13,251 .... D3
32778 Tavares⊙ 4,103 .... E3
33070 Tavernier 1,834 .... F6
33617 Temple Terrace 11,097 .... C2
33458 Tequesta 3,685 .... F5
33905 Tice 6,645 .... E5
32780 Titusville⊙ 31,910 .... F3
33740 Treasure Island 6,316 .... B3
32693 Trenton⊙ 1,131 .... D2
32784 Umatilla 1,872 .... E3
33620 University 24,514 .... C2
32580 Valparaiso 6,142 .... C6
*33595 Venice 12,153 .... D4
32462 Vernon 885 .... C6
32960 Vero Beach⊙ 16,176 .... F4
†33166 Virginia Gardens 2,098 .... B5
32970 Wabasso 2,157 .... F4
†32327 Wakulla 225 .... B1
32694 Waldo 993 .... D2
†32456 Ward Ridge 104 .... D6
32507 Warrington 15,792 .... B6
†32055 Watertown 3,804 .... D1
33873 Wauchula⊙ 2,986 .... E4
32463 Wausau 347 .... D6
33877 Waverly 1,208 .... E4
33597 Webster 856 .... D3
†33512 Weeki Wachee 8 .... D3
32093 Welaka 492 .... E2
32935 West Eau Gallie 2,591 .... F3
†32901 West Melbourne 5,078 .... F3
†33101 West Miami 6,076 .... B5
*33401 West Palm Beach⊙ 63,305 F5
West Palm Beach-Boca Raton‡ 573,125 .... F5
†32502 West Pensacola 24,371 .... B6
32464 Westville 343 .... C6
†33165 Westwood Lakes 11,478 .. B5
32465 Wewahitchka⊙ 1,742 .... D6
†32465 White City 4,110 .... F4
32096 White Springs 781 .... D1
32785 Wildwood 2,665 .... D3
32696 Williston 2,240 .... D2
33334 Wilton Manors 12,742 .... B3
33598 Wimauma 1,477 .... D4
32786 Windermere 1,302 .... E3
33880 Winter Haven 21,119 .... E3
*32789 Winter Park 22,339 .... E3
†32801 Winter Springs 10,475 .... E3
32362 Woodville 1,768 .... B1
32697 Worthington Springs 220 .. D2
32698 Yankeetown 600 .... D2
32097 Yulee 3,168 .... E1
32798 Zellwood 1,760 .... E3
33599 Zephyrhills 5,742 .... D3
33890 Zolfo Springs 1,495 .... E4

OTHER FEATURES

Alapaha (riv.) C1
Alligator (lake) E3
Amelia (isl.) E1
Anastasia (isl.) E2
Anclote (keys) D3
Apalachee (bay) B2
Apalachicola (bay) B2
Apalachicola (riv.) A1
Apopka (lake) E3
Arbuckle (lake) E4
Aucilla (riv.) C1
Banana (riv.) F3
Beresford (lake) E3
Big Cypress (swamp) E5
Big Cypress Nat'l Preserve E5
Biscayne (bay) F6
Biscayne (key) B5
Biscayne Nat'l Park F6
Blackwater (riv.) B6
Blue Cypress (lake) F4
Boca Chica (key) E7
Boca Ciega (bay) B3
Boca Grande (key) D7
Bryant (lake) E2
Caloosahatchee (riv.) E5
Captiva (isl.) D5
Casey (key) D4
Castillo de San Marcos Nat'l Mon. E2
Cecil Field Naval Air Sta. E1
Charlotte (harb.) D5
Chattahoochee (riv.) B1
Chipola (riv.) D6
Choctawhatchee (riv.) C6
Crescent (lake) E2
Cumberland Island Nat'l Seashore E1
Cypress (lake) E3
De Soto Nat'l Mem. D4
Dead (lake) D6
Dexter (lake) E2
Dog (isl.) B2
Dorr (lake) E2
Dry Tortugas (keys) D7
Dumfoundling (bay) C4
East (pt.) E6
Eglin A.F.B. 7,574 .... C6
Egmont (key) D4
Elliott (key) F6
Escambia (riv.) B6
Estero (isl.) E5
Eureka (res.) E2
Everglades, The (swamp) F6
Everglades Nat'l Park F6
Fenholloway (riv.) C1
Florida (bay) F6
Florida (cape) F6
Florida (keys) E7
Florida (strs) F7
Fort Caroline Nat'l Mem. E1
Fort Jefferson Nat'l Mon. C7
Fort Matanzas Nat'l Mon. E2
Gasparilla (isl.) D5
George (lake) E2
Grassy (key) F7
Gulf Island Nat'l Seashore B6
Harney (lake) F3
Hart (lake) E3
Hillsborough (bay) C3
Hillsborough (canal) F5
Hillsborough (riv.) C2
Homosassa (isls.) D3
Homestead A.F.B. 7,594 .... F6
Iamonia (lake) B1
Indian (riv.) F3
Iron (mt.) E4
Istokpoga (lake) E4
Jackson (lake) B1
Jackson (lake) E4
Jacksonville Naval Air Sta. E1
John F. Kennedy Space Center F3
June in Winter (lake) E4
Kennedy (Canaveral) (cape) F3
Kerr (lake) E2
Key Largo (key) F6
Key Vaca (key) E7
Key West Naval Air Sta. E7
Kissimmee (lake) E4
Kissimmee (riv.) E4
Largo (key) F6
Levy (lake) D2
Lochloosa (lake) D2
Long (key) B3
Long (key) F7
Longboat (key) D4
Lower Matecumbe (key) F7
Lowery (lake) E3
MacDill A.F.B. C3
Manatee (riv.) D4
Marco (isl.) E6
Marian (lake) E4
Marquesas (keys) D7
Matanzas (inlet) E2
Mayport Naval Air Sta. E1
McCoy A.F.B. E3
Merritt (isl.) F3
Mexico (gulf) C4
Miami (canal) F5
Miami (riv.) B5
Miccosukee (lake) B1
Monroe (lake) E3
Mosquito (lag.) F3
Mullet (key) D4
Myakka (riv.) D4
Nassau (riv.) E1
Nassau (sound) E1
New (riv.) B1
New (riv.) D1
Newnans (lake) D2
North Merritt (isl.) F3
North New River (canal) F5
Ochlockonee (riv.) B1
Okaloacoochee Slough (swamp) E5
Okeechobee (lake) F5
Okefenokee (swamp) D1
Oklawaha (riv.) E2
Old Rhodes (key) F6
Old Tampa (bay) B3
Olustee (riv.) D1
Orange (lake) D2
Patrick A.F.B. 2,843 .... F3
Peace (riv.) E4
Pensacola (bay) B6
Pensacola Naval Air Sta. B6
Perdido (riv.) B6
Pine (isl.) D5
Pine Island (sound) D5
Pine Log (creek) C6
Pinellas (pt.) C3
Piney (isl.) B1
Piney (pt.) C2
Placid (lake) E4
Plantation (key) F7
Poinsett (lake) F3
Ponce de Leon (bay) E6
Port Everglades (harb.) C4
Port Tampa (harb.) B3
Reedy (lake) E4
Romano (cape) E6
Sable (cape) E6
Saint Andrew (pt.) D6
Saint George (cape) A2
Saint George (isl.) B2
Saint George (sound) B2
Saint Johns (riv.) E2
Saint Joseph (bay) D6
Saint Joseph (pt.) D6
Saint Lucie (canal) F4
Saint Lucie (inlet) F4
Saint Marys (riv.) D1
Saint Marys Entrance (inlet) E1
Saint Vincent (isl.) D7
San Blas (cape) D7
Sand (key) B3
Sands (key) F6
Sanibel (isl.) D5
Santa Fe (lake) D2
Santa Fe (riv.) D2
Santa Rosa (isl.) B6
Santa Rosa (sound) B6
Sarasota (pt.) D4
Seminole (lake) B1
Seminole Ind. Res. E4
Seminole Ind. Res. F5
Shark (pt.) E6
Shoal (riv.) C6
Snake Creek (canal) B4
South New River (canal) F5
Stafford (lake) D2
Sugarloaf (key) E7
Suwannee (riv.) C2
Suwannee (sound) C2
Talbot (isl.) E1
Talquin (lake) B1
Tamiami (canal) E6
Tampa (bay) D4
Ten Thousand (isls.) E6
Torch (key) E7
Treasure (isl.) B3
Tsala Apopka (lake) D3
Tyndall A.F.B. 4,542 .... C6
Upper Matecumbe (key) F7
Vaca (key) E7
Virginia (key) B5
Waccasassa (bay) D2
Waccasassa (riv.) D2
Washington (lake) F3
Weir (lake) E2
Weohyakapka (lake) E4
West Palm Beach (canal) F5
Whitewater (bay) F6
Whiting Field Naval Air Sta. B6
Wimico (lake) A2
Winder (lake) F3
Withlacoochee (riv.) C1
Withlacoochee (riv.) D2
Yale (lake) E3
Yellow (riv.) B6

⊙County seat.
‡Population of metropolitan area.
† Zip of nearest p.o. * Multiple zips.

Agriculture, Industry and Resources

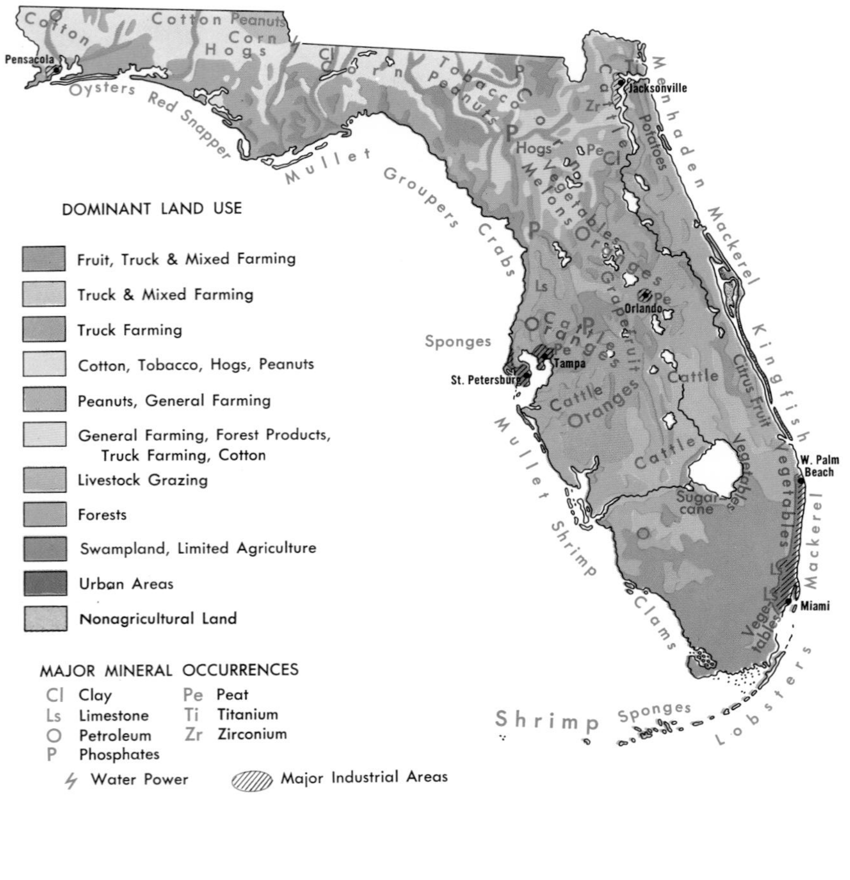
Pensacola
Jacksonville
Orlando
Tampa
St. Petersburg
W. Palm Beach
Miami
Cotton
Peanuts
Corn
Hogs
Tobacco
Oysters
Red Snapper
Mullet
Groupers
Crabs
Menhaden
Mackerel
Kingfish
Potatoes
Cattle
Vegetables
Oranges
Grapefruit
Citrus Fruit
Sugar cane
Sponges
Shrimp
Clams
Lobsters
DOMINANT LAND USE
Fruit, Truck & Mixed Farming
Truck & Mixed Farming
Truck Farming
Cotton, Tobacco, Hogs, Peanuts
Peanuts, General Farming
General Farming, Forest Products, Truck Farming, Cotton
Livestock Grazing
Forests
Swampland, Limited Agriculture
Urban Areas
Nonagricultural Land
MAJOR MINERAL OCCURRENCES
Cl Clay
Ls Limestone
O Petroleum
P Phosphates
Pe Peat
Ti Titanium
Zr Zirconium
Water Power
Major Industrial Areas

AREA 58,910 sq. mi. (152,577 sq. km.)
POPULATION 5,463,105
CAPITAL Atlanta
LARGEST CITY Atlanta
HIGHEST POINT Brasstown Bald 4,784 ft. (1458 m.)
SETTLED IN 1733
ADMITTED TO UNION January 2, 1788
POPULAR NAME Empire State of the South; Peach State
STATE FLOWER Cherokee Rose
STATE BIRD Brown Thrasher

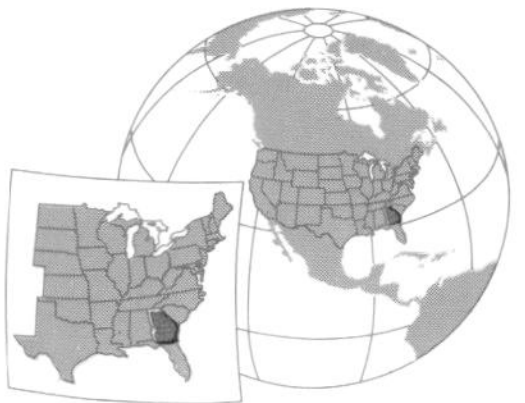

COUNTIES

Appling 15,565 .... H7
Atkinson 6,141 .... G8
Bacon 9,379 .... G7
Baker 3,808 .... D8
Baldwin 34,686 .... F4
Banks 8,702 .... E2
Barrow 21,293 .... E2
Bartow 40,760 .... C2
Ben Hill 16,000 .... F7
Berrien 13,525 .... F8
Bibb 151,085 .... E5
Bleckley 10,767 .... F6
Brantley 8,701 .... J8
Brooks 15,255 .... E9
Bryan 10,175 .... K6
Bulloch 35,785 .... J6
Burke 19,349 .... J4
Butts 13,665 .... E4
Calhoun 5,717 .... C7
Camden 13,371 .... J9
Candler 7,518 .... H6
Carroll 56,346 .... B3
Catoosa 36,991 .... B1
Charlton 7,343 .... H9
Chatham 202,226 .... K6
Chattahoochee 21,732 .... C6
Chattooga 21,856 .... B1
Cherokee 51,699 .... D2
Clarke 74,498 .... F3
Clay 3,553 .... B7
Clayton 150,357 .... D3
Clinch 6,660 .... G9
Cobb 297,694 .... C3
Coffee 26,894 .... G8
Colquitt 35,376 .... E8
Columbia 40,118 .... H3
Cook 13,490 .... F8
Coweta 39,268 .... C4
Crawford 7,684 .... E5
Crisp 19,489 .... E7
Dade 12,318 .... A1
Dawson 4,774 .... D2
Decatur 25,495 .... C9
De Kalb 483,024 .... D3
Dodge 16,955 .... F6
Dooly 10,826 .... E6
Dougherty 100,978 .... D7
Douglas 54,573 .... C3
Early 13,158 .... C8
Echols 2,297 .... G9
Effingham 18,327 .... K6
Elbert 18,758 .... G2
Emanuel 20,795 .... H5
Evans 8,428 .... J6
Fannin 14,748 .... D1
Fayette 29,043 .... C4
Floyd 79,800 .... B2
Forsyth 27,958 .... D2
Franklin 15,185 .... F2
Fulton 589,904 .... D3
Gilmer 11,110 .... D1
Glascock 2,382 .... G4
Glynn 54,981 .... J8
Gordon 30,070 .... C2
Grady 19,845 .... D9
Greene 11,391 .... F3
Gwinnett 166,903 .... D2
Habersham 25,020 .... E1
Hall 75,649 .... E2
Hancock 9,466 .... G4
Haralson 18,422 .... B3
Harris 15,464 .... C5
Hart 18,585 .... G2
Heard 6,520 .... B4
Henry 36,309 .... D4
Houston 77,605 .... E6
Irwin 8,988 .... F7
Jackson 25,343 .... E2
Jasper 7,553 .... E4
Jeff Davis 11,473 .... G7
Jefferson 18,403 .... H4
Jenkins 8,841 .... J5
Johnson 8,660 .... G5
Jones 16,579 .... E5
Lamar 12,215 .... D4
Lanier 5,654 .... F8
Laurens 36,990 .... G6
Lee 11,684 .... D7
Liberty 37,583 .... J7
Lincoln 6,949 .... H3
Long 4,524 .... J7
Lowndes 67,972 .... F9
Lumpkin 10,762 .... D1
Macon 14,003 .... D6
Madison 17,747 .... F2
Marion 5,297 .... C6
McDuffie 18,546 .... H4
McIntosh 8,046 .... K7
Meriwether 21,229 .... C4
Miller 7,038 .... C8
Mitchell 21,114 .... D8
Monroe 14,610 .... E4
Montgomery 7,011 .... G6
Morgan 11,572 .... F3
Murray 19,685 .... C1
Muscogee 170,108 .... C6
Newton 34,489 .... E3
Oconee 12,427 .... F3
Oglethorpe 8,929 .... F3
Paulding 26,042 .... C3
Peach 19,151 .... E5
Pickens 11,652 .... D2
Pierce 11,897 .... H8
Pike 8,937 .... D4
Polk 32,386 .... B3
Pulaski 8,950 .... E6
Putnam 10,295 .... F4
Quitman 2,357 .... B7
Rabun 10,466 .... F1
Randolph 9,599 .... C7
Richmond 181,629 .... H4
Rockdale 36,747 .... D3
Schley 3,433 .... D6
Screven 14,043 .... J5
Seminole 9,057 .... C9
Spalding 47,899 .... D4
Stephens 21,763 .... F1
Stewart 5,896 .... C6
Sumter 29,360 .... D6
Talbot 6,536 .... C5
Taliaferro 2,032 .... G3
Tattnall 18,134 .... J6
Taylor 7,902 .... D5
Telfair 11,445 .... G7
Terrell 12,017 .... D7
Thomas 38,098 .... E9
Tift 32,862 .... E7
Toombs 22,592 .... H6
Towns 5,638 .... E1
Treutlen 6,087 .... G6
Troup 50,003 .... B4
Turner 9,510 .... E7
Twiggs 9,354 .... F5
Union 9,390 .... E1
Upson 25,998 .... D5
Walker 56,470 .... B1
Walton 31,211 .... E3
Ware 37,180 .... H8
Warren 6,583 .... G4
Washington 18,842 .... G4
Wayne 20,750 .... J7
Webster 2,341 .... C6
Wheeler 5,155 .... G6
White 10,120 .... E1
Whitfield 65,780 .... B1
Wilcox 7,682 .... F7
Wilkes 10,951 .... G3
Wilkinson 10,368 .... F5
Worth 18,064 .... E8

CITIES and TOWNS

Zip *Name/Pop.* *Key*

31001 Abbeville⊙ 985 .... F7
30101 Acworth 3,648 .... C2
30103 Adairsville 1,739 .... C2
31620 Adel⊙ 5,592 .... F8
31002 Adrian 756 .... G5
30410 Ailey 579 .... G6
30411 Alamo⊙ 993 .... G6
31622 Alapaha 771 .... F8
*31701 Albany⊙ 74,550 .... D7
Albany‡ 112,456 .... D7
†30204 Aldora 139 .... D4
31301 Allenhurst 606 .... J7
31003 Allentown 321 .... F5
31510 Alma⊙ 3,819 .... G7
30201 Alpharetta 3,128 .... D2
30412 Alston 111 .... H6
30510 Alto 618 .... E2
†30161 Alto Park B2
31512 Ambrose 360 .... G7
31709 Americus⊙ 16,120 .... D6
31711 Andersonville 267 .... D6
30802 Appling⊙ 150 .... H3
31712 Arabi 376 .... E7
30104 Aragon 855 .... B2
†30549 Arcade 223 .... E2
†31520 Arco J8
31623 Argyle 206 .... G8
31713 Arlington 1,572 .... C8
30619 Arnoldsville 187 .... F3
31714 Ashburn⊙ 4,766 .... E7
*30601 Athens⊙ 42,549 .... F3
Athens‡ 130,015 .... F3
*30301 Atlanta (cap.)⊙ 425,022 .... K1
Atlanta‡ 2,029,618 .... K1
31715 Attapulgus 623 .... D9
30203 Auburn 692 .... E2
*30901 Augusta⊙ 47,532 .... J4
Augusta‡ 327,372 .... J4
30001 Austell 3,939 .... J1
†30557 Avalon 200 .... F1
30803 Avera 248 .... G4
30002 Avondale Estates 1,313 .... L1
31716 Baconton 763 .... D8
31717 Bainbridge⊙ 10,553 .... C9
30511 Baldwin 1,080 .... E2
30107 Ball Ground 640 .... D2
30204 Barnesville⊙ 4,887 .... D4
31625 Barney 146 .... E8
30413 Bartow 357 .... G5
31720 Barwick 413 .... E9
31513 Baxley⊙ 3,586 .... H7
†31554 Beach G8
30414 Bellville 173 .... H6
31721 Benevolence 138 .... C7
†30136 Berkeley Lake 503 .... D3
31722 Berlin 538 .... E8
30620 Bethlehem 281 .... E3
†31901 Bibb City 667 .... B5
30621 Bishop 172 .... F3
31516 Blackshear⊙ 3,222 .... H8
30512 Blairsville⊙ 530 .... E1
31723 Blakely⊙ 5,880 .... C8
31302 Bloomingdale 1,855 .... K6
30513 Blue Ridge⊙ 1,376 .... D1
31724 Bluffton 132 .... C7
30805 Blythe 367 .... H4
30622 Bogart 819 .... E3
31626 Boston 1,424 .... E9
30623 Bostwick 357 .... E3
30108 Bowdon 1,743 .... B3
30516 Bowersville 318 .... G2
30624 Bowman 890 .... G2
30517 Braselton 308 .... E2
†30153 Braswell 282 .... C3
30110 Bremen 3,966 .... B3
31725 Brinson 274 .... C9
31726 Bronwood 524 .... D7
30415 Brooklet 1,035 .... J6
30205 Brooks 199 .... D4
31519 Broxton 1,117 .... G7
31520 Brunswick⊙ 17,605 .... K8
30113 Buchanan⊙ 1,019 .... B3
30625 Buckhead 219 .... F3
31803 Buena Vista⊙ 1,544 .... C6
30518 Buford 6,578 .... D2
31006 Butler⊙ 1,959 .... D5
31007 Byromville 567 .... E6
31008 Byron 1,661 .... E5
31009 Cadwell 353 .... G6
31728 Cairo⊙ 8,777 .... D9
30701 Calhoun⊙ 5,335 .... C1
30807 Camak 283 .... G4
31730 Camilla⊙ 5,414 .... D8
30520 Canon 704 .... F2
30114 Canton⊙ 3,601 .... C2
30203 Carl 239 .... E3
30627 Carlton 291 .... F2
30521 Carnesville⊙ 465 .... F2
30117 Carrollton⊙ 14,078 .... C3
30120 Cartersville⊙ 9,247 .... C2
30124 Cave Spring 883 .... B2
31627 Cecil 280 .... F8
30125 Cedartown⊙ 8,619 .... B2
†30601 Center 330 .... F2
31028 Centerville 2,622 .... E5
†30217 Centralhatchee 240 .... B4
†31816 Chalybeate Springs 265 .... C5
30341 Chamblee 7,137 .... K1
30705 Chatsworth⊙ 2,493 .... C1
31011 Chauncey 350 .... F6
31012 Chester 409 .... F6
30707 Chickamauga 2,232 .... B1
30523 Clarkesville⊙ 1,348 .... F1
30021 Clarkston 4,539 .... L1
30417 Claxton⊙ 2,694 .... J6
30525 Clayton⊙ 1,838 .... F1
30527 Clermont 300 .... E2
30528 Cleveland⊙ 1,578 .... E1
31734 Climax 407 .... D9
31735 Cobb E7
30420 Cobbtown 494 .... H6
31014 Cochran⊙ 5,121 .... F6
30710 Cohutta 407 .... C1
30628 Colbert 498 .... F2
31736 Coleman 164 .... C7
30337 College Park 24,632 .... K2
30421 Collins 639 .... H6
31737 Colquitt⊙ 2,065 .... C8
*31901 Columbus⊙ 169,441 .... C6
Columbus‡ 239,196 .... C6
30629 Comer 930 .... F2
30529 Commerce 4,092 .... E2
30206 Concord 317 .... D4
*30207 Conyers⊙ 6,567 .... D3
31738 Coolidge 736 .... E8
31015 Cordele⊙ 11,184 .... E7
30531 Cornelia 3,203 .... E1
31739 Cotton 122 .... D8
30209 Covington⊙ 10,586 .... E3
30711 Crandall C1
30630 Crawford 498 .... F3
30631 Crawfordville⊙ 594 .... G3
†31771 Crosland E8
31016 Culloden 281 .... D5
30130 Cumming⊙ 2,094 .... D2
31805 Cusseta⊙ 1,218 .... C6
31740 Cuthbert⊙ 4,340 .... C7
30211 Dacula 1,577 .... E3
30533 Dahlonega⊙ 2,844 .... D1
30423 Daisy 174 .... J6
30132 Dallas⊙ 2,440 .... C3
30720 Dalton⊙ 20,743 .... C1
31741 Damascus 403 .... C8
30633 Danielsville⊙ 354 .... F2
31017 Danville 529 .... F5
31305 Darien⊙ 1,731 .... K8
31601 Dasher 659 .... F9
31018 Davisboro 433 .... G5
31742 Dawson⊙ 5,699 .... D7
30534 Dawsonville⊙ 342 .... D2
30808 Dearing 539 .... H4
*30030 Decatur⊙ 18,404 .... K1
†31501 Deenwood H8
31082 Deepstep 120 .... G4
30535 Demorest 1,130 .... F1
31532 Denton 286 .... G7
31743 De Soto 248 .... D7
31019 Dexter 527 .... G6
30537 Dillard 238 .... F1
31629 Dixie 259 .... E9
†31520 Dock Junction (Arco) J8
31744 Doerun 1,062 .... E8
31745 Donalsonville⊙ 3,320 .... C8
30340 Doraville 7,414 .... K1
31533 Douglas⊙ 10,980 .... G7
*30133 Douglasville⊙ 7,641 .... C3
31021 Dublin⊙ 16,083 .... G5
31022 Dudley 425 .... F5
30136 Duluth 2,956 .... D2
31630 Du Pont 267 .... G9
†31830 Durand 206 .... C5
31021 East Dublin 2,916 .... G5
30539 East Ellijay 469 .... C1

(continued on following page)

Agriculture, Industry and Resources

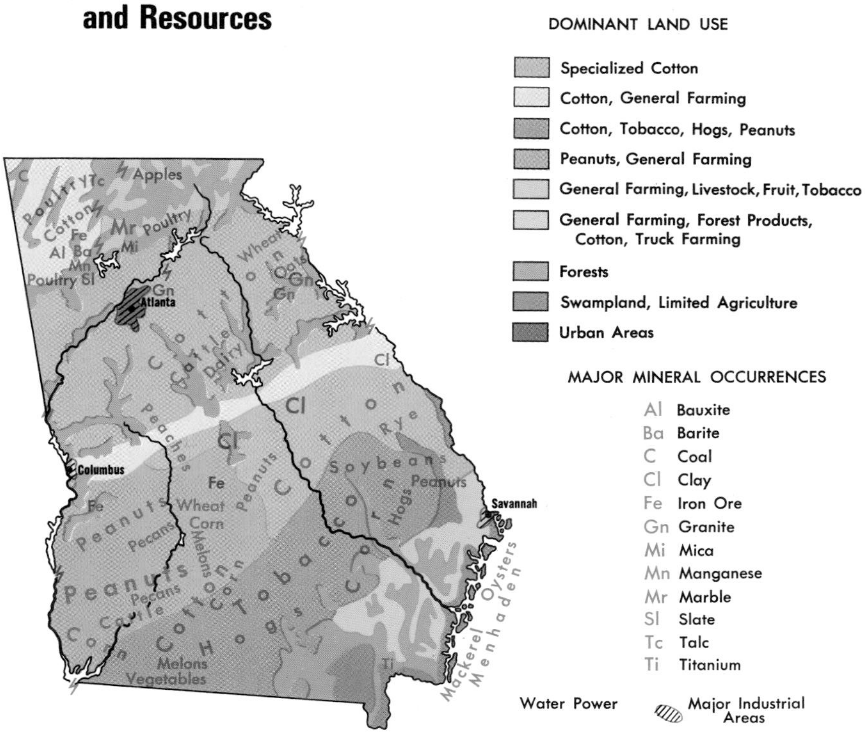

DOMINANT LAND USE
Specialized Cotton
Cotton, General Farming
Cotton, Tobacco, Hogs, Peanuts
Peanuts, General Farming
General Farming, Livestock, Fruit, Tobacco
General Farming, Forest Products, Cotton, Truck Farming
Forests
Swampland, Limited Agriculture
Urban Areas
MAJOR MINERAL OCCURRENCES
Al Bauxite
Ba Barite
C Coal
Cl Clay
Fe Iron Ore
Gn Granite
Mi Mica
Mn Manganese
Mr Marble
Sl Slate
Tc Talc
Ti Titanium
Water Power
Major Industrial Areas
Apples
Poultry
Cotton
Atlanta
Wheat
Oats
Cattle
Dairy
Peaches
Columbus
Corn
Peanuts
Pecans
Melons
Soybeans
Rye
Hogs
Tobacco
Savannah
Oysters
Menhaden
Mackerel
Vegetables

216 Georgia
(continued)

†31046 East Juliette E4
31023 Eastman⊙ 5,330 .... F6
†30263 East Newnan C4
30344 East Point 37,486 .... K2
†30677 Eastville E3
31024 Eatonton⊙ 4,833 .... F4
31307 Eden 990 .... K6
31746 Edison 1,128 .... C7
30635 Elberton⊙ 5,686 .... G2
31806 Ellaville⊙ 1,684 .... D6
31747 Ellenton 277 .... E8
31807 Ellerslie 700 .... C5
30540 Ellijay⊙ 1,507 .... C1
30137 Emerson 1,110 .... C2
31749 Enigma 574 .... F8
†30217 Ephesus 184 .... B4
30724 Eton 301 .... C1
†30120 Euharlee 477 .... C2
30809 Evans H3
30212 Experiment D4
30213 Fairburn 3,466 .... J2
30139 Fairmount 842 .... C2
30214 Fayetteville⊙ 2,715 .... C4
†31071 Finleyson 101 .... F6
31750 Fitzgerald⊙ 10,187 .... F7
†31313 Flemington 440 .... K7
30216 Flovilla 458 .... E4
30542 Flowery Branch 755 .... E2
31537 Folkston⊙ 2,243 .... H9
30050 Forest Park 18,782 .... K2
31029 Forsyth⊙ 4,624 .... E4
31751 Fort Gaines⊙ 1,260 .... C7
30742 Fort Oglethorpe 5,443 .... B1
31030 Fort Valley⊙ 9,000 .... E5
30217 Franklin⊙ 711 .... B4
30639 Franklin Springs 797 .... F2
31753 Funston 337 .... E8
30501 Gainesville⊙ 15,280 .... E2
31408 Garden City 6,895 .... K6
30425 Garfield 222 .... H5
30218 Gay 175 .... C4
31810 Geneva 232 .... C5
31754 Georgetown⊙ 935 .... B7
30810 Gibson⊙ 730 .... G4
30426 Girard 225 .... J4
30427 Glennville 4,144 .... J7
30428 Glenwood 824 .... L1
30641 Good Hope 200 .... E3
31031 Gordon 2,768 .... F5
30220 Grantville 1,110 .... C4
31032 Gray⊙ 2,145 .... F4
30221 Grayson 464 .... E3
30726 Graysville 193 .... B1
30642 Greensboro⊙ 2,985 .... F3
30222 Greenville⊙ 1,213 .... C4
30223 Griffin⊙ 20,728 .... D4
30813 Grovetown 3,491 .... H4
31312 Guyton 749 .... K6
31033 Haddock 800 .... F4
30429 Hagan 880 .... J6

31632 Hahira 1,534 .... F9
31811 Hamilton⊙ 506 .... C5
30228 Hampton 2,059 .... D4
30354 Hapeville 6,166 .... K2
30229 Haralson 123 .... C4
31034 Hardwick F4
30814 Harlem 1,485 .... H4
31035 Harrison 456 .... G5
30643 Hartwell⊙ 4,855 .... G2
31036 Hawkinsville⊙ 4,372 .... E6
31539 Hazlehurst⊙ 4,249 .... G7
30545 Helen 265 .... E1
31037 Helena 1,390 .... G6
30815 Hephzibah 1,452 .... H4
30546 Hiawassee⊙ 491 .... E1
†30410 Higgston 152 .... G6
30467 Hilltonia 515 .... J5
31313 Hinesville⊙ 11,309 .... J7
30141 Hiram 711 .... C3
31542 Hoboken 514 .... H8
30230 Hogansville 3,362 .... C4
30142 Holly Springs 687 .... D2
†31537 Homeland 683 .... H9
30547 Homer⊙ 734 .... F2
31634 Homerville⊙ 3,112 .... G8
30548 Hoschton 490 .... E2
30646 Hull 188 .... F2
31041 Ideal 619 .... D6
30647 Ila 287 .... F2
†30705 Industrial City 1,054 .... C1
31759 Iron City 367 .... C8
31042 Irwinton⊙ 841 .... F5
†31031 Ivey 455 .... F5
30233 Jackson⊙ 4,133 .... E4
31544 Jacksonville 206 .... G7
31761 Jakin 194 .... C8
30143 Jasper⊙ 1,556 .... D2
30549 Jefferson⊙ 1,820 .... F2
31044 Jeffersonville⊙ 1,473 .... F5
30234 Jenkinsburg 360 .... E4
30235 Jersey 201 .... E3
31545 Jesup⊙ 9,418 .... J7
30236 Jonesboro⊙ 4,132 .... D4
31812 Junction City 254 .... C5
30144 Kennesaw 5,095 .... C2
31548 Kingsland 2,008 .... J9
30145 Kingston 733 .... C2
31049 Kite 328 .... G5
31050 Knoxville⊙ 75 .... E5
30728 La Fayette⊙ 6,517 .... B1
30240 La Grange⊙ 24,204 .... B4
30252 Lake 2,963 .... D3
31635 Lakeland⊙ 2,647 .... F8
31636 Lake Park 448 .... F9
30553 Lavonia 2,024 .... F2
30245 Lawrenceville⊙ 8,928 .... D3
31762 Leary 783 .... C8
30146 Lebanon 800 .... D2
31763 Leesburg⊙ 1,301 .... D7
31637 Lenox 965 .... F8

31764 Leslie 470 .... D7
30648 Lexington⊙ 278 .... F3
30247 Lilburn 3,765 .... D3
31051 Lilly 202 .... E6
†30286 Lincoln Park D5
30817 Lincolnton⊙ 1,406 .... G3
30147 Lindale B2
†30728 Linwood 417 .... B1
30058 Lithonia 2,637 .... D3
30248 Locust Grove 1,479 .... D4
30249 Loganville 1,841 .... E3
30433 Lollie G6
†30230 Lone Oak 119 .... C4
†30741 Lookout Mountain 1,505 ... B1
30434 Louisville⊙ 2,823 .... H4
30250 Lovejoy 205 .... D4
31316 Ludowici⊙ 1,286 .... J7
30554 Lula 857 .... E2
31549 Lumber City 1,426 .... G7
31815 Lumpkin⊙ 1,335 .... C6
30251 Luthersville 597 .... C4
30730 Lyerly 482 .... B2
30436 Lyons⊙ 4,203 .... H6
30059 Mableton J1
*31201 Macon⊙ 116,860 .... E5
Macon‡ 254,623 .... E5
30650 Madison⊙ 2,954 .... F3
30438 Manassas 116 .... H6
31816 Manchester 4,796 .... C5
30255 Mansfield 435 .... E4
*30060 Marietta⊙ 30,805 .... J1
31057 Marshallville 1,540 .... D6
30557 Martin 305 .... F2
30671 Maxeys 205 .... F3
30558 Maysville 619 .... E2
30555 McCaysville 1,219 .... D1
30253 McDonough⊙ 2,778 .... D4
31054 McIntyre 386 .... F5
31055 McRae⊙ 3,409 .... G6
30256 Meansville 303 .... D4
30040 Mechanicsville L1
31765 Meigs 1,231 .... D8
30731 Menlo 611 .... B2
†31792 Metcalf E9
30439 Metter⊙ 3,531 .... H6
30441 Midville 670 .... H5
31320 Midway 457 .... K7
31060 Milan 1,115 .... G6
31061 Milledgeville⊙ 12,176 .... F4
30442 Millen⊙ 3,988 .... J5
30257 Milner 320 .... D4
30207 Milstead D3
30559 Mineral Bluff 130 .... D1
30820 Mitchell 214 .... G4
30258 Molena 379 .... D4
30655 Monroe⊙ 8,854 .... E3
31063 Montezuma 4,830 .... E6
31064 Monticello⊙ 2,382 .... E4
31065 Montrose 170 .... F5
30259 Moreland 358 .... C4

31766 Morgan⊙ 364 .... C7
30560 Morganton 263 .... D1
30260 Morrow 3,791 .... K2
31638 Morven 471 .... E9
31768 Moultrie⊙ 15,708 .... E8
30562 Mountain City 701 .... F1
†30075 Mountain Park 378 .... D2
30563 Mount Airy 670 .... F1
30149 Mount Berry B2
30445 Mount Vernon⊙ 1,737 .... G6
30261 Mountville 168 .... C4
30150 Mount Zion 445 .... B3
31553 Nahunta⊙ 951 .... H8
31639 Nashville⊙ 4,831 .... F8
31641 Naylor 228 .... F9
30151 Nelson 562 .... D2
30262 Newborn 391 .... E3
30446 Newington 402 .... J5
30263 Newnan⊙ 11,449 .... C4
31770 Newton⊙ 711 .... D8
31554 Nicholls 1,114 .... G7
30565 Nicholson 491 .... F2
*30071 Norcross 3,317 .... D3
31771 Norman Park 757 .... E8
†30645 North High Shoals 256 .... F3
30821 Norwood 306 .... G4
30448 Nunez 168 .... H5
31772 Oakfield 113 .... E7
30732 Oakman 150 .... C1
31903 Oak Park 256 .... H6
30566 Oakwood 723 .... E2
31773 Ochlocknee 627 .... E9
31774 Ocilla⊙ 3,436 .... F7
31067 Oconee 306 .... G5
†30222 Odessadale 142 .... C5
31555 Odum 401 .... H7
31406 Oglethorpe⊙ 1,305 .... D6
30449 Oliver 239 .... J5
31821 Omaha 169 .... C6
31775 Omega 996 .... E8
30266 Orchard Hill 162 .... D4
30267 Oxford 1,750 .... E3
30268 Palmetto 2,086 .... C3
31777 Parrott 222 .... D7
31557 Patterson 763 .... H8
31778 Pavo 830 .... E9
†31201 Payne 196 .... E5
30269 Peachtree City 6,429 .... C4
31642 Pearson⊙ 1,827 .... G8
31779 Pelham 4,306 .... D8
31321 Pembroke⊙ 1,400 .... J6
30567 Pendergrass 302 .... E2
31069 Perry⊙ 9,453 .... E6
†31794 Phillipsburg E8
31070 Pinehurst 431 .... E6
30072 Pine Lake 901 .... D3
31822 Pine Mountain 984 .... C5
†31312 Pineora 387 .... K6
†31728 Pine Park D9
31071 Pineview 564 .... F6

31072 Pitts 384 .... E7
31073 Plainfield 128 .... F6
31780 Plains 651 .... D6
30733 Plainville 281 .... C2
31322 Pooler 2,543 .... K6
30450 Portal 694 .... J5
30270 Porterdale 1,451 .... E3
31407 Port Wentworth 3,947 .... K6
31781 Poulan 818 .... E8
30073 Powder Springs 3,381 .... C3
31824 Preston⊙ 429 .... C6
30451 Pulaski 257 .... J6
31643 Quitman⊙ 5,188 .... E9
30734 Ranger 171 .... C2
31645 Ray City 658 .... F8
30660 Rayle 177 .... G3
31783 Rebecca 272 .... E7
30453 Reidsville⊙ 2,296 .... H6
31601 Remerton 443 .... F9
31075 Rentz 337 .... G6
†30518 Rest Haven 231 .... E2
31076 Reynolds 1,298 .... D5
31077 Rhine 590 .... F7
31323 Riceboro 216 .... K7
31825 Richland 1,802 .... C6
31324 Richmond Hill 1,177 .... K7
†31018 Riddleville 154 .... G5
31326 Rincon 1,988 .... K6
30736 Ringgold⊙ 1,821 .... B1
*30274 Riverdale 7,121 .... K2
†31768 Riverside 99 .... E8
†30759 Riverside B2
31078 Roberta 859 .... D5
31079 Rochelle 1,626 .... F7
30153 Rockmart 3,645 .... B2
30455 Rocky Ford 223 .... J5
30161 Rome⊙ 29,654 .... B2
30170 Roopville 229 .... B4
30741 Rossville 3,851 .... B1
*30075 Roswell 23,337 .... D2
30662 Royston 2,404 .... F2
†30680 Russell 378 .... E3
30663 Rutledge 694 .... E3
31558 Saint Marys 3,596 .... J9
31522 Saint Simons Island K8
31784 Sale City 336 .... D8
31082 Sandersville⊙ 6,137 .... G5
†20436 Santa Claus 167 .... H6
30456 Sardis 1,180 .... J5
30275 Sargent 800 .... C4
31785 Sasser 407 .... D7
*31401 Savannah⊙ 141,634 .... L6
Savannah‡ 230,728 .... L6
31083 Scotland 222 .... G6
31095 Scott 139 .... G5
31560 Screven 872 .... H7
30276 Senoia 900 .... C4
31084 Seville 209 .... E7
31085 Shady Dale 155 .... E4
30172 Shannon B2
30664 Sharon 140 .... G3
30277 Sharpsburg 194 .... C4
31786 Shellman 1,254 .... C7
31826 Shiloh 392 .... C5
30665 Siloam 446 .... F3
31787 Smithville 867 .... D7
30080 Smyrna 20,312 .... K1
30278 Snellville 8,514 .... D3
30279 Social Circle 2,591 .... E3
30457 Soperton⊙ 2,981 .... G6
31647 Sparks 1,353 .... F8
31087 Sparta⊙ 1,754 .... F4
31329 Springfield⊙ 1,075 .... K6
†30705 Spring Place 246 .... C1
30823 Stapleton 388 .... H4
31648 Statenville⊙ 700 .... G9
30458 Statesboro⊙ 14,866 .... J6
30666 Statham 1,101 .... E3
30464 Stillmore 527 .... H6
30281 Stockbridge 2,103 .... D3
*30083 Stone Mountain 4,867 .... D3
†30518 Sugar Hill 2,473 .... E2
30746 Sugar Valley C1
30466 Summertown 215 .... H5
30747 Summerville⊙ 4,878 .... B2
31789 Sumner 213 .... E7
30284 Sunny Side 338 .... D4
31563 Surrency 368 .... H7
30174 Suwanee 1,026 .... D2
30401 Swainsboro⊙ 7,602 .... H5
31790 Sycamore 474 .... E7
30467 Sylvania⊙ 3,352 .... J5
31791 Sylvester⊙ 5,860 .... E7
31827 Talbotton⊙ 1,140 .... C5
30176 Tallapoosa 2,647 .... B3
30573 Tallulah Falls 162 .... F1
30575 Talmo E2
30470 Tarrytown 145 .... H6
30178 Taylorsville 266 .... C2
30179 Temple 1,520 .... B3
31089 Tennille 1,709 .... G5
30285 The Rock 78 .... D5
30286 Thomaston⊙ 9,682 .... D5
31792 Thomasville⊙ 18,463 .... E9
30824 Thomson⊙ 7,001 .... H4
†31404 Thunderbolt 2,165 .... K6
31794 Tifton⊙ 13,749 .... F8
30576 Tiger 299 .... F1
30668 Tignall 733 .... G3
30577 Toccoa⊙ 9,104 .... F1
31090 Toomsboro 673 .... F5
30752 Trenton⊙ 1,636 .... A1
30753 Trion 1,732 .... B1
30755 Tunnel Hill 867 .... C1
30289 Turin 260 .... C4
30471 Twin City 1,402 .... H5
31328 Tybee Island 2,240 .... L6
30290 Tyrone 1,038 .... C4
31795 Ty Ty 618 .... E8
31091 Unadilla 1,566 .... E6
30291 Union City 4,780 .... J2
30669 Union Point 1,750 .... F3
†31794 Unionville F8
30473 Uvalda 646 .... H6
31601 Valdosta⊙ 37,596 .... F9
30672 Vanna F2
†30153 Van Wert 303 .... B3

30756 Varnell 288 .... C1
†31401 Vernonburg 178 .... K7
30474 Vidalia 10,393 .... H6
†30830 Vidette H4
31092 Vienna⊙ 2,886 .... E6
30180 Villa Rica 3,420 .... C3
30182 Waco 471 .... B3
30477 Wadley 2,438 .... H5
30183 Waleska 450 .... D2
†30209 Walnut Grove 387 .... E3
31333 Walthourville 905 .... J7
31830 Warm Springs 425 .... C5
31093 Warner Robins 39,893 .... E5
30828 Warrenton⊙ 2,172 .... G4
31796 Warwick 488 .... E7
30673 Washington⊙ 4,662 .... G3
30677 Watkinsville⊙ 1,240 .... E3
31831 Waverly Hall 913 .... C5
31501 Waycross⊙ 19,371 .... H8
30830 Waynesboro⊙ 5,760 .... J4
31832 Weston 109 .... C7
31833 West Point 4,294 .... B5
31797 Whigham 507 .... D9
30184 White 501 .... C2
31568 White Oak 450 .... J8
30678 White Plains 231 .... F4
30185 Whitesburg 775 .... B4
31650 Willacoochee 1,166 .... G8
30292 Williamson 250 .... D4
31410 Wilmington Island L7
30680 Winder⊙ 6,705 .... E3
31406 Windsor Forest K7
30683 Winterville 621 .... F3
31569 Woodbine⊙ 910 .... J9
30293 Woodbury 1,738 .... C5
31836 Woodland 664 .... D5
30188 Woodstock 2,699 .... D2
30670 Woodville 455 .... F3
30833 Wrens 2,415 .... H4
31096 Wrightsville⊙ 2,526 .... G5
31097 Yatesville 390 .... D5
30582 Young Harris 687 .... E1
30295 Zebulon⊙ 995 .... D4

OTHER FEATURES

Alapaha (riv.) F7
Allatoona (lake) C2
Altamaha (riv.) H7
Andersonville Nat'l Hist. Site D6
Atlanta Nav. Air Sta. J1
Banks (lake) F9
Bartletts Ferry (dam) B5
Blackshear (lake) E7
Blue Ridge (mts.) D1
Brasstown Bald (mt.) E1
Burton (lake) E1
Carters (lake) C1
Chattahoochee (riv.) B8
Chattahoochee River Nat'l Rec. Area K1
Chattooga (riv.) A2
Chattooga (riv.) F1
Chatuge (lake) E1
Chickamauga and Chattanooga Nat'l Mil. Park B1
Clark Hill (lake) H3
Coosa (riv.) A2
Coosawattee (riv.) C1
Cumberland (isl.) K9
Cumberland Island Nat'l Seashore K9
Dobbins A.F.B. J1
Doboy (sound) K8
Etowah (riv.) C2
Eufaula (Walter F. George Res.) (lake) B7
Flint (riv.) D8
Fort Benning B6
Fort Frederica Nat'l Mon. K8
Fort Gordon H4
Fort McPherson K1
Fort Pulaski Nat'l Mon. L6
Fort Stewart J7
Goat Rock (lake) B5
Harding (lake) B5
Hartwell (lake) G2
Jekyll (isl.) K8
Kennesaw Mtn. Nat'l Battlefield Park J1
Lawson A.A.F. B6
Martin Luther King, Jr., Nat'l Hist. Site K1
Moody A.F.B. F9
Nottely (lake) D1
Ochlockonee (riv.) C10
Ocmulgee (riv.) E5
Ocmulgee Nat'l Mon. F5
Oconee (riv.) F5
Ogeechee (riv.) J5
Okefenokee (swamp) H9
Oliver (lake) B5
Oostanaula (riv.) B2
Ossabaw (sound) K7
Rabun (lake) E1
Robins A.F.B. F5
Saint Andrew (sound) K9
Saint Catherines (isl.) K7
Saint Marys (riv.) J9
Saint Simons K8
Sapelo (isl.) K8
Satilla (riv.) G8
Savannah (riv.) K5
Sea (isls.) K9
Seminole (lake) B9
Sidney Lanier (lake) D2
Sinclair (lake) F4
Skidaway (isl.) L7
Springer (mt.) D1
Suwannee (riv.) G10
Tugaloo (riv.) F1
Walter F. George (res.) B7
Wassaw (sound) L7
Weiss (lake) A2
West Point (lake) B4

⊙County seat.
‡Population of metropolitan area.
† Zip of nearest p.o. * Multiple zips.

Topography

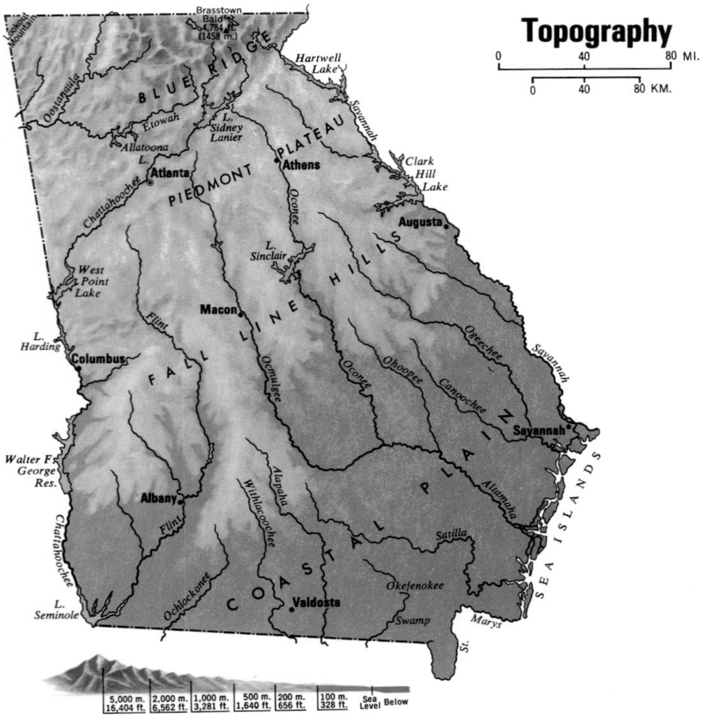

0 40 80 MI.
0 40 80 KM.
Brasstown Bald 4,784 ft. (1458 m.)
BLUE RIDGE
PIEDMONT
PLATEAU
FALL LINE HILLS
COASTAL PLAIN
SEA ISLANDS
Hartwell Lake
Clark Hill Lake
L. Sidney Lanier
Allatoona L.
Atlanta
Athens
Augusta
Macon
Columbus
Albany
Valdosta
Savannah
West Point Lake
L. Harding
L. Sinclair
Walter F. George Res.
L. Seminole
Okefenokee Swamp
Oostanaula
Etowah
Chattahoochee
Flint
Ocmulgee
Oconee
Ogeechee
Ohoopee
Canoochee
Savannah
Altamaha
Satilla
Alapaha
Withlacoochee
Ochlockonee
St. Marys
5,000 m. 16,404 ft.
2,000 m. 6,562 ft.
1,000 m. 3,281 ft.
500 m. 1,640 ft.
200 m. 656 ft.
100 m. 328 ft.
Sea Level
Below

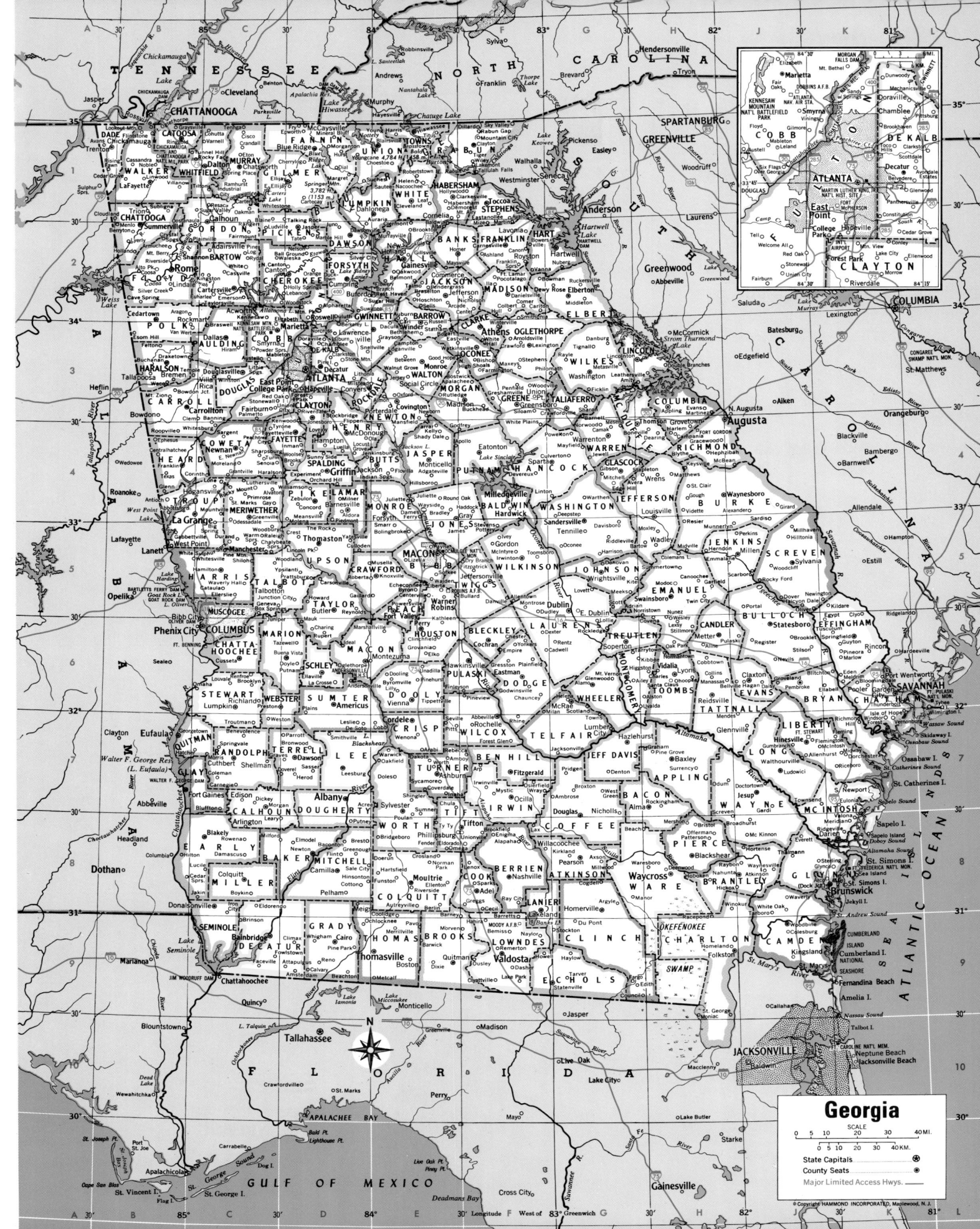

Georgia

SCALE

0 5 10   20   30   40 MI.

0 5 10   20   30   40 KM.

State Capitals .... ✪

County Seats .... ◉

Major Limited Access Hwys. _____

© Copyright HAMMOND INCORPORATED, Maplewood, N.J.

Topography

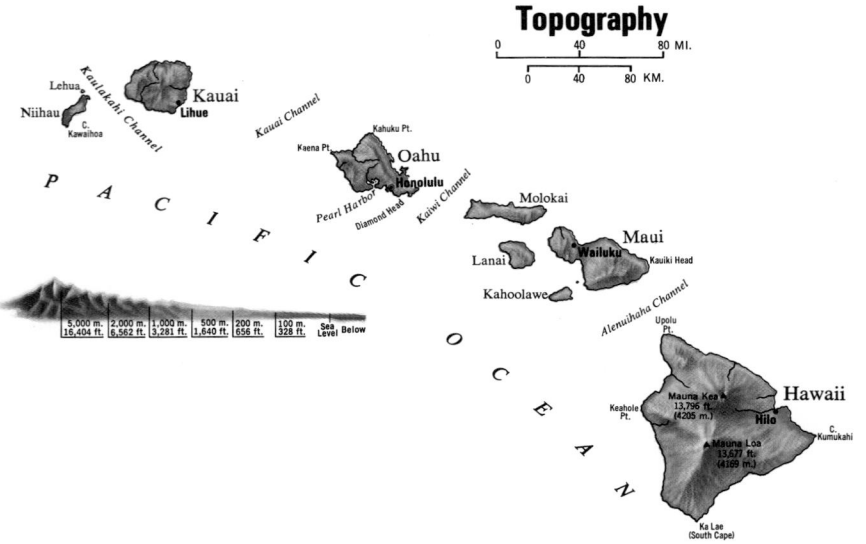

Agriculture, Industry and Resources

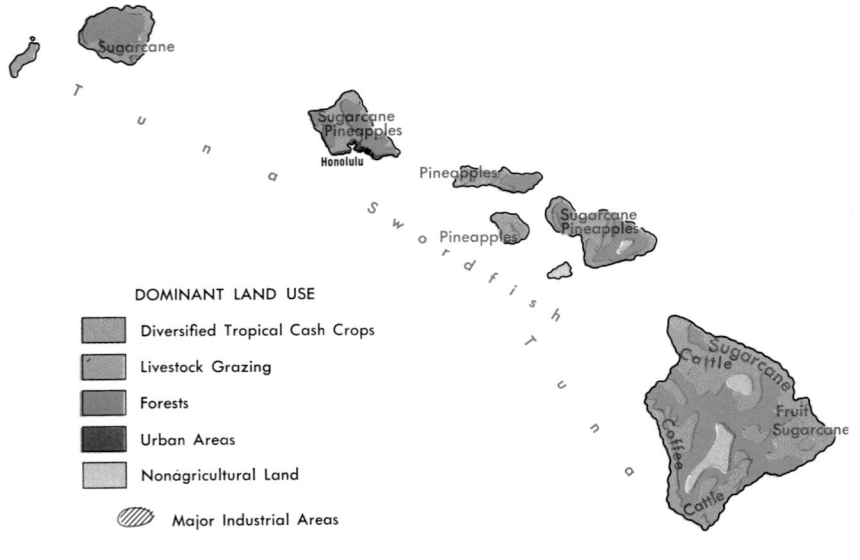

DOMINANT LAND USE

- Diversified Tropical Cash Crops
- Livestock Grazing
- Forests
- Urban Areas
- Nonagricultural Land
- Major Industrial Areas

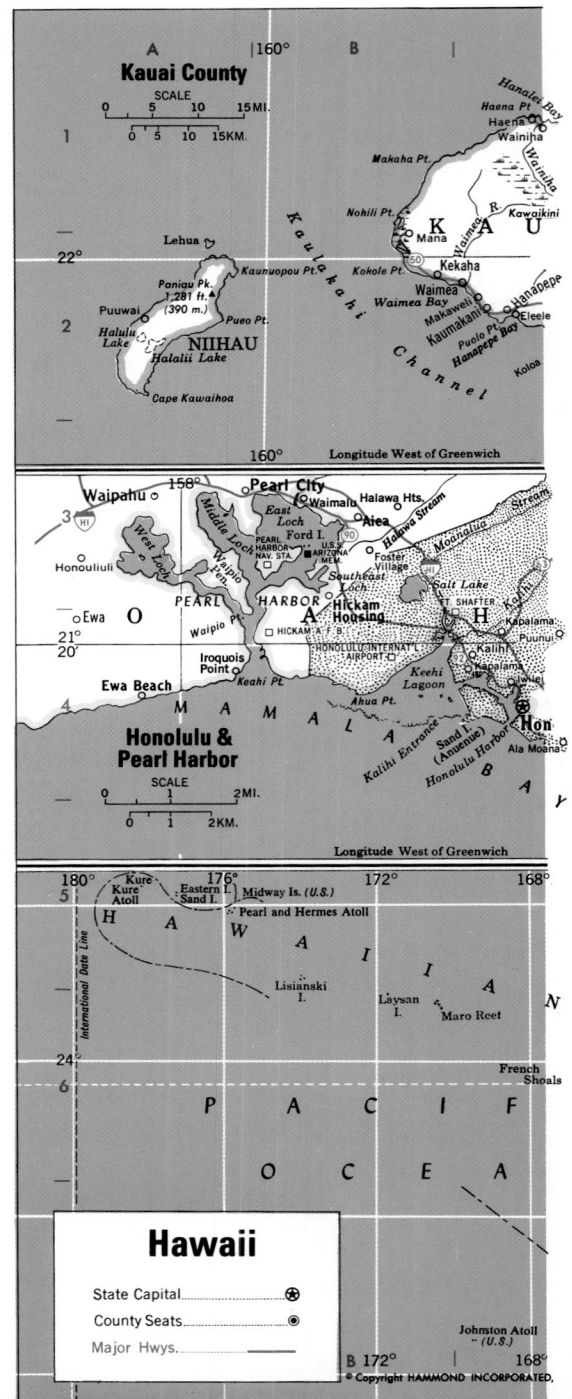

Kauai County

SCALE 0 5 10 15 MI.
0 5 10 15 KM.

Longitude West of Greenwich

Honolulu & Pearl Harbor

SCALE 0 1 2 MI.
0 1 2 KM.

Longitude West of Greenwich

Hawaii

State Capital	⊛
County Seats	⊙
Major Hwys.	▬

Johnston Atoll (U.S.)

© Copyright HAMMOND INCORPORATED,

⊙County seat.
‡Population of metropolitan area.
† Zip of nearest p.o. * Multiple zips.

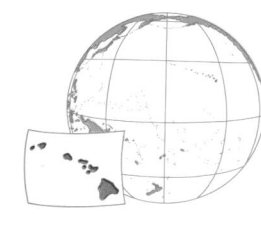

AREA 6,471 sq. mi. (16,760 sq. km.)
POPULATION 964,691
CAPITAL Honolulu
LARGEST CITY Honolulu
HIGHEST POINT Mauna Kea 13,796 ft. (4205 m.)
SETTLED IN —
ADMITTED TO UNION August 21, 1959
POPULAR NAME Aloha State
STATE FLOWER Hibiscus
STATE BIRD Nene (Hawaiian Goose)

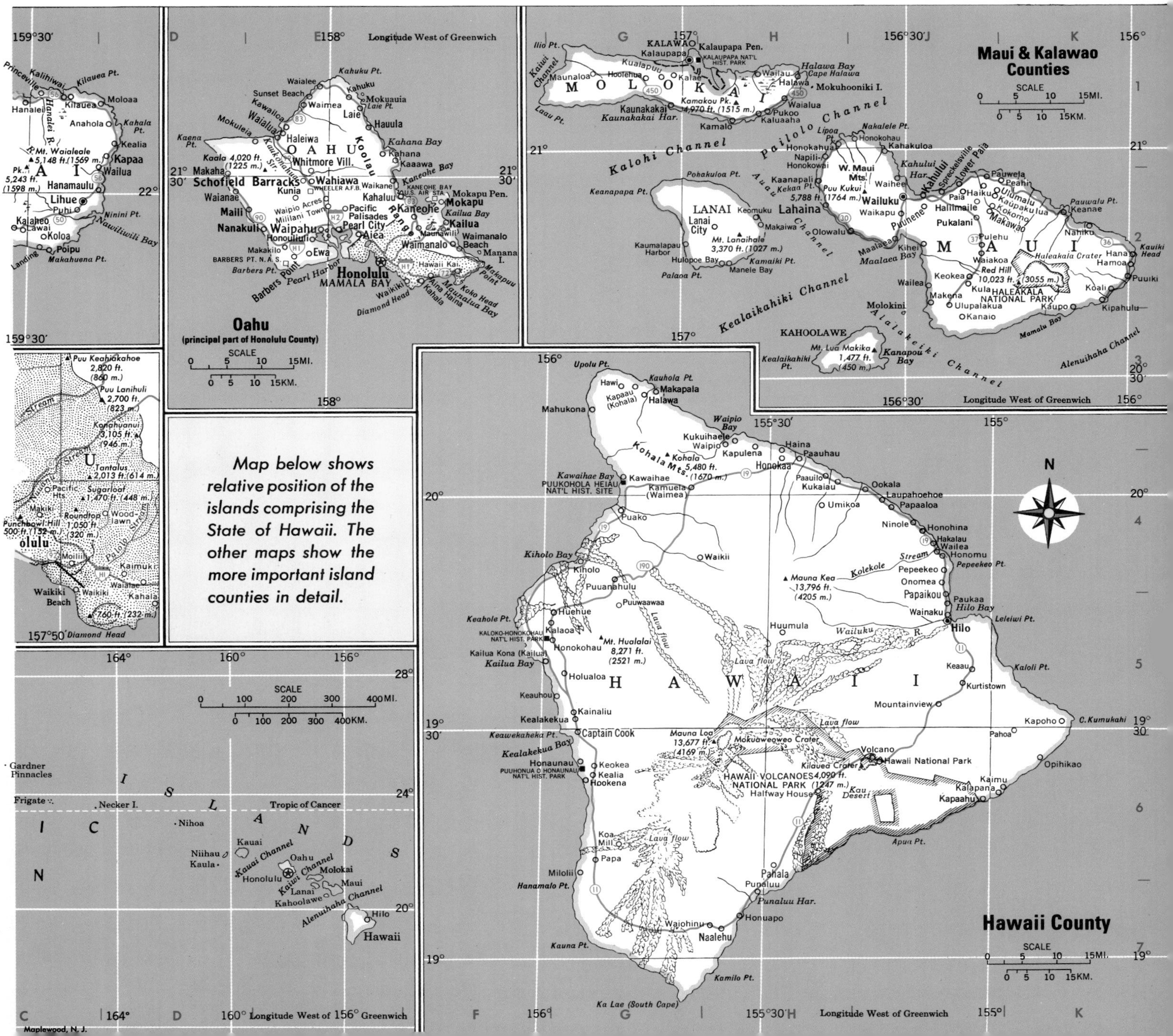

Maui & Kalawao Counties
Oahu
(principal part of Honolulu County)
Hawaii County
Map below shows relative position of the islands comprising the State of Hawaii. The other maps show the more important island counties in detail.
Longitude West of Greenwich
MOLOKAI
LANAI
KAHOOLAWE
MAUI
OAHU
KAUAI
HAWAII
Honolulu
Hilo
Tropic of Cancer
Maplewood, N. J.

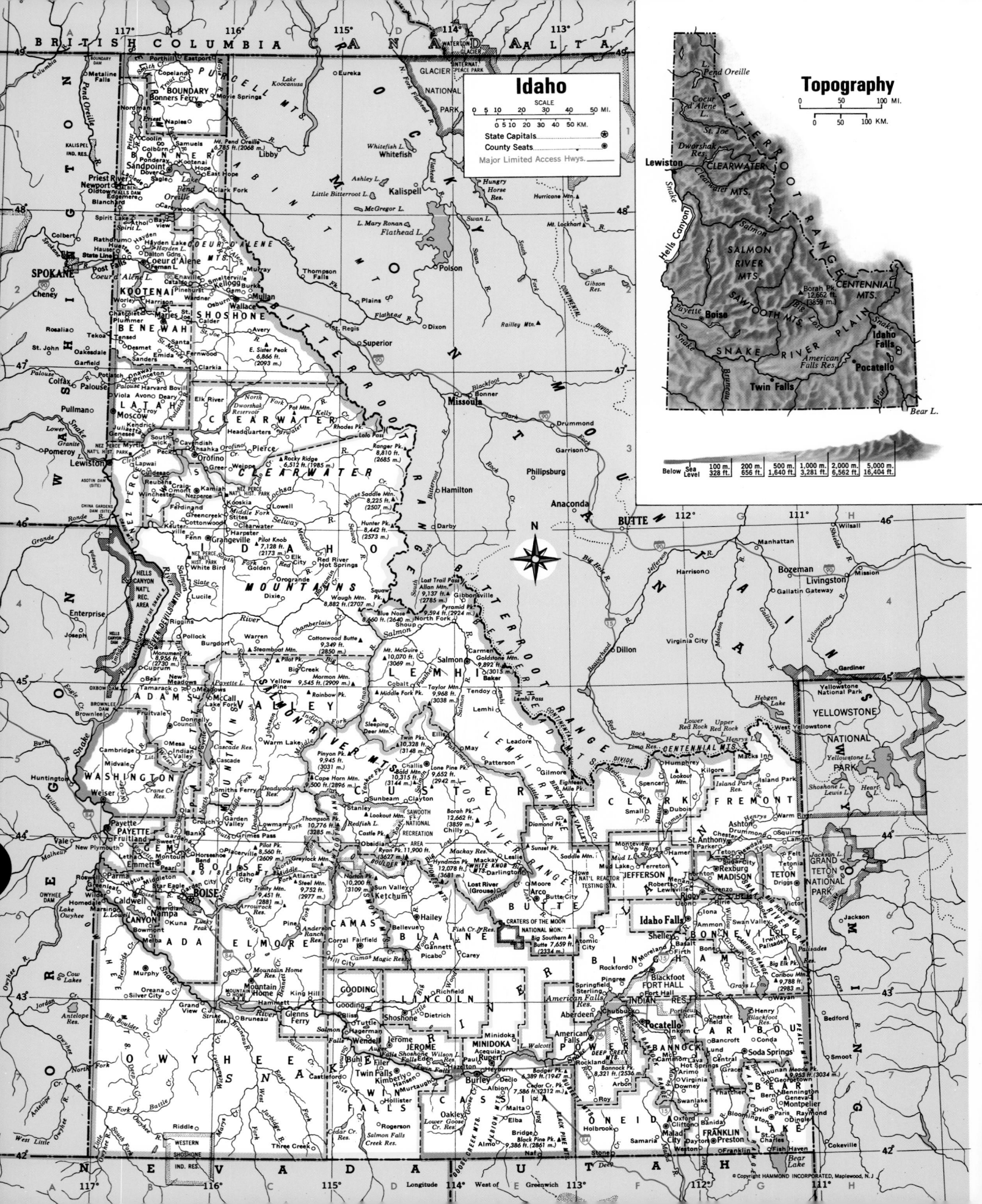

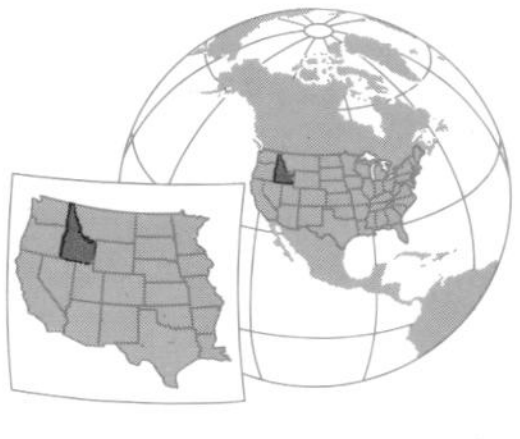

AREA 83,564 sq. mi. (216,431 sq. km.)
POPULATION 944,038
CAPITAL Boise
LARGEST CITY Boise
HIGHEST POINT Borah Pk. 12,662 ft. (3859 m.)
SETTLED IN 1842
ADMITTED TO UNION July 3, 1890
POPULAR NAME Gem State
STATE FLOWER Syringa
STATE BIRD Mountain Bluebird

COUNTIES

Ada 173,036 ..... B6
Adams 3,347 ..... B5
Bannock 65,421 ..... F7
Bear Lake 6,931 ..... G7
Benewah 8,292 ..... B2
Bingham 36,489 ..... F6
Blaine 9,841 ..... D6
Boise 2,999 ..... C6
Bonner 24,163 ..... B1
Bonneville 65,980 ..... G6
Boundary 7,289 ..... B1
Butte 3,342 ..... E6
Camas 818 ..... D6
Canyon 83,756 ..... B6
Caribou 8,695 ..... G7
Cassia 19,427 ..... E7
Clark 798 ..... F5
Clearwater 10,390 ..... C3
Custer 3,385 ..... D5
Elmore 21,565 ..... C6
Franklin 8,895 ..... G7
Fremont 10,813 ..... G5
Gem 11,972 ..... B6
Gooding 11,874 ..... D6
Idaho 14,769 ..... C4
Jefferson 15,304 ..... F6
Jerome 14,840 ..... D7
Kootenai 59,770 ..... B2
Latah 28,749 ..... B3
Lemhi 7,460 ..... D4
Lewis 4,118 ..... B3
Lincoln 3,436 ..... D6
Madison 19,480 ..... G6
Minidoka 19,718 ..... E7
Nez Perce 33,220 ..... B3
Oneida 3,258 ..... F7
Owyhee 8,272 ..... B7
Payette 15,825 ..... B5
Power 6,844 ..... F7
Shoshone 19,226 ..... B2
Teton 2,897 ..... G6
Twin Falls 52,927 ..... D7
Valley 5,604 ..... C5
Washington 8,803 ..... B5

CITIES and TOWNS

Zip Name/Pop. Key

83210 Aberdeen 1,528 ..... F7
83350 Acequia 100 ..... E7
83311 Albion 286 ..... E7
83211 American Falls⊙ 3,626 ..... E7
†83401 Ammon 4,669 ..... G6
83213 Arco⊙ 1,241 ..... E6
83214 Arimo 338 ..... F7
83420 Ashton 1,219 ..... G5
83801 Athol 312 ..... B2
83217 Bancroft 505 ..... G7
83218 Basalt 414 ..... F6
83313 Bellevue 1,016 ..... D6
83221 Blackfoot⊙ 10,065 ..... F6
83314 Bliss 208 ..... D7
83223 Bloomington 212 ..... G7
*83701 Boise (cap.)⊙ 102,160 ..... B6
Boise‡ 173,036 ..... B6
83805 Bonners Ferry⊙ 1,906 ..... B1
83806 Bovill 289 ..... B3
83316 Buhl 3,629 ..... D7
83318 Burley⊙ 8,761 ..... E7
83213 Butte City 93 ..... E6
83605 Caldwell⊙ 17,699 ..... B6
83610 Cambridge 428 ..... B5
83611 Cascade⊙ 945 ..... C5
83321 Castleford 191 ..... C7
83226 Challis⊙ 758 ..... D5
†83851 Chatcolet 181 ..... B2
83202 Chubbuck 7,052 ..... F7
83811 Clark Fork 449 ..... B1
83227 Clayton 43 ..... D5
83228 Clifton 208 ..... F7
83814 Coeur d'Alene⊙ 20,054 ..... B2
83522 Cottonwood 941 ..... B3
83612 Council⊙ 917 ..... B5
83523 Craigmont 617 ..... B3
†83622 Crouch 69 ..... B5
83524 Culdesac 261 ..... B3
†83814 Dalton Gardens 1,795 ..... B2
83232 Dayton 368 ..... F7
83823 Deary 539 ..... B3
83323 Declo 276 ..... E7
83324 Dietrich 101 ..... D7
83615 Donnelly 139 ..... B5
83234 Downey 645 ..... F7
83422 Driggs⊙ 727 ..... G6
83423 Dubois⊙ 413 ..... F5
83616 Eagle 2,620 ..... B6
†83836 East Hope 258 ..... B1
83325 Eden 355 ..... D7
83827 Elk River 265 ..... B3
83617 Emmett⊙ 4,605 ..... B6
83327 Fairfield⊙ 404 ..... D6
83526 Ferdinand 144 ..... B3
†83814 Fernan Lake 178 ..... B2
83328 Filer 1,645 ..... D7
83236 Firth 460 ..... F6
83203 Fort Hall 750 ..... F6
83237 Franklin 423 ..... G7
83619 Fruitland 2,456 ..... B6
†83704 Garden City 4,571 ..... B6
83832 Genesee 791 ..... B3
83239 Georgetown 544 ..... G7
83623 Glenns Ferry 1,374 ..... C7
83330 Gooding⊙ 2,949 ..... D7
83241 Grace 1,216 ..... G7
83624 Grand View 366 ..... B7
83530 Grangeville⊙ 3,666 ..... B4
83626 Greenleaf 663 ..... B6
83332 Hagerman 602 ..... D7
83333 Hailey⊙ 2,109 ..... D6
83425 Hamer 93 ..... F6
83334 Hansen 1,078 ..... D7
83833 Harrison 260 ..... B2
†83854 Hauser 305 ..... A2
†83835 Hayden 2,586 ..... B2
83835 Hayden Lake 273 ..... B2
83335 Hazelton 496 ..... E7
83336 Heyburn 2,889 ..... E7
†83301 Hollister 167 ..... D7
83628 Homedale 2,078 ..... A6
83836 Hope 106 ..... B1
83629 Horseshoe Bend 700 ..... B6
†83854 Huetter 65 ..... B2
83631 Idaho City⊙ 300 ..... C6
*83401 Idaho Falls⊙ 39,590 ..... F6
83245 Inkom 830 ..... F7
83427 Iona 1,072 ..... G6
83428 Irwin 113 ..... G6
83429 Island Park 154 ..... G5
83338 Jerome⊙ 6,891 ..... D7
83535 Juliaetta 522 ..... B3
83536 Kamiah 1,478 ..... B3
83837 Kellogg 3,417 ..... B2
83537 Kendrick 395 ..... B3
83340 Ketchum 2,200 ..... D6
83341 Kimberly 2,307 ..... D7
83539 Kooskia 784 ..... C3
83840 Kootenai 280 ..... B1
83634 Kuna 1,767 ..... B6
83540 Lapwai 1,043 ..... B3
83246 Lava Hot Springs 467 ..... F7
83464 Leadore 114 ..... E5
83501 Lewiston⊙ 27,986 ..... A3
83431 Lewisville 502 ..... F6
83251 Mackay 541 ..... E6
83252 Malad City⊙ 1,915 ..... F7
83342 Malta 196 ..... E7
83639 Marsing 786 ..... B6
83638 McCall 2,188 ..... C5
83250 McCammon 770 ..... F7
83641 Melba 276 ..... B6
83434 Menan 605 ..... F6
83642 Meridian 6,658 ..... B6
83644 Middleton 1,901 ..... B6
83645 Midvale 205 ..... B5
83343 Minidoka 101 ..... E7
83254 Montpelier 3,107 ..... G7
83255 Moore 210 ..... E6
83843 Moscow⊙ 16,513 ..... B3
83647 Mountain Home⊙ 7,540 ..... C6
83845 Moyie Springs 386 ..... B1
†83450 Mud Lake 243 ..... F6
83846 Mullan 1,269 ..... C2
83650 Murphy⊙ 200 ..... B6
83344 Murtaugh 114 ..... D7
83651 Nampa 25,112 ..... B6
83436 Newdale 329 ..... G6
83654 New Meadows 576 ..... B4
83655 New Plymouth 1,186 ..... B6
83543 Nezperce⊙ 517 ..... B3
83656 Notus 437 ..... B6
83346 Oakley 663 ..... D7
†99156 Oldtown 257 ..... A1
†83855 Onaway 254 ..... B3
83544 Orofino⊙ 3,711 ..... B3
83849 Osburn 2,220 ..... B2
†83263 Oxford 66 ..... F7
83261 Paris⊙ 707 ..... G7
83438 Parker 262 ..... G6
83660 Parma 1,820 ..... B6
83347 Paul 940 ..... E7
83661 Payette⊙ 5,448 ..... B5
83545 Peck 209 ..... B3
83546 Pierce 1,060 ..... C3
83850 Pinehurst 2,183 ..... B2
83851 Plummer 634 ..... B2
*83201 Pocatello⊙ 46,340 ..... F7
83852 Ponderay 399 ..... B1
83854 Post Falls 5,736 ..... A2
83855 Potlatch 819 ..... A3
83263 Preston⊙ 3,759 ..... G7
83856 Priest River 1,639 ..... A1
83858 Rathdrum 1,369 ..... A2
83548 Reubens 87 ..... B3
83440 Rexburg⊙ 11,559 ..... G6
83349 Richfield 357 ..... D6
83442 Rigby⊙ 2,624 ..... F6
83549 Riggins 527 ..... B4
83443 Ririe 555 ..... G6
83444 Roberts 466 ..... F6
83271 Rockland 283 ..... F7
83350 Rupert⊙ 5,476 ..... E7
83445 Saint Anthony⊙ 3,212 ..... G6
83272 Saint Charles 211 ..... G7
83861 Saint Maries⊙ 2,794 ..... B2
83467 Salmon⊙ 3,308 ..... D4
83864 Sandpoint⊙ 4,460 ..... B1
83274 Shelley 3,300 ..... F6
83352 Shoshone⊙ 1,242 ..... D7
†83650 Silver City 1 ..... B6
83868 Smelterville 776 ..... B2
83276 Soda Springs⊙ 4,051 ..... G7
83869 Spirit Lake 834 ..... A2
83278 Stanley 99 ..... D5
83552 Stites 253 ..... C3
83448 Sugar City 1,022 ..... G6
83353 Sun Valley 545 ..... D6
83449 Swan Valley 135 ..... G6
83870 Tensed 113 ..... B2
83451 Teton 559 ..... G6
83452 Tetonia 191 ..... G6
83871 Troy 820 ..... B3
83301 Twin Falls⊙ 26,209 ..... D7
83454 Ucon 833 ..... F6
83455 Victor 323 ..... G6
83873 Wallace⊙ 1,736 ..... C2
†83837 Wardner 423 ..... B2
83553 Weippe 828 ..... C3
83672 Weiser⊙ 4,771 ..... B5
83355 Wendell 1,974 ..... D7
83286 Weston 310 ..... F7
83554 White Bird 154 ..... B4
83676 Wilder 1,260 ..... A6
83555 Winchester 343 ..... B3
83876 Worley 206 ..... B2

OTHER FEATURES

Albeni Falls (dam) B1
Albion (mts.) E7
Allan (mt.) D4
American Falls (res.) F6
Anderson Ranch (res.) C6
Antelope (creek) E6
Arrowrock (res.) C6
Auger (falls) D7
Badger (peak) E7
Bald (mt.) D5
Bannock (creek) F7
Bannock (peak) F7
Bannock (range) F7
Bargamin (creek) C4
Battle (creek) B7
Bear (lake) G7
Bear (riv.) G7
Beaver (creek) F5
Beaverhead (mts.) E4
Big (creek) C4
Big Boulder (creek) B7
Big Elk (peak) G6
Big Hole (mts.) G6
Big Lost (riv.) E6
Big Southern (butte) E6
Big Wood (riv.) D6
Birch (creek) F5
Birch Creek (valley) E5
Bitterroot (range) D3
Blackfoot (res.) G7
Black Pine (mts.) E7
Blue Nose (mt.) D4
Boise (mts.) B6
Boise (riv.) B6
Borah (peak) E5
Boulder (mts.) D6
Brownlee (dam) B5
Bruneau (riv.) C7
Camas (creek) D5
Camas (creek) D6
Camas (creek) F5
Canyon (creek) C6
Cape Horn (mt.) C5
Caribou (mt.) G6
Caribou (range) G6
Cascade (res.) C5
Castle (creek) B7
Castle (peak) D5
Cedar Creek (peak) E7
Cedar Creek (res.) D7
Centennial (mts.) F5
Clearwater (mts.) C3
Clearwater (riv.) B3
Coeur d'Alene (lake) B2
Coeur d'Alene (mts.) C2
Coeur d'Alene (riv.) B2
Cottonwood (butte) C4
Craig (mts.) B4
Crane Creek (res.) B5
Craters of the Moon Nat'l Mon. E6
Deadwood (res.) C5
Deep (creek) B7
Deep (creek) F7
Deep Creek (mts.) F7
Diamond (peak) E5
Dworshak (res.) C3
East Sister (peak) C2
Eighteen Mile (peak) E5
Fish Creek (res.) E6
Fort Hall Ind. Res. F6
Goldstone (mt.) E4
Goose (creek) E7
Goose Creek (mts.) E7
Grand Canyon of the Snake River (canyon) B4
Grays (lake) G6
Grays Lake Outlet (creek) G6
Greylock (mt.) C6
Hayden (lake) B2
Hells (canyon) B4
Hells Canyon Nat'l Rec. Area B4
Henrys (lake) G5
Henrys Fork, Snake (riv.) G5
Hunter (peak) D3
Hyndman (peak) D6
Indian (creek) C5
Island Park (res.) G5
Jarbidge (riv.) C7
Johnson (creek) C5
Jordan (creek) A7
Kootenai (riv.) C1
Lemhi (pass) E5
Lemhi (range) E5
Lemhi (riv.) E5
Little Lost (riv.) E5
Little Owyhee (riv.) B7
Little Salmon (riv.) B4
Little Weiser (riv.) B5
Little Wood (riv.) D6
Lochsa (riv.) C3
Lolo (creek) C3
Lolo (pass) D3
Lone Pine (peak) D5
Lookout (mt.) D5
Lookout (mt.) F5
Lost River (range) E5
Lost Trail (pass) E4
Lowell (lake) B6
Lower Goose Creek (res.) D7
Lower Granite (lake) A3
Lucky Peak (lake) B6
Mackay (res.) E6
Magic (res.) D6
Malad (riv.) F7
Marsh (creek) F7
McGuire (mt.) D4
Meade (peak) G7
Meadow (creek) C4
Medicine Lodge (creek) F5
Middle Fork (peak) D5
Monument (peak) B4
Moose (creek) D3
Mores (creek) C6
Mormon (mt.) D4
Mountain Home (res.) C6
Mountain Home A.F.B. 6,403 ..... C6
Moyie (riv.) B1
Mud (lake) F6
National Reactor Testing Sta. F6
Nez Perce Nat'l Hist. Park B-C3
North Fork (riv.) B7
Norton (peak) D6
Orofino (creek) C3
Owyhee (mts.) B6
Owyhee, East Fork (riv.) B7
Oxbow (dam) B5
Pack (riv.) B1
Pahsimeroi (riv.) E5
Palisades (res.) G6
Palouse (riv.) B3
Panther (creek) D4
Payette (lake) C4
Payette (mts.) B5
Payette (riv.) B6
Peale (mts.) G7
Pend Oreille (lake) B1
Pend Oreille (mt.) B1
Pend Oreille (riv.) A1
Pilot (peak) C4
Pilot (peak) C6
Pilot Knob (mt.) C4
Pinyon (peak) C5
Pioneer (mts.) D6
Portneuf (res.) F7
Pot (mt.) C3
Potlatch (riv.) B3
Priest (lake) B1
Priest (riv.) B1
Purcell (mts.) B1
Pyramid (peak) E4
Raft (riv.) E7
Rainbow (mt.) C4
Ranger (peak) D3
Rays (lake) F6
Red (riv.) C4
Redfish (lake) D5
Reynolds (creek) B6
Rhodes (peak) D3
Rocky (mts.) D1
Rocky Ridge (mt.) C3
Ryan (peak) D6
Saddle (mt.) D3
Saddle (mt.) F6
Sailor (creek) C7
Saint Joe (riv.) B2
Saint Maries (riv.) B2
Salmon (falls) C7
Salmon (riv.) B4
Salmon Falls (creek) D7
Salmon Falls Creek (res.) D7
Salmon River (mts.) C5
Sawtooth (range) C6
Sawtooth Nat'l Rec. Area D5
Secesh (riv.) C4
Selkirk (mts.) B1
Selway (riv.) C3
Seven Devils (mts.) B4
Shoshone (falls) D7
Sleeping Deer (mt.) D5
Smith (creek) B1
Smoky (mts.) D6
Snake (riv.) A3
Snake River (plain) D7
Snake River (range) G6
Spirit (lake) B2
Squaw (creek) B5
Squaw (peak) D4
Steamboat (mt.) C4
Steel (mt.) C6
Strike, C.J. (res.) C7
Sublett (mts.) E7
Sunset (peak) E6
Taylor (mt.) D5
Teton (riv.) G6
Thompson (peak) C5
Trinity (mt.) C6
Trout (creek) B1
Twin (falls) D7
Twin Peaks (mt.) D5
Walcott (lake) E7
Wasatch (range) G7
Waugh (mt.) D4
Weiser (riv.) B5
Western Shoshone Ind. Res. B7
White Knob (mts.) E6
Wickahoney (creek) C7
Willow (creek) G6
Wilson Lake (res.) D7
Yankee Fork, Salmon (riv.) D5
Yellowstone Nat'l Park G5

⊙County seat.
‡Population of metropolitan area.
† Zip of nearest p.o.
* Multiple zips.

Agriculture, Industry and Resources

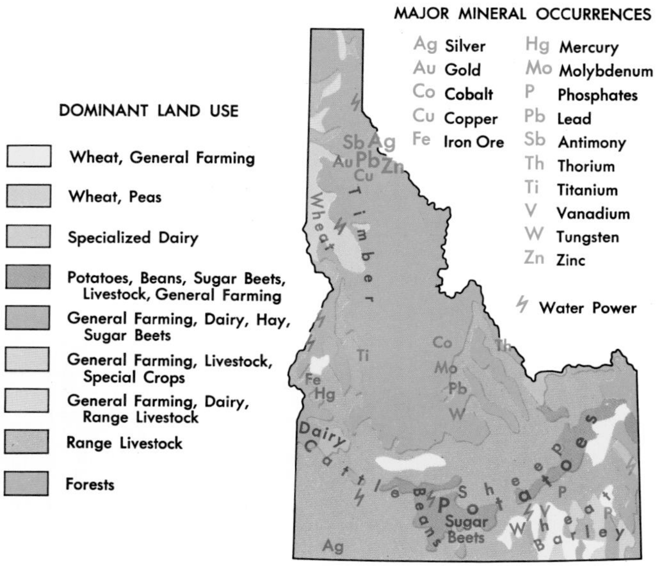
MAJOR MINERAL OCCURRENCES
Ag Silver
Au Gold
Co Cobalt
Cu Copper
Fe Iron Ore
Hg Mercury
Mo Molybdenum
P Phosphates
Pb Lead
Sb Antimony
Th Thorium
Ti Titanium
V Vanadium
W Tungsten
Zn Zinc
Water Power
DOMINANT LAND USE
Wheat, General Farming
Wheat, Peas
Specialized Dairy
Potatoes, Beans, Sugar Beets, Livestock, General Farming
General Farming, Dairy, Hay, Sugar Beets
General Farming, Livestock, Special Crops
General Farming, Dairy, Range Livestock
Range Livestock
Forests
Wheat
Timber
Dairy
Cattle
Beans
Sheep
Potatoes
Sugar Beets
Wheat
Barley

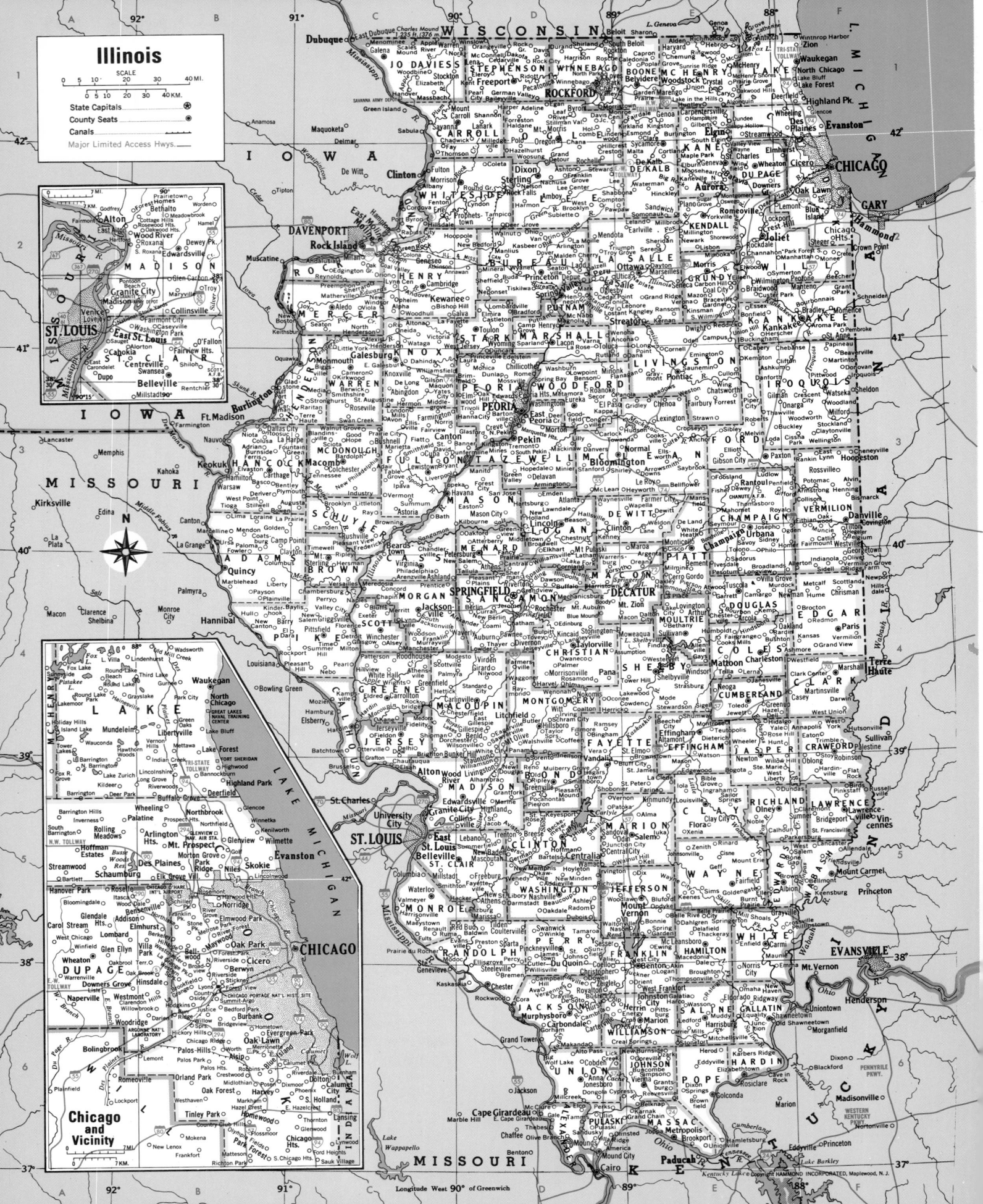

Illinois

SCALE
0 5 10 20 30 40 MI.
0 5 10 20 30 40 KM.

State Capitals ⊛
County Seats ⊙
Canals
Major Limited Access Hwys.

Chicago and Vicinity

AREA 56,345 sq. mi. (145,934 sq. km.)
POPULATION 11,426,596
CAPITAL Springfield
LARGEST CITY Chicago
HIGHEST POINT Charles Mound 1,235 ft. (376 m.)
SETTLED IN 1720
ADMITTED TO UNION December 3, 1818
POPULAR NAME Prairie State; Land of Lincoln
STATE FLOWER Native Violet
STATE BIRD Cardinal

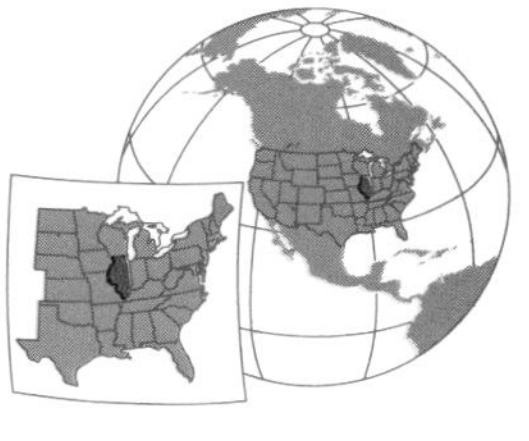

COUNTIES

Adams 71,622	B4
Alexander 12,264	D6
Bond 16,224	D5
Boone 28,630	E1
Brown 5,411	C4
Bureau 39,114	D2
Calhoun 5,867	C4
Carroll 18,779	D1
Cass 15,084	C4
Champaign 168,392	E3
Christian 36,446	D4
Clark 16,913	F4
Clay 15,283	E5
Clinton 32,617	D5
Coles 52,260	E4
Cook 5,253,655	F2
Crawford 20,818	F4
Cumberland 11,062	E4
De Kalb 74,624	E2
De Witt 18,108	E3
Douglas 19,774	E4
Du Page 658,835	E2
Edgar 21,725	F4
Edwards 7,961	E5
Effingham 30,944	E4
Fayette 22,167	D4
Ford 15,265	E3
Franklin 43,201	E5
Fulton 43,687	C3
Gallatin 7,590	E6
Greene 16,661	C4
Grundy 30,582	E2
Hamilton 9,172	E5
Hancock 23,877	B3
Hardin 5,383	E6
Henderson 9,114	C3
Henry 57,968	C2
Iroquois 32,976	F3
Jackson 61,522	D6
Jasper 11,318	E4
Jefferson 36,354	E5
Jersey 20,538	C4
Jo Daviess 23,520	C1
Johnson 9,624	E6
Kane 278,405	E2
Kankakee 102,926	F2
Kendall 37,202	E2
Knox 61,607	C3
Lake 440,372	E1
La Salle 112,033	E2
Lawrence 17,807	F5
Lee 36,328	D2
Livingston 41,381	E3
Logan 31,802	D3
Macon 131,375	E4
Macoupin 49,384	D4
Madison 247,691	D5
Marion 43,523	E5
Marshall 14,479	D2
Mason 19,492	D3
Massac 14,990	E6
McDonough 37,467	C3
McHenry 147,897	E1
McLean 119,149	E3
Menard 11,700	D3
Mercer 19,286	C2
Monroe 20,117	C5
Montgomery 31,686	D4
Morgan 37,502	C4
Moultrie 14,546	E4
Ogle 46,338	D1
Peoria 200,466	D3
Perry 21,714	D5
Piatt 16,581	E4
Pike 18,896	C4
Pope 4,404	E6
Pulaski 8,840	D6
Putnam 6,085	D2
Randolph 35,652	D5
Richland 17,587	E5
Rock Island 165,968	C2
Saint Clair 267,531	D5
Saline 28,448	E6
Sangamon 176,089	D4
Schuyler 8,365	C3
Scott 6,142	C4
Shelby 23,923	E4
Stark 7,389	D2
Stephenson 49,536	D1
Tazewell 132,078	D3
Union 17,765	D6
Vermilion 95,222	F3
Wabash 13,713	F5
Warren 21,943	C3
Washington 15,472	D5
Wayne 18,059	E5
White 17,864	E5
Whiteside 65,970	D2
Will 324,460	F2
Williamson 56,538	E6
Winnebago 250,884	D1
Woodford 33,320	D3

CITIES and TOWNS

Zip	*Name/Pop.*	*Key*
61410	Abingdon 4,210	C3
60101	Addison 29,826	B5
61230	Albany 1,014	C2
62806	Albion⊙ 2,285	E5
61231	Aledo⊙ 3,881	C2
61412	Alexis 1,076	C2
60102	Algonquin 5,834	E1
62207	Alorton 2,237	B2
61413	Alpha 815	C2
†60658	Alsip 17,134	B6
62411	Altamont 2,389	E4
62002	Alton 34,171	A2
61310	Amboy 2,377	D2
61232	Andalusia 1,238	C2
62906	Anna 5,408	D6
61234	Annawan 908	C2
60002	Antioch 4,419	E1
61910	Arcola 2,714	E4
62501	Argenta 994	E4
*60004	Arlington Heights 66,116	B5
61911	Arthur 2,122	E4
60911	Ashkum 735	E3
62612	Ashland 1,351	C4
62808	Ashley 658	D5
61912	Ashmore 883	F4
61006	Ashton 1,140	D2
62510	Assumption 1,283	E4
61501	Astoria 1,370	C3
62613	Athens 1,371	D4
61235	Atkinson 1,138	C2
61723	Atlanta 1,807	D3
61913	Atwood 1,464	E4
62615	Auburn 3,616	D4
62311	Augusta 764	C3
*60504	Aurora 81,293	E2
62907	Ava 811	D6
62216	Aviston 846	D5
61415	Avon 1,019	C3
†60015	Bannockburn 1,316	B5
60010	Barrington 9,029	A5
†60010	Barrington Hills 3,631	A5
62312	Barry 1,487	B4
60103	Bartlett 13,254	A5
61607	Bartonville 6,137	D3
60510	Batavia 12,574	E2
62618	Beardstown 6,338	C3
62219	Beckemeyer 1,119	D5
60401	Beecher 2,024	F2
*62220	Belleville⊙ 41,580	B3
60104	Bellwood 19,811	B5
61008	Belvidere⊙ 15,176	E1
61813	Bement 1,770	E4
62009	Benld 1,638	D4
60106	Bensenville 16,124	B5
62812	Benton⊙ 7,778	E6
60162	Berkeley 5,467	B5
60402	Berwyn 46,849	B6
62010	Bethalto 8,630	B2
61914	Bethany 1,550	E4
61420	Blandinsville 886	C3
60108	Bloomingdale 12,659	A5
61701	Bloomington⊙ 44,189	D3
	Bloomington-Normal‡ 119,149	D3
60406	Blue Island 21,855	B6
62513	Blue Mound 1,338	D4
62621	Bluffs 821	C4
60439	Bolingbrook 37,261	A6
60914	Bourbonnais 13,280	F2
60407	Braceville 721	E2
61421	Bradford 924	D2
60915	Bradley 11,008	F2
60408	Braidwood 3,429	E2
62230	Breese 3,516	D5
62417	Bridgeport 2,281	F5
60455	Bridgeview 14,155	B6
62012	Brighton 2,364	C4
61517	Brimfield 890	D3
60153	Broadview 8,618	B6
60513	Brookfield 19,395	B6
†62059	Brooklyn (Lovejoy) 1,233	A2
62910	Brookport 1,128	E6
61314	Buda 668	D2
†60090	Buffalo Grove 22,230	B5
62014	Bunker Hill 1,700	D4
60459	Burbank 28,462	B6
†60601	Burnham 4,030	C6
†60558	Burr Ridge 3,833	B6
61422	Bushnell 3,811	C3
61010	Byron 2,035	D1
62206	Cahokia 18,904	A3
62914	Cairo⊙ 5,931	D6
60409	Calumet City 39,697	C6
†60643	Calumet Park 8,788	C6
62915	Cambria 1,090	D6
61238	Cambridge⊙ 2,217	C2
62320	Camp Point 1,285	B3
61520	Canton 14,626	C3
61239	Carbon Cliff 1,578	C2
62901	Carbondale 26,414	D6
62626	Carlinville⊙ 5,439	D4
62231	Carlyle⊙ 3,388	D5
62821	Carmi⊙ 6,264	E5
†60187	Carol Stream 15,472	A5
60110	Carpentersville 23,272	E1
62917	Carrier Mills 2,268	E6
62016	Carrollton⊙ 2,816	C4
62918	Carterville 3,445	D6
62321	Carthage⊙ 2,978	B3
60013	Cary 6,640	E1
62420	Casey 3,026	F4
62232	Caseyville 4,308	B2
61817	Catlin 2,226	F3
61013	Cedarville 766	D1
†62801	Central City 1,505	D5
62801	Centralia 15,126	D5
62206	Centreville 9,747	B3
61818	Cerro Gordo 1,553	E4
61820	Champaign 58,133	E3
	Champaign-Urbana-Rantoul‡ 168,392	E3
62627	Chandlerville 842	C3
60410	Channahon 3,734	E2
61920	Charleston⊙ 19,355	E4
62629	Chatham 5,597	D4
60921	Chatsworth 1,187	E3
60922	Chebanse 1,191	F3
61726	Chenoa 1,847	E3
61016	Cherry Valley 946	D1
62233	Chester⊙ 8,401	D6
*60601	Chicago⊙ 3,005,072	C5
	Chicago‡ 7,102,328	C5
60411	Chicago Heights 37,026	C6
60415	Chicago Ridge 13,473	B6
61523	Chillicothe 6,176	D3
61924	Chrisman 1,413	F4
62822	Christopher 3,086	D6
60650	Cicero 61,232	B5
60924	Cissna Park 825	F3
60514	Clarendon Hills 6,870	B6
62824	Clay City 1,038	E5
62324	Clayton 889	B3
60927	Clifton 1,390	F3
61727	Clinton⊙ 8,014	E3
60416	Coal City 3,028	E2
61240	Coal Valley 3,800	C2
62920	Cobden 1,210	D6
62017	Coffeen 842	D4
62326	Colchester 1,729	C3
61728	Colfax 920	E3
62234	Collinsville 19,613	B2
61241	Colona 2,172	C2
62236	Columbia 4,269	C5
60112	Cortland 1,019	E2
62018	Cottage Hills	B2
62237	Coulterville 1,118	D5
†60525	Countryside 6,538	B6
62922	Creal Springs 845	E6
60431	Crest Hill 9,252	E2
†60445	Crestwood 10,852	B6
60417	Crete 5,417	F2
61611	Creve Coeur 6,851	D3
62827	Crossville 944	F5
60014	Crystal Lake 18,590	E1
61427	Cuba 1,648	C3
62330	Dallas City 1,408	B3
61320	Dalzell 824	D2
61732	Danvers 921	D3
61832	Danville⊙ 38,985	F3
†60559	Darien 14,536	B6
*62521	Decatur⊙ 94,081	E4
	Decatur‡ 131,375	E4
60015	Deerfield 17,430	B5
†60010	Deer Park 1,368	A5
60115	De Kalb 33,099	E2
61734	Delavan 1,973	D3
61322	Depue 1,873	D2
62924	De Soto 1,589	D6
*60016	Des Plaines 53,568	B5
62530	Divernon 1,081	D4
†60469	Dixmoor 4,175	C6
61021	Dixon⊙ 15,701	D2
60419	Dolton 24,766	C6
62926	Dongola 886	D6
60515	Downers Grove 42,572	A6
60118	Dundee (East and West Dundee) 6,169	E1
61525	Dunlap 824	D3
62239	Dupo 3,039	A3
62832	Du Quoin 6,594	D5
61024	Durand 1,073	D1
60420	Dwight 4,146	E2
60518	Earlville 1,382	E2
62024	East Alton 7,096	A2
†60411	East Chicago Heights 5,347	C6
61025	East Dubuque 2,194	C1
†60118	East Dundee (Dundee) 2,618	E1
61430	East Galesburg 928	C3
†60429	East Hazelcrest 1,362	C6
61244	East Moline 20,907	C2
61611	East Peoria 22,385	D3
*62201	East Saint Louis 55,200	A2
62531	Edinburg 1,231	D4
62025	Edwardsville⊙ 12,480	B2
62401	Effingham⊙ 11,270	E4
60119	Elburn 1,224	E2
62930	Eldorado 5,198	E6
60120	Elgin 63,981	E1
61028	Elizabeth 772	C1
62931	Elizabethtown⊙ 478	E6
60007	Elk Grove Village 28,907	B5
62932	Elkville 973	D6
60126	Elmhurst 44,276	B5
61529	Elmwood 2,117	D3
60635	Elmwood Park 24,016	B5
61738	El Paso 2,676	D3
62028	Elsah 990	C5
60421	Elwood 814	E2
62933	Energy 1,138	E6
62835	Enfield 890	E5
62934	Equality 831	E6
61250	Erie 1,725	C2
61530	Eureka⊙ 4,306	D3
*60201	Evanston 73,706	B5
62242	Evansville 863	D5
60642	Evergreen Park 22,260	B6
61739	Fairbury 3,544	E3
62837	Fairfield⊙ 5,954	E5
†62201	Fairmont City 2,313	B2
61841	Fairmount 851	F3
62208	Fairview Heights 12,414	B3
61842	Farmer City 2,252	E3
61531	Farmington 3,118	C3
62534	Findlay 868	E4
61843	Fisher 1,572	E3
61740	Flanagan 978	E3
62839	Flora 5,379	E5
60422	Flossmoor 8,423	B6
60130	Forest Park 15,177	B5
†60402	Forest View 764	B6
61741	Forrest 1,246	E3
61030	Forreston 1,384	D1
60020	Fox Lake 6,831	A4
60021	Fox River Grove 2,515	A5
60423	Frankfort 4,357	B6
61031	Franklin Grove 965	D2
60131	Franklin Park 17,507	B5
62243	Freeburg 2,989	D5
61032	Freeport⊙ 26,266	D1
61252	Fulton 3,936	C2
62935	Galatia 1,042	E6
61036	Galena⊙ 3,876	C1
61401	Galesburg⊙ 35,305	C3
61434	Galva 3,185	D2
60424	Gardner 1,322	E2
61254	Geneseo 6,373	C2
60134	Geneva⊙ 9,881	E2
60135	Genoa 3,276	E1
61846	Georgetown 4,220	F4
62245	Germantown 1,191	D5
60936	Gibson City 3,498	E3
61847	Gifford 848	E3
62033	Gillespie 3,740	D4
60938	Gilman 1,913	E3
62640	Girard 2,246	D4
61533	Glasford 1,201	D3
62034	Glen Carbon 5,197	B2
60022	Glencoe 9,200	B5
†60108	Glendale Heights 23,163	A5
60137	Glen Ellyn 23,717	A5
60025	Glenview 32,060	B5
60425	Glenwood 10,538	C6
62035	Godfrey	A2
62938	Golconda⊙ 960	E6
62939	Goreville 978	E6
62037	Grafton 1,024	C5
62942	Grand Tower 748	D6
†62701	Grandview 1,794	D4
62040	Granite City 36,815	A2
60940	Grant Park 1,038	F2
61326	Granville 1,537	D2
60030	Grayslake 5,260	B4
62844	Grayville 2,313	B4
62044	Greenfield 1,090	C4
†60048	Green Oaks 1,415	B4
†61241	Green Rock 3,324	C2
62428	Greenup 1,655	E4
61534	Green Valley 768	D3
62642	Greenview 830	D3
62246	Greenville⊙ 5,271	D5
61744	Gridley 1,246	E3
62340	Griggsville 1,301	C4
60031	Gurnee 7,179	B4
62341	Hamilton 3,509	B3
60140	Hampshire 1,735	E1
61256	Hampton 1,873	C2
61536	Hanna City 1,361	D3
61041	Hanover 1,069	C1
60103	Hanover Park 28,719	A5
62047	Hardin⊙ 1,107	C4
62946	Harrisburg⊙ 10,410	E6
62537	Harristown 1,456	D4
62048	Hartford 1,887	A2
60033	Harvard 5,126	E1
60426	Harvey 35,810	B6
60656	Harwood Heights 8,228	B5
62644	Havana⊙ 4,277	D3
†60047	Hawthorn Woods 1,658	B5
60429	Hazel Crest 13,973	B6
60034	Hebron 786	E1
†61832	Hegeler 1,853	F3
61327	Hennepin⊙ 716	D2
61537	Henry 2,740	D2
62948	Herrin 10,708	E6
60941	Herscher 1,214	E2
61745	Heyworth 1,598	E3
60457	Hickory Hills 13,778	B6
62249	Highland 7,122	D5
60035	Highland Park 30,611	B5
60040	Highwood 5,452	B5
62049	Hillsboro⊙ 4,408	D4
60162	Hillside 8,279	B5
60520	Hinckley 1,447	E2
60521	Hinsdale 16,726	B6
60525	Hodgkins 2,005	B6
60195	Hoffman Estates 37,272	A5
61849	Homer 1,279	F3
60456	Hometown 5,324	B6
60430	Homewood 19,724	B6
60942	Hoopeston 6,411	F3
61747	Hohedale 913	D3
61748	Hudson 929	E3

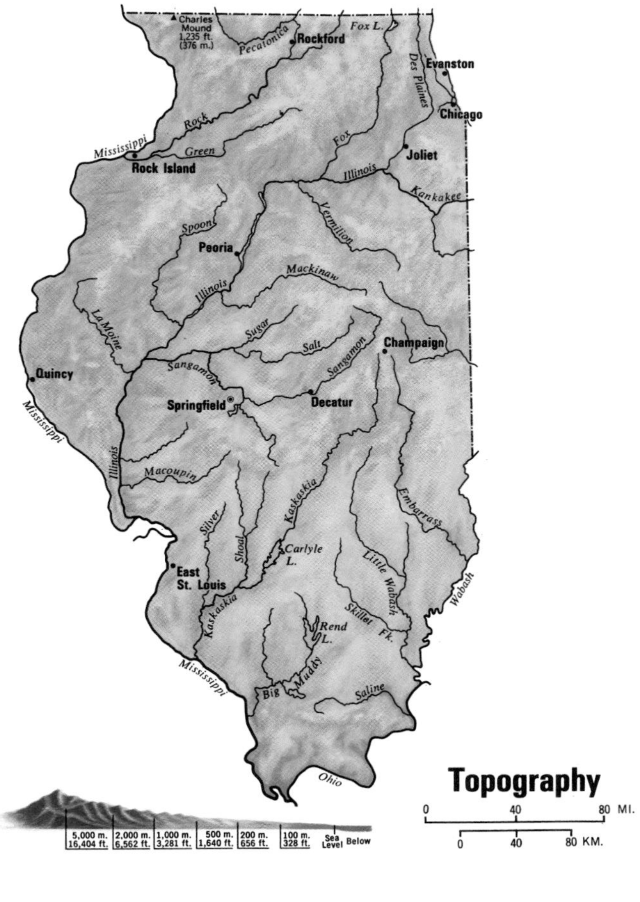
Charles Mound
1,235 ft.
(376 m.)
Rockford
Pecatonica
Fox L.
Evanston
Des Plaines
Chicago
Rock
Mississippi
Green
Fox
Joliet
Rock Island
Illinois
Kankakee
Vermilion
Spoon
Peoria
Illinois
Mackinaw
La Moine
Sugar
Salt
Sangamon
Champaign
Quincy
Sangamon
Springfield
Decatur
Mississippi
Illinois
Macoupin
Kaskaskia
Embarrass
Silver
Shoal
Carlyle L.
Little Wabash
East St. Louis
Wabash
Kaskaskia
Rend L.
Skillet Fk.
Mississippi
Big Muddy
Saline
Ohio
Topography
0 40 80 MI.
0 40 80 KM.
5,000 m. 16,404 ft.
2,000 m. 6,562 ft.
1,000 m. 3,281 ft.
500 m. 1,640 ft.
200 m. 656 ft.
100 m. 328 ft.
Sea Level
Below

(continued on following page)

Agriculture, Industry and Resources

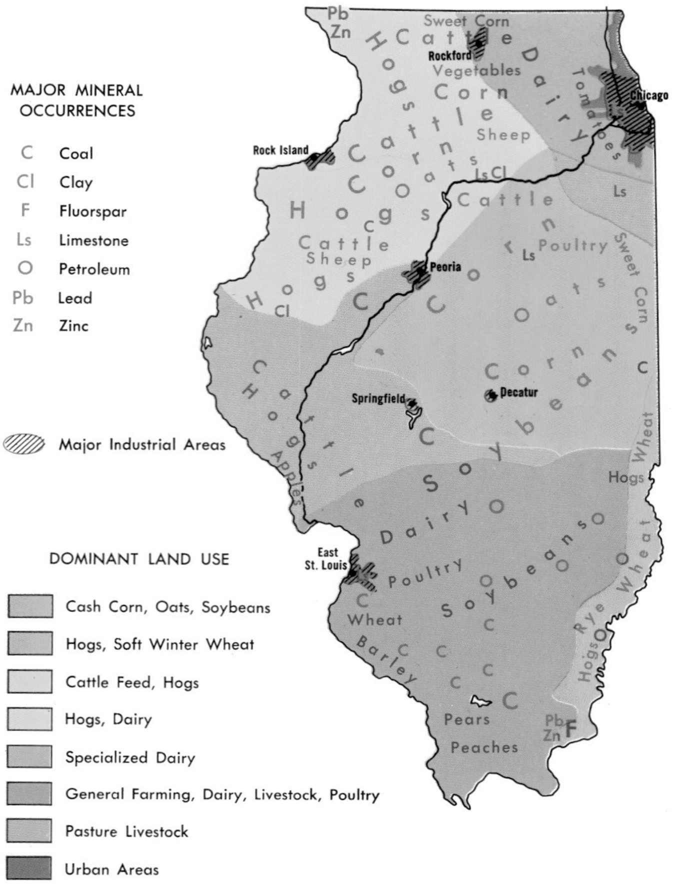
MAJOR MINERAL OCCURRENCES
C Coal
Cl Clay
F Fluorspar
Ls Limestone
O Petroleum
Pb Lead
Zn Zinc
Major Industrial Areas
DOMINANT LAND USE
Cash Corn, Oats, Soybeans
Hogs, Soft Winter Wheat
Cattle Feed, Hogs
Hogs, Dairy
Specialized Dairy
General Farming, Dairy, Livestock, Poultry
Pasture Livestock
Urban Areas
Rockford
Chicago
Rock Island
Peoria
Springfield
Decatur
East St. Louis
Sweet Corn
Vegetables
Tomatoes
Sheep
Poultry
Wheat
Barley
Pears
Peaches
Apples
Rye

60142 Huntley 1,646 ..... E1
62949 Hurst 938 ..... D6
62539 Illiopolis 1,118 ..... D4
†60067 Inverness 4,046 ..... A5
62848 Irvington 789 ..... D5
60042 Island Lake 2,293 ..... A4
60143 Itasca 7,129 ..... B5
62650 Jacksonville⊙ 20,284 ..... C4
†62701 Jerome 1,374 ..... D4
62052 Jerseyville⊙ 7,506 ..... C4
62436 Jewett 230 ..... E4
62951 Johnston City 3,873 ..... E6
*60431 Joliet⊙ 77,956 ..... E2
62952 Jonesboro⊙ 1,842 ..... D6
†60458 Justice 10,552 ..... B6
60901 Kankakee⊙ 30,141 ..... F2
Kankakee‡ 102,926 ..... F2
61933 Kansas 791 ..... F4
†63673 Kaskaskia 33 ..... C6
61442 Keithsburg 936 ..... B2
60043 Kenilworth 2,708 ..... B5
61443 Kewanee 14,508 ..... C2
†60069 Kildeer 1,609 ..... A5
62540 Kincaid 1,591 ..... D4
62854 Kinmundy 945 ..... E5
60146 Kirkland 1,155 ..... E1
61447 Kirkwood 1,008 ..... C3
61448 Knoxville 3,432 ..... C3
61540 Lacon⊙ 2,135 ..... D2
61329 Ladd 1,337 ..... D2
60525 La Grange 15,445 ..... B6
60525 La Grange Park 13,359 ..... B5
61450 La Harpe 1,471 ..... C3
†60010 Lake Barrington 2,320 ..... A5
60044 Lake Bluff 4,434 ..... B4
†60002 Lake Catherine 1,335 ..... E1
60045 Lake Forest 15,245 ..... B4
†60102 Lake in the Hills 5,651 ..... E1
60046 Lake Villa 1,462 ..... A4
62438 Lakewood 1,254 ..... E4
60047 Lake Zurich 8,225 ..... A5
61330 La Moille 734 ..... D2
61046 Lanark 1,483 ..... D1
60438 Lansing 29,039 ..... C6
61301 La Salle 10,347 ..... E2
62439 Lawrenceville⊙ 5,652 ..... F5
62254 Lebanon 3,245 ..... D5
60531 Leland 775 ..... E2
60439 Lemont 5,640 ..... B6
61048 Lena 2,295 ..... D1
61752 Le Roy 2,870 ..... E3
61542 Lewistown⊙ 2,758 ..... C3
61753 Lexington 1,806 ..... E3
60048 Libertyville 16,520 ..... B4
62656 Lincoln⊙ 16,327 ..... D3
†60015 Lincolnshire 4,151 ..... B5
†60645 Lincolnwood 11,921 ..... B5
†60046 Lindenhurst 6,220 ..... B4
60532 Lisle 13,625 ..... A6
62056 Litchfield 7,204 ..... D4
62058 Livingston 949 ..... D5
62661 Loami 770 ..... D4
60441 Lockport 9,170 ..... B6
60148 Lombard 36,897 ..... B5
60047 Long Grove 2,013 ..... B5
62858 Louisville⊙ 1,166 ..... E5
62059 Lovejoy 1,233 ..... A2
61111 Loves Park 13,192 ..... E1
61937 Lovington 1,313 ..... E4
61261 Lyndon 777 ..... D2
†60411 Lynwood 4,195 ..... C6
60534 Lyons 9,925 ..... B6
61755 Mackinaw 1,354 ..... D3
61455 Macomb⊙ 19,863 ..... C3
62544 Macon 1,300 ..... E4
62060 Madison 5,915 ..... A2
61853 Mahomet 1,986 ..... E3
60150 Malta 995 ..... E2
60442 Manhattan 1,944 ..... F2
61546 Manito 1,869 ..... D3
61854 Mansfield 921 ..... E3
60950 Manteno 3,155 ..... F2
60152 Marengo 4,361 ..... E1
62061 Marine 957 ..... D5
62959 Marion⊙ 14,031 ..... E6
62257 Marissa 2,568 ..... D5
60426 Markham 15,172 ..... B6
61756 Maroa 1,760 ..... E3
†61554 Marquette Heights 3,386 ..... D3
61341 Marseilles 4,766 ..... E2
62441 Marshall⊙ 3,655 ..... F4
62442 Martinsville 1,298 ..... F4
62062 Maryville 1,937 ..... B2
62258 Mascoutah 4,962 ..... D5
62664 Mason City 2,719 ..... D3
61263 Matherville 793 ..... C2
60443 Matteson 10,223 ..... B6
61938 Mattoon 19,055 ..... E4
60153 Maywood 27,998 ..... B5
60444 Mazon 828 ..... E2
60050 McHenry 10,908 ..... E1
†60050 McHenry Shores 1,041 ..... E1
61754 McLean 836 ..... D3
62859 McLeansboro⊙ 2,960 ..... E5
†62010 Meadowbrook 1,082 ..... B2
*60160 Melrose Park 20,735 ..... B5
62351 Mendon 979 ..... B3
61342 Mendota 7,134 ..... D2
62665 Meredosia 1,272 ..... C4
†60601 Merrionette Park 2,054 ..... B6
61548 Metamora 2,482 ..... D3
62960 Metropolis⊙ 7,171 ..... E6
60445 Midlothian 14,274 ..... B6
61264 Milan 6,264 ..... C2
60953 Milford 1,716 ..... F3
61051 Milledgeville 1,209 ..... D1
62260 Millstadt 2,736 ..... B3
61759 Minier 1,261 ..... D3
61760 Minonk 2,039 ..... D3
60447 Minooka 1,565 ..... E2
60448 Mokena 4,578 ..... B6
61265 Moline 46,278 ..... C2
60954 Momence 3,297 ..... F2
60449 Monee 993 ..... F2
61462 Monmouth⊙ 10,706 ..... C3
60538 Montgomery 3,369 ..... E2
61856 Monticello⊙ 4,753 ..... E3
60450 Morris⊙ 8,833 ..... E2
61270 Morrison⊙ 4,605 ..... C2
62546 Morrisonville 1,208 ..... D4
61550 Morton 14,178 ..... D3
60053 Morton Grove 23,747 ..... B5
62963 Mound City⊙ 1,102 ..... D6
62964 Mounds 1,669 ..... D6
62863 Mount Carmel⊙ 8,908 ..... F5
61053 Mount Carroll⊙ 1,936 ..... D1
61054 Mount Morris 2,989 ..... D1
62069 Mount Olive 2,357 ..... D4
60056 Mount Prospect 52,634 ..... B5
62548 Mount Pulaski 1,783 ..... D3
62353 Mount Sterling⊙ 2,186 ..... C4
62864 Mount Vernon⊙ 17,193 ..... E5
62549 Mount Zion 4,563 ..... E4
62550 Moweaqua 1,922 ..... E4
60060 Mundelein 17,053 ..... A4
62966 Murphysboro⊙ 9,866 ..... D6
60540 Naperville 42,601 ..... A6
62263 Nashville⊙ 3,186 ..... D5
62354 Nauvoo 1,133 ..... B3
62447 Neoga 1,736 ..... E4
60541 Newark 798 ..... E2
62264 New Athens 1,937 ..... D5
62265 New Baden 2,476 ..... D5
62670 New Berlin 834 ..... D4
61272 New Boston 731 ..... B2
60451 New Lenox 5,792 ..... B6
61942 Newman 1,079 ..... B6
62448 Newton⊙ 3,186 ..... E5
61465 New Windsor 863 ..... C2
62551 Niantic 761 ..... D4
60648 Niles 30,363 ..... B5
62868 Noble 832 ..... E5
62075 Nokomis 2,656 ..... D4
61761 Normal 35,672 ..... E3
†60656 Norridge 16,483 ..... B5
62869 Norris City 1,515 ..... E6
60542 North Aurora 5,205 ..... E2
†60010 North Barrington 1,475 ..... A5
60062 Northbrook 30,778 ..... B5
60064 North Chicago 38,774 ..... B4
60093 Northfield 5,807 ..... B5
60164 Northlake 12,166 ..... B5
†61111 North Park 15,806 ..... D1
†61554 North Pekin 1,824 ..... D3
60546 North Riverside 6,764 ..... B5
†61373 North Utica (Utica) 1,067 ..... E2
60521 Oak Brook 6,641 ..... B6
†60181 Oakbrook Terrace 2,285 ..... B5
60452 Oak Forest 26,096 ..... B6
61943 Oakland 1,035 ..... F4
*60453 Oak Lawn 60,590 ..... B6
*60303 Oak Park 54,887 ..... B5
61858 Oakwood 1,627 ..... F3
62449 Oblong 1,840 ..... F5
60460 Odell 1,083 ..... E2
62870 Odin 1,285 ..... D5
62269 O'Fallon 12,241 ..... B2
61859 Ogden 818 ..... F3
61348 Oglesby 3,979 ..... D2
62271 Okawville 1,337 ..... D5
62450 Olney⊙ 9,026 ..... E5
60461 Olympia Fields 4,146 ..... B6
60955 Onarga 1,269 ..... F3
61467 Oneida 765 ..... C2
61469 Oquawka⊙ 1,533 ..... C3
62554 Oreana 999 ..... E4
61061 Oregon⊙ 3,559 ..... D1
61273 Orion 2,013 ..... C2
60462 Orland Park 23,045 ..... B6
60543 Oswego 3,021 ..... E2
61350 Ottawa⊙ 18,166 ..... E2
60067 Palatine 32,166 ..... B5
62451 Palestine 1,718 ..... F4
62674 Palmyra 864 ..... C4
60463 Palos Heights 11,096 ..... B6
60465 Palos Hills 16,654 ..... B6
60464 Palos Park 3,150 ..... B6
62557 Pana 6,040 ..... D4
61944 Paris⊙ 9,885 ..... F4
†60085 Park City 3,673 ..... B4
60466 Park Forest 26,222 ..... B6
60466 Park Forest South 6,245 ..... F2
60068 Park Ridge 38,704 ..... B5
62558 Pawnee 2,577 ..... D4
61353 Pawpaw 839 ..... E2
60957 Paxton⊙ 4,258 ..... E3
62360 Payson 1,065 ..... B4
61063 Pecatonica 1,732 ..... D1
61554 Pekin⊙ 33,967 ..... D3
*61601 Peoria⊙ 124,160 ..... D3
Peoria‡ 365,864 ..... D3
61614 Peoria Heights 7,453 ..... D3
60468 Peotone 2,832 ..... F2
62272 Percy 1,053 ..... D5
61354 Peru 10,886 ..... D2
62675 Petersburg⊙ 2,419 ..... D4
61864 Philo 973 ..... E3
†60426 Phoenix 2,850 ..... C6
62274 Pinckneyville⊙ 3,319 ..... D5
60959 Piper City 905 ..... E3
62363 Pittsfield⊙ 4,170 ..... C4
60544 Plainfield 3,767 ..... A6
60545 Plano 4,875 ..... E2
62366 Pleasant Hill 1,112 ..... C4
62275 Pocahontas 866 ..... D5
61074 Polo 2,643 ..... D1
61764 Pontiac⊙ 11,227 ..... E3
†62040 Pontoon Beach 3,336 ..... A2
61065 Poplar Grove 818 ..... E1
61275 Port Byron 1,289 ..... C2
60469 Posen 4,642 ..... B6
61865 Potomac 874 ..... F3
61470 Prairie City 580 ..... C3
61356 Princeton⊙ 7,342 ..... D2
61559 Princeville 1,712 ..... D3
61277 Prophetstown 2,141 ..... D2
60070 Prospect Heights 11,808 ..... B5
62301 Quincy⊙ 42,554 ..... B4
62080 Ramsey 1,058 ..... D4
60960 Rankin 727 ..... F3
61866 Rantoul 20,161 ..... E3
61278 Rapids City 1,058 ..... C2
62560 Raymond 957 ..... D4
62278 Red Bud 2,850 ..... D5
60071 Richmond 1,068 ..... E1
60471 Richton Park 9,403 ..... B6
61870 Ridge Farm 1,096 ..... F4
62979 Ridgway 1,245 ..... E6
60627 Riverdale 13,233 ..... C6
60305 River Forest 12,392 ..... B5
60171 River Grove 10,368 ..... B5
60546 Riverside 9,236 ..... B6
62561 Riverton 2,783 ..... D4
†60015 Riverwoods 2,804 ..... B5
61561 Roanoke 2,001 ..... D3
60472 Robbins 8,853 ..... B6
62454 Robinson⊙ 7,285 ..... F5
61068 Rochelle 8,982 ..... D2
62563 Rochester 2,488 ..... D4
60436 Rockdale 1,913 ..... E2
61071 Rock Falls 10,633 ..... D2
*61101 Rockford⊙ 139,712 ..... D1
Rockford‡ 279,514 ..... D1
61201 Rock Island⊙ 46,928 ..... C2
Rock Island-Moline-
Davenport‡ 383,958 ..... C2
61072 Rockton 2,313 ..... E1
60008 Rolling Meadows 20,167 ..... A5
61562 Rome 2,744 ..... D3
60441 Romeoville 15,519 ..... B6
62082 Roodhouse 2,364 ..... C4
61073 Roscoe 1,388 ..... D1
60172 Roselle 16,948 ..... A5
60018 Rosemont 4,137 ..... B5
61473 Roseville 1,254 ..... C3
†62024 Rosewood Heights 5,085 ..... B2
62982 Rosiclare 1,441 ..... E6
60963 Rossville 1,363 ..... F3
60673 Round Lake 2,644 ..... A4
†60673 Round Lake Beach 12,921 ..... A4
†60673 Round Lake Heights 1,192 ..... E1
†60673 Round Lake Park 4,032 ..... A4
62084 Roxana 1,587 ..... B2
62983 Royalton 1,320 ..... D6
62681 Rushville⊙ 3,348 ..... C3
60964 Saint Anne 1,421 ..... F2
60174 Saint Charles 17,492 ..... E2
61563 Saint David 786 ..... C3
62458 Saint Elmo 1,611 ..... E4
62460 Saint Francisville 1,040 ..... F5
62281 Saint Jacob 792 ..... D5
61873 Saint Joseph 1,900 ..... E3
62881 Salem⊙ 7,813 ..... E5
62882 Sandoval 1,734 ..... D5
60548 Sandwich 5,244 ..... E2
62682 San Jose 784 ..... D3
60411 Sauk Village 10,906 ..... C6
61074 Savanna 4,529 ..... C1
61874 Savoy 2,126 ..... E3
61770 Saybrook 882 ..... E3
60194 Schaumburg 53,305 ..... A5
60176 Schiller Park 11,458 ..... B5
61360 Seneca 2,098 ..... E2
62884 Sesser 2,238 ..... D5
60550 Shabbona 851 ..... E2
61078 Shannon 938 ..... D1
62984 Shawneetown⊙ 1,841 ..... E6
61361 Sheffield 1,130 ..... D2
62565 Shelbyville⊙ 5,259 ..... E4
60966 Sheldon 1,215 ..... F3
62684 Sherman 1,501 ..... D4
61281 Sherrard 811 ..... C2
†62220 Shiloh 1,045 ..... B3
60435 Shorewood 4,714 ..... E2
61877 Sidney 886 ..... E3
61282 Silvis 7,130 ..... C2
*60076 Skokie 60,278 ..... B5
†60118 Sleepy Hollow 2,000 ..... E1
62285 Smithton 1,447 ..... C5
60552 Somonauk 1,344 ..... E2
†60010 South Barrington 1,168 ..... A5
61080 South Beloit 4,088 ..... E1
60411 South Chicago
Heights 3,932 ..... C6
60177 South Elgin 5,970 ..... E2
60473 South Holland 24,977 ..... C6
†62650 South Jacksonville 3,382 ..... C4
61564 South Pekin 1,243 ..... D3
62087 South Roxana 2,286 ..... B2
60474 South Wilmington 747 ..... E2
62286 Sparta 4,957 ..... D5
*62701 Springfield (cap.)⊙
100,054 ..... D4
Springfield‡ 187,789 ..... D4
61362 Spring Valley 5,822 ..... D2
61774 Stanford 720 ..... D3
62088 Staunton 4,744 ..... D5
62288 Steeleville 2,240 ..... D6
60475 Steger 9,269 ..... F2
61081 Sterling 16,281 ..... D2
62463 Stewardson 745 ..... E4
60402 Stickney 5,893 ..... B6
61084 Stillman Valley 961 ..... D1
61085 Stockton 1,872 ..... C1
†60160 Stone Park 4,273 ..... B5
62567 Stonington 1,184 ..... D4
60103 Streamwood 23,456 ..... A5
61364 Streator 14,795 ..... E2
61480 Stronghurst 865 ..... C3
60554 Sugar Grove 1,366 ..... E2
61951 Sullivan⊙ 4,526 ..... E4
60501 Summit-Argo 10,110 ..... B6
62466 Sumner 1,238 ..... F5
†60050 Sunnyside 1,432 ..... A4
62221 Swansea 5,347 ..... B3
60178 Sycamore⊙ 9,219 ..... E2
62888 Tamaroa 885 ..... D5
62988 Tamms 826 ..... D6
61283 Tampico 966 ..... D2
62568 Taylorville⊙ 11,386 ..... D4
62467 Teutopolis 1,414 ..... E4
62689 Thayer 759 ..... D4
61878 Thomasboro 1,242 ..... E3
61285 Thomson 911 ..... C2
60476 Thornton 3,024 ..... C6
62292 Tilden 1,025 ..... D5
†61832 Tilton 2,405 ..... F3
60477 Tinley Park 26,171 ..... B6
61368 Tiskilwa 990 ..... D2
62468 Toledo⊙ 1,284 ..... E4
61880 Tolono 2,434 ..... E3
61369 Toluca 1,471 ..... D2
61483 Toulon⊙ 1,390 ..... D2
†60010 Tower Lakes 1,177 ..... A4
61568 Tremont 2,096 ..... D3
62293 Trenton 2,504 ..... D5
62294 Troy 3,772 ..... B2
61953 Tuscola⊙ 3,839 ..... E4
61801 Urbana⊙ 35,978 ..... E3
61373 Utica 1,067 ..... E2
62891 Valier 729 ..... D5
†60120 Valley View 2,112 ..... E2
62295 Valmeyer 898 ..... C5
62471 Vandalia⊙ 5,338 ..... D5
62090 Venice 3,480 ..... A2
61484 Vermont 885 ..... C3
60061 Vernon Hills 9,827 ..... B4
62995 Vienna⊙ 1,420 ..... E6
61956 Villa Grove 2,707 ..... E4
60181 Villa Park 23,185 ..... B5
61486 Viola 1,144 ..... C2
62690 Virden 3,899 ..... D4
62691 Virginia⊙ 1,825 ..... C4
60083 Wadsworth 1,104 ..... B4
61376 Walnut 1,513 ..... D2
†62801 Wamac 1,665 ..... D5
61777 Wapella 768 ..... E3
61087 Warren 1,595 ..... C1
62573 Warrensburg 1,372 ..... D4
60555 Warrenville 7,519 ..... A6
62379 Warsaw 1,842 ..... B3
61570 Washburn 1,206 ..... D3
61571 Washington 10,364 ..... D3
62204 Washington Park 8,223 ..... B2
61488 Wataga 996 ..... C2
62298 Waterloo⊙ 4,646 ..... C5
60556 Waterman 943 ..... E2
60970 Watseka⊙ 5,543 ..... F3
60084 Wauconda 5,688 ..... A4
60085 Waukegan⊙ 67,653 ..... B4
62692 Waverly 1,537 ..... D4
60184 Wayne 940 ..... E2
62895 Wayne City 1,132 ..... E5
61377 Wenona 1,025 ..... E2
60153 Westchester 17,730 ..... B5
60185 West Chicago 12,550 ..... A5
†60118 West Dundee
(Dundee) 3,551 ..... E1
60558 Western Springs 12,876 ..... B6
62474 Westfield 733 ..... F4
62896 West Frankfort 9,437 ..... E6
†60462 Westhaven 2,784 ..... B6
60559 Westmont 16,718 ..... B6
62476 West Salem 1,145 ..... F5
61883 Westville 3,573 ..... F3
60187 Wheaton⊙ 43,043 ..... A5
60090 Wheeling 23,266 ..... B5
62092 White Hall 2,935 ..... C4
62693 Williamsville 996 ..... D4
†60521 Willowbrook 4,953 ..... B6
60480 Willow Springs 4,147 ..... B6
60091 Wilmette 28,229 ..... B5
60481 Wilmington 4,424 ..... E2
62694 Winchester⊙ 1,716 ..... C4
61957 Windsor 1,228 ..... E4
†61465 Windsor (New
Windsor) 863 ..... C2
60190 Winfield 4,422 ..... A5
61088 Winnebago 1,644 ..... D1
60093 Winnetka 12,772 ..... B5
60096 Winthrop Harbor 5,431 ..... F1
62094 Witt 1,205 ..... D4
60191 Wood Dale 11,251 ..... B5
61490 Woodhull 901 ..... C2
†60517 Woodridge 22,561 ..... B6
62095 Wood River 12,446 ..... B2
60098 Woodstock⊙ 11,725 ..... E1
62097 Worden 953 ..... B2
60482 Worth 11,592 ..... B6
61379 Wyanet 1,069 ..... D2
61491 Wyoming 1,614 ..... D2
61572 Yates City 860 ..... C3
60560 Yorkville⊙ 3,422 ..... E2
62999 Zeigler 1,858 ..... D6
60099 Zion 17,861 ..... F1

OTHER FEATURES

Apple (creek) C4
Apple (riv.) C1
Argonne Nat'l Laboratory B6
Big Bureau (riv.) D2
Big Muddy (riv.) D6
Bonpas (creek) F5
Cache (riv.) D6
Calumet (lake) C6
Carlyle (lake) D5
Chanute A.F.B. E3
Charles Mound (hill) C1
Chicago Portage Nat'l Hist. Site B6
Crab Orchard (lake) E6
Des Plaines (riv.) A6
Du Page (riv.) E2
Edwards (riv.) C2
Embarras (riv.) E4
Fort Sheridan B5
Fox (lake) A4
Fox (riv.) E2
Fox (riv.) E5
Glenview Nav. Air. Sta. B5
Granite City Army Depot A2
Great Lakes Nav. Trng. Ctr. B4
Green (riv.) D2
Henderson (riv.) C2
Illinois (riv.) C4
Illinois - Mississippi (canal) C2
Iroquois (riv.) F3
Kankakee (riv.) F2
Kaskaskia (riv.) E4
La Moine (riv.) C3
Little Wabash (riv.) E5
Mackinaw (riv.) E3
Macoupin (riv.) C4
Michigan (lake) F1
Mississippi (riv.) C5
O'Hare Field-Chicago International
Airport B5
Ohio (riv.) E6
Plum (riv.) C1
Pope (creek) C2
Rend (lake) E5
Rock (creek) D2
Rock (riv.) C2
Rock Island Arsenal C2
Saline (riv.) E6
Salt (creek) D3
Sangamon (riv.) C3
Savanna Army Depot C1
Scott A.F.B. 8,648 ..... B3
Shelbyville (lake) E4
Spoon (riv.) C3
Wabash (riv.) F5

⊙County seat.
‡Population of metropolitan area.
† Zip of nearest p.o. * Multiple zips.

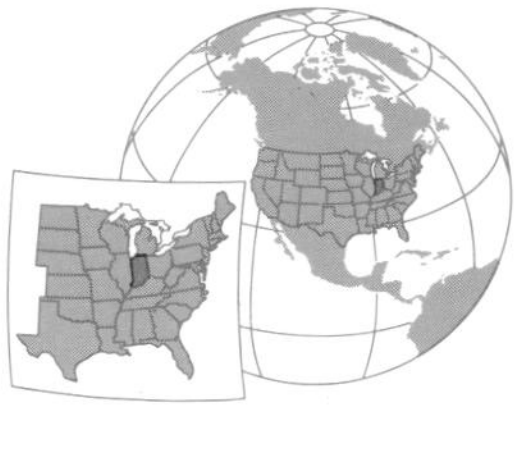

AREA 36,185 sq. mi. (93,719 sq. km.)
POPULATION 5,490,260
CAPITAL Indianapolis
LARGEST CITY Indianapolis
HIGHEST POINT 1,257 ft. (383 m.) (Wayne County)
SETTLED IN 1730
ADMITTED TO UNION December 11, 1816
POPULAR NAME Hoosier State
STATE FLOWER Peony
STATE BIRD Cardinal

COUNTIES

Adams 29,619 H3
Allen 294,335 G2
Bartholomew 65,088 F6
Benton 10,218 C3
Blackford 15,570 G4
Boone 36,446 E4
Brown 12,377 E6
Carroll 19,722 D3
Cass 40,936 E3
Clark 88,838 F8
Clay 24,862 C6
Clinton 31,545 E4
Crawford 9,820 E8
Daviess 27,836 C7
Dearborn 34,291 H6
Decatur 23,841 G6
De Kalb 33,606 H2
Delaware 128,587 G4
Dubois 34,238 D8
Elkhart 137,330 F1
Fayette 28,272 G5
Floyd 61,169 F8
Fountain 19,033 C4
Franklin 19,612 G6
Fulton 19,335 E2
Gibson 33,156 B8
Grant 80,934 F3
Greene 30,416 D6
Hamilton 82,027 E4
Hancock 43,939 F5
Harrison 27,276 E8
Hendricks 69,804 D5
Henry 53,336 G5
Howard 86,896 E4
Huntington 35,596 G3
Jackson 36,523 E7
Jasper 26,138 C2
Jay 23,239 G4
Jefferson 30,419 G7
Jennings 22,854 F7
Johnson 77,240 E6
Knox 41,838 C7
Kosciusko 59,555 F2
Lagrange 25,550 G1
Lake 522,965 C2
LaPorte 108,632 D1
Lawrence 4,272 E7
Madison 139,336 F4
Marion 765,233 E5
Marshall 39,155 E2
Martin 11,001 D7
Miami 39,820 E3
Monroe 98,785 D6
Montgomery 35,501 D4
Morgan 51,999 E6
Newton 14,844 C3
Noble 35,443 G2
Ohio 5,114 H7
Orange 18,677 E7
Owen 15,841 D6
Parke 16,372 C5
Perry 19,346 D8
Pike 13,465 C8
Porter 119,816 C2
Posey 26,414 B8
Pulaski 13,258 D2
Putnam 29,163 D5
Randolph 29,997 G4
Ripley 24,398 G6
Rush 19,604 G5
Saint Joseph 241,617 E1
Scott 20,422 F7
Shelby 39,887 F5
Spencer 19,361 C9
Starke 21,997 D2
Steuben 24,694 G1
Sullivan 21,107 C6
Switzerland 7,153 G7
Tippecanoe 121,702 D4
Tipton 16,819 E4
Union 6,860 H5
Vanderburgh 167,515 B8
Vermillion 18,229 C5
Vigo 112,385 C6
Wabash 36,640 F3
Warren 8,976 C4
Warrick 41,474 C8
Washington 21,932 E7
Wayne 76,058 G5
Wells 25,401 G3
White 23,867 D3
Whitley 26,215 F2

CITIES and TOWNS

Zip *Name/Pop.* *Key*

47240 Adams 250 F6
†46947 Adamsboro 325 E3
46102 Advance 559 D5
46910 Akron 1,045 E2
47320 Albany 2,625 G4
46701 Albion⊙ 1,637 G2
†47283 Alert 102 F6
46001 Alexandria 6,028 F4
†46738 Altona 263 G2
47917 Ambia 274 C4
46911 Amboy 450 F3
†46131 Amity 200 E6
46103 Amo 444 D5
*46011 Anderson⊙ 64,695 F4
Anderson‡ 139,336 F4
†47024 Andersonville 225 G5
46702 Andrews 1,243 F3
46703 Angola⊙ 5,486 G1
46030 Arcadia 1,801 E4
46704 Arcola 300 G2
†46624 Ardmore 800 E1
46501 Argos 1,547 E2
46104 Arlington 500 F5
46705 Ashley 841 G1
46031 Atlanta 657 E4
47918 Attica 3,841 C4
46502 Atwood 300 F2
46706 Auburn⊙ 8,122 G2
47001 Aurora 3,816 H6
47102 Austin 4,857 F7
46710 Avilla 1,272 G2
47420 Avoca 400 D7
46105 Bainbridge 644 D5
46106 Bargersville 1,647 E5
47006 Batesville 4,152 G6
47920 Battle Ground 812 D3
47421 Bedford⊙ 14,410 E7
46107 Beech Grove 13,196 E5
†46526 Benton 220 F2
46711 Berne 3,300 H3
†46111 Bethany 127 E5
46301 Beverly Shores 864 C1
47512 Bicknell 4,713 C7
46713 Bippus 300 F3
47513 Birdseye 533 D8
†46406 Black Oak C1
47831 Blanford 500 B5
47138 Blocher 400 F7
47424 Bloomfield⊙ 2,705 D6
47832 Bloomingdale 409 C5
47401 Bloomington⊙ 52,044 D6
Bloomington‡ 98,387 D6
†47360 Blountsville 213 G4
†46176 Blue Ridge 219 F5
46714 Bluffton⊙ 8,705 G3
46110 Boggstown 200 F5
46302 Boone Grove 220 C2
47601 Boonville⊙ 6,300 C8
47106 Borden 384 F8
47324 Boston 189 H5
47921 Boswell 810 C3
46504 Bourbon 1,522 E2
47833 Bowling Green 200 D6
47107 Bradford 350 E8
47834 Brazil⊙ 7,852 C5
46506 Bremen 3,565 E2
47836 Bridgeton 250 C5
†45030 Bright 450 H6
46720 Brimfield 292 G2
46913 Bringhurst 275 E3
46507 Bristol 1,203 F1
47922 Brook 926 C3
46111 Brooklyn 889 E5
†47250 Brooksburg 132 G7
47923 Brookston 1,701 D3
47012 Brookville⊙ 2,874 G6
46112 Brownsburg 6,242 E5
47220 Brownstown⊙ 2,704 F7
47325 Brownsville 250 H5
47516 Bruceville 646 C7
47326 Bryant 277 G3
47924 Buck Creek 225 D4
47647 Buckskin 200 C8
47925 Buffalo 500 D3
46914 Bunker Hill 984 E3
46508 Burket 260 F2
46915 Burlington 680 E4
47926 Burnettsville 496 D3
47222 Burney 300 F6
†46401 Burns Harbor 920 C1
46916 Burrows 250 E3
46721 Butler 2,509 H2
47223 Butlerville 300 F6
†46371 Byron 200 C5
†47362 Cadiz 180 G5
47327 Cambridge City 2,407 G5
46917 Camden 618 D3
47108 Campbellsburg 695 E7
47224 Canaan 90 G7
47519 Cannelburg 152 C7
47520 Cannelton⊙ 2,373 D9
47837 Carbon 307 C5
47838 Carlisle 717 C7
46032 Carmel 18,272 E5
46114 Cartersburg 300 E5
46115 Carthage 886 F5
47927 Cates 125 C4
47928 Cayuga 1,258 C5
47016 Cedar Grove 217 H6
46303 Cedar Lake 8,754 C2
47521 Celestine 150 D8
†47842 Centenary 150 B5
†46901 Center 310 E4
47840 Centerpoint 242 C6
46116 Centerton 250 E5
47330 Centerville 2,284 H5
47929 Chalmers 554 D3
47610 Chandler 3,043 C8
47111 Charlestown 5,596 F8
46117 Charlottesville 300 F5
†47138 Chelsea 200 F7
46017 Chesterfield 2,701 F4
46304 Chesterton 8,531 D1
47611 Chrisney 537 C8
46723 Churubusco 1,638 G2
46034 Cicero 2,557 E4
47225 Clarksburg 300 G6
47930 Clarks Hill 653 D4
47130 Clarksville 15,164 F8
47841 Clay City 883 C6
46510 Claypool 464 F2
46118 Clayton 703 D5
47426 Clear Creek 200 E6
†46737 Clear Lake 301 H1
47226 Clifford 310 F6
47842 Clinton 5,267 C5
46120 Cloverdale 1,357 D5
†47834 Cloverland 175 C6
47427 Coal City 225 D6
47845 Coalmont 450 C6
46121 Coatesville 474 D5
47931 Colburn 300 D3
46035 Colfax 823 D4
47978 Collegeville 1,059 C3
46725 Columbia City⊙ 5,091 G2
47201 Columbus⊙ 30,614 E6
47331 Connersville⊙ 17,023 G5
46919 Converse 1,279 F3
47228 Cortland 175 F7
46730 Corunna 304 G2
47112 Corydon⊙ 2,724 E8
47932 Covington⊙ 2,883 C4
†47302 Cowan 428 G4
47114 Crandall 176 E8
47522 Crane D7
47933 Crawfordsville⊙ 13,325 D4
46732 Cromwell 458 F2
47229 Crothersville 1,747 F7
46307 Crown Point⊙ 16,455 C2
46511 Culver 1,601 E2
46229 Cumberland 3,375 E5
47612 Cynthiana 874 B8
47523 Dale 1,693 D8
47334 Daleville F4
47847 Dana 803 C5
46122 Danville⊙ 4,220 D5
47940 Darlington 811 D4
47618 Darmstadt 1,280 B8
47941 Dayton 781 D4
46733 Decatur⊙ 8,649 H3
47524 Decker 256 B7
†46917 Deer Creek 250 E3
46923 Delphi⊙ 3,042 D3
46310 Demotte 2,559 C2
46926 Denver 589 E3
47230 Deputy 200 F7
47302 Desoto 385 G4
47018 Dillsboro 1,038 G6
46513 Donaldson 320 E2
†47118 Doolittle Mills 200 D8
47335 Dublin 979 G5
47525 Dubois 550 D8
47848 Dugger 1,118 C6
†46304 Dune Acres 291 C1
47336 Dunkirk 3,180 G4
†46514 Dunlap 5,397 F1
47337 Dunreith 184 F5
47231 Dupont 392 G7
46311 Dyer 9,555 C1
†46074 Eagletown 306 E4
47942 Earl Park 469 C3
46312 East Chicago 39,786 C1
47019 East Enterprise 250 H7
†47370 East Germantown (Pershing) 438 G5
47338 Eaton 1,804 G4
47116 Eckerty 108 D8
47339 Economy 237 G5
†46011 Edgewood 2,215 F4
46124 Edinburgh 4,856 E6
47528 Edwardsport 459 C7
†47150 Edwardsville 700 F8
47613 Elberfeld 640 C8
47117 Elizabeth 178 F8
47232 Elizabethtown 603 F6
46514 Elkhart 41,305 F1
Elkhart‡ 137,330 F1
47429 Ellettsville 3,328 D6
47529 Elnora 756 C7
†47018 Elrod 200 G6
†47901 Elston 500 D4
46036 Elwood 10,867 F4
46125 Eminence 200 D5
47118 English⊙ 633 E8
46524 Etna Green 522 E2
†47928 Eugene 400 B5
*47701 Evansville⊙ 130,496 C9
Evansville‡ 309,408 C9
†47331 Everton 500 G5
46126 Fairland 950 F5
46928 Fairmount 3,286 F4
†47842 Fairview Park 1,545 C5
47850 Farmersburg 1,240 C6
47340 Farmland 1,560 G4
†47421 Fayetteville 180 D7
47532 Ferdinand 2,192 D8
46128 Fillmore 550 D5
46129 Finly 400 F5
46038 Fishers 2,008 E5
47234 Flat Rock 323 F6
46929 Flora 2,303 E3
47119 Floyds Knobs 500 F8
47851 Fontanet 325 C5
46039 Forest 400 E4
47648 Fort Branch 2,504 B8
46040 Fortville 2,787 F5
*46801 Fort Wayne⊙ 172,028 G2
Fort Wayne‡ 382,961 G2
47341 Fountain City 839 H5
46130 Fountaintown 225 F5
47944 Fowler⊙ 2,319 C3
46930 Fowlerton 300 F4
47946 Francesville 944 D3
47649 Francisco 612 B8
46041 Frankfort⊙ 15,168 E4
46131 Franklin⊙ 11,563 E6
46044 Frankton 2,080 F4
47120 Fredericksburg 233 E8
47431 Freedom 100 D6
47535 Freelandville 600 C7
47235 Freetown 600 E7
46737 Fremont 1,180 H1
47432 French Lick 2,265 D7
46931 Fulton 393 E3
†47119 Galena 1,186 F8
46932 Galveston 1,822 E3
46738 Garrett 4,751 G2
*46401 Gary 151,953 C1
Gary-Hammond-East Chicago‡ 642,781 C1
46933 Gas City 6,370 F4
47342 Gaston 1,150 G4
46740 Geneva 1,430 H3
47537 Gentryville 299 C8
47122 Georgetown 1,494 F8
46133 Glenwood 370 G5
†47567 Glezen 300 C8
46045 Goldsmith 235 E4

(continued on following page)

Agriculture, Industry and Resources

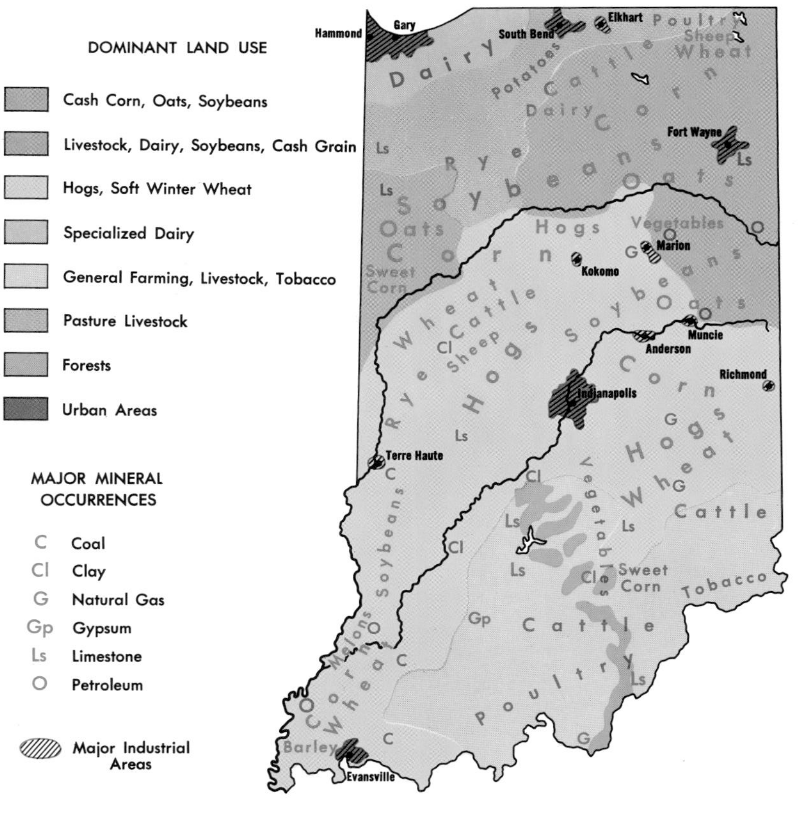
DOMINANT LAND USE
Cash Corn, Oats, Soybeans
Livestock, Dairy, Soybeans, Cash Grain
Hogs, Soft Winter Wheat
Specialized Dairy
General Farming, Livestock, Tobacco
Pasture Livestock
Forests
Urban Areas
MAJOR MINERAL OCCURRENCES
C Coal
Cl Clay
G Natural Gas
Gp Gypsum
Ls Limestone
O Petroleum
Major Industrial Areas
Hammond
Gary
South Bend
Elkhart
Fort Wayne
Marion
Kokomo
Muncie
Anderson
Richmond
Indianapolis
Terre Haute
Evansville
Poultry
Sheep
Wheat
Dairy
Potatoes
Cattle
Corn
Rye
Soybeans
Oats
Hogs
Vegetables
Sweet Corn
Tobacco
Melons
Barley

47948 Goodland 1,200 .... C3
46526 Goshen⊙ 19,665 .... F1
47433 Gosport 729 .... D6
46741 Grabill 658 .... H2
47615 Grandview 670 .... C9
46530 Granger 350 .... E1
46135 Greencastle⊙ 8,403 .... D5
†47025 Greendale 3,795 .... H6
46140 Greenfield⊙ 11,299 .... F5
47344 Greensboro 175 .... G5
47240 Greensburg⊙ 9,254 .... G6
47345 Greens Fork 426 .... H5
46936 Greentown 2,265 .... E4
47124 Greenville 537 .... F8
46142 Greenwood 19,327 .... E5
47616 Griffin 192 .... B8
46319 Griffith 17,026 .... C1
46144 Gwynneville 250 .... F5
47346 Hagerstown 1,950 .... G5
46742 Hamilton 587 .... H1
46532 Hamlet 738 .... D2
*46320 Hammond 93,714 .... B1
46340 Hanna 550 .... D2
47243 Hanover 4,054 .... F7
47125 Hardinsburg 298 .... E8
46743 Harlan 840 .... H2
47853 Harmony 613 .... C5
47434 Harrodsburg 400 .... D6
47348 Hartford City⊙ 7,622 .... G4
47244 Hartsville 379 .... F6
47617 Hatfield 800 .... C9
47639 Haubstadt 1,389 .... B8
†47546 Haysville 600 .... D8
47640 Hazleton 368 .... B8
46341 Hebron 2,696 .... C2
47436 Heltonville 400 .... E7
46937 Hemlock 300 .... F4
47126 Henryville 1,132 .... F7
46322 Highland 25,935 .... B1
47949 Hillsboro 561 .... C4
47854 Hillsdale 500 .... C5
46745 Hoagland 600 .... H3
46342 Hobart 22,987 .... C1
46047 Hobbs 200 .... F4
47541 Holland 683 .... C8
47023 Holton 487 .... G6
46146 Homer 235 .... F5
47246 Hope 2,185 .... F6
†46069 Hortonville 240 .... E4
46746 Howe 800 .... G1
46747 Hudson 447 .... G1
46552 Hudson Lake 1,347 .... D1
46748 Huntertown 1,265 .... G2
47542 Huntingburg 5,376 .... D8
46750 Huntington⊙ 16,202 .... G3
†46064 Huntsville 120 .... G4
47437 Huron 250 .... D7
47855 Hymera 1,054 .... C6
47950 Idaville 655 .... D3
*46201 Indianapolis (cap.)⊙ 700,807 .... E5
Indianapolis‡ 1,166,929 .... E5
†46601 Indian Village 151 .... E1
46048 Ingalls 909 .... F5
47545 Ireland 600 .... C8
46147 Jamestown 924 .... D5
47438 Jasonville 2,497 .... C6
47546 Jasper⊙ 9,097 .... D8
47130 Jeffersonville⊙ 21,220 .... F8
†47565 Johnson 100 .... B8
†46074 Jolietville 300 .... E4
46938 Jonesboro 2,279 .... F4
47247 Jonesville 213 .... F6
46049 Kempton 410 .... E4
46755 Kendallville 7,299 .... G2
47351 Kennard 441 .... G5
47951 Kentland⊙ 1,936 .... C3
46939 Kewanna 711 .... E2
46759 Keystone 204 .... G3
46760 Kimmell 250 .... F2
47952 Kingman 566 .... C5
46345 Kingsbury 329 .... D1
46346 Kingsford Heights 1,618 .... D2
46050 Kirklin 662 .... E4
46148 Knightstown 2,325 .... F5
47857 Knightsville 763 .... C5
46534 Knox⊙ 3,674 .... D2
46901 Kokomo⊙ 47,808 .... E4
Kokomo‡ 103,715 .... E4
†46574 Koontz Lake 1,436 .... D2
46347 Kouts 1,619 .... C2
46348 La Crosse 713 .... D2
47954 Ladoga 1,151 .... D5
*47901 Lafayette⊙ 43,011 .... D4
Lafayette-West Lafayette‡ 121,702 .... D4
46940 La Fontaine 946 .... F3
46761 Lagrange⊙ 2,164 .... F1
46941 Lagro 549 .... F3
†46157 Lake Hart 231 .... E5
†46703 Lake James 400 .... H1
46943 Laketon 500 .... F3
46349 Lake Village 900 .... C2
46536 Lakeville 629 .... E1
46944 Landess 150 .... F3
47136 Lanesville 570 .... E8
46763 Laotto 361 .... G2
46537 Lapaz 651 .... E2
46051 Lapel 1,881 .... F4
46350 LaPorte⊙ 21,796 .... D1
46764 Larwill 286 .... F2
47024 Laurel 819 .... G6
46226 Lawrence 25,591 .... E5
47025 Lawrenceburg⊙ 4,403 .... H6
47137 Leavenworth 356 .... E8
46052 Lebanon⊙ 11,456 .... D4
46538 Leesburg 629 .... F2
46945 Leiters Ford 280 .... E2
46765 Leo 500 .... G2
47551 Leopold 175 .... D8
46355 Leroy 400 .... C2
†47240 Letts 247 .... F6
47352 Lewisville 577 .... G5
47138 Lexington F7
47353 Liberty⊙ 1,844 .... H5
46766 Liberty Center 275 .... G3
46946 Liberty Mills 200 .... F2
46767 Ligonier 3,134 .... F2
47955 Linden 700 .... D4
46769 Linn Grove 175 .... H3
47441 Linton 6,315 .... C6
†46755 Lisbon 200 .... G2
47139 Little York 150 .... F7
46149 Lizton 456 .... D5
46947 Logansport⊙ 17,731 .... E3
†46360 Long Beach 2,262 .... D1
47553 Loogootee 3,100 .... D7
47354 Losantville 306 .... G4
46356 Lowell 5,827 .... C2
46950 Lucerne 135 .... E3
†46601 Lydick E1
†47874 Lyford 400 .... C5
47355 Lynn 1,250 .... H4
47619 Lynnville 566 .... C8
47443 Lyons 782 .... C7
46951 Macy 282 .... E3
47250 Madison⊙ 12,472 .... G7
47555 Magnet 75 .... D8
†47001 Manchester 250 .... H6
46150 Manilla 350 .... F5
†47872 Mansfield 200 .... C5
†47443 Marco 150 .... C7
47140 Marengo 892 .... E8
47556 Mariah Hill 300 .... D8
†46176 Marietta 234 .... F6
46952 Marion⊙ 35,874 .... F3
46770 Markle 975 .... G3
46056 Markleville 427 .... F5
47859 Marshall 413 .... C5
46151 Martinsville⊙ 11,311 .... D6
46957 Matthews 745 .... F4
46154 Maxwell 300 .... F5
46055 McCordsville 600 .... F5
47860 Mecca 482 .... C5
47957 Medaryville 731 .... D2
47260 Medora 853 .... E7
47958 Mellott 294 .... C4
47143 Memphis 300 .... F8
46539 Mentone 973 .... E2
47861 Merom 360 .... B6
46410 Merrillville 27,677 .... C2
47030 Metamora 350 .... G6
†46703 Metz 200 .... H1
46958 Mexico 850 .... E3
46959 Miami 350 .... E3
†49117 Michiana Shores 464 .... D1
46360 Michigan City 36,850 .... C1
46057 Michigantown 453 .... E4
46540 Middlebury 1,665 .... F1
47356 Middletown 2,978 .... F4
47445 Midland 250 .... C6
47031 Milan 1,566 .... G6
46542 Milford 1,153 .... F2
†47240 Milford 177 .... F6
46543 Millersburg 809 .... F1
47261 Millhousen 214 .... G6
47145 Milltown 1,006 .... E8
†47362 Millville 275 .... G5
46156 Milroy 750 .... G6
47357 Milton 729 .... G5
46544 Mishawaka 40,201 .... E1
47446 Mitchell 4,641 .... E7
47358 Modoc 243 .... G4
46771 Mongo 225 .... G1
47959 Monon 1,540 .... D3
46772 Monroe 739 .... H3
47557 Monroe City 569 .... C7
46773 Monroeville 1,372 .... H3
46157 Monrovia 800 .... E5
46960 Monterey 236 .... D2
47862 Montezuma 1,352 .... C5
47558 Montgomery 390 .... C7
47960 Monticello⊙ 5,162 .... D3
47962 Montmorenci 300 .... D4
47359 Montpelier 1,995 .... G3
47360 Mooreland 479 .... G5
47032 Moores Hill 566 .... G6
46158 Mooresville 5,349 .... E5
46160 Morgantown 897 .... E6
47963 Morocco 1,348 .... C3
47033 Morris 350 .... G6
46161 Morristown 989 .... F5
†47327 Mount Auburn 192 .... G5
47964 Mount Ayr 207 .... C3
47361 Mount Summit 357 .... G4
47620 Mount Vernon⊙ 7,656 .... B9
46058 Mulberry 1,225 .... D4
*47302 Muncie⊙ 77,216 .... G4
Muncie‡ G4
46321 Munster 20,671 .... B1
47147 Nabb 150 .... F7
47034 Napoleon 246 .... G6
46550 Nappanee 4,694 .... F2
47448 Nashville⊙ 705 .... E6
†47421 Needmore 200 .... E7
47150 New Albany⊙ 37,103 .... F8
47449 Newberry 246 .... C7
47630 Newburgh 2,906 .... C9
46552 New Carlisle 1,439 .... E1
47362 New Castle⊙ 20,056 .... G5
†46342 New Chicago 3,284 .... C1
47863 New Goshen 500 .... B5
47631 New Harmony 945 .... B8
46774 New Haven 6,714 .... H2
47366 New Lisbon 300 .... G5
†46979 New London 200 .... E4
47965 New Market 608 .... D5
46163 New Palestine 749 .... F5
46553 New Paris 1,062 .... F2
†47165 New Pekin 1,125 .... F7
47263 New Point 296 .... G6
47966 Newport⊙ 704 .... C5
†47106 New Providence (Borden) 384 .... F8
47967 New Richmond 403 .... D4
47968 New Ross 306 .... D5
†46173 New Salem 200 .... G5
47161 New Salisbury 350 .... E8
47632 Newtonville 136 .... D8
47969 Newtown 277 .... C4
47035 New Trenton 200 .... H6
47162 New Washington 800 .... F7
46961 New Waverly 162 .... E3
46184 New Whiteland 4,502 .... E5
†46122 New Winchester 180 .... D5
46060 Noblesville⊙ 12,056 .... F4
46366 North Judson 1,653 .... D2
46554 North Liberty 1,211 .... E1
46962 North Manchester 5,998 .... F3
46165 North Salem 581 .... D5
47805 North Terre Haute C5
47265 North Vernon 5,768 .... F6
46555 North Webster 709 .... F2
†47960 Norway 300 .... D3
46556 Notre Dame E1
†47331 Nulltown 235 .... G5
46965 Oakford 325 .... E4
47660 Oakland City 3,301 .... C8
47561 Oaktown 776 .... C7
47367 Oakville 220 .... G4
47562 Odon 1,463 .... C7
†46401 Ogden Dunes 1,489 .... C1
47036 Oldenburg 770 .... G6
47451 Oolitic 1,495 .... E7
†47343 Orange 200 .... G5
46063 Orestes 539 .... F4
46776 Orland 424 .... G1
47452 Orleans 2,161 .... D7
46561 Osceola 1,990 .... E1
47037 Osgood 1,554 .... G6
46777 Ossian 1,945 .... G3
46367 Otis 250 .... D1
47163 Otisco 425 .... F7
47970 Otterbein 1,118 .... C4
47564 Otwell 600 .... C8
47453 Owensburg 785 .... D7
47665 Owensville 1,261 .... B8
47971 Oxford 1,327 .... C3
†46508 Palestine 800 .... F2
47164 Palmyra 692 .... E8
47454 Paoli⊙ 3,637 .... E7
46166 Paragon 538 .... D6
47368 Parker City 1,414 .... G4
47666 Patoka 832 .... B8
47455 Patricksburg 250 .... D6
47038 Patriot 265 .... H7
47865 Paxton 200 .... C6
47165 Pekin 950 .... E7
46064 Pendleton 2,130 .... F5
47369 Pennville 805 .... G4
†46011 Perkinsville 175 .... F4
47974 Perrysville 532 .... C4
47370 Pershing 438 .... G5
†46975 Pershing 425 .... E2
46970 Peru⊙ 13,764 .... E3
47567 Petersburg⊙ 2,987 .... C7
46778 Petroleum 212 .... G3
46562 Pierceton 1,086 .... F2
47866 Pimento 150 .... C6
†46350 Pine Lake 1,676 .... D1
47975 Pine Village 257 .... C4
46167 Pittsboro 891 .... D5
†46923 Pittsburg 175 .... D3
46168 Plainfield 9,191 .... E5
47568 Plainville 556 .... C7
46779 Pleasant Lake 800 .... H1
46563 Plymouth⊙ 7,693 .... E2
47868 Poland 230 .... C6
46781 Poneto 250 .... G3
46368 Portage 27,409 .... C1
46304 Porter 2,988 .... C1
47371 Portland⊙ 7,074 .... H4
47633 Poseyville 1,247 .... B8
†46360 Pottawattamie Park 284 .... C1
47869 Prairie Creek 275 .... C6
47870 Prairieton 200 .... B6
46782 Preble 150 .... H3
†46164 Princes Lakes 937 .... E6
47670 Princeton⊙ 8,976 .... B8
46170 Putnamville 250 .... D5
47456 Quincy 250 .... D6
47573 Ragsdale 135 .... C7
46737 Ray 200 .... H1
†47274 Reddington 400 .... F6
46171 Reelsville 210 .... D5
47977 Remington 1,268 .... C3
47978 Rensselaer⊙ 4,944 .... C3
47980 Reynolds 632 .... D3
47634 Richland 500 .... C9
47374 Richmond⊙ 41,349 .... H5
47380 Ridgeville 933 .... G4
47871 Riley 269 .... C6
47040 Rising Sun⊙ 2,478 .... H7
46172 Roachdale 958 .... D5
46974 Roann 548 .... F3
46783 Roanoke 891 .... G3
46975 Rochester⊙ 5,050 .... E2
46977 Rockfield 300 .... D3
47635 Rockport⊙ 2,590 .... C9
47872 Rockville⊙ 2,785 .... C5
46371 Rolling Prairie 550 .... D1
47574 Rome 50 .... D9
46784 Rome City 1,319 .... G1
47981 Romney 250 .... D4
47874 Rosedale 744 .... C5
†46601 Roseland 832 .... E1
†46310 Roselawn 200 .... C2
46065 Rossville 1,148 .... D4
46978 Royal Center 908 .... E3
†47302 Royerton 300 .... G4
46173 Rushville⊙ 6,113 .... G5
46175 Russellville 376 .... D5
46975 Russiaville 973 .... E4
47575 Saint Anthony 470 .... D8
47875 Saint Bernice 500 .... C5
46785 Saint Joe 546 .... H2
46383 Saint John 3,974 .... C2
46373 Saint Leon 515 .... H6
47876 Saint Mary-of-the-Woods 920 .... B6
†46556 Saint Marys E1
47577 Saint Meinrad 910 .... D8
47272 Saint Paul 976 .... F6
†47012 Saint Peter 175 .... H6
†47620 Saint Philip 400 .... B9
†47638 Saint Wendel 250 .... B8
47167 Salem⊙ 5,290 .... E7
47578 Sandborn 576 .... C7
†47401 Sanders 65 .... E6
46374 San Pierre 325 .... D2
47579 Santa Claus 514 .... D8
47382 Saratoga 338 .... H4
†47283 Sardinia 133 .... F6
46375 Schererville 13,209 .... C2
46376 Schneider 364 .... C2
47580 Schnellville 250 .... D8
47273 Scipio 200 .... F6
46066 Scircleville 125 .... E4
47170 Scottsburg⊙ 5,068 .... F7
47878 Seelyville 1,374 .... C6
47172 Sellersburg 3,211 .... F8
47383 Selma 1,056 .... G4
47274 Seymour 15,050 .... F7
46068 Sharpsville 617 .... E4
47879 Shelburn 1,259 .... C6
46377 Shelby 700 .... C2
46176 Shelbyville⊙ 14,989 .... F6
47880 Shepardsville 325 .... B5
46069 Sheridan 2,200 .... E4
†47338 Shideler 275 .... G4
46565 Shipshewana 466 .... F1
47384 Shirley 919 .... F5
†46797 Shirley City (Woodburn) 1,002 .... H2
47581 Shoals⊙ 967 .... D7
46566 Sidney 194 .... F2
46982 Silver Lake 576 .... F2
46983 Sims 250 .... F3
†46142 Smith Valley E5
47458 Smithville 500 .... D6
46984 Somerset 350 .... F3
47683 Somerville 340 .... C8
*46601 South Bend⊙ 109,727 .... E1
South Bend‡ 280,772 .... E1
46786 South Milford 270 .... G1
†46201 Southport 2,266 .... E5
46787 South Whitley 1,575 .... F2
†47355 Spartanburg 201 .... H4
47172 Speed 800 .... F8
46224 Speedway 12,641 .... E5
†47808 Spelterville 200 .... C5
47460 Spencer⊙ 2,732 .... D6
46788 Spencerville 400 .... G2
47385 Spiceland 940 .... F5
†47374 Spring Grove 469 .... H5
†46140 Spring Lake 236 .... F5
47386 Springport 221 .... G4
47462 Springville 279 .... D7
47584 Spurgeon 250 .... C8
47463 Stanford 200 .... D6
46985 Star City 351 .... D3
47982 State Line 233 .... C4
47881 Staunton 607 .... C6
47585 Stendal 175 .... C8
47636 Stewartsville 225 .... B8
46180 Stilesville 350 .... D5
46351 Stillwell 225 .... D1
47464 Stinesville 227 .... D6
47983 Stockwell 310 .... D4
47387 Straughn 331 .... G5
46789 Stroh 350 .... G1
47882 Sullivan⊙ 4,774 .... C6
47388 Sulphur Springs 345 .... G4
46379 Sumava Resorts 300 .... C2
46070 Summitville 1,085 .... F4
47041 Sunman 924 .... G6
46987 Sweetser 944 .... F3
47465 Switz City 300 .... C6
46567 Syracuse 2,579 .... F2
47280 Taylorsville 1,247 .... F6
47586 Tell City 8,704 .... D9
47637 Tennyson 331 .... C8
*47801 Terre Haute⊙ 61,125 .... C6
Terre Haute‡ 176,583 .... C6
46381 Thayer 350 .... C2
46071 Thorntown 1,468 .... D4
†46975 Tiosa 100 .... E2
46570 Tippecanoe 320 .... E2
46072 Tipton⊙ 5,004 .... E4
46571 Topeka 876 .... F1
†46360 Town of Pines 962 .... D1
46181 Trafalgar 466 .... E6
†46360 Trail Creek 2,581 .... D1
†46725 Tri Lakes 1,356 .... G2
47588 Troy 550 .... D9
46988 Twelve Mile 240 .... E3
46572 Tyner 245 .... E2
47177 Underwood 550 .... F7
47390 Union City 3,908 .... H4
46791 Uniondale 303 .... G3
46382 Union Mills 650 .... D2
47468 Unionville 225 .... E6
47884 Universal 428 .... C5
46989 Upland 3,335 .... F4
46990 Urbana 400 .... F3
†47130 Utica 501 .... F8
47281 Vallonia 550 .... E7
46383 Valparaiso⊙ 22,247 .... C2
46991 Van Buren 935 .... F3
47987 Veedersburg 2,261 .... C4
47590 Velpen 375 .... C8
47282 Vernon⊙ 329 .... F7
47042 Versailles⊙ 1,560 .... G6
47043 Vevay⊙ 1,343 .... G7
†47441 Vicksburg 175 .... C6
†47170 Vienna 175 .... F7
47591 Vincennes⊙ 20,857 .... C7
46992 Wabash⊙ 12,985 .... F3
47638 Wadesville 450 .... B8
46573 Wakarusa 1,281 .... F1
46182 Waldron 850 .... F6
†47201 Walesboro 214 .... F6
46574 Walkerton 2,051 .... E2
†46802 Wallen 945 .... G2
46994 Walton 1,202 .... E3
46390 Wanatah 879 .... D2
46792 Warren 1,254 .... G3
46580 Warsaw⊙ 10,647 .... F2
47501 Washington⊙ 11,325 .... C7
46793 Waterloo 1,951 .... G2
†47130 Watson 200 .... F8
47989 Waveland 559 .... D5
46794 Wawaka 320 .... F2
47990 Waynetown 915 .... C4
47392 Webster 350 .... H5
47469 West Baden Springs 796 .... D7
†47353 West College Corner 614 .... H5
46074 Westfield 2,783 .... E4

Topography

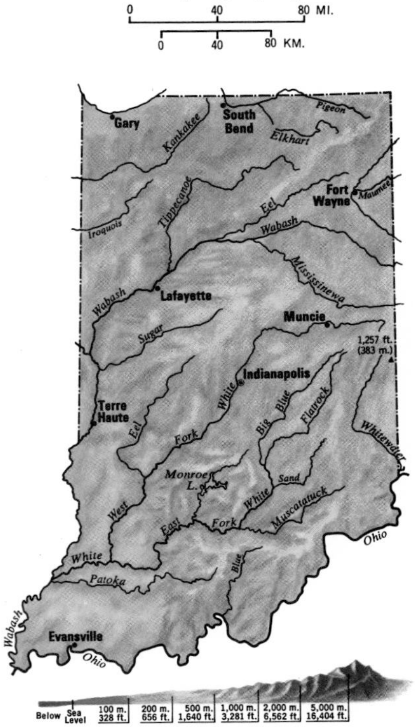

†45030 West Harrison 328 .... H6
47906 West Lafayette 21,247 .... D4
47991 West Lebanon 946 .... C4
46995 West Middleton 327 .... E4
47596 Westphalia 300 .... C7
47992 Westpoint 375 .... C4
47283 Westport 1,450 .... F6
47885 West Terre Haute 2,806 .... B6
46391 Westville 2,887 .... D1
46392 Wheatfield 755 .... C2
47597 Wheatland 532 .... C7
46393 Wheeler 540 .... C1
†47342 Wheeling 180 .... G4
46184 Whiteland 1,956 .... E5
46075 Whitestown 497 .... E5
46394 Whiting 5,630 .... C1
46186 Wilkinson 493 .... F5
47470 Williams 350 .... D7
47993 Williamsport⊙ 1,747 .... C4
46996 Winamac⊙ 2,370 .... D2
47394 Winchester⊙ 5,659 .... G4
46076 Windfall 911 .... F4
47994 Wingate 373 .... C4
46590 Winona Lake 2,827 .... F2
47598 Winslow 1,017 .... C8
47995 Wolcott 923 .... C3
46795 Wolcottville 890 .... G1
46796 Wolflake 230 .... F2
46797 Woodburn 1,002 .... H2
†46624 Woodland 400 .... E1
47471 Worthington 1,574 .... C6
46595 Wyatt 250 .... E1
†47630 Yankeetown 250 .... C9
46798 Yoder 250 .... G3
47396 Yorktown 3,945 .... G4
46998 Young America 259 .... E3
†47808 Youngstown 350 .... C6
46799 Zanesville 575 .... G3
46077 Zionsville 3,948 .... E5

OTHER FEATURES

Anderson (riv.) D8
Bass (lake) D2
Beanblossom (creek) D6
Big (creek) B8
Big Blue (riv.) F5
Big Pine (creek) C3
Big Raccoon (creek) C5
Big Walnut (creek) D5
Blue (riv.) E8
Brookville (lake) G6
Buck (creek) E8
Busseron (creek) C7
Camp (creek) E6
Cedar (creek) G2
Clifty (creek) F6
Coal (creek) C4
Crooked (creek) D2
Cypress (pond) B8
Deer (creek) E3
Deer (creek) D5
Eagle (creek) E4
Eel (riv.) C6
Eel (riv.) F3
Elkhart (riv.) F1
Fawn (riv.) G1
Flatrock (creek) F5
Fort Benjamin Harrison E5
Freeman (lake) D3
Geist (res.) F5
George Rogers Clark Nat'l Hist. Park B7
Graham (creek) F7
Grissom A.F.B. 4,676 .... E3
Huntington (lake) F3
Indian (creek) E8
Indian (creek) D6
Indiana Dunes Nat'l Lakeshore C1
Iroquois (riv.) B3
Jefferson Proving Ground G7
Kankakee (riv.) C2
Lemon (lake) E6
Lincoln Boyhood Nat'l Mem. C8
Little (riv.) G3
Little Elkhart (riv.) F1
Little Pigeon (creek) C9
Little Vermilion (riv.) B5
Lost (riv.) D7
Maria (creek) C7
Maumee (riv.) H2
Maxinkuckee (lake) E2
Michigan (lake) C1
Mill (creek) D5
Mississinewa (lake) F3
Mississinewa (riv.) F3
Monroe (lake) E6
Morse (res.) E4
Muscatatuck (riv.) E7
Ohio (riv.) B9
Patoka (riv.) C8
Pigeon (creek) C8
Pigeon (riv.) F1
Pipe (creek) F4
Prairie (creek) C7
Richland (creek) D6
Saint Joseph (riv.) E1
Saint Joseph (riv.) H2
Saint Marys (lake) H3
Saint Marys (riv.) H3
Salamonie (lake) F3
Salamonie (riv.) G4
Salt (creek) E6
Sand (creek) F6
Shafer (lake) D3
Silver (creek) F8
Sugar (creek) C5
Sugar (creek) F5
Sugar (creek) B3
Tippecanoe (riv.) E2
Vermilion (riv.) B4
Vernon Fork (creek) F7
Wabash (riv.) B7
Wawasee (lake) F2
White (riv.) B8
White, East Fork (riv.) C7
White, West Fork (riv.) C7
Whitewater (riv.) H6
Wildcat (creek) E4

⊙County seat.
‡Population of metropolitan area.
† Zip of nearest p.o. * Multiple zips.

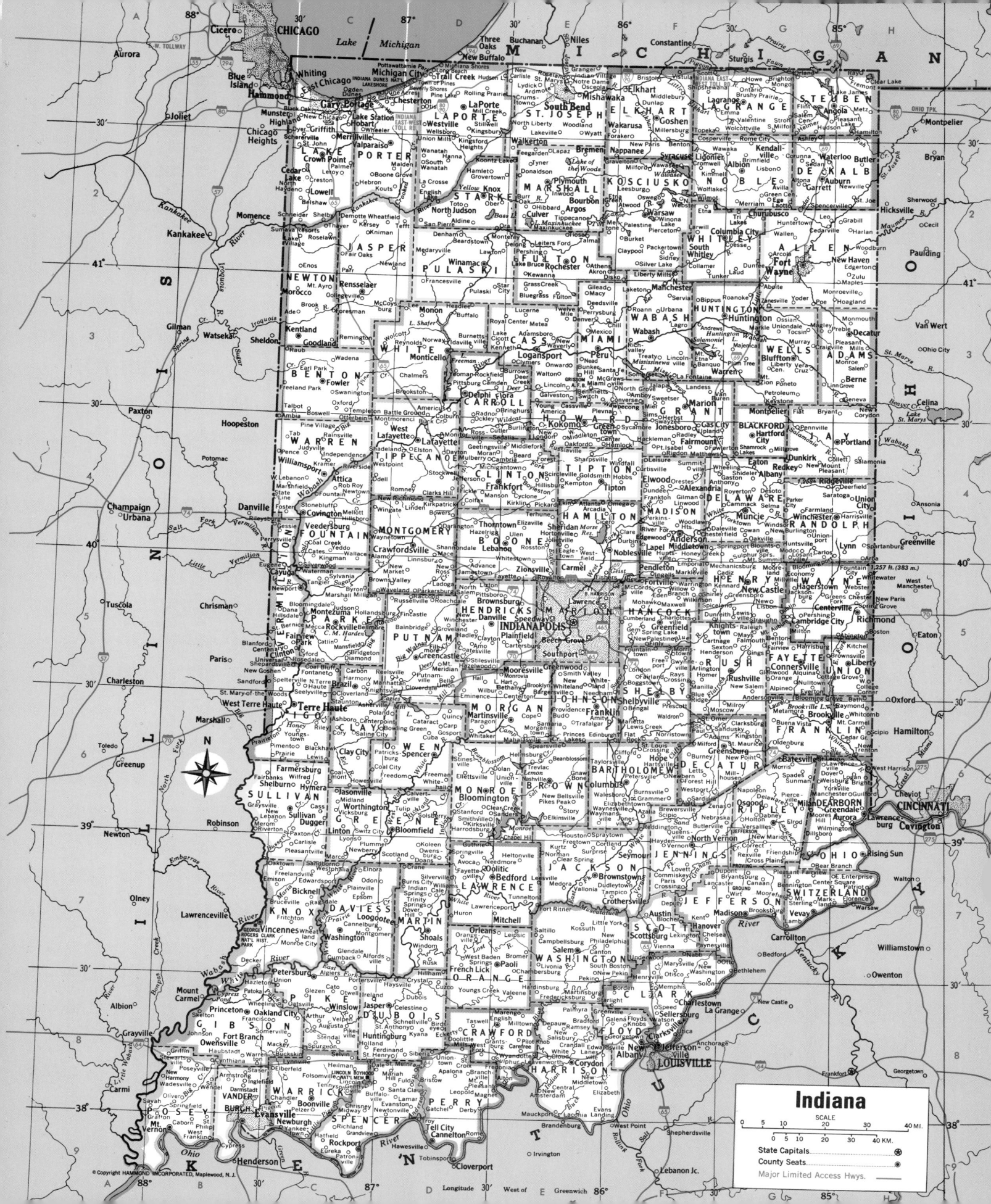

Indiana

SCALE
0 5 10   20   30   40 MI.
0 5 10   20   30   40 KM.

State Capitals........................ ⊛
County Seats......................... ⊙
Major Limited Access Hwys. _____

228 Iowa

51433 Auburn 320 ....D4
50025 Audubon⊙ 2,841 ....C5
51005 Aurelia 1,143 ....C3
50607 Aurora 248 ....K3
51521 Avoca 1,650 ....C6
50515 Ayrshire 243 ....D2
50516 Badger 653 ....E3
50026 Bagley 370 ....E5
50517 Bancroft 1,082 ....E2
50027 Barnes City 266 ....J7
52533 Batavia 525 ....J7
51006 Battle Creek 919 ....B4
50028 Baxter 951 ....G5
50029 Bayard 637 ....D5
52534 Beacon 530 ....H6
50833 Bedford⊙ 1,692 ....D7
52208 Belle Plaine 2,903 ......J5
52031 Bellevue 2,450 ....M4
50421 Belmond 2,505 ....F3
52721 Bennett 458 ....L5
50032 Berwick 600 ....G5
52722 Bettendorf 27,381 ......N5
52535 Birmingham 410 ....K7
50034 Blairsburg 288 ....F4

52209 Blairstown 695 ....J5
52536 Blakesburg 404 ....H7
51523 Blencoe 247 ....A5
50836 Blockton 280 ....D7
52537 Bloomfield⊙ 2,849 .....J7
52726 Blue Grass 1,377 ....M5
50519 Bode 406 ....E3
52620 Bonaparte 489 ....K7
50035 Bondurant 1,283 ....G5
50036 Boone⊙ 12,602 ....F4
50040 Boxholm 267 ....E4
51234 Boyden 708 ....B2
52210 Brandon 337 ....K4
51436 Breda 502 ....C4
50837 Bridgewater 233 ....D6
52540 Brighton 804 ....K6
50611 Bristow 252 ....H3
50423 Britt 2,185 ....F2
51007 Bronson 289 ....A4
52211 Brooklyn 1,509 ....J5
52728 Buffalo 1,569 ....M6
50424 Buffalo Center 1,233 ...F2
52601 Burlington⊙ 29,529 ...L7
50522 Burt 689 ....E2

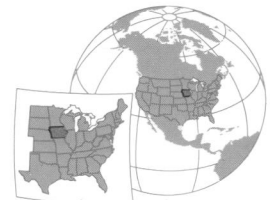

AREA 56,275 sq. mi. (145,752 sq. km.)
POPULATION 2,913,808
CAPITAL Des Moines
LARGEST CITY Des Moines
HIGHEST POINT (Osceola Co.) 1670 ft. (509 m.)
SETTLED IN 1788
ADMITTED TO UNION December 28, 1846
POPULAR NAME Hawkeye State
STATE FLOWER Wild Rose
STATE BIRD Eastern Goldfinch

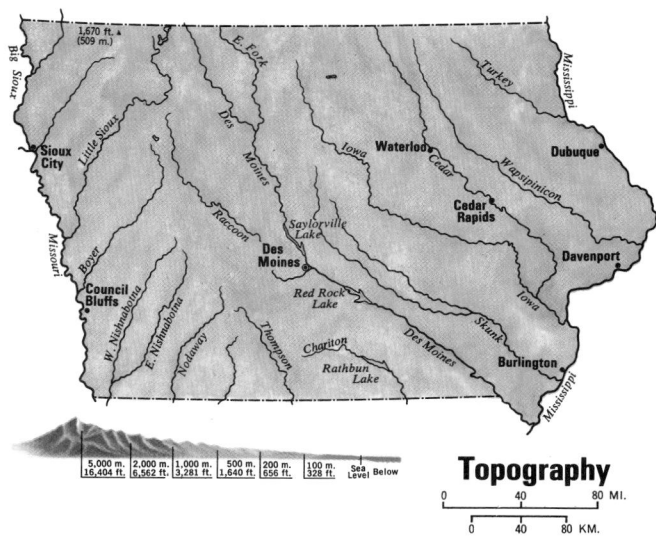

Topography

50044 Bussey 579 ....H6
52729 Calamus 452 ....M5
50523 Callender 446 ....E4
52132 Calmar 1,053 ....K2
52730 Camanche 4,725 ....N5
50046 Cambridge 732 ....G5
52542 Cantril 299 ....J7
50047 Carlisle 3,073 ....G6
51401 Carroll⊙ 9,705 ....D4
51525 Carson 716 ....C6
†68101 Carter Lake 3,438 ...E6
52033 Cascade 1,912 ....L4
50048 Casey 473 ....D5
50613 Cedar Falls 36,322 ....H3
*52401 Cedar Rapids⊙ 110,243 ..K5
 Cedar Rapids‡ 169,775 ..K5
52213 Center Point 1,591 .....K4
52544 Centerville⊙ 6,558 ....H7
52214 Central City 1,067 .....K4
50049 Chariton⊙ 4,987 ....G6
50616 Charles City 8,778 ....H2
52731 Charlotte 442 ....M5
51439 Charter Oak 615 ....C4
52215 Chelsea 376 ....J5
51012 Cherokee⊙ 7,004 ......B3
50050 Churdan 540 ....D4
52549 Cincinnati 598 ....G7
51632 Clarinda⊙ 5,458 ....C7
52216 Clarence 1,001 ....M5
50525 Clarion⊙ 3,060 ....F3
50619 Clarksville 1,424 ......H3
50840 Clearfield 433 ....D7
50428 Clear Lake 7,458 ......G2
51014 Cleghorn 275 ....B3
52134 Clermont 602 ....K3
52732 Clinton⊙ 32,828 ....N5
50318 Clive 6,064 ....F5
52217 Clutier 249 ....J4
52218 Coggon 639 ....L4
51636 Coin 316 ....C7
52035 Colesburg 463 ....L3
50054 Colfax 2,234 ....G5
51637 College Springs 307 ...C7
50055 Collins 451 ....G5
50056 Colo 808 ....G4
52737 Columbus City 367 ....L6
52738 Columbus Junction 1,429 ..L6
52739 Conesville 301 ....L6
50631 Conrad 1,133 ....H4
52220 Conroy 250 ....J5
50058 Coon Rapids 1,448 ....D5
52241 Coralville 7,687 ....K5
50841 Corning⊙ 1,939 ....D7
51016 Correctionville 935 ....B4
50430 Corwith 480 ....F3
50060 Corydon⊙ 1,818 ......G7
50431 Coulter 264 ....G3
51501 Council Bluffs⊙ 56,449 ..B6
52621 Crawfordsville 290 ....K6
51526 Crescent 547 ....B6
52136 Cresco⊙ 3,860 ....J2
50801 Creston⊙ 8,429 ....E6
50432 Crystal Lake 314 ......F2
50843 Cumberland 351 ......D6

51018 Cushing 270 ....B4
50529 Dakota City⊙ 1,072 ...E3
50062 Dallas 451 ....G6
50063 Dallas Center 1,360 ...F5
51019 Danbury 492 ....B4
52623 Danville 994 ....L7
*52801 Davenport⊙ 103,264 ..M5
 Davenport-Rock
 Island-Moline‡ 383,958 M5
50065 Davis City 327 ....F7
50530 Dayton 941 ....E4
52101 Decorah⊙ 7,991 ......K2
51440 Dedham 321 ....D5
52222 Deep River 323 ....J5
51527 Defiance 383 ....C5
52223 Delhi 511 ....L4
52037 Delmar 633 ....M4
51441 Deloit 345 ....C4
52550 Delta 482 ....J6
51442 Denison⊙ 6,675 ....C4
52624 Denmark 480 ....L7
50622 Denver 1,647 ....J3
*50301 Des Moines
 (cap.)⊙ 191,003 .....G5
 Des Moines‡ 338,048 ..G5
50069 De Soto 1,035 ....E5
50623 Dewar 230 ....J3
52742 De Witt 4,512 ....N5
50070 Dexter 678 ....E5
50845 Diagonal 362 ....E7
51333 Dickens 289 ....C2
50624 Dike 987 ....H4
52745 Dixon 312 ....M5
52746 Donahue 289 ....M5
52625 Donnellson 972 ......K7
51235 Doon 537 ....A2
52551 Douds 425 ....J7
51528 Dow City 616 ....B5
50071 Dows 771 ....F3
52001 Dubuque⊙ 62,321 .....M3
 Dubuque‡ 93,745 ......M3
50625 Dumont 815 ....H3
50532 Duncombe 504 ....E4
50626 Dunkerton 718 ....J3
51529 Dunlap 1,374 ....B5
52747 Durant 1,583 ....M5
52040 Dyersville 3,825 ......L3
52224 Dysart 1,355 ....J4
50533 Eagle Grove 4,324 ....F3
50072 Earlham 1,140 ....F6
51530 Earling 520 ....C5
52041 Earlville 844 ....L4
50535 Early 670 ....C4
52553 Eddyville 1,116 ....H6
52042 Edgewood 900 ....K3
52554 Eldon 1,255 ....J7
50627 Eldora⊙ 3,063 ....G4
52748 Eldridge 3,279 ....M5
52141 Elgin 702 ....K3
50073 Elkhart 256 ....F5
51531 Elk Horn 746 ....C6
†50700 Elk Run Heights 1,186 ..J4
51532 Elliott 493 ....C6

50075 Ellsworth 480 ....F4
50628 Elma 714 ....J2
52227 Ely 425 ....K5
51533 Emerson 502 ....C6
50536 Emmetsburg⊙ 4,621 ..D2
52045 Epworth 1,380 ....M4
51638 Essex 1,001 ....C7
51334 Estherville⊙ 7,518 ....D2
50707 Evansdale 4,798 ......J4
51338 Everly 796 ....C2
50076 Exira 978 ....D5
50629 Fairbank 980 ....K3
52228 Fairfax 683 ....K5
52556 Fairfield⊙ 9,428 ......J6
52046 Farley 1,287 ....L4
52047 Farmersburg 276 ......L3
52626 Farmington 869 ....K7
50538 Farnhamville 461 ......D4
51639 Farragut 426 ....C7
52142 Fayette 1,515 ....K3
50539 Fenton 394 ....E2
50434 Fertile 372 ....G2
50435 Floyd 408 ....H2
50540 Fonda 863 ....D3
50846 Fontanelle 805 ....E6
50436 Forest City⊙ 4,270 ...F2
52144 Fort Atkinson 374 .....J2
50501 Fort Dodge⊙ 29,423 ..E3
52627 Fort Madison⊙ 13,520 ..L7
51340 Fostoria 261 ....C2
50630 Fredericksburg 1,075 ..J3
50631 Frederika 223 ....J3
52561 Fremont 730 ....H6
52749 Fruitland 461 ....L6
51020 Galva 420 ....C3
50103 Garden Grove 297 ....F7
52049 Garnavillo 723 ....L3
50438 Garner⊙ 2,908 ....F2
52229 Garrison 411 ....J4
50632 Garwin 626 ....H4
51237 George 1,241 ....B2
50105 Gilbert 805 ....F4
50634 Gilbertville 740 ....J4
50106 Gilman 642 ....H5
50541 Gilmore City 626 ......D3
50635 Gladbrook 970 ....H4
51534 Glenwood⊙ 5,280 ....B6
51443 Glidden 1,076 ....D4
50542 Goldfield 789 ....F3
52750 Goose Lake 274 ......N5
50543 Gowrie 1,089 ....E4
51342 Graettinger 923 ......D2
50440 Grafton 255 ....G2
50107 Grand Junction 970 ...E4
52751 Grand Mound 674 ....M5
52752 Grandview 473 ....L6
50109 Granger 619 ....F5
51022 Gravity 336 ....B3
50848 Gravity 245 ....D7
52050 Greeley 313 ....L3
50636 Greene 1,332 ....H3
50849 Greenfield⊙ 2,243 ...D6
50111 Grimes 1,973 ....F5
50112 Grinnell 8,868 ....H5

(continued on following page)

© Copyright HAMMOND INCORPORATED, Maplewood, N.J.

Agriculture, Industry and Resources

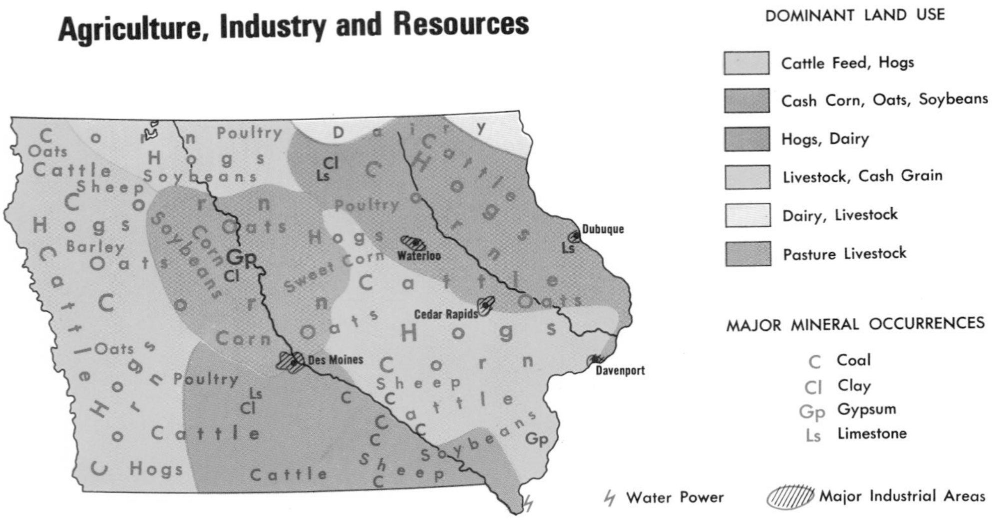
DOMINANT LAND USE
Cattle Feed, Hogs
Cash Corn, Oats, Soybeans
Hogs, Dairy
Livestock, Cash Grain
Dairy, Livestock
Pasture Livestock
MAJOR MINERAL OCCURRENCES
C Coal
Cl Clay
Gp Gypsum
Ls Limestone
Water Power
Major Industrial Areas
Poultry
Oats
Cattle
Sheep
Hogs
Soybeans
Barley
Corn
Sweet Corn
Dairy
Waterloo
Dubuque
Cedar Rapids
Des Moines
Davenport

51535 Griswold 1,176 .... C6
50638 Grundy Center⊙ 2,880 .... H4
50115 Guthrie Center⊙ 1,713 .... D5
52052 Guttenberg 2,428 .... L3
51640 Hamburg 1,597 .... B7
50441 Hampton⊙ 4,630 .... G3
51536 Hancock 254 .... C6
50544 Harcourt 347 .... E4
51537 Harlan⊙ 5,357 .... C5
52146 Harpers Ferry 258 .... L2
50118 Hartford 761 .... G6
51346 Hartley 1,700 .... C2
50119 Harvey 275 .... H6
50546 Havelock 279 .... D3
51023 Hawarden 2,722 .... A2
52147 Hawkeye 512 .... J3
50641 Hazleton 877 .... K3
52563 Hedrick 847 .... J6
51541 Henderson 236 .... B6
52233 Hiawatha 4,825 .... K4
52235 Hills 547 .... K5
52630 Hillsboro 208 .... K7
51024 Hinton 659 .... A3
50642 Holland 278 .... H4
51025 Holstein 1,477 .... B4
52053 Holy Cross 310 .... L3
52237 Hopkinton 774 .... L4
51026 Hornick 239 .... A4
51238 Hospers 655 .... B2
50122 Hubbard 852 .... G4
50643 Hudson 2,267 .... H4
51239 Hull 1,714 .... A2
50548 Humboldt 4,794 .... E3
50123 Humeston 671 .... G7
50124 Huxley 1,884 .... F5
51445 Ida Grove⊙ 2,285 .... B4
50644 Independence⊙ 6,392 .... K4
50125 Indianola⊙ 10,843 .... F6
51240 Inwood 755 .... A2
50645 Ionia 350 .... J2
52240 Iowa City⊙ 50,508 .... L5
Iowa City○‡ 81,717 .... L5
50126 Iowa Falls 6,174 .... G3
51027 Ireton 588 .... A3
51446 Irwin 427 .... C5
50128 Jamaica 275 .... E5
50647 Janesville 840 .... J3
50129 Jefferson⊙ 4,854 .... E4
50648 Jesup 2,343 .... J4
50130 Jewell 1,145 .... F4
50131 Johnston 2,617 .... F5
52247 Kalona 1,862 .... K6
50447 Kanawha 756 .... F3
50133 Kellerton 278 .... E7
50134 Kelley 237 .... F5
50135 Kellogg 654 .... H5
50448 Kensett 360 .... G2
52632 Keokuk⊙ 13,536 .... L8
52565 Keosauqua⊙ 1,003 .... J7
52248 Keota 1,034 .... K6
50136 Keswick 300 .... J6
52249 Keystone 618 .... J5
51543 Kimballton 362 .... D5
51028 Kingsley 1,209 .... A3
51448 Kiron 317 .... C4
50449 Klemme 620 .... F3
50138 Knoxville⊙ 8,143 .... G6
50139 Lacona 376 .... G6
52251 Ladora 289 .... J5
51449 Lake City 2,006 .... D4
50450 Lake Mills 2,281 .... F2
51347 Lake Park 1,123 .... C2
50588 Lakeside 589 .... C3
51450 Lake View 1,291 .... C4
50451 Lakota 330 .... E2
50140 Lamoni 2,705 .... E7
50650 Lamont 554 .... K3
52054 La Motte 322 .... M4
52151 Lansing 1,181 .... L2
50651 La Porte City 2,324 .... J4

51241 Larchwood 701 .... A2
50452 Latimer 441 .... G3
50141 Laurel 278 .... H5
50554 Laurens 1,606 .... D3
52154 Lawler 534 .... J2
51030 Lawton 447 .... A4
52753 Le Claire 2,899 .... N5
50142 Le Grand 921 .... H5
50557 Lehigh 654 .... E4
50453 Leland 274 .... F2
51031 Le Mars⊙ 8,276 .... A3
50851 Lenox 1,338 .... D7
50144 Leon⊙ 2,094 .... F7
51242 Lester 274 .... A2
52754 Letts 473 .... L6
51544 Lewis 497 .... C6
52567 Libertyville 281 .... K7
52155 Lime Springs 476 .... J2
50146 Linden 264 .... E5
50147 Lineville 319 .... G7
52253 Lisbon 1,458 .... L5
50148 Liscomb 296 .... H4
51243 Little Rock 490 .... B2
51545 Little Sioux 251 .... B5
50558 Livermore 490 .... E3
52635 Lockridge 271 .... K7
51546 Logan⊙ 1,540 .... B5
51453 Lohrville 521 .... D4
52755 Lone Tree 1,014 .... L6
52756 Long Grove 596 .... M5
50149 Lorimor 405 .... E6
52254 Lost Nation 524 .... M5
50150 Lovilia 637 .... H6
52255 Lowden 717 .... L5
52757 Low Moor 346 .... N5
52156 Luana 246 .... K2
50151 Lucas 292 .... G6
50560 Lu Verne 418 .... E3
52056 Luxemburg 271 .... L3
50153 Lynnville 406 .... H5
50561 Lytton 377 .... D4
51549 Macedonia 279 .... C6
50156 Madrid 2,281 .... F5
50157 Malcom 418 .... H5
50562 Mallard 407 .... D3
51551 Malvern 1,244 .... B7
52057 Manchester⊙ 4,942 .... L3
51454 Manilla 1,020 .... C5
50456 Manly 1,496 .... G2
51455 Manning 1,609 .... C5
50563 Manson 1,924 .... D3
51034 Mapleton 1,495 .... B4
52060 Maquoketa⊙ 6,313 .... M4
50565 Marathon 442 .... C3
50653 Marble Rock 419 .... H3
51035 Marcus 1,206 .... B3
52301 Marengo⊙ 2,308 .... J5
52302 Marion 19,474 .... K4
52158 Marquette 528 .... L2
50158 Marshalltown⊙ 26,938 .... G4
52305 Martelle 316 .... L4
50160 Martensdale 438 .... F6
50401 Mason City⊙ 30,144 .... G2
50853 Massena 518 .... D6
51036 Maurice 288 .... A3
50161 Maxwell 783 .... G5
50655 Maynard 561 .... K3
50154 McCallsburg 304 .... G4
52758 McCausland 381 .... M5
52157 McGregor 945 .... L2
52306 Mechanicsville 1,166 .... L5
52637 Mediapolis 1,685 .... L6
50162 Melbourne 732 .... G5
50163 Melcher 953 .... G6
51350 Melvin 277 .... B2
50164 Menlo 410 .... E5
51037 Meriden 233 .... B3
51038 Merrill 737 .... A3
50457 Meservey 324 .... G3
52307 Middle 335 .... K5

52638 Middletown 487 .... L7
52064 Miles 398 .... N4
51351 Milford 2,076 .... C2
50166 Milo 778 .... G6
52570 Milton 567 .... J7
50167 Minburn 390 .... E5
51553 Minden 419 .... C6
50168 Mingo 303 .... G5
51555 Missouri Valley 3,107 .... B5
50169 Mitchellville 1,530 .... G5
51556 Modale 373 .... B5
51557 Mondamin 423 .... B5
52159 Monona 1,530 .... L2
50170 Monroe 1,875 .... G5
50171 Montezuma⊙ 1,485 .... H5
52310 Monticello 3,641 .... L4
50173 Montour 387 .... H5
52759 Montpelier 250 .... M6
52639 Montrose 1,038 .... L7
51558 Moorhead 264 .... B5
50566 Moorland 257 .... E4
52571 Moravia 706 .... H7
52640 Morning Sun 959 .... L6
52760 Moscow 350 .... L5
52572 Moulton 762 .... H7
50854 Mount Ayr⊙ 1,938 .... E7
52641 Mount Pleasant⊙ 7,322 .... L7
52314 Mount Vernon 3,325 .... K5
51039 Moville 1,273 .... A4
50174 Murray 703 .... F6
52761 Muscatine⊙ 23,467 .... L6
52574 Mystic 665 .... H7
50658 Nashua 1,846 .... J3
51559 Neola 839 .... B6
50201 Nevada⊙ 5,912 .... G5
52160 New Albin 609 .... L2
50568 Newell 913 .... D3
52315 Newhall 899 .... K5
50660 New Hartford 764 .... H3
52645 New London 2,043 .... L7
51646 New Market 554 .... D7
50206 New Providence 249 .... G4
50207 New Sharon 1,225 .... H6
50208 Newton⊙ 15,292 .... H5
52065 New Vienna 430 .... L3
50210 New Virginia 512 .... F6
52766 Nichols 375 .... L6
50458 Nora Springs 1,572 .... H2
52316 North English 990 .... J5
52317 North Liberty 2,046 .... K5
50459 Northwood⊙ 2,193 .... G2
50211 Norwalk 2,676 .... F6
52318 Norway 633 .... K5
52319 Oakdale 300 .... K5
51560 Oakland 1,552 .... C6
52646 Oakville 470 .... L6
51354 Ocheyedan 599 .... B2
51458 Odebolt 1,299 .... C4
50662 Oelwein 7,564 .... K3
50212 Ogden 1,953 .... E4
51355 Okoboji 559 .... C2
52320 Olin 735 .... L5
52576 Ollie 232 .... J6
51040 Onawa⊙ 3,283 .... A4
51041 Orange City⊙ 4,588 .... A2
50858 Orient 416 .... E6
†51360 Orleans 546 .... C2
50461 Osage⊙ 3,718 .... H2
50213 Osceola⊙ 3,750 .... F6
52577 Oskaloosa⊙ 10,984 .... H6
52161 Ossian 829 .... K2
50569 Otho 692 .... E4
52501 Ottumwa⊙ 27,381 .... J6
52322 Oxford 676 .... K5
52323 Oxford Junction 600 .... M4
51561 Pacific Junction 511 .... B6
50571 Palmer 288 .... D3
52324 Palo 529 .... K4
51562 Panama 229 .... B5
50216 Panora 1,211 .... E5

50665 Parkersburg 1,968 .... H3
52325 Parnell 234 .... J5
50217 Paton 291 .... E4
51046 Paullina 1,224 .... B3
50219 Pella 8,349 .... H6
50220 Perry 7,053 .... E5
50221 Pershing 325 .... G6
51563 Persia 355 .... B5
51047 Peterson 470 .... C3
51048 Pierson 408 .... B3
51564 Pisgah 307 .... B5
50666 Plainfield 469 .... J3
50225 Pleasantville 1,531 .... G6
50464 Plymouth 463 .... G2
50574 Pocahontas⊙ 2,352 .... D3
50226 Polk City 1,658 .... F5
50575 Pomeroy 895 .... D3
51565 Portsmouth 240 .... C5
52162 Postville 1,475 .... K2
50228 Prairie City 1,278 .... G5
50859 Prescott 349 .... D6
52069 Preston 1,120 .... N4
Primghar⊙ 1,050 .... B2
52768 Princeton 965 .... N5
52163 Protivin 368 .... J2
52584 Pulaski 267 .... J7
52326 Quasqueton 599 .... K4
51049 Quimby 424 .... B3
50230 Radcliffe 593 .... G4
50465 Rake 283 .... F2
50667 Raymond 655 .... J4
50668 Readlyn 858 .... J3
50232 Reasnor 277 .... G5
50233 Redfield 959 .... E5
51566 Red Oak⊙ 6,810 .... C6
50669 Reinbeck 1,808 .... H4
50576 Rembrandt 291 .... C3
51050 Remsen 1,592 .... B3
50577 Renwick 410 .... E3
50234 Rhodes 367 .... G5
50466 Riceville 919 .... H2
52585 Richland 600 .... K6
52165 Ridgeway 308 .... K2
50578 Ringsted 557 .... D2
50235 Rippey 304 .... E5
†52722 Riverdale 462 .... N5
52327 Riverside 826 .... K6
51650 Riverton 342 .... B7
52328 Robins 726 .... K4
50468 Rockford 1,012 .... H2
51246 Rock Rapids⊙ 2,693 .... A2
51247 Rock Valley 2,706 .... A2
50469 Rockwell 1,039 .... G3
50579 Rockwell City⊙ 2,276 .... D4
50236 Roland 1,005 .... F4
50581 Rolfe 796 .... D3
50470 Rowan 259 .... F3
52329 Rowley 275 .... K4
51357 Royal 522 .... C2
50471 Rudd 460 .... H2
50237 Runnells 377 .... G5
50238 Russell 593 .... G7
51358 Ruthven 769 .... D2
52330 Ryan 390 .... K4
52070 Sabula 824 .... N4
50583 Sac City⊙ 3,000 .... C4
†52001 Sageville 291 .... M3
50472 Saint Ansgar 1,100 .... H2
50240 Saint Charles 507 .... F6
52649 Salem 463 .... K7
51052 Salix 429 .... A4
51248 Sanborn 1,398 .... B2
51053 Schaller 832 .... C4
51461 Schleswig 868 .... B4
51462 Scranton 748 .... D4
51054 Sergeant Bluff 2,416 .... A4
52590 Seymour 1,036 .... G7
50475 Sheffield 1,224 .... G3
51570 Shelby 665 .... C5
50243 Sheldahl 315 .... F5

51201 Sheldon 5,003 .... B2
50670 Shell Rock 1,478 .... H3
52332 Shellsburg 771 .... K4
51601 Shenandoah 6,274 .... C7
†52401 Shueyville 287 .... K5
51249 Sibley⊙ 3,051 .... B2
51652 Sidney⊙ 1,308 .... B7
52591 Sigourney⊙ 2,330 .... J6
51571 Silver City 291 .... B6
51250 Sioux Center 4,588 .... A2
*51101 Sioux City⊙ 82,003 .... A3
Sioux City‡ 117,457 .... A3
50585 Sioux Rapids 897 .... C3
50244 Slater 1,312 .... F5
51055 Sloan 978 .... A4
51056 Smithland 282 .... B4
51572 Soldier 257 .... B5
52333 Solon 969 .... L5
51301 Spencer⊙ 11,726 .... C2
52168 Spillville 415 .... J2
51360 Spirit Lake⊙ 3,976 .... C2
52336 Springville 1,165 .... L4
50476 Stacyville 538 .... H2
50246 Stanhope 492 .... F4
51573 Stanton 747 .... C7
52337 Stanwood 705 .... L5
50247 State Center 1,292 .... G5
50672 Steamboat Rock 387 .... G4
52651 Stockport 272 .... K7
52769 Stockton 240 .... M5
50588 Storm Lake⊙ 8,814 .... C3
50248 Story City 2,762 .... F4
50249 Stratford 806 .... F4
52076 Strawberry Point 1,463 .... K3
50250 Stuart 1,650 .... E6
50251 Sully 828 .... H5
50674 Sumner 2,335 .... J3
51058 Sutherland 897 .... B3
50590 Swea City 813 .... E2
52338 Swisher 654 .... K5
51653 Tabor 1,088 .... B7
52339 Tama 2,968 .... H5
51463 Templeton 319 .... D5
51364 Terril 420 .... C2
50478 Thompson 668 .... F2
50479 Thornton 442 .... G3
52340 Tiffin 413 .... K5
52772 Tipton⊙ 3,055 .... L5
50480 Titonka 607 .... E2
52342 Toledo⊙ 2,445 .... H4
50675 Traer 1,703 .... J4
51575 Treynor 981 .... B6
50676 Tripoli 1,280 .... J3
50257 Truro 407 .... F6
51576 Underwood 448 .... B6
50258 Union 515 .... G4
†52240 University Heights 1,069 .... K5
52595 University Park 645 .... H6
52345 Urbana 574 .... K4
50322 Urbandale 17,869 .... F5
51060 Ute 479 .... B4
51465 Vail 490 .... C4
52346 Van Horne 682 .... J4
50261 Van Meter 747 .... E5
50262 Van Wert 245 .... F7
50482 Ventura 614 .... F2
52347 Victor 1,046 .... J5
50864 Villisca 1,434 .... C7
52349 Vinton⊙ 5,040 .... J4
52077 Volga 310 .... L3
52169 Wadena 230 .... K3
†51360 Wahpeton 372 .... C2
52773 Walcott 1,425 .... M5
52351 Walford 285 .... K5
52352 Walker 733 .... K4
51365 Wallingford 256 .... D2
51466 Wall Lake 892 .... C4
51577 Walnut 897 .... C6
52653 Wapello⊙ 2,011 .... L6
52353 Washington⊙ 6,584 .... K6

51061 Washta 320 .... B3
*50701 Waterloo⊙ 75,985 .... J4
Waterloo-Cedar
Falls‡ 137,961 .... J4
52171 Waucoma 308 .... J2
50263 Waukee 2,227 .... F5
52172 Waukon⊙ 3,983 .... L2
50677 Waverly⊙ 8,444 .... J3
52654 Wayland 720 .... K6
52356 Wellman 1,125 .... K6
50680 Wellsburg 761 .... H4
50483 Wesley 598 .... E2
50597 West Bend 941 .... D3
52358 West Branch 1,867 .... L5
52655 West Burlington 3,371 .... L7
50318 West Des Moines 21,894 .... F5
50681 Westgate 263 .... K3
52776 West Liberty 2,723 .... L5
†51351 West Okoboji 435 .... C2
52656 West Point 1,133 .... K7
51467 Westside 387 .... C4
52175 West Union⊙ 2,783 .... K3
50268 What Cheer 803 .... J6
52777 Wheatland 840 .... M5
51063 Whiting 734 .... A4
50598 Whittemore 647 .... E2
50271 Williams 410 .... F3
52361 Williamsburg 2,033 .... J5
52778 Wilton 2,502 .... M5
50311 Windsor Heights 5,474 .... F5
52659 Winfield 1,042 .... L6
50273 Winterset⊙ 4,021 .... E6
50682 Winthrop 767 .... K4
50484 Woden 287 .... F2
51579 Woodbine 1,463 .... B5
50276 Woodward 1,212 .... E5
50599 Woolstock 235 .... F3
52078 Worthington 432 .... L4
52362 Wyoming 702 .... L4
50277 Yale 299 .... E5
50278 Zearing 630 .... G4

OTHER FEATURES

Big Sioux (riv.) A3
Boyer (riv.) B5
Cedar (riv.) K4
Chariton (riv.) G7
Clear (lake) G2
Eagle (lake) F2
East Nishnabotna (riv.) C6
Effigy Mounds Nat'l Mon. L2
Five Island (lake) D2
Floyd (riv.) A3
Herbert Hoover Nat'l Hist. Site L5
Iowa (riv.) H4
Little Sioux (riv.) B3
Lost Island (lake) D2
Mississippi (riv.) L7
Missouri (riv.) A4
Nodaway (riv.) D7
Palo Alto (lake) D2
Platte (riv.) D8
Raccoon (riv.) D4
Rathbun (lake) G7
Red Rock (lake) G6
Rock (riv.) A2
Sac and Fox Ind. Res. H5
Saylorville (lake) F5
Skunk (riv.) K6
Spirit (lake) C2
Storm (lake) C3
Thompson (riv.) E7
Trumbull (lake) C2
Turkey (riv.) K2
Upper Iowa (riv.) K2
Wapsipinicon (riv.) J3
West Nishnabotna (riv.) C6

⊙County seat.
‡Population of metropolitan area.
† Zip of nearest p.o. * Multiple zips.

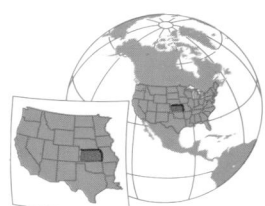

AREA 82,277 sq. mi. (213,097 sq. km.)
POPULATION 2,364,236
CAPITAL Topeka
LARGEST CITY Wichita
HIGHEST POINT Mt. Sunflower 4,039 ft. (1231 m.)
SETTLED IN 1831
ADMITTED TO UNION January 29, 1861
POPULAR NAME Sunflower State
STATE FLOWER Sunflower
STATE BIRD Western Meadowlark

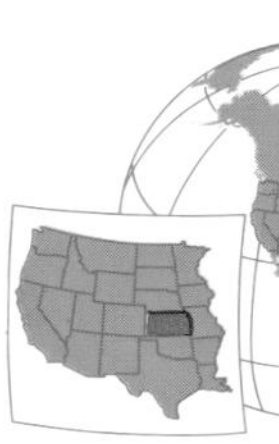

COUNTIES

Allen 15,654 .... G4
Anderson 8,749 .... G3
Atchison 18,397 .... G2
Barber 6,548 .... D4
Barton 31,343 .... D3
Bourbon 15,969 .... H4
Brown 11,955 .... G2
Butler 44,782 .... F4
Chase 3,309 .... F3
Chautauqua 5,016 .... F4
Cherokee 22,304 .... H4
Cheyenne 3,678 .... A2
Clark 2,599 .... C4
Clay 9,802 .... E2
Cloud 12,494 .... E2
Coffey 9,370 .... G3
Comanche 2,554 .... C4
Cowley 36,824 .... F4
Crawford 37,916 .... H4
Decatur 4,509 .... B2
Dickinson 20,175 .... E3
Doniphan 9,268 .... G2
Douglas 67,640 .... G3
Edwards 4,271 .... C4
Elk 3,918 .... F4
Ellis 26,098 .... C3
Ellsworth 6,640 .... D3
Finney 23,825 .... B3
Ford 24,315 .... C4
Franklin 22,062 .... G3
Geary 29,852 .... F3
Gove 3,726 .... B3
Graham 3,995 .... C2
Grant 6,977 .... A4
Gray 5,138 .... B4
Greeley 1,845 .... A3
Greenwood 8,764 .... F4
Hamilton 2,514 .... A3
Harper 7,778 .... D4
Harvey 30,531 .... E3
Haskell 3,814 .... B4
Hodgeman 2,269 .... C3
Jackson 11,644 .... G2
Jefferson 15,207 .... G2
Jewell 5,241 .... D2
Johnson 270,269 .... H3
Kearny 3,435 .... A3
Kingman 8,960 .... D4
Kiowa 4,046 .... C4
Labette 25,682 .... G4
Lane 2,472 .... B3
Leavenworth 54,809 .... G2
Lincoln 4,145 .... D2
Linn 8,234 .... H3
Logan 3,478 .... A3
Lyon 35,108 .... F3
Marion 13,522 .... E3
Marshall 12,787 .... F2
McPherson 26,855 .... E3
Meade 4,788 .... B4
Miami 21,618 .... H3
Mitchell 8,117 .... D2
Montgomery 42,281 .... G4
Morris 6,419 .... F3
Morton 3,454 .... A4
Nemaha 11,211 .... F2
Neosho 18,967 .... G4
Ness 4,498 .... C3
Norton 6,689 .... C2
Osage 15,319 .... G3
Osborne 5,959 .... D2
Ottawa 5,971 .... E2
Pawnee 8,065 .... C3
Phillips 7,406 .... C2
Pottawatomie 14,782 .... F2
Pratt 10,275 .... D4
Rawlins 4,105 .... A2
Reno 64,983 .... D4
Republic 7,569 .... E2
Rice 11,900 .... D3
Riley 63,505 .... F2
Rooks 7,006 .... C2
Rush 4,516 .... C3
Russell 8,868 .... D3
Saline 48,905 .... E3
Scott 5,782 .... B3
Sedgwick 367,088 .... E4
Seward 17,071 .... B4
Shawnee 154,916 .... G2
Sheridan 3,544 .... B2
Sherman 7,759 .... A2
Smith 5,947 .... D2
Stafford 5,694 .... D3
Stanton 2,339 .... A4
Stevens 4,736 .... A4
Sumner 24,928 .... E4
Thomas 8,451 .... A2
Trego 4,165 .... C3
Wabaunsee 6,867 .... F3
Wallace 2,045 .... A3
Washington 8,543 .... E2
Wichita 3,041 .... A3
Wilson 12,128 .... G4
Woodson 4,600 .... G4
Wyandotte 172,335 .... H2

CITIES and TOWNS

Zip *Name/Pop.* *Key*

67510 Abbyville 123 .... D4
67410 Abilene⊙ 6,572 .... E3
66830 Admire 158 .... F3
66930 Agenda 106 .... E2
67621 Agra 321 .... C2
67511 Albert 236 .... C3
67512 Alden 214 .... D3
67513 Alexander 116 .... C3
66833 Allen 205 .... F3
66401 Alma⊙ 925 .... F2
67622 Almena 517 .... C2
67330 Altamont 1,054 .... G4
66834 Alta Vista 430 .... F3
67623 Alton 135 .... D2
66710 Altoona 564 .... G4
66835 Americus 915 .... F3
67001 Andale 538 .... E4
67002 Andover 2,801 .... E4
67003 Anthony⊙ 2,661 .... D4
66711 Arcadia 460 .... H4
67004 Argonia 587 .... E4
67005 Arkansas City 13,201 .... E4
67514 Arlington 631 .... D4
66712 Arma 1,676 .... H4
67831 Ashland⊙ 1,096 .... C4
67416 Assaria 414 .... E3
66002 Atchison⊙ 11,407 .... G2
66932 Athol 90 .... D2
67008 Atlanta 256 .... F4
67009 Attica 730 .... D4
67730 Atwood⊙ 1,665 .... B2
66402 Auburn 890 .... G3
67010 Augusta 6,968 .... F4
67417 Aurora 130 .... E2
66403 Axtell 470 .... F2
66404 Baileyville 130 .... F2
66006 Baldwin City 2,829 .... G3
67418 Barnard 163 .... D2
66933 Barnes 257 .... F2
67332 Bartlett 163 .... G4
66007 Basehor 1,483 .... G2
†66749 Bassett 31 .... G4
66713 Baxter Springs 4,730 .... H4
67516 Bazine 385 .... C3
66406 Beattie 316 .... F2
67013 Belle Plaine 1,706 .... E4
66935 Belleville⊙ 2,805 .... E2
67420 Beloit⊙ 4,367 .... D2
67519 Belpre 154 .... C4
66407 Belvue 212 .... F2
66714 Benedict 111 .... G4
67422 Bennington 579 .... E2
67016 Bentley 311 .... E4
67017 Benton 609 .... E4
66408 Bern 220 .... F2
67423 Beverly 171 .... E2
67731 Bird City 546 .... A2
67520 Bison 279 .... C3
66010 Blue Mound 319 .... H3
66411 Blue Rapids 1,280 .... F2
67018 Bluff City 95 .... E4
67625 Bogue 197 .... C2
66012 Bonner Springs 6,266 .... H2
67732 Brewster 327 .... A2
66716 Bronson 414 .... H4
67425 Brookville 259 .... E3
67521 Brownell 92 .... C3
67834 Bucklin 786 .... C4
66717 Buffalo 386 .... G4
67522 Buhler 1,188 .... E3
67626 Bunker Hill 124 .... D3
67019 Burden 518 .... F4
67523 Burdett 275 .... C3
66413 Burlingame 1,239 .... G3
66839 Burlington⊙ 2,901 .... G3
66840 Burns 224 .... F3
66936 Burr Oak 366 .... D2
67020 Burrton 976 .... E3
66841 Bushong 62 .... F3
67427 Bushton 388 .... D3
67021 Byers 47 .... D4
67022 Caldwell 1,401 .... E4
67023 Cambridge 113 .... F4
67333 Caney 2,284 .... G4
67428 Canton 926 .... E3
66414 Carbondale 1,518 .... G3
67429 Carlton 49 .... E3
66842 Cassoday 122 .... F3
67430 Cawker City 640 .... D2
67628 Cedar 53 .... D2
66843 Cedar Point 66 .... F3
67024 Cedar Vale 848 .... F4
66415 Centralia 486 .... F2
66720 Chanute 10,506 .... G4
67431 Chapman 1,255 .... E3
67524 Chase 753 .... D3
67334 Chautauqua 156 .... F4
67025 Cheney 1,404 .... E4
66724 Cherokee 775 .... H4
67335 Cherryvale 2,769 .... G4
67336 Chetopa 1,751 .... G4
67835 Cimarron⊙ 1,491 .... B4
66416 Circleville 164 .... G2
67525 Claflin 764 .... D3
67432 Clay Center⊙ 4,948 .... E2
67629 Clayton 102 .... B2
67026 Clearwater 1,684 .... E4
66937 Clifton 695 .... E2
67027 Climax 81 .... F4
66938 Clyde 909 .... E2
67028 Coats 153 .... D4
67337 Coffeyville 15,185 .... G4
67701 Colby⊙ 5,544 .... A2
67029 Coldwater⊙ 989 .... C4
67631 Collyer 151 .... B2
66015 Colony 474 .... G3
66725 Columbus⊙ 3,426 .... H4
67030 Colwich 935 .... E4
66901 Concordia⊙ 6,847 .... E2
67031 Conway Springs 1,313 .... E4
67836 Coolidge 82 .... A3
67837 Copeland 323 .... B4
66417 Corning 158 .... F2
66845 Cottonwood Falls⊙ 954 .... F3
66846 Council Grove⊙ 2,381 .... F3
66939 Courtland 377 .... E2
66727 Coyville 98 .... G4
66940 Cuba 286 .... E2
†67124 Cullison 154 .... D4
67435 Culver 167 .... E3
67035 Cunningham 540 .... D4
67632 Damar 204 .... C2
67036 Danville 71 .... E4
67340 Dearing 475 .... G4
67838 Deerfield 538 .... A4
66418 Delia 181 .... G2
67436 Delphos 570 .... E2
66419 Denison 231 .... G2
66017 Denton 156 .... G2
67037 Derby 9,786 .... E4
66018 De Soto 2,061 .... H3
67038 Dexter 366 .... F4
67839 Dighton⊙ 1,390 .... B3

Agriculture, Industry and Resources

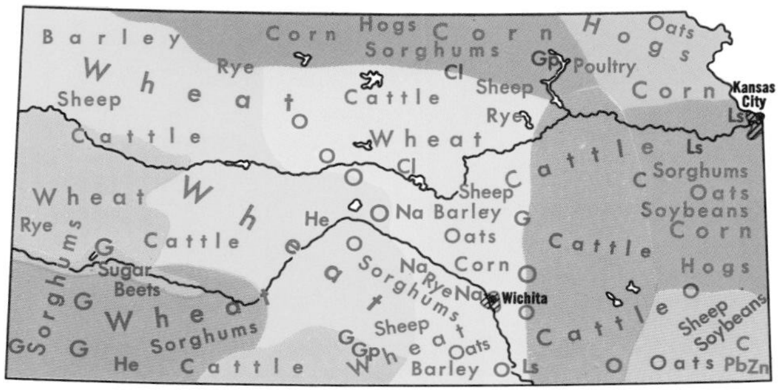

DOMINANT LAND USE

- Specialized Wheat
- Wheat, General Farming
- Wheat, Range Livestock
- Wheat, Grain Sorghums, Range Livestock
- Cattle Feed, Hogs
- Livestock, Cash Grain
- Livestock, Cash Grain, Dairy
- General Farming, Livestock, Cash Grain
- General Farming, Livestock, Special Crops
- Range Livestock

MAJOR MINERAL OCCURRENCES

C	Coal	Ls	Limestone
Cl	Clay	Na	Salt
G	Natural Gas	O	Petroleum
Gp	Gypsum	Pb	Lead
He	Helium	Zn	Zinc

Major Industrial Areas

67801 Dodge City⊙ 18,001 .... B4
67634 Dorrance 220 .... D3
67039 Douglass 1,450 .... F4
67437 Downs 1,324 .... D2
67635 Dresden 84 .... B2
66848 Dunlap 82 .... F3
67438 Durham 130 .... E3
66849 Dwight 320 .... F3
†66720 Earlton 79 .... G4
†67201 Eastborough 854 .... E4
66020 Easton 460 .... G2
66021 Edgerton 1,214 .... H3
67636 Edmond 56 .... C2
67342 Edna 537 .... G4
66113 Edwardsville 3,364 .... H2
66023 Effingham 634 .... G2
67041 Elbing 175 .... E3
67042 El Dorado⊙ 10,510 .... F4
†67361 Elgin 139 .... F4
67344 Elk City 404 .... G4
67345 Elk Falls 151 .... F4
67950 Elkhart⊙ 2,243 .... A4
67526 Ellinwood 2,508 .... D3
67637 Ellis 2,062 .... C3
67439 Ellsworth⊙ 2,465 .... D3
66850 Elmdale 109 .... F3
66732 Elsmore 104 .... G4
66024 Elwood 1,275 .... H2
66422 Emmett 223 .... F2
66801 Emporia⊙ 25,287 .... F3
67840 Englewood 111 .... C4
67841 Ensign 209 .... B4
67441 Enterprise 839 .... E3
66733 Erie⊙ 1,415 .... G4
66941 Esbon 234 .... D2
66423 Eskridge 603 .... F3
66025 Eudora 2,934 .... G3
67045 Eureka⊙ 3,425 .... F4
66424 Everest 331 .... G2
66425 Fairview 258 .... G2
†66101 Fairway 4,619 .... H2
67047 Fall River 173 .... G4
66851 Florence 729 .... E3
66026 Fontana 173 .... H3
67842 Ford 272 .... C4
66942 Formoso 166 .... D2
67843 Fort Dodge 400 .... C4
66027 Fort Leavenworth H2
66701 Fort Scott⊙ 8,893 .... H4
67844 Fowler 592 .... B4
66427 Frankfort 1,038 .... F2
66735 Franklin 400 .... H4
66736 Fredonia⊙ 3,047 .... G4
67049 Freeport 12 .... E4
66762 Frontenac 2,586 .... H4
66738 Fulton 194 .... H4
66739 Galena 3,587 .... H4
66740 Galesburg 181 .... G4
67443 Galva 651 .... E3
67846 Garden City⊙ 18,256 .... B4
67050 Garden Plain 775 .... E4
66030 Gardner 2,392 .... H3
67529 Garfield 277 .... C3
66032 Garnett⊙ 3,310 .... G3
66742 Gas 543 .... G4
67638 Gaylord 203 .... D2
67734 Gem 101 .... B2
67444 Geneseo 496 .... D3
67051 Geuda Springs 217 .... E4
66743 Girard⊙ 2,888 .... H4
67639 Glade 131 .... C2
67445 Glasco 710 .... E2
67446 Glen Elder 491 .... D2
67052 Goddard 1,427 .... E4
67053 Goessel 421 .... E3
66428 Goff 196 .... G2
67735 Goodland⊙ 5,708 .... A2
67640 Gorham 355 .... D3
67736 Gove⊙ 148 .... B3
67737 Grainfield 417 .... B2
†66441 Grandview Plaza 1,189 .... F2
66429 Grantville 220 .... G2
67530 Great Bend⊙ 16,608 .... D3
66033 Greeley 405 .... G3
67447 Green 155 .... E2
66943 Greenleaf 462 .... E2
67054 Greensburg⊙ 1,885 .... C4
67346 Grenola 335 .... F4
66852 Gridley 404 .... G3
67738 Grinnell 410 .... B2
67448 Gypsum 423 .... E3
66944 Haddam 239 .... E2
67056 Halstead 1,994 .... E4
66853 Hamilton 363 .... F4
66945 Hanover 802 .... F2
67849 Hanston 257 .... C3
67057 Hardtner 336 .... D4
67058 Harper 1,823 .... D4
66854 Hartford 551 .... F3
66431 Harveyville 280 .... F3
67347 Havana 169 .... G4
67543 Haven 1,125 .... E4
66432 Havensville 183 .... F2
67059 Haviland 770 .... C4

(continued on following page)

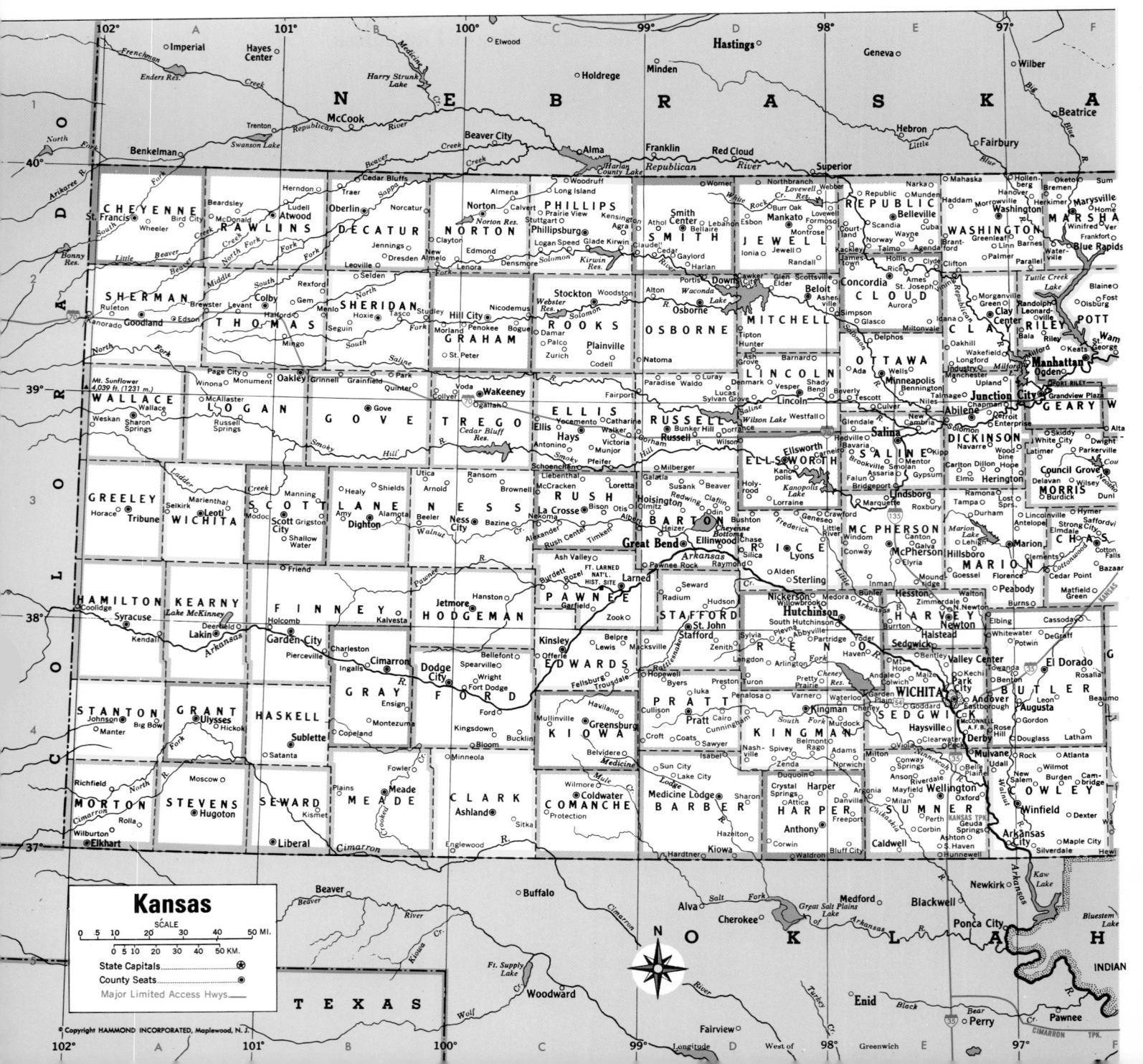

67952 Moscow 228	A4	
66056 Mound City⊙ 755	H3	
67107 Moundridge 1,453	E3	
67354 Mound Valley 381	G4	
67108 Mount Hope 791	E4	
66756 Mulberry 647	H4	
67109 Mullinville 339	C4	
67110 Mulvane 4,254	E4	
66959 Munden 152	E2	
66058 Muscotah 248	G2	
66960 Narka 120	E2	
67112 Nashville 127	D4	
67651 Natoma 515	D2	
66757 Neodesha 3,414	G4	
66758 Neosho Falls 157	F3	
66864 Neosho Rapids 289	F3	
67560 Ness City⊙ 1,769	C3	
66516 Netawaka 218	G2	
66759 New Albany 78	G4	
67470 New Cambria 175	E3	
66839 New Strawn (Strawn) 457	G3	
67114 Newton⊙ 16,332	E3	
67561 Nickerson 1,292	D3	
67355 Niotaze 104	F4	
67653 Norcatur 226	B2	
67117 North Newton 1,222	E3	
67654 Norton⊙ 3,400	C2	
66060 Nortonville 692	G2	
67118 Norwich 476	E4	
67472 Oakhill 35	E2	
67748 Oakley⊙ 2,343	B2	
67749 Oberlin⊙ 2,387	B2	
67563 Offerle 244	C4	
66517 Ogden 1,804	F2	
66518 Oketo 130	F2	
66061 Olathe⊙ 37,258	H3	
67564 Olmitz 140	D3	
66865 Olpe 477	F3	
66520 Olsburg 166	F2	
66521 Onaga 752	F2	
66522 Oneida 120	G2	
66523 Osage City 2,667	G3	
66064 Osawatomie 4,459	H3	
67473 Osborne⊙ 2,120	D2	
66066 Oskaloosa⊙ 1,092	G2	
67356 Oswego⊙ 2,218	G4	
67565 Otis 410	C3	
66067 Ottawa⊙ 11,016	G3	

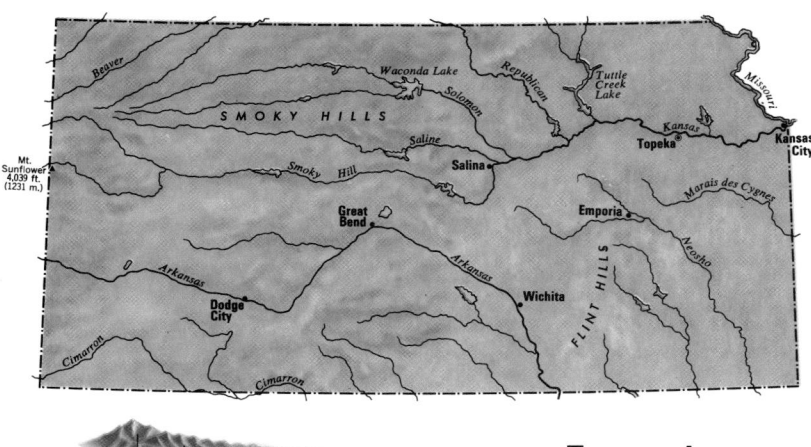

Topography

| 5,000 m. 16,404 ft. | 2,000 m. 6,562 ft. | 1,000 m. 3,281 ft. | 500 m. 1,640 ft. | 200 m. 656 ft. | 100 m. 328 ft. | Sea Level | Below |

Scale: 0 — 50 — 100 MI. / 0 — 50 — 100 KM.

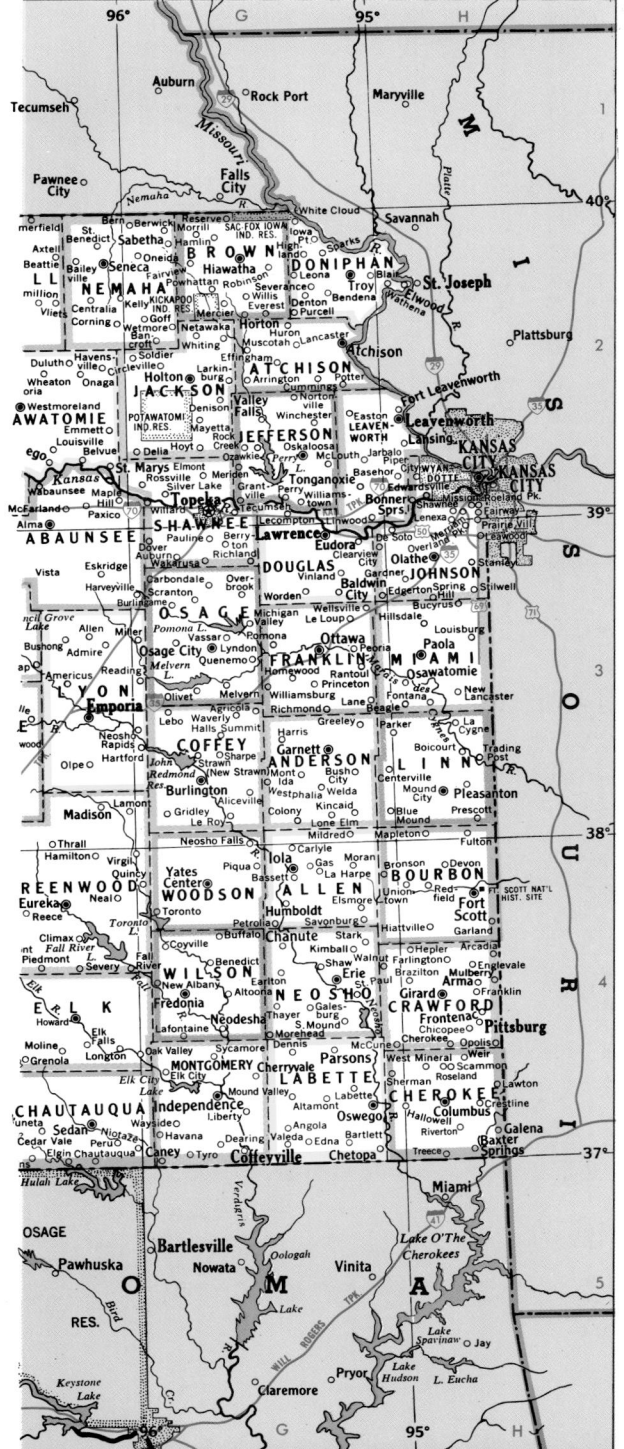

66524 Overbrook 930	G3	
66204 Overland Park 81,784	H3	
67119 Oxford 1,125	E4	
66070 Ozawkie 472	G2	
66757 Palco 329	C2	
66962 Palmer 149	E2	
66071 Paola⊙ 4,557	H3	
67658 Paradise 89	D2	
67751 Park 183	B2	
†67201 Park City 3,778	E4	
66072 Parker 270	H3	
67357 Parsons 12,898	G4	
66566 Partridge 268	D4	
67567 Pawnee Rock 409	D3	
66526 Paxico 168	F2	
66866 Peabody 1,474	E3	
67120 Peck 259	E4	
67121 Penalosa 31	D4	
66073 Perry 907	G2	
67360 Peru 286	F4	
67661 Phillipsburg⊙ 3,229	C2	
66762 Pittsburg 18,770	H4	
67869 Plains 1,044	B4	
67663 Plainville 2,458	C2	
66075 Pleasanton 1,303	H3	
67568 Plevna 115	D4	
66076 Pomona 868	G3	
67474 Portis 172	D2	
67123 Potwin 563	F4	
66527 Powhattan 95	G2	
67664 Prairie View 145	C2	
66208 Prairie Village 24,657	H2	
67124 Pratt⊙ 6,885	D4	
66767 Prescott 319	H3	
67569 Preston 227	D4	
67570 Pretty Prairie 655	D4	
66078 Princeton 244	G3	
67127 Protection 684	C4	
66528 Quenemo 413	G3	
67752 Quinter 951	B2	
67571 Radium 47	D3	
67475 Ramona 116	E3	
66963 Randall 154	D2	
66554 Randolph 131	F2	
67572 Ransom 448	C3	
66079 Rantoul 212	G3	
67573 Raymond 132	D3	
66868 Reading 244	F3	
66769 Redfield 185	H4	
66964 Republic 223	E2	
66529 Reserve 105	G2	
66753 Rexford 204	B2	
66953 Richfield 81	A4	
66080 Richmond 510	G3	
66531 Riley 779	F2	
66770 Riverton 650	H4	
66532 Robinson 324	G2	
†66205 Roeland Park 7,962	H2	
67954 Rolla 417	A4	
67133 Rose Hill 1,557	E4	
†66773 Roseland 119	H4	
66533 Rossville 1,045	G2	
67574 Rozel 219	C3	
67575 Rush Center 207	C3	
67665 Russell⊙ 5,427	D3	
67755 Russell Springs 56	A3	
66534 Sabetha 2,286	G2	
67756 Saint Francis⊙ 1,610	A2	
66535 Saint George 309	F2	
67576 Saint John⊙ 1,501	D3	
66536 Saint Marys 1,598	G2	
66771 Saint Paul 746	G4	
67401 Salina⊙ 41,843	E3	
67870 Satanta 1,117	B4	
66772 Savonburg 113	G4	
67134 Sawyer 213	D4	
66773 Scammon 501	H4	
66966 Scandia 480	E2	
67667 Schoenchen 209	C3	
67871 Scott City⊙ 4,154	B3	
66477 Scottsville 56	D2	
66537 Scranton 664	G3	
67361 Sedan⊙ 1,579	F4	
67135 Sedgwick 1,471	E4	
67757 Selden 266	B2	
66538 Seneca⊙ 2,389	F2	
66081 Severance 134	G2	
67137 Severy 447	F4	
67577 Seward 88	D3	
67138 Sharon 283	D4	
67758 Sharon Springs⊙ 982	A3	
*66202 Shawnee 29,653	H2	
66539 Silver Lake 1,350	G2	
67478 Simpson 123	E2	
66967 Smith Center⊙ 2,240	D2	
67479 Smolan 169	E3	
66540 Soldier 165	G2	
67480 Solomon 1,018	E3	
67140 South Haven 439	E4	
†67501 South Hutchinson 2,226	D3	
67876 Spearville 693	C4	
67142 Spivey 83	D4	
66083 Spring Hill⊙ 2,005	H3	
67578 Stafford 1,425	D4	
66775 Stark 143	G4	
67579 Sterling 2,312	D3	
66839 Stockton⊙ 1,825	C2	
66839 Strawn 457	G3	
66869 Strong City 675	F3	
67877 Sublette⊙ 1,293	B4	
66541 Summerfield 225	F2	
67143 Sun City 85	D4	
67481 Sylvan Grove 376	D2	
67581 Sylvia 353	D4	
67878 Syracuse⊙ 1,654	A3	
67483 Tampa 113	E3	
66542 Tecumseh 300	G2	
67484 Tescott 331	E2	
66776 Thayer 517	G4	
67582 Timken 99	C3	
67485 Tipton 321	D2	
*66601 Topeka (cap.)⊙ 115,266	G2	
Topeka‡ 185,442	G2	
66777 Toronto 466	F4	
67144 Towanda 1,332	E4	
†66075 Trading Post 35	H3	
66778 Treece 194	H4	
67879 Tribune⊙ 955	A3	
66087 Troy⊙ 1,240	G2	
67583 Turon 481	D4	
67364 Tyro 289	G4	
67146 Udall 891	E4	
67880 Ulysses⊙ 4,653	A4	
66779 Uniontown 371	H4	
67584 Utica 275	B3	
67147 Valley Center 3,300	E4	
66088 Valley Falls 1,189	G2	
66544 Vermillion 191	F2	
67671 Victoria 1,328	C3	
†66937 Vining 85	E2	
67149 Viola 199	E4	
66870 Virgil 169	F4	
67672 WaKeeney⊙ 2,388	C2	
67487 Wakefield 803	E2	
67673 Waldo 75	D2	
67150 Waldron 29	D4	
67761 Wallace 86	A3	
66780 Walnut 308	G4	
67151 Walton 269	E3	
66547 Wamego 3,159	F2	
66968 Washington⊙ 1,488	F2	
66548 Waterville 681	F2	
66090 Wathena 1,418	H2	
66871 Waverly 671	G3	
66781 Weir 705	H4	
67152 Wellington⊙ 8,212	E4	
66092 Wellsville 1,612	G3	
66782 West Mineral 206	H4	
66549 Westmoreland⊙ 598	F2	
66093 Westphalia 204	G3	
67869 West Plains (Plains) 1,044	B4	
66550 Wetmore 376	G2	
66551 Wheaton 90	F2	
66872 White City 534	F3	
66094 White Cloud 234	G2	
67154 Whitewater 751	E4	
66552 Whiting 270	G2	
*67201 Wichita⊙ 279,835	E4	
Wichita‡ 411,313	E4	
†66601 Willard 128	G2	
66095 Williamsburg 362	G3	
66435 Willis 85	G2	
†67501 Willowbrook 109	D3	
66873 Wilsey 179	F3	
67490 Wilson 978	D3	
66097 Winchester 570	G2	
67491 Windom 160	E3	
67156 Winfield⊙ 10,736	F4	
67764 Winona 258	A2	
67492 Woodbine 172	E3	
67675 Woodston 157	C2	
66783 Yates Center⊙ 1,998	G4	
67159 Zenda 146	D4	
67676 Zurich 185	C2	

OTHER FEATURES

Arkansas (riv.)	D3	
Beaver (creek)	A2	
Big Blue (riv.)	F1	
Cedar Bluff (res.)	C3	
Cheney (res.)	E4	
Cheyenne Bottoms (lake)	D3	
Chikaskia (riv.)	E4	
Cimarron (riv.)	B4	
Cottonwood (riv.)	F3	
Council Grove (lake)	F3	
Crooked (creek)	B4	
Elk (riv.)	F4	
Fall (riv.)	G4	
Fall River (lake)	F4	
Fort Larned Nat'l Hist. Site	C3	
Fort Riley-Camp Whiteside 18,233	F2	
John Redmond (res.)	G3	
Hulah (lake)	F5	
Kanopolis (lake)	D3	
Kansas (riv.)	F2	
Kickapoo Ind. Res.	G2	
Kirwin (res.)	C2	
Little Arkansas (riv.)	E3	
Little Blue (riv.)	E1	
Lovewell (res.)	D2	
Marion (lake)	E3	
McConnell A.F.B.	E4	
McKinney (lake)	A3	
Medicine Lodge (riv.)	D4	
Milford (lake)	E2	
Missouri (riv.)	G1	
Mule (creek)	C4	
Nemaha (riv.)	G1	
Neosho (riv.)	G4	
Ninnescah (riv.)	D4	
Norton (res.)	C2	
Olathe Nav. Air Sta.	H3	
Pawnee (riv.)	B3	
Perry (lake)	G2	
Pomona (lake)	G3	
Potawatomi Ind. Res.	G2	
Rattlesnake (creek)	C3	
Republican (riv.)	E2	
Sac-Fox-Iowa Ind. Res.	G2	
Saline (riv.)	D3	
Sappa (creek)	B2	
Smoky Hill (riv.)	C3	
Solomon (riv.)	D2	
Sunflower (mt.)	A2	
Toronto (lake)	F4	
Tuttle Creek (lake)	F2	
Verdigris (riv.)	G5	
Walnut (riv.)	E4	
Webster (res.)	C2	
White Rock (creek)	D2	
Wilson (res.)	D3	

⊙County seat.
‡Population of metropolitan area.
† Zip of nearest p.o.
* Multiple zips.

KENTUCKY

COUNTIES

Adair 15,233 .... L6
Allen 14,128 .... J7
Anderson 12,567 .... M5
Ballard 8,798 .... C6
Barren 34,009 .... K7
Bath 10,025 .... O4
Bell 34,330 .... O7
Boone 45,842 .... M3
Bourbon 19,405 .... N4
Boyd 55,513 .... R4
Boyle 25,066 .... M5
Bracken 7,738 .... N3
Breathitt 17,004 .... P5
Breckinridge 16,861 .... H5
Bullitt 43,346 .... K5
Butler 11,064 .... H6
Caldwell 13,473 .... F6
Calloway 30,031 .... E7
Campbell 83,317 .... N3
Carlisle 5,487 .... C7
Carroll 9,270 .... L3
Carter 25,060 .... P4
Casey 14,818 .... M6
Christian 66,878 .... F7
Clark 28,322 .... N4
Clay 22,752 .... O6
Clinton 9,321 .... L7
Crittenden 9,207 .... E6
Cumberland 7,289 .... L7
Daviess 85,949 .... G5
Edmonson 9,962 .... J6
Elliott 6,908 .... P4
Estill 14,495 .... O5
Fayette 204,165 .... N4
Fleming 12,323 .... O4
Floyd 48,764 .... R5
Franklin 41,830 .... M4
Fulton 8,971 .... C7
Gallatin 4,842 .... M3
Garrard 10,853 .... M5
Grant 13,308 .... M3
Graves 34,049 .... D7
Grayson 20,854 .... J5
Green 11,043 .... K6
Greenup 39,132 .... R3
Hancock 7,742 .... H5
Hardin 88,917 .... K5
Harlan 41,889 .... P7
Harrison 15,166 .... N4
Hart 15,402 .... K6
Henderson 40,849 .... F5
Henry 12,740 .... L4
Hickman 6,065 .... C7
Hopkins 46,174 .... F6
Jackson 11,996 .... N6
Jefferson 684,565 .... K4
Jessamine 26,065 .... M5
Johnson 24,432 .... R5
Kenton 137,058 .... M3
Knott 17,940 .... R6
Knox 30,239 .... O7
Larue 11,922 .... K5
Laurel 38,982 .... N6
Lawrence 14,121 .... R4
Lee 7,754 .... O5
Leslie 14,882 .... P6
Letcher 30,687 .... R6
Lewis 14,545 .... P3
Lincoln 19,053 .... M6
Livingston 9,219 .... E6
Logan 24,138 .... H7
Lyon 6,490 .... E6
Madison 53,352 .... N5
Magoffin 13,515 .... P5
Marion 17,910 .... L5
Marshall 25,637 .... E7
Martin 13,925 .... R5
Mason 17,765 .... O3
McCracken 61,310 .... D6
McCreary 15,634 .... N7
McLean 10,090 .... G5
Meade 22,854 .... J5
Menifee 5,117 .... O5
Mercer 19,011 .... M5
Metcalfe 9,484 .... K7
Monroe 12,353 .... K7
Montgomery 20,046 .... O4
Morgan 12,103 .... P5
Muhlenberg 32,238 .... G6
Nelson 27,584 .... K5
Nicholas 7,157 .... N4
Ohio 21,765 .... H6
Oldham 27,795 .... L4
Owen 8,924 .... M3
Owsley 5,709 .... O6
Pendleton 10,989 .... N3
Perry 33,763 .... P6
Pike 81,123 .... S6
Powell 11,101 .... O5
Pulaski 45,803 .... M6
Robertson 2,265 .... N3
Rockcastle 13,973 .... N6
Rowan 19,049 .... P4
Russell 13,708 .... L7
Scott 21,813 .... M4
Shelby 23,328 .... L4
Simpson 14,673 .... H7
Spencer 5,929 .... L4
Taylor 21,178 .... L6
Todd 11,874 .... G7
Trigg 9,384 .... F7
Trimble 6,253 .... L3
Union 17,821 .... F5
Warren 71,828 .... H6
Washington 10,764 .... L5
Wayne 17,022 .... M7
Webster 14,832 .... F5
Whitley 33,396 .... N7
Wolfe 6,698 .... O5
Woodford 17,778 .... M4

CITIES and TOWNS

Zip *Name/Pop.* *Key*

42202 Adairville 1,105 .... H7
42602 Albany⊙ 2,083 .... L7
41001 Alexandria⊙ 4,735 .... N3
41601 Allen 338 .... R5
42204 Allensville 170 .... G7
40223 Anchorage 1,726 .... L2
41101 Ashland 27,064 .... R4
Ashland-Huntington‡ 311,350 .... R4
42206 Auburn 1,467 .... H7
†40201 Audubon Park 1,571 .... J2
41002 Augusta 1,455 .... N3
41602 Auxier 900 .... R5
†40222 Bancroft 725 .... K1
41603 Banner 950 .... R5
†40201 Barbourmeade 1,038 .... K1
40906 Barbourville⊙ 3,333 .... O7
40004 Bardstown⊙ 6,155 .... L5
42023 Bardwell⊙ 988 .... D7
42024 Barlow 746 .... D6
41311 Beattyville⊙ 1,068 .... O5
42320 Beaver Dam 3,185 .... H6
40006 Bedford⊙ 835 .... L3
40359 Beechwood Village 1,462 .... K2
†40201 Bellemeade 918 .... L2
41073 Bellevue 7,678 .... S1
40807 Benham 936 .... R7
42025 Benton⊙ 3,700 .... E7
40403 Berea 8,226 .... N5
41003 Berry 287 .... N3
41605 Betsy Layne 975 .... R5
41124 Blaine 358 .... R4
40008 Bloomfield 954 .... L5
†40201 Blue Ridge Manor 465 .... L2
42713 Bonnieville 372 .... K6
†40403 Boone 300 .... N5
41314 Booneville⊙ 191 .... O6
42101 Bowling Green⊙ 40,450 .... H7
40009 Bradfordsville 331 .... L6
40108 Brandenburg⊙ 1,831 .... J4
†42025 Briensburg E7
†40201 Broadfields 311 .... K2
40409 Brodhead 686 .... N6
†41016 Bromley 844 .... S2
40109 Brooks 1,344 .... K4
41004 Brooksville⊙ 680 .... N3
†40201 Brownsboro Farm 790 .... L1
42210 Brownsville⊙ 674 .... J6
40218 Buechel 6,709 .... K2
40310 Burgin 1,008 .... M5
42717 Burkesville⊙ 2,051 .... L7
41005 Burlington⊙ 500 .... R2
42519 Burnside 775 .... M6
41006 Butler 663 .... N3
42211 Cadiz⊙ 1,661 .... F7
42327 Calhoun⊙ 1,080 .... G5
41007 California 135 .... N3
42029 Calvert City 2,388 .... E6
†40337 Camargo 1,301 .... K4
40011 Campbellsburg 714 .... L3
42718 Campbellsville⊙ 8,715 .... L6
41301 Campton⊙ 486 .... O5
42721 Caneyville 642 .... J6
40311 Carlisle⊙ 1,757 .... N4
41008 Carrollton⊙ 3,967 .... L3
42030 Carrsville 99 .... E6
†42459 Caseyville 43 .... E5
41129 Catlettsburg⊙ 3,005 .... R4
42127 Cave City 2,098 .... K6
†41522 Cedarville 81 .... S6
42328 Centertown 462 .... G6
42330 Central City 5,214 .... G6
42726 Clarkson 666 .... J6
42404 Clay 1,356 .... F6
40312 Clay City 1,276 .... O5
40313 Clearfield 1,250 .... P4
42031 Clinton⊙ 1,720 .... D7
40111 Cloverport 1,585 .... H5
†41501 Coal Run 348 .... R5
41076 Cold Spring 2,117 .... T2
42728 Columbia⊙ 3,710 .... L6
42032 Columbus 296 .... C7
41729 Combs 900 .... P6
41131 Concord 67 .... P3
40701 Corbin 8,075 .... N7
41010 Corinth 258 .... M3
42406 Corydon 874 .... F5
*41011 Covington 49,563 .... S2
40419 Crab Orchard 843 .... M6
†41016 Crescent Springs 1,951 .... R2
†41076 Crestview 528 .... S2
†41017 Crestview Hills 1,408 .... R2
40014 Crestwood 531 .... L4
41030 Crittenden 597 .... M3
42217 Crofton 823 .... G6
40823 Cumberland 3,712 .... R6
41031 Cynthiana⊙ 5,881 .... N4
40422 Danville⊙ 12,942 .... M5
42408 Dawson Springs 3,275 .... F6
41074 Dayton 6,979 .... T1
†40201 Devondale 1,164 .... K2
42036 Dexter E7
42409 Dixon⊙ 533 .... F5
†40243 Douglass Hills 4,384 .... L2
41034 Dover 305 .... O3
42337 Drakesboro 798 .... H6
41035 Dry Ridge 1,250 .... M3
42037 Dycusburg 64 .... E6
42410 Earlington 2,011 .... F6
42038 Eddyville⊙ 1,949 .... E6
†41017 Edgewood 7,230 .... S2
42129 Edmonton⊙ 1,401 .... K7
40117 Ekron 239 .... J5
42701 Elizabethtown⊙ 15,380 .... K5
41522 Elkhorn City 1,446 .... S6
42220 Elkton⊙ 1,815 .... G7
†41018 Elsmere 7,203 .... R2
40019 Eminence 2,260 .... L4
40826 Eolia 875 .... R6
41018 Erlanger 14,433 .... R2
40827 Essie 650 .... P6
42567 Eubank 207 .... M6
40828 Evarts 1,234 .... P7
41039 Ewing 144 .... O4
40118 Fairdale 7,315 .... K4
40020 Fairfield 169 .... L5
†41101 Fairview 198 .... S2
41040 Falmouth⊙ 2,482 .... N3
41524 Fedscreek 950 .... S6
42533 Ferguson 1,009 .... M6
†40222 Fincastle 804 .... L1
41139 Flatwoods 8,354 .... R4
41816 Fleming-Neon 1,195 .... R6
41041 Flemingsburg⊙ 2,835 .... O4
41042 Florence 15,586 .... R2
42343 Fordsville 561 .... H5
41527 Forest Hills 502 .... L2
40121 Fort Knox 31,055 .... K5
41017 Fort Mitchell 7,297 .... S2
41075 Fort Thomas 16,012 .... S2
†41011 Fort Wright 4,481 .... S2
41043 Foster 80 .... N3
42133 Fountain Run 340 .... K7
40601 Frankfort (cap.)⊙ 25,973 .... M4
42134 Franklin⊙ 7,738 .... J7
42411 Fredonia 535 .... E6
40322 Frenchburg⊙ 550 .... O5
†41175 Fullerton 950 .... P3
42041 Fulton 3,137 .... D7
42140 Gamaliel 456 .... K7
40324 Georgetown⊙ 10,972 .... M4
41044 Germantown 347 .... O3
41045 Ghent 439 .... L3
42044 Gilbertsville E7
42141 Glasgow⊙ 12,958 .... J7
41046 Glencoe 354 .... M3
†40222 Glenview 212 .... K1
†40222 Goose Creek 394 .... L1
42045 Grand Rivers 428 .... E7
†41005 Grant 150 .... M3
40327 Gratz 124 .... M4
†40201 Graymoor 1,167 .... K1
41143 Grayson⊙ 3,423 .... R4
42743 Greensburg⊙ 2,377 .... K6
41144 Greenup⊙ 1,386 .... R3
42345 Greenville⊙ 4,631 .... G6
42234 Guthrie 1,361 .... G7
42413 Hanson 485 .... G6
42048 Hardin 545 .... E7
40143 Hardinsburg⊙ 2,211 .... H5
41531 Hardy 900 .... S5
40831 Harlan⊙ 3,024 .... P7
40330 Harrodsburg⊙ 7,265 .... M5
42347 Hartford⊙ 2,512 .... H6
42348 Hawesville⊙ 1,036 .... H5
41701 Hazard⊙ 5,371 .... P6
42049 Hazel 465 .... E7
40949 Heidrick 400 .... O7
42420 Henderson⊙ 24,834 .... F5
42050 Hickman⊙ 2,894 .... C7
42051 Hickory D7
41076 Highland Heights 4,435 .... T2
41822 Hindman⊙ 876 .... R6
42152 Hiseville 349 .... K6
42748 Hodgenville⊙ 2,531 .... K5
†40228 Hollow Creek 1,023 .... K4
†41018 Hopeful Heights R2
42240 Hopkinsville⊙ 27,318 .... F7
42749 Horse Cave 2,045 .... K6
†40201 Houston Acres 608 .... K2
40437 Hustonville 339 .... M6
41749 Hyden⊙ 488 .... P6
41051 Independence⊙ 7,998 .... M3
†40201 Indian Hills 787 .... K1
41224 Inez⊙ 413 .... S5
40336 Irvine⊙ 2,889 .... O5
40146 Irvington 1,409 .... J5
42350 Island 532 .... G6
41642 Ivel 850 .... R5
41339 Jackson⊙ 2,651 .... P5
42629 Jamestown⊙ 1,441 .... L7
40299 Jeffersontown 15,795 .... L2
40337 Jeffersonville 1,528 .... O5
41537 Jenkins 3,271 .... R6
40440 Junction City 2,045 .... M5
40737 Keavy 900 .... N6
†41011 Kenton Vale 145 .... S2
42053 Kevil 382 .... D6
†40201 Kingsley 464 .... K2
42055 Kuttawa 560 .... E6
42056 La Center 1,044 .... C6
41643 Lackey R6
42254 La Fayette 160 .... F7
40031 La Grange⊙ 2,971 .... L4
†41017 Lakeside Park 3,038 .... R2
40444 Lancaster⊙ 3,365 .... M5
40342 Lawrenceburg⊙ 5,167 .... M4
40033 Lebanon⊙ 6,590 .... L5
40150 Lebanon Junction 1,581 .... K5
42754 Leitchfield⊙ 4,533 .... J6
42256 Lewisburg 972 .... G6
42351 Lewisport 1,832 .... H5
*40501 Lexington⊙ 204,165 .... N4
Lexington‡ 318,136 .... N4
42539 Liberty⊙ 2,206 .... M6
42352 Livermore 1,672 .... G5
40445 Livingston 334 .... N6
40036 Lockport 84 .... M4
40741 London⊙ 4,002 .... N6
42001 Lone Oak 443 .... D6
40037 Loretto 954 .... L5
41230 Louisa⊙ 1,832 .... R4
*40201 Louisville⊙ 298,840 .... J2
Louisville‡ 906,240 .... J2
40854 Loyall 1,210 .... P7
41016 Ludlow 4,959 .... S2
40855 Lynch 1,614 .... R7
†40201 Lynnview 1,157 .... K4
40040 Mackville 229 .... L5
42431 Madisonville⊙ 16,979 .... F6
40962 Manchester⊙ 1,838 .... O6
42064 Marion⊙ 3,392 .... E6
41649 Martin 827 .... R5
42066 Mayfield⊙ 10,705 .... D7
41056 Maysville⊙ 7,983 .... O3
41543 McAndrews 975 .... S5
42354 McHenry 582 .... H6
40447 McKee⊙ 759 .... O6
41835 McRoberts 1,106 .... R6
†40201 Meadow Vale 1,008 .... L1
41059 Melbourne 628 .... T2
†41060 Mentor 169 .... N3
40965 Middlesboro 12,251 .... O7
40243 Middletown 414 .... L2
40347 Midway 1,445 .... M4
40348 Millersburg 987 .... N4
40045 Milton 718 .... L3
†40201 Minor Lane Heights 1,882 .... K4
†40359 Monterey 186 .... M4
42633 Monticello⊙ 5,677 .... M7
†40223 Moorland 513 .... L2
40351 Morehead⊙ 7,789 .... P4
42437 Morganfield⊙ 3,781 .... E5
42261 Morgantown⊙ 2,000 .... H6
42440 Mortons Gap 1,201 .... F6
41064 Mount Olivet⊙ 346 .... N3
†40437 Mount Salem 50 .... M6
40353 Mount Sterling⊙ 5,820 .... N4
40456 Mount Vernon⊙ 2,334 .... N6
40047 Mount Washington 3,997 .... K4
41548 Mouthcard 900 .... S6
40155 Muldraugh 1,752 .... J5
42765 Munfordville⊙ 1,783 .... J6
42071 Murray⊙ 14,248 .... E7
42441 Nebo 269 .... F6
41840 Neon-Fleming 1,195 .... R6
40050 New Castle⊙ 832 .... L4
40051 New Haven 926 .... K5
*41071 Newport 21,587 .... S2
40356 Nicholasville⊙ 10,319 .... N5
†40201 Northfield 906 .... K1
40357 North Middletown 637 .... N4
42442 Nortonville 1,336 .... G6
42262 Oak Grove 2,088 .... G7
42159 Oakland 264 .... J6
41238 Oil Springs 900 .... P5
40219 Okolona 20,039 .... K4
41164 Olive Hill 2,539 .... P4
42301 Owensboro⊙ 54,450 .... G5
Owensboro‡ 85,949 .... G5
40359 Owenton⊙ 1,341 .... M3
40360 Owingsville⊙ 1,419 .... O4
42001 Paducah⊙ 29,315 .... D6
41240 Paintsville⊙ 3,815 .... R5
40361 Paris⊙ 7,935 .... N4
42160 Park City 614 .... J6
†41011 Park Hills 3,500 .... S2
†40201 Parkway Village 754 .... J2
42266 Pembroke 636 .... G7
40468 Perryville 841 .... M5
40056 Pewee Valley 982 .... L4
41553 Phelps 1,126 .... S6
41501 Pikeville⊙ 4,756 .... S6
42635 Pine Knot 1,389 .... M7
40977 Pineville⊙ 2,599 .... O7
†40201 Plantation 969 .... K1
40258 Pleasure Ridge Park 27,332 .... J4
40057 Pleasureville 837 .... L4
†42101 Plum Springs 393 .... J7
42367 Powderly 848 .... G6
41653 Prestonsburg⊙ 4,011 .... R5
†41008 Prestonville 205 .... L3
42445 Princeton⊙ 7,073 .... F6
40059 Prospect 1,981 .... K4
42450 Providence 4,434 .... F6
41169 Raceland 1,970 .... R3
40160 Radcliff 14,519 .... K5
40472 Ravenna 793 .... O5
40475 Richmond⊙ 21,705 .... N5
†40222 Riverwood 435 .... K1
42273 Rochester 289 .... H6

Agriculture, Industry and Resources

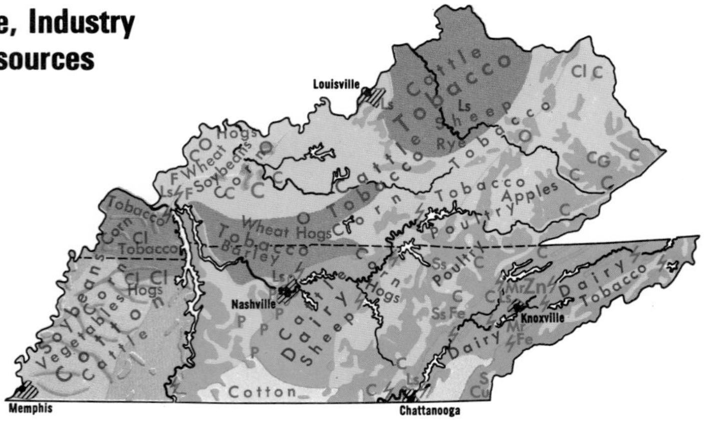

DOMINANT LAND USE

- Hogs, Soft Winter Wheat
- Tobacco, General Farming
- General Farming, Livestock, Tobacco
- General Farming, Livestock, Dairy
- General Farming, Livestock, Fruit, Tobacco
- Specialized Cotton
- Cotton, General Farming
- Cotton, Livestock
- Forests
- Swampland, Limited Agriculture

MAJOR MINERAL OCCURRENCES

C	Coal	G	Natural Gas	P	Phosphates
Cl	Clay	Ls	Limestone	S	Pyrites
Cu	Copper	Mr	Marble	Ss	Sandstone
F	Fluorspar	O	Petroleum	Zn	Zinc
Fe	Iron Ore				

ϟ Water Power   ▨ Major Industrial Areas

KENTUCKY

AREA 40,409 sq. mi. (104,659 sq. km.)
POPULATION 3,660,257
CAPITAL Frankfort
LARGEST CITY Louisville
HIGHEST POINT Black Mtn. 4,145 ft. (1263 m.)
SETTLED IN 1774
ADMITTED TO UNION June 1, 1792
POPULAR NAME Bluegrass State
STATE FLOWER Goldenrod
STATE BIRD Cardinal

TENNESSEE

AREA 42,144 sq. mi. (109,153 sq. km.)
POPULATION 4,591,120
CAPITAL Nashville
LARGEST CITY Memphis
HIGHEST POINT Clingmans Dome 6,643 ft. (2025 m.)
SETTLED IN 1757
ADMITTED TO UNION June 1, 1796
POPULAR NAME Volunteer State
STATE FLOWER Iris
STATE BIRD Mockingbird

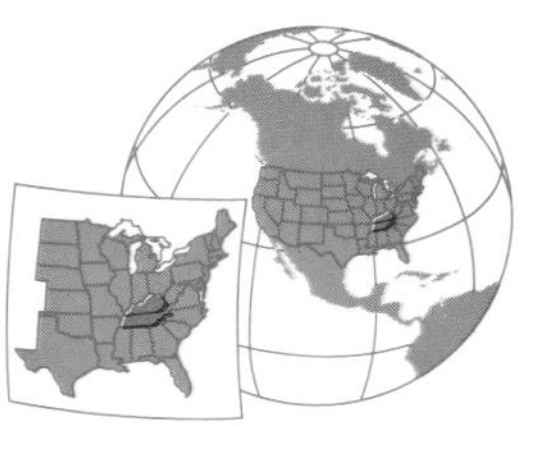

42369 Rockport 511 H6
†40201 Rolling Fields 731 K2
†40201 Rolling Hills 1,122 L1
41169 Russell 3,824 R3
42642 Russell Springs 1,831 L6
42276 Russellville⊙ 7,520 H7
†41015 Ryland Heights 252 M3
42372 Sacramento 538 G6
40370 Sadieville 253 M4
42453 Saint Charles 405 F6
40207 Saint Matthews 13,519 K2
†40201 Saint Regis Park 1,735 K2
42078 Salem 833 E6
40371 Salt Lick 347 O4
41465 Salyersville⊙ 1,352 P5
41083 Sanders 332 M3
41171 Sandy Hook⊙ 627 P4
41056 Sardis 198 O3
42553 Science Hill 655 M6
42164 Scottsville⊙ 4,278 J7
42455 Sebree 1,516 F5
†40201 Seneca Gardens 748 K2
40983 Sextons Creek 975 O6
40374 Sharpsburg 339 O4
40065 Shelbyville⊙ 5,329 L4
40165 Shepherdsville⊙ 4,454 K4
40216 Shively 16,819 K4
41085 Silver Grove 1,260 T2
40067 Simpsonville 642 L4
42456 Slaughters 269 F6
41764 Smilax 987 P6
40068 Smithfield 137 L4
42081 Smithland⊙ 512 E6
42171 Smiths Grove 767 J6
42501 Somerset⊙ 10,649 M6
42776 Sonora 416 K5
42374 South Carrollton 262 G6
41071 Southgate 2,833 T2
41174 South Portsmouth 900 P3
41175 South Shore 1,525 R3
25661 South Williamson 1,016 S5
41086 Sparta 192 M3
42458 Spottsville 914 G5
40069 Springfield⊙ 3,179 L5
†40201 Springlee 498 K2
40379 Stamping Ground 562 M4
40484 Stanford⊙ 2,764 M5
40380 Stanton⊙ 2,691 O5
42647 Stearns 1,557 N7
41567 Stone 900 S5
†40201 Strathmoor Village 466 J2
42459 Sturgis 2,293 F5
†41011 Taylor Mill 4,509 S2
40071 Taylorsville⊙ 801 L4
†40222 Thornhill 233 K1
41189 Tollesboro 808 O3
42167 Tompkinsville⊙ 4,366 K7
42286 Trenton 465 G7
41091 Union 601 M3
42461 Uniontown 1,169 F5
42784 Upton 731 K6
40272 Valley Station 24,474 K4
41179 Vanceburg⊙ 1,939 P3
41265 Van Lear 2,035 R5
†40828 Verda 1,133 P7
40383 Versailles⊙ 6,427 M4
41773 Vicco 456 P6
†41017 Villa Hills 4,402 R2
40175 Vine Grove 3,583 K5
†41063 Visalia 198 N3
40873 Wallins Creek 459 O7
41094 Walton 1,651 M3
41095 Warsaw⊙ 1,328 M3
41096 Washington 624 O3
42085 Water Valley 395 D7
42462 Waverly 434 F5
41666 Wayland 601 R6
41667 Weeksbury 850 R6
†40201 Wellington 653 K2
†40218 West Buechel 1,205 K2
41472 West Liberty⊙ 1,381 P5
40177 West Point 1,339 J4
†42501 West Somerset 850 M6
41101 Westwood 5,973 R4
†40207 Westwood 826 L1
42463 Wheatcroft 325 F5
41669 Wheelwright 865 R6
41390 Whick 280 P6
42464 White Plains 859 G6
41858 Whitesburg⊙ 1,525 R6
42378 Whitesville 788 H5
42653 Whitley City⊙ 1,683 N7
42087 Wickliffe⊙ 1,034 C7
†41071 Wilders 633 S2
40769 Williamsburg⊙ 5,560 N7
41097 Williamstown⊙ 2,502 M3
40078 Willisburg 235 L5
40390 Wilmore 3,787 M5
40391 Winchester⊙ 15,216 N5
†40201 Windy Hills 2,214 K1
42088 Wingo 606 D7
40771 Woodbine 900 N7
42170 Woodburn 330 J7
†40201 Woodland Hills 839 L2
†42001 Woodlawn-Oakdale 4,722 D6
†41071 Woodlawn 331 T2
†40201 Woodlawn Park 1,052 K2
41183 Worthington 1,948 R3
41098 Worthville 272 L3
41144 Wurtland 1,301 R3

OTHER FEATURES

Abraham Lincoln Birthplace Nat'l Hist. Site K5
Barkley (dam) E6
Barkley (lake) F7
Barren (riv.) H6
Barren River (lake) J7
Beech Fork (riv.) L5
Big Sandy (riv.) R4
Black (mt.) R7
Buckhorn (lake) O6
Chaplin (riv.) L5
Clarks, East Fork (riv.) E7
Cove Run (lake) O4
Cumberland (lake) M7
Cumberland (mt.) P7
Cumberland (riv.) K8
Cumberland Gap Nat'l Hist. Park P7
Dale Hollow (lake) L7
Dewey (lake) R5
Dix (riv.) M5
Drakes (creek) J7
Dry (creek) R3
Eagle (creek) M3
Fishtrap (lake) S6
Fort Campbell G7
Grayson (lake) P4
Green (riv.) G6
Green River (lake) L6
Herrington (lake) M5
Hinkston (creek) N4
Kentucky (dam) E7
Kentucky (lake) E8
Kentucky (riv.) M3
Land Between The Lakes Rec. Area E7
Laurel River (lake) N6
Lexington Blue Grass Army Depot N5
Licking (riv.) N3
Mammoth Cave Nat'l Park J6
Mayfield (creek) C7
Mississippi (riv.) A10
Mud (riv.) H7
Nolin (lake) K6
Nolin (riv.) J6
Obion (creek) C7
Ohio (riv.) F5
Paint Lick (riv.) M5
Panther (creek) G5
Pine (mt.) O7
Pond (riv.) G6
Red (riv.) O5
Red (riv.) G7
Rockcastle (riv.) N6
Rolling Fork (riv.) L5
Rough (riv.) H5
Rough River (lake) J5
Salt (riv.) K5
Tennessee (riv.) D6
Tradewater (riv.) F6
Tug Fork (riv.) S5

TENNESSEE

COUNTIES

Anderson 67,346 N8
Bedford 27,916 J9
Benton 14,901 E8
Bledsoe 9,478 L9
Blount 77,770 O9
Bradley 67,547 M10
Campbell 34,923 N8
Cannon 10,234 J9
Carroll 28,285 E9
Carter 50,205 S8
Cheatham 21,616 G8
Chester 12,727 D10
Claiborne 24,595 O8
Clay 7,676 K7
Cocke 28,792 P9
Coffee 38,311 J9
Crockett 14,941 C9
Cumberland 28,676 L9
Davidson 477,811 H8
Decatur 10,857 E9
De Kalb 13,589 K9
Dickson 30,037 G8
Dyer 34,663 C8
Fayette 25,305 C10
Fentress 14,826 M8
Franklin 31,983 J10
Gibson 49,467 D9
Giles 24,625 G10
Grainger 16,751 O8
Greene 54,422 R8
Grundy 13,787 K10
Hamblen 49,300 P8
Hamilton 287,740 L10
Hancock 6,887 P7
Hardeman 23,873 C10
Hardin 22,280 E10
Hawkins 43,751 P8
Haywood 20,318 C9
Henderson 21,390 E9
Henry 28,656 E8
Hickman 15,151 G9
Houston 6,871 F8
Humphreys 15,957 F8
Jackson 9,398 K8
Jefferson 31,284 P8
Johnson 13,745 T7
Knox 319,694 O9
Lake 7,455 B8
Lauderdale 24,555 B9
Lawrence 34,110 G10
Lewis 9,700 F9
Lincoln 26,483 H10
Loudon 28,553 N9
Macon 15,700 J7
Madison 74,546 D9
Marion 24,416 K10
Marshall 19,698 H10
Maury 51,095 G9
McMinn 41,878 M10
McNairy 22,525 D10
Meigs 7,431 M9
Monroe 28,700 N10
Montgomery 83,342 G8
Moore 4,510 J10
Morgan 16,604 M8
Obion 32,781 C8
Overton 17,575 L8
Perry 6,111 F9
Pickett 4,358 M7
Polk 13,602 N10
Putnam 47,690 K8
Rhea 24,235 M9
Roane 48,425 M9
Robertson 37,021 H7
Rutherford 84,058 J9
Scott 19,259 M8
Sequatchie 8,605 L10
Sevier 41,418 O9
Shelby 777,113 B10
Smith 14,935 J8
Stewart 8,665 F7
Sullivan 143,968 S7
Sumner 85,790 J8
Tipton 32,930 B9
Trousdale 6,137 J8
Unicoi 16,362 S8
Union 11,707 O8
Van Buren 4,728 L9
Warren 32,653 K9
Washington 88,755 R8
Wayne 13,946 F10
Weakley 32,896 D8
White 19,567 L9
Williamson 58,108 H9
Wilson 56,064 J8

CITIES and TOWNS

Zip Name/Pop. Key

†38301 Adair 70 D9
37010 Adams 600 G7
38310 Adamsville 1,453 E10
38001 Alamo⊙ 2,615 C9
37701 Alcoa 6,870 N9
37012 Alexandria 689 J8
38501 Algood 2,406 K8
38504 Allardt 654 M8
37301 Altamont⊙ 679 K10
38449 Ardmore 835 H10
38002 Arlington 1,778 B10
37015 Ashland City⊙ 2,329 G8
37303 Athens⊙ 12,080 M10
38004 Atoka 691 B10
38220 Atwood 1,143 D9
37016 Auburntown 204 J9
37743 Baileyton 333 R8
†37650 Banner Hill 2,913 R8
38134 Bartlett 17,170 B10
38544 Baxter 1,411 K8
37305 Beersheba Springs 643 K10
37020 Bell Buckle 450 J9
37205 Belle Meade 3,182 H8
38006 Bells 1,571 C9
37307 Benton⊙ 1,115 M10
†37201 Berry Hill 1,113 H8
†37027 Berry's Chapel 2,703 H9
38315 Bethel Springs 873 D10
38221 Big Sandy 650 E8
37709 Blaine 1,147 O8
37660 Bloomingdale 12,088 R7
37617 Blountville⊙ 2,554 S7
37618 Bluff City 1,121 S8
38008 Bolivar⊙ 6,597 C10
38010 Braden 293 B10
38316 Bradford 1,146 D8
37027 Brentwood 9,431 H8
37710 Briceville 850 N8
38011 Brighton 976 B10
37620 Bristol 23,986 S7
38012 Brownsville⊙ 9,307 C9
38317 Bruceton 1,579 E8
37711 Bulls Gap 821 P8
38015 Burlison 386 B9
37029 Burns 777 G8
38549 Byrdstown⊙ 884 L7
37309 Calhoun 590 M10
38320 Camden⊙ 3,279 E8
37030 Carthage⊙ 2,672 K8
37714 Caryville 2,039 N8
37032 Cedar Hill 420 H7
38551 Celina⊙ 1,580 K7
†37110 Centertown 300 K9
37033 Centerville⊙ 2,824 G9
37034 Chapel Hill 861 H9
37310 Charleston 756 M10
37036 Charlotte⊙ 788 G8
*37401 Chattanooga⊙ 169,558 K10
Chattanooga‡ 426,540 K10
37642 Church Hill 4,110 R7
38324 Clarksburg 400 E9
37040 Clarksville⊙ 54,777 G7
Clarksville‡ 150,220 G7
37311 Cleveland⊙ 26,415 M10
38425 Clifton 773 F10
37716 Clinton⊙ 5,245 N8
37313 Coalmont 625 K10
37315 Collegedale 4,607 M10
38017 Collierville 7,839 B10
38450 Collinwood 1,064 F10
37663 Colonial Heights 6,744 R8
38401 Columbia⊙ 26,571 G9
37720 Concord 8,569 N9
38501 Cookeville⊙ 20,535 L8
37317 Copperhill 418 N10
37047 Cornersville 722 H10
38224 Cottage Grove 117 E8
38326 Counce 975 E10
38019 Covington⊙ 6,065 B9
37318 Cowan 1,790 K10
37723 Crab Orchard 1,065 M9
37049 Cross Plains 655 H7
38555 Crossville⊙ 6,394 L9
37050 Cumberland City 276 F8
37724 Cumberland Gap 263 O8
37725 Dandridge⊙ 1,383 O8
37321 Dayton⊙ 5,913 L9
37322 Decatur⊙ 1,069 M9
38329 Decaturville⊙ 1,004 E9
37324 Decherd 2,233 J10
38391 Denmark 51 D9
37055 Dickson 7,040 G8
37058 Dover⊙ 1,197 F8
37059 Dowelltown 341 K8
38559 Doyle 344 K9
38225 Dresden⊙ 2,256 D8
37326 Ducktown 583 N10
37327 Dunlap⊙ 3,681 L10
38330 Dyer 2,419 D8
38024 Dyersburg⊙ 15,856 C8
†37801 Eagleton Village 5,331 O9
37060 Eagleville 444 H9
37412 East Ridge 21,236 L11
†38367 Eastview 552 D10
37643 Elizabethton⊙ 12,431 S8
38455 Elkton 540 H10
38029 Ellendale 850 B10
37329 Englewood 1,840 M10
38332 Enville 287 E10
37061 Erin⊙ 1,614 F8
37650 Erwin⊙ 4,739 S8
37330 Estill Springs 1,324 J10
38456 Ethridge 548 G10
37331 Etowah 3,758 M10
37062 Fairview 3,648 G9
37656 Fall Branch 1,340 R8
37334 Fayetteville⊙ 7,559 H10
38334 Finger 245 D10
38030 Finley 1,014 B8
†37201 Forest Hills 4,516 H8
37064 Franklin⊙ 12,407 H9
38034 Friendship 763 C9
37737 Friendsville 694 N9
38337 Gadsden 683 D9
38562 Gainesboro⊙ 1,119 K8
37066 Gallatin⊙ 17,191 H8
38036 Gallaway 804 B10
†38019 Garland 301 B9
38037 Gates 729 C9
37738 Gatlinburg 3,210 O9
38138 Germantown 21,482 B10
38338 Gibson 458 D9
†38015 Gilt Edge 142 B9
38229 Gleason 1,335 D8
37072 Goodlettsville 8,327 H8
38563 Gordonsville 893 K8
38039 Grand Junction 360 C10
37338 Graysville 1,380 L10
37742 Greenback 546 N9
37073 Greenbrier 3,180 H8
37743 Greeneville⊙ 14,097 R8
38230 Greenfield 2,109 D8
37339 Gruetli 910 K10
38040 Halls 2,444 C9
37658 Hampton 2,236 S8
37748 Harriman 8,303 M9
37341 Harrison 6,206 L10
37752 Harrogate-Shawanee 2,530 O8
37074 Hartsville⊙ 2,674 J8
38340 Henderson⊙ 4,449 D10
37075 Hendersonville 26,561 H8
38041 Henning 638 B9
38231 Henry 295 E8
38042 Hickory Valley 252 C10
38462 Hohenwald⊙ 3,922 F9
38342 Hollow Rock 955 E8
38232 Hornbeak 452 C8
38044 Hornsby 401 D10
38343 Humboldt 10,209 D9
38344 Huntingdon⊙ 3,962 E8
37345 Huntland 983 J10
37756 Huntsville⊙ 519 N8
37078 Hurricane Mills 850 F9
38463 Iron City 482 F10
37757 Jacksboro⊙ 1,722 N8
38301 Jackson⊙ 49,131 D9
38556 Jamestown⊙ 2,364 M8
37347 Jasper⊙ 2,633 K10
37760 Jefferson City 5,612 P8
37762 Jellico 2,798 N7
37601 Johnson City 39,753 S8
Johnson City-Kingsport-Bristol‡ 433,638 S8
37659 Jonesboro⊙ 2,829 R8
37921 Karns 1,173 N9
38233 Kenton 1,551 C8
†37347 Kimball 1,220 K10
*37660 Kingsport 32,027 R7
37763 Kingston⊙ 4,441 N9
37082 Kingston Springs 1,017 G8
*37901 Knoxville⊙ 175,045 O9
Knoxville‡ 476,517 O9
37083 Lafayette⊙ 3,808 J7
37766 La Follette 8,198 N8
38046 La Grange 185 C10
37769 Lake City 2,335 N8
†38134 Lakeland 612 B10
†37379 Lakesite 651 L10
†37138 Lakewood 2,325 H8
37086 La Vergne 5,495 H9
38464 Lawrenceburg⊙ 10,184 G10
37087 Lebanon⊙ 11,872 J8
37771 Lenoir City 5,446 N9
37091 Lewisburg⊙ 8,760 H10
38351 Lexington⊙ 5,934 E9
37095 Liberty 365 K8
37096 Linden⊙ 1,087 F9
38570 Livingston⊙ 3,372 L8
37097 Lobelville 993 F9
37350 Lookout Mountain 1,886 L11
38469 Loretto 1,612 G10
37774 Loudon⊙ 3,943 N9
37779 Luttrell 962 O8
37352 Lynchburg⊙ 668 J10
38472 Lynnville 383 G10
37354 Madisonville⊙ 2,884 N9
37355 Manchester⊙ 7,250 J10
38237 Martin 8,898 D8
37801 Maryville⊙ 17,480 O9
37806 Mascot 2,203 O8
38049 Mason 471 B10
38050 Maury City 989 C9
37807 Maynardville⊙ 924 O8
37101 McEwen 1,352 F8
38201 McKenzie 5,405 E8
38235 McLemoresville 311 D9
37110 McMinnville⊙ 10,683 K9
38355 Medina 687 D9
38356 Medon 169 D10
*38101 Memphis⊙ 646,174 B10
Memphis‡ 912,887 B10
38357 Michie 530 E10
38052 Middleton 596 D10
38358 Milan 8,083 D9
38359 Milledgeville 392 E10
38053 Millington 20,236 B10
38473 Minor Hill 564 G10
37119 Mitchellville 209 J7
37356 Monteagle 1,126 K10
38574 Monterey 2,610 L8
37357 Morrison 587 K9
†37660 Morrison City 2,032 R7
37814 Morristown⊙ 19,683 P8
38057 Moscow 499 C10
37818 Mosheim 1,539 R8
37683 Mountain City⊙ 2,125 T8
37642 Mount Carmel 3,764 R8
37122 Mount Juliet 2,879 H8
38474 Mount Pleasant 3,375 G9
38058 Munford 2,336 B10
37130 Murfreesboro⊙ 32,845 J9
*37201 Nashville (cap.)⊙ 455,651 H8
Nashville-Davidson‡ 850,505 H8
38059 Newbern 2,794 C8
†37380 New Hope 681 K11
37134 New Johnsonville 1,824 E8
37820 New Market 1,216 O8
37821 Newport⊙ 7,580 P9
37822 New Tazewell 1,677 O8
37826 Niota 765 M9
37360 Normandy 118 J10
37828 Norris 1,374 N8
37829 Oakdale 323 M9
†37201 Oak Hill 4,609 H8
38060 Oakland 472 B10
37830 Oak Ridge 27,662 N8
38240 Obion 1,282 C8
37840 Oliver Springs 3,659 N8
37841 Oneida 3,717 N7
37363 Ooltewah 950 M10
†37660 Orebank 1,284 R7
37141 Orlinda 382 H7
35740 Orme 181 K10
37365 Palmer 1,027 K10
38242 Paris⊙ 10,728 E8
37843 Parrottsville 118 P8
38363 Parsons 2,422 E9
37143 Pegram 1,081 H8
37144 Petersburg 681 H10
37845 Petros 1,286 M8
37846 Philadelphia 507 M9
37863 Pigeon Forge 1,822 O9
37367 Pikeville⊙ 2,085 L9
†38017 Piperton 746 B10
†37738 Pittman Center 488 P9
38578 Pleasant Hill 371 L9
37148 Portland 4,030 H7
37849 Powell 7,220 N8
†37397 Powells Crossroads 918 L10
38478 Pulaski⊙ 7,184 G10
38251 Puryear 624 E8
38367 Ramer 429 D10
37415 Red Bank 13,299 L10
37150 Red Boiling Springs 1,173 K7
†37641 Rheatown R8
†37380 Richard City 87 K11
38080 Ridgely 1,932 B8
†37401 Ridgeside 417 L10
37152 Ridgetop 1,225 H8
38063 Ripley⊙ 6,366 B9
38253 Rives 386 C8
37687 Roan Mountain 1,108 S8
37853 Rockford 567 O9
37854 Rockwood 5,767 M9
37857 Rogersville⊙ 4,368 P8
38053 Rosemark 950 B10
38066 Rossville 379 B10
37860 Russellville 1,069 P8
38369 Rutherford 1,378 C8
37861 Rutledge⊙ 1,058 P8
38481 Saint Joseph 897 G10
37373 Sale Creek 900 L10
38370 Saltillo 434 E10
38254 Samburg 465 C8
38371 Sardis 301 E10
38067 Saulsbury 156 C10
38372 Savannah⊙ 6,992 E10
38374 Scotts Hill 668 E10
38375 Selmer⊙ 3,979 D10
37862 Sevierville⊙ 4,556 P9
37375 Sewanee 2,298 K10
38255 Sharon 1,134 D8
37160 Shelbyville⊙ 13,530 H10
37376 Sherwood 900 K10
37377 Signal Mountain 5,818 L10
38377 Silerton 100 D10
37165 Slayden 69 G8
37166 Smithville⊙ 3,839 K9
37167 Smyrna 8,839 H9
37869 Sneedville⊙ 1,110 P7
37319 Soddy-Daisy 8,388 L10
38068 Somerville⊙ 2,264 C10
†37030 South Carthage 1,004 K8
†37311 South Cleveland 4,360 M10
†37716 South Clinton 1,671 N8
†42041 South Fulton 2,735 D8
37380 South Pittsburg 3,636 K10
37171 Southside 800 G8
38583 Sparta⊙ 4,864 K9
38585 Spencer⊙ 1,126 L9
37381 Spring City 1,951 M9
37172 Springfield⊙ 10,814 H8
37174 Spring Hill 989 H9
38069 Stanton 540 C10
38379 Stantonville 271 E10
†37660 Sullivan Gardens 2,513 R8
38483 Summertown 850 G10
37873 Surgoinsville 1,536 R8
37874 Sweetwater 4,725 N9
37877 Talbott 975 P8
37879 Tazewell⊙ 2,090 O8
37385 Tellico Plains 698 N10
37178 Tennessee Ridge 1,325 F8
38079 Tiptonville⊙ 2,438 B8
38381 Toone 355 D10
37882 Townsend 351 O9
37387 Tracy City 1,356 K10
38382 Trenton⊙ 4,601 D9
38258 Trezevant 921 D8
38259 Trimble 722 C8
38260 Troy 1,093 C8
37388 Tullahoma 15,800 J10
37743 Tusculum 1,242 R8
38261 Union City⊙ 10,436 C8
37181 Vanleer 401 G8
†37397 Victoria 800 K10
37394 Viola 149 K9

(continued on following page)

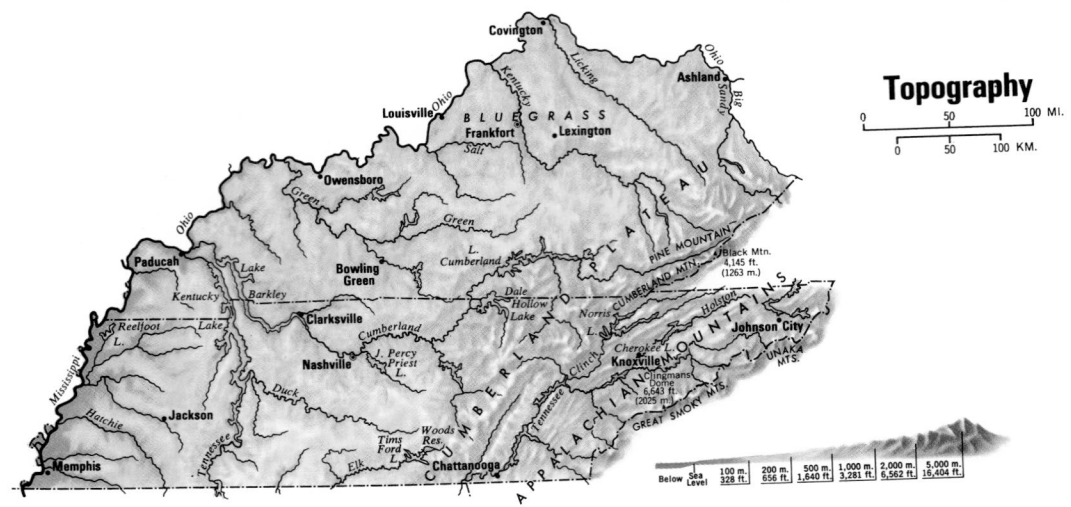
Topography

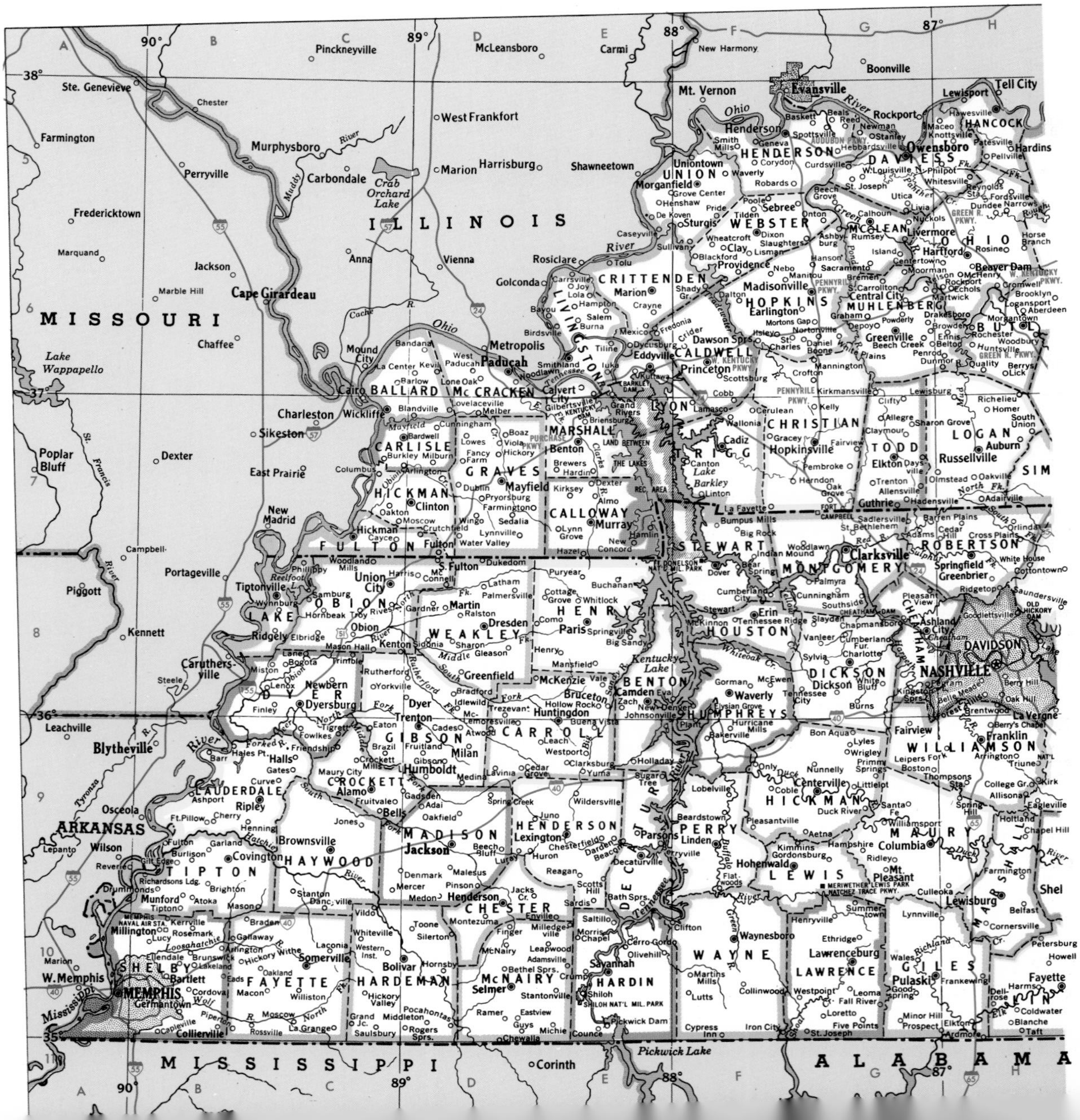

Kentucky and Tennessee

SCALE
0 5 10 20 30 40 MI
0 5 10 20 30 40 KM.

State Capitals .... ⊛
County Seats .... ⊛
Major Limited Access Hwys. ——

© Copyright HAMMOND INCORPORATED, Maplewood, N.J.

Topography

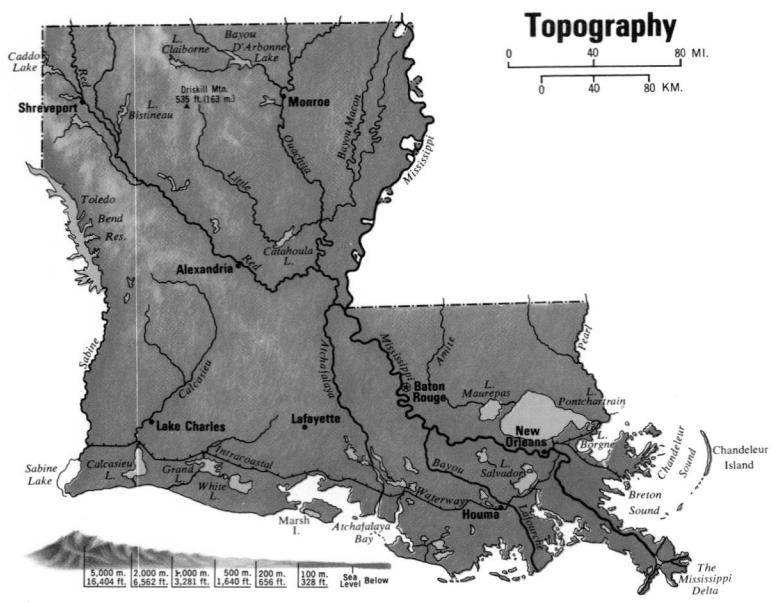

5,000 m. / 2,000 m. / 1,000 m. / 500 m. / 200 m. / 100 m. / Sea Level / Below
16,404 ft. / 6,562 ft. / 3,281 ft. / 1,640 ft. / 656 ft. / 328 ft.

PARISHES

Acadia 56,427	F6
Allen 21,390	E5
Ascension 50,068	J6
Assumption 22,084	H7
Avoyelles 41,393	G4
Beauregard 29,692	D5
Bienville 16,387	D2
Bossier 80,721	C1
Caddo 252,358	C1
Calcasieu 167,223	D6
Caldwell 10,761	F2
Cameron 9,336	D7
Catahoula 12,287	G3
Claiborne 17,095	D1
Concordia 22,981	G4
De Soto 25,727	C2
East Baton Rouge 366,191	K1
East Carroll 11,772	H1
East Feliciana 19,015	H5
Evangeline 33,343	F5
Franklin 24,141	G2
Grant 16,703	E3
Iberia 63,752	G7
Iberville 32,159	H6
Jackson 17,321	E2
Jefferson 454,592	K7
Jefferson Davis 32,168	E6
Lafayette 150,017	F6
Lafourche 82,483	K7
La Salle 17,004	F3
Lincoln 39,763	E1
Livingston 58,806	L2
Madison 15,975	H2
Morehouse 34,803	G1
Natchitoches 39,863	D3
Orleans 557,515	L6
Ouachita 139,241	F2
Plaquemines 26,049	L8
Pointe Coupee 24,045	G5
Rapides 135,282	E4
Red River 10,433	D2
Richland 22,187	G2
Sabine 25,280	C3
Saint Bernard 64,097	L7
Saint Charles 37,259	K7
Saint Helena 9,827	J5
Saint James 21,495	L3
Saint John the Baptist 31,924	M3
Saint Landry 84,128	F5
Saint Martin 40,214	G6
Saint Mary 64,253	H7
Saint Tammany 110,869	L6
Tangipahoa 80,698	K5
Tensas 8,525	H2
Terrebonne 94,393	J8
Union 21,167	F1
Vermilion 48,458	F7
Vernon 53,475	D4
Washington 44,207	K5
Webster 43,631	D1
West Baton Rouge 19,086	H6
West Carroll 12,922	H1
West Feliciana 12,186	H5
Winn 17,253	E3

CITIES and TOWNS

Zip	Name/Pop.	Key
70510	Abbeville⊙ 12,391	F7
70420	Abita Springs 1,072	L6
71316	Acme 235	G4
70710	Addis 1,320	J2
71401	Aimwell 55	G3
70421	Akers 150	N2
70711	Albany 857	M1
71301	Alexandria⊙ 51,565	E4
	Alexandria‡ 151,985	E4
†70458	Alten 500	L6
70340	Amelia 3,617	H7
70422	Amite⊙ 4,301	K5
71403	Anacoco 820	D4
70426	Angie 311	L5
70712	Angola 600	G5
70032	Arabi 10,248	P4
71001	Arcadia⊙ 3,403	E1
71218	Archibald 425	G2
70512	Arnaudville 1,679	G6
71002	Ashland 307	D2
71003	Athens 419	E1
71404	Atlanta 197	E3
70513	Avery Island 500	G7
70714	Baker 12,865	K1
70514	Baldwin 2,644	H7
71405	Ball 3,405	F4
†70401	Baptist 150	M1
70036	Barataria 1,123	K7
70515	Basile 2,635	E5
71219	Baskin 286	G2
71220	Bastrop⊙ 15,527	G1
70515	Batchelor 500	G5
*70801	Baton Rouge	
	(cap.)⊙ 219,419	K2
	Baton Rouge‡ 493,973	K2
†70360	Bayou Cane 15,723	J7
†70380	Bayou Vista 5,805	H7
71004	Belcher 436	C1
70630	Bell City 400	D6
70037	Belle Chasse 5,412	O4
71406	Belmont 350	C3
71407	Bentley 120	E3
71006	Benton⊙ 1,864	C1
70558	Bermuda 50	D3
71222	Bernice 1,869	E1
70342	Berwick 4,466	H7
71007	Bethany 300	B2
71008	Bienville 249	D2
71009	Blanchard 1,128	C1
70427	Bogalusa 16,976	L5
†71064	Bolinger 200	G1
71223	Bonita 503	G1
71320	Bordelonville 350	G4
70343	Bourg 2,073	J7
71409	Boyce 1,198	E4
70040	Braithwaite 350	P4
70516	Branch 200	F6
70517	Breaux Bridge 5,922	G6
70718	Brittany 475	L3
70518	Broussard 2,923	F6
70719	Brusly 1,762	J2
71014	Bryceland 94	E2
71321	Buckeye 280	E4
71322	Bunkie 5,364	F5
70041	Buras-Triumph 4,137	L8
70519	Cade 350	G6
71225	Calhoun 350	F2
71016	Castor 195	D2
70522	Centerville 600	H7
70043	Chalmette⊙ 33,847	P4
†70767	Chamberlin 20	J1
71324	Chase 200	G2
70524	Chataignier 431	F5
71226	Chatham 714	F2
70344	Chauvin 3,338	J8
71325	Cheneyville 865	F4
71412	Chopin 175	E4
71227	Choudrant 809	F1
70525	Church Point 4,599	F6
71414	Clarence 612	E3
71415	Clarks 931	F2
71326	Clayton 1,204	H3
70722	Clinton⊙ 1,919	J5
71416	Cloutierville 100	E3
71417	Colfax⊙ 1,680	E3
71229	Collinston 439	G1
71418	Columbia⊙ 687	F2
70723	Convent⊙ 400	L3
71419	Converse 449	C3
†71107	Cooper Road	C1
71327	Cottonport 1,911	F5
71018	Cotton Valley 1,445	D1
71019	Coushatta⊙ 2,084	D2
70433	Covington⊙ 7,892	K5
70510	Cow Island 200	F7
†70656	Cravens 200	E5
71020	Creston 135	E3
70526	Crowley⊙ 16,036	F6
71230	Crowville 400	G2
71021	Cullen 1,869	D1
70345	Cut Off 5,049	K7
71420	Cypress 55	D3
70046	Davant 600	L7
70528	Delcambre 2,216	G7
71232	Delhi 3,290	H2
71233	Delta 295	J2
70726	Denham Springs 8,563	L2
70633	De Quincy 3,966	D6
70634	De Ridder⊙ 11,057	D5
70030	Des Allemands 2,920	N4
70047	Destrehan 2,382	N4
†71055	Dixie Inn 453	D1
71422	Dodson 469	E2
70346	Donaldsonville⊙ 7,901	K3
70352	Donner 500	J7
71234	Downsville 213	F1
71023	Doyline 801	D1
70637	Dry Creek 300	D5
71423	Dry Prong 526	E3
71235	Dubach 1,161	E1
71024	Dubberly 421	D1
70353	Dulac 675	J8
71236	Dunn 225	G2
70728	Duplessis 500	K2
70529	Duson 1,253	F6
71330	Echo 525	F4
70049	Edgard⊙ 400	M3
†71019	Edgefield 312	D2
71331	Effie 300	F4
70638	Elizabeth 454	E5
71424	Elmer 200	E4
71051	Elm Grove 100	C2
70532	Elton 1,450	E6
71425	Enterprise 375	G3
71332	Eola 47	F5
71237	Epps 672	G1
70533	Erath 2,133	F7
71238	Eros 158	F2
70534	Estherwood 691	F6
70730	Ether 250	H5
70535	Eunice 12,479	F6
70639	Evans 500	D5
71333	Evergreen 272	F5
71240	Fairbanks 300	F1
71241	Farmerville⊙ 3,768	F1
70640	Fenton 491	E6

(continued)

Louisiana

SCALE
0 5 10 20 30 40 MI.
0 5 10 20 30 40 KM.

State Capitals ⊛
Parish Seats ⊙
Canals
Major Limited Access Hwys.

AREA 47,752 sq. mi. (123,678 sq. km.)
POPULATION 4,206,312
CAPITAL Baton Rouge
LARGEST CITY New Orleans
HIGHEST POINT Driskill Mtn. 535 ft. (163 m.)
SETTLED IN 1699
ADMITTED TO UNION April 30, 1812
POPULAR NAME Pelican State
STATE FLOWER Magnolia
STATE BIRD Eastern Brown Pelican

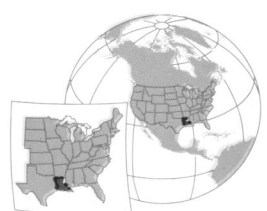

New Orleans, Baton Rouge and Vicinity

© Copyright HAMMOND INCORPORATED, Maplewood, N.J.

240 Louisiana
(continued)

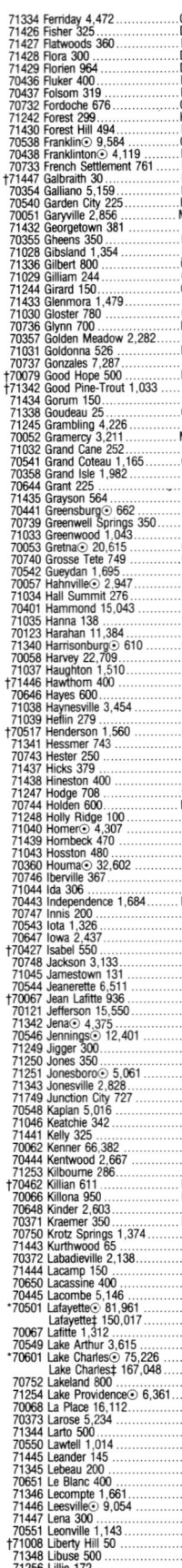

71334 Ferriday 4,472 .... G3
71426 Fisher 325 .... D4
71427 Flatwoods 360 .... E4
71428 Flora 300 .... D3
71429 Florien 964 .... D4
70436 Fluker 400 .... K5
70437 Folsom 319 .... K5
70732 Fordoche 676 .... G5
71242 Forest 299 .... H1
71430 Forest Hill 494 .... E4
70538 Franklin⊙ 9,584 .... G7
70438 Franklinton⊙ 4,119 .... K5
70733 French Settlement 761 .... L2
†71447 Galbraith 30 .... E4
70354 Galliano 5,159 .... K8
70540 Garden City 225 .... H7
70051 Garyville 2,856 .... M3
71432 Georgetown 381 .... F3
70355 Gheens 350 .... K7
71028 Gibsland 1,354 .... E1
71336 Gilbert 800 .... G2
71029 Gilliam 244 .... C1
71244 Girard 150 .... G2
71433 Glenmora 1,479 .... E5
71030 Gloster 780 .... C2
70736 Glynn 700 .... H5
70357 Golden Meadow 2,282 .... K8
71031 Goldonna 526 .... D2
70737 Gonzales 7,287 .... L2
†70079 Good Hope 500 .... N3
†71342 Good Pine-Trout 1,033 .... F3
71434 Gorum 150 .... E4
71338 Goudeau 25 .... G5
71245 Grambling 4,226 .... E1
70052 Gramercy 3,211 .... M3
71032 Grand Cane 252 .... C2
70541 Grand Coteau 1,165 .... G6
70358 Grand Isle 1,982 .... L8
70644 Grant 225 .... E5
71435 Grayson 564 .... F2
70441 Greensburg⊙ 662 .... J5
70739 Greenwell Springs 350 .... K1
71033 Greenwood 1,043 .... B2
70053 Gretna⊙ 20,615 .... O4
70740 Grosse Tete 749 .... G6
70542 Gueydan 1,695 .... E6
70057 Hahnville⊙ 2,947 .... N4
71034 Hall Summit 276 .... D2
70401 Hammond 15,043 .... N1
71035 Hanna 138 .... D3
70123 Harahan 11,384 .... O4
71340 Harrisonburg⊙ 610 .... G3
70058 Harvey 22,709 .... O4
71037 Haughton 1,510 .... C1
†71446 Hawthorn 400 .... D4
70646 Hayes 600 .... E6
71038 Haynesville 3,454 .... D1
71039 Heflin 279 .... D2
†70517 Henderson 1,560 .... G6
71341 Hessmer 743 .... F4
70743 Hester 250 .... L3
71437 Hicks 379 .... E4
71438 Hineston 400 .... E4
71247 Hodge 708 .... E2
70744 Holden 600 .... M1
71248 Holly Ridge 100 .... G2
71040 Homer⊙ 4,307 .... D1
71439 Hornbeck 470 .... D4
71043 Hosston 480 .... C1
70360 Houma⊙ 32,602 .... J7
70746 Iberville 367 .... K2
71044 Ida 306 .... C1
70443 Independence 1,684 .... M1
70747 Innis 200 .... G5
70543 Iota 1,326 .... E6
70647 Iowa 2,437 .... D6
†70427 Isabel 550 .... K5
70748 Jackson 3,133 .... H5
71045 Jamestown 131 .... D2
70544 Jeanerette 6,511 .... G7
†70067 Jean Lafitte 936 .... K7
70121 Jefferson 15,550 .... O4
71342 Jena⊙ 4,375 .... F3
70546 Jennings⊙ 12,401 .... E6
71249 Jigger 300 .... G2
71250 Jones 350 .... G1
71251 Jonesboro⊙ 5,061 .... E2
71343 Jonesville 2,828 .... G3
71749 Junction City 727 .... E1
70548 Kaplan 5,016 .... F6
71046 Keatchie 342 .... C2
71441 Kelly 325 .... F3
70062 Kenner 66,382 .... N4
70444 Kentwood 2,667 .... J5
71253 Kilbourne 286 .... H1
†70462 Killian 611 .... M2
70066 Killona 950 .... M3
70648 Kinder 2,603 .... E6
70371 Kraemer 350 .... M4
70750 Krotz Springs 1,374 .... G5
71443 Kurthwood 65 .... D4
70372 Labadieville 2,138 .... K4
71444 Lacamp 150 .... E4
70650 Lacassine 400 .... E6
70445 Lacombe 5,146 .... L6
*70501 Lafayette⊙ 81,961 .... F6
Lafayette‡ 150,017 .... F6
70067 Lafitte 1,312 .... K7
70549 Lake Arthur 3,615 .... E6
*70601 Lake Charles⊙ 75,226 .... D6
Lake Charles‡ 167,048 .... D6
70752 Lakeland 800 .... H5
71254 Lake Providence⊙ 6,361 .... H1
70068 La Place 16,112 .... N3
70373 Larose 5,234 .... K7
71344 Larto 500 .... G4
70550 Lawtell 1,014 .... F5
71445 Leander 145 .... E4
71345 Lebeau 200 .... F5
70651 Le Blanc 400 .... E5
71346 Lecompte 1,661 .... F4
71446 Leesville⊙ 9,054 .... D4
71447 Lena 300 .... E4
70551 Leonville 1,143 .... G6
†71008 Liberty Hill 50 .... E2
71348 Libuse 500 .... F4
71256 Lillie 172 .... E1

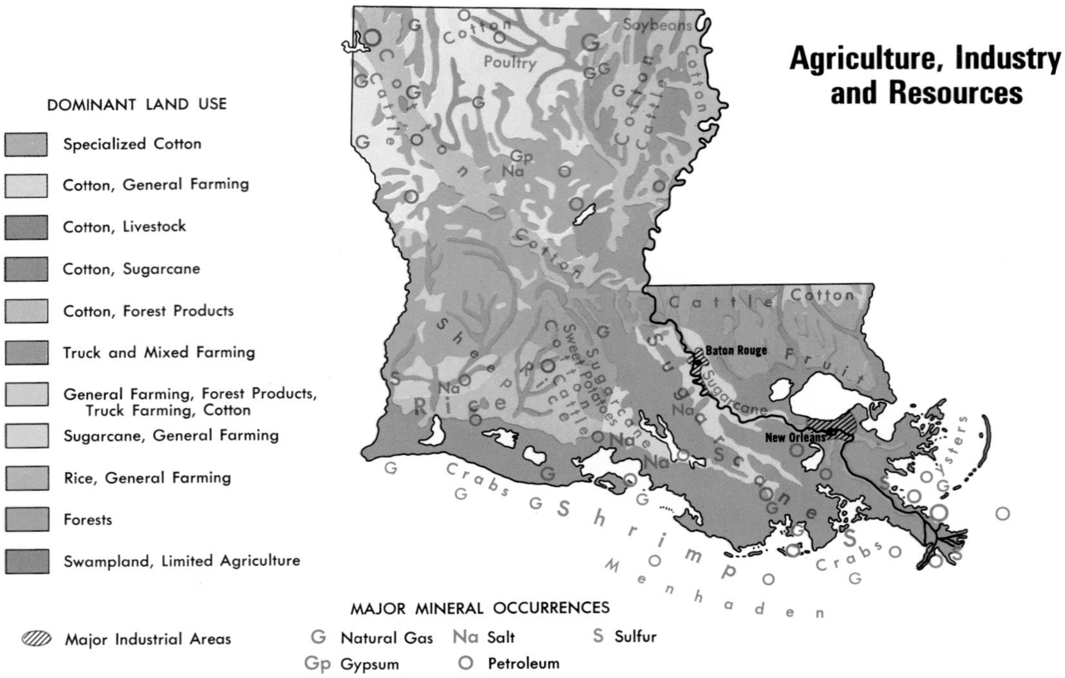
Agriculture, Industry and Resources
DOMINANT LAND USE
Specialized Cotton
Cotton, General Farming
Cotton, Livestock
Cotton, Sugarcane
Cotton, Forest Products
Truck and Mixed Farming
General Farming, Forest Products, Truck Farming, Cotton
Sugarcane, General Farming
Rice, General Farming
Forests
Swampland, Limited Agriculture
MAJOR MINERAL OCCURRENCES
Major Industrial Areas
G Natural Gas
Na Salt
S Sulfur
Gp Gypsum
O Petroleum
Soybeans
Cotton
Poultry
Cattle
Rice
Sheep
Sweet Potatoes
Sugarcane
Fruit
Baton Rouge
New Orleans
Oysters
Crabs
Shrimp
Menhaden

71257 Linville 150 .... F1
71048 Lisbon 138 .... E1
70754 Livingston⊙ 1,260 .... L1
70755 Livonia 980 .... G5
†70767 Lobdell 200 .... J1
70374 Lockport 2,424 .... K7
71049 Logansport 1,565 .... C3
71448 Longleaf 80 .... E4
71050 Longstreet 281 .... B2
70652 Longville 300 .... D5
70446 Loranger 250 .... N1
70552 Loreauville 860 .... G6
70756 Lottie 400 .... G5
†71008 Lucky 370 .... E2
70070 Luling 4,006 .... N4
70071 Lutcher 4,730 .... L3
70447 Madisonville 799 .... K6
70554 Mamou 3,194 .... F5
70448 Mandeville 6,076 .... L6
71259 Mangham 867 .... G2
71052 Mansfield⊙ 6,485 .... C2
71350 Mansura 2,074 .... G4
71449 Many⊙ 3,988 .... C3
70757 Maringouin 1,291 .... G6
71260 Marion 989 .... F1
71351 Marksville⊙ 5,113 .... G4
70072 Marrero 36,548 .... O4
†71019 Martin 584 .... D2
70555 Maurice 478 .... F6
†71433 McNary 240 .... E5
71346 Meeker 50 .... F4
71451 Melder 150 .... E4
71452 Melrose 500 .... E3
71353 Melville 1,764 .... G5
70556 Mermentau 771 .... E6
71261 Mer Rouge 802 .... G1
70653 Merryville 1,286 .... D5
*70001 Metairie 164,160 .... O4
70557 Midland 560 .... F6
70558 Milton 450 .... F6
†70070 Mimosa Park 3,737 .... N4
71055 Minden⊙ 15,074 .... D1
71059 Mira 354 .... C1
71453 Mitchell 155 .... C3
70376 Modeste 225 .... K3
*71201 Monroe⊙ 57,597 .... F1
Monroe‡ 139,241 .... F1
71454 Montgomery 843 .... E3
†70422 Montpelier 219 .... M1
71060 Mooringsport 911 .... B1
71455 Mora 427 .... E4
71355 Moreauville 853 .... G4
70380 Morgan City 16,114 .... H7
70759 Morganza 846 .... G5
71356 Morrow 600 .... F5
70559 Morse 835 .... F6
71262 Mound 40 .... H2
70450 Mount Hermon 170 .... K5
†71028 Mount Lebanon 105 .... D2
70390 Napoleonville⊙ 829 .... K4
70451 Natalbany 900 .... N1
71456 Natchez 527 .... D3
71457 Natchitoches⊙ 16,664 .... D3
71460 Negreet 400 .... C4
71357 Newellton 1,726 .... H2
70560 New Iberia⊙ 32,766 .... G6
71461 Newllano 2,213 .... D4
*70101 New Orleans⊙ 557,927 .... O4
New Orleans‡ 1,186,725 .... O4
70760 New Roads⊙ 3,924 .... G5
70078 New Sarpy 2,249 .... N4
71462 Noble 194 .... C3
70079 Norco 4,416 .... N3
†71247 North Hodge 573 .... E2
70761 Norwood 421 .... H5
71463 Oakdale 7,155 .... E5
71263 Oak Grove⊙ 2,214 .... H1
71264 Oak Ridge 257 .... G1
70655 Oberlin⊙ 1,764 .... E5
71061 Oil City 1,323 .... C1
71465 Olla 1,603 .... F3
70570 Opelousas⊙ 18,903 .... G5
70762 Oscar 650 .... H5
71466 Otis 400 .... E4
70391 Paincourtville 2,004 .... K3
71358 Palmetto 327 .... G5
70582 Parks 545 .... G6
70392 Patterson 4,693 .... H7
70452 Pearl River 1,693 .... L6
71063 Pelican 250 .... C3
70575 Perry 230 .... F7
70081 Pilottown 175 .... M8
70453 Pine Grove 570 .... J5
70576 Pine Prairie 734 .... E5
71360 Pineville 12,034 .... F4
71266 Pioneer 221 .... H1
70656 Pitkin 600 .... E5
71064 Plain Dealing 1,213 .... C1
70764 Plaquemine⊙ 7,521 .... J2
70393 Plattenville 205 .... K4
71362 Plaucheville 196 .... G5
71065 Pleasant Hill 776 .... C3
70082 Pointe a la Hache⊙ 750 .... L7
71467 Pollock 399 .... F3
70454 Ponchatoula 5,469 .... N2
70767 Port Allen⊙ 6,114 .... J2
70577 Port Barre 2,625 .... G5
70083 Port Sulphur 3,318 .... L8
†70726 Port Vincent 450 .... L2
71066 Powhatan 279 .... D3
71468 Provencal 695 .... D3
71268 Quitman 231 .... E2
70394 Raceland 6,302 .... J7
70578 Rayne 9,066 .... F6
71269 Rayville⊙ 4,610 .... G2
70580 Reddell 500 .... F5
70658 Reeves 199 .... D5
70084 Reserve 7,288 .... M3
†71282 Richmond 505 .... H2
†71201 Richwood 1,223 .... F2
†71334 Ridgecrest 895 .... G3
71068 Ringgold 1,655 .... D2
†70427 Rio 400 .... L5
70581 Roanoke 800 .... E6
71469 Robeline 238 .... D3
71069 Rodessa 337 .... B1
71364 Rosa 300 .... G5
70772 Rosedale 658 .... G6
70456 Roseland 1,346 .... J5
70659 Rosepine 953 .... D5
71365 Ruby 400 .... F4
71270 Ruston⊙ 20,585 .... E1
70457 Saint Benedict 190 .... K5
70775 Saint Francisville⊙ 1,471 .... H5
71366 Saint Joseph⊙ 1,687 .... H3
71367 Saint Landry 550 .... F5
70582 Saint Martinville⊙ 7,965 .... G6
71471 Saint Maurice 560 .... E3
71070 Saline 293 .... E2
71071 Sarepta 831 .... D1
70807 Scotlandville 15,113 .... J1
70583 Scott 2,239 .... F6
†70764 Seymourville 2,891 .... J2
71072 Shongaloo 163 .... D1
*71101 Shreveport⊙ 205,820 .... C2
Shreveport‡ 376,646 .... C2
71073 Sibley 1,211 .... D1
71368 Sicily Island 691 .... G3
71472 Sieper 226 .... E4
71473 Sikes 226 .... F2
71369 Simmesport 2,293 .... G5
71474 Simpson 534 .... D4
71275 Simsboro 553 .... E1
70660 Singer 250 .... D5
71475 Slagle 650 .... D4
70777 Slaughter 729 .... H5
70458 Slidell 26,718 .... L6
71276 Sondheimer 225 .... H1
70778 Sorrento 1,197 .... L3
†71052 South Mansfield 1,463 .... C3
71277 Spearsville 181 .... E1
71278 Spencer 50 .... F1
70462 Springfield 424 .... M2
71075 Springhill 6,516 .... D1
†71049 Stanley 151 .... C3
71280 Sterlington 1,400 .... F1
71078 Stonewall 1,175 .... C2
70662 Sugartown 375 .... D5
70663 Sulphur 19,709 .... D6
70463 Sun 404 .... L5
70584 Sunset 2,300 .... F6
70464 Talisheek 315 .... L5
71282 Tallulah⊙ 11,634 .... H2
70465 Tangipahoa 493 .... J5
71080 Taylor 500 .... D1
71476 Temple 250 .... E4
71285 Terry 50 .... H1
†70053 Terry Town 23,548 .... O4
70397 Theriot 450 .... J8
70301 Thibodaux⊙ 15,810 .... J7
70466 Tickfaw 571 .... M1
71286 Transylvania 400 .... H1
71081 Trees 327 .... B1
†70041 Triumph-Buras 4,137 .... L8
71371 Trout-Good Pine 1,033 .... F3
71479 Tullos 776 .... F3
70782 Tunica 500 .... G5
70585 Turkey Creek 366 .... F5
71480 Urania 849 .... F3
70090 Vacherie 2,169 .... L3
70467 Varnado 249 .... L5
71481 Verda 100 .... E3
71373 Vidalia⊙ 5,936 .... G3
†71270 Vienna 519 .... E1
70586 Ville Platte⊙ 9,201 .... F5
70668 Vinton 3,631 .... C6
70092 Violet 11,678 .... P4
71082 Vivian 4,146 .... B1
†71418 Vixen 40 .... F2
70784 Wakefield 400 .... H5
†70433 Waldheim 25 .... L5
70785 Walker 2,957 .... L1
71289 Warden 130 .... H1
70589 Washington 1,266 .... G5
71375 Waterproof 1,339 .... H3
70786 Watson 800 .... L1
70591 Welsh 3,515 .... E6
70669 Westlake 5,246 .... D6
71291 West Monroe 14,993 .... F1
70094 Westwego 12,663 .... O4
70787 Weyanoke 500 .... H5
70788 White Castle 2,160 .... J3
†71371 White Sulphur Springs 50 .... F3
71376 Whiteville 150 .... F5
71377 Wildsville 800 .... G3
†70040 Wills Point 150 .... L7
70789 Wilson 656 .... H5
71483 Winnfield⊙ 7,311 .... E3
71295 Winnsboro⊙ 5,921 .... G2
71378 Wisner 1,424 .... G3
71485 Woodworth 412 .... E4
70592 Youngsville 1,053 .... G6
70791 Zachary 7,297 .... K1
†71371 Zenoria 76 .... F3
†71409 Zimmerman 20 .... E4
71486 Zwolle 2,602 .... C3

OTHER FEATURES

Allemands (lake) M4
Alligator (pt.) L6
Amite (riv.) L2
Anacoco (lake) D4
Atchafalaya (bay) H8
Atchafalaya (riv.) G6
Barataria (bay) L8
Barataria (passage) L8
Barksdale A.F.B. C2
Bayou D'Arbonne (lake) F1
Bird (isl.) M8
Bistineau (lake) D2
Black (lake) D3
Black Lake (bayou) D1
Boeuf (lake) J7
Boeuf (riv.) G1
Bonnet Carré Spillway and Floodway N3
Borgne (lake) L7
Boudreau (bay) M7
Boudreaux (lake) J8
Breton (isls.) M8
Breton (sound) M7
Bundick (lake) D5
Caddo (lake) B1
Caillou (bay) J8
Calcasieu (lake) D7
Calcasieu (passage) D7
Calcasieu (riv.) E5
Catahoula (lake) F4
Cataouatche (lake) N4
Cat Island (chan.) M6
Cat Island (passage) J8
Chandeleur (isls.) N7
Chandeleur (sound) M7
Chenier (lake) F2
Chicot (pt.) M7
Claiborne (lake) E1
Clear (lake) D3
Cocodrie (lake) E5
Cotile (lake) E4
Cross (lake) C2
Curlew (isls.) M7
Dernieres (isls.) J8
Door (pt.) M6
Driskill (mt.) E2
Drum (bay) M7
East (bay) M8
East Cote Blanche (bay) G7
Edwards (lake) C2
Eloi (bay) M7
England A.F.B. E4
Fields (lake) J7
Fort Polk 14,142 .... D4
Free Mason (isls.) M7
Garden Island (bay) M8
Grand (lake) E7
Grand (lake) H8
Grand Terre (isls.) L8
Iatt (lake) E3
Jean Lafitte Nat'l Hist. Park P4
Lafourche (bayou) K8
Little (riv.) F3
Louisiana (pt.) C7
Macon (bayou) H1
Main (passage) M8
Manchac (passage) N2
Marsh (isl.) G7
Maurepas (lake) M2
Mermentau (riv.) E7
Mexico (gulf) F8
Mississippi (delta) M8
Mississippi (riv.) H3
Mississippi (sound) M6
Mississippi River Gulf Outlet (canal) L7
Mozambique (pt.) M7
Mud (lake) D7
Naval Air Sta. O4
North (isls.) M7
North (pass) N8
North (pt.) M7
Northeast (pass) M8
Ouachita (riv.) F1
Palourde (lake) H7
Pearl (riv.) L5
Point au Fer (isl.) H8
Point au Fer (pt.) H8
Pontchartrain (lake) O3
Pontchartrain Causeway O3
Raccoon (pt.) H8
Red (riv.) G4
Sabine (lake) C7
Sabine (passage) C7
Sabine (riv.) C5
Saline (lake) E3
Salvador (lake) K7
Smithport (lake) C2
South (pass) M8
South (pt.) G8
Southeast (pass) M8
Southwest (pass) L8
Tangipahoa (riv.) N1
Tensas (riv.) G3
Terrebonne (bay) J8
Tickfaw (riv.) M1
Timbalier (bay) K8
Timbalier (isl.) K8
Toledo Bend (res.) C3
Turkey Creek (lake) G3
Vermilion (bay) F7
Vernon (lake) D4
Verret (lake) H7
Wallace (lake) C2
West (bay) M8
West Cote Blanche (bay) G7
White (lake) E7

⊙Parish seat.
‡Population of metropolitan area.
† Zip of nearest p.o. * Multiple zips.

AREA 33,265 sq. mi. (86,156 sq. km.)
POPULATION 1,125,027
CAPITAL Augusta
LARGEST CITY Portland
HIGHEST POINT Katahdin 5,268 ft. (1606 m.)
SETTLED IN 1624
ADMITTED TO UNION March 15, 1820
POPULAR NAME Pine Tree State
STATE FLOWER White Pine Cone & Tassel
STATE BIRD Chickadee

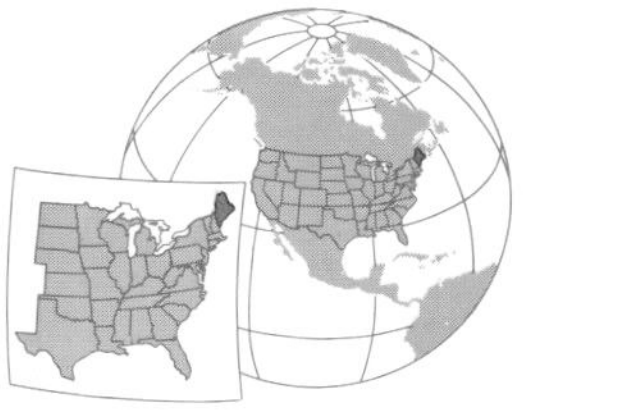

COUNTIES

Name/Pop.	Key
Androscoggin 99,657	C7
Aroostook 91,331	F2
Cumberland 215,789	C8
Franklin 27,098	B5
Hancock 41,781	G6
Kennebec 109,889	D7
Knox 32,941	E7
Lincoln 25,691	D7
Oxford 48,968	B7
Penobscot 137,015	F5
Piscataquis 17,634	E4
Sagadahoc 28,795	D7
Somerset 45,028	C4
Waldo 28,414	E6
Washington 34,963	H6
York 139,666	B9

CITIES and TOWNS

Zip	Name/Pop.	Key
04406	Abbot Village○ 576	D5
04001	Acton○ 1,228	B8
04606	Addison○ 1,061	H6
04910	Albion○ 1,551	E6
†04610	Alexander○ 385	H5
04002	Alfred○ 1,890	B9
†04774	Allagash○ 448	F1
†04938	Allens Mills 100	C6
04535	Alna○ 425	D7
†04468	Alton○ 468	F5
†04408	Amherst○ 203	G6
04216	Andover○ 850	B6
04911	Anson○ 2,226	D6
†04862	Appleton○ 818	E7
†04468	Argyle 225	F5
04732	Ashland○ 1,865	G2
04607	Ashville 36	G7
04912	Athens○ 802	D6
†04426	Atkinson○ 306	E5
04608	Atlantic 120	G7
04210	Auburn⊙ 23,128	C7
04330	Augusta (cap.)⊙ 21,819	D7
04408	Aurora○ 110	G6
04003	Bailey Island 500	D8
†04497	Bancroft○ 61	H4
04401	Bangor⊙ 31,643	F6
	Bangor‡ 83,919	F6
04609	Bar Harbor○ 4,124	G7
04609	Bar Harbor 2,685	G7
†04619	Baring○ 308	J5
04004	Bar Mills 800	C8
04653	Bass Harbor 450	G7
04530	Bath⊙ 10,246	D8
†04915	Bayside	F7
04611	Beals○ 695	H7
†04622	Beddington○ 36	H6
04915	Belfast⊙ 6,243	F7
04917	Belgrade○ 2,043	D7
†04915	Belmont○ 520	E7
04733	Benedicta○ 225	G4
†04937	Benton○ 2,188	D6
03901	Berwick○ 4,149	B9
03901	Berwick 2,378	B9
04217	Bethel○ 2,340	B7
04005	Biddeford 19,638	B9
04920	Bingham○ 1,184	D5
04920	Bingham 1,074	D5
04613	Birch Harbor 300	H7
04734	Blaine○ 922	H2
04734	Blaine-Mars Hill 1,921	H2
04614	Blue Hill○ 1,644	F7
04615	Blue Hill Falls 135	F7
04537	Boothbay○ 2,308	D8
04538	Boothbay Harbor 2,207	D8
04008	Bowdoinham○ 1,828	D7
†04481	Bowerbank○ 27	E5
04410	Bradford○ 888	F5
†04410	Bradford Center 105	F5
04411	Bradley○ 1,149	F6
04412	Brewer 9,017	F6
04735	Bridgewater○ 742	H3
04009	Bridgton○ 3,528	B7
04009	Bridgton 1,639	B7
†04990	Brighton○ 74	D5
04539	Bristol○ 2,095	D8
04616	Brooklin○ 619	F7
04921	Brooks○ 804	E6
04617	Brooksville○ 753	F7
04413	Brookton 175	H4
04010	Brownfield○ 767	B8
04414	Brownville○ 1,545	E5
04011	Brunswick○ 17,366	C8
04011	Brunswick 10,990	C8
04219	Bryant Pond 600	B7
†04232	Buckfield○ 1,333	C7
04618	Bucks Harbor 300	J6
04416	Bucksport○ 4,345	F6
04416	Bucksport 2,853	F6
04540	Burkettville 120	E7
04417	Burlington○ 322	G5
04922	Burnham○ 951	E6
†04093	Buxton○ 5,775	C8
†04275	Byron○ 114	B6
04619	Calais 4,262	J5
04923	Cambridge○ 445	E5
04843	Camden○ 4,584	F7
04843	Camden 3,743	F7
04924	Canaan○ 1,189	D6
04221	Canton○ 831	C7
03902	Cape Neddick 850	B9
04014	Cape Porpoise 500	C9
04736	Caribou 9,916	G2
04419	Carmel○ 1,695	E6
†04947	Carrabassett Valley○ 107	C5
†04487	Carroll○ 175	G5
†04224	Carthage○ 438	C6
†04465	Cary○ 229	H4
04015	Casco○ 2,243	B7
04421	Castine○ 1,304	F7
†04941	Center Montville 16	E7
†04623	Centerville○ 28	H6
†04757	Chapman○ 406	G2
04422	Charleston○ 1,037	F5
†04666	Charlotte○ 300	J5
04017	Chebeague Island 900	C8
†04345	Chelsea○ 2,522	D7
04622	Cherryfield○ 983	H6
†04458	Chester○ 434	F5
†04938	Chesterville○ 869	C6
†04478	Chesuncook 6	D3
04926	China○ 2,918	E7
†04239	Chisholm 1,796	C7
†04428	Clifton○ 462	G6
04927	Clinton○ 2,696	D6
04927	Clinton 1,305	D6
†04623	Columbia○ 275	H6
04623	Columbia Falls○ 517	H6
†04638	Cooper○ 105	H6
04624	Corea 375	H7
04928	Corinna○ 1,887	E6
04020	Cornish○ 1,047	B8
†04976	Cornville○ 838	D6
04625	Cranberry Isles○ 198	G7
†04610	Crawford○ 86	H5
†04015	Crescent Lake 325	C7
†04851	Criehaven 5	F8
04738	Crouseville 450	G2
†04747	Crystal○ 349	G4
04021	Cumberland Center○ 5,284	C8
04021	Cumberland Center 2,015	C8
04563	Cushing○ 795	E7
04626	Cutler○ 726	J6
04543	Damariscotta○ 1,493	E7
04543	Damariscotta-Newcastle 1,411	E7
04424	Danforth○ 826	H4
†04622	Deblois○ 44	H6
†04429	Dedham○ 841	F6
04627	Deer Isle○ 1,492	F7
04022	Denmark○ 672	B8
04628	Dennysville○ 296	J6
04929	Detroit○ 744	E6
04930	Dexter○ 4,286	E5
04930	Dexter 3,118	E5
04224	Dixfield○ 2,389	C6
04224	Dixfield 1,725	C6
04932	Dixmont○ 812	E6
04426	Dover-Foxcroft○ 4,323	E5
04426	Dover-Foxcroft⊙ 2,974	E5
†04426	Dover South Mills 54	E5
04342	Dresden○ 998	D7
†04747	Dyer Brook○ 275	G3
04739	Eagle Lake○ 1,019	F1
04226	East Andover 250	B6
04544	East Boothbay 800	D8
04427	East Corinth 525	F5
04227	East Dixfield 250	C6
04429	East Holden 600	F6
04027	East Lebanon 950	B9
04228	East Livermore 500	C7
04630	East Machias○ 1,233	J6
04430	East Millinocket○ 2,372	F4
04430	East Millinocket 2,361	F4
04740	Easton○ 1,305	H2
04028	East Parsonfield 400	B8
04229	East Peru 200	C7
†04210	East Poland 200	C7
04631	Eastport 1,982	K6
04231	East Stoneham 300	B7
†04607	East Sullivan 496	G6
†04220	East Sumner 120	C7
†04862	East Union 75	E7
†04428	Eddington○ 1,769	F6
†04556	Edgecomb○ 841	D8
03903	Eliot○ 4,948	B9
04605	Ellsworth⊙ 5,179	F6
04031	Emery Mills 100	B8
04433	Enfield○ 1,397	F5
04434	Etna○ 758	E6
04936	Eustis○ 582	B5
04435	Exeter○ 823	E6
†04938	Fairbanks 400	C6
04937	Fairfield○ 6,113	D6
04937	Fairfield 3,169	D6
04105	Falmouth○ 6,853	C8
04105	Falmouth 1,655	C8
†04345	Farmingdale○ 2,535	D7
†04345	Farmingdale 2,014	D7
04938	Farmington○ 6,730	C6
04938	Farmington⊙ 3,583	C6
04940	Farmington Falls 500	C6
†04349	Fayette○ 812	C7
04546	Five Islands 225	D8
04742	Fort Fairfield○ 4,376	H2
04742	Fort Fairfield 2,282	H2
04743	Fort Kent○ 4,826	F1
04743	Fort Kent 2,375	F1
04744	Fort Kent Mills 200	F1
04438	Frankfort○ 783	F6
04634	Franklin○ 979	G6
04941	Freedom○ 458	E7
04032	Freeport○ 5,863	C8
04032	Freeport 1,906	C8
04635	Frenchboro○ 43	G7
04745	Frenchville○ 1,450	G1
04547	Friendship○ 1,000	E7
04037	Fryeburg○ 2,715	A7
04037	Fryeburg 1,644	A7
04345	Gardiner 6,485	D7
04939	Garland○ 718	E5
04548	Georgetown○ 735	D8
†04217	Gilead○ 191	B7
†04401	Glenburn○ 2,319	F6
04846	Glen Cove 250	E7
04038	Gorham○ 10,101	C8
04038	Gorham 4,052	C8
†04607	Gouldsboro○ 1,574	H7
04746	Grand Isle○ 719	G1
04637	Grand Lake Stream○ 198	H5
04039	Gray○ 4,344	C8
†04408	Great Pond○ 45	G6
04236	Greene○ 3,037	C7
04441	Greenville○ 1,839	D5
04441	Greenville 1,640	D5
04442	Greenville Junction 650	D5
04443	Guilford○ 1,793	E5
04443	Guilford 1,235	E5
04347	Hallowell 2,502	D7
†04785	Hamlin○ 340	H1
04444	Hampden○ 5,250	F6
04444	Hampden 3,538	F6
04445	Hampden Highlands 950	F6
04640	Hancock○ 1,409	G6
04237	Hanover○ 256	B7
04942	Harmony○ 755	D6
†04011	Harpswell○ 3,796	D8
04643	Harrington○ 859	H6
04040	Harrison○ 1,667	B7
†04221	Hartford○ 480	C7
04943	Hartland○ 1,669	D6
04943	Hartland 1,041	D6
04446	Haynesville○ 169	G4
04238	Hebron○ 665	C7
†04401	Hermon○ 3,170	F6
04944	Hinckley 140	D6
04041	Hiram○ 1,067	B8
†04730	Hodgdon○ 1,084	H3
04042	Hollis Center○ 2,892	B8
04847	Hope○ 730	E7
04730	Houlton○ 6,766	H3
04730	Houlton⊙ 5,730	H3
04448	Howland○ 1,602	F5
04448	Howland 1,502	F5
04449	Hudson○ 797	F5
04644	Hulls Cove 200	G7
04747	Island Falls○ 981	G3
04645	Isle Au Haut○ 57	F7
04848	Islesboro○ 521	F7
04945	Jackman○ 1,003	C4
†04630	Jacksonville 200	J6
04239	Jay○ 5,080	C7
04348	Jefferson○ 1,616	D7
04648	Jonesboro○ 553	J6
04649	Jonesport○ 1,512	H6
04649	Jonesport 1,050	H6
04450	Kenduskeag○ 1,210	E6
04043	Kennebunk○ 6,621	B9
04043	Kennebunk 3,294	B9
†04043	Kennebunk Beach 200	C9
04046	Kennebunkport○ 2,952	C9
04046	Kennebunkport 1,685	C9
04349	Kents Hill 300	D7
04947	Kingfield○ 1,083	C6
04451	Kingman 281	G4
†04990	Kingsbury○ 4	D5
03904	Kittery○ 9,314	B9
03904	Kittery 5,465	B9
03905	Kittery Point 1,260	B9
†04986	Knox○ 558	E6
04453	La Grange○ 509	F5
†04463	Lake View○ 20	F5
†04605	Lamoine○ 953	G7
04455	Lee○ 688	G5
†04263	Leeds○ 1,463	C7
04456	Levant○ 1,117	F6
04240	Lewiston 40,481	C7
	Lewiston-Auburn‡ 72,378	C7
04949	Liberty○ 694	E7
04749	Lille 300	G1
04048	Limerick○ 1,356	B8
04750	Limestone○ 8,719	H2
04750	Limestone 1,334	H2
04049	Limington○ 2,203	B8
04457	Lincoln○ 5,066	G5
04457	Lincoln 3,524	G5
04849	Lincolnville○ 1,414	E7
04850	Lincolnville Center 200	E7
†04730	Linneus○ 752	H3
04250	Lisbon○ 8,769	C7
04250	Lisbon-Lisbon Center 1,865	C7
04252	Lisbon Falls 4,370	D7
04350	Litchfield○ 1,954	D7
†04627	Little Deer Isle 475	F7
04082	Little Falls-South Windham 1,366	C8
†04760	Littleton○ 1,009	H3
04253	Livermore○ 1,826	C7
04254	Livermore Falls○ 3,572	C7
04254	Livermore Falls 2,441	C7
04255	Locke Mills 600	B7
04051	Lovell○ 767	B7
†04433	Lowell○ 194	F5
04652	Lubec○ 2,045	K6
†04730	Ludlow○ 403	G3
04654	Machias○ 2,458	J6
04654	Machias⊙ 1,277	J6
04655	Machiasport○ 1,108	H6
†04451	Macwahoc○ 126	G4
04756	Madawaska○ 5,282	G1
04756	Madawaska 4,165	G1
04950	Madison○ 4,367	D6
04950	Madison 2,788	D6
†04966	Madrid○ 178	B6
†04942	Mainstream 100	D6
04351	Manchester○ 1,949	D7
04757	Mapleton○ 1,895	G2
04758	Mars Hill○ 1,892	H2
04758	Mars Hill-Blaine 1,921	H2
04759	Masardis○ 328	G3
04851	Matinicus 66	F8
04459	Mattawamkeag○ 1,000	G5
04256	Mechanic Falls○ 2,616	C7
04256	Mechanic Falls 2,198	C7
04657	Meddybemps○ 110	J5
†04453	Medford○ 163	F5
†04453	Medford Center 100	F5
04460	Medway○ 1,871	G4
04957	Mercer○ 448	D6
04257	Mexico○ 3,698	B6
04257	Mexico 3,207	B6
†04216	Middledam 10	B6
04658	Milbridge○ 1,306	H6
04461	Milford○ 2,160	F6
04461	Milford 1,688	F6
04462	Millinocket○ 7,567	F4

(continued on following page)

Agriculture, Industry and Resources

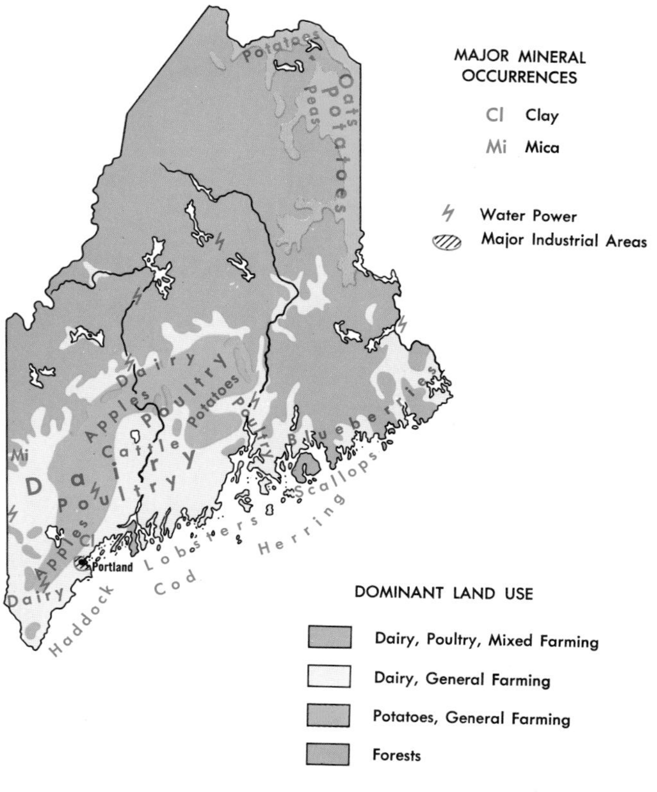

Potatoes
Oats
Potatoes
Peas
Potatoes
Dairy
Poultry
Apples
Potatoes
Poultry
Blueberries
Cattle
Dairy
Poultry
Scallops
Apples
Cl
Mi
Portland
Lobsters
Herring
Cod
Haddock
Dairy
MAJOR MINERAL OCCURRENCES
Cl Clay
Mi Mica
Water Power
Major Industrial Areas
DOMINANT LAND USE
Dairy, Poultry, Mixed Farming
Dairy, General Farming
Potatoes, General Farming
Forests

(continued)

04463 Milo○ 2,624 .... F5
04463 Milo 2,255 .... F5
04258 Minot○ 1,631 .... C7
04659 Minturn 150 .... G7
†04776 Monarda 100 .... G4
04852 Monhegan○ 109 .... E8
04259 Monmouth○ 2,888 .... D7
04951 Monroe○ 657 .... E6
04464 Monson○ 804 .... E5
04760 Monticello○ 950 .... H3
†04941 Montville○ 631 .... E7
04054 Moody 500 .... B9
†04478 Moosehead 6 .... D4
†04945 Moose River○ 252 .... C4
04952 Morrill○ 506 .... E7
04660 Mount Desert○ 2,063 .... G7
04352 Mount Vernon○ 1,021 .... D7
04055 Naples○ 1,833 .... B8
04552 Newagen 100 .... D8
†04445 Newburgh○ 1,228 .... F6
04553 Newcastle○ 1,227 .... D7
04553 Newcastle-Damariscotta 1,411 .... E7
04056 Newfield○ 644 .... B8
04260 New Gloucester○ 3,180 .... C8
04554 New Harbor 850 .... E8
04761 New Limerick○ 513 .... G3
04953 Newport○ 2,755 .... E6
04953 Newport 1,748 .... E6
04954 New Portland○ 651 .... C6
04261 Newry○ 235 .... B6
04955 New Sharon○ 969 .... C6
04762 New Sweden○ 737 .... G2
04956 New Vineyard○ 607 .... C6
04555 Nobleboro○ 1,154 .... D7
†04462 Norcross 13 .... F4
04957 Norridgewock○ 2,552 .... D6
04957 Norridgewock 1,318 .... D6
04958 North Anson 950 .... D6
03906 North Berwick○ 2,878 .... B9
03906 North Berwick 1,436 .... B9
04057 North Bridgton 300 .... B7
†04938 North Chesterville 50 .... C6
†04441 North East Carry 2 .... D4
04662 Northeast Harbor 800 .... G7
†04654 Northfield○ 88 .... H6
04853 North Haven○ 373 .... F7
04262 North Jay 800 .... C6
†04254 North Livermore 250 .... C7
04961 North New Portland 500 .... C6
†04476 North Penobscot 246 .... F7
†04849 Northport○ 958 .... E7
†04274 North Raymond 225 .... C8
04266 North Turner 350 .... C7
04962 North Vassalboro 950 .... D7
04267 North Waterford 390 .... B7
04062 North Windham 5,492 .... C8
†04219 North Woodstock 75 .... B7
†04096 North Yarmouth○ 1,919 .... C8
04268 Norway○ 4,042 .... B7
04268 Norway 2,653 .... B7
†04268 Norway Lake 75 .... B7
04763 Oakfield○ 847 .... G3
04963 Oakland○ 5,162 .... D6
04963 Oakland 3,387 .... D6
04063 Ocean Park 200 .... C9
03907 Ogunquit 1,492 .... B9
04064 Old Orchard Beach○ 6,291 .... C9
04064 Old Orchard Beach 6,023 .... C9
04468 Old Town 8,422 .... F6
04964 Oquossoc 150 .... B6
04471 Orient○ 97 .... H4
04472 Orland○ 1,645 .... F6
04473 Orono○ 10,578 .... F6
04473 Orono 9,891 .... F6
04474 Orrington○ 3,244 .... F6
04066 Orrs Island 600 .... D8
†04270 Otisfield○ 897 .... B7
04665 Otter Creek 260 .... G7
04854 Owls Head○ 1,633 .... F7
04764 Oxbow○ 84 .... G3
04270 Oxford○ 3,143 .... B7
04354 Palermo○ 760 .... E7
04965 Palmyra○ 1,485 .... E6
04271 Paris○ 4,168 .... B7
†04443 Parkman○ 621 .... D5
04475 Passadumkeag○ 430 .... F5
04765 Patten○ 1,368 .... F4
04765 Patten 1,057 .... F4
04558 Pemaquid 200 .... E8
04666 Pembroke○ 920 .... J6
04476 Penobscot○ 1,104 .... F7
04766 Perham○ 437 .... G2
04667 Perry○ 737 .... J6
04272 Peru○ 1,564 .... C6
04966 Phillips○ 1,092 .... C6
04562 Phippsburg○ 1,527 .... D8
04967 Pittsfield○ 4,125 .... E6
04967 Pittsfield 3,117 .... E6
†04345 Pittston○ 2,267 .... D7
04767 Plaisted 125 .... F1
†04925 Pleasant Pond 18 .... D5
04969 Plymouth○ 811 .... E6
04273 Poland○ 3,578 .... C7
04562 Popham Beach 40 .... D8
04768 Portage○ 562 .... G2
04855 Port Clyde 400 .... E8
04068 Porter○ 1,222 .... B8
*04101 Portland⊙ 61,572 .... C8
Portland‡ 183,625 .... C8
04069 Pownal○ 1,189 .... C8
†04487 Prentiss○ 205 .... G5
04769 Presque Isle 11,172 .... H2
04668 Princeton○ 994 .... H5
†04981 Prospect○ 511 .... F6
04669 Prospect Harbor 445 .... H7
04770 Quimby 50 .... F2
†04345 Randolph○ 1,834 .... D7
04970 Rangeley○ 1,023 .... B6
04071 Raymond○ 2,251 .... B8
04355 Readfield○ 1,943 .... D7
04357 Richmond○ 2,627 .... D7
04357 Richmond 1,578 .... D7
†04262 Riley 50 .... C6
†04930 Ripley○ 439 .... E5
04671 Robbinston○ 492 .... J5
†04734 Robinsons 160 .... H3
04841 Rockland⊙ 7,919 .... E7
04856 Rockport○ 2,749 .... F7
04478 Rockwood 265 .... D4
†04957 Rome○ 627 .... D6
†04654 Roque Bluffs○ 244 .... H6
04564 Round Pond 400 .... E8
04275 Roxbury○ 373 .... B6
04276 Rumford○ 8,240 .... B6
04276 Rumford 6,256 .... B6
04279 Rumford Point 320 .... B6
04280 Sabattus○ 3,081 .... C7
04280 Sabattus 1,234 .... C7
04072 Saco 12,921 .... C8
04772 Saint Agatha○ 1,035 .... G1
04971 Saint Albans○ 1,400 .... E6
04773 Saint David 915 .... G1
04774 Saint Francis○ 839 .... E1
04857 Saint George○ 1,948 .... E7
†04743 Saint John○ 322 .... F1
†04983 Salem 125 .... C6
†04009 Sandy Creek 132 .... B7
04972 Sandy Point 350 .... F7
04073 Sanford○ 18,020 .... B9
04073 Sanford 10,268 .... B9
04479 Sangerville○ 1,219 .... E5
†04417 Saponac 8 .... G5
04074 Scarborough○ 11,347 .... C8
04074 Scarborough 2,280 .... C8
04674 Seal Cove 215 .... G7
04675 Seal Harbor 500 .... G7
04973 Searsmont○ 782 .... E7
04974 Searsport○ 2,309 .... F7
04974 Searsport 1,348 .... F7
04075 Sebago Lake 800 .... B8
04481 Sebec○ 469 .... E5
04484 Seboeis○ 53 .... F5
†04478 Seboomook 3 .... D4
04676 Sedgwick○ 795 .... F7
04076 Shapleigh○ 1,370 .... B8
04975 Shawmut 500 .... D6
04775 Sheridan 300 .... F2
†04777 Sherman○ 1,021 .... G4
04777 Sherman Station 650 .... F4
04485 Shirley Mills○ 242 .... D5
†04330 Sidney○ 2,052 .... D7
04779 Sinclair 264 .... G1
04976 Skowhegan○ 8,098 .... D6
04976 Skowhegan⊙ 6,517 .... D6
04567 Small Point 22 .... D8
04978 Smithfield○ 748 .... D6
04780 Smyrna Mills○ 354 .... G3
04979 Solon○ 827 .... D6
†04341 Somerville○ 377 .... D7
†04660 Somesville (Mount Desert) 150 .... G7
04677 Sorrento○ 276 .... G7
03908 South Berwick○ 4,046 .... B9
†04009 South Bridgton 373 .... B8
04568 South Bristol○ 800 .... D8
04077 South Casco 750 .... B8
†03903 South Eliot 1,681 .... B9
†04928 South Exeter 100 .... E6
04080 South Hiram 350 .... B8
†04862 South Hope 200 .... E7
†04453 South La Grange 150 .... F5
†04259 South Monmouth 400 .... D7
04281 South Paris⊙ 2,128 .... C7
†04538 Southport○ 598 .... D8
04106 South Portland 22,712 .... C8
04858 South Thomaston○ 1,064 .... E7
†04864 South Union 50 .... E7
04081 South Waterford 300 .... B7
04679 Southwest Harbor○ 1,855 .... G7
04679 Southwest Harbor 1,052 .... G7
04082 South Windham (Little Falls-South Windham) 1,366 .... C8
04487 Springfield○ 443 .... G5
04083 Springvale 2,940 .... B9
04782 Stacyville○ 554 .... F4
04084 Standish○ 5,946 .... B8
†04980 Starks○ 440 .... D6
04488 Stetson○ 618 .... E6
04680 Steuben○ 970 .... H6
04489 Stillwater 700 .... F6
04783 Stockholm○ 319 .... G1
04981 Stockton Springs○ 1,230 .... F7
04681 Stonington○ 1,273 .... F7
†04058 Stow○ 186 .... A7
04982 Stratton 600 .... B5
04983 Strong○ 1,506 .... C6
†04689 Sullivan○ 967 .... G6
†04292 Sumner○ 613 .... C7
04232 Sumner-East Sumner C7
04683 Sunset 165 .... F7
†04627 Sunshine 100 .... G7
04684 Surry○ 894 .... F7
04685 Swans Island○ 337 .... G7
†04915 Swanville○ 873 .... E6
†04040 Sweden○ 163 .... B7
04984 Temple○ 518 .... C6
04860 Tenants Harbor 900 .... E8
04861 Thomaston○ 2,900 .... E7
04861 Thomaston 2,348 .... E7
04986 Thorndike○ 603 .... E6
04490 Topsfield○ 240 .... H5
04086 Topsham○ 6,431 .... D8
04086 Topsham 4,657 .... D8
†04653 Tremont○ 1,222 .... G7
†04605 Trenton○ 718 .... G7
04571 Trevett 400 .... D8
04987 Troy○ 701 .... E6
04282 Turner○ 3,539 .... C7
04862 Union○ 1,569 .... E7
04988 Unity○ 1,431 .... E6
†04293 Upper Dam 2 .... B6
04784 Upper Frenchville 405 .... G1
04261 Upton○ 65 .... B6
04785 Van Buren○ 3,557 .... G1
04785 Van Buren 3,282 .... G1
04491 Vanceboro○ 256 .... J4
04989 Vassalboro○ 3,410 .... D7
04401 Veazie○ 1,610 .... F6
04360 Vienna○ 454 .... D6
04863 Vinalhaven○ 1,211 .... F7
04492 Waite○ 130 .... H5
†04915 Waldo○ 495 .... E7
04572 Waldoboro○ 3,985 .... E7
04572 Waldoboro 1,195 .... E7
†04605 Waltham○ 186 .... G6
04864 Warren○ 2,566 .... E7
04786 Washburn○ 2,028 .... G2
04786 Washburn 1,221 .... G2
04574 Washington○ 954 .... E7
04087 Waterboro○ 2,943 .... B8
04088 Waterford○ 951 .... B7
04901 Waterville 17,779 .... D6
04284 Wayne○ 680 .... D7
04285 Weld○ 435 .... C6
04990 Wellington○ 287 .... D5
04090 Wells○ 8,211 .... B9
04686 Wesley○ 140 .... H6
†04530 West Bath○ 1,309 .... D8
04092 Westbrook 14,976 .... C8
04493 West Enfield 609 .... F5
04787 Westfield○ 647 .... G2
04985 West Forks○ 72 .... D5
†04649 West Jonesport 400 .... H6
04094 West Kennebunk 750 .... B9
†04938 West Mills 75 .... C6
04288 West Minot 400 .... C7
04095 West Newfield 300 .... B8
04424 Weston○ 155 .... H4
04289 West Paris○ 1,390 .... B7
04290 West Peru 700 .... C7
04291 West Poland 250 .... C7
04074 West Scarborough 500 .... C8
04690 West Tremont 250 .... G7
04362 Whitefield○ 1,606 .... D7
04691 Whiting○ 335 .... J6
04692 Whitneyville○ 264 .... H6
†04443 Willimantic○ 164 .... E5
04293 Wilsons Mills 50 .... B6
04294 Wilton○ 4,382 .... C6
04294 Wilton 2,262 .... C6
04363 Windsor○ 1,702 .... D7
04495 Winn○ 503 .... G5
†04901 Winslow○ 8,057 .... D6
†04901 Winslow 5,903 .... D6
04693 Winter Harbor○ 1,120 .... G7
04496 Winterport○ 2,675 .... F6
04496 Winterport 1,126 .... F6
04788 Winterville○ 235 .... F2
04364 Winthrop○ 5,889 .... C7
04364 Winthrop 3,264 .... C7
04578 Wiscasset○ 2,832 .... D7
04694 Woodland○ 1,363 .... H5
04579 Woolwich○ 2,156 .... D8
04497 Wytopitlock 130 .... G4
04096 Yarmouth○ 6,585 .... C8
04096 Yarmouth 2,981 .... C8
03909 York○ 8,465 .... B9
03909 York 4,530 .... B9
03910 York Beach 900 .... B9
03911 York Harbor 950 .... B9

OTHER FEATURES

Abraham (mt.) C5
Acadia Nat'l Park G7
Allagash (lake) D3
Allagash (riv.) E2
Androscoggin (riv.) C7
Aroostook (riv.) G2
Attean (pond) C4
Baker (lake) D3
Baskahegan (lake) H5
Bear (riv.) B6
Big (brook) E2
Big (lake) H5
Big Black (riv.) D2
Bigelow (bight) C9
Big Spencer (mt.) E4
Black (pond) D3
Blue (mt.) C6
Blue Hill (bay) G7
Bog (lake) H6
Brassua (lake) D4
Casco (bay) C8
Cathance (lake) J6
Caucomgomoc (lake) D3
Center (pond) E5
Chamberlain (lake) E3
Chemquasabamticook (lake) D3
Chesuncook (lake) E3
Chiputneticook (lakes) H4
Clayton (lake) D2
Clifford (lake) H5
Cold Stream (pond) G5
Crawford (lake) H5
Cross (isl.) J6
Cross (lake) G1
Cupsuptic (riv.) B5
Dead (riv.) C5
Deer (isl.) F7
Duck (isls.) G7
Eagle (lake) E3
Eagle (lake) F1
East Machias (riv.) H6
East Musquash (lake) H5
Elizabeth (cape) C8
Ellis (pond) B6
Ellis (riv.) B6
Embden (pond) D6
Endless (lake) F5
Englishman (bay) J6
Eskutassis (pond) G5
Fifth (lake) H5
Fish (riv.) F2
Fish River (lake) F2
Flagstaff (lake) C5
Fourth (lake) H5
Frenchman (bay) G7
Gardner (lake) J6
Georges (isls.) E8
Graham (lake) G6
Grand (lake) H4
Grand Falls (lake) H5
Grand Lake Seboeis (lake) F3
Grand Manan (chan.) K6
Great Moose (lake) D6
Great Wass (isl.) J7
Green (isl.) F8
Harrington (lake) E4
Haut (isl.) G7
Indian Pond (lake) D4
Islesboro (isl.) F7
Jo-Mary (lakes) E4
Katahdin (mt.) F4
Kennebec (riv.) D7
Kezar (lake) B7
Kezar (pond) B7
Kingsbury (pond) D5
Little Black (riv.) E1
Little Madawaska (riv.) G2
Lobster (lake) E4
Long (lake) B7
Long (lake) E2
Long (lake) G1
Long (pond) C4
Long (pond) D6
Long (pond) E5
Long (pond) C5
Long Falls (dam) B6
Longfellow (mts.) D3
Loon (lake) H2
Loring A.F.B. 6,572 .... E4
Lower Roach (pond) G5
Lower Sysladobsis (lake) J6
Machias (bay) F2
Machias (riv.) H6
Machias (riv.) J7
Machias Seal (isl.) G5
Madagascal (pond) G7
Marshall (isl.) F8
Matinicus Rock (isl.) F4
Mattamiscontis (lake) G4
Mattawamkeag (lake) G4
Mattawamkeag (riv.) G4
Meddybemps (lake) J5
Metinic (isl.) E8
Millinocket (lake) F4
Millinocket (lake) F3
Molunkus (lake) G4
Monhegan (isl.) E8
Moose (pond) B7
Moose (riv.) D4
Moosehead (lake) D4
Mooseleuk (stream) F2
Mooselookmeguntic (lake) B6
Mopang (lake) H6
Mount Desert (isl.) G7
Mount Desert Rock (isl.) G8
Moxie (lake) D5
Munsungan (lake) E3
Muscongus (bay) E8
Musquacook (lakes) E2
Nahmakanta (lake) E4
Nicatous (lake) G5
Nollesemic (lake) F4
Old (stream) H6
Onawa (lake) E5
Parlin (pond) C4
Parmachenee (lake) B5
Passamaquoddy (bay) J5
Passamaquoddy Ind. Res. J6
Pemadumcook (lake) E4
Penobscot (bay) F7
Penobscot (lake) C4
Penobscot (riv.) F5
Penobscot Ind. Res. F6
Pierce (pond) C5
Piscataqua (riv.) B9
Piscataquis (riv.) E5
Pleasant (lake) E3
Pleasant (lake) G3
Pleasant (lake) H5
Pleasant (riv.) H6
Pocomoonshine (lake) H5
Portage (lake) F2
Presque Isle A.F.B. G2
Priestly (lake) E2
Pushaw (lake) F6
Ragged (isl.) F8
Ragged (lake) E4
Rainbow (lake) E4
Rangeley (lake) B6
Richardson (lakes) B6
Rocky (lake) J6
Round (pond) E2
Rowe (lake) F2
Saco (riv.) B8
Saint Croix (riv.) J5
Saint Croix Isl. Nat'l Mon. J5
Saint Francis (riv.) E1
Saint Froid (lake) F2
Saint John (pond) D3
Saint John (riv.) G1
Salmon Falls (riv.) B9
Sandy (riv.) C6
Schoodic (lake) F5
Scraggly (lake) F3
Scraggly (lake) H5
Seal (isl.) F8
Sebago (lake) B8
Sebasticook (lake) E6
Seboeis (lake) F5
Seboeis (riv.) F3
Seboomook (lake) D4
Shallow (lake) E3
Small (cape) D8
Sourdnahunk (lake) F3
Spencer (pond) D4
Spencer (stream) C5
Spider (lake) E3
Squa Pan (lake) G2
Square (lake) G1
Sunday (riv.) B6
Swift (riv.) B6
Sysladobsis, Lower (lake) G5
Third (lake) H5
Twin (lakes) F4
Umbagog (lake) A6
Umcalcus (lake) G3
Umsaskis (lake) E2
Union, West Branch (riv.) G6
Vinalhaven (isl.) F7
Wassataquoik (stream) F4
Webb (lake) C6
Webster (brook) E3
West Grand (lake) H5
West Musquash (lake) H5
West Quoddy (head) K6
Wilson E5
Winnecook (lake) E6
Wooden Ball (isl.) F8
Wyman (lake) C5
Wytopitlock (lake) G4

⊙County seat.
‡Population of metropolitan area.
○Population of town or township.
† Zip of nearest p.o.
* Multiple zips.

Topography

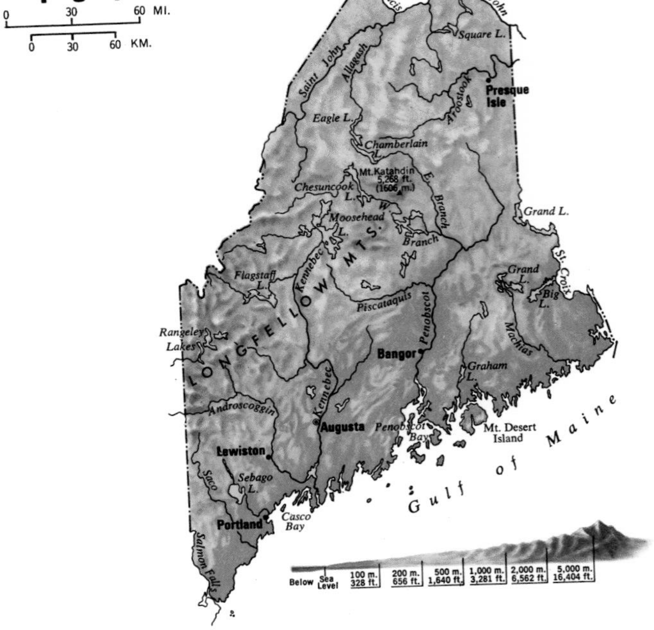

0 30 60 MI.
0 30 60 KM.
St. Francis
Saint John
Square L.
Allagash
Saint John
Presque Isle
Aroostook
Eagle L.
Chamberlain
Mt. Katahdin 5,268 ft. (1606 m.)
Chesuncook L.
E. Branch
Moosehead L.
W. Branch
Grand L.
St. Croix
Flagstaff L.
Kennebec
LONGFELLOW MTS.
Piscataquis
Penobscot
Grand L.
Big L.
Machias
Rangeley Lakes
Bangor
Graham L.
Androscoggin
Kennebec
Augusta
Penobscot Bay
Mt. Desert Island
Gulf of Maine
Lewiston
Sebago L.
Saco
Portland
Casco Bay
Salmon Falls
Below Sea Level
100 m. 328 ft.
200 m. 656 ft.
500 m. 1,640 ft.
1,000 m. 3,281 ft.
2,000 m. 6,562 ft.
5,000 m. 16,404 ft.

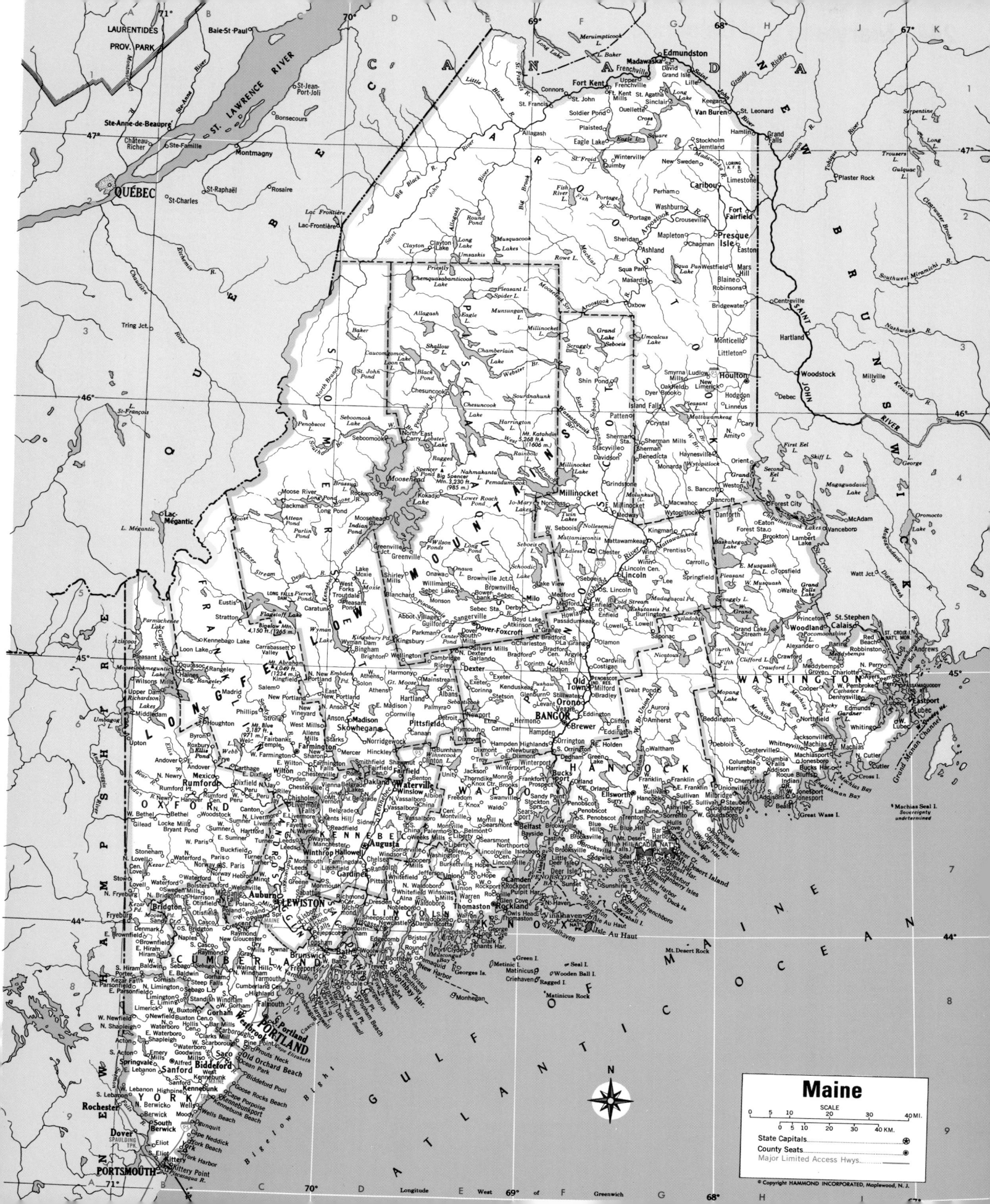

Maine

SCALE

State Capitals ⊛
County Seats ⊙
Major Limited Access Hwys.

© Copyright HAMMOND INCORPORATED, Maplewood, N.J.

244 Maryland and Delaware

MARYLAND

COUNTIES

Allegany 80,548 ....C2
Anne Arundel 370,775 ......M4
Baltimore 655,615 ....M3
Baltimore (city county) 786,775 ..M3
Calvert 34,638 ....M6
Caroline 23,143 ....K2
Carroll 96,356 ....P2
Cecil 60,430 ....K6
Charles 72,751 ....O7
Dorchester 30,623 ....J3
Frederick 114,792 ....A2
Garrett 26,498 ....N2
Harford 145,930 ....L4
Howard 118,572 ....O3
Kent 16,695 ....J4
Montgomery 579,053 ....L5
Prince Georges 665,071 ......P4
Queen Annes 25,508 ....P4
Saint Marys 59,895 ....M7
Somerset 19,188 ....R8
Talbot 25,604 ....O5
Washington 113,086 ....G2
Wicomico 64,540 ....R7
Worcester 30,889 ....S8

CITIES and TOWNS

Zip   Name/Pop.   Key

21001 Aberdeen 11,533 ....O2
21009 Abingdon 500 ....N3
21520 Accident 246 ....A2
20607 Accokeek 3,894 ....L6
*21401 Annapolis (cap.)⊙ 31,740 M5
20701 Annapolis Junction 775 M4
20608 Aquasco 950 ....L6
†21227 Arbutus 20,163 ....M4
†20785 Ardmore 500 ....G4
Aspen Hill 47,455 ....K4
*21201 Baltimore 786,775 ....M3
Baltimore‡ 2,174,023 .....M3
20610 Barstow 500 ....M6
21521 Barton 617 ....B2
21014 Bel Air⊙ 7,814 ....N2
21661 Bel Alton 800 ....L7
20705 Beltsville 12,760 ......G3
20612 Benedict 850 ....M6
21811 Berlin 2,162 ....T7
†20740 Berwyn Heights 3,135 G4
*20014 Bethesda 62,736 ......E4
21609 Bethlehem 500 ....P6
21610 Betterton 356 ....O3
20710 Bladensburg 7,691 ....G4
21523 Bloomington 486 ......B3
21713 Boonsboro 1,908 ......H2
†20027 Boulevard Heights 500 F5
20715 Bowie 33,695 ....L4
21612 Bozman 700 ....N5
20613 Brandywine 1,319 .....L6
20722 Brentwood 2,988 ......F4
21225 Brooklyn 11,508 ....M4
†21659 Brookview 78 ....P6
21716 Brunswick 4,572 ....H3
21717 Buckeystown 400 ......J3
21718 Burkittsville 202 ......H3
20618 Bushwood 750 ....L7
20731 Cabin
      John-Brookmont 5,135 .E4
20619 California 5,770 ....M7
†20705 Calverton 7,649 ......L4
21613 Cambridge⊙ 11,703 ....O6
20748 Camp Springs 16,118 ..G6
21401 Cape Saint Claire 6,022 .N4
20743 Capitol Heights 3,271 ..G5
21024 Cardiff 475 ....N2
†20028 Carmody Hills-Pepper Mill
      Village 5,571 ....G5
*21034 Castleton 750 ....N2
†21788 Catoctin Furnace 516 ..J2
21228 Catonsville 33,208 .....M3
21720 Cavetown 1,533 ....H2
21913 Cecilton 508 ....P3
21617 Centreville⊙ 2,018 ....O4
21816 Chance 600 ....P8
21914 Charlestown 720 ......P2
20622 Charlotte Hall 1,901 ...M7
21027 Chase 900 ....N3
20623 Cheltenham 950 ....L6
20732 Chesapeake Beach 1,408 .N6
21915 Chesapeake City 899 ...P2
21619 Chester 950 ....N5
21620 Chestertown⊙ 3,300 ...O4
20785 Cheverly 5,751 ....G4
20815 Chevy Chase 12,232 ...E4
†20015 Chevy Chase Section
      Four 3,189 ....E4
20783 Chillum 32,775 ....F4
21622 Church Creek 124 .....O6
21623 Church Hill 319 ....O4
21028 Churchville 500 ....N2
20734 Clarksburg 400 ....L4
21029 Clarksville 500 ....L4
21722 Clear Spring 477 .....G2
20624 Clements 800 ....L7
20735 Clinton 16,438 ....G6
21030 Cockeysville 17,013 ...M3
20904 Colesville 14,359 .....K4
20740 College Park 23,614 ...G4
†20722 Colmar Manor 1,286 ...F4
20626 Coltons Point 600 ....M8
21043 Columbia 52,518 ......L4
20627 Compton 500 ....M7
21723 Cooksville 497 ....K3
†20027 Coral Hills 11,602 ....G5
21524 Corriganville 1,020 ...C2
†20722 Cottage City 1,122 ...F4
†20611 Cox Station (Bel
      Alton) 800 ....L7
21502 Cresaptown 4,645 .....C2
21817 Crisfield 2,924 ....P9
21114 Crofton 12,009 ....M4
21032 Crownsville 950 ......M4
21502 Cumberland⊙ 25,933 ...D2
      Cumberland‡ 107,782 ...D2

20750 Damascus 4,129 ....K3
20628 Dameron 759 ....N8
21034 Darlington 850 ....N2
20751 Deale 3,008 ....P8
21821 Deal Island 800 ......A3
21784 Defense Heights G4
21875 Delmar 1,232 ....R7
21629 Denton⊙ 1,927 ....P5
20855 Derwood 413 ....K4
20753 District Heights 6,799 .G5
20747 District Heights 6,799 .G5
20630 Drayden 950 ....N8
21222 Dundalk 71,293 ....N3
†20608 Eagle Harbor 45 ......M6
21631 East New Market 230 ..P6
21601 Easton⊙ 7,536 ....O5
21528 Eckhart Mines 1,333 ...C2
21822 Eden 800 ....R7
21219 Edgemere 9,078 ......N4
†21040 Edgewood 19,455 .....N3
†20781 Edmonston 1,109 .....F4
†21784 Eldersburg 4,959 .....L3

†21659 Eldorado 93 ....P6
21920 Elk Mills 550 ....P2
21901 Elk Neck 700 ....P2
21921 Elkton⊙ 6,468 ....P2
21529 Ellerslie 950 ....C2
21043 Ellicott City⊙ 21,784 ..L3
21727 Emmitsburg 1,552 ....J2
21221 Essex 39,614 ....N3
21824 Ewell 595 ....O8
†20027 Fairmount Heights 1,616 .G5
21047 Fallston 5,572 ....N2
21632 Federalsburg 1,952 ...P6
21061 Ferndale 14,314 ......M4
21048 Finksburg 950 ....N7
21634 Fishing Creek 595 ....D2
21530 Flintstone 400 ....C2
†20001 Forest Heights 2,999 ..F5
21050 Forest Hill 450 ....G5
20028 Forestville 16,401 ....F6
†20022 Fort Foote 700 ....L6
20749 Fort Washington L6
†21163 Fountain Head 1,745 ..G2
21760 Foxville 175 ....H2
21701 Frederick⊙ 28,086 ....J3

21053 Freeland 500 ....M2
20758 Friendship 600 ....M6
21531 Friendsville 511 .....A2
21532 Frostburg 7,715 .....C2
21826 Fruitland 2,694 ......H2
21734 Funkstown 1,103 ....K4
20760 Gaithersburg 26,424 ..P3
21635 Galena 374 ....P6
†19973 Galestown 142 ......M5
20765 Galesville 600 ......L3
20765 Gamber 500 ....L3
21054 Gambrills 460 ....M4
20766 Garrett Park 1,178 ...E3
21055 Garrison 950 ....L3
20767 Germantown 9,721 ...J4
20801 Glenarden 4,993 ....G4
21061 Glen Burnie 37,263 ..M4
20768 Glen Echo 229 ......E4
21737 Glenelg 400 ....L3
21636 Goldsboro 188 ......P4
20637 Hughesville 1,208 ...L6
20639 Huntingtown 450 ....M6
21643 Hurlock 1,690 ....P6
20640 Indian Head 1,381 ...K6

21122 Green Haven 6,577 ...M4
21639 Greensboro 1,253 ....P5
21740 Hagerstown⊙ 34,132 ..G2
      Hagerstown‡ 113,086 .G2
†21740 Halfway 8,659 ....G2
21074 Hampstead 1,293 ....L2
21750 Hancock 1,887 ......F2
21201 Hanover 500 ....M4
21077 Harmans 400 ....M4
21078 Havre de Grace 8,763 .O2
21830 Hebron 714 ....R7
21640 Henderson 156 ......P4
21111 Hereford 680 ....M2
20801 Hillandale 9,686 .....F4
†20031 Hillcrest Heights 17,021 .F5
21641 Hillsboro 180 ....P5
20636 Hollywood 500 ......M7

†20685 Island Creek 400 .....M7
21084 Jarrettsville 1,485 ...M2
†21085 Joppatowne 11,348 ...N3
21756 Keedysville 476 .....H3
†20901 Kemp Mill F3
20795 Kensington 1,822 ....E4
21087 Kingsville 2,824 .....N3
21538 Kitzmiller 387 ....B3
20785 Knoxville 500 ....H3
20785 Landover 5,374 ......G4
20784 Landover Hills 1,428 .G4
20787 Langley Park 14,038 ..F4
20801 Lanham-Seabrook 15,814 .G4
21227 Lansdowne-Baltimore
      Highlands 16,759 ....M3
20646 La Plata⊙ 2,484 .....L6
20870 Largo 5,557 ....G5
20810 Laurel 12,103 ....L4
21502 La Vale-Narrows
      Park 5,523 ....C2
20760 Laytonsville 195 ....K4
21761 Le Gore 500 ....J2
†21740 Leitersburg 350 .....H2
20650 Leonardtown⊙ 1,448 ..M7

(continued)

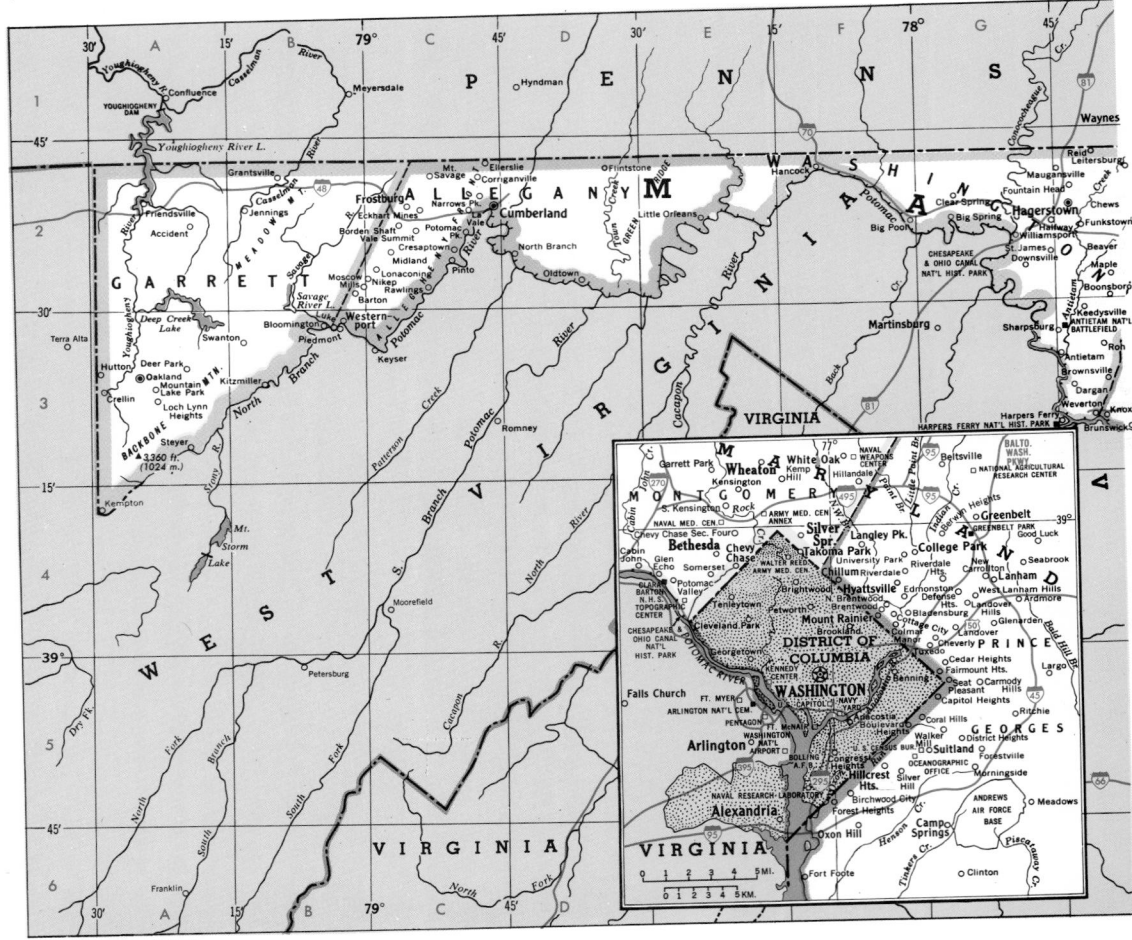

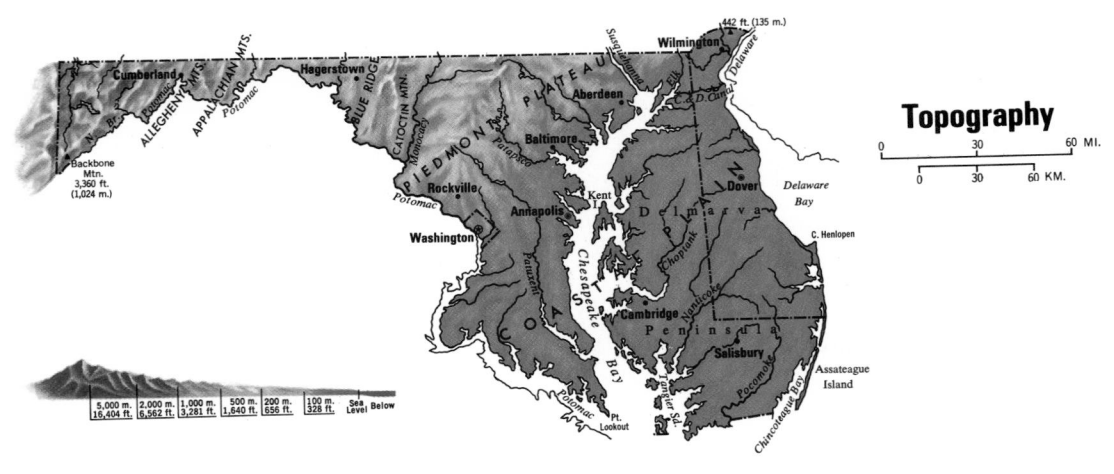

Topography

MARYLAND

AREA 10,460 sq. mi. (27,091 sq. km.)
POPULATION 4,216,975
CAPITAL Annapolis
LARGEST CITY Baltimore
HIGHEST POINT Backbone Mtn. 3,360 ft. (1024 m.)
SETTLED IN 1634
ADMITTED TO UNION April 28, 1788
POPULAR NAME Old Line State; Free State
STATE FLOWER Black-eyed Susan
STATE BIRD Baltimore Oriole

DELAWARE

AREA 2,044 sq. mi. (5,294 sq. km.)
POPULATION 594,317
CAPITAL Dover
LARGEST CITY Wilmington
HIGHEST POINT Ebright Road 442 ft. (135 m.)
SETTLED IN 1627
ADMITTED TO UNION December 7, 1787
POPULAR NAME First State; Diamond State
STATE FLOWER Peach Blossom
STATE BIRD Blue Hen Chicken

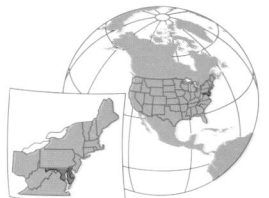

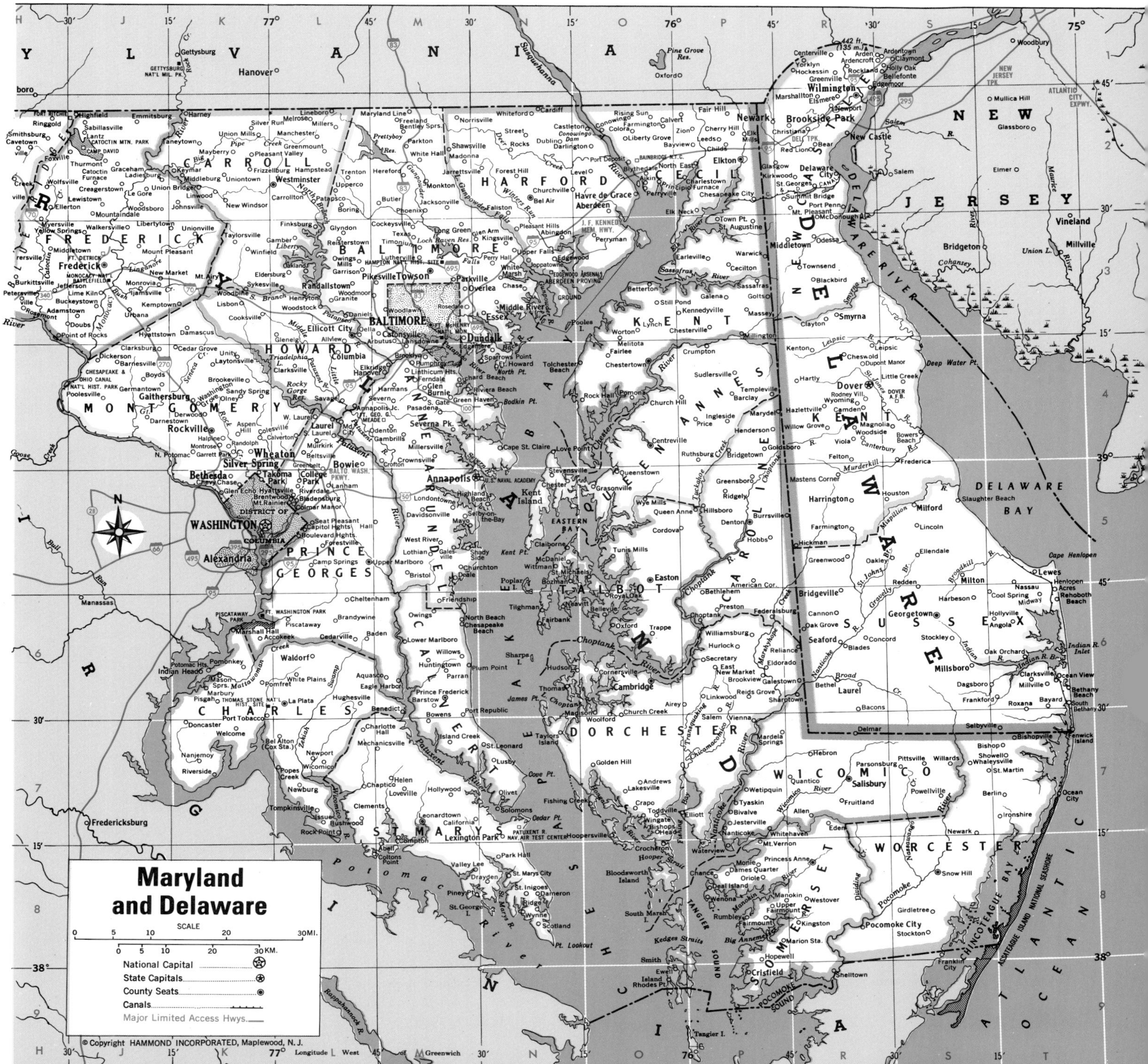

Maryland and Delaware

SCALE

0 5 10   20   30 MI.

0 5 10   20   30 KM.

National Capital ⊛
State Capitals ⊛
County Seats ⊙
Canals
Major Limited Access Hwys.

© Copyright HAMMOND INCORPORATED, Maplewood, N.J.

(continued)

21701 Lewistown 600 .... J2
20653 Lexington Park 10,361 .... M7
21762 Libertytown 400 .... J3
21090 Linthicum Heights 7,457 .... M4
21766 Little Orleans 600 .... E2
†21550 Loch Lynn Heights 503 .... A3
21539 Lonaconing 1,420 .... C2
†21035 Londontowne 6,052 .... M4
21092 Long Green 1,626 .... M3
20656 Loveville 600 .... M7
21540 Luke 329 .... B3
21093 Lutherville-Timonium 16,871 .... M3
21648 Madison 350 .... O6
21102 Manchester 1,830 .... L2
20658 Marbury 1,189 .... K6
21837 Mardela Springs 320 .... P7
21838 Marion Station 400 .... R8
†20616 Marshall Hall 325 .... K6
21649 Marydel 152 .... P4
†21113 Maryland City 6,949 .... L4
21767 Maugansville 1,707 .... H2
21106 Mayo 2,795 .... M5
20659 Mechanicsville 784 .... M7
21220 Middle River 26,756 .... N3
21769 Middletown 1,748 .... J3
21542 Midland 601 .... C2
21108 Millersville 380 .... M4
21651 Millington 546 .... P3
†20028 Morningside 1,395 .... G5
†21701 Mountaindale 400 .... J2
21550 Mountain Lake Park 1,597 .... A3
†21771 Mount Airy 2,450 .... K3
†21701 Mount Pleasant 400 .... J3
20822 Mount Rainier 7,361 .... F4
21545 Mount Savage 1,640 .... C2
†21853 Mount Vernon 900 .... P8
†20705 Muirkirk 950 .... L4
21773 Myersville 432 .... H3
21840 Nanticoke 450 .... P7
†21502 Narrows Park-La Vale 5,523 .... C2
21841 Newark 900 .... S7
20664 Newburg 550 .... L7
20784 New Carrollton 12,632 .... G4
21774 New Market 306 .... J3
21776 New Windsor 799 .... K2
20831 North Beach 1,504 .... N6
†20722 North Brentwood 580 .... F4
21901 North East 1,469 .... P2
†20854 North Potomac K4
21550 Oakland⊙ 1,994 .... A3
†21784 Oakland 2,242 .... L3
21842 Ocean City 4,946 .... T7
21113 Odenton 13,270 .... M4
†21228 Oella 600 .... L3
20832 Olney 13,026 .... K4
21206 Overlea 12,965 .... N3
20836 Owings 700 .... M6
21117 Owings Mills 9,526 .... L3
21654 Oxford 754 .... O6
20745 Oxon Hill 36,267 .... F6
20667 Park Hall 775 .... N8
21234 Parkville 35,159 .... M3
21122 Pasadena 7,439 .... M4
21128 Perry Hall 13,455 .... N3
21130 Perryman 1,819 .... O3
21903 Perryville 2,018 .... O2
21208 Pikesville 22,555 .... M3
20674 Piney Point 950 .... M8
†20735 Piscataway 500 .... L6
20640 Pisgah 650 .... K6
21850 Pittsville 519 .... S7
†21087 Pleasant Hills 2,790 .... N3
21851 Pocomoke City 3,558 .... R8
20675 Pomfret 600 .... L6
†20640 Pomonkey 410 .... K6
20837 Poolesville 3,428 .... J4
21904 Port Deposit 664 .... O2
20677 Port Tobacco 40 .... K6
20640 Potomac Heights 2,456 .... K6
†21502 Potomac Park-Bowling Green 2,275 .... C2
21852 Powellville 400 .... S7
21655 Preston 498 .... P6
20678 Prince Frederick⊙ 1,805 .... M6
21853 Princess Anne⊙ 1,499 .... P8
†21090 Pumphrey 5,666 .... M4
21657 Queen Anne 259 .... O5
21658 Queenstown 491 .... O5
21133 Randallstown 25,927 .... L3
21557 Rawlings 500 .... C2
21136 Reisterstown 19,385 .... L3
20680 Ridge 550 .... N8
21660 Ridgely 933 .... P5
21911 Rising Sun 1,160 .... O2
†20027 Ritchie 950 .... G5
†20840 Riverdale Heights G4
†21061 Riviera Beach 8,812 .... N4
21661 Rock Hall 1,511 .... O4
†21084 Rocks 450 .... N2
*20850 Rockville⊙ 43,811 .... K4
21779 Rohrersville 525 .... H3
21237 Rosedale 19,956 .... M3
†21758 Rosemont 305 .... H3
21662 Royal Oak 600 .... O6
21780 Sabillasville 450 .... J2
20684 Saint Inigoes 750 .... N8
21663 Saint Michaels 1,301 .... N5
21801 Salisbury⊙ 16,429 .... R7
20860 Sandy Spring-Ashton 2,659 .... K4
20863 Savage-Guilford 2,928 .... L4
20687 Scotland 475 .... N8
20801 Seabrook-Lanham 15,814 .... G4
20027 Seat Pleasant 5,217 .... G5
21664 Secretary 487 .... P6
†21037 Selby-on-the-Bay 3,125 .... N5
21144 Severn 20,147 .... M4
21146 Severna Park 21,253 .... M4
20867 Shady Side 2,877 .... M5
21782 Sharpsburg 721 .... G3
21861 Sharptown 654 .... R6
20023 Silver Hill-Suitland 32,164 .... F5
†21157 Silver Run 350 .... K2
*20901 Silver Spring 72,893 .... F4
21783 Smithsburg 833 .... H2
21863 Snow Hill⊙ 2,192 .... S8
†20015 Somerset 1,101 .... E4
†21113 South Gate 24,185 .... M4
†20795 South Kensington 9,344 .... E4
†20810 South Laurel 18,034 .... L4
21219 Sparrows Point N4
21666 Stevensville 500 .... N5
21667 Still Pond 350 .... O3
21864 Stockton 400 .... S8
21668 Sudlersville 443 .... P4
†20746 Suitland-Silver Hill 32,164 .... F5
21784 Sykesville 1,712 .... K3
20912 Takoma Park 16,231 .... F4
21787 Taneytown 2,618 .... K2
21669 Taylors Island 400 .... N7
21670 Templeville 96 .... P4
21788 Thurmont 2,934 .... J2
21671 Tilghman 979 .... N6
21093 Timonium-Lutherville 16,871 .... M3
21672 Toddville 500 .... O7
21204 Towson⊙ 51,083 .... M3
21673 Trappe 739 .... O6
†20780 Tuxedo 500 .... G5
21791 Union Bridge 927 .... K2
†20740 University Park 2,536 .... F4
21155 Upperco 500 .... L2
21867 Upper Fairmount 500 .... P8
21156 Upper Falls 550 .... N3
20870 Upper Marlboro⊙ 828 .... M5
20692 Valley Lee 600 .... M8
21869 Vienna 300 .... P7
20601 Waldorf 9,782 .... L6
†20023 Walker Mill 10,651 .... F5
21793 Walkersville 2,212 .... J3
21912 Warwick 550 .... P3
20880 Washington Grove 527 .... K4
20693 Welcome 438 .... K7
21562 Westernport 2,706 .... B3
†20784 West Lanham Hills 350 .... G4
21157 Westminster⊙ 8,808 .... L2
21871 Westover 450 .... R8
20902 Wheaton-Glenmont 48,598 .... E3
21160 Whiteford 500 .... N2
21161 White Hall 360 .... M2
21162 White Marsh 500 .... N3
†20901 White Oak 13,700 .... F3
20695 White Plains 5,167 .... L6
21874 Willards 540 .... S7
21795 Williamsport 2,153 .... G2
21676 Wittman 544 .... N5
21797 Woodbine 872 .... K3
21798 Woodsboro 506 .... J2
21163 Woodstock 700 .... L3
21677 Woolford 330 .... O7
21679 Wye Mills 315 .... O5
†20680 Wynne 450 .... N8
†21701 Yellow Springs 940 .... H3

OTHER FEATURES

Aberdeen Proving Ground 5,722 .... N3
Allegheny Front (mts.) C2
Andrews A.F.B. 10,064 .... G5
Antietam (creek) H2
Antietam Nat'l Battlefield H3
Army Chemical Center O3
Back (riv.) N4
Backbone (mt.) A3
Bainbridge N.T.C. O2
Bald Hill Branch (riv.) G4
Big Annemessex (riv.) P8
Big Pipe (creek) K2
Bloodsworth (isl.) O8
Blue Ridge (mts.) H3
Bodkin (pt.) N4
Bush (creek) J3
Cabin John (creek) E4
Camp David J2
Casselman (riv.) B2
Catoctin (creek) H3
Catoctin Mt. Park J2
Cedar (pt.) N7
Census Bureau F5
Chesapeake (bay) N7
Chesapeake and Delaware (canal) R2
Chesapeake and Ohio Canal Nat'l Hist. Park J4
Chester (riv.) O4
Chicamacomico (riv.) P7
Chincoteague (bay) S8
Choptank (riv.) O6
Clara Barton Nat'l Hist. Site E4
Conococheague (creek) G1
Conowingo (dam) O2
Cove (pt.) N7
Deep Creek (lake) A3
Deer (creek) N2
Dividing (creek) R8
Eastern (bay) N5
Elk (riv.) P3
Fishing (bay) O7
Fort Detrick J3
Fort George G. Meade 14,083 .... L4
Fort McHenry Nat'l Mon. M3
Fort Ritchie 1,754 .... H2
Fort Washington Park L6
Great Seneca (creek) J4
Greenbelt Park G4
Green Ridge (mts.) E2
Gunpowder (riv.) N3
Gunpowder Falls (creek) M2
Hampton Nat'l Hist. Site M3
Harpers Ferry Nat'l Hist. Park G3
Henson (creek) F6
Honga (riv.) O7
Hooper (str.) O8
Indian (creek) G4
James (pt.) N6
Kedges (strs) O8
Kent (isl.) N5
Kent (pt.) N5
Liberty (lake) L3
Linganore (creek) J3
Little Choptank (riv.) N6
Little Gunpowder Falls (creek) M2
Little Paint Branch (riv.) F4
Little Patuxent (riv.) L4
Loch Raven (res.) M3
Lookout (pt.) N8
Manokin (riv.) P8
Marshyhope (creek) P6
Mattawoman (creek) K6
Meadow (mt.) B2
Middle Patuxent (riv.) L3
Monocacy (riv.) J3
Monocacy Nat'l Battlefield J3
Nanticoke (riv.) P7
Nassawango (creek) S8
National Agricultural Research Center G3
Naval Academy, U.S. 5,367 .... N5
Naval Medical Center E4
Naval Weapons Center F3
North (pt.) N4
Oceanographic Office F5
Oxon Run (riv.) F5
Paint Branch (riv.) F4
Patapsco (riv.) M4
Patuxent (riv.) M7
Patuxent River Nav. Air Test Ctr. N7
Piscataway (creek) G6
Piscataway Park K6
Pocomoke (riv.) S8
Pocomoke (sound) P9
Pooles (isl.) O3
Poplar (isl.) N5
Potomac (riv.) M8
Prettyboy (res.) M2
Rock (creek) K4
Rocky Gorge (res.) L4
Saint George (isl.) M8
Saint Marys (riv.) N8
Sassafras (riv.) P3
Savage (riv.) B2
Savage River (lake) B2
Severn (riv.) N4
Sharps (isl.) N6
Smith (isl.) O8
South Marsh (isl.) O8
Susquehanna (riv.) N1
Tangier (sound) P8
Thomas Stone Nat'l Hist. Site K6
Tinkers (creek) F6
Topographic Center E4
Town (creek) E2
Transquaking (riv.) P7
Triadelphia (lake) L4
Tuckahoe (creek) P5
Walter Reed Army Med. Ctr. Annex E4
Wicomico (riv.) L7
Wicomico (riv.) R7
Winters Run (creek) N2
Youghiogheny (riv.) A3
Youghiogheny River (lake) A2
Zekiah Swamp (riv.) L7

DELAWARE

COUNTIES

Kent 98,219 .... R4
New Castle 398,115 .... R2
Sussex 97,983 .... S6

CITIES and TOWNS

Zip *Name/Pop.* *Key*

†19801 Arden 516 .... R1
†19810 Ardencroft 267 .... R1
†19810 Ardentown 307 .... S1
19809 Bellefonte 1,279 .... S1
19930 Bethany Beach 330 .... T6
19931 Bethel 197 .... R6
†19973 Blades 664 .... R6
†19962 Bowers Beach 198 .... S4
19993 Bridgeville 1,238 .... R6
19711 Brookside 15,255 .... R2
19934 Camden 1,757 .... R4
†19801 Centerville 800 .... R1
19936 Cheswold 269 .... R4
†19711 Christiana 500 .... R2
19937 Clarksville 350 .... T6
19703 Claymont 10,022 .... S1
19938 Clayton 1,216 .... R3
19930 Dagsboro 344 .... S6
19706 Delaware City 1,858 .... R2
19940 Delmar 948 .... R7
19901 Dover (cap.)⊙ 23,507 .... R4
†19901 Dupont Manor 1,059 .... R4
†19801 Edgemoor 7,397 .... S1
19941 Ellendale 361 .... S5
†19801 Elsmere 6,493 .... R2
19942 Farmington 141 .... R5
19943 Felton 547 .... R4
19944 Fenwick Island 114 .... T7
19945 Frankford 828 .... S6
19946 Frederica 864 .... S4
19947 Georgetown⊙ 1,710 .... S6
†19711 Glasgow 350 .... R2
19950 Greenwood 578 .... R5
19952 Harrington 2,405 .... R5
†19971 Henlopen Acres 176 .... T6
19707 Hockessin 950 .... R1
†19801 Holly Oak S1
19954 Houston 357 .... S5
19955 Kenton 243 .... R4
19708 Kirkwood 350 .... R2
19956 Laurel 3,052 .... R6
†19901 Leipsic 228 .... S4
19958 Lewes 2,197 .... T5
19960 Lincoln 757 .... S5
19961 Little Creek 230 .... S4
19962 Magnolia 197 .... R4
19709 Middletown 2,946 .... R3
19963 Milford 5,366 .... S5
19966 Millsboro 1,233 .... S6
19967 Millville 178 .... T6
19968 Milton 1,359 .... S5
19711 Newark 25,247 .... P2
19720 New Castle 4,907 .... R2
19804 Newport 1,167 .... R2
†19966 Oak Orchard 350 .... T6
19970 Ocean View 495 .... T6
19730 Odessa 384 .... R3
19971 Rehoboth Beach 1,730 .... T6
19901 Rodney Village 1,753 .... R4
19733 Saint Georges 450 .... R2
19973 Seaford 5,256 .... R6
19975 Selbyville 1,251 .... S7
†19963 Slaughter Beach 121 .... S5
19977 Smyrna 4,750 .... R3
†19930 South Bethany 115 .... T6
19734 Townsend 386 .... R3
19979 Viola 167 .... R4
*19801 Wilmington⊙ 70,195 .... R2
Wilmington‡ 524,108 .... R2
19980 Woodside 248 .... R4
19934 Wyoming 960 .... R4
19736 Yorklyn 600 .... R1

OTHER FEATURES

Broad (creek) R6
Broadkill (riv.) S5
Chesapeake and Delaware (canal) R2
Choptank (riv.) P5
Deep Water (pt.) S4
Delaware (bay) T5
Delaware (riv.) R3
Dover A.F.B. 4,391 .... S4
Henlopen (cape) T5
Indian (riv.) S6
Indian River (bay) T6
Indian River (inlet) T6
Leipsic (riv.) R4
Mispillion (riv.) S5
Murderkill (riv.) R5
Nanticoke (riv.) R6
Saint Jones (riv.) R4
Smyrna (res.) R3

DISTRICT OF COLUMBIA

CITIES and TOWNS

Zip *Name/Pop.* *Key*

20007 Georgetown E5
*20001 Washington, D.C. (cap.), U.S. 638,432 .... F5
Washington‡ 3,060,240 .... F5

OTHER FEATURES

Anacostia (riv.) F5
Bolling A.F.B. E5
Fort Lesley J. McNair E5
Kennedy Center A5
Naval Yard F5
U.S. Capitol F5
Walter Reed Army Med. Ctr. E4

⊙County seat.
‡Population of metropolitan area.
† Zip of nearest p.o.
* Multiple zips.

Agriculture, Industry and Resources

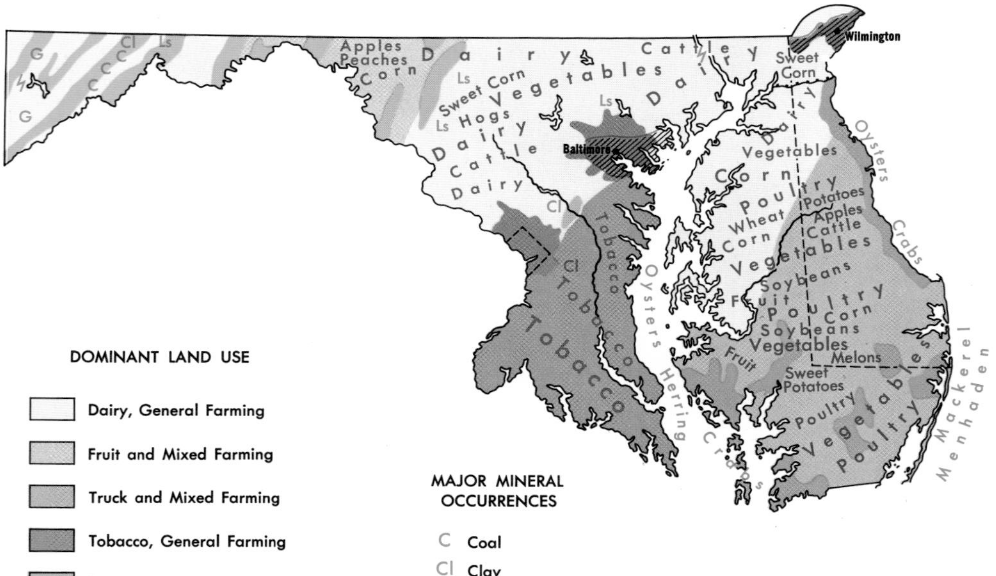

DOMINANT LAND USE

- Dairy, General Farming
- Fruit and Mixed Farming
- Truck and Mixed Farming
- Tobacco, General Farming
- Forests
- Swampland, Limited Agriculture
- Urban Areas

MAJOR MINERAL OCCURRENCES

C Coal
Cl Clay
G Natural Gas
Ls Limestone

Water Power

Major Industrial Areas

MASSACHUSETTS

AREA 8,284 sq. mi. (21,456 sq. km.)
POPULATION 5,737,037
CAPITAL Boston
LARGEST CITY Boston
HIGHEST POINT Mt. Greylock 3,491 ft. (1064 m.)
SETTLED IN 1620
ADMITTED TO UNION February 6, 1788
POPULAR NAME Bay State; Old Colony
STATE FLOWER Mayflower
STATE BIRD Chickadee

RHODE ISLAND

AREA 1,212 sq. mi. (3,139 sq. km.)
POPULATION 947,154
CAPITAL Providence
LARGEST CITY Providence
HIGHEST POINT Jerimoth Hill 812 ft. (247 m.)
SETTLED IN 1636
ADMITTED TO UNION May 29, 1790
POPULAR NAME Little Rhody; Ocean State
STATE FLOWER Violet
STATE BIRD Rhode Island Red

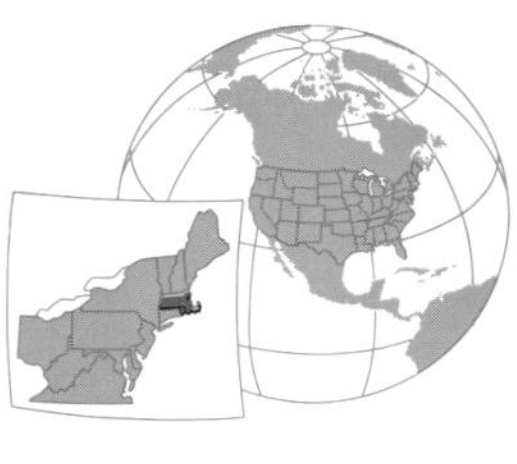

Agriculture, Industry and Resources

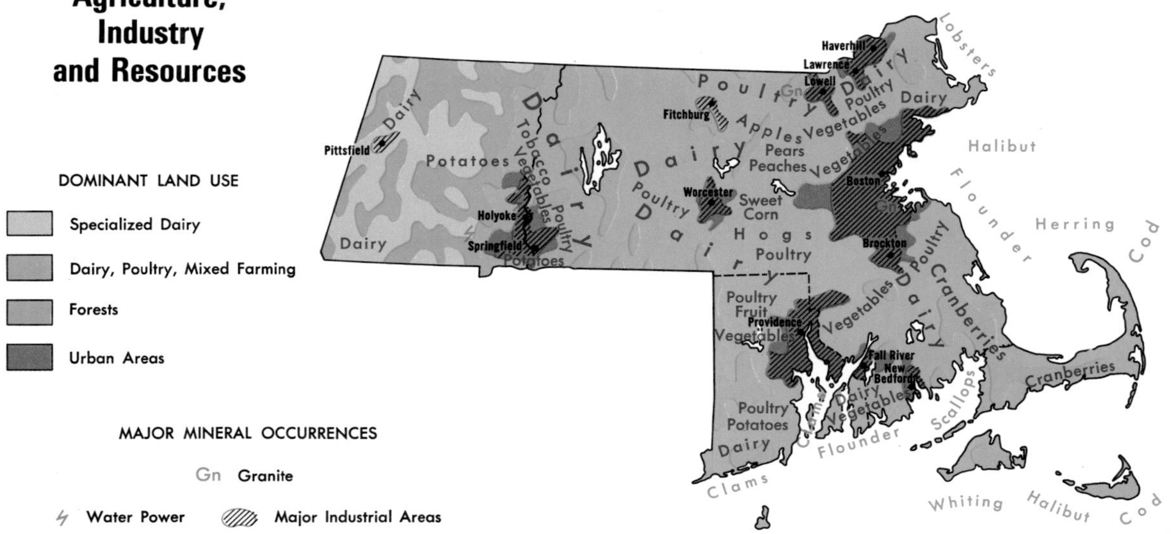
DOMINANT LAND USE
Specialized Dairy
Dairy, Poultry, Mixed Farming
Forests
Urban Areas
MAJOR MINERAL OCCURRENCES
Gn Granite
Water Power
Major Industrial Areas
Haverhill
Lawrence
Lowell
Fitchburg
Pittsfield
Worcester
Holyoke
Springfield
Boston
Brockton
Providence
Fall River
New Bedford
Dairy
Potatoes
Tobacco
Vegetables
Poultry
Apples
Pears
Peaches
Sweet Corn
Hogs
Fruit
Cranberries
Lobsters
Halibut
Flounder
Herring
Cod
Scallops
Clams
Whiting

MASSACHUSETTS

COUNTIES

Barnstable 147,925	N6
Berkshire 145,110	B3
Bristol 474,641	K5
Dukes 8,942	M7
Essex 633,632	L2
Franklin 64,317	D2
Hampden 443,018	D4
Hampshire 138,813	D3
Middlesex 1,367,034	J3
Nantucket 5,087	O7
Norfolk 606,587	K4
Plymouth 405,437	L5
Suffolk 650,142	K3
Worcester 646,352	G3

CITIES and TOWNS

Zip	*Name/Pop.*	*Key*
02351	Abington○ 13,517	L4
01720	Acton○ 17,544	J3
02743	Acushnet○ 8,704	L6
01220	Adams○ 10,381	B2
01220	Adams 6,857	B2
01001	Agawam○ 26,271	D4
†01261	Alford○ 394	A4
01913	Amesbury○ 13,971	L1
01913	Amesbury 12,236	L1
01002	Amherst○ 33,229	E3
01002	Amherst 17,773	E3
01810	Andover○ 26,370	K2
01810	Andover 8,445	K2
02174	Arlington○ 48,219	C6
01430	Ashburnham○ 4,075	G2
01430	Ashburnham 900	G2
01431	Ashby○ 2,311	G2
01330	Ashfield○ 1,458	C2
01721	Ashland○ 9,165	J3
01331	Athol○ 10,634	F2
01331	Athol 8,708	F2
02703	Attleboro 34,196	J5
01501	Auburn○ 14,845	G4
02322	Avon○ 5,026	K4
*01432	Ayer○ 6,993	H2
*01432	Ayer 3,165	H2
01436	Baldwinville 1,709	F2
02630	Barnstable○ 30,898	N6
02630	Barnstable⊙ 2,033	N6
01005	Barre○ 4,102	F3
01005	Barre 1,136	F3
01223	Becket○ 1,339	B3
01730	Bedford○ 13,067	B6
01007	Belchertown○ 8,339	E3
01007	Belchertown 2,531	E3
02019	Bellingham○ 14,300	J4
02019	Bellingham 4,454	J4
02178	Belmont○ 26,100	C6
†02780	Berkley○ 2,731	K5
01503	Berlin○ 2,215	H3
01337	Bernardston○ 1,750	D2
01915	Beverly 37,655	E5
01821	Billerica○ 36,727	J2
01504	Blackstone○ 6,570	H4
01008	Blandford○ 1,038	C4
01740	Bolton○ 2,530	H3
01009	Bondsville 1,906	E4
*02101	Boston (cap.)⊙ 562,994	D7
	Boston‡ 2,763,357	D7
02532	Bourne○ 13,874	M6
02532	Bourne 2,678	M6
01719	Boxborough○ 3,126	H3
01921	Boxford○ 5,374	L2
01921	Boxford 1,841	L2
01505	Boylston○ 3,470	H3
02184	Braintree○ 36,337	D8
02020	Brant Rock-Ocean Bluff 4,055	M4
02631	Brewster○ 5,226	O5
02631	Brewster 1,744	O5
02324	Bridgewater○ 17,202	K5
02324	Bridgewater 6,781	K5
01010	Brimfield○ 2,318	F4
*C2401	Brockton 95,172	K4
	Brockton‡ 169,374	K4
01506	Brookfield○ 2,397	F4
01506	Brookfield 1,037	F4
02146	Brookline○ 55,062	C7
01338	Buckland○ 1,864	C2
01803	Burlington○ 23,486	C5
02532	Buzzards Bay 3,375	M5
02138	Cambridge⊙ 95,322	C7
02021	Canton○ 18,182	C8
01741	Carlisle○ 3,306	J2
02330	Carver○ 6,988	M5
02632	Centerville 3,640	N6
01339	Charlemont○ 1,149	C2
01507	Charlton○ 6,719	F4
02633	Chatham○ 6,071	P6
02633	Chatham 1,922	P6
01824	Chelmsford○ 31,174	J2
02150	Chelsea 25,431	D6
01225	Cheshire○ 3,124	B2
01011	Chester○ 1,123	C3
01012	Chesterfield○ 1,000	C3
*01013	Chicopee 55,112	D4
02535	Chilmark○ 489	M7
†02054	Clicquot-Millis 3,777	A8
01510	Clinton○ 12,771	H3
01778	Cochituate 6,126	A7
02025	Cohasset○ 7,174	F7
01340	Colrain○ 1,552	D2
01742	Concord○ 16,293	B6
01341	Conway○ 1,213	D2
†01772	Cordaville 1,384	H3
01026	Cummington○ 657	C3
01226	Dalton○ 6,797	B3
01923	Danvers○ 24,100	D5
02714	Dartmouth○ 23,966	K6
02026	Dedham⊙○ 25,298	C7
01342	Deerfield○ 4,517	D2
02638	Dennis○ 12,360	O5
02639	Dennis Port 2,570	O6
02715	Dighton○ 5,352	K5
†02122	Dorchester	D7
†01516	Douglas○ 3,730	H4
02030	Dover○ 4,703	B7
02030	Dover 2,051	B7
01826	Dracut○ 21,249	J2
01570	Dudley○ 8,717	G4
01827	Dunstable○ 1,671	J2
02332	Duxbury○ 11,807	M4
02332	Duxbury 1,685	M4
02333	East Bridgewater○ 9,945	L4
01515	East Brookfield○ 1,955	G4
01515	East Brookfield 1,443	G4
01516	East Douglas 1,683	G4
02536	East Falmouth (Teaticket) 5,181	M6
02642	Eastham○ 3,472	O5
01027	Easthampton○ 15,580	D3
01028	East Longmeadow○ 12,905	E4
02334	Easton○ 16,623	K4
01437	East Pepperell 2,212	H2
02539	Edgartown○ 2,204	M7
02539	Edgartown⊙ 1,138	M7
01344	Erving○ 1,326	E2
01929	Essex○ 2,998	L2
01929	Essex 1,490	L2
02149	Everett 37,195	D6
02719	Fairhaven○ 15,759	L6
*02720	Fall River 92,574	K6
	Fall River‡ 176,831	K6
*02540	Falmouth○ 23,640	M6
*02540	Falmouth 5,720	M6
01518	Fiskdale 1,859	F4
01420	Fitchburg⊙ 39,580	G2
	Fitchburg-Leominster‡ 99,957	G2
†01247	Florida○ 730	B2
02035	Foxboro○ 14,148	J4
02035	Foxboro 5,697	J4
01701	Framingham○ 65,113	A7
02038	Franklin○ 18,217	J4
02038	Franklin 9,296	J4
01440	Gardner 17,900	G2
†02535	Gay Head○ 220	L7
01833	Georgetown○ 5,687	L2
01031	Gilbertville 1,029	F3
†01376	Gill○ 1,259	D2
01930	Gloucester 27,768	M2
01032	Goshen○ 651	C3
01519	Grafton○ 11,238	H4
01033	Granby○ 5,380	E3
01033	Granby 1,302	E3
01034	Granville○ 1,204	C4
01230	Great Barrington○ 7,405	A4
01230	Great Barrington 3,150	A4
01301	Greenfield○ 18,436	D2
01301	Greenfield⊙ 14,198	D2
02041	Green Harbor 2,002	M4
01450	Groton○ 6,154	H2
01450	Groton 1,264	H2
01830	Groveland○ 5,040	L1
01035	Hadley○ 4,125	D3
02338	Halifax○ 5,513	L5
01936	Hamilton○ 6,960	L2
01036	Hampden○ 4,745	E4
01237	Hancock○ 643	A2
02339	Hanover○ 11,358	L4
02341	Hanson○ 8,617	L4
02341	Hanson 2,120	L4
01037	Hardwick○ 2,272	F3
01451	Harvard○ 12,170	H2
02645	Harwich○ 8,971	O6
02645	Harwich 4,399	O6
01038	Hatfield○ 3,045	D3
01038	Hatfield 1,251	D3
01830	Haverhill 46,865	K1
01346	Heath○ 482	C2
02043	Hingham○ 20,339	E8
02043	Hingham 5,742	E8
01235	Hinsdale○ 1,707	B3
02343	Holbrook○ 11,140	D8
01520	Holden○ 13,336	G3
†01550	Holland○ 1,589	F4
01746	Holliston○ 12,622	A8
01040	Holyoke 44,678	D4
01747	Hopedale○ 3,905	H4
01747	Hopedale 2,810	H4
01748	Hopkinton○ 7,114	J4
01748	Hopkinton 2,542	J4
01236	Housatonic 1,314	A3
01452	Hubbardston○ 1,797	F3
01749	Hudson○ 16,408	H3
01749	Hudson 14,156	H3
02045	Hull○ 9,714	E7
01050	Huntington○ 1,804	C4
02601	Hyannis 9,118	N6
01938	Ipswich○ 11,158	L2
01938	Ipswich 4,548	L2
02364	Kingston○ 7,362	M5
02364	Kingston 4,405	M5
02346	Lakeville○ 5,931	L5
02346	Lakeville 1,948	L5
01523	Lancaster○ 6,334	H3
01237	Lanesboro○ 3,131	A2
*01840	Lawrence⊙ 63,175	K2
	Lawrence-Haverhill‡ 281,981	K2
01238	Lee○ 6,247	B3
01238	Lee 2,140	B3
01524	Leicester○ 9,446	G4
01240	Lenox○ 6,523	A3
01240	Lenox 2,668	A3
01453	Leominster 34,508	G2
01054	Leverett○ 1,471	E3
02173	Lexington○ 29,479	B6
†01301	Leyden○ 498	D2
01773	Lincoln○ 7,098	B6
01460	Littleton○ 6,970	H2
†01460	Littleton Common 3,109	J2
01106	Longmeadow○ 16,301	D4
*01850	Lowell⊙ 92,418	J2
	Lowell‡ 233,410	J2
01056	Ludlow○ 18,150	E4
01462	Lunenburg○ 8,405	H2
01462	Lunenburg 1,789	H2
*01901	Lynn 78,471	D6
01940	Lynnfield○ 11,267	D5
02148	Malden 53,386	D6
01944	Manchester○ 5,424	F5
02048	Mansfield○ 13,453	J4
02048	Mansfield 6,786	J4
01945	Marblehead○ 20,126	E7
02738	Marion○ 3,932	L6
02738	Marion 1,438	L6
01752	Marlborough 30,617	H3
02050	Marshfield○ 20,916	M4
02050	Marshfield 4,421	M4
02051	Marshfield Hills 2,308	M4
02649	Mashpee○ 3,700	M6
02739	Mattapoisett○ 5,597	L6
02739	Mattapoisett 3,159	L6
01754	Maynard○ 9,590	J3
02052	Medfield○ 10,220	B8
02052	Medfield 6,108	B8
02155	Medford 58,076	C6
02053	Medway○ 8,447	J4
02176	Melrose 30,055	D6
01756	Mendon○ 3,108	H4
01860	Merrimac○ 4,451	L1
01844	Methuen○ 36,701	K2
02346	Middleboro○ 16,404	L5
02346	Middleboro 7,012	L5
01243	Middlefield○ 385	B3
01949	Middleton○ 4,135	K2
01757	Milford○ 23,390	H4
01757	Milford 21,730	H4
01527	Millbury○ 11,808	H4
01349	Millers Falls 1,101	E2
02054	Millis○ 6,908	A8
02054	Millis-Clicquot 3,777	A8
01529	Millville○ 1,693	H4
02186	Milton○ 25,860	D7
01057	Monson○ 7,315	E4
01057	Monson 2,167	E4
01351	Montague○ 8,011	E2
01245	Monterey○ 818	B4
†12517	Mount Washington○ 93	A4
01908	Nahant○ 3,947	E6
02554	Nantucket○ 5,087	O7
02554	Nantucket⊙ 3,229	O7
01760	Natick○ 29,461	A7
02192	Needham○ 27,901	B7
*02740	New Bedford⊙ 98,478	K6
	New Bedford‡ 169,425	K6
01531	New Braintree○ 671	F3
01950	Newbury○ 4,529	L1
01950	Newburyport⊙ 15,900	L1
†01230	New Marlborough○ 1,160	B4
01355	New Salem○ 688	E2
†02158	Newton 83,622	C7
02056	Norfolk○ 6,363	J4
01247	North Adams 18,063	B2
01059	North Amherst 5,616	E3
01060	Northampton⊙ 29,286	D3
01845	North Andover○ 20,129	K2
*02760	North Attleboro○ 21,095	J5
01532	Northborough○ 10,568	H3
01532	Northborough 5,670	H3
01534	Northbridge○ 12,246	H4
01535	North Brookfield○ 4,150	F3
01535	North Brookfield 2,543	F3
02764	North Dighton 1,174	K5
02651	North Eastham 1,318	O5
01360	Northfield○ 2,386	E2
01360	Northfield 1,182	E2
02358	North Pembroke 2,215	M4
02360	North Plymouth 3,250	L5
01864	North Reading○ 11,455	C5
02060	North Scituate 5,221	F8
02766	Norton○ 12,690	K5
02766	Norton 2,035	K5
02061	Norwell○ 9,182	F8
02062	Norwood○ 29,711	B8
02557	Oak Bluffs○ 1,984	M7
02557	Oak Bluffs 1,124	M7
01068	Oakham○ 994	F3
02065	Ocean Bluff-Brant Rock 4,055	M4
†01566	Old Sturbridge Village 500	F4
02558	Onset 1,493	M6
01364	Orange○ 6,844	E2
01364	Orange 3,942	E2
02653	Orleans○ 5,306	O5
02653	Orleans 1,811	O5
02655	Osterville 1,799	N6
01253	Otis○ 963	B4
01540	Oxford○ 11,680	G4
01540	Oxford 6,369	G4
01069	Palmer○ 11,389	E4
01069	Palmer 3,854	E4
01612	Paxton○ 3,762	G3
01960	Peabody 45,976	E5
†01002	Pelham○ 1,112	E3
02359	Pembroke○ 13,487	L4
01463	Pepperell○ 8,061	H2
01463	Pepperell 2,076	H2
01366	Petersham○ 1,024	F3
†01331	Phillipston○ 953	F2
01866	Pinehurst 6,588	B5
01201	Pittsfield⊙ 51,974	A3
	Pittsfield‡ 90,505	A3
01070	Plainfield○ 425	C2
02762	Plainville○ 5,857	J4
02360	Plymouth○ 35,913	M5
02360	Plymouth⊙ 7,232	M5
02367	Plympton○ 1,974	L5
01541	Princeton○ 2,425	G3
02657	Provincetown○ 3,536	O4
02657	Provincetown 3,372	O4
02169	Quincy 84,743	D7
02368	Randolph○ 28,218	D8
02767	Raynham○ 9,085	K5
02768	Raynham Center 3,776	K5
01867	Reading○ 22,678	C5
02769	Rehoboth○ 7,570	K5
02151	Revere 42,423	D6

(continued on following page)

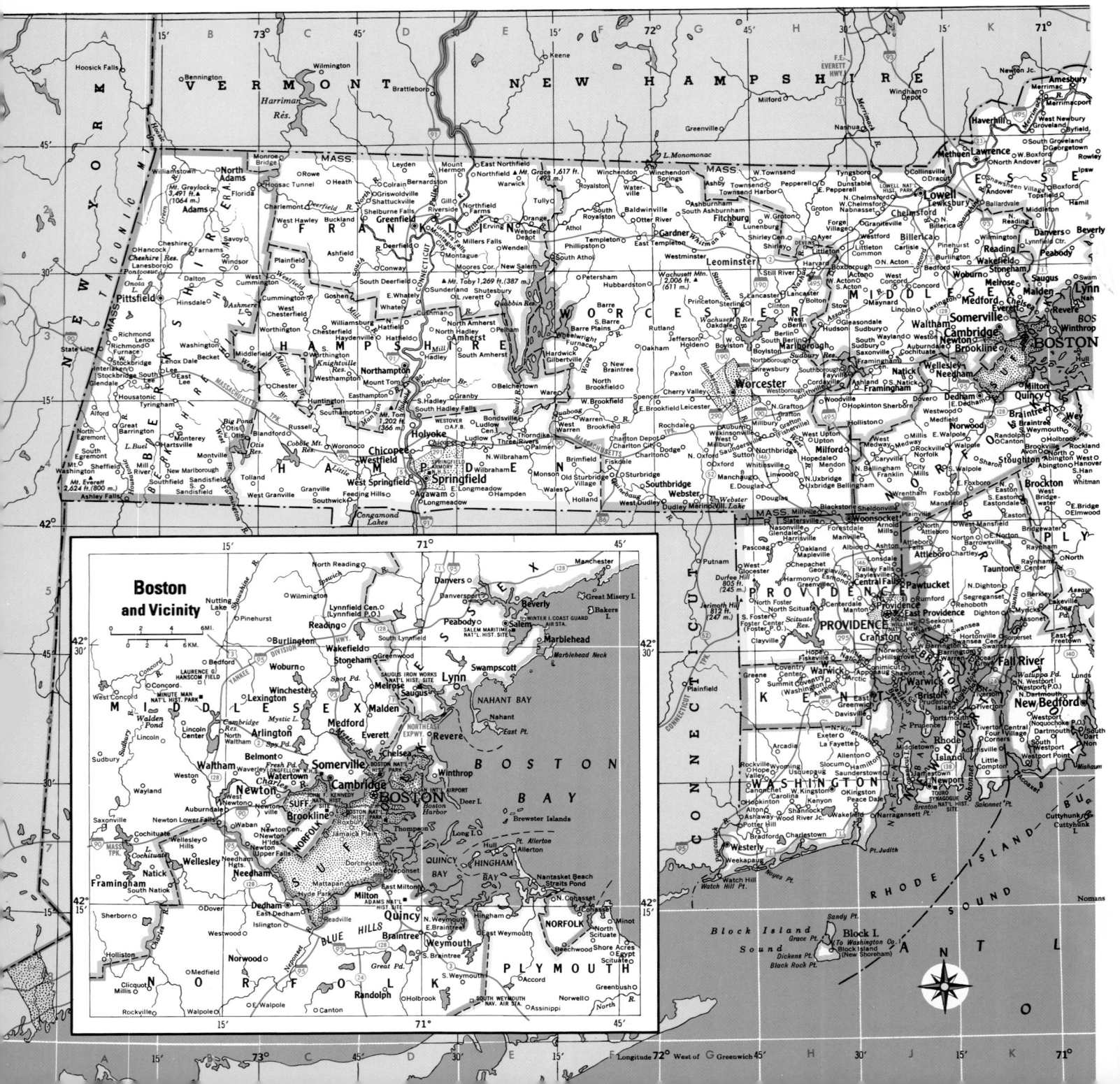

01266 West Stockbridge 1,280 ..A3
02575 West Tisbury○ 1,010...M7
01587 West Upton-Upton 2,184...H4
02576 West Wareham 1,837....L5
02090 Westwood○ 13,212 ......B8
02673 West Yarmouth 3,852 ..N6
02188 Weymouth 55,601......D8
01093 Whately○ 1,341 ....D3
01588 Whitinsville 5,379......H4
02382 Whitman○ 13,534........L4
01095 Wilbraham○ 12,053....E4
01095 Wilbraham 3,379........E4
01096 Williamsburg○ 2,237 ..C3
01267 Williamstown○ 8,741 ..B2
01267 Williamstown 4,798....B2
01887 Wilmington○ 17,471 ...C5
01475 Winchendon 7,019......F2
01475 Winchendon 4,030......F2
01890 Winchester○ 20,701....C6
01270 Windsor○ 598 ....B2

02152 Winthrop○ 19,294 ....D6
01801 Woburn 36,626 ....C6
02543 Woods Hole 1,080 ......M6
*01601 Worcester⊙ 161,799 ...H3
      Worcester‡ 372,940......H3
01098 Worthington‡ 932 ....C3
02093 Wrentham○ 7,580 ....J4
      Yarmouth 18,449 ....O6
02675 Yarmouth Port 2,490 ...N6

OTHER FEATURES

Adams Nat'l Hist. Site D7
Agawam (riv.) M5
Allerton (pt.) E7
Ann (cape) M2
Ashmere (lake) B3
Assabet (riv.) H3
Assawompset (pond) L5
Bachelor (brook) D3

Berkshire (hills) B4
Big (pond) B4
Bigelow (bight) M1
Blackstone (riv.) G3
Blue (hills) C8
Boston (bay) E6
Boston (harb.) D7
Boston Nat'l Hist. Park D6
Brewster (isls.) E7
Buel (lake) A4
Buzzards (bay) L7
Cambridge (res.) B6
Cape Cod (bay) N5
Cape Cod (canal) N5
Cape Cod Nat'l Seashore ..P5
Chappaquiddick (isl.) N7
Charles (riv.) C7
Chicopee (riv.) D4
Cobble Mountain (res.) C4
Cochituate (lake) A7

Cod (cape) O4
Concord (riv.) J2
Congamond (lkes.) D4
Connecticut (riv.) D2
Cuthyunk (isl.) L7
Deer (isl.) E7
Deerfield (riv.) C2
East (pt.) E6
East Chop (pt.) M7
Eastern (pt.) M2
Elizabeth (isls.) L7
Everett (riv.) A4
Falls (riv.) D2
Fort Devens H2
Fort Rodman L6
Fresh (pond) C6
Gammon (riv.) N6
Gay Head (prom.) L7
Grace (mt.) E2
Great (mt.) O7
Green (riv.) B2
Greylock (mt.) B2
Gurnet (pt.) M4
Hingham (bay) E7
Holyoke (range) D3
Hoosac (mts.) B2
Hoosic (riv.) A1
Housatonic (riv.) A4
Ipswich (riv.) L2
John F. Kennedy Nat'l Hist.
   Site C7
Knightville (res.) C3
Laurence G. Hanscom Field .B6
Little (riv.) C4
Logan Internat'l Airport D7
Long (isl.) E7
Long (pt.) O4
Long (pond) L5
Lowell Nat'l Hist. Park J2
Maine (gulf) M2
Manhan (riv.) D4
Manomet (pt.) N5
Marblehead (neck) F6
Martha's Vineyard (isl.) M7
Massachusetts (bay) M4
Merrimack (riv.) K1
Mill (riv.) C3
Mill (riv.) D3
Millers (riv.) E2
Minute Man Nat'l Hist. Park .B6
Mishaum (pt.) L6
Monomonac (lake) G2
Monomoy (isl.) O6
Monomoy (pt.) O6
Mount Hope (bay) K6
Muskeget (chan.) N7
Muskeget (isl.) N7
Mystic (lake) C6
Mystic (riv.) C6
Nahant (bay) E6
Nantucket (isl.) O8
Nantucket (sound) N6
Nashawena (isl.) L7
Nashua (riv.) H3
Naushon (isl.) L7
Neponset (riv.) C8
Nomans Land (isl.) L7
Nonamesset (isl.) L7
North (riv.) M6
North (riv.) D2
North (riv.) L4
Onota (lake) A3
Otis (res.) B4

Otis A.F.B. M6
Pasque (isl.) L7
Plum (isl.) L2
Plymouth (bay) M5
Poge (cape) N7
Pontoosuc (lake) A3
Quabbin (res.) E3
Quaboag (riv.) F4
Quincy (bay) D7
Quinebaug (riv.) F4
Race (pt.) N4
Salem Maritime Nat'l Hist.
   Site E5
Saugus Iron Works Nat'l Hist.
   Site D6
Shawsheen (riv.) K2
Silver (lake) L4
South (riv.) D2
Springfield Armory Nat'l Hist.
   Site D4
Squibnocket (pt.) M7
Stillwater (riv.) G3
Sudbury (riv.) H3
Sudbury (riv.) B3
Swift (riv.) A6
Taconic (mts.) E4
Taunton (riv.) A2
Thompson (isl.) D7
Toby (mt.) E3
Tom (mt.) D7
Tuckernuck (isl.) N7
Vineyard (sound) L7
Wachusett (mt.) G3
Wachusett (res.) G3
Walden (pond) A6
Ware (riv.) F3
Watuppa (pond) K6
Webster (lake) G4
Wellfleet (harb.) O5
West (riv.) H4
West Branch, Farmington
   (riv.) B4
West Chop (pt.) M7
Westfield (riv.) C3
Westover A.F.B. D4
Weweantic (riv.) L5
Whitman (riv.) G2
Winter I. Coast Guard Air Sta. .E5

RHODE ISLAND

COUNTIES

Bristol 46,942 ....J6
Kent 154,163 ....H6
Newport 81,383 ....K6
Providence 571,349 ....H5
Washington 93,317 ....H7

CITIES and TOWNS

Zip	Name/Pop.	Key
02804	Ashaway 1,747	G7
02806	Barrington○ 16,174	J6
02807	Block Island 620	H8
02808	Bradford 1,354	H7
02809	Bristol○⊙ 20,128	J6
02863	Central Falls 16,995	J5
02816	Coventry○ 27,065	H6
02910	Cranston 71,992	J5
02818	East Greenwich○⊙ 10,211	H6
02914	East Providence 50,980	J5

02822 Exeter○ 4,453 ....H6
02825 Foster○ 3,370 ....H5
02828 Greenville 7,516.......H5
02830 Harrisville 1,224.......H5
02832 Hope Valley 1,414 ....H6
02833 Hopkinton○ 6,406 ....H7
02835 Jamestown 4,040 .....J6
02835 Jamestown 2,156 .....J6
02881 Kingston 5,479 ....J7
02837 Little Compton○ 3,085 .K6
02840 Middletown 17,216 ...J6
02882 Narragansett 12,088 ..J7
02882 Narragansett 3,342 ...J7
02840 Newport⊙ 29,259 .....J7
†02807 New Shoreham (Block
      Island)○ 620............H8
02852 North Kingstown○
      29,188......................J6
02908 North Providence○
      29,188......................J5
02859 Pascoag 3,807 ....H5
*02860 Pawtucket 71,204.....J5
02883 Peace
      Dale-Wakefield 6,474 ...J7
02871 Portsmouth 14,257 ...J6
*02901 Providence
      (cap.)○⊙ 156,804.......H5
      Providence-Warwick-
      Pawtucket‡ 919,216.....H5
02878 Tiverton 13,526 ......K6
02878 Tiverton 7,653 ....K6
†02864 Valley Falls 10,892.....J5
*02879 Wakefield-Peace
      Dale 6,474.................J7
02885 Warren○ 10,640 ......J6
*02886 Warwick 87,123.......J6
02891 Westerly○ 18,580 ....G7
02891 Westerly○ 14,093......G7
02893 West Warwick 27,026 ..H6
02895 Woonsocket⊙ 45,914 ...J4

OTHER FEATURES

Black Rock (pt.) H8
Block (isl.) H8
Block Island (sound).........H8
Brenton (pt.) J7
Conanicut (isl.) J6
Dickens (pt.) H8
Durfee (hill) G5
Grace (pt.) J6
Jerimoth (hill) G5
Judith (pt.) J7
Mount Hope (bay) K6
Narragansett (bay) J6
Noyes (pt.) H7
Pawcatuck (riv.) G7
Prudence (isl.) J6
Rhode Island (isl.) J6
Rhode Island (sound) J7
Roger Williams Nat'l Mem. ...J5
Sakonnet (pt.) K7
Sakonnet (riv.) K7
Sandy (pt.) H8
Scituate (res.) H5
Stillwater (res.) C2
Touro Synagogue Nat'l Hist.
   Site J7
Watch Hill (pt.) G7
⊙County seat (Shire town).
‡Population of metropolitan area.
○Population of town or township.
† Zip of nearest p.o. * Multiple zips.

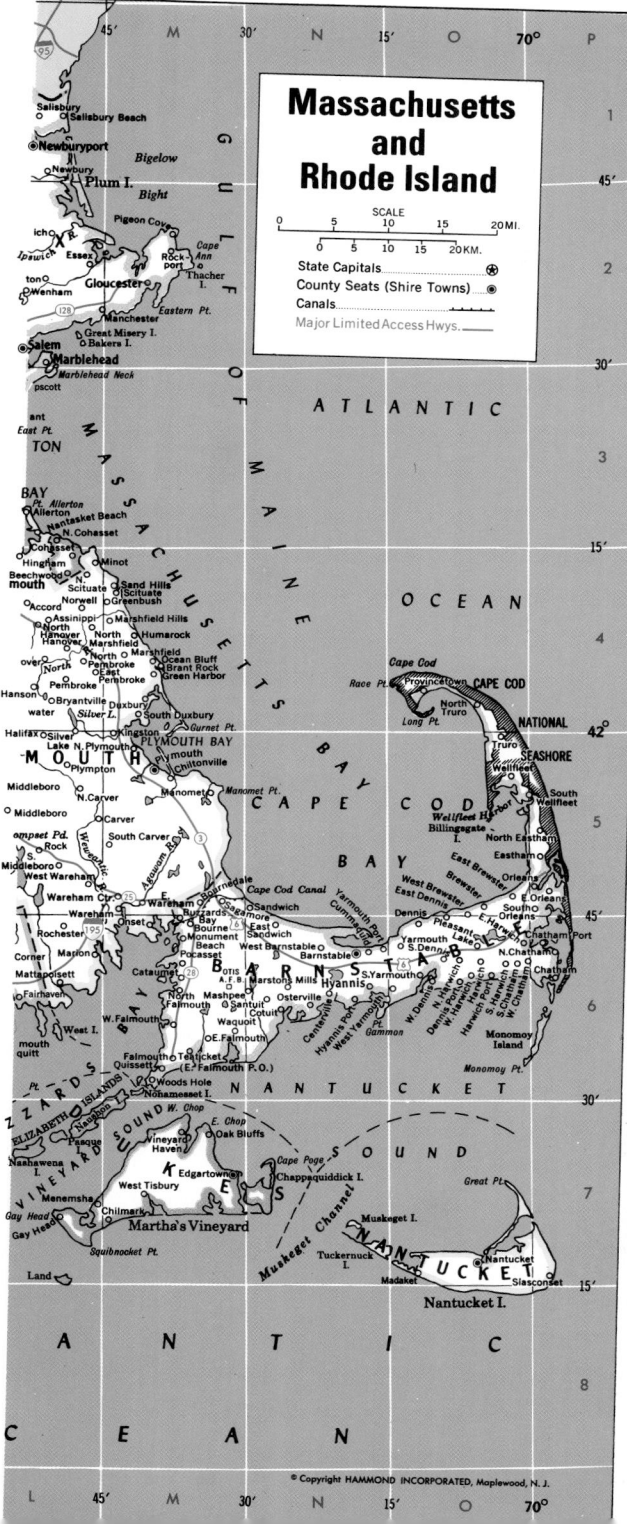

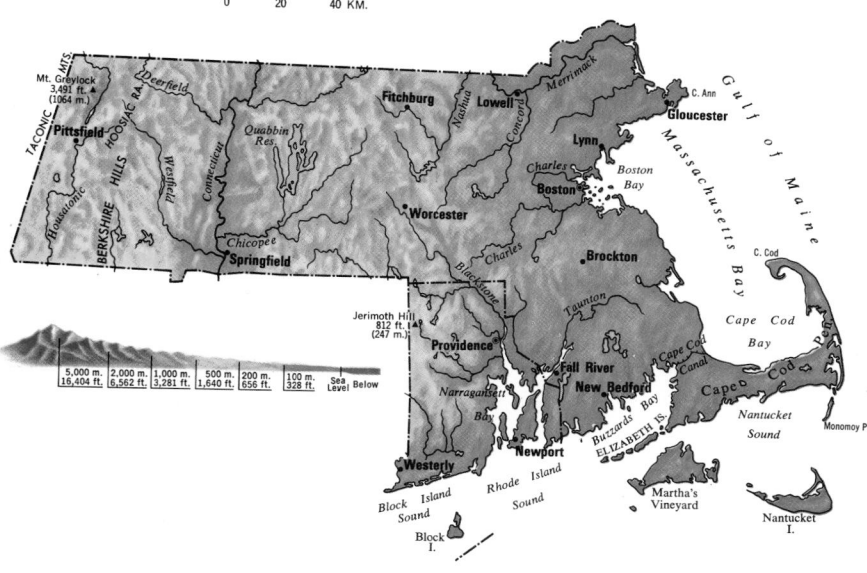

Topography

Mt. Greylock
3,491 ft.
(1,064 m.)

Jerimoth Hill
812 ft. 1.
(247 m.)

5,000 m.	2,000 m.	1,000 m.	500 m.	200 m.	100 m.	Sea	Below
16,404 ft.	6,562 ft.	3,281 ft.	1,640 ft.	656 ft.	328 ft.	Level	

© Copyright HAMMOND INCORPORATED, Maplewood, N.J.

Michigan

SCALE

0 5 10 20 30 40 50 MI.

0 5 10 20 30 40 50 KM.

State Capitals.........⊛
County Seats.........⊙
Canals.........
Major Limited Access Hwys.........

© Copyright HAMMOND INCORPORATED, Maplewood, N.J.

AREA 58,527 sq. mi. (151,585 sq. km.)
POPULATION 9,262,078
CAPITAL Lansing
LARGEST CITY Detroit
HIGHEST POINT Mt. Curwood 1,980 ft. (604 m.)
SETTLED IN 1650
ADMITTED TO UNION January 26, 1837
POPULAR NAME Wolverine State
STATE FLOWER Apple Blossom
STATE BIRD Robin

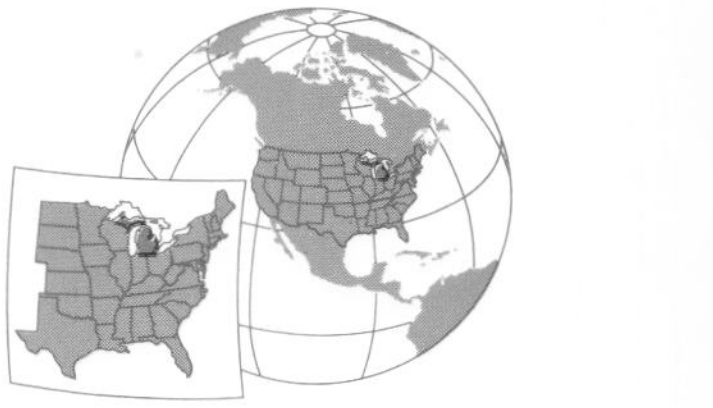

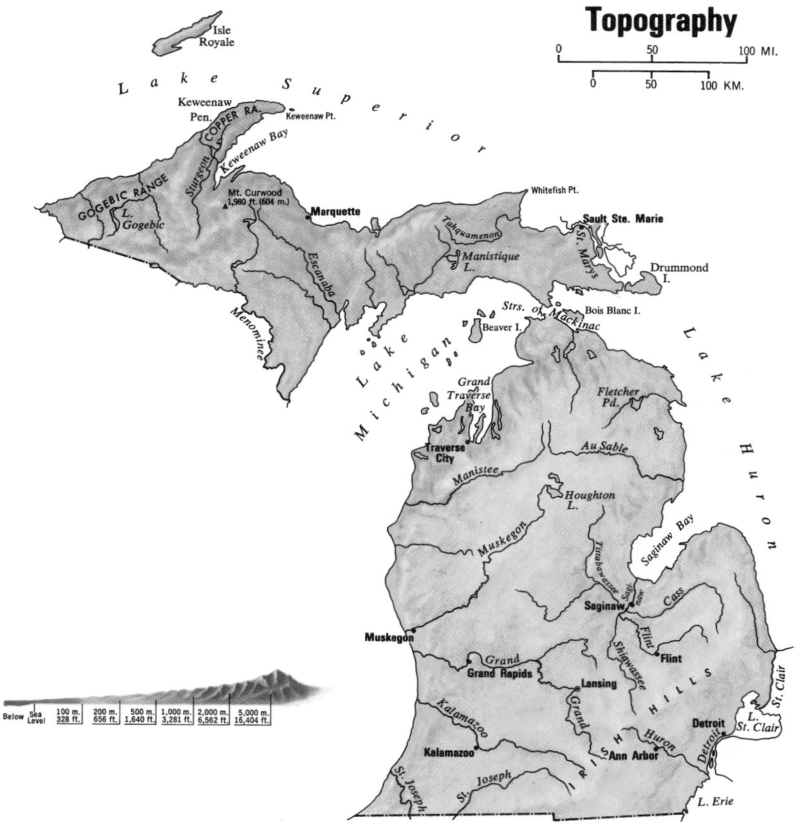
Topography
0 50 100 MI.
0 50 100 KM.
Isle Royale
Lake Superior
Keweenaw Pen.
Keweenaw Pt.
COPPER RA.
Keweenaw Bay
GOGEBIC RANGE
L. Gogebic
Sturgeon
Mt. Curwood 1,980 ft. (604 m.)
Marquette
Whitefish Pt.
Sault Ste. Marie
Tahquamenon
Manistique L.
St. Marys
Drummond I.
Escanaba
Menominee
Strs. of Mackinac
Bois Blanc I.
Beaver I.
Lake Michigan
Lake Huron
Grand Traverse Bay
Fletcher Pd.
Traverse City
Au Sable
Manistee
Houghton L.
Muskegon
Saginaw Bay
Tittabawassee
Saginaw
Cass
Muskegon
Flint
Flint
Grand
Grand Rapids
Lansing
Shiawassee
HILLS
St. Clair
L. St. Clair
Detroit
Detroit
Huron
Ann Arbor
Kalamazoo
Kalamazoo
Grand
St. Joseph
St. Joseph
L. Erie
Below Sea Level
100 m. 328 ft.
200 m. 656 ft.
500 m. 1,640 ft.
1,000 m. 3,281 ft.
2,000 m. 6,562 ft.
5,000 m. 16,404 ft.

COUNTIES

Alcona 9,740 .... F4
Alger 9,225 .... C2
Allegan 81,555 .... D6
Alpena 32,315 .... F4
Antrim 16,194 .... D3
Arenac 14,706 .... F4
Baraga 8,484 .... A2
Barry 45,781 .... D6
Bay 119,881 .... E5
Benzie 11,205 .... C4
Berrien 171,276 .... C7
Branch 40,188 .... D7
Calhoun 141,557 .... D6
Cass 49,499 .... C7
Charlevoix 19,907 .... D3
Cheboygan 20,649 .... E3
Chippewa 29,029 .... E2
Clare 23,822 .... E5
Clinton 55,893 .... E6
Crawford 9,465 .... E4
Delta 38,947 .... C2
Dickinson 25,341 .... B2
Eaton 88,337 .... E6
Emmet 22,992 .... E3
Genesee 450,449 .... F5
Gladwin 19,957 .... E4
Gogebic 19,686 .... F2
Grand Traverse 54,899 .... D4
Gratiot 40,448 .... E5
Hillsdale 42,071 .... E7
Houghton 37,872 .... G1
Huron 36,459 .... F5
Ingham 275,520 .... E6
Ionia 51,815 .... D6
Iosco 28,349 .... F4
Iron 13,635 .... G2
Isabella 54,110 .... E5
Jackson 151,495 .... E6
Kalamazoo 212,378 .... D6
Kalkaska 10,952 .... D4
Kent 444,506 .... D5
Keweenaw 1,963 .... A1
Lake 7,711 .... D5
Lapeer 70,038 .... F5
Leelanau 14,007 .... D4
Lenawee 89,948 .... E7
Livingston 100,289 .... F6
Luce 6,659 .... D2
Mackinac 10,178 .... D2
Macomb 694,600 .... G6
Manistee 23,019 .... C4
Marquette 74,101 .... B2
Mason 26,365 .... C4
Mecosta 36,961 .... D5
Menominee 26,201 .... B3
Midland 73,578 .... E5
Missaukee 10,009 .... D4
Monroe 134,659 .... F7
Montcalm 47,555 .... D5
Montmorency 7,492 .... E3
Muskegon 157,589 .... C5
Newaygo 34,917 .... D5
Oakland 1,011,793 .... F6
Oceana 22,002 .... C5
Ogemaw 16,436 .... E4
Ontonagon 9,861 .... F1
Osceola 18,928 .... D5
Oscoda 6,858 .... E4
Otsego 14,993 .... E3
Ottawa 157,174 .... C6
Presque Isle 14,267 .... F3
Roscommon 16,374 .... E4
Saginaw 228,059 .... E5
Saint Clair 138,802 .... G6
Saint Joseph 56,083 .... D7
Sanilac 40,789 .... G5
Schoolcraft 8,575 .... C2
Shiawassee 71,140 .... E6
Tuscola 56,961 .... F5
Van Buren 66,814 .... C6
Washtenaw 264,748 .... F6
Wayne 2,337,891 .... F6
Wexford 25,102 .... D4

CITIES and TOWNS

Zip *Name/Pop.* *Key*

49220 Addison 655 .... E7
49221 Adrian⊙ 21,186 .... F7
48701 Akron 538 .... F5
†48763 Alabaster 46 .... F4
49224 Albion 11,059 .... E6
48001 Algonac 4,412 .... G6
49010 Allegan⊙ 4,576 .... D6
48101 Allen Park 34,196 .... B7
48801 Alma 9,652 .... E5
48003 Almont 1,857 .... F6
49707 Alpena⊙ 12,214 .... F3
*48103 Ann Arbor⊙ 107,966 .... F6
Ann Arbor‡ 264,748 .... F6
48005 Armada 1,392 .... G6
48806 Ashley 570 .... E5
49011 Athens 960 .... D6
49709 Atlanta⊙ 475 .... E3
48611 Auburn 1,921 .... F5
48703 Au Gres 768 .... F4
49012 Augusta 913 .... D6
†48750 Au Sable 1,240 .... F4
48413 Bad Axe⊙ 3,184 .... G5
49304 Baldwin⊙ 674 .... D5
48414 Bancroft 618 .... E6
49013 Bangor 2,001 .... C6
49908 Baraga 1,055 .... G1
49101 Baroda 627 .... C7
*49014 Battle Creek 35,724 .... D6
Battle Creek‡ 187,338 .... D6
48706 Bay City⊙ 41,593 .... F5
Bay City‡ 119,881 .... F5
48612 Beaverton 1,025 .... E5
†49423 Beechwood 2,333 .... C6
48809 Belding 5,634 .... D5
49615 Bellaire⊙ 1,063 .... D4
48111 Belleville 3,366 .... F6
49021 Bellevue 1,289 .... E6
49022 Benton Harbor 14,707 .... C6
Benton Harbor‡ 171,276 .... C6
†49022 Benton Heights 6,787 .... C6
48072 Berkley 18,637 .... B6
49103 Berrien Springs 2,042 .... C7
49911 Bessemer⊙ 2,553 .... F2
49617 Beulah⊙ 454 .... C4
†48010 Beverly Hills 11,598 .... B6
49307 Big Rapids⊙ 14,361 .... D5
48415 Birch Run 1,196 .... F5
*48008 Birmingham 21,689 .... B6
49228 Blissfield 3,107 .... F7
48013 Bloomfield Hills 3,985 .... B6
49026 Bloomingdale 537 .... C6
49712 Boyne City 3,348 .... E3
48615 Breckenridge 1,495 .... E5
49106 Bridgman 2,235 .... C7
48116 Brighton 4,268 .... F6
49229 Britton 693 .... F6
49028 Bronson 2,271 .... D7
49230 Brooklyn 1,110 .... E6
48416 Brown City 1,163 .... G5
49107 Buchanan 5,142 .... C7
49030 Burr Oak 853 .... D7
48507 Burton 29,976 .... F6
48418 Byron 689 .... E6
49601 Cadillac⊙ 10,199 .... D4
49316 Caledonia 722 .... D6
49913 Calumet 1,013 .... A1
48014 Capac 1,377 .... G5
48117 Carleton 2,786 .... F6
48723 Caro⊙ 4,317 .... F5
48724 Carrollton 7,482 .... E5
48811 Carson City 1,229 .... E5
48419 Carsonville 622 .... G5
48725 Caseville 851 .... F5
49915 Caspian 1,038 .... G2
48726 Cass City 2,258 .... F5
49031 Cassopolis⊙ 1,933 .... C7
49319 Cedar Springs 2,615 .... D5
49233 Cement City 539 .... E6
48015 Center Line 9,293 .... B6
49622 Central Lake 895 .... D3
49032 Centreville⊙ 1,202 .... D7
49720 Charlevoix⊙ 3,296 .... D3
48813 Charlotte⊙ 8,251 .... E6
49721 Cheboygan⊙ 5,106 .... E3
48118 Chelsea 3,816 .... E6
48616 Chesaning 2,656 .... E5
48617 Clare 3,300 .... E5
48016 Clarkston 968 .... F6
48017 Clawson 15,103 .... B6
49034 Climax 619 .... D6
49236 Clinton 2,342 .... F6
48420 Clio 2,669 .... F5
49036 Coldwater⊙ 9,461 .... D7
48618 Coleman 1,429 .... E5
49038 Coloma 1,833 .... C6
49040 Colon 1,190 .... D7
48421 Columbiaville 953 .... F5
49041 Comstock○ 11,162 .... D6
49237 Concord 900 .... E6
49042 Constantine 1,680 .... D7
49404 Coopersville 2,889 .... C5
48817 Corunna⊙ 3,206 .... E6
48422 Croswell 2,073 .... G5
49920 Crystal Falls⊙ 1,965 .... A2
49508 Cutlerville 8,256 .... D6
48423 Davison 6,087 .... F5
*48120 Dearborn 90,660 .... B7
48127 Dearborn Heights 67,706 .... B7
49045 Decatur 1,915 .... C6
48427 Deckerville 887 .... G5
49238 Deerfield 957 .... F7
*48201 Detroit⊙ 1,203,339 .... B7
Detroit‡ 4,352,762 .... B7
†48161 Detroit Beach 2,112 .... F7
48820 De Witt 3,165 .... E6
48130 Dexter 1,524 .... F6
48821 Dimondale 1,008 .... E6
49406 Douglas 948 .... C6
49047 Dowagiac 6,307 .... D6
48020 Drayton Plains F6
49726 Drummond Island○ 746 .... F3
48428 Dryden 650 .... F6
48131 Dundee 2,575 .... F7
48429 Durand 4,241 .... E6
49924 Eagle River⊙ 20 .... A1
48021 East Detroit 38,280 .... B6
†49506 East Grand Rapids 10,914 .... D6
49727 East Jordan 2,185 .... D3
†49801 East Kingsford A3
48823 East Lansing 51,392 .... E6
48730 East Tawas 2,584 .... F4
†49001 Eastwood 7,186 .... D6
48827 Eaton Rapids 4,510 .... E6
49111 Eau Claire 573 .... C6
48229 Ecorse 14,447 .... B7
48829 Edmore 1,176 .... E5
49112 Edwardsburg 1,135 .... C7
49628 Elberta 556 .... C4
49629 Elk Rapids 1,504 .... D4
48731 Elkton 953 .... F5
48831 Elsie 1,022 .... E5
49829 Escanaba⊙ 14,355 .... C3
48732 Essexville 4,378 .... F5
49631 Evart 1,945 .... D5
48733 Fairgrove 691 .... F5
49022 Fair Plain 8,289 .... C6
*48024 Farmington 11,022 .... F6
48024 Farmington Hills 58,056 .... F6
48622 Farwell 804 .... E5
49408 Fennville 934 .... C6
48430 Fenton 8,098 .... F6
48220 Ferndale 26,227 .... B6
49409 Ferrysburg 2,440 .... C5
48134 Flat Rock 6,853 .... F6
*48501 Flint⊙ 159,611 .... F5
Flint‡ 521,589 .... F5
48433 Flushing 8,624 .... F5
48835 Fowler 1,021 .... E5
48836 Fowlerville 2,289 .... F6
48734 Frankenmuth 3,753 .... F5
49635 Frankfort 1,603 .... C4
48025 Franklin 2,864 .... B6
48026 Fraser 14,560 .... B6
48623 Freeland 1,364 .... E5
49412 Fremont 3,672 .... D5
49415 Fruitport 1,143 .... C5
49053 Galesburg 1,822 .... D6
49113 Galien 692 .... C7
48135 Garden City 35,640 .... F6
49735 Gaylord⊙ 3,011 .... E3
48173 Gibraltar 4,458 .... F6
49837 Gladstone 4,533 .... C3
48624 Gladwin⊙ 2,479 .... E5
49055 Gobles 816 .... D6
48438 Goodrich 795 .... F6
48439 Grand Blanc 6,848 .... F6
49417 Grand Haven⊙ 11,763 .... C5
48837 Grand Ledge 6,920 .... E6
*49501 Grand Rapids⊙ 181,843 .... D5
Grand Rapids‡ 601,680 .... D5
49418 Grandville 12,412 .... D6
49327 Grant 683 .... D5
49240 Grass Lake 962 .... E6
49738 Grayling⊙ 1,792 .... E4
48838 Greenville 8,019 .... D5
48138 Grosse Ile 9,320 .... B7
48236 Grosse Pointe 5,901 .... B7
†48236 Grosse Pointe Farms 10,551 .... B6
†48236 Grosse Pointe Park 13,639 B7
†48236 Grosse Pointe Shores 3,122 .... B6
†48236 Grosse Pointe Woods 18,886 .... B6
49841 Gwinn 1,408 .... B2
48212 Hamtramck 21,300 .... B6
49930 Hancock 5,122 .... G1
48441 Harbor Beach 2,000 .... G5
49740 Harbor Springs 1,567 .... D3
48225 Harper Woods 16,361 .... B6
48625 Harrison⊙ 1,700 .... E4
48740 Harrisville⊙ 559 .... F4
49420 Hart⊙ 1,888 .... C5
49057 Hartford 2,493 .... C6
48840 Haslett 7,025 .... E6
49058 Hastings⊙ 6,418 .... D6
48030 Hazel Park 20,914 .... B6
48626 Hemlock 1,362 .... E5
49421 Hesperia 876 .... D5
48203 Highland Park 27,909 .... B6
49242 Hillsdale⊙ 7,432 .... E7
49423 Holland 26,281 .... C6
48842 Holt 10,097 .... E6
49245 Homer 1,791 .... E6
49931 Houghton⊙ 7,512 .... G1
48629 Houghton Lake 2,449 .... E4
48630 Houghton Lake Heights E4
49329 Howard City 1,118 .... D5
48843 Howell⊙ 6,976 .... E6
49934 Hubbell 1,278 .... A1
49247 Hudson 2,545 .... E7
49426 Hudsonville 4,844 .... D6
48444 Imlay City 2,495 .... F5
48141 Inkster 35,190 .... B7
49643 Interlochen 600 .... D4
48846 Ionia⊙ 5,920 .... D6
49801 Iron Mountain⊙ 8,341 .... B3
49935 Iron River 2,426 .... G2
49938 Ironwood 7,741 .... F2
49849 Ishpeming 7,538 .... B2
48847 Ithaca⊙ 2,950 .... E5
*49201 Jackson⊙ 39,739 .... E6
Jackson‡ 151,495 .... E6
49428 Jenison 16,330 .... D6
49250 Jonesville 2,172 .... E6
*49001 Kalamazoo⊙ 79,722 .... D6
Kalamazoo-Portage‡ 279,192 .... D6
49646 Kalkaska⊙ 1,654 .... D4
48030 Keego Harbor 3,083 .... F6
49330 Kent City 860 .... D5
49508 Kentwood 30,438 .... D6
48445 Kinde 600 .... G5
49801 Kingsford 5,290 .... A3
49649 Kingsley 664 .... D4
48848 Laingsburg 1,145 .... E6
49651 Lake City⊙ 843 .... D4
49945 Lake Linden 1,181 .... A1
†49039 Lake Michigan Beach 2,001 C6
48849 Lake Odessa 2,171 .... D6
48035 Lake Orion 2,907 .... F6
48850 Lakeview 1,139 .... D5
†49440 Lakewood Club 695 .... C5
48144 Lambertville 6,341 .... F7
49946 L'Anse⊙ 2,500 .... G1
*48901 Lansing (cap.) 130,414 .... E6
Lansing-East Lansing‡ 468,482 .... E6
48446 Lapeer⊙ 6,198 .... F5
49913 Laurium 2,678 .... A1
49064 Lawrence 903 .... C6
49065 Lawton 1,558 .... D6
49654 Leland⊙ 776 .... D3
48449 Lennon 600 .... E5
49251 Leslie 2,110 .... E6
48450 Lexington 765 .... G5
48742 Lincoln 361 .... F4
48146 Lincoln Park 45,105 .... B7
48451 Linden 2,174 .... F6
49252 Litchfield 1,353 .... E6
*48150 Livonia 104,814 .... F6
49331 Lowell 3,707 .... D6
49431 Ludington⊙ 8,937 .... C5

(continued on following page)

48157 Luna Pier 1,443 F7
48851 Lyons 708 E6
49757 Mackinac Island 479 E3
49701 Mackinaw City 820 E3
48071 Madison Heights 35,375 B6
49659 Mancelona 1,432 E4
48158 Manchester 1,686 E6
49660 Manistee⊙ 7,566 C4
49854 Manistique⊙ 3,962 C3
49663 Manton 1,212 D4
48853 Maple Rapids 683 E5
49067 Marcellus 1,134 D6
48039 Marine City 4,414 G6
49665 Marion 816 D4
48453 Marlette 1,761 G5
49855 Marquette⊙ 23,288 B2
49068 Marshall⊙ 7,201 E6
49070 Martin 447 D6
48040 Marysville 7,345 G6
48854 Mason⊙ 6,019 E6
49071 Mattawan 2,143 D6
48744 Mayville 958 F5
49657 McBain 519 D4
48122 Melvindale 12,322 B7
48041 Memphis 1,171 G6
49072 Mendon 951 D7
49858 Menominee⊙ 10,099 B3
48637 Merrill 851 E5
48455 Metamora 552 F6
49254 Michigan Center 5,244 E6
49333 Middleville 1,797 D6
48640 Midland⊙ 37,250 E5
48160 Milan 4,182 F6
48042 Milford 5,041 F6
48746 Millington 1,237 F5
48647 Mio⊙ 975 E4
48161 Monroe⊙ 23,531 F7
49437 Montague 2,332 C5
48457 Montrose 1,706 F5
49256 Morenci 2,110 E7
49336 Morley 507 D5
48857 Morrice 733 E6
48043 Mount Clemens⊙ 18,806 G6
48458 Mount Morris 3,246 F5
48858 Mount Pleasant⊙ 23,746 E5
48860 Muir 698 D5
48861 Mulliken 550 E6
49862 Munising⊙ 3,083 C2
*49440 Muskegon⊙ 40,823 C5
Muskegon-Norton Shores-Muskegon Heights‡ 179,591 C5
49444 Muskegon Heights 14,611 C5
49261 Napoleon 1,400 E6
49073 Nashville 1,628 D6
49866 Negaunee 5,189 B2
49337 Newaygo 1,271 D5
48047 New Baltimore 5,439 G6
49868 Newberry⊙ 2,120 D2
48164 New Boston 1,200 F6
49117 New Buffalo 2,821 C7
48048 New Haven 1,871 G6
48460 New Lothrop 646 F5
49120 Niles 13,115 C7
49262 North Adams 565 E7
48461 North Branch 896 F5
49445 North Muskegon 4,024 C5
49670 Northport 611 D3
48167 Northville 5,698 F6
†49441 Norton Shores 22,025 C5
49870 Norway 2,919 B3
48050 Novi 22,525 F6
48237 Oak Park 31,537 B6
48864 Okemos 8,882 E6
49076 Olivet 1,604 E6
49765 Onaway 1,084 E3
49675 Onekama 582 C4
49265 Onsted 670 E6
49953 Ontonagon⊙ 2,182 F1
48033 Orchard Lake 1,798 F6
48462 Ortonville 1,190 F6
48750 Oscoda 2,431 F4
48463 Otisville 682 F5
49078 Otsego 3,802 D6
48866 Ovid 1,712 E5
48867 Owosso 16,455 E5
48051 Oxford 2,746 F6
49004 Parchment 1,817 D6
49269 Parma 873 E6
49079 Paw Paw⊙ 3,211 D6
†49038 Paw Paw Lake 4,193 C6
48052 Pearl Beach 3,430 G6
48466 Peck 606 G5
49769 Pellston 565 E3
49449 Pentwater 1,165 C5
48872 Perry 2,051 E6
49270 Petersburg 1,222 F7
49770 Petoskey⊙ 6,097 E3
48755 Pigeon 1,247 F5
48169 Pinckney 1,390 F6
48650 Pinconning 1,430 F5
49080 Plainwell 3,751 D6
48069 Pleasant Ridge 3,217 B6
*48170 Plymouth 9,986 F6
*48053 Pontiac⊙ 76,715 F6
49081 Portage 38,157 D6
48467 Port Austin 839 F4
48060 Port Huron⊙ 33,981 G6
48875 Portland 3,963 E6
48469 Port Sanilac 598 G5
49776 Posen 270 F3
48876 Potterville 1,502 E6
49082 Quincy 1,569 E7
49959 Ramsay F2
49451 Ravenna 951 D5
49274 Reading 1,203 E7
49677 Reed City⊙ 2,221 D5
48757 Reese 1,645 F5
48062 Richmond 3,536 G6
48218 River Rouge 12,912 B7
48192 Riverview 14,569 B7
48063 Rochester 7,203 F6
49341 Rockford 3,324 D5
48173 Rockwood 3,346 F6
49779 Rogers City⊙ 3,923 F3
48065 Romeo 3,509 F6
48174 Romulus 24,857 F6
49444 Roosevelt Park 4,015 C5
48653 Roscommon⊙ 834 E4
48654 Rose City 661 E4
48066 Roseville 54,311 B6
49452 Rothbury 522 C5
*48067 Royal Oak 70,893 B6
*48601 Saginaw⊙ 77,508 F5
Saginaw‡ 228,059 F5
48655 Saint Charles 2,276 E5
48079 Saint Clair 4,780 G6
*48080 Saint Clair Shores 76,210 B6
49781 Saint Ignace⊙ 2,632 E3
48879 Saint Johns⊙ 7,376 E6
49085 Saint Joseph⊙ 9,622 C6
48880 Saint Louis 4,107 E5
48176 Saline 6,483 F6
48471 Sandusky⊙ 2,216 G5
48657 Sanford 864 E5
48881 Saranac 1,421 E6
49453 Saugatuck 1,079 C6
49783 Sault Sainte Marie⊙ 14,448 E2
49087 Schoolcraft 1,359 D6
49454 Scottville 1,241 C5
48759 Sebewaing 2,046 F5
49455 Shelby 1,624 C5
48883 Shepherd 1,534 E5
48884 Sheridan 664 D5
†49085 Shoreham 742 C6
†49125 Shorewood 1,735 C7
*48034 Southfield 75,568 F6
48195 Southgate 32,058 F6
49090 South Haven 5,943 C6
48178 South Lyon 5,214 F6
†48161 South Monroe 4,232 F7
49963 South Range 861 G1
48179 South Rockwood 1,353 F7
†48060 Sparlingville 1,718 G6
49345 Sparta 3,373 D5
49283 Spring Arbor 2,101 E6
49015 Springfield 5,917 D6
49456 Spring Lake 2,731 C5
49284 Springport 675 E6
49964 Stambaugh 1,442 G2
48658 Standish⊙ 1,264 F5
48888 Stanton⊙ 1,315 D5
49887 Stephenson 967 B3
48659 Sterling 457 E4
48077 Sterling Heights 108,999 B6
49127 Stevensville 1,268 C6
49285 Stockbridge 1,213 E6
49091 Sturgis 9,468 D7
48890 Sunfield 591 D6
49682 Suttons Bay 504 D3
48473 Swartz Creek 5,013 F6
†48053 Sylvan Lake 1,949 F6
48763 Tawas City⊙ 1,967 F4
48180 Taylor 77,568 B7
49286 Tecumseh 7,320 E7
49092 Tekonsha 755 E6
49128 Three Oaks 1,774 C7
49093 Three Rivers 7,015 D7
49684 Traverse City⊙ 15,516 D4
48183 Trenton 22,762 B7
*48084 Troy 67,102 B6
48475 Ubly 862 G5
49094 Union City 1,667 D6
49129 Union Pier 1,039 C7
48767 Unionville 578 F5
*48087 Utica 5,282 F6
49095 Vandalia 447 D7
49795 Vanderbilt 525 E3
48768 Vassar 2,727 F5
49096 Vermontville 832 E6
48476 Vernon 1,008 F6
49097 Vicksburg 2,224 D6
49968 Wakefield 2,591 F2
49288 Waldron 570 E7
49504 Walker 15,088 D6
48088 Walled Lake 4,748 F6
*48089 Warren 161,134 B6
49098 Watervliet 1,867 C6
49348 Wayland 2,023 D6
48184 Wayne 21,159 F6
48892 Webberville 1,535 E6
49894 Wells B3
48661 West Branch⊙ 1,785 E4
48185 Westland 84,603 F6
48894 Westphalia 896 E6
49349 White Cloud⊙ 1,101 D5
49461 Whitehall 2,856 C5
49099 White Pigeon 1,478 D7
49971 White Pine 1,142 F1
48189 Whitmore Lake 2,920 F6
48770 Whittemore 438 F4
48895 Williamston 2,981 E6
48096 Wixom 6,705 F6
†49440 Wolf Lake 3,876 D5
49799 Wolverine 364 E3
†48183 Woodhaven 10,902 F6
48897 Woodland 431 D6
48192 Wyandotte 34,006 B7
49509 Wyoming 59,616 D6
48097 Yale 1,814 G5
48197 Ypsilanti 24,031 F6
49464 Zeeland 4,764 D6
†48601 Zilwaukee 2,201 F5

OTHER FEATURES

Abbaye (pt.) B2
Au Sable (pt.) C2
Au Sable (pt.) F4
Au Sable (riv.) E4
Au Train (bay) C2
Bad (riv.) E5
Barques (pt.) C3
Beaver (isl.) D3
Beaver (lake) F4
Belle (riv.) G6
Bete Grise (bay) B1
Betsy (riv.) D2
Big Bay (pt.) B2
Big Bay de Noc (bay) C3
Big Iron (riv.) F1
Big Sable (pt.) C4
Big Sable (riv.) C4
Big Star (lake) C5
Black (lake) E3
Black (riv.) E3
Black (riv.) G5
Blake (pt.) E1
Boardman (riv.) D4
Bois Blanc (isl.) E3
Bond Falls (res.) G2
Brevoort (lake) D3
Brule (riv.) A3
Burt (lake) E3
Cass (riv.) F5
Cedar (lake) F4
Charlevoix (lake) D3
Chippewa (riv.) E5
Crisp (pt.) D2
Crystal (lake) C4
Curwood (mt.) B2
Dead (riv.) B2
Deer (riv.) A2
De Tour (passage) E3
Detour (pt.) C3
Detroit (riv.) B7
Drummond (isl.) F2
Duck (lake) F4
Elk (lake) D4
Erie (lake) G7
Escanaba (riv.) B2
False Detour (chan.) F3
Fawn (riv.) D7
Fence (riv.) A2
Firesteel (riv.) G1
Fletcher (pond) F4
Flint (riv.) F5
Ford (riv.) B2
Forty Mile (pt.) F3
Fourteen Mile (pt.) F1
Garden (isl.) D3
Garden (pen.) C3
Glen (lake) C4
Gogebic (lake) F2
Good Harbor (bay) D3
Government (peak) F1
Grand (isl.) C2
Grand (lake) F3
Grand (riv.) D6
Grand Traverse (bay) D3
Granite (pt.) B2
Green (bay) B4
Gun (lake) D6
Hamlin (lake) C4
Higgins (lake) E4
High (isl.) D3
Hog (isl.) D3
Houghton (lake) E4
Hubbard (lake) F4
Huron (bay) A2
Huron (lake) G4
Huron (riv.) F6
Huron River (pt.) B2
Independence (lake) B2
Indian (lake) C2
Isle Royale Nat'l Park E1
Kalamazoo (riv.) C6
Keweenaw (bay) A1
Keweenaw (pt.) B1
K.I. Sawyer A.F.B. 7,345 B2
L'Anse Ind. Res. A2
Laughing Fish (pt.) B2
Leelanau (lake) D4
Light House (pt.) D3
Little Bay de Noc (bay) B3
Little Girl (pt.) E1
Little Sable (pt.) C5
Little Summer (isl.) C3
Little Traverse (bay) D3
Long (lake) F3
Lookingglass (riv.) E6
Mackinac (isl.) E3
Mackinac (str.) E3
Manistee (riv.) C4
Manistique (lake) D2
Manistique (riv.) C2
Manitou (isl.) B1
Maple (riv.) E5
Margrethe (lake) E4
Marquette (isl.) E3
Maumee (bay) F7
Menominee (riv.) B3
Michigamme (lake) A2
Michigamme (res.) B2
Michigamme (riv.) A2
Michigan (lake) B5
Mill (creek) G5
Millecoquins (lake) D2
Misery (bay) G1
Misery (riv.) G1
Montreal (riv.) F1
Mullett (lake) E3
Munuscong (lake) E2
Muskegon (riv.) C5
Neebish (isl.) E2
Net (riv.) G2
Ninemile (pt.) E3
North (chan.) F2
North (pt.) F3
North Fox (isl.) D3
North Manitou (isl.) C3
Oak (pt.) F5
Ontonagon (riv.) G1
Ontonagon Ind. Res. F1
Otsego (lake) E4
Paint (riv.) A2
Paradise (lake) E3
Passage (isl.) E1
Patterson (pt.) D3
Paw Paw (riv.) C6
Peninsula (pt.) C3
Perch (lake) G2
Perch (riv.) G2
Pere Marquette (riv.) D5
Pictured Rocks (cliff) C2
Pictured Rocks Nat'l Lakeshore C2
Pigeon (riv.) D7
Pigeon (riv.) E3
Pine (lake) F4
Pine (riv.) D4
Pine (riv.) E5
Platte (lake) C4
Porcupine (mts.) F1
Potagannissing (bay) F2
Poverty (isl.) C3
Prairie (riv.) D7
Presque Isle (riv.) F1
Rabbit (riv.) D6
Raisin (riv.) F7
Rapid (riv.) B2
Reedsburg (res.) E4
Rifle (riv.) E4
Royale (isl.) E1
Saginaw (bay) F5
Saginaw (riv.) F5
Saint Clair (lake) G6
Saint Clair (riv.) G6
Saint Joseph (riv.) C7
Saint Martin (bay) E3
Saint Martin (isl.) C3
Saint Marys (riv.) E2
Salt (pt.) E2
Sand (pt.) F5
Seul Choix (pt.) D3
Shiawassee (riv.) E5
Siskiwit (bay) E1
Sleeping Bear Dunes Nat'l Lakeshore C4
South (bay) C2
South (chan.) E3
South (pt.) F4
South Fox (isl.) D3
South Manitou (isl.) C3
Sturgeon (riv.) C2
Sugar (isl.) E2
Summer (isl.) C3
Superior (lake) C2
Tahquamenon (falls) D2
Tahquamenon (riv.) D2
Tawas (lake) F4
Tawas (pt.) F4
Thunder (bay) F4
Thunder Bay (riv.) F3
Tittabawassee (riv.) E5
Torch (lake) D3
Traverse (isl.) A1
Traverse (pt.) A1
Turtle (lake) F4
Two Hearted (riv.) D2
Vieux Desert (lake) G2
Walloon (lake) E3
White (riv.) C5
Whitefish (bay) E2
Whitefish (pt.) E2
Whitefish (riv.) C2
Wood (isl.) C2
Wurtsmith A.F.B. 5,166 F4
Yellow Dog (riv.) B2

⊙County seat.
‡Population of metropolitan area.
○Population of township.
† Zip of nearest p.o. * Multiple zips.

Agriculture, Industry and Resources

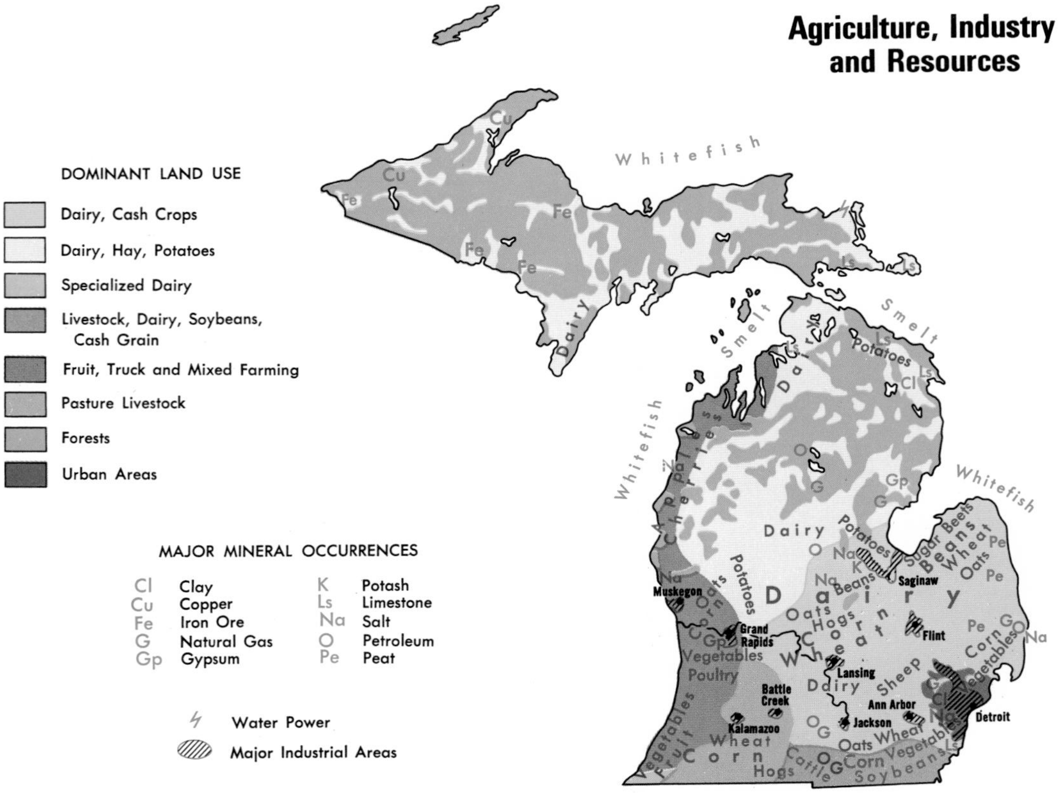
DOMINANT LAND USE
Dairy, Cash Crops
Dairy, Hay, Potatoes
Specialized Dairy
Livestock, Dairy, Soybeans, Cash Grain
Fruit, Truck and Mixed Farming
Pasture Livestock
Forests
Urban Areas
MAJOR MINERAL OCCURRENCES
Cl Clay
Cu Copper
Fe Iron Ore
G Natural Gas
Gp Gypsum
K Potash
Ls Limestone
Na Salt
O Petroleum
Pe Peat
Water Power
Major Industrial Areas
Whitefish
Smelt
Dairy
Potatoes
Cherries
Sugar Beets
Beans
Wheat
Oats
Hogs
Corn
Sheep
Vegetables
Poultry
Fruit
Cattle
Soybeans
Muskegon
Saginaw
Flint
Grand Rapids
Lansing
Battle Creek
Kalamazoo
Ann Arbor
Jackson
Detroit

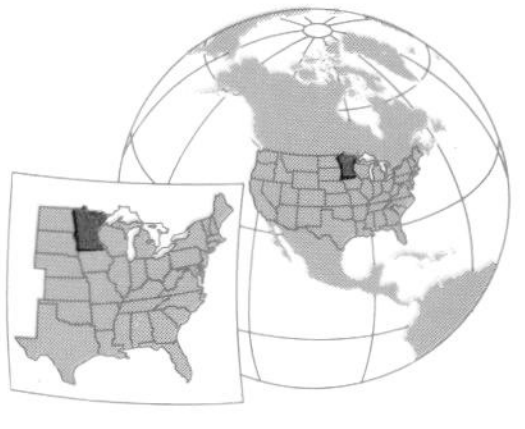

AREA 84,402 sq. mi. (218,601 sq. km.)
POPULATION 4,075,970
CAPITAL St. Paul
LARGEST CITY Minneapolis
HIGHEST POINT Eagle Mtn. 2,301 ft. (701 m.)
SETTLED IN 1805
ADMITTED TO UNION May 11, 1858
POPULAR NAME North Star State; Gopher State
STATE FLOWER Pink & White Lady's-Slipper
STATE BIRD Common Loon

COUNTIES

County	Key
Aitkin 13,404	E4
Anoka 195,998	E5
Becker 29,336	C4
Beltrami 30,982	C2
Benton 25,187	D5
Big Stone 7,716	B5
Blue Earth 52,314	D6
Brown 28,645	D6
Carlton 29,936	F4
Carver 37,046	E6
Cass 21,050	D4
Chippewa 14,941	C5
Chisago 25,717	F5
Clay 49,327	B4
Clearwater 8,761	C3
Cook 4,092	H3
Cottonwood 14,854	C6
Crow Wing 41,722	D4
Dakota 194,279	E6
Dodge 14,773	F7
Douglas 27,839	C5
Faribault 19,714	D7
Fillmore 21,930	F7
Freeborn 36,329	E7
Goodhue 38,749	F6
Grant 7,171	B5
Hennepin 941,411	E5
Houston 18,382	G7
Hubbard 14,098	D3
Isanti 23,600	E5
Itasca 43,069	E3
Jackson 13,690	C7
Kanabec 12,161	E5
Kandiyohi 36,763	C5
Kittson 6,672	B2
Koochiching 17,571	E2
Lac qui Parle 10,592	B6
Lake 13,043	G3
Lake of the Woods 3,764	D2
Le Sueur 23,434	E6
Lincoln 8,207	B6
Lyon 25,207	C6
Mahnomen 5,535	C3
Marshall 13,027	B2
Martin 24,687	D7
McLeod 29,657	D6
Meeker 20,594	D5
Mille Lacs 18,430	E5
Morrison 29,311	D4
Mower 40,390	F7
Murray 11,507	C6
Nicollet 26,929	D6
Nobles 21,840	C7
Norman 9,379	B3
Olmsted 92,006	F7
Otter Tail 51,937	C4
Pennington 15,258	B2
Pine 19,871	F4
Pipestone 11,690	B6
Polk 34,844	B3
Pope 11,657	C5
Ramsey 459,784	E5
Red Lake 5,471	B3
Redwood 19,341	C6
Renville 20,401	C6
Rice 46,087	E6
Rock 10,703	B7
Roseau 12,574	C2
Saint Louis 222,229	F3
Scott 43,784	E6
Sherburne 29,908	E5
Sibley 15,448	D6
Stearns 108,161	D5
Steele 30,328	E7
Stevens 11,322	B5
Swift 12,920	C5
Todd 24,991	D4
Traverse 5,542	B5
Wabasha 19,335	F6
Wadena 14,192	D4
Waseca 18,448	E6
Washington 113,571	F5
Watonwan 12,361	D7
Wilkin 8,454	B4
Winona 46,256	G6
Wright 58,681	D5
Yellow Medicine 13,653	B6

CITIES and TOWNS

Zip	*Name/Pop.*	*Key*
56510	Ada⊙ 1,971	B3
55909	Adams 797	F7
56110	Adrian 1,336	C7
55001	Afton 2,550	F6
56430	Ah-Gwah-Ching 400	D3
56431	Aitkin⊙ 1,770	E4
56433	Akeley 486	D3
56307	Albany 1,569	D5
56207	Alberta 145	B5
56007	Albert Lea⊙ 19,200	E7
55301	Albertville 564	E5
56009	Alden 687	E7
56308	Alexandria⊙ 7,608	C5
56111	Alpha 180	D7
55910	Altura 354	G6
56710	Alvarado 385	B2
56010	Amboy 606	D7
†55303	Andover 9,387	E5
55302	Annandale 1,568	D5
55303	Anoka⊙ 15,634	E5
56208	Appleton 1,842	C5
†55124	Apple Valley 21,818	G6
56713	Argyle 741	B2
55307	Arlington 1,779	D6
56309	Ashby 486	C4
55704	Askov 350	F4
56209	Atwater 1,128	D5
56511	Audubon 383	C4
55705	Aurora 2,670	F3
55912	Austin⊙ 23,020	E7
56114	Avoca 201	C7
56310	Avon 804	D5
55706	Babbitt 2,435	G3
56435	Backus 255	D4
56714	Badger 320	B2
56621	Bagley⊙ 1,321	C3
56115	Balaton 752	C6
56514	Barnesville 2,207	B4
55707	Barnum 464	F4
56311	Barrett 388	B5
56515	Battle Lake 708	C4
56623	Baudette⊙ 1,170	D2
†56401	Baxter 2,625	D4
55003	Bayport 2,932	F5
56211	Beardsley 344	B5
55601	Beaver Bay 283	G3
56116	Beaver Creek 260	B7
55308	Becker 601	E5
56312	Belgrade 805	C5
†55027	Bellechester 220	F6
56011	Belle Plaine 2,754	E6
56212	Bellingham 290	B5
56214	Belview 438	C6
56601	Bemidji⊙ 10,949	D3
56626	Bena 153	D3
56215	Benson⊙ 3,656	C5
56437	Bertha 510	C4
55005	Bethel 272	E5
56117	Bigelow 249	C7
56627	Big Falls 490	E2
56628	Bigfork 457	E3
55309	Big Lake 2,210	E5
56118	Bingham Lake 222	C7
55310	Bird Island 1,372	D6
55708	Biwabik 1,428	F3
56630	Blackduck 653	D3
†55433	Blaine 28,558	G5
56216	Blomkest 200	D6
55917	Blooming Prairie 1,969	E7
55420	Bloomington 81,831	G6
56013	Blue Earth⊙ 4,132	D7
56518	Bluffton 206	C4
56519	Borup 160	B3
55709	Bovey 813	E3
56314	Bowlus 276	D5
56218	Boyd 329	C6
55006	Braham 1,015	E5
56401	Brainerd⊙ 11,489	D4
†55056	Branch 1,866	F5
56315	Brandon 473	C5
56520	Breckenridge⊙ 3,909	B4
†56472	Breezy Point 384	D4
56119	Brewster 559	C7
56014	Bricelyn 487	E7
55429	Brooklyn Center 31,230	G5
†55444	Brooklyn Park 43,332	G5
56715	Brooks 173	B3
56316	Brooten 647	C5
56438	Browerville 693	D4
55918	Brownsdale 691	F7
56219	Browns Valley 887	B5
55919	Brownsville 418	G7
55312	Brownton 697	D6
56317	Buckman 171	D5
55313	Buffalo⊙ 4,560	E5
55314	Buffalo Lake 782	D6
55713	Buhl 1,284	F3
55337	Burnsville 35,674	E6
56318	Burtrum 177	D5
56120	Butterfield 634	D7
55920	Byron 1,715	F6
55921	Caledonia⊙ 2,691	G7
56521	Callaway 238	C3
55716	Calumet 469	E3
55008	Cambridge⊙ 3,287	E5
56522	Campbell 286	B4
56220	Canby 2,143	B6
55009	Cannon Falls 2,653	F6
55922	Canton 386	F7
56319	Carlos 364	C5
55718	Carlton⊙ 862	F4
55315	Carver 642	E6
56633	Cass Lake 1,001	D3
55012	Center City⊙ 458	F5
†55038	Centerville 734	E5
56121	Ceylon 543	D7
55316	Champlin 9,006	G5
56122	Chandler 344	C7
55317	Chanhassen 6,359	F6
55318	Chaska⊙ 8,346	F6
55923	Chatfield 2,055	F7
55013	Chisago City 1,634	E5
55719	Chisholm 5,930	E3
56221	Chokio 559	B5
55014	Circle Pines 3,321	G5
56222	Clara City 1,574	C6
55924	Claremont 591	E6
56440	Clarissa 663	C4
56223	Clarkfield 1,171	C6
56016	Clarks Grove 620	E7
56634	Clearbrook 579	C3
55319	Clear Lake 266	E5
55320	Clearwater 379	D5
56224	Clements 227	D6
56017	Cleveland 699	E6
56523	Climax 273	B3
56225	Clinton 622	B5
56226	Clontarf 196	C5
55720	Cloquet 11,142	F4
†55068	Coates 207	E6
55321	Cokato 2,056	D5
56320	Cold Spring 2,294	D5
55722	Coleraine 1,116	E3
55322	Cologne 545	E6
55421	Columbia Heights 20,029	G5
56019	Comfrey 548	D6
56020	Conger 183	E7
55723	Cook 800	F3
55433	Coon Rapids 35,826	G5
†55340	Corcoran 4,252	F5
56228	Cosmos 571	D6
55016	Cottage Grove 18,994	F6
56229	Cottonwood 924	C6
56021	Courtland 399	D6
55726	Cromwell 229	F4
56716	Crookston⊙ 8,628	B3
56441	Crosby 2,218	D4
56442	Crosslake 1,064	E4
†55428	Crystal 25,543	G5
55323	Crystal Bay (Orono) 6,845	F5
56123	Currie 359	C6
56323	Cyrus 334	C5
55925	Dakota 350	G7
56324	Dalton 248	C4
56230	Danube 590	C6
56231	Danvers 152	C5
56022	Darfur 139	D6
55324	Darwin 282	D5
55325	Dassel 1,066	D5
56232	Dawson 1,901	B6
55327	Dayton 4,070	E5
55391	Deephaven 3,716	G5
56527	Deer Creek 392	C4
56636	Deer River 907	E3
56444	Deerwood 580	E4
56233	De Graff 179	C5
55328	Delano 2,480	E5
56023	Delavan 262	D7
†55110	Dellwood 751	F5
56528	Dent 167	C4
56501	Detroit Lakes⊙ 7,106	C4
55926	Dexter 279	F7
56529	Dilworth 2,585	B4
55927	Dodge Center 1,816	F6
56235	Donnelly 317	B5
55929	Dover 312	F7
*55801	Duluth⊙ 92,811	F4
	Duluth-Superior‡ 266,650	F4
56236	Dumont 173	B5
55019	Dundas 422	E6
56127	Dunnell 216	D7
55111	Eagan 20,700	G6
56446	Eagle Bend 593	D4
56024	Eagle Lake 1,470	E6
†55005	East Bethel 6,626	E5
56721	East Grand Forks 8,537	B3
†56401	East Gull Lake 586	D4
56025	Easton 283	E7
56237	Echo 334	C6
55344	Eden Prairie 16,263	G6
55329	Eden Valley 763	D5
56128	Edgerton 1,123	B7
55424	Edina 46,073	G5
55931	Eitzen 226	G7
†55910	Elba 198	F6
56531	Elbow Lake⊙ 1,358	B5
55932	Elgin 667	F6
56533	Elizabeth 195	B4
55020	Elko 274	E6
55330	Elk River⊙ 6,785	E5
56026	Ellendale 555	E7
56129	Ellsworth 629	C7
56027	Elmore 882	D7
56325	Elrosa 214	C5
55731	Ely 4,820	G3
56028	Elysian 454	E6
56447	Emily 588	E4
56029	Emmons 465	E7
56534	Erhard 194	B4
56535	Erskine 585	B3
56326	Evansville 571	C4
55734	Eveleth 5,042	F3
55331	Excelsior 2,523	E6
55934	Eyota 1,244	F7
55332	Fairfax 1,405	D6
56031	Fairmont⊙ 11,506	D7
55113	Falcon Heights 5,291	G5
55021	Faribault⊙ 16,241	E6
55024	Farmington 4,370	E6
56641	Federal Dam 192	D3
56536	Felton 264	B3
56537	Fergus Falls⊙ 12,519	B4
56540	Fertile 869	B3
56448	Fifty Lakes 263	D4
55735	Finlayson 202	F4
56723	Fisher 453	B3
56328	Flensburg 256	D5
55736	Floodwood 648	E4
56329	Foley⊙ 1,606	D5
†56308	Forada 191	C5
55025	Forest Lake 4,596	F5
56330	Foreston 283	E5
56542	Fosston 1,599	C3
55935	Fountain 327	F7
56543	Foxhome 161	B4
55333	Franklin 512	D6
56544	Frazee 1,284	C4
56032	Freeborn 323	E7
56331	Freeport 563	D5
55432	Fridley 30,228	G5
56033	Frost 293	D7
56131	Fulda 1,308	C7
56332	Garfield 284	C5
56450	Garrison 174	E4
56132	Garvin 172	C6
56545	Gary 241	B3
55334	Gaylord⊙ 1,933	D6
56035	Geneva 417	E7
56239	Ghent 356	C6
55335	Gibbon 787	D6
55741	Gilbert 2,721	F3
56333	Gilman 156	E5
55336	Glencoe⊙ 4,396	D6
56036	Glenville 851	E7
56334	Glenwood⊙ 2,523	C5
56547	Glyndon 882	B4
55427	Golden Valley 22,775	G5
56644	Gonvick 362	C3
55027	Goodhue 657	F6
56725	Goodridge 191	C2
56037	Good Thunder 560	D6
55027	Goodview 2,567	G6
56240	Graceville 780	B5
56039	Granada 377	D7
55604	Grand Marais⊙ 1,289	G2
55936	Grand Meadow 965	F7
55744	Grand Rapids⊙ 7,934	E3
56241	Granite Falls⊙ 3,451	C6
55030	Grasston 123	E5
56726	Greenbush 817	B2
†55373	Greenfield 1,391	F5
55338	Green Isle 357	E6
56335	Greenwald 259	D5
56336	Grey Eagle 338	D5
56243	Grove City 596	D5
56727	Grygla 216	C2
56452	Hackensack 285	D4
56728	Hallock⊙ 1,405	A2
56548	Halstad 690	B3
55339	Hamburg 475	D6
55340	Hamel 2,623	F5
55304	Ham Lake 7,832	E5
55938	Hammond 178	F6
55031	Hampton 299	E6
56244	Hancock 877	C5
56245	Hanley Falls 265	C6
55341	Hanover 647	E5
56041	Hanska 429	D6
56134	Hardwick 279	B7
55939	Harmony 1,133	F7
55032	Harris 678	F5
56042	Hartland 322	E7
55033	Hastings⊙ 12,827	F6
56549	Hawley 1,634	B4
55940	Hayfield 1,243	F7
56043	Hayward 294	E7
55342	Hector 1,252	D6
56044	Henderson 739	E6
56136	Hendricks 737	B6
56550	Hendrum 336	B3
56551	Henning 832	C4
56248	Herman 600	B5
†55811	Hermantown 6,759	F4
56137	Heron Lake 783	C7
56453	Hewitt 299	C4
55746	Hibbing 21,193	F3
55748	Hill City 533	E4
56138	Hills 598	B7
55037	Hinckley 963	E4
56552	Hitterdal 253	B4

(continued on following page)

Agriculture, Industry and Resources

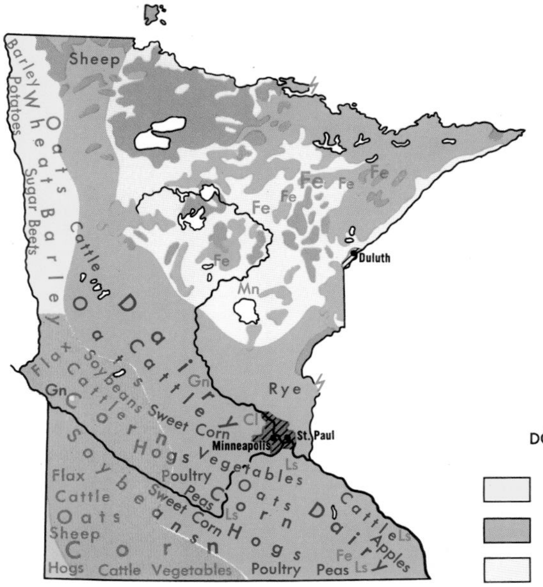

DOMINANT LAND USE

- Wheat, General Farming
- Dairy, Livestock
- Dairy, Hay, Potatoes
- Cattle Feed, Hogs
- Livestock, Cash Grain
- Forests
- Swampland, Limited Agriculture
- Urban Areas

MAJOR MINERAL OCCURRENCES

Cl	Clay	Gn	Granite
Fe	Iron Ore	Ls	Limestone
		Mn	Manganese

- Water Power
- Major Industrial Areas

56339 Hoffman 631 .... C5
55941 Hokah 686 .... G7
56340 Holdingford 635 .... D5
56139 Holland 234 .... B6
56045 Hollandale 290 .... E7
56249 Holloway 142 .... C5
55343 Hopkins 15,336 .... G5
55943 Houston 1,057 .... G7
55349 Howard Lake 1,240 .... D5
55750 Hoyt Lakes 3,186 .... F3
55038 Hugo 3,771 .... E5
55350 Hutchinson 9,244 .... D6
†55359 Independence 2,640 .... F5
56649 International Falls⊙ 5,611 .... E2
55075 Inver Grove Heights 17,171 .... E6
56141 Iona 248 .... C7
56455 Ironton 537 .... D4
55040 Isanti 858 .... E5
56342 Isle 573 .... E4
56142 Ivanhoe⊙ 761 .... B6
56143 Jackson⊙ 3,797 .... C7
56048 Janesville 1,897 .... E6
56144 Jasper 731 .... B7
56145 Jeffers 437 .... C6
56456 Jenkins 219 .... D4
55352 Jordan 2,663 .... E6
56251 Kandiyohi 447 .... D5
56732 Karlstad 934 .... B2
56050 Kasota 739 .... D6
55944 Kasson 2,827 .... F6
55753 Keewatin 1,443 .... D3
56650 Kelliher 324 .... D3
55945 Kellogg 440 .... G6
55754 Kelly Lake 900 .... F3
56733 Kennedy 405 .... B2
56343 Kensington 331 .... C5
55946 Kenyon 1,529 .... E6
56252 Kerkhoven 761 .... C5
56051 Kiester 670 .... E7
56052 Kilkenny 177 .... E6
55353 Kimball 651 .... D5
55758 Kinney 447 .... F3
55947 La Crescent 3,674 .... G7
56054 Lafayette 507 .... D6
56149 Lake Benton 869 .... B6
56734 Lake Bronson 298 .... B2
55041 Lake City 4,505 .... F6
56055 Lake Crystal 2,078 .... D6
55042 Lake Elmo 5,296 .... F6
56150 Lakefield 1,845 .... C7
†55398 Lake Fremont (Zimmerman) 1,074 .... E5
55043 Lakeland 1,812 .... F6
56253 Lake Lillian 329 .... C6
56554 Lake Park 716 .... B4
†55043 Lake Saint Croix Beach 1,176 .... F6
†56401 Lake Shore 583 .... D4
55044 Lakeville 14,790 .... E6
56151 Lake Wilson 380 .... B7
56152 Lamberton 1,032 .... C6
56735 Lancaster 368 .... B2
55949 Lanesboro 923 .... G7
56461 Laporte 160 .... D3
†55744 La Prairie 536 .... E3
56344 Lastrup 150 .... D4
†55101 Lauderdale 1,985 .... G5
56057 Le Center⊙ 1,967 .... E6
55951 Le Roy 930 .... F7
55354 Lester Prairie 1,229 .... D6
56058 Le Sueur 3,763 .... E6
55952 Lewiston 1,226 .... G7
56060 Lewisville 273 .... D7
†55014 Lexington 2,150 .... G5
†55050 Lilydale 417 .... G5
55045 Lindstrom 1,972 .... F5
†55038 Lino Lakes 4,966 .... G5
56155 Lismore 276 .... B7
55355 Litchfield⊙ 5,904 .... D5
56345 Little Falls⊙ 7,250 .... D5
56653 Littlefork 918 .... E2
†56334 Long Beach 263 .... C5
55356 Long Lake 1,747 .... F5
56347 Long Prairie⊙ 2,859 .... D5
56655 Longville 191 .... D4
55046 Lonsdale 1,160 .... E6
55357 Loretto 297 .... F5
56349 Lowry 283 .... C5
56255 Lucan 262 .... C6
56156 Luverne⊙ 4,568 .... B7
55953 Lyle 576 .... F7
56157 Lynd 304 .... C6
55954 Mabel 861 .... G7
56062 Madelia 2,130 .... D6
56256 Madison⊙ 2,212 .... B5
56063 Madison Lake 592 .... E6
56158 Magnolia 234 .... B7
56557 Mahnomen⊙ 1,283 .... C3
55115 Mahtomedi 3,851 .... F5
56001 Mankato⊙ 28,651 .... E6
55955 Mantorville⊙ 705 .... F6
†55369 Maple Grove 20,525 .... G5
55358 Maple Lake 1,132 .... D5
55359 Maple Plain 1,421 .... F5
56065 Mapleton 1,516 .... E7
†55912 Mapleview 253 .... E7
55109 Maplewood 26,990 .... G5
55764 Marble 757 .... E3
56257 Marietta 279 .... B5
55047 Marine on Saint Croix 543 .... F5
56258 Marshall⊙ 11,161 .... C6
55360 Mayer 388 .... E6
56260 Maynard 428 .... C6
55956 Mazeppa 680 .... F6
55760 McGregor 447 .... E4
56556 McIntosh 681 .... C3
55761 McKinley 230 .... F3
55049 Medford 775 .... E6
55441 Medicine Lake 419 .... G5
†55340 Medina (Hamel) 2,623 .... F5
†56352 Meire Grove 174 .... C5
56352 Melrose 2,409 .... D5
56464 Menahga 980 .... C4
55050 Mendota 219 .... G5
†55050 Mendota Heights 7,288 .... G6
56736 Mentor 219 .... B3
56737 Middle River 349 .... B2
†55033 Miesville 179 .... F6
56262 Milan 417 .... C5
55957 Millville 186 .... F6
56263 Milroy 242 .... C6
56354 Miltona 187 .... C4
*55401 Minneapolis⊙ 370,951 .... G5
Minneapolis-Saint Paul‡ 2,114,256 .... G5
56264 Minneota 1,470 .... C6
55959 Minnesota City 265 .... G6
56068 Minnesota Lake 744 .... E7
55343 Minnetonka 38,683 .... G5
†55364 Minnetrista 3,236 .... F5
56265 Montevideo⊙ 5,845 .... C6
56069 Montgomery 2,349 .... E6
55362 Monticello 2,830 .... E5
55363 Montrose 762 .... E5
56560 Moorhead⊙ 29,998 .... B4
Moorhead-Fargo‡ 137,574 B4
55767 Moose Lake 1,408 .... F4
55051 Mora⊙ 2,890 .... E5
56266 Morgan 975 .... D6
56267 Morris⊙ 5,367 .... C5
55052 Morristown 639 .... E6
56270 Morton 549 .... C6
56466 Motley 444 .... D4
55364 Mound 9,280 .... E6
†55112 Mounds View 12,593 .... G5
55768 Mountain Iron 4,134 .... F3
56159 Mountain Lake 2,277 .... D7
56271 Murdock 343 .... C5
55769 Nashwauk 1,419 .... E3
56355 Nelson 209 .... C5
55053 Nerstrand 255 .... E6
56467 Nevis 332 .... D4
55366 New Auburn 331 .... D6
55112 New Brighton 23,269 .... G5
56738 Newfolden 384 .... B2
55367 New Germany 347 .... E6
†55428 New Hope 23,087 .... G5
56273 New London 812 .... C5
55054 New Market 286 .... E6
56356 New Munich 302 .... D5
55055 Newport 3,323 .... F6
56071 New Prague 2,952 .... E6
56072 New Richland 1,263 .... E7
56073 New Ulm⊙ 13,755 .... D6
56567 New York Mills 972 .... C4
56074 Nicollet 709 .... D6
56568 Nielsville 145 .... B3
56468 Nisswa 1,407 .... D4
55056 North Branch 1,597 .... F5
55057 Northfield 12,562 .... E6
56001 North Mankato 9,145 .... D6
†55101 North Oaks 2,846 .... G5
56661 Northome 312 .... D3
56275 North Redwood 206 .... D6
56075 Northrop 269 .... D7
55109 North Saint Paul 11,921 .... G5
55368 Norwood 1,219 .... E6
†55019 Oakdale 12,123 .... E5
56276 Odessa 177 .... B5
56160 Odin 134 .... D7
56569 Ogema 215 .... C3
56358 Ogilvie 423 .... E5
56161 Okabena 263 .... C7
56742 Oklee 536 .... C3
56277 Olivia⊙ 2,802 .... C6
56359 Onamia 691 .... E4
56162 Ormsby 181 .... D7
†55323 Orono 6,845 .... F5
55960 Oronoco 574 .... F6
55771 Orr 294 .... F2
56278 Ortonville⊙ 2,550 .... B5
56360 Osakis 1,355 .... C5
56744 Oslo 379 .... A2
55369 Osseo 2,974 .... G5
55961 Ostrander 293 .... F7
56571 Ottertail 239 .... C4
55060 Owatonna⊙ 18,632 .... E6
56469 Palisade 155 .... E4
56361 Parkers Prairie 917 .... C4
56470 Park Rapids⊙ 2,976 .... D4
56362 Paynesville 2,140 .... D5
56363 Pease 174 .... E5
†56472 Pelican Lakes (Breezy Point) 384 .... D4
56572 Pelican Rapids 1,867 .... B4
56078 Pemberton 208 .... E7
56279 Pennock 410 .... C5
56472 Pequot Lakes 681 .... D4
56573 Perham 2,086 .... C4
55962 Peterson 291 .... G7
†56364 Pierz 1,018 .... D5
56473 Pillager 341 .... D4
55063 Pine City⊙ 2,489 .... F5
55963 Pine Island 1,986 .... F6
56474 Pine River 881 .... D4
56164 Pipestone⊙ 4,887 .... B7
55964 Plainview 2,416 .... F6
55370 Plato 390 .... D6
56748 Plummer 353 .... B3
†55441 Plymouth 31,615 .... G5
56280 Porter 211 .... B6
55965 Preston⊙ 1,478 .... F7
55371 Princeton 3,146 .... E5
56281 Prinsburg 557 .... C6
55372 Prior Lake 7,284 .... E6
55810 Proctor 3,180 .... F4
55967 Racine 285 .... F7
56475 Randall 527 .... D4
55065 Randolph 351 .... E6
56668 Ranier 237 .... E2
56282 Raymond 723 .... C5
56750 Red Lake Falls⊙ 1,732 .... B3
55066 Red Wing⊙ 13,736 .... F6
56283 Redwood Falls⊙ 5,210 .... C6
56672 Remer 396 .... E3
56284 Renville 1,493 .... C6
56166 Revere 158 .... C6
56367 Rice 499 .... D5
55423 Richfield 37,851 .... G6
56368 Richmond 867 .... D5
55422 Robbinsdale 14,422 .... G5
55901 Rochester⊙ 57,890 .... F6
Rochester‡ 91,971 .... F6
55067 Rock Creek 890 .... F5
55373 Rockford 2,408 .... F5
56369 Rockville 597 .... D5
55374 Rogers 652 .... E5
55969 Rollingstone 528 .... G6
56371 Roscoe 154 .... D5
56751 Roseau⊙ 2,272 .... C2
55970 Rose Creek 371 .... F7
55068 Rosemount 5,083 .... E6
55113 Roseville 35,820 .... G5
56579 Rothsay 476 .... B4
56167 Round Lake 480 .... C7
56373 Royalton 660 .... D5
55069 Rush City 1,198 .... F5
55971 Rushford 1,478 .... G7
56168 Rushmore 387 .... C7
56169 Russell 412 .... C6
56170 Ruthton 328 .... B6
55778 Rutledge 185 .... F4
56580 Sabin 446 .... B4
56285 Sacred Heart 666 .... C6
55414 Saint Anthony 7,981 .... G5
55375 Saint Bonifacius 857 .... F5
55972 Saint Charles 2,184 .... F7
56080 Saint Clair 655 .... E6
56301 Saint Cloud⊙ 42,566 .... D5
Saint Cloud‡ 163,256 .... D5
55070 Saint Francis 1,184 .... E5
56554 Saint Hilaire 388 .... B2
56081 Saint James⊙ 4,346 .... D7
56374 Saint Joseph 2,994 .... D5
55426 Saint Louis Park 42,931 .... G5
56376 Saint Martin 220 .... D5
55376 Saint Michael 1,519 .... E5
*55101 Saint Paul (cap.)⊙ 270,230 .... G6
Saint Paul-Minneapolis‡ 2,114,256 .... G5
55071 Saint Paul Park 4,864 .... G6
56082 Saint Peter⊙ 9,056 .... E6
56375 Saint Stephen 453 .... D5
56755 Saint Vincent 141 .... A2
56083 Sanborn 518 .... C6
55072 Sandstone 1,594 .... F4
56377 Sartell 3,427 .... D5
56378 Sauk Centre 3,709 .... C5
56379 Sauk Rapids 5,793 .... D5
55337 Savage 3,954 .... G6
†55720 Scanlon 1,050 .... F4
56477 Sebeka 774 .... C4
55074 Shafer 180 .... F5
55379 Shakopee⊙ 9,941 .... F6
56581 Shelly 276 .... B3
56171 Sherburn 1,275 .... D7
56676 Shevlin 193 .... C3
†55112 Shoreview 17,300 .... G5
†55331 Shorewood 4,646 .... F5
55614 Silver Bay 2,917 .... G3
55381 Silver Lake 698 .... D6
†56001 Skyline 399 .... D6
56172 Slayton⊙ 2,420 .... C7
56085 Sleepy Eye 3,581 .... D6
†56345 Sobieski 219 .... D5
55382 South Haven 205 .... D5
56679 South International Falls 2,806 .... E2
55075 South Saint Paul 21,235 .... G6
56288 Spicer 909 .... C5
56087 Springfield 2,303 .... C6
55974 Spring Grove 1,275 .... G7
†55432 Spring Lake Park 6,477 .... E5
55384 Spring Park 1,465 .... F5
55975 Spring Valley 2,616 .... F7
56681 Squaw Lake 162 .... D3
55079 Stacy 996 .... E5
56479 Staples 2,887 .... D4
56381 Starbuck 1,224 .... C5
56173 Steen 153 .... B7
56757 Stephen 898 .... A2
55385 Stewart 616 .... D6
55976 Stewartville 3,925 .... F7
55082 Stillwater⊙ 12,290 .... F5
55988 Stockton 517 .... G6
56174 Storden 341 .... C6
56758 Strandquist 136 .... B2
55783 Sturgeon Lake 222 .... F4
†55075 Sunfish Lake 344 .... E6
56382 Swanville 295 .... D5
55786 Taconite 331 .... E3
56291 Taunton 177 .... B6
55084 Taylors Falls 623 .... F5
56683 Tenstrike 159 .... D3
56701 Thief River Falls⊙ 9,105 .... B2
†56319 Thomson 152 .... F4
†55331 Tonka Bay 1,354 .... F5
55790 Tower 640 .... F3
56175 Tracy 2,478 .... C6
56176 Trimont 805 .... D7
56088 Truman 1,392 .... D7
56089 Twin Lakes 210 .... E7
56584 Twin Valley 907 .... B3
55616 Two Harbors⊙ 4,039 .... G3
56178 Tyler 1,353 .... B6
56585 Ulen 514 .... B3
56586 Underwood 332 .... C4
56384 Upsala 400 .... D5
55979 Utica 249 .... G7
†55101 Vadnais Heights 5,111 .... G5
56587 Vergas 287 .... C4
55085 Vermillion 438 .... F6
56481 Verndale 504 .... C4
56090 Vernon Center 365 .... D7
56292 Vesta 360 .... C6
55386 Victoria 1,425 .... F6
56385 Villard 275 .... C5
55792 Virginia 11,056 .... F3
55981 Wabasha⊙ 2,372 .... G6
56293 Wabasso 745 .... C6
55387 Waconia 2,638 .... E6
56482 Wadena⊙ 4,699 .... C4
56386 Wahkon 271 .... E4
56387 Waite Park 3,496 .... D5
56091 Waldorf 249 .... E7
56484 Walker⊙ 970 .... D3
56180 Walnut Grove 753 .... C6
55982 Waltham 176 .... F7
55983 Wanamingo 717 .... F6
55743 Warba 150 .... E3
56762 Warren⊙ 2,105 .... B2
56763 Warroad 1,216 .... C2
56093 Waseca⊙ 8,219 .... E6
55388 Watertown 1,818 .... E6
56096 Waterville 1,717 .... E6
55389 Watkins 757 .... D5
56295 Watson 238 .... C5
56589 Waubun 390 .... C3
55390 Waverly 470 .... E5
55391 Wayzata 3,621 .... G5
56181 Welcome 855 .... D7
56097 Wells 2,777 .... E7
56590 Wendell 216 .... B4
56183 Westbrook 978 .... C6
55985 West Concord 762 .... F6
55118 West Saint Paul 18,527 .... G5
56296 Wheaton⊙ 1,969 .... B5
55110 White Bear Lake 22,538 .... G5
55090 Willernie 654 .... G5
56686 Williams 217 .... D2
56201 Willmar⊙ 15,895 .... C5
55795 Willow River 303 .... F4
56185 Wilmont 380 .... C7
56687 Wilton 176 .... C3
56101 Windom⊙ 4,666 .... C7
56592 Winger 200 .... B3
56098 Winnebago 1,869 .... D7
55987 Winona⊙ 25,075 .... G6
55395 Winsted 1,522 .... D6
55396 Winthrop 1,376 .... D6
55796 Winton 276 .... G3
56594 Wolverton 177 .... B4
†55798 Woodbury 10,297 .... F6
56297 Wood Lake 420 .... C6
56186 Woodstock 180 .... B7
56187 Worthington⊙ 10,243 .... C7
55797 Wrenshall 333 .... F4
55798 Wright 162 .... E4
55990 Wykoff 482 .... F7
55092 Wyoming 1,559 .... F5
55397 Young America 1,237 .... E6
55398 Zimmerman 1,074 .... E5
55991 Zumbro Falls 208 .... F6
55992 Zumbrota 2,129 .... F6

OTHER FEATURES

Ash (riv.) F2
Bald Eagle (lake) G3
Basswood (lake) G2
Battle (riv.) D3
Baudette (riv.) D2
Bear (riv.) E3
Bemidji (lake) D3
Benton (lake) B6
Big Fork (riv.) E2
Big Sandy (lake) E4
Big Stone (lake) B5
Birch (lake) G3
Black (riv.) D2
Blue Earth (riv.) D7
Bois de Sioux (riv.) B4
Bowstring (lake) E3
Buffalo (riv.) B4
Burntside (lake) F3
Cass (lake) D3
Cedar (riv.) F7
Chippewa (riv.) C5
Christina (lake) C4
Clearwater (riv.) C3
Cloquet (riv.) F4
Cobb (riv.) E7
Cottonwood (riv.) C6
Crooked (creek) F4
Crooked (lake) G2
Crow (riv.) F5
Crow Wing (riv.) D4
Cuyuna (range) D4
Dead (lake) C4
Deer (lake) E3
Des Moines (riv.) C7
Eagle (mt.) G2
East Swan (riv.) F3
Elbow (lake) C3
Emily (lake) C5
Fond du Lac Ind. Res. F4
Grand Portage Ind. Res. G2
Grand Portage Nat'l Mon. G2
Green (lake) D5
Greenwood (lake) G3
Gull (lake) D4
Heron (lake) C7
Hill (riv.) C3
Independence (lake) F5
Isabella (lake) G3
Itasca (lake) C3
Kabetogama (lake) E2
Kanaranzi (creek) C7
Kettle (riv.) F4
Knife (lake) G2
La Croix (lake) F2
Lac qui Parle (lake) C5
Lac qui Parle (riv.) B6
Lake of the Woods (lake) D1
Leaf (riv.) C4
Leech (lake) D3
Leech Lake Ind. Res. D3
Lida (lake) C4
Little Fork (riv.) E2
Little Rock (creek) C7
Long (lake) D4
Long (lake) F3
Long Prairie (riv.) D4
Lost (riv.) C3
Lower Red (lake) C3
Maple (lake) B3
Maple (riv.) E7
Marsh (lake) B5
Mary (lake) C5
Mesabi (range) E3
Middle (riv.) B2
Mille Lac Ind. Res. E4
Mille Lacs (lake) E4
Miltona (lake) C4
Minneapolis-Saint Paul Airport G5
Minnesota (riv.) E6
Minnetonka (lake) F5
Minnewaska (lake) C5
Misquah (hills) F2
Mississippi (riv.) D4
Moose (riv.) C2
Mud (lake) C2
Mud (riv.) C2
Muskeg (bay) C2
Mustinka (riv.) B5
Nemadji (riv.) F4
Nett (lake) E2
Nett Lake Ind. Res. E2
North (lake) F1
Otter Tail (lake) C4
Otter Tail (riv.) B4
Partridge (riv.) G3
Pelican (lake) C4
Pelican (lake) D4
Pelican (lake) F2
Pelican (riv.) B4
Pelican (riv.) F2
Pepin (lake) F6
Pigeon (riv.) G2
Pike (riv.) F3
Pipestone Nat'l Mon. B6
Pokegama (lake) E3
Pomme de Terre (riv.) C5
Poplar (riv.) C3
Prairie (riv.) E3
Rainy (lake) E2
Rainy (riv.) D2
Rapid (riv.) D2
Redeye (riv.) D4
Red Lake (riv.) B2
Red Lake Ind. Res. C2
Red River of the North (riv.) A2
Redwood (riv.) C6
Reno (lake) C5
Rice (lake) E4
Rock (riv.) B7
Root (riv.) G7
Roseau (riv.) B2
Rum (riv.) E5
Saganaga (lake) H2
Saint Croix (riv.) F5
Saint Louis (riv.) F4
Sand (creek) F5
Sand Hill (riv.) B3
Sarah (lake) F5
Schoolcraft (riv.) C3
Shakopee (creek) C5
Shell (riv.) C4
Shetek (lake) C6
Sleepy Eye (creek) C6
Snake (riv.) A2
Snake (riv.) E4
South Fowl (lake) G1
Star (lake) C4
Sturgeon (riv.) F3
Superior (lake) G3
Swan (lake) D6
Tamarac (riv.) A2
Tamarack (riv.) D2
Thief (lake) C2
Thief (riv.) B2
Traverse (lake) B5
Trout (lake) F2
Two Rivers (riv.) A1
Upper Red (lake) D2
Vermilion (lake) F3
Vermilion (range) F3
Vermilion (riv.) F2
Voyageurs Nat'l Park F2
Wabatawangang (lake) D3
West Swan (riv.) F3
White Earth Ind. Res. C3
Whiteface (riv.) F3
Whitefish (lake) D4
White Iron (lake) G3
Wild Rice (lake) F4
Wild Rice (riv.) B3
Willow (riv.) E4
Winnibigoshish (lake) D3
Woods (lake) D1
Zumbro (riv.) F6

⊙County seat.
‡Population of metropolitan area.
† Zip of nearest p.o. * Multiple zips.

Topography

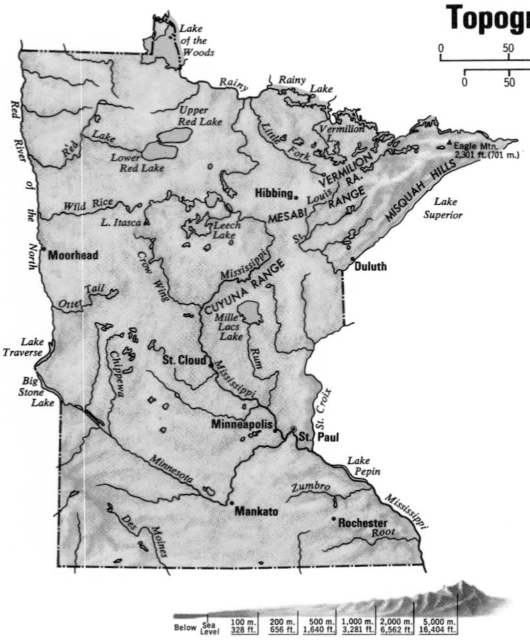
0 50 100 MI.
0 50 100 KM.
Lake of the Woods
Rainy
Rainy Lake
Red River of the North
Upper Red Lake
Red Lake
Lower Red Lake
Vermilion
Little Fork
Eagle Mtn. 2,301 ft. (701 m.)
VERMILION RA.
MISQUAH HILLS
Lake Superior
Hibbing
St. Louis
MESABI RANGE
Wild Rice
L. Itasca
Leech Lake
Moorhead
Crow Wing
Mississippi
CUYUNA RANGE
Duluth
Otter Tail
Mille Lacs Lake
Lake Traverse
Big Stone Lake
Chippewa
St. Cloud
Rum
St. Croix
Minneapolis
St. Paul
Lake Pepin
Minnesota
Zumbro
Mankato
Rochester
Root
Des Moines
Below
Sea Level
100 m. 328 ft.
200 m. 656 ft.
500 m. 1,640 ft.
1,000 m. 3,281 ft.
2,000 m. 6,562 ft.
5,000 m. 16,404 ft.

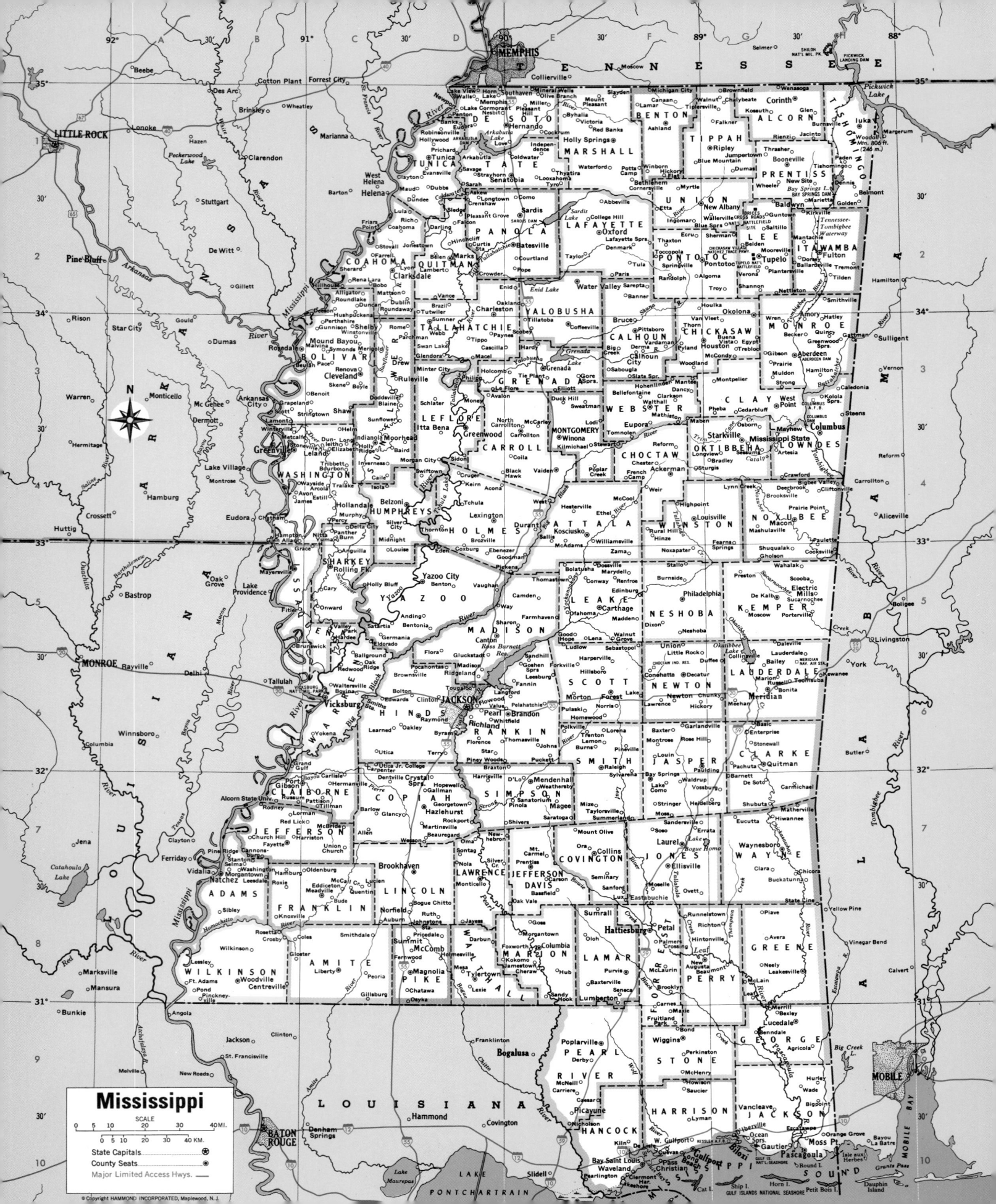

Mississippi

SCALE
0 5 10   20   30   40 MI.
0 5 10 20   30   40 KM.

State Capitals .... ⊛
County Seats .... ⊙
Major Limited Access Hwys. ___

© Copyright HAMMOND INCORPORATED, Maplewood, N. J.

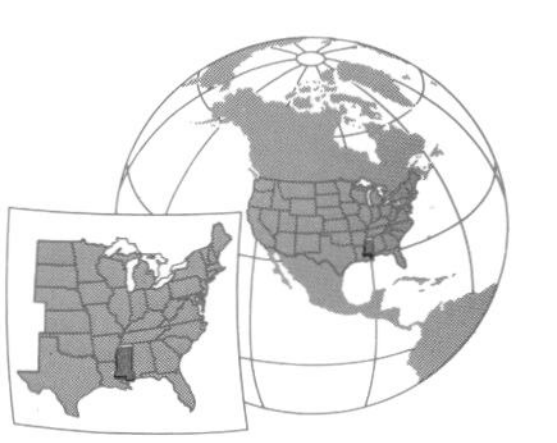

AREA 47,689 sq. mi. (123,515 sq. km.)
POPULATION 2,520,638
CAPITAL Jackson
LARGEST CITY Jackson
HIGHEST POINT Woodall Mtn. 806 ft. (246 m.)
SETTLED IN 1716
ADMITTED TO UNION December 10, 1817
POPULAR NAME Magnolia State
STATE FLOWER Magnolia
STATE BIRD Mockingbird

Topography

0 40 80 MI.
0 40 80 KM.

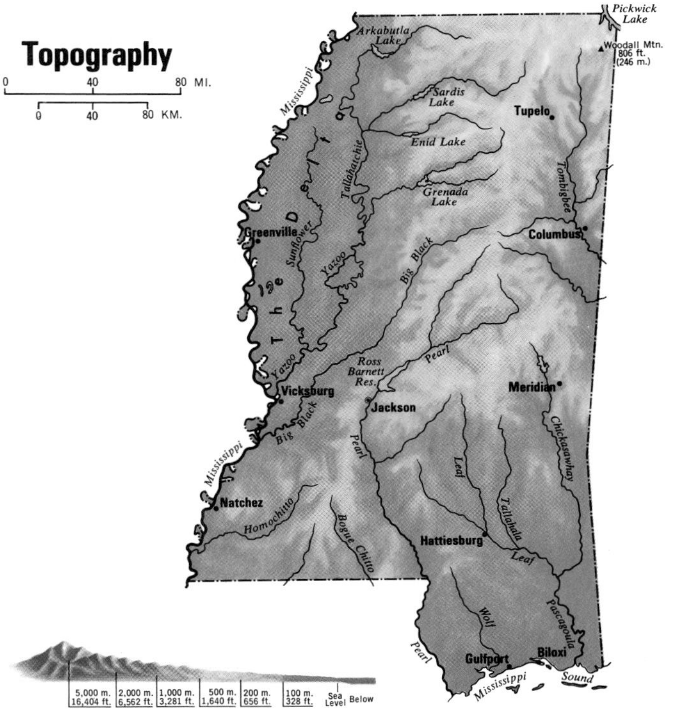

COUNTIES

Adams 38,035 B8
Alcorn 33,036 G1
Amite 13,369 C8
Attala 19,865 E4
Benton 8,153 F1
Bolivar 45,965 C3
Calhoun 15,664 F3
Carroll 9,776 E4
Chickasaw 17,853 G3
Choctaw 8,996 F4
Claiborne 12,279 C7
Clarke 16,945 G6
Clay 21,082 G3
Coahoma 36,918 C2
Copiah 26,503 D7
Covington 15,927 E7
De Soto 53,930 E1
Forrest 66,018 F8
Franklin 8,208 C8
George 15,297 G9
Greene 9,827 G8
Grenada 21,043 E3
Hancock 24,537 E10
Harrison 157,665 F10
Hinds 250,998 D6
Holmes 22,970 D4
Humphreys 13,931 C4
Issaquena 2,513 B5
Itawamba 20,518 H2
Jackson 118,015 G9
Jasper 17,265 F6
Jefferson 9,181 B7
Jefferson Davis 13,846 E7
Jones 61,912 F7
Kemper 10,148 G5
Lafayette 31,030 E2
Lamar 23,821 E8
Lauderdale 77,285 G6
Lawrence 12,518 D7
Leake 18,790 E5
Lee 57,061 G2
Leflore 41,525 D3
Lincoln 30,174 D8
Lowndes 57,304 H4
Madison 41,613 D5
Marion 25,708 E8
Marshall 29,296 E1
Monroe 36,404 H3
Montgomery 13,366 E4
Neshoba 23,789 F5
Newton 19,944 F6
Noxubee 13,212 G4
Oktibbeha 36,018 G4
Panola 28,164 E2
Pearl River 33,795 E9
Perry 9,864 G8
Pike 36,173 D8
Pontotoc 20,918 F2
Prentiss 24,025 G1
Quitman 12,636 D2
Rankin 69,427 E6
Scott 24,556 E6
Sharkey 7,964 C5
Simpson 23,441 E7
Smith 15,077 E6
Stone 9,716 F9
Sunflower 34,844 C3
Tallahatchie 17,157 D3
Tate 20,119 E1
Tippah 18,739 G1
Tishomingo 18,434 H1
Tunica 9,652 D1
Union 21,741 F2
Walthall 13,761 D8
Warren 51,627 C6
Washington 72,344 C4
Wayne 19,135 G7
Webster 10,300 F3
Wilkinson 10,021 B8
Winston 19,474 F4
Yalobusha 13,139 E2
Yazoo 27,349 D5

CITIES and TOWNS

Zip Name/Pop. Key

38601 Abbeville 448 F2
39730 Aberdeen⊙ 7,184 H3
39735 Ackerman⊙ 1,567 F4
39096 Alcorn State University B7
38820 Algoma 175 G2
†39083 Allen 15 C7
38720 Alligator 256 C2
38821 Amory 7,307 H3
38721 Anguilla 950 C5
38722 Arcola 588 C4
38602 Arkabutla 400 D1
39736 Artesia 526 G4
38603 Ashland⊙ 532 F1
38604 Askew 300 D1
†39664 Auburn 500 C8
38912 Avalon 100 D3
38723 Avon 400 B4
39320 Bailey 320 G6
38724 Baird 150 C4
38824 Baldwyn 3,427 G2
†39156 Ballground 30 C5
38913 Banner 120 F2
†39083 Barlow 20 C7
†39330 Basic 60 G6
39421 Bassfield 325 E8
38606 Batesville⊙ 4,692 E2
†39343 Baxter 75 F6
†39455 Baxterville 100 E8
39520 Bay Saint Louis⊙ 7,891 F10
39422 Bay Springs⊙ 1,884 F7
39423 Beaumont 1,112 G8
†39191 Beauregard 185 D7
38825 Becker 350 G3
38826 Belden 241 G2
38609 Belen 400 D2
39737 Bellefontaine 400 F3
38827 Belmont 1,420 H1
39038 Belzoni⊙ 2,982 C4
†39450 Benndale 500 G9
38725 Benoit 499 C3
39039 Benton 350 D5
39040 Bentonia 518 D5
†38659 Bethlehem 210 F1
38726 Beulah 431 B3
39738 Bigbee Valley 370 H4
38914 Big Creek 146 F3
†39567 Bigpoint 350 H9
*39530 Biloxi 49,311 G10
Biloxi-Gulfport‡ 191,918 G10
†38917 Black Hawk 41 E4
38727 Blaine 75 C3
38610 Blue Mountain 867 G1
38828 Blue Springs 131 G2
†38614 Bobo 200 C2
39629 Bogue Chitto 575 D8
39041 Bolton 664 D6
39550 Bond 350 F9
†39301 Bonita 300 G6
38829 Booneville⊙ 6,199 G1
†38756 Bourbon 200 C4
†39180 Bovina 50 C6
38730 Boyle 888 C3
39042 Brandon⊙ 9,626 E6
39044 Braxton 172 D6
38963 Brazil 229 D2
39601 Brookhaven⊙ 10,800 C7
39425 Brooklyn 450 F8
39739 Brooksville 1,038 G4
†38683 Brownfield 125 G1
38915 Bruce 2,208 F3
39322 Buckatunna 500 G7
39630 Bude 1,092 C8
38833 Burnsville 889 H1
38611 Byhalia 757 E1
†39205 Byram 250 D6
†38754 Caile 30 C4
39740 Caledonia 497 H3
38916 Calhoun City 2,033 F3
39045 Camden 150 E5
38612 Canaan 200 F1
39046 Canton⊙ 11,116 D5
39049 Carlisle 425 C7
†39360 Carmichael 75 G7
39050 Carpenter 200 C6
39426 Carriere 900 E9
38917 Carrollton⊙ 338 E4
39427 Carson 400 E7
39051 Carthage⊙ 3,453 E5
39054 Cary 470 C5
38920 Cascilla 230 D3
39741 Cedarbluff 175 G3
39631 Centreville 1,844 B8
38684 Chalybeate 350 G1
38921 Charleston⊙ 2,878 D2
39632 Chatawa 300 D8
38731 Chatham 150 B4
39323 Chunky 277 G6
39055 Church Hill 350 B7
39324 Clara 275 G7
38614 Clarksdale⊙ 21,137 D2
39551 Clermont Harbor 550 F10
38732 Cleveland⊙ 14,524 C3
39056 Clinton 14,660 D6
38617 Coahoma 350 C2
†38632 Cockrum 150 E1
38922 Coffeeville⊙ 1,129 E3
38923 Coila 75 E4
38618 Coldwater 1,505 E1
†39638 Coles 150 C8
†38655 College Hill 150 E2
39428 Collins⊙ 2,131 E7
39325 Collinsville 700 G6
39429 Columbia⊙ 7,733 E8
39701 Columbus⊙ 27,383 H3
38619 Como 1,378 E1
39057 Conehatta 200 F6
†39051 Conway 25 E5
38834 Corinth⊙ 13,839 G1
†38659 Cornersville 65 F1
38620 Courtland 381 E2
†39095 Coxburg 300 D5
39743 Crawford 495 G4
38621 Crenshaw 1,019 D2
39633 Crosby 349 B8
38622 Crowder 789 D2
39328 Cruger 540 D4
39059 Crystal Springs 4,902 D7
†38606 Curtis Station 350 D2
39326 Daleville 210 G5
†39643 Darbun 100 D8
38623 Darling 275 D2
39327 Decatur⊙ 1,148 F6
†39739 Deerbrook 30 G4
39328 De Kalb⊙ 1,159 G5
†39571 De Lisle 450 F10
39061 Delta City 310 C4
†38655 Denmark 40 F2
38838 Dennis 150 H1
39059 Dentville 175 C7
†39470 Derby 298 E9
38839 Derma 793 F3
†39532 D'Iberville 13,369 G10
39062 D'Lo 463 E7
38736 Doddsville 232 C3
38737 Drew 2,528 C3
38739 Dublin 100 C2
38925 Duck Hill 706 E3
†39337 Duffee 175 G6
38625 Dumas 312 G1
38740 Duncan 501 C2
38626 Dundee 600 D1
39063 Durant 2,889 E4
39436 Eastabuchie 200 F8
39064 Ebenezer 200 D5
38841 Ecru 687 F2
39634 Eddiceton 65 C8
39065 Eden 150 D5
39066 Edwards 1,515 C6
†39156 Eldorado 20 C5
39329 Electric Mills 100 G5
38742 Elizabeth 500 C4
38926 Elliott 200 E3
39437 Ellisville⊙ 4,652 F7
38927 Enid E2
39330 Enterprise 607 G6
†39440 Errata 85 F7
39552 Escatawpa 5,367 G10
39067 Ethel 486 F4
38627 Etta 75 F2
39744 Eupora 2,048 F3
†38676 Evansville 60 D1
38628 Falcon 260 D2
38629 Falkner 251 G1
38630 Farrell 300 C2
39069 Fayette⊙ 2,033 B7
39635 Fernwood 500 D8
39070 Fitler 175 B5
39071 Flora 1,507 D5
39073 Florence 1,111 D6
†39201 Flowood 943 D6
39074 Forest⊙ 5,229 F6
39076 Forkville 185 E6
39636 Fort Adams 75 B8
39483 Foxworth 800 E8
39745 French Camp 306 F4
38631 Friars Point 1,400 C2
39577 Fruitland Park 75 F9
38843 Fulton⊙ 3,238 H2
39077 Gallman D7
38844 Gattman 151 H3
39553 Gautier 8,917 G10
39078 Georgetown 343 D7
†39354 Gholson 50 G5
†39083 Glancy 25 C7
38846 Glen 100 H1
38744 Glen Allan 650 B4
38928 Glendora 220 D3
39638 Gloster 1,726 B8
†39110 Gluckstadt 150 D5
38847 Golden 292 H2
39079 Goodman 1,285 E5
38929 Gore Springs 125 E3
38745 Grace 325 C5
†38725 Grapeland 200 B3
38701 Greenville⊙ 40,613 B4
38930 Greenwood⊙ 20,115 D4
38848 Greenwood Springs 170 H3
38901 Grenada⊙ 12,641 E3
*39501 Gulfport⊙ 39,676 F10
38746 Gunnison 708 C3
38849 Guntown 359 G2
†39661 Hamburg 150 B7
39746 Hamilton 500 H3
†38901 Hardy 45 E3
39080 Harperville 200 E6
39081 Harriston 500 C7
39082 Harrisville 500 D7
†38821 Hatley 497 H3
39401 Hattiesburg⊙ 40,829 F8
39083 Hazlehurst⊙ 4,437 D7
39439 Heidelberg 1,098 F7
39086 Hermanville 750 C7
38632 Hernando⊙ 2,969 E1
†39192 Hesterville 25 E4
39332 Hickory 670 F6
38633 Hickory Flat 458 F1
39087 Hillsboro 800 E6
†38646 Hinchcliff 60 D2
†39462 Hintonville 300 F8
†39108 Hinze 30 F4
†39751 Hohenlinden 96 F3
38940 Holcomb 50 D3
38748 Hollandale 4,336 C4
39088 Holly Bluff 700 C5
38749 Holly Ridge 350 C4
38635 Holly Springs⊙ 7,285 E1
†38676 Hollywood 80 D1
†39648 Holmesville 50 D8
38637 Horn Lake 4,326 D1
38850 Houlka 710 G2
38851 Houston⊙ 3,747 G3
†39574 Howison 300 F9
†39429 Hub 80 E8
39555 Hurley 500 H9
†38774 Hushpuckena 60 C2
38638 Independence 150 E1
38751 Indianola⊙ 8,221 C4
†38652 Ingomar 150 F2
38753 Inverness 1,034 C4
38754 Isola 834 C4
38941 Itta Bena 2,904 D4
38852 Iuka⊙ 2,846 H1
†38865 Jacinto 65 H1
*39201 Jackson (cap.)⊙ 202,895 D6
Jackson‡ 320,425 D6
39641 Jayess 200 D8
38639 Jonestown 1,231 D2
†38829 Jumpertown 472 G1
†38924 Keirn 3 D4
†39364 Kewanee 250 H6
39747 Kilmichael 906 E4
39556 Kiln 800 F10
†39661 Knoxville 65 B8
39643 Kokomo 250 E8
†39740 Kolola Springs 100 H3
39090 Kosciusko⊙ 7,415 E4
38834 Kossuth 190 G1
38640 Lafayette Springs 80 F2
39092 Lake 524 F6
38641 Lake Cormorant 300 D1
39558 Lakeshore 550 F10
38642 Lamar 200 F1
38643 Lambert 1,624 D2
38755 Lamont 400 B3
39335 Lauderdale 600 G5
39440 Laurel⊙ 21,897 F7
39336 Lawrence 250 F6
39450 Leaf 250 G8
39451 Leakesville⊙ 1,120 G8
39093 Learned 113 C6
38756 Leland 6,667 C4
39094 Lena 231 E5
†39667 Lexie 40 D8
39095 Lexington⊙ 2,628 D4
39645 Liberty⊙ 669 C8
39337 Little Rock 70 F5
39560 Long Beach 7,967 F10
†39759 Longview 800 G4
39096 Lorman 350 B7
39338 Louin 338 F6
39097 Louise 400 C5
39339 Louisville⊙ 7,323 G4
†38632 Love 50 D1
39452 Lucedale⊙ 2,429 G9
39646 Lucien 75 C7
39098 Ludlow 350 E5
38644 Lula 394 C2
39455 Lumberton 2,217 E8
†39501 Lyman 500 F10
†39739 Lynn Creek 20 G4
38645 Lyon 531 D2
39750 Maben 855 F3
39341 Macon⊙ 2,396 G4
39109 Madden 450 F5
39110 Madison 2,241 D6
39111 Magee 3,497 E7
39652 Magnolia⊙ 2,461 D8
†38769 Malvina 100 C3
38855 Mantachie 732 H2
39751 Mantee 158 F3
38856 Marietta 298 H2
39342 Marion 771 G6
38646 Marks⊙ 2,260 D2
†39083 Martinsville 30 D7
†39051 Marydell 99 F5
39752 Mathiston 632 F3
38758 Mattson 200 C2
†39458 Maxie 233 F9
39113 Mayersville⊙ 378 B5
39753 Mayhew 150 G4
39107 McAdams 350 E4
†39144 McBride 2 C7
39647 McCall Creek 250 C7
38943 McCarley 250 E3
39648 McComb 12,331 D8
38854 McCondy 150 G3
39108 McCool 203 F4
39561 McHenry 660 F9
39456 McLain 688 G8
39457 McNeill 800 E9
39653 Meadville⊙ 575 C8
39114 Mendenhall⊙ 2,533 E7
39301 Meridian⊙ 46,577 G6
38759 Merigold 574 C3
†39667 Mesa 30 D8
38760 Metcalfe 952 B4
38647 Michigan City 350 F1
39115 Midnight 500 C4
38648 Mineral Wells 250 E1
38944 Minter City 150 D3
39762 Mississippi State G4
39116 Mize 363 E7
38945 Money 350 D3
39654 Monticello⊙ 1,834 D7
39754 Montpelier 175 G3
†39338 Montrose 120 F6
38857 Mooreville 200 G2
38761 Moorhead 2,358 C4
38946 Morgan City 319 D4
39484 Morgantown 325 E8
†39120 Morgantown 3,445 B7
39117 Morton 3,303 E6
†39328 Moscow 30 G5
39459 Moselle 525 F8
39460 Moss 65 F7
39563 Moss Point 18,998 G10
38762 Mound Bayou 2,917 C3
†39474 Mount Carmel 30 E7
39119 Mount Olive 993 E7
38649 Mount Pleasant 250 E1
38650 Myrtle 402 F1
39120 Natchez⊙ 22,015 B7
39461 Neely 270 G8
38651 Nesbit 366 D1
39365 Neshoba 250 F5
38858 Nettleton 1,911 G2
38652 New Albany⊙ 7,072 G2
39462 New Augusta⊙ 589 F8
39140 Newhebron 470 D7
38850 New Houlka (Houlka) 710 G2
38859 New Site 100 H1
39345 Newton 3,708 F6
39463 Nicholson 400 E10
38763 Nitta Yuma 150 C4
†39629 Norfield 75 C8
38947 North Carrollton 859 E3
39346 Noxapater 516 F5
38948 Oakland 540 E2
†39154 Oakley 133 D6
39656 Oak Vale E8
39564 Ocean Springs 14,504 G10
39141 Ofahoma 350 E5
38860 Okolona⊙ 3,409 G2
38654 Olive Branch 2,067 E1
†39482 Oloh 93 E8
†39654 Oma 200 D7
†39501 Orange Grove 13,476 H10
39657 Osyka 581 D8
39464 Ovett 600 F8
38655 Oxford⊙ 9,882 F2
38764 Pace 519 C3
39347 Pachuta 256 G6
38861 Paden 119 H1
†39401 Palmers Crossing 2,765 F8
38765 Panther Burn 300 C4
38738 Parchman 200 D3
38949 Paris 253 F2
39567 Pascagoula⊙ 29,318 G10
Pascagoula-Moss Point‡ 118,015 G10
39571 Pass Christian 5,014 F10
39144 Pattison 540 C7
39348 Paulding⊙ 630 F6
39349 Paulette 230 H4
†38920 Paynes 100 D3
39028 Pearl 18,580 D6
39572 Pearlington 500 E10
39145 Pelahatchie 1,445 E6
39573 Perkinston 950 F9
†38746 Perthshire 25 C3
39465 Petal 8,476 F8
39755 Pheba 280 G3
39350 Philadelphia⊙ 6,434 F5
38950 Philipp 975 D3
†39476 Piave 150 G8
39466 Picayune 10,361 E9
39146 Pickens 1,386 E5
39148 Piney Woods 450 D6
39149 Pinola E7

(continued on following page)

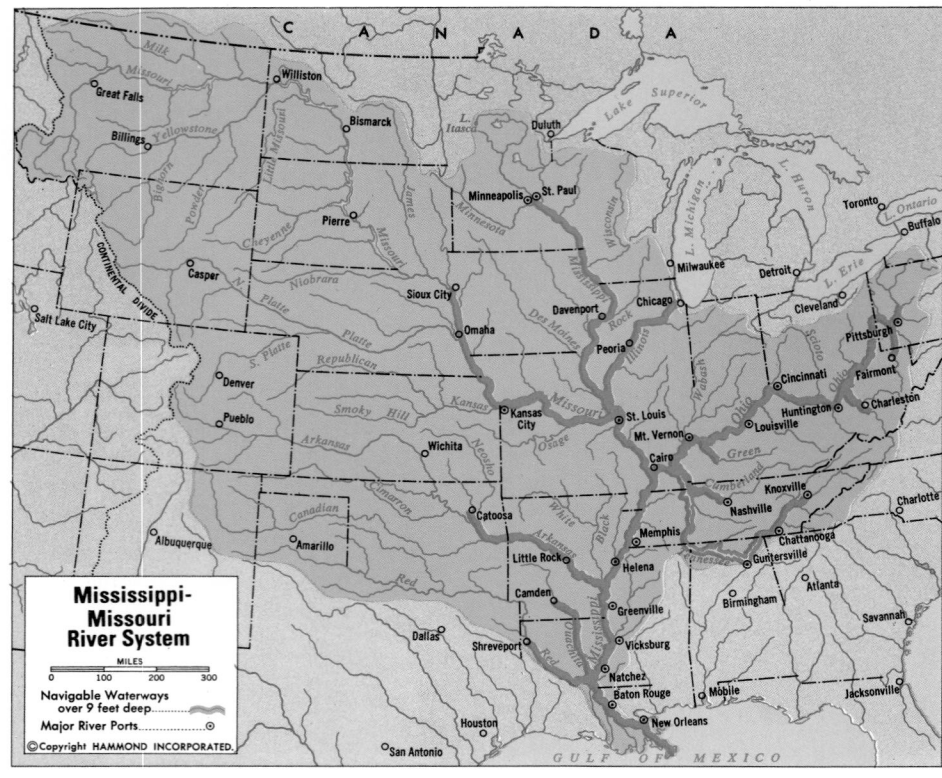

Mississippi-Missouri River System

MILES
0   100   200   300

Navigable Waterways
over 9 feet deep
Major River Ports.........⊚

©Copyright HAMMOND INCORPORATED.

38951 Pittsboro⊙ 269	F3
38862 Plantersville 920	G2
38657 Pleasant Grove 100	D2
†38651 Pleasant Hill 400	E1
39072 Pocahontas 80	D6
39118 Polkville 129	E6
38863 Pontotoc⊙ 4,723	G2
38568 Pope 208	E2
39470 Poplarville⊙ 2,562	E9
39352 Porterville 150	G5
39150 Port Gibson⊙ 2,371	B7
38659 Potts Camp 525	F1
39756 Prairie	G3
39353 Prairie Point 150	H4
39474 Prentiss⊙ 1,465	E7
39354 Preston 500	G5
†39666 Pricedale 400	D8
†38676 Prichard 50	D1
39151 Puckett 279	E6
39152 Pulaski 108	E6
39475 Purvis⊙ 2,256	F8
39647 Quentin 40	C8
39355 Quitman⊙ 2,632	G6
39153 Raleigh⊙ 998	F6
38864 Randolph	F2
39154 Raymond⊙ 1,967	D6
38661 Red Lick 100	B7
†39096 Red Banks 350	F1
39156 Redwood 80	C6
39757 Reform 100	F4
38767 Rena Lara 350	C2
39051 Renfroe 32	F5
†38732 Renova 659	C3
38662 Rich 72	D2
†39218 Richland 3,955	D6
39476 Richton 1,205	G8
39157 Ridgeland 5,461	D6
38865 Rienzi 423	G1
38663 Ripley⊙ 4,271	G1
38664 Robinsonville 285	D1
†39083 Rockport 30	D7
†39096 Rodney 100	B7
39159 Rolling Fork⊙ 2,590	C5
38768 Rome	C3
38769 Rosedale⊙ 2,793	B3
39356 Rose Hill 500	F6
†39633 Rosetta 120	B8
39661 Roxie 591	B8
38771 Ruleville 3,332	D3
†39108 Rural Hill 25	E4
†39150 Russum 200	B7
39662 Ruth 400	D8
39160 Sallis 211	E4
38866 Saltillo 1,271	G2
39112 Sanatorium 400	E7
39477 Sandersville 800	F7
39161 Sandhill 100	E5
39478 Sandy Hook 70	E8
*39479 Sanford 150	F8
38665 Sarah 150	D1
38666 Sardis⊙ 2,278	E2
38867 Sarepta 120	F2
39162 Satartia 73	C5
39574 Saucier 100	F9
38667 Savage 100	D1
38952 Schlater 429	D3
38953 Scobey 100	E3
39358 Scooba 511	G5
38772 Scott 400	B3
39359 Sebastopol 314	F5
39479 Seminary 327	E7
38668 Senatobia⊙ 5,013	E1
39758 Sessums 150	G4
38868 Shannon 680	G2
39163 Sharon 200	E5
38773 Shaw 2,461	C3
38774 Shelby 2,540	C3
38669 Sherard 150	C2
38869 Sherman 499	G2
39164 Shivers 100	E7
39360 Shubuta 626	G7
39361 Shuqualak 554	G5
39165 Sibley 350	B8
38954 Sidon 450	D4
39166 Silver City 378	C4
39663 Silver Creek 272	D7
38775 Skene 250	C3
38955 Slate Spring 102	F3
38670 Sledge 699	D2
39664 Smithdale 200	C8
38870 Smithville 866	H2
39665 Sontag 200	D7
39480 Soso 434	F7
38671 Southaven 16,071	E1
39167 Star 600	D6
39759 Starkville⊙ 15,169	G4
39362 State Line 484	G8
39766 Steens 125	H3
39767 Stewart 350	F4
38776 Stoneville 250	C4
39363 Stonewall 1,345	G6
38672 Stovall 50	C2
†38665 Strayhorn 275	D1
39481 Stringer 350	F7
38777 Stringtown 300	C3
39769 Sturgis 269	G4
39666 Summit 1,753	D8
38957 Sumner⊙ 452	D3
39482 Sumrall 1,197	E8
38778 Sunflower 1,027	C3
38958 Swan Lake 325	D3
38959 Swiftown 320	D4
39153 Sylvarena 102	F6
38673 Taylor 301	E2
39168 Taylorsville 1,387	F7
39169 Tchula 1,931	D4
39170 Terry 655	D6
38871 Thaxton 404	F2
39171 Thomastown 400	E5
†39073 Thomasville 50	E6
39172 Thornton 135	D4
†38829 Thrasher 100	G1
38960 Tie Plant 500	E3
38961 Tillatoba 106	E3
†39150 Tillman 65	C7
38674 Tiplersville 100	G1
38962 Tippo 200	D3

38873 Tishomingo 387	H1
38874 Toccopola 184	F2
39770 Tomnolen 200	F4
39364 Toomsuba 500	G6
39174 Tougaloo 800	D6
38757 Tralake 200	C4
38875 Trebloc 100	G3
38876 Tremont 379	H2
38877 Tribbett 100	C4
38675 Tula 140	F2
38676 Tunica⊙ 1,361	D1
38801 Tupelo⊙ 23,905	G2
38963 Tutwiler 1,174	D2
39667 Tylertown⊙ 1,976	D8
39365 Union 1,931	F5
39668 Union Church 75	C7
39175 Utica 865	C6
39175 Utica Junior College 40	C6
39176 Vaiden⊙ 924	E4
39564 Vancleave 1,330	G9
†38851 Van Vleet 400	G3
38878 Vardaman 1,009	F3
39179 Vaughan 210	D5
38879 Verona 2,497	G2
39180 Vicksburg⊙ 25,434	C6
38679 Victoria 800	E1
39366 Vossburg 300	F7
†39567 Wade 800	G9
39358 Wahalak 92	G5
38680 Walls 50	D1
38683 Walnut 513	G1
39189 Walnut Grove 439	F5
39771 Walthall⊙ 206	F3
39190 Washington 250	B7
38685 Waterford 400	E1
38965 Water Valley⊙ 4,147	E2
39576 Waveland 4,186	F10
39367 Waynesboro⊙ 5,349	G7
38780 Wayside 500	C4
†39114 Weathersby	E7
38966 Webb 782	D3
39772 Weir 553	F4
†38834 Wenasoga 175	G1
39191 Wesson 1,313	D7
39192 West 253	E4
†39501 West Gulfport (North Gulfport) 6,660	F10
39773 West Point⊙ 8,811	G3
38880 Wheeler 600	G1
39193 Whitfield 900	E6
39577 Wiggins⊙ 3,205	F9
†38659 Winborn 70	F1
38967 Winona⊙ 6,177	E4
38781 Winstonville 486	C3
38782 Winterville 200	B4
39776 Woodland 135	F3
†39730 Wren 150	G3
39669 Woodville⊙ 1,512	B8
39194 Yazoo City⊙ 12,092	D5
†39090 Zama 100	F5

OTHER FEATURES

Amite (riv.)	C9
Arkabutla (lake)	D1
Big Black (riv.)	C6
Black (creek)	F8
Bogue Chitto (riv.)	D8
Bogue Homo (lake)	F7
Bowie (creek)	E7
Brices Cross Roads Nat'l Battlefield Site	G2
Buttahatchee (riv.)	H3
Cat (isl.)	F10
Catalpa (creek)	G4
Chickasaw Village, Natchez Trace Pkwy.	G2
Chickasawhay (riv.)	G7
Coldwater (riv.)	D1
Columbus A.F.B. 3,650	H3
Deer (creek)	C4
Enid (lake)	E2
Grenada (lake)	E3
Gulf Islands Nat'l Seashore	G10
Homochitto (riv.)	B8
Horn (isl.)	G10
Keesler A.F.B.	G10
Leaf (riv.)	F8
Little Tallahatchie (riv.)	D2
Meridian Naval Air Sta.	G5
Mississippi (riv.)	A8
Mississippi (sound)	G10
Noxubee (riv.)	G4
Okatibbee (lake)	G5
Pascagoula (riv.)	G9
Pearl (riv.)	D8
Petit Bois (isl.)	H10
Pickwick (lake)	H1
Pierre (bayou)	C7
Ross Barnett (res.)	D6
Round (isl.)	G10
Saint Louis (bay)	F10
Sardis (lake)	E2
Ship (isl.)	G10
Skuna (riv.)	F2
Strong (riv.)	D7
Sucarnoochee (creek)	G5
Sunflower (riv.)	C5
Tallahaga (creek)	F4
Tallahala (creek)	F7
Tallahatchie (riv.)	D3
Tchula (lake)	D4
Tennessee-Tombigbee Waterway	H2
Thompson (creek)	G8
Tombigbee (riv.)	H4
Trim Cane (creek)	G4
Tupelo Nat'l Battlefield	G2
Vicksburg Nat'l Mil. Park	C6
Wolf (riv.)	F9
Woodall (mt.)	H1
Yalobusha (riv.)	E3
Yazoo (riv.)	C5
Yockanookany (riv.)	E5

⊙County seat.
‡Population of metropolitan area.
† Zip of nearest p.o.   * Multiple zips.

Agriculture, Industry and Resources

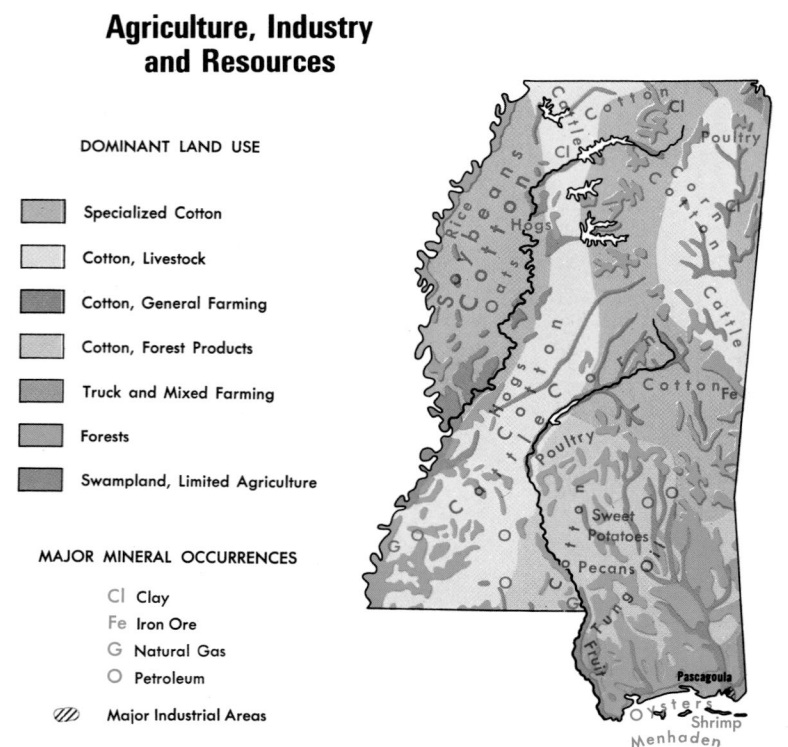

DOMINANT LAND USE

- Specialized Cotton
- Cotton, Livestock
- Cotton, General Farming
- Cotton, Forest Products
- Truck and Mixed Farming
- Forests
- Swampland, Limited Agriculture

MAJOR MINERAL OCCURRENCES

- Cl Clay
- Fe Iron Ore
- G   Natural Gas
- O   Petroleum
- ⫽⫽ Major Industrial Areas

AREA 69,697 sq. mi. (180,515 sq. km.)
POPULATION 4,916,759
CAPITAL Jefferson City
LARGEST CITY St. Louis
HIGHEST POINT Taum Sauk Mtn. 1,772 ft. (540 m.)
SETTLED IN 1764
ADMITTED TO UNION August 10, 1821
POPULAR NAME Show Me State
STATE FLOWER Hawthorn
STATE BIRD Bluebird

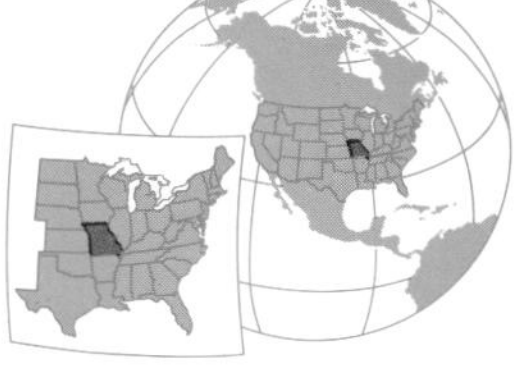

COUNTIES

Adair 24,870 .... G2
Andrew 13,980 .... C3
Atchison 8,605 .... B2
Audrain 26,458 .... J4
Barry 24,408 .... E9
Barton 11,292 .... D7
Bates 15,873 .... D6
Benton 12,183 .... F6
Bollinger 10,301 .... M8
Boone 100,376 .... H4
Buchanan 87,888 .... C3
Butler 37,693 .... M9
Caldwell 8,660 .... E3
Callaway 32,252 .... J5
Camden 20,017 .... G6
Cape Girardeau 58,837 .... N8
Carroll 12,131 .... F4
Carter 5,428 .... L9
Cass 51,029 .... D5
Cedar 11,894 .... E7
Chariton 10,489 .... F3
Christian 22,402 .... F9
Clark 8,493 .... J2
Clay 136,488 .... D4
Clinton 15,916 .... D3
Cole 56,663 .... H6
Cooper 14,643 .... G5
Crawford 18,300 .... K7
Dade 7,383 .... E8
Dallas 12,096 .... F7
Daviess 8,905 .... E3
De Kalb 8,222 .... D3
Dent 14,517 .... J7
Douglas 11,594 .... G9
Dunklin 36,324 .... M10
Franklin 71,233 .... K6
Gasconade 13,181 .... J6
Gentry 7,887 .... D2
Greene 185,302 .... F8
Grundy 11,959 .... E2
Harrison 9,890 .... E2
Henry 19,672 .... E6
Hickory 6,367 .... F7
Holt 6,882 .... B2
Howard 10,008 .... G4
Howell 28,807 .... J9
Iron 11,084 .... L7
Jackson 629,266 .... R5
Jasper 86,958 .... D8
Jefferson 146,183 .... L6
Johnson 39,059 .... E5
Knox 5,508 .... H2
Laclede 24,323 .... G7
Lafayette 29,925 .... E4
Lawrence 28,973 .... E8
Lewis 10,901 .... J2
Lincoln 22,193 .... L4
Linn 15,495 .... F3
Livingston 15,739 .... E3
Macon 16,313 .... G3
Madison 10,725 .... M8
Maries 7,551 .... J6
Marion 28,638 .... J3
McDonald 14,917 .... D9
Mercer 4,685 .... E2
Miller 18,532 .... H6
Mississippi 15,726 .... O9
Moniteau 12,068 .... G5
Monroe 9,716 .... H3
Montgomery 11,537 .... K5
Morgan 13,807 .... G6
New Madrid 22,945 .... N9
Newton 40,555 .... D9
Nodaway 21,996 .... C2
Oregon 10,238 .... K9
Osage 12,014 .... J6
Ozark 7,961 .... H9
Pemiscot 24,987 .... N10
Perry 16,784 .... N7
Pettis 36,378 .... F5
Phelps 33,633 .... J7
Pike 17,568 .... K4
Platte 46,341 .... C4
Polk 18,822 .... F7
Pulaski 42,011 .... H7
Putnam 6,092 .... F2
Ralls 8,984 .... J3
Randolph 25,460 .... G3
Ray 21,378 .... E4
Reynolds 7,230 .... L8
Ripley 12,458 .... L9
Saint Charles 144,107 .... M2
Saint Clair 8,622 .... E6
Sainte Genevieve 15,180 .... M7
Saint Francois 42,600 .... M7
Saint Louis 973,896 .... O3
Saint Louis (city county) 453,085 ... P3
Saline 24,919 .... F4
Schuyler 4,979 .... G2
Scotland 5,415 .... H2
Scott 39,647 .... N8
Shannon 7,885 .... K8
Shelby 7,826 .... H3
Stoddard 29,009 .... N9
Stone 15,587 .... F9
Sullivan 7,434 .... F2
Taney 20,467 .... F9
Texas 21,070 .... J8
Vernon 19,806 .... D7
Warren 14,900 .... K5
Washington 17,983 .... L7
Wayne 11,277 .... L8
Webster 20,414 .... G8
Worth 3,008 .... D2
Wright 16,188 .... H8

CITIES and TOWNS

Zip *Name/Pop.* *Key*

64720 Adrian 1,484 .... D6
63730 Advance 1,054 .... N8
63123 Affton 23,181 .... P4
64401 Agency 419 .... C3
64830 Alba 474 .... D8
64402 Albany⊙ 2,152 .... D2
63430 Alexandria 417 .... K2
64001 Alma 445 .... E4
65606 Alton⊙ 721 .... K9
64421 Amazonia 314 .... C3
64723 Amsterdam 231 .... D6
64831 Anderson 1,237 .... D9
63620 Annapolis 370 .... L8
63820 Anniston 320 .... O9
64724 Appleton City 1,257 .... D6
63821 Arbyrd 704 .... M10
63621 Arcadia 683 .... L7
64725 Archie 753 .... D5
65230 Armstrong 360 .... G4
63010 Arnold 19,141 .... M6
65604 Ash Grove 1,157 .... E8
65010 Ashland 1,021 .... H5
63530 Atlanta 441 .... H3
63332 Augusta 308 .... L5
65605 Aurora 6,437 .... E9
65231 Auxvasse 858 .... J4
65608 Ava⊙ 2,761 .... G9
64010 Avondale 612 .... P5
63011 Ballwin 12,656 .... N3
64011 Bates City 199 .... E5
†65619 Battlefield 1,227 .... F8
†63101 Bella Villa 758 .... R4
63735 Bell City 539 .... N8
65013 Belle 1,233 .... J6
†63137 Bellefontaine Neighbors 12,082 .... R2
63333 Bellflower 403 .... K4
†63101 Bel-Nor 2,047 .... P2
†63101 Bel-Ridge 3,682 .... P2
64012 Belton 12,708 .... C5
63736 Benton⊙ 674 .... O8
63134 Berkeley 15,922 .... P2
63822 Bernie 1,975 .... M9
63823 Bertrand 688 .... O9
64424 Bethany⊙ 3,095 .... E2
63532 Bevier 733 .... G3
65610 Billings 911 .... F8
65438 Birch Tree 622 .... K9
63624 Bismarck 1,625 .... L7
65321 Blackburn 314 .... F4
†63031 Black Jack 5,293 .... R1
65014 Bland 662 .... J6
63825 Bloomfield⊙ 1,795 .... M9
63627 Bloomsdale 397 .... M6
64015 Blue Springs 25,927 .... R6
†64101 Blue Summit R5
65613 Bolivar⊙ 5,919 .... F7
63628 Bonne Terre 3,797 .... L7
65233 Boonville⊙ 6,959 .... G5
64723 Bosworth 394 .... F4
65441 Bourbon 1,259 .... K6
63334 Bowling Green⊙ 3,022 .... K4
65616 Branson 2,550 .... F9
63533 Brashear 332 .... H2
64624 Braymer 986 .... E3
64625 Breckenridge 523 .... E3
†63114 Breckenridge Hills 5,666 .... O2
63144 Brentwood 8,209 .... P3
63044 Bridgeton 18,445 .... O2
†63044 Bridgeton Terrace 334 .... O2
64628 Brookfield 5,555 .... F3
64630 Browning 368 .... F2
65236 Brunswick 1,272 .... F4
64631 Bucklin 713 .... G3
64016 Buckner 2,848 .... R5
65622 Buffalo⊙ 2,217 .... F7
65237 Bunceton 419 .... G5
63629 Bunker 673 .... K8
64428 Burlington Junction 657 .... B2
64730 Butler⊙ 4,107 .... D6
65689 Cabool 2,090 .... H8
64632 Cainsville 496 .... E2
65239 Cairo 315 .... H4
65323 Calhoun 427 .... E6
65018 California⊙ 3,381 .... H5
63534 Callao 326 .... G3
†63101 Calverton Park 1,717 .... P2
65020 Camdenton⊙ 2,303 .... G6
64429 Cameron 4,519 .... D3
63933 Campbell 2,134 .... M9
63828 Canalou 369 .... N9
63435 Canton 2,435 .... J2
63701 Cape Girardeau 34,361 .... O8
63829 Cardwell 831 .... M10
64834 Carl Junction 3,937 .... C8
64633 Carrollton⊙ 4,700 .... E4
64835 Carterville 1,973 .... D8
64836 Carthage⊙ 11,104 .... D8
63830 Caruthersville⊙ 7,958 .... N10
65625 Cassville⊙ 2,091 .... E9
65022 Cedar City 427 .... H5
63436 Center 669 .... J3
65023 Centertown 304 .... H5
63633 Centerville⊙ 241 .... L8
65240 Centralia 3,537 .... H4
63740 Chaffee 3,241 .... N8
65024 Chamois 546 .... J5
†63101 Charlack 1,537 .... P2
63834 Charleston⊙ 5,230 .... O9
64733 Chilhowee 349 .... E5
64601 Chillicothe⊙ 9,089 .... E3
63437 Clarence 1,147 .... H3
65243 Clark 304 .... H4
65025 Clarksburg 352 .... G5
64430 Clarksdale 278 .... D3
†63017 Clarkson Valley 1,435 .... N3
63336 Clarksville 585 .... K4
63837 Clarkton 1,228 .... M10
†64119 Claycomo 1,671 .... P5
63105 Clayton⊙ 14,273 .... P3
64734 Cleveland 485 .... C5
65631 Clever 551 .... F8
64735 Clinton⊙ 8,366 .... E6
65325 Cole Camp 1,022 .... F6
65201 Columbia⊙ 62,061 .... H5
Columbia‡ 100,376 .... H5
†63128 Concord 20,896 .... P4
64020 Concordia 2,129 .... E5
65632 Conway 601 .... G7
†63101 Cool Valley 2,084 .... P2
63839 Cooter 479 .... N10
64021 Corder 483 .... E4
†64501 Country Club Village 1,234 .... C3
64437 Craig 379 .... B2
65633 Crane 1,185 .... E9
64739 Creighton 301 .... D6
†63126 Crestwood 12,815 .... O3
63141 Creve Coeur 11,757 .... O2
65452 Crocker 979 .... H7
63019 Crystal City 3,618 .... M6
†63101 Crystal Lake Park 496 .... O3
65453 Cuba 2,120 .... K6
63339 Curryville 323 .... K4
64439 Dearborn 547 .... C3
64740 Deepwater 475 .... E6
64440 De Kalb 245 .... C3
†63135 Dellwood 6,200 .... R2
63744 Delta 524 .... N8
63636 Des Arc 237 .... L8
63601 Desloge 3,481 .... M7
63020 De Soto 5,993 .... L6
63131 Des Peres 8,254 .... O3
63841 Dexter 7,043 .... N9
64840 Diamond 766 .... D9
65459 Dixon 1,402 .... H6
63935 Doniphan⊙ 1,921 .... L9
†65550 Doolittle 701 .... J7
63536 Downing 462 .... H2
64742 Drexel 908 .... C6
64841 Duenweg 703 .... D8
†64801 Duquesne 1,252 .... D8
64442 Eagleville 364 .... D2
64443 Easton 313 .... C3
63845 East Prairie 3,713 .... O9
64444 Edgerton 584 .... C3
63537 Edina⊙ 1,520 .... H2
†63101 Edmundson 1,374 .... O2
65026 Eldon 4,342 .... G6
64744 El Dorado Springs 3,868 .... E7
63638 Ellington 1,215 .... L8
†63011 Ellisville 6,233 .... M3
63937 Ellsinore 362 .... L9
63343 Elsberry 1,272 .... L4
63639 Elvins 1,548 .... L7
65466 Eminence⊙ 614 .... K8
63344 Eolia 401 .... L4
63846 Essex 545 .... N9
†63601 Esther 1,038 .... M7
63025 Eureka 3,862 .... M4
65646 Everton 317 .... E8
63440 Ewing 400 .... J2
64024 Excelsior Springs 10,424 .... R4
65647 Exeter 588 .... D9
64446 Fairfax 835 .... B2
65648 Fair Grove 863 .... F8
65649 Fair Play 384 .... E7
63345 Farber 503 .... J4
63640 Farmington⊙ 8,270 .... M7
65248 Fayette⊙ 2,983 .... G4
63026 Fenton 2,417 .... O4
63135 Ferguson 24,740 .... P2
64163 Ferrelview 447 .... O4
63028 Festus 7,574 .... M6
64449 Fillmore 265 .... C2
63940 Fisk 450 .... M9
63601 Flat River 4,443 .... M7
*63031 Florissant 55,372 .... P1
65652 Fordland 569 .... G8
64451 Forest City 387 .... B3
65653 Forsyth⊙ 1,010 .... F9
63441 Frankford 443 .... K4
63645 Fredericktown⊙ 4,036 .... M7
65035 Freeburg 554 .... J6
64746 Freeman 485 .... C5
†63101 Frontenac 3,654 .... O3
65251 Fulton⊙ 11,046 .... J5
65655 Gainesville⊙ 707 .... G9
65656 Galena⊙ 423 .... F9
64640 Gallatin⊙ 2,063 .... E3
64641 Galt 323 .... F2
64747 Garden City 1,021 .... D5
63037 Gerald 921 .... K6
63848 Gideon 1,240 .... N10
64642 Gilman City 414 .... D2
64118 Gladstone 24,990 .... P5
65254 Glasgow 1,336 .... G4
†64068 Glenaire 541 .... R5
63122 Glendale 6,035 .... P3
64748 Golden City 900 .... D8
63843 Goodman 1,030 .... C9
63543 Gorin H2
64454 Gower 1,276 .... C3
64029 Grain Valley 1,327 .... S6
64844 Granby 1,908 .... D9
64030 Grandview 24,502 .... P6
64456 Grant City⊙ 1,068 .... D2
†63155 Grantwood Village 1,002 .... O4
65037 Gravois Mills G6
63545 Green City 719 .... F2
65661 Greenfield⊙ 1,394 .... E8
65332 Green Ridge 488 .... F5
63546 Greentop 538 .... H2
63944 Greenville⊙ 393 .... M8
64034 Greenwood 1,315 .... R6
64643 Hale 529 .... F3
65255 Hallsville 624 .... H4
64644 Hamilton 1,582 .... E3
†63101 Hanley Hills 2,439 .... P2
63401 Hannibal 18,811 .... K3
64035 Hardin 688 .... E4
64701 Harrisonville⊙ 6,372 .... D5
65667 Hartville⊙ 576 .... G8
63945 Harviell M9
63349 Hawk Point 386 .... K5
63851 Hayti 3,964 .... N10
†63851 Hayti Heights 1,023 .... N10
†63736 Haywood City 425 .... N9
*63042 Hazelwood 12,935 .... P2
64036 Henrietta 424 .... E4
63048 Herculaneum 2,293 .... M6
65041 Hermann⊙ 2,695 .... K5
65668 Hermitage⊙ 384 .... F7
65257 Higbee 817 .... H4
64037 Higginsville 4,595 .... E4
63350 High Hill 254 .... K5
63050 Hillsboro⊙ 1,508 .... L6
†63101 Hillsdale 2,247 .... R2
63852 Holcomb 632 .... N10
64040 Holden 2,195 .... E5
63853 Holland 295 .... N10
65672 Hollister 1,439 .... F9
64048 Holt 276 .... D4
65043 Holts Summit 2,540 .... H5
†63879 Homestown 306 .... N10
64461 Hopkins 634 .... C1
63855 Hornersville 704 .... M10
65483 Houston⊙ 2,157 .... J8
65333 Houstonia 327 .... F5
†64152 Houston Lake 280 .... O5
†63869 Howardville 536 .... N9
65674 Humansville 907 .... E7
64752 Hume 315 .... C6
63443 Hunnewell 235 .... J3
†63101 Huntleigh 428 .... O3
65259 Huntsville⊙ 1,657 .... H4
63547 Hurdland 227 .... H2
65486 Iberia 852 .... H6
63754 Illmo 1.368 .... O8

(continued on following page)

Agriculture, Industry and Resources

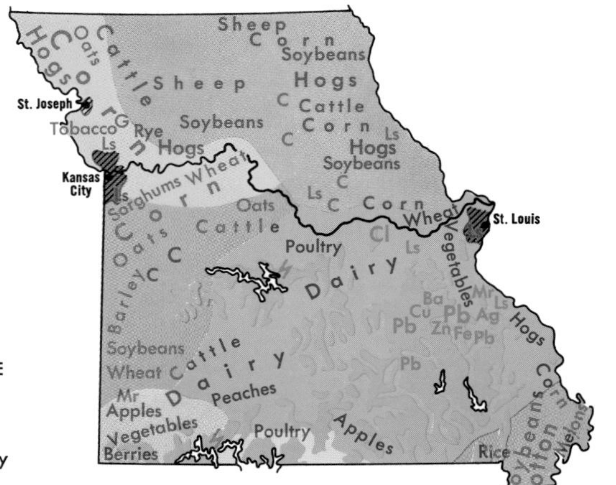

DOMINANT LAND USE

- Cattle Feed, Hogs
- Livestock, Cash Grain, Dairy
- Pasture Livestock
- Specialized Cotton
- General Farming, Dairy, Livestock, Poultry
- General Farming, Livestock, Truck Farming, Cotton
- Fruit and Mixed Farming
- Forests
- Urban Areas

MAJOR MINERAL OCCURRENCES

- Ag Silver
- Ba Barite
- C Coal
- Cl Clay
- Cu Copper
- Fe Iron Ore
- G Natural Gas
- Ls Limestone
- Mr Marble
- Pb Lead
- Zn Zinc

Water Power — Major Industrial Areas

*64050 Independence⊙ 111,806...R5
63648 Irondale 349...............L7
†64801 Iron Gates 314...........C8
63650 Ironton⊙ 1,743.............L7
63755 Jackson⊙ 7,827............N8
64648 Jamesport 651.............E3
65046 Jamestown 317............G5
64755 Jasper 1,012...............D8
65101 Jefferson City (cap.)⊙
        33,619....................H5
63136 Jennings 17,026..........R2
63351 Jonesburg 614............K5
64801 Joplin 39,023.............C8
        Joplin‡ 127,513...........C8
†63645 Junction City 238.......M7
63645 Kahoka 2,101..............J2
*64101 Kansas City 448,159....P5
        Kansas City‡ 1,327,020....P5
64060 Kearney 1,433............D4
63758 Kelso 455.................O8
63857 Kennett⊙ 10,145.........M10
65261 Keytesville⊙ 689.........G4
64649 Kidder 265................E3
65686 Kimberling City 1,285.....F9
64463 King City 1,063...........D2
64650 Kingston⊙ 280............E3
64061 Kingsville 365.............D5
63140 Kinloch 4,455.............P2
63501 Kirksville⊙ 17,167.......H2
63122 Kirkwood 27,987..........O3
65336 Knob Noster 2,040........E5
63446 Knox City 281.............H2
63447 La Belle 845...............J2
64651 Laclede 445...............F3
63352 Laddonia 726.............J4
†63124 Ladue 9,376..............P3
63448 La Grange 1,211..........K2
64063 Lake Lotawana 1,875......R6
65049 Lake Ozark 427...........G6
†63336 Lake Saint Louis 3,843....N2
63101 Lakeshire 1,593...........P4
†64015 Lake Tapawingo 925.....R6
†64152 Lake Waukomis 1,050....P5
64034 Lake Winnebago 681.....R6
64759 Lamar⊙ 4,053............D8
65337 La Monte 1,054...........F5
64847 Lanagan 440..............C9
63548 Lancaster⊙ 855...........H1
63549 La Plata 1,423.............H2
64652 Laredo 340................E2
64760 Latour 84..................D5
64062 Lawson 1,688.............D4
†63640 Leadington 238..........M7
63653 Leadwood 1,371..........L7
65535 Leasburg 304.............K6
65536 Lebanon⊙ 9,507..........G7
64063 Lee's Summit 28,741......R6
64761 Leeton 604................E5
63125 Lemay 35,424.............R4
64066 Levasy 235................S5
63452 Lewistown 502............J2
64067 Lexington⊙ 5,063.........E4
64762 Liberal 701................D7
64068 Liberty⊙ 16,251.........R5
65542 Licking 1,272..............J8
63862 Lilbourn 1,463.............N9
65338 Lincoln 819................F6
65051 Linn⊙ 1,211...............J5
65052 Linn Creek 242............G6
64653 Linneus⊙ 421.............F3
65682 Lockwood 971.............E8
64070 Lone Jack 420.............S6
63353 Louisiana 4,261...........K4
64763 Lowry City 676............E6

63762 Lutesville 865..............M8
63552 Macon⊙ 5,680.............H3
65263 Madison 656...............H4
64466 Maitland 415...............B2
63863 Malden 6,096..............M9
65339 Malta Bend 292............F4
63011 Manchester 6,191.........O3
65704 Mansfield 1,423............G8
63143 Maplewood 10,960........P3
63764 Marble Hill⊙ 601..........N8
64658 Marceline 2,938...........F3
65705 Marionville 1,920..........E8
65340 Marshall⊙ 12,781.........F4
65706 Marshfield⊙ 3,871........G8
63866 Marston 742................N9
63357 Marthasville 543...........L5
65264 Martinsburg 309...........J4
63043 Maryland Heights 5,676....O2
64468 Maryville⊙ 9,558..........C2
63857 Matthews 547.............N9
64469 Maysville⊙ 1,187.........D3
64071 Mayview 291..............E4
64659 Meadville 416..............F3
63555 Memphis⊙ 2,105..........H2
64660 Mendon 252...............F3
64661 Mercer 442................F2
65058 Meta 336..................H6
65265 Mexico⊙ 12,276..........J4
63359 Middletown 268...........J4
63556 Milan⊙ 1,947.............F2
65707 Miller 795..................E8
63952 Mill Spring 257............L8
64769 Mindenmines 318.........C8
†63801 Miner 1,182..............N9
63660 Mineral Point 358.........L7
64072 Missouri City 343..........R5
65270 Moberly 13,418...........G4
65059 Mokane 293...............J5
†63101 Moline Acres 2,774.......R2
65708 Monett 6,148..............C9
63456 Monroe City 2,557.........J3
63361 Montgomery City⊙ 2,101..K5
63457 Monticello⊙ 134..........J2
64770 Montrose 498.............E6
63868 Morehouse 1,220.........N9
63767 Morley 745.................N8
65710 Morrisville 331.............F8
64073 Mosby 284.................R4
63362 Moscow Mills 484.........K5
64470 Mound City 1,447.........B2
65711 Mountain Grove 3,974....H8
65548 Mountain View 1,664......J8
64665 Mount Moriah 162.........E2
65712 Mount Vernon⊙ 3,341....E8
†63088 Murphy 8,121..............P3
64074 Napoleon 271.............E4
63953 Naylor 602.................L9
63954 Neelyville 474.............M9
65347 Nelson 248................F4
64850 Neosho⊙ 9,493..........D9
64772 Nevada⊙ 9,044...........D7
63063 New Bloomfield 519.......J5
65550 Newburg 743..............J7
63558 New Cambria 246.........G3
63363 New Florence 731.........K5
65274 New Franklin 1,228.......G4
†63736 New Hamburg 358........O8
64471 New Hampton 358........D2
63068 New Haven 1,581.........K5
63459 New London 1,161.........K3
63869 New Madrid⊙ 3,204.......O9
65713 Niangua 376...............G8

65714 Nixa 2,662................F8
64854 Noel 1,501................D9
63621 Norborne 931.............E4
64668 Normandy 5,174..........R2
64116 North Kansas City 4,507....P5
†64152 Northmoor 506...........P5
65717 Norwood 391.............H8
63559 Novinger 626..............G2
64075 Oak Grove 4,067.........S6
65080 Oak Grove 386...........K6
†63101 Oakland 1,728...........P3
63769 Oak Ridge 252............N7
†64116 Oakview 497.............P5
63401 Oakwood 227............P5
64076 Odessa 3,088.............E5
63366 O'Fallon 8,677............L5
63369 Old Monroe 272..........L5
63124 Olivette 7,985.............O2
63771 Oran 1,266................N8
64473 Oregon⊙ 901.............C4
64855 Orrick 922.................E4
64077 Orrick 922.................E4
65065 Osage Beach 1,992.......G6
64474 Osborn 381................D3
64776 Osceola⊙ 841............E6
65548 Otterville 472..............G5
63114 Overland 19,620.........O2
65066 Owensville 2,241.........K6
65721 Ozark⊙ 2,980............F8
†63101 Pagedale 4,542..........P2
63461 Palmyra⊙ 3,469..........J3
65275 Paris⊙ 1,598.............J4
64152 Parkville 1,997............O5
64130 Parkway 254..............L6
63870 Parma 1,081..............N9
64670 Pattonsburg 502.........D2
64078 Peculiar 1,571............D5
63462 Perry 836..................J4
63069 Pacific 4,410...............L5
†63775 Perryville⊙ 7,343........N7
63070 Pevely 2,732...............M6
63957 Piedmont 2,359...........L8
65723 Pierce City 1,391..........E8
63276 Pilot Grove 745............F5
63663 Pilot Knob 722.............L7
†63120 Pine Lawn 6,662.........R2
64079 Platte City⊙ 2,114.......C4
64152 Platte Woods 467.........O5
64477 Plattsburg⊙ 2,095........D3
64080 Pleasant Hill 3,301.......D5
65725 Pleasant Hope 354........F7
†64836 Pleasant Valley 1,545.....R5
64671 Polo 583...................D3
63901 Poplar Bluff⊙ 17,139....L9
63373 Portage Des Sioux 488....M5
63873 Portageville 3,470.........N10
63664 Potosi⊙ 2,528............L7
65068 Prairie Home 279.........G5
64478 Princeton⊙ 1,264........E2
64857 Purcell 322.................D8
64078 Purdin 243.................F3
65734 Purdy 928.................E9
63960 Puxico 833................M9
63561 Queen City 783...........H2
65049 Qulin 549..................M9
†64101 Randolph 91..............P5
64479 Ravenwood 436..........C2
65555 Raymondville 388.........J8
64083 Raymore 3,154...........D5
64133 Raytown 31,759..........P6
65737 Reeds Spring 461.........F9

65738 Republic 4,485.............E8
64779 Rich Hill 1,471.............D6
65556 Richland 1,922............H7
64085 Richmond⊙ 5,499........D4
63117 Richmond Heights 11,516..P3
64481 Ridgeway 516.............D2
63874 Risco 446..................N9
63559 Rivermines 414............L7
64168 Riverside 3,206............O5
†63601 Riverview 3,367..........R2
65279 Rocheport 272............H5
65740 Rockaway Beach 292.....F9
†63119 Rock Hill 5,702...........P3
64482 Rock Port⊙ 1,511........B2
64780 Rockville 281..............D6
65742 Rogersville 741............G8
65401 Rolla⊙ 13,303............J7
63091 Rosebud 326..............K6
64483 Rosendale 223...........C3
65074 Russellville 667............H6
64864 Saginaw 293..............C8

63074 Saint Ann 15,523..........O2
63301 Saint Charles⊙ 37,379...N1
63077 Saint Clair 3,485..........K6
63670 Sainte Genevieve⊙ 4,481..M6
65075 Saint Elizabeth 312........H6
†63101 Saint George 1,545.......P4
65559 Saint James 3,328.........J6
63114 Saint John 7,854...........P2
*64501 Saint Joseph⊙ 76,691....C3
        Saint Joseph‡ 101,868....C3
*63101 Saint Louis⊙ 453,085....R3
        Saint Louis‡ 2,355,276...R3
†65101 Saint Martins 739.........H5
63673 Saint Marys 565............M7
63366 Saint Paul 561..............L5
65583 Saint Peters 15,700........N1
65560 Saint Robert 1,735.........H7
65281 Salem⊙ 4,454.............J7
65281 Salisbury 1,975............G4
63126 Sappington 11,388........O4
64862 Sarcoxie 1,381............D8
64485 Savannah⊙ 4,184.........C3

64783 Schell City 327............D6
63780 Scott City 3,262...........O8
65301 Sedalia⊙ 20,927.........F5
65745 Seligman 508.............D9
63876 Senath 1,728..............M10
64865 Seneca 1,633.............C9
65746 Seymour 1,535...........G8
65329 Shelbina 2,169............H3
63469 Shelbyville⊙ 645..........H3
64784 Sheldon 491..............D7
†63101 Shrewsbury 5,077........P3
63801 Sibley 382.................S5
63801 Sikeston 17,431...........N9
63377 Silex 287...................K4
64487 Skidmore 437.............B2
65349 Slater 2,492...............G4
63369 Smithton 559..............F5
64089 Smithville 1,873............D4
64863 South West City 516.......D9
†63138 Spanish Lake 20,632.......R1
65753 Sparta 743.................F9
64679 Spickard 389..............F2

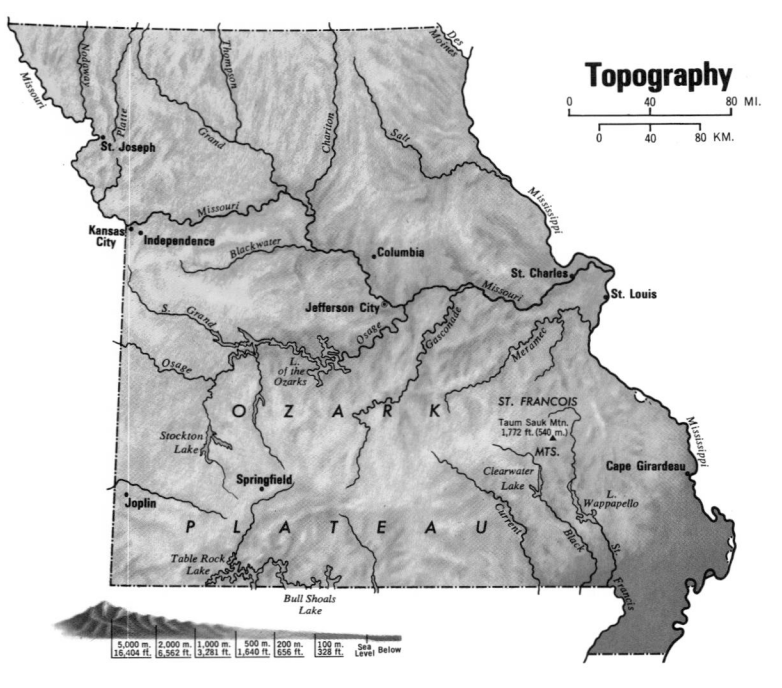

Topography

0   40   80 MI.
0   40   80 KM.

5,000 m. 2,000 m. 1,000 m. 500 m. 100 m. Sea
16,404 ft. 6,562 ft. 3,281 ft. 1,640 ft. 656 ft. Level
                                                Below

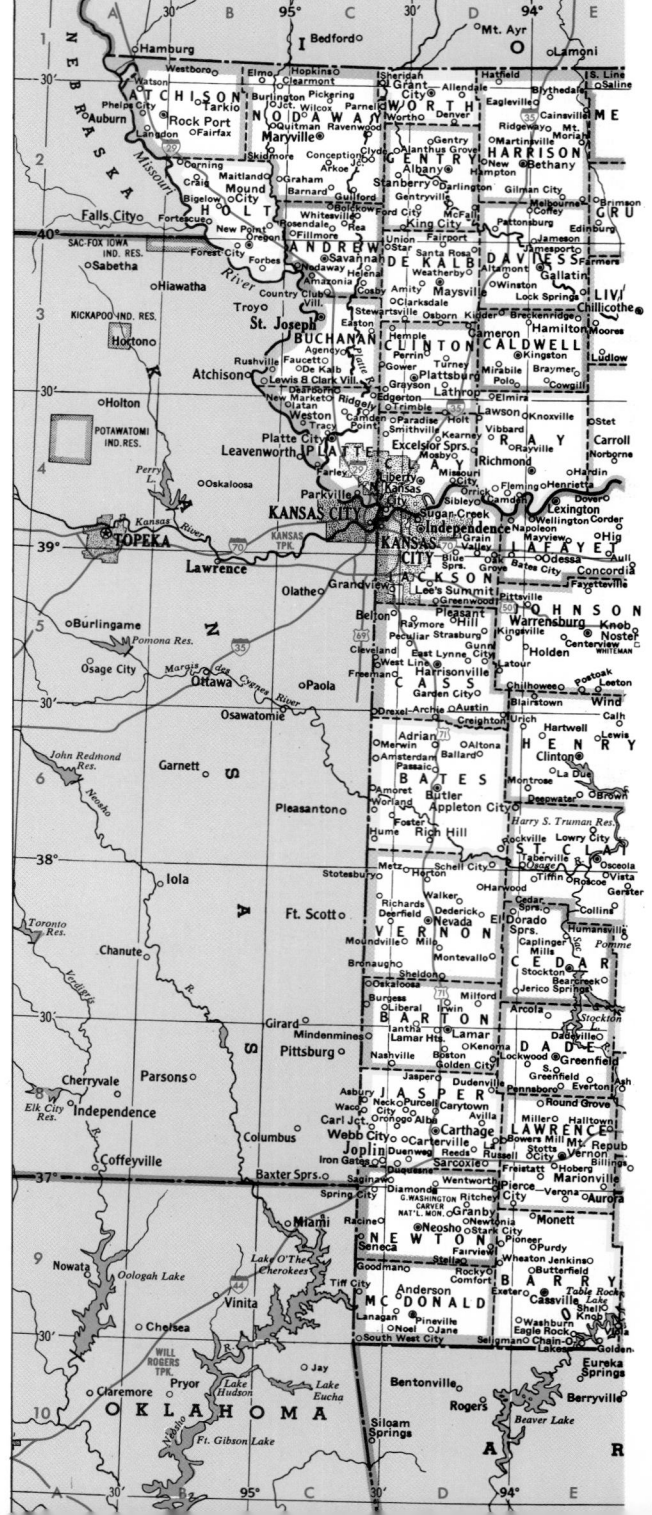

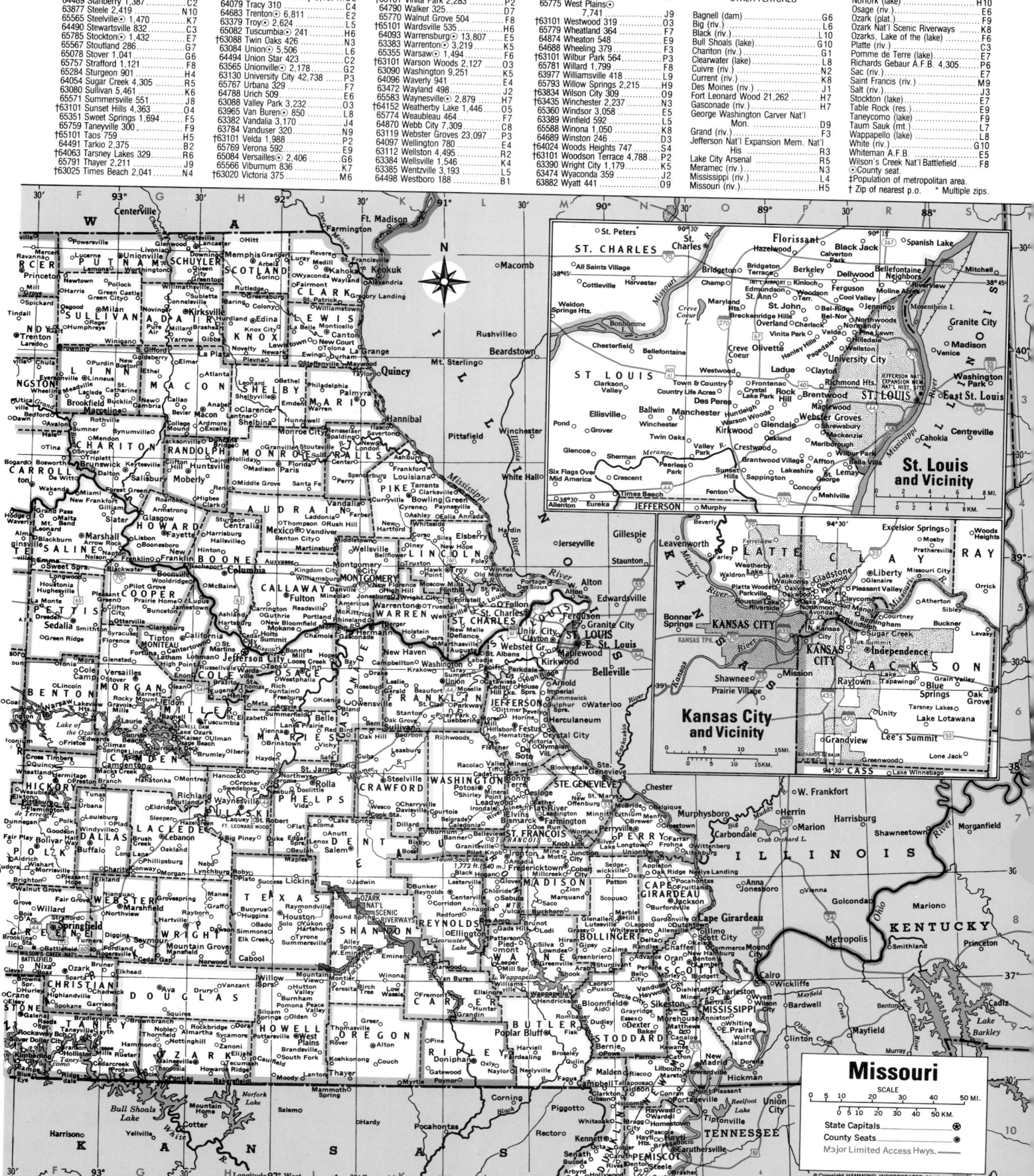

Agriculture, Industry and Resources

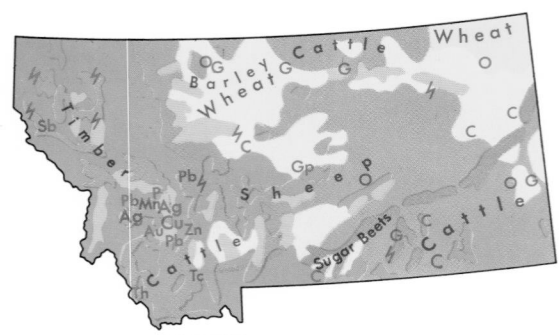

DOMINANT LAND USE

- Specialized Wheat
- Wheat, Range Livestock
- General Farming, Dairy, Range Livestock
- General Farming, Livestock, Special Crops
- Range Livestock
- Sugar Beets, Beans, Livestock, General Farming
- Forests

MAJOR MINERAL OCCURRENCES

Ag	Silver	O	Petroleum
Au	Gold	P	Phosphates
C	Coal	Pb	Lead
Cu	Copper	Sb	Antimony
G	Natural Gas	Tc	Talc
Gp	Gypsum	Th	Thorium
Mn	Manganese	Zn	Zinc

⚡ Water Power

COUNTIES

Beaverhead 8,186 ....C5
Big Horn 11,096 ....J5
Blaine 6,999 ....G2
Broadwater 3,267 ....E4
Carbon 8,099 ....G5
Carter 1,799 ....M5
Cascade 80,696 ....E3
Chouteau 6,092 ....F3
Custer 13,109 ....L4
Daniels 2,835 ....L2
Dawson 11,805 ....M3
Deer Lodge 12,518 ....C5
Fallon 3,763 ....M4
Fergus 13,076 ....F2
Flathead 51,966 ....B2
Gallatin 42,865 ....E5
Garfield 1,656 ....J3
Glacier 10,628 ....C2
Golden Valley 1,026 ....G4
Granite 2,700 ....C4
Hill 17,985 ....F2
Jefferson 7,029 ....D4
Judith Basin 2,646 ....F4
Lake 19,056 ....B3
Lewis and Clark 43,039 ....D3
Liberty 2,329 ....E2
Lincoln 17,752 ....A2
Madison 5,448 ....D5
McCone 2,702 ....L3
Meagher 2,154 ....F4
Mineral 3,675 ....B3
Missoula 76,016 ....C3
Musselshell 4,428 ....H4
Park 12,869 ....F5
Petroleum 655 ....H3
Phillips 5,367 ....J2
Pondera 6,731 ....D2
Powder River 2,520 ....L5
Powell 6,958 ....D4
Prairie 1,836 ....L4
Ravalli 22,493 ....B4
Richland 12,243 ....M3
Roosevelt 10,467 ....L2
Rosebud 9,899 ....K4
Sanders 8,675 ....A3
Sheridan 5,414 ....M2

Silver Bow 38,092 ....D5
Stillwater 5,598 ....G5
Sweet Grass 3,216 ....G5
Teton 6,491 ....D3
Toole 5,559 ....E2
Treasure 981 ....K2
Valley 10,250 ....J4
Wheatland 2,359 ....G4
Wibaux 1,476 ....M4
Yellowstone 108,035 ....H4
Yellowstone Nat'l Park 275 ....F6

CITIES and TOWNS

Zip	Name/Pop.	Key
59001	Absarokee 830	G5
59820	Alberton 368	B3
59710	Alder 120	D5
59741	Amsterdam 130	E5
59711	Anaconda-Deer Lodge County⊙ 12,518	
59312	Angela 50	K4
59211	Antelope 83	M2
59821	Arlee 200	B3
59003	Ashland 600	K5
59410	Augusta 497	D3
59713	Avon 125	D4
59411	Babb 150	C2
59212	Bainville 245	M2
59313	Baker⊙ 2,354	M4
59006	Ballantine 380	H5
59725	Bannack 2	C5
59613	Basin 380	D4
59007	Bearcreek 61	G5
59008	Belfry 300	H5
59714	Belgrade 2,336	E5
59412	Belt 825	E3
59314	Biddle 28	L5
59910	Big Arm 250	B3
59911	Bigfork 1,080	C2
59520	Big Sandy 835	G2
59011	Big Timber⊙ 1,690	G5
59101	Billings‡ 66,842	H5
	Billings‡ 108,035	H5
59012	Birney 100	K5
59414	Black Eagle 1,500	E3

59415	Blackfoot 100	D2
59823	Bonner-West Riverside 1,742	C4
59632	Boulder⊙ 1,441	E4
59521	Box Elder 300	F2
59715	Bozeman⊙ 21,645	E5
59416	Brady 450	E2
59014	Bridger 724	H5
59317	Broadus⊙ 712	L5
59015	Broadview 120	H4
59213	Brockton 374	M2
59417	Browning 1,226	C2
59016	Busby 700	J5
59701	Butte-Silver Bow County⊙ 37,205	D5
59720	Cameron 150	E5
59633	Canyon Creek 100	D4
59347	Cartersville 115	K4
59421	Cascade 773	E3
59824	Charlo 250	B3
59522	Chester⊙ 963	E2
59523	Chinook⊙ 1,660	G2
59422	Choteau⊙ 1,798	D3
59215	Circle⊙ 931	L3
59634	Clancy 550	E4
59018	Clyde Park 283	F5
59351	Coalwood 2	L5
59322	Cohagen 12	K3
59323	Colstrip 1,476	K5
59912	Columbia Falls 3,112	B2
59019	Columbus⊙ 1,439	G5
59826	Condon 300	C3
59827	Conner 420	B5
59425	Conrad⊙ 3,074	D2
59020	Cooke City 120	G5
59913	Coram 450	C2
59828	Corvallis 500	C4
59217	Crane 163	M3
59022	Crow Agency 975	J5
59218	Culbertson 887	M2
59024	Custer 300	J4
59427	Cut Bank⊙ 3,688	D2
59829	Darby 581	B4
59914	Dayton 140	B3
59830	De Borgia 300	A3
59025	Decker 150	K5
59722	Deer Lodge⊙ 4,023	D4
59430	Denton 356	G3

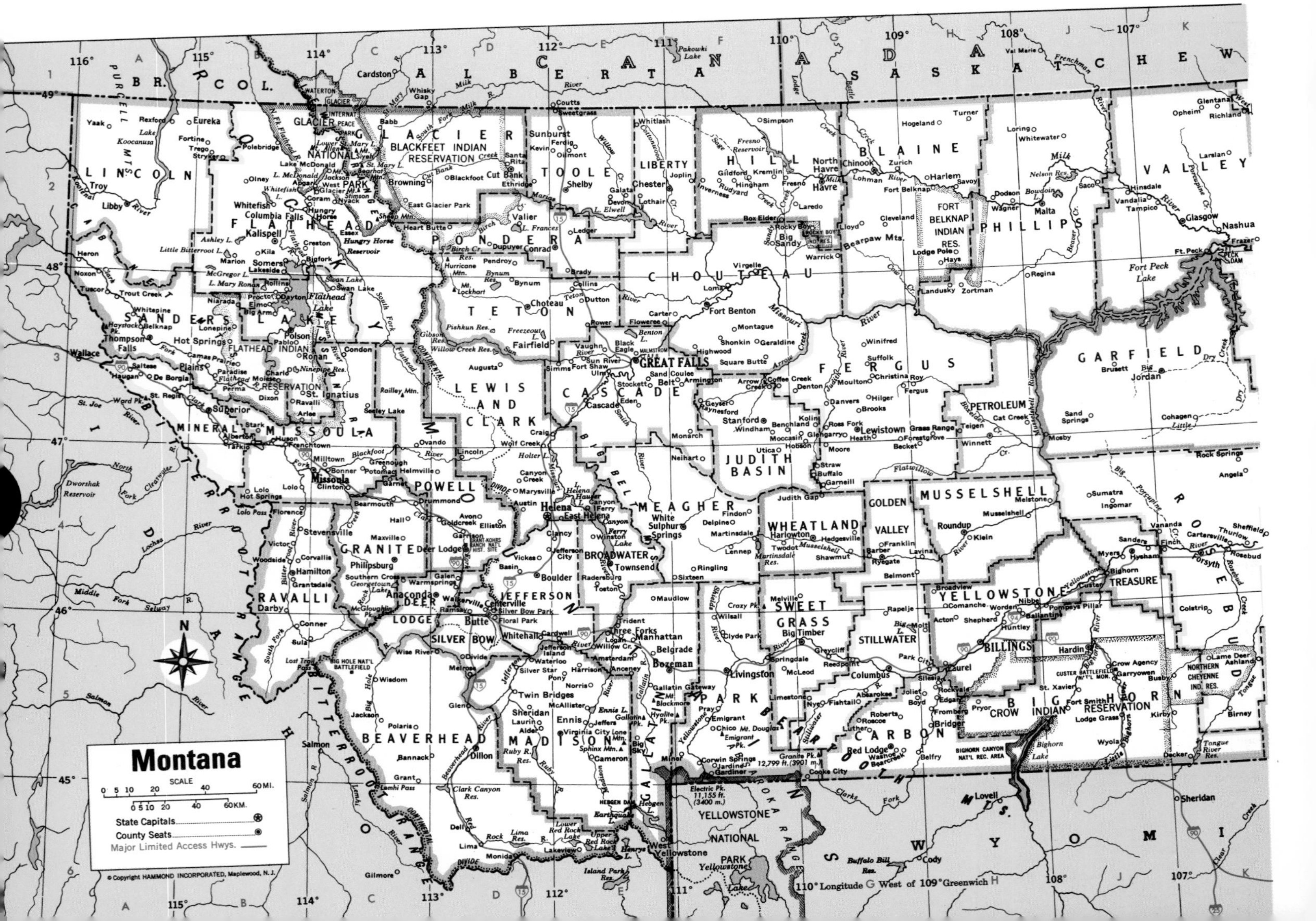

[Map: Montana]

Montana
SCALE
0 5 10   20   40   60 MI.
0 5 10 20 40   60 KM.

⊛ State Capitals
⊙ County Seats
— Major Limited Access Hwys.

© Copyright HAMMOND INCORPORATED, Maplewood, N.J.

Topography

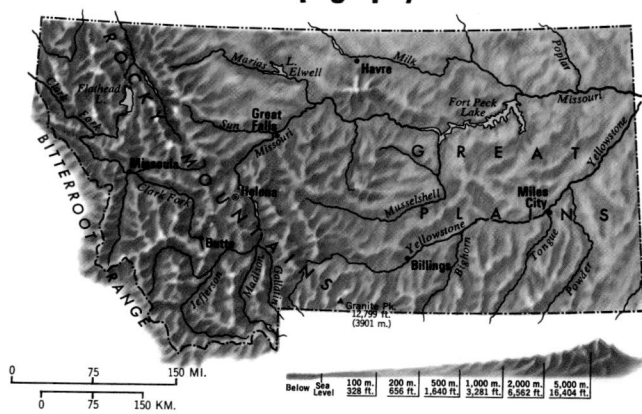

0   75   150 MI.

0   75   150 KM.

| Below Sea Level | 100 m. 328 ft. | 200 m. 656 ft. | 500 m. 1,640 ft. | 1,000 m. 3,281 ft. | 2,000 m. 6,562 ft. | 5,000 m. 16,404 ft. |

AREA 147,046 sq. mi. (380,849 sq. km.)
POPULATION 786,690
CAPITAL Helena
LARGEST CITY Billings
HIGHEST POINT Granite Pk. 12,799 ft. (3901 m.)
SETTLED IN 1809
ADMITTED TO UNION November 8, 1889
POPULAR NAME Treasure State; Big Sky Country
STATE FLOWER Bitterroot
STATE BIRD Western Meadowlark

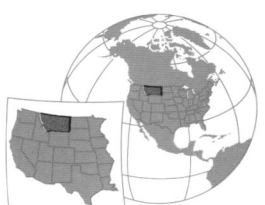

COUNTIES

Adams 30,656 F4
Antelope 8,675 F2
Arthur 513 C3
Banner 918 A3
Blaine 867 E3
Boone 7,391 F3
Box Butte 13,696 A2
Boyd 3,331 F2
Brown 4,377 E2
Buffalo 34,797 E4
Burt 8,813 H3
Butler 9,330 G3
Cass 20,297 H4
Cedar 11,375 G2
Chase 4,758 C4
Cherry 6,758 C2
Cheyenne 10,057 A3
Clay 8,106 F4
Colfax 9,890 G3
Cuming 11,664 H3
Custer 13,877 E3
Dakota 16,573 H2
Dawes 9,609 A2
Dawson 22,304 E4
Deuel 2,462 B3
Dixon 7,137 H2
Dodge 35,847 H3
Douglas 397,038 H3
Dundy 2,861 C4
Fillmore 7,920 G4
Franklin 4,377 F4
Frontier 3,647 D4
Furnas 6,486 E4
Gage 24,456 H4
Garden 2,802 B3
Garfield 2,363 F3
Gosper 2,140 E4
Grant 877 C3
Greeley 3,462 F3
Hall 47,690 F4
Hamilton 9,301 F4
Harlan 4,292 E4
Hayes 1,356 C4
Hitchcock 4,079 C4
Holt 13,552 F2
Hooker 990 C3
Howard 6,773 F3
Jefferson 9,817 G4
Johnson 5,285 H4
Kearney 7,053 F4
Keith 9,364 C3
Keya Paha 1,301 E2
Kimball 4,882 A3
Knox 11,457 G2
Lancaster 192,884 H4
Lincoln 36,455 D4
Logan 983 D3
Loup 859 E3
Madison 31,382 G3
McPherson 593 C3
Merrick 8,945 F3
Morrill 6,085 A3
Nance 4,740 F3
Nemaha 8,367 J4
Nuckolls 6,726 F4
Otoe 15,183 H4
Pawnee 3,937 H4
Perkins 3,637 C4
Phelps 9,769 E4
Pierce 8,481 G2
Platte 28,852 G3
Polk 6,320 G3
Red Willow 12,615 D4
Richardson 11,315 J4
Rock 2,383 E2
Saline 13,131 G4
Sarpy 86,015 H3
Saunders 18,716 H3
Scotts Bluff 38,344 A3
Seward 15,789 G4
Sheridan 7,544 B2
Sherman 4,226 F3
Sioux 1,845 A2
Stanton 6,549 G3
Thayer 7,582 G4
Thomas 973 D3
Thurston 7,186 H2
Valley 5,633 E3
Washington 15,508 H3
Wayne 9,858 G2
Webster 4,858 F4
Wheeler 1,060 F3
York 14,798 G4

CITIES and TOWNS

Zip *Name/Pop.* *Key*

68301 Adams 395 H4
69210 Ainsworth⊙ 2,256 D2
68620 Albion⊙ 1,997 F3
68810 Alda 601 F4
68710 Allen 390 H2
69301 Alliance⊙ 9,920 A2
68920 Alma⊙ 1,369 E4
68304 Alvo 144 H4
68812 Amherst 269 E4
68814 Ansley 644 E3
68922 Arapahoe 1,107 E4
68815 Arcadia 412 F3
68002 Arlington 1,117 H3
69120 Arnold 813 D3
69121 Arthur⊙ 124 C3
68003 Ashland 2,274 H3
68713 Atkinson 1,521 E2
68305 Auburn⊙ 3,482 J4
68818 Aurora⊙ 3,717 F4
68924 Axtell 602 E4
68004 Bancroft 552 H2
68622 Bartlett⊙ 144 F3
69020 Bartley 342 D4
68714 Bassett⊙ 1,009 E2
68715 Battle Creek 948 G3
69334 Bayard 1,435 A3
68310 Beatrice⊙ 12,891 H4
68926 Beaver City⊙ 775 E4
68313 Beaver Crossing 458 G4
68716 Beemer 853 H3
68005 Bellevue 21,813 J3
68624 Bellwood 407 G3
69021 Benkelman⊙ 1,235 C4
68317 Bennet 523 H4
68007 Bennington 631 H3
68927 Bertrand 775 E4
69122 Big Springs 505 B3
68928 Bladen 298 F4
68008 Blair⊙ 6,418 H3
68718 Bloomfield 1,393 G2
68930 Blue Hill 883 F4
68318 Blue Springs 521 H4
68010 Boys Town 622 H3
68319 Bradshaw 373 G4
69123 Brady 377 D3
68821 Brewster⊙ 46 D3
69336 Bridgeport⊙ 1,668 A3
68822 Broken Bow⊙ 3,979 E3
69127 Brule 438 C3
68322 Bruning 330 G4
68823 Burwell⊙ 1,383 E3
68722 Butte⊙ 529 F2
68824 Cairo 737 F3
68825 Callaway 579 D3
69022 Cambridge 1,206 D4
68932 Campbell 441 F4
68015 Cedar Bluffs 632 H3
68016 Cedar Creek 311 H3
68627 Cedar Rapids 447 F3
68724 Center⊙ 123 G2
68826 Central City⊙ 3,083 F3
68017 Ceresco 836 H3
69337 Chadron⊙ 5,933 B2
68725 Chambers 390 F2
68827 Chapman 349 F3
69129 Chappell⊙ 1,095 B3
68327 Chester 435 G4
68628 Clarks 445 G3
68629 Clarkson 817 G3
68328 Clatonia 273 H4
68933 Clay Center⊙ 962 F4
68726 Clearwater 409 F2
†69343 Clinton 80 B2
68727 Coleridge 673 G2
68601 Columbus⊙ 17,328 G3
68329 Cook 341 H4
68331 Cortland 403 H4
69130 Cozad 4,453 E4
69339 Crawford 1,315 A2
68729 Creighton 1,341 G2
68333 Crete 4,872 G4
68730 Crofton 948 G2
69024 Culbertson 767 C4
69025 Curtis 1,014 D4
68731 Dakota City⊙ 1,440 H2
69131 Dalton 345 B3
68831 Dannebrog 356 F3
68335 Davenport 445 G4
68632 David City⊙ 2,514 G3
68020 Decatur 723 H2
68340 Deshler 997 G4
68341 De Witt 642 G4
68342 Diller 311 H4
69133 Dix 275 A3
68633 Dodge 815 H3
68832 Doniphan 696 F4
68343 Dorchester 611 G4
68634 Duncan 410 G3
68347 Eagle 832 H4
68935 Edgar 705 F4
68636 Elgin 807 F3
68022 Elkhorn 1,344 H3
68836 Elm Creek 862 E4
68349 Elmwood 598 H4
68937 Elwood⊙ 716 E4
68733 Emerson 874 H2
68350 Endicott 198 G4
69028 Eustis 460 D4
68735 Ewing 520 F2
68351 Exeter 807 G4
68352 Fairbury⊙ 4,885 G4
68938 Fairfield 543 G4
68354 Fairmont 767 G4
68355 Falls City⊙ 5,374 J4
69029 Farnam 268 D4
68358 Firth 384 H4
68023 Fort Calhoun 641 J3
68939 Franklin⊙ 1,167 E4
68025 Fremont⊙ 23,979 H3
68359 Friend 1,079 G4
68638 Fullerton⊙ 1,506 F3
68361 Geneva⊙ 2,400 G4
68640 Genoa 1,090 G3
69341 Gering⊙ 7,760 A3
68840 Gibbon 1,531 F4
68841 Giltner 400 F4
68941 Glenvil 363 F4
69343 Gordon 2,167 B2
69138 Gothenburg 3,479 D4
68801 Grand Island⊙ 33,180 F4
69140 Grant⊙ 1,270 C4
68842 Greeley⊙ 597 F3
68366 Greenwood 587 H3
68367 Gresham 320 G3
68028 Gretna 1,609 H3
68942 Guide Rock 344 F4
68738 Hadar 286 G2
68368 Hallam 290 H4
68843 Hampton 419 G4
69346 Harrison⊙ 361 A2
68739 Hartington⊙ 1,730 G2
68944 Harvard 1,217 F4
68901 Hastings⊙ 23,045 F4
69032 Hayes Center⊙ 231 C4
69347 Hay Springs 794 B2
68370 Hebron⊙ 1,906 G4
69348 Hemingford 1,023 A2
68371 Henderson 1,072 G4
68029 Herman 340 H3
69143 Hershey 633 D3
68372 Hickman 687 H4
68947 Hildreth 394 E4
68948 Holbrook 297 D4
68949 Holdrege⊙ 5,624 E4
68030 Homer 564 H2
68031 Hooper 932 H3
68740 Hoskins 306 G2
68641 Howells 677 H3
68376 Humboldt 1,176 J4
68642 Humphrey 799 G3
69350 Hyannis⊙ 336 C3
69033 Imperial⊙ 1,941 C4
69034 Indianola 856 D4
68743 Jackson 287 H2
68378 Johnson 341 J4
68955 Juniata 703 F4
68847 Kearney⊙ 21,158 E4
68956 Kenesaw 854 F4
68034 Kennard 372 H3
69145 Kimball⊙ 3,120 A3
69035 Lamar 60 C4
68745 Laurel 1,031 G2
†68046 La Vista 9,588 J3
68957 Lawrence 350 F4
68643 Leigh 509 G3
69147 Lewellen 368 B3
68850 Lexington⊙ 7,040 E4
*68501 Lincoln (cap.)⊙ 171,932 H4
Lincoln‡ 192,884 H4
68644 Lindsay 383 G3
69149 Lodgepole 413 B3
69217 Long Pine 521 E2
68958 Loomis 447 E4
68037 Louisville 1,022 H3
68853 Loup City⊙ 1,368 E3
69352 Lyman 551 A3
68746 Lynch 357 F2
68038 Lyons 1,214 H3
68748 Madison⊙ 1,950 G3
69150 Madrid 284 C4
68402 Malcolm 355 H4
68854 Marquette 303 G4
69151 Maxwell 410 D3
69038 Maywood 332 D4
69001 McCook⊙ 8,404 D4
68401 McCool Junction 404 G4
68041 Mead 506 H3
68752 Meadow Grove 400 G2
68856 Merna 389 E3
68405 Milford 2,108 H4
68406 Milligan 332 G4
69356 Minatare 969 A3
68959 Minden⊙ 2,939 F4
69357 Mitchell 1,956 A3
68647 Monroe 294 G3
69358 Morrill 1,097 A3
69152 Mullen⊙ 720 C2
68409 Murray 465 J4
68410 Nebraska City⊙ 7,127 J4
68413 Nehawka 270 H4
68756 Neligh⊙ 1,893 G2
68961 Nelson⊙ 733 F4
68757 Newcastle 348 H2
68758 Newman Grove 930 G3
68760 Niobrara 419 G2
68962 Nora 24 G4
68701 Norfolk 19,449 G2
68649 North Bend 1,368 H3
68859 North Loup 405 F3
69101 North Platte⊙ 24,509 D3
68761 Oakdale 410 F2
68045 Oakland 1,393 H3
68415 Odell 322 H4
69153 Ogallala⊙ 5,638 C3
*68101 Omaha⊙ 313,911 J3
Omaha‡ 570,399 J3
68763 O'Neill⊙ 4,049 F2
68764 Orchard 482 F2
68862 Ord⊙ 2,658 F3
68966 Orleans 527 E4
68651 Osceola⊙ 975 G3
69154 Oshkosh⊙ 1,057 B3
68765 Osmond 871 G2
68863 Overton 633 E4
68967 Oxford 1,109 E4
69040 Palisade 401 C4
68864 Palmer 487 F3
68418 Palmyra 512 H4
68046 Papillion⊙ 6,399 J3
68420 Pawnee City⊙ 1,156 H4
69155 Paxton 568 C3
68047 Pender⊙ 1,318 H2
68421 Peru 998 J4
68652 Petersburg 381 G3
68865 Phillips 405 F4
68767 Pierce⊙ 1,535 G2
68768 Pilger 400 G2
68769 Plainview 1,483 G2
68653 Platte Center 367 G3
68048 Plattsmouth⊙ 6,295 J3
68866 Pleasanton 349 E4
68424 Plymouth 506 G4
68654 Polk 440 G3
68770 Ponca⊙ 1,057 H2
68867 Poole F4
69156 Potter 369 A3
68050 Prague 285 H3
68127 Ralston 5,143 J3
68771 Randolph 1,106 G2
68869 Ravenna 1,296 F4
68970 Red Cloud⊙ 1,300 F4
68658 Rising City 392 G3
69360 Rushville⊙ 1,217 B2
68660 Saint Edward 891 G3
68873 Saint Paul⊙ 2,094 F3
†68760 Santee 388 G2
68874 Sargent 828 E3
68661 Schuyler⊙ 4,151 G3
68875 Scotia 349 F3
69361 Scottsbluff 14,156 A3
68057 Scribner 1,011 H3
68434 Seward⊙ 5,713 H4
68662 Shelby 724 G3
68876 Shelton 1,046 F4
68436 Shickley 413 G4
69162 Sidney⊙ 6,010 B3
68663 Silver Creek 496 G3
68664 Snyder 387 H3
68776 South Sioux City 9,339 H2
68665 Spalding 645 F3
68777 Spencer 596 F2
68059 Springfield 782 H3
68778 Springview⊙ 326 E2
68779 Stanton⊙ 1,603 G3
68439 Staplehurst 306 G4
69163 Stapleton⊙ 340 D3
68442 Stella 289 J4
68443 Sterling 526 H4
69042 Stockville⊙ 45 D4
69043 Stratton 499 C4
68666 Stromsburg 1,290 G3
68780 Stuart 641 E2
68978 Superior 2,502 F4
69165 Sutherland 1,238 C3
68979 Sutton 1,416 G4
68446 Syracuse 1,638 H4
68447 Table Rock 393 H4

Agriculture, Industry and Resources

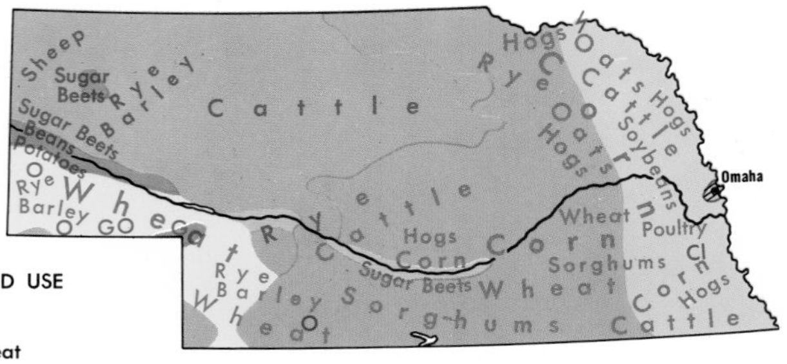

DOMINANT LAND USE

Specialized Wheat
Cattle Feed, Hogs
Livestock, Cash Grain
General Farming, Livestock, Special Crops
Sugar Beets, Dry Beans, Livestock, General Farming
Range Livestock

MAJOR MINERAL OCCURRENCES

Cl Clay
G Natural Gas
O Petroleum

Water Power
Major Industrial Areas

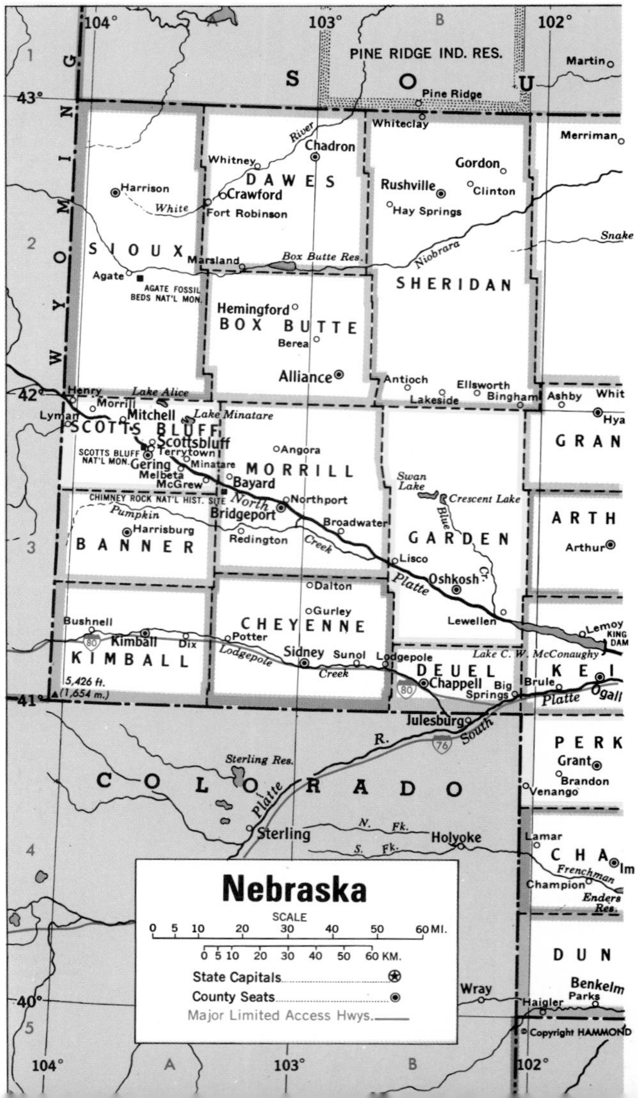

AREA 77,355 sq. mi. (200,349 sq. km.)
POPULATION 1,569,825
CAPITAL Lincoln
LARGEST CITY Omaha
HIGHEST POINT (Kimball Co.) 5,246 ft. (1654 m.)
SETTLED IN 1847
ADMITTED TO UNION March 1, 1867
POPULAR NAME Cornhusker State
STATE FLOWER Goldenrod
STATE BIRD Western Meadowlark

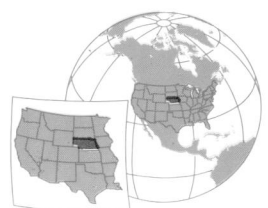

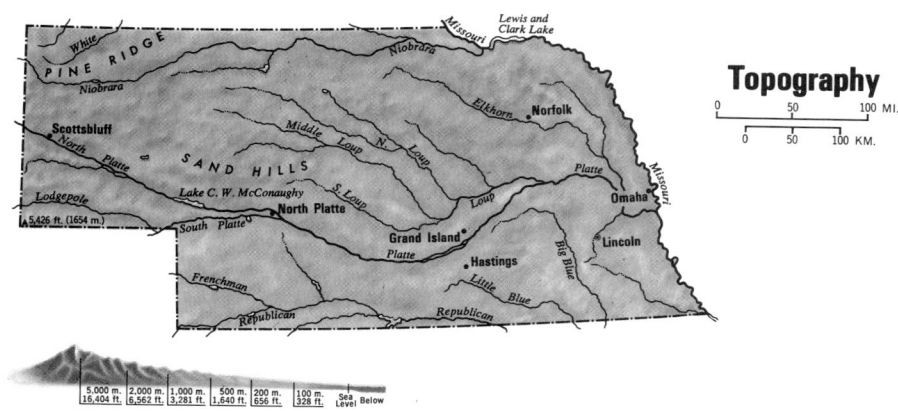

Topography

0   50   100 MI.
0   50   100 KM.

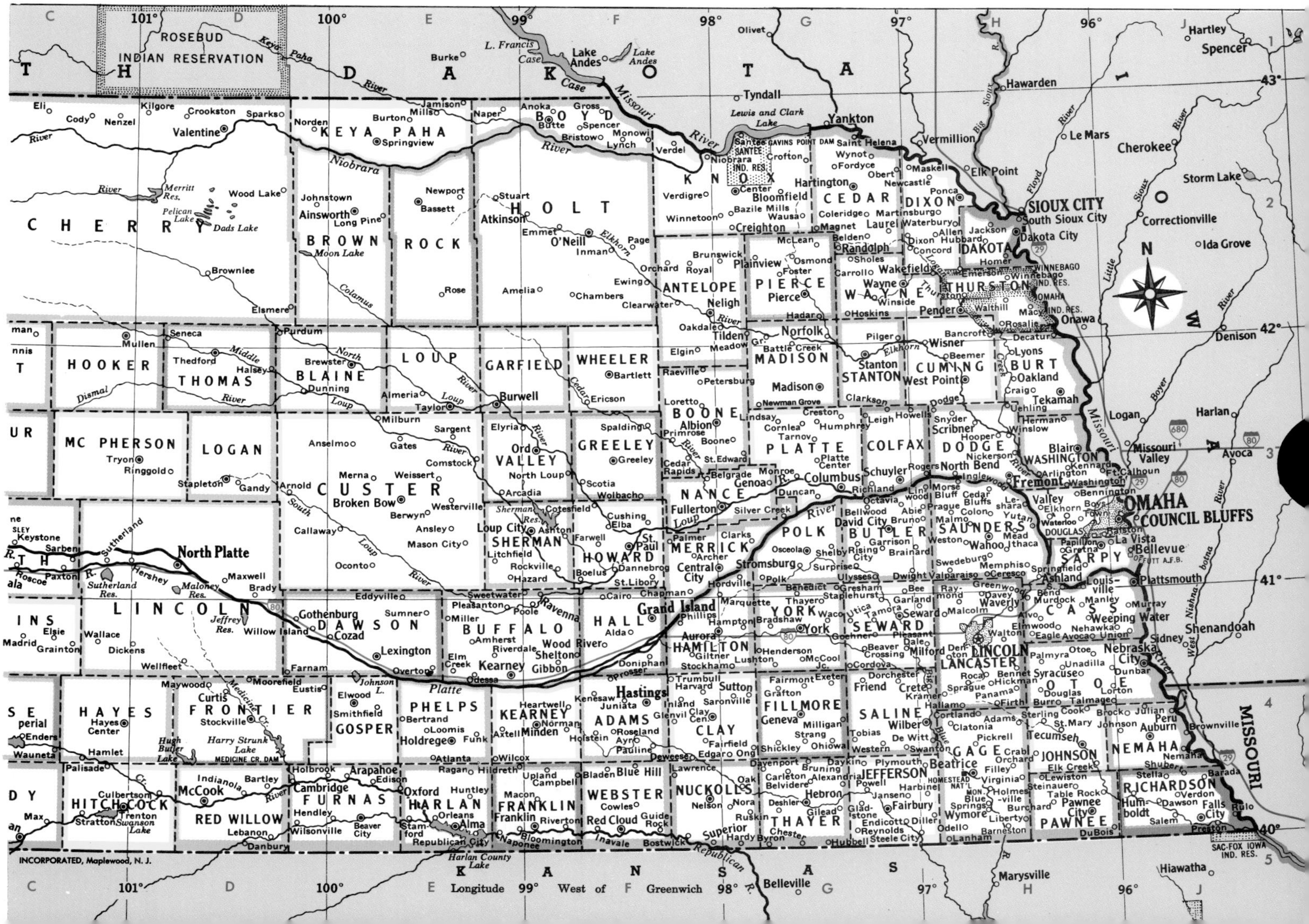

5,000 m.	2,000 m.	1,000 m.	500 m.	200 m.	100 m.	Sea
16,404 ft.	6,562 ft.	3,281 ft.	1,640 ft.	656 ft.	328 ft.	Level Below

INCORPORATED, Maplewood, N.J.

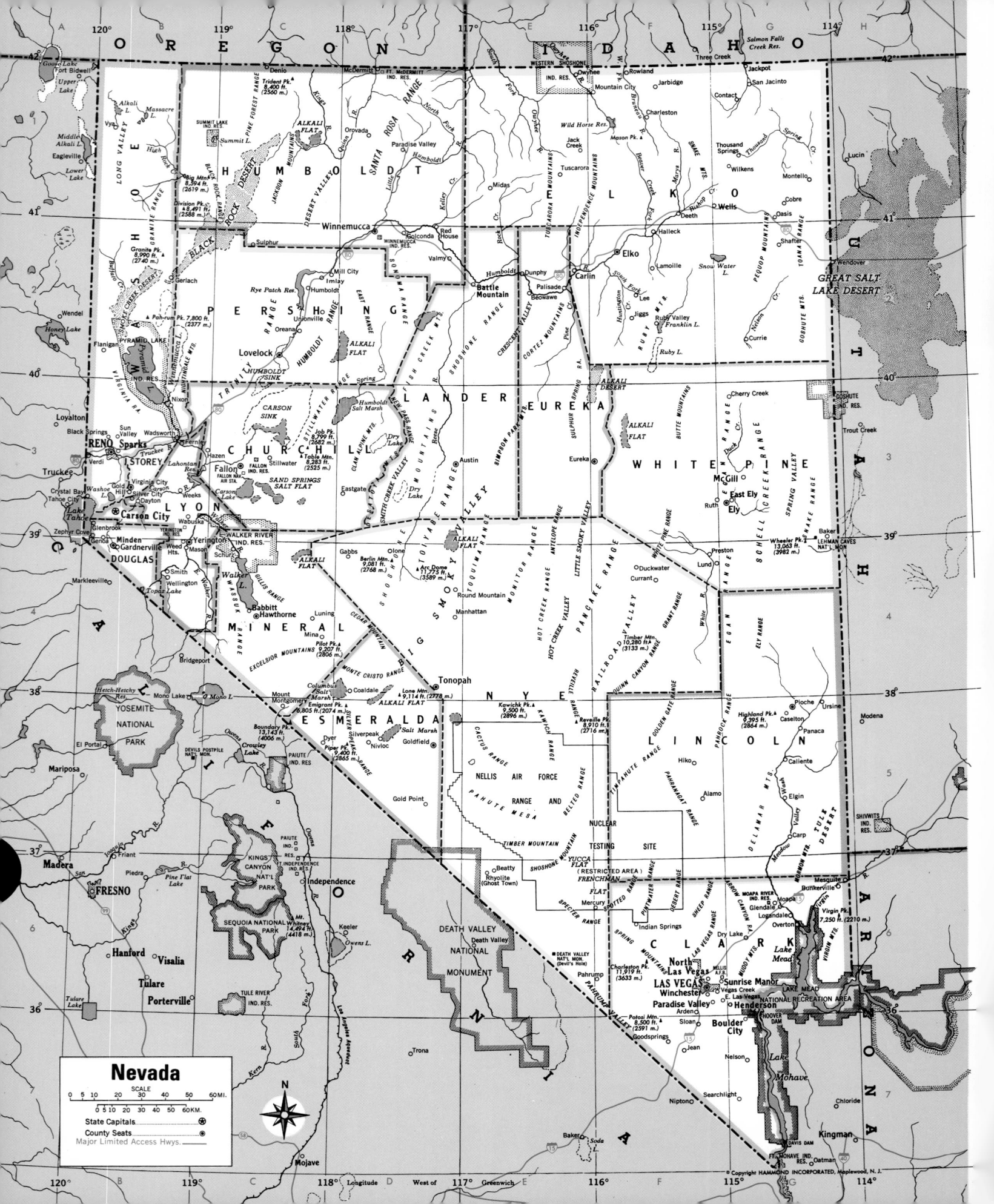

Nevada

SCALE
0 5 10 20 30 40 50 60 MI.
0 5 10 20 30 40 50 60 KM.

State Capitals........................⊛
County Seats...........................◉
Major Limited Access Hwys._____

© Copyright HAMMOND INCORPORATED, Maplewood, N. J.

AREA 110,561 sq. mi. (286,353 sq. km.)
POPULATION 800,493
CAPITAL Carson City
LARGEST CITY Las Vegas
HIGHEST POINT Boundary Pk. 13,143 ft. (4006 m.)
SETTLED IN 1850
ADMITTED TO UNION October 31, 1864
POPULAR NAME Silver State; Sagebrush State
STATE FLOWER Sagebrush
STATE BIRD Mountain Bluebird

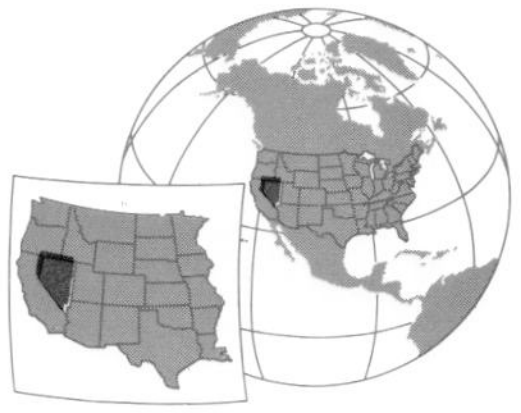

Agriculture, Industry and Resources

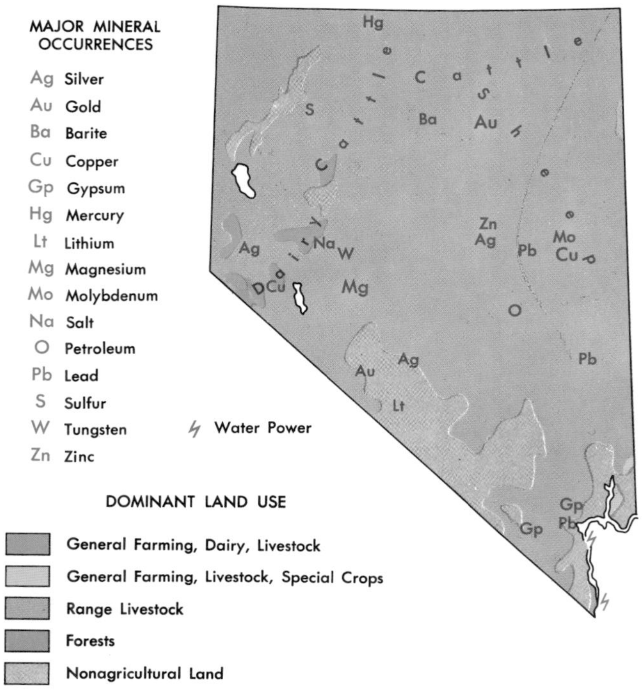
MAJOR MINERAL OCCURRENCES
Ag Silver
Au Gold
Ba Barite
Cu Copper
Gp Gypsum
Hg Mercury
Lt Lithium
Mg Magnesium
Mo Molybdenum
Na Salt
O Petroleum
Pb Lead
S Sulfur
W Tungsten
Zn Zinc
Water Power
DOMINANT LAND USE
General Farming, Dairy, Livestock
General Farming, Livestock, Special Crops
Range Livestock
Forests
Nonagricultural Land
Cattle
Sheep
Dairy Cattle

Topography

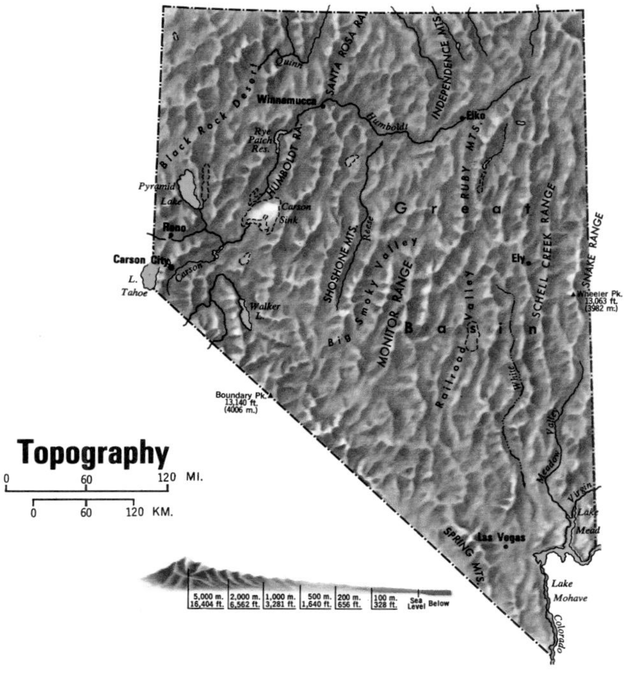
Black Rock Desert
Winnemucca
SANTA ROSA RA.
INDEPENDENCE MTS.
Humboldt
Elko
RUBY MTS.
Rye Patch Res.
HUMBOLDT RA.
Pyramid Lake
Carson Sink
Reno
Carson City
L. Tahoe
Carson
Walker L.
SHOSHONE MTS.
Great Basin
Big Smoky Valley
MONITOR RANGE
Railroad Valley
SCHELL CREEK RANGE
SNAKE RANGE
Ely
Wheeler Pk. 13,063 ft. (3982 m.)
Boundary Pk. 13,140 ft. (4006 m.)
Las Vegas
SPRING MTS.
Lake Mead
Lake Mohave
Colorado
Virgin
0 60 120 MI.
0 60 120 KM.
5,000 m. 16,404 ft.
2,000 m. 6,562 ft.
1,000 m. 3,281 ft.
500 m. 1,640 ft.
200 m. 656 ft.
100 m. 328 ft.
Sea Level
Below

COUNTIES

Carson City (city) 32,022 B 3
Churchill 13,917 C 3
Clark 463,087 F 6
Douglas 19,421 B 4
Elko 17,269 F 1
Esmeralda 777 D 5
Eureka 1,198 E 3
Humboldt 9,434 C 1
Lander 4,076 D 3
Lincoln 3,732 F 5
Lyon 13,594 B 3
Mineral 6,217 C 4
Nye 9,048 E 4
Pershing 3,408 C 2
Storey 1,503 B 3
Washoe 193,623 B 2
White Pine 8,167 F 3

CITIES and TOWNS

Zip	Name/Pop.	Key
89001	Alamo 300	F5
89310	Austin 300	E3
89416	Babbitt	C4
89311	Baker 140	G3
89820	Battle Mountain⊙ 2,749	E2
89003	Beatty 600	E6
89821	Beowawe 77	E2
†89508	Black Springs 180	B3
89005	Boulder City 9,590	G7
89007	Bunkerville 300	G6
89008	Caliente 982	G5
89822	Carlin 1,232	E2
†89008	Carp 30	G5
89701	Carson City (cap.) 32,022	B3
†89043	Caselton	G5
†89301	Cherry Creek 80	G3
89402	Crystal Bay 6,225	A3
89403	Dayton 350	B3
89823	Deeth 125	F1
89404	Denio 35	C1
89314	Duckwater 80	F4
89010	Dyer 56	C5
89315	East Ely	G3
89112	East Las Vegas 6,449	F6
89801	Elko⊙ 8,758	F2
89301	Ely⊙ 4,882	G3
89316	Eureka⊙ 300	E3
89406	Fallon⊙ 4,262	C3
89408	Fernley 750	B3
89409	Gabbs 811	D4
89410	Gardnerville 1,610	B4
89411	Genoa 254	B4
89412	Gerlach 400	B2
89413	Glenbrook 800	B3
89414	Golconda 275	D2
89013	Goldfield⊙ 500	D5
89019	Goodsprings 80	F7
89824	Halleck 68	F2
89415	Hawthorne⊙ 3,741	C4
89417	Hazen 76	C3
89015	Henderson 24,363	G6
89017	Hiko 210	F5
†89418	Humboldt 14	C2
89418	Imlay 250	C2
89018	Indian Springs 500	F6
†89310	Ione 20	D4
†89834	Jack Creek	E1
89825	Jackpot 400	G1
89826	Jarbidge 11	F1
89019	Jean 125	F7
89828	Lamoille 100	F2
*89101	Las Vegas⊙ 164,674	F6
	Las Vegas‡ 461,816	F6
89829	Lee 125	F2
89021	Logandale 410	G6
89419	Lovelock⊙ 1,680	C2
89317	Lund 380	F4
89420	Luning 90	C4
89022	Manhattan 93	E4
†89447	Mason 200	B4
89421	McDermitt 240	D1
89318	McGill 1,419	G3
89023	Mercury 900	E6
89024	Mesquite 500	G6
89422	Mina 450	C4
89423	Minden⊙ 1,029	B4
89025	Moapa 275	G6
89830	Montello 100	G1
89831	Mountain City 100	F1
†89046	Nelson 75	G7
89424	Nixon 400	B3
89030	North Las Vegas 42,739	F6
89425	Orovada 200	D1
89040	Overton 1,111	G6
89041	Pahrump 400	E6
89042	Panaca 650	G5
89119	Paradise Valley 84,818	F6
89426	Paradise Valley 115	D1
89043	Pioche⊙ 850	G5
*89501	Reno⊙ 100,756	B3
	Reno‡ 193,623	B3
†89003	Rhyolite (Ghost Town) 8	E6
89045	Round Mountain 400	E4
89833	Ruby Valley 150	F2
89319	Ruth 455	F3
89427	Schurz 800	C4
89046	Searchlight 500	F7
89428	Silver City 150	B3
89047	Silverpeak 100	D5
89430	Smith 200	B4
89431	Sparks 40,780	B3
†89406	Stillwater 150	C3
†89445	Sulphur	C2
†89110	Sunrise Manor 44,155	F6
†89431	Sun Valley 8,822	B3
†89835	Thousand Springs	G1
89049	Tonopah⊙ 1,952	D4
89834	Tuscarora 24	E1
89438	Valmy 200	D2
89121	Vegas Creek	G6
89440	Virginia City⊙ 750	B3
89442	Wadsworth 400	B3
89443	Weed Heights 8	B4
89444	Wellington 505	B4
89835	Wells 1,218	G1
†89109	Winchester 19,728	F6
89445	Winnemucca⊙ 4,140	D2
89447	Yerington⊙ 2,021	B4
89448	Zephyr Cove 1,316	A3

OTHER FEATURES

Alkali (lake) B1
Antelope (range) E3
Arc Dome (mt.) D4
Arrow Canyon (range) G6
Beaver Creek Fork, Humboldt (riv.) F1
Belted (range) E5
Berlin (mt.) D4
Big (mt.) B1
Big Smoky (valley) D4
Bishop (creek) F1
Black Rock (des.) B2
Black Rock (range) B1
Boundary (peak) C5
Buffalo (creek) B2
Butte (mts.) F3
Cactus (range) E5
Carson (lake) C3
Carson (riv.) B3
Carson (sink) C3
Cedar (mt.) D4
Charleston (peak) F6
Clan Alpine (mts.) D3
Columbus Salt (marsh) C4
Cortez (mts.) E2
Crescent (valley) E2
Davis (dam) G7
Death Valley Nat'l Mon. E6
Delamar (mts.) G5
Desatoya (mts.) D3
Desert (range) F6
Desert (valley) C1
Devil's Hole (Death Valley Nat'l Mon.) E6
Division (peak) B1
Duck (creek) G3
East (range) D2
East Walker (riv.) B4
Egan (range) G4
Ely (range) G4
Emigrant (peak) C5
Excelsior (mts.) C4
Fallon Ind. Res. C3
Fallon Nav. Air Sta. C3
Fish Creek (mts.) D2
Fort McDermitt Ind. Res. D1
Fort Mohave Ind. Res. G7
Franklin (lake) F2
Frenchman Flat (basin) F6
Gillis (range) C4
Golden Gate (range) F5
Goshute (mts.) G2
Goshute Ind. Res. G3
Granite (peak) B2
Granite (range) B2
Grant (range) F4
Great Basin Nat'l Pk. G 4
Great Salt Lake (des.) H 2
High Rock (creek) B 1
Highland (peak) G 5
Hoover (dam) G 7
Hot Creek (range) E 4
Hot Creek (valley) E 4
Humboldt (range) C 2
Humboldt (riv.) E 2
Humboldt (sink) C 2
Humboldt Salt (marsh) D 3
Huntington (creek) F 2
Independence (mts.) E 1
Jackson (mts.) C 1
Job (peak) C 3
Kawich (range) E 5
Kelley (creek) D 1
Kings (riv.) C 1
Lahontan (res.) B 3
Lake Mead Nat'l Rec. Area G 6
Las Vegas (range) F 6
Little Humboldt (riv.) D1
Little Smoky (valley) E4
Lone (mt.) D4
Long (valley) B1
Marys (riv.) F1
Mason (peak) F1
Massacre (lake) B1
Mead (lake) G6
Meadow Valley Wash (riv.) G5
Moapa River Ind. Res. G6
Mohave (lake) G7
Monitor (range) E4
Monte Cristo (range) D4
Mormon (mts.) G5
Muddy (mts.) G6
Nellis A.F.B. 7,476 F6
Nellis Air Force Range and Nuclear Testing Site E5
Nelson (creek) G2
New Pass (range) D3
Nightingale (mts.) B2
Owyhee (riv.) E1
Pahranagat (range) F5
Pahrock (range) F5
Pah-rum (peak) B2
Pahrump (valley) F6
Pahute (mesa) E5
Pancake (range) F4
Pequop (mts.) G2
Pilot (peak) C4
Pine (creek) E2
Pine Forest (range) C1
Pintwater (range) F6
Piper (peak) D5
Potosi (mt.) F7
Pyramid (lake) B2
Pyramid Lake Ind. Res. B2
Quinn (riv.) D1
Quinn Canyon (range) F4
Railroad (valley) F4
Reese (riv.) D3
Reveille (peak) E5
Reveille (range) E4
Ruby (lake) F2
Ruby (mts.) F2
Rye Patch (res.) C2
Sand Springs (salt flat) C3
Santa Rosa (range) D1
Schell Creek (range) G3
Sheep (range) F6
Shoshone (mt.) E6
Shoshone (mts.) D3
Shoshone (range) E2
Silver Peak (range) D5
Simpson Park (mts.) E3
Smith Creek (valley) D3
Smoke Creek (des.) B2
Snake (mts.) F1
Snake (range) G3
Snow Water (lake) G2
Sonoma (range) D2
Specter (range) E6
Spotted (range) F6
Spring (creek) D2
Spring (mts.) F6
Spring (valley) G3
Stillwater (range) C3
Sulphur Spring (range) E3
Summit (lake) C1
Summit Lake Ind. Res. B1
Table (mt.) C3
Tahoe (lake) B3
Thousand Spring (creek) G1
Timber (mt.) F4
Timber (mt.) E5
Timpahute (range) F5
Toana (range) G2
Toiyabe (range) D3
Topaz (lake) B4
Toquima (range) E4
Trident (peak) C1
Trinity (range) C2
Truckee (riv.) B3
Tule (des.) G5
Tuscarora (mts.) E1
Virgin (mts.) G6
Virgin (peak) G6
Virgin (riv.) G6
Virginia (range) B3
Walker (lake) C4
Walker (riv.) C3
Walker River Ind. Res. C3
Washoe (lake) B3
Wassuk (range) C4
Western Shoshone Ind. Res. E1
Wheeler (peak) G4
White (riv.) F4
White Pine (range) F3
Wild Horse (res.) E1
Winnemucca (lake) B2
Winnemucca Ind. Res. D2
Yerington Ind. Res. B3
Yucca Flat (basin) E6

⊙County seat.
‡Population of metropolitan area.
† Zip of nearest p.o.
* Multiple zips.

NEW HAMPSHIRE
AREA 9,279 sq. mi. (24,033 sq. km.)
POPULATION 920,610
CAPITAL Concord
LARGEST CITY Manchester
HIGHEST POINT Mt. Washington 6,288 ft. (1917 m.)
SETTLED IN 1623
ADMITTED TO UNION June 21, 1788
POPULAR NAME Granite State
STATE FLOWER Purple Lilac
STATE BIRD Purple Finch

VERMONT
AREA 9,614 sq. mi. (24,900 sq. km.)
POPULATION 511,456
CAPITAL Montpelier
LARGEST CITY Burlington
HIGHEST POINT Mt. Mansfield 4,393 ft. (1339 m.)
SETTLED IN 1764
ADMITTED TO UNION March 4, 1791
POPULAR NAME Green Mountain State
STATE FLOWER Red Clover
STATE BIRD Hermit Thrush

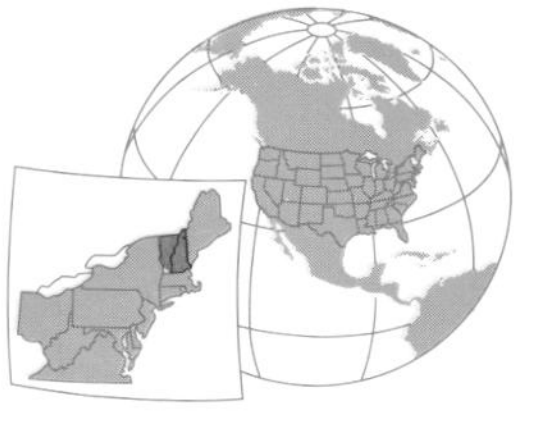

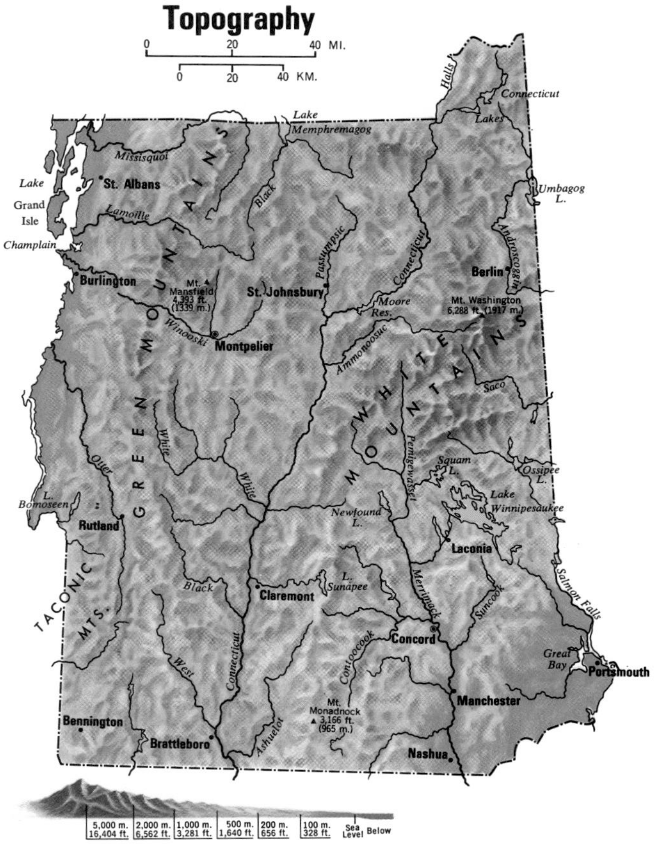
Topography
0 20 40 MI.
0 20 40 KM.
Lake Memphremagog
Missisquoi
St. Albans
Lake Champlain
Grand Isle
Lamoille
Burlington
Mt. Mansfield 4,393 ft. (1339 m.)
Winooski
Montpelier
St. Johnsbury
Passumpsic
Black
Connecticut Lakes
Halls
Umbagog L.
Androscoggin
Berlin
Mt. Washington 6,288 ft. (1917 m.)
Moore Res.
Ammonoosuc
Saco
WHITE MOUNTAINS
GREEN MOUNTAINS
White
Otter
L. Bomoseen
Rutland
Pemigewasset
Squam L.
Ossipee L.
Lake Winnipesaukee
Newfound L.
Laconia
Salmon Falls
Black
Claremont
L. Sunapee
Merrimack
Suncook
TACONIC MTS.
West
Connecticut
Contoocook
Concord
Great Bay
Portsmouth
Mt. Monadnock 3,166 ft. (965 m.)
Manchester
Bennington
Brattleboro
Ashuelot
Nashua
5,000 m. 16,404 ft.
2,000 m. 6,562 ft.
1,000 m. 3,281 ft.
500 m. 1,640 ft.
200 m. 656 ft.
100 m. 328 ft.
Sea Level
Below

NEW HAMPSHIRE

COUNTIES

Belknap 42,884 .... D4
Carroll 27,931 .... E4
Cheshire 62,116 .... C6
Coos 35,147 .... E2
Grafton 65,806 .... D4
Hillsborough 276,608 .... D6
Merrimack 98,302 .... D5
Rockingham 190,345 .... E5
Strafford 85,408 .... E5
Sullivan 36,063 .... C5

CITIES and TOWNS

Zip Name/Pop. Key

03601 Acworth○ 590 .... C5
†03864 Albany○ 383 .... E4
†03222 Alexandria○ 706 .... D4
†03275 Allenstown○ 4,398 .... E5
03602 Alstead○ 1,461 .... C5
03809 Alton○ 2,440 .... E5
03810 Alton Bay 500 .... E5
03031 Amherst○ 8,243 .... D6
03216 Andover○ 1,587 .... D5
03440 Antrim○ 2,208 .... D5
03440 Antrim 1,142 .... D5
03217 Ashland○ 1,807 .... D4
03217 Ashland 1,479 .... D4
03441 Ashuelot 810 .... C6
03811 Atkinson○ 4,397 .... E6
03032 Auburn○ 2,883 .... E5
03218 Barnstead○ 2,292 .... E5
†03825 Barrington○ 4,404 .... F5
03812 Bartlett○ 1,566 .... E3
03740 Bath○ 761 .... D3
03102 Bedford○ 9,481 .... D6
03220 Belmont○ 4,026 .... E5
03442 Bennington○ 890 .... D5
†03785 Benton○ 333 .... D3
03570 Berlin 13,084 .... E3
03574 Bethlehem○ 1,784 .... D3
03301 Boscawen○ 3,435 .... D5
03221 Bradford○ 1,115 .... D5
†03833 Brentwood○ 2,004 .... E6
†03222 Bridgewater○ 606 .... D4
03222 Bristol○ 2,198 .... D4
03222 Bristol 1,258 .... D4
†03872 Brookfield○ 385 .... E4
03033 Brookline○ 1,766 .... D6
03223 Campton○ 1,694 .... D4
03741 Canaan○ 2,456 .... C4
03034 Candia○ 2,989 .... E5
03224 Canterbury○ 1,410 .... D5
†03595 Carroll○ 647 .... D3
03813 Center Conway 558 .... E4
03226 Center Harbor○ 808 .... E4
03814 Center Ossipee 800 .... E4
03603 Charlestown○ 4,417 .... C5
03603 Charlestown 1,294 .... C5
†04037 Chatham○ 189 .... E3
03036 Chester○ 2,006 .... E6
03443 Chesterfield○ 2,561 .... C6
†03258 Chichester○ 1,492 .... E5
03817 Chocorua 575 .... E4
03743 Claremont 14,557 .... C5
†05902 Clarksville○ 262 .... E1
03576 Colebrook○ 2,459 .... E2
03576 Colebrook 1,131 .... E2
03301 Concord (cap.)⊙ 30,400 .... D5
03229 Contoocook 1,499 .... D5
03818 Conway○ 7,158 .... E4
03818 Conway 1,781 .... E4
03746 Cornish Flat 450 .... C4
†03753 Croydon○ 457 .... C5
†03598 Dalton○ 672 .... D3
03230 Danbury○ 680 .... D4
03819 Danville○ 1,318 .... E6
03037 Deerfield○ 1,979 .... E5
†03244 Deering○ 1,041 .... D5
03038 Derry○ 18,875 .... E6
03038 Derry 12,248 .... E6
†03266 Dorchester○ 244 .... D4
03820 Dover⊙ 22,377 .... F5
03444 Dublin○ 1,303 .... C6
†03588 Dummer○ 390 .... E2
†03301 Dunbarton○ 1,174 .... D5
03824 Durham○ 10,652 .... F5
03824 Durham 8,448 .... F5
03231 East Andover 500 .... D5
03826 East Hampstead 900 .... E6
03827 East Kingston○ 1,135 .... F6
†03580 Easton○ 124 .... D3
03446 East Swanzey 500 .... C6
03832 Eaton (Eaton Center)○ 256 .... E4
†03264 Ellsworth○ 53 .... D4
03748 Enfield○ 3,175 .... C4
03748 Enfield 1,581 .... C4
03042 Epping○ 3,460 .... E5
03042 Epping 1,384 .... E5
03234 Epsom○ 2,743 .... E5
03579 Errol○ 313 .... E2
03750 Etna 550 .... C4
03833 Exeter○ 11,024 .... F6
03833 Exeter⊙ 8,947 .... F6
03835 Farmington○ 4,630 .... E5
03835 Farmington 3,284 .... E5
03447 Fitzwilliam○ 1,795 .... C6
03043 Francestown○ 830 .... D6
03580 Franconia○ 743 .... D3
03235 Franklin 7,901 .... D5
03836 Freedom○ 720 .... E4
03044 Fremont○ 1,333 .... E6
†03246 Gilford○ 4,841 .... E4
03237 Gilmanton○ 1,941 .... E5
03448 Gilsum○ 652 .... C5
03838 Glen 600 .... E3
03045 Goffstown○ 11,315 .... D5
03581 Gorham○ 3,322 .... E3
03581 Gorham 2,180 .... E3
03752 Goshen○ 549 .... C5
03240 Grafton○ 739 .... D4
03753 Grantham○ 704 .... C5
03047 Greenfield○ 972 .... D6
03840 Greenland○ 2,129 .... F5
03048 Greenville○ 1,988 .... D6
03048 Greenville 1,447 .... D6
†03241 Groton○ 255 .... D4
03582 Groveton 1,389 .... D2
03754 Guild 500 .... C5
03841 Hampstead○ 3,785 .... E6
03842 Hampton○ 10,493 .... F6
03842 Hampton 6,779 .... F6
03844 Hampton Falls○ 1,372 .... F6
03449 Hancock○ 1,193 .... C6
03755 Hanover○ 9,119 .... C4
03755 Hanover 6,861 .... C4
03450 Harrisville○ 860 .... C6
03765 Haverhill○ 3,445 .... C3
03241 Hebron○ 349 .... D4
03242 Henniker○ 3,246 .... D5
03242 Henniker 1,538 .... D5
03243 Hill○ 736 .... D4
03244 Hillsboro○ 3,437 .... D5
03244 Hillsboro 1,797 .... D5
03451 Hinsdale○ 3,631 .... C6
03451 Hinsdale 1,546 .... C6
03245 Holderness○ 1,586 .... D4
03049 Hollis○ 4,679 .... D6
03106 Hooksett○ 7,303 .... E5
03106 Hooksett 1,868 .... E5
03301 Hopkinton○ 3,861 .... D5
03051 Hudson○ 14,022 .... E6
03051 Hudson 6,248 .... E6
03845 Intervale 725 .... E3
03846 Jackson○ 642 .... E3
03452 Jaffrey○ 4,349 .... C6
03452 Jaffrey 2,684 .... C6
03583 Jefferson○ 803 .... D3
03431 Keene⊙ 21,449 .... C6
03848 Kingston○ 4,111 .... E6
03246 Laconia⊙ 15,575 .... E4
03584 Lancaster○ 3,401 .... D3
03584 Lancaster⊙ 2,134 .... D3
†03585 Landaff○ 266 .... D3
†03602 Langdon○ 437 .... C5
03766 Lebanon 11,134 .... C4
†03857 Lee○ 2,111 .... F5
03606 Lempster○ 637 .... C5
03251 Lincoln○ 1,313 .... D3
03585 Lisbon○ 1,517 .... D3
03585 Lisbon 1,151 .... D3
†03051 Litchfield○ 4,150 .... E6
03561 Littleton○ 5,558 .... D3
03561 Littleton 4,480 .... D3
03053 Londonderry○ 13,598 .... E6
03301 Loudon○ 2,454 .... E5
†03585 Lyman○ 281 .... D3
03768 Lyme○ 1,289 .... C4
†03082 Lyndeborough○ 1,070 .... D6
†03820 Madbury○ 987 .... F5
03849 Madison○ 1,051 .... E4
*03101 Manchester 90,936 .... E6
Manchester‡ 160,767 .... E6
03455 Marlborough○ 1,846 .... C6
03455 Marlborough 1,184 .... C6
03456 Marlow○ 542 .... C5
03850 Melvin Village 450 .... E4
03253 Meredith○ 4,646 .... D4
03253 Meredith 1,202 .... D4
03770 Meriden 800 .... C4
03054 Merrimack○ 15,406 .... D6
†03887 Middleton○ 734 .... E5
03588 Milan○ 1,013 .... E2
03055 Milford○ 8,685 .... D6
03055 Milford 6,269 .... D6
03851 Milton○ 2,438 .... F5
03852 Milton Mills 450 .... F4
03771 Monroe○ 619 .... C3
03057 Mont Vernon○ 1,444 .... D6
03254 Moultonboro○ 2,206 .... E4
03060 Nashua⊙ 67,865 .... D6
Nashua‡ 114,221 .... D6
†03457 Nelson○ 442 .... C5
03070 New Boston○ 1,928 .... D6
03255 Newbury○ 961 .... C5
03854 New Castle○ 936 .... F5
03855 New Durham○ 1,183 .... E5
03856 Newfields○ 817 .... F5
03256 New Hampton○ 1,249 .... D4
†03801 Newington○ 716 .... F5
03071 New Ipswich○ 2,433 .... D6
03257 New London○ 2,935 .... D5
03257 New London 1,335 .... D5
03857 Newmarket○ 4,290 .... F5
03857 Newmarket 3,749 .... F5
03773 Newport○ 6,229 .... C5
03773 Newport⊙ 4,388 .... C5
03858 Newton○ 3,068 .... E6
03859 Newton Junction 450 .... E6
03860 North Conway 2,104 .... E3
†03276 Northfield○ 3,051 .... D5
†03276 Northfield-Tilton 2,574 .... D5
03862 North Hampton○ 3,425 .... F6
03590 North Stratford 600 .... D2
†03582 Northumberland○ 2,520 .... D2
03261 Northwood○ 2,175 .... E5
03262 North Woodstock 750 .... D3
03290 Nottingham○ 1,952 .... E5
†03741 Orange○ 197 .... D4
03777 Orford○ 928 .... C4
03864 Ossipee 2,465 .... E4
03076 Pelham○ 8,090 .... E6
†03275 Pembroke○ 4,861 .... E5
03458 Peterborough○ 4,895 .... D6
03458 Peterborough 2,568 .... D6
03779 Piermont○ 507 .... C4
03592 Pittsburg○ 780 .... E1
03263 Pittsfield○ 2,889 .... E5
03263 Pittsfield 1,584 .... E5
03781 Plainfield○ 1,749 .... C4
03865 Plaistow○ 5,609 .... E6
03264 Plymouth○ 5,094 .... D4
03264 Plymouth 3,628 .... D4
03801 Portsmouth 26,254 .... F5
Portsmouth-Dover-Rochester‡ 163,880 .... F5
03593 Randolph○ 274 .... E3
03077 Raymond○ 5,453 .... E5
03077 Raymond 1,192 .... E5
†03470 Richmond○ 518 .... C6
03461 Rindge○ 3,375 .... C6
03867 Rochester 21,560 .... E5
†03431 Roxbury○ 190 .... C6
03266 Rumney○ 1,212 .... D4
03870 Rye○ 4,508 .... F5
03871 Rye Beach 600 .... F6
03079 Salem○ 24,124 .... E6
03268 Salisbury○ 781 .... D5
03269 Sanbornton○ 1,679 .... D5
03872 Sanbornville 750 .... F4
03873 Sandown○ 2,057 .... E6
03270 Sandwich○ 905 .... E4
03874 Seabrook○ 5,917 .... F6
†03458 Sharon○ 184 .... D6
†03581 Shelburne○ 318 .... E3
03878 Somersworth 10,350 .... F5
†01913 South Hampton○ 660 .... F6
03462 Spofford 750 .... C6
†03284 Springfield○ 532 .... C4
†03582 Stark○ 470 .... E2
†03576 Stewartstown○ 943 .... E2
03464 Stoddard○ 482 .... C5
03884 Strafford○ 1,663 .... E5
†03590 Stratford○ 989 .... D2
03885 Stratham○ 2,507 .... F5
03585 Sugar Hill○ 397 .... D3
†03445 Sullivan○ 585 .... C5
03782 Sunapee○ 2,312 .... C5
03275 Suncook 4,698 .... D5
03431 Surry○ 656 .... C5
†03260 Sutton○ 1,091 .... D5
†03431 Swanzey○ 5,183 .... C6
03886 Tamworth○ 1,672 .... E4
03084 Temple○ 692 .... D6
†03285 Thornton○ 952 .... D4
03276 Tilton○ 3,387 .... D5
03276 Tilton-Northfield 2,574 .... D5
03465 Troy○ 2,131 .... C6
03465 Troy 1,318 .... C6
†03816 Tuftonboro○ 1,500 .... E4
03595 Twin Mountain 500 .... D3
†03743 Unity○ 1,092 .... C5
†03872 Wakefield○ 2,237 .... F4
03608 Walpole○ 3,188 .... C5
03278 Warner○ 1,963 .... D5
03279 Warren○ 650 .... D4
03280 Washington○ 411 .... C5
03223 Waterville Valley○ 180 .... D4
03281 Weare○ 3,232 .... D5
†03301 Webster○ 1,095 .... D5
03282 Wentworth○ 527 .... D4
†03579 Wentworths Location○ 49 .... E2
†03242 West Henniker 500 .... D5
03784 West Lebanon C4
03467 Westmoreland○ 1,452 .... C6
03597 West Stewartstown 700 .... E2
03469 West Swanzey 1,022 .... C6
03865 Westville 750 .... E6
03598 Whitefield○ 1,681 .... D3
03598 Whitefield 1,005 .... D3
†03287 Wilmot○ 725 .... D5
03287 Wilmot Flat 450 .... D5
03086 Wilton○ 2,669 .... D6
03086 Wilton 1,310 .... D6
03470 Winchester○ 3,465 .... C6
03470 Winchester 1,732 .... C6
03087 Windham○ 5,664 .... E6
03289 Winnisquam 500 .... E5
03894 Wolfeboro○ 3,968 .... E4
03894 Wolfeboro 2,271 .... E4
03896 Wolfeboro Falls 600 .... E4
03293 Woodstock○ 1,008 .... D4
03785 Woodsville⊙ 1,195 .... C3

OTHER FEATURES

Adams (mt.) E3
Ammonoosuc (riv.) D3
Androscoggin (riv.) E2
Ashuelot (riv.) C6
Back (lake) E1
Baker (riv.) D4
Bearcamp (riv.) E4
Beaver (brook) E6
Belknap (mt.) E5
Blackwater (res.) D5
Blue (mt.) E2
Bond (mt.) E3
Bow (lake) E5
Cabot (mt.) E2
Cannon (mt.) D3
Cardigan (mt.) D4
Carrigain (mt.) E3
Carter Dome (mt.) E3
Chocorua (mt.) E4
Cocheco (riv.) E5
Cold (riv.) C5
Comerford (dam) D3
Connecticut (riv.) B6
Contoocook (riv.) D6
Conway (lake) E4
Crawford Notch (pass) E3
Croydon (peak) C5
Croydon Branch, Sugar (riv.) C5
Crystal (lake) E5
Cube (mt.) D4
Dixville (peak) E2
Dixville Notch (pass) E2
Edward MacDowell (res.) D6
Ellis (riv.) E3
Everett (dam) D5
Exeter (riv.) E6
First Connecticut (lake) E1
Francis (lake) E1
Franconia Notch (pass) D3
Franklin Falls (res.) D4
Gale (riv.) D3
Great (bay) F5
Halls (stream) E1
Hancock (mt.) D3
Highland (lake) C5
Hutchins (mt.) E2
Indian (stream) E1
Jefferson (mt.) E3
Kearsarge (mt.) D5
Kinsman (mt.) D3
Kinsman Notch (pass) D3
Lafayette (mt.) D3
Lamprey (riv.) E5
Liberty (mt.) D3
Lincoln (mt.) D3
Long (mt.) E2
Mad (riv.) D4
Madison (mt.) E3
Mascoma (lake) C4
Massabesic (lake) E6
Merrimack (riv.) D5
Merrymeeting (lake) E5
Mohawk (riv.) E2
Monadnock (mt.) C6
Monroe (mt.) E3
Moore (dam) D3
Moore (res.) D3
Moosilauke (mt.) D3
Nash (stream) E2
Newfound (lake) D4
North Carter (mt.) E3
North Twin (mt.) D3
Nubanusit (lake) C5
Osceola (mt.) E3
Ossipee (lake) E4
Ossipee (mts.) E4
Ossipee (riv.) F4
Passaconaway (mt.) E4
Pawtuckaway (pond) E5
Pease A.F.B. F5
Pemigewasset (riv.) D4
Perry (stream) E1
Pine (riv.) E4
Pinkham Notch (pass) E3
Piscataqua (riv.) F5
Piscataquog (riv.) D5
Presidential (range) E3
Rice (mt.) E2
Saco (riv.) E3
Saint-Gaudens Nat'l Hist. Site B4
Salmon Falls (riv.) F5

(continued on following page)

Agriculture, Industry and Resources

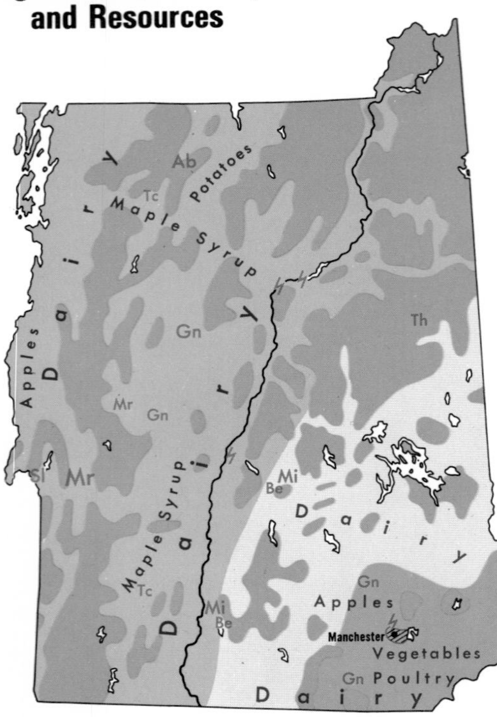

DOMINANT LAND USE

Specialized Dairy
Dairy, General Farming
Dairy, Poultry, Mixed Farming
Forests

Water Power
Major Industrial Areas

MAJOR MINERAL OCCURRENCES

Ab	Asbestos	Mr	Marble
Be	Beryl	Sl	Slate
Gn	Granite	Tc	Talc
Mi	Mica	Th	Thorium

Sandwich (mt.) E4
Sandwich (range) E4
Second (lake) E1
Shaw (mt.) E4
Shoals (isls.) F6
Smarts (mt.) C4
Souhegan (riv.) D6
South Twin (mt.) D3
Squam (lake) E4
Starr King (mt.) E3
Stub Hill (mt.) E1
Sugar (riv.) C5
Sunapee (lake) C5
Suncook (lkes) E5
Suncook (riv.) E5
Surry Mountain (lake) C5
Tarleton (lake) D4
Tecumseh (mt.) D4
Third (lake) E1
Tom (mt.) E3
Umbagog (lake) E2
Upper Ammonoosuc (riv.) E2
Warner (riv.) D5
Washington (mt.) E3
Waumbek (mt.) E3
Wentworth (lake) E4
White (isl.) F6
White (mts.) E3
Whiteface (mt.) E4
Wild Ammonoosuc (riv.) D3
Wilder (dam) C4
Winnipesaukee (lake) E4
Winnipesaukee (riv.) D5
Winnisquam (lake) D4

VERMONT

COUNTIES

Addison 29,406 .... A3
Bennington 33,345 .... A6
Caledonia 25,808 .... C2
Chittenden 115,534 .... A3
Essex 6,313 .... D2
Franklin 34,788 .... B2
Grand Isle 4,613 .... A2
Lamoille 16,767 .... B2
Orange 22,739 .... C3
Orleans 23,440 .... C2
Rutland 58,347 .... A4
Washington 52,393 .... B3
Windham 36,933 .... B5
Windsor 51,030 .... B4

CITIES and TOWNS

Zip *Name/Pop.* *Key*

05820 Albany○ 705 .... C2
05440 Alburg○ 1,352 .... A2
05440 Alburg 496 .... A2
†05143 Andover○ 350 .... B5
05250 Arlington○ 2,184 .... A5
05250 Arlington 1,309 .... A5
05441 Bakersfield○ 852 .... B2
05031 Barnard○ 790 .... B4
05821 Barnet○ 1,338 .... C3
05641 Barre 9,824 .... C3
05641 Barre○ 7,090 .... C3
05822 Barton○ 2,990 .... C2
05822 Barton 1,062 .... C2
05823 Beebe Plain 500 .... C2
05902 Beecher Falls 950 .... D2
05101 Bellows Falls 3,456 .... C5
05442 Belvidere○ 218 .... B2
05201 Bennington○ 15,815 .... A6
05201 Bennington⊙ 9,349 .... A6
05731 Benson○ 739 .... A4
†05476 Berkshire○ 1,116 .... B2
05032 Bethel○ 1,715 .... B4
05032 Bethel 1,016 .... B4
†03590 Bloomfield○ 188 .... D2
†05466 Bolton○ 715 .... B3
05732 Bomoseen 700 .... A4
05340 Bondville 500 .... B5
05033 Bradford○ 2,191 .... C3
05033 Bradford 831 .... C3
†05669 Braintree○ 1,065 .... B4
05733 Brandon○ 4,194 .... A4
05733 Brandon 1,925 .... A4
05301 Brattleboro○ 11,886 .... B6
05301 Brattleboro 8,596 .... B6
05034 Bridgewater○ 867 .... B4
05734 Bridport○ 997 .... A4
05443 Bristol○ 3,293 .... A3
05443 Bristol 1,793 .... A3
05036 Brookfield○ 959 .... B3
†05345 Brookline○ 310 .... B5
†05860 Brownington○ 708 .... C2
†05871 Burke○ 1,385 .... D2
05401 Burlington⊙ 37,712 .... A3
Burlington‡ 114,070 .... A3
05647 Cabot○ 958 .... C3
05647 Cabot 259 .... C3
05648 Calais○ 1,207 .... B3
05444 Cambridge○ 2,019 .... B2
05444 Cambridge 217 .... B2
05903 Canaan○ 1,196 .... D2
05735 Castleton○ 3,637 .... A4
05142 Cavendish○ 1,355 .... B5
05736 Center Rutland 465 .... A4
05445 Charlotte○ 2,561 .... A3
05038 Chelsea 1,091 .... C4
05143 Chester○ 2,791 .... B5
05143 Chester-Chester Depot 1,267 .... B5
05737 Chittenden○ 927 .... B4
†05759 Clarendon○ 2,372 .... A4
05446 Colchester○ 12,629 .... A2
05824 Concord○ 1,125 .... D3
05039 Corinth○ 904 .... C3
†05753 Cornwall○ 993 .... A4
05825 Coventry○ 674 .... C2
05826 Craftsbury○ 844 .... C2
05739 Danby○ 992 .... A5
05828 Danville○ 1,705 .... C3
05829 Derby○ 4,222 .... C2
05829 Derby (Derby Center) 598 .... C2
05830 Derby Line 874 .... C2
05251 Dorset○ 1,648 .... A5
†05676 Duxbury○ 877 .... B3
05252 East Arlington 600 .... A5
05649 East Barre-Graniteville 2,172 .... C3
05253 East Dorset 550 .... A5
05837 East Haven○ 280 .... D2
05740 East Middlebury 550 .... A4
05651 East Montpelier○ 2,205 .... B3
05741 East Poultney 450 .... A4
05742 East Wallingford 500 .... B5
05652 Eden○ 612 .... B2
05450 Enosburg Falls 1,207 .... B2
05451 Essex○ 14,392 .... A2
05452 Essex Junction 7,033 .... A3
05454 Fairfax○ 1,805 .... B2
05455 Fairfield○ 1,493 .... B2
05743 Fair Haven○ 2,819 .... A4
05743 Fair Haven 2,363 .... A4
05045 Fairlee○ 770 .... C4
05456 Ferrisburg○ 2,117 .... A3
†05444 Fletcher○ 626 .... B2
05745 Forest Dale 500 .... A4
05457 Franklin○ 1,006 .... B2
†05478 Georgia○ 2,818 .... A2
05904 Gilman 600 .... D3
05839 Glover○ 843 .... C2
05146 Grafton○ 604 .... B5
05840 Granby○ 70 .... D2
05458 Grand Isle○ 1,238 .... A2
05654 Graniteville-East Barre 2,172 .... C3
05747 Granville○ 288 .... B4
05841 Greensboro○ 677 .... C2
05046 Groton○ 667 .... C3
05905 Guildhall 202 .... D2
†05301 Guilford○ 1,532 .... B6
†05358 Halifax○ 488 .... B6
05748 Hancock○ 334 .... B4
05843 Hardwick○ 2,613 .... C2
05843 Hardwick 1,476 .... C2
05047 Hartford○ 7,963 .... C4
05048 Hartland○ 2,396 .... C4
†05459 Highgate○ 2,493 .... B2
05461 Hinesburg○ 2,690 .... A3
†05830 Holland○ 473 .... D2
05749 Hubbardton○ 490 .... A4
05462 Huntington○ 1,161 .... B3
05655 Hyde Park○ 2,021 .... B2
05655 Hyde Park⊙ 475 .... B2
05750 Hydeville 500 .... A4
†05777 Ira○ 354 .... A4
05845 Irasburg○ 870 .... C2
05846 Island Pond 1,216 .... D2
05463 Isle La Motte○ 393 .... A2
05342 Jacksonville 252 .... B6
05343 Jamaica○ 681 .... B5
†05859 Jay○ 302 .... C2
05464 Jeffersonville 491 .... B2
05465 Jericho○ 3,575 .... A2
05465 Jericho 1,340 .... A2
05656 Johnson○ 2,581 .... B2
05656 Johnson 1,393 .... B2
05751 Killington 700 .... B4
†05752 Leicester○ 803 .... A4
†03576 Lemington○ 108 .... D2
†05443 Lincoln○ 870 .... B3
05148 Londonderry○ 1,510 .... B5
05847 Lowell○ 573 .... C2
05149 Ludlow○ 2,414 .... B5
05149 Ludlow 1,352 .... B5
05906 Lunenburg○ 1,138 .... D3
05849 Lyndon○ 4,924 .... C2
05850 Lyndon Center C2
05851 Lyndonville 1,401 .... D2
†05905 Maidstone○ 100 .... D2
05254 Manchester○ 3,261 .... A5
05254 Manchester⊙ 563 .... A5
05255 Manchester Center 1,719 .... A5
05344 Marlboro○ 695 .... B6
05658 Marshfield○ 1,267 .... C3
05658 Marshfield 301 .... C3
†05701 Mendon○ 1,056 .... B4
05753 Middlebury○ 7,574 .... A3
05753 Middlebury⊙ 5,591 .... A3
†05602 Middlesex○ 1,235 .... B3
05757 Middletown Springs○ 603 .... A5
05468 Milton○ 6,829 .... A2
05468 Milton 1,411 .... A2
05469 Monkton○ 1,201 .... A3
05470 Montgomery○ 681 .... B2
05471 Montgomery Center 400 .... B2
05602 Montpelier (cap.)⊙ 8,241 .... B3
05660 Moretown○ 1,221 .... B3
05853 Morgan○ 460 .... D2
†05661 Morristown○ 4,448 .... B2
05661 Morrisville 2,074 .... B2
05758 Mount Holly○ 938 .... B5
†05739 Mount Tabor○ 211 .... B5
†05871 Newark○ 280 .... D2
05051 Newbury○ 1,699 .... C3
05051 Newbury 425 .... C3
05345 Newfane○ 1,129 .... B6
05345 Newfane⊙ 119 .... B6
05472 New Haven○ 1,217 .... A3
05855 Newport○ 1,319 .... C2
05855 Newport⊙ 4,756 .... C2
05257 North Bennington 1,685 .... A6
05663 Northfield○ 5,435 .... B3
05663 Northfield 2,033 .... B3
05664 Northfield Falls 600 .... B3
05052 North Hartland 500 .... C4
05474 North Hero 442 .... A2
05665 North Hyde Park 450 .... B2
05053 North Pomfret 400 .... B4
05260 North Pownal 700 .... A6
05150 North Springfield B5
05859 North Troy 717 .... C2
†05101 North Westminster 310 .... B5
05907 Norton○ 184 .... D2
05055 Norwich○ 2,398 .... C4
†05201 Old Bennington 353 .... A6
†05649 Orange○ 752 .... C3
05860 Orleans 983 .... C2
05760 Orwell○ 901 .... A4
†05491 Panton○ 537 .... A3
05761 Pawlet○ 1,244 .... A5
05862 Peacham○ 531 .... C3
05151 Perkinsville 187 .... B5
05152 Peru○ 312 .... B5
05762 Pittsfield○ 396 .... B4
05763 Pittsford○ 2,590 .... A4
05763 Pittsford 666 .... A4
05667 Plainfield○ 1,249 .... C3
05667 Plainfield 599 .... C3
05056 Plymouth○ 405 .... B4
†05067 Pomfret○ 856 .... B4
05058 Post Mills 500 .... C4
05764 Poultney○ 3,196 .... A4
05764 Poultney 1,554 .... A4
05261 Pownal○ 3,269 .... A6
05765 Proctor○ 1,998 .... A4
05153 Proctorsville 481 .... B5
05346 Putney○ 1,850 .... B6
05059 Quechee 900 .... C4
05060 Randolph○ 4,689 .... B4
05060 Randolph 2,217 .... B4
05062 Reading○ 647 .... B5
05350 Readsboro○ 638 .... B6
05350 Readsboro 402 .... B6
05476 Richford○ 2,206 .... B2
05476 Richford 1,471 .... B2
05477 Richmond○ 3,159 .... A3
05477 Richmond 865 .... A3
05766 Ripton○ 327 .... A4
05767 Rochester○ 1,054 .... B4
†05101 Rockingham○ 5,538 .... B5
05669 Roxbury○ 452 .... B3
†05068 Royalton○ 2,100 .... B4
05768 Rupert○ 605 .... A5
05701 Rutland○ 3,300 .... B4
05701 Rutland⊙ 18,436 .... B4
05042 Ryegate○ 1,000 .... C3
05478 Saint Albans○ 3,555 .... A2
05478 Saint Albans⊙ 7,308 .... A2
†05401 Saint George○ 677 .... A2
05819 Saint Johnsbury○ 7,938 .... D3
05819 Saint Johnsbury⊙ 7,150 .... D3
05863 Saint Johnsbury Center 400 .... D3
05769 Salisbury○ 881 .... A4
†05250 Sandgate○ 234 .... A5
05154 Saxtons River 593 .... B5
†05363 Searsburg○ 72 .... A6
05262 Shaftsbury○ 3,001 .... A6
05065 Sharon○ 828 .... C4
05866 Sheffield○ 435 .... C2
05482 Shelburne○ 5,000 .... A3
05483 Sheldon○ 1,618 .... B2
05770 Shoreham○ 972 .... A4
†05738 Shrewsbury○ 866 .... B4
05670 South Barre 1,301 .... B3
05401 South Burlington 10,679 .... A3
05486 South Hero○ 1,188 .... A2
05155 South Londonderry 500 .... B5
05068 South Royalton 700 .... C4
05069 South Ryegate 400 .... C3
05156 Springfield○ 10,190 .... B5
05156 Springfield 5,603 .... B5
05352 Stamford○ 773 .... A6
05487 Starksboro○ 1,336 .... A3
05772 Stockbridge○ 508 .... B4
05672 Stowe○ 2,991 .... B3
05672 Stowe 531 .... B3
05072 Strafford○ 731 .... C4
†05360 Stratton○ 122 .... B5
†05733 Sudbury○ 380 .... A4
†05250 Sunderland○ 768 .... A5
05867 Sutton○ 667 .... C2
05488 Swanton○ 5,141 .... A2
05488 Swanton 2,520 .... A2
05074 Thetford○ 2,188 .... C4
†05773 Tinmouth○ 406 .... A5
05076 Topsham○ 767 .... C3
05353 Townshend○ 849 .... B5
05868 Troy○ 1,498 .... C2
05077 Tunbridge○ 925 .... C4
05489 Underhill○ 2,172 .... B2
05490 Underhill Center 575 .... B2
05491 Vergennes 2,273 .... A3
05354 Vernon○ 1,175 .... B6
05079 Vershire○ 442 .... C4
05673 Waitsfield○ 1,300 .... B3
†05873 Walden○ 575 .... C3
05773 Wallingford○ 1,893 .... B5
05773 Wallingford 1,141 .... B5
†05491 Waltham○ 394 .... A3
05355 Wardsboro○ 505 .... B5
05674 Warren○ 956 .... B3
05675 Washington○ 855 .... C3
05676 Waterbury○ 4,465 .... B3
05676 Waterbury 1,892 .... B3
05492 Waterville○ 470 .... B2
05678 Websterville 700 .... B3
05774 Wells○ 815 .... A5
05081 Wells River 396 .... C3
05301 West Brattleboro 2,795 .... B6
05871 West Burke 338 .... C2
05356 West Dover 550 .... B6
05083 West Fairlee○ 427 .... C4
05874 Westfield○ 418 .... C2
05494 Westford○ 1,413 .... A2
05875 West Glover C2
†05743 West Haven○ 253 .... A4
05158 Westminster○ 2,493 .... C5
05158 Westminster 319 .... C5
†05860 Westmore○ 257 .... C2
05161 Weston○ 627 .... B5
05777 West Rutland○ 2,351 .... A4
05777 West Rutland 2,169 .... A4
05359 West Townshend 500 .... B5
†05753 Weybridge○ 667 .... A3
†05851 Wheelock○ 444 .... C2
05001 White River Junction 2,582 .... C4
05778 Whiting○ 379 .... A4
05361 Whitingham○ 1,043 .... B6
05088 Wilder 1,461 .... C4
05679 Williamstown○ 2,284 .... B3
05495 Williston○ 3,843 .... A3
05363 Wilmington○ 1,808 .... B6
†05359 Windham○ 223 .... B5
05089 Windsor○ 4,084 .... C5
05089 Windsor 3,478 .... C5
05404 Winooski 6,318 .... A2
05680 Wolcott○ 986 .... C2
05681 Woodbury○ 573 .... C3
†05201 Woodford○ 314 .... A6
05091 Woodstock○ 3,214 .... B4
05091 Woodstock⊙ 1,178 .... B4
05682 Worcester○ 727 .... B3

OTHER FEATURES

Abraham (mt.) B3
Arrowhead Mountain (lake) A2
Ascutney (mt.) C5
Bald (mt.) D2
Barton (riv.) C2
Batten Kill (riv.) A5
Belvidere (mt.) B2
Black (riv.) B5
Black (riv.) C2
Bloodroot (mt.) B4
Bolton (mt.) B3
Bomoseen (lake) A4
Brandon Gap (pass) B4
Bread Loaf (mt.) A3
Bromley (mt.) B5
Brown's (riv.) A2
Burke (mt.) D2
Camels Hump (mt.) B3
Carmi (lake) B2
Caspian (lake) C2
Champlain (lake) A2
Chittenden (res.) B4
Clyde (riv.) C2
Comerford (dam) D3
Connecticut (riv.) C4
Crystal (lake) C2
Dorset (peak) A5
Dunmore (lake) A4
Echo (lake) D2
Ellen (mt.) B3
Equinox (mt.) A5
Fairfield (pond) A2
Glastenbury (mt.) A6
Gore (mt.) D2
Green (mts.) B4
Green River (res.) B2
Groton (lake) C3
Hardwick (lake) C2
Harriman (res.) B6
Harveys (lake) C3
Haystack (mt.) B6
Hoosic (riv.) A6
Hortonia (lake) A4
Hunger (mt.) B3
Iroquois (lake) A3
Island (pond) D2
Jay (peak) B2
Joes (brook) C3
Killington (peak) B4
Lamoille (riv.) A2
Lewis (creek) A3
Lincoln Gap (pass) B3
Little (riv.) B3
Mad (riv.) B3
Maidstone (lake) D2
Mansfield (mt.) B2
Memphremagog (lake) C1
Mettawee (riv.) A5
Middlebury Gap (pass) B4
Mill (riv.) B4
Missisquoi (riv.) B2
Mollys Falls (pond) C3
Moore (dam) D3
Moore (res.) D3
Moose (riv.) D2
Norton (pond) D2
Nulhegan (riv.) D2
Ottauquechee (riv.) B4
Otter (creek) A3
Passumpsic (riv.) D2
Pico (peak) B4
Poultney (riv.) A4
Saint Catherine (lake) A5
Salem (lake) C2
Seymour (lake) D2
Shelburne (pond) A3
Smugglers Notch (pass) B2
Snow (mt.) B6
Somerset (res.) A5
Spruce (mt.) C3
Stratton (mt.) B5
Tabor (mt.) B5
Trout (riv.) B2
Waits (riv.) C3
Waterbury (res.) B3
Wells (riv.) C3
West (riv.) B5
White (riv.) C4
White Face (mt.) B2
Wilder (dam) C4
Willoughby (lake) D2
Winooski (riv.) B3

⊙County seat.
‡Population of metropolitan area.
○Population of town or township.
† Zip of nearest p.o. * Multiple zips.

AREA 7,787 sq. mi. (20,168 sq. km.)
POPULATION 7,364,823
CAPITAL Trenton
LARGEST CITY Newark
HIGHEST POINT High Point 1,803 ft. (550 m.)
SETTLED IN 1617
ADMITTED TO UNION December 18, 1787
POPULAR NAME Garden State
STATE FLOWER Purple Violet
STATE BIRD Eastern Goldfinch

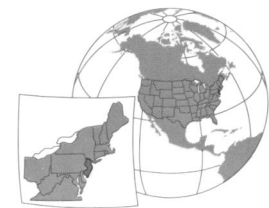

Agriculture, Industry and Resources

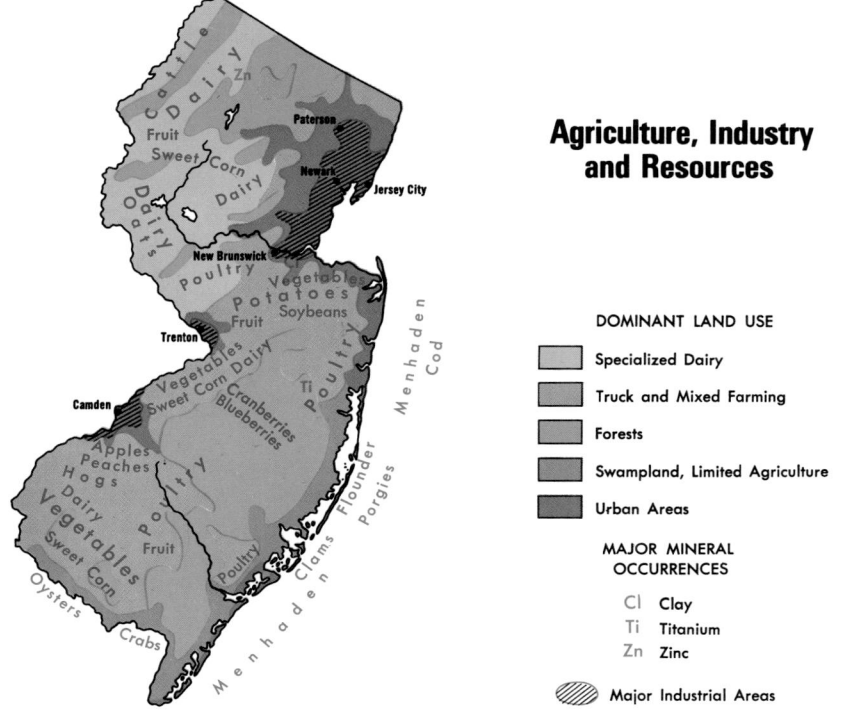

DOMINANT LAND USE

Specialized Dairy

Truck and Mixed Farming

Forests

Swampland, Limited Agriculture

Urban Areas

MAJOR MINERAL OCCURRENCES

Cl Clay
Ti Titanium
Zn Zinc

Major Industrial Areas

The Urban Northeast

Urbanized Areas
● Places with more than 10,000 inhabitants
● Places with 5,000-10,000 inhabitants
● Places with 2,500-5,000 inhabitants

© Copyright HAMMOND INCORPORATED, Maplewood, N.J.

COUNTIES

Atlantic 194,119 ....D5
Bergen 845,385 ....E2
Burlington 362,542 ....D4
Camden 471,650 ....D4
Cape May 82,266 ....D5
Cumberland 132,866 ....C5
Essex 851,116 ....E2
Gloucester 199,917 ....C4
Hudson 556,972 ....E2
Hunterdon 87,361 ....D2
Mercer 307,863 ....D3
Middlesex 595,893 ....E3
Monmouth 503,173 ....E3
Morris 407,630 ....D2
Ocean 346,038 ....E4
Passaic 447,585 ....E1
Salem 64,676 ....C4
Somerset 203,129 ....D2
Sussex 116,119 ....D1
Union 504,094 ....E2
Warren 84,429 ....C2

CITIES and TOWNS

Zip Name/Pop. Key

08201 Absecon 6,859 ....D5
07820 Allamuchy 600 ....D2
07401 Allendale 5,901 ....B1
07711 Allenhurst 912 ....F3
08501 Allentown 1,962 ....D3
08720 Allenwood E3
08001 Alloway 1,370 ....C4
08865 Alpha 2,644 ....C2
07620 Alpine 1,549 ....C1
07821 Andover 892 ....D2
08801 Annandale 1,040 ....D2
07712 Asbury Park 17,015 ....F3
  Asbury Park-Long Branch‡
  503,173 ....F3
†08033 Ashland B3
08004 Atco D4
*08401 Atlantic City 40,199 ....E5
  Atlantic City‡ 194,119 ....E5
07716 Atlantic Highlands 4,950 ..F3
08106 Audubon 9,533 ....B3
†08106 Audubon Park 1,274 ......B3
08202 Avalon 2,162 ....D5
07001 Avenel E2
07717 Avon By The Sea 2,337 ...F3
08005 Barnegat 1,012 ....E4
08006 Barnegat Light 619 ....E4
08007 Barrington 7,418 ....B3
07920 Basking Ridge D2
08742 Bay Head 1,340 ....E3
07002 Bayonne 65,047 ....B2
08008 Beach Haven 1,714 ....E4
08722 Beachwood 7,687 ....E4
07921 Bedminster○ 2,469 ....D2
08502 Belle Mead D3
07109 Belleville 35,367 ....B2
08031 Bellmawr 13,721 ....B3
07719 Belmar 6,771 ....E3
07823 Belvidere⊙ 2,475 ....C2
07621 Bergenfield 25,568 ....C1
07922 Berkeley Heights○ 12,549 ..E2
08009 Berlin 5,786 ....D4
08010 Beverly 2,919 ....D3
07924 Bernardsville 6,715 ....D2
08010 Beverly 2,919 ....D3
08012 Blackwood 5,219 ....C4
07825 Blairstown○ 4,360 ....C2
07003 Bloomfield 47,792 ....B2
07403 Bloomingdale 7,867 ....E1
08804 Bloomsbury 864 ....C2
07603 Bogota 8,344 ....B2
07005 Boonton 8,620 ....E2
08505 Bordentown 4,441 ....D3
08805 Bound Brook 9,710 ....D2
07720 Bradley Beach 4,772 ......F3
07826 Branchville 870 ....D1
08723 Breton Woods E3
08723 Brick○ 53,629 ....E3
08014 Bridgeport 750 ....C4
08302 Bridgeton⊙ 18,795 ....C5
08807 Bridgewater○ 29,175 .....D2
08730 Brielle 4,068 ....E3
08203 Brigantine 8,318 ....E5
08030 Brooklawn 2,133 ....B3
08015 Browns Mills 10,568 ......D4
07828 Budd Lake 6,523 ....D2
08310 Buena 3,642 ....D4
08016 Burlington 10,246 ....D3
07405 Butler 7,616 ....E2
07006 Caldwell 7,624 ....B2
07830 Califon 1,023 ....D2
*08101 Camden⊙ 84,910 ....B3
†08701 Candlewood 6,750 ....E3
08204 Cape May 4,853 ....D6
08210 Cape May Court House○
  3,597 ....D5
07072 Carlstadt 6,166 ....B2
08069 Carneys Point 7,574 ......C4
07008 Carteret 20,598 ....E2
07009 Cedar Grove○ 12,600 ....B2
†08723 Cedarwood Park E3

07928 Chatham 8,537 ....E2
08019 Chatsworth 700 ....D4
08879 Cheesequake E3
*08034 Cherry Hill○ 68,785 ......B3
†08089 Chesilhurst 1,590 ....D4
07930 Chester 1,433 ....D2
†08505 Chesterfield○ 3,867 ......D3
†08077 Cinnaminson○ 16,072 ...B3
07066 Clark○ 16,699 ....A3
08020 Clarksboro C4
08510 Clarksburg 800 ....E3
08312 Clayton 6,013 ....C4
08021 Clementon 5,764 ....D4
07010 Cliffside Park 21,464 .....C2
07721 Cliffwood E3
*07011 Clifton 74,388 ....B2
08809 Clinton 1,910 ....D2
07624 Closter 8,164 ....C1
08108 Collingswood 15,838 ....B3
08213 Cologne 800 ....D4
08022 Columbus 800 ....D3
07961 Convent Station E2
†08270 Corbin City 254 ....D5
†07821 Cranberry Lake 500 .....D2
08512 Cranbury 1,255 ....E3
07016 Cranford○ 24,573 ....E2
07626 Cresskill 7,609 ....C1
08515 Crosswicks 265 ....D3
07723 Deal 1,952 ....F3
08023 Deepwater 800 ....C4
08110 Delair B3
08075 Delanco○ 3,730 ....D3
08075 Delran○ 14,811 ....B3
07627 Demarest 4,963 ....C1
08214 Dennisville 890 ....D5
07834 Denville○ 14,380 ....E2
08096 Deptford○ 23,473 ....B4
08317 Dorothy 900 ....D5
07801 Dover 14,681 ....D2
07628 Dumont 18,334 ....C1
08812 Dunellen 6,593 ....E2
08816 East Brunswick○ 37,711 .E3
07936 East Hanover○ 9,319 ....E2
07734 East Keansburg E3
08873 East Millstone 950 ......D3
†07100 East Newark 1,923 ......B2
*07017 East Orange 77,690 .....B2
07073 East Rutherford 7,849 ...B2
07724 Eatontown 12,703 ......E3
07020 Edgewater 4,628 ....C2
†08010 Edgewater Park○ 9,273 .D3
*08817 Edison○ 70,193 ....E2
08215 Egg Harbor City 4,618 ..D4
07740 Elberon F3
*07201 Elizabeth⊙ 106,201 .....B2
08318 Elmer 1,569 ....C4
†07407 Elmwood Park 18,377 ...B2
08217 Elwood 1,538 ....D4
07630 Emerson 7,793 ....B1
*07631 Englewood 23,701 ......C2
07632 Englewood Cliffs 5,698 ..C2
08726 Englishtown 976 ....E3
07021 Essex Fells 2,363 ....B2
08319 Estell Manor 848 ....D5
08025 Ewan 610 ....C4
07006 Fairfield○ 7,987 ....A2
07701 Fair Haven 5,679 ....E3
07410 Fair Lawn 32,229 ....B1
08320 Fairton 1,107 ....C5
07022 Fairview 10,519 ....C2
07023 Fanwood 7,767 ....E2
07931 Far Hills 677 ....D2
07727 Farmingdale 1,348 ......E3
†08505 Fieldsboro 597 ....D3
07836 Flanders D2
08822 Flemington○ 4,132 ......D2
08518 Florence-Roebling 7,677 .D3
07932 Florham Park 9,359 ......E2
†08037 Folsom 1,892 ....D4
08863 Fords E2
08731 Forked River 900 ....E4
07024 Fort Lee 32,449 ....C2
07416 Franklin 4,486 ....D1
07417 Franklin Lakes 8,769 ....B1
†08823 Franklin Park○ 31,358 ...D3
08322 Franklinville C4
07728 Freehold⊙ 10,020 ....E3
08825 Frenchtown 1,573 ....C2
07026 Garfield 26,803 ....B2
07027 Garwood 4,752 ....E2
08026 Gibbsboro 2,510 ....B4
08027 Gibbstown C4
†08753 Gilford Park 6,528 ....E4
07933 Gillette E2
08028 Glassboro 14,574 ....C4
08029 Glendora 5,632 ....B4
08826 Glen Gardner 834 ....D2
07028 Glen Ridge 7,855 ....B2
07452 Glen Rock 11,497 ....B1
08030 Gloucester City 13,121 ..B3
07435 Green Pond 800 ....E1
07935 Green Village 800 ....D2
08323 Greenwich○ 973 ....C5
08032 Grenloch 700 ....C4

(continued on following page)

07093 Guttenberg 7,340 ... C2
*07601 Hackensack⊙ 36,039 ... B2
07840 Hackettstown 8,850 ... D2
08033 Haddonfield 12,337 ... B3
08035 Haddon Heights 8,361 ... B3
08036 Hainesport○ 3,236 ... D4
07508 Haledon 6,607 ... B1
07419 Hamburg 1,832 ... D1
08690 Hamilton Square-Mercerville 25,446 ... D3
08037 Hammonton 12,298 ... D4
08827 Hampton 1,614 ... D2
07640 Harrington Park 4,532 ... C1
07029 Harrison 12,242 ... B2
†08057 Hartford 650 ... D4
08008 Harvey Cedars 363 ... E4
07604 Hasbrouck Heights 12,166 . B2
07641 Haworth 3,509 ... C1
07507 Hawthorne 18,200 ... B2
07730 Hazlet 23,013 ... E3
08828 Helmetta 955 ... E3
07421 Hewitt 950 ... E1
08829 High Bridge 3,435 ... D2
07422 Highland Lakes 2,888 ... E1
08904 Highland Park 13,396 ... D2
07732 Highlands 5,187 ... F3
08520 Hightstown 4,581 ... D3
07642 Hillsdale 10,495 ... B1
07205 Hillside○ 21,440 ... B2
†08083 Hi-Nella 1,250 ... B4
07030 Hoboken 42,460 ... C2
07423 Ho Ho Kus 4,129 ... B1
07733 Holmdel○ 8,447 ... E3
07843 Hopatcong 15,531 ... D2
07844 Hope 310 ... D2
08525 Hopewell 2,001 ... D3
07731 Howell○ 25,065 ... E3
†07712 Interlaken 1,037 ... E3
07845 Ironia ... D2
07111 Irvington 61,493 ... B2
08830 Iselin ... E2
08732 Island Heights 1,575 ... E4
08527 Jackson○ 25,644 ... E3
08831 Jamesburg 4,114 ... E3
*07301 Jersey City⊙ 223,532 ... B2
Jersey City‡ 556,972 ... B2
07734 Keansburg 10,613 ... E3
07032 Kearny 35,735 ... B2
08824 Kendall Park 7,419 ... D3
07033 Kenilworth 8,221 ... E2
07735 Keyport 7,413 ... E3
08528 Kingston ... D3
07405 Kinnelon 7,770 ... E2
07848 Lafayette 900 ... D1
07034 Lake Hiawatha ... E2
07849 Lake Hopatcong ... D2
08733 Lakehurst 2,908 ... E3
†07871 Lake Mohawk 8,498 ... D1
08701 Lakewood 22,863 ... E3
08530 Lambertville 4,044 ... D3
07850 Landing ... D2
08734 Lanoka Harbor ... E4
08021 Laurel Springs 2,249 ... B4
08879 Laurence Harbor 6,737 ... E3
08735 Lavallette 2,072 ... E4
08045 Lawnside 3,042 ... B3
08648 Lawrenceville 19,724 ... D3
08833 Lebanon 820 ... D2
07852 Ledgewood ... D2
08327 Leesburg 700 ... D5
07737 Leonardo ... E3
07605 Leonia 8,027 ... C2
07938 Liberty Corner ... D2
07035 Lincoln Park 8,806 ... A1
07738 Lincroft ... E3
07036 Linden 37,836 ... A3
08021 Lindenwold 18,196 ... B4
08221 Linwood 6,144 ... D5
07424 Little Falls○ 11,496 ... B2
07643 Little Ferry 9,399 ... B2
07739 Little Silver 5,548 ... F3
07039 Livingston○ 28,040 ... E2
07644 Lodi 23,956 ... B2
07740 Long Branch 29,819 ... F3
Long Branch-Asbury Park‡ 503,173 ... F3
08403 Longport 1,249 ... D5
07853 Long Valley 1,682 ... D2
08048 Lumberton 600 ... D4
07071 Lyndhurst○ 20,326 ... B2
07939 Lyons ... D2
07940 Madison 15,357 ... E2
08049 Magnolia 4,881 ... B3
07430 Mahwah○ 12,127 ... E1
08328 Malaga 950 ... C4
08050 Manahawkin 1,469 ... E4
08736 Manasquan 5,354 ... E3
08738 Mantoloking 433 ... E3
08051 Mantua○ 9,193 ... C4
08835 Manville 11,278 ... D2
08052 Maple Shade○ 20,525 ... B3
07040 Maplewood○ 22,950 ... E2
08402 Margate City 9,179 ... E5
07746 Marlboro○ 17,560 ... E3
08053 Marlton 9,411 ... D4
08223 Marmora 650 ... D5
08836 Martinsville ... D2
07747 Matawan 8,837 ... E3
08330 Mays Landing⊙ 2,054 ... D5
07607 Maywood 9,895 ... B2
07428 McAfee 800 ... D1
†08232 McKee City 950 ... D5
08055 Medford ... D4
08055 Medford Lakes 4,958 ... D4
07945 Mendham 4,899 ... D2
08837 Menlo Park ... E2
08619 Mercerville-Hamilton Square 25,446 ... D3
08109 Merchantville 3,972 ... B3
08840 Metuchen 13,762 ... E2
08846 Middlesex 13,480 ... E2
07748 Middletown○ 62,574 ... E3
07432 Midland Park 7,381 ... B1
08848 Milford 1,368 ... C2
07041 Millburn○ 19,543 ... E2
07946 Millington 975 ... D2
†08876 Millstone 530 ... D2

08850 Milltown 7,136 ... E3
08332 Millville 24,815 ... C5
†07801 Mine Hill○ 3,325 ... D2
08342 Mizpah 900 ... D5
07750 Monmouth Beach 3,318 ... F3
08852 Monmouth Junction 2,579 . D3
07434 Monroe○ 15,858 ... E3
*07042 Montclair 38,321 ... B2
07645 Montvale 7,318 ... B1
07045 Montville○ 14,290 ... E2
†07070 Moonachie 2,706 ... B2
08057 Moorestown 13,695 ... B3
07950 Morris Plains 5,305 ... D2
07960 Morristown⊙ 16,614 ... D2
07046 Mountain Lakes 4,153 ... E2
07092 Mountainside 7,118 ... E2
07856 Mount Arlington 4,251 ... D2
08059 Mount Ephraim 4,863 ... B3
07970 Mount Freedom ... D2
08060 Mount Holly 10,818 ... D4
†08054 Mount Laurel○ 17,614 ... D4
†07828 Mount Olive○ 18,748 ... D2
08061 Mount Royal 900 ... C4
08062 Mullica Hill 1,050 ... C4
08087 Mystic Islands 4,929 ... E4
08063 National Park 3,552 ... B3
07752 Navesink ... E3
07753 Neptune○ 28,366 ... E3
07753 Neptune City 5,276 ... E3
07857 Netcong 3,557 ... D2
*07101 Newark⊙ 329,248 ... B2
Newark‡ 1,965,304 ... B2
*08901 New Brunswick⊙ 41,442 .. E3
New Brunswick-Perth Amboy-Sayreville‡ 595,893 ... E3
08533 New Egypt 2,111 ... E3
08344 Newfield 1,563 ... D4
07435 Newfoundland 900 ... D1
08224 New Gretna 800 ... E4
07646 New Milford 16,876 ... B1
07974 New Providence 12,426 ... E2
07860 Newton⊙ 7,748 ... D1
08346 Newtonville 950 ... D4
07976 New Vernon ... D2
07032 North Arlington 16,587 ... B2
07047 North Bergen○ 47,019 ... B2
08876 North Branch 610 ... D2
08902 North Brunswick○ 22,220 . D3
†07006 North Caldwell 5,832 ... B2
08204 North Cape May 4,029 ... C6
08225 Northfield 7,795 ... D5
07508 North Haledon 8,177 ... B1
07060 North Plainfield 19,108 ... E2
07647 Northvale 5,046 ... F1
08260 North Wildwood 4,714 ... D6
07648 Norwood 4,413 ... C1
07110 Nutley 28,998 ... B2
07755 Oakhurst ... E3
07436 Oakland 13,443 ... B1
08107 Oaklyn 4,223 ... B3
08226 Ocean City 13,949 ... D5
08740 Ocean Gate 1,385 ... E4
07756 Ocean Grove ... F3
07757 Oceanport 5,888 ... F3
07439 Ogdensburg 2,737 ... D1
08857 Old Bridge 21,815 ... E3
07675 Old Tappan 4,168 ... C1
07649 Oradell 8,658 ... B1
*07050 Orange 31,136 ... B2
08723 Osbornsville ... E3
07863 Oxford 1,587 ... C2
07470 Packanack Lake ... B1
07650 Palisades Park 13,732 ... C2
08065 Palmyra 7,085 ... B3
07652 Paramus 26,474 ... B1
07656 Park Ridge 8,515 ... B1
07054 Parsippany-Troy Hills○ 49,868 ... E2
07055 Passaic 52,463 ... E2
*07501 Paterson⊙ 137,970 ... B2
Paterson-Clifton-Passaic‡ 447,585 ... B2
08066 Paulsboro 6,944 ... C4
07977 Peapack-Gladstone 2,038 .. D2
08067 Pedricktown ... C4
08068 Pemberton 1,198 ... D4
08534 Pennington 2,109 ... D3
08110 Pennsauken○ 33,775 ... B3
08069 Penns Grove 5,760 ... C4
08070 Pennsville 12,467 ... C4
07440 Pequannock○ 13,776 ... B1
*08861 Perth Amboy 38,951 ... E2
08865 Phillipsburg 16,647 ... C2
08741 Pine Beach 1,796 ... E4
07058 Pine Brook ... E2
08021 Pine Hill 8,684 ... D4
08854 Piscataway○ 42,223 ... D2
08071 Pitman 9,744 ... C4
*07060 Plainfield 45,555 ... E2
08536 Plainsboro ... D3
08232 Pleasantville 13,435 ... D5
08742 Point Pleasant 17,747 ... E3
08742 Point Pleasant Beach 5,415 ... E3
08240 Pomona 2,358 ... D5
07442 Pompton Lakes 10,660 ... A1
07444 Pompton Plains ... B1
07758 Port Monmouth ... E3
†07850 Port Morris 616 ... D2
07865 Port Murray 250 ... D2
08349 Port Norris 1,730 ... C5
08241 Port Republic 837 ... D4
08540 Princeton 12,035 ... D3
08550 Princeton Junction 2,419 .. D3
†07885 Prospect Park 5,142 ... B1
08072 Quinton 750 ... C4
*07065 Rahway 26,723 ... E2
†08054 Ramblewood 6,475 ... D4
07446 Ramsey 12,899 ... B1
†07801 Randolph○ 17,828 ... D2
08869 Raritan 6,128 ... D2
07701 Red Bank 12,031 ... E3
07657 Ridgefield 10,294 ... B2
07660 Ridgefield Park 12,738 ... B2
*07450 Ridgewood 25,208 ... B1
08551 Ringoes 682 ... D3

07456 Ringwood 12,625 ... E1
08242 Rio Grande 2,016 ... D5
07457 Riverdale 2,530 ... A1
07661 River Edge 11,111 ... B1
08075 Riverside○ 7,941 ... B3
08077 Riverton 3,068 ... B3
07675 River Vale○ 9,489 ... B1
07662 Rochelle Park○ 5,603 ... B2
07866 Rockaway 6,852 ... D2
07647 Rockleigh 192 ... C1
08553 Rocky Hill 717 ... D3
08554 Roebling-Florence 7,677 ... D3
08555 Roosevelt 835 ... E3
07068 Roseland 5,330 ... A2
07203 Roselle 20,641 ... B2
07204 Roselle Park 13,377 ... A2
08352 Rosenhayn 950 ... C5
†07876 Roxbury○ 18,878 ... D2
07760 Rumson 7,623 ... F3
08078 Runnemede 9,461 ... B3
*07070 Rutherford 19,068 ... B2
07662 Saddle Brook○ 14,084 ... B1
07458 Saddle River 2,763 ... B1
08079 Salem⊙ 6,959 ... C4
08872 Sayreville 29,969 ... E3
07076 Scotch Plains○ 20,774 ... E2
07760 Sea Bright 1,812 ... F3
08302 Seabrook 1,411 ... C5
08750 Sea Girt 2,650 ... E3
08243 Sea Isle City 2,644 ... D5
08751 Seaside Heights 1,802 ... E4
08752 Seaside Park 1,795 ... E4
07094 Secaucus 13,719 ... B2
07077 Sewaren ... E2
08080 Sewell ... C4
08353 Shiloh 604 ... C5
08008 Ship Bottom 1,427 ... E4
07078 Short Hills ... E2
07701 Shrewsbury 2,962 ... E3
08081 Sicklerville ... D4
08558 Skillman ... D3
08201 Smithville 70 ... E5
08083 Somerdale 5,900 ... B4
08244 Somers Point 10,330 ... D5
08876 Somerville⊙ 11,973 ... D2
08879 South Amboy 8,322 ... E3
†07719 South Belmar 1,566 ... E3
08880 South Bound Brook 4,331 . E2
†08852 South Brunswick○ 17,127 . E3
07079 South Orange○ 15,864 ... A2
07080 South Plainfield 20,521 ... E2
08882 South River 14,361 ... E3
08753 South Toms River 3,954 ... E4
07871 Sparta○ 13,333 ... D1
08884 Spotswood 7,840 ... E3
07081 Springfield○ 13,955 ... E2
07762 Spring Lake 4,215 ... F3
†07762 Spring Lake Heights 5,424 . E3
07874 Stanhope 3,638 ... D2
08886 Stewartsville 950 ... C2
07980 Stirling ... E2
07460 Stockholm ... D1
08559 Stockton 643 ... D3
08247 Stone Harbor 1,187 ... D5
08084 Stratford 8,005 ... B4
†07747 Strathmore ... E3
07876 Succasunna 10,931 ... D2
07901 Summit 21,071 ... E2
08008 Surf City 1,571 ... E4
07461 Sussex 2,418 ... D1
08085 Swedesboro 2,031 ... C4
07878 Tabor ... E2
07666 Teaneck○ 39,007 ... B2
07670 Tenafly 13,552 ... C1
07608 Teterboro 19 ... B2
08086 Thorofare ... B4
08887 Three Bridges 750 ... D2
07724 Tinton Falls 7,740 ... E3
08753 Toms River⊙ 7,465 ... E4
07512 Totowa 11,448 ... B1
07082 Towaco ... E2
*08601 Trenton (cap.)⊙ 92,124 ... D3
Trenton‡ 307,863 ... D3
08087 Tuckerton 2,472 ... E4
07083 Union○ 50,184 ... A2
07735 Union Beach 6,354 ... E3
07087 Union City 55,593 ... C2
†07421 Upper Greenwood Lake 2,734 ... E1
†07458 Upper Saddle River 7,958 . B1
08406 Ventnor City 11,704 ... E5
07462 Vernon 800 ... E1
07044 Verona 14,166 ... B2
08251 Villas 5,909 ... D5
08088 Vincentown 900 ... D4
08360 Vineland 53,753 ... C5
Vineland-Millville-Bridgeton‡ 132,866 ... C5
†08043 Voorhees○ 12,919 ... B3
07463 Waldwick 10,802 ... B1
07719 Wall○ 18,952 ... E3
07057 Wallington 10,741 ... B2
†07712 Wanamassa ... E3
07465 Wanaque 10,025 ... B1
08758 Waretown 1,175 ... E4
†07060 Warren○ 9,805 ... D2
07882 Washington 6,429 ... D2
07060 Watchung 5,290 ... E2
07470 Wayne○ 46,474 ... A1
07087 Weehawken○ 13,168 ... C2
08090 Wenonah 2,303 ... C4
07006 West Caldwell 11,407 ... A2
†08204 West Cape May 1,091 ... D6
08092 West Creek 827 ... E4
†08086 West Deptford○ 18,002 ... B3
*07090 Westfield 30,447 ... E2
07764 West Long Branch 7,380 ... F3
07480 West Milford 950 ... E1
08108 Westmont 15,875 ... B3
07093 West New York 39,194 ... C2
07052 West Orange 39,510 ... A2
07424 West Paterson 11,293 ... B2
08628 West Trenton ... D3
08093 Westville 4,786 ... B3
†08260 West Wildwood 360 ... D6
07675 Westwood 10,714 ... B1
07885 Wharton 5,485 ... D2

Topography

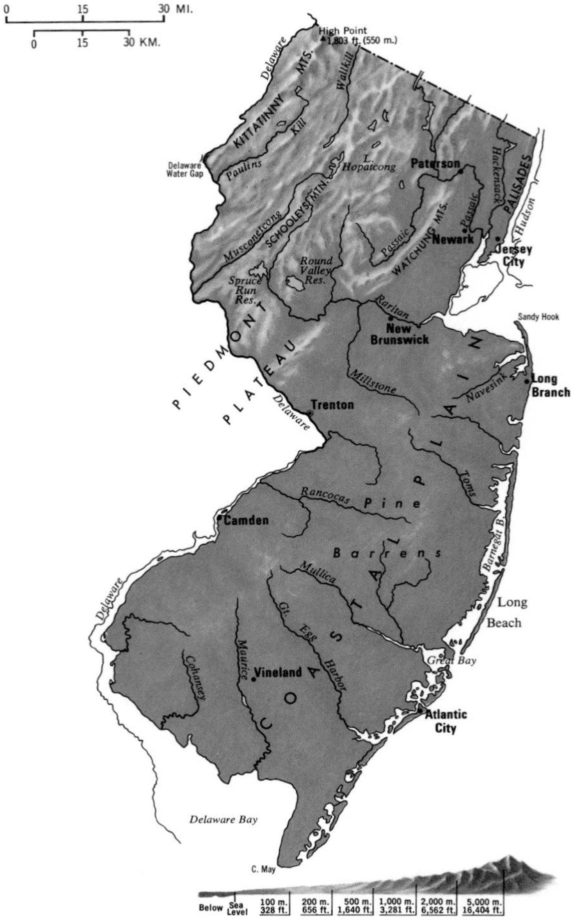
0
15
30 MI.
0
15
30 KM.
High Point
1,803 ft. (550 m.)
Delaware
KITTATINNY
MTS.
Wallkill
Kill
Paulins
Delaware Water Gap
L. Hopatcong
Paterson
Hackensack
PALISADES
Hudson
Passaic
SCHOOLEYS MTN.
Musconetcong
WATCHUNG MTS.
Newark
Jersey City
Round Valley Res.
Spruce Run Res.
Raritan
Sandy Hook
New Brunswick
PIEDMONT
PLATEAU
Millstone
Navesink
Long Branch
Trenton
Delaware
Rancocas
Pine
Toms
Camden
Barrens
Barnegat B.
Mullica
Long Beach
Delaware
Gt. Egg
Maurice
Great Bay
Vineland
Cohansey
Harbor
COASTAL
PLAIN
Atlantic City
Delaware Bay
C. May
Below
Sea Level
100 m. 328 ft.
200 m. 656 ft.
500 m. 1,640 ft.
1,000 m. 3,281 ft.
2,000 m. 6,562 ft.
5,000 m. 16,404 ft.

07981 Whippany ... E2
08889 White House Station ... D2
†07866 White Meadow Lake 8,429 D2
08252 Whitesboro 1,583 ... D5
07765 Wickatunk 950 ... E3
08260 Wildwood 4,913 ... D6
08260 Wildwood Crest 4,149 ... D6
08094 Williamstown 5,768 ... D4
08046 Willingboro○ 39,912 ... D3
†07036 Winfield○ 1,785 ... B2
08270 Woodbine 2,809 ... D5
07095 Woodbridge○ 90,074 ... E2
08096 Woodbury⊙ 10,353 ... B4
08097 Woodbury Heights 3,460 ... B4
07675 Woodcliff Lake 5,644 ... B1
†08107 Wood-Lynne 2,578 ... B3
†07885 Woodport ... D2
07075 Wood-Ridge 7,929 ... B2
08098 Woodstown 3,250 ... C4
08562 Wrightstown 3,031 ... D3
07481 Wyckoff○ 15,500 ... B1
08620 Yardville 9,414 ... D3

OTHER FEATURES

Absecon (inlet) ... E5
Alloways (creek) ... C4
Arthur Kill (str.) ... B3
Atlantic Highlands (ridge) ... E3
Barnegat (bay) ... E4
Batsto (riv.) ... D4
Bayonne Military Ocean Terminal .. B2
Beach Haven (inlet) ... E4
Beaver (brook) ... C2
Ben Davis (pt.) ... C5
Big Flat (brook) ... D1
Big Timber (creek) ... C4
Boonton (res.) ... E2
Brigantine (inlet) ... E5
Budd (lake) ... D2
Canistear (res.) ... E1
Cedar (creek) ... E4
Clinton (res.) ... E1
Cohansey (riv.) ... C5
Cold Spring (inlet) ... D6
Cooper (riv.) ... B3
Corson (inlet) ... D5
Crosswicks (creek) ... D3
Culvers (lake) ... D1
Delaware (bay) ... C5
Delaware (riv.) ... D3
Delaware Water Gap Nat'l Rec. Area ... C1
Earle Naval Weapons Sta. ... E3
Echo (lake) ... E1
Edison Nat'l Hist. Site ... A2
Egg Island (pt.) ... C5
Fort Dix 14,297 ... D3
Fort Hancock ... F3
Fort Monmouth ... E3
Gateway Nat'l Rec. Area ... E2
Great (bay) ... E4
Great Egg Harbor (inlet) ... E5
Greenwood (lake) ... E1
Hackensack (riv.) ... C1
Hereford (inlet) ... D5
High Point (mt.) ... D1
Hopatcong (lake) ... D2
Hudson (riv.) ... C1
Island (beach) ... E4
Kill Van Kull (str.) ... B2
Kittatinny (mts.) ... D1
Lakehurst Naval Air Engineering Center ... E3
Lamington (riv.) ... D2
Landing (creek) ... D4
Little Egg (harb.) ... E4
Lockatong (creek) ... C3
Long (beach) ... E4
Long Beach (isl.) ... E4
Lower New York (bay) ... E2
Manasquan (riv.) ... E3
Manumuskin (riv.) ... D5
Maurice (riv.) ... C4
May (cape) ... C6
McGuire A.F.B. 7,853 ... D3
Metedeconk (riv.) ... E3
Mill (creek) ... E4
Millstone (riv.) ... D3
Mohawk (lake) ... D1
Morristown Nat'l Hist. Park ... D2
Mullica (riv.) ... D4
Musconetcong (riv.) ... C2
Navesink (riv.) ... E3
Newark (bay) ... B2
Oak Ridge (res.) ... D1
Oldmans (creek) ... C4
Oradell (res.) ... B1
Oswego (riv.) ... E4
Owassa (lake) ... D1
Palisades ... C1
Passaic (riv.) ... E2
Paulins Kill (riv.) ... D1
Pennsauken (creek) ... B3
Pequest (riv.) ... D2
Picatinny Arsenal ... D2
Pohatcong (creek) ... C2
Pompton (lake) ... B1
Raccoon (creek) ... C4
Ramapo (riv.) ... E1
Rancocas (creek) ... D3
Raritan (bay) ... E3
Raritan (riv.) ... D2
Ridgeway Branch, Toms (riv.) ... E3
Round Valley (res.) ... D2
Saddle (riv.) ... B1
Salem (riv.) ... C4
Sandy Hook (spit) ... F3
Shoal Branch, Wading (riv.) ... D4
Spruce Run (res.) ... D2
Statue of Liberty Nat'l Mon. ... B2
Stony (brook) ... D3
Stow (creek) ... C5
Swartswood (lake) ... D1
Tappan (lake) ... C1
The Narrows (str.) ... E2
Toms (riv.) ... E3
Townsend (inlet) ... D5
Tuckahoe (riv.) ... D5
Union (lake) ... C5
Upper New York (bay) ... B2
Wading (riv.) ... D4
Wallkill (riv.) ... D1
Wanaque (res.) ... E1
Wawayanda (lake) ... E1

⊙County seat.
‡Population of metropolitan area.
○Population of town or township.
† Zip of nearest p.o. * Multiple zips.

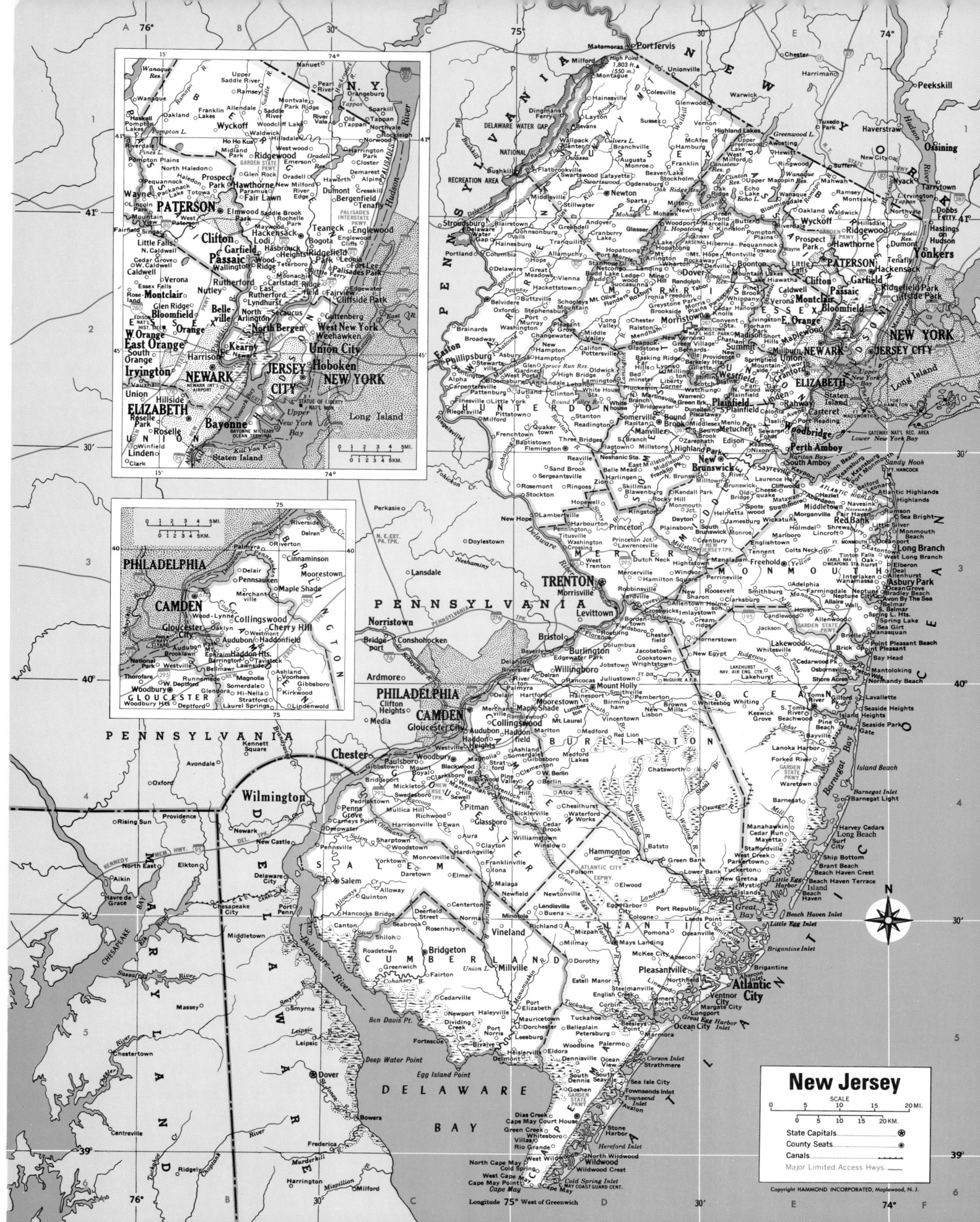

New Jersey

SCALE

0   5   10   15   20 MI.

0   5   10   15   20 KM.

State Capitals .... ⊛
County Seats .... ◉
Canals ....
Major Limited Access Hwys. _____

Copyright HAMMOND INCORPORATED, Maplewood, N.J.

Longitude 75° West of Greenwich

COUNTIES

Bernalillo 419,700 ....C4
Catron 2,720 ....A4
Chaves 51,103 ....E5
Cibola B3
Colfax 13,667 ....E2
Curry 42,019 ....F4
De Baca 2,454 ....E4
Dona Ana 96,340 ....C6
Eddy 47,855 ....E6
Grant 26,204 ....A5
Guadalupe 4,496 ....E4
Harding 987 ....F3
Hidalgo 6,049 ....A7
Lea 55,993 ....F6
Lincoln 10,997 ....D5

Los Alamos 17,599 ....C3
Luna 15,585 ....B6
McKinley 56,449 ....A3
Mora 4,205 ....E3
Otero 44,665 ....D6
Quay 10,577 ....F3
Rio Arriba 29,282 ....B2
Roosevelt 15,695 ....F4
Sandoval 34,799 ....C3
San Juan 81,433 ....A2
San Miguel 22,751 ....D3
Santa Fe 75,360 ....D3
Sierra 8,454 ....B5
Socorro 12,566 ....C5
Taos 19,456 ....D2
Torrance 7,491 ....D4
Union 4,725 ....F2
Valencia 61,115 ....C4

CITIES and TOWNS

Zip	Name/Pop.	Key
87510	Abiquiu 500	C2
†87034	Acoma 150	B4
†87034	Acomita (Pueblo of Acoma) 975	B3
88310	Alamogordo☉ 24,024	C6
*87101	Albuquerque☉ 331,767	C3
	Albuquerque‡ 454,499	C3
87511	Alcalde 975	C2
87001	Algodones 195	C3
88312	Alto 285	D5
87512	Amalia 200	D2
88021	Anthony 3,285	C6
87711	Anton Chico 400	D3
87930	Arrey 367	B6
87513	Arroyo Hondo 400	D2

87514	Arroyo Seco 500	D2
88210	Artesia 10,385	E6
87410	Aztec☉ 5,512	B2
88023	Bayard 3,036	A6
87002	Belen 5,617	C4
88314	Bent 294	D5
88024	Berino 600	C6
87412	Blanco 200	B2
87413	Blanco 4,881	A2
87005	Bluewater 300	A3
87006	Bosque (Bosque Farms) 3,353	C4
87712	Buena Vista 178	D3
87515	Canjilon 380	C2
87516	Canones 300	C2
88316	Capitan 762	D5
88414	Capulin 100	F2
88220	Carlsbad☉ 25,496	E6

88301	Carrizozo☉ 1,222	D5
87007	Casa Blanca 560	B4
88113	Causey 81	F5
87518	Cebolla 100	C2
87008	Cedar Crest 600	C3
†87410	Cedar Hill 145	B2
88026	Central 1,968	A6
87010	Cerrillos 500	D3
87519	Cerro 400	D2
87713	Chacon 310	D2
87520	Chama 1,090	C2
88027	Chamberino 700	C6
87521	Chamisal 642	D2
87522	Chimayo 1,993	D2
87714	Cimarron 888	E2
88415	Clayton☉ 2,968	F2
87715	Cleveland 450	D2
88028	Cliff 600	A6
88317	Cloudcroft 521	D6

88101	Clovis☉ 31,194	F4
87041	Cochiti 983	C3
88029	Columbus 414	B7
88416	Conchas Dam 240	E3
87523	Cordova 750	D2
88318	Corona 236	D4
87048	Corrales 2,791	C3
87524	Costilla 400	D2
87313	Crownpoint 1,134	A3
†86504	Crystal 200	A2
87013	Cuba 609	B2
87014	Cubero 300	B3
87821	Datil 150	B4
88030	Deming☉ 9,964	B6
87933	Derry 175	B6
88418	Des Moines 178	F2
88230	Dexter 882	E5
87527	Dixon 800	D2
88032	Dona Ana 800	C6

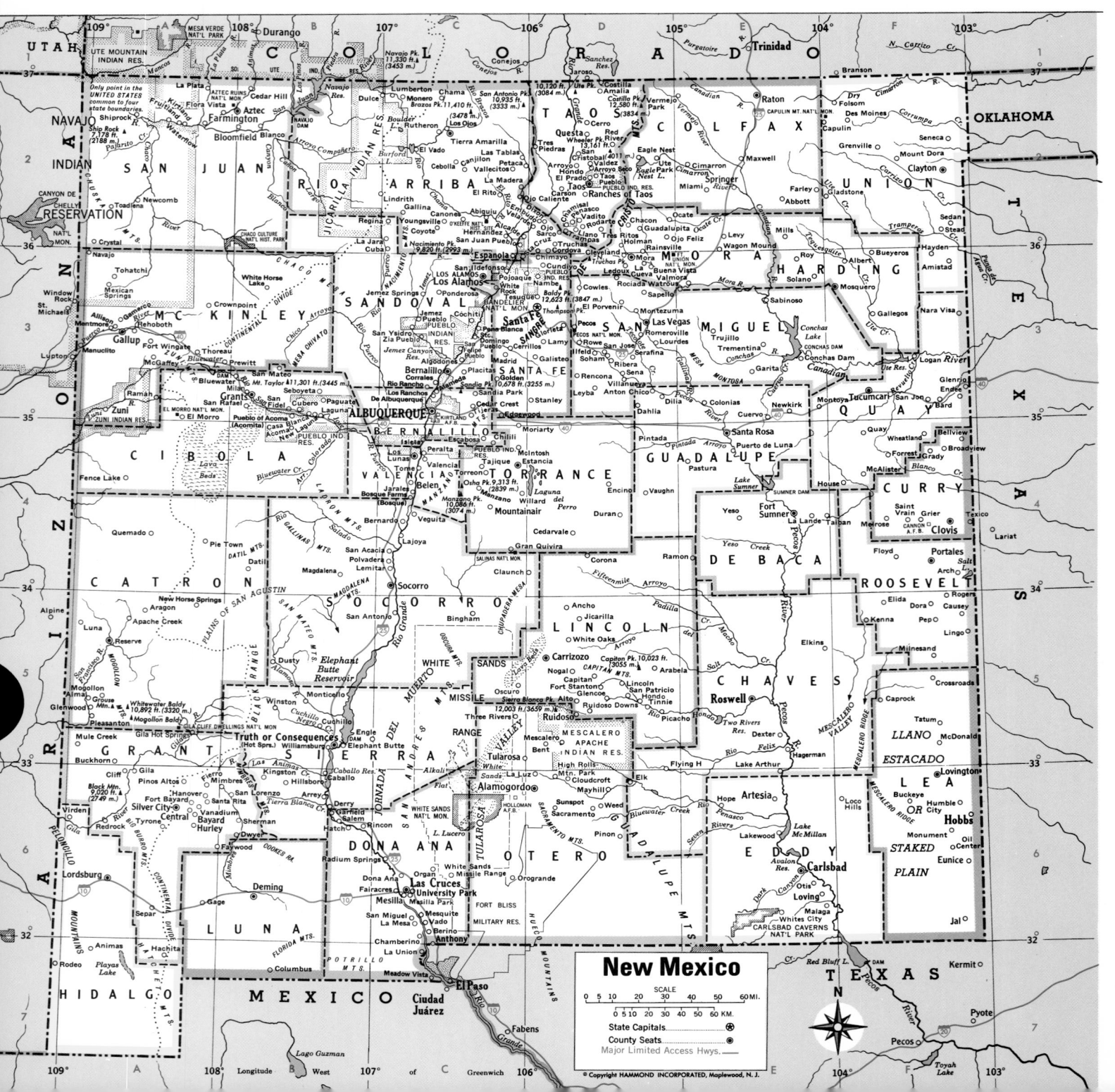

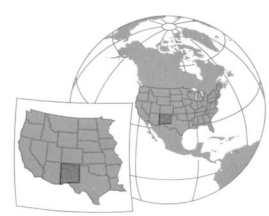

88115 Dora 168 .... F5
87528 Dulce 1,648 .... B2
87718 Eagle Nest 202 .... D2
88116 Elida 202 .... F5
87529 El Prado 200 .... D2
87530 El Rito 475 .... C2
87531 Embudo 400 .... C2
88321 Encino 155 .... D4
87532 Espanola 6,803 .... C3
87016 Estancia⊙ 830 .... D4
88231 Eunice 2,970 .... F6
88033 Fairacres 700 .... C6
87401 Farmington 31,222 .... A2
†88041 Fierro 200 .... A6
87415 Flora Vista 500 .... A2
88118 Floyd 146 .... F4
88419 Folsom 73 .... F2
88036 Fort Bayard 400 .... A6
88323 Fort Stanton 80 .... D5
88119 Fort Sumner⊙ 1,421 .... E4
87316 Fort Wingate 800 .... A3
87416 Fruitland 800 .... A2
†87540 Galisteo 125 .... D3
87017 Gallina 420 .... C2
87301 Gallup⊙ 18,167 .... A3
87317 Gamerco 800 .... A3
87936 Garfield 600 .... B6
88038 Gila 350 .... A6
88324 Glencoe 125 .... D5
88039 Glenwood 220 .... A5
87535 Glorieta 300 .... D3
88120 Grady 122 .... F4
87020 Grants 11,439 .... B3
88424 Grenville 39 .... F2
87722 Guadalupita 300 .... D2
88232 Hagerman 936 .... E5
88041 Hanover 300 .... A6
87937 Hatch 1,028 .... B6
87537 Hernandez 500 .... C2
88325 High Rolls-Mountain Park 555 .... D5
88042 Hillsboro 175 .... B6
88240 Hobbs 29,153 .... F6
87723 Holman 400 .... D2
88336 Hondo 425 .... D5
88250 Hope 111 .... E6
87901 Hot Springs (Truth or Consequences)⊙ 5,219 .... B5
88121 House 117 .... F4
88043 Hurley 1,616 .... A6
87022 Isleta 1,246 .... C4
88252 Jal 2,675 .... F6
87023 Jarales 700 .... C4
87024 Jemez Pueblo 1,503 .... C3
87025 Jemez Springs 316 .... C3
87417 Kirtland 2,358 .... A2
87026 Laguna 900 .... B3
87027 La Jara 210 .... B2
88253 Lake Arthur 327 .... E5
88337 La Luz 1,194 .... C6
87539 La Madera 200 .... C2
88044 La Mesa 900 .... C6
87418 La Plata 150 .... A2
88001 Las Cruces⊙ 45,086 .... C6
Las Cruces‡ 96,340 .... C6
87701 Las Vegas⊙ 14,322 .... D3
87725 Ledoux 300 .... D3
87823 Lemitar 800 .... B4
88338 Lincoln 100 .... D5
87543 Llano 325 .... D2
88255 Loco Hills 375 .... F6
88426 Logan 735 .... F3
88045 Lordsburg⊙ 3,195 .... A6
87544 Los Alamos⊙ 11,039 .... C3
87031 Los Lunas⊙ 3,525 .... C4
†87101 Los Ranchos De Albuquerque 2,702 .... C3
88256 Loving 1,355 .... E6
88260 Lovington⊙ 9,727 .... F6
87547 Lumberton 175 .... C2
87824 Luna 200 .... A5
87825 Magdalena 1,022 .... B4
88263 Malaga 300 .... E6
87728 Maxwell 316 .... E2
88339 Mayhill 300 .... D6
†79901 Meadow Vista 3,377 .... C7
88124 Melrose 649 .... F4
87319 Mentmore 315 .... A3
88340 Mescalero 1,259 .... D5
88046 Mesilla 2,029 .... C6
88047 Mesilla Park C6
88048 Mesquite 500 .... C6
87320 Mexican Springs 150 .... A3
87729 Miami 112 .... E2
87021 Milan 3,747 .... B3
88049 Mimbres 300 .... B6
87731 Montezuma 250 .... D3
87939 Monticello 125 .... B5
88265 Monument 300 .... F6
87732 Mora⊙ D3
87035 Moriarty 1,276 .... D4
87733 Mosquero⊙ 197 .... F3
87036 Mountainair 1,170 .... C4
†87501 Nambe 1,017 .... D3
88430 Nara Visa 250 .... F3
87328 Navajo 920 .... A3
†87325 Newcomb 500 .... A2
87038 New Laguna 250 .... B4
88266 Oil Center 236 .... F6
87549 Ojo Caliente 600 .... D2
87735 Ojo Feliz 133 .... E2
87550 Ojo Sarco 380 .... D2
88052 Organ 300 .... C6
87040 Paguate 500 .... B3
87552 Pecos 885 .... D3
87041 Pena Blanca 700 .... C3
87553 Penasco 860 .... D2
87042 Peralta 400 .... C4
88343 Picacho 100 .... D5
88053 Pinos Altos 250 .... A6
87044 Ponderosa 300 .... C3
88130 Portales⊙ 9,940 .... F4
87045 Prewitt 300 .... B3
88432 Puerto de Luna 175 .... E4
87829 Quemado 450 .... A4
87556 Questa 1,202 .... D2
88054 Radium Springs 150 .... B6
87736 Rainsville 350 .... D2
87321 Ramah 574 .... A3
87557 Ranches of Taos 1,411 .... D2
87740 Raton⊙ 8,225 .... E2
87558 Red River 332 .... D2
87322 Rehoboth 200 .... A3
87830 Reserve⊙ 439 .... A5
87560 Ribera 84 .... D3
87940 Rincon 300 .... C6
87124 Rio Rancho 9,985 .... C3
87561 Rodarte 650 .... D2
88201 Roswell⊙ 39,676 .... E5
87562 Rowe 290 .... D3
87743 Roy 381 .... E3
88345 Ruidoso 4,260 .... D5
88346 Ruidoso Downs 949 .... D5
87941 Salem 400 .... B6
87831 San Acacia 286 .... B4
87832 San Antonio 359 .... B5
87564 San Cristobal 350 .... D2
87047 Sandia Park 450 .... C3
†87001 San Felipe Pueblo 1,465 .... C3
†87501 San Ildefonso 232 .... C3
88434 San Jon 341 .... F3
87565 San Jose 150 .... D3
87566 San Juan Pueblo 870 .... C2
88041 San Lorenzo 200 .... B6
87050 San Mateo 200 .... B3
88058 San Miguel 400 .... C6
88348 San Patricio 300 .... D5
87051 San Rafael 300 .... A3
87567 Santa Cruz 754 .... D2
87501 Santa Fe (cap.)⊙ 48,953 .... C3
†88041 Santa Rita 600 .... B6
88435 Santa Rosa⊙ 2,469 .... E4
87052 Santo Domingo Pueblo 2,082 .... C3
87053 San Ysidro 199 .... C3
87745 Sapello 600 .... D3
87055 Seboyeta 125 .... B3
87568 Sena 150 .... D3
87569 Serafina 225 .... D3
87420 Shiprock 7,237 .... A2
88061 Silver City⊙ 9,887 .... A6
87801 Socorro⊙ 7,173 .... C4
†87565 Soham 104 .... D3
87747 Springer 1,657 .... E2
87057 Tajique 145 .... C4
87571 Taos⊙ 3,369 .... D2
†87571 Taos Pueblo 900 .... D2
88267 Tatum 896 .... F5
87574 Tesuque 1,014 .... C3
88135 Texico 958 .... F4
87323 Thoreau 1,099 .... A3
87575 Tierra Amarilla⊙ 850 .... C2
87059 Tijeras 311 .... C3
87324 Toadlena 200 .... A2
87325 Tohatchi 1,011 .... A3
87060 Tome 500 .... C4
87577 Tres Piedras 200 .... D2
87578 Truchas 275 .... D2
†87701 Trujillo 148 .... E3
87901 Truth or Consequences⊙ 5,219 .... B5
88401 Tucumcari⊙ 6,765 .... F3
88352 Tularosa 2,536 .... C5
88003 University Park 4,353 .... C6
87579 Vadito 400 .... D2
88072 Vado 325 .... C6
87580 Valdez 300 .... D2
†87031 Valencia 500 .... C4
87581 Vallecitos 450 .... C2
88073 Vanadium 150 .... A6
88353 Vaughn 737 .... D4
87582 Velarde 950 .... C2
87583 Villanueva 500 .... D3
†88055 Virden 246 .... A6
87752 Wagon Mound 416 .... E2
87421 Waterflow 475 .... A2
87753 Watrous 175 .... D3
87544 White Rock 6,560 .... C3
88002 White Sands Missile Range 3,120 .... C6
87063 Willard 166 .... D4
87942 Williamsburg 433 .... B5
88136 Yeso 200 .... E4
87064 Youngsville 125 .... C2
†87053 Zia Pueblo 500 .... C3
87327 Zuni 5,551 .... A3

OTHER FEATURES

Abiquiu (res.) C2
Alamosa (riv.) B5
Animas (riv.) B1

AREA 121,593 sq. mi. (314,926 sq. km.)
POPULATION 1,302,981
CAPITAL Santa Fe
LARGEST CITY Albuquerque
HIGHEST POINT Wheeler Pk. 13,161 ft. (4011 m.)
SETTLED IN 1605
ADMITTED TO UNION January 6, 1912
POPULAR NAME Land of Enchantment
STATE FLOWER Yucca
STATE BIRD Road Runner

Avalon (res.) E6
Aztec Ruins Nat'l Mon. A2
Baldy (peak) D3
Bandelier Nat'l Mon. C3
Big Burro (mts.) A6
Black (mt.) A6
Black (range) B5
Blanco (creek) F4
Bluewater (creek) B4
Bluewater (creek) D6
Bluewater (lake) A3
Boulder (lake) C2
Brazos (peak) C2
Burford (lake) C2
Caballo (res.) B6
Canadian (riv.) F3
Cannon A.F.B. 3,798 .... F4
Canyon Blanco (creek) B2
Capitan (mts.) D5
Capitan (peak) D5
Capulin Mountain Nat'l Mon. E2
Carlsbad Caverns Nat'l Park E6
Carrizo (creek) F2
Chaco (mesa) B3
Chaco (riv.) A2
Chaco Culture Nat'l Hist. Park B2
Chico Arroyo (creek) B3
Chivato (mesa) B3
Chupadera (mesa) C5
Chuska (mts.) A2
Cimarron (riv.) E2
Colorado, Arroyo (riv.) B4
Compañero, Arroyo (creek) B2
Conchas (lake) E3
Conchas (riv.) E3
Cookes (range) B6
Corrumpa (creek) F2
Costilla (peak) D2
Cuchillo Negro (creek) B5
Cuervo (creek) E3
Dark Canyon (creek) E6
Datil (mts.) B4
Dry Cimarron (riv.) F2
Eagle Nest (lake) D2
Elephant Butte (res.) B5
El Morro Nat'l Mon. A3
El Rito (riv.) C2
Fifteenmile Arroyo (creek) D4
Florida (mts.) B7
Fort Bliss Mil. Res. C6
Fort Union Nat'l Mon. E3
Gallinas (mts.) B4
Gallinas (riv.) E3
Gila (riv.) A6
Gila Cliff Dwellings Nat'l Mon. A5
Grouse (mt.) A5
Guadalupe (mts.) D6
Hatchet (mts.) A7
Holloman A.F.B. 7,245 .... C6
Hueco (mts.) D6
Jemez (riv.) C3
Jemez Canyon (res.) C3
Jicarilla Ind. Res. B2
Jornada del Muerto (valley) C5
Kirtland A.F.B. C3
Ladron (mts.) B4
La Plata (riv.) A1
Largo, Cañon (creek) B2
Las Animas (creek) B5
Llano Estacado (Staked) (plain) F5
Lucero (lake) C6
Macho, Arroyo del (creek) D5
Magdalena (mts.) B4
Manzano (mts.) C4
Manzano (peak) C4
McMillan (lake) E6
Mescalero (ridge) F6
Mescalero (valley) F5
Mescalero Apache Ind. Res. D5
Mimbres (mts.) B6
Mimbres (riv.) B6
Mogollon (mts.) A5
Mogollon Baldy (peak) A5
Montosa (mesa) E3
Mora (riv.) E3
Nacimiento (mts.) C3
Nacimiento (peak) C2
Navajo (res.) B2
Navajo Ind. Res. A2
North Truchas (peak) D3
Ocate (creek) E2
O'Keeffe Nat'l Hist. Site C2
Oscura (mts.) C5
Osha (peak) C4
Padilla (creek) D5
Pajarito (creek) A2
Pecos (riv.) E5
Pecos Nat'l Mon. D3
Peloncillo (mts.) A6
Perro (mts.) D4
Pinos, Rio de los (riv.) B2
Pintada Arroyo (creek) E4
Playas (lake) A7
Potrillo (mts.) B7
Pueblo Ind. Res. B4
Pueblo Ind. Res. D3
Pueblo Ind. Res. C4
Pueblo Ind. Res. D2
Puerco (riv.) A3
Red Bluff (lake) E7
Revuelto (creek) F3
Rio Brazos (riv.) C2
Rio Chama (riv.) C2
Rio Felix (riv.) E5
Rio Grande (riv.) C5
Rio Hondo (riv.) E5
Rio Penasco (riv.) E6
Rio Puerco (riv.) C4
Rio Salado (riv.) B4
Rocky (mts.) C1
Sacramento (mts.) D6
Salinas Nat'l Mon. C4
Salt (creek) E5
Salt (lake) F4
San Agustin (plains) B5
San Andres (mts.) C6
San Antonio (peak) C2
Sandia (peak) C3
San Francisco (riv.) A5
Sangre de Cristo (mts.) D3
San Jose (riv.) B3
San Juan (riv.) B2
San Mateo (mts.) B5
Seven Rivers (riv.) E6
Ship Rock (peak) A2
Sierra Blanca (peak) C5
Staked (Llano Estacado) (plain) F5
Sumner (lake) E4
Taylor (mt.) B3
Tecolote (creek) D3
Tequesquite (creek) E2
Thompson (peak) D3
Tierra Blanca (creek) B6
Tramperos (creek) F2
Tularosa (valley) C6
Ute (creek) F3
Ute (peak) D2
Ute (res.) F3
Ute Mountain Ind. Res. A1
Vermejo (riv.) E2
Wheeler (peak) D2
White Sands (des.) C5
White Sands Missile Range C5
White Sands Nat'l Mon. C6
Whitewater Baldy (mt.) A5
Wingate Army Depot A3
Yeso (creek) E4
Zuni (mts.) A3
Zuni (riv.) A3
Zuni Ind. Res. A3

⊙County seat.
‡Population of metropolitan area.
† Zip of nearest p.o. * Multiple zips.

Topography

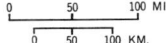

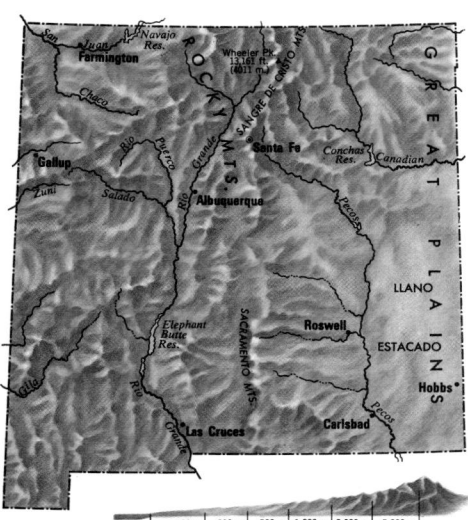

Agriculture, Industry and Resources

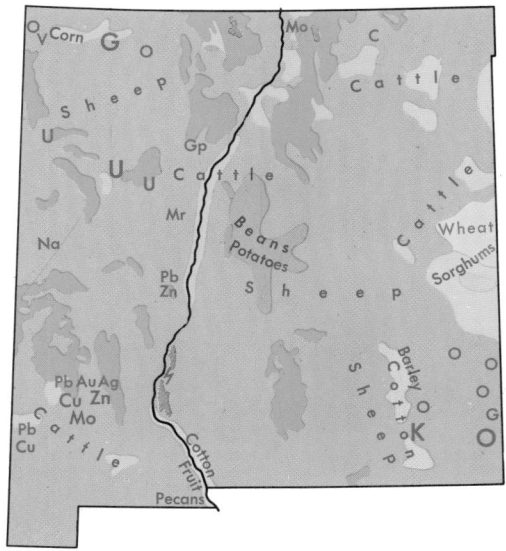

DOMINANT LAND USE

- Wheat, Grain Sorghums, Range Livestock
- General Farming, Livestock, Special Crops
- General Farming, Livestock, Cash Grain
- Dry Beans, General Farming
- Cotton, Forest Products
- Range Livestock
- Forests
- Nonagricultural Land

MAJOR MINERAL OCCURRENCES

Ag Silver
Au Gold
C Coal
Cu Copper
G Natural Gas
Gp Gypsum
K Potash
Mo Molybdenum
Mr Marble
Na Salt
O Petroleum
Pb Lead
U Uranium
V Vanadium
Zn Zinc
ϟ Water Power

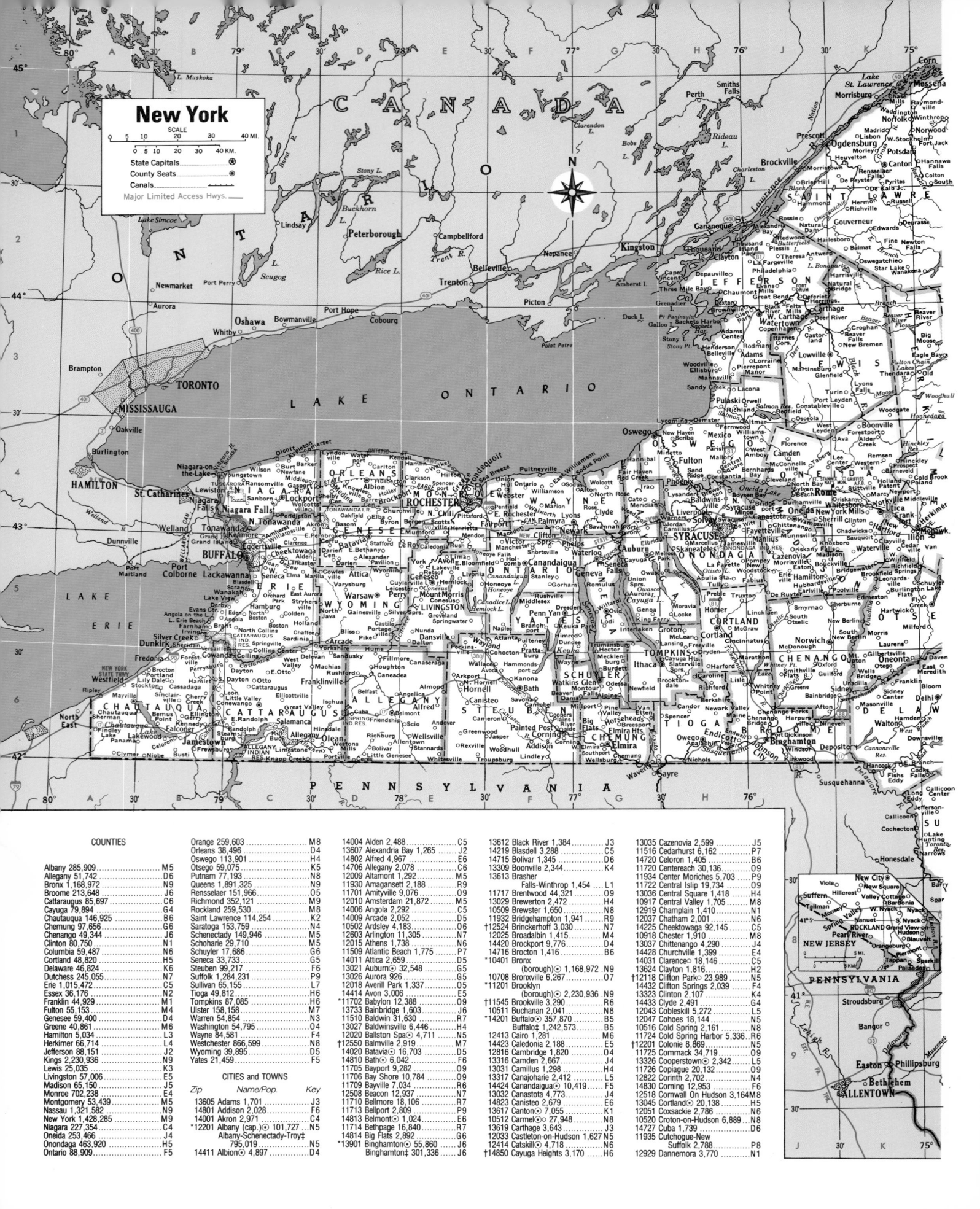

New York

SCALE
0 5 10 20 30 40 MI.
0 5 10 20 30 40 KM.

State Capitals .... ✪
County Seats .... ⊙
Canals ....
Major Limited Access Hwys. ____

COUNTIES

County	Pop.	Key
Albany 285,909		M5
Allegany 51,742		D6
Bronx 1,168,972		N9
Broome 213,648		J6
Cattaraugus 85,697		G4
Cayuga 79,894		G5
Chautauqua 146,925		B6
Chemung 49,344		G6
Chenango 59,487		K6
Clinton 80,750		N1
Columbia 59,487		N6
Cortland 48,820		H5
Delaware 46,824		K6
Dutchess 245,055		N7
Erie 1,015,472		C5
Essex 36,176		N2
Franklin 44,929		M1
Fulton 55,153		M4
Genesee 59,400		D4
Greene 40,861		M6
Hamilton 5,034		L3
Herkimer 66,714		L4
Jefferson 88,151		J2
Kings 2,230,936		N9
Lewis 25,035		K3
Livingston 57,006		E5
Madison 65,150		J5
Monroe 702,238		E4
Montgomery 53,472		M5
Nassau 1,321,582		N9
New York 1,428,285		M9
Niagara 227,354		C4
Oneida 253,466		J4
Onondaga 463,920		H5
Ontario 88,909		F5

County	Pop.	Key
Orange 259,603		M8
Orleans 38,496		D4
Oswego 123,901		H4
Otsego 59,075		K5
Putnam 77,193		N8
Queens 1,891,325		N9
Rensselaer 151,966		N5
Richmond 352,121		M9
Rockland 259,530		N8
Saint Lawrence 114,254		K2
Saratoga 153,759		N4
Schenectady 149,946		M5
Schoharie 29,710		M5
Schuyler 17,686		G6
Seneca 33,733		G5
Steuben 99,217		F6
Suffolk 1,284,231		P9
Sullivan 65,155		L7
Tioga 49,812		H6
Tompkins 87,085		H6
Ulster 158,158		M7
Warren 54,854		N3
Washington 54,795		O4
Wayne 84,581		F4
Westchester 866,599		N8
Wyoming 39,895		D5
Yates 21,459		F5

CITIES and TOWNS

Zip	Name/Pop.	Key
13605	Adams 1,701	J3
14801	Addison 2,028	F6
14001	Akron 2,971	C4
	Albany (cap.)⊙ 101,727	N5
	Albany-Schenectady-Troy‡ 795,019	N5
14411	Albion⊙ 4,897	D4
14004	Alden 2,488	C5
13607	Alexandria Bay 1,265	J2
14802	Alfred 4,967	E6
14706	Allegany 2,078	C5
12009	Altamont 1,292	M5
11930	Amagansett 2,188	R9
11701	Amityville 9,076	O9
12010	Amsterdam 21,872	M5
14006	Angola 2,292	C5
14009	Arcade 2,052	D5
10502	Ardsley 4,183	O6
12603	Arlington 11,305	N7
12015	Athens 1,738	N6
11509	Atlantic Beach 1,775	P7
14011	Attica 2,659	D5
13021	Auburn⊙ 32,548	G5
13026	Aurora 926	G5
12018	Averill Park 1,337	O5
14414	Avon 3,006	E5
14004	Alden 2,488	C5
13612	Black River 1,384	J3
14219	Blasdell 3,288	C5
14715	Bolivar 1,345	D6
13309	Boonville 2,344	K4
13613	Brasher Falls-Winthrop 1,454	L1
11717	Brentwood 44,321	O9
13029	Brewerton 2,472	H4
10509	Brewster 1,650	N8
11932	Bridgehampton 1,941	R9
†12524	Brinckerhoff 3,030	N7
12025	Broadalbin 1,415	M4
14420	Brockport 9,776	D4
14716	Brocton 1,416	B6
*10401	Bronx (borough)⊙ 1,168,972	N9
10708	Bronxville 6,267	O7
*11201	Brooklyn (borough)⊙ 2,230,936	N9
*11545	Brookville 3,290	R6
10511	Buchanan 2,041	N8
*14201	Buffalo⊙ 357,870	B5
	Buffalo‡ 1,242,573	B5
12413	Cairo 1,281	M6
14423	Caledonia 2,188	E5
12816	Cambridge 1,820	O4
13316	Camden 2,667	J4
13031	Camillus 1,298	H4
13317	Canajoharie 2,412	L5
14424	Canandaigua⊙ 10,419	F5
13032	Canastota 4,773	J4
14823	Canisteo 2,679	E6
13617	Canton⊙ 7,055	K1
13619	Carthage 3,643	J3
12033	Castleton-on-Hudson 1,627	N5
12414	Catskill⊙ 4,718	N6
†14850	Cayuga Heights 3,170	H6
13035	Cazenovia 2,599	J5
11516	Cedarhurst 6,162	P7
14720	Celoron 1,405	B6
11720	Centereach 30,136	O9
11934	Center Moriches 5,703	P9
11722	Central Islip 19,734	O9
13036	Central Square 1,418	H4
10917	Central Valley 1,705	M8
12919	Champlain 1,410	N1
12037	Chatham 2,001	N6
14225	Cheektowaga 92,145	C5
10918	Chester 1,910	M8
13037	Chittenango 4,290	J4
14428	Churchville 1,399	E4
14031	Clarence 18,146	C5
13624	Clayton 1,816	H2
†12118	Clifton Park 23,989	N5
14432	Clifton Springs 2,039	F4
13323	Clinton 2,107	K4
14433	Clyde 2,491	G4
12043	Cobleskill 5,272	L5
12047	Cohoes 18,144	N5
10516	Cold Spring 2,161	N8
11724	Cold Spring Harbor 5,336	R6
†12201	Colonie 8,869	N5
11725	Commack 34,719	O9
13326	Cooperstown⊙ 2,342	L5
11726	Copiague 20,132	O9
12822	Corinth 2,702	N4
14830	Corning 12,953	F6
12518	Cornwall On Hudson 3,164	M8
13045	Cortland⊙ 20,138	H5
12051	Coxsackie 2,786	N6
10520	Croton-on-Hudson 6,889	N8
14727	Cuba 1,739	D6
11935	Cutchogue-New Suffolk 2,788	P8
12929	Dannemora 3,770	N1

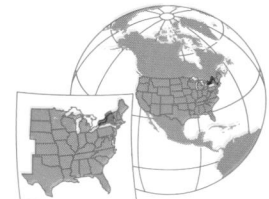

AREA 49,108 sq. mi. (127,190 sq. km.)
POPULATION 17,558,072
CAPITAL Albany
LARGEST CITY New York
HIGHEST POINT Mt. Marcy 5,344 ft. (1629 m.)
SETTLED IN 1614
ADMITTED TO UNION July 26, 1788
POPULAR NAME Empire State
STATE FLOWER Rose
STATE BIRD Bluebird

Topography

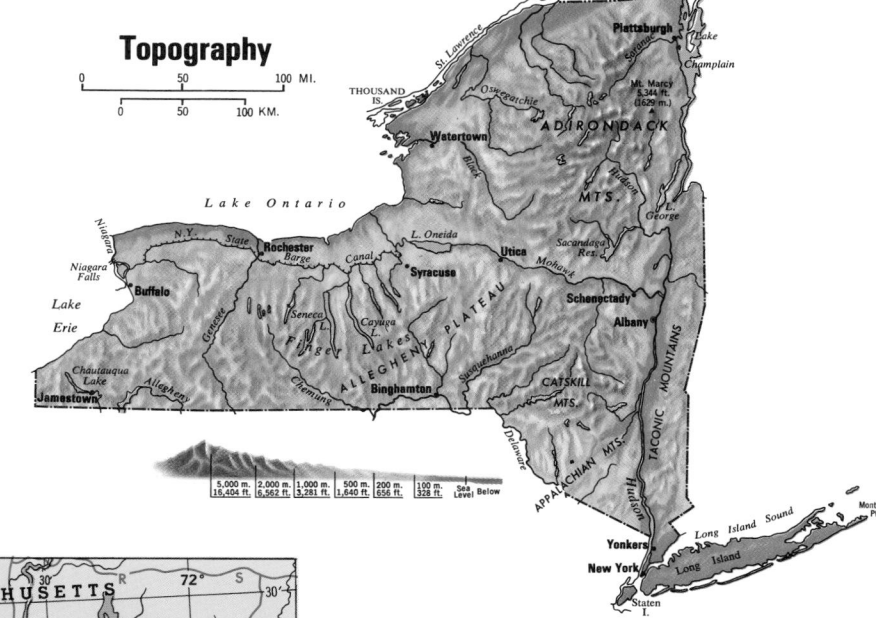

© Copyright HAMMOND INCORPORATED, Maplewood, N.J.

14437 Dansville 4,979	E5	14456 Geneva 15,133 .... G5
11729 Deer Park 30,394	O9	11542 Glen Cove 24,618 .... R6
13753 Delhi⊙ 3,374	L6	12801 Glens Falls 15,897 .... N4
12054 Delmar 8,423	N5	Glens Falls‡ 109,649 .... N4
14043 Depew 19,819	C5	12078 Gloversville 17,836 .... M4
13754 Deposit 1,897	K6	10526 Golden's Bridge 1,367 ... N8
13214 DeWitt 9,024	H4	10924 Goshen⊙ 4,874 .... M8
11746 Dix Hills 26,983	O9	13642 Gouverneur 4,285 .... K2
10522 Dobbs Ferry 10,053	O6	14070 Gowanda 2,713 .... B6
13329 Dolgeville 2,602	L4	12832 Granville 2,696 .... O4
12522 Dover Plains 1,753	O7	*11020 Great Neck 9,168 .... P6
14837 Dundee 1,556	F5	14616 Greece 16,177 .... E4
14048 Dunkirk 15,310	B5	13778 Greene 1,747 .... J6
14052 East Aurora 6,803	C5	12183 Green Island 2,696 .... N5
10709 Eastchester 20,305	P6	11944 Greenport 2,273 .... P8
11937 East Hampton 1,886	R9	12834 Greenwich 1,955 .... O4
†11576 East Hills 7,160	P7	10925 Greenwood Lake 2,809 ... M8
11554 East Meadow 39,317	R7	13073 Groton 2,313 .... H5
11731 East Northport 20,187	O9	12835 Hadley-Lake Luzerne 1,988 N4
14445 East Rochester 7,596	F4	12086 Hagaman 1,331 .... M5
11518 East Rockaway 10,917	R7	14075 Hamburg 10,582 .... C5
13057 East Syracuse 3,412	H4	13346 Hamilton 3,725 .... J5
14057 Eden 3,000	C5	11946 Hampton Bays 7,256 ...... R9
14058 Elba 750	D4	13783 Hancock 1,526 .... K7
12932 Elizabethtown⊙ 659	N2	10528 Harrison 23,046 .... P6
12428 Ellenville 4,405	M7	10530 Hartsdale 10,216 .... P6
14059 Elma 2,459	C5	10706 Hastings On Hudson 8,573 P6
*14901 Elmira⊙ 35,327	G6	11787 Hauppauge 20,960 .... O9
Elmira‡ 97,656	G6	10927 Haverstraw 8,800 .... M8
14903 Elmira Heights 4,279	G6	10532 Hawthorne 5,010 .... O6
11003 Elmont 27,592	P7	*11550 Hempstead 40,404 .... R7
10523 Elmsford 3,361	O6	13350 Herkimer⊙ 8,383 .... L4
11731 Elwood 11,847	O9	11557 Hewlett 6,986 .... P7
13760 Endicott 14,457	H6	†11557 Hewlett Harbor 1,331 .... P7
13760 Endwell 13,745	H6	*11801 Hicksville 43,245 .... R7
14450 Fairport 5,970	F4	12528 Highland 3,967 .... M7
†12601 Fairview 5,852	N7	10928 Highland Falls 4,187 ...... M8
14733 Falconer 2,778	B6	10931 Hillburn 926 .... M8
11735 Farmingdale 7,946	R7	10977 Hillcrest 5,733 .... K8
13066 Fayetteville 4,709	J4	14468 Hilton 4,151 .... E4
†12801 Fernwood 3,640	N4	14080 Holland 1,347 .... C5
12524 Fishkill 1,555	N7	14470 Holley 1,882 .... D4
†11901 Flanders-Riverside 5,400	P9	13077 Homer 3,635 .... H5
*11001 Floral Park 16,805	P7	14472 Honeoye Falls 2,410 ...... F5
10921 Florida 1,947	M8	12090 Hoosick Falls 3,609 .... O5
12068 Fonda⊙ 1,006	M5	12533 Hopewell Junction 1,754 .. N7
12937 Fort Covington 1,804	M1	14843 Hornell 10,234 .... E6
12828 Fort Edward 3,561	O4	14845 Horseheads 7,348 .... G6
13339 Fort Plain 2,555	L5	14744 Houghton 1,604 .... D6
13340 Frankfort 2,995	K4	12534 Hudson⊙ 7,986 .... N6
11010 Franklin Square 29,051	R7	12839 Hudson Falls⊙ 7,419 ...... O4
14737 Franklinville 1,887	D6	11743 Huntington 21,727 .... O9
14063 Fredonia 11,126	B6	11746 Huntington Station 28,769 . R6
11520 Freeport 38,272	R7	12443 Hurley 4,892 .... M7
14738 Frewsburg 1,908	B6	12538 Hyde Park 2,550 .... N6
14739 Friendship 1,461	D6	13357 Ilion 9,450 .... K5
13069 Fulton 13,312	H4	11696 Inwood 8,228 .... P7
11530 Garden City 22,927	R7	14617 Irondequoit 57,648 .... E4
14067 Gasport 1,339	C4	10533 Irvington 6,348 .... O6
14454 Geneseo⊙ 6,746	E5	11558 Island Park 4,847 .... R7

(continued on following page)

(continued)

11751 Islip 13,438 .... O9
14850 Ithaca⊙ 28,732 .... G6
*11401 Jamaica⊙ N9
14701 Jamestown 35,775 .... B6
11753 Jericho 12,739 .... R6
13790 Johnson City 17,126 .... J6
12095 Johnstown⊙ 9,360 .... M4
13080 Jordan 1,371 .... H4
12944 Keeseville 2,025 .... O2
14271 Kenmore 18,474 .... C5
12446 Kerhonkson 1,646 .... M7
12106 Kinderhook 1,377 .... N6
11754 Kings Park 16,131 .... O9
11024 Kings Point 5,234 .... P6
12401 Kingston⊙ 24,481 .... M7
14218 Lackawanna 22,701 .... B5
10512 Lake Carmel 7,295 .... N8
†14006 Lake Erie Beach 4,625 .... B5
12845 Lake George⊙ 1,047 .... N4
12449 Lake Katrine 2,011 .... M7
12846 Lake Luzerne-Hadley 1,988 N4
12946 Lake Placid 2,490 .... N2
12108 Lake Pleasant⊙ 700 .... M4
11040 Lake Success 2,396 .... P7
14750 Lakewood 3,941 .... B6
14086 Lancaster 13,056 .... C5
14882 Lansing 3,039 .... H5
10538 Larchmont 6,308 .... P7
12110 Latham 11,182 .... N5
†11560 Lattingtown 1,749 .... R6
11559 Lawrence 6,175 .... P7
14482 Le Roy 4,900 .... E5
11756 Levittown 57,045 .... R7
14092 Lewiston 3,326 .... B4
12754 Liberty 4,293 .... L7
14485 Lima 2,025 .... E5
11757 Lindenhurst 26,919 .... O9
13365 Little Falls 6,156 .... L4
14755 Little Valley⊙ 1,203 .... C6
13088 Liverpool 2,849 .... H4
12758 Livingston Manor 1,436 .... L7
†11743 Lloyd Harbor 3,405 .... R6
14094 Lockport⊙ 24,844 .... C4
†11791 Locust Grove 9,670 .... R6
11561 Long Beach 34,073 .... R7
13367 Lowville⊙ 3,364 .... J3
11563 Lynbrook 20,424 .... P7
14489 Lyons⊙ 4,160 .... F4
14502 Macedon 1,400 .... F4
10541 Mahopac 7,681 .... N8
12953 Malone⊙ 7,668 .... M1
11565 Malverne 9,262 .... R7
10543 Mamaroneck 17,616 .... P7
14504 Manchester 1,698 .... F5
11030 Manhasset 8,485 .... P7
*10001 Manhattan (borough) 1,428,285 .... M9
13104 Manlius 5,241 .... J5
13108 Marcellus 1,870 .... H5
12542 Marlboro 2,275 .... M7
11758 Massapequa 24,454 .... R7
11762 Massapequa Park 19,779 .... R7
13662 Massena 12,851 .... L1
11950 Mastic Beach 8,318 .... P9
11952 Mattituck 3,923 .... P9
12543 Maybrook 2,007 .... M8
14757 Mayville⊙ 1,626 .... A6
12118 Mechanicville 5,500 .... N5
14103 Medina 6,392 .... D4
†13021 Melrose Park 2,171 .... G5
11746 Melville 8,139 .... O9
†12201 Menands 4,012 .... N5
11566 Merrick 24,478 .... R7
13114 Mexico 1,621 .... H4
12122 Middleburgh 1,358 .... M5
12550 Middle Hope 3,229 .... M7
14105 Middleport 1,995 .... C4
10940 Middletown 21,454 .... L8
†12020 Milton 2,063 .... N4
11501 Mineola⊙ 20,757 .... R7
13115 Minetto 1,629 .... H4
12956 Mineville-Witherbee 1,925 .... O2
13116 Minoa 3,640 .... H4
13407 Mohawk 2,956 .... L4
10950 Monroe 5,996 .... M8
10952 Monsey 12,380 .... J8
12549 Montgomery 2,316 .... M7
12701 Monticello⊙ 6,306 .... L7
14865 Montour Falls 1,791 .... G6
13118 Moravia 1,582 .... H5
12962 Morrisonville 1,721 .... N1
13408 Morrisville 2,707 .... J5
10549 Mount Kisco 8,025 .... N8
14510 Mount Morris 3,039 .... E5
*10550 Mount Vernon 66,713 .... O7
10954 Nanuet 12,578 .... K8
12123 Nassau 1,285 .... N5
Nassau-Suffolk‡ 2,605,813 R7
14513 Newark 10,017 .... G4
13411 New Berlin 1,392 .... K5
12550 Newburgh 23,438 .... M7
Newburgh-Middletown‡ 259,603 .... M7
10956 New City⊙ 35,859 .... K8
14108 Newfane 3,120 .... C4
13413 New Hartford 2,313 .... K4
11040 New Hyde Park 9,801 .... P7
12561 New Paltz 4,938 .... M7
*10801 New Rochelle 70,794 .... P7
†10901 New Square 1,750 .... K8
12550 New Windsor 7,812 .... N8
*10001 New York⊙ 7,071,639 .... M9
New York‡ 9,119,737 .... M9
13417 New York Mills 3,549 .... K4
*14301 Niagara Falls 71,384 .... C4
†12301 Niskayuna 5,223 .... N5
13667 Norfolk 1,599 .... K1
14110 North Boston 2,743 .... C5
14111 North Collins 1,496 .... C5
11768 Northport 7,651 .... O9
13212 North Syracuse 7,970 .... H4
10591 North Tarrytown 7,994 .... O6
14120 North Tonawanda 35,760 .... C4
12134 Northville 1,304 .... M4
13815 Norwich⊙ 8,082 .... J5
13668 Norwood 1,902 .... L1
10960 Nyack 6,428 .... K8
14125 Oakfield 1,791 .... D4
11572 Oceanside 33,639 .... R7
13669 Ogdensburg 12,375 .... K1
14126 Olcott 1,571 .... C4
14760 Olean 18,207 .... D6
13421 Oneida 10,810 .... J4
13820 Oneonta 14,933 .... K6
14127 Orchard Park 3,671 .... C5
13424 Oriskany 1,680 .... K4
10562 Ossining 20,196 .... N8
13126 Oswego⊙ 19,793 .... G4
14521 Ovid⊙ 666 .... G5
13827 Owego⊙ 4,364 .... H6
13830 Oxford 1,765 .... J6
11771 Oyster Bay 6,497 .... R6
14870 Painted Post 2,196 .... F6
14522 Palmyra 3,729 .... F4
11772 Patchogue 11,291 .... P9
12564 Pawling 1,996 .... N7
10965 Pearl River 15,893 .... K8
10566 Peekskill 18,236 .... N8
10803 Pelham 6,848 .... O7
†10803 Pelham Manor 6,130 .... O7
14527 Penn Yan⊙ 5,242 .... F5
14530 Perry 4,198 .... D5
12972 Peru 1,716 .... N1
14532 Phelps 2,004 .... F5
12565 Philmont 1,539 .... N6
13135 Phoenix 2,357 .... H4
10968 Piermont 2,269 .... K8
12567 Pine Plains 1,303 .... N7
14534 Pittsford 1,568 .... E4
11803 Plainview 28,037 .... R7
12901 Plattsburgh⊙ 21,057 .... O1
10570 Pleasantville 6,749 .... N8
13140 Port Byron 1,400 .... G4
10573 Port Chester 23,565 .... P7
†13901 Port Dickinson 1,974 .... J6
12466 Port Ewen 2,813 .... N7
12974 Port Henry 1,450 .... O2
11777 Port Jefferson 6,731 .... P9
12771 Port Jervis 8,699 .... L8
11050 Port Washington 14,521 .... R6
13676 Potsdam 10,635 .... K1
*12601 Poughkeepsie⊙ 29,757 .... N7
Poughkeepsie‡ 245,055 .... N7
14873 Prattsburg○ 1,657 .... F5
13142 Pulaski 2,415 .... H3
10579 Putnam Valley○ 8,994 .... N8
*11101 Queens (borough) 1,891,325 .... N9
14772 Randolph 1,398 .... C6
14131 Ransomville 1,401 .... C4
12143 Ravena 3,091 .... N6
12571 Red Hook 1,692 .... N7
†12601 Red Oaks Mill 5,236 .... N7
12144 Rensselaer 9,047 .... N5
12572 Rhinebeck 2,542 .... N7
13439 Richfield Springs 1,561 .... K5
*10301 Richmond (Staten Island) (borough) 352,121 .... M9
11901 Riverhead⊙ 6,339 .... P9
*14601 Rochester⊙ 241,741 .... E4
Rochester‡ 971,879 .... E4
*11570 Rockville Centre 25,412 .... R7
13440 Rome 43,826 .... J4
11575 Roosevelt 14,109 .... R7
11576 Roslyn 2,134 .... R6
12979 Rouses Point 2,266 .... O1
10580 Rye 15,083 .... P6
11963 Sag Harbor 2,581 .... R8
11780 Saint James 12,122 .... O9
13452 Saint Johnsville 1,974 .... L5
14779 Salamanca 6,890 .... C6
†13132 Sand Ridge 1,293 .... H4
†11050 Sands Point 2,742 .... P6
12983 Saranac Lake 5,578 .... M2
12866 Saratoga Springs 23,906 .... N4
12477 Saugerties 3,882 .... M6
13146 Savannah○ 1,905 .... G4
11782 Sayville 12,013 .... O9
10583 Scarsdale 17,650 .... P6
*12301 Schenectady⊙ 67,972 .... M5
12157 Schoharie⊙ 1,016 .... M5
12871 Schuylerville 1,256 .... N4
12302 Scotia 7,280 .... N5
14546 Scottsville 1,789 .... E4
11579 Sea Cliff 5,364 .... R6
11783 Seaford 16,117 .... R7
13148 Seneca Falls 7,466 .... G5
13460 Sherburne 1,561 .... K5
13461 Sherrill 2,830 .... J4
14548 Shortsville 1,669 .... F5
13838 Sidney 4,861 .... K6
14136 Silver Creek 3,088 .... B5
13152 Skaneateles 2,789 .... H5
†14201 Sloan 4,529 .... C5
10974 Sloatsburg 3,154 .... M8
11787 Smithtown 30,906 .... O9
14551 Sodus 1,790 .... G4
14555 Sodus Point 1,334 .... G4
13209 Solvay 7,140 .... H4
11968 Southampton 4,000 .... R9
12779 South Fallsburg 2,196 .... L7
†12801 South Glens Falls 3,714 .... N4
†10960 South Nyack 3,602 .... K8
11971 Southold 4,770 .... P8
†14901 Southport 8,329 .... G6
14559 Spencerport 3,424 .... E4
10977 Spring Valley 20,537 .... K8
14141 Springville 4,285 .... C5
*10301 Staten Island (borough) 352,121 .... M9
12170 Stillwater 1,572 .... N5
11790 Stony Brook 16,155 .... O9
10980 Stony Point 8,686 .... M8
12172 Stottville 1,387 .... N6
10901 Suffern 10,794 .... J8
11791 Syosset 9,818 .... R6
*13201 Syracuse⊙ 170,105 .... H4
Syracuse‡ 642,375 .... H4
10983 Tappan 8,267 .... K8
10591 Tarrytown 10,648 .... O6
†11020 Thomaston 2,684 .... P7
12883 Ticonderoga 2,938 .... N3
12486 Tillson 1,529 .... M7
14150 Tonawanda 18,693 .... B4
*12180 Troy⊙ 56,638 .... N5
14886 Trumansburg 1,722 .... G5
10707 Tuckahoe 6,076 .... O7
12986 Tupper Lake 4,478 .... M2
13849 Unadilla 1,367 .... K6
11553 Uniondale 20,016 .... R7
*13501 Utica⊙ 75,632 .... K4
Utica-Rome‡ 320,180 .... K4
12184 Valatie 1,492 .... N6
10989 Valley Cottage 8,214 .... K8
*11580 Valley Stream 35,769 .... P7
13850 Vestal○ 27,238 .... H6
14564 Victor 2,370 .... F5
†10901 Viola 5,340 .... J8
12186 Voorheesville 3,320 .... M5
12586 Walden 5,659 .... M7
12589 Wallkill 2,064 .... M7
13856 Walton 3,329 .... K6
13163 Wampsville⊙ 569 .... J4
11793 Wantagh 19,817 .... R7
12590 Wappingers Falls 5,110 .... N7
12885 Warrensburg 2,834 .... N3
14569 Warsaw⊙ 3,619 .... D5
10990 Warwick 4,320 .... M8
10992 Washingtonville 2,380 .... M8
12188 Waterford 2,405 .... N5
13165 Waterloo⊙ 5,303 .... G5
13601 Watertown⊙ 27,861 .... J3
13480 Waterville 1,672 .... K5
12189 Watervliet 11,354 .... N5
14891 Watkins Glen⊙ 2,440 .... G6
14892 Waverly 4,738 .... G7
14572 Wayland 1,846 .... E5
14580 Webster 5,499 .... F4
13166 Weedsport 1,952 .... G4
14895 Wellsville 5,769 .... E6
11590 Westbury 13,871 .... R7
†13619 West Carthage 1,824 .... J3
†14901 West Elmira 5,485 .... G6
14787 Westfield 3,446 .... A6
†12801 West Glens Falls 5,331 .... N4
11977 Westhampton 2,774 .... P9
11978 Westhampton Beach 1,629 P9
12491 West Hurley 2,382 .... M6
10994 West Nyack 8,553 .... K8
14788 Westons Mills 1,837 .... D6
10996 West Point 8,105 .... M8
11796 West Sayville 8,185 .... O9
14224 West Seneca 51,210 .... C5
12887 Whitehall 3,241 .... O3
*10601 White Plains⊙ 46,999 .... P6
13492 Whitesboro 4,460 .... K4
14588 Willard 1,339 .... G5
14589 Williamson 1,768 .... F4
14221 Williamsville 6,017 .... C5
11596 Williston Park 8,216 .... R7
13865 Windsor 1,155 .... J6
13697 Winthrop-Brasher Falls 1,454 .... L1
12998 Witherbee-Mineville 1,925 .... N2
14590 Wolcott 1,496 .... G4
11598 Woodmere 17,205 .... P7
12498 Woodstock 2,280 .... M6
12790 Wurtsboro 1,128 .... L7
11798 Wyandanch 13,215 .... N9
*10701 Yonkers 195,351 .... O6
10598 Yorktown Heights 7,696 .... N8
13495 Yorkville 3,115 .... K4
14174 Youngstown 2,191 .... C4

OTHER FEATURES

Adirondack (mts.) M3
Algonquin (peak) M2
Allegany Ind. Res. 1,243 .... C6
Allegheny (res.) C7
Allegheny (riv.) C6
Ashokan (res.) M7
Ausable (riv.) N2
Batten Kill (riv.) O4
Beaver (riv.) K3
Big Moose (lake) L3
Black (lake) J1
Black (riv.) K3
Block Island (sound) S8
Blue Mountain (lake) M3
Bonaparte (lake) K2
Brandreth (lake) L3
Brant (lake) N3
Brookhaven Nat'l Lab. P9
Butterfield (lake) J2
Canandaigua (lake) F5
Canisteo (riv.) F6
Cannonsville (res.) K6
Catskill (mts.) L6
Cattaraugus (creek) C6
Cattaraugus Ind. Res. 1,994 .... C5
Cayuga (lake) G5
Champlain (lake) O1
Chateaugay, Upper (lake) M1
Chautauqua (lake) A6
Chazy (lake) N1
Chenango (riv.) J6
Cohocton (riv.) F6
Conesus (lake) E5
Conewango (creek) B6
Cranberry (lake) L2
Deer (riv.) J3
Deer (riv.) L1
Delaware (riv.) K7
East (riv.) N9
Erie (lake) A5
Fire Island Nat'l Seashore P9
Fishers (isl.) S8
Forked (lake) L3
Fort Drum J2
Fort Niagara C4
Fort Stanwix Nat'l Mon. J4
Fulton Chain (lkes) K3
Galloo (isl.) H3
Gardiners (bay) R8
Gardiners (isl.) R8
Gateway Nat'l Rec. Area M9
Genesee (riv.) E5
George (lake) N4
Grand (isl.) B5
Grass (riv.) K1
Great Sacandaga (lake) M4
Great South (bay) O9
Great South (beach) O9
Greenwood (lake) M8
Grenadier (isl.) H2
Griffiss A.F.B. K4
Haystack (mt.) N2
Hemlock (lake) E5
Hinckley (res.) K4
Honeoye (lake) F5
Honnedaga (lake) L3
Hudson (riv.) N7
Hunter (mt.) M6
Indian (lake) M3
Jones (beach) R7
Keuka (lake) F5
Lila (lake) L2
Little Tupper (lake) L2
Long (isl.) P9
Long (lake) M2
Long Island (sound) P9
Manhattan (isl.) M9
Marcy (mt.) N2
Martin Van Buren Nat'l Hist. Site N6
Meacham (lake) M1
Mohawk (riv.) L5
Montauk (pt.) S8
Moose (riv.) K3
Neversink (res.) L7
New York State Barge (canal) C4
Niagara (riv.) B4
Oil Spring Ind. Res. 6 .... D6
Oneida (lake) J4
Onondaga Ind. Res. 596 .... H5
Ontario (lake) F3
Orient (pt.) R8
Oswegatchie (riv.) K2
Oswego (riv.) H4
Otisco (lake) H5
Otsego (lake) L5
Otselic (riv.) J5
Owasco (lake) G5
Peconic (bay) R9
Peninsula (pt.) H3
Pepacton (res.) L6
Piseco (lake) M4
Placid (lake) N2
Plattsburgh A.F.B. 5,905 .... N1
Pleasant (lake) M4
Plum (isl.) R8
Poosepatuck Ind. Res. 203 .... P9
Raquette (lake) L3
Rondout (res.) M7
Round (lake) L2
Sacandaga (lake) L3
Sackets (harb.) H3
Sagamore Hill Nat'l Hist. Site R6
Saint Lawrence (lake) K1
Saint Lawrence (riv.) J2
Saint Regis (riv.) L1
Saint Regis Ind. Res. 1,802 .... M1
Salmon (res.) J3
Salmon (riv.) H3
Salmon (riv.) M1
Saranac (lkes) M2
Saranac (riv.) N1
Saratoga (lake) N4
Saratoga Nat'l Hist. Park N4
Schoharie (res.) M6
Schroon (lake) N3
Seneca (lake) G5
Seneca (riv.) G5
Shelter (isl.) R8
Shinnecock Ind. Res. 297 .... R9
Silver (lake) N1
Skaneateles (lake) H5
Skylight (mt.) M2
Slide (mt.) L6
Staten (isl.) M9
Statue of Liberty Nat'l Mon. M9
Stony (isl.) H3
Stony (pt.) H3
Susquehanna (riv.) H6
Thousand (isls.) H2
Tioughnioga (riv.) H6
Titus (lake) M1
Tomhannock (res.) O5
Tonawanda Ind. Res. 467 .... D4
Toronto (res.) L7
Tupper (lake) M2
Tuscarora Ind. Res. 921 .... B4
Unadilla (riv.) K5
Upper Chateaugay (lake) M1
Valcour (isl.) N1
Wallkill (riv.) L8
Whiteface (mt.) N2
Whitney Point (lake) J6
Woodhull (lake) L3

⊙County seat.
‡Population of metropolitan area.
○Population of town or township.
† Zip of nearest p.o. * Multiple zips.

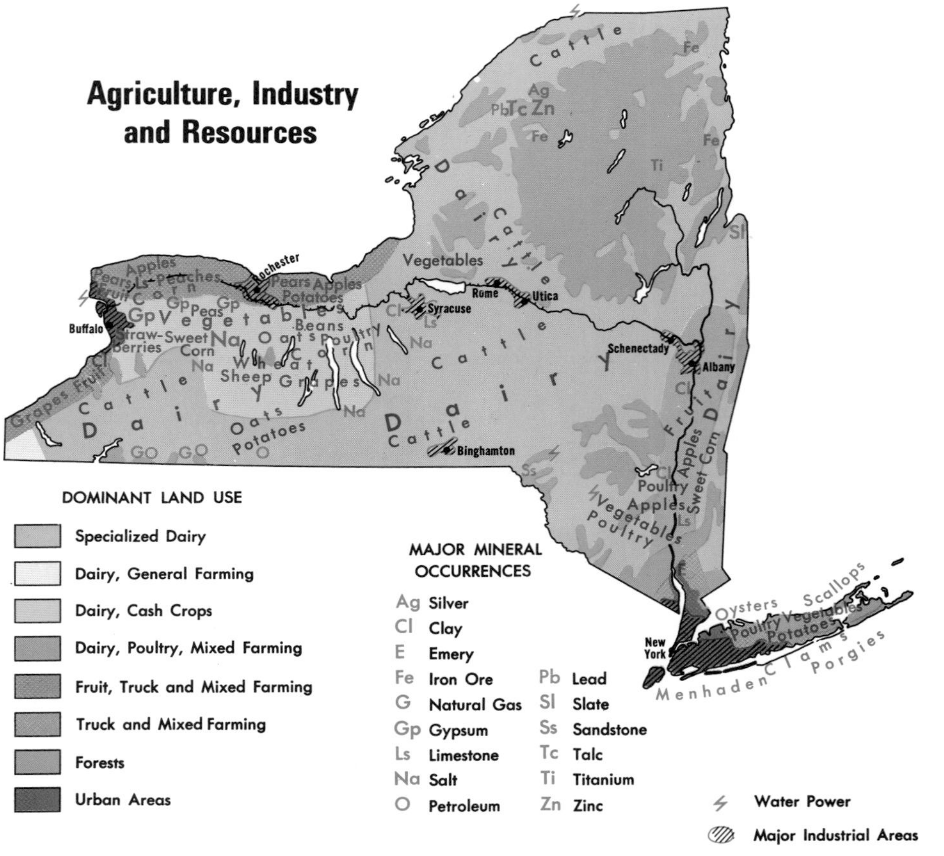

Agriculture, Industry and Resources
DOMINANT LAND USE
Specialized Dairy
Dairy, General Farming
Dairy, Cash Crops
Dairy, Poultry, Mixed Farming
Fruit, Truck and Mixed Farming
Truck and Mixed Farming
Forests
Urban Areas
MAJOR MINERAL OCCURRENCES
Ag Silver
Cl Clay
E Emery
Fe Iron Ore
G Natural Gas
Gp Gypsum
Ls Limestone
Na Salt
O Petroleum
Pb Lead
Sl Slate
Ss Sandstone
Tc Talc
Ti Titanium
Zn Zinc
Water Power
Major Industrial Areas
Cattle
Dairy
Vegetables
Rochester
Buffalo
Syracuse
Rome
Utica
Schenectady
Albany
Binghamton
New York
Grapes
Fruit
Apples
Peaches
Pears
Potatoes
Corn
Beans
Oats
Poultry
Wheat
Sheep
Grapes
Straw-berries
Sweet Corn
Oysters
Scallops
Clams
Porgies
Menhaden

AREA 52,669 sq. mi. (136,413 sq. km.)
POPULATION 5,881,813
CAPITAL Raleigh
LARGEST CITY Charlotte
HIGHEST POINT Mt. Mitchell 6,684 ft. (2037 m.)
SETTLED IN 1650
ADMITTED TO UNION November 21, 1789
POPULAR NAME Tarheel State
STATE FLOWER Flowering Dogwood
STATE BIRD Cardinal

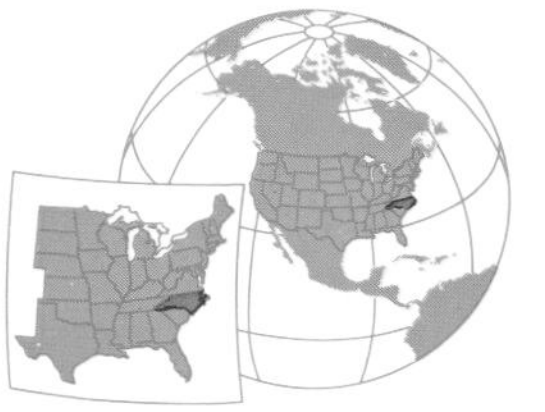

COUNTIES

Alamance 99,319 .... L3
Alexander 24,999 .... G3
Alleghany 9,587 .... G1
Anson 25,649 .... J4
Ashe 22,325 .... F2
Avery 14,409 .... F2
Beaufort 40,355 .... R4
Bertie 21,024 .... P2
Bladen 30,491 .... M5
Brunswick 35,777 .... N6
Buncombe 160,934 .... D3
Burke 72,504 .... F3
Cabarrus 85,895 .... H4
Caldwell 67,746 .... F3
Camden 5,829 .... S2
Carteret 41,092 .... R5
Caswell 20,705 .... L2
Catawba 105,208 .... G3
Chatham 33,415 .... L3
Cherokee 18,933 .... A4
Chowan 12,558 .... R2
Clay 6,619 .... B4
Cleveland 83,435 .... F4
Columbus 51,037 .... M6
Craven 71,043 .... P4
Cumberland 247,160 .... M4
Currituck 11,089 .... S2
Dare 13,377 .... T3
Davidson 113,162 .... J3
Davie 24,599 .... H3
Duplin 40,952 .... O5
Durham 152,785 .... M3
Edgecombe 55,988 .... O3
Forsyth 243,683 .... J2
Franklin 30,055 .... N2
Gaston 162,568 .... G4
Gates 8,875 .... R2
Graham 7,217 .... B4
Granville 34,043 .... M2
Greene 16,117 .... O3
Guilford 317,154 .... K3
Halifax 55,286 .... O2
Harnett 59,570 .... M4
Haywood 46,495 .... C3
Henderson 58,580 .... D4
Hertford 23,368 .... P2
Hoke 20,383 .... L4
Hyde 5,873 .... S3
Iredell 82,538 .... H3
Jackson 25,811 .... C4
Johnston 70,599 .... N4
Jones 9,705 .... P4
Lee 36,718 .... L4
Lenoir 59,819 .... O4
Lincoln 42,372 .... G3
Macon 20,178 .... B4
Madison 16,827 .... D3
Martin 25,948 .... P3
McDowell 35,135 .... E3
Mecklenburg 404,270 .... H4
Mitchell 14,428 .... E2
Montgomery 22,469 .... K4
Moore 50,505 .... L4
Nash 67,153 .... O2
New Hanover 103,471 .... O6
Northampton 22,584 .... P2
Onslow 112,784 .... P5
Orange 77,055 .... L2
Pamlico 10,398 .... R4
Pasquotank 28,462 .... S2
Pender 22,215 .... O5
Perquimans 9,486 .... S2
Person 29,164 .... M2
Pitt 90,146 .... P3
Polk 12,984 .... E4
Randolph 91,728 .... K3
Richmond 45,481 .... K4
Robeson 101,610 .... L5
Rockingham 83,426 .... K2
Rowan 99,186 .... H3
Rutherford 53,787 .... E4
Sampson 49,687 .... N4
Scotland 32,273 .... L5
Stanly 48,517 .... J4
Stokes 33,086 .... J2
Surry 59,449 .... H2
Swain 10,283 .... B3
Transylvania 23,417 .... D4
Tyrrell 3,975 .... S3
Union 70,380 .... H4
Vance 36,748 .... N2
Wake 301,327 .... M3
Warren 16,232 .... N2
Washington 14,801 .... R3
Watauga 31,666 .... F2
Wayne 97,054 .... N4
Wilkes 58,657 .... G2
Wilson 63,132 .... O3
Yadkin 28,439 .... H2
Yancey 14,934 .... E3

CITIES and TOWNS

Zip *Name/Pop.* *Key*

28315 Aberdeen 1,945 .... L4
27910 Ahoskie 4,887 .... P2
27201 Alamance 320 .... K2
28001 Albemarle⊙ 15,110 .... J4
†28043 Alexander Mills 643 .... F4
28509 Alliance 616 .... R4
28702 Almond 140 .... B4
28901 Andrews 1,621 .... B4
27501 Angier 1,709 .... M4
28007 Ansonville 794 .... J4
27502 Apex 2,847 .... M3
28510 Arapahoe 467 .... R4
27263 Archdale 5,326 .... K3
†28642 Arlington 872 .... H2
28420 Ash 150 .... N6
27203 Asheboro⊙ 15,252 .... K3
*28801 Asheville⊙ 53,583 .... D3
Asheville‡ 177,761 .... D3
†27983 Askewville 227 .... R2
28421 Atkinson 298 .... N5
28512 Atlantic Beach 941 .... R5
27805 Aulander 1,214 .... P2
27806 Aurora 698 .... R4
28318 Autryville 228 .... M4
27915 Avon 500 .... U4
28513 Ayden 4,361 .... P4
27916 Aydlett 205 .... T2
28009 Badin 1,514 .... J4
27807 Bailey 685 .... N3
28705 Bakersville⊙ 373 .... E2
28706 Balfour 1,772 .... E4
28707 Balsam 200 .... C4
28604 Banner Elk 1,087 .... F2
†27030 Bannertown 1,028 .... H1
27008 Barber 155 .... H3
†28739 Barker Heights 1,267 .... D4
28710 Bat Cave 450 .... E4
27808 Bath 207 .... R4
27809 Battleboro 632 .... O2
28515 Bayboro⊙ 759 .... R4
†27892 Beargrass 82 .... P3
28516 Beaufort⊙ 3,826 .... R5
27810 Belhaven 2,430 .... R3
27811 Bellarthur 350 .... O3
28012 Belmont 4,607 .... H4
†28451 Belville 102 .... N6
†28090 Belwood 613 .... F4
27208 Bennett 254 .... K3
27504 Benson 2,792 .... N4
28016 Bessemer City 4,787 .... G4
27812 Bethel 1,825 .... P3
28518 Beulaville 1,060 .... O5
†28803 Biltmore Forest 1,499 .... E3
27209 Biscoe 1,334 .... K4
27813 Black Creek 523 .... O3
28711 Black Mountain 4,083 .... E3
28320 Bladenboro 1,428 .... M5
27212 Blanch 200 .... L2
28605 Blowing Rock 1,337 .... F2
28092 Boger City 2,252 .... G4
28461 Boiling Spring Lakes 998 ... N7
28017 Boling Springs 2,381 .... F4
28422 Bolivia ⊙ 252 .... N6
28423 Bolton 563 .... N6
27213 Bonlee 300 .... L3
28606 Boomer 250 .... G2
28607 Boone⊙ 10,191 .... F2
27011 Boonville 1,028 .... H2
28322 Bowdens 200 .... N4
28712 Brevard⊙ 5,323 .... D4
28519 Bridgeton 461 .... R4
27505 Broadway 908 .... L4
†28601 Brookford 467 .... G3
28424 Brunswick 223 .... M6
28713 Bryson City⊙ 1,556 .... C4
27506 Buies Creek 1,939 .... M4
27507 Bullock 525 .... M2
27508 Bunn 505 .... N3
28425 Burgaw⊙ 1,738 .... N5
27215 Burlington 37,266 .... K2
Burlington‡ 99,136 .... F2
28714 Burnsville⊙ 1,452 .... E3
27509 Butner 4,240 .... M2
27312 Bynum 350 .... L3
†29566 Calabash 128 .... M7
28325 Calypso 689 .... N4
27921 Camden⊙ 300 .... S2
28326 Cameron 225 .... L4
27229 Candor 868 .... K4
28716 Canton 4,631 .... D3
†28584 Cape Carteret 944 .... P5
28428 Carolina Beach 2,000 .... O6
27510 Carrboro 7,336 .... L3
28327 Carthage⊙ 925 .... K4
27511 Cary 21,763 .... M3
28020 Casar 346 .... F3
28717 Cashiers 553 .... C4
27816 Castalia 358 .... O2
28429 Castle Hayne 1,087 .... O6
†28461 Caswell Beach 110 .... N7
28609 Catawba 509 .... G3
27230 Cedar Falls 400 .... K3
27231 Cedar Grove 250 .... L2
28520 Cedar Island 310 .... S5
†27549 Centerville 135 .... N2
28430 Cerro Gordo 295 .... M6
28431 Chadbourn 1,975 .... M6
†28445 Chadwick Acres 15 .... P6
27514 Chapel Hill 32,421 .... L3
*28201 Charlotte⊙ 314,447 .... H4
Charlotte-Gastonia‡ 637,218 .... H4
28021 Cherryville 4,844 .... G4
28023 China Grove 2,081 .... H3
28521 Chinquapin 280 .... O5
27817 Chocowinity 644 .... P4
28610 Claremont 880 .... G3
28433 Clarkton 664 .... M6
27520 Clayton 4,091 .... N3
27012 Clemmons 7,401 .... J2
27013 Cleveland 595 .... H3
28328 Clinton⊙ 7,552 .... N5
28721 Clyde 1,008 .... D3
27521 Coats 1,385 .... M4
27922 Cofield 465 .... R2
27924 Colerain 284 .... R2
27925 Columbia⊙ 758 .... S3
28722 Columbus⊙ 727 .... E4
28522 Comfort 325 .... O5
27818 Como 89 .... P1
28025 Concord⊙ 16,942 .... H4
27819 Conetoe 215 .... O3
28613 Conover 4,245 .... G3
27820 Conway 678 .... P2
27014 Cooleemee 1,448 .... H3
28031 Cornelius 1,460 .... H4
27927 Corolla 158 .... T2
28523 Cove City 500 .... P4
28032 Cramerton 1,869 .... G4
27522 Creedmoor 1,641 .... M2
27928 Creswell 426 .... S3
27852 Crisp 435 .... O3
28616 Crossnore 297 .... F2
28331 Cumberland 400 .... M5
27237 Cumnock 200 .... L3
27929 Currituck⊙ 700 .... T2
28034 Dallas 3,340 .... G4
27016 Danbury⊙ 140 .... J2
28036 Davidson 3,241 .... H4
28524 Davis 612 .... R5
27239 Denton 949 .... J3
28725 Dillsboro 179 .... C4
27017 Dobson⊙ 1,222 .... H2
†27801 Dortches 885 .... O2
28526 Dover 600 .... P4
28619 Drexel 1,392 .... F3
28332 Dublin 477 .... M5
28334 Dunn 8,962 .... M4
*27701 Durham⊙ 100,538 .... M2
Durham-Raleigh‡ 530,673 . M2
27242 Eagle Springs 280 .... K4
28038 Earl 206 .... F4
†28434 East Arcadia 461 .... N6
27018 East Bend 602 .... H2
28726 East Flat Rock 3,365 .... E4
†28723 East Laport 150 .... C4
28352 East Laurinburg 536 .... L5
†28752 East Marion 1,851 .... F3
28039 East Spencer 2,150 .... J3
27288 Eden 15,672 .... K1
27932 Edenton⊙ 5,357 .... R2
27909 Elizabeth City⊙ 14,004 .... S2
28337 Elizabethtown⊙ 3,551 .... M5
28621 Elkin 2,858 .... H2
28622 Elk Park 535 .... E2
28040 Ellenboro 560 .... F4
28338 Ellerbe 1,415 .... K4
27822 Elm City 1,561 .... O3
27244 Elon College 2,873 .... L2
†28557 Emerald Isle 865 .... P5
27823 Enfield 2,995 .... O2
28728 Enka 5,567 .... D3
28339 Erwin 2,828 .... M4
27247 Ether 425 .... K4
27935 Eure 300 .... R2
27830 Eureka 303 .... O3
27825 Everetts 213 .... P3
28438 Evergreen 310 .... M6
28439 Fair Bluff 1,095 .... M6
27826 Fairfield 900 .... S3
28340 Fairmont 2,658 .... L6
28730 Fairview 1,122 .... D3
28341 Faison 636 .... N4
28041 Faith 552 .... J3

(continued on following page)

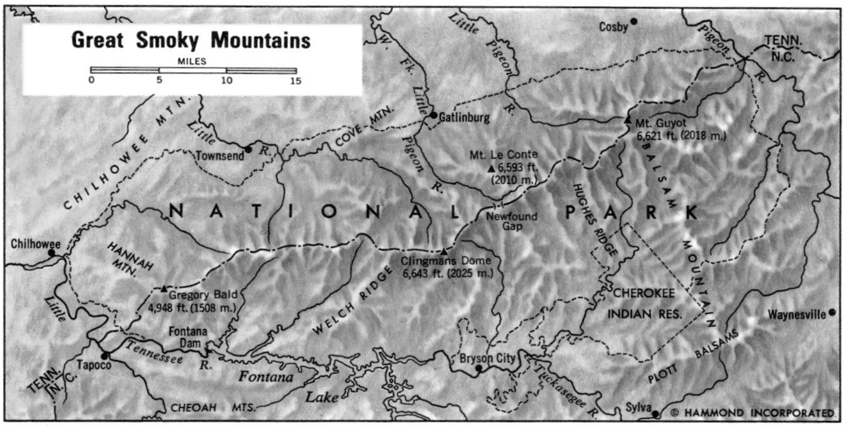

Great Smoky Mountains
MILES
0 5 10 15
Cosby
TENN.
N.C.
Little Pigeon R.
Gatlinburg
Mt. Guyot 6,621 ft. (2018 m.)
Townsend
Mt. Le Conte 6,593 ft. (2010 m.)
CHILHOWEE MTN.
COVE MTN.
BALSAM MOUNTAIN
NATIONAL PARK
Newfound Gap
HUGHES RIDGE
Chilhowee
HANNAH MTN.
Clingmans Dome 6,643 ft. (2025 m.)
Gregory Bald 4,948 ft. (1508 m.)
WELCH RIDGE
CHEROKEE INDIAN RES.
Waynesville
Fontana Dam
Tapoco
Tennessee R.
Bryson City
PLOTT BALSAMS
Tuckasegee R.
Fontana Lake
CHEOAH MTS.
Sylva
© HAMMOND INCORPORATED

Agriculture, Industry and Resources

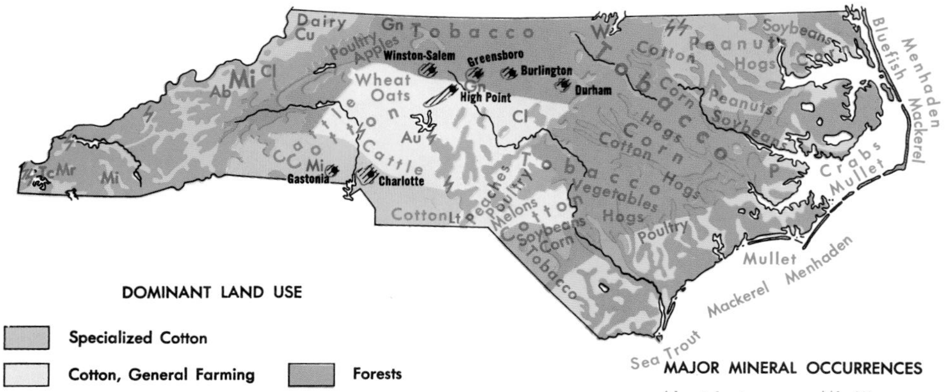

Dairy
Tobacco
Poultry
Apples
Winston-Salem
Greensboro
Burlington
Durham
High Point
Wheat
Oats
Cattle
Cotton
Peanuts
Soybeans
Hogs
Corn
Gastonia
Charlotte
Vegetables
Peaches
Melons
Crabs
Mullet
Bluefish
Menhaden
Mackerel
Sea Trout

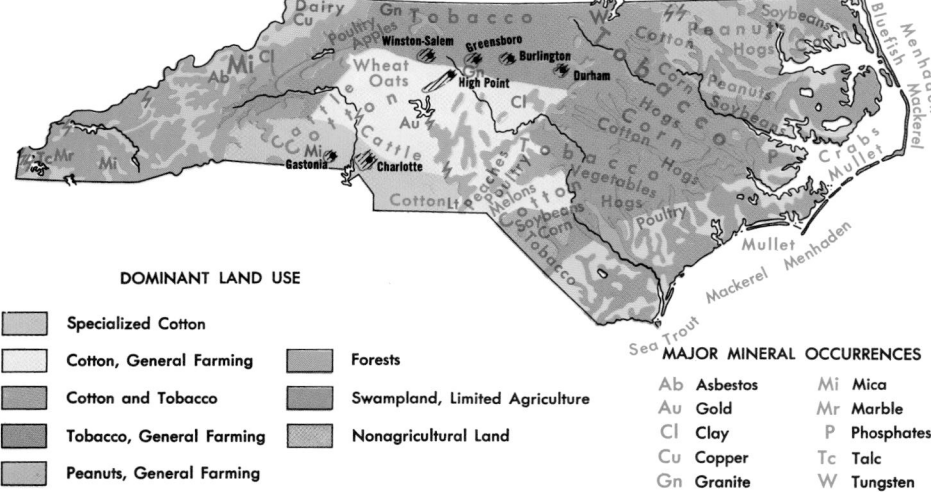

DOMINANT LAND USE

- Specialized Cotton
- Cotton, General Farming
- Cotton and Tobacco
- Tobacco, General Farming
- Peanuts, General Farming
- General Farming, Livestock, Fruit, Tobacco
- General Farming, Truck Farming, Tobacco, Livestock
- Forests
- Swampland, Limited Agriculture
- Nonagricultural Land

MAJOR MINERAL OCCURRENCES

- Ab Asbestos
- Au Gold
- Cl Clay
- Cu Copper
- Gn Granite
- Lt Lithium
- Mi Mica
- Mr Marble
- P Phosphates
- Tc Talc
- W Tungsten

- Water Power
- Major Industrial Areas

Topography

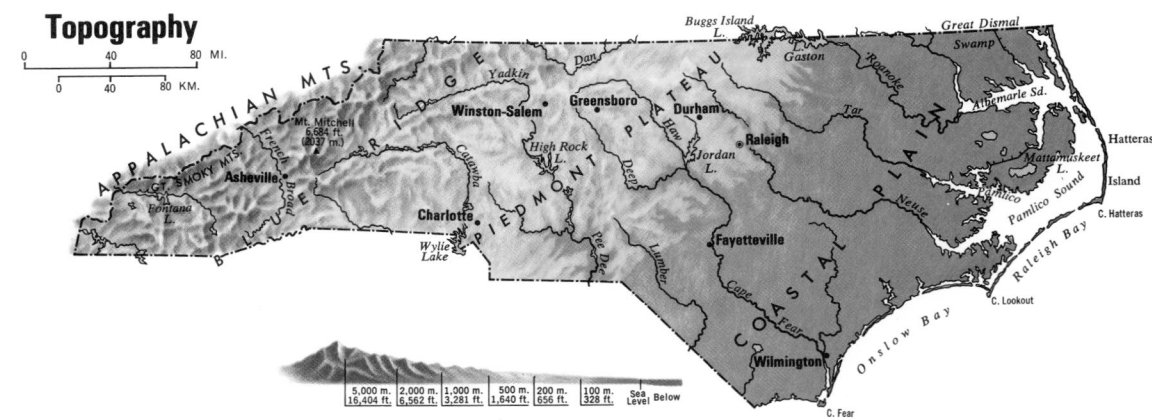

5,000 m.	2,000 m.	1,000 m.	500 m.	200 m.	100 m.	Sea Level	Below
16,404 ft.	6,562 ft.	3,281 ft.	1,640 ft.	656 ft.	328 ft.		

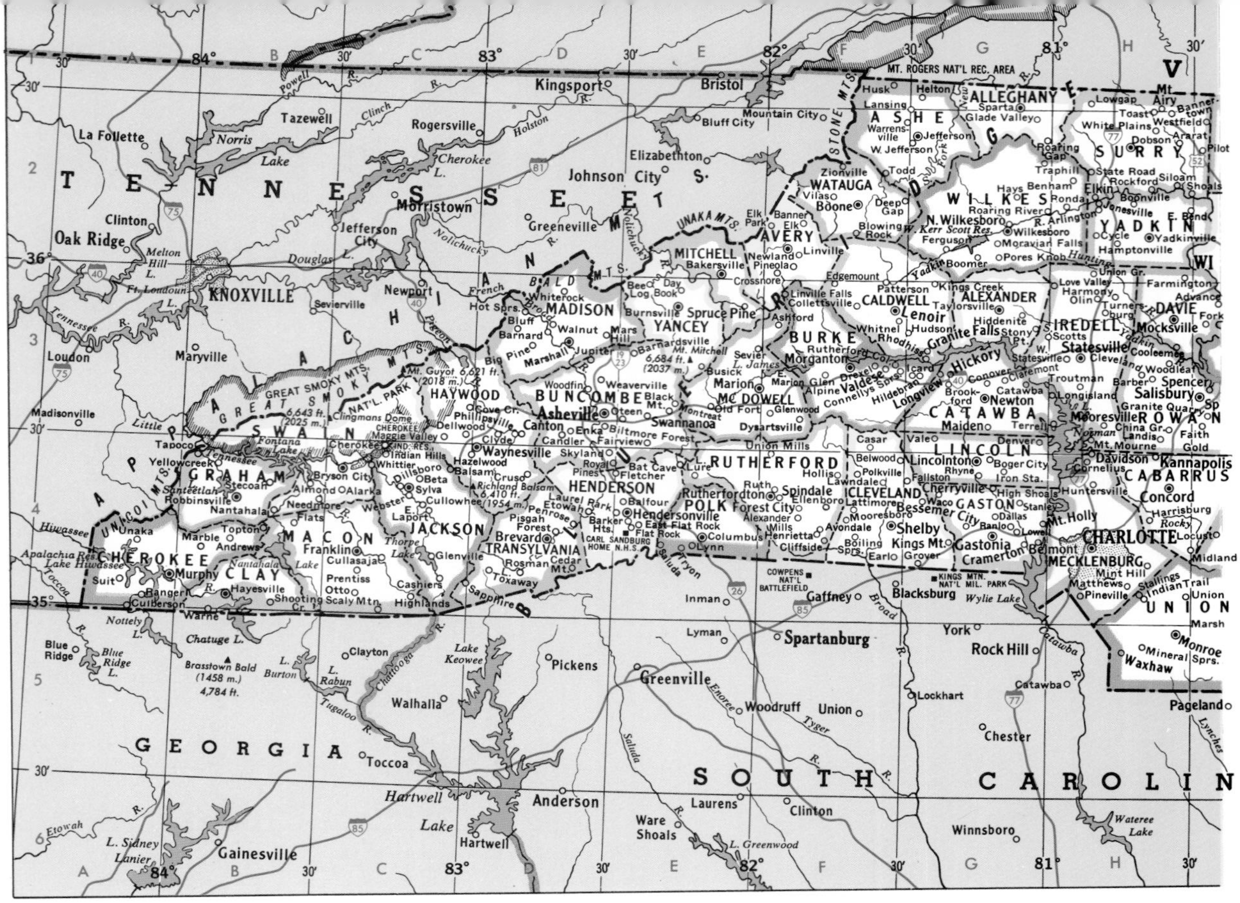

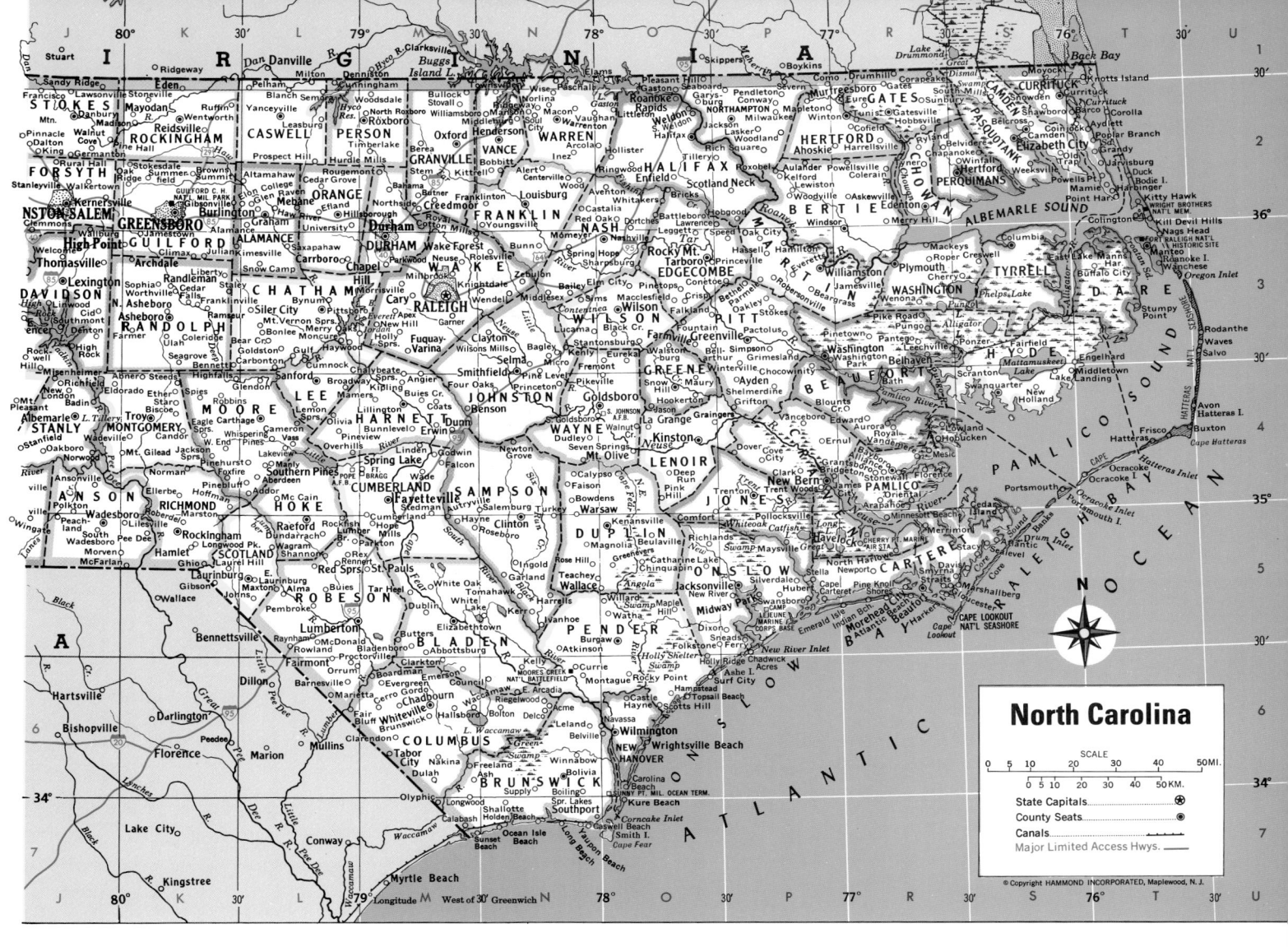

North Carolina

SCALE

0 5 10 20 30 40 50 MI.

0 5 10 20 30 40 50 KM.

State Capitals..........⊛
County Seats..........⊙
Canals..........
Major Limited Access Hwys.

© Copyright HAMMOND INCORPORATED, Maplewood, N.J.

North Dakota

SCALE

0 5 10   20   30 MI.

0 5 10   20   30 KM.

State Capitals............⊛
County Seats.............⊙
Major Limited Access Hwys._____

COUNTIES		
Adams 3,584	....	F7
Barnes 13,960	....	O5
Benson 7,944	....	M3
Billings 1,138	....	D5
Bottineau 9,239	....	J2
Bowman 4,229	....	C7
Burke 3,822	....	E2
Burleigh 54,811	....	J6
Cass 88,247	....	R5
Cavalier 7,636	....	N2
Dickey 7,207	....	N7
Divide 3,494	....	C2
Dunn 4,627	....	E5
Eddy 2,757	....	N4
Emmons 5,877	....	K7
Foster 4,611	....	N5
Golden Valley 2,391	....	C5
Grand Forks 66,100	....	P3
Grant 4,274	....	G6
Griggs 3,714	....	O5
Hettinger 4,275	....	E7
Kidder 3,833	....	L6
LaMoure 6,473	....	N7
Logan 3,493	....	L7
McHenry 7,858	....	J3
McIntosh 4,800	....	L7
McKenzie 7,132	....	D4
McLean 12,383	....	G4
Mercer 9,404	....	G5
Morton 25,177	....	H6
Mountrail 7,679	....	E3

Nelson 5,233	....	O4
Oliver 2,495	....	H5
Pembina 10,399	....	P2
Pierce 6,166	....	K3
Ramsey 13,048	....	N3
Ransom 6,698	....	P7
Renville 3,608	....	G2
Richland 19,207	....	R7
Rolette 12,177	....	L2
Sargent 5,512	....	P7
Sheridan 2,819	....	K4
Sioux 3,620	....	H7
Slope 1,157	....	C7
Stark 23,697	....	E6
Steele 3,106	....	P4
Stutsman 24,154	....	M5
Towner 4,052	....	M2
Traill 9,624	....	R5
Walsh 15,371	....	P3
Ward 58,392	....	G3
Wells 6,979	....	L4
Williams 22,237	....	C3
CITIES and TOWNS		
Zip	Name/Pop.	Key
58001 Abercrombie 260	....	S7
58210 Adams 303	....	O3
58831 Alexander 358	....	C4
58003 Alice 62	....	P6
58833 Ambrose 60	....	D2
58004 Amenia 93	....	R6
58620 Amidon⊙ 43	....	D7

58710 Anamoose 355	....	K4
58212 Aneta 341	....	P4
58213 Ardoch 78	....	P3
58835 Arnegard 193	....	D4
58006 Arthur 445	....	R5
58413 Ashley⊙ 1,192	....	M7
58007 Ayr 42	....	P5
58712 Balfour 51	....	J4
58008 Barney 70	....	S7
58216 Bathgate 67	....	P2
58621 Beach⊙ 1,381	....	C6
58316 Belcourt 1,803	....	L2
58622 Belfield 1,274	....	D6
58716 Benedict 68	....	H4
58415 Berlin 57	....	O7
58718 Berthold 485	....	G3
58523 Beulah 2,908	....	G5
58416 Binford 293	....	O5
58317 Bisbee 257	....	M2
58501 Bismarck (cap.)⊙ 44,485	....	J6
58318 Bottineau⊙ 2,829	....	J2
58721 Bowbells⊙ 587	....	F2
58623 Bowman⊙ 2,071	....	D7
58524 Braddock 86	....	K6
58320 Brinsmade 54	....	M3
58321 Brocket 74	....	O3
58722 Burlington 762	....	H3
58218 Buxton 336	....	R4
58322 Calio 60	....	N2
58323 Calvin 61	....	N2
58324 Cando⊙ 1,496	....	M3
†58241 Canton (Hensel) 68	....	P2
58725 Carpio 244	....	G3

58421 Carrington⊙ 2,641	....	M5
58529 Carson⊙ 469	....	H7
58012 Casselton 1,661	....	R6
58422 Cathay 66	....	M4
58220 Cavalier⊙ 1,505	....	P2
58013 Cayuga 75	....	P7
58530 Center⊙ 900	....	H5
58016 Clifford 51	....	R5
58017 Cogswell 227	....	P7
58727 Columbus 325	....	E2
58425 Cooperstown⊙ 1,308	....	O5
58730 Crosby⊙ 1,469	....	D2
58222 Crystal 256	....	P2
58021 Davenport 195	....	R6
58731 Deering 85	....	J3
58301 Devils Lake⊙ 7,442	....	N3
58431 Dickey 74	....	N6
58601 Dickinson⊙ 15,924	....	E6
58736 Drake 479	....	K4
58225 Drayton 1,082	....	R2
58329 Dunseith 625	....	K2
58024 Dwight 72	....	S7
58433 Edgeley 843	....	N7
58227 Edinburg 300	....	P3
58330 Edmore 416	....	O3
58436 Ellendale⊙ 1,967	....	N7
58228 Emerado 596	....	R4
58027 Enderlin 1,151	....	P6
58332 Esmond 337	....	L3
58229 Fairdale 97	....	O3
58030 Fairmount 480	....	S7
58102 Fargo⊙ 61,383	....	S6

Fargo-Moorhead‡ 137,574	....	S6
58438 Fessenden⊙ 761	....	L4
58230 Finley⊙ 718	....	P4
58535 Flasher 410	....	H7
58439 Forbes 84	....	N8
58231 Fordville 326	....	P3
58032 Forman⊙ 629	....	P7
58033 Fort Ransom 99	....	P6
58844 Fortuna 98	....	C2
58538 Fort Yates⊙ 771	....	J7
58440 Fredonia 82	....	M7
58442 Gackle 456	....	M6
58739 Gardena 66	....	J2
58036 Gardner 94	....	R5
58540 Garrison 1,830	....	H4
58235 Gilby 283	....	P3
58630 Gladstone 317	....	F6
58740 Glenburn 454	....	H2
58631 Glen Ullin 1,125	....	G6
58541 Goldenvalley 287	....	F5
58444 Goodrich 288	....	K5
58237 Grafton⊙ 5,293	....	R3
58201 Grand Forks⊙ 43,765	....	R4
Grand Forks‡ 100,944	....	R4
58741 Granville 281	....	J3
58845 Grenora 362	....	C2
58040 Gwinner 725	....	P7
58636 Halliday 355	....	F5
58041 Hankinson 1,158	....	S7
58239 Hannah 90	....	N2
58341 Harvey 2,527	....	L4
58042 Harwood 326	....	S6
58240 Hatton 787	....	R4

58637 Haynes 58	....	F8
58544 Hazelton 266	....	K7
58545 Hazen 2,365	....	G5
58638 Hebron 1,078	....	G6
58639 Hettinger⊙ 1,739	....	E7
58045 Hillsboro⊙ 1,600	....	S5
58243 Hoople 350	....	P3
58046 Hope 406	....	P5
58047 Horace 494	....	S6
58048 Hunter 369	....	R5
58244 Inkster 135	....	P3
58401 Jamestown⊙ 16,280	....	N6
58744 Karlsruhe 164	....	J3
58049 Kathryn 95	....	P6
58746 Kenmare 1,456	....	G2
58640 Killdeer 790	....	E5
58051 Kindred 568	....	R6
58343 Knox 69	....	L3
58748 Kramer 84	....	J2
58541 Kulm 570	....	N7
58344 Lakota⊙ 963	....	O3
58458 LaMoure⊙ 1,077	....	O7
58749 Landa 62	....	J2
58249 Langdon⊙ 2,335	....	O2
58750 Lansford 294	....	H2
58345 Larimore 1,524	....	P4
58459 Leal 45	....	O5
58346 Leeds 678	....	M3
58460 Lehr 254	....	M7
58052 Leonard 289	....	R6
58053 Lidgerwood 971	....	R7
58752 Lignite 332	....	F2

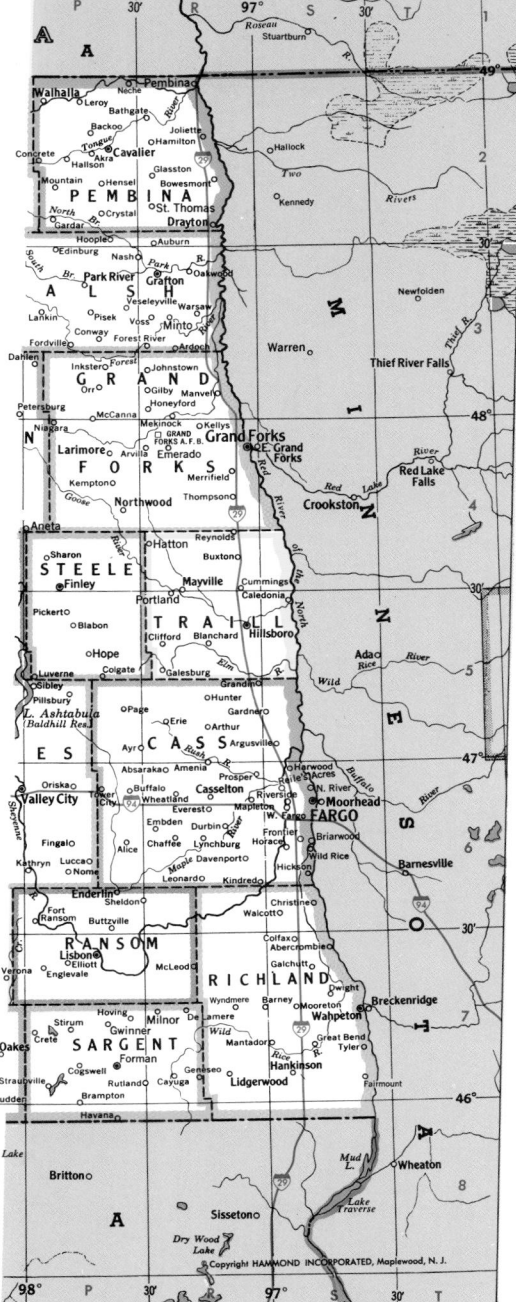

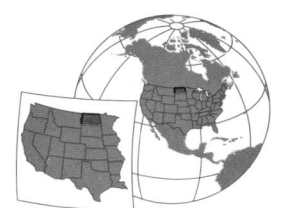

AREA 70,702 sq. mi. (183,118 sq. km.)
POPULATION 652,717
CAPITAL Bismarck
LARGEST CITY Fargo
HIGHEST POINT White Butte 3,506 ft.
 (1069 m.)
SETTLED IN 1780
ADMITTED TO UNION November 2, 1889
POPULAR NAME Flickertail State; Sioux
 State
STATE FLOWER Wild Prairie Rose
STATE BIRD Western Meadowlark

Topography

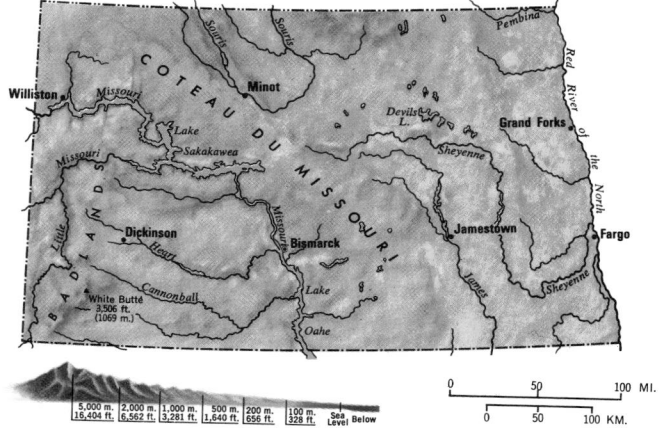

5,000 m.	2,000 m.	1,000 m.	500 m.	200 m.	100 m.	Sea Level	Below
16,404 ft.	6,562 ft.	3,281 ft.	1,640 ft.	656 ft.	328 ft.	Level	Below

Scale: 0 — 50 — 100 MI.
0 — 50 — 100 KM.

58276 Saint Thomas 528	R2
58780 Sanish	E4
58781 Sawyer 417	H3
58653 Scranton 415	D7
58568 Selfridge 273	J7
58654 Sentinel Butte 86	C6
58068 Sheldon 173	P6
58782 Sherwood 294	G2
58374♦ Sheyenne 307	M4
58655 South Heart 294	D6
58850 Spring Brook 52	D3
58784 Stanley⊙ 1,631	F3
58571 Stanton⊙ 623	H5
58482 Steele⊙ 796	L6
58573 Strasburg 623	K7
58483 Streeter 264	M6
58785 Surrey 999	H3
58487 Tappen 271	L6
58656 Taylor 239	F6
58278 Thompson 785	R4
58852 Tioga 1,597	E3
58380 Tolna 241	O4
58071 Tower City 293	P6
58788 Towner⊙ 867	K3
58575 Turtle Lake 802	J4
58576 Underwood 1,329	H5
58072 Valley City⊙ 7,774	P6
58790 Velva 1,101	J3
58792 Voltaire 65	J3
58075 Wahpeton⊙ 9,064	S7
58281 Wales 74	N2
58282 Walhalla 1,429	P2
58577 Washburn⊙ 1,767	J5
58854 Watford City⊙ 2,119	D4
58078 West Fargo 10,099	S6
58793 Westhope 741	H2
58794 White Earth 98	E3
58795 Wildrose 214	D2
58801 Williston⊙ 13,336	C3
58384 Willow City 329	K2
58579 Wilton 950	J5
58492 Wimbledon 330	O5
58495 Wishek 1,345	L7
58385 Wolford 76	L3
58081 Wyndmere 550	R7
58386 York 69	L3
58580 Zap 511	G5
58581 Zeeland 253	L8

OTHER FEATURES

Alkali (lkes)	L3	Fan (lake)	L2	Little Missouri (riv.)	D4	Smoky (lake)	K3
Alkaline (lake)	L6	Forest (riv.)	P3	Little Muddy (riv.)	C3	Souris (riv.)	J2
Apple (creek)	J6	Fort Berthold Ind. Res.	E4	Long (lake)	J4	Spring (creek)	E5
Arrowwood (lake)	N5	Fort Totten Ind. Res.	N4	Long (lake)	K6	Standing Rock Ind. Res.	J7
Ashtabula (lake)	P5	Fort Union Trading Post Nat'l Hist.		Long (lake)	L2	Strawberry (lake)	J4
Audubon (lake)	H4	Site	B3	Maple (riv.)	O8	Stump (lake)	O4
Bad Lands (reg.)	C7	Garrison (dam)	H5	Maple (riv.)	R6	Sweetwater (lake)	N3
Baldhill (Ashtabula) (res.)	P5	George (lake)	L6	Metigoshe (lake)	K2	Theodore Roosevelt Nat'l Mem. Park	
Bear (creek)	O7	Goose (riv.)	P4	Minot A.F.B. 9,880	H3		C5, D4, D6
Beaver (creek)	B5	Grand, North Fork (riv.)	E8	Missouri (riv.)	H5	Thirty Mile (creek)	F6
Beaver (creek)	K7	Grand Forks A.F.B. 9,390	R4	Muddy (creek)	G6	Tongue (riv.)	P2
Beaver (lake)	L7	Green (riv.)	D5	Myrtle (lake)	K6	Tschida (lake)	G6
Buffalo Lodge (lake)	J3	Grove (lake)	L5	North (lake)	J3	Turtle (lake)	H4
Cannonball (riv.)	G7	Heart (butte)	G6	Oahe (lake)	J7	Turtle (lake)	H4
Carpenter (lake)	L2	Heart (riv.)	F6	Oak (creek)	J7	Turtle Mountain Ind. Res.	L2
Cedar (creek)	G7	Helen (lake)	K5	Park (riv.)	R3	Upper Des Lacs (lake)	F2
Chase (lake)	M5	Horsehead (lake)	L5	Patterson, Edward A. (lake)	E6	Van (lake)	L5
Cherry (creek)	D4	International Peace Garden	K1	Pembina (riv.)	O1	Whetstone (buttes)	E7
Clark (buttes)	G7	Irvine (lake)	M3	Pipestem (riv.)	M5	White (butte)	D7
Coteau du Missouri (plain)	G3	Island (lake)	L2	Porcupine (creek)	J7	White Butte (mt.)	D7
Cranberry (lake)	J4	James (riv.)	N6	Red River of the North (riv.)	S4	White Earth (riv.)	E3
Crooked (lake)	L4	Jamestown (res.)	N6	Round (lake)	L6	Wild Rice (riv.)	R7
Cut Bank (creek)	H2	Jim (riv.)	N5	Rush (lake)	N2	Yellowstone (riv.)	B4
Darling (lake)	G2	Knife (riv.)	H5	Rush (lake)	R5		
Deep (riv.)	J1	Knife R. Indian Villages Nat'l Hist.		Sakakawea (lake)	G5	⊙County seat.	
Des Lacs (riv.)	G3	Site	H5	Sentinel (butte)	C6	‡Population of metropolitan area.	
Devils (lake)	M3	Little Deep (creek)	G2	Shell (creek)	F3	† Zip of nearest p.o.	
Dry (lake)	M3	Little Knife (riv.)	F3	Sheyenne (riv.)	O6	♦ Multiple zips.	
East Devils (lake)	N4						
Egg (creek)	H3						
Elm (riv.)	N8						
Elm (riv.)	R5						
Etta (lake)	L6						

†58501 Lincoln 656	J6
58552 Linton⊙ 1,561	K7
58054 Lisbon⊙ 2,283	P7
58461 Litchville 251	O6
58056 Luverne 65	P5
58348 Maddock 677	L4
58554 Mandan⊙ 15,513	J6
58642 Manning⊙ 75	E5
58058 Mantador 76	R7
58256 Manvel 308	R3
58059 Mapleton 306	R6
58643 Marmarth 190	B7
58759 Max 317	H4
58257 Mayville 2,255	R4
58463 McClusky⊙ 658	K4
58254 McVille 626	O4
58447 Medina 521	M6
58645 Medora⊙ 94	C6
58259 Michigan 502	O3
58060 Milnor 716	R7
58351 Minnewaukan⊙ 461	M3
58701 Minot⊙ 32,843	H3
58261 Minto 592	R3
58761 Mohall⊙ 1,049	G2
58471 Monango 59	N7
58472 Montpelier 96	N6
58646 Mott⊙ 1,315	F7
58352 Munich 300	N2
58561 Napoleon⊙ 1,103	L6
58265 Neche 471	P2
58647 New England 825	E6
58562 New Leipzig 352	G7
58356 New Rockford⊙ 1,791	N4

58563 New Salem 1,081	G6
58763 New Town 1,335	F4
58266 Niagara 76	P4
58062 Nome 67	P6
58765 Noonan 283	D2
†58102 North River 65	R4
58267 Northwood 1,240	P4
58474 Oakes 2,112	O7
58063 Oriska 125	P6
58064 Page 329	P5
58769 Palermo 97	F3
58270 Park River 1,844	P3
58770 Parshall 1,059	F4
58271 Pembina 673	R2
58476 Pingree 88	N5
58772 Portal 238	E2
58274 Portland 627	R5
58773 Powers Lake 466	E2
58849 Ray 766	D3
58649 Reeder 355	E7
58477 Regan 71	K5
58650 Regent 297	E7
58275 Reynolds 309	R4
58651 Rhame 222	C7
58652 Richardton 699	F6
†58078 Riverside 465	S6
58365 Rocklake 287	M2
58366 Rolette 667	L2
58367 Rolla⊙ 1,538	L2
58368 Rugby⊙ 3,335	L3
58479 Rogers 68	O5
58067 Rutland 250	P7
58369 Saint John 401	L2

Agriculture, Industry and Resources

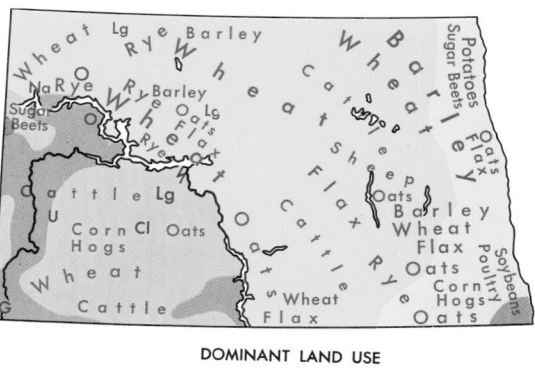

DOMINANT LAND USE

- Specialized Wheat
- Wheat, General Farming
- Wheat, Range Livestock
- Livestock, Cash Grain
- Sugar Beets, Dry Beans, Livestock, General Farming
- Range Livestock
- ⚡ Water Power

MAJOR MINERAL OCCURRENCES

- Cl Clay
- G Natural Gas
- Lg Lignite
- Na Salt
- O Petroleum
- U Uranium

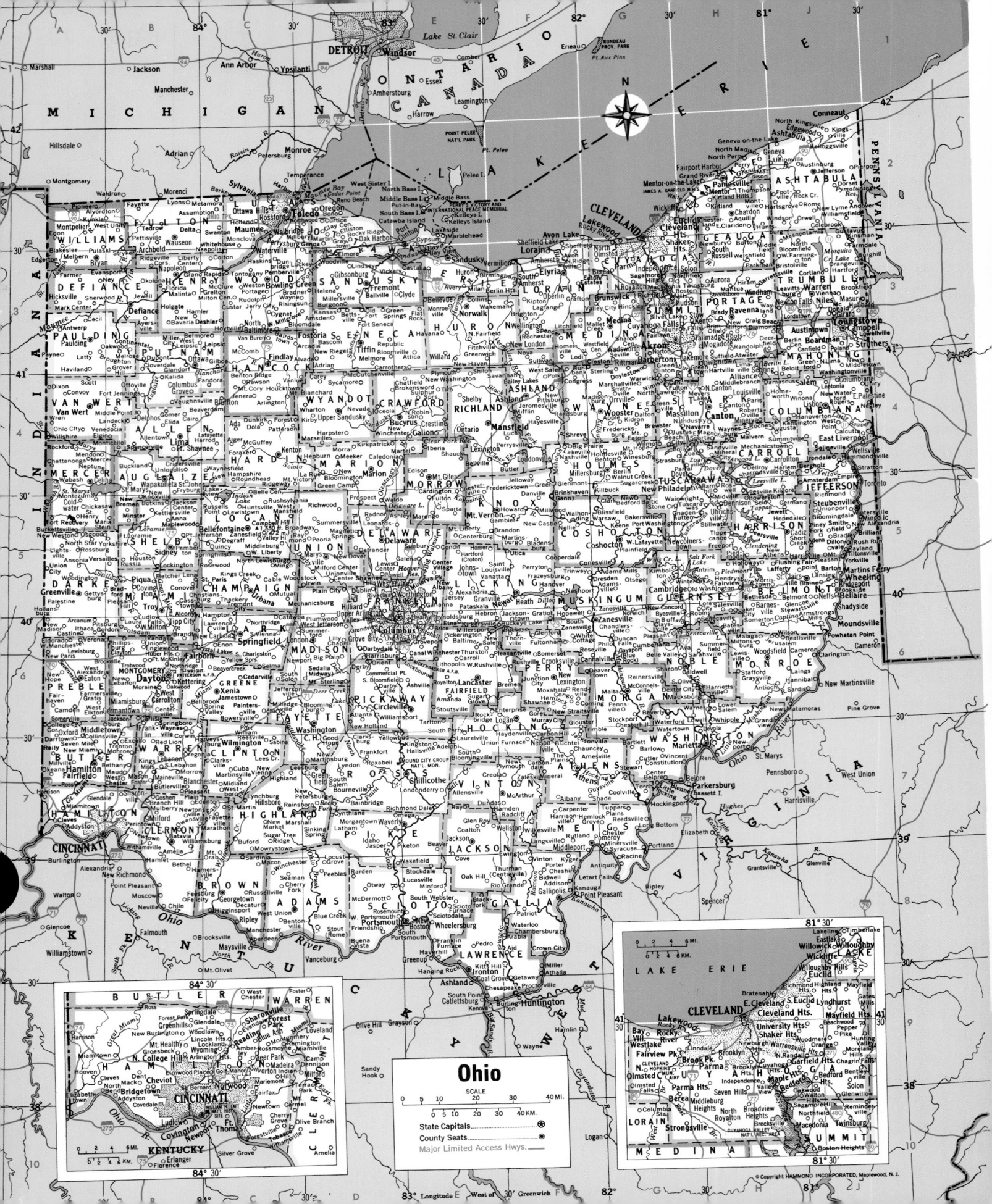

Ohio

SCALE
0 5 10   20   30   40 MI.
0 5 10 20   40 KM.

State Capitals .... ⊛
County Seats .... ◉
Major Limited Access Hwys. ____

© Copyright HAMMOND INCORPORATED, Maplewood, N.J.

AREA 41,330 sq. mi. (107,045 sq. km.)
POPULATION 10,797,624
CAPITAL Columbus
LARGEST CITY Cleveland
HIGHEST POINT Campbell Hill 1,550 ft. (472 m.)
SETTLED IN 1788
ADMITTED TO UNION March 1, 1803
POPULAR NAME Buckeye State
STATE FLOWER Scarlet Carnation
STATE BIRD Cardinal

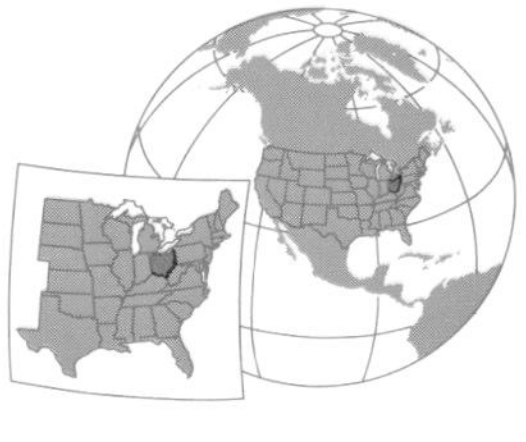

Topography

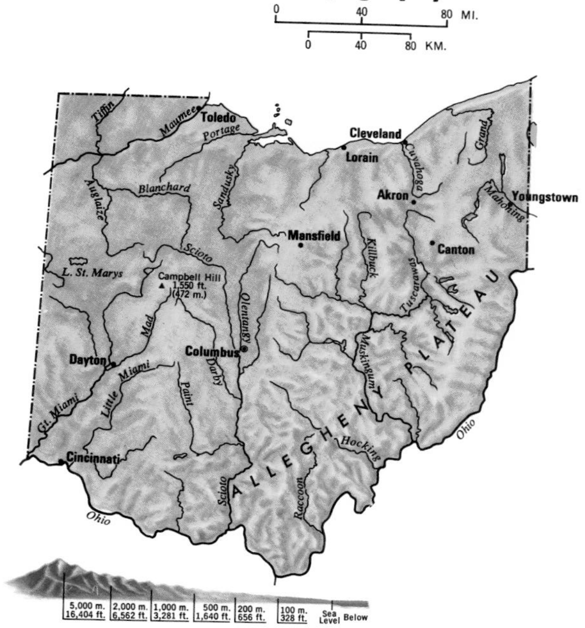
0 40 80 MI.
0 40 80 KM.
Toledo
Cleveland
Lorain
Akron
Youngstown
Mansfield
Canton
Campbell Hill 1,550 ft. (472 m.)
L. St. Marys
Dayton
Columbus
Cincinnati
Tiffin
Maumee
Portage
Auglaize
Blanchard
Sandusky
Cuyahoga
Grand
Mahoning
Scioto
Killbuck
Tuscarawas
Olentangy
Mad
Darby
Miami
Little Miami
Gt. Miami
Paint
Muskingum
Hocking
Raccoon
Ohio
ALLEGHENY PLATEAU
5,000 m. 16,404 ft.
2,000 m. 6,562 ft.
1,000 m. 3,281 ft.
500 m. 1,640 ft.
200 m. 656 ft.
100 m. 328 ft.
Sea Level
Below

COUNTIES

Adams 24,328 .... D8
Allen 112,241 .... B4
Ashland 46,178 .... F4
Ashtabula 104,215 .... J2
Athens 56,399 .... F7
Auglaize 42,554 .... B4
Belmont 82,569 .... J5
Brown 31,920 .... C8
Butler 258,787 .... A7
Carroll 25,598 .... H4
Champaign 33,649 .... C5
Clark 150,236 .... C6
Clermont 128,483 .... B7
Clinton 34,603 .... C7
Columbiana 113,572 .... J4
Coshocton 36,024 .... G5
Crawford 50,075 .... E4
Cuyahoga 1,498,400 .... G3
Darke 55,096 .... A5
Defiance 39,987 .... A3
Delaware 53,840 .... D5
Erie 79,655 .... E3
Fairfield 93,678 .... E6
Fayette 27,467 .... D6
Franklin 869,126 .... E5
Fulton 37,751 .... B2
Gallia 30,098 .... F8
Geauga 74,474 .... H3
Greene 129,769 .... C6
Guernsey 42,024 .... H5
Hamilton 873,224 .... A7
Hancock 64,581 .... C3
Hardin 32,719 .... C4
Harrison 18,152 .... H5
Henry 28,383 .... B3
Highland 33,477 .... C7
Hocking 24,304 .... F6
Holmes 29,416 .... G4
Huron 54,608 .... E3
Jackson 30,592 .... E7
Jefferson 91,564 .... J5
Knox 46,304 .... F5
Lake 212,801 .... H2
Lawrence 63,849 .... E8
Licking 120,981 .... F5
Logan 39,155 .... C5
Lorain 274,909 .... F3
Lucas 471,741 .... C2
Madison 33,004 .... D6
Mahoning 289,487 .... J4
Marion 67,974 .... D4
Medina 113,150 .... G3
Meigs 23,641 .... F7
Mercer 38,334 .... A4
Miami 90,381 .... B5
Monroe 17,382 .... H6
Montgomery 571,697 .... B6
Morgan 14,241 .... G6
Morrow 26,480 .... E4
Muskingum 83,340 .... G5
Noble 11,310 .... G6
Ottawa 40,076 .... D2
Paulding 21,302 .... A3
Perry 31,032 .... F6
Pickaway 43,662 .... D6
Pike 22,802 .... D7
Portage 135,856 .... H3
Preble 38,223 .... A6
Putnam 32,991 .... B3
Richland 131,205 .... E4
Ross 65,004 .... D7
Sandusky 63,267 .... D3
Scioto 84,545 .... D8
Seneca 61,901 .... D3
Shelby 43,089 .... B5
Stark 378,823 .... H4
Summit 524,472 .... G3
Trumbull 241,863 .... J3
Tuscarawas 84,614 .... H5
Union 29,536 .... D5
Van Wert 30,458 .... A4
Vinton 11,584 .... E7
Warren 99,276 .... B7
Washington 64,266 .... H7
Wayne 97,408 .... G4
Williams 36,369 .... A2
Wood 107,372 .... C3
Wyandot 22,651 .... D4

CITIES and TOWNS

Zip *Name/Pop.* *Key*

45101 Aberdeen 1,566 .... C8
45810 Ada 5,669 .... C4
45001 Addyston 1,195 .... B9
43101 Adelphi 472 .... E7
43901 Adena 1,062 .... J5
*44301 Akron⊙ 237,177 .... G3
Akron‡ 660,328 .... G3
45710 Albany 905 .... F7
43001 Alexandria 489 .... E5
45812 Alger 992 .... C4
44601 Alliance 24,315 .... H4
43102 Amanda 720 .... E6
†45201 Amberley 3,442 .... C9
45102 Amelia 1,108 .... D10
44001 Amherst 10,638 .... F3
43903 Amsterdam 783 .... J5
44003 Andover 1,205 .... J2
45302 Anna 1,038 .... B5
45303 Ansonia 1,267 .... A5
45813 Antwerp 1,765 .... A3
44606 Apple Creek 741 .... G4
44804 Arcadia 580 .... D3
45304 Arcanum 2,002 .... A6
43502 Archbold 3,318 .... B2
45814 Arlington 1,187 .... C4
†45201 Arlington Heights 1,082 .... C9
44805 Ashland⊙ 20,326 .... F4
43003 Ashley 1,057 .... E5
44004 Ashtabula 23,449 .... J2
43103 Ashville 2,046 .... E6
45701 Athens⊙ 19,743 .... F7
44807 Attica 865 .... E3
44201 Atwater 975 .... H3
44202 Aurora 8,177 .... H3
44010 Austinburg 900 .... J2
44515 Austintown 33,636 .... J3
44011 Avon 7,241 .... F3
44012 Avon Lake 13,222 .... F2
†43512 Ayersville 950 .... B3
†44805 Bailey Lakes 397 .... F4
45612 Bainbridge 1,042 .... D7
43804 Baltic 563 .... G5
43105 Baltimore 2,689 .... E6
44203 Barberton 29,751 .... G4
43713 Barnesville 4,633 .... H6
43905 Barton 1,039 .... J5
45103 Batavia⊙ 1,896 .... B7
†44870 Bay View 804 .... E3
44140 Bay Village 17,846 .... G9
44608 Beach City 1,083 .... G4
44122 Beachwood 9,983 .... J9
43716 Beallsville 601 .... J6
45808 Beaverdam 492 .... C4
44146 Bedford 15,056 .... H9
†44146 Bedford Heights 13,214 .... J9
43906 Bellaire 8,241 .... J5
45305 Bellbrook 5,174 .... C6
43310 Belle Center 930 .... C4
43311 Bellefontaine⊙ 11,888 .... C5
44811 Bellevue 8,187 .... E3
44813 Bellville 1,714 .... E4
43718 Belmont 714 .... J5
44609 Beloit 1,093 .... J4
45714 Belpre 7,193 .... G7
44017 Berea 19,567 .... G10
43908 Bergholz 914 .... J4
44814 Berlin Heights 756 .... F3
45106 Bethel 2,231 .... B8
43719 Bethesda 1,429 .... H5
44815 Bettsville 752 .... D3
45715 Beverly 1,471 .... G6
43209 Bexley 13,405 .... E6
45107 Blanchester 3,202 .... B7
44817 Bloomdale 744 .... D3
43106 Bloomingburg 869 .... D6
44818 Bloomville 1,019 .... D3
†45242 Blue Ash 9,506 .... C9
45817 Bluffton 3,310 .... C4
44512 Boardman 39,161 .... J3
44612 Bolivar 989 .... G4
†44264 Boston Heights 781 .... J10
45306 Botkins 1,372 .... B5
44695 Bowerston 487 .... H5
43402 Bowling Green⊙ 25,728 .... C3
45308 Bradford 2,166 .... B5
43406 Bradner 1,175 .... C3
44211 Brady Lake 470 .... H3
†44101 Bratenahl 1,485 .... H9
44141 Brecksville 10,132 .... H10
43107 Bremen 1,432 .... F6
44613 Brewster 2,321 .... G4
43912 Bridgeport 2,642 .... J5
†45211 Bridgetown 11,460 .... B9
43913 Brilliant 1,751 .... J5
†44240 Brimfield 3,161 .... H3
44402 Bristolville 900 .... J3
†44141 Broadview Heights 10,920 .... H10
44403 Brookfield 1,527 .... J3
44144 Brooklyn 12,342 .... H9
†44131 Brooklyn Heights 1,653 .... H9
44142 Brook Park 26,195 .... G9
†43912 Brookside 887 .... J5
45309 Brookville 4,322 .... B6
44212 Brunswick 28,104 .... G3
43506 Bryan⊙ 7,879 .... A3
45716 Buchtel 585 .... F7
43008 Buckeye Lake F6
44820 Bucyrus⊙ 13,433 .... E4
†45680 Burlington 900 .... F9
44021 Burton 1,401 .... H3
44822 Butler 991 .... F4
43723 Byesville 2,572 .... G6
43907 Cadiz⊙ 4,058 .... J5
45820 Cairo 596 .... B4
43920 Calcutta 1,121 .... J4
43724 Caldwell⊙ 1,935 .... G6
43314 Caledonia 759 .... D4
43725 Cambridge⊙ 13,573 .... G5
45311 Camden 1,971 .... A6
44405 Campbell 11,619 .... J3
45111 Camp Dennison 625 .... D9
44614 Canal Fulton 3,481 .... H4
43110 Canal Winchester 2,749 .... E6
44406 Canfield 5,535 .... J3
*44701 Canton⊙ 93,077 .... H4
Canton‡ 404,421 .... H4
43315 Cardington 1,665 .... E5
43316 Carey 3,674 .... D4
45005 Carlisle 4,276 .... B6
43112 Carroll 641 .... E6
44615 Carrollton⊙ 3,065 .... J4
44824 Castalia 973 .... E3
45314 Cedarville 2,799 .... C6
45822 Celina⊙ 9,137 .... A4
43011 Centerburg 1,275 .... E5
45459 Centerville 18,886 .... B6
44022 Chagrin Falls 4,335 .... J9
†45631 Chambersburg F8
44024 Chardon⊙ 4,434 .... H2
45719 Chauncey 1,050 .... F7
†45202 Cherry Grove 850 .... C10
45619 Chesapeake 1,370 .... E9
44026 Chesterland 2,301 .... H2
†45211 Cheviot 9,888 .... B9
45601 Chillicothe⊙ 23,420 .... E7
45389 Christiansburg 593 .... C5
*45201 Cincinnati⊙ 385,457 .... B9
Cincinnati‡ 1,401,403 .... B9
43113 Circleville⊙ 11,700 .... D6
43915 Clarington 558 .... J6
43115 Clarksburg 483 .... D7
45113 Clarksville 525 .... C7
45315 Clayton 752 .... B6
*44101 Cleveland⊙ 573,822 .... H9
Cleveland‡ 1,898,720 .... H9
44118 Cleveland Heights 56,438 .... H9
45002 Cleves 2,094 .... B9
44216 Clinton 1,277 .... G4
43410 Clyde 5,489 .... E3
†45638 Coal Grove 2,602 .... E9
45621 Coalton 639 .... E7
45828 Coldwater 4,220 .... A5
†44034 Colebrook 700 .... J2
44028 Columbia Station 518 .... G10
44408 Columbiana 4,987 .... J4
*43201 Columbus (cap.)⊙ 565,032 .... E6
Columbus‡ 1,093,293 .... E6
45830 Columbus Grove 2,313 .... B4
43811 Conesville 451 .... G5
44030 Conneaut 13,835 .... J2
45831 Continental 1,179 .... B3
45832 Convoy 1,140 .... A4
45723 Coolville 649 .... G7
43730 Corning 789 .... F6
44410 Cortland 5,011 .... J3
43812 Coshocton⊙ 13,405 .... G5
†45238 Covedale 5,830 .... B10
45318 Covington 2,610 .... B5
†44429 Craig Beach 1,657 .... H3
44827 Crestline 5,406 .... E4
44217 Creston 1,828 .... G3
45806 Cridersville 1,843 .... B4
43731 Crooksville 2,766 .... F6
45623 Crown City 513 .... F8
†45341 Crystal Lakes 1,463 .... C6
*44221 Cuyahoga Falls 43,890 .... G3
†44101 Cuyahoga Heights 739 .... H9
43413 Cygnet 646 .... C3
44618 Dalton 1,357 .... G4
43014 Danville 1,127 .... F5
†43123 Darbydale 825 .... D6
*45401 Dayton⊙ 193,444 .... B6
Dayton‡ 830,070 .... B6
44411 Deerfield 800 .... H3
45236 Deer Park 6,745 .... C9
43512 Defiance⊙ 16,810 .... B3
43318 Degraff 1,358 .... C5
43015 Delaware⊙ 18,780 .... E5
45833 Delphos 7,314 .... B4
43515 Delta 2,831 .... B2
44621 Dennison 3,398 .... H5
†45202 Dent 800 .... B9
43516 Deshler 1,870 .... C3
45750 Devola 2,708 .... H7
43917 Dillonvale 912 .... J5
44622 Dover 11,782 .... G4
44230 Doylestown 2,493 .... G4
43821 Dresden 1,646 .... G5
43017 Dublin 3,855 .... D5
43734 Duncan Falls 900 .... G6
45836 Dunkirk 954 .... C4
44730 East Canton 1,721 .... H4
44112 East Cleveland 36,957 .... H9
†44094 Eastlake 22,104 .... J8
43920 East Liverpool 16,687 .... J4
44413 East Palestine 5,306 .... J4
44626 East Sparta 868 .... H4
45320 Eaton⊙ 6,839 .... A6
†44035 Eaton Estates 1,806 .... G3
43517 Edgerton 1,813 .... A3
†44004 Edgewood 3,099 .... J2
43320 Edison 504 .... E4
43518 Edon 947 .... A2
45321 Eldorado 509 .... A6
45807 Elida 1,349 .... B4
43416 Elmore 1,271 .... D3
45216 Elmwood Place 2,840 .... B9
*44035 Elyria⊙ 57,538 .... F3
45322 Englewood 11,329 .... B6
45323 Enon 2,597 .... C6
44117 Euclid 59,999 .... J9
†45201 Evendale 1,954 .... C9
45042 Excello 900 .... B7
45324 Fairborn 29,702 .... B6
†45201 Fairfax 2,222 .... C9
45014 Fairfield 30,777 .... A7
44313 Fairlawn 6,100 .... G3
44077 Fairport Harbor 3,357 .... H2
44126 Fairview Park 19,311 .... G9
45325 Farmersville 950 .... A6
43521 Fayette 1,222 .... B2
45120 Felicity 929 .... B8
45840 Findlay⊙ 35,594 .... C3
45326 Fletcher 498 .... B5
43977 Flushing 1,266 .... J5
45843 Forest 1,633 .... C4
45405 Forest Park 18,675 .... B9
45230 Forestville 950 .... C10
45844 Fort Jennings 538 .... B4
45845 Fort Loramie 977 .... B5
†45426 Fort McKinley B6
45846 Fort Recovery 1,370 .... A5
†45801 Fort Shawnee 4,541 .... B4
44830 Fostoria 15,743 .... D3
45628 Frankfort 1,008 .... D7
45005 Franklin 10,711 .... B6
45629 Franklin Furnace 1,093 .... E8
43822 Frazeysburg 1,025 .... F5
44627 Fredericksburg 511 .... G4
43019 Fredericktown 2,299 .... F5
43973 Freeport 525 .... H5
43420 Fremont⊙ 17,834 .... D3
45630 Friendship 900 .... D8
43230 Gahanna 18,001 .... E5
44833 Galion 12,391 .... E4
45631 Gallipolis⊙ 5,576 .... F8
43022 Gambier 2,056 .... F5
44125 Garfield Heights 34,938 .... J9
44231 Garrettsville 1,769 .... H3
44040 Gates Mills 2,236 .... J9
44041 Geneva 6,655 .... J2
44043 Geneva-on-the-Lake 1,634 .... H2
43430 Genoa 2,213 .... D2
45121 Georgetown⊙ 3,467 .... C8
45327 Germantown 5,015 .... B6
45328 Gettysburg 545 .... A5
43431 Gibsonburg 2,479 .... D3
44420 Girard 12,517 .... J3
45848 Glandorf 746 .... B3
45246 Glendale 2,368 .... C9
†44139 Glenwillow 492 .... J10
45732 Glouster 2,211 .... F6
44629 Gnadenhutten 1,320 .... G5
†45201 Golf Manor 4,317 .... C9
45122 Goshen B7
44044 Grafton 2,231 .... F3
43522 Grand Rapids 962 .... C3
44045 Grand River 412 .... H2
†43212 Grandview Heights 7,420 .... D6
43023 Granville 3,851 .... E5
45330 Gratis 809 .... A6
43322 Green Camp 475 .... D4
45123 Greenfield 5,150 .... D7
45218 Greenhills 4,927 .... B9
44232 Greensburg 950 .... G4
44836 Green Springs 1,568 .... E3
44630 Greentown 300 .... H4
45331 Greenville⊙ 12,999 .... A5
44837 Greenwich 1,458 .... E3
43123 Grove City 16,816 .... D6
43125 Groveport 3,286 .... E6
45849 Grover Hill 486 .... B3
45634 Hamden 1,010 .... F7
45130 Hamersville 688 .... C8
*45011 Hamilton⊙ 63,189 .... A7
Hamilton-Middletown‡ 258,787 .... A7
43524 Hamler 625 .... B3
43931 Hannibal 550 .... J6
†43055 Hanover 926 .... F5
43126 Harrisburg 363 .... D6
45030 Harrison 5,855 .... A9
45850 Harrod 506 .... C4
†44085 Hartsgrove 200 .... J2
44632 Hartville 1,772 .... H4
43525 Haskins 568 .... C3
43127 Haydenville 395 .... F7
44838 Hayesville 518 .... F4
43055 Heath 6,969 .... F5
43025 Hebron 2,035 .... E6
43526 Hicksville 3,929 .... A3
†44143 Highland Heights 5,739 .... J9
43026 Hilliard 8,008 .... D5
45133 Hillsboro⊙ 6,356 .... C7
44234 Hiram 1,360 .... H3
43527 Holgate 1,315 .... B3
43528 Holland 1,048 .... C2
45033 Hooven 550 .... A9
43976 Hopedale 857 .... J5
44425 Hubbard 9,245 .... J3
45424 Huber Heights 35,480 .... B6
44236 Hudson 4,615 .... H3
†44022 Hunting Valley 786 .... J9
44839 Huron 7,123 .... E3
44131 Independence 6,607 .... H9
†45201 Indian Hill 5,521 .... C9
43932 Irondale 535 .... J4
45638 Ironton⊙ 14,290 .... E8
45640 Jackson⊙ 6,675 .... E7
45334 Jackson Center 1,310 .... B5
45740 Jacksonville 651 .... F7
45335 Jamestown 1,702 .... C6
44047 Jefferson⊙ 2,952 .... J2
†43162 Jefferson (West Jefferson) 4,448 .... D6
43128 Jeffersonville 1,252 .... C6
44840 Jeromesville 582 .... F4
43437 Jerry City 512 .... C3
43986 Jewett 972 .... H5
43031 Johnstown 3,158 .... E5
43748 Junction City 754 .... F6
45853 Kalida 1,019 .... B4
44240 Kent 26,164 .... H3
43326 Kenton⊙ 8,605 .... C4
45429 Kettering 61,186 .... B6
44637 Killbuck 937 .... G5
45034 Kings Mills 500 .... B7
45644 Kingston 1,208 .... E7
44048 Kingsville J2
44428 Kinsman 900 .... J3
43033 Kirkersville 626 .... E6
†44094 Kirtland 5,969 .... H2
43951 Lafferty 855 .... H5
44050 Lagrange 1,258 .... F3
44250 Lakemore 2,744 .... H3
43440 Lakeside 850 .... E2
43331 Lakeview 1,089 .... C4
44107 Lakewood 61,963 .... G9
43130 Lancaster⊙ 34,953 .... E6
43934 Lansing 950 .... J5
43332 La Rue 861 .... D4
43135 Laurelville 591 .... E7
†45501 Lawrenceville 307 .... C6
45036 Lebanon⊙ 9,636 .... B7
45135 Leesburg 1,019 .... D7
44431 Leetonia 2,121 .... J4
45856 Leipsic 2,171 .... C3
45338 Lewisburg 1,450 .... A6
44904 Lexington 3,823 .... E4
43532 Liberty Center 1,111 .... B3
*45801 Lima⊙ 47,381 .... B4
Lima‡ 218,244 .... B4
†45201 Lincoln Heights 5,259 .... C9
43442 Lindsey 571 .... D3
44432 Lisbon⊙ 3,159 .... J4
44253 Litchfield 650 .... F3
43136 Lithopolis 652 .... E6
45742 Little Hocking 800 .... G7
45215 Lockland 4,292 .... C9
44254 Lodi 2,942 .... F3
43138 Logan⊙ 6,557 .... F6
43140 London⊙ 6,958 .... C6
*44052 Lorain 75,416 .... F3
Lorain-Elyria‡ 274,909 .... F3
†44481 Lordstown 3,280 .... J3
44842 Loudonville 2,945 .... F4
44641 Louisville 7,996 .... H4
45140 Loveland 9,106 .... D9
45744 Lowell 729 .... H6
44436 Lowellville 1,558 .... J3
44843 Lucas 753 .... F4
45648 Lucasville 3,349 .... E8
43443 Luckey 895 .... D3
45142 Lynchburg 1,205 .... C7
44124 Lyndhurst 18,092 .... J9
43533 Lyons 596 .... B2
44056 Macedonia 6,571 .... J10
†45202 Mack B9
45243 Madeira 9,341 .... C9
44057 Madison 2,291 .... H2
44643 Magnolia 986 .... H4
43758 Malta 956 .... G6
44644 Malvern 1,032 .... H4
45144 Manchester 2,313 .... C8
*44901 Mansfield⊙ 53,927 .... F4
Mansfield‡ 131,205 .... F4
44255 Mantua 1,041 .... H3
44137 Maple Heights 29,735 .... H9
†43440 Marblehead 679 .... E2
45860 Maria Stein 950 .... A5

(continued on following page)

Agriculture, Industry and Resources

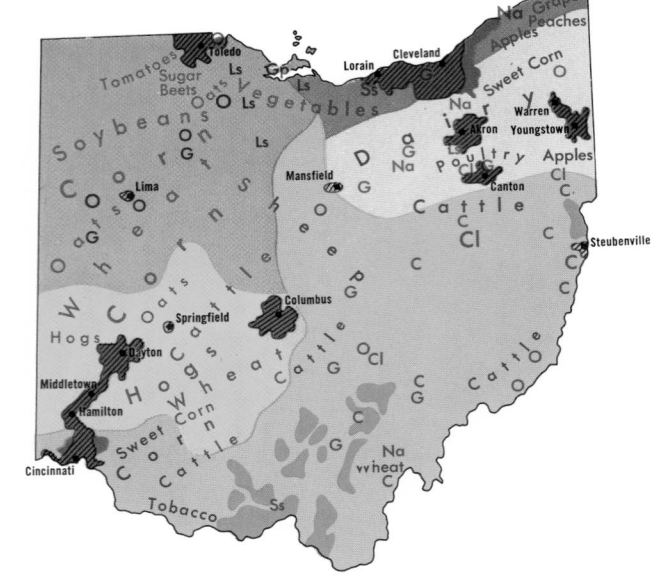

DOMINANT LAND USE

- Hogs, Soft Winter Wheat
- Livestock, Dairy, Soybeans, Cash Grain
- Dairy, General Farming
- General Farming, Livestock, Tobacco
- Fruit, Truck and Mixed Farming
- Forests
- Urban Areas

MAJOR MINERAL OCCURRENCES

- C   Coal
- Cl   Clay
- G   Natural Gas
- Gp   Gypsum
- Ls   Limestone
- Na   Salt
- O   Petroleum
- Ss   Sandstone

Major Industrial Areas

AREA 69,956 sq. mi. (181,186 sq. km.)
POPULATION 3,025,290
CAPITAL Oklahoma City
LARGEST CITY Oklahoma City
HIGHEST POINT Black Mesa 4,973 ft. (1516 m.)
SETTLED IN 1889
ADMITTED TO UNION November 16, 1907
POPULAR NAME Sooner State
STATE FLOWER Mistletoe
STATE BIRD Scissor-tailed Flycatcher

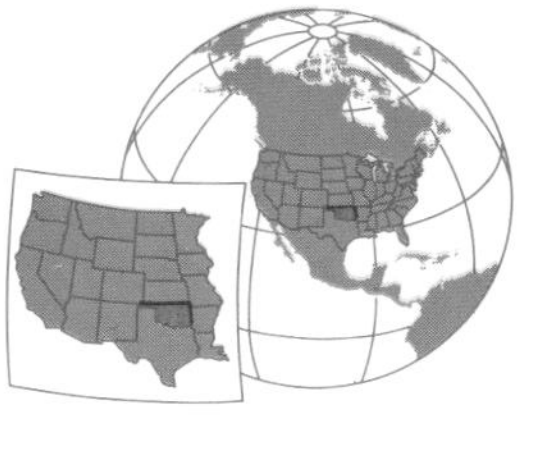

COUNTIES

Name/Pop.	Key
Adair 18,575	S3
Alfalfa 7,077	K1
Atoka 12,748	O6
Beaver 6,806	E1
Beckham 19,243	G4
Blaine 13,443	K3
Bryan 30,535	O7
Caddo 30,905	K4
Canadian 56,452	K3
Carter 43,610	M6
Cherokee 30,684	R3
Choctaw 17,203	P6
Cimarron 3,648	A1
Cleveland 133,173	M4
Coal 6,041	O5
Comanche 112,456	K5
Cotton 7,338	K6
Craig 15,014	R1
Creek 59,016	O3
Custer 25,995	H3
Delaware 23,946	S2
Dewey 5,922	H2
Ellis 5,596	G2
Garfield 62,820	L2
Garvin 27,856	M5
Grady 39,490	L5
Grant 6,518	L1
Greer 7,028	G5
Harmon 4,519	G5
Harper 4,715	G1
Haskell 11,010	R4
Hughes 14,338	O4
Jackson 30,356	H5
Jefferson 8,183	L6
Johnston 10,356	N6
Kay 49,852	M1
Kingfisher 14,187	L3
Kiowa 12,711	J5
Latimer 9,840	R5
Le Flore 40,698	S5
Lincoln 26,601	N3
Logan 26,881	M3
Love 7,469	M7
Major 8,772	K2
Marshall 10,550	N6
Mayes 32,261	R2
McClain 20,291	L5
McCurtain 36,151	S6
McIntosh 15,562	P4
Murray 12,147	M6
Muskogee 66,939	R3
Noble 11,573	M2
Nowata 11,486	P1
Okfuskee 11,125	O3
Oklahoma 568,933	M3
Okmulgee 39,169	P3
Osage 39,327	O1
Ottawa 32,870	S1
Pawnee 15,310	N2
Payne 62,435	N2
Pittsburg 40,524	P5
Pontotoc 32,598	N5
Pottawatomie 55,239	N4
Pushmataha 11,773	R6
Roger Mills 4,799	G3
Rogers 46,436	P2
Seminole 27,473	N4
Sequoyah 30,749	S3
Stephens 43,419	L6
Texas 17,727	C1
Tillman 12,398	J6
Tulsa 470,593	P2
Wagoner 41,801	P3
Washington 48,113	P1
Washita 13,798	J4
Woods 10,923	J1
Woodward 21,172	H2

CITIES and TOWNS

Zip	*Name/Pop.*	*Key*
74720	Achille 480	O7
74820	Ada⊙ 15,902	N5
74330	Adair 508	R2
73901	Adams 150	D1
73520	Addington 141	L6
74331	Afton 1,174	S1
74824	Agra 354	N3
74721	Albany 65	O7
73001	Albert 100	K4
74521	Albion 165	R5
74522	Alderson 366	P5
73002	Alex 769	L5
73716	Aline 313	K1
74825	Allen 998	O5
73521	Altus⊙ 23,101	H5
73717	Alva⊙ 6,416	J1
73004	Amber 416	L4
73718	Ames 314	K2
73719	Amorita 66	K1
73005	Anadarko⊙ 6,378	K4
74523	Antlers⊙ 2,989	P6
73006	Apache 1,560	K5
73620	Arapaho⊙ 851	H3
73401	Ardmore⊙ 23,689	M6
74901	Arkoma 2,175	T4
73832	Arnett⊙ 714	G2
74826	Asher 659	N5
74524	Ashland 72	O5
74525	Atoka⊙ 3,409	O6
74827	Atwood 225	O5
74001	Avant 461	O2
†73860	Avard 51	J1
73930	Baker 70	D1
74002	Barnsdall 1,501	O1
†74965	Baron 300	S3
74003	Bartlesville⊙ 34,568	O1
74722	Battiest 250	S6
73932	Beaver⊙ 1,939	F1
74421	Beggs 1,428	P3
†74966	Bengal 300	R5
74723	Bennington 302	P7
74331	Bernice 318	S1
73622	Bessie 245	H4
73008	Bethany 22,130	L3
74724	Bethel 350	S6
†74801	Bethel Acres 2,314	M4
74332	Big Cabin 252	R1
74630	Billings 632	M1
73009	Binger 791	K4
73720	Bison 103	L2
74008	Bixby 6,969	P3
74058	Blackburn 114	N2
74631	Blackwell 8,400	M1
73526	Blair 1,092	H5
73010	Blanchard 1,688	L4
74528	Blanco 215	P5
74529	Blocker 135	P4
†74701	Blue 150	O7
74333	Bluejacket 247	R1
73933	Boise City⊙ 1,761	B1
74726	Bokchito 628	O6
74930	Bokoshe 556	S4
74829	Boley 423	O4
74727	Boswell 702	P6
74830	Bowlegs 522	N4
74009	Bowring 115	O1
74422	Boynton 518	P3
73011	Bradley 284	L5
74423	Braggs 351	R3
74632	Braman 355	M1
73012	Bray 591	L5
73721	Breckinridge 261	L2
†73047	Bridgeport 115	K3
74010	Bristow 4,702	O3
74012	Broken Arrow 35,761	P2
74728	Broken Bow 3,965	S7
74530	Bromide 180	N6
†74873	Brooksville 46	M4
†74437	Bryant 74	P4
73834	Buffalo⊙ 1,381	G1
74931	Bunch 64	S3
74633	Burbank 161	N1
73722	Burlington 206	K1
73430	Burneyville 150	M7
73624	Burns Flat 2,431	H4
73625	Butler 388	H3
74831	Byars 353	N5
†74820	Byng 833	N5
73723	Byron 67	K1
73527	Cache 1,661	J5
74729	Caddo 923	O6
74730	Calera 1,390	O7
73014	Calumet 469	K3
74531	Calvin 315	O5
73835	Camargo 264	H2
74932	Cameron 365	T4
74425	Canadian 279	P4
74533	Caney 147	O6
73724	Canton 854	J2
73626	Canute 676	H4
73725	Capron 54	J1
74335	Cardin 500	S1
73726	Carmen 516	J1
73015	Carnegie 2,016	J4
74832	Carney 622	N3
73727	Carrier 259	K2
73627	Carter 367	H4
74934	Cartersville 79	S4
73016	Cashion 547	L3
74833	Castle 130	O4
74015	Catoosa 1,561	P2
73017	Cement 884	K5
74534	Centrahoma 166	O5
74834	Chandler⊙ 2,926	N3
73528	Chattanooga 403	J6
74426	Checotah 3,454	R4
74016	Chelsea 1,754	P1
73728	Cherokee⊙ 2,105	K1
73838	Chester 104	J2
73628	Cheyenne⊙ 1,207	G3
73018	Chickasha⊙ 15,828	L4
74635	Chilocco 400	M1
73020	Choctaw 7,520	M3
74337	Chouteau 1,559	R2
†74965	Christie 375	S3
73111	Cimarron	L3
74017	Claremore⊙ 12,085	R2
74535	Clarita 72	O6
74536	Clayton 833	R5
74835	Clearview 250	O4
73729	Cleo Springs 514	K2
74020	Cleveland 2,972	O2
73601	Clinton 8,796	H3
74538	Coalgate⊙ 2,001	O5
74733	Colbert 1,122	O7
74338	Colcord 530	S2
†73010	Cole 309	L5
73432	Coleman 200	O6
74021	Collinsville 3,556	P2
73021	Colony 185	J4
73529	Comanche 1,937	L6
74339	Commerce 2,556	R1
73022	Concho 300	L3
†73041	Cooperton 31	J5
74022	Copan 960	P1
73632	Cordell⊙ 3,301	H4
73024	Corn 542	J4
†73456	Cornish 115	L6
74428	Council Hill 141	P3
73025	Countyline 550	L6
73730	Covington 715	L2
74429	Coweta 4,554	P3
†74934	Cowlington 546	S4
73027	Coyle 345	M3
73638	Crawford 53	G3
73028	Crescent 1,651	L3
74837	Cromwell 337	N4
74430	Crowder 431	P4
†73446	Cumberland 100	N6
74023	Cushing 7,720	N3
73639	Custer City 530	J3
73029	Cyril 1,220	K5
73731	Dacoma 226	J1
74838	Dale 160	M4
74026	Davenport 974	N3
73530	Davidson 501	J6
73030	Davis 2,782	M5
74636	Deer Creek 174	L1
74027	Delaware 544	P1
73115	Del City 28,523	L4
74028	Depew 682	O3
73531	Devol 186	J6
74431	Dewar 1,048	P4
74029	Dewey 3,545	P1
73031	Dibble 348	L4
†73401	Dickson 996	M6
73641	Dill City 649	H4
74340	Disney 464	S2
73032	Dougherty 210	M6
73733	Douglas 89	L2
74341	Douthat 30	S1
73734	Dover 570	L3
73735	Drummond 482	L2
74030	Drumright 3,162	N3
73533	Duncan⊙ 22,517	L5
74701	Durant⊙ 11,972	O6
73642	Durham 30	G3
74839	Dustin 498	O4
74734	Eagletown 650	S6
73033	Eakly 452	K4
74840	Earlsboro 266	N4
†73532	East Duke 484	H5
73034	Edmond 34,637	M3
73537	Eldorado 688	G6
73538	Elgin 1,003	K5
73644	Elk City 9,579	G4
73539	Elmer 131	H6
73035	Elmore City 582	M5
73935	Elmwood 300	F1
73036	El Reno⊙ 15,486	K3
†73529	Empire City 13	L6
73701	Enid⊙ 50,363	L2
73645	Erick 1,375	G4
74342	Eucha 210	S2
74432	Eufaula⊙ 3,159	P4
74637	Fairfax 1,949	N1
74343	Fairland 1,073	S1
73736	Fairmont 419	L2
†74080	Fair Oaks 346	P2
73737	Fairview⊙ 3,370	J2
†74881	Fallis 22	M3
74935	Fanshawe 416	S5
73840	Fargo 409	G2
73540	Faxon 140	J6
73646	Fay 140	J3
73937	Felt 120	A1
74543	Finley 350	R6
74842	Fittstown 500	N5
74843	Fitzhugh 150	N5
†73569	Fleetwood 12	L7
73541	Fletcher 1,074	K5
74652	Foraker 34	Q1
†73101	Forest Park 1,148	M3
73938	Forgan 611	E1
73038	Fort Cobb 760	K4
74434	Fort Gibson 2,477	R3
73841	Fort Supply 559	G1
74735	Fort Towson 789	R7
73647	Foss 188	H4
73039	Foster 100	M5
73435	Fox 400	M6
74031	Foyil 191	R2
74844	Francis 365	N5
73542	Frederick⊙ 6,153	H6
73842	Freedom 339	H1
73843	Gage 667	G2
74936	Gans 346	S4
73738	Garber 1,215	M2
74736	Garvin 162	S7
73844	Gate 146	F1
73040	Geary 1,700	K3
73436	Gene Autry 178	N6
73543	Geronimo 726	K6
†74531	Gerty 149	O5
74032	Glencoe 490	M2
74033	Glenpool 2,706	P3
74737	Golden 300	S6
†73093	Goldsby 603	L4
73739	Goltry 305	K1
†74740	Goodwater 240	S7
73939	Goodwell 1,186	C1
74435	Gore 445	R3
73041	Gotebo 457	J4
73544	Gould 318	G5
74545	Gowen 75	R5
73042	Gracemont 503	K4
73545	Grady 85	L6
73437	Graham 200	M6
†74652	Grainola 67	N1
73546	Grandfield 1,445	J6
†74349	Grand Lake Towne 36	S1
73547	Granite 1,617	H5
†74437	Grayson 150	P3
73043	Greenfield 233	K3
74344	Grove 3,378	S1
73044	Guthrie⊙ 10,312	M3
73942	Guymon⊙ 8,492	D1
74546	Haileyville 832	P5
74034	Hallett 186	N2
†73069	Hall Park 577	M4
73650	Hammon 866	H3
74845	Hanna 157	P4
74846	Harden City 250	N5
73944	Hardesty 243	D1
73832	Harmon 27	G2
73045	Harrah 2,897	M4
†74740	Harris 192	S7
74547	Hartshorne 2,380	R5
74436	Haskell 1,953	P3
73548	Hastings 246	K6
74740	Haworth 341	S7
73549	Headrick 223	H5
73438	Healdton 3,769	M6
74937	Heavener 2,776	S5
73741	Helena 710	K1
74741	Hendrix 106	O7
73046	Hennepin 300	M5
73742	Hennessey 2,287	L2
74437	Henryetta 6,432	O4
†73086	Hickory 95	N5
73743	Hillsdale 110	K1
73047	Hinton 1,432	K4
73744	Hitchcock 172	K3
74438	Hitchita 126	P3
73651	Hobart⊙ 4,735	J5
74439	Hoffman 407	P4
74848	Holdenville⊙ 5,469	O4
73550	Hollis⊙ 2,958	G5
73551	Hollister 82	J6
74035	Hominy 3,130	O2
74549	Honobia 80	R5
73945	Hooker 1,788	D1
†74366	Hoot Owl 3	R2
73746	Hopeton 42	J1
74940	Howe 562	S5
74440	Hoyt 160	R4
74743	Hugo⊙ 7,172	P7
74441	Hulbert 633	R3
74640	Hunter 276	L1
73048	Hydro 938	J3
74745	Idabel⊙ 7,622	S7
73552	Indiahoma 364	J5
74442	Indianola 254	P4
74036	Inola 1,550	P2
73747	Isabella 113	K2
74346	Jay⊙ 2,100	S2
†73759	Jefferson 92	L1
74037	Jenks 5,876	P2
74038	Jennings 395	N2
73749	Jet 352	K1
73049	Jones 2,270	M3
74347	Kansas 491	S2
74641	Kaw City 283	N1
74039	Kellyville 960	O3

(continued on following page)

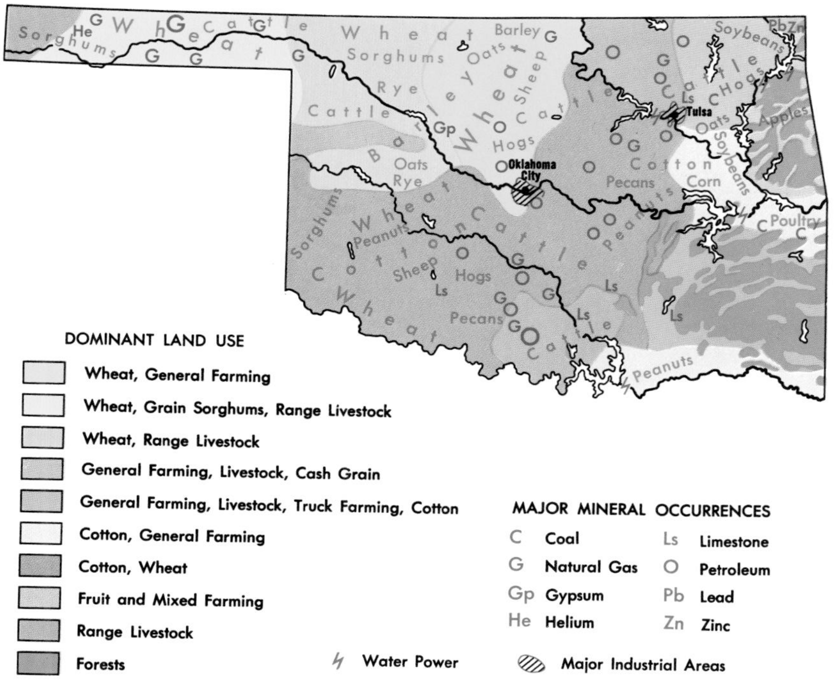

Sorghums
Wheat
Barley
Oats
Sheep
Cattle
Rye
Hogs
Soybeans
Tulsa
Apples
Oklahoma City
Cotton
Pecans
Corn
Poultry
Peanuts
DOMINANT LAND USE
Wheat, General Farming
Wheat, Grain Sorghums, Range Livestock
Wheat, Range Livestock
General Farming, Livestock, Cash Grain
General Farming, Livestock, Truck Farming, Cotton
Cotton, General Farming
Cotton, Wheat
Fruit and Mixed Farming
Range Livestock
Forests
Water Power
MAJOR MINERAL OCCURRENCES
C Coal
G Natural Gas
Gp Gypsum
He Helium
Ls Limestone
O Petroleum
Pb Lead
Zn Zinc
Major Industrial Areas

74747 Kemp 178 ....O7
†74741 Kemp City (Hendrix) 106 ...O7
74040 Kendrick 132.................N3
74748 Kenefic 140 ....O6
*74636 Kenwood 400 ....S2
74941 Keota 661 ....S4
74349 Ketchum 326 ....R1
74041 Kiefer 912 ....O3
74601 Kildare 112 ....M1
73750 Kingfisher⊙ 4,245 ....L3
73439 Kingston 1,171 ....N7
74552 Kinta 303 ....R4
74553 Kiowa 866 ....P5
73847 Knowles 44 ....F1
74849 Konawa 1,711 ....N5
74554 Krebs 1,754 ....P5
73753 Kremlin 301 ....L1
73754 Lahoma 537 ....K2
74850 Lamar 121 ....O4
†73728 Lambert 20 ....L1
74643 Lamont 571 ....R2
74350 Langley 582 ....M3
73050 Langston 443 ....G1
73848 Laverne 1,563 ....F1
73501 Lawton⊙ 80,054 ....K5
      Lawton‡ 112,456 ....K5
74351 Leach 30 ....S2
73440 Lebanon 382 ....N7
73654 Leedey 499 ....H3
74942 Leflore 322 ....S5
74556 Lehigh 284 ....O6
74042 Lenapah 350 ....P1
73441 Leon 10 ....M7
74043 Leonard 400 ....P3
74943 Lequire 250 ....R4
73051 Lexington 1,731 ....M4
†74858 Lima (New Lima) 256 ....D4
73052 Lindsay 3,454 ....L5
73442 Loco 215 ....L6
74352 Locust Grove 1,179 .....R2
73849 Logan 18 ....F1
73443 Lone Grove 3,369 ....M6
73655 Lone Wolf 613 ....H5
73755 Longdale 405 ....K2
73053 Lookeba 221 ....K4
†73842 Lookout 3 ....H1
†74063 Lotsee 7 ....O2
73553 Loveland 21 ....J6
73756 Loyal 112 ....K2
73757 Lucien 350 ....M2
73054 Luther 1,159 ....M3
†74578 Lutie 100 ....R5
74852 Macomb 58 ....N4
73446 Madill⊙ 3,173 ....N6
73758 Manchester 146 ....L1
73554 Mangum⊙ 3,833 ....G5
73555 Manitou 322 ....J5
74044 Mannford 1,610 ....O2
73447 Mannsville 568 ....N6
74045 Maramec 101 ....N2
74945 Marble City 294 ....S3
73448 Marietta⊙ 2,494 ....M7
74644 Marland 340 ....M1
73055 Marlow 5,017 ....K5
73056 Marshall 372 ....L2
73556 Martha 219 ....H5
74854 Maud 1,444 ....N4
73851 May 89 ....G1
73656 Mayfield 17 ....G4
73057 Maysville 1,396 ....M5
74353 Mazie 118 ....R2
74501 McAlester⊙ 17,255 ....P5
†74441 McBride 91 ....N7
74944 McCurtain 549 ....R4
74851 McLoud 4,061 ....M6
73445 McMillan 50 ....M6
73449 Mead 143 ....O7
73759 Medford⊙ 1,419 ....L1
73557 Medicine Park 437 .....J5
74855 Meeker 1,032 ....N4
73760 Meno 171 ....K2
73058 Meridian 78 ....M3
74354 Miami⊙ 14,237 ....S1
73110 Midwest City 49,559 ...M4
73450 Milburn 376 ....O6
74046 Milfay 200 ....N3
74856 Mill Creek 431 ....N6
74750 Millerton 262 ....S7
73451 Milo 25 ....M6
73059 Minco 1,489 ....L4
74946 Moffett 269 ....S4

74947 Monroe 150 ....S4
74444 Moodys 250 ....S2
73160 Moore 35,063 ....M4
73852 Mooreland 1,383 ......H2
74445 Morris 1,288 ....P3
73061 Morrison 671 ....M2
74941 Mounds 1,086 ....O3
73559 Mountain Park 557 ....H4
73062 Mountain View 1,189 ..J4
74557 Moyers 312 ....S4
74948 Muldrow 2,538 ....S4
73063 Mulhall 301 ....M2
74949 Muse 350 ....R3
74401 Muskogee⊙ 40,011 ....L4
73064 Mustang 7,496 ......L4
73853 Mutual 135 ....H2
74354 Narcissa 100 ....S1
74646 Nardin 88 ....M1
73761 Nash 301 ....K1
74546 Nashoba 50 ....R6
74049 New Alluwe 129 ......R1
74646 New Cordell
       (Cordell)⊙ 3,301 ...H4
†73632 New Cordell
       (Cordell)⊙ 3,301 ...H4
74647 Newkirk⊙ 2,413 ......N1
74484 New Lima 256 ....O4
74060 New Prue (Prue) 554 ..O2
74055 Nicoma Park 2,588 ...M4
†73116 Nichols Hills 4,171 ..L3
73066 Nicoma Park 2,588 ...M4
73068 Noble 3,497 ....M4
74080 Norge 87 ....K4
†73018 Norge 87 ....K4
73069 Norman⊙ 68,020 .....M4
†73701 North Enid 992 ......L2

74358 North Miami 544 ....R1
74048 Nowata⊙ 4,270 ....P1
73452 Oakland 485 ....N6
74359 Oaks 591 ....S2
73658 Oakwood 140 ....J3
74051 Ochelata 480 ....P1
74958 Octavia 30 ....S5
74052 Oilton 1,244 ....N2
73762 Okarche 1,064 ....L3
74446 Okay 554 ....R3
73763 Okeene 1,601 ....K2
74859 Okemah⊙ 3,381 ......O4
       Oklahoma City
       (cap.)⊙ 403,136 ....L4
       Oklahoma City‡ 834,088 ..L4
74447 Okmulgee⊙ 16,263 ....O3
73560 Olustee 721 ....H5
73764 Omega 50 ....K3
74053 Oologah 798 ....P2
73948 Optima 133 ....D1
73765 Orienta 25 ....J2
73073 Orlando 218 ....M2
74054 Osage 243 ....O2
73561 Oscar 60 ....L7
73453 Overbrook 443 .....M6
74055 Owasso 6,149 .....N3
74860 Paden 448 ....S4
74951 Panama 1,425 .....P4
74559 Panola 75 ....R5
73074 Paoli 573 ....M5
†74435 Paradise Hill 154 ..R3
74451 Park Hill 200 .....R3

73075 Pauls Valley⊙ 5,664 ...M5
74056 Pawhuska⊙ 4,771 .....O1
74058 Pawnee⊙ 1,688 ......N2
74301 Pensacola 82 ....R2
†66713 Peoria 165 ....S1
74059 Perkins 1,762 ......M3
73076 Pernell 110 ....M5
74864 Perry⊙ 5,796 ......M2
74862 Pharoah 100 ....O4
74538 Phillips 27 ....O6
74360 Picher 2,180 ......S1
74752 Pickens 525 ......S6
73078 Piedmont 2,016 ....L3
74873 Pink 911 ....M4
74560 Pittsburg 305 .....P5
73079 Pocasset 220 .....L4
74902 Pocola 3,268 .....T4
74601 Ponca City 26,238 ..M1
73766 Pond Creek 949 ...L1
74454 Porter 642 ....P3
74455 Porum 668 ....R4
74953 Poteau⊙ 7,089 ....S4
74864 Prague 2,208 .....N4
74456 Preston 350 ......P3
74060 Prue 554 ....O2
74361 Pryor⊙ 8,483 .....R2
73080 Purcell⊙ 4,638 ...M4
73659 Putnam 74 ....J3
74363 Quapaw 1,097 ....S1
†74085 Quay 50 ....N2
73852 Quinlan 64 ......J2
74561 Quinton 1,228 ...R4
74650 Ralston 495 .....N2
74061 Ramona 567 .....P1

†73160 Ranchwood Manor 296 ..L4
73562 Randlett 461 ....K6
73081 Ratliff City 350 .....M6
74562 Rattan 332 ....R6
74458 Ravia 487 ....N6
74458 Redbird 199 ....P3
74563 Red Oak 676 ....R5
74651 Red Rock 376 ......M2
73563 Reed 48 ....G5
†74801 Remus N4
†73759 Renfrow 27 ....L1
74459 Rentiesville 78 ......R4
73660 Reydon 252 ....G3
73456 Ringling 1,561 ......L6
73456 Ringold 200 ....R6
73768 Ringwood 389 ......K2
74062 Ripley 451 ....N2
†74932 Rock Island 160 ....T4
73661 Rocky 242 ....J4
74865 Roff 729 ....N5
74954 Roland 1,472 ......S4
73564 Roosevelt 396 .....J5
74364 Rose 100 ....R2
†74881 Rosedale 98 ....M5
73855 Rosston 66 ....G1
73457 Rubottom 35 ......M7
74755 Rufe 150 ....R6
73082 Rush Springs 1,451 ..L5
73565 Ryan 1,083 ....L6
74866 Saint Louis 109 ....N4
74365 Salina 1,115 ......R2
74955 Sallisaw⊙ 6,403 ...S4
73449 Sand Point 179 ....N7
74063 Sand Springs 13,121 ..O2

74066 Sapulpa⊙ 15,853 ......O3
74867 Sasakwa 335 ....N5
74869 Savanna 828 ....P5
74756 Sawyer 200 ....R7
73662 Sayre⊙ 3,177 ....G4
74460 Schulter 600 ....P3
73663 Seiling 1,103 ....J2
73856 Selman 25 ....H1
74888 Seminole 8,590 .....N4
73664 Sentinel 1,016 ......H4
74956 Shady Point 235 ....S4
74068 Shamrock 218 ......N3
73857 Sharon 171 ....H2
73858 Shattuck 1,759 ....G2
74801 Shawnee⊙ 26,506 ...N4
74652 Shidler 708 ....N1
†74701 Silo 43 ....N6
74069 Skedee 117 ....N2
74070 Skiatook 3,596 ...O2
73051 Slaughterville 1,953 ..M4
74071 Slick 187 ....O3
74957 Smithville 133 ....S6
74567 Snow 200 ....R6
73566 Snyder 1,848 ....J5
74072 South Coffeyville 873 .P1
74869 Spavinaw 623 ....R2
74366 Spavinaw 623 ....R2
73084 Spencer 4,064 ....M3
74760 Spencerville 275 ..R6
74073 Sperry 1,276 .....O2
74959 Spiro 2,221 ......S4
73458 Springer 679 .....M6
73567 Sterling 702 .....K5

74461 Stidham 60.........P4
74462 Stigler⊙ 2,630.........R4
74074 Stillwater⊙ 38,268.........N2
74960 Stillwell⊙ 2,369.........S3
74871 Stonewall 672.........P5
74367 Strang 126.........R2
74872 Stratford 1,459.........M5
74569 Stringtown 1,047.........P6
73665 Strong City 56.........J3
74079 Stroud 3,148.........N3
74570 Stuart 235.........O5
†73565 Sugden 76.........L6
73086 Sulphur⊙ 5,516.........N5
74966 Summerfield 150.........S5
73666 Sweetwater 85.........G4
74463 Taft 489.........R3
74464 Tahlequah⊙ 9,708.........R3
74080 Talala 191.........P1
74571 Talihina 1,387.........S5
73667 Taloga⊙ 446.........J2
†74442 Tamaha 145.........S4
73087 Tatums 281.........M6
74873 Tecumseh 5,123.........N4
73568 Temple 1,339.........K6
74081 Terlton 155.........O2
73569 Terral 604.........L7
73949 Texhoma 785.........C1
73668 Texola 106.........G4
73459 Thackerville 431.........M7
73120 The Village 11,049.........L3
73669 Thomas 1,515.........J3
†74017 Tiawah 125.........P2
73570 Tipton 1,475.........H6
73460 Tishomingo⊙ 3,212.........N6

74653 Tonkawa 3,524.........M1
†74852 Tribbey 215.........M4
†74856 Troy 92.........N6
74875 Tryon 435.........N3
74466 Tullahassee 145.........P3
*74101 Tulsa⊙ 360,919.........O2
Tulsa‡ 689,628.........O2
74572 Tupelo 542.........O5
73950 Turpin 450.........E1
74573 Tushka 358.........O6
74574 Tushkahoma 168.........R5
73088 Tussy 150.........L6
73089 Tuttle 3,051.........L4
73951 Tyrone 928.........D1
73090 Union City 558.........L4
74763 Utica 38.........O7
†73101 Valley Brook 921.........M4
74764 Valliant 927.........R6
†74820 Vanoss 130.........N5
73091 Velma 831.........L6
74082 Vera 182.........P2
73092 Verden 625.........K4
†74017 Verdigris 150.........P2
74877 Vernon 100.........P4
74962 Vian 1,521.........S4
73859 Vici 845.........H2
74301 Vinita⊙ 6,740.........R1
73571 Vinson 42.........G5
74467 Wagoner⊙ 6,191.........R3
74468 Wainwright 182.........R3
73771 Wakita 526.........L1
73572 Walters⊙ 2,778.........K6
74878 Wanette 473.........M5
74083 Wann 156.........P1

73461 Wapanucka 472.........N6
74469 Warner 1,310.........R4
73132 Warr Acres 9,940.........L3
74834 Warwick 167.........M3
73093 Washington 477.........L4
73094 Washita 180.........K4
73772 Watonga⊙ 4,139.........J3
74964 Watts 316.........S2
73773 Waukomis 1,551.........K2
73573 Waurika⊙ 2,258.........L6
73095 Wayne 621.........M5
73860 Waynoka 1,377.........J1
73096 Weatherford 9,640.........J4
74654 Webb City 157.........N1
74470 Webbers Falls 461.........R3
74369 Welch 697.........R1
74880 Weleetka 1,195.........O4
74471 Welling 115.........S3
74881 Wellston 802.........M3
74882 Welty 80.........O3
†74020 Westport 265.........O2
72761 West Siloam Springs 431..S2
74965 Westville 1,049.........S3
74883 Wetumka 1,725.........O4
74884 Wewoka⊙ 5,480.........O4
74472 Whitefield 240.........R4
74577 Whitesboro 450.........S5
74578 Wilburton⊙ 2,996.........R5
†74932 Williams 110.........T4
73673 Willow 162.........G4
73463 Wilson 1,585.........M6
74966 Wister 982.........S5
†74868 Wolf 200.........N4
73466 Woodville 94.........N7

73801 Woodward⊙ 13,610.........H2
74766 Wright City 1,168.........R6
74370 Wyandotte 336.........S1
73098 Wynnewood 2,615.........M5
74084 Wynona 780.........O1
74085 Yale 1,652.........N2
74574 Yanush 123.........R5
†74848 Yeager 138.........O4
73099 Yukon 17,112.........L3

OTHER FEATURES

Altus (res.).........H5
Altus A.F.B..........H5
Arbuckle Nat'l Rec. Area.........N6
Arbuckles, Lake of the (lake)..M6
Arkansas (riv.).........S4
Atoka (res.).........P5
Beaver (creek).........K6
Beaver (riv.).........F1
Bird (riv.).........O1
Black Bear (creek).........M2
Black Mesa (mt.).........A1
Blue (riv.).........O6
Bluestem (lake).........O1
Boston (mts.).........S3
Broken Bow (lake).........S6
Cache (creek).........K6
Canadian (riv.).........O4
Caney (riv.).........O1
Canton (lake).........J2
Carl Blackwell (lake).........M2
Cherokees, Lake O'The (lake)..S1
Chickasha (lake).........K4

Cimarron (riv.).........N2
Clear Boggy (creek).........A1
Deep Fork, North Canadian (riv.)..N3
Denison (dam).........O7
Elk (creek).........J4
Ellsworth (lake).........K5
Eucha (lake).........S2
Eufaula (lake).........P4
Fort Cobb (res.).........J4
Fort Gibson (lake).........R3
Fort Sill 15,924.........K5
Fort Supply (lake).........G1
Foss (res.).........H3
Great Salt Plains (lake).........K1
Heyburn (res.).........O3
Hudson (lake).........R6
Hugo (lake).........Q6
Hulah (lake).........O1
Illinois (riv.).........S3
Jackfork (mt.).........P5
Kaw (lake).........N1
Kerr, Robert S. (res.).........S4
Keystone (lake).........O2
Kiamichi (mts.).........R5
Kiamichi (riv.).........R5
Kiowa (creek).........F1
Lawtonka (lake).........K6
Little (riv.).........R6
McAlester (lake).........P4
Mountain Fork (riv.).........S6
Mud (riv.).........L6
Muddy Boggy (creek).........O5
Murray (lake).........M6
Neosho (riv.).........R1

North Canadian (riv.).........K3
North Carrizo (riv.).........A1
Oologah (lake).........P1
Optima (lake).........D1
Osage Ind. Res..........O1
Ouachita (mts.).........R5
Pine Creek (lake).........R6
Platt Nat'l Park.........N6
Poteau (riv.).........S5
Prairie Dog Town Fork, Red
  (riv.).........F5
Red (riv.).........R7
Red, North Fork (riv.).........H4
Salt Fork, Arkansas (riv.).........J1
Salt Fork, Red (riv.).........G5
Sans Bois (mts.).........R4
Scott (mt.).........K5
Spavinaw (lake).........S2
Tenkiller Ferry (lake).........S3
Texoma (lake).........N7
Thunderbird (lake).........M4
Tinker A.F.B..........M4
Tom Steed (res.).........J5
Vance A.F.B..........K2
Verdigris (riv.).........P2
Washita (riv.).........M5
Waurika (lake).........K6
Webbers Falls (res.).........R3
Wichita (mts.).........J5
Wildhorse (creek).........L5
Wister (lake).........S5
Wolf (creek).........G2

⊙County seat.
‡Population of metropolitan area.
† Zip of nearest p.o.   * Multiple zips.

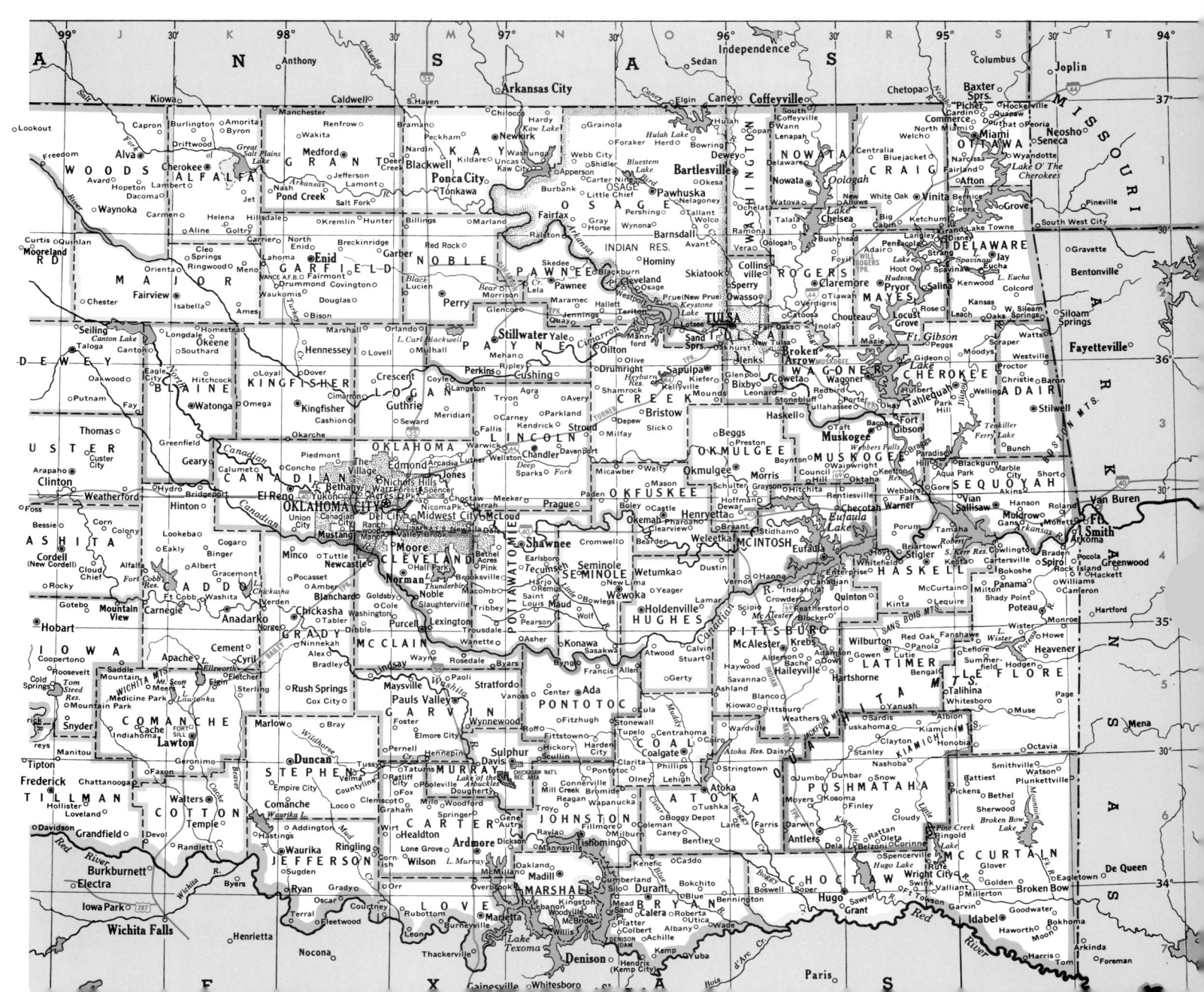

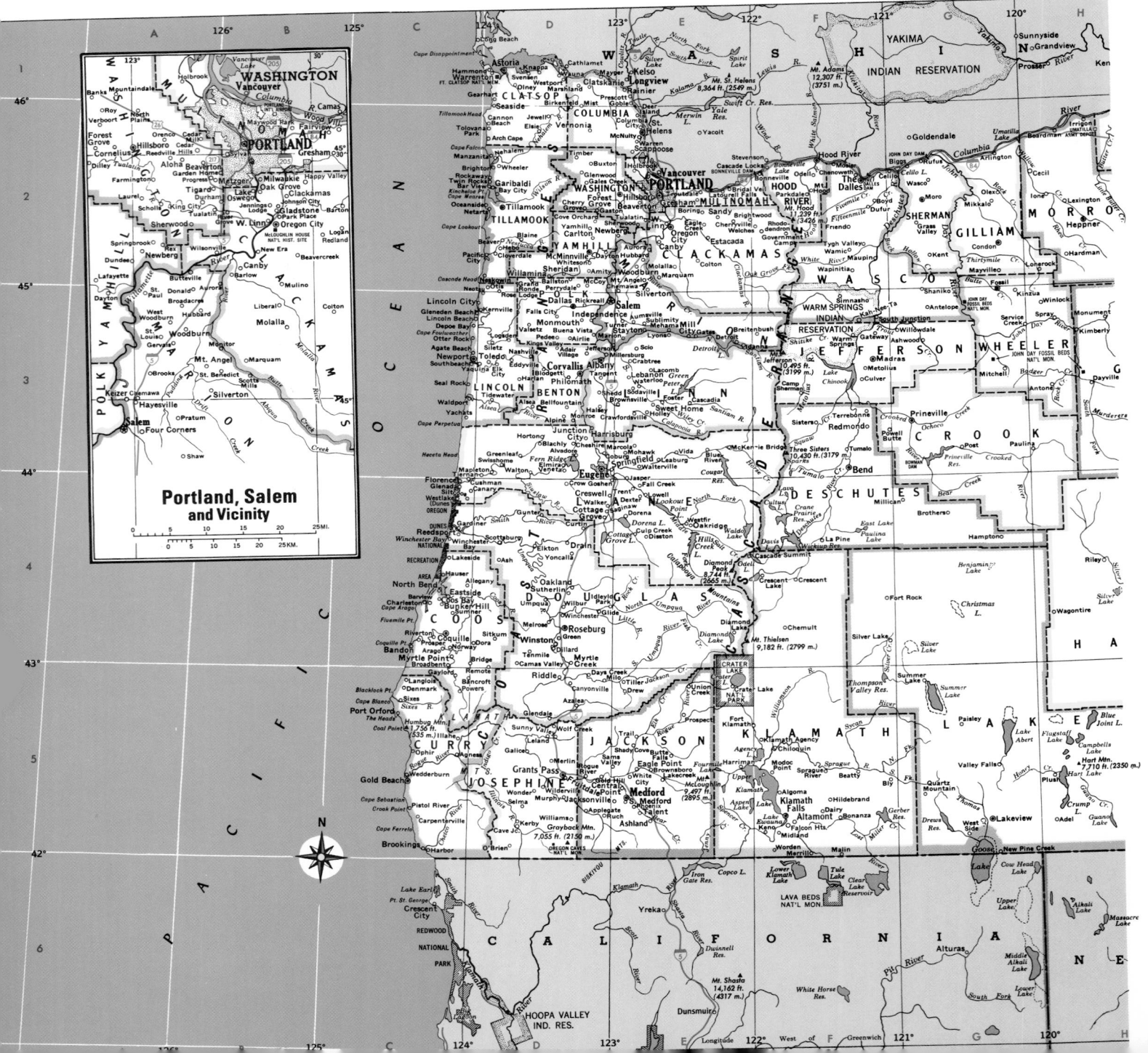

97824 Cove 451 .... K2
97335 Crabtree 200 .... E3
9732 Crane 84 .... J4
97336 Crawfordsville 350 ..... E3
97733 Crescent 750 .... F4
97425 Crescent Lake 120 ..... F4
97426 Creswell 1,770 .... D4
†97401 Crow 200 .... D4
97427 Culp Creek 600 .... E4
97734 Culver 514 .... F3
97428 Curtin 350 .... D4
†97439 Cushman 175 .... D4
97625 Dairy 80 .... F5
97338 Dallas⊙ 8,530 .... D3
97058 Dalles, The⊙ 10,820 .. F2
97429 Days Creek 550 .... D5
97114 Dayton 1,409 .... A3
97825 Dayville 199 .... H3
97054 Deer Island 225 .... E2
97341 Depoe Bay 723 .... C3
97342 Detroit 367 .... E3
97431 Dexter 500 .... E4
97432 Dillard 602 .... D4
†97116 Dilley 250 .... A2

†97427 Disston 123 .... E4
97020 Donald 267 .... A3
97434 Dorena 200 .... E4
97435 Drain 1,148 .... D4
97021 Dufur 560 .... F2
97115 Dundee 1,223 .... A2
†97493 Dunes (Westlake) 1,124 . C4
97233 Durham 707 .... A2
97905 Durkee 158 .... K3
97022 Eagle Creek 250 ...... E2
97524 Eagle Point 2,764 .... E5
97420 Eastside 1,601 .... C4
97826 Echo 624 .... H2
97343 Eddyville 564 .... D3
97827 Elgin 1,701 .... K2
97436 Elkton 155 .... D4
97828 Enterprise⊙ 2,003 .... K2
97023 Estacada 1,419 .... E2
*97401 Eugene⊙ 105,624 ... D3
      Eugene-Springfield‡
      275,226 .... D3
97024 Fairview 1,749 .... B2
†97601 Falcon Heights F5

97344 Falls City 804 .... D3
97710 Fields 150 .... J5
97439 Florence 4,411 .... C4
97116 Forest Grove 11,499 . A2
97626 Fort Klamath 200 ...... E5
97735 Fort Rock 150 .... G4
97830 Fossil⊙ 535 .... G2
97345 Foster 850 .... E3
97301 Four Corners 11,331 .. A3
97831 Fox 30 .... H3
†97526 Fruitdale-Harbeck 4,733 . D5
97117 Gales Creek 150 ...... D2
97223 Garden Home-
      Whitford 6,926 .... A2
97441 Gardiner 750 .... C4
97118 Garibaldi 999 .... D2
97119 Gaston 471 .... D2
97346 Gates 455 .... E3
†97741 Gateway 108 .... F3
97458 Gaylord 80 .... C5
97138 Gearhart 967 .... C1
97026 Gervais 799 .... A3
†97810 Gibbon 100 .... J2
97027 Gladstone 9,500 ...... B2

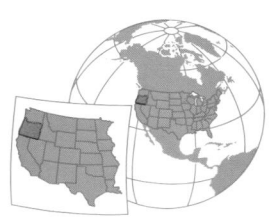

AREA 97,073 sq. mi. (251,419 sq. km.)
POPULATION 2,633,149
CAPITAL Salem
LARGEST CITY Portland
HIGHEST POINT Mt. Hood 11,239 ft.
      (3426 m.)
SETTLED IN 1810
ADMITTED TO UNION February 14, 1859
POPULAR NAME Beaver State
STATE FLOWER Oregon Grape
STATE BIRD Western Meadowlark

Topography

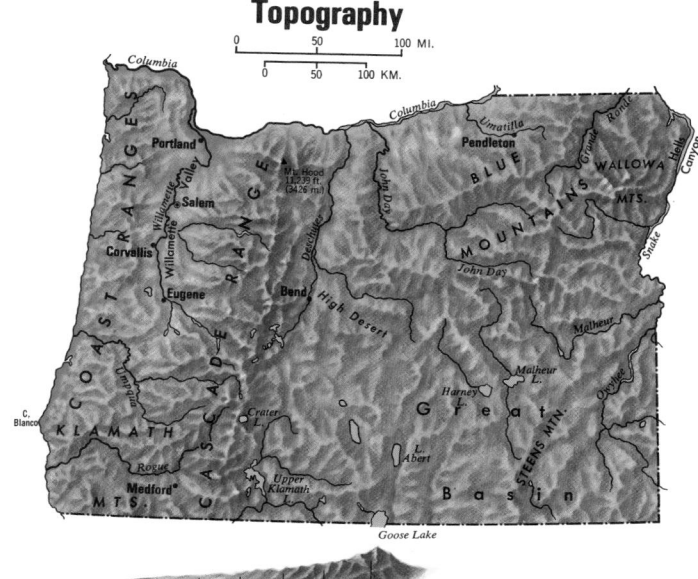

†97439 Glenada 300 .... C4
97442 Glendale 712 .... D5
97388 Gleneden Beach 400 .. C3
97120 Glenwood 225 .... D2
97443 Glide 470 .... D4
97048 Goble 108 .... E1
97444 Gold Beach⊙ 1,515 .. C5
97525 Gold Hill 904 .... D5
97401 Goshen 200 .... D4
97028 Government Camp 230 . F2
97347 Grand Ronde 289 ..... D2
†97877 Granite 17 .... J3
97526 Grants Pass⊙ 15,032 . D5
97029 Grass Valley 164 ...... G2
†97470 Green 3,897 .... D4
97030 Gresham 33,005 ...... B2
97833 Haines 341 .... J3
97834 Halfway 380 .... K3
97348 Halsey 693 .... D3
97121 Hammond 516 .... C1
97906 Harper 400 .... K4
†97601 Harriman 250 .... E5
97446 Harrisburg 1,881 ...... D3
†97459 Hauser 400 .... C4
†97301 Hayesville 9,213 ... A3
97122 Hebo 400 .... D2
97835 Helix 155 .... J2
97836 Heppner⊙ 1,498 ...... H2
97837 Hereford 128 .... K3
97838 Hermiston 9,408 ...... H2
97123 Hillsboro⊙ 27,664 ... A2
9738 Hines 1,632 .... H4
†97208 Holbrook 494 .... A1
97386 Holley 75 .... E3
97031 Hood River⊙ 4,329 .. F2
97448 Horton 175 .... D3
†97850 Hot Lake 4 .... K2
97032 Hubbard 1,640 .... A3
97907 Huntington 539 .... K3
97350 Idanha 319 .... E3
97447 Idleyld Park 300 ...... D4
97841 Imbler 292 .... J2
97351 Independence 4,024 .. D3
97843 Ione 345 .... H2
97844 Irrigon 700 .... H2
97851 Island City 477 .... K2
97530 Jacksonville 2,030 .... D5
97909 Jamieson 120 .... K3
97401 Jasper 231 .... E3
97352 Jefferson 1,702 .... D3
†97201 Jennings Lodge B2
97845 John Day 2,012 .... J3
†97027 Johnson City 378 ... B2
97910 Jordan Valley 473 .... K5
97846 Joseph 999 .... K2
97448 Junction City 3,320 ... D3
97911 Juntura 5 .... K4
97303 Keizer 18,592 .... A3

97627 Keno 500 .... F5
97033 Kent 200 .... G2
97531 Kerby 650 .... D5
97223 King City 1,853 .... A2
†97361 Kings Valley 50 ...... D3
97849 Kinzua 2 .... H3
97601 Klamath Falls⊙ 16,661 . F5
97103 Knappa 950 .... D1
†97355 Lacomb 425 .... E3
97127 Lafayette 1,215 .... A2
97850 La Grande⊙ 11,354 .. J2
†97524 Lakecreek 160 .... E5
97034 Lake Oswego 22,527 .. B2
97449 Lakeside 1,453 .... C4
97630 Lakeview⊙ 2,770 ..... G5
97450 Langlois 150 .... C5
97739 La Pine 850 .... F4
97401 Leaburg 150 .... E3
97355 Lebanon 10,413 .... E3
97839 Lexington 307 .... H2
†97042 Liberal 300 .... B3
97341 Lincoln Beach 275 .... C3
97367 Lincoln City 5,469 .... C3
97405 Logan 450 .... B2
†97823 Lonerock 26 .... H2
97850 Long Creek 252 .... H3
97857 Lostine 250 .... K2
97452 Lowell 661 .... E4
97358 Lyons 877 .... E3
†97741 Madras⊙ 2,235 ...... F3
97632 Malin 539 .... F5
97130 Manzanita 443 .... C2
97453 Mapleton 950 .... C4
97454 Marcola 400 .... E3
97359 Marion 300 .... D3
97037 Maupin 495 .... F2
†97850 May Park J2
97220 Maywood Park 1,083 .. B2
97401 McKenzie Bridge 500 .. E3
97128 McMinnville⊙ 14,080 . D2
97858 McNary 330 .... H2
†97053 McNulty 1,805 .... E2
97859 Meacham 150 .... J2
97501 Medford⊙ 39,603 ..... E5
      Medford‡ 132,456 ... E5
97384 Mehama 250 .... E3
97532 Merlin 500 .... D5
97633 Merrill 809 .... F5
†97741 Metolius 451 .... F3
†97223 Metzger 5,544 .... A2
97634 Midland 520 .... F5
97360 Mill City 1,565 .... E3
†97321 Millersburg 562 ...... E3
97417 Milo 400 .... D4
97862 Milton-Freewater 5,086 . J2
97222 Milwaukie 17,931 ..... B2
97750 Mitchell 183 .... G3
97038 Molalla 2,992 .... B3
97361 Monmouth 5,594 ...... D3
97456 Monroe 412 .... D3

97864 Monument 192 .... H3
97039 Moro⊙ 336 .... G2
97040 Mosier 340 .... F2
97362 Mount Angel 2,876 .... B3
97041 Mount Hood 200 .... F2
97865 Mount Vernon 569 .... H3
97042 Mulino 720 .... B2
97533 Murphy 500 .... D5
97457 Myrtle Creek 3,365 ... D4
97458 Myrtle Point 2,859 .... C4
97131 Nehalem 258 .... D2
97364 Neotsu 300 .... C2
97149 Neskowin 250 .... D2
97143 Netarts 975 .... C2
97132 Newberg 10,394 ...... A2
97635 New Pine Creek 400 .. G5
97365 Newport⊙ 7,519 ...... C3
97459 North Bend 9,779 ..... C4
97133 North Plains 715 ...... A2
97867 North Powder 430 .... K2
97460 Norway 150 .... C4
97913 Nyssa 2,862 .... K4
97268 Oak Grove 11,640 .... B2
97462 Oakland 886 .... D4
97463 Oakridge 3,729 .... E4
97534 O'Brien 850 .... D5
97134 Oceanside 300 .... C2
97044 Odell 450 .... F2
97914 Ontario 8,814 .... K3
97644 Ophir 275 .... C5
97045 Oregon City⊙ 14,673 .. B2
†97123 Orenco 220 .... A2
97368 Otis 200 .... D2
97369 Otter Rock 450 .... C3
97840 Oxbow 100 .... L2
97135 Pacific City 500 .... C2
97636 Paisley 343 .... G5
97041 Parkdale 950 .... F2
†97045 Park Place 500 ...... B2
97801 Pendleton⊙ 14,521 .. J2
†97101 Perrydale 200 .... D2
97370 Philomath 2,673 .... D3
97535 Phoenix 2,309 .... E5
97868 Pilot Rock 1,630 ...... J2
*97201 Portland⊙ 366,383 ... B2
      Portland‡ 1,242,187 . B2
97465 Port Orford 1,061 ..... C5
97753 Powell Butte 350 ...... G3
97466 Powers 819 .... D5
97869 Prairie City 1,106 ..... J3
97048 Prescott 73 .... D1
97721 Princeton 5 .... J4
97754 Prineville⊙ 5,276 ..... G3
†97233 Progress 100 .... A2
97536 Prospect 200 .... E5
†97411 Prosper 110 .... C4
97048 Rainier 1,655 .... E1
†97045 Redland 700 .... B2
97756 Redmond 6,452 .... G3
97467 Reedsport 4,984 ...... C4

(continued on following page)

Oregon

SCALE
0 5 10 20   30   40   50   60 MI.
0 5 10 20 30   40   50   60 KM.

State Capitals .... ⊛
County Seats .... ⊙
Major Limited Access Hwys. ....

© Copyright HAMMOND INCORPORATED, Maplewood, N.J.

Agriculture, Industry and Resources

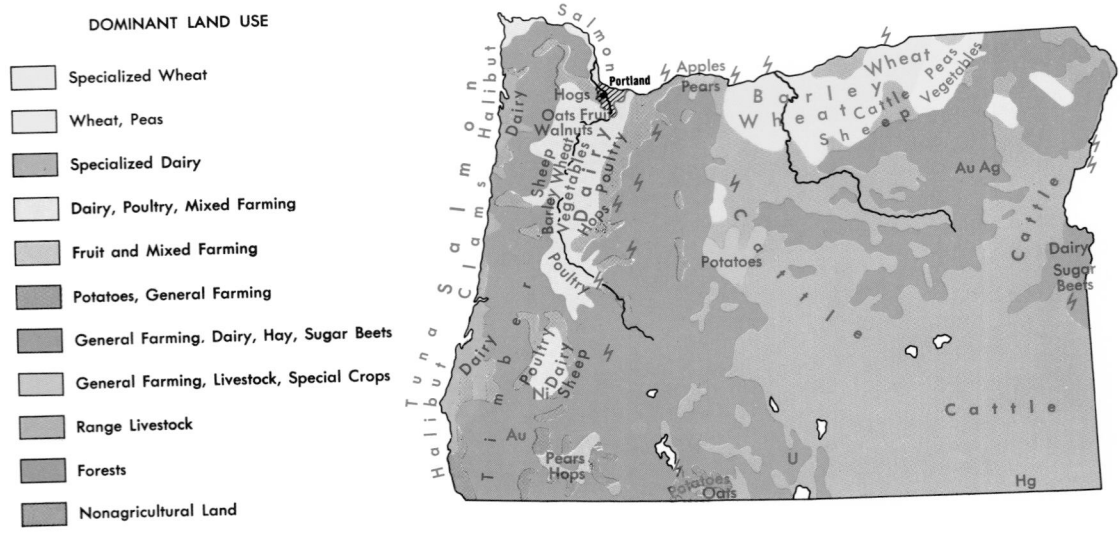

DOMINANT LAND USE

- Specialized Wheat
- Wheat, Peas
- Specialized Dairy
- Dairy, Poultry, Mixed Farming
- Fruit and Mixed Farming
- Potatoes, General Farming
- General Farming, Dairy, Hay, Sugar Beets
- General Farming, Livestock, Special Crops
- Range Livestock
- Forests
- Nonagricultural Land

MAJOR MINERAL OCCURRENCES

Ag Silver   Hg Mercury

Au Gold   Ni Nickel

U Uranium

⚡ Water Power

▨ Major Industrial Areas

†97005 Reedville 850	A2
97870 Richland 181	K3
97371 Rickreall 700	D3
97469 Riddle 1,265	D5
†97801 Rieth 300	J2
97758 Riley 100	H4
†97223 River Grove 314	B2
†97423 Riverton 150	C4
97136 Rockaway 906	C2
97537 Rogue River 1,308	D5
97470 Roseburg ⊙ 16,644	D4
97372 Rose Lodge 300	D3
†97106 Roy 200	A2
97050 Rufus 352	G2
97472 Saginaw 150	E4
97051 Saint Helens ⊙ 7,064	A2
†97026 Saint Louis 102	A3
97137 Saint Paul 312	A3
*97301 Salem (cap.) ⊙ 89,233	A3
Salem‡ 249,895	A3
†97525 Sams Valley 100	E5
97055 Sandy 2,905	E2
97056 Scappoose 3,213	E3
97374 Scio 579	D4
97473 Scottsburg 300	D4
97375 Scotts Mills 249	B3
97376 Seal Rock 430	C3
97138 Seaside 5,193	D2
97538 Selma 150	D5
97873 Seneca 285	J3
97539 Shady Cove 1,097	E5
97057 Shaniko 30	G3
†97325 Shaw 800	A3
97377 Shedd 850	D3
97378 Sheridan 2,249	D2
97140 Sherwood 2,386	A2
97380 Siletz 1,001	D3
97638 Silver Lake 200	F4
97381 Silverton 5,168	B3
97759 Sisters 696	F3
97476 Sixes 300	C5
†97355 Sodaville 171	E3
97366 Southbeach 300	C3
†97501 South Medford 2,898	E5
97639 Sprague River 200	F5
97874 Spray 155	H3
†97132 Springbrook 500	A2
97477 Springfield 41,621	E3
97875 Stanfield 1,568	H2
97383 Stayton 4,396	E3
97385 Sublimity 1,077	E3
97876 Summerville 143	K2
†97420 Sumner 100	C4
97877 Sumpter 133	J3
97478 Sunny Valley 159	D5
97479 Sutherlin 4,560	D1
97103 Svensen 950	D1
97386 Sweet Home 6,921	E3
97480 Swisshome 350	D3
†97201 Sylvan	B2

97540 Talent 2,577	E5
97389 Tangent 478	D3
97481 Tenmile 500	D4
97760 Terrebonne 521	F3
97058 The Dalles ⊙ 10,820	F2
97223 Tigard 14,286	A2
97141 Tillamook ⊙ 3,981	C2
97484 Tiller 300	E5
97144 Timber 175	D2
97391 Toledo 3,151	C3
97145 Tolovana Park 165	C2
97541 Trail 350	E5
†97431 Trent 100	E4
†97060 Troutdale 5,908	E2
97062 Tualatin 7,483	A2
†97701 Tumalo 500	F3
97392 Turner 1,116	E3
†97136 Twin Rocks 450	C2
97063 Tygh Valley 663	F2
97880 Ukiah 249	J2
97881 Umapine 100	J2
97882 Umatilla 3,199	H2
97486 Umpqua 705	D4
97883 Union 2,062	K2
97884 Unity 115	J3
97918 Vale ⊙ 1,558	K4
97393 Valsetz 320	D3
97487 Veneta 2,449	D3
†97116 Verboort 280	A2
97064 Vernonia 1,785	D2
97488 Vida 300	E3
97394 Waldport 1,274	C3
97885 Wallowa 847	K2
97489 Walterville 250	E3
97490 Walton 300	D3
97063 Wamic 255	F2
97761 Warm Springs 550	F3
97053 Warren 750	E2
97016 Warrenton 2,493	C1
97065 Wasco 415	G2
†97355 Waterloo 221	E3
97491 Wedderburn 700	C5
†97067 Welches 300	E2
97492 Westfir 312	E4
97493 Westlake 1,124	C4
97068 West Linn 12,956	B2
97886 Weston 719	J2
97016 Westport 400	D1
†97071 West Woodburn 600	A3
97147 Wheeler 319	D2
97503 White City 5,445	E5
†97128 Whiteson 100	D2
97494 Wilbur 476	D4
97543 Williams 200	D5
97396 Willamina 1,749	D2
97544 Williams 750	D5
97070 Wilsonville 2,920	A2
97495 Winchester 300	D4
97467 Winchester Bay 535	C4
97496 Winston 3,359	D4

97497 Wolf Creek 500	D5
97071 Woodburn 11,196	A3
†97060 Wood Village 2,253	B2
97498 Yachats 482	C3
97148 Yamhill 690	D2
†97365 Yaquina 175	C3
97499 Yoncalla 805	D4

OTHER FEATURES

Abert (lake)	G5
Abiqua (creek)	B3
Agency (lake)	E5
Alsea (riv.)	D3
Alvord (lake)	J5
Antelope (creek)	K5
Arago (cape)	C5
Aspen (lake)	E5
Badger (creek)	H3
Battle (creek)	K5
Bear (creek)	E5
Bear (creek)	K2
Bear (creek)	G4
Benjamin (lake)	G4
Beulah (res.)	J4
Blacklock (pt.)	C5
Blanco (cape)	C5
Blue (mts.)	J3
Bonneville (dam)	E2
Brownlee (dam)	L3
Buck Hollow (creek)	G2
Bully (creek)	K3
Burnt (riv.)	K3
Butte (creek)	G2
Butte (creek)	B3
Butter (creek)	H2
Calapooia (riv.)	E3
Calapooya (mts.)	E4
Camp (creek)	J4
Campbells (lake)	H5
Cascade (head)	C2
Cascade (range)	E4
Celilo (lake)	G2
Chetco (riv.)	C5
Clackamas (riv.)	E2
Clover (creek)	K3
Coal (pt.)	C5
Coast (ranges)	D5
Columbia (riv.)	G2
Coos (riv.)	C4
Coquille (pt.)	C4
Cottage Grove (lake)	E4
Cottonwood (creek)	K4
Cougar (res.)	E3
Cow (creek)	K4
Crane (creek)	J4
Crane Prairie (res.)	F4
Crater (lake)	E5

Crater Lake Nat'l Park	E5
Crook (pt.)	C5
Crooked (creek)	K5
Crooked (riv.)	G3
Cultus (lake)	F4
Dalles, The (dam)	F2
Davis (lake)	F4
Deschutes (riv.)	G2
Detroit (lake)	E3
Diamond (lake)	E4
Donner and Blitzen (riv.)	J4
Dorena (lake)	E4
Drews (res.)	G5
Drift (creek)	B3
Eagle (creek)	K3
East (lake)	F4
Elk (creek)	E5
Ewauna (lake)	E5
Falcon (cape)	C2
Fern Ridge (lake)	D5
Ferrelo (cape)	C5
Fifteenmile (creek)	F4
Fish (lake)	E5
Fivemile (creek)	F4
Fivemile (creek)	C4
Flagstaff (lake)	H5
Fort Clatsop Nat'l Mem.	C1
Foulweather (cape)	C3
Fourmile (lake)	E5
Gerber (res.)	F5
Goose (lake)	G5
Grand Canyon, Snake R. (canyon)	L2
Grande Ronde (riv.)	K2
Green Peter (lake)	E3
Guano (creek)	H5
Guano (lake)	H5
Harney (lake)	H4
Hart (lake)	H5
Hart (mt.)	H5
Heads, The (prom.)	C3
Hells Canyon (canyon)	L2
Hells Canyon Nat'l Rec. Area	K2
Hills Creek (lake)	E4
Honey (creek)	G5
Hood (mt.)	F2
Hood (riv.)	F2
Horse (creek)	E3
Illinois (riv.)	D5
Imnaha (riv.)	L2
Indigo (creek)	D5
Jackson (creek)	E5
Jefferson (mt.)	F3
Jenny (creek)	E5
John Day (dam)	G2
John Day (riv.)	G2
John Day Fossil Beds Nat'l Mon.	G3
Jordan (creek)	K5
Joseph (creek)	K2
Keeny (creek)	K4

Kiger (creek)	J5
Kincheloe (pt.)	C2
Klamath (mts.)	C5
Lake (creek)	J3
Lava (lake)	F4
Lightning (creek)	L2
Little (riv.)	E4
Little Butter (creek)	H2
Little Sheep (creek)	K2
Lookout (cape)	C2
Lookout Point (lake)	E4
Lost (riv.)	F5
Malheur (lake)	J4
Malheur (riv.)	J4
McCoy (creek)	J5
McKay (creek)	J2
McKenzie, South Fork (riv.)	E3
McLoughlin (mt.)	E5
McLoughlin House Nat'l Hist. Site	B2
McNary (dam)	H2
Meares (cape)	C2
Metolius (riv.)	F3
Miller (creek)	F5
Molalla (riv.)	B3
Mud (creek)	K2
Murderers (creek)	H3
Nehalem (riv.)	D2
Nestucca (riv.)	D2
North Santiam (riv.)	E3
North Umpqua (riv.)	E4
Ochoco (creek)	G3
Odell (lake)	E4
Oregon (creek)	K5
Oregon Caves Nat'l Mon.	D5
Oregon Dunes Nat'l Rec. Area	C4
Owyhee (dam)	K4
Owyhee (lake)	K4
Owyhee (mts.)	K5
Owyhee, North Fork (riv.)	L3
Oxbow (dam)	L3
Paulina (lake)	F4
Perpetua (cape)	C3
Pine (creek)	L3
Pine (creek)	J4
Portland Int'l Airport	B2
Powder (riv.)	K3
Prineville (res.)	G3
Pudding (riv.)	A3
Pueblo (mts.)	J5
Rattlesnake (creek)	K5
Rhea (creek)	H2
Rock (creek)	E4
Rock (creek)	H3
Rock (creek)	G2
Rogue (riv.)	C5
Salt (creek)	E4
Sebastian (cape)	C5

Sheep (creek)	L2
Shitike (creek)	F3
Silver (creek)	H4
Silver (creek)	C5
Silver (lake)	G4
Silver (lake)	H4
Siletz (riv.)	C3
Siskiyou (mts.)	D6
Siuslaw (riv.)	D3
Sixes (riv.)	C5
Smith (riv.)	D4
Snake (riv.)	K3
South Santiam (riv.)	E3
South Umpqua (riv.)	E4
Sparks (lake)	F3
Spencer (creek)	E5
Sprague (riv.)	F5
Squaw (creek)	F3
Steens (mt.)	J5
Succor (creek)	K4
Summer (lake)	G5
Summit (creek)	J3
Sycan (riv.)	F5
Tenmile (creek)	K5
The Dalles (dam)	F2
Thielsen (mt.)	F4
Thirtymile (creek)	G2
Thomas (creek)	K5
Three Sisters (mt.)	F3
Tillamook (head)	C2
Trout (creek)	J5
Trout (creek)	F3
Tualatin (riv.)	A2
Tumalo (creek)	F3
Tumtum (lake)	J5
Umatilla (lake)	G2
Umatilla (riv.)	H2
Umatilla Army Depot	H2
Umatilla Ind. Res.	J2
Umpqua (riv.)	D4
Upper Klamath (lake)	E5
Waldo (lake)	E4
Walla Walla (riv.)	J1
Wallowa (mts.)	K2
Wallowa (riv.)	K2
Wallula (lake)	H1
Warm Springs (res.)	J4
Warm Springs Ind. Res.	F3
White (riv.)	F2
Wickiup (res.)	F4
Wiley (creek)	E3
Willamette (riv.)	A3
Willamette, Middle Fork (riv.)	E4
Williamson (riv.)	F5
Willow (creek)	H2
Willow (creek)	K3
Wilson (riv.)	D2
Winchester (bay)	C4

⊙County seat.

‡Population of metropolitan area.

† Zip of nearest p.o.   * Multiple zips.

AREA 45,308 sq. mi. (117,348 sq. km.)
POPULATION 11,863,895
CAPITAL Harrisburg
LARGEST CITY Philadelphia
HIGHEST POINT Mt. Davis 3,213 ft. (979 m.)
SETTLED IN 1682
ADMITTED TO UNION December 12, 1787
POPULAR NAME Keystone State
STATE FLOWER Mountain Laurel
STATE BIRD Ruffed Grouse

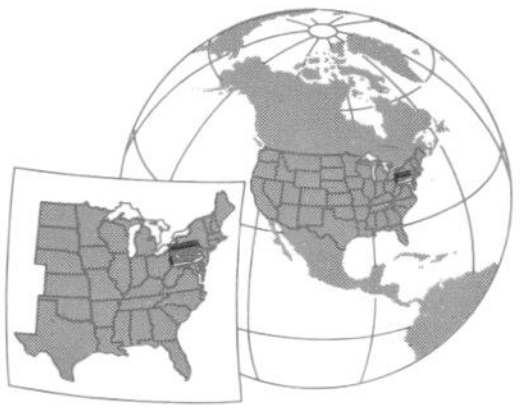

DOMINANT LAND USE

- Specialized Dairy
- Dairy, General Farming
- Fruit and Mixed Farming
- Fruit, Truck and Mixed Farming
- General Farming, Livestock, Tobacco
- General Farming, Livestock, Fruit, Tobacco
- Forests
- Urban Areas

MAJOR MINERAL OCCURRENCES

C Coal
Cl Clay
Co Cobalt
Fe Iron Ore
G Natural Gas
Ls Limestone
O Petroleum
Sl Slate
Ss Sandstone
Zn Zinc

Water Power
Major Industrial Areas

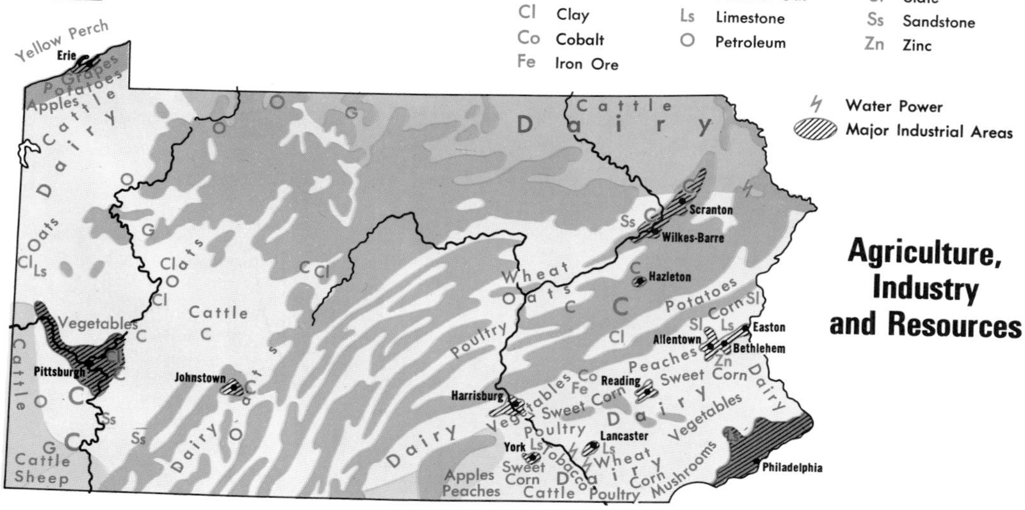

Agriculture, Industry and Resources

COUNTIES

Adams 68,292 ..... H6
Allegheny 1,450,085 ..... B5
Armstrong 77,768 ..... D4
Beaver 204,441 ..... B4
Bedford 46,784 ..... E6
Berks 312,509 ..... K5
Blair 136,621 ..... F4
Bradford 62,919 ..... J2
Bucks 479,211 ..... M5
Butler 147,912 ..... C4
Cambria 183,263 ..... E4
Cameron 6,674 ..... F3
Carbon 53,285 ..... L4
Centre 112,760 ..... G4
Chester 316,660 ..... L6
Clarion 43,362 ..... D3
Clearfield 83,578 ..... F3
Clinton 38,971 ..... G3
Columbia 61,967 ..... K3
Crawford 88,869 ..... B2
Cumberland 178,541 ..... H5
Dauphin 232,317 ..... J5
Delaware 555,007 ..... M6
Elk 38,338 ..... E3
Erie 279,780 ..... B2
Fayette 159,417 ..... C6
Forest 5,072 ..... D2
Franklin 113,629 ..... G6
Fulton 12,842 ..... F6
Greene 40,476 ..... B6
Huntingdon 42,253 ..... F5
Indiana 92,281 ..... D4
Jefferson 48,303 ..... D3
Juniata 19,188 ..... H4
Lackawanna 227,908 ..... L3
Lancaster 362,346 ..... K5
Lawrence 107,150 ..... B4
Lebanon 108,582 ..... K5
Lehigh 272,349 ..... L4
Luzerne 343,079 ..... L3
Lycoming 118,416 ..... H3
McKean 50,635 ..... E2
Mercer 128,299 ..... B3
Mifflin 46,908 ..... G4
Monroe 69,409 ..... M3
Montgomery 643,621 ..... M5
Montour 16,675 ..... J3
Northampton 225,418 ..... M4
Northumberland 100,381 ..... J4
Perry 35,718 ..... H5
Philadelphia (city county) 1,688,210 ..... M6
Pike 18,271 ..... M3
Potter 17,726 ..... G2
Schuylkill 160,630 ..... K4
Snyder 33,584 ..... H4
Somerset 81,243 ..... D6
Sullivan 6,349 ..... J3
Susquehanna 37,876 ..... L2
Tioga 40,973 ..... H2
Union 32,870 ..... H4
Venango 64,444 ..... C3
Warren 47,449 ..... D2
Washington 217,074 ..... B5
Wayne 35,237 ..... M2
Westmoreland 392,294 ..... D5
Wyoming 26,433 ..... K2
York 312,963 ..... J6

CITIES and TOWNS

Zip Name/Pop. Key

19001 Abington○ 59,084 ..... M5
19501 Adamstown 1,119 ..... K5
17501 Akron 3,471 ..... K5
16401 Albion 1,818 ..... B2
18011 Alburtis 1,428 ..... L5
†19018 Aldan 4,671 ..... M7
15001 Aliquippa 17,094 ..... B4
*18101 Allentown⊙ 103,758 ..... L4
Allentown-Bethlehem-Easton‡ 636,714 ..... L4
15101 Allison Park 10,000 ..... C4
*16601 Altoona 57,078 ..... F4
Altoona‡ 136,621 ..... F4
19002 Ambler 6,628 ..... M5
15003 Ambridge 9,575 ..... B4
17003 Annville 4,493 ..... J5
15613 Apollo 2,212 ..... C4
18403 Archbald 6,295 ..... F6
19003 Ardmore M6
15068 Arnold 6,853 ..... C4
17921 Ashland 4,235 ..... K4
18706 Ashley 3,512 ..... E7
15215 Aspinwall 3,284 ..... C6
18810 Athens 3,622 ..... K2
17851 Atlas 1,162 ..... K4
15202 Avalon 6,240 ..... B6
15312 Avella 900 ..... B5
17721 Avis 1,718 ..... H3
18641 Avoca 3,536 ..... F7
19311 Avondale 891 ..... L6
15618 Avonmore 1,234 ..... C4
15005 Baden 5,318 ..... B4
19004 Bala-Cynwyd N6
†15208 Baldwin 24,598 ..... B7
19503 Bally 1,051 ..... L5
18013 Bangor 5,006 ..... M4
15714 Barnesboro 2,741 ..... E4
18014 Bath 1,953 ..... M4
15009 Beaver⊙ 5,441 ..... B4
15921 Beaverdale 1,187 ..... E5
15010 Beaver Falls 12,525 ..... B4
18216 Beaver Meadows 1,078 ..... L4
15522 Bedford⊙ 3,326 ..... F5
16823 Bellefonte⊙ 6,300 ..... G4
15012 Belle Vernon 1,489 ..... C5
17004 Belleville 1,689 ..... G4
15202 Bellevue 10,128 ..... B6
16617 Bellwood 2,114 ..... F4
†15202 Ben Avon 2,314 ..... B6
15314 Bentleyville 2,525 ..... B5
15530 Berlin 1,999 ..... E6
19506 Bernville 798 ..... K5
18603 Berwick 11,850 ..... K3
19312 Berwyn 5,246 ..... L5
16112 Bessemer 1,293 ..... B4
15102 Bethel Park 34,755 ..... B7
*18015 Bethlehem 70,419 ..... M4
19508 Birdsboro 3,481 ..... L5
15716 Black Lick 1,313 ..... D4
15717 Blairsville 4,166 ..... D5
18447 Blakely 7,438 ..... F6
15238 Blawnox 1,653 ..... C6
17068 Bloomfield (New Bloomfield)⊙ 1,109 ..... H5
17815 Bloomsburg⊙ 11,717 ..... J3
16912 Blossburg 1,757 ..... H2
16827 Boalsburg 2,295 ..... G4
15315 Bobtown 1,008 ..... B6
17007 Boiling Springs 2,223 ..... H5
15923 Bolivar 706 ..... D5
15531 Boswell 1,480 ..... E5
18030 Bowmanstown 1,078 ..... L4
19512 Boyertown 3,979 ..... L5
15014 Brackenridge 4,297 ..... C4
15104 Braddock 5,634 ..... C7
16701 Bradford 11,211 ..... E2
15227 Brentwood 11,907 ..... B7
19405 Bridgeport 4,843 ..... M5
15017 Bridgeville 6,154 ..... B5
19007 Bristol 10,867 ..... N5
19007 Bristol○ 58,733 ..... N5
15824 Brockway 2,376 ..... E3
19015 Brookhaven 7,912 ..... M7
15825 Brookville⊙ 4,568 ..... D3
19008 Broomall M6
15417 Brownsville 4,043 ..... C5
19010 Bryn Mawr M5
15021 Burgettstown 1,867 ..... A5
17009 Burnham 2,457 ..... H4
16001 Butler⊙ 17,026 ..... C4
15924 Cairnbrook 1,081 ..... E5
15419 California 5,703 ..... C5
16403 Cambridge Springs 2,102 ..... C2
17011 Camp Hill 8,422 ..... H5
15317 Canonsburg 10,459 ..... B5
17724 Canton 1,959 ..... J2
18407 Carbondale 11,255 ..... L2
17013 Carlisle⊙ 18,314 ..... H5
15106 Carnegie 10,099 ..... B7
15722 Carrolltown 1,395 ..... E4
15234 Castle Shannon 10,164 ..... B7
18032 Catasauqua 6,711 ..... M4
17820 Catawissa 1,568 ..... K4
16404 Centerville 4,207 ..... B6
15926 Central City 1,496 ..... E5
17927 Centralia 1,017 ..... K4
16828 Centre Hall 1,233 ..... G4
18914 Chalfont 2,802 ..... M5
17201 Chambersburg⊙ 16,174 ..... G6
15022 Charleroi 5,717 ..... C5
19012 Cheltenham○ 35,509 ..... M5
*19013 Chester 45,794 ..... L7
19017 Chester Heights 1,302 ..... L7
†16866 Chester Hill 1,054 ..... F4
15024 Cheswick 2,336 ..... C6
16025 Chicora 1,192 ..... C4
17509 Christiana 1,183 ..... K6
†15235 Churchill 4,285 ..... C7
15025 Clairton 12,188 ..... C7
16214 Clarion⊙ 6,664 ..... D3
†18411 Clarks Green 1,862 ..... F6
18411 Clarks Summit 5,272 ..... F6
16625 Claysburg 1,346 ..... F5
15323 Claysville 1,029 ..... B5
16830 Clearfield⊙ 7,580 ..... F3
19018 Clifton Heights 7,320 ..... M7
15728 Clymer 1,761 ..... E4
18218 Coaldale 2,762 ..... L4
19320 Coatesville 10,698 ..... L5
16314 Cochranton 1,240 ..... B2
19426 Collegeville 3,406 ..... M5
19023 Collingdale 9,539 ..... N7
17512 Columbia 10,466 ..... K5
15927 Colver 1,165 ..... E4
†19023 Colwyn 2,851 ..... N7
15425 Connellsville 10,319 ..... C5
19428 Conshohocken 8,475 ..... M5
15027 Conway 2,747 ..... B4
18219 Conyngham 2,242 ..... K3
18036 Coopersburg 2,595 ..... M5
18037 Coplay 3,130 ..... L4
15108 Coraopolis 7,308 ..... B4
17016 Cornwall 2,653 ..... K5
16407 Corry 7,149 ..... C2
16915 Coudersport⊙ 2,791 ..... G2
15624 Crabtree 900 ..... D5
15205 Crafton 7,623 ..... B7
16630 Cresson 2,184 ..... E5
17929 Cressona 1,810 ..... K4
16833 Curwensville 3,116 ..... E4
†15901 Dale 1,906 ..... E5
18612 Dallas 2,679 ..... E7
17313 Dallastown 3,949 ..... J6
18414 Dalton 1,383 ..... L2
17821 Danville⊙ 5,239 ..... J4
19023 Darby 11,513 ..... M7
18327 Delaware Water Gap 597 ..... M4
15626 Delmont 2,159 ..... D5
17517 Denver 2,018 ..... K5
15627 Derry 3,072 ..... D5
18519 Dickson City 6,699 ..... F7
17019 Dillsburg 1,733 ..... J5
15033 Donora 7,524 ..... C5
15216 Dormont 11,275 ..... B7
17315 Dover 1,910 ..... J6
19335 Downingtown 7,650 ..... L5
18901 Doylestown⊙ 8,717 ..... M5
15034 Dravosburg 2,511 ..... C7
19026 Drexel Hill M6
18221 Drifton 1,786 ..... L3
18917 Dublin 1,565 ..... M5
15801 DuBois 9,290 ..... E3
†17701 Duboistown 1,218 ..... H3
15431 Dunbar 1,369 ..... C6
17020 Duncannon 1,645 ..... H5
16635 Duncansville 1,355 ..... F5
18512 Dunmore 16,781 ..... F7
18641 Dupont 3,460 ..... F7
15110 Duquesne 10,094 ..... C7
18642 Duryea 5,415 ..... F7
17316 East Berlin 1,054 ..... J6
†18603 East Berwick 2,324 ..... K3
16028 East Brady 1,153 ..... C3
15909 East Conemaugh 2,128 ..... E5
†17701 East Faxon 3,951 ..... J3
18041 East Greenville 2,456 ..... L5
†19050 East Lansdowne 2,806 ..... M7
18042 Easton⊙ 26,027 ..... M4
17520 East Petersburg 3,600 ..... K5
18301 East Stroudsburg 8,039 ..... M4
†15301 East Washington 2,241 ..... B5
15931 Ebensburg⊙ 4,096 ..... E5
†15005 Economy 9,538 ..... B4
†19013 Eddystone 2,555 ..... M7
†15218 Edgewood 4,382 ..... B7
†15143 Edgeworth 1,738 ..... B4
16412 Edinboro 6,324 ..... B2
18704 Edwardsville 5,729 ..... E7
16731 Eldred 965 ..... F2
15037 Elizabeth 1,892 ..... C5
17022 Elizabethtown 8,233 ..... J5
17023 Elizabethville 1,531 ..... J4
16920 Elkland 1,974 ..... H1
15331 Ellsworth 1,228 ..... B5
16117 Ellwood City 9,998 ..... B4
17824 Elysburg 1,447 ..... K4
17318 Emigsville 2,413 ..... J5
16373 Emlenton 807 ..... C3
18049 Emmaus 11,001 ..... M4
15834 Emporium⊙ 2,837 ..... F2
15202 Emsworth 3,074 ..... B6
17025 Enola J5
17522 Ephrata 11,095 ..... K5
*16501 Erie⊙ 119,123 ..... B1
Erie‡ 279,780 ..... B1
17815 Espy 1,571 ..... K4
15223 Etna 4,534 ..... B6
16033 Evans City 2,299 ..... B4
15537 Everett 1,828 ..... F5
15631 Everson 1,032 ..... C5
15632 Export 1,143 ..... C5
15436 Fairchance 2,106 ..... C6
19030 Fairless Hills 16,000 ..... N5
16415 Fairview 1,855 ..... B1
15840 Falls Creek 1,208 ..... E3
16121 Farrell 8,645 ..... A3
17222 Fayetteville 3,202 ..... G6
18921 Ferndale 2,204 ..... E5
19522 Fleetwood 3,422 ..... L5
†17745 Flemington 1,416 ..... G3
19032 Folcroft 8,231 ..... M7
16226 Ford City 3,923 ..... D4
18421 Forest City 1,924 ..... L2
†15221 Forest Hills 8,198 ..... C7
18704 Forty Fort 5,590 ..... F7
†18015 Fountain Hill 4,805 ..... L4
†15238 Fox Chapel 5,049 ..... C6
17931 Frackville 5,308 ..... K4
16323 Franklin⊙ 8,146 ..... C3
†16335 Fredericksburg 1,202 ..... B2
15333 Fredericktown 1,052 ..... C6
15042 Freedom 2,272 ..... B4
18224 Freeland 4,285 ..... L3
†18017 Freemansburg 1,879 ..... M4
16229 Freeport 2,381 ..... C4
16922 Galeton 1,462 ..... G2
16641 Gallitzin 2,315 ..... E4
†17701 Garden View 2,777 ..... H3
15904 Geistown 3,304 ..... E5
17325 Gettysburg⊙ 7,194 ..... H6
17934 Gilberton 1,096 ..... K4
16417 Girard 2,615 ..... B2
17935 Girardville 2,268 ..... K4
15045 Glassport 6,242 ..... C7
18617 Glen Lyon 2,352 ..... E7
19036 Glenolden 7,633 ..... M7
17327 Glen Rock 1,662 ..... J6
19038 Glenside M5
15634 Grapeville C5
18821 Great Bend 740 ..... L2
17225 Greencastle 3,679 ..... G6
15601 Greensburg⊙ 17,558 ..... D5
15242 Greentree 5,722 ..... B7
16125 Greenville 7,730 ..... B3
16127 Grove City 8,162 ..... B3
17032 Halifax 909 ..... J5
17406 Hallam 1,428 ..... J6
18822 Hallstead 1,280 ..... L2
19526 Hamburg 4,011 ..... L4
17331 Hanover 14,890 ..... J6
16037 Harmony 1,334 ..... B4
*17101 Harrisburg (cap.)⊙ 53,264 ..... H5
Harrisburg‡ 446,072 ..... H5
16038 Harrisville 1,033 ..... B3
18618 Harveys Lake 2,318 ..... E7
16646 Hastings 1,574 ..... E4
19040 Hatboro 7,579 ..... M5
19440 Hatfield 2,533 ..... M5
19041 Haverford○ 52,349 ..... M6
19083 Havertown M6
16840 Hawk Run 1,960 ..... F4
18428 Hawley 1,181 ..... M3
18201 Hazleton 27,318 ..... L4
15106 Heidelberg 1,606 ..... B7
17406 Hellam (Hallam) 1,428 ..... J6
18055 Hellertown 6,025 ..... M4
17033 Hershey 13,249 ..... J5
†17044 Highland Park 1,879 ..... H4
17034 Highspire 2,959 ..... J5
16648 Hollidaysburg⊙ 5,892 ..... F5
15748 Homer City 2,248 ..... D4
15120 Homestead 5,092 ..... B7
18431 Honesdale⊙ 5,128 ..... M2
19344 Honey Brook 1,164 ..... L5
15936 Hooversville 863 ..... E5
15445 Hopwood 2,420 ..... C6
15342 Houston 1,568 ..... B5
16651 Houtzdale 1,222 ..... F4
†18640 Hughestown 1,783 ..... F7
17737 Hughesville 2,174 ..... J3
17036 Hummelstown 4,267 ..... J5
16652 Huntingdon⊙ 7,042 ..... G5
16843 Hyde 1,791 ..... F4
15545 Hyndman 1,106 ..... E6
15126 Imperial 3,207 ..... B5
15701 Indiana⊙ 16,051 ..... D4
15052 Industry 2,417 ..... B4
†15205 Ingram 4,346 ..... B7
15642 Irwin 4,995 ..... C5
17407 Jacobus 1,396 ..... J6
15644 Jeannette 13,106 ..... C5
†15025 Jefferson 8,643 ..... B7
19046 Jenkintown 4,942 ..... M5
18433 Jermyn 2,411 ..... L2
15937 Jerome 1,196 ..... D5
17740 Jersey Shore 4,631 ..... H3
18434 Jessup 4,974 ..... F6
18229 Jim Thorpe⊙ 5,263 ..... L4
15845 Johnsonburg 3,938 ..... E3
*15901 Johnstown 35,496 ..... D5
Johnstown‡ 264,506 ..... D5
16735 Kane 4,916 ..... E2
†19607 Kenhorst 3,187 ..... L5
19348 Kennett Square 4,715 ..... L6
18704 Kingston 15,681 ..... F7
16201 Kittanning⊙ 5,432 ..... D4
16232 Knox 1,364 ..... C3
16136 Koppel 1,146 ..... B4
17834 Kulpmont 3,675 ..... J4
19530 Kutztown 4,040 ..... L4
16423 Lake City 2,384 ..... B1
*17601 Lancaster⊙ 54,725 ..... K5
Lancaster‡ 362,346 ..... K5

(continued on following page)

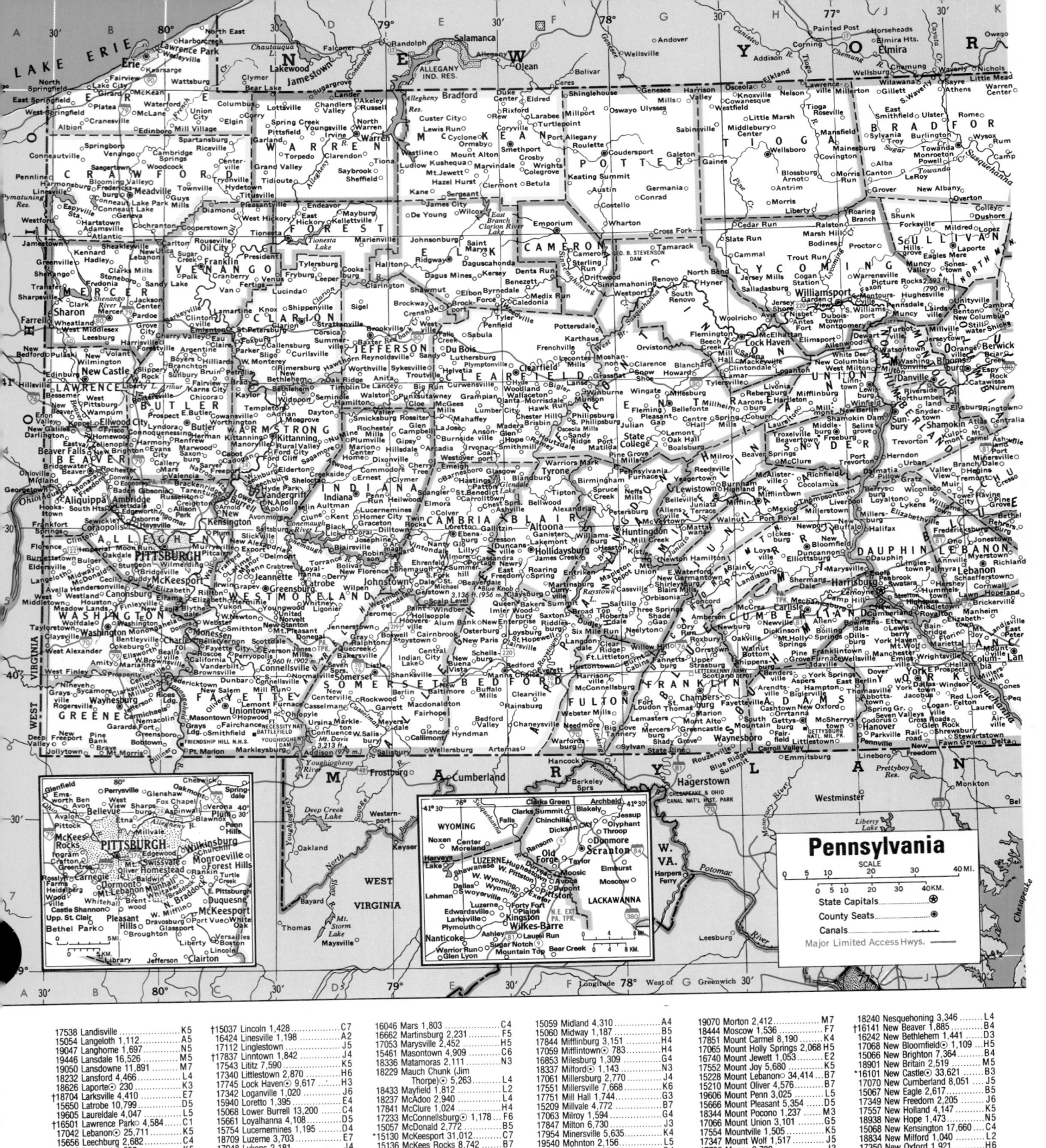

Pennsylvania

SCALE
0 5 10 20 30 40 MI.
0 5 10 20 30 40 KM.

State Capitals ⊛
County Seats ⊙
Canals
Major Limited Access Hwys. ———

16823 Pleasant Gap 1,859 ....G4
15236 Pleasant Hills 9,676 ....B7
16341 Pleasantville 1,099 ....C2
15239 Plum 25,390 ....C5
18651 Plymouth 7,605 ....E7
15474 Point Marion 1,642 ....C6
16342 Polk 1,884 ....C3
15946 Portage 3,510 ....E5
16743 Port Allegany 2,593 ....F2
17965 Port Carbon 2,576 ....K4
†15133 Port Vue 5,316 ....C7
19464 Pottstown 22,729 ....L5
17901 Pottsville⊙ 18,195 ....K4
19076 Prospect Park 6,593 ....M7
15767 Punxsutawney 7,479 ....E4
18951 Quakertown 8,867 ....L5
17566 Quarryville 1,558 ....K6
†19601 Reading⊙ 78,686 ....L5
  Reading‡ 312,509 ....L5
17567 Reamstown 1,308 ....K5
18076 Red Hill 1,727 ....L5
17356 Red Lion 5,824 ....J6
17084 Reedsville 1,023 ....G4
17764 Renovo 1,812 ....G3
15851 Reynoldsville 3,016 ....D3
17087 Richland 1,470 ....K5
18955 Richlandtown 1,180 ....M5
15853 Ridgway⊙ 5,604 ....E3
19078 Ridley Park 7,889 ....M7
18077 Riegelsville 993 ....M4
16248 Rimersburg 1,096 ....D3
17868 Riverside 2,266 ....J4
16673 Roaring Spring 2,962 ....F5
19551 Robesonia 1,748 ....K5
15074 Rochester 4,759 ....B4
15557 Rockwood 1,058 ....D6
15477 Roscoe 1,123 ....C5
18013 Roseto 1,484 ....M4
19065 Rose Valley 1,038 ....L7
17250 Rouzerville 1,371 ....G6
19468 Royersford 4,243 ....L5
16249 Rural Valley 1,033 ....D4
15076 Russelton 1,878 ....C5
17970 Saint Clair 4,037 ....K4
15857 Saint Marys 6,417 ....E3
15951 Saint Michael 1,445 ....E5
15681 Saltsburg 964 ....D4
†15081 Sandy 1,835 ....E3
16056 Saxonburg 1,336 ....C4
18840 Sayre 6,951 ....K2
†15963 Scalp Level 1,186 ....E5
17972 Schnecksville 1,041 ....L5
19473 Schwenksville 1,041 ....L5
15683 Scottdale 5,833 ....C5
18501 Scranton⊙ 88,117 ....F7
  Scranton (Northeast
  Pa.)‡ 640,396 ....F7
17870 Selinsgrove 5,227 ....J4
18960 Sellersville 3,143 ....M5
15143 Sewickley 4,778 ....B4
17872 Shamokin 10,357 ....J4
17876 Shamokin Dam 1,622 ....J4
16146 Sharon 19,057 ....B3
  Sharon‡ 128,299 ....B3
19079 Sharon Hill 6,221 ....N7
15215 Sharpsburg 4,351 ....B6
16150 Sharpsville 5,375 ....A3
16347 Sheffield 1,471 ....D2
17976 Shenandoah 7,589 ....K4
18655 Shickshinny 1,192 ....K3
19607 Shillington 5,601 ....K5
16748 Shinglehouse 1,310 ....F2
17257 Shippensburg 5,261 ....H5
19555 Shoemakersville 1,391 .....K4
17361 Shrewsbury 2,688 ....J6
19608 Sinking Spring 2,617 ....K5
18080 Slatington 4,277 ....L4
15684 Slickville 1,178 ....C4
16057 Slippery Rock 3,047 ....B3
16749 Smethport 1,797 ....F2
15478 Smithfield 1,084 ....C6
15501 Somerset⊙ 6,474 ....D6
18964 Souderton 6,657 ....M5
15425 South Connellsville 2,296 ..C6
15956 South Fork 1,401 ....C5
†18840 South Waverly 1,176 ......J2

17701 South Williamsport 6,581 ..J3
15775 Spangler 2,399 ....E4
19475 Spring City 3,389 ....L5
15144 Springdale 4,418 ....C6
19064 Springfield⊙ 25,326 ....M7
17362 Spring Grove 1,832 ....J6
16801 State College 36,130 ......G4
  State College‡ 112,760 .....G4
17263 State Line 1,253 ....G6
17113 Steelton 6,484 ....J5
17363 Stewartstown 1,072 ....K6
16153 Stoneboro 1,177 ....B3
19464 Stowe 3,860 ....L5
17579 Strasburg 1,999 ....K6
18360 Stroudsburg⊙ 5,148 ....M4
15082 Sturgeon 1,312 ....B5
†16323 Sugar Creek 5,954 ....C3
18706 Sugar Notch 1,191 ....E7
18250 Summit Hill 3,418 ....L4
17801 Sunbury⊙ 12,292 ....J4
18847 Susquehanna 1,994 ....L2
19081 Swarthmore 5,950 ....M7
†17111 Swatara⊙ 18,796 ....J5
15218 Swissvale 11,345 ....C7
18704 Swoyersville 5,795 ....E7
15865 Sykesville 1,537 ....E3
18252 Tamaqua 8,843 ....L4
15084 Tarentum 6,419 ....C4
18517 Taylor 7,246 ....F7
18969 Telford 3,507 ....M5
19560 Temple 1,486 ....L5
17581 Terre Hill 1,217 ....L5
18512 Throop 4,166 ....F7
16351 Tidioute 844 ....D2
16353 Tionesta⊙ 659 ....D2
16684 Tipton 1,348 ....F4
16354 Titusville 6,884 ....C2
19562 Topton 1,818 ....L5
19374 Toughkenamon 1,111 ....L6
18848 Towanda⊙ 3,526 ....J2
17980 Tower City 1,667 ....J4
15085 Trafford 3,662 ....C5
†19013 Trainer 2,056 ....L7
17981 Tremont 1,796 ....K4
18254 Tresckow 1,128 ....K4
17881 Trevorton 2,192 ....J4
16947 Troy 1,381 ....J2
19007 Tullytown 2,079 ....N6
15145 Turtle Creek 6,959 ....C7
16686 Tyrone 6,346 ....F4
16438 Union City 3,623 ....C2
15401 Uniontown⊙ 14,510 ....C6
†19013 Upland 3,458 ....L7
*19082 Upper Darby⊙ 84,054 ....M6
15241 Upper Saint Claire⊙ 19,023 B7
19481 Valley Forge 400 ....L5
17983 Valley View 1,722 ....J4
15690 Vandergrift 6,623 ....D4
15147 Verona 3,174 ....C7
15132 Versailles 2,150 ....C7
19085 Villanova M6
18088 Walnutport 2,007 ....L4
16365 Warren⊙ 12,146 ....D2
16441 Waterford 1,568 ....B2
17777 Watsontown 2,366 ....J3
19087 Wayne M6
17268 Waynesboro 9,726 ....G6
15370 Waynesburg⊙ 4,482 ......B6
18255 Weatherly 2,891 ....L4
16901 Wellsboro⊙ 3,805 ....H2
19565 Wernersville 1,811 ....K5
16510 Wesleyville 3,998 ....C1
15417 West Brownsville 1,433 ....C5
19380 West Chester⊙ 17,435 ...L6
16950 Westfield 1,268 ....H2
19390 West Grove 1,820 ....L6
18201 West Hazleton 4,871 ......K4
†16201 West Kittanning 1,591 ....C4
15656 West Leechburg 1,395 ....C4
16159 West Middlesex 1,064 .....B3
15122 West Mifflin 26,279 ....C7
†15905 Westmont 6,113 ....D5
15089 West Newton 3,387 ....C5
16160 West Pittsburg 1,133 ......B4
18643 West Pittston 5,980 ....F7
15229 West View 7,648 ....B6

18644 West Wyoming 3,288 ......E7
†17401 West York 4,526 ....J6
15120 Whitaker 1,615 ....C7
†15234 Whitehall 15,206 ....B7
18661 White Haven 1,921 ....L3
15131 White Oak 9,480 ....C7
17097 Wiconisco 1,321 ....J4
*18701 Wilkes-Barre⊙ 51,551 .....F7
15221 Wilkinsburg 23,669 ....C7
16693 Williamsburg 1,400 ....F5
17701 Williamsport⊙ 33,401 .....H3
  Williamsport‡ 118,416 .....H3
17098 Williamstown 1,664 ....J4
19090 Willow Grove M5
15148 Wilmerding 2,421 ....C5
15025 Wilson 7,564 ....M4
15963 Windber 5,585 ....E5
18091 Windgap 2,651 ....M4
19567 Womelsdorf 1,827 ....K5
19094 Woodlyn M7
17368 Wrightsville 2,365 ....J5
18644 Wyoming 3,655 ....F7
19610 Wyomissing 6,551 ....K5
19067 Yardley 2,533 ....N5
19050 Yeadon 11,727 ....N7
17099 Yeagertown 1,305 ....G4
*17401 York⊙ 44,619 ....J6
  York‡ 381,255 ....J6
16371 Youngsville 2,006 ....D2
15697 Youngwood 3,749 ....D5
16063 Zelienople 3,502 ....B4

OTHER FEATURES

Allegheny (res.) E2
Allegheny (riv.) D2
Allegheny Front (mts.) E5
Appalachian (mts.) H4
Ararat (mt.) M2
Arthur (lake) C4
Beaver (riv.) B4
Blue (mt.) G5
Blue Knob (mt.) E5
Casselman (riv.) D6
Clarion (riv.) D3
Conemaugh (riv.) D5
Conemaugh River (lake) D4
Conewago (creek) D1
Davis (mt.) D6
Delaware (riv.) N3
Delaware Water Gap Nat'l Rec.
  Area N3
Erie (lake) B1
Fort Necessity Nat'l
  Battlefield C6
George B. Stevenson (dam) G3
Gettysburg Nat'l Mil. Park H6
Glendale (lake) F4
Juniata (riv.) G5
Laurel Hill (mt.) D5
Lehigh (riv.) L3
Letterkenny Army Depot G6
Licking (creek) F6
Little Tinicum (isl.) M7
Lycoming (creek) H3
Monongahela (riv.) C6
North (mt.) K3
Ohio (riv.) A4
Oil (creek) C2
Pine (creek) H2
Pine Grove (res.) K6
Pocono (mts.) M3
Pymatuning (res.) A2
Redbank (creek) E3
Schuylkill (riv.) K5
Shenango River (lake) B3
Sinnemahoning (creek) F3
South (mt.) H6
Susquehanna (riv.) K6
Tioga (riv.) H1
Tionesta Creek (lake) D3
Towanda (creek) J2
Tuscarora (riv.) G5
Wallenpaupack (lake) M3
Youghiogheny River (lake) D6

⊙County seat.
‡Population of metropolitan area.
⊙Population of town or township.
† Zip of nearest p.o. * Multiple zips.

18067 Northampton 8,240 ....M4
15673 North Apollo 1,487 ....D4
15104 North Braddock 8,711 ......C7
†18032 North Catasauqua 2,554 ...L4
16428 North East 4,568 ....C1
17857 Northumberland 3,636 .....J4
19454 North Wales 3,391 ....M5
15674 Norvelt 2,541 ....D5
19074 Norwood 6,647 ....M7
15071 Oakdale 1,955 ....B5
15139 Oakmont 7,039 ....C6
†15059 Ohioville 4,217 ....B4
16301 Oil City 13,881 ....C3
18518 Old Forge 9,304 ....F7
15472 Oliver 3,777 ....C6
18447 Olyphant 5,204 ....F7
17961 Orwigsburg 2,700 ....K4
16666 Osceola Mills 1,466 ....F4
19363 Oxford 3,633 ....K6
†15963 Paint 1,177 ....E5
18071 Palmerton 5,455 ....L4
17078 Palmyra 7,228 ....J5
19301 Paoli 5,277 ....M5

17562 Paradise 1,107 ....K5
19365 Parkesburg 2,578 ....L6
†19013 Parkside 2,464 ....M7
†17331 Parkville 5,009 ....J6
16668 Patton 2,441 ....E4
18072 Pen Argyl 3,388 ....M4
17103 Penbrook 3,006 ....J5
19047 Penndel 2,703 ....N5
18073 Pennsburg 2,339 ....M5
†17331 Pennville 1,398 ....J6
†19151 Penn Wynne M6
18944 Perkasie 5,241 ....M5
15473 Perryopolis 2,139 ....C5
*19101 Philadelphia⊙ 1,688,210 ...N6
  Philadelphia‡ 4,716,818 ...N6
16866 Philipsburg 3,533 ....F4
19460 Phoenixville 14,165 ....L5
17963 Pine Grove 2,244 ....K4
16868 Pine Grove Mills 1,030 .....G4
15140 Pitcairn 4,175 ....C5
*15201 Pittsburgh⊙ 423,938 ......B7
  Pittsburgh‡ 2,263,894 .....B7
*18640 Pittston 9,930 ....F7
†18701 Plains 5,455 ....F7

Topography

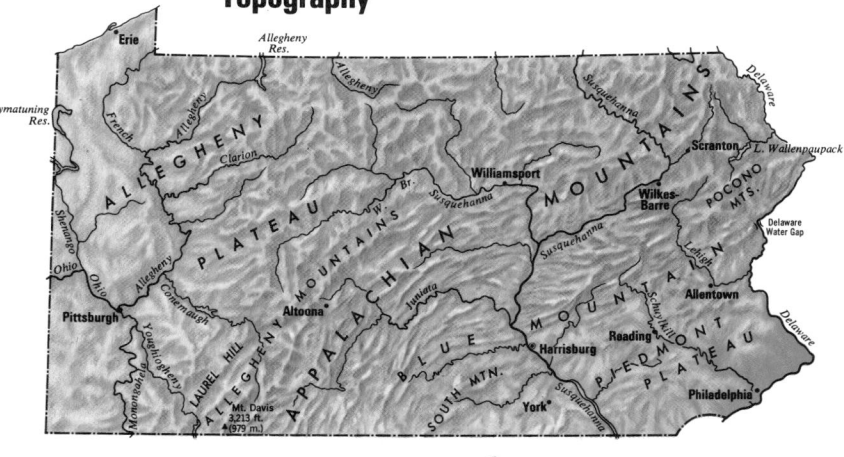

0   30   60 MI.
0   30   60 KM.

5,000 m. 2,000 m. 1,000 m. 500 m. 200 m. 100 m. Sea
16,404 ft. 6,562 ft. 3,281 ft. 1,640 ft. 656 ft. 328 ft. Level Below

South Carolina

SCALE
0 5 10 20 30 40 MI.
0 10 20 30 40 KM.

State Capitals............⊛
County Seats............⊙
Canals...................
Major Limited Access Hwys. ....

© Copyright HAMMOND

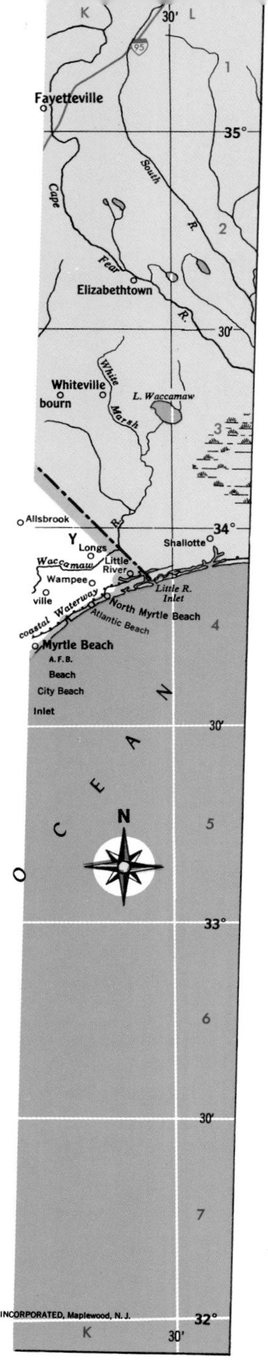
Fayetteville
Cape Fear R.
South R.
Elizabethtown
Whiteville
L. Waccamaw
White Marsh
Allsbrook
Longs
Shallotte
Waccamaw
Little River
Wampee
Little R. Inlet
North Myrtle Beach
Atlantic Beach
coastal Waterway
Myrtle Beach A.F.B.
OCEAN
INCORPORATED, Maplewood, N.J.

29554 Hemingway 853 .... J4
†29706 Hemlock (Eureka) 1,627 .... E2
29717 Hickory Grove 344 .... E2
29813 Hilda 355 .... E5
29928 Hilton Head Island 11,344 . F7
29653 Hodges 154 .... C3
29059 Holly Hill 1,785 .... G5
29449 Hollywood 729 .... G6
29654 Honea Path 4,114 .... C3
29349 Inman 1,554 .... C1
29063 Irmo 3,957 .... E3
†29720 Irwin 1,373 .... F2
29451 Isle of Palms 3,421 .... H6
29655 Iva 1,369 .... B3
29831 Jackson 1,771 .... D5
29453 Jamestown 193 .... H5
†29483 Jedburg 900 .... G5
29718 Jefferson 651 .... G2
29351 Joanna 1,839 .... D3
29555 Johnsonville 1,421 .... J4
29832 Johnston 2,624 .... D4
29353 Jonesville 1,201 .... D2
29067 Kershaw 1,993 .... G2
29556 Kingstree⊙ 4,147 .... H4
29814 Kline 315 .... E5
29456 Ladson 13,246 .... G6
29560 Lake City 6,731 .... H4
29563 Lake View 939 .... J3
29069 Lamar 1,333 .... G3
29720 Lancaster⊙ 9,703 .... F2

Agriculture, Industry and Resources

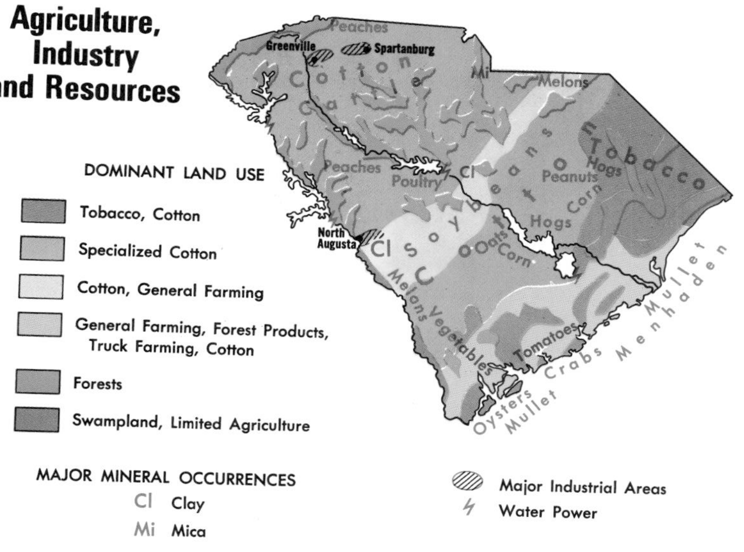
DOMINANT LAND USE
Tobacco, Cotton
Specialized Cotton
Cotton, General Farming
General Farming, Forest Products, Truck Farming, Cotton
Forests
Swampland, Limited Agriculture
MAJOR MINERAL OCCURRENCES
Cl Clay
Mi Mica
Major Industrial Areas
Water Power
Greenville
Spartanburg
Peaches
Cotton
Cattle
Melons
Tobacco
Soybeans
Poultry
Peanuts
Hogs
Corn
Oats
North Augusta
Vegetables
Tomatoes
Oysters
Mullet
Crabs
Menhaden

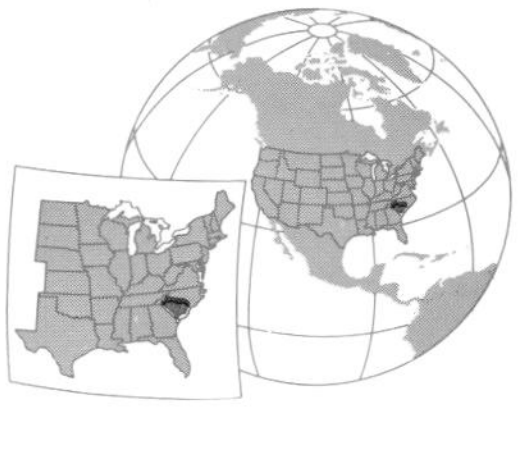

AREA 31,113 sq. mi. (80,583 sq. km.)
POPULATION 3,121,833
CAPITAL Columbia
LARGEST CITY Columbia
HIGHEST POINT Sassafras Mtn. 3,560 ft. (1085 m.)
SETTLED IN 1670
ADMITTED TO UNION May 23, 1788
POPULAR NAME Palmetto State
STATE FLOWER Carolina (Yellow) Jessamine
STATE BIRD Carolina Wren

†29720 Lancaster Mills 2,096 .... F2
29356 Landrum 2,141 .... C1
29564 Lane 554 .... H5
29834 Langley 1,714 .... D4
29565 Latta 1,804 .... J3
29902 Laurel Bay 5,238 .... F7
29360 Laurens⊙ 10,587 .... C3
29070 Leesville 2,296 .... E4
†29730 Lesslie 1,102 .... E2
29072 Lexington⊙ 2,131 .... E4
29657 Liberty 3,167 .... B2
†29483 Lincolnville 808 .... G6
29075 Little Mountain 282 .... E3
29076 Livingston 166 .... E4
29364 Lockhart 85 .... E2
29082 Lodge 145 .... F5
29569 Loris 2,193 .... K3
29659 Lowndesville 197 .... B3
†29706 Lowrys 225 .... E2
29078 Lugoff 2,939 .... F3
29932 Luray 149 .... E6
29325 Lydia Mills 925 .... D3
29365 Lyman 1,067 .... C2
29080 Lynchburg 534 .... G3
†29829 Madison 1,150 .... D4
29102 Manning⊙ 4,746 .... G4
29661 Marietta-Slater 1,834 .... C1
29571 Marion⊙ 7,700 .... J3
29662 Mauldin 8,143 .... C2
29104 Mayesville 663 .... G4
29101 McBee 774 .... G3
29458 McClellanville 436 .... H5
29570 McColl 2,677 .... H2
29726 McConnells 171 .... E2
29835 McCormick⊙ 1,725 .... C4
29460 Meggett 249 .... G6
†29379 Monarch Mills 2,353 .... D2
29461 Moncks Corner⊙ 3,699 .... G5
29105 Monetta 167 .... D4
29840 Mount Carmel 182 .... C3
29727 Mount Croghan 146 .... G2
29464 Mount Pleasant 14,209 .... H6
29574 Mullins 6,068 .... J3
29576 Murrells Inlet 2,410 .... K4
29577 Myrtle Beach 18,446 .... K4
29107 Neeses 557 .... E4
29108 Newberry⊙ 9,866 .... D3
29809 New Ellenton 2,628 .... D5
†29536 New Town 950 .... J3
29581 Nichols 606 .... J3
29666 Ninety Six 2,249 .... C3
29667 Norris 903 .... B2
29112 North 1,304 .... E4
29841 North Augusta 13,593 .... C5
29406 North Charleston 62,534 ... G6
†29550 North Hartsville 2,650 .... G3
29582 North Myrtle Beach 3,960 .. K4
29113 Norway 518 .... E5
29114 Olanta 699 .... H4
29843 Olar 381 .... E5
29115 Orangeburg⊙ 14,933 .... F4
29372 Pacolet 1,556 .... D2
29373 Pacolet Mills 1,051 .... D2
29728 Pageland 2,720 .... G2
29583 Pamplico 1,213 .... H4
29844 Parksville 157 .... C4
29584 Patrick 375 .... G2
29102 Paxville 244 .... G4
29122 Peak 82 .... E3
29123 Pelion 213 .... E4
29669 Pelzer 130 .... B2
29670 Pendleton 3,154 .... B2
29124 Perry 273 .... E4
29671 Pickens⊙ 3,199 .... B2
29673 Piedmont 2,992 .... C2
29934 Pineland 800 .... E6
†29169 Pineridge 1,287 .... E4
29468 Pineville 900 .... H5
29125 Pinewood 689 .... G4
29469 Pinopolis 788 .... G5
29845 Plum Branch 73 .... C4
29126 Pomaria 271 .... E3
29935 Port Royal 2,977 .... F7
29127 Prosperity 803 .... D3
†29501 Quinby 952 .... H3
29470 Ravenel 1,655 .... G6

29471 Reevesville 241 .... F5
29729 Richburg 269 .... E2
29936 Ridgeland⊙ 1,143 .... E7
29129 Ridge Spring 969 .... D4
29472 Ridgeville 603 .... G5
29130 Ridgeway 343 .... F3
29730 Rock Hill 35,344 .... E2
Rock Hill‡ 106,720 .... E2
29133 Rowesville 388 .... F5
29741 Ruby 256 .... G2
29407 Saint Andrews 9,908 .... G6
29477 Saint George⊙ 2,134 .... F5
29135 Saint Matthews⊙ 2,496 .... F4
29479 Saint Stephen 1,850 .... H5
29676 Salem 194 .... A2
29137 Salley 584 .... E4
29138 Saluda⊙ 2,752 .... D4
29142 Santee 612 .... F5
†29301 Saxon 4,383 .... D2
29939 Scotia 72 .... E6
29591 Scranton 861 .... H4
29592 Sellers 388 .... H3
29678 Seneca 7,436 .... A2
29742 Sharon 323 .... E2
29145 Silverstreet 200 .... D3
29681 Simpsonville 9,037 .... C2
29682 Six Mile 470 .... B2
29683 Slater-Marietta 1,834 .... C1
29481 Smoaks 165 .... F5
29743 Smyrna 47 .... E1
†29812 Snelling 111 .... E5
29593 Society Hill 848 .... H2
†29512 South Bennettsville 1,065 .. H2
†29169 South Congaree 2,113 .... E4
*29301 Spartanburg⊙ 43,826 .... C1
29169 Springdale 2,985 .... E4
†29720 Springdale 2,570 .... F2
29146 Springfield 604 .... E4
†29067 Spring Mills 1,419 .... F2
29684 Starr 241 .... B3
29377 Startex 1,006 .... C2
29554 Stuckey 222 .... H4
29482 Sullivans Island 1,867 .... H6
29148 Summerton 1,173 .... G4
29483 Summerville 6,706 .... G5
†29054 Summit 172 .... E4
29150 Sumter⊙ 24,890 .... G4
29577 Surfside Beach 2,522 .... K4
29160 Swansea 888 .... E4
29846 Sycamore 261 .... E5
29594 Tatum 101 .... H2
29687 Taylors 15,801 .... C2
29688 Tigerville 975 .... C1
29161 Timmonsville 2,112 .... H3
29690 Travelers Rest 3,017 .... C2
29847 Trenton 404 .... D4
29848 Troy 705 .... C4
29162 Turbeville 549 .... G4
29849 Ulmer 91 .... E5
29379 Union⊙ 10,523 .... D2
†29678 Utica 1,501 .... B2
29163 Vance 89 .... G5
29944 Varnville 1,948 .... E6
†29607 Wade-Hampton 20,180 .... C2
29164 Wagener 903 .... E4
29691 Walhalla⊙ 3,977 .... A2
29488 Walterboro⊙ 6,209 .... F6
29166 Ward 98 .... D4
29692 Ware Shoals 2,370 .... C3
29851 Warrenville 1,029 .... D4
29384 Waterloo 200 .... C3
†29360 Watts Mills 1,324 .... D2
29385 Wellford 2,143 .... C2
29169 West Columbia 10,409 .... E4
29693 Westminster 3,114 .... A2
29669 West Pelzer 944 .... B2
29696 West Union 300 .... B2
†29301 Westview 1,999 .... C2
29178 Whitmire 2,038 .... D3
29303 Whitney 4,052 .... D1
29493 Williams 205 .... F5
29697 Williamston 4,310 .... B2
29853 Williston 3,173 .... E5
29856 Windsor 55 .... E5
†29501 Windy Hill 1,622 .... H3
29180 Winnsboro⊙ 2,919 .... E3

†29180 Winnsboro Mills 1,890 .... E3
†29112 Woodford 206 .... E4
29388 Woodruff 5,171 .... D2
29945 Yemassee 789 .... F6
29745 York⊙ 6,412 .... E1

OTHER FEATURES

Ashepoo (riv.) F6
Ashley (riv.) G6
Bay Point (isl.) F7
Beaufort Marine Air Sta. F7
Big Black (creek) G2
Black (riv.) H4
Blue Ridge (mts.) B1
Broad (riv.) E2
Broad (riv.) F7
Buck (creek) J3
Bull (isl.) H6
Bullock (creek) E2
Bulls (bay) H6
Bush (riv.) D3
Buzzard Roost (dam) D3
Cape (isl.) J5
Capers (isl.) H6
Catawba (riv.) F2
Catfish (creek) J3
Charleston A.F.B. G6
Chattooga (riv.) A2
Clark Hill (dam) C4
Clark Hill (lake) C4
Combahee (riv.) F6
Congaree (riv.) F4
Congaree Nat'l Mon. F4
Cooper (riv.) H6
Coosaw (riv.) G7
Coosawhatchie (riv.) E6
Cowpens Nat'l Battlefield D1
Crooked (creek) H2
Deep (creek) B2
Dewees (isl.) H6
Donaldson A.F.B. C2

Edisto (isl.) G6
Edisto (riv.) G7
Enoree (riv.) C2
Fort Jackson F4
Fort Sumter Nat'l Mon. H6
Four Hole Swamp (creek) F5
Fripp (isl.) G7
Great Pee Dee (riv.) J4
Greenwood (lake) D3
Hartwell (dam) B3
Hartwell (lake) A3
Hilton Head (isl.) F7
Hunting (isl.) G7
Intracoastal Waterway H5
James (isl.) H6
Johns (isl.) G6
Juniper (creek) H2
Keowee (lake) B2
Keowee (riv.) B2
Kiawah (isl.) G6
Kings Mountain Nat'l Mil. Park E1
Little (riv.) C3
Little (riv.) D3
Little Lynches (riv.) G3
Little Pee Dee (riv.) J4
Little River (inlet) L4
Lumber (riv.) J3
Lynches (riv.) H3
Marion (lake) G5
Morris (isl.) H6
Moultrie (lake) G5
Murphy (isl.) J5
Murray (lake) D4
Myrtle Beach A.F.B. K4
Naval Base H6
New (riv.) E6
Ninety Six Nat'l Hist. Site C3
North (inlet) J5
North (isl.) J5
North Edisto (riv.) G6
Pacolet (riv.) D1
Palms, Isle of (isl.) H6

Parris Island Marine Base F7
Pee Dee (riv.) H2
Pinopolis (dam) G5
Pocotaligo (riv.) G4
Port Royal (sound) F7
Pritchards (isl.) G7
Reedy (riv.) C2
Robinson (lake) G3
Romain (cape) J6
Saint Helena (isl.) F7
Saint Helena (sound) G7
Salkehatchie (riv.) E5
Saluda (riv.) D3
Sandy (pt.) H6
Sandy (riv.) E2
Santee (dam) G4
Santee (riv.) H5
Sassafras (mt.) B1
Savannah (riv.) E6
Savannah River Plant D5
Sea (isls.) G7
Seabrook (isl.) G6
Seneca (riv.) B2
Shaw A.F.B. 6,939 .... F4
South (isl.) J5
Stevens (creek) C4
Stono (inlet) H6
Thompsons (creek) G2
Tugaloo (riv.) A2
Turkey (creek) E2
Tybee Roads (chan.) F7
Tyger (riv.) D2
Waccamaw (riv.) J5
Wadmalaw (isl.) G6
Wando (riv.) H6
Wateree (lake) F3
Wateree (riv.) F3
Winyah (bay) J5
Wylie (lake) E1

⊙County seat.
‡Population of metropolitan area.
† Zip of nearest p.o. * Multiple zips.

Topography

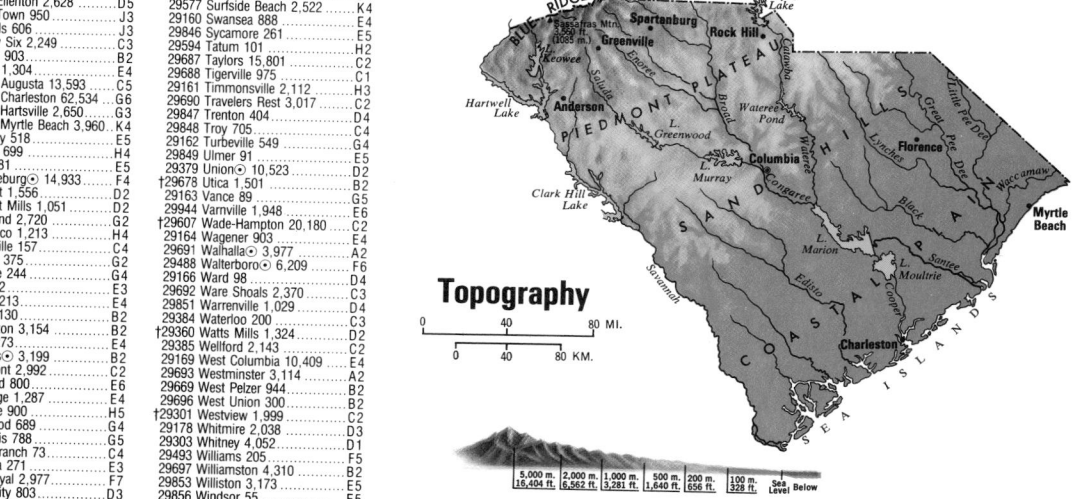

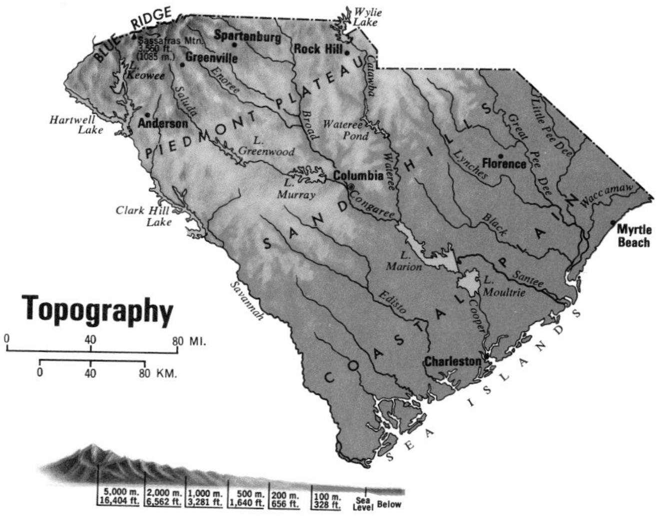
BLUE RIDGE
Sassafras Mtn. 3,560 ft. (1085 m.)
Spartanburg
Rock Hill
Wylie Lake
Greenville
Keowee
Hartwell Lake
Anderson
PIEDMONT PLATEAU
L. Greenwood
Wateree Pond
Columbia
L. Murray
Clark Hill Lake
SAND HILLS
Florence
Myrtle Beach
L. Marion
L. Moultrie
COASTAL PLAIN
Charleston
SEA ISLANDS
0 40 80 MI.
0 40 80 KM.
5,000 m. 16,404 ft.
2,000 m. 6,562 ft.
1,000 m. 3,281 ft.
500 m. 1,640 ft.
200 m. 656 ft.
100 m. 328 ft.
Sea Level
Below

SOUTH DAKOTA
COUNTIES

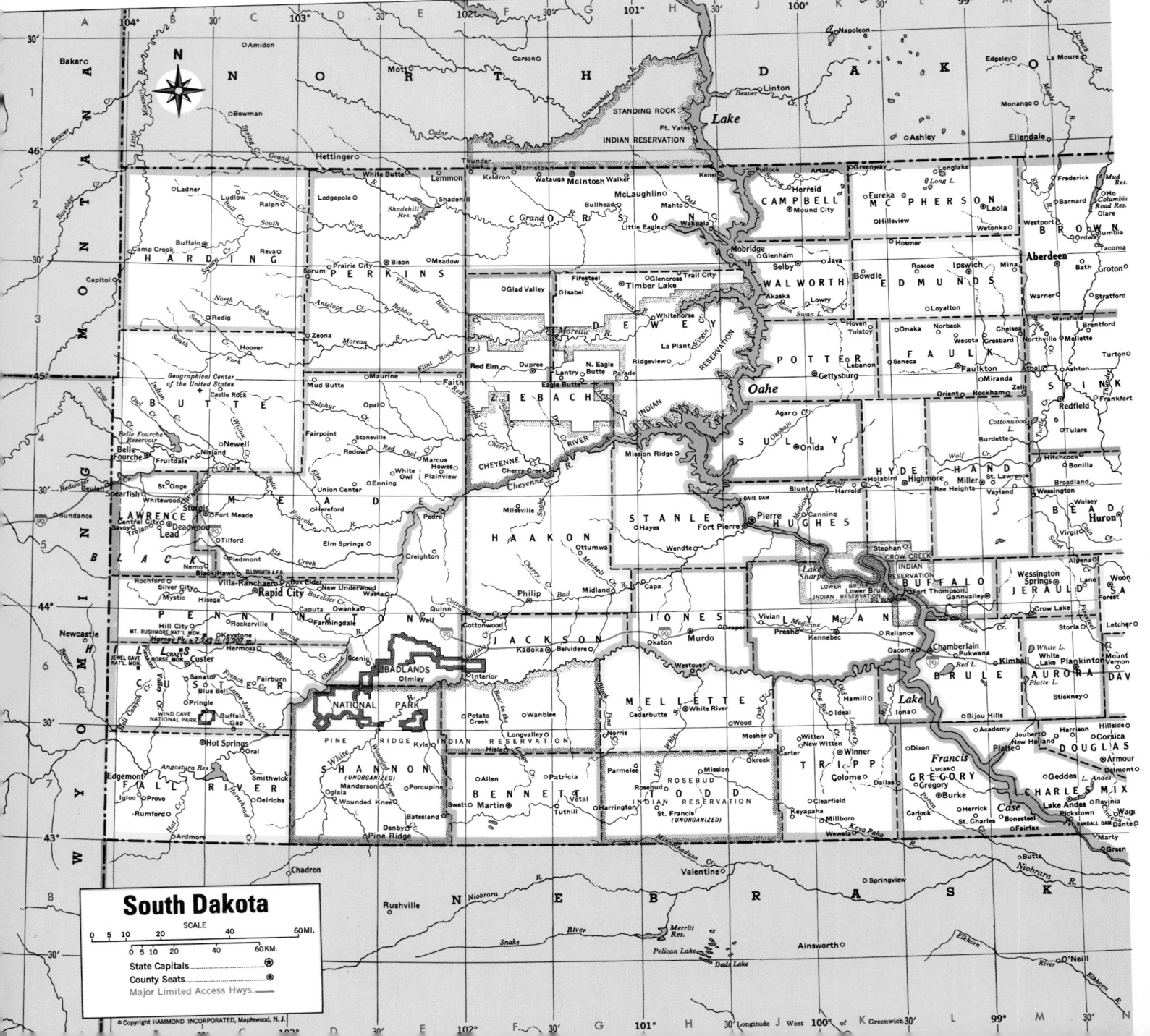

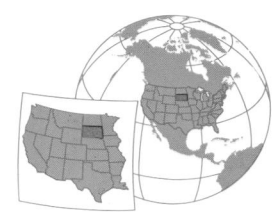

AREA 77,116 sq. mi. (199,730 sq. km.)
POPULATION 690,768
CAPITAL Pierre
LARGEST CITY Sioux Falls
HIGHEST POINT Harney Pk. 7,242 ft.
(2207 m.)
SETTLED IN 1856
ADMITTED TO UNION November 2, 1889
POPULAR NAME Coyote State; Sunshine
State
STATE FLOWER Pasqueflower
STATE BIRD Ring-necked Pheasant

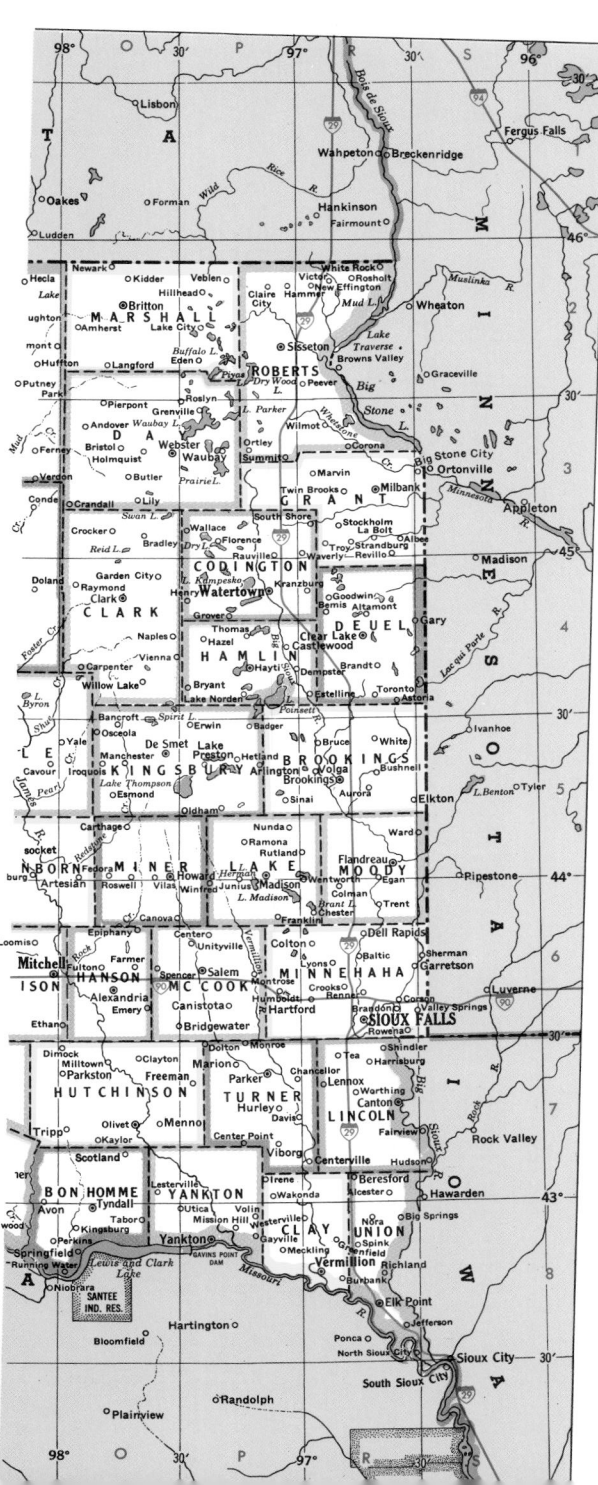

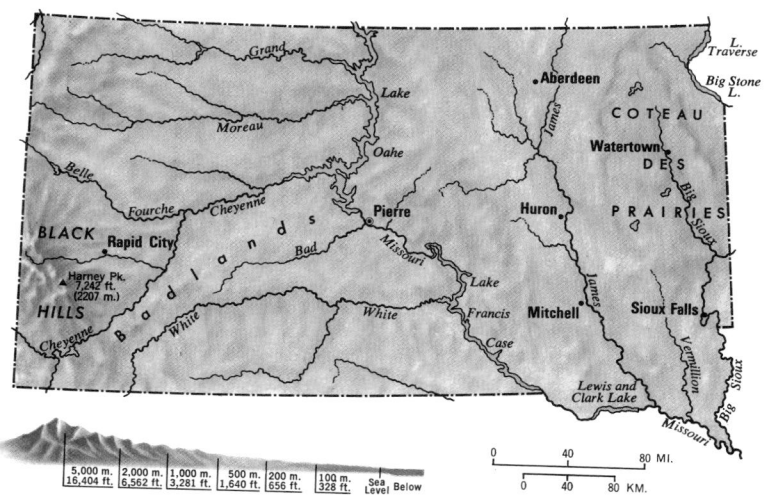

5,000 m.	2,000 m.	1,000 m.	500 m.	200 m.	100 m.	Sea
16,404 ft.	6,562 ft.	3,281 ft.	1,640 ft.	656 ft.	328 ft.	Level Below

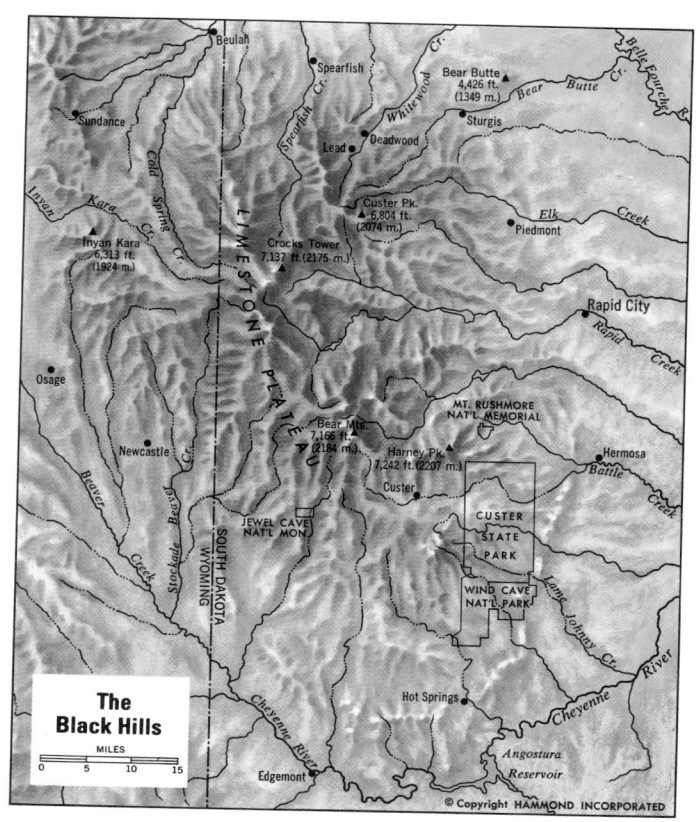

The Black Hills

MILES
0 5 10 15

© Copyright HAMMOND INCORPORATED

Agriculture, Industry and Resources

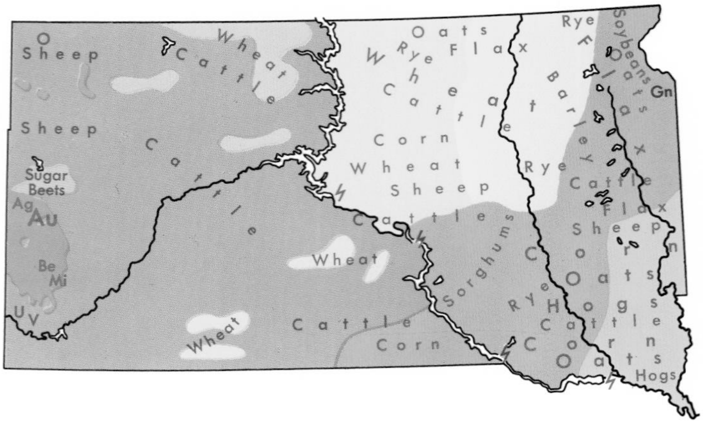

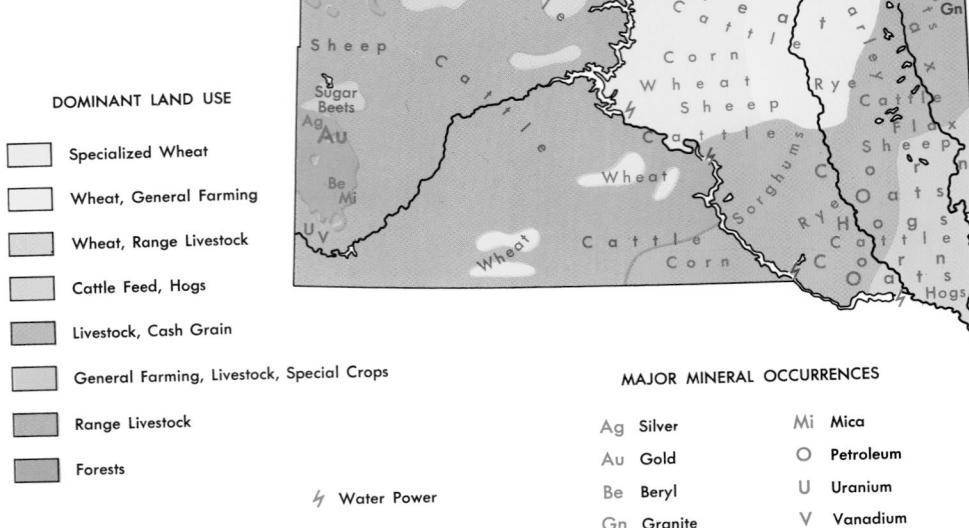

DOMINANT LAND USE

- Specialized Wheat
- Wheat, General Farming
- Wheat, Range Livestock
- Cattle Feed, Hogs
- Livestock, Cash Grain
- General Farming, Livestock, Special Crops
- Range Livestock
- Forests

ϟ Water Power

MAJOR MINERAL OCCURRENCES

Ag Silver
Au Gold
Be Beryl
Gn Granite
Mi Mica
O Petroleum
U Uranium
V Vanadium

57235 Florence 190 .... P3
57338 Forestburg 100 .... N5
57532 Fort Pierre⊙ 1,789 .... H5
57339 Fort Thompson 750 .... L5
57440 Frankfort 209 .... N4
57441 Frederick 307 .... N2
57029 Freeman 1,462 .... O7
57742 Fruitdale 88 .... B4
57340 Fulton 108 .... O6
57341 Gannvalley⊙ 70 .... L5
57236 Garden City 104 .... O4
57030 Garretson 963 .... S6
57237 Gary 354 .... S4
57031 Gayville 407 .... P8
57342 Geddes 303 .... M7
57442 Gettysburg⊙ 1,623 .... K3
57629 Glad Valley 75 .... F3
57630 Glencross 150 .... H3
57631 Glenham 169 .... J2
57238 Goodwin 139 .... R4
57533 Gregory 1,503 .... L7
57239 Grenville 119 .... O3
57445 Groton 1,230 .... N3
57534 Hamill 25 .... K6
57032 Harrisburg 558 .... R7
57344 Harrison 89 .... M7
57536 Harrold 196 .... K4
57033 Hartford 1,207 .... P6
57537 Hayes 25 .... H5
57241 Hayti⊙ 371 .... P4
57242 Hazel 94 .... P4
57446 Hecla 435 .... N2
57243 Henry 217 .... P4
57743 Hereford 50 .... D5
57744 Hermosa 251 .... C6
57632 Herreid 570 .... K2
57538 Herrick 115 .... L7
57244 Hetland 66 .... P5
57345 Highmore⊙ 1,055 .... L4
57745 Hill City 535 .... B6
†57437 Hillsview 9 .... L2
57348 Hitchcock 132 .... M4
57540 Holabird 30 .... K4
†57274 Holmquist 25 .... O3
57448 Hosmer 385 .... L2
57747 Hot Springs⊙ 4,742 .... C7
57449 Houghton 80 .... N2
57450 Hoven 615 .... K3
57349 Howard⊙ 1,169 .... P5
57748 Howes 4 .... E4
57034 Hudson 388 .... R7
57035 Humboldt 487 .... P6
57036 Hurley 419 .... P7
57350 Huron⊙ 13,000 .... N5
57541 Ideal 250 .... K6
57750 Interior 62 .... F6
57542 Iona 4 .... L6
57451 Ipswich⊙ 1,153 .... L3
57037 Irene 523 .... P7
57353 Iroquois 348 .... O5
57633 Isabel 332 .... G3
57452 Java 261 .... K3
57038 Jefferson 592 .... S8
57543 Kadoka⊙ 832 .... F6
57354 Kaylor 120 .... O7
57634 Keldron 17 .... F2
57544 Kennebec⊙ 334 .... K6
57545 Keyapaha 4 .... J7
57751 Keystone 295 .... C6
57355 Kimball 752 .... M6
57245 Kranzburg 136 .... R4
57752 Kyle 600 .... E7
57246 La Bolt 94 .... R3
57356 Lake Andes⊙ 1,029 .... M7
57247 Lake City 46 .... O2
57248 Lake Norden 417 .... P4
57249 Lake Preston 789 .... P5
57358 Lane 83 .... N5

57454 Langford 307 .... O2
57636 Lantry 200 .... G3
57754 Lead 4,330 .... B5
57455 Lebanon 129 .... K3
57638 Lemmon 1,871 .... E2
57039 Lennox 1,827 .... R7
57456 Leola⊙ 645 .... M2
57040 Lesterville 156 .... O7
57359 Letcher 221 .... N6
57250 Lily 38 .... O3
57639 Little Eagle 150 .... H2
57640 Lodgepole 20 .... D2
57457 Longlake 117 .... L2
57547 Longvalley 15 .... F7
57360 Loomis 55 .... N6
†57472 Lowry 22 .... K3
†57471 Loyalton 6 .... L3
57755 Ludlow 10 .... C2
57041 Lyons 100 .... R6
57042 Madison⊙ 6,210 .... P6
57643 Mahto 9 .... H2
57756 Manderson 450 .... D7
57460 Mansfield 120 .... N3
57757 Marcus 5 .... E4
57043 Marion 830 .... P7
57551 Martin⊙ 1,018 .... F7
57361 Marty 250 .... N8
57251 Marvin 52 .... R3
57641 McIntosh⊙ 418 .... G2
57642 McLaughlin 754 .... H2
57644 Meadow 21 .... E2
57044 Meckling 108 .... R8
57461 Mellette 192 .... N3
57045 Menno 793 .... P7
57552 Midland 277 .... G5
57252 Milbank⊙ 4,120 .... R3
57553 Milesville 6 .... F5
57554 Millboro 12 .... K7
57362 Miller⊙ 1,931 .... L4
57462 Mina 29 .... M3
57463 Miranda 30 .... M4
57555 Mission 748 .... H7
57046 Mission Hill 197 .... P8
57557 Mission Ridge 46 .... H4
57301 Mitchell⊙ 13,916 .... N6
57601 Mobridge 4,174 .... J2
57047 Monroe 170 .... P7
57048 Montrose 396 .... P6
57645 Morristown 127 .... F2
57558 Mosher 9 .... J7
57646 Mound City⊙ 111 .... K2
57363 Mount Vernon 402 .... N6
57758 Mud Butte 3 .... D4
57559 Murdo⊙ 723 .... H6
†57271 Naples 45 .... O4
57759 Nemo 42 .... B5
57255 New Effington 261 .... R2
57760 Newell 638 .... C4
57364 New Holland 125 .... M7
57761 New Underwood 517 .... D5
†57584 New Witten 134 .... K7
57762 Nisland 216 .... C4
57560 Norris 25 .... G7
†57625 North Eagle Butte 1,354 .... G3
57049 North Sioux City 1,992 .... R8
57465 Northville 138 .... M3
57050 Nunda 60 .... P5
57365 Oacoma 289 .... L6
57763 Oelrichs 124 .... C7
57764 Oglala 475 .... D7
57562 Okaton 30 .... H6
57563 Okreek 500 .... J7
57051 Oldham 222 .... P5
57052 Olivet⊙ 96 .... O7
57466 Onaka 70 .... L3
57564 Onida⊙ 851 .... K4
57765 Opal 5 .... D4
57766 Oral 60 .... C7

57467 Orient 87 .... L4
57256 Ortley 80 .... P3
57565 Ottumwa 3 .... G5
57767 Owanka 18 .... D5
57647 Parade 2 .... G3
57053 Parker⊙ 999 .... P7
57366 Parkston 1,545 .... O7
57566 Parmelee 600 .... G7
57257 Peever 232 .... R2
57567 Philip⊙ 1,088 .... F5
57367 Pickstown 225 .... M7
57769 Piedmont 500 .... C5
57468 Pierpont 184 .... O3
57501 Pierre (cap.)⊙ 11,973 .... J5
57770 Pine Ridge 3,059 .... E7
57771 Plainview 2 .... E4
57368 Plankinton⊙ 644 .... N6
57369 Platte 1,334 .... M7
57648 Pollock 355 .... J2
57772 Porcupine 260 .... E7
57649 Prairie City 50 .... D2
57568 Presho 760 .... J6
57773 Pringle 105 .... B6
57774 Provo 60 .... B7
57370 Pukwana 234 .... L6
57775 Quinn 80 .... E5
57650 Ralph 12 .... C2
57054 Ramona 241 .... P5
57701 Rapid City⊙ 46,492 .... C5
Rapid City‡ 90,850 .... C5
57357 Ravinia 88 .... N7
57258 Raymond 106 .... O4
57469 Redfield⊙ 3,027 .... N4
57776 Redig 50 .... C3
57777 Redowl 10 .... D4
57371 Ree Heights 88 .... L4
57569 Reliance 190 .... K6
57055 Renner 320 .... R6
57651 Reva 8 .... C2
57259 Revillo 158 .... R3
57652 Ridgeview 75 .... H3
†57701 Rockerville 28 .... C6
57470 Rockham 52 .... M4
57471 Roscoe 370 .... L3
57570 Rosebud 900 .... H7
57260 Rosholt 446 .... R2
57261 Roslyn 261 .... P2
57372 Roswell 19 .... O6
57056 Rowena 100 .... R6
57057 Rutland 30 .... P5
57571 Saint Charles 25 .... L7
57572 Saint Francis 766 .... H7
57373 Saint Lawrence 223 .... M4
57779 Saint Onge 250 .... B4
57058 Salem⊙ 1,486 .... P6
57780 Scenic 26 .... D6
57059 Scotland 1,022 .... O7
57472 Selby⊙ 884 .... J3
57473 Seneca 103 .... L3
57060 Sherman 100 .... S6
57781 Silver City 31 .... B5
57061 Sinai 129 .... P5
*57101 Sioux Falls⊙ 81,343 .... R6
Sioux Falls‡ 109,435 .... R6
57262 Sisseton⊙ 2,789 .... R2
57782 Smithwick 50 .... C7
57654 Sorum 2 .... D3
57263 South Shore 241 .... P3
57783 Spearfish 5,251 .... B5
57374 Spencer 380 .... O6
†57010 Spink 75 .... R8
57062 Springfield 1,377 .... N8
57346 Stephan 30 .... K5
57375 Stickney 409 .... M6
57264 Stockholm 95 .... R3
57784 Stoneville 20 .... D4
†57359 Storla 19 .... M6
57265 Strandburg 79 .... R3

57474 Stratford 82 .... N3
57785 Sturgis⊙ 5,184 .... B5
57266 Summit 290 .... P3
57063 Tabor 460 .... O8
†57433 Tacoma Park 20 .... N2
57064 Tea 729 .... R7
†57242 Thomas 12 .... P4
†57638 Thunder Hawk 26 .... F2
†57769 Tilford 75 .... C5
57656 Timber Lake⊙ 660 .... H3
57475 Tolstoy 97 .... K3
57268 Toronto 236 .... R4
57657 Trail City 68 .... H3
57065 Trent 197 .... R6
57376 Tripp 804 .... N7
†57754 Trojan 40 .... B5
†57265 Troy 18 .... R3
57476 Tulare 238 .... N4
57477 Turton 101 .... N3
57574 Tuthill 75 .... G7
57269 Twin Brooks 87 .... R3
57066 Tyndall⊙ 1,253 .... O8
57787 Union Center 63 .... D4
†57058 Unityville 20 .... P6
57067 Utica 100 .... P8
57788 Vale 160 .... C4
57068 Valley Springs 801 .... S6
†57381 Vayland 3 .... M5
57270 Veblen 368 .... P2
57478 Verdon 7 .... N3
57069 Vermillion⊙ 10,136 .... R8
57575 Vetal 19 .... G7
57070 Viborg 812 .... P7
†57260 Victor 9 .... R2
57271 Vienna 90 .... O4
†57349 Vilas 28 .... O6
†57701 Villa Ranchaero 1,666 .... C5
57379 Virgil 37 .... N5
57576 Vivian 95 .... J6
57071 Volga 1,221 .... R5
57072 Volin 156 .... P8
57380 Wagner 1,453 .... N7
57073 Wakonda 383 .... P7
57658 Wakpala 500 .... H2
57659 Walker 12 .... G2
57790 Wall 770 .... E6
57272 Wallace 90 .... P3
57577 Wanblee 550 .... F6
57074 Ward 43 .... R5
57479 Warner 322 .... M3
57791 Wasta 99 .... D5
57660 Watauga 50 .... F2
57201 Watertown⊙ 15,649 .... P4
57273 Waubay 675 .... P3
57202 Waverly 30 .... R3
57274 Webster⊙ 2,417 .... P3
57480 Wecota 30 .... L3
57075 Wentworth 193 .... R6
57381 Wessington 327 .... M5
57382 Wessington Springs⊙ 1,203 .... M5
†57069 Westerville 21 .... P8
57481 Westport 122 .... M2
57482 Wetonka 22 .... M2
57578 Wewela 6 .... K7
57276 White 474 .... R5
†57638 White Butte 21 .... E2
57661 Whitehorse 196 .... H3
57383 White Lake 414 .... M6
57792 White Owl 6 .... E4
57579 White River⊙ 561 .... H6
†57260 White Rock 10 .... R2
57793 Whitewood 821 .... B5
57278 Willow Lake 375 .... O4
57279 Wilmot 507 .... R3
57076 Winfred 81 .... P6
57580 Winner⊙ 3,472 .... K7
57584 Witten 134 .... J7

57384 Wolsey 437 .... N5
57585 Wood 134 .... J6
57385 Woonsocket⊙ 799 .... N5
57077 Worthing 388 .... R7
57794 Wounded Knee 376 .... D7
57386 Yale 136 .... O5
57078 Yankton⊙ 12,011 .... P8
57483 Zell 60 .... M4
57795 Zeona 2 .... D3

OTHER FEATURES

Aeber (creek) G4
Andes (lake) N7
Angostura (res.) B7
Antelope (creek) D3
Bad (riv.) G5
Badlands Nat'l Mon. E6
Battle (creek) C6
Bear in the Lodge (creek) F6
Beaver (creek) A6
Belle Fourche (res.) B4
Belle Fourche (riv.) C4
Big Bend (dam) K5
Big Sioux (riv.) S7
Big Stone (lake) R3
Black Hills (mts.) B5
Black Pine (creek) G6
Bois de Sioux (riv.) R1
Boxelder (creek) D5
Brant (lake) R6
Buffalo (creek) F6
Buffalo (lake) P2
Bull (creek) C2
Bull (creek) K6
Byron (lake) N4
Cain (creek) N5
Cherry (creek) F4
Cherry (creek) F5
Cheyenne (riv.) F4
Cheyenne River Ind. Res. F4
Choteau (creek) N7
Columbia Road (res.) N2
Cottonwood (creek) E5
Cottonwood (lake) M4
Crazy Horse Mon. B6
Crow (creek) A4
Crow Creek Ind. Res. L5
Dog Ear (creek) K6
Dry (creek) G4
Dry (lake) P3
Dry Wood (lake) P2
Elk (creek) C5
Ellsworth A.F.B. 4,766 .... C5
Elm (creek) D4
Elm (riv.) M2
Firesteel (creek) N6
Flint Rock (creek) E3
Fort Randall (dam) N7
Foster (creek) N4
Francis Case (lake) L7
French (creek) C6
Gavins Point (dam) P8
Geographical Center of U.S. B4
Grand (riv.) F2
Harney (peak) B6
Hat (creek) B7
Hell Canyon (creek) B6
Herman (lake) P5
Horsehead (creek) C7
Indian (creek) B4
James (riv.) N5
Jewel Cave Nat'l Mon. B6
Kampeska (lake) P4
Keya Paha (riv.) K7
Lame Johnny (creek) C6
Lewis and Clark (lake) O8
Little Missouri (riv.) B1
Little Moreau (riv.) G3
Little White (riv.) H7
Long (lake) L2
Lower Brule Ind. Res. K5
Madison (lake) P6
Maple (riv.) M1
Medicine (creek) J6
Medicine Knoll (creek) J5
Minnechaduza (creek) H7
Minnesota (riv.) S3
Missouri (riv.) P8
Mitchell (creek) G5
Moreau (riv.) G3
Mount Rushmore Nat'l Mem. B6
Mud (creek) N3
Mud (lake) R2
Mud Lake (res.) N2
Nasty (creek) C2
Oahe (dam) J5
Oahe (lake) J1
Oak (creek) H2
Oak (creek) J6
Okobojo (creek) J4
Old Lodge (creek) K6
Owl (creek) B4
Parker (lake) P3
Pearl (creek) N5
Pine Ridge Ind. Res. D7
Piyas (lake) P2
Platte (lake) M6
Pleasant Valley (creek) B6
Poinsett (lake) P4
Ponca (creek) L7
Prairie (lake) P3
Rabbit (creek) E3
Red (lake) L6
Red Owl (creek) E4
Red Scaffold (creek) F4
Redstone (creek) O5
Redwater (creek) A4
Reid (lake) O3
Rock (creek) O6
Rosebud Ind. Res. H7
Sand (creek) C2
Sand (creek) M5
Shadehill (res.) E2
Sharpe (lake) J5
Shue (creek) N5
Smith (creek) L6
Snake (creek) F4
Snake (creek) F5
Snake (creek) M3
Spirit (lake) O4
Spring (creek) C6
Spring (creek) J2
Squaw (creek) B3
Sulphur (creek) D4
Swan (creek) J3
Swan (lake) O3
Swan (lake) K3
Thompson (lake) O5
Thunder (creek) N4
Thunder Butte (creek) E3
Traverse (lake) R2
Turtle (creek) M4
Vermillion (riv.) P6
Virgin (creek) H3
Waubay (lake) O3
Whetstone (creek) R3
White (lake) M6
White (riv.) D7
Whitewood (creek) B4
Willow (creek) C4
Wind Cave Nat'l Park B6
Wolf (creek) L4
Wounded Knee (creek) E7

⊙County seat.
‡Population of metropolitan area.
† Zip of nearest p.o. * Multiple zips.

COUNTIES

Anderson 38,381 .... J6
Andrews 13,323 .... B5
Angelina 64,172 .... K6
Aransas 14,260 .... H10
Archer 7,266 .... F4
Armstrong 1,994 .... C3
Atascosa 25,055 .... F9
Austin 17,726 .... H8
Bailey 8,168 .... B3
Bandera 7,084 .... E8
Bastrop 24,726 .... G7
Baylor 4,919 .... E4
Bee 26,030 .... G9
Bell 157,820 .... G6
Bexar 988,798 .... F8
Blanco 4,681 .... F8
Borden 859 .... C5
Bosque 13,401 .... G6
Bowie 75,301 .... K4
Brazoria 169,587 .... J8
Brazos 93,588 .... H7
Brewster 7,573 .... A8
Briscoe 2,579 .... C3
Brooks 8,428 .... F11
Brown 33,057 .... F6
Burleson 12,313 .... H7
Burnet 17,803 .... F7
Caldwell 23,637 .... G8
Calhoun 19,574 .... H9
Callahan 10,992 .... E5
Cameron 209,727 .... G11
Camp 9,275 .... K5
Carson 6,672 .... C2
Cass 29,430 .... K4
Castro 10,556 .... B3
Chambers 18,538 .... K8
Cherokee 38,127 .... J6
Childress 6,950 .... D3
Clay 9,582 .... F4
Cochran 4,825 .... B4
Coke 3,196 .... D6
Coleman 10,439 .... E6
Collin 144,576 .... H4
Collingsworth 4,648 .... D3
Colorado 18,823 .... H8
Comal 36,446 .... F8
Comanche 12,617 .... F5
Concho 2,915 .... E6
Cooke 27,656 .... G4
Coryell 56,767 .... G6
Cottle 2,947 .... D3
Crane 4,600 .... B6
Crockett 4,608 .... C7
Crosby 8,859 .... C4
Culberson 3,315 .... C11
Dallam 6,531 .... B1
Dallas 1,556,390 .... H5
Dawson 16,184 .... C5
Deaf Smith 21,165 .... B3
Delta 4,839 .... J4
Denton 143,126 .... G4
De Witt 18,903 .... G9
Dickens 3,539 .... D4
Dimmit 11,367 .... E9
Donley 4,075 .... D2
Duval 12,517 .... F10
Eastland 19,480 .... F5
Ector 115,374 .... B6
Edwards 2,033 .... D7
Ellis 59,743 .... H5
El Paso 479,899 .... A10
Erath 22,560 .... F5
Falls 17,946 .... H6
Fannin 24,285 .... H4
Fayette 18,832 .... H8
Fisher 5,891 .... D5
Floyd 9,834 .... C3
Foard 2,158 .... E3
Fort Bend 130,846 .... J8
Franklin 6,893 .... J4
Freestone 14,830 .... H6
Frio 13,785 .... E9
Gaines 13,150 .... B5
Galveston 195,940 .... K8
Garza 5,336 .... C4
Gillespie 13,532 .... F7
Glasscock 1,304 .... C6
Goliad 5,193 .... G9
Gonzales 15,949 .... G8
Gray 26,386 .... D2
Grayson 89,796 .... H4
Gregg 99,495 .... K5
Grimes 13,580 .... J7
Guadalupe 46,708 .... G8
Hale 37,592 .... C3
Hall 5,594 .... D3
Hamilton 8,297 .... F6
Hansford 6,209 .... C1
Hardeman 6,368 .... E3
Hardin 40,721 .... K7
Harris 2,409,547 .... J8
Harrison 52,265 .... K5
Hartley 3,987 .... B2
Haskell 7,725 .... E4
Hays 40,594 .... F7
Hemphill 5,304 .... D2
Henderson 42,606 .... J5
Hidalgo 283,323 .... F11
Hill 25,024 .... G5
Hockley 23,230 .... B4
Hood 17,714 .... G5
Hopkins 25,247 .... J4
Houston 22,299 .... J6
Howard 33,142 .... C5
Hudspeth 2,728 .... B10
Hunt 55,248 .... H4
Hutchinson 26,304 .... C2
Irion 1,386 .... C6
Jack 7,408 .... F4
Jackson 13,352 .... H9
Jasper 30,781 .... K7
Jeff Davis 1,647 .... C11
Jefferson 250,938 .... K8
Jim Hogg 5,168 .... F11
Jim Wells 36,498 .... F10
Johnson 67,649 .... G5
Jones 17,268 .... E5
Karnes 13,593 .... G9
Kaufman 39,029 .... H5
Kendall 10,635 .... F8
Kenedy 543 .... G11
Kent 1,145 .... D4
Kerr 28,780 .... E7
Kimble 4,063 .... E7
King 425 .... D4
Kinney 2,279 .... D8
Kleberg 33,358 .... G10
Knox 5,329 .... E4
Lamar 42,156 .... J4
Lamb 18,669 .... B3
Lampasas 12,005 .... F6
La Salle 5,514 .... E9
Lavaca 19,004 .... H8
Lee 10,952 .... H7
Leon 9,594 .... J6
Liberty 47,088 .... K7
Limestone 20,224 .... H6
Lipscomb 3,766 .... D1
Live Oak 9,606 .... F9
Llano 10,144 .... F7
Loving 91 .... A6
Lubbock 211,651 .... C4
Lynn 8,605 .... C4
Madison 10,649 .... J6
Marion 10,360 .... K5
Martin 4,684 .... C5
Mason 3,683 .... E7
Matagorda 37,828 .... H9
Maverick 31,398 .... D9
McCulloch 8,735 .... E6
McLennan 170,755 .... G6
McMullen 789 .... F9
Medina 23,164 .... E8
Menard 2,346 .... E7
Midland 82,636 .... B6
Milam 22,732 .... H7
Mills 4,477 .... F6
Mitchell 9,088 .... D5
Montague 17,410 .... G4
Montgomery 128,487 .... J7
Moore 16,575 .... C2
Morris 14,629 .... K4

AREA 266,807 sq. mi. (691,030 sq. km.)
POPULATION 14,229,288
CAPITAL Austin
LARGEST CITY Houston
HIGHEST POINT Guadalupe Pk. 8,749 ft. (2667 m.)
SETTLED IN 1686
ADMITTED TO UNION December 29, 1845
POPULAR NAME Lone Star State
STATE FLOWER Bluebonnet
STATE BIRD Mockingbird

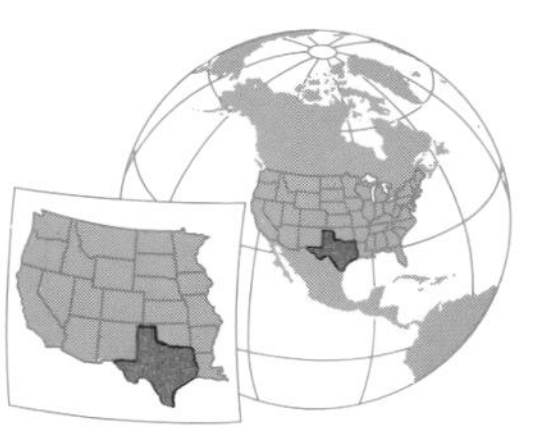

Motley 1,950 .... D3
Nacogdoches 46,786 .... K6
Navarro 35,323 .... H5
Newton 13,254 .... L7
Nolan 17,359 .... D5
Nueces 268,215 .... G10
Ochiltree 9,588 .... D1
Oldham 2,283 .... B2
Orange 83,838 .... L7
Palo Pinto 24,062 .... F5
Panola 20,724 .... K5
Parker 44,609 .... G5
Parmer 11,038 .... B3
Pecos 14,618 .... B7
Polk 24,407 .... K7
Potter 98,637 .... C2
Presidio 5,188 .... C12
Rains 4,839 .... J5
Randall 75,062 .... C2
Reagan 4,135 .... C6
Real 2,469 .... E8
Red River 16,101 .... J4
Reeves 15,801 .... D11
Refugio 9,289 .... G9
Roberts 1,187 .... D2
Robertson 14,653 .... H6
Rockwall 14,528 .... H5
Runnels 11,872 .... E6
Rusk 41,382 .... K5
Sabine 8,702 .... L6
San Augustine 8,785 .... K6
San Jacinto 11,434 .... J7
San Patricio 58,013 .... G10
San Saba 6,204 .... F6
Schleicher 2,820 .... D7
Scurry 18,192 .... D5
Shackelford 3,915 .... E5
Shelby 23,084 .... K6
Sherman 3,174 .... C1
Smith 128,366 .... J5
Somervell 4,154 .... G5
Starr 27,266 .... F11
Stephens 9,926 .... F5
Sterling 1,206 .... C6
Stonewall 2,406 .... D4
Sutton 5,130 .... D7
Swisher 9,723 .... C3
Tarrant 860,880 .... G5
Taylor 110,932 .... E5
Terrell 1,595 .... B7
Terry 14,581 .... B4
Throckmorton 2,053 .... E4
Titus 21,442 .... K4
Tom Green 84,784 .... D6
Travis 419,573 .... G7
Trinity 9,450 .... J6
Tyler 16,223 .... K7
Upshur 28,595 .... K5
Upton 4,619 .... B6
Uvalde 22,441 .... E8
Val Verde 35,910 .... C8
Van Zandt 31,426 .... J5
Victoria 68,807 .... H9
Walker 41,789 .... J7
Waller 19,798 .... J8
Ward 13,976 .... A6
Washington 21,998 .... H7
Webb 99,258 .... E10
Wharton 40,242 .... H8
Wheeler 7,137 .... D2
Wichita 121,082 .... F3
Wilbarger 15,931 .... E3
Willacy 17,495 .... G11
Williamson 76,507 .... G7
Wilson 16,756 .... F8
Winkler 9,944 .... A6
Wise 26,575 .... G4
Wood 24,697 .... J5
Yoakum 8,299 .... B4
Young 19,083 .... F4
Zapata 6,628 .... E11
Zavala 11,666 .... E9

CITIES and TOWNS

Zip Name/Pop. Key

*79601 Abilene⊙ 98,315 .... E5
Abilene‡ 139,192 .... E5
78516 Alamo 5,831 .... F11
78209 Alamo Heights 6,252 .... K10
76430 Albany⊙ 2,450 .... E5
78332 Alice⊙ 20,961 .... F10
75002 Allen 8,314 .... H1
79830 Alpine⊙ 5,465 .... D12
77511 Alvin 16,515 .... J3
*79101 Amarillo⊙ 149,230 .... C2
Amarillo‡ 173,699 .... C2
77514 Anahuac⊙ 1,840 .... K8
77830 Anderson⊙ 500 .... J7
79714 Andrews⊙ 11,061 .... B5
77515 Angleton⊙ 13,929 .... J8
79501 Anson⊙ 2,831 .... E5
78336 Aransas Pass 7,173 .... G10
76351 Archer City⊙ 1,862 .... F4
*76010 Arlington 160,123 .... F2
79502 Aspermont⊙ 1,357 .... D4
75751 Athens⊙ 10,197 .... J5
75551 Atlanta 6,272 .... K4
*78701 Austin (cap.)⊙ 345,496 .... G7
Austin‡ 536,450 .... G7
76020 Azle 5,822 .... E2
77518 Bacliff 4,851 .... K2
79504 Baird⊙ 1,696 .... E5
75180 Balch Springs 13,746 .... H2
†78201 Balcones Heights 2,511 .... J10
76821 Ballinger⊙ 4,207 .... E6
78003 Bandera⊙ 947 .... F8
77532 Barrett 3,183 .... K1
78602 Bastrop⊙ 3,789 .... G7
77414 Bay City⊙ 17,837 .... H9
77520 Baytown 56,923 .... L2
*77701 Beaumont⊙ 118,102 .... K7
Beaumont-Port Arthur-Orange‡ 375,497 .... K7
76021 Bedford 20,821 .... F2
78102 Beeville⊙ 14,574 .... G9
77401 Bellaire 14,950 .... J2
76704 Bellmead 7,569 .... H6
77418 Bellville⊙ 2,860 .... H8
76513 Belton⊙ 10,660 .... G7
76126 Benbrook 13,579 .... E2
79505 Benjamin⊙ 257 .... E4
76932 Big Lake⊙ 3,404 .... C6
79720 Big Spring⊙ 24,804 .... C5
78006 Boerne⊙ 3,229 .... J10
75418 Bonham⊙ 7,338 .... H4
79007 Borger 15,837 .... C2
75557 Boston⊙ 400 .... K4
76230 Bowie 5,610 .... G4
78832 Brackettville⊙ 1,676 .... D8
76825 Brady⊙ 5,969 .... E6
77422 Brazoria 3,025 .... J9
76024 Breckenridge⊙ 6,921 .... F5
77833 Brenham⊙ 10,966 .... H7
77611 Bridge City 7,667 .... L7
79316 Brownfield⊙ 10,387 .... B4
*78520 Brownsville⊙ 84,997 .... G12
Brownsville-Harlingen-San Benito‡ 209,680 .... G12
76801 Brownwood⊙ 19,396 .... F6
77801 Bryan⊙ 44,337 .... H7
Bryan-College Station‡ 93,588 .... H7
76354 Burkburnett 10,668 .... F3
76028 Burleson 11,734 .... F3
78611 Burnet⊙ 3,410 .... F7
77836 Caldwell⊙ 2,953 .... H7
76520 Cameron⊙ 5,721 .... H7
79014 Canadian⊙ 3,491 .... D2
75103 Canton⊙ 2,845 .... J5
79015 Canyon⊙ 10,724 .... C3
78834 Carrizo Springs⊙ 6,886 .... E9
*75006 Carrollton 40,595 .... G2
75633 Carthage⊙ 6,447 .... K5
†78213 Castle Hills 4,773 .... J10
75104 Cedar Hill 6,849 .... G3
75935 Center⊙ 5,827 .... K6
75833 Centerville⊙ 799 .... H6
77530 Channelview 17,471 .... K1
79018 Channing⊙ 304 .... B2
79201 Childress⊙ 5,817 .... D3
76437 Cisco 4,517 .... E5
79226 Clarendon⊙ 2,220 .... C3
75426 Clarksville⊙ 4,917 .... K4
79019 Claude⊙ 1,112 .... C2
†77565 Clear Lake Shores 755 .... K2
76031 Cleburne⊙ 19,218 .... G5
77327 Cleveland 5,977 .... K7
77531 Clute 9,577 .... J9
77331 Coldspring⊙ 569 .... J7
76834 Coleman⊙ 5,960 .... E6
77840 College Station 37,272 .... H7
76034 Colleyville 6,700 .... F2
79512 Colorado City⊙ 5,405 .... C5
78934 Columbus⊙ 3,923 .... H8
76442 Comanche⊙ 4,075 .... F6
75428 Commerce 8,136 .... J4
*77301 Conroe⊙ 18,034 .... J7
78109 Converse 5,150 .... K11
75432 Cooper⊙ 2,338 .... J4
76522 Copperas Cove 19,469 .... G6
*78401 Corpus Christi⊙ 231,999 .... G10
Corpus Christi‡ 326,228 .... G10
75110 Corsicana⊙ 21,712 .... H5
78014 Cotulla⊙ 3,912 .... E9
79731 Crane⊙ 3,622 .... B6
75835 Crockett⊙ 7,405 .... J6
79322 Crosbyton⊙ 2,289 .... C4
79227 Crowell⊙ 1,509 .... E4
76036 Crowley 5,852 .... E3
78839 Crystal City⊙ 8,334 .... E9
77954 Cuero⊙ 7,124 .... G8
75638 Daingerfield⊙ 3,030 .... K4
79022 Dalhart⊙ 6,854 .... B1
*75201 Dallas⊙ 904,078 .... G2
Dallas-Ft. Worth‡ 2,974,878 .... G2
77535 Dayton 4,908 .... J7
76234 Decatur⊙ 4,104 .... G4
77536 Deer Park 22,648 .... K2
76444 De Leon 2,478 .... F5
78840 Del Rio⊙ 30,034 .... D8
75020 Denison 23,884 .... H4
76201 Denton⊙ 48,063 .... G4

(continued on following page)

Agriculture, Industry and Resources

DOMINANT LAND USE

- Wheat, Grain Sorghums, Range Livestock
- Cotton, Wheat
- Specialized Cotton
- Cotton, General Farming
- Cotton, Forest Products
- Cotton, Range Livestock
- Rice, General Farming
- Peanuts, General Farming
- General Farming, Livestock, Cash Grain
- General Farming, Forest Products, Truck Farming, Cotton
- Fruit, Truck and Mixed Farming
- Range Livestock
- Forests
- Swampland, Limited Agriculture
- Nonagricultural Land
- Urban Areas

MAJOR MINERAL OCCURRENCES

At	Asphalt	He	Helium
Cl	Clay	Ls	Limestone
Fe	Iron Ore	Na	Salt
G	Natural Gas	O	Petroleum
Gn	Granite	S	Sulfur
Gp	Gypsum	Tc	Talc
Gr	Graphite	U	Uranium

Water Power
Major Industrial Areas

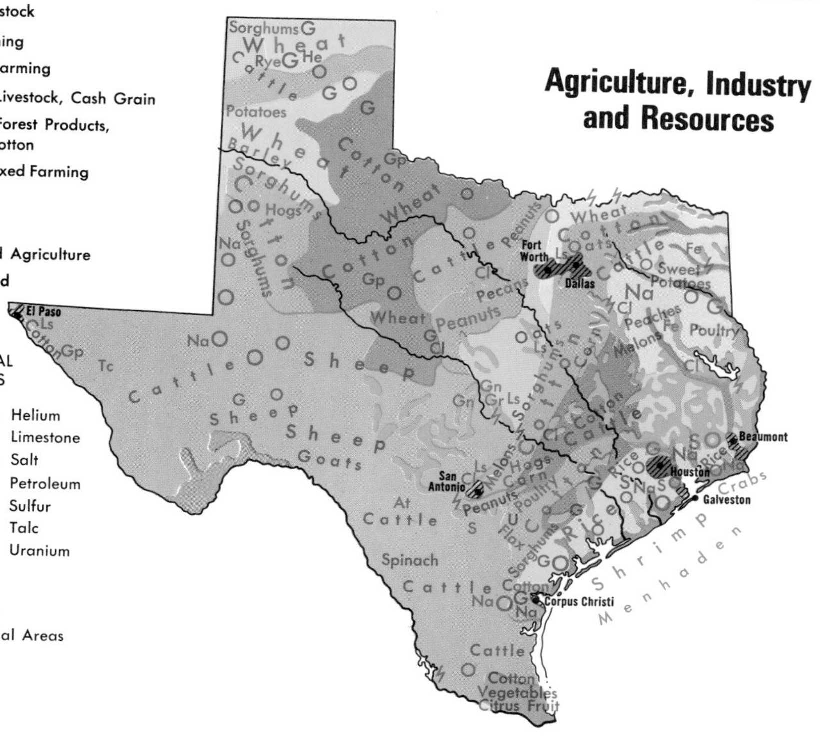

79323 Denver City 4,704 .... B4
75115 De Soto 15,538 .... G3
78016 Devine 3,756 .... E8
75941 Diboll 5,227 .... K6
79229 Dickens⊙ 409 .... D4
77539 Dickinson 7,505 .... K3
79027 Dimmitt⊙ 5,019 .... B3
78537 Donna 9,952 .... F11
79029 Dumas⊙ 12,194 .... C2
75116 Duncanville 27,781 .... G3
78852 Eagle Pass⊙ 21,407 .... D9
76448 Eastland⊙ 3,747 .... F5
78539 Edinburg⊙ 24,075 .... F11
77957 Edna⊙ 5,650 .... H9
77437 El Campo 10,462 .... H8
76936 Eldorado⊙ 2,061 .... D7
78621 Elgin 4,535 .... G7
*79901 El Paso⊙ 425,259 .... A10
El Paso‡ 479,899 .... A10
78543 Elsa 5,061 .... G11
75440 Emory⊙ 813 .... J5
75119 Ennis 12,110 .... H5
76039 Euless 24,002 .... F2
76140 Everman 5,387 .... F3
79838 Fabens 4,285 .... B10
75840 Fairfield⊙ 3,505 .... H6
78355 Falfurrias⊙ 6,103 .... F10
75234 Farmers Branch 24,863 .... G2
79325 Farwell⊙ 1,354 .... A3
78114 Floresville⊙ 4,381 .... K11
†75067 Flower Mound 4,402 .... F1
79235 Floydada⊙ 4,193 .... C3
†76119 Forest Hill 11,684 .... F2
79734 Fort Davis⊙ 900 .... D11
79735 Fort Stockton⊙ 8,688 .... A7
*76101 Fort Worth⊙ 385,164 .... F2
77856 Franklin⊙ 1,349 .... H7
78624 Fredericksburg⊙ 6,412 .... E7
76842 Fredonia 50 .... E7
77541 Freeport 13,444 .... J9
77546 Friendswood 10,719 .... J2
79035 Friona 3,809 .... B3
75034 Frisco 3,499 .... H4
79738 Gail⊙ 171 .... C5
76240 Gainesville⊙ 14,081 .... G4
77547 Galena Park 9,879 .... J1
*77550 Galveston⊙ 61,902 .... L3
Galveston-Texas City‡ 195,940 .... L3
79739 Garden City⊙ 350 .... C6
*75040 Garland 138,857 .... H2
76528 Gatesville⊙ 6,260 .... G6
78626 Georgetown⊙ 9,468 .... G7
78022 George West⊙ 2,627 .... F9
78942 Giddings⊙ 3,950 .... H7
75644 Gilmer⊙ 5,167 .... J5
75647 Gladewater 6,548 .... K5
76043 Glen Rose⊙ 2,075 .... G5
76844 Goldthwaite⊙ 1,783 .... F6
77963 Goliad⊙ 1,990 .... G9
78629 Gonzales⊙ 7,152 .... G8
76046 Graham⊙ 9,170 .... F4
76048 Granbury⊙ 3,332 .... G5
*75050 Grand Prairie 71,462 .... G2
76051 Grapevine 11,801 .... F2
75401 Greenville⊙ 22,161 .... H4
76642 Groesbeck⊙ 3,373 .... H6
77619 Groves 17,090 .... L8
75845 Groveton⊙ 1,262 .... J7
79236 Guthrie⊙ 170 .... D4
77964 Hallettsville⊙ 2,865 .... G8
76117 Haltom City 29,014 .... F2
76531 Hamilton⊙ 3,189 .... G6
78550 Harlingen 43,543 .... G11
79521 Haskell⊙ 3,782 .... E4
77859 Hearne 5,418 .... H7
78361 Hebbronville⊙ 4,684 .... F10
75948 Hemphill⊙ 1,353 .... L6
77445 Hempstead⊙ 3,456 .... J7
75652 Henderson⊙ 11,473 .... K5
76365 Henrietta⊙ 3,149 .... F4
79045 Hereford⊙ 15,853 .... B3
†75201 Highland Park 8,909 .... G2
77562 Highlands 6,467 .... K1
76645 Hillsboro⊙ 7,397 .... G5
77563 Hitchcock 6,655 .... K3
78861 Hondo⊙ 6,057 .... E8
*77001 Houston⊙ 1,595,138 .... J2
Houston‡ 2,905,350 .... J2
*77338 Humble 6,729 .... J7
†77001 Hunters Creek Village 4,215 .... J1
77340 Huntsville⊙ 23,936 .... J7
76053 Hurst 31,420 .... F2
76367 Iowa Park 6,184 .... F4
*75061 Irving 109,943 .... G2
77029 Jacinto City 8,953 .... J1
76056 Jacksboro⊙ 4,000 .... F4
75766 Jacksonville 12,264 .... J5
75951 Jasper⊙ 6,959 .... L7
79528 Jayton⊙ 638 .... D4
75657 Jefferson⊙ 2,643 .... K5
†77001 Jersey Village 4,084 .... J1
78636 Johnson City⊙ 872 .... F7
78026 Jourdanton⊙ 2,743 .... F9
76849 Junction⊙ 2,593 .... E7
78118 Karnes City⊙ 3,296 .... G9
77450 Katy 5,660 .... J8
75142 Kaufman⊙ 4,658 .... H5
76248 Keller 4,156 .... F2
78119 Kenedy 4,356 .... G9
79745 Kermit⊙ 8,015 .... B6
78028 Kerrville⊙ 15,276 .... E7
75662 Kilgore 11,006 .... K5
76541 Killeen 46,296 .... G6
Killeen-Temple‡ 214,656 .... G6
78363 Kingsville⊙ 28,808 .... G10
†78109 Kirby 6,435 .... K11
77625 Kountze⊙ 2,716 .... K7
78945 La Grange⊙ 3,768 .... G8
77566 Lake Jackson 19,102 .... J8
76135 Lake Worth 4,394 .... E2
77568 La Marque 15,372 .... K3
79331 Lamesa⊙ 11,790 .... C5
76550 Lampasas⊙ 6,165 .... F6
*75146 Lancaster 14,807 .... G3
77571 La Porte 14,062 .... K2

*78040 Laredo⊙ 91,449 .... E10
Laredo‡ 99,258 .... E10
77573 League City 16,578 .... K2
78873 Leakey⊙ 468 .... E8
†78201 Leon Valley 9,088 .... J10
79336 Levelland⊙ 13,809 .... B4
*75067 Lewisville 24,273 .... G1
77575 Liberty⊙ 7,945 .... K7
75563 Linden⊙ 2,443 .... K4
79056 Lipscomb⊙ 52 .... D1
79339 Littlefield⊙ 7,409 .... B4
†78201 Live Oak 8,183 .... K10
77351 Livingston⊙ 4,928 .... K7
78643 Llano⊙ 3,071 .... F7
78644 Lockhart⊙ 7,953 .... G8
79241 Lockney 2,334 .... C3
*75601 Longview⊙ 62,762 .... K5
Longview-Marshall‡ 151,752 .... K5
*79401 Lubbock⊙ 173,979 .... C4
Lubbock‡ 211,651 .... C4
75901 Lufkin⊙ 28,562 .... K6
78648 Luling 5,039 .... G8
77864 Madisonville⊙ 3,660 .... J7
76063 Mansfield 8,092 .... F3
77578 Manvel 3,549 .... J3
79843 Marfa⊙ 2,466 .... C12
76661 Marlin⊙ 7,099 .... H6
75670 Marshall⊙ 24,921 .... K5
76856 Mason⊙ 2,153 .... E7
79244 Matador⊙ 1,052 .... D3
78368 Mathis 5,667 .... G9
78501 McAllen 66,281 .... F11
McAllen-Pharr-Edinburg‡ 283,229 .... F11
76657 McGregor 4,513 .... G6
75069 McKinney⊙ 16,256 .... H4
†77520 McNair K1
79245 Memphis⊙ 3,352 .... D3
76859 Menard⊙ 1,697 .... E7
79754 Mentone⊙ 50 .... D10
78570 Mercedes 11,851 .... F12
76665 Meridian⊙ 1,330 .... G6
76941 Mertzon⊙ 687 .... C6
*75149 Mesquite 67,053 .... H2
76667 Mexia 7,094 .... H6
79059 Miami⊙ 813 .... D2
*79701 Midland⊙ 70,525 .... C6
Midland‡ 82,636 .... C6
76065 Midlothian 3,219 .... G5
75773 Mineola 4,346 .... J5
76067 Mineral Wells 14,468 .... F5
78572 Mission 22,653 .... F11
77459 Missouri City 24,533 .... J2
79756 Monahans⊙ 8,397 .... B6
76251 Montague⊙ 1,253 .... G4
79346 Morton⊙ 2,674 .... B4
75455 Mount Pleasant⊙ 11,003 .... K4
75457 Mount Vernon⊙ 2,025 .... J4
79347 Muleshoe⊙ 4,842 .... B3
75961 Nacogdoches⊙ 27,149 .... J6
†77598 Nassau Bay 4,526 .... K2
77868 Navasota 5,971 .... J7
77627 Nederland 16,855 .... K8
75570 New Boston 4,628 .... K4
78130 New Braunfels⊙ 22,402 .... K10
75966 Newton⊙ 1,620 .... L7
76118 North Richland Hills 30,592 .... F2
79760 Odessa⊙ 90,027 .... B6
Odessa‡ 115,374 .... B6
76374 Olney 4,060 .... F4
77630 Orange⊙ 23,628 .... L7
76943 Ozona⊙ 3,766 .... C7
79248 Paducah⊙ 2,216 .... D4
76866 Paint Rock⊙ 256 .... E6
77465 Palacios 4,667 .... H9
75801 Palestine⊙ 15,948 .... J6
76072 Palo Pinto⊙ 350 .... F5
79065 Pampa⊙ 21,396 .... D2
79068 Panhandle⊙ 2,226 .... C2
75460 Paris⊙ 25,498 .... J4
*77501 Pasadena 112,560 .... J2
77581 Pearland 13,248 .... J2
78061 Pearsall⊙ 7,383 .... E9
79772 Pecos⊙ 12,855 .... D10
79070 Perryton⊙ 7,991 .... D1
78577 Pharr 21,381 .... F11
75686 Pittsburg⊙ 4,245 .... J4
79355 Plains⊙ 1,457 .... B4
79072 Plainview⊙ 22,187 .... C3
75074 Plano 72,331 .... G1
78064 Pleasanton 6,346 .... F9
77640 Port Arthur 61,251 .... K8
78578 Port Isabel 3,769 .... G11
78374 Portland 12,023 .... G10
77979 Port Lavaca⊙ 10,911 .... H9
77651 Port Neches 13,944 .... K7
79356 Post⊙ 3,961 .... C4
78065 Poteet 3,086 .... F8
77445 Prairie View 3,993 .... J7
79845 Presidio 1,723 .... C12
79252 Quanah⊙ 3,890 .... E3
76470 Ranger 3,142 .... F5
79778 Rankin⊙ 1,216 .... B6
78580 Raymondville⊙ 9,493 .... G11
78377 Refugio⊙ 3,898 .... G9
75080 Richardson 72,496 .... G2
76118 Richland Hills 7,977 .... F2
77469 Richmond⊙ 9,692 .... J8
78582 Rio Grande City⊙ 8,930 .... F11
77019 River Oaks 6,890 .... E2
76945 Robert Lee⊙ 1,202 .... D6
78380 Robstown 12,100 .... G10
79543 Roby⊙ 814 .... D5
76567 Rockdale 5,611 .... G7
78382 Rockport⊙ 3,686 .... H9
78880 Rocksprings⊙ 1,317 .... D8
75087 Rockwall⊙ 5,939 .... H5
78584 Roma-Los Saenz 3,384 .... E11
77471 Rosenberg 17,995 .... J8
78664 Round Rock 12,740 .... G7
75088 Rowlett 7,522 .... H2
75785 Rusk⊙ 4,681 .... J6
76179 Saginaw 5,736 .... E2
*76901 San Angelo⊙ 73,240 .... D6
San Angelo‡ 84,784 .... D6

Topography

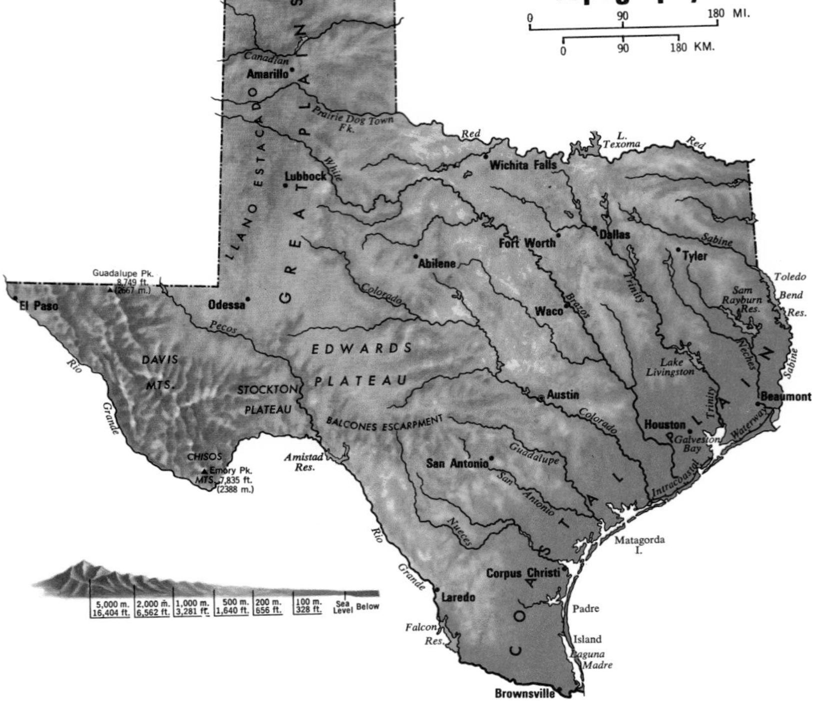

*78201 San Antonio⊙ 786,023 .... J11
San Antonio‡ 1,071,954 .... J11
75972 San Augustine⊙ 2,930 .... K6
78586 San Benito 17,988 .... G12
79848 Sanderson⊙ 1,241 .... B7
78384 San Diego⊙ 5,225 .... F10
76266 Sanger 2,574 .... G4
78589 San Juan 7,608 .... F11
78666 San Marcos⊙ 23,420 .... F8
76877 San Saba⊙ 2,847 .... F6
†76101 Sansom Park Village 3,921 .... E2
†77510 Santa Fe 6,172 .... K3
78385 Sarita⊙ 200 .... G10
78154 Schertz 7,262 .... K10
77586 Seabrook 4,670 .... K2
75159 Seagoville 7,304 .... H3
77474 Sealy 3,875 .... H8
78155 Seguin⊙ 17,854 .... G8
79360 Seminole⊙ 6,080 .... B5
†78357 Seven Sisters 2 .... F9
76380 Seymour⊙ 3,657 .... E4
75090 Sherman⊙ 30,413 .... H4
Sherman-Denison‡ 89,796 .... H4
79851 Sierra Blanca⊙ 800 .... B11
77656 Silsbee 7,684 .... K7
79257 Silverton⊙ 918 .... C3
78387 Sinton⊙ 6,044 .... G9
79364 Slaton 6,804 .... C4
78957 Smithville 3,470 .... G7
79549 Snyder⊙ 12,705 .... D5
76950 Sonora⊙ 3,856 .... D7
77587 South Houston 13,293 .... J2
79081 Spearman⊙ 3,413 .... C1
*77373 Spring J7
†77001 Spring Valley 3,353 .... J1
77477 Stafford 4,755 .... J2
79553 Stamford 4,542 .... E5
79782 Stanton⊙ 2,314 .... C5
76401 Stephenville⊙ 11,881 .... F5
76951 Sterling City⊙ 915 .... D6
79083 Stinnett⊙ 2,222 .... C2
79084 Stratford⊙ 1,917 .... C1
77478 Sugar Land 8,826 .... J8
75482 Sulphur Springs⊙ 12,804 .... J4
77480 Sweeny 3,538 .... J8
79556 Sweetwater⊙ 12,242 .... D5
78390 Taft 3,686 .... G9
79373 Tahoka⊙ 3,262 .... C4
76574 Taylor 10,619 .... G7
†77586 Taylor Lake Village 3,669 .... K2
75860 Teague 3,390 .... H6
76501 Temple 42,354 .... G6
79852 Terlingua 100 .... D12
75160 Terrell 13,269 .... H5
†78201 Terrell Hills 4,644 .... K11
*75501 Texarkana 31,271 .... L4
Texarkana, Tex.-Texarkana, Ark.‡ 27,019 .... L4
77590 Texas City 41,403 .... K3
73949 Texhoma 358 .... C1
The Colony 11,586 .... G1
76083 Throckmorton⊙ 1,174 .... F4
78072 Tilden⊙ 450 .... F9
77375 Tomball 3,996 .... J7
75862 Trinity 2,620 .... J7
79088 Tulia⊙ 5,033 .... C3
*75701 Tyler⊙ 70,508 .... J5
Tyler‡ 128,366 .... J5
78148 Universal City 10,720 .... K10
†75205 University Park 22,254 .... G2
78801 Uvalde⊙ 14,178 .... E8
75095 Van Alstyne 1,860 .... H4

79855 Van Horn⊙ 2,772 .... C11
79092 Vega⊙ 900 .... B2
76384 Vernon⊙ 12,695 .... E3
77901 Victoria⊙ 50,695 .... H9
Victoria‡ 68,807 .... H9
77662 Vidor 11,834 .... L7
*76701 Waco⊙ 101,261 .... G6
Waco‡ 170,755 .... G6
75501 Wake Village 3,865 .... K4
75165 Waxahachie⊙ 14,624 .... H5
76086 Weatherford⊙ 12,049 .... G5
79095 Wellington⊙ 3,043 .... D3
78596 Weslaco 19,331 .... F11
77486 West Columbia 4,109 .... J8
77630 West Orange 4,610 .... L7
†77005 West University Place 12,010 .... J2
†76101 Westworth 3,651 .... E2
77488 Wharton⊙ 9,033 .... J8
79096 Wheeler⊙ 1,584 .... D2
75693 White Oak 4,415 .... K5
76273 Whitesboro 3,197 .... H4
76108 White Settlement 13,508 .... E2
*76301 Wichita Falls⊙ 94,201 .... F4
Wichita Falls‡ 130,664 .... F4
†78201 Windcrest 5,332 .... K11
75494 Winnsboro 3,458 .... J5
79567 Winters 3,061 .... E6
75979 Woodville⊙ 2,821 .... K7
75098 Wylie 3,152 .... H1
78076 Zapata⊙ 3,831 .... E11

OTHER FEATURES

Amistad (res.) C8
Amistad Nat'l Rec. Area D8
Angelina (riv.) K6
Apache (mts.) C11
Aransas (passage) H10
Arlington (lake) F2
Baffin (bay) G10
Balcones Escarpment (plat.) E8
Beals (creek) C5
Benbrook (lake) E3
Bergstrom A.F.B. G7
Big Bend Nat'l Park A8
Bolivar (pen.) K8
Brazos (riv.) H7
Brownwood (lake) E6
Buchanan (lake) F7
Buck (creek) D3
Caddo (lake) L5
Canadian (riv.) D1
Carrizo (creek) A1
Carswell A.F.B. E2
Cathedral (mt.) D12
Cavallo (passage) H9
Cedar (lake) B5
Cerro Alto (mt.) B10
Chamizal Nat'l Mem. A10
Chase N.A.S. G9
Chinati (mts.) C12
Chinati (peak) C12
Chisos (mts.) A8
Cibolo (creek) K11
Clear Fork, Brazos (riv.) D5
Coldwater (creek) B1
Colorado (riv.) F7
Copano (bay) G9
Corpus Christi (lake) F9
Corpus Christi N.A.S. G10
Cottonwood Draw (dry riv.) C10
Davis (mts.) C11
Deep (creek) C5
Delaware (creek) C10
Delaware (mts.) C10
Denison (dam) H4
Devils (riv.) D7
Diablo, Sierra (mts.) C10
Double Mountain Fork, Brazos (riv.) C4
Dyess A.F.B. D5
Eagle (peak) C11
Eagle Mountain (lake) E2
Edwards (plat.) C7
Elephant (mt.) D12
Ellington A.F.B. K2
Elm Fork, Trinity (riv.) G2
Emory (peak) A8
Falcon (res.) E11
Finlay (mts.) B10
Fort Bliss 12,687 .... A10
Fort Davis Nat'l Hist. Site D11
Fort Hood 31,250 .... G6
Frio (riv.) E8
Galveston (bay) L2
Galveston (isl.) K8
Glass (mts.) A7
Goodfellow A.F.B. D6
Grapevine (lake) F2
Guadalupe (mts.) C10
Guadalupe (peak) B10
Guadalupe (riv.) G8
Guadalupe Mts. Nat'l Park C10
Houston (lake) J8
Houston Ship (chan.) K2
Howard (creek) C7
Hubbard Creek (lake) F5
Hueco (mts.) B10
Intracoastal Waterway J9
Johnson Draw (dry riv.) C7
Kelly A.F.B. J11
Kemp (lake) E4
Kingsville N.A.S. G10
Kiowa (creek) D1
Lackland A.F.B. 14,459 .... J11
Lake Meredith Nat'l Rec. Area C2
Lampasas (riv.) G6
Laughlin A.F.B. 2,994 .... D8
Lavon (lake) H1
Leon (riv.) F6
Livermore (mt.) C11
Livingston (lake) K7
Llano (riv.) D7
Llano Estacado (plain) B4
Locke (mt.) D11
Los Olmos (creek) F10
Los Olmos (creek) F11
Lyndon B. Johnson Nat'l Hist. Site F7
Lyndon B. Johnson Space Ctr. K2
Madre (lag.) G11
Maravillas (creek) A7
Matagorda (bay) H9
Matagorda (isl.) H9
Matagorda (pen.) J9
Matagorda Isl. Bombing and Gunnery Range H9
Medina (lake) E8
Medina (riv.) J11
Mexico (gulf) K9
Middle Concho (riv.) C6
Mountain Creek (lake) G2
Mustang (creek) A1
Mustang (isl.) G10
Mustang Draw (dry riv.) B5
Navasota (riv.) H7
Navidad (riv.) H8
Neches (riv.) K6
North Concho (riv.) C6
North Pease (riv.) D3
Nueces (riv.) F9
Padre (isl.) G10
Padre Island Nat'l Seashore G11
Palo Duro (creek) B2
Palo Duro (creek) C1
Pease (riv.) D3
Pecos (riv.) C7
Pedernales (riv.) F7
Possum Kingdom (lake) F5
Prairie Dog Town Fork, Red (riv.) C3
Quitman (mts.) B11
Red (riv.) F3
Red Bluff (lake) A6
Reese A.F.B. 1,934 .... B4
Rio Grande (riv.) D9
Rita Blanca (creek) B2
Sabine (riv.) L7
Salt Fork, Red (riv.) D3
Sam Rayburn (res.) K6
San Antonio (bay) H9
San Antonio (mt.) B10
San Antonio Missions Nat'l Hist. Park J11
San Francisco (creek) B8
San Luis (passage) K8
San Martine Draw (dry riv.) C11
San Saba (riv.) D7
Santa Isabel (creek) E10
Santiago (mts.) A8
Santiago (peak) D12
Sheppard A.F.B. F3
Sierra Diablo (mts.) C10
Sierra Vieja (mts.) C11
Staked (Llano Estacado) (plain) B4
Stamford (lake) E4
Stockton (plat.) B7
Sulphur (riv.) J4
Sulphur Draw (dry riv.) B4
Sulphur Springs (creek) B4
Tenmile (creek) G3
Terlingua (creek) D12
Texoma (lake) H3
Tierra Blanca (creek) B3
Toledo Bend (res.) L6
Toyah (creek) A6
Toyah (lake) A6
Travis (lake) G7
Trinity (bay) L2
Trinity (riv.) H5
Trinity, West Fork (riv.) G2
Trujillo (creek) A2
Vieja, Sierra (mts.) C11
Walnut (creek) F3
Washita (riv.) D2
West (bay) K3
White (riv.) C3
White River (lake) C4
White Rock (creek) G2
Wichita (riv.) F4
Wolf (creek) D1
Worth (lake) E2

⊙County seat.
‡Population of metropolitan area.
† Zip of nearest p.o. * Multiple zips.

Texas

State Capitals .... ⊛
County Seats .... ⊙
Major Limited Access Hwys. ─────

© Copyright HAMMOND INCORPORATED, Maplewood, N.J.

Western Part of Texas
Same scale as main map

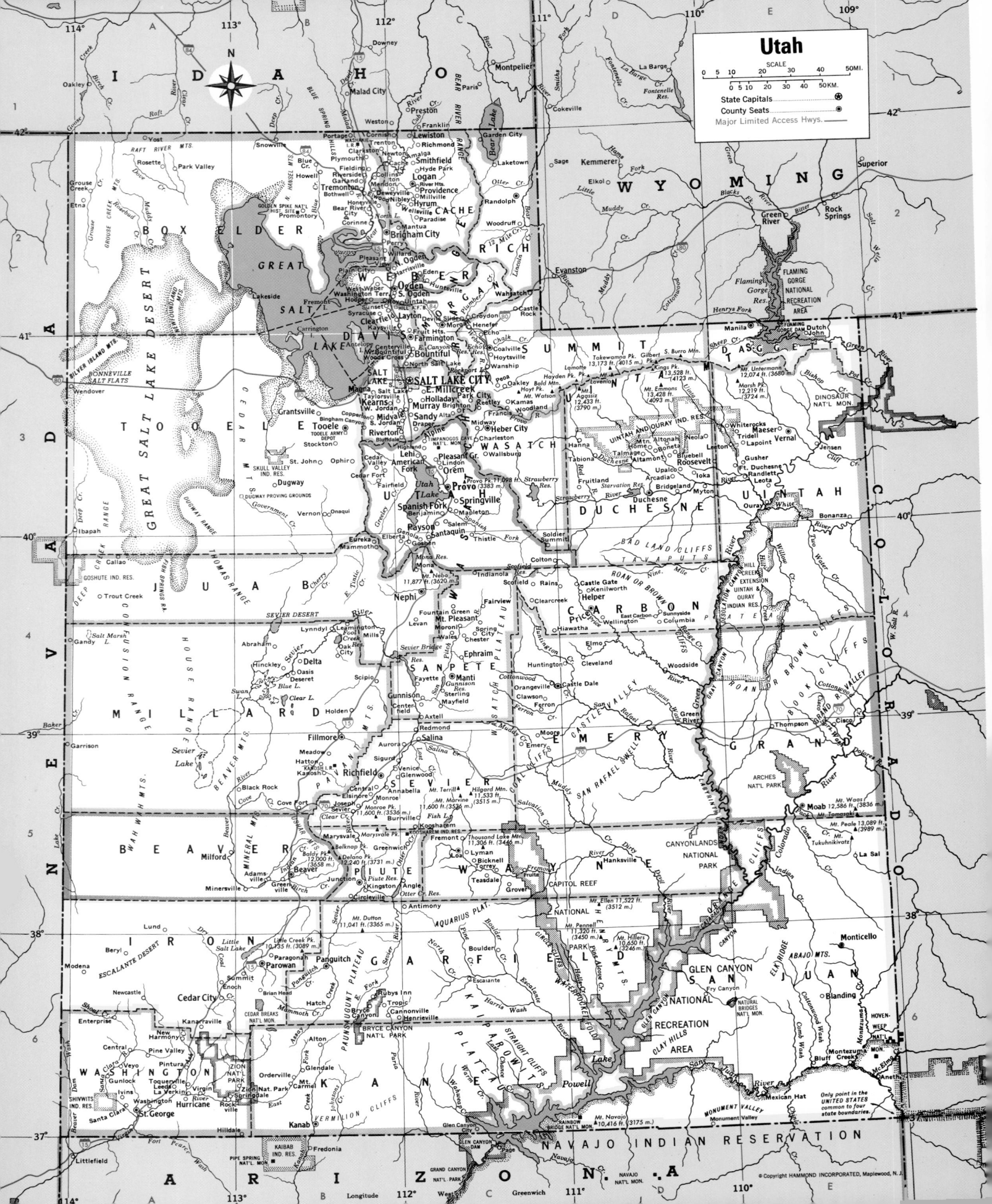

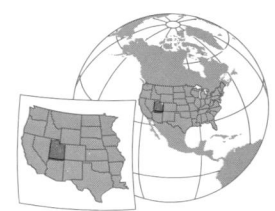

AREA 84,899 sq. mi. (219,888 sq. km.)
POPULATION 1,461,037
CAPITAL Salt Lake City
LARGEST CITY Salt Lake City
HIGHEST POINT Kings Pk. 13,528 ft. (4123 m.)
SETTLED IN 1847
ADMITTED TO UNION January 4, 1896
POPULAR NAME Beehive State
STATE FLOWER Sego Lily
STATE BIRD Sea Gull

Agriculture, Industry and Resources

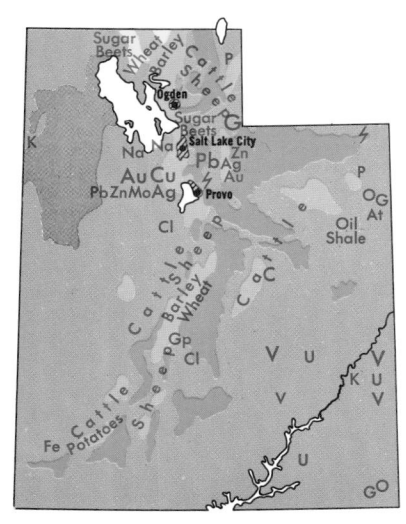

DOMINANT LAND USE

- Wheat, General Farming
- General Farming, Livestock, Special Crops
- Range Livestock
- Forests
- Nonagricultural Land

MAJOR MINERAL OCCURRENCES

Ag	Silver	Fe	Iron Ore
At	Asphalt	G	Natural Gas
Au	Gold	Gp	Gypsum
C	Coal	K	Potash
Cl	Clay	Mo	Molybdenum
Cu	Copper	Na	Salt

O	Petroleum
P	Phosphates
Pb	Lead
U	Uranium
V	Vanadium
Zn	Zinc

⚡ Water Power

▨ Major Industrial Areas

Topography

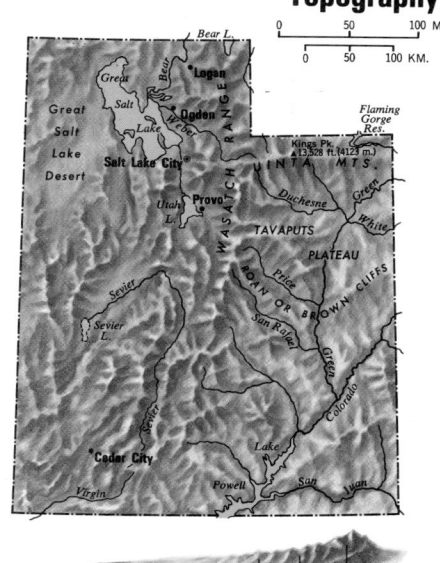

Topography

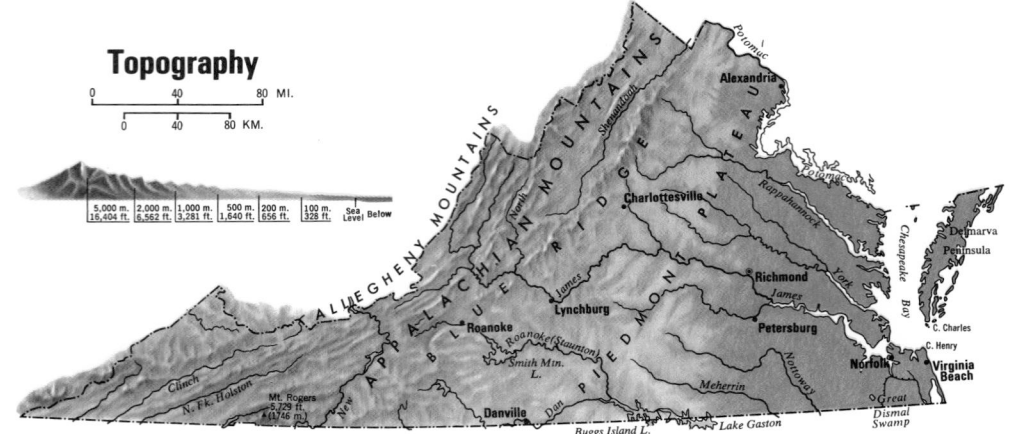

5,000 m. / 16,404 ft.   2,000 m. / 6,562 ft.   1,000 m. / 3,281 ft.   500 m. / 1,640 ft.   200 m. / 656 ft.   100 m. / 328 ft.   Sea Level   Below

0   40   80 MI.
0   40   80 KM.

*22901	Charlottesville (I.C.)⊙ 39,916	M4	
	Charlottesville‡ 113,568	M4	
23924	Chase City 2,749	M7	
24531	Chatham⊙ 1,390	K7	
23316	Cheriton 695	R6	
*23320	Chesapeake (I.C.) 114,486	R7	
23831	Chester 11,728	O6	
23832	Chesterfield⊙ 950	N6	
22623	Chester Gap 400	M3	
24319	Chilhowie 1,269	E7	
23336	Chincoteague 1,607	T5	
24073	Christiansburg 10,345	H6	
23032	Church View 200	P5	
23899	Claremont 380	P6	
23927	Clarksville 1,468	L7	
†23061	Clay Bank 200	P6	
23139	Clayville 200	N6	
†22624	Clear Brook 300	M2	
24225	Cleveland 360	D7	
24422	Clifton Forge (I.C.) 5,046	J5	
24321	Clinchburg 250	E7	
24226	Clinchco 900	D6	
24244	Clinchport 89	C7	
24228	Clintwood⊙ 1,369	D6	
24534	Clover 215	L7	
24077	Cloverdale 850	J6	
24535	Cluster Springs 350	L7	
23035	Cobbs Creek 700	R6	
24230	Coeburn 2,625	D7	
24536	Coleman Falls 250	K6	
†24450	Collierstown 300	J5	
24078	Collinsville 7,517	J7	
22443	Colonial Beach 2,474	P4	
23834	Colonial Heights (I.C.) 16,509	O6	
23038	Columbia 111	M5	
24538	Concord 500	K6	
23837	Courtland⊙ 976	O7	
22931	Covesville 475	L5	
24426	Covington (I.C.)⊙ 9,063	H5	
24430	Craigsville 845	J4	
23930	Crewe 2,325	M6	
24431	Crimora 450	L4	
24322	Cripple Creek 200	F7	
24323	Crockett 200	F7	
22932	Crozet 2,553	L4	
23039	Crozier 300	N5	
24539	Crystal Hill 475	L7	
23934	Cullen 725	L6	
22701	Culpeper⊙ 6,621	M4	
24083	Daleville 450	J6	
24236	Damascus 1,330	E7	
24237	Dante 1,083	D7	
*24540	Danville (I.C.) 45,642	J7	
	Danville‡ 111,789	J7	

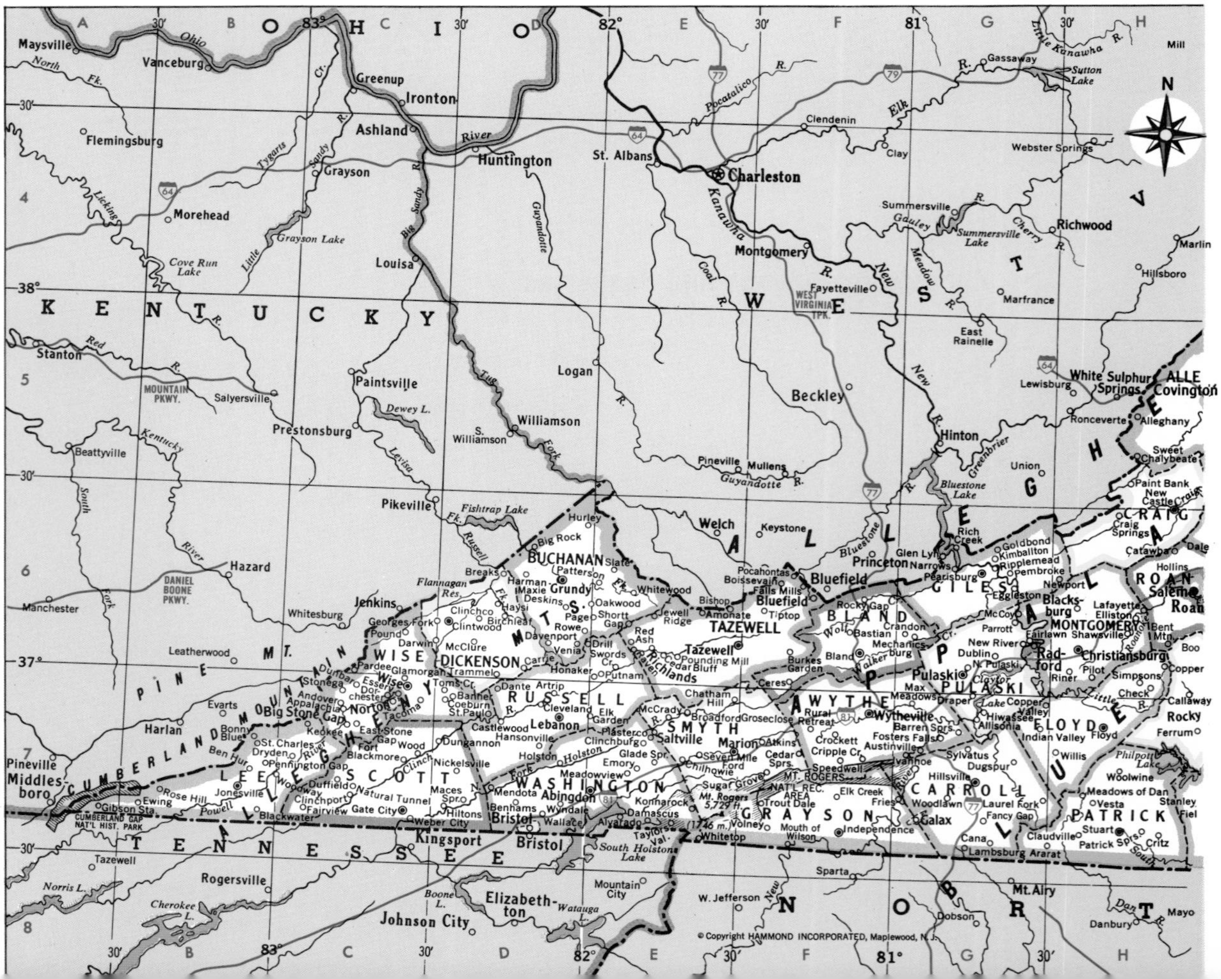

COUNTIES

Accomack 31,268	S5	
Albemarle 55,783	L5	
Alleghany 14,333	H5	
Amelia 8,405	M6	
Amherst 29,122	K5	
Appomattox 11,971	L6	
Arlington 152,599	S2	
Augusta 53,732	K4	
Bath 5,860	J6	
Bedford 34,927	J6	
Bland 6,349	F6	
Botetourt 23,270	J5	
Brunswick 15,632	N7	
Buchanan 37,989	D6	
Buckingham 11,751	L5	
Campbell 45,424	K6	
Caroline 17,904	O4	
Carroll 27,270	G7	
Charles City 6,692	O6	
Charlotte 12,266	L6	
Chesterfield 141,372	N6	
Clarke 9,965	M2	
Craig 3,948	H6	
Culpeper 22,620	M3	
Cumberland 7,881	M6	
Dickenson 19,806	D6	
Dinwiddie 22,602	N6	
Essex 8,864	P5	
Fairfax 596,901	O3	
Fauquier 35,889	N3	
Floyd 11,563	H7	
Fluvanna 10,244	M5	
Franklin 35,740	J6	
Frederick 34,150	M2	
Giles 17,810	G6	
Gloucester 20,107	P6	
Goochland 11,761	N5	
Grayson 16,579	F7	
Greene 7,625	M4	
Greensville 10,903	N7	
Halifax 30,599	L7	
Hanover 50,398	N5	
Henrico 180,735	O6	
Henry 57,654	J7	
Highland 2,937	J4	
Isle of Wight 21,603	P7	
James City 22,763	P6	
King and Queen 5,968	P5	
King George 10,543	O4	
King William 9,334	O5	
Lancaster 10,129	R5	
Lee 25,956	B7	
Loudoun 57,427	N2	
Louisa 17,825	N5	
Lunenburg 12,124	M7	
Madison 10,232	M4	
Mathews 7,995	R6	
Mecklenburg 29,444	M7	
Middlesex 7,719	R5	
Montgomery 63,516	H6	
Nelson 12,204	L5	
New Kent 8,781	P5	
Northampton 14,625	S6	
Northumberland 9,828	R5	
Nottoway 14,666	M6	
Orange 18,063	M4	
Page 19,401	M3	
Patrick 17,647	H7	
Pittsylvania 66,147	K7	
Powhatan 13,062	N5	
Prince Edward 16,456	M6	
Prince George 25,733	O6	
Prince William 144,703	O3	
Pulaski 35,229	G6	
Rappahannock 6,093	M3	
Richmond 6,952	P5	
Roanoke 72,945	H6	
Rockbridge 17,911	K5	
Rockingham 57,038	L4	
Russell 31,761	D7	
Scott 25,068	C7	
Shenandoah 27,559	L3	
Smyth 33,366	E7	
Southampton 18,731	O7	
Spotsylvania 34,435	N4	
Stafford 40,470	O4	
Surry 6,046	P6	
Sussex 10,874	O7	
Tazewell 50,511	E6	
Warren 21,200	M3	
Washington 46,487	D7	
Westmoreland 14,041	P4	
Wise 43,863	C6	
Wythe 25,522	F7	
York 35,463	P6	

CITIES and TOWNS

Zip	Name/Pop.	Key
24210	Abingdon⊙ 4,318	D7
23301	Accomac⊙ 522	S5
23001	Achilles 525	R6
22920	Afton 350	L4
23821	Alberta 394	N7
*22301	Alexandria (I.C.)⊙ 103,217	S3
24310	Allisonia 325	G7
24517	Altavista 3,849	K6
24520	Alton 500	K7
23002	Amelia Court House⊙ 500	N6
24521	Amherst⊙ 1,135	K5
24601	Amonate 350	E6
22003	Annandale 49,524	S3
24216	Appalachia 2,418	C7
24522	Appomattox⊙ 1,345	L6
24053	Ararat 500	G7
*22201	Arlington⊙ 152,599	T3
22922	Arrington 500	L5
23004	Arvonia 500	M5
23005	Ashland 4,640	N5
22011	Ashburn 345	O2
24311	Atkins 1,352	F7
24411	Augusta Springs 600	K4
22920	Austinville 750	F7
24054	Axton 540	J7
22041	Bailey's Crossroads 12,564	S3
24230	Banner 327	D7
22923	Barboursville 600	M4
24055	Bassett 2,034	J7
24314	Bastian 600	F6
22924	Batesville 575	L5
23015	Beaverdam 500	N5
24523	Bedford (I.C.)⊙ 5,991	J6
23306	Belle Haven 589	S5
24218	Ben Hur 400	B7
22610	Bentonville 500	M3
22611	Berryville⊙ 1,752	M2
24526	Big Island 500	K5
24603	Big Rock 900	D6
24219	Big Stone Gap 4,748	C7
24220	Birchleaf 650	D6
23307	Birdsnest 736	S6
24604	Bishop 600	E6
24060	Blacksburg 30,638	H6
23824	Blackstone 3,624	N6
24527	Blairs 500	K7
24315	Bland⊙ 950	F6
23308	Bloxom 407	S5
24605	Bluefield 5,946	F6
24064	Blue Ridge 2,347	J6
24606	Boissevain 975	E6
24065	Boones Mill 344	J6
23235	Bon Air 16,224	N5
22713	Boston 400	M3
22427	Bowling Green⊙ 665	O4
22620	Boyce 401	M2
23917	Boydton⊙ 486	M7
23827	Boykins 791	O7
22714	Brandy Station 400	N4
24607	Breaks 550	D6
22812	Bridgewater 3,289	K4
24201	Bristol (I.C.) 19,042	D7
24316	Broadford 500	E7
22815	Broadway 1,234	L3
23920	Brodnax 492	N7
24430	Brooke 245	O4
24528	Brookneal 1,454	L6
24415	Brownsburg 300	K5
22610	Browntown 300	M3
24222	Brucetown 250	M3
24066	Buchanan 1,205	J5
23921	Buckingham⊙ 200	L5
24416	Buena Vista (I.C.) 6,717	K5
22015	Burke 33,835	R3
24608	Burkes Garden 267	F6
23922	Burkeville 606	M6
22435	Callao 500	P5
24067	Callaway 225	H7
22016	Calverton 500	N3
23310	Cape Charles 1,512	R6
23313	Capeville 325	R6
23829	Capron 238	O7
23315	Carrsville 300	P7
23830	Carson 500	O6
22017	Casanova 370	N3
24069	Cascade 835	J7
24224	Castlewood 2,420	D7
24070	Catawba 350	H6
22019	Catlett 500	N3
24609	Cedar Bluff 1,550	E6
22437	Center Cross 360	P5
†22441	Chancellorsville 40	N4
22021	Chantilly 12,259	O3
23030	Charles City⊙ 5	O6
23923	Charlotte Court House⊙ 568	L6

© Copyright HAMMOND INCORPORATED, Maplewood, N.J.

24239 Davenport 230 .... D6
22821 Dayton 1,017 .... L4
24432 Deerfield 500 .... K4
23043 Deltaville 1,082 .... R5
23839 Dendron 307 .... P6
†24520 Denniston 200 .... L7
23936 Dillwyn 637 .... M5
23841 Dinwiddie⊙ 500 .... N6
23842 Disputanta 800 .... O6
23937 Drakes Branch 617 .... L7
23844 Drewryville 200 .... O7
24243 Dryden 400 .... B7
24549 Dry Fork 200 .... K7
24084 Dublin 2,368 .... G6
24244 Duffield 148 .... C7
22026 Dumfries 3,214 .... O3
23938 Dundas 200 .... M7
24245 Dungannon 339 .... D7
22027 Dunn Loring 6,077 .... S2
22454 Dunnsville 800 .... P5
24085 Eagle Rock 750 .... J5
22936 Earlysville 210 .... M4
24246 East Stone Gap 240 .... C7
23347 Eastville⊙ 238 .... R6
23845 Ebony 400 .... N7
22824 Edinburg 752 .... M3
24086 Eggleston 350 .... G6
22827 Elkton 1,520 .... L4
24087 Elliston-Lafayette 1,172 .... H6
24327 Emory-Meadowview 2,292 .... E7
23847 Emporia (I.C.)⊙ 4,840 .... N7
22937 Esmont 950 .... L5
24274 Esserville 750 .... G2
23803 Ettrick 4,890 .... O6
23939 Evergreen 300 .... L6
24248 Ewing 800 .... B7
23350 Exmore 1,300 .... S5
22030 Fairfax (I.C.)⊙ 19,390 .... R3
22039 Fairfax Station R3
24435 Fairfield 465 .... K5
24141 Fairlawn 1,794 .... G6
*22040 Falls Church (I.C.) 9,515 .... S2
24613 Falls Mills 800 .... F6
22401 Falmouth 3,271 .... O4
24328 Fancy Gap 200 .... G7
23901 Farmville⊙ 6,067 .... M6
24088 Ferrum 200 .... H7
24089 Fieldale 1,190 .... H7
24090 Fincastle⊙ 282 .... J6
22939 Fishersville 975 .... K4
22627 Flint Hill 750 .... M3
24091 Floyd⊙ 411 .... H7
24551 Forest 497 .... K6
23055 Fork Union 350 .... M5
24437 Fort Defiance 600 .... L4
22578 Foxwells 400 .... R5
22310 Franconia 8,476 .... S3
23851 Franklin (I.C.) 7,308 .... P7
23354 Franktown 500 .... S6
*22401 Fredericksburg (I.C.) 15,322 .... N4
24330 Fries 758 .... F7
22630 Front Royal⊙ 11,126 .... M3
22065 Gainesville 600 .... N3
24333 Galax (I.C.) 6,524 .... G7
22463 Garrisonville 200 .... N4
24251 Gate City⊙ 2,494 .... C7
†24228 Georges Fork 200 .... C6
24340 Glade Spring 1,722 .... E7
24554 Gladys 500 .... K6
24555 Glasgow 1,259 .... K5
23060 Glen Allen 6,202 .... N5
24093 Glen Lyn 235 .... G6
†24541 Glenwood 2,276 .... K7
23061 Gloucester⊙ 1,545 .... P6
23062 Gloucester Point 5,841 .... R6
24094 Goldbond 250 .... G6
22720 Goldvein 500 .... N4
23063 Goochland⊙ 800 .... N5
24556 Goode 200 .... K6
22942 Gordonsville 1,421 .... M4
22637 Gore 500 .... M2
24439 Goshen 134 .... K5
23692 Grafton 500 .... P6
23356 Greenbackville 300 .... T5
23942 Green Bay 500 .... M6
23357 Greenbush 200 .... S5
24440 Greenville 400 .... K5
22943 Greenwood 800 .... L4
24557 Gretna 1,255 .... K7
24441 Grottoes 1,369 .... L4
†22306 Groveton 18,860 .... T3
24614 Grundy⊙ 1,699 .... D6
23066 Gwynn 205 .... R5
22469 Hague 425 .... P4
24558 Halifax⊙ 772 .... L7
23359 Hallwood 243 .... S5
22068 Hamilton 598 .... N2
23943 Hampden-Sydney 1,011 .... L6
*23601 Hampton (I.C.) 122,617 .... R6
23069 Hanover⊙ 500 .... O5
23389 Harborton 200 .... S5
24101 Hardy 325 .... J6
24618 Harman-Maxie 650 .... D6
22801 Harrisonburg (I.C.)⊙ 19,671 .... K4
23071 Hartfield 700 .... R5
22069 Haymarket 230 .... N3
22472 Haynesville 500 .... P5
24256 Haysi 371 .... D6
22473 Heathsville⊙ 300 .... P5
24102 Henry 300 .... J7
*22070 Herndon 11,449 .... O3
23075 Highland Springs 12,146 .... O5
22132 Hillsboro 115 .... N2
24343 Hillsville⊙ 2,123 .... G7
24258 Hiltons 300 .... D7
24347 Hiwassee 250 .... G7
24020 Hollins College 12,295 .... H6
24260 Honaker 1,475 .... D6
23860 Hopewell (I.C.) 23,397 .... O6
23395 Horntown 400 .... T5
24445 Hot Springs 300 .... J4
24104 Huddleston 200 .... K6

(continued on following page)

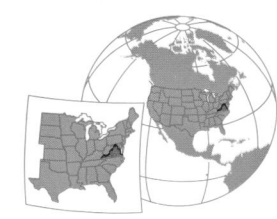

AREA 40,767 sq. mi. (105,587 sq. km.)
POPULATION 5,346,818
CAPITAL Richmond
LARGEST CITY Norfolk
HIGHEST POINT Mt. Rogers 5,729 ft. (1746 m.)
SETTLED IN 1607
ADMITTED TO UNION June 26, 1788
POPULAR NAME Old Dominion
STATE FLOWER Dogwood
STATE BIRD Cardinal

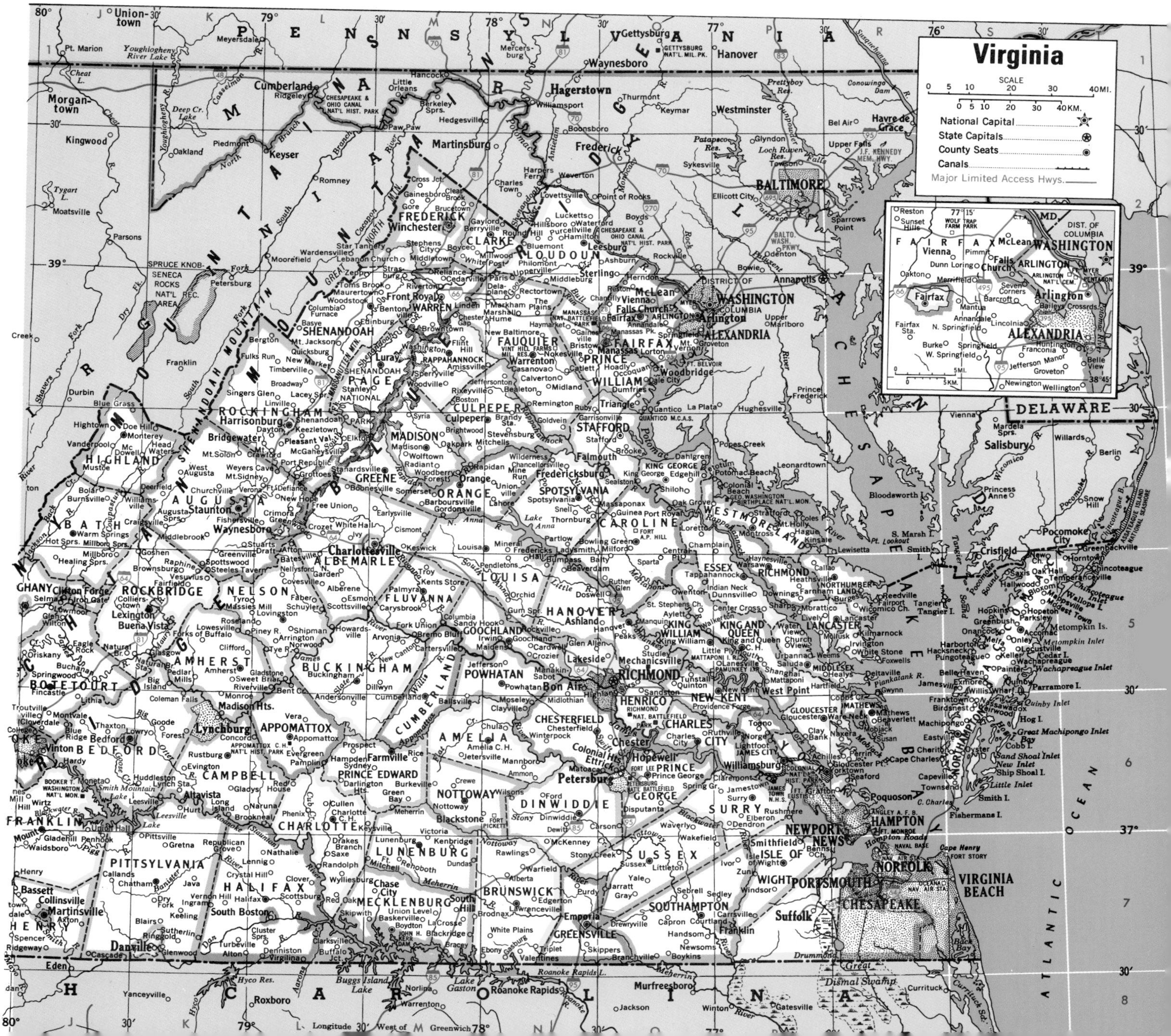

Agriculture, Industry and Resources

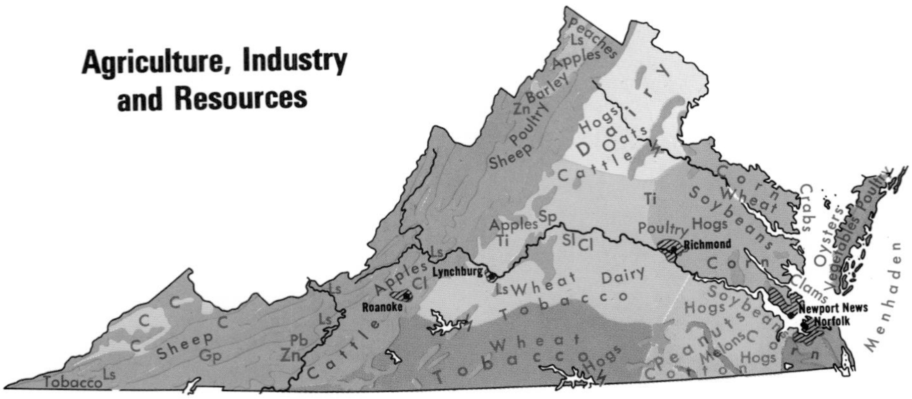
Peaches
Apples
Barley
Poultry
Sheep
Hogs
Dairy
Oats
Cattle
Wheat
Soybeans
Corn
Crabs
Oysters
Vegetables
Poultry
Clams
Menhaden
Richmond
Lynchburg
Roanoke
Newport News
Norfolk
Tobacco
Peanuts
Cotton
Melons

MAJOR MINERAL OCCURRENCES

C Coal
Cl Clay
Gp Gypsum
Ls Limestone
Pb Lead
Sl Slate
Sp Soapstone
Ti Titanium
Zn Zinc
Water Power
Major Industrial Areas

DOMINANT LAND USE

Dairy, General Farming
General Farming, Livestock, Dairy
General Farming, Livestock, Tobacco
General Farming, Livestock, Fruit, Tobacco
General Farming, Truck Farming, Tobacco, Livestock
Tobacco, General Farming
Peanuts, General Farming
Fruit and Mixed Farming
Truck and Mixed Farming
Forests
Swampland, Limited Agriculture

22639 Hume 350 N3
†22301 Huntington 5,813 S3
24620 Hurley 850 D6
24563 Hurt 1,481 K6
24348 Independence⊙ 1,112 F7
24105 Indian Valley 300 G7
24448 Iron Gate 620 J5
22480 Irvington 567 R5
23397 Isle of Wight⊙ 185 P7
24350 Ivanhoe 900 G7
23866 Ivor 403 P7
22945 Ivy 900 L4
23081 Jamestown 12 P6
23398 Jamesville 500 S5
23867 Jarratt 614 O7
22303 Jefferson Manor S3
22724 Jeffersonton 300 N3
24622 Jewell Ridge 600 E6
24263 Jonesville⊙ 874 B7
24566 Keeling 680 K7
22832 Keezletown 975 L4
23401 Keller 236 S5
23944 Kenbridge 1,352 M7
24265 Keokee 300 C7
22947 Keswick 300 M4
23947 Keysville 704 M6
22482 Kilmarnock 945 R5
23085 King and Queen Court House⊙ 500 P5
22485 King George⊙ 575 O4
23086 King William⊙ 100 O5
22488 Kinsale 250 P4
23950 La Crosse 734 M7
22501 Ladysmith 360 N4
24108 Lafayette-Elliston 1,172 H6
†22041 Lake Barcroft 8,725 S3
23228 Lakeside 12,289 N5
24351 Lambsburg 800 G7
22503 Lancaster⊙ 110 R5
24352 Laurel Fork 300 G7
23868 Lawrenceville⊙ 1,484 N7
24266 Lebanon⊙ 3,206 D7
22641 Lebanon Church 300 L2
22075 Leesburg⊙ 8,357 N2
24450 Lexington (I.C.)⊙ 7,292 J5
†22313 Lincolnia 10,350 S3
22642 Linden 320 M3
22834 Linville 500 L3
22507 Lively 400 P5
22079 Lorton 5,813 O3
23093 Louisa⊙ 932 M4
22080 Lovettsville 613 N2
22949 Lovingston⊙ 600 L5
22951 Lowesville 500 K5
24457 Lowmoor 700 J5
†22075 Lucketts 500 N2
23952 Lunenburg⊙ 13 M7
22835 Luray⊙ 3,584 M3
*24501 Lynchburg (I.C.) 66,743 K6
Lynchburg‡ 153,260 K6
24571 Lynch Station 500 K6
23405 Machipongo 400 S6
22727 Madison⊙ 267 M4
24572 Madison Heights 14,146 K6
23103 Manakin-Sabot 200 N5
22110 Manassas (I.C.)⊙ 15,438 O3
22110 Manassas Park (I.C.) 6,524 O3
23106 Manquin 576 O5
†22030 Mantua 6,523 S3
23407 Mappsville 700 T5
24354 Marion⊙ 7,029 E7
22643 Markham 300 N3
22115 Marshall 800 N3
24112 Martinsville (I.C.)⊙ 18,149 J7
22954 Massies Mill 225 K5
23109 Mathews⊙ 500 R6
23803 Matoaca 1,967 N6
23110 Mattaponi 300 P5
24360 Max Meadows 782 G6
24269 McClure 300 D6
24111 McCoy 600 G6
22840 McGaheysville 600 L4
23872 McKenney 473 N7
*22101 McLean 35,664 S2
24361 Meadowview-Emory 2,292 D7
†24315 Mechanicsburg 350 G6
23111 Mechanicsville 9,269 O5
23954 Meherrin 400 M6
23410 Melfa 391 S5
24270 Mendota 375 D7
22116 Merrifield 7,525 S3
22117 Middleburg 619 N3
22645 Middletown 841 M2
22728 Midland 600 N3
23113 Midlothian 950 N6
22514 Milford 650 O4
24460 Millboro 400 J5
24460 Millboro Springs 200 J4
22646 Millwood 400 N2
23117 Mineral 399 N4
22568 Mine Run 450 N4
23118 Mobjack 210 R6
23412 Modest Town 225 T5
22517 Mollusk 800 P5
24121 Moneta 300 J6
24574 Monroe 500 K6
24465 Monterey⊙ 247 K4
22520 Montross⊙ 456 P4
24122 Montvale 900 J6
22523 Morattico 225 P5
23120 Moseley 210 N6
22841 Mount Crawford 315 L4
22524 Mount Holly 200 P4
22842 Mount Jackson 1,419 L3
24467 Mount Sidney 500 K4
22121 Mount Vernon 24,058 O3
24363 Mouth of Wilson 400 F7
24124 Narrows 2,516 G6
23413 Nassawadox 630 S6
24577 Nathalie 200 L7
24578 Natural Bridge 200 J5
24579 Natural Bridge Sta. 450 K5
23122 Naxera 300 R6
22958 Nellysford 290 L5
24127 New Castle⊙ 213 H5
23415 New Church 427 S5
24469 New Hope 200 L4
22122 Newington 8,313 S3
23124 New Kent⊙ 25 P5
22844 New Market 1,118 L3
24128 Newport 600 H6
*23601 Newport News (I.C.) 144,903 P6
Newport News-Hampton‡ 364,449 P6
24129 New River 500 G6
23874 Newsoms 368 O7
24271 Nickelsville 464 D7
22123 Nokesville 520 N3
24272 Nora 550 D6
*23501 Norfolk (I.C.) 266,979 R7
Norfolk-Virginia Beach-Portsmouth ‡ 806,691 R7
23127 Norge 750 P6
22959 North Garden 200 L5
†24301 North Pulaski 1,405 G6
22151 North Springfield 9,538 S3
24273 Norton (I.C.) 4,757 C7
23955 Nottoway⊙ 170 M6
23416 Oak Hall 221 S5
22124 Oakton 19,150 R3
24631 Oakwood 715 E6
22125 Occoquan 241 O3
23417 Onancock 1,461 S5
23418 Onley 526 S5
22960 Orange⊙ 2,631 M4
23419 Oyster 200 S6
24131 Paint Bank 235 H5
23420 Painter 321 S5
22963 Palmyra⊙ 250 M5
23958 Pamplin 273 L6
23421 Parksley 979 S5
24132 Parrott 750 G6
24133 Patrick Springs 800 H7
†23069 Peaks 500 O5
24134 Pearisburg⊙ 2,128 G6
24136 Pembroke 1,302 G6
24137 Penhook 500 J7
24277 Pennington Gap 1,716 C7
23803 Petersburg (I.C.) 41,055 N6
Petersburg-Colonial Heights-Hopewell‡ 129,296 N6
23959 Phenix 250 L6
22131 Philomont 265 N2
24138 Pilot 360 H6
22043 Pimmit 6,658 S2
22964 Piney River 778 L5
24139 Pittsville 600 K7
24635 Pocahontas 708 F6
23662 Poquoson (I.C.) 8,726 R6
22535 Port Royal 291 O4
*23701 Portsmouth (I.C.) 104,577 R7
24279 Pound 1,086 C6
24637 Pounding Mill 399 E6
23139 Powhatan⊙ 600 N5
23875 Prince George⊙ 150 O6
23960 Prospect 275 L6
23140 Providence Forge 500 P6
24301 Pulaski⊙ 10,106 G6
23422 Pungoteague 500 S5
22132 Purcellville 1,567 N2
†23847 Purdy 350 N7
22134 Quantico 621 O3
23423 Quinby 350 S5
24141 Radford (I.C.) 13,225 G6
22732 Radiant 250 M4
24472 Raphine 500 K5
24639 Raven 4,000 E6
23876 Rawlings 200 N7
22140 Rectortown 225 N3
24640 Red Ash 300 E6
23964 Red Oak 250 L7
22539 Reedville 400 R5
22734 Remington 425 N3
22090 Reston 36,407 R2
24147 Rich Creek 746 G6
24641 Richlands 5,796 E6
*23201 Richmond (cap.) (I.C.)⊙ 219,214 O5
Richmond‡ 632,015 O5
24148 Ridgeway 858 J7
24149 Riner 360 H6
24150 Ripplemead 600 G6
22651 Riverton 500 M3
*24001 Roanoke (I.C.) 100,220 H6
Roanoke‡ 224,341 H6
23146 Rockville 290 N5
24366 Rocky Gap 200 F6
24151 Rocky Mount⊙ 4,198 J7
24280 Rosedale 760 E7
24281 Rose Hill 700 B7
22967 Roseland 300 K5
22141 Round Hill 510 N2
24368 Rural Retreat 1,083 F7
†23430 Rushmere 1,070 P6
24588 Rustburg⊙ 650 K6
22546 Ruther Glen 200 O5
23147 Ruthville 300 P6
24282 Saint Charles 241 B7
24283 Saint Paul 973 D7
23148 St. Stephens Church 500 O5
24153 Salem (I.C.)⊙ 23,958 H6
24370 Saltville 2,376 E7
23149 Saluda⊙ 150 P5
23150 Sandston O5
23153 Sandy Hook 700 M5
23427 Saxis 415 S5
22969 Schuyler 250 L5
24589 Scottsburg 335 L7
24590 Scottsville 250 L5
23696 Seaford R6
22547 Sealston 200 O4
23878 Sedley 523 P7
24474 Selma 500 J5
22044 Seven Corners 6,058 S3
24373 Seven Mile Ford 425 E7
24162 Shawsville 950 H6
22849 Shenandoah 1,861 L4
22971 Shipman 350 L5
23430 Smithfield 3,718 P7
22553 Snell 300 N4
22972 Somerset 200 M4
24592 South Boston (I.C.) 7,093 L7
23970 South Hill 4,347 M7
22552 Sparta 485 O4
24374 Speedwell 650 F8
24165 Spencer 500 J7
22740 Sperryville 500 M3
22553 Spotsylvania⊙ 350 N4
*22150 Springfield 21,435 S3
22554 Stafford⊙ 750 O4
22973 Stanardsville⊙ 284 L4
22851 Stanley 1,204 L3
24168 Stanleytown 1,761 H7
22654 Star Tannery 500 L2
24401 Staunton (I.C.)⊙ 21,857 K4
24476 Steeles Tavern 200 K5
22655 Stephens City 1,179 M2
22170 Sterling 16,080 O2
24285 Stonega 275 C7
23882 Stony Creek 329 N7
22657 Strasburg 2,311 M3
24171 Stuart⊙ 1,131 H7
24477 Stuarts Draft 1,776 L4
23162 Studley 500 O5
*23432 Suffolk (I.C.) 47,621 P7
24375 Sugar Grove 1,027 E7
22090 Sunset Hills R2
23883 Surry⊙ 237 P6
23163 Susan 500 R6
23884 Sussex⊙ 75 O7
24595 Sweet Briar 900 K5
24649 Swords Creek 315 E6
†24343 Sylvatus 200 G7
23602 Tabb R6
23440 Tangier 771 R5
22560 Tappahannock⊙ 1,821 O5
24651 Tazewell⊙ 4,468 E6
23442 Temperanceville 400 T5
24174 Thaxton 450 K6
22171 The Plains 382 N3
22853 Timberville 1,510 L3
23168 Toano 950 P6
22660 Toms Brook 226 L3
23443 Townsend 525 R6
24289 Trammel 450 D6
22172 Triangle 4,770 O3
23886 Triplet 300 N7
24378 Trout Dale 248 F7
24175 Troutville 496 J6
22567 Unionville 500 N4
22176 Upperville 250 N2
23175 Urbanna 518 P5
23887 Valentines 400 N7
24656 Vansant 2,708 D6
24597 Vernon Hill 250 K7
24482 Verona 2,782 K4
24177 Vesta 350 H7
24483 Vesuvius 500 K5
23974 Victoria 2,004 M6
22180 Vienna 15,469 R2
24179 Vinton 8,027 J6
*23450 Virginia Beach (I.C.) 262,199 S7
23480 Wachapreague 404 S5
23888 Wakefield 1,355 O7
23177 Walkerton 985 O5
24484 Warm Springs⊙ 325 J4
22186 Warrenton⊙ 3,907 N3
22572 Warsaw⊙ 771 P5
22747 Washington⊙ 247 M3
22190 Waterford 350 N2
23180 Water View 265 P5
23890 Waverly 2,284 O6
22980 Waynesboro (I.C.) 15,329 K4
24251 Weber City 1,543 C7
22576 Weems 500 P5
23484 Weirwood 300 S6
24485 West Augusta 325 K4
23181 West Point 2,726 P5
22153 West Springfield 25,012 S3
24486 Weyers Cave 300 L4
22987 White Hall 250 L4
22578 White Stone 409 R5
24292 Whitetop 860 E7
24657 Whitewood 350 E6
22579 Wicomico Church 500 R5
†22553 Wilderness 200 N4
23185 Williamsburg (I.C.)⊙ 9,870 P6
23486 Willis Wharf 360 S5
22601 Winchester (I.C.)⊙ 20,217 M2
23487 Windsor 985 P7
24184 Wirtz 500 J6
24293 Wise⊙ 3,894 C7
22748 Wolftown 350 M4
22989 Woodberry Forest 450 M4
*22191 Woodbridge 24,004 O3
24381 Woodlawn 1,689 G7
22664 Woodstock⊙ 2,627 L3
†24277 Woodway 400 C7
23976 Wylliesburg 213 L7
24382 Wytheville⊙ 7,135 G7
23690 Yorktown⊙ 550 R6
23898 Zuni 300 P7

OTHER FEATURES

Aarons (creek) L7
Allegheny (mts.) H5
Anna (lake) N4
Appalachian (mts.) J5
Appomattox (riv.) M6
Appomattox Court House Nat'l Hist. Park K6
Arlington Nat'l Cemetery T3
Assateague Island Nat'l Seashore T4
Back (bay) S7
Back (creek) J4
Banister (riv.) K7
Big Otter (riv.) K6
Blackwater (riv.) J6
Blackwater (riv.) O6
Blue Ridge (mts.) J6
Bluestone (lake) G5
Booker T. Washington Nat'l Mon. J6
Buggs Island (lake) L8
Bull Run (creek) N3
Cedar (isl.) S5
Central Intelligence Agency (C.I.A.) S2
Charles (cape) R6
Chesapeake (bay) R5
Chesapeake and Ohio Canal Nat'l Mon. O2
Chincoteague (bay) T4
Chincoteague (inlet) T5
Claytor (lake) G6
Clinch (riv.) C7
Cobb (isl.) S6
Colonial Nat'l Hist. Park P6
Cowpasture (riv.) J4
Craig (creek) H5
Cub (creek) L6
Cumberland (mt.) B7
Cumberland Gap Nat'l Hist. Pk. A7
Dan (riv.) K7
Drummond (lake) P7
Fishermans (isl.) S6
Flannagan (res.) C6
Flat (creek) M6
Fort Belvoir 7,726 O3
Fort Eustis P6
Fort A.P. Hill O4
Fort Lee 9,784 O6
Fort Monroe R6
Fort Myer T2
Fort Pickett N6
Fort Story S7
Gaston (lake) M8
George Washington Birthplace Nat'l Mon. P4
Goose (creek) J6
Goose (creek) N3
Great Machipongo (inlet) S6
Great North (mt.) L2
Hampton Roads (est.) R7
Henry (cape) R7
Hog (isl.) S6
Hog Island (bay) S6
Holston, North Fork (riv.) D7
Hyco (riv.) K8
Jackson (riv.) J4
James (riv.) O6
Jamestown Nat'l Hist. Site P6
John H. Kerr (dam) M7
Langley A.F.B. R6
Leesville (lake) K6
Levisa Fork (riv.) C5
Little (inlet) S6
Little (riv.) N5
Little (riv.) H7
Manassas Nat'l Battlefield Pk. K3
Massanutten (mt.) L3
Mattaponi (riv.) O5
Mattaponi Ind. Res. P5
Maury (riv.) K5
Meherrin (riv.) M7
Metompkin (inlet) T5
Metompkin (isl.) T5
Mobjack (bay) R6
Mount Rogers Nat'l Rec. Area F7
Naval Air Station R7
New (inlet) S6
New (riv.) F8
Ni (riv.) N4
North Anna (riv.) M4
Nottoway (riv.) O7
Oceana N.A.S. S7
Pamunkey (riv.) O5
Pamunkey Ind. Res. P5
Parramore (isl.) S5
Pentagon T3
Petersburg Nat'l Battlefield O6
Philpott (lake) H7
Piankatank (riv.) R5
Pigg (riv.) J7
Po (riv.) N4
Pocomoke (sound) S5
Potomac (riv.) O4
Powell (riv.) B7
Quantico Marine Corps Air Sta. 7,121 O4
Quinby (inlet) S6
Rapidan (riv.) M4
Rappahannock (riv.) P4
Richmond Nat'l Battlefield Pk. O6
Rivanna (riv.) M5
Roanoke (riv.) N8
Rogers (mt.) E7
Russell Fork (riv.) C5
Sand Shoal (inlet) S6
Shenandoah (mt.) K3
Shenandoah (riv.) N2
Shenandoah Nat'l Park L3
Ship Shoal (isl.) S6
Slate (riv.) L5
Smith (isl.) S6
Smith (riv.) J7
Smith Mountain (lake) J6
South Anna (riv.) N5
South Holston (lake) E7
South Mayo (riv.) H7
Staunton (Roanoke) (riv.) K6
Stony (creek) N6
Swift (creek) O6
Tangier (isl.) R5
Tangier (sound) S5
Tug Fork (riv.) D5
U.S. Naval Base R7
Vint Hill Farms Mil. Res. N3
Wachapreague (inlet) T6
Walker (creek) F6
Wallops (isl.) T5
Willis (riv.) M5
Wolf (creek) F6
Wolf Trap Farm Park S2
York (riv.) P6

I.C. Independent City.
⊙County seat.
‡Population of metropolitan area.
† Zip of nearest p.o * Multiple zips.

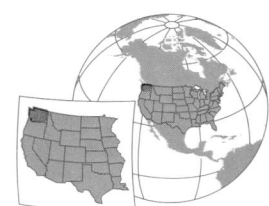

AREA 68,139 sq. mi. (176,480 sq. km.)
POPULATION 4,132,180
CAPITAL Olympia
LARGEST CITY Seattle
HIGHEST POINT Mt. Rainier 14,410 ft. (4392 m.)
SETTLED IN 1811
ADMITTED TO UNION November 11, 1889
POPULAR NAME Evergreen State
STATE FLOWER Western Rhododendron
STATE BIRD Willow Goldfinch

COUNTIES

Adams 13,267 .... G3
Asotin 16,823 .... H4
Benton 109,444 .... F4
Chelan 45,061 .... E3
Clallam 51,648 .... B2
Clark 192,227 .... C5
Columbia 4,057 .... H4
Cowlitz 79,548 .... C4
Douglas 22,144 .... F3
Ferry 5,811 .... G2
Franklin 35,025 .... G4
Garfield 2,468 .... H4
Grant 48,522 .... F3
Grays Harbor 66,314 .... B3
Island 44,048 .... C2
Jefferson 15,965 .... B3
King 1,269,749 .... D3
Kitsap 147,152 .... C3
Kittitas 24,877 .... E3
Klickitat 15,822 .... E5
Lewis 56,028 .... C4
Lincoln 9,604 .... G3
Mason 31,184 .... B3
Okanogan 30,639 .... F2
Pacific 17,237 .... B4
Pend Oreille 8,580 .... H2
Pierce 485,667 .... C3
San Juan 7,838 .... C2
Skagit 64,138 .... D2
Skamania 7,919 .... D5

CITIES and TOWNS

Zip   Name/Pop.   Key

Snohomish 337,720 .... D2
Spokane 341,835 .... H3
Stevens 28,979 .... H2
Thurston 124,264 .... C4
Wahkiakum 3,832 .... B4
Walla Walla 47,435 .... G4
Whatcom 106,701 .... D2
Whitman 40,103 .... H4
Yakima 172,508 .... E4

98520 Aberdeen 18,739 .... B3
98220 Acme 500 .... C2
99001 Airway Heights 1,730 .... H3
99102 Albion 631 .... H4
†98328 Alder 300 .... C4
98002 Algona 1,467 .... C3
98524 Allyn 850 .... C3
99103 Almira 330 .... G3
98526 Amanda Park 495 .... A3
98601 Amboy 480 .... C5
98221 Anacortes 9,013 .... C2
98603 Ariel 386 .... C5
98223 Arlington 3,282 .... C2
98304 Ashford 300 .... C4
99402 Asotin⊙ 943 .... H4
98002 Auburn 26,417 .... C3
98110 Bainbridge Island-Winslow
       (Winslow) 2,196 .... A2
98604 Battle Ground 2,774 ..... C5

†98004 Beaux Arts Village 328 ...... B2
98305 Beaver 450 .... A2
98528 Belfair 500 .... C3
*98004 Bellevue 73,903 .... B2
98225 Bellingham⊙ 45,794 .... C2
       Bellingham‡ 106,701 ...... C2
99320 Benton City 1,980 .... F4
98605 Bingen 644 .... D5
98010 Black Diamond 1,170 .... C3
98230 Blaine 2,363 .... C2
†98390 Bonney Lake 5,328 .... C3
98011 Bothell 7,943 .... B1
98310 Bremerton 36,208 .... A2
       Bremerton‡ 146,609 ...... A2
98812 Brewster 1,337 .... F2
98813 Bridgeport 1,174 .... F3
†98036 Brier 2,915 .... C2
98320 Brinnon 500 .... B3
†98101 Bryn Mawr-Skyway 11,754 . B2
98321 Buckley 3,143 .... C3
98530 Bucoda 519 .... C4
98921 Buena 590 .... E4
98166 Burien 23,189 .... A2
98233 Burlington 3,894 ..... C2
98013 Burton 650 .... C3
98607 Camas 5,681 .... C5
98323 Carbonado 456 .... D3
98324 Carlsborg 500 .... B2
98814 Carlton 410 .... F2
98014 Carnation 913 ...... D3
98610 Carson 500 .... D5
98815 Cashmere 2,240 .... E3

98611 Castle Rock 2,162 ...... B4
98612 Cathlamet⊙ 635 .... B4
98531 Centralia 11,555 ...... C4
98520 Central Park 2,709 ..... B3
98532 Chehalis⊙ 6,100 ...... C4
98816 Chelan 2,802 .... E3
99004 Cheney 7,630 .... H3
98109 Chewelah 1,888 ...... H2
98614 Chinook 928 .... B4
98326 Clallam Bay 600 .... A2
99403 Clarkston 6,903 .... H4
98235 Clearlake 750 ...... C2
98922 Cle Elum 1,773 .... E3
98236 Clinton 900 .... C3
†98004 Clyde Hill 3,229 .. B2
†98055 Coalfield 500 ..... B2
99111 Colfax⊙ 2,780 .... H4
99324 College Place 5,771 . G4
99113 Colton 307 .... H4
†98632 Columbia Heights 2,515 .. C4
99114 Colville⊙ 4,510 .. H2
98819 Conconully 157 .... F2
98237 Concrete 592 ..... D2
99326 Connell 1,981 .... G4
98535 Copalis Beach 600 .. A3
98536 Copalis Crossing 500 . B3
98537 Cosmopolis 1,575 .. B4
99115 Coulee City 510 ... F3
99116 Coulee Dam 1,412 .. G3
98239 Coupeville⊙ 1,006 . C2
99117 Creston 309 .... G3
99119 Cusick 246 .... H2

98240 Custer 300 .... C2
98617 Dallesport 600 .... D5
98241 Darrington 1,064 .... D2
99122 Davenport⊙ 1,559 .... G3
99328 Dayton⊙ 2,565 .... H4
98243 Deer Harbor 400 .... B2
99006 Deer Park 2,140 .... H3
98188 Des Moines 7,378 .... C3
99213 Dishman 10,169 .... H3
99329 Dixie 210 .... G4
98821 Dryden 500 .... E3
†98382 Dungeness 675 .... B2
98327 Du Pont 559 .... C3
98019 Duvall 729 .... D3
98245 Eastsound 800 .... B2
98801 East Wenatchee 1,640 . E3
98328 Eatonville 998 .... C4
98020 Edmonds 27,679 ... C3
99123 Electric City 927 . F3
98926 Ellensburg⊙ 11,752 . E3
98541 Elma 2,720 .... B4
99124 Elmer City 312 .... G2
98513 Endicott 290 ...... H4
†98310 Enetai 2,638 ..... A2
98822 Entiat 445 ...... E3
98022 Enumclaw 5,427 .. D3
98823 Ephrata⊙ 5,359 . F3
†98310 Erlands Point 1,254 . A2
*98201 Everett⊙ 54,413 . C3
98247 Everson 898 ..... C2
99012 Fairfield 582 .... H3
†98901 Fairview-Sumach 2,788 . E4
98024 Fall City 1,528 . D3
99128 Farmington 176 .. H3
98248 Ferndale 3,855 .. C2
98424 Fife 1,823 ...... C3
98466 Fircrest 5,477 .. C3
†98531 Fords Prairie 2,582 . B4
98331 Forks 3,060 .... A3
99014 Four Lakes 500 . H3
98250 Friday Harbor⊙ 1,200 . B2
†98901 Fruitvale 3,967 . E4
99130 Garfield 599 .... H3
†99362 Garrett 1,134 ... G4
98824 George 261 ...... F3
98335 Gig Harbor 2,429 . C3
98336 Glenoma 500 ..... C4
98619 Glenwood 626 .... D4
98251 Gold Bar 794 .... D3
98620 Goldendale⊙ 3,575 . E5
98337 Gorst 750 .... A2
99133 Grand Coulee 1,180 . G3
98930 Grandview 5,615 . F4
98932 Granger 1,812 ... E4
98252 Granite Falls 911 . D2
98547 Grayland 750 .... A4
98621 Grays River 350 . B4
98253 Greenbank 600 ... C2
98339 Hadlock-Irondale 1,752 . C2
98255 Hamilton 268 .... D2
†98366 Harper 300 ...... A2
99933 Harrah 343 ...... E4
99134 Harrington 507 .. G3
99135 Hartline 165 .... F3
99332 Hatton 81 .... G4
98025 Hoodsport 500 ... D3
98548 Hoodsport 500 ... B3
98550 Hoquiam 9,719 ... A3
†98004 Hunts Point 480 . B2
98624 Ilwaco 604 ...... A4
98256 Index 147 .... D3
98342 Indianola 800 ... A1
99139 Ione 594 .... H2
98027 Issaquah 5,536 .. C3
98343 Joyce 375 .... B2
99033 Juanita 17,232 .. B1
99335 Kahlotus 203 .... G4
98625 Kalama 1,216 .... C4
98344 Kapowsin 500 .... C4
98626 Kelso⊙ 11,129 ... C4
98028 Kenmore 7,281 ... B1
99336 Kennewick 34,397 . F4
98031 Kent 23,152 ..... C3
98345 Keyport 900 ..... A2
98346 Kingston 950 .... C3
98033 Kirkland 18,779 . B2
98934 Kittitas 782 .... E4
98628 Klickitat 750 ... D5
†98832 Krupp (Marlin) 83 . F3
98629 La Center 439 ... C5
98503 Lacey 13,940 .... C3
98257 La Conner 633 ... C2
99143 Lacrosse 373 .... H4
†98101 Lake Forest Park 2,485 . B1
98258 Lake Stevens 1,660 . D3
99017 Lamont 101 ...... H3
98260 Langley 650 ..... C2
98350 La Push 500 ..... A3
99018 Latah 155 .... H3
98826 Leavenworth 1,522 . E3
99019 Liberty Lake 1,599 . J3
98555 Lilliwaup 75 .... B3
99341 Lind 567 .... G4
98556 Littlerock 850 .. B4
98631 Long Beach 1,199 . A4

98351 Longbranch 640 .... C3
98642 Longview 31,052 .... B4
99148 Loon Lake 500 .... H2
98262 Lummi Island 675 .... C2
98635 Lyle 580 .... D5
98263 Lyman 285 .... D2
98264 Lynden 4,022 .... C2
98036 Lynnwood 22,641 .... C3
98935 Mabton 1,248 .... E4
99149 Malden 200 .... H3
98829 Malott 350 .... F2
98353 Manchester 400 ... A2
98830 Mansfield 315 .... F3
98266 Maple Falls 300 .. D2
98038 Maple Valley 900 . C3
99151 Marcus 174 ...... H2
98268 Marietta-Alderwood 2,324 . C2
98832 Marlin 83 .... F3
98270 Marysville 5,080 . C2
98837 Mattawa 299 ..... F4
98557 McCleary 1,419 .. B3
99022 Medical Lake 3,600 . H3
98039 Medina 3,220 .... B2
98040 Mercer Island
       (city) 21,522 .... B2
99343 Mesa 278 .... G4
99152 Metaline 190 .... H2
99153 Metaline Falls 296 . H2
†99210 Millwood 1,717 . H3
98354 Milton 3,162 ... C3
98832 Mineral 550 .... C4
98562 Moclips 500 .... A3
98836 Monitor 650 .... E3
98272 Monroe 2,869 ... D3
98563 Montesano⊙ 3,247 . B4
98356 Morton 1,264 ... C4
98837 Moses Lake 10,629 . F3
98564 Mossyrock 463 .. C4
98043 Mountlake Terrace 16,534 . B1
98273 Mount Vernon⊙ 13,009 . C2
98936 Moxee City 687 . E4
98275 Mukilteo 1,426 . C3
98937 Naches 644 ..... E4
98565 Napavine 611 ... C4
98638 Naselle 500 .... B4
†98310 Navy Yard City 2,594 . A2
98357 Neah Bay 800 ... A2
99155 Nespelem 284 ... G2
†98283 Newhalem 350 .. D2
99156 Newport⊙ 1,665 . H2
†98501 Nisqually 500 . C3
98276 Nooksack 429 .. C2
98358 Nordland 706 .. C2
†98100 Normandy Park 4,268 . A2
98045 North Bend 1,701 . D3
98639 North Bonneville 394 . C5
99157 Northport 368 . H2
99158 Oakesdale 444 . H3
98277 Oak Harbor 12,271 . C2
98568 Oakville 537 .. B4
98569 Ocean City 350 . A3
98640 Ocean Park 918 . A4
98551 Ocean Shores 1,692 . A3
†98520 Ocosta 369 ... B4
99159 Odessa 1,009 .. G3
98840 Okanogan⊙ 2,302 . F2
98359 Olalla 500 ... A2
*98501 Olympia (cap.)⊙ 27,447 . C3
       Olympia‡ 124,264 .... C3
98841 Omak 4,007 ... F2
98570 Onalaska 600 . C4
99214 Opportunity 21,241 . H3
98662 Orchards 8,828 . C5
98844 Oroville 1,483 . F2
98360 Orting 1,787 . C3
99344 Othello 4,454 . F4
99027 Otis Orchards-East
       Farms 4,597 .... H3
98938 Outlook 300 .. E4
98047 Pacific 2,261 . C3
98571 Pacific Beach 900 . A4
98361 Packwood 800 . D4
99161 Palouse 1,005 . H4
98939 Parker 500 ... E4
98444 Parkland 23,355 . C3
99301 Pasco⊙ 18,425 . F4
98846 Pateros 555 .. E2
98572 Pe Ell 617 .. B4
98847 Peshastin 500 . E3
98281 Point Roberts 500 . B2
99347 Pomeroy⊙ 1,716 . H4
98362 Port Angeles⊙ 17,311 . B2
†98101 Port Blakely 600 . A2
98366 Port Orchard⊙ 4,787 . A2
98368 Port Townsend⊙ 6,067 . C2
†98584 Potlatch 100 . B3
98370 Poulsbo 3,453 . A1
99348 Prescott 341 . G4
98050 Preston 500 .. D3
99350 Prosser⊙ 3,896 . F4
99163 Pullman 23,579 . H4
98371 Puyallup 18,251 . C3
98376 Quilcene 900 . B3
98575 Quinault 450 . B3
98848 Quincy 3,525 . F3
98576 Rainier 891 .. C4

(continued on following page)

Agriculture, Industry and Resources

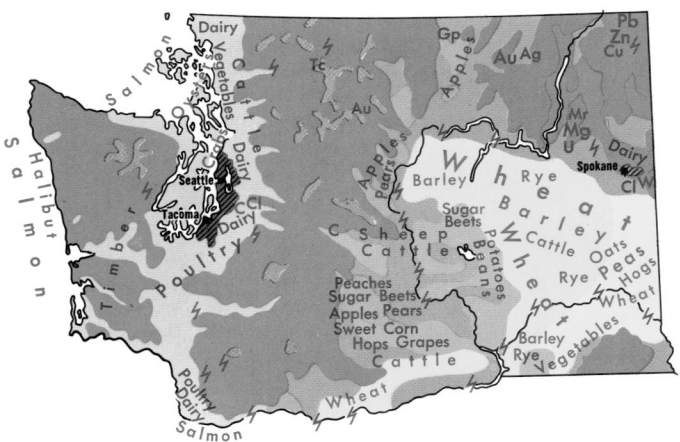

DOMINANT LAND USE

Specialized Wheat
Wheat, Peas
Dairy, Poultry, Mixed Farming
Fruit and Mixed Farming
General Farming, Dairy, Range Livestock
General Farming, Livestock, Special Crops
Range Livestock
Forests
Urban Areas
Nonagricultural Land

MAJOR MINERAL OCCURRENCES

Ag Silver   Mr Marble
Au Gold   Pb Lead
C   Coal   Tc Talc
Cl Clay   U   Uranium
Cu Copper   W   Tungsten
Gp Gypsum   Zn Zinc
Mg Magnesium

⚡ Water Power
▨ Major Industrial Areas

Washington

SCALE

0 5 10 20 30 40 MI.

0 5 10 20 30 40 KM.

State Capitals .... ✪

County Seats .... ◉

Major Limited Access Hwys. ———

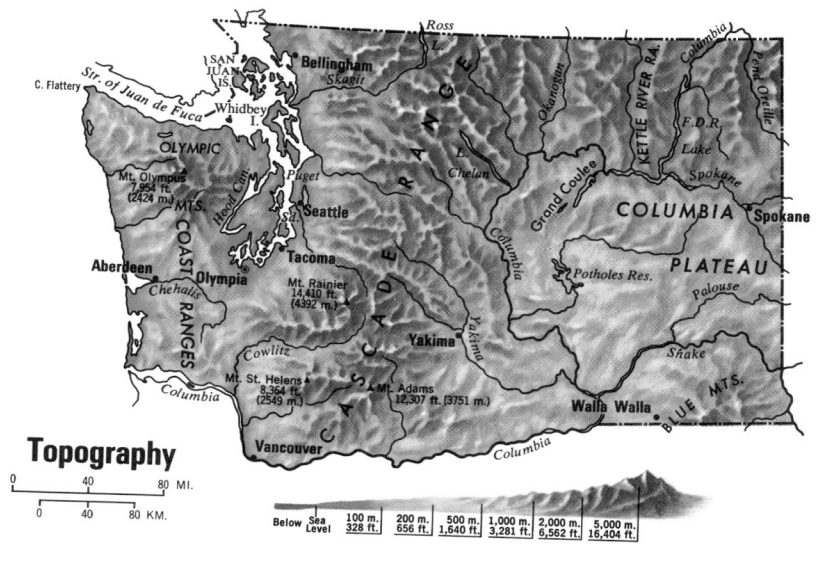

Topography

| 0 | 40 | 80 MI. |
| 0 | 40 | 80 KM. |

| Below Sea Level | 100 m. 328 ft. | 200 m. 656 ft. | 500 m. 1,640 ft. | 1,000 m. 3,281 ft. | 2,000 m. 6,562 ft. | 5,000 m. 16,404 ft. |

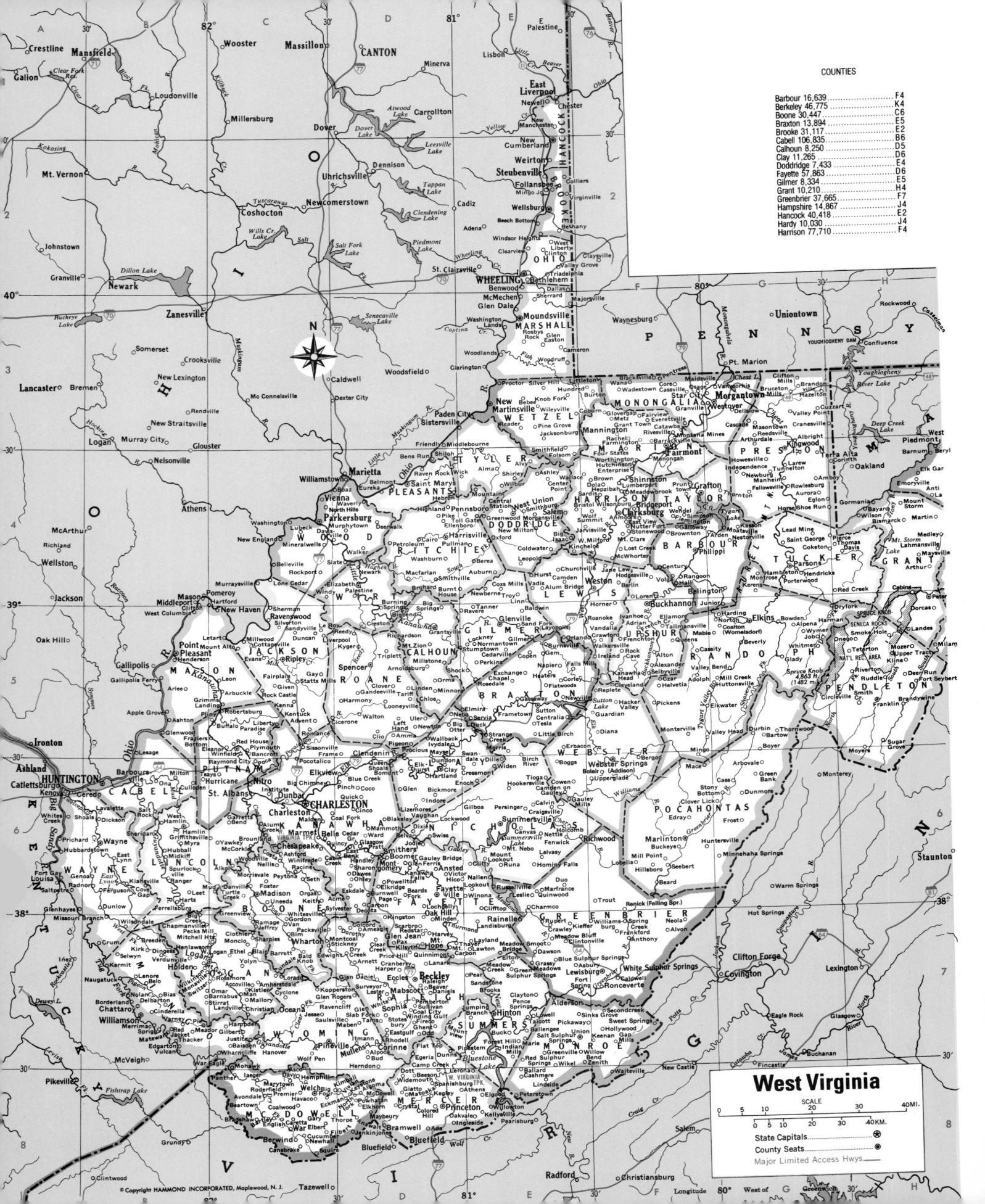

West Virginia

COUNTIES

Barbour 16,639 .... F4
Berkeley 46,775 .... K4
Boone 30,447 .... C6
Braxton 13,894 .... E5
Brooke 31,117 .... B6
Cabell 106,835 .... D5
Calhoun 8,250 .... D6
Clay 11,265 .... E4
Doddridge 7,433 .... E4
Fayette 57,863 .... E5
Gilmer 8,334 .... E4
Grant 10,210 .... H4
Greenbrier 37,665 .... F7
Hampshire 14,867 .... J4
Hancock 40,418 .... E2
Hardy 10,030 .... J4
Harrison 77,710 .... F4

SCALE
State Capitals
County Seats
Major Limited Access Hwys

Jackson 25,794 ... C5
Jefferson 30,302 ... L4
Kanawha 231,414 ... C6
Lewis 18,813 ... E4
Lincoln 23,675 ... B6
Logan 50,679 ... C7
Marion 65,789 ... F4
Marshall 41,608 ... E3
Mason 27,045 ... B5
McDowell 49,899 ... C8
Mercer 73,942 ... D8
Mineral 27,234 ... J4
Mingo 37,336 ... B7
Monongalia 75,024 ... F3
Monroe 12,873 ... E7
Morgan 10,711 ... K3
Nicholas 28,126 ... E6
Ohio 61,389 ... E2
Pendleton 7,910 ... H5
Pleasants 8,236 ... D4
Pocahontas 9,919 ... F6
Preston 30,460 ... G4
Putnam 38,181 ... C6
Raleigh 86,821 ... D7
Randolph 28,734 ... G5
Ritchie 11,442 ... D4
Roane 15,952 ... D5
Summers 15,875 ... E7
Taylor 16,584 ... F4
Tucker 8,675 ... F4
Tyler 11,320 ... E4
Upshur 23,427 ... F5
Wayne 46,021 ... B6
Webster 12,245 ... F6
Wetzel 21,874 ... E3
Wirt 4,922 ... D4
Wood 93,648 ... D4
Wyoming 35,993 ... C7

AREA 24,231 sq. mi. (62,758 sq. km.)
POPULATION 1,950,279
CAPITAL Charleston
LARGEST CITY Charleston
HIGHEST POINT Spruce Knob 4,863 ft. (1482 m.)
SETTLED IN 1774
ADMITTED TO UNION June 20, 1863
POPULAR NAME Mountain State
STATE FLOWER Big Rhododendron
STATE BIRD Cardinal

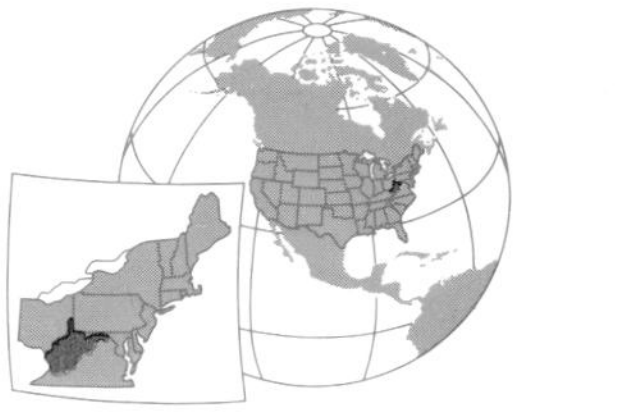

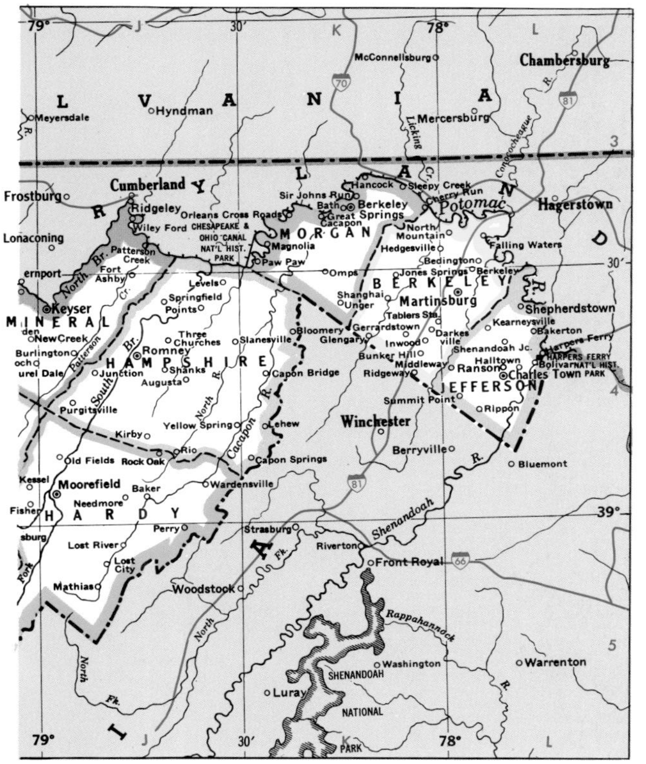

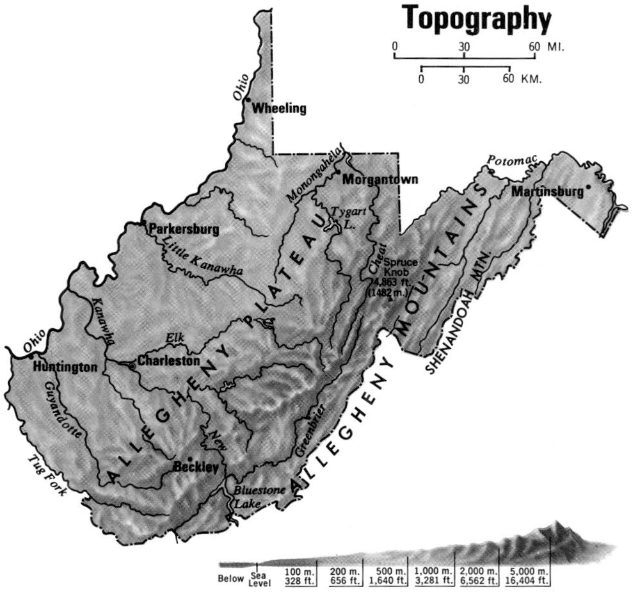

CITIES and TOWNS

Zip *Name/Pop.* *Key*

25606 Accoville 975 ... C7
†26288 Addison (Webster Springs)⊙ 939 ... F6
26210 Adrian 510 ... F5
26519 Albright 357 ... G3
24910 Alderson 1,375 ... E7
24807 Algoma 200 ... D8
25501 Alkol 500 ... C6
26320 Alma 197 ... E4
24710 Alpoca 200 ... D7
26321 Alum Bridge 150 ... E4
25003 Alum Creek 900 ... C6
26322 Alvy 150 ... E4
25004 Ameagle 230 ... D7
25607 Amherstdale 1,075 ... C7
25005 Amma 200 ... D5
24808 Anawalt 652 ... D8
26323 Anmoore 865 ... F4
25812 Ansted 1,952 ... D6
25502 Apple Grove 900 ... B5
24915 Arbovale 610 ... G6
26816 Arthur 350 ... H4
26520 Arthurdale 1,063 ... G3
24916 Asbury 280 ... E7
24809 Asco 175 ... C8
25009 Ashford 400 ... C6
25503 Ashton 259 ... B5
24712 Athens 1,147 ... E8
26325 Auburn 116 ... E4
26704 Augusta 750 ... J4
26705 Aurora 250 ... G4
24811 Avondale 250 ... C8
25608 Baisden 500 ... C7
26801 Baker 200 ... J4
25410 Bakerton 125 ... L4
25010 Bald Knob 356 ... C7
26326 Baldwin 92 ... E5
25011 Bancroft 528 ... C5
25504 Barboursville 2,871 ... B6
25609 Barnabus 750 ... C7
26559 Barrackville 1,815 ... F3
25013 Barrett 950 ... C7
24813 Bartley 900 ... C8
24920 Bartow 500 ... G5
†25411 Bath (Berkeley Springs) 789 ... K3
26707 Bayard 540 ... H4
25014 Beards Fork 400 ... D6
25813 Beaver (Glen Hedrick) 1,122 ... D7
25801 Beckley⊙ 20,492 ... D7
26030 Beech Bottom 507 ... E2
24714 Beeson 300 ... D8
26250 Belington 2,038 ... F4
25015 Belle 1,621 ... C6
26133 Belleville 105 ... C4
26134 Belmont 887 ... D4
26656 Belva 275 ... D6
26135 Bens Run 85 ... D4
26031 Benwood 1,994 ... E2
26298 Bergoo 220 ... F6
25411 Berkeley Springs (Bath)⊙ 789 ... K3
24815 Berwind 615 ... C8
26032 Bethany 1,336 ... E2
†26003 Bethlehem 3,045 ... E2
26253 Beverly 475 ... G5
25019 Bickmore 300 ... D6
26136 Bigbend 120 ... D5
25302 Big Chimney 450 ... C6
25505 Big Creek 500 ... B7
26137 Big Springs 485 ... D5
25021 Bim 500 ... C7
26610 Birch River 650 ... E6
26521 Blacksville 248 ... F3
25022 Blair 800 ... C7
26817 Bloomery 200 ... K4
25026 Blue Creek 650 ... D6
24701 Bluefield 16,060 ... D8
26288 Bolair 450 ... F6
†25425 Bolivar 672 ... L4
25030 Bomont 170 ... D6
25031 Boomer 1,051 ... D6
24817 Bradshaw 1,002 ... C8
24715 Bramwell 989 ... D8
26523 Brandonville 92 ... G3
26802 Brandywine 300 ... H5
25666 Breeden 600 ... B7
26330 Bridgeport 6,604 ... F4
26138 Brohard 80 ... D4
25957 Brooks 196 ... E7
26334 Brownton 400 ... F4
26525 Bruceton Mills 296 ... G3
24924 Buckeye 125 ... F6
26201 Buckhannon⊙ 6,820 ... F5
24716 Bud 400 ... D7
25033 Buffalo 1,034 ... C5
25413 Bunker Hill 600 ... K4
26710 Burlington 300 ... J4
26335 Burnsville 531 ... E5
26336 Burnt House 175 ... D4
26562 Burton 200 ... F3
25035 Cabin Creek 900 ... C6
26337 Cairo 428 ... D4
24925 Caldwell 795 ... F7
26660 Calvin 400 ... E6
26208 Camden on Gauley 236 ... E6
26033 Cameron 1,474 ... E3
24819 Canebrake 300 ... C8
26662 Canvas 300 ... E6
26711 Capon Bridge 191 ... K4
26823 Capon Springs 580 ... K4
25037 Carbon 300 ... D6
24821 Caretta 650 ... C8
24927 Cass 148 ... G6
26527 Cassville 800 ... F3
25039 Cedar Grove 1,479 ... D6
26339 Center Point 250 ... E4
26612 Centralia 100 ... E5
26340 Central Station 200 ... E4
26214 Century 250 ... F4
25507 Ceredo 2,255 ... B6
25508 Chapmanville 1,164 ... B7
*25301 Charleston (cap.)⊙ 63,968 ... C6
Charleston‡ 269,595 ... C6
25414 Charles Town⊙ 2,857 ... L4
25958 Charmco 800 ... E6
25667 Chattaroy 1,383 ... B7
25418 Cherry Run 120 ... L3
†25301 Chesapeake 2,364 ... C6
26034 Chester 3,297 ... E1
26301 Clarksburg⊙ 22,371 ... F4
25043 Clay⊙ 940 ... D6
25044 Clear Creek 300 ... D7
†26003 Clearview 740 ... E2
25045 Clendenin 1,373 ... D5
26215 Cleveland 74 ... F5
25822 Clifftop 100 ... E6
25237 Clifton 325 ... B5
24928 Clintonville 250 ... E7
25046 Clio 300 ... D5
25047 Clothier 900 ... C7
25823 Coal City 2,324 ... D7
25306 Coal Fork 2,775 ... D6
26257 Coalton 306 ... G5
24824 Coalwood 650 ... C8
25048 Colcord 600 ... D7
26035 Colliers 864 ... E2
26615 Copen 50 ... E5
25826 Corinne 900 ... D7
25051 Costa 250 ... C6
25239 Cottageville 300 ... C5
25509 Cove Gap 650 ... B6
26206 Cowen 723 ... E6
26342 Coxs Mills 275 ... E4
26205 Craigsville 1,562 ... E6
25828 Cranberry 315 ... D7
24931 Crawley 395 ... E7
25669 Crum 500 ... B7
24826 Cucumber 274 ... C8
25510 Culloden 2,931 ... B6
24827 Cyclone 500 ... C7
26036 Dallas 450 ... E2
25832 Daniels 1,959 ... D7
25053 Danville 727 ... C6
†25428 Darkesville 150 ... L4
26260 Davis 979 ... H4
24828 Davy 882 ... C8
25054 Dawes 800 ... D6
24932 Dawson 300 ... E7
25670 Delbarton 981 ... B7
26531 Dellslow 300 ... G3
26217 Diana 300 ... F5
26617 Dille 300 ... E6
25671 Dingess 600 ... B7
25059 Dixie 985 ... D6
25060 Dorothy 400 ... D7
24721 Dott 100 ... D8
25062 Dry Creek 441 ... D7
26263 Dryfork 425 ... H5
25063 Duck 500 ... E5
25064 Dunbar 9,285 ... C6
24934 Dunmore 280 ... G6
26264 Durbin 379 ... G5
25067 East Bank 1,155 ... D6
25835 Eastgulf 300 ... D7
25512 East Lynn 150 ... B6
†26301 East View 1,222 ... F4
25836 Eccles 1,162 ... D7
24829 Eckman 750 ... C8
25672 Edgarton 415 ... B7
26716 Eglon 70 ... G4
24830 Elbert 400 ... C8
25070 Eleanor 1,282 ... C5
26143 Elizabeth⊙ 856 ... D4
26717 Elk Garden 291 ... H4
26241 Elkins⊙ 8,536 ... G5
25071 Elkview 1,161 ... C6
26267 Ellamore 250 ... F5
26346 Ellenboro 357 ... D4
25965 Elton 200 ... E7
24832 English 500 ... C8
26568 Enterprise 1,110 ... F4
25075 Eskdale 400 ... D6
25076 Ethel 450 ... C7
26144 Eureka 125 ... D4
25241 Evans 400 ... C5
26533 Everettville 175 ... F3
26554 Fairmont 23,863 ... F4
26570 Fairview 759 ... F3
†24966 Falling Spring (Renick) 240 ... F6
26571 Farmington 583 ... F3
25840 Fayetteville⊙ 2,366 ... D6
26202 Fenwick 500 ... E6
24835 Filbert 130 ... D8
26818 Fisher 500 ... H4
25841 Flat Top 550 ... D7
26621 Flatwoods 405 ... E5
26347 Flemington 452 ... F4
26037 Follansbee 3,994 ... E2
26348 Folsom 360 ... E4
24935 Forest Hill 314 ... E7
26719 Fort Ashby 1,205 ... J4
25514 Fort Gay 886 ... A6
26806 Fort Seybert 200 ... H5
24936 Fort Spring 250 ... E7
25081 Foster 500 ... C6
26572 Four States 500 ... F4
25071 Frame 76 ... C5
26623 Frametown 150 ... E5
26807 Franklin⊙ 780 ... H5
25082 Fraziers Bottom 250 ... B5
26219 Frenchton 102 ... F5
26146 Friendly 242 ... D3
25515 Gallipolis Ferry 325 ... B5
26349 Galloway 500 ... F4
25243 Gandeeville 150 ... D5
24941 Gap Mills 300 ... F7
24836 Gary 2,233 ... C8
26624 Gassaway 1,225 ... E5
25085 Gauley Bridge 1,177 ... D6
26240 Gauley Mills 165 ... E6
25244 Gay 300 ... C5
25420 Gerrardstown 240 ... K4
25843 Ghent 500 ... D7
25621 Gilbert 757 ... C7
26671 Gilboa 500 ... E6
26350 Gilmer 110 ... E5
26268 Glady 175 ... G5
25086 Glasgow 1,031 ... D6
25088 Glen 175 ... D6
26038 Glen Dale 1,875 ... E3
26039 Glen Easton 100 ... E3
25090 Glen Ferris 200 ... D6
25421 Glengary 250 ... K4
†25813 Glen Hedrick (Beaver) 1,122 ... D7
25846 Glen Jean ... D7
25848 Glen Rogers 500 ... D7
26351 Glenville⊙ 2,155 ... E5
25849 Glen White 300 ... D7
25520 Glenwood 400 ... B5
†26585 Glovergap 100 ... F3
25093 Gordon 300 ... C7
26720 Gormania 100 ... H4
26354 Grafton⊙ 6,845 ... G4
26147 Grantsville⊙ 788 ... D5
26574 Grant Town 987 ... F3
26534 Granville 992 ... F3
24943 Grassy Meadows 100 ... E7
25422 Great Cacapon 750 ... K3
24944 Green Bank 115 ... G6
25966 Green Sulphur Springs 225 ... E7
24945 Greenville 125 ... E7
26360 Greenwood 750 ... E4
25095 Grimms Landing 350 ... B5
26221 Guardian 175 ... F5
26222 Hacker Valley 440 ... F5
25423 Halltown 375 ... L4
26269 Hambleton 403 ... G4
25523 Hamlin⊙ 1,219 ... B6
25623 Hampden 300 ... C7
25424 Hancock 175 ... K3
25102 Handley 633 ... D6
†26250 Harding 100 ... G5
26270 Harman 181 ... G5
25246 Harmony 600 ... D5
25851 Harper 400 ... D7
25425 Harpers Ferry 361 ... L4
26362 Harrisville⊙ 1,673 ... E4
25247 Hartford 556 ... C4
25524 Harts 400 ... B6
25852 Harvey 300 ... D7
24841 Havaco 350 ... C8
26627 Heaters 440 ... E5
25427 Hedgesville 217 ... K3
26224 Helvetia 130 ... F5
24842 Hemphill 700 ... C8
25106 Henderson 604 ... B5
26271 Hendricks 390 ... G4
25624 Henlawson 900 ... B7
26369 Hepzibah 600 ... F4
24726 Herndon 500 ... D7
25854 Hico 750 ... D6
24946 Hillsboro 276 ... F6
25951 Hinton⊙ 4,622 ... E7
25625 Holden 2,036 ... B7
26372 Horner 125 ... F5
26769 Horse Shoe Run 500 ... G4
†25506 Hubball 145 ... B6
26575 Hundred 485 ... E3
*25701 Huntington⊙ 63,684 ... A6
Huntington-Ashland‡ 311,350 ... A6
25526 Hurricane 3,751 ... C6
26273 Huttonsville 242 ... G5
24844 Iaeger 833 ... C8
26374 Independence 200 ... G4
24949 Indian Mills 150 ... E7
25111 Indore 300 ... D6
25112 Institute ... C6
25428 Inwood 1,159 ... K4
24847 Itmann 600 ... D7
25113 Ivydale 800 ... D5
26377 Jacksonburg 400 ... E3
26378 Jane Lew 406 ... F4
25114 Jeffrey 900 ... C7
24848 Jenkinjones 750 ... D8
24849 Jesse 400 ... C7
26674 Jodie 440 ... D6
25969 Jumping Branch 700 ... E7
26824 Junction 75 ... J4

(continued on following page)

Agriculture, Industry and Resources

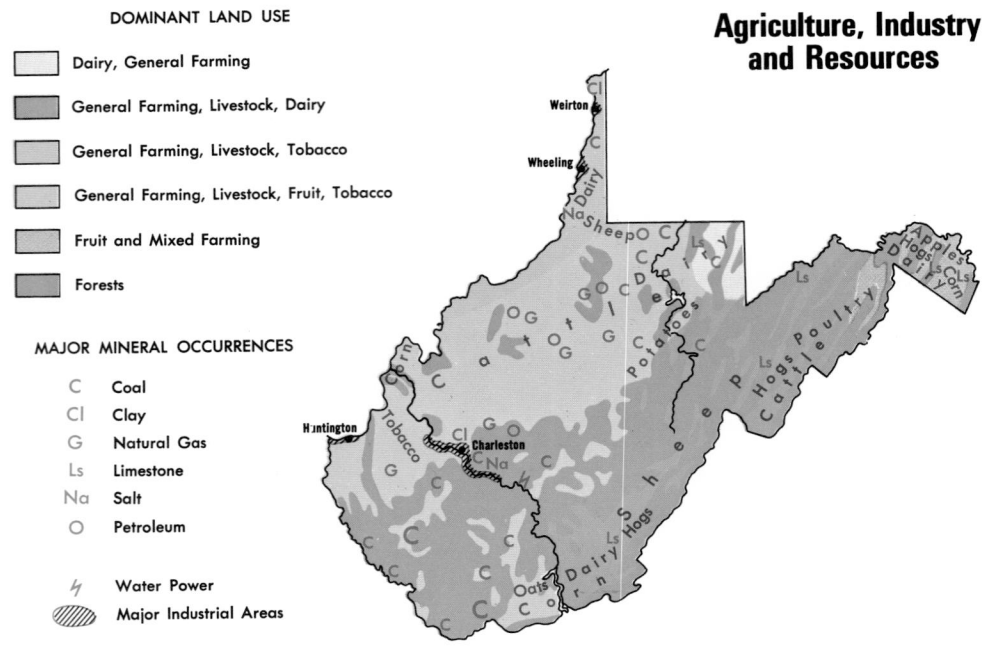

DOMINANT LAND USE

- Dairy, General Farming
- General Farming, Livestock, Dairy
- General Farming, Livestock, Tobacco
- General Farming, Livestock, Fruit, Tobacco
- Fruit and Mixed Farming
- Forests

MAJOR MINERAL OCCURRENCES

- C Coal
- Cl Clay
- G Natural Gas
- Ls Limestone
- Na Salt
- O Petroleum

- ϟ Water Power
- Major Industrial Areas

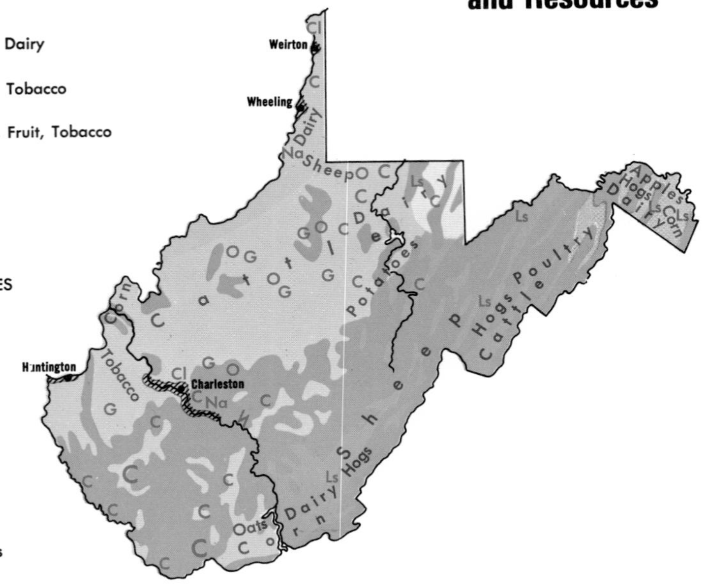

26275 Junior 591 ... G5
24851 Justice 600 ... C7
25115 Kanawha Falls 105 ... D6
25430 Kearneysville 250 ... L4
24731 Kegley 900 ... D8
24732 Kellysville 165 ... E8
25248 Kenna 150 ... C5
25530 Kenova 4,454 ... A6
25249 Kentuck 200 ... C5
25674 Kermit 705 ... B7
26726 Keyser⊙ 6,569 ... J4
24852 Keystone 902 ... D8
24950 Kieffer 135 ... E7
25859 Kilsyth 200 ... D7
24853 Kimball 871 ... C8
25120 Kingston 189 ... D7
26537 Kingwood⊙ 2,877 ... G4
26729 Kirby 110 ... J4
25628 Kistler 200 ... C7
26579 Knob Fork 106 ... E3
24854 Kopperston 700 ... C7
26731 Lahmansville 200 ... H4
25860 Lanark 559 ... D7
25629 Landville 400 ... C7
25535 Lavalette 600 ... B6
25863 Lawton 100 ... E7
25864 Layland 500 ... E7
†26430 Layopolis (Sand Fork) 280 ... E5
25251 Left Hand 700 ... D5
26676 Leivasy 200 ... E6
25676 Lenore 800 ... B7
25123 Leon 228 ... C5
25971 Lerona 550 ... D8
25537 Lesage 600 ... B5
25972 Leslie 350 ... E6
25865 Lester 626 ... D7
25253 Letart 350 ... C5
25431 Levels 180 ... J4
24901 Lewisburg⊙ 3,065 ... E7
26384 Linn 165 ... E4
26629 Little Birch 400 ... E5
26581 Littleton 335 ... F3
25125 Lizemores 400 ... D6
25866 Lochgelly 250 ... D6
25258 Lockney 190 ... E5
25601 Logan⊙ 3,029 ... B7
25630 Lorado 400 ... C7
†26201 Lorentz 200 ... F4
26810 Lost City 130 ... J5
26385 Lost Creek 604 ... F4
26811 Lost River 500 ... J5
†26101 Lubeck 1,356 ... C4
26386 Lumberport 939 ... F4
25631 Lundale 525 ... C7
25870 Maben 450 ... D7
26278 Mabie 550 ... F5
25871 Mabscott 1,668 ... D7
26148 Macfarlan 436 ... D4
25130 Madison⊙ 3,228 ... C6
26541 Maidsville 500 ... F3
25306 Malden 900 ... C6
25634 Mallory 1,330 ... C7
25132 Mammoth 563 ... D6
25635 Man 1,333 ... C7
26582 Mannington 3,036 ... F3
25975 Marfrance 225 ... E6
24954 Marlinton⊙ 1,352 ... F6
25315 Marmet 2,196 ... C6
25401 Martinsburg⊙ 13,063 ... K4
25260 Mason 1,432 ... B4
26542 Masontown 1,052 ... G3
25678 Matewan 822 ... B7
24736 Matoaka 613 ... D8
24861 Maybeury 300 ... D8
26833 Maysville 150 ... H4
24858 McDowell 500 ... D8
26040 McMechen 2,402 ... E3
26401 McWhorter 150 ... F4
24958 Meadow Bluff 250 ... E7
25976 Meadow Bridge 530 ... E7
26404 Meadowbrook 500 ... F4
25977 Meadow Creek 300 ... E7
26585 Metz 150 ... F3
26149 Middlebourne⊙ 941 ... E3
25540 Midkiff 650 ... B6
26280 Mill Creek 801 ... G5
24959 Mill Point 148 ... F6
25261 Millstone 850 ... D5
25262 Millwood 800 ... C5
25541 Milton 2,178 ... B6
25879 Minden 800 ... D7
26150 Mineralwells 325 ... C4
26281 Mingo 350 ... F5
25263 Minnora 500 ... D5
26405 Moatsville 150 ... G4
25636 Monaville 950 ... B7
26554 Monongah 1,132 ... F4
26586 Montana Mines 200 ... F3
25135 Montcoal 150 ... D7
26282 Monterville 250 ... F5
25136 Montgomery 3,104 ... D6
26283 Montrose 129 ... G4
26836 Moorefield⊙ 2,257 ... J4
26505 Morgantown⊙ 27,605 ... G3
25542 Morrisvale 450 ... C6
26041 Moundsville⊙ 12,419 ... E3
26407 Mountain 200 ... E4
25264 Mount Alto 200 ... C5
25139 Mount Carbon 450 ... D7
26408 Mount Clare 950 ... F4
25637 Mount Gay 4,366 ... C7
25880 Mount Hope 1,849 ... D7
26678 Mount Lookout 500 ... E6
26679 Mount Nebo 535 ... E6
26739 Mount Storm 500 ... H4
25882 Mullens 2,919 ... D7
26680 Nallen 250 ... E6
26631 Napier 158 ... E5
25685 Naugatuck 500 ... B7
25141 Nebo 200 ... D5
25142 Nellis 600 ... C6
24961 Neola 300 ... F7
26681 Nettie 500 ... E6
26410 Newburg 418 ... G4
26047 New Cumberland⊙ 1,752 ... E2
26050 Newell 2,032 ... E1
26154 New England 335 ... C4
24866 Newhall 400 ... C8
25265 New Haven 1,723 ... C5
26056 New Manchester 800 ... E1
26155 New Martinsville⊙ 7,109 ... E3
25266 Newton 390 ... D5
26632 Newville 160 ... E5
25143 Nitro 8,074 ... C6
25687 Nolan 250 ... B7
25267 Normantown 112 ... E5
24868 Northfork 1,105 ... D8
†26101 North Hills 940 ... D4
26285 Norton 400 ... G5
26301 Nutter Fort 2,078 ... F4
25901 Oak Hill 7,120 ... D6
24739 Oakvale 208 ... D8
24870 Oceana 2,143 ... C7
25902 Odd 500 ... D7
25147 Ohley 450 ... D6
25638 Omar 900 ... C7
26886 Onego 400 ... H5
25148 Orgas 500 ... C6
26412 Orlando 700 ... E5
25268 Orma ... D5
26543 Osage 285 ... F3
25151 Packsville 225 ... C7
26159 Paden City 3,671 ... D3
25152 Page 600 ... D6
26160 Palestine 110 ... D4
24872 Panther 450 ... C8
26101 Parkersburg⊙ 39,967 ... D4
Parkersburg-Marietta‡ 162,836 ... D4
26287 Parsons⊙ 1,937 ... G4
26746 Patterson Creek 157 ... J3
25434 Paw Paw 644 ... K3
25904 Pax 274 ... D7
†25955 Pear 100 ... E7
25547 Pecks Mill 350 ... B7
25905 Pemberton 300 ... D7
24962 Pence Springs 300 ... E7
26415 Pennsboro 1,652 ... E4
26544 Pentress 250 ... F3
26847 Petersburg⊙ 2,084 ... H5
24963 Peterstown 648 ... E8
25154 Peytona 175 ... C6
26416 Philippi⊙ 3,194 ... G4
24964 Pickaway 225 ... E7
26230 Pickens 240 ... F5
25689 Pie 250 ... B7
26750 Piedmont 1,491 ... H4
25156 Pinch 800 ... D6
26419 Pine Grove 767 ... E3
24874 Pineville⊙ 1,140 ... C7
25158 Pliny 900 ... B5
25159 Poca 1,142 ... C6
†25301 Pocotalico 2,420 ... C6
25550 Point Pleasant⊙ 5,682 ... B5
25437 Points 250 ... J4
25161 Powellton 1,339 ... D6
24877 Powhatan 400 ... D8
25162 Pratt 821 ... D6
24878 Premier 400 ... C8
†25880 Price Hill 175 ... D7
25555 Prichard 500 ... A6
24740 Princeton⊙ 7,493 ... D8
25164 Procious 600 ... D5
26055 Proctor 350 ... E3
26421 Pullman 196 ... D4
26852 Purgitsville 450 ... J4
25045 Quick 400 ... D6
†25015 Quincy 150 ... C6
25981 Quinwood 460 ... E6
26587 Rachel 550 ... F3
25165 Racine 725 ... C6
25556 Radnor 300 ... A6
25962 Rainelle 1,983 ... E7
25911 Raleigh 900 ... D7
25166 Ramage 350 ... C7
25557 Ranger 300 ... B6
25438 Ranson 2,471 ... L4
25913 Ravencliff 350 ... C7
26164 Ravenswood 4,126 ... C5
26167 Reader 950 ... E3
26289 Red Creek 125 ... H4
25168 Red House 600 ... C5
25692 Red Jacket 850 ... B7
26547 Reedsville 564 ... G3
25270 Reedy 338 ... D5
24966 Renick 240 ... F6
25915 Rhodell 472 ... D7
26261 Richwood 3,568 ... F6
26753 Ridgeley 994 ... J3
25440 Ridgeway 200 ... K4
26755 Rio 140 ... J4
25271 Ripley⊙ 3,464 ... C5
25441 Rippon 500 ... L4
26588 Rivesville 1,327 ... F3
26234 Rock Cave 400 ... F5
24881 Roderfield 900 ... C8
26757 Romney⊙ 2,094 ... J4
24970 Ronceverte 2,312 ... F7
26636 Rosedale 400 ... E5
25643 Rossmore 200 ... C7
26425 Rowlesburg 966 ... G4
26688 Runa 150 ... E6
25984 Rupert 1,276 ... E7
26689 Russellville 280 ... E6
25177 Saint Albans 12,402 ... C6
26290 Saint George 150 ... G4
26170 Saint Marys⊙ 2,219 ... D4
26426 Salem 2,706 ... E4
25559 Salt Rock 350 ... B6
26430 Sand Fork 280 ... E5
25985 Sandstone 300 ... E7
25275 Sandyville 500 ... C5
25876 Saulsville 250 ... C7
25917 Scarbro 800 ... D7
24975 Seebert 100 ... F6
25181 Seth 950 ... C6
26761 Shanks 500 ... J4
25182 Sharon 450 ... D6
25183 Sharples 250 ... C7
25443 Shepherdstown 1,791 ... L4
26173 Sherman 104 ... C5
26431 Shinnston 3,059 ... F4
26434 Shirley 275 ... E4
25562 Shoals 150 ... B6
26638 Shock 200 ... D5
†26164 Silverton 250 ... C5
26435 Simpson 250 ... F4
24976 Sinks Grove 156 ... F7
25320 Sissonville 450 ... C5
26175 Sistersville 2,367 ... D3
25920 Slab Fork 210 ... D7
25444 Slanesville 250 ... K4
26436 Smithburg 130 ... E4
25186 Smithers 1,482 ... D6
26437 Smithfield 278 ... E4
26178 Smithville 200 ... D4
24977 Smoot 300 ... E7
25921 Sophia 1,216 ... D7
25303 South Charleston 15,968 ... C6
25922 Spanishburg 550 ... D8
25276 Spencer⊙ 2,799 ... D5
25693 Sprigg 225 ... B7
26763 Springfield 250 ... J4
25565 Spurlockville 250 ... B6
24884 Squire 900 ... C8
26505 Star City 1,464 ... F3
25279 Statts Mills 400 ... C5
25188 Stickney 150 ... D7
25645 Stirrat 250 ... C7
26301 Stonewood 2,058 ... F4
24979 Stony Bottom 50 ... F6
25280 Stumptown 125 ... E5
26651 Summersville⊙ 2,972 ... E6
25446 Summit Point 455 ... K4
25932 Surveyor 300 ... D7
26601 Sutton⊙ 1,192 ... E5
26690 Swiss 500 ... D6
25647 Switzer 1,034 ... B7
25193 Sylvester 256 ... C6
24981 Talcott 800 ... E7
26237 Tallmansville 140 ... F5
26179 Tanner 375 ... E5
26764 Terra Alta 1,946 ... H4
26640 Tesla 300 ... E5
25694 Thacker 525 ... B7
26292 Thomas 747 ... H4
26440 Thornton 200 ... G4
24888 Thorpe 600 ... D8
26765 Three Churches 350 ... J4
25936 Thurmond 67 ... D7
26691 Tioga 825 ... E6
26059 Triadelphia 1,461 ... E2
26443 Troy 110 ... E4
26444 Tunnelton 510 ... G4
25203 Turtle Creek 566 ... C6
25205 Uneeda 700 ... C6
25447 Unger 300 ... K4
24983 Union⊙ 743 ... E7
26266 Upperglade 750 ... F6
26866 Upper Tract 155 ... H5
26445 Vadis 130 ... E4
26293 Valley Bend 950 ... F5
26060 Valley Grove 597 ... E2
26294 Valley Head 900 ... G5
25206 Van 800 ... C7
25696 Varney 750 ... B7
25649 Verdunville 950 ... B7
25938 Victor 500 ... D6
26105 Vienna 11,618 ... D4
24891 Vivian 500 ... D8
26238 Volga 125 ... F4
25697 Vulcan 130 ... B7
26589 Wadestown 300 ... F3
24984 Waiteville 230 ... F8
26180 Walker 100 ... D4
26448 Wallace 325 ... E4
25286 Walton 550 ... D5
26590 Wana 150 ... F3
24892 War 2,158 ... C8
26851 Wardensville 241 ... J4
26181 Washington 450 ... C4
26184 Waverly 500 ... D4
25570 Wayne⊙ 1,495 ... B6
26288 Webster Springs⊙ 939 ... F6
26062 Weirton 25,371 ... E2
Weirton-Steubenville‡ 163,099 ... E2
24801 Welch⊙ 3,885 ... C8
26070 Wellsburg⊙ 3,963 ... E2
25287 West Columbia 245 ... B5
25571 West Hamlin 643 ... B6
26074 West Liberty 744 ... E2
25601 West Logan 630 ... C7
26451 West Milford 510 ... F4
26452 Weston⊙ 6,250 ... F4
26505 Westover 4,884 ... G3
26456 West Union⊙ 1,090 ... E4
25651 Wharncliffe 900 ... C7
25208 Wharton 450 ... C7
26003 Wheeling⊙ 43,070 ... E2
Wheeling‡ 185,566 ... E2
24986 White Sulphur Springs 3,371 ... F7
25209 Whitesville 689 ... C6
26296 Whitmer 400 ... G5
25211 Widen 230 ... E6
26767 Wiley Ford 1,224 ... J3
26186 Wileyville 175 ... E3
25653 Wilkinson 975 ... B7
24991 Williamsburg 350 ... F7
25661 Williamson⊙ 5,219 ... B7
26187 Williamstown 3,095 ... C4
26461 Wilsonburg 350 ... F4
25699 Wilsondale 250 ... B7
26075 Windsor Heights 800 ... E2
25213 Winfield⊙ 329 ... C5
25214 Winifrede 750 ... C6
25942 Winona 250 ... E6
26462 Wolf Summit 750 ... F4
†26257 Womelsdorf (Coalton) 306 ... G5
25572 Woodville 300 ... C6
26591 Worthington 329 ... F4
25573 Yawkey 985 ... C6
26865 Yellow Spring 280 ... J4
25654 Yolyn 400 ... C7

OTHER FEATURES

Big Sandy (riv.) ... A6
Bluestone (lake) ... E7
Buckhannon (riv.) ... F5
Cacapon (riv.) ... J4
Cheat (riv.) ... G3
Cherry (riv.) ... E6
Chesapeake and Ohio Canal Nat'l Hist. Pa ... J3
Clear Fork, Guyandotte (riv.) ... C7
Coal (riv.) ... C6
Dry Fork (riv.) ... C8
Dry Fork (riv.) ... G5
East Lynn (lake) ... B6
Elk (riv.) ... D6
Fish (creek) ... E3
Gauley (riv.) ... D6
Greenbrier (riv.) ... F6
Guyandotte (riv.) ... B6
Harpers Ferry Nat'l Hist. Park ... L4
Hughes (riv.) ... D4
Kanawha (riv.) ... C5
Little Kanawha (riv.) ... D5
Meadow (riv.) ... E6
Mill (creek) ... C5
Monongahela (riv.) ... G3
Mount Storm (lake) ... H4
Mud (riv.) ... B6
New (riv.) ... E7
North (riv.) ... J4
Ohio (riv.) ... B5
Patterson (creek) ... J4
Pigeon (creek) ... B7
Pocatalico (riv.) ... C5
Pond Fork (riv.) ... C6
Potomac (riv.) ... L3
Potts (creek) ... F7
Reedy (creek) ... D5
Shavers Fork (riv.) ... G5
Shenandoah (riv.) ... K4
Spruce Knob (mt.) ... G5
Spruce Knob-Seneca Rocks Nat'l Rec. Area ... H5
Stony (riv.) ... H4
Summersville (lake) ... E6
Sutton (lake) ... F5
Tug Fork (riv.) ... B7
Twelvepole (creek) ... A6
Tygart (lake) ... G4
Tygart Valley (riv.) ... F5
West Fork (riv.) ... E5
Williams (riv.) ... F6

⊙County seat.
‡Population of metropolitan area.
† Zip of nearest p.o. * Multiple zips.

AREA 56,153 sq. mi. (145,436 sq. km.)
POPULATION 4,705,521
CAPITAL Madison
LARGEST CITY Milwaukee
HIGHEST POINT Timms Hill 1,951 ft. (595 m.)
SETTLED IN 1670
ADMITTED TO UNION May 29, 1848
POPULAR NAME Badger State
STATE FLOWER Wood Violet
STATE BIRD Robin

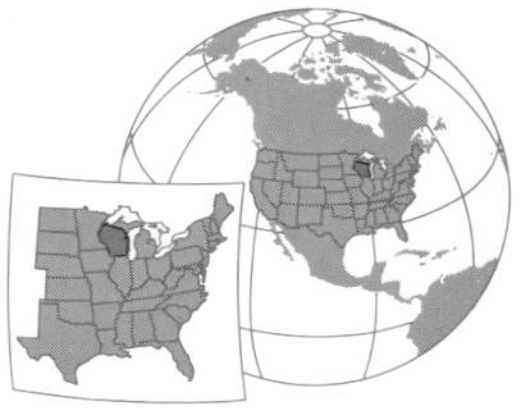

COUNTIES

Adams 13,457 ..... G7
Ashland 16,783 ..... E3
Barron 38,730 ..... C5
Bayfield 13,822 ..... D3
Brown 175,280 ..... L7
Buffalo 14,309 ..... C7
Burnett 12,340 ..... B4
Calumet 30,867 ..... K7
Chippewa 52,127 ..... D5
Clark 32,910 ..... E6
Columbia 43,222 ..... H9
Crawford 16,556 ..... E9
Dane 323,545 ..... H9
Dodge 75,064 ..... J9
Door 25,029 ..... M6
Douglas 44,421 ..... C3
Dunn 34,314 ..... C6
Eau Claire 78,805 ..... D6
Florence 4,172 ..... K4
Fond du Lac 88,964 ..... K8
Forest 9,044 ..... J4
Grant 51,736 ..... E10
Green 30,012 ..... G10
Green Lake 18,370 ..... H8
Iowa 19,802 ..... F9
Iron 6,730 ..... F3
Jackson 16,831 ..... E7
Jefferson 66,152 ..... J9
Juneau 21,039 ..... F8
Kenosha 123,137 ..... K10
Kewaunee 19,539 ..... L6
La Crosse 91,056 ..... D8
Lafayette 17,412 ..... F10
Langlade 19,978 ..... H5
Lincoln 26,555 ..... G5
Manitowoc 82,918 ..... L7
Marathon 111,270 ..... G6
Marinette 39,314 ..... K5
Marquette 11,672 ..... H8
Menominee 3,373 ..... J5
Milwaukee 964,988 ..... L9
Monroe 35,074 ..... E8
Oconto 28,947 ..... K6
Oneida 31,216 ..... G4
Outagamie 128,799 ..... K7
Ozaukee 66,981 ..... L9
Pepin 7,477 ..... C6
Pierce 31,149 ..... B6
Polk 32,351 ..... B5
Portage 57,420 ..... G6
Price 15,788 ..... F4
Racine 173,132 ..... K10
Richland 17,476 ..... F9
Rock 139,420 ..... H10
Rusk 15,589 ..... D5
Saint Croix 43,262 ..... B5
Sauk 43,469 ..... G9
Sawyer 12,843 ..... D4
Shawano 35,928 ..... J6
Sheboygan 100,935 ..... L8
Taylor 18,817 ..... E5
Trempealeau 26,158 ..... D7
Vernon 25,642 ..... E8
Vilas 16,535 ..... G3
Walworth 71,507 ..... J10
Washburn 13,174 ..... C4
Washington 84,848 ..... K9
Waukesha 280,080 ..... K9
Waupaca 42,831 ..... J6
Waushara 18,526 ..... H7
Winnebago 131,722 ..... J8
Wood 72,799 ..... F7

CITIES and TOWNS

Zip *Name/Pop.* *Key*

54405 Abbotsford 1,901 ..... F6
53910 Adams 1,744 ..... G8
53001 Adell 545 ..... L8
53501 Afton 225 ..... H10
53502 Albany 1,051 ..... G10
†53534 Albion 300 ..... H10
54201 Algoma 3,656 ..... M6
53002 Allenton 915 ..... K9
†54301 Allouez 14,882 ..... L7
54610 Alma⊙ 876 ..... C7
54611 Alma Center 454 ..... E7
54805 Almena 526 ..... B5
54909 Almond 477 ..... G7
54720 Altoona 4,393 ..... C6
54102 Amberg 875 ..... K5
54001 Amery 2,404 ..... B5
54406 Amherst 701 ..... H7
54407 Amherst Junction 225 ..... H7
54408 Aniwa 273 ..... H6
54409 Antigo⊙ 8,653 ..... H5
54911 Appleton⊙ 58,913 ..... J7
Appleton-Oshkosh‡ 291,325 J7
†54568 Arbor Vitae 900 ..... G4
54612 Arcadia 2,109 ..... D7
53503 Arena 451 ..... G9
54511 Argonne 600 ..... J4
53504 Argyle 720 ..... G10
54721 Arkansaw 400 ..... B6
53911 Arlington 440 ..... H9
54103 Armstrong Creek 615 ..... K4
54410 Arpin 361 ..... G6
53003 Ashippun 750 ..... H1
54806 Ashland⊙ 9,115 ..... E2
54304 Ashwaubenon 14,486 ..... K7
54411 Athens 988 ..... G5
54412 Auburndale 641 ..... F6
54722 Augusta 1,560 ..... D6
53506 Avoca 505 ..... F9
†53520 Avon 120 ..... H10
54413 Babcock 250 ..... F7
53801 Bagley 317 ..... D10
54202 Baileys Harbor 250 ..... M5
54002 Baldwin 1,620 ..... B6
54810 Balsam Lake⊙ 749 ..... B5
54921 Bancroft 355 ..... G7
54614 Bangor 1,012 ..... E8
53913 Baraboo⊙ 8,081 ..... G9
†54873 Barnes 225 ..... D3
53507 Barneveld 579 ..... F10
54812 Barron⊙ 2,595 ..... C5
†53001 Batavia 125 ..... K8
54723 Bay City 543 ..... B6
54814 Bayfield 778 ..... E2
†53201 Bayside 4,724 ..... M1
54922 Bear Creek 454 ..... J6
53916 Beaver Dam 14,149 ..... J9
53802 Beetown 150 ..... E10
53004 Belgium 892 ..... L8
†54631 Bell Center 124 ..... E9
53508 Belleville 1,302 ..... G10
53510 Belmont 826 ..... F10
53511 Beloit 35,207 ..... H10
53803 Benton 983 ..... F10
54923 Berlin 5,478 ..... H8
†54410 Bethel 210 ..... F6
†54440 Bevent 200 ..... H6
53103 Big Bend 1,345 ..... K2
54926 Big Falls 107 ..... H6
54817 Birchwood 437 ..... C4
54414 Birnamwood 688 ..... H6
†54494 Biron 698 ..... G7
54106 Black Creek 1,097 ..... K7
53515 Black Earth 1,145 ..... G9
54615 Black River Falls⊙ 3,434 ..... E7
†54541 Blackwell 550 ..... J4
54616 Blair 1,142 ..... D7
53516 Blanchardville 803 ..... G10
54617 Bloom City 167 ..... E8
54724 Bloomer 3,342 ..... D5
53804 Bloomington 743 ..... E10
53517 Blue Mounds 387 ..... G9
53518 Blue River 412 ..... E9
†53581 Boaz 161 ..... E9
†53105 Bohners Lake 1,507 ..... K10
54107 Bonduel 1,160 ..... K6
53805 Boscobel 2,662 ..... E9
54512 Boulder Junction 780 ..... G3
54416 Bowler 339 ..... J6
54725 Boyceville 862 ..... C5
54726 Boyd 660 ..... E6
54203 Branch 300 ..... L7
53919 Brandon 862 ..... J8
54513 Brantwood 500 ..... F4
53920 Briggsville 250 ..... H8
54110 Brillion 2,907 ..... L7
53520 Brodhead 3,153 ..... G10
54417 Brokaw 298 ..... G5
53005 Brookfield 34,035 ..... K1
53521 Brooklyn 627 ..... H10
53209 Brown Deer 12,921 ..... L1
†53105 Brown's Lake 1,648 ..... K3
53006 Brownsville 433 ..... J8
53522 Browntown 284 ..... G10
54819 Bruce 905 ..... D5
54820 Brule 335 ..... C2
54204 Brussels 500 ..... L6
†54622 Buffalo 894 ..... C7
53105 Burlington 8,385 ..... K10
53922 Burnett 260 ..... J9
53007 Butler 2,059 ..... K1
54514 Butternut 438 ..... E3
53009 Byron 40 ..... K8
54821 Cable 227 ..... D3
54727 Cadott 1,247 ..... D6
53923 Cambria 680 ..... H8
53523 Cambridge 844 ..... H9
54822 Cameron 1,115 ..... C5
†53019 Campbellsport 1,740 ..... K8
54618 Camp Douglas 589 ..... F8
53109 Camp Lake 2,060 ..... K10
54823 Canton 100 ..... C5
54928 Caroline 450 ..... J6
53011 Cascade 615 ..... K8
54205 Casco 484 ..... L6
54619 Cashton 827 ..... E8
53806 Cassville 1,270 ..... E10
54620 Cataract 200 ..... E7
54515 Catawba 205 ..... E4
54206 Cato 85 ..... L7
53924 Cazenovia 259 ..... F8
54111 Cecil 445 ..... K6
53012 Cedarburg 9,005 ..... L9
53013 Cedar Grove 1,420 ..... L8
54824 Centuria 711 ..... A5
54621 Chaseburg 279 ..... D8
54419 Chelsea 120 ..... F5
†53029 Chenequa 532 ..... J1
54728 Chetek 1,931 ..... C5
54420 Chili 185 ..... F6
53014 Chilton⊙ 2,965 ..... K7
54729 Chippewa Falls⊙ 12,270 ..... D6
54004 Clayton 425 ..... B5
54005 Clear Lake 899 ..... B5
53015 Cleveland 1,270 ..... L8
53525 Clinton 1,751 ..... J10
54929 Clintonville 4,567 ..... J6
53016 Clyman 317 ..... J9
53526 Cobb 409 ..... F10
54622 Cochrane 512 ..... C7
54421 Colby 1,496 ..... F6
54112 Coleman 852 ..... L5
54730 Colfax 1,149 ..... C6
54930 Coloma 367 ..... H7
53925 Columbus 4,049 ..... H9
54113 Combined Locks 2,573 ..... K7
†53147 Como 1,376 ..... K10
54519 Conover 480 ..... H3
54731 Conrath 86 ..... E5
54623 Coon Valley 758 ..... E8
54732 Cornell 1,583 ..... D5
54827 Cornucopia 250 ..... D2
54520 Crandon⊙ 1,969 ..... H4
54114 Crivitz 1,041 ..... L5
53528 Cross Plains 2,156 ..... G9
53807 Cuba City 2,129 ..... F10
53110 Cudahy 19,547 ..... M2
54829 Cumberland 1,983 ..... C4
54422 Curtiss 127 ..... F6
54006 Cushing 150 ..... A4
54931 Dale 410 ..... J7
54733 Dallas 477 ..... C5
53926 Dalton 300 ..... H8
53529 Dane 518 ..... G9
53114 Darien 1,152 ..... J10
53530 Darlington⊙ 2,300 ..... F10
53531 Deerfield 1,466 ..... H9
54007 Deer Park 232 ..... B5
53532 De Forest 3,367 ..... H9
53018 Delafield 4,083 ..... J1
53115 Delavan 5,684 ..... J10
†53115 Delavan Lake 2,082 ..... J10
†54856 Delta 35 ..... D3
54208 Denmark 1,475 ..... L7
54115 De Pere 14,892 ..... K7
†54663 De Soto 318 ..... D9
†54014 Diamond Bluff 100 ..... A6
53808 Dickeyville 1,156 ..... E10
54625 Dodge 185 ..... D7
53533 Dodgeville⊙ 3,458 ..... F10
54425 Dorchester 613 ..... F5
53118 Dousman 1,153 ..... J1
54734 Downing 242 ..... B5
54735 Downsville 200 ..... C6
53928 Doylestown 294 ..... H9
54009 Dresser 670 ..... A5
54832 Drummond 200 ..... D3
54736 Durand⊙ 2,047 ..... C6
53119 Eagle 1,008 ..... H2
54521 Eagle River⊙ 1,326 ..... H4
54626 Eastman 371 ..... D9
53120 East Troy 2,385 ..... J2
54701 Eau Claire⊙ 51,509 ..... D6
Eau Claire‡ 130,507 ..... D6
53019 Eden 534 ..... K8
54426 Edgar 1,194 ..... G6
53534 Edgerton 4,335 ..... H10
54209 Egg Harbor 238 ..... M5
54427 Eland 230 ..... H6
54428 Elcho 500 ..... H5
54429 Elderon 191 ..... H6
54932 Eldorado 200 ..... J8
54738 Eleva 593 ..... D6
53020 Elkhart Lake 1,054 ..... L8
53121 Elkhorn⊙ 4,605 ..... J10
54739 Elk Mound 737 ..... C6
54210 Ellison Bay 112 ..... M5
54011 Ellsworth⊙ 2,143 ..... A6
53122 Elm Grove 6,735 ..... K1
54740 Elmwood 885 ..... B6
†53401 Elmwood Park 483 ..... M3
53929 Elroy 1,504 ..... F8
54430 Elton 150 ..... J5
54933 Embarrass 496 ..... J6
53930 Endeavor 335 ..... G8
54211 Ephraim 319 ..... M5
54627 Ettrick 462 ..... D7
53536 Evansville 2,835 ..... H10
54835 Exeland 219 ..... D4
54741 Fairchild 577 ..... D6
53931 Fair Water 310 ..... J8
54742 Fall Creek 1,148 ..... D6
53932 Fall River 850 ..... H9
†54840 Falun 95 ..... A4
54120 Fence 200 ..... K4
53809 Fennimore 2,212 ..... E9
54431 Fenwood 165 ..... F6
54628 Ferryville 227 ..... D9
54524 Fifield 310 ..... F4
54212 Fish Creek 119 ..... M5
54121 Florence⊙ 780 ..... K4
54935 Fond du Lac⊙ 35,863 ..... K8
53125 Fontana 1,764 ..... J10
53537 Footville 794 ..... H10
54123 Forest Junction 140 ..... K7
54213 Forestville 455 ..... L6
53538 Fort Atkinson 9,785 ..... J10
54629 Fountain City 963 ..... C7
54836 Foxboro 360 ..... B2
53933 Fox Lake 1,373 ..... J8
†53117 Fox Point 7,649 ..... M1
54214 Francis Creek 589 ..... L7
53132 Franklin 16,871 ..... L2
54837 Frederic 1,039 ..... B4
53021 Fredonia 1,437 ..... L8
54940 Fremont 510 ..... J7
53934 Friendship⊙ 744 ..... G8
53935 Friesland 267 ..... H8
54630 Galesville 1,239 ..... D7
54631 Gays Mills 627 ..... E9
53127 Genesee Depot 350 ..... J2
54632 Genoa 283 ..... D8
53128 Genoa City 1,202 ..... K11
53022 Germantown 10,729 ..... K1
54124 Gillett 1,356 ..... K6
54433 Gilman 436 ..... E5
54743 Gilmanton 300 ..... C7
54435 Gleason 200 ..... G5
53023 Glenbeulah 423 ..... L8
†53209 Glendale 13,882 ..... M1
54526 Glen Flora 83 ..... E4
53810 Glen Haven 160 ..... E10
54013 Glenwood City 950 ..... B5
54527 Glidden 940 ..... E3
54125 Goodman 875 ..... K4
54838 Gordon 600 ..... C3
53540 Gotham 250 ..... F9
53024 Grafton 8,381 ..... L9
53936 Grand Marsh 725 ..... G8
54839 Grand View 447 ..... D3
54436 Granton 399 ..... E6
54840 Grantsburg⊙ 1,153 ..... A4
53541 Gratiot 280 ..... F10
*54301 Green Bay⊙ 87,899 ..... K6
Green Bay‡ 175,280 ..... K6
53129 Greendale 16,928 ..... L2
53220 Greenfield 31,467 ..... L2
54941 Green Lake⊙ 1,208 ..... H8
54126 Greenleaf 300 ..... L7
54942 Greenville 900 ..... J7
54437 Greenwood 1,124 ..... E6
54128 Gresham 534 ..... J6
54014 Hager City 110 ..... A6
53130 Hales Corners 7,110 ..... K2
54015 Hammond 991 ..... A6
54943 Hancock 419 ..... G7
54529 Harshaw 87 ..... G4
53027 Hartford 7,046 ..... K9
53029 Hartland 5,559 ..... J1
54440 Hatley 300 ..... H6
54841 Haugen 251 ..... C4
54530 Hawkins 407 ..... E4
54842 Hawthorne 200 ..... C3
54843 Hayward⊙ 1,698 ..... D3
53811 Hazel Green 1,282 ..... F11
54531 Hazelhurst 630 ..... G4
†53538 Hebron 450 ..... J10
53137 Helenville 300 ..... J10
54844 Herbster 100 ..... D2
54441 Hewitt 470 ..... F6
53543 Highland 860 ..... F9
54129 Hilbert 1,176 ..... K7
†54511 Hiles 350 ..... J4

(continued on following page)

Agriculture, Industry and Resources

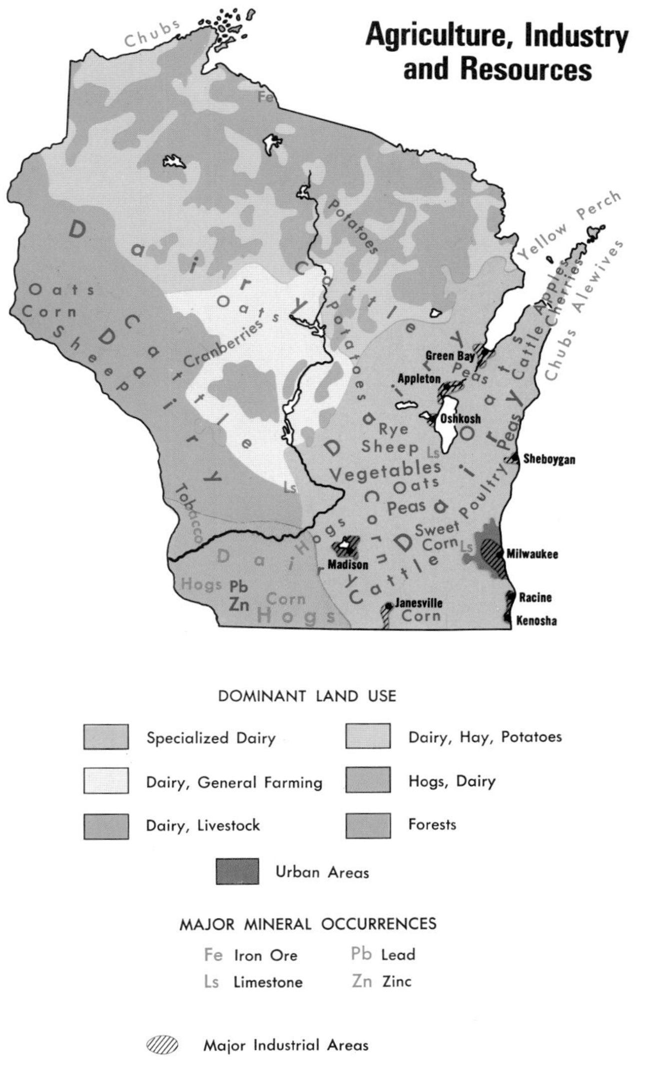

Chubs
Fe
Potatoes
Yellow Perch
Alewives
Apples
Cherries
Chubs
Dairy
Oats
Corn
Sheep
Cattle
Cranberries
Green Bay
Appleton
Oshkosh
Peas
Rye
Sheep
Ls
Vegetables
Oats
Peas
Sweet Corn
Poultry
Sheboygan
Tobacco
Hogs
Madison
Milwaukee
Racine
Kenosha
Janesville
Pb
Zn
Corn
DOMINANT LAND USE
Specialized Dairy
Dairy, Hay, Potatoes
Dairy, General Farming
Hogs, Dairy
Dairy, Livestock
Forests
Urban Areas
MAJOR MINERAL OCCURRENCES
Fe Iron Ore
Pb Lead
Ls Limestone
Zn Zinc
Major Industrial Areas

54634 Hillsboro 1,263 .... F8
53031 Hingham 250 .... K8
54635 Hixton 364 .... E7
54745 Holcombe 200 .... D5
53544 Hollandale 271 .... G10
54636 Holmen 2,411 .... D8
53138 Honey Creek 300 .... J3
53032 Horicon 3,584 .... J9
54944 Hortonville 2,016 .... J7
†55082 Houlton 915 .... A5
54303 Howard 8,240 .... K6
53081 Howards Grove-Millersville 1,838 . L8
53033 Hubertus 600 .... K1
54016 Hudson⊙ 5,434 .... A6
54746 Humbird 190 .... E6
54534 Hurley⊙ 2,015 .... F3
53034 Hustisford 874 .... J9
54637 Hustler 170 .... F8
54747 Independence 1,180 .... D7
54945 Iola 957 .... H6
54536 Iron Belt 300 .... F3
53035 Iron Ridge 766 .... K9
54847 Iron River 878 .... D2
†53941 Ironton 206 .... F8
53036 Ixonia 525 .... H1
53037 Jackson 1,817 .... K9
†54235 Jacksonport 150 .... M6
53545 Janesville⊙ 51,071 .... H10
Janesville-Beloit‡ 139,420 H10
53549 Jefferson⊙ 5,647 .... J10
54748 Jim Falls 100 .... D5
53038 Johnson Creek 1,136 .... J9
53550 Juda 500 .... H10
54443 Junction City 523 .... G6
53039 Juneau⊙ 2,045 .... J9
53139 Kansasville 150 .... L3
54130 Kaukauna 11,310 .... K7
†53050 Kekoskee 224 .... J8
54215 Kellnersville 369 .... L7
54638 Kendall 486 .... F8
54537 Kennan 194 .... F5
*53140 Kenosha⊙ 77,685 .... M3
Kenosha‡ 123,137 .... M3
54135 Keshena⊙ 980 .... J6
53040 Kewaskum 2,381 .... K8
54216 Kewaunee⊙ 2,801 .... M7
53042 Kiel 3,083 .... L8
53812 Kieler 800 .... E10
54136 Kimberly 5,881 .... K7
53939 Kingston 328 .... H8
54749 Knapp 419 .... B6
†54455 Knowlton 127 .... G6
53044 Kohler 1,651 .... L8
53147 Krakow 345 .... K6
54538 Lac du Flambeau 500 .... G4
†53066 Lac La Belle 289 .... H1
54601 La Crosse⊙ 48,347 .... D8
La Crosse‡ 91,056 .... D8
54848 Ladysmith⊙ 3,826 .... D5
54639 La Farge 746 .... E8
53940 Lake Delton 1,158 .... G8
53147 Lake Geneva 5,612 .... K10
53551 Lake Mills 3,670 .... H9
54849 Lake Nebagamon 780 .... C3
54539 Lake Tomahawk 600 .... H4
†54494 Lake Wazeecha 2,176 .... G7
†54729 Lake Wissota 1,788 .... D6
54138 Lakewood 425 .... K5
53813 Lancaster⊙ 4,076 .... E10
54540 Land O'Lakes 786 .... H3
53046 Lannon 987 .... K1
53941 La Valle 412 .... F8
53047 Lebanon 250 .... H1
54139 Lena 585 .... K6
†54656 Leon 100 .... E8
54948 Leopolis 200 .... J6
54851 Lewis 200 .... B4
53942 Limeridge 191 .... F9
53553 Linden 395 .... F10
54140 Little Chute 7,907 .... K7
53554 Livingston 642 .... E10
53555 Lodi 1,959 .... G9
53943 Loganville 239 .... F9
†54970 Lohrville 336 .... H7
53048 Lomira 1,446 .... J8
53556 Lone Rock 577 .... F9
54542 Long Lake 150 .... J4
53557 Lowell 326 .... J9
54446 Loyal 1,252 .... E6
54447 Lublin 142 .... E5
54853 Luck 997 .... B4
54217 Luxemburg 1,040 .... L6
53944 Lyndon Station 375 .... F8
54640 Lynxville 174 .... D9
53148 Lyons 550 .... K10
*53701 Madison (cap.)⊙ 170,616 . H9
Madison‡ 323,545 .... H9
54750 Maiden Rock 172 .... B6
54949 Manawa 1,205 .... J7
54220 Manitowoc⊙ 32,547 .... L7
54226 Maplewood 200 .... M6
54448 Marathon 1,552 .... G6
54855 Marengo 130 .... E3
54227 Maribel 363 .... L7
54143 Marinette⊙ 11,965 .... L5
54950 Marion 1,348 .... J6
53946 Markesan 1,446 .... J8
53947 Marquette 204 .... H8
53559 Marshall 2,363 .... H9
54449 Marshfield 18,290 .... F6
54856 Mason 102 .... D3
54450 Mattoon 382 .... J5
53948 Mauston⊙ 3,284 .... F8
53050 Mayville 4,333 .... K9
53560 Mazomanie 1,248 .... G9
53558 McFarland 3,783 .... H10
54543 McNaughton 450 .... H4
54451 Medford⊙ 4,035 .... F5
54546 Mellen 1,046 .... E3
54642 Melrose 507 .... E7
54619 Melvina 117 .... E8
54952 Menasha 14,728 .... J7
53051 Menomonee Falls 27,845 . K1
54751 Menomonie⊙ 12,769 .... C6
53092 Mequon 16,193 .... L1
54452 Merrill⊙ 9,578 .... G5

54754 Merrillan 587 .... E7
53561 Merrimac 365 .... G9
53056 Merton 1,045 .... K1
53562 Middleton 11,848 .... G9
54857 Mikana 200 .... C4
54453 Milan 153 .... F6
†53038 Milford 35 .... J9
54454 Milladore 250 .... G6
54643 Millston 110 .... E7
54858 Milltown 732 .... B4
53563 Milton 4,092 .... J10
*53201 Milwaukee⊙ 636,236 .... M1
Milwaukee‡ 1,397,143 .... M1
54644 Mindoro 200 .... D7
53565 Mineral Point 2,259 .... F10
54548 Minocqua 950 .... G4
54859 Minong 557 .... C3
54228 Mishicot 1,503 .... L7
54755 Mondovi 2,545 .... C6
54549 Monico 250 .... H4
53716 Monona 8,809 .... H9
53566 Monroe⊙ 10,027 .... G10
53949 Montello⊙ 1,273 .... H8
53569 Montfort 616 .... E10
53570 Monticello 1,021 .... G10
54550 Montreal 887 .... F3
53571 Morrisonville 375 .... G9
54455 Mosinee 3,015 .... G6
54149 Mountain 250 .... K5
53057 Mount Calvary 585 .... K8
53816 Mount Hope 197 .... D10
53572 Mount Horeb 3,251 .... G10
54645 Mount Sterling 223 .... D9
†53572 Mount Vernon 138 .... G10
53149 Mukwonago 4,014 .... J2
53573 Muscoda 1,331 .... F9
53150 Muskego 15,277 .... K2
53058 Nashotah 513 .... J1
54646 Necedah 773 .... F7
54956 Neenah 22,432 .... J7
54456 Neillsville⊙ 2,780 .... E6
54457 Nekoosa 2,519 .... G7
54756 Nelson 389 .... C7
54458 Nelsonville 199 .... H7
54150 Neopit 1,065 .... J6
53059 Neosho 575 .... J9
54960 Neshkoro 386 .... H8
54551 Newald 375 .... J4
54757 New Auburn 466 .... D5
53151 New Berlin 30,529 .... K2
53060 Newburg 783 .... K9
†61075 New Diggings 65 .... F10
54229 New Franken 150 .... L6
53574 New Glarus 1,763 .... G10
53061 New Holstein 3,412 .... K8
53950 New Lisbon 1,390 .... F8
54961 New London 6,210 .... J7
54017 New Richmond 4,306 .... A5
54151 Niagara 2,079 .... K4
54152 Nichols 267 .... K6
†53401 North Bay 219 .... M3
†54935 North Fond du Lac 3,844 . J8
53951 North Freedom 616 .... G9
†54016 North Hudson 2,218 .... A5
53064 North Lake 400 .... J1
53217 North Shore 14,930 .... M1
54648 Norwalk 517 .... E8
53154 Oak Creek 16,932 .... M2
54649 Oakdale 150 .... F8
53065 Oakfield 990 .... J8
53066 Oconomowoc 9,909 .... H1
†53066 Oconomowoc Lake 524 .... H1
54153 Oconto⊙ 4,505 .... L6
54154 Oconto Falls 2,500 .... K6
54962 Ogdensburg 214 .... J7
54459 Ogema 238 .... F5
53069 Okauchee 3,958 .... J1
†53555 Okee 250 .... H9
†54880 Oliver 253 .... B2
54963 Omro 2,763 .... J7
54650 Onalaska 9,249 .... D8
54155 Oneida 900 .... K7
54651 Ontario 398 .... E8
53070 Oostburg 1,647 .... L8
53575 Oregon 3,876 .... H10
53576 Orfordville 1,143 .... H10
54020 Osceola 1,581 .... A5
54901 Oshkosh⊙ 49,620 .... J8
54758 Osseo 1,474 .... D6
54460 Owen 998 .... F6
53952 Oxford 432 .... H8
53953 Packwaukee 271 .... G8
†53168 Paddock Lake 2,207 .... K10
53156 Palmyra 1,515 .... H2
53954 Pardeeville 1,594 .... H8
54552 Park Falls 3,192 .... F4
†54481 Park Ridge 643 .... H6
53817 Patch Grove 259 .... D10
53157 Pell Lake 1,826 .... K10
54553 Pence 234 .... F3
54759 Pepin 890 .... B7
54157 Peshtigo 2,807 .... L5
53072 Pewaukee 4,637 .... K1
54554 Phelps 950 .... H3
54555 Phillips⊙ 1,522 .... E4
54464 Phlox 150 .... J5
54465 Pickerel 107 .... J5
54760 Pigeon Falls 338 .... D7
54466 Pittsville 810 .... F7
53577 Plain 676 .... F9
54966 Plainfield 813 .... G7
†53017 Plat 120 .... K1
53818 Platteville 9,580 .... F10
53158 Pleasant Prairie 950 .... L10
54467 Plover 5,310 .... G7
54761 Plum City 505 .... B6
53073 Plymouth 6,027 .... L8
†54423 Polonia 200 .... H6
54864 Poplar 569 .... C2
53901 Portage⊙ 7,896 .... G8
54469 Port Edwards 2,077 .... G7
53074 Port Washington⊙ 8,612 . L9
54865 Port Wing 290 .... D2
53820 Potosi 736 .... E10
54160 Potter 330 .... K7
54161 Pound 407 .... L5
53955 Poynette 1,447 .... G9

54967 Poy Sippi 425 .... J7
53821 Prairie du Chien⊙ 5,859 . D9
53578 Prairie du Sac 2,145 .... G9
54762 Prairie Farm 387 .... C5
54556 Prentice 605 .... F4
54021 Prescott 2,654 .... A6
54968 Princeton 1,479 .... H8
54162 Pulaski 1,875 .... K6
54164 Pulcifer 35 .... K6
*53401 Racine⊙ 85,725 .... M3
Racine‡ 173,132 .... M3
54867 Radisson 280 .... D4
53956 Randolph 1,691 .... H8
53075 Random Lake 1,287 .... K8
†53126 Raymond 300 .... L2
54652 Readstown 396 .... E9
54970 Redgranite 976 .... J7
53959 Reedsburg 5,038 .... G8
54230 Reedsville 1,134 .... L7
53579 Reeseville 649 .... J9
53580 Rewey 233 .... F10
54501 Rhinelander⊙ 7,873 .... H4
54470 Rib Lake 945 .... F5
54868 Rice Lake 7,691 .... C5
53581 Richland Center⊙ 4,997 . F9
54763 Ridgeland 300 .... B5
53582 Ridgeway 503 .... F10
53960 Rio 785 .... H9
54971 Ripon 7,111 .... J8
54022 River Falls 9,019 .... A6
†53201 River Hills 1,642 .... M1
54023 Roberts 833 .... A6
53167 Rochester 746 .... K3
†53523 Rockdale 200 .... J10
53077 Rockfield 200 .... L1
54653 Rockland 383 .... D8
53961 Rock Springs 426 .... F8
†53178 Rome 200 .... H1
54974 Rosendale 725 .... J8
54473 Rosholt 520 .... H6
54474 Rothschild 3,338 .... G6
†53583 Roxbury 260 .... G9
54475 Rudolph 392 .... G7
†54751 Rusk 40 .... C6
53079 Saint Cloud 560 .... K8
54024 Saint Croix Falls 1,497 .... A5
†53207 Saint Francis 10,042 .... M2
†54601 Saint Joseph Ridge 450 . D8
54232 Saint Nazianz 738 .... L7
54765 Sand Creek 225 .... C5
53583 Sauk City 2,703 .... G9
53080 Saukville 3,494 .... L9
54559 Saxon 375 .... F3
54977 Scandinavia 292 .... H7
54476 Schofield 2,226 .... H6
†54843 Seeley 68 .... D3
54654 Seneca 235 .... E9
53584 Sextonville 225 .... F9
54165 Seymour 2,530 .... K6
53585 Sharon 1,280 .... J11
54166 Shawano⊙ 7,013 .... J6
53081 Sheboygan⊙ 48,085 .... L8
Sheboygan‡ 100,935 .... L8
53085 Sheboygan Falls 5,253 .... L8
54766 Sheldon 292 .... D5
54871 Shell Lake⊙ 1,135 .... C4
54169 Sherwood 372 .... K7
54170 Shiocton 805 .... K7
53211 Shorewood 14,327 .... M1
†53701 Shorewood Hills 1,837 .... G9
53586 Shullsburg 1,484 .... F10
53170 Silver Lake 1,598 .... K10
54872 Siren 896 .... B4
54234 Sister Bay 564 .... M5
53086 Slinger 1,612 .... K9
54655 Soldiers Grove 622 .... E9
54873 Solon Springs 590 .... C3
54025 Somerset 860 .... A5
53172 South Milwaukee 21,069 . M2
53587 South Wayne 495 .... G10
54656 Sparta⊙ 6,934 .... E8
54479 Spencer 1,754 .... F6
54801 Spooner 2,365 .... B4
53588 Spring Green 1,265 .... G9
54767 Spring Valley 982 .... B6
54768 Stanley 2,095 .... E6
54026 Star Prairie 420 .... A5
54480 Stetsonville 487 .... F5
54657 Steuben 175 .... E9
54481 Stevens Point⊙ 22,970 .... G7
54172 Stiles 300 .... L6
53825 Stitzer 190 .... E10
53088 Stockbridge 567 .... K7
54769 Stockholm 104 .... B7
54658 Stoddard 762 .... D8
54876 Stone Lake 210 .... C4
53589 Stoughton 7,589 .... H10
54484 Stratford 1,385 .... F6
54770 Strum 944 .... D6
54235 Sturgeon Bay⊙ 8,847 .... M6
53177 Sturtevant 4,130 .... M3
54173 Suamico 900 .... K6
53178 Sullivan 434 .... H1
54485 Summit Lake 250 .... H5
53590 Sun Prairie 12,931 .... H9
54880 Superior⊙ 29,571 .... C2
Superior-Duluth‡ 266,650 . C2
†54880 Superior Village 580 .... B2
54174 Suring 581 .... K5
53089 Sussex 3,482 .... K1
53090 Taycheedah 350 .... K8
54659 Taylor 411 .... E7
†53820 Tennyson 476 .... E10
53091 Theresa 766 .... K8
53092 Thiensville 3,341 .... L1
54771 Thorp 1,635 .... E6
54562 Three Lakes 950 .... H4
54486 Tigerton 865 .... H6
54240 Tisch Mills 315 .... L7
54660 Tomah 7,204 .... F8
54487 Tomahawk 3,527 .... G5
53573 Tony 146 .... E5
54888 Trego 280 .... C4
54661 Trempealeau 956 .... C8
54662 Tunnel City 200 .... E7
54889 Turtle Lake 762 .... B5
53181 Twin Lakes 3,474 .... K11

Topography

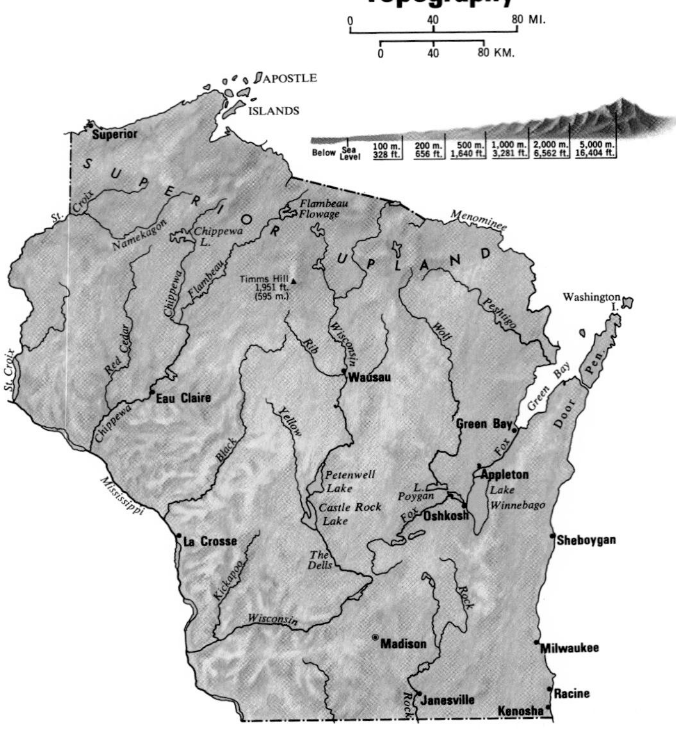

54241 Two Rivers 13,354 .... M7
53962 Union Center 216 .... F8
53182 Union Grove 3,517 .... L3
54488 Unity 418 .... F6
54245 Valders 984 .... L7
53593 Verona 3,336 .... G9
54489 Vesper 554 .... F7
54664 Viola 696 .... E8
54665 Viroqua⊙ 3,716 .... D8
54566 Wabeno 800 .... J5
53093 Waldo 416 .... L8
53183 Wales 1,992 .... J1
53184 Walworth 1,607 .... J10
54666 Warrens 300 .... E7
54890 Wascott 70 .... C3
54891 Washburn⊙ 2,080 .... D2
54246 Washington Island 550 .... M5
53185 Waterford 2,051 .... K3
53594 Waterloo 2,393 .... J9
53094 Watertown 18,113 .... J9
53021 Waubeka 450 .... L9
53186 Waukesha⊙ 50,365 .... K1
53597 Waunakee 3,866 .... G9
54981 Waupaca⊙ 4,472 .... H7
53963 Waupun 8,132 .... J8
54401 Wausau⊙ 32,426 .... G6
Wausau‡ 111,270 .... G6
54177 Wausaukee 648 .... K5
54982 Wautoma⊙ 1,629 .... H7
53226 Wauwatosa 51,308 .... L1
53826 Wauzeka 580 .... E9
†54126 Wayside 140 .... L7
54893 Webster 610 .... B4
53214 West Allis 63,982 .... L1
†53913 West Baraboo 846 .... G9
53095 West Bend⊙ 21,484 .... K9
54490 Westboro 750 .... F5
54667 Westby 1,797 .... E8
53964 Westfield 1,033 .... H8
†53201 West Milwaukee 3,535 .... L1
†54476 Weston 8,775 .... G6
54669 West Salem 3,276 .... D8
54983 Weyauwega 1,549 .... H7
54895 Weyerhaeuser 313 .... D5
54772 Wheeler 231 .... C5
54773 Whitehall⊙ 1,530 .... D7
54491 White Lake 309 .... J5
54247 Whitelaw 649 .... L7
53190 Whitewater 11,520 .... J10
†54481 Whiting 2,050 .... H7
54984 Wild Rose 741 .... H7
53191 Williams Bay 1,763 .... J10
54027 Wilson 155 .... B6
54670 Wilton 465 .... F8
54567 Winchester 300 .... G3
53185 Wind Lake 900 .... K2
†53401 Wind Point 1,695 .... M2
53598 Windsor 827 .... H9
54985 Winnebago 1,433 .... J8
54986 Winneconne 1,935 .... J7
54896 Winter 376 .... E4
53965 Wisconsin Dells 2,521 .... G8
54494 Wisconsin Rapids⊙ 17,995 G7

54498 Withee 509 .... E6
54499 Wittenberg 997 .... H6
53968 Wonewoc 842 .... F8
53827 Woodman 116 .... E9
54568 Woodruff 850 .... G4
54028 Woodville 725 .... B6
54180 Wrightstown 1,169 .... K7
54671 Wyeville 163 .... F7
53969 Wyocena 548 .... H9
54182 Zachow 135 .... K6

OTHER FEATURES

Apostle (isls.) F2
Apostle Islands Nat'l Lakeshore E1
Apple (riv.) A5
Bad River Ind. Res. E2
Bardon (lake) C3
Bear (isl.) E1
Beaver Dam (lake) J9
Beulah (lake) J2
Big Eau Pleine (res.) G6
Big Muskego (lake) L2
Big Rib (riv.) G5
Black (riv.) E7
Butternut (lake) J4
Castle Rock (lake) G8
Cat (isl.) E1
Chambers (isl.) M5
Chequamegon (bay) E2
Chetac (lake) D4
Chippewa (lake) D4
Chippewa (riv.) B7
Clam (lake) B4
Clam (riv.) A4
Dells, The (valley) G8
Denoon (lake) K2
Du Bay (lake) G6
Eagle (lake) H2
Eagle (lake) K3
Eau Claire (riv.) D6
Flambeau (riv.) E4
Flambeau Flowage (res.) F3
Fox (riv.) K2
Fox (riv.) K7
General Mitchell Field M2
Geneva (lake) K10
Golden (lake) H1
Green (bay) L6
Grindstone (lake) C4
Holcombe Flowage (res.) D5
Jump (riv.) E5
Kegonsa (lake) H10
Kickapoo (riv.) E9
Koshkonong (lake) H10
La Belle (lake) H1
Lac Court Oreilles Ind. Res. D4
Lac du Flambeau Ind. Res. G3
Long (lake) C4
Madeline (isl.) E2
Mendota (lake) H9
Menominee (riv.) L5
Metonga (lake) J4

Michigan (isl.) F2
Michigan (lake) M9
Mississippi (riv.) D10
Montreal (riv.) F2
Moose (lake) E3
Moose (lake) F3
Nagawicka (lake) J1
Namekagon (lake) D3
Namekagon (riv.) C3
North (lake) J1
Oak (isl.) E2
Oconomowoc (lake) H1
Oconto (riv.) K5
Okauchee (lake) J1
Outer (isl.) F1
Owen (lake) D3
Pecatonica (riv.) H11
Pelican (lake) H4
Pepin (lake) B7
Peshtigo (riv.) K5
Petenwell (lake) G7
Pewaukee (lake) K1
Phantom (lake) J2
Pine (lake) J1
Porte des Morts (str.) N5
Poygan (lake) J7
Puckaway (lake) H8
Red Cedar (riv.) C5
Red Cliff Ind. Res. E2
Rib (mt.) G6
Rock (riv.) J9
Round (lake) F4
Round (lake) D3
Saint Croix (lake) A6
Saint Croix (riv.) A4
Saint Croix Flowage (res.) C3
Saint Louis (riv.) A2
Sand (isl.) D2
Shawano (lake) K6
Shell (lake) C4
Spider (lake) D3
Stockbridge Ind. Res. J6
Stockton (isl.) F2
Sugar (riv.) H10
Sugarbush Hill (mt.) J4
Superior (lake) F1
Thunder (lake) H4
Tichigan (lake) K2
Timms Hill (mt.) F5
Trempealeau (riv.) C7
Trout (lake) G3
Vieux Desert (lake) J3
Washington (isl.) M5
Willow (res.) F4
Wind (lake) K2
Winnebago (lake) K7
Wisconsin (riv.) E9
Wolf (riv.) J5
Yellow (lake) B4
Yellow (riv.) F7

⊙County seat.
‡Population of metropolitan area.
† Zip of nearest p.o. * Multiple zips.

Wisconsin

SCALE
0 5 10   20   30   40 MI.
0 5 10 20 30 40 KM.

State Capitals............... ⊛
County Seats................. ⊚
Canals.......................
Major Limited Access Hwys. _____

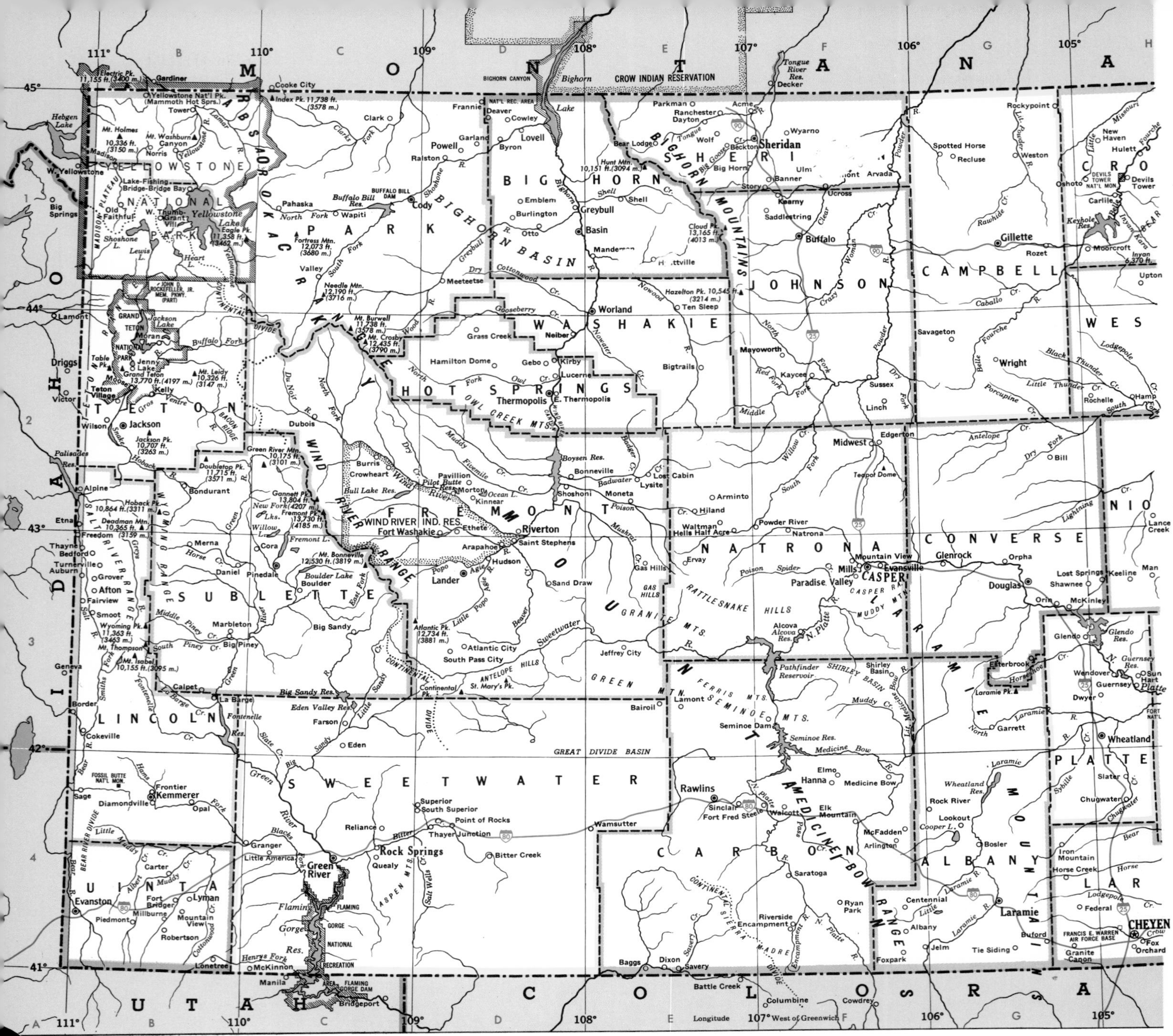

Agriculture, Industry and Resources

DOMINANT LAND USE

- Specialized Wheat
- Specialized Dairy
- General Farming, Livestock, Special Crops
- Sugar Beets, Dry Beans, Livestock, General Farming
- Range Livestock
- Forests
- Nonagricultural Land

MAJOR MINERAL OCCURRENCES

C	Coal	G	Natural Gas	So	Soda Ash
Cl	Clay	O	Petroleum	U	Uranium
Fe	Iron Ore	P	Phosphates	V	Vanadium
		⚡	Water Power		

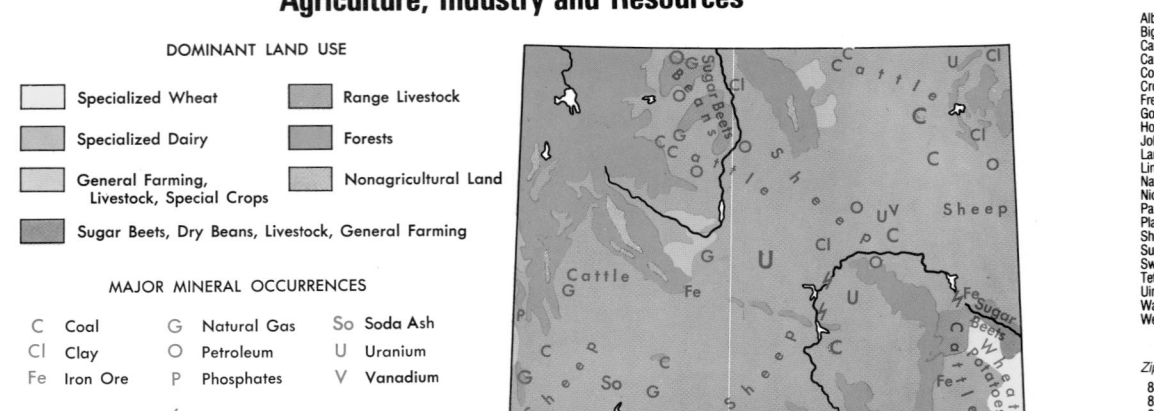

COUNTIES

Albany 29,062	G4
Big Horn 11,896	E1
Campbell 24,367	G1
Carbon 21,896	F4
Converse 14,069	G3
Crook 5,308	H1
Fremont 38,992	D2
Goshen 12,040	H4
Hot Springs 5,710	D2
Johnson 6,700	F1
Laramie 68,649	H4
Lincoln 12,177	B3
Natrona 71,856	F3
Niobrara 2,924	H2
Park 21,639	C1
Platte 11,975	H4
Sheridan 25,048	F1
Sublette 4,548	C3
Sweetwater 41,723	D4
Teton 9,355	B2
Uinta 13,021	B4
Washakie 9,496	E2
Weston 7,106	H2

CITIES and TOWNS

Zip	Name/Pop.	Key
83110	Afton 1,481	B3
82050	Albin 128	H4
82620	Alcova 275	F3

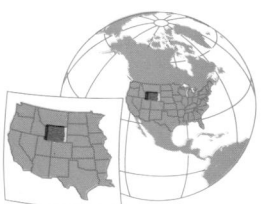

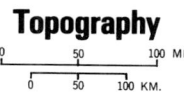

AREA 97,809 sq. mi. (253,325 sq. km.)
POPULATION 469,557
CAPITAL Cheyenne
LARGEST CITY Casper
HIGHEST POINT Gannett Pk. 13,804 ft. (4207 m.)
SETTLED IN 1834
ADMITTED TO UNION July 10, 1890
POPULAR NAME Equality State
STATE FLOWER Indian Paintbrush
STATE BIRD Meadowlark

Topography

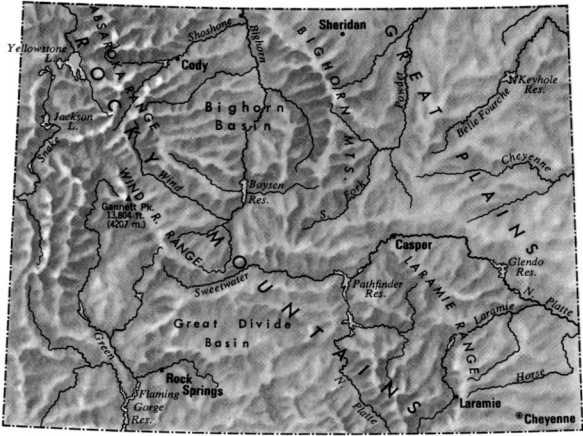

82510 Arapahoe 682	D3	82926 Eden 198	C3
83111 Auburn 360	A3	82635 Edgerton 510	F2
82321 Baggs 433	E4	82324 Elk Mountain 338	F4
82322 Bairoil 300	E3	82325 Encampment 611	F4
82410 Basin⊙ 1,349	E1	83118 Etna 200	A2
†82801 Beckton 110	E1	82930 Evanston⊙ 6,421	B4
83112 Bedford 350	A3	82636 Evansville 2,335	F3
82712 Beulah 184	H1	83119 Fairview 150	A3
82833 Big Horn 350	E1	82932 Farson 350	C3
83113 Big Piney 530	B3	82933 Fort Bridger 300	B4
82051 Bosler 195	G4	82212 Fort Laramie 356	H3
82834 Buffalo⊙ 3,799	F1	82514 Fort Washakie 400	C2
82411 Burlington 300	D1	†82001 Fox Farm 2,850	H4
82053 Burns 268	H4	82423 Frannie 138	D1
82412 Byron 633	D1	83120 Freedom 400	A3
82601 Casper⊙ 51,016	F3	83121 Frontier 150	B4
82055 Centennial 140	F4	82501 Gas Hills 150	D2
82001 Cheyenne (cap.)⊙ 47,283	H4	82716 Gillette⊙ 12,134	G1
82210 Chugwater 282	H4	82213 Glendo 367	G3
82835 Clearmont 191	F1	82637 Glenrock 2,736	G3
82414 Cody⊙ 6,790	D1	82934 Granger 177	C4
83114 Cokeville 515	B3	82425 Grass Creek 152	D2
82420 Cowley 455	D1	82935 Green River⊙ 12,807	C4
82512 Crowheart 200	C2	82426 Greybull 2,277	E1
83115 Daniel 130	B3	83122 Grover 425	A3
82836 Dayton 701	E1	82214 Guernsey 1,512	H3
82421 Deaver 178	D1	82327 Hanna 2,288	F4
82323 Dixon 82	E4	82215 Hartville 149	H3
82633 Douglas⊙ 6,030	G3	82060 Hillsdale 160	H4
82513 Dubois 1,067	C2	82061 Horse Creek 225	G4
†82443 East Thermopolis 359	D2	82515 Hudson 514	D2
		82720 Hulett 291	H1

83001 Jackson⊙ 4,511	B2	82842 Story 637	F1
82310 Jeffrey City 1,882	E3	82729 Sundance⊙ 1,087	H1
82639 Kaycee 271	F2	82945 Superior 500	D4
83011 Kelly 100	B2	82442 Ten Sleep 407	E1
83101 Kemmerer⊙ 3,273	B4	83127 Thayne 256	A3
82516 Kinnear 145	D2	82443 Thermopolis⊙ 3,852	D2
82430 Kirby 129	D2	82240 Torrington⊙ 5,441	H3
83123 La Barge 302	B3	82730 Upton 1,193	H1
82221 Lagrange 232	H4	82242 Van Tassell 10	H3
82520 Lander⊙ 7,867	D3	82335 Walcott 200	F4
82070 Laramie⊙ 24,410	G4	82336 Wamsutter 681	E4
82640 Linch 187	F2	82201 Wheatland⊙ 5,816	H3
82223 Lingle 475	H3	83014 Wilson 480	B2
82929 Little America 175	C4	82401 Worland⊙ 6,391	E1
†82642 Lost Cabin 25	E2	82732 Wright 1,117	G2
82224 Lost Springs 9	G3	82190 Yellowstone Nat'l Pk. 350	B1
82431 Lovell 2,447	D1	82244 Yoder 110	H4
†82443 Lucerne 240	D2	
82225 Lusk⊙ 1,650	H3	**OTHER FEATURES**
82937 Lyman 2,284	B4	
82642 Lysite 175	E2	Absaroka (range)	C1
†82190 Mammoth Hot Springs		Antelope (creek)	G2
(Yellowstone Nat'l Park 350	B1	Antelope (hills)	D3
82432 Manderson 174	E1	Aspen (mts.)	C4
82227 Manville 94	H3	Atlantic (peak)	D3
†83113 Marbleton 537	B3	Badwater (creek)	E2
82938 McKinnon 135	C4	Bear (creek)	H4
82329 Medicine Bow 953	F4	Bear (riv.)	B4
82433 Meeteetse 512	D1	Bear Lodge (mts.)	H1
82643 Midwest 638	F2	Bear River Divide (mts.)	B4
82644 Mills 2,139	F3	Beaver (creek)	D3
82721 Moorcroft 1,014	H1	Beaver (creek)	H2
83012 Moose 150	B2	Belle Fourche (riv.)	H1
83013 Moran 200	B2	Big Goose (creek)	E1
†82601 Mountain View	F3	Bighorn (basin)	D1
82930 Mountain View 628	B4	Bighorn (lake)	E1
82701 Newcastle⊙ 3,596	H2	Bighorn (mts.)	E1
82190 Old Faithful 75	B1	Bighorn (riv.)	D1
†82001 Orchard Valley 3,327	H4	Bighorn Canyon Nat'l Rec. Area	D1
82723 Osage 500	H2	Big Sandy (riv.)	C3
†82601 Paradise Valley	F3	Bitter (creek)	C4
82523 Pavillion 287	D2	Blacks Fork, Green (riv.)	C4
82082 Pine Bluffs 1,077	H4	Black Thunder (creek)	G2
82941 Pinedale⊙ 1,066	C3	Bonneville (creek)	C3
82942 Point of Rocks 425	D4	Boysen (res.)	D2
82435 Powell 5,310	D1	Buffalo Bill (dam)	C1
82839 Ranchester 655	E1	Buffalo Bill (res.)	C1
82301 Rawlins⊙ 11,547	E4	Buffalo Fork, Snake (riv.)	B2
82725 Recluse 225	G1	Burwell (mt.)	C2
82943 Reliance 325	C4	Caballo (creek)	G3
†82325 Riverside 55	F4	Casper (range)	F3
82501 Riverton 9,247	D2	Cheyenne (riv.)	H2
82944 Robertson 142	B4	Chugwater (creek)	H4
82083 Rock River 415	G4	Clarks Fork (riv.)	C1
82901 Rock Springs 19,458	C4	Clear (creek)	F1
82331 Saratoga 2,410	F4	Cloud (peak)	E1
82801 Sheridan⊙ 15,146	F1	Cottonwood (creek)	G2
82615 Shirley Basin 195	F3	Crazy Woman (creek)	F1
82649 Shoshoni 879	D2	Crosby (mt.)	C2
82334 Sinclair 586	E4	Crow (creek)	H4
83126 Smoot 310	B3	Deadman (mt.)	B2
†82945 South Superior 586	D4	Devils Tower Nat'l Mon.	H1

Doubletop (peak)	B2	Lodgepole (creek)	H2
Dry (creek)	C2	Lodgepole (creek)	H4
Dry Cottonwood (creek)	D1	Madison (plat.)	B1
Eagle (peak)	B1	Medicine Bow (range)	F4
Fivemile (creek)	D2	Medicine Bow (riv.)	F3
Flaming Gorge (res.)	C4	Middle Piney (creek)	B3
Flaming Gorge Nat'l Rec. Area	C4	Muddy (creek)	D2
Fontenelle (creek)	B3	Muskrat (creek)	E2
Fontenelle (res.)	B3	Needle (mt.)	C1
Fort Laramie Nat'l Hist. Site	H3	Niobrara (riv.)	J3
Fortress (mt.)	C1	North Laramie (riv.)	G3
Fossil Butte Nat'l Mon.	B4	North Platte (riv.)	H3
Francis E. Warren A.F.B. 3,627	G4	Nowater (creek)	E2
Fremont (lake)	C2	Nowood (riv.)	E1
Fremont (peak)	C2	Owl, North Fork (creek)	D2
Gannett (peak)	C2	Owl Creek (mts.)	D2
Gas (hills)	E3	Palisades (res.)	A2
Glendo (res.)	H3	Pass (creek)	F4
Gooseberry (creek)	D1	Pathfinder (res.)	F3
Grand Teton (mt.)	B2	Poison (creek)	E2
Grand Teton Nat'l Park	B2	Poison Spider (creek)	F3
Granite (mt.)	E3	Popo Agie (riv.)	D3
Great Divide (basin)	E3	Powder (riv.)	F2
Green (mt.)	E3	Rattlesnake (range)	E3
Green (riv.)	C4	Rawhide (creek)	G1
Green, East Fork (riv.)	C3	Rawhide (creek)	H3
Green River (mt.)	C2	Rocky (mts.)	C1
Greybull (riv.)	D1	Salt (riv.)	B3
Greys (riv.)	B3	Salt River (range)	B3
Gros Ventre (riv.)	B2	Salt Wells (creek)	D4
Guernsey (res.)	H3	Seminoe (mts.)	E3
Hams Fork (riv.)	B4	Seminoe (res.)	F3
Hazelton (peak)	E1	Shell (creek)	E1
Henrys Fork, Green (riv.)	C4	Shirley (basin)	F3
Hoback (peak)	B2	Shoshone (lake)	B1
Hoback (riv.)	B2	Shoshone (riv.)	D1
Holmes (mt.)	B1	Sierra Madre (mts.)	E4
Horse (creek)	H4	Slate (creek)	C3
Horseshoe (creek)	G3	Smiths Fork (riv.)	B3
Hunt (mt.)	E1	Snake (riv.)	B2
Index (peak)	C1	South Cheyenne (riv.)	H2
Inyan Kara (creek)	H1	South Piney (creek)	B3
Inyan Kara (mt.)	H1	Sweetwater (riv.)	D3
Isabel (mt.)	B3	Sybille (creek)	G4
Jackson (lake)	B2	Teapot Dome (mt.)	F2
Jackson (mt.)	B2	Teton (range)	B2
John D. Rockefeller, Jr., Mem.		Tongue (riv.)	E1
Pkwy.	B1	Washburn (mt.)	B1
Keyhole (res.)	H1	Wheatland (res.)	G4
Lamar (riv.)	B1	Willow (creek)	F2
Lance (creek)	H2	Wind (riv.)	C2
Laramie (mts.)	G3	Wind River (canyon)	D2
Laramie (peak)	G3	Wind River (range)	C2
Laramie (riv.)	G4	Wind River Ind. Res.	C2
Leidy (mt.)	B2	Wood (riv.)	D1
Lewis (lake)	B1	Wyoming (peak)	B3
Lightning (creek)	G2	Wyoming (range)	B2
Little Missouri (riv.)	H1	Yellowstone (lake)	B1
Little Muddy (riv.)	B4	Yellowstone (riv.)	B1
Little Powder (riv.)	G1	Yellowstone Nat'l Park	B1
Little Sandy (creek)	C3	⊙County seat.
Little Thunder (creek)	G2	† Zip of nearest p.o. * Multiple zips.

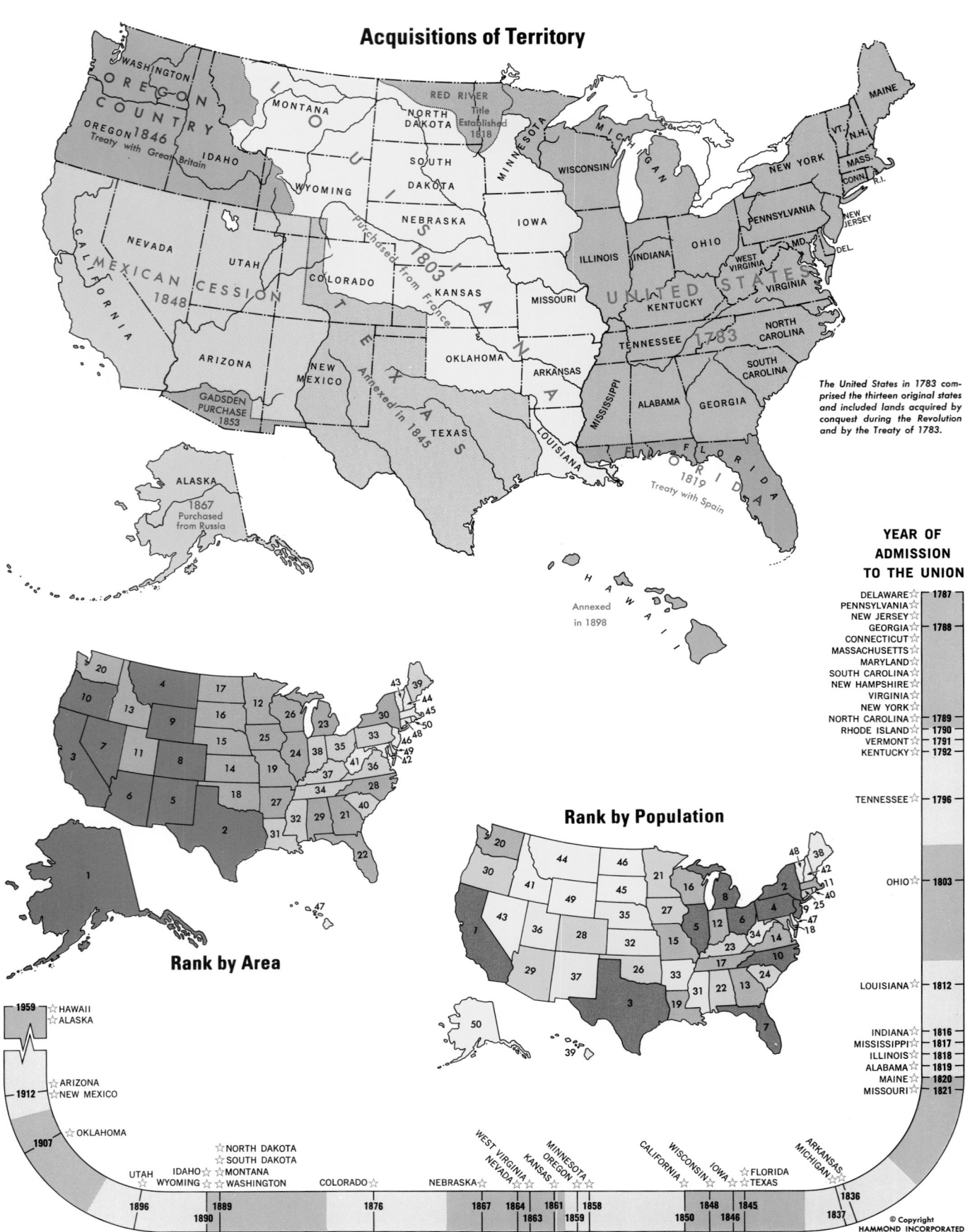

Acquisitions of Territory

WASHINGTON
OREGON COUNTRY
OREGON 1846 Treaty with Great Britain
IDAHO
MONTANA
NORTH DAKOTA
RED RIVER Title Established 1818
MINNESOTA
MICHIGAN
WISCONSIN
MAINE
VT. N.H.
NEW YORK
MASS.
CONN. R.I.
PENNSYLVANIA
NEW JERSEY
SOUTH DAKOTA
WYOMING
NEBRASKA
IOWA
ILLINOIS
INDIANA
OHIO
WEST VIRGINIA
MD.
DEL.
CALIFORNIA
NEVADA
UTAH
COLORADO
KANSAS
MISSOURI
KENTUCKY
VIRGINIA
UNITED STATES
MEXICAN CESSION 1848
ARIZONA
NEW MEXICO
OKLAHOMA
ARKANSAS
TENNESSEE
NORTH CAROLINA
1783
SOUTH CAROLINA
GADSDEN PURCHASE 1853
Annexed in 1845
TEXAS
MISSISSIPPI
ALABAMA
GEORGIA
LOUISIANA
Purchased from France
LOUISIANA 1803
FLORIDA 1819 Treaty with Spain

ALASKA 1867 Purchased from Russia

HAWAII Annexed in 1898

The United States in 1783 comprised the thirteen original states and included lands acquired by conquest during the Revolution and by the Treaty of 1783.

Rank by Area

Rank by Population

YEAR OF ADMISSION TO THE UNION

DELAWARE ☆	1787
PENNSYLVANIA ☆	
NEW JERSEY ☆	
GEORGIA ☆	1788
CONNECTICUT ☆	
MASSACHUSETTS ☆	
MARYLAND ☆	
SOUTH CAROLINA ☆	
NEW HAMPSHIRE ☆	
VIRGINIA ☆	
NEW YORK ☆	
NORTH CAROLINA ☆	1789
RHODE ISLAND ☆	1790
VERMONT ☆	1791
KENTUCKY ☆	1792
TENNESSEE ☆	1796
OHIO ☆	1803
LOUISIANA ☆	1812
INDIANA ☆	1816
MISSISSIPPI ☆	1817
ILLINOIS ☆	1818
ALABAMA ☆	1819
MAINE ☆	1820
MISSOURI ☆	1821

1959 ☆ HAWAII ☆ ALASKA
1912 ☆ ARIZONA ☆ NEW MEXICO
1907 ☆ OKLAHOMA
UTAH ☆ WYOMING ☆ 1896 1890 IDAHO ☆ MONTANA ☆ 1889 WASHINGTON ☆
☆ NORTH DAKOTA ☆ SOUTH DAKOTA
COLORADO ☆ 1876
NEBRASKA ☆ 1867
WEST VIRGINIA ☆ NEVADA ☆ 1864 1863
KANSAS ☆ 1861
MINNESOTA ☆ OREGON ☆ 1858 1859
CALIFORNIA ☆ 1850
WISCONSIN ☆ 1848
IOWA ☆ 1846
☆ FLORIDA ☆ TEXAS 1845
MICHIGAN ☆ 1837
ARKANSAS ☆ 1836

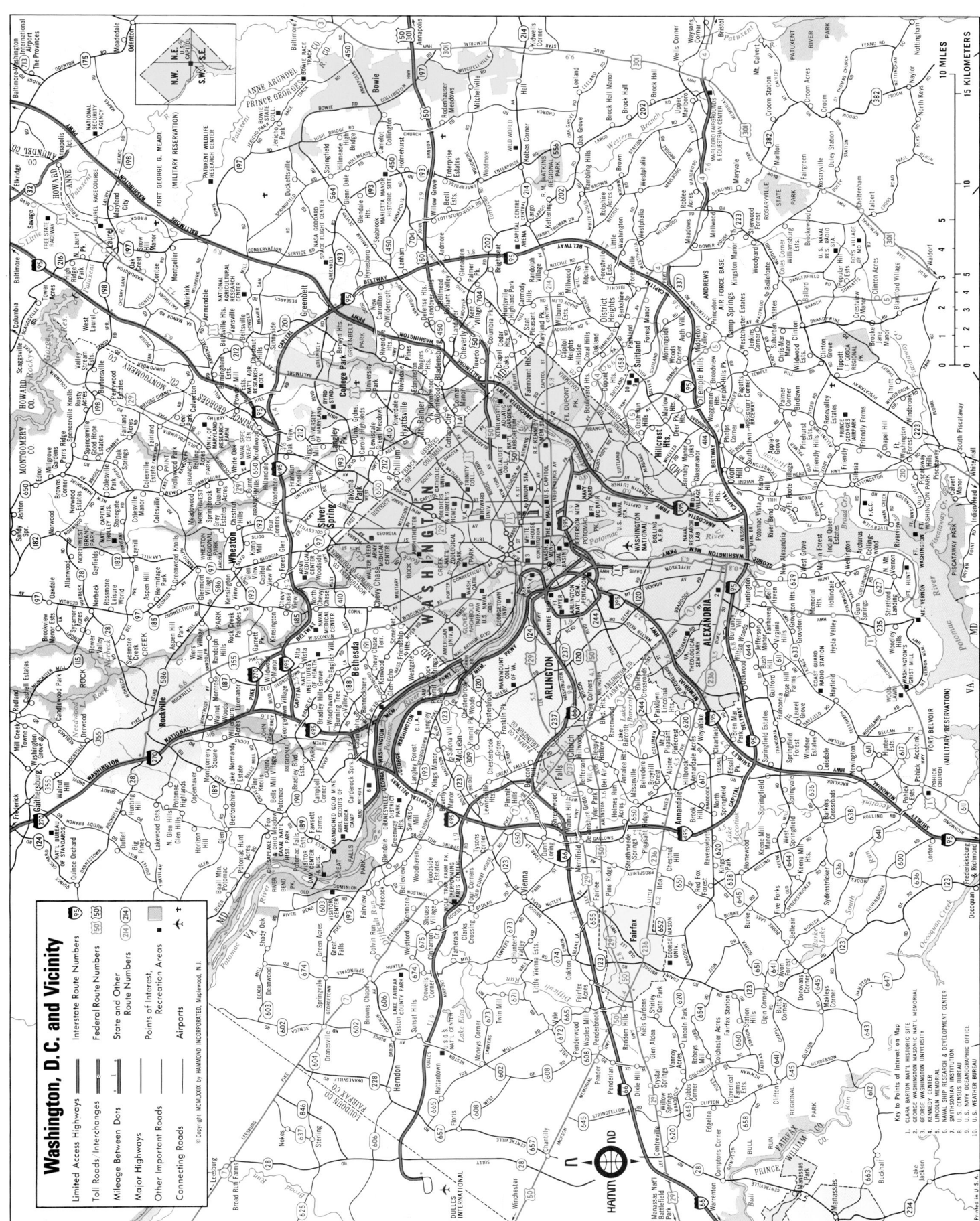

Washington, D.C. and Vicinity

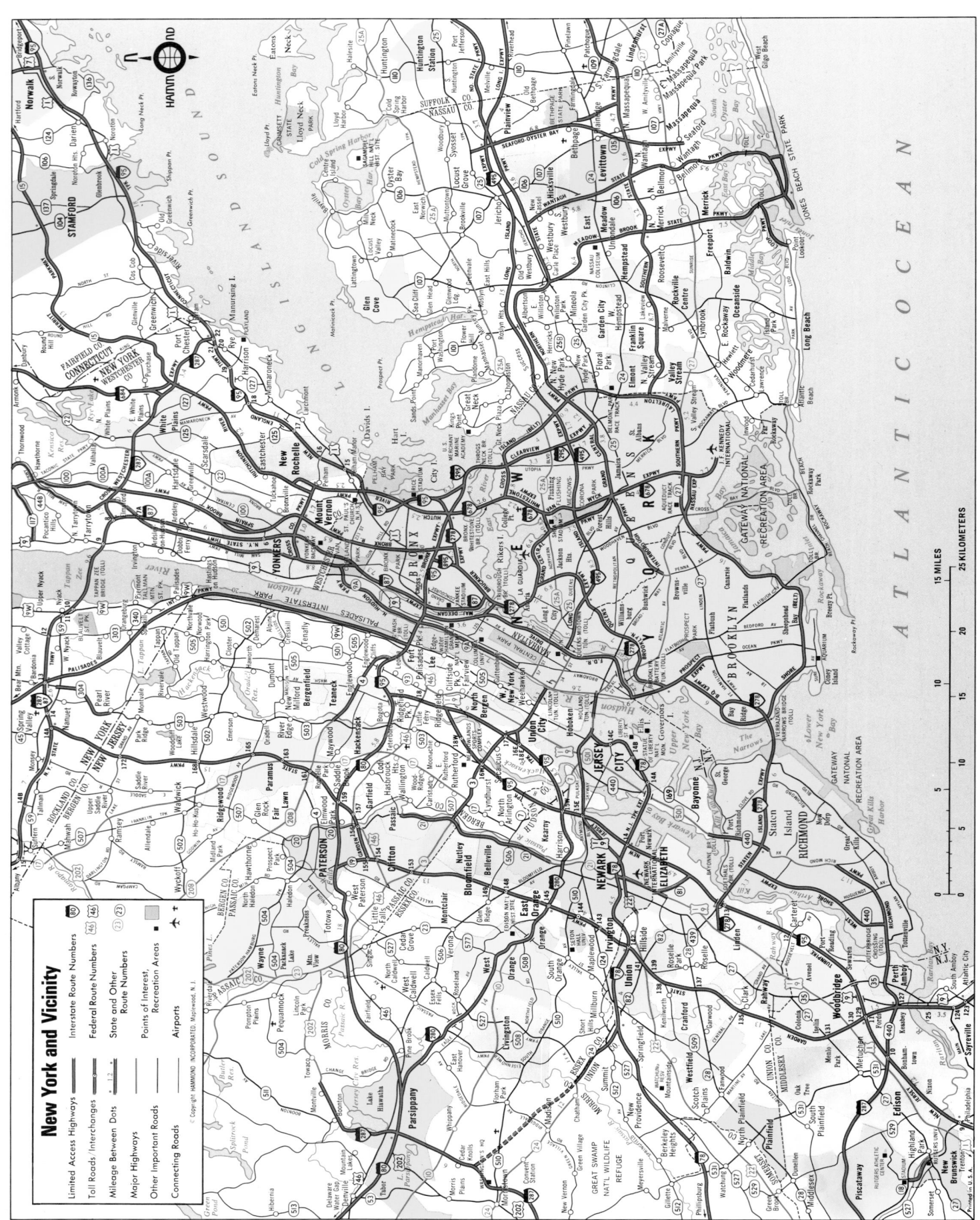

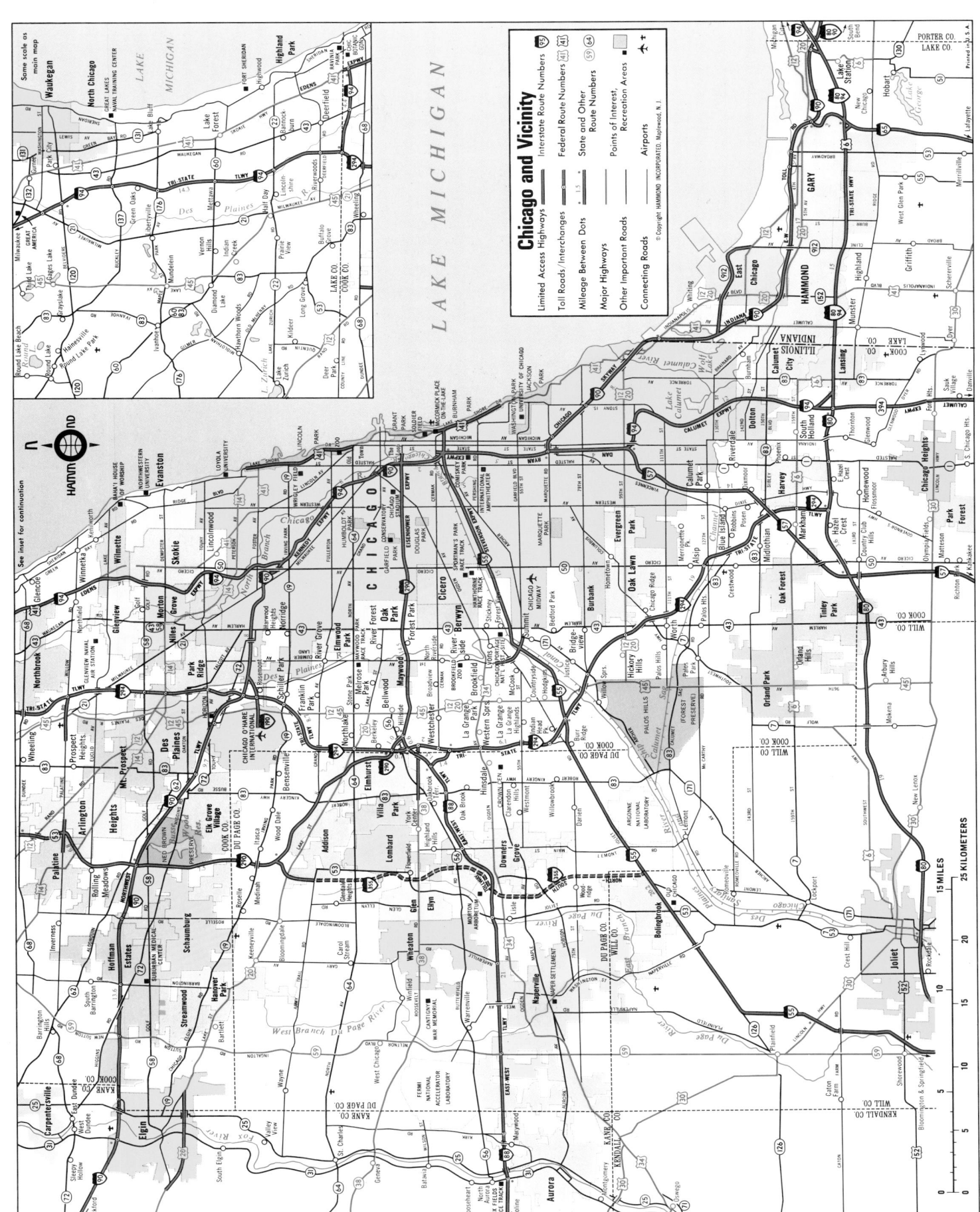

Chicago and Vicinity

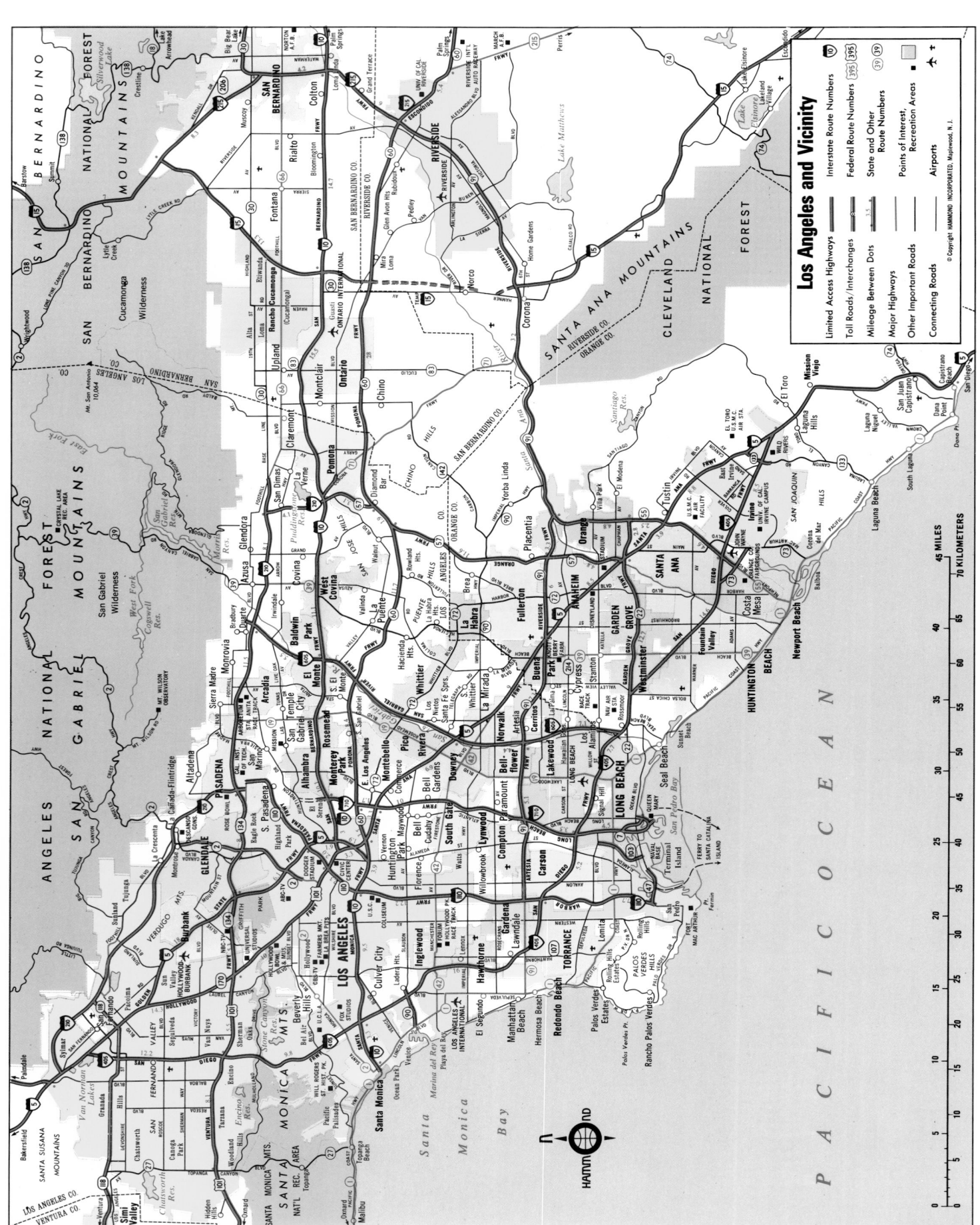

INDEX OF THE WORLD

Introduction

This index contains a complete alphabetical listing of more than one hundred thousand names shown on all the maps included in this atlas. Names not found in the individual indexes accompanying the maps appear here. The user who is unfamiliar with the location of a country, town, or physical feature, or who is in doubt as to which country, state or province a place belongs will find the answers to his questions in this index. Entries are indexed to all maps or insets showing the place.

The name of the feature sought will be found in its proper alphabetical sequence, followed by the name of the political division in which it is located, the page number of the map on which it will be found, and the key reference necessary for finding its location on the map. After noting the key reference letter-number combination for the place name, turn to the page number indicated. The place name will be found within the square formed by the two lines of latitude and the two lines of longitude which enclose the coordinates—i.e., the marginal letters and numbers. An open circle (○) after the name signifies a township — better known as a town — in the northeastern U.S.

All index entries for cities and towns in the United States are followed by a five-digit postal ZIP code number applying to the community. This useful feature permits the reader to address his mail so that it will be routed and delivered more efficiently and quickly by the U.S. Postal Service. A dagger (†) designates those places that do not possess a post office. The ZIP code number listed in such cases refers to that of the nearest post office. An asterisk (*) marks those larger cities which are divided into multiple ZIP code areas. Using the single ZIP code number listed in such cases will direct your letter to the proper city with dispatch. However, if the precise ZIP code number of the address within the city is needed, it is suggested that the reader refer to the latest National ZIP Code Directory at his local post office. This detailed guide lists every street in a multiple ZIP code city with the proper ZIP code for the street.

Because of limitations of space on the map, place names do not always appear in their complete form on the map. The complete forms are, however, given in the index. Variant spellings of names and alternate names are also given in this index. The alternate form or spelling of the name appears first, followed in parentheses by the name as it appears on the map. Physical features are usually listed under their proper names and not according to their generic terms; that is to say, Rio Negro will be found under Negro and not under Rio Negro. Exceptions are familiar names such as Rio Grande.

The abbreviations for the political division names and geographical features are explained on page XVI of the atlas. In addition, reference can be made to the Gazetteer-Index appearing on pages IX through XIII in which area, population, capital, map reference and population source data may be found for all major political and physical divisions of the world. Population figures for most entries are also included in the comprehensive individual indexes accompanying each map.

A

Aa (riv.), Switzerland 39/F3
Aachen, W. Germany 22/B3
Aadorf, Switzerland 39/G2
Aalen, W. Germany 22/D4
Aalsmeer, Netherlands 27/F4
Aalst, Belgium 27/D7
Aalten, Netherlands 27/K5
Aalter, Belgium 27/C6
Äänekoski, Finland 18/O5
Aarau, Switzerland 39/F2
Aarberg, Switzerland 39/D2
Aarburg, Switzerland 39/E2
Aardenburg, Netherlands 27/C6
Aare (riv.), Switzerland 39/E3
Aargau (canton), Switzerland 39/F2
Aarlen (Arlon), Belgium 27/H9
Aarons (creek), Va. 307/L7
Aaronsburg, Pa. (16820) 294/H4
Aarschot, Belgium 27/F7
Aat (Ath), Belgium 27/D7
Aba, China 77/F5
Aba, Hungary 41/E3
Aba, Nigeria 106/F7
Aba, Nigeria 102/C4
Aba, Zaire 115/F3
Aba as Sa'ud, Saudi Arabia 59/D6
Abacaxis (riv.), Brazil 132/B4
Abadan, Iran 54/F6
Abadan, Iran 66/F5
Abadan, Iran 59/F3
Abadeh, Iran 66/H5
Abadeh, Iran 59/F2
Abadla, Algeria 106/D2
Abádszalók, Hungary 41/F3
Abaeté, Brazil 132/E7
Abaetetuba, Brazil 132/D3
Abaetetuba, Brazil 120/E3
Abagnar (Silinhot), China 77/J3
Abai, Paraguay 144/E4
Abaiang (atoll), Kiribati 87/H5
'Abaila, Saudi Arabia 59/F5
Abajo (mts.), Utah 304/E6
Abakan, U.S.S.R. 54/L5
Abakan, U.S.S.R. 48/K4
Abala, Congo 115/C4
Abalos (pt.), Cuba 158/A2
Abana, Turkey 63/F2
Abancay, Peru 120/B4
Abancay, Peru 128/F9
Abapó, Bolivia 136/B6
Abaq, China 77/J3
Abarqu, Iran 59/F3
Abarqu, Iran 66/H5
'Abasan, Gaza Strip 65/A5
Abashiri, Japan 81/M1
Abashiri (riv.), Japan 81/M1
Abau, Papua N.G. 85/C7
Abaújszántó, Hungary 41/F2
Abay (riv.), Ethiopia 111/G5
Abay, U.S.S.R. 48/H5
Abaya (lake), Ethiopia 111/G6
Abaza, U.S.S.R. 48/J4

Abbaye (pt.), Mich. 250/B2
Abbe (lake), Djibouti 111/H5
Abbeville, Ala. (36310) 195/H7
Abbeville, France 28/D2
Abbeville, Georgia (31001) 217/F7
Abbeville, La. (70510) 238/F7
Abbeville, Miss. (38601) 256/F2
Abbeville (co.), S.C. 296/B3
Abbeville, S.C. (29620) 296/C3
Abbey, Sask. 181/C5
Abbey (head), Scotland 15/E6
Abbeydorney, Ireland 17/B7
Abbeyfeale, Ireland 10/B4
Abbeyfeale, Ireland 17/C7
Abbeylara, Ireland 17/F4
Abbeyleix, Ireland 17/G6
Abbotsford, Br. Col. 184/L3
Abbotsford, Wis. (54405) 317/F6
Abbott, Ark. (†72944) 202/B3
Abbott, N. Mex. (†87747) 274/E2
Abbott, Texas (76621) 303/G6
Abbottabad, Pakistan 68/C2
Abbottabad, Pakistan 59/K3
Abbottsburg, N.C. (28321) 281/M5
Abbottsford, Georgia (†30240) 217/B4
Abbottstown, Pa. (17301) 294/J6
Abbot Village○, Maine (04406) 243/D5
Abbyville, Kansas (67510) 232/D4
'Abdul 'Aziz, Jebel (mts.), Syria 63/J4
Abdulino, U.S.S.R. 52/H4
Abéché, Chad 102/D3
Abéché, Chad 111/D5
Abee, Alberta 182/D2
Abell, Md. (20606) 245/M8
Abemama (atoll), Kiribati 87/H5
Abengourou, Ivory Coast 106/D7
Abengourou, Ivory Coast 102/B4
Åbenrå, Denmark 18/F9
Åbenrå, Denmark 21/C7
Abeokuta, Niger 106/E7
Abeokuta, Nigeria 102/C4
Aberaeron, Wales 13/C5
Aberaeron, Wales 10/D4
Abercarn, Wales 13/B6
Aberchirder, Scotland 15/F3
Abercorn, Québec 172/E4
Abercorn (Mbala), Zambia 115/F5
Abercrombie, N. Dak. (58001) 282/S7
Abercrombie, Nova Scotia 168/F3
Abercrombie (mt.), Wash. 310/H2
Aberdare, Wales 13/A6
Aberdare, Wales 10/E5
Aberdaron, Wales 13/C5
Aberdeen, Idaho (83210) 220/F7
Aberdeen, Ky. (42201) 237/H6
Aberdeen, Md. (21001) 245/O2
Aberdeen, Miss. (39730) 256/H3
Aberdeen○, N.J. (†07747) 273/E3
Aberdeen, N.S. Wales 97/F3
Aberdeen, N.C. (28315) 281/L4
Aberdeen (lake), N.W. Terrs. 187/J3
Aberdeen, Ohio (45101) 284/C8
Aberdeen, Sask. 181/E3
Aberdeen, Scotland 7/D3

Aberdeen, Scotland 15/F3
Aberdeen, Scotland 10/F2
Aberdeen (trad. co.), Scotland 15/B5
Aberdeen, S. Africa 118/C6
Aberdeen, S. Dak. 146/J5
Aberdeen, S. Dak. 188/G1
Aberdeen, S. Dak. (57401) 298/M3
Aberdeen, Wash. 188/B1
Aberdeen, Wash. (98520) 310/B3
Aberdeen Proving Ground, Md. 245/N3
Aberdour, Scotland 15/D1
Aberfeldy, Sask. 181/B2
Aberfeldy, Scotland 10/D2
Aberfeldy, Scotland 15/E4
Aberfoyle, Scotland 15/D4
Abergavenny, Wales 13/B6
Abergavenny, Wales 10/E5
Abergele, Wales 13/D4
Aberlady, Scotland 15/F4
Aberlour, Scotland 15/E3
Abernant, Ala. (35440) 195/D4
Abernathy, Texas (79311) 303/B4
Abernethy, Sask. 181/H5
Abernethy, Scotland 15/E4
Aberporth, Wales 13/C5
Abert (lake), Oreg. 188/C2
Abert (lake), Oreg. 291/G5
Abertillery, Wales 13/B6
Abertillery, Wales 10/E5
Aberystwyth, Wales 13/C5
Aberystwyth, Wales 10/D4
Abez', U.S.S.R. 52/K1
Abha, Saudi Arabia 59/D6
Abha, Saudi Arabia 54/F8
Abhar, Iran 66/F2
Abiad, Ras el (Blanc) (cape), Tunisia 106/G1
Abibe, Serranía de (mts.), Colombia 126/B3
'Abidiya, Sudan 59/B6
Abidjan (cap.), Ivory Coast 2/J5
Abidjan (cap.), Ivory Coast 102/B4
Abidjan (cap.), Ivory Coast 106/D7
Abie, Nebr. (68001) 264/H3
Abilene, Kansas (67410) 232/E3
Abilene, Texas 146/J6
Abilene, Texas (*79601) 303/E5
Abilene, Texas 188/G4
Abingdon, England 13/F6
Abingdon, England 13/F6
Abingdon, Ill. (61410) 222/C3
Abingdon, Iowa (†52533) 229/J6
Abingdon, Md. (21009) 245/N3
Abingdon, Va. (24210) 307/D7
Abingdon Downs, Queensland 95/B3
Abington, Conn. (06230) 210/G1
Abington, Ind. (†47330) 227/H5
Abington○, Mass. (02351) 249/L4
Abington, Pa. (19001) 294/M5
Abington, Scotland 15/E5
Abiqua (creek), Oreg. 291/B3
Abiquiu, N. Mex. (87510) 274/C2
Abiquiu (res.), N. Mex. 274/C2
Abita Springs, La. (70420) 238/L6
Abitibi (riv.), Ont. 162/H5

Abitibi (lake), Ont. 162/H6
Abitibi (lake), Ontario 175/E3
Abitibi (riv.), Ontario 175/D2
Abitibi (riv.), Ontario 177/J5
Abitibi (county), Québec 174/B2
Abitibi (terr.), Québec 174/B3
Abkhaz A.S.S.R., U.S.S.R. 48/E5
Abkhaz A.S.S.R., U.S.S.R. 52/F6
Abminga, S. Australia 94/D2
Abner, N.C. (†27371) 281/K4
Abnûb, Egypt 111/J4
Åbo (Turku), Finland 18/N6
Aboisso, Ivory Coast 106/D7
Aboite, Ind. (†46783) 227/G3
Abomey, Benin 106/E7
Abong-Mbang, Cameroon 115/B3
Abony, Hungary 41/E3
Abor (hills), India 68/G3
Aborlan, Philippines 82/B6
Abou Deïa, Chad 111/C5
Aboyne, Scotland 15/F3
Abqaiq, Saudi Arabia 59/F4
Abra (prov.), Philippines 82/C2
Abra (riv.), Philippines 82/C2
Abraham (lake), Alberta 182/B3
Abraham (mt.), Maine 243/C5
Abraham, Utah (†84635) 304/B4
Abraham (mt.), Vt. 268/B3
Abraham Lincoln Birthplace Nat'l Hist. Site, Ky. 237/K5
Abrams, Wis. (54101) 317/L6
Abrantes, Portugal 33/B3
Abra Pampa, Argentina 143/C1
Abreus, Cuba 158/D2
'Abri, Sudan 111/E6
Abricots, Haiti 158/A6
Abruzzi (reg.), Italy 34/D3
Absaraka, N. Dak. (58002) 282/P6
Absaroka (range), Mont. 262/F5
Absaroka (range), Wyo. 319/C1
Absarokee, Mont. (59001) 262/G5
Absecon, N.J. (08201) 273/D5
Absecon (inlet), N.J. 273/E5
Abu, India 68/C4
Abu 'Arish, Saudi Arabia 124/D3
Abu Dara, Ras (cape), Sudan 59/D6
Abu Dara, Ras (cape), Sudan 111/G3
Abu Deleiq, Sudan 59/B6
Abu Dhabi (cap.), U.A.E. 54/G7
Abu Dhabi (cap.), U.A.E. 59/F5
Abu ed Duhur, Syria 63/G5
Abu Habl, Wadi (dry riv.), Sudan 111/F5
Abu Hadriya, Saudi Arabia 59/E4
Abu Hamed, Sudan 111/F4
Abu Hamed, Sudan 59/B6
Abuja (cap.), Niger 106/F7
Abu Kemal, Syria 59/D3
Abu Kemal, Syria 63/J5
Abukuma (riv.), Japan 81/K4
Abu-Mad, Ras (cape), Saudi Arabia 59/C5
Abu Matariq, Sudan 111/E5
Abumombazi, Zaire 115/D3
Abuná (riv.), Bolivia 136/B2
Abunã, Brazil 132/H10

Abunã (riv.), Brazil 132/G10
Abu Qir (bay), Egypt 111/J2
Abu Qurqâs, Egypt 111/J4
Abu Road, India 68/C4
Abu Rujmein, Jebel (mts.), Syria 63/H5
Abu Shagara, Ras (cape), Sudan 111/G3
Abu Shagara, Ras (cape), Sudan 59/C5
Abut (head), N. Zealand 100/B5
Abu Tabari (well), Sudan 111/E4
Abuyog, Philippines 82/E5
Abu Zabad, Sudan 59/A7
Abu Zabad, Sudan 111/E5
Abwong, Sudan 111/F6
Aby (lag.), Ivory Coast 106/D8
Åbybro, Denmark 21/C3
Abydos (ruins), Egypt 111/F2
Abydos (ruins), Turkey 63/B6
Abyei, Sudan 111/E6
A'Chralaig (mt.), Scotland 15/C3
Aci (lake), Turkey 63/C4
Acigöl, Turkey 63/F3
Acipayam, Turkey 63/C4
Acireale, Italy 34/E6
Ackerly, Texas (79713) 303/C5
Ackerman, Miss. (39735) 256/F4
Ackerville, Ala. (†36778) 195/D6
Ackley, Iowa (50601) 229/G3
Acklins (isl.), Bahamas 146/L7
Acklins (isl.), Bahamas 156/C2
Ackworth, Iowa (50001) 229/G6
Aclare, Ireland 17/D3
Acle, England 13/J5
Acme, Alberta 182/D4
Acme, La. (†71316) 238/G4
Acme, Mich. (49610) 250/D4
Acme, N.C. (†28456) 281/N6
Acme, Texas (†79252) 303/E3
Acme, Wash. (98220) 310/C2
Acme, W. Va. (†25122) 312/D6
Acme, Wyo. (82839) 319/E1
Acoaxet, Mass. (†02837) 249/K7
Acobamba, Peru 128/E10
Acolla, Peru 128/E8
Acoma, N. Mex. (†87034) 274/B4
Acomayo, Cusco, Peru 128/G9
Acomayo, Huánuco, Peru 128/E7
Acomita (Pueblo of Acoma), N. Mex. (†87034) 274/B3
Acona, Miss. (†39095) 256/F4
Aconcagua (riv.) 120/C6
Aconcagua, Cerro (mt.), Argentina 143/C3
Aconcagua, Chile 138/A9
Aconcagua (riv.), Chile 138/F2
Aconchi, Mexico 150/D2
Acopiara, Brazil 132/G4
Acora, Peru 128/H11
Acorizal, Brazil 132/C6
Acoyapa, Nicaragua 154/E5
Acqui Terme, Italy 34/B2
Acraman (lake), S. Australia 94/D5
Acre (state), Brazil 132/B4
Acre, Brazil 132/G10
Acre, Israel 65/C2

Allgäu 327

Alabat (isl.), Philippines 82/D3
Alaca, Turkey 63/F2
Alacahan, Turkey 63/G3
Alaçam, Turkey 63/F2
Alachua (co.), Fla. 212/D2
Alachua, Fla. (32615) 212/D2
Alacrán (reef), Mexico 150/P5
Alacranes, Cuba 158/D1
Aladağ (mt.), Turkey 63/F4
Aladagh, Kuh-i- (mt.), Iran 59/G2
'Aladagh, Kuh-e (mts.), Iran 66/K2
Aladdin, Wyo. (82710) 319/H1
Alaejos, Spain 33/D2
Alagir, U.S.S.R. 52/F6
Alagoa Grande, Brazil 132/H4
Alagoas (state), Brazil 132/G5
Alagoinhas, Brazil 120/F4
Alagoinhas, Brazil 132/G6
Alagón, Spain 33/F2
Alagón (riv.), Spain 33/C2
Alah (riv.), Philippines 82/E7
Al Ahqaf (Bahr es Safi) (des.), Saudi Arabia 59/E6
Al 'Ain, Saudi Arabia 59/C4
Alajuela, C. Rica 154/E6
Alakanuk, Alaska (99554) 196/E2
Alakol' (lake), U.S.S.R. 48/J5
Al 'Ala, Saudi Arabia 59/C4
Alalakeiki (chan.), Hawaii 218/J3
Alalapadu, Suriname 131/C4
Alamagan (isl.), No. Marianas 87/E4
Alamance (co.), N.C. 281/L3
Alamance, N.C. (27201) 281/K2
Alameda (co.), Calif. 204/D6
Alameda, Calif. (94501) 204/J2
Alameda (creek), Calif. 204/K3
Alameda, N. Mex. (87114) 274/C3
Alameda, Sask. 181/J6
Alamikamba, Nicaragua 154/E4
Alamo (lake), Ariz. 198/B4
Alamo (riv.), Calif. 204/K10
Alamo, Georgia (30411) 217/G6
Alamo, Ind. (47916) 227/C5
Alamo, Mexico 150/L6
Alamo, Nev. (89001) 266/F5
Alamo, N. Dak. (58830) 282/D2
Alamo, Tenn. (38001) 237/C9
Alamo, Texas (78516) 303/F11
Ala Moana, Hawaii 218/C4
Alamo-Danville, Calif. (94507) 204/K2
Alamogordo, N. Mex. 188/E4
Alamogordo, N. Mex. (88310) 274/C6
Alamo Heights, Texas (78209) 303/K10
Álamos, Mexico 150/E3
Alamosa (co.), Colo. 208/H7
Alamosa, Colo. (81101) 208/H8
Alamosa (creek), Colo. 208/G8
Alamosa (riv.), N. Mex. 274/B5
Alamota, Kansas (67830) 232/B3
Åland (Ahvenanmaa) (prov.), Finland 18/L6
Åland (isls.), Finland 7/F2
Åland (isls.), Finland 18/L6
Alanje, Panama 154/F6
Alanreed, Texas (79002) 303/D2
Alanson, Mich. (49706) 250/E3
Alanthus Grove, Mo. (†64489) 261/D2
Alanya, Turkey 59/B2
Alanya, Turkey 63/D4
Alaotra (lake), Madagascar 118/H3
Alapaha (riv.), Fla. 212/C1
Alapaha, Georgia (31622) 217/F8
Alapaha (riv.), Georgia 217/F7
Alaqua (creek), Fla. 212/C6
Alarcón (res.), Spain 33/E3
Alarka, N.C. (†28713) 281/C4
Alas (str.), Indonesia 85/F7
Alaşehir, Turkey 63/C3
Alashtar, Iran 66/E4
Alaska (reg.) 4/C17
Alaska 188/C5
Alaska (gulf) 146/D4
ALASKA 196
Alaska (gulf), Alaska 188/D6
Alaska (pen.), Alaska 188/C6
Alaska (range), Alaska 188/C6
Alaska (range), Alaska 146/C3
Alaska (pen.), Alaska 146/C4
Alaska (gulf), Alaska 196/K3
Alaska (pen.), Alaska 196/G3
Alaska (range), Alaska 196/H2
Alaska, Mich. (†49316) 250/D6
Alaska (state), U.S. 2/B2
Alaska (state), U.S. 146/C3
Alaska (range), U.S. 4/C17
Alaska (pen.), U.S. 4/D18
Alaska (gulf), U.S. 4/D17
Alaska Highway, Yukon 187/E3
Alassio, Italy 34/A2
Alatna, Alaska (†99720) 196/H1
Alatna (riv.), Alaska 196/H1
Alatri, Italy 34/D4
Alatyr', U.S.S.R. 52/G4
Al 'Auda, Saudi Arabia 59/E4
Alausí, Ecuador 128/C4
Álava (prov.), Spain 33/E1
Alava (cape), Wash. 188/A1
Alava (cape), Wash. 310/A2
Alaverdi, U.S.S.R. 52/F6
Alavus, Finland 18/N5
Alayor, Spain 33/J3
Al 'Azair, Iraq 66/E5
Alazeya (riv.), U.S.S.R. 48/Q3
Al'Aziziya, Iraq 59/E3
Al 'Aziziya, Iraq 66/D4
Alba, Italy 34/B2
Alba, Mich. (49611) 250/E4
Alba, Mo. (64830) 261/D8
Alba, Pa. (16910) 294/J2
Alba, Texas (75410) 303/J5
Albacete (prov.), Spain 33/E3
Albacete, Spain 7/D5
Albacete, Spain 33/F3
Alba de Tormes, Spain 33/D2
Albaida, Spain 33/F3
Alba Iulia, Romania 45/F2
Albalate del Arzobispo, Spain 33/F2
Alban, Ontario 177/D1
Albanel, Québec 172/E1
Albanel (lake), Québec 174/C2
Albania 2/K3
Albania 7/G4
ALBANIA 45/E5
Albano (lake), Italy 34/F7
Albano Laziale, Italy 34/F7
Albany, Australia 87/B9
Albany, Calif. (94706) 204/J2
Albany, Ga. 146/K6
Albany, Georgia (*31701) 217/D7
Albany, Ill. (61230) 222/C2
Albany, Ind. (47320) 227/G4
Albany, Jamaica 158/J6
Albany, Ky. (42602) 237/L7
Albany, La. (70711) 238/M1
Albany, Minn. (56307) 255/D5
Albany, Mo. (64402) 261/D2
Albany○, N.H. (†03864) 268/E4
Albany (cap.), N.Y. 188/M2
Albany (cap.), N.Y. 146/L5
Albany (co.), N.Y. 276/M5
Albany (cap.), N.Y. (*12201) 276/N5
Albany, N. Zealand 100/B1
Albany, Nova Scotia 168/C4
Albany, Ohio (45710) 284/F7
Albany, Okla. (74721) 288/O7
Albany (riv.), Ont. 146/K4
Albany (riv.), Ont. 162/H5
Albany (riv.), Ontario 175/C2
Albany, Oreg. 188/B2
Albany, Oreg. (97321) 291/D3
Albany, Pr. Edward I. 168/E2
Albany, Texas (76430) 303/E5
Albany, Vt. (05820) 268/C2
Albany○, Vt. (05820) 268/C2
Albany, W. Australia 88/B6
Albany, W. Australia 92/B6
Albany, Wis. (53502) 317/G10
Albany (co.), Wyo. 319/G4
Albany, Wyo. (†82055) 319/F4
Albany Creek, Queensland 88/J2
Albardon, Argentina 143/C3
Albarracín, Spain 33/F2
Albatross (pt.), N. Zealand 100/E3
Albatross (bay), Queensland 88/G2
Albatross (bay), Queensland 95/B2
Albay (prov.), Philippines 82/D4
Albay (gulf), Philippines 82/D4
Albee, S. Dak. (57210) 298/S3
Albemarle (pt.), Ecuador 128/B9
Albemarle (sound), N.C. 188/L3
Albemarle, N.C. (28001) 281/J4
Albemarle (sound), N.C. 281/S2
Albemarle (co.), Va. 307/L5
Albenga, Italy 34/B3
Albeni Falls (dam), Idaho 220/B1
Alberdi, Paraguay 144/D5
Alberene, Va. (†22959) 307/L5
Alberga, S. Australia 94/D2
Alberga, The (riv.), S. Australia 94/D2
Alberga, The (riv.), S. Australia 88/E5
Alberhill, Calif. (†92330) 204/E11
Alberni (inlet), Br. Col. 184/H3
Albers, Ill. (62215) 222/D5
Albert (canal), Belgium 27/F6
Albert, France 28/E2
Albert, Kansas (67511) 232/C3
Albert (co.), New Bruns. 170/F3
Albert, N. Mex. (87733) 274/F3
Albert, N.S. Wales 97/D3
Albert, Okla. (73001) 288/K4
Albert (lake), Québec 172/C3
Albert (Mobuto Sese Seko) (lake), Uganda 115/F3
Albert (creek), Wyo. 319/B4
Albert (Mobute Sese Seko) (lake), Zaire 115/F3
Alberta (prov.) 162/E5
Alberta (prov.) Canada 146/G4
Alberta, Ala. (36720) 195/D6
ALBERTA 182
Alberta (mt.), Alberta 182/B3
Alberta (mt.), Alta. 162/E5
Alberta, La. (†71016) 238/D2
Alberta, Minn. (56207) 255/B5
Alberta, Va. (23821) 307/N7
Alberta Beach, Alberta 182/C3
Albert City, Iowa (50510) 229/C3
Albert Edward (bay), N.W. Terrs. 187/H3
Albert Head, Br. Col. 184/J4
Alberti, Argentina 143/G7
Albertirsa, Hungary 41/E3
Albert Lea, Minn. (56007) 255/E7
Albert Mines, New Bruns. 170/F3
Alberton, Mont. (59820) 262/B3
Alberton, Pr. Edward I. 168/E2
Alberton, S. Africa 118/H6
Albert Town, Jamaica 158/H6
Albertville, Ala. (35950) 195/F2
Albertville, France 28/G5
Albertville, Minn. (55301) 255/E5
Albertville, Sask. 181/F2
Albeuve, Switzerland 39/D3
Albi, France 28/E6
Albia, Iowa (52531) 229/H6
Albin, Wyo. (82050) 319/H4
Albina, Suriname 131/D3
Albino, Italy 34/B2
Albion, Calif. (95410) 204/B4
Albion, Idaho (83311) 220/E7
Albion (mts.), Idaho 220/E7
Albion, Ill. (62806) 222/E5
Albion, Ind. (46701) 227/G2
Albion, Iowa (50005) 229/H4
Albion○, Maine (04910) 243/E6
Albion, Mich. (49224) 250/E6
Albion, Nebr. (68620) 264/F3
Albion, N.Y. (14411) 276/D4
Albion, Okla. (74521) 288/R5
Albion, Pa. (16401) 294/B2
Albion, R.I. (02802) 249/H5
Albion, Wash. (99102) 310/H4
Albion, Wis. (†53534) 317/H10
Al Birk, Saudi Arabia 59/D6
Albocácer, Spain 33/F2
Alborán (isl.), Spain 7/D5
Alborán (isl.), Spain 33/E5
Ålborg, Denmark 7/F3
Ålborg, Denmark 18/G8
Ålborg (bay), Denmark 21/D4
Alborn, Minn. (55702) 255/F4
Albox, Spain 33/E4
Albreda, Br. Col. 184/H4
Albright, W. Va. (26519) 312/G3
Albrightsville, Pa. (18210) 294/L3
Albristhorn (mt.), Switzerland 39/D4
Albufeira, Portugal 33/B4
Albuñol, Spain 33/E4
Albuquerque (cays), Colombia 126/A10
Albuquerque, N. Mex. 146/H6
Albuquerque, N. Mex. 188/E3
Albuquerque, N. Mex. (*87101) 274/C3
Alburg, Vt. (05440) 268/A2
Alburg○, Vt. (05440) 268/A2
Alburnett, Iowa (52202) 229/K4
Alburquerque, Spain 33/C3
Alburtis, Pa. (18011) 294/L5
Albury, Australia 87/E9
Albury, N. S. Wales 88/H7
Albury, N.S. Wales 97/D5
Albury, N. Zealand 100/C6
Alca, Peru 128/F10
Alcácer do Sal, Portugal 33/B3
Alcalá, Bolivia 136/C6
Alcalá de Chivert, Spain 33/G2
Alcalá de Guadaira, Spain 33/D4
Alcalá de Henares, Spain 33/G4
Alcalá de los Gazules, Spain 33/D4
Alcalá la Real, Spain 33/E4
Alcalde, N. Mex. (87511) 274/C2
Alcamo, Italy 34/D6
Alcanar, Spain 33/G2
Alcañices, Spain 33/C2
Alcañiz, Spain 33/F2
Alcántara, Portugal 33/A1
Alcántara, Spain 33/C3
Alcántara (res.), Spain 33/C3
Alcántaratara (res.), Portugal 33/C3
Alcantarilla, Spain 33/F4
Alcaraz, Argentina 143/G5
Alcaraz, Spain 33/E3
Alcaraz, Sierra de (range), Spain 33/E3
Alcatraz (isl.), Calif. 204/J2
Alcaudete, Spain 33/E4
Alcázar de San Juan, Spain 33/E3
Alcester, S. Dak. (57001) 298/R7
Alcida, New Bruns. 170/E1
Alcira, Spain 33/F3
Alco, Ark. (72610) 202/F2
Alco, La. (71402) 238/D4
Alcoa, Tenn. (37701) 237/N9
Alcobaça, Brazil 132/G7
Alcobaça, Portugal 33/B3
Alcolu, S.C. (29001) 296/G4
Alcomdale, Alberta 182/C3
Alcona (co.), Mich. 250/F4
Alcona Beach, Ontario 177/E3
Alcones, Chile 138/F5
Alcony, Ohio (†45373) 284/B5
Alcora, Spain 33/F2
Alcorisa, Spain 33/F2
Alcorn, Ky. (†40447) 237/O5
Alcorn (co.), Miss. 256/G1
Alcorn State University, Miss. (39096) 256/B7
Alcorta, Argentina 143/F6
Alcoutim, Portugal 33/C4
Alcova, Wyo. (82620) 319/F3
Alcova (res.), Wyo. 319/F3
Alcoy, Spain 33/F3
Alcudia (bay), Spain 33/H3
Alda, Nebr. (68810) 264/F4
Aldabra (isls.), Seychelles 102/G5
Aldabra (isls.), Seychelles 118/H1
Aldama, Chihuahua, Mexico 150/G2
Aldama, Tamaulipas, Mexico 150/L5
Aldan, Pa. (†19018) 294/M7
Aldan, U.S.S.R. 54/O4
Aldan (riv.), U.S.S.R. 54/P3
Aldan, U.S.S.R. 48/N4
Aldan (plat.), U.S.S.R. 48/N4
Aldan (riv.), U.S.S.R. 48/O3
Aldeburgh, England 13/J5
Aldeburgh, England 10/G4
Aldeia Carajá, Brazil 132/D6
Aldeia Nova de São Bento, Portugal 33/C4
Alden, Ill. (60001) 222/E1
Alden, Iowa (50006) 229/G4
Alden, Kansas (67512) 232/D3
Alden, Mich. (49612) 250/D4
Alden, Minn. (56009) 255/E7
Alden, N.Y. (14004) 276/C5
Alden Bridge, La. (†71006) 238/C1
Aldenville, Pa. (18401) 294/M2
Alder, Mont. (59710) 262/D5
Alder, Wash. (†98328) 310/C4
Alder (lake), Wash. 310/C4
Alder Creek, N.Y. (13301) 276/K4
Alder Flats, Alberta 182/C3
Alderley, Wis. (†53066) 317/J1
Alderney (isl.), Chan. Is. 10/E6
Alderney (isl.), Chan. Is. 13/E8
Alderpoint, Calif. (95411) 204/B3
Alder Point, Nova Scotia 168/H2
Aldershot, England 10/F5
Aldershot, England 13/G8
Aldershot, Nova Scotia 168/D3
Alderson, Okla. (74522) 288/P5
Alderson, W. Va. (24910) 312/E7
Aldersyde, Alberta 182/C4
Aldine, Ind. (†46366) 227/D2
Aldora, Georgia (†30204) 217/D4
Aldouane, New Bruns. 170/E2
Aldrich, Ala. (†35115) 195/E4
Aldrich, Minn. (56434) 255/C4
Aldrich, Mo. (65601) 261/F7
Aldridge Brownhills, England 10/G3
Aldridge Brownhills, England 13/E5
Aledo, Ill. (61231) 222/C2
Aledo, Texas (76008) 303/E2
Aleg, Mauritania 106/B5
Alegre, Brazil 135/F2
Alegre, Brazil 132/F8
Alegrete, Brazil 132/B10
Alegrete, Brazil 120/D5
'Aleih, Lebanon 63/F6
Alejandra, Argentina 143/F5
Alejandría, Bolivia 136/C3
Alejandro Selkirk (isl.), Chile 120/A6
Aleknagik, Alaska (99555) 196/G3
Aleksandriya, U.S.S.R. 52/D5
Aleksandrov Gay, U.S.S.R. 52/G4
Aleksandrovsk, U.S.S.R. 52/J3
Aleksandrovsk-Sakhalinsky, U.S.S.R. 54/R4
Aleksandrovsk-Sakhalinskiy, U.S.S.R. 48/P5
Aleksandrów Kujawski, Poland 47/D2
Aleksandrów Łódzki, Poland 47/D3
Alekseyevka, U.S.S.R. 48/H4
Alekseyevka, U.S.S.R. 52/E4
Aleksin, U.S.S.R. 52/E4
Aleksinac, Yugoslavia 45/E4
Além Paraíba, Brazil 135/E2
Alençon, France 28/D3
Alenquer, Brazil 132/C3
Alenquer, Brazil 120/D3
Alenuihaha (chan.), Hawaii 218/E7
Aleppo (prov.), Syria 63/G4
Aleppo, Syria 54/E6
Aleppo, Syria 59/C2
Aleppo, Syria 63/G4
Aléria, France 28/B6
Alert, Canada 4/A12
Alert, Ind. (†47283) 227/F6
Alert, N.C. (†27589) 281/N2
Alert, N.W.T. 162/N3
Alert, N.W. Terrs. 187/M1
Alert (pt.), N.W. Terrs. 187/K1
Alert Bay, Br. Col. 184/D5
Alès, France 28/E5
Alessandria (prov.), Italy 34/B2
Alessandria, Italy 34/B2
Ålestrup, Denmark 21/C4
Ålesund, Norway 7/E2
Ålesund, Norway 18/D5
Aletschhorn (mt.), Switzerland 39/F4
Aleutian (isls.), Alaska 188/D6
Aleutian (isls.), Alaska 196/J4
Aleutian (range), Alaska 196/G3
Aleutian (isls.), U.S. 4/D18
Aleutian (isls.), U.S. 2/A3
Alex, Okla. (73002) 288/L5
Alexander (arch.), Alaska 146/E4
Alexander (arch.), Alaska 196/L1
Alexander (isl.) 5/B15
Alexander, Ark. (72002) 202/F4
Alexander (lake), Conn. 210/H1
Alexander, Georgia (30801) 217/J4
Alexander (co.), Ill. 222/D6
Alexander, Ill. (62601) 222/D4
Alexander, Iowa (50420) 229/G3
Alexander, Kansas (67513) 232/C3
Alexander○, Maine (†04610) 243/H5
Alexander, Manitoba 179/B5
Alexander, N.Y. (14005) 276/D5
Alexander (co.), N.C. 281/G3
Alexander, N. Dak. (58831) 282/C4
Alexander (cape), Solomon Is. 86/D2
Alexander (arch.), U.S. 4/D16
Alexander, W. Va. (26218) 312/F5
Alexander Bay, S. Africa 102/D7
Alexander Bay, S. Africa 118/B5
Alexander City, Ala. (35010) 195/G5
Alexander Mills, N.C. (†28043) 281/F4
Alexandra, N. Zealand 100/B6
Alexandra, S. Africa 118/H6
Alexandra, Victoria 97/C5
Alexandra Land (isl.), U.S.S.R. 4/A8
Alexandra Land (isl.), U.S.S.R. 48/E1
Alexandretta (Iskenderun), Turkey 63/G4
Alexandretta (gulf), Turkey 63/F4
Alexandria, Ala. (36250) 195/G3
Alexandria, Br. Col. 184/F4
Alexandria, Egypt 2/L4
Alexandria, Egypt 102/E1
Alexandria, Egypt 59/A3
Alexandria, Egypt 111/J2
Alexandria, Ind. (46001) 227/F4
Alexandria, Jamaica 158/J6
Alexandria, Ky. (41001) 237/N3
Alexandria, La. 146/J6
Alexandria, La. 188/H4
Alexandria, La. (71301) 238/E4
Alexandria, Minn. (56308) 255/C5
Alexandria, Mo. (63430) 261/K2
Alexandria, Nebr. (68303) 264/G4
Alexandria○, N.H. (†03222) 268/D4
Alexandria, North. Terr. 93/E5
Alexandria, Ohio (43001) 284/E5
Alexandria, Ontario 177/K2
Alexandria, Pa. (16611) 294/F4
Alexandria, Romania 45/G3
Alexandria, Scotland 15/A1
Alexandria, Scotland 10/A1
Alexandria, S. Dak. (57311) 298/O6
Alexandria, Tenn. (37012) 237/J8
Alexandria, Va. 188/L3
Alexandria (I.C.), Va. (*22301) 307/S3
Alexandria Bay, N.Y. (13607) 276/J2
Alexandrina (lake), S. Australia 94/F6
Alexandroúpolis, Greece 45/H5
Alexis, Ill. (61412) 222/C2
Alexis (riv.), Newf. 166/C3
Alexis Creek, Br. Col. 184/F4
Aleysk, U.S.S.R. 48/J4
Aleza Lake, Br. Col. 184/G3
Alfalfa (co.), Okla. 288/K1
Alfalfa, Okla. (†73015) 288/J4
Al Falluja, Iraq 59/D3
Al Falluja, Iraq 66/C4
Alfaro, Spain 33/F1
Alfatar, Bulgaria 45/H4
Al Fatha, Iraq 59/D2
Al Fatha, Iraq 66/C3
Alfeld, W. Germany 22/C2
Alfenas, Brazil 135/D2
Alférez (riv.), Uruguay 145/E5
Alford, England 13/H4
Alford, Fla. (32420) 212/D6
Alford○, Mass. (†01261) 249/A4
Alford, Scotland 15/F3
Alford, Scotland 10/E2
Alfordsville, Ind. (†47553) 227/C7
Alfred, Maine (04002) 243/B9
Alfred○, Maine (04002) 243/B9
Alfred, N.Y. (14802) 276/E6
Alfred, N. Dak. (58411) 282/N6
Alfred, Ontario 177/K2
Alfredton, N. Zealand 100/F4
Alfreton, England 13/F4
Alga, U.S.S.R. 48/F5
Ålgård, Norway 18/D7
Algarrobo, Chile 138/F5
Algarrobo (pt.), P. Rico 161/A2
Algarrobo del Águila, Argentina 143/C4
Algeciras, Colombia 126/C6
Algeciras, Spain 33/D4
Algemesí, Spain 33/F3
Alger (co.), Mich. 250/C2
Alger, Mich. (48610) 250/E4
Alger, Ohio (45812) 284/C4
Algeria 2/J4
Algeria 102/C2
ALGERIA 106/D3
Algés, Portugal 33/A1
Algete, Spain 33/G4
Alghero, Italy 34/B4
Algiers (cap.), Algeria 102/C1
Algiers (cap.), Algeria 106/E1
Algiers (cap.), Algeria 2/K4
Algiers, Ind. (†47567) 227/C7
Algoa, Ark. (†72112) 202/B6
Algoa (bay), S. Africa 118/D6
Algoa, Texas (†77511) 303/K3
Algodones, N. Mex. (87001) 274/C3
Algoma, Miss. (38820) 256/G2
Algoma (terr. dist.), Ontario 177/J5
Algoma (terr. dist.), Ontario 175/D3
Algoma, Oreg. (†97601) 291/F5
Algoma, W. Va. (24807) 312/D8
Algoma, Wis. (54201) 317/M6
Algoma Mills, Ontario 177/B1
Algona, Iowa (50511) 229/E2
Algona, Wash. (98002) 310/C3
Algonac, Mich. (48001) 250/G6
Algonquin, Ill. (60102) 222/E1
Algonquin (peak), N.Y. 276/M2
Algonquin Park, Ontario 177/F2
Algonquin Prov. Park, Ontario 177/F2
Algonquin Prov. Park, Ontario 175/E3
Algood, Tenn. (38501) 237/K8
Algorta, Uruguay 145/B3
Algrove, Sask. 181/H3
Alhama de Granada, Spain 33/E4
Alhama de Murcia, Spain 33/F4
Alhambra, Alberta 182/C3
Alhambra, Calif. (*91801) 204/C10
Alhambra, Ill. (62001) 222/D5
Al Hawtah, P.D.R. Yemen 59/E6
Al Hilla, Saudi Arabia 59/E5
Al Hoceima, Morocco 106/D1
Alhos Vedros, Portugal 33/B3
Alhué, Estero de (riv.), Chile 138/F4
Alia, Spain 33/D3
'Aliabad, Kuh-e (mt.), Iran 59/F3
'Aliabad, Kuh-e (mt.), Iran 66/G3
Aliağa, Turkey 63/B3
Alibag, India 68/C5
Alibates Flint Quarries Nat'l Mon., Texas 303/C2
Ali-Bayramly, U.S.S.R. 52/G7
Alibeyköyü, Turkey 63/D6
Alicante (prov.), Spain 33/F3
Alicante, Spain 33/F3
Alicante, Spain 7/D5
Alice (lake), Nebr. 264/A2
Alice, N. Dak. (58003) 282/P6
Alice (lake), N. Dak. 282/M3
Alice, Ontario 177/G2
Alice (chan.), Philippines 82/B8
Alice (riv.), Queensland 95/C4
Alice, Texas (78332) 303/F10
Alice Arm, Br. Col. 184/C2
Alicel, Oreg. (†97824) 291/J2
Alice Springs, Australia 87/D8
Alice Springs, North. Terr. 88/E4
Alice Springs, North. Terr. 93/D7
Aliceville, Ala. (35442) 195/B4
Aliceville (dam), Ala. 195/B4
Aliceville, Kansas (66832) 232/G3
Alicia, Ark. (72410) 202/H2
Alicia (bank), Colombia 126/B8
Alicudi (isl.), Italy 34/E5
Alida, Minn. (†56676) 255/C3
Alida, Sask. 181/K6
Aligarh, India 68/D3
'Ali Gharbi, Iraq 66/E4
Alijó, Portugal 33/C2
Alima (riv.), Congo 115/B4
Alimodian, Philippines 82/D5
Alindao, Cent. Afr. Rep. 115/D2
Aline, Georgia (†30420) 217/H6
Aline, Okla. (73716) 288/K1
Alingly, Sask. 181/E2
Alingsås, Sweden 18/H7
Alipore, India 68/F2
Aliquippa, Pa. (15001) 294/B4
Ali Sabieh, Djibouti 111/H5
'Ali Sharqi, Iraq 66/E4
Aliskerovo, U.S.S.R. 48/R3
Alivérion, Greece 45/G6
Aliwal North, S. Africa 118/D6
Alix, Alberta 182/D3
Alix, Ark. (72820) 202/C3
Aljezur, Portugal 33/B4
Aljojuca, Mexico 150/O1
Aljustrel, Portugal 33/B4
Alkabo, N. Dak. (58832) 282/C2
Alkali (lakes), Calif. 204/E2
Alkali (lake), Nev. 266/B1
Alkali (lakes), N. Dak. 282/L3
Alkali Lake, Br. Col. 184/F4
Alkaline (lake), N. Dak. 282/L6
Alken, Belgium 27/G7
Alkmaar, Netherlands 27/F3
Alkmaardermeer (lake), Netherlands 27/F3
Alkol, W. Va. (25501) 312/C6
Al Kufa, Iraq 66/D4
Al Kumait, Iraq 66/E4
Al Kuwait (cap.), Kuwait 59/E4
Al Kuwait (cap.), Kuwait 54/F7
Allagash○, Maine (†04774) 243/F1
Allagash (lake), Maine 243/D3
Allagash (riv.), Maine 243/E2
Allahabad, India 68/E3
Allahabad, India 54/K7
Allaine (riv.), Switzerland 39/D2
Allaire, N.J. (†07727) 273/E3
Allakaket, Alaska (99720) 196/H1
Allakh-Yun', U.S.S.R. 48/O3
Allamakee (co.), Iowa 229/L2
Allaman, Switzerland 39/B4
All American (canal), Calif. 204/K11
Allamoore, Texas (†79855) 303/C11
Allamuchy, N.J. (07820) 273/D2
Allan (mt.), Idaho 220/D4
Allan, Sask. 181/E4
Allan (hills), Sask. 181/E4
Allanmyo, Burma 72/B3
Allanwater, Ontario 175/C2
Allanwater, Ontario 177/G4
'Allaqi, Wadi (dry riv.), Egypt 111/F3
Allard (lake), Québec 174/E2
Allardt, Tenn. (38504) 237/M8
Allardville, New Bruns. 170/E1
Allariz, Spain 33/C1
Allatoona (lake), Georgia 217/C2
Alle, Switzerland 39/D2
Alleene, Ark. (71820) 202/B6
Allegan (co.), Mich. 250/D6
Allegan, Mich. (49010) 250/D6
Allegany (co.), Md. 245/C2
Allegany (co.), N.Y. 276/D6
Allegany, N.Y. (14706) 276/C6
Allegany, Oreg. (97407) 291/D4
Allegany Ind. Res., N.Y. 276/C6
Alleghany, Calif. (95910) 204/E4
Alleghany (co.), N.C. 281/G1
Alleghany (co.), Va. 307/H5
Alleghany, Va. (†24426) 307/H5
Allegheny (res.), N.Y. 276/C7
Allegheny (riv.), N.Y. 276/C6
Allegheny (co.), Pa. 294/B5
Allegheny (res.), Pa. 294/E2
Allegheny (riv.), Pa. 294/D2
Allegheny (mts.), Va. 307/H5
Allegheny Front (mts.), Md. 245/C2
Allegheny Front (mts.), Pa. 294/E5
Allègre (pt.), Guadeloupe 161/A6
Allegre, Ky. (42203) 237/G7
Alleman, Iowa (50007) 229/F5
Allemands (lake), La. 238/M4
Allen, Ala. (36419) 195/C7
Allen, Argentina 143/C4
Allen (co.), Ind. 227/G2
Allen, Lough (lake), Ireland 10/C3
Allen (lake), Ireland 17/E3
Allen, Bog of (marsh), Ireland 17/H5
Allen (co.), Kansas 232/G4
Allen, Kansas (66833) 232/F3
Allen (co.), Ky. 237/J7
Allen, Ky. (41601) 237/R5
Allen (par.), La. 238/E5
Allen, La. (†71469) 238/D3
Allen, Md. (21810) 245/R7
Allen, Mich. (49227) 250/E7
Allen, Miss. (†39083) 256/C7
Allen (mt.), Mont. 262/C2
Allen, Nebr. (68710) 264/H2
Allen (co.), Ohio 284/B4
Allen, Okla. (74825) 288/O5
Allen, Pa. (†17007) 294/H5
Allen, S. Dak. (57714) 298/F7
Allen, Texas (75002) 303/H1
Allendale, England 13/E3
Allendale, Ill. (62410) 222/F5
Allendale, Mo. (†64456) 261/D2
Allendale, N.J. (07401) 273/B1
Allendale (co.), S.C. 296/E6
Allendale, S.C. (29810) 296/E5
Allende, Coahuila, Mexico 150/J2
Allende, Nuevo León, Mexico 150/J4
Allendorf, Iowa (51330) 229/B2
Allenford, Ontario 177/C3
Allenhurst, Georgia (31301) 217/J7
Allenhurst, N.J. (07711) 273/F3
Allen Park, Mich. (48101) 250/B7
Allens Mills, Maine (†04938) 243/C6
Allenspark, Colo. (80510) 208/J2
Allen Springs, Ky. (†42122) 237/J7
Allenstein (Olsztyn), Poland 47/E2
Allenstown○, N.H. (†03275) 268/E5
Allensville, Ky. (42204) 237/G7
Allensville, Ohio (45611) 284/E7
Allensville, Pa. (17002) 294/G4
Allenton, Mo. (63001) 261/M4
Allenton, R.I. (†02852) 249/H6
Allenton, Wis. (53002) 317/K9
Allentown, Georgia (31003) 217/F5
Allentown, N.J. (08501) 273/D3
Allentown, N.Y. (14707) 276/E6
Allentown, Ohio (†45801) 284/B4
Allentown, Pa. 188/L2
Allentown, Pa. (*18101) 294/L4
Allentsteig, Austria 41/C2
Allenville, Ill. (†61951) 222/E4
Allenville, Mo. (†63740) 261/N8
Allenwood, N.J. (08720) 273/E3
Allenwood, Pa. (17810) 294/H3
Alleppey-Cochin, India 68/D7
Aller (riv.), W. Germany 22/C2
Allerton, Ill. (61810) 222/F4
Allerton, Iowa (50008) 229/G7
Allerton, Mass. (02045) 249/E7
Allerton (pt.), Mass. 249/E7
Alley, Jamaica 158/J7
Alley Spring, Mo. (†65466) 261/J8
Allgäu (reg.), W. Germany 22/D5

Antsiranana 329

Amritsar, India 68/C2
Amrum (isl.), W. Germany 22/C1
Amsden, Ohio (44803) 284/D3
Amstelveen, Netherlands 27/B5
Amsterdam (isl.) 2/N7
Amsterdam, Georgia (31734) 217/D9
Amsterdam, Mo. (64723) 261/D6
Amsterdam, Mont. (†59741) 262/E5
Amsterdam (cap.), Netherlands 27/B4
Amsterdam (cap.), Netherlands 7/E3
Amsterdam, N.Y. (12010) 276/M5
Amsterdam, Ohio (43903) 284/J5
Amsterdam, Sask. 181/J4
Amstetten, Austria 41/C2
Amston, Conn. (06231) 210/F2
Am-Timan, Chad 111/D5
Amuay, Venezuela 124/C2
Amudar'ya (riv.) 2/N3
Amudar'ya (riv.), U.S.S.R. 54/H5
Amudar'ya (riv.), U.S.S.R. 48/G5
Amukta (isl.), Alaska 196/D4
Amukta (passage), Alaska 196/D4
Amuku (mts.), Guyana 131/B4
Amulet, Sask. 181/G6
Amund Ringnes (isl.), N.W.T. 162/M3
Amund Ringnes (isl.), N.W. Terrs. 187/J2
Amundsen (sea) 2/D10
Amundsen (bay) 5/C3
Amundsen (sea) 5/B13
Amundsen (gulf), Canada 4/B16
Amundsen (gulf), N.W.T. 162/D1
Amundsen (gulf), N.W.T. 146/F2
Amundsen (gulf), N.W. Terrs. 187/F2
Amundsen-Scott Station 5/A14
Amuntai, Indonesia 85/F6
Amur (riv.) 2/R3
Amur (riv.) 54/P5
Amur (Heilong Jiang) (riv.), China 77/L2
'Amur, Wadi (dry riv.), Sudan 111/G4
Amur (riv.), U.S.S.R. 48/O4
Amurang, Indonesia 85/G5
Amursk, U.S.S.R. 48/O4
Amy, Kansas (†67850) 232/B3
Amya (pass), Burma 72/C4
Amya (pass), Thailand 72/C4
Amyun, Lebanon 63/F5
An, Burma 72/B3
'Ana, Iraq 66/B3
'Ana, Iraq 59/D3
Anaa (atoll), Fr. Poly. 87/M7
Anabar (riv.), U.S.S.R. 48/M2
Anabel, Mo. (63431) 261/H3
Ana Branch, Darling (riv.), N.S. Wales 97/A3
'Anabta, West Bank 65/C3
Anacapa (isl.), Calif. 204/F10
Anaco, Venezuela 124/F3
Anacoco, La. (71403) 238/D4
Anacoco (lake), La. 238/D4
Anaconda, Mont. 188/D1
Anaconda-Deer Lodge County, Mont. (59711) 262/C4
Anacortes, Wash. (98221) 310/C2
Anacostia, D.C. (20020) 245/F5
Anacostia (riv.), D.C. 245/F5
Anadarko, Okla. (73005) 288/K4
Anadia, Portugal 33/B2
Anadolufeneri, Turkey 63/D5
Anadoluhisarı, Turkey 63/D6
Anadyr', U.S.S.R 2/T2
Anadyr', U.S.S.R. 4/C1
Anadyr' (gulf), U.S.S.R. 4/C18
Anadyr' (gulf), U.S.S.R. 54/V3
Anadyr' (riv.), U.S.S.R. 54/U3
Anadyr' (riv.), U.S.S.R. 4/C1
Anadyr', U.S.S.R. 48/S3
Anadyr' (gulf), U.S.S.R. 48/T3
Anadyr' (range), U.S.S.R. 48/S3
Anadyr' (riv.), U.S.S.R. 48/S3
Anadyr' U.S.S.R. 54/U3
Anáfi (isl.), Greece 45/G7
Anagance, New Bruns. 170/E3
Anaheim, Calif. 188/C4
Anaheim, Calif. (*92801) 204/D11
Anahim Lake, Br. Col. 184/E4
Anahola, Hawaii (96703) 218/C1
Anáhuac, Chihuahua, Mexico 150/F2
Anáhuac, Nuevo León, Mexico 150/J3
Anahuac, Texas (77514) 303/K8
Anaï (well), Algeria 106/G4
Anai Mudi (mt.), India 68/D6
'Anaiza, Saudi Arabia 59/D4
'Anaiza, Saudi Arabia 54/F7
Anak, N. Korea 81/B4
Anakapalle, India 68/E5
Anaktalik Brook (riv.), Newf. 166/B2
Anaktuvuk Pass, Alaska (99721) 196/H1
Analalava, Madagascar 118/H2
Ana María (gulf), Cuba 158/F3
Anambas (isls.), Indonesia 85/D5
Anambra (state), Nigeria 106/F7
Anamoose, N. Dak. (58710) 282/K4
Anamosa, Iowa (52205) 229/L4
Anamur, Turkey 63/E4
Anamur (cape), Turkey 59/B2
Anamur (cape), Turkey 63/E5
Anan, Japan 81/G7
Anandale, La. (†71301) 238/F4
Ananea, Bolivia 136/A4
Anantapur, India 68/D6
Anantnag, India 68/D2
Anapa, U.S.S.R. 52/E6
Anápolis, Brazil 132/D7
Anápolis, Brazil 120/E4
Anar, Iran 66/J5
Anar, Iran 59/G3
Anarak, Iran 66/H4
Anarak, Iran 59/F3
Anar Darreh, Afghanistan 59/H3
Anar Darreh, Afghanistan 68/A2
Añasco, P. Rico 161/A1
Añasco, P. Rico 156/F1
Añasco (bay), P. Rico 161/A1
Anastasia (isl.), Fla. 212/E2
Anatahan (isl.), No. Marianas 87/E4
Anatolia (reg.), Turkey 63/D3
Anatone, Wash. (99401) 310/H4
Añatuya, Argentina 143/D2
Anauá (riv.), Brazil 132/B2
Anawalt, W. Va. (24808) 312/D8
Anaye (well), Niger 106/G5
Anbar (gov.), Iraq 66/B4
Ancash (dept.), Peru 128/D7
Ancaster, Ontario 177/D4
Anceney, Mont. (†59741) 262/E5
Ancenis, France 28/C4
Anchieta, Brazil 132/F8
Ancho, N. Mex. (†88301) 274/D5
Anchor, Ill. (61720) 222/E3
Anchorage, Alaska 188/D6
Anchorage, Alaska 146/D3
Anchorage, Alaska (*99501) 196/B1
Anchorage, Ky. (40223) 237/L2
Anchorage, U.S. 2/B2
Anchorage, U.S. 4/D17
Anchorena, Argentina 143/C4
Anchor Point, Alaska (99556) 196/B2
Anchor Point, Newf. 166/C3
Anchorville, Mich. (48004) 250/G6
Anchovy, Jamaica 158/H5
Ancienne-Lorette, Québec 172/H3
Ancitas (cay), Cuba 158/F3
Anclote (keys), Fla. 212/D3
Anco, Ky. (41711) 237/P6
Ancohuma (mt.), Bolivia 120/C4
Ancohuma, Nevada (mt.), Bolivia 136/A4
Ancón, Peru 128/D8
Ancona, Ill. (61311) 222/E2
Ancona (prov.), Italy 34/D3
Ancona, Italy 34/D3
Ancona, Italy 7/F4
Ancón de Sardinas (bay), Colombia 126/A7
Ancón de Sardinas (bay), Ecuador 128/C2
Ancoraimes, Bolivia 136/A4
Ancram, N.Y. (12502) 276/N6
Ancroft, England 13/F2
Ancrum, Scotland 15/F5
Ancud, Chile 120/B7
Ancud, Chile 138/D4
Ancud (gulf), Chile 138/D4
Anda (Anta), China 77/L2
Andacollo, Argentina 143/B4
Andacollo, Chile 138/A8
Andado, North. Terr. 93/D8
Andahuaylas, Peru 128/F9
Andale, Kansas (67001) 232/E4
Andalgalá, Argentina 143/C2
Åndalsnes, Norway 18/F5
Andalusia, Ala. (36420) 195/E8
Andalusia, Ill. (61232) 222/C2
Andalusia, Pa. (†19020) 294/N5
Andalusia (reg.), Spain 33/C4
Andaman (sea) 54/L8
Andaman (sea), Burma 72/B4
Andaman (isls.), India 2/P5
Andaman (isls.), India 54/L8
Andaman (isls.), India 68/G6
Andaman (sea), India 68/G6
Andaman and Nicobar Isls. (terr.), India 68/G6
Andamarca, Bolivia 136/B6
Andamarca, Peru 128/E8
Andamooka, S. Australia 94/E4
Andapa, Madagascar 118/H2
Andaraí, Brazil 132/F6
Andau, Austria 41/D3
Andeer, Switzerland 39/H3
Andelfingen, Switzerland 39/G1
Andenne, Belgium 27/G8
Anderlecht, Belgium 27/B9
Anderlues, Belgium 27/E8
Andermatt, Switzerland 39/G3
Andernach, W. Germany 22/B3
Anderson, Ala. (35610) 195/D1
Anderson, Alaska (†99760) 196/H2
Anderson, Argentina 143/F7
Anderson, Calif. (96007) 204/C3
Anderson, Ind. 188/J2
Anderson, Ind. (*46011) 227/F4
Anderson (riv.), Ind. 227/D8
Anderson, Iowa (†51652) 229/B7
Anderson (co.), Kansas 232/G3
Anderson (co.), Ky. 237/M5
Anderson (lake), Manitoba 179/D2
Anderson (pt.), Manitoba 179/F3
Anderson, Mo. (64831) 261/D9
Anderson (riv.), N.W.T. 162/D2
Anderson (riv.), N.W. Terrs. 187/F3
Anderson, S.C. 188/K4
Anderson (co.), S.C. 296/B2
Anderson, S.C. (*29621) 296/B2
Anderson (bay), Tasmania 99/D2
Anderson (co.), Tenn. 237/N8
Anderson, Tenn. (†37376) 237/K10
Anderson (co.), Texas 303/J6
Anderson, Texas (77830) 303/J7
Anderson Ranch (res.), Idaho 220/C6
Andersonville, Georgia (31711) 217/D6
Andersonville, Ind. (†47024) 227/G5
Andersonville, Tenn. (37705) 237/O8
Andersonville, Va. (23911) 307/L6
Andersonville Nat'l Hist. Site, Georgia 217/D6
Andes (range), 120/B2-6
Andes, Cordillera de los (mts.), Argentina 143/C2
Andes, Cordillera de los (mts.), Chile 138/C5,E
Andes, Colombia 126/C5
Andes, Mont. (†59218) 262/M3
Andes, N.Y. (13731) 276/L6
Andes, Cordillera de los (mts.), Peru 128/F10
Andes (lake), S. Dak. 298/N7
Andheri, India 68/B7
Andhra Pradesh (state), India 68/D5
Andijk, Netherlands 27/G3
Andikíthira (isl.), Greece 45/F8
Andilamena, Madagascar 118/H3
Andimeshk, Iran 66/F4
Anding, Miss. (†39040) 256/D5
Andırın, Turkey 63/G4
Ándissa, Greece 45/H6
Andizhan, U.S.S.R. 54/J5
Andizhan, U.S.S.R. 48/H5
Andkhvoy, Afghanistan 68/A1
Andkhvoy, Afghanistan 59/H2
Andoas Nuevo, Ecuador 128/D4
Andoma, Zaire 115/E3
Andong, S. Korea 81/D5
Andorra 7/E4
ANDORRA 33/G1
Andorra, Spain 33/F2
Andorra la Vella (cap.), Andorra 33/G1
Andover○, Conn. (06232) 210/F2
Andover, England 10/F5
Andover, England 13/F6
Andover, Ill. (61233) 222/C2
Andover, Iowa (52701) 229/N5
Andover, Kansas (67002) 232/E4
Andover, Maine (04216) 243/B6
Andover○, Maine (04216) 243/B6
Andover, Mass. (01810) 249/K2
Andover○, Mass. (01810) 249/K2
Andover, Minn. (†55303) 255/E5
Andover○, N.H. (03216) 268/D5
Andover, N.J. (07821) 273/D2
Andover, N.Y. (14806) 276/E6
Andover, Ohio (44003) 284/J2
Andover, S. Dak. (57422) 298/O3
Andover○, Vt. (†05143) 268/B5
Andover, Va. (24215) 307/C7
Andøya (isl.), Norway 18/J2
Andradas, Brazil 135/C3
Andradina, Brazil 132/D8
Andraitx, Spain 33/H3
Andravídha, Greece 45/E6
Andre (lake), Newf. 166/A3
Andreafski (Saint Marys), Alaska (†99658) 196/F2
Andreanof (isls.), Alaska 196/L4
Andreas (cape), Cyprus 63/F5
Andrelândia, Brazil 135/D2
Andrés, Nicaragua 154/F3
Andrespol, Poland 47/D3
Andrew, Alberta 182/D3
Andrew, Iowa (52030) 229/M4
Andrew, La. (†70548) 238/F6
Andrew (co.), Mo. 261/C3
Andrew (isl.), Nova Scotia 168/H3
Andrew Johnson Nat'l Hist. Site, Tenn. 237/R8
Andrews, (†21626) 245/O7
Andrews, Ind. (46702) 227/F3
Andrews, N.C. (28901) 281/B4
Andrews, Oreg. (†97732) 291/J5
Andrews, S.C. (29510) 296/H5
Andrews (co.), Texas 303/B5
Andrews, Texas (79714) 303/B5
Andrews A.F.B., Md. 245/G5
Andreyevka, U.S.S.R. 52/H4
Andria, Italy 34/F4
Androka, Madagascar 118/G5
Andros (isl.), Bahamas 146/L7
Andros (isl.), Bahamas 156/B1
Ándros, Greece 45/G7
Ándros (isl.), Greece 45/G7
Androscoggin (co.), Maine 243/C7
Androscoggin (riv.), Maine 243/C7
Androscoggin (riv.), N.H. 268/E2
Andrott (isl.), India 68/C6
Andrychów, Poland 47/D4
Andsfjorden (fjord), Norway 18/K2
Andújar, Spain 33/D3
Andul, India 68/F2
Andulo, Angola 102/D6
Andulo, Angola 115/C6
Anéfis, Mali 106/E5
Anegada (isl.), Virgin Is. (Br.) 156/H1
Anegada (passage), Virgin Is. (Br.) 156/F3
Anécho (Anécho), Togo 106/E7
Aneityum (Anatom) (isl.), Vanuatu 87/H8
'Aneiza, Jebel (mt.), Iraq 66/A4
'Aneiza, Jebel (mt.), Iraq 59/C3
'Aneiza, Jebel (mt.), Jordan 59/C3
'Aneiza, Jebel (mt.), Saudi Arabia 59/C3
Añelo, Argentina 143/C4
Anerley, Sask. 181/D4
Aneroid, Sask. 181/D6
Aneta, N. Dak. (58212) 282/P4
Aneth, Utah (84510) 304/E6
Aneto (peak), Spain 33/G1
Angaki (Quirino), Philippines 82/C2
Angamos (isl.), Chile 138/D8
Angamos (pt.), Chile 138/A4
Angara (riv.), U.S.S.R. 54/L4
Angara (riv.), U.S.S.R. 48/K4
Angarsk, U.S.S.R. 54/M4
Angarsk, U.S.S.R. 48/L4
Angas Downs, North. Terr. 93/C8
Angaston, S. Australia 94/F6
Angaur (isl.), Belau 87/D5
Ånge, Sweden 18/J5
Ange-Gardien, Québec 172/E4
Angel (isl.), Calif. 204/J2
Angel (falls), Venezuela 120/C2
Angel (falls), Venezuela 124/G5
Angela, Mont. (59312) 262/K4
Ángel de la Guarda (isl.), Mexico 150/C2
Angeles, Philippines 82/C3
Ángeles, P. Rico 161/B2
Ängelholm, Sweden 18/H8
Angélica, Argentina 143/E5
Angelica, N.Y. (14709) 276/E6
Angelica, Wis. (†54162) 317/K6
Angelina (co.), Texas 303/K6
Angelina (riv.), Texas 303/K6
Angelo, Wis. (†54656) 317/E8
Angels Camp, Calif. (95222) 204/E5
Angelus, S.C. (†29718) 296/G2
Angerman (riv.), Sweden 7/F2
Ångermanälven (riv.), Sweden 18/K5
Angermünde, E. Germany 22/E2
Angers, France 7/D4
Angers, France 28/C4
Angers, Québec 172/B4
Angicos, Brazil 132/G4
Angie, La. (70426) 238/L5
Angier, N.C. (27501) 281/M4
Angijak (isl.), N.W. Terrs. 187/M3
Angikuni (lake), N.W. Terrs. 187/J3
Angkor Wat (ruins), Cambodia 72/E4
Angle, Utah (†84712) 304/C5
Angle Inlet, Minn. (56711) 255/C1
Anglem (mt.), N. Zealand 100/A7
Anglesey (isl.), Wales 13/C4
Anglesey (isl.), Wales 10/D4
Angleton, Texas (77515) 303/J8
Anglia, Sask. 181/C4
Angliers, Québec 174/B3
Angmagssalik, Greenl. 4/C11
Angmagssalik, Greenland 146/Q3
Ango, Zaire 115/E3
Angoche, Mozambique 118/G3
Angoche, Mozambique 102/G6
Angoche (isl.), Mozambique 118/G3
Angol, Chile 138/D1
Angola 2/K6
Angola 102/D6
ANGOLA 115/C6
Angola, Del. (†19966) 245/T6
Angola, Ind. (46703) 227/G1
Angola, Kansas (67331) 232/G4
Angola, La. (70712) 238/G5
Angola, N.Y. (14006) 276/C5
Angola (swamp), N.C. 281/O5
Angola on the Lake, N.Y. (†14006) 276/B5
Angoon, Alaska (99820) 196/M1
Angora, Minn. (55703) 255/F3
Angora, Nebr. (69331) 264/A3
Angoram, Papua N.G. 85/B6
Angostura (falls), Colombia 120/B2
Angostura (falls), Colombia 126/E6
Angostura, Mexico 150/E4
Angostura (res.), S. Dak. 298/B7
Angoulême, France 28/D5
Angoumois (trad. prov.), France, 29
Angra do Heroísmo (dist.), Portugal 33/C1
Angra do Heroísmo, Portugal 33/C1
Angra dos Reis, Brazil 135/D3
Angren, U.S.S.R. 48/H5
Ang Thong, Thailand 72/C4
Anguil, Argentina 143/D4
Anguilla (isl.) 146/M8
ANGUILLA 156
Anguilla, Anguilla 156/F3
Anguilla, Miss. (38721) 256/C5
Anguillara Sabazia, Italy 34/F6
Anguille (cape), Newf. 166/C4
Angurugu, North. Terr. 93/E3
Angus, Iowa (†50220) 229/E5
Angus, Minn. (56712) 255/B2
Angus, Ontario 177/E3
Angus (trad. prov.), Scotland, 15/B5
Angusville, Manitoba 179/A4
Angwin, Calif. (94508) 204/C5
Anhée, Belgium 27/F8
Anholt, Denmark 21/E4
Anholt (isl.), Denmark 21/E4
Anholt (isl.), Denmark 18/G8
Anhua, China 77/H6
Anhui (Anhwei), China 77/J5
Aniak, Alaska (99557) 196/G2
Aniakchak (vol.), Alaska 196/G3
Aniakchak Nat'l Mon., Alaska 196/G3
Aniakchak Nat'l Preserve, Alaska 196/G3
Anicuns, Brazil 132/D7
Aniene (riv.), Italy 34/F6
Animas (riv.), Colo. 208/D8
Animas, N. Mex. (88020) 274/A7
Animas (riv.), N. Mex. 274/B1
Añimbo, Bolivia 136/C7
Anin, Burma 72/C4
Anin, West Bank 65/C3
Anina, Romania 45/E3
Anita, Iowa (50020) 229/D6
Anita, Pa. (15711) 294/D3
Aniva (cape), U.S.S.R. 48/P5
Aniwa, Wis. (54408) 317/H6
'Anjara, Jordan 65/D3
Anjidiv (Angediva) (isl.), India 68/C6
Anjou (trad. prov.), France, 29
Anjou, Québec 172/H4
Anjouan (isl.), Comoros 102/G6
Anjouan (isl.), Comoros 118/G2
Anju, N. Korea 81/B4
Anjum, Netherlands 27/J2
Ankang, China 77/G5
Ankara (prov.), Turkey 63/E3
Ankara (cap.), Turkey 63/E3
Ankara (cap.), Turkey 2/L4
Ankara (cap.), Turkey 54/E5
Ankara (cap.), Turkey 59/B2
Ankara (riv.), Turkey 63/D3
Ankazoabo, Madagascar 118/G4
Ankeny, Iowa (50021) 229/F5
Anker (riv.), England 10/G3
Ankerton, Alberta 182/D3
Ankhor, Somalia 115/J1
Anking (Anqing), China 77/J5
Anklam, E. Germany 22/E2
Ankober, Ethiopia 111/H6
Ankona, Fla. (†33450) 212/F4
Ankoro, Zaire 115/E5
An Loc (Binh Long), Vietnam 72/E5
Anlu, China 77/H5
Anmoore, W. Va. (26323) 312/F4
Ann (cape), Mass. 249/M2
Anna, Ill. (62906) 222/D6
Anna, Ky. (†42270) 237/J6
Anna, Ohio (45302) 284/B5
Anna, Texas (75003) 303/H4
Anna (lke), Va. 307/N4
Annaba, Algeria 102/C1
Annaba, Algeria 106/F1
Annabella, Utah (84711) 304/B5
Annaberg-Buchholz, E. Germany 22/E3
Anna Creek, S. Australia 94/D3
Annada, Mo. (63330) 261/L4
Annadel, Tenn. (†37770) 237/M8
Annagry, Ireland 17/E1
Annaheim, Sask. 181/G3
Annai, Guyana 131/B4
An Najaf (gov.), Iraq 66/C5
An Najaf, Iraq 59/D3
An Najaf, Iraq 66/D5
An Najaf, Iraq 54/F6
Annalee (riv.), Ireland 17/G3
Annalong, N. Ireland 17/K3
Annaly (bay), Virgin Is. (U.S.) 161/E3
Anna Maria, Fla. (33501) 212/D4
Annan, Scotland 15/E6
Annan, Scotland 10/E3
Annan (riv.), Scotland 15/E5
Annandale, Minn. (55302) 255/D5
Annandale, N.J. (08801) 273/D2
Annandale, Va. (22003) 307/S3
Annandale-on-Hudson, N.Y. (12504) 276/N6
Anna Plains, W. Australia 92/C2
Annapolis, Calif. (95412) 204/B5
Annapolis, Ill. (62413) 222/F4
Annapolis (cap.), Md. (*21401) 245/M5
Annapolis (cap.), Md. 188/L3
Annapolis, Mo. (63620) 261/L8
Annapolis (co.), Nova Scotia 168/C4
Annapolis (basin), Nova Scotia 168/C4
Annapolis (riv.), Nova Scotia 168/C4
Annapolis Junction, Md. (20701) 245/M4
Annapolis Royal, Nova Scotia 168/C4
Annapurna (mt.), Nepal 68/E3
Ann Arbor, Mich. 188/K2
Ann Arbor, Mich. (*48103) 250/F6
Anna Regina, Guyana 131/B2
Annascaul, Ireland 17/B7
An Nasiriya, Iraq 59/E3
An Nasiriya, Iraq 66/D5
Annat, Scotland 15/C3
Annaville, Québec 172/E3
Annawan, Ill. (61234) 222/C2
Annbank Station, Scotland 15/D5
Anne (mt.), Tasmania 99/C4
Anne Arundel (co.), Md. 245/M4
Annecy, France 28/G5
Annemanie, Ala. (36721) 195/D6
Anner (riv.), Ireland 17/F7
Anneta, Ky. (†42754) 237/J6
Annette, Alaska (99920) 196/N2
An Nhon, Vietnam 72/F4
Annieopscotch (mts.), Newf. 166/C4
Anniston, Ala. 188/J4
Anniston, Ala. (36201) 195/G3
Anniston, Mo. (63820) 261/O9
Anniston Army Depot, Ala. 195/F3
Annobon (isl.), Equat. Guinea 102/C5
Annona, Texas (75550) 303/K4
Annonay, France 28/F5
Annotto Bay, Jamaica 156/C3
Annotto Bay, Jamaica 158/K6
Annville, Ky. (40402) 237/O6
Annville, Pa. (17003) 294/J5
Annweiler am Trifels, W. Germany 22/B4
Anoka (co.), Minn. 255/E5
Anoka, Minn. (55303) 255/E5
Anoka, Nebr. (†68722) 264/F2
Anola, Manitoba 179/F5
Ano Nuevo (pt.), Calif. 204/J4
Áno Viánnos, Greece 45/G8
Anóyia, Greece 45/G8
Anqing (Anking), China 77/J5
Ans, Belgium 27/H7
Ansager, Denmark 21/B6
Ansai, China 77/G4
Ansbach, W. Germany 22/D4
Anse à Galets, Haiti 158/B6
Anse-à-Pitre, Haiti 158/C6
Anse-au-Griffon, Québec 172/D1
Anse-aux-Gascons, Québec 172/D2
Anse-à-Veau, Haiti 158/B6
Anse-Bertrand, Guadeloupe 161/A5
Anse-Bleue, New Bruns. 170/E1
Anse Boileau, Seychelles 118/H5
Anse-d'Hainault, Haiti 158/A6
Anse la Raye, St. Lucia 161/F6
Anselmo, Nebr. (68813) 264/E3
Anser Group (isls.), Tasmania 99/C1
Anserma, Colombia 126/B5
Anse Rouge, Haiti 158/B5
Anse Royale, Seychelles 118/H5
Anshan, China 77/K3
Anshan, China 54/O5
Anshun, China 77/G6
Ansley, Ala. (36001) 195/F7
Ansley, La. (†71228) 238/E2
Ansley, Nebr. (68814) 264/E3
Anson, Kansas (†67103) 232/E4
Anson, Maine (04911) 243/D6
Anson○, Maine (04911) 243/D6
Anson (pt.), Norfolk I. 88/K5
Anson (bay), Norfolk I. 88/K5
Anson (co.), N.C. 281/J4
Anson (bay), North. Terr. 88/D2
Anson, Texas (79501) 303/E5
Ansŏng, S. Korea 81/C5
Ansongo, Mali 106/E5
Ansonia, Conn. (06401) 210/C3
Ansonia, Ohio (45303) 284/A5
Ansonville, N.C. (28007) 281/J4
Ansonville, Pa. (†16656) 294/E4
Ansted, W. Va. (25812) 312/D6
Anta, Peru 128/F9
Antabamba, Peru 128/F10
Antakya, Turkey 59/C2
Antakya, Turkey 63/G4
Antalaha, Madagascar 118/J2
Antalaha, Madagascar 102/H6
Antalya (prov.), Turkey 63/D4
Antalya, Turkey 54/D6
Antalya, Turkey 63/D4
Antalya, Turkey 59/B2
Antalya (gulf), Turkey 63/D4
Antalya (gulf), Turkey 59/B2
Antananarivo (prov.), Madagascar 118/H3
Antananarivo (cap.), Madagascar 2/M6
Antananarivo (cap.), Madagascar 102/G6
Antananarivo (cap.), Madagascar 118/H3
Antarctic (pen.), Ant. 2/G9
Antarctic (pen.) 5/C15
Antarctica 2/E11
ANTARCTICA 5
Antarctic Circle 2/A9
An Teallach (mt.), Scotland 15/C3
Antelope (creek), Idaho 220/E6
Antelope, Kansas (66836) 232/F3
Antelope, Mont. (59211) 262/M2
Antelope (co.), Nebr. 264/F2
Antelope (range), Nev. 266/E3
Antelope, Oreg. (97001) 291/G3
Antelope (creek), Oreg. 291/K5
Antelope (res.), Oreg. 291/K5
Antelope, Sask. 181/C5
Antelope (lake), Sask. 181/C5
Antelope (creek), S. Dak. 298/D3
Antelope, Texas (76350) 303/F4
Antelope (isl.), Utah 304/B3
Antelope (creek), Wyo. 319/G2
Antelope (hills), Wyo. 319/D3
Antequera, Paraguay 144/D4
Antequera, Spain 33/D4
Antero (mt.), Colo. 208/G5
Antero (res.), Colo. 208/H5
Antes Fort, Pa. (17720) 294/H3
Anthon, Iowa (51004) 229/B4
Anthony, Fla. (32617) 212/D2
Anthony, Ind. (†47302) 227/G4
Anthony, Kansas (67003) 232/D4
Anthony, N. Mex. (88021) 274/C6
Anthony, R.I. (†02816) 249/H6
Anthony, Texas (88021) 303/A10
Anthony, W. Va. (24914) 312/F7
Anthony Lagoon, North. Terr. 88/E3
Anthony Lagoon, North. Terr. 93/D4
Anthracite, Alberta 182/C4
Anti-Atlas (ranges), Morocco 106/C3
Antibes, France 28/G6
Anticosti (isl.), Que. 146/M5
Anticosti (isl.), Que. 162/K6
Anticosti (isl.), Québec 174/E3
Antietam, Md. (†21782) 245/H3
Antietam (creek), Md. 245/H2
Antietam Nat'l Battlefield, Md. 245/H3
Antigo, Wis. (54409) 317/H5
Antigonish (co.), Nova Scotia 168/F3
Antigonish, Nova Scotia 168/F3
Antigonish (harb.), Nova Scotia 168/G3
Antigua (isl.) 146/M8
ANTIGUA & BARBUDA 156
ANTIGUA & BARBUDA 161
Antigua (isl.), Ant. & Bar. 161/E11
Antigua (isl.), Ant. & Bar. 156/G3
Antigua, Guatemala 154/B3
Antigua (riv.), Mexico 150/Q1
Antigua, Spain 33/B4
Antigues (pt.), Guadeloupe 161/A5
Antiguo Morelos, Mexico 150/K5
Antilla, Cuba 156/C2
Antilla, Cuba 158/J3
Antilles, Greater (isls.), W. Indies 156/B2
Antilles, Lesser (isls.), W. Indies 156/E4
Antimony, Utah (84712) 304/C5
Antioch, Calif. (94509) 204/L1
Antioch, Georgia (†30240) 217/B4
Antioch, Ill. (60002) 222/E1
Antioch, Nebr. (69340) 264/B2
Antioch, Ohio (43710) 284/H6
Antioch, S.C. (†29020) 296/F3
Antioch (Antakya), Turkey 63/G4
Antioch, W. Va. (†26743) 312/H4
Antioquia (dept.), Colombia 126/B4
Antioquia, Colombia 126/B4
Antique (prov.), Philippines 82/D5
Antiquity, Ohio (†45771) 284/G8
Antisana (mt.), Ecuador 128/D3
Anti-Taurus (mts.), Turkey 63/G3
Antler, N. Dak. (58771) 282/H2
Antler, Sask. 181/K6
Antler (riv.), Sask. 181/K6
Antler Lake, Alberta 182/D3
Antlers, Okla. (74523) 288/P6
Antofagasta (reg.), Chile 138/B4
Antofagasta, Chile 120/B5
Antofagasta, Chile 2/F7
Antofagasta, Chile 138/A4
Antofagasta de la Sierra, Argentina 143/C2
Antoine, Ark. (71922) 202/D5
Antoing, Belgium 27/C7
Anton, Colo. (80801) 208/N3
Antón, Panama 154/G6
Anton, Texas (79313) 303/B4
Anton Chico, N. Mex. (87711) 274/D3
Antone, Oreg. (†97750) 291/H3
Antongil (bay), Madagascar 118/J3
Antonina, Brazil 135/B4
Antonino, Kansas (67624) 232/C3
Antonito, Colo. (81120) 208/H8
Antony, France 28/B2
Antora (peak), Colo. 208/G6
Antreville, S.C. (†29620) 296/B3
Antrim (co.), Mich. 250/D3
Antrim, Mich. (†49659) 250/D4
Antrim, N.H. (03440) 268/D5
Antrim○, N.H. (03440) 268/D5
Antrim (dist.), N. Ireland 17/J2
Antrim, N. Ireland 10/C3
Antrim, N. Ireland 17/J2
Antrim, Ohio (†43973) 284/H5
Antrim, Pa. (†16901) 294/H2
Antsalova, Madagascar 118/G3
Antsirabe, Madagascar 102/G7
Antsirabe, Madagascar 118/H3
Antsiranana (prov.), Madagascar 118/H2
Antsiranana, Madagascar 118/H2
Antsiranana, Madagascar 102/G6

330 Antsia

Antsla, U.S.S.R. 53/D2
Antsohihy, Madagascar 118/H2
Antu, China 77/L3
An Tuc (An Khe), Vietnam 72/F4
Antwerp (prov.), Belgium 27/F6
Antwerp, Belgium 7/E3
Antwerp, Belgium 27/E6
Antwerp, N.Y. (13608) 276/J2
Antwerp, Ohio (45813) 284/A3
Antwerpen (Antwerp), Belgium 27/E6
An Uaimh, Ireland 10/C4
An Uaimh, Ireland 17/H4
Anuenue (Sand) (isl.), Hawaii 218/C4
Anuradhapura, Sri Lanka 68/E7
Anutt, Mo. (†65401) 261/J7
Anvik, Alaska (99558) 196/F2
Anvil (peak), Alaska 196/K4
Anxi, China 77/E3
Anxious (bay), S. Australia 94/D5
Anyang, China 77/H4
A'nyêmaqên Shan (mts.), China 77/E5
Anykščiai, U.S.S.R. 53/C3
Anzá, Colombia 126/C4
'Anza, West Bank 65/C3
Anzac, Alberta 182/E1
Anzaldo, Bolivia 136/C5
Anzhero-Sudzhensk, U.S.S.R. 54/K4
Anzhero-Sudzhensk, U.S.S.R. 48/J4
Anzio, Italy 34/D4
Anzoátegui (state), Venezuela 124/F3
Aoiz, Spain 33/F1
Aoji-ri, N. Korea 81/E2
Aomori (pref.), Japan 81/K3
Aomori, Japan 54/R5
Aomori, Japan 81/K3
Ao Paray (riv.), Paraguay 144/A5
Aosta (reg.), Italy 34/A2
Aosta (prov.), Italy 34/A2
Aosta, Italy 34/A2
Aouara, Fr. Guiana 131/E3
Aouinet Bel Egrâ (well), Algeria 106/C3
Aoulef, Algeria 106/E3
Aozou, Chad 111/C3
Apa (riv.), Paraguay 144/D3
Apache (co.), Ariz. 198/F3
Apache (lake), Ariz. 198/D5
Apache, Okla. (73006) 288/K5
Apache (mts.), Texas 303/C11
Apache Creek, N. Mex. (†87830) 274/A5
Apache Junction, Ariz. (85220) 198/D5
Apalachee (bay), Fla. 188/K5
Apalachee (bay), Fla. 212/B2
Apalachee, Georgia (†30650) 217/E3
Apalachia (res.), N.C. 281/A4
Apalachicola, Fla. (32320) 212/A2
Apalachicola (bay), Fla. 212/B2
Apalachicola (riv.), Fla. 212/A1
Apalachin, N.Y. (13732) 276/H6
Apalona, Ind. (†47576) 227/D8
Apan, Mexico 150/M1
Apaporis (riv.), Colombia 126/F8
Aparecida, Brazil 135/D3
Aparri, Philippines 82/C1
Aparri, Philippines 85/G2
Aparurén, Venezuela 124/G5
Apataki (atoll), Fr. Poly. 87/M7
Apatin, Yugoslavia 45/D3
Apatity, U.S.S.R. 52/D1
Apatzingán de la Constitución, Mexico 150/H7
Ape, U.S.S.R. 53/D2
Apeldoorn, Netherlands 27/H4
Apennines (mts.), Italy 7/F4
Apennines, Central (range), Italy 34/D3
Apennines, Northern (range), Italy 34/B2
Apennines, Southern (range), Italy 34/E4
Apere (riv.), Bolivia 136/C4
Apex, N.C. (27502) 281/M3
Apgar, Mont. (†59936) 262/B2
Apia (cap.), W. Samoa 2/A6
Apia (cap.), W. Samoa 87/J7
Apia (cap.), W. Samoa 86/M8
Apiaí, Brazil 135/B4
Apishapa (riv.), Colo. 208/L8
Apison, Tenn. (37302) 237/L10
Ap Iwan, Cerro (mt.), Chile 138/E6
Apizaco, Mexico 150/N1
Aplao, Peru 128/F11
Aplin, Ark. (†72126) 202/E4
Aplington, Iowa (50604) 229/H3
Ap Long Ha, Vietnam 72/F5
Apo (vol.), Philippines 82/E7
Apohaqui, New Bruns. 170/E3
Apolda, E. Germany 22/D3
Apolima (str.), W. Samoa 86/L8
Apollo, Georgia (†31024) 217/F4
Apollo, Pa. (15613) 294/C4
Apollo Bay, Victoria 97/B6
Apollo Beach, Fla. (33570) 212/C3
Apolo, Bolivia 136/A4
Aponguao (riv.), Venezuela 124/H5
Apopka, Fla. (32703) 212/E3
Apopka (lake), Fla. 212/E3
Aporé (riv.), Brazil 132/D7
Apostle (isls.), Wis. 317/F2
Apostle Islands Nat'l Lakeshore, Wis. 317/E1
Apóstoles, Argentina 143/E2
Apoteri, Guyana 131/B3
Appalachia, Va. (24216) 307/C7
Appalachian (mts.) 188/K3
Appalachian (mts.), N.C. 281/D2
Appalachian (mts.), Pa. 294/H4
Appalachian (mts.), Tenn. 237/M10
Appalachian (mts.), U.S. 146/K6
Appalachian (mts.), Va. 307/J5
Appam, N. Dak. (†58830) 282/C2
Appanoose (co.), Iowa 229/H7
Appelscha, Netherlands 27/J3
Appenzell, Ausser Rhoden (canton), 39/H2
Appenzell, Inner Rhoden (canton), Switzerland 39/H2
Appenzell, Switzerland 39/H2
Apperson, Okla. (†74633) 288/N1
Appin, Ontario 177/C5
Appin (dist.), Scotland 15/C4
Appingedam, Netherlands 27/K2
Apple (creek), Ill. 222/C4
Apple (riv.), Ill. 222/C1
Apple (creek), N. Dak. 282/J6
Apple (riv.), Wis. 317/A5
Appleby, England 13/E3
Appleby, England 10/E3
Appleby, Texas (75961) 303/K6
Apple Creek, Ohio (44606) 284/G4
Applecross, Scotland 15/C3
Appledale, Br. Col. 184/J5
Applegate, Calif. (95703) 204/E5
Applegate, Mich. (48401) 250/G5
Applegate, Oreg. (97530) 291/D5
Apple Grove, W. Va. (25502) 312/B5
Apple Hill, Ontario 177/K2
Apple River, Ill. (61001) 222/C1
Apple River, Nova Scotia 168/D3
Apples, Switzerland 39/B3
Appleton, Ark. (72822) 202/E3
Appleton, Maine (†04540) 243/E7
Appleton○, Maine (†04862) 243/E7
Appleton, Minn. (56208) 255/C5
Appleton (Old Appleton), Mo. (†63770) 261/N7
Appleton, N.Y. (14008) 276/C4
Appleton, Ontario 177/H2
Appleton, S.C. (†29836) 296/E5
Appleton, Wash. (98602) 310/D5
Appleton, Wis. 188/J2
Appleton, Wis. (54911) 317/J7
Appleton City, Mo. (64724) 261/D6
Apple Valley, Calif. (92307) 204/H9
Apple Valley, Minn. (†55124) 255/G6
Appling (co.), Georgia 217/H7
Appling, Georgia (30802) 217/H3
Appomattox (co.), Va. 307/L6
Appomattox, Va. (24522) 307/L6
Appomattox (riv.), Va. 307/M6
Appomattox Court House Nat'l Hist. Park, Va. 307/K6
Apponaug, R.I. (†02887) 249/J6
Approuague (riv.), Fr. Guiana 131/E4
Apra (harb.), Guam 86/K7
Aprilia, Italy 34/D4
Apsheron (pen.), U.S.S.R. 52/H6
Apsheronsk, U.S.S.R. 52/F6
Apsley, Ontario 177/F3
Apsley, Victoria 97/A5
Apt, France 28/F6
Aptos, Calif. (95003) 204/K4
Apua (pt.), Hawaii 218/J6
Apulia (Puglia) (reg.), Italy 34/F4
Apulia Station, N.Y. (13020) 276/H5
Apure (state), Venezuela 124/D4
Apure (riv.), Venezuela 124/E4
Apurímac (dept.), Peru 128/F10
Apurímac (riv.), Peru 120/B4
Apurímac (riv.), Peru 128/F9
Apurito, Venezuela 124/D4
Ap Vinh Hao, Vietnam 72/F5
Aqaba (gulf) 54/E7
'Aqaba (gulf), Egypt 111/G2
'Aqaba (gulf), Egypt 59/C4
'Aqaba (gulf), Israel 65/D6
'Aqaba, Jordan 65/D6
'Aqaba, Jordan 59/C4
Aqaba (gulf), Jordan 65/D6
'Aqaba (gulf), Saudi Arabia 59/C4
Aqcheh, Afghanistan 68/B1
Aqcheh, Afghanistan 59/J2
Aq Darband, Iran 66/M2
'Aqiq, Sudan 111/G4
'Aqqaba, West Bank 65/C3
Aqqikkol Hu (lake), China 77/C4
'Aqra, Iraq 66/D2
'Aqraba, West Bank 65/C3
Aqsu (Aksu), China 77/B3
Aquades Beach, Sask. 181/C2
Aquaforte, Newf. 166/D2
Aqua Park, Okla. (†74435) 288/R3
Aquarius (range), Ariz. 198/B4
Aquarius (plat.), Utah 304/C5
Aquasco, Md. (20608) 245/L6
Aquia, Peru 128/D8
Aquidabán (riv.), Paraguay 144/D3
Aquidauana, Brazil 120/D5
Aquidauana, Brazil 132/C8
Aquila, Mexico 150/H7
Aquila, Switzerland 39/G3
Aquiles Serdán, Mexico 150/G2
Aquilla, Ohio (†44024) 284/H2
Aquin, Haiti 158/B6
Ara (riv.), Japan 81/O2
Arab, Ala. (35016) 195/E2
'Arab, Shatt-al- (riv.), Iran 59/E4
'Arab, Shatt-al- (riv.), Iran 66/F5
'Arab, Shatt-al- (riv.), Iraq 59/E4
'Arab, Shatt-al- (riv.), Iraq 66/F5
Arab, Mo. (63733) 261/M8
'Araba, Wadi (valley), Israel 65/D5
'Araba, Wadi (valley), Jordan 65/D5
Arabela, N. Mex. (†88351) 274/D5
Arabella, Sask. 181/K3
Arabi, Georgia (31712) 217/E7
'Arabi (isl.), Iran 66/G7
Arabi, La. (70032) 238/P4
Arabia, Ky. (†40437) 237/M6
Arabia, Ohio (†45659) 284/F8
Arabian (sea) 54/H8
Arabian (sea) 2/N5
Arabian (des.), Egypt 111/F2
Arabian (des.), Egypt 59/B4
Arabian (sea), India 68/B5
Arabian (sea), Pakistan 68/B5
Arabian (sea), P.D.R. Yemen 59/H5
Arabopó, Venezuela 124/H5
Araç, Turkey 63/E2
Araca, Bolivia 136/B5
Aracaju, Brazil 120/F4
Aracaju, Brazil 132/G5
Aracataca, Colombia 126/D2
Aracati, Brazil 132/G4
Araçatuba, Brazil 132/D8
Araçatuba, Brazil 135/A2
Araceli, Philippines 82/C5
Aracena, Spain 33/C4
Araçuaí, Brazil 132/F7
Arad, Israel 65/C5
Arad, Romania 7/G4
Arad, Romania 45/E2
Arada, Chad 111/D4
'Aradah, U.A.E. 59/F5
Aradan, Iran 66/H3
Arafat, Jebel (mt.), Saudi Arabia 59/D5
Arafura (sea) 87/D6
Arafura (sea) 2/R6
Arafura (sea) 88/E2
Arafura (sea), Indonesia 85/J8
Arafura (sea), North. Terr. 93/D1
Arago, Minn. (†56470) 255/C3
Arago, Oreg. (97458) 291/C4
Arago (cape), Oreg. 291/C4
Aragon, Georgia (30104) 217/B2
Aragon, N. Mex. (87820) 274/A5
Aragón (reg.), Spain 33/F2
Aragón (riv.), Spain 33/F1
Aragona, Italy 34/D6
Aragua (state), Venezuela 124/E3
Araguacema, Brazil 132/D5
Aragua de Barcelona, Venezuela 124/F3
Aragua de Maturín, Venezuela 124/G3
Araguaia (riv.), Brazil 120/E3
Araguaia (riv.), Brazil 132/D4
Araguaiana, Brazil 132/C6
Araguaina, Brazil 120/E3
Araguari, Brazil 120/E4
Araguari, Brazil 132/D7
Araguari (riv.), Brazil 132/D2
Araioses, Brazil 132/F3
Arak, Algeria 106/E3
Arak, Iran 54/G6
Arak, Iran 59/E3
Arak, Iran 66/F3
Arakan (state), Burma 72/B3
Arakan Yoma (mts.), Burma 72/B3
Araks (riv.) 54/F6
Araks (riv.), Iran 59/E2
Araks (Aras) (riv.), Iran 66/E1
Araks (riv.), Turkey 63/K2
Araks (riv.), U.S.S.R. 7/J5
Araks (riv.), U.S.S.R. 52/G7
Aral (sea), U.S.S.R. 54/G5
Aral (sea), U.S.S.R. 48/F5
Aralık, Turkey 63/L3
Aral Sea (lake), U.S.S.R. 2/M3
Aral'sk, U.S.S.R. 54/H5
Aral'sk, U.S.S.R. 48/G5
Aramac, Queensland 95/C4
Aramberri, Mexico 150/J5
Arampampa, Bolivia 136/B5
Aran (isl.), Ireland 10/B3
Aran (isl.), Ireland 17/D2
Aran (isls.), Ireland 17/B5
Aran (isls.), Ireland 10/B4
Aranda de Duero, Spain 33/E2
Arandas, Mexico 150/H6
Aran Fawddwy (mt.), Wales 13/C5
Arani, Bolivia 136/C5
Aranjuez, Spain 33/E2
Aransas (co.), Texas 303/H10
Aransas (passage), Texas 303/H10
Aransas Pass, Texas (78336) 303/G10
Araoua (mts.), Fr. Guiana 131/E4
Araouane, Mali 106/D5
Araouane, Mali 102/B3
Arapaho, Okla. (73620) 288/H3
Arapahoe (co.), Colo. 208/L3
Arapahoe, Colo. (80802) 208/P5
Arapahoe (peak), Colo. 208/H2
Arapahoe, Nebr. (68922) 264/E4
Arapahoe, N.C. (28510) 281/R4
Arapahoe, Wyo. (82510) 319/D3
Arapaho Nat'l Rec. Area, Colo. 208/G2
Arapey, Uruguay 145/B1
Arapey Chico (riv.), Uruguay 145/B1
Arapey Grande (riv.), Uruguay 145/B2
Arapicos, Ecuador 128/D3
Arapiraca, Brazil 120/F3
Arapkir, Turkey 63/H3
Arapkir, Turkey 59/C2
'Ar'ar, Wadi (dry riv.), Iraq 66/B5
'Ar'ar, Wadi (dry riv.), Iraq 59/D3
'Ar'ar, Wadi (dry riv.), Saudi Arabia 59/D3
Araracuara, Colombia 126/E8
Araracuara, Cerros de (mts.), Colombia 126/E7
Araranguá, Brazil 132/D10
Araraquara, Brazil 132/E8
Araraquara, Brazil 135/B2
Araras, Brazil 135/C3
Ararat, Ala. (†36921) 195/B7
Ararat, N.C. (27007) 281/H2
Ararat (mt.), Pa. 294/M2
Ararat (mt.), Turkey 54/F6
Ararat (mt.), Turkey 63/L3
Ararat (mt.), Turkey 59/D2
Ararat, Victoria 88/G7
Ararat, Victoria 97/B5
Ararat, Va. (24053) 307/G7
Arari, Brazil 132/E3
Araruama (lake), Brazil 135/E3
Aras (Araks) (riv.), Iran 66/E1
Aras (Araks) (riv.), Iran 59/E2
Aratürük (Yiwu), China 77/D3
Arauca (riv.) 120/C2
Arauca (inten.), Colombia 126/E4
Arauca, Colombia 120/B2
Arauca, Colombia 126/E4
Arauca (riv.), Colombia 126/E4
Arauca (riv.), Venezuela 124/E4
Arauco, Chile 138/D1
Arauco (gulf), Chile 138/D1
Arauquita, Colombia 126/E4
Araure, Venezuela 124/D3
Aravaca, Spain 33/F4
Aravaipa (creek), Ariz. 198/E6
Arawa, Papua N.G. 86/C2
Arawe, Papua N.G. 86/B2
Arax (Araks)(riv), Asia 59/E2
Araxá, Brazil 132/E7
Araya, Venezuela 124/F2
Arba, Ind. (†47355) 227/H4
Arba Mench, Ethiopia 111/G6
Arba Mench, Ethiopia 102/F4
Arbeca, Spain 33/G2
Arbedo-Castione, Switzerland 39/G4
Arbela (Erbil), Iraq 59/D2
Arbela (Erbil), Iraq 66/D2
Arbela, Mo. (63432) 261/H2
Arboga, Sweden 18/J7
Arbois, France 28/F4
Arbon, Idaho (83212) 220/F7
Arbon, Switzerland 39/H1
Arborea, Italy 34/B5
Arborfield, Sask. 181/H2
Arborg, Manitoba 179/E4
Arbor Vitae, Wis. (†54568) 317/G4
Arbovale, W. Va. (24915) 312/G6
Arbrå, Sweden 18/K6
Arbroath, Scotland 15/F4
Arbroath, Scotland 10/E2
Arbroth, La. (†70736) 238/H5
Arbucias, Spain 33/H2
Arbuckle, Calif. (95912) 204/C4
Arbuckle (lake), Fla. 212/E4
Arbuckle, W. Va. (25006) 312/C5
Arbuckles, Lake of the (lake), Okla. 288/M6
Arbuthnot, Sask. 181/E6
Arbutus, Md. (†21227) 245/M4
Arbyrd, Mo. (63821) 261/M10
Arcachon, France 28/C5
Arcachon (bay), France 28/C5
Arcade, Georgia (†30549) 217/E2
Arcade, N.Y. (14009) 276/D5
Arcadia, Calif. (91006) 204/C10
Arcadia, Fla. (33821) 212/E4
Arcadia, Ind. (46030) 227/E4
Arcadia, Iowa (51430) 229/C4
Arcadia, Kansas (66711) 232/H4
Arcadia, La. (71001) 238/E1
Arcadia, Mich. (49613) 250/C4
Arcadia, Mo. (63621) 261/L7
Arcadia, Nebr. (68815) 264/F3
Arcadia, Nova Scotia 168/B5
Arcadia, Ohio (44804) 284/D3
Arcadia, Okla. (73007) 288/M3
Arcadia, Pa. (15712) 294/E4
Arcadia, R.I. (†02832) 249/H6
Arcadia, S.C. (29320) 296/C2
Arcadia, Texas (77517) 303/K3
Arcadia, Utah (†84012) 304/D3
Arcadia, Wis. (54612) 317/D7
Arcadia Lakes, S.C. (†29201) 296/F3
Arcahaie, Haiti 158/C6
Arcanum, Ohio (45304) 284/A6
Arcas (cay), Mexico 150/N6
Arcata, Calif. (95521) 204/A3
Arc Dome (mt.), Nev. 266/D4
Arcelia, Mexico 150/J7
Arch, N. Mex. (†88130) 274/F4
Archambault (lake), Québec 172/C3
Archangel, U.S.S.R. 4/C7
Archangel, U.S.S.R. 2/M2
Archangel, U.S.S.R. 7/J2
Archangel (Arkhangel'sk), U.S.S.R. 48/E3
Archangel (Arkhangel'sk), U.S.S.R. 52/F2
Archbald, Pa. (18403) 294/F6
Archbold, Ohio (43502) 284/B2
Arch Cape, Oreg. (97102) 291/D2
Archdale, N.C. (27263) 281/K3
Archena, Spain 33/F3
Archer, Fla. (32618) 212/D2
Archer, Iowa (51231) 229/B2
Archer, Nebr. (68816) 264/F3
Archer (fiord), N.W. Terrs. 187/M1
Archer (riv.), Queensland 95/B2
Archer (co.), Texas 303/F4
Archer City, Texas (76351) 303/F4
Archerfield, Queensland 88/K3
Archerfield, Queensland 95/D3
Archerwill, Sask. 181/H3
Arches Nat'l Park, Utah 304/E5
Archibald, La. (71218) 238/G2
Archidona, Ecuador 128/D3
Archidona, Spain 33/D4
Archie, La. (†71343) 238/G3
Archie, Mo. (64725) 261/D5
Archiestown, Scotland 15/E3
Archuleta (co.), Colo. 208/E8
Archydal, Sask. 181/F5
Arcis-sur-Aube, France 28/F3
Arckaringa (creek), S. Australia 94/D2
Arco, Georgia (†31520) 217/J8
Arco, Idaho (83213) 220/E6
Arco, Idaho 188/D2
Arco, Minn. (56113) 255/B6
Arcola, Ill. (61910) 222/E4
Arcola, Ind. (46704) 227/G2
Arcola, La. (†70456) 238/K5
Arcola, Miss. (38722) 256/C4
Arcola, Mo. (65603) 261/E7
Arcola, N.C. (†27589) 281/N2
Arcola, Sask. 181/J6
Arcopongo, Bolivia 136/B5
Arcosanti, Ariz. (†86333) 198/C4
Arcos de Jalón, Spain 33/E2
Arcos de la Frontera, Spain 33/D4
Arcos de Valdevez, Portugal 33/B2
Arcot, India 68/D6
Arcoverde, Brazil 132/G5
Arctic (ocean) 54/C1
Arctic (ocean) 146/B2
Arctic (plain), Alaska 196/G1
Arctic, R.I. (†02893) 249/J6
Arctic Bay, Canada 4/B14
Arctic Bay, N.W.T. 162/H1
Arctic Bay, N.W. Terrs. 187/K2
Arctic Circle 2/J2
Arctic Ocean 2/B2
Arctic Ocean 4/A15
Arctic Ocean, U.S.S.R. 48/K1
Arctic Red (riv.), N.W. Terrs. 187/E3
Arctic Red River, N.W.T. 162/C2
Arctic Red River, N.W. Terrs. 187/E3
Arctic Village, Alaska (99722) 196/K1
Arda (riv.), Greece 45/G5
Ardabil, Iran 54/F6
Ardabil, Iran 59/E2
Ardabil, Iran 66/F1
Ardagh, Limerick, Ireland 17/C7
Ardagh, Longford, Ireland 17/F4
Ardahan, Turkey 59/D1
Ardahan, Turkey 63/K2
Ardal, Iran 66/G4
Årdal, Norway 18/F7
Årdalstangen, Norway 18/F6
Ardanuç, Turkey 63/K2
Ardara, Ireland 17/E2
Ardath, Sask. 181/D4
Ardavasar, Scotland 15/B3
Ardbeg, Ontario 177/D2
Ardèche (dept.), France 28/F5
Ardee, Ireland 17/H4
Ardee, Ireland 10/C4
Arden, Ark. (†71822) 202/B6
Arden, Del. (†19801) 245/R1
Arden, Denmark 21/C4
Arden, Manitoba 179/C4
Arden, Ontario 177/G3
Arden, Wash. (†99114) 310/H2
Arden, W. Va. (†26405) 312/G4
Arden-Arcade, Calif. (95825) 204/B8
Ardencroft, Del. (†19810) 245/R1
Ardennes (for.), Belgium 27/F9
Ardennes (dept.), France 28/F3
Ardenode, Alberta 182/D3
Ardentown, Del. (†19810) 245/S1
Ardenvoir, Wash. (98811) 310/E3
Ardersier, Scotland 15/E3
Ardeşen, Turkey 63/J2
Ardestan, Iran 59/F3
Ardestan, Iran 66/H4
Ardez, Switzerland 39/K3
Ardfert, Ireland 17/B7
Ardfinnan, Ireland 17/F7
Ardgay, Scotland 15/D3
Ardglass, N. Ireland 17/K3
Ardgour (dist.), Scotland 15/C4
Ardhéa, Greece 45/F5
Ardila (riv.), Spain 33/C3
Ardill, Sask. 181/F6
Ardino, Bulgaria 45/G5
Ardivachar (pt.), Scotland 15/A3
Ardle (riv.), Scotland 15/E4
Ardlethan, N.S. Wales 97/D4
Ardmore, Ala. (35805) 195/E1
Ardmore, Alberta 182/E2
Ardmore, Ind. (†46624) 227/E1
Ardmore, Ireland 17/F8
Ardmore, Md. (†20785) 245/G4
Ardmore, Mo. (†65247) 261/H3
Ardmore, Okla. 188/G4
Ardmore, Okla. (73401) 288/M6
Ardmore, Pa. (19003) 294/M6
Ardmore, S. Dak. (57715) 298/B7
Ardmore, Tenn. (38449) 237/H10
Ardnamurchan (pen.), Scotland 15/B4
Ardnamurchan (pt.), Scotland 15/B4
Ardoch, N. Dak. (58213) 282/R3
Ardon, Switzerland 39/D4
Ardooie, Belgium 27/C7
Ardrahan, Ireland 17/D5
Ardrishaig, Scotland 15/C4
Ardrossan, Alberta 182/D3
Ardrossan, Scotland 10/D3
Ardrossan, Scotland 15/D5
Ards (dist.), N. Ireland 17/K2
Ardsley, N.Y. (10502) 276/O6
Åre, Sweden 18/H5
Arecibo (dist.), P. Rico 161/C1
Arecibo, P. Rico 156/G1
Arecibo, P. Rico 161/B1
Aredale, Iowa (50605) 229/H3
Areguá, Paraguay 144/B4
Areia Branca, Brazil 132/G4
Arelee, Sask. 181/D3
Arena (pt.), Calif. 188/B3
Arena (pt.), Calif. 204/B5
Arena (pt.), Mexico 150/E5
Arena, N. Dak. (58412) 282/K5
Arena (isl.), Philippines 82/C6
Arena, Wis. (53503) 317/G9
Arenac (co.), Mich. 250/F4
Arenales, Cerro (mt.), Chile 138/D7
Arenas (pt.), Argentina 143/C7
Arenas (cay), Mexico 150/O5
Arenas (pt.), P. Rico 161/F2
Arenas de San Pedro, Spain 33/D2
Arendal, Norway 18/F7
Arendjelovac, Yugoslavia 45/E3
Arendonk, Belgium 27/G6
Arendtsville, Pa. (17303) 294/H6
Arenillas, Ecuador 128/B4
Arenys de Mar, Spain 33/H2
Arenzville, Ill. (62611) 222/C4
Areópolis, Greece 45/F7
Arequipa (dept.), Peru 128/F10
Arequipa, Peru 128/G11
Arequipa, Peru 120/B4
Arequipa, Peru 128/72
Aresji, Neth. Ant. 161/D9
Areuse (riv.), Switzerland 39/C3
Arévalo, Spain 33/D2
Areyonga, North. Terr. 88/E4
Areyonga, North. Terr. 93/C8
Arezzo (prov.), Italy 34/C3
Arezzo, Italy 34/C3
Arfa Deh, Iran 66/H3
Arga (riv.), Spain 33/F1
Argadargada, North. Terr. 93/E6
Argalant, Mongolia 77/G3
Argalastí, Greece 45/F6
Argamasilla de Alba, Spain 33/E3
Arganda, Spain 33/G4
Argao, Philippines 82/D6
Argenta, Br. Col. 184/J5
Argenta, Ill. (62501) 222/E4
Argenta, Italy 34/D2
Argentan, France 28/D3
Argentat, France 28/D5
Argenteuil, France 28/A1
Argenteuil (co.), Québec 172/C4
Argentia, Newf. 166/C2
Argentina 2/F7
Argentina 120/C6
ARGENTINA 143
Argentine, Pa. (†16040) 294/C3
Argentino (lake), Argentina 143/B7
Argenton-sur-Creusot, France 28/D4
Argeş (riv.), Romania 45/G3
Argo, Ala. (†35173) 195/E3
Argo, Sudan 111/F4
Argo, Sudan 59/B6
Argolis (gulf), Greece 45/F7
Argonia, Kansas (67004) 232/E4
Argonne, Wis. (54511) 317/J4
Argonne Nat'l Laboratory, Ill. 222/B6
Árgos, Greece 45/F7
Argos, Ind. (46501) 227/E2
Argos (cape), Nova Scotia 168/G3
Argostólion, Greece 45/E6
Arguello (pt.), Calif. 204/E9
Arguin (bay), Mauritania 106/A4
Argun (riv.) 54/N4
Argun' (Ergun He) (riv.), China 77/K1
Argun' (riv.), U.S.S.R. 48/M4
Argungu, Nigeria 106/E6
Argus (range), Calif. 204/H7
Argusville, N. Dak. (58005) 282/R5
Arguvan, Turkey 63/H3
Argyle, Fla. (32422) 212/C6
Argyle, Georgia (31623) 217/G8
Argyle, Iowa (52619) 229/K7
Argyle, Maine (†04468) 243/F5
Argyle, Manitoba 179/E4
Argyle, Mich. (48410) 250/G5
Argyle, Minn. (56713) 255/B2
Argyle, Mo. (65001) 261/J6
Argyle, New Bruns. 170/C2
Argyle, N.Y. (12809) 276/O4
Argyle, Texas (76226) 303/F1
Argyle (lake), W. Australia 88/D3
Argyle (lake), W. Australia 92/E2
Argyle, Wis. (53504) 317/G10
Argyle Downs, W. Australia 92/E2
Argyll (dist.), Scotland 15/C4
Argyll (trad. co.), Scotland 15/B5
Arhangay, Mongolia 77/F2
Arhavi, Turkey 63/J2
Arhli (Arlit), Niger 106/F4
Ar Horqin, China 77/K3
Århus (co.), Denmark 21/D5
Århus, Denmark 7/E3
Århus, Denmark 21/D5
Århus, Denmark 18/F8
Aria, N. Zealand 100/E3
Ariah Park, N.S. Wales 97/D4
Ariail, S.C. (†29640) 296/B2
Ariano Irpino, Italy 34/E4
Ariari (riv.), Colombia 126/D6
Aribinda, Upper Volta 106/D6
Arica, Chile 120/B4
Arica, Chile 138/A1
Arica, Colombia 126/E9
Aricagua, Venezuela 124/C3
Ariccia, Italy 34/F7
Arichat, Nova Scotia 168/H3
Arichuna, Venezuela 124/E4
Arichuna (riv.), Venezuela 124/D4
Arid (cape), W. Australia 88/C6
Arid (cape), W. Australia 92/C6
Ariège (dept.), France 28/D6
Ariel, Wash. (98603) 310/C5
Ariguaní (riv.), Colombia 126/D3
Ariha (Jericho), West Bank 65/C4
Arikaree (riv.), Colo. 208/O3
Arima, Trin. & Tob. 156/G5
Arima, Trin. & Tob. 161/B10
Arimo, Idaho (83214) 220/F7
Arinagour, Scotland 15/B4
Aringa, Uganda 115/F3
Arinos (riv.), Brazil 132/B5
Ario de Rosales, Mexico 150/J7
Arion, Iowa (51520) 229/B5
Aripao, Venezuela 124/F4
Aripeka, Fla. (33502) 212/D3
Aripine, Ariz. (†85901) 198/E4
Aripo, El Cerro del (mt.), Trin. & Tob. 161/B10
Ariporo (riv.), Colombia 126/E4
Aripuanã, Brazil 120/C3
Aripuanã, Brazil 132/A5
Aripuanã (riv.), Brazil 120/D3
Aripuanã (riv.), Brazil 132/A4
Arisaig, Scotland 15/C4
Arisaig (sound), Scotland 15/C4
Arismendi, Venezuela 124/D3
Arispe, Iowa (50831) 229/E7
Aristazabal (isl.), Br. Col. 184/C4
Aritao, Philippines 82/C2
Ariton, Ala. (36311) 195/G7
Arivaca, Ariz. (85601) 198/D7
Arivonimamo, Madagascar 118/H3
Arixang (Wenquan), China 77/B3
Ariza, Spain 33/E2
Arizaro, Salar de (salt dep.), Argentina 143/C2
Arizona 188/D4
ARIZONA 198
Arizona (state), U.S. 146/G6
Arizona City, Ariz. (85223) 198/D6
Arizona Sunsites, Ariz. (85625) 198/F7
Arizpe, Mexico 150/D1
Årjäng, Sweden 18/H7
Arjay, Ky. (40902) 237/O7
Arjeplog, Sweden 18/L3
Arjona, Colombia 126/C2
Arkabutla, Miss. (38602) 256/D1
Arkabutla (dam), Miss. 256/D1
Arkabutla (lake), Miss. 256/D1
Arkadelphia, Ala. (35033) 195/E3
Arkadelphia, Ark. (71923) 202/D5
Arkaig, Loch (lake), Scotland 15/C4
Arkaig, Loch (lake), Scotland 10/D2
Arkalyk, U.S.S.R. 48/G4
Arkansas 188/H3
Arkansas (riv.) 188/H3
ARKANSAS 202
Arkansas (co.), Ark. 202/H5

Atchison 331

Arkansas (riv.), Ark. 202/G5
Arkansas (riv.), Colo. 208/P6
Arkansas (riv.), Kansas 232/D3
Arkansas (riv.), Okla. 288/S4
Arkansas (state), U.S. 146/J6
Arkansas (riv.), U.S. 2/E4
Arkansas (riv.), U.S. 146/J6
Arkansas City, Ark. (71630) 202/H6
Arkansas City, Kans. 188/G3
Arkansas City, Kansas (67005) 232/E4
Arkansas Divide (mts.), Colo. 208/L4
Arkansas Post Nat'l Mem., Ark. 202/H5
Arkansaw, Wis. (54721) 317/B6
Arkdale, Wis. (54613) 317/G7
Arkhángelos, Greece 45/J7
Arkhipo-Osipovka, U.S.S.R. 52/E6
Arkinda, Ark. (71821) 202/B6
Arklow, Ireland 10/C4
Arklow, Ireland 17/J6
Arklow (bank), Ireland 17/K6
Arkoe, Mo. (†64468) 261/C2
Arkoma, Okla. (74901) 288/T4
Arkona (cape), E. Germany 22/E1
Arkona, Ontario 177/C4
Arkport, N.Y. (14807) 276/E6
Arkticheskiy Institut (isls.), U.S.S.R. 48/H2
Arkville, N.Y. (12406) 276/L6
Arkwright, S.C. (†29301) 296/C2
Arlee, Mont. (59821) 262/B3
Arlee, W. Va. (†25106) 312/B5
Arles, France 28/F6
Arley, Ala. (35541) 195/D2
Arlington, Ala. (36722) 195/C6
Arlington, Ariz. (85322) 198/C5
Arlington, Colo. (81021) 208/N6
Arlington, Georgia (31713) 217/C8
Arlington, Ill. (61312) 222/D2
Arlington, Ind. (46104) 227/F5
Arlington, Iowa (50606) 229/K3
Arlington, Kansas (67514) 232/D4
Arlington, Ky. (42021) 237/D7
Arlington○, Mass. (02174) 249/C6
Arlington, Minn. (55307) 255/D6
Arlington, Nebr. (68002) 264/H3
Arlington, N.Y. (12603) 276/N7
Arlington, N.C. (†28642) 281/H2
Arlington, Ohio (45814) 284/C4
Arlington, Oreg. (97812) 291/G2
Arlington, S. Dak. (57212) 298/P5
Arlington, Tenn. (38002) 237/B10
Arlington, Tex. 188/G4
Arlington, Texas (*76010) 303/F2
Arlington (lake), Texas 303/F2
Arlington, Vt. (05250) 268/A5
Arlington○, Vt. (05250) 268/A5
Arlington (co.), Va. 307/S2
Arlington, Va. (*22201) 307/T3
Arlington, Wash. (98223) 310/C2
Arlington, Wis. (53911) 317/H9
Arlington, Wyo. (†82080) 319/F4
Arlington Beach, Sask. 181/F4
Arlington Heights, Ill. (*60004) 222/B5
Arlington Heights, Ohio (†45201) 284/C9
Arlington Nat'l Cemetery, Va. 307/T3
Arlit (Arhli), Niger 106/F4
Arló, Hungary 41/F2
Arlon, Belgium 27/H9
Arltunga, North. Terr. 93/D7
Arm (riv.), Sask. 181/F5
Arma, Kansas (66712) 232/H4
Arma (plat.), Saudi Arabia 59/E4
Armada, Alberta 182/D4
Armada, Mich. (48005) 250/G6
Armadale, Scotland 15/C2
Armadale, Scotland 10/B1
Armagh (dist.), N. Ireland 17/H3
Armagh, N. Ireland 10/C3
Armagh, N. Ireland 17/H3
Armagh, Pa. (15920) 294/E5
Armagh, Québec 172/G3
Armathwaite, Tenn. (38506) 237/M8
Armavir, U.S.S.R. 7/J4
Armavir, U.S.S.R. 48/E5
Armavir, U.S.S.R. 52/F5
Armena, Alberta 182/D3
Armenia, Colombia 120/B2
Armenia, Colombia 126/B5
Armenian S.S.R., U.S.S.R. 7/J4
Armenian S.S.R., U.S.S.R. 52/F6
Armenian S.S.R., U.S.S.R. 48/E6
Armentières, France 28/E2
Armería, Mexico 150/G7
Armero, Colombia 126/C5
Armidale, Australia 87/F9
Armidale, N. S. Wales 88/J6
Armidale, N.S. Wales 97/F2
Armington, Ill. (61721) 222/D3
Armington, Mont. (†59412) 262/F3
Arminto, Wyo. (82630) 319/E2
Armistead, La. (†71019) 238/D3
Armit (lake), Manitoba 179/A2
Armley, Sask. 181/G2
Armona, Calif. (93202) 204/F7
Armorel, Ark. (72310) 202/L2
Armour, S. Dak. (57313) 298/N7
Armourdale, N. Dak. (†58365) 282/M2
Armoy, N. Ireland 17/J1
Armstrong, Br. Col. 184/H5
Armstrong, Ill. (61812) 222/F3
Armstrong, Ind. (†47708) 227/B8
Armstrong, Iowa (50514) 229/D2
Armstrong, Mo. (65230) 261/G4
Armstrong, Ont. 162/H5
Armstrong, Ontario 175/C2
Armstrong, Ontario 177/H4
Armstrong (co.), Pa. 294/D4
Armstrong (co.), Texas 303/C3
Armstrong, Texas (78338) 303/G11
Armstrong Brook, New Bruns. 170/E1
Armstrong Creek, Wis. (54103) 317/K4
Armstrongs Mills, Ohio (43904) 284/J6
Armuchee, Georgia (30105) 217/B2
Army Chemical Center, Md. 245/O3
Army Med. Ctr. Annex (Walter Reed), Md. 245/E4
Arnaia, Greece 45/F5
Arnaud, Manitoba 179/E5
Arnaud (riv.), Québec 174/F1
Arnaudville, La. (70512) 238/G6
Arnauti (cape), Cyprus 59/B2
Arnauti (cape), Cyprus 63/E5
Arnavutköy, Turkey 63/D6
Arnedo, Spain 33/E1
Arnegard, N. Dak. (58835) 282/D4
Årnes, Norway 18/G6
Arnett, Okla. (73832) 288/G2
Arnett, W. Va. (25007) 312/D7
Arney (riv.), N. Ireland 17/F3
Arnheim, Mich. (†49958) 250/G1
Arnhem (cape), Australia 87/D7
Arnhem, Netherlands 27/H4
Arnhem (cape), North. Terr. 88/F2
Arnhem (cape), North. Terr. 93/E2
Arnhem Land (reg.), Australia 87/D7
Arnhem Land (reg.), North. Terr. 88/E2
Arnhem Land (reg.), North. Terr. 93/D2
Arnhem Land Aboriginal Reserve, North. Terr. 88/E2
Arnhem Land Aboriginal Res., North. Terr. 93/C2
Arno (riv.), Italy 34/C3
Arno (atoll), Marshall Is. 87/H5
Arnold, Calif. (95223) 204/E5
Arnold, England 13/F4
Arnold, Kansas (67515) 232/B3
Arnold, Mich. (49819) 250/B2
Arnold, Minn. (†55801) 255/F4
Arnold, Mo. (63010) 261/M6
Arnold, Nebr. (69120) 264/D3
Arnold (riv.), North. Terr. 93/D3
Arnold, Pa. (15068) 294/C4
Arnold Mills, R.I. (†02864) 249/J5
Arnoldsburg, W. Va. (25234) 312/D5
Arnold's Cove, Newf. 166/C2
Arnolds Park, Iowa (51331) 229/C2
Arnoldstein, Austria 41/B3
Arnoldsville, Georgia (30619) 217/F3
Arnot, Pa. (16911) 294/H2
Arnøya (isl.), Norway 18/M1
Arnprior, Ontario 177/H2
Arnsberg, W. Germany 22/C3
Arnstadt, E. Germany 22/D3
Årø (isl.), Denmark 21/C7
Aro (riv.), Venezuela 124/F4
Aroa, Venezuela 124/D2
Aroab, Namibia 118/B5
Aroche, Spain 33/C4
Arock, Oreg. (97902) 291/K5
Aroland, Ontario 177/H4
Aroland, Ontario 175/C2
Arolla, Switzerland 39/E4
Arolsen, W. Germany 22/C3
Aroma, Bolivia 136/B6
Aroma, Sudan 111/G4
Aroma Park, Ill. (60910) 222/F2
Aromas, Calif. (95004) 204/D7
Aroostook (co.), Maine 243/F2
Aroostook (riv.), Maine 243/G2
Aroostook, New Bruns. 170/C2
Arorae (atoll), Kiribati 87/H6
Aroroy, Philippines 82/D4
Arosa, Ria de (est.), Spain 33/B1
Arosa, Switzerland 39/J3
Aroser Rothorn (mt.), Switzerland 39/J3
Årøsund, Denmark 21/C7
Arouca, Trin. & Tob. 161/B10
Arp, Georgia (†31783) 217/F7
Arp, Texas (75750) 303/J5
Arpa (riv.), Turkey 63/K2
Arpaçay, Turkey 63/K2
Arpin, Wis. (54410) 317/G6
Arque, Bolivia 136/B5
'Arraba, West Bank 65/C3
'Arrabe, Israel 65/C2
Arrah, India 68/E3
Ar Rahhaliya, Iraq 66/C4
Ar Rahhaliya, Iraq 59/D3
Arraias, Brazil 132/E6
Arran, Fla. (†32327) 212/B1
Arran, Sask. 181/K4
Arran (isl.), Scotland 15/C5
Arran (isl.), Scotland 10/D3
Arras, Br. Col. 184/G2
Arras, France 28/E2
Arrecifal, Colombia 126/F6
Arrecife, Spain 106/B3
Arrecife, Spain 33/C4
Arrecife de la Media Luna (reefs), Honduras 154/F3
Arrecifes, Argentina 143/F7
Arrecifes (riv.), Argentina 143/G6
Arrey, N. Mex. (87930) 274/B6
Arriaga, Mexico 150/N8
Arriba, Colo. (80804) 208/N4
Arribeños, Argentina 143/F7
Arrington, Kansas (†66436) 232/G2
Arrington, Tenn. (37014) 237/H9
Arrington, Va. (22922) 307/L5
Arriola, Colo. (†81323) 208/B8
Arrochar, Scotland 15/D4
Arronches, Portugal 33/C3
Arrow (lake), Ireland 17/E3
Arrow (creek), Mont. 262/F3
Arrow Canyon (range), Nev. 266/G6
Arrow Creek, Mont. (†59424) 262/F3
Arrowhead Mountain (lake), Vt. 268/A2
Arrow River, Manitoba 179/B4
Arrowrock (res.), Idaho 220/C6
Arrow Rock, Mo. (65320) 261/F4
Arrowsmith, Ill. (61722) 222/E3
Arrowtown, N. Zealand 100/B6
Arrowwood, Alberta 182/D4
Arrowwood (lake), N. Dak. 282/N5
Arroyas, Los (lake), Bolivia 136/C3
Arroyo, P. Rico 161/E3
Arroyo, P. Rico 156/G1
Arroyo Blanco, Cuba 158/F2
Arroyo de la Luz, Spain 33/C3
Arroyo del Valle (dry riv.), Calif. 204/L3
Arroyo Grande, Bolivia 136/A2
Arroyo Grande, Calif. (93420) 204/E8
Arroyo Hondo (dry riv.), Calif. 204/L3
Arroyo Hondo, N. Mex. (87513) 274/D2
Arroyo Mocho (dry riv.), Calif. 204/L2
Arroyo Seco, Argentina 143/F6
Arroyo Seco (dry riv.), Calif. 204/K10
Arroyo Seco, N. Mex. (87514) 274/D2
Arroyos y Esteros, Paraguay 144/B4
Ar Rumaila, Iraq 66/E5
Års, Denmark 21/C4
Ars-en-Ré, France 28/C4
Arsen'yev, U.S.S.R. 48/O5
Arsin, Turkey 63/H2
Arslanköy, Turkey 63/F4
Árta, Greece 45/E6
Artá, Spain 33/H3
Artas, S. Dak. (57423) 298/K2
Artawiya, Saudi Arabia 59/E4
Arteaga, Mexico 150/H7
Artem, U.S.S.R. 48/O5
Artemas, Pa. (17211) 294/E6
Artemisa, Cuba 158/B1
Artemisa, Cuba 156/A2
Artemovskiy, U.S.S.R. 48/M4
Artemus, Ky. (40903) 237/O7
Artena, Italy 34/F7
Artesia, Calif. (90701) 204/C11
Artesia, Miss. (39736) 256/G4
Artesia, N. Mex. 188/F4
Artesia, N. Mex. (88210) 274/E6
Artesian, S. Dak. (57314) 298/O6
Artesia Wells, Texas (78001) 303/E9
Arth, Switzerland 39/F2
Arthabaska (co.), Québec 172/E4
Arthabaska, Québec 172/F3
Arthur, Ill. (61911) 222/E4
Arthur, Ind. (†47598) 227/C8
Arthur, Iowa (51431) 229/C4
Arthur (co.), Nebr. 264/C3
Arthur, Nebr. (69121) 264/C3
Arthur (range), N. Zealand 100/D4
Arthur, N. Dak. (58006) 282/R5
Arthur, Ontario 177/D4
Arthur (lake), Pa. 294/C4
Arthur (lake), Tasmania 99/D4
Arthur (range), Tasmania 99/C5
Arthur (riv.), Tasmania 99/B3
Arthur, Tenn. (37707) 237/O7
Arthur (riv.), W. Australia 92/B2
Arthur, W. Va. (26816) 312/H4
Arthurdale, W. Va. (26520) 312/G3
Arthuret, England 13/E2
Arthurette, New Bruns. 170/C2
Arthur Kill (str.), N.J. 273/B3
Arthur's (pass), N. Zealand 100/C5
Arthurstown, Ireland 17/H7
Artibonite (dept.), Haiti 158/C5
Artibonite (riv.), Haiti 158/C5
Artigas (dept.), Uruguay 145/B1
Artigas, Uruguay 145/C1
Artillery (lake), N.W. Terrs. 187/H3
Artland, Sask. 181/B3
Artois, Calif. (95913) 204/C4
Artois (trad. prov.), France 29
Artova, Turkey 63/G2
Artux (Atushi), China 77/A4
Artvin (prov.), Turkey 63/J2
Artvin, Turkey 59/D1
Artvin, Turkey 63/J2
Aru (isls.), Indonesia 85/K7
Aru, Zaire 115/F3
Arua, Uganda 115/F3
Aruba (isl.), Neth. Ant. 161/E9
Aruba (isl.), Neth. Ant. 156/E4
Arucas, Spain 33/B5
Arunachal Pradesh (terr.), India 68/G3
Arundel, England 13/G7
Arundel, England 10/F5
Arundel, Québec 172/C4
Årup, Denmark 21/D7
Aruppukkottai, India 68/D7
'Arura, West Bank 65/C3
Arus, P. Rico 161/C3
Arusha (reg.), Tanzania 115/G4
Arusha, Tanzania 102/F5
Arusha, Tanzania 115/G4
Arusi (prov.), Ethiopia 111/G6
Aruwimi (riv.), Zaire 115/E3
Arva, Ireland 17/F4
Arva, Ontario 177/C4
Arvada, Colo. (*80001) 208/J3
Arvada, Wyo. (82831) 319/F1
Arvayheer, Mongolia 77/F2
Arvel, Ky. (†40447) 237/O5
Arvi, India 68/D4
Arvida, Québec 172/F1
Arvidsjaur, Sweden 18/L4
Arvika, Sweden 18/H7
Arvilla, N. Dak. (58214) 282/P4
Arvin, Calif. (93203) 204/G8
Arvonia, Va. (23004) 307/M5
Arwad (Ruad) (isl.), Syria 63/F5
Arxan, China 77/K2
Arys', U.S.S.R. 48/G5
Arzamas, U.S.S.R. 48/E4
Arzamas, U.S.S.R. 52/F3
Arzúa, Spain 33/B1
As, Belgium 27/H6
Aš, Czech. 41/B1
Aså, Denmark 21/D3
Asaba, Nigeria 106/F7
Asadabad, Iran 66/F3
Asahan (riv.), Indonesia 85/B5
Asahi, Japan 81/K6
Asahi (mt.), Japan 81/J4
Asahikawa, Japan 81/L2
Asahikawa, Japan 54/P5
Asama (mt.), Japan 81/J5
Asansol, India 68/F4
Åsarna, Sweden 18/J5
Asau, W. Samoa 86/L8
Asbest, U.S.S.R. 48/G4
Asbestos, Québec 172/F4
Asbury, Iowa (†52001) 229/M4
Asbury, Mo. (64832) 261/C8
Asbury, N.J. (08802) 273/C2
Asbury, W. Va. (24916) 312/E7
Asbury Park, N.J. (07712) 273/F3
As Busaiya, Iraq 66/E5
Ascención (Añez), Bolivia 136/D4
Ascensión, Argentina 143/F7
Ascension (par.), La. 238/J6
Ascensión, Mexico 150/E1
Ascension, Neth. Ant. 161/F8
Ascension (isl.), St. Helena 102/A5
Ascension (isl.), St. Helena 2/J6
Aschaffenburg, W. Germany 22/C4
Aschendorf, W. Germany 22/B2
Aschersleben, E. Germany 22/D3
Asco, W. Va. (24809) 312/C8
Ascog, Scotland 15/A2
Ascoli Piceno (prov.), Italy 34/D3
Ascoli Piceno, Italy 34/D3
Ascona, Switzerland 39/G4
Ascope, Peru 128/C6
Ascot, Queensland 88/K2
Ascot, Queensland 95/E2
Ascotán, Chile 138/B3
Ascotán, Salar de (salt dep.), Chile 138/B3
Ascot Corner, Québec 172/F4
Ascrib (isls.), Scotland 15/B3
Ascutney, Vt. (05030) 268/C5
Ascutney (mt.), Vt. 268/C5
Åseda, Sweden 18/J8
Åsele, Sweden 18/K4
Asenovgrad, Bulgaria 45/G5
Asèr, Ras (cape), Somalia 2/M5
Asèr, Ras (cape), Somalia 115/K1
Ash (riv.), Minn. 255/F2
Ash, N.C. (28420) 281/N6
Ash, Oreg. (†97473) 291/D4
Ash (creek), Utah 304/A6
'Ashaira, Saudi Arabia 59/D5
Ashanti (reg.), Ghana 102/B4
Ashanti (reg.), Ghana 106/D7
Ashaway, R.I. (02804) 249/G7
Ashboro, Ind. (†47840) 227/C6
Ashburn, Georgia (31714) 217/E7
Ashburn, Mo. (63433) 261/K3
Ashburn, Va. (22011) 307/O2
Ashburnham, Mass. (01430) 249/G2
Ashburnham○, Mass. (01430) 249/G2
Ashburton (riv.), Australia 87/B8
Ashburton, England 13/D7
Ashburton, N. Zealand 100/C5
Ashburton (riv.), W. Australia 88/B4
Ashburton (riv.), W. Australia 92/A3
Ashburton Downs, W. Australia 88/B4
Ashby, Ala. (†35035) 195/E4
Ashby○, Mass. (01431) 249/G2
Ashby, Minn. (56309) 255/C4
Ashby, Nebr. (69333) 264/C2
Ashbyburg, Ky. (†42456) 237/G5
Ash Creek, Minn. (†56173) 255/B7
Ashcroft, Br. Col. 184/G5
Ashdale, Maine (†04565) 243/D8
Ashdod, Israel 65/B4
Ashdot Ya'aqov, Israel 65/D2
Ashdown, Ark. (71822) 202/B6
Ashe (co.), N.C. 281/F2
Ashe (isl.), N.C. 281/P6
Asheboro, N.C. (27203) 281/K3
Ashepoo, S.C. (†29446) 296/G6
Ashepoo (riv.), S.C. 296/F6
Asher, Okla. (74826) 288/N5
Ashern, Manitoba 179/D3
Asherton, Texas (78827) 303/E9
Asherville, Ind. (†47834) 227/C6
Asherville, Kansas (67420) 232/D2
Asheville, N.C. 188/K3
Asheville, N.C. (*28801) 281/D3
Asheweig (riv.), Ontario 175/C2
Ashfield○, Mass. (01330) 249/C2
Ashfield, N. S. Wales 88/K4
Ashfield, N.S. Wales 97/J3
Ash Flat, Ark. (72513) 202/G1
Ashford, Ala. (36312) 195/H8
Ashford○, Conn. (06278) 210/G1
Ashford, England 10/G5
Ashford, England 13/H6
Ashford, Ireland 17/J5
Ashford, N.S. Wales 97/F1
Ashford, N.C. (†28752) 281/F3
Ashford, Wash. (98304) 310/C4
Ashford, W. Va. (25009) 312/C6
Ashford P.O. (Warrenville), Conn. (06278) 210/G1
Ash Fork, Ariz. (86320) 198/C3
Ash Grove, Kansas (†67455) 232/D2
Ash Grove, Mo. (65604) 261/E8
Ashgrove, Queensland 88/K2
Ashhurst, N. Zealand 100/E4
Ashibetsu, Japan 81/L2
Ashikaga, Japan 81/J5
Ashington, England 13/F2
Ashington, England 10/F3
Ashippun, Wis. (53003) 317/H1
Ashiya, Japan 81/H8
Ashizuri (cape), Japan 81/F7
Ashkhabad, U.S.S.R. 54/G6
Ashkhabad, U.S.S.R. 48/F6
Ashkum, Ill. (60911) 222/E3
Ash Lake, Minn. (†55771) 255/F2
Ashland, Ala. (36251) 195/G4
Ashland, Calif. (†94577) 204/K2
Ashland, Georgia (†30521) 217/F2
Ashland, Ill. (62612) 222/C4
Ashland, Kansas (67831) 232/C4
Ashland, Ky. (41101) 237/R4
Ashland, Ky. 188/K3
Ashland, La. (71002) 238/D2
Ashland, Maine (04732) 243/G2
Ashland○, Maine (04732) 243/G2
Ashland○, Mass. (01721) 249/J3
Ashland, Miss. (38603) 256/F1
Ashland, Mo. (65010) 261/H5
Ashland, Mont. (59003) 262/K5
Ashland, Nebr. (68003) 264/H3
Ashland, N.H. (03217) 268/D4
Ashland○, N.H. (03217) 268/D4
Ashland, N.J. (†08033) 273/B3
Ashland, N.Y. (12407) 276/M6
Ashland (co.), Ohio 284/F4
Ashland, Ohio (44805) 284/F4
Ashland, Okla. (74524) 288/O5
Ashland, Oreg. (97520) 291/E5
Ashland, Pa. (17921) 294/K4
Ashland, Va. (23005) 307/N5
Ashland (co.), Wis. 317/E3
Ashland, Wis. (54806) 317/E2
Ashland City, Tenn. (37015) 237/G8
Ashley (co.), Ark. 202/G7
Ashley, Ill. (62808) 222/D5
Ashley, Ind. (46705) 227/G1
Ashley, Mich. (48806) 250/E5
Ashley, Mo. (†63334) 261/K4
Ashley (lake), Mont. 262/B2
Ashley, N.S. Wales 97/E1
Ashley, N. Dak. (58413) 282/M7
Ashley, Ohio (43003) 284/E5
Ashley, Pa. (18706) 294/E7
Ashley (riv.), S.C. 296/G6
Ashley, W. Va. (†26339) 312/E4
Ashley Falls, Mass. (01222) 249/A4
Ashmere (lake), Mass. 249/B3
Ashmont, Alberta 182/E2
Ashmore, Ill. (61912) 222/F4
Ashmore, Nova Scotia 168/C4
Ashmore (isls.), Terr. of Ashmore and Cartier Is. 88/C2
Ashmore and Cartier Is., Terr. of, 88/C2
Ashokan, N.Y. (†12491) 276/M7
Ashokan (res.), N.Y. 276/M7
Ashport, Tenn. (†38063) 237/B9
Ashqelon, Israel 65/A4
Ash Shabicha, Iraq 66/C5
Ashtabula (lake), N. Dak. 282/P5
Ashtabula (co.), Ohio 284/J2
Ashtabula, Ohio (44004) 284/J2
Ashton, Idaho (83420) 220/G5
Ashton, Ill. (61006) 222/D2
Ashton, Iowa (51232) 229/B2
Ashton, Kansas (†67051) 232/E4
Ashton, Mich. (†49677) 250/D5
Ashton, Nebr. (68817) 264/F3
Ashton, R.I. (02864) 249/J5
Ashton, S.C. (†29082) 296/E5
Ashton, S. Dak. (57424) 298/N3
Ashton, W. Va. (25503) 312/B5
Ashton Creek, Br. Col. 184/H5
Ashton-under-Lyne, England 13/H2
Ashton-under-Lyne, England 10/G2
Ashuanipi (lake), Newf. 166/A3
Ashuanipi (riv.), Newf. 166/A3
Ashuanipi, Newf. 166/A3
Ashuelot, N.H. (03441) 268/C6
Ashuelot (riv.), N.H. 268/C6
Ash Valley, Kansas (†67550) 232/C3
Ashville, Ala. (35953) 195/F3
Ashville, Maine (04607) 243/G7
Ashville, Manitoba 179/B3
Ashville, Ohio (43103) 284/E6
Ashville, Pa. (16613) 294/F4
Ashwaubenon, Wis. (54304) 317/K7
Ashwood, Oreg. (97711) 291/G3
'Asi (Orontes) (riv.), Syria 63/G5
Asia 2/P3
Asia (isls.), Indonesia 85/J5
Asid (gulf), Philippines 82/D4
Asidonhoppo, Suriname 131/D4
Asilah, Morocco 106/C1
Asinara (gulf), Italy 34/B4
Asinara (isl.), Italy 34/B4
Asino, U.S.S.R. 48/J4
'Asir (reg.), Saudi Arabia 59/D6
Aşkale, Turkey 63/J3
Askeaton, Ireland 17/D6
Askew, Miss. (38604) 256/D1
Askewville, N.C. (†27983) 281/R2
Askim, Norway 18/E4
Askim, Sweden 18/G8
Aski Mosul, Iraq 66/C2
Askival (mt.), Scotland 15/B4
Askov, Denmark 21/C7
Askov, Minn. (55704) 255/F4
Askvoll, Norway 18/D6
Asmara, Ethiopia 111/G4
Asmara, Ethiopia 59/C6
Asmara, Ethiopia 102/F3
Asnaes, Denmark 21/E6
Åsnen (lake), Sweden 18/J8
Asnières-sur-Seine, France 28/A1
Aso (mt.), Japan 81/E7
Aso National Park, Japan 81/E7
Asosa, Ethiopia 111/F5
Asoteriba, Jebel (mt.), Sudan 111/G3
Asotin (co.), Wash. 310/H4
Asotin, Wash. (99402) 310/H4
Asotin (creek), Wash. 310/J4
Asotin (dam), Wash. 310/J4
Aspang Markt, Austria 41/D3
Aspatria, England 13/D3
Aspe, Spain 33/F3
Aspelund, Minn. (†55946) 255/F6
Aspen, Colo. (81611) 208/F4
Aspen, Nova Scotia 168/F3
Aspen (lake), Oreg. 291/E5
Aspen (mts.), Wyo. 319/C4
Aspen Grove, Br. Col. 184/G5
Aspen Hill, Md. 245/K4
Aspermont, Texas (79502) 303/D4
Aspers, Pa. (17304) 294/H6
Aspetuck, Conn. (†06880) 210/B4
Aspetuck (res.), Conn. 210/B4
Aspetuck (riv.), Conn. 210/B3
Aspinwall, Iowa (51432) 229/C5
Aspinwall, Pa. (15215) 294/C6
Aspiring (mt.), N. Zealand 100/B6
Aspley, Queensland 88/K2
Aspy (bay), Nova Scotia 168/H2
Asquith, Sask. 181/D3
Assab, Ethiopia 59/D7
Assab, Ethiopia 111/H5
Assaba (reg.), Mauritania 106/B5
Assabet (riv.), Mass. 249/H3
Assad, Bahrat (lake), Syria 63/H4
Assakarai (dry riv.), Niger 106/F5
Assale (lake), Ethiopia 111/H5
As Salman, Iraq 59/E3
As Salman, Iraq 66/D5
Assam (state), India 68/G3
Assapan (riv.), Manitoba 179/G2
Assaria, Kansas (67416) 232/E3
Assateague Island Nat'l Seashore, Va. 307/T4
Assawompset (pond), Mass. 249/L5
Assay (creek), Utah 304/B6
Asse, Belgium 27/E7
Asselar (well), Mali 106/D5
Asselle, Ethiopia 102/F4
Asselle, Ethiopia 111/G6
Assen, Netherlands 27/K3
Assenede, Belgium 27/D6
Assens, Århus, Denmark 21/D4
Assens, Fyn, Denmark 21/D7
Assesse, Belgium 27/G8
Assigny (lake), Newf. 166/A3
Assiniboia, Sask. 181/E6
Assiniboine (mt.), Alberta 182/C4
Assiniboine (mt.), Br. Col. 184/K5
Assiniboine (riv.), Manitoba 179/C5
Assiniboine (riv.), Sask. 181/J3
Assinica (lake), Québec 174/C3
Assinika (lake), Manitoba 179/G2
Assinika (riv.), Manitoba 179/G2
Assinippi, Mass. (02339) 249/E8
Assis, Brazil 132/D8
Assis, Brazil 135/A3
Assisi, Italy 34/D3
Assonet, Mass. (02702) 249/K5
Assumption, Ill. (62510) 222/E4
Assumption (par.), La. 238/H7
Assumption, Ohio (†43540) 284/B2
Assumption (isl.), Seychelles 118/H1
Assynt (dist.), Scotland 15/C2
Assynt, Loch (lake), Scotland 15/D2
Assyria, Mich. (†49021) 250/D6
Astara, U.S.S.R. 52/G7
Astatula, Fla. (32705) 212/E3
Asten, Netherlands 27/H6
Asterabad (Gorgan), Iran 59/F2
Asterabad (Gorgan), Iran 66/J2
Asti, Calif. (95413) 204/C5
Asti (prov.), Italy 34/B2
Asti, Italy 34/B2
Astillero, Peru 128/H9
Astipálaia, Greece 45/H7
Astipálaia (isl.), Greece 45/H7
Astle, New Bruns. 170/D2
Aston (bay), N.W. Terrs. 187/J2
Aston-Jonction, Québec 172/E3
Astor, Fla. (32002) 212/E2
Astorga, Spain 33/C1
Astoria, Ill. (61501) 222/C3
Astoria, Oreg. 188/B1
Astoria, Oreg. (97103) 291/D1
Astoria, S. Dak. (57213) 298/S4
Astorville, Ontario 177/E1
Astove (isl.), Seychelles 102/G6
Astove (isl.), Seychelles 118/H2
Astra, Argentina 143/C6
Astrakhan', U.S.S.R. 7/J4
Astrakhan', U.S.S.R. 52/G5
Astrakhan', U.S.S.R. 48/E5
Astray (lake), Newf. 166/A3
Astudillo, Spain 33/D1
Asturias (reg.), Spain 33/C1
Asunción, Bolivia 136/B2
Asuncion (isl.), No. Marianas 87/E4
Asunción, Paraguay 144/A4
Asunción (cap.), Paraguay 2/F7
Asunción (dept.), Paraguay 144/A4
Asunción (cap.), Paraguay 120/D5
Asuncion (passage), Philippines 82/D5
Asunción Mita, Guatemala 154/C3
Asunción Nochixtlán, Mexico 150/L8
Asunta, Bolivia 136/B5
Aswad, Ras al (cape), Saudi Arabia 59/C5
Aswân, Egypt 111/F3
Aswân, Egypt 59/B5
Aswân, Egypt 102/F2
Aswân (dam), Egypt 59/B5
Aswân (dam), Egypt 111/F3
Aswân High (dam), Egypt 102/F2
Aswân High (dam), Egypt 111/F3
Asyût, Egypt 111/J4
Asyût, Egypt 102/F2
Asyût, Egypt 59/B4
Aszód, Hungary 41/E3
Atabapo (riv.), Colombia 126/G6
Atabapo (riv.), Venezuela 124/E6
Atacama, Puna de (reg.), Argentina 143/C2
Atacama (reg.), Chile 138/B6
Atacama (des.), Chile 120/C5
Atacama (des.), Chile 138/B4
Atacama, Salar de (salt dep.), Chile 138/C4
Atafu (atoll), Tokelau Is. 87/J6
Atahona, Uruguay 145/B4
Atakora (mts.), Benin 106/E6
Atakpamé, Togo 106/E7
Atalándi, Greece 45/F6
Atalaya, Peru 128/E8
Atalissa, Iowa (52720) 229/L5
Atambua, Indonesia 85/G7
Atami, Japan 81/J6
Atapirire, Venezuela 124/F3
Atar, Mauritania 106/B4
Atar, Mauritania 102/A2
Ataran (riv.), Burma 72/C4
Atascadero, Calif. (93422) 204/E8
Atascosa (co.), Texas 303/F9
Atascosa, Texas (78002) 303/J11
Atbara (riv.), Ethiopia 111/G4
Atbara, Sudan 111/F4
Atbara, Sudan 59/B6
Atbara, Sudan 102/F3
Atbara (riv.), Sudan 59/C6
Atbara (riv.), Sudan 111/G4
Atbasar, U.S.S.R. 48/G4
Atchafalaya (bay), La. 238/H8
Atchafalaya (riv.), La. 238/G6
Atchison, Kans. 188/G3

334 Baliangao

Baliangao, Philippines 82/D6
Balicuatro (isls.), Philippines 82/E4
Balige, Indonesia 85/B5
Balıkesir (prov.), Turkey 63/B3
Balıkesir, Turkey 63/B3
Balıkesir, Turkey 59/A2
Balikpapan, Indonesia 54/N10
Balikpapan, Indonesia 85/F6
Balık-Uzun (lake), Turkey 63/G2
Balimbing (Bato-Bato), Philippines 82/C8
Baling, Malaysia 72/D6
Balingasag, Philippines 82/E6
Balingen, W. Germany 22/C4
Balintang (chan.), Philippines 82/A2
Balintang (isls.), Philippines 82/A2
Baljennie, Sask. 181/C3
Balk, Netherlands 27/H3
Balkan (mts.) 7/G4
Balkan (mts.), Bulgaria 45/G4
Balkan, Ky. (40804) 237/O7
Balkány, Hungary 41/G3
Balkbrug, Netherlands 27/J3
Balkh, Afghanistan 68/B1
Balkh, Afghanistan 59/J2
Balkhash, U.S.S.R. 54/J5
Balkhash (lake), U.S.S.R. 2/N3
Balkhash (lake), U.S.S.R. 54/J5
Balkhash, U.S.S.R. 48/H5
Balkhash (lake), U.S.S.R. 48/H5
Balko, Okla. (73931) 288/E1
Ball (mt.), Conn. 210/C1
Ball (pond), Conn. 210/A3
Ball, La. (71405) 238/F4
Ball (bay), Norfolk I. 88/L6
Balla, Ireland 17/C4
Balladonia, W. Australia 92/D6
Ballaghaderreen, Ireland 17/E4
Ballaigues, Switzerland 39/B3
Ballantine, Mont. (59006) 262/J5
Ballantrae, Scotland 15/C5
Ballantyne (str.), N.W. Terrs. 187/G2
Ballarat, Australia 87/E9
Ballarat, Victoria 88/G7
Ballarat, Victoria 97/C5
Ballard (co.), Ky. 237/C6
Ballard, Mo. (†64730) 261/D6
Ballard (cape), Newf. 166/D2
Ballard (lake), W. Australia 88/B5
Ballard, W. Va. (24918) 312/E8
Ballardsville, Miss. (†38801) 256/H2
Ballardvale, Mass. (01810) 249/K2
Ballater, Scotland 10/E2
Ballater, Scotland 15/F3
Ball Club, Minn. (†56636) 255/E3
Ballenas (bay), Mexico 150/C3
Ballenero (chan.), Chile 138/E11
Ballengee, W. Va. (†24981) 312/E7
Ballens, Switzerland 39/B3
Ballenstedt, E. Germany 22/D3
Ballentine, S.C. (29002) 296/E3
Balleny (isls.), Ant. 2/S9
Balleny (isls.) 5/C9
Ballerup, Denmark 21/F6
Ballesteros, Philippines 82/C1
Balleza, Mexico 150/F3
Ball Ground, Georgia (30107) 217/D2
Ballground, Miss. (†39156) 256/C5
Ballia, India 68/E3
Ballidu, W. Australia 92/B5
Ballina, Mayo, Ireland 17/C3
Ballina, Tipperary, Ireland 17/E6
Ballina, Ireland 10/B3
Ballina, N.S. Wales 97/G1
Ballinagh, Ireland 17/G4
Ballinakill, Ireland 17/G6
Ballinamore, Ireland 17/F3
Ballinasloe, Ireland 10/B4
Ballinasloe, Ireland 17/E5
Ballincollig-Carrigrohane, Ireland 17/D8
Ballindine, Ireland 17/C4
Ballineen, Ireland 17/D8
Ballingarry, Limerick, Ireland 17/D7
Ballingarry, Tipperary, Ireland 17/F6
Ballinger, Texas (76821) 303/E6
Ballingry, Scotland 15/D1
Ballinlough, Ireland 17/D4
Ballinluig, Scotland 15/E4
Ballinrobe, Ireland 10/B4
Ballinrobe, Ireland 17/C4
Ballinskelligs (bay), Ireland 17/A8
Ballintober, Ireland 17/E4
Ballintra, Ireland 17/E2
Ballisodare, Ireland 17/E3
Ballivor, Ireland 17/H4
Balloch, Highland, Scotland 15/D3
Balloch, Strathclyde, Scotland 15/B1
Ballouville, Conn. (06233) 210/H1
Ballston, Oreg. (†97378) 291/D2
Ballston Spa, N.Y. (12020) 276/N5
Ballsville, Va. (†29139) 307/M6
Balltown, Iowa (†52073) 229/M3
Ballville, Ohio (†43420) 284/D3
Ballwin, Mo. (63011) 261/N3
Bally, India 68/F1
Bally, Pa. (19503) 294/L5
Ballybay, Ireland 17/G3
Ballybofey-Stranorlar, Ireland 17/F2
Ballybunio, Ireland 10/B4
Ballybunion, Ireland 17/B7
Ballycanew, Ireland 17/J6
Ballycarney, Ireland 17/J6
Ballycarry, N. Ireland 17/K2
Ballycastle, Ireland 17/C3
Ballycastle, N. Ireland 10/C3
Ballycastle, N. Ireland 17/J1
Ballyclare, N. Ireland 17/J2
Ballyconnell, Ireland 17/F3
Ballycotton, Ireland 17/F8
Ballycotton (bay), Ireland 17/F8
Ballydehob, Ireland 17/C8
Ballyduff, Ireland 17/B7
Ballygally, N. Ireland 17/K2
Ballygar, Ireland 17/E4
Ballygawley, N. Ireland 17/G3
Ballygeary, Ireland 17/J7
Ballygrant, Scotland 15/B5
Ballyhaise, Ireland 17/G3
Ballyhaunis, Ireland 17/D4
Ballyheige (bay), Ireland 17/B7
Ballyheigue, Ireland 17/B7
Ballyhoura (hills), Ireland 17/E7
Ballyjamesduff, Ireland 17/G4
Ballykelly, N. Ireland 17/G1
Ballylanders, Ireland 17/E7
Ballylongford, Ireland 17/B6
Ballymahon, Ireland 17/F4
Ballymakeery, Ireland 17/C8
Ballymena (dist.), N. Ireland 17/J2
Ballymena, N. Ireland 17/J2
Ballymena, N. Ireland 10/C3
Ballymoney (dist.), N. Ireland 17/J1
Ballymoney, N. Ireland 10/C3
Ballymoney, N. Ireland 17/J1
Ballymore, Ireland 17/F5
Ballymore Eustace, Ireland 17/J5
Ballymote, Ireland 17/D3
Ballymote, Ireland 10/B3
Ballynahinch, N. Ireland 17/J3
Ballynakill (harb.), Ireland 17/A4
Ballyporeen, Ireland 17/E7
Ballyragget, Ireland 17/G6
Ballyroan, Ireland 17/G6
Ballysadare (bay), Ireland 17/D3
Ballyshannon, Ireland 10/B3
Ballyshannon, Ireland 17/E3
Ballyteige (bay), Ireland 17/H7
Ballytore, Ireland 17/H5
Ballywalter, N. Ireland 17/K2
Balmaceda, Chile 138/E6
Balmat, N.Y. (13609) 276/K2
Balmazújváros, Hungary 41/F3
Balmertown, Ontario 175/B2
Balmhorn (mt.), Switzerland 39/E4
Balmoral, Manitoba 179/E4
Balmoral, New Bruns. 170/D1
Balmoral, Queensland 88/K2
Balmoral, Queensland 95/E2
Balmoral, Victoria 97/A5
Balmoral Castle, Scotland 10/
Balmoral Castle, Scotland 15/E3
Balmorhea, Texas (79718) 303/D11
Balmville, N.Y. (†12550) 276/M7
Balnearia, Argentina 143/D3
Balneario El Tesoro, Uruguay 145/E5
Balneario La Barra, Uruguay 145/E5
Balneario Solis, Uruguay 145/D5
Balombo, Angola 115/B6
Balonne (riv.), Queensland 88/H5
Balonne (riv.), Queensland 95/D6
Balotra, India 68/C3
Baloy (mt.), Philippines 82/D5
Balpunga, N.S. Wales 97/A3
Balrampur, India 68/E3
Balranald, N.S. Wales 88/G6
Balranald, N.S. Wales 97/B4
Balş, Romania 45/G3
Balsam, N.C. (28707) 281/C4
Balsam (lake), Ontario 177/F3
Balsam Creek, Ontario 177/E1
Balsam Lake, Wis. (54810) 317/B5
Balsapuerto, Peru 128/D5
Balsas, Brazil 120/E3
Balsas, Brazil 132/E4
Balsas (riv.), Brazil 132/E5
Balsas (riv.), Mexico 146/H8
Balsas (riv.), Mexico 150/J7
Bålsta, Sweden 18/G1
Balsthal, Switzerland 39/E2
Balta, N. Dak. (58313) 282/K3
Baltanás, Spain 33/D2
Baltasar Brum, Uruguay 145/B1
Baltasound, Scotland 15/G2
Baltic (sea) 2/K3
Baltic (sea) 7/F3
Baltic, Conn. (06330) 210/G2
Baltic (sea), Denmark 21/E9
Baltic (sea), E. Germany 22/E1
Baltic (sea), Finland 18/K9
Baltic, Mich. (†49905) 250/G1
Baltic, Ohio (43804) 284/G5
Baltic (sea), Poland 47/B1
Baltic, S. Dak. (57003) 298/R6
Baltic (sea), Sweden 18/K9
Baltic (sea), U.S.S.R. 52/B3
Baltic (sea), U.S.S.R. 48/B4
Baltimore, Ireland 10/B5
Baltimore, Ireland 17/C9
Baltimore (city county), Md. 245/M3
Baltimore (co.), Md. 245/M3
Baltimore, Md. (*21201) 245/M3
Baltimore, Md. 188/L3
Baltimore, Md. 146/L6
Baltimore, Ohio (43105) 284/E6
Baltimore, Ontario 177/F3
Baltinglass, Ireland 17/H6
Baltistan (reg.), Pakistan 68/D1
Baltit, Pakistan 68/C1
Baltiysk, U.S.S.R. 52/A4
Baltra (isl.), Ecuador 128/B9
Baltray, Ireland 17/J4
Baltrum (isl.), W. Germany 22/B2
Balty, Va. (†22546) 307/O5
Baluchistan (reg.), Iran 66/M7
Baluchistan (prov.), Pakistan 68/B3
Baluchistan (reg.), Pakistan 59/J4
Balurghat, India 68/F3
Balvi, U.S.S.R. 53/D2
Balwina Aboriginal Reserve, W. Australia 88/D4
Balwina Aboriginal Res., W. Australia 92/E3
Balya, Turkey 63/B3
Balykshi, U.S.S.R. 48/F5
Balzac, Alberta 182/C4
Balzar, Ecuador 128/C3
Bam, Iran 54/G7
Bam, Iran 66/L6
Bam, Iran 59/G4
Bam, U.S.S.R. 48/N4
Bama, Nigeria 106/G6
Bamako (cap.), Mali 2/J5
Bamako (cap.), Mali 106/C6
Bamako (cap.), Mali 102/B3
Bamba, Mali 106/D5
Bambamarca, Peru 128/C6
Bamban, Philippines 82/C3
Bambari, Cent. Afr. Rep. 102/E4
Bambari, Cent. Afr. Rep. 115/D2
Bamberg (co.), S.C. 296/E5
Bamberg, S.C. (29003) 296/E5
Bamberg, W. Germany 22/D4
Bambesa, Zaire 115/E3
Bambili, Zaire 115/E3
Bambio, Cent. Afr. Rep. 115/C3
Bamble, Norway 18/F7
Bamboo, Jamaica 158/J6
Bamboo Creek, W. Australia 92/C3
Bambuí, Brazil 132/E8
Bambuí, Brazil 135/C2
Bamenda, Cameroon 115/B2
Bamfield, Br. Col. 184/E6
Bamian, Afghanistan 59/J3
Bamian, Afghanistan 68/B2
Bamingui, Cent. Afr. Rep. 115/D2
Bamingui (riv.), Cent. Afr. Rep. 115/C2
Bamoa, Mexico 150/E4
Bampur, Iran 59/H4
Bampur, Iran 66/M7
Bampur (riv.), Iran 66/M7
Bamyili-Beswick, North. Terr. 93/C3
Banaba (isl.), Kiribati 87/G6
Bañado de Medina, Uruguay 145/E3
Bañado de Rocha, Uruguay 145/C2
Banagher, Ireland 17/F5
Banagüises, Cuba 158/D1
Banahao (mt.), Philippines 82/C3
Banalia, Zaire 115/E3
Banam, Cambodia 72/E5
Banamba, Mali 106/C6
Banamba, Mali 102/B3
Banamichi, Mexico 150/D2
Banana (riv.), Fla. 212/F3
Banana, Zaire 115/B5
Bananal (isl.), Brazil 120/D4
Bananal (isl.), Brazil 132/D5
Bananier, Guadeloupe 161/A7
Banao, Cuba 158/F2
Ban Aranyaprathet, Thailand 72/D4
Bânâs, Ras (cape), Egypt 111/G3
Bânâs, Ras (cape), Egypt 59/C5
Banas (riv.), India 68/D3
Banaz, Turkey 63/C3
Banaz (riv.), Turkey 63/C3
Banbar, China 77/E5
Ban Boun Tai, Laos 72/D2
Banbridge, N. Ireland 17/J3
Banbury, England 10/F4
Banbury, England 13/F5
Bancalan (isl.), Philippines 82/A6
Bancannia (lake), N.S. Wales 97/A2
Banchory, Scotland 10/E2
Banchory, Scotland 15/F3
Bancoran (isl.), Philippines 82/B7
Bancroft, Idaho (83217) 220/G7
Bancroft, Iowa (50517) 229/E2
Bancroft, Kansas (†66428) 232/G2
Bancroft, Ky. (†40222) 237/K1
Bancroft, La. (†70653) 238/C5
Bancroft, Maine (†04497) 243/H4
Bancroft, Maine (†04497) 243/H4
Bancroft, Mich. (48414) 250/E6
Bancroft, Nebr. (68004) 264/H2
Bancroft, Ontario 177/G2
Bancroft, Oreg. (†97458) 291/D5
Bancroft, S. Dak. (57316) 298/O4
Bancroft, W. Va. (25011) 312/C5
Bancroft, Wis. (54921) 317/G7
Bancroft (Chililabombwe), Zambia 115/E6
Banda, Gabon 115/B4
Banda, India 68/D3
Banda (sea), Indonesia 54/O10
Banda (isls.), Indonesia 85/H6
Banda (sea), Indonesia 85/H7
Banda Aceh, Indonesia 85/A4
Banda Aceh, Indonesia 54/L9
Bandai (mt.), Japan 81/K5
Bandai-Asahi National Park, Japan 81/J4
Bandama (riv.), Ivory Coast 106/C7
Bandana, Ky. (42022) 237/D6
Bandanaira, Indonesia 85/H6
Bandar (Machilipatnam), India 68/E5
Bandar 'Abbas, Iran 66/J7
Bandar 'Abbas, Iran 54/G7
Bandar 'Abbas, Iran 59/G4
Bandar-e Deylam, Iran 66/G5
Bandar-e Lengeh, Iran 66/J7
Bandar-e Lengeh, Iran 59/F4
Bandar-e Ma'shur, Iran 66/F5
Bandar-e Pahlavi (Enzeli), Iran 59/E2
Bandar-e Pahlavi (Enzeli), Iran 66/F2
Bandar-e Rig, Iran 59/F4
Bandar-e Rig, Iran 66/G6
Bandar-e Torkaman, Iran 66/H2
Bandar-e Torkaman, Iran 59/F2
Bandar Khomeini, Iran 66/F5
Bandar Khomeini, Iran 59/E3
Bandar Maharani (Muar), Malaysia 72/D7
Bandar Penggaram (Batu Pahat), Malaysia 72/D7
Bandar Seri Begawan, Brunei 85/E4
Bandar Seri Begawan (cap.), Brunei 54/N9
Bandar Shahpur, Iran 66/F5
Bandawe, Malawi 115/F6
Bande, Spain 33/B1
Bandeira (mt.), Brazil 120/E5
Bandeira, Pico da (mt.), Brazil 132/F8
Bandeira (mt.), Brazil 135/E2
Bandelier Nat'l Mon., N. Mex. 274/C3
Bandera, Argentina 143/D2
Bandera (co.), Texas 303/E8
Bandera, Texas (78003) 303/F8
Banderas (bay), Mexico 150/G6
Banderilla, Mexico 150/P1
Bandholm, Denmark 21/E8
Bandiagara, Mali 106/D6
Bandırma, Turkey 59/A1
Bandırma, Turkey 63/B2
Bandon, Ireland 10/B5
Bandon, Ireland 17/D8
Bandon (riv.), Ireland 17/D8
Bandon, Oreg. (97411) 291/C4
Bandra, India 68/B7
Bandundu (prov.), Zaire 115/C4
Bandundu, Zaire 102/D5
Bandundu, Zaire 115/C4
Bandung, Indonesia 54/M10
Bandung, Indonesia 85/H2
Bandy, Va. (24602) 307/E6
Bandya, W. Australia 92/C4
Banes, Cuba 156/C2
Banes, Cuba 158/J3
Banff, Alberta 182/C4
Banff, Alta. 162/E5
Banff, Scotland 15/F3
Banff, Scotland 10/E2
Banff (trad. co.), Scotland 15/A5
Banff Nat'l Park, Alberta 182/B4
Banff Nat'l Park, Alta. 162/E5
Banfora, Upper Volta 106/D6
Bangalore, India 2/N5
Bangalore, India 54/J8
Bangalore, India 68/D6
Bangalow, N.S. Wales 97/G1
Bangar, Philippines 82/C2
Bangassou, Centr. Afr. Rep. 102/E4
Bangassou, Cent. Afr. Rep. 115/D3
Banggai, Indonesia 85/G6
Banggai (arch.), Indonesia 85/G6
Banggi (isl.), Malaysia 85/F4
Bangil, Indonesia 85/K2
Bangka (isl.), Indonesia 54/M10
Bangka (isl.), Indonesia 85/D6
Bangka (str.), Indonesia 85/C6
Bangkalan, Indonesia 85/K2
Bangkok (cap.), Thailand 2/P5
Bangkok (cap.), Thailand 72/D4
Bangkok (cap.), Thailand 54/M8
Bangladesh 2/P4
Bangladesh 54/L7
BANGLADESH 68/G4
Bang Lamung, Thailand 72/D4
Bangong Co (lake), China 77/A5
Bangor, Calif. (95914) 204/D4
Bangor, Maine 146/M5
Bangor, Maine (04401) 243/F6
Bangor, Maine 188/N2
Bangor, Mich. (49013) 250/C6
Bangor, N.Y. (12966) 276/M1
Bangor, N. Ireland 17/K2
Bangor, Pa. (18013) 294/M4
Bangor, Sask. 181/J5
Bangor, Wales 13/C4
Bangor, Wales 10/D4
Bangor, Wis. (54614) 317/E8
Bangs, Texas (76823) 303/E6
Bang Saphan, Thailand 72/C5
Bangued, Philippines 85/G2
Bangued, Philippines 82/C2
Banguezane (mt.), Niger 106/F5
Bangui (cap.), Cent. Afr. Rep. 102/D4
Bangui (cap.), Centr. Afr. Rep. 2/K5
Bangui (cap.), Cent. Afr. Rep. 115/C3
Bangui, Philippines 85/G2
Bangui, Philippines 82/C1
Bangui (bay), Philippines 82/C1
Bangweulu (lake), Zambia 115/F6
Ban Houayxay, Laos 72/D2
Baní, Dom. Rep. 158/E6
Baní, Dom. Rep. 156/D3
Bani (riv.), Mali 106/C6
Bani, Jebel (mts.), Morocco 106/C3
Bani, Philippines 82/B2
Bania, Cent. Afr. Rep. 115/C3
Baniara, Papua N.G. 85/C7
Bánica, Dom. Rep. 156/D3
Bánica, Dom. Rep. 158/D5
Banida, Idaho (†83263) 220/G7
Banister (riv.), Va. 307/K7
Bani Suheila, Gaza Strip 65/A5
Baniyas, Syria 63/F5
Banja Luka, Yugoslavia 7/F4
Banja Luka, Yugoslavia 45/C3
Banjarmasin, Indonesia 54/N10
Banjarmasin, Indonesia 85/E6
Banjul (cap.), Gambia 102/A3
Banjul (cap.), Gambia 106/A6
Banka Banka, North. Terr. 93/C5
Ban Kantang, Thailand 72/C6
Ban Kapong, Thailand 72/C5
Bankass, Mali 106/D6
Bankend, Sask. 181/H4
Ban Kèngkok, Laos 72/E3
Bankfoot, Scotland 15/E4
Bankhead (lake), Ala. 195/D4
Bankhead, Scotland 15/F3
Ban Khlong Yai, Thailand 72/D5
Ban Khon, Laos 72/E4
Banks, Ala. (36005) 195/G7
Banks (pt.), Alaska 196/H3
Banks, Ark. (71631) 202/F6
Banks (isl.), Br. Col. 184/B3
Banks (isl.), Canada 2/C2
Banks (isl), Canada 4/B16
Banks (bay), Ecuador 128/B9
Banks (co.), Georgia 217/E2
Banks (lake), Georgia 217/F9
Banks, Idaho (83602) 220/B5
Banks, Miss. (†38664) 256/D1
Banks (cape), N. S. Wales 88/L4
Banks (cape), N.S. Wales 97/K4
Banks (pen.), N. Zealand 100/D5
Banks (isl.), N.W.T. 146/F2
Banks (isl.), N.W.T. 162/D1
Banks (isl.), N.W. Terrs. 187/F2
Banks, Oreg. (97106) 291/A1
Banks (isl.), Queensland 88/G2
Banks (isl.), Queensland 95/B1
Banks (str.), Tasmania 88/H8
Banks (str.), Tasmania 99/D2
Banks (isls.), Vanuatu 87/G7
Banks (lake), Wash. 310/F3
Bankston, Ala. (35542) 195/C3
Bankston, Iowa (†52045) 229/L3
Bankstown, N. S. Wales 88/K4
Bankstown, N.S. Wales 97/J3
Ban Kui Nua, Thailand 72/D4
Bankura, India 68/F4
Ban Lahanam, Laos 72/E3
Ban Me Thuot, Vietnam 72/F4
Bann (riv.), Ireland 17/J6
Bann (riv.), N. Ireland 17/H2
Bannack, Mont. (†59725) 262/C5
Banner, Ill. (†61520) 222/D3
Banner, Ky. (41603) 237/R5
Banner, Miss. (38913) 256/F2
Banner, Mo. (†63623) 261/L7
Banner (co.), Nebr. 264/A3
Banner, Va. (24230) 307/D7
Banner, Wyo. (82832) 319/F1
Banner Elk, N.C. (28604) 281/F2
Banner Hill, Tenn. (†37650) 237/R8
Banner Springs, Tenn. (†38556) 237/M8
Bannertown, N.C. (†27030) 281/H1
Ban Ngon, Thailand 72/D3
Banning, Calif. (92220) 204/J10
Banning, Georgia (†30185) 217/C3
Bannister, Mich. (48807) 250/E5
Bannock (co.), Idaho 220/F7
Bannock (creek), Idaho 220/F7
Bannock (peak), Idaho 220/F7
Bannock (range), Idaho 220/F7
Bannockburn, Ill. (†60015) 222/B5
Bannockburn, Ontario 177/G3
Bannockburn, Scotland 15/C1
Bannockburn, Scotland 10/B1
Bannow, Ireland 17/H7
Bannu, Pakistan 59/K3
Bannu, Pakistan 68/C2
Bañolas, Spain 33/H1
Bánovce nad Bebravou, Czech. 41/E2
Ban Pak Phanang, Thailand 72/D5
Banphot Phisai, Thailand 72/C3
Ban Pua, Thailand 72/D3
Banquo, Ind. (†46940) 227/F3
Ban Sattahip, Thailand 72/D4
Bansberia, India 68/F1
Bansha, Ireland 17/E7
Banská Bystrica, Czech. 41/E2
Banská Štiavnica, Czech. 41/E2
Bansko, Bulgaria 45/F5
Banstead, England 13/H8
Banstead, England 10/B6
Bansud, Philippines 82/C4
Banswara, India 68/C4
Bantam, Conn. (06750) 210/B2
Bantam (lake), Conn. 210/C2
Bantam (riv.), Conn. 210/B2
Bantayan, Philippines 82/D5
Bantayan (isl.), Philippines 82/D5
Ban Tha Uthen, Thailand 72/D3
Banton, Philippines 82/D4
Banton (isl.), Philippines 82/D4
Bantry, Ireland 10/B5
Bantry, Ireland 17/C8
Bantry (bay), Ireland 10/A5
Bantry (bay), Ireland 17/B8
Bantry, N. Dak. (58713) 282/J3
Bantul, Indonesia 85/J2
Bañuelo (mt.), Spain 33/D3
Banyak (isls.), Indonesia 85/B5
Banyo, Cameroon 115/B2
Banyo, Queensland 88/K2
Banyumas, Indonesia 85/J2
Banyuwangi, Indonesia 85/L2
Banzare Coast (reg.) 5/C7
Baode, China 77/H4
Baoding (Paoting), China 77/J4
Bao Ha, Vietnam 72/D2
Baoji (Paoki), China 77/G5
Baoji, China 54/M6
Bao Lac, Vietnam 72/E2
Baoshan, China 77/E7
Baoting, China 77/G8
Baotou (Paotow), China 77/G3
Baotou, China 54/M5
Baoulé (riv.), Ivory Coast 106/C6
Baoulé (dry riv.), Mali 106/C6
Baoulé (riv.), Mali 106/C6
Bapaume, Sask. 181/D2
Bapchule, Ariz. (85221) 198/D5
Bapsfontein, S. Africa 118/J6
Baptist, La. (†70401) 238/M1
Baptiste (lake), Ontario 177/G2
Baptistown, N.J. (08803) 273/D2
Baqên, China 77/D5
Ba'quba, Iraq 59/D3
Ba'quba, Iraq 66/D4
Baquedano, Chile 138/A4
Baquerizo Moreno, Ecuador 128/C9
Baqura, Jordan 65/D2
Bar, Yugoslavia 45/D4
Bara, Sudan 111/F5
Bara, Sudan 59/B7
Barabai, Indonesia 85/F6
Barabinsk, U.S.S.R. 48/H4
Baraboo, Wis. (53913) 317/G9
Baracaldo, Spain 33/E1
Barachois, New Bruns. 170/F2
Barachois (pt.), Nova Scotia 168/G4
Barachois, Québec 172/D1
Barachois Pond Prov. Park, Newf. 166/C4
Baracoa, Cuba 158/K4
Baracoa, Cuba 156/C2
Barada, Nebr. (†68457) 264/J4
Baradères, Haiti 158/B6
Baradères (bay), Haiti 158/B6
Baradero, Argentina 143/G6
Baradine, N.S. Wales 97/E2
Baradine (creek), N.S. Wales 97/E2
Baraga (co.), Mich. 250/A2
Baraga, Mich. (49908) 250/G1
Baragoi, Kenya 115/G3
Baraguá, Cuba 158/F2
Baragua, Venezuela 124/D2
Barahona (prov.), Dom. Rep. 158/D6
Barahona, Dom. Rep. 158/D6
Barahona, Dom. Rep. 156/D3
Barajas, Spain 33/F4
Barak, Turkey 63/G4
Baraka (riv.), Ethiopia 111/G4
Baraka (riv.), Sudan 111/G4
Baraka (riv.), Sudan 59/C6
Baraka, Zaire 115/E4
Baraki Barak, Afghanistan 59/J3
Baraki Barak, Afghanistan 68/B2
Baralzon (lake), Manitoba 179/J1
Barama (riv.), Guyana 131/A2
Baramanni, Guyana 131/B2
Baramati, India 68/C5
Baramita, Guyana 131/A2
Baramula, India 68/C2
Baranagar, India 68/F1
Barankwa, Sudan 59/B7
Baranoa, Colombia 126/C2
Baranof (isl.), Alaska 196/M1
Baranovichi, U.S.S.R. 7/G3
Baranovichi, U.S.S.R. 48/C4
Baranovichi, U.S.S.R. 52/C4
Baranya (co.), Hungary 41/E4
Barão de Cocais, Brazil 135/E1
Baras, Philippines 82/E4
Barasat, India 68/F1
Baratang (isl.), India 68/G6
Barataria, La. (70036) 238/K7
Barataria (bay), La. 238/L8
Barataria (passage), La. 238/L8
Barawa (Brava), Somalia 115/H3
Baraya, Colombia 126/C6
Barbacena, Brazil 120/E5
Barbacena, Brazil 135/E2
Barbacena, Brazil 132/F8
Barbacoas, Colombia 126/A7
Barbacoas, Venezuela 124/E3
Barbados 2/G5
Barbados 146/N8
BARBADOS 156/G4
BARBADOS 161/B8
Barbar (isls.), Indonesia 85/J7
Barbas (cape), Western Sahara 106/A4
Barbastro, Spain 33/F1
Barbate (riv.), Spain 33/D4
Barbeau, Mich. (49710) 250/E2
Barbeau (peak), N.W. Terrs. 187/L1
Barber, Ark. (72922) 202/B3
Barber (co.), Kansas 232/D4
Barber, Mont. (†59074) 262/G4
Barber, N.C. (27008) 281/H3
Barbers (pt.), Hawaii 218/E2
Barbers Point, Hawaii (†96706) 218/E2
Barbers Point Nav. Air Sta., Hawaii 218/E2
Barberton, Ohio (4r203) 284/G4
Barberton, S. Africa 118/E5
Barberville, Fla. (32005) 212/E2
Barbezieux-St-Hilaire, France 28/C5
Barbil, India 68/F4
Barbizon, France 28/E3
Barbosa, Colombia 126/D5
Barbour (co.), Ala. 195/H7
Barbour (co.), W. Va. 312/F4
Barbourmeade, Ky. (†40201) 237/K1
Barboursville, Va. (22923) 307/M4
Barboursville, W. Va. (25504) 312/B6
Barbourville, Ky. (40906) 237/O7
Barbuda (isl.) 146/M8
Barbuda (isl.), Ant. & Bar. 156/G3
Barcaldine, Queensland 88/G4
Barcaldine, Queensland 95/C4
Barcaldine, Scotland 15/C4
Barcarrota, Spain 33/C3
Barce (El Marj), Libya 111/D1
Barcellona Pozzo di Gotto, Italy 34/E5
Barcelona (prov.), Spain 33/G2
Barcelona, Spain 7/E4
Barcelona, Spain 33/H2
Barcelona, Venezuela 124/F2
Barcelona, Venezuela 120/C2
Barceloneta, P. Rico 161/C1
Barcelonnette, France 28/G5
Barcelos, Brazil 120/C3
Barcelos, Brazil 132/H9
Barcelos, Portugal 33/B2
Barclay, Md. (21607) 245/P4
Barco, N.C. (27917) 281/T2
Barcoo (creek), Queensland 88/G4
Barcoo (creek), Queensland 95/B5
Barcoo (creek), S. Australia 88/F5
Barcoo (creek), S. Australia 94/F3
Barcos (pt.), Cuba 158/B2
Barcs, Hungary 41/D4
Barczewo, Poland 47/E2
Bard, Calif. (92222) 204/L11
Bard, N. Mex. (88411) 274/F3
Bardai, Chad 111/C3
Bardai, Chad 102/D2
Bardejov, Czech. 41/F2
Bardera, Somalia 115/H3
Bardera, Somalia 102/G4
Bardney, England 13/G4
Bardolph, Ill. (61416) 222/C3
Bardon (lake), Wis. 317/C3
Bardonia, N.Y. (†10954) 276/K8
Bardsey (isl.), Wales 13/C5
Bardstown, Ky. (40004) 237/L5
Barduelv (riv.), Norway 18/L2
Bardwell, Ky. (42023) 237/D7
Bardwell, Texas (75101) 303/H5
Bareilly, India 54/K7
Bareilly, India 68/D3
Barellan, N.S. Wales 97/D4
Bärenhorn (mt.), Switzerland 39/H3
Barents (sea) 2/L2
Barents (sea) 7/J1
Barents (sea) 4/B8
Barents (sea), U.S.S.R. 48/D2
Barents (sea), U.S.S.R. 52/E1
Barentsburg, Norway 18/C2
Barentsøya (isl.), Norway 18/D2
Båretswil, Switzerland 39/G2
Barfield, Ark. (†72315) 202/L2
Barfleur, France 28/C3
Barfleur (pt.), France 28/C3
Barga, China 77/B5
Bargal, Somalia 115/K1
Bargamin (creek), Idaho 220/C4
Bargersville, Ind. (46106) 227/E5
Bargo, N.S. Wales 97/F4
Bargrax (Bohu), China 77/C3

Bering 337

BELGIUM 27
Belgium, Ill. (†61883) 222/F3
Belgium, Wis. (53004) 317/L8
Belgorod, U.S.S.R. 7/H3
Belgorod, U.S.S.R. 52/E4
Belgorod, U.S.S.R. 48/D4
Belgorod-Dnestrovskiy, U.S.S.R. 52/D5
Belgrade, Maine (04917) 243/D7
Belgrade○, Maine (04917) 243/D7
Belgrade, Minn. (56312) 255/C5
Belgrade, Mo. (63622) 261/L7
Belgrade, Mont. (59714) 262/E5
Belgrade, Nebr. (68623) 264/G3
Belgrade (cap.), Yugoslavia 7/G4
Belgrade (cap.), Yugoslavia 2/K3
Belgrade (cap.), Yugoslavia 45/E3
Belgrade Lakes, Maine (04918) 243/D6
Belgrave, Ontario 177/C4
Belgrave Heights, Victoria 97/J5
Belgrave South, Victoria 97/K5
Belgreen, Ala. (†35653) 195/C2
Belhaven, N.C. (27810) 281/R3
Belic, Cuba 158/G4
Belice (riv.), Italy 34/D6
Beli Manastir, Yugoslavia 45/D3
Belington, W. Va. (26250) 312/F4
Belitung (Billiton) (isl.), Indonesia 85/D6
Belize 2/E5
Belize 146/K8
BELIZE 154/C2
Belize (riv.), Belize 154/C2
Belize City, Belize 154/C2
Bélizon, Fr. Guiana 131/E3
Belk, Ala. (35545) 195/C3
Belknap, Ill. (†62995) 222/E6
Belknap, Iowa (†52537) 229/J7
Belknap, Mont. (†59874) 262/A3
Belknap (co.), N.H. 268/D4
Belknap (mt.), N.H. 268/E5
Belknap (peak), Utah 304/B5
Belkofski, Alaska (†99612) 196/F3
Bell, Calif. (90201) 204/C11
Bell, Fla. (32619) 212/D2
Bell (co.), Ky. 237/O7
Bell (isl.), Newf. 166/D2
Bell (isl.), Newf. 166/C3
Bell (isl.), Newf. 162/L5
Bell (pen.), N.W. Terrs. 187/K3
Bell (riv.), Que. 162/J6
Bell (riv.), Québec 174/B3
Bell (co.), Texas 303/G6
Bella Bella, Br. Col. 184/D4
Bellac, France 28/D4
Bellaco, Uruguay 145/B3
Bella Coola, Br. Col. 184/D4
Bella Coola (riv.), Br. Col. 184/D4
Belladère, Haiti 158/C6
Bella Flor, Bolivia 136/A2
Bellaghy, N. Ireland 17/H2
Bellagio, Italy 34/B2
Bellaire, Kansas (66934) 232/D2
Bellaire, Mich. (49615) 250/D4
Bellaire, Ohio (43906) 284/J5
Bellaire, Texas (77401) 303/J2
Bellamy, Ala. (36901) 195/B6
Bellarmin, Québec 172/G4
Bellarthur, N.C. (27811) 281/O3
Bellary, India 68/D5
Bellata, N.S. Wales 97/E1
Bella Unión, Uruguay 145/B1
Bella Villa, Mo. (†63101) 261/R4
Bella Vista, Corrientes, Argentina 143/E2
Bella Vista, Tucumán, Argentina 143/D2
Bella Vista, Ark. (†72712) 202/B1
Bella Vista, Bolivia 136/E3
Bella Vista, Salar de (salt dep.), Chile 138/B3
Bella Vista, Paraguay 144/D3
Bella Vista, Paraguay 144/E5
Bellavista, Peru 128/C5
Bell Bay, Tasmania 99/C3
Bellbird-Cessnock, N.S. Wales 97/F3
Bellbrook, Ohio (45305) 284/C6
Bell Buckle, Tenn. (37020) 237/J9
Bellburns, Newf. 166/C3
Bell Center, Wis. (†54631) 317/E9
Bell City, La. (70630) 238/D6
Bell City, Mo. (63735) 261/N8
Belle (riv.), Mich. 250/G6
Belle, Mo. (65013) 261/J6
Belle, W. Va. (25015) 312/C6
Belleair, Fla. (33540) 212/B2
Belleair Beach, Fla. (†33540) 212/B2
Belleair Bluffs, Fla. (33540) 212/B3
Belleair Shores, Fla. (†33540) 212/B3
Belle-Anse, Haiti 158/C6
Belle Center, Ohio (43310) 284/C4
Belle Chasse, La. (70037) 238/O4
Bellechasse (co.), Québec 172/G3
Bellechester, Minn. (†55027) 255/F6
Belle Côte, Nova Scotia 168/G2
Belle D'Eau, La. (†71330) 238/F4
Belledune, New Bruns. 170/E1
Belleek, N. Ireland 17/E3
Bellefleur, New Bruns. 170/C1
Bellefond, New Bruns. 170/E1
Bellefont, Kansas (†67876) 232/C4
Bellefontaine, Martinique 161/C6
Bellefontaine, Miss. (39737) 256/F3
Bellefontaine, Mo. (†63017) 261/N2
Bellefontaine, Ohio (43311) 284/C5
Bellefontaine Neighbors, Mo. (†63137) 261/R2
Bellefonte, Ark. (†72601) 202/D1
Bellefonte, Del. (19809) 245/S1
Bellefonte, Pa. (16823) 294/G4
Belle Fourche (riv.) 188/F2
Belle Fourche, S. Dak. (57717) 298/B4
Belle Fourche (res.), S. Dak. 298/B4
Belle Fourche (riv.), S. Dak. 298/C4
Belle Fourche (riv.), Wyo. 319/H1
Bellegarde, Sask. 181/K6
Belle Glade, Fla. (33430) 212/F5
Belle Glade Camp, Fla. (†33430) 212/F5
Belle Haven, Va. (23306) 307/S5
Belle-Île (isl.), France 28/B4
Belle Isle (str.), Canada 146/N5
Belle Isle (str.), Canada 2/G3
Belle Isle, Fla. (†32801) 212/E3
Belleisle (bay), New Bruns. 170/E3
Belle Isle (isl.), Newf. 166/C3
Belle Isle (str.), Newf. 166/C3
Belle Isle (str.), Newf. 162/L5
Belleisle Creek, New Bruns. 170/E3
Belle-Marche, Nova Scotia 168/H2
Belle Mead, N.J. (08502) 273/D3
Bellemeade, Ky. (†40201) 237/K2
Belle Meade, Tenn. (37205) 237/H8
Belle Mina, Ala. (35615) 195/E1
Bellemont, Ariz. (86015) 198/D3
Belleoram, Newf. 166/C4
Belleplain, N.J. (†08270) 273/D5
Belleplaine, Barbados 161/B8
Belle Plaine, Iowa (52208) 229/J5
Belle Plaine, Kansas (67013) 232/E4
Belle Plaine, Minn. (56011) 255/E6
Belle Plaine, Sask. 181/F5
Belle Prairie City, Ill. (†62828) 222/E5
Belle Rive, Ill. (62810) 222/E5
Belle River, Minn. (†56319) 255/C5
Belle River, Ontario 177/B5
Belle Rose, La. (70341) 238/K3
Bellerose, N.Y. (11426) 276/P7
Belle Terre, N.Y. (†11777) 276/O9
Belleterre, Québec 174/B3
Belle Union, Ind. (†46121) 227/D5
Belle Valley, Ohio (43717) 284/G6
Belle Vernon, Pa. (15012) 294/C5
Belleview, Fla. (32620) 212/D2
Belleview, Manitoba 179/B5
Belleview, Mo. (63623) 261/L7
Belle View, Va. (22307) 307/T3
Belleville, Ark. (72824) 202/D3
Belleville, Fla. (†31636) 212/C1
Belleville, France 28/F4
Belleville, Ill. 188/J3
Belleville, Ill. (*62220) 222/B3
Belleville, Kansas (66935) 232/E2
Belleville, Mich. (48111) 250/F6
Belleville, N.J. (07109) 273/B2
Belleville, N.Y. (13611) 276/H3
Belleville, Ontario 177/G3
Belleville, Pa. (17004) 294/G4
Belleville, W. Va. (26133) 312/C4
Belleville, Wis. (53508) 317/G10
Bellevue, Alberta 182/C5
Bellevue, Idaho (83313) 220/D6
Bellevue, Iowa (52031) 229/M4
Bellevue, Ky. (41073) 237/S1
Bellevue, Md. (†21662) 245/O6
Bellevue, Mich. (49021) 250/E6
Bellevue, Nebr. (68005) 264/J3
Bellevue, Newf. 166/D2
Bellevue, Ohio (44811) 284/E3
Bellevue, Pa. (15202) 294/B6
Bellevue, Sask. 181/F3
Bellevue, Texas (76228) 303/F4
Bellevue, Wash. (*98004) 310/B2
Belley, France 28/F5
Bell Farm, Ky. (†42647) 237/M7
Bellflower, Calif. (90706) 204/C11
Bellflower, Ill. (61724) 222/E3
Bellflower, Mo. (63333) 261/K4
Bellfountain, Oreg. (†97456) 291/D3
Bell Gardens, Calif. (90201) 204/C11
Bellin, Que. 162/J3
Bellin, Québec 174/F1
Bellingen, N.S. Wales 97/G2
Bellingham, England 13/E2
Bellingham, Mass. (02019) 249/J4
Bellingham○, Mass. (02019) 249/J4
Bellingham, Minn. (56212) 255/B5
Bellingham, Wash. 188/B1
Bellingham, Wash. (98225) 310/C2
Bellingham, Wash. 310/80
Bellingshausen (sea), Ant. 2/E9
Bellingshausen (sea) 5/C14
Bellinzona, Switzerland 39/H4
Bell-Irving (riv.), Br. Col. 184/C2
Bellis, Alberta 182/D2
Belliveau Cove, Nova Scotia 168/B4
Bellmawr, N.J. (08031) 273/B3
Bellmead, Texas (76704) 303/H6
Bellmont, Ill. (62811) 222/F5
Bellmore, Ind. (47830) 227/C5
Bellmore, N.Y. (11710) 276/R7
Bello, Colombia 126/C4
Bello, Colombia 120/B2
Bellona (reefs), New Caled. 87/G8
Bellona (isl.), Solomon Is. 86/D3
Bellot (str.), N.W.T. 162/G1
Bellot (str.), N.W. Terrs. 187/J2
Bellows Falls, Vt. (05101) 268/C5
Belloy, Alberta 182/A2
Bellport, N.Y. (11713) 276/P9
Bell Rock, N.W. Terrs. 187/G3
Bell Rock (isl.), Scotland 15/F4
Bells, Tenn. (38006) 237/C9
Bells, Texas (75414) 303/H4
Bellsbank, Scotland 15/D5
Bellshill, Scotland 15/C2
Bellsite, Manitoba 179/B2
Bellsund, Norway 18/C2
Belluno (prov.), Italy 34/D1
Belluno, Italy 34/D1
Bellview, Ala. (†36452) 195/D7
Bellview, N. Mex. (88111) 274/F4
Bell Ville, Argentina 143/D3
Bell Ville, Argentina 120/C6
Bellville, Georgia (30414) 217/H6
Bellville, Ohio (44813) 284/E4
Bellville, S. Africa 118/F6
Bellville, Texas (77418) 303/H8
Bellvue, Colo. (80512) 208/J1
Bellwald, Switzerland 39/F4
Bellwood, Ala. (36313) 195/G8
Bellwood, Ill. (60104) 222/B5
Bellwood, La. (†71468) 238/D3
Bellwood, Nebr. (68624) 264/G3
Bellwood, Pa. (16617) 294/F4
Belly (riv.), Alberta 182/D5
Belmar, N.J. (07719) 273/E3
Bélmez, Spain 33/D3
Belmond, Iowa (50421) 229/F3
Belmont, Ala. (†35450) 195/C5
Belmont, Calif. (94002) 204/J3
Belmont, Georgia (†30501) 217/E2
Belmont, Kansas (67014) 232/D4
Belmont, Ky. (40105) 237/K5
Belmont, La. (71406) 238/C3
Belmont○, Maine (†04915) 243/E7
Belmont, Manitoba 179/C5
Belmont○, Mass. (02178) 249/C6
Belmont, Miss. (38827) 256/H1
Belmont, Mont. (†59046) 262/G4
Belmont○, N.H. (03220) 268/E5
Belmont, N.Y. (14813) 276/E6
Belmont, N. Zealand 100/B2
Belmont, N.C. (28012) 281/H4
Belmont, Nova Scotia 168/E3
Belmont (co.), Ohio 284/J5
Belmont, Ohio (43718) 284/J5
Belmont, Ontario 177/C5
Belmont, Wash. (99104) 310/H3
Belmont, W. Va. (26134) 312/D4
Belmont, Wis. (53510) 317/F10
Belmonte, Brazil 132/G6
Belmonte, Portugal 33/C2
Belmonte, Spain 33/E3
Belmopan (cap.), Belize 146/K8
Belmopan (cap.), Belize 154/C2
Belmore, N.S. Wales 97/J3
Belmore, Ohio (45815) 284/B3
Belmullet, Ireland 17/B3
Bel-Nor, Mo. (†63101) 261/P2
Belo, W. Va. (†25661) 312/B7
Beloeil, Belgium 27/D7
Beloeil, Québec 172/D4
Belogorsk, U.S.S.R. 54/O4
Belogorsk, U.S.S.R. 48/N4
Belogradchik, Bulgaria 45/F4
Belo Horizonte, Brazil 2/G6
Belo Horizonte, Brazil 120/E4
Belo Horizonte, Brazil 132/F7
Belo Horizonte, Brazil 135/D1
Beloit, Ala. (†36759) 195/D6
Beloit, Kansas (67420) 232/D2
Beloit, Ohio (44609) 284/J4
Beloit, Wis. 188/J2
Beloit, Wis. (53511) 317/H10
Belomorsk, U.S.S.R. 48/D3
Belomorsk, U.S.S.R. 52/D2
Belorado, Spain 33/E1
Belorechensk, U.S.S.R. 52/E6
Beloretsk, U.S.S.R. 52/J4
Beloretsk, U.S.S.R. 48/F4
Belo-Tsiribihina, Madagascar 118/G3
Belovo, U.S.S.R. 48/J4
Beloye (lake), U.S.S.R. 48/D3
Beloye (lake), U.S.S.R. 52/E2
Belozersk, U.S.S.R. 52/E3
Belp, Switzerland 39/D3
Belpre, Kansas (67519) 232/C4
Belpre, Ohio (45714) 284/G7
Bel-Ridge, Mo. (†63101) 261/P2
Belshaw, Ind. (†46356) 227/C2
Belt, Mont. (59412) 262/E3
Belted (range), Nev. 266/E5
Belterra, Brazil 132/C3
Belton, Ky. (42324) 237/H6
Belton, Mo. (64012) 261/C5
Belton, S.C. (29627) 296/C2
Belton, Texas (76513) 303/G7
Beltra (lake), Ireland 17/C4
Beltrami (co.), Minn. 255/C2
Beltrami, Minn. (56517) 255/B3
Beltsville, Md. (20705) 245/G3
Bel'tsy, U.S.S.R. 7/G4
Bel'tsy, U.S.S.R. 52/C5
Belturbet, Ireland 17/G3
Beluga (lake), Alaska 196/B1
Belumut, Gunong (mt.), Malaysia 72/D7
Belush'ya Guba, U.S.S.R. 4/B7
Belush'ya Guba, U.S.S.R. 52/H1
Belva, W. Va. (26656) 312/D6
Belvedere, Calif. (94920) 204/H2
Belvedere, Georgia (†30032) 217/L1
Belvidere, Ill. (61008) 222/E1
Belvidere, Kansas (67015) 232/C4
Belvidere, Nebr. (68315) 264/G4
Belvidere, N.J. (07823) 273/C2
Belvidere, N.C. (27919) 281/S2
Belvidere, S. Dak. (57521) 298/G6
Belvidere, Tenn. (37306) 237/J10
Belvidere○, Vt. (05442) 268/B2
Belvidere (mt.), Vt. 268/B2
Belvidere Center, Vt. (05442) 268/B2
Belvidere Junction, Vt. (†05492) 268/B2
Belview, Minn. (56214) 255/C6
Belville, N.C. (†28451) 281/N6
Belvue, Kansas (66407) 232/F2
Belwood, N.C. (†28090) 281/F4
Belwood, Ontario 177/D4
Belyando (riv.), Queensland 88/H4
Belyando (riv.), Queensland 95/C4
Belyy (isl.), U.S.S.R. 4/B6
Belyy (isl.), U.S.S.R. 48/G2
Belzoni, Miss. (39038) 256/C4
Belzoni, Okla. (†74523) 288/R6
Bełżyce, Poland 47/F3
Bem, Mo. (†65066) 261/K6
Bembe, Angola 115/B5
Bemboka, N.S. Wales 97/E5
Bement, Ill. (61813) 222/E4
Bemersyde, Sask. 181/J5
Bemidji, Minn. (56601) 255/D3
Bemidji (lake), Minn. 255/D3
Bemis, S. Dak. (57215) 298/R4
Bemiss, Georgia (†31601) 217/F9
Bemmel, Netherlands 27/H5
Bemus Point, N.Y. (14712) 276/B6
Bena, Minn. (56626) 255/D3
Benabarre, Spain 33/G1
Bena-Dibele, Zaire 115/D4
Ben Alder (mt.), Scotland 15/D4
Benalla, Victoria 97/D5
Benalto, Alberta 182/C3
Benanee, N.S. Wales 97/B4
Benares (Varanasi), India 68/E3
Benavente, Spain 33/D1
Benavides, Texas (78341) 303/F10
Ben Avon, Pa. (†15202) 294/B6
Ben Avon (mt.), Scotland 15/E3
Ben Barvas (mt.), Scotland 15/B2
Benbecula (isl.), Scotland 15/A3
Benbecula (isl.), Scotland 10/C2
Benbrook, Texas (76126) 303/E2
Benbrook (lake), Texas 303/E3
Benchland, Mont. (†59462) 262/F3
Ben Cruachan (mt.), Scotland 15/C4
Bencubbin, W. Australia 92/B5
Bend, Oreg. 188/B2
Bend, Oreg. (97701) 291/F3
Bend, Texas (76824) 303/F7
Ben Dash (hill), Ireland 17/C6
Ben Davis (pt.), N.J. 273/C5
Bendel (state), Nigeria 106/F7
Bendemeer, N.S. Wales 97/F2
Bendena, Kansas (66008) 232/G2
Bender Beila, Somalia 115/K2
Bender Beila, Somalia 102/G4
Bender Cassim (Bosaso), Somalia 115/J1
Bendersville, Pa. (17306) 294/H6
Bendery, U.S.S.R. 52/C5
Bendigo, Australia 87/E9
Bendigo, Victoria 88/G7
Bendigo, Victoria 97/C5
Bendoc, Victoria 97/E5
Bendon, Mich. (†49643) 250/D4
Bendorf, W. Germany 22/B3
Bene Beraq, Israel 65/B3
Benedict (pond), Conn. 210/C1
Benedict, Kansas (66714) 232/G4
Benedict, Md. (20612) 245/M6
Benedict, Minn. (56436) 255/D3
Benedict, Nebr. (68316) 264/G3
Benedict (mt.), Newf. 166/C3
Benedict, N. Dak. (58716) 282/H4
Benedicta○, Maine (04733) 243/G4
Beneditinos, Brazil 132/F4
Benenitra, Madagascar 118/H4
Benešov, Czech. 41/C2
Benevenan, Loch (lake), Scotland 15/D3
Benevento (prov.), Italy 34/E4
Benevento, Italy 34/E4
Benevolence, Georgia (31721) 217/C7
Benewah (co.), Idaho 220/B2
Benezett, Pa. (15821) 294/F3
Benfica, Portugal 33/A1
Benfleet, England 13/J8
Benga, Mozambique 118/E3
Bengal (bay) 54/K8
Bengal, Bay of (sea), Bangladesh 68/F5
Bengal, Bay of (sea) 2/P5
Bengal, Bay of (sea), Burma 72/B3
Bengal, Bay of (sea), India 68/F5
Bengal, Ind. (†46131) 227/F6
Bengal, Okla. (†74966) 288/R5
Ben Gardane, Tunisia 106/G2
Bengbis, Cameroon 115/B3
Bengbu (Pengpu), China 77/J5
Benge, Wash. (99105) 310/G4
Benggala (str.), Indonesia 85/A4
Benghazi, Libya 2/L4
Benghazi, Libya 102/D1
Benghazi (cap.), Libya 111/C1
Ben Ghnema, Jebel (mts.), Libya 111/C2
Bengkalis, Indonesia 85/C5
Bengkayang, Indonesia 85/E5
Bengkulu, Indonesia 85/C6
Bengo (dist.), Angola 115/B5
Bengough, Sask. 181/F6
Ben Griam More (mt.), Scotland 15/D2
Bengtsfors, Sweden 18/H7
Benguela (dist.), Angola 115/B6
Benguela, Angola 115/B6
Benguela, Angola 102/D6
Ben Guerdane (well), Mauritania 106/B3
Benguet (prov.), Philippines 82/C2
Benha, Egypt 111/J3
Benham, Ky. (40807) 237/R7
Benham, N.C. (†28621) 281/G2
Benhams, Va. (†24201) 307/D7
Ben Hee (mt.), Scotland 15/D2
Ben Hill (co.), Georgia 217/F7
Ben Hope (mt.), Scotland 15/D2
Ben Horn (mt.), Scotland 15/D2
Ben Hur, Va. (24218) 307/B7
Beni, El (dept.), Bolivia 136/C3
Beni (riv.), Bolivia 120/C4
Beni (riv.), Bolivia 136/B2
Beni, Zaire 115/E3
Beni Abbès, Algeria 106/D2
Benicarló, Spain 33/G2
Benicia, Calif. (94510) 204/K1
Benicito (riv.), Bolivia 136/C3
Beni Mazar, Egypt 111/J4
Beni Mellal, Morocco 106/C2
Beni Mellal, Morocco 102/B1
Benin 2/K5
Benin 102/C4
BENIN 106/E7
Benin (bight), Benin 106/E8
Benin (bight), Ghana 106/E8
Benin (bight), Nigeria 106/E8
Benin (bight), Togo 106/E8
Benin City, Nigeria 106/F7
Benin City, Nigeria 102/C4
Beni Ounif, Algeria 106/D2
Beni Saf, Algeria 106/D1
Beni Suef, Egypt 111/J3
Beni Suef, Egypt 102/E2
Beni Suef, Egypt 59/B4
Benito, Manitoba 179/A3
Beni Ulid, Libya 111/B1
Benjamín (isl.), Chile 138/D5
Benjamin, New Bruns. 170/D1
Benjamin (lake), Oreg. 291/G4
Benjamin, Texas (79505) 303/E4
Benjamin, Utah (†84660) 304/C3
Benjamin Aceval, Paraguay 144/C4
Benjamin Constant, Brazil 132/G9
Benjamin Constant, Brazil 120/B3
Benjamin Hill, Mexico 150/D1
Benkelman, Nebr. (69021) 264/C4
Ben Kilbreck (mt.), Scotland 15/D2
Ben Lawers (mt.), Scotland 15/D4
Benld, Ill. (62009) 222/D4
Ben Lomond, Ark. (71823) 202/B6
Ben Lomond, Calif. (95005) 204/K4
Ben Lomond, New Bruns. 170/E3
Ben Lomond (mt.), Scotland 15/D4
Ben Loyal (mt.), Scotland 15/D2
Ben Lui (mt.), Scotland 15/D4
Ben Macdhui (mt.), Scotland 15/E3
Ben Mhor (mt.), Scotland 15/A3
Ben More (mt.), Scotland 15/D4
Ben More (mt.), Scotland 15/B4
Ben More Assynt (mt.), Scotland 15/D2
Bennan (head), Scotland 15/C5
Bennane (head), Scotland 15/C5
Benndale, Miss. (†39450) 256/G9
Bennet, Nebr. (68317) 264/H4
Bennett, Br. Col. 184/J1
Bennett, W.A.C. (dam), Br. Col. 184/F2
Bennett, Colo. (80102) 208/L3
Bennett (peak), Colo. 208/G7
Bennett (creek), Idaho 220/C6
Bennett, Iowa (52721) 229/L5
Bennett, N.C. (27208) 281/K3
Bennett (lake), North. Terr. 93/B7
Bennett (co.), S. Dak. 298/F7
Bennett, Wis. (54815) 317/C3
Bennettsbridge, Ireland 17/G6
Bennetts Point, S.C. (†29446) 296/G6
Bennetts Switch, Ind. (†46901) 227/E3
Bennettsville, S.C. (29512) 296/H2
Bennettville, Minn. (†56431) 255/E4
Ben Nevis (mt.), Scotland 7/D3
Ben Nevis (mt.), Scotland 15/D4
Ben Nevis (mt.), Scotland 10/D2
Bennington, Idaho (†83254) 220/G7
Bennington, Ind. (47011) 227/G7
Bennington, Kansas (67422) 232/E2
Bennington, Nebr. (68007) 264/H3
Bennington○, N.H. (03442) 268/D5
Bennington, Okla. (74723) 288/P7
Bennington (co.), Vt. 268/A6
Bennington, Vt. (05201) 268/A6
Bennington○, Vt. (05201) 268/A6
Benns Church, Va. (†23430) 307/P7
Benoit, Miss. (38725) 256/C3
Benoit, Wis. (54816) 317/D3
Benom, Gunong (mt.), Malaysia 72/D7
Benoni, S. Africa 118/J6
Bensenville, Ill. (60106) 222/B5
Bensheim, W. Germany 22/C4
Benson, Ariz. (85602) 198/E7
Benson, Ill. (61516) 222/D3
Benson, La. (†71419) 238/C3
Benson, Minn. (56215) 255/C5
Benson, N.C. (27504) 281/N4
Benson (co.), N. Dak. 282/M3
Benson (Hollsopple), Pa. (15935) 294/E5
Benson, Sask. 181/J6
Benson○, Vt. (05731) 268/A4
Benson Landing, Vt. (†05731) 268/A4
Bens Run, W. Va. (26135) 312/D4
Bent (co.), Colo. 208/N7
Bent, N. Mex. (88314) 274/D5
Bent Creek, Va. (†24553) 307/L5
Benteng, Indonesia 85/F7
Bentham, England 13/E3
Bentheim, W. Germany 22/B2
Bentinck (isl.), Burma 72/C5
Bentinck (isl.), Queensland 88/F3
Bentinck (isl.), Queensland 95/A3
Bentiu, Sudan 111/E6
Bentley, Alberta 182/C3
Bentley, Ill. (†62321) 222/B3
Bentley, Iowa (†51559) 229/B6
Bentley, Kansas (67016) 232/E4
Bentley, La. (71407) 238/E3
Bentley, Mich. (48613) 250/E5
Bentley, N. Dak. (58522) 282/F7
Bentley, Okla. (†74525) 288/O6
Bentley Springs, Md. (21019) 245/M2
Bentleyville, Ohio (†44022) 284/J9
Bentleyville, Pa. (15314) 294/B5
Bentley with Arksey, England 13/F4
Bent Mountain, Va. (24059) 307/H6
Bento Gonçalves, Brazil 132/C10
Benton, Ala. (36785) 195/E6
Benton, Alberta 182/E4
Benton (co.), Ark. 202/B1
Benton, Ark. (72015) 202/E4
Benton, Calif. (93512) 204/G6
Benton, Ill. (62812) 222/E6
Benton (co.), Ind. 227/C3
Benton, Ind. (†46526) 227/F2
Benton (co.), Iowa 229/J4
Benton, Iowa (50835) 229/E7
Benton, Kansas (67017) 232/E4
Benton, Ky. (42025) 237/E7
Benton, La. (71006) 238/C1
Benton○, Maine (†04937) 243/D6
Benton (co.), Minn. 255/D5
Benton, Minn. (†55322) 255/F6
Benton (lake), Minn. 255/B6
Benton (co.), Miss. 256/F1
Benton, Miss. (39039) 256/D5
Benton (co.), Mo. 261/F6
Benton, Mo. (63736) 261/O8
Benton (lake), Mont. 262/E3
Benton, New Bruns. 170/C3
Benton○, N.H. (†03785) 268/D3
Benton, Ohio (44654) 284/G4
Benton (co.), Oreg. 291/D3
Benton, Pa. (17814) 294/K3
Benton (co.), Tenn. 237/E8
Benton, Tenn. (37307) 237/M10
Benton (co.), Wash. 310/F4
Benton, Wis. (53803) 317/F10
Benton City, Mo. (65232) 261/J4
Benton City, Wash. (99320) 310/F4
Bentong, Malaysia 72/D7
Benton Harbor, Mich. (49022) 250/C6
Benton Heights, Mich. (†49022) 250/C6
Bentonia, Miss. (39040) 256/D5
Benton Ridge, Ohio (45816) 284/C4
Bentonsport, Iowa (†52565) 229/K7
Bentonville, Ark. (72712) 202/B1
Bentonville, Ind. (47322) 227/G5
Bentonville, Ohio (45105) 284/C8
Bentonville, Va. (22610) 307/M3
Bent's Old Fort Nat'l Hist. Site, Colo. 208/M6
Benué (riv.), Cameroon 115/A2
Benue (state), Nigeria 106/F7
Benue (riv.), Nigeria 102/C4
Benue (riv.), Nigeria 106/F7
Ben Vorlich (mt.), Scotland 15/D4
Ben Vrackie (mt.), Scotland 15/E4
Benwee (head), Ireland 17/B3
Benwood, W. Va. (26031) 312/E2
Ben Wyvis (mt.), Scotland 15/D3
Benxi (Penki), China 77/K3
Benxi, China 54/O5
Benzie (co.), Mich. 250/C4
Benzonia, Mich. (49616) 250/D4
Beo, Indonesia 85/H5
Beograd (Belgrade) (cap.), Yugoslavia 45/E3
Beowawe, Nev. (89821) 266/E2
Beppu, Japan 81/E7
Bequia (isl.), St. Vin. & Grens. 156/G4
Beragh, N. Ireland 17/G2
Berar (reg.), India 68/D4
Berat, Albania 45/D5
Berau (bay), Indonesia 85/J6
Berber, Sudan 111/F4
Berber, Sudan 59/B6
Berber, Sudan 102/F3
Berbera, Somalia 115/J1
Berbera, Somalia 102/G3
Berberati, Cent. Afr. Rep. 102/D4
Berberati, Cent. Afr. Rep. 115/C3
Berbice (riv.), Guyana 131/B3
Berchem, Belgium 27/F6
Berchem-Sainte-Agathe, Belgium 27/B9
Bercher, Switzerland 39/C3
Berchtesgaden, W. Germany 22/E5
Berck, France 28/D2
Berclair, Texas (78107) 303/G9
Berdichev, U.S.S.R. 48/C5
Berdichev, U.S.S.R. 52/C5
Berdsk, U.S.S.R. 48/J4
Berdyansk, U.S.S.R. 7/H4
Berdyansk, U.S.S.R. 52/E5
Berea, Ky. (40403) 237/N5
Berea, Nebr. (†69301) 264/A2
Berea, N.C. (†27565) 281/M2
Berea, Ohio (44017) 284/G10
Berea, S.C. (29611) 296/C2
Berea, Spain 33/C1
Berea, W. Va. (26327) 312/E4
Bereda, Somalia 115/K1
Bereda, Somalia 102/H3
Beregovo, U.S.S.R. 52/B5
Berekum, Ghana 106/D7
Berenguela, Bolivia 136/A5
Berenice (ruins), Egypt 111/F3
Berens (riv.), Man. 162/G5
Berens (isl.), Manitoba 179/E2
Berens (riv.), Manitoba 179/F2
Berens (riv.), Ontario 175/A2
Berens River, Man. 162/G5
Berens River, Manitoba 179/F2
Beresford (lake), Fla. 212/E3
Beresford, New Bruns. 170/E1
Beresford, S. Dak. (57004) 298/R7
Beresford Lake, Manitoba 179/G4
Berești Tîrg, Romania 45/H2
Berettyó (riv.), Hungary 41/F3
Berettyóújfalu, Hungary 41/F3
Berezina (riv.), U.S.S.R. 52/C4
Bereznik, U.S.S.R. 52/F2
Berezniki, U.S.S.R. 7/K3
Berezniki, U.S.S.R. 48/F4
Berezniki, U.S.S.R. 52/J3
Berezovo, U.S.S.R. 48/G3
Berg, Norway 18/K2
Berg, Switzerland 39/H1
Berga, Algeria 106/E3
Berga, Spain 33/G1
Bergama, Turkey 63/B3
Bergama, Turkey 59/A2
Bergamo (prov.), Italy 34/B2
Bergamo, Italy 34/B2
Bergeijk, Netherlands 27/G6
Bergen (Mons), Belgium 27/E8
Bergen, E. Germany 22/E1
Bergen, Minn. (†56101) 255/D7
Bergen, Netherlands 27/F3
Bergen (co.), N.J. 273/E2
Bergen, N.Y. (14416) 276/E4
Bergen, N. Dak. (58792) 282/J3
Bergen, Norway 18/D6
Bergen, Norway 7/E2
Berg en Dal, Suriname 131/D3
Bergenfield, N.J. (07621) 273/C1
Bergen op Zoom, Netherlands 27/E5
Berger, Mo. (63014) 261/K5
Bergerac, France 28/D5
Bergholz, Ohio (43908) 284/J4
Bergisch Gladbach, W. Germany 22/B3
Bergland, Mich. (49910) 250/F1
Bergman, Ark. (72615) 202/E1
Bergoo, W. Va. (26298) 312/F6
Bergos (riv.), Turkey 63/C6
Bergshamra, Sweden 18/L7
Bergsjö, Sweden 18/K5
Bergstrom A.F.B., Texas 303/G7
Bergton, Va. (22811) 307/L3
Berguent, Morocco 106/D2
Bergum, Netherlands 27/H2
Bergumermeer (lake), Netherlands 27/J2
Bergün-Bravuogn, Switzerland 39/J3
Berhala (str.), Indonesia 85/C6
Berhampore, India 68/F4
Berhampur, India 68/F5
Berhida, Hungary 41/E3
Bering (sea) 2/A3

Blandburg 339

Big Spencer (mt.), Maine 243/E4
Big Spring, Georgia (†30240) 217/C5
Big Spring, Ky. (40106) 237/J5
Big Spring, Md. (21722) 245/G2
Big Spring, Tenn. (37323) 237/M10
Big Spring, Texas 188/F4
Big Spring, Texas (79720) 303/C5
Big Springs, Nebr. (69122) 264/B3
Big Springs, S. Dak. (†57001) 298/S8
Big Springs, W. Va. (26137) 312/D5
Big Star (lake), Mich. 250/C5
Bigstick (lake), Sask. 181/B5
Big Stone, Alberta 182/E4
Bigstone (lake), Manitoba 179/J3
Bigstone (pt.), Manitoba 179/E2
Bigstone (riv.), Manitoba 179/J3
Big Stone (co.), Minn. 255/B5
Big Stone (lake), Minn. 255/B5
Big Stone (lake), S. Dak. 298/R3
Big Stone City, S. Dak. (57216) 298/S3
Big Stone Gap, Va. (24219) 307/C7
Big Sur, Calif. (93920) 204/D7
Big Thicket Nat'l Preserve, Texas 303/K7
Big Thompson (riv.), Colo. 208/H2
Big Timber, Mont. (59011) 262/G5
Big Timber (creek), N.J. 273/C4
Big Tracadie (riv.), New Bruns. 170/E1
Bigtrails, Wyo. (†82442) 319/E2
Big Trout (lake), Ontario 177/F2
Big Trout (lake), Ontario 175/B2
Big Trout Lake, Ontario 175/C2
Big Valley, Alberta 182/D3
Big Walnut (creek), Ind. 227/D5
Big Walnut (creek), Ohio 284/E5
Big Wells, Texas (78830) 303/E9
Big Whiteshell Lake, Manitoba 179/G4
Big Wood (riv.), Idaho 220/D6
Bihać, Yugoslavia 45/B3
Bihar (state), India 68/F4
Bihar, India 68/F3
Biharamulo, Tanzania 115/F4
Biharkeresztes, Hungary 41/F3
Biharnagybajom, Hungary 41/F3
Bijagós (isls.), Guinea-Biss. 106/A6
Bijagós (isls.), Guinea-Biss. 102/A3
Bijapur, Karnataka, India 68/D5
Bijapur, Madhya Pradesh, India 68/E5
Bijar, Iran 66/E3
Bijeljina, Yugoslavia 45/D3
Bijelo Polje, Yugoslavia 45/D4
Bijiang, China 77/E6
Bijie, China 77/G6
Bijnor, India 68/D3
Bijou (creek), Colo. 208/L3
Bijou Hills, S. Dak. (†57310) 298/L6
Bikaner, India 54/J7
Bikaner, India 68/C3
Bikar (atoll), Marshall Is. 87/H4
Bikin, U.S.S.R. 48/O5
Bikini (atoll), Marshall Is. 87/G4
Bikoro, Zaire 115/C4
Bikoro, Zaire 102/D5
Bilaspur, India 68/E4
Bilauktaung (range), Burma 72/C4
Bilauktaung (range), Thailand 72/C4
Bilbao, Spain 33/E1
Bilbao, Spain 7/D4
Bileća, Yugoslavia 45/D4
Bilecik (prov.), Turkey 63/D2
Bilecik, Turkey 59/A1
Bilecik, Turkey 63/D2
Biłgoraj, Poland 47/F3
Bilibino, U.S.S.R. 4/C1
Bilibino, U.S.S.R. 48/R3
Bilin, Burma 72/C3
Bilina, Czech. 41/B1
Biliran (isl.), Philippines 82/E5
Bill, Wyo. (82631) 319/G2
Billate (riv.), Ethiopia 111/G6
Billerica○, Mass. (01821) 249/J2
Billings (lake), Conn. 210/H2
Billings, Mo. (65610) 261/F8
Billings, Mont. 146/H5
Billings, Mont. 188/E1
Billings, Mont. (*59101) 262/H5
Billings (co.), N. Dak. 282/D5
Billings, Okla. (74630) 288/M1
Billingsgate (isl.), Mass. 249/O5
Billingshurst, England 13/G6
Billingsley, Ala. (36006) 195/E5
Billiton (isl.), Indonesia 54/M10
Billiton (isl.), Indonesia 85/D6
Bill Williams (riv.), Ariz. 198/B4
Billy Clapp (lake), Wash. 310/F3
Bilma, Niger 102/D3
Bilma, Niger 106/G5
Biloela, Queensland 88/J4
Biloela, Queensland 95/D5
Biloku, Guyana 131/B5
Biloxi, Miss. 146/K6
Biloxi, Miss. 188/J4
Biloxi, Miss. (*39530) 256/G10
Biltine, Chad 111/D5
Biltine, Chad 102/D3
Biltmore Forest, N.C. (†28803) 281/E3
Bilwaskarma, Nicaragua 154/F3
Bilzen, Belgium 27/G7
Bim, W. Va. (25021) 312/C7
Biminis, The (isls.), Bahamas 156/B1
Bina-Itawa, India 68/D4
Binalbagan, Philippines 82/D5
Binalong, N.S. Wales 97/E4
Binboğa (mts.), Turkey 63/G3
Binbrook, Ontario 177/E4
Binche, Belgium 27/E8
Binda, N.S. Wales 97/E4
Bindloss, Alberta 182/E4
Bindoon, W. Australia 92/B1
Bindura, Zimbabwe 118/E3
Binéfar, Spain 33/G2
Binevenagh (mt.), N. Ireland 17/H1
Binford, N. Dak. (58416) 282/O4
Binga (mt.), Mozambique 118/E3
Bingara, N.S. Wales 97/F1
Bingen, Wash. (98605) 310/D5
Bingen, W. Germany 22/B4
Binger, Okla. (73009) 288/K4
Bingerville, Ivory Coast 106/D7
Bingham (co.), Idaho 220/F6
Bingham, Ill. (62011) 222/D4
Bingham, Maine (04920) 243/D5
Bingham○, Maine (04920) 243/D5
Bingham, Nebr. (69335) 264/B2
Bingham, N. Mex. (87815) 274/C5
Bingham, S.C. (†29565) 296/H3
Bingham Lake, Minn. (56118) 255/C7
Binghamton, N.Y. 188/L2
Binghamton, N.Y. (*13901) 276/J6
Bingöl (prov.), Turkey 63/J3
Bingöl (Çapakçur), Turkey 63/J3
Bingöl Dağları (mts.), Turkey 63/J3
Binhai, China 77/K5
Binh Long (An Loc), Vietnam 72/E5
Binh Son, Vietnam 72/F4
Binjai, Indonesia 85/B5
Binn, Switzerland 39/F4
Binnaway, N.S. Wales 97/E2
Binningen, Switzerland 39/D1
Binongko (isl.), Indonesia 85/G7
Binscarth, Manitoba 179/A4
Bintan (isl.), Indonesia 85/C5
Bintuhan, Indonesia 85/C6
Bintulu, Malaysia 85/E5
Binyamina, Israel 65/B2
Binyang, China 77/G7
Biobío (reg.), Chile 138/E1
Bío-Bío (riv.), Chile 138/E2
Biograd, Yugoslavia 45/B4
Bioko (isl.), Equat. Guinea 102/C4
Bioko (terr.), Equat. Guinea 115/A3
Bioko (isl.), Equat. Guinea 115/A3
Biola, Calif. (93606) 204/E7
Bippus, Ind. (46713) 227/F3
Bir, India 68/D5
Bira, U.S.S.R. 48/O5
Birag, Kuh-e (mts.), Iran 66/M7
Bir 'Ali, P.D.R. Yemen 59/E7
Birama (pt.), Cuba 158/G4
Birao, Cent. Afr. Rep. 115/D1
Biratnagar, Nepal 68/F3
Biratori, Japan 81/L2
Bir Bala, Iran 66/L8
Bir Bala, Iran 59/G4
Bircao, Somalia 115/H4
Birch (creek), Alaska 196/J1
Birch (hills), Alberta 182/A2
Birch (lake), Alberta 182/E3
Birch (mts.), Alberta 182/B5
Birch (riv.), Alberta 182/B5
Birch (creek), Idaho 220/F5
Birch (isl.), Manitoba 179/C2
Birch (lake), Minn. 255/G3
Birch (creek), Mont. 262/D2
Birch (lake), Sask. 181/C2
Birch (creek), Utah 304/B5
Birch (pt.), Wash. 310/C2
Birch Creek, Alaska (†99740) 196/J1
Birch Creek (valley), Idaho 220/E5
Birch Creek (res.), Mont. 262/D2
Birchdale, Minn. (56629) 255/D2
Birch Harbor, Maine (04613) 243/H7
Birch Hills, Sask. 181/F3
Birchip, Victoria 97/B4
Birch Island, Br. Col. 184/H4
Birchleaf, Va. (24220) 307/D6
Birch River, Manitoba 179/A2
Birch River, W. Va. (26610) 312/E6
Birch Run, Mich. (48415) 250/F5
Birchtown, Nova Scotia 168/C5
Birch Tree, Mo. (65438) 261/K9
Birchwood, Md. (†20021) 245/F5
Birchwood, Tenn. (37308) 237/M10
Birchwood, Wis. (54817) 317/C4
Birchy Bay, Newf. 166/D4
Bird (isl.), La. 238/M8
Bird (creek), Okla. 288/O1
Bird City, Kansas (67731) 232/A2
Bird Cove, Newf. 166/C3
Bird Island, Minn. (55310) 255/D6
Birds, Ill. (62415) 222/F5
Birdsboro, Pa. (19508) 294/L5
Birdseye, Ind. (47513) 227/D8
Birds Hill, Manitoba 179/F4
Birdsnest, Va. (23307) 307/S6
Birdsong, Ark. (†72386) 202/K3
Birdsville, Ky. (†42081) 237/D6
Birdsville, Queensland 88/F5
Birdsville, Queensland 95/A5
Birdtail, Manitoba 179/B4
Birdum, North. Terr. 93/C3
Birdwood, S. Australia 94/C7
Birecik, Turkey 63/H4
Bir el Khzaim (well), Mauritania 106/C4
Bireuen, Indonesia 85/B4
Bir Ganduz (well), Western Sahara 106/A4
Birganj, Nepal 68/F3
Bir Hakeim (ruins), Libya 111/D1
Birigui, Brazil 135/A2
Birjand, Iran 66/L4
Birjand, Iran 59/G3
Birjand, Iran 54/G6
Birken, Br. Col. 184/F5
Birkenfeld, Oreg. (97016) 291/D1
Birkenfeld, W. Germany 22/B4
Birkenhead, England 13/G2
Birkenhead, England 10/F2
Birkenhead, N. Zealand 100/B1
Birkenhead Lake Prov. Park, Br. Col. 184/F5
Birkerød, Denmark 21/F6
Birket Qârûn (lake), Egypt 111/J3
Bir Ksaib Ounane (well), Mali 106/C4
Birksgate (range), S. Australia 94/A2
Bîrlad, Romania 45/H2
Bîrlad (riv.), Romania 45/H2
Birmingham, Ala. 146/K6
Birmingham, Ala. 188/J4
Birmingham, Ala. 195/D3
Birmingham, England 7/D3
Birmingham, England 10/G3
Birmingham, England 13/F5
Birmingham, Iowa (52535) 229/K7
Birmingham, Mich. (*48008) 250/B6
Birmingham, Mo. (†64068) 261/R5
Birmingham, N.J. (08011) 273/D4
Birmingham, Ohio (44816) 284/F3
Birmingham, Pa. (†16686) 294/F4
Birmingham, Sask. 181/H5
Birmitrapur, India 68/E4
Bir Mogreïn, Mauritania 106/B3
Birnam, Scotland 15/E4
Birnamwood, Wis. (54414) 317/H6
Birney, Mont. (59012) 262/K5
Birnie, Manitoba 179/C4
Birnin Kebbi, Nigeria 106/E6
Birni-N'Konni, Niger 106/E6
Birni-N'Konni, Niger 102/C3
Bir Nzaran (well), Western Sahara 106/B4
Birobidzhan, U.S.S.R. 54/O5
Birobidzhan, U.S.S.R. 48/O5
Biron, Wis. (†54494) 317/G7
Bir Ounane (well), Mali 106/D4
Birqin, West Bank 65/C3
Birr, Ireland 17/F5
Birr, Ireland 10/B4
Birregurra, Victoria 97/B6
Birrie (riv.), N. S. Wales 88/H5
Birrie (riv.), N.S. Wales 97/D1
Birrimbah, North. Terr. 93/C3
Birrindudu, North. Terr. 93/A5
Birriwa, N.S. Wales 97/E3
Birs (riv.), Switzerland 39/D2
Birsay, Sask. 181/D4
Birsk, U.S.S.R. 52/J3
Birta, Ark. (†72853) 202/D3
Bir Taba, Egypt 59/B4
Bir Taba (well), Egypt 111/F2
Birtle, Manitoba 179/B4
Biru, China 77/D5
Biruaca, Venezuela 124/E4
Biruni, U.S.S.R. 48/G5
Biržai, U.S.S.R. 53/C2
Bir Zeit, West Bank 65/C4
Bisbee, Ariz. 188/E4
Bisbee, Ariz. (85603) 198/F7
Bisbee, N. Dak. (58317) 282/M2
Biscarrosse (lake), France 28/C5
Biscay (bay) 2/J3
Biscay (bay) 7/D4
Biscay (bay), France 28/B5
Biscay, Minn. (†55336) 255/D6
Biscay (bay), Spain 33/E1
Biscay Bay (riv.), Newf. 166/D2
Biscayne (bay), Fla. 212/F6
Biscayne (key), Fla. 212/B5
Biscayne Nat'l Park, Fla. 212/F6
Biscayne Park, Fla. (33152) 212/B4
Bisceglie, Italy 34/F4
Bischofshofen, Austria 41/B3
Bischofswerda, E. Germany 22/F3
Bischofszell, Switzerland 39/H1
Biscoe (isls.) 5/C15
Biscoe, Ark. (72017) 202/H4
Biscoe, N.C. (27209) 281/K4
Biscotasing, Ontario 177/J5
Biscotasing, Ontario 175/D3
Biscucuy, Venezuela 124/D3
Bisha, Saudi Arabia 59/D5
Bisha, Wadi (dry riv.), Saudi Arabia 59/D5
Bishiara (well), Libya 111/D3
Bisho (cap.), Ciskei, S. Africa 102/E8
Bishop, Calif. (93514) 204/G6
Bishop, Georgia (30621) 217/F3
Bishop, Md. (†21813) 245/S7
Bishop (creek), Nev. 266/F1
Bishop, Texas (78343) 303/G10
Bishop (creek), Utah 304/E3
Bishop, Va. (24604) 307/E6
Bishop Auckland, England 10/E3
Bishop Auckland, England 13/E3
Bishopbriggs, Scotland 15/B2
Bishop Hill, Ill. (61419) 222/C2
Bishopric, Sask. 181/F5
Bishop's Falls, Newf. 166/C4
Bishops Head, Md. (21611) 245/O7
Bishops Mitre (mt.), Newf. 166/B2
Bishop's Stortford, England 10/G5
Bishop's Stortford, England 13/H6
Bishopton, Québec 172/F4
Bishopton, Scotland 15/B2
Bishopville, Md. (21813) 245/T7
Bishopville, S.C. (29010) 296/G3
Bishri, Jebel el (mts.), Syria 63/H5
Biskra, Algeria 106/F2
Biskra, Algeria 102/C1
Biskupiec, Poland 47/E2
Bislig, Philippines 85/H4
Bislig, Philippines 82/F6
Bismarck, Ark. (71929) 202/D5
Bismarck, Ill. (61814) 222/F3
Bismarck, Mo. (63624) 261/L7
Bismarck (cap.), N. Dak. 146/H5
Bismarck (cap.), N. Dak. 188/G1
Bismarck (cap.), N. Dak. (58501) 282/J6
Bismarck (arch.), Papua N.G. 87/E6
Bismarck (arch.), Papua N.G. 86/B1
Bismarck (sea), Papua N.G. 86/B1
Bismarck (arch.), Papua N.G. 2/S6
Bismarck, W. Va. (†26739) 312/H4
Bismil, Turkey 63/J4
Bison (lake), Alberta 182/B1
Bison, Kansas (67520) 232/C3
Bison, Okla. (73720) 288/L2
Bison, S. Dak. (57620) 298/E2
Bispgården, Sweden 18/K5
Bissau (cap.), Guinea-Biss. 106/A6
Bissau (cap.), Guinea-Biss. 102/A3
Bissett, Manitoba 179/G4
Bistineau (lake), La. 238/D2
Bistrița, Romania 45/G2
Bita (riv.), Colombia 126/F5
Bitagron, Suriname 131/C3
Bitam, Gabon 115/B3
Bitburg, W. Germany 22/B4
Bitely, Mich. (49309) 250/D5
Bithlo, Fla. (†32801) 212/E3
Bitkine, Chad 111/C5
Bitlis (prov.), Turkey 63/J3
Bitlis, Turkey 63/J3
Bitlis, Turkey 59/D2
Bitola, Yugoslavia 45/E5
Bitola, Yugoslavia 7/G4
Bitonto, Italy 34/F4
Bitter (lakes), Egypt 111/K3
Bitter (lake), Sask. 181/B5
Bitter (creek), Wyo. 319/C4
Bitter Creek, Wyo. (†82901) 319/D4
Bitterfeld, E. Germany 22/E3
Bitterfontein, S. Africa 118/B6
Bittern (lake), Alberta 182/D3
Bittern Lake, Alberta 182/D3
Bitterroot (range) 188/D1
Bitterroot (range), Idaho 220/D3
Bitterroot (range), Mont. 262/B4
Bitterroot (riv.), Mont. 262/B4
Bitterroot (range), U.S. 146/G5
Bitti, Italy 34/B4
Bitumount, Alberta 182/E1
Bitung, Indonesia 85/H5
Biu, Nigeria 106/G6
Biu (plat.), Nigeria 106/G6
Bivalve, Md. (21814) 245/P7
Bivalve, N.J. (08301) 273/C5
Bivolari, Romania 45/H2
Biwa (lake), Japan 81/H6
Biwabik, Minn. (55708) 255/F3
Bixby, Minn. (55916) 255/E7
Bixby, Mo. (65439) 261/K7
Bixby, Okla. (74008) 288/P3
Biyang, China 77/H5
Biysk, U.S.S.R. 54/K4
Biysk, U.S.S.R. 48/J4
Bizcocho, Uruguay 145/B4
Bizerte, Tunisia 106/F1
Bizerte, Tunisia 102/C1
Bjargtangar (pt.), Iceland 21/A1
Bjelovar, Yugoslavia 45/C3
Bjerringbro, Denmark 21/C5
Bjorkdale, Sask. 181/H3
Bjørnafjorden (fjord), Norway 18/D6
Bjorne (pen.), N.W. Terrs. 187/K2
Bjornøya (isl.), Norway 18/D3
Blabon, N. Dak. (†58046) 282/P5
Blachly, Oreg. (97412) 291/D3
Black (sea) 2/L3
Black (sea) 54/E5
Black (sea) 7/H4
Black, Ala. (36314) 195/G8
Black (riv.), Alaska 196/K1
Black (mesa), Ariz. 198/E2
Black (mts.), Ariz. 198/A3
Black (riv.), Ariz. 198/E5
Black (riv.), Ark. 202/H2
Black (sea), Bulgaria 45/J4
Black (pond), Conn. 210/G1
Black (pt.), Conn. 210/G3
Black (mts.), England 13/D6
Black (creek), Fla. 212/E1
Black (head), Ireland 17/C5
Black (riv.), Jamaica 158/H6
Black (mt.), Ky. 237/R7
Black (lake), La. 238/D3
Black (pond), Maine 243/D3
Black (isl.), Manitoba 179/F3
Black (riv.), Manitoba 179/F4
Black (lake), Mich. 250/E3
Black (riv.), Mich. 250/E3
Black (riv.), Mich. 250/G5
Black (riv.), Minn. 255/D2
Black (creek), Miss. 256/F8
Black, Mo. (63625) 261/L7
Black (riv.), Mo. 261/L10
Black (mt.), N. Mex. 274/A6
Black (range), N. Mex. 274/B5
Black (lake), N.Y. 276/J1
Black (riv.), N.Y. 276/K3
Black (riv.), N.C. 281/N5
Black (riv.), Ohio 284/F3
Black (riv.), Ontario 177/E3
Black (sea), Romania 45/J4
Black (lake), Sask. 181/M2
Black (riv.), S.C. 296/H4
Black (sea), Turkey 63/E1
Black (sea), U.S.S.R. 48/D5
Black (sea), U.S.S.R. 52/D6
Black (creek), Vt. 268/B2
Black (riv.), Vt. 268/C2
Black (riv.), Vt. 268/B5
Black (riv.), Vietnam 72/D2
Black (mts.), Wales 13/D6
Black (for.), W. Germany 22/C4
Black (riv.), Wis. 317/E7
Black (riv.), Yukon 187/D3
Blackall, Australia 87/E8
Blackall, Queensland 88/H4
Blackall, Queensland 95/C5
Black Bear (creek), Okla. 288/M2
Blackberry (riv.), Conn. 210/B1
Blackbird, Del. (†19734) 245/R3
Blackbourne (pt.), Norfolk I. 88/L6
Black Branch, Nulhegan (riv.), Vt. 268/D2
Blackburn (mt.), Alaska 196/K2
Blackburn, England 13/H1
Blackburn, England 10/G1
Blackburn, La. (†71038) 238/D1
Blackburn, Mo. (65321) 261/F4
Blackburn, Okla. (74058) 288/N2
Blackburn, Ontario 177/J2
Blackburn, Scotland 15/D5
Black Butte (lake), Calif. 204/C4
Black Canyon City, Ariz. (85324) 198/C4
Black Canyon of the Gunnison Nat'l Mon., Colo. 208/D5
Black Creek, Br. Col. 184/E5
Black Creek, N.C. (27813) 281/O3
Black Creek, Wis. (54106) 317/K7
Black Diamond, Alberta 182/C4
Black Diamond, Wash. (98010) 310/D3
Blackduck, Minn. (56630) 255/D3
Black Duck (riv.), Ontario 175/C1
Black Eagle, Mont. (59414) 262/E3
Black Earth, Wis. (53515) 317/G9
Black Elster (riv.), E. Germany 22/E3
Blackey, Ky. (41804) 237/R6
Blackfalds, Alberta 182/D3
Blackfeet Ind. Res., Mont. 262/D2
Blackfoot, Alberta 182/E3
Blackfoot, Idaho (83221) 220/F6
Blackfoot (res.), Idaho 220/G7
Blackfoot (riv.), Idaho 220/G6
Blackfoot, Mont. (59415) 262/D2
Blackfoot (riv.), Mont. 262/C4
Blackford (co.), Ind. 227/G4
Blackford, Ky. (42403) 237/F6
Blackford, Scotland 15/E4
Black Forest, Colo. (80908) 208/K4
Blackfork, Ohio (45615) 284/E8
Black Fork, Mohican (riv.), Ohio 284/F4
Blackgum, Okla. (†74962) 288/S3
Black Hall, Conn. (†06371) 210/F3
Black Hawk, Colo. (80422) 208/J3
Blackhawk, Ind. (†47866) 227/C6
Black Hawk (co.), Iowa 229/J4
Black Hawk, Miss. (†38917) 256/E4
Black Hawk, S. Dak. (57718) 298/C5
Blackhead (bay), Newf. 166/D2
Blackhead Road, Newf. 166/D2
Black Hills (mts.) 188/F2
Black Hills (mts.), S. Dak. 298/B5
Blackie, Alberta 182/D4
Black Isle (pen.), Scotland 15/D3
Black Jack, Mo. (†63031) 261/R1
Black Lake (bayou), La. 238/D1
Black Lake, Québec 172/F3
Black Lake, Sask. 181/M2
Blackledge (riv.), Conn. 210/F2
Black Lick, Pa. (15716) 294/D4
Blacklock (pt.), Oreg. 291/C5
Black Mesa (mt.), Okla. 288/A1
Blackmore (mt.), Mont. 262/F5
Black Mountain, N.C. (28711) 281/E3
Black Oak, Ark. (72414) 202/K2
Black Oak, Ind. (†46406) 227/C1
Black Pine (mts.), Idaho 220/E7
Black Pine (peak), Idaho 220/E7
Black Pine (creek), S. Dak. 298/G6
Black Point, Calif. (†94947) 204/J1
Black Point, Conn. (†06357) 210/G3
Black Point, New Bruns. 170/D1
Blackpool, England 13/G1
Blackpool, England 10/F1
Blackridge, Va. (23916) 307/M7
Black River, Jamaica 158/H6
Black River, Jamaica 156/B3
Black River (bay), Jamaica 158/G6
Black River, Mich. (48721) 250/F4
Black River, New Bruns. 170/E3
Black River (pond), Newf. 166/C2
Black River, N.Y. (13612) 276/J3
Black River Bridge, New Bruns. 170/E2
Black River Falls, Wis. (54615) 317/E7
Black Rock, Ark. (72415) 202/H1
Black Rock (des.), Nev. 266/B2
Black Rock (range), Nev. 266/B1
Black Rock (pt.), R.I. 249/H8
Black Rock, Utah (†84751) 304/B5
Blacksburg, S.C. (29702) 296/D1
Blacksburg, Va. (24060) 307/H6
Blacks Fork, Green (riv.), Wyo. 319/C4
Blacks Harbour, New Bruns. 170/D3
Blackshear, Georgia (31516) 217/H8
Blackshear (lake), Georgia 217/E7
Blacksher, Ala. (†36507) 195/C8
Blacksod (bay), Ireland 17/A3
Black Springs, Ark. (†71960) 202/C5
Black Springs, Nev. (†89508) 266/B3
Black Squirrel (creek), Colo. 208/L5
Blackstairs (mt.), Ireland 17/H6
Blackstock, Ontario 177/F3
Blackstock, S.C. (29014) 296/E2
Blackstone○, Mass. (01504) 249/H4
Blackstone (riv.), Mass. 249/G3
Blackstone, Va. (23824) 307/N6
Blacksville, W. Va. (26521) 312/F3
Black Thunder (creek), Wyo. 319/G2
Black Tickle, Newf. 166/C3
Blackton, Ark. (†72069) 202/H4
Blacktown, N. S. Wales 88/K4
Blacktown, N.S. Wales 97/H3
Blackville, New Bruns. 170/E2
Blackville, S.C. (29817) 296/E5
Black Volta (riv.) 102/B3
Black Volta (riv.), Ghana 106/D6
Black Volta (riv.), Ivory Coast 106/D6
Black Volta (riv.), Upper Volta 106/D6
Black Warrior (riv.), Ala. 195/C5
Blackwater (riv.), England 13/H6
Blackwater (riv.), Fla. 212/B6
Blackwater, Ireland 17/J7
Blackwater (riv.), Ireland 10/B4
Blackwater (riv.), Ireland 17/D7
Blackwater (riv.), Ireland 17/H4
Blackwater, Mo. (65322) 261/G5
Blackwater (res.), N.H. 268/D5
Blackwater (riv.), N. Ireland 17/H3
Blackwater, Queensland 95/D4
Blackwater, Queensland 88/H4
Blackwater (res.), Scotland 15/D4
Blackwater, Va. (24221) 307/B7
Blackwater (riv.), Va. 307/J6
Blackwater (riv.), Va. 307/O6
Blackwell, Ark. (72019) 202/E3
Blackwell (brook), Conn. 210/H1
Blackwell, Okla. (74631) 288/M1
Blackwell, Texas (79506) 303/D5
Blackwell, Wis. (†54541) 317/J4
Blackwood (Ngunju) (cape), Indonesia 85/F8
Blackwood, N.J. (08012) 273/C4
Blackwood Terrace, N.J. (†08096) 273/C4
Bladen, Nebr. (68928) 264/F4
Bladen (co.), N.C. 281/M5
Bladenboro, N.C. (28320) 281/M5
Bladensburg, Md. (20710) 245/G4
Bladensburg, Ohio (43005) 284/F5
Blades, Del. (†19973) 245/R6
Bladon Springs, Ala. (36902) 195/B7
Bladworth, Sask. 181/E4
Blaeberry, Br. Col. 184/J4
Blaenavon, Wales 13/B6
Blagodarnoye, U.S.S.R. 52/F5
Blagoevgrad, Bulgaria 45/F5
Blagoveshchensk, U.S.S.R. 54/O4
Blagoveshchensk, U.S.S.R. 48/N4
Blagoveshchensk, U.S.S.R. 52/J4
Blain, France 28/C4
Blain, Pa. (17006) 294/H5
Blaine, Georgia (†30175) 217/C1
Blaine (co.), Idaho 220/D6
Blaine, Kansas (66410) 232/F2
Blaine, Ky. (41124) 237/R4
Blaine○, Maine (04734) 243/H2
Blaine, Mich. (†48032) 250/G5
Blaine, Minn. (†55433) 255/G5
Blaine, Miss. (38727) 256/C3
Blaine (co.), Mont. 262/G2
Blaine (co.), Nebr. 264/E3
Blaine, Ohio (43909) 284/J5
Blaine (co.), Okla. 288/K3
Blaine, Oreg. (†97108) 291/D2
Blaine, Tenn. (37709) 237/O8
Blaine, Wash. (98230) 310/C2
Blaine Lake, Sask. 181/D3
Blaine-Mars Hill, Maine (04734) 243/H2
Blainville, Québec 172/H4
Blair, Kansas (†66090) 232/H2
Blair, Nebr. (68008) 264/H3
Blair, Okla. (73526) 288/H5
Blair (co.), Pa. 294/F4
Blair, S.C. (29015) 296/E3
Blair, W. Va. (25022) 312/C7
Blair, Wis. (54616) 317/D7
Blair Athol, Queensland 95/C4
Blair Atholl, Scotland 10/E2
Blair Atholl, Scotland 15/E4
Blairgowrie and Rattray, Scotland 15/E4
Blairgowrie and Rattray, Scotland 10/E2
Blairmore, Alberta 182/C5
Blairs, Va. (24527) 307/K7
Blairsburg, Iowa (50034) 229/F4
Blairsden, Calif. (96103) 204/E4
Blairs Mills, Ky. (41402) 237/P4
Blairs Mills, Pa. (17213) 294/G5
Blairstown, Iowa (52209) 229/J5
Blairstown, Mo. (64726) 261/E5
Blairstown○, N.J. (07825) 273/C2
Blairsville, Georgia (30512) 217/E1
Blairsville, Pa. (15717) 294/D5
Blaisdell, N. Dak. (58720) 282/F3
Blaj, Romania 45/F2
Blake (pt.), Mich. 250/E1
Blakeley, Minn. (†56011) 255/E6
Blakeley, W. Va. (†25160) 312/D6
Blakely, Georgia (31723) 217/C8
Blakely, Pa. (18447) 294/F6
Blakesburg, Iowa (52536) 229/H7
Blakeslee, Ohio (43505) 284/A2
Blakeslee, Pa. (18610) 294/L3
Blaketown, Newf. 166/D2
Blalock, Ala. (†36773) 195/D6
Blalock, Georgia (†30525) 217/E1
Blalock (isl.), Wash. 310/F5
Blanc (cape) 2/J4
Blanc (mt.), France 7/E4
Blanc (mt.), France 28/G5
Blanc (mt.), Italy 34/A2
Blanc (cape), Mauritania 102/A2
Blanc (cape), Mauritania 106/A4
Blanc (cape), Tunisia 106/G1
Blanc (cape), Western Sahara 106/A4
Blanca (bay), Argentina 120/C6
Blanca (bay), Argentina 143/D4
Blanca (lag.), Chile 138/E10
Blanca (peak), Colo. 188/F3
Blanca, Colo. (81123) 208/H8
Blanca (peak), Colo. 208/H7
Blanca (pt.), C. Rica 154/F5
Blanca, Cordillera (mts.), Peru 128/D7
Blanch, N.C. (27212) 281/L2
Blanchard, Idaho (83804) 220/A1
Blanchard, Iowa (51630) 229/C7
Blanchard, La. (71009) 238/C1
Blanchard○, Maine (†04406) 243/D5
Blanchard, Mich. (49310) 250/D5
Blanchard, N. Dak. (58009) 282/R5
Blanchard (riv.), Ohio 284/C4
Blanchard, Okla. (73010) 288/L4
Blanchard, Pa. (16826) 294/G3
Blanchard, Wash. (†98232) 310/C2
Blanchardstown, Ireland 17/H5
Blanchardville, Wis. (53516) 317/G10
Blanche, Ky. (†40902) 237/O7
Blanche (riv.), Québec 172/E2
Blanche (lake), S. Australia 88/F5
Blanche (lake), S. Australia 94/F3
Blanche, Tenn. (†38488) 237/H10
Blanche (lake), W. Australia 88/C4
Blanche Marie (fall), Suriname 131/C3
Blanchester, Ohio (45107) 284/B7
Blanchisseuse, Trin. & Tob. 161/B10
Blanco (riv.), Argentina 143/C2
Blanco (riv.), Bolivia 136/D4
Blanco (lake), Chile 138/F10
Blanco (cape), C. Rica 154/E6
Blanco (peak), C. Rica 154/F6
Blanco (riv.), Mexico 150/Q2
Blanco, N. Mex. (87412) 274/B2
Blanco (creek), N. Mex. 274/F4
Blanco, Okla. (74528) 288/P5
Blanco (cape), Oreg. 188/A2
Blanco (cape), Oreg. 291/C5
Blanco (cape), Peru 128/B5
Blanco (riv.), Peru 128/F6
Blanco (co.), Texas 303/F8
Blanco, Texas (78606) 303/F7
Blanc-Sablon, Québec 174/F2
Bland, Mo. (65014) 261/J6
Bland (co.), Va. 307/F6
Bland, Va. (24315) 307/F6
Blandburg, Pa. (16619) 294/F4

340 Blandford

Blandford○, Mass. (01008) 249/C4
Blandford, Nova Scotia 168/D4
Blandford Forum, England 13/E7
Blandford Forum, England 10/E5
Blanding, Utah (84511) 304/E6
Blandinsville, Ill. (61420) 222/C3
Blandville, Ky. (42026) 237/D7
Blanefield, Scotland 15/B1
Blanes, Spain 33/H2
Blaney Park, Mich. (†49836) 250/D2
Blanford, Ind. (47831) 227/B5
Blankenberge, Belgium 27/C6
Blankenburg am Harz, E. Germany 22/D3
Blanket, Texas (76432) 303/F6
Blanquillo, Uruguay 145/D3
Blansko, Czech. 41/D2
Blanton, Ala. (†36872) 195/H5
Blanton, Fla. (†33525) 212/D3
Blantyre, Malawi 115/F7
Blantyre, Malawi 102/F6
Blantyre, Scotland 15/B2
Blarney, Ireland 10/B5
Blarney, Ireland 17/D8
Blas (peak), Switzerland 39/G3
Blasdell, N.Y. (14219) 276/C5
Blasket (isls.), Ireland 10/A4
Blasket (isls.), Ireland 17/A7
Blatná, Czech. 41/B2
Blato, Yugoslavia 45/C4
Blatten, Switzerland 39/E4
Blaubeuren, W. Germany 22/C4
Blauvelt, N.Y. (10913) 276/K8
Blåvands Huk (pt.), Denmark 21/A6
Blawenburg, N.J. (08504) 273/D3
Blawnox, Pa. (15238) 294/C6
Blaydon, England 10/F3
Blaydon, England 13/H3
Blaye, France 28/C5
Blayney, N.S. Wales 97/E3
Blaze (pt.), North. Terr. 88/D2
Blaze (pt.), North. Terr. 93/A2
Bleckley (co.), Georgia 217/F6
Bled, Yugoslavia 45/A2
Bledsoe (co.), Tenn. 237/L9
Bledsoe, Texas (79314) 303/A4
Bleecker, Ala. (†36874) 195/H5
Blekinge (co.), Sweden 18/J8
Blencoe, Iowa (51523) 229/A5
Blenheim, N. Zealand 100/D4
Blenheim, Ontario 177/C5
Blenheim, S.C. (29516) 296/H2
Blenker, Wis. (54415) 317/F6
Blennerhassett (isl.), Ohio 284/G7
Blerick, Netherlands 27/J6
Blesbok (riv.), S. Africa 118/J7
Blessing, Texas (77419) 303/H9
Blessington, Ireland 17/J5
Blevins, Ark. (71825) 202/C6
Blewett, Texas (†78801) 303/D8
Blida, Algeria 106/E1
Blida, Algeria 102/C1
Bligh (sound), N. Zealand 100/A6
Bligh Water (bay), Fiji 86/P10
Blind Channel, Br. Col. 184/E5
Blind River, Ont. 162/H6
Blind River, Ontario 177/J5
Blind River, Ontario 175/D3
Blinman, S. Australia 88/F6
Blinman, S. Australia 94/F4
Blinnenhorn (mt.), Switzerland 39/F4
Bliss, Idaho (83314) 220/D7
Bliss, N.Y. (14024) 276/D5
Blissfield, Mich. (49228) 250/F7
Blissfield, New Bruns. 170/D2
Blissfield, Ohio (43805) 284/G5
Blitar, Indonesia 85/K2
Blitchton, Georgia (†31308) 217/J6
Blocher, Ind. (47138) 227/F7
Block (isl.), R.I. 249/H8
Blocker, Okla. (74529) 288/P4
Block House, Nova Scotia 168/D4
Block Island (sound), N.Y. 276/S8
Block Island, R.I. (02807) 249/H8
Block Island (sound), R.I. 249/H8
Blockton, Iowa (50836) 229/D7
Blodgett, Mo. (63824) 261/08
Blodgett, Oreg. (97326) 291/D3
Blodgett Landing, N.H. (†03255) 268/D5
Bloemendaal, Netherlands 27/E4
Bloemfontein, S. Africa 102/E7
Bloemfontein, S. Africa 118/C5
Blois, France 28/D4
Blokzijl, Netherlands 27/H3
Blomkest, Minn. (56216) 255/D6
Blonie, Poland 47/E2
Bloodroot (mt.), Vt. 268/B4
Bloodsworth (isl.), Md. 245/08
Bloodvein (riv.), Manitoba 179/F3
Bloodvein (riv.), Ontario 175/A2
Bloodvein River, Manitoba 179/F3
Bloody Foreland (prom.), Ireland 17/E1
Bloody Foreland (prom.), Ireland 10/B3
Bloom, Kansas (67833) 232/C4
Bloom, N. Dak. (†58401) 282/N6
Bloomburg, Texas (75556) 303/L4
Bloom City, Wis. (54617) 317/E8
Bloomdale, Ohio (44817) 284/D3
Bloomer, Ark. (†72933) 202/B3
Bloomer, Wis. (54724) 317/D5
Bloomery, W. Va. (26817) 312/K4
Bloomfield, Sierra (mts.), Bolivia 136/D4
Bloomfield○, Conn. (06002) 210/E1
Bloomfield, Ind. (47424) 227/D6
Bloomfield, Iowa (52537) 229/J7
Bloomfield, Ky. (40008) 237/L5
Bloomfield, Mo. (63825) 261/M9
Bloomfield, Mont. (59315) 262/M3
Bloomfield, Nebr. (68718) 264/G2
Bloomfield, Newf. 166/D2
Bloomfield, N.J. (07003) 273/B2
Bloomfield, N. Mex. (87413) 274/A2
Bloomfield, Ontario 177/G4
Bloomfield (New Bloomfield), Pa. (17068) 294/H5
Bloomfield○, Vt. (†03590) 268/D2
Bloomfield Hills, Mich. (48013) 250/B6
Bloomfield Ridge, New Bruns. 170/D2
Bloomfield Station, New Bruns. 170/E3
Bloomingburg, N.Y. (12721) 276/L7
Bloomingburg, Ohio (43106) 284/D6
Bloomingdale, Georgia (31302) 217/K6
Bloomingdale, Ill. (60108) 222/A5
Bloomingdale, Ind. (47832) 227/C5
Bloomingdale, Mich. (49026) 250/C6
Bloomingdale, N.J. (07403) 273/E1
Bloomingdale, N.Y. (12913) 276/M2
Bloomingdale, Ohio (43910) 284/J5
Bloomingdale, Tenn. (37660) 237/R7
Bloomingdale, Wis. (†54667) 317/E8
Blooming Grove, Ind. (†47012) 227/G5
Blooming Grove, Pa. (†18428) 294/M3
Blooming Grove, Texas (76626) 303/H5
Bloomingport, Ind. (†47355) 227/G5
Blooming Prairie, Minn. (55917) 255/E7
Bloomington, Calif. (92316) 204/E10
Bloomington, Idaho (83223) 220/G7
Bloomington, Ill. 188/J2
Bloomington, Ill. (61701) 222/D3
Bloomington, Ind. (47401) 227/D6
Bloomington, Md. (21523) 245/B3
Bloomington, Minn. (55420) 255/G6
Bloomington, Nebr. (68929) 264/F4
Bloomington, Texas (77951) 303/H9
Bloomington, Wis. (53804) 317/E10
Bloomington Springs, Tenn. (38545) 237/K8
Blooming Valley, Pa. (†16335) 294/B2
Bloomsburg, Pa. (17815) 294/J3
Bloomsbury, Alberta 182/C2
Bloomsbury, N.J. (08804) 273/C2
Bloomsdale, Mo. (63627) 261/M6
Bloomville, N.Y. (13739) 276/L6
Bloomville, Ohio (44818) 284/D3
Blora, Indonesia 85/K2
Blossburg, Pa. (16912) 294/H2
Blossom, Texas (75416) 303/J4
Bloubergstrand, S. Africa 118/E6
Blount (co.), Ala. 195/E2
Blount (co.), Tenn. 237/O9
Blounts Creek, N.C. (27814) 281/P4
Blount Springs, Ala. (†35079) 195/E3
Blountstown, Fla. (32424) 212/A1
Blountsville, Ala. (35031) 195/E2
Blountsville, Ind. (†47360) 227/G4
Blountville, Tenn. (37617) 237/S7
Blowering (res.), N.S. Wales 97/E4
Blowing Rock, N.C. (28605) 281/F2
Bloxom, Va. (23308) 307/S5
Bludenz, Austria 41/A3
Blue, Ariz. (85922) 198/F5
Blue (riv.), Ariz. 198/F5
Blue (mt.), Colo. 208/B2
Blue (riv.), Colo. 208/G3
Blue (riv.), Ind. 227/E8
Blue (mts.), Jamaica 158/J6
Blue (mt.), Maine 243/C6
Blue (hills), Mass. 249/C8
Blue (creek), Nebr. 264/B3
Blue (mt.), New Bruns. 170/D1
Blue (mt.), N.H. 268/E2
Blue (mts.), N.S. Wales 88/H6
Blue (mts.), N.S. Wales 97/F3
Blue, Okla. (†74701) 288/O7
Blue (riv.), Okla. 288/O6
Blue (mts.), Oreg. 291/J3
Blue (mt.), Pa. 294/G5
Blue (creek), Utah 304/B2
Blue (lake), Utah 304/B4
Blue (lake), Wash. 310/F3
Blue (mts.), Wash. 310/H4
Blue Ash, Ohio (†45242) 284/C9
Blue Ball, Ark. (†72866) 202/C4
Blue Bell, S. Dak. (†57773) 298/C6
Bluebell, Utah (84007) 304/D3
Blueberry Creek, Br. Col. 184/J5
Blueberry Mountain, Alberta 182/A2
Blue Creek, Ohio (45616) 284/D8
Blue Creek, Utah (†84337) 304/B2
Bluecreek, Wash. (†99109) 310/H2
Blue Creek, W. Va. (25026) 312/D6
Blue Cypress (lake), Fla. 212/F4
Blue Diamond, Ky. (41718) 237/P6
Blue Earth (co.), Minn. 255/D6
Blue Earth, Minn. (56013) 255/D7
Blue Earth (riv.), Minn. 255/D7
Blue Eye, Ark. (65611) 202/D1
Blue Eye, Mo. (65611) 261/F9
Bluefield, Va. (24605) 307/F6
Bluefield, W. Va. 188/K3
Bluefield, W. Va. (24701) 312/D8
Bluefields, Jamaica 158/G6
Bluefields, Nicaragua 154/F4
Bluegrass, Ind. (†46939) 227/E3
Blue Grass, Iowa (52726) 229/M5
Blue Grass, Minn. (†56477) 255/C4
Blue Grass, Va. (24413) 307/J3
Blue Heron, Sask. 181/E2
Blue Hill, Maine (04614) 243/F7
Blue Hill○, Maine (04614) 243/F7
Blue Hill (bay), Maine 243/G7
Blue Hill, Nebr. (68930) 264/F4
Blue Hill Falls, Maine (04615) 243/F7
Blue Hills, Conn. (06112) 210/E1
Blue Island, Ill. (60406) 222/B6
Bluejacket, Okla. (74333) 288/R1
Blue Jay, Calif. (92317) 204/H9
Blue Joint (lake), Oreg. 291/H5
Blue Knob (mt.), Pa. 294/E5
Blue Lake, Calif. (95525) 204/A3
Blue Mesa (res.), Colo. 208/E5
Bluemont, Va. (22012) 307/N2
Blue Mound, Ill. (62513) 222/D4
Blue Mound, Kansas (66010) 232/H3
Blue Mound, Texas (†76101) 303/E2
Blue Mounds, Wis. (53517) 317/G9
Blue Mountain, Ala. (36201) 195/G3
Blue Mountain, Ark. (72826) 202/C3
Blue Mountain (lake), Ark. 202/C3
Blue Mountain (peak), Jamaica 158/K6
Blue Mountain (peak), Jamaica 156/C3
Blue Mountain, Miss. (38610) 256/G1
Blue Mountain (lake), N.Y. 276/M3
Blue Mountain Lake, N.Y. (12812) 276/M3
Blue Mountains, Australia 87/E9
Blue Mountains, N. S. Wales 88/J6
Blue Mountains, N.S. Wales 97/F3
Blue Nile (riv.) 102/F3
Blue Nile (Abay) (riv.), Ethiopia 111/G5
Blue Nile (prov.), Sudan 111/F5
Blue Nile (riv.), Sudan 59/B6
Blue Nile (riv.), Sudan 111/F5
Blue Nose (mt.), Idaho 220/D4
Bluenose (lake), N.W. Terrs. 187/G3
Blue Rapids, Kansas (66411) 232/F2
Blue Ridge, Alberta 182/C2
Blue Ridge, Georgia (30513) 217/D1
Blue Ridge (lake), Georgia 217/D1
Blue Ridge (mts.), Georgia 217/D1
Blue Ridge, Ind. (†46176) 227/F5
Blue Ridge (mts.), Md. 245/H3
Blue Ridge (mts.), N.C. 281/E3
Blue Ridge (mts.), S.C. 296/B1
Blue Ridge, Va. (24064) 307/J6
Blue Ridge (mts.), Va. 307/J6
Blue Ridge Manor, Ky. (†40201) 237/L2
Blue Ridge Summit, Pa. (17214) 294/G6
Blue River, Br. Col. 184/H4
Blue River, Colo. (†80424) 208/G4
Blue River, Oreg. (97413) 291/E3
Blue River, Wis. (53518) 317/E9
Blue Rock, Nova Scotia 168/D4
Blue Rock (Gaysport), Ohio (43720) 284/G6
Blue Sea Lake, Québec 172/A3
Bluesky, Alberta 182/A1
Blue Spring (hills), Utah 304/B1
Blue Springs, Ala. (†36017) 195/G7
Blue Springs, Miss. (38828) 256/G2
Blue Springs, Mo. (64015) 261/R6
Blue Springs, Nebr. (68318) 264/H4
Blue Stack (mts.), Ireland 17/E2
Bluestem (lake), Okla. 288/O1
Bluestone (lake), Va. 307/G5
Bluestone (lake), W. Va. 312/E7
Blue Sulphur Springs, W. Va. (†25545) 312/E7
Blue Summit, Mo. (†64101) 261/R5
Bluevale, Ontario 177/C4
Bluewater, N. Mex. (87005) 274/A3
Bluewater (creek), N. Mex. 274/B4
Bluewater (creek), N. Mex. 274/D6
Bluewater (lake), N. Mex. 274/A3
Bluff (cape), Newf. 166/C3
Bluff, N. Zealand 100/B7
Bluff, N.C. (†28743) 281/D3
Bluff, Utah (84512) 304/E6
Bluff City, Ark. (71722) 202/D6
Bluff City, Ill. (†62624) 222/E5
Bluff City, Kansas (67018) 232/E4
Bluff City, Tenn. (37618) 237/S8
Bluff Dale, Texas (76433) 303/F5
Bluffdale, Utah (†84065) 304/B3
Bluff Knoll (mt.), W. Australia 92/B6
Bluff Park, Ala. (35226) 195/E4
Bluffs, Ill. (62621) 222/C4
Bluffsprings, Fla. (†32535) 212/B5
Bluffton, Alberta 182/C3
Bluffton, Ark. (72827) 202/C4
Bluffton, Georgia (31724) 217/C7
Bluffton, Ind. (46714) 227/G3
Bluffton, Minn. (56518) 255/C4
Bluffton, Ohio (45817) 284/C4
Bluffton, S.C. (29910) 296/F7
Bluford, Ill. (62814) 222/E5
Blum, Texas (76627) 303/G5
Blumenau, Brazil 132/D9
Blumenau, Brazil 120/E5
Blumenfeld, Manitoba 179/D5
Blumenheim, Sask. 181/E3
Blumenhof, Sask. 181/D5
Blumenort, Manitoba 179/E5
Blumenort, Manitoba 179/F5
Blumenort, Sask. 181/D6
Blumenstein, Switzerland 39/E3
Blumenthal, Sask. 181/E3
Blümlisalp (mt.), Switzerland 39/E3
Blunt, S. Dak. (57522) 298/J4
Bly, Oreg. (97622) 291/F5
Blying (sound), Alaska 196/C1
Blyn, Wash. (†98382) 310/B3
Blyth, England 13/F2
Blyth, England 10/F3
Blyth, Ontario 177/C4
Blyth Bridge, Scotland 15/E5
Blythe, Calif. (92225) 204/L10
Blythe, Georgia (30805) 217/H4
Blythedale, Md. (†21904) 245/O2
Blythedale, Mo. (64426) 261/E2
Blythedale, Pa. (†15018) 294/C5
Blytheswood, Ontario 177/B5
Blytheville, Ark. 188/H3
Blytheville, Ark. (72315) 202/L2
Blytheville A.F.B., Ark. 202/K2
Blythewood, S.C. (29016) 296/E3
Bo, S. Leone 102/A4
Bo, S. Leone 106/B7
Boac, Philippines 82/C4
Boaco, Nicaragua 154/E4
Boa Esperança, Brazil 135/D2
Boalsburg, Pa. (16827) 294/G4
Boano (isl.), Indonesia 85/H6
Boa Nova, Brazil 132/B5
Board Camp, Ark. (71932) 202/B4
Boardman (riv.), Mich. 250/D4
Boardman, N.C. (†28438) 281/M6
Boardman, Ohio (44512) 284/J3
Boardman, Oreg. (97818) 291/H2
Boardman, Wis. (†54016) 317/A5
Boardmans Bridge, Conn. (†06776) 210/B2
Boas (riv.), N.W. Terrs. 187/K3
Boat Basin, Br. Col. 184/D5
Boat Harbour, Tasmania 99/B2
Boat of Garten, Scotland 15/E3
Boa Vista, Brazil 120/C2
Boa Vista, Brazil 132/H8
Boa Vista (isl.), C. Verde 106/B8
Boayan (isl.), Philippines 82/B5
Boaz, Ala. (35957) 195/F2
Boaz, Ky. (42027) 237/D7
Boaz, Mo. (†65631) 261/F8
Boaz, W. Va. (†26187) 312/D4
Boaz, Wis. (†53581) 317/E9
Bobadah, N.S. Wales 97/D3
Bobai, China 77/H7
Bobaomby (cape), Madagascar 102/G6
Bobaomby (Amber) (cape), Madagascar 118/H2
Bobare, Venezuela 124/D2
Bobbili, India 68/E5
Bobbitt, N.C. (†27544) 281/N2
Bobcaygeon, Ontario 177/F3
Bobigny, France 28/B1
Böblingen, W. Germany 22/C4
Bobo, Miss. (†38614) 256/C2
Bobo Dioulasso, Upper Volta 106/D6
Bobo Dioulasso, Upper Volta 102/B3
Bobon, Philippines 82/F7
Bobonaza (riv.), Ecuador 128/D3
Bobonong, Botswana 118/D4
Bobotov Kuk (mt.), Yugoslavia 45/D4
Bobr (riv.), Poland 47/B3
Bobrov, U.S.S.R. 52/F4
Bobruysk, U.S.S.R. 7/G3
Bobruysk, U.S.S.R. 52/C4
Bobruysk, U.S.S.R. 48/C4
Bobs (lake), Ontario 177/H3
Bobtown, Pa. (15315) 294/B6
Bobures, Venezuela 124/C3
Boby, Pic (mt.), Madagascar 118/H4
Bocabec, New Bruns. 170/C3
Boca Chica, Dom. Rep. 158/E6
Boca Chica (key), Fla. 212/E7
Boca Ciega (bay), Fla. 212/B3
Boca de Aroa, Venezuela 124/D2
Boca del Mangle, Venezuela 124/D2
Boca del Pao, Venezuela 124/F3
Boca del Pepé, Colombia 126/B5
Boca del Río, Mexico 150/Q2
Boca del Soco, Dom. Rep. 158/F6
Boca do Acre, Brazil 132/G10
Boca Grande, Fla. (33921) 212/D5
Boca Grande (key), Fla. 212/D7
Boca Grande (passage), Trin. & Tob. 161/A10
Boca Grande (gulf), Venezuela 124/H3
Bocaiúva, Brazil 132/E7
Bocaranga, Cent. Afr. Rep. 115/C2
Boca Raton, Fla. (*33432) 212/F5
Bocas del Toro, Panama 154/F6
Bocay, Nicaragua 154/E3
Bochnia, Poland 47/E4
Bocholt, Belgium 27/H6
Bocholt, W. Germany 22/B3
Bochov, Czech. 41/B1
Bochum, W. Germany 22/B3
Bock, Minn. (56313) 255/E5
Boco, Chile 138/F2
Boconó, Venezuela 124/C3
Boda, Cent. Afr. Rep. 115/C3
Bodalla, N.S. Wales 97/F5
Bodaybo, U.S.S.R. 54/N4
Bodaybo, U.S.S.R. 48/M4
Bodcaw, Ark. (†71858) 202/D6
Boddam, Scotland 15/G3
Boddington, W. Australia 92/B2
Bode, Iowa (50519) 229/E3
Bodega (bay), Calif. 204/B5
Bodega (head), Calif. 204/B5
Bodega Bay, Calif. (94923) 204/B5
Bodegraven, Netherlands 27/F4
Bodélé (depr.), Chad 102/D3
Bodélé (depr.), Chad 111/C4
Boden, Sweden 18/M4
Bodensee (Constance) (lake), Austria 41/A3
Bodensee (Constance) (lake), Switzerland 39/H1
Bodensee (Constance) (lake), W. Germany 22/C5
Boderg (lake), Ireland 17/E4
Bodfish, Calif. (93205) 204/G8
Bodhan, India 68/D5
Bodie (isl.), N.C. 281/T2
Bodinayakkanur, India 68/D6
Bodines, Pa. (17722) 294/H3
Bodio, Switzerland 39/G4
Bodkin (pt.), Md. 245/N4
Bodmin, England 13/C7
Bodmin, England 10/D5
Bodmin, Sask. 181/D2
Bodo, Alberta 182/E3
Bodø, Norway 18/J3
Bodø, Norway 7/F2
Bodrum, Turkey 63/B4
Bodrum, Turkey 59/A2
Bo Duc, Vietnam 72/E4
Bódvaszilas, Hungary 41/F2
Boelus, Nebr. (68820) 264/F3
Boende, Zaire 115/D4
Boerne, Texas (78006) 303/J10
Boeuf (lake), La. 238/J7
Boeuf (riv.), La. 238/G1
Boffa, Guinea 106/B6
Bog (lake), Maine 243/H6
Bogalusa, La. 188/H4
Bogalusa, La. (70427) 238/L5
Bogan (riv.), N.S. Wales 97/D2
Bogandé, Upper Volta 106/E6
Bogan Gate, N.S. Wales 97/D3
Bogantungan, Queensland 95/C4
Bogard, Mo. (64622) 261/E4
Bogart, Georgia (30622) 217/E3
Bogata, Texas (75417) 303/J4
Bogatynia, Poland 47/B3
Boğazlıyan, Turkey 63/F3
Bogen, W. Germany 22/E4
Bogenfels, Namibia 118/B5
Bogense, Denmark 21/D6
Boger City, N.C. (28092) 281/G4
Boggabilla, N.S. Wales 97/F1
Boggabri, N.S. Wales 97/F2
Boggeragh (mts.), Ireland 17/D7
Boggs, W. Va. (26299) 312/E6
Boggstown, Ind. (46110) 227/F5
Boggy (peak), Ant. & Bar. 161/D11
Boggy Creek, Manitoba 179/A3
Boggy Depot, Okla. (†74525) 288/O6
Bogia, Papua N.G. 85/B6
Bogie (riv.), Scotland 15/F3
Bognor Regis, England 13/G7
Bognor Regis, England 10/F5
Bogny-sur-Meuse, France 28/F3
Bogo, Philippines 82/E5
Bogon (riv.), N. S. Wales 88/H6
Bogong (mt.), Victoria 97/D5
Bogor, Indonesia 54/M10
Bogor, Indonesia 85/H2
Bogoslof (isl.), Alaska 196/E4
Bogotá (cap.), Colombia 126/D5
Bogotá (cap.), Colombia 120/B2
Bogotá (cap.), Colombia 2/F5
Bogota, Ill. (†62448) 222/E5
Bogota, N.J. (07603) 273/B2
Bogota, Tenn. (38007) 237/C8
Bogra, Bangladesh 68/F4
Boguchar, U.S.S.R. 52/F5
Bogue, Kansas (67625) 232/C2
Bogué, Mauritania 106/B5
Bogue Chitto, Miss. (39629) 256/D8
Bogue Chitto (riv.), Miss. 256/D8
Bogue Homo (lake), Miss. 256/F7
Boguszów-Gorce, Poland 47/B3
Bog Walk, Jamaica 158/J6
Bo Hai (gulf), China 77/J4
Boharm, Sask. 181/F5
Bohemian (for.), Czech. 41/B2
Bohemian (for.), W. Germany 22/E4
Bohemian-Moravian Heights (hills), Czech. 41/C2
Boherbue, Ireland 17/C7
Bohners Lake, Wis. (†53105) 317/K10
Bohodleh, Somalia 115/J2
Bohol (prov.), Philippines 82/E6
Bohol (isl.), Philippines 85/G4
Bohol (isl.), Philippines 82/E6
Bohol (sea), Philippines 82/E6
Bohol (str.), Philippines 82/D6
Böhönye, Hungary 41/D3
Bohu (Bagrax), China 77/C3
Boicourt, Kansas (†66075) 232/H3
Boiestown, New Bruns. 170/D2
Boiling Spring Lakes, N.C. (28461) 281/N7
Boiling Springs, N.C. (28017) 281/F4
Boiling Springs, Pa. (17007) 294/H5
Bois Blanc (isl.), Mich. 250/E3
Boischatel, Québec 172/J3
Boisdale, Nova Scotia 168/H2
Boisdale, Loch (inlet), Scotland 15/A3
Bois D'Arc, Mo. (65612) 261/F8
Bois-des-Filion, Québec 172/H4
Bois de Sioux (riv.), Minn. 255/B4
Bois de Sioux (riv.), S. Dak. 298/R1
Boise (co.), Idaho 220/C6
Boise (cap.), Idaho 146/G5
Boise (cap.), Idaho (*83701) 220/B6
Boise (cap.), Idaho 188/C2
Boise (mts.), Idaho 220/B6
Boise (riv.), Idaho 220/B6
Boise City, Okla. (73933) 288/B1
Boissevain, Man. 162/G6
Boissevain, Manitoba 179/C5
Boissevain, Va. (24606) 307/F6
Boistfort, Wash. (†98532) 310/B4
Boisvert (pt.), Québec 172/J1
Boizenburg an der Elbe, E. Germany 22/D2
Bojador (cape), W. Sahara 102/A2
Bojador (cape), Western Sahara 106/B3
Bojeador (cape), Philippines 82/C1
Bojnurd, Iran 66/K2
Bojnurd, Iran 59/G2
Bojonegoro, Indonesia 85/J2
Bokchito, Okla. (74726) 288/O6
Boké, Guinea 106/B6
Bokeelia, Fla. (33922) 212/D5
Bokel (cay), Belize 154/D2
Bokhara (riv.), N.S. Wales 97/D1
Bokhoma, Okla. (†71821) 288/S7
Boknafjord (fjord), Norway 18/D7
Boko, Congo 115/B4
Bokoro, Chad 111/C5
Bokoshe, Okla. (74930) 288/S4
Bokote, Zaire 115/D4
Bokpyin, Burma 72/C5
Boksburg, S. Africa 118/J6
Bokungu, Zaire 115/D4
Bol, Chad 111/B5
Bol, Chad 102/D3
Bolair, W. Va. (26288) 312/F6
Bolama, Guinea-Biss. 106/A6
Bolan (pass), Pakistan 68/B3
Bolangir, India 68/E4
Bolar, Va. (24414) 307/J4
Bolatusha, Miss. (†39160) 256/E5
Bolayır, Turkey 63/C5
Bolbec, France 28/D3
Bolckow, Mo. (64427) 261/C2
Bolderslev, Denmark 21/C8
Bolding, Ark. (†71747) 202/F7
Boldman, Ky. (†41501) 237/R5
Boldon, England 13/J3
Bolduc, Québec 172/G4
Bole, China 77/B3
Bole, Ghana 106/D7
Boles, Ark. (72926) 202/B4
Bolesławiec, Poland 47/B3
Boley, Okla. (74829) 288/O4
Bolgatanga, Ghana 106/D6
Boli, China 77/M2
Boligee, Ala. (35443) 195/C5
Bolinao, Philippines 82/B2
Bolinao (cape), Philippines 82/B2
Bolinas, Calif. (94924) 204/H1
Boling, Texas (77420) 303/H8
Bolingbroke, Georgia (31004) 217/E5
Bolingbrook, Ill. (60439) 222/A6
Bolinger, Ala. (36903) 195/B7
Bolinger, La. (†71064) 238/C1
Bolivar, Argentina 143/D4
Bolivar, Bolivia 136/B3
Bolivar (dept.), Colombia 126/C3
Bolivar, Antioquia, Colombia 126/C5
Bolivar, Cauca, Colombia 126/B7
Bolivar (prov.), Ecuador 128/C3
Bolivar, Ecuador 128/C2
Bolivar (co.), Miss. 256/C3
Bolivar, Mo. (65613) 261/F7
Bolivar, N.Y. (14715) 276/D6
Bolivar, Ohio (44612) 284/G4
Bolivar, Pa. (15923) 294/D5
Bolivar, Peru 128/D6
Bolivar, Tenn. (38008) 237/C10
Bolivar (pen.), Texas 303/K8
Bolivar (state), Venezuela 124/F7
Bolivar, Cerro (mt.), Venezuela 124/G4
Bolivar, Pico (peak), Venezuela 124/C3
Bolivar, W. Va. (†25425) 312/L4
Bolivia 2/F6
Bolivia 120/C4
BOLIVIA 136
Bolivia, N.C. (28422) 281/N6
Bolkar (mts.), Turkey 63/F4
Bolkhov, U.S.S.R. 52/E4
Bolligen, Switzerland 39/E3
Bolling, Ala. (36007) 195/E7
Bolling A.F.B., D.C. 245/E5
Bollinger (co.), Mo. 261/M8
Bollington, England 10/G2
Bollington, England 13/H2
Bollnäs, Sweden 18/K6
Bollon, Queensland 95/C6
Bollon, Queensland 88/H5
Bollstabruk, Sweden 18/L5
Bolmen (lake), Sweden 18/H8
Bolobo, Zaire 115/C4
Bologna (prov.), Italy 34/C2
Bologna, Italy 34/C2
Bologna, Italy 7/F4
Bolognesi, Peru 128/F8
Bolognesi, Peru 128/F6
Bologoye, U.S.S.R. 52/D3
Bolomba, Zaire 115/C3
Bolonchén de Rejón, Mexico 150/O7
Bolondrón, Cuba 156/B2
Bolondrón, Cuba 158/D1
Bolovens (plat.), Laos 72/E4
Bolpebra, Bolivia 136/A2
Bolsena (lake), Italy 34/C3
Bol'shevik (isl.) U.S.S.R. 54/N2
Bol'shevik (isl.), U.S.S.R. 4/A4
Bol'shevik (isl.), U.S.S.R. 48/K2
Bol'shoy Lyakhov (isl.), U.S.S.R. 54/R2
Bol'shoy Lyakhovskiy (isl.), U.S.S.R. 48/P2
Bolsover, England 13/J2
Bolsters Mills, Maine (†04040) 243/B7
Bolsward, Netherlands 27/H2
Boltaña, Spain 33/F1
Boltigen, Switzerland 39/D3
Bolton○, Conn. (06040) 210/F1
Bolton, England 10/G2
Bolton, England 13/H2
Bolton○, Mass. (01740) 249/H3
Bolton, Miss. (39041) 256/D6
Bolton, N.C. (28423) 281/N6
Bolton○, Vt. (†05466) 268/B3
Bolton (mt.), Vt. 268/B3
Bolton Landing, N.Y. (12814) 276/N3
Bolu (prov.), Turkey 63/D2
Bolu, Turkey 59/B1
Bolu, Turkey 63/D2
Bolus (head), Ireland 17/A8
Bolvadin, Turkey 63/D3
Bolvanskiy Nos (cape), U.S.S.R. 52/K1
Bolvanskiy Nos (cape), U.S.S.R. 48/G2
Bolzano (Bolzen), Italy 34/C1
Bolzano, Italy 7/F4
Bolzano-Bozen (prov.), Italy 34/C1
Bolzen (Bolzano), Italy 34/C1
Boma, Zaire 102/D5
Boma, Zaire 115/B5
Bomaderry-Nowra, N.S. Wales 97/F4
Bomarton, Texas (†76380) 303/E4
Bomba (gulf), Libya 111/D1
Bombala, N.S. Wales 97/E5
Bombardopolis, Haiti 158/B5
Bombay, India 54/J8
Bombay, India 2/N5
Bombay (harb.), India 68/B7
Bombay, Minn. (†55946) 255/F6
Bombay, N.Y. (12914) 276/M1
Bomboma, Zaire 115/C3
Bom Conselho, Brazil 132/G5
Bom Despacho, Brazil 135/D1
Bom Despacho, Brazil 132/E7
Bomdila, India 68/G3
Bom Futuro, Brazil 120/C4
Bom Futuro, Brazil 132/A5
Bomi, China 77/E6
Bom Jesus, Brazil 132/E5
Bom Jesus da Lapa, Brazil 120/E4
Bom Jesus da Lapa, Brazil 132/F6
Bom Jesus do Itabapoana, Brazil 135/F2
Bomongo, Zaire 115/C3
Bomont, W. Va. (25030) 312/D6
Bomoseen, Vt. (05732) 268/A4
Bomoseen (lake), Vt. 268/A4
Bom Retiro, Brazil 132/D10
Bom Sucesso, Brazil 135/D2
Bomu (riv.), Cent. Afr. Rep. 102/E4
Bomu (riv.), Cent. Afr. Rep. 115/D3
Bomu (riv.), Zaire 115/D3
Bon (cape), Tunisia 102/D1
Bon (cape), Tunisia 106/G1
Bona (mt.), Alaska 196/K2
Bonabéri, Cameroon 115/A3
Bonacca (Guanaja) (isl.), Honduras 154/E2
Bon Accord, Alberta 182/D3
Bonaduz, Switzerland 39/H3
Bon Air, Ala. (35032) 195/F4
Bonair, Iowa (†52155) 229/J2
Bon Air, Tenn. (†38583) 237/L9
Bon Air, Va. (23235) 307/N5
Bonaire (isl.), Neth. Ant. 156/E4
Bonaire (isl.), Neth. Ant. 161/E9
Bonalbo, N.S. Wales 97/G1

Boyne City 341

Bonanza, Alberta 182/A2
Bonanza, Ark. (†72901) 202/B3
Bonanza, Colo. (†81155) 208/G6
Bonanza, Nicaragua 154/E4
Bonanza, Oreg. (97623) 291/F5
Bonanza, Utah (84008) 304/E3
Bonanza (peak), Wash. 310/E2
Bonao, Dom. Rep. 158/E6
Bonaparte, Iowa (52620) 229/K7
Bonaparte (lake), N.Y. 276/K2
Bonaparte (creek), Wash. 310/F2
Bonaparte (mt.), Wash. 310/F2
Bonaparte (arch.), W. Australia 88/C2
Bonaparte (arch.), W. Australia 92/D1
Bon Aqua, Tenn. (37025) 237/G9
Bonar Bridge, Scotland 15/D3
Bonaventure (cape), Newf. 166/D2
Bonaventure (co.), Québec 172/C2
Bonaventure (county), Québec 174/D3
Bonaventure, Québec 172/C2
Bonaventure (isl.), Québec 172/D1
Bonaventure (riv.), Québec 172/C1
Bonavista, Newf. 166/D2
Bonavista (bay), Newf. 166/D1
Bonavista (cape), Newf. 166/D1
Bonavista, Newf. 162/L6
Boncarbo, Colo. (81024) 208/K8
Bonchester Bridge, Scotland 15/F5
Boncourt, Switzerland 39/C2
Bond, Colo. (80423) 208/F3
Bond (co.), Ill. 222/D5
Bond, Ky. (40407) 237/N6
Bond, Miss. (39550) 256/F9
Bond (mt.), N.H. 268/E3
Bondeno, Italy 34/C2
Bond Falls (res.), Mich. 250/G2
Bondi (beach), N.S. Wales 97/K3
Bondiss, Alberta 182/D2
Bondo, Zaire 115/D3
Bondoukou, Ivory Coast 106/D7
Bondowoso, Indonesia 85/L2
Bondsville, Mass. (01009) 249/E4
Bonduel, Wis. (54107) 317/K6
Bondurant, Iowa (50035) 229/G5
Bondurant, Wyo. (82922) 319/B2
Bondville, Ill. (61815) 222/E3
Bondville, Ky. (40308) 237/M5
Bondville, Vt. (05340) 268/B5
Bondy, France 28/B1
Bône (Annaba), Algeria 106/F1
Bone, Idaho (†83401) 220/G6
Bone (gulf), Indonesia 54/O10
Bone (gulf), Indonesia 85/G7
Bone Cave, Tenn. (†38581) 237/L9
Bone Gap, Ill. (62815) 222/F5
Bo'ness, Scotland 10/C1
Bo'ness, Scotland 15/C1
Bonesteel, S. Dak. (57317) 298/M7
Bonet (riv.), Ireland 17/E3
Boneta, Utah (†84051) 304/D3
Bonete (dam), Uruguay 145/C3
Bonetraill, N. Dak. (†58801) 282/C3
Boneville, Georgia (30806) 217/G4
Bonfield, Ill. (60913) 222/E2
Bonfield, Ontario 177/E1
Bonfol, Switzerland 39/D2
Bong (range), Liberia 106/B7
Bongabong, Philippines 82/C4
Bongandanga, Zaire 115/D3
Bonggaw, Philippines 82/B8
Bongo (isl.), Philippines 82/D7
Bongor, Chad 111/C5
Bongor, Chad 102/D3
Bong Son (Hoai Nhon), Vietnam 72/F4
Bonham, Texas (75418) 303/H4
Bonhill, Scotland 15/B1
Bonhomme (isl.), Mo. 261/N2
Bon Homme (co.), S. Dak. 298/O7
Bonifacio, France 28/B7
Bonifacio (str.), France 28/B7
Bonifacio (str.), Italy 34/B4
Bonifay, Fla. (32425) 212/C5
Bönigen, Switzerland 39/E3
Bonilla, S. Dak. (†57348) 298/N4
Bonin (isls.), Japan 2/S4
Bonin (isls.), Japan 54/R7
Bonin (isls.), Japan 87/E3
Bonin (isls.), Japan 81/M3
Bonita, Ariz. (†85643) 198/E6
Bonita (pt.), Calif. 204/H2
Bonita, La. (71223) 238/G1
Bonita, Miss. (†39301) 256/G6
Bonita Springs, Fla. (33923) 212/E5
Bonlee, N.C. (27213) 281/L3
Bonn (cap.), W. Germany 7/E3
Bonn (cap.), W. Germany 22/B3
Bonne (bay), Newf. 166/C4
Bonneau, S.C. (29431) 296/H5
Bonner (co.), Idaho 220/B1
Bonners Ferry, Idaho (83805) 220/B1
Bonner Springs, Kansas (66012) 232/H2
Bonner-West Riverside, Mont. (59823) 262/C4
Bonnet (lake), Manitoba 179/G4
Bonnétable, France 28/D3
Bonnet Carré Spillway and Floodway, La. 238/N3
Bonne Terre, Mo. (63628) 261/L7
Bonnet Plume (riv.), Yukon 187/E3
Bonneville, France 28/G4
Bonneville (co.), Idaho 220/G6
Bonneville, Oreg. (97008) 291/F2
Bonneville (dam), Oreg. 291/E2
Bonneville (salt flats), Utah 304/A3
Bonneville (dam), Wash. 310/D5
Bonneville (lake), Wash. 310/D5
Bonneville, Wyo. (†82649) 319/E2
Bonneville (mt.), Wyo. 319/C3
Bonney Lake, Wash. (†98390) 310/C3
Bonnie, Ill. (62816) 222/E5
Bonnieville, Ky. (42713) 237/K6
Bonnots Mill, Mo. (65016) 261/J5
Bonny (res.), Colo. 208/P3
Bonny, Nigeria 106/F8
Bonny (bight), Nigeria 106/F8
Bonnybridge, Scotland 15/C1
Bonnyman, Ky. (41719) 237/P6
Bonnyrigg, N. S. Wales 88/K4
Bonnyrigg, N.S. Wales 97/H3
Bonnyrigg and Lasswade, Scotland 10/C1
Bonnyrigg and Lasswade, Scotland 15/D2
Bonny River, New Bruns. 170/D3
Bonnyville, Alberta 182/E2
Bono, Ark. (72416) 202/J2
Bono, Ohio (†43445) 284/D2
Bonorva, Italy 34/B4
Bonpas (creek), Ill. 222/F5
Bonpland (mt.), N. Zealand 100/A6
Bon Secour, Ala. (36511) 195/C10
Bon Secour (bay), Ala. 195/C10
Bonsecours, Québec 172/E4
Bonshaw, Pr. Edward I. 168/E2
Bonthain, Indonesia 85/F7
Bonthe, S. Leone 106/B7
Bontoc, Philippines 85/G2
Bontoc, Philippines 82/C2
Bon Wier, Texas (75928) 303/L7
Bonyhád, Hungary 41/E3
Boody, Ill. (62514) 222/D4
Book (cliffs), Utah 304/E4
Booker, Texas (79005) 303/D1
Booker T. Washington Nat'l Mon., Va. 307/J6
Boolaloo, W. Australia 92/B3
Booligal, N.S. Wales 97/C3
Boom, Belgium 27/E6
Boom, Tenn. (†38573) 237/L7
Boomer, N.C. (28606) 281/G2
Boomer, W. Va. (25031) 312/D6
Boomi, N. S. Wales 88/H5
Boomi, N.S. Wales 97/E1
Boon (pt.), Ant. & Bar. 161/E11
Boon, Mich. (49618) 250/D4
Boondall, Queensland 88/K2
Boone (co.), Ark. 202/D1
Boone, Colo. (81025) 208/L6
Boone (co.), Ill. 222/E1
Boone (co.), Ind. 227/E4
Boone (co.), Iowa 229/F5
Boone, Iowa (50036) 229/F4
Boone (co.), Ky. 237/M3
Boone, Ky. (†40403) 237/N5
Boone (co.), Mo. 261/H4
Boone (co.), Nebr. 264/F3
Boone, Nebr. (68625) 264/F3
Boone, N.C. (28607) 281/F2
Boone (lake), Tenn. 237/S8
Boone (co.), W. Va. 312/C6
Boone Grove, Ind. (46302) 227/C2
Boonesboro, Mo. (†65250) 261/G4
Boones Mill, Va. (24065) 307/J6
Boonesville, Va. (†22935) 307/L4
Booneville, Ark. (72927) 202/C3
Booneville, Ky. (41314) 237/O6
Booneville, Miss. (38829) 256/G1
Boonsboro, Md. (21713) 245/H2
Boonton, N.J. (07005) 273/E2
Boonton (res.), N.J. 273/E2
Boonville, Calif. (95415) 204/B5
Boonville, Ind. (47601) 227/C8
Boonville, Mo. (65233) 261/G5
Boonville, N.Y. (13309) 276/K4
Boonville, N.C. (27011) 281/H2
Boopi (riv.), Bolivia 136/B4
Boorooban, N.S. Wales 97/C4
Boorowa, N.S. Wales 97/E4
Boort, Victoria 97/B5
Booth, Ala. (36008) 195/E6
Boothbay, Maine (04537) 243/D8
Boothbay○, Maine (04537) 243/D8
Boothbay Harbor, Maine (04538) 243/D8
Boothia (pen.), Canada 4/B14
Boothia (gulf), Canada 4/B14
Boothia (pen.), N.W.T. 146/J2
Boothia (gulf), N.W.T. 146/J2
Boothia (isthmus), N.W.T. 162/G2
Boothia (pen.), N.W.T. 162/G1
Boothia (gulf), N.W.T. 162/G1
Boothia (gulf), N.W. Terrs. 187/K3
Boothia (pen.), N.W. Terrs. 187/J2
Boothville, La. (70038) 238/M8
Boothwyn, Pa. (19061) 294/L7
Bootle, England 10/F2
Bootle, England 13/G2
Booué, Gabon 115/B3
Bophuthatswana (bantustan), S. Africa 102/E7
Bophuthatswana (rep.), S. Africa 118/D5
Boppard, W. Germany 22/B3
Boquerón, Cuba 158/K4
Boquerón, Cuba 156/C3
Boquerón, (dept.), Paraguay 144/B3
Boquerón, El (pass), Peru 128/E7
Boquerón, P. Rico 156/F1
Boquerón, P. Rico 161/A3
Boquerón (bay), P. Rico 161/A3
Boquilla del Carmen, Mexico 150/H2
Bor, Czech. 41/B2
Bor, Sudan 111/F6
Bor, Turkey 63/F4
Bor, U.S.S.R. 52/F3
Bor, Yugoslavia 45/E3
Bora-Bora (isl.), Fr. Poly. 87/L7
Borah (peak), Idaho 188/D2
Borah (peak), Idaho 220/E5
Borama, Somalia 115/H1
Borås, Sweden 7/F3
Borås, Sweden 18/H8
Borazjan, Iran 66/G6
Borazjan, Iran 59/F4
Borba, Brazil 120/D3
Borba, Brazil 132/H9
Borba, Portugal 33/C3
Borbón, Venezuela 124/F4
Borçka, Turkey 63/J2
Borculo, Netherlands 27/J4
Bordeaux, France 28/C5
Bordeaux, France 7/D4
Bordeaux, S.C. (†29835) 296/C4
Bordeaux (mt.), Virgin Is. (U.S.) 161/C4
Bordelonville, La. (71320) 238/G4
Borden (isl.), Canada 4/B15
Borden, Ind. (47106) 227/F8
Borden (isl.), N.W. Terrs. 187/G2
Borden (pen.), N.W. Terrs. 187/K2
Borden, Pr. Edward I. 168/E2
Borden, Sask. 181/D3
Borden, S.C. (29017) 296/G3
Borden, Wyo. (†83114) 319/B3
Borden (co.), Texas 303/C5
Borden, W. Australia 92/B6
Borden Shaft, Md. (†21532) 245/B2
Borden Springs, Ala. (†36262) 195/H3
Bordentown, N.J. (08505) 273/D3
Border, Minn. (†56623) 255/D2
Border, Wyo. (†83114) 319/B3
Borderland, W. Va. (25665) 312/B7
Borders (reg.), Scotland 15/E5
Bordertown, S. Australia 88/F7
Bordertown, S. Australia 94/G7
Bordighera, Italy 34/A3
Bordj Bou Arreridj, Algeria 106/E1
Bordj Fly Sainte Marie, Algeria 106/D3
Bordj Omar Driss, Algeria 106/F3
Bordj Omar Driss, Algeria 102/C2
Bordulac, N. Dak. (58417) 282/N5
Boreing, Ky. (†40740) 237/N6
Boreray (isl.), Scotland 15/A2
Boreray (isl.), Scotland 15/A3
Borgå, Finland 18/O6
Borge, Norway 18/H2
Borger, Netherlands 27/K3
Borger, Texas (79007) 303/C2
Borger, Texas 188/F3
Borgerhout, Belgium 27/E6
Borgholm, Sweden 18/K8
Borghorst, W. Germany 22/B2
Borgloon, Belgium 27/G7
Borgne (lake), La. 238/L7
Borgne (riv.), Switzerland 39/D4
Borgo, Italy 34/C1
Borgomanero, Italy 34/B2
Borgo San Lorenzo, Italy 34/C2
Borgworm (Waremme), Belgium 27/G7
Borikan, Laos 72/D3
Boring, Md. (21020) 245/L2
Boring, Oreg. (97009) 291/E2
Borinquen (pt.), P. Rico 156/F1
Borinquen (pt.), P. Rico 161/A1
Borislav, U.S.S.R. 52/B5
Borisoglebsk, U.S.S.R. 48/E4
Borisoglebsk, U.S.S.R. 52/F4
Borisov, U.S.S.R. 52/C4
Borisovka, U.S.S.R. 52/E4
Bo River Post, Sudan 111/E6
Borja, Peru 128/D5
Borja, Spain 33/F2
Borjas Blancas, Spain 33/G2
Borken, W. Germany 22/B3
Børkop, Denmark 21/C6
Borku, Chad 111/C4
Borkum, W. Germany 22/B2
Borkum (isl.), W. Germany 22/B2
Borlänge, Sweden 18/J6
Borna, E. Germany 22/E3
Borndiep (chan.), Netherlands 27/H2
Borne, Netherlands 27/K4
Borneo (isl.) 2/Q6
Borneo (isl.) 54/N9
Borneo (isl.), Indonesia 85/E5
Borneo (isl.), Malaysia 85/E5
Bornheim, W. Germany 22/B3
Bornholm (co.), Denmark 21/F9
Bornholm (isl.), Denmark 7/F3
Bornholm (isl.), Denmark 18/J9
Bornholm (isl.), Denmark 21/F9
Borno (state), Nigeria 106/G6
Bornova, Turkey 63/B3
Borocay (isl.), Philippines 82/D5
Borojó, Venezuela 124/C2
Boron, Calif. (93516) 204/H8
Borongan, Philippines 82/E5
Borot Kidod (well), Israel 65/C5
Borovichi, U.S.S.R. 52/D3
Borradaile, Alberta 182/E3
Borre, Norway 18/D4
Borrego Springs, Calif. (92004) 204/J10
Borris, Ireland 17/H6
Borris-in-Ossory, Ireland 17/F6
Borrisokane, Ireland 17/E6
Borrisoleigh, Ireland 17/E6
Borroloola, North. Terr. 88/F3
Borroloola, North. Terr. 93/E4
Borşa, Romania 45/G2
Borsod-Abaúj-Zemplén (co.), Hungary 41/F2
Bortala (Bole), China 77/B3
Borth, Wales 13/C5
Bort-les-Orgues, France 28/E5
Boruca, C. Rica 154/F6
Borujerd, Iran 59/E3
Borujerd, Iran 66/F4
Borup, Denmark 21/E7
Borup, Minn. (56519) 255/B3
Börzsöny (mts.), Hungary 41/E3
Borzya, U.S.S.R. 48/M4
Bosa, Italy 34/B4
Bosanska Dubica, Yugoslavia 45/C3
Bosanska Gradiška, Yugoslavia 45/C3
Bosanska Kostajnica, Yugoslavia 45/B3
Bosanska Krupa, Yugoslavia 45/C3
Bosanski Brod, Yugoslavia 45/D3
Bosanski Novi, Yugoslavia 45/C3
Bosanski Petrovac, Yugoslavia 45/C3
Bosanski Šamac, Yugoslavia 45/D3
Bosaso, Somalia 115/J1
Bosaso, Somalia 102/G3
Boscawen○, N.H. (03301) 268/D5
Bosch, van den (cape), Indonesia 85/J6
Bosco, La. (†71201) 238/F2
Boscobel, Wis. (53805) 317/E9
Bose, China 77/G7
Boshan, China 77/J4
Boskoop, Netherlands 27/F4
Boskovice, Czech. 41/D2
Bosler, Wyo. (82051) 319/G4
Bosna (riv.), Yugoslavia 45/D3
Bosnia and Hercegovina (rep.), Yugoslavia 45/C3
Boso (pen.), Japan 81/K6
Bosobolo, Zaire 115/D3
Bosporus (str.), Turkey 7/G4
Bosporus (str.), Turkey 59/A1
Bosporus (str.), Turkey 63/C2
Bosque (Bosque Farms), N. Mex. (87006) 274/C4
Bosque (co.), Texas 303/G6
Boss, Mo. (65440) 261/K7
Bossangoa, Cent. Afr. Rep. 102/D4
Bossangoa, Cent. Afr. Rep. 115/C2
Bossburg, Wash. (†99126) 310/H2
Bossé, New Bruns. 170/B1
Bossembele, Cent. Afr. Rep. 115/C2
Bossier (par.), La. 238/C1
Bossier City, La. (*71111) 238/C1
Bosso, Niger 106/G6
Bostan, Iran 66/F5
Bostan, Pakistan 68/B2
Bostanabad-e-Bala, Iran 66/E2
Bosten (Bagrax) Hu (lake), China 77/C3
Boston (mts.), Ark. 202/B2
Boston, England 13/G5
Boston, England 10/F4
Boston, Georgia (31626) 217/E9
Boston, Ind. (47324) 227/H5
Boston, Ky. (40107) 237/K5
Boston (cap.), Mass. 146/L5
Boston (cap.), Mass. 188/M2
Boston (cap.), Mass. (*02101) 249/D7
Boston (bay), Mass. 249/E6
Boston (harb.), Mass. 249/D7
Boston, Mo. (†64759) 261/D8
Boston, N.Y. (14025) 276/C5
Boston (mts.), Okla. 288/S3
Boston, Pa. (15135) 294/C7
Boston, Tenn. (†37064) 237/G9
Boston, Texas (75557) 303/K4
Boston, U.S. 2/F3
Boston, Va. (22713) 307/M3
Boston Bar, Br. Col. 184/G5
Boston Heights, Ohio (†44264) 284/J10
Bostonnais (isl.), Québec 172/E3
Bostonnais, Grand Lac (lake), Québec 172/E2
Bostonnais (riv.), Québec 172/E2
Boston Nat'l Hist. Park, Mass. 249/D6
Bostwick, Fla. (32007) 212/E2
Bostwick, Georgia (30623) 217/E3
Bostwick, Nebr. (†68978) 264/F4
Boswell, Ark. (72516) 202/F1
Boswell, Br. Col. 184/J5
Boswell, Ind. (47921) 227/C3
Boswell, Okla. (74727) 288/P6
Boswell, Pa. (15531) 294/E5
Boswell Bay, Alaska (†99574) 196/J2
Boswil, Switzerland 39/F2
Bosworth, Mo. (64723) 261/F4
Bot (riv.), S. Africa 118/G7
Botany, N. S. Wales 88/L4
Botany (bay), N. S. Wales 88/L4
Botany, N.S. Wales 97/J4
Botany (bay), N.S. Wales 97/J4
Botene, Laos 72/D3
Botetourt (co.), Va. 307/J5
Botevgrad, Bulgaria 45/F4
Botha, Alberta 182/D3
Botha (riv.), Alberta 182/B1
Bothell, Wash. (98011) 310/B1
Bothnia (gulf) 7/G2
Bothnia (gulf), Finland 18/M5
Bothnia (gulf), Sweden 18/N4
Bothwell, Ontario 177/C5
Bothwell, Tasmania 99/C4
Bothwell, Utah (†84337) 304/B2
Botkins, Ohio (45306) 284/B5
Botna, Iowa (†51454) 229/C5
Botoşani, Romania 45/H2
Botrange (mt.), Belgium 27/J8
Botrivier, S. Africa 118/F7
Botsford, Conn. (06404) 210/C3
Botswana 2/L7
Botswana 102/E7
BOTSWANA 118/C4
Bottesford, England 13/G4
Bottineau (co.), N. Dak. 282/J2
Bottineau, N. Dak. (58318) 282/J2
Bottrel, Alberta 182/C4
Bottrop, W. Germany 22/B3
Botucatu, Brazil 135/B3
Botucatu, Brazil 132/D8
Botwood, Newf. 166/C4
Bouaflé, Ivory Coast 106/C7
Bouaké, Ivory Coast 102/B4
Bouaké, Ivory Coast 106/D7
Bouali, Cent. Afr. Rep. 115/C3
Bouar, Cent. Afr. Rep. 102/D4
Bouar, Cent. Afr. Rep. 115/C2
Bou Arfa, Morocco 106/D2
Bouca, Cent. Afr. Rep. 115/C2
Boucaut (bay), North. Terr. 93/D1
Boucherville, Québec 172/J4
Boucherville (isl.), Québec 172/J4
Bouches-du-Rhône (dept.), France 28/F6
Bouchette, Québec 172/A3
Bouckville, N.Y. (13310) 276/J5
Bou Djebeha, Mali 106/D5
Boudreau (bay), La. 238/M7
Boudreaux, La. (†70353) 238/J8
Boudreaux (lake), La. 238/J8
Boudry, Switzerland 39/C3
Boufarik, Algeria 106/E1
Bougainville (reef), 95/C2
Bougainville (reef), Coral Sea Is. Terr. 88/H3
Bougainville (isl.), Papua N.G. 87/F6
Bougainville (isl.), Papua N.G. 86/C2
Bougainville (str.), Papua N.G. 86/D2
Bougainville (str.), Solomon Is. 86/D2
Bougainville (cape), W. Australia 88/D2
Bougainville (cape), W. Australia 92/D1
Bougaroun (cape), Algeria 106/F1
Boughton (isl.), Pr. Edward I. 168/F2
Bougie (Béjaïa), Algeria 106/F1
Bougouni, Mali 106/C6
Bouillante, Guadeloupe 161/A6
Bouillon, Belgium 27/G9
Bou Izakarn, Morocco 106/C3
Boujad, Morocco 106/C2
Boulaide, Cent. Afr. Rep. 115/C3
Boulanger, Québec 172/E1
Boularderie (isl.), Nova Scotia 168/H2
Boulder, Australia 87/C9
Boulder, Colo. 188/E2
Boulder, Colo. 146/H6
Boulder (co.), Colo. 208/J2
Boulder, Colo. (*80301) 208/J2
Boulder (mts.), Idaho 220/D6
Boulder, Mont. (59632) 262/E4
Boulder (lake), N. Mex. 274/C2
Boulder, Utah (84716) 304/C6
Boulder (creek), Utah 304/C6
Boulder, W. Australia 88/C6
Boulder, Wyo. (82923) 319/C3
Boulder (lake), Wyo. 319/C3
Boulder City, Nev. (89005) 266/G7
Boulder Creek, Calif. (95006) 204/J4
Boulder Junction, Wis. (54512) 317/G3
Boulder-Kalgoorlie, W. Australia 92/C5
Boulevard, Calif. (92005) 204/J11
Boulevard Heights, Md. (†20027) 245/F5
Boulia, Queensland 95/A4
Boulia, Queensland 88/F4
Boulogne, Fla. (†32046) 212/E1
Boulogne-Billancourt, France 28/A2
Boulogne-sur-Mer, France 28/D2
Bouna, Ivory Coast 106/D7
Boundary, Alaska (†99732) 196/K2
Boundary (co.), Idaho 220/B1
Boundary (peak), Nev. 266/C5
Boundary (plat.), Sask. 181/B6
Boundary (bay), Wash. 310/C1
Boundary (dam), Wash. 310/H2
Boundary (lake), Wash. 310/H2
Boundary Bend, Victoria 97/B4
Bound Brook, N.J. (08805) 273/D2
Boundiali, Ivory Coast 106/C7
Boundji, Congo 115/C4
Boun Nua, Laos 72/D2
Bountiful, Utah (84010) 304/C3
Bounty (isls.), N. Zealand 87/H10
Bounty, Sask. 181/D4
Bourail, New Caled. 87/G8
Bourail, New Caled. 86/G4
Bourbon, Ill. (†61953) 222/E4
Bourbon, Ind. (46504) 227/E2
Bourbon (co.), Kansas 232/H4
Bourbon (co.), Ky. 237/N4
Bourbon, Miss. (†38756) 256/C4
Bourbon, Mo. (65441) 261/K6
Bourbonnais (trad. prov.), France 29
Bourbonnais, Ill. (60914) 222/F2
Bourem, Mali 106/E5
Bourg, La. (70343) 238/J7
Bourganeuf, France 28/D5
Bourg-des-Saintes, Guadeloupe 161/A7
Bourg-en-Bresse, France 28/F4
Bourgeois, New Bruns. 170/F2
Bourges, France 28/E4
Bourget, Ontario 177/J2
Bourg-Léopold (Leopoldsburg), Belgium 27/G6
Bourgoin-Jallieu, France 28/F5
Bourg Saint-Pierre, Switzerland 39/D5
Bourke, N. S. Wales 88/H6
Bourke, N.S. Wales 97/D2
Bourne, England 13/G5
Bourne, Mass. (02532) 249/M6
Bourne○, Mass. (02532) 249/M6
Bournedale, Mass. (†02532) 249/M5
Bournemouth, England 13/F7
Bournemouth, England 10/F5
Bourneville, Ohio (45617) 284/D7
Bou Saâda, Algeria 106/E1
Bouse, Ariz. (85325) 198/A5
Bouse Wash (dry riv.), Ariz. 198/A4
Boussac, France 28/D4
Bousso, Chad 111/C5
Boussu, Belgium 27/D8
Boutilimit, Mauritania 106/B5
Boutilimit, Mauritania 102/A3
Bouton, Iowa (50039) 229/E5
Boutte, La. (70039) 238/N4
Bouvard (cape), W. Australia 92/A2
Bouvet (isl.) 5/D1
Bouvetøya (Bouvet) (isl.) 5/D1
Boven Bolivia, Neth. Ant. 161/E8
Boves, Italy 34/A2
Bovey, Minn. (55709) 255/E3
Bovey Tracey, England 13/D7
Bovill, Idaho (83806) 220/B3
Bovina, Miss. (†39180) 256/C6
Bovina, Texas (79009) 303/A3
Bovril, Argentina 143/G5
Bow (riv.), Alberta 182/D4
Bow (riv.), Alta. 162/E5
Bow (lake), N.H. 268/E5
Bow, Wash. (98232) 310/C2
Bowbells, N. Dak. (58721) 282/F2
Bow City, Alberta 182/D4
Bowden, Alberta 182/C4
Bowden, Jamaica 158/K6
Bowden, W. Va. (26254) 312/G5
Bowdens, N.C. (28322) 281/N4
Bowdle, S. Dak. (57428) 298/K3
Bowdoin (lake), Mont. 262/J2
Bowdoinham○, Maine (04008) 243/D7
Bowdon, Georgia (30108) 217/B3
Bowdon, N. Dak. (58418) 282/L5
Bowdon Junction, Georgia (30109) 217/B3
Bowell, Alberta 182/E4
Bowen, Australia 87/E7
Bowen, Ill. (62316) 222/B3
Bowen, Ky. (40309) 237/O5
Bowen, Queensland 95/D3
Bowen, Queensland 88/H3
Bowen Island, Br. Col. 184/K3
Bowens, Md. (†20678) 245/M6
Bowerbank○, Maine (†04481) 243/E5
Bowers, Ind. (†47940) 227/D4
Bowers Beach, Del. (†19962) 245/S4
Bowers Mill, Mo. (†64848) 261/E8
Bowerston, Ohio (44695) 284/H5
Bowersville, Georgia (30516) 217/G2
Bowersville, Ohio (44695) 284/C6
Bowes, England 13/F3
Bowesmont, N. Dak. (58217) 282/R2
Bowie, Ariz. (85605) 198/F6
Bowie, Colo. (†81428) 208/D5
Bowie, Md. (20715) 245/L4
Bowie (creek), Miss. 256/E7
Bowie (co.), Texas 303/K4
Bowie, Texas (76230) 303/G4
Bow Island, Alberta 182/E5
Bowkan, Iran 66/E2
Bowlegs, Okla. (74830) 288/N4
Bowler, Wis. (54416) 317/J6
Bowling Green, Fla. (33834) 212/E4
Bowling Green, Ind. (47833) 227/D6
Bowling Green, Ky. (42101) 237/H7
Bowling Green, Ky. 188/J3
Bowling Green, Mo. (63334) 261/K4
Bowling Green, Ohio (43402) 284/C3
Bowling Green (cape), Queensland 88/H3
Bowling Green (cape), Queensland 95/C3
Bowling Green, S.C. (29703) 296/E1
Bowling Green, Va. (22427) 307/O4
Bowlus, Minn. (56314) 255/D5
Bowman, Calif. (95604) 204/C8
Bowman, Georgia (30624) 217/G2
Bowman (co.), N. Dak. 282/C7
Bowman, N. Dak. (58623) 282/D7
Bowman (bay), N.W.T. 162/J2
Bowman (bay), N.W. Terrs. 187/L3
Bowman (dam), Oreg. 291/G3
Bowman, S.C. (29018) 296/F5
Bowmansdale, Pa. (17008) 294/J5
Bowmanstown, Pa. (18030) 294/L4
Bowmansville, Pa. (17507) 294/L5
Bow Mills, N.H. (†03301) 268/D5
Bowmont, Idaho (†83651) 220/B6
Bowmore, Scotland 15/B5
Bowmore, Scotland 10/C3
Bowral, N.S. Wales 97/F4
Bowraville, N.S. Wales 97/G2
Bowring, Okla. (74009) 288/O1
Bowron Lake Prov. Park, Br. Col. 184/G3
Bowser, Br. Col. 184/H2
Bowser (lake), Br. Col. 184/C2
Bowsman, Manitoba 179/A2
Bowstring, Minn. (56631) 255/E3
Bowstring (lake), Minn. 255/E3
Boxborough○, Mass. (01719) 249/H3
Box Butte (co.), Nebr. 264/A2
Box Butte (res.), Nebr. 264/A2
Box Canyon (dam), Wash. 310/H2
Box Elder (creek), Colo. 208/K4
Box Elder, Mont. (59521) 262/F2
Boxelder (creek), Mont. 262/M5
Boxelder (creek), Mont. 262/H3
Box Elder, S. Dak. (57719) 298/D5
Boxelder (creek), S. Dak. 298/D5
Box Elder (co.), Utah 304/A2
Boxford, Mass. (01921) 249/L2
Boxford○, Mass. (01921) 249/L2
Box Hill, Victoria 97/J5
Box Hill, Victoria 88/L7
Boxholm, Iowa (50040) 229/E4
Bo Xian (Pohsien), China 77/J5
Boxley, Ark. (†72742) 202/D2
Boxmeer, Netherlands 27/H5
Box Springs, Georgia (31801) 217/C5
Boxtel, Netherlands 27/G5
Boyabat, Turkey 63/F2
Boyacá (dept.), Colombia 126/D5
Boyama (Stanley) (falls), Zaire 102/E5
Boyama (Stanley) (falls), Zaire 115/D3
Boyanup, W. Australia 92/A2
Boyce, La. (71409) 238/E4
Boyce, Va. (22620) 307/M2
Boyceville, Wis. (54725) 317/C5
Boyd, Ala. (†35470) 195/B5
Boyd, Fla. (†32347) 212/C1
Boyd (co.), Ky. 237/R4
Boyd, Minn. (56218) 255/C6
Boyd, Mont. (59013) 262/G5
Boyd (co.), Nebr. 264/F2
Boyd, Okla. (†73931) 288/E1
Boyd, Oreg. (†97021) 291/F2
Boyd, Texas (76023) 303/E1
Boyd, Wis. (54726) 317/E6
Boydell, Ark. (†71658) 202/H7
Boyden, Iowa (51234) 229/B2
Boyden Arbor, S.C. (†29128) 296/F3
Boyd Lake, Maine (†04463) 243/F5
Boyds, Md. (20720) 245/J4
Boyds, Wash. (99107) 310/G2
Boydton, Va. (23917) 307/M7
Boyer (riv.), Alberta 182/A5
Boyer, Iowa (†51448) 229/C4
Boyer (riv.), Iowa 229/B5
Boyer, W. Va. (†24915) 312/G5
Boyer Ahmadiyeh and Kohkiluyeh (gov.), Iran 66/G5
Boyero, Colo. (80821) 208/N5
Boyers, Pa. (16020) 294/C3
Boyertown, Pa. (19512) 294/L5
Boyes, Mont. (59316) 262/M5
Boykin, Georgia (†31737) 217/C8
Boykin, S.C. (†29128) 296/F3
Boykins, Va. (23827) 307/O7
Boyle, Alberta 182/D2
Boyle, Ireland 17/E4
Boyle, Ireland 10/B3
Boyle (co.), Ky. 237/M5
Boyle, Miss. (38730) 256/C3
Boyleston, Ind. (†46057) 227/E4
Boylston○, Mass. (01505) 249/H3
Boylston, Nova Scotia 168/G3
Boyne (riv.), Ireland 17/J4
Boyne City, Mich. (49712) 250/E3

342 Boyne Falls

Boyne Falls, Mich. (49713) 250/E3
Boyne Lake, Alberta 182/E5
Boynton, Okla. (74422) 288/P3
Boynton Beach, Fla. (*33435) 212/F5
Boy River, Minn. (56632) 255/D3
Boysen (res.), Wyo. 319/D2
Boysen Bay, N.Y. (†13212) 276/H4
Boys Ranch, Texas (79010) 303/B2
Boys Town, Nebr. (68010) 264/H3
Boyuibe, Bolivia 136/D7
Bozcaada (isl.), Turkey 63/A3
Bozdoğan, Turkey 63/C4
Bozeman, Mont. 188/D1
Bozeman, Mont. (59715) 262/E5
Bozkır, Turkey 63/E4
Bozkurt, Turkey 63/F2
Bozman, Md. (21612) 245/N5
Bozoum, Cent. Afr. Rep. 115/C2
Bozova, Turkey 63/H4
Bozqush, Kuh-e (mts.), Iran 66/E2
Bozüyük, Turkey 59/B2
Bozüyük, Turkey 63/C3
Bra, Italy 34/A2
Brabant (prov.), Belgium 27/F7
Brabant Lake, Sask. 181/M3
Brač (isl.), Yugoslavia 45/C4
Bracadale, Loch (inlet), Scotland 15/B3
Bracciano, Italy 34/C3
Bracciano (lake), Italy 34/D3
Bracebridge, Ontario 177/E2
Braceville, Ill. (60407) 222/E2
Bracey, Va. (23919) 307/M7
Bräcke, Sweden 18/J5
Bracken (co.), Ky. 237/N3
Bracken, Sask. 181/C6
Brackendale, Br. Col. 184/F5
Brackenridge, Pa. (15014) 294/C4
Brackett, Wis. (†54742) 317/D6
Brackettville (canton), Texas 303/D8
Brackley, England 10/F4
Brackley, England 13/F5
Bracknell, England 13/G8
Bracknell, Tasmania 99/C3
Brackney, Pa. (18812) 294/K2
Brackwede, W. Germany 22/C3
Braço Maior do Araguaia (riv.), Brazil 132/D5
Braço Menor do Araguaia (riv.), Brazil 132/D6
Brad, Romania 45/F2
Bradbury, Calif. (91010) 204/D10
Braddock, N. Dak. (58524) 282/K6
Braddock, Pa. (15104) 294/C7
Braddock, Sask. 181/D5
Braddyville, Iowa (51631) 229/D7
Braden, Okla. (†74959) 288/S4
Braden, Tenn. (38010) 237/B10
Bradenton, Fla. (*33506) 212/D4
Bradenton Beach, Fla. (33510) 212/D4
Bradford, Ark. (72020) 202/G3
Bradford, England 13/J1
Bradford, England 10/H1
Bradford (co.), Fla. 212/D2
Bradford, Ill. (61421) 222/D2
Bradford, Ind. (47107) 227/E8
Bradford, Iowa (50041) 229/G3
Bradford, Ky. (†41043) 237/N3
Bradford, Maine (04410) 243/F5
Bradford○, Maine (04410) 243/F5
Bradford○, N.H. (03221) 268/D5
Bradford, Ohio (45308) 284/B5
Bradford, Ontario 177/E3
Bradford (co.), Pa. 294/J2
Bradford, Pa. (16701) 294/E2
Bradford, R.I. (02808) 249/H7
Bradford, Tenn. (38316) 237/D8
Bradford, Vt. (05033) 268/C3
Bradford○, Vt. (05033) 268/C3
Bradford Center, Maine (†04410) 243/F5
Bradford-on-Avon, England 13/E6
Bradfordsville, Ky. (40009) 237/L6
Bradgate, Iowa (50520) 229/E3
Bradley (co.), Ark. 202/F7
Bradley, Ark. (71826) 202/C7
Bradley, Calif. (93426) 204/E8
Bradley, Fla. (33835) 212/D4
Bradley, Georgia (†31032) 217/E4
Bradley, Ill. (60915) 222/F2
Bradley○, Maine (04411) 243/F6
Bradley, Miss. (†39759) 256/G4
Bradley, Ohio (†43917) 284/J5
Bradley, Okla. (73011) 288/L5
Bradley, S.C. (29819) 296/C3
Bradley, S. Dak. (57217) 298/O3
Bradley (co.), Tenn. 237/M10
Bradley, Wis. (†54487) 317/G4
Bradley Beach, N.J. (07720) 273/F3
Bradleyton, Ala. (†36041) 195/F7
Bradleyville, Mo. (65614) 261/F9
Bradner, Ohio (43406) 284/C3
Bradshaw, Nebr. (68319) 264/G4
Bradshaw, Texas (†79567) 303/D5
Bradshaw, W. Va. (24817) 312/C8
Bradwardine, Manitoba 179/B5
Bradwell, Sask. 181/E4
Brady (glac.), Alaska 196/M1
Brady, Mont. (59416) 262/E2
Brady, Nebr. (69123) 264/D3
Brady (mt.), S. Australia 94/D3
Brady, Texas (76825) 303/E6
Brady Lake, Ohio (44211) 284/H3
Bradyville, Tenn. (37026) 237/J9
Brae, Scotland 15/G2
Braedstrup, Denmark 21/C6
Braemar, Scotland 15/E3
Braemar, Scotland 10/E2
Braemar (dist.), Scotland 15/E3
Braemar, Tenn. (37658) 237/S8
Braeside, Ontario 177/H2
Braeside, W. Australia 92/C3
Braga (dist.), Portugal 33/B2
Braga, Portugal 7/D4
Braga, Portugal 33/B2
Bragado, Argentina 143/F7
Bragança, Brazil 120/E3
Bragança, Brazil 132/E3
Bragança (dist.), Portugal 33/C2
Bragança, Portugal 33/C2
Bragança Paulista, Brazil 135/C3
Bragança Paulista, Brazil 132/E8
Braggadocio, Mo. (63826) 261/N10
Bragg City, Mo. (63827) 261/N10
Bragg Creek, Alberta 182/C4
Braggs, Ala. (†36761) 195/E6
Braggs, Okla. (74423) 288/R3
Bragman's Bluff (Puerto Cabezas), Nicaragua 154/F3
Braham, Minn. (55006) 255/E5
Brahmaputra (riv.) 54/L7
Brahmaputra (riv.), Bangladesh 68/G3
Brahmaputra (riv.), India 68/G3
Braich-y-Pwll (prom.), Wales 10/D4
Braich-y-Pwll (prom.), Wales 13/C5
Braidwood, Ill. (60408) 222/E2
Braidwood, N.S. Wales 97/E4
Brăila, Romania 7/G4
Brăila, Romania 45/H3
Brăila (marshes), Romania 45/H3
Brainard, Nebr. (68626) 264/G3
Brainards, N.J. (08865) 273/C2
Braine-l'Alleud, Belgium 27/E7
Braine-le-Comte, Belgium 27/D7
Brainerd, Minn. 188/H1
Brainerd, Minn. (56401) 255/D4
Braintree○, Mass. (02184) 249/D8
Braintree (West Braintree), Vt. 268/B4
Braintree○, Vt. (†05669) 268/B4
Braintree and Bocking, England 13/H6
Braintree and Bocking, England 10/G5
Braithwaite, La. (70040) 238/P4
Brak, Libya 102/D2
Brak, Libya 111/B2
Brake, W. Germany 22/C2
Brakna (reg.), Mauritania 106/B5
Brakpan, S. Africa 118/J6
Bralorne, Br. Col. 184/F5
Braman, Okla. (74632) 288/M1
Bramber, Nova Scotia 168/D3
Bramberg am Wildkogel, Austria 41/B3
Bramble (bay), Queensland 95/E2
Bramming, Denmark 21/B7
Bramon, Venezuela 124/B4
Brampton, England 13/E3
Brampton, Mich. (49810) 250/B3
Brampton, N. Dak. (58010) 282/P7
Brampton, Ontario 177/J4
Bramsche, W. Germany 22/B2
Bramwell, W. Va. (24715) 312/D8
Bran (riv.), Scotland 15/D3
Brancepeth, Sask. 181/F2
Branch, Ark. (72928) 202/C3
Branch, La. (70516) 238/F6
Branch (co.), Mich. 250/D7
Branch, Mich. (49402) 250/D5
Branch, Minn. (†55056) 255/F5
Branch, Mo. (†65786) 261/G7
Branch, Newf. 166/D2
Branch (riv.), Newf. 166/C2
Branch, Wis. (54203) 317/L7
Branch Dale, Pa. (17923) 294/K4
Branchport, N.Y. (14418) 276/F5
Branchton, Pa. (16021) 294/C3
Branchville, Ala. (†35120) 195/F3
Branchville, Conn. (†06829) 210/B3
Branchville, Ind. (47514) 227/D8
Branchville, N.J. (07826) 273/D1
Branchville, S.C. (29432) 296/F5
Branchville, Va. (23828) 307/O7
Branco (riv.), Brazil 120/C2
Branco (riv.), Brazil 132/H8
Brandberg (mt.), Namibia 118/A4
Brande, Denmark 21/B6
Brandenburg, E. Germany 22/E2
Brandenburg (reg.), E. Germany 22/E2
Brandenburg, Ky. (40108) 237/J4
Brandon, Colo. (81026) 208/P6
Brandon, England 13/H5
Brandon, Fla. (33511) 212/D4
Brandon, Iowa (52210) 229/K4
Brandon (bay), Ireland 17/A7
Brandon (head), Ireland 17/A7
Brandon (mt.), Ireland 17/A7
Brandon, Man. 146/H4
Brandon, Man. 162/F6
Brandon, Manitoba 179/C5
Brandon, Minn. (56315) 255/C5
Brandon, Miss. (39042) 256/E6
Brandon, Nebr. (69102) 264/C4
Brandon, Ohio (†43050) 284/F5
Brandon, S. Dak. (57005) 298/R6
Brandon, Vt. (05733) 268/A4
Brandon○, Vt. (05733) 268/A4
Brandon, Wis. (53919) 317/J8
Brandon Gap (pass), Vt. 268/B4
Brandonville, W. Va. (26523) 312/G3
Brandreth (lake), N.Y. 276/L3
Brandsville, Mo. (65688) 261/J9
Brandt, Ohio (†45371) 284/B6
Brandt, S. Dak. (57218) 298/R4
Brandvlei, S. Africa 118/B6
Brandýs nad Labem-Stará Boleslavv, Czech. 41/C1
Brandy Station, Va. (22714) 307/N4
Brandywine, Md. (20613) 245/L6
Brandywine, W. Va. (26802) 312/H5
Branford, Conn. (06405) 210/D3
Branford○, Conn. (06405) 210/D3
Branford (harb.), Conn. 210/D4
Branford (riv.), Conn. 210/D3
Branford, Fla. (32008) 212/D2
Braniewo, Poland 47/D1
Brannock (isls.), Ireland 17/A5
Bransfield (str.) 5/C16
Branson, Colo. (81027) 208/M8
Branson, Mo. (65616) 261/F9
Brant, Alberta 182/D4
Brant, Mich. (48614) 250/E5
Brant, N.Y. (14027) 276/B5
Brant (lake), N.Y. 276/N3
Brant (county), Ontario 177/D4
Brant (lake), S. Dak. 298/R6
Brant Beach, N.J. (†08008) 273/E4
Brantford, Kansas (†66938) 232/E2
Brantford, N. Dak. (†58356) 282/N4
Brantford, Ontario 177/D4
Brant Lake, N.Y. (12815) 276/N3
Brantley, Ala. (36009) 195/F7
Brantley (co.), Georgia 217/J8
Brant Rock-Ocean Bluff, Mass. (02020) 249/M4
Brantville, New Bruns. 170/E1
Brantwood, Wis. (54513) 317/F4
Branxholm, Tasmania 99/D3
Branxholme, Victoria 97/A5
Branxton-Greta, N.S. Wales 97/F3
Bras d'Or, Nova Scotia 168/H2
Bras d'Or (lake), Nova Scotia 168/H3
Braselton, Georgia (30517) 217/E2
Brasfield, Ark. (†72017) 202/H4
Brashear, Mo. (63533) 261/H2
Brasher, Mo. (†63830) 261/N10
Brasher Falls-Winthrop, N.Y. (13613) 276/L1
Brasiléia, Brazil 132/G10
Brasília (cap.), Brazil 2/G6
Brasília (cap.), Brazil 120/E4
Brasília (cap.), Brazil 132/E6
Brasília de Minas, Brazil 132/F7
Braşov, Romania 45/G3
Braşov, Romania 7/G4
Brass, Nigeria 106/F8
Brass (isls.), Virgin Is. (U.S.) 161/A4
Brassey (range), W. Australia 92/C4
Brasstown Bald (mt.), Georgia 217/E1
Brassua (lake), Maine 243/D4
Braswell, Georgia (†30153) 217/C3
Brate, Norway 18/G7
Bratenahl, Ohio (†44101) 284/H9
Bratislava, Czech. 7/F4
Bratislava (city), Czech. 41/D2
Bratislava, Czech. 41/D2
Bratsk, U.S.S.R. 54/M4
Bratsk, U.S.S.R. 48/L4
Bratsk (res.), U.S.S.R. 48/L4
Brattleboro, Vt. (05301) 268/B6
Brattleboro○, Vt. (05301) 268/B6
Bratton, Sask. 181/D4
Braunau am Inn, Austria 41/B2
Braunlage, W. Germany 22/D3
Braunschweig (Brunswick), W. Germany 22/D2
Braunton, England 13/C6
Brava (isl.), C. Verde 106/B8
Brava, Somalia 115/H3
Brava, Somalia 102/G4
Brava (pt.), Uruguay 145/B7
Brave, Pa. (15316) 294/B6
Bravo (riv.), Chile 138/D7
Bravo (Grande) (riv.), Mexico 150/G2
Brawley, Calif. 188/C4
Brawley, Calif. (92227) 204/K11
Braxton, Miss. (39044) 256/D6
Braxton (co.), W. Va. 312/E5
Bray, Ireland 17/K5
Bray, Ireland 10/C4
Bray (head), Ireland 17/A8
Bray (isl.), N.W. Terrs. 187/L3
Bray, Okla. (73012) 288/L5
Braymer, Mo. (64624) 261/E3
Brayton, Iowa (50042) 229/D5
Brazeau (dam), Alberta 182/C3
Brazeau (mt.), Alberta 182/B3
Brazeau (riv.), Alberta 182/B3
Brazil 2/F6
Brazil 120/D4
BRAZIL 132, 135
Brazil, Ind. (47834) 227/C5
Brazil, Miss. (38963) 256/D2
Brazil, Tenn. (†38382) 237/C9
Brazilian Highlands (plat.), Brazil 120/E4
Brazilton, Kansas (†66743) 232/H4
Brazito, Mo. (†65101) 261/H6
Brazoria (co.), Texas 303/J8
Brazoria, Texas (77422) 303/J9
Brazos (peak), N. Mex. 274/C2
Brazos (co.), Texas 303/H7
Brazos (riv.), Texas 188/G4
Brazos (riv.), Texas 146/J6
Brazos (riv.), Texas 303/H7
Brazo Sur, Pilcomayo (riv.), Argentina 143/E1
Brazzaville (cap.), Congo 115/C4
Brazzaville (cap.), Congo 2/K6
Brazzaville (cap.), Congo 102/D5
Brčko, Yugoslavia 45/D3
Brda (riv.), Poland 47/C2
Brea, Calif. (92621) 204/D11
Breadalbane (dist.), Scotland 15/D4
Bread Loaf, Vt. (05753) 268/B4
Bread Loaf (mt.), Vt. 268/A3
Breakabeen, N.Y. (†12122) 276/M5
Breakeyville, Québec 172/J3
Breaks, Va. (24607) 307/D6
Breaksea (sound), N. Zealand 100/A6
Bream (bay), N. Zealand 100/E1
Breasclete, Scotland 15/B2
Breathitt (co.), Ky. 237/P5
Breau-Village, New Bruns. 170/F2
Breaux Bridge, La. (70517) 238/G6
Brebes, Indonesia 85/H2
Brébeuf, Québec 172/C3
Brébeuf (lake), Québec 172/G1
Brechin, Ontario 177/E3
Brechin, Scotland 10/E2
Brechin, Scotland 15/F4
Brecht, Belgium 27/F6
Breckenridge, Colo. (80424) 208/G4
Breckenridge, Mich. (48615) 250/E5
Breckenridge, Minn. (56520) 255/B4
Breckenridge, Mo. (64625) 261/E3
Breckenridge, Texas (76024) 303/F5
Breckenridge Hills, Mo. (†63114) 261/O2
Breckinridge (co.), Ky. 237/H5
Breckinridge, Okla. (73721) 288/L2
Brecknock (Brecon), Wales 13/D6
Brecksville, Ohio (44141) 284/H10
Břeclav, Czech. 41/D2
Brecon, Wales 13/D6
Brecon, Wales 10/E5
Brecon Beacons (mt.), Wales 13/D6
Brecon Beacons National Park, Wales 13/D6
Breda, Iowa (51436) 229/C4
Breda, Netherlands 27/F5
Bredasdorp, S. Africa 118/B6
Bredasdorp Nat'l Park, S. Africa 118/C6
Bredbo, N.S. Wales 97/E4
Bredbyn, Sweden 18/L5
Bredebro, Denmark 21/B7
Bredenbury, Sask. 181/K5
Bredene, Belgium 27/B6
Bredstedt, W. Germany 22/C1
Bree, Belgium 27/H6
Breed, Wis. (†54174) 317/K5
Breeden, W. Va. (25666) 312/B7
Breeding, Ky. (42715) 237/L7
Breedsville, Mich. (49027) 250/C6
Breese, Ill. (62230) 222/D5
Breesport, N.Y. (14816) 276/G6
Breezand, Netherlands 27/F3
Breezy Point, Minn. (†56472) 255/D4
Bregenz, Austria 41/A3
Bregovo, Bulgaria 45/F3
Breidhafjördhur (fjord), Iceland 7/B2
Breidhafjördhur (fjord), Iceland 21/B1
Breien, N. Dak. (58525) 282/H7
Breil-Brigels, Switzerland 39/H3
Breil-sur-Roya, France 28/G6
Breisach am Rhein, W. Germany 22/B4
Breisgau (reg.), W. Germany 22/B5
Breitenbach, Switzerland 39/E2
Breitenbush, Oreg. (†97342) 291/F3
Breithorn (mt.), Switzerland 39/E5
Breithorn (mt.), Switzerland 39/E4
Brejo, Brazil 132/F3
Bremanger (isl.), Norway 18/D6
Bremen, Ala. (35033) 195/E3
Bremen, Georgia (30110) 217/B3
Bremen, Ill. (†62233) 222/D6
Bremen, Ind. (46506) 227/E2
Bremen, Kansas (66412) 232/F2
Bremen, Ky. (42325) 237/G6
Bremen, N. Dak. (58319) 282/M4
Bremen, Ohio (43107) 284/F6
Bremen, Sask. 181/E3
Bremen, W. Germany 7/E3
Bremen (state), W. Germany 22/C2
Bremen, W. Germany 22/C2
Bremer (co.), Iowa 229/J3
Bremer, Iowa (†50677) 229/J3
Bremerhaven, W. Germany 22/C2
Bremerton, Wash. 188/B1
Bremerton, Wash. (98310) 310/A2
Bremervörde, W. Germany 22/C2
Bremgarten, Switzerland 39/F2
Bremo Bluff, Va. (23022) 307/M5
Bremond, Texas (76629) 303/H6
Brenham, Texas (77833) 303/H7
Brenner (pass), Austria 41/A3
Brenner (pass), Italy 34/C1
Brent, Ala. (35034) 195/D5
Brent, England 13/H8
Brent, England 10/B5
Brent, Ontario 177/F1
Brentford, S. Dak. (57429) 298/N3
Brenton (pt.), R.I. 249/J7
Brentwood, Ark. (†72959) 202/B2
Brentwood, Calif. (94513) 204/L2
Brentwood, England 10/C5
Brentwood, England 13/J8
Brentwood, Md. (20722) 245/F4
Brentwood, Mo. (63144) 261/P3
Brentwood○, N.H. (†03833) 268/E6
Brentwood, N.Y. (11717) 276/O9
Brentwood, Pa. (15227) 294/B7
Brentwood, Tenn. (37027) 237/H8
Brentwood Park, S. Africa 118/J6
Brereton Lake, Manitoba 179/G5
Bresaylor, Sask. 181/C3
Brescia (prov.), Italy 34/C2
Brescia, Italy 7/E4
Brescia, Italy 34/C2
Breskens, Netherlands 27/C6
Breslau (Wrocław), Poland 47/C3
Bressanone, Italy 34/C1
Bressay (isl.), Scotland 15/G2
Bressay (isl.), Scotland 10/G1
Bressuire, France 28/C4
Brest, France 7/D4
Brest, France 28/A3
Brest, Georgia (†31716) 217/D8
Brest, New Bruns. 170/E2
Brest, U.S.S.R. 7/G3
Brest, U.S.S.R. 48/C4
Brest, U.S.S.R. 52/B4
Bretaña, Peru 128/E5
Brethren, Mich. (49619) 250/D4
Breton, Alberta 182/C3
Breton (isls.), La. 238/M8
Breton (sound), La. 238/M7
Breton (cape), Nova Scotia 168/J3
Breton Cove, Nova Scotia 168/H2
Breton Woods, N.J. (08723) 273/E3
Brett (cape), N. Zealand 100/E1
Bretten, W. Germany 22/C4
Bretton Woods, N.H. (03575) 268/E3
Brevard (co.), Fla. 212/F3
Brevard, N.C. (28712) 281/D4
Breves, Brazil 132/D3
Brevig Mission, Alaska (99785) 196/E1
Brevik, Minn. (†56655) 255/D3
Brevoort (lake), Mich. 250/D3
Brevoort (isl.), N.W. Terrs. 187/M3
Brevort, Mich. (†49760) 250/E2
Brewarrina, N.S. Wales 88/H5
Brewarrina, N.S. Wales 97/D1
Brewer, Maine (04412) 243/F6
Brewer, Mo. (†63775) 261/N7
Brewers, Ky. (†42025) 237/E7
Brewers Mills, New Bruns. 170/C2
Brewersville, Ind. (†47265) 227/F6
Brewerton, N.Y. (13029) 276/H4
Brewster (pond), Conn. 210/F2
Brewster, Kansas (67732) 232/A2
Brewster, Mass. (02631) 249/O5
Brewster○, Mass. (02631) 249/O5
Brewster (isls.), Mass. 249/E7
Brewster, Minn. (56119) 255/C7
Brewster, Nebr. (68821) 264/D3
Brewster (lake), N.S. Wales 97/D3
Brewster, N.Y. (10509) 276/N8
Brewster, Ohio (44613) 284/G4
Brewster, Cerro (mt.), Panama 154/H6
Brewster (co.), Texas 303/A8
Brewster, Wash. (98812) 310/F2
Brewton, Ala. (36426) 195/D8
Breynat, Alberta 182/D2
Brežice, Yugoslavia 45/B3
Brezina, Algeria 106/E2
Březnice, Czech. 41/B2
Breznik, Bulgaria 45/F4
Brezno, Czech. 41/E2
Bria, Cent. Afr. Rep. 102/E4
Bria, Cent. Afr. Rep. 115/D2
Briançon, France 28/G5
Brian Head, Utah (84719) 304/B6
Briar, Texas (†76023) 303/E1
Briar Creek, Pa. (†18603) 294/K3
Briare, France 28/E4
Briartown, Okla. (†74455) 288/R4
Briarwood, (†58102) 282/S6
Bribbaree, N.S. Wales 97/D3
Brice, Ohio (43109) 284/E6
Bricelyn, Minn. (56014) 255/E7
Brices Cross Roads Nat'l Battlefield Site, Miss.256/G2
Briceville, Tenn. (37710) 237/N8
Brí Chualann (Bray), Ireland 17/K5
Brick○, N.J. (08723) 273/E3
Brickaville (Vohibinany), Madagascar 118/H3
Brickerville, Pa. (†17543) 294/K5
Brickeys, Ark. (72320) 202/J4
Bricks, N.C. (†27891) 281/O2
Brickton, Nova Scotia 168/C4
Bridal Veil, Oreg. (97010) 291/E2
Bride (riv.), Ireland 17/E7
Bridesville, Br. Col. 184/H6
Bridge, Idaho (†83342) 220/E7
Bridge, Oreg. (†97458) 291/D4
Bridgeboro, Georgia (31705) 217/E8
Bridge City, Texas (77611) 303/L7
Bridgedale, New Bruns. 170/F3
Bridgeford, Sask. 181/E5
Bridgehampton, N.Y. (11932) 276/R9
Bridge Lake, Br. Col. 184/G4
Bridgeland, Utah (84012) 304/D3
Bridgend, Wales 13/A7
Bridgenorth, Ontario 177/F3
Bridge of Allan, Scotland 10/B1
Bridge of Allan, Scotland 15/C1
Bridge of Don, Scotland 15/F3
Bridge of Weir, Scotland 15/A2
Bridgeport, Ala. (35740) 195/G1
Bridgeport, Calif. (93517) 204/F5
Bridgeport, Conn. 188/M2
Bridgeport, Conn. (*06601) 210/C4
Bridgeport, Ill. (62417) 222/F5
Bridgeport, Kansas (67416) 232/E3
Bridgeport, Mich. (48722) 250/F5
Bridgeport, Nebr. (69336) 264/A3
Bridgeport, N.J. (08014) 273/C4
Bridgeport, N.Y. (13030) 276/J4
Bridgeport, Ohio (43912) 284/J5
Bridgeport, Okla. (†73047) 288/K3
Bridgeport, Oreg. (97819) 291/K3
Bridgeport, Pa. (19405) 294/M5
Bridgeport, Texas (76026) 303/G4
Bridgeport, Wash. (98813) 310/F3
Bridgeport, W. Va. (26330) 312/F4
Bridgeport, Wis. (†53821) 317/D9
Bridger, Mont. (59014) 262/H5
Bridgeton, Ind. (47836) 227/C5
Bridgeton, Mich. (†49327) 250/D5
Bridgeton, Mo. (63044) 261/O2
Bridgeton, N.J. (08302) 273/C5
Bridgeton, N.C. (28519) 281/R4
Bridgeton Terrace, Mo. (†63044) 261/O2
Bridgetown (cap.), Barbados 156/G4
Bridgetown (cap.), Barbados 161/B9
Bridgetown, Md. (†21640) 245/P4
Bridgetown, Nova Scotia 168/C4
Bridgetown, Ohio (†45211) 284/B9
Bridgetown, W. Australia 88/B6
Bridgetown, W. Australia 92/B6
Bridgeview, Ill. (60455) 222/B6
Bridgeville, Calif. (95526) 204/B3
Bridgeville, Del. (19993) 245/R6
Bridgeville, Nova Scotia 168/F3
Bridgeville, Pa. (15017) 294/B5
Bridgeville, Québec 172/D1
Bridgewater○, Conn. (06752) 210/B2
Bridgewater, Iowa (50837) 229/D6
Bridgewater○, Maine (04735) 243/H3
Bridgewater, Mass. (02324) 249/K5
Bridgewater○, Mass. (02324) 249/K5
Bridgewater○, N.H. (†03222) 268/D4
Bridgewater○, N.J. (08807) 273/D2
Bridgewater, N.Y. (13313) 276/K5
Bridgewater, N.S. 162/K7
Bridgewater, Nova Scotia 168/D4
Bridgewater, Pa. (15009) 294/B4
Bridgewater, S. Dak. (57319) 298/P6
Bridgewater, Tasmania 99/D4
Bridgewater○, Vt. (05034) 268/B4
Bridgewater (cape), Victoria 97/A6
Bridgewater, Va. (22812) 307/K4
Bridgewater Center, Vt. (†05034) 268/B4
Bridgewater Corners, Vt. (05035) 268/B4
Bridgman, Mich. (49106) 250/C7
Bridgnorth, England 13/E5
Bridgnorth, England 10/E4
Bridgton, Maine (04009) 243/B7
Bridgton○, Maine (04009) 243/B7
Bridgwater, England 10/E5
Bridgwater, England 13/E6
Bridlington, England 13/G3
Bridlington, England 10/F3
Bridlington (bay), England 13/G3
Bridport, England 13/E7
Bridport, England 10/E5
Bridport, Tasmania 99/D3
Bridport○, Vt. (05734) 268/A4
Brieg (Brzeg), Poland 47/C3
Brielle, Netherlands 27/E5
Brielle, N.J. (08730) 273/E3
Briensburg, Ky. (†42025) 237/E7
Brienz, Switzerland 39/F3
Brienzer Rothorn (mt.), Switzerland 39/F3
Brienzersee (lake), Switzerland 39/F3
Brier (isl.), Nova Scotia 168/B4
Brier, Wash. (†98036) 310/C3
Briercrest, Sask. 181/F5
Brierfield, Ala. (35035) 195/E4
Brier Hill, N.Y. (13614) 276/J1
Brig, Switzerland 39/F4
Brigantine, N.J. (08203) 273/E5
Brigantine (inlet), N.J. 273/E5
Brigden, Ontario 177/B5
Brigg, England 13/G4
Briggs, Texas (78608) 303/F7
Briggs Corner, New Bruns. 170/E2
Briggsdale, Colo. (80611) 208/L1
Briggsville, Ark. (72828) 202/C4
Briggsville, Wis. (53920) 317/H8
Brigham City, Utah 188/D2
Brigham City, Utah (84302) 304/C2
Brighouse, England 13/J1
Bright, Ind. (†45030) 227/H6
Bright, Victoria 97/D5
Brightlingsea, England 13/J6
Brightlingsea, England 10/G5
Brighton, Ala. (35020) 195/D4
Brighton, Colo. (80601) 208/K3
Brighton, England 10/F5
Brighton, England 13/G7
Brighton, Fla. (†33472) 212/E4
Brighton, Ill. (62012) 222/C4
Brighton, Ind. (†46746) 227/G1
Brighton, Iowa (52540) 229/K6
Brighton○, Maine (†04990) 243/D5
Brighton, Mich. (48116) 250/F6
Brighton, Mo. (65617) 261/F8
Brighton, Nova Scotia 168/C4
Brighton, Ohio (†44090) 284/F3
Brighton, Ontario 177/G3
Brighton, Oreg. (†97136) 291/C2
Brighton, S. Australia 88/D8
Brighton, S. Australia 94/A8
Brighton, Tasmania 99/D4
Brighton, Tenn. (38011) 237/B10
Brighton, Utah (†84101) 304/C3
Brighton, Victoria 97/J5
Brighton, Victoria 88/L7
Brighton, Wis. (†53139) 317/K3
Brightons, Scotland 15/C1
Brightsand (lake), Sask. 181/B2
Brights Grove, Ontario 177/B4
Brightshade, Ky. (40962) 237/O7
Brightstar, Ark. (†75556) 202/C7
Brightwood, D.C. (20011) 245/F4
Brightwood, Oreg. (97001) 291/E2
Brightwood, Va. (22715) 307/M4
Brignoles, France 28/G6
Brigus, Newf. 166/D2
Brihuega, Spain 33/E2
Brikama, Gambia 106/A6
Brill, Wis. (54818) 317/C4
Brilliant, Ala. (35548) 195/C2
Brilliant, Ohio (43913) 284/J5
Brillion, Wis. (54110) 317/L7
Brilon, W. Germany 22/C3
Brimfield, Ill. (61517) 222/D3
Brimfield, Ind. (46720) 227/G2
Brimfield○, Mass. (01010) 249/F4
Brimfield, Ohio (†44240) 284/H3
Brimley, Mich. (49715) 250/E2
Brimson, Minn. (55602) 255/F3
Brimson, Mo. (64642) 261/E2
Brimstone (hill), St. Chris.-Nevis 161/C10
Brinckerhoff, N.Y. (†12524) 276/N7
Brindakit, U.S.S.R. 48/O4
Brindisi (prov.), Italy 34/G4
Brindisi, Italy 7/F4
Brindisi, Italy 34/G4
Bringhurst, Ind. (46913) 227/E3
Brinkhaven, Ohio (43006) 284/F5
Brinkley, Ark. (72021) 202/H4
Brinkman, Okla. (†73673) 288/G4
Brinktown, Mo. (65443) 261/J6
Brinnon, Wash. (98320) 310/B3
Brinsmade, N. Dak. (58320) 282/M3
Brinson, Georgia (31725) 217/C9
Briny Breezes, Fla. (†33435) 212/G5
Brione, Switzerland 39/G4
Brioude, France 28/E5
Brisbane, Australia 2/S7
Brisbane, Calif. (94005) 204/J2
Brisbane (cap.), Queensland 95/D2
Brisbane (cap.), Queensland 88/K3
Brisbane (riv.), Queensland 88/J3
Brisbane (riv.), Queensland 95/D2
Brisbane Airport, Queensland 95/E2
Brisbane International Airport, Queensland 88/K2
Brisbane Water, N.S. Wales 88/J6
Brisbane Water, N.S. Wales 97/F3
Brisbin, Pa. (16620) 294/F4
Brisco, Br. Col. 184/J5
Briscoe (co.), Texas 303/C3
Briscoe, Texas (79011) 303/D2
Brisighella, Italy 34/C2
Brissago, Switzerland 39/G4
Bristol (bay), Alaska 188/C6
Bristol (bay), Alaska 146/B4
Bristol (bay), Alaska 196/F3
Bristol (lake), Calif. 204/K9
Bristol, Colo. (81028) 208/P6
Bristol, Conn. (06010) 210/D2
Bristol, England 13/E6
Bristol, England 7/D3
Bristol, England 10/E5
Bristol (chan.), England 13/C6
Bristol (chan.), England 10/E5
Bristol, Fla. (32321) 212/B1
Bristol, Georgia (31518) 217/H8
Bristol, Ind. (46507) 227/F1

Budaörs 343

Bristol, Maine (04539) 243/D8
Bristol○, Maine (04539) 243/D8
Bristol, Md. (†20820) 245/M5
Bristol (co.), Mass. 249/K5
Bristol, Mich. (†49688) 250/D4
Bristol, New Bruns. 170/C2
Bristol, N.H. (03222) 268/D4
Bristol○, N.H. (03222) 268/D4
Bristol, Pa. (19007) 294/N5
Bristol○, Pa. (19007) 294/N5
Bristol (co.), R.I. 249/J6
Bristol, R.I. (02809) 249/J6
Bristol, S. Dak. (57219) 298/O3
Bristol, Tenn. 188/K3
Bristol, Tenn. (37620) 237/S7
Bristol (bay), U.S. 4/D18
Bristol, Va. 188/K3
Bristol, Vt. (05443) 268/A3
Bristol○, Vt. (05443) 268/A3
Bristol (I.C.), Va. (24201) 307/D7
Bristol (chan.), Wales 13/C6
Bristol (chan.), Wales 10/E5
Bristol, W. Va. (26332) 312/F4
Bristolville, Ohio (44402) 284/J3
Bristow, Ind. (47515) 227/D8
Bristow, Iowa (50611) 229/H3
Bristow, Nebr. (68719) 264/F2
Bristow, Okla. (74010) 288/O3
Bristow, Va. (22013) 307/N3
Britannia Beach, Br. Col. 184/K2
British (mts.), Alaska 196/K1
British (mts.), Yukon 187/D3
British Columbia (prov.) 162/D4
BRITISH COLUMBIA 184
British Columbia (prov.), Canada 146/F4
British Indian Ocean Territory 2/N6
British Indian Ocean Territory 54/J10
British Isles 7/D3
Brits, S. Africa 118/D5
Britstown, S. Africa 118/C6
Britt, Iowa (50423) 229/F2
Britt, Minn. (55710) 255/F3
Britt, Ontario 177/D2
Brittany (trad. prov.), France 29
Brittany, La. (70718) 238/L3
Brittnau, Switzerland 39/E2
Britton, Mich. (49229) 250/F6
Britton, S. Dak. (57430) 298/O2
Brive-la-Gaillarde, France 28/D5
Briviesca, Spain 33/E1
Brno, Czech. 7/F4
Brno, Czech. 41/D2
Broa (inlet), Cuba 158/C1
Broach (Bharuch), India 68/C4
Broad (brook), Conn. 210/H2
Broad (creek), Del. 245/R6
Broad (riv.), N.C. 281/E4
Broad (sound), Queensland 88/H4
Broad (sound), Queensland 95/D4
Broad (bay), Scotland 15/B2
Broad (riv.), S.C. 296/F7
Broad (riv.), S.C. 296/E2
Broadacres, Oreg. (†97032) 291/A3
Broadacres, Sask. 181/B3
Broadalbin, N.Y. (12025) 276/M4
Broad Arrow, W. Australia 88/C6
Broad Arrow, W. Australia 92/C5
Broadback (riv.), Québec 174/B2
Broadbent, Oreg. (97414) 291/C4
Broad Brook, Conn. (06016) 210/E1
Broad Cove, Newf. 166/D2
Broad Cove, Nova Scotia 168/D4
Broaddus, Texas (75929) 303/K6
Broadfields, Ky. (†40201) 237/K2
Broadford, Ireland 17/C7
Broadford, Scotland 15/B3
Broadford, Victoria 97/C5
Broadford, Va. (24316) 307/E7
Broad Haven (harb.), Ireland 17/B3
Broadhurst, Georgia (†31545) 217/J8
Broadkill (riv.), Del. 245/S5
Broadland, S. Dak. (†57350) 298/N4
Broadlands, Ill. (61816) 222/E4
Broad Law (mt.), Scotland 15/E5
Broadmeadows, Victoria 88/L6
Broadmeadows, Victoria 97/H4
Broadstairs and Saint Peter's, England 13/J6
Broad Top, Pa. (16621) 294/F5
Broadus, Mont. (59317) 262/L5
Broad Valley, Manitoba 179/E4
Broadview, Ill. (60153) 222/B6
Broadview, Mont. (59015) 262/H4
Broadview, N. Mex. (88112) 274/F4
Broadview, Sask. 181/J5
Broadview Heights, Ohio (†44141) 284/H10
Broadview Park, Fla. (†33314) 212/B4
Broadwater (co.), Mont. 262/E4
Broadwater, Nebr. (69125) 264/B3
Broadway, N.J. (08808) 273/C2
Broadway, N.C. (27505) 281/L4
Broadway, Ohio (43007) 284/C5
Broadway, Va. (22815) 307/L3
Broadwell, Ill. (62623) 222/D3
Broager, Denmark 21/C8
Broc, Switzerland 39/D3
Brochet, Man. 162/F4
Brochet, Manitoba 179/H2
Brock (isl.), N.W.T. 162/M3
Brock, Nebr. (68320) 264/H4
Brock (isl.), N.W. Terrs. 187/G2
Brock, Sask. 181/C4
Brockdell, Tenn. (†37367) 237/L10
Brocken (mt.), E. Germany 22/D3
Brocket, Alberta 182/D5
Brocket, N. Dak. (58321) 282/O3
Brockington, Sask. 181/G2
Brockport, N.Y. (14420) 276/D4
Brockport, Pa. (15823) 294/E3
Brockton, Mass. (*02401) 249/K4
Brockton, Mont. (59213) 262/M2
Brockville, Ontario 177/J3
Brockway, Mont. (59214) 262/L3
Brockway, New Bruns. 170/C3
Brockway, Pa. (15824) 294/E3
Brocton, Ill. (61917) 222/F4
Brocton, N.Y. (14716) 276/B6
Broderick, Sask. 181/E4
Broderick-Bryte, Calif. (95605) 204/B8
Brodeur (pen.), Canada 4/B14
Brodeur (pen.), N.W.T. 146/K2
Brodeur (pen.), N.W.T. 162/H1
Brodeur (pen.), N.W. Terrs. 187/K2
Brodhead, Ky. (40409) 237/N6
Brodhead, Wis. (53520) 317/G10
Brodheadsville, Pa. (18322) 294/M4
Brodick, Scotland 15/C5
Brodick, Scotland 10/D3
Brodnax, Va. (23920) 307/N7
Brodnica, Poland 47/D2
Broek in Waterland, Netherlands 27/C4
Brogan, Oreg. (97903) 291/K3
Brohard, W. Va. (26138) 312/D4
Brohman, Mich. (49312) 250/D5
Brokaw, Wis. (54417) 317/G5
Broken (bay), N.S. Wales 97/F3
Broken Arrow, Okla. (74012) 288/P2
Broken Bow, Nebr. (68822) 264/E3
Broken Bow, Okla. (74728) 288/S7
Broken Bow (lake), Okla. 288/S6
Broken Hill, Australia 87/E9
Broken Hill, N. S. Wales 88/G6
Broken Hill, N.S. Wales 97/A3
Broken Hill (Kabwe), Zambia 115/E6
Brokensword, Ohio (†44820) 284/E4
Brokopondo (dist.), Suriname 131/D4
Brokopondo, Suriname 131/D3
Brome (co.), Québec 172/E4
Brome, Québec 172/E4
Brome (lake), Québec 172/E4
Bromer, Ind. (†47452) 227/E7
Bromhead, Sask. 181/H6
Bromide, Okla. (74530) 288/N6
Bromley, England 13/H8
Bromley, England 10/C5
Bromley, Ky. (†41016) 237/S2
Bromley (mt.), Vt. 268/B5
Bromont, Québec 172/E4
Brompton (lake), Québec 172/E4
Bromptonville, Québec 172/F4
Bromsgrove, England 13/E5
Bromyard, England 13/E5
Bronaugh, Mo. (64728) 261/C7
Bronco, Texas (†79355) 303/B4
Brønderslev, Denmark 18/F8
Brønderslev, Denmark 21/C3
Brønnøysund, Norway 18/G4
Brøns, Denmark 21/B7
Bronson, Fla. (32621) 212/D2
Bronson, Iowa (51007) 229/A4
Bronson, Kansas (66716) 232/H4
Bronson, Mich. (49028) 250/D7
Bronson (lake), Sask. 181/B2
Bronson, Texas (75930) 303/L6
Bronston, Ky. (42518) 237/M7
Bronte, Italy 34/E6
Bronte, Texas (76933) 303/D6
Bronwood, Georgia (31726) 217/D7
Bronx (co.), N.Y. 276/N9
Bronx (borough), N.Y. (*10401) 276/N9
Bronxville, N.Y. (10708) 276/O7
Brook, Ind. (47922) 227/C3
Brookdale, Calif. (95007) 204/J4
Brookdale, Manitoba 179/C4
Brookdale, Nova Scotia 168/D3
Brooke, Va. (22430) 307/O4
Brooke (co.), W. Va. 312/E2
Brookeborough, N. Ireland 17/G3
Brookeland, Texas (75931) 303/L6
Brooker, Fla. (32622) 212/D2
Brooke's Point, Philippines 82/A6
Brookeville, Md. (20729) 245/K4
Brookfield○, Conn. (06804) 210/B3
Brookfield, Georgia (31727) 217/F8
Brookfield, Ill. (60513) 222/B6
Brookfield, Mass. (01506) 249/F4
Brookfield○, Mass. (01506) 249/F4
Brookfield, Mo. (64628) 261/F3
Brookfield○, N.H. (†03872) 268/E4
Brookfield, N.Y. (13314) 276/K5
Brookfield, Nova Scotia 168/E3
Brookfield, Ohio (44403) 284/J3
Brookfield○, Vt. (05036) 268/B3
Brookfield, Wis. (53005) 317/K1
Brookfield Center, Conn. (06805) 210/B3
Brookford, N.C. (†28601) 281/G3
Brookhaven, Georgia (†30304) 217/K1
Brookhaven, Miss. (39601) 256/C7
Brookhaven, Pa. (19015) 294/M7
Brookhaven Nat'l Lab., N.Y. 276/P9
Brookings, Oreg. (97415) 291/C5
Brookings (co.), S. Dak. 298/R5
Brookings, S. Dak. (57006) 298/R5
Brookland, Ark. (72417) 202/J2
Brookland, D.C. (20017) 245/F4
Brooklawn, N.J. (08030) 273/B3
Brooklet, Georgia (30415) 217/J6
Brookley Air Force Base, Ala. 195/B9
Brooklin○, Maine (04616) 243/F7
Brookline○, Mass. (02146) 249/C7
Brookline○, N.H. (03033) 268/D6
Brookline○, Vt. (†05345) 268/B5
Brookline Station (Brookline), Mo. (65619) 261/F8
Brooklyn, Ala. (36429) 195/E8
Brooklyn○, Conn. (06234) 210/H1
Brooklyn, Georgia (†31814) 217/C6
Brooklyn (Lovejoy), Ill. (†62059) 222/A2
Brooklyn, Ill. (†62367) 222/C3
Brooklyn, Ind. (46111) 227/E5
Brooklyn, Iowa (52211) 229/J5
Brooklyn, Ky. (42209) 237/H6
Brooklyn, Md. (21225) 245/M4
Brooklyn, Mich. (49230) 250/E6
Brooklyn, Miss. (39425) 256/F8
Brooklyn, Newf. 166/D2
Brooklyn (borough), N.Y. (*11201) 276/N9
Brooklyn, Nova Scotia 168/D4
Brooklyn, Ohio (44144) 284/H9
Brooklyn, Pa. (18813) 294/L2
Brooklyn, Wash. (†98537) 310/B4
Brooklyn, Wis. (53521) 317/H10
Brooklyn Center, Minn. (55429) 255/G5
Brooklyn Heights, Ohio (†44131) 284/H9
Brooklyn Park, Minn. (†55444) 255/G5
Brookmere, Br. Col. 184/G5
Brookneal, Va. (24528) 307/L6
Brook Park, Minn. (55007) 255/F5
Brook Park, Ohio (44142) 284/G9
Brookport, Ill. (62910) 222/E6
Brooks (range), Alaska 146/C3
Brooks (range), Alaska 188/C5
Brooks (range), Alaska 196/G1
Brooks, Alberta 182/E4
Brooks (pen.), Br. Col. 184/D5
Brooks, Calif. (95606) 204/C5
Brooks (co.), Georgia 217/E9
Brooks, Georgia (30205) 217/D4
Brooks, Iowa (†50841) 229/D7
Brooks, Ky. (40109) 237/K4
Brooks○, Maine (04921) 243/E6
Brooks, Minn. (56715) 255/B3
Brooks, Mont. (†59457) 262/G3
Brooks, Oreg. (97305) 291/A3
Brooks (co.), Texas 303/F11
Brooks (range), U.S. 4/C17
Brooks, W. Va. (25957) 312/E7
Brooks, Wis. (53921) 317/G8
Brooks A.F.B., Texas 303/K11
Brooksburg, Ind. (†47250) 227/G7
Brooksby, Sask. 181/G2
Brookshire, Texas (77423) 303/J8
Brookside, Ala. (35036) 195/E3
Brookside, Colo. (†81212) 208/J6
Brookside, Del. (19711) 245/R2
Brookside, N.J. (07926) 273/D2
Brookside, Ohio (†43912) 284/J5
Brookside Village, Texas (77581) 303/J2
Brookston, Ind. (47923) 227/D3
Brookston, Minn. (55711) 255/F4
Brooksville, Ala. (†35031) 195/F2
Brooksville, Fla. (33512) 212/D3
Brooksville, Ky. (41004) 237/N3
Brooksville, Maine (04617) 243/F7
Brooksville○, Maine (04617) 243/F7
Brooksville, Miss. (39739) 256/G4
Brooksville, Okla. (†74873) 288/M4
Brookton, Georgia (†30501) 217/E2
Brookton, Maine (04413) 243/H4
Brookton, W. Australia 92/B2
Brooktondale, N.Y. (14817) 276/H6
Brookview, Md. (†21659) 245/P6
Brook Village, Nova Scotia 168/G2
Brookville, Ind. (47012) 227/G6
Brookville (lake), Ind. 227/G6
Brookville, Kansas (67425) 232/E3
Brookville, Mass. (†02343) 249/K4
Brookville, N.Y. (†11545) 276/R6
Brookville, Ohio (45309) 284/B6
Brookville, Pa. (15825) 294/D3
Brookwood, Ala. (35444) 195/D4
Broom, Loch (inlet), Scotland 15/C3
Broomall, Pa. (19008) 294/M6
Broome, Australia 87/C7
Broome (co.), N.Y. 276/J6
Broome, W. Australia 88/C3
Broome, W. Australia 92/C2
Broomfield, Colo. (80020) 208/J3
Broomhill, Manitoba 179/B5
Brooten, Minn. (56316) 255/C5
Brora, Scotland 15/E2
Brora (riv.), Scotland 15/D2
Brørup, Denmark 21/C7
Broseley, Mo. (63932) 261/M9
Brosna, Ireland 17/C7
Brosna (riv.), Ireland 17/F5
Brossard, Québec 172/H4
Brosseau, Alberta 182/E3
Brothers, Oreg. (97712) 291/G4
Brotherton, Tenn. (†38501) 237/L8
Brothertown, Wis. (†53014) 317/K7
Brou, France 28/D3
Brough (head), Scotland 15/E1
Brough Ness (prom.), Scotland 15/F2
Broughshane, N. Ireland 17/J2
Broughton, Ill. (62817) 222/E6
Broughton, Ohio (†45855) 284/B3
Broughton, Pa. (†15236) 294/B7
Broughton, Scotland 15/E5
Broughton Island, N.W. Terrs. 187/M3
Broumov, Czech. 41/D1
Brounland, W. Va. (†25314) 312/C6
Brouse, Br. Col. 184/J5
Broussard, La. (70518) 238/F6
Brouwershaven, Netherlands 27/D5
Brovst, Denmark 21/C3
Broward (co.), Fla. 212/F5
Browardale, Fla. (†33311) 212/B4
Browder, Ky. (42326) 237/H6
Browerville, Minn. (56438) 255/D4
Brown (co.), Ill. 222/C4
Brown (co.), Ind. 227/E6
Brown (co.), Kansas 232/G2
Brown (co.), Minn. 255/D6
Brown (co.), Nebr. 264/E2
Brown (lake), N.W. Terrs. 187/J3
Brown (co.), Ohio 284/C8
Brown (reefs), Philippines 85/F3
Brown (co.), S. Dak. 298/N2
Brown (co.), Texas 303/F6
Brown (Roan) (cliffs), Utah 304/E4
Brown (pt.), Wash. 310/A4
Brown, W. Va. (†26448) 312/F4
Brown (co.), Wis. 317/L7
Brownbranch, Mo. (65608) 261/G9
Brown City, Mich. (48416) 250/G5
Brown Deer, Wis. (53209) 317/L1
Browndell, Texas (†75931) 303/L7
Browne (bay), N.W. Terrs. 187/J2
Brownell, Kansas (67521) 232/C3
Browney (riv.), England 13/H3
Brownfield, Alberta 182/E3
Brownfield, Ill. (62911) 222/E6
Brownfield, Maine (04010) 243/B8
Brownfield○, Maine (04010) 243/B8
Brownfield, Miss. (†38683) 256/G1
Brownfield, Texas (79316) 303/B4
Browning, Ill. (62624) 222/C3
Browning, Mo. (64630) 261/F2
Browning, Mont. (59417) 262/C2
Browning, N.S. Wales 97/E4
Browning, Sask. 181/J6
Browning Entrance (str.), Br. Col. 184/B3
Brownington, Mo. (†64740) 261/E6
Brownington○, Vt. (†05860) 268/C2
Brownlee (dam), Idaho 220/B5
Brownlee, Nebr. (69126) 264/D2
Brownlee, Oreg. (†97840) 291/L3
Brownlee (dam), Oreg. 291/L3
Brownlee, Sask. 181/F5
Browns, Ala. (36724) 195/D6
Browns, Ill. (62818) 222/F5
Brown's (riv.), Vt. 268/A2
Brownsboro, Ala. (35741) 195/F1
Brownsboro, Oreg. (†97524) 291/E5
Brownsboro, Texas (75656) 303/J5
Brownsboro Farm, Ky. (†40201) 237/L1
Brownsburg, Ind. (46112) 227/E5
Brownsburg, Québec 172/C4
Brownsburg, Va. (24415) 307/K5
Brownsdale, Minn. (55918) 255/F7
Brownsdale, Newf. 166/D2
Browns Flat, New Bruns. 170/D3
Brown's Lake, Wis. (†53105) 317/K3
Browns Mills, N.J. (08015) 273/D4
Browns Spring, Mo. (†65610) 261/F9
Browns Summit, N.C. (27214) 281/K2
Brownstown, Ill. (62418) 222/E5
Brownstown, Ind. (47220) 227/F7
Browns Town, Jamaica 158/J6
Brownstown, Pa. (17508) 294/K5
Brownstown, Wash. (98920) 310/E4
Browns Valley, Ind. (†47933) 227/C5
Browns Valley, Minn. (56219) 255/B5
Browns Village, Fla. (†33142) 212/B4
Brownsville, Ind. (47325) 227/H5
Brownsville, Ky. (42210) 237/J6
Brownsville, Md. (21715) 245/H3
Brownsville, Minn. (55919) 255/G7
Brownsville, Miss. (†39041) 256/D6
Brownsville, Oreg. (97327) 291/E3
Brownsville, Pa. (15417) 294/C5
Brownsville, Tenn. (38012) 237/C9
Brownsville, Texas (*78520) 303/G12
Brownsville, Texas 188/G5
Brownsville, Texas 146/J7
Brownsville, Vt. (05037) 268/B5
Brownsville, Wash. (†98310) 310/A2
Brownsville, Wis. (53006) 317/J8
Brownton, Minn. (55312) 255/D6
Brownton, W. Va. (26334) 312/F4
Browntown, Va. (22610) 307/M3
Browntown, Wis. (53522) 317/G10
Brownvale, Alberta 182/B1
Brownville, Ala. (†35476) 195/C4
Brownville, Fla. (†33821) 212/E4
Brownville, Maine (04414) 243/E5
Brownville○, Maine (04414) 243/E5
Brownville, Nebr. (68321) 264/J4
Brownville, N.Y. (13615) 276/H3
Brownville Junction, Maine (04415) 243/E5
Brown Willy (mt.), England 13/C7
Brownwood, Texas (76801) 303/F6
Brownwood (lake), Texas 303/E6
Browse (isl.), W. Australia 88/C2
Browse (isl.), W. Australia 92/C1
Broxburn, Scotland 15/D1
Broxton, Georgia (31519) 217/G7
Broye (riv.), Switzerland 39/C3
Broyle (cape), Newf. 166/D2
Brozas, Spain 33/C3
Brozville, Miss. (†39095) 256/D4
Brtnice, Czech. 41/C2
Bruay-en-Artois, France 28/E2
Bruce, Alberta 182/E3
Bruce (mt.), Australia 87/C8
Bruce, Fla. (32455) 212/C6
Bruce, Miss. (38915) 256/F3
Bruce (mts.), N.W. Terrs. 187/L2
Bruce (county), Ontario 177/C3
Bruce (pen.), Ontario 177/C2
Bruce, S. Dak. (57220) 298/R5
Bruce (mt.), W. Australia 88/B4
Bruce (mt.), W. Australia 92/B3
Bruce, Wis. (54819) 317/D5
Bruce Crossing, Mich. (49912) 250/G2
Brucefield, Ontario 177/C4
Bruce Lake, Ontario 175/B2
Bruce Mines, Ontario 177/J5
Bruce Mines, Ontario 175/D3
Bruce Rock, W. Australia 88/B6
Bruce Rock, W. Australia 92/B5
Bruceton, Tenn. (38317) 237/E8
Bruceton Mills, W. Va. (26525) 312/G3
Brucetown, Va. (22622) 307/M2
Bruceville, Ind. (47516) 227/C7
Bruchsal, W. Germany 22/C4
Bruck an der Leitha, Austria 41/D2
Bruck an der Mur, Austria 41/C3
Bruderheim, Alberta 182/D3
Bruff, Ireland 17/D7
Bruges, Belgium 27/C6
Brugg, Switzerland 39/F2
Brugge (Bruges), Belgium 27/C6
Brühl, W. Germany 22/B3
Bruin, Ky. (41125) 237/P4
Bruin (cape), New Bruns. 170/G2
Bruin, Pa. (16022) 294/C3
Bruins, Ark. (†72348) 202/K4
Brûlé, Alberta 182/B3
Brule (riv.), Mich. 250/A3
Brule, Nebr. (69127) 264/C3
Brule, Nova Scotia 168/E3
Brûlé (lake), Québec 172/C3
Brûlé (lake), Québec 172/B2
Brule (co.), S. Dak. 298/L6
Brule (mt.), Switzerland 39/D4
Brule, Wis. (54820) 317/C2
Brumado, Brazil 120/E4
Brumado, Brazil 132/F6
Brumley, Mo. (65017) 261/H6
Brummen, Netherlands 27/J4
Brundidge, Ala. (36010) 195/G7
Bruneau, Idaho (83604) 220/C7
Bruneau (riv.), Idaho 220/C7
Brunei 2/Q5
Brunei 54/N9
BRUNEI 85/E4
Bruner, Mo. (65620) 261/F8
Brunete, Spain 33/F4
Brunette (isl.), Newf. 166/C4
Brunflo, Sweden 18/J5
Bruni, Texas (78344) 303/F10
Brunico, Italy 34/D1
Bruning, Nebr. (68322) 264/G4
Brunkild, Manitoba 179/E5
Brunner, N. Zealand 100/C5
Brunner (lake), N. Zealand 100/C5
Bruno, Ark. (72618) 202/E1
Bruno, Minn. (55712) 255/F4
Bruno, Nebr. (68014) 264/G3
Bruno, Sask. 181/F3
Brunot, Mo. (†63636) 261/M8
Brunsbüttel, W. Germany 22/C2
Brunson, S.C. (29911) 296/E6
Brunssum, Netherlands 27/J7
Brunsville, Iowa (51008) 229/A3
Brunswick (pen.), Chile 138/E10
Brunswick, Ga. 188/K4
Brunswick, Georgia (31520) 217/K8
Brunswick, Maine (04011) 243/C8
Brunswick○, Maine (04011) 243/C8
Brunswick, Md. (21716) 245/H3
Brunswick, Minn. (†55051) 255/E5
Brunswick, Miss. (†39180) 256/C5
Brunswick, Mo. (65236) 261/F4
Brunswick, Nebr. (68720) 264/G2
Brunswick (co.), N.C. 281/N6
Brunswick, N.C. (28424) 281/M6
Brunswick, Ohio (44212) 284/G3
Brunswick, Tenn. (38014) 237/B10
Brunswick, Victoria 88/K7
Brunswick, Victoria 97/H5
Brunswick (co.), Va. 307/N7
Brunswick (bay), W. Australia 88/C3
Brunswick, W. Germany 7/E3
Brunswick (bay), W. Australia 92/D1
Brunswick, W. Germany 22/D2
Brunswick Heads, N.S. Wales 97/G1
Brunswick Junction, W. Australia 92/A2
Bruntál, Czech. 41/D2
Bruree, Ireland 17/D7
Brus (lag.), Honduras 154/E2
Brusett, Mont. (59318) 262/J3
Brush, Colo. (80723) 208/M2
Brush Creek, Minn. (†56014) 255/E7
Brush Creek, Mo. (†65536) 261/G7
Brush Creek, Tenn. (38547) 237/J8
Brush Prairie, Wash. (98606) 310/C5
Brushton, N.Y. (12916) 276/L1
Brushy Prairie, Ind. (†46761) 227/G1
Brusio, Switzerland 39/K4
Brus Laguna, Honduras 154/E3
Brusly, La. (70719) 238/J2
Brusque, Brazil 132/D9
Brussels (cap.), Belgium 7/E3
Brussels, Ill. (62013) 222/C5
Brussels, Ontario 177/C4
Brussels, Wis. (54204) 317/L6
Bruthen, Victoria 97/D5
Brutus, Mich. (49716) 250/E3
Bruxelles, Manitoba 179/C5
Bruzual, Venezuela 124/D3
Bryan (co.), Georgia 217/K6
Bryan, Ohio (43506) 284/A3
Bryan (co.), Okla. 288/O7
Bryan, Texas 188/G4
Bryan, Texas (77801) 303/H7
Bryan (lake), Wash. 310/H4
Bryansk, U.S.S.R. 7/H3
Bryansk, U.S.S.R. 52/D4
Bryansk, U.S.S.R. 48/D4
Bryanston, Ontario 177/C4
Bryant, Ala. (35958) 195/G1
Bryant, Ark. (72022) 202/F4
Bryant, Fla. (33439) 212/F5
Bryant (lake), Fla. 212/E2
Bryant, Ill. (61519) 222/C3
Bryant, Ind. (47326) 227/G3
Bryant, Iowa (52727) 229/N5
Bryant, Okla. (†74437) 288/P4
Bryant, S. Dak. (57221) 298/P4
Bryant, Wis. (54418) 317/J5
Bryant Pond, Maine (04219) 243/B7
Bryantsburg, Ind. (†47250) 227/G7
Bryantsville, Ky. (40410) 237/M5
Bryantville, Mass. (02327) 249/L4
Bryce (mt.), Br. Col. 184/J4
Bryce Canyon, Utah (84717) 304/B6
Bryce Canyon Nat'l Park, Utah 304/B6
Bryceland, La. (71014) 238/E2
Bryceville, Fla. (32009) 212/D1
Bryn Athyn, Pa. (19009) 294/M5
Brynica (riv.), Poland 47/B4
Bryn Mawr, Pa. (19010) 294/M5
Brynmawr, Wales 10/E5
Brynmawr, Wales 13/B6
Bryn Mawr-Skyway, Wash. (†98101) 310/B2
Bryrup, Denmark 21/C5
Bryson, Texas (76027) 303/F4
Bryson City, N.C. (28713) 281/C4
Bryte-Broderick, Calif. (95605) 204/B8
Brzeg, Poland 47/C3
Brzeg Dolny, Poland 47/C3
Brzesko, Poland 47/E3
Brzozów, Poland 47/F4
B-Say-Tah, Sask. 181/G5
Bua Chum, Thailand 72/D4
Buad (isl.), Philippines 82/E5
Buba, Guinea-Biss. 106/B6
Bubali, Neth. Ant. 161/D10
Bubaque, Guinea-Biss. 106/A6
Bubendorf, Switzerland 39/E2
Bubikon, Switzerland 39/G2
Bubiyan (isl.), Kuwait 59/E4
Bucak, 63/D4
Bucaramanga, Colombia 120/B2
Bucaramanga, Colombia 126/D4
Bucareli (bay), Alaska 196/M2
Bucas Grande (isl.), Philippines 82/F6
Bucasia, Queensland 95/D4
Buccaneer (arch.), W. Australia 88/C3
Buccaneer (arch.), W. Australia 92/C2
Buchan (gulf), N.W. Terrs. 187/L2
Buchan (dist.), Scotland 15/F3
Buchanan, Georgia (30113) 217/B3
Buchanan (co.), Iowa 229/K4
Buchanan, Iowa (†52772) 229/L5
Buchanan, Ky. (†41129) 237/R4
Buchanan, Liberia 106/B7
Buchanan, Liberia 102/A4
Buchanan, Mich. (49107) 250/C7
Buchanan (co.), Mo. 261/C3
Buchanan, N.Y. (10511) 276/N8
Buchanan, N. Dak. (58420) 282/N5
Buchanan, Sask. 181/J4
Buchanan, Tenn. (38222) 237/E8
Buchanan (lake), Texas 303/F7
Buchanan (co.), Va. 307/D6
Buchanan, Va. (24066) 307/J5
Buchan Ness (prom.), Scotland 15/G3
Buchans, Newf. 166/C4
Bucharest (cap.), Romania 7/G4
Bucharest (cap.), Romania 2/L3
Bucharest (București) (cap.), Romania 45/G3
Buchegg (mts.), Switzerland 39/D2
Buchholz in der Nordheide, W. Germany 22/C2
Buchlyvie, Scotland 15/B1
Buchon (pt.), Calif. 204/D8
Buchs, Switzerland 39/H2
Buchtel, Ohio (45716) 284/F7
Buck (creek), Ind. 227/E8
Buck (creek), S.C. 296/J3
Buck (creek), Texas 303/D3
Buck (isl.), Virgin Is. (U.S.) 161/G3
Buck, W. Va. (†24935) 312/E7
Buckatunna, Miss. (39322) 256/G7
Buck Creek, Alberta 182/C3
Buck Creek, Ind. (47924) 227/D4
Bückeburg, W. Germany 22/C2
Buckeye, Ariz. (85326) 198/C5
Buckeye, Iowa (50043) 229/G4
Buckeye, La. (71321) 238/F4
Buckeye, N. Mex. (†88260) 274/F6
Buckeye (lake), Ohio 284/F6
Buckeye, W. Va. (24924) 312/F6
Buckeye Lake, Ohio (43008) 284/F6
Buckeystown, Md. (21717) 245/J3
Buckfastleigh, England 13/C7
Buckfield○, Maine (†04232) 243/C7
Buck Grove, Iowa (†51442) 229/C5
Buckhannon, W. Va. (26201) 312/F5
Buckhannon (riv.), W. Va. 312/F5
Buckhaven and Methil, Scotland 15/F4
Buckhaven and Methil, Scotland 10/E2
Buckhead, Georgia (30625) 217/F3
Buck Hollow (creek), Oreg. 291/G2
Buckholts, Texas (76518) 303/H7
Buckhorn (lake), Ky. 237/O6
Buckhorn, Mo. (†63655) 261/M8
Buckhorn, N. Mex. (88025) 274/A5
Buckhorn, Ontario 177/F3
Buckhorn (lake), Ontario 177/F3
Buckie, Scotland 15/E3
Buckie, Scotland 10/E2
Buckingham, Colo. (†80742) 208/L1
Buckingham, Conn. (†06033) 210/E2
Buckingham, England 13/G6
Buckingham, England 10/F5
Buckingham, Ill. (60917) 222/E2
Buckingham, Iowa (50612) 229/J4
Buckingham, Québec 172/B4
Buckingham, Texas (†75080) 303/H2
Buckingham (co.), Va. 307/L5
Buckingham, Va. (23921) 307/L5
Buckinghamshire (co.), England 13/G6
Buck Island (chan.), Virgin Is. (U.S.) 161/F3
Buck Island Reef Nat'l Mon., Virgin Is. (U.S.) 161/G3
Buck Lake, Alberta 182/C3
Buckland, Alaska (99727) 196/F1
Buckland, Conn. (06040) 210/E1
Buckland○, Mass. (01338) 249/C2
Buckland, Ohio (45819) 284/B4
Buckland, Québec 172/G3
Buckley, Ill. (60918) 222/F3
Buckley, Mich. (49620) 250/D4
Buckley, Wales 13/G2
Buckley, Wash. (98321) 310/C3
Bucklin, Kansas (67834) 232/C4
Bucklin, Mo. (64631) 261/G3
Buckman, Minn. (56317) 255/D5
Buckner, Ark. (71827) 202/D7
Buckner, Ill. (62819) 222/E6
Buckner, Ky. (40010) 237/L4
Buckner, Mo. (64016) 261/R5
Bucks, Ala. (36512) 195/B8
Bucks (co.), Pa. 294/M5
Bucksburn, Scotland 15/F3
Bucks Harbor, Maine (04618) 243/J6
Buckskin (mts.), Ariz. 198/B4
Buckskin, Ind. (47647) 227/C8
Bucksport, Maine (04416) 243/F6
Bucksport○, Maine (04416) 243/F6
Bucksport, S.C. (29527) 296/J4
Buckville, Ark. (71934) 202/D4
Bucoda, Mo. (†63876) 261/M10
Bucoda, Wash. (98530) 310/C4
Buco-Zau, Angola 111/B4
Buctouche, New Bruns. 170/F2
Buctouche (harb.), New Bruns. 170/F2
Buctouche (riv.), New Bruns. 170/F2
București (Bucharest) (cap.), Romania 45/G3
Bucyrus, Kansas (66013) 232/H3
Bucyrus, Mo. (65444) 261/H8
Bucyrus, N. Dak. (58624) 282/E7
Bucyrus, Ohio (44820) 284/E4
Bud, Ind. (†46131) 227/E6
Bud, W. Va. (24716) 312/D7
Buda, Ill. (61314) 222/D2
Buda, Texas (78610) 303/G7
Budafok, Hungary 41/E3
Budakeszi, Hungary 41/E3
Budaörs, Hungary 41/E3

344 Budapest

Budapest (city), Hungary 41/E3
Budapest (cap.), Hungary 41/E3
Budapest (cap.), Hungary 7/F4
Budaun, India 68/D3
Budd (lake), N.J. 273/D2
Budd Coast (reg.) 5/C6
Budd Lake, N.J. (07828) 273/D2
Buddon Ness (prom.), Scotland 15/F4
Bude (bay), England 13/C7
Bude, Miss. (39630) 256/C8
Bude-Stratton, England 13/C7
Budge-Budge, India 68/F2
Budgewoi Lake, N.S. Wales 97/F3
Budia, Spain 33/E2
Büdingen, W. Germany 22/C3
Budišov, Czech. 41/D2
Budjala, Zaire 115/C3
Budleigh Salterton, England 13/D7
Budrio, Italy 34/C2
Budva, Yugoslavia 45/D4
Buea, Cameroon 115/A3
Buechel, Ky. (40218) 237/K2
Buel (lake), Mass. 249/A4
Buellton, Calif. (93427) 204/E9
Buena, N.J. (08310) 273/D4
Buena, Wash. (98921) 310/E4
Buena Esperanza, Argentina 143/C3
Buena Park, Calif. (*90622) 204/D11
Buenaventura, Colombia 126/B6
Buenaventura, Colombia 120/B2
Buenaventura (bay), Colombia 126/B6
Buenaventura, Cuba 158/H3
Buenaventura, Mexico 150/F2
Buena Vista, Ala. (†36425) 195/D7
Buena Vista, Ark. (†71764) 202/D7
Buena Vista, Bolivia 136/D5
Buena Vista, Idaho (83316) 220/D7
Buena Vista (lake), Calif. 204/F8
Buena Vista, Colo. (81211) 208/G5
Buenavista, Cuba 158/F2
Buenavista (bay), Cuba 158/F2
Buena Vista, Georgia (31803) 217/C6
Buena Vista (co.), Iowa 229/C3
Buena Vista, Miss. (†38851) 256/G3
Buena Vista, N. Mex. (87712) 274/D3
Buena Vista, Ohio (†45684) 284/D8
Buena Vista, Oreg. (†97351) 291/D3
Buena Vista, Paraguay 144/D5
Buenavista, Philippines 82/E6
Buena Vista, Sask. 181/F5
Buena Vista, Tenn. (38318) 237/E9
Buena Vista, Uruguay 145/E3
Buena Vista, Anzoátegui, Venezuela 124/F3
Buena Vista, Apure, Venezuela 124/D4
Buena Vista, Falcón, Venezuela 124/D2
Buena Vista (I.C.), Va. (24416) 307/K5
Buendía (res.), Spain 33/E2
Bueno (riv.), Chile 138/D3
Buenos Aires (lake) 120/B7
Buenos Aires (prov.), Argentina 143/D4
Buenos Aires (cap.), Argentina 120/C6
Buenos Aires (cap.), Argentina 143/H7
Buenos Aires (cap.), Argentina 2/F7
Buenos Aires (lake), Argentina 143/B6
Buenos Aires (lake), Chile 138/E6
Buenos Aires, Amazonas, Colombia 126/F9
Buenos Aires, Caquetá, Colombia 126/D7
Buenos Aires, C. Rica 154/F6
Buesaco, Colombia 126/B7
Buey Arriba, Cuba 158/H4
Bueyeros, N. Mex. (88412) 274/F3
Buffalo, Ala. (†36862) 195/H5
Buffalo, Alberta 182/E4
Buffalo (lake), Alberta 182/D3
Buffalo (riv.), Ark. 202/E2
Buffalo, Ill. (62515) 222/D4
Buffalo, Ind. (47925) 227/D3
Buffalo, Iowa (52728) 229/M6
Buffalo, Kansas (66717) 232/G4
Buffalo, Ky. (42716) 237/K6
Buffalo (bay), Manitoba 179/G5
Buffalo, Minn. (55313) 255/E5
Buffalo (riv.), Minn. 255/B4
Buffalo, Mo. (65622) 261/F7
Buffalo, Mont. (59418) 262/G4
Buffalo (co.), Nebr. 264/E4
Buffalo (creek), Nev. 266/B2
Buffalo, N.Y. 146/L5
Buffalo, N.Y. 188/L2
Buffalo, N.Y. (*14201) 276/B5
Buffalo, N. Dak. (58011) 282/R6
Buffalo, Ohio (43722) 284/G6
Buffalo, Okla. (73834) 288/G1
Buffalo, S.C. (29321) 296/D2
Buffalo (co.), S. Dak. 298/L5
Buffalo, S. Dak. (57720) 298/B2
Buffalo (creek), S. Dak. 298/F6
Buffalo (lake), S. Dak. 298/P2
Buffalo (riv.), Tenn. 237/F9
Buffalo, Texas (75831) 303/J6
Buffalo, W. Va. (25033) 312/C5
Buffalo (co.), Wis. 317/C7
Buffalo, Wis. (†54622) 317/C7
Buffalo, Wyo. (82834) 319/F1
Buffalo Bill (dam), Wyo. 319/C1
Buffalo Bill (res.), Wyo. 319/C1
Buffalo Center, Iowa (50424) 229/F2
Buffalo City, Ark. (†72653) 202/E1
Buffalo City, N.C. (†27931) 281/T3
Buffalo Creek, Br. Col. 184/G4
Buffalo Creek, Colo. (80425) 208/J4
Buffalo Fork, Snake (riv.), Wyo. 319/B2
Buffalo Gap, Sask. 181/F6
Buffalo Gap, S. Dak. (57722) 298/C6
Buffalo Gap, Texas (79508) 303/E5
Buffalo Grove, Ill. (†60090) 222/B5
Buffalo Head (hills), Alberta 182/B5
Buffalo Junction, Va. (24529) 307/L7
Buffalo Lake, Minn. (55314) 255/D6
Buffalo Lodge (lake), N. Dak. 282/J3
Buffalo Mills, Pa. (15534) 294/E6
Buffalo Narrows, Sask. 181/L3
Buffalo Nat'l River, Ark. 202/E1
Buffalo Pound Prov. Park, Sask. 181/F5
Buffalo River Junction, N.W. Terrs. 187/G3
Buffalo Valley, Tenn. (38548) 237/K8
Buffaloville, Ind. (47518) 227/D8
Buff Bay, Jamaica 158/K6
Buford, Alberta 182/D3
Buford, Georgia (30518) 217/D2
Buford, N. Dak. (†58853) 282/C3
Buford, Ohio (45110) 284/C7
Buford, Wyo. (82052) 319/G4
Bug (riv.) 7/G3
Bug (riv.), Poland 47/F2
Bug (riv.), U.S.S.R. 7/G4
Bug (riv.), U.S.S.R. 52/B4
Bug (riv.), U.S.S.R. 52/D5
Buga, Colombia 126/B6
Bugaboo Glacier Prov. Park, Br. Col. 184/J5
Bugak, Hungary 41/E3
Bugaldie, N.S. Wales 97/E2
Bugasong, Philippines 82/C5
Buggs Island (lake), N.C. 281/M1
Buggs Island (lake), Va. 307/L8
Bugiougio (isl.), Portugal 33/B2
Bugojno, Yugoslavia 45/C3
Bugrino, U.S.S.R. 52/G1
Bugsuk (isl.), Philippines 85/F4
Bugsuk (isl.), Philippines 82/A6
Bugt, China 77/K2
Bugui (pt.), Philippines 82/D4
Bugul'ma, U.S.S.R. 7/K3
Bugul'ma, U.S.S.R. 52/H4
Bugul'ma, U.S.S.R. 48/F4
Buguruslan, U.S.S.R. 52/H4
Buhl, Ala. (35446) 195/C4
Buhl, Idaho (83316) 220/D7
Buhl, Minn. (55713) 255/F3
Bühl, W. Germany 22/C4
Buhler, Kansas (67522) 232/E3
Buhuşi, Romania 45/H2
Buie, Loch (inlet), Scotland 15/C4
Buies, N.C. (†28377) 281/L5
Buies Creek, N.C. (27506) 281/M4
Buiksloot, Netherlands 27/C4
Builth Wells, Wales 13/D5
Builth Wells, Wales 10/E4
Buin, Chile 138/G4
Buin, Papua N.G. 86/C2
Buin (peak), Switzerland 39/K3
Buinsk, U.S.S.R. 52/G4
Bujalance, Spain 33/D4
Bujumbura (cap.), Burundi 102/F5
Bujumbura (cap.), Burundi 115/E4
Buka, Papua N.G. 87/F6
Buka (isl.), Papua N.G. 86/C2
Buka (passage), Papua N.G. 86/C2
Bukachacha, U.S.S.R. 48/M4
Bukama, Zaire 115/E5
Buka Passage, Papua N.G. 86/C2
Bukavu, Zaire 102/E5
Bukavu, Zaire 115/E4
Bukene, Tanzania 115/F4
Bukhara, U.S.S.R. 54/H5
Bukhara, U.S.S.R. 48/G5
Bukidnon (prov.), Philippines 82/E6
Bukittinggi, Indonesia 85/B6
Bükk (mts.), Hungary 41/F2
Bukoba, Tanzania 115/F4
Bukowno, Poland 47/C4
Bul, Kuh-e (mt.), Iran 66/H5
Bula, Indonesia 85/J6
Bula, Texas (79320) 303/B4
Bulacan (prov.), Philippines 82/C3
Bülach, Switzerland 39/G1
Bulahdelah, N.S. Wales 97/G3
Bulak (Bole), China 77/B3
Bulalakao, Philippines 82/C4
Bulan, Ky. (41722) 237/P6
Bulan, Philippines 82/D4
Bulancak, Turkey 63/H2
Bulanık, Turkey 63/K3
Bûlaq, Egypt 111/F2
Bûlaq, Egypt 59/B4
Bulawayo, Zimbabwe 118/D3
Bulawayo, Zimbabwe 102/E7
Buldan, Turkey 59/A2
Buldan, Turkey 63/C3
Buldibuyo, Peru 128/D7
Buldir (isl.), Alaska 196/J3
Bulgan, Mongolia 77/F2
Bulgan, Ömnögovĭ, Mongolia 77/F3
Bulgan, Hovd, Mongolia 77/D2
Bulgan, Bulgan, Mongolia 77/F2
Bulgaria 2/L3
Bulgaria 7/G4
BULGARIA 45/G4
Bulger, Pa. (15019) 294/B5
Bulgroo, Queensland 95/B5
Bulgroo, Queensland 88/G5
Bulhar, Somalia 115/H1
Buli, Indonesia 85/H5
Buliluyan (cape), Philippines 85/F4
Buliluyan (cape), Philippines 82/A6
Bulimba (creek), Queensland 95/E3
Bulkley (riv.), Br. Col. 184/D2
Bull, The (isl.), Ireland 17/A8
Bull (isl.), Newf. 166/D2
Bull (isl.), S.C. 296/H6
Bull (creek), S. Dak. 298/K6
Bull (creek), S. Dak. 298/C2
Bullard, Georgia (†31020) 217/F5
Bullard, Texas (75757) 303/J5
Bull Arm (inlet), Newf. 166/D2
Bullas, Spain 33/F4
Bulldog (isl.), Newf. 166/C3
Bulle, Switzerland 39/D3
Bullen (bay), Neth. Ant. 161/F8
Buller (riv.), N. Zealand 100/D4
Buller (mt.), Victoria 97/D5
Bullfinch, W. Australia 92/B5
Bull Harbour, Br. Col. 184/C5
Bullhead, S. Dak. (57621) 298/G2
Bullhead City-Riviera, Ariz. (86430) 198/A3
Bullitt (co.), Ky. 237/K5
Bull Lake (res.), Wyo. 319/C2
Bulloch (co.), Georgia 217/J6
Bullock (co.), Ala. 195/G6
Bullock, N.C. (27507) 281/M2
Bullock (creek), S.C. 296/E2
Bulloo (riv.), Queensland 88/G5
Bulloo (lake), Queensland 95/B6
Bulloo (riv.), Queensland 95/B6
Bulloo Downs, Queensland 88/G5
Bull Run (creek), Va. 307/N3
Bulls, N. Zealand 100/E4
Bulls (bay), S.C. 296/H6
Bull Savanna-Junction, Jamaica 158/H6
Bulls Bridge, Conn. (†06785) 210/B2
Bulls Gap, Tenn. (37711) 237/P8
Bull Shoals, Ark. (72619) 202/E1
Bull Shoals (lake), Ark. 202/E1
Bull Shoals (lake), Mo. 261/G10
Bully (creek), Oreg. 291/K3
Bulnes, Chile 138/E1
Bulo Burti, Somalia 115/J3
Bulolo, Papua N.G. 85/B7
Bulpitt, Ill. (62517) 222/D4
Buluan (lake), Philippines 82/E7
Bulukumba, Indonesia 85/G7
Bulun, U.S.S.R. 4/B3
Bulun, U.S.S.R. 48/N2
Bulungu, Zaire 115/C4
Bulusan, Philippines 82/E4
Bulusan (vol.), Philippines 82/D4
Bulyea, Sask. 181/G5
Bumba, Zaire 115/D3
Bumble Bee, Ariz. (†86301) 198/C4
Bumiayu, Indonesia 85/H2
Bumpass, Va. (23024) 307/N5
Bumping (lake), Wash. 310/D4
Bumpus Mills, Tenn. (37028) 237/F7
Bumthang, Bhutan 68/G3
Buna, Kenya 115/G3
Buna, Papua N.G. 85/C7
Buna, Texas (77612) 303/L7
Bunavista, Texas (†79007) 303/C2
Bunawan, Philippines 82/E6
Bunbeg-Derrybeg, Ireland 17/E1
Bunbury, Australia 87/B9
Bunbury, Pr. Edward I. 168/F2
Bunbury, W. Australia 88/B6
Bunbury, W. Australia 92/A2
Bunceton, Mo. (65237) 261/G5
Bunch, Iowa (†52552) 229/H7
Bunch, Okla. (74931) 288/S3
Bunche Park, Fla. (†33054) 212/B4
Bunclody-Carrickduff, Ireland 17/H6
Buncombe, Ill. (62912) 222/E6
Buncombe (co.), N.C. 281/D3
Buncrana, Ireland 17/G1
Buncrana, Ireland 10/C3
Bundaberg, Australia 87/E8
Bundaberg, Queensland 88/J4
Bundaberg, Queensland 95/D5
Bundanoon, N.S. Wales 97/F4
Bundarra, N.S. Wales 97/F2
Bünde, W. Germany 22/C2
Bundi, India 68/D3
Bundick (lake), La. 238/D5
Bundooma, North. Terr. 93/D8
Bundoora, Victoria 97/J4
Bundoran, Ireland 17/E3
Bunessan, Scotland 15/B4
Bunga (pt.), Philippines 82/E4
Bungalaut (chan.), Indonesia 85/B6
Bungay, England 10/G4
Bungay, England 13/J5
Bungee (brook), Conn. 210/G1
Bu Ngem, Libya 111/C1
Bungendore, N.S. Wales 97/E4
Bungo (str.), Japan 81/F7
Bunguran (Great Natuna) (isl.), Indonesia 85/D5
Bunguran (Natuna) (isls.), Indonesia 85/D5
Bunia, Zaire 115/E3
Bunia, Zaire 102/E4
Bunji, Pakistan 68/D1
Bunker, Mo. (63629) 261/K8
Bunker Group (isls.), Queensland 95/E4
Bunker Hill, Ill. (62014) 222/D4
Bunker Hill, Ind. (46914) 227/E3
Bunker Hill, Kansas (67626) 232/D3
Bunker Hill, Oreg. (†97420) 291/C4
Bunker Hill, W. Va. (25413) 312/K4
Bunker Hill Village, Texas (†77001) 303/J1
Bunkerville, Nev. (89007) 266/G6
Bunkeya, Zaire 115/E6
Bunkie, La. (71322) 238/F5
Bunn, N.C. (27508) 281/N3
Bunnell, Fla. (32010) 212/E2
Bunnlevel, N.C. (28323) 281/M4
Buntok, Indonesia 85/F6
Bunyala, Kenya 115/F3
Bünyan, Turkey 63/G3
Bunyan's Cove, Newf. 166/C2
Bunyu (isl.), Indonesia 85/F5
Buochs, Switzerland 39/F3
Buol, Indonesia 85/G5
Buq, Iran 66/M6
Bura, Kenya 115/H4
Bur Acaba, Somalia 115/H3
Bur Acaba, Somalia 102/G4
Buraida, Saudi Arabia 59/D4
Buraimi, Oman 59/G5
Buraimi, U.A.E. 59/G5
Buram, Sudan 111/E5
Burang, China 77/B5
Burao, Somalia 102/G4
Burao, Somalia 115/J2
Buras-Triumph, La. (70041) 238/L8
Burauen, Philippines 82/E5
Buraz, Turkey 63/B6
Burbank, Calif. (*91501) 204/C10
Burbank, Ill. (60459) 222/B6
Burbank, Ohio (44214) 284/F4
Burbank, Okla. (74633) 288/N1
Burbank, S. Dak. (57010) 298/R8
Burbank, Wash. (99323) 310/G4
Burchard, Minn. (†56115) 255/C6
Burchard, Nebr. (68323) 264/H4
Burcher, N.S. Wales 97/D3
Burchinal, Iowa (†50469) 229/G2
Burdekin (riv.), Queensland 88/H3
Burdekin (riv.), Queensland 95/C3
Burden, Kansas (67019) 232/F4
Burdett, Alberta 182/E5
Burdett, Kansas (67523) 232/C3
Burdett, N.Y. (14818) 276/G6
Burdette, Ark. (72321) 202/L2
Burdette, S. Dak. (†57476) 298/M4
Burdick, Kansas (66838) 232/F3
Burdur (prov.), Turkey 63/D4
Burdur, Turkey 59/A2
Burdur, Turkey 63/D4
Burdur (lake), Turkey 63/D4
Burdwan, India 68/F4
Bureå, Sweden 18/M4
Bureau (co.), Ill. 222/D2
Bureau, Ill. (61315) 222/D2
Burei, Ethiopia 111/G6
Büren, W. Germany 22/C3
Büren an der Aare, Switzerland 39/D2
Bürentsogt, Mongolia 77/H2
Burford (lake), N. Mex. 274/C2
Burford, Ontario 177/D4
Burfordville, Mo. (63739) 261/N8
Burgas, Bulgaria 45/H4
Burgas, Bulgaria 7/G4
Burg auf Fehmarn, W. Germany 22/D1
Burgaw, N.C. (28425) 281/N5
Burgaz (isl.), Turkey 63/D6
Burg bei Magdeburg, E. Germany 22/D2
Burgdorf, Switzerland 39/E2
Burgenland (prov.), Austria 41/D3
Burgeo, Newf. 166/C4
Burgersdorp, S. Africa 118/D6
Burgess, Mo. (†66756) 261/C7
Burgess, S.C. (†29576) 296/J4
Burgess, Va. (22432) 307/R5
Burgess (mt.), Yukon 187/D3
Burgess Hill, England 13/G7
Burgessville, Ontario 177/D4
Burgettstown, Pa. (15021) 294/A5
Burghausen, W. Germany 22/E4
Burghead, Scotland 10/E2
Burghead, Scotland 15/E3
Burghill, Ohio (44404) 284/J3
Burgin, Ky. (40310) 237/M5
Burgis, Sask. 181/J4
Bürglen, Thurgau, Switzerland 39/H1
Bürglen, Uri, Switzerland 39/G3
Burglengenfeld, W. Germany 22/D4
Burgoon, Ohio (43407) 284/D3
Burgos, Mexico 150/K4
Burgos (prov.), Spain 33/E1
Burgos, Spain 7/D4
Burgos, Spain 33/E1
Burg Stargard, E. Germany 22/E2
Burgsteinfurt, W. Germany 22/B2
Burgsvik, Sweden 18/K8
Burgundy (trad. prov.), France 29
Burhaniye, Turkey 63/B3
Burhanpur, India 68/D4
Buri, Brazil 135/B3
Buri (pen.), Ethiopia 111/H4
Burias (isl.), Philippines 82/D4
Burias (passage), Philippines 82/D4
Buribay, U.S.S.R. 52/J4
Burica (pt.), C. Rica 154/F6
Burica, Punta (cape), Panama 154/F6
Burien, Wash. (98166) 310/A2
Burin, Newf. 166/C4
Burin (pen.), Newf. 166/C4
Buriram, Thailand 72/D4
Buriti, Brazil 132/F3
Buriti Alegre, Brazil 132/D7
Buriti dos Lopes, Brazil 132/F3
Burj al Hattaba, Tunisia 106/F2
Burkburnett, Texas (76354) 303/F3
Burke (chan.), Br. Col. 184/D4
Burke (co.), Georgia 217/J4
Burke, Idaho (†83873) 220/C2
Burke, N.Y. (12917) 276/M1
Burke (co.), N.C. 281/F3
Burke (co.), N. Dak. 282/E2
Burke, S. Dak. (57523) 298/L7
Burke, Texas (75941) 303/K6
Burke○, Vt. (†05871) 268/D2
Burke (mt.), Vt. 268/D2
Burke, Va. (22015) 307/R3
Bürkelkopf (mt.), Switzerland 39/K3
Burkes Garden, Va. (24608) 307/F6
Burkesville, Ky. (42717) 237/L7
Burket, Ind. (46508) 227/F2
Burketown, Queensland 95/A3
Burketown, Queensland 88/F3
Burkett, Texas (76828) 303/E5
Burkettsville, Ohio (45310) 284/A5
Burkettville, Maine (04540) 243/E7
Burkeville, Texas (75932) 303/L7
Burkeville, Va. (23922) 307/M6
Burkittsville, Md. (21718) 245/H3
Burkley, Ky. (†42021) 237/C7
Burk's Falls, Ontario 177/E2
Burkville, Ala. (36725) 195/E6
Burleigh (co.), N. Dak. 282/J6
Burleson (co.), Texas 303/H7
Burleson, Texas (76028) 303/F3
Burley, Idaho (83318) 220/E7
Burley, Wash. (98322) 310/C3
Burlingame, Calif. (94010) 204/J2
Burlingame, Kansas (66413) 232/G3
Burlington, Colo. (80807) 208/P4
Burlington○, Conn. (06013) 210/D1
Burlington, Ill. (60109) 222/E1
Burlington, Ind. (46915) 227/E4
Burlington, Iowa (52601) 229/L7
Burlington, Iowa 188/H2
Burlington, Kansas (66839) 232/G3
Burlington, Ky. (41005) 237/R2
Burlington○, Maine (04417) 243/G5
Burlington○, Mass. (01803) 249/C5
Burlington, Mich. (49029) 250/D6
Burlington (co.), N.J. 273/D4
Burlington, N.J. (08016) 273/D3
Burlington, N.C. (27215) 281/K2
Burlington, N. Dak. (58722) 282/H3
Burlington, Ohio (†45680) 284/F9
Burlington, Okla. (73722) 288/K1
Burlington, Ontario 177/E4
Burlington, Pa. (18814) 294/J2
Burlington, Vt. (05401) 268/A3
Burlington, Vt. 146/L5
Burlington, Vt. 188/M2
Burlington, Wash. (98233) 310/C2
Burlington, W. Va. (26710) 312/J4
Burlington, Wis. (53105) 317/K10
Burlington, Wyo. (82411) 319/D1
Burlington Flats, N.Y. (13315) 276/K5
Burlington Junction, Mo. (64428) 261/B2
Burlison, Tenn. (38015) 237/B9
Burma 2/P4
Burma 54/L7
BURMA 72
Burmis, Alberta 182/C5
Burna, Ky. (42028) 237/E6
Burnaby, Br. Col. 184/K3
Burnaby (isl.), Br. Col. 184/B4
Burnet (co.), Texas 303/F7
Burnet, Texas (78611) 303/F7
Burnett, Minn. (†55727) 255/F4
Burnett (co.), Wis. 317/B4
Burnett, Wis. (53922) 317/J9
Burnettown, S.C. (†29834) 296/D5
Burnettsville, Ind. (47926) 227/D3
Burney, Calif. (96013) 204/D3
Burney (mt.), Chile 138/D9
Burney, Ind. (47222) 227/F6
Burneyville, Okla. (73430) 288/M7
Burnham, Ill. (†60601) 222/C6
Burnham○, Maine (04922) 243/E6
Burnham, Mo. (†65793) 261/J9
Burnham, Pa. (17009) 294/H4
Burnham-on-Crouch, England 13/H6
Burnham-on-Sea, England 13/D6
Burnie, Tasmania 99/B3
Burnie-Somerset, Tasmania 88/H8
Burning Springs, Ky. (40922) 237/O6
Burning Springs, W. Va. (26139) 312/D5
Burnips, Mich. (49314) 250/D6
Burnley, England 10/G1
Burnley, England 13/H1
Burnmouth, Scotland 15/F5
Burns, Colo. (80426) 208/F3
Burns, Kansas (66840) 232/F3
Burns, Miss. (†39153) 256/E6
Burns, N.S. Wales 97/A3
Burns, Oreg. (97720) 291/H4
Burns, Tenn. (37029) 237/G8
Burns, Wyo. (82053) 319/H4
Burns City, Ind. (47553) 227/D7
Burns Flat, Okla. (73624) 288/H4
Burns Harbor, Ind. (†46401) 227/C1
Burnside, Conn. (†06108) 210/E1
Burnside, Ill. (62318) 222/B3
Burnside, Iowa (50521) 229/E4
Burnside, Ky. (42519) 237/M6
Burnside, La. (70738) 238/L3
Burnside, Miss. (†39350) 256/F5
Burnside (riv.), N.W. Terrs. 187/G3
Burnside, Pa. (15721) 294/E4
Burnside, S. Australia 88/E8
Burnside, S. Australia 94/B8
Burnside, Suriname 131/C2
Burns Junction, Oreg. (†97902) 291/K5
Burns Lake, Br. Col. 162/D5
Burns Lake, Br. Col. 184/D3
Burnstad, N. Dak. (58526) 282/L7
Burnsville, Ala. (†36701) 195/E6
Burnsville, Ind. (†47201) 227/F6
Burnsville, Minn. (55337) 255/E6
Burnsville, Miss. (38833) 256/H1
Burnsville, New Bruns. 170/E1
Burnsville, N.C. (28714) 281/E3
Burnsville, Va. (24420) 307/J4
Burnsville, W. Va. (26335) 312/E5
Burnt (lakes), Alberta 182/C1
Burnt (lake), Newf. 166/B3
Burnt (riv.), Ontario 177/F3
Burnt (riv.), Oreg. 291/K3
Burnt (lake), Québec 174/E2
Burnt Cabins, Pa. (17215) 294/G5
Burnt Corn, Ala. (36431) 195/D7
Burnt House, W. Va. (26336) 312/D4
Burnt Island (lake), Ontario 177/F2
Burntisland, Scotland 15/D1
Burntisland, Scotland 10/C1
Burnt Islands, Newf. 166/C4
Burnt Point, Newf. 166/D2
Burnt Prairie, Ill. (62820) 222/E5
Burnt River, Ontario 177/F3
Burntroot (lake), Ontario 177/F2
Burntside (lake), Minn. 255/F3
Burntwood, England 13/F5
Burntwood, England 10/G2
Burntwood (riv.), Manitoba 179/J2
Burnwell, W. Va. (25034) 312/D6
Burqa, West Bank 65/C3
Burqin, China 77/C2
Burr (pond), Conn. 210/C1
Burr, Minn. (†56220) 255/B6
Burr, Nebr. (68324) 264/H4
Burr, Sask. 181/F3
Burra, S. Australia 94/F5
Burraboi, N.S. Wales 97/C4
Burramurra, North. Terr. 93/E6
Burray (isl.), Scotland 15/F2
Burrel, Albania 45/D5
Burren Junction, N.S. Wales 97/E2
Burriana, Spain 33/G3
Burringbar, N.S. Wales 97/G1
Burrinjuck (res.), N.S. Wales 97/E4
Burris, Wyo. (†82501) 319/C2
Burro (creek), Ariz. 198/B4
Burro (mts.), Mexico 150/J2
Burr Oak, Ind. (46509) 227/E2
Burr Oak, Iowa (52131) 229/K2
Burr Oak, Kansas (66936) 232/D2
Burr Oak, Mich. (49030) 250/D7
Burro-Burro (riv.), Guyana 131/B3
Burrow (head), Scotland 15/D6
Burrows, Ind. (46916) 227/E3
Burrows, Sask. 181/K5
Burr Ridge, Ill. (†60558) 222/B6
Burrsville, Md. (†21629) 245/P5
Burrton, Kansas (67020) 232/E3
Burrville, Conn. (†06790) 210/C1
Burrville, Tenn. (†37872) 237/M8
Burrville, Utah (†84701) 304/C5
Burrwood, La. (†70091) 238/M8
Burry Port, Wales 13/C6
Bursa (prov.), Turkey 63/C2
Bursa, Turkey 63/C2
Bursa, Turkey 59/A1
Bursa, Turkey 54/D5
Bur Sa'id (Port Said), Egypt 111/K2
Bur Said (Port Said), Egypt 59/B3
Burstall, Sask. 181/B5
Burt, Iowa (50522) 229/E2
Burt, Mich. (48417) 250/F5
Burt (lake), Mich. 250/E3
Burt (co.), Nebr. 264/H3
Burt, N.Y. (14028) 276/C4
Burt, N. Dak. (†58646) 282/F7
Burta, N.S. Wales 97/A3
Burt Lake, Mich. (49717) 250/E3
Burton, Br. Col. 184/H5
Burton (lake), Georgia 217/E1
Burton, Mich. (48507) 250/F6
Burton, Nebr. (†68778) 264/E2
Burton, New Bruns. 170/D3
Burton, Ohio (44021) 284/H3
Burton, S.C. (29902) 296/F7
Burton, Texas (77835) 303/H7
Burton, Wash. (98013) 310/C3
Burton, W. Va. (26562) 312/F3
Burtonport, Ireland 17/E2
Burtonport, Ireland 10/B3
Burton upon Trent, England 13/F5
Burton upon Trent, England 10/G2
Burtonville, Ky. (†41179) 237/P4
Burträsk, Sweden 18/M4
Burtrum, Minn. (56318) 255/D5
Burtts Corner, New Bruns. 170/D2
Buru (isl.), Indonesia 54/O10
Buru (isl.), Indonesia 85/H6
Buru (sea), Indonesia 85/H6
Burultokay (Fuhai), China 77/C2
Burundi 2/L6
Burundi 102/F5
BURUNDI 115/E4
Bururi, Burundi 115/F4
Burutu, Nigeria 106/F7
Burwash Landing, Yukon 187/D3
Burwell, Nebr. (68823) 264/E3
Burwell (mt.), Wyo. 319/C2
Burwood, N. S. Wales 88/K4
Burwood, N.S. Wales 97/J3
Bury, England 13/H2
Bury, England 10/G2
Bury, Québec 172/F4
Buryat A.S.S.R., U.S.S.R. 48/M4
Burye, Ethiopia 102/F3
Burye, Ethiopia 111/G5
Bury Saint Edmunds, England 13/H5
Bury Saint Edmunds, England 10/G4
Busby, Alberta 182/C3
Busby, Mont. (59016) 262/J5
Buseno, Switzerland 39/H4
Bush, Ill. (†62924) 222/D6
Bush, Ky. (40724) 237/O6
Bush, La. (70431) 238/L5
Buh (creek), Md. 245/J3
Bush (riv.), N. Ireland 17/H1
Bush (riv.), S.C. 296/D3
Bush City, Kansas (†66032) 232/G3
Bushehr (prov.), Iran 66/G6
Bushehr (Bushire), Iran 66/G6
Bushehr, Iran 59/F4
Bushell, Sask. 181/L2
Bushey, England 10/B5
Bushey, England 13/H7
Bushire, Iran 54/G7
Bushiribana, Neth. Ant. 161/E10
Bush Island, Nova Scotia 168/D4
Bushkill, Pa. (18324) 294/M3
Bushland, Texas (79012) 303/B2
Bushmills, N. Ireland 17/J1
Bushnell, Fla. (33513) 212/D3
Bushnell, Ill. (61422) 222/C3
Bushnell, Nebr. (69128) 264/A3
Bushnell, S. Dak. (†57276) 298/R5
Bushong, Kansas (66841) 232/F3
Bushton, Ill. (†61920) 222/E4
Bushton, Kansas (67427) 232/D3
Bushwood, Md. (20618) 245/L7
Bushyhead, Okla. (†74016) 288/P2
Bushy Park, Tasmania 99/C4
Busick, N.C. (†28714) 281/E3
Businga, Zaire 115/D3
Buskerud (co.), Norway 18/F6
Buskirk, Ky. (41406) 237/P5
Busko Zdrój, Poland 47/E3
Busra, Syria 63/G6
Busselton, W. Australia 88/A6
Busselton, W. Australia 92/A6
Busseron (creek), Ind. 227/C7
Busse Woods (res.), Ill. 222/B5
Bussey, Iowa (50044) 229/H6
Bussigny-près-Lausanne, Switzerland 39/B3
Bussum, Netherlands 27/G4
Bustard (isls.), Ontario 177/C2
Busti, N.Y. (†14701) 276/B6
Bustinza, Argentina 143/F6
Busto Arsizio, Italy 34/B2
Busuanga (isl.), Philippines 82/B4
Busuanga (isl.), Philippines 85/F3
Busu-Djanoa, Zaire 115/D3
Büsum, W. Germany 22/C1
Buta, Zaire 102/E4
Buta, Zaire 115/D3
Buta-Ranquil, Argentina 143/C4
Butare, Rwanda 115/E4
Butaritari (atoll), Kiribati 87/H5
Butcher (isl.), India 68/B7
Bute (inlet), Br. Col. 184/E5
Bute (isl.), Scotland 15/C5
Bute (trad. co.), Scotland 15/A5
Bute (sound), Scotland 15/C5
Butedale, Br. Col. 184/C3
Butembo, Zaire 115/E3
Butembo, Zaire 102/E5
Butha, China 77/K2
Butiaba, Uganda 115/F3

Caltagirone 345

Butler (co.), Ala. 195/E7
Butler, Ala. (36904) 195/B6
Butler, Georgia (31006) 217/D5
Butler, Ill. (62015) 222/D4
Butler, Ind. (46721) 227/H2
Butler (co.), Iowa 229/H3
Butler (co.), Kansas 232/F4
Butler (co.), Ky. 237/H6
Butler, Ky. (41006) 237/N3
Butler, Md. (21023) 245/M2
Butler, Minn. (†56567) 255/C4
Butler (co.), Mo. 261/M9
Butler, Mo. (64730) 261/D6
Butler (co.), Nebr. 264/G3
Butler, N.J. (07405) 273/E2
Butler (co.), Ohio 284/A7
Butler, Ohio (44822) 284/F4
Butler, Okla. (73625) 288/H3
Butler (co.), Pa. 294/C4
Butler, Pa. (16001) 294/C4
Butler, S. Dak. (57222) 298/O3
Butler, Tenn. (37640) 237/T8
Butler (bay), Virgin Is. (U.S.) 161/E4
Butler, Wis. (53007) 317/K1
Butler Springs, Ala. (†36030) 195/E7
Butlerville, Ark. (†72176) 202/G4
Butlerville, Ind. (47223) 227/F6
Butlerville, Ohio (†45162) 284/B7
Butner, N.C. (27509) 281/M2
Bütschelegg (mt.), Switzerland 39/D3
Bütschwil, Switzerland 39/H2
Buttahatchee (riv.), Ala. 195/B3
Buttahatchee (riv.), Miss. 256/H3
Butte (co.), Calif. 204/D4
Butte (co.), Idaho 220/E6
Butte, Mont. 146/G5
Butte, Mont. 188/D1
Butte, Nebr. (68722) 264/F2
Butte (mts.), Nev. 266/F3
Butte, N. Dak. (58723) 282/J4
Butte (creek), Oreg. 291/G2
Butte (creek), Oreg. 291/B3
Butte (co.), S. Dak. 298/B4
Butte City, Calif. (95920) 204/C4
Butte City, Idaho (83213) 220/E6
Butte Des Morts, Wis. (†54901) 317/J7
Butte Falls, Oreg. (97522) 291/E5
Butter (creek), Oreg. 291/H2
Butterfield, Ark. (†72104) 202/E5
Butterfield, Minn. (56120) 255/D7
Butterfield, Mo. (65623) 261/E9
Butterfield (lake), N.Y. 276/J2
Butternut, Mich. (†48811) 250/E5
Butternut, Wis. (54514) 317/E3
Butternut (lake), Wis. 317/J4
Butter Pot Prov. Park, Newf. 166/D2
Butters, N.C. (28324) 281/M5
Butterworth, Malaysia 72/D6
Butterworth (Gcuwa), S. Africa 118/D6
Buttes, Switzerland 39/C3
Butte-Silver Bow County, Mont. (59701) 262/D5
Buttevant, Ireland 17/D7
Butteville, Oreg. (†97002) 291/A2
Butt of Lewis (prom.), Scotland 15/B2
Button (isls.), N.W. Terrs. 187/M3
Buttonwillow, Calif. (93206) 204/F8
Butts (co.), Georgia 217/E4
Buttzville, N.J. (07829) 273/D2
Buttzville, N. Dak. (†58054) 282/P6
Butuan, Philippines 82/E6
Butuan, Philippines 85/H4
Butuan, Philippines 54/O9
Butuan (bay), Philippines 82/E6
Butumi, U.S.S.R. 7/J4
Butung (isl.), Indonesia 54/O10
Butung (isl.), Indonesia 85/G6
Buturlinovka, U.S.S.R. 52/F4
Butzbach, W. Germany 22/C3
Bützow, E. Germany 22/E2
Buxtehude, W. Germany 22/C2
Buxton, England 10/G2
Buxton, England 13/J2
Buxton○, Maine (†04093) 243/C8
Buxton, N.C. (27920) 281/U4
Buxton, N. Dak. (58218) 282/R4
Buxton, Oreg. (97109) 291/D2
Buxton Center, Maine (†04093) 243/B8
Buy, U.S.S.R. 52/F3
Buyck, Minn. (55771) 255/F2
Buynaksk, U.S.S.R. 52/G6
Büyükada, Turkey 63/D6
Büyük Ağrı (Ararat) (mt.), Turkey 63/L3
Büyük Ağrı (Ararat) (mt.), Turkey 59/D2
Büyükanafarta, Turkey 63/B6
Büyükdere, Turkey 63/D5
Büyük Hasan Dağı, Turkey 63/E3
Büyük Menderes (riv.), Turkey 59/A2
Buzău, Romania 45/H3
Buzău (riv.), Romania 45/H3
Buzeima (well), Libya 111/D3
Buziaş, Romania 45/E3
Buzios (cape), Brazil 135/F3
Buzuluk, U.S.S.R. 52/H4
Buzuluk, U.S.S.R. 48/F4
Buzzard Roost (dam), S.C. 296/D3
Buzzards (bay), Mass. 249/L7
Buzzards Bay, Mass. (02532) 249/M5
Byala, Bulgaria 45/G4
Byala Slatina, Bulgaria 45/F4
Byam Martin (chan.), N.W. Terrs. 187/H2
Byam Martin (isl.), N.W. Terrs. 187/H2
Byars, Okla. (74831) 288/N5
Bybee, Tenn. (37713) 237/P8
Bydgoszcz (prov.), Poland 47/C2
Bydgoszcz, Poland 47/C2
Bydgoszcz, Poland 7/F3
Byemoor, Alberta 182/D4
Byers, Colo. (80103) 208/L3
Byers, Kansas (67021) 232/D4
Byers, Texas (76357) 303/F3
Byesville, Ohio (43723) 284/G6
Byfield, Mass. (01922) 249/L1
Byford, W. Australia 88/B2
Bygland, Minn. (†56723) 255/B3
Bygland, Norway 18/F7
Byhalia, Miss. (38611) 256/E1
Bykhov, U.S.S.R. 52/C4
Bylas, Ariz. (85530) 198/E5
Bylot (isl.), N.W.T. 146/L2
Bylot (isl.), N.W.T. 162/J1
Bylot (isl.), N.W. Terrs. 187/L2
Byng, Okla. (†74820) 288/N5
Byng Inlet, Ontario 177/D2
Byng Inlet, Ontario 175/D3
Bynum, Mont. (59419) 262/D3
Bynum (res.), Mont. 262/D2
Bynum, N.C. (27312) 281/L3
Bynumville, Mo. (†65281) 261/G3
Byram, Conn. (06830) 210/A4
Byram (pt.), Conn. 210/A4
Byram (riv.), Conn. 210/A4
Byram, Miss. (†39205) 256/D6
Byrd Station 5/A12
Byrdstown, Tenn. (38549) 237/L7
Byrnedale, Pa. (15827) 294/E3
Byrock, N.S. Wales 97/D2
Byromville, Georgia (31007) 217/E6
Byron, Calif. (94514) 204/L2
Byron (isl.), Chile 138/D7
Byron, Georgia (31008) 217/E5
Byron, Ill. (61010) 222/D1
Byron, Ind. (†46371) 227/C5
Byron, Maine (†04275) 243/B6
Byron○, Maine (†04275) 243/B6
Byron, Mich. (48418) 250/E6
Byron, Minn. (55920) 255/F6
Byron, Nebr. (68325) 264/G4
Byron (bay), Newf. 166/C3
Byron (cape), N. S. Wales 88/J5
Byron (cape), N.S. Wales 97/G1
Byron, N.Y. (14422) 276/D4
Byron, Okla. (73723) 288/K1
Byron (lake), S. Dak. 298/N4
Byron, Wis. (53009) 317/K8
Byron, Wyo. (82412) 319/D1
Byron Bay, N.S. Wales 97/G1
Byron Center, Mich. (49315) 250/D6
Byrum, Denmark 21/E3
Byskeälv (riv.), Sweden 18/L4
Bystřice nad Pernštejnem, Czech. 41/D2
Bystřice pod Hostýnem, Czech. 41/D2
Bystrzyca Kłodzka, Poland 47/C3
Bytča, Czech. 41/E2
Bytom, Poland 47/A3
Bytów, Poland 47/C1

C

Caacupé, Paraguay 144/B5
Caaguazú (dept.), Paraguay 144/D-E4
Caaguazú, Paraguay 144/D4
Caála, Angola 115/C6
Caamaño (sound), Br. Col. 184/C4
Caapucú, Paraguay 144/D5
Caatingas (for.), Brazil 120/E3
Caazapá (dept.), Paraguay 144/D-E5
Caazapá, Paraguay 144/D5
Caba, Philippines 82/C2
Cabadbaran, Philippines 82/E6
Cabaiguán, Cuba 158/E2
Cabalasan (mt.), Philippines 82/E5
Caballero, Paraguay 144/B5
Caballo, N. Mex. (87931) 274/B6
Caballo (res.), N. Mex. 274/B6
Caballo (creek), Wyo. 319/G1
Caballococha, Peru 128/G4
Caballones (chan.), Cuba 158/F3
Cabana, Peru 128/C7
Cabañaquinta, Spain 33/D1
Cabañas, Cuba 158/B1
Cabanatuan, Philippines 54/O8
Cabanatuan, Philippines 82/C3
Cabanatuan, Philippines 85/G2
Cabanes, Spain 33/F2
Cabano, Québec 172/J2
Cabarroquis, Philippines 82/C2
Cabarrus (co.), N.C. 281/H4
Cabazon, Calif. (92230) 204/J10
Cabbage Tree (creek), Queensland 95/D2
Cabedelo, Brazil 132/H4
Cabell (co.), W. Va. 312/B6
Cabery, Ill. (60919) 222/E3
Cabet, Pitons du (mt.), Martinique 161/C6
Cabeza del Buey, Spain 33/D3
Cabezas, Bolivia 136/D6
Cabezas, Cuba 158/D1
Cabildo, Chile 138/A9
Cabimas, Venezuela 120/B1
Cabimas, Venezuela 124/C2
Cabin Creek, W. Va. (25035) 312/C6
Cabinda (dist.), Angola 115/B5
Cabinda, Angola 115/B5
Cabinda, Angola 102/D5
Cabinet (mts.), Mont. 262/A2
Cabin John (creek), Md. 245/E4
Cabin John-Brookmont, Md. (20731) 245/E4
Cabins, W. Va. (26855) 312/H4
Cable, Minn. (†56301) 255/D5
Cable, Ohio (43009) 284/C5
Cable, Wis. (54821) 317/D3
Cabo Blanco, Peru 128/B5
Cabo Delgado (prov.), Mozambique 118/F2
Cabo Frio, Brazil 132/F8
Cabo Frio, Brazil 135/F3
Cabo Gracias a Dios, Nicaragua 154/F3
Cabonga (res.), Québec 174/B3
Cabool, Mo. (65689) 261/H8
Cabora Bassa (dam), Mozambique 118/E3
Caborn, Ind. (†47620) 227/B9
Cabo Rojo, P. Rico 161/A2
Cabo San Lucas, Mexico 150/E5
Cabot (str.) 162/K6
Cabot, Ark. (72023) 202/F4
Cabot (str.), Canada 146/N5
Cabot (lake), Newf. 166/B2
Cabot (str.), Newf. 166/B4
Cabot (mt.), N.H. 268/E2
Cabot (head), Ontario 177/C2
Cabot, Pa. (16023) 294/C4
Cabot, Vt. (05647) 268/C3
Cabot○, Vt. (05647) 268/C3
Cabo Virgenes, Argentina 143/C7
Cabra, Spain 33/D4
Cabra de Santo Cristo, Spain 33/E4
Cabral, Dom. Rep. 158/D6
Cabral (lag.), Paraguay 144/A5
Cabrera, Dom. Rep. 158/E5
Cabrera (isl.), Spain 33/H3
Cabri, Sask. 181/C5
Cabri (lake), Sask. 181/B4
Cabrillo Nat'l Mon., Calif. 204/H11
Cabrits (isl.), Martinique 161/D7
Cabrón (cape), Dom. Rep. 158/F5
Cabruta, Venezuela 124/E4
Cabudare, Venezuela 124/D3
Cabugao, Philippines 82/C2
Cabulauan (isls.), Philippines 82/C5
Cabullones (pt.), P. Rico 161/C3
Caburai (mt.), Guyana 131/A3
Cabure, Venezuela 124/D2
Caçador, Brazil 132/D9
Cacahoatán, Mexico 150/N9
Čačak, Yugoslavia 45/E4
Caçapava, Brazil 135/D3
Caçapava do Sul, Brazil 132/C10
Cacapon (riv.), W. Va. 312/J4
Cáceres (lag.), Bolivia 136/G6
Cáceres, Brazil 132/B7
Cáceres, Brazil 120/D4
Cáceres, Colombia 126/C4
Cáceres (prov.), Spain 33/C3
Cáceres, Spain 33/C3
Cáceres, Spain 7/D5
Cachapoal (riv.), Chile 138/G5
Cache (riv.), Ark. 202/H3
Cache (riv.), Ill. 222/D6
Cache, Okla. (73527) 288/J5
Cache (creek), Okla. 288/K6
Cache (co.), Utah 304/C2
Cache Bay, Ontario 177/D1
Cache Creek, Br. Col. 184/G5
Cache Junction, Utah (84304) 304/C2
Cache la Poudre (riv.), Colo. 208/H1
Cacheu, Guinea-Biss. 106/A6
Cachi, Argentina 143/C2
Cachina, Quebrada (riv.), Chile 138/A5
Cachipo, Venezuela 124/G3
Cachoeira, Brazil 132/G6
Cachoeira de Itapemirim, Brazil 120/E5
Cachoeira do Arari, Brazil 132/D3
Cachoeira do Sul, Brazil 132/C10
Cachoeira do Sul, Brazil 120/D6
Cachoeiro de Itapemirim, Brazil 132/G8
Cachorras, Colombia 126/D8
Cachos (pt.), Chile 138/A6
Cachuela Esperanza, Bolivia 136/C2
Cachuma (lake), Calif. 204/F9
Cacocum, Cuba 158/H3
Cacocum, Cuba 156/C2
Cacolo, Angola 115/C6
Caconda, Angola 115/B6
Cacouna, Québec 172/H2
Cactus (range), Nev. 266/E5
Cactus (hills), Sask. 181/F5
Cactus, Texas (79013) 303/B1
Cactus Lake, Sask. 181/B3
Cacuri, Venezuela 124/F5
Cacuso, Angola 115/C5
Čadca, Czech. 41/E2
Caddo (riv.), Ark. 202/D5
Caddo (par.), La. 238/C1
Caddo (lake), La. 238/B1
Caddo (co.), Okla. 288/K4
Caddo, Okla. (74729) 288/O6
Caddo, Texas (76029) 303/F5
Caddo (lake), Texas 303/L5
Caddo Gap, Ark. (71935) 202/C5
Caddo Valley, Ark. (†71923) 202/D5
Caddy Lake, Manitoba 179/G5
Cade, La. (70519) 238/G6
Cadereyta Jiménez, Mexico 150/K4
Cades, S.C. (29518) 296/H4
Cades, Tenn. (†38358) 237/D9
Cades Cove, Tenn. (†37882) 237/O9
Cadet, Mo. (63630) 261/L6
Cadibarrawirracanna (lake), S. Australia 94/D3
Cadillac, Mich. (49601) 250/D4
Cadillac, Québec 174/B3
Cadillac, Sask. 181/D6
Cadiz, Calif. (92319) 204/K9
Cadiz (lake), Calif. 204/K9
Cadiz, Ind. (†47362) 227/G5
Cadiz, Ky. (42211) 237/F7
Cadiz, Ohio (43907) 284/J5
Cadiz, Philippines 82/D5
Cádiz (prov.), Spain 33/D4
Cádiz, Spain 33/C4
Cádiz, Spain 7/D5
Cádiz (gulf), Spain 33/C4
Cádizadiz (gulf), Portugal 33/C4
Cadogan, Alberta 182/E3
Cadogan○, Pa. (16212) 294/C4
Cadomin, Alberta 182/B3
Cadott, Wis. (54727) 317/D6
Cadotte (lake), Alberta 182/B1
Cadotte (riv.), Alberta 182/B1
Cadotte Lake, Alberta 182/B1
Cadron (creek), Ark. 202/F3
Caduruan (pt.), Philippines 82/D5
Cadwell, Georgia (31009) 217/G6
Cadyville, N.Y. (12918) 276/N1
Caen, France 28/C3
Caen, France 7/D4
Caerleon, Wales 13/B6
Caernarfon, Wales 13/C4
Caernarfon, Wales 10/D4
Caernarfon (bay), Wales 13/C4
Caernarfon (bay), Wales 10/D4
Caerphilly, Wales 13/B6
Caerphilly, Wales 10/E5
Caesar, Miss. (†39466) 256/E9
Caesarea, Ontario 177/F3
Caesars Head, S.C. (†29635) 296/B1
Caeté, Brazil 135/E1
Caetité, Brazil 132/F6
Cafayate, Argentina 143/C2
Cafelândia, Brazil 135/B2
Cagayan (prov.), Philippines 82/C1
Cagayan (isls.), Philippines 82/C6
Cagayan (isls.), Philippines 85/F4
Cagayan (riv.), Philippines 82/C2
Cagayancillo, Philippines 82/C6
Cagayan de Oro, Philippines 82/E6
Cagayan de Oro, Philippines 85/G4
Cagayan Sulu (isl.), Philippines 85/F4
Cagayan Sulu (isl.), Philippines 82/B7
Cagle, Tenn. (†37327) 237/L10
Cagles Mill (lake), Ind. 227/D6
Cagli, Italy 34/D3
Cagliari (prov.), Italy 34/B5
Cagliari, Italy 7/E5
Cagliari, Italy 34/B5
Cagliari (gulf), Italy 34/B5
Cagua (vol.), Philippines 82/D1
Cagua, Venezuela 124/E2
Caguán (riv.), Colombia 126/C7
Caguas, P. Rico 161/E2
Caguas, P. Rico 156/G1
Caha (mts.), Ireland 17/B8
Cahaba, Ala. (†36767) 195/D6
Cahaba (riv.), Ala. 195/D5
Cahabón, Guatemala 154/C3
Cahir, Ireland 10/B4
Cahir, Ireland 17/F7
Cahirciveen, Ireland 17/A8
Cahirciveen, Ireland 10/A5
Cahokia, Ill. (62206) 222/A3
Cahone, Colo. (81320) 208/B7
Cahore (pt.), Ireland 17/J6
Cahors, France 28/D5
Cahuapanas, Peru 128/D5
Cahuilla Ind. Res., Calif. 204/J10
Cahuinari (riv.), Colombia 126/E8
Cahuita (pt.), C. Rica 154/F6
Caiapônia, Brazil 132/C7
Caibarién, Cuba 158/F2
Caibarién, Cuba 156/B2
Caibiran, Philippines 82/E5
Caicara, Venezuela 124/G3
Caicara de Orinoco, Venezuela 124/E4
Caicedonia, Colombia 126/C5
Caicó, Brazil 120/F3
Caicó, Brazil 132/G4
Caicos (passage), Bahamas 156/D2
Caicos (bank), Turks & Caicos 156/D2
Caicos (isls.), Turks & Caicos 156/D2
Caicos (passage), Turks & Caicos 156/D2
Caile, Miss. (†38754) 256/C4
Cailloma, Peru 128/G10
Caillou (bay), La. 238/J8
Caimanera, Cuba 158/J4
Caimanera, Cuba 156/C3
Cain (creek), S. Dak. 298/N5
Cainde, Angola 115/B7
Cains (riv.), New Bruns. 170/D2
Cains Store, Ky. (42520) 237/M6
Cainsville, Mo. (64632) 261/E2
Cainsville, Tenn. (†37085) 237/J9
Caird Coast (reg.) 5/B17
Cairnbaan, Scotland 15/C4
Cairnbrook, Pa. (15924) 294/E5
Cairndow, Scotland 15/D4
Cairn Gorm (mt.), Scotland 15/E3
Cairngorm (mts.), Scotland 15/E3
Cairnryan, Scotland 15/D6
Cairns, Australia 87/E7
Cairns, Queensland 95/C3
Cairns, Queensland 88/H3
Cairnsmore (mt.), Scotland 15/D5
Cairn Toul (mt.), Scotland 15/E3
Cairo (cap.), Egypt 102/F2
Cairo (cap.), Egypt 111/J3
Cairo (cap.), Egypt 2/L4
Cairo, Egypt 59/B4
Cairo, Georgia (31728) 217/D9
Cairo, Ill. 188/J3
Cairo, Ill. (62914) 222/D6
Cairo, Kansas (†67035) 232/D4
Cairo, Mo. (65239) 261/H4
Cairo, Nebr. (68824) 264/F3
Cairo, N.Y. (12413) 276/M6
Cairo, Ohio (45820) 284/B4
Cairo, Okla. (†74538) 288/O5
Cairo, W. Va. (26337) 312/D4
Caissie (pt.), New Bruns. 170/F2
Caister-on-Sea, England 13/J5
Caistor, England 13/G4
Caithness (trad. co.), Scotland 15/B4
Caiundo, Angola 102/D6
Caiundo, Angola 115/C7
Caiza, Bolivia 136/C7
Cajabamba, Ecuador 128/C3
Cajabamba, Peru 128/C6
Cajacay, Peru 128/D8
Caja de Muertos (isl.), P. Rico 161/C3
Cajamarca (dept.), Peru 128/C6
Cajamarca, Peru 128/C6
Cajamarca, Peru 120/B3
Cajatambo, Peru 128/D8
Cajazeiras, Brazil 132/G4
Cajidiocan, Philippines 82/D4
Cajuata, Bolivia 136/B5
Cajuru, Brazil 135/C2
Čakovec, Yugoslavia 45/C2
Çal, Turkey 63/C3
Çala, Turkey 63/K2
Calabar, Nigeria 102/D4
Calabar, Nigeria 106/F7
Calabash, N.C. (†29566) 281/M7
Calabazar de Sagua, Cuba 158/E1
Calabogie, Ontario 177/H2
Calabozo, Venezuela 124/E3
Calabria (reg.), Italy 34/F5
Cala Burras (pt.), Spain 33/D4
Calacalte, Spain 33/G2
Calacoto, Bolivia 136/A5
Caladesi (isl.), Fla. 212/B2
Calafat, Romania 45/F3
Calafate, Argentina 143/B7
Calafquén (lake), Chile 138/E3
Calagnaan (isl.), Philippines 82/D5
Calagua (isls.), Philippines 82/D3
Calahoo, Alberta 182/D3
Calahorra, Spain 33/E1
Calais, Alberta 182/B2
Calais, France 28/D2
Calais, France 7/E3
Calais (Dover) (str.), France 28/D2
Calais, Maine 188/N1
Calais, Maine (04619) 243/J5
Calais○, Vt. (05648) 268/B3
Calama, Brazil 132/H10
Calama, Chile 120/C5
Calama, Chile 138/B3
Calamar, Bolívar, Colombia 126/C2
Calamar, Vaupés, Colombia 126/D7
Calamarca, Bolivia 136/A5
Calamba, Laguna, Philippines 82/C3
Calamba, Misamis Occ., Philippines 82/D6
Calamian Group (isls.), Philippines 85/F3
Calamian Group (isls.), Philippines 82/B4
Calamine, Ark. (72418) 202/H1
Calamocha, Spain 33/F2
Calamus, Iowa (52729) 229/M5
Calanasan, Philippines 82/C1
Calancasca (riv.), Switzerland 39/H4
Calanda, Spain 33/F2
Calang, Indonesia 85/B5
Calansho, Serir (des.), Libya 111/D2
Calansho Sand Sea (des.), Libya 111/D2
Calapan, Philippines 82/C4
Calapan, Philippines 85/G3
Calapooia (riv.), Oreg. 291/E3
Calapooya (mts.), Oreg. 291/E4
Călăraşi, Romania 45/H3
Calarcá, Colombia 126/C5
Calasparra, Spain 33/F3
Calatayud, Spain 33/F2
Calatorao, Spain 33/F2
Calauag, Philippines 82/D4
Calaveras (co.), Calif. 204/E5
Calaveras (res.), Calif. 204/L3
Calaveras (lake), Texas 303/K11
Calavite (cape), Philippines 82/C4
Calayan, Philippines 82/A2
Calayan (isl.), Philippines 82/A2
Calbayog, Philippines 82/E4
Calbe, E. Germany 22/D3
Calbuco, Chile 138/D4
Calca, Peru 128/G9
Calcasieu (par.), La. 238/D6
Calcasieu, La. (71433) 238/E4
Calcasieu (lake), La. 238/D7
Calcasieu (passage), La. 238/D7
Calcasieu (riv.), La. 238/E5
Calceta, Ecuador 128/C3
Calchaquí, Argentina 143/F5
Calcis, Ala. (†35178) 195/F4
Calcutta, India 68/F2
Calcutta, India 54/K7
Calcutta, India 2/P4
Calcutta, Ohio (43920) 284/J4
Calcutta, Suriname 131/C3
Caldas (dept.), Colombia 126/C5
Caldas da Rainha, Portugal 33/B3
Caldas Novas, Brazil 132/D7
Calder, Idaho (83808) 220/B2
Calder, Sask. 181/K4
Calder, Loch (lake), Scotland 15/E2
Caldera, Chile 120/B5
Caldera, Chile 138/A6
Calderas (bay), Dom. Rep. 158/D6
Calderas, Venezuela 124/C3
Calderwood, Tenn. (†37801) 237/N9
Caldicot, Wales 13/E6
Çaldıran, Turkey 63/K3
Caldwell, Ark. (72322) 202/J3
Caldwell, Idaho (83605) 220/B6
Caldwell, Idaho 188/C2
Caldwell, Kansas (67022) 232/E4
Caldwell (co.), Ky. 237/F6
Caldwell (par.), La. 238/F2
Caldwell (co.), Mo. 261/E3
Caldwell, N.J. (07006) 273/B2
Caldwell (co.), N.C. 281/F3
Caldwell, Ohio (43724) 284/G6
Caldwell (co.), Texas 303/G8
Caldwell, Texas (77836) 303/H7
Caldwell, W. Va. (24925) 312/F7
Caldwell, Wis. (†53149) 317/J2
Caldy (isl.), Wales 13/C6
Cale, Ark. (71828) 202/D6
Cale, Ind. (†47544) 227/D7
Caledon, N. Ireland 17/H3
Caledon, Ontario 177/E4
Caledon, S. Africa 118/G7
Caledonia, Ill. (61011) 222/E1
Caledonia, Mich. (49316) 250/D6
Caledonia, Minn. (55921) 255/G7
Caledonia, Miss. (39740) 256/H3
Caledonia, Mo. (63631) 261/L7
Caledonia, N.Y. (14423) 276/E5
Caledonia, N. Dak. (58219) 282/S5
Caledonia, Guysborough, Nova Scotia 168/F3
Caledonia, Queens, Nova Scotia 168/C4
Caledonia, Ohio (43314) 284/D4
Caledonia, Pa. (†15868) 294/F3
Caledonia (co.), Vt. 268/C2
Caledonia, Wis. (53108) 317/L2
Caledonian (canal), Scotland 15/D3
Calella, Spain 33/H2
Calenzana, France 28/B6
Calera, Ala. (35040) 195/E4
Calera, Okla. (74730) 288/O7
Calera de Tango, Chile 138/G4
Caleta Barquito, Chile 138/A6
Caleta Clarencia, Chile 138/E10
Caleta Olivia, Argentina 143/C6
Caleta Olivia, Argentina 120/C7
Caleta Pan de Azúcar, Chile 138/A5
Caleu, Chile 138/G2
Caleufú, Argentina 143/C4
Calexico, Calif. (92231) 204/K11
Calf of Man (isl.), I. of Man 13/C3
Calfsound, Scotland 15/F1
Calgary, Alberta 182/C4
Calgary, Alta. 162/E5
Calgary (cap.), Alta.. 146/G4
Calgary, Canada 2/D3
Calhan, Colo. (80808) 208/L4
Calheta, Portugal 33/A2
Calhoun (co.), Ala. 195/G3
Calhoun, Ala. (†36047) 195/F6
Calhoun (co.), Ark. 202/E6
Calhoun (co.), Fla. 212/D6
Calhoun (co.), Georgia 217/C7
Calhoun, Georgia (30701) 217/C1
Calhoun (co.), Ill. 222/C4
Calhoun, Ill. (62419) 222/E5
Calhoun (co.), Iowa 229/D4
Calhoun, Ky. (42327) 237/G5
Calhoun, La. (71225) 238/F2
Calhoun (co.), Mich. 250/D6
Calhoun (co.), Miss. 256/F3
Calhoun, Mo. (65323) 261/E6
Calhoun (co.), S.C. 296/F4
Calhoun, Tenn. (37309) 237/M10
Calhoun (co.), Texas 303/H9
Calhoun (co.), W. Va. 312/D5
Calhoun City, Miss. (38916) 256/F3
Calhoun Falls, S.C. (29628) 296/B3
Cali, Colombia 126/B6
Cali, Colombia 120/B2
Calicito, Cuba 158/H4
Calicoan (isl.), Philippines 82/E5
Calico Rock, Ark. (72519) 202/F1
Calicut (Kozhikode), India 68/D6
Caliente, Nev. (89008) 266/G5
Califon, N.J. (07830) 273/D2
California 188/B3
CALIFORNIA 204
California, Ky. (41007) 237/N3
California, Md. (20619) 245/M7
California (gulf), Mexico 146/G7
California (gulf), Mexico 150/D3
California, Mo. (65018) 261/H5
California, Pa. (15419) 294/C5
California, Trin. & Tob. 161/A11
California (state), U.S. 146/G6
California Aqueduct, Calif. 204/E7
California City, Calif. (93505) 204/H8
California Hot Springs, Calif. (93207) 204/G8
California Junction, Iowa (†51555) 229/B5
Calimete, Cuba 158/D1
Calio, N. Dak. (58322) 282/N2
Calion, Ark. (71724) 202/E7
Calipatria, Calif. (92233) 204/K10
Calistoga, Calif. (94515) 204/C5
Calixa-Lavallée, Québec 172/J4
Calkiní, Mexico 150/O6
Çalköy, Turkey 63/C3
Call, Texas (75933) 303/L7
Callabonna (lake), S. Australia 88/G5
Callabonna (lake), S. Australia 94/F3
Callafo, Ethiopia 111/H6
Callahan, Calif. (96014) 204/C2
Callahan, Fla. (32011) 212/E1
Callahan (co.), Texas 303/E5
Callalli, Peru 128/G10
Callan, Ireland 17/G7
Callan, Ireland 10/C4
Callander, Ont. 162/H6
Callander, Ontario 177/E1
Callander, Scotland 10/D2
Callander, Scotland 15/D4
Callands, Va. (24530) 307/J7
Callantsoog, Netherlands 27/F3
Callao, Mo. (63534) 261/G3
Callao (prov.), Peru 128/D9
Callao, Peru 128/D9
Callao, Peru 2/F6
Callao, Peru 120/B4
Callao, Utah (†84034) 304/A4
Callao, Va. (22435) 307/P5
Callapa, Bolivia 136/A5
Callaway, Minn. (56521) 255/C3
Callaway (co.), Mo. 261/J5
Callaway, Nebr. (68825) 264/D3
Callaway, Va. (24067) 307/H7
Calle Larga, Chile 138/G2
Callender, Iowa (50523) 229/E4
Callensburg, Pa. (16213) 294/D3
Callery, Pa. (16024) 294/C4
Calleuque, Chile 138/F5
Calliaqua, St. Vin. & Grens. 161/A9
Callicoon, N.Y. (12723) 276/K7
Callicoon Center, N.Y. (12724) 276/L7
Callihan, Texas (78007) 303/F9
Callimont, Pa. (†15552) 294/E6
Calling (lake), Alberta 182/D2
Callis, Somalia 115/J2
Callison, S.C. (29819) 296/C3
Callosa de Ensarriá, Spain 33/G3
Calloway, Fla. (32401) 212/D6
Calloway (co.), Ky. 237/E7
Calmar, Alberta 182/D3
Calmar, Iowa (52132) 229/K2
Calmer, Ark. (†71665) 202/F6
Calnali, Mexico 150/K6
Calne, England 13/F6
Calobre, Panama 154/G6
Caloosahatchee (riv.), Fla. 212/E5
Caloundra, Queensland 88/J5
Caloundra, Queensland 95/E5
Čalovo, Czech. 41/D3
Calpella, Calif. (95418) 204/B4
Calpet, Wyo. (†83123) 319/B3
Calpulálpan, Mexico 150/M1
Calstock, England 13/C7
Caltagirone, Italy 34/E6

Carseland 347

Cap (isl.), Philippines 82/C8
Cap (pt.), St. Lucia 161/G5
Capa, S. Dak. (57525) 298/H5
Capac, Mich. (48014) 250/G5
Capachica, Peru 128/H10
Çapakçur, Turkey 59/D2
Çapakçur, Turkey 63/J3
Cap-à-l'Aigle, Québec 172/G2
Capalonga, Philippines 82/D3
Capanaparo (riv.), Venezuela 124/E4
Capanema, Brazil 132/E3
Capannori, Italy 34/C3
Capão Bonito, Brazil 132/D9
Capão Bonito, Brazil 135/B4
Caparica, Portugal 33/A1
Caparo (riv.), Venezuela 124/C4
Capasin, Sask. 181/D2
Capatárida, Venezuela 124/C2
Capay, Calif. (95607) 204/C5
Cap-Bateau, New Bruns. 170/F1
Cap-Chat, Que. 162/K6
Cap-Chat, Québec 172/B1
Cap-Chat, Québec 174/D3
Cap-de-la-Madeleine, Québec 172/E3
Cap-des-Rosiers, Québec 172/D1
Cap d'Or (cape), Nova Scotia 168/D3
Cape (pen.), S. Africa 118/E7
Cape (pt.), S. Africa 118/F7
Cape (isl.), S.C. 296/J5
Cape Barren (isl.), Tasmania 88/H8
Cape Barren (isl.), Tasmania 99/E2
Cape Breton (isl.), N.S. 146/N5
Cape Breton (isl.), N.S. 162/K6
Cape Breton (co.), Nova Scotia 168/H3
Cape Breton (isl.), Nova Scotia 168/J2
Cape Breton Highlands Nat'l Park, Nova Scotia168/H2
Cape Broyle, Newf. 166/D2
Cape Canaveral, Fla. (32920) 212/F3
Cape Carteret, N.C. (†28584) 281/P5
Cape Charles, Newf. 166/C3
Cape Charles, Va. (23310) 307/R6
Cape Coast, Ghana 106/D7
Cape Coast, Ghana 102/B4
Cape Cod (bay), Mass. 249/N5
Cape Cod (canal), Mass. 249/N5
Cape Cod Nat'l Seashore, Mass. 249/P5
Cape Coral, Fla. (33904) 212/E5
Cape Dorset, N.W.T. 162/J3
Cape Dorset, N.W. Terrs. 187/L3
Cape Dyer, N.W. Terrs. 187/M3
Cape Fanshaw, Alaska (†99833) 196/N1
Cape Fear (riv.), N.C. 188/L4
Cape Fear (riv.), N.C. 281/M5
Cape George, Nova Scotia 168/F3
Cape Girardeau (co.), Mo. 261/N8
Cape Girardeau, Mo. (63701) 261/O8
Cape Girardeau, Mo. 188/H3
Cape Hatteras Nat'l Seashore, N.C. 281/T4
Cape Horn (mt.), Idaho 220/C5
Cape Krusenstern Nat'l Mon., Alaska 196/F1
Capel, W. Australia 92/A2
Capela, Brazil 132/G5
Cape Lisburne, Alaska (†99766) 196/E1
Capella, Queensland 95/D4
Capella (isls.), Virgin Is. (U.S.) 161/B5
Capelle, Netherlands 27/F5
Capelongo, Angola 115/C6
Cape Lookout Nat'l Seashore, N.C. 281/S5
Cape May (co.), N.J. 273/D5
Cape May, N.J. (08204) 273/D6
Cape May Coastguard Ctr., N.J. 273/D6
Cape May Court House, N.J. (08210) 273/D5
Cape May Point, N.J. (08212) 273/D6
Capenda-Camulemba, Angola 115/C5
Capenda-Camulemba, Angola 102/D5
Cape Neddick, Maine (03902) 243/B9
Cape Negro (isl.), Nova Scotia 168/C5
Cape North, Nova Scotia 168/H2
Cape of Good Hope (prov.), S. Africa 102/E8
Cape of Good Hope (prov.), S. Africa 118/C6
Cape Pole, Alaska (†99901) 196/M2
Cape Porpoise, Maine (04014) 243/C9
Cape Ray, Newf. 166/C4
Capers (isl.), S.C. 296/H6
Cape Sable (isl.), Nova Scotia 168/C5
Cape Saint Claire, Md. (21401) 245/N4
Cape Smith, N.W. Terrs. 187/L3
Capesterre, Basse-Terre, Guadeloupe 161/A7
Capesterre, Marie-Galante, Guadeloupe 161/B7
Cape Tormentine, New Bruns. 170/G2
Cape Town (cap.), S. Africa 2/L7
Cape Town (cap.), S. Africa 102/D8
Cape Town (cap.), S. Africa 118/E6
Cape Verde 2/H5
CAPE VERDE 106/A8
Capeville, Va. (23313) 307/R6
Cape Vincent, N.Y. (13618) 276/H2
Cape Yakataga, Alaska (99560) 196/K2
Cape York (pen.), Australia 87/E7
Cape York, Queensland 95/B1
Cape York (pen.), Queensland 88/G2
Cape York (pen.), Queensland 95/B2
Cap-Haïtien, Haiti 158/C5
Cap-Haïtien, Haiti 156/D3
Capiatá, Paraguay 144/B4
Capibara, Venezuela 124/E6
Capilla de Farruco, Uruguay 145/D3
Capim (riv.), Brazil 132/D3
Capinota, Bolivia 136/B5
Capira, Panama 154/G6
Capirenda, Bolivia 136/D7
Capistrano Beach, Calif. (92624) 204/H10
Capitan, N. Mex. (88316) 274/D5
Capitan (mts.), N. Mex. 274/D5
Capitan (peak), N. Mex. 274/D5
Capitán Aracena (isl.), Chile 138/E10
Capitán Bado, Paraguay 144/E3
Capitan Grande Ind. Res., Calif. 204/J11
Capitán Meza, Paraguay 144/E5
Capitán Pastene, Chile 138/D2
Capitán Ustarés, Cerro (mt.), Bolivia 136/E6
Capitol, Mont. (59319) 262/M5
Capitola, Calif. (95010) 204/K4
Capitola, Fla. (†32302) 212/B1
Capitol Heights, Md. (20743) 245/G5
Capitol Hill (cap.), No. Marianas 87/E4
Capitol Reef Nat'l Park, Utah 304/C5
Capiz (prov.), Philippines 82/D5
Caplan, Québec 172/C2
Capleville, Tenn. (†38101) 237/B10
Caplin Cove, Newf. 166/D2
Caplinger Mills, Mo. (65607) 261/E7
Čapljina, Yugoslavia 45/C4
Cap Lumière, New Bruns. 170/F2
Capon Bridge, W. Va. (26711) 312/K4
Capon Springs, W. Va. (26823) 312/K4
Capotoan (mt.), Philippines 82/E4
Cappahayden, Newf. 166/D2
Cappamore, Ireland 17/E6
Cappawhite, Ireland 17/E6
Cap-Pelé, New Bruns. 170/F2
Cappoquin, Ireland 17/F7
Capps, Ala. (†36353) 195/H8
Capraia (isl.), Italy 34/B3
Capreol, Ontario 175/D3
Capreol, Ontario 177/K5
Capri (isl.), Italy 34/E4
Capricorn (chan.), Queensland 95/D4
Capricorn Group (isls.), Queensland 88/J4
Capricorn Group (isls.), Queensland 95/E4
Caprivi Strip (reg.), Namibia 102/E6
Caprivi Strip (reg.), Namibia 118/C3
Caprock, N. Mex. (88213) 274/F5
Capron, Ill. (61012) 222/E1
Capron, Okla. (73725) 288/J1
Capron, Va. (23829) 307/O7
Cap-Rouge, Québec 172/H3
Cap-Saint-Ignace, Québec 172/G2
Cap-Santé, Québec 172/F3
Cap-Seize, Québec 172/C1
Capshaw, Ala. (35742) 195/E1
Capstan (cape), Nova Scotia 168/D3
Capstick, Nova Scotia 168/H1
Captain Bermúdez, Argentina 143/F6
Captain Cook, Hawaii (96704) 218/G5
Captains Flat, N.S. Wales 97/E4
Captieux, France 28/C5
Captina (creek), Ohio 284/J6
Captiva, Fla. (33924) 212/D5
Captiva (isl.), Fla. 212/D5
Capua, Italy 34/E4
Capuchin (cape), Dominica 161/E5
Capulhuac de Mirafuentes, Mexico 150/K1
Capulin, Colo. (81124) 208/G8
Capulin, N. Mex. (88414) 274/F2
Capulin Mountain Nat'l Mon., N. Mex. 274/E2
Caputa, S. Dak. (57725) 298/D5
Caquetá (inten.), Colombia 126/C7
Caquetá (riv.), Colombia 120/B2
Caquetá (riv.), Colombia 126/E8
Caquiaviri, Bolivia 136/A5
Carabao (isl.), Philippines 82/D4
Carabelas, Argentina 143/F6
Carabobo (state), Venezuela 124/D2
Carabobo, Bolivar, Venezuela 124/H4
Carabobo, Carabobo, Venezuela 124/D3
Carabuco, Bolivia 136/A4
Caracal, Romania 45/G3
Caracaraí, Brazil 120/C2
Caracas (bay), Neth. Ant. 161/G9
Caracas (cap.), Venezuela 120/C2
Caracas (cap.), Venezuela 124/E2
Caracas (cap.), Venzuela 2/F5
Carache, Venezuela 124/C3
Caracollo, Bolivia 136/B5
Caraga, Philippines 82/F7
Caragabal, N.S. Wales 97/D3
Caraguatá, Uruguay 145/D3
Caraguatá (riv.), Uruguay 145/D3
Caraguatatuba, Brazil 135/D3
Caraguatay, Paraguay 144/B4
Carahue, Chile 138/D2
Carajás, Serra dos (range), Brazil 132/D4
Caramat, Ontario 177/H5
Caramat, Ontario 175/C3
Caramoan, Philippines 82/D4
Caranavi, Bolivia 136/B4
Carandaí, Brazil 135/E2
Carandaiti, Bolivia 136/D7
Carandotta, Queensland 95/A4
Carangola, Brazil 135/E2
Caransebeş, Romania 45/F3
Carapa (riv.), Paraguay 144/E4
Carapa, Venezuela 124/G3
Caraparaná (riv.), Colombia 126/D8
Caraparí, Bolivia 136/D7
Carapeguá, Paraguay 144/B5
Carapichaima, Trin. & Tob. 161/B10
Caraquet, New Bruns. 170/E1
Caraquet (isl.), New Bruns. 170/F1
Carás, Peru 128/D7
Caratasca, Honduras 154/F3
Caratasca (cays), Honduras 154/F2
Caratasca (lag.), Honduras 154/F3
Caratinga, Brazil 132/F7
Caratinga, Brazil 135/E1
Caratunk, Maine (04925) 243/C5
Caratunk○, Maine (04925) 243/C5
Carauari, Brazil 120/C3
Carauari, Brazil 132/G9
Caraúbas, Brazil 132/G4
Caravaca de la Cruz, Spain 33/E3
Caravaggio, Italy 34/B2
Caravelas, Brazil 132/G7
Caravelí, Peru 128/F10
Caravelle (pen.), Martinique 161/D6
Caraway, Ark. (72419) 202/K2
Carayaó, Paraguay 144/C4
Carazinho, Brazil 132/C10
Carballino, Spain 33/B1
Carballo, Spain 33/B1
Carberry, Manitoba 179/C5
Carbo, Mexico 150/D2
Carbon, Alberta 182/D4
Carbon (peak), Colo. 208/E5
Carbon, Ind. (47837) 227/C5
Carbon, Iowa (50839) 229/D6
Carbon (co.), Mont. 262/G5
Carbon (co.), Pa. 294/L4
Carbon, Texas (76435) 303/F5
Carbon (co.), Utah 304/D4
Carbon, W. Va. (25037) 312/D6
Carbon (co.), Wyo. 319/F4
Carbonado, Wash. (98323) 310/D3
Carbonara (cape), Italy 34/B5
Carbon Cliff, Ill. (61239) 222/C2
Carbondale, Alberta 182/D3
Carbondale, Colo. (81623) 208/E4
Carbondale, Ill. (62901) 222/D6
Carbondale, Kansas (66414) 232/G3
Carbondale, Ohio (45717) 284/F7
Carbondale, Pa. (18407) 294/L2
Carbonear, Newf. 166/D2
Carbon Hill, Ala. (35549) 195/D3
Carbon Hill, Ill. (†60416) 222/E2
Carbon Hill, Ohio (43111) 284/F7
Carbonia, Italy 34/B5
Carbonton, N.C. (†27330) 281/L3
Carbost, Scotland 15/B3
Carbury, Ireland 17/H5
Carbury, N. Dak. (58724) 282/J2
Carcagente, Spain 33/F3
Carcans (lake), France 28/C5
Carcaraña, Argentina 143/F6
Carcaraña (riv.), Argentina 143/F6
Carcassonne, France 28/D6
Carchi (prov.), Ecuador 128/C2
Carcoar, N.S. Wales 97/E3
Carcross, Yukon 187/E3
Çardak, Turkey 63/C6
Cardal, Uruguay 145/C5
Cardale, Manitoba 179/B4
Cárdenas, Cuba 158/D1
Cárdenas, Cuba 156/B2
Cárdenas (bay), Cuba 158/D1
Cárdenas, San Luis Potosí, Mexico 150/K6
Cárdenas, Tabasco, Mexico 150/N8
Cardenden, Scotland 15/D1
Cardiel (lake), Argentina 143/B6
Cardiff, Ala. (35041) 195/E3
Cardiff, Md. (21024) 245/N2
Cardiff, Wales 7/D3
Cardiff, Wales 13/B7
Cardiff, Wales 10/E5
Cardiff-by-the-Sea, Calif. (92007) 204/H10
Cardigan (mt.), N.H. 268/D4
Cardigan, Pr. Edward I. 168/F2
Cardigan (bay), Pr. Edward I. 168/F2
Cardigan, Wales 13/C5
Cardigan, Wales 10/D4
Cardigan (bay), Wales 10/D4
Cardigan (bay), Wales 13/C5
Cardin, Okla. (74335) 288/S1
Cardinal (lake), Alberta 182/B1
Cardinal, Manitoba 179/D5
Cardinal, Ontario 177/J3
Cardington, Ohio (43315) 284/E5
Cardona, Uruguay 145/B4
Cardoso (isl.), Brazil 135/C4
Cardozo, Uruguay 145/C3
Cardross, Sask. 181/F6
Cardston, Alberta 182/D5
Cardston, Alta. 162/E6
Cardville, Maine (04418) 243/F5
Cardwell, Mo. (63829) 261/M10
Cardwell, Mont. (59721) 262/E5
Cardwell, Queensland 95/C3
Cardwell, Va. (†23039) 307/N5
Carefree, Ariz. (85331) 198/C5
Carefree, Ind. (†47137) 227/E8
Carei, Romania 45/F2
Carén, Chile 138/A8
Carencro, La. (70520) 238/G6
Carentan, France 28/C3
Caretta, W. Va. (24821) 312/C8
Carey, Idaho (83320) 220/E6
Carey, Ohio (43316) 284/D4
Carey (lake), W. Australia 88/C5
Carey (lake), W. Australia 92/C5
Careywood, Idaho (83809) 220/B1
Cargill, Ontario 177/C3
Carhuás, Peru 128/D7
Cariaco, Venezuela 124/G2
Cariamanga, Ecuador 128/C5
Caribbean (sea) 2/F5
Caribbean (sea) 146/K8
Caribbean (sea), 156/B4
Caribbean (sea), Ant. & Bar. 156/B4
Caribbean (sea), Cayman Is. 156/B4
Caribbean (sea), Cuba 156/B4
Caribbean (sea), Dominica 156/B4
Caribbean (sea), Dom. Rep. 156/B4
Caribbean (sea), Grenada 156/B4
Caribbean (sea), Guadeloupe 156/B4
Caribbean (sea), Haiti 156/B4
Caribbean (sea), Jamaica 156/B4
Caribbean (sea), Martinique 156/B4
Caribbean (sea), Neth. Ant. 156/B4
Caribbean (sea), P. Rico 156/B4
Caribbean (sea), St. Chris.-Nevis 156/B4
Caribbean (sea), St. Lucia 156/B4
Caribbean (sea), St. Vin. & Grens. 156/B4
Caribbean (sea), Virgin Is. (Br.) 156/B4
Caribbean (sea), Virgin Is. (U.S.) 156/B4
Caribén, Venezuela 124/E4
Cariboo (mts.), Br. Col. 184/G3
Caribou (mts.), Alberta 182/B5
Caribou (co.), Idaho 220/G7
Caribou (mt.), Idaho 220/G6
Caribou (range), Idaho 220/G6
Caribou, Maine 188/N1
Caribou, Maine (04736) 243/G2
Caribou (riv.), Manitoba 179/J1
Caribou, Nova Scotia 168/F3
Caribou (isl.), Nova Scotia 168/F3
Caribou (isl.), Ontario 175/C3
Caribou (lake), Ontario 177/H4
Caribou (lake), Québec 172/D3
Caribou River, Nova Scotia 168/F3
Carib Reserve, Dominica 161/F6
Caribrod (Dimitrovgrad), Yugoslavia 45/F4
Carichic, Mexico 150/F2
Carievale, Sask. 181/K6
Carigara, Philippines 82/E5
Carignan, Québec 172/J4
Carignan (lake), Québec 172/E2
Carillon, Québec 172/C4
Carina, Queensland 88/K3
Carinda, N.S. Wales 97/D2
Cariñena, Spain 33/F2
Carinhanha, Brazil 132/E6
Carini, Italy 34/D5
Carinthia (prov.), Austria 41/B3
Caripe, Venezuela 124/G2
Caripito, Venezuela 124/G2
Cariquima, Chile 138/B2
Carirubana, Venezuela 124/C2
Carite (lake), P. Rico 161/E2
Cark (mt.), Ireland 17/F2
Carl, Georgia (30203) 217/E3
Carl Blackwell (lake), Okla. 288/M2
Carlea, Sask. 181/H2
Carleton, Mich. (48117) 250/F6
Carleton, Nebr. (68326) 264/G4
Carleton (co.), New Bruns. 170/C2
Carleton (mt.), New Bruns. 170/D1
Carleton, Nova Scotia 168/C4
Carleton (riv.), Nova Scotia 168/C4
Carleton, Québec 172/C2
Carleton Place, Ontario 177/H2
Carlile, Wyo. (82713) 319/H1
Carlin, Nev. (89822) 266/E2
Carlingford, Ireland 17/J3
Carlingford (inlet), Ireland 17/J3
Carlingford (mt.), Ireland 17/J3
Carlingford, New Bruns. 170/C2
Carlinville, Ill. (62626) 222/D4
Carlisle, Ark. (72024) 202/G4
Carlisle (bay), Barbados 161/B9
Carlisle, England 13/D3
Carlisle, England 10/E3
Carlisle, Ind. (47838) 227/C7
Carlisle, Iowa (50047) 229/G6
Carlisle (co.), Ky. 237/C7
Carlisle, Ky. (40311) 237/N4
Carlisle, La. (70042) 238/L7
Carlisle○, Mass. (01741) 249/J2
Carlisle, Minn. (56538) 255/B4
Carlisle, Miss. (39049) 256/C7
Carlisle, New Bruns. 170/C2
Carlisle, N.Y. (12031) 276/L5
Carlisle, Ohio (45005) 284/B6
Carlisle, Ontario 177/D4
Carlisle, Pa. (17013) 294/H5
Carlisle, S.C. (29031) 296/D2
Carl Junction, Mo. (64834) 261/C8
Carlock, Ill. (61725) 222/D3
Carlock, S. Dak. (†57533) 298/L7
Carloforte, Italy 34/B5
Carlos, Ind. (†47355) 227/G4
Carlos, Minn. (56319) 255/C5
Carlos Casares, Argentina 143/F7
Carlos Reyles, Uruguay 145/C4
Carlos Tejedor, Argentina 143/D4
Carlow (co.), Ireland 17/H6
Carlow, Ireland 17/H6
Carlow, Ireland 10/C4
Carloway, Scotland 15/B2
Carlowrie, Manitoba 179/E5
Carlowville, Ala. (†36761) 195/D6
Carl Sandburg Home Nat'l Hist. Site, N.C. 281/D4
Carlsbad, (92008) 204/H10
Carlsbad, N. Mex. 188/F4
Carlsbad, N. Mexico 146/H6
Carlsbad, N. Mex. (88220) 274/E6
Carlsbad, Texas (76934) 303/D6
Carlsbad Caverns Nat'l Park, N. Mex. 274/E6
Carlsbad Springs, Ontario 177/J2
Carlsborg, Wash. (98324) 310/B2
Carlshend, Mich. (49811) 250/B2
Carlstadt, N.J. (07072) 273/B2
Carlton, Ala. (36515) 195/C8
Carlton, Barbados 161/B8
Carlton, England 13/F5
Carlton, Georgia (30627) 217/F2
Carlton, Kansas (67429) 232/E3
Carlton (co.), Minn. 255/F4
Carlton, Minn. (55718) 255/F4
Carlton, N.Y. (†14411) 276/D4
Carlton, Oreg. (97111) 291/D2
Carlton, Pa. (16311) 294/C3
Carlton, Sask. 181/E3
Carlton, Texas (76436) 303/F6
Carlton, Wash. (98814) 310/F2
Carlton (pass), Wash. 310/D4
Carltonville, S. Africa 118/G7
Carluke, Scotland 15/E5
Carluke, Scotland 10/B1
Carlyle, Ill. (62231) 222/D5
Carlyle (lake), Ill. 222/D5
Carlyle, Kansas (66718) 232/G4
Carlyle, Mont. (59320) 262/M4
Carlyle, Sask. 181/J6
Carlyle Lake Resort, Sask. 181/J6
Carmacks, Yukon 187/E3
Carmagnola, Italy 34/A2
Carman, Ill. (61425) 222/B3
Carman, Man. 162/G6
Carman, Manitoba 179/D5
Carmangay, Alberta 182/D4
Carmanville, Newf. 166/D4
Carmarthen, Wales 13/C6
Carmarthen, Wales 10/D5
Carmarthen (bay), Wales 10/D5
Carmarthen (bay), Wales 13/C6
Carmaux, France 28/E5
Carmel, Calif. (93923) 204/D7
Carmel, Ind. (46032) 227/E5
Carmel (cape), Israel 65/B2
Carmel (mt.), Israel 65/C2
Carmel○, Maine (04419) 243/E6
Carmel○, N.Y. (10512) 276/N8
Carmel, Sask. 181/F3
Carmel (head), Wales 13/C4
Carmelo, Uruguay 145/A4
Carmelo, Venezuela 124/C2
Carmel Valley, Calif. (93924) 204/D7
Carmen, Ariz. (†85640) 198/D7
Carmen, Bolivia 136/B2
Carmen (riv.), Chile 138/B7
Carmen, C. Rica 154/F5
Carmen, Idaho (83462) 220/E4
Carmen (isl.), Mexico 150/D3
Carmen, Okla. (73726) 288/J1
Carmen, Bohol, Philippines 82/E6
Carmen, North Cotabato, Philippines 82/E7
Carmen, Uruguay 145/D4
Carmen de Areco, Argentina 143/F7
Carmen del Paraná, Paraguay 144/D5
Carmen de Patagones, Argentina 143/D5
Carmensa, Argentina 143/C4
Carmi, Br. Col. 184/H5
Carmi, Ill. (62821) 222/E5
Carmi (lake), Vt. 268/B2
Carmichael, Calif. (95608) 204/C8
Carmichael, Miss. (†39360) 256/G7
Carmichael, Sask. 181/C5
Carmichaels, Pa. (15320) 294/B6
Carmiel, Israel 65/C2
Carmila, Queensland 95/D4
Carmine, Texas (78932) 303/H7
Carmody Hills-Pepper Mill Village, Md. (†20028)245/G5
Carmona, Spain 33/D4
Carnac, France 28/B4
Carnadero (creek), Calif. 204/L4
Carnamah, W. Australia 92/A5
Carnarvon, Australia 87/B8
Carnarvon, Iowa (51437) 229/C4
Carnarvon, Ontario 177/F2
Carnarvon (range), Queensland 95/D5
Carnarvon, S. Africa 118/C6
Carnarvon, W. Australia 88/A4
Carnarvon, W. Australia 92/A4
Carnation, Wash. (98014) 310/D3
Carnaxide, Portugal 33/A1
Carn Ban (mt.), Scotland 15/D3
Carndonagh, Ireland 17/G1
Carnduff, Sask. 181/K6
Carnegie, Georgia (†31740) 217/C7
Carnegie, Okla. (73015) 288/J4
Carnegie, Pa. (15106) 294/B7
Carnegie (lake), W. Australia 88/C5
Carnegie (lake), W. Australia 92/C4
Carn Eige (mt.), Scotland 15/C3
Carneiro, Kansas (†67425) 232/D3
Carnes, Miss. (†39455) 256/F8
Carnesville, Georgia (30521) 217/F2
Carnew, Ireland 17/H6
Carney, Mich. (49812) 250/B3
Carney, Okla. (74832) 288/N3
Carneys Point, N.J. (08069) 273/C4
Carnic Alps (mts.), Austria 41/B3
Carnic Alps (range), Italy 34/D1
Car Nicobar (isl.), India 68/G7
Carnlough, N. Ireland 17/K2
Carn More (mt.), Scotland 15/E3
Carnot, Cent. Afr. Rep. 115/C3
Carnoustie, Scotland 15/F4
Carnoustie, Scotland 10/E2
Carnsore (pt.), Ireland 10/C4
Carnsore (pt.), Ireland 17/J7
Carnwath (riv.), N.W. Terrs. 187/F3
Carnwath, Scotland 15/E5
Carnwood, Alberta 182/C3
Caro, Mich. (48723) 250/F5
Caroga Lake, N.Y. (12032) 276/L4
Carol City, Fla. (33055) 212/B4
Carolina, Ala. (†36420) 195/E8
Carolina, Brazil 132/E4
Carolina, P. Rico 161/E1
Carolina, R.I. (02812) 249/H7
Carolina Beach, N.C. (28428) 281/O6
Caroline, Alberta 182/C3
Caroline (isl.), Kiribati 87/M7
Caroline (co.), Md. 245/P5
Caroline, N.Y. (†14817) 276/H6
Caroline (isls.), Pac. Is. Terr. 87/E5
Caroline (isls.), Pacific Is. Terr. 2/S5
Caroline (co.), Va. 307/O4
Caroline, Wis. (54928) 317/J6
Carol Stream, Ill. (†60187) 222/A5
Caron, Sask. 181/F5
Caron Brook, New Bruns. 170/B1
Carondelet, Ecuador 128/C2
Caroni, Trin. & Tob. 161/B10
Caroní (riv.), Venezuela 120/C2
Caroní (riv.), Venezuela 124/G4
Carora, Venezuela 124/C2
Carouge, Switzerland 39/B4
Carp, Ind. (†47460) 227/D6
Carp, Minn. (†56623) 255/D2
Carp, Nev. (†89008) 266/G5
Carp, Ontario 177/H2
Carpathian (mts.) 7/G4
Carpathian (mts.), Romania 45/G2
Carpentaria (gulf) 88/F2
Carpentaria (gulf), Australia 87/D7
Carpentaria (gulf), North. Terr. 93/E3
Carpentaria (gulf), Queensland 95/A2
Carpenter (lake), Br. Col. 184/F5
Carpenter, Iowa (50426) 229/H2
Carpenter, Ky. (†40769) 237/O7
Carpenter, Miss. (39050) 256/C6
Carpenter (lake), N. Dak. 282/L2
Carpenter, Ohio (†47518) 284/F7
Carpenter, S. Dak. (57322) 298/O4
Carpenter, Wyo. (82054) 319/H4
Carpentersville, Ill. (60110) 222/E1
Carpentersville, N.J. (†08865) 273/C2
Carpenterville, Oreg. (†97415) 291/C5
Carpentras, France 28/F5
Carpertee (riv.), N.S. Wales 97/F3
Carpi, Italy 34/C2
Carpinteria, Calif. (93013) 204/F9
Carpio, N. Dak. (58725) 282/G3
Carp Lake, Mich. (49718) 250/E3
Carp Lake Prov. Park, Br. Col. 184/F3
Carr, Colo. (80612) 208/K1
Carra (lake), Ireland 17/C4
Carrabassett Valley○, Maine (†04947) 243/C5
Carrabelle, Fla. 212/B2
Carradale, Scotland 15/C5
Carragana, Sask. 181/J3
Carraguao (pt.), Cuba 158/B2
Carraipía, Colombia 126/D2
Carraizo (lake), P. Rico 161/E1
Carranglan, Philippines 82/C3
Carrantuohill (mt.), Ireland 10/B5
Carrantuohill (mt.), Ireland 17/B7
Carranza, Venustiano (res.), Mexico 150/J3
Carrao (riv.), Venezuela 124/G5
Carrara, Italy 34/C2
Carrasco, Uruguay 145/B7
Carrasquero, Venezuela 124/B2
Carrathool, N. S. Wales 88/G6
Carrathool, N.S. Wales 97/C4
Carrboro, N.C. (27510) 281/L3
Carrbridge, Scotland 15/E3
Carrera de Yeguas, Dom. Rep. 158/D6
Carrera Pinto, Chile 138/B6
Carreta (pt.), C. Rica 154/F6
Carreto, Panama 154/J6
Carriacou (isl.), Grenada 156/G4
Carrick, Manitoba 179/F5
Carrick (dist.), Scotland 15/D5
Carrickfergus (dist.), N. Ireland 17/K2
Carrickfergus, N. Ireland 10/D3
Carrickfergus, N. Ireland 17/K2
Carrickmacross, Ireland 10/C3
Carrickmacross, Ireland 17/H4
Carrick-on-Shannon, Ireland 17/F4
Carrick-on-Shannon, Ireland 10/C4
Carrick-on-Suir, Ireland 17/F7
Carrick-on-Suir, Ireland 10/C4
Carrier, Okla. (73727) 288/K2
Carriere, Miss. (39426) 256/E9
Carrier Mills, Ill. (62917) 222/E6
Carrigaholt, Ireland 17/B6
Carrigain (mt.), N.H. 268/E3
Carrigaline, Ireland 17/E8
Carrigallen, Ireland 17/F4
Carrigan (head), Ireland 17/D2
Carrigart, Ireland 17/F1
Carrigtwohill, Ireland 17/E8
Carrington, Mo. (†65251) 261/H5
Carrington, N. Dak. (58421) 282/M5
Carrión de los Condes, Spain 33/D1
Carrizal, Colombia 126/D1
Carrizal Bajo, Chile 138/A7
Carrizo (creek), Ariz. 198/E4
Carrizo (mts.), Ariz. 198/G2
Carrizo (creek), N. Mex. 274/F2
Carrizo (creek), Texas 303/A1
Carrizo Springs, Texas (78834) 303/E9
Carrizozo, N. Mex. (88301) 274/D5
Carroll (co.), Ark. 202/C1
Carroll (co.), Georgia 217/B3
Carroll (co.), Ill. 222/D1
Carroll (co.), Ind. 227/D3
Carroll (co.), Iowa 229/D4
Carroll, Iowa (51401) 229/D4
Carroll (co.), Ky. 237/L3
Carroll○, Maine (†04487) 243/G5
Carroll, Manitoba 179/B5
Carroll (lake), Manitoba 179/G3
Carroll (co.), Md. 245/K2
Carroll (co.), Miss. 256/E4
Carroll (co.), Mo. 261/F4
Carroll, Nebr. (68723) 264/G2
Carroll (co.), N.H. 268/E4
Carroll○, N.H. (†03595) 268/D3
Carroll, N.S. Wales 97/F2
Carroll (co.), Ohio 284/H4
Carroll, Ohio (43112) 284/E6
Carroll (co.), Tenn. 237/E9
Carroll (co.), Va. 307/G7
Carrolls, Wash. (98609) 310/C4
Carrolls Crossing, New Bruns. 170/D2
Carrollton, Ala. (35447) 195/B4
Carrollton, Georgia (30117) 217/C3
Carrollton, Ill. (62016) 222/C4
Carrollton, Iowa (†51440) 229/D5
Carrollton, Ky. (41008) 237/L3
Carrollton, Md. (†21157) 245/L2
Carrollton, Mich. (48724) 250/E5
Carrollton, Miss. (38917) 256/E4
Carrollton, Mo. (64633) 261/E4
Carrollton, Ohio (44615) 284/J4
Carrollton, Texas (*75006) 303/G2
Carrolltown, Pa. (15722) 294/E4
Carroll Valley, Pa. (†17320) 294/H6
Carron, Scotland 15/C1
Carron (riv.), Scotland 15/D3
Carron (riv.), Scotland 15/C3
Carron (riv.), Scotland 15/C1
Carron Valley (res.), Scotland 15/B1
Carrot (riv.), Sask. 181/J2
Carrot Creek, Alberta 182/B3
Carrothers, Ohio (44823) 284/D3
Carrot River, Sask. 181/H2
Carrowdore, N. Ireland 17/K2
Carrowkeel, Ireland 17/G1
Carrowmore (lake), Ireland 17/B3
Carrsville, Ky. (42030) 237/E6
Carrsville, Va. (23315) 307/P7
Carruthers, Sask. 181/B3
Carrville, Ala. (†36023) 195/G5
Carryduff, N. Ireland 17/K2
Carryville, Ark. (†72454) 202/K1
Çarşamba, Turkey 63/G2
Carseland, Alberta 182/D4

Changyŏn 349

Ceclavín, Spain 33/C3
Cedar (pt.), Ala. 195/B10
Cedar, Br. Col. 184/J3
Cedar (creek), Colo. 208/M1
Cedar (lake), Conn. 210/E3
Cedar (creek), Ind. 227/G2
Cedar (co.), Iowa 229/L5
Cedar, Iowa (52543) 229/H6
Cedar (riv.), Iowa 188/H2
Cedar (riv.), Iowa 229/K4
Cedar, Kansas (67628) 232/D2
Cedar (lake), Manitoba 179/B1
Cedar (pt.), Md. 245/N7
Cedar, Mich. (49621) 250/D4
Cedar (lake), Mich. 250/F4
Cedar (riv.), Minn. 255/F7
Cedar (co.), Mo. 261/E7
Cedar (co.), Nebr. 264/G2
Cedar (riv.), Nebr. 264/F3
Cedar (mt.), Nev. 266/D4
Cedar (creek), N.J. 273/E4
Cedar (creek), N. Dak. 282/G7
Cedar (pt.), Ohio 284/D2
Cedar (lake), Ontario 177/F1
Cedar (lake), Texas 303/B5
Cedar (mts.), Utah 304/B3
Cedar (isl.), Va. 307/S5
Cedar (riv.), Wash. 310/B2
Cedar Bluff, Ala. (35959) 195/G2
Cedar Bluff, Iowa (†52772) 229/L5
Cedar Bluff (res.), Kansas 232/C3
Cedarbluff, Miss. (39741) 256/G3
Cedar Bluff, Va. (24609) 307/E6
Cedar Bluffs, Kansas (†67749) 232/B2
Cedar Bluffs, Nebr. (68015) 264/H3
Cedar Breaks Nat'l Mon., Utah 304/B6
Cedar Brook, N.J. (08018) 273/D4
Cedarburg, Wis. (53012) 317/L9
Cedarbutte, S. Dak. (57527) 298/H6
Cedar City, Mo. (65022) 261/H5
Cedar City, Utah 188/D3
Cedar City, Utah (84720) 304/A6
Cedar Cove, Ala. (†35453) 195/D4
Cedar Creek, Ark. (†72950) 202/C4
Cedar Creek (peak), Idaho 220/E7
Cedar Creek (res.), Idaho 220/D7
Cedarcreek, Mo. (†65680) 261/G9
Cedar Creek, Nebr. (68016) 264/H3
Cedar Crest, N. Mex. (87008) 274/C3
Cedaredge, Colo. (81413) 208/D5
Cedar Falls, Iowa (50613) 229/H3
Cedar Falls, N.C. (27230) 281/K3
Cedar Falls, Wash. (†98045) 310/D3
Cedar Falls, Wis. (†54751) 317/C6
Cedar Fort, Utah (†84013) 304/B3
Cedar Gap, Mo. (†65746) 261/G8
Cedar Grove, Ant. & Bar. 161/E11
Cedar Grove, Fla. (†32401) 212/D6
Cedar Grove, Georgia (†30727) 217/L2
Cedar Grove, Ind. (47016) 227/H6
Cedar Grove, Md. (†20767) 245/K4
Cedar Grove○, N.J. (07009) 273/B2
Cedar Grove, N.C. (27231) 281/L2
Cedar Grove, Tenn. (38321) 237/D9
Cedar Grove, W. Va. (25039) 312/D6
Cedar Grove, Wis. (53013) 317/L8
Cedar Heights, Md. (†20027) 245/G5
Cedar Hill, N. Mex. (†87410) 274/B2
Cedar Hill, Tenn. (37032) 237/H7
Cedar Hill, Texas (75104) 303/G3
Cedar Hill Lakes, Mo. (63016) 261/L6
Cedar Hills, Oreg. (97225) 291/A2
Cedarhurst, N.Y. (11516) 276/P7
Cedar Island, N.C. (28520) 281/S5
Cedar Key, Fla. (32625) 212/C2
Cedar Knolls, N.J. (07927) 273/E2
Cedar Lake, Ind. (46303) 227/C2
Cedar Lake, Minn. (†56431) 255/E4
Cedar Mill, Oreg. (†97005) 291/A2
Cedar Mills, Minn. (55351) 255/D6
Cedar Mountain, N.C. (28718) 281/D4
Cedar Park, Texas (78613) 303/G7
Cedar Point, Ill. (61316) 222/D2
Cedar Point, Kansas (66843) 232/F3
Cedar Rapids, Iowa 188/H2
Cedar Rapids, Iowa (*52401) 229/K5
Cedar Rapids, Iowa 146/J5
Cedar Rapids, Nebr. (68627) 264/F3
Cedar River, Mich. (49813) 250/B3
Cedar Run, N.J. (†08092) 273/E4
Cedar Run, Pa. (17727) 294/H2
Cedar Springs, Georgia (31732) 217/C8
Cedar Springs, Mich. (49319) 250/D5
Cedar Springs, Mo. (†64744) 261/E7
Cedar Springs, Ontario 177/B5
Cedar Springs, Va. (†24368) 307/F7
Cedar Swamp (pond), Conn. 210/G2
Cedartown, Georgia (30125) 217/B2
Cedarvale, Br. Col. 184/C2
Cedar Vale, Kansas (67024) 232/F4
Cedarvale, N. Mex. (87009) 274/D4
Cedar Valley, Utah (84013) 304/B3
Cedarville, Ark. (72932) 202/B2
Cedarville, Calif. (96104) 204/E2
Cedarville, Ill. (61013) 222/D1
Cedarville, Ind. (†46741) 227/G2
Cedarville, Ky. (†41522) 237/S6
Cedarville, Md. (†20613) 245/L6
Cedarville, Mich. (49719) 250/E2
Cedarville, N.J. (08311) 273/C5
Cedarville, N.Y. (†13357) 276/K5
Cedarville, Ohio (45314) 284/C6
Cedarville, Va. (†22630) 307/M3
Cedarville, W. Va. (26611) 312/E5
Cedarwood Park, N.J. (†08723) 273/E3
Cedonia, Wash. (99137) 310/G2
Cedoux, Sask. 181/H6
Cedral, Mexico 150/J5
Cedros, Honduras 154/D3
Cedros (isl.), Mexico 146/G7
Cedros (isl.), Mexico 150/B2
Cedros, Trin. & Tob. 161/A11
Ceduna, S. Australia 88/E6
Ceduna, S. Australia 94/D5
Cee Vee, Texas (79223) 303/D3
Cefalù, Italy 34/E5
Cegléd, Hungary 41/E3
Ceglie Messapico, Italy 34/F4
Cehegín, Spain 33/F3
Ceiba, P. Rico 161/F2
Çekerek, Turkey 63/F2
Çekerek (riv.), Turkey 63/F3
Cela, Angola 115/C6
Celada Cué, Paraguay 144/D3
Celano, Italy 34/D3
Celanova, Spain 33/B1
Celaya, Mexico 150/J6
Celbridge, Ireland 17/H5
Celebes (sea) 54/O9
Celebes (isl.), Indonesia 54/N10
Celebes (isl.), Indonesia 2/R6
Celebes (Sulawesi) (isl.), Indonesia 85/G5
Celebes (sea), Indonesia 85/G5
Celebes (sea), Philippines 82/D8
Celendín, Peru 128/D6
Celerigna-Schlarigna, Switzerland 39/J3
Celeste, Texas (75423) 303/H4
Celestine, Ind. (47521) 227/D8
Celestún, Mexico 150/O6
Celica, Ecuador 128/B4
Céligny, Switzerland 39/B4
Çelikhan, Turkey 63/H3
Celilo, Oreg. (†97058) 291/G2
Celilo (lake), Oreg. 291/G2
Celilo (lake), Wash. 310/E5
Celina, Minn. (†55788) 255/E3
Celina, Ohio (45822) 284/A4
Celina, Tenn. (38551) 237/K7
Celina, Texas (75009) 303/H4
Celista, Br. Col. 184/H5
Celje, Yugoslavia 45/B2
Cella, Spain 33/F2
Cellar (head), Scotland 15/B2
Celldömölk, Hungary 41/D3
Celle, W. Germany 22/D2
Celorico da Beira, Portugal 33/C2
Celoron, N.Y. (14720) 276/B6
Cement, Okla. (73017) 288/K5
Cement City, Mich. (49233) 250/E6
Çemişkezek, Turkey 63/H3
Cemmaes (head), Wales 13/C5
Cenderawasih (bay), Indonesia 85/K6
Ceneri (mt.), Switzerland 39/G4
Cenia, Spain 33/G2
Census Bureau, Md. 245/F5
Centenary, Ind. (†47842) 227/B5
Centenary, S.C. (29519) 296/J3
Centennial (mts.), Idaho 220/F5
Centennial, Wyo. (82055) 319/F4
Centennial Wash (dry riv.), Ariz. 198/B5
Center, Colo. (81125) 208/G7
Center, Georgia (†30601) 217/F2
Center, Ind. (†46901) 227/E4
Center, Ky. (42214) 237/K6
Center (pond), Maine 243/E5
Center, Mo. (63436) 261/J3
Center, Nebr. (68724) 264/G2
Center, N. Dak. (58530) 282/H5
Center, Okla. (†74820) 288/N5
Center, S. Dak. (†57058) 298/P6
Center, Texas (75935) 303/K6
Center Barnstead, N.H. (03225) 268/E5
Center Belpre, Ohio (†45714) 284/G7
Centerbrook, Conn. (06409) 210/F3
Centerburg, Ohio (43011) 284/E5
Center City, Minn. (55012) 255/F5
Center Conway, N.H. (03813) 268/E4
Center Cross, Va. (22437) 307/P5
Centerdale, R.I. (02911) 249/H5
Centereach, N.Y. (11720) 276/O9
Centerfield, Utah (84622) 304/C4
Center Groton, Conn. (†06340) 210/G3
Center Harbor○, N.H. (03226) 268/E4
Center Hill, Ark. (72143) 202/G3
Center Hill, Fla. (33514) 212/D3
Center Hill (lake), Tenn. 237/K9
Center Junction, Iowa (52212) 229/L4
Center Line, Mich. (48015) 250/B6
Center Lovell, Maine (04016) 243/B7
Center Montville, Maine (†04941) 243/E7
Center Moreland, Pa. (18657) 294/E7
Center Moriches, N.Y. (11934) 276/P9
Center Ossipee, N.H. (03814) 268/E4
Center Point, Ark. (71830) 202/C5
Centerpoint, Ind. (47840) 227/C6
Center Point, Iowa (52213) 229/K4
Center Point, La. (71323) 238/F4
Center Point, S. Dak. (†57070) 298/P7
Center Point, Texas (78010) 303/E8
Center Point, W. Va. (26339) 312/E4
Center Ridge, Ark. (72027) 202/E3
Center Rutland, Vt. (05736) 268/A4
Center Sandwich, N.H. (03227) 268/D4
Center Square, Ind. (†47043) 227/H7
Center Strafford, N.H. (03815) 268/E5
Centerton, Ark. (72719) 202/B1
Centerton, Ind. (46116) 227/E5
Centerton, N.J. (†08318) 273/C4
Centertown, Ky. (42328) 237/G6
Centertown, Mo. (65023) 261/H5
Centertown, Tenn. (†37110) 237/K9
Center Tuftonboro, N.H. (03816) 268/E4
Centerview, Mo. (64019) 261/E5
Center Village, Ohio (†43021) 284/E5
Centerville, Ark. (72829) 202/D3
Centerville, Del. (†19801) 245/R1
Centerville, Georgia (31028) 217/E5
Centerville, Ind. (47330) 227/H5
Centerville, Iowa (52544) 229/H7
Centerville, Kansas (66014) 232/H3
Centerville, Ky. (†41522) 237/S6
Centerville, La. (70522) 238/H7
Centerville○, Maine (†04623) 243/H6
Centerville, Mass. (02632) 249/N6
Centerville, Minn. (†55038) 255/E5
Centerville, Mo. (63633) 261/L8
Centerville, N.C. (†27549) 281/N2
Centerville, Ohio (45459) 284/B6
Centerville, Pa. (15417) 294/B6
Centerville, Pa. (16404) 294/C2
Centerville, S. Dak. (57014) 298/R7
Centerville, Tenn. (37033) 237/G9
Centerville, Texas (75833) 303/H6
Centerville, Utah (84014) 304/C3
Centerville, Wash. (98613) 310/D5
Centrahoma, Okla. (74534) 288/O5
Central, Ala. (36014) 195/F5
Central (sen. dist.), Alaska 196/H2
Central, Alaska (99730) 196/J1
Central, Ariz. (85531) 198/F6
Central, Cordillera (range), Bolivia 136/C6
Central, Cordillera (range), Colombia 126/C5
Central, Cordillera (range), Dom. Rep. 158/D5
Central, Idaho (†83241) 220/G7
Central, Ind. (47110) 227/E8
Central (Markazi) (prov.), Iran 66/G3
Central (dist.), Israel 65/B3
Central (prov.), Kenya 115/G4
Central, La. (†70723) 238/L3
Central, N. Mex. (88026) 274/A6
Central (dept.), Paraguay 144/D4
Central (Baganga), Philippines 82/F7
Central, Cordillera (range), P. Rico 161/C2
Central (reg.), Scotland 15/D4
Central, S.C. (29630) 296/B2
Central, Utah (†84701) 304/A6
Central, Utah (84722) 304/B5
Central Aboriginal Reserve, W. Australia 88/D4
Central Aboriginal Res., W. Australia 92/E3
Central African Republic 2/K5
Central African Republic 102/D4
CENTRAL AFRICAN REPUBLIC 115/C2
Central Aguirre, P. Rico 161/D3
Central Amancio Rodríguez, Cuba 158/G3
Central America 2/E5
Central América, Cuba 158/J4
Central Bedeque, Pr. Edward I. 168/E2
Central Blissville, New Bruns. 170/D3
Central Bolivia, Cuba 158/G2
Central Brasil, Cuba 158/G2
Central Bridge, N.Y. (12035) 276/M5
Central Butte, Sask. 181/E5
Central Cándido González, Cuba 158/G3
Central City, Ark. (†72923) 202/B3
Central City, Colo. (80427) 208/J3
Central City, Ill. (†62801) 222/D5
Central City, Iowa (52214) 229/K4
Central City, Ky. (42330) 237/G6
Central City, Nebr. (68826) 264/F3
Central City, Pa. (15926) 294/E5
Central City, S. Dak. (†57754) 298/B5
Central Colombia, Cuba 158/G3
Central Falls, R.I. (02863) 249/J5
Central Frank País, Cuba 158/K3
Central Greece and Euboea (reg.), Greece 45/F6
Central Guatemala, Cuba 158/J3
Central Haití, Cuba 158/G3
Centralhatchee, Georgia (†30217) 217/B4
Central Heights-Midland City, Ariz. (†85501) 198/E5
Centralia, Ill. (62801) 222/D5
Centralia, Iowa (†52068) 229/M4
Centralia, Kansas (66415) 232/F2
Centralia, Mo. (65240) 261/H4
Centralia, Okla. (74336) 288/R1
Centralia, Pa. (17927) 294/K4
Centralia, Texas (75834) 303/K6
Centralia, Wash. 188/B1
Centralia, Wash. (98531) 310/C4
Centralia, W. Va. (26612) 312/E5
Central Intelligence Agency (C.I.A.), Va. 307/S2
Central Islip, N.Y. (11722) 276/O9
Central Lake, Mich. (49622) 250/D3
Central Los Reynaldos, Cuba 158/J4
Central Loynaz Echevarría, Cuba 158/J3
Central Manuel Tames, Cuba 158/K4
Central Niágara, Cuba 158/B1
Central Pacolet, S.C. (†29372) 296/D2
Central Park, Wash. (98520) 310/B3
Central Patricia, Ontario 175/B2
Central Point, Oreg. (97502) 291/D5
Central Point, Va. (†22427) 307/O4
Central Saanich, Br. Col. 184/K3
Central Square, N.Y. (13036) 276/H4
Central Station, W. Va. (26340) 312/E4
Central Ural (mts.), U.S.S.R. 52/J2
Central Valley, Calif. (96019) 204/C3
Central Valley, N.Y. (10917) 276/M8
Central Village, Conn. (06332) 210/H2
Central Village, Mass. (02790) 249/K6
Central Wedge (mt.), North. Terr. 93/C7
Centre, Ala. (35960) 195/G2
Centre (co.), Pa. 294/G4
Centre Hall, Pa. (16828) 294/G4
Centre Island, N.Y. (†11771) 276/R6
Centre-Saint-Simon, New Bruns. 170/E1
Centreville, Ala. (35042) 195/D5
Centreville, Ill. (62206) 222/B3
Centreville, Md. (21617) 245/O4
Centreville, Mich. (49032) 250/D7
Centreville, Miss. (39631) 256/B8
Centreville, New Bruns. 170/C2
Centreville, Digby, Nova Scotia 168/B4
Centreville, Kings, Nova Scotia 168/D3
Centreville (Thurman), Ohio (†45685) 284/F8
Centuria, Wis. (54824) 317/A5
Centurión, Uruguay 145/F3
Century, Fla. (32535) 212/B5
Century, W. Va. (26214) 312/F4
Cephalonia (Kefallinía) (isl.), Greece 45/E6
Ceram (isl.), Indonesia 54/P10
Ceram (isl.), Indonesia 85/H6
Cerbat (mts.), Ariz. 198/A3
Cercal, Portugal 33/B4
Cerca la Source, Haiti 158/C5
Cereal, Alberta 182/E4
Ceredo, W. Va. (25507) 312/B6
Ceres, Argentina 143/D2
Ceres, Brazil 132/D6
Ceres, Brazil 120/E4
Ceres, Calif. (95307) 204/D6
Ceres, N.Y. (14721) 276/D6
Ceres, S. Africa 118/B6
Ceres, Va. (24318) 307/F6
Ceresco, Nebr. (68017) 264/H3
Céret, France 28/E6
Cereté, Colombia 126/C3
Cerf (lake), Québec 172/B3
Cerf (isl.), Seychelles 118/H5
Cerfontaine, Belgium 27/E8
Cerignola, Italy 34/E4
Çerkeş, Turkey 63/E2
Çerkezköy, Turkey 63/C2
Çermik, Turkey 63/H3
Cernavodă, Romania 45/J3
Cernier, Switzerland 39/C2
Cernobbio, Italy 34/B2
Cerralvo (isl.), Mexico 150/E4
Cerrillos, N. Mex. (87010) 274/D3
Cerrillos, Uruguay 145/A6
Cerrito, Paraguay 144/D5
Cerritos, Calif. (†90701) 204/C11
Cerritos, Mexico 150/J5
Cerro, N. Mex. (87519) 274/D2
Cerro Aconcagua (mt.) 120/C6
Cerro Alto (mt.), Texas 303/B10
Cêrro Azul, Brazil 135/B4
Cerro Azul, Mexico 150/L6
Cerro Azul, Peru 128/D9
Cerro Castillo, Chile 138/E9
Cerro Chato, Cerro Largo, Uruguay 145/F3
Cerro Chato, Rivera, Uruguay 145/D2
Cerro Chato, Treinta y Tres, Uruguay 145/D4
Cerro Colorado, Uruguay 145/D4
Cerro Corá, Paraguay 144/E3
Cerro de las Armas, Uruguay 145/B5
Cerro de las Cuentas, Uruguay 145/E3
Cerro de Pasco, Peru 120/B4
Cerro de Pasco, Peru 128/D8
Cerro de San Antonio, Colombia 126/C
Cerro Gordo, Ill. (61818) 222/E4
Cerro Gordo (co.), Iowa 229/G2
Cerro Gordo, N.C. (28430) 281/M6
Cerro Gordo (pt.), P. Rico 161/D1
Cerro Gordo, Tenn. (38322) 237/E10
Cerro Largo (dept.), Uruguay 145/E3
Cerro Manantiales, Chile 138/F10
Cerulean, Ky. (42215) 237/F7
Cervera, Spain 33/G2
Cervera del Río Alhama, Spain 33/E1
Cervera de Pisuerga, Spain 33/D1
Cerveteri, Italy 34/E6
Cervione, France 28/B6
Cesano, Italy 34/F6
César (dept.), Colombia 126/D3
César (riv.), Colombia 126/D2
Cesena, Italy 34/D2
Cesenatico, Italy 34/D2
Cēsis, U.S.S.R. 53/C2
Cēsis, U.S.S.R. 52/C3
Česká Kamenice, Czech. 41/C1
Česká Lípa, Czech. 41/C1
Česká Třebová, Czech. 41/D2
České Budějovice, Czech. 41/C2
Český Brod, Czech. 41/C1
Český Krumlov, Czech. 41/C2
Český Těšín, Czech. 41/E2
Çeşme, Turkey 63/B3
Céspedes, Cuba 158/G2
Cessford, Alberta 182/E4
Cessnock-Bellbird, N.S. Wales 88/J6
Cessnock-Bellbird, N.S. Wales 97/F3
Cestos (riv.), Liberia 106/C7
Cetinje, Yugoslavia 45/D4
Çetinkaya, Turkey 63/G3
Ceuta, Spain 106/C1
Ceuta, Spain 7/D5
Ceuta, Spain 102/B1
Ceuta, Spain 33/D5
Cévennes (mts.), France 28/E5
Cevio, Switzerland 39/G4
Cevizli, Turkey 63/D4
Ceyhan, Turkey 63/F4
Ceyhan (riv.), Turkey 63/F4
Ceyhan (riv.), Turkey 59/C2
Ceylânpınar, Turkey 63/H4
Ceylon (Sri Lanka) 54/K9
Ceylon, Minn. (56121) 255/D7
Ceylon, Sask. 181/G6
Chabás, Argentina 143/F6
Chaca, Chile 138/B1
Chacabuco, Argentina 143/F7
Chacabuco, Chile 138/G2
Chacachacare (isl.), Trin. & Tob. 161/A10
Chacahoula, La. (†70395) 238/J7
Chacalluta, Chile 138/A1
Chachacomani, Bolivia 136/A6
Chachapoyas, Peru 128/D6
Chachapoyas, Peru 120/B3
Chachoengsao, Thailand 72/D4
Chachro, Pakistan 68/C3
Chaco (prov.), Argentina 143/D2
Chaco (mesa), N. Mex. 274/B3
Chaco (riv.), N. Mex. 274/A2
Chaco (dept.), Paraguay 144/B-C2
Chaco Austral (reg.), Argentina 143/D2
Chaco Boreal (reg.), Paraguay 144/B2-3
Chaco Central (reg.), Argentina 143/D1
Chaco Culture Nat'l Hist. Park, N. Mex. 274/B2
Chacoma, Bolivia 136/A6
Chacon (cape), Alaska 196/N2
Chacon, N. Mex. (87713) 274/D2
Chacuaco (creek), Colo. 208/M8
Chad 2/K5
Chad 102/D3
Chad (lake) 102/D3
CHAD 111/C4
Chad (lake), Chad 111/C5
Chad (lake), Niger 106/G6
Chad (lake), Nigeria 106/G6
Chadan, U.S.S.R. 48/K4
Chadbourn, N.C. (28431) 281/M6
Chadron, Nebr. (69337) 264/B2
Chadwick, Ill. (61014) 222/D1
Chadwick, Mo. (65629) 261/G9
Chadwick Acres, N.C. (†28445) 281/P6
Chadwicks, N.Y. (13319) 276/K4
Chadyr-Lunga, U.S.S.R. 52/C5
Chaffee (co.), Colo. 208/G5
Chaffee, Mo. (63740) 261/N8
Chaffee, N.Y. (14030) 276/C5
Chaffee, N. Dak. (58014) 282/R6
Chaffers (isl.), Chile 138/D5
Chafurray, Colombia 126/D6
Chagai (hills), Afghanistan 68/A3
Chagai, Pakistan 59/H4
Chagai, Pakistan 68/A3
Chagai (hills), Pakistan 68/A3
Chagai (hills), Pakistan 59/H4
Chagda, U.S.S.R. 48/O4
Chaghcharan, Afghanistan 68/B2
Chagoda, U.S.S.R. 52/E3
Chagoness, Sask. 181/G3
Chagos (arch.), Br. Ind. Ocean Terr. 2/N6
Chagos (arch.), Br. Ind. Ocean Terr. 54/J10
Chagrin (riv.), Ohio 284/J8
Chagrin Falls, Ohio (44022) 284/J9
Chaguanas, Trin. & Tob. 161/B10
Chaguaramas, Trin. & Tob. 161/A10
Chaguaramas, Venezuela 124/E3
Chaguaya, Bolivia 136/C7
Chagulak (isl.), Alaska 196/D4
Chahal, Guatemala 154/C3
Chahar Borjak, Afghanistan 59/H3
Chahar Borjak, Afghanistan 68/A2
Chah Bahar, Afghanistan 59/H4
Chah Bahar, Iran 66/M8
Chahuites, Mexico 150/M8
Chai Badan, Thailand 72/D4
Chaibasa, India 68/F4
Chai Buri, Thailand 72/D3
Chainat, Thailand 72/D4
Chain-O-Lakes, Mo. (†65641) 261/E9
Chaira, Laguna (lake), Colombia 126/C7
Chaires, Fla. (†32302) 212/B1
Chaitén, Chile 138/E4
Chaiya, Thailand 72/C5
Chaiyaphum, Thailand 72/D4
Chajarí, Argentina 143/G5
Chajul, Guatemala 154/B3
Chake Chake, Tanzania 115/H5
Chala, Peru 128/E10
Chalais, Switzerland 39/E4
Chalatenango, El Salvador 154/C3
Chalchihuites, Mexico 150/G5
Chalco de Díaz Covarrubias, Mexico 150/M1
Chaleur (bay), New Bruns. 170/E1
Chaleur (bay), Québec 172/C2
Chaleur (bay), Québec 174/D3
Chalfont, Pa. (18914) 294/M5
Chalhuanca, Peru 128/F10
Chaling, China 77/H6
Chalk (creek), Utah 304/C3
Chalk River, Ontario 175/E3
Chalk River, Ontario 177/G1
Chalkyitsik, Alaska (99788) 196/K1
Challacollo, Bolivia 136/B6
Challana, Bolivia 136/A4
Challapata, Bolivia 136/B6
Challenger (mts.), N.W. Terrs. 187/L1
Challis, Idaho (83226) 220/D5
Challviri (salt dep.), Bolivia 136/B8
Chalmers, Ind. (47929) 227/D3
Chalmette, La. (70043) 238/P4
Chalna Port, Bangladesh 68/F4
Chalonnes-sur-Loire, France 28/C4
Châlons-sur-Marne, France 28/F3
Chalon-sur-Saône, France 28/F4
Chaltel, Cerro (mt.), Chile 138/E8
Chalus, Iran 59/F2
Chalus, Iran 66/G2
Chalybeate, Miss. (38684) 256/G1
Chalybeate Springs, Georgia (†31816) 217/C5
Chalybeate Springs, N.C. (†27526) 281/M3
Cham, Switzerland 39/F2
Cham, W. Germany 22/E4
Chama, Colo. (81126) 208/J8
Chama, N. Mex. (87520) 274/C2
Chaman, Pakistan 68/B2
Chaman, Pakistan 59/J3
Chamba, India 68/D2
Chambal (riv.), India 68/D3
Chambas, Cuba 158/F2
Chamberino, N. Mex. (88027) 274/C6
Chamberlain (creek), Idaho 220/C4
Chamberlain (lake), Maine 243/E3
Chamberlain, Sask. 181/F5
Chamberlain, S. Dak. (57325) 298/L6
Chamberlain, Uruguay 145/C3
Chamberlin, La. (†70767) 238/J1
Chambers (co.), Ala. 195/H5
Chambers, Ariz. (86502) 198/F3
Chambers, Nebr. (68725) 264/F2
Chambers (co.), Texas 303/K8
Chambers (isl.), Wis. 317/M5
Chambersburg, Ill. (62323) 222/C4
Chambersburg, Ind. (†47454) 227/E7
Chambersburg, Ohio (†45631) 284/F8
Chambersburg, Pa. (17201) 294/G6
Chambéry, France 28/F5
Chambeshi (riv.), Zambia 115/F6
Chambeyron (mt.), France 28/G5
Chambeyron (mt.), Italy 34/A2
Chambi, Jebel (mt.), Tunisia 106/F2
Chamblee, Georgia (30341) 217/K1
Chambly (co.), Québec 172/J4
Chambly, Québec 172/J4
Chambord, France 28/D4
Chambord, Québec 172/E1
Chamdo (Qamdo), China 77/E5
Chame (pt.), Panama 154/H6
Chamela (bay), Mexico 150/G7
Chamical, Argentina 143/C3
Chamisal, N. Mex. (87521) 274/D2
Chamizal Nat'l Mem., Texas 303/A10
Chamizo, Uruguay 145/D5
Chamo (lake), Ethiopia 111/G6
Chamois, Mo. (65024) 261/J5
Chamonix-Mont-Blanc, France 28/G5
Chamoson, Switzerland 39/D4
Champ, Mo. (†63042) 261/O2
Champagne (trad. prov.), France 29
Champagne, Yukon 187/E3
Champaign, Ill. 188/J2
Champaign (co.), Ill. 222/E3
Champaign, Ill. (61820) 222/E3
Champaign (co.), Ohio 284/C5
Champasak, Laos 72/E4
Champdani, India 68/F1
Champerico, Guatemala 154/A3
Champéry, Switzerland 39/C4
Champex, Switzerland 39/D4
Champigny-sur-Marne, France 28/C2
Champion, Alberta 182/D4
Champion, Mich. (49814) 250/B2
Champion, Nebr. (69023) 264/C4
Champlain (lake) 188/M2
Champlain, N.Y. (12919) 276/N1
Champlain (lake), N.Y. 276/O1
Champlain (county), Québec 174/C3
Champlain (co.), Québec 172/E2
Champlain, Québec 172/E3
Champlain (lake), Québec 172/D4
Champlain (lake), Vt. 268/A2
Champlain, Va. (22438) 307/O4
Champlain-Park, N.Y. (†12901) 276/O1
Champlin, Minn. (55316) 255/G5
Champney's West, Newf. 166/D2
Champotón, Mexico 150/O7
Chamusa, Sierra (mts.), Colombia 126/C6
Chamusca, Portugal 33/B3
Chan, Ko (isl.), Thailand 72/C5
Chana, Ill. (61015) 222/D2
Chañaral, Chile 120/B5
Chañaral, Chile 138/A6
Chañaral (isl.), Chile 138/A7
Chancay, Peru 128/D8
Chance, Ala. (36729) 195/C7
Chance, Ky. (†42728) 237/L7
Chance, Md. (21816) 245/P8
Chance Cove, Newf. 166/D2
Chance Cove (cape), Newf. 166/D2
Chance Harbour, New Bruns. 170/D3
Chancellor, Ala. (36316) 195/G8
Chancellor, Alberta 182/D4
Chancellor, S. Dak. (57015) 298/R7
Chancellorsville, Va. (†22401) 307/N4
Chanco, Chile 138/A11
Chancy, Switzerland 39/A4
Chandalar, Alaska (†99726) 196/J1
Chandalar (riv.), Alaska 196/J1
Chandalar, East Fork (riv.), Alaska 196/J1
Chandeleur (isls.), La. 238/N7
Chandeleur (sound), La. 238/M7
Chanderi, India 68/D4
Chandernagore, India 68/F1
Chandigarh (terr.), India 68/D2
Chandigarh, India 68/D2
Chandler, Ariz. (85224) 198/D5
Chandler, Ind. (47610) 227/C8
Chandler, Minn. (56122) 255/C7
Chandler, Okla. (74834) 288/N3
Chandler, Que. 162/K6
Chandler, Québec 174/E3
Chandler, Québec 172/D2
Chandler, Texas (75758) 303/J5
Chandler Springs, Ala. (†35160) 195/F4
Chandlers Valley, Pa. (16312) 294/D2
Chandlersville, Ohio (43727) 284/G6
Chandlerville, Ill. (62627) 222/C3
Chandmanī, Mongolia 77/E2
Chandolin, Switzerland 39/E4
Chandos (lake), Ontario 177/G3
Chandrapur, India 68/D5
Chaneysville, Pa. (†21530) 294/F6
Chang, Ko (isl.), Thailand 72/D4
Changane (riv.), Mozambique 118/E4
Changbaek-sanmaek (mts.), N. Korea 81/D2
Changchih (Changzhi), China 77/H4
Changchow (Zhangzhou), China 77/J7
Changchow (Changzhou), China 77/J5
Changchun, China 77/K3
Changchun, China 54/O5
Changchun, China 2/R3
Changde (Changteh), China 77/H6
Changde, China 54/N7
Change Islands, Newf. 166/D4
Changewater, N.J. (07831) 273/D2
Changhua, China 77/K7
Changhŭng, S. Korea 81/C6
Changji, China 77/C3
Changjiang, China 77/G8
Chang Jiang (Yangtze) (riv.), China 2/Q4
Chang Jiang (Yangtze) (riv.), China 54/N6
Chang Jiang (Yangtze) (riv.), China 77/K5
Changjin (res.), N. Korea 81/C3
Chang Khoeng, Thailand 72/C3
Changling, China 77/K3
Changsha, China 77/H6
Changsha, China 2/Q4
Changsha, China 54/N7
Changshu, China 77/G6
Changsŏng, S. Korea 81/C6
Changteh (Changde), China 77/H6
Changuinola, Panama 154/F6
Changwu, China 77/G4
Changyang, China 77/H5
Changyeh (Zhangye), China 77/F4
Changyŏn, N. Korea 81/B4

Coleman 353

Cleveland, Mo. (64734) 261/C5
Cleveland, Mont. (†59523) 262/G2
Cleveland, N. Mex. (87715) 274/D2
Cleveland, N.Y. (13042) 276/J4
Cleveland (co.), N.C. 281/F4
Cleveland, N.C. (27013) 281/H3
Cleveland, N. Dak. (58424) 282/M6
Cleveland, Ohio 188/K2
Cleveland, Ohio (*44101) 284/H9
Cleveland, Ohio 146/K5
Cleveland (co.), Okla. 288/M4
Cleveland, Okla. (74020) 288/O2
Cleveland, S.C. (29635) 296/C1
Cleveland, Tenn. (37311) 237/M10
Cleveland, Texas (77327) 303/K7
Cleveland, Utah (84518) 304/D4
Cleveland, Va. (24225) 307/D7
Cleveland, W. Va. (26215) 312/F5
Cleveland, Wis. (53015) 317/L8
Cleveland Heights, Ohio (44118) 284/H9
Cleveland-Hopkins Mun. Airport, Ohio 284/G9
Clevelândia do Norte, Brazil 132/D2
Cleveland Park, D.C. (20008) 245/E4
Clever, Mo. (65631) 261/F8
Cleves, Iowa (†50601) 229/G4
Cleves, Ohio (45002) 284/B9
Clew (bay), Ireland 17/B4
Clew (bay), Ireland 10/B4
Clewiston, Fla. (33440) 212/E5
Clichy, France 28/B1
Clicquot-Millis, Mass. (†02054) 249/A8
Clifden, Ireland 10/B4
Clifden, Ireland 17/B5
Cliff, N. Mex. (88028) 274/A6
Cliff (cape), Nova Scotia 168/E3
Cliff (creek), Utah 304/E3
Cliffdell, Wash. (†98937) 310/E4
Clifford, Ind. (47226) 227/F6
Clifford, Ky. (41208) 237/S4
Clifford (lake), Maine 243/H5
Clifford, Mich. (48727) 250/F5
Clifford, N. Dak. (58016) 282/R5
Clifford, Ontario 177/D4
Clifford, Pa. (18413) 294/L2
Clifford, Va. (24533) 307/K5
Clifford, Wis. (†54564) 317/F4
Cliffordvale, New Bruns. 170/C2
Cliffside, N.C. (28024) 281/F4
Cliffside Park, N.J. (07010) 273/C2
Clifftop, W. Va. (25822) 312/E6
Cliffwood, N.J. (07721) 273/E3
Clifton, Ariz. (85533) 198/F5
Clifton, Colo. (81520) 208/C4
Clifton, Idaho (83228) 220/F7
Clifton, Ill. (60927) 222/F3
Clifton, Kansas (66937) 232/E2
Clifton, La. (†70438) 238/K5
Clifton○, Maine (†04428) 243/G6
Clifton, New Bruns. 170/E1
Clifton, N.J. (*07011) 273/B2
Clifton, S.C. (29324) 296/D2
Clifton, Tenn. (38425) 237/F10
Clifton, Texas (76634) 303/G6
Clifton, W. Va. (25237) 312/B5
Clifton, Wis. (†54618) 317/F8
Clifton City, Mo. (†65348) 261/G5
Clifton Dartmouth Hardness, England 10/E5
Clifton Dartmouth Hardness, England 13/D7
Clifton Forge (I.C.), Va. (24422) 307/J5
Clifton Heights, Pa. (19018) 294/M7
Clifton Hill, Mo. (65244) 261/G4
Clifton Hills, S. Australia 94/F2
Clifton Mills, W. Va. (†26525) 312/G3
Clifton Park○, N.Y. (†12118) 276/N5
Clifton Springs, N.Y. (14432) 276/F4
Cliftonville, Miss. (†39739) 256/H4
Clifty, Ark. (†72756) 202/C1
Clifty (creek), Ind. 227/F6
Clifty, Ky. (42216) 237/G7
Clifty, Tenn. (†38583) 237/L9
Clifty, W. Va. (†25854) 312/E6
Climax, Colo. (80429) 208/G4
Climax, Georgia (31734) 217/D9
Climax, Kansas (67027) 232/F4
Climax, Ky. (40413) 237/N6
Climax, Mich. (49034) 250/D6
Climax, Minn. (56523) 255/B3
Climax, N.C. (27233) 281/K3
Climax, Sask. 181/C6
Climax Springs, Mo. (65324) 261/G6
Climbing Hill, Iowa (51015) 229/B4
Clinch (co.), Georgia 217/G9
Clinch (riv.), Tenn. 237/N9
Clinch (riv.), Va. 307/C7
Clinchburg, Va. (24321) 307/E7
Clinchco, Va. (24226) 307/D6
Clinchfield, Georgia (31013) 217/E6
Clinchmore, Tenn. (†37714) 237/N8
Clinchport, Va. (24244) 307/C7
Cline Settlement, Alberta 182/B3
Clingmans Dome (mt.), N.C. 281/C3
Clingmans Dome (mt.), Tenn. 237/P10
Clint, Texas (79836) 303/B10
Clinton, Ala. (35448) 195/C5
Clinton, Ark. (72031) 202/F2
Clinton, Br. Col. 184/G4
Clinton, Conn. (06413) 210/E3
Clinton○, Conn. (06413) 210/E3
Clinton (co.), Ill. 222/D5
Clinton, Ill. (61727) 222/E3
Clinton (co.), Ind. 227/E4
Clinton, Ind. (47842) 227/C5
Clinton (co.), Iowa 229/M5
Clinton, Iowa 188/J2
Clinton, Iowa (52732) 229/N5
Clinton (co.), Ky. 237/L7
Clinton, Ky. (42031) 237/D7
Clinton, La. (70722) 238/J5
Clinton, Maine (04927) 243/D6
Clinton○, Maine (04927) 243/D6
Clinton, Md. (20735) 245/G6
Clinton○, Mass. (01510) 249/H3
Clinton (co.), Mich. 250/E6
Clinton, Mich. (49236) 250/F6
Clinton, Minn. (56225) 255/B5
Clinton, Miss. (39056) 256/D6
Clinton (co.), Mo. 261/D3
Clinton, Mo. (64735) 261/E6
Clinton, Mont. (59825) 262/C4
Clinton, Nebr. (†69343) 264/B2
Clinton, N.J. (08809) 273/D2
Clinton (res.), N.J. 273/E1
Clinton (co.), N.Y. 276/N1
Clinton, N.Y. (13323) 276/K4
Clinton, N. Zealand 100/B7
Clinton, N.C. (28328) 281/N5
Clinton (co.), Ohio 284/C7
Clinton, Ohio (44216) 284/G4
Clinton, Okla. (73601) 288/H3
Clinton, Ontario 177/C4
Clinton (co.), Pa. 294/G3
Clinton, Pa. (15026) 294/B5
Clinton, S.C. (29325) 296/D3
Clinton, Tenn. (37716) 237/N8
Clinton, Wash. (98236) 310/C3
Clinton, W. Va. (†26058) 312/E2
Clinton, Wis. (53525) 317/J10
Clinton-Colden (lake), N.W. Terrs. 187/H3
Clinton Corners, N.Y. (12514) 276/N7
Clinton Creek, Yukon 187/D3
Clintondale, N.Y. (12515) 276/M7
Clintondale, Pa. (†17751) 294/H3
Clinton Falls, Minn. (†55060) 255/E6
Clintonville, Conn. (†06473) 210/D3
Clintonville, Ky. (†40361) 237/N4
Clintonville, Pa. (16372) 294/C3
Clintonville, W. Va. (24928) 312/E7
Clintonville, Wis. (54929) 317/J6
Clintwood, Va. (24228) 307/D6
Clio, Ala. (36017) 195/G7
Clio, Iowa (50052) 229/G7
Clio, La. (†70462) 238/M2
Clio, Mich. (48420) 250/F5
Clio, S.C. (29525) 296/H2
Clio, W. Va. (25046) 312/D5
Clipper, Wash. (98244) 310/C2
Clipperton (isl.) 146/H8
Clipperton (isl.) 2/D5
Clisham (mt.), Scotland 15/B3
Clitherall, Minn. (56524) 255/C4
Clitheroe, England 13/H1
Clitheroe, England 10/G1
Clive, Alberta 182/D3
Clive, Iowa (50318) 229/F5
Clive, N. Zealand 100/F3
Cliza, Bolivia 136/C5
Cloan, Sask. 181/C3
Cloates (pt.), W. Australia 92/A3
Clode (sound), Newf. 166/D2
Cloe, Pa. (†15767) 294/E4
Cloghan, Ireland 17/F5
Clogh-Chatsworth, Ireland 17/G6
Clogheen, Ireland 17/F7
Clogher, N. Ireland 17/G3
Clogherhead, Ireland 17/J4
Cloghy, N. Ireland 17/K3
Clonakilty, Ireland 10/B5
Clonakilty, Ireland 17/D8
Clonakilty (bay), Ireland 17/D8
Clonaslee, Ireland 17/F5
Cloncurry, Australia 87/E8
Cloncurry, Queensland 95/B4
Cloncurry, Queensland 88/G4
Cloncurry (riv.), Queensland 95/B4
Clondalkin, Ireland 17/J5
Clonegal, Ireland 17/H6
Clones, Ireland 10/C3
Clones, Ireland 17/G3
Clonfert, Ireland 17/E5
Clonmany, Ireland 17/G1
Clonmel, Ireland 17/F7
Clonmel, Ireland 10/C4
Clonmellon, Ireland 17/H4
Clonroche, Ireland 17/H7
Clontarf, Minn. (56226) 255/C5
Clontuskert, Ireland 17/E4
Cloone, Ireland 17/F4
Cloppenburg, W. Germany 22/B2
Clopton, Ala. (36317) 195/G7
Cloquet, Minn. (55720) 255/F4
Cloquet (riv.), Minn. 255/F4
Cloridorme, Québec 172/D1
Clorinda, Argentina 143/E2
Closeburn, Scotland 15/E5
Closplint, Ky. (40927) 237/P7
Closter, N.J. (07624) 273/C1
Clothier, W. Va. (25047) 312/C7
Clotho, Minn. (†56347) 255/C4
Cloud (co.), Kansas 232/E2
Cloud (peak), Wyo. 319/E1
Cloud Chief, Okla. (†73632) 288/J4
Cloudcroft, N. Mex. (88317) 274/D6
Cloudland, Georgia (30709) 217/A1
Cloudy (bay), N. Zealand 100/E4
Cloudy, Okla. (74537) 288/R6
Cloughjordan, Ireland 17/E6
Cloughmills, N. Ireland 17/J2
Cloutierville, La. (71416) 238/E3
Clova, Québec 174/B3
Clover (creek), Oreg. 291/K3
Clover, S.C. (29710) 296/E1
Clover, Va. (24534) 307/L7
Clover, W. Va. (†25276) 312/D5
Clover Bar, Alberta 182/D3
Clover Bend, Ark. (†72433) 202/H2
Clover Bottom, Ky. (40447) 237/N5
Cloverdale, Ala. (35617) 195/C1
Cloverdale, Calif. (95425) 204/B5
Cloverdale, Ind. (46120) 227/D5
Cloverdale, Minn. (†55037) 255/F4
Cloverdale, Ohio (45827) 284/B3
Cloverdale, Oreg. (97112) 291/D2
Cloverdale, Va. (24077) 307/J6
Cloverland, Ind. (†47834) 227/C6
Cloverland, Wash. (†99402) 310/H4
Cloverleaf, Manitoba 179/F5
Clover Lick, W. Va. (†24979) 312/F6
Clover Pass, Alaska (†99901) 196/N2
Cloverport, Ky. (40111) 237/H5
Cloverton, Minn. (†55048) 255/F4
Clovis, Calif. (93612) 204/F7
Clovis, N.Mex. 188/F4
Clovis, N. Mex. (88101) 274/F4
Clovulin, Scotland 15/C4
Cloyne, Ireland 17/E8
Cloyne, Ontario 177/G3
Cluanie, Loch (lake), Scotland 15/C3
Club (isl.), Ontario 177/C2
Cluff Lake, Sask. 181/L2
Cluj-Napoca, Romania 45/F2
Cluj-Napoca, Romania 7/G4
Clun, England 10/E4
Clun, England 13/D6
Clune, Pa. (15727) 294/D4
Clunes, Victoria 97/B5
Cluny, Alberta 182/D4
Cluny, France 28/F4
Cluses, France 28/G4
Clusone-Fiorine, Italy 34/C2
Cluster Springs, Va. (24535) 307/L7
Clute, Texas (77531) 303/J9
Clutha (riv.), N. Zealand 100/B6
Clutier, Iowa (52217) 229/J4
Clwyd (co.), Wales 13/D4
Clyattville, Georgia (31604) 217/F9
Clyde, Alberta 182/D2
Clyde (lake), Alberta 182/E2
Clyde, Canada 4/B13
Clyde (riv.), Dominica 161/F6
Clyde, Kansas (66938) 232/E2
Clyde, Mo. (64432) 261/C2
Clyde, N.Y. (14433) 276/G4
Clyde, N.C. (28721) 281/D3
Clyde, N. Dak. (†58352) 282/N2
Clyde, N.W.T. 162/J1
Clyde (inlet), N.W.T. 162/K1
Clyde, N.W. Terrs. 187/M2
Clyde (inlet), N.W. Terrs. 187/M2
Clyde (riv.), Nova Scotia 168/C5
Clyde, Ohio (43410) 284/E3
Clyde (firth), Scotland 15/D5
Clyde (firth), Scotland 10/D3
Clyde (riv.), Scotland 10/E3
Clyde (riv.), Scotland 15/D5
Clyde (riv.), Tasmania 99/D4
Clyde, Texas (79510) 303/E5
Clyde (riv.), Vt. 268/C2
Clyde, Wash. (†99348) 310/G4
Clydebank, Scotland 15/B2
Clydebank, Scotland 10/A1
Clyde Hill, Wash. (†98004) 310/B2
Clyde Park, Mont. (59018) 262/F5
Clyde River, Nova Scotia 168/C5
Clyman, Wis. (53016) 317/J9
Clymer, N.Y. (14724) 276/A6
Clymer, Pa. (15728) 294/E4
Clymers, Ind. (†46947) 227/E3
Clyo, Georgia (31303) 217/K6
Cnoc May (mt.), Scotland 15/C5
Coachella, Calif. (92236) 204/J10
Coachella (canal), Calif. 204/K10
Coachford, Ireland 17/D8
Coahoma (co.), Miss. 256/C2
Coahoma, Miss. (38617) 256/C2
Coahoma, Texas (79511) 303/C5
Coahuila (state), Mexico 150/H3
Coakley, Ky. (†42782) 237/K6
Coal (creek), Ind. 227/C4
Coal, Mo. (†64735) 261/E6
Coal (co.), Okla. 288/O5
Coal (pt.), Oreg. 291/C5
Coal (butte), Utah 304/C5
Coal (creek), Wash. 310/G3
Coal (riv.), W. Va. 312/C6
Coal Bluff, Ind. (†47874) 227/C5
Coal Branch, New Bruns. 170/E2
Coalburn, Scotland 15/E5
Coal City, Ill. (60416) 222/E2
Coal City, Ind. (47427) 227/D6
Coal City, W. Va. (25823) 312/D7
Coalcomán de Matamoros, Mexico 150/H7
Coal Creek, Alaska (†99701) 196/K1
Coal Creek, Colo. (81221) 208/J6
Coal Creek, Ind. (†47932) 227/C4
Coal Creek, New Bruns. 170/E2
Coaldale, Alberta 182/D5
Coaldale, Colo. (81222) 208/H6
Coaldale, Nev. (†89049) 266/D4
Coaldale, Pa. (18218) 294/L4
Coaldale (Six Mile Run), Pa. (16679) 294/F5
Coalfield, Tenn. (37719) 237/N8
Coalfield, Wash. (†98055) 310/B2
Coal Fork, W. Va. (25306) 312/D6
Coalgate, Okla. (74538) 288/O5
Coal Grove, Ohio (†45638) 284/E9
Coal Harbour, Br. Col. 184/D5
Coal Hill, Ark. (72832) 202/C3
Coalhurst, Alberta 182/D5
Coaling, Ala. (35449) 195/D4
Coalinga, Calif. (93210) 204/E7
Coalisland, N. Ireland 17/H2
Coalmont, Br. Col. 184/G5
Coalmont, Colo. (80430) 208/F1
Coalmont, Ind. (47845) 227/C6
Coalmont, Tenn. (37313) 237/K10
Coalport, Pa. (16627) 294/E4
Coalridge, Mont. (†59219) 262/M2
Coal Run, Ky. (†41501) 237/R5
Coalspur, Alberta 182/B3
Coalton, Ill. (†62075) 222/D4
Coalton, Ohio (45621) 284/E7
Coalton, W. Va. (26257) 312/G5
Coal Valley, Alberta 182/B3
Coal Valley, Ill. (61240) 222/C2
Coalville, England 13/F5
Coalville, Iowa (†50501) 229/E4
Coalville, Utah (84017) 304/C3
Coalwood, Mont. (†59351) 262/L5
Coalwood, W. Va. (24824) 312/C8
Coambo, Angola 115/C5
Coambo, Angola 102/D5
Coamo, P. Rico 161/D2
Coamo, P. Rico 156/G1
Coamo (res.), P. Rico 161/D3
Coamo (riv.), P. Rico 161/D3
Coari, Brazil 120/C3
Coari, Brazil 132/H9
Coarsegold, Calif. (93614) 204/F6
Coast (mts.) 162/C4
Coast (ranges) 188/B2
Coast (mts.), Alaska 196/N1
Coast (mts.), Br. Col. 146/E4
Coast (mts.), Br. Col. 184/D3
Coast (ranges), Calif. 204/D7
Coast (prov.), Kenya 115/G4
Coast (ranges), Oreg. 291/D5
Coast (ranges), U.S. 146/F5
Coast (ranges), Wash. 310/B3
Coast Guard Academy, Conn. 210/G3
Coatbridge, Scotland 10/B1
Coatbridge, Scotland 15/C2
Coatepec, Mexico 150/P1
Coatepeque, Guatemala 154/A3
Coates, Minn. (†55068) 255/E6
Coatesville, Ind. (46121) 227/D5
Coatesville, Pa. (19320) 294/L5
Coatetelco, Mexico 150/L2
Coaticook, Québec 172/F4
Coatopa, Ala. (35450) 195/B6
Coats, Kansas (67028) 232/D4
Coats, N.C. (27521) 281/M4
Coats (isl.), N.W.T. 162/H3
Coats (isl.), N.W.T. 146/K3
Coats (isl.), N.W. Terrs. 187/K3
Coatsburg, Ill. (62325) 222/B3
Coats Land (reg.), Ant. 2/H10
Coats Land (reg.) 5/B17
Coatsville, Mo. (63535) 261/G1
Coatzacoalcos, Mexico 146/J8
Coatzacoalcos, Mexico 150/M7
Coatzingo, Mexico 150/N2
Cobalt, Conn. (06414) 210/E2
Cobalt, Idaho (83229) 220/D4
Cobalt, Ont. 162/H6
Cobalt, Ontario 177/K5
Cobalt, Ontario 175/D3
Cobalt City, Mo. (†63645) 261/M7
Cobán, Guatemala 154/B3
Cobar, N. S. Wales 88/H6
Cobar, N.S. Wales 97/C2
Cobargo, N.S. Wales 97/E5
Cobb (co.), Georgia 217/C3
Cobb, Georgia (31735) 217/E7
Cobb, Ky. (42405) 237/F6
Cobb (riv.), Minn. 255/E7
Cobb (isl.), Va. 307/S6
Cobb, Wis. (53526) 317/F10
Cobbadah, N.S. Wales 97/F2
Cobble Hill, Br. Col. 184/K3
Cobble Mountain (res.), Mass. 249/C4
Cobbs Creek, Va. (23035) 307/R6
Cobbtown, Georgia (30420) 217/H6
Cobden, Ill. (62920) 222/D6
Cobden, Minn. (†56085) 255/D6
Cobden, Ontario 177/H2
Cobden, Victoria 97/B6
Cobequid (bay), Nova Scotia 168/E3
Cóbh, Ireland 10/B5
Cóbh, Ireland 17/E8
Cobham (riv.), Manitoba 179/G1
Cobham (riv.), Ontario 175/A2
Cobija, Bolivia 136/A2
Cobija, Brazil 120/C4
Coble, Tenn. (†37033) 237/F9
Cobleskill, N.Y. (12043) 276/L5
Coboconk, Ontario 177/F3
Cobourg (pen.), North. Terr. 88/E2
Cobourg (pen.), North. Terr. 93/C1
Cobourg, Ontario 177/F4
Cobquecura, Chile 138/D1
Cobram, Victoria 97/C4
Cobre, Nev. (†89830) 266/G1
Cóbuè, Mozambique 118/F2
Coburg, Iowa (†51566) 229/C7
Coburg (isl.), N.W. Terrs. 187/L2
Coburg, Oreg. (97401) 291/E3
Coburg, Victoria 88/K7
Coburg, Victoria 97/H5
Coburg, W. Germany 22/D3
Coburn, Pa. (16832) 294/H4
Coburn, W. Va. (26562) 312/F3
Coca, Ecuador 128/D3
Cocachacra, Peru 128/G11
Cocagne, New Bruns. 170/F2
Cocagne (isl.), New Bruns. 170/F2
Cocagne (riv.), New Bruns. 170/F2
Cocagne Cape, New Bruns. 170/F2
Cocama, Peru 128/G8
Cocanada (Kakinada), India 68/E5
Cocani, Bolivia 136/B7
Cocapata, Bolivia 136/B5
Cocentaina, Spain 33/F3
Cochabamba (dept.), Bolivia 136/C5
Cochabamba, Bolivia 120/C4
Cochabamba, Bolivia 136/C5
Cochamó, Chile 138/E3
Coche (isl.), Venezuela 124/F2
Cocheco (riv.), N.H. 268/E5
Cochecton, N.Y. (12726) 276/K7
Cochem, W. Germany 22/B3
Cochenour, Ontario 175/B2
Cochetopa (creek), Colo. 208/F6
Cochimbo, Serra do (mts.), Brazil 132/C5
Cochin, Sask. 181/C2
Cochin-Alleppey, India 68/D6
Cochinos (bay), Cuba 158/D2
Cochise (co.), Ariz. 198/F7
Cochise, Ariz. (85606) 198/F6
Cochiti, N. Mex. (†87041) 274/C3
Cochituate, Mass. (01778) 249/A7
Cochituate (lake), Mass. 249/A7
Cochran, Georgia (31014) 217/F6
Cochran (co.), Texas 303/B4
Cochrane, Ala. (†35442) 195/B4
Cochrane, Alberta 182/C4
Cochrane (lake), Chile 138/E7
Cochrane, Cerro (mt.), Chile 138/E7
Cochrane (riv.), Manitoba 179/H2
Cochrane, Ont. 146/K5
Cochrane, Ont. 162/H6
Cochrane (terr. dist.), Ontario 177/J4
Cochrane (terr. dist.), Ontario 175/D2
Cochrane, Ontario 177/K5
Cochrane, Ontario 175/D3
Cochrane (riv.), Sask. 181/N2
Cochrane, Wis. (54622) 317/C7
Cochranton, Pa. (16314) 294/B2
Cochranville, Pa. (19330) 294/L6
Cockburn (chan.), Chile 138/E11
Cockburn (isl.), Ontario 177/A2
Cockburn, S. Australia 94/G5
Cockburn (sound), W. Australia 88/B2
Cockburn Harbour, Turks & Caicos 156/D2
Cockburnspath, Scotland 15/F5
Cocke (co.), Tenn. 237/P9
Cockenoe (isl.), Conn. 210/B4
Cockenzie and Port Seton, Scotland 15/D1
Cockermouth, England 13/D3
Cockermouth, England 10/E3
Cockeysville, Md. (21030) 245/M3
Cockrell Hill, Texas (75211) 303/G2
Cockrum, Miss. (†38632) 256/E1
Coclé del Norte, Panama 154/G6
Coco (chan.), Burma 72/B4
Coco (cay), Cuba 158/G1
Coco (riv.), Honduras 154/E3
Coco (chan.), India 68/G6
Coco (riv.), Nicaragua 154/E3
Coco, W. Va. (†25071) 312/D6
Cocoa, Fla. (32922) 212/F3
Cocoa Beach, Fla. (32931) 212/F3
Cocobeach, Gabon 115/B3
Cocodrie (lake), La. 238/E5
Cocolamus, Pa. (17014) 294/H4
Coconino (co.), Ariz. 198/C3
Coconino (plat.), Ariz. 198/C3
Coconut Creek, Fla. (†33060) 212/F5
Cocopah Ind. Res., Ariz. 198/A6
Cocorit, Mexico 150/E3
Cocos (isls.), Australia 2/P6
Cocos (isls.), Australia 54/L11
Cocos (isl.), C. Rica 146/K9
Cocos (isl.), Guam 86/K7
Cocos (bay), Trin. & Tob. 161/B10
Cocuy, Sierra Nevada del (mts.), Colombia 126/D4
Cod (cape), Mass. 146/M5
Cod (cape), Mass. 188/N2
Cod (cape), Mass. 249/O4
Cod (isl.), Newf. 166/B2
Codajás, Brazil 120/C3
Codajás, Brazil 132/H9
Coddle (harb.), Nova Scotia 168/G3
Codegua, Chile 138/G4
Codell, Kansas (67630) 232/C2
Coden, Ala. (36523) 195/B10
Codera (cape), Venezuela 124/F2
Coderre, Sask. 181/E5
Codesa, Alberta 182/B2
Codes Corner, Ontario 177/H3
Codette, Sask. 181/H2
Codfish (isl.), N. Zealand 100/A7
Codigua, Chile 138/F4
Codington (co.), S. Dak. 298/P4
Codó, Brazil 120/E3
Codó, Brazil 132/E4
Codorus, Pa. (17311) 294/J6
Codpa, Chile 138/B1
Codrington, Ant. & Bar. 156/G3
Codrington, Barbados 161/B8
Codroipo, Italy 34/D2
Codroy, Newf. 166/C4
Cody, Nebr. (69211) 264/C2
Cody, Wyo. (82414) 319/D1
Codys, New Bruns. 170/E3
Coe, Ind. (†47598) 227/C8
Coeburn, Va. (24230) 307/D7
Coe Hill, Ontario 177/G3
Coelemu, Chile 138/D1
Coello, Ill. (62825) 222/D6
Coen, Queensland 88/G2
Coen, Queensland 95/B2
Coeroeni (riv.), Suriname 131/C4
Coesfeld, W. Germany 22/B3
Coesse, Ind. (†46725) 227/G2
Coeur d'Alene, Idaho (83814) 220/B2
Coeur d'Alene, Idaho 188/C1
Coeur d'Alene (lake), Idaho 220/B2
Coeur d'Alene (mts.), Idaho 220/C2
Coeur d'Alene (riv.), Idaho 220/B2
Coevorden, Netherlands 27/K3
Coeymans, N.Y. (12045) 276/N6
Coffee (co.), Ala. 195/G8
Coffee (co.), Georgia 217/G8
Coffee (co.), Tenn. 237/J9
Coffee Creek, Mont. (59424) 262/F3
Coffeen, Ill. (62017) 222/D4
Coffee Springs, Ala. (36318) 195/G8
Coffeeville, Ala. (36524) 195/B7
Coffeeville (dam), Ala. 195/B7
Coffeeville, Miss. (38922) 256/E3
Coffey (co.), Kansas 232/G3
Coffey, Mo. (64636) 261/E2
Coffeyville, Kans. 188/G3
Coffeyville, Kansas (67337) 232/G4
Coffin (bay), S. Australia 94/D6
Coffin Bay (pen.), S. Australia 94/D6
Coffs Harbour, N. S. Wales 88/J6
Coffs Harbour, N.S. Wales 97/G2
Cofield, N.C. (27922) 281/R2
Cogan Station, Pa. (†17728) 294/H3
Cogar, Okla. (†73059) 288/K4
Cogdell, Georgia (31628) 217/G8
Cogealac, Romania 45/J3
Coggon, Iowa (52218) 229/L4
Coghinas (riv.), Italy 34/B4
Cogliano (Hohe Warte) (mt.), Austria 41/B3
Cognac, France 28/C5
Cogolludo, Spain 33/E2
Cogotí, Chile 138/A8
Cogswell, N. Dak. (58017) 282/P7
Cogton, Philippines 82/E6
Cohagen, Mont. (59322) 262/K3
Cohansey (riv.), N.J. 273/C5
Cohasset, Ala. (†36474) 195/E8
Cohasset○, Mass. (02025) 249/F7
Cohasset, Minn. (55721) 255/E3
Cohoctah, Mich. (48816) 250/F6
Cohocton, N.Y. (14826) 276/F5
Cohocton (riv.), N.Y. 276/F6
Cohoe, Alaska (†99669) 196/B1
Cohoes, N.Y. (12047) 276/N5
Cohoni, Bolivia 136/B5
Cohuna, Victoria 97/C4
Cohutta, Georgia (30710) 217/C1
Coiba, Isla de (isl.), Panama 154/F7
Coihaique, Chile 138/E6
Coihaique Alto, Chile 138/E6
Coihueco, Chile 138/A11
Coila, Miss. (38923) 256/E4
Coill Dubh, Ireland 17/H5
Coimbatore, India 54/J8
Coimbatore, India 68/D6
Coimbra (dist.), Portugal 33/B2
Coimbra, Portugal 7/D4
Coimbra, Portugal 33/B2
Coin, Iowa (51636) 229/C7
Coín, Spain 33/D4
Coinco, Chile 138/G5
Coinjock, N.C. (27923) 281/S2
Coipasa, Bolivia 136/A6
Coipasa (lake), Bolivia 136/B6
Coipasa (salt dep.), Bolivia 136/A6
Coire, Loch (lake), Scotland 15/D2
Cojata, Peru 128/H10
Cojedes (state), Venezuela 124/D3
Cojedes (riv.), Venezuela 124/D3
Cojimíes, Ecuador 128/B3
Cojoro, Venezuela 124/C2
Cojutepeque, El Salvador 154/C4
Cokato, Minn. (55321) 255/D5
Coke (co.), Texas 303/D6
Cokeburg, Pa. (15324) 294/B5
Cokedale, Colo. (81032) 208/K8
Coker, Ala. (35452) 195/C4
Cokercreek, Tenn. (37314) 237/N10
Coketon, W. Va. (†26292) 312/G4
Cokeville, Wyo. (83114) 319/B3
Colaba (pt.), India 68/B7
Colac, Victoria 88/G7
Colac, Victoria 97/B6
Colachel, India 68/D7
Colair (lake), India 68/E5
Colamus (riv.), Nebr. 264/E2
Colasay, Peru 128/C5
Colatina, Brazil 120/E4
Colatina, Brazil 132/F7
Colbeck (cape) 5/B10
Colbert (co.), Ala. 195/C1
Colbert, Georgia (30628) 217/F2
Colbert, Okla. (74733) 288/O7
Colbert, Wash. (99005) 310/H3
Colborne, Ontario 177/G4
Colbún, Chile 138/A11
Colburn, Idaho (83865) 220/B1
Colburn, Ind. (47931) 227/D3
Colby, Kansas (67701) 232/A2
Colby, Wash. (†98366) 310/A2
Colby, Wis. (54421) 317/F6
Colcamar, Peru 128/D6
Colchester, Conn. (06415) 210/F2
Colchester○, Conn. (06415) 210/F2
Colchester, England 13/H6
Colchester, England 10/G5
Colchester, Ill. (62326) 222/C3
Colchester (co.), Nova Scotia 168/E3
Colchester, Ontario 177/B6
Colchester○, Vt. (05446) 268/A2
Colcord, Okla. (74338) 288/S2
Colcord, W. Va. (25048) 312/D7
Cold (bay), Alaska 196/F4
Cold (lake), Alberta 182/E2
Cold (riv.), N.H. 268/C5
Cold Bay, Alaska (99571) 196/F3
Cold Brook, N.Y. (13324) 276/L4
Coldbrook Station, Nova Scotia 168/D3
Colden, N.Y. (14033) 276/C5
Coldingham, Scotland 15/F5
Cold Lake, Alberta 182/E2
Cold Spring, Ky. (41076) 237/T2
Cold Spring, Minn. (56320) 255/D5
Cold Spring, N.J. (†08204) 273/D6
Cold Spring (inlet), N.J. 273/D6
Cold Spring, N.Y. (10516) 276/N8
Coldspring (head), Nova Scotia 168/E3
Coldspring, Texas (77331) 303/J7
Cold Spring Harbor, N.Y. (11724) 276/R6
Cold Springs, Okla. (†73564) 288/J5
Coldstream, Br. Col. 184/H5
Cold Stream (pond), Maine 243/G5
Coldstream, New Bruns. 170/C2
Coldstream, Scotland 10/E3
Coldstream, Scotland 15/F5
Coldstream, Victoria 97/K4
Coldwater, Kansas (67029) 232/C4
Coldwater, Mich. (49036) 250/D7
Coldwater, Miss. (38618) 256/E1
Coldwater (riv.), Miss. 256/D1
Coldwater, Ohio (45828) 284/A5
Coldwater, Ontario 177/E3
Coldwater, Tenn. (†37334) 237/H10
Coldwater (creek), Texas 303/B1
Coldwater, W. Va. (†26411) 312/E4
Cole (co.), Mo. 261/H6
Cole (harb.), Nova Scotia 168/E4
Cole, Okla. (†73010) 288/L5
Colebrook○, Conn. (06021) 210/C1
Colebrook, N.H. (03576) 268/E2
Colebrook○, N.H. (03576) 268/E2
Colebrook, Ohio (†44034) 284/J2
Colebrook, Tasmania 99/D4
Colebrook River (lake), Conn. 210/C1
Cole Camp, Mo. (65325) 261/F6
Coleen (riv.), Alaska 196/K1
Colegrove, Pa. (†16749) 294/F2
Coleharbor, N. Dak. (58531) 282/H4
Coleman, Alberta 182/C5
Coleman, Alta. 162/E6
Coleman, Fla. (33521) 212/D3
Coleman, Georgia (31736) 217/C7
Coleman, Mich. (48618) 250/E5
Coleman, Okla. (73432) 288/O6
Coleman (riv.), Queensland 95/B2
Coleman (co.), Texas 303/E6
Coleman, Texas (76834) 303/E6

354 Coleman

Coleman, Wis. (54112) 317/L5
Coleman Falls, Va. (24536) 307/K6
Colemans Lake, Georgia (†30441) 217/H5
Çölemerik, Turkey 63/K4
Colerain, N.C. (27924) 281/R2
Coleraine, Minn. (55722) 255/E3
Coleraine (dist.), N. Ireland 17/H1
Coleraine, N. Ireland 17/H1
Coleraine, N. Ireland 10/C3
Coleraine, Québec 172/F4
Coleraine, Victoria 97/A5
Coleridge, Nebr. (68727) 264/G2
Coleridge (lake), N. Zealand 100/C5
Coleridge, N.C. (27234) 281/K3
Coles (co.), Ill. 222/E4
Coles, Miss. (†39638) 256/C8
Coles (pt.), Peru 128/G11
Colesberg, S. Africa 118/D6
Colesburg, Georgia (†31569) 217/J9
Colesburg, Iowa (52035) 229/L3
Colesburg, Ky. (†40150) 237/K5
Coles Island, New Bruns. 170/E3
Coles Point, Va. (22442) 307/P4
Colesville, Md. (20904) 245/K4
Colesville, N.J. (†07461) 273/D1
Coleta, Ill. (61017) 222/D2
Coleville, Calif. (96107) 204/F5
Coleville, Sask. 181/B4
Colfax, Calif. (95713) 204/E4
Colfax, Ill. (61728) 222/E3
Colfax, Ind. (46035) 227/D4
Colfax, Iowa (50054) 229/G5
Colfax, La. (71417) 238/E3
Colfax (co.), Nebr. 264/G3
Colfax (co.), N. Mex. 274/E2
Colfax, N. Dak. (58018) 282/S7
Colfax, Sask. 181/H6
Colfax, Wash. (99111) 310/H4
Colfax, Wis. (54730) 317/C6
Colgan, N. Dak. (†58844) 282/C2
Colgate, N. Dak. (†58046) 282/P5
Colgate (cape), N.W. Terrs. 187/J1
Colgate, Sask. 181/H6
Colgate, Wis. (53017) 317/K1
Colhué Huapi (lake), Argentina 143/C6
Co Lieu, Vietnam 72/E3
Colignan, Victoria 97/B4
Colijnsplaat, Netherlands 27/D5
Colima (state), Mexico 150/G7
Colima, Mexico 150/H7
Colina, Chile 138/G3
Colina (riv.), Chile 138/G3
Colinas, Brazil 132/F4
Colinet, Newf. 166/D2
Colington, N.C. (†27949) 281/T3
Colinton, Alberta 182/D2
Coll, Scotland 15/B2
Coll (isl.), Scotland 15/B4
Coll (isl.), Scotland 10/C2
Collaguasi, Chile 138/B3
Collamer, Ind. (†46787) 227/F2
Collarenebri, N.S. Wales 97/E1
Collbran, Colo. (81624) 208/C4
Colle di Val d'Elsa, Italy 34/C3
College, Alaska (99701) 196/J1
College Bridge, New Bruns. 170/F3
College City, Ark. (72476) 202/J1
College Corner, Ohio (45003) 284/A6
Collegedale, Tenn. (37315) 237/M10
College Grove, Tenn. (37046) 237/H9
College Heights, Alberta 182/D3
College Hill, Ky. (40416) 237/N5
College Hill, Miss. (†38655) 256/E2
College Mound, Mo. (†65247) 261/G3
College Park, Georgia (30337) 217/K2
College Park, Md. (20740) 245/G4
College Place, Wash. (99324) 310/G4
College Springs, Iowa (51637) 229/C7
College Station, Texas (77840) 303/H7
Collegeville, Ind. (47978) 227/C3
Collegeville, Minn. (56321) 255/D5
Collegeville, Pa. (19426) 294/M5
Colle Sestriere, Italy 34/A2
Colleton (co.), S.C. 296/F6
Collett, Ind. (†47371) 227/H4
Collette, New Bruns. 170/E2
Collettsville, N.C. (28611) 281/F3
Colley, Pa. (†18614) 294/K2
Colleyville, Texas (76034) 303/F2
Collie, Australia 87/B9
Collie, N.S. Wales 97/E2
Collie, W. Australia 88/B6
Collie, W. Australia 92/B2
Collier (co.), Fla. 212/E5
Collier (bay), W. Australia 88/C3
Collier (bay), W. Australia 92/C1
Colliers, Newf. 166/D2
Colliers, S.C. (†29838) 296/C4
Colliers, W. Va. (26035) 312/E2
Collierstown, Va. (†24450) 307/J5
Collierville, Tenn. (38017) 237/B10
Colliguay, Chile 138/F3
Collin (co.), Texas 303/H4
Collingdale, Pa. (19023) 294/N7
Collingswood, N.J. (08108) 273/B3
Collingsworth (co.), Texas 303/D3
Collingwood, N. Zealand 100/D4
Collingwood, Ontario 177/D3
Collingwood, Victoria 97/J5
Collingwood, Victoria 88/L7
Collingwood Corner, Nova Scotia 168/E3
Collins, Ark. (71634) 202/G6
Collins, Georgia (30421) 217/H6
Collins, Iowa (50055) 229/G5
Collins, Miss. (39428) 256/E7
Collins, Mo. (64738) 261/E7
Collins, Mont. (†59433) 262/E3
Collins, N.Y. (14034) 276/C6
Collins (head), Norfolk I. 88/L6
Collins, Ohio (44826) 284/E3
Collins, Ontario 177/G4
Collins (riv.), Tenn. 237/K9
Collins Bay, Ontario 177/H3
Collins Bay, Sask. 181/M2
Collins Center, N.Y. (14035) 276/C6
Collinston, La. (71229) 238/G1
Collinston, Utah (84306) 304/B2
Collinsville, Ala. (35961) 195/G2
Collinsville, Calif. (†94585) 204/L1
Collinsville, Conn. (06022) 210/D1
Collinsville, Ill. (62234) 222/B2
Collinsville, Mass. (†01826) 249/J2
Collinsville, Miss. (39325) 256/G6
Collinsville, Ohio (45004) 284/A6
Collinsville, Okla. (74021) 288/P2
Collinsville, Queensland 88/H4
Collinsville, Queensland 95/C4
Collinsville, Va. (24078) 307/J7
Collinwood, Tenn. (38450) 237/F10
Collipulli, Chile 138/E2
Collirene, Ala. (†36785) 195/E6
Collis, Minn. (†56236) 255/B5
Collison, Ill. (61831) 222/F3
Collista, Ky. (†41222) 237/R5
Collombey-Muraz, Switzerland 39/C4
Collon, Ireland 17/J4
Collon (mt.), Switzerland 39/D5
Collonge-Bellerive, Switzerland 39/B4
Collooney, Ireland 17/E3
Collpa, Bolivia 136/C6
Collyer, Kansas (67631) 232/B2
Colma, Calif. (94014) 204/J2
Colman, S. Dak. (57017) 298/R6
Colmar, France 28/G3
Colmar, Pa. (18915) 294/M5
Colmar Manor, Md. (†20722) 245/F4
Colmenar, Spain 33/D4
Colmenar de Oreja, Spain 33/G5
Colmenar Viejo, Spain 33/F4
Colmesneil, Texas (75938) 303/K7
Colmonell, Scotland 15/D5
Colne, England 10/G1
Colne, England 13/H1
Colne (riv.), England 10/B5
Colne (riv.), England 13/G8
Colne Valley, England 10/G2
Colne Valley, England 13/J2
Colo, Iowa (50056) 229/G4
Colo (riv.), N.S. Wales 97/F3
Cologne, Minn. (55322) 255/E6
Cologne, N.J. (08213) 273/D4
Cologne, W. Germany 7/E3
Cologne, W. Germany 22/B3
Coloma, Calif. (95613) 204/D5
Coloma, Mich. (49038) 250/C6
Coloma, Wis. (54930) 317/H7
Colombes, France 28/A1
Colombia 2/F5
Colombia 120/B2
COLOMBIA 126
Colombia, Colombia 126/C6
Colombo (cap.), Sri Lanka 54/J9
Colombo (cap.), Sri Lanka 2/N5
Colombo (cap.), Sri Lanka 68/D7
Colome, S. Dak. (57528) 298/K7
Colón, Buenos Aires, Argentina 143/F6
Colón, Entre Ríos, Argentina 143/G6
Colón, Colombia 120/B1
Colón, Colombia 126/B7
Colón, Cuba 158/D1
Colón, Cuba 156/B2
Colón, Archipiélago de (terr.), Ecuador 128/C8
Colón (mts.), Honduras 154/E3
Colón, Mexico 150/K6
Colon, Mich. (49040) 250/D7
Colon, Nebr. (68018) 264/H3
Colón, Pan. 146/K9
Colón, Panama 154/H6
Colón, Isla de (isl.), Panama 154/G6
Colón, Lavalleja, Uruguay 145/E4
Colón, Montevideo, Uruguay 145/B7
Colón, Venezuela 124/E6
Colona, Colo. (†81401) 208/D6
Colona, Ill. (61241) 222/C2
Colonarie, St. Vin. & Grens. 161/A9
Colonarie (pt.), St. Vin. & Grens. 161/A9
Colonel Light Gardens, S. Australia 88/D8
Colonel Light Gardens, S. Australia 94/A8
Colonia, N.J. (07067) 273/E2
Colonia (dept.), Uruguay 145/B5
Colonia, Uruguay 145/B5
Colonia Agraciada, Uruguay 145/A4
Colonia Arrué, Uruguay 145/B5
Colonia Artigas, Uruguay 145/B1
Colonia Concordia, Uruguay 145/A4
Colonia Elisa, Argentina 143/E2
Colonia Itacumbú, Uruguay 145/B1
Colonia Josefa, Argentina 143/D4
Colonia Las Heras, Argentina 143/C6
Colonia Lavalleja, Uruguay 145/C2
Colonial Beach, Va. (22443) 307/P4
Colonial Heights, Tenn. (37663) 237/R8
Colonial Heights (I.C.), Va. (23834) 307/O6
Colonial Nat'l Hist. Park, Va. 307/P6
Colonia Neuland, Paraguay 144/B3
Colonia Palma, Uruguay 145/B1
Colonia Pte. Stroessner, Paraguay 144/D3
Colonia Rossel y Rius, Uruguay 145/D4
Colonias, N. Mex. (†88435) 274/E3
Colonia San Alfredo, Paraguay 144/D3
Colonia Sgto. José E. López, Paraguay 144/D3
Colonia Valdense, Uruguay 145/B5
Colonia Yby Yu, Paraguay 144/E3
Colonie, N.Y. (†12201) 276/N5
Colonne (cape), Italy 34/F5
Colonsay, Sask. 181/F4
Colonsay (isl.), Scotland 10/C2
Colonsay (isl.), Scotland 15/B4
Colony, Kansas (66015) 232/G3
Colony, Mo. (†63563) 261/H2
Colony, Okla. (73021) 288/J4
Colony, Wyo. (†57717) 319/H1
Colora, Md. (21917) 245/O2
Colorada (lag.), Bolivia 136/A8
Colorado 188/E3
COLORADO 208
Colorado (riv.) 188/D4
Colorado (riv.), Argentina 2/F5
Colorado (riv.), Argentina 120/C6
Colorado (riv.), Argentina 143/D4
Colorado (riv.), Ariz. 198/A5
Colorado (riv.), Calif. 204/L8
Colorado (riv.), Colo. 208/A5
Colorado (riv.), Mexico 150/B1
Colorado, Arroyo (riv.), N. Mex. 274/B4
Colorado (co.), Texas 303/H8
Colorado (riv.), Texas 188/G4
Colorado (riv.), Texas 146/H6
Colorado (riv.), Texas 303/F7
Colorado (state), U.S. 146/H6
Colorado (riv.), U.S. 146/G6
Colorado (riv.), U.S. 2/D4
Colorado (riv.), Utah 304/E5
Colorado City, Ariz. (86021) 198/B2
Colorado City, Colo. (81019) 208/K6
Colorado City, Texas (79512) 303/C5
Colorado Nat'l Mon., Colo. 208/B4
Colorado River Aqueduct, Calif. 204/K10
Colorado River Ind. Res., Ariz. 198/A5
Colorado River Ind. Res., Calif. 204/L10
Colorados, Los (arch.), Cuba 158/A1
Colorado Springs, Colo. 146/H6
Colorado Springs, Colo. 188/F3
Colorado Springs, Colo. (*80901) 208/K5
Colored Hill, W. Va. (†24740) 312/D8
Colotlán, Mexico 150/H5
Colp, Ill. (62921) 222/D6
Colpoy (bay), Ontario 177/C3
Colpoys Bay, Ontario 177/C3
Colquechaca, Bolivia 136/B6
Colquiri, Bolivia 136/B5
Colquitt (co.), Georgia 217/E8
Colquitt, Georgia (31737) 217/C8
Colrain○, Mass. (01340) 249/D2
Colson, Ky. (†41858) 237/R6
Colstrip, Mont. (59323) 262/K5
Colt, Ark. (72326) 202/J3
Coltauco, Chile 138/F5
Colton, Calif. (92324) 204/E10
Colton, N.Y. (13625) 276/L1
Colton, Ohio (43510) 284/C3
Colton, Oreg. (97017) 291/B3
Colton, S. Dak. (57018) 298/P6
Colton, Utah (†84601) 304/C4
Colton, Wash. (99113) 310/H4
Coltons Point, Md. (20626) 245/M8
Colts Neck, N.J. (07722) 273/E3
Coluene (riv.), Brazil 120/D4
Columbia (riv.) 188/B1
Columbia, Ala. (36319) 195/H8
Columbia (glac.), Alaska 196/C1
Columbia (mt.), Alberta 182/B3
Columbia (co.), Ark. 202/D7
Columbia (lake), Br. Col. 184/K5
Columbia (mt.), Br. Col. 184/J4
Columbia (riv.), Br. Col. 184/H4
Columbia, Calif. (95310) 204/E5
Columbia (cape), Canada 4/A13
Columbia○, Conn. (06237) 210/F2
Columbia (co.), Fla. 212/D1
Columbia, Fla. (†32055) 212/D1
Columbia (co.), Georgia 217/H3
Columbia, Ill. (62236) 222/C5
Columbia, Iowa (50057) 229/G6
Columbia, Ky. (42728) 237/L6
Columbia, La. (71418) 238/F2
Columbia○, Maine (†04623) 243/H6
Columbia, Md. (21043) 245/L4
Columbia, Miss. (39429) 256/E8
Columbia, Mo. (65201) 261/H5
Columbia, Mo. 188/H3
Columbia, N.J. (07832) 273/C2
Columbia (co.), N.Y. 276/N6
Columbia, N.C. (27925) 281/S3
Columbia (cape), N.W.T. 162/N3
Columbia (cape), N.W. Terrs. 187/M1
Columbia (co.), Oreg. 291/D2
Columbia (riv.), Oreg. 291/G2
Columbia (co.), Pa. 294/K3
Columbia, Pa. (17512) 294/K5
Columbia (cap.), S.C. 146/K6
Columbia (cap.), S.C. 188/K4
Columbia (cap.), S.C. (*29201) 296/F4
Columbia, S. Dak. (57433) 298/N2
Columbia, Tenn. 188/J3
Columbia, Tenn. (38401) 237/G9
Columbia (riv.), U.S. 146/F5
Columbia, Utah (†84501) 304/D4
Columbia, Va. (23038) 307/M5
Columbia (co.), Wash. 310/H4
Columbia (riv.), Wash. 310/B4
Columbia (co.), Wis. 317/H9
Columbia City, Ind. (46725) 227/G2
Columbia City, Oreg. (97018) 291/E2
Columbia Falls○, Maine (04623) 243/H6
Columbia Falls, Mont. (59912) 262/B2
Columbia Furnace, Va. (†22824) 307/L3
Columbia Heights, Minn. (55421) 255/G5
Columbia Heights, Wash. (†98632) 310/C4
Columbiana, Ala. (35051) 195/E4
Columbiana (co.), Ohio 284/J4
Columbiana, Ohio (44408) 284/J4
Columbia Road (res.), S. Dak. 298/N2
Columbia Station, Ohio (44028) 284/G10
Columbiaville, Mich. (48421) 250/F5
Columbine, Colo. (†80428) 208/E1
Columbretes (isls.), Spain 33/G3
Columbus (dam), 256/H3
Columbus, Ark. (71831) 202/C6
Columbus, Ga. 188/K4
Columbus, Ga. 146/K6
Columbus, Georgia (*31901) 217/C6
Columbus, Ill. (62328) 222/B4
Columbus, Ind. (47201) 227/E6
Columbus, Kansas (66725) 232/H4
Columbus, Ky. (42032) 237/C7
Columbus, Miss. 188/J4
Columbus, Miss. (39701) 256/H3
Columbus, Mont. (59019) 262/G5
Columbus, Nebr. (68601) 264/G3
Columbus, N.J. (08022) 273/D3
Columbus, N. Mex. (88029) 274/B7
Columbus (co.), N.C. 281/M6
Columbus, N.C. (28722) 281/E4
Columbus, N. Dak. (58727) 282/E2
Columbus (cap.), Ohio 188/K3
Columbus (cap.), Ohio 146/K6
Columbus (cap.), Ohio (*43201) 284/E6
Columbus, Pa. (16405) 294/C2
Columbus, Texas (78934) 303/H8
Columbus, Wis. (53925) 317/J9
Columbus A.F.B., Miss. 256/H3
Columbus City, Iowa (52737) 229/L6
Columbus Grove, Ohio (45830) 284/B4
Columbus Junction, Iowa (52738) 229/L6
Columbus Salt (marsh), Nev. 266/C4
Colusa (co.), Calif. 204/C4
Colusa, Calif. (95932) 204/C4
Colusa, Ill. (62329) 222/B3
Colver, Pa. (15927) 294/E4
Colville (riv.), Alaska 188/C5
Colville (riv.), Alaska 196/G1
Colville (cape), N. Zealand 100/E2
Colville (bay), N.W. Terrs. 187/K3
Colville (lake), N.W. Terrs. 187/F3
Colville, Wash. (99114) 310/H2
Colville (riv.), Wash. 310/H2
Colville Ind. Res., Wash. 310/G2
Colville Lake, N.W. Terrs. 187/F3
Colwell, Iowa (50620) 229/H2
Colwich, Kansas (67030) 232/E4
Colwyn, Pa. (†19023) 294/N7
Colwyn Bay, Wales 10/E4
Colwyn Bay, Wales 13/D4
Comacchio, Italy 34/D2
Comai, China 77/D6
Comal (co.), Texas 303/F8
Comala, Mexico 150/H7
Comalapa, Guatemala 154/B3
Comalapa, Nicaragua 154/E4
Comalcalco, Mexico 150/N7
Comanche (co.), Kansas 232/C4
Comanche, Mont. (†59015) 262/H4
Comanche (co.), Okla. 288/K5
Comanche, Okla. (73529) 288/L6
Comanche (co.), Texas 303/F5
Comanche, Texas (76442) 303/F6
Comandante Fontana, Argentina 143/D2
Comandante Luis Piedrabuena, Argentina 143/C6
Comanești, Romania 45/H2
Comarapa, Bolivia 136/C5
Comayagua, Honduras 154/D3
Combahee (riv.), S.C. 296/F6
Combarbalá, Chile 138/A8
Comber, N. Ireland 17/K2
Comber, Ontario 177/B5
Combermere (bay), Burma 72/B3
Combermere, Ontario 177/G2
Combine, Texas (†75159) 303/H3
Combined Locks, Wis. (54113) 317/K7
Comblain-au-Pont, Belgium 27/G8
Combourg, France 28/C3
Comboyne, N.S. Wales 97/G2
Combs, Ark. (72721) 202/C2
Combs, Ky. (41729) 237/P6
Comb Wash (creek), Utah 304/E6
Comeauville, Nova Scotia 168/B4
Come By Chance, Newf. 166/C2
Come-by-Chance, N.S. Wales 97/E2
Comendador, Dom. Rep. 158/C6
Comer, Ala. (†36053) 195/H6
Comer, Georgia (30629) 217/F2
Comeragh (mts.), Ireland 17/F7
Comerford (dam), N.H. 268/D3
Comerford (dam), Vt. 268/D3
Comerío, P. Rico 161/D2
Comet (riv.), Queensland 88/H4
Comet (riv.), Queensland 95/D5
Comfort, N.C. (28522) 281/O5
Comfort (cape), N.W. Terrs. 187/K3
Comfort, Texas (78013) 303/F7
Comfrey, Minn. (56019) 255/D6
Comilla, Bangladesh 68/G4
Comines, Belgium 27/B7
Comino (isl.), Malta 34/E7
Comins, Mich. (48619) 250/E4
Comiso, Italy 34/E6
Comitán de Domínguez, Mexico 150/O8
Comite, La. (†70739) 238/K1
Commack, N.Y. (11725) 276/O9
Commentry, France 28/E4
Commerce, Calif. (90040) 204/C10
Commerce, Georgia (30529) 217/E2
Commerce, Mo. (63742) 261/O8
Commerce, Okla. (74339) 288/R1
Commerce, Texas (75428) 303/J4
Commerce City, Colo. (80022) 208/K3
Commercial Point, Ohio (43116) 284/E6
Commercy, France 28/F3
Commewijne (dist.), Suriname 131/D3
Commewijne (riv.), Suriname 131/D3
Commiskey, Ind. (47227) 227/F7
Commissaires (lake), Québec 172/E1
Commissioner (isl.), Manitoba 179/E2
Committee (bay), N.W.T. 162/H2
Committee (bay), N.W. Terrs. 187/K3
Commodore, Pa. (15729) 294/D4
Commodore (reef), Philippines 85/F4
Commonwealth, Wis. (†54121) 317/K4
Communism (mt.), U.S.S.R. 54/J6
Communism (peak), U.S.S.R. 48/H6
Como, Colo. (80432) 208/H4
Como (prov.), Italy 34/B2
Como, Italy 7/E4
Como, Italy 34/B2
Como (lake), Italy 34/B1
Como, La. (†71295) 238/G2
Como, Miss. (38619) 256/E1
Como, N.C. (27818) 281/P1
Como, Tenn. (38223) 237/E8
Como, Texas (75431) 303/J4
Como, Wis. (†53147) 317/K10
Comodoro Rivadavia, Argentina 143/C6
Comodoro Rivadavia, Argentina 120/C7
Comoé (riv.), Ivory Coast 106/D7
Comoé (riv.), Upper Volta 106/D7
Comorin (cape), India 54/J9
Comorin (cape), India 2/N5
Comorin (cape), India 68/D7
Comoros 2/M6
Comoros 102/G6
COMOROS 118/G2
Comox, Br. Col. 184/H2
Compañero, Arroyo (creek), N. Mex. 274/B2
Compass Lake, Fla. (32448) 212/D6
Compeer, Alberta 182/E4
Compiègne, France 28/E3
Compostela, Mexico 150/G6
Comprida (isl.), Brazil 135/C4
Comptche, Calif. (95427) 204/B4
Compton, Calif. (*90220) 204/C11
Compton, Ill. (61318) 222/D2
Compton, Md. (20627) 245/M7
Compton (co.), Québec 172/F4
Compton, Québec 172/F4
Comrie, Scotland 15/E4
Comstock, Mich. (49041) 250/D6
Comstock, Minn. (56525) 255/B4
Comstock, Nebr. (68828) 264/E3
Comstock, N.Y. (12821) 276/O4
Comstock, Texas (78837) 303/C8
Comstock, Wis. (54826) 317/C5
Comstocks Bridge, Conn. (†06424) 210/F2
Comté (riv.), Fr. Guiana 131/E3
Comunidad, Venezuela 124/E6
Cona, China 77/D6
Conaica, Peru 128/E9
Conakry (cap.), Guinea 102/A4
Conanicut (isl.), R.I. 249/J6
Conara Junction, Tasmania 99/D3
Conargo, N.S. Wales 97/C4
Conasauga, Tenn. (37316) 237/M10
Conasauga (riv.), Tenn. 237/M11
Concarneau, France 28/A4
Conceição da Barra, Brazil 132/G7
Conceição do Araguaia, Brazil 132/D5
Conceição do Araguaia, Brazil 120/D3
Concepción, Corrientes, Argentina 143/E2
Concepción, Tucumán, Argentina 143/C2
Concepción, El Beni, Bolivia 136/B2
Concepción, Santa Cruz, Bolivia 136/D5
Concepción (lag.), Bolivia 136/E5
Concepción, Chile 138/D1
Concepción, Chile 120/B6
Concepción (chan.), Chile 138/D9
Concepción (bay), Mexico 150/D3
Concepción (dept.), Paraguay 144/D3
Concepción, Paraguay 144/D3
Concepción, Paraguay 120/D5
Concepción, Peru 128/E8
Concepcion, Texas (78349) 303/F10
Concepción de la Sierra, Argentina 143/E2
Concepción del Oro, Mexico 150/J4
Concepción del Uruguay, Argentina 143/G6
Concepción de María, Honduras 154/D4
Conception (pt.), Calif. 188/B4
Conception (pt.), Calif. 204/E9
Conception (bay), Newf. 166/D2
Conception Harbour, Newf. 166/D2
Conception Junction, Mo. (64434) 261/C2
Conchas (res.), N. Mex. 188/F3
Conchas (dam), N. Mex. 274/E3
Conchas (lake), N. Mex. 274/E3
Conchas (riv.), N. Mex. 274/E3
Conchas Dam, N. Mex. (88416) 274/E3
Conche, Newf. 166/C3
Conchi, Chile 138/B3
Conchillas, Uruguay 145/B5
Conchi Viejo, Chile 138/B3
Concho, Ariz. (85924) 198/F4
Concho, Okla. (73022) 288/L3
Concho (co.), Texas 303/E6
Conchos (riv.), Mexico 146/H7
Conchos (riv.), Mexico 150/G2
Concise, Switzerland 39/C3
Concón, Chile 138/F2
Conconully, Wash. (98819) 310/F2
Concord, Ark. (72523) 202/G2
Concord, Calif. (*94520) 204/K1
Concord, Del. (†19973) 245/R6
Concord, Fla. (†32333) 212/B1
Concord, Georgia (30206) 217/D4
Concord, Ill. (62631) 222/C4
Concord, Ky. (41131) 237/P3
Concord○, Mass. (01742) 249/B6
Concord (riv.), Mass. 249/J2
Concord, Mich. (49237) 250/E6
Concord, Mo. (†63128) 261/P4
Concord, Nebr. (68728) 264/H2
Concord (cap.), N.H. 146/L5
Concord (cap.), N.H. 188/M2
Concord (cap.), N.H. (03301) 268/D5
Concord, N. S. Wales 88/K4
Concord, N.S. Wales 97/J3
Concord, N.C. (28025) 281/H4
Concord, Pa. (17217) 294/G5
Concord, Tenn. (37720) 237/N9
Concord○, Vt. (05824) 268/D3
Concord, Va. (24538) 307/K6
Concord, Wis. (†53066) 317/H1
Concordia, Argentina 143/G5
Concordia, Argentina 120/D6
Concórdia, Brazil 132/D9
Concordia, Honduras 154/D3
Concordia, Kansas (66901) 232/E2
Concordia, Ky. (†40157) 237/J4
Concordia (par.), La. 238/G4
Concordia, Mexico 150/G5
Concordia, Mo. (64020) 261/E5
Concordia, Peru 128/E5
Concordville, Pa. (19331) 294/M6
Concrete, N. Dak. (58221) 282/P2
Concrete, Wash. (98237) 310/D2
Con Cuong, Vietnam 72/E3
Conda, Idaho (83230) 220/G7
Condado, Cuba 158/E2
Condamine (riv.), Queensland 88/H5
Condamine (riv.), Queensland 95/D5
Condar, Colombia 126/D8
Conde, Brazil 132/G5
Conde, S. Dak. (57434) 298/N3
Condega, Nicaragua 154/D4
Condit, Ohio (†43074) 284/E5
Condo, Bolivia 136/B6
Condoblin, N.S. Wales 97/D3
Condobolin, N. S. Wales 88/H6
Condom, France 28/D6
Condon, Mont. (59826) 262/C3
Condon, Oreg. (97823) 291/G2
Condor, Alberta 182/C3
Cóndor, Cordillera del (range), Ecuador 128/C5
Cóndor, Cordillera del (range), Peru 128/C5
Condoto, Colombia 126/B5
Cone, Texas (79321) 303/C4
Conecuh (co.), Ala. 195/E8
Conecuh (riv.), Ala. 195/D8
Conegliano, Italy 34/D2
Conehatta, Miss. (39057) 256/F6
Conejos (co.), Colo. 208/G8
Conejos, Colo. (81129) 208/G8
Conejos (peak), Colo. 208/G8
Conejos (riv.), Colo. 208/G8
Conemaugh (riv.), Pa. 294/D5
Conemaugh River (lake), Pa. 294/D4
Conestee, S.C. (29636) 296/C2
Conestoga, Pa. (17516) 294/K6
Conesus, N.Y. (14435) 276/E5
Conesus (lake), N.Y. 276/E5
Conesville, Iowa (52739) 229/L6
Conesville, Ohio (43811) 284/G5
Conetoe, N.C. (27819) 281/O3
Conewango, N.Y. (†14726) 276/C6
Conewango (creek), N.Y. 276/B6
Conewango (creek), Pa. 294/D1
Confidence, Iowa (†52569) 229/G7
Confluence, Ky. (41730) 237/P6
Confluence, Pa. (15424) 294/D6
Confolens, France 28/D4
Confusion (range), Utah 304/A4
Confuso (riv.), Paraguay 144/C4
Cong, Ireland 17/C4
Congamond (lakes), Conn. 210/E1
Congamond (lakes), Mass. 249/D4
Congaree (riv.), S.C. 296/F4
Congaree Nat'l Mon., S.C. 296/F4
Conger, Minn. (56020) 255/E7
Conger (range), N.W. Terrs. 187/K1
Congerville, Ill. (61729) 222/D3
Conghua, China 77/H7
Congleton, England 13/H2
Congo 2/K6
Congo 102/D5
Congo (riv.) 102/D5
Congo (riv.) 2/L5
Congo (riv.), Angola 115/C4
CONGO 115/C3
Congo (riv.), Congo 115/C4
Congo, Ohio (†43730) 284/F6
Congo (riv.), Zaire 115/C4
Congonhas, Brazil 135/E2
Congress, Ariz. (85332) 198/C4
Congress, Ohio (†44287) 284/F4
Congress, Sask. 181/E6
Congress Heights, D.C. (20032) 245/F5
Cónico, Cerro (mt.), Argentina 143/B5
Cónico, Cerro (mt.), Chile 138/E4
Conimicut, R.I. (02889) 249/J6
Coningsby, England 13/G4
Coniston, North. Terr. 93/C7
Conjuror (bay), N.W. Terrs. 187/G3
Conklin, Alberta 182/E2
Conklin, Mich. (49403) 250/D5
Conley, Georgia (30027) 217/K2
Conn, Lough (lake), Ireland 10/B3
Conn (lake), Ireland 17/C3
Conn (lake), N.W. Terrs. 187/L2
Connacht (prov.), Ireland 17/C4
Connacht (trad. prov.), Ireland 17
Connah's Quay, Wales 13/G2
Connaught Heights, Sask. 181/G3
Conneaut, Ohio (44030) 284/J2
Conneaut Lake, Pa. (16316) 294/B2
Conneaut Lake Park, Pa. (16316) 294/B2
Conneautville, Pa. (16406) 294/A2
Connecticut 188/M2
Connecticut (riv.) 188/M2
CONNECTICUT 210
Connecticut (riv.), Conn. 210/E2
Connecticut (riv.), Mass. 249/D2
Connecticut (riv.), N.H. 268/B6
Connecticut (state), U.S. 146/L5
Connecticut (riv.), Vt. 268/C4
Connel, Scotland 15/C4
Connell, New Bruns. 170/C2
Connell, Wash. (99326) 310/G4
Connell Creek, Sask. 181/H2
Connellsville, Pa. (15425) 294/C5
Connellys Springs, N.C. (28612) 281/F3
Connelsville, Mo. (†63559) 261/G2
Connemara (dist.), Ireland 17/B5
Conner, Mont. (59827) 262/B5
Conner (mt.), North. Terr. 93/B8
Connersville, Ind. (47331) 227/G5
Connerville, Okla. (74836) 288/N6
Connétable (isls.), Fr. Guiana 131/F3
Connoquenessing, Pa. (16027) 294/B4
Connors, New Bruns. 170/B1
Conoble, N.S. Wales 97/C3
Conococheague (creek), Md. 245/G1
Cononbridge, Scotland 15/D3
Conover, N.C. (28613) 281/G3
Conover, Ohio (45317) 284/B5
Conover, Wis. (54519) 317/H3
Conowingo, Md. (21918) 245/O2
Conowingo (dam), Md. 245/O2
Conquerall Bank, Nova Scotia 168/D4
Conquest, Sask. 181/D4
Conquista, Bolivia 136/B2
Conrad, Alberta 182/D5
Conrad, Iowa (50631) 229/H4
Conrad, Mont. (59425) 262/E2
Conrad, Pa. (†16720) 294/G2
Conran, Mo. (63873) 261/N10
Conrath, Wis. (54731) 317/E5

Cotonou 355

Conroe, Texas (*77301) 303/J7
Conroy, Iowa (52220) 229/J5
Consecon, Ontario 177/G3
Conselheiro Lafaiete, Brazil 135/E2
Conselheiro Lafaiete, Brazil 132/E8
Consett, England 13/H3
Conshohocken, Pa. (19428) 294/M5
Consolación del Norte, Cuba 158/B1
Consolación del Sur, Cuba 158/B2
Consolación del Sur, Cuba 156/A2
Consort, Alberta 182/E3
Constable, N.Y. (12926) 276/M1
Constableville, N.Y. (13325) 276/J3
Constance (lake), Austria 41/A3
Constance, Ky. (41009) 237/R2
Constance, Sask. 181/F6
Constance (lake), Switzerland 39/H1
Constance (mt.), Wash. 310/B3
Constance (lake), W. Germany 22/C5
Constancia, Uruguay 145/B3
Constant, Morne (hill), Guadeloupe 161/B7
Constanţa, Romania 7/G4
Constanţa, Romania 45/J3
Constantia, N.Y. (13044) 276/H4
Constantia, S. Africa 118/E6
Constantina, Spain 33/D4
Constantine (cape), Alaska 196/G3
Constantine, Algeria 102/C1
Constantine, Algeria 106/F1
Constantine, Mich. (49042) 250/D7
Constanza, Argentina 143/G6
Constanza, Dom. Rep. 158/D6
Constitución, Chile 138/A11
Constitución, Uruguay 145/A2
Constitution, Georgia 217/K2
Constitution, Ohio (45722) 284/G7
Consuegra, Spain 33/E3
Consul, Ala. (†36783) 195/C6
Consul, Sask. 181/B6
Contact, Nev. (†89825) 266/G1
Contamana, Peru 128/E6
Contas (riv.), Brazil 132/F6
Contentnea (creek), N.C. 281/N3
Conthey, Switzerland 39/D4
Continental, Ariz. (†85640) 198/D7
Continental, Ohio (45831) 284/B3
Continental (peak), Wyo. 319/D3
Contla, Mexico 150/N1
Contoocook, N.H. (03229) 268/D5
Contoocook (riv.), N.H. 268/D6
Contra Costa (co.), Calif. 204/D6
Contramaestre, Cuba 158/G3
Contratación, Colombia 126/D4
Contrecoeur, Québec 172/D4
Contreras (isl.), Chile 138/D9
Contreras (isls.), Panama 154/F7
Controller (bay), Alaska 196/J3
Contulmo, Chile 138/D2
Contumazá, Peru 128/C6
Contwoyto (lake), N.W.T. 162/E2
Contwoyto (lake), N.W. Terrs. 187/H3
Convención, Colombia 126/D3
Convent, La. (70723) 238/L3
Convent Station, N.J. (07961) 273/E2
Conversano, Italy 34/F4
Converse (hill), Conn. 210/F1
Converse, Ind. (46919) 227/F3
Converse, La. (71419) 238/C3
Converse, S.C. (29329) 296/D2
Converse, Texas (78109) 303/K11
Converse (co.), Wyo. 319/G3
Convoy, Ireland 17/F2
Convoy, Ohio (45832) 284/A4
Conway (co.), Ark. 202/E3
Conway, Ark. (72032) 202/F3
Conway (lake), Ark. 202/F3
Conway, Iowa (50834) 229/D7
Conway, Kansas (67434) 232/E3
Conway, Ky. (40417) 237/N6
Conway○, Mass. (01341) 249/D2
Conway, Mich. (49722) 250/E3
Conway, Miss. (†39051) 256/E5
Conway, Mo. (65632) 261/G7
Conway, N.H. (03818) 268/E4
Conway○, N.H. (03818) 268/E4
Conway (lake), N.H. 268/E4
Conway, N.C. (27820) 281/P2
Conway, N. Dak. (†58233) 282/P3
Conway, Nova Scotia 168/C4
Conway, Pa. (15027) 294/B4
Conway, S.C. (29526) 296/J4
Conway, Texas (†79068) 303/C2
Conway, Wash. (98238) 310/C2
Conway Springs, Kansas (67031) 232/E4
Conwy, Wales 10/E4
Conwy, Wales 13/D4
Conwy (bay), Wales 13/C4
Conyers, Georgia (*30207) 217/D3
Conyngham, Pa. (18219) 294/K3
Coober Pedy, S. Australia 88/E5
Coober Pedy, S. Australia 94/D3
Cooch Behar, India 68/F3
Coogee, N.S. Wales 97/K3
Cook (isls.) 87/K7
Cook (inlet), Alaska 196/B1
Cook (mt.), Alaska 196/K2
Cook (cape), Br. Col. 184/C5
Cook (bay), Chile 138/E11
Cook (co.), Georgia 217/F8
Cook (co.), Ill. 222/F2
Cook (co.), Minn. 255/H3
Cook, Minn. (55723) 255/F3
Cook, Nebr. (68329) 264/H4
Cook (isls.), N. Zealand 2/B6
Cook (mt.), N. Zealand 87/G10
Cook (str.), N. Zealand 87/H10
Cook (mt.), N. Zealand 100/C5
Cook (str.), N. Zealand 100/E4
Cook, S. Australia 88/E6
Cook, S. Australia 94/B4
Cook (inlet), U.S. 4/D17
Cook (pt.), Victoria 97/H5
Cook (pt.), Victoria 88/K7
Cook, Wash. (98605) 310/D5
Cooke (co.), Texas 303/G4
Cooke City, Mont. (59020) 262/G5
Cookes (range), N. Mex. 274/B6
Cookeville, Tenn. (38501) 237/L8
Cooking Lake, Alberta 182/D3
Cook's (Paopao) (bay), Fr. Poly. 86/S12
Cooks, Mich. (49817) 250/C3
Cooksburg, Pa. (16217) 294/D3
Cooks Falls, N.Y. (12728) 276/K7
Cook's Harbour, Newf. 166/C3
Cookshire, Québec 172/F4
Cooks Mills, Ill. (†61931) 222/E4
Cook Station, Mo. (65449) 261/K7
Cookstown, N.J. (08511) 273/D3
Cookstown (dist.), N. Ireland 17/H2
Cookstown, N. Ireland 10/C3
Cookstown, N. Ireland 17/H2
Cookstown, Ontario 177/E3
Cooksville, Ill. (61730) 222/E3
Cooksville, Md. (21723) 245/K3
Cooksville, Miss. (†39341) 256/H5
Cooktown, Australia 87/E7
Cooktown, Queensland 95/C2
Cooktown, Queensland 88/H3
Cool, Texas (†76086) 303/G5
Coolabah, N.S. Wales 97/D2
Cooladdi, Queensland 95/C5
Cooladdi, Queensland 88/H5
Coolah, N.S. Wales 97/E2
Coolamon, N.S. Wales 97/D4
Coolaney, Ireland 17/D3
Coolatai, N.S. Wales 97/F1
Cooleemee, N.C. (27014) 281/H3
Cooley, Minn. (†55769) 255/E3
Coolgardie, W. Australia 88/C6
Coolgardie, W. Australia 92/C5
Coolgreany, Ireland 17/J6
Coolibah, North. Terr. 93/B3
Coolidge, Ariz. (85228) 198/D6
Coolidge (dam), Ariz. 198/E5
Coolidge, Georgia (31738) 217/E8
Coolidge, Kansas (67836) 232/A3
Coolidge, Texas (76635) 303/H6
Coolidge Dam, Ariz. (†85542) 198/E5
Coolin, Idaho (83821) 220/B1
Cool Spring, Del. (†19951) 245/T6
Cool Valley, Mo. (†63101) 261/P2
Coolville, Ohio (45723) 284/G7
Cooma, N. S. Wales 88/H7
Cooma, N.S. Wales 97/E5
Coombs, Br. Col. 184/H3
Coonabarabran, N.S. Wales 97/E2
Coonamble, N. S. Wales 88/H6
Coonamble, N.S. Wales 97/E2
Coondapoor, India 68/C6
Coon Rapids, Iowa (50058) 229/D5
Coon Rapids, Minn. (55433) 255/G5
Coon Valley, Wis. (54623) 317/E8
Cooper, Ala. (†35045) 195/E5
Cooper (pt.), Calif. 204/D7
Cooper, Iowa (50059) 229/E5
Cooper, Ky. (†42633) 237/M7
Cooper, Maine (†04638) 243/H6
Cooper○, Maine (†04638) 243/H6
Cooper (co.), Mo. 261/G5
Cooper (riv.), N.J. 273/B3
Cooper, S.C. (†29560) 296/H4
Cooper (riv.), S.C. 296/H6
Cooper, Texas (75432) 303/J4
Cooper (lake), Wyo. 319/G4
Co-Operative, Ky. (42610) 237/M7
Cooper City, Fla. (33328) 212/B4
Cooperdale, Ohio (†43842) 284/F5
Cooper Landing, Alaska (99572) 196/C1
Coopers (Barcoo) (creek), Queensland 95/B5
Coopers (Barcoo) (creek), S. Australia 88/G5
Coopers (Barcoo) (creek), S. Australia 94/F3
Coopersburg, Pa. (18036) 294/M5
Coopers Mills, Maine (04341) 243/E7
Coopers Plains, N.Y. (14827) 276/F6
Coopers Plains, Queensland 95/D3
Coopers Plains, Queensland 88/K3
Cooperstown, N.Y. (13326) 276/L5
Cooperstown, N. Dak. (58425) 282/O5
Cooperstown, Pa. (16317) 294/C2
Coopersville, Ky. (42611) 237/M7
Coopersville, Mich. (49404) 250/C5
Cooperton, Okla. (†73041) 288/J5
Coorabie, S. Australia 88/E6
Coorabie, S. Australia 94/B4
Coorong, The (lag.), S. Australia 94/F6
Coorow, W. Australia 92/B5
Coos (co.), N.H. 268/E2
Coos (co.), Oreg. 291/C4
Coos (riv.), Oreg. 291/D4
Coosa (co.), Ala. 195/F5
Coosa (riv.), Ala. 195/F4
Coosa, Georgia (30129) 217/B2
Coosa (riv.), Georgia 217/A2
Coosada, Ala. (36020) 195/F5
Coosaw (riv.), S.C. 296/G7
Coosawattee (riv.), Georgia 217/C1
Coosawhatchie, S.C. (29912) 296/F6
Coosawhatchie (riv.), S.C. 296/E6
Coos Bay, Oreg. 188/A2
Coos Bay, Oreg. (97420) 291/C4
Cootamundra, N. S. Wales 88/H6
Cootamundra, N.S. Wales 97/D4
Cootehill, Ireland 17/G3
Cootehill, Ireland 10/C3
Cooter, Mo. (63839) 261/N10
Copacabana, Argentina 143/C2
Copacabana, Bolivia 136/A5
Copake, N.Y. (12516) 276/N6
Copake Falls, N.Y. (12517) 276/N6
Copala, Mexico 150/K8
Copalis Beach, Wash. (98535) 310/A3
Copalis Crossing, Wash. (98536) 310/B3
Copan, Okla. (74022) 288/P1
Copano (bay), Texas 303/G9
Copco (lake), Calif. 204/C2
Cope, Colo. (80812) 208/O3
Cope, Ind. (†46151) 227/E6
Cope, S.C. (29038) 296/E5
Cope (cape), Spain 33/F4
Copeland, Ala. (†36558) 195/B7
Copeland, Fla. (33926) 212/E6
Copeland, Idaho (†83805) 220/B1
Copeland, Kansas (67837) 232/B4
Copeland (isl.), N. Ireland 17/K2
Copemish, Mich. (49625) 250/D4
Copen, W. Va. (26615) 312/E5
Copenhagen (commune), Denmark 21/F6
Copenhagen (cap.), Denmark 7/F3
Copenhagen (cap.), Denmark 21/F6
Copenhagen (cap.), Denmark 18/G9
Copenhagen, N.Y. (13626) 276/J3
Copere, Bolivia 136/D6
Copiague, N.Y. (11726) 276/O9
Copiah (co.), Miss. 256/D7
Copiapó, Chile 120/B5
Copiapó, Chile 138/B6
Copiapó (bay), Chile 138/A6
Copiapó (riv.), Chile 138/A6
Copinsay (isl.), Scotland 15/F2
Coplay, Pa. (18037) 294/L4
Copley, S. Australia 94/F4
Copmanhurst, N.S. Wales 97/G1
Coporito, Venezuela 124/H3
Coporolo (riv.), Angola 115/B6
Coppell, Texas (75019) 303/G2
Coppename (riv.), Suriname 131/C3
Copper (riv.), Alaska 196/J2
Copper (mts.), Ariz. 198/B6
Copperas Cove, Texas (76522) 303/G6
Copper Canyon, Texas (†76226) 303/F1
Copper Center, Alaska (99573) 196/J2
Copper City, Mich. (49917) 250/A1
Copperfield, W. Australia 88/C5
Copperfield, W. Australia 92/B5
Copper Harbor, Mich. (49918) 250/B1
Copperhill, Tenn. (37317) 237/N10
Copper Hill, Va. (24079) 307/H6
Coppermine, Canada 4/C15
Coppermine, N.W.T. 162/E2
Coppermine (riv.), N.W.T. 162/E2
Coppermine, N.W. Terrs. 187/G3
Coppermine (riv.), N.W. Terrs. 187/G3
Copper Mountain, Br. Col. 184/G5
Copperton, Utah (†84006) 304/B3
Copper Valley, Va. (†24141) 307/G7
Coppet, Switzerland 39/B4
Coppock, Iowa (†52654) 229/K6
Coqên, China 77/C5
Coquet (riv.), England 13/F2
Coquí, P. Rico 161/D3
Coquille, Oreg. (97423) 291/C4
Coquille (pt.), Oreg. 291/C4
Coquimatlán, Mexico 150/G7
Coquimbo (reg.), Chile 138/A8
Coquimbo, Chile 120/B6
Coquimbo, Chile 138/A8
Coquitlam, Br. Col. 184/K3
Cora, Ill. (†62280) 222/D6
Cora, Wyo. (82925) 319/C3
Corabia, Romania 45/G4
Coracora, Peru 128/F10
Corail, Haiti 158/A6
Coraki, N.S. Wales 97/G1
Coral (sea) 87/F7
Coral (sea) 88/H2
Coral (sea) 2/S6
Coral, Mich. (49322) 250/D5
Coral (sea), New Caled. 86/G4
Coral (sea), Papua N.G. 85/B7
Coral, Pa. (15731) 294/D5
Coral (bay), Philippines 82/A6
Coral (sea), Queensland 95/C1
Coral (bay), Virgin Is. (U.S.) 161/C4
Coral Cove, Fla. (†33559) 212/D4
Coral Gables, Fla. (33134) 212/B5
Coral Harbour, N.W.T. 162/H2
Coral Harbour, N.W. Terrs. 187/K3
Coral Hills, Md. (†20027) 245/G5
Coral Sea Islands (terr.), Australia 87/E7
CORAL SEA ISLANDS TERR. 95/C2
Coral Sea Islands Territory, /J3
Coral Springs, Fla. (33060) 212/F5
Coralville, Iowa (52241) 229/K5
Coralville (lake), Iowa 229/K5
Coram, Mont. (59913) 262/C2
Coramba, N.S. Wales 97/G2
Corangamite (lake), Victoria 97/B6
Corantijn (riv.), Suriname 131/C3
Coraopolis, Pa. (15108) 294/B4
Corapeake, N.C. (27926) 281/R1
Corato, Italy 34/F4
Corbeil, Ontario 177/E1
Corberrie, Nova Scotia 168/C4
Corbigny, France 28/E4
Corbin, Kansas (67032) 232/E4
Corbin, Ky. (40701) 237/N7
Corbin City, N.J. (†08270) 273/D5
Corbridge, England 13/E3
Corby, England 13/G5
Corcelles-près-Payerne, Switzerland 39/C3
Corcoran, Calif. (93212) 204/F7
Corcoran, Minn. (†55340) 255/F5
Corcovado (gulf), Chile 120/B7
Corcovado (gulf), Chile 138/D4
Corcovado (vol.), Chile 138/D5
Corcubión, Spain 33/B1
Cord, Ark. (72524) 202/H2
Cordaville, Mass. (†01772) 249/H3
Cordele, Georgia (31015) 217/E7
Cordelia, Calif. (†94585) 204/K1
Cordell, Okla. (73632) 288/H4
Cordell Hull (res.), Tenn. 237/K8
Corder, Mo. (64021) 261/E4
Cordesville, S.C. (29434) 296/H5
Cordillera (dept.), Paraguay 144/D4
Cordillo Grounds, S. Australia 94/G2
Córdoba (prov.), Argentina 143/D3
Córdoba, Argentina 2/F7
Córdoba, Argentina 143/D3
Córdoba, Argentina 120/C6
Córdoba (dept.), Colombia 126/C3
Córdoba, Mexico 150/P2
Córdoba (prov.), Spain 33/D3
Córdoba, Spain 33/D4
Córdoba, Spain 7/D5
Cordobés (riv.), Uruguay 145/D3
Cordova, Ala. (35550) 195/D3
Cordova, Alaska (99574) 196/D1
Cordova, Alaska 188/D6
Cordova, Alaska 146/D3
Cordova (bay), Alaska 196/M2
Cordova, Ill. (61242) 222/C2
Cordova, Manitoba 179/C4
Cordova, Md. (21625) 245/O5
Cordova, Nebr. (68330) 264/G4
Cordova, N. Mex. (87523) 274/D2
Córdova, Peru 128/E10
Cordova, S.C. (29039) 296/F5
Cordova, Tenn. (38018) 237/B10
Cordova, U.S. 4/C17
Cordova Mines, Ontario 177/G3
Core (banks), N.C. 281/S5
Core (sound), N.C. 281/S5
Core, W. Va. (26529) 312/F3
Corea, Maine (04624) 243/H7
Coredó (Humboldt) (bay), Colombia 126/B4
Coree South, N.S. Wales 97/C4
Corella, Spain 33/F1
Corey, La. (†71201) 238/F2
Corfield, Queensland 88/G4
Corfield, Queensland 95/B4
Corfu (Kérkira) (isl.), Greece 45/D6
Corfu, N.Y. (14036) 276/D5
Corgémont, Switzerland 39/D2
Cori, Italy 34/F7
Coria, Spain 33/C3
Coria del Río, Spain 33/C4
Corigliano Calabro, Italy 34/F5
Corinda, Queensland 88/K3
Corinda, Queensland 95/A3
Corinda, Queensland 95/D3
Coringa (islets), Australia 87/F7
Coringa (isls.), Coral Sea Is. Terr. 88/H3
Corinna○, Maine (04928) 243/E6
Corinne, Okla. (†74751) 288/R6
Corinne, Sask. 181/G5
Corinne, Utah (84307) 304/B2
Corinne, W. Va. (25826) 312/D7
Corinth, Ark. (†72833) 202/C3
Corinth, Georgia (†30230) 217/B4
Corinth, Greece 45/F7
Corinth (gulf), Greece 45/F6
Corinth, Ky. (41010) 237/M3
Corinth, Miss. (38834) 256/G1
Corinth, N.Y. (12822) 276/N4
Corinth, N. Dak. (†58830) 282/D2
Corinth○, Vt. (05039) 268/C3
Corinth, W. Va. (26713) 312/H4
Corinto, Brazil 132/E7
Corinto, Colombia 126/B6
Corinto, Nicaragua 154/D4
Coriole, Somalia 115/H3
Coripata, Bolivia 136/B5
Corisco (isl.), Equat. Guinea 115/A3
Cork (co.), Ireland 17/D7
Cork, Ireland 7/D3
Cork, Ireland 10/B5
Cork, Ireland 17/E8
Cork (harb.), Ireland 17/E8
Cork (harb.), Ireland 10/B5
Cork, New Bruns. 170/D3
Corker (cay), Belize 154/D2
Corleone, Italy 34/D6
Corley, W. Va. (26616) 312/E5
Çorlu, Turkey 63/B2
Cormorant, Manitoba 179/H3
Cormorant (lake), Manitoba 179/H3
Cormorant, Minn. (†56572) 255/B4
Corn (creek), Ariz. 198/E3
Corn, Okla. (73024) 288/J4
Cornaca, Bolivia 136/C7
Corncake (inlet), N.C. 281/O7
Cornelia, Georgia (30531) 217/E1
Cornélio Procópio, Brazil 132/D8
Cornelius, N.C. (28031) 281/H4
Cornelius, Oreg. (97113) 291/A2
Cornell, Ill. (61319) 222/E3
Cornell, Mich. (49818) 250/B3
Cornell, Wis. (54732) 317/D5
Corner (inlet), Victoria 97/D6
Corner Brook, Newf. 166/C4
Corner Brook, Newf. 162/K6
Cornerstone, Ark. (†72004) 202/G5
Cornersville, Md. (†21613) 245/O6
Cornersville, Miss. (†38659) 256/F1
Cornersville, Tenn. (37047) 237/H10
Cornerville, Ark. (†71667) 202/G6
Cornettes de Bise (mts.), Switzerland 39/C4
Cornfield (pt.), Conn. 210/F3
Cornfields, Ariz. (†86505) 198/F3
Cornhill, New Bruns. 170/E3
Cornhill, Scotland 15/F3
Corning, Ark. (72422) 202/J1
Corning, Calif. (96021) 204/C4
Corning, Iowa (50841) 229/D7
Corning, Kansas (66417) 232/F2
Corning, Mo. (64435) 261/B2
Corning, N.Y. (14830) 276/F6
Corning, Ohio (43730) 284/F6
Corning, Sask. 181/J6
Cornish, Colo. (†80611) 208/L2
Cornish○, Maine (04020) 243/B8
Cornish, Okla. (†73456) 288/L6
Cornish, Utah (84308) 304/B2
Cornish Flat, N.H. (03746) 268/C4
Cornishville, Ky. (40314) 237/M5
Cornland, Ill. (62519) 222/D4
Cornlea, Nebr. (68630) 264/G3
Corno (mt.), Italy 34/D3
Cornucopia, Wis. (54827) 317/D2
Cornville, Ariz. (86325) 198/D4
Cornville○, Maine (†04976) 243/D6
Cornwall○, Conn. (06753) 210/B1
Cornwall (co.), England 13/C7
Cornwall (cape), England 13/B7
Cornwall (isl.), N.W.T. 162/M3
Cornwall (isl.), N.W. Terrs. 187/J2
Cornwall, Ont. 162/J7
Cornwall, Ontario 177/K2
Cornwall, Pa. (17016) 294/K5
Cornwall, Pr. Edward I. 168/E2
Cornwall, Tasmania 99/E3
Cornwall○, Vt. (†05753) 268/A4
Cornwall Bridge, Conn. (06754) 210/B1
Cornwall Center, Conn. (†06796) 210/B1
Cornwall Hollow, Conn. (†06031) 210/B1
Cornwallis (isl.), N.W.T. 162/F1
Cornwallis (isl.), N.W. Terrs. 187/J2
Cornwall On Hudson, N.Y. (12518) 276/M8
Cornwell, Fla. (33836) 212/E4
Coro, Venezuela 124/D2
Coro, Venezuela 120/C1
Coroatá, Brazil 132/F3
Corocoro, Bolivia 120/C4
Corocoro, Bolivia 136/A5
Corofin, Ireland 17/C6
Coroico, Bolivia 136/B5
Corolla, N.C. (27927) 281/T2
Coromandel, Brazil 132/E7
Coromandel, N. Zealand 100/E2
Coromandel (pen.), N. Zealand 100/F2
Coromandel (range), N. Zealand 100/E2
Coromandel Coast (reg.), India 68/E6
Coron, Philippines 82/C4
Coron (isl.), Philippines 82/C5
Corona, Ala. (†35546) 195/C3
Corona, Calif. (91720) 204/E11
Corona, N. Mex. (88318) 274/D4
Corona, S. Dak. (57227) 298/R3
Coronaca, S.C. (†29646) 296/C3
Coronach, Sask. 181/F6
Coronado (bay), C. Rica 154/F6
Coronado, Calif. (92118) 204/H11
Coronado (pt.), Philippines 82/C7
Coronado Nat'l Memorial, Ariz. 198/E7
Coronados (gulf), Chile 138/D4
Coronation (isl.), Alaska 196/M2
Coronation, Alberta 182/E3
Coronation (isl.) 5/C16
Coronation (gulf), N.W.T. 162/E2
Coronation (gulf), N.W. Terrs. 187/G3
Coronda, Argentina 143/F6
Coronel, Chile 138/D1
Coronel, Chile 120/B6
Coronel Bogado, Argentina 143/F6
Coronel Bogado, Paraguay 144/D5
Coronel Brandsen, Argentina 143/H7
Coronel Dorrego, Argentina 143/D4
Coronel F. Gabrera, Bolivia 136/E6
Coronel F. Cabrera (mt.), Paraguay 144/B1
Coronel Martínez, Paraguay 144/B5
Coronel Moldes, Argentina 143/C2
Coronel Oviedo, Paraguay 144/C5
Coronel Pringles, Argentina 143/D4
Coronel Suárez, Argentina 143/D4
Coronel Vidal, Argentina 143/E4
Corongo, Peru 128/D7
Coronie (dist.), Suriname 131/C3
Coropuna, Nudo (mt.), Peru 128/F10
Cororooke, Victoria 97/B6
Çorovodë, Albania 45/E5
Corowa, N.S. Wales 97/D4
Corozal, Colombia 126/C3
Corozal, P. Rico 161/D1
Corozal Town, Belize 154/C1
Corozo Pando, Venezuela 124/E3
Corpach, Scotland 15/C4
Corpus Christi, Texas 188/G5
Corpus Christi, Texas 146/J7
Corpus Christi, Texas (*78401) 303/G10
Corpus Christi (bay), Texas 188/G5
Corpus Christi (lake), Texas 303/F9
Corpus Christi N.A.S., Texas 303/G10
Corque, Bolivia 136/B6
Corquín, Honduras 154/C3
Corral, Chile 138/D3
Corral, Idaho (83322) 220/D6
Corral City, Texas (†76226) 303/F1
Corral de Almaguer, Spain 33/E3
Corral de Bustos, Argentina 143/D3
Corrales, N. Mex. (87048) 274/C3
Corralillo, Cuba 158/D1
Corralitos, Calif. (†95076) 204/L4
Corral Viejo, P. Rico 161/C2
Correct, Ind. (†47042) 227/G7
Correctionville, Iowa (51016) 229/B4
Correggio, Italy 34/C2
Corregidor (isl.), Philippines 82/C3
Correll, Minn. (56227) 255/B5
Corrente, Brazil 132/E5
Corrente (riv.), Brazil 132/E6
Correntina, Brazil 132/E6
Corrèze (dept.), France 28/D5
Corrib (lake), Ireland 17/C5
Corrib, Lough (lake), Ireland 10/B4
Corridon, Mo. (†63633) 261/L8
Corrie, Scotland 15/C5
Corrientes (prov.), Argentina 143/E2
Corrientes, Argentina 143/E2
Corrients, Argentina 120/D5
Corrientes (riv.), Argentina 143/E2
Corrientes (cape), Colombia 120/B2
Corrientes (cape), Colombia 126/B5
Corrientes (cape), Cuba 158/A2
Corrientes (inlet), Cuba 158/A2
Corrientes (cape), Mexico 146/H7
Corrientes (cape), Mexico 150/F6
Corrientes (riv.), Peru 128/E4
Corrigan, Texas (75939) 303/K7
Corriganville, Md. (21524) 245/C2
Corrigin, W. Australia 92/B6
Corriverton, Guyana 131/C3
Corrumpa (creek), N. Mex. 274/F2
Corry, Pa. (16407) 294/C2
Corryong, Victoria 97/D5
Corryton, Tenn. (37721) 237/O8
Corse (cape), France 28/B6
Corse du Sud (dept.), France 28/B6
Corserine (mt.), Scotland 15/D5
Corsewall (pt.), Scotland 15/C5
Corsham, England 13/E6
Corsica (isl.), France 7/E4
Corsica (isl.), France 28/B6
Corsica, Pa. (15829) 294/D3
Corsica, S. Dak. (57328) 298/N7
Corsicana, Texas 188/G4
Corsicana, Texas (75110) 303/H5
Corso, Mo. (63377) 261/K4
Corson (inlet), N.J. 273/D5
Corson (co.), S. Dak. 298/G2
Corson, S. Dak. (57019) 298/R6
Cortaro, Ariz. (85230) 198/D6
Corte, France 28/B6
Corte Madera, Calif. (94925) 204/J2
Cortés, Cuba 158/A2
Cortés (inlet), Cuba 158/B2
Cortez, Colo. (81321) 208/B8
Cortez, Fla. (33522) 212/D4
Cortez (mts.), Nev. 266/E2
Cortina d'Ampezzo, Italy 34/D1
Cortland, Ill. (60112) 222/E2
Cortland, Ind. (47228) 227/F7
Cortland, Nebr. (68331) 264/H4
Cortland (co.), N.Y. 276/H5
Cortland, N.Y. (13045) 276/H5
Cortland, Ohio (44410) 284/J3
Cortona, Italy 34/C3
Coruche, Portugal 33/B3
Çoruh (riv.), Turkey 59/D1
Çoruh (riv.), Turkey 63/J2
Çorum (prov.), Turkey 63/F2
Çorum, Turkey 59/B1
Çorum, Turkey 63/F2
Çorum (riv.), Turkey 63/F2
Corumbá, Brazil 120/D4
Corumbá, Brazil 132/B7
Corunna, Ind. (46730) 227/G2
Corunna, Mich. (48817) 250/E6
Corunna, Ontario 177/B5
Corvallis, Mont. (59828) 262/C4
Corvallis, Oreg. 188/B2
Corvallis, Oreg. (97330) 291/D3
Corvo (isl.), Portugal 33/A1
Corvuso, Minn. (†56228) 255/D6
Corwen, Wales 10/E4
Corwen, Wales 13/D5
Corwin, Kansas (†67061) 232/D4
Corwin, Ohio (†45068) 284/B6
Corwin Springs, Mont. (59021) 262/F5
Corwith, Iowa (50430) 229/F3
Cory, Ind. (47846) 227/C6
Corydon, Ind. (47112) 227/E8
Corydon, Iowa (50060) 229/G7
Corydon, Ky. (42406) 237/F5
Coryell (co.), Texas 303/G6
Coryville, Pa. (†16731) 294/F2
Corzoneso, Switzerland 39/G4
Cosalá, Mexico 150/F4
Cosamaloapan de Carpio, Mexico 150/M7
Cosapa, Bolivia 136/A6
Cosautlán de Carvajal, Mexico 150/P1
Cosby, Mo. (64436) 261/C3
Cosby, Tenn. (37722) 237/P9
Cos Cob, Conn. (06807) 210/A4
Coscomatepec de Bravo, Mexico 150/P2
Cosegüina (pt.), Nicaragua 154/D4
Cosenza (prov.), Italy 34/F5
Cosenza, Italy 34/F5
Cosenza, Italy 7/F5
Coshocton (co.), Ohio 284/G5
Coshocton, Ohio (43812) 284/G5
Cosine, Sask. 181/A3
Cosío, Mexico 150/H5
Cosmoledo (isls.), Seychelles 102/G5
Cosmoledo (isls.), Seychelles 118/H1
Cosmo Newbery Aboriginal Reserve, W. Australia 88/C5
Cosmo Newbery Aboriginal Res., W. Australia 92/C5
Cosmopolis, Wash. (98537) 310/B4
Cosmos, Minn. (56228) 255/D6
Cosne-Cours-sur-Loire, France 28/E4
Cosperville, Ind. (†46794) 227/F1
Cosquín, Argentina 143/D3
Cossonay, Switzerland 39/B3
Costa, W. Va. (25051) 312/C6
Costa Azul, Uruguay 145/E5
Costa Brava (reg.), Spain 33/H2
Costa da Caparica, Portugal 33/A1
Costa de Sola (Costa del Sol) (reg.), Spain 33/D4
Costa Mesa, Calif. (*92626) 204/D11
Costa Rica 2/E5
Costa Rica 146/K8
Costa Rica, Bolivia 136/A2
COSTA RICA 154/E5
Costa Rica, Mexico 150/F4
Costa Smeralda (reg.), Italy 34/B4
Costa Verde (reg.), Italy 34/B5
Costello, Pa. (†16720) 294/G2
Costessey, England 13/J5
Costeşti, Romania 45/G3
Costigan, Maine (04423) 243/F5
Costilla (co.), Colo. 208/J8
Costilla, N. Mex. (87524) 274/D2
Costilla (peak), N. Mex. 274/D2
Cosumnes (riv.), Calif. 204/C9
Coswig, Dresden, E. Germany 22/E3
Coswig, Halle, E. Germany 22/E3
Cotabato, Philippines 85/G4
Cotabato, Philippines 82/D7
Cotacajes (riv.), Bolivia 136/B5
Cotagaita, Bolivia 136/C7
Cotahuasi, Peru 128/F10
Cotati, Calif. (94928) 204/C5
Coteau, N. Dak. (58728) 282/F2
Coteau (hills), Sask. 181/D4
Coteau-du-Lac, Québec 172/C4
Coteau du Missouri (plain), N. Dak. 282/G3
Coteau-Landing, Québec 172/C4
Coteaux, Haiti 158/A6
Côte-d'Or (dept.), France 28/F4
Côte-d'Or (mts.), France 28/F4
Cotentin (pen.), France 28/C3
Côte-Saint-Luc, Québec 172/H4
Côtes de Fer, Haiti 158/B6
Côtes-du-Nord (dept.), France 28/B3
Cotesfield, Nebr. (68829) 264/F3
Cotija de la Paz, Mexico 150/H7
Cotile (lake), La. 238/E4
Coto, Argentina 143/D2
Cotoca, Bolivia 136/D5
Coto Laurel, P. Rico 161/C2
Cotonou, Benin 102/C4

356 Cotonou

Cotonou, Benin 106/E7
Cotopaxi, Colo. (81223) 208/H6
Cotopaxi (prov.), Ecuador 128/C3
Cotopaxi (mt.), Ecuador 128/C3
Cotswold (hills), England 13/E6
Cottage City, Md. (†20722) 245/F4
Cottage Grove, Ala. (†35089) 195/F5
Cottage Grove, Ind. (†47353) 227/H5
Cottage Grove, Minn. (55016) 255/F6
Cottage Grove, Oreg. (97424) 291/D4
Cottage Grove (lake), Oreg. 291/E4
Cottage Grove, Tenn. (38224) 237/E8
Cottagehill, Fla. (32533) 212/B6
Cottage Hills, Ill. (62018) 222/B2
Cottageville, S.C. (29435) 296/G6
Cottageville, W. Va. (25239) 312/C5
Cottam, Ontario 177/B5
Cottbus (dist.), E. Germany 22/F3
Cottbus, E. Germany 22/F3
Cotter, Ark. (72626) 202/E1
Cotter, Iowa (52221) 229/L6
Cottesloe, W. Australia 88/B2
Cottian Alps (range), France 28/G5
Cottian Alps (range), Italy 34/A2
Cottica, Suriname 131/D4
Cottica (riv.), Suriname 131/D3
Cottle, Ky. (41412) 237/P5
Cottle (co.), Texas 303/D3
Cottleville, Mo. (63338) 261/M2
Cotton, Georgia (31739) 217/D8
Cotton, Minn. (55724) 255/F3
Cotton (co.), Okla. 288/K6
Cottonburg, Ky. (†40475) 237/N5
Cotton Center, Texas (79021) 303/C4
Cottondale, Ala. (35453) 195/D4
Cottondale, Fla. (32431) 212/D6
Cotton Ground, St. Chris.-Nevis 161/C11
Cotton Plant, Ark. (72036) 202/H3
Cottonport, La. (71327) 238/F5
Cottonton, Ala. (36851) 195/H6
Cottontown, Tenn. (37048) 237/H8
Cotton Valley, La. (71018) 238/D1
Cottonwood, Ala. (36320) 195/H8
Cottonwood, Ariz. (86326) 198/D4
Cottonwood (cliffs), Ariz. 198/B3
Cottonwood, Br. Col. 184/G3
Cottonwood, Calif. (96022) 204/C3
Cottonwood (creek), Calif. 204/C3
Cottonwood, Idaho (83522) 220/B3
Cottonwood (butte), Idaho 220/C4
Cottonwood (riv.), Kansas 232/F3
Cottonwood (co.), Minn. 255/C6
Cottonwood, Minn. (56229) 255/C6
Cottonwood (riv.), Minn. 255/C6
Cottonwood (creek), Mont. 262/E2
Cottonwood (creek), Oreg. 291/K4
Cottonwood, S. Dak. (57775) 298/F6
Cottonwood (creek), S. Dak. 298/E5
Cottonwood (lake), S. Dak. 298/M4
Cottonwood, Texas (†79504) 303/D5
Cottonwood (creek), Utah 304/C4
Cottonwood (creek), Utah 304/E4
Cottonwood (creek), Wyo. 319/B4
Cottonwood Draw (dry riv.), Texas 303/C10
Cottonwood Falls, Kansas (66845) 232/F3
Cottonwood Wash (dry riv.), Ariz. 198/E4
Cottonwood Wash (creek), Utah 304/E6
Cotuí, Dom. Rep. 158/E5
Cotuit, Mass. (02635) 249/N6
Cotulla, Texas (78014) 303/E9
Couch, Mo. (65690) 261/K9
Couchiching (lake), Ontario 177/E3
Couchwood, La. (†71018) 238/D1
Coudekerque-Branche, France 28/E2
Couderay, Wis. (54828) 317/D4
Coudersport, Pa. (16915) 294/G2
Coudres (isl.), Québec 172/G2
Cougar (res.), Oreg. 291/E3
Cougar, Wash. (98616) 310/C4
Coughlan, New Bruns. 170/E2
Coulee, N. Dak. (†58746) 282/F2
Coulee City, Wash. (99115) 310/F3
Coulee Dam, Wash. (99116) 310/G3
Coulee Dam Nat'l Rec. Area, Wash. 310/G2
Coulihaut, Dominica 161/E6
Coulommiers, France 28/E3
Coulter, Iowa (50431) 229/G3
Coulter, Manitoba 179/B5
Coulterville, Calif. (95311) 204/E6
Coulterville, Ill. (62237) 222/D5
Counamama, Fr. Guiana 131/E3
Counce, Tenn. (38326) 237/E10
Council, Alaska (†99784) 196/F2
Council, Georgia (†31631) 217/G9
Council, Idaho (83612) 220/B5
Council, N.C. (28434) 281/M6
Council Bluffs, Iowa (51501) 229/B6
Council Bluffs, Iowa 188/G2
Council Grove, Kansas (66846) 232/F3
Council Grove (lake), Kansas 232/F3
Council Hill, Okla. (74428) 288/P3
Countess, Alberta 182/D4
Country (harb.), Nova Scotia 168/G3
Country Club Hills, Ill. (60477) 222/B6
Country Club Village, Mo. (†64501) 261/C3
Country Harbour Mines, Nova Scotia 168/G3
Country Life Acres, Mo. (†63101) 261/N3
Countryside, Ill. (†60525) 222/B6
County Line, Ala. (†35172) 195/E3
County Line, Ala. (†36467) 195/F8
Countyline, Okla. (73025) 288/L6
Coupar Angus, Scotland 10/E2
Coupar Angus, Scotland 15/E4
Coupeville, Wash. (98239) 310/C2
Courantyne (riv.) 120/D2
Courantyne (riv.), Guyana 131/C3
Courbevoie, France 28/A1
Courcelles, Belgium 27/E8
Courcelles, Québec 172/G4
Courgenay, Switzerland 39/D2
Courmayeur, Italy 34/A2
Courrendlin, Switzerland 39/D2
Courroux, Switzerland 39/D2
Courtelary, Switzerland 39/C2
Courtenay, Br. Col. 162/D6
Courtenay, Br. Col. 184/E5
Courtenay, N. Dak. (58426) 282/N5
Courtételle, Switzerland 39/D2
Courtland, Ala. (35618) 195/D1
Courtland, Calif. (95615) 204/B9
Courtland, Kansas (66939) 232/E2
Courtland, Minn. (56021) 255/D6
Courtland, Miss. (38620) 256/E2
Courtland, Ontario 177/D5
Courtland, Va. (23837) 307/O7
Courtmacsherry, Ireland 17/D8
Courtmacsherry (bay), Ireland 17/D8
Courtney, Mo. (†64051) 261/R5
Courtney, Okla. (†73456) 288/L7
Courtois, Mo. (65451) 261/K7
Courtown (Este Sudeste) (cays), Colombia 126/A10
Courtown Harbour, Ireland 17/J6
Courtrai (Kortrijk), Belgium 27/C7
Courtright, Ontario 177/B5
Courval, Sask. 181/E5
Courville, Québec 172/J3
Coushatta, La. (71019) 238/D2
Coutances, France 28/C3
Coutras, France 28/C5
Coutts, Alberta 182/D5
Coutts (inlet), N.W. Terrs. 187/L2
Couva, Trin. & Tob. 161/B10
Couvet, Switzerland 39/C3
Couvin, Belgium 27/F8
Cova da Piedade, Portugal 33/A1
Cove, Ark. (71937) 202/B5
Cove (pt.), Md. 245/N7
Cove, Minn. (†56359) 255/E4
Cove, Ohio (†45640) 284/E8
Cove (isl.), Ontario 177/C2
Cove, Oreg. (97824) 291/K2
Cove, Texas (†77580) 303/L1
Cove (creek), Utah 304/B5
Cove and Kilcreggan, Scotland 15/A1
Cove Bay, Scotland 15/F3
Cove City, N.C. (28523) 281/P4
Cove Creek, N.C. (†28786) 281/D3
Covedale, Ohio (†45238) 284/B10
Cove Fort, Utah (†84713) 304/B5
Cove Gap, W. Va. (25509) 312/B6
Covelo, Calif. (95428) 204/B4
Covena, Georgia (30422) 217/H6
Covendo, Bolivia 136/B4
Cove Neck, N.Y. (†11771) 276/R6
Coventry○, Conn. (06238) 210/F1
Coventry, England 13/F5
Coventry, England 10/F4
Coventry○, R.I. (02816) 249/H6
Coventry○, Vt. (05825) 268/C2
Coventry Center, R.I. (02816) 249/H6
Cove Orchard, Oreg. (†97148) 291/D2
Coverdale, Georgia (†31714) 217/E7
Coverdale, Ontario 177/F4
Covert, Mich. (49043) 250/C6
Cove Run (lake), Ky. 237/O4
Covesville, Va. (22931) 307/L5
Covilhã, Portugal 33/C2
Covin, Ala. (†35555) 195/C3
Covina, Calif. (*91722) 204/D10
Covington (co.), Ala. 195/F8
Covington, Georgia (30209) 217/E3
Covington, Ind. (47932) 227/C4
Covington, Iowa (†52324) 229/K5
Covington, Ky. (*41011) 237/S2
Covington, Ky. 188/J3
Covington, La. (70433) 238/K5
Covington, Mich. (49919) 250/G2
Covington (co.), Miss. 256/E7
Covington, Ohio (45318) 284/B5
Covington, Okla. (73730) 288/L2
Covington, Pa. (16917) 294/J2
Covington, Tenn. (38019) 237/B9
Covington (I.C.), Va. (24426) 307/H5
Cow (creek), Mont. 262/G2
Cow (creek), Oreg. 291/K4
Cow (lake), Oreg. 291/K4
Cow (creek), Wash. 310/G3
Cowal (lake), N.S. Wales 97/D3
Cowal (dist.), Scotland 15/C4
Cowan, Ind. (†47302) 227/G4
Cowan, Ky. (†41039) 237/O4
Cowan, Manitoba 179/B2
Cowan (lake), Sask. 181/D2
Cowan, Tenn. (37318) 237/K10
Cowan (lake), W. Australia 88/C6
Cowan (lake), W. Australia 92/C5
Cowanesque, Pa. (16918) 294/H2
Cowangie, Victoria 97/A4
Cowansville, Pa. (16218) 294/C4
Cowansville, Québec 172/E4
Cowaramup, W. Australia 92/A6
Coward, S.C. (29530) 296/H4
Coward Springs, S. Australia 94/E3
Cowarie, S. Australia 94/F2
Cowarts, Ala. (36321) 195/H8
Cow Bay, Nova Scotia 168/E4
Cowbridge, Wales 13/A7
Cowcreek, Ky. (†41314) 237/O6
Cowden, Ill. (62422) 222/E4
Cowdenbeath, Scotland 10/C1
Cowdenbeath, Scotland 15/D1
Cowdrey, Colo. (80434) 208/G1
Cowell, S. Australia 88/F6
Cowell, S. Australia 94/E5
Cowen, W. Va. (26206) 312/E6
Cowes, England 10/F5
Cowes, England 13/F7
Coweta (co.), Georgia 217/C4
Coweta, Okla. (74429) 288/P3
Cowgill, Mo. (64637) 261/E3
Cow Head, Newf. 166/C4
Cowichan (lake), Br. Col. 184/J3
Cowiche, Wash. (98923) 310/E4
Cowie, Scotland 15/C1
Cowikee, North Fork (creek), Ala. 195/H6
Cow Island, La. (†70510) 238/F7
Cowles, Nebr. (†68930) 264/F4
Cowles, N. Mex. (†87535) 274/D3
Cowlesville, N.Y. (14037) 276/D5
Cowley, Alberta 182/D5
Cowley (co.), Kansas 232/F4
Cowley, Wyo. (82420) 319/D1
Cowley, Yukon 187/E3
Cowlington, Okla. (†74934) 288/S4
Cowlitz (co.), Wash. 310/C4
Cowlitz (pass), Wash. 310/D4
Cowlitz (riv.), Wash. 310/C4
Cowpasture (riv.), Va. 307/J4
Cowpens, S.C. (29330) 296/D1
Cowpens Nat'l Battlefield, S.C. 296/D1
Cowra, N. S. Wales 88/H6
Cowra, N.S. Wales 97/E3
Cox (bight), Tasmania 99/C5
Coxburg, Miss. (†39095) 256/D5
Cox City, Okla. (†73082) 288/L5
Coxim, Brazil 132/C7
Coxsackie, N.Y. (12051) 276/N6
Cox's Bazar (Maheshkhali), Bangladesh 68/G4
Cox's Cove, Newf. 166/C4
Coxs Mills, W. Va. (26342) 312/E4
Cox Station (Bel Alton), Md. (†20611) 245/L7
Coxton, Ky. (40831) 237/P7
Coy, Ala. (36435) 195/D7
Coy, Ark. (72037) 202/G4
Coyame, Mexico 150/G2
Coyle (riv.), Argentina 143/B7
Coyle, Okla. (73027) 288/M3
Coyoacán, Mexico 150/L1
Coyote (creek), Calif. 204/L3
Coyote (res.), Calif. 204/L4
Coyote, N. Mex. (87012) 274/C2
Coyotepec, Mexico 150/L1
Coyuca (riv.), Mexico 150/O1
Coyuca de Benítez, Mexico 150/J8
Coyuca de Catalán, Mexico 150/J7
Coyutla, Mexico 150/L6
Coyville, Kansas (66727) 232/G4
Cozad, Nebr. (69130) 264/E4
Cozumel, Mexico 150/Q6
Cozumel (isl.), Mexico 150/Q6
Crab (creek), Wash. 310/F3
Crab Hill, Barbados 161/B8
Crab Orchard (lake), Ill. 222/E6
Crab Orchard, Ky. (40419) 237/M6
Crab Orchard, Nebr. (68332) 264/H4
Crab Orchard, Tenn. (37723) 237/M9
Crabtree, Oreg. (97335) 291/E3
Crabtree, Pa. (15624) 294/D5
Crabtree, Québec 172/D4
Cracow (city), Poland 47/E4
Cracow (Kraków) (prov.), Poland 47/E4
Cracow, Poland 47/E4
Cracow, Poland 7/F3
Cradle (mt.), Tasmania 99/B3
Cradle Mt. Lake St. Clair Nat'l Park, Tasmania 99/B3
Cradock, S. Africa 102/E8
Cradock, S. Africa 118/D6
Crafers-Bridgewater, S. Australia 88/E8
Crafers-Bridgewater, S. Australia 94/B8
Crafton, Pa. (15205) 294/B7
Craftsbury○, Vt. (05826) 268/C2
Craftsbury Common, Vt. (05827) 268/C2
Cragford, Ala. (36255) 195/G4
Craig, Alaska (99921) 196/M2
Craig, Colo. (81625) 208/D2
Craig (mts.), Idaho 220/B4
Craig, Iowa (51017) 229/A3
Craig, Mo. (64437) 261/B2
Craig, Mont. (†59648) 262/D3
Craig, Nebr. (68019) 264/H3
Craig (co.), Okla. 288/R1
Craig (co.), Va. 307/H6
Craig (creek), Va. 307/H5
Craigavon (dist.), N. Ireland 17/J3
Craigavon, N. Ireland 10/C3
Craigavon, N. Ireland 17/J3
Craig Beach, Ohio (†44429) 284/H3
Craigellachie, Scotland 15/E3
Craighead (co.), Ark. 202/J2
Craighouse, Scotland 15/C5
Craigieburn, Victoria 97/C5
Craigleith, Ontario 177/D3
Craigmont, Idaho (83523) 220/B3
Craigmyle, Alberta 182/D4
Craignish (hills), Nova Scotia 168/G3
Craignure, Scotland 15/C4
Craigs (Sainte Rita), Manitoba 179/F5
Craig Springs, Va. (†24127) 307/H6
Craigsville, Va. (24430) 307/J4
Craigsville, W. Va. (26205) 312/E6
Craigville, Ind. (46731) 227/G3
Craigville, Minn. (†56639) 255/E3
Craik, Sask. 181/F4
Crail, Scotland 15/F4
Crail, Scotland 10/E2
Crailsheim, W. Germany 22/D4
Craiova, Romania 45/F3
Craiova, Romania 7/G4
Cramerton, N.C. (28032) 281/G4
Cramond (isl.), Scotland 15/D1
Cranberry (lake), N.Y. 276/L2
Cranberry (lake), N. Dak. 282/L3
Cranberry, Pa. (16319) 294/C3
Cranberry, W. Va. (25828) 312/D7
Cranberry Isles, Maine (04625) 243/G7
Cranberry Isles○, Maine (04625) 243/G7
Cranberry Lake, N. J. (†07821) 273/D2
Cranberry Lake, N.Y. (12927) 276/L2
Cranberry Portage, Manitoba 179/H3
Cranbourne, Victoria 97/C6
Cranbourne, Victoria 88/M8
Cranbrook, Br. Col. 162/E6
Cranbrook, Br. Col. 184/K5
Cranbrook, Tasmania 99/D4
Cranbrook, W. Australia 92/B6
Cranbury, Conn. (†06856) 210/B4
Cranbury, N.J. (08512) 273/E3
Crandall, Georgia (30711) 217/C1
Crandall, Ind. (47114) 227/E8
Crandall, Manitoba 179/B4
Crandall, S. Dak. (†57434) 298/O3
Crandall, Texas (75114) 303/H5
Crandon, Va. (†24315) 307/G6
Crandon, Wis. (54520) 317/H4
Crane, Barbados 161/C9
Crane, Ind. (47522) 227/D7
Crane, Mo. (65633) 261/E9
Crane, Mont. (59217) 262/M3
Crane, Oreg. (97732) 291/J4
Crane (creek), Oreg. 291/J4
Crane (lake), Sask. 181/B5
Crane (co.), Texas 303/B6
Crane, Texas (79731) 303/B6
Crane Creek (res.), Idaho 220/B5
Crane Hill, Ala. (35053) 195/D2
Crane Lake, Minn. (55725) 255/F2
Crane Nest, Ky. (40928) 237/O7
Crane Prairie (res.), Oreg. 291/F4
Crane River, Manitoba 179/C3
Cranesville, Pa. (16410) 294/B2
Cranesville, W. Va. (†26764) 312/G3
Crane Valley, Sask. 181/F6
Cranfills Gap, Texas (76637) 303/G6
Cranford○, N.J. (07016) 273/E2
Cranleigh, England 13/G6
Cransac, France 28/E5
Cranston, Iowa (52741) 229/L6
Cranston, R.I. (02910) 249/J5
Crapaud, Pr. Edward I. 168/E2
Crapo, Md. (21626) 245/O7
Crary, N. Dak. (58327) 282/N3
Craster, England 13/F2
Crater (lake), Oreg. 291/E5
Crater Lake, Oreg. (97604) 291/E5
Crater Lake Nat'l Park, Oreg. 291/E5
Craters of the Moon Nat'l Mon., Idaho 220/E6
Crateús, Brazil 132/F4
Crateús, Brazil 120/E3
Crati (riv.), Italy 34/F5
Crato, Brazil 132/G4
Crato, Brazil 120/E3
Crato e Mártires, Portugal 33/C3
Crauford (cape), N.W. Terrs. 187/K2
Craven (co.), N.C. 281/P4
Craven, Sask. 181/G5
Cravens, La. (†70656) 238/E5
Cravo Norte, Colombia 126/F4
Cravo Norte (riv.), Colombia 126/E4
Cravo Sur (riv.), Colombia 126/E5
Crawford (co.), Ark. 202/B2
Crawford, Colo. (81415) 208/D5
Crawford (co.), Georgia 217/E5
Crawford, Georgia (30630) 217/F3
Crawford (co.), Ill. 222/F4
Crawford (co.), Ind. 227/E8
Crawford (co.), Iowa 229/C4
Crawford (co.), Kansas 232/H4
Crawford, Kansas (†67444) 232/E3
Crawford○, Maine (†04610) 243/H5
Crawford (lake), Maine 243/H5
Crawford (co.), Mich. 250/E4
Crawford, Miss. (39743) 256/G4
Crawford (co.), Mo. 261/K7
Crawford, Nebr. (69339) 264/A2
Crawford (co.), Ohio 284/E4
Crawford, Okla. (73638) 288/G3
Crawford (co.), Pa. 294/B2
Crawford, Scotland 15/E5
Crawford, Tenn. (38554) 237/L8
Crawford, Texas (76638) 303/G6
Crawford, W. Va. (26343) 312/F5
Crawford (co.), Wis. 317/E9
Crawford Bay, Br. Col. 184/J5
Crawford House, N.H. (†03595) 268/E3
Crawford Notch (pass), N.H. 268/E3
Crawfordsville, Ark. (72327) 202/K3
Crawfordsville, Ind. 227/D4
Crawfordsville, Iowa (52621) 229/K6
Crawfordsville, Oreg. (97336) 291/E3
Crawfordville, Fla. (32327) 212/B1
Crawfordville, Georgia (30631) 217/G3
Crawley, England 13/G6
Crawley, W. Va. (24931) 312/E7
Crayne, Ky. (42033) 237/E6
Crazy (peak), Mont. 262/F4
Crazy Horse Mon., S. Dak. 298/B6
Crazy Woman (creek), Wyo. 319/F1
Creach Bheinn (mt.), Scotland 15/C4
Creagerstown, Md. (†21788) 245/J2
Creag Meagaidh (mt.), Scotland 15/D4
Creal Springs, Ill. (62922) 222/E6
Cream (hill), Conn. 210/B1
Cream, Wis. (†54610) 317/C7
Creamridge, N.J. (08514) 273/E3
Crean (lake), Sask. 181/E1
Creciente (isl.), Mexico 150/D5
Credenhill, England 13/E5
Crediton, England 13/D7
Crediton, England 10/E5
Crediton, Ontario 177/C4
Cree (lake), Sask. 162/F4
Cree (lake), Sask. 181/L3
Cree (riv.), Sask. 181/M2
Cree (riv.), Scotland 15/D5
Creede, Colo. (81130) 208/E7
Creedmoor, N.C. (27522) 281/M2
Creek (co.), Okla. 288/O3
Creekside, Pa. (15732) 294/D4
Creek Stand, Ala. (†36070) 195/G6
Creekville, Ky. (†40963) 237/P6
Creel, Mexico 150/E3
Cree Lake, Sask. 181/L3
Creelman, Sask. 181/H6
Creelsboro, Ky. (†42629) 237/L7
Creemore, Ontario 177/D3
Creeslough, Ireland 17/F1
Creetown, Scotland 15/D6
Creighton, Mo. (64739) 261/D6
Creighton, Nebr. (68729) 264/G2
Creighton, Pa. (15030) 294/C4
Creighton, Sask. 181/N4
Creighton, S. Dak. (57729) 298/E5
Creignish, Nova Scotia 168/G3
Creil, France 28/E3
Crellin, Md. (21525) 245/A3
Crema, Italy 34/B2
Cremona, Alberta 182/C4
Cremona (prov.), Italy 34/B2
Cremona, Italy 34/B2
Crenshaw (co.), Ala. 195/F7
Crenshaw, Miss. (38621) 256/D2
Crenshaw, Pa. (†15824) 294/E3
Creola, Ala. (36525) 195/B9
Creola, Ohio (45622) 284/E7
Creole, La. (70632) 238/D7
Crépy-en-Valois, France 28/E3
Creran, Loch (inlet), Scotland 15/C4
Cres (isl.), Yugoslavia 45/B3
Cresaptown, Md. (21502) 245/C2
Cresbard, S. Dak. (57435) 298/M3
Crescent (isls.), China 85/E2
Crescent (lake), Fla. 212/E2
Crescent, Iowa (51526) 229/B6
Crescent, La. (†70764) 238/J2
Crescent, Mo. (63018) 261/N4
Crescent (lake), Nev. 264/B3
Crescent (valley), Nev. 266/E2
Crescent, Okla. (73028) 288/L3
Crescent, Oreg. (97733) 291/F4
Crescent (lake), Tasmania 99/D4
Crescent (lake), Wash. 310/B2
Crescent Beach, Conn. (†06537) 210/G3
Crescent City, Calif. (95531) 204/A2
Crescent City, Fla. (32012) 212/E2
Crescent City, Ill. (60928) 222/F3
Crescent Head, N.S. Wales 97/G2
Crescent Lake, Maine (†04015) 243/C7
Crescent Lake, Oreg. (97425) 291/F4
Crescent Lake, Sask. 181/J4
Crescent Mills, Calif. (95934) 204/E3
Crescent Springs, Ky. (†41016) 237/R2
Cresco, Iowa (52136) 229/J2
Cresco, Pa. (18326) 294/M3
Crespo, Argentina 143/F6
Cresskill, N.J. (07626) 273/C1
Cressmont, W. Va. (†25074) 312/E6
Cresson, Pa. (16630) 294/E5
Cresson, Texas (76035) 303/G5
Cressona, Pa. (17929) 294/K4
Cressy, Tasmania 99/C3
Crest, France 28/F5
Crest, Georgia (†30286) 217/D5
Crested Butte, Colo. (81224) 208/E5
Crest Hill, Ill. (60431) 222/E2
Crestline, Calif. (92325) 204/H9
Crestline, Kansas (66728) 232/H4
Crestline, Ohio (44827) 284/E4
Creston, Br. Col. 184/J5
Creston, Calif. (93432) 204/E8
Creston, Ill. (60113) 222/D2
Creston, Ind. (†46356) 227/C2
Creston, Iowa (50801) 229/E6
Creston, Ky. (42524) 237/L6
Creston, La. (71020) 238/E3
Creston, Mont. (59902) 262/C2
Creston, Nebr. (68631) 264/G3
Creston, Newf. 166/C4
Creston, Ohio (44217) 284/G3
Creston, S.C. (†29030) 296/F4
Creston, Wash. (99117) 310/G3
Creston, W. Va. (26141) 312/D5
Crestone, Colo. (81131) 208/H7
Crestone (peak), Colo. 208/H7
Crestview, Fla. (32536) 212/C6
Crestview, Ky. (†41076) 237/S2
Crestview Hills, Ky. (†41017) 237/R2
Crestwood, Ill. (†60445) 222/B6
Crestwood, Ky. (40014) 237/L4
Crestwood, Mo. (†63126) 261/O3
Crestwynd, Sask. 181/F5
Creswell, N.C. (27928) 281/S3
Creswell (bay), N.W. Terrs. 187/J2
Creswell, Oreg. (97426) 291/D4
Creswell Downs, North. Terr. 93/E4
Creswick, Victoria 97/B5
Crete (reg.), Greece 45/G8
Crete (isl.), Greece 7/G5
Crete (isl.), Greece 45/G8
Crete (sea), Greece 45/G7
Crete, Ill. (60417) 222/F2
Crete, Nebr. (68333) 264/G4
Crete, N. Dak. (58020) 282/P7
Créteil, France 28/B2
Cretin (cape), Papua N.G. 86/B2
Creus (cape), Spain 33/H1
Creuse (dept.), France 28/D4
Creuse (riv.), France 28/D4
Creve Coeur, Ill. (61611) 222/D3
Creve Coeur, Mo. (63141) 261/O2
Crevillente, Spain 33/F3
Crewe, Va. (23930) 307/M6
Crewe and Nantwich, England 13/E4
Crewe and Nantwich, England 10/F2
Crewkerne, England 13/E7
Crewkerne, England 10/E5
Crews, Ala. (†35586) 195/B3
Crianlarich, Scotland 15/D4
Criccieth, Wales 13/C5
Criccieth, Wales 10/D4
Crichton, Sask. 181/D6
Criciúma, Brazil 132/D10
Crider, Ky. (†42445) 237/F6
Cridersville, Ohio (45806) 284/B4
Crieff, Scotland 15/E4
Crieff, Scotland 10/E2
Criehaven, Maine (†04851) 243/F8
Crillon (mt.), Alaska 196/L1
Crimea (pen.), U.S.S.R. 7/H4
Crimea (pen.), U.S.S.R. 48/D5
Crimea (pen.), U.S.S.R. 52/D5
Crimean Oblast, U.S.S.R. 52/D6
Crimmitschau, E. Germany 22/E3
Crimond, Scotland 15/G3
Crimora, Va. (24431) 307/L4
Crinan, Scotland 15/C4
Cripple Creek, Colo. 188/F3
Cripple Creek, Colo. (80813) 208/J5
Cripple Creek, Va. (24322) 307/F7
Crisfield, Md. (21817) 245/P9
Crisp (co.), Georgia 217/E7
Crisp (pt.), Mich. 250/E2
Crisp, N.C. (27852) 281/O3
Crissolo, Italy 34/A2
Cristal, Sierra del (mts.), Cuba 158/J3
Cristalina, Brazil 132/E7
Cristóbal (mt.), Colombia 120/B1
Cristóbal (pt.), Ecuador 128/B9
Cristóbal, Panama 154/G6
Cristóbal Colón, Pico (peak), Colombia 126/D2
Crişul Alb (riv.), Romania 45/F2
Crişul Repede (riv.), Romania 45/F2
Crittenden (co.), Ark. 202/K3
Crittenden (co.), Ky. 237/E6
Crittenden, Ky. (41030) 237/M3
Critz, Va. (24082) 307/H7
Crivitz, Wis. (54114) 317/L5
Croagh Patrick (mt.), Ireland 17/C4
Croatan (sound), N.C. 281/T3
Croatia (rep.), Yugoslavia 45/C3
Croche (riv.), Québec 172/E2
Crocheron, Md. (21627) 245/O8
Crochu, Grenada 161/D8
Crocker, Mo. (65452) 261/H7
Crocker, S. Dak. (57229) 298/O3
Crocketford, Scotland 15/E5
Crockett, Calif. (94525) 204/J1
Crockett (co.), Tenn. 237/C9
Crockett (co.), Texas 303/C7
Crockett, Texas (75835) 303/J6
Crockett, Va. (24323) 307/F7
Crockett Mills, Tenn. (38021) 237/C9
Crocketts Bluff, Ark. (72038) 202/H5
Crocketville, S.C. (29913) 296/E6
Crocodile (riv.), S. Africa 118/H6
Croft, Kansas (†67028) 232/D4
Crofton, Br. Col. 184/J3
Crofton, Ky. (42217) 237/G6
Crofton, Md. (21114) 245/M4
Crofton, Nebr. (68730) 264/G2
Croghan, N.Y. (13327) 276/K3
Croix des Bouquets, Haiti 158/C6
Croker (cape), North. Terr. 88/E2
Croker (cape), North. Terr. 93/C1
Croker (bay), N.W. Terrs. 187/K2
Croker (cape), Ontario 177/D3
Croker Island Mission, North. Terr. 88/E2
Croker Island Mission, North. Terr. 93/C1
Cromarty, Scotland 15/E3
Cromarty, Scotland 10/D2
Cromarty (firth), Scotland 15/D3
Cromdale, Scotland 15/E3
Cromer, England 13/J5
Cromer, England 10/G4
Cromer, Manitoba 179/A5
Cromwell, Ala. (36906) 195/B6
Cromwell○, Conn. (06416) 210/E2
Cromwell, Ind. (46732) 227/F2
Cromwell, Iowa (50842) 229/E6
Cromwell, Ky. (42333) 237/H6
Cromwell, Minn. (55726) 255/F4
Cromwell, N. Zealand 100/B6
Cromwell, Okla. (74837) 288/N4
Cronulla, N. S. Wales 88/L5
Cronulla, N.S. Wales 97/J4
Crook, Colo. (80726) 208/O1
Crook (co.), Oreg. 291/G3
Crook (pt.), Oreg. 291/C5
Crook (co.), Wyo. 319/H1
Crook and Willington, England 13/E3
Crooked (isl.), Bahamas 156/D2
Crooked (creek), Ind. 227/D2
Crooked (creek), Kansas 232/B4
Crooked (lake), Minn. 255/F4
Crooked (lake), Minn. 255/G2
Crooked (lake), N. Dak. 282/J4
Crooked (creek), Oreg. 291/K5
Crooked (riv.), Oreg. 291/G3
Crooked (creek), S.C. 296/H2
Crooked Creek, Alaska (99575) 196/G2
Crooked Creek, Alberta 182/B2
Crooked Island (passage), Bahamas 156/C2
Crooked River, Sask. 181/H3
Crookhaven, Ireland 17/B9
Crooks, S. Dak. (57020) 298/R6
Crookston, Minn. 188/G1
Crookston, Minn. (56716) 255/B3
Crookston, Nebr. (69212) 264/D2
Crooksville, Ohio (43731) 284/F6
Crookwell, N.S. Wales 97/E4
Croom, Ireland 17/D6
Cropper, Ky. (40015) 237/L4
Cropsey, Ill. (61731) 222/E3
Crosby, Ala. (†36343) 195/H8
Crosby, England 13/G2
Crosby, England 10/F2
Crosby, Minn. (56441) 255/D4
Crosby, Miss. (39633) 256/B8
Crosby, N. Dak. (58730) 282/D2
Crosby, Pa. (16724) 294/F2
Crosby (co.), Texas 303/C4
Crosby, Texas (77532) 303/J8
Crosby (mt.), Wyo. 319/C2
Crosbyton, Texas (79322) 303/C4
Crosland, Georgia (†31771) 217/E8
Cross (sound), Alaska 196/L1
Cross (co.), Ark. 202/J3
Cross (riv.), Cameroon 115/A2
Cross (lake), La. 238/C2
Cross (isl.), Maine 243/J6
Cross (lake), Maine 243/G1
Cross (bay), Manitoba 179/C1
Cross (lake), Manitoba 179/J3
Cross (cape), Namibia 118/A4
Cross (riv.), Nigeria 106/F7
Cross (isl.), Nova Scotia 168/D4
Cross, S.C. (29436) 296/G5
Cross Anchor, S.C. (29331) 296/D2
Crossapoll, Scotland 15/B4
Cross City, Fla. (32628) 212/C2
Cross Creek, New Bruns. 170/D2
Crossett, Ark. (71635) 202/G7
Crossfarnoge (pt.), Ireland 17/J7
Cross Fell (mt.), England 13/E3
Crossfield, Alberta 182/C4
Cross Fork, Pa. (17729) 294/G3

Cyrenaica 357

Crossgar, N. Ireland 17/K3
Crosshaven, Ireland 17/E8
Crosshill, Scotland 15/D5
Cross Hill, S.C. (29332) 296/D3
Cross Junction, Va. (22625) 307/M2
Cross Keys, S.C. (†29379) 296/D2
Cross Lake, Manitoba 179/J3
Crosslake, Minn. (56442) 255/E4
Crossley (mt.), N. Zealand 100/D5
Crossmaglen, N. Ireland 17/H3
Crossmichael, Scotland 15/D6
Crossmolina, Ireland 17/C3
Crossnore, N.C. (28616) 281/F2
Cross Plains, Ind. (47017) 227/G7
Cross Plains, Tenn. (37049) 237/H7
Cross Plains, Texas (76443) 303/E5
Cross Plains, Wis. (53528) 317/G9
Cross River (state), Nigeria 106/F7
Cross Roads, Calif. (†92242) 204/L9
Crossroads, N. Mex. (88114) 274/F5
Cross Roads, Pa. (†17322) 294/J6
Cross Timbers, Mo. (65634) 261/F6
Crosstown, Mo. (†63775) 261/N7
Cross Village, Mich. (49723) 250/D3
Crossville, Ala. (35962) 195/G2
Crossville, Ill. (62827) 222/F5
Crossville, Tenn. (38555) 237/L9
Crosswicks, N.J. (08515) 273/D3
Crosswicks (creek), N.J. 273/D3
Croswell, Mich. (48422) 250/G5
Crotch (lake), Ontario 177/H3
Crothersville, Ind. (47229) 227/F7
Croton (Hartford), Ohio (43013) 284/E5
Crotone, Italy 34/F5
Croton Falls, N.Y. (10519) 276/N8
Croton-on-Hudson, N.Y. (10520) 276/N8
Crouch, Idaho (†83622) 220/B5
Crouseville, Maine (04738) 243/G2
Crow (creek), Colo. 208/L1
Crow (riv.), Minn. 255/F5
Crow, Oreg. (†97401) 291/D4
Crow (creek), S. Dak. 298/A4
Crow (creek), Wyo. 319/H4
Crow Agency, Mont. (59022) 262/J5
Crowborough, England 13/H6
Crow Creek Ind. Res., S. Dak. 298/L5
Crowder, Miss. (38622) 256/D2
Crowder, Okla. (74430) 288/P4
Crowduck (lake), Manitoba 179/G4
Crowdy (head), N.S. Wales 97/G2
Crowell, Texas (79227) 303/E4
Crowfoot, Alberta 182/D4
Crowheart, Wyo. (82512) 319/C2
Crow Ind. Res., Mont. 262/H5
Crowl (creek), N.S. Wales 97/C2
Crow Lake, S. Dak. (†57382) 298/M6
Crowle, England 13/G4
Crowley (lake), Calif. 204/G6
Crowley (co.), Colo. 208/M6
Crowley, Colo. (81033) 208/M6
Crowley, La. (70526) 238/F6
Crowley, Texas (76036) 303/E3
Crowley Lake, Calif. (93546) 204/G6
Crowley's Ridge (mt.), Ark. 202/J2
Crown, Minn. (†55005) 255/E5
Crown (mt.), Virgin Is. (U.S.) 161/A4
Crown City, Ohio (45623) 284/F8
Crown King, Ariz. (86333) 198/C4
Crown Point, Ind. (46307) 227/C2
Crownpoint, N. Mex. (87313) 274/A3
Crown Point, N.Y. (12928) 276/N3
Crown Prince Frederik (isl.), N.W. Terrs. 187/K3
Crownsville, Md. (21032) 245/M4
Crows Landing, Calif. (95313) 204/D6
Crowsnest (pass), Alberta 182/C5
Crowsnest, Br. Col. 184/K5
Crowsnest (pass), Br. Col. 184/K5
Crowville, La. (71230) 238/G2
Crow Wing (co.), Minn. 255/D4
Crow Wing (riv.), Minn. 255/D4
Croydon, England 13/H8
Croydon, England 10/B6
Croydon○, N.H. (†03753) 268/C5
Croydon (peak), N.H. 268/C5
Croydon, Queensland 88/G3
Croydon, Queensland 95/B3
Croydon, Utah (84018) 304/C2
Croydon, Victoria 88/M7
Croydon, Victoria 97/K5
Croydon Branch, Sugar (riv.), N.H. 268/C5
Crozet (isls.) 2/M8
Crozet, Va. (22932) 307/L4
Crozier (chan.), N.W. Terrs. 187/G2
Crozier, Va. (23039) 307/N5
Cruces, Cuba 158/E2
Cruces, Cuba 156/B2
Cruden Bay, Scotland 15/G3
Cruger, Miss. (38924) 256/D4
Cruillas, Mexico 150/K4
Crum (creek), Pa. 294/M7
Crum, W. Va. (25669) 312/B7
Crumlin, N. Ireland 17/J2
Crum Lynne, Pa. (19022) 294/M7
Crummies, Ky. (40821) 237/P7
Crump, Mich. (†48634) 250/E5
Crump (lake), Oreg. 291/H5
Crump, Tenn. (38327) 237/E10
Crumpton (pt.), Dominica 161/F5
Crumpton, Md. (21628) 245/P4
Crumrod, Ark. (72328) 202/H5
Crumstown, Ind. (†46554) 227/E1
Crusheen, Ireland 17/D6
Cruso, N.C. (†28716) 281/D4
Cruta, Honduras 154/F3
Crutchfield, Ky. (42034) 237/D7
Crutwell, Sask. 181/E2
Cruz (cape), Cuba 156/C3
Cruz (cape), Cuba 158/G4
Cruz Alta, Brazil 120/D5
Cruz Alta, Brazil 132/C10
Cruz Bay, Virgin Is. (U.S.) 161/C4
Cruz del Eje, Argentina 143/C3
Cruz del Eje, Argentina 120/C6
Cruz de Piedra, Uruguay 145/E3
Cruz de San Pedro, Uruguay 145/E2
Cruzeiro, Brazil 135/D3
Cruzeiro do Sol, Brazil 120/B3
Cruzeiro do Sul, Brazil 132/G10
Cruz Grande, Chile 138/A7
Crysler, Ontario 177/J2
Crystal (mts.), Congo 115/B4
Crystal (lake), Conn. 210/F1
Crystal (pond), Conn. 210/G1
Crystal (bay), Fla. 212/D3
Crystal (mts.), Gabon 115/B4
Crystal, Ind. (†47527) 227/D8
Crystal○, Maine (†04747) 243/G4
Crystal, Mich. (48818) 250/E5
Crystal (lake), Mich. 250/C4
Crystal, Minn. (†55428) 255/G5
Crystal, N.H. (†03591) 268/E2
Crystal (lake), N.H. 268/E5
Crystal, N. Mex. (†86504) 274/A2
Crystal, N. Dak. (58222) 282/P2
Crystal (lake), Vt. 268/C2
Crystal, W. Va. (†24747) 312/D8
Crystal Bay (Orono), Minn. (55323) 255/F5
Crystal Bay, Nev. (89402) 266/A3
Crystal Beach, Texas (77650) 303/K8
Crystal Brook, S. Australia 94/E5
Crystal City, Manitoba 179/C5
Crystal City, Mo. (63019) 261/M6
Crystal City, Texas (78839) 303/E9
Crystal Falls, Mich. (49920) 250/A2
Crystal Falls, Ontario 177/E1
Crystal Hill, Va. (24539) 307/L7
Crystal Lake, Conn. (†06066) 210/F1
Crystal Lake, Fla. (†32463) 212/D6
Crystal Lake, Ill. (60014) 222/E1
Crystal Lake, Iowa (50432) 229/F2
Crystal Lake Park, Mo. (†63101) 261/O3
Crystal Lakes, Ohio (†45341) 284/C6
Crystal River, Fla. (32629) 212/D3
Crystal Springs, Ark. (†71968) 202/D5
Crystal Springs (res.), Calif. 204/J3
Crystal Springs, Fla. (33524) 212/D3
Crystal Springs, Georgia (†30105) 217/B2
Crystal Springs, Kansas (†67058) 232/D4
Crystal Springs, Miss. (39059) 256/D7
Crystal Springs, N. Dak. (58427) 282/L6
Crystal Springs, Sask. 181/F3
Crystal Valley, Mich. (†49420) 250/C5
Csabrendek, Hungary 41/D3
Csákvár, Hungary 41/E3
Csanádpalota, Hungary 41/F3
Csenger, Hungary 41/G3
Csepel, Hungary 41/E3
Csepelsziget (isl.), Hungary 41/E3
Csepreg, Hungary 41/D3
Csongrád (co.), Hungary 41/F3
Csongrád, Hungary 41/E3
Csorna, Hungary 41/D3
Csorvás, Hungary 41/F3
Csurgó, Hungary 41/D3
Ctesiphon (ruins), Iraq 66/D4
Cúa, Venezuela 124/E2
Cuadro Nacional, Argentina 143/C3
Cuamba, Mozambique 118/F2
Cuando (riv.), Angola 115/C7
Cuando (riv.), Zambia 115/D7
Cuando Cubango (dist.), Angola 115/C7
Cuangar, Angola 115/C7
Cuango (riv.) 102/D5
Cuango, Angola 115/C5
Cuango (riv.), Angola 115/C5
Cuanza (riv.), Angola 102/D6
Cuanza (riv.), Angola 115/C5
Cuanza-Norte (dist.), Angola 115/B5
Cuanza-Sul (dist.), Angola 115/C6
Cuao (riv.), Venezuela 124/E5
Cua Rao, Vietnam 72/E3
Cuareim (riv.), Uruguay 145/B1
Cuaró, Uruguay 145/D2
Cuatrociénagas de Carranza, Mexico 150/H3
Cuatro Compañeros, Cuba 158/G3
Cuatro Ojos, Bolivia 136/D5
Cuauhtémoc, Mexico 150/F2
Cuautepec de Hinojosa, Mexico 150/K6
Cuautitlán de Romero Rubio, Mexico 150/L1
Cuautla Morelos, Mexico 150/L2
Cub (creek), Utah 304/C1
Cub (creek), Va. 307/L6
Cuba 2/E4
Cuba 146/L7
Cuba, Ala. (36907) 195/B6
CUBA 156/B2
CUBA 158
Cuba, Ill. (61427) 222/C3
Cuba, Ind. (†47460) 227/D6
Cuba, Kansas (66940) 232/E2
Cuba, Mo. (65453) 261/K6
Cuba, N. Mex. (87013) 274/B2
Cuba, N.Y. (14727) 276/D6
Cuba (chan.), N. Zealand 100/D7
Cuba, Ohio (45114) 284/C7
Cuba, Portugal 33/C3
Cuba City, Wis. (53807) 317/F10
Cubage, Ky. (40822) 237/O7
Cubagua (isl.), Venezuela 124/F2
Cuballing, W. Australia 92/B2
Cubango (riv.), Angola 102/D6
Cubango (riv.), Angola 115/C7
Cubango (riv.), Namibia 118/B3
Cubatão, Brazil 135/C3
Cube (mt.), N.H. 268/D4
Cubero, N. Mex. (87014) 274/B3
Cubiro, Venezuela 124/D3
Cub Run, Ky. (42729) 237/J6
Çubuk, Turkey 63/E2
Cubulco, Guatemala 154/B3
Cuchara, Colo. (81055) 208/J8
Cuchi, Angola 115/C1
Cuchi, Angola 102/D6
Cuchillo, N. Mex. (87932) 274/B5
Cuchillo-Có, Argentina 143/D4
Cuchillo Negro (creek), N. Mex. 274/B5
Cuchivero, Venezuela 124/F4
Cuchivero (riv.), Venezuela 124/F4
Cuckfield, England 13/G6
Cuckfield, England 10/F5
Cucumber, W. Va. (24826) 312/C8
Cúcuta, Colombia 126/D4
Cúcuta, Colombia 120/B2
Cudahy, Calif. (90201) 204/C5
Cudahy, Wis. (53110) 317/M2
Cudal, N.S. Wales 97/E3
Cuddalore, India 68/E6
Cuddapah, India 68/D6
Cuddeback (lake), Calif. 204/H8
Cuddy, Pa. (15031) 294/B5
Cudgewa, Victoria 97/D5
Cudillero, Spain 33/C1
Cudjoe (key), Fla. 212/E7
Cudrefin, Switzerland 39/D3
Cudworth, Sask. 181/F3
Cue, W. Australia 88/B5
Cue, W. Australia 92/B4
Cuéllar, Spain 33/D2
Cuéllar-Baza, Spain 33/E4
Cuemaní (riv.), Colombia 126/D7
Cuenca, Ecuador 120/B3
Cuenca, Ecuador 128/C4
Cuenca (prov.), Spain 33/E2
Cuenca, Spain 33/E2
Cuenca, Sierra de (range), Spain 33/F3
Cuencamé de Ceniceros, Mexico 150/H4
Cuernavaca, Mexico 150/L2
Cuero, Texas (77954) 303/G8
Cuervo, N. Mex. (88417) 274/E3
Cuervo (creek), N. Mex. 274/E3
Cueto, Cuba 158/J3
Cuevas, Miss. (†39571) 256/F10
Cuevas del Almanzora, Spain 33/F4
Cuevas de Vinromá, Spain 33/F2
Cuevo, Bolivia 136/D7
Cufré, Uruguay 145/B5
Cuiabá, Brazil 120/D4
Cuiabá, Brazil 132/C6
Cuiabá (riv.), Brazil 132/B7
Cuicatlán, Mexico 150/L8
Cuicuina, Nicaragua 154/E4
Cuilapa, Guatemala 154/B3
Cuilapa Miravalles (vol.), C. Rica 154/E5
Cuilcagh (mt.), Ireland 17/F3
Cuilco, Guatemala 154/B3
Cuillin (hills), Scotland 15/B3
Cuillin (sound), Scotland 10/C2
Cuillin (sound), Scotland 15/B3
Cuilo, Angola 115/C5
Cuitlahuac, Mexico 150/P2
Cuito (riv.), Angola 115/C7
Cuito-Cuanavale, Angola 115/C7
Cuitzeo (lake), Mexico 150/J7
Cuivre (riv.), Mo. 261/N2
Cujmir, Romania 45/F3
Cukmantl, Czech. 41/D1
Çukur, Turkey 63/F3
Çukurca, Turkey 63/K4
Culaba, Philippines 82/E5
Cu Lao, Hon (isls.), Vietnam 72/F5
Culberson, N.C. (28903) 281/A4
Culberson (co.), Texas 303/C11
Culbertson, Mont. (59218) 262/M2
Culbertson, Nebr. (69024) 264/C4
Culcairn, N.S. Wales 97/D4
Culdaff, Ireland 17/G1
Culdaff (bay), Ireland 17/G1
Culdesac, Idaho (83524) 220/B3
Cul-de-Sac du Marin (bay), Martinique 161/D7
Culebra (creek), Colo. 208/H8
Culebra (peak), Colo. 208/J8
Culebra, P. Rico 161/G1
Culebra (isl.), P. Rico 161/G1
Culebra (isl.), P. Rico 156/G1
Culebras, Peru 128/C7
Culebrinas (riv.), P. Rico 161/A1
Culebrita (isl.), P. Rico 161/G2
Culemborg, Netherlands 27/G5
Culgoa (riv.), N.S. Wales 97/D1
Culgoa (riv.), Queensland 95/C6
Culiacán, Mexico 150/F4
Culiacán, Mexico 146/H7
Culion, Philippines 82/C5
Culion (isl.), Philippines 82/B5
Cullasaja, N.C. (†28734) 281/C4
Cullburra-Orient Point, N.S. Wales 97/F4
Cullen, La. (71021) 238/D1
Cullen, Sask. 181/J6
Cullen, Scotland 15/F3
Cullen, Va. (23934) 307/L6
Cullen Bullen, N.S. Wales 97/F3
Culleoka, Tenn. (38451) 237/G10
Cullera, Spain 33/F3
Cullin (lake), Ireland 17/C4
Cullison, Kansas (†67124) 232/D4
Cullman (co.), Ala. 195/E2
Cullman, Ala. (35055) 195/E2
Culloden, Georgia (31016) 217/D5
Culloden, W. Va. (25510) 312/B6
Cullom, Ill. (60929) 222/E3
Cullomburg, Ala. (36920) 195/B7
Cullompton, England 13/D7
Cullowhee, N.C. (28723) 281/C4
Cully, Switzerland 39/C4
Cullybackey, N. Ireland 17/J2
Culotte (lake), Québec 172/C2
Culp, Alberta 182/B2
Culp Creek, Oreg. (97427) 291/E4
Culpeper (co.), Va. 307/M3
Culpeper, Va. (22701) 307/M4
Culpepper (isl.), Ecuador 128/B8
Culpina, Bolivia 136/C7
Culross, Manitoba 179/E5
Culross, Scotland 10/B1
Culross, Scotland 15/C1
Culta, Bolivia 136/B6
Cults, Scotland 15/F3
Cultus (lake), Oreg. 291/F4
Cultus Lake, Br. Col. 184/M3
Culuene (riv.), Brazil 132/C6
Culver, Ind. (46511) 227/E2
Culver, Kansas (67435) 232/E3
Culver, Minn. (55727) 255/F4
Culver, Oreg. (97734) 291/F3
Culver (pt.), W. Australia 88/D6
Culver (pt.), W. Australia 92/D6
Culver City, Calif. (90230) 204/B10
Culverden, N. Zealand 100/D5
Culvers (lake), N.J. 273/D1
Culverton, Georgia (†31087) 217/G4
Cuma, Angola 115/B6
Cumaná, Venezuela 120/C2
Cumaná, Venezuela 124/F2
Cumanacoa, Venezuela 124/F2
Cumanayagua, Cuba 158/E2
Cumaria, Peru 128/F7
Cumback, Ind. (†47501) 227/C7
Cumbal, Colombia 126/B7
Cumberland (riv.) 188/J3
Cumberland (plat.), Ala. 195/F1
Cumberland, Br. Col. 184/E5
Cumberland (sound), Canada 4/C13
Cumberland (isl.), Georgia 217/K9
Cumberland (co.), Ill. 222/E4
Cumberland, Ind. (46229) 227/E5
Cumberland, Iowa (50843) 229/D6
Cumberland (co.), Ky. 237/L7
Cumberland, Ky. (40823) 237/R6
Cumberland (lake), Ky. 237/M7
Cumberland (mt.), Ky. 237/P7
Cumberland (riv.), Ky. 237/K8
Cumberland (co.), Maine 243/C8
Cumberland, Md. (21502) 245/D2
Cumberland, Md. 245/80
Cumberland, Md. 188/L3
Cumberland (basin), New Bruns. 170/F3
Cumberland (co.), N.J. 273/C5
Cumberland (co.), N.C. 281/M4
Cumberland, N.C. (28331) 281/M5
Cumberland (pen.), N.W.T. 162/K2
Cumberland (pen.), N.W. Terrs. 187/M3
Cumberland (sound), N.W.T. 146/N3
Cumberland (sound), N.W.T. 162/K2
Cumberland (sound), N.W. Terrs. 187/M3
Cumberland (co.), Nova Scotia 168/D3
Cumberland (basin), Nova Scotia 168/D3
Cumberland, Ohio (43732) 284/G6
Cumberland, Okla. (†73446) 288/N6
Cumberland, Ontario 177/J2
Cumberland (co.), Pa. 294/H5
Cumberland (isls.), Queensland 88/H4
Cumberland (isls.), Queensland 95/D4
Cumberland (bay), St. Vin. & Grens. 161/A8
Cumberland (lake), Sask. 181/J1
Cumberland (co.), Tenn. 237/L9
Cumberland (plat.), Tenn. 237/L9
Cumberland (riv.), Tenn. 237/K8
Cumberland (co.), Va. 307/M6
Cumberland, Va. (23040) 307/M6
Cumberland (mt.), Va. 307/B7
Cumberland, Wash. (†98022) 310/D3
Cumberland, Wis. (54829) 317/C4
Cumberland Bay, New Bruns. 170/E2
Cumberland Beach, Ontario 177/E3
Cumberland Center, Maine (04021) 243/C8
Cumberland Center○, Maine (04021) 243/C8
Cumberland City, Tenn. (37050) 237/F8
Cumberland Furnace, Tenn. (37051) 237/G8
Cumberland Gap, Tenn. (37724) 237/O8
Cumberland Gap Nat'l Hist. Park, Ky. 237/P7
Cumberland Gap Nat'l Hist. Park, Tenn. 237/O7
Cumberland Gap Nat'l Hist. Park, Va. 307/A7
Cumberland House, Sask. 181/J2
Cumberland Island Nat'l Seashore, Georgia 217/K9
Cumbernauld, Scotland 15/C1
Cumbre del Laudo (mt.), Argentina 143/C2
Cumbre Negra, Cerro (mt.), Argentina 143/C5
Cumbre Negra, Cerro (mt.), Chile 138/E5
Cumbria (co.), England 13/D3
Cumbrian (mts.), England 13/D3
Cumbum, India 68/D5
Cumby, Texas (75433) 303/J4
Cuming (co.), Nebr. 264/H3
Cummaquid, Mass. (02637) 249/N6
Cumming, Georgia (30130) 217/D2
Cumming, Iowa (50061) 229/F6
Cummings, Kansas (66016) 232/G2
Cummings, N. Dak. (58223) 282/S4
Cummings, S.C. (†29944) 296/E6
Cummingsville, Tenn. (†38583) 237/L9
Cummington○, Mass. (01026) 249/C3
Cummins, S. Australia 94/D6
Cumnock, N.S. Wales 97/E3
Cumnock, N.C. (27237) 281/L3
Cumnock and Holmhead, Scotland 10/D3
Cumnock and Holmhead, Scotland 15/D5
Cumpas, Mexico 150/E1
Çumra, Turkey 63/E4
Cuñapirú, Uruguay 145/D2
Cuñapirú, Arroyo (riv.), Uruguay 145/D2
Cunapo, Trin. & Tob. 161/B10
Cuñare, Colombia 126/D7
Cunaviche, Venezuela 124/E4
Cunco, Chile 138/E2
Cuncumén, Coquimbo, Chile 138/A9
Cuncumén, Santiago, Chile 138/F4
Cundeelee Aboriginal Reserve, W. Australia 88/C6
Cundeelee Aboriginal Res., W. Australia 92/C5
Cunderdin, W. Australia 92/B5
Cundiff, Ky. (42730) 237/L7
Cundinamarca (dept.), Colombia 126/C5
Cundiyo, N. Mex. (87522) 274/D3
Cunduacán, Mexico 150/N7
Cundys Harbor, Maine (04011) 243/D8
Cunene (riv.) 102/D6
Cunene (dist.), Angola 115/C7
Cunene (dam), Angola 115/B7
Cunene (riv.), Angola 115/B7
Cuneo (prov.), Italy 34/A2
Cuneo, Italy 34/A2
Çüngüş, Turkey 63/H3
Cunnamulla, Australia 87/E8
Cunnamulla, Queensland 95/C5
Cunnamulla, Queensland 88/H5
Cunningham, Kansas (67035) 232/D4
Cunningham, Ky. (42035) 237/D7
Cunningham, N.C. (†27343) 281/L1
Cunningham, Tenn. (37052) 237/G8
Cunningham, Wash. (99327) 310/G4
Cuorgnè, Italy 34/A2
Cupar, Sask. 181/G5
Cupar, Scotland 15/E4
Cupar, Scotland 10/E2
Cupertino, Calif. (95014) 204/K3
Cupica (gulf), Colombia 126/B4
Cupids, Newf. 166/D2
Ćuprija, Yugoslavia 45/E4
Cuprum, Idaho (†83612) 220/B4
Cupsuptic (riv.), Maine 243/B5
Cuquenán (riv.), Venezuela 124/H5
Cuquiari (riv.), Colombia 126/E7
Curaçá, Brazil 132/G5
Curaçao (isl.), Neth. Ant. 161/G7
Curaçao (isl.), Neth. Ant. 156/E4
Curacautín, Chile 138/E2
Curacaví, Chile 138/G3
Curahuara de Carangas, Bolivia 136/A5
Curahuara de Pacajes, Bolivia 136/A5
Curanilahue, Chile 138/D1
Curaray (riv.), Ecuador 128/D3
Curaumilla (pt.), Chile 138/E2
Curdsville, Ky. (42334) 237/G5
Curecanti Nat'l Rec. Area, Colo. 208/F6
Curepipe, Mauritius 118/G5
Curepto, Chile 138/A10
Curiapo, Venezuela 124/H3
Curiche, Bolivia 136/D6
Curicó, Chile 120/B6
Curicó, Chile 138/A10
Curieuse (isl.), Seychelles 118/H5
Curitiba, Brazil 132/D9
Curitiba, Brazil 120/F5
Curitiba, Brazil 135/B4
Curlew, Iowa (50527) 229/D3
Curlew (isls.), La. 238/M7
Curlew, Wash. (99118) 310/G2
Curlew (lake), Wash. 310/G2
Curlewis, N.S. Wales 97/F2
Curllsville, Pa. (16221) 294/D3
Curnamona, S. Australia 94/F4
Curragh, The, Ireland 17/H5
Curragh, The (racecourse), Ireland 10/C4
Currais Novos, Brazil 132/G4
Curran, Ill. (62632) 222/D4
Curran, Mich. (48728) 250/F4
Currant, Nev. (†89314) 266/F4
Currawilla, Queensland 95/B5
Current (riv.), Ark. 202/J1
Current (riv.), Mo. 261/K8
Currie, Minn. (56123) 255/C6
Currie, Nev. (†89301) 266/G2
Currie, N.C. (28435) 281/N6
Currie, Scotland 15/D2
Currie, Tasmania 99/A1
Currituck (co.), N.C. 281/S2
Currituck, N.C. (27929) 281/T2
Currituck (sound), N.C. 281/T2
Curry, Alaska (†99676) 196/J2
Curry (co.), N. Mex. 274/F4
Curry (co.), Oreg. 291/C5
Curryville, Mo. (63339) 261/K4
Curryville, Pa. (16631) 294/F5
Curtea de Argeş, Romania 45/G3
Curtice, Ohio (43412) 284/D2
Curtin, Oreg. (97428) 291/D4
Curtina, Uruguay 145/C3
Curtis, Ark. (71728) 202/D6
Curtis, La. (†71101) 238/C2
Curtis, Mich. (49820) 250/D2
Curtis, Nebr. (69025) 264/D4
Curtis, Okla. (†73852) 288/H2
Curtis (isl.), Queensland 88/J4
Curtis (isl.), Queensland 95/D4
Curtis, Wash. (98538) 310/B4
Curtis Group (isls.), Tasmania 99/C1
Curtiss, Wis. (54422) 317/F6
Curtis Station, Miss. (†38606) 256/D2
Curtisville, Ind. (†46036) 227/F4
Curuá (riv.), Brazil 132/C4
Curuçá, Brazil 132/E3
Curuguaty, Paraguay 144/E4
Curup, Indonesia 85/C6
Cururú, Bolivia 136/D4
Cururupu, Brazil 132/E3
Curutú (riv.), Venezuela 124/G5
Curuzú Cuatiá, Argentina 143/G5
Curuzú Cuatiá, Argentina 120/D5
Curve, Tenn. (†38063) 237/B9
Curvelo, Brazil 132/E7
Curwensville, Pa. (16833) 294/E4
Curwood (mt.), Mich. 250/A2
Cusachón (isl.), Colombia 126/D1
Cusco, Peru 120/B4
Cusco (dept.), Peru 128/F9
Cusco (Cuzco), Peru 128/F9
Cushendall, N. Ireland 17/J1
Cushing, Iowa (51018) 229/B4
Cushing○, Maine (04563) 243/E7
Cushing, Minn. (56443) 255/D4
Cushing, Nebr. (†68873) 264/F3
Cushing, Okla. (74023) 288/N3
Cushing, Texas (75760) 303/J6
Cushing, Wis. (54006) 317/A4
Cushman, Ark. (72526) 202/G2
Cushman, Mass. (01002) 249/D3
Cushman, Oreg. (†97439) 291/D4
Cushman (lake), Wash. 310/B3
Cusiana (riv.), Colombia 126/D5
Cusick, Wash. (99119) 310/H2
Cuslett, Newf. 166/C2
Cusset, France 28/E4
Cusseta, Ala. (36852) 195/H5
Cusseta, Georgia (31805) 217/C6
Cusson, Minn. (†55771) 255/F2
Custar, Ohio (43511) 284/C3
Custer (co.), Colo. 208/J6
Custer (co.), Idaho 220/D5
Custer, Ky. (40115) 237/J5
Custer, Mich. (49405) 250/C5
Custer (co.), Mont. 262/L4
Custer, Mont. (59024) 262/J4
Custer (co.), Nebr. 264/E3
Custer (co.), Okla. 288/H3
Custer (co.), S. Dak. 298/B6
Custer, S. Dak. (57730) 298/B6
Custer, Wash. (98240) 310/C2
Custer Battlefield Nat'l Mon., Mont. 262/J5
Custer City, Okla. (73639) 288/J3
Custer City, Pa. (16725) 294/E2
Custer Park, Ill. (60418) 222/E2
Cut Bank, Mont. (59427) 262/D2
Cut Bank (creek), Mont. 262/D2
Cut Bank (creek), N. Dak. 282/H2
Cutbank, Sask. 181/E4
Cutchogue-New Suffolk, N.Y. (11935) 276/P8
Cutervo, Peru 128/C6
Cuthbert, Georgia (31740) 217/C7
Cut Knife, Sask. 181/B3
Cutler, Calif. (93615) 204/F7
Cutler, Ill. (62238) 222/D5
Cutler, Ind. (46920) 227/D4
Cutler, Maine (04626) 243/J6
Cutler○, Maine (04626) 243/J6
Cutler, Ohio (45724) 284/G7
Cutler Ridge, Fla. (33157) 212/F6
Cutlerville, Mich. (49508) 250/D6
Cut Off, La. (70345) 238/K7
Cutra (lake), Ireland 17/D5
Cutral-Có, Argentina 143/C4
Cutshin, Ky. (41732) 237/P6
Cuttaburra (creek), N.S. Wales 97/C1
Cuttack, India 54/K7
Cuttack, India 68/F4
Cutten, Calif. (95534) 204/A3
Cuttingsville, Vt. (05738) 268/B4
Cuttyhunk, Mass. (02713) 249/L7
Cuttyhunk (isl.), Mass. 249/L7
Cuvier (isl.), N. Zealand 100/E2
Cuvier (cape), W. Australia 88/A4
Cuvier (cape), W. Australia 92/A4
Cuvo (riv.), Angola 115/B6
Cuxhaven, W. Germany 22/C2
Cuya, Chile 138/B2
Cuyabeno, Ecuador 128/E3
Cuyahoga (co.), Ohio 284/G3
Cuyahoga (riv.), Ohio 284/H10
Cuyahoga Falls, Ohio (*44221) 284/G3
Cuyahoga Heights, Ohio (†44101) 284/H9
Cuyama, Calif. (93214) 204/F9
Cuyama (riv.), Calif. 204/E8
Cuyapaipe Ind. Res., Calif. 204/J11
Cuyk, Netherlands 27/H5
Cuylerville, N.Y. (†14481) 276/E5
Cuyo, Philippines 82/C5
Cuyo (isl.), Philippines 82/C5
Cuyo (isls.), Philippines 82/C5
Cuyo (isls.), Philippines 85/G3
Cuyocuyo, Peru 128/H10
Cuyo East (passage), Philippines 82/C5
Cuyo West (passage), Philippines 82/C5
Cuyuna, Minn. (†56444) 255/E4
Cuyuna (range), Minn. 255/D4
Cuyuni (riv.) 120/C2
Cuyuni (riv.), Guyana 131/B2
Cuyuni (riv.), Venezuela 124/H4
Cuyu Tigni, Nicaragua 154/F3
Cuzco, Ind. (†47432) 227/D8
Cuzzart, W. Va. (26530) 312/H3
Čvrsnica (mt.), Yugoslavia 45/C4
Cwmamman, Wales 13/D6
Cwmbran, Wales 13/B6
Cyangugu, Rwanda 115/E4
Cyclades (isls.), Greece 45/G7
Cycle, N.C. (27015) 281/H2
Cyclone, Ind. (†46041) 227/E4
Cyclone, Pa. (16726) 294/E2
Cyclone, W. Va. (24827) 312/C7
Cygnet, Ohio (43413) 284/C3
Cygnet, Tasmania 99/C5
Cylinder, Iowa (50528) 229/D2
Cylon, Wis. (†54017) 317/B5
Cymric, Sask. 181/G4
Cynthia, Alberta 182/C3
Cynthiana, Ind. (47612) 227/B8
Cynthiana, Ky. (41031) 237/N4
Cynthiana, Ohio (45624) 284/D7
Cypert, Ark. (†72366) 202/J5
Cypress, Ala. (35454) 195/C5
Cypress (hills), Alberta 182/E5
Cypress (bayou), Ark. 202/F3
Cypress, Calif. (90630) 204/D11
Cypress, Fla. (32432) 212/A1
Cypress (lake), Fla. 212/E3
Cypress, Ill. (62923) 222/D6
Cypress, Ind. (†47708) 227/B9
Cypress (pond), Ind. 227/B8
Cypress, La. (71420) 238/D3
Cypress (hills), Sask. 181/B6
Cypress (lake), Sask. 181/B6
Cypress Gardens, Fla. (33880) 212/E3
Cypress Hills Prov. Park, Alberta 182/E5
Cypress Hills Prov. Park, Sask. 181/B6
Cypress Inn, Tenn. (38452) 237/F10
Cypress Prov. Park, Br. Col. 184/K3
Cypress Quarters, Fla. (†33472) 212/F4
Cypress River, Manitoba 179/D5
Cyprus 2/L4
Cyprus 54/E6
CYPRUS 59/B2
CYPRUS 63/E5
Cyrenaica (reg.), Libya 102/E1
Cyrenaica (reg.), Libya 111/D1

358 Cyrene

Cyrene (Shahat), Libya 111/D1
Cyrene, Mo. (†63334) 261/K4
Cyril, Okla. (73029) 288/K5
Cyrus, Minn. (56323) 255/C5
Czar, Alberta 182/E3
Czar, W. Va. (†26224) 312/F5
Czarna Białostocka, Poland 47/F2
Czarnków, Poland 47/C2
Czechoslovakia 2/K3
Czechoslovakia 7/F4
CZECHOSLOVAKIA 41
Czechowice-Dziedzice, Poland 47/D4
Czech Socialist Rep., Czech. 41/B1
Czeladź, Poland 47/B4
Czersk, Poland 47/D2
Częstochowa (prov.), Poland 47/D3
Częstochowa, Poland 47/D3
Częstochwa, Poland 7/F3
Człuchów, Poland 47/C2

D

Da'an (Talai), China 77/K2
Daaquam, Québec 172/H3
Dabajuro, Venezuela 124/C2
Dabakala, Ivory Coast 106/D7
Dabas, Hungary 41/E3
Daba Shan (range), China 77/G5
Dabeiba, Colombia 126/B4
Dabhoi, India 68/C4
Dabney, Ind. (†47023) 227/G6
Dabob (bay), Wash. 310/C3
Dabola, Guinea 106/B6
Dabou, Ivory Coast 106/D7
Daboya, Ghana 106/D7
Dąbrowa Górnicza, Poland 47/B3
Dąbrowa Tarnowska, Poland 47/E3
Dăbuleni, Romania 45/F4
Dacca (cap.), Bangladesh 54/L7
Dacca (cap.), Bangladesh 68/G4
Dachau, W. Germany 22/D4
Dačice, Czech. 41/C2
Dac Lac, Cao Nguyen (plat.), Vietnam 72/F4
Dacoma, Okla. (73731) 288/J1
Dacono, Colo. (80514) 208/K2
Dacre, Ontario 177/G2
Dacula, Georgia (30211) 217/E3
Dacusville, S.C. (†29640) 296/B2
Dadanawa, Guyana 131/B4
Daday, Turkey 63/E2
Dade (co.), Fla. 212/F6
Dade (co.), Georgia 217/A1
Dade (co.), Mo. 261/E8
Dade City, Fla. (33525) 212/D3
Dadeville, Ala. (36853) 195/G5
Dadeville, Mo. (65635) 261/E8
Dadra and Nagar Haveli (terr.), India 68/C4
Dads (lake), Nebr. 264/D2
Dadu, Pakistan 68/B3
Dadu, Pakistan 59/J4
Dăeni, Romania 45/J3
Daer (res.), Scotland 15/E5
Daet, Philippines 85/G3
Daet, Philippines 82/D3
Dafang, China 77/G6
Dafna, Israel 65/D1
Dafoe, Sask. 181/G4
Dafter, Mich. (49724) 250/E2
Dagabur, Ethiopia 111/H6
Dagana, Senegal 106/A5
Dagda, U.S.S.R. 53/D2
Dagelet (Ullŭng) (isl.), S. Korea 81/E5
Dagestan A.S.S.R., U.S.S.R. 48/E5
Dagestan A.S.S.R., U.S.S.R. 52/G6
Dagestanskiye Ogni, U.S.S.R. 52/G6
Daggett, Calif. (92327) 204/H9
Daggett, Mich. (49821) 250/B3
Daggett (co.), Utah 304/E3
Dagmar, Mont. (59219) 262/M2
Dagö (Hiiumaa) (isl.), U.S.S.R. 52/B3
Dagsboro, Del. (19930) 245/S6
Dagua, Colombia 126/B6
Daguan, China 77/F6
D'Aguilar (range), Tasmania 99/B4
Dagupan, Philippines 82/C2
Daguscahonda, Pa. (†15853) 294/E3
Dagus Mines, Pa. (15831) 294/E3
Dahab, Egypt 111/F2
Dahana (des.), Saudi Arabia 54/F7
Dahana (des.), Saudi Arabia 59/E4
Dahinda, Ill. (61428) 222/C3
Dahinda, Sask. 181/G6
Da Hingan Ling (Great Khingan) (range), China 54/O5
Da Hingan Ling (range), China 77/J3
Dahlak (arch.), Ethiopia 111/H4
Dahlak (arch.), Ethiopia 59/D6
Dahlak (isl.), Ethiopia 59/D6
Dahlak (isl.), Ethiopia 111/H4
Dahlem, W. Germany 22/E4
Dahlen, N. Dak. (58224) 282/P3
Dahlgren, Ill. (62828) 222/E5
Dahlgren, Va. (22448) 307/O4
Dahlia, N. Mex. (†87711) 274/D3
Dahlonega, Georgia (30533) 217/D1
Dahme, E. Germany 22/E3
Dai (mt.), Japan 81/F6
Dailekh, Nepal 68/E3
Dailey, Colo. (†80728) 208/O1
Dailly, Scotland 15/D5
Daimanji (mt.), Japan 81/F5
Daimiel, Spain 33/E3
Daingean, Ireland 17/G5
Daingerfield, Texas (75638) 303/K4
Daio (cape), Japan 81/H6
Daiquirí, Cuba 158/J4
Daireaux, Argentina 143/D4
Dairût, Egypt 111/J4
Dairy, Oreg. (97625) 291/F5
Dairy Flat-Redvale, N. Zealand 100/B1
Dairyland, Wis. (†54830) 317/B3
Daisen-Oki National Park, Japan 81/F6
Daisetsu (mt.), Japan 81/L2
Daisetsu-Zan National Park, Japan 81/L2
Daisetta, Texas (77533) 303/K7
Daisy, Ark. (†71950) 202/C5
Daisy, Georgia (30423) 217/J6
Daisy, Ky. (41733) 237/P6
Daisy, Mo. (63743) 261/N7
Daisy, Okla. (74540) 288/P5
Daisy, Wash. (†99167) 310/G2
Daito, Japan 81/J8
Daito (isls.), Japan 54/P7
Dajabón (prov.), Dom. Rep. 158/D5
Dajabón, Dom. Rep. 158/D5
Dajarra, Queensland 88/F4
Dajarra, Queensland 95/A4
Dakar (cap.), Senegal 2/J5
Dakar (cap.), Senegal 102/A3
Dakar (cap.), Senegal 106/A6
Dakhla (oasis), Egypt 111/E2
Dakhla (oasis), Egypt 59/A4
Dakhla, W. Sahara 102/A2
Dakhla, Western Sahara 106/A4
Dakoro, Niger 106/F6
Dakota, Georgia (†31714) 217/E7
Dakota, Ill. (61018) 222/D1
Dakota (co.), Minn. 255/E6
Dakota, Minn. (55925) 255/G7
Dakota (co.), Nebr. 264/H2
Dakota City, Iowa (50529) 229/E3
Dakota City, Nebr. (68731) 264/H2
Dal (riv.), Sweden 7/F2
Dala, Angola 115/D6
Dalaba, Guinea 106/B6
Dalälven (riv.), Sweden 18/K6
Dalaman (riv.), Turkey 63/C4
Dalandzadgad, Mongolia 77/G3
Dalanganem (isls.), Philippines 82/C5
Dalark, Ark. (†71923) 202/E5
Da Lat, Vietnam 72/F5
Dalavich, Scotland 15/C4
Dalbandin, Pakistan 68/A3
Dalbandin, Pakistan 59/H4
Dalbeattie, Scotland 10/E3
Dalbeattie, Scotland 15/E6
Dalbo, Minn. (55017) 255/E5
Dalby, Queensland 95/D5
Dalby, Queensland 88/J5
Dalby, Sweden 18/H6
Dalcahue, Chile 138/D4
Dalcour, La. (†70040) 238/P4
Dale (co.), Ala. 195/G8
Dale, Ill. (62829) 222/E6
Dale, Ind. (47523) 227/D8
Dale, Minn. (†56549) 255/B4
Dale, Norway 18/E6
Dale, Okla. (74838) 288/M4
Dale, Oreg. (97880) 291/J3
Dale, Pa. (†15901) 294/E5
Dale, S.C. (29914) 296/F6
Dale (mt.), W. Australia 88/B2
Dale (mt.), W. Australia 92/B1
Dale, Wis. (54931) 317/J7
Dale City, Va. (22193) 307/O3
Dale Hollow (lake), Ky. 237/L7
Dale Hollow (lake), Tenn. 237/L7
Dalemead, Alberta 182/D4
Dalen, Netherlands 27/K3
Daleside, S. Africa 118/H7
Daleville, Ala. (36322) 195/G8
Daleville, Ind. (47334) 227/F4
Daleville, Miss. (39326) 256/G5
Daleville, Va. (24083) 307/J6
Dale West, W. Australia 92/B2
Dalhart, Texas (79022) 303/B1
Dalhousie, New Bruns. 170/D1
Dalhousie (cape), N.W. Terrs. 187/E2
Dalhousie (mt.), Nova Scotia 168/E3
Dalhousie East, Nova Scotia 168/D4
Dalhousie Junction, New Bruns. 170/D1
Dalhousie West, Nova Scotia 168/C4
Dali, China 77/E6
Dallas, Spain 33/E4
Daliburgh, Scotland 15/A3
Dalizi, China 77/L3
Dalkeith, Ontario 177/K2
Dalkeith, Scotland 10/C1
Dalkeith, Scotland 15/D2
Dalkena, Wash. (†99156) 310/H2
Dall (isl.), Alaska 196/M2
Dall (mt.), Alaska 196/H2
Dallam (co.), Texas 303/B1
Dallas (co.), Ala. 195/D6
Dallas (co.), Ark. 202/E6
Dallas, Georgia (30132) 217/C3
Dallas (co.), Iowa 229/E5
Dallas, Iowa (50062) 229/G6
Dallas, Manitoba 179/E3
Dallas (co.), Mo. 261/F7
Dallas, N.C. (28034) 281/G4
Dallas, Oreg. (97338) 291/D3
Dallas, Pa. (18612) 294/E7
Dallas, Scotland 15/E3
Dallas, S. Dak. (57529) 298/K7
Dallas (co.), Texas 303/H5
Dallas, Texas (*75201) 303/G2
Dallas, Texas 188/G4
Dallas, Texas 146/J6
Dallas, U.S. 2/E4
Dallas, W. Va. (26036) 312/E2
Dallas, Wis. (54733) 317/C5
Dallas Center, Iowa (50063) 229/E5
Dallas City, Ill. (62330) 222/B3
Dallas Naval Air Sta., Texas 303/G2
Dallastown, Pa. (17313) 294/J6
Dalles, The, Oreg. (97058) 291/F2
Dalles, The (dam), Oreg. 291/F2
Dalles, The (dam), Wash. 310/D5
Dallesport, Wash. (98617) 310/D5
Dallol, Ethiopia 111/G5
Dallol Bosso (dry riv.), Niger 106/E6
Dalmaj, Hor (lake), Iraq 66/D4
Dalmally, Scotland 10/D2
Dalmally, Scotland 15/D4
Dalmatia, Pa. (17017) 294/J4
Dalmatia (reg.), Yugoslavia 45/C4
Dalmellington, Scotland 15/D5
Dalmellington, Scotland 10/D3
Dalmeny, Sask. 181/E3
Dal'negorsk, U.S.S.R. 48/O5
Dal'nerechensk, U.S.S.R. 48/O5
Daloa, Ivory Coast 106/C7
Daloa, Ivory Coast 102/B4
Dalroy, Alberta 182/D4
Dalry, Scotland 10/A1
Dalry, Scotland 15/D5
Dalrymple, Scotland 15/D5
Dalton, Ark. (72423) 202/H1
Dalton, Georgia (30720) 217/C1
Dalton, Ky. (†42445) 237/F6
Dalton○, Mass. (01226) 249/B3
Dalton, Mich. (†49445) 250/C5
Dalton, Minn. (56324) 255/C4
Dalton, Mo. (65246) 261/F4
Dalton, Nebr. (69131) 264/B3
Dalton○, N.H. (†03598) 268/D3
Dalton, N.Y. (14836) 276/E5
Dalton, N.C. (†27043) 281/J2
Dalton, Ohio (44618) 284/G4
Dalton, Pa. (18414) 294/L2
Dalton, Wis. (53926) 317/H8
Dalton City, Ill. (61925) 222/E4
Daltonganj, India 68/E4
Dalton Gardens, Idaho (†83814) 220/B2
Dalton-in-Furness, England 13/D3
Dalupiri (isl.), Philippines 82/A3
Dalwallinu, W. Australia 88/B6
Dalwallinu, W. Australia 92/B5
Dalwhinnie, Scotland 15/D4
Dalworthington Gardens, Texas (†76101) 303/F2
Daly (cape) 5/C4
Daly (riv.), North. Terr. 88/E2
Daly (riv.), North. Terr. 93/B2
Daly (bay), N.W. Terrs. 187/K3
Dalyat al-Karmel, Israel 65/B2
Daly City, Calif. (*94014) 204/H2
Daly River, North. Terr. 88/E2
Daly River, North. Terr. 93/B2
Daly River Aboriginal Reserve, North. Terr. 88/D2
Daly River Aboriginal Res., North. Terr. 93/A2
Dalyup, W. Australia 92/C6
Daly Waters, Australia 87/D7
Daly Waters, North. Terr. 88/E3
Daly Waters, North. Terr. 93/C4
Dalzell, Ill. (61320) 222/D2
Dalzell, S.C. (29040) 296/G3
Dam, Saudi Arabia 59/D5
Daman (dist.), India 68/C4
Damanhur, Egypt 111/J3
Damanhur, Egypt 59/A3
Damar (isl.), Indonesia 85/H7
Damar (isls.), Indonesia 85/H7
Damar, Kansas (67632) 232/C2
Damara, Cent. Afr. Rep. 115/C2
Damaraland (reg.), Namibia 118/B4
Damariscotta○, Maine (04543) 243/E7
Damariscotta-Newcastle, Maine (04543) 243/E7
Damascus, Ark. (72039) 202/F3
Damascus, Georgia (31741) 217/C8
Damascus, Md. (20750) 245/K3
Damascus, Ohio (44619) 284/J4
Damascus, Pa. (18415) 294/M2
Damascus (prov.), Syria 63/G6
Damascus (cap.), Syria 59/C3
Damascus (cap.), Syria 54/E6
Damascus (cap.), Syria 63/G6
Damascus, Va. (24236) 307/E7
Damavand, Iran 66/H3
Damavand (mt.), Iran 54/G6
Damavand (mt.), Iran 59/F2
Damavend (Demavend) (mt.), Iran 66/G3
Damazin (Ed Damazin), Sudan 111/F5
Damba, Angola 115/B5
Dam Doi, Vietnam 72/E5
Dame Marie, Haiti 158/A6
Dame Marie (cape), Haiti 158/A6
Dame Marie (cape), Haiti 156/C3
Dameron, Md. (20628) 245/N8
Dames Ferry, Georgia (†31046) 217/E4
Dames Quarter, Md. (21820) 245/P8
Damghan, Iran 59/F2
Damghan, Iran 66/J2
Damh, Loch (lake), Scotland 15/C3
Damietta, Egypt 102/F1
Damietta, Egypt 111/J3
Damietta, Egypt 59/B3
Damiya, Jordan 65/D3
Dammam, Saudi Arabia 59/F4
Dammastock (mt.), Switzerland 39/F3
Damme, Belgium 27/C6
Damodar (riv.), India 68/F4
Damoh, India 68/D4
Damongo, Ghana 106/D7
Dampier (str.), Indonesia 85/J6
Dampier (str.), Papua N.G. 86/B2
Dampier (str.), Papua N.G. 85/C7
Dampier, W. Australia 88/B4
Dampier (arch.), W. Australia 88/B4
Dampier, W. Australia 92/B3
Dampier (arch.), W. Australia 92/B3
Dampier Downs, W. Australia 92/C2
Dampier Land (reg.), W. Australia 88/C3
Dampier Land (reg.), W. Australia 92/C2
Damqut, P.D.R. Yemen 59/F6
Damvant, Switzerland 39/C2
Dan, Israel 65/D1
Dan (riv.), N.C. 281/L1
Dan (riv.), Va. 307/K7
Dana, Ill. (61321) 222/E3
Dana, Ind. (47847) 227/C5
Dana, Iowa (50064) 229/E4
Dana, Jordan 65/E5
Dana, Sask. 181/F3
Danakil (reg.), Ethiopia 111/H5
Danané, Ivory Coast 106/C7
Da Nang, Vietnam 72/E3
Da Nang, Vietnam 54/M8
Da Nang, Mui (cape), Vietnam 72/F3
Danao, Philippines 82/D5
Dana Point, Calif. (92629) 204/H10
Danba, China 77/F5
Danburg, Georgia (30668) 217/G3
Danbury, Conn. (06810) 210/B3
Danbury, Iowa (51019) 229/B4
Danbury, Nebr. (69026) 264/D4
Danbury○, N.H. (03230) 268/D4
Danbury, N.C. (27016) 281/J2
Danbury, Sask. 181/J4
Danbury, Texas (77534) 303/J8
Danbury, Wis. (54830) 317/B3
Danbury P.O. (South Danbury), N.H. (03230) 268/D5
Danby (lake), Calif. 204/K9
Danby○, Vt. (05739) 268/A5
Dancing (pt.), Manitoba 179/D2
Dancy, Ala. (†35442) 195/B4
Dancy, Miss. (†39751) 256/F3
Dancy, Wis. (†54455) 317/G6
Dancyville, Tenn. (†38069) 237/C10
Dand, Manitoba 179/B5
Dandaragan, W. Australia 88/B6
Dandaragan, W. Australia 92/A5
Dandenong, Victoria 97/K5
Dandenong, Victoria 88/M7
Dandenong (creek), Victoria 97/K5
Dandenong (mt.), Victoria 97/K5
Dandenong (creek), Victoria 88/M7
Danderyd, Sweden 18/H1
Dandong (Tantung), China 77/K3
Dandong, China 54/O5
Dandridge, Tenn. (37725) 237/O8
Dane (riv.), England 13/H2
Dane (co.), Wis. 317/H9
Dane, Wis. (53529) 317/G9
Daneborg, Greenl. 4/B10
Danford Lake, Québec 172/A4
Danforth, Ill. (60930) 222/E3
Danforth, Maine (04424) 243/H4
Danforth○, Maine (04424) 243/H4
Danger (Pukapuka) (atoll), Cook Is. 87/K7
Dangila, Ethiopia 111/G5
Dangrek (mts.), Cambodia 72/D4
Dangrek (Dong Rak) (mts.), Thailand 72/D4
Dangriga (Stann Creek), Belize 153/C2
Dania, Fla. (33004) 212/B4
Daniel (mt.), Wash. 310/D3
Daniel, Wyo. (83115) 319/B3
Daniel Boone, Ky. (†42442) 237/G6
Daniel-Johnson (dam), Québec 174/D2
Daniels, Md. (†21043) 245/L3
Daniels (co.), Mont. 262/L2
Daniels, W. Va. (25832) 312/D7
Daniel's Harbour, Newf. 166/C3
Danielson, Conn. (06239) 210/H1
Danielson Prov. Park, Sask. 181/E4
Danielstown, Guyana 131/B2
Danielsville, Georgia (30633) 217/F2
Danielsville, Pa. (18038) 294/M4
Danilov, U.S.S.R. 52/E3
Dankov, U.S.S.R. 52/E4
Danlí, Honduras 154/D3
Danmarkshavn, Greenl. 4/B10
Dannebrog, Nebr. (68831) 264/F3
Dannelly (res.), Ala. 195/D6
Dannemora, N.Y. (12929) 276/N1
Dannemora, Sweden 18/K6
Dannenberg, W. Germany 22/D2
Danner, Oreg. (†97910) 291/K5
Dannevirke, N. Zealand 100/F4
Dan Sai, Thailand 72/D3
Dansville, Mich. (48819) 250/E6
Dansville, N.Y. (14437) 276/E5
Dante (Hafun), Somalia 115/K1
Dante, S. Dak. (57329) 298/N7
Dante, Va. (24237) 307/D7
Danube (riv.) 7/G4
Danube (riv.), Austria 41/C2
Danube (riv.), Bulgaria 45/H4
Danube (riv.), Czech. 41/C2
Danube (riv.), Hungary 41/E3
Danube, Minn. (56230) 255/C6
Danube (delta), Romania 45/J3
Danube (riv.), Romania 45/H4
Danube (riv.), W. Germany 22/C4
Danube (riv.), Yugoslavia 45/E3
Danubyu, Burma 72/B3
Danvers, Ill. (61732) 222/D3
Danvers○, Mass. (01923) 249/D5
Danvers, Minn. (56231) 255/C5
Danvers, Mont. (59429) 262/G3
Danversport, Mass. (†01923) 249/E5
Danville, Ala. (35619) 195/D2
Danville, Ark. (72833) 202/D3
Danville, Calif. (94526) 204/K2
Danville, Georgia (31017) 217/F5
Danville, Ill. 188/J3
Danville, Ill. (61832) 222/F3
Danville, Ind. (46122) 227/D5
Danville, Iowa (52623) 229/L7
Danville, Kansas (67036) 232/E4
Danville, Ky. (40422) 237/M5
Danville, La. (†71008) 238/E2
Danville, Mo. (†63361) 261/J5
Danville○, N.H. (03819) 268/E6
Danville, Ohio (43014) 284/F5
Danville, Pa. (17821) 294/J4
Danville, Québec 172/E4
Danville○, Vt. (05828) 268/C3
Danville, Va. 188/L3
Danville, Va. 146/L6
Danville (I.C.), Va. (*24540) 307/J7
Danville, Wash. (99121) 310/G2
Danville, W. Va. (25053) 312/C6
Danville, Wis. (†53925) 317/J9
Dan Xian, China 77/G8
Danzig (Gdańsk), Poland 47/D1
Danzig (Gdańsk) (gulf), Poland 47/D1
Daocheng, China 77/F6
Dao Xian, China 77/H6
Dapa, Philippines 82/E6
Dapaong, Togo 106/E6
Daphne, Ala. (36526) 195/C9
Daphne, Sask. 181/G3
Dapitan, Philippines 82/D6
Dapoli, India 68/C5
Dapp, Alberta 182/C2
Da Qaidam, China 77/E4
Darab, Iran 59/G4
Darab, Iran 66/J6
Darabani, Romania 45/H1
Dar al Hamra, Saudi Arabia 59/C4
Daram (isl.), Philippines 82/E5
Daran, Iran 66/G4
Darbandikhan (dam), Iraq 66/D3
Darbhanga, India 68/F3
Darbun, Miss. (†39643) 256/D8
Darby (cape), Alaska 196/F2
Darby, Mont. (59829) 262/B4
Darby (creek), Ohio 284/D5
Darby, Pa. (19023) 294/M7
Darby (creek), Pa. 294/M6
Darby, Victoria 97/D6
Darbydale, Ohio (†43123) 284/D6
Darbyville, Ohio (†43164) 284/D6
D'Arcy, Br. Col. 184/F5
D'Arcy, Sask. 181/C4
Dardanelle, Ark. (72834) 202/D3
Dardanelle (lake), Ark. 202/D3
Dardanelles (str.), Turkey 7/G5
Dardanelles (str.), Turkey 59/A2
Dardanelles (str.), Turkey 63/B6
Darden, Tenn. (38328) 237/E9
Dare (co.), N.C. 281/T3
Dar-el-Beida (Casablanca), Morocco 106/C2
Darende, Turkey 63/G3
Dar es Salaam (cap.), Tanzania 102/F5
Dar es Salaam (cap.), Tanzania 2/M6
Dar es Salaam (cap.), Tanzania 115/G5
Dareton, N.S. Wales 97/B4
Daretown, N.J. (†08318) 273/C4
Darfur, Minn. (56022) 255/D6
Darfur, Northern (prov.), Sudan 111/D5
Darfur, Southern (prov.), Sudan 111/E5
Dargan, Md. (†25425) 245/H3
Dargaville, N. Zealand 100/D1
Dar Hamid (reg.), Sudan 111/F5
Darham Mumînggan Lianheqi, China 77/H3
Darhan (Darkhan), Mongolia 77/G2
Darien○, Conn. (06820) 210/B4
Darien, Georgia (31305) 217/K8
Darien, Ill. (†60559) 222/B6
Darien, N.Y. (†14040) 276/B5
Darién (mts.), Panama 154/J6
Darien, Wis. (53114) 317/J10
Darien Center, N.Y. (14040) 276/D5
Dariense, Cordillera (range), Nicaragua 154/E4
Darjeeling, India 68/F3
Dark (head), St. Vin. & Grens. 161/A8
Darkan, W. Australia 92/B2
Dark Canyon (creek), N. Mex. 274/E6
Dark Cove, Newf. 166/D4
Darke (co.), Ohio 284/A5
Darkesville, W. Va. (†25428) 312/L4
Darkin (riv.), W. Australia 88/B2
Darlag, China 77/E5
Darling (river), Australia 87/E9
Darling, Miss. (38623) 256/D2
Darling (riv.), N. S. Wales 88/G6
Darling (riv.), N. S. Wales 97/B3
Darling (lake), N. Dak. 282/G2
Darling, Pa. (†19063) 294/L7
Darling (range), W. Australia 88/B6
Darling (range), W. Australia 92/A1
Darling Downs, Queensland 95/D5
Darlingford, Manitoba 179/D5
Darlington, Ala. (36730) 195/D7
Darlington, England 10/F3
Darlington, England 13/F3
Darlington, Fla. (†32464) 212/C5
Darlington, Idaho (83231) 220/E6
Darlington, Ind. (47940) 227/D4
Darlington, La. (†70441) 238/J5
Darlington, Md. (21034) 245/N2
Darlington, Mo. (64438) 261/D2
Darlington, New Bruns. 170/D1
Darlington, Pa. (16115) 294/A4
Darlington (co.), S.C. 296/H3
Darlington, S.C. (29532) 296/H3
Darlington, Wis. (53530) 317/F10
Darlington Heights, Va. (23935) 307/L6
Darlington Point, N.S. Wales 97/C4
Darliston, Jamaica 158/H6
Darłowo, Poland 47/C1
Dar Masalit (reg.), Sudan 111/D5
Darmody, Sask. 181/E5
Darmstadt, Ill. (†62255) 222/D5
Darmstadt, Ind. (†47618) 227/B8
Darmstadt, W. Germany 22/C4
Darnell, La. (71231) 238/G1
Darnestown, Md. (†20760) 245/J4
Darnick, N.S. Wales 97/B3
Darnley (cape) 5/C4
Darnley (bay), N.W. Terrs. 187/F3
Daroca, Spain 33/F2
Darra, Queensland 88/K3
Darreh Gaz, Iran 66/L2
Darrington, Wash. (98241) 310/D2
Dar Rounga (reg.), Cent. Afr. Rep. 115/D2
Darrouzett, Texas (79024) 303/D1
Darrow, La. (70725) 238/K3
Darrtown, Ohio (†45056) 284/A7
Darsser Ort (pt.), E. Germany 22/E1
Dart (cape) 5/B12
Dart (riv.), England 13/D7
D'Artagnan, Québec 172/J3
Dartford, England 13/J8
Dartford, England 10/C5
Dartmoor, Victoria 97/A5
Dartmoor National Park, England 13/C7
Dartmouth (Clifton Dartmouth Hardness), England 10/E5
Dartmouth (Clifton Dartmouth Hardness), England 13/D7
Dartmouth○, Mass. (02714) 249/K6
Dartmouth, N.S. 162/K7
Dartmouth, Nova Scotia 168/E4
Dartmouth (riv.), Québec 172/D1
Darton, England 13/J2
Dartuch (cape), Spain 33/H3
Daru, Papua N.G. 87/E6
Daru, Papua N.G. 85/B7
Daruvar, Yugoslavia 45/C3
Darvel, Scotland 15/D5
Darwell, Alberta 182/C3
Darwen, England 10/G1
Darwen, England 13/H1
Darwin, Australia 2/R6
Darwin, Australia 87/D7
Darwin, Calif. (93522) 204/H7
Darwin (bay), Chile 138/D6
Darwin, Cordillera (mts.), Chile 138/D8
Darwin, Cordillera (mts.), Chile 138/E11
Darwin (Culpepper) (isl.), Ecuador 128/B8
Darwin, Ill. (†62477) 222/F4
Darwin, Minn. (55324) 255/D5
Darwin (cap.), North. Terr. 88/E2
Darwin (cap.), North. Terr. 93/B2
Darwin, Okla. (†74523) 288/P6
Das (isl.), U.A.E. 59/F4
Dash, Ben (hill), Ireland 17/C6
Dashan, Ras (mt.), Ethiopia 59/C7
Dashbalbar, Mongolia 77/H2
Dasher, Georgia (31601) 217/F9
Dashinchilen, Mongolia 77/F2
Dasht (riv.), Pakistan 68/A3
Dasht (riv.), Pakistan 59/H4
Dashtiari, Iran 66/M8
Dashtiari, Iran 59/H4
Dashwood, Br. Col. 184/H3
Dashwood, Ontario 177/C4
Dasol (bay), Philippines 82/B3
Dassel, Minn. (55325) 255/D5
Datça, Turkey 63/B4
Dateland, Ariz. (85333) 198/B6
Datia, India 68/D3
Datil, N. Mex. (87821) 274/B4
Datil (mts.), N. Mex. 274/B4
Datong, Qinghai, China 77/F4
Datong (Tatung), Shanxi, China 77/H3
Datto, Ark. (72424) 202/J1
Datu Piang, Philippines 82/E7
Daua (riv.), Kenya 115/H3
Daufuskie Island, S.C. (29915) 296/F7
Daugava (Western Dvina) (riv.), U.S.S.R. 53/D2
Daugavpils, U.S.S.R. 7/G3
Daugavpils, U.S.S.R. 53/D3
Daugavpils, U.S.S.R. 48/C4
Daugavpils, U.S.S.R. 52/C3
Daule, Ecuador 128/B3
Daulnay, New Bruns. 170/E1
Daun, W. Germany 22/B3
Daung Kyun (isl.), Burma 72/C4
Dauphin, Man. 162/F5
Dauphin, Manitoba 179/B3
Dauphin (lake), Manitoba 179/C3
Dauphin (riv.), Manitoba 179/D3
Dauphin (cape), Nova Scotia 168/H2
Dauphin (co.), Pa. 294/J5
Dauphin, Pa. (17018) 294/J5
Dauphin, St. Lucia 161/G5
Dauphiné (trad. prov.), France 29
Dauphin Island, Ala. (36528) 195/B10
Daus, Tenn. (†37327) 237/L10
Davangere, India 68/D6
Davant, La. (70046) 238/L7
Davao, Philippines 85/H4
Davao, Philippines 54/O9
Davao, Philippines 2/R5
Davao, Philippines 82/E7
Davao (gulf), Philippines 82/E7
Davao (gulf), Philippines 85/H4
Davao del Norte (prov.), Philippines 82/E7
Davao del Sur (prov.), Philippines 82/E7
Davao Oriental (prov.), Philippines 82/F7
Daveluyville, Québec 172/E3
Davenport, Calif. (95017) 204/K4
Davenport, Fla. (33837) 212/E3
Davenport, Iowa (*52801) 229/M5
Davenport, Iowa 188/H2
Davenport, Nebr. (68335) 264/G4
Davenport, N.Y. (13750) 276/L6
Davenport, N. Dak. (58021) 282/R6
Davenport (mt.), North. Terr. 93/B7
Davenport, Okla. (74026) 288/N3
Davenport, Va. (24239) 307/D6
Davenport, Wash. (99122) 310/G3
Daventry, England 13/F5
Davey, Nebr. (68336) 264/H4
Davey (riv.), Tasmania 99/B4
David (pt.), Grenada 161/D8
David, Ky. (41616) 237/R5
David, Panama 154/F6
David City, Nebr. (68632) 264/G3
Davidson (mts.), Alaska 196/K1
Davidson, Maine (†04782) 243/F4
Davidson (co.), N.C. 281/J3
Davidson, N.C. (28036) 281/H4
Davidson, Okla. (73530) 288/J6
Davidson, Sask. 181/E4
Davidson (co.), Tenn. 237/H8
Davidson (mts.), Yukon 187/D3
Davidsonville, Md. (21035) 245/M5
Davie, Fla. (33314) 212/B4
Davie (co.), N.C. 281/H3
Daviess (co.), Ind. 227/C7
Daviess (co.), Ky. 237/G5
Daviess (co.), Mo. 261/E3
Davik, Norway 18/D6
Davilla, Texas (76523) 303/G7
Davin, Sask. 181/H5
Daviot, Scotland 15/D3
Davis (str.) 2/G2
Davis (str.) 146/N3
Davis (str.) 4/C12
Davis (sea) 5/C5
Davis (dam), Ariz. 198/A3
Davis, Calif. (95616) 204/B8
Davis (isl.), Fla. 212/C3
Davis, Ill. (61019) 222/D1

Dent d'Hérens 359

Davis (co.), Iowa 229/J7
Davis (dam), Nev. 266/G7
Davis, N.C. (28524) 281/R5
Davis (str.), N.W.T. 162/K1
Davis (str.), N.W. Terrs. 187/M3
Davis, Okla. (73030) 288/M5
Davis (lake), Oreg. 291/F4
Davis (mt.), Pa. 294/D6
Davis, Sask. 181/F2
Davis, S. Dak. (57021) 298/P7
Davis (mts.), Texas 303/C11
Davis (co.), Utah 304/B3
Davis, W. Va. (26260) 312/H4
Davisboro, Georgia (31018) 217/G5
Davis City, Iowa (50065) 229/F7
Davis Cove, Newf. 166/D4
Davis Creek, Calif. (96108) 204/E2
Davis Dam, Ariz. (†86430) 198/A3
Davis Inlet, Newf. 166/B2
Davis Junction, Ill. (61020) 222/D1
Davis-Monthan A.F.B., Ariz. 198/E6
Davison, Mich. (48423) 250/F5
Davison (co.), S. Dak. 298/N6
Davis Station 5/C4
Davis Station, S.C. (29041) 296/G4
Daviston, Ala. (36256) 195/G4
Davisville, Mo. (65456) 261/K7
Davisville, R.I. (02854) 249/H6
Davisville, W. Va. (26142) 312/C4
Davlekanovo, U.S.S.R. 52/H4
Davos, Switzerland 39/J3
Davos (valley), Switzerland 39/J3
Davy, W. Va. (24828) 312/C8
Dawa (riv.), Ethiopia 111/G7
Dawasir, Hadhb (range), Saudi Arabia 59/D5
Dawasir, Wadi (dry riv.), Saudi Arabia 59/E5
Dawes (co.), Nebr. 264/A2
Dawes, W. Va. (25054) 312/D6
Dawlish, England 13/D7
Dawn, Mo. (64638) 261/E3
Dawn, Texas (79025) 303/B3
Dawna (range), Burma 72/C3
Dawson, Ala. (35963) 195/G2
Dawson, Canada 4/C16
Dawson (isl.), Chile 138/E10
Dawson (co.), Georgia 217/D2
Dawson, Georgia (31742) 217/D7
Dawson, Ill. (62520) 222/D4
Dawson, Iowa (50066) 229/E5
Dawson (bay), Manitoba 179/B2
Dawson, Minn. (56232) 255/B6
Dawson, Mo. (†65548) 261/H8
Dawson (co.), Mont. 262/M3
Dawson (co.), Nebr. 264/E4
Dawson, Nebr. (68337) 264/J4
Dawson, N. Dak. (58428) 282/L6
Dawson (inlet), N.W. Terrs. 187/J3
Dawson (riv.), Queensland 88/H4
Dawson (riv.), Queensland 95/D5
Dawson (co.), Texas 303/C5
Dawson, Texas (76639) 303/H6
Dawson, W. Va. (24932) 312/E7
Dawson, Yukon 146/E3
Dawson, Yukon 162/C3
Dawson, Yukon 187/E3
Dawson Bay, Manitoba 179/B2
Dawson Creek, Br. Col. 146/F4
Dawson Creek, Br. Col. 162/D4
Dawson Creek, Br. Col. 184/G2
Dawson Springs, Ky. (42408) 237/F6
Dawsonville, Georgia (30534) 217/D2
Dawsonville, New Bruns. 170/C1
Dawu, China 77/H5
Dawu, China 77/F5
Dax, France 28/C6
Da Xian, China 77/G5
Day, Fla. (32013) 212/C1
Day, Minn. (†55006) 255/E5
Day (co.), S. Dak. 298/O3
Day Book, N.C. (†28714) 281/E3
Daykin, Nebr. (68338) 264/G4
Daylesford, Victoria 97/C5
Daylight, Tenn. (†37110) 237/K9
Daymán, Uruguay 145/B2
Daymán (range), Uruguay 145/B2
Daymán (riv.), Uruguay 145/B2
Dayong, China 77/H6
Days Creek, Oreg. (97429) 291/D5
Daysland, Alberta 182/D3
Daysville, Ky. (†42276) 237/G7
Dayton, Ala. (36731) 195/C6
Dayton, Idaho (83232) 220/F7
Dayton, Ill. (†61350) 222/E2
Dayton, Ind. (47941) 227/D4
Dayton, Iowa (50530) 229/E4
Dayton, Ky. (41074) 237/T1
Dayton, Mich. (†49113) 250/C7
Dayton, Minn. (55327) 255/E5
Dayton, Mont. (59914) 262/B3
Dayton, Nev. (89403) 266/B3
Dayton, N.J. (08810) 273/D3
Dayton, N.Y. (4041) 276/C6
Dayton, Ohio (*45401) 284/B6
Dayton, Ohio 146/K6
Dayton, Ohio 188/K3
Dayton, Oreg. (97114) 291/A3
Dayton, Pa. (16222) 294/D4
Dayton, Tenn. (37321) 237/L9
Dayton, Texas (77535) 303/J7
Dayton, Va. (22821) 307/L4
Dayton, Wash. (99328) 310/H4
Dayton, Wis. (†53508) 317/H10
Dayton, Wyo. (82836) 319/E1
Daytona Beach, Fla. 188/K5
Daytona Beach, Fla. 146/K7
Daytona Beach, Fla. (*32014) 212/F2
Daytona Beach Shores, Fla. (32016) 212/F2
Dayu, China 77/H6
Dayville, Conn. (06241) 210/H1
Dayville, Oreg. (97825) 291/H3
Dazey, N. Dak. (58429) 282/O5
Dazhai, China 77/H4
Dazkırı, Turkey 63/D4
De Aar, S. Africa 118/C6
Dead (lake), Fla. 212/D6
Dead (sea), Israel 65/C4
Dead (sea), Israel 59/C3
Dead (sea), Jordan 59/C3
Dead (sea), Jordan 65/C4
Dead (riv.), Maine 243/C5
Dead (riv.), Mich. 250/B2
Dead (lake), Minn. 255/C4
Dead (sea), West Bank 59/C3
Deadhorse, Alaska (†99723) 196/J1
Deadman (creek), Wash. 310/H4
Deadman (mt.), Wyo. 319/B2
Deadwood, Alberta 182/B1
Deadwood (res.), Idaho 220/C5
Deadwood (riv.), Idaho 220/C5
Deadwood, S. Dak. (57732) 298/B5
Deaf Smith (co.), Texas 303/B3
Deal, England 13/J6
Deal, England 10/G5
Deal, N.J. (07723) 273/F3
Deal (isl.), Tasmania 99/D1
Deale, Md. (20751) 245/M5
Deal Island, Md. (21821) 245/P8
Dean (chan.), Br. Col. 184/D4
Dean (riv.), Br. Col. 184/D4
Dean, Nova Scotia 168/F3
Deán Funes, Argentina 143/D3
Deanville, Texas (77852) 303/H7
Dearborn (co.), Ind. 227/H6
Dearborn, Mich. (*48120) 250/B7
Dearborn, Mo. (64439) 261/C3
Dearborn Heights, Mich. (48127) 250/B7
Dearing, Georgia (30808) 217/H4
Dearing, Kansas (67340) 232/G4
De Armanville, Ala. (36257) 195/G3
Dearne, England 13/K2
Deary, Idaho (83823) 220/B3
Dease (inlet), Alaska 196/H1
Dease (lake), Br. Col. 184/K2
Dease (riv.), Br. Col. 184/K2
Dease (str.), N.W.T. 146/G3
Dease (str.), N.W.T. 162/F2
Dease (str.), N.W. Terrs. 187/H3
Dease Arm (inlet), N.W. Terrs. 187/F3
Death (valley), Calif. 204/H7
Death Valley (depr.), Calif. 188/C3
Death Valley, Calif. (92328) 204/J7
Death Valley Junction, Calif. (92328) 204/J7
Death Valley Nat'l Mon., Calif. 204/H7
Death Valley Nat'l Mon., Nev. 266/E6
Deatsville, Ala. (36022) 195/F5
Deauville, France 28/C3
Deauville, Québec 172/E4
Deaver, Wyo. (82421) 319/D1
Deavertown, Ohio (†43731) 284/G6
De Baca (co.), N. Mex. 274/E4
Deba Habe, Nigeria 106/G6
Debar, Yugoslavia 45/E5
De Bary, Fla. (32713) 212/E3
Debden, Sask. 181/E2
Débé, Trin. & Tob. 161/B11
Debec, New Bruns. 170/C2
De Beque, Colo. (81630) 208/C4
De Berry, Texas (75639) 303/L5
Debert, Nova Scotia 168/E3
Dębica, Poland 47/E3
De Bilt, Netherlands 27/G4
Dęblin, Poland 47/E3
Deblois○, Maine (†04622) 243/H6
Dębno, Poland 47/B2
Debo (lake), Mali 106/D5
Debolt, Alberta 182/B2
De Borgia, Mont. (59830) 262/A3
Debra Birhan, Ethiopia 111/G6
Debra Markos, Ethiopia 111/G5
Debra Markos, Ethiopia 102/F3
Debra Tabor, Ethiopia 111/G5
Debrecen, Hungary 41/F3
Debrecen, Hungary 7/G4
Decatur, Ala. (*35601) 195/D1
Decatur, Ark. (72722) 202/A1
Decatur (co.), Georgia 217/C9
Decatur, Georgia (*30030) 217/K1
Decatur, Ill. 188/J3
Decatur, Ill. 146/K6
Decatur, Ill. (*62521) 222/E4
Decatur (co.), Ind. 227/G6
Decatur, Ind. (46733) 227/H3
Decatur (co.), Iowa 229/F7
Decatur, Iowa (50067) 229/F7
Decatur (co.), Kansas 232/B2
Decatur, Mich. (49045) 250/C6
Decatur, Miss. (39327) 256/F6
Decatur, Nebr. (68020) 264/H2
Decatur, Ohio (45115) 284/C8
Decatur (co.), Tenn. 237/E9
Decatur, Tenn. (37322) 237/M9
Decatur, Texas (76234) 303/G4
Decaturville, Tenn. (38329) 237/E9
Decazeville, France 28/E5
Deccan (plat.), India 68/D6
Decherd, Tenn. (37324) 237/J10
Děčín, Czech. 41/C1
Decision (cape), Alaska 196/M2
Decize, France 28/E4
Decker, Ind. (47524) 227/B7
Decker, Manitoba 179/B4
Decker, Mich. (48426) 250/F5
Decker, Mont. (59025) 262/K5
Decker Lake, Br. Col. 184/E3
Deckers, Colo. (†80135) 208/J4
Deckerville, Ark. (†72386) 202/K3
Deckerville, Mich. (48427) 250/G5
Declo, Idaho (83323) 220/E7
Decorah, Iowa (52101) 229/K2
Decota, W. Va. (†25122) 312/D6
Decoy, Ky. (41321) 237/P5
Dededo, Guam 86/K6
Dedegül Dağı (mt.), Turkey 63/D4
Dedemsvaart, Netherlands 27/J3
Dederick, Mo. (†64744) 261/D7
Dedham, Iowa (51440) 229/D5
Dedham, Maine (†04429) 243/F6
Dedham○, Maine (†04429) 243/F6
Dedham, Mass. (02026) 249/C7
Dédougou, Upper Volta 106/D6
Dedza, Malawi 115/F6
Dee (riv.), England 13/D4
Dee (riv.), England 10/E4
Dee (riv.), Ireland 17/H4
Dee (riv.), Scotland 15/D5
Dee (riv.), Scotland 15/F3
Dee (riv.), Scotland 10/E2
Dee (riv.), Tasmania 99/C4
Dee (riv.), Wales 10/E4
Dee (riv.), Wales 13/D4
Deedsville, Ind. (46921) 227/E3
Deel (riv.), Ireland 17/C3
Deel (riv.), Ireland 17/G4
Deel (riv.), Ireland 17/D7
Deele (riv.), Ireland 17/F2
Deenwood, Georgia (†31501) 217/H8
Deep (creek), Idaho 220/F7
Deep (creek), Idaho 220/B7
Deep (inlet), Newf. 166/B2
Deep (riv.), N.C. 281/K3
Deep (riv.), N. Dak. 282/J1
Deep (creek), S.C. 296/B2
Deep (creek), Texas 303/C5
Deep (creek), Utah 304/B1
Deep (creek), Utah 304/A3
Deep Bight, Newf. 166/C2
Deep Brook, Nova Scotia 168/C4
Deep Creek (mts.), Idaho 220/F7
Deep Creek (lake), Md. 245/A3
Deep Creek (range), Utah 304/A4
Deepcreek, Wash. (†99010) 310/H3
Deepdale, Manitoba 179/A3
Deep Fork, North Canadian (riv.), Okla. 288/N3
Deep Gap, N.C. (28618) 281/F2
Deephaven, Minn. (55391) 255/G5
Deeping Saint James, England 13/G5
Deep River, Conn. (06417) 210/F3
Deep River○, Conn. (06417) 210/F3
Deep River (res.), Conn. 210/F2
Deep River, Iowa (52222) 229/J5
Deep River, Ontario 177/G1
Deep River, Ontario 175/E3
Deep River, Wash. (†98638) 310/B4
Deep Run, N.C. (28525) 281/O4
Deep Springs, Calif. (†93513) 204/H6
Deepstep, Georgia (31082) 217/G4
Deep Valley, Pa. (†15352) 294/A6
Deep Water (pt.), Del. 245/S4
Deepwater, Mo. (64740) 261/E6
Deepwater, N.J. (08023) 273/C4
Deepwater, N.S. Wales 97/F1
Deer (isl.), Alaska 196/F4
Deer, Ariz. (72628) 202/D2
Deer (creek), Ind. 227/D5
Deer (creek), Ind. 227/E3
Deer (isl.), Maine 243/F7
Deer (creek), Md. 245/N2
Deer (isl.), Mass. 249/E7
Deer (riv.), Mich. 250/A2
Deer (lake), Minn. 255/E3
Deer (creek), Miss. 256/C4
Deer (isl.), New Bruns. 170/D4
Deer (harb.), Newf. 166/D2
Deer (riv.), N.Y. 276/L1
Deer (riv.), N.Y. 276/J3
Deer (creek), Ohio 284/D6
Deer (lake), Wash. 310/H2
Deerbrook, Miss. (†39739) 256/G4
Deerbrook, Wis. (54424) 317/H5
Deer Creek, Ill. (61733) 222/D3
Deer Creek, Ind. (†46917) 227/E3
Deer Creek, Minn. (56527) 255/C4
Deer Creek (lake), Ohio 284/D6
Deer Creek, Okla. (74636) 288/L1
Deerfield, Ill. (60015) 222/B5
Deerfield, Ind. (†47380) 227/H4
Deerfield, Kansas (67838) 232/A4
Deerfield○, Mass. (01342) 249/D2
Deerfield (riv.), Mass. 249/C2
Deerfield, Mich. (49238) 250/F7
Deerfield, Mo. (64741) 261/D7
Deerfield○, N.H. (03037) 268/E5
Deerfield, Ohio (44411) 284/H3
Deerfield (riv.), Vt. 268/B6
Deerfield, Va. (24432) 307/K4
Deerfield, Wis. (53531) 317/H9
Deerfield Beach, Fla. (33441) 212/F5
Deerfield Street, N.J. (08313) 273/C4
Deerford, La. (†70791) 238/K1
Deer Grove, Ill. (61243) 222/D2
Deer Harbor, Wash. (98243) 310/B2
Deerhorn, Manitoba 179/E4
Deering, Alaska (99736) 196/F1
Deering○, N.H. (†03244) 268/D5
Deering, N. Dak. (58731) 282/J3
Deer Island, Oreg. (97054) 291/E2
Deer Isle, Maine (04627) 243/F7
Deer Isle○, Maine (04627) 243/F7
Deer Lake, Newf. 166/C4
Deer Lake, Ontario 175/B2
Deer Lodge (co.), Mont. 262/C5
Deer Lodge, Mont. (59722) 262/D4
Deer Lodge, Tenn. (37726) 237/M8
Deer Park, Ala. (36529) 195/B8
Deer Park, Calif. (94576) 204/C5
Deer Park, Fla. (†32901) 212/F3
Deer Park, Ill. (†60010) 222/A5
Deer Park, Md. (21550) 245/A3
Deer Park, N.Y. (11729) 276/O9
Deer Park, Ohio (45236) 284/C9
Deer Park, Texas (77536) 303/K2
Deer Park, Wash. (99006) 310/H3
Deer Park, Wis. (54007) 317/B5
Deer River, Minn. (56636) 255/E3
Deer River, N.Y. (13627) 276/J3
Deer Run, W. Va. (†26807) 312/H5
Deersville, Ohio (44693) 284/H5
Deerton, Mich. (49822) 250/B2
Deer Trail, Colo. (80105) 208/M3
Deerwalk, W. Va. (†26180) 312/D4
Deerwood, Minn. (56444) 255/E4
Deesa, India 68/C4
Deeson, Miss. (†38740) 256/C2
Deeth, Nev. (89823) 266/F1
Dee Why, N.S. Wales 88/L4
Dee Why, N.S. Wales 97/J3
Defense Heights, Md. (†20784) 245/G4
Deferiet, N.Y. (13628) 276/J2
Defiance (plat.), Ariz. 198/F3
Defiance, Iowa (51527) 229/C5
Defiance, Mo. (63341) 261/L5
Defiance (co.), Ohio 284/A3
Defiance, Ohio (43512) 284/B3
De Fluessen (lake), Netherlands 27/G3
Defoe, Ky. (40017) 237/L4
Deford, Mich. (48729) 250/F5
De Forest, Wis. (53532) 317/H9
Defoy, Québec 172/E3
De Funiak Springs, Fla. (32433) 212/C6
Dégelis, Québec 172/J2
Degema, Nigeria 106/F8
Degersheim, Switzerland 39/H2
Deggendorf, W. Germany 22/E4
De Graff, Kansas (†66840) 232/F4
De Graff, Minn. (56233) 255/C5
Degraff, Ohio (43318) 284/C5
Degrasse, N.Y. (13629) 276/L2
De Gray (lake), Ark. 202/D5
De Grey, W. Australia 88/B4
De Grey, W. Australia 92/B3
De Grey (riv.), W. Australia 88/C4
De Grey (riv.), W. Australia 92/B3
De Haan, Belgium 27/C6
Deh Bid, Iran 66/H5
Dehdez, Iran 66/G5
Deheq, Iran 66/G4
Dehiwala-Mt. Lavinia, Sri Lanka 68/D7
Dehkhvareqan, Iran 66/D2
Dehlco, La. (†71269) 238/G2
De Honte (bay), Netherlands 27/D6
Dehra Dun, India 68/D2
Dehua, China 77/J6
Deim Zubeir, Sudan 111/E6
Deinze, Belgium 27/C7
Deir Abu Sa'id, Jordan 65/D3
Deir Ballut, West Bank 65/C3
Deir el Balah, Gaza Strip 65/A5
Deir ez Zor (prov.), Syria 63/H5
Deir ez Zor, Syria 63/H5
Deir ez Zor, Syria 59/C2
Deir Sharaf, West Bank 65/C3
Dej, Romania 45/F2
De Kalb (co.), Ala. 195/G2
De Kalb (co.), Georgia 217/D3
De Kalb (co.), Ill. 222/E2
De Kalb, Ill. (60115) 222/E2
De Kalb (co.), Ind. 227/H2
De Kalb, Miss. (39328) 256/G5
De Kalb (co.), Mo. 261/D3
De Kalb, Mo. (64440) 261/C3
De Kalb (co.), Tenn. 237/K9
De Kalb, Texas (75559) 303/K4
De Kalb Junction, N.Y. (13630) 276/K2
Dekese, Zaire 115/D4
Dekoa, Cent. Afr. Rep. 115/C2
De Koog, Netherlands 27/F2
De Koven, Ky. (†42459) 237/E5
Dela, Okla. (†74523) 288/P6
Delacour, Alberta 182/D4
Delacroix, La. (†70085) 238/L7
Delafield, Ill. (†62859) 222/E5
Delafield, Wis. (53018) 317/J1
Delagoa (bay), Mozambique 118/E5
Delair, N.J. (08110) 273/B3
Delamar (mts.), Nev. 266/G5
De Lamere, N. Dak. (58022) 282/R7
DeLancey, Pa. (15733) 294/D4
Delanco○, N.J. (08075) 273/D3
De Land, Fla. (32720) 212/E2
De Land, Ill. (61839) 222/E3
Delaney, Ark. (†72727) 202/C2
Delano, Calif. (93215) 204/F8
Delano, Minn. (55328) 255/E5
Delano, Pa. (18220) 294/K4
Delano, Tenn. (37325) 237/M10
Delano (peak), Utah 304/B5
Delanson, N.Y. (12053) 276/M5
Delaplaine, Ark. (72425) 202/J1
Delaplane, Va. (22025) 307/N3
Delaram, Afghanistan 59/H3
Delaram, Afghanistan 68/A2
Delaronde (lake), Sask. 181/E1
Delavan, Ill. (61734) 222/D3
Delavan, Kansas (66847) 232/F3
Delavan, Minn. (56023) 255/D7
Delavan, Wis. (53115) 317/J10
Delavan Lake, Wis. (†53115) 317/J10
Delaware 188/L3
Delaware (bay) 188/M3
Delaware, Ark. (72835) 202/D3
DELAWARE 245
Delaware (bay), Del. 245/T5
Delaware (riv.), Del. 245/R3
Delaware (co.), Ind. 227/G4
Delaware, Ind. (†47037) 227/G6
Delaware (co.), Iowa 229/L4
Delaware, Iowa (52036) 229/L4
Delaware, N.J. (07833) 273/C2
Delaware (bay), N.J. 273/C5
Delaware (riv.), N.J. 273/D3
Delaware (co.), N.Y. 276/K6
Delaware (riv.), N.Y. 276/K7
Delaware (co.), Ohio 284/D5
Delaware, Ohio (43015) 284/E5
Delaware (lake), Ohio 284/E5
Delaware (co.), Okla. 288/S2
Delaware, Okla. (74027) 288/P1
Delaware, Ontario 177/C5
Delaware (co.), Pa. 294/M6
Delaware (riv.), Pa. 294/N3
Delaware (creek), Texas 303/C10
Delaware (mts.), Texas 303/C10
Delaware (state), U.S. 146/L6
Delaware City, Del. (19706) 245/R2
Delaware Water Gap Nat'l Rec. Area, N.J. 273/C1
Delaware Water Gap, Pa. (18327) 294/M4
Delaware Water Gap Nat'l Rec. Area, Pa. 294/N3
Delbarton, W. Va. (25670) 312/B7
Del Bonita, Alberta 182/D5
Delburne, Alberta 182/D3
Delcambre, La. (70528) 238/G7
Del City, Okla. (73115) 288/L4
Delco, N.C. (28436) 281/N6
Deldoul, Algeria 106/E3
Deleau, Manitoba 179/B5
Delegate, N.S. Wales 97/E5
Delémont, Switzerland 39/D2
De Leon, Texas (76444) 303/F5
De Leon Springs, Fla. (32028) 212/E2
Delevan, N.Y. (14042) 276/D6
Delfí, Greece 45/F6
Delft, Minn. (56124) 255/C7
Delft, Netherlands 27/E4
Delfzijl, Netherlands 27/K2
Delgada (pt.), Argentina 143/D5
Delgada (pt.), Calif. 204/A3
Delgada (pt.), Mexico 150/L7
Delgado (cape), Mozambique 102/G6
Delgado (cape), Mozambique 118/G2
Delgado Chalbaud, Cerro (mt.), Venezuela 124/G6
Delgertsogt, Mongolia 77/G2
Delgo, Sudan 111/F3
Delhi, Calif. (95315) 204/E6
Delhi, Colo. (†81059) 208/M7
Delhi, Ill. (†62052) 222/C4
Delhi (terr.), India 68/D3
Delhi, India 68/D3
Delhi, India 54/J7
Delhi, India 2/N4
Delhi, Iowa (52223) 229/L4
Delhi, La. (71232) 238/H2
Delhi, Minn. (56234) 255/C6
Delhi, N.Y. (13753) 276/L6
Delhi, Okla. (†73662) 288/G4
Delhi, Ontario 177/D5
Delia, Alberta 182/D4
Delia, Kansas (66418) 232/G2
Delice, Dominica 161/F7
Delice, Turkey 63/E3
Delice (riv.), Turkey 63/F3
Délices, Fr. Guiana 131/E3
Delicias, Cuba 158/H3
Delicias, Venezuela 124/B4
Delight, Ark. (71940) 202/C5
Delijan, Iran 66/G4
Delingha, China 77/E4
De Lisle, Miss. (†39571) 256/F10
Delisle, Québec 172/F1
Delisle, Sask. 181/D4
Delitzsch, E. Germany 22/E3
Dell, Ark. (72426) 202/K2
Dell, Mont. (59724) 262/D6
Dell City, Texas (79837) 303/C10
Dell Rapids, S. Dak. (57022) 298/R6
Dellrose, Tenn. (38453) 237/H10
Dellroy, Ohio (44620) 284/H4
Dells, The (valley), Wis. 317/G8
Dellslow, W. Va. (26531) 312/G3
Dellwood, Minn. (†55110) 255/F5
Dellwood, Mo. (†63135) 261/R2
Dellwood, N.C. (†28786) 281/C3
Dellwood, Wis. (53927) 317/G7
Dellys, Algeria 106/E1
Delmar, Ala. (35551) 195/C2
Del Mar, Calif. (92014) 204/H11
Delmar, Del. (19940) 245/R7
Delmar, Iowa (52037) 229/M4
Delmar, Md. (21875) 245/R7
Delmar, N.Y. (12054) 276/N5
Delmas, Sask. 181/C3
Delmas, S. Africa 118/J6
Delmenhorst, W. Germany 22/C2
Delmont, N.J. (08314) 273/C5
Delmont, Pa. (15626) 294/D5
Delmont, S. Dak. (57330) 298/N7
Del Norte (co.), Calif. 204/B2
Del Norte, Colo. (81132) 208/G7
Del Norte (peak), Colo. 208/F7
Deloit, Iowa (51441) 229/C4
DeLong (mts.), Alaska 196/F1
De Long, Ill. (†61436) 222/C3
Delong, Ind. (46922) 227/E2
Deloraine, Man. 162/G6
Deloraine, Manitoba 179/B5
Deloraine, Tasmania 99/C3
Delorme (lake), Québec 174/C2
Deloro, Ontario 177/G3
Delphi, Ind. (46923) 227/D3
Delphia, Ky. (41735) 237/P6
Delphos, Iowa (50844) 229/E7
Delphos, Kansas (67436) 232/E2
Delphos, Ohio (45833) 284/B4
Delpine, Mont. (†59053) 262/F4
Delran○, N.J. (08075) 273/B3
Delray Beach, Fla. (*33444) 212/F5
Del Rey Oaks, Calif. (93940) 204/D7
Del Rio, Tenn. (37727) 237/P9
Del Rio, Texas 188/F5
Del Rio, Texas 146/H7
Del Rio, Texas (78840) 303/D8
Del Rosa, Calif. (92404) 204/E10
Delson, Québec 172/H4
Delta, Ala. (36258) 195/G4
Delta, Br. Col. 184/K3
Delta (co.), Colo. 208/D5
Delta, Colo. (81416) 208/D5
Delta, Iowa (52550) 229/J6
Delta, La. (71233) 238/J2
Delta, Manitoba 179/D4
Delta (co.), Mich. 250/C2
Delta, Mo. (63744) 261/N8
Delta, Ohio (43515) 284/B2
Delta, Ontario 177/H3
Delta, Pa. (17314) 294/K6
Delta (co.), Texas 303/J4
Delta, Utah (84624) 304/B4
Delta, Wis. (†54856) 317/D3
Delta Amacuro (terr.), Venezuela 124/H3
Delta City, Miss. (39061) 256/C4
Delta Junction, Alaska (99737) 196/J2
Deltaville, Va. (23043) 307/R5
Delton, Mich. (49046) 250/D6
Deltona, Fla. (32725) 212/E3
Delungra, N.S. Wales 97/F1
Del Valle, Argentina 143/F7
Del Valle (lake), Calif. 204/L3
Delvin, Ireland 17/G4
Delvinákion, Greece 45/E6
Delvinë, Albania 45/D6
Delwin, Mich. (†48858) 250/E5
Demaine, Sask. 181/D5
Demak, Indonesia 85/J2
Demanda, Sierra de la (range), Spain 33/E1
Demarcation (pt.), Alaska 196/K1
Demarest, N.J. (07627) 273/C1
Demavend (Damavend) (mt.), Iran 66/G3
Demba, Zaire 115/D5
Dembidollo, Ethiopia 111/F6
Demchok, India 68/D2
Demerara (riv.), Guyana 131/B3
Demidov, U.S.S.R. 52/D3
Deming, N. Mex. (88030) 274/B6
Deming, Wash. (98244) 310/C2
Demini (riv.), Brazil 132/H8
Demirci, Turkey 63/C3
Demirkent, Turkey 63/E4
Demirköy, Turkey 63/B2
Demir Qapu, Syria 63/J4
Demmin, E. Germany 22/E2
Democracia, Venezuela 124/E6
Demopolis, Ala. (36732) 195/C6
Demopolis (dam), Ala. 195/C5
Demopolis (lake), Ala. 195/C5
Demorest, Georgia (30535) 217/F1
De Mossville, Ky. (41033) 237/N3
Demotte, Ind. (46310) 227/C2
Dempo (mt.), Indonesia 85/C6
Dempster, S. Dak. (57230) 298/R4
Demster, N.Y. (†13126) 276/H3
Demta, Indonesia 85/L6
Denain, France 28/E2
Denali, Alaska (†99729) 196/J2
Denali Nat'l Park, Alaska 196/H2
Denali Nat'l Preserve, Alaska 196/H2
Denare Beach, Sask. 181/M4
Denau, U.S.S.R. 48/G6
Denbigh (cape), Alaska 196/F2
Denbigh, N. Dak. (58732) 282/J3
Denbigh, Ontario 177/G2
Denbigh, Wales 13/D4
Denbigh, Wales 10/E4
Den Burg, Netherlands 27/F2
Denby, S. Dak. (57733) 298/E7
Denby Dale, England 13/J2
Den Chai, Thailand 72/C3
Dender (riv.), Belgium 27/D7
Denderleeuw, Belgium 27/E7
Dendermonde, Belgium 27/E6
Dendron, Va. (23839) 307/P6
Denekamp, Netherlands 27/L4
Denezhkin Kamen' (mt.), U.S.S.R. 52/J2
Dengkou, China 77/G3
Dêngqên, China 77/E5
Denham, Ind. (46925) 227/D2
Denham, Minn. (55728) 255/F4
Denham, W. Australia 92/A4
Denham Springs, La. (70726) 238/L2
Den Helder, Netherlands 27/F3
Denhoff, N. Dak. (58430) 282/K5
Denholm, Sask. 181/C3
Denholm, Scotland 15/F5
Denia, Spain 33/G3
Deniliquin, N. S. Wales 88/G7
Deniliquin, N.S. Wales 97/C4
Denio, Nev. (89404) 266/C1
Denison, Iowa (51442) 229/C4
Denison, Kansas (66419) 232/G2
Denison (dam), Okla. 288/O7
Denison (range), Tasmania 99/C4
Denison, Texas 188/G4
Denison, Texas (75020) 303/H4
Denison (dam), Texas 303/H4
Denison, Wash. (†99006) 310/H3
Denizli (prov.), Turkey 63/C4
Denizli, Turkey 63/C4
Denizli, Turkey 59/A2
Denman, N.S. Wales 97/F3
Denman Island, Br. Col. 184/H2
Denmark 2/K3
Denmark 7/E3
Denmark (strait) 4/C11
Denmark (str.) 146/S3
Denmark (str.) 7/B2
DENMARK 18/D9
DENMARK 21/E6
Denmark, Iowa (52624) 229/L7
Denmark, Kansas (†67455) 232/D2
Denmark○, Maine (04022) 243/B8
Denmark, Miss. (†38655) 256/F2
Denmark (bay), N.W. Terrs. 187/H2
Denmark, Oreg. (†97450) 291/C5
Denmark, S.C. (29042) 296/E5
Denmark, Tenn. (38391) 237/D9
Denmark, W. Australia 88/B7
Denmark, W. Australia 92/B6
Denmark, Wis. (54208) 317/L7
Dennard, Ark. (72629) 202/E2
Dennehotso, Ariz. (86535) 198/F2
Dennery, St. Lucia 161/G6
Denning, Ark. (†72821) 202/C3
Dennis (hill), Conn. 210/C1
Dennis, Kansas (67341) 232/G4
Dennis○, Mass. (02638) 249/O5
Dennis, Miss. (38838) 256/H1
Dennis (head), Scotland 15/F1
Dennison, Minn. (55018) 255/E6
Dennison, Ohio (44621) 284/H5
Dennis Port, Mass. (02639) 249/O6
Denniston, Va. (†24520) 307/L7
Dennisville, N.J. (08214) 273/D5
Dennisvile, Sask. 181/K6
Denny and Dunipace, Scotland 10/B1
Denny and Dunipace, Scotland 15/C1
Dennysville○, Maine (04628) 243/J6
Den Oever, Netherlands 27/G3
Denoon (lake), Wis. 317/K2
Denpasar, Indonesia 85/E7
Densmore, Kansas (67633) 232/C2
Dent, Minn. (56528) 255/C4
Dent (co.), Mo. 261/J7
Dent, Ohio (†45202) 284/B9
Dent Blanche (mt.), Switzerland 39/E4
Dent de Lys (mt.), Switzerland 39/D4
Dent de Ruth (mt.), Switzerland 39/D3
Dent d'Hérens (mt.), Switzerland 39/E5

Dovray 361

Disko (isl.), Greenland 146/N3
Disko, Ind. (†46982) 227/E2
Disley, Sask. 181/F5
Dismal (riv.), Nebr. 264/C3
Dismal (Great) (swamp), N.C. 281/S1
Disney, Okla. (74340) 288/S2
Dison, Belgium 27/H7
Dispur, India 68/G3
Disputanta, Va. (23842) 307/O6
Disraeli (bay), N.W. Terrs. 187/L1
Disraëli, Québec 172/F4
Diss, England 13/J5
Diss, England 10/G4
Disston (lake), Fla. 212/E2
Disston, Oreg. (†97427) 291/E4
District Heights, Md. (20747) 245/G5
District of Columbia 146/L6
District of Columbia 188/L3
DISTRICT OF COLUMBIA 245
Distrito Especial, Colombia 126/C5
Distrito Federal, Argentina 143/H7
Distrito Federal, Mexico 150/L1
Distrito Federal, Venezuela 124/E2
Distrito Nacional, Dom. Rep. 158/E6
Disûq, Egypt 111/J3
Dittmer, Mo. (63023) 261/L6
Ditton (riv.), Québec 172/F4
Diu, India 68/C4
Diu (dist.), India 68/C4
Diuata (mts.), Philippines 82/E6
Divernon, Ill. (62530) 222/D4
Divide, Colo. (80814) 208/J5
Divide, Mont. (59727) 262/D5
Divide (co.), N. Dak. 282/C2
Dividing (creek), Md. 245/R8
Dividing Creek, N.J. (08315) 273/C5
Divino, Brazil 135/E2
Divinópolis, Brazil 132/E8
Divinópolis, Brazil 120/E5
Divinópolis, Brazil 135/D2
Divis (mt.), N. Ireland 17/J2
Divisa Nova, Brazil 135/C2
Division (peak), Nev. 266/B1
Divo, Ivory Coast 106/C7
Divriği, Turkey 63/H3
Divriği, Turkey 59/C2
Dix, Ill. (62830) 222/E5
Dix (riv.), Ky. 237/M5
Dix, Nebr. (69133) 264/A3
Dixfield, Maine (04224) 243/C6
Dixfield○, Maine (04224) 243/C6
Dix Hills, N.Y. (11746) 276/O9
Dixie, Ala. (†36420) 195/E8
Dixie (co.), Fla. 212/C2
Dixie, Georgia (31629) 217/E9
Dixie, Idaho (83525) 220/C4
Dixie, La. (†71107) 238/C1
Dixie, Wash. (99329) 310/G4
Dixie, W. Va. (25059) 312/D6
Dixie Inn, La. (†71055) 238/D1
Dixmont, Maine (04932) 243/E6
Dixmont○, Maine (04932) 243/E6
Dixmoor, Ill. (†60469) 222/C6
Dixmude (Diksmuide), Belgium 27/B6
Dixon, Calif. (95620) 204/B9
Dixon, Ill. (61021) 222/D2
Dixon, Iowa (52745) 229/M5
Dixon, Ky. (42409) 237/F5
Dixon, Miss. (†39350) 256/F5
Dixon, Mo. (65459) 261/H6
Dixon, Mont. (59831) 262/B3
Dixon (co.), Nebr. 264/H2
Dixon, Nebr. (68732) 264/H2
Dixon, N. Mex. (87527) 274/D2
Dixon, N.C. (†28445) 281/O5
Dixon, Ohio (†46773) 284/A4
Dixon, S. Dak. (57530) 298/L7
Dixon, Wyo. (82323) 319/E4
Dixon Entrance (chan.) 146/E4
Dixon Entrance (chan.), Alaska 196/M2
Dixon Entrance (chan.), Br. Col. 184/A3
Dixons Mills, Ala. (36736) 195/C6
Dixon Springs, Ill. (†62911) 222/E6
Dixon Springs, Tenn. (37057) 237/J8
Dixonville, Ala. (†36426) 195/E8
Dixonville, Alberta 182/B1
Dixonville, Pa. (15734) 294/D4
Dixville (peak), N.H. 268/E2
Dixville, Québec 172/F4
Dixville Notch, N.H. (†03576) 268/E2
Dixville Notch (pass), N.H. 268/E2
Diyadin, Turkey 63/K3
Diyala (heads), Iraq 66/D4
Diyala (riv.), Iraq 66/D4
Diyarbakır (prov.), Turkey 63/H4
Diyarbakır, Turkey 54/F6
Diyarbakır, Turkey 63/H4
Diyarbakır, Turkey 59/C2
Dizful (Dezful), Iran 66/F4
Dja (riv.), Cameroon 115/B3
Dja (riv.), Congo 115/B3
Djado (plat.) 102/D2
Djado, Niger 102/D2
Djado, Niger 106/G4
Djado (plat.), Niger 106/G4
Djakarta (Jakarta) (cap.), Indonesia 85/H1
Djakovica, Yugoslavia 45/E4
Djakovo, Yugoslavia 45/D3
Djambala, Congo 115/B4
Djambi (Jambi), Indonesia 85/C6
Djanet, Algeria 106/F4
Djanet, Algeria 102/C2
Djelfa, Algeria 106/E2
Djema, Cent. Afr. Rep. 115/E2
Djemaa, Algeria 106/F2
Djenné, Mali 102/B3
Djenné, Mali 106/D6
Djerba (isl.), Tunisia 106/G2
Djerid, Shott el (salt lake), Tunisia 106/F2
Djibo, Upper Volta 106/D6
Djibouti 2/L5
Djibouti 102/G3
DJIBOUTI 111/H5
Djibouti (cap.), Djibouti 111/H5
Djibouti (cap.), Djibouti 102/G3
Djokjakarta (Yogyakarta), Indonesia 85/J2
Djolu, Zaire 115/D3
Djouf, El (des.), Mauritania 106/C4
Djougou, Benin 106/E7
Djoum, Cameroon 115/B3
Djugu, Zaire 115/F3
D'Lo, Miss. (39062) 256/E7
Dmitriya Lapteva (str.), U.S.S.R. 4/B2
Dmitriya Lapteva (str.), U.S.S.R. 48/O2
Dneprodzerzhinsk, U.S.S.R. 7/H4
Dneprodzerzhinsk, U.S.S.R. 52/D5
Dnepropetrovsk, U.S.S.R. 7/H4
Dnepropetrovsk, U.S.S.R. 48/D5
Dnepropetrovsk, U.S.S.R. 52/D5
Dnieper (riv.), U.S.S.R. 7/H3
Dnieper (riv.), U.S.S.R. 48/D5
Dnieper (riv.), U.S.S.R. 52/D5
Dniester (riv.), U.S.S.R. 7/G4
Dniester (riv.), U.S.S.R. 52/C5
Dniester (riv.), U.S.S.R. 48/C5
Dno, U.S.S.R. 52/D3
Doaghbeg, Ireland 17/F1
Doaktown, New Bruns. 170/D2
Doans, Ind. (†47424) 227/D7
Doba, Chad 111/C6
Doba, Chad 102/D4
Dobbie (mt.), North. Terr. 93/E7
Dobbin (bay), N.W. Terrs. 187/L2
Dobbins A.F.B., Georgia 217/J1
Dobbs Ferry, N.Y. (10522) 276/O6
Dobbyn, Queensland 95/A3
Dobele, U.S.S.R. 53/B2
Döbeln, E. Germany 22/E3
Doberai (pen.), Indonesia 85/J6
Dobiegniew, Poland 47/B2
Doblas, Argentina 143/D4
Dobo, Indonesia 85/J7
Doboj, Yugoslavia 45/C3
Doboy (sound), Georgia 217/K8
Dobřany, Czech. 41/B2
Dobre Miasto, Poland 47/E2
Dobrich (Tolbukhin), Bulgaria 45/H4
Dobříš, Czech. 41/C2
Dobrush, U.S.S.R. 52/D4
Dobruška, Czech. 41/D1
Dobryanka, U.S.S.R. 52/J3
Dobšiná, Czech. 41/F2
Dobson, N.C. (27017) 281/H2
Doce (riv.), Brazil 135/E2
Doce (riv.), Brazil 132/F7
Doce Leguas (cays), Cuba 158/F3
Docker River, North. Terr. 93/A8
Docking, England 13/H5
Dock Junction (Arco), Georgia (†31520) 217/J8
Doctor Arroyo, Mexico 150/K5
Doctor Cecilio Báez, Paraguay 144/D4
Doctor Juan L. Mallorquín, Paraguay 144/E4
Doctor Juan Manuel Frutos, Paraguay 144/E4
Doctor M. Irala, Paraguay 144/E4
Doctor Pedro P. Peña, Paraguay 144/A3
Doctors Inlet, Fla. (32030) 212/E1
Doctortown, Georgia (†31545) 217/J7
Doddridge, Ark. (71834) 202/C1
Doddridge (co.), W. Va. 312/E4
Dodds, Alberta 182/D3
Doddsville, Miss. (38736) 256/C3
Dodecanese (isls.), Greece 45/H8
Dodge (co.), Georgia 217/F6
Dodge, Mass. (†01507) 249/G4
Dodge (co.), Minn. 255/F7
Dodge (co.), Nebr. 264/H3
Dodge, Nebr. (68633) 264/H3
Dodge, N. Dak. (58625) 282/F5
Dodge, Texas (77334) 303/J7
Dodge (co.), Wis. 317/J9
Dodge, Wis. (54625) 317/D7
Dodge Center, Minn. (55927) 255/F6
Dodge City, Kans. 188/F3
Dodge City, Kansas (67801) 232/B4
Dodgeville, Wis. (53533) 317/F10
Dodgingtown, Conn. (†06470) 210/B3
Dodman (pt.), England 13/C7
Dodoma (reg.), Tanzania 115/G5
Dodoma, Tanzania 102/F5
Dodoma, Tanzania 115/G5
Dodsland, Sask. 181/C4
Dodson, La. (71422) 238/E2
Dodson, Mont. (59524) 262/H2
Dodson, Texas (79230) 303/D3
Doe (lake), Ontario 177/E2
Doe (bay), Wash. 310/C2
Doe Bay, Wash. (†98279) 310/C2
Doe Hill, Va. (24433) 307/K4
Doering, Wis. (†54435) 317/G5
Doerun, Georgia (31744) 217/E8
Doe Run, Mo. (63637) 261/M7
Doesburg, Netherlands 27/J4
Doetinchem, Netherlands 27/J5
Dog (pond), Conn. 210/C1
Dog (isl.), Fla. 212/B2
Dog (lake), Manitoba 179/D3
Dog (isl.), Newf. 166/B2
Dog (lake), Ontario 177/G5
Dogai Coring (lake), China 77/C5
Doğanbey, Turkey 63/D4
Doğanhisar, Turkey 63/D3
Doğanşehir, Turkey 63/G3
Dog Creek, Br. Col. 184/G4
Dog Ear (creek), S. Dak. 298/K6
Döger, Turkey 63/D3
Dogo (isl.), Japan 81/F5
Dogondoutchi, Niger 106/E6
Dogondoutchi, Niger 102/C3
Dogpatch, Ark. (72648) 202/D1
Dog Pound, Alberta 182/C4
Dogskin (lake), Manitoba 179/G3
Doğubeyazıt, Turkey 63/K3
Dogwood (pt.), St. Chris.-Nevis 161/D11
Doha (cap.), Qatar 54/G7
Doha (cap.), Qatar 59/F4
Dohad, India 68/C4
Doheny, Québec 172/E2
Dohuk (gov.), Iraq 66/C2
Dohuk, Iraq 66/C2
Doi Inthanon (mt.), Thailand 72/C3
Doilungdeqen, China 77/C6
Doi Pha Hom Pok (mt.), Thailand 72/C2
Doi Pia Fai (mt.), Thailand 72/D4
Doische, Belgium 27/F8
Dois Córregos, Brazil 135/B3
Dois Irmãos, Serra (range), Brazil 132/F5
Dokkum, Netherlands 27/H2
Doksy, Czech. 41/C1
Dokterstuin, Neth. Ant. 161/F8
Dola, Ohio (45835) 284/C4
Dola, W. Va. (†26386) 312/F4
Dolan, Ind. (†47401) 227/E6
Doland, S. Dak. (57436) 298/N4
Dolan Springs, Ariz. (86441) 198/A3
Dolavon, Argentina 143/C5
Dolbeau, Québec 174/C3
Dolbeau, Québec 172/E1
Doldenhorn (mt.), Switzerland 39/E4
Dole, France 28/F4
Dolega, Panama 154/F6
Dolent (mt.), Switzerland 39/C5
Doles, Georgia (†31791) 217/E7
Dolgellau, Wales 13/D5
Dolgellau, Wales 10/E4
Dolgeville, N.Y. (13329) 276/L4
Dolgiy (isl.), U.S.S.R. 52/J1
Dolinsk, U.S.S.R. 48/P5
Dollar, Scotland 10/B1
Dollar, Scotland 15/E4
Dollar Bay, Mich. (49922) 250/G1
Dollard (bay), Netherlands 27/L2
Dollard, Sask. 181/C6
Dollard-des-Ormeaux, Québec 172/H4
Dollart (est.), W. Germany 22/B2
Dollarville, Mich. (†49868) 250/D2
Dolliver, Iowa (50531) 229/D2
Dolný Kubín, Czech. 41/E2
Dolo, Ethiopia 111/H7
Dolomite, Ala. (35061) 195/D4
Dolomite Alps (range), Italy 34/C1
Dolores, Argentina 143/E4
Dolores, Argentina 120/D6
Dolores (co.), Colo. 208/C7
Dolores, Colo. (81323) 208/C8
Dolores (riv.), Colo. 208/B5
Dolores, Guatemala 154/C2
Dolores, Philippines 82/E4
Dolores, Spain 33/F3
Dolores, Uruguay 145/A4
Dolores (riv.), Utah 304/E5
Dolores, Venezuela 124/D3
Dolores Hidalgo de la Independencia Nacional, Mexico 150/J6
Dolphin and Union (str.), N.W. Terrs. 187/G3
Dölsach, Austria 41/B3
Dolton, Ill. (60419) 222/C6
Dolton, S. Dak. (57023) 298/P7
Dom (mt.), Switzerland 39/E4
Domain, Manitoba 179/E5
Domanic, Turkey 63/C3
Domar (dry riv.), Chad 111/C4
Domat-Ems, Switzerland 39/H3
Domažlice, Czech. 41/B2
Dombås, Norway 18/F5
Dombe Grande, Angola 115/B6
Dombóvár, Hungary 41/E3
Dombrád, Hungary 41/F2
Dombresson, Switzerland 39/C2
Domburg, Netherlands 27/C5
Domburg, Suriname 131/D3
Dome, Ariz. (†85364) 198/A6
Dome Creek, Br. Col. 184/G3
Domeiko, Chile 138/A7
Domeyko, Cordillera (mts.), Chile 138/B4
Domínguez, Argentina 143/G6
Dominica 2/F5
Dominica 146/M8
DOMINICA 156/G4
DOMINICA 161/E7
Dominica (passage), Dominica 161/E5
Dominican Republic 2/F4
Dominican Republic 146/L8
DOMINICAN REPUBLIC 156/D3
DOMINICAN REPUBLIC 158
Dominion (lake), Newf. 166/B3
Dominion (cape), N.W. Terrs. 187/L3
Dominion, Nova Scotia 168/J2
Dominion City, Manitoba 179/E5
Domino, Newf. 166/C3
Dömitz, E. Germany 22/D2
Domjor, India 68/F1
Domleschg (valley), Switzerland 39/E2
Dommel (riv.), Netherlands 27/H6
Domo, Ethiopia 111/J6
Domodossola, Italy 34/A1
Dom Pedrito, Brazil 132/C10
Dompu, Indonesia 85/F7
Domremy, Sask. 181/F3
Domrémy-la-Pucelle, France 28/F3
Dom Silvério, Brazil 135/E2
Dömsöd, Hungary 41/E3
Domuyo (vol.), Argentina 143/B4
Don (riv.), England 10/F4
Don (riv.), England 13/F4
Don (riv.), Ontario 177/J4
Don (riv.), Scotland 15/F3
Don (riv.), Scotland 10/E2
Don (riv.), U.S.S.R. 7/J4
Don (riv.), U.S.S.R. 48/E5
Don (riv.), U.S.S.R. 52/F5
Dona Ana (Mutarara), Mozambique 118/F3
Dona Ana (co.), N. Mex. 274/C6
Dona Ana, N. Mex. (88032) 274/C6
Donabate, Ireland 17/J5
Donaghadee, N. Ireland 17/K2
Donahue, Iowa (52746) 229/M5
Donald, Br. Col. 184/J4
Donald, Oreg. (97020) 291/A3
Donald, Victoria 97/B5
Donald, Wash. (†98951) 310/E4
Donald, Wis. (†54433) 317/E5
Donalda, Alberta 182/D3
Donalds, S.C. (29638) 296/C3
Donaldson, Ark. (71941) 202/E5
Donaldson, Ind. (46513) 227/E2
Donaldson, Minn. (56720) 255/B2
Donaldson A.F.B., S.C. 296/C2
Donaldsonville, La. (70346) 238/K3
Donalsonville, Georgia (31745) 217/C8
Donansburg, Ky. (†42743) 237/K6
Donath, Switzerland 39/H3
Donatville, Alberta 182/D2
Donau (Danube) (riv.), Austria 41/D2
Donau (Danube) (riv.), W. Germany 22/C4
Donaueschingen, W. Germany 22/C5
Donauwörth, W. Germany 22/D4
Donavon, Sask. 181/D4
Donbar, Queensland 95/B3
Don Benito, Spain 33/C3
Doncaster, England 13/F4
Doncaster, England 10/F4
Doncaster, Md. (†20646) 245/K7
Doncaster and Templestowe, Victoria 88/L7
Doncaster and Templestowe, Victoria 97/J5
Dondo, Angola 115/B5
Dondo, Mozambique 118/F3
Dondra (head), Sri Lanka 68/E7
Dondra Head (cape), Sri Lanka 54/K9
Donegal (co.), Ireland 17/K2
Donegal, Ireland 10/B3
Donegal, Ireland 17/F2
Donegal (bay), Ireland 17/D3
Donegal (bay), Ireland 10/B3
Donegal (harb.), Ireland 17/E2
Donegal (pt.), Ireland 17/B6
Donegal, Pa. (15628) 294/D5
Donel, Honduras 154/E3
Doneraile, Ireland 17/D7
Doneraile, S.C. (†29532) 296/H3
Donets (riv.), U.S.S.R. 7/H4
Donets (riv.), U.S.S.R. 48/D5
Donets (riv.), U.S.S.R. 52/E5
Donetsk, U.S.S.R. 7/H4
Donetsk, U.S.S.R. 48/D5
Donetsk, U.S.S.R. 52/E5
Donga (riv.), Cameroon 115/B2
Donga, Nigeria 106/G7
Donga (riv.), Nigeria 106/G7
Dongara, W. Australia 92/A5
Dongchuan, China 77/F6
Dongen, Netherlands 27/F5
Dongfang, China 77/G8
Dongfanghong, China 77/M2
Donggala, Indonesia 85/F6
Dõnghén, Laos 72/E3
Dong Hoi, Vietnam 72/E3
Dongio, Switzerland 39/H4
Dongning, China 77/M3
Dongo, Zaire 115/C3
Dongola, Ill. (62926) 222/D6
Dongola, Sudan 102/E3
Dongola, Sudan 59/B6
Dongola, Sudan 111/F4
Dongou, Congo 115/C3
Dong Rak (mts.), Thailand 72/D4
Dongsha (isl.), China 77/J7
Dongsheng, China 77/H4
Dongtai, China 77/K5
Dongting (lake), China 54/N7
Dongting Hu (riv.), China 77/H6
Dong Ujimqin, China 77/J2
Dongwe (riv.), Zambia 115/D6
Donie, Texas (75838) 303/H6
Doñihue, Chile 138/G5
Doniphan (co.), Kansas 232/G2
Doniphan, Mo. (63935) 261/L9
Doniphan, Nebr. (68832) 264/F4
Donji Vakuf, Yugoslavia 45/C3
Donkin, Nova Scotia 168/J2
Donley (co.), Texas 303/D2
Dønna (isl.), Norway 18/H3
Donna, Texas (78537) 303/F11
Donnacona, Québec 172/F3
Donnan, Iowa (52139) 229/K3
Donnellson, Ill. (62019) 222/D4
Donnellson, Iowa (52625) 229/K7
Donnelly, Alberta 182/B2
Donnelly, Idaho (83615) 220/B5
Donnelly, Minn. (56235) 255/B5
Donner (pass), Calif. 204/E4
Donner, La. (70352) 238/J7
Donner and Blitzen (riv.), Oreg. 291/J4
Donnybrook, N. Dak. (58734) 282/G2
Donnybrook, Queensland 95/D5
Donnybrook, W. Australia 92/A2
Donora, Pa. (15033) 294/C5
Donovan, Georgia (†31096) 217/G5
Donovan, Ill. (60931) 222/F3
Donsol, Philippines 82/D4
Donwell, Sask. 181/J4
Donzère, France 28/F5
Dooagh-Keel, Ireland 17/A4
Doole, Texas (76836) 303/E6
Dooling, Georgia (†31063) 217/E6
Doolittle (pond), Conn. 210/C1
Doolittle, Mo. (†65550) 261/J7
Doolittle Mills, Ind. (†47118) 227/D8
Dooly (co.), Georgia 217/E6
Doon, Iowa (51235) 229/A2
Doon, Ireland 17/E6
Doon, Loch (lake), Scotland 15/D5
Doon (riv.), Scotland 15/D5
Doonerak (mt.), Alaska 196/H1
Doonside, Sask. 181/K6
Door (pt.), La. 238/M6
Door (co.), Wis. 317/M6
Door (pen.), Wis. 317/M6
Doorn, Netherlands 27/G4
Doornik (Tournai), Belgium 27/C7
Doqa, Saudi Arabia 59/D6
Dor, Israel 65/B2
Dora, Ala. (35062) 195/D3
Dora, Mo. (65637) 261/H9
Dora, N. Mex. (88115) 274/F5
Dora, Oreg. (†97458) 291/D4
Dora (lake), W. Australia 88/C4
Dora (lake), W. Australia 92/C3
Dora Baltea (riv.), Italy 34/A2
Dorado, P. Rico 161/D1
Dora Lake, Minn. (†56661) 255/D3
Doran, Minn. (56530) 255/B4
Dora Riparia (riv.), Italy 34/A2
Doraville, Georgia (30340) 217/K1
D'Orbigny, Bolivia 136/D7
Dorbiljin (Emin), China 77/B2
Dorbod, China 77/K2
Dorcas, W. Va. (26835) 312/H5
Dorchester, England 10/E5
Dorchester, England 13/E7
Dorchester, Georgia (†31317) 217/K7
Dorchester, Ill. (62020) 222/D4
Dorchester, Iowa (52140) 229/L2
Dorchester (co.), Md. 245/O7
Dorchester, Mass. (†02122) 249/D7
Dorchester, Nebr. (68343) 264/G4
Dorchester, New Bruns. 170/F3
Dorchester○, N.H. (†03266) 268/D4
Dorchester, N.J. (08316) 273/D5
Dorchester (cape), N.W. Terrs. 187/L3
Dorchester, Ontario 177/C5
Dorchester (co.), Québec 172/C3
Dorchester (co.), S.C. 296/G5
Dorchester, S.C. (29437) 296/G5
Dorchester, Wis. (54425) 317/F5
Dorchester Crossing, New Bruns. 170/F2
Dordogne (dept.), France 28/D5
Dordogne (riv.), France 7/E4
Dordogne (riv.), France 28/D5
Dordrecht, Netherlands 27/F5
Doré (lake), Ontario 177/G2
Doré (lake), Sask. 181/L3
Dore Alps (mts.), France 28/E5
Doré Lake, Sask. 181/L4
Dorena, Mo. (†63845) 261/O9
Dorena, Oreg. (97434) 291/E4
Dorena (lake), Oreg. 291/E4
Dorenlee, Alberta 182/D3
Dores, Scotland 15/D3
Dores do Indaiá, Brazil 132/E7
Dorgali, Italy 34/B4
Dörgön Nuur (lake), Mongolia 77/D2
Dori, Mali 102/B3
Dori, Upper Volta 106/D6
Doring (riv.), S. Africa 118/B6
Dorintosh, Sask. 181/L4
Dorion, Ontario 177/H5
Dorion, Québec 172/C4
Dorking, England 13/G8
Dorking, England 10/F5
Dormont, Pa. (15216) 294/B7
Dornach, Switzerland 39/E2
Dornbirn, Austria 41/A3
Dornie, Scotland 15/C3
Dornoch, Scotland 10/D2
Dornoch, Scotland 15/D3
Dornoch (firth), Scotland 15/E3
Dornoch (firth), Scotland 10/E2
Dornod, Mongolia 77/H2
Dornogovĭ, Mongolia 77/G3
Dorog, Hungary 41/E3
Dorohoi, Romania 45/H2
Dorotea, Sweden 18/K4
Dorothy, Alberta 182/D4
Dorothy, Minn. (†56750) 255/B3
Dorothy, N.J. (08317) 273/D5
Dorothy, W. Va. (25060) 312/D7
Dorr (lake), Fla. 212/E2
Dorr, Mich. (49323) 250/D6
Dorrance, Kansas (67634) 232/D3
Dorre (isl.), W. Australia 88/A5
Dorre (isl.), W. Australia 92/A4
Dorreen, Br. Col. 184/C3
Dorrigo, N.S. Wales 97/G2
Dorris, Calif. (96023) 204/D2
Dorset (co.), England 13/E7
Dorset, Minn. (†56470) 255/D4
Dorset, Ohio (44032) 284/J2
Dorset○, Vt. (05251) 268/A5
Dorset (peak), Vt. 268/A5
Dorset Heights (hills), England 13/E7
Dorsey, Miss. (†38801) 256/H2
Dorsten, W. Germany 22/B3
Dortches, N.C. (†27801) 281/O2
Dortmund, W. Germany 7/E3
Dortmund, W. Germany 22/B3
Dorton, Ky. (41520) 237/R6
Dörtyol, Turkey 63/F4
Doruma, Zaire 115/E3
Dorval, Québec 172/H4
Dory Point, N.W. Terrs. 187/G3
Dos Bahías (cape), Argentina 143/D5
Dos Cabezas, Ariz. (†85643) 198/F6
Dos Caminos, Cuba 158/J4
Dos de Mayo, Peru 128/E6
Dos Hermanas, Spain 33/D4
Dos Palos, Calif. (93620) 204/E6
Dosquet, Québec 172/F3
Dos Reyes (pt.), Chile 138/A5
Dos Ríos, Cuba 158/J4
Dosso, Niger 106/E6
Dossor, U.S.S.R. 48/F5
Dossville, Miss. (†39051) 256/F5
Doswell, Va. (23047) 307/N5
Dothan, Ala. 188/J4
Dothan, Ala. (*36303) 195/H8
Doti, Nepal 68/E3
Dot Klish (canyon), Ariz. 198/E2
Dot Lake, Alaska (99737) 196/K2
Dott, W. Va. (24721) 312/D8
Döttingen, Switzerland 39/F1
Doty, Wash. (98539) 310/B4
Douai, France 28/E2
Douala, Cameroon 115/B3
Douala, Cameroon 102/D4
Douarnenez, France 28/A3
Double Branches, Georgia (†30817) 217/H3
Double Mer (lake), Newf. 166/C3
Double Mountain Fork, Brazos (riv.), Texas 303/C4
Double Oak, Texas (†76226) 303/F1
Double Springs, Ala. (35553) 195/D2
Doubletop (peak), Wyo. 319/B2
Doubs (dept.), France 28/G4
Doubs (riv.), France 28/G4
Doubs, Md. (†21710) 245/J3
Doubs (riv.), Switzerland 39/C2
Doubtful (sound), N. Zealand 100/A6
Doubtless (bay), N. Zealand 100/D1
Doucette, Texas (79542) 303/K7
Douds, Iowa (52551) 229/J7
Doué-la-Fontaine, France 28/C4
Douentza, Mali 106/D6
Douentza, Mali 102/B3
Dougherty (co.), Georgia 217/D7
Dougherty, Iowa (50433) 229/G3
Dougherty, Okla. (73032) 288/M6
Dougherty, Texas (79231) 303/C4
Douglas, Ala. (35964) 195/F2
Douglas (mt.), Alaska 196/H3
Douglas, Ariz. 146/G6
Douglas, Ariz. 188/E4
Douglas, Ariz. (85607) 198/F7
Douglas (chan.), Br. Col. 184/C3
Douglas (co.), Colo. 208/K4
Douglas (creek), Colo. 208/B3
Douglas (bay), Dominica 161/E5
Douglas (co.), Georgia 217/C3
Douglas, Georgia (31533) 217/G7
Douglas (co.), Ill. 222/E4
Douglas, Ireland 17/D8
Douglas (cap.), I. of Man 13/C3
Douglas (cap.), I. of Man 10/D3
Douglas (co.), Kansas 232/G3
Douglas, Manitoba 179/C5
Douglas○, Mass. (†01516) 249/H4
Douglas, Mich. (49406) 250/C6
Douglas (co.), Minn. 255/C5
Douglas, Minn. (†55960) 255/F6
Douglas (co.), Mo. 261/G9
Douglas (mt.), Mont. 262/F5
Douglas (co.), Nebr. 264/H3
Douglas, Nebr. (68344) 264/H4
Douglas (co.), Nev. 266/B4
Douglas, N. Dak. (58735) 282/G4
Douglas, North. Terr. 93/B2
Douglas, Okla. (73733) 288/L2
Douglas, Ontario 177/H2
Douglas (pt.), Ontario 177/C3
Douglas (co.), Oreg. 291/D4
Douglas, Scotland 15/E5
Douglas, S. Africa 118/C5
Douglas (co.), S. Dak. 298/N7
Douglas (lake), Tenn. 237/P9
Douglas (co.), Wash. 310/F3
Douglas, Wash. (†98858) 310/F3
Douglas (co.), Wis. 317/C3
Douglas, Wyo. (82633) 319/G3
Douglas Harbour, New Bruns. 170/D3
Douglas Lake, Br. Col. 184/H5
Douglas Prov. Park, Sask. 181/E4
Douglass, Kansas (67039) 232/F4
Douglass, Texas (75943) 303/K6
Douglass Hills, Ky. (†40243) 237/L2
Douglassville, Pa. (19518) 294/L5
Douglastown, New Bruns. 170/E1
Douglastown, Québec 172/D1
Douglasville, Georgia (*30133) 217/C3
Doullens, France 28/E2
Doulus (head), Ireland 17/A8
Doumé, Cameroon 115/B3
Dounby, Scotland 15/E1
Doune, Scotland 15/D4
Dour, Belgium 27/D8
Dourados, Brazil 120/D5
Dourados, Brazil 132/C8
Douro (riv.), Portugal 7/D4
Douro (riv.), Portugal 33/B2
Douro (riv.), Spain 33/C2
Dousman, Wis. (53118) 317/J1
Douthat, Okla. (74341) 288/S1
Douville, Québec 172/D4
Dove (riv.), England 13/J2
Dove (creek), Utah 304/A2
Dove Creek, Colo. (81324) 208/A7
Dover, Ark. (72837) 202/D3
Dover (cap.), Del. 146/L6
Dover (cap.), Del. 188/L3
Dover (cap.), Del. (19901) 245/R4
Dover, England 7/E3
Dover, England 10/G5
Dover, England 13/J6
Dover (str.), England 13/J7
Dover (str.), England 10/G5
Dover, Fla. (33527) 212/D4
Dover, Georgia (30424) 217/J5
Dover, Idaho (83825) 220/B1
Dover, Ill. (61323) 222/D2
Dover, Ind. (†46052) 227/H6
Dover, Kansas (66420) 232/G3
Dover, Ky. (41034) 237/O3
Dover, Mass. (02030) 249/B7
Dover○, Mass. (02030) 249/B7
Dover, Minn. (55929) 255/F7
Dover, Mo. (64022) 261/E4
Dover, N.H. (03820) 268/F5
Dover, N.J. (07801) 273/D2
Dover, N.C. (28526) 281/P4
Dover, Ohio (44622) 284/G4
Dover (lake), Ohio 284/H4
Dover, Okla. (73734) 288/L3
Dover, Pa. (17315) 294/J6
Dover, Tasmania 99/C5
Dover, Tenn. (37058) 237/F8
Dover (pt.), W. Australia 88/D6
Dover (pt.), W. Australia 92/D6
Dover A.F.B., Del. 245/S4
Doverel, Georgia (†31742) 217/D7
Dover-Foxcroft, Maine (04426) 243/E5
Dover-Foxcroft○, Maine (04426) 243/E5
Dover Hill, Ind. (†47581) 227/D7
Dover Plains, N.Y. (12522) 276/O7
Dover South Mills, Maine (†04426) 243/E5
Dovesville, S.C. (29540) 296/H3
Dovey (riv.), Wales 10/D4
Dovey (riv.), Wales 13/D5
Dovns Klint (cliff), Denmark 21/D8
Dovray, Minn. (56125) 255/C6

362 Dovre

Dovre, Norway 18/F6
Dovrefjell (hills), Norway 18/F5
Dow (Xau) (lake), Botswana 118/C4
Dow, Ill. (62022) 222/C4
Dow, Okla. (†74547) 288/P5
Dowa, Malawi 115/F6
Dowagiac, Mich. (49047) 250/D6
Dow City, Iowa (51528) 229/B5
Dowell, Ill. (62927) 222/D6
Dowelltown, Tenn. (37059) 237/K8
Dowlatabad, Afghanistan 59/H3
Dowlatabad, Afghanistan 68/A2
Dowlatabad, Kerman, Iran 66/K6
Dowlatabad, Khorasan, Iran 66/M2
Dowlat Yar, Afghanistan 59/J3
Dowlat Yar, Afghanistan 68/B2
Dowling, Alberta 182/E4
Dowling (lake), Alberta 182/D4
Dowling, Mich. (49050) 250/D6
Dowling Park, Fla. (32060) 212/C1
Down (dist.), N. Ireland 17/K3
Downe, Sask. 181/C4
Downer, Minn. (†56514) 255/B4
Downers Grove, Ill. (60515) 222/A6
Downey, Calif. (*90240) 204/C11
Downey, Idaho (83234) 220/F7
Downey, Iowa (†52358) 229/L5
Downfall (creek), Queensland 95/D2
Downham Market, England 13/H5
Downham Market, England 10/G4
Downieville, Calif. (95936) 204/E4
Downing, Mo. (63536) 261/H2
Downing, Wis. (54734) 317/B5
Downings, Va. (†22460) 307/P5
Downingtown, Pa. (19335) 294/L5
Downpatrick (head), Ireland 17/C3
Downpatrick, N. Ireland 10/C3
Downpatrick, N. Ireland 17/K3
Downs, Ill. (61736) 222/E3
Downs, Kansas (67437) 232/D2
Downsville, La. (71234) 238/F1
Downsville, Md. (†21795) 245/G2
Downsville, N.Y. (13755) 276/L6
Downsville, Wis. (54735) 317/C6
Downton, England 13/F6
Dows, Iowa (50071) 229/F3
Dowshi, Afghanistan 59/J2
Dowshi, Afghanistan 68/B1
Doyle, Calif. (96109) 204/E3
Doyle, Georgia (†31803) 217/D6
Doyle, Tenn. (38559) 237/K9
Doylestown, Ohio (44230) 284/G4
Doylestown, Pa. (18901) 294/M5
Doylestown, Wis. (53928) 317/H9
Doyleville, Colo. (†81239) 208/F6
Doyline, La. (71023) 238/D1
Doyon, N. Dak. (58328) 282/O3
Dozen (isls.), Japan 81/F5
Dozier, Ala. (36028) 195/F7
Dozier, Texas (†79079) 303/D2
Dozois (res.), Québec 174/B3
Dra, Wadi (dry riv.), Morocco 106/C3
Drachten, Netherlands 27/J2
Dracut○, Mass. (01826) 249/J2
Drăgănesti Olt, Romania 45/G3
Drăgăsani, Romania 45/F3
Dragonera (isl.), Spain 33/H3
Dragons Mouth (str.), Trin. & Tob. 156/F5
Dragons Mouth (str.), Trin. & Tob. 161/A10
Dragons Mouth (str.), Venezuela 124/H2
Dragoon, Ariz. (85609) 198/F6
Dragoon (mts.), Ariz. 198/F7
Draguignan, France 28/G6
Drain, Oreg. (97435) 291/D4
Drake (passage) 2/F8
Drake (passage) 5/C15
Drake (passage), Chile 138/E11
Drake, Colo. (80515) 208/J2
Drake, Mo. (†65066) 261/K6
Drake, N. Dak. (58736) 282/K4
Drake, Sask. 181/G4
Drakensberg (range), Lesotho 118/D6
Drakensberg (range), S. Africa 118/D6
Drakensberg (range), Swaziland 118/D6
Drakes (creek), Ky. 237/J7
Drakesboro, Ky. (42337) 237/H6
Drakes Branch, Va. (23937) 307/L7
Drakesville, Iowa (52552) 229/J7
Draketown, Georgia (†30179) 217/B3
Dráma, Greece 45/F5
Drammen, Norway 7/E3
Drammen, Norway 18/C4
Drance (riv.), Switzerland 39/D4
Drancy, France 28/B1
Drang, Ia (riv.), Cambodia 72/E4
Draper, S. Dak. (57531) 298/J6
Draper, Utah (84020) 304/C3
Draper, Va. (24324) 307/G7
Draper, Wis. (†54852) 317/E4
Draperstown, N. Ireland 17/H2
Draperstown, N. Ireland 10/C3
Drasco, Ark. (72530) 202/G2
Drau (riv.), Austria 41/C3
Drava (riv.) 7/F4
Dráva (riv.), Hungary 41/D3
Drava (riv.), Yugoslavia 45/C3
Dravosburg, Pa. (15034) 294/C7
Drawsko Pomorskie, Poland 47/B2
Drax Hall, Barbados 161/B8
Drayden, Md. (20630) 245/N8
Drayton, N. Dak. (58225) 282/R2
Drayton, Ontario 177/D4
Drayton Plains, Mich. (48020) 250/F6
Drayton Valley, Alberta 182/C3
Drenthe (prov.), Netherlands 27/K3
Dresbach, Minn. (55930) 255/G7
Dresden, E. Germany 7/F3
Dresden (dist.), E. Germany 22/E3
Dresden, E. Germany 22/E3
Dresden, Kansas (67635) 232/B2
Dresden○, Maine (04342) 243/D7
Dresden, Mo. (†65301) 261/F5
Dresden, N.Y. (14441) 276/F5
Dresden, N. Dak. (†58249) 282/O2
Dresden, Ohio (43821) 284/G5
Dresden, Ontario 177/B5
Dresden, Tenn. (38225) 237/D8
Dresden Station, N.Y. (†12887) 276/O3
Dresser, Wis. (54009) 317/A5
Dreux, France 28/D3
Drew (co.), Ark. 202/G6
Drew, Miss. (38737) 256/C3
Drew, Oreg. (†97484) 291/E5
Drewry, Ala. (†36460) 195/D8
Drewryville, Va. (23844) 307/O7
Drews (res.), Oreg. 291/G5
Drewsey, Oreg. (97904) 291/J4
Drewsville, N.H. (03604) 268/C5
Drexel, Mo. (64742) 261/C6
Drexel, N.C. (28619) 281/F3
Drexel Hill, Pa. (19026) 294/M6
Dreyfus, Ky. (40426) 237/N5
Drezdenko, Poland 47/B2
Driebergen, Netherlands 27/G4
Driffield, England 13/G3
Driffield, England 10/F4
Drift (creek), Oreg. 291/B3
Drifton, Pa. (18221) 294/L3
Driftwood, Okla. (†73722) 288/K1
Driftwood, Pa. (15832) 294/F3
Driggs, Ark. (†72943) 202/C3
Driggs, Idaho (83422) 220/G6
Drill, Va. (†24260) 307/E6
Drimoleague, Ireland 17/C8
Drin (riv.), Albania 45/E4
Drina (riv.), Yugoslavia 45/D3
Drinkwater, Sask. 181/F5
Dripping Springs, Texas (78620) 303/F7
Driscoll, N. Dak. (58532) 282/K6
Driscoll, Texas (78351) 303/G10
Drishane, Ireland 17/C7
Driskill (mt.), La. 238/E2
Drøbak, Norway 18/D4
Drobeta-Turnu Severin, Romania 45/F3
Drogenbos, Belgium 27/B10
Drogheda, Ireland 17/J4
Drogheda, Ireland 10/C4
Drogobych, U.S.S.R. 52/B5
Drogobych, U.S.S.R. 48/C5
Droichead Nua, Ireland 10/C4
Droichead Nua, Ireland 17/H5
Droitwich, England 13/E5
Dromahair, Ireland 17/E3
Drome (dept.), France 28/F5
Drome (riv.), France 28/F5
Dromore, Bainbridge, N. Ireland 17/J3
Dromore, Omagh, N. Ireland 17/G3
Dromore West, Ireland 17/D3
Dronfield, England 13/J2
Drongan, Scotland 15/D5
Dronne (riv.), France 28/D5
Dronninglund, Denmark 21/D3
Dronten (prov.), Netherlands 27/H4
Dronten, Netherlands 27/H3
Dropmore, Manitoba 179/A3
Drouin, Victoria 97/C6
Druid, Sask. 181/C4
Druif, Neth. Ant. 161/D10
Drum (hills), Ireland 17/F7
Drum (bay), La. 238/M7
Drum (inlet), N.C. 281/S5
Drumaness, N. Ireland 17/K3
Drumbeg, Scotland 15/C2
Drumbo, Ontario 177/D4
Drumcar, Ireland 17/J4
Drumconrath, Ireland 17/H4
Drumheller, Alberta 182/D4
Drumheller, Alta. 162/E5
Drumhill, N.C. (†27937) 281/R1
Drumkeerin, Ireland 17/E3
Drumlish, Ireland 17/F4
Drummond, Idaho (†83420) 220/G5
Drummond (isl.), Mich. 250/F2
Drummond, Mont. (59832) 262/D4
Drummond, New Bruns. 170/C1
Drummond (mt.), North. Terr. 93/E5
Drummond, Okla. (73735) 288/L2
Drummond (co.), Québec 172/E4
Drummond (range), Queensland 88/H4
Drummond (range), Queensland 95/C5
Drummond (lake), Va. 307/P7
Drummond, Wis. (54832) 317/D3
Drummond Island, Mich. (49726) 250/F3
Drummonds, Tenn. (38023) 237/A10
Drummondville, Québec 172/E4
Drummondville-Nord, Québec 172/E4
Drummondville-Sud, Québec 172/E4
Drummore, Scotland 15/D6
Drummoyne, N. S. Wales 88/K4
Drummoyne, N.S. Wales 97/J3
Drumnadrochit, Scotland 15/D3
Drumquin, N. Ireland 17/F2
Drumright, Okla. (74030) 288/N3
Drums, Pa. (18222) 294/K3
Drumshanbo, Ireland 17/E3
Drury, Mo. (65638) 261/H9
Druskininkai, U.S.S.R. 53/C3
Druten, Netherlands 27/H5
Druz, Jebel ed (mts.), Syria 63/G6
Druzhba, U.S.S.R. 48/J5
Druzhina, U.S.S.R. 48/P3
Drvar, Yugoslavia 45/C3
Dry (bay), Alaska 196/L3
Dry (creek), Ky. 237/R3
Dry (lake), N. Dak. 282/M3
Dry (riv.), North. Terr. 88/E3
Dry (riv.), North. Terr. 93/C3
Dry (creek), S. Dak. 298/G4
Dry (lake), S. Dak. 298/P3
Dry (creek), Wyo. 319/C2
Dryad, Wash. (†98532) 310/B4
Dryanovo, Bulgaria 45/G4
Dry Branch, Georgia (31020) 217/F5
Dry Cimarron (riv.), N. Mex. 274/F2
Dry Coal (creek), Utah 304/A6
Dry Cottonwood (creek), Wyo. 319/D1
Dry Creek, La. (70637) 238/D5
Dry Creek, W. Va. (25062) 312/D7
Dryden, Ark. (†72401) 202/J2
Dryden, Maine (04225) 243/C6
Dryden, Mich. (48428) 250/F6
Dryden, N.Y. (13053) 276/H6
Dryden, Ontario 177/G4
Dryden, Ontario 175/B3
Dryden, Texas (78851) 303/C7
Dryden, Va. (24243) 307/B7
Dryden, Wash. (98821) 310/E3
Dry Falls (dam), Wash. 310/F3
Dry Fork, Va. (24549) 307/K7
Dryfork, W. Va. (26263) 312/H5
Dry Fork (riv.), W. Va. 312/G5
Dry Fork (riv.), W. Va. 312/C8
Dry Fork, Cheyenne (riv.), Wyo. 319/G2
Dry Fork, Powder (riv.), Wyo. 319/F2
Dry Lake, Nev. (†89040) 266/G6
Drymen, Scotland 15/B1
Dry Mills, Maine (†04039) 243/C8
Dry Prong, La. (71423) 238/E3
Dry Ridge, Ky. (41035) 237/M3
Dry Run, Pa. (17220) 294/G5
Drysdale (riv.), W. Australia 88/D3
Drysdale (riv.), W. Australia 92/D1
Dry Tortugas (keys), Fla. 212/D7
Drytown, Calif. (95699) 204/C8
Dry Wood (lake), S. Dak. 298/P2
Dschang, Cameroon 115/A2
Duaca, Venezuela 124/D2
Duaringa, Queensland 95/D4
Duart, Ontario 177/C5
Duarte, Calif. (91010) 204/D10
Duarte (prov.), Dom. Rep. 158/E5
Duarte (peak), Dom. Rep. 158/D5
Dubach, La. (71235) 238/E1
Dubai, U.A.E. 59/F4
Dubawnt (lake), N.W.T. 162/F3
Dubawnt (lake), N.W.T. 146/H3
Dubawnt (lake), N.W. Terrs. 187/H3
Dubawnt (riv.), N.W.T. 162/F3
Dubawnt (riv.), N.W. Terrs. 187/H3
Du Bay (lake), Wis. 317/G6
Dubberly, La. (71024) 238/D1
Dubbo, N. S. Wales 88/H6
Dubbo, N.S. Wales 97/E3
Dubbs, Miss. (†38626) 256/D1
Dübendorf, Switzerland 39/G2
Dublin, Calif. (94566) 204/K2
Dublin, Georgia (31021) 217/G5
Dublin, Ind. (47335) 227/G5
Dublin (co.), Ireland 17/J5
Dublin (cap.), Ireland 7/D3
Dublin (cap.), Ireland 17/K5
Dublin (cap.), Ireland 10/C4
Dublin (bay), Ireland 10/C4
Dublin (bay), Ireland 17/J5
Dublin, Ky. (†42039) 237/D7
Dublin, Md. (†21154) 245/N2
Dublin, Mich. (†49689) 250/D4
Dublin, Miss. (38739) 256/C2
Dublin○, N.H. (03444) 268/C6
Dublin, N.C. (28332) 281/M5
Dublin, Ohio (43017) 284/D5
Dublin, Ontario 177/C4
Dublin, Pa. (18917) 294/M5
Dublin, Texas (76446) 303/F5
Dublin, Va. (24084) 307/G6
Dubna, U.S.S.R. 52/E4
Dubna, U.S.S.R. 52/E3
Dubnica nad Váhom, Czech. 41/E2
Dubno, U.S.S.R. 52/C4
Dubois, Idaho (83423) 220/F5
Dubois, Ill. (62831) 222/D5
Dubois (co.), Ind. 227/D8
Dubois, Ind. (47527) 227/D8
Du Bois, Nebr. (68345) 264/H4
DuBois, Pa. (15801) 294/E3
Dubois, Wyo. (82513) 319/C2
Duboistown, Pa. (†17701) 294/H3
Dubréka, Guinea 106/B7
Dubreuilville, Ontario 177/J5
Dubrovnik, Yugoslavia 45/C4
Dubrueilville, Ontario 175/D3
Dubuc, Sask. 181/J5
Dubuque (co.), Iowa 229/M4
Dubuque, Iowa 188/H2
Dubuque, Iowa (52001) 229/M3
Duchcov, Czech. 41/B1
Duchesne (co.), Utah 304/D3
Duchesne, Utah (84021) 304/D3
Duchesne (riv.), Utah 304/D3
Duchess, Alberta 182/E4
Duchess, Queensland 88/F4
Duchess, Queensland 95/A4
Ducie (isl.), Pitcairn Is. 87/O8
Duck (isls.), Maine 243/G7
Duck (lake), Mich. 250/F4
Duck (creek), Nev. 266/G3
Duck, N.C. (†27949) 281/T2
Duck (creek), Ohio 284/H6
Duck (isl.), Ontario 177/H4
Duck (isls.), Ontario 177/A2
Duck (riv.), Tenn. 237/F9
Duck, W. Va. (25063) 312/E5
Duck Bay, Manitoba 179/B2
Duck Hill, Miss. (38925) 256/E3
Duck Lake, Sask. 181/E3
Duck Lake Hist. Park, Sask. 181/E3
Duck Lake Post, Manitoba 179/J2
Duck Mountain Prov. Park, Manitoba 179/B3
Duck Mountain Prov. Park, Sask. 181/K4
Duck River, Tenn. (38454) 237/G9
Ducktown, Georgia (†30130) 217/D2
Ducktown, Tenn. (37326) 237/N10
Duckwater, Nev. (89314) 266/F4
Duclos, Québec 172/A4
Ducor, Calif. (93218) 204/G8
Ducos, Martinique 161/D6
Dudelange, Luxembourg 27/J10
Dudenville, Mo. (†64748) 261/D8
Duderstadt, W. Germany 22/D3
Dudhi, India 68/E4
Dudignac, Argentina 143/F7
Düdingen, Switzerland 39/D3
Dudinka, U.S.S.R. 54/K3
Dudinka, U.S.S.R. 4/B5
Dudinka, U.S.S.R. 48/J3
Dudley, England 13/E5
Dudley, England 10/G3
Dudley, Georgia (31022) 217/F5
Dudley○, Mass. (01570) 249/G4
Dudley, Mo. (63936) 261/M9
Dudley, N.C. (28333) 281/N4
Dudley, Pa. (16634) 294/F5
Dudley (lake), Québec 172/B3
Dudleytown, Ind. (†47274) 227/F7
Dudváh (riv.), Czech. 41/D2
Dudweiler, W. Germany 22/B4
Dueñas, Spain 33/D2
Duenweg, Mo. (64841) 261/D8
Duero (Douro) (riv.), Spain 33/C2
Due West, S.C. (29639) 296/C3
Duff, Sask. 181/H5
Duff, Tenn. (37729) 237/N8
Duffee, Miss. (†39337) 256/G6
Duffel, Belgium 27/F6
Dufferin (county), Ontario 177/D3
Duffield, Alberta 182/C3
Duffield, Va. (24244) 307/C7
Dufftown, Scotland 10/E2
Dufftown, Scotland 15/E3
Dufourspitze (mt.), Switzerland 39/E5
Dufresne, Manitoba 179/F5
Dufrost, Manitoba 179/E5
Dufur, Oreg. (97021) 291/F2
Dugald, Manitoba 179/F5
Dugger, Ind. (47848) 227/C6
Dugi Otok (isl.), Yugoslavia 45/B3
Dugspur, Va. (24325) 307/G7
Duguayville, New Bruns. 170/E1
Du Gué (riv.), Québec 174/C1
Dugway, Utah (84022) 304/B3
Dugway (range), Utah 304/A3
Dugway Proving Grounds, Utah 304/B3
Duhamel, Alberta 182/D3
Duhamel, Québec 172/B3
Duich, Loch (inlet), Scotland 15/C3
Duida, Cerro (mt.), Venezuela 124/F6
Duifken (pt.), Queensland 88/G2
Duifken (pt.), Queensland 95/B2
Duiker (pt.), S. Africa 118/E6
Duinain (riv.), Scotland 15/D3
Duirinish (dist.), Scotland 15/B3
Duisburg, W. Germany 22/B3
Duitama, Colombia 126/D5
Duiveland (isl.), Netherlands 27/D5
Duivendrecht, Netherlands 27/C5
Duke, Ala. (†36279) 195/G3
Duke (isl.), Alaska 196/N2
Duke, Mo. (65461) 261/H7
Duke, Okla. (73532) 288/G5
Duke Center, Pa. (16729) 294/F2
Dukedom, Tenn. (38226) 237/D8
Duke of Gloucester (isls.), Fr. Poly. 87/M8
Dukes (co.), Mass. 249/M7
Dukes, Mich. (†49885) 250/B2
Dukhan, Qatar 59/F4
Duki, Pakistan 68/B2
Dukla (pass), Czech. 41/F2
Dukla (pass), Poland 47/E4
Dukou, China 77/F6
Dulac, La. (70353) 238/J8
Dulah, N.C. (†28463) 281/M6
Dulan, China 77/E4
Dulce (riv.), Argentina 143/D2
Dulce (gulf), C. Rica 154/F6
Dulce, N. Mex. (87528) 274/B2
Duleek, Ireland 17/J4
Dulgalakh (riv.), U.S.S.R. 48/O3
Dülmen, W. Germany 22/B3
Dulunguin (pt.), Philippines 82/C7
Duluth, Georgia (30136) 217/D2
Duluth, Kansas (66421) 232/F2
Duluth, Minn. 146/J5
Duluth, Minn. 188/H1
Duluth, Minn. (*55801) 255/F4
Dulverton, England 13/D6
Duma, Syria 63/G6
Duma, West Bank 65/C3
Dumagasa (pt.), Philippines 82/C7
Dumaguete, Philippines 82/D6
Dumaguete, Philippines 85/G4
Dumanquilas (bay), Philippines 82/D7
Dumaran (isl.), Philippines 85/G3
Dumaran (isl.), Philippines 82/C5
Dumaresq (riv.), N.S. Wales 97/F1
Dumas, Ark. (71639) 202/H6
Dumas, Miss. (38625) 256/G1
Dumas, Sask. 181/J6
Dumas, Texas (79029) 303/C2
Dumbarton, New Bruns. 170/C3
Dumbarton, Scotland 10/A1
Dumbarton, Scotland 15/B1
Dum Dum, India 68/F1
Dume (pt.), Calif. 204/G10
Dumeir, Syria 63/G6
Dumfoundling (bay), Fla. 212/C4
Dumfries, New Bruns. 170/C3
Dumfries, Scotland 15/E5
Dumfries, Scotland 10/E3
Dumfries (trad. co.), Scotland, 15/B5
Dumfries, Va. (22026) 307/O3
Dumfries and Galloway (reg.), Scotland 15/E5
Dumlu, Turkey 63/J2
Dummer○, N.H. (†03588) 268/E2
Dummer, Sask. 181/G6
Dümmersee (lake), W. Germany 22/C2
Dumont, Iowa (50625) 229/H3
Dumont, Minn. (56236) 255/B5
Dumont, N.J. (07628) 273/C1
Dumont, Texas (79232) 303/D4
Dumont d'Urville Station 5/C7
Dumyât (Damietta), Egypt 111/J3
Dumyat (Damietta), Egypt 59/B3
Dun (isl.), Scotland 15/A2
Duna (Danube) (riv.), Hungary 41/E3
Dunaff (head), Ireland 17/F1
Dunaföldvár, Hungary 41/E3
Dunaharaszti, Hungary 41/E3
Dunajec (riv.), Czech. 41/F2
Dunajec (riv.), Poland 47/E4
Dunajská Streda, Czech. 41/D3
Dunakeszi, Hungary 41/E3
Dunalley, Tasmania 99/D4
Dunany (pt.), Ireland 17/J4
Dunaszekcsö, Hungary 41/E3
Dunaújváros, Hungary 41/E3
Dunav (Danube) (riv.), Bulgaria 45/H4
Dunavecse, Hungary 41/E3
Dunbar, Iowa (†50158) 229/H5
Dunbar, Nebr. (68346) 264/J4
Dunbar, Okla. (†74557) 288/P6
Dunbar, Pa. (15431) 294/C6
Dunbar, Scotland 10/E2
Dunbar, Scotland 15/F4
Dunbar, S.C. (†29525) 296/H2
Dunbar, W. Va. (25064) 312/C6
Dunbar, Wis. (54119) 317/K4
Dunbarton○, N.H. (†03301) 268/D5
Dunbarton (trad. co.), Scotland 15/A5
Dunbarton Center, N.H. (†03301) 268/D5
Dunbeath, Scotland 15/E2
Dunbeg, Scotland 15/C4
Dunblane, Sask. 181/D4
Dunblane, Scotland 15/E4
Dunblane, Scotland 10/D2
Dunbridge, Ohio (43414) 284/C3
Duncan, Ariz. (85534) 198/F6
Duncan, Br. Col. 184/J3
Duncan (riv.), Br. Col. 184/J5
Duncan (isls.), China 85/E2
Duncan, Ill. (†61559) 222/D3
Duncan (passage), India 68/G6
Duncan, Miss. (38740) 256/C2
Duncan, Nebr. (68634) 264/G3
Duncan, Okla. (73533) 288/L5
Duncan (lake), Québec 174/B2
Duncan, S.C. (29334) 296/C2
Duncan, W. Va. (25240) 312/C5
Duncan Falls, Ohio (43734) 284/G6
Duncannon, Ireland 17/H7
Duncannon, Pa. (17020) 294/H5
Duncans, Jamaica 158/H5
Duncans Bridge, Mo. (†63437) 261/H3
Duncansby (head), Scotland 15/F2
Duncansby (head), Scotland 10/E1
Duncansville, Pa. (16635) 294/F5
Duncanville, Ala. (35456) 195/D4
Duncanville, Texas (75116) 303/G3
Dunchurch, Ontario 177/E2
Duncombe, Iowa (50532) 229/E4
Duncombe (bay), Norfolk I. 88/L5
Dundaga, U.S.S.R. 53/B2
Dundalk, Ireland 17/H3
Dundalk, Ireland 10/C4
Dundalk (bay), Ireland 10/C4
Dundalk (bay), Ireland 17/J4
Dundalk, Md. (21222) 245/N3
Dundalk, Ontario 177/D3
Dundarrach, N.C. (†28386) 281/L5
Dundas (isl.), Br. Col. 184/B3
Dundas, Greenl. 4/B13
Dundas, Greenland 146/M2
Dundas, Ill. (62425) 222/E5
Dundas, Minn. (55019) 255/E6
Dundas (str.), North. Terr. 88/E2
Dundas (str.), North. Terr. 93/B1
Dundas (pen.), N.W. Terrs. 187/G2
Dundas, Ohio (45625) 284/E7
Dundas (county), Ontario 177/J2
Dundas, Ontario 177/D4
Dundas, Va. (23938) 307/M7
Dundas (lake), W. Australia 88/C6
Dundas (lake), W. Australia 92/C6
Dundee, Fla. (33838) 212/E3
Dundee (East and West Dundee), Ill. (60118) 222/E1
Dundee, Ind. (†47348) 227/F4
Dundee, Iowa (52038) 229/L3
Dundee, Ky. (42338) 237/H5
Dundee, Mich. (48131) 250/F7
Dundee, Minn. (56126) 255/C7
Dundee, Miss. (38626) 256/D1
Dundee, N.Y. (14837) 276/F5
Dundee, Oreg. (97115) 291/A2
Dundee, Scotland 7/D3
Dundee, Scotland 15/F4
Dundee, Scotland 10/E2
Dundee, S. Africa 118/E5
Dundee, Texas (76358) 303/F4
Dundgovĭ, Mongolia 77/G2
Dundon, W. Va. (†25043) 312/D6
Dundonald, Scotland 15/D5
Dundrum, N. Ireland 17/K3
Dundrum (bay), N. Ireland 17/K3
Dundurn, Sask. 181/E4
Dundy (co.), Nebr. 264/C4
Dune Acres, Ind. (†46304) 227/C1
Dunedin, Fla. (33528) 212/B2
Dunedin, N. Zealand 2/T8
Dunedin, N. Zealand 100/C6
Dunedoo, N.S. Wales 97/E3
Dunellen, N.J. (08812) 273/D2
Dunes (Westlake), Oreg. (†97493) 291/C4
Dunfanaghy, Ireland 17/F1
Dunfee, Ind. (†46802) 227/G2
Dunfermline, Ill. (61524) 222/D3
Dunfermline, Sask. 181/D3
Dunfermline, Scotland 15/D1
Dunfermline, Scotland 10/C1
Dungalear Station, N.S. Wales 97/D1
Dungannon (dist.), N. Ireland 17/H3
Dungannon, N. Ireland 17/H3
Dungannon, Ontario 177/C4
Dungannon, Va. (24245) 307/D7
Dungarpur, India 68/C4
Dungarvan, Ireland 10/C4
Dungarvan, Ireland 17/F7
Dungarvan (harb.), Ireland 10/C4
Dungarvan (harb.), Ireland 17/G7
Dungarvon (riv.), New Bruns. 170/D2
Dungeness (pt.), Argentina 143/C7
Dungeness (pt.), Chile 138/F10
Dungeness (prom.), England 13/J7
Dungeness (prom.), England 10/G5
Dungeness, Wash. (†98382) 310/B2
Dungiven, N. Ireland 17/H2
Dungloe, Ireland 17/E2
Dungog, N.S. Wales 97/F3
Dungu, Zaire 115/E3
Dungunab, Sudan 59/C5
Dungunab, Sudan 111/G3
Dunham, Québec 172/E4
Dunhua (Tunhwa), China 77/L3
Dunhuang, China 77/E3
Dunkeld, Queensland 95/D5
Dunkeld, Scotland 15/E4
Dunkeld, Victoria 97/B5
Dunkellin (riv.), Ireland 17/D5
Dunkerton, Iowa (50626) 229/J3
Dunkery (hill), England 13/D6
Dunkineely, Ireland 17/E2
Dunkirk (riv.), Alberta 182/D1
Dunkirk (Dunkerque), France 28/E2
Dunkirk, France 28/E2
Dunkirk, Ind. (47336) 227/G4
Dunkirk, N.Y. (14048) 276/B5
Dunkirk, Ohio (45836) 284/C4
Dunkley, Br. Col. 184/F3
Dunklin (co.), Mo. 261/M10
Dunkwa, Ghana 106/D7
Dún Laoghaire, Ireland 10/D4
Dún Laoghaire, Ireland 17/K5
Dunlap, Ill. (61525) 222/D3
Dunlap, Ind. (†46514) 227/F1
Dunlap, Iowa (51529) 229/B5
Dunlap, Kansas (66848) 232/F3
Dunlap, Tenn. (37327) 237/L10
Dunlavin, Ireland 17/H5
Dunleath, Sask. 181/K4
Dunleer, Ireland 17/J4
Dunleith, Miss. (†38756) 256/C4
Dunlow, W. Va. (25511) 312/B6
Dunloy, N. Ireland 17/J1
Dunmanus (bay), Ireland 17/B8
Dunmanway, Ireland 17/C8
Dunmanway, Ireland 10/B5
Dunmor, Ky. (42339) 237/G6
Dunmore, Alberta 182/E5
Dunmore, Ireland 17/D4
Dunmore, Pa. (18512) 294/F7
Dunmore (lake), Vt. 268/A4
Dunmore, W. Va. (24934) 312/G6
Dunmore East, Ireland 17/G7
Dunn, La. (71236) 238/G2
Dunn, N.C. (28334) 281/M4
Dunn (co.), N. Dak. 282/E5
Dunn, Texas (79516) 303/D5
Dunn (co.), Wis. 317/C6
Dunnamanagh, N. Ireland 17/G2
Dunn Center, N. Dak. (58626) 282/E5
Dunnegan, Mo. (65640) 261/E7
Dunnell, Minn. (56127) 255/D7
Dunnellon, Fla. (32630) 212/D2
Dunnet, Scotland 15/E2
Dunnet (bay), Scotland 15/E2
Dunnet (head), Scotland 10/E1
Dunnet (head), Scotland 15/E2
Dunnigan, Calif. (95937) 204/C5
Dunning, Nebr. (68833) 264/D3
Dunning, Scotland 15/E4
Dunn Loring, Va. (22027) 307/S2
Dunnottar, Manitoba 179/E4
Dunnottar, S. Africa 118/J6
Dunns, W. Va. (†25841) 312/D7
Dunnsville, Va. (22454) 307/P5
Dunnville, Ky. (42528) 237/M6
Dunnville, Ontario 177/E5
Du Noir (riv.), Wyo. 319/C2
Dunolly, Victoria 97/B5
Dunoon, Scotland 15/A2
Dunoon, Scotland 10/A1
Dunphy, Nev. (†89821) 266/E2
Dunragit, Scotland 15/D6
Dunrea, Manitoba 179/C5
Dunreith, Ind. (47337) 227/F5
Duns, Scotland 10/E3
Duns, Scotland 15/F5
Dunscore, Scotland 15/E5
Dunseith, N. Dak. (58329) 282/K2
Dunshaughlin, Ireland 17/H5
Dunsmuir, Calif. (96025) 204/C2
Dunstable, England 10/F5
Dunstable, England 13/G6
Dunstable○, Mass. (01827) 249/J2
Dunster, Br. Col. 184/G3
Duntochter, Scotland 15/B2
Dunure, Scotland 15/D5
Dunvegan, Nova Scotia 168/F4
Dunvegan, Scotland 15/B3
Dunvegan, Loch (inlet), Scotland 15/B3
Dunville, Newf. 166/D2
Dunwoody, Georgia (†30338) 217/K1
Duo, W. Va. (†25984) 312/E6
Duolun, China 77/J3
Duong Dong, Vietnam 72/D5
Du Page (co.), Ill. 222/E2
Du Page, East Branch (riv.), Ill. 222/A6
Du Page, West Branch (riv.), Ill. 222/A6
Du Page (riv.), Ill. 222/E2
Duparquet, Québec 174/B3
Duperow, Sask. 181/C4
Duplessis, La. (70728) 238/K2
Duplin (co.), N.C. 281/O5
Dupo, Ill. (62239) 222/A3
Du Pont, Georgia (31630) 217/G9
Dupont, Ind. (47231) 227/G7
Dupont, Ohio (45837) 284/B3
Dupont, Pa. (18641) 294/F7
Du Pont, Wash. (98327) 310/C3
Dupont Manor, Del. (†19901) 245/R4
Dupree, S. Dak. (57623) 298/F3
Dupuis Corner, New Bruns. 170/F2
Dupuy, Québec 174/B3
Dupuyer, Mont. (59432) 262/D2
Duque de Bragança, Angola 115/C5
Duque de Caxias, Brazil 135/E3
Duque de York (isl.), Chile 138/C9
Duquesne, Mo. (†64801) 261/D8
Duquesne, Pa. (15110) 294/C7
Duquette, Minn. (55729) 255/F4
Du Quoin, Ill. (62832) 222/D5
Duquoin, Kansas (†67058) 232/D4
Dura, West Bank 65/C4
Durack (range), W. Australia 88/D3
Durağan, Turkey 63/F2
Duran, N. Mex. (88319) 274/D4
Durance (riv.), France 28/F6

Eastsound 363

Durand, Georgia (†31830) 217/C5
Durand, Ill. (61024) 222/D1
Durand, Mich. (48429) 250/E6
Durand, Wis. (54736) 317/C6
Durango, Colo. 188/E3
Durango, Colo. (81301) 208/D8
Durango, Iowa (52039) 229/M3
Durango (state), Mexico 150/G4
Durango, Mexico 146/H7
Durango, Mexico 150/G4
Durango, Spain 33/E1
Duranillin, W. Australia 92/B2
Durant, Iowa (52747) 229/M5
Durant, Miss. (39063) 256/E4
Durant, Okla. 188/G4
Durant, Okla. (74701) 288/O6
Duratón (riv.), Spain 33/E2
Durazno (dept.), Uruguay 145/C3
Durazno, Uruguay 145/C4
Durazno, Grande del (range), Uruguay 145/D4
Durban, Manitoba 179/A3
Durban, S. Africa 2/L7
Durban, S. Africa 102/F7
Durban, S. Africa 118/E5
Durbanville, S. Africa 118/F6
Durbe, U.S.S.R. 53/A2
Durbin, Ind. (†46060) 227/F4
Durbin, N. Dak. (58023) 282/R6
Durbin, W. Va. (26264) 312/G5
Durbuy, Belgium 27/H8
Düren, W. Germany 22/B3
Durfee (hill), R.I. 249/G5
Durg, India 68/E4
Durgapur, India 68/F4
Durgerdam, Netherlands 27/C4
Durham, Ark. (†72701) 202/C2
Durham, Calif. (95938) 204/D4
Durham, Conn. (06422) 210/E3
Durham○, Conn. (06422) 210/E3
Durham (co.), England 13/F3
Durham, England 13/J3
Durham, England 10/F3
Durham, Kansas (67438) 232/E3
Durham, Mo. (63438) 261/J3
Durham, N.H. (03824) 268/F5
Durham○, N.H. (03824) 268/F5
Durham (pt.), N. Zealand 100/D7
Durham, N.C. 188/L3
Durham (co.), N.C. 281/M3
Durham, N.C. (*27701) 281/M2
Durham, Okla. (73642) 288/G3
Durham (reg. munic.), Ontario 177/F3
Durham, Ontario 177/D3
Durham, Oreg. (†97233) 291/A2
Durham Bridge, New Bruns. 170/D2
Durham Center, Conn. (†06422) 210/E3
Durham Downs, Queensland 95/B5
Durham-Sud, Québec 172/E4
Durhamville, N.Y. (13054) 276/J4
Duri, N.S. Wales 97/F2
Durkee, Oreg. (97905) 291/K3
Durness, Scotland 15/D2
Durnford (pt.), Western Sahara 106/A4
Dürnten, Switzerland 39/G2
Duror, Scotland 15/C4
Durrell, Newf. 166/D4
Dürrenroth, Switzerland 39/E2
Durrës (Durazzo), Albania 45/D5
Durrës, Albania 7/F4
Durrington, England 13/F6
Durrow, Laoighis, Ireland 17/G6
Durrow, Offaly, Ireland 17/F5
Dursey (isl.), Ireland 17/A8
Dursunbey, Turkey 63/C3
Duruh, Iran 59/H3
Duruh, Iran 66/M4
D'Urville (isl.), N. Zealand 100/D4
Duryea, Pa. (18642) 294/F7
Dusa Marreb, Somalia 115/J2
Dūsh, Egypt 59/B5
Dūsh, Egypt 111/F3
Dushan, China 77/G6
Dushanbe, U.S.S.R. 54/H6
Dushanbe, U.S.S.R. 2/N4
Dushanbe, U.S.S.R. 48/G6
Dushore, Pa. (18614) 294/K2
Dusky (sound), N. Zealand 100/A6
Duson, La. (70529) 238/F6
Düsseldorf, W. Germany 7/E3
Düsseldorf, W. Germany 22/B3
Dustin, Okla. (74839) 288/O4
Dusty, N. Mex. (87934) 274/B5
Dusty, Wash. (†99143) 310/H4
Dutch (creek), Ark. 202/C4
Dutch Cap (cay), Virgin Is. (U.S.) 161/A4
Dutchess (co.), N.Y. 276/N7
Dutch Flat, Calif. (95714) 204/E4
Dutch Harbor, Alaska (†99685) 196/E4
Dutch John, Utah (84023) 304/E3
Dutch Mills, Ark. (†72744) 202/B2
Dutch Neck, N.J. (†08550) 273/D3
Dutchtown, Mo. (63745) 261/N8
Dutton, Ala. (35744) 195/G1
Dutton, Ark. (†72760) 202/C2
Dutton (mt.), Conn. 210/C1
Dutton, Mont. (59433) 262/E3
Dutton, Ontario 177/C5
Dutton (mt.), Utah 304/B5
Duval (co.), Fla. 212/E1
Duval, Sask. 181/G4
Duval (co.), Texas 303/F10
Duvalierville, Haiti 158/C6
Duvall, Wash. (98019) 310/D3
Duvergé, Dom. Rep. 158/D6
Duvernay, Alberta 182/E3
Duwadami, Saudi Arabia 59/D5
Duxbury (pt.), Calif. 204/H2
Duxbury, Mass. (02332) 249/M4
Duxbury○, Mass. (02332) 249/M4
Duxbury○, Vt. (†05676) 268/B3
Duyun (Tuyün), China 77/G6
Düzce, Turkey 63/D2
Duzdab (Zahedan), Iran 66/M6
Dvina, (bay), U.S.S.R. 52/E2
Dvina, Northern (riv.), U.S.S.R. 4/C7
Dvina, Northern (riv.), U.S.S.R. 7/J2
Dvina, Northern (riv.), U.S.S.R. 48/E3
Dvina, Northern (riv.), U.S.S.R. 52/F2
Dvina, Western (riv.) U.S.S.R. 53/C2
Dvina, Western (riv.), U.S.S.R. 48/C4
Dvina, Western (riv.), U.S.S.R. 52/C3
Dvina, Western (riv.), U.S.S.R. 7/G3
Dvinsk (Daugavpils), U.S.S.R. 52/C3
Dvory nad Žitavou, Czech. 41/E3
Dvůr Králové nad Labem, Austria 41/C1
Dwale, Ky. (41621) 237/R5
Dwarka, India 68/B4
Dwellingup, W. Australia 92/B2
Dwight, Ill. (60420) 222/E2
Dwight, Kansas (66849) 232/F3
Dwight, Nebr. (68635) 264/G3
Dwight, N. Dak. (58024) 282/S7
Dwight, Ontario 177/F2
Dworshak (res.), Idaho 220/C3
Dwyer, N. Mex. (†88034) 274/B6
Dwyer, Wyo. (82211) 319/G3
Dyas, Ala. (†36507) 195/C9
Dyat'kovo, U.S.S.R. 52/D4
Dybvad, Denmark 21/D3
Dyce, Scotland 15/F3
Dyckesville, Wis. (†54217) 317/L6
Dycusburg, Ky. (42037) 237/E6
Dyer, Ark. (72935) 202/B3
Dyer, Ind. (46311) 227/C1
Dyer, Ky. (†40115) 237/J5
Dyer, Nev. (89010) 266/C5
Dyer (cape), N.W.T. 162/K2
Dyer (cape), N.W. Terrs. 187/M3
Dyer (co.), Tenn. 237/C8
Dyer, Tenn. (38330) 237/D8
Dyer Brook○, Maine (†04747) 243/G3
Dyersburg, Tenn. (38024) 237/C8
Dyersville, Iowa (52040) 229/L3
Dyess, Ark. (72330) 202/K2
Dyess A.F.B., Texas 303/D5
Dyfed, Wales 13/C6
Dyje (riv.), Czech. 41/D2
Dyke (lake), Newf. 166/A3
Dykh-Tau (mt.), U.S.S.R. 52/F6
Dyle (riv.), Belgium 27/F7
Dysart, Iowa (52224) 229/J4
Dysart, Sask. 181/H5
Dysartsville, N.C. (†28761) 281/F3
Dzamïn Üüd, Mongolia 77/H3
Dzaoudzi (cap.), Comoros 118/H2
Dzavhan, Mongolia 77/E2
Dzavhan Gol (riv.), Mongolia 77/D2
Dzerzhinsk, U.S.S.R. 7/J3
Dzerzhinsk, U.S.S.R. 48/E4
Dzerzhinsk, U.S.S.R. 52/F3
Dzhalal-Abad, U.S.S.R. 48/H5
Dzhalilabad, U.S.S.R. 52/G7
Dzhalinda, U.S.S.R. 48/N4
Dzhambul, U.S.S.R. 54/J5
Dzhambul, U.S.S.R. 48/H5
Dzhankoy, U.S.S.R. 52/D5
Dzhelinda, U.S.S.R. 48/M2
Dzhetygara, U.S.S.R. 48/G4
Dzhezkazgan, U.S.S.R. 54/H5
Dzhezkazgan, U.S.S.R. 48/G5
Dzhugdzhur (range), U.S.S.R. 54/P4
Dzhugdzhur (range), U.S.S.R. 48/O4
Dzhul'fa, U.S.S.R. 52/G7
Dzhusaly, U.S.S.R. 48/G5
Działdowo, Poland 47/E2
Dzibalchén, Mexico 150/P7
Dzibichaltún (ruin), Mexico 150/P6
Dzidzantún, Mexico 150/P6
Dzierzoniów, Poland 47/C3
Dzilam de Bravo, Mexico 150/P6
Dzitbalché, Mexico 150/P6
Dzurh, Mongolia 77/E2
Dzüünharaa, Mongolia 77/G2
Dzuunmod, Mongolia 77/G2

E

Eabamet (lake), Ontario 175/C2
Eads, Colo. (81036) 208/O6
Eads, Tenn. (38028) 237/B10
Eadytown, S.C. (†29468) 296/G5
Eagan, Minn. (55111) 255/G6
Eagan, Tenn. (37730) 237/O7
Eagar, Ariz. (85925) 198/F4
Eagarville, Ill. (†62033) 222/D4
Eagle, Alaska 188/D5
Eagle, Alaska (99738) 196/K2
Eagle (creek), Ariz. 198/F5
Eagle (lake), Calif. 204/E3
Eagle (peak), Calif. 204/E2
Eagle (co.), Colo. 208/F3
Eagle, Colo. (81631) 208/F3
Eagle (riv.), Colo. 208/E3
Eagle, Idaho (83616) 220/B6
Eagle (creek), Ind. 227/E4
Eagle (lake), Iowa 229/F2
Eagle (creek), Ky. 237/M3
Eagle (lake), Maine 243/F1
Eagle (lake), Maine 243/E3
Eagle, Mich. (48822) 250/E6
Eagle (mt.), Minn. 255/G2
Eagle, Nebr. (68347) 264/H4
Eagle (riv.), Newf. 166/C3
Eagle, Ontario 177/C5
Eagle (lake), Ontario 177/F5
Eagle (lake), Ontario 177/E2
Eagle (creek), Oreg. 291/K3
Eagle (hills), Sask. 181/C3
Eagle (peak), Texas 303/C11
Eagle (mt.), Virgin Is. (U.S.) 161/E4
Eagle, Wis. (53119) 317/H2
Eagle (lake), Wis. 317/H2
Eagle (lake), Wis. 317/K3
Eagle (peak), Wyo. 319/B1
Eagle Bay, N.Y. (13331) 276/L3
Eagle Bend, Minn. (56446) 255/D4
Eagle Bridge, N.Y. (12057) 276/O5
Eagle Butte, S. Dak. (57625) 298/G4
Eagle City, Okla. (73658) 288/J3
Eagle Crags (mt.), Calif. 204/J8
Eagle Creek, Oreg. (97022) 291/E2
Eagle Grove, Iowa (50533) 229/F3
Eagle Harbor, Md. (†20608) 245/M6
Eagle Harbor, Mich. (49951) 250/A1
Eaglehawk, Victoria 97/C5
Eaglehill (creek), Sask. 181/D4
Eagle Lake, Fla. (33839) 212/E4
Eagle Lake, Maine (04739) 243/F1
Eagle Lake○, Maine (04739) 243/F1
Eagle Lake, Minn. (56024) 255/E6
Eagle Lake, Ontario 177/F2
Eagle Lake, Texas (77434) 303/H8
Eagle Mills, Ark. (71729) 202/E6
Eagle Mountain, Calif. (92241) 204/K10
Eagle Mountain (lake), Texas 303/E2
Eagle Nest, N. Mex. (87718) 274/D2
Eagle Nest (lake), N. Mex. 274/D2
Eagle Pass, Texas (78852) 303/D9
Eagle Point, Oreg. (97524) 291/E5
Eagle River, Alaska (99577) 196/C1
Eagle River, Mich. (49924) 250/A1
Eagle River, Wis. (54521) 317/H4
Eagle Rock, Mo. (65641) 261/E9
Eagle Rock, Va. (24085) 307/J5
Eaglesfield, Scotland 15/E5
Eaglesham, Alberta 182/B2
Eaglesham, Scotland 15/D5
Eagles Mere, Pa. (17731) 294/J3
Eagle Springs, N.C. (27242) 281/K4
Eagleton Village, Tenn. (†37801) 237/O9
Eagletown, Ind. (†46074) 227/E4
Eagletown, Okla. (74734) 288/S6
Eagleville, Calif. (96110) 204/E2
Eagleville, Conn. (†06268) 210/F1
Eagleville, Mo. (64442) 261/D2
Eagleville, Tenn. (37060) 237/H9
Eakly, Okla. (73033) 288/K4
Ealing, England 13/H8
Ealing, England 10/B5
Ear (lake), Sask. 181/B3
Earby, England 13/H1
Eardley (lake), Manitoba 179/F2
Ear Falls, Ontario 175/B2
Earl (lake), Calif. 204/A2
Earl, N.C. (28038) 281/F4
Earl, Wis. (54833) 317/C4
Earle, Ark. (72331) 202/K3
Earle Naval Weapons Sta., N.J. 273/E3
Earleton, Fla. (32631) 212/D2
Earleville, Md. (21919) 245/P3
Earl Grey, Sask. 181/G5
Earlham, Iowa (50072) 229/E6
Earlimart, Calif. (93219) 204/F8
Earling, Iowa (51530) 229/C5
Earlington, Ky. (42410) 237/F6
Earl Park, Ind. (47942) 227/C3
Earlsboro, Okla. (74840) 288/N4
Earlston, Scotland 15/F5
Earlton, Kansas (†66720) 232/G4
Earlton, Ontario 177/K5
Earltown, Nova Scotia 168/E3
Earlville, Ill. (60518) 222/E2
Earlville, Iowa (52041) 229/L4
Earlville, N.Y. (13332) 276/J5
Early (co.), Georgia 217/C8
Early, Iowa (50535) 229/C4
Early Branch, S.C. (29916) 296/F6
Earlysville, Va. (22936) 307/M4
Earn, Loch (lake), Scotland 15/D4
Earn (riv.), Scotland 15/E4
Earnslaw (mt.), N. Zealand 100/B6
Earp, Calif. (92242) 204/L9
Earth, Texas (79031) 303/B3
Earthquake (lake), Mont. 262/E6
Easby, N. Dak. (†58249) 282/O2
Easington, England 13/J3
Easingwold, England 13/F3
Eask (lake), Ireland 17/E2
Easky, Ireland 17/D3
Easley, S.C. (29640) 296/B2
East (cape), Alaska 196/K4
East (riv.), Conn. 210/E3
East (pt.), Fla. 212/E6
East (bay), La. 238/M8
East (pt.), Mass. 249/E6
East (range), Nev. 266/D2
East (pt.), N.S. Wales 97/J2
East (riv.), N.Y. 276/N9
East (cape), N. Zealand 87/H9
East (cape), N. Zealand 100/G2
East (bay), Nova Scotia 168/H3
East (riv.), Nova Scotia 168/F3
East (lake), Oreg. 291/F4
East (pt.), Pr. Edward I. 168/G2
East (Dezhnev) (cape), U.S.S.R. 4/C18
East (pt.), Virgin Is. (U.S.) 161/G4
Eastaboga, Ala. (36260) 195/F3
Eastabuchie, Miss. (39436) 256/F8
East Albany, Vt. (†05820) 268/C2
East Alburg, Vt. (†05440) 268/A2
East Aldfield, Québec 172/A4
East Alligator (riv.), North. Terr. 93/C2
East Alton, Ill. (62024) 222/A2
East Andover, Maine (04226) 243/B6
East Andover, N.H. (03231) 268/D5
East Angus, Québec 172/F4
Eastanollee, Georgia (30538) 217/F1
East Arcadia, N.C. (†28434) 281/N6
East Arlington, Vt. (05252) 268/A5
East Arrow Park, Br. Col. 184/J5
East Aspetuck (riv.), Conn. 210/B2
East Aurora, N.Y. (14052) 276/C5
East Baldwin, Maine (04024) 243/B8
East Bangor, Pa. (18013) 294/M4
East Bank, W. Va. (25067) 312/D6
East Barnet, Vt. (†05821) 268/C3
East Barre-Graniteville, Vt. (05649) 268/C3
East Barrington, N.H. (03825) 268/F5
East Baton Rouge (par.), La. 238/K1
East Bay, Nova Scotia 168/H2
East Bay (hills), Nova Scotia 168/H3
East Bend, N.C. (27018) 281/H2
East Berbice-Corantyne (dist.), Guyana 131/C3
East Berkshire, Vt. (05447) 268/B2
East Berlin, Conn. (06023) 210/E2
East Berlin, Pa. (17316) 294/J6
East Bernard, Texas (77435) 303/H8
East Bernstadt, Ky. (40729) 237/N6
East Berwick, Pa. (†18603) 294/K3
East Bethany, N.Y. (14054) 276/D5
East Bethel, Minn. (†55005) 255/E5
East Bethel, Vt. (†05032) 268/B4
East Bloomfield, N.Y. (14443) 276/E5
East Blue Hill, Maine (04629) 243/G7
East Blythe, Calif. (†92225) 204/L10
East Boothbay, Maine (04544) 243/D8
Eastborough, Kansas (†67201) 232/E4
Eastbourne, England 13/H7
Eastbourne, England 10/G5
Eastbourne, N. Zealand 100/B3
East Brady, Pa. (16028) 294/C3
East Braintree, Manitoba 179/G5
East Braintree, Mass. (†02184) 249/D8
East Braintree, Vt. (†05060) 268/B3
East Branch, N.Y. (13756) 276/K7
East Branch, Rocky (riv.), Ohio 284/G10
East Brewster, Mass. (†02631) 249/O5
East Brewton, Ala. (36426) 195/E8
East Bridgewater○, Mass. (02333) 249/L4
East Brisbane, Queensland 88/K3
East Brisbane, Queensland 95/E3
East Brookfield, Mass. (01515) 249/G4
East Brookfield○, Mass. (01515) 249/G4
East Brookfield, Vt. (†05036) 268/C3
East Brooklyn, Conn. (†06239) 210/H1
East Broughton, Québec 172/F3
East Broughton Station, Québec 172/F3
East Brownfield, Maine (†04010) 243/B8
East Brunswick○, N.J. (08816) 273/E3
East Burke, Vt. (05832) 268/D2
East Butler, Pa. (16029) 294/C4
East Calais, Vt. (05650) 268/C3
East Calder, Scotland 15/D2
East Camden, Ark. (71701) 202/E6
East Canaan, Conn. (06024) 210/B1
East Candia, N.H. (03040) 268/E5
East Canton, Ohio (44730) 284/H4
East Canyon (res.), Utah 304/C3
East Cape Girardeau, Ill. (†62957) 222/D6
East Carbon, Utah (84520) 304/D4
East Carondelet, Ill. (62240) 222/A3
East Carroll (par.), La. 238/H1
East Chain, Minn. (†56031) 255/D7
East Charleston, Vt. (05833) 268/D2
Eastchester, N.Y. (10709) 276/P6
East Chester, Nova Scotia 168/D4
East Chevington, England 13/F2
East Chezzetcook, Nova Scotia 168/E4
East Chicago, Ind. (46312) 227/C1
East Chicago Heights, Ill. (†60411) 222/C6
East China (sea) 54/O7
East China (sea), China 77/L6
East China (sea), Japan 81/C8
East China (sea), S. Korea 81/C8
East Chop (pt.), Mass. 249/M7
East Claridon, Ohio (44033) 284/H2
East Cleveland, Ohio (44112) 284/H9
East Coast Bays, N. Zealand 100/B1
East Concord, Vt. (†05906) 268/D3
East Conemaugh, Pa. (15909) 294/E5
East Corinth, Maine (04427) 243/F5
East Corinth, Vt. (05040) 268/C3
East Cote Blanche (bay), La. 238/G7
East Coulée, Alberta 182/D4
East Craftsbury, Vt. (†05826) 268/C2
East Dedham, Mass. (02026) 249/C8
East Demerara-West Coast Berbice (dist.), Guyana 131/C2
East Dennis, Mass. (02641) 249/O5
East Dereham, England 13/H5
East Dereham, England 10/G4
East Derry, N.H. (03041) 268/E6
East Detroit, Mich. (48021) 250/B6
East Devils (lake), N. Dak. 282/N4
East Dixfield, Maine (04227) 243/C6
East Dixmont, Maine (†04932) 243/E6
East Dorset, Vt. (05253) 268/A5
East Douglas, Mass. (01516) 249/G4
East Dover, Vt. (05341) 268/B6
East Dublin, Georgia (31021) 217/G5
East Dubuque, Ill. (61025) 222/C1
East Duke, Okla. (†73532) 288/H5
East Dundee (Dundee), Ill. (†60118) 222/E1
East Durham, N.Y. (12423) 276/M6
East Eddington, Maine (04428) 243/F6
East Ellijay, Georgia (30539) 217/C1
East Ely, Nev. 266/G3
Eastend, Sask. 181/C6
Eastend, Virgin Is. (U.S.) 161/D4
East Enterprise, Ind. (47019) 227/H7
Easter (isl.), Chile 87/Q8
Easter (isl.), Chile 2/D7
Eastern (pt.), Conn. 210/G3
Eastern (Arabian) (des.), Egypt 111/F2
Eastern (prov.), Kenya 115/G4
Eastern (bay), Md. 245/N5
Eastern (pt.), Mass. 249/M2
Eastern (creek), N.S. Wales 97/H3
Eastern Channel (str.), Japan 81/D7
Eastern Ghats (mts.), India 68/D6
Eastern Samar (prov.), Philippines 82/E5
Eastern Scheldt (est.), Netherlands 27/D5
Eastern Taurus (mts.), Turkey 63/J3
Eastern Wolf (isl.), New Bruns. 170/D4
Easterville, Manitoba 179/C1
East Fairfield, Vt. (05448) 268/B2
East Falkland (isl.), 143/E7
East Falkland (isl.), Falk. Is. 120/D8
East Falmouth (Teaticket), Mass. (02536) 249/M6
East Farnham, Québec 172/E4
East Faxon, Pa. (†17701) 294/J3
East Feliciana (par.), La. 238/H5
East Ferry, Nova Scotia 168/B4
East Flanders (prov.), Belgium 27/D7
East Flat Rock, N.C. (28726) 281/E4
Eastford○, Conn. (06242) 210/G1
East Fork, Little Miami (riv.), Ohio 284/C7
East Fork, Green (riv.), Wyo. 319/C3
East Foxboro, Mass. (†02035) 249/K4
East Franklin, Maine (†04634) 243/G6
East Franklin, Vt. (†05457) 268/B2
East Freedom, Pa. (16637) 294/E5
East Freetown, Mass. (02717) 249/L5
East Friesland (reg.), W. Germany 22/B2
East Frisian (isls.), W. Germany 22/B2
East Gaffney, S.C. (†29340) 296/D1
East Galesburg, Ill. (61430) 222/C3
Eastgate, Nev. (†89406) 266/D3
East Georgia, Vt. (†05455) 268/A2
East Germantown (Pershing), Ind. (†47370) 227/G5
East Germany 7/F3
EAST GERMANY 22
East Gillespie, Ill. (†62033) 222/D4
East Glacier Park, Mont. (59434) 262/C2
East Glastonbury, Conn. (06025) 210/E2
East Grafton, N.H. (†03240) 268/D4
East Granby○, Conn. (06026) 210/E1
East Grand Forks, Minn. (56721) 255/B3
East Grand Rapids, Mich. (†49506) 250/D6
East Granville, Vt. (†05669) 268/B3
East Greenbush, N.Y. (12061) 276/N5
East Green Harbour, Nova Scotia 168/C5
East Greenville, Ohio (†44666) 284/G4
East Greenville, Pa. (18041) 294/L5
East Greenwich, R.I. (02818) 249/H6
East Grinstead, England 10/G5
East Grinstead, England 13/G6
Eastgulf, W. Va. (25835) 312/D7
East Gull Lake, Minn. (†56401) 255/D4
East Haddam○, Conn. (06423) 210/F3
Eastham○, Mass. (02642) 249/O5
East Hampstead, N.H. (03826) 268/E6
East Hampton, Conn. (06424) 210/E2
East Hampton○, Conn. (06424) 210/E2
Easthampton○, Mass. (01027) 249/D3
East Hampton, N.Y. (11937) 276/R9
East Hanover○, N.J. (07936) 273/E2
East Hardin, Ill. (†62031) 222/C4
East Hardwick, Vt. (05836) 268/C2
East Hartford○, Conn. (06108) 210/E1
East Hartland, Conn. (06027) 210/D1
East Harwich, Mass. (†02645) 249/O6
East Haven○, Conn. (06512) 210/D3
East Haven○, Vt. (05837) 268/D2
East Haverhill, N.H. (†03780) 268/D3
East Hazelcrest, Ill. (†60429) 222/C6
East Hebron, N.H. (03232) 268/D4
East Helena, Mont. (59635) 262/E4
East Hereford, Québec 172/F4
East Herkimer, N.Y. 276/L4
East Hickory, Pa. (16321) 294/D2
East Hills, N.Y. (†11576) 276/R7
East Hiram, Maine (†04041) 243/B8
East Hodge, La. (†71247) 238/E2
East Holden, Maine (04429) 243/F6
East Hope, Idaho (†83836) 220/B1
East Jackson, Maine (†04986) 243/E6
East Jamaica, Vt. (†05343) 268/B5
East Jordan, Mich. (49727) 250/D3
East Juliette, Georgia (†31046) 217/E4
East Keansburg, N.J. (†07734) 273/E3
East Kelowna, Br. Col. 184/H5
East Kent, Conn. (†06785) 210/B2
East Kilbride, Scotland 15/B2
East Killingly, Conn. (06243) 210/H1
East Kingsford, Mich. (†49801) 250/A3
East Kingston○, N.H. (03827) 268/F6
East Knox, Maine (†04921) 243/E7
East Korea (bay), N. Korea 81/D4
East Lake, Mich. (49626) 250/C4
East Lake, Minn. (†55760) 255/E4
East Lake, N.C. (27931) 281/S3
Eastlake, Ohio (†44094) 284/J8
East Lake-Orient Park, Fla. (†33601) 212/C2
Eastland, Tenn. (†38583) 237/L9
Eastland (co.), Texas 303/F5
Eastland, Texas (76448) 303/F5
East Lansdowne, Pa. (†19050) 294/M7
East Lansing, Mich. (48823) 250/E6
East Laport, N.C. (†28723) 281/C4
East Las Vegas, Nev. (89112) 266/F6
East Laurinburg, N.C. (28352) 281/L5
East Lebanon, Maine (04027) 243/B9
East Lee, Mass. (†01238) 249/B3
Eastleigh, England 13/F7
Eastleigh, England 10/F5
East Lempster, N.H. (03605) 268/C5
East Limington, Maine (†04049) 243/B8
East Linton, Scotland 15/F5
East Litchfield, Conn. (†06759) 210/C1
East Livermore, Maine (04228) 243/C7
East Liverpool, Ohio (43920) 284/J4
East Loch (inlet), Hawaii 218/B3
East Loch Tarbert (inlet), Scotland 15/B3
East London, S. Africa 102/E8
East London, S. Africa 118/D6
East Longmeadow○, Mass. (01028) 249/E4
East Los Angeles, Calif. (90022) 204/C10
East Lowell, Maine (†04433) 243/G5
East Lyme○, Conn. (06333) 210/G3
East Lynn, Ill. (60932) 222/F3
East Lynn, W. Va. (25512) 312/B6
East Lynn (lake), W. Va. 312/B6
East Lynne, Mo. (64743) 261/D5
East Machias, Maine (04630) 243/J6
East Machias○, Maine (04630) 243/J6
East Machias (riv.), Maine 243/H6
East Madison, Maine (†04950) 243/D6
East Madison, N.H. (†03849) 268/E4
Eastmain, Que. 162/J5
Eastmain (riv.), Que. 146/L4
Eastmain (riv.), Que. 162/J5
Eastmain, Québec 174/B2
Eastmain (riv.), Québec 174/B2
Eastman, Georgia (31023) 217/F6
Eastman, Québec 172/E4
Eastman, Wis. (54626) 317/D9
East Marion, N.C. (†28752) 281/F3
East Meadow, N.Y. (11554) 276/R7
East Meredith, N.Y. (13757) 276/L6
East Middlebury, Vt. (05740) 268/A4
East Millcreek, Utah (84109) 304/C3
East Millinocket, Maine (04430) 243/F4
East Millinocket○, Maine (04430) 243/F4
East Millstone, N.J. (08873) 273/D3
East Milton, Mass. (†02186) 249/D7
East Mines, Nova Scotia 168/E3
East Moline, Ill. (61244) 222/C2
East Montpelier○, Vt. (05651) 268/B3
East Moriches, N.Y. (11940) 276/P9
East Morris, Conn. (†06763) 210/C2
East Murton, England 13/J3
East Musquash (lake), Maine 243/H5
East Naples, Fla. (†33940) 212/E5
East Newark, N.J. (†07100) 273/B2
East New Market, Md. (21631) 245/P6
East Newnan, Georgia (†30263) 217/C4
East New Portland, Maine (†04954) 243/D6
East Nishnabotna (riv.), Iowa 229/C6
East Northfield, Mass. (†01360) 249/E2
East Northport, N.Y. (11731) 276/O9
East Norton, Mass. (†02766) 249/K5
East Norwalk, Conn. (†06856) 210/B4
East Olympia, Wash. (98540) 310/B4
Easton, Calif. (93706) 204/F7
Easton○, Conn. (06612) 210/B4
Easton (res.), Conn. 210/B3
Easton, Ill. (62633) 222/D3
Easton, Kansas (66020) 232/G2
Easton, La. (†70586) 238/F5
Easton○, Maine (04740) 243/H2
Easton, Md. (21601) 245/O5
Easton○, Mass. (02334) 249/K4
Easton, Minn. (56025) 255/E7
Easton, Mo. (64443) 261/C3
Easton○, N.H. (†03580) 268/D3
Easton, Pa. (18042) 294/M4
Easton, Wash. (98925) 310/D3
Easton, Wis. (†53936) 317/G8
Eastondale, Mass. (†02375) 249/K4
East Orange, N.J. (*07017) 273/B2
East Orland, Maine (04431) 243/F6
East Orleans, Mass. (02643) 249/P5
East Otis, Mass. (01029) 249/B4
East Otisfield, Maine (†04270) 243/B7
East Otto, N.Y. (14729) 276/C6
Eastover, S.C. (29044) 296/F4
East Palatka, Fla. (32031) 212/E2
East Palestine, Ohio (44413) 284/J4
East Park (res.), Calif. 204/C4
East Parsonfield, Maine (04028) 243/B8
East Peacham, Vt. (†05821) 268/C3
East Pembroke, Mass. (†02359) 249/M4
East Pembroke, N.Y. (14056) 276/D5
East Peoria, Ill. (61611) 222/D3
East Pepperell, Mass. (01437) 249/H2
East Peru (Peru), Iowa (†50222) 229/F6
East Peru, Maine (04229) 243/C7
East Petersburg, Pa. (17520) 294/K5
East Pleasant Plain, Iowa (†52540) 229/K6
Eastpoint, Fla. (32328) 212/B2
East Point, Georgia (30344) 217/K2
East Point, Ky. (41216) 237/R5
East Point, La. (71025) 238/D2
East Poland, Maine (†04210) 243/C7
East Poplar, Sask. 181/F6
Eastport, Idaho (83826) 220/B1
Eastport, Maine 188/N2
Eastport, Maine (04631) 243/K6
Eastport, Mich. (49627) 250/D3
Eastport, Newf. 166/D1
Eastport, N.Y. (11941) 276/P9
East Poultney, Vt. (05741) 268/A4
East Prairie, Mo. (63845) 261/O9
East Preston, England 13/G7
East Prospect, Pa. (17317) 294/J6
East Providence, R.I. (02914) 249/J5
East Putnam, Conn. (†06260) 210/H1
East Randolph, N.Y. (14730) 276/C6
East Randolph, Vt. (05041) 268/B4
East Retford, England 13/G4
East Retford, England 10/F4
East Richford, Vt. (†05476) 268/B2
East Ridge, Tenn. (37412) 237/L11
Eastriggs, Scotland 15/E5
East Rindge, N.H. (†03461) 268/D6
East River, Conn. (†06443) 210/E3
East River Saint Marys, Nova Scotia 168/F3
East Riverside-Kingshurst, New Bruns. 170/E3
East Rochester, N.Y. (14445) 276/F4
East Rochester, Ohio (44625) 284/H4
East Rockaway, N.Y. (11518) 276/R7
East Rutherford, N.J. (07073) 273/B2
Eastry, England 13/J6
East Ryegate, Vt. (05042) 268/C3
East Saint Louis, Ill. 188/J3
East Saint Louis, Ill. (*62201) 222/A2
East Sandwich, Mass. (02537) 249/N6
East Saugus, Mass. (†01906) 249/D6
East Sebago, Maine (04029) 243/B8
East Selkirk, Manitoba 179/F4
East Shoal (lake), Manitoba 179/E4
East Siberian (sea), U.S.S.R. 4/B1
East Siberian (sea), U.S.S.R. 54/T2
East Siberian (sea), U.S.S.R. 48/S2
Eastside, Oreg. (97420) 291/C4
East Side, Pa. (18634) 294/L3
East Sister (peak), Idaho 220/C2
East Sister (isl.), Tasmania 99/E1
East Smithfield, Pa. (18817) 294/J2
Eastsound, Wash. (98245) 310/B2

364 East Sparta

East Sparta, Ohio (44626) 284/H4
East Spencer, N.C. (28039) 281/J3
East Springfield, N.Y. (13333) 276/L5
East Springfield, Pa. (16411) 294/A2
East Stone Gap, Va. (24246) 307/C7
East Stoneham, Maine (04231) 243/B7
East Stroudsburg, Pa. (18301) 294/M4
East Sullivan, Maine (†04607) 243/G6
East Sullivan, N.H. (03445) 268/C6
East Sumner, Maine (†04220) 243/C7
East Sussex (co.), England 13/H7
East Swan (riv.), Minn. 255/F3
East Swanzey, N.H. (03446) 268/C6
East Syracuse, N.Y. (13057) 276/H4
East Tawas, Mich. (48730) 250/F4
East Templeton, Mass. (01438) 249/G2
East Thermopolis, Wyo. (†82443) 319/D2
East Thetford, Vt. (05043) 268/C4
East Thompson, Conn. (†06255) 210/H1
East Tintic (creek), Utah 304/B4
East Tohopekaliga (lake), Fla. 212/E3
East Troy, Wis. (53120) 317/J2
East Union, Maine (†04862) 243/E7
Eastvale, Pa. (†15010) 294/B4
Eastvale, Texas (†75067) 303/G1
East Vassalboro, Maine (04935) 243/D7
East Verde (riv.), Ariz. 198/D4
Eastview, Tenn. (†38367) 237/D10
East View, W. Va. (†26301) 312/F4
East Village, Conn. (†06468) 210/C3
Eastville, Georgia (†30677) 217/E3
Eastville, Va. (23347) 307/R6
East Wakefield, N.H. (03830) 268/E4
East Walker (riv.), Nev. 266/B4
East Wallingford, Vt. (05742) 268/B5
East Walpole, Mass. (02032) 249/C8
East Wareham, Mass. (02538) 249/M5
East Washington, Pa. (†15301) 294/B5
East Waterboro, Maine (04030) 243/B8
East Waterford, Pa. (17021) 294/G5
East Wenatchee, Wash. (98801) 310/E3
East Weymouth, Mass. (†02189) 249/E8
East Whately, Mass. (†01373) 249/D3
East Williamson, N.Y. (14449) 276/F4
East Willington, Conn. (†06279) 210/G1
East Wilton, Maine (04234) 243/C6
East Windsor○, Conn. (†06088) 210/E1
East Windsor Hill, Conn. (06028) 210/E1
East Winn, Maine (†04495) 243/G5
East Wolfeboro, N.H. (†03894) 268/E4
Eastwood, Mich. (†49001) 250/D6
Eastwood, N. S. Wales 88/K4
Eastwood, N.S. Wales 97/J3
Eastwood, Ontario 177/D4
East Woodstock, Conn. (06244) 210/H1
East Worcester, N.Y. (12064) 276/L5
East York, Ontario 177/J4
Eaton, Colo. (80615) 208/K1
Eaton, Ill. (†62454) 222/F4
Eaton, Ind. (47338) 227/G4
Eaton, Maine (†04424) 243/H4
Eaton (co.), Mich. 250/E6
Eaton (Eaton Center)○, N.H. (03832) 268/E4
Eaton, N.Y. (13334) 276/J5
Eaton, Ohio (45320) 284/A6
Eaton, Tenn. (38331) 237/C9
Eaton Center, N.H. (03832) 268/E4
Eaton Estates, Ohio (†44035) 284/G3
Eatonia, Sask. 181/B4
Eaton Rapids, Mich. (48827) 250/E6
Eatonton, Georgia (31024) 217/F4
Eatontown, N.J. (07724) 273/E3
Eatonville, Fla. (32751) 212/E3
Eatonville, Wash. (98328) 310/C4
Eau Claire, Mich. (49111) 250/C6
Eau Claire, Pa. (16030) 294/C3
Eau Claire, Lac à l' (lake), Que. 162/J4
Eau Claire (lake), Québec 174/C1
Eau Claire, Wis. 188/H2
Eau Claire (co.), Wis. 317/D6
Eau Claire, Wis. (54701) 317/D6
Eau Claire (riv.), Wis. 317/D6
Eau Galle, Wis. (54737) 317/B6
Eauripik (atoll), Micronesia 87/E5
Ebal (mt.), Jordan 65/C3
Ebano, Mexico 150/K5
Ebb, Fla. (†32331) 212/C1
Ebb and Flow (lake), Manitoba 179/C3
Ebbw Vale, Wales 13/B6
Ebbw Vale, Wales 10/E5
Ebeltoft, Denmark 21/D5
Ebeltoft, Denmark 18/G8
Ebenezer, Miss. (39064) 256/D5
Ebenezer, Sask. 181/J4
Ebenfurth, Austria 41/D3
Eben Junction, Mich. (49825) 250/B2
Ebensburg, Pa. (15931) 294/E5
Ebensee, Austria 41/B3
Eberbach, W. Germany 22/C4
Ebersbach, E. Germany 22/F3
Eberswalde-Finow, E. Germany 22/E2
Ebetsu, Japan 81/K2
Ebingen, W. Germany 22/C4
Ebinur Hu (lake), China 77/B2
Ebnat-Kappel, Switzerland 39/H2
Eboli, Italy 34/E4
Ebolowa, Cameroon 102/D4
Ebolowa, Cameroon 115/B3
Ebon (atoll), Marshall Is. 87/G5
Ebony, Va. (23845) 307/N7
Ebor, Manitoba 179/A5
Ebrach, W. Germany 22/D4
Ebrié (lag.), Ivory Coast 106/D8
Ebro, Fla. (32437) 212/C6
Ebro, Minn. (†56621) 255/C3
Ebro (riv.), Spain 7/D4
Ebro (riv.), Spain 33/G2
Ecatepec de Morelos, Mexico 150/L1
Ecaussinnes, Belgium 27/E7
Ecclefechan, Scotland 15/E5
Eccles, W. Va. (25836) 312/D7
Ecclesville, Trin. & Tob. 161/B11
Eceabat, Turkey 63/B6
Echallens, Switzerland 39/C3
Echarate, Peru 128/F9
Echeconnee, Georgia (†31008) 217/E5
Echmiadzin, U.S.S.R. 52/F6
Echo, Ala. (†36360) 195/G8
Echo (cliffs), Ariz. 198/D2
Echo, La. (71330) 238/F4
Echo, Minn. (56237) 255/C6
Echo (lake), N.J. 273/E1
Echo, Oreg. (97826) 291/H2
Echo (lake), Tasmania 99/C4
Echo, Utah (84024) 304/C3
Echo (res.), Utah 304/C3
Echo (lake), Vt. 268/D2
Echo Bay, Ontario 177/J5
Echo Bay, Ontario 175/D3
Echola, Ala. (35457) 195/C4
Echo Lake, N.J. (†07435) 273/E1
Echo Lake, Nova Scotia 168/E4
Echols (co.), Georgia 217/G9
Echols, Ky. (42340) 237/H6
Echo Valley Prov. Park, Sask. 181/G5
Echt, Netherlands 27/H6
Echternach, Luxembourg 27/J9
Echuca, Victoria 97/C5
Echuca, Victoria 88/G7
Écija, Spain 33/D4
Eck, Loch (lake), Scotland 15/A1
Eckelson, N. Dak. (58432) 282/O6
Eckerman, Mich. (49728) 250/E2
Eckernförde, W. Germany 22/D1
Eckerty, Ind. (47116) 227/D8
Eckhart Mines, Md. (21528) 245/C2
Eckley, Colo. (80727) 208/P2
Eckman, N. Dak. (†58760) 282/H2
Eckman, W. Va. (24829) 312/C8
Eckville, Alberta 182/C3
Eclectic, Ala. (36024) 195/F5
Eclipse (harb.), Newf. 166/B2
Eclipse (sound), N.W. Terrs. 187/L2
Economy, Ind. (47339) 227/G5
Economy, Nova Scotia 168/D3
Economy, Pa. (†15005) 294/B4
Écorce (lake), Québec 172/A2
Écorces (riv.), Québec 172/F1
Ecorse, Mich. (48229) 250/B7
Écrins, Les (mt.), France 28/G5
Ecru, Miss. (38841) 256/F2
Ector (co.), Texas 303/B6
Ecuador 2/D6
Ecuador 120/B3
ECUADOR 128
Ecublens, Switzerland 39/B3
Ecum Secum, Nova Scotia 168/F3
Ecum Secum Bridge, Nova Scotia 168/F4
Edam, Sask. 181/C2
Edam-Volendam, Netherlands 27/G4
Eday (isl.), Scotland 10/E1
Eday (isl.), Scotland 15/F1
Edberg, Alberta 182/D3
Edcouch, Texas (78538) 303/G11
Edd, Ethiopia 111/H5
Edd, Ethiopia 59/D7
Ed Da'ein, Sudan 111/E5
Ed Damazin, Sudan 111/F5
Ed Damer, Sudan 111/F4
Ed Damer, Sudan 59/B6
Ed Damer, Sudan 102/F3
Ed Debba, Sudan 111/F4
Ed Debba, Sudan 59/B6
Edderton, Scotland 15/D3
Eddiceton, Miss. (39634) 256/C8
Eddington, Maine (†04428) 243/F6
Eddington○, Maine (†04428) 243/F6
Eddington, Pa. (19020) 294/N5
Eddleston, Scotland 15/E5
Eddontenajon, Br. Col. 184/K2
Eddrachillis (bay), Scotland 15/C2
Ed Dueim, Sudan 59/B7
Ed Dueim, Sudan 111/F5
Ed Dueim, Sudan 102/F3
Eddy (co.), N. Mex. 274/E6
Eddy (co.), N. Dak. 282/N4
Eddy, Texas (76524) 303/G6
Eddystone (rocks), England 13/C7
Eddystone (rocks), England 10/D5
Eddystone, Manitoba 179/C3
Eddystone, Pa. (†19013) 294/M7
Eddystone (pt.), Tasmania 88/H8
Eddystone (pt.), Tasmania 99/E2
Eddyville, Ill. (62928) 222/E6
Eddyville, Iowa (52553) 229/H6
Eddyville, Ky. (42038) 237/E6
Eddyville, Nebr. (68834) 264/E3
Eddyville, Oreg. (97343) 291/D3
Ede, Netherlands 27/H4
Ede, Nigeria 106/E7
Edéa, Cameroon 115/B3
Edelény, Hungary 41/F2
Edelstein, Ill. (61526) 222/D3
Eden, Ariz. (85535) 198/F6
Edén, Ecuador 128/E3
Eden (riv.), England 13/E3
Eden (riv.), England 10/E3
Eden, Georgia (31307) 217/K6
Eden, Idaho (83325) 220/D7
Eden, Ind. (†46140) 227/F5
Eden, Manitoba 179/C4
Eden, Md. (21822) 245/R7
Eden, Miss. (39065) 256/D5
Eden, Mont. (†59401) 262/E3
Eden, N.S. Wales 97/E5
Eden, N.Y. (14057) 276/C5
Eden, N.C. (27288) 281/K1
Eden (riv.), Scotland 15/F4
Eden, S. Dak. (57232) 298/P2
Eden, Texas (76837) 303/E6
Eden, Utah (84310) 304/C2
Eden○, Vt. (05652) 268/B2
Eden, Wis. (53019) 317/K8
Eden, Wyo. (82926) 319/C3
Edenburg, Sask. 181/E3
Edenburg, S. Africa 118/D5
Edendale, S. Africa 118/D5
Edenderry, Ireland 10/C4
Edenderry, Ireland 17/G5
Edenhope, Victoria 97/A5
Eden Mills, Ontario 177/D4
Eden Mills, Vt. (05653) 268/C2
Eden Prairie, Minn. (55344) 255/G6
Edenton, N.C. (27932) 281/R2
Edenton, Ohio (†45122) 284/C7
Edenvale, S. Africa 118/H6
Eden Valley, Minn. (55329) 255/D5
Eden Valley (res.), Wyo. 319/C3
Edenville, Mich. (48620) 250/E5
Edenwold, Sask. 181/G5
Eder (res.), W. Germany 22/C3
Eder (riv.), W. Germany 22/C3
Ederney and Kesh, N. Ireland 17/F2
Edgar (co.), Ill. 222/F4
Edgar, Mont. (59026) 262/H5
Edgar, Nebr. (68935) 264/F4
Edgar, Wis. (54426) 317/G6
Edgard, La. (70049) 238/M3
Edgar Springs, Mo. (65462) 261/J7
Edgarton, W. Va. (25672) 312/B7
Edgartown, Mass. (02539) 249/M7
Edgartown○, Mass. (02539) 249/M7
Edge (isl.), Norway 4/B8
Edgecliff, Texas (†76101) 303/E2
Edgecomb○, Maine (†04556) 243/D8
Edgecombe (co.), N.C. 281/O3
Edgecumbe (cape), Alaska 196/L1
Edgecumbe, N. Zealand 100/F2
Edgefield, La. (†71019) 238/D2
Edgefield (co.), S.C. 296/D4
Edgefield, S.C. (29824) 296/C4
Edge Hill, Georgia (†30810) 217/G4
Edgehill, Va. (†22485) 307/O4
Edgeley, N. Dak. (58433) 282/N7
Edgeley, Sask. 181/H5
Edgell (isl.), N.W. Terrs. 187/M3
Edgemere, Idaho (†83856) 220/B1
Edgemere, Md. (†21219) 245/N4
Edgemont, Ark. (72044) 202/F2
Edgemont, S. Dak. (57735) 298/B7
Edgemoor, Del. (†19801) 245/S1
Edgemoor, S.C. (29712) 296/E2
Edgemount, N.C. (28645) 281/F2
Edgeøya (isl.), Norway 18/E2
Edgerly, La. (†70668) 238/C6
Edgerton, Alberta 182/E3
Edgerton, Ind. (†46797) 227/H2
Edgerton, Kansas (66021) 232/H3
Edgerton, Minn. (56128) 255/B7
Edgerton, Mo. (64444) 261/C3
Edgerton, Ohio (43517) 284/A3
Edgerton, Va. (†23868) 307/N7
Edgerton, Wis. (53534) 317/H10
Edgerton, Wyo. (82635) 319/F2
Edgewater, Br. Col. 184/J5
Edgewater, Colo. (80214) 208/J3
Edgewater, Fla. (32032) 212/F3
Edgewater, N.J. (07020) 273/C2
Edgewater, Wis. (54834) 317/D4
Edgewater Park○, N.J. (†08010) 273/D3
Edgewood, Br. Col. 184/H5
Edgewood, Calif. (96094) 204/C2
Edgewood, Fla. (†32801) 212/E3
Edgewood, Ill. (62426) 222/E5
Edgewood, Ind. (†46011) 227/F4
Edgewood, Iowa (52042) 229/K3
Edgewood, Ky. (†41017) 237/S2
Edgewood, Md. (21040) 245/N3
Edgewood, N. Mex. (87015) 274/C3
Edgewood, Ohio (†44004) 284/J2
Edgewood, Pa. (†15218) 294/B7
Edgeworth, Pa. (†15143) 294/B4
Edgington, Ill. (†61284) 222/C2
Édhessa, Greece 45/F5
Edievale, N. Zealand 100/B6
Edina, Minn. (55424) 255/G5
Edina, Mo. (63537) 261/H2
Edinboro, Pa. (16412) 294/B2
Edinburg, Ill. (62531) 222/D4
Edinburg, Miss. (†39051) 256/F5
Edinburg, Mo. (†64683) 261/E2
Edinburg, N. Dak. (58227) 282/P3
Edinburg, Pa. (16116) 294/B3
Edinburg, Texas (78539) 303/F11
Edinburg, Va. (22824) 307/M3
Edinburgh, Ind. (46124) 227/E6
Edinburgh (cap.), Scotland 7/D3
Edinburgh (cap.), Scotland 15/D1
Edinburgh (cap.), Scotland 10/C1
Edingen (Enghien), Belgium 27/D7
Edime (prov.), Turkey 63/B2
Edirne, Turkey 7/G4
Edirne, Turkey 63/B2
Edirne, Turkey 59/A1
Edison, Calif. (93220) 204/G8
Edison (lake), Calif. 204/F6
Edison, Georgia (31746) 217/C7
Edison, Nebr. (68936) 264/E4
Edison○, N.J. (*08817) 273/E2
Edison, Ohio (43320) 284/E4
Edison, Wash. (98246) 310/C2
Edison Nat'l Hist. Site, N.J. 273/A2
Edisto (isl.), S.C. 296/G6
Edisto (riv.), S.C. 296/G7
Edisto Beach, S.C. (†29438) 296/G7
Edisto Island, S.C. (29438) 296/G6
Edith, Georgia (†31631) 217/G9
Edithburgh, S. Australia 94/E6
Ediz Hook (pen.), Wash. 310/B2
Edjeleh, Algeria 106/F3
Edmeston, N.Y. (13335) 276/K5
Edmond, Kansas (67636) 232/C2
Edmond, Okla. (73034) 288/M3
Edmonds, Wash. (98020) 310/C3
Edmondson, Ark. (72332) 202/K3
Edmondt, Fr. Guiana 131/E3
Edmonson (co.), Ky. 237/J6
Edmonson, Texas (79032) 303/C3
Edmonston, Md. (†20781) 245/F4
Edmonton (cap.), Alberta 182/D3
Edmonton, Alta. 146/G4
Edmonton (cap.), Alta. 162/E5
Edmonton, Canada 2/D3
Edmonton, Ky. (42129) 237/K7
Edmonton Beach, Alberta 182/C3
Edmore, Mich. (48829) 250/E5
Edmore, N. Dak. (58330) 282/O3
Edmore, Sask. 181/H4
Edmund, Wis. (†53533) 317/F9
Edmunds, Maine (†04628) 243/J6
Edmunds, N. Dak. (†58746) 282/M5
Edmunds (co.), S. Dak. 298/L3
Edmundson, Mo. (†63101) 261/O2
Edmundston, N. Br. 162/K6
Edmundston, New Bruns. 170/B1
Edna, Ala. (†36922) 195/B6
Edna, Iowa (†51246) 229/A2
Edna, Kansas (67342) 232/G4
Edna, Texas (77957) 303/H9
Edna Bay, Alaska (†99901) 196/M2
Edo (riv.), Japan 81/P2
Edolo, Italy 34/C1
Edom, Texas (†75656) 303/J5
Edon, Ohio (43518) 284/A2
Édouard (lake), Québec 172/E2
Edrans, Manitoba 179/C4
Edray, W. Va. (†24954) 312/F6
Edremit, Turkey 63/B3
Edremit, Turkey 59/A2
Edremit (gulf), Turkey 63/B3
Edri, Libya 111/B2
Edsbyn, Sweden 18/J6
Edson, Alberta 182/B3
Edson, Alta. 162/E5
Edson, Kansas (67733) 232/A2
Eduardo Castex, Argentina 143/D4
Edwall, Wash. (99008) 310/H3
Edwand, Alberta 182/D2
Edward (lake) 102/E5
Edward, N.C. (27821) 281/R4
Edward (lake), Uganda 115/E4
Edward (lake), Zaire 115/E4
Edward MacDowell (res.), N.H. 268/D6
Edwards, Colo. (81632) 208/F3
Edwards (co.), Ill. 222/E5
Edwards, Ill. (61528) 222/D3
Edwards (riv.), Ill. 222/C2
Edwards (co.), Kansas 232/C4
Edwards (lake), La. 238/C2
Edwards, Miss. (39066) 256/C6
Edwards, Mo. (65326) 261/F6
Edwards, N.Y. (13635) 276/K2
Edwards (co.), Texas 303/D7
Edwards (plat.), Texas 303/C7
Edwards A.F.B., Calif. 204/H9
Edwardsburg, Mich. (49112) 250/C7
Edwardsport, Ind. (47528) 227/C7
Edwardsville, Ala. (36261) 195/H3
Edwardsville, Ill. (62025) 222/B2
Edwardsville, Ind. (†47150) 227/F8
Edwardsville, Kansas (66113) 232/H2
Edwardsville, Pa. (18704) 294/E7
Edward VII (pen.) 5/B11
Edward VIII (bay) 5/C4
Edwight, W. Va. (†25189) 312/C7
Edwin, Ala. (†36317) 195/H7
Edwin, Manitoba 179/D5
Edzell, Scotland 15/F4
Eefde, Netherlands 27/J4
Eek, Alaska (99578) 196/F2
Eeklo, Belgium 27/D6
Eel (riv.), Calif. 204/B4
Eel (riv.), Ind. 227/C6
Eel (riv.), Ind. 227/F3
Eel River Bridge, New Bruns. 170/F1
Eel River Crossing, New Bruns. 170/D1
Eems (riv.), Netherlands 27/K2
Eersteriver, S. Africa 118/F6
Efate (isl.), Vanuatu 87/G7
Eferding, Austria 41/B2
Effie, La. (71331) 238/F4
Effie, Minn. (56639) 255/E3
Effigy Mounds Nat'l Mon., Iowa 229/L2
Effingham (co.), Georgia 217/K6
Effingham (co.), Ill. 222/E4
Effingham, Ill. (62401) 222/E4
Effingham, Kansas (66023) 232/G2
Effingham, S.C. (29541) 296/H3
Effingham Falls, N.H. (†03814) 268/E4
Effort, Pa. (18330) 294/M4
Efland, N.C. (27243) 281/L2
Eflâni, Turkey 63/E2
Egadi (isls.), Italy 34/C6
Egan, Ill. (61026) 222/D1
Egan (range), Nev. 266/G4
Egan, S. Dak. (57024) 298/R6
Egaña, Uruguay 145/B4
Eganville, Ontario 177/G2
Egbert, Wyo. (†82053) 319/H4
Ege, Ind. (†46763) 227/G2
Egegik, Alaska (99579) 196/G3
Egeland, N. Dak. (58331) 282/M2
Eger, Hungary 41/F3
Egeria, W. Va. (†25902) 312/D7
Egernsund, Denmark 21/C8
Egerton (mt.), W. Australia 92/B4
Egg (isl.), Manitoba 179/E3
Egg (creek), N. Dak. 282/H3
Egg, Switzerland 39/G2
Eggenburg, Austria 41/C2
Eggertsville, N.Y. (†14226) 276/C5
Egg Harbor, Wis. (54209) 317/M5
Egg Harbor City, N.J. (08215) 273/D4
Egg Island (pt.), N.J. 273/C5
Eggiwil, Switzerland 39/E3
Egg Lagoon, Tasmania 99/A1
Eggleston, Va. (24086) 307/G6
Egham, England 13/G8
Egham, England 10/B5
Éghezée, Belgium 27/F7
Egilsay (isl.), Scotland 15/F1
Eglin A.F.B., Fla. 212/C6
Eglington (isl.), N.W.T. 162/L3
Eglinton (cape), N.W. Terrs. 187/M2
Eglinton (isl.), N.W. Terrs. 187/F2
Eglisau, Switzerland 39/G1
Eglon, W. Va. (26716) 312/G4
Egmond aan Zee, Netherlands 27/E3
Egmondville, Ontario 177/C4
Egmont (key), Fla. 212/D4
Egmont (cape), N. Zealand 100/D3
Egmont (mt.), N. Zealand 100/D3
Egmont (cape), Nova Scotia 168/H2
Egmont (bay), Pr. Edward I. 168/D2
Egmont (cape), Pr. Edward I. 168/D2
Egnach, Switzerland 39/H1
Egnar, Colo. (81325) 208/B7
Egremont, Alberta 182/D2
Egremont, England 13/D3
Eğridir, Turkey 63/D4
Eğridir (lake), Turkey 59/B2
Eğridir (lake), Turkey 63/D4
Egtved, Denmark 21/C6
Egvekinot, U.S.S.R. 48/S3
Egyek, Hungary 41/F3
Egypt 2/L4
Egypt 102/E2
EGYPT 111/E2
EGYPT 59/A4
Egypt, Georgia (†31329) 217/K6
Egypt, Miss. (†38860) 256/G3
Egypt Lake, Fla. (†33614) 212/C2
Eha Amufu, Nigeria 106/F7
Ehime (pref.), Japan 81/F7
Ehingen, W. Germany 22/G4
Ehrenberg (range), North. Terr. 93/B7
Ehrenburg, Ariz. (85334) 198/A5
Ehrenfeld, Pa. (†15956) 294/E5
Ehrhardt, S.C. (29081) 296/E5
Ehrwald, Austria 41/A3
Eiao (isl.), Fr. Poly. 87/M6
Eibar, Spain 33/E1
Eichstätt, W. Germany 22/D4
Eider (riv.), W. Germany 22/C1
Eidfjord, Norway 18/E6
Eidsfoss, Norway 18/C4
Eidson, Tenn. (37731) 237/P7
Eidsvold, Queensland 95/D5
Eidsvoll, Norway 18/G6
Eielson A.F.B., Alaska 196/J2
Eigenbrakel (Braine-l'Alleud), Belgium 27/E7
Eigersund, Norway 18/D7
Eigg (mt.), Nova Scotia 168/F3
Eigg (isl.), Scotland 15/B4
Eigg (isl.), Scotland 10/C2
Eigg (sound), Scotland 15/B4
Eight Degree (chan.), India 68/C7
Eighteen Mile (peak), Idaho 220/E5
Eight Mile (brook), Conn. 210/C3
Eight Mile (riv.), Conn. 210/F3
Eights Coast (reg.) 5/B14
Eighty Eight, Ky. (42130) 237/K7
Eighty Mile (beach), W. Australia 88/C3
Eighty Mile (beach), W. Australia 92/C2
Eijerlandsche Gat (str.), Netherlands 27/F2
Eil, Loch (lake), Scotland 15/C4
Eil, Somalia 115/J2
Eildon, Victoria 97/C5
Eildon (lake), Victoria 97/C5
Eileen, Ill. (†60416) 222/E2
Eileen (lake), N.W.T. 162/F3
Eilenburg, E. Germany 22/E3
Eilerts de Haan (mts.), Suriname 131/C4
Eina, Norway 18/G6
Einbeck, W. Germany 22/C3
Eindhoven, Netherlands 27/G6
'Ein Gedi, Israel 65/C5
'Ein Harod, Israel 65/C2
'Ein Netafim (well), Israel 65/D5
Einsiedeln, Switzerland 39/G2
Eirunepé, Brazil 132/G10
Eirunepé, Brazil 120/B3
Eisenach, E. Germany 22/D3
Eisenberg, E. Germany 22/D3
Eisenerz, Austria 41/C3
Eisenhower (mt.), Alberta 182/C4
Eisenhüttenstadt, E. Germany 22/F2
Eisenkappel-Vellach, Austria 41/C3
Eisenstadt, Austria 41/D3
Eiserfeld, W. Germany 22/C3
Eishort, Loch (inlet), Scotland 15/B3
Eisleben, E. Germany 22/D3
Eisling (mts.), Luxembourg 27/H9
Eitzen, Minn. (55931) 255/G7
Ejby, Denmark 21/C7
Ejea de los Caballeros, Spain 33/F1
Ejido, Venezuela 124/C3
Ejin, China 77/F3
Ejin Horo, China 77/G4
Ejutla de Crespo, Mexico 150/L8
Ekalaka, Mont. (59324) 262/M5
Ekenäs, Finland 18/N6
Ekeren, Belgium 27/E6
Eketahuna, N. Zealand 100/E4
Ekibastuz, U.S.S.R. 48/H4
Ekibin, Queensland 88/K3
Ekimchan, U.S.S.R. 48/O4
Ekin, Ind. (†46072) 227/E4
Ekonk, Conn. (†06384) 210/H2
Ekron, Ky. (40117) 237/J5
Eksjö, Sweden 18/J8
Ekuk, Alaska (†99569) 196/G3
Ekwan (riv.), Ont. 162/H5
Ekwan (riv.), Ontario 175/C2
Ekwok, Alaska (99580) 196/G3
El Aaiún (Laayoune), Morocco 102/A2
El Aaiún (Laayoune), Western Sahara 106/B3
El Abbasiya, Sudan 111/F5
El Abiar, Libya 111/D1
El Abiod Sidi Cheikh, Algeria 106/E2
El Agheila, Libya 111/C1
Elaine, Ark. (72333) 202/J5
El 'Al, Jordan 65/D4
El 'Alamein, Egypt 111/E1
El 'Alamein, Egypt 59/A3
El Almacén, Venezuela 124/G4
El Amparo de Apure, Venezuela 124/C4
Elams, N.C. (†23919) 281/O1
Elamton, Ky. (41420) 237/P5
Elamville, Ala. (†36311) 195/G7
Eland, Wis. (54427) 317/H6
El Ángel, Ecuador 128/C2
El Arahal, Spain 33/D4
El 'Arish, Egypt 59/B3
El 'Arish, Egypt 111/F1
El Asiento, Bolivia 136/B6
El Asnam, Algeria 106/E1
El Asnam, Algeria 102/C1
Elassón, Greece 45/F6
Elat, Israel 65/D6
Elath (Elat), Israel 65/D6
Elath, Israel 59/B4
El Athale (Itala), Somalia 115/J3
Elato (atoll), Micronesia 87/E5
El 'Atrun (oasis), Sudan 111/E4
El 'Auja, Israel 65/D5
Elâzığ (prov.), Turkey 63/H3
Elâzığ, Turkey 59/C2
Elâzığ, Turkey 63/H3
El Azizia, Libya 111/B1
El Azúcar (res.), Mexico 150/K3
Elba, Ala. (36323) 195/F8
Elba, Idaho (83326) 220/E7
Elba (isl.), Italy 7/E4
Elba (isl.), Italy 34/C3
Elba, Minn. (†55910) 255/F6
Elba, Nebr. (68835) 264/F3
Elba, N.Y. (14058) 276/D4
Elba, Ohio (45728) 284/H6
El Bab, Syria 63/G4
El Balqa (dist.), Jordan 65/D4
El Banco, Colombia 126/D3
El Barco, Spain 33/C1
El Barco de Ávila, Spain 33/D2
El Bardi, Libya 111/D1
El Barkat, Libya 111/B3
Elbasan, Albania 45/E5
El Baúl, Venezuela 124/D3
El Bawiti, Egypt 111/E2
El Bawiti, Egypt 102/E2
El Bawiti, Egypt 59/A4
El Bayadh, Algeria 106/E2
El Bayadh, Algeria 102/C1
Elbe (riv.) 7/F3
Elbe (riv.), E. Germany 22/D2
Elbe, Wash. (98330) 310/C4
Elbe (riv.), W. Germany 22/C2
El Beida, Yemen Arab Rep. 59/E7
El Beni (dept.), Bolivia 136/C3
Elberfeld, Ind. (47613) 227/C8
Elberon, Iowa (52225) 229/J4
Elberon, N.J. (07740) 273/F3
Elberon, Va. (23846) 307/P6
Elbert (mt.), Colo. 188/E3
Elbert (co.), Colo. 208/L4
Elbert, Colo. (80106) 208/L4
Elbert (mt.), Colo. 208/G4
Elbert (co.), Georgia 217/G2
Elbert, Texas (76359) 303/E4
Elbert, W. Va. (24830) 312/C8
Elberta, Ala. (36530) 195/C10
Elberta, Georgia (†31093) 217/E5
Elberta, Mich. (49628) 250/C4
Elberta, Utah (84626) 304/B4
Elberton, Georgia (30635) 217/G2
Elberton, Wash. (†99130) 310/H4
Elbeuf, France 28/D3
Elbing, Kansas (67041) 232/E3
Elbing (Elbląg), Poland 47/D1
El Bira, West Bank 65/C4
Elbistan, Turkey 63/G3
Elbląg (prov.), Poland 47/D1
Elbląg, Poland 47/D1
Elbląg, Poland 7/F3
El Bolsón, Argentina 143/B5
Elbon, Pa. (†15823) 294/E3
El Bonillo, Spain 33/E3
El Boquerón (pass), Peru 128/E7
El Borma, Tunisia 106/F2
Elbow (riv.), Alberta 182/C4
Elbow (lake), Manitoba 179/G4
Elbow (lake), Minn. 255/C3
Elbow, Sask. 181/E4
Elbow Lake, Minn. (56531) 255/B5
Elbridge, N.Y. (13060) 276/G4
Elbridge, Tenn. (38227) 237/C8
El'brus (mt.), U.S.S.R. 7/J4
El'brus (mt.), U.S.S.R. 52/F6
El Buheyrat (prov.), Sudan 111/E6
El Bur, Somalia 115/J3
Elburg, Netherlands 27/H4
El Burgo de Osma, Spain 33/E2
Elburn, Ill. (60119) 222/E2
Elburz (mts.), Iran 59/F2
Elburz (mts.), Iran 66/G2
El Cajon, Calif. (*92020) 204/J11
El Callao, Venezuela 124/G4
El Calvario, Venezuela 124/E3
El Campo, Texas (77437) 303/H8
El Caney, Cuba 158/J4
El Carmen, El Beni, Bolivia 136/D3
El Carmen, Santa Cruz, Bolivia 136/F6
El Carmen, Ñuble, Chile 138/A11
El Carmen, O'Higgins, Chile 138/F5
El Carmen, Chocó, Colombia 126/B5
El Carmen, Nariño, Colombia 126/A6
El Carmen, Norte de Santander, Colombia 126/D3
El Carmen de Bolívar, Colombia 126/C3
El Carre, Ethiopia 111/H6
El Centro, Calif. 188/C4
El Centro, Calif. (92243) 204/K11
El Centro, Colombia 126/D4
El Cercado, Dom. Rep. 158/D6
El Cerrito, Calif. (94530) 204/J2
El Cerrito, Colombia 126/B6
El Cerro, Bolivia 136/E5
El Chaparro, Venezuela 124/F3
Elche, Spain 33/F3
Elche de la Sierra, Spain 33/E3
Elcho (isl.), North. Terr. 93/D1
Elcho, Wis. (54428) 317/H5
El Chocón (res.), Argentina 143/C4
Elcho Island Mission, North. Terr. 93/D1
El Choro, Bolivia 136/B6
El Chorro, Argentina 143/D1
Elco, Ill. (62929) 222/D6
El Cobre, Chile 138/A4
El Cobre, Cuba 158/J4
El Cocuy, Colombia 126/D4
El Convento, Chile 138/F4
El Corazón, Ecuador 128/C3
El Cristo, Venezuela 124/G4
El Cuey, Dom. Rep. 158/F6
El Cuy, Argentina 143/C4
Elda, Spain 33/F3
El Dara, Ill. (†62312) 222/B4

Elvira 365

Elde (riv.), E. Germany 22/D2
Elden (mt.), Ariz. 198/D3
El Der, Ethiopia 111/H6
Elderbank, Nova Scotia 168/E4
El Dere, Somalia 115/J3
El Dere, Somalia 102/G4
Elderon, Wis. (54429) 317/H6
Eldersburg, Md. (†21784) 245/L3
Eldersley, Sask. 181/H3
Elderslie, Scotland 15/B2
Eldersville, Pa. (15036) 294/A5
Elderton, Pa. (15736) 294/D4
El Diente (peak), Colo. 208/C7
El'dikan, U.S.S.R. 48/O3
Eldivan, Turkey 63/E2
El Diviso, Colombia 126/A7
El Djem, Tunisia 106/G1
El Djezair (Algiers) (cap.), Algeria 106/E1
El Djouf (des.) 102/B2
Eldon, Iowa (52554) 229/J7
Eldon, Mo. (65026) 261/G6
Eldon, Wash. (†98555) 310/B3
Eldora, Colo. (†80466) 208/H3
Eldora, Iowa (50627) 229/G4
Eldora, N.J. (†08270) 273/D5
Eldorado, Argentina 143/F2
El Dorado, Ark. 188/H4
El Dorado, Ark. (71730) 202/E7
Eldorado, Brazil 135/B4
El Dorado (co.), Calif. 204/E5
El Dorado, Calif. (95623) 204/C8
Eldorado (Fender), Georgia (†31794) 217/E8
Eldorado, Ill. (62930) 222/E6
Eldorado, Iowa (52175) 229/K2
El Dorado, Kansas (67042) 232/F4
Eldorado, Md. (†21659) 245/P6
Eldorado, Mexico 150/E4
Eldorado, Miss. (†39156) 256/C5
Eldorado, N.C. (†27371) 281/K4
Eldorado, Ohio (45321) 284/A6
Eldorado, Okla. (73537) 288/G6
Eldorado, Sask. 181/L2
Eldorado, Texas (76936) 303/D7
El Dorado, Venezuela 124/H4
Eldorado, Wis. (54932) 317/J8
El Dorado Hills, Calif. (95630) 204/C8
El Dorado Springs, Mo. (64744) 261/E7
Eldorendo, Georgia (†31737) 217/C8
Eldoret, Kenya 102/F4
Eldoret, Kenya 115/G3
Eldred, Ill. (62027) 222/C4
Eldred, Minn. (56532) 255/B3
Eldred, Pa. (16731) 294/F2
Eldridge, Ala. (35554) 195/C3
Eldridge, Iowa (52748) 229/M5
Eldridge, Mo. (65463) 261/G7
Eldridge, N. Dak. (58435) 282/N6
El Dulce Nombre, Honduras 154/E3
Eleanor, W. Va. (25070) 312/C5
Electra, Texas (76360) 303/F4
Electric (peak), Mont. 262/F6
Electric City, Wash. (99123) 310/F3
Electric Mills, Miss. (39329) 256/G5
Electron, Wash. (†98360) 310/C4
Eleele, Hawaii (96705) 218/C2
Elefantes (gulf), Chile 138/D6
Elek, Hungary 41/F3
Elektrostal', U.S.S.R. 7/H3
Elektrostal', U.S.S.R. 52/E3
El Empedrado, Venezuela 124/C3
Elena, Bulgaria 45/G4
Elephant (isl.) 5/D16
Elephant (riv.), Namibia 118/B5
Elephant (mt.), Texas 303/D12
Elephanta (isl.), India 68/B7
Elephant Butte, N. Mex. (87935) 274/B5
Elephant Butte (res.), N. Mex. 188/E4
Elephant Butte (res.), N. Mex. 274/B5
Eleroy, Ill. (61027) 222/D1
Eleşkirt, Turkey 63/K3
El Espinar, Spain 33/D2
El Estor, Guatemala 154/C3
Eleuthera (isl.), Bahamas 146/L7
Eleuthera (isl.), Bahamas 156/C1
Eleva, Wis. (54738) 317/D6
Eleven Mile Canyon (res.), Colo. 208/H5
Elevtheroúpolis, Greece 45/G5
El Faiyûm, Egypt 111/J3
El Faiyûm, Egypt 59/B4
El Faiyûm, Egypt 102/E2
El Fasher, Sudan 111/E5
El Fasher, Sudan 102/E3
El Fashn, Egypt 111/J4
El Ferrol, Spain 7/D4
Elfers, Fla. (33531) 212/D3
El Fifi, Sudan 111/D5
Elfin Cove, Alaska (99825) 196/M1
El Fogaha, Libya 111/C2
Elfrida, Ariz. (†85617) 198/F7
Elfros, Sask. 181/H4
El Fuerte, Mexico 150/E3
El Furat (riv.), Syria 63/H4
El Gallo, Nicaragua 154/E4
El Gatrun, Libya 111/B3
El Gatrun, Libya 102/D2
El Geneina, Sudan 111/D5
El Geneina, Sudan 102/E3
El Geteina, Sudan 111/F5
El Geteina, Sudan 59/B7
El Gezira, Libya 111/D2
El Gezira (prov.), Sudan 111/F5
Elgg, Switzerland 39/G2
El Gheria esh Sherqia, Libya 111/B1
El Ghor (reg.), Jordan 65/C6
Elgin, Ariz. (†85637) 198/E7
Elgin, Ill. 188/J2
Elgin, Ill. (60120) 222/E1
Elgin, Iowa (52141) 229/K3
Elgin, Kansas (†67361) 232/F4
Elgin, Manitoba 179/B5
Elgin, Minn. (55932) 255/F6
Elgin, Nebr. (68636) 264/F3
Elgin, Nev. (†89009) 266/G5
Elgin, New Bruns. 170/E3
Elgin, N. Dak. (58533) 282/G7
Elgin, Ohio (45838) 284/A4
Elgin, Okla. (73538) 288/K5
Elgin (county), Ontario 177/C5
Elgin, Ontario 177/H3
Elgin, Oreg. (97827) 291/K2
Elgin, Pa. (16413) 294/C2
Elgin, Scotland 10/E2
Elgin, Scotland 15/E3
Elgin, S.C. (29045) 296/F3
Elgin, Tenn. (37732) 237/M8
Elgin, Texas (78621) 303/G7
El Golea, Algeria 102/C1
El Goléa, Algeria 106/E2
Elgon (mt.) 102/F4
Elgon (mt.), Kenya 115/F3
Elgon (mt.), Uganda 115/F3
Elgood, W. Va. (24723) 312/E8
El Granada, Calif. (94018) 204/H3
El Guapo, Venezuela 124/F2
El Guayabo, Dom. Rep. 158/E5
El Hamad (des.), Iraq 59/D3
El Hammam, Egypt 111/E1
El Hammam, Egypt 59/A3
El Hamurre, Somalia 115/J2
El Haseke, Syria 59/D2
El Haseke, Syria 63/J4
El Hilla, Sudan 111/E5
El Huecu, Argentina 143/B4
El Husn, Jordan 65/D3
Eli, Nebr. (69213) 264/C2
Elias, Ky. (40186) 237/O6
Elida, N. Mex. (88116) 274/F5
Elida, Ohio (45807) 284/B4
Elie, Manitoba 179/E5
Elie and Earlsferry, Scotland 15/F4
Elihu, Ky. (42530) 237/M6
Elijah, Mo. (†65626) 261/H9
Elila (riv.), Zaire 115/E4
Elim, Alaska (99739) 196/F2
Elimsport, Pa. (†17810) 294/H3
El Indio, Texas (78860) 303/D9
Eling, England 13/F7
Elin Pelin, Bulgaria 45/F4
Eliot○, Maine (03903) 243/B9
Eliot (mt.), Newf. 166/B2
Elisa, Argentina 143/F5
Eliska, Ala. (†36480) 195/C8
El Iskandariya (Alexandria), Egypt 59/A3
El Iskandariya (Alexandria), Egypt 111/J2
Elista, U.S.S.R. 7/J4
Elista, U.S.S.R. 48/E5
Elista, U.S.S.R. 52/F5
Elizabeth, Ark. (72531) 202/F1
Elizabeth, Colo. (80107) 208/K4
Elizabeth, Georgia (30060) 217/J1
Elizabeth, Ill. (61028) 222/C1
Elizabeth, Ind. (47117) 227/F8
Elizabeth, La. (70638) 238/E5
Elizabeth (cape), Maine 243/C8
Elizabeth (isls.), Mass. 249/L7
Elizabeth, Minn. (56533) 255/B4
Elizabeth, Miss. (38742) 256/C4
Elizabeth (mt.), New Bruns. 170/D1
Elizabeth, N.J. (*07201) 273/B2
Elizabeth, Pa. (15037) 294/C5
Elizabeth, S. Australia 88/E7
Elizabeth, S. Australia 94/B7
Elizabeth, W. Va. (26143) 312/D4
Elizabeth City, N.C. (27909) 281/S2
Elizabethton, Tenn. (37643) 237/S8
Elizabethtown, Ill. (62931) 222/E6
Elizabethtown, Ind. (47232) 227/F6
Elizabethtown, Ky. (42701) 237/K5
Elizabethtown, N.Y. (12932) 276/N2
Elizabethtown, N.C. (28337) 281/M5
Elizabethtown, Ohio (†45052) 284/A9
Elizabethtown, Pa. (17022) 294/J5
Elizabethville, Pa. (17023) 294/J4
Elizaville, Ind. (†46052) 227/E4
Elizaville, Ky. (41037) 237/O4
Elizondo, Spain 33/F1
El Jadida, Morocco 102/B1
El Jadida, Morocco 106/C2
El Jauf, Libya 102/B1
El Jauf, Libya 111/D3
El Jicaral, Nicaragua 154/D4
El Jícaro, Nicaragua 154/E4
Elk (riv.), Ala. 195/D1
Elk (riv.), Br. Col. 184/K5
Elk, Calif. (95432) 204/B4
Elk (riv.), Colo. 208/F1
Elk (co.), Kansas 232/F4
Elk (riv.), Kansas 232/F4
Elk (isl.), Manitoba 179/F4
Elk (riv.), Md. 245/P3
Elk (lake), Mich. 250/D4
Elk, N. Mex. (†88210) 274/D6
Elk (creek), Okla. 288/H4
Elk (creek), Oreg. 291/E5
Elk (co.), Pa. 294/E3
Ełk, Poland 47/F2
Elk (creek), S. Dak. 298/C5
Elk (riv.), Tenn. 237/H10
Elk (ridge), Utah 304/E6
Elk, Wash. (99009) 310/H2
Elk (riv.), W. Va. 312/D6
Elkader, Iowa (52043) 229/L3
El Kamlin, Sudan 59/B7
El Karak (dist.), Jordan 65/E5
El Karak, Jordan 59/C3
El Karak, Jordan 65/E4
El Karnak, Egypt 111/F2
El Karnak, Egypt 59/B4
Elkatawa, Ky. (41322) 237/P5
Elk City, Idaho (83525) 220/C4
Elk City, Kansas (67344) 232/G4
Elk City (lake), Kansas 232/F4
Elk City, Okla. (73644) 288/G4
Elk City, Oreg. (†97391) 291/D3
Elk Creek, Calif. (95939) 204/C4
Elk Creek, Ky. (†40071) 237/L4
Elk Creek, Mo. (65464) 261/H8
Elk Creek, Nebr. (68348) 264/H4
Elk Creek, Va. (24326) 307/F7
Elk Creek, Wis. (†54747) 317/C7
El Kef, Tunisia 106/F1
El Kelaa des Srarhna, Morocco 106/C2
Elk Falls, Kansas (67345) 232/F4
Elkford, Br. Col. 184/K5
Elkfork, Ky. (41421) 237/P5
Elk Garden, Va. (†24266) 307/E7
Elk Garden, W. Va. (26717) 312/H4
Elk Grove, Calif. (95624) 204/B9
Elk Grove Village, Ill. (60007) 222/B5
El Khalil (Hebron), West Bank 65/C4
El Khandaq, Sudan 59/B6
El Khandaq, Sudan 111/E4
El Khârga, Egypt 111/F2
El Khârga, Egypt 102/E2
El Khârga, Egypt 59/B4
Elkhart, Ill. (62634) 222/D3
Elkhart, Ind. 188/J2
Elkhart (co.), Ind. 227/F1
Elkhart, Ind. (46514) 227/F1
Elkhart (riv.), Ind. 227/F1
Elkhart, Iowa (50073) 229/F5
Elkhart, Kansas (67950) 232/A4
Elkhart, Texas (75839) 303/J6
Elkhart Lake, Wis. (53020) 317/L8
Elkhead, Mo. (65753) 261/G8
Elk Horn, Iowa (51531) 229/C5
Elkhorn, Manitoba 179/A5
Elkhorn, Nebr. (68022) 264/H3
Elkhorn (riv.), Nebr. 264/G3
Elkhorn, W. Va. (24831) 312/D8
Elkhorn, Wis. (53121) 317/J10
Elkhorn City, Ky. (41522) 237/S6
Elkhovo, Bulgaria 45/H4
Elkhurst, W. Va. (†25043) 312/D6
Elkin, N.C. (28621) 281/H2
Elkins, Ark. (72727) 202/C1
Elkins, N. Mex. (†88101) 274/E5
Elkins, W. Va. (26241) 312/G5
Elkinsville, Ind. (†47448) 227/E6
Elk Island Nat'l Park, Alberta 182/D3
Elk Island Nat'l Pk., Alta 162/E5
El Kitta, Jordan 65/D3
Elk Lake, Ontario 177/K5
Elk Lake, Ontario 175/D3
Elk Lakes Prov. Park, Br. Col. 184/K5
Elkland, Mo. (65644) 261/F8
Elkland, Pa. (16920) 294/H1
Elk Mills, Md. (21920) 245/P2
Elkmont, Ala. (35620) 195/E1
Elkmont, Tenn. (†37862) 237/O9
Elk Mound, Wis. (54739) 317/C6
Elk Mountain, Wyo. (82324) 319/F4
Elk Neck, Md. (†21901) 245/P2
Elko, Br. Col. 184/K5
Elko, Georgia (31025) 217/E6
Elko, Minn. (55020) 255/E6
Elko, Nev. 188/C2
Elko, Nev. 146/G6
Elko (co.), Nev. 266/F1
Elko, Nev. (89801) 266/F2
Elko, S.C. (29826) 296/E5
Elk Park, N.C. (28622) 281/E2
Elk Point, Alberta 182/E3
Elk Point, S. Dak. (57025) 298/R8
Elkport, Iowa (52044) 229/L3
Elk Rapids, Mich. (49629) 250/D4
Elkridge, Md. (†21227) 245/M4
Elkridge, W. Va. (†24868) 312/D6
Elk River, Idaho (83827) 220/B3
Elk River, Minn. (55330) 255/E5
Elk Run Heights, Iowa (†50700) 229/J4
Elk Springs, Colo. (81633) 208/C2
Elkton, Alberta 182/C4
Elkton, Fla. (32033) 212/E2
Elkton, Ky. (42220) 237/G7
Elkton, Md. (21921) 245/P2
Elkton, Mich. (48731) 250/F5
Elkton, Minn. (55933) 255/F7
Elkton, Mo. (†65650) 261/F7
Elkton, Oreg. (97436) 291/D4
Elkton, S. Dak. (57026) 298/S5
Elkton, Tenn. (38455) 237/H10
Elkton, Va. (22827) 307/L4
Elk Valley, Tenn. (†37848) 237/N7
Elkview, W. Va. (25071) 312/C6
Elkville, Ill. (62932) 222/D6
Elkwater, Alberta 182/E5
Elkwater, W. Va. (†26273) 312/G5
Ellabell, Georgia (31308) 217/K6
El Ladhiqiya (Latakia), Syria 59/C2
El Ladhiqiya (Latakia), Syria 63/F5
El Lago, Texas (†77586) 303/K2
Ellamar, Alaska (†99695) 196/D1
Ellamore, W. Va. (26267) 312/F5
Ellaville, Fla. (†32060) 212/C1
Ellaville, Georgia (31806) 217/D6
Ellef Ringnes (isl.), Canada 4/B15
Ellef Ringnes (isl.), N.W.T. 146/H2
Ellef Ringnes (isl.), N.W.T. 162/M3
Ellef Ringnes (isl.), N.W. Terrs. 187/H2
Ellen (mt.), Utah 304/D5
Ellen (mt.), Vt. 268/B3
Ellenboro, N.C. (28040) 281/F4
Ellenboro, W. Va. (26346) 312/D4
Ellenboro, Wis. (†53813) 317/E10
Ellenburg Center, N.Y. (12934) 276/N1
Ellenburg Depot, N.Y. (12935) 276/N1
Ellendale, Del. (19941) 245/S5
Ellendale, Minn. (56026) 255/E7
Ellendale, N. Dak. (58436) 282/N7
Ellendale, Tasmania 99/C4
Ellendale, Tenn. (38029) 237/B10
Ellendale, W. Australia 92/D2
Ellensburg, Wash. (98926) 310/E3
Ellenton, Georgia (31747) 217/E8
Ellenville, N.Y. (12428) 276/M7
Ellenwood, Georgia (30049) 217/L2
Ellerbe, N.C. (28338) 281/K4
Ellershouse, Nova Scotia 168/D4
Ellerslie, Georgia (31807) 217/C5
Ellerslie, Md. (21529) 245/C2
Ellerslie, N. Zealand 100/C1
Ellerslie, Pr. Edward I. 168/D2
Ellerton, Barbados 161/B9
Ellerton, Md. (†21773) 245/H2
Ellery, Ill. (62833) 222/E5
Ellesmere (isl.), Canada 4/B14
Ellesmere (isl.), Canada 2/F1
Ellesmere, England 13/E5
Ellesmere (lake), N. Zealand 100/D5
Ellesmere (isl.), N.W.T. 146/K1
Ellesmere (isl.), N.W.T. 162/N3
Ellesmere (isl.), N.W. Terrs. 187/K2
Ellesmere Port, England 13/G2
Ellesmere Port, England 10/F2
Ellettsville, Ind. (47429) 227/D6
Ellezelles, Belgium 27/D7
El Libertador General Bernardo O'Higgins (reg.), Chile 138/A10
Ellice (riv.), N.W. Terrs. 187/H3
Ellicott City, Md. (21043) 245/L3
Ellicottville, N.Y. (14731) 276/C6
Ellijay, Georgia (30540) 217/C1
El Limón, Nicaragua 154/E4
Ellington○, Conn. (06029) 210/F1
Ellington, Mo. (63638) 261/L8
Ellington, N.Y. (14732) 276/B6
Ellington A.F.B., Texas 303/K2
Ellinwood, Kansas (67526) 232/D3
Elliot (lake), Manitoba 179/G2
Elliot, S. Africa 118/D6
Elliot Lake, Ontario 177/B1
Elliot Lake, Ontario 175/D3
Elliott, Ark. (†71701) 202/E7
Elliott (key), Fla. 212/F6
Elliott, Ill. (60933) 222/E3
Elliott, Iowa (51532) 229/C6
Elliott (co.), Ky. 237/P4
Elliott, Md. (21823) 245/P7
Elliott, Miss. (38926) 256/E3
Elliott, N. Dak. (58025) 282/P7
Elliott, North. Terr. 88/E3
Elliott, North. Terr. 93/C4
Elliott, S.C. (29046) 296/G3
Elliott, Tasmania 99/B3
Elliott (bay), Tasmania 99/B5
Elliottsburg, Pa. (17024) 294/H5
Elliottville, Ky. (40317) 237/P4
Ellis, Idaho (83235) 220/D5
Ellis (co.), Kansas 232/C3
Ellis, Kansas (67637) 232/C3
Ellis (pond), Maine 243/B6
Ellis (riv.), Maine 243/B6
Ellis (riv.), N.H. 268/E3
Ellis (co.), Okla. 288/G2
Ellis (co.), Texas 303/H5
El Lisan (pen.), Jordan 65/C5
Ellisburg, N.Y. (13636) 276/H3
Ellis Grove, Ill. (62241) 222/D5
Ellison Bay, Wis. (54210) 317/M5
Elliston, Mont. (59728) 262/D4
Elliston, Newf. 166/D2
Elliston, Ohio (43432) 284/D2
Elliston, S. Australia 88/E6
Elliston, S. Australia 94/D5
Elliston-Lafayette, Va. (24087) 307/H6
Ellisville, Ill. (61431) 222/C3
Ellisville, Miss. (39437) 256/F7
Ellisville, Mo. (†63011) 261/M3
Ellisville, Wis. (†54217) 317/L7
Ellon, Scotland 10/E2
Ellon, Scotland 15/F3
Elloree, S.C. (29047) 296/F4
Elloughton, England 13/G4
Ells (riv.), Alberta 182/D1
Ellscott, Alberta 182/D2
Ellsinore, Mo. (63937) 261/L9
Ellston, Iowa (50074) 229/E7
Ellsworth (hill), Conn. 210/B1
Ellsworth, Ill. (61737) 222/E3
Ellsworth, Iowa (50075) 229/F4
Ellsworth (co.), Kansas 232/D3
Ellsworth, Kansas (67439) 232/D3
Ellsworth, Maine (04605) 243/F6
Ellsworth, Mich. (49729) 250/D3
Ellsworth, Minn. (56129) 255/C7
Ellsworth, Nebr. (69340) 264/B2
Ellsworth○, N.H. (†03264) 268/D4
Ellsworth (lake), Okla. 288/K5
Ellsworth, Pa. (15331) 294/B5
Ellsworth, Wis. (54011) 317/A6
Ellsworth A.F.B., S. Dak. 298/C5
Ellsworth Land (reg.) 5/B14
Ellwangen, W. Germany 22/D4
Ellwood City, Pa. (16117) 294/B4
Elm (riv.), N. Dak. 282/R5
Elm (riv.), N. Dak. 282/N8
Elm (creek), S. Dak. 298/D4
Elm (riv.), S. Dak. 298/M2
Elm, Switzerland 39/H3
Elma, Iowa (50628) 229/J2
Elma, Manitoba 179/G5
Elma, N.Y. (14059) 276/C5
Elma, Wash. (98541) 310/B4
El Macao, Dom. Rep. 158/F6
El Madwar, Jordan 65/E3
El Mafraq, Jordan 65/E3
El Mahalla el Kubra, Egypt 111/J3
El Maitén, Argentina 143/B5
El Majdal, Jordan 65/D3
Elmalı, Turkey 63/C4
El Managil, Sudan 111/F5
El Mansûra, Egypt 111/K3
El Mansûra, Egypt 59/B3
El Manteco, Venezuela 124/G4
El Manzano, Chile 138/F5
El Ma'qil, Iraq 66/E5
El Marj, Libya 102/E1
El Marj, Libya 111/D1
El Marmol, Mexico 150/B2
Elm City, N.C. (27822) 281/O3
Elm Creek, Manitoba 179/E5
Elm Creek, Nebr. (68836) 264/E4
Elmdale, Kansas (66850) 232/F3
Elmdale, Minn. (†56314) 255/D5
Elmendorf, Texas (78112) 303/K11
Elmendorf A.F.B., Alaska 196/B1
Elmer, La. (71424) 238/E4
Elmer, Minn. (†55765) 255/F3
Elmer, Mo. (63538) 261/G3
Elmer, N.J. (08318) 273/C4
Elmer, Okla. (73539) 288/H6
Elmer City, Wash. (99124) 310/G2
Elm Fork, Trinity (riv.), Texas 303/G2
Elm Grove, La. (71051) 238/C2
Elm Grove, Wis. (53122) 317/K1
Elmhurst, Ill. (60126) 222/B5
Elmhurst, Pa. (18416) 294I)F7
El Miamo, Venezuela 124/H4
El Milagro, Argentina 143/C3
Elmina, Ghana 106/D8
El Minya, Egypt 102/F2
El Minya, Egypt 59/B4
El Minya, Egypt 111/J4
Elmira, Ill. (†61483) 222/D2
Elmira, Mich. (49730) 250/E3
Elmira, Mo. (†64062) 261/D3
Elmira, N.Y. 188/L2
Elmira, N.Y. (*14901) 276/G6
Elmira, Ontario 177/D4
Elmira, Oreg. (97437) 291/D3
Elmira, Pr. Edward I. 168/F2
Elmira, W. Va. (26618) 312/E5
El Mirage, Ariz. (85335) 198/C5
Elmira Heights, N.Y. (14903) 276/G6
El Misti (mt.), Peru 128/G11
Elmo, Kansas (†67451) 232/E3
Elmo, Mo. (64445) 261/B1
Elmo, Mont. (59915) 262/B3
Elmo, Texas (75118) 303/H5
Elmo, Utah (84521) 304/D4
Elmo, Wyo. (†82327) 319/F4
Elmodel, Georgia (31748) 217/D8
Elmont, Kansas (†66603) 232/G2
Elmont, N.Y. (11003) 276/P7
El Monte, Calif. (*91731) 204/D10
El Monte, Chile 138/G4
Elmora, Pa. (15737) 294/E4
Elmore (co.), Ala. 195/F5
Elmore, Ala. (36025) 195/F5
Elmore (co.), Idaho 220/C6
Elmore, Minn. (56027) 255/D7
Elmore, Ohio (43416) 284/D3
Elmore City, Okla. (73035) 288/M5
El Morro, N. Mex. (†87321) 274/A3
El Morro Nat'l Mon., N. Mex. 274/A3
Elm Park, La. (†70775) 238/H5
El Mraiti (well), Mali 106/D5
El Mrayer (well), Mauritania 106/C4
El Mreïti (well), Mauritania 106/C4
Elmrock, Ky. (41624) 237/P6
Elmsdale, Nova Scotia 168/E4
Elmsdale, Pr. Edward I. 168/D2
Elmsford, N.Y. (10523) 276/O6
Elmshorn, W. Germany 22/C2
Elm Springs, Ark. (72728) 202/B1
Elm Springs, S. Dak. (57736) 298/D5
Elmsvale, Nova Scotia 168/E3
Elmvale, Ontario 177/E3
Elmville, Conn. (†06239) 210/H1
Elmwood, Conn. (06110) 210/D2
Elmwood, Ill. (61529) 222/D3
Elmwood, Mass. (02337) 249/L4
Elmwood, Nebr. (68349) 264/H4
Elmwood, Okla. (73935) 288/F1
Elmwood, Ontario 177/C3
Elmwood, Wis. (54740) 317/B6
Elmwood Park, Ill. (60635) 222/B5
Elmwood Park, N.J. (†07407) 273/B2
Elmwood Park, Wis. (†53401) 317/M3
Elmwood Place, Ohio (45216) 284/B9
Elmworth, Alberta 182/A2
Elne, France 28/E6
El Nido, Calif. (95317) 204/E6
El Nido, Philippines 82/B5
El Ñilhue, Chile 138/G2
Elnora, Alberta 182/D3
Elnora, Ind. (47529) 227/C7
El Obeid, Sudan 102/E3
El Obeid, Sudan 59/B7
El Obeid, Sudan 111/E5
Elobey (isls.), Equat. Guinea 115/A3
El Odaiya, Sudan 111/E5
Eloff, S. Africa 118/J6
Eloi (bay), La. 238/M7
Elon, Ala. (†35760) 195/F1
Elon College, N.C. (27244) 281/L2
Elora, Ontario 177/D4
Elora, Tenn. (37328) 237/J10
El Oro (prov.), Ecuador 128/C4
Elortondo, Argentina 143/F6
Elorza, Venezuela 124/D4
El Oso, Venezuela 124/H5
El Oued, Algeria 106/F2
Eloy, Ariz. (85231) 198/D6
El Pájaro, Colombia 126/D2
El Palmar, Chuquisaca, Bolivia 136/D7
El Palmar, Santa Cruz, Bolivia 136/D5
El Palmar, Tarija, Bolivia 136/D7
El Palmar, Venezuela 124/G4
El Pao, Anzoátegui, Venezuela 124/F3
El Pao, Bolívar, Venezuela 124/G3
El Pao, Cojedes, Venezuela 124/D3
El Paraíso, Colombia 126/C7
El Paraíso, Copán, Honduras 154/C3
El Paraíso, El Paraíso, Honduras 154/D4
El Pardo, Spain 33/F4
El Paso, Ark. (72045) 202/F3
El Paso (co.), Colo. 208/K5
El Paso, Ill. (61738) 222/D3
El Paso (co.), Texas 303/A10
El Paso, Texas 146/H6
El Paso, Texas 188/E4
El Paso, Texas (*79901) 303/A10
El Paso, U.S. 2/D4
El Pato, Colombia 126/C6
El Perú, Bolivia 136/B3
El Perú, Venezuela 124/H4
Elphin, Ireland 17/E4
Elphinstone, Manitoba 179/B4
El Pico, Bolivia 136/C4
El Pilar, Cuba 158/G3
El Pilar, Venezuela 124/G2
El Pintado, Argentina 143/D1
El Piquete, Argentina 143/D1
El Portal, Calif. (95318) 204/F6
El Portal, Fla. (†33101) 212/B4
El Portugués, Peru 128/C7
El Porvenir, Honduras 154/D3
El Porvenir, Mexico 150/G1
El Porvenir, N. Mex. (†87731) 274/D3
El Porvenir, Panama 154/H6
El Potosí, Mexico 150/J4
El Pozo, Dom. Rep. 158/E5
El Prado, N. Mex. (87529) 274/D2
El Progreso, Ecuador 128/C9
El Progreso, Guatemala 154/B3
El Progreso, Honduras 154/D3
El Puente, Santa Cruz, Bolivia 136/D5
El Puente, Tarija, Bolivia 136/C7
El Puerto de Santa María, Spain 33/C4
El Pun, Ecuador 128/D2
El Qâhira (Cairo) (cap.), Egypt 59/B4
El Qâhira (Cairo) (cap.), Egypt 111/J3
El Qantara, Egypt 111/K3
El Qantara, Egypt 59/B3
El Qasr, Egypt 111/E2
El Qasr, Egypt 59/A4
El Quadmus, Syria 63/F5
El Quebrachal, Argentina 143/D2
Elqui (riv.), Chile 138/A8
El Quisco, Chile 138/E3
El Quneitra (prov.), Syria 63/F6
El Quneitra, Syria 63/F6
El Quryatein, Syria 63/G5
El Quseir, Egypt 102/F2
El Quseir, Egypt 59/B4
El Quseir, Egypt 111/F2
El Quseir, Syria 63/G5
El Quweira, Jordan 65/E5
Elrama, Pa. (15038) 294/C5
El Rashid, Syria 63/H5
El Rashid, Syria 59/C2
El Rastro, Venezuela 124/E3
El Real de Santa María, Panama 154/J6
El Realejo, Nicaragua 154/D4
El Reno, Okla. (73036) 288/K3
El Rio, Calif. (†93030) 204/F9
El Rito, N. Mex. (87530) 274/C2
El Rito (riv.), N. Mex. 274/C2
Elrod, Ala. (35458) 195/C4
Elrod, Ind. (†47018) 227/G6
El Roque, Venezuela 124/E2
Elrosa, Minn. (56325) 255/C5
El Rosario, Estero (riv.), Chile 138/F3
El Rosario, Mexico 150/B1
Elrose, Sask. 181/D4
Elroy, Wis. (53929) 317/F8
Elsa, Texas (78543) 303/G11
Elsa, Yukon 187/E3
Elsah, Ill. (62028) 222/C5
El Salado, Dom. Rep. 158/F6
El Salto, Mexico 150/G5
El Salvador 2/E5
El Salvador 146/J8
El Salvador, C. Rica 154/F5
EL SALVADOR 154/C4
El Samán de Apure, Venezuela 124/D4
El Santo, Cuba 158/E1
Elsas, Ontario 175/D3
El Sauce, Nicaragua 154/D4
Elsberry, Mo. (63343) 261/L4
Elsburg, S. Africa 118/H6
El Segundo, Calif. (90245) 204/B11
El Seibo (prov.), Dom. Rep. 158/F6
El Seibo, Dom. Rep. 158/F6
Elsey, Mo. (†65633) 261/E9
Elsie, Mich. (48831) 250/E5
Elsie, Nebr. (69134) 264/C4
Elsie, Oreg. (†97138) 291/D2
Elsiesrivier, S. Africa 118/F6
Elsinore (lake), Calif. 204/E11
Elsinore, Utah (84724) 304/B5
Elsmere, Del. (†19801) 245/R2
Elsmere, Ky. (†41018) 237/R2
Elsmere, Nebr. (69135) 264/D2
Elsmore, Kansas (66732) 232/G4
El Socorro, Venezuela 124/F3
El Sollum (gulf), Egypt 111/E1
El Sombrero, Venezuela 124/E3
Elst, Netherlands 27/H5
Elster, Black (riv.), E. Germany 22/E3
Elster, White (riv.), E. Germany 22/E3
Elston, Ind. (†47901) 227/D4
Elstow, Sask. 181/E4
El Tabo, Chile 138/F3
El Tambo, Colombia 126/B6
El Teleno (mt.), Spain 33/C1
Eltham, N. Zealand 100/E3
Eltham, Victoria 97/J4
Eltham, Victoria 88/L6
El Tiemblo, Spain 33/D2
El Tigre, Venezuela 120/C2
El Tigre, Venezuela 124/F3
El Tocuyo, Venezuela 124/C3
El Tofo, Chile 138/A7
Elton, La. (70532) 238/E6
El'ton, U.S.S.R. 52/G5
Elton, W. Va. (25965) 312/E7
Elton, Wis. (54430) 317/J5
Eltopia, Wash. (99330) 310/G4
El Toro, Calif. (92630) 204/E11
El Toro (mt.), P. Rico 161/F2
El Toro, Venezuela 124/H3
El Toro Marine Air Sta., Calif. 204/D11
El Tránsito, Chile 138/B7
El Triunfo, Honduras 154/D4
El Tucuche (mt.), Trin. & Tob. 161/B10
El Tûr, Egypt 111/F2
El Tur, Egypt 59/B4
Eluru, India 68/E5
El' Uweinat, Libya 111/B2
Elva, Manitoba 179/A5
Elva, U.S.S.R. 53/D1
El Vado, N. Mex. (†87575) 274/C2
Elvas, Portugal 33/C3
Elvaston, Ill. (62334) 222/B3
Elverson, Pa. (19520) 294/L5
Elverum, Norway 18/G6
El Viejo, Nicaragua 154/D4
El Vigía, Venezuela 124/C3
El Vinculo, Venezuela 124/D1
Elvins, Mo. (63639) 261/L7
Elvira, Iowa (†52732) 229/N5

366 Elvira

Elvira (isl.), N.W. Terrs. 187/H2
El Volcán, Chile 138/B10
El Wak, Kenya 115/H3
El War (well), Niger 106/G4
El Wasta, Egypt 111/J3
Elwell, Mich. (48832) 250/E5
Elwell (lake), Mont. 262/E2
Elwha (riv.), Wash. 310/B3
Elwood, Ill. (60421) 222/E2
Elwood, Ind. (46036) 227/F4
Elwood, Iowa (52226) 229/M4
Elwood, Kansas (66024) 232/H2
Elwood, Nebr. (68937) 264/E4
Elwood, N.J. (08217) 273/D4
Elwood, N.Y. (11731) 276/O9
Elwood, Utah (†84337) 304/B2
Ely, England 13/H5
Ely, England 10/G4
Ely, Iowa (52227) 229/K5
Ely, Minn. (55731) 255/G3
Ely, Nev. 188/D3
Ely, Nev. (89301) 266/G3
Ely (range), Nev. 266/G4
Ely, Vt. (05044) 268/C4
Ely (riv.), Wales 13/B7
El Yaduda, Jordan 65/D4
El Yagual, Venezuela 124/D4
Elyakim, Israel 65/C2
Elyashiv, Israel 65/B3
Elyria, Kansas (†67460) 232/E3
Elyria, Nebr. (68837) 264/E3
Elyria, Ohio (*44035) 284/F3
Elysburg, Pa. (17824) 294/K4
Elysian, Minn. (56028) 255/E6
Elysian Fields, Texas (75642) 303/L5
Elysian Grove, Tenn. (†37185) 237/F8
El Yunque (mt.), P. Rico 161/F1
El Zacatón, Mexico 150/J5
Elze, W. Germany 22/C2
Emanguk (Emmonak), Alaska (99581) 196/E2
Emanuel (co.), Georgia 217/H5
Emba, U.S.S.R. 48/F5
Emba (riv.), U.S.S.R. 48/F5
Embar, Newf. 166/A3
Embarcación, Argentina 143/D1
Embarras (riv.), Ill. 222/E4
Embarras Airport, Alberta 182/C5
Embarrass, Minn. (55732) 255/F3
Embarrass, Wis. (54933) 317/J6
Embden (pond), Maine 243/D6
Embden, N. Dak. (†58079) 282/R6
Emblem, Wyo. (82422) 319/D1
Embo, Scotland 15/E3
Emboscada, Paraguay 144/B4
Embree, Newf. 166/C4
Embreeville, Pa. (†19320) 294/L6
Embreeville Junction, Tenn. (†37601) 237/R8
Embro, Ontario 177/C4
Embrun, France 28/G5
Embrun, Ontario 177/J2
Embu, Kenya 115/G4
Embudo, N. Mex. (87531) 274/C2
Emden, Ill. (62635) 222/D3
Emden, Mo. (63439) 261/J3
Emden, W. Germany 22/B2
Emeigh, Pa. (15738) 294/E4
Emelle, Ala. (35459) 195/B5
Emerado, N. Dak. (58228) 282/R4
Emerald (isl.), N.W. Terrs. 187/G2
Emerald, Queensland 88/H4
Emerald, Queensland 95/C4
Emerald, Wis. (54012) 317/B5
Emerald Isle, N.C. (†28557) 281/P5
Emero (riv.), Bolivia 136/B3
Emerson, Ark. (71740) 202/D7
Emerson, Georgia (30137) 217/C2
Emerson, Iowa (51533) 229/C6
Emerson, Man. 162/G6
Emerson, Manitoba 179/E5
Emerson, Nebr. (68733) 264/H2
Emerson, N.J. (07630) 273/B1
Emerson, N.C. (28433) 281/M6
Emery, S. Dak. (57332) 298/O6
Emery (co.), Utah 304/D4
Emery, Utah (84522) 304/C5
Emery Mills, Maine (04031) 243/B8
Emeryville, Calif. (94608) 204/J2
Emeryville, Ontario 177/B5
Emet, Turkey 63/C3
Emida, Idaho (†83861) 220/B2
Emigrant, Mont. (59027) 262/F5
Emigrant (peak), Mont. 262/F5
Emigrant (peak), Nev. 266/C5
Emigsville, Pa. (17318) 294/J5
Emi Koussi (mt.), Chad 102/D3
Emi Koussi (mt.), Chad 111/C4
Emilia-Romagna (reg.), Italy 34/C2
Emilio Ayarza, Argentina 143/F7
Emily, Minn. (56447) 255/E4
Emily (lake), Minn. 255/C5
Emin (Dorbiljin), China 77/B2
Emine (cape), Bulgaria 45/J4
Eminence, Ind. (46125) 227/D5
Eminence, Ky. (40019) 237/L4
Eminence, Mo. (65466) 261/K8
Emington, Ill. (60934) 222/E3
Emirau (isl.), Papua N.G. 86/B1
Emirdağ, Turkey 63/D3
Emir Dağı (mt.), Turkey 63/D3
Emir Daği (mt.), Turkey 59/B2
Emirgazi, Turkey 63/E4
Emison, Ind. (47530) 227/C7
Emita, Tasmania 99/D2
Emlenton, Pa. (16373) 294/C3
Emlyn, Ky. (40730) 237/N7
Emma, Ill. (62834) 222/E6
Emma, Ind. (†46571) 227/F1
Emma, Ky. (41625) 237/R5
Emma, Mo. (65327) 261/F5
Emma (range), Suriname 131/C4
Emmaboda, Sweden 18/J8
Emmalane, Georgia (†30442) 217/H5
Emmastad, Neth. Ant. 161/F9
Emmaus, Pa. (18049) 294/M4
Emmaus, Virgin Is. (U.S.) 161/C4
Emmaville, N.S. Wales 97/F1
Emmeloord, Netherlands 27/H3
Emmen, Netherlands 27/K3
Emmen, Switzerland 39/F2
Emmendingen, W. Germany 22/B4
Emmental (riv.), Switzerland 39/E3
Emmerich, W. Germany 22/B3
Emmet, Ark. (71835) 202/D6
Emmet (co.), Iowa 229/D2
Emmet (co.), Mich. 250/E3
Emmet, Nebr. (68734) 264/F2
Emmet, N. Dak. (58534) 282/G4
Emmet, Queensland 88/G4
Emmet, Queensland 95/C5
Emmetsburg, Iowa (50536) 229/D2
Emmett, Idaho (83617) 220/B6
Emmett, Kansas (66422) 232/F2
Emmett, Mich. (48022) 250/G6
Emmitsburg, Md. (21727) 245/J2
Emmonak, Alaska (99581) 196/E2
Emmons, Minn. (56029) 255/E7
Emmons (co.), N. Dak. 282/K7
Emmons (mt.), Utah 304/D3
Emneth, England 13/H5
Emo, Ontario 175/B3
Emo, Ontario 177/F5
Emory (riv.), Tenn. 237/M8
Emory, Texas (75440) 303/J5
Emory (peak), Texas 303/A8
Emory Gap, Tenn. (37735) 237/M9
Emory-Meadowview, Va. (24327) 307/E7
Emoryville, W. Va. (†26717) 312/H4
Empalme, Mexico 150/D2
Empalme Olmos, Uruguay 145/B6
Empangeni, S. Africa 118/E5
Empedrado, Argentina 143/E2
Empedrado, Chile 138/A11
Empexa (salt dep.), Bolivia 136/A7
Empire, Ala. (35063) 195/D3
Empire, Calif. (95319) 204/D6
Empire, Colo. (80438) 208/H3
Empire (res.), Colo. 208/L2
Empire, Georgia (31026) 217/F6
Empire, La. (70050) 238/L8
Empire, Mich. (49630) 250/C4
Empire, Ohio (43926) 284/J5
Empire City, Okla. (†73529) 288/L6
Empire Landing, Ariz. (85344) 198/A4
Empoli, Italy 34/C3
Emporia, Fla. (†32080) 212/E2
Emporia, Ind. (†46056) 227/F5
Emporia, Kans. 188/G3
Emporia, Kansas (66801) 232/F3
Emporia (I.C.), Va. (23847) 307/N7
Emporium, Pa. (15834) 294/F2
Empress, Alberta 182/E4
Empress Augusta (bay), Papua N.G. 86/C2
'Emrani, Iran 66/L3
Emrick, N. Dak. (†58422) 282/L4
Ems (riv.), W. Germany 22/B2
Emsdale, Ontario 177/E2
Emsdetten, W. Germany 22/B2
Emsworth, Pa. (15202) 294/B6
Emyvale, Ireland 17/G3
Enarotali, Indonesia 85/K6
Enard (bay), Scotland 15/C2
Enaville, Idaho (83829) 220/B2
Encampment, Wyo. (82325) 319/F4
Encampment (riv.), Wyo. 319/F4
Encarnación, Paraguay 120/D5
Encarnación, Paraguay 144/E5
Encarnación de Díaz, Mexico 150/H6
Enchant, Alberta 182/D4
Enchi, Ghana 106/D7
Encinal, Texas (78019) 303/E9
Encinitas, Calif. (92024) 204/H10
Encino, Calif. (91316) 204/B10
Encino, N. Mex. (88321) 274/D4
Encino, Texas (78353) 303/F11
Enciso, Colombia 126/E7
Encontrados, Venezuela 124/B3
Encounter (bay), S. Australia 88/F7
Encounter (bay), S. Australia 94/F6
Encrucijada, Cuba 158/E1
Endako, Br. Col. 184/E3
Ende, Indonesia 85/G7
Endeavor, Pa. (16322) 294/D2
Endeavor (str.), Queensland 88/G2
Endeavor, Wis. (53930) 317/G8
Endeavour (str.), Queensland 95/B1
Endeavour, Sask. 181/J3
Endee, N. Mex. (†88411) 274/F3
Endelave (isl.), Denmark 21/D6
Enderbury (isl.), Kiribati 87/J6
Enderby, Br. Col. 184/H5
Enderby Land (reg.) Ant. 2/M9
Enderby Land (reg.) 5/B3
Enderlin, N. Dak. (58027) 282/P6
Enders, Nebr. (69027) 264/C4
Enders (res.), Nebr. 264/C4
Endiang, Alberta 182/D4
Endicott (mts.), Alaska 196/H1
Endicott, Nebr. (68350) 264/G4
Endicott, N.Y. (13760) 276/H6
Endicott, S. Africa 118/J6
Endicott, Wash. (99125) 310/H4
Endless (lake), Maine 243/F4
Endrick Water (riv.), Scotland 15/B1
Endrőd, Hungary 41/F3
Endwell, N.Y. (13760) 276/H6
Ene (riv.), Peru 128/E8
Energy, Ill. (62933) 222/E6
Enes, Hungary 41/F2
Enetai, Wash. (†98310) 310/A2
Enewetak (Eniwetok) (atoll), Marshall Is. 87/G4
Enez, Turkey 63/B2
Enfield, Conn. (06082) 210/E1
Enfield○, Conn. (06082) 210/E1
Enfield, England 13/H7
Enfield, England 10/B5
Enfield, Ill. (62835) 222/E5
Enfield, Maine (04433) 243/F5
Enfield○, Maine (04433) 243/F5
Enfield, Minn. (†55362) 255/E5
Enfield, N.H. (03748) 268/C4
Enfield○, N.H. (03748) 268/C4
Enfield, N.C. (27823) 281/O2
Enfield, Nova Scotia 168/E4
Enfield, S. Australia 88/D7
Enfield, S. Australia 94/B7
Enfield Center, N.H. (03749) 268/C4
Enfield P.O. (Thompsonville), Conn. (06082) 210/E1
Engadine, Mich. (49827) 250/D2
Engadine (valley), Switzerland 39/K3
Engaño (cape), Dom. Rep. 158/F6
Engaño (cape), Philippines 82/D1
Engaño (cape), Philippines 54/O8
Engelberg, Switzerland 39/F3
Engelhard, N.C. (27824) 281/T3
Engelhartszell, Austria 41/B2
Engel's, U.S.S.R. 7/J3
Engel's, U.S.S.R. 52/G4
Engel's, U.S.S.R. 48/E4
Engen, Br. Col. 184/E3
Enggano (isl.), Indonesia 85/C7
Enghien, Belgium 27/D7
Engi, Switzerland 39/H3
England, Ark. (72046) 202/G4
ENGLAND 13
ENGLAND 10/F5
England, U.K. 7/D3
England A.F.B., La. 238/E4
Engle, N. Mex. (†87935) 274/B5
Englee, Newf. 166/C3
Englefeld, Sask. 181/G3
Englehart, Ont. 162/H6
Englehart, Ontario 177/K5
Englehart, Ontario 175/E3
Englevale, Kansas (†66756) 232/H4
Englevale, N. Dak. (58028) 282/P7
Englewood, Colo. (†80110) 208/K3
Englewood, Fla. (33533) 212/D5
Englewood, Kansas (67840) 232/C4
Englewood, N.J. (*07631) 273/C2
Englewood, Ohio (45322) 284/B6
Englewood, Tenn. (37329) 237/M10
Englewood Cliffs, N.J. (07632) 273/C2
English (chan.) 7/D4
English (chan.), Chan. Is. 13/D8
English (chan.), England 13/D8
English (chan.), England 10/E6
English (chan.), France 28/B3
English, Ind. (47118) 227/E8
English, Ky. (†41008) 237/L3
English (riv.), Ontario 175/B2
English, W. Va. (24832) 312/C8
English Bay, Alaska (99603) 196/B2
English Bazar, India 68/F3
English Coast (reg.) 5/B15
English Creek, N.J. (†08330) 273/D5
English Harbour, Newf. 166/D2
English Harbour West, Newf. 166/C4
English Lake, Ind. (46366) 227/D2
Englishman (bay), Maine 243/J6
English River, Ontario 177/G5
English River, Ontario 175/B3
Englishtown, N.J. (07726) 273/E3
Englishtown, Nova Scotia 168/H2
Énguera, Spain 33/F3
Enid, Miss. (38927) 256/E2
Enid (lake), Miss. 256/E2
Enid, Mont. (59220) 262/M3
Enid, Okla. 188/G3
Enid, Okla. (73701) 288/L2
Enid (mt.), W. Australia 92/B3
Enigma, Georgia (31749) 217/F8
Enilda, Alberta 182/B2
Eniwa, Japan 81/K2
Enka, N.C. (28728) 281/D3
Enkeldoorn, Zimbabwe 118/E3
Enkhuizen, Netherlands 27/G3
Enköping, Sweden 18/G1
Enmore, Guyana 131/C2
Enna (prov.), Italy 34/E6
Enna, Italy 34/E6
Ennadai (lake), N.W. Terrs. 187/H3
En Nahud, Sudan 111/E5
En Nahud, Sudan 102/E3
En Naqura, Lebanon 63/F6
En Nebk, Syria 59/C3
En Nebk, Syria 63/G5
Ennedi (plat.), Chad 111/D4
Ennell (lake), Ireland 17/G5
Ennenda, Switzerland 39/H3
Ennery, Haiti 158/C5
Enngonia, N.S. Wales 97/C1
Enning, S. Dak. (57737) 298/E4
Ennis, Ireland 10/B4
Ennis, Ireland 17/D6
Ennis, Ky. (†42337) 237/H6
Ennis, Mont. (59729) 262/E5
Ennis (lake), Mont. 262/E5
Ennis, Texas (75119) 303/H5
Enniscorthy, Ireland 17/J7
Enniscorthy, Ireland 10/C4
Enniskerry, Ireland 17/J5
Enniskillen, New Bruns. 170/D3
Enniskillen, N. Ireland 10/C3
Enniskillen, N. Ireland 17/F3
Ennistymon, Ireland 10/B4
Ennistymon, Ireland 17/C6
Enns, Austria 41/C2
Enns (riv.), Austria 41/C3
Enoch, Utah (†84720) 304/A6
Enoch, W. Va. (†25043) 312/E6
Enochs, Texas (79324) 303/B4
Enoggera, Queensland 88/K2
Enoggera (creek), Queensland 95/D2
Enola, Ark. (72047) 202/F3
Enola, Pa. (17025) 294/J5
Enon, Mo. (†65074) 261/G6
Enon, Ohio (45323) 284/C6
Enontekiö, Finland 18/N2
Enon Valley, Pa. (16120) 294/B4
Enoree, S.C. (29335) 296/D2
Enoree (riv.), S.C. 296/C2
Enos, Ind. (†47963) 227/C2
Enosburg Falls, Vt. (05450) 268/B2
Enrage (cape), New Bruns. 170/F3
Enrile, Philippines 82/C2
Enrique Carbó, Argentina 143/G6
Enriquillo, Dom. Rep. 158/D7
Enriquillo, Dom. Rep. 156/D3
Enriquillo (lake), Dom. Rep. 158/C6
Ens, Sask. 181/F3
Enschede, Netherlands 27/K4
Ensenada, Argentina 143/H7
Ensenada, Mexico 150/A1
Ensenada, P. Rico 161/B3
Enshi, China 77/G5
Ensign, Alberta 182/D4
Ensign, Kansas (67841) 232/B4
Ensign, Mich. (†49878) 250/C3
Ensley, Fla. (32504) 212/B6
Ent A.F.B., Colo. 208/K5
Entebbe, Uganda 115/F4
Entebbe, Uganda 102/F5
Enterprise, Ala. (36330) 195/G8
Enterprise, Calif. (96001) 204/C3
Enterprise, Guyana 131/B2
Enterprise, Kansas (67441) 232/E3
Enterprise, La. (71425) 238/G3
Enterprise, Miss. (39330) 256/G6
Enterprise, N.W. Terrs. 187/G3
Enterprise, Ohio (†43138) 284/F6
Enterprise, Okla. (†74561) 288/R4
Enterprise, Ontario 177/H3
Enterprise, Oreg. (97828) 291/K2
Enterprise, Utah (84725) 304/A6
Enterprise, W. Va. (26568) 312/F4
Entiat, Wash. (98822) 310/E3
Entiat (lake), Wash. 310/E3
Entiat (mts.), Wash. 310/E2
Entiat (riv.), Wash. 310/E3
Entlebuch, Switzerland 39/F3
Entrance, Alberta 182/B3
Entrejo, Neth. Ant. 161/E8
Entrelacs, Québec 172/C3
Entrepeñas (res.), Spain 33/E2
Entre Ríos (prov.), Argentina 143/E3
Entre Ríos, Bolivia 136/C7
Entre Rios, Brazil 132/C4
Entre Rios de Minas, Brazil 135/D2
Entriken, Pa. (16638) 294/F5
Entwistle, Alberta 182/C3
Enugu, Nigeria 102/C4
Enugu, Nigeria 106/F7
Enumclaw, Wash. (98022) 310/D3
Envigado, Colombia 126/C4
Enville, Tenn. (38332) 237/E10
Enwarak (mt.), Guyana 131/B3
Enyellé, Congo 115/C3
Enying, Hungary 41/E3
Enzeli, Iran 66/F2
Enzeli, Iran 59/E2
Eola, La. (71332) 238/F5
Eola, Texas (76937) 303/E6
Eolia, Ky. (40826) 237/R6
Eolia, Mo. (63344) 261/L4
Eoline, Ala. (35042) 195/D4
Epe, Netherlands 27/H4
Epéna, Congo 115/C3
Epéna, Congo 102/D4
Epenarra, North. Terr. 93/D6
Épernay, France 28/E3
Epes, Ala. (35460) 195/B5
Ephesus, Georgia (†30217) 217/B4
Ephesus (ruins), Turkey 63/B3
Ephraim, Utah (84627) 304/C4
Ephraim, Wis. (54211) 317/M5
Ephrata, Pa. (17522) 294/K5
Ephrata, Wash. (98823) 310/F3
Ephratah, N.Y. (†13339) 276/L4
Épinal, France 28/G3
Épinay-sur-Seine, France 28/B1
Epiphany, S. Dak. (†57321) 298/O6
Epira, Guyana 131/C3
Epirus (reg.), Greece 45/E6
Episkopi, Cyprus 63/E5
Eport, Loch (inlet), Scotland 15/A3
Epoufette, Mich. (†49762) 250/D2
Epping, England 13/H7
Epping, England 10/C5
Epping, N.H. (03042) 268/E5
Epping○, N.H. (03042) 268/E5
Epping, N. Dak. (58843) 282/D3
Epps, La. (71237) 238/G1
Epsie, Mont. (†59317) 262/L5
Epsom, Ind. (†47568) 227/C7
Epsom○, N.H. (03234) 268/E5
Epsom and Ewell, England 13/G8
Epsom and Ewell, England 10/B6
Epukiro, Namibia 118/B4
Epworth, Georgia (30541) 217/D1
Epworth, Iowa (52045) 229/M4
Equality, Ala. (36026) 195/F5
Equality, Ill. (62934) 222/E6
Equateur (prov.), Zaire 115/D3
Equator 2/H5
Equatoria, Eastern (prov.), Sudan 111/F6
Equatoria, Western (prov.), Sudan 111/E6
Equatorial Guinea 2/K5
Equatorial Guinea 102/C4
EQUATORIAL GUINEA 115/A3
Equinox (mt.), Vt. 268/A5
Equinunk, Pa. (18417) 294/M2
Era, Ohio (†43143) 284/D6
Era, Texas (76238) 303/G4
Eran, Philippines 82/A6
Erath, La. (70533) 238/F7
Erath (co.), Texas 303/F5
Erbaa, Turkey 63/G2
Erbach, W. Germany 22/C4
Erbacon, W. Va. (26203) 312/E5
Erbil (gov.), Iraq 66/C3
Erbil, Iraq 59/D2
Erbil, Iraq 54/F6
Erbil, Iraq 66/D2
Erçek (lake), Turkey 63/K3
Ercilla, Chile 138/E2
Erciş, Turkey 59/D2
Erciş, Turkey 63/K3
Erciyas Dağı (mt.), Turkey 63/F3
Érd, Hungary 41/E3
Erdahl, Minn. (†56531) 255/C5
Erdek, Turkey 63/B2
Erdemli, Turkey 63/F4
Erdenetsagaan, Mongolia 77/J2
Erdőtelek, Hungary 41/F3
Erebato (riv.), Venezuela 124/F5
Ereen, Mongolia 77/H2
Ereğli, Turkey 63/D2
Ereğli, Turkey 59/B2
Ereğli, Turkey 63/F4
Erenhot, China 77/H3
Erenhot, China 54/N5
Erenköy, Turkey 63/D6
Eresma (riv.), Spain 33/D2
Erexim, Brazil 132/C9
Érezée, Belgium 27/G8
Erfoud, Morocco 106/D2
Erfurt, E. Germany 7/F3
Erfurt (dist.), E. Germany 22/D3
Erfurt, E. Germany 22/D3
Ergani, Turkey 63/H3
Ergene (riv.), Turkey 63/B2
Ërgli, U.S.S.R. 53/C2
Ergun He (Argun') (riv.), China 77/K1
Ergun Youqi, China 77/K1
Ergun Zuoqi, China 77/K1
Ergun Zuoqi, China 54/O4
Er Hai (lake), China 77/F6
Erhard, Minn. (56534) 255/B4
Eriboll, Loch (inlet), Scotland 15/D2
Erica, Netherlands 27/K3
Erica, Victoria 97/D5
Erice, Italy 34/D5
Ericeira, Portugal 33/B3
Erichsen (lake), N.W. Terrs. 187/K2
Ericht, Loch (lake), Scotland 15/D4
Erick, Okla. (73645) 288/G4
Erickson, Br. Col. 184/J5
Erickson, Manitoba 179/C4
Ericsburg, Minn. (†56649) 255/E2
Ericson, Nebr. (68637) 264/F3
Erie (lake) 146/K5
Erie (lake) 188/K2
Erie (lake) 162/H7
Erie, Colo. (80516) 208/K2
Erie, Ill. (61250) 222/C2
Erie, Kansas (66733) 232/G4
Erie, Mich. (48133) 250/F7
Erie (lake), Mich. 250/G7
Erie (co.), N.Y. 276/C5
Erie (lake), N.Y. 276/A5
Erie, N. Dak. (58029) 282/R5
Erie (co.), Ohio 284/E3
Erie (lake), Ohio 284/H1
Erie (lake), Ontario 177/E5
Erie, Pa. 188/K2
Erie, Pa. 146/L5
Erie (co.), Pa. 294/B2
Erie, Pa. (*16501) 294/B1
Erie (lake), Pa. 294/B1
Erie, Tenn. (†37846) 237/M9
Erieau, Ontario 177/C5
Erie Beach, Ontario 177/B5
Erieville, N.Y. (13061) 276/J5
Erigabo, Somalia 115/J1
Eriksdale, Manitoba 179/D4
Erimo (cape), Japan 81/L3
Erin, Ontario 177/D4
Erin, Tenn. (37061) 237/F8
Erin (bay), Trin. & Tob. 161/A11
Erin (pt.), Trin. & Tob. 161/A11
Erinferry, Sask. 181/D2
Erinview, Manitoba 179/E4
Eriskay (isl.), Scotland 15/A3
Erisort, Loch (inlet), Scotland 15/B2
Erith, Alberta 182/B3
Eritrea (prov.), Ethiopia 111/G4
Eritrea (reg.), Ethiopia 102/F3
Eritrea (reg.), Ethiopia 59/C6
Erivan, U.S.S.R. 7/J4
Erivan, U.S.S.R. 48/E6
Erivan, U.S.S.R. 52/F6
Erkilet, Turkey 63/F3
Erkina (riv.), Ireland 17/G6
Erkowit, Sudan 59/C6
Erlach, Switzerland 39/D2
Erlands Point, Wash. (†98310) 310/A2
Erlangen, W. Germany 22/D4
Erlanger, Ky. (41018) 237/R2
Erldunda, North. Terr. 93/C8
Erlenbach im Simmental, Switzerland 39/E3
Erling (lake), Ark. 202/C7
Ermatingen, Switzerland 39/H1
Ermelo, Netherlands 27/H4
Ermelo, S. Africa 118/E5
Ermenak, Turkey 63/E4
Ermeran Station, N.S. Wales 97/D3
Ermoúpolis, Greece 45/G7
Ernabella, S. Australia 94/C2
Ernakulam, India 54/J8
Erne (riv.), Ireland 17/E3
Erne (lake), N. Ireland 17/F3
Erne, Lough (lake), N. Ireland 10/C3
Ernée, France 28/C3
Ernen, Switzerland 39/F4
Ernest, Pa. (15739) 294/D4
Ernfold, Sask. 181/D5
Ernul, N.C. (28527) 281/P4
Erode, India 68/D6
Eromanga, Queensland 88/G5
Eromanga, Queensland 95/B5
Eros, La. (71238) 238/F2
Erquelinnes, Belgium 27/E8
Err (peak), Switzerland 39/J3
Er Rafid, Jordan 65/D2
Er Rahad, Sudan 111/F5
Er Rahad, Sudan 59/B7
Er Ramtha, Jordan 65/E2
Er Ras, Saudi Arabia 59/D4
Errata, Miss. (†39440) 256/F7
Errego, Mozambique 118/F3
Er Rif (range), Morocco 106/D2
Errigal (mt.), Ireland 17/E1
Er Rihiya, West Bank 65/C5
Errington, Br. Col. 184/J3
Erris (head), Ireland 10/A3
Erris (head), Ireland 17/A3
Errol○, N.H. (03579) 268/E2
Errol, Scotland 15/E4
Erromanga (isl.), Vanuatu 87/H7
Er Roseires, Sudan 111/F5
Er Rumman, Jordan 65/D3
Er Ruseifa, Jordan 65/E3
Ersekë, Albania 45/E5
Erskine, Alberta 182/D3
Erskine, Minn. (56535) 255/B3
Erstein, France 28/G3
Erstfeld, Switzerland 39/G3
Ertai, China 77/C2
Ertil', U.S.S.R. 52/F4
Eruh, Turkey 63/K4
Erval, Brazil 132/C11
Ervay, Wyo. (†82638) 319/E3
Erving○, Mass. (01344) 249/E2
Erwin, N.C. (28339) 281/M4
Erwin, S. Dak. (57233) 298/P5
Erwin, Tenn. (37650) 237/S8
Erwinna, Pa. (18920) 294/N5
Erwinville, La. (70729) 238/H5
Erwood, Sask. 181/J3
Eryuan, China 77/F6
Erzgebirge (mts.), Czech. 41/B1
Erzgebirge (mts.), E. Germany 22/E3
Erzin, Turkey 63/G4
Erzincan (prov.), Turkey 63/H3
Erzincan, Turkey 63/H3
Erzincan, Turkey 59/C2
Erzurum (prov.), Turkey 63/J3
Erzurum, Turkey 59/D2
Erzurum, Turkey 54/E5
Erzurum, Turkey 63/J3
Esan (pt.), Japan 81/K3
Esashi, Iwate, Japan 81/K4
Esashi, Hokkaido, Japan 81/J3
Esashi, Hokkaido, Japan 81/L1
Esbjerg, Denmark 21/B7
Esbjerg, Denmark 7/E3
Esbjerg, Denmark 18/F9
Esbon, Kansas (66941) 232/D2
Escabosa, N. Mex. (†87059) 274/C4
Escalante, Philippines 82/D5
Escalante, Utah (84726) 304/C6
Escalante (des.), Utah 304/A6
Escalante (riv.), Utah 304/C6
Escalon, Calif. (95320) 204/E6
Escalón, Mexico 150/G3
Escalona, Spain 33/D2
Escambia (co.), Ala. 195/D8
Escambia (creek), Ala. 195/D8
Escambia (riv.), Ala. 195/D8
Escambia (co.), Fla. 212/B6
Escambia (riv.), Fla. 212/B6
Escanaba, Mich. (49829) 250/C3
Escanaba (riv.), Mich. 250/B2
Escarcega, Mexico 150/O7
Escatawpa (riv.), 256/H8
Escatawpa, Ala. (†36584) 195/B8
Escatawpa (riv.), Ala. 195/B9
Escatawpa, Miss. (39552) 256/G10
Eschenbach, Switzerland 39/G2
Escholzmatt, Switzerland 39/E3
Esch-sur-Alzette, Luxembourg 27/J9
Esch-sur-Sûre, Luxembourg 27/H9
Eschwege, W. Germany 22/C3
Eschweiler, W. Germany 22/B3
Escobar, Argentina 143/G7
Escobar, Paraguay 144/B5
Escocesa (bay), Dom. Rep. 158/E5
Escoma, Bolivia 136/A4
Escondido, Calif. (*92025) 204/J10
Escondido (riv.), Nicaragua 154/F4
Escoumins, Québec 172/H1
Escudo de Veraguas (isl.), Panama 154/G6
Escuinapa de Hidalgo, Mexico 150/G5
Escuintla, Guatemala 154/B3
Escuintla, Mexico 150/N9
Escuminac, New Bruns. 170/F1
Escuminac (bay), New Bruns. 170/D1
Escuminac (pt.), New Bruns. 170/F1
Esdaile, Wis. (†54723) 317/A6
Eséka, Cameroon 115/B3
Eşen, Turkey 63/C4
Esfahan (Isfahan) (prov.), Iran 66/H4
Esfahan (Isfahan), Iran 66/G4
Esfandak, Iran 66/N7
Esh, England 13/H3
Esher, England 13/H8
Esher, England 10/B6
Eshowe, S. Africa 118/E5
Esh Shaubak, Jordan 65/D5
Esk (riv.), England 13/D2
Esk, Queensland 95/E5
Esk, Sask. 181/G4
Esk (riv.), Scotland 15/F5
Eska, Alaska (†99674) 196/B1
Eskdale, W. Va. (25075) 312/D6
Esker, Newf. 166/A3
Eskilstuna, Sweden 18/K7
Eskimalatya, Turkey 63/H3
Eskimo (lkes), N.W. Terrs. 187/E3
Eskimo Point, N.W.T. 162/G3
Eskimo Point, N.W. Terrs. 187/J3
Eskipazar, Turkey 63/E2
Eskişehir (prov.), Turkey 63/D3
Eskişehir, Turkey 54/D6
Eskişehir, Turkey 59/B2
Eskişehir, Turkey 63/D3
Esko, Minn. (55733) 255/F4
Eskridge, Kansas (66423) 232/F3
Eskutassis (pond), Maine 243/G5
Esla (riv.), Spain 33/D2
Eslöv, Sweden 18/H9
Esme, Sask. 181/D6
Eşme, Turkey 63/C3
Esmeralda (isl.), Chile 138/C8
Esmeralda, Cuba 158/G1
Esmeralda (co.), Nev. 266/D5
Esmeraldas (prov.), Ecuador 128/C2
Esmeraldas, Ecuador 120/A2
Esmeraldas, Ecuador 128/B2
Esmeraldas (riv.), Ecuador 128/C2
Esmond, Ill. (60129) 222/E1
Esmond, N. Dak. (58332) 282/L3
Esmond, R.I. (02917) 249/H5
Esmond, S. Dak. (†57353) 298/O5
Esmont, Va. (22937) 307/L5
Esmoraca, Bolivia 136/B7
Esneux, Belgium 27/H7
Esom Hill, Georgia (30138) 217/B3

Fairhaven 367

Espada (pt.), Colombia 126/E1
Espada (pt.), Dom. Rep. 158/F6
Espagnol (pt.), St. Vin. & Grens. 161/A8
Espaillat (prov.), Dom. Rep. 158/E5
Espalion, France 28/E5
Española (isl.), Ecuador 128/C10
Espanola, Fla. (†32010) 212/E2
Espanola, N. Mex. (87532) 274/C3
Espanola, Ontario 177/J5
Espanola, Ontario 175/D3
Espanola, Wash. (†99022) 310/H3
Esparta, C. Rica 154/E5
Esparto, Calif. (95627) 204/C5
Espejo, Chile 138/G3
Espejo, Spain 33/D4
Espelkamp, W. Germany 22/C2
Espenberg (cape), Alaska 196/F1
Esperança, Brazil 132/G4
Esperance, Australia 87/C9
Esperance, N.Y. (12066) 276/M5
Esperance, W. Australia 88/C6
Esperance, W. Australia 92/C6
Esperance (bay), W. Australia 92/C6
Esperanza, Argentina 143/F5
Esperanza, Br. Col. 184/D5
Esperanza, Cuba 158/E2
Esperanza, Dom. Rep. 158/D5
Esperanza (mts.), Honduras 154/E3
Esperanza, Puebla, Mexico 150/O2
Esperanza, Sonora, Mexico 150/E3
Esperanza, Peru 128/G7
Esperanza, P. Rico 161/G2
Esperanza, Texas (†79841) 303/B11
Esperanza, Venezuela 124/E6
Espichel (cape), Portugal 33/B3
Espigão Mestre (Geral de Goiás) (range), Brazil 132/E6
Espinal, Colombia 126/C5
Espinhaço (mts.), Brazil 120/E4
Espinhaço, Serra do (range), Brazil 132/F7
Espinho, Portugal 33/B2
Espinillo, Argentina 143/E2
Espinillo (pt.), Uruguay 145/A7
Espino, Venezuela 124/F3
Espírito Santo (state), Brazil 132/F7
Espírito Santo (state), Brazil 135/F2
Espíritu Santo (isl.), Mexico 150/D4
Espiritu Santo (cape), Philippines 85/H3
Espiritu Santo (cape), Philippines 82/E4
Espiritu Santo (isl.), Vanuatu 87/G7
Espita, Mexico 150/Q6
Espiye, Turkey 63/H2
Esplanada, Brazil 132/G5
Espluga de Francolí, Spain 33/G2
Espoir (bay), Newf. 166/C4
Espoo, Finland 18/O6
Esposende, Portugal 33/B2
Esprit-Saint, Québec 172/J1
Espungabera, Mozambique 118/E4
Espy, Pa. (17815) 294/K4
Spyville Station, Pa. (16414) 294/B2
Esqueda, Mexico 150/E1
Esquel, Argentina 143/B5
Esquel, Argentina 120/B7
Esquimalt, Br. Col. 184/K4
Esquina, Argentina 143/G5
Esquipulas, Nicaragua 154/E4
Es Sahab, Jordan 65/E4
Es Salt, Jordan 65/D3
Es Salt, Jordan 59/C3
Essaouira, Morocco 106/B2
Essaouira, Morocco 102/A1
Essé, Cameroon 115/B3
Essen, Belgium 27/F6
Essen, W. Germany 7/E3
Essen, W. Germany 22/B3
Essendon, Victoria 88/K7
Essendon, Victoria 97/H5
Essequibo (riv.), Guyana 120/D2
Essequibo (riv.), Guyana 131/B3
Esserville, Va. (24274) 307/G2
Essex, Calif. (92332) 204/K9
Essex, Conn. (06426) 210/F3
Essex○, Conn. (06426) 210/F3
Essex (co.), England 13/H6
Essex, Ill. (60935) 222/E2
Essex, Iowa (51638) 229/C7
Essex, Md. (21221) 245/N3
Essex (co.), Mass. 249/L2
Essex, Mass. (01929) 249/L2
Essex○, Mass. (01929) 249/L2
Essex, Mo. (63846) 261/N9
Essex, Mont. (59916) 262/C2
Essex (co.), N.J. 273/E2
Essex (co.), N.Y. 276/N2
Essex, N.Y. (12936) 276/O2
Essex (county), Ontario 177/B5
Essex, Ontario 177/B5
Essex (co.), Vt. 268/D2
Essex○, Vt. (05451) 268/A2
Essex (co.), Va. 307/P5
Essex Fells, N.J. (07021) 273/B2
Essex Junction, Vt. (05452) 268/A3
Essexville, Mich. (48732) 250/F5
Es Sidr, Libya 111/C1
Essie, Ky. (40827) 237/P6
Essig, Minn. (56030) 255/D6
Essington, Pa. (19029) 294/M7
Esslingen am Neckar, W. Germany 22/C4
Essonne (dept.), France 28/E3
Es Sukhna, Jordan 65/E3
Es Sukhne, Syria 59/C3
Es Sukhne, Syria 63/H5
Es Suki, Sudan 59/B7
Es Suweida (prov.), Syria 63/G6
Es Suweida, Syria 59/C3
Es Suweida, Syria 63/G6
Est (pt.), Haiti 158/C4
Est (lake), Québec 172/H2
Estacada, Oreg. (97023) 291/E2
Estaca de Vares (pt.), Spain 33/C1
Estación Atlántida, Uruguay 145/B6
Estación Cuaró, Uruguay 145/C1
Estación J.J. Castro, Uruguay 145/C4
Estación José Ignacio, Uruguay 145/E5
Estación La Floresta, Uruguay 145/C7
Estación Lasala, Uruguay 145/C7
Estación Laureles, Uruguay 145/C2
Estación Margat, Uruguay 145/B6
Estación Migues, Uruguay 145/C6
Estación Pampa, Uruguay 145/C3
Estación Puma, Uruguay 145/D5
Estación Rincón, Uruguay 145/F3
Estación Sosa Díaz, Uruguay 145/C6
Estación Tapia, Uruguay 145/C6
Estación Villasboas, Uruguay 145/C4
Estación Yí, Uruguay 145/C4
Estados (isl.), Argentina 120/C8
Estados, Los (isl.), Argentina 143/D7
Estahbanat, Iran 59/F4
Estahbanat, Iran 66/J6
Estaire, Ontario 177/D1
Estampuis, Belgium 27/C7
Estância, Brazil 132/G5
Estância, Brazil 120/F4
Estancia, N. Mex. (87016) 274/D4
Estancia Caleta Josefina, Chile 138/F10
Estancia Laguna Blanca, Chile 138/E9
Estancia Morro Chico, Chile 138/E9
Estancia Punta Delgada, Chile 138/E9
Estancia San Gregorio, Chile 138/E9
Estancia Springhill (Cerro Manantiales), Chile 138/F10
Estanzuela, Uruguay 145/B5
Estanzuelas, El Salvador 154/C4
Estarca, Bolivia 136/C7
Estats (peak), Spain 33/G1
Estavayer-le-Lac, Switzerland 39/C3
Estcourt, S. Africa 118/D5
Este (pt.), Cuba 158/C3
Este, Italy 34/C2
Este (pt.), P. Rico 161/G2
Este (pt.), Uruguay 120/D6
Este (pt.), Uruguay 145/D6
Esteban Rams, Argentina 143/F5
Estelí, Nicaragua 154/D4
Estella, Spain 33/E1
Estelline, S. Dak. (57234) 298/R4
Estelline, Texas (79233) 303/D3
Estell Manor, N.J. (08319) 273/D5
Estepa, Spain 33/D4
Estepona, Spain 33/D4
Ester, Alaska (99725) 196/J2
Esterbrook, Wyo. (†82633) 319/G3
Estérel, Québec 172/C3
Esterhazy, Sask. 181/K5
Estero (bay), Calif. 204/D8
Estero (pt.), Calif. 204/D8
Estero, Fla. (33928) 212/E5
Estero (isl.), Fla. 212/E5
Estes Park, Colo. (80517) 208/J2
Este Sudeste (cays), Colombia 126/A10
Estevan, Sak. 162/F6
Estevan, Sask. 181/J6
Estevan Point, Br. Col. 184/D5
Estey, Mich. (†48652) 250/E5
Esther (isl.), Alaska 196/C1
Esther, Alberta 182/E4
Esther, La. (†70510) 238/F7
Esther, Mo. (†63601) 261/M7
Estherville, Iowa (51334) 229/D2
Estherwood, La. (70534) 238/F6
Estill (co.), Ky. 237/O5
Estill, Miss. (†38748) 256/C4
Estill, S.C. (29918) 296/E6
Estillfork, Ala. (35745) 195/F1
Estill Springs, Tenn. (37330) 237/J10
Estlin, Sask. 181/G5
Esto, Fla. (32425) 212/C5
Eston, England 13/F3
Eston, Sask. 162/F5
Eston, Sask. 181/C4
ESTONIA 53
Estonian S.S.R., U.S.S.R. 7/G3
Estonian S.S.R., U.S.S.R. 48/C4
Estonian S.S.R, U.S.S.R. 52/C3
Estoril, Portugal 33/B3
Estral Beach, Mich. (†48166) 250/F7
Estreito (res.), Brazil 135/C2
Estrela, Serra da (mts.), Portugal 33/C2
Estrella (riv.), Calif. 204/E8
Estremadura (reg.), Spain 33/C3
Estremoz, Portugal 33/C3
Estrondo, Serra do (range), Brazil 132/D4
Estuary, Sask. 181/B5
Esztergom, Hungary 41/E3
Etadunna, S. Australia 94/F3
Étalle, Belgium 27/H9
Étampes, France 28/E3
Étaples, France 28/D2
Etawah, India 68/D3
Etawney (lake), Manitoba 179/J2
Etchojoa, Mexico 150/E3
Ethan, S. Dak. (57334) 298/N6
Ethel, Ark. (72048) 202/H5
Ethel (mt.), Colo. 208/F1
Ethel, La. (70730) 238/H5
Ethel, Miss. (39067) 256/F4
Ethel, Mo. (63539) 261/G3
Ethel, Ontario 177/C4
Ethel, Wash. (98542) 310/C4
Ethel, W. Va. (25076) 312/C7
Ethelbert, Manitoba 179/B3
Ethel Creek, W. Australia 92/C3
Ethelsville, Ala. (35461) 195/B4
Ethelton, Sask. 181/G3
Ether, N.C. (27247) 281/K4
Ethete, Wyo. (82520) 319/D2
Ethiopia 2/L5
Ethiopia 102/F4
ETHIOPIA 59/C7
ETHIOPIA 111/G5
Ethridge, Mont. (59435) 262/D2
Ethridge, Tenn. (38456) 237/G10
Etive, Loch (inlet), Scotland 15/C4
Etiwanda, Calif. (91739) 204/E10
Etna, Calif. (96027) 204/C2
Etna, Ind. (†46725) 227/F2
Etna (vol.), Italy 7/F5
Etna (vol.), Italy 34/E6
Etna○, Maine (04434) 243/E6
Etna, N.H. (03750) 268/C4
Etna, Ohio (43018) 284/E6
Etna, Pa. (15223) 294/B6
Etna, Utah (†84313) 304/A2
Etna, Wyo. (83118) 319/A2
Etna Green, Ind. (46524) 227/E2
Etobicoke, Ontario 177/J4
Etoile, Ky. (42131) 237/K7
Etoile, Zaire 115/E6
Etolin (isl.), Alaska 196/N2
Etolin (str.), Alaska 196/E2
Etomami (riv.), Manitoba 179/F2
Etomami (riv.), Sask. 181/J3
Eton, England 10/F5
Eton, England 13/G8
Eton, Georgia (30724) 217/C1
Etosha Pan (salt pan), Namibia 118/B3
Etosha Salt Pan, Namibia 102/D6
Etoumbi, Congo 115/B3
Etowah (co.), Ala. 195/F2
Etowah, Ark. (72428) 202/K2
Etowah (riv.), Georgia 217/C2
Etowah, N.C. (28729) 281/D4
Etowah, Tenn. (37331) 237/M10
Étretat, France 28/D3
Etta, Miss. (38627) 256/F2
Etta (lake), N. Dak. 282/L6
Et Tafila, Jordan 65/E5
Et Taiyiba, Jordan 65/D2
Ettelbruck, Luxembourg 27/J9
Et Tell el Abyad, Syria 63/H4
Etten-Leur, Netherlands 27/F5
Etter, Minn. (†55033) 255/F6
Etterbeek, Belgium 27/B9
Etters, Pa. (17319) 294/J5
Etters Beach, Sask. 181/F4
Ettington, Sask. 181/F6
Ettlingen, W. Germany 22/C4
Ettrick, Scotland 15/E5
Ettrick, Va. (23803) 307/O6
Ettrick, Wis. (54627) 317/D7
Ettrick Pen (mt.), Scotland 15/E5
Etty, Ky. (41523) 237/R6
Etzatlán, Mexico 150/G6
Etzikom, Alberta 182/E5
Etzikom Coulee (riv.), Alberta 182/E5
Eu, France 28/D3
Euabalong, N.S. Wales 97/D3
Eubank, Ky. (42567) 237/M6
Euboea (Évvoia) (isl.), Greece 45/G6
Eucha, Okla. (74342) 288/S2
Eucha (lake), Okla. 288/S2
Eucla, W. Australia 92/E5
Euclid, Minn. (56722) 255/B3
Euclid, Ohio (44117) 284/J9
Eucumbene (lake), N.S. Wales 97/E5
Eudora, Miss. (†39360) 256/G7
Eudora, Ark. (71640) 202/H7
Eudora, Kansas (66025) 232/G3
Eudora, Miss. (†38632) 256/D1
Eudora, Mo. (65645) 261/E7
Eufaula, Ala. (36027) 195/H7
Eufaula (Walter F. George Res.) (lake), Ala 195/H7
Eufaula (Walter F. George Res.) (lake), Georgia 217/B7
Eufaula (res.), Ohio 284/L4
Eufaula, Okla. (74432) 288/P4
Eufaula (lake), Okla. 288/P4
Eugene, Ind. (†47928) 227/B5
Eugene, Mo. (65032) 261/H6
Eugene, Oreg. 188/B2
Eugene, Oreg. 146/F5
Eugene, Oreg. (*97401) 291/D3
Eugene O'Neill Nat'l Hist. Site, Calif. 204/K2
Eugowra, N.S. Wales 97/E3
Euharlee, Georgia (†30120) 217/C2
Euless, Texas (76039) 303/F2
Eulo, Queensland 95/C6
Eulonia, Georgia (†31331) 217/K7
Eumungerie, N.S. Wales 97/E2
Eunice, La. (70535) 238/F6
Eunice, N. Mex. (88231) 274/F6
Eunola, Ala. (†36340) 195/G8
Eupen, Belgium 27/J7
Euphrates (riv.) 54/F6
Euphrates (riv.), Iran 59/E3
Euphrates (riv.), Iraq 59/E3
Euphrates (riv.), Iraq 66/D4
Euphrates (riv.), Syria 59/E3
Euphrates (El Furat) (riv.), Syria 63/H4
Euphrates (Fırat) (riv.), Turkey 63/G4
Eupora, Miss. (39744) 256/F3
Eure (dept.), France 28/D3
Eure (riv.), France 28/D3
Eure, N.C. (27935) 281/R2
Eure-et-Loir (dept.), France 28/D3
Eureka, Calif. 188/B2
Eureka, Calif. 146/F5
Eureka, Calif. (95501) 204/A3
Eureka, Canada 4/A14
Eureka, Colo. (†81433) 208/D7
Eureka (res.), Fla. 212/E2
Eureka, Ill. (61530) 222/D3
Eureka, Ind. (†47635) 227/C9
Eureka, Kansas (67045) 232/F4
Eureka, Mo. (63025) 261/M4
Eureka, Mont. (59917) 262/B2
Eureka (co.), Nev. 266/E3
Eureka, Nev. (89316) 266/E3
Eureka, N.C. (27830) 281/O3
Eureka, N.W.T. 146/K2
Eureka, N.W.T. 162/N3
Eureka, N.W. Terrs. 187/K2
Eureka (sound), N.W. Terrs. 187/K2
Eureka, Nova Scotia 168/F3
Eureka, S.C. (†29706) 296/E2
Eureka, S.C. (†29847) 296/D4
Eureka, S. Dak. (57437) 298/K2
Eureka, Utah (84628) 304/B4
Eureka, Wash. (†99348) 310/G4
Eureka, W. Va. (26144) 312/D4
Eureka Lodge, Alaska (†99588) 196/C1
Eureka Springs, Ark. (72632) 202/C1
Euroa, Victoria 97/C5
Europa (pt.), Gibraltar 33/D4
Europa (isl.), Réunion 102/G7
Europa (isl.), Réunion 118/G4
Europe 2/K3
Europoort, Netherlands 27/E5
Eusebio Ayala, Paraguay 144/B4
Euskirchen, W. Germany 22/B3
Eustace, Texas (75124) 303/H5
Eustis, Fla. (32726) 212/E3
Eustis, Maine (04936) 243/B5
Eustis○, Maine (04936) 243/B5
Eustis, Nebr. (69028) 264/D4
Euston, N.S. Wales 97/B4
Eutaw, Ala. (35462) 195/C5
Eutawville, S.C. (29048) 296/G5
Eutin, W. Germany 22/D1
Eutsuk (lake), Br. Col. 184/D3
Eva, Ala. (35621) 195/E2
Eva (lake), Alberta 182/B5
Eva, La. (†71354) 238/G4
Eva, Okla. (†73949) 288/C1
Eva, Tenn. (38333) 237/E8
Evadale, Texas (77615) 303/L7
Eva Downs, North. Terr. 93/D5
Évain, Québec 174/B3
Evan, Minn. (56238) 255/D6
Evan (lake), Québec 174/B2
Evandale, New Bruns. 170/D3
Evandale, Tasmania 99/D3
Evangeline (par.), La. 238/F5
Evangeline, La. (70537) 238/F6
Evangeline, New Bruns. 170/F1
Evans, Colo. (80620) 208/K2
Evans (mt.), Colo. 208/H3
Evans (co.), Georgia 217/J6
Evans, Georgia (30809) 217/H3
Evans, La. (70639) 238/D5
Evans (head), N.S. Wales 97/G1
Evans (str.), N.W.T. 162/H3
Evans (str.), N.W. Terrs. 187/K3
Evans, Wash. (99126) 310/H2
Evans, W. Va. (25241) 312/C5
Evansburg, Alberta 182/C3
Evans Center, N.Y. (†14006) 276/B5
Evans City, Pa. (16033) 294/B4
Evansdale, Iowa (50707) 229/J4
Evans Head, N.S. Wales 97/G1
Evans Mills, N.Y. (13637) 276/J2
Evansport, Ohio (43519) 284/B3
Evanston, Ill. (*60201) 222/B5
Evanston, Ind. (47531) 227/D8
Evanston, Wyo. 188/D2
Evanston, Wyo. (82930) 319/B4
Evansville (Bettles Field), Alaska (†99726) 196/H1
Evansville, Ark. (72729) 202/B2
Evansville, Ill. (62242) 222/D5
Evansville, Ind. 188/J3
Evansville, Ind. 146/K6
Evansville, Ind. (*47701) 227/C9
Evansville, Minn. (56326) 255/C4
Evansville, Miss. (†38676) 256/D1
Evansville, Pa. (19521) 294/L5
Evansville, Wis. (53536) 317/H10
Evansville, Wyo. (82636) 319/F3
Evant, Texas (76525) 303/G6
Evanton, Scotland 15/D3
Evart, Mich. (49631) 250/D5
Evarts, Ky. (40828) 237/P7
Evaton, S. Africa 118/H7
Evaz, Iran 66/J7
Eveleth, Minn. (55734) 255/F3
Evelyn, La. (†71052) 238/D3
Evendale, Ohio (†45201) 284/C9
Evening Shade, Ark. (72532) 202/G1
Evenki Aut. Okr., U.S.S.R. 48/K3
Evensk, U.S.S.R. 4/C1
Evensk, U.S.S.R. 48/Q3
Evensville, Tenn. (37332) 237/M9
Even Yehuda, Israel 65/B3
Everard (lake), S. Australia 88/E6
Everard (lake), S. Australia 94/D4
Everard (ranges), S. Australia 94/C2
Evere, Belgium 27/C9
Everest (mt.) 54/K7
Everest (mt.), China 77/C6
Everest, Kansas (66424) 232/G2
Everest (mt.), Nepal 68/F3
Everest, N. Dak. (†58023) 282/R6
Everett, Georgia (31536) 217/J8
Everett, Mass. (02149) 249/D6
Everett (mt.), Mass. 249/A4
Everett, New Bruns. 170/C1
Everett (dam), N.H. 268/D5
Everett (mts.), N.W. Terrs. 187/M3
Everett, Ontario 177/E3
Everett, Pa. (15537) 294/F5
Everett, Wash. 188/B1
Everett, Wash. (*98201) 310/C3
Everetts, N.C. (27825) 281/P3
Everettville, W. Va. (26533) 312/F3
Evergem, Belgium 27/D6
Everglades, The (swamp), Fla. 212/F6
Everglades, The (swamp), Fla. 188/K5
Everglades City, Fla. (33929) 212/E6
Everglades Nat'l Park, Fla. 212/F6
Evergreen, Ala. (36401) 195/E8
Evergreen, Colo. (80439) 208/J3
Evergreen, La. (71333) 238/F5
Evergreen, N.C. (28438) 281/M6
Evergreen, Va. (23939) 307/L6
Evergreen Park, Ill. (60642) 222/B6
Everly, Iowa (51338) 229/C2
Everman, Texas (76140) 303/F3
Everson, Pa. (15631) 294/C5
Everson, Wash. (98247) 310/C2
Eversonville, Mo. (†64688) 261/F3
Everton, Ark. (72633) 202/E1
Everton, Ind. (†47331) 227/G5
Everton, Mo. (65646) 261/E8
Evesham, England 10/E4
Evesham, England 13/F5
Evesham, Sask. 181/B3
Evington, Va. (24550) 307/K6
Evolène, Switzerland 39/D4
Évora (dist.), Portugal 33/C3
Évora, Portugal 7/D5
Évora, Portugal 33/C3
Évreux, France 28/D3
Évros (riv.), Greece 45/H5
Évry, France 28/E3
Évvoia (isl.), Greece 7/G5
Évvoia (isl.), Greece 45/G6
Ewa, Hawaii (96706) 218/A4
Ewab (Kai) (isls.), Indonesia 85/J7
Ewa Beach, Hawaii (96706) 218/A4
Ewan, N.J. (08025) 273/C4
Ewan, Wash. (99127) 310/H3
Ewaninga, North. Terr. 93/D7
Ewart, Iowa (†50171) 229/H5
Ewarton, Jamaica 156/C3
Ewarton, Jamaica 158/J6
Ewauna (lake), Oreg. 291/F5
Ewe, Loch (inlet), Scotland 15/C3
Ewell, Md. (21824) 245/O9
Ewen, Mich. (49925) 250/F2
Ewing, Ill. (62836) 222/E5
Ewing, Ky. (41039) 237/O4
Ewing, Mo. (63440) 261/J2
Ewing, Nebr. (68735) 264/F2
Ewing (mt.), North. Terr. 93/E7
Ewing, Va. (24248) 307/B7
Ewington, Ohio (45627) 284/F8
Ewo, Congo 115/B4
Exaltación, Bolivia 136/C3
Excel, Ala. (36439) 195/D8
Excel, Alberta 182/E4
Excello, Mo. (65247) 261/H3
Excello, Ohio (45042) 284/B7
Excelsior, Minn. (55331) 255/E6
Excelsior (mts.), Nev. 266/C4
Excelsior, Wis. (†53518) 317/E9
Excelsior Springs, Mo. (64024) 261/R4
Exchange, W. Va. (26619) 312/E5
Excursion Inlet, Alaska (†99826) 196/M1
Exe (riv.), England 13/D7
Exe (riv.), England 10/E5
Executive Committee (range) 5/B12
Exeland, Wis. (54835) 317/D4
Exeter, Calif. (93221) 204/F7
Exeter, Conn. (†06249) 210/F2
Exeter, England 13/D7
Exeter, England 10/E5
Exeter, Ill. (†62694) 222/C4
Exeter, Maine (04435) 243/E6
Exeter○, Maine (04435) 243/E6
Exeter, Mo. (65647) 261/D9
Exeter, Nebr. (68351) 264/G4
Exeter, N.H. (03833) 268/F6
Exeter○, N.H. (03833) 268/F6
Exeter (riv.), N.H. 268/E6
Exeter (sound), N.W. Terrs. 187/M3
Exeter, Ontario 177/C4
Exeter○, R.I. (02822) 249/H6
Exeter, Tasmania 99/C3
Exira, Iowa (50076) 229/D5
Exline, Iowa (52555) 229/H7
Exminster, England 13/D7
Exmoor National Park, England 13/D6
Exmore, Va. (23350) 307/S5
Exmouth, England 13/D7
Exmouth, England 10/E5
Exmouth, W. Australia 88/A4
Exmouth (gulf), W. Australia 88/A4
Exmouth, W. Australia 92/A3
Exmouth (gulf), W. Australia 92/A3
Expanse, Sask. 181/E6
Experiment, Georgia (30212) 217/D4
Exploits (riv.), Newf. 166/C4
Export, Pa. (15632) 294/C5
Exshaw, Alberta 182/C4
Extension, Br. Col. 184/J3
Extension, La. (71239) 238/G3
Exu, Brazil 132/G4
Exuma (cays), Bahamas 156/C1
Exuma (sound), Bahamas 156/C1
Eyasi (lake), Tanzania 115/F4
Eye, England 10/G4
Eye, England 13/J5
Eye (pen.), Scotland 15/B2
Eyebrow, Sask. 181/E5
Eyebrow (lake), Sask. 181/E5
Eyehill (creek), Sask. 181/B3
Eyemouth, Scotland 15/F5
Eyemouth, Scotland 10/F3
Eynesil, Turkey 63/H2
Eynhallow (sound), Scotland 15/E1
Eynort, Loch (inlet), Scotland 15/A3
Eyota, Minn. (55934) 255/F7
Eyre (lake), Australia 87/D8
Eyre (bay), Chile 138/D8
Eyre (mts.), N. Zealand 100/B6
Eyre (riv.), Queensland 88/F5
Eyre (lake), S. Australia 88/F5
Eyre (pen.), S. Australia 88/F6
Eyre (lake), S. Australia 94/E3
Eyre (pen.), S. Australia 94/D5
Eyre, W. Australia 92/D6
Eyrecourt, Ireland 17/E5
Eyre North (lake), S. Australia 94/E3
Eyre South (lake), S. Australia 94/E3
Eysturoy (isl.), Denmark 21/B3
Eyüp, Turkey 63/D6
Ezel, Ky. (41425) 237/P5
Ezequiel Montes, Mexico 150/K6
Ezibider, Turkey 63/H2
Ezine, Turkey 63/B3
Ezna, Iran 66/F4
Ez Zababida, West Bank 65/C3
Ez Zarqa', Jordan 65/E3
Ez Zuetina, Libya 111/D1

F

Faaa, Fr. Poly. 86/S13
Fabens, Texas (79838) 303/B10
Faber (lake), N.W. Terrs. 187/G3
Faber, Va. (22938) 307/L5
Fabius, Ala. (35965) 195/G1
Fabius, N.Y. (13063) 276/J5
Fåborg, Denmark 21/D7
Fåborg, Denmark 18/G9
Fabriano, Italy 34/D3
Fabyan, Alberta 182/E3
Fabyan, Conn. (06245) 210/H1
Fabyan House, N.H. (†03595) 268/E3
Facatativá, Colombia 126/C5
Faceville, Georgia (†31717) 217/C9
Fachi, Niger 106/G5
Fackler, Ala. (35746) 195/G1
Factoryville, Pa. (18419) 294/L2
Facundo, Argentina 143/C6
Fada, Chad 111/D4
Fada-N'Gourma, Upper Volta 106/E6
Fadd, Hungary 41/E3
Faddeyevskiy (isl.), U.S.S.R. 4/B2
Faddeyevskiy (isl.), U.S.S.R. 48/P2
Faden, Newf. 166/A3
Faenza, Italy 34/D2
Faerøe (isls.), Den. 4/C10
Faerøe (isls.), Denmark 7/D2
Faerøe (isls.), Denmark 21/B2
FAERØE ISLANDS, Denmark 21/B2
Faerøe Islands, Denmark 21/B2
Fafan (riv.), Ethiopia 111/H6
Fafe, Portugal 33/B2
Fagan, Ky. (†40322) 237/O5
Făgăraş, Romania 45/G3
Fagernes, Norway 18/F6
Fagersta, Sweden 18/J6
Fagnano (lake), Argentina 143/C7
Fagnano (lake), Chile 138/F11
Faguibine (lake), Mali 106/D5
Fagundes, Brazil 132/C4
Fagus, Mo. (63938) 261/M9
Fahan, Ireland 17/G1
Fahrej (Iranshahr), Iran 66/M7
Fahrej (Iranshahr), Iran 59/H4
Faial (isl.), Portugal 33/B1
Faid, Saudi Arabia 59/D4
Faido, Switzerland 39/G4
Fainaven (mt.), Scotland 15/D2
Fair (head), N. Ireland 17/J1
Fair (isl.), Scotland 10/F1
Fairacres, N. Mex. (88033) 274/C6
Fairbank, Ariz. (85612) 198/E7
Fairbank, Iowa (50629) 229/K3
Fairbank, Md. (†21671) 245/N6
Fairbanks, Alaska 146/D3
Fairbanks, Alaska (99701) 196/J2
Fairbanks, Alaska 188/D5
Fairbanks, Fla. (†32601) 212/D2
Fairbanks, Ind. (47849) 227/B6
Fairbanks, La. (71240) 238/F1
Fairbanks, Maine (†04938) 243/C6
Fairbanks, Minn. (†55602) 255/G3
Fairbanks, U.S. 4/C17
Fairbanks, U.S. 2/C2
Fair Bluff, N.C. (28439) 281/M6
Fairborn, Ohio (45324) 284/B6
Fairburn, Georgia (30213) 217/J2
Fairburn, S. Dak. (57738) 298/C6
Fairbury, Ill. (61739) 222/E3
Fairbury, Nebr. (68352) 264/G4
Fairchance, Pa. (15436) 294/C6
Fairchild, Wis. (54741) 317/D6
Fairchild A.F.B., Wash. 310/H3
Fairdale, Ill. (†60146) 222/E1
Fairdale, Ky. (40118) 237/K4
Fairdale, N. Dak. (58229) 282/O3
Fairdealing, Mo. (63939) 261/L9
Fairfax, Ala. (36854) 195/H5
Fairfax, Calif. (94930) 204/H1
Fairfax, Iowa (52228) 229/K5
Fairfax, Manitoba 179/B5
Fairfax, Minn. (55332) 255/D6
Fairfax, Mo. (64446) 261/B2
Fairfax, Ohio (†45201) 284/C9
Fairfax, Okla. (74637) 288/N1
Fairfax, S.C. (29827) 296/E6
Fairfax, S. Dak. (57335) 298/M7
Fairfax○, Vt. (05454) 268/B2
Fairfax (co.), Va. 307/O3
Fairfax (I.C.), Va. (22030) 307/R3
Fairfax, Wash. (†98323) 310/C4
Fairfax Station, Va. (22039) 307/R3
Fairfield, Ala. (35064) 195/E4
Fairfield, Calif. (94533) 204/K1
Fairfield (co.), Conn. 210/B3
Fairfield○, Conn. (06430) 210/B4
Fairfield, Fla. (32634) 212/D2
Fairfield, Idaho (83327) 220/D6
Fairfield, Ill. (62837) 222/E5
Fairfield, Iowa (52556) 229/J6
Fairfield, Ky. (40020) 237/L5
Fairfield, Maine (04937) 243/D6
Fairfield○, Maine (04937) 243/D6
Fairfield, Mont. (59436) 262/D3
Fairfield, Nebr. (68938) 264/G4
Fairfield, New Bruns. 170/E3
Fairfield○, N.J. (07006) 273/A2
Fairfield, N.S. Wales 88/K4
Fairfield, N.S. Wales 97/H3
Fairfield, N. Zealand 100/C6
Fairfield, N.C. (27826) 281/S3
Fairfield, N. Dak. (58627) 282/D5
Fairfield (co.), Ohio 284/E6
Fairfield, Ohio (45014) 284/A7
Fairfield, Pa. (17320) 294/H6
Fairfield (co.), S.C. 296/E3
Fairfield, Tenn. (†37183) 237/J9
Fairfield, Texas (75840) 303/H6
Fairfield, Utah (†84013) 304/B3
Fairfield○, Vt. (05455) 268/B2
Fairfield (pond), Vt. 268/A2
Fairfield, Va. (24435) 307/K5
Fairfield, Wash. (99012) 310/H3
Fairfield Center, Maine (†04937) 243/D6
Fairford, Ala. (†36553) 195/B8
Fairford, Manitoba 179/D3
Fairgrange, Ill. (†61920) 222/E4
Fairgrove, Mich. (48733) 250/F5
Fair Grove, Mo. (65648) 261/F8W
Fair Harbour, Br. Col. 184/D5
Fairhaven○, Mass. (02719) 249/L6
Fair Haven, Mich. (48023) 250/G6
Fairhaven, Minn. (†55382) 255/D5
Fairhaven, New Bruns. 170/C4

368 Fair Haven

Fair Haven, N.J. (07701) 273/E3
Fair Haven, N.Y. (13064) 276/G4
Fairhaven, Ohio (†45003) 284/A6
Fair Haven, Vt. (05743) 268/A4
Fair Haven○, Vt. (05743) 268/A4
Fair Hill, Md. (†21921) 245/P2
Fairholme, Sask. 181/C2
Fairhope, Ala. (36532) 195/C10
Fairhope, Pa. (15538) 294/E6
Fairisle, New Bruns. 170/E1
Fair Isle (isl.), Scotland 15/F3
Fairland, Ind. (46126) 227/F5
Fairland, Okla. (74343) 288/S1
Fair Lawn, N.J. (07410) 273/B1
Fairlawn, Ohio (44313) 284/G3
Fairlawn, Va. (24141) 307/G6
Fairlee, Md. (†21620) 245/O4
Fairlee○, Vt. (05045) 268/C4
Fairless Hills, Pa. (19030) 294/N5
Fairlie, N. Zealand 100/C6
Fairlie, Scotland 15/D5
Fairlight, Sask. 181/K6
Fairmead, Calif. (†93610) 204/E6
Fairmont, Ill. (†62002) 222/A2
Fairmont, Minn. (56031) 255/D7
Fairmont, Mo. (†63474) 261/J2
Fairmont, Nebr. (68354) 264/G4
Fairmont, N.C. (28340) 281/L6
Fairmont, Okla. (73736) 288/L2
Fairmont, W. Va. 188/K3
Fairmont, W. Va. (26554) 312/F4
Fairmont City, Ill. (†62201) 222/B2
Fairmont Hot Springs, Br. Col. 184/J5
Fairmount, Georgia (30139) 217/C2
Fairmount, Ill. (61841) 222/F3
Fairmount, Ind. (46928) 227/F4
Fairmount, Md. (†21871) 245/P8
Fairmount, N. Dak. (58030) 282/S7
Fairmount, Sask. 181/B4
Fairmount Heights, Md. (†20027) 245/G5
Fair Oaks, Ark. (72397) 202/J3
Fair Oaks, Calif. (95628) 204/C8
Fair Oaks, Georgia (†30060) 217/J1
Fair Oaks, Ind. (47943) 227/C2
Fair Oaks, Okla. (†74080) 288/P2
Fair Plain, Mich. (49022) 250/C6
Fairplain, W. Va. (†25271) 312/C5
Fairplay, Colo. (80440) 208/H4
Fairplay, Ky. (42735) 237/L7
Fair Play, Mo. (65649) 261/E7
Fair Play, S.C. (29643) 296/A2
Fairpoint, Ohio (43927) 284/J5
Fairpoint, S. Dak. (†57785) 298/D4
Fairport, Iowa (†52761) 229/M6
Fairport, Kansas (†67665) 232/C2
Fairport, Mo. (64447) 261/D2
Fairport, N.Y. (14450) 276/F4
Fairport, Va. (†22539) 307/R5
Fairport Harbor, Ohio (44077) 284/H2
Fairton, N.J. (08320) 273/C5
Fairvale, New Bruns. 170/E3
Fairview, Ala. (35208) 195/E2
Fairview, Alberta 182/A1
Fairview, Ill. (61432) 222/B3
Fairview, Ind. (†46127) 227/G5
Fairview, Ind. (†47018) 227/G7
Fairview, Kansas (66425) 232/G2
Fairview, Ky. (†41101) 237/S2
Fairview, Ky. (42221) 237/G7
Fairview, Mich. (48621) 250/F4
Fairview, Mo. (64842) 261/D9
Fairview, Mont. (59221) 262/M3
Fairview, N.J. (07022) 273/C2
Fairview, N.Y. (†12601) 276/N7
Fairview, N.C. (28730) 281/D3
Fairview, Ohio (43736) 284/H5
Fairview, Okla. (73737) 288/J2
Fairview, Oreg. (97024) 291/B2
Fairview, Pa. (16415) 294/B1
Fairview, Pa. (†16041) 294/C3
Fairview, S. Dak. (57027) 298/R7
Fairview, Tenn. (37062) 237/G9
Fairview, Utah (84629) 304/C4
Fairview, W. Va. (26570) 312/F3
Fairview, Wyo. (83119) 319/B3
Fairview Heights, Ill. (62208) 222/B3
Fairview Park, Ind. (†47842) 227/C5
Fairview Park, Ohio (44126) 284/G9
Fairview-Sumach, Wash. (†98901) 310/E4
Fair Water, Wis. (53931) 317/J8
Fairway, Kansas (†66101) 232/H2
Fairweather (cape), Alaska 196/L1
Fairweather (mt.), Alaska 196/L1
Fairweather (mt.), Br. Col. 184/H1
Fairy Glen, Sask. 181/G2
Fais (isl.), Micronesia 87/E5
Faisalabad, Pakistan 54/J6
Faisalabad, Pakistan 59/K3
Faisalabad, Pakistan 68/C2
Faison, N.C. (28341) 281/N4
Faith, Minn. (†56584) 255/B3
Faith, N.C. (28041) 281/J3
Faith, S. Dak. (57626) 298/E4
Faithorn, Mich. (†49892) 250/B3
Faizabad-cum-Ayodhya, India 68/E3
Fajami, Syria 63/J5
Fajardo, P. Rico 161/F1
Fajardo (riv.), P. Rico 161/F1
Fajou (isl.), Guadeloupe 161/A6
Fakaofo (atoll), Tokelau Is. 87/J6
Fakarava (atoll), Fr. Poly. 87/M7
Fakenham, England 13/H5
Fakfak, Indonesia 85/J6
Fakılı, Turkey 63/F3
Fakse, Denmark 21/F7
Fakse (bay), Denmark 21/F7
Fakse Ladeplads, Denmark 21/F7
Falaise, France 28/C3
Falam, Burma 72/B2
Falama, West Bank 65/C3
Falcarragh, Ireland 17/E1
Fălçiu, Romania 45/J2
Falcon, Ky. (41426) 237/P5
Falcon (lake), Manitoba 179/G5
Falcón (res.), Mexico 150/K3
Falcon, Miss. (38628) 256/D2
Falcon, N.C. (28342) 281/M4
Falcon (cape), Oreg. 291/C2
Falcon (res.), Texas 188/G5
Falcon (dam), Texas 303/E11
Falcon (res.), Texas 303/E11
Falcón (state), Venezuela 124/D2
Falcone (cape), Italy 34/B4
Falconer, N.Y. (14733) 276/B6
Falcon Heights, Minn. (55113) 255/G5
Falcon Heights, Oreg. (†97601) 291/F5
Falcon Lake, Manitoba 179/G5
Falémé (riv.), Mali 106/B6
Falémé (riv.), Senegal 106/B6
Faleolo, W. Samoa 86/L8
Falfurrias, Texas (78355) 303/F10
Falher, Alberta 182/B2
Falkenberg, Sweden 18/H8
Falkensee, E. Germany 22/E3
Falkenstein, E. Germany 22/E3
Falkirk, N. Dak. (†58577) 282/H5
Falkirk, Scotland 10/B1
Falkirk, Scotland 15/C1
Falkland (isls.) 2/G8
Falkland (isls.), 143/D7
Falkland (sound), 143/D7
Falkland, Br. Col. 184/H5
Falkland, N.C. (27827) 281/O3
Falkland, Scotland 15/E4
FALKLAND ISLANDS 143
Falkland Islands 120/D8
Falkner, Miss. (38629) 256/G1
Falknov (Sokolov), Czech. 41/B1
Falköping, Sweden 18/H7
Falkville, Ala. (35622) 195/E2
Fall (riv.), Kansas 232/G4
Falla, Cuba 158/F2
Fall Branch, Tenn. (37656) 237/R8
Fallbrook, Calif. (92028) 204/H10
Fall City, Wash. (98024) 310/D3
Fall Creek, Oreg. (97438) 291/E4
Fall Creek, Wis. (54742) 317/D6
Fallin, Scotland 15/C1
Falling Spring (Renick), W. Va. (†24966) 312/F6
Falling Waters, W. Va. (25419) 312/L3
Fallis, Okla. (†74881) 288/M3
Fall Mills, Tenn. (†37345) 237/J10
Fallon (co.), Mont. 262/M4
Fallon, Mont. (59326) 262/L4
Fallon, Nev. (89406) 266/C3
Fallon Ind. Res., Nev. 266/C3
Fallon Nav. Air Sta., Nev. 266/C3
Fall River, Kansas (67047) 232/G4
Fall River (lake), Kansas 232/F4
Fall River, Mass. 188/M2
Fall River, Mass. (*02720) 249/K6
Fall River, Nova Scotia 168/E4
Fall River (co.), S. Dak. 298/B7
Fall River, Tenn. (†38468) 237/G10
Fall River, Wis. (53932) 317/H9
Fall River Mills, Calif. (96028) 204/D3
Falls (riv.), Mass. 249/D2
Falls, Pa. (18615) 294/E6
Falls (co.), Texas 303/H6
Falls Church (I.C.), Va. (*22040) 307/S2
Falls City, Nebr. (68355) 264/J4
Falls City, Oreg. (97344) 291/D3
Falls City, Texas (78113) 303/G9
Falls Creek, Pa. (15840) 294/E3
Falls Mill, W. Va. (26620) 312/E5
Falls Mills, Va. (24613) 307/F6
Falls of Rough, Ky. (40119) 237/J5
Fallston, Md. (21047) 245/N2
Fallston, N.C. (28042) 281/K3
Falls Village, Conn. (06031) 210/B1
Fallsville, Ark. (†72861) 202/D2
Falmouth, Ant. & Bar. 161/E11
Falmouth, Ant. & Bar. 156/F3
Falmouth, England 10/D5
Falmouth, England 13/B7
Falmouth (bay), England 13/B7
Falmouth, Ind. (46127) 227/G5
Falmouth, Jamaica 158/H5
Falmouth, Jamaica 156/C3
Falmouth, Ky. (41040) 237/N3
Falmouth, Maine (04105) 243/C8
Falmouth○, Maine (04105) 243/C8
Falmouth, Mass. (*02540) 249/M6
Falmouth○, Mass. (*02540) 249/M6
Falmouth, Mich. (49632) 250/E4
Falmouth, Nova Scotia 168/D3
Falmouth, Va. (22401) 307/O4
False (bay), S. Africa 118/F7
False Detour (chan.), Mich. 250/F3
False Divi (pt.), India 68/E5
False Pass, Alaska (99583) 196/F4
Falso (cape), Dom. Rep. 158/C7
Falso (cape), Honduras 154/F3
Falso (cape), Mexico 150/D5
Falster (isl.), Denmark 21/F8
Fălticeni, Romania 45/H2
Falun, Kansas (67442) 232/E3
Falun, Sweden 18/J6
Falun, Sweden 7/F2
Falun, Wis. (†54840) 317/A4
Famagusta, Cyprus 63/F5
Famagusta, Cyprus 59/B3
Famagusta (bay), Cyprus 63/F5
Famaka, Sudan 111/F5
Famatina, Argentina 143/C2
Famatina, Sierra de (mts.), Argentina 143/C2
Family (lake), Manitoba 179/G3
Famoso, Calif. (†93280) 204/F8
Fan (lake), N. Dak. 282/L2
Fanad (head), Ireland 17/F1
Fancy Farm, Ky. (42039) 237/D7
Fancy Gap, Va. (24328) 307/G7
Fancy Prairie, Ill. (62637) 222/D4
Fandriana, Madagascar 118/H4
Fangak, Sudan 111/F6
Fang Xian, China 77/G5
Fangzheng, China 77/L2
Fannettsburg, Pa. (17221) 294/G5
Fannich, Loch (lake), Scotland 15/D3
Fannin (co.), Georgia 217/D1
Fannin, Miss. (†39042) 256/E6
Fannin (co.), Texas 303/H4
Fannin, Texas (77960) 303/G9
Fanning (isl.), Kiribati 87/L5
Fanning (isl.), Kiribati 2/B5
Fanning Springs (Suwannee River), Fla. (†32693) 212/D2
Fanny Bay, Br. Col. 184/H2
Fannystelle, Manitoba 179/E5
Fanø (isl.), Denmark 21/B7
Fanø (isl.), Denmark 18/F9
Fano, Italy 34/D3
Fanshawe, Okla. (74935) 288/S5
Fan Si Pan (mt.), Vietnam 72/D2
Fantasque (pt.), Haiti 158/B6
Fanwood, N.J. (07023) 273/E2
Fao, Iraq 66/F6
Faradje, Zaire 115/E3
Faradofay, Madagascar 102/G7
Faradofay, Madagascar 118/H5
Farafangana, Madagascar 102/G7
Farafangana, Madagascar 118/H4
Farâfra (oasis), Egypt 111/E2
Farâfra (oasis), Egypt 59/A4
Farah, Afghanistan 68/A2
Farah, Afghanistan 54/H6
Farah, Afghanistan 59/H3
Farah Rud (riv.) 54/H6
Farah Rud (riv.), Afghanistan 59/H3
Farah Rud (riv.), Afghanistan 68/A2
Farallon (isls.), Calif. 204/B6
Farallon de Pajaros (isl.), No. Marianas 87/E3
Farallons, The (gulf), Calif. 204/H2
Faranah, Guinea 106/B6
Farasan (isls.), Saudi Arabia 59/D6
Faraulep (atoll), Micronesia 87/E5
Farber, Mo. (63345) 261/J4
Farciennes, Belgium 27/E8
Fareham, England 10/F5
Fareham, England 13/F7
Farewell, Alaska (†99629) 196/H2
Farewell (cape), Greenl. 4/D12
Farewell (cape), Greenland 146/P4
Farewell (cape), Greenland 2/G3
Farewell (cape), N. Zealand 100/D4
Farfa, Italy 34/D3
Farfán, Ecuador 128/D2
Fargo, Ark. (†72021) 202/H4
Fargo, Georgia (31631) 217/G9
Fargo, Mich. (†48006) 250/G5
Fargo, N. Dak. 146/J5
Fargo, N. Dak. 188/G1
Fargo, N. Dak. (58102) 282/S6
Fargo, Okla. (73840) 288/G2
Fargo, Texas (†76384) 303/E3
Far Hills, N.J. (07931) 273/D2
Faribault, Minn. 188/H2
Faribault (co.), Minn. 255/D7
Faribault, Minn. (55021) 255/E6
Faridabad, India 68/D3
Faridpur, Bangladesh 68/F4
Fariman, Iran 66/L3
Farina, Ill. (62838) 222/E5
Farisita, Colo. (81037) 208/J7
Fariston, Ky. (†40741) 237/N6
Färjestaden, Sweden 18/K8
Farler, Ky. (41742) 237/P6
Farley, Iowa (52046) 229/L4
Farley, Mo. (64028) 261/O4
Farley, N. Mex. (†87747) 274/E2
Farlin, Iowa (50077) 229/E4
Farlington, Kansas (66734) 232/H4
Farm (riv.), Conn. 210/D3
Farmdale, Ohio (44417) 284/J3
Farmer, N.C. (27203) 281/K3
Farmer (isl.), N.W. Terrs. 187/K4
Farmer, Ohio (43520) 284/A3
Farmer, S. Dak. (57336) 298/O6
Farmer City, Ill. (61842) 222/E3
Farmers, Ky. (40319) 237/P4
Farmers Branch, Texas (75234) 303/G2
Farmersburg, Ind. (47850) 227/C6
Farmersburg, Iowa (52047) 229/L3
Farmersville, Ala. (36737) 195/E6
Farmersville, Calif. (93223) 204/F7
Farmersville, Ill. (62533) 222/D4
Farmersville, Mo. (†64683) 261/E3
Farmersville, Ohio (45325) 284/A6
Farmersville, Texas (75031) 303/H4
Farmerville, La. (71241) 238/F1
Farmhaven, Miss. (†39046) 256/E5
Farmill (riv.), Conn. 210/C3
Farmingdale, Maine (†04345) 243/D7
Farmingdale○, Maine (†04345) 243/D7
Farmingdale, N.J. (07727) 273/E3
Farmingdale, N.Y. (11735) 276/R7
Farmingdale, S. Dak. (†57725) 298/D6
Farmington, Ark. (72730) 202/B1
Farmington, Br. Col. 184/G2
Farmington, Calif. (95230) 204/E6
Farmington○, Conn. (06032) 210/D2
Farmington (riv.), Conn. 210/D1
Farmington, Del. (19942) 245/R5
Farmington, Georgia (30638) 217/F3
Farmington, Ill. (61531) 222/C3
Farmington, Iowa (52626) 229/K7
Farmington, Ky. (42040) 237/D7
Farmington, Maine (04938) 243/C6
Farmington○, Maine (04938) 243/C6
Farmington, Md. (†21911) 245/O2
Farmington, Mich. (*48024) 250/F6
Farmington, Minn. (55024) 255/E6
Farmington, Mo. (63640) 261/M7
Farmington, N.H. (03835) 268/E5
Farmington○, N.H. (03835) 268/E5
Farmington, N. Mex. 188/E3
Farmington, N. Mex. (87401) 274/A2
Farmington, N.C. (†27028) 281/H3
Farmington, Oreg. (†97123) 291/A2
Farmington, Tenn. (†37091) 237/H9
Farmington, Utah (84025) 304/C3
Farmington, Wash. (99128) 310/H3
Farmington, W. Va. (26571) 312/F3
Farmington, Wis. (†54020) 317/A5
Farmington Falls, Maine (04940) 243/C6
Farmington Hills, Mich. (48024) 250/F6
Farmland, Ind. (47340) 227/G4
Farmville, N.C. (27828) 281/O3
Farmville, Va. (23901) 307/M6
Farnam, Nebr. (69029) 264/D4
Farnams, Mass. (†01225) 249/B2
Farnborough, England 13/G8
Farner, Tenn. (37333) 237/N10
Farnham, England 13/G8
Farnham, England 10/F5
Farnham, N.Y. (14061) 276/B6
Farnham, Québec 172/E4
Farnham, Va. (22460) 307/P5
Farnhamville, Iowa (50538) 229/D4
Farnsworth, Texas (79033) 303/C1
Farnworth, England 13/H2
Faro, Brazil 132/B3
Faro (dist.), Portugal 33/B4
Faro, Portugal 7/D5
Faro, Portugal 33/B4
Fårö (isl.), Sweden 18/L8
Faro, Yukon 187/E3
Faro, Yukon 162/C3
Fårösund, Sweden 18/L8
Farquhar (cape), W. Australia 88/A4
Farquhar (cape), W. Australia 92/A3
Farr (bay) 5/C5
Farragut, Iowa (51639) 229/C7
Farrar, Georgia (†31085) 217/E4
Farrar, Iowa (†50161) 229/G5
Farrar, Mo. (63740) 261/N7
Farrar (riv.), Scotland 15/D3
Farrashband, Iran 66/G6
Farrell (lake), Alberta 182/D4
Farrell, Miss. (38630) 256/C2
Farrell, Pa. (16121) 294/A3
Farrellton, Québec 172/A4
Farris, Okla. (74542) 288/P6
Farrow, Alberta 182/D4
Farrukhabad-cum-Fatehgarh, India 68/D3
Fars (prov.), Iran 66/H6
Fársala, Greece 45/F6
Farsi, Afghanistan 68/A2
Farsi, Afghanistan 59/H3
Farsi (isl.), Iran 66/G7
Farsø, Denmark 21/C4
Farson, Iowa (†52563) 229/J6
Farson, Wyo. (82932) 319/C3
Farsund, Norway 18/E7
Fartak, Ras (cape), P.D.R. Yemen 59/F6
Farum, Denmark 21/F6
Farwell, Mich. (48622) 250/E5
Farwell, Minn. (56327) 255/C5
Farwell, Nebr. (68838) 264/F3
Farwell, Texas (79325) 303/A3
Fasa, Iran 66/H6
Fasa, Iran 59/F4
Fasano, Italy 34/F4
Fashoda (Kodok), Sudan 111/F6
Fassett, Québec 172/C4
Fastnet Rock (isl.), Ireland 17/B9
Fastov, U.S.S.R. 52/C4
Fatagar Tuting (cape), Indonesia 85/J6
Fatehpur, Rajasthan, India 68/C3
Fatehpur, Uttar Pradesh, India 68/E3
Fatih, Turkey 63/D6
Fátima, Portugal 33/B3
Fatsa, Turkey 63/G2
Fatshan (Foshan), China 77/H7
Fatuhiva (isl.), Fr. Poly. 87/N7
Faubush, Ky. (42532) 237/M6
Faucett, Mo. (64448) 261/C3
Faucilles (mts.), France 28/G3
Fauldhouse, Scotland 10/C1
Fauldhouse, Scotland 15/C2
Faulk (co.), S. Dak. 298/L3
Faulkner (co.), Ark. 202/F3
Faulkner, Iowa (†50601) 229/G3
Faulkner, Manitoba 179/D3
Faulkton, S. Dak. (57438) 298/L3
Faunsdale, Ala. (36738) 195/C6
Fauquier, Ontario 177/J5
Fauquier, Ontario 175/D3
Fauquier (co.), Va. 307/N3
Făurei, 45/H3
Faust, Alberta 182/C2
Favara, Italy 34/D6
Faversham, England 13/H6
Faversham, England 10/G5
Favignana (isl.), Italy 34/D6
Fawcett, Alberta 182/C2
Fawn (riv.), Ind. 227/G1
Fawn (riv.), Mich. 250/D7
Fawn (lake), Ont. 162/H5
Fawn (riv.), Ontario 175/C2
Fawn Grove, Pa. (17321) 294/J6
Fawnskin, Calif. (92333) 204/J9
Faxaflói (bay), Iceland 21/B1
Faxon, Okla. (73540) 288/J6
Fay, Ill. (†61285) 222/C2
Fay, Okla. (73646) 288/J3
Faya-Largeau, Chad 102/D3
Faya-Largeau, Chad 111/C4
Fayette (co.), Ala. 195/C3
Fayette, Ala. (35555) 195/C3
Fayette (co.), Georgia 217/C4
Fayette (co.), Ill. 222/D4
Fayette (co.), Ind. 227/G5
Fayette, Ind. (†46052) 227/E5
Fayette (co.), Iowa 229/K3
Fayette, Iowa (52142) 229/K3
Fayette (co.), Ky. 237/N4
Fayette○, Maine (†04349) 243/C7
Fayette, Miss. (39069) 256/B7
Fayette, Mo. (65248) 261/G4
Fayette (co.), Ohio 284/D6
Fayette, Ohio (43521) 284/B2
Fayette (co.), Pa. 294/C6
Fayette (co.), Tenn. 237/C10
Fayette (co.), Texas 303/H8
Fayette, Utah (84630) 304/C4
Fayette (co.), W. Va. 312/D6
Fayette City, Pa. (15438) 294/C5
Fayetteville, Ala. (†35150) 195/F4
Fayetteville, Ark. 188/H3
Fayetteville, Ark. (72701) 202/B1
Fayetteville, Georgia (30214) 217/C4
Fayetteville, Ill. (†62258) 222/D5
Fayetteville, Ind. (†47421) 227/D7
Fayetteville, Mo. (†64093) 261/E5
Fayetteville, N.Y. (13066) 276/J4
Fayetteville, N.C. 188/L3
Fayetteville, N.C. (*28301) 281/M4
Fayetteville, Ohio (45118) 284/C7
Fayetteville, Pa. (17222) 294/G6
Fayetteville, Tenn. (37334) 237/H10
Fayetteville, Texas (78940) 303/H8
Fayetteville, W. Va. (25840) 312/D6
Fayville, Mass. (01745) 249/H3
Faywood, N. Mex. (88034) 274/B6
Fdérik (Fort-Gouraud), Mauritania 106/B4
Feakle, Ireland 17/D6
Feale (riv.), Ireland 17/C7
Fear (cape), N.C. 188/L4
Fear (cape), N.C. 281/O7
Fearer, Md. (†21531) 245/A2
Fearns Springs, Miss. (†39339) 256/G4
Feather (riv.), Calif. 204/D4
Feather Falls, Calif. (95940) 204/D4
Featherston, N. Zealand 100/E4
Featherston, Okla. (†74561) 288/P4
Fécamp, France 28/D3
Fédala (Mohammedia), Morocco 106/C2
Federación, Argentina 143/G5
Federal, Alberta 182/E3
Federal, Wyo. (†82001) 319/G4
Federal Dam, Minn. (56641) 255/D3
Federal District, Brazil 132/E6
Federal Heights, Colo. (†80221) 208/J3
Federalsburg, Md. (21632) 245/P6
Federal Territory (state), Laos 72/D7
Fedora, S. Dak. (57337) 298/O5
Fedscreek, Ky. (41524) 237/S6
Feeagh (lake), Ireland 17/B4
Feeding Hills, Mass. (01030) 249/D4
Feeny, N. Ireland 17/H2
Feesburg, Ohio (45119) 284/B8
Fegyvernek, Hungary 41/F3
Fehérgyarmat, Hungary 41/G3
Fehmarn (isl.), Denmark 21/E8
Fehmarn (str.), Denmark 21/E8
Fehmarn (isl.), W. Germany 22/D1
Fehmarn (str.), W. Germany 22/D1
Feia (lake), Brazil 135/F3
Feijó, Brazil 132/G10
Feilding, N. Zealand 100/E4
Feio (riv.), Brazil 135/B2
Feira, Portugal 33/B2
Feira (Luangwa), Zambia 115/E7
Feira de Santana, Brazil 132/G5
Feira de Santana, Brazil 120/F4
Fejér (co.), Hungary 41/E3
Fejø (isl.), Denmark 21/E8
Feke, Turkey 63/G4
Felanitx, Spain 33/H3
Felch, Mich. (49831) 250/B3
Felchville (Reading), Vt. (†05062) 268/B5
Felda, Fla. (33930) 212/E5
Feldbach, Austria 41/C3
Feldberg (mt.), W. Germany 22/C5
Feldkirch, Austria 41/A3
Feldkirchen in Kärnten, Austria 41/B3
Feliciano (riv.), Argentina 143/G5
Felicité (isl.), Seychelles 118/J5
Felicity, Ohio (45120) 284/B8
Felipe Carillo Puerto, Mexico 150/P7
Felipe Matiauda, Paraguay 144/D4
Felipe Yofré, Argentina 143/G4
Felix (cape), N.W. Terrs. 187/J3
Felixstowe, England 10/G5
Felixstowe, England 13/J6
Fellbach, W. Germany 22/C4
Felletin, France 28/E5
Felling, England 13/J3
Fellows, Calif. (93224) 204/F8
Fellowsville, W. Va. (†26410) 312/G4
Fellsburg, Kansas (67048) 232/C4
Fellsmere, Fla. (32948) 212/F4
Fels am Wagram, Austria 41/C2
Felsberg, Switzerland 39/H3
Felsenthal, Ark. (†71747) 202/F7
Felt, Idaho (83424) 220/G6
Felt, Okla. (73937) 288/A1
Felton, Ark. (†72360) 202/J4
Felton, Calif. (95018) 204/K4
Felton, Del. (19943) 245/R4
Felton, Georgia (30140) 217/B3
Felton, Minn. (56536) 255/B3
Felton, Pa. (17322) 294/J6
Feltre, Italy 34/C1
Felts Mills, N.Y. (13638) 276/J3
Feltwell, England 13/H5
Felty, Ky. (†40962) 237/O6
Femø (isl.), Denmark 21/E8
Femundsjø (lake), Norway 18/G5
Fence (riv.), Mich. 250/A2
Fence, Wis. (54120) 317/K4
Fence Lake, N. Mex. (87315) 274/A4
Fender, Georgia (†31794) 217/E8
Fenelon Falls, Ontario 177/F3
Fengcheng, China 77/K3
Fengjie, China 77/G5
Fengning, China 77/J3
Fengqing, China 77/E7
Fengtai, China 77/J5
Feng Xian, China 77/G5
Fengxiang, China 77/G5
Fengyang, China 77/H4
Fengzhen, China 77/H3
Fen He (riv.), China 77/H4
Fenholloway (riv.), Fla. 212/C1
Feni (isls.), Papua N.G. 86/C2
Fenimore (passage), Alaska 196/L4
Fenit, Ireland 17/B7
Fenn, Alberta 182/D3
Fenn, Idaho (83531) 220/B4
Fenner, Calif. (†92332) 204/K9
Fennimore, Wis. (53809) 317/E9
Fennville, Mich. (49408) 250/C6
Fenoarivo, Fianarantsoa, Madagascar 118/H4
Fenoarivo, Toamasina, Madagascar 118/H3
Fens, The (reg.), England 13/G5
Fenton (riv.), Conn. 210/G1
Fenton, Ill. (61251) 222/C2
Fenton, Iowa (50539) 229/E2
Fenton, La. (70640) 238/E6
Fenton, Mich. (48430) 250/F6
Fenton, Mo. (63026) 261/O4
Fenton, Sask. 181/F2
Fentress (co.), Tenn. 237/M8
Fenwick, Conn. (†06475) 210/F3
Fenwick, Mich. (48834) 250/D5
Fenwick, Nova Scotia 168/D3
Fenwick, W. Va. (26202) 312/E6
Fenwick Island, Del. (19944) 245/T7
Fenwood, Sask. 181/H4
Fenwood, Wis. (54431) 317/F6
Feodosiya, U.S.S.R. 52/D5
Ferbane, Ireland 17/F5
Ferdig, Mont. (59437) 262/E2
Ferdinand, Idaho (83526) 220/B3
Ferdinand, Ind. (47532) 227/D8
Ferdows, Iran 59/G3
Ferdows, Iran 66/K3
Ferfer, Somalia 115/J2
Fergana, U.S.S.R. 54/J6
Fergana, U.S.S.R. 48/H5
Fergus (riv.), Ireland 17/D6
Fergus (co.), Mont. 262/G3
Fergus, Mont. (59451) 262/H3
Fergus, Ontario 177/D4
Fergus Falls, Minn. (56537) 255/B4
Ferguson, Br. Col. 184/J5
Ferguson, Iowa (50078) 229/H5
Ferguson, Ky. (42533) 237/M6
Ferguson, Mo. (63135) 261/P2
Ferguson, N.C. (28624) 281/G2
Ferguson, W. Va. (†25511) 312/B6
Ferintosh, Alberta 182/D3
Ferkessédougou, Ivory Coast 106/D7
Ferlach, Austria 41/C3
Ferland, Ontario 177/H4
Ferland, Ontario 175/C2
Ferland, Québec 172/G1
Ferland, Sask. 181/D6
Ferlo (reg.), Senegal 106/B6
Fermanagh (dist.), N. Ireland 17/F3
Ferme-Neuve, Québec 172/B3
Fermeuse, Newf. 166/D2
Fermo, Italy 34/D3
Fermont, Québec 174/D2
Fermoselle, Spain 33/C2
Fermoy, Ireland 17/E7
Fermoy, Ireland 10/B4
Fernald, Iowa (†50201) 229/G4
Fernández, Argentina 143/D2
Fernandina (isl.), Ecuador 128/B9
Fernandina Beach, Fla. (32034) 212/E1
Fernando de la Mora, Paraguay 144/B4
Fernando Po (Bioko) (isl.), Equat. Guinea 102/C4
Fernando Po (Bioko) (isl.), Equat. Guinea 115/A3
Fernandópolis, Brazil 135/A2
Fernan Lake, Idaho (†83814) 220/B2
Fernbank, Ala. (35558) 195/B3
Fernberg, Queensland 88/K3
Ferndale, Calif. (95536) 204/A3
Ferndale, Md. (21061) 245/M4
Ferndale, Mich. (48220) 250/B6
Ferndale, Pa. (18921) 294/M4
Ferndale, Pa. (15905) 294/E5
Ferndale, Wash. (98248) 310/C2
Fernelmont, Belgium 27/F7
Ferness, Scotland 15/E3
Ferney, S. Dak. (57439) 298/N3
Fernie, Br. Col. 162/E6
Fernie, Br. Col. 184/K5
Fernley, Nev. (89408) 266/B3
Fern Ridge (lake), Oreg. 291/D3
Ferns, Ireland 17/J6
Fern Tree Gully, Victoria 97/K5
Fernwood, Idaho (83830) 220/B2
Fernwood, Miss. (39635) 256/D8
Fernwood, N.Y. (†12801) 276/N4
Fernwood, N.Y. (†13142) 276/H4
Ferolle (pt.), Newf. 166/C3
Ferrandina, Italy 34/F4
Ferrara (prov.), Italy 34/C2
Ferrara, Italy 7/F4
Ferrara, Italy 34/C2
Ferré (cape), Martinique 161/E7
Ferreira do Alentejo, Portugal 33/B3
Ferreira Gomes, Brazil 132/D2
Ferrellsburg, W. Va. (25513) 312/B6
Ferrelo (cape), Oreg. 291/C5
Ferrelview, Mo. (64163) 261/O4
Ferreñafe, Peru 128/C6
Ferriday, La. (71334) 238/G3
Ferrier, Alberta 182/C3
Ferrières, Belgium 27/H8
Ferris, Ill. (62336) 222/B3
Ferris, Texas (75125) 303/H3
Ferris (mts.), Wyo. 319/E3
Ferrisburg○, Vt. (05456) 268/A3
Ferrol (pen.), Peru 128/C7
Ferrol del Caudillo, Spain 33/B1
Ferron, Utah (84523) 304/C4
Ferron (creek), Utah 304/C4
Ferros, Brazil 132/F7
Ferrum, Va. (24088) 307/H7
Ferry, Guadeloupe 161/A6
Ferry, Mich. (49455) 250/C5
Ferry (co.), Wash. 310/G2
Ferryden, Scotland 15/F4
Ferryland, Newf. 166/D2
Ferryland (cape), Newf. 166/D2
Ferry Road, New Bruns. 170/E1
Ferrysburg, Mich. (49409) 250/C5
Ferryville, Wis. (54628) 317/D9
Fertigs, Pa. (†16364) 294/C3
Fertile, Iowa (50434) 229/G2
Fertile, Minn. (56540) 255/B3
Fertile, Sask. 181/K6
Fertilia, Italy 34/B4
Fertő tó (Neusiedler See) (lake), Austria 41/D3
Fertő tó (Neusiedler See) (lake), Hungary 41/D3
Fès (Fez), Morocco 106/D2
Fès, Morocco 102/B1

Fontaine 369

Feshi, Zaire 115/C5
Fessenden, N. Dak. (58438) 282/L4
Fesserton, Ontario 177/E3
Festina, Iowa (52143) 229/K2
Festus, Mo. (63028) 261/M6
Fetești, Romania 45/H3
Fethard, Tipperary, Ireland 17/F7
Fethard, Wexford, Ireland 17/H7
Fethiye, Turkey 63/C4
Fethiye, Turkey 59/A2
Fetlar (isl.), Scotland 15/G2
Fetlar (isl.), Scotland 10/H1
Feudal, Sask. 181/D4
Feuerkogel (mt.), Austria 41/B3
Feuerthalen, Switzerland 39/G1
Feuilles (riv.), Que. 162/J4
Feuilles (riv.), Que. 146/L4
Feuilles (riv.), Québec 174/C1
Feversham, Ontario 177/D3
Fevzipaşa, Turkey 63/G4
Feyzabad, Afghanistan 54/H6
Feyzabad, Afghanistan 59/K2
Feyzabad, Afghanistan 68/C1
Fezzan (reg.), Libya 102/D2
Fezzan (reg.), Libya 111/B2
Ffestiniog, Wales 10/E4
Ffestiniog, Wales 13/D5
Fiambalá, Argentina 143/C2
Fianarantsoa (prov.), Madagascar 118/H4
Fianarantsoa, Madagascar 102/G7
Fianarantsoa, Madagascar 118/H4
Fianga, Chad 111/C6
Fiat, Ind. (†47326) 227/G3
Fiatt, Ill. (61433) 222/C3
Fichtelberg (mt.), E. Germany 22/E3
Fichtelgebirge (range), W. Germany 22/D3
Fickle, Ind. (†46035) 227/D4
Ficklin, Georgia (†30673) 217/G3
Ficksburg, S. Africa 118/D5
Fidalgo (isl.), Wash. 310/C2
Fidelity, Ill. (62030) 222/C4
Fidenza, Italy 34/B2
Fieberbrunn, Austria 41/B3
Field, Br. Col. 184/J4
Field, Ky. (40934) 237/O7
Field, Ontario 177/E1
Fieldale, Va. (24089) 307/H7
Field Creek, Texas (†76869) 303/F7
Fielding, New Bruns. 170/C2
Fielding, Sask. 181/D3
Fielding, Utah (84311) 304/B2
Fieldon, Ill. (62031) 222/C4
Fields, La. (70641) 238/C5
Fields (lake), La. 238/J7
Fields, Oreg. (97710) 291/J5
Fieldsboro, N.J. (†08505) 273/D3
Fieldton, Texas (79326) 303/B3
Fier, Albania 45/D5
Fierro, N. Mex. (†88041) 274/A6
Fiesch, Switzerland 39/F4
Fiesole, Italy 34/C3
Fife (lake), Sask. 181/E6
Fife (reg.), Scotland 15/E4
Fife (trad. co.), Scotland 15/B5
Fife, Wash. (98424) 310/C3
Fife Lake, Mich. (49633) 250/D4
Fife Lake, Sask. 181/F6
Fife Ness (prom.), Scotland 15/F4
Fifield, N.S. Wales 97/D3
Fifield, Wis. (54524) 317/F4
Fifteenmile (creek), Oreg. 291/F2
Fifteenmile Arroyo (creek), N. Mex. 274/D4
Fifth (lake), Maine 243/H5
Fifth Cataract, Sudan 111/F4
Fifth Cataract, Sudan 59/B6
Fifth Cataract (dam), Sudan 102/F3
Fifty Lakes, Minn. (56448) 255/D4
Fiftysix, Ark. (72533) 202/F2
Fig (riv.), Newf. 166/B3
Figeac, France 28/D5
Figueira da Foz, Portugal 33/B2
Figueras, Spain 33/H1
Figuig, Morocco 102/B1
Figuig, Morocco 106/D2
Figuras (pt.), P. Rico 161/E3
Fiji 2/A6
Fiji 87/H8
FIJI 86/P11
Filadelfia, Bolivia 136/A2
Filadelfia, C. Rica 154/E5
Filadelfia, Paraguay 144/B3
Fil'akovo, Czech. 41/E2
Filbert, S.C. (†29745) 296/E1
Filbert, W. Va. (24835) 312/D8
Filchner Ice Shelf, Ant. 2/H10
Filchner Ice Shelf, Ant. 5/B16
Fil di Remia (peak), Switzerland 39/H4
File (hills), Sask. 181/H5
Filer, Idaho (83328) 220/D7
Filer City, Mich. (49634) 250/C4
Filey, England 13/G3
Filey, England 10/F3
Filiátes, Greece 45/E6
Filiatrá, Greece 45/E7
Filicudi (isl.), Italy 34/E5
Filingué, Niger 106/E6
Filion, Mich. (48432) 250/G5
Filippiás, Greece 45/E6
Filipstad, Sweden 18/H7
Filisur, Switzerland 39/J3
Filley, Nebr. (68357) 264/H4
Fillmore, Calif. (93015) 204/G9
Fillmore, Ill. (62032) 222/D4
Fillmore, Ind. (46128) 227/D5
Fillmore (co.), Minn. 255/F7
Fillmore, Minn. (†55990) 255/F7
Fillmore, Mo. (64449) 261/C2
Fillmore (co.), Nebr. 264/G4
Fillmore, N.Y. (14735) 276/D6
Fillmore, N. Dak. (58333) 282/L3
Fillmore, Okla. (†73450) 288/N6
Fillmore, Sask. 181/H6
Fillmore, Utah (84631) 304/B5
Filtu, Ethiopia 111/H6
Filyos (riv.), Turkey 63/D2
Fimi (riv.), Zaire 115/C4
Finale Emilia, Italy 34/C2
Finale Ligure, Italy 34/B2
Fiñana, Spain 33/E4
Fincastle, Ind. (†46172) 227/D5
Fincastle, Ky. (†40222) 237/L1
Fincastle, Va. (24090) 307/J6
Finch, Mont. (†59076) 262/K4
Finch, Ontario 177/J2
Finchburg, Ala. (†36444) 195/D7
Finchville, Ky. (40022) 237/L4
Findhorn, Scotland 15/E3
Findhorn (riv.), Scotland 15/E3
Fındıklı, Turkey 63/J2
Findlater, Sask. 181/F5
Findlay, Ill. (62534) 222/E4
Findlay, Ohio (45840) 284/C3
Findley Lake, N.Y. (14736) 276/A6
Findochty, Scotland 15/E3
Findon, Mont. (†59053) 262/F4
Fine, N.Y. (13639) 276/K2
Finesville, N.J. (†08865) 273/C2
Fingal, N. Dak. (58031) 282/P6
Fingal, Ontario 177/C5
Fingal, Tasmania 99/E3
Finger (lake), Ontario 175/B2
Finger, Tenn. (38334) 237/D10
Fingerville, S.C. (29338) 296/D1
Fingoè, Mozambique 118/E2
Finhaut, Switzerland 39/C4
Finike, Turkey 63/D4
Finistère (dept.), France 28/A3
Finisterre (cape), Spain 7/C4
Finisterre (cape), Spain 33/B1
Finke (riv.), North. Terr. 88/E5
Finke (riv.), North. Terr. 93/C8
Finke (riv.), S. Australia 94/C1
Finksburg, Md. (21048) 245/L3
Finland 2/L2
Finland 4/C8
Finland 7/G2
Finland (gulf) 7/G3
FINLAND 18
Finland (gulf), Finland 18/P7
Finland, Minn. (55603) 255/G3
Finland (gulf), U.S.S.R. 52/C3
Finland (gulf), U.S.S.R. 48/C4
Finland (gulf), U.S.S.R. 53/D1
Finlay (riv.), Br. Col. 162/D4
Finlay (riv.), Br. Col. 184/E1
Finlay (mts.), Texas 303/B10
Finlayson, Minn. (55735) 255/F4
Finley, Ky. (42736) 237/L6
Finley, N. S. Wales 88/H7
Finley, N.S. Wales 97/C4
Finley, N. Dak. (58230) 282/P4
Finley, Okla. (74543) 288/R6
Finley, Tenn. (38030) 237/B8
Finley, Wash. (†99336) 310/F4
Finleyson, Georgia (†31071) 217/F6
Finleyville, Pa. (15332) 294/B5
Finly, Ind. (46129) 227/F5
Finn (riv.), Ireland 17/F2
Finn (riv.), Ireland 17/G3
Finnegan, Alberta 182/E4
Finney (co.), Kansas 232/B3
Finnmark (co.), Norway 18/O2
Finschhafen, Papua N.G. 86/B2
Finschhafen, Papua N.G. 85/C7
Finspång, Sweden 18/J7
Finsteraarhorn (mt.), Switzerland 39/F3
Finstermünz (pass), Switzerland 39/K3
Finsterwalde, E. Germany 22/E3
Finstown, Scotland 15/E1
Fintona, N. Ireland 17/G3
Fintry, Scotland 15/B1
Fionn Loch (lake), Scotland 15/C3
Fir (riv.), Sask. 181/J2
Firat (riv.), Turkey 63/G4
Fircrest, Wash. (98466) 310/C3
Fire (isl.), Alaska 196/B1
Firebag (riv.), Alberta 182/E1
Firebaugh, Calif. (93622) 204/E7
Firebrick, Ky. (41137) 237/P3
Fireco, W. Va. (†25856) 312/D7
Fire Island National Seashore, N.Y. 276/P9
Firenze (Florence), Italy 34/C3
Fires (bay), Tasmania 99/E3
Firesteel (riv.), Mich. 250/G1
Firesteel, S. Dak. (57628) 298/G3
Firesteel (creek), S. Dak. 298/N6
Firestone, Colo. (80520) 208/K2
Firgrove, S. Africa 118/F6
Firmat, Argentina 143/F6
Firminy, France 28/F5
Fir Mountain, Sask. 181/E6
Firozabad, India 68/D3
Firozpur, India 68/C2
First (lake), New Bruns. 170/B1
First Cataract, Egypt 59/B5
First Connecticut (lake), N.H. 268/E1
First Eel (lake), New Bruns. 170/C3
Firstview, Colo. (†80810) 208/O5
Firth (riv.), Alaska 196/K1
Firth, Idaho (83236) 220/F6
Firth, Nebr. (68358) 264/H4
Firth (riv.), Yukon 187/D3
Firuzabad, Iran 66/H6
Firuzkuh, Iran 66/H3
Fischot Islands, Newf. 166/C3
Fish (creek), Ind. 227/H2
Fish (riv.), Maine 243/F2
Fish (riv.), Namibia 118/B5
Fish (creek), Oreg. 291/E4
Fish (lake), Utah 304/C5
Fish (creek), W. Va. 312/E3
Fish Camp, Calif. (93623) 204/F6
Fish Creek (res.), Idaho 220/E6
Fish Creek (mts.), Nev. 266/D2
Fish Creek, Wis. (54212) 317/M5
Fisher, Ark. (72429) 202/J2
Fisher (isl.), Fla. 212/B5
Fisher, Ill. (61843) 222/E3
Fisher, La. (71426) 238/D4
Fisher (bay), Manitoba 179/E3
Fisher (riv.), Manitoba 179/E3
Fisher, Minn. (56723) 255/B3
Fisher (str.), N.W.T. 162/H3
Fisher (str.), N.W. Terrs. 187/K3
Fisher (lake), Nova Scotia 168/C4
Fisher, S. Australia 94/B4
Fisher (co.), Texas 303/D5
Fisher, W. Va. (26818) 312/H4
Fisher Bay, Manitoba 179/E3
Fisher Branch, Manitoba 179/E3
Fishermans (isl.), Va. 307/S6
Fishers, Ind. (46038) 227/E5
Fishers (isl.), N.Y. 276/S8
Fishers Island, N.Y. (06390) 276/R8
Fishersville, Va. (22939) 307/K4
Fisherville (South Grafton), Mass. (01560) 249/H4
Fishguard and Goodwick, Wales 13/B5
Fishguard and Goodwick, Wales 10/D4
Fish Haven, Idaho (83261) 220/G7
Fishing (lake), Manitoba 179/G2
Fishing (bay), Md. 245/O7
Fishing (creek), N.C. 281/O2
Fishing Creek, Md. (21634) 245/N7
Fishing Lake, Alberta 182/E3
Fishing Ships Harbour, Newf. 166/C3
Fishkill, N.Y. (12524) 276/N7
Fish River (lake), Maine 243/F2
Fishs Eddy, N.Y. (13774) 276/K8
Fish Springs (range), Utah 304/A4
Fishtail, Mont. (59028) 262/G5
Fishtoft, England 13/H5
Fishtrap, Ky. (41525) 237/S6
Fishtrap (lake), Ky. 237/S6
Fisk, Mo. (63940) 261/M9
Fiskdale, Mass. (01518) 249/F4
Fiske, Sask. 181/C4
Fiskeville, R.I. (02823) 249/H6
Fitch Bay, Québec 172/E4
Fitchburg, Mass. (01420) 249/G2
Fitchville, Conn. (06334) 210/G2
Fitchville, Ohio (†44851) 284/E3
Fithian, Ill. (61844) 222/F3
Fitler, Miss. (39070) 256/B5
Fitri (lake), Chad 111/C5
Fittstown, Okla. (74842) 288/N5
Fitzcarrald, Peru 128/G8
Fitzgerald, Alberta 182/C4
Fitzgerald, Georgia (31750) 217/F7
Fitzgerald, N.W.T. 162/E4
Fitzhugh (sound), Br. Col. 184/D4
Fitzhugh, Okla. (74843) 288/N5
Fitzmaurice (riv.), North. Terr. 93/B3
Fitzpatrick, Ala. (36029) 195/G6
Fitzpatrick, Georgia (†31044) 217/F5
Fitzroy (riv.), Australia 87/C7
Fitz Roy (Chaltel) (mt.), Chile 138/E8
Fitzroy, North. Terr. 93/B4
Fitzroy (riv.), Queensland 88/J4
Fitzroy (riv.), Queensland 95/D4
Fitzroy, Victoria 97/H5
Fitzroy, Victoria 88/L7
Fitzroy (riv.), W. Australia 88/C3
Fitzroy (riv.), W. Australia 92/D2
Fitzroy Crossing, W. Australia 88/D3
Fitzroy Crossing, W. Australia 92/D2
Fitzroy Harbour, Ontario 177/H2
Fitzwilliam◯, N.H. (03447) 268/C6
Fitzwilliam (isl.), Ontario 177/C2
Fitzwilliam Depot, N.H. (03447) 268/C6
Fiume (Rijeka), Yugoslavia 45/B3
Fiumicino, Italy 34/F7
Five (isls.), Nova Scotia 168/D3
Five Fingers, New Bruns. 170/C1
Five Island (lake), Iowa 229/D2
Five Islands, Maine (04546) 243/D8
Five Islands, Nova Scotia 168/D3
Five Mile (riv.), Conn. 210/H1
Fivemile (creek), Oreg. 291/E2
Fivemile (pt.), Oreg. 291/C4
Fivemile (creek), Wyo. 319/D2
Fivemiletown, N. Ireland 17/G3
Five Points, Ala. (36855) 195/H4
Five Points, Fla. (32922) 212/D1
Five Points, Tenn. (38457) 237/G10
Five Stars, Guyana 131/A2
Fivizzano, Italy 34/B2
Fizi, Zaire 115/E4
Fjerritslev, Denmark 21/C3
Flagler, Colo. (80815) 208/N4
Flagler (co.), Fla. 212/E2
Flagler Beach, Fla. (32036) 212/E2
Flag Pond, Tenn. (37657) 237/R8
Flagstaff, Ariz. 146/G6
Flagstaff, Ariz. 188/D3
Flagstaff, Ariz. (86001) 198/D3
Flagstaff (lake), Maine 243/C5
Flagstaff (lake), Oreg. 291/H5
Flagtown, N.J. (08821) 273/D2
Flambeau (riv.), Wis. 317/E4
Flambeau Flowage (res.), Wis. 317/F3
Flamborough (head), England 13/G3
Flamborough (head), England 10/G3
Flamenco de San Pedro, Cuba 158/F3
Flaming Gorge (dam), Utah 304/E3
Flaming Gorge (res.), Utah 304/E3
Flaming Gorge (res.), Wyo. 319/C4
Flaming Gorge Nat'l Rec. Area, Utah 304/E2
Flaming Gorge Nat'l Rec. Area, Wyo. 319/C4
Flamingo (cay), Bahamas 156/C2
Flanagan, Ill. (61740) 222/E3
Flanagan (passage), Virgin Is. (Br.) 161/D4
Flanagan (passage), Virgin Is. (U.S.) 161/D4
Flanagin Town, Trin. & Tob. 161/B10
Flanders, Conn. (†06757) 210/B1
Flanders (trad. prov.) France 29
Flanders, N.J. (07836) 273/D2
Flanders, Ontario 175/B3
Flanders-Riverside, N.Y. (†11901) 276/P9
Flandreau, S. Dak. (57028) 298/R5
Flanigan, Nev. (†89501) 266/B2
Flannagan (res.), Va. 307/C6
Flannan (isls.), Scotland 15/A2
Flannan (isls.), Scotland 10/C1
Flasher, N. Dak. (58535) 282/H7
Flat, Ky. (41325) 237/O5
Flat, Mo. (†65550) 261/J7
Flat (isl.), Philippines 85/F3
Flat, Texas (76526) 303/G6
Flat (creek), Va. 307/M6
Flat (cays), Virgin Is. (U.S.) 161/A4
Flat Bay, Newf. 166/C4
Flatbrookville, N.J. (†07832) 273/D1
Flatbush, Alberta 182/C2
Flat Creek, Tenn. (†37160) 237/H10
Flat Creek-Wegra, Ala. (†35129) 195/D3
Flat Fork, Ky. (41427) 237/P5
Flatgap, Ky. (41219) 237/R5
Flathead (riv.), Br. Col. 184/K6
Flathead (co.), Mont. 262/B2
Flathead (lake), Mont. 188/D1
Flathead (lake), Mont. 262/C3
Flathead (riv.), Mont. 262/B2
Flathead, North Fork (riv.), Mont. 262/B2
Flathead, South Fork (riv.), Mont. 262/C3
Flathead Ind. Res., Mont. 262/B3
Flatlands, New Bruns. 170/D1
Flat Lick, Ky. (40935) 237/O7
Flatonia, Texas (78941) 303/G8
Flat River, Mo. (63601) 261/M7
Flat Rock, Ala. (35966) 195/G1
Flat Rock, Ill. (62427) 222/F5
Flat Rock, Ind. (47234) 227/F6
Flatrock (creek), Ind. 227/F5
Flat Rock, Ky. (†42634) 237/M7
Flat Rock, Mich. (48134) 250/F6
Flat Rock, Newf. 166/D2
Flat Rock, N.C. (†27043) 281/E4
Flat Rock, Ohio (44828) 284/E3
Flats, N.C. (†28781) 281/B4
Flattery (cape), Br. Col. 162/D6
Flattery (cape), Queensland 88/H2
Flattery (cape), Queensland 95/C2
Flattery (cape), Wash. 146/F5
Flattery (cape), Wash. 188/A1
Flattery (cape), Wash. 310/A2
Flat Top, W. Va. (25841) 312/D7
Flatwillow (creek), Mont. 262/H4
Flatwood, Ala. (†36739) 195/C6
Flatwoods, Ky. (41139) 237/R4
Flatwoods, La. (71427) 238/E4
Flatwoods, Tenn. (38458) 237/F9
Flatwoods, W. Va. (26621) 312/E5
Flawil, Switzerland 39/H2
Flaxcombe, Sask. 181/B4
Flaxman (isl.), Alaska 196/J1
Flaxton, N. Dak. (58737) 282/F2
Flaxville, Mont. (59222) 262/L2
Fleet, Alberta 182/E3
Fleet, England 13/G8
Fleet, Loch (inlet), Scotland 15/D3
Fleetwood, England 10/E4
Fleetwood, England 13/D4
Fleetwood, Okla. (†73569) 288/L7
Fleetwood, Pa. (19522) 294/L5
Fleischmanns, N.Y. (12430) 276/L6
Flekkefjord, Norway 18/E7
Flémalle, Belgium 27/G7
Fleming, Colo. (80728) 208/O1
Fleming, Georgia (31309) 217/K7
Fleming (co.), Ky. 237/O4
Fleming, Mo. (†64077) 261/D4
Fleming, Pa. (19375) 294/G4
Fleming, Sask. 181/K5
Fleming-Neon, Ky. (41816) 237/R6
Flemingsburg, Ky. (41041) 237/O4
Flemington, Georgia (†31313) 217/K7
Flemington, Mo. (65650) 261/F7
Flemington, N.J. (08822) 273/D2
Flemington, Pa. (†17745) 294/G3
Flemington, W. Va. (26347) 312/F4
Flen, Sweden 18/K7
Flensburg, Minn. (56328) 255/D5
Flensburg, W. Germany 22/C1
Flers, France 28/C3
Flesherton, Ontario 177/D3
Flesk (riv.), Ireland 17/C7
Fleta, Ala. (†36043) 195/F6
Fletcher (pond), Mich. 250/F4
Fletcher, Mo. (63030) 261/L6
Fletcher, N.C. (28732) 281/E4
Fletcher, Ohio (45326) 284/B5
Fletcher, Okla. (73541) 288/K5
Fletcher◯, Vt. (†05444) 268/B2
Fletschhorn (mt.), Switzerland 39/F4
Fleurance, France 28/D6
Fleur de Lys, Newf. 166/C3
Fleur-de-May (lake), Newf. 166/B3
Fleurier, Switzerland 39/C3
Fleurus, Belgium 27/E8
Flevoland Polders, Netherlands 27/G4
Flims, Switzerland 39/H3
Flinders (reefs), 95/D3
Flinders (riv.), Australia 87/E7
Flinders (reef), Coral Sea Is. Terr. 88/H3
Flinders (riv.), Queensland 88/G3
Flinders (riv.), Queensland 95/B3
Flinders (range), S. Australia 88/F6
Flinders (range), S. Australia 94/F4
Flinders (isl.), Tasmania 88/H7
Flinders (isl.), Tasmania 99/D1
Flinders (bay), W. Australia 88/A6
Flinders (bay), W. Australia 92/A6
Flin Flon, Man. 146/H4
Flin Flon, Manitoba 179/H3
Flin Flon, Man.-Sask. 162/F4
Flin Flon, Sask. 181/N4
Flint (riv.), Ga. 188/K4
Flint, Georgia (†31716) 217/D8
Flint (riv.), Georgia 217/D8
Flint, Ind. (†46703) 227/G1
Flint (isl.), Kiribati 87/L7
Flint, Mich. 146/K5
Flint, Mich. 188/K2
Flint, Mich. (*48501) 250/F5
Flint (riv.), Mich. 250/F5
Flint (lake), N.W. Terrs. 187/L3
Flint, Wales 13/G2
Flint City, Ala. (†35601) 195/D1
Flinthill, Mo. (63346) 261/L5
Flint Hill, Va. (22627) 307/M3
Flinton, Ontario 177/G3
Flint Rock (creek), S. Dak. 298/E3
Flintstone, Georgia (30725) 217/B1
Flintstone (lake), Manitoba 179/G4
Flintstone, Md. (21530) 245/D2
Flintville, Tenn. (37335) 237/H10
Flippen, Georgia (30215) 217/D3
Flippin, Ark. (72634) 202/E1
Flippin, Ky. (42132) 237/K7
Flix, Spain 33/G2
Flom, Minn. (56541) 255/B3
Flomaton, Ala. (36441) 195/D8
Flomot, Texas (79234) 303/D3
Flood, Br. Col. 184/M3
Floodwood, Minn. (55736) 255/E4
Flora, Ill. (62839) 222/E5
Flora, Ind. (46929) 227/E3
Flora, La. (71428) 238/D3
Flora, Miss. (39071) 256/D5
Flora, N. Dak. (†58348) 282/M4
Flora (riv.), North. Terr. 93/B3
Flora, Norway 18/D6
Flora, Oreg. (†97828) 291/K2
Florac, France 28/E5
Florahome, Fla. (32635) 212/E2
Floral, Ark. (72534) 202/G2
Florala, Ala. (36442) 195/F8
Floral City, Fla. (32636) 212/D3
Floral Park, N.Y. (*11001) 276/P7
Floraville, Queensland 95/B3
Flora Vista, N. Mex. (87415) 274/A2
Floreana (Sta. María), Ecuador 128/B10
Floreana (Santa María) (isl.), Ecuador 128/B10
Florence, Ala. 188/J4
Florence, Ala. (*35630) 195/C1
Florence, Ariz. (85232) 198/D5
Florence, Ark. (†71655) 202/G6
Florence (lake), Calif. 204/G6
Florence, Colo. (81226) 208/J6
Florence, Ill. (†62363) 222/C4
Florence, Ind. (47020) 227/H7
Florence (prov.), Italy 34/C3
Florence, Italy 7/F4
Florence, Italy 34/C3
Florence, Kansas (66851) 232/E3
Florence, Ky. (41042) 237/R2
Florence, Minn. (56130) 255/B6
Florence, Miss. (39073) 256/D6
Florence, Mo. (65329) 261/G5
Florence, Mont. (59833) 262/B4
Florence, N.Y. (†13316) 276/J4
Florence, N.C. (†28556) 281/R4
Florence, Nova Scotia 168/H2
Florence, Ontario 177/B5
Florence, Oreg. (97439) 291/C4
Florence, Pa. (†15021) 294/A5
Florence, S.C. 188/L4
Florence (co.), S.C. 296/H3
Florence, S.C. (29501) 296/H3
Florence, S. Dak. (57235) 298/P3
Florence (riv.), Tasmania 99/C4
Florence, Tenn. (†37130) 237/H9
Florence, Texas (76527) 303/G7
Florence, Vt. (05744) 268/A4
Florence (co.), Wis. 317/K4
Florence, Wis. (54121) 317/K4
Florence Junction, Ariz. (†85220) 198/D5
Florence-Roebling, N.J. (08518) 273/D3
Florenceville, New Bruns. 170/C2
Florencia, Colombia 126/C7
Florencia, Colombia 120/B2
Florencia, Cuba 158/F2
Florennes, Belgium 27/F8
Florenton, Minn. (†55792) 255/F3
Florenville, Belgium 27/G9
Flores, Las (riv.), Argentina 143/G7
Flores, Brazil 132/G4
Flores (isl.), Br. Col. 184/D5
Flores, Guatemala 154/C2
Flores (isl.), Indonesia 54/O10
Flores (isl.), Indonesia 85/G7
Flores (sea), Indonesia 2/Q6
Flores (sea), Indonesia 54/N10
Flores (sea), Indonesia 85/F7
Flores (isl.), Portugal 33/A1
Flores (dept.), Uruguay 145/C4
Flores (isl.), Uruguay 145/D5
Floresville, Texas (78114) 303/K11
Florey, Texas (†79714) 303/B5
Florham Park, N.J. (07932) 273/E2
Floriano, Brazil 132/F4
Floriano, Brazil 120/E3
Florianópolis, Brazil 132/E9
Florianópolis, Brazil 120/E5
Florida 188/K5
FLORIDA 212
Florida (strs.) 146/K7
Florida, Bolivia 136/D6
Florida, Cuba 158/G3
Florida (str.), Cuba 156/B1
Florida (bay), Fla. 188/K6
Florida (bay), Fla. 212/F6
Florida (cape), Fla. 212/F6
Florida (keys), Fla. 188/K6
Florida (keys), Fla. 212/E7
Florida (strs.), Fla. 188/K6
Florida (strs.), Fla. 212/F7
Florida◯, Mass. (†01247) 249/B2
Florida, Mo. (†65283) 261/J4
Florida (mts.), N. Mex. 274/B7
Florida, N.Y. (10921) 276/M8
Florida, Ohio (†43545) 284/B3
Florida, P. Rico 161/C1
Florida (isls.), Solomon Is. 86/E3
Florida (state), U.S. 146/K7
Florida (dept.), Uruguay 145/D4
Florida, Uruguay 145/C5
Florida City, Fla. (33034) 212/F6
Florida Ridge, Fla. (†32960) 212/F4
Floridia, Italy 34/E6
Florien, La. (71429) 238/D4
Florin, Calif. (95828) 204/B8
Florin, Pa. (†17552) 294/J5
Flórina, Greece 45/E5
Floris, Iowa (52560) 229/J7
Florissant, Colo. (80816) 208/J5
Florissant, Mo. (*63031) 261/P1
Florissant Fossil Beds Nat'l Mon., Colo. 208/J5
Flossmoor, Ill. (60422) 222/B6
Flovilla, Georgia (30216) 217/E4
Flowerdale, Tasmania 99/B2
Floweree, Mont. (59440) 262/E3
Flower Mound, Texas (†75067) 303/F1
Flowerpot (isl.), Ontario 177/C2
Flowers (bay), Newf. 166/B2
Flowers Cove, Newf. 166/C3
Flowery Branch, Georgia (30542) 217/E2
Flowood, Miss. (†39201) 256/D6
Floyd (co.), Georgia 217/B2
Floyd, Georgia (30059) 217/J1
Floyd (co.), Ind. 227/F8
Floyd (co.), Iowa 229/H2
Floyd, Iowa (50435) 229/H2
Floyd (riv.), Iowa 229/A3
Floyd (co.), Ky. 237/R5
Floyd, La. (†71266) 238/H1
Floyd, N. Mex. (88118) 274/F4
Floyd (co.), Texas 303/C3
Floyd (co.), Va. 307/H7
Floyd, Va. (24091) 307/H7
Floydada, Texas (79235) 303/C3
Floyd Dale, S.C. (29542) 296/J3
Floyds Knobs, Ind. (47119) 227/F8
Fluchthorn (mt.), Switzerland 39/K3
Flüela (pass), Switzerland 39/J3
Flüelen, Switzerland 39/G3
Fluhberg (mt.), Switzerland 39/G2
Fluker, La. (70436) 238/K5
Flums, Switzerland 39/H2
Flushing, Mich. (48433) 250/F5
Flushing, Netherlands 27/C6
Flushing, Ohio (43977) 284/J5
Fluvanna, Texas (79517) 303/D5
Fluvanna (co.), Va. 307/M5
Fly, Ohio (45730) 284/H6
Fly (riv.), Papua N.G. 87/E6
Fly (riv.), Papua N.G. 85/A7
Fly Creek, N.Y. (13337) 276/K5
Flying H, N. Mex. (88322) 274/E5
Flying Shot, Alberta 182/A2
Flynns Lick, Tenn. (†38562) 237/K8
Foam Lake, Sask. 181/H4
Foard (co.), Texas 303/E3
Foça, Turkey 63/B3
Foča, Yugoslavia 45/D4
Fochabers, Scotland 15/E3
Focșani, Romania 45/H3
Foge (isl.), Nigeria 106/E6
Foggia (prov.), Italy 34/E4
Foggia, Italy 7/F4
Foggia, Italy 34/E4
Fogo (isl.), C. Verde 106/B8
Fogo, Newf. 166/D4
Fogo (isl.), Newf. 166/D4
Fogo (isl.), Newf. 162/L6
Fohnsdorf, Austria 41/C3
Föhr (isl.), W. Germany 22/C1
Foisy, Alberta 182/E3
Foix, France 28/D6
Foix (trad. prov.) France 29
Folcroft, Pa. (19032) 294/M7
Folda (fjord), Norway 18/J3
Folda (fjord), Norway 18/G4
Földeák, Hungary 41/F3
Földes, Hungary 41/F2
Foley, Ala. (36535) 195/C10
Foley, Fla. (†32347) 212/C1
Foley, Minn. (56329) 255/D5
Foley, Mo. (63347) 261/L4
Foley (isl.), N.W. Terrs. 187/L3
Foleyet, Ontario 177/J5
Foleyet, Ontario 175/D3
Folgares, Angola 115/C6
Foligno, Italy 34/D3
Folkestone, England 13/J6
Folkestone, England 10/G5
Folkston, Georgia (31537) 217/H9
Folkstone, N.C. (†28445) 281/O5
Follansbee, W. Va. (26037) 312/E2
Follett, Texas (79034) 303/D1
Föllinge, Sweden 18/J5
Folly Beach, S.C. (29439) 296/H6
Folsom, Calif. (95630) 204/C8
Folsom (lake), Calif. 204/C8
Folsom, La. (70437) 238/K5
Folsom, N.J. (†08037) 273/D4
Folsom, N. Mex. (88419) 274/F2
Folsom, Pa. (19033) 294/M7
Folsom, W. Va. (26348) 312/E4
Folsomville, Ind. (47614) 227/C8
Foltești, Romania 45/H3
Fomboni, Comoros 118/G2
Fomento, Cuba 158/E2
Fonda, Iowa (50540) 229/D3
Fonda, N.Y. (12068) 276/M5
Fonda, N. Dak. (†58366) 282/K2
Fond d'Or (bay), St. Lucia 161/G6
Fond-du-Lac (riv.), Sask. 162/F4
Fond du Lac, Sask. 181/L2
Fond du Lac (riv.), Sask. 181/M2
Fond du Lac, Wis. 188/J2
Fond du Lac (co.), Wis. 317/K8
Fond du Lac, Wis. (54935) 317/K8
Fond du Lac Ind. Res., Minn. 255/F4
Fonde, Ky. (40937) 237/O7
Fondi, Italy 34/D4
Fond-Lahaye, Martinique 161/C6
Fond-Saint-Denis, Martinique 161/C6
Fond Verrettes, Haiti 158/C6
Fonehill, Sask. 181/J4
Fongafale (cap.), Tuvalu 87/H6
Fonsagrada, Spain 33/C1
Fonseca, Colombia 126/D2
Fonseca (gulf), El Salvador 154/D4
Fonseca (gulf), Honduras 154/D4
Fonseca (gulf), Nicaragua 154/D4
Fontaine, New Bruns. 170/F2

Front 371

Foster (riv.), Sask. 181/M3
Foster (creek), S. Dak. 298/N4
Foster, W. Va. (25081) 312/C6
Foster, Wis. (†54758) 317/D6
Foster Center (Foster P.O.), R.I. (†02825) 249/H5
Foster City, Calif. (94404) 204/J2
Foster City, Mich. (49834) 250/B3
Fosters, Ala. (35463) 195/C4
Fosters, Mich. (†48415) 250/F5
Fosters Falls, Va. (24329) 307/G7
Fosterton, Sask. 181/C5
Foster Village, Hawaii (†96701) 218/B3
Fosterville, New Bruns. 170/C3
Fosterville, Tenn. (37063) 237/J9
Fostoria, Ala. (†36737) 195/E6
Fostoria, Iowa (51340) 229/C2
Fostoria, Kansas (66426) 232/F2
Fostoria, Mich. (48435) 250/F5
Fostoria, Ohio (44830) 284/D3
Fougamou, Gabon 115/A4
Fougères, France 28/C3
Fouke, Ark. (71837) 202/C7
Foul (bay), Egypt 111/G3
Foul (sound), Ireland 17/B5
Foula (isl.), Scotland 15/F2
Foula (isl.), Scotland 10/G1
Foules, La. (†71326) 238/G3
Foulness Island (pen.), England 13/J6
Foulpointe, Madagascar 118/H3
Foulweather (cape), Oreg. 291/C3
Foulwind (cape), N. Zealand 100/C4
Foumban, Cameroon 115/B2
Foumban, Cameroon 102/D4
Fountain, Ala. (36460) 195/D7
Fountain, Colo. (80817) 208/K5
Fountain (creek), Colo. 208/K5
Fountain, Fla. (32438) 212/D6
Fountain (co.), Ind. 227/C4
Fountain, Ind. (†47918) 227/C4
Fountain, Mich. (49410) 250/C4
Fountain, Minn. (55935) 255/F7
Fountain, N.C. (27829) 281/O3
Fountain City, Ind. (47341) 227/H5
Fountain City, Wis. (54629) 317/C7
Fountain Green, Ill. (†62321) 222/C3
Fountain Green, Utah (84632) 304/C4
Fountain Head, Md. (†21740) 245/G2
Fountain Head, Tenn. (†37148) 237/J7
Fountain Hill, Ark. (71642) 202/G7
Fountain Hill, Pa. (†18015) 294/L4
Fountain Inn, S.C. (29644) 296/C2
Fountain Run, Ky. (42133) 237/K7
Fountaintown, Ind. (46130) 227/F5
Fountain Valley, Calif. (92708) 204/D11
Four (peaks), Newf. 166/B2
Four Buttes, Mont. (59224) 262/L2
Fourche, Ariz. (†72016) 202/E4
Fourche LaFave (riv.), Ark. 202/D4
Four Corners, Oreg. (97301) 291/A3
Four Corners, Wyo. (82715) 319/H1
Four Falls, New Bruns. 170/C2
Four Hole Swamp (creek), S.C. 296/F5
Four Lakes, Wash. (99014) 310/H3
Fourmies, France 28/F2
Four Mile (riv.), Conn. 210/F3
Fourmile (lake), Oreg. 291/E5
Four Mountains (isls.), Alaska 196/E4
Fournier (cape), N. Zealand 100/E7
Fournier, Ontario 177/K2
Four Oaks, N.C. (27524) 281/M4
Four Paths, Jamaica 158/J6
Four Peaks (mt.), Ariz. 198/D5
Four States, W. Va. (26572) 312/F4
Fourteen Mile (pt.), Mich. 250/F1
Fourth (lake), Maine 243/H5
Fourth Cataract, Sudan 111/F4
Fourth Cataract, Sudan 59/B6
Fourth Cataract (dam), Sudan 102/F3
Foveaux (str.), N. Zealand 87/G10
Foveaux (str.), N. Zealand 100/A7
Fowler, Calif. (93625) 204/F7
Fowler, Colo. (81039) 208/L6
Fowler, Ill. (62338) 222/B3
Fowler, Ind. (47944) 227/C3
Fowler, Kansas (67844) 232/B4
Fowler, Mich. (48835) 250/E5
Fowlerton, Ind. (46930) 227/F4
Fowlerton, Texas (78021) 303/F9
Fowlerville, Mich. (48836) 250/F6
Fowlkes, Tenn. (38033) 237/C9
Fowlstown, Georgia (31752) 217/D9
Fowman, Iran 66/F2
Fowyang (Fuyang), China 77/J5
Fox (isls.), Alaska 196/E4
Fox, Ark. (72051) 202/F2
Fox (lake), Ill. 222/A4
Fox (riv.), Ill. 222/E5
Fox (riv.), Ill. 222/E2
Fox (riv.), Manitoba 179/K2
Fox, Mich. (†49813) 250/B3
Fox (isl.), New Bruns. 170/F1
Fox, Okla. (73435) 288/M6
Fox, Oreg. (97831) 291/H3
Fox (riv.), Wis. 317/K7
Fox (riv.), Wis. 317/K2
Foxboro, Mass. (02035) 249/J4
Foxboro○, Mass. (02035) 249/J4
Foxboro, Ontario 177/G3
Foxboro, Wis. (54836) 317/B2
Foxburg, Pa. (16036) 294/C3
Fox Chapel, Pa. (†15238) 294/C6
Fox Creek, Alberta 182/B2
Foxe (basin), Canada 4/C13
Foxe (basin), N.W.T. 146/L3
Foxe (basin), N.W.T. 162/J2
Foxe (basin), N.W. Terrs. 187/L3
Foxe (chan.), N.W.T. 162/H2
Foxe (chan.), N.W.T. 146/K3
Foxe (chan.), N.W. Terrs. 187/K3
Foxe (pen.), N.W.T. 146/L3
Foxe (pen.), N.W.T. 162/J3
Foxe (pen.), N.W. Terrs. 187/L3
Fox Farm, Wyo. (†82001) 319/H4
Foxfire, N.C. (†28373) 281/K4
Foxford, Ireland 17/C4
Foxford, Sask. 181/F2
Fox Glacier, N. Zealand 100/B5
Fox Harbour, Newf. 166/D2
Fox Harbour, Newf. 166/C3
Foxholm, N. Dak. (58738) 282/G3
Foxhome, Minn. (56543) 255/B4
Fox Lake, Alberta 182/B5
Fox Lake, Ill. (60020) 222/A4
Fox Lake, Wis. (53933) 317/J8
Foxon, Conn. (†06512) 210/D3
Foxpark, Wyo. (82057) 319/F4
Fox Point, Wis. (†53117) 317/M1
Fox River, Nova Scotia 168/D3
Fox River Grove, Ill. (60021) 222/A5
Foxton, Colo. (80441) 208/J4
Foxton, N. Zealand 100/E4
Fox Valley, Sask. 181/B5
Foxville, Md. (†21760) 245/H2
Foxwarren, Manitoba 179/A4
Foxwells, Va. (22578) 307/R5
Foxworth, Miss. (39483) 256/E8
Foyers, Scotland 15/D3
Foyil, Okla. (74031) 288/R2
Foyle (inlet), Ireland 17/G1
Foyle, Lough (inlet), Ireland 10/C3
Foyle (riv.), Ireland 17/G2
Foyle, Lough (inlet), N. Ireland 10/C3
Foyle (inlet), N. Ireland 17/G1
Foyle (riv.), N. Ireland 17/G2
Foynes, Ireland 10/B4
Foynes, Ireland 17/C6
Foz do Breu, Brazil 132/F10
Foz do Cunene, Angola 115/B7
Foz do Iguaçu, Brazil 132/C9
Frackville, Pa. (17931) 294/K4
Fraga, Spain 33/G2
Fragoso (cay), Cuba 158/F1
Fraile Muerto, Uruguay 145/E3
Frailes, Los (isl.), Dom. Rep. 158/C7
Fram, Paraguay 144/E5
Framboise, Nova Scotia 168/H3
Framboise Cove (bay), Nova Scotia 168/H3
Frame, W. Va. (25071) 312/C5
Frameries, Belgium 27/D8
Frametown, W. Va. (26623) 312/E5
Framingham○, Mass. (01701) 249/A7
Framingham Center, Mass. (01701) 249/J3
Framlingham, England 13/J5
Frampton, Québec 172/G3
Franca, Brazil 135/C2
Franca, Brazil 132/E8
Francavilla Fontana, Italy 34/F4
France 2/J3
France 7/E4
FRANCE 28
Francés (cape), Cuba 158/B2
Francés (cape), Cuba 158/A2
Frances (lake), Mont. 262/D2
Frances, Wash. (†98577) 310/B4
Frances (lake), Yukon 187/E3
Francestown○, N.H. (03043) 268/D6
Francés Viejo (cape), Dom. Rep. 158/E5
Francesville, Ind. (47946) 227/D3
Franceville, Gabon 115/B4
Franche Comté (trad. prov.), France 29
Francia, Uruguay 145/C3
Francis (lake), N.H. 268/E1
Francis, Okla. (74844) 288/N5
Francis, Sask. 181/H5
Francis, Utah (†84036) 304/C3
Francis Case (lake), S. Dak. 188/F2
Francis Case (lake), S. Dak. 146/J5
Francis Case (lake), S. Dak. 298/L7
Francisco, Ala. (†37345) 195/F1
Francisco, Ind. (47649) 227/B8
Francisco, N.C. (†27053) 281/J2
Francisco de Orellana, Peru 128/F4
Francisco I. Madero, Mexico 150/H4
Francis Creek, Wis. (54214) 317/L7
Francis E. Warren A.F.B., Wyo. 319/G4
Francistown, Botswana 118/D4
Francoeur, Québec 172/F3
François (lake), Br. Col. 162/D5
François (lake), Br. Col. 184/D3
François, Newf. 166/C4
François Lake, Br. Col. 184/D3
Franconia○, N.H. (03580) 268/D3
Franconia, Va. (22310) 307/S3
Franconian Jura (range), W. Germany 22/D4
Franconia Notch (pass), N.H. 268/D3
Franeker, Netherlands 27/H2
Frank, Alberta 182/C5
Frankel City, Texas (79737) 303/B5
Frankenberg-Eder, W. Germany 22/C3
Frankenmarkt, Austria 41/B3
Frankenmuth, Mich. (48734) 250/F5
Frankenthal, W. Germany 22/C4
Frankenwald (for.), W. Germany 22/D3
Frankewing, Tenn. (38459) 237/H10
Frankfield, Jamaica 158/H6
Frankford, Del. (19945) 245/S6
Frankford (Kilcormac), Ireland 17/F5
Frankford, Mo. (63441) 261/K4
Frankford, Ontario 177/G3
Frankford, W. Va. (24938) 312/F7
Frankfort, Ala. (†35653) 195/C1
Frankfort, Ill. (60423) 222/B6
Frankfort, Ind. (46041) 227/E4
Frankfort, Kansas (66427) 232/F2
Frankfort (cap.), Ky. (40601) 237/M4
Frankfort (cap.), Ky. 188/K3
Frankfort (cap.), Ky. 146/K6
Frankfort○, Maine (04438) 243/F6
Frankfort, Mich. (49635) 250/C4
Frankfort, N.Y. (13340) 276/K4
Frankfort, Ohio (45628) 284/D7
Frankfort, S. Dak. (57440) 298/N4
Frankfort Springs, Pa. (†15050) 294/A4
Frankfurt (dist.), E. Germany 22/F2
Frankfurt, W. Germany 7/E3
Frankfurt am Main, W. Germany 22/C3
Frankfurt an der Oder, E. Germany 22/F2
Frankland (cape), Tasmania 99/D1
Frankland (range), Tasmania 99/B4
Franklin (co.), Ala. 195/C2
Franklin, Ala. (36444) 195/G6
Franklin (pt.), Alaska 196/G1
Franklin, Ariz. (85534) 198/F6
Franklin (co.), Ark. 202/C2
Franklin, Ark. (72536) 202/G1
Franklin○, Conn. (†06254) 210/G2
Franklin (co.), Fla. 212/B2
Franklin (co.), Georgia 217/F2
Franklin, Georgia (30217) 217/B4
Franklin (co.), Idaho 220/G7
Franklin, Idaho (83237) 220/G7
Franklin (co.), Ill. 222/E5
Franklin, Ill. (62638) 222/C4
Franklin (co.), Ind. 227/G6
Franklin, Ind. (46131) 227/E6
Franklin (co.), Iowa 229/G3
Franklin, Iowa (†52625) 229/L7
Franklin (co.), Kansas 232/G3
Franklin, Kansas (66735) 232/H4
Franklin (co.), Ky. 237/M4
Franklin, Ky. (42134) 237/J7
Franklin (par.), La. 238/G2
Franklin, La. (70538) 238/G7
Franklin (co.), Maine 243/B5
Franklin, Maine (04634) 243/G6
Franklin○, Maine (04634) 243/G6
Franklin, Manitoba 179/C4
Franklin (co.), Mass. 249/D2
Franklin, Mass. (02038) 249/J4
Franklin○, Mass. (02038) 249/J4
Franklin, Mich. (48025) 250/B6
Franklin, Minn. (†55792) 255/F3
Franklin, Minn. (55333) 255/D6
Franklin (co.), Miss. 256/C8
Franklin (co.), Mo. 261/K6
Franklin, Mo. (65250) 261/G4
Franklin, Mont. (†59074) 262/G4
Franklin (co.), Nebr. 264/F4
Franklin, Nebr. (68939) 264/E4
Franklin (lake), Nev. 266/F2
Franklin, N.H. (03235) 268/D5
Franklin, N.J. (07416) 273/D1
Franklin (co.), N.Y. 276/M1
Franklin, N.Y. (13775) 276/K6
Franklin (co.), N.C. 281/N2
Franklin, N.C. (28734) 281/C4
Franklin (dist.), N.W.T. 162/H1
Franklin (bay), N.W. Terrs. 187/F2
Franklin (lake), N.W. Terrs. 187/J3
Franklin (mts.), N.W. Terrs. 187/F3
Franklin (str.), N.W.T. 162/G1
Franklin (str.), N.W. Terrs. 187/J2
Franklin (co.), Ohio 284/E5
Franklin, Ohio (45005) 284/B6
Franklin (co.), Pa. 294/G6
Franklin, Pa. (16323) 294/C3
Franklin, S. Dak. (†57042) 298/P6
Franklin, Tasmania 99/C5
Franklin (riv.), Tasmania 99/B4
Franklin (co.), Tenn. 237/J10
Franklin, Tenn. (37064) 237/H9
Franklin (co.), Texas 303/J4
Franklin, Texas (77856) 303/H7
Franklin (co.), Vt. 268/B2
Franklin○, Vt. (05457) 268/B2
Franklin (co.), Va. 307/J6
Franklin (I.C.), Va. (23851) 307/P7
Franklin (co.), Wash. 310/G4
Franklin, W. Va. (26807) 312/H5
Franklin, Wis. (53132) 317/L2
Franklin D. Roosevelt (lake), Wash. 310/G2
Franklin Falls (res.), N.H. 268/D4
Franklin Furnace, Ohio (45629) 284/E8
Franklin Grove, Ill. (61031) 222/D2
Franklin Lakes, N.J. (07417) 273/B1
Franklin Park, Ill. (60131) 222/B5
Franklin Park○, N.J. (†08823) 273/D3
Franklin River, Br. Col. 184/H3
Franklin Springs, Georgia (30639) 217/F2
Franklin Square, N.Y. (11010) 276/R7
Franklinton, La. (70438) 238/K5
Franklinton, N.C. (27525) 281/N2
Franklintown, Pa. (17323) 294/H5
Franklinville, N.J. (08322) 273/C4
Franklinville, N.Y. (14737) 276/D6
Franklinville, N.C. (27248) 281/K3
Franks (pond), Newf. 166/D2
Frankslake, Sask. 181/G5
Frankston, Texas (75763) 303/J5
Franksville, Wis. (53126) 317/M3
Frankton, Ind. (46044) 227/F4
Franktown, Colo. (80116) 208/K4
Franktown, Ontario 177/H2
Franktown, Va. (23354) 307/S6
Frankville, Ala. (36538) 195/B7
Frankville, Iowa (†52162) 229/K2
Frankville, Nova Scotia 168/G3
Frankville, Ontario 177/J2
Frannie, Wyo. (82423) 319/D1
Franquelin, Québec 172/B1
Franquia, Uruguay 145/B1
Franschhoek, S. Africa 118/F6
Fransfontein, Namibia 118/A4
Františkovy Lázně, Czech. 41/B1
Franz, Ontario 177/J5
Franz, Ontario 175/D3
Franz Josef Land (isls.), U.S.S.R. 2/L1
Franz Josef Land (isls.), U.S.S.R. 4/A7
Franz Josef Land (isls.), U.S.S.R. 48/F1
Frascati, Italy 34/F7
Fraser (isl.), Australia 87/F8
Fraser (riv.), Br. Col. 146/F4
Fraser (riv.), Br. Col. 162/D5
Fraser (lake), Br. Col. 184/E3
Fraser (riv.), Br. Col. 184/F4
Fraser, Colo. (80442) 208/H3
Fraser, Iowa (†50036) 229/E4
Fraser, Mich. (48026) 250/B6
Fraser, Minn. (†55719) 255/F3
Fraser (riv.), Newf. 166/B2
Fraser (isl.), Queensland 88/J4
Fraser (isl.), Queensland 95/E5
Fraserburgh, Scotland 15/G3
Fraserburgh, Scotland 10/E2
Fraserdale, Ontario 175/D3
Fraserdale, Ontario 177/J5
Fraser Lake, Br. Col. 184/E3
Fraser Mills, Br. Col. 184/K3
Fraser Reach (chan.), Br. Col. 184/C3
Frasertown, N. Zealand 100/F3
Fraserwood, Manitoba 179/E4
Frasnes-lez Anvaing, Belgium 27/D7
Frauenfeld, Switzerland 39/G1
Frauenkirchen, Austria 41/D3
Fray Benito, Cuba 158/J3
Fray Bentos, Uruguay 145/A4
Fray Marcos, Uruguay 145/D5
Frazee, Minn. (56544) 255/C4
Frazer, Mont. (59225) 262/K2
Frazeysburg, Ohio (43822) 284/F5
Frazier Park, Calif. (93225) 204/F9
Fraziers Bottom, W. Va. (25082) 312/B5
Frechen, W. Germany 22/B3
Fred, Texas (77616) 303/K7
Freda, N. Dak. (†58569) 282/H7
Fredensborg, Denmark 21/F6
Fredensdal, Virgin Is. (U.S.) 161/F4
Frederic, Mich. (49733) 250/E4
Frederic, Wis. (54837) 317/B4
Frederica, Del. (19946) 245/S4
Fredericia, Denmark 21/C6
Fredericia, Denmark 18/F9
Frederick (sound), Alaska 196/N1
Frederick, Colo. (80530) 208/K2
Frederick, Ill. (62639) 222/C3
Frederick, Kansas (†67444) 232/D3
Frederick (co.), Md. 245/J3
Frederick, Md. (21701) 245/J3
Frederick, Okla. (73542) 288/H6
Frederick, S. Dak. (57441) 298/N2
Frederick (co.), Va. 307/M2
Fredericksburg, Ind. (47120) 227/E8
Fredericksburg, Iowa (50630) 229/J3
Fredericksburg, Ohio (44627) 284/G4
Fredericksburg, Pa. (17026) 294/J5
Fredericksburg, Pa. (†16335) 294/B2
Fredericksburg, Texas (78624) 303/E7
Fredericksburg (I.C.), Va. (*22401) 307/N4
Fredericks Hall, Va. (†23117) 307/N4
Frederickton, N.S. Wales 97/G2
Fredericktown, Mo. (63645) 261/M7
Fredericktown, Ohio (43019) 284/F5
Fredericktown, Pa. (15333) 294/C6
Fredericton, N. Br. 146/M5
Fredericton, N. Br. 162/K6
Fredericton (cap.), New Bruns. 170/D3
Fredericton Junction, New Bruns. 170/D3
Frederika, Iowa (50631) 229/J3
Frederik Hendrik (Kolepom) (isl.), Indonesia 85/K7
Frederiksberg (commune), Denmark 21/F6
Frederiksberg, Denmark 21/F6
Frederiksborg (co.), Denmark 21/E5
Frederikshåb, Greenl. 4/C12
Frederikshåb, Greenland 146/N3
Frederikshavn, Denmark 18/G8
Frederikshavn, Denmark 21/D3
Frederikssund, Denmark 21/E6
Frederiksted, Virgin Is. (U.S.) 161/E4
Frederiksted, Virgin Is. (U.S.) 156/G2
Frederiksvaerk, Denmark 21/E6
Frederiksvaerk, Denmark 18/G8
Frederik Willem IV (falls), Suriname 131/C4
Fredonia, Ala. (†31833) 195/H5
Fredonia, Ariz. (86022) 198/C2
Fredonia (Biscoe), Ark. (72017) 202/H4
Fredonia, Ind. (†47137) 227/E8
Fredonia, Iowa (†52738) 229/L6
Fredonia, Kansas (66736) 232/G4
Fredonia, Ky. (42411) 237/E6
Fredonia, N.Y. (14063) 276/B6
Fredonia, N. Dak. (58440) 282/M7
Fredonia, Pa. (16124) 294/B3
Fredonia, Texas (76842) 303/E7
Fredonia, Wis. (53021) 317/L8
Fredric, Iowa (†52531) 229/H6
Fredrika, Sweden 18/L4
Fredrikstad, Norway 18/D4
Freeborn (co.), Minn. 255/E7
Freeborn, Minn. (56032) 255/E7
Freeburg, Ill. (62243) 222/D5
Freeburg, Minn. (†55921) 255/G7
Freeburg, Mo. (65035) 261/J6
Freeburg, Pa. (17827) 294/H4
Freeburn, Ky. (41528) 237/S5
Freedhem, Minn. (†56345) 255/D4
Freedom, Calif. (95019) 204/L4
Freedom, Ind. (47431) 227/D6
Freedom, Ky. (†42157) 237/K7
Freedom○, Maine (04941) 243/E7
Freedom○, N.H. (03836) 268/E4
Freedom, Okla. (73842) 288/H1
Freedom, Pa. (15042) 294/B4
Freedom, Wyo. (83120) 319/B3
Freehold, N.J. (07728) 273/E3
Freehold, N.Y. (12431) 276/N6
Freel (peak), Calif. 204/F5
Freeland, Md. (21053) 245/M2
Freeland, Mich. (48623) 250/E5
Freeland, N.C. (28440) 281/N6
Freeland, Pa. (18224) 294/L3
Freeland, Wash. (98249) 310/C2
Freeland Park, Ind. (†47944) 227/C3
Freelandville, Ind. (47535) 227/C7
Freels (cape), Newf. 166/D3
Freelton, Ontario 177/D4
Freeman (riv.), Alberta 182/C2
Freeman, Ind. (†47460) 227/D6
Freeman (lake), Ind. 227/D3
Freeman, Mo. (64746) 261/C5
Freeman, S. Dak. (57029) 298/O7
Freeman, Wash. (99015) 310/H3
Freemansburg, Pa. (†18017) 294/M4
Freemanville, Ala. (†36502) 195/D8
Free Mason (isls.), La. 238/M7
Freemont, Calif. 188/B3
Freemont, Sask. 181/B3
Freeport, Bahamas 156/B1
Freeport, Fla. (32439) 212/C6
Freeport, Ill. 188/J2
Freeport, Ill. (61032) 222/D1
Freeport, Ind. (†46161) 227/F5
Freeport, Kansas (67049) 232/E4
Freeport, Maine (04032) 243/C8
Freeport○, Maine (04032) 243/C8
Freeport, Mich. (49325) 250/D6
Freeport, Minn. (56331) 255/D5
Freeport, N.Y. (11520) 276/R7
Freeport, Nova Scotia 168/B4
Freeport, Ohio (43973) 284/H5
Freeport, Pa. (16229) 294/C4
Freeport, Texas (77541) 303/J9
Freer, Texas (78357) 303/F10
Free Soil, Mich. (49411) 250/C4
Freestone (co.), Texas 303/H6
Freetown, Ant. & Bar. 161/E11
Freetown, Ind. (47235) 227/E7
Freetown, N.Y. (†11937) 276/R9
Freetown (cap.), S. Leone 102/A4
Freetown (cap.), S. Leone 106/B7
Free Union, Va. (22940) 307/L4
Freeville, N.Y. (13068) 276/H5
Freezeout (lake), Mont. 262/D3
Fregenal de la Sierra, Spain 33/C3
Fregene, Italy 34/F6
Freiberg, E. Germany 22/E3
Freiburg, W. Germany 7/E4
Freiburg im Breisgau, W. Germany 22/B5
Freidberg, Austria 41/D3
Freienbach, Switzerland 39/G2
Freire, Chile 138/E2
Freirina, Chile 138/A7
Freising, W. Germany 22/D4
Freistadt, Austria 41/C2
Freistatt, Mo. (65654) 261/E8
Freital, E. Germany 22/E3
Freixo de Espada à Cinta, Portugal 33/C2
Fréjus, France 28/G6
Fréjus (pass), France 28/G5
Fréjus (pass), Italy 34/A2
Frelighsburg, Québec 172/E4
Fremantle, Australia 2/Q7
Fremantle, Australia 87/B9
Fremantle, W. Australia 88/B6
Fremantle, W. Australia 92/A1
Fremington, England 13/C6
Fremont, Calif. (*94536) 204/K3
Fremont (peak), Calif. 204/H8
Fremont (co.), Colo. 208/J5
Fremont (co.), Idaho 220/G5
Fremont, Ind. (46737) 227/H1
Fremont (co.), Iowa 229/B7
Fremont, Iowa (52561) 229/H6
Fremont, Mich. (49412) 250/D5
Fremont, Mo. (63941) 261/K9
Fremont, Nebr. 188/G2
Fremont, Nebr. (68025) 264/H3
Fremont○, N.H. (03044) 268/E6
Fremont, N.C. (27830) 281/N3
Fremont, Ohio (43420) 284/D3
Fremont, Utah (84727) 304/C5
Fremont (isl.), Utah 304/B2
Fremont (riv.), Utah 304/C5
Fremont, Wis. (54940) 317/J7
Fremont (co.), Wyo. 319/D2
Fremont (lake), Wyo. 319/C3
Fremont (peak), Wyo. 319/C2
French, Argentina 143/F7
French (riv.), Conn. 210/H1
French (riv.), Ontario 177/D1
French (creek), Pa. 294/C2
French (creek), S. Dak. 298/C6
French (isl.), Victoria 97/C6
Frenchboro○, Maine (04635) 243/G7
French Broad (riv.), N.C. 281/D3
French Broad (riv.), Tenn. 237/R9
Frenchburg, Ky. (40322) 237/O5
French Camp, Miss. (39745) 256/F4
French Creek, W. Va. (26218) 312/F5
French Frigate (shoal), Hawaii 188/F6
French Frigate (shoals), Hawaii 87/K3
French Frigate (shoals), Hawaii 218/C6
Frenchglen, Oreg. (97736) 291/H5
French Guiana 2/G5
French Guiana 120/D2
FRENCH GUIANA 131/E3
French Lick, Ind. (47432) 227/D7
Frenchman (creek), Colo. 208/P1
Frenchman (bay), Maine 243/G7
Frenchman (riv.), Mont. 188/E1
Frenchman (riv.), Mont. 262/J1
Frenchman (creek), Nebr. 264/C4
Frenchman (riv.), Sask. 181/C6
Frenchman (cay), Virgin Is. (Br.) 161/C4
Frenchman Butte, Sask. 181/B2
Frenchman Flat (basin), Nev. 266/F6
Frenchmans Cap (mt.), Tasmania 99/B4
Frenchmans Island, Newf. 166/C3
Frenchpark, Ireland 17/E4
French Polynesia 87/L8
French River, Minn. (†55801) 255/G4
French River, Ontario 177/D1
French Settlement, La. (70733) 238/L2
Frenchton, W. Va. (26219) 312/F5
Frenchtown, Mont. (59834) 262/B3
Frenchtown, N.J. (08825) 273/C2
Frenchville, Maine (04745) 243/G1
Frenchville○, Maine (04745) 243/G1
Frenchville, Pa. (16836) 294/F3
Frenštát pod Radhoštěm, Czech. 41/E2
Fresco, Ivory Coast 106/C7
Fresh (pond), Mass. 249/G6
Freshford, Ireland 17/G6
Freshwater, Calif. (†95501) 204/B3
Freshwater (Guffey), Colo. (80820) 208/H5
Freshwater, England 13/F7
Freshwater, Newf. 166/D2
Fresia, Chile 138/D3
Fresillo, Mexico 146/H7
Fresnillo de González Echeverría, Mexico 150/H5
Fresno (co.), Calif. 204/E7
Fresno, Calif. 146/G6
Fresno, Calif. 188/C3
Fresno, Calif. (*93706) 204/F7
Fresno (riv.), Calif. 204/E7
Fresno, Colombia 126/C5
Fresno, Mont. (†59532) 262/G2
Fresno (res.), Mont. 262/F2
Fresno, Texas (77545) 303/J2
Freudenstadt, W. Germany 22/C4
Frew, Ky. (41744) 237/P6
Frewena, North. Terr. 93/D5
Frewsburg, N.Y. (14738) 276/B6
Freycinet (pen.), Tasmania 99/E4
Fria, Guinea 106/B6
Fria (cape), Namibia 102/D6
Fria (cape), Namibia 118/A3
Friant, Calif. (93626) 204/F7
Friant-Kern (canal), Calif. 204/F8
Friars Point, Miss. (38631) 256/C2
Frías, Argentina 143/D2
Fribourg (canton), Switzerland 39/D3
Fribourg, Switzerland 39/D3
Frick, Switzerland 39/E1
Friday Harbor, Wash. (98250) 310/B2
Fridley, Minn. (55432) 255/G5
Fried, N. Dak. (†58401) 282/N5
Friedberg, W. Germany 22/C3
Friedland, E. Germany 22/E2
Friedrichshafen, W. Germany 22/C5
Friedrichstadt, W. Germany 22/C1
Friend, Kansas (67845) 232/B3
Friend, Nebr. (68359) 264/G4
Friend, Oreg. (97021) 291/F2
Friendly, W. Va. (26146) 312/D3
Friendship, Ark. (71942) 202/E5
Friendship, Ind. (47021) 227/G7
Friendship, Maine (04547) 243/E7
Friendship○, Maine (04547) 243/E7
Friendship, Md. (20758) 245/M6
Friendship, N.Y. (14739) 276/D6
Friendship, Ohio (45630) 284/D8
Friendship, Tenn. (38034) 237/C9
Friendship, Wis. (53934) 317/G8
Friendship Hill Nat'l Hist. Site, Pa. 294/C6
Friendsville, Ill. (†62863) 222/F5
Friendsville, Md. (21531) 245/A2
Friendsville, Pa. (18818) 294/L2
Friendsville, Tenn. (37737) 237/N9
Friendswood, Texas (77546) 303/J2
Frienisberg (mt.), Switzerland 39/D2
Frierson, La. (71027) 238/C2
Fries, Va. (24330) 307/F7
Friesach, Austria 41/C3
Friesche Gat (chan.), Netherlands 27/J2
Friesland, Minn. (†55037) 255/E4
Friesland (prov.), Netherlands 27/H2
Friesland, Wis. (53935) 317/H8
Frigate (isl.), Seychelles 118/J5
Frigate Bay, St. Chris.-Nevis 161/C10
Frimley and Camberley, England 13/G8
Frink, Fla. (†32430) 212/D6
Frinton and Walton, England 10/G5
Frinton and Walton, England 13/J6
Frio (cape), Brazil 120/E5
Frio (cape), Brazil 135/F3
Frio (co.), Texas 303/E9
Frio (riv.), Texas 303/E8
Friockheim, Scotland 15/F4
Friol, Spain 33/C1
Friona, Texas (79035) 303/B3
Fripp (isl.), S.C. 296/G7
Frisches Haff (lag.), Poland 47/D1
Frisco, Colo. (80443) 208/G3
Frisco, N.C. (27936) 281/T4
Frisco, Pa. (†16117) 294/B4
Frisco, Texas (75034) 303/H4
Frisco City, Ala. (36445) 195/D8
Frisian (isls.) 7/E3
Frisian, North (isls.), Denmark 21/B7
Frisian, West (isls.), Netherlands 27/G2
Frisian, East (isls.), W. Germany 22/B2
Frisian, North (isls.), W. Germany 22/B1
Frissell (mt.), Conn. 210/B1
Fristoe, Mo. (†65355) 261/F6
Fritch, Texas (79036) 303/C2
Fritchton, Ind. (†47591) 227/C7
Fritz Creek, Alaska (†99603) 196/B2
Fritzlar, W. Germany 22/C3
Friuli-Venezia Giulia (reg.), Italy 34/D1
Frizzellburg, Md. (†21157) 245/K2
Frobisher (bay), N.W.T. 162/K3
Frobisher (bay), N.W. Terrs. 187/M3
Frobisher, Sask. 181/J6
Frobisher (lake), Sask. 181/L3
Frobisher Bay, N.W.T. 162/K3
Frobisher Bay, N.W. Terrs. 187/M3
Froelich, Iowa (†52047) 229/L2
Frog (lake), Alberta 182/E3
Frog Lake, Alberta 182/E3
Frogmore, S.C. (29920) 296/F7
Frogue, Ky. (†42714) 237/L7
Frohavet (bay), Norway 18/F5
Frohna, Mo. (63748) 261/N7
Frohnleiten, Austria 41/C3
Froid, Mont. (59226) 262/M2
Froidchapelle, Belgium 27/E8
Frolovo, U.S.S.R. 48/E5
Frolovo, U.S.S.R. 52/F5
Fromberg, Mont. (59029) 262/H5
Frome (lake), Australia 87/E9
Frome, England 10/E5
Frome, England 13/E6
Frome, Jamaica 158/G6
Frome (lake), S. Australia 88/G6
Frome (lake), S. Australia 94/G4
Front (range), Colo. 208/H1

372 Fronteira

Fronteira, Portugal 33/C3
Fronteiras, Brazil 132/F4
Frontenac, Kansas (66762) 232/H4
Frontenac, Minn. (55026) 255/F6
Frontenac, Mo. (†63101) 261/O3
Frontenac (county), Ontario 177/H3
Frontenac (co.), Québec 172/G4
Frontera, Mexico 150/N7
Frontier, Mich. (49239) 250/E7
Frontier (co.), Nebr. 264/D4
Frontier, N. Dak. (†58102) 282/S6
Frontier, Sask. 181/C6
Frontier, Wyo. (83121) 319/B4
Front Royal, Va. (22630) 307/M3
Frosinone (prov.), Italy 34/D4
Frosinone, Italy 34/D4
Frösö, Sweden 18/J5
Frost, La. (†70753) 238/L2
Frost, Minn. (56033) 255/D7
Frost, Texas (76641) 303/H5
Frost, W. Va. (†24954) 312/G6
Frostburg, Md. (21532) 245/C2
Frostproof, Fla. (33843) 212/E4
Froude, Sask. 181/H6
Frövi, Sweden 18/J7
Frøya (isl.), Norway 18/F5
Frozen (str.), N.W.T. 162/H2
Frozen (str.), N.W. Terrs. 187/K3
Fruita, Colo. (81521) 208/B4
Fruita, Utah (†84775) 304/C5
Fruitdale, Ala. (36539) 195/B8
Fruitdale, S. Dak. (57742) 298/B4
Fruitdale-Harbeck, Oreg. (†97526) 291/D5
Fruitgrove, Queensland 88/K3
Fruit Heights, Utah (†84037) 304/C2
Fruithurst, Ala. (36262) 195/G3
Fruitland, Idaho (83619) 220/B6
Fruitland, Iowa (52749) 229/L6
Fruitland, Md. (21826) 245/R7
Fruitland, Mo. (†63755) 261/N8
Fruitland, N. Mex. (87416) 274/A2
Fruitland, Tenn. (†38343) 237/D9
Fruitland, Utah (84027) 304/D3
Fruitland, Wash. (99129) 310/G2
Fruitland Park, Fla. (32731) 212/D3
Fruitland Park, Miss. (39577) 256/F9
Fruitport, Mich. (49415) 250/C5
Fruitvale, Br. Col. 184/J5
Fruitvale, Idaho (83620) 220/B5
Fruitvale, Tenn. (38336) 237/C9
Fruitvale, Wash. (†98901) 310/E4
Fruitville, Fla. (33578) 212/D4
Frunze, U.S.S.R. 54/J5
Frunze, U.S.S.R. 48/H5
Frutal, Brazil 135/B2
Frutigen, Switzerland 39/E3
Frutillar, Chile 138/D3
Fry, Georgia (37317) 217/D1
Fryburg, N. Dak. (†58622) 282/D6
Fryburg, Ohio (†45895) 284/B4
Fryburg, Pa. (16326) 294/D3
Fry Canyon, Utah (†84511) 304/D6
Frýdek-Místek, Czech. 41/E2
Frýdlant nad Ostravicí, Czech. 41/E2
Frýdlant v. Čechách, Czech. 41/C1
Frye, Maine (04235) 243/B6
Fryeburg, La. (†71039) 238/D2
Fryeburg, Maine (04037) 243/A7
Fryeburg◯, Maine (04037) 243/A7
Fu'an, China 77/K6
Fuchu, Hiroshima, Japan 81/F6
Fuchu, Tokyo, Japan 81/O2
Fuding, China 77/K6
Fuengirola, Spain 33/D4
Fuensalida, Spain 33/D2
Fuente-Álamo, Spain 33/F4
Fuente de Cantos, Spain 33/C3
Fuentelapeña, Spain 33/D2
Fuente Obejuna, Spain 33/D3
Fuenterrabía, Spain 33/E1
Fuentesaúco, Spain 33/D2
Fuentes de Andalucía, Spain 33/D4
Fuentes de Oñoro, Spain 33/C2
Fuerte (isl.), Colombia 126/B3
Fuerte (riv.), Mexico 150/E3
Fuerte Bulnes, Chile 138/E10
Fuerte Olimpo, Argentina 120/D5
Fuerte Olimpo, Paraguay 144/C2
Fuerteventura (isl.), Spain 102/A2
Fuerteventura (isl.), Spain 106/B3
Fuerteventura (isl.), Spain 33/C4
Fuga (isl.), Philippines 82/A3
Fuglebjerg, Denmark 21/E7
Fugu, China 77/H4
Fuhai (Burultokay), China 77/C2
Fuik, Neth. Ant. 161/G9
Fujairah, U.A.E. 59/G4
Fuji, Japan 81/J6
Fuji (mt.), Japan 81/J6
Fuji (riv.), Japan 81/J6
Fujian (Fukien), China 77/J6
Fujieda, Japan 81/J6
Fuji-Hakone-Izu National Park, Japan 81/H6
Fujin, China 77/M2
Fujisawa, Japan 81/O3
Fukagawa, Japan 81/L2
Fukang, China 77/C3
Fukuchiyama, Japan 81/G6
Fukue, Japan 81/D7
Fukui (pref.), Japan 81/G5
Fukui, Japan 81/G5
Fukuoka (pref.), Japan 81/D7
Fukuoka, Japan 54/O6
Fukuoka, Japan 81/D7
Fukushima (pref.), Japan 81/K5
Fukushima, Japan 81/K5
Fukuyama, Japan 81/F6
Fulbourn, England 13/H5
Fulbright, Texas (75436) 303/J4
Fulda, Ind. (47536) 227/D8
Fulda, Minn. (56131) 255/C7
Fulda, Sask. 181/F3
Fulda, W. Germany 22/C3
Fulda (riv.), W. Germany 22/C3
Fulford, England 13/F4
Fulford Harbour, Br. Col. 184/K3
Fuling, China 77/G6
Fulks Run, Va. (22830) 307/L3
Fullarton, Trin. & Tob. 161/A11
Fullerton, Calif. (*92631) 204/D11
Fullerton, Ky. (†41175) 237/P3
Fullerton, La. (70642) 238/D4
Fullerton, Nebr. (68638) 264/F3
Fullerton, N. Dak. (58441) 282/O7
Fully, Switzerland 39/D4
Fulnek, Czech. 41/D2
Fulpmes, Austria 41/A3
Fulton, Ala. (36446) 195/C7
Fulton (co.), Ark. 202/G1
Fulton, Ark. (71838) 202/C6
Fulton (co.), Georgia 217/D3
Fulton (co.), Ill. 222/C3
Fulton, Ill. (61252) 222/C2
Fulton (co.), Ind. 227/E2
Fulton, Ind. (46931) 227/E3
Fulton, Iowa (†52060) 229/M4
Fulton, Kansas (66738) 232/H4
Fulton (co.), Ky. 237/C7
Fulton, Ky. (42041) 237/D7
Fulton, Mich. (49052) 250/D6
Fulton, Miss. (38843) 256/H2
Fulton, Mo. (65251) 261/J5
Fulton (co.), N.Y. 276/M4
Fulton, N.Y. (13069) 276/H4
Fulton (co.), Ohio 284/B2
Fulton, Ohio (43321) 284/E5
Fulton (co.), Pa. 294/F6
Fulton, S. Dak. (57340) 298/O6
Fulton, Tenn. (†38041) 237/B9
Fulton, Texas (78358) 303/H9
Fulton Chain (lakes), N.Y. 276/K3
Fultondale, Ala. (35068) 195/E3
Fultonham, Ohio (43738) 284/F6
Fultonville, N.Y. (12072) 276/M5
Fults, Ill. (62244) 222/C5
Fulwood, England 10/G1
Fulwood, England 13/G1
Funabashi, Japan 81/P2
Funafuti (atoll), Tuvalu 87/H6
Funchal (cap.), Madeira, Port. 102/A1
Funchal (dist.), Portugal 33/A2
Funchal (cap.), Madeira, Portugal 106/A2
Funchal, Portugal 33/A2
Fundación, Colombia 126/C2
Fundão, Portugal 33/C2
Fundy (bay) 162/K7
Fundy (bay), New Bruns. 170/E3
Fundy (bay), Nova Scotia 168/C3
Fundy Nat'l Park, New Bruns. 170/E3
Funhalouro, Mozambique 118/E4
Funing, China 77/K5
Funk, Nebr. (68940) 264/E4
Funk (isl.), Newf. 166/D4
Funkley, Minn. (†56630) 255/D3
Funkstown, Md. (21734) 245/H2
Funston, Georgia (31753) 217/E8
Funter, Alaska (†99801) 196/M1
Funtua, Nigeria 106/F6
Fuping, China 77/H4
Fuquay-Varina, N.C. (27526) 281/M3
Furancungo, Mozambique 118/E2
Furka (pass), Switzerland 39/F3
Furman, Ala. (36741) 195/E6
Furman, S.C. (29921) 296/E6
Furmanov, U.S.S.R. 52/F3
Furnace, Ky. (†40472) 237/O5
Furnace, Mass. (†01031) 249/F3
Furnace, Scotland 15/C4
Furnas (res.), Brazil 120/E5
Furnas (dam), Brazil 135/C2
Furnas (co.), Nebr. 264/E4
Furneaux Group (isls.), Australia 87/E9
Furneaux Group (isls.), Tasmania 88/H8
Furneaux Group (isls.), Tasmania 99/E1
Furnes (Veurne), Belgium 27/B6
Furness, Sask. 181/B2
Furry Creek, Br. Col. 184/K2
Fürstenberg, E. Germany 22/E2
Fürstenfeld, Austria 41/C3
Fürstenfeldbruck, W. Germany 22/D4
Fürstenwalde, E. Germany 22/F2
Fürth, W. Germany 22/D4
Furth im Wald, W. Germany 22/E4
Furukawa, Japan 81/K4
Fury and Hecla (str.), N.W.T. 162/H2
Fury and Hecla (str.), N.W. Terrs. 187/K3
Fusagasugá, Colombia 126/C5
Fushun, China 77/K3
Fushun, China 54/O5
Fusilier, Sask. 181/B4
Fusin (Fuxin), China 77/K3
Fusingchen (Simao), China 77/F7
Fusio, Switzerland 39/G4
Fusong, China 77/L3
Füssen, W. Germany 22/D5
Futa Jallon (mts.), Guinea 106/B6
Futaleufú, Chile 138/E4
Futrono, Chile 138/E3
Futuna (Hoorn) (isls.), Wallis and Futuna 87/J7
Fu Xian, Liaoning, China 77/K4
Fu Xian, Shaanxi, China 77/G4
Fuxin (Fusin), China 77/K3
Fuxin, China 54/O5
Fuyang (Fowyang), China 77/J5
Fuyu, Heilongjiang, China 77/K2
Fuyu, Jilin, China 77/L2
Fuyuan, Heilongjiang, China 77/M2
Fuyuan, Yunnan, China 77/F6
Fuyun, China 77/C2
Füzesabony, Hungary 41/F3
Füzesgyarmat, Hungary 41/F3
Fuzhou (Foochow), Fujian, China 77/J6
Fuzhou, Jiangxi, China 77/J6
Fuzhou, China 2/R4
Fuzhou, China 54/N7
Fyffe, Ala. (35971) 195/G2
Fylingdales, England 13/G3
Fyn (co.), Denmark 21/D7
Fyn (isl.), Denmark 21/D7
Fyn (isl.), Denmark 18/G9
Fyne, Loch (inlet), Scotland 10/D2
Fyne, Loch (inlet), Scotland 15/C5
Fyns Hoved (pt.), Denmark 21/D6
Fyvie, Scotland 15/F3
Fyzabad, Trin. & Tob. 161/A11

G

Gaastra, Mich. (49927) 250/G2
Gabarus, Nova Scotia 168/H3
Gabarus (bay), Nova Scotia 168/H3
Gabarus (cape), Nova Scotia 168/J3
Gabbettville, Georgia (†30240) 217/B5
Gabbs, Nev. (89409) 266/D4
Gabela, Angola 115/B6
Gabès, Tunisia 106/F2
Gabès, Tunisia 102/D1
Gabès (gulf), Tunisia 106/G2
Gabgaba, Wadi (dry riv.), Sudan 111/F3
Gable, S.C. (29051) 296/G4
Gabon 2/K6
Gabon 102/D4
GABON 115/B4
Gaborone (cap.), Botswana 2/L7
Gaborone (cap.), Botswana 118/D4
Gaborone (cap.), Botswana 102/E7
Gabras, Sudan 111/E5
Gabredarre, Ethiopia 111/H6
Gabriel (str.), N.W. Terrs. 187/M3
Gabrik (riv.), Iran 66/L7
Gabriola, Br. Col. 184/J3
Gabrovo, Bulgaria 45/G4
Gachalá, Colombia 126/D5
Gach Saran, Iran 59/F3
Gach Saran, Iran 66/G5
Gackle, N. Dak. (58442) 282/M6
Gacko, Yugoslavia 45/D4
Gadag-Betgeri, India 68/D5
Gäddede, Sweden 18/J4
Gadê, China 77/E5
Gadebusch, E. Germany 22/D2
Gadmen, Switzerland 39/F3
Gadsby, Alberta 182/D3
Gadsden, Ala. 188/J4
Gadsden, Ala. (*35901) 195/G2
Gadsden, Ariz. (85336) 198/A6
Gadsden (co.), Fla. 212/B1
Gadsden, S.C. (29052) 296/F4
Gadsden, Tenn. (38337) 237/D9
Gads Hill, Mo. (†63957) 261/L8
Gadston (pt.), Fla. 212/C3
Gadwal, India 68/D5
Gadyach, U.S.S.R. 52/D4
Găeşti, Romania 45/G3
Gaeta, Italy 34/D4
Gaeta (gulf), Italy 34/D4
Gaferut (isl.), Micronesia 87/E5
Gaffney, S.C. (29340) 296/D1
Gafsa, Tunisia 106/F2
Gagarin, U.S.S.R. 52/D3
Gage, Alberta 182/A1
Gage (co.), Nebr. 264/H4
Gage, N. Mex. (†88030) 274/A6
Gage, Okla. (73843) 288/G2
Gagetown, Mich. (48735) 250/F5
Gagetown, New Bruns. 170/D3
Gaggenau, W. Germany 22/C4
Gagnoa, Ivory Coast 102/B4
Gagnoa, Ivory Coast 106/C7
Gagnon, Que. 162/K5
Gagnon, Québec 174/D2
Gagnon (lake), Québec 172/B3
Gagny, France 28/C1
Gagra, U.S.S.R. 52/E6
Gahanna, Ohio (43230) 284/E5
Gaiba (lag.), Bolivia 136/F5
Gail, Saudi Arabia 59/E5
Gail, Texas (79738) 303/C5
Gaillac, France 28/D6
Gaillard (lake), Conn. 210/D3
Gaillard, Georgia (†31078) 217/D5
Gaima, Papua N.G. 85/B7
Gaiman, Argentina 143/C5
Gaines, Mich. (48436) 250/F6
Gaines, Pa. (16921) 294/G2
Gaines (co.), Texas 303/B5
Gainesboro, Tenn. (38562) 237/K8
Gainesboro, Va. (†22601) 307/M2
Gainestown, Ala. (36540) 195/C8
Gainesville, Ala. (35464) 195/B5
Gainesville (dam), Ala. 195/B5
Gainesville, Fla. 188/K5
Gainesville, Fla. (*32601) 212/D2
Gainesville, Georgia (30501) 217/E2
Gainesville, Mo. (65655) 261/G9
Gainesville, N.Y. (14066) 276/D5
Gainesville, Texas (76240) 303/G4
Gainesville, Va. (22065) 307/N3
Gainsborough, England 10/F4
Gainsborough, England 13/G4
Gainsborough, Sask. 181/K6
Gairdner (lake), Australia 87/D9
Gairdner (lake), S. Australia 88/F6
Gairdner (lake), S. Australia 94/D4
Gairloch, Scotland 15/C3
Gairloch, Loch (inlet), Scotland 15/C3
Gais, Switzerland 39/H2
Gaithersburg, Md. (20760) 245/K4
Gajdel, Czech. 41/E2
Gakona, Alaska (99586) 196/K2
Galadi, Ethiopia 111/J6
Galahad, Alberta 182/E3
Galana (riv.), Kenya 115/G4
Galand, Iran 66/J2
Galanta, Czech. 41/D2
Galápagos (isls.), Ecuador 2/E6
Galápagos (isls.), Ecuador 128/C8
Galashiels, Scotland 10/E3
Galashiels, Scotland 15/F5
Galata, Mont. (59444) 262/E2
Galata, Turkey 63/C6
Galaţi, Romania 7/G4
Galaţi, Romania 45/H3
Galatia, Ill. (62935) 222/E6
Galatia, Kansas (†67567) 232/D3
Galatina, Italy 34/G4
Galatone, Italy 34/F4
Galax (I.C.), Va. (24333) 307/G7
Galbally, Ireland 17/E7
Galbraith, La. (†71447) 238/E4
Galcaio, Somalia 102/G4
Galcaio, Somalia 115/J2
Galchutt, N. Dak. (58034) 282/S7
Gale, Ill. (62936) 222/D6
Gale (riv.), N.H. 268/D3
Galeana, Chihuahua, Mexico 150/F1
Galeana, Nuevo León, Mexico 150/J4
Galela, Indonesia 85/H5
Galen, Mont. (†59722) 262/D4
Galena, Alaska (99741) 196/G2
Galena, Ill. (61036) 222/C1
Galena, Ind. (†47119) 227/F8
Galena, Kansas (66739) 232/H4
Galena, Md. (21635) 245/P3
Galena, Mo. (65656) 261/F9
Galena, Ohio (43021) 284/E5
Galena Park, Texas (77547) 303/J1
Galeota (pt.), Trin. & Tob. 161/B11
Galera (pt.), Chile 138/D3
Galera (pt.), Ecuador 128/B2
Galera (pt.), Trin. & Tob. 161/C10
Galera (pt.), Trin. & Tob. 156/G5
Galesburg, Ill. 188/H2
Galesburg, Ill. (61401) 222/C3
Galesburg, Kansas (66740) 232/G4
Galesburg, Mich. (49053) 250/D6
Galesburg, N. Dak. (58035) 282/R5
Gales Creek, Oreg. (97117) 291/D2
Gales Ferry, Conn. (06335) 210/G3
Galestown, Md. (†19973) 245/P6
Galesville, Md. (20765) 245/M5
Galesville, Wis. (54630) 317/D7
Galeton, Colo. (80622) 208/K1
Galeton, Pa. (16922) 294/G2
Galetta, Ontario 177/H2
Galgenberg (hill), Netherlands 27/H4
Galguduud (prov.), Somalia 115/J2
Galiano, Br. Col. 184/K3
Galiano (isl.), Br. Col. 184/K3
Galice, Oreg. (†97532) 291/D5
Galich, U.S.S.R. 52/F3
Galicia (reg.), Spain 33/B1
Galien, Mich. (49113) 250/C7
Galilee, Sea of (lake), Israel 59/C3
Galilee, Sea of (Tiberias) (lake), Israel 65/D2
Galilee (reg.), Israel 65/C2
Galilee (lake), Queensland 95/C4
Galina (pt.), Jamaica 158/J6
Galion (bay), Martinique 161/D6
Galion, Ohio (44833) 284/E4
Galisteo, N. Mex. (†87540) 274/D3
Galiuro (mts.), Ariz. 198/E6
Galivants Ferry, S.C. (29544) 296/J3
Gallabat, Sudan 111/G5
Gallan (head), Scotland 15/A2
Gallant, Ala. (35972) 195/F2
Gallarate, Italy 34/B2
Gallatin (co.), Ill. 222/E6
Gallatin (co.), Ky. 237/M3
Gallatin, Mo. (64640) 261/E3
Gallatin (co.), Mont. 262/E5
Gallatin (peak), Mont. 262/E5
Gallatin (riv.), Mont. 262/E5
Gallatin, Tenn. (37066) 237/H8
Gallatin Gateway, Mont. (59730) 262/E5
Galloway, Tenn. (38036) 237/B10
Galle, Sri Lanka 54/J9
Galle, Sri Lanka 68/D7
Gallegos (riv.), Argentina 143/B7
Gallegos, N. Mex. (†87733) 274/F3
Galley (head), Ireland 17/D9
Gallia (co.), Ohio 284/F8
Galliano, La. (70354) 238/K8
Gallina, N. Mex. (87017) 274/C2
Gallinas (pt.), Colombia 120/B1
Gallinas (pt.), Colombia 126/E1
Gallinas (mts.), N. Mex. 274/B4
Gallinas (riv.), N. Mex. 274/E3
Gallion, Ala. (36742) 195/C6
Gallion, La. (†71223) 238/G1
Gallipoli, Italy 34/F4
Gallipoli, Turkey 59/A1
Gallipoli, Turkey 63/C5
Gallipolis, Ohio (45631) 284/F8
Gallipolis Ferry, W. Va. (25515) 312/B5
Gallitzin, Pa. (16641) 294/E4
Gällivare, Sweden 18/M3
Gallman, Miss. (39077) 256/D7
Gallo (pt.), Chile 138/E3
Gallo (mt.), Dom. Rep. 158/D5
Gällö, Sweden 18/J5
Galloo (isl.), N.Y. 276/H3
Galloway, Ark. (†72114) 202/F4
Galloway, Br. Col. 184/K5
Galloway (dist.), Scotland 15/D5
Galloway, Mull of (prom.), Scotland 15/D6
Galloway, Mull of (prom.), Scotland 10/D3
Galloway, W. Va. (26349) 312/F4
Galloway, Wis. (54432) 317/H6
Gallup, N. Mex. 188/E3
Gallup, N. Mex. (87301) 274/A3
Gallur, Spain 33/F2
Galole, Kenya 115/G4
Gal'on, Israel 65/B4
Galston, Scotland 10/D3
Galston, Scotland 15/D5
Galt, Calif. (95632) 204/C9
Galt, Iowa (50101) 229/F3
Galt, Mo. (64641) 261/E2
Galtee (mts.), Ireland 17/E7
Galtymore (mt.), Ireland 17/E7
Galva, Ill. (61434) 222/D2
Galva, Iowa (51020) 229/C3
Galva, Kansas (67443) 232/E3
Galván (mt.), Paraguay 144/C3
Galvarino, Chile 138/D2
Galveston, Ind. (46932) 227/E3
Galveston (co.), Texas 303/K8
Galveston, Texas 146/J7
Galveston, Texas 188/H5
Galveston, Texas (*77550) 303/L3
Galveston (bay), Texas 188/H5
Galveston (bay), Texas 303/L2
Galveston (isl.), Texas 303/K8
Gálvez, Argentina 143/F6
Galvez, La. (†70769) 238/L2
Gálvez, Spain 33/D3
Galvin, Wash. (98544) 310/B4
Galway (co.), Ireland 17/D5
Galway, Ireland 17/C5
Galway, Ireland 7/D3
Galway, Ireland 10/B4
Galway (bay), Ireland 17/C5
Galway (bay), Ireland 10/B4
Galway, N.Y. (12074) 276/N4
Gamaliel, Ky. (42140) 237/K7
Gamarra, Colombia 126/D3
Gamas Ab (riv.), Iran 66/E3
Gamay, Philippines 82/E4
Gamay (bay), Philippines 82/E4
Gamba, China 77/C6
Gambaga, Ghana 106/D6
Gambela, Ethiopia 111/F6
Gambell, Alaska (99742) 196/D2
Gamber, Md. (†21048) 245/L3
Gambia 2/J5
Gambia 102/A3
GAMBIA 106/A6
Gambia (riv.), Gambia 106/B6
Gambia (riv.), Senegal 106/B6
Gambier (isls.), Fr. Poly. 87/N8
Gambier, Ohio (43022) 284/F5
Gambo, Newf. 166/D4
Gamboma, Congo 115/C4
Gambos, Angola 115/B6
Gambrills, Md. (21054) 245/M4
Gamerco, N. Mex. (87317) 274/A3
Gaming, Austria 41/C3
Gamleby, Sweden 18/J8
Gammon (riv.), Manitoba 179/G3
Gammon (pt.), Mass. 249/N6
Gampel, Switzerland 39/E4
Gamu-Gofa (prov.), Ethiopia 111/G6
Gamvik, Norway 18/Q1
Ganado, Ariz. (86505) 198/F3
Ganado, Texas (77962) 303/H8
Ganale Dorya (riv.), Ethiopia 111/H6
Gananoque, Ontario 177/H3
Ganassi, Philippines 82/D7
Ganaveh, Iran 66/G6
Ganda, Angola 115/B6
Gandajika, Zaire 115/D5
Gandara, Philippines 82/E4
Gándara, Spain 33/C1
Gandava, Pakistan 68/B3
Gandava, Pakistan 59/J4
Gandeeville, W. Va. (25243) 312/D5
Gander, Newf. 166/D4
Gander (lake), Newf. 166/D4
Gander (riv.), Newf. 166/D4
Gander, Newf. 162/L6
Gandesa, Spain 33/G2
Gandhinagar, India 68/C4
Gandia, Spain 33/F3
Gandy, Nebr. (†69163) 264/D3
Gandy, Utah (†84728) 304/A4
Gandzha (Kirovabad), U.S.S.R. 52/G6
Ganga (Ganges) (riv.), India 68/F3
Gan Gan, Argentina 143/C5
Ganganagar, India 68/C3
Gangapur, India 68/D3
Gangara, Niger 106/F6
Gangaw, Burma 72/B2
Gangca, China 77/F4
Gangdisê Shan (range), China 77/B5
Ganges (riv.) 54/K7
Ganges (riv.) 2/P4
Ganges, Mouths of the (delta), Bangladesh 68/F3
Ganges (riv.), Bangladesh 68/F3
Ganges, Br. Col. 184/K3
Ganges, Mouths of the (delta), India 68/F4
Ganges (riv.), India 68/F3
Gangtok, India 68/F3
Gan He (riv.), China 77/K2
Gani, Indonesia 85/H6
Ganister, Pa. (†16693) 294/F5
Ganmain, N.S. Wales 97/D4
Gann (Brinkhaven), Ohio (†43006) 284/F5
Gannat, France 28/E4
Gannett, Idaho (†83313) 220/D6
Gannett (peak), Wyo. 188/D2
Gannett (peak), Wyo. 319/C2
Gannvalley, S. Dak. (57341) 298/L5
Ganquan, China 77/H4
Gans, Okla. (74936) 288/S4
Gänserndorf, Austria 41/D2
Gansevoort, N.Y. (12831) 276/N4
Ganshoren, Belgium 27/B9
Gansu (Kansu), China 77/E3
Gansville, La. (†71422) 238/E2
Gantt, Ala. (36038) 195/E8
Gantt, S.C. (†29609) 296/C2
Ganzhou (Kanchow), China 77/H6
Gao (mt.), Cent. Afr. Rep. 115/C2
Gao, Mali 102/C3
Gao, Mali 106/E5
Gao'an, China 77/H6
Gaolan, China 77/F4
Gaotai, China 77/F4
Gaoua, Upper Volta 106/D6
Gaoual, Guinea 106/B6
Gaoyou Hu (lake), China 77/J5
Gap, France 28/G5
Gap, Pa. (17527) 294/L6
Gap (creek), Sask. 181/B6
Gapan, Philippines 82/C3
Gapcreek, Ky. (†42603) 237/M7
Gap Mills, W. Va. (24941) 312/F7
Gar, China 77/B5
Gara (lake), Ireland 17/D4
Gara, Lough (lake), Ireland 10/B4
Garachiné, Panama 154/H6
Garad, Somalia 115/J2
Garadice (lake), Ireland 17/F3
Garah, N.S. Wales 97/E1
Garamba Nat'l Park, Zaire 115/E3
Garanhuns, Brazil 120/F3
Garanhuns, Brazil 132/G5
Garards Fort, Pa. (15334) 294/B6
Garbahaarrey, Somalia 115/H3
Garba Tula, Kenya 115/G3
Garber, Iowa (52048) 229/L3
Garber, Okla. (73738) 288/M2
Garberville, Calif. (95440) 204/B3
Garbosh, Kuh-e (mt.), Iran 66/G4
Garbsen, W. Germany 22/C2
Garça, Brazil 135/B3
Garcia, Colo. (81134) 208/J8
García de Sola (res.), Spain 33/D3
Garcitas, Venezuela 124/C3
Gard (dept.), France 28/F6
Gard (riv.), France 28/F5
Garda (lake), Italy 34/C2
Gardanne, France 28/F6
Gardar, N. Dak. (58234) 282/P2
Gardelegen, E. Germany 22/D2
Garden, Mich. (49835) 250/C3
Garden (isl.), Mich. 250/D3
Garden (pen.), Mich. 250/C3
Garden (co.), Nebr. 264/B3
Garden (isl.), W. Australia 88/A2
Garden (isl.), W. Australia 92/A1
Gardena, Calif. (*90747) 204/C11
Gardena, Idaho (†83629) 220/B5
Gardena, N. Dak. (58739) 282/J2
Garden City, Ala. (35070) 195/E2
Garden City, Georgia (31408) 217/K6
Garden City, Idaho (†83704) 220/B6
Garden City, Iowa (50102) 229/G4
Garden City, Kans. 188/F3
Garden City, Kansas (67846) 232/B4
Garden City, La. (70540) 238/H7
Garden City, Mich. (48135) 250/F6
Garden City, Minn. (56034) 255/D6
Garden City, Mo. (64747) 261/D5
Garden City, N.Y. (11530) 276/R7
Garden City, S. Dak. (57236) 298/O4
Garden City, Texas (79739) 303/C6
Garden City, Utah (84028) 304/C2
Garden City Beach, S.C. (29576) 296/K4
Gardendale, Ala. (35071) 195/E3
Garden Grove, Calif. (*92640) 204/D11
Garden Grove, Iowa (50103) 229/F7
Garden Home-Whitford, Oreg. (97223) 291/A2
Garden Island (bay), La. 238/M8
Garden Plain, Kansas (67050) 232/E4
Garden Prairie, Ill. (61038) 222/E1
Garden Reach, India 68/F2
Garden River, Alberta 182/B5
Gardenstown, Scotland 15/F3
Gardenton, Manitoba 179/F5
Garden Valley, Idaho (83622) 220/C5
Garden View, Pa. (†17701) 294/H3
Garden Village, Ontario 177/E1
Gardez, Afghanistan 59/J3
Gardez, Afghanistan 68/B2
Gardi, Georgia (†31545) 217/J7
Gardiner, Maine (04345) 243/D7
Gardiner, Mont. (59030) 262/F5
Gardiner, Oreg. (97441) 291/C4
Gardiner (dam), Sask. 181/D4
Gardiner, Wash. (98334) 310/B2
Gardiners (bay), N.Y. 276/R8
Gardiners (isl.), N.Y. 276/R8
Gardner (canal), Br. Col. 184/C3
Gardner, Colo. (81040) 208/J7
Gardner (lake), Conn. 210/G2
Gardner, Fla. (†33890) 212/E4
Gardner, Ill. (60424) 222/E2
Gardner, Kansas (66030) 232/H3
Gardner (isl.), Kiribati 87/J6
Gardner (lake), Maine 243/J6
Gardner, Mass. (01440) 249/G2
Gardner, N. Dak. (58036) 282/R5
Gardner, Tenn. (†38237) 237/D8
Gardner (mt.), Wash. 310/E2
Gardner Creek, New Bruns. 170/E3
Gardner Pinnacles (isls.), Hawaii 87/K3
Gardner Pinnacles (isls.), Hawaii 188/F6
Gardner Pinnacles (isls.), Hawaii 218/C6
Gardnerville, Nev. (89410) 266/B4
Gardo, Somalia 115/J2
Gardula, Ethiopia 111/G6
Gare Loch (inlet), Scotland 15/A1
Garelochhead, Scotland 15/A1
Garelochhead, Scotland 10/A1
Gareloi (isl.), Alaska 196/K4
Garessio, Italy 34/A2
Garfield, Ark. (72732) 202/C1
Garfield (co.), Colo. 208/C3
Garfield, Colo. (81227) 208/G5
Garfield, Georgia (30425) 217/H5
Garfield, Kansas (67529) 232/C3
Garfield, Ky. (40140) 237/J5
Garfield, Minn. (56332) 255/C5
Garfield (co.), Mont. 262/J3
Garfield (co.), Nebr. 264/F3
Garfield, N.J. (07026) 273/B2
Garfield, N. Mex. (87936) 274/B6
Garfield (co.), Okla. 288/L2
Garfield (co.), Utah 304/C6
Garfield (co.), Wash. 310/H4
Garfield, Wash. (99130) 310/H3
Garfield Heights, Ohio (44125) 284/J9
Gargaliánoi, Greece 45/E7
Gargunnock, Scotland 15/B1
Garibaldi, Br. Col. 184/F5
Garibaldi, Oreg. (97118) 291/D2
Garibaldi Prov. Park, Br. Col. 184/F5
Garies, S. Africa 118/B6
Garioch (dist.), Scotland 15/F3
Garissa, Kenya 115/G4
Garita, N. Mex. (88421) 274/E3
Garland, Ala. (†36456) 195/E7
Garland (co.), Ark. 202/D4

Ghemines 373

Garland, Ark. (71839) 202/C7
Garland, Kansas (66741) 232/H4
Garland, Maine (04939) 243/E5
Garland○, Maine (04939) 243/E5
Garland, Manitoba 179/B3
Garland, Nebr. (68360) 264/G4
Garland, N.C. (28441) 281/N5
Garland, Pa. (16416) 294/C2
Garland, Tenn. (†38019) 237/B9
Garland, Tex. 188/G4
Garland, Texas (*75040) 303/H2
Garland, Utah (84312) 304/B2
Garland, Wyo. (†82435) 319/D1
Garlandville, Miss. (†39345) 256/F6
Garlieston, Scotland 15/D6
Garlin, Ky. (†42728) 237/L6
Garmisch-Partenkirchen, W. Germany 22/D5
Garmouth, Scotland 15/E3
Garmsar, Iran 59/F2
Garmsar, Iran 66/H3
Garnavillo, Iowa (52049) 229/L3
Garneill, Mont. (59445) 262/G4
Garner, Ark. (72052) 202/G3
Garner, Iowa (50438) 229/F2
Garner (lake), Manitoba 179/G4
Garner, N.C. (27529) 281/M3
Garnet, Mich. (†49762) 250/D2
Garnet, Mont. (†59832) 262/C4
Garnet (bay), N.W. Terrs. 187/L3
Garnett, Kansas (66032) 232/G3
Garnett, S.C. (29922) 296/E6
Garnish, Newf. 166/C4
Garoe, Somalia 115/J2
Garonne (riv.), France 7/D4
Garonne (riv.), France 28/C5
Garoua, Cameroon 102/D4
Garoua, Cameroon 115/B2
Garrabost, Scotland 15/B2
Garrard (co.), Ky. 237/M5
Garretson, S. Dak. (57030) 298/S6
Garrett, Ill. (†61913) 222/E4
Garrett, Ind. (46738) 227/G2
Garrett, Ky. (41630) 237/R6
Garrett (co.), Md. 245/A2
Garrett, Pa. (15542) 294/D6
Garrett, Wash. (†99362) 310/G4
Garrett, Wyo. (82058) 319/G3
Garrett Park, Md. (20766) 245/E3
Garretts Bend, W. Va. (†25523) 312/C6
Garrettsville, Ohio (44231) 284/H3
Garrick, Sask. 181/G2
Garrison, Iowa (52229) 229/J4
Garrison, Ky. (41141) 237/P3
Garrison, Md. (21055) 245/L3
Garrison, Minn. (56450) 255/E4
Garrison, Mo. (65657) 261/F9
Garrison, Mont. (59731) 262/D4
Garrison, Nebr. (68632) 264/G3
Garrison, N.Y. (10524) 276/N8
Garrison, N. Dak. (58540) 282/H4
Garrison (dam), N. Dak. 282/H5
Garrison, Texas (75946) 303/K6
Garrison, Utah (84728) 304/A5
Garrisonville, Va. (22463) 307/N4
Garron (pt.), N. Ireland 17/K1
Garrovillas, Spain 33/C3
Garry (lake), Canada 4/C14
Garry (lake), N.W.T. 162/G2
Garry (lake), N.W. Terrs. 187/H3
Garry, Loch (lake), Scotland 15/D3
Garry (riv.), Scotland 15/D4
Garryowen, Mont. (59031) 262/J5
Garsen, Kenya 115/G4
Garske, N. Dak. (†58382) 282/N3
Garson (lake), Alberta 182/E1
Garson, Manitoba 179/F4
Garstang, England 13/G1
Gartan (lake), Ireland 17/F2
Gartmore, Scotland 15/B1
Garulia, India 68/F1
Garut, Indonesia 85/H2
Garvagh, N. Ireland 17/H2
Garvan (isls.), Ireland 17/G1
Garvin, Minn. (56132) 255/C6
Garvin (co.), Okla. 288/M5
Garvin, Okla. (74736) 288/S7
Garwin, Iowa (50632) 229/H4
Garwolin, Poland 47/E3
Garwood, Mo. (†63965) 261/L8
Garwood, N.J. (07027) 273/E2
Garwood, Texas (77442) 303/H8
Gary, Ind. 146/K5
Gary, Ind. 188/J2
Gary, Ind. (*46401) 227/C1
Gary, Minn. (56545) 255/B3
Gary, S. Dak. (57237) 298/S4
Gary, Texas (75643) 303/K5
Gary, W. Va. (24836) 312/C8
Garyarsa (Gartok), China 77/B5
Garyarsa, China 54/K6
Garysburg, N.C. (27831) 281/O2
Garyville, La. (70051) 238/M3
Garza (co.), Texas 303/C4
Garzê, China 77/F5
Garzón, Colombia 126/C6
Garzón, Uruguay 145/E5
Garzón (lag.), Uruguay 145/E5
Gas, Kansas (66742) 232/G4
Gas (hills), Wyo. 319/E3
Gasan-Kuli, U.S.S.R. 48/F6
Gasburg, Va. (23857) 307/N7
Gas City, Ind. (46933) 227/F4
Gasconade (co.), Mo. 261/J6
Gasconade, Mo. (65036) 261/J5
Gasconade (riv.), Mo. 261/H7
Gascony (trad. prov.), France 29
Gascoyne (riv.), Australia 87/B8
Gascoyne, N. Dak. (58629) 282/D7
Gascoyne (riv.), W. Australia 88/A4
Gascoyne (riv.), W. Australia 92/B4
Gascoyne Junction, W. Australia 92/A4
Gash (Mareb) (riv.), Ethiopia 59/C7
Gash (riv.), Sudan 59/C6
Gashaka, Nigeria 106/G7
Gas Hills, Wyo. (82501) 319/E3
Gash Mareb (riv.), Ethiopia 111/G5
Gasht, Iran 66/M7
Gasker (isl.), Scotland 15/A3
Gaskiers, Newf. 166/D2
Gasmata, Papua N.G. 86/B2
Gaspar, Cuba 158/F2
Gaspar Hernández, Dom. Rep. 158/E5
Gasparilla (isl.), Fla. 212/D5
Gaspé, Que. 162/K6
Gaspé, Québec 172/D1
Gaspé, Québec 174/E3
Gaspé (bay), Québec 172/D1
Gaspé (cape), Québec 172/D1
Gaspé (pen.), Québec 172/D2
Gaspé-Est (county), Québec 174/E3
Gaspé-Est (co.), Québec 172/D1
Gaspé-Ouest (co.), Québec 172/C1
Gaspé-Ouest (county), Québec 174/D3
Gaspereau (riv.), New Bruns. 170/D2
Gaspereau (lake), Nova Scotia 168/D4
Gaspésie Prov. Park, Québec 174/D3
Gaspésie Prov. Park, Québec 172/C1
Gasport, N.Y. (14067) 276/C4
Gasque, Ala. (†36542) 195/C10
Gassan (mt.), Japan 81/J4
Gassaway, Tenn. (†37095) 237/K9
Gassaway, W. Va. (26624) 312/E5
Gassetts, Vt. (†05144) 268/B5
Gassville, Ark. (72635) 202/F1
Gaston, Ind. (47342) 227/G4
Gaston (co.), N.C. 281/G4
Gaston, N.C. (27832) 281/O1
Gaston (res.), N.C. 281/O2
Gaston, Oreg. (97119) 291/D2
Gaston, S.C. (29053) 296/E4
Gaston (lake), Va. 307/M8
Gastonburg, Ala. (†36728) 195/C6
Gastonia, N.C. 188/K3
Gastonia, N.C. (28052) 281/G4
Gastre, Argentina 143/C5
Gat, Israel 65/B4
Gata (cape), Cyprus 59/B3
Gata (cape), Cyprus 63/E5
Gata (cape), Spain 33/F4
Gata (mts.), Spain 33/C2
Gatchel, Ind. (†47586) 227/D8
Gatchina, U.S.S.R. 52/C3
Gate, Okla. (73844) 288/F1
Gate, Wash. (†98579) 310/B4
Gate City, Va. (24251) 307/C7
Gatehouse of Fleet, Scotland 10/E3
Gatehouse of Fleet, Scotland 15/D6
Gates, Nebr. (68839) 264/E3
Gates (co.), N.C. 281/R2
Gates, N.C. (27937) 281/R2
Gates, Oreg. (97346) 291/E3
Gates, Tenn. (38037) 237/C9
Gateshead, England 10/F3
Gateshead, England 13/J3
Gateshead (isl.), N.W. Terrs. 187/J2
Gates Mills, Ohio (44040) 284/J9
Gates of the Arctic Nat'l Park, Alaska 196/H1
Gates of the Arctic Nat'l Preserve, Alaska 196/H1
Gatesville, N.C. (27938) 281/R2
Gatesville, Texas (76528) 303/G6
Gateswood, Ala. (†36507) 195/C9
Gateway, Ark. (72733) 202/B1
Gateway, Colo. (81522) 208/B5
Gateway, Oreg. (†97741) 291/F3
Gateway Nat'l Rec. Area, N.J. 273/E2
Gateway Nat'l Rec. Area, N.Y. 276/M9
Gatewood, Mo. (63942) 261/K9
Gatico, Chile 138/A4
Gatineau (co.), Québec 172/B3
Gatineau (county), Québec 174/B3
Gatineau, Québec 172/B4
Gatineau (riv.), Québec 172/B3
Gatliff, Ky. (†40769) 237/O7
Gatlinburg, Tenn. (37738) 237/O9
Gatooma, Zimbabwe 118/D3
Gatooma, Zimbabwe 102/E6
Gatow, W. Germany 22/E4
Gatteville-le-Phare, France 28/C3
Gattman, Miss. (38844) 256/H3
Gatton, Queensland 88/J5
Gatton, Queensland 95/E5
Gatun (lake), Panama 154/G6
Gatzke, Minn. (56724) 255/C2
Gaucín, Spain 33/D4
Gauhati, India 68/G3
Gauhati, India 54/L7
Gauja (riv.), U.S.S.R. 53/C2
Gauley (riv.), W. Va. 312/D6
Gauley Bridge, W. Va. (25085) 312/D6
Gauley Mills, W. Va. (26240) 312/E6
Gaultois, Newf. 166/C4
Gausdale, Ky. (40906) 237/N7
Gause, Texas (77857) 303/H7
Gaussberg (mt.) 5/C5
Gautier, Miss. (39553) 256/G10
Gavater, Iran 59/H5
Gavater, Iran 66/M8
Gávdhos (isl.), Greece 45/F8
Gave de Pau (riv.), France 28/C6
Gavião, Portugal 33/C3
Gavins Point (dam), Nebr. 264/G2
Gavins Point (dam), S. Dak. 298/P8
Gaviota, Calif. (†93017) 204/E9
Gavkhuni (lake), Iran 59/F3
Gavkhuni (marsh), Iran 66/H4
Gävle, Sweden 7/F2
Gävle, Sweden 18/K6
Gävleborg (co.), Sweden 18/K6
Gawai, Burma 72/C1
Gawler, S. Australia 88/F6
Gawler (ranges), S. Australia 88/F6
Gawler, S. Australia 94/B6
Gawler (ranges), S. Australia 94/E5
Gawler (riv.), S. Australia 94/B6
Gay, Georgia (30218) 217/C4
Gay, Mich. (49928) 250/A1
Gay, U.S.S.R. 52/J4
Gay, W. Va. (25244) 312/C5
Gaya, India 68/F4
Gaya, Niger 106/E6
Gay Head○, Mass. (†02535) 249/L7
Gay Head (prom.), Mass. 249/L7
Gay Hill, Texas (†77833) 303/H7
Gayle, Jamaica 158/J6
Gaylesville, Ala. (35973) 195/G2
Gaylord, Kansas (67638) 232/D2
Gaylord, Mich. (49735) 250/E3
Gaylord, Minn. (55334) 255/D6
Gaylord, Oreg. (97458) 291/C5
Gaylord, Va. (†22611) 307/M2
Gaylordsville, Conn. (06755) 210/A2
Gayndah, Queensland 95/D5
Gayndah, Queensland 88/J5
Gayny, U.S.S.R. 52/H2
Gays, Ill. (61928) 222/E4
Gaysin, U.S.S.R. 52/C5
Gays Mills, Wis. (54631) 317/E9
Gaysport, Ohio (†43720) 284/G6
Gaysville, Vt. (05746) 268/B4
Gayville, S. Dak. (57031) 298/P8
Gaza, Cent. Afr. Rep. 115/C3
Gaza, Egypt 59/B3
Gaza, Gaza Strip 65/A5
Gaza, Iowa (†51245) 229/B2
Gaza (prov.), Mozambique 118/E4
Gaza, N.H. (†03269) 268/D4
GAZA STRIP 59/B3
Gaza Strip 65/A5
Gazelle, Calif. (96034) 204/C2
Gazelle (pen.), Papua N.G. 86/B2
Gaziantep (prov.), Turkey 63/G4
Gaziantep, Turkey 54/E6
Gaziantep, Turkey 63/G4
Gaziantep, Turkey 59/C2
Gazik, Iran 66/L4
Gazipaşa, Turkey 63/E4
Gbarnga, Liberia 106/C7
Gbarnga, Liberia 102/B4
Gbogo, Nigeria 106/F7
Gcuwa, S. Africa 118/D6
Gdańsk (prov.), Poland 47/D1
Gdańsk, Poland 7/F3
Gdańsk, Poland 47/D1
Gdov, U.S.S.R. 52/C3
Gdynia, Poland 7/F3
Gdynia, Poland 47/D1
Gearhart, Oreg. (97138) 291/C1
Geary (co.), Kansas 232/F3
Geary, New Bruns. 170/D3
Geary, Okla. (73040) 288/K3
Geashill, Ireland 17/G5
Geauga (co.), Ohio 284/H3
Gebe (isl.), Indonesia 85/H6
Gebeit Mine, Sudan 111/G3
Gebo, Wyo. (†82430) 319/D2
Gebze, Turkey 63/C2
Gedaref, Sudan 111/G5
Gedaref, Sudan 59/C7
Gedaref, Sudan 102/F3
Geddes, S. Dak. (57342) 298/M7
Gede (mt.), Indonesia 85/H2
Gedera, Israel 65/B4
Gedi (ruins), Kenya 115/G4
Gedinne, Belgium 27/F9
Gediz, Turkey 63/C3
Gediz (riv.), Turkey 63/C3
Gedo, Ethiopia 111/G6
Gedo (prov.), Somalia 115/H3
Gedser, Denmark 21/F8
Gedser Odde (pt.), Denmark 21/E8
Gedsted, Denmark 21/C4
Geebung, Queensland 88/K2
Geebung, Queensland 95/E2
Geel, Belgium 27/F6
Geelong, Victoria 88/L7
Geelong, Victoria 97/C6
Geelong West, Victoria 88/G7
Geelong West, Victoria 97/C6
Geelvink (Cenderawasih) (bay), Indonesia 85/K6
Geelvink (chan.), W. Australia 88/A5
Geelvink (chan.), W. Australia 92/A5
Geertruidenberg, Netherlands 27/F5
Geesthacht, W. Germany 22/D2
Geetingsville, Ind. (†46041) 227/D4
Geeveston, Tasmania 99/C5
Geff, Ill. (62842) 222/E5
Gê'gyai, China 77/B5
Geh, Iran 59/H4
Geh, Iran 66/L7
Gehua, Papua N.G. 85/C8
Geidam, Nigeria 106/G6
Geiger, Ala. (†35459) 195/B5
Geiger Heights, Wash. (†99219) 310/H3
Geikie (riv.), Sask. 181/M3
Geilo, Norway 18/F6
Geiranger, Norway 18/E5
Geislingen an der Steige, W. Germany 22/C4
Geismar, La. (70734) 238/K3
Geist (res.), Ind. 227/F5
Geistown, Pa. (15904) 294/E5
Geita, Tanzania 115/F4
Gejiu (Kokiu), China 77/F7
Gejiu, China 54/M7
Gela, Italy 34/E6
Gelang, Tanjong (pt.), Malaysia 72/D6
Geldenaken (Jodoigne), Belgium 27/F7
Gelderland (prov.), Netherlands 27/H4
Geldermalsen, Netherlands 27/G5
Geldern, W. Germany 22/B3
Geldrop, Netherlands 27/H6
Geleen, Netherlands 27/H7
Gelendzhik, U.S.S.R. 52/E6
Gelgia (riv.), Switzerland 39/J3
Gelibolu (Gallipoli), Turkey 63/C5
Gelidonya (cape), Turkey 59/B2
Gelidonya (cape), Turkey 63/D4
Gelligaer, Wales 13/A6
Gelnhausen, W. Germany 22/C3
Gelnica, Czech. 41/F2
Gelså (riv.), Denmark 21/C7
Gelsenkirchen, W. Germany 22/B3
Gelsted, Denmark 21/C7
Gelterkinden, Switzerland 39/E2
Gem, Alberta 182/D4
Gem (co.), Idaho 220/B6
Gem, Idaho (†83873) 220/C2
Gem, Ind. (†46140) 227/F5
Gem, Kansas (67734) 232/B2
Gem (lake), Manitoba 179/G4
Gem, W. Va. (26625) 312/E5
Gemas, Malaysia 72/D7
Gembloux-sur-Orneau, Belgium 27/F7
Gemena, Zaire 115/D3
Gemena, Zaire 102/E4
Gemerek, Turkey 63/G3
Gemert, Netherlands 27/H5
Gemlik, Turkey 63/C2
Gemmell, Minn. (†56660) 255/D3
Gemona, Italy 34/D1
Gemsa, Egypt 111/F2
Genç, Turkey 63/J3
Gendringen, Netherlands 27/J5
Gene Autry, Okla. (73436) 288/N6
Genemuiden, Netherlands 27/H3
General Acha, Argentina 143/C4
General Alvear, Buenos Aires, Argentina 143/F7
General Alvear, Mendoza, Argentina 143/C3
General Arenales, Argentina 143/F7
General Artigas, Paraguay 144/D5
General Belgrano, Argentina 143/G7
General Bravo, Mexico 150/K4
General Campos, Argentina 143/G5
General Cepeda, Mexico 150/J4
General Conesa, Argentina 143/C5
General Elizardo Aquino, Paraguay 144/D4
General Enrique Martínez, Uruguay 145/F4
General Eugenio A. Garay, Paraguay 144/A2
General Galarza, Argentina 143/C6
General Grant Grove Section (King's Canyon), Calif. 204/G7
General Güemes, Argentina 143/D1
General Guido, Argentina 143/E4
General José de San Martín, Argentina 143/E2
General Juan Madariaga, Argentina 143/E4
General Lagos, Chile 138/B1
General La Madrid, Argentina 143/D4
General Las Heras, Argentina 143/G7
General Lavalle, Argentina 143/E4
General Manuel Belgrano, Cerro (mt.), Argentina 143/C2
General Mitchell Field, Wis. 317/M2
General O'Brien, Argentina 143/F7
General Paz, Argentina 143/E2
General Paz, Argentina 143/H7
General Paz (lake), Chile 138/E5
General Pico, Argentina 143/D4
General Ramírez, Argentina 143/F6
General Roca, Argentina 143/C4
General Saavedra, Bolivia 136/D5
General San Martín, Argentina 143/D4
General San Martín, Argentina 143/G4
General Santos, Philippines 82/E7
General Terán, Mexico 150/K4
General Tinio, Philippines 82/C3
General-Toshevo, Bulgaria 45/H4
General Viamonte, Argentina 143/F7
General Villegas, Argentina 143/D4
Generoso (mt.), Switzerland 39/H5
Genesee, Idaho (83832) 220/B3
Genesee (co.), Mich. 250/F5
Genesee (co.), N.Y. 276/D4
Genesee (riv.), N.Y. 276/E5
Genesee, Pa. (16923) 294/G2
Genesee, Wis. (†53127) 317/J2
Genesee Depot, Wis. (53127) 317/J2
Geneseo, Ill. (61254) 222/C2
Geneseo, Kansas (67444) 232/D3
Geneseo, N.Y. (14454) 276/E5
Geneseo, N. Dak. (58037) 282/R7
Geneva (lake) 7/E4
Geneva (co.), Ala. 195/G8
Geneva, Ala. (36340) 195/G8
Geneva, Fla. (32732) 212/E3
Geneva (lake), France 28/G4
Geneva, Georgia (31810) 217/C5
Geneva, Idaho (83238) 220/G7
Geneva, Ill. (60134) 222/E2
Geneva, Ind. (46740) 227/H3
Geneva, Iowa (50633) 229/G3
Geneva, Ky. (†42406) 237/F5
Geneva, Minn. (56035) 255/E7
Geneva, Nebr. (68361) 264/G4
Geneva, N.Y. (14456) 276/G5
Geneva, Ohio (44041) 284/J2
Geneva, Pa. (16316) 294/B2
Geneva (Genève) (canton), Switzerland 39/B4
Geneva (Genève), Switzerland 39/B4
Geneva, Switzerland 7/E4
Geneva (lake), Switzerland 39/C4
Geneva, Texas (75947) 303/L6
Geneva (lake), Wis. 317/K10
Geneva-on-the-Lake, Ohio (44043) 284/H2
Genezin, Turkey 63/F3
Genichesk, U.S.S.R. 52/E5
Genil (riv.), Spain 33/D4
Genk, Belgium 27/H7
Gennargentu, Monti del (mt.), Italy 34/B5
Gennep, Netherlands 27/H5
Gennevilliers, France 28/B1
Genoa, Ark. (71840) 202/C7
Genoa, Colo. (80818) 208/N4
Genoa, Ill. (60135) 222/E1
Genoa (prov.), Italy 34/B2
Genoa, Italy 7/E4
Genoa, Italy 34/B2
Genoa (gulf), Italy 34/B2
Genoa, Nebr. (68640) 264/G3
Genoa, Nev. (89411) 266/B4
Genoa, N.Y. (13071) 276/G5
Genoa, Ohio (43430) 284/D2
Genoa, W. Va. (25517) 312/A6
Genoa, Wis. (54632) 317/D8
Genoa City, Wis. (53128) 317/K11
Genola, Minn. (†56364) 255/D5
Genola, Utah (†84655) 304/C4
Genova (Genoa), Italy 34/B2
Genovesa (isl.), Ecuador 128/C9
Gent (Ghent), Belgium 27/D6
Genthin, E. Germany 22/E2
Gentilly, France 28/B2
Gentilly, Minn. (†56716) 255/B3
Genting, Indonesia 85/D5
Gentofte, Denmark 21/F6
Gentry, Ark. (72734) 202/A1
Gentry (co.), Mo. 261/D2
Gentry, Mo. (64453) 261/D2
Gentryville, Ind. (47537) 227/C8
Gentryville, Mo. (†64402) 261/D2
Genzano di Roma, Italy 34/F7
Geographe (chan.), W. Australia 88/A4
Geographe (bay), W. Australia 92/A6
Geographe (chan.), W. Australia 92/A4
Geographical Center of North America, N. Dak. 282/K3
Geographical Center of U.S., S. Dak. 298/B4
George (isl.), 143/E7
George (lake), Fla. 212/E2
George, Iowa (51237) 229/B2
George (isl.), Manitoba 179/E2
George (lake), Manitoba 179/G4
George (co.), Miss. 256/G9
George (isl.), Newf. 166/C3
George (lake), N.S. Wales 97/E4
George (lake), N.Y. 276/N4
George (sound), N. Zealand 100/A6
George (lake), N. Dak. 282/L6
George (cape), Nova Scotia 168/G3
George (lake), Nova Scotia 168/B5
George (riv.), Que. 162/K4
George (riv.), Que. 146/M4
George (riv.), Québec 174/F2
George, S. Africa 118/C6
George (lake), Uganda 115/F4
George, Wash. (98824) 310/F3
George A.F.B., Calif. 204/H9
George B. Stevenson (dam), Pa. 294/G3
George Land (isl.), U.S.S.R. 4/B7
George Land (isl.), U.S.S.R. 48/E1
George Rogers Clark Nat'l Hist. Park, Ind. 227/B7
Georges (isls.), Maine 243/E8
Georges (riv.), N. S. Wales 88/K4
Georges (riv.), N. S. Wales 97/H4
Georges Brook, Newf. 166/D2
George's Cove, Newf. 166/C3
Georges Fork, Va. (†24228) 307/C6
Georges Mills, N.H. (03751) 268/C5
Georgetown, Ark. (72054) 202/G3
Georgetown, Calif. (95634) 204/E5
George Town (cap.), Cayman Is. 156/B3
Georgetown, Colo. (80444) 208/H3
Georgetown, Conn. (06829) 210/B4
Georgetown, Del. (19947) 245/S6
Georgetown, D.C. (20007) 245/E5
Georgetown, Fla. (32039) 212/E2
Georgetown, Gambia 106/A6
Georgetown, Georgia (31754) 217/B7
Georgetown (cap.), Guyana 2/G5
Georgetown (cap.), Guyana 131/C2
Georgetown (cap.), Guyana 120/D2
Georgetown, Idaho (83239) 220/G7
Georgetown, Ill. (61846) 222/F4
Georgetown, Ind. (47122) 227/F8
Georgetown, Ky. (40324) 237/M4
Georgetown, La. (71432) 238/F3
Georgetown, Maine (04548) 243/D8
Georgetown○, Maine (04548) 243/D8
George Town (Pinang), Malaysia 72/C6
George Town, Malaysia 54/M9
Georgetown, Mass. (01833) 249/L2
Georgetown○, Mass. (01833) 249/L2
Georgetown, Minn. (56546) 255/B3
Georgetown, Miss. (39078) 256/D7
Georgetown (lake), Mont. 262/C4
Georgetown, Ohio (45121) 284/C8
Georgetown, Pa. (15043) 294/A4
Georgetown, Pr. Edward I. 168/F2
Georgetown, Queensland 88/G3
Georgetown, Queensland 95/B3
Georgetown, St. Vin. & Grens. 161/A8
Georgetown, St. Vin. & Grens. 156/G4
Georgetown (co.), S.C. 296/J5
Georgetown, S.C. 188/L4
Georgetown, S.C. (29440) 296/J5
George Town, Tasmania 99/C3
George Town, Tasmania 88/H8
Georgetown, Tenn. (37336) 237/L10
Georgetown, Texas (78626) 303/G7
George V Coast (reg.) 5/C8
Georgeville, Minn. (†56312) 255/C5
Georgeville, Nova Scotia 168/F3
George Washington Carver Nat'l Mon., Mo. 261/D9
George Washington Birthplace Nat'l Mon., Va. 307/P4
George West, Texas (78022) 303/F9
Georgia 188/K4
GEORGIA 217
Georgia (str.), Br. Col. 184/J3
Georgia (state), U.S. 146/K6
Georgia○, Vt. (†05478) 268/A2
Georgia (str.), Wash. 310/B2
Georgia Center, Vt. (†05478) 268/A2
Georgian (bay), Ont. 162/H6
Georgian (bay), Ontario 177/D2
Georgian (bay), Ontario 175/D3
Georgiana, Ala. (36033) 195/E7
Georgian Bay Is. Nat'l Park, Ontario 177/C2D3
Georgian S.S.R., U.S.S.R. 7/J4
Georgian S.S.R., U.S.S.R. 52/F6
Georgian S.S.R., U.S.S.R. 48/D5
Georgiaville, R.I. (†02917) 249/H5
Georgina (riv.), North. Terr. 93/E6
Georgina (isl.), Ontario 177/E3
Georgina (riv.), Queensland 88/F4
Georgina (riv.), Queensland 95/A4
Georgiu-Dezh, U.S.S.R. 52/E4
Georgsmarienhütte, W. Germany 22/B2
Gera (dist.), E. Germany 22/D3
Gera, E. Germany 22/E3
Geraardsbergen, Belgium 27/D7
Gerald, Mo. (63037) 261/K6
Gerald, Sask. 181/K5
Geral de Goiás, Serra (range), Brazil 132/E6
Geraldine, Ala. (35974) 195/G2
Geraldine, Mont. (59446) 262/F3
Geraldine, N. Zealand 100/C6
Geraldton, Australia 87/B8
Geraldton, Ont. 162/H6
Geraldton, Ontario 177/H5
Geraldton, Ontario 175/C3
Geraldton, W. Australia 88/A5
Geraldton, W. Australia 92/A5
Gerar (dry riv.), Israel 65/B5
Gerber, Calif. (96035) 204/C3
Gerber (res.), Oreg. 291/F5
Gercüş, Turkey 63/J4
Gerdine (mt.), Alaska 196/A1
Gerede, Turkey 63/E2
Gereshk, Afghanistan 59/H3
Gereshk, Afghanistan 68/A2
Geretsried, W. Germany 22/D5
Gérgal, Spain 33/E4
Gerger, Turkey 63/H3
Gerik, Malaysia 72/D6
Gering, Nebr. (69341) 264/A3
Gerlach, Nev. (89412) 266/B2
Gerlachovka (mt.), Czech. 41/E2
Gerlogubi, Ethiopia 111/H6
Germania, Miss. (†39162) 256/C5
Germania, Pa. (16922) 294/G2
Germania, Wis. (†54968) 317/H8
Germano, Ohio (†43825) 284/J5
Germansen (lake), Br. Col. 184/E2
Germansen Landing, Br. Col. 184/E2
Germanton, N.C. (27019) 281/J2
Germantown, Ill. (62245) 222/D5
Germantown, Ky. (41044) 237/O3
Germantown, Md. (20767) 245/J4
Germantown, New Bruns. 170/F3
Germantown, N.Y. (12526) 276/N6
Germantown, Ohio (45327) 284/B6
Germantown, Tenn. (38138) 237/B10
Germantown, Wis. (53022) 317/K1
German Valley, Ill. (61039) 222/D1
Germany (East) 2/K3
Germany (West) 2/K3
GERMANY, EAST 22/E2
GERMANY, WEST 22
Germencik, Turkey 63/B4
Germersheim, W. Germany 22/C4
Germfask, Mich. (49836) 250/C2
Germiston, S. Africa 102/E7
Germiston, S. Africa 118/H6
Gerofit, Israel 65/D5
Gerolstein, W. Germany 22/B3
Gerona (prov.), Spain 33/H1
Gerona, Spain 33/H2
Geronimo, Ariz. (†85536) 198/F5
Geronimo, Okla. (73543) 288/K6
Gerpinnes, Belgium 27/F8
Gerpir (cape), Iceland 21/D1
Gerra, Switzerland 39/G4
Gerrardstown, W. Va. (25420) 312/K4
Gerringong, N.S. Wales 97/F4
Gerrish, N.H. (†03301) 268/D5
Gerry, N.Y. (14740) 276/B6
Gers (dept.), France 28/D6
Gers (riv.), France 28/D6
Gersau, Switzerland 39/G2
Gersfeld, W. Germany 22/C3
Gerster, Mo. (†64776) 261/E7
Gerty, Okla. (†74531) 288/O5
Gervais, Oreg. (97026) 291/A3
Gervasio, Uruguay 145/F4
Gêrzê, China 77/B5
Gerze, Turkey 63/F2
Geser, Indonesia 85/J6
Gesher, Israel 65/C2
Gesher Haziv, Israel 65/C1
Gessie, Ind. (†47974) 227/C4
Getafe, Spain 33/F4
Getaway, Ohio (†45675) 284/F9
Gettysburg, Ohio (45328) 284/A5
Gettysburg, Pa. (17325) 294/H6
Gettysburg, S. Dak. (57442) 298/K3
Gettysburg Nat'l Mil. Park, Pa. 294/H6
Getulio Vargas, Uruguay 145/F3
Getz Ice Shelf 5/B12
Geuda Springs, Kansas (67051) 232/E4
Geurie, N.S. Wales 97/E3
Gevar'am, Israel 65/B4
Gevaş, Turkey 63/K3
Gevgelija, Yugoslavia 45/F5
Gex, France 28/G4
Geyser, Mont. (59447) 262/F3
Geyserville, Calif. (95441) 204/B5
Geyve, Turkey 63/D2
Gezira, El (reg.), Sudan 111/F5
Ghabaghib, Syria 63/H5
Ghadames, Libya 102/D2
Ghadames, Libya 111/A2
Ghaghra (riv.), India 68/E3
Ghaida, P.D.R. Yemen 59/F6
Ghalla, Wadi el (dry riv.), Sudan 111/E5
Ghana 2/J5
Ghana 102/B4
GHANA 106/D7
Ghanzi, Botswana 118/C4
Ghard Abu Muharik (des.), Egypt 111/J4
Ghardaïa, Algeria 106/E2
Ghardaïa, Algeria 102/C1
Gharian, Libya 102/D1
Gharian, Libya 111/B1
Gharib, Jebel (mt.), Egypt 59/B4
Ghat, Libya 102/D2
Ghat, Libya 111/B3
Ghat Kopar, India 68/B7
Ghazaouet, Algeria 106/D2
Ghaziabad, India 68/D3
Ghazipur, India 68/E3
Ghazni, Afghanistan 68/B2
Ghazni, Afghanistan 59/J3
Ghea (riv.), India 68/F1
Gheen, Minn. (55740) 255/F3
Gheens, La. (70355) 238/K7
Ghemines, Libya 111/C1

Gramercy 375

Gobabis, Namibia 118/B4
Gobabis, Namibia 102/D7
Gobernador Crespo, Argentina 143/F5
Gobernador Gregores, Argentina 143/C6
Gobernador Mansilla, Argentina 143/G6
Gobi (des.) 54/M5
Gobi (des.), China 77/G3
Gobi (des.), Mongolia 77/G3
Goble, Oreg. (97048) 291/E1
Gobler, Mo. (63849) 261/N10
Gobles, Mich. (49055) 250/D6
Gobo, Japan 81/G7
Gobwen, Somalia 115/H4
Goch, W. Germany 22/B3
Go Cong, Vietnam 72/E5
Godahl, Minn. (†56081) 255/D6
Godalming, England 13/G8
Godalming, England 10/F5
Godavari (riv.), India 54/J8
Godavari (riv.), India 68/D5
Godbout, Québec 174/D3
Godbout, Québec 172/B1
Goddard, Kansas (67052) 232/E4
Godech, Bulgaria 45/F4
Goderich, Ontario 177/C4
Godfrey, Georgia (30650) 217/F4
Godfrey, Ill. (62035) 222/A2
Godhavn, Greenl. 4/C12
Godhavn, Greenland 146/N3
Godhra, India 68/C4
Gödöllő, Hungary 41/E3
Godoy Cruz, Argentina 143/C3
Gods (lake), Man. 162/G5
Gods (lake), Manitoba 179/K3
Gods (riv.), Man. 162/G4
Gods (riv.), Manitoba 179/K3
Gods Mercy (bay), N.W. Terrs. 187/K3
Gods River, Manitoba 179/K3
Godthåb (Nûk) (cap.), Greenl. 4/C12
Godthåb (Nûk) (cap.), Greenland 2/G2
Godthåb (Nûk) (cap.), Greenland 146/N3
Godwin, N.C. (28344) 281/M4
Godwin Austen (K2) (mt.), Pakistan 68/D1
Godwinsville, Georgia (†31023) 217/F6
Goehner, Nebr. (68364) 264/G4
Goéland (lake), Québec 174/B3
Goélands (lake), Québec 174/E1
Goeree (isl.), Netherlands 27/D5
Goes, Netherlands 27/D6
Goessel, Kansas (67053) 232/E3
Goetzville, Mich. (49736) 250/E2
Goff, Kansas (66428) 232/G2
Goff (creek), Okla. 288/C1
Goffstown◯, N.H. (03045) 268/D5
Gogama, Ontario 175/D3
Gogama, Ontario 177/J5
Gogebic (co.), Mich. 250/F2
Gogebic (lake), Mich. 250/F2
Göggingen, W. Germany 22/D4
Gogrial, Sudan 111/E6
Goi, Ben (bay), Vietnam 72/F4
Goiana, Brazil 132/H4
Goiandira, Brazil 132/E7
Goiânia, Brazil 132/D7
Goiânia, Brazil 120/D4
Goiás (state), Brazil 132/D6
Goiás, Brazil 132/D6
Goiás, Brazil 120/D4
Goil, Loch (lake), Scotland 15/A1
Goin, Tenn. (†37825) 237/O8
Goirle, Netherlands 27/G5
Góis, Portugal 33/B2
Gojjam (prov.), Ethiopia 111/G5
Gökçe, Turkey 63/B2
Gökçeada (isl.), Turkey 59/A1
Gökçeada (isl.), Turkey 63/A2
Gökırmak (riv.), Turkey 63/F2
Göksu (riv.), Turkey 63/E4
Göksun, Turkey 63/G3
Gokteik, Burma 72/C2
Gol, Norway 18/F6
Gola (isl.), Ireland 17/E1
Golan Heights (reg.), West Bank 65/D1
Gölbaşı, Turkey 63/G4
Golborne, England 13/G2
Gol'chikha, U.S.S.R. 48/J2
Golconda, Ill. (62938) 222/E6
Golconda (ruins), India 68/D5
Golconda, Nev. (89414) 266/D2
Gölcük, Turkey 63/C2
Golčův Jeníkov, Czech. 41/C2
Gold (riv.), Nova Scotia 168/D4
Goldap, Poland 47/F1
Gold Bar, Wash. (98251) 310/D3
Gold Beach, Oreg. (97444) 291/C5
Goldbond, Va. (24094) 307/G6
Goldboro, Nova Scotia 168/G3
Gold Bridge, Br. Col. 184/F5
Gold Coast (reg.), Ghana 106/D8
Gold Coast, Queensland 95/E6
Gold Coast, Queensland 88/J5
Goldcreek, Mont. (59733) 262/D4
Golden, Br. Col. 184/J4
Golden, Colo. (80401) 208/J3
Golden, Idaho (†83530) 220/C4
Golden, Ill. g)62339) 222/B3
Golden, Ireland 17/F7
Golden, Miss. (38847) 256/H2
Golden, Mo. (65658) 261/E9
Golden, N. Mex. (†87047) 274/C3
Golden (bay), N. Zealand 100/D4
Golden, Okla. (74737) 288/S6
Golden (lake), Ontario 177/G2
Golden (lake), Wis. 317/H1
Golden Beach, Fla. (†33160) 212/C4
Golden City, Mo. (64748) 261/D8
Goldendale, Wash. (98620) 310/E5
Golden Ears Prov. Park, Br. Col. 184/L2
Golden Gate (chan.), Calif. 188/B3
Golden Gate (chan.), Calif. 204/H2
Golden Gate, Fla. (33999) 212/E5
Golden Gate, Ill. (62843) 222/E5
Golden Gate (range), Nev. 266/F5
Golden Gate Nat'l Rec. Area, Calif. 204/H2
Golden Grove, Jamaica 158/K6
Golden Hill, Md. (†21622) 245/O7
Golden Lake, Ontario 177/G2
Golden Meadow, La. (70357) 238/K8
Golden Prairie, Sask. 181/B5
Golden Rock, St. Chris.-Nevis 161/C10
Golden's Bridge, N.Y. (10526) 276/N8
Golden Shores, Ariz. (†86436) 198/A4
Golden Spike Nat'l Hist. Site, Utah 304/B2
Golden Vale (plain), Ireland 17/E7
Golden Valley, Minn. (55427) 255/G5
Golden Valley (co.), Mont. 262/G4
Golden Valley (co.), N. Dak. 282/C5
Goldenvalley, N. Dak. (58541) 282/F5
Golden Valley, Ontario 177/E2
Goldfield, Iowa (50542) 229/F3
Goldfield, Nev. 188/C3
Goldfield, Nev. (89013) 266/D5
Gold Hill, Ala. (†36879) 195/G5
Gold Hill, Nev. (†89440) 266/B3
Gold Hill, N.C. (28071) 281/J3
Gold Hill, Oreg. (97525) 291/D5
Goldonna, La. (71031) 238/D2
Gold Point, Nev. (†89013) 266/D5
Gold River, Br. Col. 184/D5
Goldsberry, Mo. (†63539) 261/G3
Goldsboro, Md. (21636) 245/P4
Goldsboro, N.C. 188/L3
Goldsboro, N.C. (27530) 281/O4
Goldsboro (Etters), Pa. (17319) 294/J5
Goldsby, Okla. (†73093) 288/L4
Goldsmith, Ind. (46045) 227/E4
Goldsmith, Texas (79741) 303/B5
Goldston, N.C. (27252) 281/L3
Goldstone (mt.), Idaho 220/E4
Goldsworthy, W. Australia 88/C4
Goldsworthy, W. Australia 92/B3
Goldthwaite, Texas (76844) 303/F6
Goldvein, Va. (22720) 307/N4
Goldville, Ala. (†35010) 195/G4
Göle, Turkey 63/K2
Goleniów, Poland 47/B2
Goleta, Calif. (93117) 204/F9
Golf, Fla. (†33444) 212/F5
Golf, Ill. (60029) 222/B5
Golfito, C. Rica 154/F6
Golf Manor, Ohio (†45201) 284/C9
Golfo Santa Clara, Mexico 150/B1
Gölhisar, Turkey 63/C4
Goliad (co.), Texas 303/G9
Goliad, Texas (77963) 303/G9
Gölköy, Turkey 63/G2
Golling an der Salzach, Austria 41/B3
Gölmarmara, Turkey 63/C3
Golmud (Golmo), China 77/D4
Golmud, China 54/L6
Golo (riv.), France 28/B6
Golo (isl.), Philippines 82/C4
Golovin, Alaska (99762) 196/F2
Golpayegan, Iran 59/F3
Golpayegan, Iran 66/G4
Gölpazarı, Turkey 63/D2
Golshan (Tabas), Iran 66/K4
Golspie, Scotland 15/E3
Goltry, Okla. (73739) 288/K1
Golts, Md. (21637) 245/P3
Golub-Dobrzyn, Poland 47/D2
Golungo Alto, Angola 115/B5
Golva, N. Dak. (58632) 282/C6
Goma, Zaire 115/E4
Goma, Zaire 102/E5
Gombari, Zaire 115/E3
Gombe, Nigeria 106/G6
Gomel', U.S.S.R. 7/H3
Gomel', U.S.S.R. 48/D4
Gomel', U.S.S.R. 52/D4
Gomer, Ohio (45809) 284/B4
Gomera (isl.), Spain 106/A3
Gomera (isl.), Spain 33/B5
Gometra (isl.), Scotland 15/B4
Gomez, Fla. (†33455) 212/F4
Gómez Farías, Mexico 150/F2
Gómez Palacio, Mexico 150/G4
Gomishan, Iran 66/J2
Goms (valley), Switzerland 39/F4
Gona, Papua N.G. 85/C7
Gonabad, Iran 59/G3
Gonabad, Iran 66/L3
Gonaïves, Haiti 158/B5
Gonaïves, Haiti 156/D3
Gonâve (gulf), Haiti 158/B5
Gonâve (isl.), Haiti 158/B6
Gonâve (isl.), Haiti 156/D3
Gonbad-e Kavus, Iran 66/J2
Gonbadli, Iran 66/M2
Gönc, Hungary 41/F2
Gonda, India 68/E3
Gondal, India 68/C4
Gondar, Ethiopia 102/F3
Gondar, Ethiopia 59/C7
Gondar, Ethiopia 111/G5
Gondia, India 68/E4
Gondola Point, New Bruns. 170/D3
Gondomar, Portugal 33/B2
Gönen, Turkey 63/B2
Gonggar, China 77/D6
Gongga Shan (mt.), China 77/F6
Gonghe, China 77/F4
Gongliu, China 77/B3
Gongola (state), Nigeria 106/G7
Gongola (riv.), Nigeria 106/G6
Gongolgan, N.S. Wales 97/D2
Góngora (mt.), C. Rica 154/E5
Goñi, Uruguay 145/C4
Gonjo, China 77/E5
Gonvick, Minn. (56644) 255/C3
Gonzaga, Philippines 82/D1
Gonzales, Calif. (93926) 204/D7
Gonzales, La. (70737) 238/L2
Gonzales (co.), Texas 303/G8
Gonzales, Texas (78629) 303/G8
Gonzalez, Fla. (32560) 212/B6
González, Mexico 150/K5
González, Riacho (riv.), Paraguay 144/C3
Goobies, Newf. 166/D2
Goochland (co.), Va. 307/N5
Goochland, Va. (23063) 307/N5
Goodbee, La. (†70433) 238/K6
Goode (mt.), Alaska 196/C1
Goode, Va. (24556) 307/K6
Goodell, Iowa (50439) 229/F3
Goodenough (cape) 5/C7
Gooderham, Ontario 177/F3
Goodeve, Sask. 181/H4
Goodfare, Alberta 182/A2
Goodfellow A.F.B., Texas 303/D6
Goodfield, Ill. (61742) 222/D3
Good Harbor (bay), Mich. 250/D3
Good Hart, Mich. (49737) 250/D3
Good Hope, Ala. (†36024) 195/E2
Goodhope (bay), Alaska 196/F1
Good Hope, Georgia (30641) 217/E3
Good Hope, Ill. (61438) 222/C3
Good Hope, La. (†70079) 238/N3
Good Hope, Miss. (†39094) 256/E5
Good Hope, Ohio (43121) 284/D7
Good Hope (cape), S. Africa 102/D8
Good Hope (cape), S. Africa 2/K7
Good Hope (cape), S. Africa 118/E7
Goodhue (co.), Minn. 255/F6
Goodhue, Minn. (55027) 255/F6
Gooding (co.), Idaho 220/D6
Gooding, Idaho (83330) 220/D7
Goodland, Fla. (33933) 212/E6
Goodland, Ind. (47948) 227/C3
Goodland, Kansas (67735) 232/A2
Goodland, Minn. (55742) 255/E3
Goodlands, Manitoba 179/B5
Goodlettsville, Tenn. (37072) 237/H8
Goodlow, Br. Col. 184/G2
Good Luck, Md. (†20715) 245/G4
Goodman, Miss. (39079) 256/E5
Goodman, Mo. (63843) 261/C9
Goodman, Wis. (54125) 317/K4
Goodnews Bay, Alaska (99589) 196/F3
Goodnight, Texas (†79226) 303/C3
Goodnoe Hills, Wash. (†99356) 310/E5
Goodooga, N.S. Wales 97/D1
Good Pine, La. (†71342) 238/F3
Goodrich, Colo. (†80653) 208/M2
Goodrich, Mich. (48438) 250/F6
Goodrich, N. Dak. (58444) 282/K5
Goodrich, Texas (77335) 303/K7
Goodrich, Wis. (†54451) 317/G5
Goodridge, Alberta 182/E2
Goodridge, Minn. (56725) 255/C2
Goodsoil, Sask. 181/L4
Goodson, Mo. (65659) 261/F7
Good Spirit (lake), Sask. 181/J4
Goodspirit Lake Prov. Park, Sask. 181/J4
Goodsprings, Tenn. (38460) 237/G10
Goodsprings, Ala. (35560) 195/D3
Goodsprings, Nev. (89019) 266/F7
Good Thunder, Minn. (56037) 255/D6
Goodview, Minn. (55027) 255/G6
Goodwater, Ala. (35072) 195/F4
Goodwater, Okla. (†74740) 288/S7
Goodwater, Sask. 181/H6
Goodway, Ala. (36449) 195/D8
Goodwell, Okla. (73939) 288/C1
Goodwin, Ark. (72340) 202/J4
Goodwin, S. Dak. (57238) 298/R4
Goodwins Mills, Maine (†04005) 243/B8
Goodwood, Ontario 177/E3
Goodwood, S. Africa 118/F6
Goodyear, Ariz. (85323) 198/C5
Gooik, Belgium 27/E7
Goole, England 10/F4
Goole, England 13/G4
Goolgowi, N.S. Wales 97/C3
Gooloogong, N.S. Wales 97/E3
Goomalling, W. Australia 88/B6
Goomalling, W. Australia 92/B1
Goombalie, N.S. Wales 97/C1
Goondiwindi, Queensland 88/H5
Goondiwindi, Queensland 95/D6
Goor, Netherlands 27/K4
Goose (lake) 188/B2
Goose (lake), Calif. 204/E1
Goose (creek), Idaho 220/E7
Goose (riv.), Newf. 166/B3
Goose (riv.), N. Dak. 282/P4
Goose (isl.), Nova Scotia 168/F4
Goose (isl.), Nova Scotia 168/G3
Goose (lake), Oreg. 291/G5
Goose (creek), Va. 307/J6
Goose (creek), Va. 307/N3
Goose Airport P.O. (Goose Bay), Newf. 162/K5
Goose Bay, Newf. 162/K5
Goose Bay, Newf. 146/M4
Goose Bay-Happy Valley, Newf. 166/B3
Gooseberry (creek), Wyo. 319/D1
Gooseberry Cove, Newf. 166/C2
Goose Cove, Newf. 166/C2
Goose Cove, Newf. 166/C3
Goose Cove, Nova Scotia 168/H2
Goose Creek (mts.), Idaho 220/E7
Goose Creek, Ky. (†40222) 237/L1
Goose Creek, S.C. (29445) 296/H6
Goose Lake, Iowa (52750) 229/N5
Gooseprairie, Wash. (†98937) 310/D4
Goose Rock, Ky. (40944) 237/O6
Goose Rocks Beach, Maine (†04046) 243/C9
Göppingen, W. Germany 22/C4
Góra, Poland 47/C3
Gorakhpur, India 68/E3
Gorchs, Argentina 143/G7
Gorda (pt.), Cuba 158/C2
Gorda (bank), Honduras 154/F3
Gorda (cay), Honduras 154/F3
Gorda (pt.), Nicaragua 154/F5
Gorda (pt.), Panama 154/H6
Gördes, Turkey 63/C3
Gordevio, Switzerland 39/G4
Gørding, Denmark 21/B7
Gordo, Ala. (35466) 195/C4
Gordola, Switzerland 39/G4
Gordon, Ala. (36343) 195/H8
Gordon (lake), Alberta 182/E1
Gordon (riv.), Br. Col. 184/H3
Gordon (isl.), Chile 138/E11
Gordon (co.), Georgia 217/C2
Gordon, Georgia (31031) 217/F5
Gordon, Kansas (†67010) 232/F4
Gordon, Nebr. (69343) 264/B2
Gordon, Ohio (45329) 284/B6
Gordon, Scotland 15/F5
Gordon, Tasmania 99/G5
Gordon (lake), Tasmania 99/C4
Gordon (riv.), Tasmania 99/B4
Gordon, Texas (76543) 303/F5
Gordon, W. Va. (25093) 312/C7
Gordon, Wis. (54838) 317/C3
Gordondale, Alberta 182/A2
Gordon Downs, W. Australia 92/E2
Gordon's Bay, S. Africa 118/F7
Gordonsburg, Tenn. (†38462) 237/F9
Gordonsville, Ala. (†36040) 195/E6
Gordonsville, Minn. (†56036) 255/E7
Gordonsville, Tenn. (38563) 237/K8
Gordonsville, Va. (22942) 307/M4
Gordonvale, Queensland 88/H3
Gordonvale, Queensland 95/C3
Gordonville, Mo. (63752) 261/N8
Gore (pt.), Alaska 196/C2
Goré, Chad 111/C6
Gore (range), Colo. 208/G3
Gore, Ethiopia 111/G6
Gore, Ethiopia 102/F4
Gore, N. Zealand 100/B7
Gore, Ohio (†43188) 284/F6
Gore, Okla. (74435) 288/R3
Gore (mt.), Vt. 268/D2
Gore, Va. (22637) 307/M2
Gore Bay, Ontario 177/B2
Gorebridge, Scotland 10/C1
Gorebridge, Scotland 15/D2
Goree, Texas (76363) 303/E4
Goregaon, India 68/B7
Görele, Turkey 63/H2
Gore Springs, Miss. (38929) 256/E3
Goreville, Ill. (62939) 222/E6
Gorey, Chan. Is. 13/F8
Gorey, Ireland 17/J6
Gorey, Ireland 10/C4
Gorgan, Iran 54/G6
Gorgan, Iran 59/F2
Gorgan (Gurgan), Iran 66/J2
Gorgan (riv.), Iran 66/J2
Gorgan (riv.), Iran 59/F2
Gorgas, Ala. (†35580) 195/D3
Gorgol (reg.), Mauritania 106/B5
Gorgona (isl.), Colombia 126/A6
Gorgona (isl.), Italy 34/B3
Gorham, Ill. (62940) 222/D6
Gorham, Kansas (67640) 232/D3
Gorham, Maine (04038) 243/C8
Gorham◯, Maine (04038) 243/C8
Gorham, N.H. (03581) 268/E3
Gorham◯, N.H. (03581) 268/E3
Gorham, N.Y. (14461) 276/F5
Gorham, N. Dak. (†58627) 282/D5
Gori, U.S.S.R. 52/F6
Gorin, Mo. (63543) 261/H2
Gorinchem, Netherlands 27/G5
Gorizia (prov.), Italy 34/D2
Gorizia, Italy 34/D2
Gorki, U.S.S.R. 52/D4
Gor'kiy, U.S.S.R. 2/M3
Gor'kiy, U.S.S.R. 7/J3
Gor'kiy, U.S.S.R. 48/E4
Gor'kiy, U.S.S.R. 52/F3
Gørlev, Denmark 21/E7
Gorlice, Poland 47/E4
Görlitz, E. Germany 22/F3
Görlitz, E. Germany 7/F3
Gorlitz, Sask. 181/J4
Gorlovka, U.S.S.R. 7/J4
Gorlovka, U.S.S.R. 52/E5
Gorman, Calif. (93243) 204/G9
Gorman, Tenn. (†37101) 237/F8
Gorman, Texas (76454) 303/F5
Gormania, W. Va. (26720) 312/H4
Gormanston, Ireland 17/J4
Gormanston, Tasmania 99/B4
Gorna Oryakhovitsa, Bulgaria 45/G4
Gornji Milanovac, Yugoslavia 45/D3
Gornji Vakuf, Yugoslavia 45/C4
Gorno-Altay Aut. Obl., U.S.S.R. 48/J4
Gorno-Altaysk, U.S.S.R. 48/J4
Gorno-Badakhshan Aut. Obl., U.S.S.R. 48/H6
Gornyak, U.S.S.R. 48/J4
Gorodets, U.S.S.R. 52/F3
Gorodok, U.S.S.R. 52/D3
Goroka, Papua N.G. 85/B7
Goroke, Victoria 97/A5
Gorong (isl.), Indonesia 85/J6
Gorong (isls.), Indonesia 85/J6
Gorongosa Nat'l Park, Mozambique 118/E3
Gorontalo, Indonesia 85/G5
Gorrahei, Ethiopia 111/H6
Gorredijk, Netherlands 27/J2
Gorrie, Ontario 177/C4
Gorst, Wash. (98337) 310/C3
Gort, Ireland 10/B4
Gort, Ireland 17/D5
Gortin, N. Ireland 17/G2
Gorum, La. (71434) 238/E4
Gorumna (isl.), Ireland 17/B5
Goryn' (riv.), U.S.S.R. 52/C4
Gorzów (prov.), Poland 47/B2
Gorzów Wielkopolski, Poland 47/B2
Gorzów Wielkopolski, Poland 7/F3
Göschenen, Switzerland 39/G3
Gose, Japan 81/J8
Gosen, Japan 81/J5
Goshen, Ala. (36035) 195/F7
Goshen, Ark. (72735) 202/C1
Goshen, Calif. (93227) 204/F7
Goshen◯, Conn. (06756) 210/C1
Goshen (pt.), Conn. 210/G3
Goshen, Ind. (46526) 227/F1
Goshen, Ky. (40026) 237/K4
Goshen◯, Mass. (01032) 249/C3
Goshen◯, N.H. (03752) 268/C5
Goshen, N.J. (08218) 273/D5
Goshen, N.Y. (10924) 276/M8
Goshen, Nova Scotia 168/G3
Goshen, Ohio (45122) 284/B7
Goshen, Oreg. (97401) 291/D4
Goshen, Utah (84633) 304/C4
Goshen, Va. (24439) 307/K5
Goshen (co.), Wyo. 319/H4
Goshen Springs, Miss. (†39042) 256/E6
Goshogawara, Japan 81/K3
Goshute (mts.), Nev. 266/G2
Goshute Ind. Res., Nev. 266/G3
Goshute Ind. Res., Utah 304/A4
Gosier, Guadeloupe 161/B6
Goslar, W. Germany 22/D3
Gosnell, Ark. (†72315) 202/K2
Gosper (co.), Nebr. 264/E4
Gospić, Yugoslavia 45/B3
Gosport, Ala. (†36482) 195/C7
Gosport, England 13/F7
Gosport, England 10/F5
Gosport, Ind. (47433) 227/D6
Goss, Miss. (†39429) 256/E8
Gossau, Switzerland 39/H2
Gossville, N.H. (†03234) 268/E5
Gostivar, Yugoslavia 45/E5
Gostyń, Poland 47/C3
Gostynin, Poland 47/D2
Göta (canal), Sweden 18/J7
Göta (riv.), Sweden 18/H7
Gotebo, Okla. (73041) 288/J4
Göteborg, Sweden 7/F3
Göteborg, Sweden 18/G8
Göteborg och Bohus (co.), Sweden 18/G7
Gotha, E. Germany 22/D3
Gotham, Wis. (53540) 317/F9
Gothenburg, Nebr. (69138) 264/D4
Gothic (mesa), Ariz. 198/F2
Gotland (co.), Sweden 18/L8
Gotland (isl.), Sweden 7/F3
Gotland (isl.), Sweden 18/L8
Goto (isls.), Japan 81/D7
Goto (lake), Neth. Ant. 161/D8
Gotse Delchev, Bulgaria 45/F5
Gotska Sandön (isl.), Sweden 18/L7
Gotsu, Japan 81/F6
Göttingen, W. Germany 22/D3
Gottwaldov, Czech. 41/D2
Götzis, Austria 41/A3
Goubere, Cent. Afr. Rep. 115/E2
Gouda, Netherlands 27/F4
Goudeau, La. (71338) 238/G5
Gough (lake), Alberta 182/D3
Gough, Georgia (30811) 217/H4
Gough (isl.), St. Helena 2/J8
Gouin (res.), Que. 162/J6
Gouin (res.), Québec 174/C3
Goulburn, N. S. Wales 88/J6
Goulburn, N.S. Wales 97/E4
Goulburn (isls.), North. Terr. 88/E2
Goulburn (isls.), North. Terr. 93/C1
Goulburn (riv.), Victoria 97/C5
Goulburn Island, North. Terr. 93/C1
Gould, Ark. (71643) 202/G6
Gould, Colo. (†80480) 208/G2
Gould, Okla. (73544) 288/G5
Gould, Québec 172/F4
Gould City, Mich. (49838) 250/D2
Goulding, Fla. (†32502) 212/B6
Goulds, Fla. (33170) 212/F6
Goulds, Newf. 166/D2
Gouldsboro, Maine (†04607) 243/H7
Gouldsboro◯, Maine (†04607) 243/H7
Gouldsboro, Pa. (18424) 294/L3
Gouldtown, Sask. 181/D5
Goulmima, Morocco 106/C2
Goumbou, Mali 106/C6
Gounamitz (riv.), New Bruns. 170/C1
Goundam, Mali 106/D5
Goundam, Mali 102/B3
Gourara (oasis), Algeria 106/E3
Gourbeyre, Guadeloupe 161/A7
Gourdon, France 28/D5
Gouré, Niger 106/G6
Gourma-Rharous, Mali 106/D5
Gournay-en-Bray, France 28/D3
Gouro, Chad 111/C4
Gourock, Scotland 10/A1
Gourock, Scotland 15/A1
Gouveia, Portugal 33/C2
Gouverneur, N.Y. (13642) 276/K2
Gouvy, Belgium 27/H8
Gouyave, Grenada 161/C8
Gouyave, Grenada 156/F4
Govan, Sask. 181/G4
Govan, S.C. (†29843) 296/E5
Gove (co.), Kansas 232/B3
Gove, Kansas (67736) 232/B3
Gove (Nhulunbuy), North. Terr. 93/E2
Govena (cape), U.S.S.R. 48/R4
Govenlock, Sask. 181/B6
Governador Valadares, Brazil 132/F7
Governador Valadares, Brazil 120/E4
Government (mt.), Ariz. 198/C3
Government (peak), Mich. 250/F1
Government (creek), Utah 304/B3
Government Camp, Oreg. (97028) 291/F2
Governor (lake), Nova Scotia 168/F3
Govĭ-Altay, Mongolia 77/E3
Gowan, Minn. (†55736) 255/F4
Gowanda, N.Y. (14070) 276/B6
Gowd-e Zerreh (depr.), Afghanistan 59/H4
Gowen, Mich. (49326) 250/D5
Gowen, Okla. (74545) 288/R5
Gowensville, S.C. (†29356) 296/C1
Gower, Mo. (64454) 261/C3
Gower (isl.), N.S. Wales 97/J2
Gower (mt.), N.S. Wales 97/J2
Gower (pen.), Wales 13/C6
Gowna (lake), Ireland 17/G4
Gowran, Ireland 17/G6
Gowrie, Iowa (50543) 229/E4
Gowrie Park, Tasmania 99/C3
Goya, Argentina 120/D5
Goya, Argentina 143/G4
Goyave, Guadeloupe 161/A6
Goyder (riv.), North. Terr. 93/D2
Goyders (lag.), S. Australia 94/F2
Göynücek, Turkey 63/F2
Göynük, Turkey 63/D2
Goz Beïda, Chad 111/D5
Gozo (isl.), Malta 34/E6
Goz Regeb, Sudan 111/G4
Graaff-Reinet, S. Africa 118/C6
Graal-Müritz, E. Germany 22/E1
Graauw, Netherlands 27/E6
Grabill, Ind. (46741) 227/H2
Grabouw, S. Africa 118/F7
Grabs, Switzerland 39/H2
Gračac, Yugoslavia 45/B3
Gračanica, Yugoslavia 45/D3
Grace, Idaho (83241) 220/G7
Grace (mt.), Mass. 249/E2
Grace, Miss. (38745) 256/C5
Grace (pt.), R.I. 249/H8
Grace City, N. Dak. (58445) 282/N4
Gracefield, Québec 172/A3
Graceham, Md. (†21788) 245/J2
Gracemont, Okla. (73042) 288/K4
Graceton, Minn. (†56686) 255/D2
Graceton, Pa. (15743) 294/D4
Graceville, Fla. (32440) 212/D5
Graceville, Minn. (56240) 255/B5
Graceville, Queensland 88/K3
Gracewood, Georgia (30812) 217/H4
Gracey, Ky. (42232) 237/F7
Grächen, Switzerland 39/E4
Gracias, Honduras 154/C3
Gracias a Dios (cape), Nic. 146/K8
Gracias a Dios (cape), Nicaragua 154/F3
Graciosa (isl.), Portugal 33/C1
Gradačac, Yugoslavia 45/D3
Gradaús, Brazil 120/D3
Gradaús, Brazil 132/D4
Gradaús, Serra dos (range), Brazil 132/D4
Grado, Spain 33/D1
Grady, Ala. (36036) 195/F7
Grady, Ark. (71644) 202/G5
Grady (co.), Georgia 217/D9
Grady (isl.), Newf. 166/C3
Grady, N. Mex. (88120) 274/F4
Grady (co.), Okla. 288/L5
Grady, Okla. (73545) 288/L6
Gradyville, Ky. (42742) 237/L6
Graeagle, Calif. (96103) 204/E4
Graested, Denmark 21/F5
Graettinger, Iowa (51342) 229/D2
Graf, Iowa (†52039) 229/M3
Grafenau, W. Germany 22/E4
Grafenwöhr, W. Germany 22/D4
Graff, Mo. (65660) 261/H8
Graff-Reinet, S. Africa 102/E8
Graford, Texas (76045) 303/F5
Grafton, Australia 87/F8
Grafton (isls.), Chile 138/D10
Grafton, Ill. (62037) 222/C5
Grafton, Ind. (†47620) 227/B9
Grafton, Iowa (50440) 229/G2
Grafton◯, Mass. (01519) 249/H4
Grafton, Nebr. (68365) 264/G4
Grafton, New Bruns. 170/C2
Grafton (co.), N.H. 268/D4
Grafton◯, N.H. (03240) 268/D4
Grafton, N. S. Wales 88/J5
Grafton, N.S. Wales 97/G1
Grafton, N.Y. (12082) 276/N5
Grafton, N. Dak. (58237) 282/R3
Grafton, Ohio (44044) 284/F3
Grafton, Ontario 177/G4
Grafton◯, Vt. (05146) 268/B5
Grafton, Va. (23692) 307/P6
Grafton, W. Va. (26354) 312/G4
Grafton, Wis. (53024) 317/L9
Grafton Center, N.H. (†03240) 268/D4
Graham, Ala. (36263) 195/H4
Graham (lake), Alberta 182/C1
Graham (co.), Ariz. 198/E6
Graham (mt.), Ariz. 198/F6
Graham (isl.), Br. Col. 184/A3
Graham (peak), Colo. 208/E8
Graham, Fla. (32042) 212/D2
Graham, Georgia (†31513) 217/H7
Graham (creek), Ind. 227/F7
Graham (co.), Kansas 232/C2
Graham, Ky. (42344) 237/G6
Graham (lake), Maine 243/G6
Graham, Mo. (64455) 261/C2
Graham (co.), N.C. 281/B4
Graham, N.C. (27253) 281/L2
Graham (isl.), N.W.T. 162/M3
Graham (isl.), N.W. Terrs. 187/J2
Graham, Okla. (73437) 288/M6
Graham, Ontario 175/B3
Graham, Ontario 177/G5
Graham, Texas (76046) 303/F4
Graham Bell (isl.), U.S.S.R. 4/A6
Graham Bell (isl.), U.S.S.R. 48/G1
Grahamdale, Manitoba 179/D3
Graham Land (reg.), Ant. 2/G9
Graham Land (reg.) 5/C15
Graham Reach (chan.), Br. Col. 184/C3
Grahamstown, S. Africa 102/E8
Grahamstown, S. Africa 118/D6
Grahamsville, N.Y. (12740) 276/L7
Grahn, Ky. (41142) 237/P4
Graian Alps (range), France 28/G5
Graian Alps (range), Italy 34/A2
Graiguenamanagh-Tinnahinch, Ireland 17/H6
Grain Coast (reg.), Liberia 106/B8
Grainfield, Kansas (67737) 232/B2
Grainger (co.), Tenn. 237/O8
Graingers, N.C. (†28501) 281/O4
Grainola, Okla. (†74652) 288/N1
Grainton, Nebr. (69169) 264/C4
Grain Valley, Mo. (64029) 261/S6
Grajaú, Brazil 132/E4
Grajaú (riv.), Brazil 132/E4
Grajewo, Poland 47/F2
Gram, Denmark 21/C7
Gramalote, Colombia 126/D4
Gramat, France 28/D5
Grambling, La. (71245) 238/E1
Gramercy, La. (70052) 238/M3

376 Gramling

Gramling, S.C. (29348) 296/C1
Grammer, Ind. (47236) 227/F6
Grammont (Geraardsbergen), Belgium 27/D7
Grampian, Pa. (16838) 294/E4
Grampian (reg.), Scotland 15/F3
Grampian (mts.), Scotland 15/D4
Gramsbergen, Netherlands 27/K3
Gran, Norway 18/G6
Granada, Colo. (81041) 208/P6
Granada, Minn. (56039) 255/D7
Granada, Nicaragua 154/E5
Granada (prov.), Spain 33/E4
Granada, Spain 33/E4
Granada, Spain 7/D5
Granada Hills, Calif. (91344) 204/B10
Granados, Mexico 150/E2
Granard, Ireland 17/F4
Granbury, Texas (76048) 303/G5
Granby, Colo. (80446) 208/H2
Granby (lake), Colo. 208/G2
Granby, Conn. (06035) 210/D1
Granby◯, Conn. (06035) 210/D1
Granby, Mass. (01033) 249/E3
Granby◯, Mass. (01033) 249/E3
Granby, Mo. (64844) 261/D9
Granby, Québec 172/E4
Granby◯, Vt. (05840) 268/D2
Gran Canaria (isl.), Spain 33/B5
Gran Chaco (reg.) 120/C5
Gran Chaco (reg.), Argentina 143/D1
Gran Chaco (reg.), Paraguay 144/B2-3
Gran Couva, Trin. & Tob. 161/B11
Grand (canal), China 54/N6
Grand (canal), China 77/J4
Grand (co.), Colo. 208/G2
Grand (bay), Dominica 161/F7
Grand (canal), Ireland 17/G5
Grand (lake), La. 188/H4
Grand (lake), La. 238/H8
Grand (lake), La. 238/E7
Grand (lake), Maine 243/H4
Grand (isl.), Mich. 250/C2
Grand (lake), Mich. 250/F3
Grand (riv.), Mich. 250/D6
Grand (riv.), Mo. 261/F3
Grand (bay), New Bruns. 170/D3
Grand (lake), New Bruns. 170/D3
Grand (lake), New Bruns. 170/C3
Grand (lake), Newf. 166/B3
Grand (lake), Newf. 166/C4
Grand (isl.), N.Y. 276/B5
Grand (riv.), Ohio 284/H2
Grand (riv.), Ontario 177/D4
Grand (riv.), S. Dak. 298/F2
Grand (co.), Utah 304/E5
Grand Anse, Grenada 161/C9
Grand Bahama (isl.), Bahamas 146/L7
Grand Bahama (isl.), Bahamas 156/B1
Grand Bank, Newf. 166/C4
Grand-Bassam, Ivory Coast 106/D7
Grand Bay, Ala. (36541) 195/B10
Grand Bay, Dominica 161/F7
Grand Bay, New Bruns. 170/D3
Grand Bayou, La. (†71052) 238/C2
Grand Beach, Manitoba 179/F4
Grand Beach, Mich. (†49117) 250/C7
Grand Bend, Ontario 177/C4
Grand Blanc, Mich. (48439) 250/F6
Grand-Bourg, Guadeloupe 161/B7
Grand Bruit, Newf. 166/C4
Grand Caicos (isl.), Turks & Caicos 156/D2
Grand Caille (pt.), St. Lucia 161/F6
Grand Canary (isl.), Spain 102/A2
Grand Canary (isl.), Spain 106/A3
Grand Cane, La. (71032) 238/C2
Grand Canyon, Ariz. 188/D3
Grand Canyon, Ariz. (86023) 198/C2
Grand Canyon, Snake R. (canyon), Oreg. 291/L2
Grand Canyon Nat'l Mon., Ariz. 198/C2
Grand Canyon Nat'l Park, Ariz. 188/D3
Grand Canyon Nat'l Park, Ariz. 198/C2
Grand Canyon of the Snake River (canyon), Idaho 220/B4
Grand Cayman (isl.), Cayman Is. 156/B3
Grand Centre, Alberta 182/E2
Grand Cess, Liberia 106/C8
Grand Chain, Ill. (62941) 222/E6
Grand Chenier, La. (70643) 238/E7
Grand Combin (mt.), Switzerland 39/D5
Grand Comoro (isl.), Comoros 102/G6
Grand Comoro (isl.), Comoros 118/G2
Grand Coteau, La. (70541) 238/G6
Grand Coulee, Sask. 181/G5
Grand Coulee, Wash. (99133) 310/G3
Grand Coulee (canyon), Wash. 310/F3
Grand Coulee (dam), Wash. 310/F3
Grandcour, Switzerland 39/C3
Grand Cul de Sac (riv.), St. Lucia 161/G6
Grand Cul-de-Sac Marin (bay), Guadeloupe 161/A6
Grand Desert, Nova Scotia 168/E4
Grand Detour, Ill. (†61021) 222/D2
Grande (bay), Argentina 120/C8
Grande (bay), Argentina 143/C7
Grande (falls), Argentina 143/E3
Grande (riv.), Argentina 143/C4
Grande (marsh), Bolivia 136/F5
Grande (riv.), Bolivia 136/C6
Grande (riv.), Bolivia 136/C4
Grande (isl.), Brazil 132/C8
Grande (isl.), Brazil 135/D3
Grande (riv.), Brazil 120/E5
Grande (riv.), Brazil 132/D8
Grande (riv.), Brazil 132/E5
Grande (riv.), Brazil 135/B2
Grande (isl.), Chile 138/A6
Grande (riv.), Chile 138/F10
Grande, Salar (salt dep.), Chile 138/B3
Grande, Salto (falls), Colombia 126/D8
Grande (isl.), Colombia 126/B4
Grande (riv.), Guatemala 154/A3
Grande (riv.), Jamaica 158/K6
Grande (riv.), Mexico 150/G2
Grande (riv.), Mexico 150/N8
Grande (riv.), New Bruns. 170/C1
Grande (riv.), Nicaragua 154/E4
Grande (riv.), Peru 128/E10
Grande (range), Uruguay 145/D4
Grande, Arroyo (riv.), Uruguay 145/B4
Grande-Anse, New Bruns. 170/E1
Grande-Anse, Québec 172/E2
Grande Cache, Alberta 182/A3
Grande-Cascapédia, Québec 172/C2
Grande Cayemite (isl.), Haiti 158/B6
Grande-Clairière, Manitoba 179/B5
Grande de Añasco (riv.), P. Rico 161/B2
Grande de Arecibo (riv.), P. Rico 161/C1
Grande de Lípez (riv.), Bolivia 136/B7
Grande de Loíza (riv.), P. Rico 161/E1
Grande de Manatí (riv.), P. Rico 161/C1
Grande de Santiago (riv.), Mexico 150/G6
Grande de Tierra del Fuego (isl.), Argentina 143/C7
Grande de Tierra del Fuego (isl.), Chile 138/E11
Grande Dixence (dam), Switzerland 39/D4
Grande-Grève, Québec 172/D1
Grande Inferior (range), Uruguay 145/C4
Grande Pointe, Manitoba 179/F5
Grande Prairie, Alberta 182/A2
Grande Prairie, Alta. 162/E4
Grande-Prairie, Alta. 146/G4
Grande Prairie, Texas (*75050) 303/G2
Grand Erg Occidental (des.), Algeria 102/C1
Grand Erg Occidental (des.), Algeria 106/E2
Grand Erg Oriental (des.), Algeria 102/C1
Grand Erg Oriental (des.), Algeria 106/F2
Grand Erg Oriental (des.), Tunisia 106/F2
Grande' Rivière, Martinique 161/C5
Grande-Rivière, Québec 172/D2
Grande-Rivière, La (riv.), Que. 146/L4
Grande Rivière, La (riv.), Québec 174/B2
Grande Rivière, Trin. & Tob. 161/B10
Grande Rivière du Nord, Haiti 158/C5
Grande Ronde (riv.), Oreg. 291/K2
Grande Ronde (riv.), Wash. 310/H5
Grande Saline, Haiti 158/B5
Grandes-Bergeronnes, Québec 172/H1
Grandes-Piles, Québec 172/E3
Grand-Étang, Nova Scotia 168/G2
Grande-Terre, Guadeloupe 161/B6
Grande-Vallée, Québec 172/D1
Grande Vigie, Guadeloupe 161/B5
Grand Falls (lake), Maine 243/H5
Grand Falls, New Bruns. 170/C1
Grand Falls, Newf. 166/C4
Grand Falls, Newf. 146/N5
Grand Falls, Newf. 162/L6
Grandfalls, Texas (79742) 303/B6
Grand Falls Hill, New Bruns. 170/C1
Grandfield, Okla. (73546) 288/J6
Grand Forks, Br. Col. 184/H6
Grand Forks, N. Dak. 146/J5
Grand Forks, N. Dak. 188/G1
Grand Forks (co.), N. Dak. 282/P3
Grand Forks, N. Dak. (58201) 282/R4
Grand Forks A.F.B., N. Dak. 282/R4
Grand Glaise, Ark. (†72020) 202/G3
Grand Goâve, Haiti 158/B6
Grand Gorge, N.Y. (12434) 276/L6
Grand Gosier, Haiti 158/C6
Grand Gulf, Miss. (†39150) 256/B6
Grand Harbour, New Bruns. 170/D4
Grand Haven, Mich. (49417) 250/C5
Grand-Îlet (isl.), Guadeloupe 161/A7
Grandin, Fla. (32638) 212/E2
Grandin, Mo. (63943) 261/L9
Grandin, N. Dak. (58038) 282/R5
Grand Island, Nebr. 146/J5
Grand Island, Nebr. 188/G2
Grand Island, Nebr. (68801) 264/F4
Grand Island, N.Y. (14072) 276/B5
Grand Isle, La. (70358) 238/L8
Grand Isle, Maine (04746) 243/G1
Grand Isle, Maine 243/G18
Grand Isle (co.), Vt. 268/A2
Grand Isle◯, Vt. (05458) 268/A2
Grand Junction, Colo. 146/H6
Grand Junction, Colo. 188/E3
Grand Junction, Colo. (81501) 208/B4
Grand Junction, Iowa (50107) 229/E4
Grand Junction, Mich. (49056) 250/C6
Grand Junction, Tenn. (38039) 237/C10
Grand-Lahou, Ivory Coast 106/C8
Grand Lake, Ark. (†71640) 202/H7
Grand Lake, Colo. (80447) 208/H2
Grand Lake, La. (†70601) 238/D6
Grand Lake, Nova Scotia 168/E4
Grand Lake Seboeis (lake), Maine 243/F3
Grand Lake Stream◯, Maine (04637) 243/H5
Grand Lake Towne, Okla. (†74349) 288/S1
Grand Ledge, Mich. (48837) 250/E6
Grand-Lieu (lake), France 28/C4
Grand Manan (chan.), Maine 243/K6
Grand Manan (chan.), New Bruns. 170/C4
Grand Manan (isl.), New Bruns. 170/D4
Grand Marais, Manitoba 179/F4
Grand Marais, Mich. (49839) 250/D2
Grand Marais, Minn. (55604) 255/G2
Grand Marsh, Wis. (53936) 317/G8
Grand Meadow, Minn. (55936) 255/F7
Grand'Mère, Québec 172/E3
Grand Mound, Iowa (52751) 229/M5
Grand Mound, Wash. (†98531) 310/C4
Grand Muveran (mt.), Switzerland 39/D4
Grand Narrows, Nova Scotia 168/H3
Grândola, Portugal 33/B3
Grandora, Sask. 181/E3
Grand Pass, Mo. (65331) 261/F4
Grand-Popo, Benin 106/E7
Grand Portage, Minn. (55617) 255/G2
Grand Portage Ind. Res., Minn. 255/G2
Grand Portage Nat'l Mon., Minn. 255/G2
Grand Pré, Nova Scotia 168/D3
Grand Rapids, Manitoba 179/C1
Grand Rapids, Mich. 146/K5
Grand Rapids, Mich. 188/K2
Grand Rapids, Mich. (*49501) 250/D5
Grand Rapids, Minn. (55744) 255/E3
Grand Rapids, N. Dak. (†58458) 282/N7
Grand Rapids, Ohio (43522) 284/C3
Grand-Remous, Québec 172/B3
Grand Ridge, Fla. (32442) 212/A1
Grand Ridge, Ill. (61325) 222/E2
Grand River, Iowa (50108) 229/F7
Grand River, Nova Scotia 168/H3
Grand River, Ohio (44045) 284/H2
Grand River (valley), Utah 304/E4
Grand Rivers, Ky. (42045) 237/E7
Grand Ronde, Oreg. (97347) 291/D2
Grand Roy, Grenada 161/C8
Grand Saline, Texas (75140) 303/J5
Grand Santi, Fr. Guiana 131/D3
Grandson, Switzerland 39/C3
Grand Terrace, Calif. (92324) 204/E10
Grand Terre (isls.), La. 238/L8
Grand Teton (mt.), Wyo. 319/B2
Grand Teton Nat'l Park, Wyo. 319/B2
Grand Tower, Ill. (62942) 222/D6
Grand Traverse (co.), Mich. 250/D4
Grand Traverse (bay), Mich. 250/D3
Grand Turk (isl.), Turks & Caicos 156/D2
Grand Valley, Ontario 177/D4
Grand Valley, Pa. (16420) 294/C2
Grandview, Ark. (72637) 202/C1
Grand View, Idaho (83624) 220/B7
Grandview, Ill. (†62701) 222/D4
Grand View, Ill. (†61944) 222/F4
Grandview, Ind. (47615) 227/C9
Grandview, Iowa (52752) 229/L6
Grandview, Manitoba 179/B3
Grandview, Mo. (64030) 261/P6
Grandview, Ohio (†45767) 284/H7
Grandview, Tenn. (37337) 237/M9
Grandview, Texas (76050) 303/G5
Grandview, Wash. (98930) 310/F4
Grand View, Wis. (54839) 317/D3
Grandview Heights, Ohio (†43212) 284/D6
Grand View-on-Hudson, N.Y. (†10960) 276/K8
Grandview Plaza, Kansas (†66441) 232/F2
Grandville, Mich. (49418) 250/D6
Grand Wash (butte), Ariz. 198/B2
Grand Wash (riv.), Ariz. 198/B2
Grandy, Minn. (55029) 255/E5
Grandy, N.C. (27939) 281/T2
Graneros, Chile 138/G5
Grange, England 13/E3
Grange, N.H. (†03584) 268/E3
Grangeburg, Ala. (†36343) 195/H8
Grange City, Ky. (†41049) 237/O4
Grangemouth, Scotland 10/B1
Grangemouth, Scotland 15/C1
Granger, Ind. (46530) 227/E1
Granger, Iowa (50109) 229/F5
Granger, Minn. (55937) 255/F7
Granger, Mo. (63442) 261/H2
Granger, Texas (76530) 303/G7
Granger, Wash. (98932) 310/E4
Granger, Wyo. 188/D2
Granger, Wyo. (82934) 319/C4
Grangeville, Idaho (83530) 220/B4
Grangeville, La. (†70422) 238/J5
Granisle, Br. Col. 184/D3
Granite, Colo. (81228) 208/G4
Granite, Md. (†21163) 245/L3
Granite (pt.), Mich. 250/B2
Granite (co.), Mont. 262/C4
Granite (peak), Mont. 262/F5
Granite (peak), Nev. 266/B2
Granite (range), Nev. 266/B2
Granite, Okla. (73547) 288/H5
Granite, Oreg. (†97877) 291/J3
Granite (mts.), Wyo. 319/E3
Granite Bay, Br. Col. 184/E5
Granite Canon, Wyo. (82059) 319/G4
Granite City, Ill. (62040) 222/A2
Granite City Army Depot, Ill. 222/A2
Granite Falls, Minn. (56241) 255/C6
Granite Falls, N.C. (28630) 281/G3
Granite Falls, Wash. (98252) 310/D2
Granite Quarry, N.C. (28072) 281/H3
Graniteville, Mass. (01829) 249/J2
Graniteville, Mo. (†63650) 261/L7
Graniteville, S.C. (29829) 296/D4
Graniteville-East Barre, Vt. (05654) 268/C3
Granitique, Chaîne (range), Fr. Guiana 131/E4
Granity, N. Zealand 100/C4
Granja, Brazil 132/F3
Granma (prov.), Cuba 158/H4
Gränna, Sweden 18/J8
Grannis, Ark. (71944) 202/B5
Grano, N. Dak. (†58750) 282/G2
Granollers, Spain 33/H2
Gran Paradiso (mt.), Italy 34/A2
Gran Piedra (mt.), Cuba 158/J4
Gran Quivira, N. Mex. (†87036) 274/D4
Gran Sabana, La (plain), Venezuela 124/G5
Grant, Ala. (35747) 195/F1
Grant (co.), Ark. 202/F5
Grant, Colo. (80448) 208/H4
Grant, Fla. (32949) 212/F4
Grant (co.), Ind. 227/F3
Grant, Iowa (50847) 229/C6
Grant (co.), Kansas 232/A4
Grant (co.), Ky. 237/M3
Grant, Ky. (†41005) 237/M3
Grant (par.), La. 238/E3
Grant, La. (70644) 238/E5
Grant, Mich. (49327) 250/D5
Grant (co.), Minn. 255/B5
Grant, Mont. (†59725) 262/C5
Grant (co.), Nebr. 264/C3
Grant, Nebr. (69140) 264/C4
Grant (range), Nev. 266/F4
Grant (co.), N. Mex. 274/A5
Grant (co.), N. Dak. 282/G6
Grant (co.), Okla. 288/L1
Grant, Okla. (74738) 288/R7
Grant (co.), Oreg. 291/J3
Grant (co.), S. Dak. 298/R3
Grant (co.), Wash. 310/F3
Grant (co.), W. Va. 312/H4
Grant (co.), Wis. 317/E10
Grant Center, Iowa (†51026) 229/A4
Grant City, Mo. (64456) 261/D2
Grantfork, Ill. (†62249) 222/D5
Grantham, Alberta 182/E4
Grantham, England 13/G5
Grantham, England 10/F4
Grantham◯, N.H. (03753) 268/C5
Granthams Landing, Br. Col. 184/J3
Grant-Kohrs Ranch Nat'l Hist. Site, Mont. 262/D4
Granton, Ontario 177/C4
Granton, Wis. (54436) 317/E6
Grantown-on-Spey, Scotland 10/E2
Grantown-on-Spey, Scotland 15/E3
Grant Park, Ill. (60940) 222/F2
Grants, N. Mex. (87020) 274/B3
Grantsboro, N.C. (28529) 281/R4
Grantsburg, Ill. (62943) 222/E6
Grantsburg, Ind. (47123) 227/E8
Grantsburg, Wis. (54840) 317/A4
Grantsdale, Mont. (59835) 262/B4
Grants Pass (chan.), Ala. 195/B10
Grants Pass, Oreg. 188/B2
Grants Pass, Oreg. (97526) 291/D5
Grantsville, Md. (21536) 245/B2
Grantsville, Utah (84029) 304/B3
Grantsville, W. Va. (26147) 312/D5
Grant Town, W. Va. (26574) 312/F3
Grantville, Alberta 182/D4
Grantville, Georgia (30220) 217/C4
Grantville, Kansas (66429) 232/G2
Grantwood Village, Mo. (†63155) 261/O4
Granum, Alberta 182/D5
Granville, France 28/C3
Granville, Ill. (61326) 222/D2
Granville, Iowa (51022) 229/B3
Granville (lake), Man. 162/G4
Granville (lake), Manitoba 179/H2
Granville◯, Mass. (01034) 249/C4
Granville, Mo. (†65275) 261/H3
Granville, N.Y. (12832) 276/O4
Granville (co.), N.C. 281/M2
Granville, N. Dak. (58741) 282/J3
Granville, Ohio (43023) 284/E5
Granville, Tenn. (38564) 237/K8
Granville◯, Vt. (05747) 268/B4
Granville, W. Va. (26534) 312/F3
Granville Centre, Nova Scotia 168/C4
Granville Ferry, Nova Scotia 168/C4
Granville Lake, Manitoba 179/H2
Grapeland, Miss. (†38725) 256/B3
Grapeland, Texas (75844) 303/J6
Grapeview, Wash. (98546) 310/C3
Grapeville, Pa. (15634) 294/C5
Grapevine, Ark. (72057) 202/F5
Grapevine (mts.), Calif. 204/H7
Grapevine, Texas (76051) 303/F2
Grapevine (lake), Texas 303/F2
Grasmere, Br. Col. 184/K5
Grasmere, N.H. (†03045) 268/D5
Grasmere, S. Africa 118/H7
Gräsö (isl.), Sweden 18/L6
Grasonville, Md. (21638) 245/O5
Grass (riv.), Manitoba 179/J3
Grass (riv.), N.Y. 276/K1
Grass (pt.), Virgin Is. (U.S.) 161/G4
Grass Creek, Ind. (46935) 227/E3
Grass Creek, Wyo. (82425) 319/D2
Grasse, France 28/G6
Grassflat, Pa. (16839) 294/F3
Grassington, England 13/F3
Grass Lake, Mich. (49240) 250/E6
Grassland, Alberta 182/D2
Grass Patch, W. Australia 92/C6
Grass Range, Mont. (59032) 262/H3
Grass River Prov. Park, Manitoba 179/H3
Grasston, Minn. (55030) 255/E5
Grass Valley, Calif. 188/B3
Grass Valley, Calif. (95945) 204/D4
Grass Valley, Oreg. (97029) 291/G2
Grassy (key), Fla. 212/F7
Grassy, Mo. (63753) 261/M8
Grassy Butte, N. Dak. (58634) 282/D5
Grassy Lake, Alberta 182/E5
Grassy Meadows, W. Va. (24943) 312/E7
Grassy Park, S. Africa 118/E6
Grassy Plains, Br. Col. 184/E3
Gråsten, Denmark 21/C8
Grates (pt.), Newf. 166/D2
Grates Cove, Newf. 166/D2
Gratiot (co.), Mich. 250/E5
Gratiot, Ohio (43740) 284/F6
Gratiot, Wis. (53541) 317/F10
Gratis, Ohio (4533) 284/A6
Graton, Calif. (95444) 204/C5
Gratwein, Austria 41/C3
Gratz, Ky. (40327) 237/M4
Gratz, Pa. (17030) 294/J4
Graubünden (Grisons) (canton), Switzerland 39/H3
Grauehörner (mts.), Switzerland 39/H3
Graulhet, France 28/E6
Graus, Spain 33/G1
Grauspitz (mt.), Liecht. 39/J2
Grave (pt.), France 28/C5
Grave, Netherlands 27/H5
Gravelbourg, Sask. 181/E6
Gravelly, Ark. (72838) 202/C4
Gravelly Beach, Tasmania 99/C3
Gravelly Branch, Nanticoke (riv.), Del. 245/R6
Gravel Switch, Ky. (40328) 237/L5
Gravelton, Ind. (†46542) 227/F2
Gravenhurst, Ontario 177/E3
Graves, Georgia (31755) 217/C7
Graves (co.), Ky. 237/D7
Gravesend, England 10/C5
Gravesend, England 13/J8
Gravette, Ark. (72736) 202/B1
Gravina (isl.), Alaska 196/N2
Gravina in Puglia, Italy 34/F4
Gravity, Iowa (50848) 229/D7
Gravois (pt.), Haiti 158/A7
Gravois Mills, Mo. (65037) 261/G6
Grawn, Mich. (49637) 250/D4
Gray, France 28/F4
Gray, Georgia (31032) 217/F4
Gray, Iowa (50110) 229/D5
Gray (co.), Kansas 232/B4
Gray, Ky. (40734) 237/O7
Gray, La. (70359) 238/J7
Gray, Maine (04039) 243/C8
Gray◯, Maine (04039) 243/C8
Gray, Pa. (15544) 294/D5
Gray, Sask. 181/G5
Gray (co.), Texas 303/D2
Gray (canyon), Utah 304/D4
Gray, Va. (†23897) 307/O7
Grayback (mt.), Oreg. 291/D5
Gray Court, S.C. (29645) 296/C2
Gray Hawk, Ky. (40434) 237/N6
Gray Horse, Okla. (†74637) 288/N1
Grayland, Wash. (98547) 310/A4
Grayling, Alaska (99590) 196/G2
Grayling, Mich. (49738) 250/E4
Graymont, Ill. (61743) 222/E3
Graymoor, Ky. (†40201) 237/K1
Gray Rapids, New Bruns. 170/E2
Grayridge, Mo. (63850) 261/N9
Grays, Ark. (†72101) 202/H3
Grays (lake), Idaho 220/G6
Grays, S.C. (†29916) 296/E6
Grays (harb.), Wash. 310/A4
Graysbranch, Ky. (†41144) 237/R3
Grays Harbor (co.), Wash. 310/B3
Grayslake, Ill. (60030) 222/B4
Grays Lake Outlet (creek), Idaho 220/G6
Grays Landing, Pa. (15461) 294/C6
Grayson, Georgia (30221) 217/E3
Grayson (co.), Ky. 237/J5
Grayson, Ky. (41143) 237/R4
Grayson (lake), Ky. 237/P4
Grayson, La. (71435) 238/F2
Grayson, Mo. (†64492) 261/D3
Grayson, Okla. (†74437) 288/P3
Grayson, Sask. 181/J5
Grayson (co.), Texas 303/H4
Grayson (co.), Va. 307/F7
Grays River, Wash. (98621) 310/B4
Gray Summit, Mo. (63039) 261/L6
Graysville, Ala. (35073) 195/D3
Graysville, Georgia (30726) 217/B1
Graysville, Ind. (47852) 227/B6
Graysville, Manitoba 179/D5
Graysville, Ohio (45734) 284/H6
Graysville, Pa. (15337) 294/B6
Graysville, Tenn. (37338) 237/L10
Graytown, Ohio (43432) 284/D2
Grayville, Ill. (62844) 222/B4
Graz, Austria 7/F4
Graz, Austria 41/C3
Grazalema, Spain 33/D4
Greaney, Minn. (†55740) 255/F3
Great (lakes) 2/E3
Great (sound), Bermuda 156/G3
Great (fall), Guyana 131/B3
Great (chan.), India 68/G7
Great (riv.), Jamaica 158/H6
Great (pond), Mass. 249/D8
Great (pt.), Mass. 249/O7
Great (bay), N.H. 268/F5
Great (bay), N.J. 273/E4
Great (isl.), N. Zealand 100/D1
Great (lake), N.C. 281/P5
Great (lake), Tasmania 99/C3
Great (pond), Virgin Is. (U.S.) 161/F4
Great Abaco (isl.), Bahamas 146/L7
Great Abaco (isl.), Bahamas 156/C1
Great Alföld (plain), Hungary 41/F3
Great Australian (bight) 88/D6
Great Australian (bight), Australia 87/C9
Great Australian (bight), S. Australia 94/A5
Great Australian (bight), W. Australia 92/E6
Great Averill (pond), Vt. 268/D2
Great Bacolet (pt.), Grenada 161/D8
Great Baddow, England 13/J7
Great Bahama (bank), Bahamas 156/B1
Great Barrier (reef) 88/H2
Great Barrier (reef), 95/C2
Great Barrier (reef), Australia 87/E7
Great Barrier (isl.), N. Zealand 100/E2
Great Barrington, Mass. (01230) 249/A4
Great Barrington◯, Mass. (01230) 249/A4
Great Barton, England 13/H5
Great Bear (lake), Canada 4/C16
Great Bear (lake), N.W.T. 162/D2
Great Bear (lake), N.W.T. 146/H3
Great Bear (lake), N.W. Terrs. 187/F3
Great Bear (riv.), N.W. Terrs. 187/F3
Great Bend, Kansas (67530) 232/D3
Great Bend, N.Y. (13643) 276/J2
Great Bend, N. Dak. (58039) 282/S7
Great Bend, Pa. (18821) 294/L2
Great Blasket (isl.), Ireland 17/A7
Great Bras d'Or (chan.), Nova Scotia 168/H2
Great Burnt (lake), Newf. 166/C4
Great Cacapon, W. Va. (25422) 312/K3
Great Coco (isl.), Burma 72/B4
Great Colinet (isl.), Newf. 166/D2
Great Corn (isl.), Nicaragua 154/F4
Great Cornard, England 13/H5
Great Cumbrae (isl.), Scotland 15/A2
Great Dismal (swamp), N.C. 281/S1
Great Dismal (swamp), Va. 307/R8
Great Divide (basin), Wyo. 319/E3
Great Dividing (range), N. S. Wales 88/J6
Great Dividing (range), N.S. Wales 97/E3
Great Dividing (range), Queensland 88/H4
Great Dividing (range), Queensland 95/C4
Great Egg Harbor (inlet), N.J. 273/E5
Great Egg Harbor (riv.), N.J. 273/D4
Greater Antilles (isls.) 146/K7
Greater London, England 13/H8
Greater Manchester (co.), England 13/H2
Greaterville, Ariz. (†85637) 198/E7
Great Exhibition (bay), N. Zealand 100/D1
Great Exuma (isl.), Bahamas 146/L7
Great Exuma (isl.), Bahamas 156/C2
Great Falls, Manitoba 179/F4
Great Falls, Mont. 188/D1
Great Falls, Mont. 146/G5
Great Falls, Mont. (59401) 262/E3
Great Falls, S.C. (29055) 296/F2
Great Falls (dam), Tenn. 237/K9
Great Fish (riv.), S. Africa 118/D6
Great Harwood, England 13/H1
Greathead (bay), St. Vin. & Grens. 161/A9
Great Inagua (isl.), Bahamas 146/L7
Great Inagua (isl.), Bahamas 156/D2
Great Indian (des.), India 68/C3
Great Isaac (isl.), Bahamas 156/B1
Great Kai (isl.), Indonesia 85/J7
Great Karoo (reg.), S. Africa 118/C6
Great Kei (riv.), S. Africa 118/D6
Great Khingan (range), China 54/O5
Great Lakes Nav. Trng. Ctr., Ill. 222/B4
Great Machipongo (inlet), Va. 307/S6
Great Meadows, N.J. (07838) 273/D2
Great Mercury (isl.), N. Zealand 100/F2
Great Miami (riv.), Ohio 284/A7
Great Misery (isl.), Mass. 249/F5
Great Moose (lake), Maine 243/D6
Great Namaland (reg.), Namibia 118/B4
Great Natuna (isl.), Indonesia 85/D5
Great Neck, N.Y. (*11020) 276/P6
Great Nicobar (isl.), India 68/G7
Great North (mt.), Va. 307/L2
Great Ormes (head), Wales 13/C4
Great Ouse (riv.), England 13/H5
Great Ouse (riv.), England 10/G4
Great Pedro Bluff (prom.), Jamaica 158/H6
Great Pee Dee (riv.), S.C. 296/J4
Great Pond◯, Maine (†04408) 243/G6
Great Pond (bay), Virgin Is. (U.S.) 161/F4
Great Pubnico (lake), Nova Scotia 168/C5
Great Ruaha (riv.), Tanzania 115/G5
Great Sacandaga (lake), N.Y. 276/M4
Great Saint Bernard (pass), Italy 34/A2
Great Saint Bernard (mt.), Switzerland 39/D5
Great Saint Bernard (pass), Switzerland 39/D5
Great Saint Bernard (tunnel), Switzerland 39/D5
Great Salt (pond), St. Chris.-Nevis 161/D10
Great Salt (lake), Utah 188/D2
Great Salt (lake), Utah 146/G6
Great Salt (lake), Utah 304/B2
Great Salt Lake (des.), Nev. 266/H2
Great Salt Lake (des.), Utah 304/A3
Great Salt Plains (lake), Okla. 288/K1
Great Sand (hills), Sask. 181/B5
Great Sand Dunes Nat'l Mon., Colo. 208/H7
Great Sand Sea (des.), Egypt 111/D2
Great Sand Sea (des.), Libya 111/D2
Great Sandy (desert), Australia 87/C8
Great Sandy (Fraser) (isl.), Queensland 88/J5
Great Sandy (Fraser) (isl.), Queensland 95/E5
Great Sandy (des.), W. Australia 88/C4
Great Sandy (des.), W. Australia 92/C3
Great Seneca (creek), Md. 245/J4
Great Sitkin (isl.), Alaska 196/L4
Great Slave (lake), Canada 4/C15
Great Slave (lake), N.W.T. 162/E3
Great Slave (lake), N.W.T. 146/H3
Great Slave (lake), N.W. Terrs. 187/G3
Great Slave Lake Highway, N.W. Terrs. 187/G3
Great Smoky (mts.), N.C. 281/B3
Great Smoky (mts.), Tenn. 237/P9
Great Smoky Mountains Nat'l Park, Tenn. 237/P9
Great Smoky Mts. Nat'l Park, N.C. 281/B3
Great South (bay), N.Y. 276/O9
Great South (beach), N.Y. 276/O9
Great Tenasserim (riv.), Burma 72/C4
Great Thatch (isl.), Virgin Is. (Br.) 161/C4
Great Tobago (isl.), Virgin Is. (Br.) 161/B3

Guadalupe Bravo 377

Great Torrington, England 10/D5
Great Torrington, England 13/C7
Great Valley, N.Y. (14741) 276/C6
Great Victoria (des.) 88/D5
Great Victoria (desert), Australia 87/C8
Great Victoria (des.), S. Australia 94/B3
Great Victoria (des.), W. Australia 92/D5
Great Village, Nova Scotia 168/E3
Great Wall (ruins), China 54/N5
Great Wall (ruins), China 77/G4,J
Great Wass (isl.), Maine 243/J7
Great Western Tiers (mts.), Tasmania 99/C3
Great Yarmouth, England 13/J5
Great Yarmouth, England 10/G4
Great Zab (riv.), Iraq 66/C2
Grecco, Uruguay 145/B3
Grecia, C. Rica 154/E5
Greco (cape), Cyprus 63/F5
Gredos, Sierra de (range), Spain 33/D2
Greece 2/L4
Greece 7/G5
GREECE 45/F6
Greece, N.Y. (14616) 276/E4
Greeley, Colo. 188/F2
Greeley, Colo. (80631) 208/K2
Greeley, Iowa (52050) 229/L3
Greeley (co.), Kansas 232/A3
Greeley, Kansas (66033) 232/G3
Greeley (co.), Nebr. 264/F3
Greeley, Nebr. (68842) 264/F3
Greeley, Pa. (18425) 294/N3
Greeley (creek), Utah 304/B3
Greeleyville, S.C. (29056) 296/H4
Greely (fjord), N.W. Terrs. 187/K1
Greely, Ontario 177/J2
Green (bay) 188/J1
Green (riv.) 188/D3
Green (isl.), Ant. & Bar. 161/E11
Green (riv.), Colo. 208/A2
Green (isl.), Grenada 161/D8
Green (riv.), Ill. 222/D2
Green, Kansas (67447) 232/E2
Green (co.), Ky. 237/K6
Green (riv.), Ky. 237/G6
Green (isl.), Maine 243/F8
Green (riv.), Mass. 249/B2
Green, Mich. (†49953) 250/F1
Green (bay), Mich. 250/B4
Green (lake), Minn. 255/D5
Green (riv.), New Bruns. 170/B1
Green (cape), N.S. Wales 97/F5
Green (swamp), N.C. 281/N6
Green (riv.), N. Dak. 282/D5
Green (pt.), Nova Scotia 168/C5
Green (isl.), Ontario 177/A2
Green, Oreg. (†97470) 291/D4
Green (isls.), Papua N.G. 86/C2
Green (lake), Sask. 181/D1
Green (riv.), Tenn. 237/F10
Green (riv.), U.S. 146/H6
Green (riv.), Utah 304/D4
Green (mts.), Vt. 268/B4
Green (cay), Virgin Is. (U.S.) 161/F4
Green (lake), Wash. 310/A2
Green (riv.), Wash. 310/C3
Green (co.), Wis. 317/G10
Green (bay), Wis. 317/L6
Green (mt.), Wyo. 319/E3
Green (riv.), Wyo. 319/C4
Greenacres, Calif. (93308) 204/F8
Green Acres, Sask. 181/F2
Greenacres, Wash. (99016) 310/J3
Greenacres City, Fla. (33463) 212/F5
Greenan, Sask. 181/C4
Greenback, Tenn. (37742) 237/N9
Greenbackville, Va. (23356) 307/T5
Green Bank, N.J. (†08215) 273/D4
Greenbank, Wash. (98253) 310/C2
Green Bank, W. Va. (24944) 312/G6
Green Bay, N. Zealand 100/B1
Green Bay, Va. (23942) 307/M6
Green Bay, Wis. 188/J2
Green Bay, Wis. 146/J5
Green Bay, Wis. (*54301) 317/K6
Greenbelt, Md. (20770) 245/G4
Greenbelt Park, Md. 245/G4
Greenbrier, Ala. (†35758) 195/E1
Greenbrier, Ark. (72058) 202/F3
Greenbrier, Mo. (†63730) 261/M8
Greenbrier, Tenn. (37073) 237/H8
Greenbrier (co.), W. Va. 312/F7
Greenbrier (riv.), W. Va. 312/F6
Green Brook, N.J. (08812) 273/D2
Greenbush, Mass. (02040) 249/F8
Greenbush, Mich. (48738) 250/F4
Greenbush, Minn. (56726) 255/B2
Greenbush, Va. (23357) 307/S5
Green Camp, Ohio (43322) 284/D4
Greencastle, Ind. (46135) 227/D5
Greencastle, Ireland 17/H1
Green Castle, Mo. (63544) 261/G2
Greencastle, Pa. (17225) 294/G6
Green Center, Ind. (†46701) 227/G2
Green City, Mo. (63545) 261/F2
Green Court, Alberta 182/C2
Green Cove Springs, Fla. (32043) 212/E2
Greencreek, Idaho (83533) 220/B3
Green Creek, N.J. (08219) 273/D5
Greendale, Ind. (†47025) 227/H6
Greendale, Wis. (53129) 317/L2
Greendell, N.J. (07839) 273/D2
Greene (co.), Ala. 195/C5
Greene (co.), Ark. 202/J1
Greene (co.), Georgia 217/F3
Greene (co.), Ill. 222/C4
Greene (co.), Ind. 227/D6
Greene (co.), Iowa 229/E5
Greene, Iowa (50636) 229/H3
Greene○, Maine (04236) 243/C7
Greene (co.), Miss. 256/G8
Greene (co.), Mo. 261/F8
Greene (co.), N.Y. 276/M6
Greene, N.Y. (13778) 276/J6
Greene (co.), N.C. 281/O3
Greene, N. Dak. (†58787) 282/G2
Greene (co.), Ohio 284/C6
Greene (co.), Pa. 294/B6
Greene, R.I. (02827) 249/G6
Greene (co.), Tenn. 237/R8
Greene (co.), Va. 307/M4
Greenevers, N.C. (†28521) 281/O5
Greeneville, Tenn. (37743) 237/R8
Greenfield, Calif. (93927) 204/D7
Greenfield, Ill. (62044) 222/C4
Greenfield, Ind. (46140) 227/F5
Greenfield, Iowa (50849) 229/D6
Greenfield, Mass. (01301) 249/D2
Greenfield○, Mass. (01301) 249/D2
Greenfield, Minn. (†55373) 255/F5
Greenfield, Mo. (65661) 261/E8
Greenfield○, N.H. (03047) 268/D6
Greenfield, Nova Scotia 168/D4
Greenfield, Ohio (45123) 284/D7
Greenfield, Okla. (73043) 288/K3
Greenfield, S. Dak. (†57010) 298/R8
Greenfield, Tenn. (38230) 237/D8
Greenfield, Wis. (53220) 317/L2
Greenfield Hill, Conn. (†06430) 210/B4
Greenfield Park, Québec 172/J4
Greenford, Ohio (44422) 284/J4
Green Forest, Ark. (72638) 202/D1
Green Hall, Ky. (41328) 237/O6
Green Harbor, Mass. (02041) 249/M4
Green Haven, Md. (21122) 245/M4
Greenhills, Ohio (45218) 284/B9
Greenhorn, Oreg. (†97877) 291/J3
Green Island, Iowa (52051) 229/N4
Green Island, Jamaica 158/G6
Green Island, N.Y. (12183) 276/N5
Green Island, N. Zealand 100/C7
Greenisland, N. Ireland 17/K2
Green Island (bay), Philippines 82/B5
Green Island Cove, Newf. 166/C3
Green Isle, Minn. (55338) 255/E6
Green Lake, Maine (†04429) 243/F6
Green Lake, Sask. 181/L4
Green Lake (co.), Wis. 317/H8
Green Lake, Wis. (54941) 317/H8
Greenland 2/G2
Greenland 4/B12
Greenland 146/P2
Greenland (sea) 146/T2
Greenland (sea) 4/B10
Greenland, Ark. (72737) 202/B1
Greenland, Barbados 161/B8
Greenland, Colo. (†80118) 208/K4
Greenland, Mich. (49929) 250/G1
Greenland○, N.H. (03840) 268/F5
Greenlaw, Scotland 15/F5
Greenleaf, Idaho (83626) 220/B6
Greenleaf, Kansas (66943) 232/E2
Greenleaf, Minn. (†55355) 255/D6
Greenleaf, Oreg. (97445) 291/D3
Greenleaf, Wis. (54126) 317/L7
Greenleafton, Minn. (†55965) 255/F7
Greenlee (co.), Ariz. 198/F5
Green Lowther (mt.), Scotland 15/E5
Greenmount, Ky. (†40741) 237/N6
Greenmount, Md. (†21074) 245/L2
Green Mountain (res.), Colo. 208/G3
Green Mountain, Iowa (50637) 229/H4
Green Mountain, N.C. (28740) 281/E3
Green Mountain Falls, Colo. (80819) 208/K5
Green Oaks, Ill. (†60048) 222/B4
Greenock, Scotland 10/A1
Greenock, Scotland 15/A2
Greenore, Ireland 17/J4
Greenore (pt.), Ireland 17/J7
Greenough (mt.), Alaska 196/K1
Greenough, Georgia (†31716) 217/D8
Greenough, Mont. (59836) 262/C4
Green Peter (lake), Oreg. 291/E3
Green Pond, Ala. (35074) 195/D4
Green Pond, N.J. (07435) 273/E1
Green Pond, S.C. (29446) 296/F6
Greenport, N.Y. (11944) 276/P8
Green Ridge (mts.), 245/E2
Green Ridge, Mo. (65332) 261/F5
Green River (lake), Ky. 237/L6
Green River, Utah (84525) 304/D4
Green River (res.), Vt. 268/B2
Green River, Wyo. 188/E2
Green River, Wyo. (82935) 319/C4
Green River (mt.), Wyo. 319/C2
Green Rock, Ill. (†61241) 222/C2
Greens (peak), Ariz. 198/F4
Greensboro, Ala. (36744) 195/C5
Greensboro, Fla. (32330) 212/B1
Greensboro, Georgia (30642) 217/F3
Greensboro, Ind. (47344) 227/G5
Greensboro, Md. (21639) 245/P5
Greensboro, N.C. 146/L6
Greensboro, N.C. 188/K3
Greensboro, N.C. (*27401) 281/K2
Greensboro, Pa. (15338) 294/B6
Greensboro○, Vt. (05841) 268/C2
Greensburg, Ind. (47240) 227/G6
Greensburg, Kansas (67054) 232/C4
Greensburg, Ky. (42743) 237/K6
Greensburg, La. (70441) 238/J5
Greensburg, Mo. (†63531) 261/H2
Greensburg, Ohio (44232) 284/G4
Greensburg, Pa. (15601) 294/D5
Green Sea, S.C. (29545) 296/J3
Greens Farms, Conn. (06436) 210/B4
Greens Fork, Ind. (47345) 227/H5
Green's Harbour, Newf. 166/D2
Greenshields, Alberta 182/E3
Greenslopes, Queensland 88/K3
Greenslopes, Queensland 95/E3
Greenspond, Newf. 166/D4
Green Springs, Ohio (44836) 284/E3
Greenstone (pt.), Scotland 15/C3
Greenstreet, Sask. 181/A2
Green Sulphur Springs, W. Va. (25966) 312/E7
Greensville (co.), Va. 307/N7
Greentop, Mo. (63546) 261/H2
Greentown, Ind. (46936) 227/E4
Greentown, Ohio (44630) 284/H4
Greentree, Pa. (15242) 294/B7
Greenup, Ill. (62428) 222/E4
Greenup (co.), Ky. 237/R3
Greenup, Ky. (41144) 237/R3
Greenvale, Queensland 95/C3
Green Valley, Ariz. (85614) 198/D7
Green Valley, Ill. (61534) 222/D3
Green Valley, Minn. (†56258) 255/C6
Green Valley, Ontario 177/K2
Green Valley, Wis. (54127) 317/K6
Greenview, Calif. (96037) 204/B2
Greenview, Ill. (62642) 222/D3
Greenview, W. Va. (†25166) 312/C6
Green Village, N.J. (07935) 273/D2
Greenville, Ala. (36037) 195/E7
Greenville, Calif. (95947) 204/E3
Greenville, Del. (19807) 245/R1
Greenville, Fla. (32331) 212/C1
Greenville, Georgia (30222) 217/C4
Greenville, Ill. (62246) 222/D5
Greenville, Ind. (47124) 227/F8
Greenville, Iowa (51343) 229/C3
Greenville, Ky. (42345) 237/G6
Greenville, Liberia 106/C8
Greenville, Maine (04441) 243/D5
Greenville○, Maine (04441) 243/D5
Greenville, Mich. (48838) 250/D5
Greenville, Miss. 146/J6
Greenville, Miss. 188/H4
Greenville, Miss. (38701) 256/B4
Greenville, Mo. (63944) 261/M8
Greenville, N.H. (03048) 268/D6
Greenville○, N.H. (03048) 268/D6
Greenville, N.C. (27834) 281/P3
Greenville, Ohio (45331) 284/A5
Greenville, Pa. (16125) 294/B3
Greenville, R.I. (02828) 249/H5
Greenville, S.C. 146/K6
Greenville, S.C. 188/K4
Greenville (co.), S.C. 296/C2
Greenville, S.C. (*29601) 296/C2
Greenville, Texas 188/G4
Greenville, Texas (75401) 303/H4
Greenville, Utah (84731) 304/B5
Greenville, Va. (24440) 307/K5
Greenville, W. Va. (24945) 312/E7
Greenville, Wis. (54942) 317/J7
Greenville Junction, Maine (04442) 243/D5
Greenwald, Minn. (56335) 255/D5
Greenwater Lake, Sask. 181/H3
Greenwater Lake Prov. Park, Sask. 181/H3
Greenway, Ark. (72430) 202/K1
Greenway, Manitoba 179/C5
Greenway, S. Dak. (†57437) 298/K2
Greenwell Springs, La. (70739) 238/K1
Greenwich○, Conn. (06830) 210/A4
Greenwich (pt.), Conn. 210/A4
Greenwich, England 13/H8
Greenwich, England 10/B5
Greenwich (Kapingamarangi) (atoll), Micronesia 87/F5
Greenwich○, N.J. (08323) 273/C5
Greenwich, N.Y. (12834) 276/O4
Greenwich, Ohio (44837) 284/E3
Greenwich, Utah (84732) 304/B5
Greenwood, Ark. (72936) 202/B3
Greenwood, Br. Col. 184/H5
Greenwood, Calif. (95635) 204/E5
Greenwood, Del. (19950) 245/R5
Greenwood, Fla. (32443) 212/A1
Greenwood, Ind. (46142) 227/E5
Greenwood (co.), Kansas 232/F4
Greenwood, Ky. (†42634) 237/N7
Greenwood, La. (71033) 238/B2
Greenwood, Mass. (01880) 249/D6
Greenwood (lake), Minn. 255/G3
Greenwood, Miss. (38930) 256/D4
Greenwood, Mo. (64034) 261/R6
Greenwood, Nebr. (68366) 264/H3
Greenwood (lake), N.J. 273/E1
Greenwood, N.Y. (14839) 276/E6
Greenwood (lake), N.Y. 276/M8
Greenwood, S.C. 188/K4
Greenwood (co.), S.C. 296/C3
Greenwood, S.C. (29646) 296/C3
Greenwood (lake), S.C. 296/D3
Greenwood, S. Dak. (†57380) 298/N8
Greenwood, Va. (22943) 307/L4
Greenwood, W. Va. (26360) 312/E4
Greenwood, Wis. (54437) 317/E6
Greenwood Lake, N.Y. (10925) 276/M8
Greenwood Springs, Miss. (38848) 256/H3
Greer, Ariz. (85927) 198/F4
Greer, Idaho (†83544) 220/B3
Greer, Mo. (†65606) 261/K9
Greer, Ohio (†44628) 284/F4
Greer (co.), Okla. 288/G5
Greer, S.C. (29651) 296/C2
Greers Ferry, Ark. (†72067) 202/F2
Greers Ferry (lake), Ark. 202/G2
Greeson (lake), Ark. 202/C5
Gregg (co.), Texas 303/K5
Greggs, Georgia (†31620) 217/F8
Gregory, Ark. (72059) 202/H3
Gregory, Mich. (48137) 250/E6
Gregory (range), Queensland 95/B3
Gregory (riv.), Queensland 88/F3
Gregory (riv.), Queensland 95/A3
Gregory (lake), S. Australia 88/F5
Gregory (lake), S. Australia 94/F3
Gregory (co.), S. Dak. 298/L7
Gregory, S. Dak. (57533) 298/L7
Gregory (lake), W. Australia 92/C4
Gregory Landing, Mo. (†63435) 261/K2
Gregory's (sound), Ireland 17/B5
Greian (head), Scotland 15/A3
Greifensee (lake), Switzerland 39/G2
Greifswald, E. Germany 22/E1
Grein, Austria 41/C2
Greina (pass), Switzerland 39/G3
Greiz, E. Germany 22/E3
Grelton, Ohio (43523) 284/C3
Gremikha, U.S.S.R. 52/E1
Gremyachinsk, U.S.S.R. 52/J3
Grenå, Denmark 21/D5
Grenå, Denmark 18/G8
Grenada 2/F5
Grenada 146/M8
Grenada, Calif. (96038) 204/C2
GRENADA 161/D9
GRENADA 156/G4
Grenada (isl.), Grenada 156/G4
Grenada (co.), Miss. 256/E3
Grenada, Miss. (38901) 256/E3
Grenada (lake), Miss. 256/E3
Grenadier (isl.), N.Y. 276/H2
Grenadines (isls.), Grenada 156/G4
Grenadines (isls.), St. Vin. & Grens. 156/G4
Grenchen, Switzerland 39/D2
Grenfell, N.S. Wales 97/E3
Grenfell, Sask. 181/J5
Grenloch, N.J. (08032) 273/C4
Grenoble, France 7/E4
Grenoble, France 28/F5
Grenola, Kansas (67346) 232/F4
Grenora, N. Dak. (58845) 282/C2
Grenville (chan.), Br. Col. 184/C3
Grenville, Grenada 161/D8
Grenville (bay), Grenada 161/D8
Grenville, N. Mex. (88424) 274/F2
Grenville (county), Ontario 177/J3
Grenville, Québec 172/C4
Grenville (cape), Queensland 88/G2
Grenville (cape), Queensland 95/B1
Grenville, S. Dak. (57239) 298/O3
Grenville (pt.), Wash. 310/A3
Gresham, Nebr. (68367) 264/G3
Gresham, Oreg. (97030) 291/B2
Gresham, S.C. (29546) 296/J4
Gresham, Wis. (54128) 317/J6
Greshamville, Georgia (†30650) 217/F3
Gresik, Indonesia 85/K2
Gresston, Georgia (†31023) 217/F6
Greta-Branxton, N.S. Wales 97/F3
Greta East, N.S. Wales 97/F3
Gretna, Fla. (32332) 212/B1
Gretna, La. (70053) 238/O4
Gretna, Manitoba 179/E5
Gretna, Nebr. (68028) 264/H3
Gretna, Scotland 10/E3
Gretna, Scotland 15/E5
Gretna, Tasmania 99/D4
Gretna, Va. (24557) 307/K7
Grevelingen (str.), Netherlands 27/E5
Greven, W. Germany 22/B2
Grevená, Greece 45/E5
Grevenbroich, W. Germany 22/B3
Grevenmacher, Luxembourg 27/J9
Grevesmühlen, E. Germany 22/D2
Greville (bay), Nova Scotia 168/D3
Grey (isls.), Newf. 166/C3
Grey (riv.), N. Zealand 100/C5
Grey (cape), North. Terr. 88/F2
Grey (cape), North. Terr. 93/E2
Grey (county), Ontario 177/D3
Grey (range), Queensland 88/G5
Grey (range), Queensland 95/B5
Grey Abbey, N. Ireland 17/K2
Greybull, Wyo. (82426) 319/E1
Greybull (riv.), Wyo. 319/D1
Greycliff, Mont. (59033) 262/G5
Grey Eagle, Minn. (56336) 255/D5
Grey Forest, Texas (†78201) 303/J10
Grey Islands, Newf. 166/C3
Greylock (mt.), Idaho 220/C6
Greylock (mt.), Mass. 249/B2
Greymouth, N. Zealand 100/C5
Greymouth, N. Zealand 87/G10
Grey River, Newf. 166/C4
Greys (riv.), Wyo. 319/B3
Greystone, Colo. (†81640) 208/B1
Greystone, Conn. (†06786) 210/C2
Greystone Park, N.J. (07950) 273/D2
Greystones-Delgany, Ireland 10/D4
Greystones-Delgany, Ireland 17/K5
Greytown, N. Zealand 100/E4
Greytown (San Juan del Norte), Nicaragua 154/F5
Greytown, S. Africa 118/E5
Grez-Doiceau, Belgium 27/F7
Gribbles Settlement, North. Terr. 93/B1
Gridley, Calif. (95948) 204/D4
Gridley (mt.), Conn. 210/B1
Gridley, Ill. (61744) 222/E3
Gridley, Kansas (66852) 232/G3
Gridone (mt.), Switzerland 39/G4
Griend (isl.), Netherlands 27/G2
Grier, N. Mex. (†88101) 274/F4
Gries am Brenner, Austria 41/A3
Griesheim, W. Germany 22/C4
Grieskirchen, Austria 41/B2
Griffin, Georgia (30223) 217/D4
Griffin, Ind. (47616) 227/B8
Griffin, Sask. 181/H6
Griffiss A.F.B., N.Y. 276/K4
Griffith, Ind. (46319) 227/C1
Griffith, N.S. 88/H6
Griffith, N.S. Wales 97/C4
Griffith (isl.), Ontario 177/D3
Griffithsville, W. Va. (25521) 312/B6
Griffithville, Ark. (72060) 202/G3
Grifton, N.C. (28530) 281/P4
Griggs (co.), N. Dak. 282/O5
Griggs, Okla. (†73949) 288/B1
Griggsville, Ill. (62340) 222/C4
Grigston, Kansas (†67871) 232/B3
Grijalva (riv.), Mexico 150/N7
Grim (cape), Tasmania 99/A2
Grimari, Cent. Afr. Rep. 115/C2
Grimbergen, Belgium 27/E7
Grimes, Ala. (†36350) 195/H8
Grimes, Calif. (95950) 204/C4
Grimes, Iowa (50111) 229/F5
Grimes, Okla. (†73628) 288/G4
Grimes (co.), Texas 303/J7
Grimesland, N.C. (27837) 281/P3
Griminish, Scotland 15/A3
Grimma, E. Germany 22/E3
Grimmen, E. Germany 22/E1
Grimms Landing, W. Va. (25095) 312/B5
Grimsby, England 13/G4
Grimsby, England 10/F4
Grimsby, Ontario 177/E4
Grimsel (pass), Switzerland 39/F3
Grímsey (isl.), Iceland 21/C1
Grimshaw, Alberta 182/B1
Grimsley, Tenn. (38565) 237/L2
Grimstad, Norway 18/F7
Grindelwald, Switzerland 39/E3
Grindrod, Br. Col. 184/H5
Grindsted, Denmark 21/B6
Grindstone, Maine (†04460) 243/F4
Grindstone (isl.), New Bruns. 170/F3
Grindstone (lake), Wis. 317/C4
Grind Stone City, Mich. (48467) 250/G4
Grindstone Prov. Rec. Park, Manitoba 179/F3
Grinnell, Iowa (50112) 229/H5
Grinnell, Kansas (67738) 232/B2
Grinnell (pen.), N.W. Terrs. 187/J2
Grippon, Guadeloupe 161/B6
Griqualand West (reg.), S. Africa 118/C5
Griquatown, S. Africa 118/C5
Grise Fiord, Canada 4/B13
Grise Fiord, N.W.T. 162/H1
Grise Fiord, N.W. Terrs. 187/K2
Gris-Nez (cape), France 28/D2
Grisons (Graubünden) (elec. div.), Switzerland 39/H3
Grissom A.F.B., Ind. 227/E3
Griswold, Iowa (51535) 229/C6
Griswold, Manitoba 179/B5
Griswoldville, Mass. (01345) 249/D2
Griva, U.S.S.R. 53/D3
Grizzly (bay), Calif. 204/K1
Grizzly Flats, Calif. (95636) 204/E5
Groais (isl.), Newf. 166/C3
Grobiņa, U.S.S.R. 53/A2
Grodno, U.S.S.R. 7/G3
Grodno, U.S.S.R. 48/C4
Grodno, U.S.S.R. 52/B4
Grodzisk Mazowiecki, Poland 47/E2
Grodzisk Wielkopolski, Poland 47/C2
Groenlo, Netherlands 27/K4
Groesbeck, Ohio (45239) 284/B9
Groesbeck, Texas (76642) 303/H6
Groesbeek, Netherlands 27/H5
Groix (isl.), France 28/B4
Grójec, Poland 47/E3
Grömitz, W. Germany 22/D1
Gronau, W. Germany 22/B2
Grondines, Québec 172/E3
Grong, Norway 18/H4
Grong Grong, N.S. Wales 97/D4
Groningen, Minn. (†55072) 255/E4
Groningen (prov.), Netherlands 27/K2
Groningen, Netherlands 27/K2
Groningen, Suriname 131/D2
Groninger Wad (sound), Netherlands 27/J2
Gronlid, Sask. 181/G2
Grønnedal, Greenl. 4/C12
Grono, Switzerland 39/H4
Groom, Texas (79039) 303/C2
Groomsport, N. Ireland 17/K2
Groot-Drakenstein, S. Africa 118/F6
Groote (isl.), North. Terr. 88/F2
Groote (riv.), S. Africa 118/C6
Groote Eylandt (isl.), Australia 87/D7
Groote Eylandt (isl.), North. Terr. 93/E3
Groote IJ Polder, Netherlands 27/B4
Grootfontein, Namibia 118/B3
Groot Sint Joris, Neth. Ant. 161/G9
Gros (pt.), Grenada 161/C8
Gros Islet, St. Lucia 161/G5
Gros Islet (bay), St. Lucia 161/G5
Grosmont (Island Lake), Alberta 182/D2
Gros Morne, Haiti 158/B5
Gros-Morne, Martinique 161/D6
Gros Morne (mt.), Newf. 166/C4
Gros-Morne, Québec 172/C1
Gros Morne Nat'l Park, Newf. 166/C4
Gros Piton (mt.), St. Lucia 161/G6
Gross, Nebr. (†68719) 264/F2
Grosse Ile, Mich. (48138) 250/B7
Grosse Isle, Manitoba 179/E4
Gross Emme (riv.), Switzerland 39/E2
Grossenbrode, W. Germany 22/D1
Grossenhain, E. Germany 22/E3
Grosse Pointe, Mich. (48236) 250/B7
Grosse Pointe Farms, Mich. (†48236) 250/B6
Grosse Pointe Park, Mich. (†48236) 250/B7
Grosse Pointe Shores, Mich. (†48236) 250/B6
Grosse Pointe Woods, Mich. (†48236) 250/B6
Grosser Arber (mt.), W. Germany 22/E4
Grosser Peilstein (mt.), Austria 41/C2
Grosses Coques, Nova Scotia 168/B4
Grosses-Roches, Québec 172/B1
Grosse Tete, La. (70740) 238/G6
Grosseto (prov.), Italy 34/C3
Grosseto, Italy 34/C3
Grossglockner (mt.), Austria 41/B3
Gross Litzner (mt.), Switzerland 39/K3
Grossräschen, E. Germany 22/E3
Grosssiegharts, Austria 41/C2
Grosswangen, Switzerland 39/F2
Grosvenor Dale, Conn. (06246) 210/H1
Gros Ventre (riv.), Wyo. 319/B2
Groswater (bay), Newf. 166/C3
Groton, Conn. (06340) 210/G3
Groton○, Conn. (06340) 210/G3
Groton, Mass. (01450) 249/H2
Groton○, Mass. (01450) 249/H2
Groton○, N.H. (†03241) 268/D4
Groton, N.Y. (13073) 276/H5
Groton, S. Dak. (57445) 298/N3
Groton○, Vt. (05046) 268/C3
Groton (lake), Vt. 268/C3
Groton Long (pt.), Conn. 210/H3
Groton Long Point, Conn. (†06340) 210/G3
Grottaferrata, Italy 34/F7
Grottaglie, Italy 34/F4
Grotto, Wash. (98288) 310/D3
Grottoes, Va. (24441) 307/L4
Grouard, Alberta 182/B2
Grouard Mission, Alberta 182/C2
Grouard Mission, Alta. 162/E4
Groundhog (riv.), Ontario 175/D3
Grouse (Lost River), Idaho (†83255) 220/E6
Grouse (mt.), N. Mex. 274/A5
Grouse (creek), Utah 304/A2
Grouse Creek, Utah (84313) 304/A2
Grouse Creek (mts.), Utah 304/A2
Grouw, Netherlands 27/H2
Grovania, Georgia (†31036) 217/E6
Grove, Maine (04638) 243/J5
Grove (lake), N. Dak. 282/L5
Grove, Okla. (74344) 288/S1
Grove Beach, Conn. (†06413) 210/E3
Grove Center, Ky. (†42437) 237/F5
Grove City, Fla. (33533) 212/D5
Grove City, Minn. (56243) 255/D5
Grove City, Ohio (43123) 284/D6
Grove City, Pa. (16127) 294/B3
Grovedale, Alberta 182/A2
Grove Hill, Ala. (36451) 195/C7
Groveland, Calif. (95321) 204/E6
Groveland, Fla. (32736) 212/E3
Groveland, Georgia (†31321) 217/J6
Groveland, Ind. (†46121) 227/D5
Groveland○, Mass. (01830) 249/L1
Groveland, N.Y. (14462) 276/E5
Groveoak, Ala. (35975) 195/F2
Grove Place, Virgin Is. (U.S.) 161/E4
Groveport, Ohio (43125) 284/E6
Grover, Colo. (80729) 208/L1
Grover, Mo. (63040) 261/M3
Grover, N.C. (28073) 281/G4
Grover, Pa. (17735) 294/J2
Grover, S.C. (29447) 296/F5
Grover, S. Dak. (†57201) 298/P4
Grover, Utah (†84773) 304/C5
Grover, Wyo. (83122) 319/B3
Grover City, Calif. (93433) 204/E8
Grover Hill, Ohio (45849) 284/B3
Grovertown, Ind. (46531) 227/D2
Groves, Texas (77619) 303/L8
Grovespring, Mo. (65662) 261/G8
Groveton, N.H. (03582) 268/D2
Groveton, Texas (75845) 303/J7
Groveton, Va. (†22306) 307/T3
Grovetown, Georgia (30813) 217/H4
Groveville, N.J. (†08601) 273/D3
Growler (mts.), Ariz. 198/B6
Groznyy, U.S.S.R. 7/J4
Groznyy, U.S.S.R. 48/E5
Groznyy, U.S.S.R. 52/G6
Grubbs, Ark. (72431) 202/H2
Grubišno Polje, Yugoslavia 45/C3
Grudovo, Bulgaria 45/H4
Grudziądz, Poland 47/D2
Gruenthal, Sask. 181/E3
Gruetli, Tenn. (37339) 237/K10
Gruinard (bay), Scotland 15/C3
Grulla, Texas (78548) 303/F11
Grünberg (Zielona Góra), Poland 47/B3
Grünburg, Austria 41/C3
Grundy (co.), Ill. 222/E2
Grundy (co.), Iowa 229/H4
Grundy (co.), Mo. 261/E2
Grundy (co.), Tenn. 237/K10
Grundy, Va. (24614) 307/D6
Grundy Center, Iowa (50638) 229/H4
Grunthal, Manitoba 179/F5
Gruver, Iowa (51344) 229/D2
Gruver, Texas (79040) 303/C1
Gruyères, Switzerland 39/D3
Gryazi, U.S.S.R. 52/F4
Gryazovets, U.S.S.R. 52/F3
Gryfice, Poland 47/B2
Gryfino, Poland 47/B2
Grygla, Minn. (56727) 255/C2
Gryon, Switzerland 39/D4
Grytviken 5/D17
Gstaad, Switzerland 39/D4
Gsteig, Switzerland 39/D4
Guacamaya, Colombia 126/C6
Guacamayo, Colombia 126/F6
Guacanayabo (gulf), Cuba 156/C2
Guacanayabo (gulf), Cuba 158/G4
Guacara, Venezuela 124/D2
Guachara, Venezuela 124/D4
Gu Achi, Ariz. (†85634) 198/C6
Guácimo, C. Rica 154/F5
Guacui, Brazil 135/F2
Guadalajara, Mexico 2/D5
Guadalajara, Mexico 150/H6
Guadalajara, Mexico 146/H7
Guadalajara (prov.), Spain 33/E2
Guadalajara, Spain 33/E2
Guadalcanal (isl.), Solomon Is. 87/F7
Guadalcanal (isl.), Solomon Is. 86/D3
Guadalcanal, Spain 33/D3
Guadalimar (riv.), Spain 33/E3
Guadaloupe (isl.), Mexico 146/G7
Guadalquivir (riv.), Spain 7/D5
Guadalquivir (riv.), Spain 33/C4
Guadalupe, Potosí, Bolivia 136/B7
Guadalupe, Santa Cruz, Bolivia 136/C6
Guadalupe, Calif. (93434) 204/E9
Guadalupe (riv.), Calif. 204/K3
Guadalupe, Nuevo León, Mexico 150/K4
Guadalupe, Zacatecas, Mexico 150/H5
Guadalupe (co.), N. Mex. 274/E4
Guadalupe (mts.), N. Mex. 274/D6
Guadalupe, Peru 128/E9
Guadalupe, Spain 33/D3
Guadalupe, Sierra de (range), Spain 33/D3
Guadalupe (co.), Texas 303/G8
Guadalupe (mts.), Texas 303/C10
Guadalupe (peak), Texas 303/B10
Guadalupe (riv.), Texas 303/G8
Guadalupe Bravo, Mexico 150/F1

378 Guadalupe

Guadalupe Mts. Nat'l Park, Texas 303/C10
Guadalupe Victoria, Durango, Mexico 150/H4
Guadalupe Victoria, Puebla, Mexico 150/O1
Guadalupe y Calvo, Mexico 150/F3
Guadalupita, N. Mex. (87722) 274/D2
Guadarrama, Sierra de (range), Spain 33/E2
Guadarrama (riv.), Spain 33/F4
Guadarrama, Venezuela 124/D3
Guadeloupe (isl.) 146/M8
GUADELOUPE 161/A5
GUADELOUPE 156/F3
Guadeloupe (isl.), Guadeloupe 161/B6
Guadeloupe (isl.), Guadeloupe 156/F3
Guadeloupe (passage), Guadeloupe 161/A5
Guadeloupe Nat'l Park, Guadeloupe 161/A6
Guadiana (riv.) 7/D5
Guadiana (riv.), Portugal 33/C4
Guadiana (riv.), Spain 33/D3
Guadix, Spain 33/E4
Guafo (gulf), Chile 138/D5
Guafo (isl.), Chile 138/D5
Guage, Ky. (41329) 237/P5
Guaicanamar, Cuba 158/G3
Guaico, Trin. & Tob. 161/B10
Guaimaca, Honduras 154/D3
Guáimaro, Cuba 158/G3
Guaina, Venezuela 124/G5
Guainía (riv.) 120/C2
Guainía (comm.), Colombia 126/F6
Guainía (riv.), Colombia 126/F6
Guainía (riv.), Venezuela 124/E6
Guaira (dept.), Paraguay 144/D4
Guairá (falls), Paraguay 144/E4
Guaitecas (isls.), Chile 138/D5
Guajaba (cay), Cuba 158/G2
Guajará-Mirim, Brazil 132/H10
Guajará-Mirim, Brazil 120/C4
Guajataca (lake), P. Rico 161/B1
Guajira (pen.) 120/B1
Guajira, La (dept.), Colombia 126/D2
Guajira (pen.), Colombia 126/E1
Gualaca, Panama 154/F6
Gualaceo, Ecuador 128/C4
Gualala, Calif. (95445) 204/B5
Gualán, Guatemala 154/C3
Gualaquiza, Ecuador 128/C4
Guale, Ecuador 128/B3
Gualeguay, Argentina 143/G6
Gualeguay (riv.), Argentina 143/G5
Gualeguaychú, Argentina 143/G6
Gualpatanta, Honduras 154/E3
Guam (isl.) 87/E4
GUAM 86/K7
Guam (isl.), U.S. 2/S5
Guamal, Magdalena, Colombia 126/C3
Guamal, Meta, Colombia 126/D6
Guamblin (isl.), Chile 138/D5
Guamo, Cuba 158/H3
Guamote, Ecuador 128/C4
Guampí, Sierra de (mts.), Venezuela 124/F4
Guamúchil, Mexico 150/E4
Guana, Venezuela 124/G5
Guanabacoa, Cuba 158/C1
Guanabacoa, Cuba 156/B2
Guanabara (bay), Brazil 135/E3
Guanaceví, Mexico 150/G4
Guanahacabibes (gulf), Cuba 158/A2
Guanahacabibes (pen.), Cuba 158/A2
Guanaja, Honduras 154/E2
Guanaja (isl.), Honduras 154/E2
Guanajay, Cuba 158/B1
Guanajay, Cuba 156/A2
Guanajibo (pt.), P. Rico 161/A2
Guanajibo (riv.), P. Rico 161/A2
Guanajuato (state), Mexico 150/J6
Guanajuato, Mexico 150/J6
Guanambi, Brazil 120/E4
Guañape (isls.), Peru 128/C7
Guanare, Venezuela 124/D3
Guanare (riv.), Venezuela 124/D3
Guanare Viejo (riv.), Venezuela 124/D3
Guanarito, Venezuela 124/D3
Guandacol, Argentina 143/C2
Guane, Cuba 158/A2
Guane, Cuba 156/A2
Guangdong (Kwangtung) (prov.), China 77/H7
Guangnam, China 77/G7
Guangshan, China 77/J5
Guangxi Zhuangzu (Kwangsi Chuang Aut. Reg.), China 77/G7
Guangyuan, China 77/G5
Guangze, China 77/J6
Guangzhou (Canton), China 77/H7
Guangzhou (Canton), China 54/N7
Guánica, P. Rico 161/B3
Guánica, P. Rico 156/F1
Guánica (lake), P. Rico 161/B3
Guanipa (riv.), Venezuela 124/G3
Guaniquilla (pt.), P. Rico 161/A2
Guano, Ecuador 128/C3
Guano (creek), Oreg. 291/H5
Guano (lake), Oreg. 291/H5
Guanoco, Venezuela 124/G2
Guanta, Venezuela 124/F2
Guantánamo (prov.), Cuba 158/K4
Guantánamo, Cuba 146/L7
Guantánamo, Cuba 158/K4
Guantánamo, Cuba 156/C2
Guantánamo (bay), Cuba 158/J4
Guantánamo (bay), Cuba 156/C3
Guantánamo Bay U.S. Nav. Reserve, Cuba 158/K4
Guan Xian, China 77/F5
Guape, Colombia 126/D6
Guapí, Colombia 126/B6
Guapi (bay), Colombia 126/A6
Guápiles, C. Rica 154/F5
Guapo (bay), Trin. & Tob. 161/A11
Guaporé (riv.) 120/C4
Guaporé (riv.), Bolivia 136/C3
Guaporé (riv.), Brazil 132/H10
Guaqui, Bolivia 136/A5
Guarambaré, Paraguay 144/B5
Guaranda, Ecuador 128/C3
Guarapuava, Brazil 132/C9
Guaratinguetá, Brazil 135/D3
Guaratinguetá, Brazil 132/E8
Guarda (dist.), Portugal 33/C2
Guarda, Portugal 33/C2
Guardatinajas, Venezuela 124/E3
Guardiagrele, Italy 34/E3
Guardia Mitre, Argentina 143/D5
Guardian (bank), C. Rica 154/D6
Guardian, W. Va. (26221) 312/F5
Guareña, Spain 33/C3
Guarenésia, Brazil 135/C2
Guarero, Venezuela 124/B2
Guarico (pt.), Cuba 158/K3
Guárico (state), Venezuela 124/E3
Guarico, Venezuela 124/D3
Guárico (res.), Venezuela 124/E3
Guárico (riv.), Venezuela 124/E3
Guariquén, Venezuela 124/G2
Guarita, Honduras 154/C3
Guaro, Cuba 158/J3
Guarujá, Brazil 135/C4
Guarulhos, Brazil 135/C3
Guasave, Mexico 150/E4
Guasdualito, Venezuela 124/C4
Guasimal, Cuba 158/E2
Guasimal, Venezuela 124/D4
Guasipati, Venezuela 124/H4
Guastalla, Italy 34/C2
Guatemala 2/D5
Guatemala 146/J8
Guatemala (cap.), Guat. 146/J8
GUATEMALA 154/B3
Guatemala (cap.), Guatemala 154/B3
Guateque, Colombia 126/D5
Guatuaro (pt.), Trin. & Tob. 161/B11
Guaviare (riv.), Colombia 120/B2
Guaviare (riv.), Colombia 126/F6
Guaxupé, Brazil 135/C2
Guayabal, Cuba 158/G3
Guayabal (lake), P. Rico 161/C2
Guayabal, Amazonas, Venezuela 124/E6
Guayabal, Guárico, Venezuela 124/E3
Guayabero (riv.), Colombia 126/D6
Guayacán, Chile 138/A8
Guayaguayare, Trin. & Tob. 161/B11
Guayama (dist.), P. Rico 161/D2
Guayama, P. Rico 161/E3
Guayama, P. Rico 156/G1
Guayaneco (arch.), Chile 138/D7
Guayanés (pt.), P. Rico 161/F2
Guayanés (riv.), P. Rico 161/E2
Guayanilla, P. Rico 161/B3
Guayanilla, P. Rico 156/F1
Guayanilla (bay), P. Rico 161/B3
Guayape, Honduras 154/D3
Guayapo, Serranía (mts.), Venezuela 124/E5
Guayaquil, Ecuador 2/E6
Guayaquil, Ecuador 128/B4
Guayaquil, Ecuador 120/A3
Guayaquil (gulf), Ecuador 120/A3
Guayaquil (gulf), Ecuador 128/B4
Guayaquilaró (riv.), Argentina 143/G5
Guayaramerín, Bolivia 136/C2
Guayas (prov.), Ecuador 128/B4
Guayas (riv.), Ecuador 128/C4
Guaymas, Mexico 146/G7
Guaymas, Mexico 150/D3
Guaynabo, P. Rico 161/D1
Guayo (lake), P. Rico 161/B2
Guayos, Cuba 158/F2
Guayubín, Dom. Rep. 158/D5
Guazú-cuá, Paraguay 144/D5
Gubakha, U.S.S.R. 48/F4
Gubakha, U.S.S.R. 52/J3
Guban (reg.), Somalia 115/H1
Gubat, Philippines 82/E4
Gubbio, Italy 34/D3
Guben (Wilhelm-Pieck-Stadt), E. Germany 22/F3
Guben (Gubin), Poland 47/B3
Gubin, Poland 47/B3
Gubkin, U.S.S.R. 52/E4
Guckeen, Minn. (†56013) 255/D7
Gúdar, Sierra de (range), Spain 33/F2
Gudauta, U.S.S.R. 52/F6
Gudenå (riv.), Denmark 21/C5
Gudermes, U.S.S.R. 52/G6
Güdül, Turkey 63/E2
Gudur, India 68/D6
Guebwiller, France 28/G4
Guéckédou, Guinea 106/B7
Guelma, Algeria 106/F1
Guelph, N. Dak. (58447) 282/O7
Guelph, Ont. 162/H7
Guelph, Ontario 177/D4
Guelta de Zemmur (well), Western Sahara 106/B3
Guemar, Algeria 102/C1
Guemar, Algeria 106/F2
Güémez, Mexico 150/K5
Güeppi, Peru 128/E3
Guerara, Algeria 106/E2
Güere (riv.), Venezuela 124/F3
Guéréda, Chad 111/D5
Guéret, France 28/D4
Guerneville, Calif. (95446) 204/B5
Guernica y Luno, Spain 33/E1
Guernsey (isl.), Chan. Is. 13/E8
Guernsey (isl.), Chan. Is. 10/E6
Guernsey, Iowa (50172) 229/J5
Guernsey (co.), Ohio 284/H5
Guernsey, Sask. 181/F4
Guernsey, Wyo. (82214) 319/H3
Guernsey (res.), Wyo. 319/H3
Guerra, Texas (78360) 303/F11
Guerrero (state), Mexico 150/J8
Guerzim, Algeria 106/D3
Gueydan, La. (70542) 238/E6
Guffey, Colo. (80820) 208/H5
Gugerd, Kuh-e (mts.), Iran 66/H3
Guggisberg, Switzerland 39/D3
Gughe (mt.), Ethiopia 111/G6
Guiana (isl.), Ant. & Bar. 161/E11
Guiana Highlands (plat.) 120/C2
Guichi, China 77/J5
Guichón, Uruguay 145/B3
Guidder, Cameroon 115/B2
Guide, China 77/F4
Guide Rock, Nebr. (68942) 264/F4
Guidonia, Italy 34/F6
Guiglo, Ivory Coast 106/C7
Guihulngan, Philippines 82/D5
Güija (lake), El Salvador 154/C3
Güija (lake), Guatemala 154/C3
Guija, Mozambique 118/E4
Guijuelo, Spain 33/D2
Guilarte (mt.), P. Rico 161/B2
Guild, N.H. (03754) 268/C5
Guildford, England 13/G8
Guildford, England 10/F5
Guildford Junction, Tasmania 99/B3
Guildhall, Vt. (05905) 268/D2
Guilford, Conn. (06437) 210/E3
Guilford○, Conn. (06437) 210/E3
Guilford, Ind. (47022) 227/H6
Guilford, Maine (04443) 243/E5
Guilford○, Maine (04443) 243/E5
Guilford, Mo. (64457) 261/C2
Guilford, N.Y. (13780) 276/J6
Guilford (co.), N.C. 281/K3
Guilford○, Vt. (†05301) 268/B6
Guilin (Kweilin), China 77/G6
Guilin, China 54/N7
Guillaume-Delisle (lake), Québec 174/B1
Guimarães, Brazil 132/E3
Guimarães, Portugal 33/B2
Guimaras (isl.), Philippines 82/D5
Guimaras (str.), Philippines 82/D5
Guimba, Philippines 82/C3
Guin, Ala. (35563) 195/C3
Guinan, China 77/F4
Guinda, Calif. (95637) 204/C5
Guinea 2/J5
Guinea 102/A3
GUINEA 106/B6
Guinea (gulf) 2/K5
Guinea (gulf) 102/C4
Guinea (gulf), Benin 106/E8
Guinea (gulf), Ghana 106/E8
Guinea (gulf), Guinea-Biss. 106/E8
Guinea (gulf), Ivory Coast 106/E8
Guinea (gulf), Nigeria 106/E8
Guinea (gulf), Togo 106/E8
Guinea, Va. (†22580) 307/O4
Guinea-Bissau 2/H5
Guinea-Bissau 102/A3
GUINEA-BISSAU 106/A6
Güines, Cuba 158/C1
Güines, Cuba 156/B2
Guingamp, France 28/B3
Guion, Ark. (72540) 202/G2
Guionos (pt.), C. Rica 154/E6
Guiping, China 77/G7
Guipúzcoa (prov.), Spain 33/E1
Güira de Melena, Cuba 158/C1
Guiratinga, Brazil 132/C7
Guir Hamada (des.), Algeria 106/D2
Güiria, Venezuela 124/G2
Guisa, Cuba 158/H4
Guisanbourg, Fr. Guiana 131/F3
Guisborough, England 13/F3
Guise, France 28/E3
Guitiriz, Spain 33/C1
Guiuan, Philippines 82/E5
Guixi, China 77/J6
Gui Xian, China 77/G7
Guiyang (Kweiyang), Guizhou, China 77/G6
Guiyang, Hunan, China 77/H6
Guiyang, China 54/M7
Guizhou (Kweichow) (prov.), China 77/G6
Gujarat (state), India 68/C4
Gujranwala, Pakistan 59/K3
Gujranwala, Pakistan 68/C2
Gujrat, Pakistan 59/K3
Gujrat, Pakistan 68/C2
Gukovo, U.S.S.R. 52/F5
Gulang, China 77/F4
Gulargambone, N.S. Wales 97/E2
Gulbarga, India 68/D5
Gulbene, U.S.S.R. 53/D2
Gulch (cape), Newf. 166/B2
Gulen, Norway 18/D6
Gulf (co.), Fla. 212/D7
Gulf, N.C. (27256) 281/L3
Gulf Breeze, Fla. (32561) 212/B6
Gulf Crest, Ala. (†36521) 195/B8
Gulf Hammock, Fla. (32639) 212/D2
Gulf Harbors, Fla. (†33552) 212/D3
Gulf Island Nat'l Seashore, Fla. 212/B6
Gulf Islands Nat'l Seashore, Miss. 256/G10
Gulfport, Fla. (33737) 212/B3
Gulf Port, Ill. (†52601) 222/B3
Gulfport, Miss. 188/J4
Gulfport, Miss. (*39501) 256/F10
Gulf Shores, Ala. (36542) 195/C10
Gulf Stream, Fla. (†33444) 212/F5
Gulgong, N.S. Wales 97/E3
Gulian, China 77/K1
Gulin, China 77/G6
Gulistan, 48/G5
Gulja (Yining), China 77/B3
Gulkana, Alaska (†99586) 196/J2
Gull (lake), Alberta 182/C3
Gull (lake), Minn. 255/D4
Gull (isl.), Newf. 166/D2
Gullane, Scotland 15/F4
Gull Bay, Ontario 177/H5
Gull Bay, Ontario 175/C3
Gullfoot (lake), Ontario 177/F3
Gull Island, Newf. 166/D2
Gull Island (pt.), Newf. 166/D2
Gulliver, Mich. (49840) 250/D2
Gull Lake, Alberta 182/D3
Gull Lake, Sask. 181/C5
Gully, Minn. (56646) 255/C3
Gülnar, Turkey 63/E4
Gulnare, Colo. (81042) 208/K8
Gulnare, Ky. (41530) 237/S5
Gulquac (lake), New Bruns. 170/D2
Gulquac (riv.), New Bruns. 170/C2
Gülşehir, Turkey 63/F3
Gulu, Uganda 115/F3
Gulvain (mt.), Scotland 15/C4
Guma (Pishan), China 77/A4
Gumaca, Philippines 82/D4
Gumare, Botswana 118/C3
Gumbranch, Georgia (†31313) 217/J7
Gumel, Nigeria 106/F6
Gumeracha, S. Australia 94/C7
Gumma (pref.), Japan 81/J5
Gummersbach, W. Germany 22/B3
Gummi, Nigeria 106/F6
Gum Spring, Va. (23065) 307/N5
Gum Springs, Ark. (†71923) 202/D5
Gümüş, Turkey 63/F2
Gümüşhacıköy, Turkey 63/F2
Gümüşhane (prov.), Turkey 63/H2
Gümüşhane, Turkey 59/C1
Gümüşhane, Turkey 63/H2
Gun (cay), Bahamas 156/B1
Gun (lake), Mich. 250/D6
Guna, India 68/D4
Gunbower, Victoria 97/C4
Gundagai, N.S. Wales 97/D4
Gunderbooka (ranges), N.S. Wales 97/C2
Gündoğmuş, Turkey 63/D4
Güney, Turkey 63/C3
Gunflint Trail, Minn. (†55604) 255/F1
Gungu, Zaire 115/C5
Gunisao (lake), Manitoba 179/J3
Gunlock, Utah (84733) 304/A6
Gunn, Alberta 182/C3
Gunna (isl.), Scotland 15/B4
Gunnbjørn (mt.), Greenl. 4/C11
Gunn City, Mo. (†64760) 261/D5
Gunnedah, N. S. Wales 88/H6
Gunnedah, N.S. Wales 97/F2
Gunning, N.S. Wales 97/E4
Gunnison (co.), Colo. 208/E5
Gunnison, Colo. (81230) 208/E5
Gunnison (riv.), Colo. 208/C5
Gunnison (tunnel), Colo. 208/D6
Gunnison, Miss. (38746) 256/C3
Gunnison, Utah (84634) 304/C4
Gunnison (res.), Utah 304/C4
Gunnworth, Sask. 181/C4
Gunpowder (riv.), Md. 245/N3
Gunpowder, Queensland 95/A3
Gunpowder, Queensland 88/F3
Gunpowder Falls (creek), Md. 245/M2
Guntakal, India 68/D5
Gunter, Ontario 177/G3
Gunter, Oreg. (†97436) 291/D4
Gunter Air Force Base, Ala. 195/F6
Guntersville, Ala. (35976) 195/F2
Guntersville (dam), Ala. 195/F2
Guntersville (lake), Ala. 195/F2
Gunton, Manitoba 179/E4
Guntown, Miss. (38849) 256/G2
Guntur, India 54/K8
Guntur, India 68/D5
Gunungapi (isl.), Indonesia 85/H7
Günzburg, W. Germany 22/D4
Gunzenhausen, W. Germany 22/D4
Gurabo, P. Rico 161/E2
Gurais, India 68/D2
Gurdon, Ark. (71743) 202/D6
Gurgan (Gorgan), Iran 66/J2
Gurguéia (riv.), Brazil 132/E5
Guri, Venezuela 124/G4
Guri (dam), Venezuela 120/C2
Guri (res.), Venezuela 120/C2
Guri (res.), Venezuela 124/G4
Gurk, Austria 41/C3
Gurla Mandhada (mt.), China 77/B5
Gurley, Ala. (35748) 195/F1
Gurley, La. (†70730) 238/H5
Gurley, Nebr. (69141) 264/B3
Gurley, N.S. Wales 97/E1
Gurley, S.C. (†29569) 296/J3
Gurleyville, Conn. (†06268) 210/G1
Gurnee, Ill. (60031) 222/B4
Gurnet (pt.), Mass. 249/M4
Gurney, Wis. (54528) 317/F3
Gurneyville, Alberta 182/E2
Guro, Mozambique 118/E3
Gürpınar, Turkey 63/K3
Gurteen, Ireland 17/D3
Gurtnellen, Switzerland 39/G3
Gürün, Turkey 63/G3
Gurupá, Brazil 132/D3
Gurupi, Brazil 132/D5
Gurupi, Brazil 120/E4
Gurupi, Serra do (range), Brazil 132/E4
Gurupi (riv.), Brazil 132/E3
Gur'yev, U.S.S.R. 54/G5
Gur'yev, U.S.S.R. 48/F5
Gusau, Nigeria 106/F6
Gusau, Nigeria 102/C3
Gusher, Utah (84030) 304/E3
Gusinje, Yugoslavia 45/D4
Gusinoozersk, U.S.S.R. 48/L4
Gus'-Khrustal'nyy, U.S.S.R. 52/F3
Güssing, Austria 41/D3
Gustavo Díaz Ordaz, Mexico 150/K3
Gustavus, Alaska (99826) 196/M1
Gustavus, Ohio (†44417) 284/J3
Gustine, Calif. (95322) 204/D6
Gustine, Texas (76455) 303/F6
Guston, Ky. (40142) 237/J5
Güstrow, E. Germany 22/E2
Gütersloh, W. Germany 22/C3
Guthrie, Ind. (†47421) 227/D7
Guthrie (co.), Iowa 229/D5
Guthrie, Ky. (42234) 237/G7
Guthrie, Minn. (56451) 255/D3
Guthrie, Mo. (†65063) 261/H5
Guthrie, Okla. 188/G3
Guthrie, Okla. (73044) 288/M3
Guthrie, Texas (79236) 303/D4
Guthrie Center, Iowa (50115) 229/D5
Gutiérrez Zamora, Mexico 150/L6
Guttannen, Switzerland 39/F3
Guttenberg, Iowa (52052) 229/L3
Guttenberg, N.J. (07093) 273/C2
Guttingen, Switzerland 39/H1
Gu-Win, Ala. (†35563) 195/C3
Guy, Alberta 182/B2
Guy, Ark. (72061) 202/F3
Guyana 2/G5
Guyana 120/D2
GUYANA 131/B3
Guyandotte (riv.), W. Va. 312/B6
Guyang, China 77/G3
Guymon, Okla. (73942) 288/D1
Guyot (glac.), Alaska 196/K2
Guyot (mt.), N.C. 281/C3
Guyot (mt.), Tenn. 237/P9
Guyra, N.S. Wales 97/F2
Guys, Tenn. (38339) 237/D10
Guysborough (co.), Nova Scotia 168/F3
Guysborough, Nova Scotia 168/G3
Guysborough (riv.), Nova Scotia 168/G3
Guys Mills, Pa. (16327) 294/C2
Guysville, Ohio (45735) 284/G7
Guyton, Georgia (31312) 217/K6
Guyuan, China 77/G4
Guzmán (lake), Mexico 150/F1
Guzmán Blanco, Venezuela 124/E6
Guzmanes (cays), Cuba 158/B2
Gwa, Burma 72/B3
Gwaai, Zimbabwe 118/D3
Gwabegar, N.S. Wales 97/E2
Gwadabawa, Nigeria 106/F6
Gwadar, Pakistan 59/H5
Gwadar, Pakistan 68/A4
Gwalior, India 54/J7
Gwalior, India 68/D3
Gwanda, Zimbabwe 118/D4
Gwda (riv.), Poland 47/C2
Gweebarra (bay), Ireland 17/D2
Gweebarra (riv.), Ireland 17/E2
Gwelo, (Gweru) Zimbabwe 118/D3
Gwelo, Zimbabwe 102/F6
Gwent, Wales 13/D6
Gwersyllt, Wales 13/E4
Gwinn, Mich. (49841) 250/B2
Gwinner, N. Dak. (58040) 282/P7
Gwinnett (co.), Georgia 217/D2
Gwydir (riv.), N.S. Wales 97/E1
Gwynedd, Wales 13/C4
Gwynn, Va. (23066) 307/R5
Gwynne, Alberta 182/D3
Gwynneville, Ind. (46144) 227/F5
Gyaca, China 77/D6
Gyangzê, China 77/C6
Gyaring Co (lake), China 77/C5
Gyaring Hu (lake), China 77/E5
Gyasikan, Ghana 106/D7
Gyda (pen.), U.S.S.R. 54/J2
Gyda (pen.), U.S.S.R. 4/C6
Gyda, U.S.S.R. 48/H2
Gyda (pen.), U.S.S.R. 48/H2
Gydan (Kolyma) (range), U.S.S.R. 48/Q3
Gyirong, China 77/B6
Gylling, Denmark 21/D6
Gympie, Australia 87/F8
Gympie, Queensland 88/J5
Gympie, Queensland 95/E5
Gyobingauk, Burma 72/C3
Gyoma, Hungary 41/F3
Gyöngyös, Hungary 41/E3
Gyönk, Hungary 41/E3
Győr, Hungary 7/F4
Győr, Hungary 41/D3
Győr-Sopron (co.), Hungary 41/D3
Gypsum, Colo. (81637) 208/F3
Gypsum, Kansas (67448) 232/E3
Gypsum (lake), Manitoba 179/D3
Gypsum, Ohio (43433) 284/E2
Gypsumville, Manitoba 179/D3
Gyrfalcon (isls.), N.W. Terrs. 187/M4
Gyula, Hungary 41/F3

H

Haacht, Belgium 27/F7
Haag, Austria 41/C2
Haakon (co.), S. Dak. 298/F5
Haamstede, Netherlands 27/D5
Ha'apai Group (isls.), Tonga 87/J8
Haapajärvi, Finland 18/O5
Haapamäki, Finland 18/O5
Haapsalu, U.S.S.R. 53/B1
Haar, W. Germany 22/D4
Haarlem, Netherlands 27/F4
Haarlemmermeer (Hoofddorp), Netherlands 27/F4
Haarlemmermeer Polder, Netherlands 27/B5
Haast, N. Zealand 100/B5
Haast (pass), N. Zealand 100/B6
Haast (riv.), N. Zealand 100/B5
Haasts Bluff, North. Terr. 88/E4
Haasts Bluff, North. Terr. 93/B7
Haasts Bluff Aboriginal Reserve, North. Terr. 88/E5
Haasts Bluff Aboriginal Res., North. Terr. 93/B7
Hab (riv.), Pakistan 68/B3
Hab (riv.), Pakistan 59/J4
Habahe, China 77/C2
Habana, La (Havana) (prov.), Cuba 158/C1
Habana, Cuba 158/C1
Habay, Alberta 182/A5
Habay, Belgium 27/H9
Habban, P.D.R. Yemen 59/E7
Habbaniya, Iraq 59/D3
Habbaniya, Iraq 66/C4
Habbaniya, Hor al (lake), Iraq 66/C4
Habersham (co.), Georgia 217/E1
Habersham, Georgia (30544) 217/F1
Habersham, Tenn. (†37766) 237/N8
Habiganj, Bangladesh 68/G4
Habikino, Japan 81/J8
Habomai (isls.), Japan 81/N2
Habonim, Israel 65/B2
Haboro, Japan 81/K1
Hachenburg, W. Germany 22/B3
Hachinohe, Japan 81/K3
Hachioji, Japan 81/O2
Hachiro (lag.), Japan 81/J3
Hachita, N. Mex. (88040) 274/A7
Hacıbektaş, Turkey 63/F3
Hacienda Village, Fla. (†33301) 212/B4
Hacılar, Turkey 63/F3
Hack (mt.), S. Australia 94/F4
Hackberry, Ariz. (86411) 198/B3
Hackberry, La. (70645) 238/D7
Hackensack, Minn. (56452) 255/D4
Hackensack, N.J. (*07601) 273/B2
Hackensack (riv.), N.J. 273/C1
Hacker Valley, W. Va. (26222) 312/F5
Hacketstown, Ireland 17/H6
Hackett, Ark. (72937) 202/B3
Hacketts Cove, Nova Scotia 168/E4
Hackettstown, N.J. (07840) 273/D2
Hackleburg, Ala. (35564) 195/C2
Hackleman, Ind. (†46928) 227/F4
Hackney, England 13/H8
Hackney, England 10/B5
Hacksneck, Va. (23358) 307/S5
Hacoda, Ala. (†36442) 195/F8
Hadano, Japan 81/O3
Hadar, Nebr. (68738) 264/G2
Hadarba, Ras (cape), Sudan 111/G3
Hadashville, Manitoba 179/G5
Hadd, Ras al (cape), Oman 59/G5
Hadd, Ras al (cape), Oman 54/H7
Haddam○, Conn. (06438) 210/E3
Haddam, Kansas (66944) 232/E2
Haddam Neck, Conn. (†06424) 210/E2
Haddar, Saudi Arabia 59/E5
Haddington, Scotland 10/E3
Haddington, Scotland 15/F5
Haddix, Ky. (41331) 237/P6
Haddock, Georgia (31033) 217/F4
Haddonfield, N.J. (08033) 273/B3
Haddon Heights, N.J. (08035) 273/B3
Hadejia, Nigeria 106/G6
Hadejia (riv.), Nigeria 106/F6
Hadensville, Ky. (†42234) 237/G7
Hadera, Israel 65/B3
Hadera (dry riv.), Israel 65/B3
Haderslev, Denmark 21/C7
Haderslev, Denmark 18/F9
Hadhar, Iraq 66/C3
Hadhramaut (reg.), P.D.R. Yemen 54/F8
Hadhramaut (dist.), P.D.R. Yemen 59/E7
Hadhramaut, Wadi (dry riv.), P.D.R. Yemen 59/F7
Hadibu, P.D.R. Yemen 54/G8
Hadibu, P.D.R. Yemen 59/F7
Hadım, Turkey 63/E4
Haditha, Iraq 66/C3
Haditha, Iraq 59/D3
Hadiya, Saudi Arabia 59/C4
Hadleigh, England 13/H5
Hadley, Ind. (†46122) 227/D5
Hadley, Ky. (42235) 237/H6
Hadley○, Mass. (01035) 249/D3
Hadley, Minn. (56133) 255/C7
Hadley (bay), N.W. Terrs. 187/H2
Hadley, Pa. (16130) 294/B3
Hadley-Lake Luzerne, N.Y. (12835) 276/N4
Hadlock-Irondale, Wash. (98339) 310/C2
Hadlyme, Conn. (06439) 210/F3
Hadselfjorden (fjord), Norway 18/J2
Hadspen, Tasmania 99/D3
Hadsten, Denmark 21/C5
Hadsund, Denmark 21/D4
Haedo (range), Uruguay 145/C2
Haeju, N. Korea 81/B4
Haena, Hawaii (†96714) 218/C1
Haena (pt.), Hawaii 218/C1
Hafar al Batin, Saudi Arabia 59/E4
Haffe, Syria 63/G5
Hafford, Sask. 181/D3
Hafik, Turkey 63/G3
Haflong, India 68/G3
Hafnarfjördhur, Iceland 21/B2
Haft Gel, Iran 66/F5
Hafun, Somalia 115/K1
Hafun, Ras (cape), Somalia 115/K1
Hagaman, N.Y. (12086) 276/M5
Hagan, Georgia (30429) 217/J6
Hagar, Ontario 177/D1
Hagari (riv.), India 68/D6
Hagarstown, Ill. (62247) 222/D5
Hagarville, Ark. (72839) 202/D2
Hagemeister (isl.), Alaska 196/F3
Hagen, Sask. 181/F3
Hagen, W. Germany 22/B3
Hagenow, E. Germany 22/D2
Hagensborg, Br. Col. 184/D4
Hager City, Wis. (54014) 317/A6
Hagerman, Idaho (83332) 220/D7
Hagerman, N. Mex. (88232) 274/E5
Hagerstown, Ind. (47346) 227/G5
Hagerstown, Md. (21740) 245/G2
Hagerstown, Md. 188/L3
Hagfors, Sweden 18/H6
Hagi, Japan 81/E6
Ha Giang, Vietnam 72/E2
Hagley, Tasmania 99/C3
Hagood, S.C. (†29128) 296/F3
Hags (head), Ireland 17/B6
Hague, Fla. (†32601) 212/D2
Hague (cape), France 28/C3
Hague, The (cap.), Netherlands 7/E3
Hague, The (cap.), Netherlands 27/E4
Hague, N.Y. (12836) 276/N3
Hague, N. Dak. (58542) 282/L7
Hague, Sask. 181/E3
Hague, Va. (22469) 307/P4
Haguenau, France 28/G3
Haha (isl.), Japan 87/E3
Haha (isl.), Japan 81/M3
Ha! Ha! (lake), Qué. 172/G1

Hardesty 379

Ha! Ha! (riv.) Qué. 172/G1
Hahatonka, Mo. (†65020) 261/G7
Hahira, Georgia (31632) 217/F9
Hahndorf, S. Australia 94/C8
Hahnville, La. (70057) 238/N4
Hai, Iraq 59/E3
Hai, Iraq 66/E4
Haifa (dist.), Israel 65/C2
Haifa, Israel 65/B2
Haifa, Israel 59/B3
Haifa (bay), Israel 65/C2
Haifeng, China 77/J7
Haig (lake), Alberta 182/B1
Haight, Alberta 182/D3
Haigler, Nebr. (69030) 264/C4
Haikang, China 77/G7
Haikou (Hoihow), China 77/H7
Haikou, China 54/N8
Haiku, Hawaii (96708) 218/J2
Hail, Saudi Arabia 54/F7
Hail, Saudi Arabia 59/D4
Hailar, China 77/J2
Hailar He (riv.), China 77/K2
Haile, La. (†71260) 238/F1
Hailesboro, N.Y. (13645) 276/K2
Hailey, Idaho (83333) 220/D6
Haileybury, Ontario 177/K5
Haileybury, Ontario 175/D3
Haileyville, Okla. (74546) 288/P5
Hailong, China 77/L3
Hailsham, England 13/H7
Hailun, China 77/L2
Hailuoto, Finland 18/O4
Hailuoto (isl.), Finland 18/O4
Haina, Hawaii (96727) 218/H3
Hainan (isl.), China 2/Q5
Hainan (isl.), China 54/N8
Hainan (isl.), China 77/H8
Hainaut (prov.), Belgium 27/D7
Hainburg an der Donau, Austria 41/D2
Haines, Alaska (99827) 196/M1
Haines, Oreg. (97833) 291/J3
Hainesburg, N.J. (†07832) 273/C2
Haines City, Fla. (33844) 212/E3
Haines Junction, Yukon 187/E3
Haines Landing, Maine (†04964) 243/B6
Hainesport○, N.J. (08036) 273/D4
Hainesville, Ill. (†60030) 222/A4
Hainesville, N.J. (†07826) 273/D1
Hainfeld, Austria 41/C2
Haiphong, Vietnam 54/M7
Hairy Hill, Alberta 182/D3
Haiti 2/F5
Haiti 146/L8
HAITI 158
HAITI 156/D3
Haiwee, Calif. 204/H7
Haiya Junction, Sudan 59/C6
Haiya Junction, Sudan 111/G4
Haiyan, China 77/F4
Haiyang, China 77/K4
Haiyuan, China 77/G4
Hajara, Al (plain), Iraq 66/D5
Hajarain, P.D.R. Yemen 59/E6
Hajdú-Bihar (co.), Hungary 41/F3
Hajdúböszörmény, Hungary 41/F3
Hajdudorog, Hungary 41/F3
Hajdúhadház, Hungary 41/F3
Hajdúnánás, Hungary 41/F3
Hajdúsámson, Hungary 41/F3
Hajdúszoboszló, Hungary 41/F3
Haji Ibraham (mt.), Iraq 66/D2
Hajja, Yemen Arab Rep. 59/D6
Hajnowka, Poland 47/F2
Hajós, Hungary 41/E3
Haka, Burma 72/B2
Hakalau, Hawaii (96710) 218/J4
Hakkâri (prov.), Turkey 63/K4
Hakkâri (Çölemerik), Turkey 63/K4
Hakkâri (mts.), Turkey 63/K4
Hakken (mt.), Japan 81/H6
Hakodate, Japan 81/K3
Hakodate, Japan 54/R5
Haku (mt.), Japan 81/H5
Hakui, Japan 81/H5
Hakusan National Park, Japan 81/H5
Hal (Halle), Belgium 27/E7
Halabja, Iraq 66/D3
Halachó, Mexico 150/O6
Halaib, Sudan 59/C5
Halaib, Sudan 111/G3
Halalii (lake), Hawaii 218/A2
Halaula, Hawaii 188/G5
Halawa, Hawaii, Hawaii (†96711) 218/G3
Halawa, Molokai, Hawaii (†96748) 218/H1
Halawa (bay), Hawaii 218/H1
Halawa (cape), Hawaii 218/H1
Halawa (stream), Hawaii 218/B3
Halawa Heights, Hawaii (†96701) 218/B3
Halberstadt, E. Germany 22/D3
Halbrite, Sask. 181/H6
Halbur, Iowa (51444) 229/D4
Halcon (mt.), Philippines 82/C4
Halcyon Dale, Georgia (†30467) 217/J5
Haldane, Ill. (†61030) 222/D1
Haldeman, Ky. (40329) 237/P4
Halden, Norway 18/G7
Haldensleben, E. Germany 22/D2
Haldimand, Ontario 177/E5
Haldimand-Norfolk (reg. munic.), Ontario 177/E5
Hale (co.), Ala. 195/C5
Hale, Argentina 143/F7
Hale, Colo. (80730) 208/P3
Hale, Camp, Colo. 208/G4
Hale, England 13/H2
Hale, Iowa (52230) 229/L4
Hale, Mich. (48739) 250/F4
Hale, Mo. (64643) 261/F3
Hale (riv.), North. Terr. 93/D8
Hale (co.), Texas 303/C3
Hale (mt.), W. Australia 92/B4
Haleakala (crater), Hawaii 218/K2
Haleakala Nat'l Park, Hawaii 218/K2
Haleb (Aleppo), Syria 59/C2
Haleb (Aleppo), Syria 63/G4
Haleburg, Ala. (†36319) 195/H8
Hale Center, Texas (79041) 303/C3
Haledon, N.J. (07508) 273/B1
Haleiwa, Hawaii (96712) 218/E1
Halen, Belgium 27/G7
Hales Corners, Wis. (53130) 317/K2
Halesowen, England 13/E5
Halesowen, England 10/G3
Hales Point, Tenn. (†38040) 237/B9
Halesworth, England 13/J5
Haley, N. Dak. (†58629) 282/D8
Haley Station, Ontario 177/H2
Haleyville, Ala. (35565) 195/C2
Haleyville, N.J. (†08349) 273/C5
Half Assini, Ghana 106/D8
Halfeti, Turkey 63/H4
Half Island Cove, Nova Scotia 168/G3
Half Moon (cay), Belize 154/D2
Halfmoon Bay, Alberta 182/C3
Halfmoon Bay, Br. Col. 184/J2
Half Moon Bay, Calif. (94019) 204/H3
Half Moon Bay (Oban), N. Zealand 100/B7
Half Moon Lake, Alberta 182/D2
Halford, Kansas (†67701) 232/B2
Halfway (riv.), Br. Col. 184/F2
Halfway, Ky. (42150) 237/J7
Halfway, Md. (†21740) 245/G2
Half Way, Mo. (65663) 261/F7
Halfway, Oreg. (97834) 291/K3
Halfway House, Hawaii (†96718) 218/H6
Halfway House, S. Africa 118/H6
Halfweg, Netherlands 27/B4
Halhul, West Bank 65/C4
Haliburton (county), Ontario 177/F2
Haliburton, Ontario 177/F2
Haliburton (lake), Ontario 177/F2
Halieli, Turkey 63/B6
Halifax, Canada 2/F3
Halifax, England 13/J1
Halifax, England 10/G1
Halifax (harb.), Grenada 161/C8
Halifax○, Mass. (02338) 249/L5
Halifax (co.), N.C. 281/O2
Halifax, N.C. (27839) 281/O2
Halifax (co.), Nova Scotia 168/E4
Halifax (cap.), N.S. 162/K7
Halifax (cap.), N.S. 146/M5
Halifax (cap.), Nova Scotia 168/E4
Halifax (harb.), Nova Scotia 168/E4
Halifax, Pa. (17032) 294/J5
Halifax (bay), Queensland 88/H3
Halifax (bay), Queensland 95/C3
Halifax○, Vt. (†05358) 268/B6
Halifax (co.), Va. 307/L7
Halifax, Va. (24558) 307/L7
Halifax Center, Vt. (†05358) 268/B6
Haliimaile, Hawaii (96787) 218/J2
Halil (riv.), Iran 59/G4
Halin, Somalia 115/J2
Halkett (cape), Alaska 196/H1
Halkirk, Alberta 182/D3
Halkirk, Scotland 10/E1
Halkirk, Scotland 15/E2
Hall (isl.), Alaska 196/D2
Hall (co.), Georgia 217/E2
Hall, Ind. (†46157) 227/D5
Hall, Ky. (†41840) 237/R6
Hall, Md. (†20716) 245/L5
Hall (isls.), Micronesia 87/F5
Hall, Mont. (59837) 262/C4
Hall (co.), Nebr. 264/F4
Hall (basin), N.W. Terrs. 187/M1
Hall (lake), N.W. Terrs. 187/K3
Hall (pen.), N.W.T. 162/K3
Hall (pen.), N.W. Terrs. 187/M3
Hall (riv.), Québec 172/C2
Hall (co.), Texas 303/D3
Hall, W. Va. (†26201) 312/F4
Halla (mt.), S. Korea 81/C7
Hallam, Nebr. (68368) 264/H4
Hallam, Victoria 97/K5
Halland (co.), Sweden 18/H8
Hallandale, Fla. (33009) 212/B4
Hallandale (riv.), Scotland 15/E2
Hallaniya (isl.), P.D.R. Yemen 59/G6
Hallau, Switzerland 39/F1
Hall Beach, N.W. Terrs. 187/K3
Hallboro, Manitoba 179/C4
Halle, Belgium 27/E7
Halle, E. Germany 7/F3
Halle (dist.), E. Germany 22/D3
Halle, E. Germany 22/D3
Halleck, Nev. (89824) 266/F2
Hallefors, Sweden 18/J7
Hallein, Austria 41/B3
Halle-Neustadt, E. Germany 22/D3
Hallett, Okla. (74034) 288/N2
Hallettsville, Texas (77964) 303/G8
Halley, Ark. (†71638) 202/H6
Halliday, N. Dak. (58636) 282/F5
Hallie, Wis. (†54729) 317/D6
Halligen (isls.), W. Germany 22/C1
Hall Meadow (brook), Conn. 210/C1
Hallock, Minn. (56728) 255/A2
Hallonquist, Sask. 181/D5
Hallowell, Kansas (66744) 232/H4
Hallowell, Maine (04347) 243/D7
Hall Park, Okla. (†73069) 288/M4
Halls (stream), N.H. 268/E1
Halls, Tenn. (38040) 237/C9
Halls (creek), Utah 304/D6
Hallsberg, Sweden 18/J7
Hallsboro, N.C. (28442) 281/M6
Halls Creek, Australia 87/C7
Halls Creek, W. Australia 88/D3
Halls Creek, W. Australia 92/D2
Halls Crossroads, Tenn. (37918) 237/O8
Hallson, N. Dak. (†58220) 282/P2
Halls Summit, Kansas (†66871) 232/G3
Hallstahammar, Sweden 18/K7
Hallstatt, Austria 41/B3
Hallstavik, Sweden 18/L6
Hallstead, Pa. (18822) 294/L2
Hall Summit, La. (71034) 238/D2
Hallsville, Ill. (†61727) 222/D3
Hallsville, Mo. (65255) 261/H4
Hallsville, Ohio (45633) 284/E7
Hallsville, Texas (75650) 303/K5
Hallton, Pa. (†15860) 294/E3
Halltown, Mo. (65664) 261/E8
Halltown, W. Va. (25423) 312/L4
Hallum, Netherlands 27/H2
Hallwilersee (lake), Switzerland 39/F2
Hallwood, Va. (23359) 307/S5
Halma, Minn. (56729) 255/B2
Halmahera (isl.), Indonesia 54/O9
Halmahera (isl.), Indonesia 85/H5
Halmahera (sea), Indonesia 85/H5
Halmstad, Sweden 18/H8
Halpine, Md. (†20852) 245/K4
Halq el Oued, Tunisia 106/G1
Hals, Denmark 21/D3
Halsell, Ala. (†36912) 195/B6
Halsey, Nebr. (69142) 264/D3
Halsey, Oreg. (97348) 291/D3
Halstad, Minn. (56548) 255/B3
Halstead, England 13/H6
Halstead, England 10/G5
Halstead, Kansas (67056) 232/E4
Haltdalen, Norway 18/G5
Haltemprice, England 13/G4
Haltemprice, England 10/F4
Haltern, W. Germany 22/B3
Haltiatunturi (mt.), Finland 18/M2
Haltom City, Texas (76117) 303/F2
Halton (reg. munic.), Ontario 177/E4
Halton Hills, Ontario 177/E4
Haltwhistle, England 13/E2
Halulu (lake), Hawaii 218/A2
Ham, Chad 111/C5
Ham, France 28/E3
Hama (prov.), Syria 63/G5
Hama, Syria 63/G5
Hama, Syria 59/C2
Hamada, Jebel (mt.), Egypt 59/B5
Hamada, Japan 81/E6
Hamadan (gov.), Iran 66/F3
Hamadan, Iran 66/F3
Hamadan, Iran 59/E3
Hamadan, Iran 54/F6
Hamamatsu, Japan 54/P6
Hamamatsu, Japan 81/H6
Hamar, N. Dak. (58336) 282/N4
Hamar, Norway 18/G6
Hamar, Saudi Arabia 59/E5
Hambantota, Sri Lanka 68/E7
Hamberg, N. Dak. (58337) 282/L4
Hamber Prov. Park, Br. Col. 184/H4
Hamblen (co.), Tenn. 237/P8
Hambleton, W. Va. (26269) 312/G4
Hamburg, Ark. (71646) 202/G7
Hamburg, Conn. (†06371) 210/F3
Hamburg, Ill. (62045) 222/C4
Hamburg, Iowa (51640) 229/B7
Hamburg, Mich. (48139) 250/F6
Hamburg, Minn. (55339) 255/D6
Hamburg, Miss. (†39661) 256/B7
Hamburg, N.J. (07419) 273/D1
Hamburg, N.Y. (14075) 276/C5
Hamburg, Pa. (19526) 294/L4
Hamburg, W. Germany 7/F3
Hamburg (state), W. Germany 22/D2
Hamburg, W. Germany 22/D2
Hamburg, Wis. (54438) 317/G5
Hamda, Saudi Arabia 59/D6
Hamden○, Conn. (06514) 210/D3
Hamden, N.Y. (13782) 276/K6
Hamden, Ohio (45634) 284/F7
Häme (prov.), Finland 18/O6
Hämeenlinna, Finland 18/O6
Hamel, Ill. (62046) 222/B2
Hamel, Minn. (55340) 255/F5
Hamel, Québec 172/G3
Hamelin Pool, W. Australia 88/A5
Hamelin Pool, W. Australia 92/A4
Hameln, W. Germany 22/C2
Hamer, Idaho (83425) 220/F6
Hamer, S.C. (29547) 296/J3
Hamersley (range), W. Australia 88/B4
Hamersley (range), W. Australia 92/B3
Hamersville, Ohio (45130) 284/C8
Hamhŭng, N. Korea 81/C4
Hami (Kumul), China 77/D3
Hami, China 54/L5
Hamill, S. Dak. (57534) 298/K6
Hamilton, Ala. (35570) 195/C2
Hamilton (lake), Ark. 202/D5
Hamilton (cap.), Bermuda 156/G3
Hamilton (mt.), Calif. 204/L3
Hamilton, Colo. (81638) 208/D2
Hamilton (co.), Fla. 212/D1
Hamilton, Georgia (31811) 217/C5
Hamilton (co.), Ill. 222/E5
Hamilton, Ill. (62341) 222/B3
Hamilton (co.), Ind. 227/E4
Hamilton, Ind. (46742) 227/H1
Hamilton (co.), Iowa 229/F4
Hamilton, Iowa (50116) 229/H6
Hamilton (co.), Kansas 232/A3
Hamilton, Kansas (66853) 232/F4
Hamilton○, Mass. (01936) 249/L2
Hamilton, Mich. (49419) 250/C6
Hamilton, Miss. (39746) 256/H3
Hamilton, Mo. (64644) 261/E3
Hamilton, Mont. (59840) 262/B4
Hamilton (co.), Nebr. 264/F4
Hamilton (inlet), Newf. 166/C3
Hamilton (inlet), Newf. 146/N4
Hamilton (inlet), Newf. 162/L5
Hamilton (sound), Newf. 166/D4
Hamilton (co.), N.Y. 276/L3
Hamilton, N.Y. (13346) 276/J5
Hamilton, N. Zealand 100/E2
Hamilton, N.C. (27840) 281/P3
Hamilton, N. Dak. (58238) 282/R2
Hamilton (co.), Ohio 284/A7
Hamilton, Ohio 188/K3
Hamilton, Ohio (*45011) 284/A7
Hamilton, Ont. 146/K5
Hamilton, Ont. 162/H7
Hamilton, Ontario 177/E4
Hamilton, Oreg. (†97856) 291/H3
Hamilton, Pa. (15744) 294/D4
Hamilton (riv.), Queensland 95/B4
Hamilton, R.I. (†02852) 249/J6
Hamilton, Scotland 15/C2
Hamilton, Scotland 10/B1
Hamilton, The (riv.), S. Australia 94/D2
Hamilton, The (riv.), S. Australia 88/E5
Hamilton, Tasmania 99/C4
Hamilton (co.), Tenn. 237/L10
Hamilton (co.), Texas 303/F6
Hamilton, Texas (76531) 303/G6
Hamilton, Victoria 88/G7
Hamilton, Victoria 97/B5
Hamilton, Va. (22068) 307/N2
Hamilton, Wash. (98255) 310/D2
Hamilton City, Calif. (95951) 204/C4
Hamilton Dome, Wyo. (82427) 319/D2
Hamilton Square-Mercerville, N.J. (08690) 273/D3
Hamilton-Wentworth (reg. munic.), Ontario 177/D4
Hamina, Finland 18/P6
Hamiota, Manitoba 179/B4
Ham Lake, Minn. (55304) 255/E5
Hamler, Ohio (43524) 284/B3
Hamlet, Ind. (46532) 227/D2
Hamlet, Nebr. (69031) 264/C4
Hamlet, N.Y. (†14138) 276/B6
Hamlet, N.C. (28345) 281/K5
Hamlet, N. Dak. (†58795) 282/E2
Hamlet, Ohio (†45102) 284/B8
Hamletsburg, Ill. (62944) 222/E6
Hamlin, Alberta 182/D2
Hamlin, Iowa (50117) 229/D5
Hamlin, Kansas (†66434) 232/G2
Hamlin, Ky. (42046) 237/E7
Hamlin○, Maine (†04785) 243/H1
Hamlin (lake), Mich. 250/C4
Hamlin, N.Y. (14464) 276/E4
Hamlin, Pa. (18427) 294/M3
Hamlin, Sask. 181/C3
Hamlin (co.), S. Dak. 298/P4
Hamlin, Texas (79520) 303/E5
Hamlin, W. Va. (25523) 312/B6
Hamm, W. Germany 22/B3
Hammamet (gulf), Tunisia 106/G1
Hammar, Hor al (lake), Iraq 66/E5
Hammarstrand, Sweden 18/J5
Hamme, Belgium 27/E6
Hammel, Denmark 21/C5
Hammelburg, W. Germany 22/C3
Hammer, S. Dak. (†57255) 298/R2
Hammerdal, Sweden 18/J5
Hammerfest, Norway 4/B9
Hammerfest, Norway 18/N1
Hammerfest, Norway 7/G1
Hammersmith, England 10/B5
Hammersmith, England 13/H8
Hammerum, Denmark 21/C5
Hammett, Idaho (83627) 220/C7
Hammon, Okla. (73650) 288/H3
Hammonasset (pt.), Conn. 210/E3
Hammonasset (res.), Conn. 210/E3
Hammonasset (riv.), Conn. 210/E3
Hammond, Ill. (61929) 222/E4
Hammond, Ind. (*46320) 227/B1
Hammond, Ky. (†40935) 237/O7
Hammond, La. (70401) 238/N1
Hammond, Minn. (55938) 255/F6
Hammond, Mo. (†65762) 261/G9
Hammond, Mont. (59332) 262/M5
Hammond (riv.), New Bruns. 170/E3
Hammond, N.Y. (13646) 276/J2
Hammond, Oreg. (97121) 291/C1
Hammond, Wis. (54015) 317/A6
Hammondsport, N.Y. (14840) 276/F6
Hammondsville, Ohio (43930) 284/J4
Hammondvale, New Bruns. 170/E3
Hammondville, Ala. (†35989) 195/G1
Hammonton, N.J. (08037) 273/D4
Hamnavoe, Scotland 15/G2
Ham-Nord, Québec 172/F4
Hamoa, Hawaii (†96713) 218/K2
Hamois, Belgium 27/G8
Hamont-Achel, Belgium 27/H6
Hampden, Maine (04444) 243/F6
Hampden○, Maine (04444) 243/F6
Hampden (co.), Mass. 249/D4
Hampden○, Mass. (01036) 249/E4
Hampden, Newf. 166/C4
Hampden, N. Zealand 100/C6
Hampden, N. Dak. (58338) 282/N2
Hampden, W. Va. (25623) 312/C7
Hampden Highlands, Maine (04445) 243/F6
Hampden-Sydney, Va. (23943) 307/L6
Hampshire (co.), England 13/F6
Hampshire, Ill. (60140) 222/E1
Hampshire (co.), Mass. 249/D3
Hampshire, Tenn. (38461) 237/G9
Hampshire (co.), W. Va. 312/J4
Hampshire, Wyo. (†82701) 319/H2
Hampstead, Dominica 161/E5
Hampstead, Md. (21074) 245/L2
Hampstead, New Bruns. 170/D3
Hampstead○, N.H. (03841) 268/E6
Hampstead, N.C. (28443) 281/O6
Hampstead, Québec 172/H4
Hampton, Ark. (71744) 202/F6
Hampton○, Conn. (06247) 210/G1
Hampton, Fla. (32044) 212/D2
Hampton, Georgia (30228) 217/D4
Hampton, Ill. (61256) 222/C2
Hampton, Iowa (50441) 229/G3
Hampton, Ky. (42047) 237/E6
Hampton, Minn. (55031) 255/E6
Hampton, Miss. (†38744) 256/B4
Hampton, Nebr. (68843) 264/G4
Hampton, New Bruns. 170/E3
Hampton, N.H. (03842) 268/F6
Hampton○, N.H. (03842) 268/F6
Hampton, N.J. (08827) 273/D2
Hampton, N.Y. (12837) 276/O3
Hampton, Nova Scotia 168/C4
Hampton, Oreg. (†97712) 291/G4
Hampton, Pa. (†17350) 294/H6
Hampton (co.), S.C. 296/E6
Hampton, S.C. (29924) 296/E6
Hampton, Tenn. (37658) 237/S8
Hampton (I.C.), Va. (*23601) 307/R6
Hampton Bays, N.Y. (11946) 276/R9
Hampton Beach, N.H. (03842) 268/F6
Hampton Falls○, N.H. (03844) 268/F6
Hampton Nat'l Hist. Site, Md. 245/M3
Hampton Park, Victoria 97/K6
Hampton Park, Victoria 88/M8
Hampton Roads (est.), Va. 307/R7
Hampton Springs, Fla. (†32347) 212/C1
Hamptonville, N.C. (27020) 281/H2
Hamrat esh Sheikh, Sudan 111/E5
Hamrin, Jabal (mts.), Iraq 66/D3
Hams Bluff (prom.), Virgin Is. (U.S.) 161/E3
Hams Fork (riv.), Wyo. 319/B4
Ham-Sud, Québec 172/F4
Hamtramck, Mich. (48212) 250/B6
Hamur, Turkey 63/K3
Han (riv.), China 54/N6
Han (riv.), S. Korea 81/C5
Hana, Hawaii 188/F5
Hana, Hawaii (96713) 218/K2
Hanac, Turkey 63/K2
Hanaford (Logan), Ill. (†62856) 222/E6
Hanagita (peak), Alaska 196/K2
Hanahan, S.C. (29410) 296/H6
Hanakiya, Saudi Arabia 59/D5
Hanalei, Hawaii (96714) 218/C1
Hanalei (bay), Hawaii 218/C1
Hanalei (riv.), Hawaii 218/C1
Hanamaki, Japan 81/K4
Hanamalo (pt.), Hawaii 218/F7
Hanamaulu, Hawaii (96715) 218/C1
Hanapepe, Hawaii (96716) 218/C2
Hanapepe (bay), Hawaii 218/C2
Hanau, W. Germany 22/C3
Hanbogd, Mongolia 77/G3
Hanceville, Ala. (35077) 195/E2
Hancheng, China 77/H4
Hanchung (Hanzhong), China 77/G5
Hancock, Conn. (†06786) 210/C2
Hancock (co.), Georgia 217/G4
Hancock (co.), Ill. 222/B3
Hancock (co.), Ind. 227/F5
Hancock (co.), Iowa 229/F2
Hancock, Iowa (51536) 229/C6
Hancock (co.), Ky. 237/H5
Hancock (co.), Maine 243/G6
Hancock○, Maine (04640) 243/G6
Hancock, Md. (21750) 245/F2
Hancock○, Mass. (01237) 249/A2
Hancock, Mich. (49930) 250/G1
Hancock, Minn. (56244) 255/C5
Hancock (co.), Miss. 256/E10
Hancock, Mo. (†65452) 261/H7
Hancock○, N.H. (03449) 268/C6
Hancock (mt.), N.H. 268/D3
Hancock, N.Y. (13783) 276/K7
Hancock (co.), Ohio 284/C3
Hancock (co.), Tenn. 237/P7
Hancock○, Vt. (05748) 268/B4
Hancock (co.), W. Va. 312/E2
Hancock, W. Va. (25424) 312/K3
Hancock, Wis. (54943) 317/G7
Hancocks Bridge, N.J. (08038) 273/C4
Hand (co.), S. Dak. 298/L4
Handa (isl.), Scotland 15/C2
Handan (Hantan), China 77/H4
Handan, China 54/N6
Handel, Sask. 181/C3
Handeni, Tanzania 115/G5
Handies (peak), Colo. 208/E7
Handley, W. Va. (25102) 312/D6
Handlová, Czech. 41/E2
Handsom, Va. (23859) 307/O7
Handsworth, Sask. 181/J6
Haney, Br. Col. 184/L3
Hanford, Calif. (93230) 204/F7
Hanford Reservation, Wash. 310/F4
Hangayn Nuruu (mts.), Mongolia 77/E2
Hangchow (Hangzhou), China 77/J5
Hanggin, China 77/G4
Hanging Rock, Ohio (45635) 284/E8
Hangklip (cape), S. Africa 118/F7
Hangö, Finland 18/N7
Hangöudd (prom.), Finland 18/N7
Hangzhou (Hangchow), China 77/J5
Hangzhou, China 54/N6
Hangzhou Wan (bay), China 77/K5
Hanh, Mongolia 77/F1
Hani, Turkey 63/J3
Haniqra, Rosh (cape), Israel 65/C1
Hanish (isls.), Yemen Arab Rep. 59/D7
Hankinson, N. Dak. (58041) 282/S7
Hanko (Hangö), Finland 18/N7
Hanks, N. Dak. (†58856) 282/C2
Hanksville, Utah (84734) 304/D5
Hanle, India 68/D2
Hanley, Sask. 181/E4
Hanley Falls, Minn. (56245) 255/C6
Hanley Hills, Mo. (†63101) 261/P2
Hanlontown, Iowa (50444) 229/G2
Hanmer, N. Zealand 100/D5
Hann (mt.), W. Australia 92/D1
Hanna, Alberta 182/E4
Hanna, Alta. 162/E5
Hanna, Ind. (46340) 227/D2
Hanna, La. (71035) 238/D3
Hanna, Okla. (74845) 288/P4
Hanna, Utah (84031) 304/D3
Hanna, Wyo. (82327) 319/F4
Hanna City, Ill. (61536) 222/D3
Hannaford, N. Dak. (58448) 282/O5
Hannah, N. Dak. (58239) 282/N2
Hannah (bay), Ontario 175/D2
Hannawa Falls, N.Y. (13647) 276/L1
Hannibal, Mo. (63401) 261/K3
Hannibal, Mo. 188/H3
Hannibal, N.Y. (13074) 276/G4
Hannibal, Ohio (43931) 284/J6
Hannibal, Wis. (54439) 317/E5
Hanno, Japan 81/O2
Hannover, N. Dak. (58543) 282/H5
Hannover, W. Germany 7/E3
Hannover, W. Germany 22/C2
Hannuit (Hannut), Belgium 27/G7
Hannut, Belgium 27/G7
Hanöbukten (bay), Sweden 18/J9
Hanoi (cap.), Vietnam 2/Q4
Hanoi (cap.), Vietnam 54/M7
Hanover (isl.), Chile 120/B8
Hanover (isl.), Chile 138/D9
Hanover, Conn. (06350) 210/G2
Hanover, Ill. (61041) 222/C1
Hanover, Ind. (47243) 227/F7
Hanover, Kansas (66945) 232/F2
Hanover○, Maine (04237) 243/B7
Hanover, Md. (21201) 245/M4
Hanover○, Mass. (02339) 249/L4
Hanover, Mich. (49241) 250/E6
Hanover, Minn. (55341) 255/E5
Hanover, N.H. (03755) 268/C4
Hanover○, N.H. (03755) 268/C4
Hanover, N. Mex. (88041) 274/A6
Hanover, Ohio (†43055) 284/F5
Hanover, Ontario 177/C3
Hanover, Pa. (17331) 294/J6
Hanover (co.), Va. 307/N5
Hanover, Va. (23069) 307/O5
Hanover, W. Va. (24839) 312/C7
Hanover Park, Ill. (60103) 222/A5
Hanoverton, Ohio (44423) 284/J4
Hansboro, N. Dak. (58339) 282/M2
Hansell, Iowa (50640) 229/G3
Hansen, Idaho (83334) 220/D7
Hansford (co.), Texas 303/C1
Han Shui (riv.), China 77/H5
Hanska, Minn. (56041) 255/D6
Hans Lollik (isls.), Virgin Is. (U.S.) 161/B4
Hanson, Ky. (42413) 237/G6
Hanson, Mass. (02341) 249/L4
Hanson○, Mass. (02341) 249/L4
Hanson (bay), N. Zealand 100/E7
Hanson (riv.), North. Terr. 93/C6
Hanson, Okla. (†74955) 288/S4
Hanson (co.), S. Dak. 298/O6
Hansonville, Va. (†24266) 307/D7
Hanstholm, Denmark 21/B3
Hanston, Kansas (67849) 232/C3
Hansville, Wash. (98340) 310/C3
Hantan (Handan), China 77/H4
Hants (co.), Nova Scotia 168/D4
Hant's Harbour, Newf. 166/D2
Hantsport, Nova Scotia 168/D3
Hantzsch (riv.), N.W. Terrs. 187/L3
Hanumangarh, India 68/C3
Hanwood, N.S. Wales 97/C4
Hanyuan, China 77/F6
Hanzhong (Hanchung), China 77/G5
Hao (atoll), Fr. Poly. 87/N7
Haouach, Wadi (dry riv.), Chad 111/C4
Haparanda, Sweden 18/N4
Hapeville, Georgia (30354) 217/K2
Happy, Ky. (41746) 237/P6
Happy, Texas (79042) 303/C3
Happy Adventure, Newf. 166/D2
Happy Camp, Calif. (96039) 204/B2
Happy Jack, Ariz. (86024) 198/D4
Happy Jack, La. (†70083) 238/L7
Happy Valley, Oreg. (†97222) 291/B2
Happy Valley-Goose Bay, Newf. 166/B3
Haql, Saudi Arabia 59/C4
Harad, Saudi Arabia 59/E5
Harads, Sweden 18/M3
Harahan, La. (70123) 238/O4
Haraja, Saudi Arabia 59/D6
Haralson (co.), Georgia 217/B3
Haralson, Georgia (30229) 217/C4
Haramachi, Japan 81/K5
Harar (prov.), Ethiopia 111/H6
Harar, Ethiopia 111/H6
Harar, Ethiopia 102/G4
Harardera, Somalia 115/J3
Harare (Salisbury) (cap.), Zimbabwe 102/E6
Haraz, Chad 111/C5
Harbel, Liberia 106/B7
Harbeson, Del. (19951) 245/S6
Harbin, China 77/L2
Harbin, China 2/R3
Harbin, China 54/O5
Harbine, Nebr. (†68377) 264/G4
Harbinger, N.C. (27941) 281/T2
Harboør, Denmark 21/B4
Harbor, Oreg. (97415) 291/C5
Harbor Beach, Mich. (48441) 250/G5
Harbor City, Calif. (90710) 204/C11
Harborcreek, Pa. (16421) 294/C1
Harbor Springs, Mich. (49740) 250/D3
Harborton, Va. (23389) 307/S5
Harbor View, Ohio (43434) 284/C2
Harbour (isl.), Bahamas 156/C1
Harbour Breton, Newf. 166/C4
Harbour Deep, Newf. 166/C3
Harbour Grace, Newf. 166/D2
Harbour Grace, Newf. 162/L6
Harbour Main, Newf. 166/D2
Harbourton, N.J. (†08530) 273/D3
Harbourville, Nova Scotia 168/D3
Harburg-Wilhelmsburg, W. Germany 22/C2
Hårby, Denmark 21/D7
Harco, Ill. (†62935) 222/E6
Harcourt, Iowa (50544) 229/E4
Harcourt, New Bruns. 170/E2
Harcourt, Ontario 177/F2
Harcuvar (mts.), Ariz. 198/B5
Harda, India 68/D4
Hardangerfjord (fjord), Norway 18/D7
Hardangerfjord (fjord), Norway 7/E3
Hardangervidda (plat.), Norway 18/E6
Hardaway, Ala. (36039) 195/G6
Hardburly, Ky. (41747) 237/P6
Hardee (co.), Fla. 212/E4
Hardee, Miss. (†39177) 256/C5
Hardeeville, S.C. (29927) 296/E7
Hardeman (co.), Tenn. 237/C10
Hardeman (co.), Texas 303/E3
Hardenberg, Netherlands 27/J3
Harden City, Okla. (74846) 288/N5
Harderwijk, Netherlands 27/H4
Hardesty, Okla. (73944) 288/D1

380 Hardieville

Hardieville, Alberta 182/D5
Hardin (co.), Ill. 222/E6
Hardin, Ill. (62047) 222/C4
Hardin (co.), Iowa 229/G4
Hardin (co.), Ky. 237/K5
Hardin, Ky. (42048) 237/E7
Hardin, Mo. (64035) 261/E4
Hardin, Mont. (59034) 262/J5
Hardin (co.), Ohio 284/C4
Hardin (co.), Tenn. 237/E10
Hardin (co.), Texas 303/K7
Harding (co.), Ohio 284/C4
Harding (lake), Ala. 195/H5
Harding (lake), Georgia 217/B5
Harding, Manitoba 179/B5
Harding, Minn. (56364) 255/E4
Harding (co.), N. Mex. 274/F3
Harding (pt.), Nova Scotia 168/D5
Harding (co.), S. Dak. 298/B2
Harding, W. Va. (†26250) 312/G5
Harding Icefield, Alaska 196/C2
Hardingville, N.J. (†08343) 273/C4
Hardinsburg, Ind. (47125) 227/E8
Hardinsburg, Ky. (40143) 237/H5
Hardin Springs, Ky. (†42712) 237/J5
Hardinville, Ill. (†62449) 222/F5
Hardinxveld-Giessendam, Netherlands 27/G5
Hardisty, Alberta 182/E3
Hardisty (lake), N.W. Terrs. 187/G3
Hardman, Oreg. (†97836) 291/H2
Hardoi, India 68/E3
Hardshell, Ky. (41348) 237/P6
Hardt (mts.), W. Germany 22/C4
Hardtner, Kansas (67057) 232/D4
Hardwar, India 68/D2
Hardwick (Midway-Hardwick), Georgia (31034) 217/F4
Hardwick○, Mass. (01037) 249/F3
Hardwick, Minn. (56134) 255/B7
Hardwick, Vt. (05843) 268/C2
Hardwick○, Vt. (05843) 268/C2
Hardwick (lake), Vt. 268/C2
Hardwicke, New Bruns. 170/E1
Hardwicke Island, Br. Col. 184/E5
Hardwood Ridge, New Bruns. 170/D2
Hardy, Ark. (72542) 202/H1
Hardy (pen.), Chile 138/F11
Hardy, Iowa (50545) 229/E3
Hardy, Ky. (41531) 237/S5
Hardy, Miss. (†38901) 256/E3
Hardy, Nebr. (68943) 264/G4
Hardy, Okla. (†74641) 288/N1
Hardy, Sask. 181/G6
Hardy, Va. (24101) 307/J6
Hardy (co.), W. Va. 312/J4
Hardyville, Ky. (42746) 237/K6
Hare (bay), Newf. 166/C3
Hare (fjord), N.W. Terrs. 187/K1
Hare Bay, Newf. 166/D4
Harelbeke, Belgium 27/C7
Harfleur, France 28/D3
Harford (co.), Md. 245/N2
Harford, N.Y. (13784) 276/H6
Harford, Pa. (18823) 294/L2
Hargeysa, Somalia 115/H2
Hargeysa, Somalia 102/G4
Hargill, Texas (78549) 303/F11
Hargrave, Manitoba 179/A5
Hargwen, Alberta 182/B3
Har Hu (lake), China 77/E4
Hari (riv.), Indonesia 85/C6
Harib, Yemen Arab Rep. 59/E7
Haricha Hamada (des.), Mali 106/D4
Harim, Syria 63/G4
Harima (sea), Japan 81/G6
Harima, Jordan 65/D2
Haringey, England 10/B5
Haringey, England 13/H8
Haringvliet (str.), Netherlands 27/E5
Hariq, Saudi Arabia 59/E5
Harirud (riv.), Afghanistan 68/A1
Harirud (riv.), Afghanistan 59/H3
Hari Rud (riv.), Iran 66/M3
Haris, West Bank 65/C3
Harjavalta, Finland 18/M6
Harjo, Okla. (†74854) 288/N4
Harkaway, Victoria 97/K5
Harkers Island, N.C. (28531) 281/R5
Harkiko, Ethiopia 111/G4
Harlan, Ind. (46743) 227/H2
Harlan, Iowa (51537) 229/C5
Harlan, Kansas (67641) 232/D2
Harlan (co.), Ky. 237/P7
Harlan, Ky. (40831) 237/P7
Harlan (co.), Nebr. 264/E4
Harlan, Oreg. (†97343) 291/D3
Harlan County (lake), Nebr. 264/E5
Harlech, Wales 10/E4
Harlech, Wales 13/C5
Harlem, Fla. (33440) 212/F5
Harlem, Georgia (30814) 217/H4
Harlem, Mont. (59526) 262/H2
Harlem Springs, Ohio (44631) 284/J4
Harleston, England 13/J5
Harleton, Texas (75651) 303/K5
Hårlev, Denmark 21/F7
Harleyville, S.C. (29448) 296/G5
Harlingen, Netherlands 27/G2
Harlingen, N.J. (†08502) 273/D3
Harlingen, Texas (78550) 303/G11
Harlingen, Texas 188/G5
Harlow, England 13/H7
Harlow, N. Dak. (58340) 282/M3
Harlowton, Mont. (59036) 262/F4
Harman, W. Va. (26270) 312/G5
Harman-Maxie, Va. (24618) 307/D6
Harmans, Md. (21077) 245/M4
Harmattan, Alberta 182/C4
Harmon, Ill. (61042) 222/D2
Harmon (co.), Okla. 288/G5
Harmon, Okla. (73832) 288/G2
Harmonsburg, Pa. (16422) 294/B2
Harmony, Ark. (†72830) 202/D2
Harmony, Ind. (47853) 227/C5
Harmony, Maine (04942) 243/D6
Harmony○, Maine (04942) 243/D6
Harmony, Minn. (55939) 255/F7
Harmony, N.C. (28634) 281/H3
Harmony, Pa. (16037) 294/B4
Harmony, R.I. (02829) 249/H5
Harmony, W. Va. (25246) 312/D5
Harms, Tenn. (†37334) 237/H10
Harned, Ky. (40144) 237/J5
Harnett (co.), N.C. 281/M4
Harney (lake), Fla. 212/F3
Harney, Md. (†21787) 245/K2
Harney (co.), Oreg. 291/H4
Harney (lake), Oreg. 188/C2
Harney, Oreg. (†97720) 291/J4
Harney (lake), Oreg. 291/H4
Harney (peak), S. Dak. 298/B6
Härnösand, Sweden 18/L5
Haro, Spain 33/E1
Haro (str.), Wash. 310/B2
Harold, Fla. (32563) 212/B6
Harold, Ky. (41635) 237/R5
Harp (lake), Newf. 166/B2
Harper, Ill. (†61030) 222/D1
Harper, Iowa (52231) 229/J6
Harper (co.), Kansas 232/D4
Harper, Kansas (67058) 232/D4
Harper, Liberia 106/C8
Harper, Liberia 102/B4
Harper (co.), Okla. 288/G1
Harper, Oreg. (97906) 291/K4
Harper, Texas (78631) 303/E7
Harper, Wash. (†98366) 310/A2
Harper, W. Va. (25851) 312/D7
Harpers Ferry, Iowa (52146) 229/L2
Harpers Ferry, W. Va. (25425) 312/L4
Harpers Ferry Nat'l Hist. Park, Md. 245/G3
Harpers Ferry Nat'l Hist. Park, W. Va. 312/L4
Harpersville, Ala. (35078) 195/F4
Harperville, Miss. (39080) 256/E6
Harper Woods, Mich. (48225) 250/B6
Harpeth (riv.), Tenn. 237/G8
Harpster, Idaho (†83521) 220/C4
Harpster, Ohio (43323) 284/D4
Harpswell○, Maine (†04011) 243/D8
Harpswell Center, Maine (†04011) 243/D8
Harpursville, N.Y. (13787) 276/J6
Harput, Turkey 63/H3
Harquahala (mts.), Ariz. 198/B5
Harrah, Okla. (73045) 288/M4
Harrah, Wash. (98933) 310/E4
Harran, Turkey 63/H4
Harrell, Ark. (71745) 202/F7
Harrells, N.C. (28444) 281/N5
Harrellsville, N.C. (27942) 281/R2
Harricana (riv.), Québec 174/B3
Harriet, Ark. (72939) 202/E2
Harrietsfield, Nova Scotia 168/E4
Harrietta, Mich. (49638) 250/D4
Harriettsville, Ohio (†45745) 284/H6
Harrigan Cove, Nova Scotia 168/F4
Harriman, N.Y. (10926) 276/M8
Harriman, Oreg. (†97601) 291/E5
Harriman, Tenn. (37748) 237/M9
Harriman (res.), Vt. 268/B6
Harrington (sound), Bermuda 156/G3
Harrington, Del. (19952) 245/R5
Harrington○, Maine (04643) 243/H6
Harrington (lake), Maine 243/E4
Harrington, N.S. Wales 97/G2
Harrington, S. Dak. (†57551) 298/G7
Harrington, Wash. (99134) 310/G3
Harrington Harbour, Québec 174/F2
Harrington Park, N.J. (07640) 273/C1
Harris, Calif. (†95440) 204/B3
Harris (co.), Georgia 217/C5
Harris, Iowa (51345) 229/C2
Harris, Kansas (†66032) 232/G3
Harris, Mich. (49845) 250/B3
Harris, Minn. (55032) 255/F5
Harris, Mo. (64645) 261/F2
Harris, Okla. (†74740) 288/S7
Harris, Sask. 181/D4
Harris (dist.), Scotland 15/B3
Harris (dist.), Scotland 10/C2
Harris (sound), Scotland 15/A3
Harris (sound), Scotland 10/C2
Harris (lake), S. Australia 94/D4
Harris, Tenn. (†38261) 237/C8
Harris (co.), Texas 303/J8
Harrisburg, Ark. (72432) 202/J2
Harrisburg, Ill. (62946) 222/E6
Harrisburg, Ind. (†47331) 227/G5
Harrisburg, Mo. (65256) 261/H4
Harrisburg, Nebr. (69345) 264/A3
Harrisburg, N.C. (28075) 281/H4
Harrisburg, Ohio (43126) 284/D6
Harrisburg, Oreg. (97446) 291/D3
Harrisburg (cap.), Pa. 188/L2
Harrisburg (cap.), Pa. 146/L5
Harrisburg (cap.), Pa. (*17101) 294/H5
Harrisburg, S. Dak. (57032) 298/R7
Harrismith, S. Africa 118/D5
Harrison (bay), Alaska 196/H1
Harrison, Ark. (72601) 202/D1
Harrison (lake), Br. Col. 184/M2
Harrison, Georgia (31035) 217/G5
Harrison, Idaho (83833) 220/B2
Harrison, Ill. (†61072) 222/D1
Harrison (co.), Ind. 227/E8
Harrison (co.), Iowa 229/B5
Harrison (co.), Ky. 237/N4
Harrison○, Maine (04040) 243/B7
Harrison, Mich. (48625) 250/E4
Harrison (co.), Miss. 256/F10
Harrison (co.), Mo. 261/E2
Harrison, Mont. (59735) 262/E5
Harrison, Nebr. (69346) 264/A2
Harrison (cape), Newf. 166/C3
Harrison (cape), Newf. 162/L5
Harrison, N.J. (07029) 273/B2
Harrison, N.Y. (10528) 276/P6
Harrison (co.), Ohio 284/H5
Harrison, Ohio (45030) 284/A9
Harrison, S. Dak. (57344) 298/M7
Harrison, Tenn. (37341) 237/L10
Harrison (co.), Texas 303/K5
Harrison (co.), W. Va. 312/F4
Harrison, Wis. (†54435) 317/G5
Harrisonburg, La. (71340) 238/G3
Harrisonburg (I.C.), Va. (22801) 307/K4
Harrison Hot Springs, Br. Col. 184/M3
Harrison Valley, Pa. (16927) 294/G2
Harrisonville, Ill. (†62295) 222/C5
Harrisonville, Mo. (64701) 261/D5
Harrisonville, N.J. (08039) 273/C4
Harrisonville, Ohio (†45769) 284/F7
Harrisonville, Pa. (17228) 294/F6
Harriston, Miss. (39081) 256/C7
Harriston, Ontario 177/D4
Harristown, Ill. (62537) 222/D4
Harrisville, Ind. (†47390) 227/H4
Harrisville, Mich. (48740) 250/F4
Harrisville, Miss. (39082) 256/D7
Harrisville○, N.H. (03450) 268/C6
Harrisville, N.Y. (13648) 276/K2
Harrisville, Ohio (43974) 284/J5
Harrisville, Pa. (16038) 294/B3
Harrisville, R.I. (02830) 249/H5
Harrisville, Utah (†84401) 304/C2
Harrisville, W. Va. (26362) 312/E4
Harris Wash (creek), Utah 304/C6
Harrod, Ohio (45850) 284/C4
Harrodsburg, Ind. (47434) 227/D6
Harrodsburg, Ky. (40330) 237/M5
Harrods Creek, Ky. (40027) 237/K4
Harrogate, Br. Col. 184/J5
Harrogate, England 13/J1
Harrogate, England 10/F4
Harrogate-Shawanee, Tenn. (37752) 237/O8
Harrold, S. Dak. (57536) 298/K4
Harrold, Texas (76364) 303/F3
Harrop (lake), Manitoba 179/G2
Harrow, England 13/G8
Harrow, England 10/B5
Harrow, Ontario 177/B5
Harrow, Victoria 97/A5
Harrowby, Manitoba 179/A4
Harrowsmith, Ontario 177/H3
Harry Strunk (lake), Nebr. 264/D4
Harsens Island, Mich. (48028) 250/G6
Harshaw, Wis. (54529) 317/G4
Harstad, Norway 18/K2
Hart (lake), Fla. 212/E3
Hart (co.), Georgia 217/G2
Hart (co.), Ky. 237/K6
Hart, Mich. (49420) 250/C5
Hart (lake), Oreg. 291/H5
Hart (mt.), Oreg. 291/H5
Hart, Texas (79043) 303/B3
Hart (riv.), Yukon 187/E3
Hartbees (riv.), S. Africa 118/C5
Hartberg, Austria 41/C3
Harte, Manitoba 179/C4
Harte (mt.), Manitoba 179/A2
Hartell, Alberta 182/C4
Hartfield, Va. (23071) 307/R5
Hartford, Ala. (36344) 195/G8
Hartford, Ark. (72938) 202/B3
Hartford (co.), Conn. 210/D1
Hartford (cap.), Conn. 146/L5
Hartford (cap.), Conn. 188/M2
Hartford (cap.), Conn. (*06101) 210/E1
Hartford, Ill. (62048) 222/A2
Hartford, Iowa (50118) 229/G6
Hartford, Kansas (66854) 232/F3
Hartford, Ky. (42347) 237/H6
Hartford○, Maine (†04221) 243/C7
Hartford, Mich. (49057) 250/C6
Hartford, N.J. (†08057) 273/D4
Hartford, N.Y. (12838) 276/O4
Hartford, Ohio (†43013) 284/E5
Hartford, Ohio (44424) 284/J3
Hartford, S. Dak. (57033) 298/P6
Hartford, Tenn. (37753) 237/P9
Hartford○, Vt. (05047) 268/C4
Hartford, W. Va. (25247) 312/C4
Hartford, Wis. (53027) 317/K9
Hartford City, Ind. (47348) 227/G4
Harthill, Scotland 15/C2
Hartington, Nebr. (68739) 264/G2
Hartington, Ontario 177/H3
Hartland○, Conn. (†06091) 210/D1
Hartland, England 13/C7
Hartland (pt.), England 13/C6
Hartland (pt.), England 10/D5
Hartland, Maine (04943) 243/D6
Hartland○, Maine (04943) 243/D6
Hartland, Mich. (48029) 250/F6
Hartland, Minn. (56042) 255/E7
Hartland, New Bruns. 170/C2
Hartland○, Vt. (05048) 288/C4
Hartland, W. Va. (†25043) 312/D6
Hartland, Wis. (53029) 317/J1
Hartland Four Corners, Vt. (05049) 268/C4
Hartlepool, England 10/F3
Hartlepool, England 13/F3
Hartleton, Pa. (17829) 294/H4
Hartley, Iowa (51346) 229/C2
Hartley (co.), Texas 303/B2
Hartley, Texas (79044) 303/B2
Hartley, Zimbabwe 118/E3
Hartleyville, Alberta 182/D5
Hartline, Wash. (99135) 310/F3
Hartly, Del. (19953) 245/R4
Hartman, Ark. (72840) 202/C3
Hartman, Colo. (81043) 208/P6
Hartney, Manitoba 179/B5
Harts (pass), Wash. 310/E2
Harts, W. Va. (25524) 312/B6
Hartsburg, Ill. (62643) 222/D3
Hartsburg, Mo. (65039) 261/H5
Hartsdale, N.Y. (10530) 276/P6
Hartsel, Colo. (80449) 208/H4
Hartselle, Ala. (35640) 195/E2
Hartsfield, Georgia (31756) 217/E8
Hartsgrove, Ohio (†44085) 284/J2
Hartshorn, Mo. (65479) 261/J8
Hartshorne, Okla. (74547) 288/R5
Harts Range, North. Terr. 88/F4
Harts Range, North. Terr. 93/D7
Hartstown, Pa. (16131) 294/B2
Hartsville, Ind. (47244) 227/F6
Hartsville, Mass. (†01230) 249/B4
Hartsville, S.C. (29550) 296/G3
Hartsville, Tenn. (37074) 237/J8
Hartville, Mo. (65667) 261/G8
Hartville, Ohio (44632) 284/H4
Hartville, Wyo. (82215) 319/H3
Hartwell, Georgia (30643) 217/G2
Hartwell (dam), Georgia 217/G2
Hartwell (lake), Georgia 217/G2
Hartwell, Mo. (†64788) 261/E6
Hartwell (dam), S.C. 296/B3
Hartwell (lake), S.C. 296/A3
Hartwick, Iowa (52232) 229/J5
Hartwick, N.Y. (13348) 276/K5
Hartz (mt.), Tasmania 99/C5
Harug el Asued, El (mts.), Libya 111/C2
Haruniye, Turkey 63/G4
Har Us Nuur (lake), Mongolia 77/D2
Harvard (mt.), Colo. 208/G5
Harvard, Idaho (83834) 220/B3
Harvard, Ill. (60033) 222/E1
Harvard, Iowa (†50008) 229/G7
Harvard○, Mass. (01451) 249/H2
Harvard, Nebr. (68944) 264/F4
Harvel, Ill. (62538) 222/D4
Harvest, Ala. (35749) 195/E1
Harvester, Mo. (63303) 261/N2
Harvey, Ill. (60426) 222/B6
Harvey, Iowa (50119) 229/H6
Harvey (co.), Kansas 232/E3
Harvey, La. (70058) 238/O4
Harvey, Albert, New Bruns. 170/F3
Harvey, York, New Bruns. 170/D3
Harvey (lake), New Bruns. 170/C3
Harvey (mt.), New Bruns. 170/D3
Harvey, N. Dak. (58341) 282/L4
Harvey, W. Australia 88/B6
Harvey, W. Australia 92/A2
Harvey, W. Va. (25852) 312/D7
Harvey Cedars, N.J. (08008) 273/E4
Harveys (lake), Vt. 268/C3
Harveysburg, Ohio (45032) 284/C7
Harveys Lake, Pa. (18618) 294/E7
Harveyton, Ky. (†41718) 237/P6
Harveyville, Kansas (66431) 232/F3
Harviell, Mo. (63945) 261/M9
Harwich, England 13/J6
Harwich, England 10/G5
Harwich, Mass. (02645) 249/O6
Harwich○, Mass. (02645) 249/O6
Harwich Port, Mass. (02646) 249/O6
Harwinton, Conn. (06791) 210/C1
Harwinton○, Conn. (06791) 210/C1
Harwood, Mo. (64750) 261/D7
Harwood, N. Dak. (58042) 282/S6
Harwood, Ontario 177/F3
Harwood, Texas (78632) 303/G8
Harwood Heights, Ill. (60656) 222/B5
Harwood Island, N.S. Wales 97/G1
Harworth, England 13/F4
Haryana (state), India 68/D3
Harz (mts.), E. Germany 22/D3
Harz (mts.), W. Germany 22/D3
Harzgerode, E. Germany 22/D3
Hasa, Wadi el (dry riv.), Jordan 65/E5
Hasan Dağı, Büyük (mt.), Turkey 63/E3
Hasbrouck Heights, N.J. (07604) 273/B2
Hase (riv.), W. Germany 22/B2
Haseke (prov.), Syria 63/J4
Haselünne, W. Germany 22/B2
Hasenkamp, Argentina 143/F5
Hashtpar, Iran 66/F2
Haskeir (isl.), Scotland 15/A3
Haskell, Ark. (†72015) 202/E4
Haskell (co.), Kansas 232/B4
Haskell, N.J. (07420) 273/A1
Haskell (co.), Okla. 288/R4
Haskell, Okla. (74436) 288/P3
Haskell (co.), Texas 303/E4
Haskell, Texas (79521) 303/E4
Haskett, Manitoba 179/D5
Haskins, Iowa (†52201) 229/K6
Haskins, Ohio (43525) 284/C3
Haslach an der Mühl, Austria 41/C2
Hasle, Denmark 21/F8
Haslemere, England 13/G6
Haslemere, England 10/F5
Haslet, Texas (76052) 303/E2
Haslett, Mich. (48840) 250/E6
Haslev, Denmark 21/E7
Haslingden, England 13/H1
Hassa, Turkey 63/G4
Hassan, India 68/D6
Hassayampa (riv.), Ariz. 198/C5
Hasse, Texas (76456) 303/F6
Hassel (sound), N.W. Terrs. 187/J2
Hassel (isl.), Virgin Is. (U.S.) 161/B4
Hassell, N.C. (27841) 281/P3
Hasselt, Belgium 27/G7
Hasselt, Netherlands 27/J3
Hassfurt, W. Germany 22/D3
Hassi Messaoud, Algeria 106/F2
Hassi R'Mel, Algeria 106/E2
Hässleholm, Sweden 18/H8
Hassloch, W. Germany 22/C4
Haster, Scotland 15/E2
Hastière, Belgium 27/F8
Hastings, England 10/G5
Hastings, England 13/H7
Hastings, Fla. (32045) 212/E2
Hastings, Iowa (51540) 229/C6
Hastings, Mich. (49058) 250/D6
Hastings, Minn. (55033) 255/F6
Hastings, Nebr. 188/G2
Hastings, Nebr. (68901) 264/F4
Hastings, N. Zealand 100/F3
Hastings, N. Dak. (†58049) 282/O6
Hastings, Okla. (73548) 288/K6
Hastings (county), Ontario 177/G3
Hastings, Ontario 177/G3
Hastings, Pa. (16646) 294/E4
Hastings On Hudson, N.Y. (10706) 276/O6
Hasty, Ark. (72640) 202/D1
Hasty, Colo. (81044) 208/O6
Hasvik, Norway 18/M1
Haswell, Colo. (81045) 208/N6
Hat (peak), Calif. 204/E2
Hat (creek), S. Dak. 298/B7
Hatay (prov.), Turkey 63/G4
Hatay (Antakya), Turkey 63/G4
Hatboro, Pa. (19040) 294/M5
Hatch, N. Mex. (87937) 274/B6
Hatch, Utah (84735) 304/B6
Hatchechubbee, Ala. (36858) 195/H6
Hatcher, Georgia (†31754) 217/B7
Hatches Creek, North. Terr. 88/F4
Hatches Creek, North. Terr. 93/D6
Hatchet (mts.), N. Mex. 274/A7
Hatchett (pt.), Conn. 210/G3
Hatchie (riv.), Tenn. 237/B9
Hatchineha (lake), Fla. 212/E3
Hațeg, Romania 45/F3
Hatfield, Ark. (71945) 202/B5
Hatfield, England 13/H7
Hatfield, Ind. (47617) 227/C9
Hatfield, Ky. (†41514) 237/S5
Hatfield, Mass. (01038) 249/D3
Hatfield○, Mass. (01038) 249/D3
Hatfield, Minn. (56135) 255/B7
Hatfield, Mo. (64458) 261/D1
Hatfield, N.S. Wales 97/B3
Hatfield, Pa. (19440) 294/M5
Hatfield, Sask. 181/F4
Hatfield, Wis. (†54754) 317/E7
Hatfield Point, New Bruns. 170/E3
Hatgal, Mongolia 77/E1
Hathaway, Mont. (59333) 262/K4
Hatherleigh, Sask. 181/C2
Hathras, India 68/D3
Hatiba, Ras (cape), Saudi Arabia 59/C5
Ha Tien, Vietnam 72/E5
Hatillo, P. Rico 161/B1
Ha Tinh, Vietnam 72/E3
Hatira (mt.), Israel 65/B6
Hatley, Miss. (†38821) 256/H3
Hatley, Québec 172/F4
Hatley, Wis. (54440) 317/H6
Hato, Neth. Ant. 161/G8
Hato del Volcán, Panama 154/F6
Hato Mayor, Dom. Rep. 158/F6
Hato Rey, P. Rico 161/E1
Hatseva, Israel 65/D5
Hattem, Netherlands 27/H4
Hatteras (cape), N.C. 146/L6
Hatteras (cape), N.C. 188/M3
Hatteras, N.C. (27943) 281/T4
Hatteras (cape), N.C. 281/U4
Hatteras (inlet), N.C. 281/T4
Hatteras (isl.), N.C. 281/U4
Hatteras (cape), U.S. 2/F4
Hattiesburg, Miss. 188/H4
Hattiesburg, Miss. (39401) 256/F8
Hattieville, Ark. (72063) 202/E3
Hattieville, Belize 154/C2
Hatton, Ala. (†35672) 195/D1
Hatton, N. Dak. (58240) 282/R4
Hatton, Sask. 181/B5
Hatton, Scotland 15/G3
Hatton, Utah (†84637) 304/B5
Hatton, Wash. (99332) 310/G4
Hatuey, Cuba 158/G3
Hatvan, Hungary 41/E3
Hat Yai, Thailand 72/C6
Hatzic, Br. Col. 184/L3
Hau Bon, Vietnam 72/E4
Haubstadt, Ind. (47639) 227/B8
Haud (reg.), Ethiopia 111/J6
Haud (plat.), Somalia 115/J2
Haugan, Mont. (59842) 262/A3
Hauge, Norway 18/E7
Haugen, Wis. (54841) 317/C4
Haugesund, Norway 7/E3
Haugesund, Norway 18/D7
Haughton, La. (71037) 238/C1
Hauhungaroa (range), N. Zealand 100/E3
Haukivesi (lake), Finland 18/Q5
Haultain (riv.), Sask. 181/L3
Haunstetten, W. Germany 22/D4
Hauppauge, N.Y. (11787) 276/O9
Haura, P.D.R. Yemen 59/E7
Hauraki (gulf), N. Zealand 100/C1
Hauran, Wadi (dry riv.), Iraq 59/D3
Hauran, Wadi (dry riv.), Iraq 66/B4
Hauroko (lake), N. Zealand 100/A6
Hauru (pt.), Fr. Poly. 86/S12
Hauser, Idaho (†83854) 220/A2
Hauser (lake), Mont. 262/E4
Hauser, Oreg. (†97459) 291/C4
Hausstock (mt.), Switzerland 39/H3
Haut (isl.), Maine 243/G7
Haute (isl.), Nova Scotia 168/C3
Haute-Corse (dept.), France 28/B6
Haute-Garonne (dept.), France 28/D6
Haute-Loire (dept.), France 28/E5
Haute-Marne (dept.), France 28/F3
Hauterive, Québec 172/A1
Hauterive, Québec 174/D3
Hautes-Alpes (dept.), France 28/G5
Haute-Saône (dept.), France 28/G4
Haute-Savoie (dept.), France 28/G5
Hautes-Pyrénées (dept.), France 28/D6
Haute-Vienne (dept.), France 28/D5
Hautmont, France 28/F2
Haut-Rhin (dept.), France 28/G4
Hauts-de-Seine (dept.), France 28/A2
Haut-Zaïre (prov.), Zaire 115/E3
Hauula, Hawaii (96717) 218/E1
Havaco, W. Va. (24841) 312/C8
Havana, Ala. (35467) 195/C5
Havana, Ark. (72842) 202/D3
Havana (cap.), Cuba 156/A2
Havana (cap.), Cuba 2/E4
Havana (cap.), Cuba 146/K7
Havana (cap.), Cuba 158/C1
Havana, Fla. (32333) 212/B1
Havana, Ill. (62644) 222/D3
Havana, Kansas (67347) 232/G4
Havana, Minn. (†55060) 255/E6
Havana, N. Dak. (58043) 282/P8
Havana, Ohio (†44890) 284/E3
Havannah (chan.), New Caled. 86/H5
Havant and Waterloo, England 13/G7
Havasu (lake) 188/D4
Havasu (lake), Ariz. 198/A4
Havasu (lake), Calif. 204/L9
Havasu (lake), U.S. 146/G6
Havasupai Ind. Res., Ariz. 198/C2
Havdrup, Denmark 21/F6
Havel (riv.), E. Germany 22/E2
Havelange, Belgium 27/G8
Havelberg, E. Germany 22/D2
Havelock, Iowa (50546) 229/D3
Havelock, New Bruns. 170/E3
Havelock, N. Zealand 100/D4
Havelock, N.C. (28532) 281/P5
Havelock, N. Dak. (†58647) 282/E7
Havelock, Ontario 177/G3
Havelock North, N. Zealand 100/F3
Haven, Kansas (67543) 232/E4
Havensville, Kansas (66432) 232/F2
Haverford○, Pa. (19041) 294/M6
Haverfordwest, Wales 10/D5
Haverfordwest, Wales 13/B6
Haverhill, England 13/H5
Haverhill, Iowa (50120) 229/H5
Haverhill, Mass. (01830) 249/K1
Haverhill○, N.H. (03765) 268/C3
Haverhill, Ohio (45636) 284/E8
Havering, England 10/C5
Havering, England 13/J8
Haverstraw, N.Y. (10927) 276/M8
Havertown, Pa. (19083) 294/M6
Haviland, Kansas (67059) 232/C4
Haviland, Ohio (45851) 284/A3
Havillah, Wash. (†98855) 310/F2
Havířov, Czech. 41/E2
Havlíčkův Brod, Czech. 41/C2
Havran, Turkey 63/B3
Havre, Mont. 146/G5
Havre, Mont. 188/E1
Havre, Mont. (59501) 262/G2
Havre Boucher, Nova Scotia 168/G3
Havre de Grace, Md. (21078) 245/O2
Havre-Saint-Pierre, Québec 174/E2
Havre-St-Pierre, Que. 162/K5
Havsa, Turkey 63/B2
Havza, Turkey 63/F2
Haw (riv.), N.C. 281/K2
Hawaii 188/F5
HAWAII 218
Hawaii (co.), Hawaii 218/K7
Hawaii (isl.), Hawaii 87/L4
Hawaii (isl.), Hawaii 188/F6
Hawaii (isl.), Hawaii 218/H5
Hawaii (state), U.S. 2/B4
Hawaii (state), U.S. 87/K4
Hawaiian (isls.) 87/J3
Hawaii Kai, Hawaii (96825) 218/F2
Hawaii Nat'l Park, Hawaii (96718) 218/J6
Hawaii Volcanoes Nat'l Park, Hawaii 218/H6
Hawara, Jordan 65/D2
Hawarden, Iowa (51023) 229/A2
Hawarden, N. Zealand 100/D5
Hawarden, Sask. 181/E4
Hawarden, Wales 13/G2
Hawea (lake), N. Zealand 100/B6
Hawera, N. Zealand 100/E3
Hawes, England 13/E3
Hawesville, Ky. (42348) 237/H5
Hawi, Hawaii (96719) 218/G3
Hawick, Minn. (56246) 255/D5
Hawick, Scotland 10/E3
Hawick, Scotland 15/F5
Hawk (hills), Alberta 182/B1
Hawke (hills), Newf. 166/D2
Hawke (isl.), Newf. 166/C3
Hawke (riv.), Newf. 166/C3
Hawke (bay), N. Zealand 100/F3
Hawker, S. Australia 88/F6
Hawker, S. Australia 94/F4
Hawke's Bay, Newf. 166/C3
Hawkesbury (isl.), Br. Col. 184/C3
Hawkesbury, Ontario 177/K2
Hawkestone, Ontario 177/E3
Hawkeye, Iowa (52147) 229/J3
Hawkins, Mich. (†49677) 250/D5
Hawkins (co.), Tenn. 237/P8
Hawkins, Texas (75765) 303/J5
Hawkins, Wis. (54530) 317/E4
Hawkinsville, Georgia (31036) 217/E6
Hawk Junction, Ontario 175/D3
Hawk Junction, Ontario 177/J5
Hawk Point, Mo. (63349) 261/K5
Hawk Run, Pa. (16840) 294/F4
Hawks, Mich. (49743) 250/F3
Hawk Springs, Wyo. (82217) 319/H4
Hawley, Minn. (56549) 255/B4
Hawley, Pa. (18428) 294/M3
Hawley, Texas (79525) 303/E5
Hawleyville, Conn. (06440) 210/B3
Haworth, N.J. (07641) 273/C1
Haworth, Okla. (74740) 288/S7
Hawston, S. Africa 118/G7
Hawthorn, La. (†71446) 238/D4
Hawthorn, Pa. (16230) 294/D3
Hawthorn, Victoria 97/J5
Hawthorne, Calif. (90250) 204/C11
Hawthorne, Fla. (32640) 212/D2
Hawthorne, Nev. (89415) 266/C4
Hawthorne, N.J. (07507) 273/B2
Hawthorne, N.Y. (10532) 276/O6
Hawthorne, Victoria 88/L7
Hawthorne, Wis. (54842) 317/C3
Hawthorn Woods, Ill. (†60047) 222/B5
Haxby, England 13/F3
Haxtun, Colo. (80731) 208/O1
Hay (riv.) 162/E4
Hay (lake), Alberta 182/A5
Hay (riv.), Alberta 182/A5
Hay (riv.), Canada 146/G4
Hay, N. S. Wales 88/H6
Hay, N.S. Wales 97/C4
Hay (dry riv.), North. Terr. 88/F4
Hay (cape), North. Terr. 93/A3
Hay (dry riv.), North. Terr. 93/E7
Hay (lake), Ontario 177/F2

382 Herowabad

Herowabad, Iran 66/F2
Herradura, Argentina 143/E2
Herradura, Cuba 158/B1
Herreid, S. Dak. (57632) 298/K2
Herrera, Argentina 143/D2
Herrera del Duque, Spain 33/D3
Herrera de Pisuerga, Spain 33/D1
Herrero (pt.), Mexico 150/Q7
Herrick, Ill. (62431) 222/D4
Herrick, S. Dak. (57538) 298/L7
Herrick, Tasmania 99/D3
Herrick Center, Pa. (18430) 294/L2
Herrin, Ill. (62948) 222/E6
Herring Cove, Nova Scotia 168/E4
Herrings, N.Y. (13653) 276/J2
Herrington (lake), Ky. 237/M5
Herron, Mich. (49744) 250/F3
Herronton, Alberta 182/D4
Hersbruck, W. Germany 22/D4
Herschel, Sask. 181/C4
Herschel (isl.), Yukon 187/E3
Herscher, Ill. (60941) 222/E2
Herselt, Belgium 27/F6
Hersey, Mich. (49639) 250/D5
Hersey, Wis. (†54027) 317/B6
Hershey, Nebr. (69143) 264/D3
Hershey, Pa. (17033) 294/J5
Hersman, Ill. (†62353) 222/C4
Herstal, Belgium 27/H7
Hertel, Wis. (54845) 317/B4
Hertford, England 13/H7
Hertford, England 10/G5
Hertford (co.), N.C. 281/P2
Hertford, N.C. (27944) 281/S2
Hertfordshire (co.), England 13/G6
Hervás, Spain 33/D2
Herve, Belgium 27/H7
Hervey Bay, Queensland 88/J5
Hervey Bay, Queensland 95/E5
Hervey (bay), Queensland 88/J4
Hervey (bay), Queensland 95/E5
Herzberg, E. Germany 22/E3
Herzeliyya, Israel 65/B3
Herzogenbuchsee, Switzerland 39/E2
Herzogenburg, Austria 41/C2
Heshui, China 77/G4
Hesketh, Alberta 182/D4
Hesper, Iowa (†52101) 229/K2
Hesper, N. Dak. (†58348) 282/L4
Hesperange, Luxembourg 27/J9
Hesperia, Calif. (92345) 204/H9
Hesperia, Mich. (49421) 250/D5
Hespero, Alberta 182/C3
Hesperus, Colo. (81326) 208/C8
Hesperus (mt.), Colo. 208/C8
Hess, Okla. (†73539) 288/H6
Hess (riv.), Yukon 187/E3
Hesse (state), W. Germany 22/C3
Hessel, Mich. (49745) 250/E2
Hessmer, La. (71341) 238/F4
Hesston, Kansas (67062) 232/E3
Hesston, Pa. (16647) 294/F5
Hester, La. (70743) 238/L3
Hester, Okla. (†73554) 288/H5
Hesterville, Miss. (†39192) 256/E4
Hetch Hetchy (res.), Calif. 204/F6
Heth, Ark. (72346) 202/K3
Het IJ (est.), Netherlands 27/C4
Hetland, S. Dak. (57244) 298/P5
Hettick, Ill. (62649) 222/C4
Hettinger (co.), N. Dak. 282/E7
Hettinger, N. Dak. (58639) 282/E8
Hetton, England 13/J3
Hettstedt, E. Germany 22/D3
Heusden, Netherlands 27/G5
Heuvelland, Belgium 27/B7
Heuvelton, N.Y. (13654) 276/K1
Heves (co.), Hungary 41/F3
Heves, Hungary 41/F3
Heward, Sask. 181/H6
Hewins, Kansas (67024) 232/F4
Hewitt, Minn. (56453) 255/C4
Hewitt, N.J. (07421) 273/E1
Hewitt, Wis. (54441) 317/F6
Hewlett, N.Y. (11557) 276/P7
Hewlett Harbor, N.Y. (†11557) 276/P7
Hexham, England 13/E3
Hexham, England 10/E3
He Xian, China 77/H7
Hexigten, China 77/J3
Hext, Texas (76848) 303/E7
Heybeli (isl.), Turkey 63/D6
Heybridge, Tasmania 99/C3
Heyburn, Idaho (83336) 220/E7
Heyburn (res.), Okla. 288/O3
Heyden, Ontario 177/J5
Heyfield, Victoria 97/D6
Heyuan, China 77/H7
Heywood (chan.), Burma 72/B3
Heywood, England 13/H2
Heywood, Victoria 97/A6
Heyworth, Ill. (61745) 222/E3
Heze, China 77/J4
Hezuo, China 77/F5
Hialeah, Fla. 188/K5
Hialeah, Fla. (*33010) 212/B4
Hialeah Gardens, Fla. (†33010) 212/B4
Hiattville, Kansas (66747) 232/H4
Hiawassee, Georgia (30546) 217/E1
Hiawatha, Iowa (52233) 229/K4
Hiawatha, Kansas (66434) 232/G2
Hiawatha, Mich. (†49854) 250/C2
Hiawatha, Utah (84527) 304/D4
Hibbard, Ind. (†46511) 227/E2
Hibbing, Minn. 188/H1
Hibbing, Minn. (55746) 255/F3
Hibbs (pt.), Tasmania 99/B4
Hibernia, N.J. (07842) 273/E2
Hibuson (isl.), Philippines 82/E5
Hicacos (pen.), Cuba 158/D1
Hicacos (pt.), Cuba 158/D1
Hickam A.F.B., Hawaii 218/B4
Hickam Housing, Hawaii (96824) 218/B4
Hickman, Ark. (†72315) 202/L2
Hickman, Del. (†21629) 245/R5
Hickman (co.), Ky. 237/C7
Hickman, Ky. (42050) 237/C7
Hickman, Nebr. (68372) 264/H4
Hickman (co.), Tenn. 237/G9
Hickman, Tenn. (38567) 237/K8
Hickman's Harbour, Newf. 166/D2
Hickok, Kansas (†67880) 232/A4
Hickory, Ky. (42051) 237/D7
Hickory, Miss. (39332) 256/F6
Hickory (co.), Mo. 261/F7
Hickory, N.C. (28601) 281/G3
Hickory, Okla. (†73086) 288/N5
Hickory Corners, Mich. (49060) 250/D6
Hickory Creek, Texas (†75423) 303/F1
Hickory Flat, Ala. (†36274) 195/H4
Hickory Flat, Miss. (38633) 256/F1
Hickory Grove, S.C. (29717) 296/E2
Hickory Hills, Ill. (60457) 222/B6
Hickory Plains, Ark. (72066) 202/G3
Hickory Ridge, Ark. (72347) 202/J3
Hickory Valley, Tenn. (38042) 237/C10
Hickory Withe, Tenn. (38043) 237/B10
Hickox, Georgia (†31553) 217/H8
Hicks, La. (71437) 238/E4
Hickson, N. Dak. (†58047) 282/S6
Hickson, Ontario 177/D4
Hicksville, N.Y. (*11801) 276/R7
Hicksville, Ohio (43526) 284/A3
Hico, La. (†71235) 238/E1
Hico, Texas (76457) 303/F6
Hico, W. Va. (25854) 312/D6
Hida (riv.), Japan 81/H6
Hidalgo, Ill. (62432) 222/E4
Hidalgo, Ky. (42622) 237/M7
Hidalgo (state), Mexico 150/K6
Hidalgo, Coahuila, Mexico 150/K3
Hidalgo, Tamaulipas, Mexico 150/K4
Hidalgo (co.), N. Mex. 274/A7
Hidalgo (co.), Texas 303/F11
Hidalgo, Texas (78557) 303/F11
Hidalgo del Parral (Parral), Mexico 150/G3
Hidden Hills, Calif. (†91302) 204/B10
Hiddenite, N.C. (28636) 281/G3
Hiddensee (isl.), E. Germany 22/E1
Hieflau, Austria 41/C3
Hienghene, New Caled. 86/G4
Hierro (isl.), Spain 106/A3
Hierro (isl.), Spain 33/A5
Higashiosaka, Japan 81/J8
Higbee, Mo. (65257) 261/H4
Higden, Ark. (72067) 202/F2
Higdon, Ala. (35979) 195/G1
Higganum, Conn. (06441) 210/E2
Higgins (lake), Mich. 250/E4
Higgins, Texas (79046) 303/D1
Higgins Lake, Mich. (48627) 250/E4
Higginson, Ark. (72068) 202/G3
Higginsport, Ohio (45131) 284/C8
Higginsville, Mo. (64037) 261/E4
Higgston, Georgia (†30410) 217/G6
High, Iowa (†52203) 229/K5
High (isl.), Ireland 17/A4
High (isl.), Mich. 250/D3
High Atlas (ranges), Morocco 106/C2
High Bluff, Manitoba 179/D4
High Bridge, Ky. (40333) 237/M5
High Bridge, N.J. (08829) 273/D2
High Bridge, Wis. (54846) 317/E3
Highbury, W. Australia 92/B2
High Falls, N.Y. (12440) 276/M7
Highfalls, N.C. (27259) 281/K4
Highfield-Cascade, Md. (21753) 245/J2
Highfill, Ark. (†72734) 202/B1
Highgate, Jamaica 158/J6
Highgate, Ontario 177/C5
Highgate○, Vt. (†05459) 268/B2
Highgate Center, Vt. (05459) 268/B2
Highgate Falls, Vt. (†05459) 268/A2
Highgate Springs, Vt. (05460) 268/A2
Highgrove, Calif. (92507) 204/E10
High Hill, Mo. (63350) 261/K5
High Island, Texas (77623) 303/K8
Highland, Calif. (92346) 204/H9
Highland (lake), Conn. 210/C1
Highland (pt.), Fla. 212/E6
Highland, Ill. (62249) 222/D5
Highland, Ind. (46322) 227/B1
Highland, Kansas (66035) 232/G2
Highland (peak), Nev. 266/G5
Highland (lake), N.H. 268/C5
Highland, N.Y. (12528) 276/M7
Highland (co.), Ohio 284/C7
Highland, Ohio (45132) 284/C7
Highland (reg.), Scotland 15/D3
Highland, Utah (†84043) 304/C3
Highland (co.), Va. 307/J4
Highland, W. Va. (†26346) 312/D4
Highland, Wis. (53543) 317/F9
Highland Beach, Fla. (33431) 212/F5
Highland Beach, Md. (†21401) 245/M5
Highland Center, Iowa (52564) 229/J6
Highland City, Fla. (33846) 212/E4
Highland Falls, N.Y. (10928) 276/M8
Highland Heights, Ky. (41076) 237/T2
Highland Heights, Ohio (†44143) 284/J9
Highland Home, Ala. (36041) 195/F7
Highland Lake, Ala. (†35013) 195/F3
Highland Lake, Maine (†04082) 243/C8
Highland Lakes, N.J. (07422) 273/E1
Highland Park, Conn. (†06040) 210/F1
Highland Park, Fla. (32401) 212/E4
Highland Park, Ill. (60035) 222/B5
Highland Park, Mich. (48203) 250/B6
Highland Park, N.J. (08904) 273/D2
Highland Park, Pa. (†17044) 294/H4
Highland Park, Texas (†75201) 303/G2
Highlands (co.), Fla. 212/E4
Highlands, N.J. (07732) 273/F3
Highlands, N.C. (28741) 281/C4
Highlands, Texas (77562) 303/K1
Highland Springs, Va. (23075) 307/O5
Highland Village, Texas (†75205) 303/F1
Highlandville, Iowa (52149) 229/K2
Highlandville, Mo. (65669) 261/F9
High Level, Alberta 182/A5
Highmore, S. Dak. (57345) 298/L4
Highpine, Maine (†04090) 243/B9
High Plateaus (ranges), Algeria 106/D2
High Point, Fla. (†33515) 212/B3
Highpoint, Miss. (†39339) 256/F4
High Point, Mo. (65042) 261/G5
High Point (mt.), N.J. 273/D1
High Point, N.C. 188/K3
High Point, N.C. (*27260) 281/J3
High Prairie, Alberta 182/B2
Highridge, Alberta 182/D2
High Ridge, Mo. (63049) 261/M6
High River, Alberta 182/D4
High River, Alta. 162/E5
High Rock (creek), Nev. 266/B1
High Rock, N.C. (27239) 281/J3
High Rock (lake), N.C. 281/J3
High Rocky (pt.), Tasmania 99/B4
High Rolls-Mountain Park, N. Mex. (88325) 274/D5
High Shoals, N.C. (28077) 281/G4
Highspire, Pa. (17034) 294/J5
Highsplint, Ky. (†40828) 237/P7
High Springs, Fla. (32643) 212/D2
High Tatra (range), Poland 47/D4
Hightower, Ala. (†36264) 195/H3
Hightown, Va. (24444) 307/J4
Hightstown, N.J. (08520) 273/D3
Highway, Ky. (†42602) 237/L7
High Willhays (mt.), England 13/C7
Highwood (riv.), Alberta 182/C4
Highwood, Ill. (60040) 222/B5
Highwood, Mont. (59450) 262/F3
Highworth, England 13/F6
High Wycombe, England 13/G8
High Wycombe, England 10/F5
Higley, Ariz. (85236) 198/D5
Higuerote, Venezuela 124/F2
Higüey, Dom. Rep. 158/F6
Hiiraan (prov.), Somalia 115/J3
Hiiumaa (isl.), U.S.S.R. 7/G3
Hiiumaa (isl.), U.S.S.R. 52/B3
Hiiumaa (isl.), U.S.S.R. 53/B1
Hiiumaa (isl.), U.S.S.R. 48/C4
Híjar, Spain 33/F2
Hijuelas, Chile 138/F2
Hiko, Nev. (89017) 266/F5
Hikone, Japan 81/H6
Hikueru (atoll), Fr. Poly. 87/M7
Hikurangi, N. Zealand 100/E1
Hikurangi (mt.), N. Zealand 100/G2
Hiland, Wyo. (82638) 319/E2
Hiland Park, Fla. (32405) 212/C6
Hilbert, Wis. (54129) 317/K7
Hilbre, Manitoba 179/D3
Hilda, Alberta 182/E4
Hilda, S.C. (29813) 296/E5
Hildburghausen, E. Germany 22/D3
Hildebran, N.C. (28637) 281/F3
Hildebrand, Oreg. (†97625) 291/F5
Hilden, Nova Scotia 168/E3
Hildesheim, W. Germany 22/D2
Hildreth, Nebr. (68947) 264/E4
Hiles, Wis. (†54511) 317/J4
Hilgard (mt.), Utah 304/C5
Hilger, Mont. (59451) 262/G3
Hilham, Tenn. (38568) 237/L8
Hill (riv.), Minn. 255/C3
Hill (co.), Mont. 262/F2
Hill○, N.H. (03243) 268/D4
Hill (co.), Texas 303/G5
Hill (creek), Utah 304/E4
Hilla, Iraq 66/D4
Hilla, Iraq 59/D3
Hill A.F.B., Utah 304/C2
Hillaby (mt.), Barbados 161/B8
Hillandale, Md. (†20903) 245/F4
Hill Bank, Belize 154/C2
Hillburn, N.Y. (10931) 276/M8
Hill City, Idaho (83337) 220/D6
Hill City, Kansas (67642) 232/C2
Hill City, Minn. (55748) 255/E4
Hill City, S. Dak. (57745) 298/B6
Hill Country Village, Texas (†78232) 303/K10
Hill Creek Ext., Uintah and Ouray Ind. Res., Utah 304/E4
Hillcrest, Alberta 182/C5
Hillcrest, Ill. (†61244) 222/D2
Hillcrest, N.Y. (†10977) 276/K8
Hillcrest, Texas (†77511) 303/J3
Hillcrest Heights, Fla. (†33827) 212/E4
Hillcrest Heights, Md. (†20031) 245/F5
Hilldale, Utah (†84767) 304/A6
Hillegom, Netherlands 27/E4
Hillemann, Ark. (†72101) 202/H3
Hill End, N.S. Wales 97/E3
Hillerød, Denmark 18/H9
Hillerød, Denmark 21/F6
Hillers (mt.), Utah 304/D6
Hillham, Ind. (†47432) 227/D7
Hillhead, S. Dak. (†57270) 298/O2
Hillhouse, Miss. (†38720) 256/C2
Hilliard, Alberta 182/D3
Hilliard, Fla. (32046) 212/E1
Hilliard, Ohio (43026) 284/D5
Hilliards, Pa. (16040) 294/C3
Hilliardville, Fla. (†32327) 212/B1
Hillingdon, England 10/B5
Hillingdon, England 13/G8
Hillisburg, Ind. (46046) 227/E4
Hill Island (lake), N.W. Terrs. 187/H3
Hillman, Mich. (49746) 250/F3
Hillman, Minn. (56338) 255/E4
Hillman, New Bruns. 170/C2
Hillmond, Sask. 181/B2
Hill of Fearn, Scotland 15/D3
Hillridge, Manitoba 179/C3
Hillrose, Colo. (80733) 208/N2
Hills, Iowa (52235) 229/K5
Hills, Minn. (56138) 255/B7
Hillsboro, Ala. (35643) 195/D1
Hillsboro, Georgia (31038) 217/E4
Hillsboro, Ill. (62049) 222/D4
Hillsboro, Ind. (47949) 227/C4
Hillsboro, Iowa (52630) 229/K7
Hillsboro, Kansas (67063) 232/E3
Hillsboro, Ky. (41049) 237/O4
Hillsboro, Md. (21641) 245/P5
Hillsboro, Miss. (39087) 256/E6
Hillsboro, Mo. (63050) 261/L6
Hillsboro, N.H. (03244) 268/D5
Hillsboro○, N.H. (03244) 268/D5
Hillsboro, N. Mex. (88042) 274/B6
Hillsboro, N. Dak. (58045) 282/S5
Hillsboro, Ohio (45133) 284/C7
Hillsboro, Oreg. (97123) 291/A2
Hillsboro, Tenn. (37342) 237/K10
Hillsboro, Texas (76645) 303/G5
Hillsboro, Va. (22132) 307/N2
Hillsboro, W. Va. (24946) 312/F6
Hillsboro, Wis. (54634) 317/F8
Hillsboro Beach, Fla. (†33060) 212/F5
Hillsboro Lower Village, N.H. (†03244) 268/D5
Hillsborough, Calif. (94010) 204/J2
Hillsborough (co.), Fla. 212/D4
Hillsborough (bay), Fla. 212/C3
Hillsborough (canal), Fla. 212/F5
Hillsborough (riv.), Fla. 212/C2
Hillsborough, New Bruns. 170/F3
Hillsborough (co.), N.H. 268/D6
Hillsborough, N.C. (27278) 281/L2
Hillsborough, N. Ireland 17/J3
Hillsborough (bay), Pr. Edward I. 168/E2
Hillsboro Upper Village, N.H. (†03244) 268/D5
Hillsburgh, Ontario 177/D4
Hillsburn, Nova Scotia 168/C4
Hills Creek (lake), Oreg. 291/E4
Hillsdale, Ill. (61257) 222/C2
Hillsdale, Ind. (47854) 227/C5
Hillsdale, Kansas (66036) 232/H3
Hillsdale (co.), Mich. 250/E7
Hillsdale, Mich. (49242) 250/E7
Hillsdale, Mo. (†63101) 261/R2
Hillsdale, N.J. (07642) 273/B1
Hillsdale, N.Y. (12529) 276/O6
Hillsdale, Okla. (73743) 288/K1
Hillsdale, Ontario 177/E3
Hillsdale, Pa. (15746) 294/E4
Hillsdale, Wis. (54744) 317/C5
Hillsdale, Wyo. (82060) 319/H4
Hillsgrove, Pa. (18619) 294/J3
Hillsgrove, R.I. (†02887) 249/J6
Hillside, Ariz. (†86301) 198/B4
Hillside, Colo. (81232) 208/H6
Hillside, Ill. (60162) 222/B5
Hillside○, N.J. (07205) 273/B2
Hillside, Scotland 15/F4
Hillside, S. Dak. (†57328) 298/N7
Hillside Beach, Manitoba 179/F4
Hillsport, Ontario 175/C3
Hillsport, Ontario 177/H5
Hill Spring, Alberta 182/D5
Hillston, N. S. Wales 88/G6
Hillston, N.S. Wales 97/C3
Hillsview, S. Dak. (†57437) 298/L2
Hillsville, Pa. (16132) 294/A4
Hillsville, Va. (24343) 307/G7
Hillswick, Scotland 15/G2
Hilltonia, Georgia (30467) 217/J5
Hilltop, Ariz. (†85632) 198/F6
Hilltown, N. Ireland 17/J3
Hillview, Ill. (62050) 222/C4
Hillview, Minn. (†56477) 255/C4
Hillview, Newf. 166/D2
Hilmar-Irwin, Calif. (95324) 204/E6
Hilo, Hawaii 87/L4
Hilo, Hawaii (96720) 218/J5
Hilo, Hawaii 188/G6
Hilo (bay), Hawaii 218/J5
Hilongos, Philippines 82/E5
Hilshire Village, Texas (†77001) 303/J1
Hilt, Calif. (†96044) 204/C2
Hilterfingen, Switzerland 39/E3
Hilton (inlet) 5/B16
Hilton, Georgia (†31723) 217/C8
Hilton, Manitoba 179/C5
Hilton, N.Y. (14468) 276/E4
Hilton Beach, Ontario 177/J5
Hilton Head (isl.), S.C. 296/F7
Hilton Head Island, S.C. (29928) 296/F7
Hiltons, Va. (24258) 307/D7
Hilvan, Turkey 63/H4
Hilvarenbeek, Netherlands 27/G6
Hilversum, Netherlands 27/G4
Hima, Ky. (40951) 237/O6
Himachal Pradesh (state), India 68/D2
Himalaya (mts.) 54/L7
Himalaya (mts.), Bhutan 68/E2
Himalaya (mts.), China 77/C6
Himalaya (mts.), India 68/D2
Himalaya (mts.), Nepal 68/D2
Himanka, Finland 18/N5
Himeji, Japan 81/G6
Himi, Japan 81/H5
Himlerville (Beauty), Ky. (†41203) 237/S5
Himrod, N.Y. (14842) 276/F5
Himyar, Ky. (40952) 237/O7
Hinatuan, Philippines 82/F6
Hinchcliff, Miss. (†38646) 256/D2
Hinche, Haiti 158/C5
Hinche, Haiti 156/D3
Hinchinbrook (isl.), Alaska 196/D1
Hinchinbrook (isl.), Queensland 88/H3
Hinchinbrook (isl.), Queensland 95/C3
Hinchinbrook Entrance (chan.), Alaska 196/J3
Hinchliffe, Sask. 181/J3
Hinckley, England 10/F4
Hinckley, England 13/F5
Hinckley, Ill. (60520) 222/E2
Hinckley, Maine (04944) 243/D6
Hinckley, Minn. (55037) 255/E4
Hinckley, N.Y. (13352) 276/K4
Hinckley (res.), N.Y. 276/K4
Hinckley, Ohio (44233) 284/G3
Hinckley, Utah (84635) 304/B4
Hindeloopen, Netherlands 27/G3
Hindenburg (Zabrze), Poland 47/A4
Hinderwell, England 13/G3
Hindiya, Iraq 66/C4
Hindman, Ky. (41822) 237/R6
Hindmarsh, S. Australia 88/D8
Hindmarsh, S. Australia 94/A7
Hindmarsh (lake), Victoria 97/A5
Hinds (co.), Miss. 256/D6
Hinds, N. Zealand 100/C6
Hindsboro, Ill. (61930) 222/E4
Hindsville, Ark. (72738) 202/C1
Hindubagh, Pakistan 68/B2
Hindu Kush (mts.) 54/J6
Hindu Kush (mts.), Afghanistan 68/B1
Hindu Kush (mts.), Afghanistan 59/J2
Hindu Kush (mts.), India 68/C1
Hindu Kush (mts.), Pakistan 68/B1
Hindupur, India 68/D6
Hi-Nella, N.J. (†08083) 273/B4
Hines, Minn. (56647) 255/D3
Hines, Oreg. (97738) 291/H4
Hinesburg○, Vt. (05461) 268/A3
Hines Creek, Alberta 182/A1
Hines Creek, Alta. 162/E4
Hineston, La. (71438) 238/E4
Hinesville, Georgia (31313) 217/J7
Hinganghat, India 68/D4
Hingham, Mass. (02043) 249/E8
Hingham○, Mass. (02043) 249/E8
Hingham (bay), Mass. 249/E7
Hingham, Mont. (59528) 262/F2
Hingham, Wis. (53031) 317/K8
Hingoli, India 68/D5
Hinigaran, Philippines 82/D5
Hinis, Turkey 63/J3
Hinkley, Calif. (92347) 204/H9
Hinkston (creek), Ky. 237/N4
Hinlopenstreten (str.), Norway 18/C1
Hinnerup, Denmark 21/D5
Hinnøya (isl.), Norway 18/K2
Hino, Japan 81/O2
Hinojosa del Duque, Spain 33/D3
Hinsdale (co.), Colo. 208/E7
Hinsdale, Ill. (60521) 222/B6
Hinsdale○, Mass. (01235) 249/B3
Hinsdale, Mont. (59241) 262/K2
Hinsdale, N.H. (03451) 268/C6
Hinsdale○, N.H. (03451) 268/C6
Hinsdale, N.Y. (14743) 276/D6
Hinson, Fla. (†32333) 212/B1
Hinsonton, Georgia (†31779) 217/D8
Hinterrhein (riv.), Switzerland 39/H3
Hinton, Alberta 182/B3
Hinton, Iowa (51024) 229/A3
Hinton, Mo. (†65201) 261/H4
Hinton, Okla. (73047) 288/K4
Hinton, W. Va. (25951) 312/E7
Hintonville, Miss. (†39462) 256/F8
Hinwil, Switzerland 39/G2
Hinze, Miss. (†39108) 256/F4
Hippolytushoef, Netherlands 27/G3
Hipswell, England 13/F3
Hirakata, Japan 81/J7
Hiram, Georgia (30141) 217/C3
Hiram, Ky. (†40823) 237/P7
Hiram, Maine (04041) 243/B8
Hiram○, Maine (04041) 243/B8
Hiram, Mo. (63947) 261/M8
Hiram, Ohio (44234) 284/H3
Hirara, Japan 81/L7
Hirata, Japan 81/F6
Hiratsuka, Japan 81/O3
Hîrlău, Romania 45/H2
Hiroo, Japan 81/L2
Hirosaki, Japan 81/K3
Hiroshima (pref.), Japan 81/E6
Hiroshima, Japan 54/P6
Hiroshima, Japan 81/E6
Hirsch, Sask. 181/J6
Hirschberg (Jelenia Góra), Poland 47/B3
Hirson, France 28/F3
Hîrşova, Romania 45/J3
Hirtshals, Denmark 21/C2
Hisarönü, Turkey 63/E2
Hisban, Jordan 65/D4
Hisega, S. Dak. (†57701) 298/C5
Hiseville, Ky. (42152) 237/K6
Hisle, S. Dak. (†57577) 298/F7
Hispaniola (isl.) 146/L7
Hispaniola (isl.), Dom. Rep. 156/D2
Hispaniola (isl.), Haiti 156/D2
Hispaniola (isl.), W. Indies 156/D2
Hissar, India 68/D3
Hissop, Ala. (35081) 195/F5
Hit, Iraq 59/D3
Hit, Iraq 66/C4
Hitachi, Japan 81/K5
Hitachiota, Japan 81/K5
Hitchcock (lkes), Conn. 210/D2
Hitchcock (co.), Nebr. 264/C4
Hitchcock, Okla. (73744) 288/K3
Hitchcock, Sask. 181/J6
Hitchcock, S. Dak. (57348) 298/M4
Hitchcock, Texas (77563) 303/K3
Hitchin, England 13/G6
Hitchin, England 10/F5
Hitchins, Ky. (41146) 237/R4
Hitchita, Okla. (74438) 288/P3
Hiteman, Iowa (†52531) 229/H6
Hitoyoshi, Japan 81/E7
Hitra (isl.), Norway 18/F5
Hitt, Mo. (†63555) 261/H1
Hitterdal, Minn. (56552) 255/B4
Hitzacker, W. Germany 22/D2
Hitzkirch, Switzerland 39/F2
Hivaoa (isl.), Fr. Poly. 87/N6
Hiwannee, Miss. (†39367) 256/G7
Hiwasse, Ark. (72739) 202/B1
Hiwassee (lake), N.C. 281/A4
Hiwassee (riv.), N.C. 281/A4
Hiwassee (riv.), Tenn. 237/O10
Hiwassee, Va. (24347) 307/G7
Hixon, Br. Col. 184/F3
Hixson, Tenn. (37343) 237/L10
Hixton, Wis. (54635) 317/E7
Hizan, Turkey 63/K3
Hjallerup, Denmark 21/C3
Hjälmaren (lake), Sweden 18/J7
Hjerm, Denmark 21/B5
Hjerting, Denmark 21/B6
Hjo, Sweden 18/J7
Hjørring, Denmark 18/F8
Hjørring, Denmark 21/C3
Hka, Nam (riv.), Burma 72/C2
Hkakabo Razi (mt.), Burma 72/C1
Hlinsko, Czech. 41/D2
Hlohovec, Czech. 41/D2
Hlučín, Czech. 41/E2
Hmawbi, Burma 72/C3
Hnúšťa-Likier, Czech. 41/E2
Ho, Ghana 106/E7
Hoa Binh, Vietnam 72/E2
Hoa Da, Vietnam 72/F5
Hoadley, Alberta 182/C3
Hoadly, Va. (†22191) 307/O3
Hoagland, Ind. (46745) 227/H3
Hoai Nhon, Vietnam 72/F4
Hoaksbergen, Netherlands 27/K4
Hoare (bay), N.W. Terrs. 187/M3
Hoback (peak), Wyo. 319/B2
Hoback (riv.), Wyo. 319/B2
Hobart, Australia 2/S8
Hobart, Ind. (46342) 227/C1
Hobart, N.Y. (13788) 276/L6
Hobart, Okla. (73651) 288/J5
Hobart (cap.), Tasmania 88/H8
Hobart (cap.), Tasmania 99/D4
Hobart, Wash. (98025) 310/D3
Hobbema, Alberta 182/D3
Hobbs, Ind. (46047) 227/F4
Hobbs (lake), Manitoba 179/G3
Hobbs, Md. (†21629) 245/P5
Hobbs, N. Mex. 188/F4
Hobbs, N. Mex. (88240) 274/F6
Hobbs Coast (reg.) 5/B12
Hobbs Island, Ala. (†35804) 195/F1
Hobbsville, N.C. (27946) 281/R2
Hoberg, Mo. (†65712) 261/E8
Hobe Sound, Fla. (33455) 212/F4
Hobgood, N.C. (27843) 281/P2
Hoboken, Belgium 27/E6
Hoboken, Georgia (31542) 217/H8
Hoboken, N.J. (07030) 273/C2
Hoboksar, China 77/C2
Hobro, Denmark 21/C4
Hobro, Denmark 18/F8
Hobson (lake), Br. Col. 184/H4
Hobson, Mont. (59452) 262/G4
Hobson City, Ala. (†36201) 195/G3
Hobsons (bay), Victoria 97/H5
Hobsons (bay), Victoria 88/L7
Hobucken, N.C. (28537) 281/S4
Hoburgen (cliff), Sweden 18/L8
Hochdorf, Switzerland 39/F2
Hochfeld, Manitoba 179/E5
Hochgolling (mt.), Austria 41/B3
Ho Chi Minh City, Vietnam 2/Q5
Ho Chi Minh City, Vietnam 54/M8
Hochwan (Hechuan), China 77/G5
Hochwang (mt.), Switzerland 39/J3
Hockaday, Mich. (†48624) 250/E4
Hockanum, Conn. (†06108) 210/E2
Hockanum (riv.), Conn. 210/E1
Hockenheim, W. Germany 22/C4
Hockerville, Okla. (†74363) 288/S1
Hockessin, Del. (19707) 245/R1
Hocking (co.), Ohio 284/F6
Hocking (riv.), Ohio 284/F7
Hockingport, Ohio (45739) 284/G7
Hockley (co.), Texas 303/B4
Hodaka (mt.), Japan 81/H5
Hodder (riv.), England 13/H1
Hoddesdon, England 13/H7
Hodeida, Yemen Arab Rep. 54/F8
Hodeida, Yemen Arab Rep. 59/D7
Hodgdon○, Maine (†04730) 243/H3
Hodge, La. (71247) 238/E2
Hodge, Mo. (†64096) 261/E4
Hodgeman (co.), Kansas 232/C3
Hodgen, Okla. (74939) 288/S5
Hodgenville, Ky. (42748) 237/K5
Hodges, Ala. (35571) 195/C2
Hodges, Mont. (†59353) 262/M4
Hodges, S.C. (29653) 296/C3
Hodge's Cove, Newf. 166/D2
Hodgesville, W. Va. (†26201) 312/F4
Hodgeville, Sask. 181/E6
Hodgkins, Ill. (60525) 222/B6
Hodgson, Manitoba 179/E3
Hodh (reg.), Mauritania 106/C5
Hod Hasharon, Israel 65/B3
Hodiyya, Israel 65/B4
Hódmezővásárhely, Hungary 41/F3
Hodonín, Czech. 41/D2
Hoehne, Colo. (81046) 208/L8
Hoei (Huy), Belgium 27/G8
Hoek, Netherlands 27/D6
Hoek van Holland (Hook of Holland), Netherlands 27/D4
Hoek van Holland (cape), Netherlands 27/D5
Hoensbroek, Netherlands 27/H7
Hoeryŏng, N. Korea 81/D2
Hoeselt, Belgium 27/G7
Hoey, Sask. 181/F3
Hof, W. Germany 22/D3
Hofei (Hefei), China 77/J5
Hoffman (mt.), Calif. 204/D2
Hoffman, Ill. (62250) 222/D5
Hoffman, Minn. (56339) 255/C5
Hoffman, N.C. (28347) 281/K4
Hoffman, Okla. (74439) 288/P4
Hoffman Estates, Ill. (60195) 222/A5
Hofgeismar, W. Germany 22/C3
Hofors, Sweden 18/K6
Hofs (glac.), Iceland 21/C1
Hofu, Japan 81/E6
Hofuf, Saudi Arabia 59/E4
Hofuf, Saudi Arabia 54/F7
Hog (isl.), Mich. 250/D3
Hog (isl.), Pr. Edward I. 168/E2
Hog (isl.), Va. 307/S6
Hogan, Mo. (†63646) 261/L7
Hogan (lake), Ontario 177/F2
Höganäs, Sweden 18/H8
Hogan Group (isls.), Tasmania 99/D1
Hogansburg, N.Y. (13655) 276/L1
Hogansville, Georgia (30230) 217/C4

Horwich 383

Hogarth (mt.), North. Terr. 93/E6
Hogatza, Alaska (99744) 196/G1
Hogeland, Mont. (59529) 262/H2
Hog Island (bay), Va. 307/S6
Hog River (Hogatza), Alaska (99744) 196/G1
Hogshead (pt.), Conn. 210/E3
Hőgyész, Hungary 41/E3
Hoh (head), Wash. 310/A3
Hoh (riv.), Wash. 310/A3
Hohenau, Paraguay 144/E5
Hohenau an der March, Austria 41/D2
Hohenberg, Austria 41/C3
Hohenems, Austria 41/A3
Hohenlinden, Miss. (†39751) 256/F3
Hohen Neuendorf, E. Germany 22/E2
Hohen Solms, La. (†70788) 238/K3
Hohenstollen (mt.), Switzerland 39/F3
Hohenwald, Tenn. (38462) 237/F9
Hohe Tauern (range), Austria 41/B3
Hohe Venn (plat.), Belgium 27/H8
Hohe Warte (mt.), Austria 41/B3
Hohhot (Huhehot), China 77/H3
Hohhot, China 54/N5
Hoh Ind. Res., Wash. 310/A3
Hohokam Pima Nat'l Mon., Ariz. 198/D5
Ho Ho Kus, N.J. (07423) 273/B1
Hoholitna (riv.), Alaska 196/G2
Hoh Xil Shan (mts.), China 77/C4
Hoi An, Vietnam 72/F4
Hoihow (Haikou), China 77/H7
Hoima, Uganda 115/F3
Hoisington, Kansas (67544) 232/D3
Hoi Xuan, Vietnam 72/E2
Højer, Denmark 21/B8
Højslev, Denmark 21/C4
Hokah, Minn. (55941) 255/G7
Hokang (Hegang), China 77/L2
Hoke (co.), N.C. 281/L4
Hokes Bluff, Ala. (35903) 195/G3
Hokianga (harb.), N. Zealand 100/D1
Hokitika, N. Zealand 100/C5
Hokkaido (pref.), Japan 81/K2
Hokkaido (isl.), Japan 2/S3
Hokkaido (isl.), Japan 54/R5
Hokkaido (isl.), Japan 81/L2
Holabird, S. Dak. (57540) 298/K4
Holbaek, Denmark 21/E6
Holbaek, Denmark 18/G9
Holbeach, England 10/F4
Holbeach, England 13/H5
Holbein, Sask. 181/E2
Holberg, Br. Col. 184/C5
Holbrook, Ariz. (86025) 198/E4
Holbrook, Idaho (83243) 220/F7
Holbrook, Iowa (†52325) 229/K5
Holbrook○, Mass. (02343) 249/D8
Holbrook, Nebr. (68948) 264/D4
Holbrook, N.S. Wales 97/D4
Holbrook, Oreg. (†97208) 291/A1
Holcomb, Ill. (61043) 222/D1
Holcomb, Kansas (67851) 232/B3
Holcomb, Miss. (38940) 256/D3
Holcomb, Mo. (63852) 261/N10
Holcomb, N.Y. (14469) 276/F5
Holcomb, W. Va. (26262) 312/E6
Holcombe, Wis. (54745) 317/D5
Holcombe Flowage (res.), Wis. 317/D5
Holden, Alberta 182/D3
Holden, La. (70744) 238/M1
Holden○, Mass. (01520) 249/G3
Holden, Mo. (64040) 261/E5
Holden, Utah (84636) 304/B4
Holden, W. Va. (25625) 312/B7
Holden Beach, N.C. (28462) 281/N7
Holdenville, Okla. (74848) 288/O4
Holder, Fla. (32645) 212/D3
Holderness (pen.), England 13/G4
Holderness○, N.H. (03245) 268/D4
Holdfast, Sask. 181/F5
Holdingford, Minn. (56340) 255/D5
Holdrege, Nebr. (68949) 264/E4
Holeby, Denmark 21/E8
Holen, Norway 18/D4
Holešov, Czech. 41/D2
Holetown, Barbados 161/B8
Holgate, Ohio (43527) 284/B3
Holguín (prov.), Cuba 158/J3
Holguín, Cuba 146/L7
Holguín, Cuba 158/J3
Holguín, Cuba 156/C2
Holič, Czech. 41/D2
Holice, Czech. 41/C1
Holiday Hills, Ill. (†60050) 222/A4
Holijsloot, Netherlands 27/C4
Holitna (riv.), Alaska 196/G2
Hollabrunn, Austria 41/D2
Holladay, Tenn. (38341) 237/E9
Holladay, Utah (84117) 304/C3
Hollam's Bird (isl.), Namibia 118/A4
Holland, Georgia (†30730) 217/B2
Holland, Ind. (47541) 227/C8
Holland, Iowa (50642) 229/H4
Holland, Ky. (42153) 237/J7
Holland, Manitoba 179/D5
Holland○, Mass. (†01550) 249/F4
Holland, Mich. (49423) 250/C6
Holland, Minn. (56139) 255/B6
Holland, Mo. (63853) 261/N10
Holland, N.Y. (14080) 276/C5
Holland, Ohio (43528) 284/C2
Holland, Texas (76534) 303/G7
Holland○, Vt. (†05830) 268/D2
Hollandale, Minn. (56045) 255/E7
Hollandale, Miss. (38748) 256/C4
Hollandale, Wis. (53544) 317/G10
Holland Centre, Ontario 177/D3
Hollandia (Jayapura), Indonesia 85/K6
Holland Landing, Ontario 177/E3
Holland Park, Queensland 88/K3
Holland Park, Queensland 95/E3
Holland Patent, N.Y. (13354) 276/K4
Hollandsburg, Ind. (†47872) 227/C5
Hollandstoun, Scotland 15/F1
Hollansburg, Ohio (45332) 284/A5
Hollenbeck (riv.), Conn. 210/B1
Hollenberg, Kansas (66946) 232/F2
Holley, N.Y. (14470) 276/D4
Holley, Oreg. (†97386) 291/E3
Hollick-Kenyon (plat.) 5/B13
Holliday, Mo. (65258) 261/H3
Holliday, Texas (76366) 303/F4
Hollidaysburg, Pa. (16648) 294/F5
Hollins, Ala. (35082) 195/F4
Hollins College, Va. (24020) 307/H6
Hollis, Ark. (†72857) 202/D4
Hollis, Kansas (†66901) 232/E2
Hollis○, N.H. (03049) 268/D6
Hollis, N.C. (†28040) 281/F4
Hollis, Okla. (73550) 288/G5
Hollis Center○, Maine (04042) 243/B8
Hollister, Calif. (95023) 204/D7
Hollister, Fla. (32047) 212/E2
Hollister, Idaho (†83301) 220/D7
Hollister, Mo. (65672) 261/F9
Hollister, N.C. (27844) 281/O2
Hollister, Okla. (73551) 288/J6
Hollister, Wis. (†54491) 317/J5
Holliston○, Mass. (01746) 249/A8
Holloman A.F.B., N. Mex. 274/C6
Holloway, Minn. (56249) 255/C5
Holloway, Ohio (43985) 284/H5
Hollowayville, Ill. (†61356) 222/D2
Hollow Creek, Ky. (†40228) 237/K4
Hollow Rock, Tenn. (38342) 237/E8
Hollsopple, Pa. (15935) 294/E5
Hollum, Netherlands 27/H2
Holly, Colo. (81047) 208/P6
Holly, Mich. (48442) 250/F6
Holly, Wash. (†98310) 310/C3
Holly Bluff, Miss. (39088) 256/C5
Holly Grove, Ark. (72069) 202/H4
Holly Hill, Fla. (32017) 212/E2
Holly Hill, S.C. (29059) 296/G5
Holly Oak, Del. (†19801) 245/S1
Holly Pond, Ala. (35083) 195/E2
Holly Ridge, La. (71248) 238/G2
Holly Ridge, Miss. (38749) 256/C4
Holly Ridge, N.C. (28445) 281/O6
Holly Shelter (swamp), N.C. 281/O6
Holly Springs, Ark. (71746) 202/E6
Holly Springs, Georgia (30142) 217/D2
Holly Springs, Miss. (38635) 256/E1
Holly Springs, N.C. (27540) 281/M3
Hollytree, Ala. (35751) 195/F1
Hollyville, Del. (†19951) 245/T6
Hollywood, Ala. (35752) 195/G1
Hollywood, Ark. (†71923) 202/D5
Hollywood, Calif. (90028) 204/C10
Hollywood, Fla. 188/K5
Hollywood, Fla. (*33020) 212/B4
Hollywood, Georgia (30523) 217/E1
Hollywood, La. (†70663) 238/D6
Hollywood, Md. (20636) 245/M7
Hollywood, Miss. (†38676) 256/D1
Hollywood, Mo. (†63821) 261/M10
Hollywood, S.C. (29449) 296/G6
Hollywood, W. Va. (†24983) 312/F7
Hollywood Park, Texas (†78201) 303/K10
Holman, N. Mex. (87723) 274/D2
Holman (isl.), N.W.T. 162/D1
Holman Island, Canada 4/B15
Holman Island, N.W. Terrs. 187/G2
Holmdel○, N.J. (07733) 273/E3
Holmen, Wis. (54636) 317/D8
Holmes (reef), 95/C3
Holmes (reef), Coral Sea Is. Terr. 88/H3
Holmes (co.), Fla. 212/C5
Holmes (creek), Fla. 212/D5
Holmes, Iowa (†50525) 229/F3
Holmes (co.), Miss. 256/D4
Holmes (co.), Ohio 284/G4
Holmes (mt.), Wyo. 319/B1
Holmes Beach, Fla. (33509) 212/D4
Holmes City, Minn. (56341) 255/C5
Holmeson, N.J. (†08526) 273/E3
Holmestrand, Norway 18/C4
Holmesville, Miss. (†39648) 256/D8
Holmesville, Nebr. (68374) 264/H4
Holmesville, New Bruns. 170/C2
Holmesville, Ohio (44633) 284/G4
Holmesville, Ontario 177/C4
Holmfield, Manitoba 179/C5
Holmfirth, England 13/J2
Holmquist, S. Dak. (†57274) 298/O3
Holmsbu, Norway 18/D4
Holmsund, Sweden 18/M5
Holmwood, La. (†70647) 238/D6
Holon, Israel 65/B3
Holopaw, Fla. (†32901) 212/E3
Holroyd, N.S. Wales 97/H3
Holroyd (riv.), Queensland 95/B2
Holstebro, Denmark 18/F8
Holstebro, Denmark 21/B5
Holsted, Denmark 21/B6
Holstein, Iowa (51025) 229/B4
Holstein, Mo. (†63378) 261/K5
Holstein, Nebr. (68950) 264/F4
Holstein, Ontario 177/D3
Holsteinsborg, Greenl. 4/C12
Holston (riv.), Tenn. 237/O8
Holston, Va. (†24210) 307/D7
Holston, North Fork (riv.), Va. 307/D7
Holston Valley, Tenn. (†37620) 237/S7
Holsworthy, England 10/D5
Holsworthy, England 13/C7
Holt, Ala. (35404) 195/D4
Holt (dam), Ala. 195/D4
Holt, Calif. (95234) 204/D6
Holt, England 13/J5
Holt, Fla. (32564) 212/C6
Holt, Mich. (48842) 250/E6
Holt, Minn. (†56738) 255/B2
Holt (co.), Mo. 261/B2
Holt, Mo. (64048) 261/D4
Holt (co.), Nebr. 264/F2
Holte, Denmark 21/F6
Holter (lake), Mont. 262/D4
Holtland, Tenn. (†37034) 237/H9
Holton, Ind. (47023) 227/G6
Holton, Kansas (66436) 232/G2
Holton, La. (†70422) 238/K5
Holton, Mich. (49425) 250/C5
Holton, Newf. 166/C3
Holts Summit, Mo. (65043) 261/H5
Holtville, Ala. (†36022) 195/F5
Holtville, Calif. (92250) 204/K11
Holtville, New Bruns. 170/D2
Holtwood, Pa. (17532) 294/K6
Holualoa, Hawaii (96725) 218/G5
Holualoa, Hawaii 188/F6
Holwerd, Netherlands 27/H2
Holy (isl.), England 13/F2
Holy (isl.), England 10/F3
Holy (isl.), Scotland 15/C5
Holy (isl.), Wales 10/D4
Holy (isl.), Wales 13/C4
Holy City, Calif. (95026) 204/K4
Holy Cross, Alaska (99602) 196/G2
Holy Cross (mt.), Colo. 208/F4
Holy Cross, Iowa (52053) 229/L3
Holycross, Ireland 17/F6
Holy Cross, Wis. (†53004) 317/L9
Holyhead, Wales 10/D4
Holyhead, Wales 13/C4
Holy Loch (inlet), Scotland 15/A1
Holyoke, Colo. (80734) 208/P1
Holyoke, Mass. (01040) 249/D4
Holyoke (range), Mass. 249/D3
Holyoke, Minn. (55749) 255/F4
Holyrood, Kansas (67450) 232/D3
Holyrood, Newf. 166/D2
Holyrood (bay), Newf. 166/D2
Holyrood (pond), Newf. 166/D2
Holyroyd, N. S. Wales 88/K4
Holy Trinity, Ala. (36859) 195/H6
Holywell, Wales 13/G2
Holywood, N. Ireland 17/K2
Holzminden, W. Germany 22/C3
Homalin, Burma 72/B1
Homathko (riv.), Br. Col. 184/E4
Homayunshahr, Iran 66/G4
Hombori, Mali 106/D5
Hombori (mts.), Mali 106/D5
Homburg, W. Germany 22/B4
Home (bay) 162/K2
Home, Kansas (66438) 232/F2
Home (isl.), Newf. 166/B1
Home (bay), N.W. Terrs. 187/M3
Home, Pa. (15747) 294/D4
Homedale, Idaho (83628) 220/A6
Home Gardens, Calif. (†91720) 204/E11
Home Hill, Queensland 88/H3
Home Hill, Queensland 95/C3
Homeland, Calif. (92348) 204/H10
Homeland, Georgia (†31537) 217/H9
Home Place, La. (†70083) 238/L8
Homer, Alaska (99603) 196/B2
Homer, Georgia (30547) 217/F2
Homer, Ill. (61849) 222/F3
Homer, Ind. (46146) 227/F5
Homer, Ky. (†42276) 237/H7
Homer, La. (71040) 238/D1
Homer, Mich. (49245) 250/E6
Homer, Minn. (55942) 255/G6
Homer, Nebr. (68030) 264/H2
Homer, N.Y. (13077) 276/H5
Homer, Ohio (43027) 284/E5
Homer City, Pa. (15748) 294/D4
Homerville, Georgia (31634) 217/G8
Homerville, Ohio (44235) 284/F3
Homestead, Fla. (*33030) 212/F6
Homestead, Iowa (52236) 229/K5
Homestead, Mont. (59242) 262/M2
Homestead, Okla. (†73763) 288/K2
Homestead, Pa. (15120) 294/B7
Homestead, Queensland 95/C4
Homestead A.F.B., Fla. 212/F6
Homestead Nat'l Mon., Nebr. 264/H4
Homestown, Mo. (†63879) 261/N10
Hometown, Ill. (60456) 222/B6
Home Valley, Wash. (†98648) 310/D5
Homewood, Ala. (35209) 195/E4
Homewood, Calif. (95718) 204/E4
Homewood, Ill. (60430) 222/B6
Homewood, Kansas (†66095) 232/G3
Homewood, Manitoba 179/E5
Homewood, Miss. (†39152) 256/E6
Homewood, Pa. (15208) 294/B4
Homeworth, Ohio (44634) 284/J4
Hominy, Okla. (74035) 288/O2
Hominy Falls, W. Va. (†26651) 312/E6
Homochitto (riv.), Miss. 256/B8
Homoine, Mozambique 118/E4
Homonhon (isl.), Philippines 82/E5
Homosassa, Fla. (32646) 212/D3
Homosassa (isls.), Fla. 212/D3
Homosassa Springs, Fla. (32647) 212/D3
Homra, Hamada el (des.), Libya 111/B2
Homs, Libya 102/D1
Homs, Libya 111/B1
Homs (prov.), Syria 63/G5
Homs, Syria 59/C3
Homs, Syria 63/G5
Homs, Syria 54/E6
Hon, Ark. (†72958) 202/B4
Hon, Libya 102/D2
Hon, Libya 111/C2
Honaker, Va. (24260) 307/D6
Honan (Henan) (prov.), China 77/H5
Honaunau, Hawaii (96726) 218/G6
Honavar, India 68/C6
Honaz Dağı (mt.), Turkey 63/C4
Hon Chong, Vietnam 72/E5
Honda, Colombia 126/C5
Honda (bay), Cuba 158/B1
Honda (bay), Philippines 82/B6
Honda (bay), P. Rico 161/F2
Hondo (riv.), Belize 154/C1
Hondo, Japan 81/E7
Hondo (riv.), Mexico 150/P7
Hondo, N. Mex. (88336) 274/D5
Hondo, Texas (78861) 303/E8
Hondsrug (hills), Netherlands 27/K3
Honduras 2/E5
Honduras 146/K8
HONDURAS 154
Honduras (gulf) 146/K8
Honduras (gulf), Belize 154/D2
Honduras (gulf), Guatemala 154/D2
Honduras (cape), Honduras 154/E2
Honduras (gulf), Honduras 154/D2
Honea Path, S.C. (29654) 296/C3
Honegg (mt.), Switzerland 39/E3
Honeoye, N.Y. (14471) 276/F5
Honeoye (lake), N.Y. 276/F5
Honeoye Falls, N.Y. (14472) 276/F5
Honesdale, Pa. (18431) 294/M2
Honey (lake), Calif. 204/E3
Honey (creek), Ind. 227/C6
Honey (creek), Oreg. 291/G5
Honey Brook, Pa. (19344) 294/L5
Honey Creek, Ind. (†47356) 227/F4
Honey Creek, Iowa (51542) 229/B6
Honey Creek, Wis. (53138) 317/J3
Honeydale, New Bruns. 170/C3
Honeyford, N. Dak. (†58242) 282/R3
Honey Grove, Texas (75446) 303/J4
Honey Harbour, Ontario 177/E3
Honey Hill, S.C. (†29479) 296/H5
Honey Island, Texas (†77625) 303/K7
Honeymoon Bay, Br. Col. 184/J3
Honeyville, Utah (84314) 304/B2
Honeywood, Ontario 177/D3
Honfleur, France 28/D3
Honfleur, Québec 172/G3
Høng, Denmark 21/E7
Honga (riv.), Md. 245/O7
Hon Gai, Vietnam 72/E2
Hongch'ŏn, S. Korea 81/D5
Hong Kong 54/N7
Hong Kong 2/Q4
HONG KONG 77
Hongliuhe, China 77/E3
Hongor, Mongolia 77/H2
Hongshui He (riv.), China 77/G7
Hongsŏng, S. Korea 81/C5
Hongtong, China 77/H4
Honguedo (passage), Québec 174/E3
Hongwŏn, N. Korea 81/C3
Hongze Hu (lake), China 77/J5
Honiara (cap.), Solomon Is. 86/D3
Honiara (cap.), Solomon Is. 87/F6
Honiton, England 10/E5
Honiton, England 13/D7
Honjo, Japan 81/J4
Honnedaga (lake), N.Y. 276/L3
Honnelles, Belgium 27/D8
Honningsvag, Norway 18/O1
Honobia, Okla. (74549) 288/R5
Honohina, Hawaii (†96710) 218/J4
Honokaa, Hawaii 188/G5
Honokaa, Hawaii (96727) 218/H4
Honokahua, Hawaii (†96761) 218/H1
Honokohau, Hawaii, Hawaii (†96740) 218/G5
Honokohau, Maui, Hawaii (†96725) 218/J1
Honolulu (co.), Hawaii 218/D3
Honolulu (cap.), Hawaii 87/L3
Honolulu (cap.), Hawaii 188/F5
Honolulu (cap.), Hawaii (*96801) 218/C4
Honolulu (harb.), Hawaii 218/C4
Honolulu, U.S. 2/B5
Honolulu Int'l Airport, Hawaii 218/B4
Honomu, Hawaii (96728) 218/J4
Honor, Mich. (49640) 250/D4
Honoraville, Ala. (36042) 195/F7
Honouliuli, Hawaii (†96706) 218/A3
Honshu (isl.), Japan 2/S4
Honshu (isl.), Japan 54/P6
Honshu (isl.), Japan 81/J5
Honuapo, Hawaii (†96772) 218/H7
Hood, Calif. (95639) 204/B9
Hood (riv.), N.W. Terrs. 187/G3
Hood (mt.), Oreg. 291/F2
Hood (riv.), Oreg. 291/F2
Hood (co.), Texas 303/G5
Hood (canal), Wash. 310/B3
Hood River (co.), Oreg. 291/F2
Hood River, Oreg. (97031) 291/F2
Hoodsport, Wash. (98548) 310/B3
Hoofddorp (Haarlemmermeer), Netherlands 27/F4
Hoogeveen, Netherlands 27/J3
Hoogezand-Sappemeer, Netherlands 27/K2
Hooghly (riv.), India 68/F2
Hooghly-Chinsura, India 68/F1
Hoogkarspel, Netherlands 27/G3
Hoogstraten, Belgium 27/F6
Hook (head), Ireland 17/H7
Hook (isl.), Queensland 88/H4
Hook (isl.), Queensland 95/D4
Hookena, Hawaii (†96704) 218/G6
Hooker (co.), Nebr. 264/C3
Hooker, Okla. (73945) 288/D1
Hooker Creek, North. Terr. 88/E3
Hooker Creek, North. Terr. 93/B5
Hooker Creek Aboriginal Reserve, North. Terr. 88/E3
Hookersville, W. Va. (†26651) 312/E6
Hookerton, N.C. (28538) 281/O4
Hook of Holland, Netherlands 27/D4
Hooks, Texas (75561) 303/K4
Hooksett, N.H. (03106) 268/E5
Hooksett○, N.H. (03106) 268/E5
Hookstown, Pa. (15050) 294/B4
Hoolehua, Hawaii 188/F5
Hoolehua, Hawaii (96729) 218/G1
Hoonah, Alaska (99829) 196/M1
Hoonah (sound), Alaska 196/M1
Hoopa, Calif. (95546) 204/B2
Hoopa Valley Ind. Res., Calif. 204/A2
Hooper, Colo. (81136) 208/H7
Hooper (str.), Md. 245/O8
Hooper, Nebr. (68031) 264/H3
Hooper, Utah (84315) 304/B2
Hooper, Wash. (99333) 310/G4
Hooper Bay, Alaska (99604) 196/E2
Hooper Bay, Alaska 188/C5
Hoopersville, Md. (21642) 245/O7
Hoopeston, Ill. (60942) 222/F3
Hoople, N. Dak. (58243) 282/P2
Hooppole, Ill. (61258) 222/D2
Hoorn, Netherlands 27/G3
Hoorn (isls.), Wallis and Futuna 87/J7
Hoosac (mts.), Mass. 249/B2
Hoosac Tunnel, Mass. (†01339) 249/C2
Hoosic (riv.), Mass. 249/A1
Hoosic (riv.), Vt. 268/K6
Hoosick Falls, N.Y. (12090) 276/O5
Hoosier, Sask. 181/B4
Hoot Owl, Okla. (†74366) 288/R2
Hooven, Ohio (45033) 284/A9
Hoover, Ala. (†35216) 195/E4
Hoover (dam), Ariz. 198/A2
Hoover (dam), Nev. 266/G7
Hoover (res.), Ohio 284/E5
Hoover, S. Dak. (†57760) 298/C3
Hooversville, Pa. (15936) 294/E5
Hop (riv.), Conn. 210/F1
Hopa, Turkey 63/J2
Hopatcong, N.J. (07843) 273/D2
Hopatcong (lake), N.J. 273/D2
Hop Bottom, Pa. (18824) 294/L2
Hope, Alaska (99605) 196/C1
Hope (pt.), Alaska 196/E1
Hope (bay) 5/C16
Hope, Ark. (71801) 202/C6
Hope, Br. Col. 162/D6
Hope, Br. Col. 184/M3
Hope, Idaho (83836) 220/B1
Hope, Ind. (47246) 227/F6
Hope, Kansas (67451) 232/E3
Hope, Ky. (40334) 237/O4
Hope, Maine (04847) 243/E7
Hope○, Maine (04847) 243/E7
Hope, Mich. (48628) 250/E5
Hope, Minn. (56045) 255/E7
Hope, Mo. (†65061) 261/J5
Hope (lake), Newf. 166/B3
Hope, N.J. (07844) 273/D2
Hope, N. Mex. (88250) 274/E6
Hope, N. Dak. (58046) 282/P5
Hope (isl.), Norway 4/B8
Hope, R.I. (02831) 249/H6
Hope, Loch (lake), Scotland 15/D2
Hope Bay, Jamaica 158/K6
Hopedale, Ill. (61747) 222/D3
Hopedale, Mass. (01747) 249/H4
Hopedale○, Mass. (01747) 249/H4
Hopedale, Newf. 166/B2
Hopedale, Newf. 162/L4
Hopedale, Newf. 146/N4
Hopedale, Ohio (43976) 284/J5
Hopeful Heights, Ky. (†41018) 237/R2
Hope Hull, Ala. (36043) 195/F6
Hopei (Hebei) (prov.), China 77/J4
Hopeland, Pa. (17533) 294/K5
Hopelchén, Mexico 150/P7
Hopeman, Scotland 15/E3
Hope Mills, N.C. (28348) 281/M5
Hopen (isl.), Norway 18/E2
Hopes Advance (cape), Québec 174/F1
Hopeton, Okla. (73746) 288/J1
Hopeton, Va. (†23421) 307/S5
Hopetoun, Victoria 97/B4
Hopetoun, W. Australia 92/C6
Hopetown, Québec 172/D2
Hopetown, S. Africa 118/C5
Hopetown, W. Australia 88/C6
Hope Valley, R.I. (02832) 249/H6
Hope Valley (res.), S. Australia 88/E7
Hopeville, Iowa (†50174) 229/F7
Hopewell, Ala. (†36264) 195/H3
Hopewell, Jamaica 158/G5
Hopewell, Kansas (†67557) 232/D4
Hopewell, Md. (†21817) 245/P8
Hopewell, Miss. (†39059) 256/D7
Hopewell, N.J. (08525) 273/D3
Hopewell (isls.), N.W. Terrs. 187/L4
Hopewell, Nova Scotia 168/F3
Hopewell, Ohio (43746) 284/F6
Hopewell, Pa. (16650) 294/F5
Hopewell (I.C.), Va. (23860) 307/O6
Hopewell Cape, New Bruns. 170/F3
Hopewell Hill, New Bruns. 170/F3
Hopewell Junction, N.Y. (12533) 276/N7
Hopfgarten in Nordtirol, Austria 41/B3
Hopi (buttes), Ariz. 198/E3
Hopi Ind. Res., Ariz. 198/E2
Hopkins (co.), Ky. 237/F6
Hopkins, Mich. (49328) 250/D6
Hopkins, Minn. (55343) 255/G5
Hopkins, Mo. (64461) 261/C1
Hopkins (lake), North. Terr. 93/A8
Hopkins, S.C. (29061) 296/F4
Hopkins (co.), Texas 303/J4
Hopkins (riv.), Victoria 97/B5
Hopkins, Va. (†23421) 307/S5
Hopkins (lake), W. Australia 88/D4
Hopkins (lake), W. Australia 92/E4
Hopkinsville, Ky. (42240) 237/F7
Hopkinton, Iowa (52237) 229/L4
Hopkinton, Mass. (01748) 249/J4
Hopkinton○, Mass. (01748) 249/J4
Hopkinton○, N.H. (03301) 268/D5
Hopkinton, N.Y. (12940) 276/L1
Hopkinton○, R.I. (02833) 249/H7
Hopland, Calif. (95449) 204/B5
Hoppo (Hepu), China 77/G7
Hop River, Conn. (†06237) 210/F2
Hopwood, Pa. (15445) 294/C6
Hoquiam, Wash. 188/B1
Hoquiam, Wash. (98550) 310/A3
Horace, Kansas (†67879) 232/A3
Horace, N. Dak. (58047) 282/S6
Horasan, Turkey 63/K2
Horatio, Ark. (71842) 202/B3
Horatio, S.C. (29062) 296/F3
Horažďovice, Czech. 41/B2
Horche, Spain 33/E2
Horconcitos, Panama 154/F6
Hordaland (co.), Norway 18/E6
Horden, England 13/J4
Hordio, Somalia 115/K1
Hordville, Nebr. (68846) 264/G3
Horgen, Switzerland 39/G2
Hořice v Podkrkonoší, Czech. 41/C1
Horicon, Wis. (53032) 317/J9
Horine, Mo. (†63070) 261/M6
Horizon, Sask. 181/F6
Horley, England 13/H8
Hormigüeros, P. Rico 161/A2
Hormoz, Iran 66/J7
Hormoz (isl.), Iran 66/J7
Hormozgan (prov.), Iran 66/J7
Hormuz (str.), Iran 59/G4
Hormuz (str.), Iran 66/K7
Hormuz (str.), Oman 59/G4
Horn (cape) 2/F8
Horn, Austria 41/C2
Horn (cape), Chile 120/C8
Horn (cape), Chile 138/F11
Horn (cape), Iceland 7/B2
Horn (cape), Iceland 21/B1
Horn (head), Ireland 17/E1
Horn (isl.), Miss. 256/G10
Horn (mts.), N.W. Terrs. 187/G3
Horn (riv.), N.W. Terrs. 187/G3
Hornád (riv.), Czech. 41/F2
Hornaday (riv.), N.W. Terrs. 187/F3
Hornafjördhur (fjord), Iceland 21/D1
Horná Štubňa, Czech. 41/E2
Horn-Bad Meinberg, W. Germany 22/C3
Hornbeak, Tenn. (38232) 237/C8
Hornbeck, Alberta 182/B3
Hornbeck, La. (71439) 238/D4
Hornbrook, Calif. (96044) 204/C2
Hornby, N. Zealand 100/D5
Hornby (bay), N.W. Terrs. 187/G3
Hornby Island, Br. Col. 184/H2
Horncastle, England 13/G4
Horncastle, England 10/F4
Horndean, Manitoba 179/E5
Hörnefors, Sweden 18/L5
Hornell, N.Y. (14843) 276/E6
Hornepayne, Ontario 175/C3
Hornepayne, Ontario 177/J5
Horner, W. Va. (26372) 312/F5
Hornerstown, N.J. (†08514) 273/E3
Hornersville, Mo. (63855) 261/M10
Horn Hill, Ala. (†36467) 195/F8
Horní Benešov, Czech. 41/D2
Hornick, Iowa (51026) 229/A4
Horní Libina, Czech. 41/D2
Hornings Mills, Ontario 177/D3
Hornitos, Calif. (95325) 204/E6
Horn Lake, Miss. (38637) 256/D1
Hörnli (mt.), Switzerland 39/G2
Hornos, Falso (cape), Chile 138/F11
Hornsby, N. S. Wales 88/K3
Hornsby, N.S. Wales 97/J3
Hornsby, Tenn. (38044) 237/D10
Hornsea, England 13/G4
Hornsea, England 10/F4
Hornslandet (pen.), Sweden 18/K6
Hornslet, Denmark 21/D5
Horns Road, Nova Scotia 168/H2
Hornsund (bay), Norway 18/C2
Horntown, Va. (23395) 307/T5
Hořovice, Czech. 41/C2
Horqin Youyi Qianqi (Ulanhot), China 77/K2
Horqueta, Paraguay 144/D3
Horry (co.), S.C. 296/J4
Horse (lake), Calif. 204/E3
Horse (creek), Colo. 208/M5
Horse (creek), Fla. 212/E4
Horse (isls.), Newf. 166/C3
Horse (creek), Oreg. 291/F3
Horse (creek), Wyo. 319/H4
Horse (creek), Wyo. 319/B3
Horse Branch, Ky. (42349) 237/H6
Horse Cave, Ky. (42749) 237/K6
Horse Chops (head), Newf. 166/D2
Horse Creek, Calif. (96045) 204/C2
Horse Creek (res.), Colo. 208/N6
Horse Creek, Wyo. (82061) 319/G4
Horsefly, Br. Col. 184/G4
Horsefly (lake), Br. Col. 184/G4
Horsehead (lake), N. Dak. 282/L5
Horsehead (creek), S. Dak. 298/C7
Horseheads, N.Y. (14845) 276/G6
Horsens, Denmark 18/F9
Horsens, Denmark 21/C6
Horsens (fjord), Denmark 21/D6
Horseshoe (lake), Ariz. 198/D5
Horseshoe (pt.), Fla. 212/C2
Horseshoe (lake), Manitoba 179/G2
Horse Shoe (pt.), St. Chris.-Nevis 161/C11
Horseshoe (creek), Wyo. 319/G3
Horseshoe Beach, Fla. (32648) 212/C2
Horseshoe Bend, Ark. (72512) 202/G1
Horseshoe Bend, Idaho (83629) 220/B6
Horseshoe Bend Nat'l Mil. Park, Ala. 195/G5
Horseshoe Lake, Ontario 177/E2
Horse Shoe Run, W. Va. (26769) 312/G4
Horsetooth (res.), Colo. 208/J1
Horsham, England 10/F5
Horsham, England 13/G6
Horsham, Sask. 181/B5
Horsham, Victoria 97/B5
Horsham, Victoria 88/G7
Hørsholm, Denmark 21/F6
Horšovský Týn, Czech. 41/B2
Horst, Netherlands 27/H6
Horta (dist.), Portugal 33/A1
Horta, Portugal 33/B1
Hortaleza, Spain 33/G4
Horten, Norway 18/D4
Hortense, Georgia (31543) 217/J8
Hortensfjord (fjord), Norway 18/G4
Horton, Ala. (35980) 195/F2
Horton, Iowa (†50677) 229/J3
Horton, Kansas (66439) 232/G2
Horton, Mich. (49246) 250/E6
Horton, Mo. (64751) 261/D7
Horton (riv.), N.S. Wales 97/F2
Horton (riv.), N.W. Terrs. 187/F3
Horton, Oreg. (97448) 291/D3
Horton Bay, Mich. (†49712) 250/D3
Hortonia (lake), Vt. 268/A4
Hortonville, Ind. (†46069) 227/E4
Hortonville, Mass. (†02777) 249/K5
Hortonville, Wis. (54944) 317/J7
Hørve, Denmark 21/E6
Horwich, England 10/G2
Horwich, England 13/G2

384 Hoschton

Hoschton, Georgia (30548) 217/E2
Hoselaw, Alberta 182/E2
Hosenofu (well), Libya 111/D3
Hosford, Fla. (32334) 212/B1
Hoshab, Pakistan 68/A3
Hoshab, Pakistan 59/H4
Hoshangabad, India 68/D4
Hoskins, Nebr. (68740) 264/G2
Hosmer, Br. Col. 184/K5
Hosmer, S. Dak. (57448) 298/L2
Hospental, Switzerland 39/F3
Hospers, Iowa (51238) 229/B2
Hospet, India 68/D5
Hospital, Chile 138/G4
Hospital, Ireland 17/E7
Hospitalet, Spain 33/H2
Hosseina, Ethiopia 111/G6
Hosston, La. (71043) 238/C1
Hoste (isl.), Chile 120/B8
Hoste (isl.), Chile 138/F11
Hostinné, Czech. 41/C1
Hoswick, Scotland 15/G2
Hot, Thailand 72/C3
Hotan, China 77/B4
Hotan, China 54/K6
Hotan He (riv.), China 77/B4
Hotchkiss, Alberta 182/B1
Hotchkiss, Colo. (81419) 208/D5
Hotchkissville, Conn. (†06798) 210/C2
Hot Creek (range), Nev. 266/E4
Hot Creek (valley), Nev. 266/E4
Hotevilla, Ariz. (86030) 198/E3
Hotham (inlet), Alaska 196/F1
Hoting, Sweden 18/K4
Hot Lake, Oreg. (†97850) 291/K2
Hot Spring (co.), Ark. 202/E5
Hot Springs, Mont. (59845) 262/B3
Hot Springs (Truth or Consequences), N. Mex. (8790 274/B5
Hot Springs, N.C. (28743) 281/D3
Hot Springs, S. Dak. 188/F2
Hot Springs, S. Dak. (57747) 298/C7
Hot Springs, Va. (24445) 307/J4
Hot Springs (co.), Wyo. 319/D2
Hot Springs Cove, Br. Col. 184/D5
Hot Springs National Park, Ark. 188/H4
Hot Springs National Park, Ark. (71901) 202/D4
Hot Springs Nat'l Park, Ark. 202/D4
Hot Sulphur Springs, Colo. (80451) 208/H2
Hottah (lake), N.W.T. 162/E2
Hottah (lake), N.W. Terrs. 187/G3
Hottentot (bay), Namibia 118/A5
Hotton, Belgium 27/G8
Hou, Nam (riv.), Laos 72/D2
Houck, Ariz. (86506) 198/F3
Houcktown, Ohio (†45840) 284/C4
Houffalize, Belgium 27/H8
Houghton, Iowa (52631) 229/K7
Houghton, Maine (†04275) 243/B6
Houghton, Mich. 188/J1
Houghton (co.), Mich. 250/G1
Houghton, Mich. (49931) 250/G1
Houghton (lake), Mich. 250/E4
Houghton, N.Y. (14744) 276/D6
Houghton, S. Dak. (57449) 298/N2
Houghton Lake, Mich. (48629) 250/E4
Houghton Lake Heights, Mich. (48630) 250/E4
Houghton-le-Spring, England 13/J3
Houhoek, S. Africa 118/F7
Houlka, Miss. (38850) 256/G2
Houlton, Maine 188/N1
Houlton, Maine (04730) 243/H3
Houlton○, Maine (04730) 243/H3
Houlton, Wis. (†55082) 317/A5
Houma, China 77/H4
Houma, La. (70360) 238/J7
Houndé, Upper Volta 106/D6
Hounslow, England 13/G8
Hounslow, England 10/B5
Hourn, Loch (inlet), Scotland 15/C3
Housatonic (riv.), Conn. 210/C3
Housatonic, Mass. (01236) 249/A3
Housatonic (riv.), Mass. 249/A4
House (mt.), Alberta 182/C2
House (riv.), Alberta 182/D2
House, N. Mex. (88121) 274/F4
House (range), Utah 304/A4
House Springs, Mo. (63051) 261/L6
Houston (co.), Ala. 195/H8
Houston, Ala. (35572) 195/D2
Houston, Alaska (†99687) 196/B1
Houston, Ark. (72070) 202/E3
Houston, Br. Col. 184/D3
Houston, Del. (19954) 245/S5
Houston, Fla. (†32060) 212/D1
Houston (co.), Georgia 217/E6
Houston, Ind. (†47235) 227/E6
Houston (co.), Minn. 255/G7
Houston, Minn. (55943) 255/G7
Houston, Miss. (38851) 256/G3
Houston, Mo. (65483) 261/J8
Houston, Ohio (45333) 284/B5
Houston, Pa. (15342) 294/B5
Houston (co.), Tenn. 237/F8
Houston (co.), Texas 303/J6
Houston, Texas (*77001) 303/J2
Houston, Texas 188/G5
Houston, Texas 146/J7
Houston (lake), Texas 303/J8
Houston, U.S. 2/E4
Houston Acres, Ky. (†40201) 237/K2
Houstonia, Mo. (65333) 261/F5
Houston Lake, Mo. (†64152) 261/O5
Houston Ship (chan.), Texas 303/K2
Hout (bay), S. Africa 118/E6
Houtbaai, S. Africa 118/E6
Houtman Abrolhos (isls.), W. Australia 88/A5
Houtman Abrolhos (isls.), W. Australia 92/A5
Houtrak Polder, Netherlands 27/A4
Houtzdale, Pa. (16651) 294/F4
Hov, Denmark 21/D6
Hovd, Mongolia 77/D2
Hovd (Kobdo, Jirgalanta), Mongolia 77/D2
Hovd, Mongolia 54/L5
Hovd Gol (riv.), Mongolia 77/D2
Hove, England 13/G7
Hove, England 10/F5
Hoven, S. Dak. (57450) 298/K3
Hovenweep Nat'l Mon., Colo. 208/A8
Hovenweep Nat'l Mon., Utah 304/E6
Hoveyzeh, Iran 66/F5
Hoving, N. Dak. (†58060) 282/P7
Hovland, Minn. (55606) 255/G2
Hövsgöl, Mongolia 77/E1
Hövsgöl Nuur (lake), Mongolia 77/F1
Howar, Wadi (dry riv.), Sudan 111/E4
Howard (pass), Alaska 196/G1
Howard (co.), Ark. 202/C5
Howard, Colo. (81233) 208/H6
Howard, Georgia (31039) 217/D5
Howard (co.), Ind. 227/E4
Howard (co.), Iowa 229/J2
Howard, Kansas (67349) 232/F4
Howard (co.), Md. 245/L4
Howard (co.), Mo. 261/G4
Howard (co.), Nebr. 264/F3
Howard, New Bruns. 170/E2
Howard, Ohio (43028) 284/F5
Howard, Pa. (16841) 294/G3
Howard, S. Dak. (57349) 298/P5
Howard (co.), Texas 303/C5
Howard (creek), Texas 303/C7
Howard, Wis. (54303) 317/K6
Howard A. Hanson (res.), Wash. 310/D3
Howard City, Mich. (49329) 250/D5
Howard City (Boelus), Nebr. (68820) 264/F3
Howard Lake, Minn. (55349) 255/D5
Howards Grove-Millersville, Wis. (53081) 317/L8
Howards Ridge, Mo. (†65655) 261/H9
Howardstown, Ky. (40028) 237/K5
Howardsville, Va. (24562) 307/L5
Howardville, Mo. (†63869) 261/N9
Howden, England 13/G4
Howe (cape), Australia 87/F9
Howe (sound), Br. Col. 184/K2
Howe, Idaho (83244) 220/F6
Howe, Ind. (46746) 227/G1
Howe (cape), N. S. Wales 88/J7
Howe (cape), N.S. Wales 97/F5
Howe, Okla. (74940) 288/S5
Howe, Texas (75059) 303/H4
Howell, Ark. (72071) 202/H3
Howell, Georgia (†31636) 217/F9
Howell, Mich. (48843) 250/E6
Howell (co.), Mo. 261/J9
Howell○, N.J. (07731) 273/E3
Howell, Tenn. (†37334) 237/H10
Howell, Utah (84316) 304/B2
Howells, Nebr. (68641) 264/H3
Howes, S. Dak. (57748) 298/E4
Howesville, Ind. (†47438) 227/C6
Howesville, W. Va. (†26444) 312/G4
Howey In The Hills, Fla. (32737) 212/E3
Howick, N. Zealand 100/C1
Howick, Québec 172/D4
Howick, S. Africa 118/E5
Howison, Miss. (†39574) 256/F9
Howland, Maine (04448) 243/F5
Howland○, Maine (04448) 243/F5
Howland (isl.), Pacific 87/J5
Howland Ridge, New Bruns. 170/C2
Howley, Newf. 166/C4
Howlong, N.S. Wales 97/D4
Howrah, India 68/F2
Howrah, India 54/K7
Howser, Br. Col. 184/J5
Hoxeyville, Mich. (49641) 250/D4
Hoxie, Ark. (72433) 202/H1
Hoxie, Kansas (67740) 232/B2
Höxter, W. Germany 22/C3
Hoxud, China 77/C3
Hoy (isl.), Scotland 15/E2
Hoy (isl.), Scotland 10/E1
Hoy (sound), Scotland 15/E2
Hoyerswerda, E. Germany 22/F3
Hoylake, England 13/G2
Hoylake, England 10/F2
Hoyland Nether, England 13/J2
Hoyleton, Ill. (62803) 222/D5
Hoyos, Spain 33/C2
Hoyran (lake), Turkey 63/D3
Hoyt, Colo. (80641) 208/L2
Hoyt, Kansas (66440) 232/G2
Hoyt, New Bruns. 170/D3
Hoyt, Okla. (74440) 288/R4
Hoyt (peak), Utah 304/C3
Hoyt Lakes, Minn. (55750) 255/F3
Hoytsville, Utah (†84017) 304/C3
Hoytville, Ohio (43529) 284/C3
Hozat, Turkey 59/C2
Hozat, Turkey 63/H3
Hradec Králové, Czech. 41/C1
Hranice, Czech. 41/D2
Hrinova, Czech. 41/E2
Hron (riv.), Czech. 41/E2
Hronov, Czech. 41/D1
Hrubieszów, Poland 47/F3
Hrušovany, Czech. 41/D2
Hsewi, Burma 72/C2
Hsipaw, Burma 72/C2
Hsüchang (Xuchang), China 77/H5
Htawgaw, Burma 72/C1
Huacaraje, Bolivia 136/D3
Huacareta, Bolivia 136/C7
Huacaya, Bolivia 136/D7
Huachacalla, Bolivia 136/A6
Huachi, Bolivia 136/D4
Huachi, China 77/G4
Huachipato, Chile 138/D1
Huacho, Peru 120/B4
Huacho, Peru 128/D8
Huachuca (peak), Ariz. 198/E7
Huachuca City, Ariz. (85616) 198/E7
Huacrachuco, Peru 128/D7
Huade, China 77/H3
Huadian, China 77/L3
Hua Hin, Thailand 72/D4
Huahine (isl.), Fr. Poly. 87/L7
Huaibei, China 77/J5
Huaibin, China 77/H5
Huaide (Hwaiteh), China 77/K3
Huaiji, China 77/H7
Huainan, China 77/J5
Huainan, China 54/N6
Huairen, China 77/H4
Huajuapan de León, Mexico 150/L8
Hualaihué, Chile 138/E4
Hualalai (mt.), Hawaii 218/G5
Hualañé, Chile 138/A10
Hualapai (mts.), Ariz. 198/B4
Hualapai (peak), Ariz. 198/B3
Hualapai Ind. Res., Ariz. 198/B3
Hualgayoc, Peru 128/C6
Hualien, China 77/K7
Hualla, Peru 128/F9
Huallaga (riv.), Peru 120/B3
Huallaga (riv.), Peru 128/D5
Huallanca, Ancash, Peru 128/D7
Huallanca, Huánuco, Peru 128/D7
Huallen, Alberta 182/A2
Huamachuco, Peru 128/D6
Huamantla, Mexico 150/N1
Huambo (dist.), Angola 115/C6
Huambo, Angola 102/D6
Huambo, Angola 115/C6
Huambo, Angola 2/K6
Huanaqui, Bolivia 136/A7
Huanay, Bolivia 136/B4
Huancabamba, Peru 128/C5
Huancané, Bolivia 136/B6
Huancané, Peru 128/H10
Huancapi, Peru 128/E9
Huancavelica (dept.), Peru 128/E9
Huancavelica, Peru 120/B4
Huancavelica, Peru 128/E9
Huancayo, Peru 128/E9
Huancayo, Pru 120/B4
Huanchaca, Bolivia 136/B7
Huanchaca, Cerro (mt.), Bolivia 136/B7
Huanchaca, Serranía de (mts.), Bolivia 136/E4
Huanchaco, Peru 128/C7
Huanggang, China 77/J5
Huang He (riv.), China 2/Q4
Huang He (Hwang Ho) (riv.), China 54/N6
Huang He (Ma Qu) (riv.), China 77/F5
Huang He (Yellow) (riv.), China 77/J4
Huangling, China 77/G4
Huangliu, China 77/G8
Huangshi, China 77/J5
Huangzhong, China 77/F4
Huanqueros, Argentina 143/F5
Huanta, Peru 128/E9
Huánuco (dept.), Peru 128/D7
Huánuco, Peru 128/E7
Huánuco, Peru 120/B3
Huanuni, Bolivia 136/B6
Huanuni, Bolivia 120/C4
Huan Xian, China 77/G4
Huapai, N. Zealand 100/B1
Huapí (mts.), Nicaragua 154/E4
Huaquechula, Mexico 150/M2
Huara, Chile 138/B2
Huaral, Peru 128/D8
Huaráz, Peru 128/D7
Huaráz, Peru 120/B3
Huari, Bolivia 136/B6
Huari, Peru 128/D7
Huariaca, Peru 128/E8
Huarina, Bolivia 136/A5
Huarmey, Peru 128/C8
Huarochirí, Peru 128/D9
Huarocondo, Peru 128/F9
Huásabas, Mexico 150/E2
Huasaga (riv.), Peru 128/D4
Huascarán (mt.), Peru 120/B3
Huascarán (mt.), Peru 128/D7
Huasco, Chile 138/A7
Huasco (riv.), Chile 138/A7
Huatabampo, Mexico 150/D3
Huatunas (lag.), Bolivia 136/B3
Huatusco de Chicuellar, Mexico 150/P2
Huauchinango, Mexico 150/L6
Huaura, Peru 128/D8
Huautla de Jiménez, Mexico 150/L7
Huayabamba (riv.), Peru 128/D6
Huaylas, Peru 128/C7
Huayllas, Bolivia 136/C6
Hub, Miss. (†39429) 256/E8
Hubball, W. Va. (†25506) 312/B6
Hubbard, Iowa (50122) 229/G4
Hubbard (lake), Mich. 250/F4
Hubbard (co.), Minn. 255/D3
Hubbard, Minn. (†56470) 255/C4
Hubbard, Nebr. (68741) 264/H2
Hubbard, Ohio (44425) 284/J3
Hubbard, Oreg. (97032) 291/A3
Hubbard, Sask. 181/H4
Hubbard, Texas (76648) 303/H6
Hubbard Creek (lake), Texas 303/F5
Hubbard Lake, Mich. (49747) 250/F4
Hubbards, Nova Scotia 168/D4
Hubbardston○, Mass. (01452) 249/F3
Hubbardston, Mich. (48845) 250/E5
Hubbardstown, W. Va. (†25555) 312/A6
Hubbardsville, N.Y. (13355) 276/J5
Hubbardton○, Vt. (05749) 268/A4
Hubbart (pt.), Manitoba 179/K2
Hubbell, Mich. (49934) 250/A1
Hubbell, Nebr. (68375) 264/G4
Hubbell Trading Post Nat'l Hist. Site, Ariz. 198/F3
Hub City, Wis. (†53581) 317/F9
Hubei (Hupei) (prov.), China 77/H5
Huberdeau, Québec 172/C4
Huber Heights, Ohio (45424) 284/B6
Hubert, N.C. (28539) 281/P5
Hubertus, Wis. (53033) 317/K1
Hubli-Dharwar, India 68/C5
Hubli-Dharwar, India 54/J8
Huch'ang, N. Korea 81/C3
Hückelhoven, W. Germany 22/B3
Hucknall, England 13/F4
Huddersfield, England 10/G2
Huddersfield, England 13/J2
Huddinge, Sweden 18/H1
Huddleston, Va. (24104) 307/K6
Huddy, Ky. (41535) 237/S5
Hudiksvall, Sweden 18/K6
Hudson (bay) 162/H3
Hudson (str.) 162/J3
Hudson (bay), Canada 2/E3
Hudson (str.), Canada 146/L3
Hudson (bay), Canada 146/K3
Hudson, Colo. (80642) 208/K2
Hudson, Fla. (33568) 212/D3
Hudson, Ill. (61748) 222/E3
Hudson, Ind. (46747) 227/G1
Hudson, Iowa (50643) 229/H4
Hudson, Kansas (67545) 232/D3
Hudson, Ky. (40145) 237/J5
Hudson○, Maine (04449) 243/F5
Hudson (bay), Manitoba 179/K2
Hudson, Md. (†21613) 245/N6
Hudson, Mass. (01749) 249/H3
Hudson○, Mass. (01749) 249/H3
Hudson, Mich. (49247) 250/E7
Hudson, N.H. (03051) 268/E6
Hudson○, N.H. (03051) 268/E6
Hudson (co.), N.J. 273/E2
Hudson (riv.), N.J. 273/C1
Hudson, N.Y. (12534) 276/N6
Hudson (riv.), N.Y. 276/N7
Hudson, N.C. (28638) 281/G3
Hudson (bay), N.W. Terrs. 187/K3
Hudson (str.), N.W. Terrs. 187/L3
Hudson, Ohio (44236) 284/H3
Hudson (lake), Okla. 288/R2
Hudson, Ontario 175/B2
Hudson, Ontario 177/G4
Hudson (bay), Ontario 175/D1
Hudson, Québec 172/C4
Hudson (bay), Québec 174/A1
Hudson (str.), Québec 174/F1
Hudson, S. Dak. (57034) 298/R7
Hudson, Wis. (54016) 317/A6
Hudson, Wyo. (82515) 319/D3
Hudson Bay, Sask. 181/J3
Hudson Falls, N.Y. (12839) 276/O4
Hudson Hope, Br. Col. 184/F2
Hudson Lake, Ind. (46552) 227/D1
Hudsons Bay, Alberta 182/E4
Hudsonville, Mich. (49426) 250/D6
Hudspeth (co.), Texas 303/B10
Hudwin (lake), Manitoba 179/G1
Hue, Vietnam 54/M8
Hue, Vietnam 72/E3
Hueco (mts.), N. Mex. 274/D6
Hueco (mts.), Texas 303/B10
Huedin, Romania 45/F2
Huehue, Hawaii (†96740) 218/G5
Huehuetenango, Guatemala 154/B3
Huehuetlán el Chico, Mexico 150/M2
Huejotzingo, Mexico 150/M1
Huejutla, Mexico 150/K6
Huelma, Spain 33/E4
Huelva (prov.), Spain 33/C4
Huelva, Spain 33/C4
Huelva, Spain 7/D5
Huelva (riv.), Spain 33/C4
Huentelauquén, Chile 138/A8
Huercal-Overa, Spain 33/F4
Huerfano (co.), Colo. 208/K7
Huerfano (riv.), Colo. 208/L7
Huesca (prov.), Spain 33/F1
Huesca, Spain 33/F1
Huéscar, Spain 33/E4
Huetamo, Mexico 150/J7
Huete, Spain 33/E2
Huetter, Idaho (†83854) 220/B2
Huey, Ill. (62252) 222/D5
Hueyotlipan de Hidalgo, Mexico 150/M1
Hueytown, Ala. (35020) 195/D4
Huff, N. Dak. (58555) 282/J6
Huffman, Ark. (†72315) 202/L2
Huffton, S. Dak. (†57432) 298/N2
Huger, S.C. (29450) 296/H5
Huggins, Mo. (65484) 261/H8
Hugh Butler (lake), Nebr. 264/D4
Hughenden, Alberta 182/E3
Hughenden, Australia 87/E8
Hughenden, Queensland 88/G4
Hughenden, Queensland 95/B4
Hughes, Alaska (99745) 196/H1
Hughes, Ark. (72348) 202/J4
Hughes (co.), Okla. 288/O4
Hughes, S. Australia 94/A4
Hughes (co.), S. Dak. 298/J5
Hughes (riv.), W. Va. 312/D4
Hughes Springs, Texas (75656) 303/K5
Hughestown, Pa. (†18640) 294/F7
Hughesville, Md. (20637) 245/L6
Hugheville, Mo. (65334) 261/F5
Hughesville, Pa. (17737) 294/J3
Hughson, Calif. (95326) 204/E6
Hughton, Sask. 181/D4
Hugh Town, England 13/A8
Hugo, Colo. (80821) 208/N4
Hugo, Minn. (55038) 255/E5
Hugo, Okla. (74743) 288/P7
Hugo (lake), Okla. 288/R6
Hugo Stroessner, Paraguay 144/C4
Hugoton, Kansas (67951) 232/A4
Huhehot (Hohhot), China 77/H3
Huiarau (range), N. Zealand 100/F3
Hŭich'ŏn, N. Korea 81/C3
Huila (dist.), Angola 115/B7
Huila (dept.), Colombia 126/C6
Huila (mt.), Colombia 120/B2
Huila, Nevado del (mt.), Colombia 126/C6
Huimanguillo, Mexico 150/N8
Huimin, China 77/J4
Huinca Renancó, Argentina 143/D3
Huining, China 77/G4
Huissen, Netherlands 27/H5
Huitzilán, Mexico 150/O1
Huitzuco de los Figueroa, Mexico 150/K7
Huixcolotla, Mexico 150/N2
Huixtepec, Mexico 150/L8
Huixtla, Mexico 150/N9
Huize, China 77/F6
Huizen, Netherlands 27/G4
Huizhou, China 77/H7
Hulaco, Ala. (†35087) 195/E2
Hulah (lake), Kansas 232/F5
Hulah, Okla. (†67333) 288/O1
Hulah (lake), Okla. 288/O1
Hulan, China 77/L2
Hulbert, Mich. (49748) 250/D2
Hulbert, Okla. (74441) 288/R3
Hulberton, N.Y. (14473) 276/D4
Hulett, Wyo. (82720) 319/H1
Hulin, China 77/M2
Hull, England 7/E3
Hull, England 10/F4
Hull, England 13/G4
Hull, Fla. (†33842) 212/E4
Hull, Georgia (30646) 217/F2
Hull, Ill. (62343) 222/B4
Hull, Iowa (51239) 229/A2
Hull (isl.), Kiribati 87/J6
Hull○, Mass. (02045) 249/E7
Hull, N. Dak. (†58542) 282/K7
Hull, Que. 162/J6
Hull (co.), Québec 172/B4
Hull, Québec 172/B4
Hulls Cove, Maine (04644) 243/G7
Hulopee (bay), Hawaii 218/G2
Hulopoe Bay, Hawaii (†96763) 218/H2
Hulst, Netherlands 27/E6
Hultsfred, Sweden 18/K8
Hulun Nur (lake), China 77/J2
Huma, China 77/L1
Humacao (dist.), P. Rico 161/F2
Humacao, P. Rico 161/E2
Humacao, P. Rico 156/G1
Humacao (riv.), P. Rico 161/E2
Huma He (riv.), China 77/K1
Humahuaca, Argentina 143/C1
Humaitá, Bolivia 136/B2
Humaitá, Brazil 132/H10
Humaitá, Brazil 120/C3
Humaitá, Brazil 132/G10
Humaitá, Paraguay 144/C5
Humansdorp, S. Africa 118/C6
Humansville, Mo. (65674) 261/E7
Humarock, Mass. (02047) 249/M4
Humber (riv.), England 13/G4
Humber (riv.), England 10/G4
Humber (riv.), Newf. 166/C4
Humber (riv.), Ontario 177/J3
Humberside (co.), England 13/G4
Humberto, Argentina 143/F5
Humbird, Wis. (54746) 317/E6
Humble, Texas (*77338) 303/J7
Humble City, N. Mex. (†88240) 274/F6
Humboldt, Ariz. (86329) 198/C4
Humboldt (co.), Calif. 204/B3
Humboldt (bay), Calif. 204/A3
Humboldt (bay), Colombia 126/B4
Humboldt, Ill. (61931) 222/E4
Humboldt (co.), Iowa 229/E3
Humboldt, Iowa (50548) 229/E3
Humboldt, Kansas (66748) 232/G4
Humboldt, Minn. (56731) 255/A2
Humboldt, Nebr. (68376) 264/J4
Humboldt (co.), Nev. 266/C1
Humboldt, Nev. (†89418) 266/C2
Humboldt (range), Nev. 266/C2
Humboldt (riv.), Nev. 188/C2
Humboldt (riv.), Nev. 266/E2
Humboldt (sink), Nev. 266/C2
Humboldt (mt.), New Caled. 86/H4
Humboldt, Sask. 162/F5
Humboldt, Sask. 181/F3
Humboldt, S. Dak. (57035) 298/P6
Humboldt, Tenn. (38343) 237/D9
Humboldt Salt (marsh), Nev. 266/D3
Humbug (mt.), Oreg. 291/C5
Hume, Ill. (61932) 222/F4
Hume, Mo. (64752) 261/C6
Hume (res.), N.S. Wales 97/D4
Hume, N.Y. (14745) 276/D5
Hume, Sask. 181/H6
Hume (lake), Victoria 97/D4
Hume, Va. (22639) 307/N3
Humenné, Czech. 41/G2
Humeston, Iowa (50123) 229/G7
Humlum, Denmark 21/B4
Hummelstown, Pa. (17036) 294/J5
Hummock (isl.), Tasmania 99/D2
Humnoke, Ark. (72072) 202/G4
Humphrey (pt.), Alaska 196/K1
Humphrey, Ark. (72073) 202/G5
Humphrey, Idaho (†83446) 220/F5
Humphrey, Nebr. (68642) 264/G3
Humphreys (peak), Ariz. 198/D3
Humphreys, La. (†70356) 238/J7
Humphreys (co.), Miss. 256/C4
Humphreys, Mo. (64646) 261/F2
Humphreys, Okla. (†73521) 288/H5
Humphreys (co.), Tenn. 237/F8
Humpolec, Czech. 41/C2
Humptulips, Wash. (98552) 310/A3
Humptulips (riv.), Wash. 310/B3
Humpty Doo, North. Terr. 93/B2
Húnaflói (bay), Iceland 7/B2
Húnaflói (bay), Iceland 21/B1
Hunan (prov.), China 77/H6
Hunchun, China 77/M3
Hundested, Denmark 21/E6
Hundred, W. Va. (26575) 312/E3
Hunedoara, Romania 7/G4
Hunedoara, Romania 45/F3
Hünfeld, W. Germany 22/C3
Hungary 2/K3
Hungary 7/F4
HUNGARY 41
Hunger (mt.), Vt. 268/B3
Hungerford, Queensland 95/B6
Hŭngnam, N. Korea 54/O6
Hungry Horse, Mont. (59919) 262/C2
Hungry Horse (res.), Mont. 262/C2
Hungtow (isl.), China 77/K7
Hunjiang, China 77/L3
Hunmanby, England 13/G3
Hunnewell, Kansas (†67140) 232/E4
Hunnewell, Mo. (63443) 261/J3
Hunse (riv.), Netherlands 27/K3
Hunsrück (mts.), W. Germany 22/B4
Hunstanton, England 13/H5
Hunstanton, England 10/G4
Hunt, Ill. (†62480) 222/E4
Hunt (co.), Texas 303/H4
Hunt (mt.), Wyo. 319/E1
Hunte (riv.), W. Germany 22/C2
Hunter, Ark. (72074) 202/H3
Hunter (isl.), Br. Col. 184/C4
Hunter (peak), Idaho 220/D3
Hunter, Kansas (67452) 232/D2
Hunter, Mo. (†63943) 261/L9
Hunter (riv.), N.S. Wales 97/F3
Hunter, N.Y. (12442) 276/M6
Hunter (mt.), N.Y. 276/M6
Hunter (mts.), N. Zealand 100/A6
Hunter, N. Dak. (58048) 282/R5
Hunter, Okla. (74640) 288/L1
Hunter (isls.), Tasmania 88/G8
Hunter (isl.), Tasmania 99/A2
Hunter (isls.), Tasmania 99/B2
Hunterdon (co.), N.J. 273/D2
Hunter River, Pr. Edward I. 168/E2
Hunters, Wash. (99137) 310/G2
Hunters Creek Village, Texas (†77001) 303/J1
Hunters Hill, N. S. Wales 88/K4
Hunters Hill, N.S. Wales 97/J3
Huntersville, Ky. (†42602) 237/L7
Huntersville, Minn. (†56464) 255/D4
Huntersville, N.C. (28078) 281/H4
Huntersville, W. Va. (†24954) 312/G6
Huntertown, Ind. (46748) 227/G2
Hunterville, N. Zealand 100/E3
Hunting (riv.), N.C. 281/H2
Hunting (isl.), S.C. 296/G7
Huntingburg, Ind. (47542) 227/D8
Huntingdon, Br. Col. 184/L3
Huntingdon (isl.), Newf. 166/C3
Huntingdon (co.), Pa. 294/F5
Huntingdon, Pa. (16652) 294/G5
Huntingdon (co.), Québec 172/C4
Huntingdon, Québec 172/C4
Huntingdon, Tenn. (38344) 237/E8
Huntingdon and Godmanchester, England 13/G5
Huntingdon and Godmanchester, England 10/F4
Huntington, Ark. (72940) 202/B3
Huntington, Conn. (†06484) 210/C3
Huntington, England 13/G3
Huntington (co.), Ind. 227/G3
Huntington, Ind. (46750) 227/G3
Huntington (lake), Ind. 227/F3
Huntington, Iowa (†51334) 229/D2
Huntington○, Mass. (01050) 249/C4
Huntington (creek), Nev. 266/F2
Huntington, N.J. (†08865) 273/C2
Huntington, N.Y. (11743) 276/R6
Huntington, Oreg. (97907) 291/K3
Huntington, Texas (75949) 303/K6
Huntington, Utah (84528) 304/C4
Huntington (creek), Utah 304/C4
Huntington○, Vt. (05462) 268/B3
Huntington, Va. (†22301) 307/S3
Huntington, W. Va. 188/K3
Huntington, W. Va. (*25701) 312/A6
Huntington Beach, Calif. (*92646) 204/C11
Huntington Center, Vt. (†05462) 268/B3
Huntington Park, Calif. (90255) 204/C11
Huntington Station, N.Y. (11746) 276/R6
Huntingtown, Md. (20639) 245/M6
Hunting Valley, Ohio (†44022) 284/J9
Huntland, Tenn. (37345) 237/J10
Huntleigh, Mo. (†63101) 261/O3
Huntley, Ill. (60142) 222/E1
Huntley, Minn. (56047) 255/D7
Huntley, Mont. (59037) 262/H5
Huntley, Nebr. (68951) 264/E4
Huntley, Wyo. (82218) 319/H4
Huntly, N. Zealand 100/E2
Huntly, Scotland 10/E2
Huntly, Scotland 15/F3
Huntoon, Sask. 181/H6
Huntsburg, Ohio (44046) 284/H2
Hunts Inlet, Br. Col. 184/B3
Hunts Point, Nova Scotia 168/D5
Hunts Point, Wash. (†98004) 310/B2
Huntsville, Ala. 188/J4
Huntsville, Ala. (*35801) 195/E1
Huntsville, Ark. (72740) 202/C1
Huntsville, Conn. (†06031) 210/B1
Huntsville, Ind. (†47358) 227/F4
Huntsville, Ind. (†46064) 227/G4
Huntsville, Ky. (42251) 237/H6
Huntsville, Mo. (65259) 261/H4
Huntsville, Ohio (43324) 284/C5
Huntsville, Ontario 177/E2
Huntsville, Ontario 175/E3
Huntsville, Tenn. (37756) 237/N8
Huntsville, Texas (77340) 303/J7
Huntsville, Utah (84317) 304/C2
Huntsville, Wash. (99328) 310/G4
Hunucmá, Mexico 150/O6
Hunza (Baltit), Pakistan 68/C1
Huocheng, China 77/B3
Huon (isls.), New Caled. 87/G7
Huon (gulf), Papua N.G. 87/E6
Huon (gulf), Papua N.G. 85/C7
Huon (pen.), Papua N.G. 86/A2
Huon (riv.), Tasmania 99/C5
Huong Khe, Vietnam 72/E3
Huonville-Ranelagh, Tasmania 99/C5
Huoshan, China 77/J5
Huot, Minn. (†56716) 255/B3
Huo Xian, China 77/H4
Hupei (Hubei) (prov.), China 77/H5
Hurbanovo, Czech. 41/E3
Hurd (cape), Ontario 177/C2
Hurdland, Mo. (63547) 261/H2
Hurdle Mills, N.C. (27541) 281/L2
Hurdsfield, N. Dak. (58451) 282/L5

Indianola 385

Hure, China 77/K3
Hureidha, P.D.R. Yemen 59/E6
Hurghada, Egypt 111/F2
Hurghada, Egypt 59/B4
Hurlburt, Fla. (†32548) 212/B6
Hurley, Miss. (39555) 256/H9
Hurley, Mo. (65675) 261/F9
Hurley, N. Mex. (88043) 274/A6
Hurley, N.Y. (12443) 276/M7
Hurley, S. Dak. (57036) 298/P7
Hurley, Va. (24620) 307/D6
Hurley, Wis. (54534) 317/F3
Hurleyville, N.Y. (12747) 276/L7
Hurlford, Scotland 15/D5
Hurlock, Md. (21643) 245/P6
Huron (lake) 146/K5
Huron (lake) 162/H7
Huron, Calif. (93234) 204/E7
Huron, Ind. (47437) 227/D7
Huron, Kansas (66038) 232/G2
Huron (lake), Mich. 188/K2
Huron (co.), Mich. 250/F5
Huron (bay), Mich. 250/A2
Huron (lake), Mich. 250/G4
Huron (riv.), Mich. 250/F6
Huron (co.), Ohio 284/E3
Huron, Ohio (44839) 284/E3
Huron (riv.), Ohio 284/E3
Huron (county), Ontario 177/C4
Huron (lake), Ontario 177/B3
Huron (lake), Ontario 175/D3
Huron, S. Dak. 188/G2
Huron, S. Dak. (57350) 298/N5
Huron, Tenn. (38345) 237/E9
Huron City, Mich. (†48467) 250/G4
Huron Mountain, Mich. (†49808) 250/B2
Huron Park, Ontario 177/C4
Huron River (pt.), Mich. 250/B2
Hurricane, Ala. (†36507) 195/C9
Hurricane (cliffs), Ariz. 198/B2
Hurricane (mt.), Mont. 262/D2
Hurricane, Utah (84737) 304/A6
Hurricane, W. Va. (25526) 312/C6
Hurricane Deck, Mo. (†65079) 261/G6
Hurricane Mills, Tenn. (37078) 237/F9
Hurst, Georgia (†30560) 217/D1
Hurst, Ill. (62949) 222/D6
Hurst, Texas (76053) 303/F2
Hurst, W. Va. (†26445) 312/E4
Hurstville, Iowa (†52060) 229/M4
Hurstville, N. S. Wales 88/K4
Hurstville, N.S. Wales 97/J4
Hurt, Va. (24563) 307/K6
Hürth, W. Germany 22/B3
Hurtsboro, Ala. (36860) 195/H6
Hurunui (riv.), N. Zealand 100/D5
Hurup, Denmark 21/B4
Húsavík, Iceland 21/C1
Husher, Wis. (†53108) 317/L2
Hushpuckena, Miss. (†38774) 256/C2
Huşi, Romania 45/J2
Husk, N.C. (28639) 281/F1
Huskisson, N.S. Wales 97/F4
Huslia, Alaska (99746) 196/G1
Huson, Mont. (59846) 262/B3
Hussar, Alberta 182/D4
Hustisford, Wis. (53034) 317/J9
Hustler, Wis. (54637) 317/F8
Hustontown, Pa. (17229) 294/F5
Hustonville, Ky. (40437) 237/M6
Hustopeče, Czech. 41/D2
Husum, Sweden 18/L5
Husum, Wash. (98623) 310/D5
Husum, W. Germany 22/C1
Hutchins (mt.), N.H. 268/E2
Hutchins, Texas (75141) 303/G3
Hutchins, Wis. (†54450) 317/H6
Hutchinson, Kans. 188/G3
Hutchinson, Kansas (67501) 232/D3
Hutchinson, Kansas 146/J6
Hutchinson, Minn. (55350) 255/D6
Hutchinson (co.), S. Dak. 298/O7
Hutchinson (co.), Texas 303/C2
Hutchinson, W. Va. (†26591) 312/F4
Huth, Yemen Arab Rep. 59/D6
Hutsonville, Ill. (62433) 222/F4
Hutt (riv.), N. Zealand 100/C2
Hüttenberg, Austria 41/C3
Hüttental, W. Germany 22/C3
Hutte Sauvage (lake), Québec 174/E1
Huttig, Ark. (71747) 202/F7
Hutto, Texas (78634) 303/G7
Hutton, La. (†71402) 238/D4
Hutton, Md. (†21550) 245/A3
Huttonsville, W. Va. (26273) 312/G5
Hutton Valley, Mo. (†65793) 261/J9
Huttwil, Switzerland 39/E2
Hutubi, China 77/C3
Huumula, Hawaii (†96743) 218/H5
Huutokoski, Finland 18/P5
Huwelijkszorg, Suriname 131/C2
Huxford, Ala. (36543) 195/D8
Hu Xian, China 77/G5
Huxley, Alberta 182/D4
Huxley, Iowa (50124) 229/F5
Huxley, Texas (†75973) 303/L6
Huy, Belgium 27/G8
Huyton-with-Roby, England 13/G2
Hvannadalshnúkur (mt.), Iceland 21/C1
Hvar (isl.), Yugoslavia 45/C4
Hvidbjerg, Denmark 21/B4
Hvide Sande, Denmark 21/A6
Hviding, Denmark 21/B7
Hvitá (riv.), Iceland 21/B1
Hwainan (Huainan), China 77/J5
Hwaiteh (Huaide), China 77/K3
Hwange (Wankie), Zimbabwe 118/D3
Hwang Ho (riv.), China 54/N6
Hwangju, N. Korea 81/C4
Hwangshih (Huangshi), China 77/J5
Hyak, Wash. (98068) 310/D3
Hyalite (peak), Mont. 262/E5
Hyannis, Mass. (02601) 249/N6
Hyannis, Nebr. (69350) 264/C3
Hyannis Port, Mass. (02647) 249/N6
Hyargas, Mongolia 77/D2
Hyargas Nuur (lake), Mongolia 77/D2
Hyas, Sask. 181/J4
Hyattstown, Md. (20734) 245/J3
Hyattsville, Md. (*20780) 245/F4
Hyattville, Wyo. (82428) 319/E1
Hybart, Ala. (36452) 195/D7
Hybord, Manitoba 179/C1
Hyco (riv.), N.C. 281/L2
Hyco (riv.), Va. 307/K8
Hydaburg, Alaska (99922) 196/M2
Hyde, England 13/H2
Hyde, England 10/G2
Hyde, N. Zealand 100/C6
Hyde (co.), N.C. 281/S3
Hyde, Pa. (16843) 294/F4
Hyde (co.), S. Dak. 298/K4
Hyden, Ky. (41749) 237/P6
Hyden, W. Australia 92/B6
Hyde Park, Mass. (02136) 249/C7
Hyde Park, N.Y. (12538) 276/N6
Hyde Park, Ontario 177/C4
Hyde Park, Pa. (15641) 294/D4
Hyde Park, Utah (84318) 304/C2
Hyde Park, Vt. (05655) 268/B2
Hyde Park○, Vt. (05655) 268/B2
Hyder, Alaska (99923) 196/P2
Hyderabad, India 2/N5
Hyderabad, India 68/D5
Hyderabad, India 54/J8
Hyderabad, Pakistan 68/B3
Hyderabad, Pakistan 59/J4
Hyderabad, Pakistan 54/H7
Hydesville, Calif. (95547) 204/B3
Hydetown, Pa. (16328) 294/C2
Hydeville, Vt. (05750) 268/A4
Hydraulic, Br. Col. 184/F4
Hydro, Okla. (73048) 288/J3
Hye, Texas (78635) 303/F7
Hyères, France 28/G6
Hyères (isls.), France 28/G6
Hyesan, N. Korea 81/D3
Hygiene, Colo. (80533) 208/J2
Hyland (riv.), Yukon 187/F3
Hylo, Alberta 182/D2
Hyltebruk, Sweden 18/H8
Hyman, S.C. (†29583) 296/H4
Hymer, Kansas (†66869) 232/F3
Hymera, Ind. (47855) 227/C6
Hyndman (peak), Idaho 220/D6
Hyndman, Pa. (15545) 294/E6
Hyner, Pa. (17738) 294/G3
Hynish (bay), Scotland 15/B4
Hyogo (pref.), Japan 81/H7
Hypoluxo, Fla. (†33460) 212/F5
Hyrra Banda, Cent. Afr. Rep. 115/D2
Hyrum, Utah (84319) 304/C2
Hyrynsalmi, Finland 18/Q4
Hysham, Mont. (59038) 262/J4
Hythe, Alberta 182/A2
Hythe, Alta. 162/E4
Hythe, England 10/G5
Hythe, England 13/H6
Hythe, Tasmania 99/C5
Hytop, Ala. (35753) 195/F1
Hyuga, Japan 81/E7
Hyvinkää, Finland 18/O6

I

Ia Drang (riv.), Vietnam 72/E4
Iaeger, W. Va. (24844) 312/C8
Ialomiţa (marshes), Romania 45/J3
Ialomiţa (riv.), Romania 45/H3
Iamonia (lake), Fla. 212/B1
Iantha, Mo. (64753) 261/D8
Iar Connacht (dist.), Ireland 17/C5
Iaşi, Romania 7/G4
Iaşi, Romania 45/H2
Iatan, Mo. (†64098) 261/C4
Iatt (lake), La. 238/E3
Iba, Philippines 85/F2
Iba, Philippines 82/B3
Ibadan, Nigeria 2/K5
Ibadan, Nigeria 102/C4
Ibadan, Nigeria 106/E7
Ibagué, Colombia 126/C5
Ibagué, Colombia 120/B2
Ibaiti, Brazil 135/A3
Ibapah, Utah (84034) 304/A3
Ibar (riv.), Yugoslavia 45/E4
Ibaraki (pref.), Japan 81/K5
Ibaraki, Japan 81/J7
Ibarra, Ecuador 128/D2
Ibarra, Ecuador 120/B2
Ibarreta, Argentina 143/D2
Ibb, Yemen Arab Rep. 59/D7
Ibbenbüren, W. Germany 22/B2
'Ibbin, Jordan 65/D3
Iberia (par.), La. 238/G7
Iberia, Mo. (65486) 261/H6
Iberia, Ohio (43325) 284/E4
Iberia, Peru 128/F5
Iberville (par.), La. 238/H6
Iberville, La. (70746) 238/K2
Iberville (co.), Québec 172/D4
Iberville, Québec 172/D4
Iberville, D' (lake), Québec 174/C1
Ibi, Nigeria 106/F7
Ibiá, Brazil 132/E7
Ibibobo, Bolivia 136/D7
Ibicaraí, Brazil 132/G6
Ibicuí (riv.), Brazil 132/C10
Ibicuy, Argentina 143/G6
Ibipetuba, Brazil 132/F5
Ibitinga, Brazil 135/B2
Ibiza, Spain 33/G3
Ibiza (isl.), Spain 7/E5
Ibiza (isl.), Spain 33/G3
Ibo, Bolivia 136/D7
Ibo, Mozambique 118/G2
Ibounzi (mt.), Gabon 115/B4
Ibra, Oman 59/G5
Ibra, Wadi (dry riv.), Sudan 111/D5
Ibrány, Hungary 41/F2
'Ibri, Oman 59/G5
Ibusuki, Japan 81/E8
Içá (riv.), Brazil 120/C3
Içá (riv.), Brazil 132/G9
Ica (dept.), Peru 128/E10
Ica, Peru 128/E10
Ica, Peru 120/B4
Ica (riv.), Peru 128/E10
Icabarú, Venezuela 124/H5
Icabarú (riv.), Venezuela 124/G5
Icacos (pt.), Trin. & Tob. 161/A11
Icaño, Catamarca, Argentina 143/C2
Icaño, Santiago del Estero, Argentina 143/D2
Icard, N.C. (28666) 281/G3
Ice Harbor (dam), Wash. 310/G4
Içel (prov.), Turkey 63/F4
Içel (Mersin), Turkey 63/F4
Iceland 2/J2
Iceland 7/C2
Iceland 4/C10
ICELAND 21/B1
Ichang (Yichang), China 77/H5
Ichchapuram, India 68/F5
Ichhapur, India 68/F1
Ichihara, Japan 81/P3
Ichikawa, Japan 81/P2
Ichilo (riv.), Bolivia 136/C5
Ichinohe, Japan 81/K3
Ichinomiya, Japan 81/H6
Ichinoseki, Japan 81/K4
Ichnya, U.S.S.R. 52/D4
Ichoa (riv.), Bolivia 136/C4
Ichoca, Bolivia 136/B5
Ichtegem, Belgium 27/B6
Ichun (Yichun), China 77/L2
Ichuña, Peru 128/G11
Icicle (creek), Wash. 310/E3
Ickesburg, Pa. (17037) 294/H5
Icla, Bolivia 136/C6
Içme, Turkey 63/H3
Icó, Brazil 132/G4
Iconium, Mo. (†64776) 261/E6
Icy (bay), Alaska 196/K3
Icy (cape), Alaska 196/F1
Icy (cape), Alaska 196/K3
Icy (pt.), Alaska 196/L1
Icy (str.), Alaska 196/M1
Ida (co.), Iowa 229/C4
Ida, La. (71044) 238/C1
Ida, Mich. (48140) 250/F7
Idabel, Okla. (74745) 288/S7
Ida Grove, Iowa (51445) 229/B4
Idaho 188/D2
IDAHO 220
Idaho (co.), Idaho 220/C4
Idaho, 202
Idaho, Ohio (45661) 284/D7
Idaho (state), U.S. 146/G5
Idaho City, Idaho (83631) 220/C6
Idaho Falls, Idaho 146/G5
Idaho Falls, Idaho 188/D2
Idaho Falls, Idaho (*83401) 220/F6
Idaho Springs, Colo. (80452) 208/H3
Idahue, Chile 138/F5
Idalia, Colo. (80735) 208/P3
Idalou, Texas (79329) 303/C4
Idana, Kansas (67432) 232/E2
Idanha, Oreg. (97350) 291/E3
Idanha-a-Nova, Portugal 33/C3
Idar-Oberstein, W. Germany 22/B4
Idaville, Ind. (47950) 227/D3
Idaville, Pa. (17337) 294/H5
Iddan, Somalia 115/J2
Iddesleigh, Alberta 182/E4
Ide, Japan 81/J7
Ideal, Georgia (31041) 217/D6
Ideal, S. Dak. (57541) 298/K6
Idehan Murzuk (des.), Libya 111/B2
Idehan Ubari (des.), Libya 111/B2
Idelès, Algeria 106/F4
Ider, Ala. (35981) 195/G1
Ider Gol (riv.), Mongolia 77/E2
Idfu, Egypt 111/F3
Idfu, Egypt 59/B5
Ídhi (mt.), Greece 45/G8
Ídhra, Greece 45/F7
Idi, Indonesia 85/B4
Idil, Turkey 63/J4
Idiofa, Zaire 115/C4
Idlewild, Mich. (49642) 250/D5
Idlewild, Tenn. (38346) 237/D8
Idleyld Park, Oreg. (97447) 291/D4
Idlib (prov.), Syria 63/G5
Idlib, Syria 63/G5
Idna, West Bank 65/B4
Idrigill (pt.), Scotland 15/B3
Idyllwild-Pine Cove, Calif. (92349) 204/J10
Ie (isl.), Japan 81/N6
Ieper, Belgium 27/B7
Ierápetra, Greece 45/G8
Iet, Somalia 115/H3
Ifakara, Tanzania 115/G5
Ifalik (atoll), Micronesia 87/E5
Ifanadiana, Madagascar 118/H4
Ife, Nigeria 106/E7
Iférouane, Niger 102/C3
Iférouane, Niger 106/F5
Iffley, Sask. 181/C3
Ifni, Morocco 106/B3
Ifni, Morocco 102/B2
Ifugao (prov.), Philippines 82/C2
Igal, Hungary 41/D3
Igara-Paraná (riv.), Colombia 126/D8
Igarapava, Brazil 135/C2
Igarapé-Miri, Brazil 132/D3
Igarka, U.S.S.R. 4/C5
Igarka, U.S.S.R. 54/K3
Igarka, U.S.S.R. 48/J3
Iğdır, Turkey 63/K3
Iggesund, Sweden 18/K6
Igis, Switzerland 39/J3
Igiugig, Alaska (†99613) 196/G3
Iglesias, Italy 34/B5
Igli, Algeria 106/D2
Igloo, S. Dak. (†57774) 298/B7
Igloolik, Canada 4/B14
Igloolik, N.W.T. 162/H2
Igloolik, N.W. Terrs. 187/K3
Iglosiatik (isl.), Newf. 166/B2
Ignace, Ont. 162/G6
Ignace, Ontario 175/B3
Ignace, Ontario 177/G5
Ignacio, Calif. (94947) 204/H1
Ignacio, Colo. (81137) 208/D8
Ignacio Agramonte, Cuba 158/G3
Ignacio de la Llave, Mexico 150/Q2
İğneada (cape), Turkey 63/C2
Igoumenítsa, Greece 45/E6
Igra, U.S.S.R. 52/H3
Igrim, U.S.S.R. 48/G3
Iguaçu (riv.) 120/D5
Iguaçu (riv.), Brazil 132/C9
Igualada, Spain 33/G2
Iguala de la Independencia, Mexico 150/K7
Iguape, Brazil 135/C4
Iguassú (falls) 120/D5
Iguatu, Brazil 120/F3
Iguatu, Brazil 132/G4
Iguazú (falls), Argentina 143/F2
Iguazú (falls), Brazil 132/C9
Iguazú (falls), Paraguay 144/E4
Iguazú Nat'l Park, Argentina 143/E2
Iguéla, Gabon 115/A4
Iguidi, Erg (des.), 102/B2
Iguidi, Erg (des.), Algeria 106/C3
Iguidi, Erg (des.), Mauritania 106/C3
Iheya (isl.), Japan 81/N6
Ihlen, Minn. (56140) 255/B7
Ihosy, Madagascar 118/H4
Ihu, Papua N.G. 85/B7
Ii (riv.), Finland 7/G2
Iida, Japan 81/H6
Iijoki (riv.), Finland 18/O4
Iisalmi, Finland 18/P5
Iizuka, Japan 81/E7
Ijamsville, Md. (21754) 245/J3
Ijebu-Ode, Nigeria 106/E7
IJlst, Netherlands 27/H2
IJmeer (bay), Netherlands 27/C4
IJmuiden, Netherlands 27/E4
IJssel (riv.), Netherlands 27/J4
IJsselmeer (lake), Netherlands 27/G3
IJsselstein, Netherlands 27/F4
Ijuí, Brazil 132/C10
IJzendijke, Netherlands 27/D6
Ikaalinen, Finland 18/N6
Ikaría (isl.), Greece 45/G7
Ikast, Denmark 21/C5
Ikeda, Hokkaido, Japan 81/L2
Ikeda, Osaka, Japan 81/H7
Ikeja, Nigeria 106/E7
Ikela, Zaire 115/D4
Ikelemba, Congo 115/C3
Ikhtiman, Bulgaria 45/F4
Iki (isl.), Japan 81/D7
Ikom, Nigeria 106/F7
Ikoma, Japan 81/J8
Ikopa (riv.), Madagascar 118/H3
Ikpikpuk (riv.), Alaska 196/H1
Iksal, Israel 65/C2
Ikuno, Japan 81/G6
Ila, Georgia (30647) 217/F2
Ilagan, Philippines 82/C2
Ilam (gov.), Iran 66/E4
Ilam, Iran 66/E4
Ilam, Nepal 68/F3
Ilan, China 77/K7
Ilanskiy, U.S.S.R. 48/K4
Ilanz, Switzerland 39/H3
Ilaro, Nigeria 106/E7
Ilasco, Mo. (†63401) 261/K3
Ilava, Czech. 41/E2
Ilave, Peru 128/H11
Iława, Poland 47/D2
Ilderton, Ontario 177/C4
Île-à-la-Crosse, Sask. 181/L3
Île-à-la-Crosse (lake), Sask. 181/L3
Île-Bizard, Québec 172/H4
Ilebo, Zaire 115/D4
Île de France (trad. prov.), France, 29
Île-de-Montréal (co.), Québec 172/H4
Île des Chênes, Manitoba 179/F5
Île-Jésus (co.), Québec 172/H4
Ilek (riv.), U.S.S.R. 52/J4
Île-Perrot, Québec 172/G4
Îles (lake), Québec 172/B3
Ilesha, Nigeria 106/F7
Ilfeld, N. Mex. (87538) 274/D3
Ilfis (riv.), Switzerland 39/E3
Ilford, Manitoba 179/J2
Ilford, N.S. Wales 97/E3
Ilfracombe, England 10/D5
Ilfracombe, England 13/C6
Ilgaz, Turkey 63/E2
Ilgaz (mts.), Turkey 63/E2
Ilgın, Turkey 63/D3
Ilha Grande (bay), Brazil 135/D3
Ílhavo, Portugal 33/B2
Ilhéus, Brazil 120/F4
Ilhéus, Brazil 132/G6
Ili (riv.), U.S.S.R. 54/J5
Ili (riv.), U.S.S.R. 48/H5
Iliamna, Alaska (99606) 196/G3
Iliamna (lake), Alaska 188/C6
Iliamna (lake), Alaska 196/G3
Iliamna (vol.), Alaska 196/H2
Iliç, Turkey 63/H3
Ilica, Turkey 63/J3
Iliff, Colo. (80736) 208/N1
Iligan, Philippines 82/E6
Iligan (bay), Philippines 82/E6
Ilin (isl.), Philippines 82/C4
Ilio (pt.), Hawaii 218/G1
Ilion, N.Y. (13357) 276/K5
Ilium (ruins), Turkey 63/B6
Ilkeston, England 13/F5
Ilkeston, England 10/F4
Illabo, N.S. Wales 97/D4
Illahe, Oreg. (†97406) 291/C5
Illampu, Nevada (mt.), Bolivia 136/A4
Illana (bay), Philippines 82/D7
Illana, Spain 33/E2
Illapel, Chile 138/A8
Ille-et-Vilaine (dept.), France 28/C3
Illéla, Niger 106/F6
Iller (riv.), W. Germany 22/D4
Illescas, Spain 33/D2
Illescas, Uruguay 145/D4
Ille-sur-Têt, France 28/E6
Illimani, Nevada (mt.), Bolivia 136/B5
Illinois 188/J3
ILLINOIS 222
Illinois (bayou), Ark. 202/D3
Illinois (riv.), Colo. 208/G1
Illinois (riv.), Ill. 188/H2
Illinois (riv.), Ill. 222/C4
Illinois (riv.), Okla. 288/S3
Illinois (riv.), Oreg. 291/D5
Illinois (state), U.S. 146/K6
Illinois - Mississippi (canal), Ill. 222/C2
Illiopolis, Ill. (62539) 222/D4
Illizi, Algeria 106/F3
Illizi, Algeria 102/C2
Illmo, Mo. (63754) 261/O8
Illnau, Switzerland 39/G2
Illora, Spain 33/E4
Illuka, N.S. Wales 97/G1
Il'men (lake), U.S.S.R. 7/H3
Il'men' (lake), U.S.S.R. 52/D3
Ilmenau, E. Germany 22/D3
Ilmenau (riv.), W. Germany 22/D2
Ilminster, England 13/D7
Ilo, Peru 128/G11
Ilobasco, El Salvador 154/C4
Ilocos Norte (prov.), Philippines 82/C1
Ilocos Sur (prov.), Philippines 82/C2
Iloilo (prov.), Philippines 82/D5
Iloilo, Philippines 85/G3
Iloilo, Philippines 82/D5
Iloilo, Philippines 54/O8
Iloilo (str.), Philippines 82/D5
Ilomantsi, Finland 18/R5
Ilorin, Nigeria 106/E7
Ilorin, Nigeria 102/C4
Ilpendam, Netherlands 27/C4
Ilsley, Ky. (†42408) 237/F6
Ilubabor (prov.), Ethiopia 111/F6
Ilūkste, U.S.S.R. 53/D3
Ilwaco, Wash. (98624) 310/A4
Iłża, Poland 47/E3
Imabari, Japan 81/F6
Imandra (lake), U.S.S.R. 48/D3
Imandra (lake), U.S.S.R. 52/D1
Imari, Japan 81/D7
Imataca, Serranía (mts.), Venezuela 124/H4
Imatra, Finland 18/Q6
Imazu, Japan 81/G6
Imbâba, Egypt 111/J3
Imbabura (prov.), Ecuador 128/C2
Imbaimadai, Guyana 131/A3
Imbert, Dom. Rep. 158/D5
Imbituba, Brazil 132/D10
Imbituva, Brazil 135/A4
Imbler, Oreg. (97841) 291/J2
Imboden, Ark. (72434) 202/H1
Imeri, Sierra (mts.), Venezuela 124/F7
Imese, Zaire 115/C3
Imi, Ethiopia 111/H6
Imías, Cuba 158/K4
Imilac, Chile 138/B4
Imishli, U.S.S.R. 52/G7
Imlay, Nev. (89418) 266/C2
Imlay, S. Dak. (†57780) 298/E6
Imlay City, Mich. (48444) 250/F5
Imlaystown, N.J. (08526) 273/D3
Imler, Pa. (16655) 294/E5
Immaculata, Pa. (19345) 294/L6
Immenstadt im Allgäu, W. Germany 22/C5
Immingham, England 13/G4
Immokalee, Fla. (33934) 212/E5
Imnaha, Oreg. (97842) 291/L2
Imnaha (riv.), Oreg. 291/L2
Imo (state), Nigeria 106/F7
Imogene, Iowa (51645) 229/C7
Imola, Italy 34/C2
Impach, Wash. (†99138) 310/G2
Imperatriz, Brazil 120/E3
Imperatriz, Brazil 132/E4
Imperia (prov.), Italy 34/B3
Imperia, Italy 34/B3
Imperial (dam), Ariz. 198/A6
Imperial (res.), Ariz. 198/A6
Imperial (co.), Calif. 204/K10
Imperial, Calif. (92251) 204/K11
Imperial (dam), Calif. 204/L11
Imperial (res.), Calif. 204/L10
Imperial (valley), Calif. 204/K10
Imperial (riv.), Chile 138/D2
Imperial, Mo. (63052) 261/M6
Imperial, Nebr. (69033) 264/C4
Imperial, Pa. (15126) 294/B5
Imperial, Peru 128/D9
Imperial, Sask. 181/F4
Imperial, Texas (79743) 303/B6
Imperial Beach, Calif. (92032) 204/H11
Imperial Mills, Alberta 182/E2
Impfondo, Congo 115/C3
Imphal, India 54/L7
Imphal, India 68/G4
Impora, Bolivia 136/C7
Imralı (isl.), Turkey 63/C2
Imranlı, Turkey 63/H2
Imroz (Gökçeada) (isl.), Turkey 63/A2
Imst, Austria 41/A3
Imuris, Mexico 150/D1
Imuruan (bay), Philippines 82/B5
Imuruk (basin), Alaska 196/E1
'Imwas, West Bank 65/B4
Ina, Ill. (62846) 222/E5
Ina, Japan 81/H6
Ina (riv.), Japan 81/H7
Inaha, Georgia (†31790) 217/E7
Inala, Queensland 88/K3
Inala, Queensland 95/D3
Inambari, Peru 128/H9
Inambari (riv.), Peru 128/H9
In Amenas, Algeria 106/F3
In Amguel, Algeria 106/E4
Inangahua Junction, N. Zealand 100/C4
Iñapari, Peru 128/H8
Inarajan, Guam 86/K7
Inari, Finland 18/P2
Inari (lake), Finland 7/G2
Inari (lake), Finland 18/P2
Inavale, Nebr. (68952) 264/F4
Inawashiro (lake), Japan 81/K5
In Azaoua (well), Niger 106/F4
Inca, Spain 33/H3
Incacamachi, Cerro (mt.), Bolivia 136/A6
Inca de Oro, Chile 138/B6
Incaguasi, Nevada (mt.), Chile 138/C6
Incahuasi, Cerro de (mt.), Argentina 143/C2
Ince (cape), Turkey 63/F1
Incekum (cape), Turkey 63/F4
Incesu, Turkey 63/F3
Inchard, Loch (inlet), Scotland 15/C2
Inchcape (Bell Rock) (isl.), Scotland 15/F4
Inchelium, Wash. (99138) 310/G2
Inchigeelagh, Ireland 17/C8
Inchiri (reg.), Mauritania 106/A5
Inchkeith, Sask. 181/J5
Inchkeith (isl.), Scotland 15/D1
Inchnadamph, Scotland 15/D2
Inch'ŏn, S. Korea 54/O6
Inch'ŏn, S. Korea 81/C5
Indaal, Loch (inlet), Scotland 15/B5
In Dagouber (well), Mali 106/D4
Indalsälven (riv.), Sweden 18/H5
Indawgyi (lake), Burma 72/C1
Indé, Mexico 150/G4
Independence (co.), Ark. 202/G2
Independence, Belize 154/C2
Independence, Calif. (93526) 204/H7
Independence, Ind. (†47918) 227/C4
Independence, Iowa (50644) 229/K4
Independence, Kansas (67301) 232/G4
Independence, Ky. (41051) 237/M3
Independence, La. (70443) 238/M1
Independence (lake), Mich. 250/B2
Independence, Minn. (†55359) 255/F5
Independence (lake), Minn. 255/F5
Independence, Miss. (38638) 256/E1
Independence, Mo. (*64050) 261/R5
Independence (mts.), Nev. 266/E1
Independence, Ohio (44131) 284/H9
Independence, Oreg. (97351) 291/D3
Independence, Va. (24348) 307/F7
Independence, W. Va. (26374) 312/G4
Independence, Wis. (54747) 317/D7
Independencia, Bolivia 136/B5
Independencia, Brazil 132/C6
Independencia (prov.), Dom. Rep. 158/D6
Independencia (bay), Peru 128/D10
Independencia (isl.), Peru 128/D10
Independencia, Venezuela 124/B4
Index, Wash. (98256) 310/D3
Index (peak), Wyo. 319/C1
India 2/N4
India 54/J7
INDIA 68/D4
Indiahoma, Okla. (73552) 288/J5
Indialantic, Fla. (32903) 212/F3
India Muerta (riv.), Uruguay 145/E4
Indian (ocean) 54/H10
Indian (ocean) 102/G7
Indian (mt.), Conn. 210/B1
Indian (pond), Conn. 210/A1
Indian (riv.), Del. 245/S6
Indian (riv.), Fla. 212/F3
Indian (creek), Idaho 220/C5
Indian (creek), Ind. 227/D6
Indian (creek), Ind. 227/E8
Indian (creek), Md. 245/G4
Indian (lake), Mich. 250/C2
Indian (stream), N.H. 268/E1
Indian (lake), N.Y. 276/M3
Indian (harb.), Nova Scotia 168/G3
Indian (lake), Ohio 284/C5
Indian (creek), S. Dak. 298/B4
Indian (creek), Utah 304/B5
Indian (creek), Utah 304/E5
Indiana 188/J3
INDIANA 227
Indiana (co.), Pa. 294/D4
Indiana, Pa. (15701) 294/D4
Indiana (state), U.S. 146/K6
Indiana Dunes Nat'l Lakeshore, Ind. 227/C1
Indianapolis (cap.), Ind. 146/K5
Indianapolis (cap.), Ind. 188/J3
Indianapolis (cap.), Ind. (*46201) 227/E5
Indian Bay, Manitoba 179/G5
Indian Beach, N.C. (†28575) 281/R5
Indian Brook, Nova Scotia 168/H2
Indian Cabins, Alberta 182/B4
Indian Creek, Fla. (†33139) 212/B4
Indian Creek, Ill. (†60069) 222/B4
Indian Harbour Beach, Fla. (†32901) 212/F3
Indian Head, Md. (20640) 245/K6
Indian Head, Sask. 162/F5
Indian Head, Sask. 181/H5
Indian Hill, Ohio (†45201) 284/C9
Indian Hills, Ky. (†40201) 237/K1
Indian Hills, N.C. (†28719) 281/C4
Indian Lake, N.Y. (12842) 276/M3
Indian Lake, Pa. (†15560) 294/E5
Indian Mills, W. Va. (24949) 312/E7
Indian Mound, Tenn. (37079) 237/F7
Indian Neck, Conn. (†06405) 210/D3
Indian Neck, Va. (23077) 307/O5
Indian Ocean 2/N6
Indian Ocean 5/C3
Indian Ocean, Indonesia 85/E8
Indian Ocean, S. Australia 94/E7
Indian Ocean, Tasmania 99/A4
Indian Ocean, Victoria 97/B6
Indian Ocean, W. Australia 92/A5
Indianola, Ill. (61850) 222/F4
Indianola, Iowa (50125) 229/F6

386 Indianola

Indianola, Miss. (38751) 256/C4
Indianola, Nebr. (69034) 264/D4
Indianola, Okla. (74442) 288/P4
Indianola, Utah (†84629) 304/C4
Indianola, Wash. (98342) 310/A1
Indian Pond (lake), Maine 243/D4
Indian River (bay), Del. 245/T6
Indian River (inlet), Del. 245/T6
Indian River (co.), Fla. 212/F4
Indian River, Maine (†04649) 243/H6
Indian River, Mich. (49749) 250/E3
Indian River, Ontario 177/F3
Indian River Shores, Fla. (32960) 212/F4
Indian Rocks Beach, Fla. (33535) 212/B3
Indian Shores, Fla. (†33535) 212/B3
Indian Springs, Georgia (30231) 217/E4
Indian Springs, Ind. (47544) 227/D7
Indian Springs, Nev. (89018) 266/F6
Indiantown, Fla. (33456) 212/F4
Indian Trail, N.C. (28079) 281/H4
Indian Valley, Idaho (83632) 220/B5
Indian Valley, Va. (24105) 307/G7
Indian Village, Ind. (†46601) 227/E1
Indian Village, La. (†70764) 238/H6
Indian Wells, Ariz. (86031) 198/E3
Indian Wells, Calif. (†92260) 204/J10
Indiga, U.S.S.R. 48/E3
Indiga, U.S.S.R. 52/G1
Indigirka, U.S.S.R. 54/R3
Indigirka (riv.), U.S.S.R. 4/C2
Indigirka (riv.), U.S.S.R. 48/P3
Indigo (crek), Oreg. 291/D5
Indio, Calif. (92201) 204/J10
Indios (chan.), Cuba 158/B2
Indispensable (str.), Solomon Is. 86/E3
Indochina (reg.), Vietnam 72/D2
Indonesia 2/Q6
Indonesia 54/M10
INDONESIA 85
Indooroopilly, Queensland 95/D3
Indooroopilly, Queensland 88/K3
Indore, India 68/D4
Indore, India 54/J7
Indore, W. Va. (25111) 312/D6
Indramayu, Indonesia 85/H2
Indramayu (pt.), Indonesia 85/H1
Indravati (riv.), India 68/E5
Indre (dept.), France 28/D4
Indre (riv.), France 28/D4
Indre-et-Loire (dept.), France 28/D4
Indus (riv.) 2/N4
Indus (riv.) 54/H7
Indus, Alberta 182/D4
Indus (riv.), India 68/B3
Indus, Minn. (†56629) 255/E2
Indus, Mouths of the (delta), Pakistan 68/B4
Indus (riv.), Pakistan 59/J4
Indus (riv.), Pakistan 68/B3
Industrial City, Georgia (†30705) 217/C1
Industry, Ill. (61440) 222/C3
Industry, Kansas (†67410) 232/E2
Industry, Pa. (15052) 294/B4
Industry, Texas (78944) 303/H7
Inebolu, Turkey 59/B1
Inebolu, Turkey 63/E2
Inegöl, Turkey 63/C2
In Eker, Algeria 106/F4
Ineu, Romania 45/E2
Inez, Ky. (41224) 237/S5
Inez, N.C. (27589) 281/N2
Inezgane, Morocco 106/C2
In Ezzane (well), Algeria 106/G4
Infanta, Philippines 82/C3
Infieles (pt.), Chile 138/A6
Infiesto, Spain 33/D1
In-Gall, Niger 106/F5
Ingalls, Ark. (71648) 202/F7
Ingalls (mt.), Calif. 204/E3
Ingalls, Ind. (46048) 227/F5
Ingalls, Kansas (67853) 232/B4
Ingalls, Mich. (49848) 250/B3
Ingavi, Bolivia 136/B2
Ingelmunster, Belgium 27/C7
Ingelow, Manitoba 179/C5
Ingenbohl, Switzerland 39/G2
Ingende, Zaire 115/C4
Ingende, Zaire 102/D5
Ingeniero Huergo, Argentina 143/C4
Ingeniero Jacobacci, Argentina 143/C5
Ingeniero Luiggi, Argentina 143/D4
Ingeniero Montero Hoyos (Tocomechi), Bolivia 136/D5
Ingersoll, Ontario 177/C4
Ingham (co.), Mich. 250/E6
Ingham, Queensland 88/H3
Ingham, Queensland 95/C3
Inglefield, Ind. (47618) 227/B8
Inglés (pt.), Cuba 158/G4
Inglesa (bay), Chile 138/A6
Ingleside, Md. (21644) 245/P4
Ingleside, Ontario 177/J2
Ingleside, W. Va. (†24740) 312/E8
Inglewood, Calif. (*90301) 204/B11
Inglewood, Nebr. (†68025) 264/H3
Inglewood, N. Zealand 100/E3
Inglewood, Victoria 97/B5
Inglis, Fla. (32649) 212/D2
Inglis, Manitoba 179/A4
Ingold, N.C. (28446) 281/N5
Ingoldsby, Ontario 177/F3
Ingolstadt, W. Germany 22/D4
Ingomar, Miss. (†38652) 256/F2
Ingomar, Mont. (59039) 262/J4
Ingomar, Nova Scotia 168/C5
Ingomar, Pa. (15127) 294/C4
Ingonish, Nova Scotia 168/H2
Ingonish Beach, Nova Scotia 168/H2
Ingonish North (bay), Nova Scotia 168/H2
Ingornachoix (bay), Newf. 166/C3
Ingraham (lake), Fla. 212/E6
Ingraham, Ill. (62434, 222/E5
Ingram, Pa. (†15205) 294/B7
Ingram, Texas (78025) 303/E7
Ingram, Va. (24564) 307/K7
Ingram, Wis. (†54530) 317/E5
Ingre, Bolivia 136/D7
In Guezzam, Algeria 106/F5
Ingwavuma, S. Africa 118/E5
Inhambane (prov.), Mozambique 118/E4
Inhambane, Mozambique 118/F4
Inhambane, Mozambique 102/F7
Inhaminga, Mozambique 118/F3
Inharrime, Mozambique 118/F4
Inharrime, Mozambique 102/F7
Inhumas, Brazil 132/D7
Iniesta, Spain 33/F3
Inini, Fr. Guiana 131/E4
Inini (riv.), Fr. Guiana 131/E4
Inírida, Colombia 120/C2
Inírida, Colombia 126/F6
Inírida (riv.), Colombia 126/F6
Inishannon, Ireland 17/D8
Inishbofin (isl.), Ireland 17/A4
Inishbofin (isl.), Ireland 10/A4
Inishbofin (isl.), Ireland 17/E1
Inisheer (isl.), Ireland 17/B5
Inishmaan (isl.), Ireland 17/C5
Inishmore (isl.), Ireland 17/B5
Inishmurray (isl.), Ireland 17/D3
Inishowen (head), Ireland 17/H1
Inishowen (pen.), Ireland 17/G1
Inishshark (isl.), Ireland 17/A4
Inishtrahull (isl.), Ireland 17/G1
Inishtrahull (sound), Ireland 17/G1
Inishturk (isl.), Ireland 10/A4
Inishturk (isls.), Ireland 17/A4
Inistioge, Ireland 17/G7
Injune, Queensland 95/D5
Injune, Queensland 88/H5
Inkerman, New Bruns. 170/F1
Inklin (riv.), Br. Col. 184/J2
Inkom, Idaho (83245) 220/F7
Inkster, Mich. (48141) 250/B7
Inkster, N. Dak. (58244) 282/P3
Inland (lake), Ala. 195/E3
Inland (lake), Alaska 196/G1
Inland (lake), Manitoba 179/C2
Inland, Nebr. (68954) 264/F4
Inle (lake), Burma 72/C2
Inlet, N.Y. (13360) 276/L3
Inman, Georgia (30232) 217/D4
Inman, Kansas (67546) 232/E3
Inman, Nebr. (68742) 264/F2
Inman, S.C. (29349) 296/C1
Inn (riv.), Austria 41/B2
Inn (riv.), Switzerland 39/K3
Inn (riv.), W. Germany 22/E4
Innamincka, S. Australia 94/G2
Innellan, Scotland 15/A2
Inner (sound), Scotland 10/D2
Inner (sound), Scotland 15/C3
Inner Hebrides (isls.), Scotland 15/B4
Innerkip, Ontario 177/D4
Innerleithen, Scotland 10/E3
Innerleithen, Scotland 15/E5
Inner Mongolia (reg.), China 54/N5
Inner Mongolia (reg.), China 77/H3
Inner Mongolian Aut. Reg. (Nei Monggol), China 77/H3
Innertkirchen, Switzerland 39/F3
Innes (lake), N.S. Wales 97/G2
Innis, La. (70747) 238/G5
Inniscrone, Ireland 17/C3
Innisfail, Alberta 182/D3
Innisfail, Queensland 95/C3
Innisfail, Queensland 88/H3
Innisfree, Alberta 182/E3
Innisville, Ontario 177/H2
Innoko (riv.), Alaska 196/G2
Innsbruck, Austria 7/F4
Innsbruck, Austria 41/A3
Inny (riv.), Ireland 17/F4
Inny (riv.), Ireland 17/A8
Inola, Okla. (74036) 288/P2
Inongo, Zaire 115/C4
Inönü, Turkey 63/D3
Inoucdjouac, Que. 162/H4
Inoucdjouac, Québec 174/E1
Inowrocław, Poland 47/D2
Inquisivi, Bolivia 136/B5
In Rhar, Algeria 106/E3
Ins, Switzerland 39/D2
In Salah, Algeria 106/E3
In Salah, Algeria 102/C2
Insch, Scotland 15/F3
Insein, Burma 72/C3
Inset, Norway 18/G5
Insinger, Sask. 181/H4
Inspiration, Ariz. (85537) 198/D5
Institute, W. Va. (25112) 312/C6
Instow, Sask. 181/C6
Inta, U.S.S.R. 7/K2
Inta, U.S.S.R. 52/K1
Inta, U.S.S.R. 48/G3
Intake, Mont. (†59330) 262/M3
Intelewa, Suriname 131/D4
Intendente Alvear, Argentina 143/D4
Intepe, Turkey 63/B6
Intercession City, Fla. (33848) 212/E3
Intercourse, Pa. (17534) 294/K5
Interior, S. Dak. (57750) 298/F6
Interlachen, Fla. (32048) 212/E2
Interlaken, Mass. (†01266) 249/A3
Interlaken, N.J. (†07712) 273/E3
Interlaken, N.Y. (14847) 276/G5
Interlaken, Switzerland 39/E3
Interlochen, Mich. (49643) 250/D4
International Airport, Georgia 217/K2
International Airport, Mo. 261/P2
International Airport (Dallas-Ft. Worth), Texas 303/F2
International Falls, Minn. 188/H1
International Falls, Minn. (56649) 255/E2
International Peace Garden, Manitoba 179/B5
International Peace Garden, N. Dak. 282/K1
Intervale, N.H. (03845) 268/E3
Interview (isl.), India 68/G6
Inthanon, Doi (mt.), Thailand 72/C3
Intipucá, El Salvador 154/D4
Intracoastal Waterway, S.C. 296/H5
Intracoastal Waterway, Texas 303/J9
Intragna, Switzerland 39/G4
Intutu, Peru 128/E4
Inubo (cape), Japan 81/K6
Inútil (bay), Chile 138/E10
Inuvik, Canada 4/C16
Inuvik, N.W.T. 146/E3
Inuvik, N.W.T. 162/C2
Inuvik (dist.), N.W. Terrs. 187/F3
Inuvik, N.W. Terrs. 187/E3
Inver (bay), Ireland 17/E2
Inveraray, Scotland 10/D2
Inveraray, Scotland 15/C4
Inverbervie, Scotland 10/E2
Inverbervie, Scotland 15/F4
Invercargill, N. Zealand 100/B7
Invercassley, Scotland 15/D3
Inverell, N. S. Wales 88/J5
Inverell, N.S. Wales 97/F1
Invergarry, Scotland 15/D3
Invergordon, Scotland 10/D2
Invergordon, Scotland 15/D3
Invergowrie, Scotland 15/E4
Inver Grove Heights, Minn. (55075) 255/E6
Inverhuron, Ontario 177/C3
Inverie, Scotland 15/C3
Inverkeilor, Scotland 15/F4
Inverkeithing, Scotland 15/D1
Inverkeithing, Scotland 10/C1
Inverloch, Victoria 97/C6
Invermay, Ontario 177/C3
Invermay, Sask. 181/J4
Invermere, Br. Col. 184/J5
Invermoriston, Scotland 15/D3
Inverness, Ala. (†36089) 195/G6
Inverness, Calif. (94937) 204/B5
Inverness, Fla. (32650) 212/D3
Inverness, Ill. (†60067) 222/A5
Inverness, Miss. (38753) 256/C4
Inverness, Mont. (59530) 262/F2
Inverness, N.S. 162/K6
Inverness (co.), Nova Scotia 168/G2
Inverness, Nova Scotia 168/G2
Inverness, Québec 172/F3
Inverness, Scotland 15/D3
Inverness, Scotland 7/D3
Inverness, Scotland 10/D2
Inverness, (trad. co.), Scotland, 15/A5
Inverurie, Scotland 15/F3
Inverurie, Scotland 10/E2
Inverway, North. Terr. 93/A4
Investigator (shoal), Philippines 85/E4
Investigator (str.), S. Australia 88/F7
Investigator (str.), S. Australia 94/E6
Investigator Group (isls.), S. Australia 88/E6
Investigator Group (isls.), S. Australia 94/D5
Inwood, Ind. (46533) 227/E2
Inwood, Iowa (51240) 229/A2
Inwood, Manitoba 179/E4
Inwood, N.Y. (11696) 276/P7
Inwood, Ontario 177/C5
Inwood, W. Va. (25428) 312/K4
Inyanga, Zimbabwe 118/E3
Inyan Kara (creek), Wyo. 319/H1
Inyan Kara (mt.), Wyo. 319/H1
Inyo (co.), Calif. 204/H7
Inyo (mts.), Calif. 204/G6
Inyokern, Calif. (93527) 204/H8
Inza, U.S.S.R. 52/G4
Inzana (lake), Br. Col. 184/E3
Ioánnina, Greece 7/G4
Ioánnina, Greece 45/E6
Ioco, Br. Col. 184/K3
Ioka, Utah (†84052) 304/D3
Iola, Ill. (62847) 222/E5
Iola, Kansas (66749) 232/G4
Iola, Texas (77861) 303/H7
Iola, Wis. (54945) 317/H6
Iolotan', U.S.S.R. 48/G6
Ioma, Papua N.G. 85/C7
Iona, Angola 115/B7
Iona, Idaho (83427) 220/G6
Iona, Minn. (56141) 255/C7
Iona (isls.), Newf. 166/C2
Iona, N.J. (†08322) 273/C4
Iona, Nova Scotia 168/H3
Iona, Ontario 177/C5
Iona (isl.), Scotland 15/B4
Iona (isl.), Scotland 10/C2
Iona, S. Dak. (57542) 298/L6
Ione, Ark. (†72927) 202/B3
Ione, Calif. (95640) 204/C9
Ione, Nev. (†89310) 266/D4
Ione, Oreg. (97843) 291/H2
Ione, Wash. (99139) 310/H2
Ionia, Iowa (50645) 229/J2
Ionia, Kansas (66947) 232/D2
Ionia (co.), Mich. 250/D6
Ionia, Mich. (48846) 250/D6
Ionia, Mo. (65335) 261/F6
Ionian (sea) 7/F5
Ionian (isls.), Greece 7/F5
Ionian (sea), Greece 45/D7
Ionian (sea), Italy 34/F6
Ionian Islands (reg.), Greece 45/D6
Íos, Greece 45/G7
Íos (isl.), Greece 45/G7
Iosco (co.), Mich. 250/F4
Iosegun (lake), Alberta 182/B2
Iosegun (riv.), Alberta 182/B2
Iota, La. (70543) 238/E6
Iowa 188/H2
IOWA 229
Iowa (co.), Iowa 229/J5
Iowa (riv.), Iowa 188/H2
Iowa (riv.), Iowa 229/H4
Iowa, La. (70647) 238/D6
Iowa (state), U.S. 146/J5
Iowa (co.), Wis. 317/F9
Iowa City, Iowa 188/H2
Iowa City, Iowa (52240) 229/L5
Iowa Colony, Texas (†77583) 303/J2
Iowa Falls, Iowa (50126) 229/G3
Iowa Park, Texas (76367) 303/F4
Iowa Point, Kansas (†66035) 232/G2
Ipala, Guatemala 154/C3
Ipameri, Brazil 132/E7
Ipanema, Brazil 135/F1
Iparia, Peru 128/E7
Ipatovo, U.S.S.R. 52/F5
Ipava, Ill. (61441) 222/C3
Ipel' (riv.), Czech. 41/E2
Iphigenia (bay), Alaska 196/M2
Ipiales, Colombia 126/B7
Ipil, Philippines 82/D7
Ipin (Yibin), China 77/F6
Ipoh, Malaysia 54/M9
Ipoh, Malaysia 72/D6
Ipoly (riv.), Hungary 41/E2
Iporá, Brazil 120/D4
Ipperwash Prov. Park, Ontario 177/C4
Ippy, Cent. Afr. Rep. 115/D2
Ipsala, Turkey 63/B2
Ipsile, Turkey 63/G2
Ipswich, Australia 87/F8
Ipswich, England 13/J5
Ipswich, England 10/G4
Ipswich, Mass. (01938) 249/L2
Ipswich○, Mass. (01938) 249/L2
Ipswich (riv.), Mass. 249/L2
Ipswich, Queensland 88/J3
Ipswich, Queensland 95/E5
Ipswich, S. Dak. (57451) 298/L3
Ipu, Brazil 132/F4
Iquique, Chile 120/B5
Iquique, Chile 138/A2
Iquitos, Peru 120/B3
Iquitos, Peru 128/F4
Ira, Iowa (50127) 229/G5
Ira, N.Y. (†13033) 276/G4
Ira, Texas (79527) 303/C5
Ira○, Vt. (†05777) 268/A4
Iraan, Texas (79744) 303/B7
Iracoubo, Fr. Guiana 131/E3
Iraël', U.S.S.R. 52/H2
Iráklion, Greece 45/G8
Iráklion, Greece 7/G5
Iran 2/M4
Iran 54/G7
IRAN 66
IRAN 59/F3
Iran (mts.), Malaysia 85/E5
Iranshahr, Iran 66/M7
Iranshahr, Iran 59/H4
Irapa, Venezuela 124/G2
Irapuato, Mexico 150/J6
Iraq 2/M4
Iraq 54/F6
IRAQ 59/D3
IRAQ 66
Irasburg○, Vt. (05845) 268/C2
Irati, Brazil 132/D9
Irati, Brazil 135/A4
Irawan, Philippines 82/B6
Irazú (mt.), C. Rica 154/F6
Irbid, Jordan 65/D2
Irby, Wash. (99159) 310/G3
Irecê, Brazil 120/E4
Iredell (co.), N.C. 281/H3
Iredell, Texas (76649) 303/G6
Ireland 2/J3
Ireland 7/D3
Ireland (isl.), Bermuda 156/G3
Ireland, Ind. (47545) 227/C8
IRELAND 17
IRELAND 10/B4
IRELAND, NORTHERN 10, 17
Ireland, Texas (76536) 303/F6
Ireland, W. Va. (26376) 312/F5
Ireland's Eye (isl.), Ireland 17/K5
Ireland's Eye (isl.), Newf. 166/D2
Irene, S. Africa 118/H6
Irene, S. Dak. (57037) 298/P7
Ireng (riv.), Guyana 131/B3
Ireton, Iowa (51027) 229/A3
Irharhar, Wadi (dry riv.), Algeria 106/F3
Iri, S. Korea 81/C6
Irian Jaya (reg.), Indonesia 2/R6
Irian Jaya (reg.), Indonesia 85/J6
Iriba, Chad 111/D4
Iriga, Philippines 82/D4
Iringa (reg.), Tanzania 115/G5
Iringa, Tanzania 102/F5
Iringa, Tanzania 115/G5
Iriomote (isl.), Japan 81/K7
Irion (co.), Texas 303/C6
Iriona, Honduras 154/E2
Iriri (riv.), Brazil 132/C4
Irish (sea) 7/D3
Irish (sea), England 13/B4
Irish (sea), England 10/D4
Irish (sea), Ireland 10/D4
Irish (sea), Ireland 17/K4
Irish (sea), I. of Man 13/B4
Irish (sea), Wales 13/B4
Irish (sea), Wales 10/D4
Irishtown, New Bruns. 170/F2
Irishtown, Tasmania 99/B2
Irish Vale, Nova Scotia 168/H3
Irkutsk, U.S.S.R. 2/Q3
Irkutsk, U.S.S.R. 54/M4
Irkutsk, U.S.S.R. 48/L4
Irma, Alberta 182/E3
Irma, Wis. (54442) 317/G5
Irmo, S.C. (29063) 296/E3
Iro (cape), Japan 81/J6
Irois (cape), Haiti 158/A6
Iron (mt.), Fla. 212/E4
Iron (co.), Mich. 250/G2
Iron, Minn. (55751) 255/F3
Iron (co.), Mo. 261/L7
Iron (mts.), Tenn. 237/S8
Iron (co.), Utah 304/A6
Iron (co.), Wis. 317/F3
Iron Belt, Wis. (54536) 317/F3
Ironbound (isls.), Newf. 166/C2
Iron Bridge, Ontario 177/A1
Iron City, Georgia (31759) 217/C8
Iron City, Tenn. (38463) 237/F10
Irondale, Ala. (35210) 195/E3
Irondale, Mo. (63648) 261/L7
Irondale, Ohio (43932) 284/J4
Irondequoit, N.Y. (14617) 276/E4
Iron Gate (res.), Calif. 204/C2
Iron Gate, Va. (24448) 307/J5
Iron Gates, Mo. (†64801) 261/C8
Ironia, N.J. (07845) 273/D2
Iron Knob, S. Australia 88/F6
Iron Knob, S. Australia 94/E5
Iron Mountain, Mich. (49801) 250/B3
Iron Mountain, Wyo. (82062) 319/G4
Iron Range, Queensland 95/B2
Iron Ridge, Wis. (53035) 317/K9
Iron River, Alberta 182/E2
Iron River, Mich. (49935) 250/G2
Iron River, Wis. (54847) 317/D2
Irons, Mich. (49644) 250/D4
Ironshire, Md. (†21811) 245/T7
Ironside, Oreg. (97908) 291/K3
Ironspring (creek), Sask. 181/G3
Iron Springs, Alberta 182/D5
Iron Springs, Ariz. (86330) 198/C4
Iron Station, N.C. (28080) 281/G4
Ironton, Minn. (56455) 255/D4
Ironton, Mo. (63650) 261/L7
Ironton, Ohio (45638) 284/E8
Ironton, Wis. (†53941) 317/F8
Ironwood, Mich. (49938) 250/F2
Iroquois (co.), Ill. 222/F3
Iroquois, Ill. (60945) 222/F3
Iroquois (riv.), Ill. 222/F3
Iroquois (riv.), Ind. 227/B3
Iroquois, Ontario 177/J3
Iroquois, S. Dak. (57353) 298/O5
Iroquois (lake), Vt. 268/A3
Iroquois Falls, Ont. 162/H6
Iroquois Falls, Ontario 175/D3
Iroquois Falls, Ontario 177/J5
Iroquois Point, Hawaii (†96706) 218/A4
'Irqa, P.D.R. Yemen 59/E7
Irrara (creek), N.S. Wales 97/C1
Irrawaddy (div.), Burma 72/B3
Irrawaddy, Mouths of the (delta), Burma 72/B4
Irrawaddy (riv.), Burma 54/L7
Irrawaddy (riv.), Burma 72/B3
Irricana, Alberta 182/D4
Irrigon, Oreg. (97844) 291/H2
Irtysh (riv.), U.S.S.R. 54/J4
Irtysh (riv.), U.S.S.R. 48/H4
Irumu, Zaire 115/E3
Irún, Spain 33/F1
Irupana, Bolivia 136/B5
Iruya, Argentina 143/D1
Irvine, Alberta 182/E5
Irvine, Calif. (92713) 204/D11
Irvine, Ky. (40336) 237/O5
Irvine (lake), N. Dak. 282/M3
Irvine, Pa. (16329) 294/D2
Irvine, Scotland 15/D5
Irvine, Scotland 10/D3
Irvinestown, N. Ireland 17/F3
Irving, Ill. (62051) 222/D4
Irving, Iowa (†52225) 229/J5
Irving, N.Y. (14081) 276/B5
Irving, Texas (*75061) 303/G2
Irvington, Ala. (36544) 195/B9
Irvington, Ill. (62848) 222/D5
Irvington, Iowa (50550) 229/E3
Irvington, Ky. (40146) 237/J5
Irvington, N.J. (07111) 273/B2
Irvington, N.Y. (10533) 276/O6
Irvington, Va. (22480) 307/R5
Irvin's (bay), Grenada 161/D8
Irvona, Pa. (16656) 294/E4
Irwin (co.), Georgia 217/F7
Irwin, Idaho (83428) 220/G6
Irwin, Iowa (51446) 229/C5
Irwin, Mo. (64754) 261/D7
Irwin, Ohio (43029) 284/D5
Irwin, Pa. (15642) 294/C5
Irwin, S.C. (†29720) 296/F2
Irwin, Va. (23063) 307/N5
Irwin, W. Australia 88/A5
Irwinton, Georgia (31042) 217/F5
Irwinville, Georgia (31760) 217/F7
Isa, Nigeria 106/F6
Isaac (lake), Br. Col. 184/G3
Isaacs (riv.), Queensland 88/H4
Isaacs (riv.), Queensland 95/D4
Isaac's Harbour North, Nova Scotia 168/G3
Isabel (bay), Ecuador 128/B9
Isabel, Kansas (67065) 232/D4
Isabel, La. (†70427) 238/K5
Isabel, S. Dak. (57633) 298/G3
Isabel (mt.), Wyo. 319/B3
Isabela (bay), Dom. Rep. 158/D5
Isabela (cape), Dom. Rep. 158/D5
Isabela (isl.), Ecuador 128/B9
Isabela (prov.), Philippines 82/C2
Isabela, Philippines 82/C7
Isabela, P. Rico 156/F1
Isabela, P. Rico 161/A1
Isabela de Sagua, Cuba 158/E1
Isabelia, Cordillera (range), Nicaragua 154/E4
Isabella (lake), Calif. 204/G8
Isabella, Manitoba 179/B4
Isabella (co.), Mich. 250/E5
Isabella, Mich. (†49878) 250/C3
Isabella, Minn. (55607) 255/G3
Isabella (lake), Minn. 255/G3
Isabella (riv.), Minn. 255/G3
Isabella (bay), N.W. Terrs. 187/M3
Isabella, Okla. (73747) 288/K2
Isabella, Tenn. (37346) 237/N10
Isabel Segunda, P. Rico 161/G2
Isaccea, Romania 45/J3
Isachsen, Canada 4/B15
Isachsen, N.W. Terrs. 187/H2
Isachsen (cape), N.W. Terrs. 187/H2
Isachsens, N.W.T. 146/H2
Ísafjördhardjúp (fjord), Iceland 21/A1
Ísafjördhur, Iceland 7/B2
Ísafjördhur, Iceland 21/B1
Isahaya, Japan 81/D7
Isana (riv.), Colombia 126/F7
Isangi, Zaire 115/D3
Isanti (co.), Minn. 255/E5
Isanti, Minn. (55040) 255/E5
Isar (riv.), W. Germany 22/E4
Isarog (mt.), Philippines 82/D4
Isbell, Ala. (†35653) 195/C2
Iscar, Spain 33/D2
Ischia (isl.), Italy 34/D4
Ischua, N.Y. (14746) 276/D6
Iscuandé, Colombia 126/A6
Ise, Japan 81/H6
Ise (bay), Japan 81/H6
Isefjord (fjord), Denmark 21/E6
Iselin, N.J. (08830) 273/E2
Iselin, Pa. (†15681) 294/D4
Isenthal, Switzerland 39/F3
Iseo (lake), Italy 34/C2
Isère (dept.), France 28/F5
Isère (riv.), France 28/F5
Iserlohn, W. Germany 22/B3
Isernia (prov.), Italy 34/E4
Isernia, Italy 34/E4
Ise-Shima National Park, Japan 81/H6
Iseyin, Nigeria 106/E7
Isfahan (prov.), Iran 66/H4
Isfahan, Iran 54/G6
Isfahan, Iran 66/G4
Isfahan, Iran 59/F3
Isfjorden (fjord), Norway 18/C2
Isham, Sask. 181/C4
Isherton, Guyana 131/B4
Ishigaki, Japan 81/L7
Ishigaki (isl.), Japan 81/L7
Ishige, Japan 81/P2
Ishikari (bay), Japan 81/K2
Ishikari (riv.), Japan 81/L2
Ishikawa (pref.), Japan 81/H5
Ishim (riv.), U.S.S.R. 54/H4
Ishim, U.S.S.R. 48/H4
Ishim (riv.), U.S.S.R. 48/G4
Ishimbay, U.S.S.R. 52/J4
Ishinomaki, Japan 81/K4
Ishioka, Japan 81/K5
Ishizuchi (mt.), Japan 81/F7
Ishpeming, Mich. (49849) 250/B2
Isiboro (riv.), Bolivia 136/C5
Isil'kul', U.S.S.R. 48/H4
Isimu, Indonesia 85/G5
Isiolo, Kenya 115/G3
Isiro, Zaire 102/E4
Isiro, Zaire 115/E3
Isisford, Queensland 88/G4
Isisford, Queensland 95/C5
Iskenderun, Turkey 59/C2
Iskenderun, Turkey 63/G4
Iskilip, Turkey 63/F2
Iskŭr (riv.), Bulgaria 45/G4
Iskut (riv.), Br. Col. 184/B2
Isla, Salar de la (salt dep.), Chile 138/B5
Isla, Veracruz, Mexico 150/M7
Isla (riv.), Scotland 15/E4
Isla Cristina, Spain 33/C4
Isla de Aguada, Mexico 150/O7
Isla de Maipo, Chile 138/G4
Islâhiye, Turkey 63/G4
Isla Holbox, Mexico 150/Q6
Islamabad (cap.), Pakistan 68/C2
Islamabad (cap.), Pakistan 2/N4
Islamabad (cap.), Pakistan 54/J6
Islamabad (cap.), Pakistan 59/K3
Islamabad District, Pakistan 68/C2
Islamorada, Fla. (33036) 212/F7
Isla Mujeres, Mexico 150/Q6
Island, Ky. (42350) 237/G6
Island (lake), Man. 162/G5
Island (lake), Manitoba 179/K3
Island (beach), N.J. 273/E4
Island (lake), N. Dak. 282/L2
Island (bay), Philippines 82/B6
Island (lag.), S. Australia 94/E4
Island (pond), Vt. 268/D2
Island (co.), Wash. 310/C2
Island City, Oreg. (97851) 291/K2
Island Creek, Md. (†20685) 245/M7
Island Falls○, Maine (04747) 243/G3
Island Falls, Ontario 175/D3
Island Grove, Fla. (32654) 212/D2
Island Heights, N.J. (08732) 273/E4
Islandia, Fla. (†33101) 212/F6
Island Lake, Ill. (60042) 222/A4
Island Lake, Manitoba 179/J3
Island Lake, Wis. (†54757) 317/D5
Island Park, Idaho (83429) 220/G5
Island Park (res.), Idaho 220/G5
Island Park, N.Y. (11558) 276/R7
Island Park, R.I. (†02871) 249/J6
Island Pond, Vt. (05846) 268/D2
Islands (bay), Newf. 166/C4
Islands (bay), Newf. 166/C2
Islands (bay), N. Zealand 100/E1
Islandton, S.C. (29929) 296/F6
Island View, Minn. (†56649) 255/E2
Island View, New Bruns. 170/D3
Isla Patrulla, Uruguay 145/E3
Isla Pucú, Paraguay 144/B4
Isla Umbú, Paraguay 144/C5
Isla Vista, Calif. (93117) 204/E9
Islay, Alberta 182/E3
Islay (isl.), Scotland 15/B5
Islay (isl.), Scotland 10/C3
Islay (sound), Scotland 15/C5
Isle (riv.), France 28/D5
Isle, Minn. (56342) 255/E4
Isle Au Haut○, Maine (04645) 243/F7
Isle-aux-Coudres, Québec 172/G2
Isle-aux-Grues, Québec 172/G2
Isle aux Morts, Newf. 166/C4
Isle La Motte○, Vt. (05463) 268/A2
Isle of Hope, Georgia (†31406) 217/K7
ISLE OF MAN 13/C3
ISLE OF MAN 10/D3

Isle of Palms, S.C. (29451) 296/H6
Isle of Whithorn, Scotland 15/D6
Isle of Wight (co.), England 13/F7
Isle of Wight (co.), Va. 307/P7
Isle of Wight, Va. (23397) 307/P7
Isle Pierre, Br. Col. 184/F3
Isle Royale (isl.), Mich. 250/D1
Isle Royale National Park, Mich. (†55605) 250/E1
Isle Royale Nat'l Park, Mich. 250/E1
Islesboro, Maine (04848) 243/F7
Islesboro○, Maine (04848) 243/F7
Islesboro (isl.), Maine 243/F7
Islesford, Maine (04646) 243/G7
Isles of Scilly, England 13/A7
Isleta, N. Mex. (87022) 274/C4
Isleton, Calif. (95641) 204/L1
Islington, England 10/B5
Islington, England 13/H8
Islington, Mass. (02090) 249/C8
Islip, N.Y. (11751) 276/O9
Ismailia, Egypt 111/K3
Ismailia, Egypt 59/B3
Ismay, Mont. (59336) 262/M4
Isna, Egypt 111/F2
Isna, Egypt 59/B4
Isney, Ala. (†36919) 195/B7
Isny im Allgäu, W. Germany 22/D5
Isojoki, Finland 18/M5
Isoka, Zambia 115/F6
Isola, Miss. (38754) 256/C4
Isonville, Ky. (41149) 237/P4
Isparta (prov.), Turkey 63/D4
Isparta, Turkey 63/D4
Isparta, Turkey 59/B2
Isperikh, Bulgaria 45/H4
Ispir, Turkey 63/J2
Israel 2/L4
Israel 54/E6
ISRAEL 59/B3
ISRAEL 65
Issano, Guyana 131/B3
Issaouane Erg (des.), Algeria 106/F3
Issaquah, Wash. (98027) 310/C3
Issaquena (co.), Miss. 256/B5
Issia, Ivory Coast 106/C7
Issineru, Guyana 131/A2
Issoire, France 28/E5
Issoudun, France 28/D4
Issue, Md. (20645) 245/L7
Issyk-Kul' (lake), U.S.S.R. 54/J5
Issyk-Kul' (lake), U.S.S.R. 48/H5
Issy-les-Moulineaux, France 28/A2
Istanbul (prov.), Turkey 63/C2
Istanbul, Turkey 2/L3
Istanbul, Turkey 7/G4
Istanbul, Turkey 63/D6
Istanbul, Turkey 59/A1
Isthmus (bay), Ontario 177/C2
Istiaia, Greece 45/F6
Istmina, Colombia 126/B5
Istokpoga (lake), Fla. 212/E4
Istranca (mts.), Turkey 63/B2
Istres, France 28/F6
Istria (pen.), Yugoslavia 45/A3
Isulan, Philippines 82/E7
Itá, Paraguay 144/B5
Itabaiana, Paraíba, Brazil 132/H4
Itabaiana, Sergipe, Brazil 132/G5
Itaberaba, Brazil 132/F6
Itabira, Brazil 120/E4
Itabira, Brazil 132/F7
Itabirito, Brazil 135/E2
Itabuna, Brazil 132/G6
Itabuna, Brazil 120/F4
Itacoatiara, Brazil 132/B3
Itacoatiara, Brazil 120/D3
Itacurubí, Paraguay 144/B5
Itacurubí del Rosario, Paraguay 144/D4
Itaguara, Brazil 135/D2
Itaguatins, Brazil 132/D4
Itagüí, Colombia 126/C4
Itaí, Brazil 135/B3
Itaipu (dam) 120/D5
Itaipu (dam), Brazil 132/C9
Itaipu (dam), Paraguay 144/E4
Itaituba, Brazil 132/C4
Itajaí, Brazil 120/E5
Itajaí, Brazil 132/D9
Itajubá, Brazil 135/D3
Itajubá, Brazil 132/E8
Itala, Somalia 115/J3
Italy 2/K3
Italy 7/F4
ITALY 34
Italy, Texas (76651) 303/H5
Itamarandiba, Brazil 132/F7
Itami, Japan 81/H7
Itanagar, India 68/G3
Itanhaém, Brazil 135/C4
Itapagipe, Brazil 135/B1
Itapé, Paraguay 144/C5
Itapeby, Uruguay 145/B2
Itapecerica, Brazil 135/D2
Itapecuru (riv.), Brazil 132/F4
Itapecuru-Mirim, Brazil 132/F3
Itapemirim, Brazil 132/F8
Itaperuna, Brazil 135/F2
Itapetinga, Brazil 120/F4
Itapetinga, Brazil 132/G6
Itapetininga, Brazil 135/B3
Itapetininga, Brazil 132/D8
Itapeva, Brazil 132/D8
Itapeva, Brazil 135/B3
Itapi (riv.), Brazil 132/B3
Itapicuru, Brazil 132/G5
Itapicuru (riv.), Brazil 132/G5
Itapipoca, Brazil 132/G3
Itapira, Brazil 135/C3
Itapiranga, Brazil 132/B3
Itápolis, Brazil 132/D8
Itápolis, Brazil 135/B2
Itaporanga, Brazil 132/G4
Itapúa (dept.), Paraguay 144/E5
Itaqui, Brazil 132/B10
Itaquyry, Paraguay 144/E4
Itararé, Brazil 132/D9
Itararé, Brazil 135/B4
Itararé (riv.), Brazil 135/B3
Itariri, Brazil 135/C4
Itarsi, India 68/D4
Itasca, Ill. (60143) 222/B5
Itasca (co.), Minn. 255/E3
Itasca (lake), Minn. 255/C3
Itasca, Texas (76055) 303/G5
Itasy (lake), Madagascar 118/H3
Itata (riv.), Chile 138/A11
Itatí, Argentina 143/E2
Itatiba, Brazil 135/C3
Itaú, Bolivia 136/D7
Itauguá, Paraguay 144/B5
Itaúna, Brazil 135/D2
Itawamba (co.), Miss. 256/H2
Itbayat (isl.), Philippines 82/A2
Itchen (lake), N.W. Terrs. 187/G3
Iténez (Guaporé) (riv.), Bolivia 136/C3
Ithaca, Mich. (48847) 250/E5
Ithaca, Nebr. (68033) 264/H3
Ithaca, N.Y. (14850) 276/G6
Ithaca, Ohio (†45329) 284/A6
Ithaca, Queensland 88/K2
Ithaca, Wis. (†53581) 317/F9
Itháki, Greece 45/E6
Itháki (Ithaca) (isl.), Greece 45/E6
Itigi, Tanzania 115/F5
Itimbiri (riv.), Zaire 115/D3
Itkillik (riv.), Alaska 196/H1
Itmann, W. Va. (24847) 312/D7
Itnay (riv.), Fr. Guiana 120/D2
Ito, Japan 81/J6
Itoigawa, Japan 81/H5
Itoman, Japan 81/N6
Itonamas (riv.), Bolivia 136/C3
Itta Bena, Miss. (38941) 256/D4
Ittre, Belgium 27/E7
Itu, Brazil 135/C3
Ituaçu, Brazil 132/F6
Ituango, Colombia 126/C4
Ituberá, Brazil 132/G6
Ituiutaba, Brazil 132/D7
Itumbiara, Brazil 120/E4
Itumbiara, Brazil 132/D7
Ituna, Sask. 181/H4
Ituni, Guyana 131/B3
Itupiranga, Brazil 132/D4
Iturama, Brazil 135/A1
Iturbe, Paraguay 144/C5
Ituri (for.), Zaire 115/E3
Iturup (isl.), U.S.S.R. 54/R5
Iturup (isl.), U.S.S.R. 48/P5
Ituverava, Brazil 135/C2
Ituzaingó, Argentina 143/E2
Ituzaingó, Uruguay 145/A6
Itzehoe, W. Germany 22/C2
Iuka, Ill. (62849) 222/E5
Iuka, Kansas (67066) 232/D4
Iuka, Ky. (42052) 237/E6
Iuka, Miss. (38852) 256/H1
Iul'tin, U.S.S.R. 48/T3
Iva, S.C. (29655) 296/B3
Ivaí (riv.), Brazil 132/C8
Ivalo, Finland 18/P2
Ivalojoki (riv.), Finland 18/P2
Ivan, Ark. (71748) 202/F6
Ivan, La. (†71006) 238/C1
Ivančice, Czech. 41/D2
Ivangrad, Yugoslavia 45/E4
Ivanhoe, Calif. (93235) 204/F7
Ivanhoe, Minn. (56142) 255/B6
Ivanhoe, N. S. Wales 88/G6
Ivanhoe, N.S. Wales 97/C3
Ivanhoe, N.C. (28447) 281/N5
Ivanhoe, Va. (24350) 307/G7
Ivanhoe, W. Australia 92/E1
Ivanhoe, W. Va. (†26201) 312/F5
Ivanjica, Yugoslavia 45/E4
Ivanof, Alaska (†99502) 196/G3
Ivano-Frankovsk, U.S.S.R. 7/G4
Ivano-Frankovsk, U.S.S.R. 48/C5
Ivano-Frankovsk, U.S.S.R. 52/B5
Ivanovo, U.S.S.R. 7/J3
Ivanovo, U.S.S.R. 48/E4
Ivanovo, U.S.S.R. 52/E3
Ivarib, Namibia 118/B4
Ivaylovgrad, Bulgaria 45/H5
Ivdel, U.S.S.R. 48/G3
Ivel, Ky. (41642) 237/R5
Ives (mesa), Ariz. 198/E3
Ivesdale, Ill. (61851) 222/E4
Ivey, Georgia (†31031) 217/F5
Ivigtut, Greenl. 4/D12
Ivindo (riv.), Cameroon 115/B3
Ivindo (riv.), Congo 115/B3
Ivindo (riv.), Gabon 115/B3
Ivins, Utah (84738) 304/A6
Ivohibe, Madagascar 118/H4
Ivón, Bolivia 136/C2
Ivor, Va. (23866) 307/P7
Ivory Coast 2/J5
Ivory Coast 102/B4
IVORY COAST 106/C7
Ivory Coast (reg.), Ivory Coast 106/C8
Ivoryton, Conn. (06442) 210/F3
Ivrea, Italy 34/B2
Ivrindi, Turkey /B3
Ivry-sur-Seine, France 28/B2
Ivujivik, Que. 162/J3
Ivujivik, Québec 174/E1
Ivy, Va. (22945) 307/L4
Ivybridge, England 13/D7
Ivydale, W. Va. (25113) 312/D5
Ivyland, Pa. (†18974) 294/M5
Ivy Mountain (brook), Conn. 210/C1
Ivyton, Ky. (41444) 237/P5
Ivyton, Tenn. (†38543) 237/L8
Iwaizumi, Japan 81/K4
Iwaki, Japan 54/R6
Iwaki, Japan 81/K5
Iwaki (mt.), Japan 81/K3
Iwakuni, Japan 81/E6
Iwami, Japan 81/G6
Iwamizawa, Japan 81/L2
Iwanai, Japan 81/K2
Iwasaki, Japan 81/J3
Iwata, Japan 81/H6
Iwate (pref.), Japan 81/K4
Iwate (mt.), Japan 81/K4
Iwatsuki, Japan 81/O2
Iwilei, Hawaii (†96801) 218/C4
Iwo (isl.), Japan 87/E3
Iwo (isl.), Japan 81/M4
Iwo, Nigeria 106/E7
Iwŏn, N. Korea 81/D3
Ixelles, Belgium 27/C9
Ixiamas, Bolivia 136/A3
Ixmiquilpan, Mexico 150/K6
Ixonia, Wis. (53036) 317/H1
Ixtapa, Mexico 150/J8
Ixtapalapa, Mexico 150/L1
Ixtenco, Mexico 150/N1
Ixtepec, Mexico 150/M8
Ixtlán del Río, Mexico 150/G6
Iyo, Japan 81/F7
Iyo (sea), Japan 81/E7
Izabal (lake), Guatemala 154/C3
Izamal, Mexico 150/P6
Izard (co.), Ark. 202/G1
Izberbash, U.S.S.R. 52/G6
Izegem, Belgium 27/C7
Izeh, Iran 66/F5
Izhevsk, U.S.S.R. 7/K3
Izhevsk, U.S.S.R. 48/F4
Izhevsk, U.S.S.R. 52/H3
Izhma (riv.), U.S.S.R. 52/H2
Izigan (cape), Alaska 196/E4
Izmail, U.S.S.R. 48/C5
Izmail, U.S.S.R. 52/C5
Izmir (prov.), Turkey 63/B3
Izmir, Turkey 54/D6
Izmir, Turkey 63/B3
Izmir, Turkey 59/A2
Izmir (gulf), Turkey 63/B3
Izmit, Turkey 59/A1
Izmit, Turkey 63/D2
Iznájar, Spain 33/D4
Iznalloz, Spain 33/E4
Iznik, Turkey 63/C2
Iznik (lake), Turkey 63/C2
Izozog, Bolivia 136/D6
Izozog (swamp), Bolivia 136/E6
Izra, Syria 63/G6
Izsák, Hungary 41/E3
Izsófalva, Hungary 41/F2
Iztapa, Guatemala 154/B4
Izu (isls.), Japan 81/J6
Izu (pen.), Japan 81/J6
Izúcar de Matamoros, Mexico 150/M2
Izuhara, Japan 81/D6
Izumi, Japan 81/J8
Izumiotsu, Japan 81/J8
Izumisano, Japan 81/G6
Izumo, Japan 81/F6
Izyum, U.S.S.R. 52/E5

J

Jaba, West Bank 65/C3
Jabaliya, Gaza Strip 65/A4
Jabalpur, India 54/K7
Jabalpur, India 68/D4
Jabe Rud (riv.), Iran 66/L2
Jabbeke, Belgium 27/C6
Jabir, Jordan 65/E2
Jablonec nad Nisou, Czech. 41/C1
Jablonica, Czech. 41/D2
Jablunka (pass), Czech. 41/E2
Jablunkov, Czech. 41/E2
Jaboatão, Brazil 120/F3
Jaboatão, Brazil 132/H5
Jaboticabal, Brazil 135/B2
Jaboticabal, Brazil 132/D8
Jabrin, Saudi Arabia 59/E5
Jaca, Spain 33/F1
Jacaguas (riv.), P. Rico 161/C2
Jacaleapa, Honduras 154/D3
Jacaltenango, Guatemala 154/B3
Jacaréacanga, Brazil 132/B4
Jacareí, Brazil 132/E8
Jacareí, Brazil 135/D3
Jacarezinho, Brazil 135/A3
Jacarezinho, Brazil 132/D8
Jáchal, Argentina 143/C3
Jachin, Ala. (36910) 195/B6
Jáchymov, Czech. 41/B1
Jacinto, Miss. (†38865) 256/H1
Jacinto City, Texas (77029) 303/J1
Jack, Ala. (36346) 195/F7
Jack (creek), Minn. 255/C7
Jack (lake), Ontario 177/F3
Jack (co.), Texas 303/F4
Jack (mt.), Wash. 310/E2
Jack Creek, Nev. (†89834) 266/E1
Jackfish (riv.), Alberta 182/B5
Jackfish (lake), Sask. 181/C2
Jackfish Lake, Sask. 181/C2
Jackfork (mt.), Okla. 288/P5
Jackman, Maine (04945) 243/C4
Jackman○, Maine (04945) 243/C4
Jackpot, Nev. (89825) 266/G1
Jacksboro, Tenn. (37757) 237/N8
Jacksboro, Texas (76056) 303/F4
Jacks Creek, Tenn. (38347) 237/D10
Jacks Fork (riv.), Mo. 261/J8
Jackson (co.), Ala. 195/F1
Jackson, Ala. (36545) 195/C8
Jackson (co.), Ark. 202/H2
Jackson, Calif. (95642) 204/C9
Jackson (co.), Colo. 208/G1
Jackson (co.), Fla. 212/D5
Jackson (lake), Fla. 212/B1
Jackson (lake), Fla. 212/E4
Jackson (co.), Georgia 217/E2
Jackson, Georgia (30233) 217/E4
Jackson (lake), Georgia 217/E4
Jackson (co.), Ill. 222/D6
Jackson (co.), Ind. 227/E7
Jackson (co.), Iowa 229/M4
Jackson (co.), Kansas 232/G2
Jackson (co.), Ky. 237/N6
Jackson, Ky. (41339) 237/P5
Jackson (par.), La. 238/E2
Jackson, La. (70748) 238/H5
Jackson (co.), Mich. 250/E6
Jackson, Mich. 188/J2
Jackson, Mich. (*49201) 250/E6
Jackson (co.), Minn. 255/C7
Jackson, Minn. (56143) 255/C7
Jackson (co.), Miss. 256/G9
Jackson (cap.), Miss. 146/K6
Jackson (cap.), Miss. 188/J4
Jackson (cap.), Miss. (*39201) 256/D6
Jackson (co.), Mo. 261/R5
Jackson, Mo. (63755) 261/N8
Jackson, Mont. (59736) 262/C5
Jackson (mt.), Mont. 262/C2
Jackson, Nebr. (68743) 264/H2
Jackson (mts.), Nev. 266/C1
Jackson○, N.H. (03846) 268/E3
Jackson○, N.J. (08527) 273/E3
Jackson (bay), N. Zealand 100/B5
Jackson (co.), N.C. 281/C4
Jackson, N.C. (27845) 281/P2
Jackson (co.), Ohio 284/E7
Jackson, Ohio (45640) 284/E7
Jackson (co.), Okla. 288/H5
Jackson (co.), Oreg. 291/E5
Jackson (creek), Oreg. 291/E5
Jackson, Pa. (18825) 294/L2
Jackson, S.C. (29831) 296/D5
Jackson (co.), S. Dak. 298/F6
Jackson (co.), Tenn. 237/K8
Jackson, Tenn. 188/J3
Jackson, Tenn. (38301) 237/D9
Jackson (co.), Texas 303/H9
Jackson (riv.), Va. 307/J4
Jackson (co.), W. Va. 312/C5
Jackson (co.), Wis. 317/E7
Jackson, Wis. (53037) 317/K9
Jackson (lake), Wyo. 188/E2
Jackson, Wyo. (83001) 319/B2
Jackson (lake), Wyo. 319/B2
Jackson (peak), Wyo. 319/B2
Jacksonboro, S.C. (29452) 296/G6
Jacksonburg, Ind. (†47327) 227/G5
Jacksonburg, Ohio (†45067) 284/B6
Jacksonburg, W. Va. (26377) 312/E3
Jackson Center, Ohio (45334) 284/B5
Jackson Center, Pa. (16133) 294/B3
Jackson Junction, Iowa (52150) 229/K2
Jackson Lake (res.), Colo. 208/L2
Jacksonport, Ark. (72075) 202/H2
Jacksonport, Wis. (†54235) 317/M6
Jackson's Arm, Newf. 166/C4
Jacksons Gap, Ala. (36861) 195/G5
Jackson Springs, N.C. (27281) 281/K4
Jacksontown, Ohio (43030) 284/F6
Jacksonville, Ala. (36265) 195/G3
Jacksonville, Ark. (72076) 202/F4
Jacksonville, Fla. 146/K6
Jacksonville, Fla. 188/K4
Jacksonville, Fla. (*32201) 212/E1
Jacksonville, Georgia (31544) 217/G7
Jacksonville, Ill. (62650) 222/C4
Jacksonville, Maine (†04630) 243/J6
Jacksonville, Md. (†21131) 245/M2
Jacksonville, Mo. (65260) 261/G3
Jacksonville, New Bruns. 170/C2
Jacksonville, N.C. (28540) 281/O5
Jacksonville, Ohio (45740) 284/F7
Jacksonville, Oreg. (97530) 291/D5
Jacksonville (Kent), Pa. (15752) 294/D4
Jacksonville, Texas (75766) 303/J5
Jacksonville, Vt. (05342) 268/B6
Jacksonville Beach, Fla. (32250) 212/E1
Jacksonville Naval Air Sta., Fla. 212/E1
Jacmel, Haiti 158/C6
Jacmel, Haiti 156/D3
Jacobabad, Pakistan 59/J4
Jacobabad, Pakistan 68/B3
Jacobina, Brazil 120/E4
Jacobina, Brazil 132/F5
Jacob Lake, Ariz. (86051) 198/C2
Jacobson, Minn. (55752) 255/E4
Jacobstown, N.J. (†08562) 273/D3
Jacobsville, Mich. (†49945) 250/A1
Jacobus, Pa. (17407) 294/J6
Jacques-Cartier (lake), Québec 172/F2
Jacques-Cartier (mt.), Québec 172/C1
Jacques-Cartier (passage), Québec 174/E3
Jacques-Cartier (riv.), Québec 172/F2
Jacquet (riv.), New Bruns. 170/D1
Jacquet River, New Bruns. 170/E1
Jacquinot (bay), Papua N.G. 86/B2
Jacuípe (riv.), Brazil 132/F5
Jacumba, Calif. (92034) 204/J11
Jacupiranga, Brazil 135/B4
Jaddi, Ras (cape), Pakistan 59/H4
Jaddi, Ras (pt.), Pakistan 68/A4
Jade (bay), W. Germany 22/C2
Jadwin, Mo. (65501) 261/K8
Jaén, Peru 128/C5
Jaén (prov.), Spain 33/E4
Jaén, Spain 7/D5
Jaén, Spain 33/E4
Jaffa (cape), S. Australia 94/F7
Jaffna, Sri Lanka 68/E7
Jaffna, Sri Lanka 54/K9
Jaffray, Br. Col. 184/K5
Jaffrey, N.H. (03452) 268/C6
Jaffrey○, N.H. (03452) 268/C6
Jaffrey Center, N.H. (03454) 268/C6
Jafura (des.), Saudi Arabia 59/F5
Jagdalpur, India 68/E5
Jagdaqi, China 77/K1
Jagersfontein, S. Africa 118/D5
Jagfontein, S. Africa 118/G7
Jaghbub (Jarabub), Libya 111/D2
Jagin (riv.), Iran 66/L8
Jagna, Philippines 82/E6
Jagtial, India 68/D5
Jagua, Cuba 158/D2
Jaguaquara, Brazil 132/F6
Jaguara (res.), Brazil 135/C2
Jaguarão, Brazil 132/C11
Jaguarialva, Brazil 132/D9
Jaguarialva, Brazil 135/B4
Jaguaribe (riv.), Brazil 132/G4
Jagüey Grande, Cuba 158/D2
Jagüey Grande, Cuba 156/B2
Jahrom, Iran 59/F4
Jahrom, Iran 66/H6
Jaicoa, Cordillera (mts.), P. Rico 161/B1
Jaicós, Brazil 132/F4
Jailolo, Indonesia 85/H5
Jainca, China 77/F4
Jaipur, India 54/J7
Jaipur, India 68/D3
Jaisalmer, India 68/C3
Jajarm, Iran 66/K2
Jajce, Yugoslavia 45/C3
Jajpur, India 68/F4
Jakarta (cap.), Indonesia 2/Q6
Jakarta (cap.), Indonesia 54/M10
Jakarta (cap.), Indonesia 85/H1
Jakin, Georgia (31761) 217/C8
Jakobstad, Finland 18/N5
Jakubany, Czech. 41/F2
Jal, N. Mex. (88252) 274/F6
Jala, Mexico 150/G6
Jalacingo, Mexico 150/P1
Jalaid, China 77/K2
Jalalabad, Afghanistan 68/B2
Jalalabad, Afghanistan 59/K3
Jalama, West Bank 65/C3
Jalapa, Guatemala 154/B3
Jalapa, Ind. (†46952) 227/F3
Jalapa, Nicaragua 154/E4
Jalapa, S.C. (†29108) 296/D3
Jalapa Enríquez, Mexico 146/J8
Jalapa Enríquez, Mexico 150/P1
Jalbun, West Bank 65/C3
Jaleswar, Nepal 68/F3
Jalgaon, India 68/D4
Jalingo, Nigeria 106/G7
Jalisco (state), Mexico 150/H6
Jalkot, Pakistan 59/K2
Jalna, India 68/D4
Jalo, Libya 111/D2
Jalo (oasis), Libya 111/D2
Jalón (riv.), Spain 33/E2
Jalor, India 68/C3
Jalpa, Mexico 150/H6
Jalpa de Méndez, Mexico 150/N7
Jalpaiguri, India 68/F3
Jalpan, Mexico 150/K6
Jalq, Iran 66/N7
Jáltipan de Morelos, Mexico 150/M8
Jalud, West Bank 65/C3
Jaluit (atoll), Marshall Is. 87/G5
Jam, Iran 66/H7
Jama, Ecuador 128/B3
Jamaica 2/F5
Jamaica 146/L8
Jamaica, Cuba 158/K4
Jamaica (chan.), Haiti 156/C3
Jamaica, Iowa (50128) 229/E5
JAMAICA 158
JAMAICA 156/C3
Jamaica (chan.), Jamaica 156/C3
Jamaica, N.Y. (*11401) 276/N9
Jamaica○, Vt. (05343) 268/B5
Jamaica Plain, Mass. (02130) 249/C7
Jamaiké, Suriname 131/D4
Jamalpur, Bangladesh 68/F4
Jamalpur, India 68/F3
Jamama, Somalia 115/H3
Jamanota (mt.), Neth. Ant. 161/E10
Jamanxim (riv.), Brazil 132/C4
Jambi, Indonesia 85/C6
Jambi, Indonesia 54/M10
Jambuair (cape), Indonesia 85/B4
James (bay) 162/H5
James (riv.) 188/G2
James (bay), Canada 146/K4
James (isl.), Chile 138/D5
James (peak), Colo. 208/H3
James, Georgia (†31032) 217/E5
James, Iowa (†51101) 229/A3
James (pt.), Md. 245/N6
James, Miss. (†38748) 256/B4
James (lake), N.C. 281/E3
James (riv.), N. Dak. 282/N6
James (bay), Ontario 175/D2
James (bay), Québec 174/A2
James (isl.), S.C. 296/H6
James (riv.), S. Dak. 298/N5
James (riv.), Va. 307/O6
James A. Garfield Nat'l Hist. Site, Ohio 284/G2
James Bay, Ontario 177/E2
Jamesburg, N.J. (08831) 273/E3
James City, N.C. (28550) 281/R4
James City, Pa. (16734) 294/E2
James City (co.), Va. 307/P6
James Creek, Pa. (16657) 294/F5
Jameson, Mo. (64647) 261/E2
Jameson Park, S. Africa 118/J7
Jamesport, Mo. (64648) 261/E3
James Ross (isl.) 5/C16
James Ross (str.), N.W.T. 162/G1
James Ross (str.), N.W. Terrs. 187/J3
Jamestown, Ala. (†35973) 195/G2
Jamestown, Ark. (†72501) 202/G2
Jamestown, Calif. (95327) 204/E6
Jamestown, Colo. (80455) 208/J2
Jamestown, Ill. (†62238) 222/D5
Jamestown, Ind. (46147) 227/D5
Jamestown, Kansas (66948) 232/E2
Jamestown, Ky. (42629) 237/L7
Jamestown, La. (71045) 238/D2
Jamestown, Miss. (†39483) 256/E8
Jamestown, Mo. (65046) 261/G5
Jamestown, N.Y. 188/L2
Jamestown, N.Y. (14701) 276/B6
Jamestown, N.C. (27282) 281/K3
Jamestown, N.Dak. 188/G1
Jamestown, N. Dak. (58401) 282/N6
Jamestown (dam), N. Dak. 282/N6
Jamestown (res.), N. Dak. 282/N6
Jamestown, Ohio (45335) 284/C6
Jamestown, Pa. (16134) 294/A3
Jamestown, R.I. (02835) 249/J6
Jamestown○, R.I. (02835) 249/J6
Jamestown, S. Australia 88/F6
Jamestown, S. Australia 94/F5
Jamestown, S.C. (29453) 296/H5
Jamestown, Tenn. (38556) 237/M8
Jamestown, Va. (23081) 307/P6
Jamestown Nat'l Hist. Site, Va. 307/P6
Jamesville, N.Y. (13078) 276/H5
Jamesville, N.C. (27846) 281/R3
Jamesville, Va. (23398) 307/S5
Jamieson, Fla. (†32333) 212/B1
Jamieson, Oreg. (97909) 291/K3
Jamison, Nebr. (†68759) 264/E2
Jamison, S.C. (†29115) 296/F4
Jamma, Somalia 102/G4
Jammerbugt (bay), Denmark 21/C3
Jammu, India 54/J6
Jammu, India 68/D2
Jammu and Kashmir (state), India 68/D2
Jamnagar, India 68/B4
Jamnagar, India 54/H7
Jampur, Pakistan 59/K4
Jämsä, Finland 18/O6
Jamshedpur, India 54/K7
Jamshedpur, India 68/F4
Jämtland (co.), Sweden 18/J5
Jamursba (cape), Indonesia 85/J5
Janakpur, Nepal 68/F3
Jandaq, Iran 66/J3
Jandowae, Queensland 95/D5
Jane, Mo. (64846) 261/D9
Jane Lew, W. Va. (26378) 312/F4
Janesville, Calif. (96114) 204/E3
Janesville, Ill. (62435) 222/E4
Janesville, Iowa (50647) 229/J3
Janesville, Minn. (56048) 255/E6
Janesville (Smithmill), Pa. (16680) 294/F4
Janesville, Wis. 188/J2
Janesville, Wis. (53545) 317/H10
Janesville-Beloit, Wis. 317/80
Janetstown, Scotland 15/E2
Janeville, New Bruns. 170/E1
Jánico, Dom. Rep. 158/D5
Janikowo, Poland 47/C2
Janiuay, Philippines 82/D5
Jan Mayen (isl.), Norway 4/B10
Jan Mayen (isl.), Norway 7/D1
Janos, Mexico 150/F1
Jánoshalma, Hungary 41/E3
Jánosháza, Hungary 41/D3
Janów Lubelski, Poland 47/F3
Jansen, Colo. (†81082) 208/K8
Jansen, Nebr. (68377) 264/G4
Jansen, Sask. 181/G4
Jantetelco, Mexico 150/L2
Januária, Brazil 120/E4
Januária, Brazil 132/E6
Janvrin (isl.), Nova Scotia 168/G3
Jaora, India 68/D4
Japan 2/S4
Japan 54/R6
Japan (sea) 2/R4
Japan (sea) 54/P6
JAPAN 81
Japan (sea), Japan 81/G4
Japan (sea), N. Korea 81/G4
Japan (sea), S. Korea 81/G4
Japan (sea), U.S.S.R. 48/O6
Japurá, Brazil 132/G9
Japurá (riv.), Brazil 120/C3
Japurá (riv.), Brazil 132/G9
Jaquet (pt.), Dominica 161/E5
Jara, Cerrito (mt.), Bolivia 136/F6
Jara (hill), Paraguay 144/C1
Jarabacoa, Dom. Rep. 158/E5
Jarabub, Libya 102/E2
Jarabub, Libya 111/D2
Jaragua, Dom. Rep. 158/D6
Jaraíz de la Vera, Spain 33/D2
Jarales, N. Mex. (87023) 274/C4
Jarama (riv.), Spain 33/E2
Jaramillo, Argentina 143/C6
Jarandilla de la Vera, Spain 33/D2
Jarash, Jordan 65/D3
Jarbalo, Kansas (†66048) 232/G2
Jarbidge (riv.), Idaho 220/C7
Jarbidge, Nev. (89826) 266/F1
Jardim, Brazil 132/G4
Jardine, Mont. (†59030) 262/F5
Jardines de la Reina (arch.), Cuba 158/F3
Jardines de la Reina (arch.), Cuba 156/B2
Jargalant, Mongolia 77/J2
Jari (riv.), Brazil 120/D2
Jari (riv.), Brazil 132/C3
Järna, Sweden 18/G2
Jarnac, France 28/C5
Jaro, Philippines 82/E5
Jarocin, Poland 47/C3
Jaroměř, Czech. 41/C1
Jarosław, Poland 47/F4
Jaroso, Colo. (81138) 208/H8
Järpen, Sweden 18/H5
Jarrahdale, W. Australia 88/B3
Jarrahdale, W. Australia 92/B2
Jarratt, Va. (23867) 307/O7
Jarrettsville, Md. (21084) 245/M2
Jarrow, Alberta 182/E3
Jarrow, England 13/J3
Jarrow, England 10/F3
Jars (plain), Laos 72/D3
Jartai, China 77/G4
Jaruco, Cuba 158/C1
Jarud, China 77/K3
Järvenpää, Finland 18/O6
Jarvie, Alberta 182/D2
Jarvis (isl.), Pacific 87/K6
Jarvisburg, N.C. (27947) 281/T2
Jarvisville, W. Va. (†26462) 312/F4
Järvsö, Sweden 18/K6
Jask, Iran 59/G4

Jask, Iran 54/G7
Jask, Iran 66/K8
Jasło, Poland 47/E4
Jasmin, Sask. 181/H4
Jasmine Estates, Fla. (†33568) 212/D3
Jason (isls.), 143/D7
Jason, Ky. (†41714) 237/O6
Jason, N.C. (†28580) 281/O4
Jasonville, Ind. (47438) 227/C6
Jasper, Ala. (35501) 195/D3
Jasper, Alberta 182/B3
Jasper, Alta. 162/E5
Jasper, Ark. (72641) 202/D1
Jasper, Fla. (32052) 212/D1
Jasper (co.), Georgia 217/E4
Jasper, Georgia (30143) 217/D2
Jasper (co.), Ill. 222/E4
Jasper (co.), Ind. 227/C2
Jasper, Ind. (47546) 227/D8
Jasper (co.), Iowa 229/G5
Jasper, Mich. (49248) 250/E7
Jasper, Minn. (56144) 255/B7
Jasper (co.), Miss. 256/F6
Jasper (co.), Mo. 261/D8
Jasper, Mo. (64755) 261/D8
Jasper, N.Y. (14855) 276/F6
Jasper, Ohio (45642) 284/D7
Jasper, Ontario 177/H3
Jasper, Oreg. (97401) 291/E3
Jasper (co.), S.C. 296/E6
Jasper, Tenn. (37347) 237/K10
Jasper (co.), Texas 303/K7
Jasper, Texas (75951) 303/L7
Jasper Nat'l Park, Alberta 182/A3
Jasper Nat'l Park, Alta. 162/E5
Jastrowie, Poland 47/C2
Jastrzębie Zdroj, Poland 47/D3
Jászapáti, Hungary 41/E3
Jászárokszállás, Hungary 41/E3
Jászberény, Hungary 41/E3
Jászfényszaru, Hungary 41/E3
Jászkarajenő, Hungary 41/E3
Jászkisér, Hungary 41/F3
Jászladány, Hungary 41/F3
Jataí, Brazil 120/D4
Jataí, Brazil 132/D7
Jatibonico, Cuba 158/F2
Jatibonico del Sur (riv.), Cuba 158/F3
Játiva, Spain 33/F3
Jaú, Brazil 132/D8
Jaú, Brazil 135/B3
Jauaperi (riv.), Brazil 132/A2
Jauari, Serra (mts.), Brazil 132/C3
Jauco, Cuba 158/K4
Jauf, Saudi Arabia 54/F7
Jauf, Saudi Arabia 59/C4
Jauja, Peru 128/E8
Jaumave, Mexico 150/K5
Jaun, Switzerland 39/D3
Jaunjelgava, U.S.S.R. 53/C2
Jaunpur, India 68/E3
Jauri, Iran 66/M6
Java (head), Indonesia 85/C7
Java (isl.), Indonesia 2/Q6
Java (isl.), Indonesia 54/M10
Java (isl.), Indonesia 85/J2
Java (sea), Indonesia 2/Q6
Java (sea), Indonesia 54/M10
Java (sea), Indonesia 85/D6
Java, S. Dak. (57452) 298/K3
Java, Va. (24565) 307/K7
Javari (riv.), Brazil 132/F9
Jávea, Spain 33/G3
Javier de Viana, Uruguay 145/C1
Jaworzno, Poland 47/B4
Jay, Fla. (32565) 212/B5
Jay (co.), Ind. 227/G4
Jay, Maine (04239) 243/C7
Jay○, Maine (04239) 243/C7
Jay, N.Y. (12941) 276/N2
Jay, Okla. (74346) 288/S2
Jay○, Vt. (†05859) 268/C2
Jay (peak), Vt. 268/B2
Jaya, Puncak (mt.), Indonesia 85/K6
Jayanca, Peru 128/B6
Jayapura, Indonesia 85/L6
Jayawijaya (range), Indonesia 85/K6
Jay Creek, North. Terr. 88/E4
Jay Em, Wyo. (82219) 319/H3
Jayess, Miss. (39641) 256/D8
Jayton, Texas (79528) 303/D4
Jayuya, P. Rico 156/G1
Jayuya, P. Rico 161/C2
Jaz Murian, Hamun-e (marsh), Iran 66/L7
Jaz Murian, Hamun-e (marsh), Iran 59/G4
Jean, Nev. (89019) 266/F7
Jean, Texas (†76374) 303/F4
Jean Côté, Alberta 182/B2
Jeanerette, La. (70544) 238/G7
Jeanette (bay), Newf. 166/C3
Jean Lafitte, La. (†70067) 238/K7
Jean Lafitte Nat'l Hist. Park, La. 238/P4
Jean-Marie River, N.W. Terrs. 187/F3
Jeanne Mance, New Bruns. 170/E1
Jeannette, Pa. (15644) 294/C5
Jean-Rabel, Haiti 158/B5
Jean-Rabel (pt.), Haiti 158/B5
Jebba, Nigeria 106/E7
Jebel Abyad (plat.), Sudan 111/E4
Jebel Aulia (dam), Sudan 102/F3
Jebel Aulia (dam), Sudan 111/F4
Jebel Dhanna, U.A.E. 59/F5
Jeberos, Peru 128/D5
Jeble, Syria 63/F5
Jedburg, S.C. (†29483) 296/G5
Jedburgh, Sask. 181/J4
Jedburgh, Scotland 10/E3
Jedburgh, Scotland 15/F5
Jeddah (Jidda), Saudi Arabia 59/C5
Jeddito, Ariz. (†86025) 198/E3
Jeddo, Mich. (48032) 250/G5
Jeddo, Pa. (†18224) 294/L3
Jeddore (cape), Nova Scotia 168/E4
Jeddore (harb.), Nova Scotia 168/F4
Jędrzejów, Poland 47/E3
Jefara (reg.), Libya 111/B1
Jefara (reg.), Tunisia 106/G2
Jeff, Ala. (†35804) 195/E1
Jeff, Ky. (41751) 237/P6
Jeff Davis (co.), Georgia 217/G7
Jeff Davis (co.), Texas 303/C11
Jeffers, Minn. (56145) 255/C6
Jeffers, Mont. (†59729) 262/E5
Jefferson (co.), Ala. 195/E3
Jefferson, Ala. (36745) 195/C6
Jefferson (co.), Ark. 202/G5
Jefferson, Ark. (72079) 202/F5
Jefferson (co.), Colo. 208/J3
Jefferson, Colo. (80456) 208/H4
Jefferson (co.), Fla. 212/C1
Jefferson (co.), Georgia 217/H4
Jefferson, Georgia (30549) 217/F2
Jefferson (co.), Idaho 220/F6
Jefferson (co.), Ill. 222/E5
Jefferson (co.), Ind. 227/G7
Jefferson, Ind. (†46041) 227/D4
Jefferson (co.), Iowa 229/K6
Jefferson, Iowa (50129) 229/E4
Jefferson (co.), Kansas 232/G2
Jefferson (co.), Ky. 237/K4
Jefferson (par.), La. 238/K7
Jefferson○, Maine (04348) 243/D7
Jefferson, Md. (21755) 245/J3
Jefferson, Mass. (01522) 249/G3
Jefferson (co.), Miss. 256/B7
Jefferson (co.), Mo. 261/L6
Jefferson (co.), Mont. 262/D4
Jefferson (riv.), Mont. 262/D5
Jefferson (co.), Nebr. 264/G4
Jefferson○, N.H. (03583) 268/D3
Jefferson (mt.), N.H. 268/E3
Jefferson (co.), N.Y. 276/J2
Jefferson, N.Y. (12093) 276/L6
Jefferson, N.C. (28640) 281/G2
Jefferson (co.), Ohio 284/J5
Jefferson (West Jefferson), Ohio (†43162) 284/D6
Jefferson, Ohio (44047) 284/J2
Jefferson (co.), Okla. 288/L6
Jefferson, Okla. (†73759) 288/L1
Jefferson (co.), Oreg. 291/F3
Jefferson, Oreg. (97352) 291/D3
Jefferson (mt.), Oreg. 291/F3
Jefferson (co.), Pa. 294/D3
Jefferson, Pa. (†15025) 294/B7
Jefferson, Pa. (15344) 294/B6
Jefferson (Codorus), Pa. (†17311) 294/J6
Jefferson, S.C. (29718) 296/G2
Jefferson, S. Dak. (57038) 298/S8
Jefferson (co.), Tenn. 237/P8
Jefferson (co.), Texas 303/K8
Jefferson, Texas (75657) 303/J5
Jefferson, Va. (†23139) 307/N5
Jefferson (co.), Wash. 310/B3
Jefferson (co.), W. Va. 312/L4
Jefferson (co.), Wis. 317/J9
Jefferson, Wis. (53549) 317/J10
Jefferson City (cap.), Mo. (65101) 261/H5
Jefferson City (cap.), Mo. 146/J6
Jefferson City (cap.), Mo. 188/H3
Jefferson City, Mont. (59638) 262/E4
Jefferson City, Tenn. (37760) 237/P8
Jefferson Davis (par.), La. 238/E6
Jefferson Davis (co.), Miss. 256/E7
Jefferson Heights, La. (70121) 238/O4
Jefferson Island, Mont. (†59721) 262/E5
Jefferson Manor, Va. (22303) 307/S3
Jefferson Nat'l Expansion Mem. Nat'l Hist. Site, Mo. 261/R3
Jefferson Proving Ground, Ind. 227/G7
Jeffersonton, Va. (22724) 307/N3
Jeffersontown, Ky. (40299) 237/L2
Jeffersonville, Georgia (31044) 217/F5
Jeffersonville, Ind. (47130) 227/F8
Jeffersonville, Ky. (40337) 237/O5
Jeffersonville, N.Y. (12748) 276/L7
Jeffersonville, Ohio (43128) 284/C6
Jeffersonville, Vt. (05464) 268/B2
Jeffrey (res.), Nebr. 264/D4
Jeffrey, W. Va. (25114) 312/C7
Jeffrey City, Wyo. (82310) 319/E3
Jeffrey's, Newf. 166/C4
Jef Jef es Seghin (plat.), Chad 111/D3
Jef Jef es Seghin (plat.), Libya 111/D3
Jega, Nigeria 106/E6
Jegenstorf, Switzerland 39/D2
Jeinemeni, Cerro (mt.), Chile 138/E6
Jeiseyville, Ill. (†62568) 222/D4
Jejuí-Guazú (riv.), Paraguay 144/D4
Jēkabpils, U.S.S.R. 53/C2
Jēkabpils, U.S.S.R. 52/C3
Jekyll (isl.), Georgia 217/K8
Jeleń, Poland 47/B4
Jelenia Góra (prov.), Poland 47/B3
Jelenia Góra, Poland 47/B3
Jelgava, U.S.S.R. 7/G3
Jelgava, U.S.S.R. 53/B2
Jelgava, U.S.S.R. 52/B3
Jellico, Tenn. (37762) 237/N7
Jellico Creek, Ky. (†40769) 237/N7
Jellicoe, Ontario 177/H5
Jelling, Denmark 21/C6
Jelloway, Ohio (†43014) 284/F4
Jelm, Wyo. (82063) 319/G4
Jelšava, Czech. 41/F2
Jemaja (isl.), Indonesia 85/D5
Jemappes, Belgium 27/D8
Jember, Indonesia 85/K2
Jemez (riv.), N. Mex. 274/C3
Jemez Canyon (res.), N. Mex. 274/C3
Jemez Pueblo, N. Mex. (87024) 274/C3
Jemez Springs, N. Mex. (87025) 274/C3
Jeminay, China 77/C2
Jemison, Ala. (35085) 195/E5
Jemnice, Czech. 41/C2
Jemseg, New Bruns. 170/D3
Jemtland, Maine (†04783) 243/G1
Jena, E. Germany 22/D3
Jena, La. (71342) 238/F3
Jenaz, Switzerland 39/J3
Jenbach, Austria 41/A3
Jendouba, Tunisia 106/F1
Jeneponto, Indonesia 85/F7
Jenera, Ohio (45841) 284/C4
Jenifer, Ala. (†36268) 195/G3
Jenin, West Bank 65/C3
Jenison, Mich. (49428) 250/D6
Jenkinjones, W. Va. (24848) 312/D8
Jenkins (co.), Georgia 217/J5
Jenkins, Ky. (41537) 237/R6
Jenkins, Minn. (56456) 255/D4
Jenkins, Mo. (65677) 261/E9
Jenkinsburg, Georgia (30234) 217/E4
Jenkinsville, S.C. (29065) 296/E3
Jenkintown, Pa. (19046) 294/M5
Jenks, Okla. (74037) 288/P2
Jenner, Alberta 182/E4
Jennersdorf, Austria 41/C3
Jennerstown, Pa. (15547) 294/D5
Jennie, Ark. (71649) 202/H7
Jennie, Suriname 131/C3
Jennings, Ant. & Bar. 161/D11
Jennings, Fla. (32053) 212/C1
Jennings (co.), Ind. 227/F7
Jennings, Kansas (67643) 232/B2
Jennings, La. (70546) 238/E6
Jennings, Md. (†21536) 245/B2
Jennings, Mich. (†49651) 250/D4
Jennings, Mo. (63136) 261/R2
Jennings, N.S. Wales 97/F1
Jennings, Okla. (74038) 288/N2
Jennings Lodge, Oreg. (†97201) 291/B2
Jenny (creek), Oreg. 291/E5
Jenny Lake, Wyo. (†83012) 319/B2
Jenny Lind, Ark. (†72901) 202/B3
Jenny Lind, Calif. (†95252) 204/C9
Jenny Lind (isl.), N.W. Terrs. 187/H3
Jenolan Caves, N.S. Wales 97/E3
Jenpeg, Manitoba 179/J2
Jensen, Utah (84035) 304/E3
Jensen Beach, Fla. (33457) 212/F4
Jens Munk (isl.), N.W.T. 162/H2
Jens Munk (isl.), N.W. Terrs. 187/K3
Jepara, Indonesia 85/J2
Jequié, Brazil 120/E4
Jequié, Brazil 132/F6
Jequitinhonha, Brazil 132/F7
Jequitinhonha (riv.), Brazil 120/E4
Jequitinhonha (riv.), Brazil 132/F7
Jerablus, Syria 63/G4
Jerada, Morocco 106/D2
Jerauld (co.), S. Dak. 298/M5
Jérémie, Haiti 156/C3
Jérémie, Haiti 158/A6
Jeremoabo, Brazil 132/G5
Jeremy (riv.), Conn. 210/F2
Jerez, Spain 7/D5
Jerez de García Salinas, Mexico 150/H5
Jerez de la Frontera, Spain 33/C4
Jerez de los Caballeros, Spain 33/C3
Jericho, Ark. (†72327) 202/K3
Jericho, N.Y. (11753) 276/R6
Jericho, Queensland 95/C4
Jericho, Vt. (05465) 268/A2
Jericho○, Vt. (05465) 268/A2
Jericho, West Bank 65/C4
Jericho Center, Vt. (05465) 268/B3
Jerico Springs, Mo. (64756) 261/E7
Jeriel, Ky. (†41143) 237/R4
Jerilderie, N.S. Wales 97/C4
Jerimoth (hill), R.I. 249/G5
Jermyn, Pa. (18433) 294/L2
Jermyn, Texas (76057) 303/F4
Jerome, Ariz. (86331) 198/C4
Jerome, Ark. (71650) 202/G7
Jerome (co.), Idaho 220/D7
Jerome, Idaho (83338) 220/D7
Jerome, Ill. (†62701) 222/D4
Jerome, Mo. (65529) 261/J7
Jerome, Pa. (15937) 294/D5
Jeromesville, Ohio (44840) 284/F4
Jerry City, Ohio (43437) 284/C3
Jersey, Ark. (71651) 202/F7
Jersey (isl.), Chan. Is. 13/E8
Jersey (isl.), Chan. Is. 10/E6
Jersey, Georgia (30235) 217/E3
Jersey (co.), Ill. 222/C4
Jersey, Ohio (†43062) 284/E5
Jersey (bay), Virgin Is. (U.S.) 161/B4
Jersey City, N.J. 188/M2
Jersey City, N.J. (*07301) 273/B2
Jersey Mills, Pa. (17739) 294/H3
Jersey Shore, Pa. (17740) 294/H3
Jerseyside, Newf. 166/B3
Jerseytown, Pa. (†17815) 294/J3
Jersey Village, Texas (†77001) 303/J1
Jerseyville, Ill. (62052) 222/C4
Jerslev, Denmark 21/D3
Jerumenha, Brazil 132/F4
Jerusalem, Ark. (72080) 202/E3
Jerusalem (dist.), Israel 65/B4
Jerusalem (cap.), Israel 54/E6
Jerusalem (cap.), Israel 65/C4
Jerusalem (cap.), Israel 59/C3
Jerusalem, Ohio (43747) 284/H6
Jervis (inlet), Br. Col. 184/E5
Jervis (mt.), Chile 138/D8
Jervis Bay, Aust. Cap. Terr. 97/F4
Jervois Range, North. Terr. 88/F4
Jesenice, Yugoslavia 45/A2
Jeseník, Czech. 41/D1
Jeseníky (mts.), Czech. 41/D1
Jesenské, Czech. 41/F2
Jesi, Italy 34/D3
Jessamine (co.), Ky. 237/M5
Jesse, W. Va. (24849) 312/C7
Jessie, N. Dak. (58452) 282/O4
Jessieville, Ark. (71949) 202/D4
Jessnitz, E. Germany 22/E3
Jessore, Bangladesh 68/F4
Jessup, Pa. (18434) 294/F6
Jesterville, Md. (†21814) 245/P7
Jesuit Bend, La. (†70113) 238/K7
Jesup, Georgia (31545) 217/J7
Jesup, Iowa (50648) 229/J4
Jesús, Paraguay 144/E5
Jesús de Machaca, Bolivia 136/A5
Jesús de Otoro, Honduras 154/C3
Jesús María, Argentina 143/D3
Jesús María (reef), Mexico 150/L4
Jet, Okla. (73749) 288/K1
Jetersville, Va. (23083) 307/M6
Jetmore, Kansas (67854) 232/B3
Jett, Ky. (†40601) 237/M4
Jette, Belgium 27/B9
Jetts Creek, Ky. (†41382) 237/O6
Jever, W. Germany 22/B2
Jevíčko, Czech. 41/D2
Jewel Cave Nat'l Mon., S. Dak. 298/B6
Jewell, Georgia (31045) 217/G4
Jewell, Iowa (50130) 229/F4
Jewell (co.), Kansas 232/D2
Jewell, Kansas (66949) 232/D2
Jewell, Ohio (43530) 284/B3
Jewell, Oreg. (†97138) 291/D2
Jewell Ridge, Va. (24622) 307/E6
Jewett, Ill. (62436) 222/E4
Jewett, Ohio (43986) 284/H5
Jewett, Texas (75846) 303/H6
Jewett City, Conn. (06351) 210/H2
Jewish Aut. Obl., U.S.S.R. 48/O5
Jeypore, India 68/E5
Jhalawar, India 68/D4
Jhal Jhao, Pakistan 59/H4
Jhal Jhao, Pakistan 68/B3
Jhang Sadar, Pakistan 59/K3
Jhang Sadar, Pakistan 68/C2
Jhansi, India 68/D3
Jharsuguda, India 68/E4
Jhelum (riv.), India 68/C2
Jhelum, Pakistan 68/C2
Jhelum, Pakistan 59/K3
Jhelum (riv.), Pakistan 68/C2
Jhudo, Pakistan 68/B3
Jhunjhunu, India 68/D3
Jialing (riv.), China 54/M6
Jiamusi (Kiamusze), China 77/M2
Ji'an (Kian), China 77/J6
Jiande, China 77/J6
Jiangcheng, China 77/F7
Jiangmen (Kongmoon), China 77/H7
Jiangsu (Kiangsu) (prov.), China 77/K5
Jiangxi (Kiangsi) (prov.), China 77/J6
Jiangyou, China 77/G5
Jian'ou, China 77/J6
Jianshi, China 77/H5
Jianshui, China 77/F7
Jianyang, China 77/J6
Jiaohe, China 77/L3
Jiao Xian, China 77/K4
Jiaozuo (Tsiaotso), China 77/H4
Jiashan, China 77/J5
Jia Xian, China 77/H4
Jiaxing (Kashing), China 77/K5
Jiayin, China 77/M2
Jiayu, China 77/H6
Jiayuguan, China 77/E4
Jibaro, Cuba 158/F2
Jibhalanta (Uliastay), Mongolia 77/E2
Jibóia, Brazil 132/G8
Jibou, Romania 45/F2
Jibsh, Ras (cape), Oman 59/G5
Jicarilla, N. Mex. (†88313) 274/D5
Jicarilla Ind. Res., N. Mex. 274/B2
Jicarón (isl.), Panama 154/F7
Jičín, Czech. 41/C1
Jico, Mexico 150/P1
Jidda, Saudi Arabia 54/E7
Jidda, Saudi Arabia 59/C5
Jiexiu, China 77/H4
Jieyang, China 77/J7
Jifna, West Bank 65/C4
Jigalong Aboriginal Reserve, W. Australia 88/C4
Jigger, La. (71249) 238/G2
Jiggs, Nev. (†89801) 266/F2
Jiguaní, Cuba 158/H4
Jiguero (pt.), P. Rico 156/F1
Jiguero (pt.), P. Rico 161/A1
Jigüey (bay), Cuba 158/G2
Jigzhi, China 77/F5
Jihlava, Czech. 41/C2
Jihlava (riv.), Czech. 41/D2
Jihočeský (reg.), Czech. 41/C2
Jihomoravský (reg.), Czech. 41/D2
Jijel, Algeria 106/F1
Jijia (riv.), Romania 45/H2
Jijiga, Ethiopia 111/H6
Jijona, Spain 33/F3
Jilemnice, Czech. 41/C1
Jilib, Somalia 115/H3
Jilin (Kirin) (prov.), China 77/L3
Jilin (Kirin), China 77/L3
Jilin, China 54/O5
Jilotepec de Abasolo, Mexico 150/K7
Jim (lake), N. Dak. 282/N5
Jimaní, Dom. Rep. 158/C6
Jimbolia, Romania 45/E3
Jimena de la Frontera, Spain 33/D4
Jiménez, Chihuahua, Mexico 150/G3
Jiménez, Coahuila, Mexico 150/J2
Jim Falls, Wis. (54748) 317/D5
Jim Hogg (co.), Texas 303/F11
Jimma, Ethiopia 111/G6
Jimma, Ethiopia 102/F4
Jimsar, China 77/C3
Jim Thorpe, Pa. (18229) 294/L4
Jim Wells (co.), Texas 303/F10
Jim Woodruff (dam), Georgia 217/C9
Jinan (Tsinan), China 77/J4
Jinan, China 54/N6
Jincheng, China 77/H4
Jinchuan, China 77/F5
Jind, India 68/D3
Jindabyne, N.S. Wales 97/E5
Jindabyne (lake), N.S. Wales 97/E5
Jindalee, N.S. Wales 97/E4
Jindřichův Hradec, Czech. 41/C2
Jingbian, China 77/G4
Jingdezhen (Kingtehchen), China 77/J6
Jingellic, N.S. Wales 97/D4
Jinggu, China 77/F7
Jinghe, China 77/B3
Jinghong, China 77/F7
Jingtai, China 77/F4
Jingxi, China 77/G7
Jing Xian, Anhui, China 77/J5
Jing Xian, Hunan, China 77/H6
Jingyuan, China 77/F4
Jinhua (Kinhwa), China 77/J6
Jining (Tsining), Nei Monggol, China 77/H3
Jining (Tsining), Shandong, China 77/J4
Jinja, Uganda 115/F3
Jinja, Uganda 102/F4
Jinmen (Quemoy) (isl.), China 77/J7
Jinotega, Nicaragua 154/E4
Jinotepe, Nicaragua 154/D5
Jinping, China 77/G6
Jinsha Jiang (Yangtze) (riv.), China 77/E5
Jinshi (Tsingshih), China 77/H6
Jintotolo (chan.), Philippines 82/D5
Jinxi (Chinsi), China 77/K3
Jin Xian, China 77/K4
Jinzhou (Chinchow), China 77/K3
Jinzhou, China 54/N5
Jipijapa, Ecuador 128/B3
Jiran, Ethiopia 111/G6
Jirgalanta (Hovd), Mongolia 77/D2
Jiřkov, Czech. 41/B1
Jish, Israel 65/C1
Jishou, China 77/H6
Jisr esh Shughur, Syria 63/G5
Jiu (riv.), Romania 45/F3
Jiujiang (Kiukiang), China 77/J6
Jiulong, China 77/F6
Jiuquan (Kiuchüan), China 77/E4
Jixi (Kisi), China 77/M2
Jixi, China 54/P5
Ji Xian, China 77/H4
Jizan (Qizan), Saudi Arabia 59/D6
Jizera (riv.), Czech. 41/C1
Joaçaba, Brazil 132/D9
Joachimsthal, E. Germany 22/E2
Joachín, Mexico 150/Q2
Joana Peres, Brazil 132/D3
Joanico, Uruguay 145/B6
Joanna, S.C. (29351) 296/D3
João Monlevade, Brazil 135/E1
João Pessoa, Brazil 120/F3
João Pessoa, Brazil 132/H4
João Pinheiro, Brazil 132/E7
Joaquim Távora, Brazil 135/B3
Joaquin, Texas (75954) 303/L5
Joaquín Suárez, Canelones, Uruguay 145/B6
Joaquín Suárez, Colonia, Uruguay 145/B5
Joaquín V. González, Argentina 143/D2
Job (peak), Nev. 266/C3
Job, W. Va. (26274) 312/G5
Jobabo, Cuba 158/H3
Jobos, P. Rico 161/D3
Jobos (bay), P. Rico 161/D3
Job's Cove, Newf. 166/D2
Jobstown, N.J. (08041) 273/D3
Joch (pass), Switzerland 39/F3
Jódar, Spain 33/E4
Jo Daviess (co.), Ill. 222/C1
Jodhpur, India 54/J7
Jodhpur, India 68/C3
Jodie, W. Va. (26674) 312/D6
Jodoigne, Belgium 27/F7
Joe Batt's Arm, Newf. 166/D4
Joensuu, Finland 7/H2
Joensuu, Finland 18/R5
Joes, Colo. (80822) 208/O3
Joes (brook), Vt. 268/C3
Joetsu, Japan 81/H5
Joffre, Alberta 182/D3
Jofra (oasis), Libya 111/C2
Jõgeva, U.S.S.R. 53/D1
Joggins, Nova Scotia 168/D3
Joghatay, Kuh-e (mts.), Iran 66/K2
Jogjakarta (Yogyakarta), Indonesia 85/J2
Jogues, Ontario 175/D3
Johannesburg, Calif. (93528) 204/H8
Johannesburg, Mich. (49751) 250/E4
Johannesburg, S. Africa 102/E7
Johannesburg, S. Africa 2/L7
Johannesburg, S. Africa 118/H6
Johanngeorgenstadt, E. Germany 22/E3
John (riv.), Alaska 196/H1
John (cape), Nova Scotia 168/E3
John D. Rockefeller, Jr., Mem. Pkwy., Wyo. 319/B1
John Day, Oreg. (97845) 291/J3
John Day (dam), Oreg. 291/G2
John Day (riv.), Oreg. 291/G2
John Day (dam), Wash. 310/E5
John Day Fossil Beds Nat'l Mon., Oreg. 291/G3
John d'Or Prairie, Alberta 182/B5
Johnetta, Ky. (40439) 237/N6
John F. Kennedy Space Center, Fla. 212/F3
John F. Kennedy Nat'l Hist. Site, Mass. 249/C7
John H. Kerr (dam), Va. 307/M7
John Jay (mt.), Br. Col. 184/B2
John Martin (res.), Colo. 208/N6
John Muir Nat'l Hist. Site, Calif. 204/K1
John O'Groats, Scotland 15/E2
John Redmond (res.), Kansas 232/G3
Johns, Miss. (†39042) 256/E6
Johns, N.C. (†28352) 281/K5
Johns (isl.), S.C. 296/G6
Johnsburg, Minn. (†55909) 255/F7
Johnsburg, N.Y. (12843) 276/M3
Johnshaven, Scotland 15/F4
Johns Island, S.C. (29455) 296/G6
Johnson (co.), Ark. 202/C2
Johnson, Ark. (72741) 202/B1
Johnson (isl.), Chile 138/D5
Johnson (co.), Georgia 217/G5
Johnson (creek), Idaho 220/C5
Johnson (co.), Ill. 222/E6
Johnson (co.), Ind. 227/E6
Johnson, Ind. (†47565) 227/B8
Johnson (co.), Iowa 229/K5
Johnson (co.), Kansas 232/H3
Johnson, Kansas (67855) 232/A4
Johnson (co.), Ky. 237/R5
Johnson, Minn. (56250) 255/B5
Johnson (co.), Mo. 261/E5
Johnson (co.), Nebr. 264/H4
Johnson, Nebr. (68378) 264/J4
Johnson (lake), Nebr. 264/E4
Johnson (co.), Tenn. 237/T7
Johnson (co.), Texas 303/G5
Johnson, Vt. (05656) 268/B2
Johnson○, Vt. (05656) 268/B2
Johnson (co.), Wyo. 319/F1
Johnsonburg, N.J. (07846) 273/D2
Johnsonburg, Pa. (15845) 294/E3
Johnson City, N.Y. (13790) 276/J6
Johnson City, Oreg. (†97027) 291/B2
Johnson City, Tenn. (37601) 237/S8
Johnson City, Texas (78636) 303/F7
Johnson Creek, Wis. (53038) 317/J9
Johnsondale, Calif. (93238) 204/G8
Johnson Draw (dry riv.), Texas 303/C7
Johnsons (creek), Utah 304/B6
Johnsons Bayou, La. (†70631) 238/C7
Johnson's Crossing, Yukon 187/E3
Johnsons Landing, Br. Col. 184/J5
Johnsons Point, Ant. & Bar. 161/D11
Johnsonville, Ill. (62850) 222/E5
Johnsonville, N.Y. (12094) 276/O5
Johnsonville, S.C. (29555) 296/J4
Johnston (key), Fla. 212/E7
Johnston, Iowa (50131) 229/F5
Johnston (co.), N.C. 281/N4
Johnston (co.), Okla. 288/N6
Johnston (atoll), Pacific 87/K4
Johnston, S.C. (29832) 296/D4
Johnston (lakes), W. Australia 88/C6
Johnston, The (lakes), W. Australia 92/C6
Johnston City, Ill. (62951) 222/E6
Johnstone (str.), Br. Col. 184/D5
Johnstone, Scotland 10/A1
Johnstone, Scotland 15/B2
Johnstons Station, Miss. (†39666) 256/D8
Johnstown, Colo. (80534) 208/K2
Johnstown, Ireland 17/G6
Johnstown, Nebr. (69214) 264/D2
Johnstown, N.Y. (12095) 276/M4
Johnstown, N. Dak. (58245) 282/R3
Johnstown, Ohio (43031) 284/E5
Johnstown, Ontario 177/J3
Johnstown, Pa. 188/L2
Johnstown, Pa. (*15901) 294/D5
Johnsville, Ark. (†71648) 202/F7
Johnsville, Md. (†21791) 245/K2
Johor (Johore) (state), Malaysia 72/D7
Johor, Sungai (riv.), Malaysia 72/F5
Johor Baharu (Johore Bharu), Malaysia 72/F5
Johore (str.), Malaysia 72/E6
Johore Baharu, Malaysia 54/M9
Joice, Iowa (50446) 229/G2
Joigny, France 28/E3
Joiner, Ark. (72350) 202/K3
Joinvile, Brazil 120/E5
Joinvile, Brazil 132/D9
Joinville (isl.) 5/C16
Jojutla de Juárez, Mexico 150/L2
Jokkmokk, Sweden 18/L3
Jökulsá (riv.), Iceland 21/C1
Joli (pt.), Nova Scotia 168/D5
Jolicure, New Bruns. 170/F3
Joliet, Ill. 188/J2
Joliet, Ill. (*60431) 222/E2
Joliet, Mont. (59041) 262/G5
Joliette, N. Dak. (58246) 282/R2
Joliette (county), Québec 174/B3
Joliette (co.), Québec 172/C3
Joliette, Québec 172/D3
Jolietville, Ind. (†46074) 227/E4
Jolley, Iowa (50551) 229/D4
Jollytown, Pa. (†15352) 294/B6
Jolo, Philippines 82/C8
Jolo (isl.), Philippines 85/G4
Jolo (isl.), Philippines 82/C7
Jolon, Calif. (93928) 204/D7
Jomalig (isl.), Philippines 82/D3
Jo-Mary (lkes), Maine 243/E4
Jombang, Indonesia 85/K2
Jomda, China 77/E5
Jona, Switzerland 39/G2
Jonacatepec, Mexico 150/M2
Jonava, U.S.S.R. 53/C3
Jones (plain), Cambodia 72/E5
Jones (plain), Vietnam 72/E5
Jones, Ala. (36749) 195/E5
Jones (isls.), Alaska 196/J1
Jones (co.), Georgia 217/E5
Jones (co.), Iowa 229/L4
Jones, La. (71250) 238/G1
Jones, Mich. (49061) 250/D7
Jones (co.), Miss. 256/F7
Jones (beach), N.Y. 276/R7
Jones (co.), N.C. 281/P4
Jones (sound), N.W. Terrs. 187/K2
Jones (sound), N.W.T. 146/K2
Jones (sound), N.W.T. 162/M3
Jones, Okla. (73049) 288/M3
Jones (co.), S. Dak. 298/H6
Jones, Tenn. (†38006) 237/C9
Jones (co.), Texas 303/E5
Jonesboro, Ark. 188/H3
Jonesboro, Ark. (72401) 202/J2
Jonesboro, Georgia (30236) 217/D4
Jonesboro, Ill. (62952) 222/D6
Jonesboro, Ind. (46938) 227/F4
Jonesboro, La. (71251) 238/E2
Jonesboro○, Maine (04648) 243/J6
Jonesboro, Tenn. (37659) 237/R8
Jonesborough, N. Ireland 17/J3
Jonesburg, Mo. (63351) 261/K5

Kamienna Góra 389

Jones Creek, Texas (†77541) 303/J9
Jonesdale, Wis. (†53565) 317/F10
Jones Mills, Ark. (72105) 202/E5
Jones Mills, Pa. (15646) 294/D5
Jonesport, Maine (04649) 243/H6
Jonesport○, Maine (04649) 243/H6
Jones Springs, W. Va. (25427) 312/K4
Jonestown, Miss. (38639) 256/D2
Jonestown, Pa. (17038) 294/K5
Jonesville, Alaska (†99674) 196/B1
Jonesville, Ind. (47247) 227/F6
Jonesville, Ky. (41052) 237/M3
Jonesville, La. (71343) 238/G3
Jonesville, Mich. (49250) 250/E6
Jonesville, N.C. (28642) 281/H2
Jonesville, S.C. (29353) 296/D2
Jonesville, Vt. (05466) 268/B3
Jonesville, Va. (24263) 307/B7
Jonglei, Sudan 111/F6
Joniškis, U.S.S.R. 53/B2
Jönköping (co.), Sweden 18/H8
Jönköping, Sweden 18/H8
Jönköping, Sweden 7/F3
Jonquière, Que. 162/J6
Jonquière, Québec 172/F1
Jonquière, Québec 174/C3
Jonuta, Mexico 150/N7
Jonzac, France 28/C5
Joplin, Mo. (64801) 261/C8
Joplin, Mo. 146/J6
Joplin, Mo. 188/H3
Joplin, Mont. (59531) 262/F2
Joppa, Ala. (35087) 195/E2
Joppa, Ill. (62953) 222/E6
Joppa, Tenn. (†37861) 237/O8
Joppatowne, Md. (†21085) 245/N3
Jorat (mt.), Switzerland 39/C3
Jordan 2/L4
Jordan 54/E6
JORDAN 59/C3
Jordan (dam), Ala. 195/F5
Jordan (lake), Ala. 195/F5
Jordan, (creek) Idaho 220/A7
Jordan, Iowa (†50036) 229/F4
Jordan (riv.), Israel 65/D3
Jordan (riv.), Jordan 65/D3
Jordan, Minn. (55352) 255/E6
Jordan, Mont. (59337) 262/J3
Jordan, N.Y. (13080) 276/H4
Jordan, B. Everett (lake), N.C. 281/M3
Jordan (bay), Nova Scotia 168/C5
Jordan (lake), Nova Scotia 168/C4
Jordan (riv.), Nova Scotia 168/C5
Jordan (creek), Oreg. 291/K5
Jordan, S.C. (†29102) 296/G4
Jordan (riv.), Utah 304/C3
Jordan Falls, Nova Scotia 168/C5
Jordan River, Sask. 181/H2
Jordan Valley, Oreg. (97910) 291/K5
Jorge Montt (isl.), Chile 138/D9
Jorhat, India 68/G3
Jorm, Afghanistan 68/C1
Jorm, Afghanistan 59/K2
Jörn, Sweden 18/M4
Jornada del Muerto (valley), N. Mex. 274/C5
Jorquera (riv.), Chile 138/B6
Jörva-Jaani, U.S.S.R. 53/D1
Jos, Nigeria 106/F7
Jos, Nigeria 102/C4
Jos (plat.), Nigeria 106/F7
Jose Abad Santos, Philippines 82/E8
José Agustín Palacios, Bolivia 136/B3
José Batlle y Ordóñez, Uruguay 145/D4
José Cardel, Mexico 150/Q1
José de San Martín, Argentina 143/B5
José Enrique Rodó, Uruguay 145/B4
José Ignacio (lag.), Uruguay 145/E5
José M. Micheo, Argentina 143/G7
Jose Panganiban, Philippines 82/D3
José Pedro Varela, Uruguay 145/E4
Joseph (lake), Newf. 166/B3
Joseph (lake), Ontario 177/E2
Joseph, Oreg. (97846) 291/K2
Joseph (creek), Oreg. 291/K2
Joseph, Utah (84739) 304/B5
Joseph Bonaparte (gulf) 88/D2
Joseph Bonaparte (gulf), Australia 87/C7
Joseph Bonaparte (gulf), North. Terr. 93/A3
Joseph Bonaparte (gulf), W. Australia 92/E1
Joseph City, Ariz. (86032) 198/E4
Josephine, Ala. (†36530) 195/C10
Josephine (co.), Oreg. 291/D5
Josephine, Pa. (15750) 294/D5
Joshinetsu-Kogen National Park, Japan 81/J5
Joshua (pt.), Conn. 210/E4
Joshua Tree, Calif. (92252) 204/J9
Joshua Tree Nat'l Mon., Calif. 204/J10
Jostedal, Norway 18/E6
Jostedalsbreen (glac.), Norway 18/E6
Jost Van Dyke (isl.), Virgin Is. (Br.) 161/C3
Jost Van Dyke (isl.), Virgin Is. (Br.) 156/G1
Joubert, S. Dak. (†57344) 298/M7
Jourdanton, Texas (78026) 303/F9
Joure, Netherlands 27/H3
Joussard, Alberta 182/B2
Joux (lake), Switzerland 39/B3
Jovellanos, Cuba 156/B2
Jovellanos, Cuba 158/D1
Joveyn (riv.), Iran 66/K2
Joy, Ill. (61260) 222/C2
Joy, Ky. (†42047) 237/E6
Joyce, La. (71440) 238/E3
Joyce, Wash. (98343) 310/B2
Joyce's Country (dist.), Ireland 17/B4
Joyo, Japan 81/J7
Juab (co.), Utah 304/A4
Juana Díaz, P. Rico 161/C2
Juan Aldama, Mexico 150/H4
Juan D. Jackson, Uruguay 145/C4
Juan de Fuca (str.) 146/F5
Juan de Fuca (str.), Br. Col. 162/D6
Juan de Fuca (str.), Br. Col. 184/J4
Juan de Fuca (str.), Wash. 188/A1
Juan de Fuca (str.), Wash. 310/A2
Juan de Mena, Paraguay 144/D4
Juan de Nova (isl.), Réunion 102/G6
Juan de Nova (isl.), Réunion 118/G3
Juan Fernández (isls.), Chile 2/E7
Juan Fernández (isls.), Chile 120/B6
Juangriego, Venezuela 124/G2
Juani (isl.), Tanzania 115/G5
Juanita, N. Dak. (58453) 282/N4
Juanita, Wash. (98033) 310/B1
Juanjuí, Peru 128/D6
Juan L. Lacaze, Uruguay 145/B5
Juan Stuven (isl.), Chile 138/D7
Juárez, Argentina 143/D4
Juárez, Mexico 150/J3
Juazeiro, Brazil 132/G5
Juàzeiro, Brazil 120/E3
Juazeiro do Norte, Brazil 132/F4
Juàzeiro do Norte, Brazil 120/F3
Juba, Sudan 111/F7
Juba, Sudan 102/F4
Jubail, Saudi Arabia 59/F4
Jubba, Saudi Arabia 59/D4
Jubbada Hoose (prov.), Somalia 115/H3
Jubbulpore (Jabalpur), India 68/D4
Jubilee (lake), W. Australia 88/D5
Juby (cape), Morocco 106/B3
Júcar (riv.), Spain 7/D5
Júcar (riv.), Spain 33/F3
Júcaro, Cuba 158/F2
Juchipila, Mexico 150/H6
Juchique de Ferrer, Mexico 150/Q1
Juchitán de Zaragoza, Mexico 150/M8
Jucuarán, El Salvador 154/C4
Jud, N. Dak. (58454) 282/N6
Juda, Wis. (53550) 317/H10
Judaea (reg.), Israel 65/B5
Judaea (reg.), Jordan 65/C4
Judas (pt.), C. Rica 154/E6
Judenburg, Austria 41/C3
Judibana, Venezuela 124/C2
Judique, Nova Scotia 168/G3
Judith (riv.), Mont. 262/G3
Judith (pt.), R.I. 249/J7
Judith Basin (co.), Mont. 262/F4
Judith Gap, Mont. (59453) 262/G4
Judson, Ind. (47856) 227/C5
Judson, Minn. (†56055) 255/D6
Judson, N. Dak. (†58563) 282/H6
Judsonia, Ark. (72081) 202/G3
Judyville, Ind. (†47993) 227/C4
Juelsminde, Denmark 21/D6
Juhu, India 68/B7
Juichin (Ruijin), China 77/J6
Juigalpa, Nicaragua 154/E4
Juist (isl.), W. Germany 22/B2
Juiz de Fora, Brazil 120/E5
Juiz de Fora, Brazil 135/E2
Juiz de Fora, Brazil 132/F8
Jujuy (prov.), Argentina 143/C1
Jujuy, Argentina 143/C1
Jujuy, Argentina 120/C5
Jukskei (riv.), S. Africa 118/H6
Julesburg, Colo. (80737) 208/P1
Juli, Peru 128/H11
Juliaca, Peru 120/B4
Juliaca, Peru 128/G10
Julia Creek, Queensland 88/G4
Julia Creek, Queensland 95/B4
Juliaetta, Idaho (83535) 220/B3
Julian, Calif. (92036) 204/J10
Julian, Nebr. (68379) 264/J4
Julian, N.C. (27283) 281/K3
Julian, Pa. (16844) 294/G4
Julian Alps (range), Italy 34/D1
Julianatop (mt.), Suriname 131/C4
Julianehåb, Greenl. 4/D12
Julianehåb, Greenland 2/G2
Julianehåb, Greenland 146/P3
Jülich, W. Germany 22/B3
Juliette, Georgia (31046) 217/E4
Juliff, Texas (†77583) 303/J3
Julio María Sanz, Uruguay 145/E4
Juliustown, N.J. (08042) 273/D3
Jullundur, India 68/D2
Jumbilla, Peru 128/C5
Jumbo, Okla. (†74523) 288/P6
Jumilla, Spain 33/F3
Jumla, Nepal 68/E3
Jumna (riv.), India 68/E3
Jump (riv.), Wis. 317/E5
Jumpertown, Miss. (†38829) 256/G1
Jumping Branch, W. Va. (25969) 312/E7
Jump River, Wis. (54434) 317/E5
Junagadh, India 68/B4
Junaina, Saudi Arabia 59/D5
Juncal, Argentina 143/F6
Juncos, P. Rico 161/E2
Juncos, P. Rico 156/G1
Junction, Ill. (62954) 222/E6
Junction, Texas (76849) 303/E7
Junction, Utah (84740) 304/B5
Junction, W. Va. (26824) 312/J4
Junction City, Ark. (71749) 202/E7
Junction City, Georgia (31812) 217/C5
Junction City, Ill. (†61601) 222/D5
Junction City, Kansas (66441) 232/E2
Junction City, Ky. (40440) 237/M5
Junction City, La. (71749) 238/E1
Junction City, Mo. (†63645) 261/M7
Junction City, Ohio (43748) 284/F6
Junction City, Oreg. (97448) 291/D3
Junction City, Wis. (54443) 317/G6
Jundah, Queensland 95/B5
Jundah, Queensland 88/G4
Jundiaí, Brazil 135/C3
Jundiaí, Brazil 132/E8
Juneau, Alaska 146/E4
Juneau (cap.), Alaska 188/E6
Juneau (cap.), Alaska (99801) 196/N1
Juneau, U.S. 4/D16
Juneau, U.S. 2/C3
Juneau (co.), Wis. 317/F8
Juneau, Wis. (53039) 317/J9
Juneda, Spain 33/G2
Junee, N.S. Wales 97/D4
June in Winter (lake), Fla. 212/E4
June Lake, Calif. (93529) 204/G6
June Park, Fla. (†32901) 212/F3
Jungar, China 77/H4
Jungfrau (mt.), Switzerland 39/E3
Jungfraujoch, Switzerland 39/E3
Junggar Pendi (desert basin), China 77/C2
Junglei (prov.), Sudan 111/F6
Juniata, Nebr. (68955) 264/F4
Juniata (co.), Pa. 294/H4
Juniata (riv.), Pa. 294/G5
Juniata Terrace, Pa. (†17044) 294/G4
Junín, Argentina 143/F7
Junín, Argentina 120/C6
Junín (dept.), Peru 128/E8
Junín, Peru 128/E8
Junín (lake), Peru 128/E8
Junín de los Andes, Argentina 143/B4
Junior, W. Va. (26275) 312/G5
Juniper (mts.), Ariz. 198/C3
Juniper (mt.), Colo. 208/C1
Juniper, Georgia (31801) 217/C6
Juniper, New Bruns. 170/C2
Juniper (creek), S.C. 296/H2
Junius, S. Dak. (†57042) 298/P6
Juniye, Lebanon 63/F5
Junlian, China 77/F6
Juno, Georgia (30534) 217/D2
Juno, North. Terr. 93/C5
Juno, Tenn. (†38351) 237/E9
Juno, Texas (76943) 303/C7
Juno Beach, Fla. (†33404) 212/F5
Junosuando, Sweden 18/N3
Juntura, Oreg. (97911) 291/K4
Jun Xian, China 77/H5
Juojärvi (lake), Finland 18/Q5
Jupiter, Fla. (33458) 212/F5
Jupiter, N.C. (28787) 281/D3
Jupiter Island, Fla. (†33455) 212/F4
Juquiá, Brazil 135/C4
Jur (riv.), Sudan 111/E6
Jura (dept.), France 28/F4
Jura (mts.), France 28/F4
Jura (isl.), Scotland 10/D3
Jura (isl.), Scotland 15/C5
Jura (sound), Scotland 15/C5
Jura (sound), Scotland 10/D3
Jura (canton), Switzerland /D2
Jura (mts.), Switzerland 39/B3
Juradó, Colombia 126/B4
Jurbarkas, U.S.S.R. 53/B3
Jurmala, U.S.S.R. 53/B2
Jurmala, U.S.S.R. 52/B3
Jurong, Singapore 72/E6
Juruá (riv.), Brazil 120/C3
Juruá (riv.), Brazil 132/G10
Juruá (riv.), Peru 128/F7
Juruena, Brazil 132/B6
Juruena (riv.), Brazil 120/D4
Juruena (riv.), Brazil 132/B5
Juruti, Brazil 132/B3
Jusepín, Venezuela 124/G3
Juskatla, Br. Col. 184/A3
Jussy, Switzerland 39/B4
Justice, Ill. (†60458) 222/B6
Justice, Manitoba 179/C4
Justice, W. Va. (24851) 312/C7
Justiceburg, Texas (79330) 303/C5
Justin, Texas (76247) 303/F1
Justus, Ohio (†44662) 284/G4
Jutaí (riv.), Brazil 132/G9
Jüterbog, E. Germany 22/E3
Jutiapa, Guatemala 154/B3
Jutiapa, Honduras 154/D3
Juticalpa, Honduras 154/D3
Jutland (pen.), Denmark 21/C5
Jutland (pen.), Denmark 18/F9
Jutland, N.J. (08809) 273/D2
Juuka, Finland 18/Q5
Juventud (municipio especial), Cuba 158/C2
Juventud (isl.), Cuba 146/K7
Juventud, Isla de la (Pines), Cuba 158/B3
Juventud (Pines) (isl.), Cuba 156/A2
Juwara, Oman 59/G6
Ju Xian, China 77/J4
Juye, China 77/J4
Jyderup, Denmark 21/E6
Jylland (Jutland) (pen.), Denmark 21/C5
Jyske Ås (hills), Denmark 21/D3
Jyväskylä, Finland 7/G2
Jyväskylä, Finland 18/O5

K

K2 (mt.) 54/J6
K2 (mt.), Pakistan 68/D1
Kaaawa, Hawaii (96730) 218/F1
Kaabong, Uganda 115/F3
Kaala (mt.), Hawaii 218/D1
Kaanapali, Hawaii (†96761) 218/H2
Kaba (Habahe), China 77/C2
Kaba, Hungary 41/F2
Kabacan, Philippines 82/E7
Kabaena (isl.), Indonesia 85/G7
Kabala, S. Leone 106/B7
Kabale, Uganda 115/E4
Kabalo, Zaire 115/E5
Kabambare, Zaire 115/E4
Kabardin-Balkar A.S.S.R., U.S.S.R. 48/E5
Kabardin-Balkar A.S.S.R., U.S.S.R. 52/F6
Kabare, Zaire 115/E4
Kabarega Nat'l Park, Uganda 115/F3
Kabasalan, Philippines 82/D7
Kabba, Nigeria 106/F7
Kabetogama, Minn. (†56669) 255/F2
Kabetogama (lake), Minn. 255/E2
Kabinakagami (riv.), Ontario 177/J5
Kabin Buri, Thailand 72/D4
Kabinda, Zaire 115/D5
Kabir Kuh (mts.), Iran 66/E4
Kabompo, Zambia 115/D6
Kabompo (riv.), Zambia 115/D6
Kabong, Malaysia 85/E5
Kabongo, Zaire 115/E5
Kabud Gonbad, Iran 66/L2
Kabul (cap.), Afghanistan 68/B2
Kabul (cap.), Afghanistan 59/J3
Kabul (cap.), Afghanistan 54/H6
Kabul (cap.), Afghanistan 2/N4
Kabul (riv.), Afghanistan 68/C2
Kabul (riv.), Afghanistan 59/K3
Kabul (riv.), Pakistan 68/C2
Kabunda, Zaire 115/E6
Kabwe, Zambia 102/E6
Kabwe, Zambia 115/E6
Kabylia (reg.), Algeria 106/E1
Kachemak, Alaska (†99663) 196/B2
Kachemak (bay), Alaska 196/B2
Kachess (lake), Wash. 310/D3
Kachin (state), Burma 72/C1
Kachug, U.S.S.R. 48/L4
Kaçkar Dağı (mt.), Turkey 63/J2
Kackley, Kansas (†66948) 232/E2
Kadaň, Czech. 41/B1
Kadan Kyun (isl.), Burma 72/C4
Kadavu (Kandavu) (isl.), Fiji 87/H7
Kadayanallur, India 68/D7
Kadei (riv.), Cameroon 115/C3
Kadei (riv.), Cent. Afr. Rep. 115/C3
Kadei (riv.), Congo 115/C3
Kadıköy, Turkey 63/D6
Kadina, S. Australia 88/F6
Kadina, S. Australia 94/F5
Kadınhanı, Turkey 63/E3
Kadiolo, Mali 106/C6
Kadiri, India 68/D6
Kadirli, Turkey 63/F4
Kadiyevka (Stakhanov), U.S.S.R. 52/E5
Kadmat (isl.), India 68/C6
Kadoka, S. Dak. (57543) 298/F6
Kadoma, Japan 81/J7
Kadoma (Gatooma), Zimbabwe 118/D3
Kadugli, Sudan 111/E5
Kadugli, Sudan 102/E3
Kaduna (state), Nigeria 106/F6
Kaduna, Nigeria 102/C3
Kaduna, Nigeria 106/F6
Kaduna (riv.), Nigeria 106/F7
Kadzherom, U.S.S.R. 52/J2
Kaech'ŏn, N. Korea 81/B4
Kaédi, Mauritania 106/B5
Kaédi, Mauritania 102/A3
Kaélé, Cameroon 115/B1
Kaena (pt.), Hawaii 218/D1
Kaeo, N. Zealand 100/D1
Kaesŏng, N. Korea 81/C4
Kaf, Saudi Arabia 59/C3
Kafan, U.S.S.R. 52/G7
Kafar Kanna, Israel 65/C2
Kaffa (prov.), Ethiopia 111/G6
Kaffrine, Senegal 106/A6
Kafia Kingi, Sudan 111/D6
Kafirévs (cape), Greece 45/G6
Kafr Yasif, Israel 65/C2
Kafue, Zambia 115/E7
Kafue (riv.), Zambia 115/E7
Kafue Nat'l Park, Zambia 115/E6
Kaga, Japan 81/H5
Kaga Bandoro, Cent. Afr. Rep. 115/C2
Kagalaska (isl.), Alaska 196/L4
Kagan, U.S.S.R. 48/G6
Kagawa (pref.), Japan 81/G6
Kagawong, Ontario 177/B2
Kagawong (lake), Ontario 177/B2
Kagera Nat'l Park, Rwanda 115/F4
Kağıthane, Turkey 63/D6
Kağızman, Turkey 63/K2
Kagoshima (pref.), Japan 81/E8
Kagoshima, Japan 81/E8
Kagoshima, Japan 54/O6
Kagoshima (bay), Japan 81/E8
Kagul, U.S.S.R. 52/C5
Kaguyak, Alaska (†99608) 196/H3
Kahakuloa, Hawaii (†96793) 218/J1
Kahala, Hawaii (†96801) 218/D5
Kahala (pt.), Hawaii 218/D1
Kahaluu, Hawaii (†96744) 218/E2
Kahama, Tanzania 115/F4
Kahana, Hawaii (†96717) 218/F1
Kahana (bay), Hawaii 218/F1
Kahayan (riv.), Indonesia 85/E6
Kahemba, Zaire 115/C5
Kahiltna (riv.), Alaska 196/B1
Kahlotus, Wash. (99335) 310/G4
Kah-Nee-Ta, Oreg. (†97761) 291/F3
Kahoka, Mo. (63445) 261/J2
Kahoolawe (isl.), Hawaii 188/F5
Kahoolawe (isl.), Hawaii 87/L4
Kahoolawe (isl.), Hawaii 218/H3
Kahouanne (isl.), Guadeloupe 161/A6
Kahramanmaraş (prov.), Turkey 63/G4
Kâhta, Turkey 63/H4
Kahuku, Hawaii (96731) 218/E1
Kahuku, Hawaii 188/F5
Kahuku (pt.), Hawaii 218/E1
Kahului, Hawaii (96732) 218/J2
Kahului, Hawaii 188/F5
Kahului (harb.), Hawaii 218/J1
Kai (isls.), Indonesia 85/J7
Kaiama, Nigeria 106/E7
Kaiapit, Papua N.G. 85/B7
Kaiapoi, N. Zealand 100/D5
Kaibab (plat.), Ariz. 198/C2
Kaibab Ind. Res., Ariz. 198/C2
Kaibito, Ariz. (86053) 198/D2
Kaibito (plat.), Ariz. 198/D2
Kaieteur (fall), Guyana 131/B3
Kaifeng, China 77/H5
Kaifeng, China 54/N6
Kaikohe, N. Zealand 100/D1
Kaikoura, N. Zealand 100/D5
Kaikoura (pen.), N. Zealand 100/E5
Kaikoura (range), N. Zealand 100/D5
Kaili, China 77/G6
Kailu, China 77/K3
Kailua (Kailua Kona), Hawaii, Hawaii (96740) 218/F5
Kailua, Oahu, Hawaii (96734) 218/F2
Kailua (bay), Hawaii 218/F2
Kailua (bay), Hawaii 218/F5
Kailua Kona, Hawaii (96740) 218/F5
Kaimana, Indonesia 85/J6
Kaimanawa (range), N. Zealand 100/E3
Kaimu, Hawaii (†96778) 218/J6
Kaimuki, Hawaii (96816) 218/D4
Kainaliu, Hawaii (†96750) 218/G5
Kainaliu, Hawaii 188/F6
Kainan (bay) 5/B10
Kaingaroa, N. Zealand 100/E7
Kainji (res.), Nigeria 106/E6
Kaipara (harb.), N. Zealand 100/D2
Kaipara (riv.), N. Zealand 100/A1
Kaiparowits (plat.), Utah 304/C6
Kaipokok (bay), Newf. 166/B2
Kaipokok (riv.), Newf. 166/B3
Kairouan, Tunisia 106/F1
Kairuku, Papua N.G. 85/B7
Kaiser, Mo. (65047) 261/G6
Kaiseregg (mt.), Switzerland 39/D3
Kaiserslautern, W. Germany 22/B4
Kaiserstuhl (mt.), W. Germany 22/B4
Kaitaia, N. Zealand 100/D1
Kaitangata, N. Zealand 100/C7
Kaitumälv (riv.), Sweden 18/M3
Kaiwi (chan.), Hawaii 218/E6
Kaiyuan, Liaoning, China 77/K3
Kaiyuan, Yunnan, China 77/F7
Kaiyuh (mts.), Alaska 196/G2
Kaizuka, Japan 81/H8
Kajaani, Finland 7/G2
Kajaani, Finland 18/P4
Kajabbi, Queensland 88/G3
Kajabbi, Queensland 95/A4
Kajiado, Kenya 115/G4
Kajok, Sudan 111/E6
Kaka, Cent. Afr. Rep. 115/E2
Kaka, Sudan 111/F5
Kakabeka Falls, Ontario 177/G5
Kakabeka Falls, Ontario 175/B3
Kakamega, Kenya 115/F3
Kake, Alaska (99830) 196/M1
Kakhk, Iran 66/L3
Kakhonak, Alaska (†99647) 196/H3
Kakhovka, U.S.S.R. 52/D5
Kakhovka (res.), U.S.S.R. 48/D5
Kakhovka (res.), U.S.S.R. 52/D5
Kakinada, India 54/K8
Kakinada, India 68/E5
Kakisa, N.W. Terrs. 187/G3
Kakkiviak (cape), Newf. 166/B1
Kakogawa, Japan 81/G6
Kaktovik, Alaska (99747) 196/K1
Kakwa (riv.), Alberta 182/A2
Kalaa-Kebira, Tunisia 106/F1
Kalabahi, Indonesia 85/G7
Kalabo, Zambia 115/D6
Kalach, U.S.S.R. 52/F4
Kalachinsk, U.S.S.R. 48/H4
Kalach-na-Donu, U.S.S.R. 52/F5
Kaladan (riv.), Burma 72/B2
Kaladar, Ontario 177/H3
Kalae, Hawaii (†96757) 218/G1
Ka Lae (cape), Hawaii 218/G7
Kalahari (des.) 102/E7
Kalahari (des.), Botswana 118/C4
Kalahari (des.), Namibia 118/C4
Kalahari Gemsbok Nat'l Park, S. Africa 118/C5
Kalaheo, Hawaii (96741) 218/C2
Kalajoki, Finland 18/N4
Kalajoki (riv.), Finland 18/O4
Kalakan, U.S.S.R. 48/M4
Kalaloch, Wash. (†98331) 310/A3
Kalam, Pakistan 68/C1
Kalama, Wash. (98625) 310/C4
Kalama (riv.), Wash. 310/C4
Kalámai, Greece 7/G5
Kalámai, Greece 45/F7
Kalamazoo, Mich. 188/J2
Kalamazoo (co.), Mich. 250/D6
Kalamazoo, Mich. (*49001) 250/D6
Kalamazoo (riv.), Mich. 250/C6
Kalambo (falls), Tanzania 115/F5
Kalambo (falls), Zambia 115/F5
Kalamo, Mich. (†49096) 250/D6
Kalampáka, Greece 45/E6
Kalamunda, W. Australia 88/B2
Kalan, Turkey 63/H3
Kalao (isl.), Indonesia 85/G7
Kalaoa, Hawaii (†96740) 218/G5
Kalaotoa (isl.), Indonesia 85/G5
Kalapana, Hawaii (†96778) 218/J6
Kalasin, Thailand 72/D3
Kalat (Qalat), Afghanistan 68/B2
Kalat (Qalat), Afghanistan 59/J3
Kalat, Pakistan 54/H7
Kalat, Pakistan 59/J4
Kalat, Pakistan 68/B3
Kalâtdlit-Nunât (Greenland) 4/B12
Kalâtdlit-Nunât (Greenland) 146/P2
Kalaupapa, Hawaii (96742) 218/G1
Kalaupapa (pen.), Hawaii 218/H1
Kalaupapa Nat'l Hist. Park, Hawaii 218/H1
Kalávrita, Greece 45/F6
Kalawao (co.), Hawaii 218/G1
Kalbarri, W. Australia 92/A4
Kale, Turkey 63/C4
Kalecik, Turkey 63/E2
Kaleden, Br. Col. 184/H5
Kalegauk (isl.), Burma 72/C4
Kalehe, Zaire 115/E4
Kaleida, Manitoba 179/D5
Kalemie, Zaire 115/E5
Kalemie, Zaire 102/E5
Kalemyo, Burma 72/B2
Kaleva, Mich. (49645) 250/C4
Kalevala, U.S.S.R. 52/D1
Kalewa, Burma 72/B2
Kalgan (Zhangjiakou), China 77/J3
Kalgin (isl.), Alaska 196/B1
Kalgoorlie, Australia 2/R7
Kalgoorlie, W. Australia 88/C6
Kalgoorlie, W. Australia 92/C5
Kalgoorlie-Boulder, W. Australia 92/C5
Kaliakra (cape), Bulgaria 45/J4
Kalianda, Indonesia 85/D7
Kalibo, Philippines 82/D5
Kalida, Ohio (45853) 284/B4
Kalihi, Hawaii (†96801) 218/C4
Kalihi (stream), Hawaii 218/C3
Kalihi Entrance (str.), Hawaii 218/B4
Kalihiwai, Hawaii (†96754) 218/C1
Kalima, Zaire 115/E4
Kalimantan (reg.), Indonesia 85/E5
Kálimnos, Greece 45/H7
Kálimnos (isl.), Greece 45/H7
Kalinga, Queensland 88/K2
Kalinga-Apayao (prov.), Philippines 82/C1
Kalinin, U.S.S.R. 7/H3
Kalinin, U.S.S.R. 48/D4
Kalinin, U.S.S.R. 52/E3
Kaliningrad, U.S.S.R. 7/G3
Kaliningrad, U.S.S.R. 48/B4
Kaliningrad, Kaliningrad, U.S.S.R. 52/B4
Kaliningrad, Moscow Oblast, U.S.S.R. 52/E3
Kalininsk, U.S.S.R. 52/F4
Kalinkovichi, U.S.S.R. 52/C4
Kalispel Ind. Res., Wash. 310/H2
Kalispell, Mont. 188/C1
Kalispell, Mont. (59901) 262/B2
Kalisz (prov.), Poland 47/D3
Kalisz, Poland 7/F3
Kalisz, Poland 47/D3
Kaliua, Tanzania 115/F5
Kalix, Sweden 18/N4
Kalixälv (riv.), Sweden 18/N3
Kalkaska (co.), Mich. 250/D4
Kalkaska, Mich. (49646) 250/D4
Kalkfeld, Namibia 118/B4
Kalkfontein, Botswana 118/C4
Kallaste, U.S.S.R. 53/D1
Kallavesi (lake), Finland 18/P5
Kallsjö (lake), Sweden 18/H5
Kalmalo, Nigeria 106/F6
Kalmar (co.), Sweden 18/K8
Kalmar, Sweden 7/F3
Kalmar, Sweden 18/K8
Kalmarsund (sound), Sweden 18/K8
Kalmthout, Belgium 27/F6
Kalmuck A.S.S.R., U.S.S.R. 52/F5
Kalmuck A.S.S.R., U.S.S.R. 48/E5
Kalmunai, Sri Lanka 68/E7
Kalmykovo, U.S.S.R. 48/F5
Kalo, Iowa (†50569) 229/E4
Kalocsa, Hungary 41/E3
Kalohi (chan.), Hawaii 218/G1
Kaloko-Honokohau Nat'l Hist. Park, Hawaii 218/F6
Kaloli (pt.), Hawaii 218/K5
Kalomo, Zambia 115/E7
Kalona, Iowa (52247) 229/K6
Kalpeni (isl.), India 68/C7
Kalpin, China 77/A3
Kalskag, Alaska (99607) 196/F2
Kaltag, Alaska (99748) 196/G2
Kaltbrunn, Switzerland 39/H2
Kaluaaha, Hawaii (†96748) 218/H1
Kaluga, U.S.S.R. 7/H3
Kaluga, U.S.S.R. 48/D4
Kaluga, U.S.S.R. 52/E4
Kalumburu Mission, W. Australia 88/D2
Kalumburu Mission, W. Australia 92/D1
Kalundborg, Denmark 21/D6
Kalundborg, Denmark 18/G9
Kalush, U.S.S.R. 52/B5
Kalutara, Sri Lanka 68/D7
Kalvarija, U.S.S.R. 53/B3
Kalvesta, Kansas (67856) 232/B3
Kalyan, India 68/C5
Kama, Burma 72/B3
Kama (res.), U.S.S.R. 52/J3
Kama (riv.), U.S.S.R. 7/K3
Kama (riv.), U.S.S.R. 52/H2
Kama, Zaire 115/E4
Kamaiki (pt.), Hawaii 218/H2
Kamaing, Burma 72/C1
Kamaishi, Japan 81/L4
Kamakou (peak), Hawaii 218/H1
Kamakura, Japan 81/O3
Kamakusa, Guyana 131/A3
Kamalino, Hawaii (†96769) 218/A2
Kamalo, Hawaii (†96748) 218/H1
Kaman, Turkey 63/E3
Kamaniskeg (lake), Ontario 177/G2
Kamanjab, Namibia 118/A3
Kamaran (isl.), P.D.R. Yemen 59/D6
Kamarang, Guyana 131/A3
Kamarhati, India 68/F1
Kamaria (falls), Guyana 131/B2
Kamas, Utah (84036) 304/C3
Kamay, Texas (76369) 303/F4
Kambalda, W. Australia 88/C6
Kambalda, W. Australia 92/C5
Kambia, S. Leone 106/B7
Kambove, Zaire 115/E6
Kambove, Zaire 102/E6
Kamchatka (pen.), U.S.S.R. 54/S4
Kamchatka (pen.), U.S.S.R. 2/T3
Kamchatka (pen.), U.S.S.R. 48/Q4
Kamela, Oreg. (†97859) 291/J2
Kamenets-Podol'skiy, U.S.S.R. 52/C5
Kamenice, Czech. 41/C2
Kamenjak (cape), Yugoslavia 45/A3
Kamenka, Arkhangel, U.S.S.R. 52/F1
Kamenka, Penza, U.S.S.R. 52/F4
Kamen'-na-Obi, U.S.S.R. 48/H4
Kamenskoye, U.S.S.R. 48/R3
Kamensk-Shakhtinskiy, U.S.S.R. 52/F5
Kamensk-Ural'skiy, U.S.S.R. 48/G4
Kamenz, E. Germany 22/F3
Kameoka, Japan 81/J7
Kames, Scotland 15/C5
Kamet (mt.), India 68/D2
Kamiah, Idaho (83536) 220/B3
Kamienna Góra, Poland 47/B3

Khachmas 391

Kazan-retto (Volcano) (isls.), Japan 81/M4
Kazatin, U.S.S.R. 52/C5
Kazbek (mt.), U.S.S.R. 52/F6
Kazerun, Iran 66/G6
Kazerun, Iran 59/F4
Kazhim, U.S.S.R. 52/H2
Kazimierza Wielka, Poland 47/E3
Kazımkarabekir, Turkey 63/E4
Kazincbarcika, Hungary 41/F2
Kazlu-Rūda, U.S.S.R. 53/B3
Kazumba, Zaire 115/D5
Kazvin (Qazvin), Iran 66/F2
Kbenhaven (co.), Denmark 21/F6
Kbenhavn (Copenhagen) (commune), Denmark 21/F6
Kdyně, Czech. 41/B2
Kéa, Greece 45/G7
Kéa (isl.), Greece 45/G7
Keaau, Hawaii 188/G6
Keaau, Hawaii (96749) 218/J5
Keady, N. Ireland 17/H3
Keahi (pt.), Hawaii 218/A4
Keahole (pt.), Hawaii 218/F5
Kealaikahiki (chan.), Hawaii 218/H3
Kealaikahiki (pt.), Hawaii 218/H3
Kealakekua, Hawaii (96750) 218/G5
Kealakekua (bay), Hawaii 218/F6
Kealia, Hawaii (†96704) 218/G6
Kealia, Kauai, Hawaii (96751) 218/D1
Keams Canyon, Ariz. (86034) 198/E3
Keanae, Hawaii (†96708) 218/K2
Keanapapa (pt.), Hawaii 218/G2
Keansburg, N.J. (07734) 273/E3
Kearney, Mo. (64060) 261/D4
Kearney, Nebr. 188/G2
Kearney (co.), Nebr. 264/F4
Kearney, Nebr. (68847) 264/E4
Kearney, Ontario 177/E2
Kearneysville, W. Va. (25430) 312/L4
Kearns, Utah (84118) 304/B3
Kearny, Ariz. (85237) 198/E5
Kearny (co.), Kansas 232/A3
Kearny, N.J. (07032) 273/B2
Kearny, Wyo. (†82832) 319/F1
Kearsarge, N.H. (03847) 268/E3
Kearsarge (mt.), N.H. 268/D5
Kearsarge, Pa. (†16501) 294/B1
Keasbey, N.J. (08832) 273/E2
Keatchie, La. (71046) 238/C2
Keating, Oreg. (†97814) 291/K3
Keating Summit, Pa. (16737) 294/F2
Keatley, Sask. 181/D3
Keaton, Ky. (41226) 237/P5
Keats, Kansas (†66502) 232/F2
Keats (mt.), W. Australia 92/A2
Keauhou, Hawaii (†96725) 218/F5
Keavy, Ky. (40737) 237/N6
Keawekaheka (pt.), Hawaii 218/F5
Keban, Turkey 63/H3
Kebang (mt.), S. Korea 81/D5
Ke Bao, Vietnam 72/E2
Kebbi (riv.), Nigeria 106/E6
Kebnekaise (mt.), Sweden 7/F2
Kebnekaise (mt.), Sweden 18/L3
Kebock (head), Scotland 15/B2
Kebumen, Indonesia 85/J2
Kecel, Hungary 41/E3
Kechi, Kansas (67067) 232/E4
Kechika (riv.), Br. Col. 184/L2
Keçiborlu, Turkey 63/D4
Kecskemét, Hungary 7/F4
Kecskemét, Hungary 41/E3
Kedah (state), Malaysia 72/D6
Kedainiai, U.S.S.R. 53/C3
Keddie, Calif. (95952) 204/E3
Kedges (strs), Md. 245/O8
Kedgwick, New Bruns. 170/C1
Kedgwick (riv.), New Bruns. 170/C1
Kedgwick Ouest, New Bruns. 170/C1
Kedgwick River, New Bruns. 170/C1
Kediri, Indonesia 85/K2
Kédougou, Senegal 106/B6
Kedron (brook), Queensland 95/D2
Kedzierzyn-Koźle, Poland 47/C3
Keechelus (lake), Wash. 310/D3
Keedysville, Md. (21756) 245/H3
Keefers, Br. Col. 184/G5
Keefton, Okla. (†74401) 288/R3
Keegan, Maine (†04785) 243/G1
Keego Harbor, Mich. (48030) 250/F6
Keehi (lag.), Hawaii 218/B4
Keel-Dooagh, Ireland 17/A4
Keele (riv.), N.W. Terrs. 187/F3
Keele (peak), Yukon 187/E3
Keeler, Calif. (93530) 204/H7
Keeler, Sask. 181/F5
Keeline, Wyo. (82220) 319/H3
Keeling (Cocos) (isls.), Australia 2/P6
Keeling, Va. (24566) 307/K7
Keels, Newf. 166/D1
Keelung, China 77/K6
Keenan, W. Va. (†24983) 312/F7
Keenan Siding, New Bruns. 170/E2
Keene, Calif. (93531) 204/G8
Keene, Ky. (40339) 237/M5
Keene, N.H. (03431) 268/C6
Keene, N.Y. (12942) 276/N2
Keene, N. Dak. (58847) 282/E4
Keene, Ohio (43828) 284/G5
Keene, Ontario 177/F3
Keene, Texas (76059) 303/G5
Keener, Ala. (†35954) 195/G2
Keenes, Ill. (62851) 222/E5
Keenesburg, Colo. (80643) 208/L2
Keene Valley, N.Y. (12943) 276/N2
Keensburg, Ill. (62852) 222/F5
Keeny (creek), Oreg. 291/K4
Keeper (hill), Ireland 17/E6
Keerweer (cape), Queensland 88/G2
Keerweer (cape), Queensland 95/B2
Keeseville, N.Y. (12944) 276/O2
Keesler A.F.B., Miss. 256/G10
Keetley, Utah (†84060) 304/C3
Keetmanshoop, Namibia 118/B5
Keetmanshoop, Namibia 102/D7
Keewatin, Minn. (55753) 255/E3
Keewatin (dist.), N.W.T. 162/G3
Keewatin (dist.), N.W. Terrs. 187/J3
Keewatin, Ontario 177/F5
Keewatin, Ontario 175/A3
Keewong, N.S. Wales 97/C3
Keezletown, Va. (22832) 307/L4
Kefallinía (isl.), Greece 45/E6
Kefar Blum, Israel 65/D1
Kefar Gil'adi, Israel 65/C1
Kefar Ruppin, Israel 65/D3
Kefar Sava, Israel 65/B3
Kefar Vitkin, Israel 65/B3
Kefar Zekhariya, Israel 65/B4
Keffi, Nigeria 106/F7
Keflavík, Iceland 21/B1
Kégashka, Québec 174/E2
Kegley, W. Va. (24731) 312/D8
Kegonsa (lake), Wis. 317/H10
Keg River, Alberta 182/A5
Kehl, W. Germany 22/B4
Kehoe, Ky. (†41144) 237/P4
Kehra, U.S.S.R. 53/C1
Keila, U.S.S.R. 53/C1
Keilor, Victoria 88/K7
Keilor, Victoria 97/H5
Keimoes, S. Africa 118/C5
Keirn, Miss. (†38924) 256/D4
Keiser, Ark. (72351) 202/K2
Keiss, Scotland 15/E2
Keitele (lake), Finland 18/O5
Keith (co.), Nebr. 264/C3
Keith, Scotland 10/E2
Keith, Scotland 15/F3
Keith, S. Australia 94/G7
Keith, W. Va. (†25148) 312/C6
Keith Arm (inlet), N.W. Terrs. 187/F3
Keithley Creek, Br. Col. 184/G4
Keithsburg, Ill. (61442) 222/B2
Keithville, La. (71047) 238/C2
Keizer, Oreg. (97303) 291/A3
Kejimkujik (lake), Nova Scotia 168/C4
Kejimkujik Nat'l Park, Nova Scotia 168/C4
Kekaa (pt.), Hawaii 218/H2
Kekaha, Hawaii (96752) 218/C2
Kekaha, Hawaii 188/E5
Kekertaluk (isl.), N.W. Terrs. 187/M3
Kékes (mt.), Hungary 41/E3
Kekoskee, Wis. (†53050) 317/J8
Kelang, Malaysia 72/D7
Kelantan (state), Malaysia 72/D6
Kelantan, Sungai (riv.), Malaysia 72/D6
Kelasa (str.), Indonesia 85/D6
Keldron, S. Dak. (57634) 298/F2
Keles, Turkey 63/C3
Kelfield, Sask. 181/C4
Kelford, N.C. (27847) 281/P2
Kelheim, W. Germany 22/D4
Kelkit, Turkey 63/H2
Kelkit (riv.), Turkey 59/C1
Kelkit (riv.), Turkey 63/G2
Kell, Ill. (62853) 222/E5
Kellé, Congo 115/B4
Keller (lake), N.W. Terrs. 187/F3
Keller, Texas (76248) 303/F2
Keller, Va. (23401) 307/S5
Keller, Wash. (99140) 310/G2
Kellerberrin, W. Australia 88/B6
Kellerberrin, W. Australia 92/B5
Kellerman, Ala. (35468) 195/D4
Kellerton, Iowa (50133) 229/E7
Kellerville, Texas (79057) 303/D2
Kellett (cape), N.W.T. 162/D1
Kellett (cape), N.W. Terrs. 187/F2
Kellett (str.), N.W. Terrs. 187/G2
Kellettville, Pa. (†16353) 294/D2
Kelley, Iowa (50134) 229/F5
Kelley (creek), Nev. 266/D1
Kelleys (isl.), Ohio 284/E2
Kelleys Island, Ohio (43438) 284/E2
Kelligrews, Newf. 166/D2
Kelliher, Minn. (56650) 255/D3
Kelliher, Sask. 181/H4
Kellnersville, Wis. (54215) 317/L7
Kellogg (mt.), Ariz. 198/E6
Kellogg, Idaho (83837) 220/B2
Kellogg, Iowa (50135) 229/H5
Kellogg, Minn. (55945) 255/G6
Kelloggsville, Ohio (†44048) 284/J2
Kelloselkä, Finland 18/Q3
Kells (Ceanannus Mór), Ireland 17/G4
Kells, Ireland 17/G6
Kells, N. Ireland 17/J2
Kelly, Georgia (31048) 217/E4
Kelly (creek), Idaho 220/C3
Kelly, Kansas (66446) 232/G2
Kelly, Ky. (†42240) 237/G7
Kelly, La. (71441) 238/F3
Kelly, N.C. (28448) 281/N6
Kelly, Wyo. (83011) 319/B2
Kelly A.F.B., Texas 303/J11
Kelly Lake, Br. Col. 184/G4
Kelly Lake, Minn. (55754) 255/F3
Kellys, N. Dak. (†58201) 282/R4
Kellysville, W. Va. (24732) 312/E8
Kellyton, Ala. (35089) 195/F5
Kellyville, Okla. (74039) 288/O3
Kelme, U.S.S.R. 53/B3
Kélo, Chad 111/C6
Kélo, Chad 102/D4
Kelowna, Br. Col. 146/G4
Kelowna, Br. Col. 162/E6
Kelowna, Br. Col. 184/H5
Kelsey, Alberta 182/D3
Kelsey, Minn. (55755) 255/F3
Kelsey Bay, Br. Col. 184/D5
Kelseyville, Calif. (95451) 204/C5
Kelso, Ark. (†71674) 202/H6
Kelso, Calif. (92351) 204/K8
Kelso, Mo. (63758) 261/O8
Kelso, Sask. 181/K6
Kelso, Scotland 10/E3
Kelso, Scotland 15/F5
Kelso, Tenn. (37348) 237/J10
Kelso, Wash. (98626) 310/C4
Kelstern, Sask. 181/E5
Kelston West, N. Zealand 100/B1
Keltie (cape) 5/C7
Keltner, Ky. (†42761) 237/K6
Kelton, S.C. (†29353) 296/D2
Kelty, Scotland 10/C1
Kelty, Scotland 15/D1
Keluang, Malaysia 72/D7
Kelvington, Sask. 181/H3
Kelwood, Manitoba 179/C4
Kem', U.S.S.R. 7/H2
Kem', U.S.S.R. 4/C8
Kem', U.S.S.R. 52/D2
Kem', U.S.S.R. 48/D3
Ké-Macina, Mali 106/C6
Kemah, Texas (77565) 303/K2
Kemah, Turkey 63/H3
Kemaliye, Turkey 63/H3
Kemalpaşa, Turkey 63/J2
Kemano, Br. Col. 184/D3
Kemasik, Malaysia 72/D6
Kembe, Cent. Afr. Rep. 115/D3
Kemble, Ontario 177/D3
Kemboma, Gabon 115/B3
Kemecse, Hungary 41/F2
Kemer, Turkey 63/D4
Kemerburgaz, Turkey 63/D5
Kemerovo, U.S.S.R. 54/K4
Kemerovo, U.S.S.R. 48/J4
Kemi, Finland 7/G2
Kemi, Finland 18/O4
Kemi (riv.), Finland 7/G2
Kemijärvi, Finland 18/P3
Kemijärvi (lake), Finland 18/Q3
Kemijoki (riv.), Finland 18/O3
Kemiklı, Büyük (cape), Turkey 63/B6
Kemirhisar, Turkey 63/F4
Kemmerer, Wyo. (83101) 319/B4
Kemnay, Manitoba 179/B5
Kemnay, Scotland 15/F3
Kemp, Ill. (†61910) 222/E4
Kemp, Okla. (74747) 288/O7
Kemp, Texas (75143) 303/H5
Kemp (lake), Texas 303/E4
Kemp City (Hendrix), Okla. (†74741) 288/O7
Kemp Coast (reg.) 5/C3
Kemper (co.), Miss. 256/G5
Kemp Mill, Md. (†20901) 245/F3
Kempsey, N. S. Wales 88/J6
Kempsey, N. S. Wales 97/G2
Kempster, Wis. (54444) 317/H5
Kempston, England 13/G5
Kempt, Nova Scotia 168/C4
Kempt (lake), Québec 172/C2
Kempten, W. Germany 22/D5
Kempton, Ill. (60946) 222/E3
Kempton, Ind. (46049) 227/E4
Kempton, Md. (†26292) 245/A4
Kempton, N. Dak. (†58267) 282/P4
Kempton, Pa. (19529) 294/L4
Kempton, Tasmania 99/D4
Kempton Park, S. Africa 118/J6
Kemptown, Md. (†21770) 245/J3
Kemptown, Nova Scotia 168/E3
Kemptville, Nova Scotia 168/C4
Kemptville, Ontario 177/J2
Ken, Afghanistan 68/A2
Ken, Afghanistan 59/H3
Kenadsa, Algeria 106/D2
Kenai, Alaska (99611) 196/B1
Kenai (lake), Alaska 196/C1
Kenai (mt.), Alaska 196/C2
Kenai (pen.), Alaska 196/C2
Kenai Fjords Nat'l Park, Alaska 196/C3
Kenamu (riv.), Newf. 166/B3
Kenansville, Fla. (32739) 212/F4
Kenansville, N.C. (28349) 281/O5
Kenaston, N. Dak. (†58746) 282/F2
Kenaston, Sask. 181/E4
Kenbridge, Va. (23944) 307/M7
Kendal, Barbados 161/B8
Kendal, England 13/E3
Kendal, England 10/E3
Kendal, Indonesia 85/J2
Kendal, Sask. 181/H5
Kendall, Fla. (33156) 212/B5
Kendall (co.), Ill. 222/E2
Kendall, Kansas (67857) 232/A4
Kendall, N.S. Wales 97/G2
Kendall, N.Y. (14476) 276/E4
Kendall (cape), N.W. Terrs. 187/K3
Kendall (co.), Texas 303/F8
Kendall, Wash. (†98244) 310/C2
Kendall, Wis. (54638) 317/F8
Kendall Park, N.J. (08824) 273/D3
Kendallville, Ind. (46755) 227/G2
Kendallville, Iowa (†52136) 229/K2
Kendari, Indonesia 85/G6
Kendawangan, Indonesia 85/D6
Kendrapara, India 68/F4
Kendrick (peak), Ariz. 198/D3
Kendrick, Fla. (†32670) 212/D2
Kendrick, Idaho (83537) 220/B3
Kendrick, Okla. (74040) 288/N3
Kenduskeag◯, Maine (04450) 243/E6
Kenedy (co.), Texas 303/G11
Kenedy, Texas (78119) 303/G9
Kenefic, Okla. (74748) 288/O6
Kenel, S. Dak. (†57642) 298/H2
Kenema, S. Leone 102/A4
Kenema, S. Leone 106/B7
Kenesaw, Nebr. (68956) 264/F4
Kengah (isls.), Indonesia 85/F7
Kenge, Zaire 115/C4
Keng Hkam, Burma 72/C2
Keng Tung, Burma 72/C2
Kenhardt, S. Africa 118/C5
Kenhorst, Pa. (†19607) 294/L5
Kéniéba, Mali 106/B6
Kenilworth, England 13/F5
Kenilworth, Ill. (60043) 222/B5
Kenilworth, N.J. (07033) 273/E2
Kenilworth, Ontario 177/D4
Kenilworth, Utah (84529) 304/D4
Keningau, Malaysia 85/F4
Kenitra, Morocco 102/B1
Kenitra, Morocco 106/C2
Kenli, China 77/J4
Kenly, N.C. (27542) 281/N3
Kenmare, Ireland 10/B5
Kenmare, Ireland 17/B8
Kenmare (riv.), Ireland 17/A8
Kenmare, N. Dak. (58746) 282/G2
Kenmore, N.Y. (14217) 276/C5
Kenmore, Queensland 88/J3
Kenmore, Scotland 15/E4
Kenmore, Wash. (98028) 310/B1
Kenna, N. Mex. (88122) 274/F5
Kenna, W. Va. (25248) 312/C5
Kennah, Wis. (54537) 317/F5
Kennard, Ind. (47351) 227/G5
Kennard, Nebr. (68034) 264/H3
Kennard, Pa. (†16125) 294/B3
Kennard, Texas (75847) 303/J6
Kennebago Lake, Maine (†04970) 243/B5
Kennebec (co.), Maine 243/D7
Kennebec (riv.), Maine 243/D7
Kennebec, S. Dak. (57544) 298/K6
Kennebecasis (bay), New Bruns. 170/E3
Kennebecasis (riv.), New Bruns. 170/E3
Kennebunk, Maine (04043) 243/B9
Kennebunk◯, Maine (04043) 243/B9
Kennebunk Beach, Maine (†04043) 243/C9
Kennebunkport, Maine (04046) 243/C9
Kennebunkport◯, Maine (04046) 243/C9
Kennedale, Texas (76060) 303/F3
Kennedy, Ala. (35574) 195/B3
Kennedy (Canaveral) (cape), Fla. 212/F3
Kennedy, Minn. (56733) 255/B2
Kennedy, N.Y. (14747) 276/B6
Kennedy (chan.), N.W.T. 162/N3
Kennedy (chan.), N.W. Terrs. 187/M1
Kennedy, Sask. 181/J5
Kennedy Center, D.C. 245/A5
Kennedy Entrance (str.), Alaska 196/H3
Kennedyville, Md. (21645) 245/P3
Kenner, La. (70062) 238/N4
Kennesaw, Georgia (30144) 217/C2
Kennesaw Mtn. Nat'l Battlefield Park, Georgia 217/J1
Kennet (riv.), England 13/F6
Kennetcook, Nova Scotia 168/E3
Kennetcook (riv.), Nova Scotia 168/E3
Kenneth, Ind. (†46947) 227/E3
Kenneth, Minn. (56147) 255/B7
Kenneth City, Fla. (33709) 212/B3
Kennett, Mo. (63857) 261/M10
Kennett Square, Pa. (19348) 294/L6
Kennewick, Wash. (99336) 310/F4
Kenney (dam), Br. Col. 184/E3
Kenney, Ill. (61749) 222/D3
Kennisis (lake), Ontario 177/F2
Keno, Oreg. (97627) 291/F5
Kenogami (riv.), Ont. 162/H6
Kenogami (riv.), Ontario 177/H4
Kenogami (riv.), Ontario 175/C2
Kénogami (lake), Québec 172/F1
Keno Hill, Yukon 187/E3
Kenoma, Mo. (†64759) 261/D8
Kenora (terr. dist.), Ont. 177/G5
Kenora (terr. dist.), Ont. 175/C2
Kenora, Ont. 146/J4
Kenora, Ont. 162/G5
Kenora, Ontario 175/B3
Kenora, Ontario 177/F4
Kenosee Park, Sask. 181/J6
Kenosha (co.), Wis. 317/K10
Kenosha, Wis. (*53140) 317/M3
Kenova, W. Va. (25530) 312/A6
Kensal, N. Dak. (58455) 282/N5
Kenscoff, Haiti 158/C6
Kensett, Ark. (72082) 202/G3
Kensett, Iowa (50448) 229/G2
Kensington, Calif. (†94701) 204/J2
Kensington, Conn. (06037) 210/D2
Kensington, Kansas (66951) 232/C2
Kensington, Md. (20795) 245/E4
Kensington, Minn. (56343) 255/C5
Kensington, N.S. Wales 97/J4
Kensington, Ohio (44427) 284/J4
Kensington, Pr. Edward I. 168/E2
Kensington and Chelsea, England 13/G8
Kensington and Chelsea, England 10/B5
Kensington and Norwood, S. Australia 88/E8
Kensington and Norwood, S. Australia 94/B8
Kent, Ala. (36045) 195/G5
Kent, Br. Col. 184/M3
Kent◯, Conn. (06757) 210/B2
Kent (co.), Del. 245/R4
Kent (co.), England 13/H6
Kent, Ill. (61044) 222/D1
Kent, Ind. (†47250) 227/F7
Kent, Iowa (50850) 229/E7
Kent (co.), Md. 245/O3
Kent (isl.), Md. 245/N5
Kent (pt.), Md. 245/N5
Kent (co.), Mich. 250/D5
Kent, Minn. (56553) 255/B4
Kent (co.), New Bruns. 170/E2
Kent (pen.), N.W. Terrs. 187/H3
Kent, Ohio (44240) 284/H3
Kent (county), Ontario 177/B5
Kent, Oreg. (97033) 291/G2
Kent, Pa. (15752) 294/D4
Kent (co.), R.I. 249/H6
Kent (co.), Texas 303/D4
Kent, Texas (79855) 303/C11
Kent, Wash. (98031) 310/C3
Kentau, U.S.S.R. 48/G5
Kent Bridge, Ontario 177/B5
Kent City, Mich. (49330) 250/D5
Kent Furnace, Conn. (†06757) 210/B2
Kent Group (isls.), Tasmania 99/D1
Kent Junction, New Bruns. 170/E2
Kent Lake, New Bruns. 170/E2
Kentland, Ind. (47951) 227/C3
Kenton, Del. (19955) 245/R4
Kenton (co.), Ky. 237/M3
Kenton, Ky. (41053) 237/N3
Kenton, Manitoba 179/B5
Kenton, Mich. (49943) 250/G2
Kenton, Ohio (43326) 284/C4
Kenton, Okla. (73946) 288/A1
Kenton, Tenn. (38233) 237/C8
Kenton Vale, Ky. (†41011) 237/S2
Kents Hill, Maine (04349) 243/D7
Kents Store, Va. (23084) 307/M5
Kentuck, W. Va. (25249) 312/C5
Kentucky 188/J3
Kentucky (lake) 188/J3
KENTUCKY 237
Kentucky (dam), Ky. 237/E7
Kentucky (lake), Ky. 237/E8
Kentucky (riv.), Ky. 237/M3
Kentucky (lake), Tenn. 237/E8
Kentucky (state), U.S. 146/K6
Kentville, Nova Scotia 168/D3
Kentwood, La. (70444) 238/J5
Kentwood, Mich. (49508) 250/D6
Kenville, Manitoba 179/A3
Kenvir, Ky. (40847) 237/P7
Kenwood, Georgia (†30214) 217/D3
Kenwood, Okla. (†74365) 288/S2
Kenya 2/L5
Kenya 102/F4
KENYA 115/G3
Kenya (mt.), Kenya 102/F4
Kenya (mt.), Kenya 115/G4
Kenyon, Minn. (55946) 255/E6
Kenyon, R.I. (02836) 249/H7
Kenyonville, Conn. (†06281) 210/G1
Keo, Ark. (72083) 202/G4
Keokea, Hawaii, Hawaii (†96704) 218/G6
Keokea, Maui, Hawaii (†96790) 218/J2
Keokee, Va. (24265) 307/C7
Keokuk (co.), Iowa 229/J6
Keokuk, Iowa 188/H2
Keokuk, Iowa (52632) 229/L8
Keoma, Alberta 182/D4
Keomah, Iowa (†52577) 229/J6
Keomuku, Hawaii (†96763) 218/H2
Keonjhar, India 68/F4
Keosauqua, Iowa (52565) 229/J7
Keota, Colo. (†80729) 208/L1
Keota, Iowa (52248) 229/K6
Keota, Okla. (74941) 288/S4
Keowee (lake), S.C. 296/B2
Keowee (riv.), S.C. 296/B2
Kepez, Turkey 63/B6
Kepi, Indonesia 85/K7
Kępno, Poland 47/C3
Keppel (harb.), Singapore 72/F6
Kepsut, Turkey 63/C3
Kerala (state), India 68/D6
Kerama (isls.), Japan 81/M6
Kerang, Victoria 97/B4
Kerava, Finland 18/O6
Kerby, Oreg. (97531) 291/D5
Kerch', U.S.S.R. 7/H4
Kerch', U.S.S.R. 52/E5
Kerchoual, Mali 106/E5
Kerema, Papua N.G. 85/B7
Keremeos, Br. Col. 184/G5
Kerempe (cape), Turkey 63/E1
Keren, Ethiopia 59/C6
Keren, Ethiopia 111/G4
Kerens, Texas (75144) 303/H5
Kerens, W. Va. (26276) 312/G4
Keret', U.S.S.R. 52/D1
Kerguélen (isl.), 2/N8
Kerhonkson, N.Y. (12446) 276/M7
Kericho, Kenya 115/F4
Kerinci (mt.), Indonesia 85/C6
Keriya (Yutian), China 77/B4
Keriya He (riv.), China 77/B4
Keriya Shankou (pass), China 77/B4
Kerkdriel, Netherlands 27/G5
Kerkennah (isls.), Tunisia 106/G2
Kerkhoven, Minn. (56252) 255/C5
Kerki, U.S.S.R. 48/G6
Kérkira, Greece 45/D6
Kérkira (isl.), Greece 7/F5
Kérkira (isl.), Greece 45/D6
Kerkrade, Netherlands 27/J7
Kerlin, Ark. (†71753) 202/D7
Kerma, Sudan 111/F4
Kerma, Sudan 59/B6
Kermadec (isls.), N. Zealand 2/T7
Kermadec (isls.), N. Zealand 87/J9
Kerman, Calif. (93600) 204/E7
Kerman (prov.), Iran 66/K6
Kerman, Iran 54/G6
Kerman, Iran 59/G3
Kerman, Iran 66/K5
Kermanshah, Iran 54/F6
Kermanshah, Iran 59/E3
Kermanshah, Iran 66/E3
Kermanshahan (prov.), Iran 66/E3
Kerme (gulf), Turkey 63/B4
Kermit, Texas (79745) 303/B6
Kermit, W. Va. (25674) 312/B7
Kern (co.), Calif. 204/G8
Kern (riv.), Calif. 204/G8
Kernan, Ill. (†61364) 222/E2
Kernersville, N.C. (27284) 281/J2
Kerns, Switzerland 39/F3
Kernville, Calif. (93238) 204/G8
Kernville, Oreg. (†97367) 291/D3
Kérouané, Guinea 106/C7
Kerr (lake), Fla. 212/E2
Kerr, N.C. (†28444) 281/N5
Kerr, W. Scott (res.), N.C. 281/G2
Kerr, Robert S. (res.), Okla. 288/S4
Kerr (co.), Texas 303/E7
Kerrera (isl.), Scotland 15/C4
Kerrick, Minn. (55756) 255/F4
Kerrick, Texas (79051) 303/B1
Kerrobert, Sask. 181/C4
Kerrville, Tenn. (†38053) 237/B10
Kerrville, Texas (78028) 303/E7
Kerry (co.), Ireland 17/B7
Kerry (head), Ireland 17/A7
Kerry, Wales 13/D5
Kersey, Colo. (80644) 208/L2
Kersey, Ind. (†46310) 227/C2
Kersey, Pa. (15846) 294/E3
Kershaw (co.), S.C. 296/F3
Kershaw, S.C. (29067) 296/G2
Kersley, Br. Col. 184/F4
Kerteminde, Denmark 21/D7
Kerulen (riv.) 54/N5
Kerulen (riv.), Mongolia 77/H2
Kerwood, Ontario 177/C5
Kerzaz, Algeria 106/D3
Kerzers, Switzerland 39/D3
Kesagami (lake), Ontario 175/E2
Keşan, Turkey 63/B2
Keşap, Turkey 63/H2
Kesch (peak), Switzerland 39/J3
Kesennuma, Japan 81/K4
Kesgrave, England 13/J5
Kesh, N. Ireland 17/F3
Keshena, Wis. (54135) 317/J6
Keşiş Tepesi (mt.), Turkey 63/H3
Keskin, Turkey 63/E3
Keski-Suomi (prov.), Finland 18/O5
Kesley, Iowa (50649) 229/H3
Kessel, W. Va. (†26818) 312/H4
Kesten'ga, U.S.S.R. 52/D1
Kesteren, Netherlands 27/G5
Keswick, England 13/D3
Keswick, England 10/E3
Keswick, Iowa (50136) 229/J6
Keswick, New Bruns. 170/D3
Keswick (riv.), New Bruns. 170/C2
Keswick, Ontario 177/E3
Keswick, Va. (22947) 307/M4
Keswick Grove, N.J. (†08759) 273/E4
Keszthely, Hungary 41/D3
Keta, Ghana 106/E7
Ketapang, Indonesia 85/E6
Ketchen, Sask. 181/J3
Ketch Harbour, Nova Scotia 168/E4
Ketchikan, Alaska 146/E4
Ketchikan, Alaska 188/E6
Ketchikan, Alaska (99901) 196/N2
Ketchum, Idaho (83340) 220/D6
Ketchum, Okla. (74349) 288/R1
Kétegyháza, Hungary 41/F3
Kete Krachi, Ghana 106/E7
Kętrzyn, Poland 47/E1
Kettering, England 13/G5
Kettering, England 10/F4
Kettering, Ohio (45429) 284/B6
Kettering, Tasmania 99/D5
Kettle (riv.), Br. Col. 184/H5
Kettle (riv.), Minn. 255/F4
Kettle (pt.), Ontario 177/B4
Kettle (riv.), Wash. 310/G2
Kettle Falls, Wash. (99141) 310/H2
Kettleman City, Calif. (93239) 204/E7
Kettle River, Minn. (55757) 255/E4
Kettle River (range), Wash. 310/G2
Kettlersville, Ohio (45336) 284/B5
Kettle Valley, Br. Col. 184/H5
Keuka (lake), N.Y. 276/F5
Keuka Park, N.Y. (14478) 276/F5
Keuterville, Idaho (83538) 220/B3
Kevelaer, W. Germany 22/B3
Kevil, Ky. (42053) 237/D6
Kevin, Mont. (59454) 262/D2
Kevisville, Alberta 182/C4
Kew, Victoria 88/L7
Kew, Victoria 97/J5
Kewa, Wash. (†99138) 310/G2
Kewanee, Ill. (61443) 222/C2
Kewanee, Miss. (†39364) 256/H6
Kewanee, Mo. (63860) 261/N9
Kewanna, Ind. (46939) 227/E2
Kewaskum, Wis. (53040) 317/K8
Kewaunee (co.), Wis. 317/L6
Kewaunee, Wis. (54216) 317/M7
Keweenaw (co.), Mich. 250/A1
Keweenaw (bay), Mich. 250/A1
Keweenaw (pt.), Mich. 250/B1
Keweenaw Bay, Mich. (49944) 250/G1
Key, Ala. (†35960) 195/G2
Key (lake), Ireland 17/E3
Keya Paha (co.), Nebr. 264/E2
Keya Paha (riv.), Nebr. 264/D1
Keyapaha, S. Dak. (57545) 298/J7
Keya Paha (riv.), S. Dak. 298/K7
Key Biscayne, Fla. (33149) 212/B5
Key Colony Beach, Fla. (33051) 212/F7
Keyes, Calif. (95328) 204/E6
Keyes, Manitoba 179/C4
Keyes, Okla. (73947) 288/B1
Keyesport, Ill. (62253) 222/D5
Keyhole (res.), Wyo. 319/H1
Key Largo, Fla. (33037) 212/F6
Key Largo (key), Fla. 212/F6
Keymar, Md. (21757) 245/K2
Keynsham, England 13/E6
Keyport, N.J. (07735) 273/E3
Keyport, Wash. (98345) 310/A2
Keysbrook, W. Australia 88/B3
Keyser, W. Va. (26726) 312/J4
Keystone, Ind. (46759) 227/G3
Keystone, Iowa (52249) 229/J5
Keystone, Nebr. (69144) 264/C3
Keystone (res.), Ohio 284/K2
Keystone (lake), Okla. 288/O2
Keystone, S. Dak. (57751) 298/C6
Keystone, W. Va. (24852) 312/D8
Keystone Heights, Fla. (32656) 212/E2
Keystown, Sask. 181/F5
Keysville, Georgia (30816) 217/H4
Keysville, Va. (23947) 307/M6
Keytesville, Mo. (65261) 261/G4
Key Vaca (key), Fla. 212/E7
Key West, Fla. 146/K7
Key West, Fla. 188/K6
Key West, Fla. (33040) 212/E7
Key West Naval Air Sta., Fla. 212/E7
Kezar (lake), Maine 243/B7
Kezar (pond), Maine 243/B7
Kezar Falls, Maine (04047) 243/B8
Kežmarok, Czech. 41/F2
Khabake (Habahe), China 77/C2
Khabarovsk, U.S.S.R. 54/P5
Khabarovsk, U.S.S.R. 2/R3
Khabarovsk, U.S.S.R. 48/O5
Khabur (riv.), Syria 63/J5
Khabur (riv.), Syria 59/D2
Khachmas, U.S.S.R. 52/G6

392 Khadyzhensk

Khadyzhensk, U.S.S.R. 52/E6
Khaf, Iran 66/L3
Khaibar, 'Asir, Saudi Arabia 59/D5
Khaibar, Hejaz, Saudi Arabia 59/C4
Khairpur, Pakistan 68/B3
Khairpur, Pakistan 59/J4
Khakass Aut. Obl., U.S.S.R. 48/J4
Khálki (isl.), Greece 45/H7
Khalkís, Greece 45/F6
Khal'mer-Yu, U.S.S.R. 52/K1
Khaluf, Oman 59/G5
Khamgaon, India 68/D4
Khamis Mushait, Saudi Arabia 59/D6
Khamkeut, Laos 72/E3
Khamman, India 68/D5
Khanabad, Afghanistan 59/J2
Khanabad, Afghanistan 68/B1
Khanaqin, Iraq 59/D3
Khanaqin, Iraq 66/D3
Khancoban, N.S. Wales 97/E5
Khandwa, India 68/D4
Khandyga, U.S.S.R. 48/O3
Khan esh Shamat, Syria 63/G6
Khanewal, Pakistan 68/C2
Khanh Hoa, Vietnam 72/F4
Khanh Hung, Vietnam 72/E5
Khaniá, Greece 45/G8
Khaniá, Greece 7/G5
Khaniá (gulf), Greece 45/G8
Khanka (lake) 54/P5
Khanka (lake), China 77/M3
Khanka (lake), U.S.S.R. 48/O5
Khanpur, Pakistan 68/C3
Khanpur, Pakistan 59/K4
Khan Sheikhun, Syria 63/G5
Khanty-Mansi Aut. Okr., U.S.S.R. 48/H3
Khanty-Mansiysk, U.S.S.R. 54/J3
Khanty-Mansiysk, U.S.S.R. 48/H3
Khanu, Thailand 72/C3
Khan Yunis, Gaza Strip 65/A5
Khao Luang (mt.), Burma 72/C5
Khao Luang (mt.), Thailand 72/C5
Khapcheranga, U.S.S.R. 48/M5
Kharagpur, India 68/F4
Kharan, Pakistan 59/J4
Kharan Kalat, Pakistan 68/A3
Kharas, West Bank 65/C4
Kharasavey (cape), U.S.S.R. 48/G2
Khardah, India 68/F1
Khârga (oasis), Egypt 111/F2
Khârga (oasis), Egypt 59/B4
Khark (Kharg) (isl.), Iran 66/G6
Khar'kov, U.S.S.R. 7/H4
Khar'kov, U.S.S.R. 2/L3
Khar'kov, U.S.S.R. 52/E5
Khar'kov, U.S.S.R. 48/D4
Kharmanli, Bulgaria 45/H5
Kharovsk, U.S.S.R. 48/D3
Kharovsk, U.S.S.R. 52/F3
Khartoum (prov.), Sudan 111/F4
Khartoum (cap.), Sudan 2/L5
Khartoum (cap.), Sudan 59/B6
Khartoum (cap.), Sudan 111/F4
Khartoum (cap.), Sudan 102/F3
Khartoum North, Sudan 102/F3
Khartoum North, Sudan 59/B6
Khartoum North, Sudan 111/F4
Khasab, Oman 59/G4
Khasavyurt, U.S.S.R. 52/G6
Khash, Afghanistan 68/A2
Khash, Afghanistan 59/H3
Khash, Iran 59/H4
Khash, Iran 66/M6
Khashm el Girba, Sudan 111/G5
Khashuri, U.S.S.R. 52/F6
Khasi (hills), India 68/G3
Khaskovo, Bulgaria 45/G5
Khatanga, U.S.S.R. 4/B4
Khatanga, U.S.S.R. 54/M2
Khatanga, U.S.S.R. 48/L2
Khatuniye, Syria 63/J4
Khay, Saudi Arabia 59/D6
Khedive, Sask. 181/G6
Khemis Miliana, Algeria 106/E1
Khemmarat, Thailand 72/E4
Khenifra, Morocco 106/C2
Kherson, U.S.S.R. 7/H4
Kherson, U.S.S.R. 48/D5
Kherson, U.S.S.R. 52/D5
Khe Sanh, Vietnam 72/E3
Kheta (riv.), U.S.S.R. 48/K2
Khilok, U.S.S.R. 48/M4
Khíos, Greece 45/G6
Khíos (isl.), Greece 45/G6
Khirbet Qumran (site), Jordan 65/D4
Khiva, 48/F5
Khiyav, Iran 66/E1
Khmel'nitskiy, U.S.S.R. 7/G4
Khmel'nitskiy, U.S.S.R. 52/C5
Khoai, Hon (isl.), Vietnam 72/E5
Khodzheyli, U.S.S.R. 48/F5
Kholm, Afghanistan 68/B1
Kholm, Afghanistan 59/J2
Kholm, U.S.S.R. 52/D3
Kholmsk, U.S.S.R. 48/P5
Khoman, Iran 66/F2
Khon Kaen, Thailand 72/D3
Khoper (riv.), U.S.S.R. 52/F4
Khorasan (prov.), Iran 66/K3
Khora Sfakion, Greece 45/G8
Khorat (Nakhon Ratchasima), Thailand 72/D4
Khoreyver, U.S.S.R. 52/J1
Khorixas, Namibia 118/A4
Khorog, U.S.S.R. 48/H6
Khorol, U.S.S.R. 52/D5
Khorramabad, Iran 59/E3
Khorramabad, Iran 66/F4
Khorramshahr, Iran 59/E3
Khorramshahr, Iran 66/F5
Khotan (Hotan), China 77/B4
Khotin, U.S.S.R. 52/C5
Khouribga, Morocco 106/C2
Khowst, Afghanistan 68/B2
Khromtau, U.S.S.R. 48/F4
Khuaf, Iran 59/H3
Khugiani, Afghanistan 68/B2
Khugiani, Afghanistan 59/J3
Khuis, Botswana 118/C5
Khu Khan, Thailand 72/E4
Khulna, Bangladesh 68/F4
Khurda, India 68/F4
Khurma, Saudi Arabia 59/D5
Khusf Rud (riv.), Iran 66/L4
Khushab, Pakistan 68/C2
Khust, U.S.S.R. 52/B5
Khuzdar, Pakistan 59/J4
Khuzestan (prov.), Iran 66/F5
Khvaf, Iran 66/L3
Khvalynsk, U.S.S.R. 52/G4
Khvojeh Lak, Kuh-e (mt.), Iran 66/E3
Khvonsar, Iran 66/F4
Khvor, Iran 59/G3
Khvor, Iran 66/J4
Khvoy, Iran 59/E2
Khvoy (Khoi), Iran 66/D1
Khwae Noi, Mae Nam (riv.), Thailand 72/C4
Khyber (pass) 54/J6
Khyber (pass), Pakistan 59/K3
Khyber (pass), Pakistan 68/C2
Kia, Solomon Is. 86/D2
Kiahsville, W. Va. (25534) 312/B6
Kiama, N.S. Wales 97/F4
Kiamba, Philippines 82/E8
Kiambi, Zaire 115/E5
Kiambu, Kenya 115/G4
Kiamichi, Okla. (†74574) 288/R5
Kiamichi (mts.), Okla. 288/R5
Kiamichi (riv.), Okla. 288/R6
Kiamika, Québec 172/B3
Kiamika (lake), Québec 172/B3
Kiamika (riv.), Québec 172/B3
Kiamusze (Jiamusi), China 77/M2
Kian (Ji'an), China 77/J6
Kiana, Alaska (99749) 196/F1
Kiangsi (Jiangxi) (prov.), China 77/J6
Kiangsu (Jiangsu) (prov.), China 77/K5
Kiantajärvi (lake), Finland 18/Q4
Kiáton, Greece 45/F6
Kiawah (isl.), S.C. 296/G6
Kibaek, Denmark 21/B5
Kibangou, Congo 115/B4
Kibara, Tanzania 115/F4
Kibaya, Tanzania 115/G5
Kibbee, Georgia (†30474) 217/H6
Kibler, Ark. (†72956) 202/B3
Kibombo, Zaire 115/E4
Kibondo, Tanzania 115/F4
Kibre Mengist, Ethiopia 111/G6
Kibwezi, Kenya 115/G4
Kičevo, Yugoslavia 45/E5
Kickapoo (riv.), Wis. 317/E9
Kickapoo Ind. Res., Kansas 232/G2
Kickinghorse (pass), Alberta 182/B4
Kicking Horse (pass), Br. Col. 184/J4
Kidal, Mali 102/C3
Kidal, Mali 106/E5
Kidapawan, Philippines 82/E7
Kidder, Mo. (64649) 261/D3
Kidder (co.), N. Dak. 282/L6
Kidder, S. Dak. (†57430) 298/O2
Kidderminster, England 10/G3
Kidderminster, England 13/E5
Kidepo Nat'l Park, Uganda 115/F3
Kidnappers (cape), N. Zealand 100/F3
Kidron, Ohio (44636) 284/G4
Kidsgrove, England 13/E4
Kidwelly, Wales 13/C6
Kidwelly, Wales 10/D5
Kief, N. Dak. (58747) 282/J4
Kiefer, Okla. (74041) 288/O3
Kieffer, W. Va. (24950) 312/E7
Kiel, W. Germany 7/E3
Kiel, W. Germany 22/D1
Kiel (bay), W. Germany 22/D1
Kiel (Nord-Ostsee) (canal), W. Germany 22/C1
Kiel, Wis. (53042) 317/L8
Kielce (prov.), Poland 47/E3
Kielce, Poland 47/E3
Kielce, Poland 7/G3
Kieler, Wis. (53812) 317/E10
Kien Hung, Vietnam 72/E5
Kienyang (Qianyang), China 77/H6
Kiester, Minn. (56051) 255/E7
Kieta, Papua N.G. 86/C2
Kieta, Papua N.G. 87/F6
Kiev, U.S.S.R. 2/L3
Kiev, U.S.S.R. 7/H3
Kiev, U.S.S.R. 48/D4
Kiev, U.S.S.R. 52/D4
Kiev (res.), U.S.S.R. 52/C4
Kiffa, Mauritania 106/B5
Kifri, Iraq 66/D3
Kigali (cap.), Rwanda 115/F4
Kigali (cap.), Rwanda 102/F5
Kiger (creek), Oreg. 291/J5
Kiği, Turkey 63/J3
Kiglapait (cape), Newf. 166/B2
Kiglapait (mts.), Newf. 166/B2
Kigoma (reg.), Tanzania 115/F4
Kigoma-Ujiji, Tanzania 115/E4
Kigoma-Ujiji, Tanzania 102/F5
Kihei, Hawaii (96753) 218/J2
Kihnu (isl.), U.S.S.R. 53/B1
Kiholo, Hawaii (†96740) 218/G4
Kiholo (bay), Hawaii 218/F4
Kii (chan.), Japan 81/G7
Kiiminki, Finland 18/P4
Kikai (isl.), Japan 81/O5
Kikiktaksoak (isl.), Newf. 166/B2
Kikinda, Yugoslavia 45/E3
Kikino, Alberta 182/D2
Kikkertavak (isl.), Newf. 166/B2
Kikoira, N.S. Wales 97/D3
Kikonai, Japan 81/K3
Kikori, Papua N.G. 85/B7
Kikwit, Zaire 115/C5
Kikwit, Zaire 102/D5
Kila, Mont. (59920) 262/B2
Kilafors, Sweden 18/K6
Kilauea, Hawaii 188/E5
Kilauea, Hawaii (96754) 218/C1
Kilauea (crater), Hawaii 218/H6
Kilauea (pt.), Hawaii 218/C1
Kilbaha, Ireland 17/B6
Kilbarchan, Scotland 15/A2
Kilbeggan, Ireland 17/G5
Kilbirnie, Scotland 15/A2
Kilbourne, Ill. (62655) 222/D3
Kilbourne, La. (71253) 238/H1
Kilbrannan (sound), Scotland 15/C5
Kilbride, Newf. 166/D2
Kilbuck (mts.), Alaska 196/G2
Kilburn, New Bruns. 170/C2
Kilcar, Ireland 17/D2
Kilchoan, Scotland 15/B4
Kilchu, N. Korea 81/D3
Kilcock, Ireland 17/H5
Kilconnell, Ireland 17/E5
Kilcoole, Ireland 17/K5
Kilcormac, Ireland 17/F5
Kilcoy, Queensland 95/E5
Kilcullen, Ireland 17/H5
Kildare, Georgia (†30449) 217/K5
Kildare (co.), Ireland 17/H5
Kildare, Ireland 10/C4
Kildare, Ireland 17/H5
Kildare, Okla. (74601) 288/M1
Kildare (cape), Pr. Edward I. 168/E2
Kildare, Texas (75562) 303/K5
Kildeer, Ill. (†60069) 222/A5
Kil'din (isl.), U.S.S.R. 52/D1
Kildonan, Br. Col. 184/E5
Kildonan, Scotland 15/E2
Kildonan, Zimbabwe 118/E3
Kildurk, North. Terr. 93/A4
Kildysart, Ireland 17/C6
Kilembe, Uganda 115/F3
Kilembe, Zaire 115/C5
Kilfenora, Ireland 17/C6
Kilfinane, Ireland 17/D7
Kilgarvan, Ireland 17/B8
Kilgore, Idaho (†83423) 220/G5
Kilgore, Nebr. (69216) 264/D2
Kilgore, Ohio (†44615) 284/H5
Kilgore, Texas (75662) 303/K5
Kili (isl.), Marshall Is. 87/G5
Kilifi, Kenya 115/G4
Kilimanjaro (reg.), Tanzania 115/G4
Kilimanjaro (mt.), Tanzania 102/G5
Kilimanjaro (mt.), Tanzania 115/G4
Kilimli, Turkey 63/D2
Kilinailau (isls.), Papua N.G. 86/C2
Kilingi-Nõmme, U.S.S.R. 53/C1
Kilis, Turkey 63/G4
Kilitbahir, Turkey 63/B6
Kiliya, U.S.S.R. 52/C5
Kilkee, Ireland 10/B4
Kilkee, Ireland 17/B6
Kilkeel, N. Ireland 17/K3
Kilkelly, Ireland 17/D4
Kilkenny (co.), Ireland 17/G6
Kilkenny, Ireland 10/C4
Kilkenny, Ireland 17/G6
Kilkenny, Minn. (56052) 255/E6
Kilkieran (bay), Ireland 17/B5
Kilkis, Greece 45/F5
Killala, Ireland 17/C3
Killala (bay), Ireland 17/C3
Killaloe, Ireland 10/B4
Killaloe, Ireland 17/D6
Killaloe Station, Ontario 177/G2
Killaly, Sask. 181/J5
Killam, Alberta 182/E3
Killam, New Bruns. 170/E2
Killarney, Ireland 10/B4
Killarney, Ireland 17/C7
Killarney (lakes), Ireland 10/B4
Killarney, Man. 162/G6
Killarney, Manitoba 179/C5
Killarney, North. Terr. 93/B4
Killarney, Ontario 177/C2
Killarney Prov. Park, Ontario 177/C1
Killary (harb.), Ireland 17/A4
Killavullen, Ireland 17/D7
Killbear Point Prov. Park, Ontario 177/D2
Kill Buck, N.Y. (14748) 276/C6
Killbuck, Ohio (44637) 284/G5
Killbuck (creek), Ohio 284/G4
Killdeer, N. Dak. (58640) 282/E5
Killdeer, Sask. 181/E6
Kill Devil Hills, N.C. (27948) 281/T3
Killduff, Iowa (50137) 229/H5
Killearn, Scotland 15/B1
Killeen, Texas (76541) 303/G6
Killen, Ala. (35645) 195/D1
Killenaule, Ireland 17/F6
Killeshandra, Ireland 17/F3
Killian, La. (†70462) 238/M2
Killimor, Ireland 17/E5
Killin, Scotland 15/D4
Killinaboy, Ireland 17/C6
Killingly○, Conn. (†06241) 210/H1
Killington, Vt. (05751) 268/B4
Killington (peak), Vt. 268/B4
Killingworth○, Conn. (†06413) 210/E3
Killona, La. (70066) 238/M3
Killorglin, Ireland 17/B7
Killough, N. Ireland 17/K3
Killucan-Rathwire, Ireland 17/G4
Kill Van Kull (str.), N.J. 273/B2
Killybegs, Ireland 17/E2
Killyclogher, N. Ireland 17/G2
Killyleagh, N. Ireland 17/K3
Kilmacolm, Scotland 15/A2
Kilmacrennan, Ireland 17/F1
Kilmacthomas, Ireland 17/G7
Kilmallock, Ireland 17/D7
Kilmarnock, Scotland 15/D5
Kilmarnock, Scotland 10/D3
Kilmarnock, Va. (22482) 307/R5
Kilmaurs, Scotland 15/D5
Kilmeadan, Ireland 17/G7
Kilmichael, Miss. (39747) 256/E4
Kilmihill, Ireland 17/C6
Kilmoganny, Ireland 17/G7
Kilmore, Victoria 97/C5
Kilmore Quay, Ireland 17/H7
Kilmurry, Ireland 17/C6
Kiln, Miss. (39556) 256/F10
Kilnaleck, Ireland 17/G4
Kilninver, Scotland 15/C4
Kilo, Zaire 115/E3
Kilombero (riv.), Tanzania 115/G5
Kilosa, Tanzania 115/G5
Kilpisjärvi (lake), Finland 18/M2
Kilpisjärvi (lake), Sweden 18/M2
Kilrea, N. Ireland 17/H2
Kilrenny and Anstruther, Scotland 15/F4
Kilrenny and Anstruther, Scotland 10/E2
Kilronan, Ireland 17/B5
Kilrush, Ireland 10/B4
Kilrush, Ireland 17/C6
Kilsheelan, Ireland 17/F7
Kilsyth, Scotland 15/B1
Kilsyth, Scotland 10/B1
Kilsyth, W. Va. (25859) 312/D7
Kiltan (isl.), India 68/C6
Kiltimagh, Ireland 17/C4
Kilwa, Zaire 115/E5
Kilwa Kivinje, Tanzania 115/G5
Kilwa Masoko, Tanzania 115/G5
Kilwinning, Sask. 181/E2
Kilwinning, Scotland 15/D5
Kilworth, Ireland 17/E7
Kilyos, Turkey 63/D5
Kim, Colo. (81049) 208/N8
Kimba, S. Australia 88/F6
Kimba, S. Australia 94/E5
Kimball (mt.), Alaska 196/K2
Kimball, Alberta 182/D5
Kimball, Kansas (†66733) 232/G4
Kimball, Minn. (55353) 255/D5
Kimball (co.), Nebr. 264/A3
Kimball, Nebr. (69145) 264/A3
Kimball, S. Dak. (57355) 298/M6
Kimball, Tenn. (†37347) 237/K10
Kimball, W. Va. (24853) 312/C8
Kimballton, Iowa (51543) 229/D5
Kimballton, Va. (†24150) 307/G6
Kimbe, Papua N.G. 86/B2
Kimbe, Papua N.G. 87/F6
Kimberley, Br. Col. 184/K5
Kimberley, S. Africa 102/E7
Kimberley, S. Africa 118/C5
Kimberley (plat.), W. Australia 88/D3
Kimberley (plat.), W. Australia 92/D2
Kimberley Research Station, W. Australia 88/D3
Kimberling City, Mo. (65686) 261/F9
Kimberlin Heights, Tenn. (37920) 237/O9
Kimberly, Ala. (35091) 195/E3
Kimberly, Idaho (83341) 220/D7
Kimberly, Minn. (†56431) 255/E4
Kimberly, Oreg. (97848) 291/H3
Kimberly, Wis. (54136) 317/K7
Kimble (co.), Texas 303/E7
Kimbolton, Ohio (43749) 284/G5
Kimbrough, Ala. (36746) 195/C6
Kimch'aek, N. Korea 81/D3
Kimch'ŏn, S. Korea 81/D5
Kimesville, N.C. (†27298) 281/L3
Kimhae, Pakistan 81/D6
Kími, Greece 45/F6
Kimitsu, Japan 81/O3
Kimiwan (lake), Alberta 182/B2
Kimje, S. Korea 81/C6
Kimmell, Ind. (46760) 227/F2
Kimmins, Tenn. (38462) 237/F9
Kimmswick, Mo. (63053) 261/M6
Kimolos (isl.), Greece 45/G7
Kimovsk, U.S.S.R. 52/E4
Kimry, U.S.S.R. 52/E3
Kimsquit, Br. Col. 184/D4
Kinabalu (mt.), Malaysia 85/F4
Kinalı (isl.), Turkey 63/D6
Kinalung, N.S. Wales 97/B3
Kinango, Kenya 115/G4
Kinard, Fla. (32449) 212/D6
Kinards, S.C. (29355) 296/D3
Kinbrace, Scotland 15/E2
Kinbrae, Minn. (†56126) 255/C7
Kinburn, Ontario 177/H2
Kincaid, Ill. (62540) 222/D4
Kincaid, Kansas (66039) 232/G3
Kincaid, Sask. 181/D6
Kincardine, Ontario 177/C3
Kincardine, Scotland 10/B1
Kincardine, Scotland 15/C1
Kincardine, (trad. co.), Scotland, 15/A5
Kincheloe (pt.), Oreg. 291/C2
Kincheloe, W. Va. (†26378) 312/E4
Kincolith, Br. Col. 184/B2
Kincraig, Scotland 15/E3
Kinda, Zaire 115/D5
Kindama, Congo 115/C4
Kindberg, Austria 41/C3
Kinde, Mich. (48445) 250/G5
Kinder, La. (70648) 238/E6
Kinderhook, Ill. (62345) 222/B4
Kinderhook, N.Y. (12106) 276/N6
Kindersley, Sask. 162/F5
Kindersley, Sask. 181/B4
Kindia, Guinea 106/B6
Kindia, Guinea 102/A3
Kindred, N. Dak. (58051) 282/R6
Kinel', U.S.S.R. 52/H4
Kinel' (riv.), U.S.S.R. 52/H4
Kineshma, U.S.S.R. 7/J3
Kineshma, U.S.S.R. 52/F3
King (isl.), Alaska 196/E1
King (isl.), Australia 87/E10
King (isl.), Br. Col. 184/D4
King, Ky. (†40906) 237/O7
King (pt.), N.S. Wales 97/J2
King (cays), Nicaragua 154/F4
King, N.C. (27021) 281/J2
King (isl.), Tasmania 88/G7
King (isl.), Tasmania 99/A1
King (riv.), Tasmania 99/B4
King (co.), Texas 303/D4
King (co.), Wash. 310/D3
King (sound), W. Australia 88/C3
King (sound), W. Australia 92/C2
King, Wis. (54946) 317/H7
King and Queen (co.), Va. 307/P5
King and Queen Court House, Va. (23085) 307/P5
Kingaroy, Queensland 95/D5
Kingaroy, Queensland 88/J5
King Christian (isl.), N.W. Terrs. 187/H2
King Christian IX Land (reg.), Greenl. 4/C11
King Christian IX Land (reg.), Greenland 146/Q3
King Christian X Land (reg.), Greenl. 4/B11
King Christian X Land (reg.), Greenland 146/R2
King City, Calif. (93930) 204/D7
King City, Mo. (64463) 261/D2
King City, Ontario 177/J3
King City, Oreg. (97223) 291/A2
Kingcome Inlet, Br. Col. 184/D4
King Cove, Alaska (99612) 196/F4
Kingdom City, Mo. (65262) 261/J5
King Ferry, N.Y. (13081) 276/G5
Kingfield○, Maine (04947) 243/C6
Kingfisher (co.), Okla. 288/L3
Kingfisher, Okla. (73750) 288/L3
King Frederik VI Coast (reg.), Greenland 146/P3
King Frederik VIII Land (reg.), Greenl. 4/B11
King Frederik VIII Land (reg.), Greenland 146/R2
King George (isl.) 5/C16
King George (isls.), N.W. Terrs. 187/L4
King George (co.), Va. 307/O4
King George, Va. (22485) 307/O4
King George's (falls), S. Africa 118/B5
King Hill, Idaho (83633) 220/C6
Kinghorn, Scotland 15/D1
Kingisepp (Kuressaare), U.S.S.R. 53/B1
King Leopold (range), W. Australia 88/D3
King Leopold (range), W. Australia 92/D2
Kingman, Alberta 182/D3
Kingman, Ariz. (86401) 198/A3
Kingman, Ind. (47952) 227/C5
Kingman (co.), Kansas 232/D4
Kingman, Kansas (67068) 232/D4
Kingman, Maine (04451) 243/G4
Kingman (reef), Pacific 87/K5
Kingoonya, S. Australia 88/E6
Kingoonya, S. Australia 94/D4
Kings (co.), Calif. 204/G8
Kings (riv.), Calif. 204/F7
Kings (riv.), Nev. 266/C1
King's (co.), New Bruns. 170/E3
Kings (co.), N.Y. 276/N9
Kings (co.), Nova Scotia 168/D4
Kings (co.), Pr. Edward I. 168/F2
Kings (peak), Utah 304/D3
King Salmon, Alaska (99613) 196/G3
Kings Beach, Calif. (95719) 204/F4
Kingsbridge, England 13/D7
Kingsburg, Calif. (93631) 204/F7
Kingsburg, S.C. (†29555) 296/H4
Kingsburg, S. Dak. (†57062) 298/O8
Kingsbury, Ind. (46345) 227/D1
Kingsbury○, Maine (†04990) 243/D5
Kingsbury (pond), Maine 243/D5
Kingsbury, Québec 172/E4
Kingsbury (co.), S. Dak. 298/O5
Kingsbury, Texas (78638) 303/G8
Kings Canyon Nat'l Park, Calif. 204/G7
Kingsclear, New Bruns. 170/D3
Kingscliff, N.S. Wales 97/G1
Kingscote, S. Australia 88/F7
Kingscote, S. Australia 94/E6
Kingscourt, Ireland 17/H4
Kingscourt, Ireland 10/C4
King's Cove, Newf. 166/D1
Kings Creek, N.C. (†28645) 281/G3
Kings Creek, Ohio (†43078) 284/C5
Kings Creek, S.C. (29719) 296/E1
Kingsdale, Minn. (†55015) 255/F4
Kingsdown, Kansas (67858) 232/C4
Kingsey Falls, Québec 172/E4
Kingsford, Mich. (49801) 250/A3
Kingsford Heights, Ind. (46346) 227/D2
Kingsford-Smith Airport, N.S. Wales 88/L4
Kingsford-Smith Airport, N.S. Wales 97/J4
Kingsgate, Br. Col. 184/K5
Kingshill, Virgin Is. (U.S.) 161/F4
Kingsland, Ark. (71652) 202/F6
Kingsland, Georgia (31548) 217/J9
Kingsland, Texas (78639) 303/F7
Kings Landing, Ala. (†36775) 195/D6
King's Landing, New Bruns. 170/C3
Kingsley (lake), Fla. 212/E2
Kingsley, Iowa (51028) 229/A3
Kingsley, Ky. (†40201) 237/K2
Kingsley, Mich. (49649) 250/D4
Kingsley (dam), Nebr. 264/C3
Kingsley, New Bruns. 170/D2
King's Lynn, England 13/H5
King's Lynn, England 10/G4
Kingsmere (lake), Sask. 181/E1
Kingsmill, Texas (†79065) 303/D2
Kings Mills, Ohio (45034) 284/B7
Kings Mountain, Ky. (40442) 237/M6
Kings Mountain, N.C. (28086) 281/G4
Kings Mountain Nat'l Mil. Park, S.C. 296/E1
Kings Park, N.Y. (11754) 276/O9
King's Point, Newf. 166/C4
Kings Point, N.Y. (11024) 276/P6
Kingsport, Nova Scotia 168/D3
Kingsport, Tenn. (*37660) 237/R7
Kingston, Ark. (72742) 202/C1
Kingston, Australia 87/G8
Kingston, Georgia (30145) 217/C2
Kingston, Ill. (60145) 222/E1
Kingston, Ind. (†47240) 227/G6
Kingston, Iowa (†52637) 229/L7
Kingston (cap.), Jamaica 146/L8
Kingston (cap.), Jamaica 156/C3
Kingston (cap.), Jamaica 158/K6
Kingston, La. (†71032) 238/C2
Kingston, Md. (21834) 245/R8
Kingston, Mass. (02364) 249/M5
Kingston○, Mass. (02364) 249/M5
Kingston, Mich. (48741) 250/F5
Kingston, Minn. (55326) 255/D5
Kingston, Mo. (64650) 261/E3
Kingston○, N.H. (03848) 268/E6
Kingston, N.J. (08528) 273/D3
Kingston, N. Mex. (†88042) 274/B6
Kingston, N.Y. (12401) 276/M7
Kingston, N. Zealand 100/B6
Kingston, Norfolk I. 88/L6
Kingston, Nova Scotia 168/D4
Kingston, Ohio (45644) 284/E7
Kingston, Okla. (73439) 288/N7
Kingston, Ont. 162/J7
Kingston, Ont. 146/L5
Kingston, Ontario 177/H3
Kingston, Pa. (18704) 294/F7
Kingston, R.I. (02881) 249/J7
Kingston, S. Australia 94/G7
Kingston, Tasmania 99/D4
Kingston, Tenn. (37763) 237/N9
Kingston, Utah (84743) 304/B5
Kingston, Wash. (98346) 310/C3
Kingston, W. Va. (25120) 312/D7
Kingston, Wis. (53939) 317/H8
Kingston Mines, Ill. (61539) 222/D3
Kingston Springs, Tenn. (37082) 237/G8
Kingston upon Thames, England 10/B6
Kingston upon Thames, England 13/H8
Kingstown (Dún Laoghaire), Ireland 17/K5
Kingstown, N.S. Wales 97/F2
Kingstown (cap.), St. Vin. & Grens. 161/A9
Kingstown (cap.), St. Vin. & Grens. 156/G4
Kingstown (bay), St. Vin. & Grens. 161/A9
Kingstree, S.C. (29556) 296/H4
Kings Valley, Oreg. (†97361) 291/D3
Kingsville, Md. (21087) 245/N3
Kingsville, Mo. (64061) 261/D5
Kingsville, Ohio (44048) 284/J2
Kingsville, Ontario 177/B6
Kingsville, Texas (78363) 303/G10
Kingsville N.A.S., Texas 303/G10
Kingswood, England 13/E6
Kingswood, Ky. (†40144) 237/J5
Kingtehchen (Jingdezhen), China 77/J6
Kington, England 13/E5
Kington, England 10/E4
Kingurutik (mesa), Newf. 166/B2
Kingussie, Scotland 15/D3
Kingussie, Scotland 10/D2
Kingville, S.C. (†29052) 296/F4
King William (isl.), N.W.T. 162/G2
King William (isl.), N.W. Terrs. 187/J3
King William (lake), Tasmania 99/C4
King William (co.), Va. 307/O5
King William, Va. (23086) 307/O5
King William's Town, S. Africa 102/E8
King William's Town, S. Africa 118/D6
Kingwood, W. Va. (26537) 312/G4
Kinhwa (Jinhua), China 77/J6
Kiniama, Zaire 115/E6
Kınık, Turkey 63/B3
Kinistino, Sask. 181/F3
Kinkala, Congo 115/B4
Kinkora, Pr. Edward I. 168/E2
Kinley, Sask. 181/D3
Kinloch, Mo. (63140) 261/P2
Kinlochbervie, Scotland 15/D2
Kinlochewe, Scotland 15/C3
Kinlochleven, Scotland 15/D4
Kinloch Rannoch, Scotland 15/D4
Kinloss, Scotland 15/E3
Kinlough, Ireland 17/E3
Kinmount, Minn. (†55771) 255/F2
Kinmount, Ontario 177/F3
Kinmundy, Ill. (62854) 222/E5
Kinna, Sweden 18/H8
Kinnairds (head), Scotland 10/F2
Kinnairds (head), Scotland 15/G3
Kinnear, Wyo. (82516) 319/D2
Kinnegad, Ireland 17/G5
Kinnelon, N.J. (07405) 273/E2
Kinneret, Israel 65/D2
Kinney, Minn. (55758) 255/F3
Kinney (co.), Texas 303/D8
Kinnitty, Ireland 17/F5
Kino (riv.), Japan 81/G6
Kinoosao, Sask. 181/N3
Kinosota, Manitoba 179/D4
Kinrooi, Belgium 27/H6
Kinross, Iowa (52250) 229/J6
Kinross, Scotland 15/E4
Kinross, Scotland 10/E2
Kinross (trad. co.), Scotland, 15/A5
Kinsale, Ireland 10/B5
Kinsale, Ireland 17/D8
Kinsale (harb.), Ireland 17/E8
Kinsale, Old Head of (head), Ireland 17/E8
Kinsale, Va. (22488) 307/P4
Kinsella, Alberta 182/E3
Kinsey, Ala. (†36301) 195/H8
Kinsey, Mont. (59338) 262/L4
Kinshasa (prov.), Zaire 115/C4
Kinshasa (cap.), Zaire 2/K6
Kinshasa (cap.), Zaire 115/C4
Kinshasa (cap.), Zaire 102/D5
Kinsley, Kansas (67547) 232/C4
Kinsman, Ill. (60437) 222/E2
Kinsman (mt.), N.H. 268/D3
Kinsman, Ohio (44428) 284/J3
Kinsman Notch (pass), N.H. 268/D3
Kinston, Ala. (36453) 195/F8
Kinston, N.C. (28501) 281/O4
Kinta, Okla. (74552) 288/R4

394 Kongsberg

Kongsberg, Norway 18/F7
Kongsfjorden (fjord), Norway 18/B2
Kongsvinger, Norway 18/H6
Kongur Shan (mt.), China 77/A4
Kongwa, Tanzania 115/G5
Koni (pen.), U.S.S.R. 48/Q4
Koniecpol, Poland 47/D3
Königsberg (Kaliningrad), U.S.S.R. 52/B4
Königssee (lake), W. Germany 22/E5
Königswiesen, Austria 41/C2
Königswinter, W. Germany 22/B3
Königs Wusterhausen, E. Germany 22/E2
Konin (prov.), Poland 47/D2
Konin, Poland 47/D2
Kónitsa, Greece 45/E5
Koniuji (isls.), Alaska 196/G3
Köniz, Switzerland 39/D3
Konjic, Yugoslavia 45/D4
Konkiep, Namibia 118/B5
Konnagar, India 68/F1
Konolfingen, Switzerland 39/E3
Konomoc (lake), Conn. 210/G3
Konosha, U.S.S.R. 52/F2
Konotop, U.S.S.R. 52/D4
Konqi He (riv.), China 77/C3
Końskie, Poland 47/E3
Konstantinovka, U.S.S.R. 52/E5
Konstantynów Łódzki, Poland 47/D3
Konstanz, W. Germany 22/C5
Kontagora, Nigeria 106/F6
Kontcha, Cameroon 115/B2
Kontich, Belgium 27/E6
Kontiomäki, Finland 18/Q4
Kontum, Vietnam 72/E4
Kontum (plat.), Vietnam 72/E4
Konya (prov.), Turkey 63/E4
Konya, Turkey 63/E4
Konya, Turkey 59/B2
Konya, Turkey 54/E6
Konza, Kenya 115/G4
Koocanusa (lake), Br. Col. 184/K6
Koocanusa (lake), Mont. 262/A2
Koochiching (co.), Minn. 255/E2
Koog aan de Zaan, Netherlands 27/A4
Koolan (isl.), W. Australia 88/C3
Koolan (isl.), W. Australia 92/C1
Koolau (range), Hawaii 218/E2
Kooline Station, W. Australia 92/B3
Koolpinyah, North. Terr. 93/B2
Koolyanobbing, W. Australia 88/B6
Koolyanobbing, W. Australia 92/B5
Koondrook, Victoria 97/B4
Koonibba, S. Australia 88/E6
Koonibba, S. Australia 94/C4
Koontz Lake, Ind. (†46574) 227/D2
Koorawatha, N.S. Wales 97/E4
Koosharem, Utah (84744) 304/C5
Koosharem Ind. Res., Utah 304/C5
Kooskia, Idaho (83539) 220/C3
Koostatak, Manitoba 179/E3
Kootenai (co.), Idaho 220/B2
Kootenai, Idaho (83840) 220/B1
Kootenai (riv.), Idaho 220/C1
Kootenai (riv.), Mont. 262/A2
Kootenay (lake), Br. Col. 162/E5
Kootenay (lake), Br. Col. 184/J5
Kootenay (riv.), Br. Col. 184/K5
Kootenay Nat'l Park, Br. Col. 184/J4
Kootenay Nat'l Pk., Br. Col. 162/E5
Kootingal, N.S. Wales 97/F2
Kópavogur, Iceland 21/B1
Köpenick, E. Germany 22/F4
Koper, Yugoslavia 45/A3
Kopervik, Norway 18/D7
Kopeysk, U.S.S.R. 48/G4
Köping, Sweden 18/J7
Koppal, India 68/D5
Koppang, Norway 18/G6
Kopparberg (co.), Sweden 18/J6
Kopparberg, Sweden 18/J7
Koppel, Pa. (16136) 294/B4
Kopperston, W. Va. (24854) 312/C7
Koprivnica, Yugoslavia 45/C2
Köprü (riv.), Turkey 63/D4
Kor (riv.), Iran 66/H6
Korab (mt.), Albania 45/E5
Korab (mt.), Yugoslavia 45/E5
Koraka (cape), Turkey 63/B3
Koran, La. (†71037) 238/D2
Koraput, India 68/E5
Korba, India 68/E4
Korbach, W. Germany 22/C3
Korbel, Calif. (95550) 204/B3
Korçë, Albania 45/E5
Korčula (isl.), Yugoslavia 45/C4
Kordestan (Kurdistan) (prov.), Iran 66/E3
Kord Kuy, Iran 66/J2
Kordofan, Southern (prov.), Sudan 111/E5
Kordofan, Northern (prov.), Sudan 111/E5
Korea (North) 2/R4
KOREA (NORTH) 81
Korea (South) 2/R4
KOREA (SOUTH) 81
Korea (bay), N. Korea 81/B4
Korea (str.), S. Korea 81/D6
Korenovsk, U.S.S.R. 52/E5
Korf, U.S.S.R. 54/T3
Korf, U.S.S.R. 4/C1
Korf, U.S.S.R. 48/R3
Korhogo, Ivory Coast 106/C7
Korhogo, Ivory Coast 102/B4
Kőrishegy (mt.), Hungary 41/D3
Koriyama, Japan 81/K5
Korkuteli, Turkey 63/D4
Korla, China 77/C3
Kormakiti (cape), Cyprus 59/B2
Kormakiti (cape), Cyprus 63/E5
Körmend, Hungary 41/D3
Kornat (isl.), Yugoslavia 45/B4
Korneuburg, Austria 41/D2
Kornsjø, Norway 18/G7
Kornwestheim, W. Germany 22/C4
Koro (isl.), Fiji 86/Q10
Koro (sea), Fiji 86/Q10
Köroğlu (mts.), Turkey 63/E2
Köroğlu Dağı (mt.), Turkey 63/E2
Korogwe, Tanzania 115/G5
Koroit, Victoria 97/B6
Korona, Fla. (†32010) 212/E2
Koronadal, Philippines 82/E7
Koronowo, Poland 47/C2
Koropi, Greece 45/G7
Koror (cap.), Belau 87/D5
Kororoit (creek), Victoria 97/H5
Kororoit (creek), Victoria 88/K7
Körös (riv.), Hungary 41/F3
Körösladány, Hungary 41/F3
Korosten', U.S.S.R. 52/C4
Korostyshev, U.S.S.R. 52/C4
Koro Toro, Chad 111/C4
Korpilombolo, Sweden 18/N3
Korsakov, U.S.S.R. 48/P5
Korsnäs, Finland 18/M5
Korsør, Denmark 21/E7
Korsør, Denmark 18/G9
Kortemark, Belgium 27/C6
Korti, Sudan 111/F4
Korti, Sudan 59/B6
Kortrijk, Belgium 27/C7
Korumburra, Victoria 97/D6
Koryak (range), U.S.S.R. 54/U3
Koryak (range), U.S.S.R. 48/S3
Koryak Aut. Okr., U.S.S.R. 48/R3
Koryazhma, U.S.S.R. 52/G2
Kos, Greece 45/H7
Kos (isl.), Greece 45/H7
Kościan, Poland 47/C2
Kościerzyna, Poland 47/C1
Kosciusko (mt.), Australia 87/F9
Kosciusko (co.), Ind. 227/F2
Kosciusko, Miss. (39090) 256/E4
Kosciusko (mt.), N. S. Wales 88/H7
Kosciusko (mt.), N.S. Wales 97/E5
Koshigaya, Japan 81/P2
Koshiki (isls.), Japan 81/D8
Koshke-e Kohneh, Afghanistan 68/A2
Koshkonong, Mo. (65692) 261/J9
Koshkonong (lake), Wis. 317/H10
Košice, Czech. 7/G4
Košice, Czech. 41/F2
Koslan, U.S.S.R. 48/E3
Koslan, U.S.S.R. 52/G2
Köslin (Koszalin), Poland 47/C1
Kosoma, Okla. (†74557) 288/P6
Kosŏng, N. Korea 81/D4
Kosovo (aut. reg.), Yugoslavia 45/E4
Kosovska Mitrovica, Yugoslavia 45/E4
Kosrae (isl.), Micronesia 87/G5
Kosse, Texas (76653) 303/H6
Kössen, Austria 41/B3
Kossou, Lac de (lake), Ivory Coast 106/C7
Kossuth, Ind. (†47167) 227/E7
Kossuth (co.), Iowa 229/E2
Kossuth, Miss. (38834) 256/G1
Kostajnica, Yugoslavia 45/C3
Kostelec nad Černými Lesy, Czech. 41/C2
Kostelec nad Orlicí, Czech. 41/D1
Kosti, Sudan 59/B7
Kosti, Sudan 111/F5
Kosti, Sudan 102/F3
Kostopol', U.S.S.R. 52/C4
Kostroma, U.S.S.R. 7/J3
Kostroma, U.S.S.R. 52/F3
Kostroma, U.S.S.R. 48/E4
Kostrzyń, Poland 47/B2
Koszalin (prov.), Poland 47/C1
Koszalin, Poland 7/F3
Koszalin, Poland 47/C1
Kőszeg, Hungary 41/D3
Koszta, Iowa (†52208) 229/J5
Kota, India 68/D3
Kota, India 54/J7
Kotaagung, Indonesia 85/C7
Kotabaharu, Indonesia 85/E6
Kota Baharu, Malaysia 54/M9
Kota Baharu, Malaysia 72/D6
Kotabaru, Indonesia 85/F6
Kotabumi, Indonesia 85/C7
Kota Kinabalu, Malaysia 54/N9
Kota Kinabalu, Malaysia 85/F4
Kotamobagu, Indonesia 85/G5
Kota Tinggi, Malaysia 72/F5
Kotawaringin, Indonesia 85/E6
Kotcho (lake), Br. Col. 184/M2
Kotcho (riv.), Br. Col. 184/M2
Kotel, Bulgaria 45/H4
Kotel'nich, U.S.S.R. 52/G3
Kotel'nikovo, U.S.S.R. 52/F5
Kotel'nyy (isl.), U.S.S.R. 4/B2
Kotel'nyy (isl.), U.S.S.R. 48/O2
Köthen, E. Germany 22/E3
Kotido, Uganda 115/F3
Kotka, Finland 7/G2
Kotka, Finland 18/P6
Kotlas, U.S.S.R. 7/J2
Kotlas, U.S.S.R. 48/E3
Kotlas, U.S.S.R. 52/G2
Kotlik, Alaska (99620) 196/F2
Kotor, Yugoslavia 45/D4
Kotovo, U.S.S.R. 52/G4
Kotovsk, Odessa, U.S.S.R. 52/C5
Kotovsk, Tambov, U.S.S.R. 52/F4
Kotri, Pakistan 68/B3
Kötschach-Mauthen, Austria 41/B3
Kottaguden, India 68/E5
Kottayam, India 68/D7
Kotto (riv.), Cent. Afr. Rep. 115/D2
Kotturu, India 68/D6
Kotuy (riv.), U.S.S.R. 4/B4
Kotuy (riv.), U.S.S.R. 54/M2
Kotuy (riv.), U.S.S.R. 48/L3
Kotzebue, Alaska (99752) 196/F1
Kotzebue, Alaska 146/B3
Kotzebue, Alaska 188/C5
Kotzebue (sound), Alaska 196/F1
Kotzebue, U.S. 4/C18
Kouango, Cent. Afr. Rep. 115/D2
Kouchibouguac, New Bruns. 170/F2
Kouchibouguac (bay), New Bruns. 170/F2
Kouchibouguacis (riv.), New Bruns. 170/E2
Kouchibouguac Nat'l Park, New Bruns. 170/F2
Koudougou, Upper Volta 106/D6
Kouilou (riv.), Congo 115/B4
Koukdjuak (riv.), N.W. Terrs. 187/L3
Kouki, Cent. Afr. Rep. 115/C2
Koula-Moutou, Gabon 115/B4
Koula-Moutou, Gabon 102/D5
Koulikoro, Mali 106/C6
Koulikoro, Mali 102/B3
Koumala, Queensland 95/D4
Koumbi Saleh (ruins), Mauritania 106/C5
Koumra, Chad 102/D4
Koumra, Chad 111/C6
Koundara, Guinea 106/B6
Kounde, Cent. Afr. Rep. 115/B2
Kouno, Chad 111/C6
Kounradskiy, U.S.S.R. 48/H5
Kountze, Texas (77625) 303/K7
Koupela, Upper Volta 106/D6
Kourou, Fr. Guiana 131/E3
Kourouba, Mali 106/B6
Kouroussa, Guinea 106/C6
Kousseri, Cameroon 115/B1
Koutiala, Mali 106/C6
Koutiala, Mali 102/B3
Kouts, Ind. (46347) 227/C2
Kouvola, Finland 18/P6
Kovdor, U.S.S.R. 52/D1
Kovel', U.S.S.R. 52/C4
Kovel', U.S.S.R. 48/C4
Kovrov, U.S.S.R. 52/F3
Kovrov, U.S.S.R. 48/E4
Kovur, India 68/E6
Kovylkino, U.S.S.R. 52/F4
Kowary, Poland 47/B3
Kowst, Afghanistan 59/J3
Kowt-e 'Ashrow, Afghanistan 68/B2
Koyama, Japan 81/E8
Köyceğiz, Turkey 63/C4
Köyceğiz (lake), Turkey 63/C4
Koyuk, Alaska (99753) 196/F1
Koyukuk, Alaska (99754) 196/G1
Koyukuk (riv.), Alaska 188/C5
Koyukuk (riv.), Alaska 196/G1
Koyulhisar, Turkey 63/G2
Kozaklı, Turkey 63/F3
Kozan, Turkey 63/F4
Kozáni, Greece 45/F5
Kozhevnikovo, U.S.S.R. 48/L2
Kozhikode, India 68/D6
Kozhikode, India 54/J8
Kozhva, U.S.S.R. 52/J1
Kozienice, Poland 47/E3
Kozlu, Turkey 63/D2
Kozluk, Turkey 63/J3
Kozmin, Poland 47/C3
Kozuchów, Poland 47/B3
Kpalimé, Togo 106/E7
Kpandu, Ghana 106/D7
Kpémé, Togo 106/E7
Kra (isth.), Thailand 72/C5
Kraaifontein, S. Africa 118/F6
Kraainem, Belgium 27/C9
Krabi, Thailand 72/C5
Kra Buri, Thailand 72/C5
Kracheh, Cambodia 72/E4
Kraemer, La. (70371) 238/M4
Kragan, Indonesia 85/K2
Kragerø, Norway 18/F7
Kragujevac, Yugoslavia 45/E3
Kragujevac, Yugoslavia 7/G4
Krakatau (Rakata) (isl.), Indonesia 85/C7
Krakow, Mo. (†63090) 261/K6
Kraków (Cracow), Poland 47/E4
Krakow, Wis. (53147) 317/K6
Kralendijk (cap.), Bonaire, Neth. Ant. 161/E8
Kralendijk, Neth. Ant. 156/E4
Králíky, Czech. 41/D1
Kraljevo, Yugoslavia 45/E4
Kralovice, Czech. 41/B2
Král'ovský Chlmec, Czech. 41/G2
Kralupy nad Vltavou, Czech. 41/C1
Kramatorsk, U.S.S.R. 52/E5
Kramer, Ind. (†47918) 227/C4
Kramer, Nebr. (†68333) 264/H4
Kramer, N. Dak. (58748) 282/J2
Kramfors, Sweden 18/L5
Kranídhion, Greece 45/F7
Kranj, Yugoslavia 45/B2
Kranzburg, S. Dak. (57245) 298/R4
Krapkowice, Poland 47/D3
Krasino, U.S.S.R. 52/H1
Krasino, U.S.S.R. 48/F2
Krāslava, U.S.S.R. 53/D3
Kraslice, Czech. 41/B1
Krásná Lípa, Czech. 41/C1
Kraśnik Fabryczny, Poland 47/F3
Krasnoarmeysk, U.S.S.R. 52/G4
Krasnoborsk, U.S.S.R. 52/G2
Krasnodar, U.S.S.R. 7/H4
Krasnodar, U.S.S.R. 48/E5
Krasnodar, U.S.S.R. 52/E6
Krasnograd, U.S.S.R. 52/E5
Krasnokamensk, U.S.S.R. 48/M4
Krasnokamsk, U.S.S.R. 52/H3
Krasnokamsk, U.S.S.R. 48/F4
Krasnoperekopsk, U.S.S.R. 52/D5
Krasnoslobodsk, U.S.S.R. 52/G5
Krasnotur'insk, U.S.S.R. 48/G3
Krasnoural'sk, U.S.S.R. 48/G4
Krasnovishersk, U.S.S.R. 52/J2
Krasnovodsk, U.S.S.R. 54/G5
Krasnovodsk, U.S.S.R. 48/F5
Krasnoyarsk, U.S.S.R. 54/L4
Krasnoyarsk, U.S.S.R. 2/P3
Krasnoyarsk, U.S.S.R. 48/K4
Krasnystaw, Poland 47/F3
Krasnyy Kut, U.S.S.R. 52/G4
Krasnyy Luch, U.S.S.R. 52/E5
Krasnyy Sulin, U.S.S.R. 52/F5
Krasnyy Yar, U.S.S.R. 52/G5
Kraulshavn, Greenl. 4/B13
Krause Lagoon (chan.), Virgin Is. (U.S.) 161/F4
Krawang, Indonesia 85/H2
Krebs, Okla. (74554) 288/P5
Krefeld, W. Germany 22/B3
Kremenchug, U.S.S.R. 7/H4
Kremenchug, U.S.S.R. 48/D5
Kremenchug, U.S.S.R. 52/D5
Kremlin, Mont. (59532) 262/F2
Kremlin, Okla. (73753) 288/L1
Kremmling, Colo. (80459) 208/G2
Kremnica, Czech. 41/E2
Krems an der Donau, Austria 41/C2
Krenitzin (isls.), Alaska 196/E4
Kresgeville, Pa. (18333) 294/L4
Kress, Texas (79052) 303/C3
Kretinga, U.S.S.R. 53/A3
Kreutztal, W. Germany 22/C3
Kreuzlingen, Switzerland 39/H1
Kribi, Cameroon 115/B3
Krichev, U.S.S.R. 52/D4
Kriens, Switzerland 39/F2
Krimml, Austria 41/B3
Krimpen aan den IJssel, Netherlands 27/F5
Kriós (cape), Greece 45/F8
Krishna (Kistna) (riv.), India 68/D5
Krishnanagar, India 68/F4
Kristiansand, Norway 18/F8
Kristiansand, Norway 7/E3
Kristianstad (co.), Sweden 18/J8
Kristianstad, Sweden 18/J9
Kristiansund, Norway 7/E2
Kristiansund, Norway 18/E5
Kristiinankaupunki (Kristinestad), Finland 18/N5
Kristinehamn, Sweden 18/H7
Kristinestad, Finland 18/N5
Kríti (Crete) (isl.), Greece 45/G8
Krivoy Rog, U.S.S.R. 7/H4
Krivoy Rog, U.S.S.R. 48/D5
Krivoy Rog, U.S.S.R. 52/D5
Križevci, Yugoslavia 45/C2
Krk, Yugoslavia 45/B3
Krk (isl.), Yugoslavia 45/B3
Krnov, Czech. 41/D1
Krolevets, U.S.S.R. 52/D4
Kroměříž, Czech. 41/D2
Krompachy, Czech. 41/F2
Kronach, W. Germany 22/D3
Kronau, Sask. 181/G5
Krong Kaoh Kong, Cambodia 72/D4
Krong Keb, Cambodia 72/E5
Kronoberg (co.), Sweden 18/J8
Kronshtadt, U.S.S.R. 52/C3
Kroonstad, S. Africa 118/D5
Kropotkin, U.S.S.R. 52/F5
Kroschel, Minn. (†55037) 255/E4
Krosno (prov.), Poland 47/E4
Krosno, Poland 47/E4
Krosno Odrzanskie, Poland 47/B2
Krotoszyn, Poland 47/C3
Krotz Springs, La. (70750) 238/G5
Krško, Yugoslavia 45/B3
Kru Coast (reg.), Liberia 106/C8
Kruger Nat'l Park, S. Africa 118/E4
Krugersdorp, S. Africa 118/H6
Krugloi (pt.), Alaska 196/J3
Kruis (riv.), S. Africa 118/F6
Krujë, Albania 45/D5
Krum, Texas (76249) 303/G4
Krumbach, W. Germany 22/D4
Krummenau, Switzerland 39/H2
Krumovgrad, Bulgaria 45/G5
Krung Thep (Bangkok) (cap.), Thailand 72/D4
Krupina, Czech. 41/E2
Krupka, Czech. 41/B1
Krupp (Marlin), Wash. (†98832) 310/F3
Krusenstern (cape), Alaska 196/F1
Krusenstern (cape), N.W. Terrs. 187/G3
Kruševac, Yugoslavia 45/E4
Krušné Hory (Erzgebirge) (mts.), Czech. 41/B1
Kruszwica, Poland 47/D2
Kruzof (isl.), Alaska 196/M1
Krydor, Sask. 181/D3
Krymsk, U.S.S.R. 52/E5
Krynica, Poland 47/E4
Krypton, Ky. (41754) 237/P6
Krzyz, Poland 47/C2
Ksar el Boukhari, Algeria 106/E1
Ksar el Kebir, Morocco 106/C2
Ksar es Souk, Morocco 106/D2
Ktima, Cyprus 63/E5
Kuala Dungun, Malaysia 72/D6
Kualakapuas, Indonesia 85/E6
Kuala Kerai, Malaysia 72/D6
Kualakurun, Indonesia 85/E6
Kuala Lipis, Malaysia 72/D6
Kuala Lumpur (cap.), Malaysia 72/D7
Kuala Lumpur (cap.), Malaysia 54/M9
Kuala Lumpur (cap.), Malaysia 2/P5
Kuala Pilah, Malaysia 72/D7
Kualapuu, Hawaii (96757) 218/G1
Kuala Rompin, Malaysia 72/D7
Kuala Selangor, Malaysia 72/D7
Kuala Terengganu, Malaysia 72/D6
Kuancheng, China 77/J3
Kuantan, Malaysia 72/D7
Kuba, U.S.S.R. 52/G6
Kubachi, U.S.S.R. 52/G6
Kubaisa, Iraq 66/C4
Kuban' (riv.), U.S.S.R. 7/J4
Kuban' (riv.), U.S.S.R. 52/E5
Kubbum, Sudan 111/D5
Kubeno (lake), U.S.S.R. 52/E3
Küblis, Switzerland 39/J3
Kubohama, Japan 81/F7
Kubrat, Bulgaria 45/H4
Kuching, Malaysia 54/N9
Kuching, Malaysia 85/E5
Kuchino (isl.), Japan 81/O4
Kuçovë (Stalin), Albania 45/D5
Küçükköy, Turkey 63/C6
Kudarebe (pt.), Neth. Ant. 161/D9
Kudat, Malaysia 85/F4
Kudowa Zdrój, Poland 47/B3
Kudus, Indonesia 85/J2
Kudymkar, U.S.S.R. 48/F4
Kudymkar, U.S.S.R. 52/H3
Kufra (oasis), Libya 102/E2
Kufra (oasis), Libya 111/D3
Kufrinja, Jordan 65/D3
Kufstein, Austria 41/A3
Kuh (cape), Iran 66/K8
Kuhak, Iran 66/N7
Kuhestan, Afghanistan 59/H3
Kuhestan, Afghanistan 68/A2
Kühlungsborn, E. Germany 22/D1
Kuhmo, Finland 18/Q4
Kuhpayeh, Iran 66/H4
Kuilsrivier, S. Africa 118/F6
Kuiseb (riv.), Namibia 118/B4
Kuiu (isl.), Alaska 196/M2
Kuivaniemi, Finland 18/O4
Kuji, Japan 81/K3
Kuju (mt.), Japan 81/E7
Kuk (riv.), Alaska 196/G1
Kukaiau, Hawaii (†96775) 218/H4
Kukaklek (lake), Alaska 196/G3
Kukalar, Kuh-e (mt.), Iran 59/F3
Kukalar, Kuh-e (mt.), Iran 66/G5
Kukalaya (riv.), Nicaragua 154/F4
Kukawa, Nigeria 106/G6
Kukës, Albania 45/E4
Kuki, Japan 81/O2
Kukpowruk (riv.), Alaska 196/F1
Kukui (riv.), Guyana 131/A3
Kukuihaele, Hawaii (96727) 218/H3
Kula, Bulgaria 45/F4
Kula, Hawaii (96790) 218/J2
Kula, Turkey 63/C3
Kulai, Malaysia 72/F5
Kula Kangri (mt.), Bhutan 68/G3
Kuldīga, U.S.S.R. 53/A2
Kuldja (Yining), China 77/B3
Kulebaki, U.S.S.R. 52/F3
Kulen, Cambodia 72/E4
Kulen Vakuf, Yugoslavia 45/B3
Kulgera, North. Terr. 88/E5
Kulgera, North. Terr. 93/C8
Kulkyne (creek), N.S. Wales 97/C1
Kulm, N. Dak. (58456) 282/N7
Kulmbach, W. Germany 22/D3
Kuloy, U.S.S.R. 52/F2
Kulp, Turkey 63/J3
Kulpmont, Pa. (17834) 294/J4
Kulpsville, Pa. (19443) 294/M5
Kul'sary, U.S.S.R. 48/F5
Kulu, India 68/D2
Kulu, Turkey 63/E3
Kulunda, U.S.S.R. 48/H4
Kulyab, U.S.S.R. 48/H6
Kŭm (riv.), S. Korea 81/C5
Kuma (riv.), U.S.S.R. 7/J4
Kuma (riv.), U.S.S.R. 48/E5
Kuma (riv.), U.S.S.R. 52/G5
Kumagaya, Japan 81/J5
Kumai, Indonesia 85/E6
Kumaka, Guyana 131/B4
Kumamoto (pref.), Japan 81/E7
Kumamoto, Japan 54/P6
Kumamoto, Japan 81/E7
Kumano, Japan 81/G7
Kumanovo, Yugoslavia 45/E4
Kumara, N. Zealand 100/C5
Kumasi, Ghana 106/D7
Kumasi, Ghana 102/B4
Kumba, Cameroon 115/A3
Kumbakonam, India 68/D6
Kumbo, Cameroon 115/B2
Kum-Dag, U.S.S.R. 48/F6
Kume (isl.), Japan 81/M6
Kumertau, U.S.S.R. 52/J4
Kumeu, N. Zealand 100/B1
Kŭmgang (mt.), N. Korea 81/D4
Kumiyama, Japan 81/J7
Kumkale, Turkey 63/B6
Kumköy, Turkey 63/B6
Kumla, Sweden 18/J7
Kumluca, Turkey 63/D4
Kummerowersee (lake), E. Germany 22/E2
Kumo (riv.), Finland 7/G2
Kumo, Nigeria 106/G7
Kumphawapi, Thailand 72/D3
Kumta, India 68/C6
Kumukahi (cape), Hawaii 218/K5
Kumul (Hami), China 77/D3
Kuna, Idaho (83634) 220/B6
Kunágota, Hungary 41/F3
Kunashir (isl.), U.S.S.R. 54/R5
Kunda, U.S.S.R. 52/C3
Kunda, U.S.S.R. 53/D1
Kundiawa, Papua N.G. 85/B7
Kundl, Austria 41/A3
Künes (Xinyuan), China 77/B3
Künes He (riv.), China 77/B3
Kungälv, Sweden 18/G8
Kunghit (isl.), Br. Col. 184/B4
Kungsbacka, Sweden 18/G8
Kungu, Zaire 102/D4
Kungu, Zaire 115/C3
Kungur, U.S.S.R. 7/K3
Kungur, U.S.S.R. 48/F4
Kungur, U.S.S.R. 52/J3
Kunhegyes, Hungary 41/F3
Kunia, Hawaii (96759) 218/E2
Kuningan, Indonesia 85/H2
Kunkle, Ohio (43531) 284/A2
Kunkletown, Pa. (18058) 294/M4
Kunlong, Burma 72/C2
Kunlun (range), China 54/K6
Kunlun (range), India 68/D1
Kunlun Shan (range), China 77/B4
Kunmadaras, Hungary 41/F3
Kunming, China 77/F6
Kunming, China 2/Q4
Kunming, China 54/M7
Kunsan, S. Korea 81/C6
Kunszentmárton, Hungary 41/F3
Kunszentmiklós, Hungary 41/E3
Kununurra, W. Australia 88/D3
Kununurra, W. Australia 92/E2
Kuolayarvi, U.S.S.R. 52/D1
Kuopio (prov.), Finland 18/P5
Kuopio, Finland 7/G2
Kuopio, Finland 18/Q5
Kupa (riv.), Yugoslavia 45/B3
Kupang, Indonesia 54/O11
Kupang, Indonesia 85/G8
Kuparuk (riv.), Alaska 196/H1
Kupino, U.S.S.R. 48/H4
Kupiškis, U.S.S.R. 53/C3
Kupreanof (isl.), Alaska 196/N1
Kupyansk, U.S.S.R. 52/E5
Kuqa, China 77/B3
Kur (isl.), Indonesia 85/J7
Kura (riv.), U.S.S.R. 48/E6
Kura (riv.), U.S.S.R. 52/G6
Kuraiyima, Jordan 65/D3
Kurang (riv.), Iran 66/G4
Kurashiki, Japan 81/F6
Kurayoshi, Japan 81/F6
Kurdistan (Kordestan) (prov.), Iran 66/E3
Kurdistan (reg.), Iran 59/D2
Kurdistan (reg.), Iran 66/D2
Kurdistan (reg.), Iraq 59/D2
Kurdistan (reg.), Iraq 66/C2
Kurdistan (reg.), Turkey 59/D2
Kŭrdzhali, Bulgaria 45/G5
Kure (atoll), Hawaii 87/J3
Kure (atoll), Hawaii 218/A5
Kure (isl.), Hawaii 218/A5
Kure, Japan 81/F6
Küre, Turkey 63/E2
Küre (mts.), Turkey 63/E2
Kure Beach, N.C. (28449) 281/O7
Kuressaare, U.S.S.R. 53/B1
Kuressaare, U.S.S.R. 52/B3
Kurgan, U.S.S.R. 54/H4
Kurgan, U.S.S.R. 48/G4
Kurgan-Tyube, U.S.S.R. 48/G6
Kuria Muria (isls.), Oman 54/G8
Kuria Muria (isls.), Oman 59/G6
Kurikka, Finland 18/M5
Kuril (isls.), U.S.S.R. 2/S3
Kuril (isls.), U.S.S.R. 54/R5
Kuril (isls.), U.S.S.R. 48/P5
Kuril'sk, U.S.S.R. 48/P5
Ku-ring-gai, N. S. Wales 88/K4
Kuring Kuru, Namibia 118/B3
Kurla, India 68/B7
Kurmuk, Sudan 111/F5
Kurnell (pen.), N.S. Wales 97/J4
Kurnool, India 54/J8
Kurnool, India 68/D5
Kuroiso, Japan 81/K5
Kuroki, Sask. 181/H4
Kurow, N. Zealand 100/C6
Kurri Kurri-Weston, N.S. Wales 97/F3
Kuršenai, U.S.S.R. 53/B2
Kursk, U.S.S.R. 7/H3
Kursk, U.S.S.R. 48/D4
Kursk, U.S.S.R. 52/E4
Kurşunlu, Turkey 63/E2
Kurtalan, Turkey 63/J3
Kurthwood, La. (71443) 238/D4
Kurtistown, Hawaii (96760) 218/J5
Kurtz, Ind. (47249) 227/E7
Kurucaşile, Turkey 63/E2
Kuruçay (riv.), Turkey 63/K2
Kuruktag Shan (range), China 77/C3
Kuruman, S. Africa 118/C5
Kurume, Japan 81/E7
Kurundi, North. Terr. 93/D6
Kurunegala, Sri Lanka 68/E7
Kurungiku (mts.), Guyana 131/B3
Kurupukari, Guyana 131/B3
Kuş (lake), Turkey 63/B2
Kuşada (gulf), Turkey 63/B4
Kuşadası, Turkey 63/B4
Kushchevskaya, U.S.S.R. 52/E5
Kushequa, Pa. (†16735) 294/E2
Kushikino, Japan 81/E8
Kushima, Japan 81/E8
Kushimoto, Japan 81/G7
Kushiro, Japan 54/R5
Kushiro, Japan 81/M2
Kushka, U.S.S.R. 48/G6
Kushog (lake), Ontario 177/F2
Kuskokwim (bay), Alaska 196/F3
Kuskokwim (mts.), Alaska 196/G2
Kuskokwim (riv.), Alaska 188/C6
Kuskokwim (riv.), Alaska 196/G2
Kuskokwim (riv.), Alaska 146/C3
Kuskokwim, North Fork (riv.), Alaska 196/H2
Kuskokwim, South Fork (riv.), Alaska 196/H2
Kuskokwim (riv.), U.S. 4/C17
Küsnacht, Switzerland 39/G2
Kusŏng, N. Korea 81/B4
Küssnacht am Rigi, Switzerland 39/F2
Kustanay, U.S.S.R. 54/H4
Kustanay, U.S.S.R. 48/G4
Kustatan, Alaska (†99682) 196/B1
Küstrin, Poland 47/B2
Kut, Iraq 59/E3
Kut, Iraq 66/D4
Kut, Ko (isl.), Thailand 72/D5
Kuta, Nigeria 106/F7
Kütahya (prov.), Turkey 63/C3
Kütahya, Turkey 59/B2
Kütahya, Turkey 63/C3
Kutaisi, U.S.S.R. 7/J4
Kutaisi, U.S.S.R. 48/E5
Kutaisi, U.S.S.R. 52/F6
Kutaraja (Banda Aceh), Indonesia 85/A4
Kutari (riv.), Guyana 131/C4
Kutari (riv.), Suriname 131/C4
Kutch, Colo. (†80832) 208/M5
Kutch (gulf), India 68/B4
Kutch (reg.), India 68/B4
Kutch, Rann of (salt marsh), 54/H7
Kutch, Rann of (salt marsh), India 68/B4
Kutch, Rann of (salt marsh), Pakistan 68/B4
Kutch, Rann of (salt lake), Pakistan 59/K5
Kutcharo (lake), Japan 81/M2

Lead Mine 397

La Palma, El Salvador 154/C3
La Palma, Panama 154/H6
La Palma (isl.), Spain 102/A2
La Palma (isl.), Spain 106/A3
La Palma (isl.), Spain 33/A4
La Palma del Condado, Spain 33/C4
La Paloma, Uruguay 145/F5
La Pampa (prov.), Argentina 143/C4
La Paragua, Venezuela 124/G4
Laparan (isl.), Philippines 82/B8
Laparan (isls.), Philippines 82/B8
La Passe, Ontario 177/H2
La Patrie, Québec 172/F4
La Paz, Entre Ríos, Argentina 143/G5
La Paz, Mendoza, Argentina 143/C3
La Paz (dept.), Bolivia 136/A4
La Paz (cap.), Bolivia 136/B5
La Paz (cap.), Bolivia 2/F6
La Paz (cap.), Bolivia 120/C4
La Paz, Honduras 154/D3
Lapaz, Ind. (46537) 227/E2
La Paz, Mexico 146/G7
La Paz, Baja California Sur, Mexico 150/D5
La Paz, San Luis Potosí, Mexico 150/J5
La Paz (bay), Mexico 150/D4
La Paz, Philippines 82/E6
La Paz, Canelones, Uruguay 145/B6
La Paz, Colonia, Uruguay 145/B5
La Paz Central, Nicaragua 154/D4
La Paz de Oriente, Nicaragua 154/E5
La Pêche, Québec 172/B4
La Pedrera, Colombia 126/F8
La Pedrera, Uruguay 145/F5
Lapeer (co.), Mich. 250/F5
Lapeer, Mich. (48446) 250/F5
Lapel, Ind. (46051) 227/F4
La Pelada, Argentina 143/F5
La Pérade, Québec 172/E3
La Pérouse (str.) 54/R5
La Perouse, N.S. Wales 88/L4
La Perouse, N.S. Wales 97/J4
La Pérouse (str.), U.S.S.R. 48/P5
La Pesca, Mexico 150/L4
Lapeyrère (lake), Québec 172/E2
La Piedad Cavadas, Mexico 150/H6
Lapine, Ala. (36046) 195/F7
La Pine, Oreg. (97739) 291/F4
Lapinin (isl.), Philippines 82/E5
La Pintada, Panama 154/G6
Lapithos, Cyprus 63/E5
La Place, Ill. (61936) 222/E4
La Place, La. (70068) 238/N3
La Plaine, Dominica 161/F6
Lapland (reg.) 7/G2
Lapland (reg.), Finland 18/O2
Lapland (reg.), Norway 18/K2
Lapland (reg.), Sweden 18/M2
Lapland (reg.), U.S.S.R. 52/D1
La Plant, S. Dak. (57637) 298/H3
Laplante, New Bruns. 170/E1
La Plata (est.) 120/D6
La Plata, Argentina 143/H7
La Plata, Argentina 120/D6
La Plata, Río de (est.), Argentina 143/E4
La Plata, Colombia 126/C6
La Plata (co.), Colo. 208/D8
La Plata (peak), Colo. 208/G4
La Plata (riv.), Colo. 208/C8
La Plata, Md. (20646) 245/L6
La Plata, Mo. (63549) 261/H2
La Plata, N. Mex. (87418) 274/A2
La Plata (riv.), N. Mex. 274/A1
La Plume, Pa. (18440) 294/L2
La Pobla de Lillet, Spain 33/G1
La Pocatière, Québec 172/H2
La Poile, Newf. 166/C4
La Poile (bay), Newf. 166/C4
Lapoint, Utah (84039) 304/E3
La Pointe, Wis. (54850) 317/E2
La Porte, Calif. (95981) 204/D4
Laporte, Colo. (80535) 208/J1
LaPorte (co.), Ind. 227/D1
LaPorte, Ind. (46350) 227/D1
Laporte, Mich. (†48623) 250/E5
Laporte, Minn. (56461) 255/D3
Laporte, Pa. (18626) 294/K3
Laporte, Sask. 181/B4
La Porte, Texas (77571) 303/K2
La Porte City, Iowa (50651) 229/J4
Lappajärvi, Finland 18/O5
Lappajärvi (lake), Finland 18/O5
Lappeenranta, Finland 7/G2
Lappeenranta, Finland 18/P6
Lappi (prov.), Finland 18/P3
La Prairie, Ill. (62346) 222/B3
La Prairie, Minn. (†55744) 255/E3
Laprairie (co.), Québec 172/H4
La Prairie, Québec 172/J4
Laprida, Argentina 143/D4
La Protección, Honduras 154/D3
La Providence, Québec 172/E4
La Pryor, Texas (78872) 303/E9
Lâpseki, Turkey 63/C6
Laptev (sea), U.S.S.R. 4/B3
Laptev (sea), U.S.S.R. 54/O2
Laptev (sea), U.S.S.R. 48/N2
Lapua, Finland 18/N5
Lapuanjoki (riv.), Finland 18/N5
La Puebla, Spain 33/H3
La Puebla de Montalbán, Spain 33/D3
La Puente, Calif. (*91744) 204/D10
La Puerta, Cuba 158/H3
Lapu-Lapu, Philippines /E5
La Puntilla (cape), Ecuador 128/B4
La Purísima, Mexico 150/D3
La Push, Wash. (98350) 310/A3
Lapwai, Idaho (83540) 220/B3
Lapy, Poland 47/F2
Laqiya 'Umran (well), Sudan 111/E3
Laquey, Mo. (65534) 261/H7
La Quiaca, Argentina 143/C1
L'Aquila (prov.), Italy 34/D3
L'Aquila, Italy 34/D3
Lar, Iran 59/F4
Lar, Iran 66/J7
Lara (state), Venezuela 124/C2
Lara, Victoria 97/C6
Larabee, Pa. (†16731) 294/F2
Larache, Morocco 106/C1
Laracor, Ireland 17/H4
Larak (isl.), Iran 66/K7
La Rambla, Spain 33/D4
Laramie (mts.), Colo. 208/H1
Laramie (riv.), Colo. 208/H1
Laramie (co.), Wyo. 319/H4
Laramie, Wyo. 146/H5
Laramie, Wyo. 188/E2
Laramie, Wyo. (82070) 319/G4
Laramie (mts.), Wyo. 319/G3
Laramie (peak), Wyo. 319/G3
Laramie (riv.), Wyo. 319/G4
Laranjeiras do Sul, Brazil 132/C9
Larantuka, Indonesia 85/G7
Larat (isl.), Indonesia 85/J7
Larbert, Scotland 10/B1
Larbert, Scotland 15/C1
Lärbro, Sweden 18/L8
Larchmont, N.Y. (10538) 276/P7
Larchwood, Iowa (51241) 229/A2
Lardeau, Br. Col. 184/J5
Larder Lake, Ontario 175/E3
Larder Lake, Ontario 177/K5
L'Ardoise West, Nova Scotia 168/H3
La Rédemption, Québec 172/B2
Laredo (sound), Br. Col. 184/C4
Laredo, Mo. (64652) 261/E2
Laredo, Mont. (†59501) 262/G2
Laredo, Spain 33/E1
Laredo, Texas (*78040) 303/E10
Laredo, Texas 188/G5
Laredo, Texas 146/J7
La Reine, Québec 174/B3
Laren, Netherlands 27/G4
Larena, Philippines 82/D6
La Réole, France 28/C5
Lares, P. Rico 161/B2
Lares, P. Rico 156/F1
La Retuca, Chile 138/F3
Larew, W. Va. (†26537) 312/G4
Largentière, France 28/F5
Largo (cay), Cuba 158/D2
Largo (cay), Cuba 156/B2
Largo, Fla. (*33540) 212/B3
Largo (key), Fla. 212/F6
Largo, Md. (†20870) 245/G5
Largo, Cañon (creek), N. Mex. 274/B2
Largs, Scotland 15/A2
Largs, Scotland 10/A1
Lariat, Texas (79335) 303/B3
Larimer (co.), Colo. 208/H1
Larimer, Pa. (15647) 294/C5
Larimore, N. Dak. (58251) 282/P4
Larino, Italy 34/E4
La Rioja (prov.), Argentina 143/C2
La Rioja, Argentina 120/C5
La Rioja, Argentina 143/C2
La Rioja, Cuba 158/H3
Lárisa, Greece 45/F6
Lárisa, Greece 7/G5
Laristan (reg.), Iran 66/J7
La Rivière, Manitoba 179/D5
Lark, N. Dak. (58550) 282/H7
Larkana, Pakistan 59/J4
Larkana, Pakistan 68/B3
Larkhall, Scotland 10/B1
Larkhall, Scotland 15/E5
Lark Harbour, Newf. 166/C4
Larkinburg, Kansas (†66436) 232/G2
Larkinsville, Ala. (†35768) 195/F1
Larkspur, Calif. (94939) 204/H1
Larkspur, Colo. (80118) 208/K4
Larksville, Pa. (†18704) 294/E7
Larnaca, Cyprus 59/B3
Larnaca, Cyprus 63/E5
Larnaca (bay), Cyprus 63/E5
Larne (dist.), N. Ireland 17/K2
Larne, N. Ireland 17/K2
Larne, N. Ireland 10/D3
Larne (inlet), N. Ireland 17/K2
Larned, Kansas (67550) 232/C3
La Robla, Spain 33/D1
La Roche, Switzerland 39/D3
La Roche-en-Ardenne, Belgium 27/G8
La Rochelle, France 7/D4
La Rochelle, France 28/C4
La Rochelle, Manitoba 179/F5
La Roche-sur-Yon, France 28/C4
La Roda, Spain 33/E3
La Romana (prov.), Dom. Rep. 158/F6
La Romana, Dom. Rep. 158/F6
La Romana, Dom. Rep. 156/E3
La Ronge, Sask. 181/L3
La Rose, Ill. (61541) 222/D3
Larose, La. (70373) 238/K7
Larouche, Québec 172/F1
Larrabee, Iowa (51029) 229/B3
Larrimah, North. Terr. 88/E3
Larrimah, North. Terr. 93/C3
Larroque, Argentina 143/F5
Larry's River, Nova Scotia 168/G3
Larsen (sound), N.W. Terrs. 187/J2
Larsen Bay, Alaska (99624) 196/H3
Larsen Ice Shelf, Ant. 2/F9
Larsen Ice Shelf, Ant. 5/C16
Larslan, Mont. (59244) 262/K2
Larsmont, Minn. (†55616) 255/G4
Larson, N. Dak. (58751) 282/E2
Larto, La. (71344) 238/G4
Larue (co.), Ky. 237/K5
La Rue, Ohio (43332) 284/D4
Laruns, France 28/C6
La Russell, Mo. (64848) 261/D8
Larvik, Norway 18/C4
Larwill, Ind. (46764) 227/F2
La Sal, Utah (84530) 304/E5
La Salle, Colo. (80645) 208/K2
La Salle (co.), Ill. 222/E2
La Salle, Ill. (61301) 222/E2
La Salle (par.), La. 238/F3
La Salle, Manitoba 179/E5
La Salle (riv.), Manitoba 179/E5
La Salle, Mich. (48145) 250/F7
La Salle, Minn. (56056) 255/D6
La Salle, Québec 172/H4
Lasalle (lake), Québec 172/E2
La Salle (co.), Texas 303/E9
Las Animas (co.), Colo. 208/L8
Las Animas, Colo. (81054) 208/N6
Las Animas (creek), N. Mex. 274/B5
Las Anod, Somalia 115/J2
La Sarraz, Switzerland 39/C3
La Sarre, Que. 162/J6
La Sarre, Québec 174/B3
Lasauces, Colo. (†81151) 208/H8
Las Aves (isls.), Venezuela 124/E2
Las Bonitas, Venezuela 124/F4
Las Breas, Chile 138/B7
Lasca, Ala. (†36784) 195/C6
Las Cabras, Chile 138/F5
Lascahobas, Haiti 156/D3
Lascahobas, Haiti 158/C6
Lascano, Uruguay 145/E4
Las Carreras, Bolivia 136/C7
Lascassas, Tenn. (37085) 237/J9
L'Ascension, Labelle, Québec 172/C3
L'Ascension, Lac-St-Jean-E., Québec 172/F1
L'Ascension-de-Patapédia, Québec 172/B2
Las Choapas, Mexico 150/M7
La Scie, Newf. 166/C4
Las Cruces, Chile 138/F3
Las Cruces, N. Mex. 146/H6
Las Cruces, N. Mex. 188/E4
Las Cruces, N. Mex. (88001) 274/C6
Las Dureh, Somalia 115/J1
La Selva Beach, Calif. (95076) 204/K4
La Serena, Chile 120/B5
La Serena, Chile 138/A8
La Seyne-sur-Mer, France 28/F6
Las Flores, Argentina 143/E4
Las Flores, Uruguay 145/D5
Las Hadas, Mexico 150/G7
Lashburn, Sask. 181/B2
Lash-e Joveyn, Afghanistan 68/A2
Lash-e Joveyn, Afghanistan 59/H3
Lashio, Burma 72/C2
Lashkar Gah, Afghanistan 68/A2
Lashkar Gah, Afghanistan 59/H3
La Sierra, Uruguay 145/D5
L'Asile, Haiti 158/B6
Las Juntas, Colombia 126/E6
Las Juntas, C. Rica 154/E5
Łask, Poland 47/D3
Lasker, N.C. (27848) 281/P2
La Skhirra, Tunisia 106/G2
Las Khoreh, Somalia 115/J1
Las Lajas, Argentina 143/B4
Las Lajitas, Venezuela 124/F4
Las Lomitas, Argentina 143/D1
Las Marias, P. Rico 161/B2
Las Martinas, Cuba 158/A2
Las Matas de Farfán, Dom. Rep. 158/D6
Las Matas de Farfán, Dom. Rep. 156/D3
Las Mercedes, Venezuela 124/E3
Las Navas del Marqués, Spain 33/D2
Lasne, Belgium 27/F7
Las Nieves, Mexico 150/G3
La Solana, Spain 33/E3
La Sorcière (mt.), St. Lucia 161/G6
La Souterraine, France 28/D4
Las Palmas, Argentina 143/E2
Las Palmas (cap.), Canary Is., 102/A2
Las Palmas, Panama 154/G6
Las Palmas (prov.), Spain 33/C4
Las Palmas de Gran Canaria, Spain 33/B4
Las Palmas de Gran Canaria, Spain 106/B3
Las Pampitas, Bolivia 136/C3
Las Parejas, Argentina 143/F6
Las Pedroñeras, Spain 33/E3
Las Petas, Bolivia 136/F5
La Spezia (prov.), Italy 34/B2
La Spezia, Italy 34/B2
La Spezia, Italy 7/E4
Las Piedras, Peru 128/H9
Las Piedras, P. Rico 161/E2
Las Piedras, Uruguay 145/B6
Las Piedras, Falcón, Venezuela 124/C2
Las Piedras, Zulia, Venezuela 124/B2
Las Plumas, Argentina 143/C5
Lasqueti Island, Br. Col. 184/J2
Las Rosas, Argentina 143/F6
Las Rosas, Mexico 150/N8
Lassen (co.), Calif. 204/E3
Lassen (peak), Calif. 204/D3
Lassen Volcanic Nat'l Park, Calif. 204/D3
L'Assomption (co.), Québec 172/D4
L'Assomption, Québec 172/D4
L'Assomption (riv.), Québec 172/D3
Las Tablas, N. Mex. (87541) 274/C2
Las Tablas, Panama 154/G7
Lastarria (vol.), Chile 138/B5
La Station-du-Coteau, Québec 172/C4
Last Chance (creek), Utah 304/C6
Las Termas, Argentina 143/D2
Last Mountain (lake), Sask. 181/F4
Las Toscas, Uruguay 145/E3
Lastoursville, Gabon 115/B4
Lastovo (Lagosta) (isl.), Yugoslavia 45/C4
Las Trincheras, Venezuela 124/F4
Las Truchas, Mexico 150/H7
Lastrup, Minn. (56344) 255/D4
Las Tunas (prov.), Cuba 158/H3
Las Varillas, Argentina 143/D3
Las Vegas, Nev. 146/G6
Las Vegas, Nev. 188/C3
Las Vegas, Nev. (*89101) 266/F6
Las Vegas (range), Nev. 266/F6
Las Vegas, N.Mex. 188/E3
Las Vegas, N. Mex. (87701) 274/D3
Las Vegas, Venezuela 124/D3
Las Yaras, Peru 128/G11
Las Yungas (reg.), Bolivia 136/B5
La Tabatière, Québec 174/F2
Latacunga, Ecuador 128/C3
La Tagua, Colombia 126/C8
Latah (co.), Idaho 220/B3
Latah, Wash. (99018) 310/H3
Latah (creek), Wash. 310/H3
Latakia (prov.), Syria 63/G5
Latakia, Syria 54/E6
Latakia, Syria 63/F5
Latakia, Syria 59/C2
La Taste, Grenada 161/D8
Latchford, Ontario 177/K5
Laterrière, Québec 172/F1
Latexo, Texas (75849) 303/J6
Latham, Ala. (†36579) 195/C8
Latham, Ill. (62543) 222/D4
Latham, Kansas (67072) 232/F4
Latham, Mo. (65050) 261/G5
Latham, N.Y. (12110) 276/N5
Latham, Ohio (45646) 284/D7
Latham, Tenn. (†38225) 237/D8
Lathrop, Calif. (95330) 204/D6
Lathrop, Mich. (†49880) 250/B2
Lathrop, Mo. (64465) 261/D3
La Tigra, Venezuela 124/H4
Latimer, Iowa (50452) 229/G3
Latimer, Kansas (†67449) 232/F3
Latimer (co.), Okla. 288/R5
Latimers (brook), Conn. 210/G3
Latina (prov.), Italy 34/D4
Latina, Italy 34/D4
La Tina, Peru 128/B5
Latium (Lazio) (reg.), Italy 34/D3
La Tola, Ecuador 128/C2
La Toma, Argentina 143/C3
Laton, Calif. (93242) 204/F7
Latorica (riv.), Czech. 41/F2
La Tortuga (isl.), Venezuela 124/F2
Latouche Treville (cape), W. Australia 88/C3
Latouche Treville (cape), W. Australia 92/C2
Latour, Mo. (64760) 261/D5
La Tour-de-Peilz, Switzerland 39/C4
La Tour-du-Pin, France 28/F5
Latourell Falls, Oreg. (†97060) 291/E2
La Trinidad, Nicaragua 154/D4
La Trinidad, Philippines 82/C2
La Trinidad, Venezuela 124/D3
La Trinidad de Arauca, Venezuela 124/D4
La Trinidad de Orichuna, Venezuela 124/D4
La Trinité, Martinique 161/D6
La Trinité-des-Monts, Québec 172/J1
Latrobe, Pa. (15650) 294/D5
Latrobe, Tasmania 99/C3
Latta, S.C. (29565) 296/J3
Lattimore, N.C. (28089) 281/F4
Lattingtown, N.Y. (†11560) 276/R6
Latty, Ohio (45855) 284/A3
La Tuque, Que. 162/J6
La Tuque, Québec 172/E2
La Tuque, Québec 174/C3
Latur, India 68/D5
LATVIA 53/B2
Latvian S.S.R., U.S.S.R. 7/G3
Latvian S.S.R., U.S.S.R. 52/B3
Latvian S.S.R., U.S.S.R. 48/C4
Lauca (riv.), Bolivia 136/A6
Lauca (riv.), Chile 138/B1
Lauchhammer, E. Germany 22/E3
Laud, Ind. (†46725) 227/G2
Laudat, Dominica 161/E6
Lauder, Manitoba 179/B5
Lauder, Scotland 10/E3
Lauder, Scotland 15/F5
Lauderdale (co.), Ala. 195/C1
Lauderdale, Minn. (†55101) 255/G5
Lauderdale (co.), Miss. 256/G6
Lauderdale, Miss. (39335) 256/G5
Lauderdale, Tasmania 99/D4
Lauderdale (co.), Tenn. 237/B9
Lauderdale-by-the-Sea, Fla. (33308) 212/C3
Lauderdale Lakes, Fla. (†33313) 212/B3
Lauderhill, Fla. (33313) 212/B3
Lauenburg an der Elbe, W. Germany 22/D2
Lauenen, Switzerland 39/D4
Lauf an der Pegnitz, W. Germany 22/D4
Läufelfingen, Switzerland 39/E2
Laufen, Switzerland 39/D2
Laufen, W. Germany 22/E5
Laufenburg, Switzerland 39/F1
Laughery (creek), Ind. 227/G6
Laughing Fish (pt.), Mich. 250/B2
Laughlin A.F.B., Texas 303/D8
Lau Group (isls.), Fiji 87/J7
Lauingen, W. Germany 22/D4
Launceston, England 13/C7
Launceston, England 10/D5
Launceston, Tasmania 99/C3
Launceston, Tasmania 88/H8
Laune (riv.), Ireland 17/B7
Launglon Bok (isls.), Burma 72/C4
La Unión, Chile 138/D3
La Unión, Colombia 126/B7
La Unión, El Salvador 154/D4
La Unión, Mexico 150/J8
La Union, N. Mex. (†88021) 274/C7
La Unión, Peru 128/D7
La Union (prov.), Philippines 82/C2
La Unión, Spain 33/F4
La Unión, Venezuela 124/E3
Laupahoehoe, Hawaii (96764) 218/J4
Laupen, Switzerland 39/D3
Lauperswil, Switzerland 39/E3
Laura, Ill. (61451) 222/D3
Laura, Ohio (45337) 284/B6
Laura, Queensland 88/G3
Laura, Queensland 95/C2
Laura, Sask. 181/D4
Laura, S. Australia 94/F5
La Urbana, Venezuela 124/E4
Laurel, Del. (19956) 245/R6
Laurel, Fla. (33545) 212/D4
Laurel, Ind. (47024) 227/G6
Laurel, Iowa (50141) 229/H5
Laurel (co.), Ky. 237/N6
Laurel, Md. (*20810) 245/L4
Laurel, Miss. 188/J4
Laurel, Miss. (39440) 256/F7
Laurel, Mont. (59044) 262/H5
Laurel, Nebr. (68745) 264/G2
Laurel, Oreg. (†97123) 291/A2
Laurel, Pa. (†17322) 294/K6
Laurel, Wash. (†98672) 310/D5
Laurel (mt.), W. Va. 312/G4
Laurel Bay, S.C. (29902) 296/F7
Laurel Bloomery, Tenn. (37680) 237/T7
Laureldale, Pa. (19605) 294/L5
Laurel Dale, W. Va. (†26743) 312/H4
Laureles, Paraguay 144/D5
Laurel Fork, Va. (24352) 307/G7
Laurel Hill, Fla. (32567) 212/C5
Laurel Hill, N.C. (28351) 281/K5
Laurel Hill (mt.), Pa. 294/D5
Laurel Park, N.C. (†28739) 281/D4
Laurel River (lake), Ky. 237/N6
Laurel Run, Pa. (†18701) 294/F7
Laurel Springs, N.J. (08021) 273/B4
Laurelton, Pa. (17835) 294/H4
Laurelville, Ohio (43135) 284/E7
Laurence G. Hanscom Field, Mass. 249/B6
Laurence Harbor, N.J. (08879) 273/E3
Laurencekirk, Scotland 10/E2
Laurencekirk, Scotland 15/F4
Laurens (co.), Georgia 217/G6
Laurens, Iowa (50554) 229/D3
Laurens, N.Y. (13796) 276/K5
Laurens (co.), S.C. 296/D2
Laurens, S.C. (29360) 296/C3
Laurentides, Québec 172/D4
Laurentides Prov. Park, Québec 174/C3
Laurentides Prov. Park, Québec 172/F2
Lauria, Italy 34/E4
Laurie (lake), Manitoba 179/A3
Laurie, Mo. (65038) 261/G6
Laurier, Manitoba 179/C4
Laurier, Wash. (99146) 310/G2
Laurier-Station, Québec 172/F3
Laurierville, Québec 172/F3
Laurieston, Scotland 15/D6
Laurin, Mont. (†59749) 262/D5
Laurinburg, N.C. (28352) 281/K5
Lauritsala, Finland 18/Q6
Laurium, Mich. (49913) 250/A1
Laurot (Laut Kecil) (isls.), Indonesia 85/E7
Lausanne, Switzerland 39/C3
Lauscha, E. Germany 22/D3
Laut (isl.), Indonesia 85/F6
Laut (North Natuna) (isl.), Indonesia 85/D5
Lautaro, Chile 138/E2
Lauterbach, W. Germany 22/C3
Lauterbrunnen, Switzerland 39/E3
Lauterique, Honduras 154/D4
Laut Kecil (isls.), Indonesia 85/E7
Lautoka, Fiji 86/P10
Lauwers (chan.), Netherlands 27/J1
Lauwers Zee (bay), Netherlands 27/J2
Lauzon, Québec 172/J3
Lava (lake), Oreg. 291/F4
Lava Beds Nat'l Mon., Calif. 204/D2
Lavaca, Ala. (36911) 195/B6
Lavaca, Ark. (72941) 202/B3
Lavaca (co.), Texas 303/H8
Lavaca (bay), Texas 303/H9
Lava Hot Springs, Idaho (83246) 220/F7
Laval, France 28/C3
Laval, Québec 172/H4
Laval (bay), Québec 172/J1
La Vale-Narrows Park, Md. (21502) 245/C2
Lavalette, W. Va. (25535) 312/B6
Lavalle, Argentina 143/G4
La Valle, Wis. (53941) 317/F8
Lavalleja (dept.), Uruguay 145/D5
Lavallette, N.J. (08735) 273/E4
Lavalley, Colo. (†81153) 208/J8
Lavaltrie, Québec 172/D4
Lavamünd, Austria 41/C3
Lavapié (pt.), Chile 138/D1
Lavaur, France 28/D6
La Vecilla de Curueño, Spain 33/D1
Laveen, Ariz. (85339) 198/C5
La Vega (prov.), Dom. Rep. 158/D6
La Vega, Dom. Rep. 158/E5
La Vega, Dom. Rep. 156/D3
La Vega, Spain 33/C1
La Vela (cape), Colombia 126/D1
La Vela de Coro, Venezuela 124/D2
Lavelanet, France 28/E6
Lavello, Italy 34/E4
Lavenham, Manitoba 179/D5
L'Avenir, Québec 172/E4
La Vergne, Tenn. (37086) 237/H9
La Verkin, Utah (84745) 304/A6
La Verne, Calif. (91750) 204/D10
Laverne, Okla. (73848) 288/G1
La Vernia, Texas (78121) 303/K11
Laverton, Australia 87/C8
Laverton, W. Australia 88/C5
Laverton, W. Australia 92/C5
La Veta, Colo. (81055) 208/J8
Lavey-Morcles, Switzerland 39/D4
Lavezares, Philippines 82/E4
La Victoria, Colombia 126/A7
La Victoria, Apure, Venezuela 124/D4
La Victoria, Apure, Venezuela 124/C4
La Victoria, Aragua, Venezuela 124/E2
Lavieille (lake), Ontario 177/F2
La Vieja (pt.), Chile 138/A11
Lavik, Norway 18/D6
Lavillette, New Bruns. 170/E1
Lavina, Mont. (59046) 262/H4
Lavinia, Manitoba 179/B4
Lavinia, Tenn. (38348) 237/D9
La Vista, Nebr. (†68046) 264/J3
Lavon (lake), Texas 303/H1
Lavongai (isl.), Papua N.G. 87/F6
Lavongai (isls.), Papua N.G. 86/B1
Lavonia, Georgia (30553) 217/F2
Lavos, Portugal 33/B2
Lavoy, Alberta 182/E3
Lavras, Brazil 132/E8
Lavras, Brazil 135/D2
Lávrion, Greece 45/G7
Lawa (riv.), Fr. Guiana 131/D4
Lawa (riv.), Suriname 131/D4
Lawai, Hawaii (96765) 218/C2
Lawang, Indonesia 85/K2
Lawen, Oreg. (97740) 291/J4
Lawler, Iowa (52154) 229/J2
Lawler, Minn. (†55760) 255/E4
Lawlers, W. Australia 92/C5
Lawley, Ala. (36793) 195/E5
Lawn, Newf. 166/C4
Lawn, Pa. (17041) 294/J5
Lawn, Texas (79530) 303/E5
Lawndale, Calif. (90260) 204/B11
Lawndale, Ill. (61751) 222/D3
Lawndale, Minn. (†56579) 255/B4
Lawndale, N.C. (28090) 281/F4
Lawnhill, Br. Col. 184/A3
Lawn Hill, Queensland 95/A3
Lawnside, N.J. (08045) 273/B3
Lawra, Ghana 106/D6
Lawrence (co.), Ala. 195/D1
Lawrence (co.), Ark. 202/H1
Lawrence (co.), Ill. 222/F5
Lawrence (co.), Ind. 227/E7
Lawrence, Ind. (46226) 227/E5
Lawrence, Kans. 188/G3
Lawrence, Kansas (66044) 232/G3
Lawrence (co.), Ky. 237/R4
Lawrence, Mass. 188/M2
Lawrence, Mass. (*01840) 249/K2
Lawrence, Mich. (49064) 250/C6
Lawrence (co.), Miss. 256/D7
Lawrence, Miss. (39336) 256/F6
Lawrence (co.), Mo. 261/E8
Lawrence, Nebr. (68957) 264/F4
Lawrence, N.Y. (11559) 276/P7
Lawrence, N. Zealand 100/B6
Lawrence, N.C. (†27886) 281/O2
Lawrence (co.), Ohio 284/E8
Lawrence (co.), Pa. 294/B4
Lawrence (co.), S. Dak. 298/B5
Lawrence (co.), Tenn. 237/G10
Lawrenceburg, Ind. (47025) 227/H6
Lawrenceburg, Ky. (40342) 237/M4
Lawrenceburg, Tenn. (38464) 237/G10
Lawrence Park○, Pa. (†16501) 294/C1
Lawrenceport, Ind. (†47446) 227/D7
Lawrence Station, New Bruns. 170/C3
Lawrencetown, Nova Scotia 168/C4
Lawrenceville, Georgia (30245) 217/D3
Lawrenceville, Ill. (62439) 222/F5
Lawrenceville, Ind. (†47041) 227/H6
Lawrenceville○, N.J. (08648) 273/D3
Lawrenceville, N.Y. (12949) 276/L1
Lawrenceville, Ohio (†45501) 284/C6
Lawrenceville, Pa. (16929) 294/H2
Lawrenceville, Québec 172/E4
Lawrenceville, Va. (23868) 307/N7
Lawson, Ark. (71750) 202/F7
Lawson, Colo. (†80452) 208/H3
Lawson, Mo. (64062) 261/D4
Lawson, Sask. 181/E5
Lawsonville, N.C. (27022) 281/J2
Lawtell, La. (70550) 238/F5
Lawtey, Fla. (32058) 212/D1
Lawton, Ind. (†46996) 227/D2
Lawton, Iowa (51030) 229/A4
Lawton, Kansas (66752) 232/H4
Lawton, Ky. (41153) 237/P4
Lawton, Mich. (49065) 250/D6
Lawton, N. Dak. (58345) 282/O3
Lawton, Okla. 146/J6
Lawton, Okla. 188/G4
Lawton, Okla. (73501) 288/K5
Lawton, Pa. (18828) 294/K2
Lawton, W. Va. (25863) 312/E7
Lawtonka (lake), Okla. 288/K5
Lawu (mt.), Indonesia 85/J2
Lax, Georgia (†31650) 217/F8
Lax, Switzerland 39/F4
Laxå, Sweden 18/J7
Laxey, I. of Man 13/C3
Laxford, Loch (inlet), Scotland 15/C2
Lay (dam), Ala. 195/E5
Lay (lake), Ala. 195/F4
Lay (pt.), Alaska 196/F1
Lay, Colo. (†81625) 208/D2
Lay, Mui (cape), Vietnam 72/E3
Layang Layang, Malaysia 72/E5
Layland, W. Va. (25864) 312/E7
Layopolis (Sand Fork), W. Va. (†26430) 312/E5
Layou (riv.), Dominica 161/E6
Layou, St. Vin. & Grens. 161/A9
Laysan (isl.), Hawaii 87/J3
Laysan (isl.), Hawaii 188/E6
Laysan (isl.), Hawaii 218/B5
Laysville, Conn. (†06371) 210/F3
Layton, Fla. (†33050) 212/F7
Layton, N.J. (07851) 273/D1
Layton, Utah (84041) 304/C2
Laytonsville, Md. (20760) 245/K4
Laytonville, Calif. (95454) 204/B4
Laytown-Bettystown-Mornington, Ireland 17/J4
Lazarev Station, Ant. 5/C1
Lazdijai, U.S.S.R. 53/B3
Lazear, Colo. (81420) 208/D5
Lazi, Philippines 82/D6
Łaziska Górne, Poland 47/A4
Lazy Lake, Fla. (†33301) 212/B3
Lea (riv.), England 13/G6
Lea (co.), N. Mex. 274/F6
Leaburg, Oreg. (97401) 291/E3
Leach, Okla. (74351) 288/S2
Leach, Tenn. (38349) 237/E9
Leachville, Ark. (72438) 202/K2
Leacross, Sask. 181/H2
Lead, S. Dak. 188/F2
Lead, S. Dak. (57754) 298/B5
Leadbetter (pt.), Wash. 310/A4
Leader, Minn. (56462) 255/D4
Leader, Sask. 181/B5
Lead Hill, Ark. (72644) 202/D1
Leadington, Mo. (†63640) 261/M7
Leadmine (brook), Conn. 210/C1
Lead Mine, W. Va. (†26290) 312/G4

Lingshan 399

Leti (isls.), Indonesia 85/H7
Leticia, Colombia 126/F10
Leticia, Colombia 120/B3
L'Etivaz, Switzerland 39/D4
Letka, U.S.S.R. 52/H3
Leto, Fla. (†33614) 212/C2
Letohatchee, Ala. (36047) 195/E6
Leton, La. (†71072) 238/D1
Letona, Ark. (72085) 202/G3
Letong, Indonesia 85/D5
Le Touquet-Paris-Plage, France 28/D2
Letpadan, Burma 72/C3
Le Tréport, France 28/D2
Letsôk-aw Kyun (isl.), Burma 72/C5
Lette, N.S. Wales 97/B4
Letterkenny, Ireland 10/B3
Letterkenny, Ireland 17/F2
Letterkenny Army Depot, Pa. 294/G6
Lettermullan (isl.), Ireland 17/B5
Letts, Ind. (†47240) 227/F6
Letts, Iowa (52754) 229/L6
Lettsworth, La. (70753) 238/G5
Leucadia, Calif. (92024) 204/H10
Leucate (mts.), France 28/E6
Leuchars, Scotland 15/F4
Leuk, Switzerland 39/E4
Leukerbad, Switzerland 39/E4
Leupp, Ariz. (86035) 198/E3
Leurbost, Scotland 15/B2
Leuser (mt.), Indonesia 85/B5
Leuven, Belgium 27/F7
Leuze-en-Hainaut, Belgium 27/D7
Levádhia, Greece 45/F6
Levallois-Perret, France 28/A1
Levan, Utah (84639) 304/C4
Levanger, Norway 18/G5
Levant, Kansas (67743) 232/A2
Levant○, Maine (04456) 243/F6
Levanzo (isl.), Italy 34/D5
Levasy, Mo. (64066) 261/S5
Le Vauclin, Martinique 161/D6
Levee, Ky. (†40337) 237/O5
Level, Md. (†21078) 245/O2
Level Green, Ky. (†40456) 237/N6
Level Land, S.C. (†29655) 296/C3
Levelland, Texas (79336) 303/B4
Levelock, Alaska (99625) 196/G3
Level Plains, Ala. (†36322) 195/G8
Levels, W. Va. (25431) 312/J4
Leven, Scotland 10/E2
Leven, Scotland 15/F4
Leven, Loch (inlet), Scotland 15/D4
Leven (lake), Scotland 15/E4
Leven (riv.), Tasmania 99/B3
Leveque (cape), Australia 87/C7
L'Eveque (cape), N. Zealand 100/D7
Lévêque (cape), W. Australia 88/C3
Lévêque (cape), W. Australia 92/C2
Leverburgh, Scotland 15/B3
Le Verdon-sur-Mer, France 28/C5
Leverett○, Mass. (01054) 249/E3
Levering, Mich. (49755) 250/E3
Leverkusen, W. Germany 22/B3
Levesque, New Bruns. 170/C1
Levice, Czech. 41/E2
Levick (mt.) 5/B8
Levie, France 28/B7
Le Vigan, France 28/E5
Levin, N. Zealand 100/E4
Lévis (co.), Québec 172/J3
Lévis, Québec 172/J3
Lévis, Québec 174/C3
Levisa Fork (riv.), Va. 307/C5
Levítha (isl.), Greece 45/H7
Levittown, N.Y. (11756) 276/R7
Levittown, Pa. (*19053) 294/N5
Levittown, P. Rico 161/D1
Levkás, Greece 45/E6
Levkás (isl.), Greece 45/E6
Levoča, Czech. 41/F2
Lévrier (bay), Mauritania 106/A4
Levuka, Fiji 87/H7
Levukaa, Fiji 86/Q10
Levy (co.), Fla. 212/D2
Levy (lake), Fla. 212/D2
Levy, N. Mex. (†87752) 274/E2
Lewe, Burma 72/B3
Lewellen, Nebr. (69147) 264/B3
Lewes, Del. (19958) 245/T5
Lewes, England 13/H7
Lewes, England 10/G5
Lewis, Colo. (81327) 208/B8
Lewis (isl.), Fla. 212/B3
Lewis (co.), Idaho 220/B3
Lewis, Ind. (47858) 227/C6
Lewis, Iowa (51544) 229/C6
Lewis, Kansas (67552) 232/C4
Lewis (co.), Ky. 237/P3
Lewis, Manitoba 179/F5
Lewis (lake), Manitoba 179/G2
Lewis (co.), Mo. 261/J2
Lewis, Mo. (†64735) 261/E6
Lewis (range), Mont. 262/C2
Lewis (co.), N.Y. 276/K3
Lewis, N.Y. (12950) 276/N2
Lewis (dist.), Scotland 15/B2
Lewis (dist.), Scotland 10/C1
Lewis, Butt of (prom.), Scotland 15/B2
Lewis, Butt of (prom.), Scotland 10/C1
Lewis, S.C. (†29706) 296/E2
Lewis (co.), Tenn. 237/F9
Lewis (creek), Vt. 268/A3
Lewis (co.), Wash. 310/C4
Lewis (riv.), Wash. 310/C5
Lewis (co.), W. Va. 312/E4
Lewis, Wis. (54851) 317/B4
Lewis (lake), Wyo. 319/B1
Lewis and Clark (co.), Mont. 262/D3
Lewis and Clark (lake), Nebr. 264/G2
Lewis and Clark (lake), S. Dak. 298/O8
Lewis and Clark Village, Mo. (†64484) 261/C3
Lewisberry, Pa. (17339) 294/J5
Lewisburg, Ky. (42256) 237/G6
Lewisburg, La. (†70525) 238/F6
Lewisburg, Ohio (45338) 284/A6
Lewisburg, Pa. (17837) 294/J4
Lewisburg, Tenn. (37091) 237/H10
Lewisburg, W. Va. (24901) 312/E7
Lewis Center, Ohio (43035) 284/D5
Lewis Creek, Ind. (†47234) 227/F6
Lewisetta, Va. (22505) 307/R4
Lewisham, England 10/B5
Lewisham, England 13/H8
Lewis Hill (mt.), Newf. 166/C4
Lewisport, Ky. (42351) 237/H5
Lewisporte, Newf. 166/C4
Lewis Run, Pa. (16738) 294/E2
Lewis Smith (dam), Ala. 195/D3
Lewis Smith (lake), Ala. 195/D2
Lewiston, Calif. (96052) 204/C3
Lewiston, Idaho 188/C1
Lewiston, Idaho (83501) 220/A3
Lewiston, Maine 188/N2
Lewiston, Maine (04240) 243/C7
Lewiston, Mich. (49756) 250/E4
Lewiston, Minn. (55952) 255/G7
Lewiston, Nebr. (68380) 264/H4
Lewiston, N.Y. (14092) 276/B4
Lewiston, N.C. (27849) 281/P2
Lewiston, Utah (84320) 304/C2
Lewiston, Vt. (†05055) 268/C4
Lewistown, Ill. (61542) 222/C3
Lewistown, Md. (21701) 245/J2
Lewistown, Mo. (63452) 261/J2
Lewistown, Mont. (59457) 262/G3
Lewistown, Ohio (43333) 284/C5
Lewistown, Pa. (17044) 294/G4
Lewisville, Ark. (71845) 202/C7
Lewisville, Idaho (83431) 220/F6
Lewisville, Ind. (47352) 227/G5
Lewisville, Minn. (56060) 255/D7
Lewisville, Ohio (43754) 284/H6
Lewisville (Ulysses), Pa. (16948) 294/G2
Lewisville, Pa. (19351) 294/L6
Lewisville, Texas (*75067) 303/G1
Lewisville (lake), Texas 303/G1
Lewvan, Sask. 181/H5
Lexa, Ark. (72355) 202/J4
Lexie, Miss. (†39667) 256/D8
Lexington, Ala. (35648) 195/D1
Lexington, Ark. (†72153) 202/F2
Lexington, Georgia (30648) 217/F3
Lexington, Ill. (61753) 222/E3
Lexington, Ind. (47138) 227/F7
Lexington, Ky. (*40501) 237/N4
Lexington, Ky. 146/K6
Lexington, Ky. 188/K3
Lexington○, Mass. (02173) 249/B6
Lexington, Mich. (48450) 250/G5
Lexington, Minn. (†55014) 255/G5
Lexington, Miss. (39095) 256/D4
Lexington, Mo. (64067) 261/E4
Lexington, Nebr. (68850) 264/E4
Lexington, N.Y. (12452) 276/M6
Lexington, N.C. (27292) 281/J3
Lexington, Ohio (44904) 284/E4
Lexington, Okla. (73051) 288/M4
Lexington, Oreg. (97839) 291/H2
Lexington (co.), S.C. 296/E4
Lexington, S.C. (29072) 296/E4
Lexington, Tenn. (38351) 237/E9
Lexington, Texas (78947) 303/G7
Lexington (I.C.), Va. (24450) 307/J5
Lexington Blue Grass Army Depot, Ky. 237/N5
Lexington Park, Md. (20653) 245/M7
Lexsy, Georgia (†30401) 217/H6
Leyba, N. Mex. (87542) 274/D3
Leyburn, England 13/F3
Leyden○, Mass. (†01301) 249/D2
Lye, China 77/G7
Leyland, England 13/G1
Leyland, England 10/F1
Leyond (riv.), Manitoba 179/F3
Leysin, Switzerland 39/C4
Leyte (prov.), Philippines 82/E5
Leyte (isl.), Philippines 54/O8
Leyte (gulf), Philippines 82/E5
Leyte (isl.), Philippines 85/H3
Leyte (isl.), Philippines 82/E5
Lezajsk, Poland 47/F3
Lezama, Argentina 143/H7
Lézarde (riv.), Martinique 161/D6
Lezhë, Albania 45/D5
Lézignan-Corbières, France 28/E6
Lezuza, Spain 33/E3
L'gov, U.S.S.R. 52/E4
Lhanbryde, Scotland 15/E3
Lhari, China 77/D5
Lhasa, China 77/D6
Lhasa, China 2/P4
Lhasa, China 54/L7
Lhazê (Lhatse), China 77/C6
Lhazhong, China 77/C5
Lhokseumawe, Indonesia 85/B4
Lhorong, China 77/E5
Lhozhag, China 77/D6
Lhünzê, China 77/D6
Lhünzhub, China 77/D5
Liancheng, China 77/J6
Lianga, Philippines 82/E6
Lianga (bay), Philippines 82/F6
Lianping, China 77/H7
Lian Xian, China 77/H7
Lianyungang (Lienyünkang), China 77/J5
Lianyunggang, China 54/N6
Liao (riv.), China 54/O5
Liaodong Bandao (pen.), China 77/K3
Liao He (riv.), China 77/K3
Liaoning (prov.), China 77/K3
Liaoyang, China 77/K3
Liaoyuan, China 77/K3
Liard (riv.) 162/D3
Liard (riv.), Br. Col. 184/L2
Liard (riv.), Canada 146/F3
Liard (riv.), N.W. Terrs. 187/F4
Liard (riv.), Yukon 187/E3
Liard River, Br. Col. 184/L2
Libáň, Czech. 41/C1
Líbano, Colombia 126/C5
Libau, Manitoba 179/F4
Libby, Minn. (†55760) 255/E4
Libby, Mont. (59923) 262/A2
Libenge, Zaire 115/C3
Liberal, Kansas (67901) 232/B4
Liberal, Mo. (64762) 261/D7
Liberal, Oreg. (†97042) 291/B3
Liberdade, Brazil 135/D3
Liberec, Czech. 41/C1
Liberia 2/J5
Liberia 102/B4
LIBERIA 106/C7
Liberia, C. Rica 154/E5
Liberta, Ant. & Bar. 161/E11
Libertad, Belize 154/C1
Libertad, Uruguay 145/C5
Libertad, Barinas, Venezuela 124/D3
Libertad, Cojedes, Venezuela 124/D3
Liberty, Ariz. (†85326) 198/C5
Liberty (co.), Fla. 212/B1
Liberty (co.), Georgia 217/J7
Liberty, Ill. (62347) 222/B4
Liberty, Ind. (47353) 227/H5
Liberty, Kansas (67351) 232/G4
Liberty, Ky. (42539) 237/M6
Liberty, Maine (04949) 243/E7
Liberty○, Maine (04949) 243/E7
Liberty (lake), Md. 245/L3
Liberty, Miss. (39645) 256/C8
Liberty, Mo. (64068) 261/R5
Liberty (co.), Mont. 262/E2
Liberty, Nebr. (68381) 264/H4
Liberty (mt.), N.H. 268/D3
Liberty, N.Y. (12754) 276/L7
Liberty, N.C. (27298) 281/K3
Liberty, Pa. (16930) 294/H2
Liberty, Pa. (†15100) 294/C7
Liberty, Sask. 181/F4
Liberty, S.C. (29657) 296/B2
Liberty, Tenn. (37095) 237/K8
Liberty (co.), Texas 303/K7
Liberty, Texas (77575) 303/K7
Liberty, Wash. (†98922) 310/E3
Liberty, W. Va. (25124) 312/C5
Liberty Center, Ind. (46766) 227/G3
Liberty Center, Iowa (50145) 229/F6
Liberty Center, Ohio (43532) 284/B3
Liberty Corner, N.J. (07938) 273/D2
Liberty Grove, Md. (†21918) 245/O2
Liberty Hill, Conn. (†06249) 210/G2
Liberty Hill, La. (†71008) 238/E2
Liberty Hill, S.C. (29074) 296/F3
Liberty Lake, Wash. (99019) 310/J3
Liberty Mills, Ind. (46946) 227/F2
Liberty Pole, Wis. (†54665) 317/D8
Libertytown, Md. (21762) 245/J3
Libertyville, Ala. (†36420) 195/F8
Libertyville, Ill. (60048) 222/B4
Libertyville, Iowa (52567) 229/K7
Libiaz, Poland 47/D3
Libin, Belgium 27/G9
Libochovice, Czech. 41/B1
Libon, Philippines 82/D4
Libong, Ko (isl.), Thailand 72/C6
Libourne, France 28/C5
Libramont-Chevigny, Belgium 27/G9
Library, Pa. (15129) 294/B7
Libres, Mexico 150/O1
Libreville (cap.), Gabon 2/K6
Libreville (cap.), Gabon 115/A3
Libreville (cap.), Gabon 102/C4
Libuse, La. (71348) 238/F4
Libya 2/K4
Libya 102/D2
LIBYA 111/B2
Libyan (des.) 102/E2
Libyan (des.), Egypt 111/E2
Libyan (plat.), Egypt 111/E1
Libyan (des.), Libya 111/D2
Libyan (plat.), Libya 111/D1
Libyan (des.), Sudan 111/E3
Licancábur, Cerro (mt.), Chile 138/B4
Licantén, Chile 138/A10
Licata, Italy 34/D6
Lice, Turkey 63/J3
Lichfield, England 13/F5
Lichfield, England 10/G2
Lichinga, Mozambique 102/F6
Lichinga, Mozambique 118/F2
Lichtenberg, E. Germany 22/F4
Lichtenfels, W. Germany 22/D3
Lichtenrade, W. Germany 22/F4
Lichterfelde, W. Germany 22/E4
Lichtervelde, Belgium 27/C6
Lick (creek), Tenn. 237/R8
Lick Creek, Ill. (†62912) 222/D6
Licking, North Fork (riv.), Ky. 237/O3
Licking, South Fork (riv.), Ky. 237/N3
Licking (riv.), Ky. 237/N3
Licking, Mo. (65542) 261/J8
Licking (co.), Ohio 284/F5
Licking (riv.), Ohio 284/F5
Licking (creek), Pa. 294/F6
Licosa (cape), Italy 34/E4
Lida, Ky. (†40741) 237/O6
Lida (lake), Minn. 255/C4
Lida, U.S.S.R. 52/C4
Lidcombe, N.S. Wales 97/J3
Liddel Water (riv.), Scotland 15/F5
Lidderdale, Iowa (51452) 229/D4
Liddes, Switzerland 39/D5
Liddon (gulf), N.W. Terrs. 187/G4
Lidgerwood, N. Dak. (58053) 282/R7
Lidice, Czech. 41/C1
Lidingö, Sweden 18/H1
Lidköping, Sweden 18/H7
Lido di Ostia, Italy 34/F7
Lido di Venezia, Italy 34/D2
Lidzbark, Poland 47/D2
Lidzbark Warmiński, Poland 47/E1
Liebenthal, Kansas (67553) 232/C3
Liebenthal, Sask. 181/B5
Liechtensteig, Switzerland 39/H2
Liechtenstein 7/F4
LIECHTENSTEIN 39/J2
Liedekerke, Belgium 27/D7
Liége (riv.), Alberta 182/D1
Liège (prov.), Belgium 27/H7
Liège, Belgium 7/E3
Liège, Belgium 27/H7
Liegnitz (Legnica), Poland 47/C3
Lieksa, Finland 18/R5
Lienyünkang (Lianyungang), China 77/J5
Lienz, Austria 41/B3
Liepāja, U.S.S.R. 7/F3
Liepāja, U.S.S.R. 53/A2
Liepāja, U.S.S.R. 48/B4
Liepāja, U.S.S.R. 52/B3
Lier, Belgium 27/F6
Lierneux, Belgium 27/H8
Lierre (Lier), Belgium 27/F6
Liestal, Switzerland 39/E2
Liévin, France 28/E2
Lièvre (riv.), Québec 172/B4
Lièvres (isl.), Québec 172/H2
Liezen, Austria 41/C3
Liffey (riv.), Ireland 17/H5
Liffey (riv.), Ireland 10/C4
Lifford, Ireland 10/C3
Lifford, Ireland 17/F2
Lifu (isl.), New Caled. 87/G8
Lifu (isl.), New Caled. 86/H4
Ligao, Philippines 82/D4
Ligatne, U.S.S.R. 53/C2
Liggett, Ky. (†40831) 237/P7
Lightfoot, Va. (23090) 307/P6
Lighthouse (pt.), Fla. 212/B2
Light House (pt.), Mich. 250/D3
Lighthouse Point, Fla. (33064) 212/F5
Lightning (creek), Oreg. 291/L2
Lightning (creek), Wyo. 319/G2
Lightning Ridge, N.S. Wales 97/E1
Lightsville, Ohio (†45362) 284/A5
Lignite, N. Dak. (58752) 282/F2
Ligon, Ky. (41646) 237/R6
Ligonha (riv.), Mozambique 118/F3
Ligonier, Ind. (46767) 227/F2
Ligonier, Pa. (15658) 294/D5
Liguria (reg.), Italy 34/B2
Ligurian (sea), Italy 34/B3
Lihir Group (isls.), Papua N.G. 86/C1
Lihou (cays), Coral Sea Is. Terr. 88/J3
Lihue, Hawaii (96766) 218/C2
Lihue, Hawaii 188/E5
Lihula, U.S.S.R. 53/C1
Lijiang, China 77/F6
Likasi, Panda-, Zaire 115/E6
Likati, Zaire 115/D3
Likely, Br. Col. 184/G4
Likely, Calif. (96116) 204/E2
Likhoslavl', U.S.S.R. 52/E3
Likouala (riv.), Congo 115/C3
Lila (lake), N.Y. 276/L2
Lilac, Sask. 181/D3
Lilbourn, Mo. (63862) 261/N9
Lilburn, Georgia (30247) 217/D3
Lileah, Tasmania 99/B2
L'Île-Rousse, France 28/B6
Liles (pt.), Chile 138/F2
Lilesville, N.C. (28091) 281/K5
Lilienfeld, Austria 41/C3
Lille, France 7/E3
Lille, France 28/E2
Lille, Maine (04749) 243/G1
Lilleå (riv.), Denmark 21/B5
Lille Baelt (chan.), Denmark 21/C7
Lillehammer, Norway 18/F6
Lillesand, Norway 18/F7
Lillestrøm, Norway 18/E3
Lillian, Ala. (36549) 195/D10
Lillie, La. (71256) 238/E1
Lilliesleaf, Scotland 15/F5
Lillington, N.C. (27546) 281/M4
Lillinonah (lake), Conn. 210/B3
Lilliwaup, Wash. (98555) 310/B3
Lillo, Spain 33/E3
Lillooet, Br. Col. 162/D5
Lillooet, Br. Col. 184/G5
Lillooet (riv.), Br. Col. 184/F5
Lilly, Georgia (31051) 217/E6
Lilly, Ill. (†61755) 222/D3
Lilly, Pa. (15938) 294/E5
Lilly Chapel, Ohio (†43162) 284/D6
Lillydale, Victoria 97/J4
Lilongwe (cap.), Malawi 2/L6
Lilongwe (cap.), Malawi 102/F6
Lilongwe (cap.), Malawi 115/F6
Liloy, Philippines 82/D6
Lily, Ky. (40740) 237/N6
Lily, S. Dak. (57250) 298/O3
Lily, Wis. (54445) 317/J5
Lilydale, Minn. (†55050) 255/G5
Lily Dale, N.Y. (14752) 276/B6
Lilydale, Tasmania 99/D3
Lily Plain, Sask. 181/E2
Lim (fjord), Denmark 18/E8
Lim (riv.), Yugoslavia 45/D4
Lima, Ill. (62348) 222/B3
Lima (isls.), Indonesia 85/F7
Lima, Pulau (isl.), Malaysia 72/F6
Lima, Mont. (59739) 262/D6
Lima (res.), Mont. 262/D6
Lima, N.Y. (14485) 276/E5
Lima, Ohio (*45801) 284/B4
Lima, Ohio 188/K2
Lima (New Lima), Okla. (†74858) 288/D4
Lima, Paraguay 144/D3
Lima, Pa. (†19037) 294/L7
Lima (dept.), Peru 128/D8
Lima (cap.), Peru 2/F6
Lima (cap.), Peru 120/B4
Lima (cap.), Peru 128/D8
Lima (riv.), Portugal 33/B2
Lima (pt.), P. Rico 161/F2
Lima Center, Wis. (†53190) 317/J10
Limache, Chile 138/F2
Lima Duarte, Brazil 135/E2
Limal, Bolivia 136/C8
Limanowa, Poland 47/E4
Limarí (riv.), Chile 138/A8
Limasawa (isl.), Philippines 82/E6
Limassol, Cyprus 59/B3
Limassol, Cyprus 63/E5
Limavady (dist.), N. Ireland 17/H1
Limavady, N. Ireland 10/C3
Limavady, N. Ireland 17/H1
Limaville, Ohio (44640) 284/H4
Limay (riv.), Argentina 120/C6
Limay (riv.), Argentina 143/C4
Limbach-Oberfrohna, E. Germany 22/E3
Limbani, Peru 128/H10
Limbaži, U.S.S.R. 53/C2
Limbé, Haiti 158/C5
Limbourg, Belgium 27/J7
Limbunya, North. Terr. 93/B4
Limburg (prov.), Belgium 27/G7
Limburg (Limbourg), Belgium 27/J7
Limburg (prov.), Netherlands 27/H6
Limburg an der Lahn, W. Germany 22/C3
Lime, Oreg. (†97907) 291/K3
Limedsforsen, Sweden 18/H6
Limeira, Brazil 132/E8
Limeira, Brazil 135/C3
Lime Kiln, Md. (†21701) 245/J3
Limekilns, Scotland 15/D1
Limenária, Greece 45/G5
Limerick (co.), Ireland 17/D7
Limerick, Ireland 17/D6
Limerick, Ireland 10/B4
Limerick, Ireland 7/D3
Limerick○, Maine (04048) 243/B8
Limerick, Sask. 181/E6
Limeridge, Wis. (53940) 317/F9
Lime Rock, Conn. (†06039) 210/B1
Lime Springs, Iowa (52155) 229/J2
Limestone (co.), Ala. 195/E1
Limestone, Ark. (72628) 202/D2
Limestone, Fla. (†33865) 212/E4
Limestone, Maine (04750) 243/H2
Limestone○, Maine (04750) 243/H2
Limestone, Mont. (†59028) 262/F5
Limestone, N.Y. (14753) 276/C6
Limestone, Tenn. (37681) 237/R8
Limestone (co.), Texas 303/H6
Lime Village, Alaska (†99673) 196/G2
Limfjorden (fjord), Denmark 21/D4
Limfjorden (fjord), Denmark 21/A4
Limington, Maine (04049) 243/B8
Limington○, Maine (04049) 243/B8
Limmat (riv.), Switzerland 39/F2
Limmen (bight), North. Terr. 88/F2
Limmen (bight), North. Terr. 93/D3
Limmen Bight (riv.), North. Terr. 88/F3
Limmen Bight (riv.), North. Terr. 93/D4
Límni, Greece 45/F6
Límnos (isl.), Greece 45/G6
Limoeiro, Brazil 132/H4
Limoeiro do Norte, Brazil 132/G4
Limoges, France 7/E4
Limoges, France 28/D5
Limoges, Ontario 177/J2
Limon, Colo. (80828) 208/M4
Limón, C. Rica 146/K8
Limón, C. Rica 154/F6
Limón, Honduras 154/E3
Limonade, Haiti 158/C5
Limonar, Cuba 158/D1
Limoquije, Bolivia 136/C4
Limousin (trad. prov.), France, 29
Limousin (reg.), France 28/D5
Limoux, France 28/E6
Limpio, Paraguay 144/B4
Limpopo (riv.) 102/E7
Limpopo (riv.), Botswana 118/D4
Limpopo (riv.), Mozambique 118/E4
Limpopo (riv.), S. Africa 118/D4
Lim Rock, Ala. (†35776) 195/F1
Linapacan (isl.), Philippines 82/B5
Linapacan (str.), Philippines 82/B5
Linard (peak), Switzerland 39/K3
Linares, Chile 138/A11
Linares, Chile 120/B6
Linares, Mexico 150/K4
Linares, Spain 33/E3
Linares, Spain 7/D5
Linaria, Alberta 182/C2
Lincang, China 77/E7
Linch, Wyo. (82640) 319/F2
Lincklaen, N.Y. (†13052) 276/J5
Lincoln (sea) 146/M1
Lincoln (sea) 4/A12
Lincoln, Ala. (35096) 195/F3
Lincoln, Argentina 143/F7
Lincoln (co.), Ark. 202/G6
Lincoln, Ark. (72744) 202/B2
Lincoln, Calif. (95648) 204/B8
Lincoln (isl.), China 85/E2
Lincoln (co.), Colo. 208/M5
Lincoln (mt.), Colo. 208/G4
Lincoln, Del. (19960) 245/S5
Lincoln, England 13/G4
Lincoln, England 10/F4
Lincoln (co.), Georgia 217/H3
Lincoln (co.), Idaho 220/D6
Lincoln, Ill. (62656) 222/D3
Lincoln, Ind. (†46994) 227/E3
Lincoln, Iowa (50652) 229/H4
Lincoln (co.), Kansas 232/D2
Lincoln, Kansas (67455) 232/D2
Lincoln (co.), Ky. 237/M6
Lincoln (par.), La. 238/E1
Lincoln (co.), Maine 243/D7
Lincoln, Maine (04457) 243/G5
Lincoln○, Maine (04457) 243/G5
Lincoln○, Mass. (01773) 249/B6
Lincoln, Mich. (48742) 250/F4
Lincoln (co.), Minn. 255/B6
Lincoln (co.), Miss. 256/D8
Lincoln (co.), Mo. 261/L4
Lincoln, Mo. (65338) 261/F6
Lincoln (co.), Mont. 262/A2
Lincoln, Mont. (59639) 262/D4
Lincoln (co.), Nebr. 264/D4
Lincoln (cap.), Nebr. 146/J5
Lincoln (cap.), Nebr. 188/G2
Lincoln (cap.), Nebr. (*68501) 264/H4
Lincoln (co.), Nev. 266/F5
Lincoln○, N.H. (03251) 268/D3
Lincoln (mt.), N.H. 268/D3
Lincoln (co.), N. Mex. 274/D5
Lincoln, N. Mex. (88338) 274/D5
Lincoln (co.), N.C. 281/G3
Lincoln, N. Dak. (†58501) 282/J6
Lincoln (sea), N.W. Terrs. 187/M1
Lincoln (co.), Okla. 288/N3
Lincoln, Ontario 177/E4
Lincoln (co.), Oreg. 291/D3
Lincoln, Pa. (†15037) 294/C7
Lincoln (co.), S. Dak. 298/R7
Lincoln (co.), Tenn. 237/H10
Lincoln, Texas (78948) 303/H7
Lincoln (creek), Utah 30r/C2
Lincoln○, Vt. (†05443) 268/B3
Lincoln (co.), Wash. 310/G3
Lincoln, Wash. (99147) 310/G3
Lincoln (co.), W. Va. 312/B6
Lincoln (co.), Wis. 317/G5
Lincoln (co.), Wyo. 319/B3
Lincoln Beach, Oreg. (†97341) 291/C3
Lincoln Boyhood Nat'l Mem., Ind. 227/C8
Lincoln Center, Maine (04458) 243/G5
Lincoln Center, Mass. (01773) 249/B6
Lincoln City, Ind. (47552) 227/C8
Lincoln City, Oreg. (97367) 291/C3
Lincoln Gap (pass), Vt. 268/B3
Lincoln Heights, Ohio (†45201) 284/C9
Lincolnia, Va. (†22313) 307/S3
Lincoln Park, Colo. (†81212) 208/J6
Lincoln Park, Georgia (†30286) 217/D5
Lincoln Park, Mich. (48146) 250/B7
Lincoln Park, N.J. (07035) 273/A1
Lincolnshire (co.), England 13/G4
Lincolnshire, Ill. (†60015) 222/B5
Lincolnton, Georgia (30817) 217/G3
Lincolnton, N.C. (28092) 281/G4
Lincoln University, Pa. (19352) 294/L6
Lincolnville, Ind. (†46992) 227/F3
Lincolnville, Kansas (66858) 232/F3
Lincolnville, Maine (04849) 243/E7
Lincolnville○, Maine (04849) 243/E7
Lincolnville, Nova Scotia 168/G3
Lincolnville, S.C. (†29483) 296/G6
Lincolnville Center, Maine (04850) 243/E7
Lincoln Wolds (hills), England 13/G4
Lincolnwood, Ill. (†60645) 222/B5
Lincroft, N.J. (07738) 273/E3
L'Incudine (mt.), France 28/B7
Lind, Wash. (99341) 310/G4
Linda, Calif. (†95901) 204/D4
Lindale, Alberta 182/C3
Lindale, Georgia (30147) 217/B2
Lindale, Texas (75771) 303/J5
Lindau, W. Germany 22/C5
Lindberg, Alberta 182/E3
Linden, Ala. (36748) 195/C6
Linden, Alberta 182/D4
Linden, Ariz. (†85901) 198/E4
Linden, Calif. (95236) 204/D5
Linden, Guyana 131/L2
Linden, Ind. (47955) 227/D4
Linden, Iowa (50146) 229/E5
Linden, Mich. (48451) 250/F6
Linden, N.J. (07036) 273/A3
Linden, N.C. (28356) 281/M4
Linden (mts.), Switzerland 39/F2
Linden, Tenn. (37096) 237/F9
Linden, Texas (75563) 303/K4
Linden, Va. (22642) 307/M3
Linden, W. Va. (25256) 312/D5
Linden, Wis. (53553) 317/F10
Linden Beach, Ontario 177/B6
Lindenhurst, Ill. (†60046) 222/B4
Lindenhurst, N.Y. (11757) 276/O9
Lindenwold, N.J. (08021) 273/B4
Lindenwood, Ill. (61049) 222/D1
Lindesberg, Sweden 18/J7
Lindesnes (cape), Norway 7/E3
Lindesnes (cape), Norway 18/E8
Lindi (reg.), Tanzania 115/G5
Lindi, Tanzania 102/F5
Lindi, Tanzania 115/G5
Lindi (riv.), Zaire 115/E3
Lindisfarne (Holy) (dist.), England 13/F2
Lindisfarne (Holy) (isl.), England 10/F3
Lindley, N.Y. (14858) 276/F6
Lindon, Colo. (80740) 208/N3
Lindon, Utah (†84062) 304/C3
Lindos, Greece 45/J7
Lindrith, N. Mex. (87029) 274/C2
Lindsay, Calif. (93247) 204/F7
Lindsay, La. (†70748) 238/H5
Lindsay, Mont. (59339) 262/L3
Lindsay, Nebr. (68644) 264/G3
Lindsay, Okla. (73052) 288/L5
Lindsay, Ontario 177/F3
Lindsborg, Kansas (67456) 232/E3
Lindsey, Ohio (43442) 284/D3
Lindsey, Wis. (†54449) 317/F6
Lindside, W. Va. (24951) 312/E8
Lindstrom, Minn. (55045) 255/F5
Line (isls.) 2/B6
Line (isls.), Pacific 87/K5
Lineboro, Md. (21088) 245/L2
Linesville, Pa. (16424) 294/A2
Lineville, Ala. (36266) 195/G4
Lineville, Iowa (50147) 229/G7
Linfen, China 77/H4
Linfield, Pa. (19468) 294/L5
Linganore (creek), Md. 245/J3
Lingao, China 77/G8
Lingayen, Philippines 85/F2
Lingayen, Philippines 82/C2
Lingayen (gulf), Philippines 82/C2
Lingen, W. Germany 22/B2
Lingga (arch.), Indonesia 85/D5
Lingga (isl.), Indonesia 85/D6
Lingle, Wyo. (82223) 319/H3
Linglestown, Pa. (17112) 294/J5
Lingling, China 77/H6
Lingo, N. Mex. (88123) 274/F5
Lingqui, China 77/H4
Lingshan, China 77/G7

400 Lingshui

Lingshui, China 77/H8
Linguère, Senegal 106/B5
Lingwu, China 77/G4
Linhai, China 77/K6
Linhares, Brazil 132/F7
Linhe, China 77/G3
Linière, Québec 172/G3
Linkebeek, Belgium 27/C10
Linköping, Sweden 18/K7
Linköping, Sweden 7/F3
Linkou, China 77/M2
Linkwood, Md. (21835) 245/P6
Linlithgow, Scotland 10/B1
Linlithgow, Scotland 15/C1
Linn (co.), Iowa 229/K4
Linn (co.), Kansas 232/H3
Linn, Kansas (66953) 232/E2
Linn (co.), Mo. 261/F3
Linn, Mo. (65051) 261/J5
Linn (co.), Oreg. 291/E3
Linn, Texas (78563) 303/F11
Linn, W. Va. (26384) 312/E4
Linn Creek, Mo. (65052) 261/G6
Linndale, Ohio (†44101) 284/G9
Linneus○, Maine (†04730) 243/H3
Linneus, Mo. (64653) 261/F3
Linn Grove, Ind. (46769) 227/H3
Linn Grove, Iowa (51033) 229/C3
Linnhe, Loch (inlet), Scotland 10/D2
Linnhe, Loch (inlet), Scotland 15/C4
Linnsburg, Ind. (†47933) 227/D5
Linntown, Pa. (†17837) 294/J4
Lino Lakes, Minn. (†55038) 255/G5
Linosa (isl.), Italy 34/D7
Linqing (Lintsing), China 77/J4
Lins, Brazil 132/D8
Lins, Brazil 135/B2
Linstead, Jamaica 158/J6
Linter, Belgium 27/G7
Linth (riv.), Switzerland 39/G3
Linthal, Switzerland 39/H3
Linthicum Heights, Md. (21090) 245/M4
Lintlaw, Sask. 181/H3
Linton, Georgia (†31087) 217/F4
Linton, Ind. (47441) 227/C6
Linton, Ky. (†42211) 237/F7
Linton, N. Dak. (58552) 282/K7
Linville, La. (71257) 238/F1
Linville, N.C. (28646) 281/F2
Linville, Va. (22834) 307/L3
Linville Falls, N.C. (28647) 281/F3
Linwood, Georgia (†30728) 217/B1
Linwood, Ind. (†46001) 227/F4
Linwood, Kansas (66052) 232/G2
Linwood, Ky. (†42765) 237/K6
Linwood, Md. (21764) 245/K2
Linwood, Mass. (01525) 249/H4
Linwood, Mich. (48634) 250/F5
Linwood, Nebr. (68036) 264/H3
Linwood, N.J. (08221) 273/D5
Linwood, N.C. (27299) 281/J3
Linwood, Ontario 177/D4
Linwood, Pa. (19061) 294/L7
Linwood, Scotland 15/B2
Linxi, China 77/J3
Linxia (Linsia), China 77/F4
Linyi, China 77/J4
Linz, Austria 7/F4
Linz, Austria 41/C2
Linze, China 77/F4
Linzee (cape), Nova Scotia 168/G2
Lionel, Scotland 15/B2
Lionel Town, Jamaica 158/J7
Lions (gulf) 7/E4
Lions (gulf), France 28/F6
Lion's Bay, Br. Col. 184/K3
Lion's Head, Ontario 177/C2
Lipa, Philippines 82/C4
Lipan, Texas (76462) 303/F5
Lipari, Italy 34/E5
Lipari (isl.), Italy 34/E5
Lipari (isls.), Italy 34/E5
Lipetsk, U.S.S.R. 7/H3
Lipetsk, U.S.S.R. 48/E4
Lipetsk, U.S.S.R. 52/E4
Lipez, Cordillera de (range), Bolivia 136/B8
Liping, China 77/G6
Lipník nad Bečvou, Czech. 41/D2
Lipno (res.), Czech. 41/C2
Lipno, Poland 47/D2
Lipoa (pt.), Hawaii 218/H1
Lipova, Romania 45/E2
Lippe (riv.), W. Germany 22/C3
Lippstadt, W. Germany 22/C3
Lipscomb, Ala. (35020) 195/E4
Lipscomb (co.), Texas 303/D1
Lipscomb, Texas (79056) 303/D1
Lipton, Sask. 181/H5
Liptovský Hrádok, Czech. 41/E2
Liptovský Mikuláš, Czech. 41/E2
Lipu, China 77/H7
Lira, Uganda 115/F3
Lircay, Peru 128/E9
Liri (riv.), Italy 34/D4
Liria, Spain 33/F3
Lisala, Zaire 115/D3
Lisbellaw, N. Ireland 17/K2
Lisbon○, Conn. (06351) 210/G2
Lisbon, Ill. (†60541) 222/E2
Lisbon, Ind. (†46755) 227/G2
Lisbon, Iowa (52253) 229/L5
Lisbon, La. (71048) 238/E1
Lisbon○, Maine (04250) 243/C7
Lisbon, Md. (21765) 245/K3
Lisbon, Mo. (†65254) 261/G4
Lisbon, N.H. (03585) 268/D3
Lisbon○, N.H. (03585) 268/D3
Lisbon, N.Y. (13658) 276/K1
Lisbon, N. Dak. (58054) 282/P7
Lisbon, Ohio (44432) 284/J4
Lisbon (dist.), Portugal 33/A1
Lisbon (cap.), Portugal 2/J4
Lisbon (cap.), Portugal 7/D5
Lisbon (Lisboa) (cap.), Portugal 33/A1
Lisbon Falls, Maine (04252) 243/D7
Lisbon-Lisbon Center, Maine (04250) 243/C7
Lisburn, Alberta 182/C3
Lisburn (dist.), N. Ireland 17/J2
Lisburn, N. Ireland 10/D3
Lisburn, N. Ireland 17/J2
Lisburne (cape), Alaska 196/E1
Lisburne (pen.), Alaska 196/E1
Liscannor (bay), Ireland 17/B6
Liscarroll, Ireland 17/D7
Lisco, Nebr. (69148) 264/B3
Liscomb, Iowa (50148) 229/H4
Liscomb (isl.), Nova Scotia 168/G4
Lisdoonvarna, Ireland 17/C5
Lishi, China 77/H4
Lishui, China 77/K6
Lisianski (isl.), Hawaii 188/E6
Lisianski (isl.), Hawaii 87/J3
Lisianski (isl.), Hawaii 218/B5
Lisichansk, U.S.S.R. 52/E5
Lisieux, France 28/D3
Lisieux, Sask. 181/E6
Liskeard, England 13/C7
Liskeard, England 10/D5
Lisle, Ill. (60532) 222/A6
Lisle, N.Y. (13797) 276/H6
Lisle, Ontario 177/E3
L'Islet (co.), Québec 172/G2
L'Islet, Québec 172/G2
L'Islet-sur-Mer, Québec 172/G2
L'Isle-Verte, Québec 172/G1
Lisman, Ala. (36912) 195/B6
Lisman, Ky. (†42404) 237/F6
Lismore, Australia 87/F8
Lismore, Ireland 10/B4
Lismore, Ireland 17/F7
Lismore, La. (†71343) 238/G3
Lismore, Minn. (56155) 255/B7
Lismore, N. S. Wales 88/J5
Lismore, N.S. Wales 97/G1
Lismore (isl.), Scotland 15/C4
Lisnaskea, N. Ireland 17/G3
Lišov, Czech. 41/C2
Lispeszentadorján, Hungary 41/D3
Lisse, Netherlands 27/F4
Lista (pen.), Norway 18/E7
Lister (mt.) 5/B8
Listie, Pa. (15549) 294/D5
Listowel, Ireland 17/C7
Listowel, Ireland 10/B4
Listowel, Ontario 177/D4
Litang, China 77/F6
Litani (riv.), Fr. Guiana 131/D4
Litani (riv.), Lebanon 63/F6
Litani (riv.), Suriname 131/D4
Litchfield (co.), Conn. 210/B1
Litchfield, Conn. (06759) 210/C2
Litchfield○, Conn. (06759) 210/C2
Litchfield, Ill. (62056) 222/D4
Litchfield○, Maine (04350) 243/D7
Litchfield, Mich. (49252) 250/E6
Litchfield, Minn. (55355) 255/D5
Litchfield, Nebr. (68852) 264/E3
Litchfield○, N.H. (†03051) 268/E6
Litchfield, North. Terr. 93/B2
Litchfield, Ohio (44253) 284/F3
Litchfield Park, Ariz. (85340) 198/C5
Litchville, N. Dak. (58461) 282/O6
Lith, Netherlands 27/G5
Litherland, England 13/G2
Litherland, England 10/F2
Lithgow, Australia 87/F9
Lithgow, N. S. Wales 88/J6
Lithgow, N.S. Wales 97/F3
Lithia, Va. (24066) 307/J6
Lithia Springs, Georgia (30057) 217/C3
Lithium, Mo. (†63775) 261/N7
Lithonia, Georgia (30058) 217/D3
Lithopolis, Ohio (43136) 284/E6
LITHUANIA 53/B3
Lithuanian S.S.R., U.S.S.R. 7/G3
Lithuanian S.S.R., U.S.S.R. 48/C4
Lithuanian S.S.R., U.S.S.R. 52/B3
Lititz, Pa. (17543) 294/K5
Litókhoron, Greece 45/F5
Litoměřice, Czech. 41/C1
Litomyšl, Czech. 41/D2
Litovel, Czech. 41/D2
Littau, Switzerland 39/F2
Littcarr, Ky. (41834) 237/R6
Little (riv.), Ala. 195/G2
Little (riv.), Ala. 195/C8
Little (riv.), Ark. 202/B6
Little (riv.), Conn. 210/G2
Little (riv.), Conn. 210/H1
Little (riv.), Ind. 227/G3
Little (riv.), La. 238/F3
Little (riv.), Mass. 249/C4
Little (riv.), New Bruns. 170/D2
Little (riv.), N.C. 281/N3
Little (riv.), N.C. 281/L4
Little (riv.), Okla. 288/R6
Little (riv.), Oreg. 291/E4
Little (riv.), S.C. 296/D3
Little (riv.), S.C. 296/C3
Little (riv.), Vt. 268/B3
Little (inlet), Va. 307/S6
Little (riv.), Va. 307/N5
Little (riv.), Va. 307/H7
Little Alföld (plain), Hungary 41/D3
Little America, Ant. 2/B10
Little America 5/B10
Little America, Wyo. (82929) 319/C4
Little Andaman (isl.), India 68/G6
Little Arkansas (riv.), Kansas 232/E3
Little Barrier (isl.), N. Zealand 100/E2
Little Bay de Noc (bay), Mich. 250/B3
Little Bay Islands, Newf. 166/C4
Little Beaver (creek), Kansas 232/A2
Little Beaver (creek), Ohio 284/J4
Little Bighorn (riv.), Mont. 262/J5
Little Birch (lake), Manitoba 179/E3
Little Birch, W. Va. (26629) 312/E5
Little Bitterroot (lake), Mont. 262/B2
Little Black (riv.), Maine 243/E1
Little Black, Wis. (†54451) 317/F5
Little Blue (riv.), Kansas 232/E1
Little Blue (riv.), Nebr. 264/H5
Little Boars Head, N.H. (†03871) 268/F6
Little Bow (riv.), Alberta 182/D4
Little Britain, Ontario 177/F3
Little Brook, Nova Scotia 168/B4
Little Brosna (riv.), Ireland 17/E5
Little Buffalo Lake, Alberta 182/B1
Little Bullhead, Manitoba 179/F3
Little Butter (creek), Oreg. 291/H2
Little Cadotte (riv.), Alberta 182/B1
Little Cape, New Bruns. 170/F2
Little Catalina, Newf. 166/D2
Little Cayman (isl.), Cayman Is. 156/B3
Little Cedar, Iowa (50454) 229/H2
Little Chief, Okla. (†74637) 288/N1
Little Choptank (riv.), Md. 245/N6
Little Chute, Wis. (54140) 317/K7
Little Coco (isl.), Burma 72/B4
Little Colorado (riv.), Ariz. 188/D3
Little Colorado (riv.), Ariz. 198/D3
Little Compton○, R.I. (02837) 249/K6
Little Corn (isl.), Nicaragua 154/F4
Little Creek, Del. (19961) 245/S4
Little Creek, La. (†71371) 238/F3
Little Creek (peak), Utah 304/B6
Little Current, Ontario 177/B2
Little Current (riv.), Ontario 175/C2
Little Deep (creek), N. Dak. 282/G2
Little Deer Isle, Maine (†04627) 243/F7
Little Diomede (isl.), Alaska 196/E1
Little Dover, Nova Scotia 168/G3
Little Dry (creek), Mont. 262/K3
Little Eagle, S. Dak. (57639) 298/H2
Little Egg (harb.), N.J. 273/E4
Little Egg (inlet), N.J. 273/E5
Little Elkhart (riv.), Ind. 227/F1
Little Falls, Minn. (56345) 255/D5
Little Falls○, N.J. (07424) 273/B2
Little Falls, N.Y. (13365) 276/L4
Little Falls-South Windham, Maine (04082) 243/C8
Little Farms, La. (†70123) 238/N4
Little Ferry, N.J. (07643) 273/B2
Littlefield, Ariz. (86432) 198/B2
Littlefield, Texas (79339) 303/B4
Little Flock, Ark. (†72712) 202/B1
Littlefork, Minn. (56653) 255/E2
Little Fork (riv.), Minn. 255/E2
Little Genesee, N.Y. (14754) 276/D6
Little Girl (pt.), Mich. 250/E1
Little Goose (dam), Wash. 310/G4
Little Grand Rapids, Manitoba 179/G2
Little Gunpowder Falls (creek), Md. 245/M2
Littlehampton, England 13/G7
Littlehampton, England 10/F5
Little Harbour, Nova Scotia 168/D5
Little Heart's Ease, Newf. 166/D2
Little Hocking, Ohio (45742) 284/G7
Little Humboldt (riv.), Nev. 266/D1
Little Inagua (isl.), Bahamas 156/D2
Little Kai (isl.), Indonesia 85/J7
Little Kanawha (riv.), W. Va. 312/D5
Little Knife (riv.), N. Dak. 282/F3
Little Lake, Calif. (93542) 204/H8
Little Lake, Mich. (49833) 250/B2
Little Laramie (riv.), Wyo. 319/G4
Little London, Jamaica 158/G6
Little Lorraine, Nova Scotia 168/J3
Little Lost (riv.), Idaho 220/E5
Littlelot, Tenn. (†38454) 237/G9
Little Lynches (riv.), S.C. 296/G3
Little Madawaska (riv.), Maine 243/G2
Little Makin (atoll), Kiribati 87/H5
Little Manitou (lake), Sask. 181/F4
Little Marais, Minn. (55611) 255/G3
Little Marsh, Pa. (16931) 294/H2
Little Meadows, Pa. (18830) 294/K2
Little Mecatina (riv.), Newf. 166/B3
Little Medicine Bow (riv.), Wyo. 319/F3
Little Miami (riv.), Ohio 284/B6
Little Minch (sound), Scotland 10/C2
Little Minch (sound), Scotland 15/B3
Little Missouri (riv.) 188/F1
Little Missouri (riv.), Ark. 202/D6
Little Missouri (riv.), Mont. 262/M5
Little Missouri (riv.), N. Dak. 282/D4
Little Missouri (riv.), S. Dak. 298/B1
Little Missouri (riv.), Wyo. 319/H1
Littlemore, England 13/F6
Little Moreau (riv.), S. Dak. 298/G3
Little Mountain, S.C. (29075) 296/E3
Little Muddy (riv.), N. Dak. 282/C3
Little Muddy (creek), Wyo. 319/B4
Little Muskingum (riv.), Ohio 284/H6
Little Narrows, Nova Scotia 168/H3
Little Nicobar (isl.), India 68/G7
Little Orleans, Md. (21766) 245/E2
Little Owyhee (riv.), Idaho 220/B7
Little Paint Branch (riv.), Md. 245/F4
Little Para (riv.), S. Australia 88/D7
Little Para (riv.), S. Australia 94/B7
Little Patuxent (riv.), Md. 245/L4
Little Pee Dee (riv.), N.C. 281/L6
Little Pee Dee (riv.), S.C. 296/J4
Little Pigeon (creek), Ind. 227/C9
Little Plymouth, Va. (23091) 307/P5
Little Popo Agie (riv.), Wyo. 319/D3
Littleport, England 13/H5
Littleport, Iowa (52055) 229/L3
Little Powder (riv.), Wyo. 319/G1
Little Prairie, Wis. (†53149) 317/H2
Little Red (riv.), Ark. 202/G3
Little River, Ala. (36550) 195/C8
Little River (co.), Ark. 202/B6
Littleriver, Calif. (95456) 204/B4
Little River, Kansas (67457) 232/E3
Little River, N. Zealand 100/D5
Little River, Nova Scotia 168/B4
Little River (harb.), Nova Scotia 168/B5
Little River, S.C. (29566) 296/K4
Little River (inlet), S.C. 296/L4
Little Rock (cap.), Ark. 188/H4
Little Rock (cap.), Ark. 202/F4
Little Rock (cap.), Ark. (*72201) 202/F4
Little Rock, Iowa (51243) 229/B2
Little Rock, Minn. (†56373) 255/D5
Little Rock (creek), Minn. 255/C7
Little Rock, Miss. (39337) 256/F5
Little Rock, S.C. (29567) 296/J3
Littlerock, Wash. (98556) 310/B4
Little Rock A.F.B., Ark. 202/F4
Little Sable (pt.), Mich. 250/C5
Little Saint Bernard (pass), France 28/G5
Little Saint George (isl.), Fla. 212/B2
Little Salmon (riv.), Idaho 220/B4
Little Salt (lake), Utah 304/A6
Little Sandy (creek), Wyo. 319/C3
Little Sauk, Minn. (56346) 255/D5
Little Sevogle (riv.), New Bruns. 170/D1
Little Shawmut, Ala. (†36876) 195/H5
Little Sheep (creek), Oreg. 291/K2
Little Shippegan, New Bruns. 170/F1
Little Silver, N.J. (07739) 273/F3
Little Sioux, Iowa (51545) 229/B5
Little Sioux (riv.), Iowa 229/B3
Little Sitkin (isl.), Alaska 196/K4
Little Smoky, Alberta 182/B2
Little Smoky (riv.), Alberta 182/B2
Little Smoky (valley), Nev. 266/E4
Little Southwest Miramichi (riv.), New Bruns. 170/D2
Little Spokane (riv.), Wash. 310/H3
Littlestown, Pa. (17340) 294/H6
Little Suamico, Wis. (54141) 317/L6
Little Summer (isl.), Mich. 250/C3
Little Tallahatchie (riv.), Miss. 256/D2
Little Tennessee (riv.), N.C. 281/B4
Little Tennessee (riv.), Tenn. 237/N10
Little Thunder (creek), Wyo. 319/G2
Little Tinicum (isl.), Pa. 294/M7
Little Tobago (isl.), Virgin Is. (Br.) 161/B3
Little Tobique (riv.), New Bruns. 170/C1
Littleton, Colo. (*80120) 208/K3
Littleton, Ill. (61452) 222/C3
Littleton, Iowa (†50648) 229/K3
Littleton, Ireland 17/F6
Littleton○, Maine (†04760) 243/H3
Littleton○, Mass. (01460) 249/H2
Littleton, N.H. (03561) 268/D3
Littleton○, N.H. (03561) 268/D3
Littleton, N.C. (27850) 281/O2
Littleton, Va. (†23890) 307/O7
Littleton, W. Va. (26581) 312/F3
Littleton Common, Mass. (†01460) 249/J2
Little Traverse (bay), Mich. 250/D3
Little Trout River (pond), Newf. 166/C4
Little Tupper (lake), N.Y. 276/L2
Little Valley, N.Y. (14755) 276/C6
Little Vermilion (riv.), Ind. 227/B5
Littleville, Ala. (†35653) 195/C1
Little Wabash (riv.), Ill. 222/E5
Little Weiser (riv.), Idaho 220/B5
Little White (riv.), S. Dak. 298/H7
Little Wood (riv.), Idaho 220/D6
Little Yenisey (riv.), U.S.S.R. 48/K4
Little York, Ill. (61453) 222/C2
Little York, Ind. (47139) 227/F7
Little York, N.J. (08834) 273/C2
Little Zab (riv.), Iraq 66/C3
Lituya (bay), Alaska 196/L1
Litvínov, Czech. 41/B1
Liuba, China 77/G5
Liukang Tenggaja (isls.), Indonesia 85/F7
Liuli, Tanzania 115/F6
Liuzhou (Liuchow), China 77/G7
Liuzhou, China 54/M7
Līvāni, U.S.S.R. 53/D2
Livelong, Sask. 181/C2
Lively (isl.), 143/E7
Lively, Va. (22507) 307/P5
Livengood, Alaska (†99701) 196/J1
Live Oak, Calif. (†95073) 204/K4
Live Oak, Calif. (95953) 204/D4
Live Oak, Fla. (32060) 212/D1
Live Oak (co.), Texas 303/F9
Live Oak, Texas (†78201) 303/K10
Liveringa, W. Australia 88/C3
Liveringa, W. Australia 92/D2
Livermore, Calif. (94550) 204/L2
Livermore, Colo. (80536) 208/J1
Livermore, Iowa (50558) 229/E3
Livermore, Ky. (42352) 237/G5
Livermore, Maine (04253) 243/C7
Livermore○, Maine (04253) 243/C7
Livermore (mt.), Texas 303/C11
Livermore Falls, Maine (04254) 243/C7
Livermore Falls○, Maine (04254) 243/C7
Livermore Falls, N.H. (†03264) 268/D4
Liverpool (swamp), Bolivia 136/D4
Liverpool, England 10/F2
Liverpool, England 13/G2
Liverpool, England 7/D3
Liverpool (bay), England 13/D4
Liverpool, Ill. (61543) 222/C3
Liverpool, N. S. Wales 88/K4
Liverpool, N.S. Wales 97/H4
Liverpool (range), N.S. Wales 97/F2
Liverpool, N.Y. (13088) 276/H4
Liverpool (bay), N.W. Terrs. 187/E2
Liverpool (cape), N.W. Terrs. 187/L2
Liverpool, Nova Scotia 168/D4
Liverpool (bay), Nova Scotia 168/D5
Liverpool, Pa. (17045) 294/H4
Liverpool, Texas (77577) 303/J3
Liverpool, W. Va. (25257) 312/C5
Livia, Ky. (†42376) 237/G5
Livigno, Italy 34/C1
Livingston, Ala. (35470) 195/B5
Livingston, Calif. (95334) 204/E6
Livingston, Guatemala 154/C3
Livingston (co.), Ill. 222/E3
Livingston, Ill. (62058) 222/D5
Livingston (co.), Ky. 237/E6
Livingston, Ky. (40445) 237/N6
Livingston (par.), La. 238/L2
Livingston, La. (70754) 238/L1
Livingston (co.), Mich. 250/F6
Livingston (co.), Mo. 261/E3
Livingston, Mont. 188/D1
Livingston, Mont. (59047) 262/F5
Livingston○, N.J. (07039) 273/E2
Livingston (co.), N.Y. 276/E5
Livingston, Scotland 15/C2
Livingston, Scotland 10/C1
Livingston, S.C. (29076) 296/E4
Livingston, Tenn. (38570) 237/L8
Livingston, Texas (77351) 303/K7
Livingston (lake), Texas 303/K7
Livingston, Wis. (53554) 317/E10
Livingstone (range), Alberta 182/C4
Livingstone (falls), Zaire 115/B5
Livingstone, Zambia 115/E7
Livingstone, Zambia 102/E6
Livingstonia, Malawi 115/F6
Livingston Manor, N.Y. (12758) 276/L7
Livingstonville, N.Y. (†12122) 276/M6
Livno, Yugoslavia 45/C4
Livny, U.S.S.R. 52/E4
Livona, N. Dak. (58501) 282/K6
Livonia, Ind. (†47108) 227/E7
Livonia, La. (70755) 238/G5
Livonia, Mich. (*48150) 250/F6
Livonia, Mo. (63551) 261/G1
Livonia, N.Y. (14487) 276/E5
Livonia, Pa. (†16872) 294/H4
Livorno (Leghorn), Italy 34/C3
Livry-Gargan, France 28/C1
Liwale, Tanzania 115/G5
Li Xian, China 77/H6
Lixoúrion, Greece 45/E6
Lizard, The (pen.), England 13/B8
Lizard (pt.), England 10/D6
Lizard (pt.), England 13/B8
Lizella, Georgia (31052) 217/E5
Lizemores, W. Va. (25125) 312/D6
Lizton, Ind. (46149) 227/D5
Ljubinje, Yugoslavia 45/D4
Ljubljana, Yugoslavia 45/B3
Ljubljana, Yugoslavia 7/F4
Ljubuški, Yugoslavia 45/C4
Ljugarn, Sweden 18/L8
Ljungan (riv.), Sweden 18/K5
Ljungby, Sweden 18/J8
Ljusdal, Sweden 18/J6
Ljusna (riv.), Sweden 7/F2
Ljusnan (riv.), Sweden 18/H5
Ljusne, Sweden 18/K6
Llagostera, Spain 33/H2
Llaima (vol.), Chile 138/E2
Llallagua, Bolivia 136/B6
Llallagua, Bolivia 120/C4
Llamara, Salar de (salt dep.), Chile 138/B3
Llanarth, Wales 13/C5
Llancanelo (lag.), Argentina 143/C4
Llancanelo, Salina y Laguna (salt dep.), Argentina 143/C4
Llandeilo, Wales 13/C6
Llandovery, Wales 13/D5
Llandovery, Wales 10/D5
Llandrindod Wells, Wales 10/E4
Llandrindod Wells, Wales 13/D5
Llandudno, Wales 13/D4
Llandudno, Wales 10/E4
Llandybie, Wales 13/C6
Llandyssul, Wales 13/C5
Llanelli, Wales 13/C6
Llanelli, Wales 10/D5
Llanes, Spain 33/D1
Llanfair Caereinion, Wales 13/D5
Llanfairfechan, Wales 13/D4
Llanfyllin, Wales 10/E4
Llanfyllin, Wales 13/D5
Llangefni, Wales 13/C4
Llangollen, Wales 13/D5
Llangollen, Wales 10/E4
Llanguicke, Wales 13/D6
Llanidloes, Wales 13/D5
Llanidloes, Wales 10/E4
Llanllyfni, Wales 13/C4
Llannon, Wales 13/C6
Llano, N.Mex. (87543) 274/D2
Llano (co.), Texas 303/F7
Llano, Texas (78643) 303/F7
Llano (riv.), Texas 303/D7
Llano Estacado (Staked) (plain), N. Mex. 274/F5
Llano Estacado (plain), Texas 303/B4
Llanon, Wales 13/C5
Llanos (plain) 120/B2
Llanos (plains), Colombia 126/D5
Llanquera, Bolivia 136/A6
Llanquihue (lake), Chile 138/E3
Llanrhaeadr, Wales 13/D5
Llanrhystyd, Wales 13/C5
Llanrian, Wales 13/B6
Llanrwst, Wales 13/D4
Llanrwst, Wales 10/E4
Llantrisant, Wales 13/A7
Llantwit Major, Wales 13/A7
Llanwnog, Wales 13/D5
Llanwrtyd Wells, Wales 13/D5
Llata, Peru 128/D7
Llay-Llay, Chile 138/G2
Llera de Canales, Mexico 150/K5
Llerena (pt.), C. Rica 154/F6
Llerena, Spain 33/C3
Lleyn (pen.), Wales 13/C5
Llica, Bolivia 136/A6
Llico, Chile 138/A10
Llivia, Spain 33/G1
Llobregat (riv.), Spain 33/H2
Llodio, Spain 33/E1
Llolleo, Chile 138/F4
Llorente, Philippines 82/E5
Lloyd, Fla. (32337) 212/C1
Lloyd (res.), Ga. 188/K4
Lloyd, Ky. (41156) 237/R3
Lloyd, Mont. (59535) 262/G2
Lloyd Harbor, N.Y. (†11743) 276/R6
Lloydminster, Alberta 182/E3
Lloydminster, Alta.-Sask. 162/E5
Lloydminster, Sask. 181/A2
Lluchmayor, Spain 33/H3
Lluidas Vale, Jamaica 158/J6
Llullaillaco (mt.) 120/C5
Llullaillaco (vol.), Argentina 143/C1
Llullaillaco (vol.), Chile 138/B5
Lluta (riv.), Chile 138/B1
Llwchwr, Wales 13/D6
Loa (riv.), Chile 120/C5
Loa (riv.), Chile 138/B3
Loa, Utah (84747) 304/C5
Loachapoka, Ala. (36865) 195/G5
Loami, Ill. (62661) 222/D4
Loange (riv.), Angola 115/C5
Loange (riv.), Zaire 115/C5
Loanhead, Scotland 10/C1
Loanhead, Scotland 15/D2
Lobatse, Botswana 118/D5
Löbau, E. Germany 22/F3
Lobaye (riv.), Cent. Afr. Rep. 115/C2
Lobdell, La. (†70767) 238/J1
Lobeco, S.C. (29931) 296/F6
Lobelia, W. Va. (†24946) 312/F6
Lobelville, Tenn. (37097) 237/F9
Lobenstein, E. Germany 22/D3
Lobería, Argentina 143/E4
Lobethal, S. Australia 94/C7
Łobez, Poland 47/B2
Lobito, Angola 115/B6
Lobito, Angola 102/D6
Lobitos, Peru 128/B5
Lobo, Philippines 82/C4
Lobo (cay), P. Rico 161/G1
Lobos, Argentina 143/G7
Lobos (pt.), Chile 138/A3
Lobos (cape), Mexico 150/C2
Lobos (pt.), Mexico 150/D3
Lobos (isl.), Uruguay 145/E6
Lobos de Afuera (isls.), Peru 128/B6
Lobos de Tierra (isl.), Peru 128/B6
Lobster (lake), Maine 243/E4
Locarno, Switzerland 39/G4
Locate, Mont. (†59336) 262/L4
Lochaber, Nova Scotia 168/F3
Lochaber (dist.), Scotland 15/D4
Lochailort, Scotland 15/C4
Lochaline, Scotland 15/C4
Lochans, Scotland 15/D6
Locharbriggs, Scotland 15/E5
Lochawe, Scotland 15/C4
Lochboisdale, Scotland 15/A3
Lochbuie, Colo. (†80601) 208/K2
Lochcarron, Scotland 10/D2
Lochcarron, Scotland 15/C3
Lochearnhead, Scotland 15/D4
Lochem, Netherlands 27/J4
Lochend, Scotland 15/D3
Loches, France 28/D4
Lochgelly, Scotland 10/C1
Lochgelly, Scotland 15/D1
Lochgelly, W. Va. (25866) 312/D6
Lochgilphead, Scotland 10/D2
Lochgilphead, Scotland 15/C4
Lochgoilhead, Scotland 15/D4
Lochindorb (lake), Scotland 15/E3
Lochinver, Scotland 10/D1
Lochinver, Scotland 15/C2
Lochloosa, Fla. (32662) 212/E2
Lochloosa (lake), Fla. 212/D2
Loch Lynn Heights, Md. (†21550) 245/A3
Lochmaben, Scotland 10/E3
Lochmaben, Scotland 15/E5
Lochmaddy, Scotland 15/A3
Lochmere, N.H. (03252) 268/D5
Lochnagar (mt.), Scotland 15/E4
Lochore, Scotland 15/D1
Lochranza, Scotland 15/C5
Loch Raven (res.), Md. 245/M3
Lochristi, Belgium 27/D6
Lochsa (riv.), Idaho 220/C3
Lochwinnoch, Scotland 15/A2
Lochy, Loch (lake), Scotland 15/D3
Lochy, Loch (lake), Scotland 10/D2
Lock, S. Australia 94/D5
Lockatong (creek), N.J. 273/C3
Lockbourne, Ohio (43137) 284/E6
Locke, Calif. (†95690) 204/B9
Locke, N.Y. (13092) 276/H5
Locke (mt.), Texas 303/D11
Lockeford, Calif. (95237) 204/C9
Locke Mills, Maine (04255) 243/B7
Lockeport, Nova Scotia 168/C5
Lockerbie, Scotland 10/E3
Lockerbie, Scotland 15/E5
Lockesburg, Ark. (71846) 202/B6
Lockhart, Ala. (36455) 195/F8
Lockhart, Minn. (†56510) 255/B3
Lockhart (mt.), Mont. 262/D3
Lockhart, N.S. Wales 97/D4
Lockhart (riv.), N.W. Terrs. 187/H3
Lockhart, S.C. (29364) 296/E2
Lockhart, Texas (78644) 303/G8
Lock Haven, Pa. (17745) 294/H3
Lockington, Ohio (†45356) 284/B5
Lockland, Ohio (45215) 284/C9
Lockney, Texas (79241) 303/C3
Lockney, W. Va. (25258) 312/E5
Lockport, Ill. (60441) 222/B6
Lockport, Ky. (40036) 237/M4
Lockport, La. (70374) 238/K7
Lockport, Manitoba 179/F4
Lockport, N.Y. (14094) 276/C4
Lockridge, Iowa (52635) 229/K7
Lock Springs, Mo. (64654) 261/E3
Lockwood, Mo. (65682) 261/E8
Lockwood, Sask. 181/G4
Lockwood, W. Va. (†26651) 312/D6
Loc Ninh, Vietnam 72/E5
Loco, Okla. (73442) 288/L6
Loco Hills, N. Mex. (88255) 274/F6

Locumba, Peru 128/G11
Locumba (riv.), Peru 128/G11
Locust, N.C. (28097) 281/J4
Locust Bayou, Ark. (†71701) 202/E6
Locust Fork, Ala. (35097) 195/E3
Locust Fork (riv.), Ala. 195/E3
Locust Grove, Ark. (72550) 202/G2
Locust Grove, Georgia (30248) 217/D4
Locust Grove, N.Y. (†11791) 276/R6
Locust Grove, Ohio (†45660) 284/D8
Locust Grove, Okla. (74352) 288/R2
Locust Hill, Ky. (40151) 237/J5
Locustville, Va. (23404) 307/S5
Lod (Lydda), Israel 65/B4
Loda, Ill. (60948) 222/E3
Lodar, P.D.R. Yemen 59/E7
Loddon, England 13/J5
Loddon (riv.), Victoria 97/B5
Loddon (riv.), Victoria 88/G7
Lodève, France 28/E6
Lodeynoye Pole, U.S.S.R. 52/D2
Lodge (creek), Mont. 262/G1
Lodge (creek), Sask. 181/B6
Lodge, S.C. (29082) 296/F5
Lodge Bay, Newf. 166/C3
Lodge Grass, Mont. (59050) 262/J5
Lodge Hill, Barbados 161/B8
Lodgepole, Alberta 182/C3
Lodge Pole, Mont. (†59524) 262/H2
Lodgepole, Nebr. (69149) 264/B3
Lodgepole (creek), Nebr. 264/A3
Lodgepole, S. Dak. (57640) 298/D2
Lodgepole (creek), Wyo. 319/H2
Lodgepole (creek), Wyo. 319/H4
Lodi, Calif. 188/B3
Lodi, Calif. (95240) 204/C9
Lodi, Italy 34/B2
Lodi, Miss. (†39767) 256/E3
Lodi, Mo. (63950) 261/M8
Lodi, N.J. (07644) 273/B2
Lodi, N.Y. (14860) 276/G5
Lodi, Ohio (44254) 284/F3
Lodi (cape), Tasmania 99/E3
Lodi, Texas (75564) 303/K5
Lodi, Wis. (53555) 317/G9
Lødingen, Norway 18/J2
Lodja, Zaire 102/E5
Lodja, Zaire 115/D4
Lodosa, Spain 33/E1
Lodrino, Switzerland 39/G4
Lodwar, Kenya 115/G3
Łódź (prov.), Poland 47/D3
Łódź (city), Poland 47/D3
Łódź, Poland 7/F3
Łódź, Poland 47/D3
Loei, Thailand 72/D3
Loen, Norway 18/E6
Lofer, Austria 41/B3
Lofoten (isls.), Norway 4/C9
Lofoten (isls.), Norway 7/F2
Lofoten (isls.), Norway 18/H2
Loftus, England 13/G3
Loftus, England 10/F3
Lofty (mt.), S. Australia 88/E8
Lofty (mt.), S. Australia 94/B8
Lofty (range), Tasmania 99/B3
Logan, Ala. (35098) 195/E2
Logan (lake), Alberta 182/E2
Logan (co.), Ark. 202/C3
Logan (mt.), Canada 4/C17
Logan (co.), Colo. 208/N1
Logan (co.), Ill. 222/D3
Logan, Ill. (62856) 222/E6
Logan, Ind. (†45030) 227/H6
Logan, Iowa (51546) 229/B5
Logan (co.), Kansas 232/A3
Logan, Kansas (67646) 232/C2
Logan (co.), Ky. 237/H7
Logan, Mont. (†59741) 262/E5
Logan (co.), Nebr. 264/D3
Logan (creek), Nebr. 264/H2
Logan, N. Mex. (88426) 274/F3
Logan (co.), N. Dak. 282/L7
Logan, N. Dak. (†58701) 282/H3
Logan (co.), Ohio 284/C5
Logan, Ohio (43138) 284/F6
Logan (co.), Okla. 288/M3
Logan, Okla. (73849) 288/F1
Logan, Oreg. (†97405) 291/B2
Logan, Utah (84321) 304/C2
Logan, Utah 188/D2
Logan (mt.), Wash. 310/E2
Logan (co.), W. Va. 312/C7
Logan, W. Va. (25601) 312/B7
Logan (mt.), Yukon 162/B3
Logan (mt.), Yukon 187/D3
Logan (mts.), Yukon 187/F3
Logandale, Nev. (89021) 266/G6
Logan Internat'l Airport, Mass. 249/D7
Logan Lake, Br. Col. 184/G5
Logan Martin (lake), Ala. 195/F4
Logansport, Ind. (46947) 227/E3
Logansport, Ky. (42258) 237/H6
Logansport, La. (71049) 238/C3
Loganton, Pa. (17747) 294/H3
Loganville, Georgia (30249) 217/E3
Loganville, Pa. (17342) 294/J6
Loganville, Wis. (53943) 317/F9
Loge (riv.), Angola 115/B5
Loggieville, New Bruns. 170/E1
Log Lane Village, Colo. (†80701) 208/M2
Logone (riv.) 102/D3
Logone (riv.), Cameroon 115/C2
Logone (riv.), Chad 111/C5
Logroño (prov.), Spain 33/E1
Logroño, Spain 7/D4
Logroño, Spain 33/E1
Logrosán, Spain 33/D3
Logsden, Oreg. (97357) 291/D3
Løgstør, Denmark 21/C4
Løgstør, Denmark 18/F8
Løgstør Bredning (fjord), Denmark 21/C4
Løgumkloster, Denmark 21/B7
Lohals, Denmark 21/D7
Lohardaga, India 68/E4
Lohatlha, S. Africa 118/C5
Lohman, Mo. (65053) 261/H5
Lohman, Mont. (†59523) 262/G2
Lohn, Texas (76852) 303/E6
Löhne, W. Germany 22/C2
Loho (Luohe), China 77/H5
Lohr am Main, W. Germany 22/C4
Lohrville, Iowa (51453) 229/D4
Lohrville, Wis. (†54970) 317/H7
Loica, Chile 138/F4
Loi-kaw, Burma 72/C3
Loi Leng (mt.), Burma 72/C2
Loimaa, Finland 18/N6
Loir (riv.), France 28/D4
Loire (dept.), France 28/F5
Loire (riv.), France 7/E4
Loire (riv.), France 28/C4
Loire-Atlantique (dept.), France 28/C4
Loiret (dept.), France 28/E4
Loir-et-Cher (dept.), France 28/D4
Loíza, P. Rico 161/E1
Loíza Aldea, P. Rico 161/E1
Loja (prov.), Ecuador 128/C4
Loja, Ecuador 128/C4
Loja, Ecuador 120/B3
Loja, Spain 33/D4
Løjt Kirkeby, Denmark 21/C7
Loka, Sudan 111/F7
Lokeren, Belgium 27/D6
Lokitaung, Kenya 115/G3
Lokka (res.), Finland 18/Q3
Løkken, Denmark 21/C3
Løkken, Norway 18/F5
Lokoja, Nigeria 106/F7
Lokolama, Zaire 115/D4
Lokoro (riv.), Zaire 115/C4
Lököshaza, Hungary 41/F3
Lokossa, Benin 106/E7
Loksa, U.S.S.R. 53/C1
Loks Land (isl.), N.W. Terrs. 187/M3
Lol (dry riv.), Sudan 111/E6
Lola, Ky. (42059) 237/E6
Loleta, Calif. (95551) 204/A3
Lolgorien, Kenya 115/G4
Lolita, Texas (77971) 303/H9
Lolland (isl.), Denmark 18/G9
Lolland (isl.), Denmark 21/E8
Lollie, Georgia (30433) 217/G6
Lolo (creek), Idaho 220/C3
Lolo (pass), Idaho 220/D3
Lolo, Mont. (59847) 262/B4
Lolo (pass), Mont. 262/B4
Lolo Hot Springs, Mont. (†59847) 262/B4
Lom, Bulgaria 45/F4
Lom (riv.), Cameroon 115/B2
Lom, Norway 18/F6
Loma, Colo. (81524) 208/B4
Loma, Mont. (59460) 262/F3
Loma, N. Dak. (†58311) 282/O2
Loma, Mansa (lag.), S. Leone 106/B7
Loma Alta, Bolivia 136/B2
Loma Bonita, Mexico 150/M7
Loma Linda, Calif. (92354) 204/F10
Loma Mar, Calif. (94021) 204/J3
Lomami (riv.), Zaire 115/D4
Loman, Minn. (56654) 255/E2
Loma Plata, Paraguay 144/C3
Lomas, Peru 128/E10
Lomas de Zamora, Argentina 143/G7
Lomax, Ala. (†35045) 195/E5
Lomax, Ill. (61454) 222/B3
Lomax, Texas (†77571) 303/K2
Lombard, Ill. (60148) 222/B5
Lombarda, Serra (mts.), Brazil 132/D2
Lombardville, Ill. (†61421) 222/D2
Lombardy (reg.), Italy 34/B2
Lombardy, S. Africa 118/H6
Lombez, France 28/D6
Lomblen (isl.), Indonesia 85/G7
Lombok (isl.), Indonesia 54/N10
Lombok (isl.), Indonesia 85/F7
Lombok (str.), Indonesia 85/E7
Lomé (cap.), Togo 102/C4
Lomé (cap.), Togo 106/E7
Lomela, Zaire 115/D4
Lomela (riv.), Zaire 115/D4
Lometa, Texas (76853) 303/F6
Lomié, Cameroon 115/B3
Lomira, Wis. (53048) 317/J8
Lo Miranda, Chile 138/G5
Lomita, Calif. (90717) 204/C11
Lommel, Belgium 27/G6
Lomnice, Czech. 41/C2
Lomond, Alberta 182/D4
Lomond, Loch (lake), Nova Scotia 168/H3
Lomond, Loch (lake), Scotland 15/D4
Lomond, Loch (lake), Scotland 10/A1
Lompoc, Calif. (93436) 204/E9
Lom Sak, Thailand 72/D3
Łomza (prov.), Poland 47/F2
Łomza, Poland 47/F2
Lonaconing, Md. (21539) 245/C2
Loncoche, Chile 138/D2
Loncopué, Argentina 143/B4
London, Ark. (72847) 202/D3
London, Greater, England 13/H8
London (cap.), England 7/D3
London (cap.), England 10/B5
London (cap.), England 13/H8
London, Ind. (†46126) 227/F5
London, Ky. (40741) 237/N6
London, Minn. (56061) 255/E7
London, Ohio (43140) 284/C6
London, Ont. 146/K5
London, Ont. 162/H7
London, Ontario 177/C5
London, Texas (76854) 303/E7
London (cap.), U.K. 2/J3
London, Wis. (†53523) 317/H9
Londonderry (isl.), Chile 138/E11
Londonderry○, N.H. (03053) 268/E6
Londonderry, N. Ireland 7/D3
Londonderry (dist.), N. Ireland 17/G2
Londonderry, N. Ireland 10/C3
Londonderry, N. Ireland 17/G2
Londonderry, Nova Scotia 168/E3
Londonderry, Ohio (45647) 284/E7
Londonderry○, Vt. (05148) 268/B5
Londonderry (cape), W. Australia 88/D2
Londonderry (cape), W. Australia 92/D1
Londonderry Station, Nova Scotia 168/E3
London Mills, Ill. (61544) 222/C3
Londontowne, Md. (†21035) 245/M4
Londrina, Brazil 132/D8
Londrina, Brazil 120/D5
Lone (mt.), Mont. 262/E5
Lone (mt.), Nev. 266/D4
Lone Butte, Br. Col. 184/G4
Lone Cedar, W. Va. (†26153) 312/C4
Lone Cone (mt.), Colo. 208/C7
Lone Elm, Kansas (†66039) 232/G3
Lone Grove, Okla. (73443) 288/M6
Lone Jack, Mo. (64070) 261/S6
Lonely (lake), Manitoba 179/C3
Lonely (isl.), Ontario 177/C2
Lone Mountain, Tenn. (†37879) 237/O8
Lone Oak, Georgia (†30230) 217/C4
Lone Oak, Ky. (42001) 237/D6
Lone Oak, Texas (75453) 303/H5
Lone Pine, Alberta 182/C2
Lone Pine, Calif. (93545) 204/H7
Lone Pine (peak), Idaho 220/D5
Lonepine, La. (†71367) 238/F5
Lonepine, Mont. (59848) 262/B3
Lone Prairie, Br. Col. 184/G2
Lone Rock, Iowa (50559) 229/E2
Lonerock, Oreg. (†97823) 291/H2
Lone Rock, Sask. 181/A2
Lone Rock, Wis. (53556) 317/F9
Lone Star, S.C. (29077) 296/F4
Lone Tree (creek), Colo. 208/K1
Lone Tree, Iowa (52755) 229/L6
Lonetree, N. Dak. (†58718) 282/G3
Lonetree, Wyo. (82936) 319/B4
Lone Wolf, Okla. (73655) 288/H5
Long, Alaska (†99768) 196/G2
Long (isl.), Alaska 196/M2
Long (isl.), Ant. & Bar. 161/E11
Long (isl.), Bahamas 146/L7
Long (cay), Bahamas 156/C2
Long (isl.), Bahamas 156/C2
Long (bay), Barbados 161/B9
Long (mt.), Conn. 210/B2
Long (pond), Conn. 210/H3
Long (key), Fla. 212/F7
Long (key), Fla. 212/B3
Long (pond), Fla. 212/D2
Long (co.), Georgia 217/J7
Long (bay), Jamaica 158/H7
Long (lake), Maine 243/E2
Long (lake), Maine 243/G1
Long (lake), Maine 243/B7
Long (pond), Maine 243/E5
Long (pond), Maine 243/D6
Long (pond), Maine 243/C4
Long (lake), Manitoba 179/G4
Long (pt.), Manitoba 179/D1
Long (pt.), Manitoba 179/D4
Long (isl.), Martinique 161/D6
Long (isl.), Mass. 249/D7
Long (pond), Mass. 249/L5
Long (pt.), Mass. 249/O4
Long (lake), Mich. 250/F3
Long (lake), Minn. 255/D4
Long (lake), Minn. 255/F3
Long, Miss. (†38828) 256/C4
Long (valley), Nev. 266/B1
Long (isl.), New Bruns. 170/D3
Long (lake), New Bruns. 170/D1
Long (isl.), Newf. 166/C2
Long (isl.), Newf. 166/D2
Long (lake), Newf. 166/A3
Long (lake), Newf. 166/B3
Long (pt.), Newf. 166/C4
Long (mt.), N.H. 268/E2
Long (beach), N.J. 273/E4
Long (isl.), N.Y. 188/M2
Long (isl.), N.Y. 276/P9
Long (lake), N.Y. 276/M2
Long (isl.), N. Zealand 100/A7
Long (lake), N.C. 281/P5
Long (lake), N. Dak. 282/K6
Long (lake), N. Dak. 282/J4
Long (lake), N. Dak. 282/L2
Long (isl.), Nova Scotia 168/B4
Long (lake), Ontario 177/H5
Long (lake), Ontario 175/C3
Long (pt.), Ontario 177/D5
Long (isl.), Papua N.G. 85/B7
Long (isl.), Papua N.G. 86/A2
Long (creek), Sask. 181/H6
Long, Loch (inlet), Scotland 10/A1
Long, Loch (inlet), Scotland 15/D4
Long (lake), S. Dak. 298/L2
Long (pt.), Tasmania 99/E3
Long (str.), U.S.S.R. 48/S2
Long (pt.), Virgin Is. (U.S.) 161/B4
Long (pt.), Virgin Is. (U.S.) 161/E4
Long (isl.), Wash. 310/A4
Long (lake), Wash. 310/H3
Long (reef), W. Australia 92/D1
Long (lake), Wis. 317/C4
Longa, Angola 115/C6
Longa (isl.), Scotland 15/C3
Longaví, Chile 138/A11
Long Bay, Jamaica 158/K6
Long Beach, Br. Col. 184/E5
Long Beach, Calif. 146/F6
Long Beach, Calif. 188/C4
Long Beach, Calif. (*90801) 204/C11
Long Beach (pen.), Conn. 210/C4
Long Beach, Ind. (†46360) 227/D1
Long Beach, Minn. (†56334) 255/C5
Long Beach, Miss. (39560) 256/F10
Long Beach (isl.), N.J. 273/E4
Long Beach, N.Y. (11561) 276/R7
Long Beach, N.C. (28461) 281/N7
Long Beach, Ontario 177/E5
Long Beach, Wash. (98631) 310/A4
Longbenton, England 13/J3
Longboat (key), Fla. 212/D4
Longboat Key, Fla. (33548) 212/D4
Long Bottom, Ohio (45743) 284/G7
Long Branch, N.J. (07740) 273/F3
Longbranch, Wash. (98351) 310/C3
Longchuan, China 77/J7
Long Cove, Maine (†04857) 243/E8
Long Creek, Oreg. (97856) 291/H3
Longcreek, S.C. (29658) 296/A2
Longdale, Okla. (73755) 288/K2
Longde, China 77/G4
Long Eaton, England 13/F5
Long Eddy, N.Y. (12760) 276/K7
Long Falls (dam), Maine 243/C5
Longfellow (mts.), Maine 243/B6
Longford (co.), Ireland 17/F4
Longford, Ireland 10/C4
Longford, Ireland 17/F4
Longford, Kansas (67458) 232/E2
Longford, Ontario 177/E3
Longford, Tasmania 99/C3
Longford, Virgin Is. (U.S.) 161/F4
Long Green, Md. (21092) 245/M3
Long Grove, Ill. (60047) 222/B5
Long Grove, Iowa (52756) 229/M5
Long Harbour, Newf. 166/D2
Long Hill, Conn. (†06611) 210/C3
Longhua, China 77/J3
Longhui, China 77/H6
Longido, Tanzania 115/G4
Longiram, Indonesia 85/F5
Long Island (sound), Conn. 210/C4
Long Island (bay), Ireland 17/B9
Long Island, Kansas (67647) 232/C2
Long Island (sound), N.Y. 276/P9
Longisland, N.C. (28648) 281/H3
Long Island, Tenn. (†37662) 237/S7
Long Island, Va. (24569) 307/K6
Longjiang, China 77/K2
Long Key, Fla. (33001) 212/F7
Longkou, China 77/J4
Longlac, Ontario 177/H5
Longlac, Ontario 175/C3
Long Lake, Mich. (48743) 250/F4
Long Lake, Minn. (55356) 255/F5
Long Lake, N.Y. (12847) 276/L3
Longlake, S. Dak. (57457) 298/L2
Long Lake, Wis. (54542) 317/J4
Long Lane, Mo. (65590) 261/G7
Longleaf, La. (71448) 238/E4
Long Meadow (pond), Conn. 210/C2
Longmeadow○, Mass. (01106) 249/D4
Longmire, Wash. (98397) 310/D4
Longmont, Colo. 188/E2
Longmont, Colo. (80501) 208/J2
Longnan, China 77/J7
Longnawan, Indonesia 85/F5
Long Neck (pt.), Conn. 210/B4
Long Pine, Nebr. (69217) 264/E2
Long Point, Ill. (61333) 222/E3
Long Point, Nova Scotia 168/G3
Long Point (bay), Ontario 177/D5
Long Point Beach, Ontario 177/D5
Long Pond, Maine (†04945) 243/C4
Long Pond, Pa. (18334) 294/L3
Longport, N.J. (08403) 273/D5
Long Prairie, Minn. (56347) 255/D5
Long Prairie (riv.), Minn. 255/D4
Long Range (mts.), Newf. 166/C4
Long Rapids, Mich. (†49753) 250/F3
Longreach, Australia 87/E8
Long Reach (inlet), New Bruns. 170/D3
Longreach, Queensland 88/G4
Longreach, Queensland 95/B4
Long Reef (pt.), N.S. Wales 97/K3
Longridge, England 13/H1
Longridge, England 10/G1
Longs (peak), Colo. 208/H2
Longs, S.C. (29568) 296/K4
Long Sault, Ontario 177/K2
Longshan, China 77/G6
Long Siding, Minn. (†55371) 255/E5
Long Society, Conn. (†06360) 210/G2
Long Spruce, Manitoba 179/K2
Longstreet, La. (71050) 238/B2
Longton, Kansas (67352) 232/F4
Longtown, Miss. (†38665) 256/D1
Longtown, Mo. (†63775) 261/N7
Longtown, S.C. (†29130) 296/F3
Longueuil, Québec 172/J4
Long Valley, N.J. (07853) 273/D2
Longvalley, S. Dak. (57547) 298/F7
Longview, Ala. (†35137) 195/E4
Longview, Alberta 182/C4
Longview, Colo. (†80135) 208/J4
Longview, Ill. (61852) 222/E4
Longview, Miss. (†39759) 256/G4
Longview, N.C. (28601) 281/F3
Longview, Texas 188/G4
Longview, Texas (*75601) 303/K5
Longview, Wash. 188/B1
Longview, Wash. (98632) 310/B4
Longville, La. (70652) 238/D5
Longville, Minn. (56655) 255/D4
Longwood, Fla. (32750) 212/E3
Longwood, Mo. (†65301) 261/F5
Longwood, N.C. (28452) 281/M7
Longwood Park, N.C. (†28345) 281/K5
Longworth, Br. Col. 184/G3
Longworth, Texas (†79604) 303/D5
Longwy, France 28/F3
Long Xian, China 77/G5
Long Xuyen, Vietnam 72/E5
Longyan, China 77/J6
Longyearbyen, Norway 18/D2
Longyearbyen, Norway 4/B8
Longzhen (Lungchen), China 77/L2
Loni Beach, Manitoba 179/F4
Lonigo, Italy 34/C2
Lonneker, Netherlands 27/K4
Lonoke (co.), Ark. 202/G4
Lonoke, Ark. (72086) 202/G4
Lonquimay, Chile 138/E2
Lonsdale, Ark. (72087) 202/E4
Lonsdale, Minn. (55046) 255/E6
Lonsdale, R.I. (†02864) 249/J5
Lons-le-Saunier, France 28/F4
Lonton, Burma 72/B1
Lontzen, Belgium 27/H9
Looe, England 13/C7
Loogootee, Ind. (47553) 227/D7
Lookeba, Okla. (73053) 288/K4
Lookingglass (riv.), Mich. 250/E6
Lookout (mt.), Ala. 195/G2
Lookout (ridge), Alaska 196/G1
Lookout, Calif. (96054) 204/D2
Lookout (mt.), Idaho 220/F5
Lookout (mt.), Idaho 220/D5
Lookout, Ky. (41542) 237/S6
Lookout (pt.), Md. 245/N8
Lookout (cape), N.C. 188/L4
Lookout (cape), N.C. 281/S5
Lookout, Okla. (†73842) 288/H1
Lookout (cape), Oreg. 188/B1
Lookout (cape), Oreg. 291/C2
Lookout, Pa. (†18417) 294/M2
Lookout, W. Va. (25868) 312/E6
Lookout, Wyo. (†82051) 319/G4
Lookout Mountain, Georgia (†30741) 217/B1
Lookout Mountain, Tenn. (37350) 237/L11
Lookout Point (lake), Oreg. 291/E4
Looma, Alberta 182/D3
Loomis, Calif. (95650) 204/C8
Loomis, Nebr. (68958) 264/E4
Loomis, Sask. 181/C6
Loomis, S. Dak. (57360) 298/N8
Loomis, Wash. (98827) 310/F2
Loomis, Wis. (†54157) 317/K5
Loon (lake), Alberta 182/C1
Loon (riv.), Alberta 182/C1
Loon (lake), Maine 243/D3
Loon (lake), Ontario 177/F3
Loon (creek), Sask. 181/G4
Loon (lake), Wash. 310/H2
Looneyville, W. Va. (25259) 312/D5
Loon Lake, Alberta 182/C1
Loon Lake, Maine (†04970) 243/B5
Loon Lake, N.Y. (†12968) 276/M1
Loon Lake, Sask. 181/B1
Loon Lake, Wash. (99148) 310/H2
Loon op Zand, Netherlands 27/G5
Loon Strait, Manitoba 179/F3
Loop (head), Ireland 17/A6
Loop (head), Ireland 10/A4
Loop, Texas (79342) 303/B5
Loos, Br. Col. 184/G3
Loosahatchie (riv.), Tenn. 237/B10
Loose Creek, Mo. (65054) 261/J5
Lo Ovalle, Chile 138/F3
Looxahoma, Miss. (†38668) 256/E1
Looz (Borgloon), Belgium 27/G7
Lopatka (cape), U.S.S.R. 54/S4
Lopatka (cape), U.S.S.R. 48/Q4
Lop Buri, Thailand 72/D4
Lopeno, Texas (78564) 303/E11
Lopez (pt.), Calif. 204/D7
Lopez (cape), Gabon 102/C5
Lopez (cape), Gabon 115/A4
Lopez, Pa. (18628) 294/K3
Lopez, Wash. (98261) 310/C2
Lopez (isl.), Wash. 310/C2
Lopi, Congo 115/C3
Lop Nor (Lop Nur) (lake), China 77/D3
Lopnur (Yuli), China 77/C3
Lop Nur (lake), China 54/L5
Lopphavet (bay), Norway 18/M1
Lora, Hamun-i- (swamp), Pakistan 68/B3
Lora, Hamun-i- (swamp), Pakistan 59/J4
Lora del Río, Spain 33/D4
Lorado, W. Va. (25630) 312/C7
Lorain (co.), Ohio 284/F3
Lorain, Ohio (*44052) 284/F3
Loraine, Ill. (62349) 222/B3
Loraine, N. Dak. (58761) 282/G2
Loraine, Texas (79532) 303/D5
Loraine, Wis. (†54825) 317/B4
Loralai, Pakistan 68/B2
Loralai, Pakistan 59/J3
Loramie (lake), Ohio 284/B5
Loranger, La. (70446) 238/N1
Lorca, Spain 33/F4
Lord Howe (isl.), Australia 87/G9
Lord Howe (isl.), Australia 2/T7
Lord Howe (isl.), N.S. Wales 97/J2
Lord Howe (Ontong Java) (isl.), Solomon Is. 87/G6
Lord Howe (Ontong Java) (isl.), Solomon Is. 86/D2
Lord Mayor (bay), N.W. Terrs. 187/J3
Lordsburg, N. Mex. (88045) 274/A6
Lords Point, Conn. (†06378) 210/H3
Lordstown, Ohio (†44481) 284/J3
Lords Valley, Pa. (†18428) 294/M3
Loreauville, La. (70552) 238/G6
Loreburn, Sask. 181/E4
Lore City, Ohio (43755) 284/H6
Lorena, Brazil 135/D3
Lorena, Miss. (†39153) 256/F6
Lorengau, Papua N.G. 86/A1
Lorengau, Papua N.G. 87/E6
Lo-Reninge, Belgium 27/B7
Lorentz, W. Va. (†26201) 312/F4
Lorenzo, Idaho (†83442) 220/G6
Lorenzo, Texas (79343) 303/C4
Lorenzo Geyres, Uruguay 145/B3
Lorestan (Luristan) (governorate), Iran 66/F4
Loreto, Bolivia 136/C4
Loreto, Colombia 126/E9
Loreto, Ecuador 128/D3
Loreto, Baja California, Mexico 150/D4
Loreto, Zacatecas, Mexico 150/J5
Loreto, Paraguay 144/D3
Loreto (dept.), Peru 128/E5
Loreto, Agusan del Sur, Philippines 82/E6
Loreto, Surigao del Norte, Philippines 82/E5
Loretta, Kansas (†67520) 232/C3
Loretta, Wis. (54852) 317/E4
Lorette, Manitoba 179/F5
Loretteville, Québec 172/H3
Loretto, Ky. (40037) 237/L5
Loretto, Mich. (49852) 250/B3
Loretto, Minn. (55357) 255/F5
Loretto, Nebr. (68646) 264/F3
Loretto, Pa. (15940) 294/E4
Loretto, Tenn. (38469) 237/G10
Loretto, Va. (22509) 307/O4
Lorian (swamp), Kenya 115/G3
Lorica, Colombia 126/C3
Lorida, Fla. (33857) 212/E4
Lorient, France 7/D4
Lorient, France 28/B4
L'Orignal, Ontario 177/K2
Lorimor, Iowa (50149) 229/E6
Lőrinci, Hungary 41/E3
Loring, Mont. (59537) 262/J2
Loring, Ontario 177/D2
Loring A.F.B., Maine 243/H2
Loris, S.C. (29569) 296/K3
Lorlie, Sask. 181/H5
Lorman, Miss. (39096) 256/B7
Lorne, New Bruns. 170/D1
Lorne, Nova Scotia 168/F3
Lorne (dist.), Scotland 15/C4
Lorne (firth), Scotland 10/D2
Lorne (firth), Scotland 15/C4
Loros (pt.), Chile 138/E3
Lörrach, W. Germany 22/B5
Lorrain (riv.), Martinique 161/D5
Lorraine (trad. prov.), France 29
Lorraine, Kansas (67459) 232/D3
Lorraine, N.Y. (13659) 276/J3
Lorraine, Québec 172/H4
Lorrainville, Québec 174/B3
Lorrha, Ireland 17/E5
Lort (riv.), W. Australia 88/C6
Lorton, Nebr. (68382) 264/H4
Lorton, Va. (22079) 307/O3
Lorze (riv.), Switzerland 39/F2
Los (isls.), Guinea 106/B7
Losada (riv.), Colombia 126/C6
Los Alamitos, Calif. (90720) 204/D11
Los Alamos, Calif. (93440) 204/E9
Los Alamos, N. Mex. 188/E3
Los Alamos (co.), N. Mex. 274/C3
Los Alamos, N. Mex. (87544) 274/C3
Los Alerces Nat'l Park, Argentina 143/C5
Los Algodones, Mexico 150/B1
Los Altos, Calif. (94022) 204/K3
Los Altos Hills, Calif. (94022) 204/J3
Los Amates, Guatemala 154/C3
Los Andes, Chile 138/B9
Los Andes, Colombia 126/B7
Los Angeles, Calif. 146/G6
Los Angeles, Calif. 188/C4
Los Angeles (co.), Calif. 204/G9
Los Angeles, Calif. (*90001) 204/C10
Los Ángeles, Chile 138/D1
Los Angeles, Chile 120/B6
Los Angeles, Texas (78051) 303/F9
Los Angeles, U.S. 2/D4
Los Angeles Aqueduct, Calif. 204/G8
Los Antiguos, Argentina 143/B6
Losantville, Ind. (47354) 227/G4
Los Arabos, Cuba 158/E1
Los Arroyos, Cuba 158/A2
Los Banos, Calif. (93635) 204/E6
Los Barcos (pt.), Cuba 158/B2
Los Canarreos (arch.), Cuba 158/C2
Los Castillos, Venezuela 124/G3
Los Choros (riv.), Chile 138/A7
Los Colorados (arch.), Cuba 158/A1
Los Conquistadores, Argentina 143/G5
Los Coyotes Ind. Res., Calif. 204/J10
Los Cusis, Bolivia 136/D4
Los Estados (isl.), Argentina 143/D7
Los Frailes (isl.), Dom. Rep. 158/C7
Los Fresnos, Texas (78566) 303/G11
Los Gatos, Calif. (95030) 204/K4
Los Glaciares Nat'l Park, Argentina 143/B6
Loshan (Leshan), China 77/F6
Los Hermanos (isls.), Venezuela 124/F2
Łosice, Poland 47/F2
Los Indios, Cuba 158/B2
Lošinj (isl.), Yugoslavia 45/B3
Los Lagos (reg.), Chile 138/D3
Los Lagos, Chile 138/D3
Los Llanos, Dom. Rep. 158/F6
Los Loros, Chile 138/B8
Los Lunas, N. Mex. (87031) 274/C4
Los Menucos, Argentina 143/C5
Los Mochis, Mexico 150/E4
Los Molinos, Calif. (96055) 204/D3
Los Monjes (isls.), Venezuela 124/C1
Los Muermos, Chile 138/D3
Los Navalmorales, Spain 33/D3
Los Navalucillos, Spain 33/D3
Los Negros, Cuba 158/F2
Løsning, Denmark 21/C6
Los Novillos, Uruguay 145/D2
Los Ojos, N. Mex. (87551) 274/C2
Los Olivos, Calif. (93441) 204/E9
Los Olmos (creek), Texas 303/F10
Los Olmos (creek), Texas 303/F11
Los Osos-Baywood Park, Calif. (†93402) 204/E8
Los Palacios, Cuba 158/B1
Los Palacios, Cuba 156/A2
Los Perales de Tapihue, Chile 138/F3
Los Pinos (riv.), Colo. 208/G8
Los Ranchos De Albuquerque, N. Mex. (†87101) 274/C3
Los Reyes de Salgado, Mexico 150/H7
Los Ríos (prov.), Ecuador 128/C3
Los Roques (isls.), Venezuela 124/E2
Los Santos, Panama 154/G7
Los Santos de Maimona, Spain 33/C3
Los Sauces, Chile 138/D2
Losser, Netherlands 27/L4
Lossiemouth and Branderburgh, Scotland 15/E3
Lossiemouth and Branderburgh, Scotland 10/E2
Lost (riv.), Calif. 204/D1

402 Lost

Lost (riv.), Ind. 227/D7
Lost (riv.), Minn. 255/C3
Lost (riv.), Oreg. 291/F5
Lost (creek), Utah 304/C5
Lostallo, Switzerland 39/H4
Lostant, Ill. (61334) 222/D2
Los Taques, Venezuela 124/C2
Lost Cabin, Wyo. (†82642) 319/E2
Lost City, W. Va. (26810) 312/J5
Lost Creek, Ky. (41348) 237/P6
Lost Creek, Wash. (†99180) 310/H2
Lost Creek, W. Va. (26385) 312/F4
Los Teques, Venezuela 120/C2
Los Teques, Venezuela 124/E2
Los Testigos (isls.), Venezuela 124/G2
Lost Hills, Calif. (93249) 204/F8
Lostine, Oreg. (97857) 291/K2
Lost Island (lake), Iowa 229/D2
Lost Nation, Iowa (52254) 229/M5
Lost River, Idaho (†83255) 220/E6
Lost River (range), Idaho 220/E5
Lost River, W. Va. (26811) 312/J5
Lost Springs, Kansas (66859) 232/E3
Lost Springs, Wyo. (82224) 319/G3
Lost Trail (pass), Idaho 220/E4
Lost Trail (pass), Mont. 262/B5
Lostwood, N. Dak. (†58784) 282/F3
Los Vilos, Chile 138/A9
Los Yébenes, Spain 33/E3
Lot (dept.), France 28/D5
Lot (riv.), France 28/D5
Lota, Chile 138/D1
Lotagipi Swamp (plain), Sudan 111/F6
Lotbinière (co.), Québec 172/F3
Lotbinière, Québec 172/F3
Lot-et-Garonne (dept.), France 28/D5
Lothair, Ky. (†41701) 237/P6
Lothair, Mont. (59461) 262/E2
Lothian, Md. (20820) 245/M5
Lothian (reg.), Scotland 15/E5
Lothain (trad. co.), Scotland 15/A5
Loto, Zaire 115/D4
Lötschberg (tunnel), Switzerland 39/E4
Lotsee, Okla. (†74063) 288/O2
Lott, Texas (76656) 303/H6
Lottie, Ala. (†36552) 195/C8
Lottie, La. (70756) 238/G5
Lottsville, Pa. (†16402) 294/D2
Lotus, Calif. (95651) 204/C8
Lotzwil, Switzerland 39/E2
Louang Namtha, Laos 72/D2
Louangphrabang, Laos 72/D3
Louangphrabang, Laos 54/M7
Louann, Ark. (71751) 202/E7
Loubomo, Congo 115/B4
Loubomo, Congo 102/D5
Loudéac, France 28/B3
Loudima, Congo 115/B4
Loudon○, N.H. (03301) 268/E5
Loudon (co.), Tenn. 237/N9
Loudon, Tenn. (37774) 237/N9
Loudonville, Ohio (44842) 284/F4
Loudoun (co.), Va. 307/N2
Loudun, France 28/D4
Louellen, Ky. (40853) 237/P7
Louga, Senegal 106/A5
Loughborough, England 13/F5
Loughborough, England 10/F4
Loughbrickland, N. Ireland 17/J3
Lougheed, Alberta 182/E3
Lougheed (isl.), N.W. Terrs. 187/H2
Loughman, Fla. (33858) 212/E3
Loughrea, Ireland 17/E5
Loughrea, Ireland 10/B4
Loughros More (bay), Ireland 17/D2
Louin, Miss. (39338) 256/F6
Louisa (co.), Iowa 229/L6
Louisa, Ky. (41230) 237/R4
Louisa, La. (†70538) 238/G7
Louisa (lake), Ontario 177/F2
Louisa (co.), Va. 307/N5
Louisa, Va. (23093) 307/M4
Louisbourg, Nova Scotia 168/J3
Louisbourg Nat'l Hist. Park, Nova Scotia 168/J3
Louisburg, Kansas (66053) 232/H3
Louisburg, Minn. (56254) 255/B5
Louisburg, Mo. (65685) 261/F7
Louisburg, N.C. (27549) 281/N2
Louisburgh, Ireland 17/B4
Louis Creek, Br. Col. 184/H4
Louisdale, Nova Scotia 168/G3
Louise (lake), Alaska 196/C1
Louise (isl.), Br. Col. 184/B4
Louise, Miss. (39097) 256/C5
Louise (lake), Québec 172/C4
Louise, Texas (77455) 303/H8
Louiseville, Québec 172/E3
Louisiade (arch.), Papua N.G. 87/F7
Louisiade (arch.), Papua N.G. 85/D8
Louisiana 188/H4
LOUISIANA 238
Louisiana (pt.), La. 238/C7
Louisiana, Mo. (63353) 261/K4
Louisiana (state), U.S. 146/J6
Louis Trichardt, S. Africa 118/E4
Louisville, Ala. (36048) 195/G7
Louisville, Colo. (80027) 208/J3
Louisville, Georgia (30434) 217/H4
Louisville, Ill. (62858) 222/E5
Louisville, Kansas (66450) 232/F2
Louisville, Ky. (*40201) 237/J2
Louisville, Ky. 146/K6
Louisville, Miss. (39339) 256/G4
Louisville, Nebr. (68037) 264/H3
Louisville, Ohio (44641) 284/H4
Louisville, Tenn. (37777) 237/N9
Louisville, Ky. 188/J3
Louis XIV (pt.), Que. 162/H5
Louis XIV (pt.), Québec 174/B2
Loukhi, U.S.S.R. 52/D1
Loulé, Portugal 33/B4
Louny, Czech. 41/B1
Loup (co.), Nebr. 264/E3
Loup (riv.), Nebr. 264/F3
Loup (riv.), Québec 172/H2
Loup City, Nebr. (68853) 264/E3
Lourdes, France 28/C6
Lourdes, Newf. 166/C4
Lourdes, N. Mex. (†87701) 274/D3
Lourdes, Québec 172/F3
Louriçal, Portugal 33/B3
Lourinhã, Portugal 33/B3
Lousã, Portugal 33/B2
Lousana, Alberta 182/D3
Louth, England 13/H4
Louth, England 10/F4
Louth (co.), Ireland 17/J4
Louth, Ireland 17/J4
Louth, N.S. Wales 97/C2
Loutrá Aidhipsoú, Greece 45/F6
Louvain (Leuven), Belgium 27/F7
Louvale, Georgia (31814) 217/C6
Louviers, Colo. (80131) 208/K4
Louviers, France 28/D3
Lövånger, Sweden 18/M4
Lovango (cay), Virgin Is. (U.S.) 161/C4
Lovat' (riv.), U.S.S.R. 52/D3
Love, Miss. (†38632) 256/D1
Love (co.), Okla. 288/M7
Love, Sask. 181/G2
Lovech, Bulgaria 45/G4
Lovejoy, Georgia (30250) 217/D4
Lovejoy, Ill. (62059) 222/A2
Lovelaceville, Ky. (42060) 237/D7
Lovelady, Texas (75851) 303/J6
Loveland, Colo. 188/E2
Loveland, Colo. (80537) 208/J2
Loveland, Iowa (†51555) 229/B6
Loveland, Ohio (45140) 284/D9
Loveland, Okla. (73553) 288/J6
Lovell, Maine (04051) 243/B7
Lovell○, Maine (04051) 243/B7
Lovell, Okla. (†73028) 288/L2
Lovell, Wyo. (82431) 319/D1
Lovells, Mich. (†49738) 250/E4
Lovelock, Nev. (89419) 266/C2
Lovely, Ky. (41231) 237/S5
Lovenia (mt.), Utah 304/D3
Love Point, Md. (†21617) 245/N4
Loverna, Sask. 181/B4
Loves Park, Ill. (61111) 222/E1
Lovett, Georgia (†31021) 217/G5
Lovett, Ind. (†47265) 227/F7
Lovettsville, Va. (22080) 307/N2
Love Valley, N.C. (28677) 281/H3
Loveville, Md. (20656) 245/M7
Lovewell, Kansas (†66942) 232/D2
Lovewell (res.), Kansas 232/D2
Lovilia, Iowa (50150) 229/H6
Loving, N. Mex. (88256) 274/E6
Loving (co.), Texas 303/A6
Lovingston, Va. (22949) 307/L5
Lovington, Ill. (61937) 222/E4
Lovington, N. Mex. (88260) 274/F6
Lovisa, Finland 18/P6
Lövö, Hungary 41/D3
Lovosice, Czech. 41/C1
Lóvua, Angola 115/D5
Low (cape), N.W.T. 162/H3
Low (cape), N.W. Terrs. 187/K3
Low, Québec 172/B4
Lowa (riv.), Zaire 115/E4
Low Bush River, Ontario 177/K5
Low Bush River, Ontario 175/E3
Lowden, Iowa (52255) 229/L5
Lowder, Ill. (62662) 222/D4
Lowe Farm, Manitoba 179/E5
Lowell, Ark. (72745) 202/B1
Lowell, Fla. (32663) 212/D2
Lowell, Idaho (†83539) 220/C3
Lowell (lake), Idaho 220/B6
Lowell, Ind. (46356) 227/C2
Lowell, Iowa (†52645) 229/L7
Lowell, Maine (†04433) 243/F5
Lowell○, Maine (†04433) 243/F5
Lowell, Mass. 188/M2
Lowell, Mass. (*01850) 249/J2
Lowell, Mich. (49331) 250/D6
Lowell, N.C. (28098) 281/G4
Lowell, Ohio (45744) 284/H6
Lowell, Oreg. (97452) 291/E4
Lowell○, Vt. (05847) 268/C2
Lowell, W. Va. (†24910) 312/E7
Lowell, Wis. (53557) 317/J9
Lowell Nat'l Hist. Park, Mass. 249/J2
Lowellville, Ohio (44436) 284/J3
Lower Alkali (lake), Calif. 204/E2
Lower Argyle, Nova Scotia 168/C5
Lower Arrow (lake), Br. Col. 184/H5
Lower Austria (prov.), Austria 41/C2
Lower Bank, N.J. (†08215) 273/E4
Lower Barneys River, Nova Scotia 168/F3
Lower Brule, S. Dak. (57548) 298/K5
Lower Brule Ind. Res., S. Dak. 298/K5
Lower Burrell, Pa. (15068) 294/C4
Lower Cabot, Vt. (†05658) 268/C3
Lower California (pen.), Mexico 2/D4
Lower California (pen.), Mexico 146/G7
Lower California (pen.), Mexico 150/C3
Lower Cloverdale, New Bruns. 170/F2
Lower Crab (creek), Wash. 310/F4
Lower Derby, New Bruns. 170/E2
Lower Durham, New Bruns. 170/D2
Lower East Pubnico, Nova Scotia 168/C5
Lower Elwah Ind. Res., Wash. 310/B2
Lower Engadine (valley), Switzerland 39/K3
Lower Goose Creek (res.), Idaho 220/D7
Lower Granite (lake), Idaho 220/A3
Lower Granite (dam), Wash. 310/H4
Lower Granite (lake), Wash. 310/H4
Lower Hainesville, New Bruns. 170/C2
Lower Hutt, N. Zealand 100/B2
Lower Island Cove, Newf. 166/D2
Lower Kalskag, Alaska (99626) 196/F2
Lower Kars, New Bruns. 170/E3
Lower Klamath (lake), Calif. 204/D2
Lower Lake, Calif. (95457) 204/C5
Lower L'Ardoise, Nova Scotia 168/H3
Lower Marlboro, Md. (†20836) 245/M6
Lower Matecumbe (key), Fla. 212/F7
Lower Millstream, New Bruns. 170/E3
Lower Montague, Pr. Edward I. 168/F2
Lower Monumental (dam), Wash. 310/G4
Lower Monumental (lake), Wash. 310/G4
Lower New York (bay), N.J. 273/E2
Lower Nicola, Br. Col. 184/G5
Lower Ohio, Nova Scotia 168/C5
Lower Paia, Hawaii (†96779) 218/J1
Lower Peach Tree, Ala. (36751) 195/C7
Lower Post, Br. Col. 184/K1
Lower Red (lake), Minn. 255/C3
Lower Red Rock (lake), Mont. 262/E6
Lower Rhine (riv.), Netherlands 27/H5
Lower Roach (pond), Maine 243/E4
Lower Saint Mary (lake), Mont. 262/C2
Lower Salem, Ohio (45745) 284/H6
Lower Sapin, New Bruns. 170/F2
Lower Saranac (lake), N.Y. 276/M2
Lower Saxony (state), W. Germany 22/C2
Lower Southampton, New Bruns. 170/C2
Lower South River, Nova Scotia 168/F3
Lower Sysladobsis (lake), Maine 243/G5
Lower Tonsina, Alaska (†99566) 196/J2
Lower Tunguska (riv.), U.S.S.R. 54/L3
Lower Tunguska (riv.), U.S.S.R. 48/K3
Lower Waterford, Vt. (05848) 268/D3
Lower Wedgeport, Nova Scotia 168/C5
Lower West Pubnico, Nova Scotia 168/C5
Lower Woods Harbour, Nova Scotia 168/C5
Lowery, Ala. (†36453) 195/F8
Lowery (lake), Fla. 212/E3
Lowes, Ky. (42061) 237/D7
Lowestoft, England 13/J5
Lowestoft, England 10/G4
Lowesville, Va. (22951) 307/K5
Lowgap, N.C. (27024) 281/H1
Łowicz, Poland 47/D2
Lowland, N.C. (28552) 281/S4
Lowman, Idaho (83637) 220/C5
Lowmansville, Ky. (41232) 237/R5
Low Moor, Iowa (52757) 229/N5
Lowmoor, Va. (24457) 307/J5
Lowndes (co.), Ala. 195/E6
Lowndes (co.), Georgia 217/F9
Lowndes (co.), Miss. 256/H4
Lowndes, Mo. (63951) 261/M8
Lowndesboro, Ala. (36752) 195/E6
Lowndesville, S.C. (29659) 296/B3
Lowpoint, Ill. (61545) 222/D3
Low Rocky (pt.), Tasmania 99/B4
Lowry, Minn. (56349) 255/C5
Lowry, S. Dak. (†57472) 298/K3
Lowry, Va. (24570) 307/K6
Lowry A.F.B., Colo. 208/K3
Lowry City, Mo. (64763) 261/E6
Lowrys, S.C. (†29706) 296/E2
Lowther (isl.), N.W. Terrs. 187/J2
Lowville, N.Y. (13367) 276/J3
Low Wassie, Mo. (†65588) 261/K9
Loxahatchee, Fla. (33470) 212/F5
Loxley, Ala. (36551) 195/C9
Loxton, S. Australia 94/G6
Loxton North, S. Australia 94/G6
Loyal, Okla. (73756) 288/K3
Loyal, Loch (lake), Scotland 15/D2
Loyal, Wis. (54446) 317/E6
Loyalhanna, Pa. (15661) 294/D5
Loyalist, Alberta 182/E4
Loyall, Ky. (40854) 237/P7
Loyalton, Calif. (96118) 204/E4
Loyalton, Pa. (†17048) 294/J4
Loyalton, S. Dak. (†57471) 298/L3
Loyalty (isls.), New Caled. 87/G8
Loyalty (isls.), New Caled. 86/H4
Loyang (Luoyang), China 77/H5
Loyd, Wis. (†53924) 317/F9
Loyne, Loch (lake), Scotland 15/C3
Loysburg, Pa. (16659) 294/F5
Loysville, Pa. (17047) 294/H5
Lozeau (lake), Newf. 166/B3
Lozère (dept.), France 28/E5
Loznica, Yugoslavia 45/D3
Lozovaya, U.S.S.R. 52/E5
Lua (riv.), Zaire 115/C3
Luacano, Angola 115/D6
Luachimo, Angola 115/D5
Lualaba (riv.), Zaire 102/E5
Lualaba (riv.), Zaire 115/E4
Lua Makika (mt.), Hawaii 218/J3
Lu'an, China 77/J5
Luana, Iowa (52156) 229/K2
Luana (pt.), Jamaica 158/G6
Luanchuan, China 77/H5
Luanda (dist.), Angola 115/B5
Luanda (cap.), Angola 2/K6
Luanda (cap.), Angola 115/B5
Luanda (cap.), Angola 102/D5
Luang, Thale (lag.), Thailand 72/D6
Luang (mt.), Thailand 72/C5
Luang Prabang (Loungphrabang), Laos 72/D3
Luangwa (Feira), Zambia 115/E7
Luangwa (riv.), Zambia 115/F6
Luanshya, Zambia 115/E6
Luanshya, Zambia 102/E6
Luao, Angola 115/D6
Luapula (riv.), Zaire 115/E6
Luapula (riv.), Zambia 115/E6
Luarca, Spain 33/C1
Luashi, Zaire 115/D6
Luba, Equat. Guinea 115/A3
Lubaczów, Poland 47/F3
Lubań, Poland 47/B3
Lubāna (lake), U.S.S.R. 53/D2
Lubang, Philippines 82/C4
Lubang (isls.), Philippines 85/F3
Lubang (isls.), Philippines 82/B4
Lubango, Angola 115/B6
Lubango, Angola 102/D6
Lubartów, Poland 47/F3
Lubawa, Poland 47/D2
Lübben, E. Germany 22/E3
Lübbenau, E. Germany 22/F3
Lubbock (co.), Texas 303/C4
Lubbock, Texas 146/H6
Lubbock, Texas (*79401) 303/C4
Lubbock, Texas 188/F4
Lubec, Maine (04652) 243/K6
Lubec○, Maine (04652) 243/K6
Lübeck, W. Germany 7/E3
Lübeck, W. Germany 22/D2
Lubeck, W. Va. (†26101) 312/C4
Lubefu, Zaire 115/D4
Lubero, Zaire 115/E4
L'ubica, Czech. 41/F2
Lubicon (lake), Alberta 182/C1
Lubien Kujawski, Poland 47/D2
Lubilash (riv.), Zaire 115/D5
Lubin, Poland 47/C3
Lublin (prov.), Poland 47/F3
Lublin, Poland 47/F3
Lublin, Poland 7/G3
Lublin, Wis. (54447) 317/E5
Lubliniec, Poland 47/D3
Lubny, U.S.S.R. 52/D4
Luboń, Poland 47/C2
Lubrín, Spain 33/F4
Lubsko, Poland 47/B3
Lubuagan, Philippines 82/C2
Lubudi, Zaire 115/E5
Lubuklinggau, Indonesia 85/C6
Lubuksikaping, Indonesia 85/B5
Lubumbashi, Zaire 2/L6
Lubumbashi, Zaire 115/E6
Lubumbashi, Zaire 102/E6
Lubutu, Zaire 115/E4
Lübz, E. Germany 22/D2
Lucama, N.C. (27851) 281/N3
Lucan, Minn. (56255) 255/C6
Lucan, Ontario 177/C4
Luc An Chau, Vietnam 72/E2
Lucan-Doddsborough, Ireland 17/J5
Lucas (co.), Iowa 229/G6
Lucas, Iowa (50151) 229/G6
Lucas, Kansas (67648) 232/D2
Lucas, Ky. (42156) 237/K7
Lucas, Mich. (†49657) 250/D4
Lucas (co.), Ohio 284/C2
Lucas, Ohio (44843) 284/F4
Lucas, S. Dak. (57549) 298/L7
Lucas, Texas (†75069) 303/H1
Lucas E. de Peña, Dom. Rep. 158/D5
Lucas González, Argentina 143/G6
Lucasville, Ohio (45648) 284/E8
Lucban, Philippines 82/C3
Lucca (prov.), Italy 34/C3
Lucca, Italy 34/C3
Lucca, N. Dak. (†58027) 282/P6
Luce (co.), Mich. 250/D2
Luce, Minn. (†56573) 255/C4
Luce (bay), Scotland 10/D3
Luce (bay), Scotland 15/D6
Lucea, Jamaica 158/G5
Lucedale, Miss. (39452) 256/G9
Lucena, Philippines 85/G3
Lucena, Philippines 82/C4
Lucena, Spain 33/D4
Lucena del Cid, Spain 33/F2
Lučenec, Czech. 41/E2
Lucens, Switzerland 39/C3
Lucera, Italy 34/E4
Lucerna, Peru 128/H9
Lucerne, Calif. (95458) 204/C4
Lucerne, Colo. (80646) 208/K2
Lucerne, Ind. (46950) 227/E3
Lucerne, Mo. (64655) 261/F2
Lucerne, Québec 172/B4
Lucerne (Luzern) (canton), Switzerland 39/F2
Lucerne, Switzerland 39/F2
Lucerne (lake), Switzerland 39/F3
Lucerne, Wash. (†98816) 310/E2
Lucerne, Wyo. (†82443) 319/D2
Lucernemines, Pa. (15754) 294/D4
Lucerne Valley, Calif. (92356) 204/J9
Lucero (lake), N. Mex. 274/C6
Luceville, Québec 172/J1
Luchow (Luzhou), China 77/G6
Lüchow, W. Germany 22/D2
Lucia, Calif. (†93920) 204/D7
Lucie (riv.), Suriname 131/C4
Lucien, Miss. (39646) 256/C7
Lucien, Okla. (73757) 288/M2
Lucile, Georgia (†31723) 217/C8
Lucile, Idaho (83542) 220/B4
Lucile, Ky. (†41171) 237/P4
Lucinda, Pa. (16235) 294/D3
Lucira, Angola 115/B6
Luck, Wis. (54853) 317/B4
Luckau, E. Germany 22/E3
Luckenwalde, E. Germany 22/E2
Lucketts, Va. (†22075) 307/N2
Luckey, Ohio (43443) 284/D3
Lucknow, India 68/E3
Lucknow, India 54/K7
Lucknow, Ontario 177/C4
Lucky, La. (†71008) 238/E2
Lucky Lake, Sask. 181/D5
Lucky Peak (lake), Idaho 220/B6
Luçon, France 28/C4
Lucrecia (cape), Cuba 158/J3
Lucy, La. (†70049) 238/M3
Lucy, Tenn. (†38053) 237/B10
Lucy Creek, North. Terr. 93/E7
Lüda (Lüta), China 77/K4
Lüda, China 2/R4
Lüda, China 54/O6
Ludden, N. Dak. (58462) 282/O7
Ludell, Kansas (67744) 232/B2
Lüdenscheid, W. Germany 22/B3
Lüderitz, Namibia 118/A5
Lüderitz, Namibia 102/D7
Lüderitz (bay), Namibia 118/A5
Ludhiana, India 54/J6
Ludhiana, India 68/D2
Ludington, Mich. (49431) 250/C5
Ludlow, Calif. (†92365) 204/J9
Ludlow, England 10/E4
Ludlow, England 13/E5
Ludlow, Ill. (60949) 222/E3
Ludlow, Ky. (41016) 237/S2
Ludlow○, Maine (†04730) 243/G3
Ludlow○, Mass. (01056) 249/E4
Ludlow, Miss. (39098) 256/E5
Ludlow, Mo. (64656) 261/E3
Ludlow, New Bruns. 170/D2
Ludlow, Pa. (16333) 294/E2
Ludlow, S. Dak. (57755) 298/C2
Ludlow, Vt. (05149) 268/B5
Ludlow○, Vt. (05149) 268/B5
Ludlow (mt.), Vt. 268/B5
Ludlow Center, Mass. (†01056) 249/E4
Ludlow Falls, Ohio (45339) 284/B6
Ludowici, Georgia (31316) 217/J7
Luduş, Romania 45/G2
Ludvika, Sweden 18/J6
Ludville, Georgia (†30175) 217/C2
Ludwigsburg, W. Germany 22/C4
Ludwigshafen am Rhein, W. Germany 22/C4
Ludwigslust, E. Germany 22/D2
Ludza, U.S.S.R. 53/D2
Lue, N.S. Wales 97/E3
Luebbering, Mo. (63061) 261/L6
Luebo, Zaire 115/D5
Lueders, Texas (79533) 303/E5
Luella, Georgia (†30248) 217/D4
Luena, Angola 115/C6
Luepa, Venezuela 124/H5
Lüeyang, China 77/G5
Lufeng, China 77/J7
Lufira (riv.), Zaire 115/E5
Lufkin, Texas (75901) 303/K6
Luga, U.S.S.R. 52/C3
Luga, U.S.S.R. 48/D4
Lugano, Switzerland 39/G4
Lugano (lake), Switzerland 39/H5
Luganville, Vanuatu 87/G7
Lugareño, Cuba 158/G3
Lugenda (riv.), Mozambique 118/F2
Lugerville, Wis. (†54555) 317/E4
Lugnaquillia (mt.), Ireland 17/J5
Lugo, Italy 34/D2
Lugo (prov.), Spain 33/C1
Lugo, Spain 33/C1
Lugoff, S.C. (29078) 296/F3
Lugoj, Romania 45/E3
Luhaiya, Yemen Arab Rep. 59/D6
Luiana, Angola 115/D7
Luiana, Angola 102/E6
Luik (Liège), Belgium 27/H7
Luilaka (riv.), Zaire 115/C4
Luimneach (Limerick), Ireland 10/B4
Luimneach (Limerick), Ireland 17/D6
Luina, Tasmania 99/B3
Luing (isl.), Scotland 15/C4
Luís Correia, Brazil 132/F3
Luis de Saboya, Cerro (mt.), Chile 138/F11
Luishia, Zaire 115/E6
Luitpold Coast (reg.) 5/B17
Luiza, Zaire 115/D5
Luján, Argentina 143/G7
Lujiang, China 77/J5
Lukachukai, Ariz. (86507) 198/F2
Lukachukai (mts.), Ariz. 198/F2
Lukapa, Angola 115/D5
Luke, Md. (21540) 245/B3
Luke A.F.B., Ariz. 198/C5
Lukenie (riv.), Zaire 115/D4
Lukeville, Ariz. (85341) 198/C7
Lukolela, Equateur, Zaire 115/C4
Lukolela, Kasai-Oriental, Zaire 115/D5
Lukovit, Bulgaria 45/G4
Łuków, Poland 47/F3
Lukuga (riv.), Zaire 115/E5
Lukula, Zaire 115/B5
Lukulu, Zambia 115/D6
Lula, Georgia (30554) 217/E2
Łula, Miss. (38644) 256/C2
Lula, Okla. (†74825) 288/O5
Lule (riv.), Sweden 7/G2
Luleå, Sweden 7/G2
Luleå, Sweden 18/N4
Luleälv (riv.), Sweden 18/M4
Lüleburgaz, Turkey 63/B2
Lules, Argentina 143/C2
Luling, La. (70070) 238/N4
Luling, Texas (78648) 303/G8
Lulu, Fla. (32061) 212/D1
Lulua (riv.), Zaire 115/D5
Lum, Mich. (48452) 250/F5
Lumajang, Indonesia 85/K2
Lumajangdong Co (lake), China 77/B5
Lumbala, Angola 115/D6
Lumber (riv.), N.C. 281/L6
Lumber (riv.), S.C. 296/J3
Lumber Bridge, N.C. (28357) 281/L5
Lumber City, Georgia (31549) 217/G7
Lumber City, Pa. (†16833) 294/E4
Lumberport, W. Va. (26386) 312/F4
Lumberton, Miss. (39455) 256/E8
Lumberton, N.J. (08048) 273/D4
Lumberton, N. Mex. (87547) 274/C2
Lumberton, N.C. (28358) 281/L5
Lumberton, Texas (†77656) 303/K7
Lumberville, Pa. (18933) 294/N5
Lumbo, Mozambique 118/G3
Lumbrales, Spain 33/C2
Lumbrein, Switzerland 39/H3
Lumby, Br. Col. 184/H5
Lumding, India 68/G3
Lummen, Belgium 27/G7
Lummi (isl.), Wash. 310/C2
Lummi Ind. Res., Wash. 310/C2
Lummi Island, Wash. (98262) 310/C2
Lumphat, Cambodia 72/E4
Lumpkin (co.), Georgia 217/D1
Lumpkin, Georgia (31815) 217/C6
Lumsden, Newf. 166/D4
Lumsden, N. Zealand 100/B6
Lumsden, Sask. 181/G5
Lumsden, Scotland 15/F3
Lumsden Beach, Sask. 181/F5
Lumut, Malaysia 72/D6
Luna, Ark. (†71653) 202/H7
Luna (co.), N. Mex. 274/B6
Luna, N. Mex. (87824) 274/A5
Luna Pier, Mich. (48157) 250/F7
Luncarty, Scotland 15/E4
Lund, Br. Col. 184/E5
Lund, Idaho (†83241) 220/G7
Lund, Nev. (89317) 266/F4
Lund, Sweden 18/H9
Lund, Utah (†84720) 304/A5
Lundale, W. Va. (25631) 312/C7
Lunda Norte (dist.), Angola 115/C5
Lundar, Manitoba 179/D4
Lunda Sul (dist.), Angola 115/D5
Lundazi, Zambia 115/F6
Lundbreck, Alberta 182/C5
Lundby, Denmark 21/E7
Lundell, Ark. (†72367) 202/H5
Lunderskov, Denmark 21/C7
Lundi (riv.), Zimbabwe 118/E4
Lunds Corner, Mass. (02745) 249/L6
Lundsvalley, N. Dak. (†58724) 282/E3
Lundy (isl.), England 13/C6
Lundy (isl.), England 10/D5
Lune (riv.), England 13/E3
Lüneburg, W. Germany 22/D2
Lüneburger Heide (dist.), W. Germany 22/C2
Lunel, France 28/E6
Lünen, W. Germany 22/B3
Lunenburg, Mass. (01462) 249/H2
Lunenburg○, Mass. (01462) 249/H2
Lunenburg, N.S. 162/K7
Lunenburg (co.), Nova Scotia 168/D4
Lunenburg, Nova Scotia 168/D4
Lunenburg (bay), Nova Scotia 168/D4
Lunenburg○, Vt. (05906) 268/D3
Lunenburg (co.), Va. 307/M7
Lunenburg, Va. (23952) 307/M7
Lunéville, France 28/G3
Lung (riv.), Ireland 17/D4
Lungchen (Longzhen), China 77/L2
Lungdo, China 77/B5
Lungern, Switzerland 39/F3
Lungi, S. Leone 106/B7
Lungleh, India 68/G4
Lungwebungu (riv.), Angola 115/D6
Lungwebungu (riv.), Zambia 115/D6
Luni (riv.), India 68/C3
Luninets, U.S.S.R. 52/C4
Luning, Nev. (89420) 266/C4
Lunita, La. (†70661) 238/C6
Lunsford, Ark. (†72437) 202/K2
Luocheng, China 77/G7
Luodian, China 77/G6
Luoding, China 77/H7
Luohe, China 77/H5
Luoyang (Loyang), China 77/H5
Luoyang, China 54/N6
Luozi, Zaire 115/B5
Lupeni, Romania 45/F3
Luperón, Dom. Rep. 158/D5
Lupon, Philippines 82/E7
Lupton, Ariz. (86508) 198/F3
Lupton, Mich. (48635) 250/F4
Lupus, Mo. (†65046) 261/H5
Luputa, Zaire 115/D5
Luqu, China 77/F5
Luque, Paraguay 144/B4
Luquillo, P. Rico 161/F1
Luquillo, Sierra de (mts.), P. Rico 161/E2
Lurah (riv.), Afghanistan 68/B2
Lurah (riv.), Afghanistan 59/J3
Luray, Kansas (67649) 232/D2
Luray, Mo. (63453) 261/J2
Luray, S.C. (29932) 296/E6
Luray, Tenn. (38352) 237/D9
Luray, Va. (22835) 307/M3
Lure, France 28/G4
Lurgan, N. Ireland 17/J3
Luribay, Bolivia 136/B5
Lurín, Peru 128/D9
Lúrio, Mozambique 118/G2
Lúrio (riv.), Mozambique 118/F2
Luristan (Lorestan) (gov.), Iran 66/F4
Lurton, Ark. (†72856) 202/D2
Lusaka (cap.), Zambia 115/E7
Lusaka (cap.), Zambia 102/E6
Lusaka (cap.), Zambia 2/L6
Lusambo, Zaire 102/E5
Lusambo, Zaire 115/D4
Lusatia (reg.), E. Germany 22/F3
Lusby, Md. (20657) 245/N7
Luseland, Sask. 181/B3
Lushi, China 77/H5
Lushnje, Albania 45/D5
Lushoto, Tanzania 115/G4
Lushton, Nebr. (†68371) 264/G4
Lushui, China 77/E6
Lüshun, China 77/K4
Lusk, Ireland 17/J4
Lusk, Wyo. (82225) 319/H3
Luso, Angola 102/E6
Luss, Scotland 15/A1
Lustenau, Austria 41/A3
Lustre, Mont. (59225) 262/K2
Lut, Dasht-e (des.), Iran 59/G3
Lut, Dasht-e (des.), Iran 66/L5
Lüta (Lüda), China 77/K4
Lutcher, La. (70071) 238/L3
Lutesville, Mo. (63762) 261/M8
Luther, Iowa (50152) 229/F5
Luther, Mich. (49656) 250/D4
Luther, Mont. (59051) 262/G5
Luther, Okla. (73054) 288/M3
Luther, Tenn. (†37869) 237/P8
Luthern, Switzerland 39/E2
Luthersburg, Pa. (15848) 294/E3
Luthersville, Georgia (30251) 217/C4
Lutherville-Timonium, Md. (21093) 245/M3
Lutie, Okla. (†74578) 288/R5
Luton, England 13/G6
Luton, England 10/F5
Luton, Iowa (†51052) 229/A4
Lutry, Switzerland 39/C3

Magaguadavic 403

Lutsen, Minn. (55612) 255/F2
Lutsk, U.S.S.R. 7/G3
Lutsk, U.S.S.R. 52/B4
Lutsk, U.S.S.R. 48/C4
Luttrell, Tenn. (37779) 237/O8
Lutts, Tenn. (38471) 237/F10
Lutz, Fla. (33549) 212/D3
Lützelflüh, Switzerland 39/E3
Lützow-Holm (bay) 5/C3
Luuq, Somalia 115/H3
Luverne, Ala. (36049) 195/F7
Lu Verne, Iowa (50560) 229/E3
Luvernen Minn. (56156) 255/B7
Luverne, N. Dak. (58056) 282/P5
Luvua (riv.), Zaire 115/E5
Luwingu, Zambia 115/E6
Luwuk, Indonesia 85/G6
Lux, Miss. (†39401) 256/F8
Luxembourg 7/E4
Luxembourg (prov.), Belgium 27/G9
LUXEMBOURG 27/J9
Luxembourg (cap.), Luxembourg 27/J9
Luxemburg, Iowa (52056) 229/L3
Luxemburg, Minn. (†56301) 255/D5
Luxemburg, Wis. (54217) 317/L6
Luxeuil-les-Bains, France 28/G4
Luxi, China 77/E7
Luxi, China 77/F7
Luxor, Egypt 102/F2
Luxor, Egypt 59/B4
Luxor, Egypt 111/F2
Luxora, Ark. (72358) 202/K2
Luz, Brazil 135/D1
Luz (isl.), Chile 138/D6
Luza, U.S.S.R. 52/G2
Luzein, Switzerland 39/J3
Luzern (canton), Switzerland 39/F2
Luzern (Lucerne), Switzerland 39/F2
Luzerne, Iowa (52257) 229/J5
Luzerne, Mich. (48636) 250/E4
Luzerne (co.), Pa. 294/L3
Luzerne, Pa. (18709) 294/E7
Luzhai, China 77/G7
Luzhi, China 77/G6
Luzhou (Luchow), China 77/G6
Luziânia, Brazil 132/E7
Luzilândia, Brazil 132/F3
Lužnice (riv.), Czech. 41/C2
Luzon (isl.), Philippines 2/R5
Luzon (isl.), Philippines 54/O8
Luzon (isl.), Philippines 82/C3
Luzon (isl.), Philippines 85/G2
Luzon (sea), Philippines 82/B4
Luzon (str.), Philippines 82/A2
Luz-Saint-Sauveur, France 28/C6
L'vov, U.S.S.R. 7/G4
L'vov, U.S.S.R. 48/C4
L'vov (Lwów), U.S.S.R. 52/B5
Lyakhov (isls.), U.S.S.R. 4/B3
Lyal (isl.), Ontario 177/C3
Lyallpur (Faisalabad), Pakistan 68/C2
Lyallpur (Faisalabad), Pakistan 59/K3
Lyalta, Alberta 182/D4
Lyatkhovskiye (isls.), U.S.S.R. 48/O2
Lybster, Scotland 10/E1
Lybster, Scotland 15/E2
Lycan, Colo. (†81054) 208/P7
Lycksele, Sweden 18/L4
Lycoming, N.Y. (13093) 276/H3
Lycoming (co.), Pa. 294/H3
Lycoming (creek), Pa. 294/H3
Lydallville, Conn. (†06040) 210/F1
Lydd, England 13/H7
Lydda, Israel 65/B4
Lydenburg, S. Africa 118/E4
Lydia, Minn. (†55352) 255/E6
Lydia, S.C. (29079) 296/G3
Lydia Mills, S.C. (29325) 296/D3
Lydick, Ind. (†46601) 227/E1
Lyell (mt.), Alberta 182/B4
Lyell (isl.), Br. Col. 184/B4
Lyell (mt.), Br. Col. 184/J4
Lyell (mt.), Tasmania 99/B4
Lyerly, Georgia (30730) 217/B2
Lyford, Ind. (†47874) 227/C5
Lyford, Texas (78569) 303/G11
Lykens, Pa. (17048) 294/J4
Lyle, Minn. (55953) 255/F7
Lyle, Wash. (98635) 310/D5
Lyles, Tenn. (37098) 237/G9
Lyleton, Manitoba 179/A5
Lyman, Miss. (†39501) 256/F10
Lyman, Nebr. (69352) 264/A3
Lyman○, N.H. (†03585) 268/D3
Lyman, S.C. (29365) 296/C2
Lyman (co.), S. Dak. 298/J6
Lyman, Utah (84749) 304/C5
Lyman, Wash. (98263) 310/D2
Lyman, Wyo. (82937) 319/B4
Lyme (bay), England 13/D7
Lyme (bay), England 10/E5
Lyme○, N.H. (03768) 268/C4
Lyme Center, N.H. (03769) 268/C4
Lyme Regis, England 13/E7
Lyme Regis, England 10/E5
Lymington, England 10/F5
Lymington, England 13/F7
Lymm, England 13/H2
Lymm, England 10/G2
Lyn, Ontario 177/J3
Lyna (riv.), Poland 47/E1
Lynbrook, N.Y. (11563) 276/P7
Lynch, Ky. (40855) 237/R7
Lynch, Md. (21646) 245/O3
Lynch, Nebr. (68746) 264/F2
Lynchburg, Mo. (65543) 261/H7
Lynchburg, N. Dak. (†58023) 282/R6
Lynchburg, Ohio (45142) 284/C7
Lynchburg, S.C. (29080) 296/G3
Lynchburg, Tenn. (37352) 237/J10
Lynchburg, Va. 188/L3
Lynchburg, Va. 146/K6
Lynchburg (I.C.), Va. (*24501) 307/K6
Lynches (riv.), S.C. 296/H3
Lynch Station, Va. (24571) 307/K6
Lynd, Minn. (56157) 255/C6
Lynd, Queensland 95/C3
Lyndeborough○, N.H. (†03082) 268/D6
Lynden, Ontario 177/D4
Lynden, Wash. (98264) 310/C2
Lyndhurst○, N.J. (07071) 273/B2
Lyndhurst, N.S. Wales 97/E3
Lyndhurst, Ohio (44124) 284/J9
Lyndhurst, Ontario 177/H3
Lyndhurst, S. Australia 88/F6
Lyndhurst, S. Australia 94/E4
Lyndoch, S. Australia 94/C6
Lyndon, Ill. (61261) 222/D2
Lyndon, Kansas (66451) 232/G3
Lyndon, Ohio (45649) 284/D7
Lyndon○, Vt. (05849) 268/C2
Lyndon, W. Australia 92/A3
Lyndon B. Johnson Nat'l Hist. Site, Texas 303/F7
Lyndon B. Johnson Space Ctr., Texas 303/K2
Lyndon Center, Vt. (05850) 268/C2
Lyndon Station, Wis. (53944) 317/F8
Lyndonville, N.Y. (14098) 276/D4
Lyndonville, Vt. (05851) 268/D2
Lyndora, Pa. (16045) 294/B4
Lynedoch, Ontario 177/D5
Lyness, Scotland 15/E2
Lyngby, Denmark 21/F6
Lynhurst, Ontario 177/C5
Lynn, Ala. (35575) 195/C2
Lynn, Ark. (72440) 202/H2
Lynn, Ind. (47355) 227/H4
Lynn, Mass. (*01901) 249/D6
Lynn, N.C. (28750) 281/E4
Lynn (co.), Texas 303/C4
Lynn, Wis. (†54436) 317/F6
Lynn Canal (inlet), Alaska 196/M1
Lynn Center, Ill. (61262) 222/C2
Lynn Creek, Miss. (†39739) 256/G4
Lynndyl, Utah (84640) 304/B4
Lynnfield○, Mass. (01940) 249/D5
Lynnfield Center (Lynnfield P.O.), Mass. (†01940) 249/C5
Lynn Grove, Ky. (42062) 237/E7
Lynn Haven, Fla. (32444) 212/C6
Lynn Lake, Man. 162/G4
Lynn Lake, Man. 146/H4
Lynn Lake, Manitoba 179/H2
Lynnview, Ky. (†40201) 237/K4
Lynnville, Ill. (†62650) 222/C4
Lynnville, Ind. (47619) 227/C8
Lynnville, Iowa (50153) 229/H5
Lynnville, Ky. (42063) 237/D7
Lynnville, Tenn. (38472) 237/G10
Lynnwood, Wash. (98036) 310/C3
Lynton, England 10/E5
Lynton, England 13/D6
Lynwood, Calif. (90262) 204/C11
Lynwood, Ill. (†60411) 222/C6
Lynx (lake), N.W. Terrs. 187/H3
Lynxville, Wis. (54640) 317/D9
Lyon, France 7/E4
Lyon, France 28/F5
Lyon (co.), Iowa 229/A2
Lyon (co.), Kansas 232/F3
Lyon (co.), Ky. 237/E6
Lyon (co.), Minn. 255/C6
Lyon, Miss. (38645) 256/D2
Lyon (co.), Nev. 266/B3
Lyon (inlet), N.W. Terrs. 187/K3
Lyon, Loch (lake), Scotland 15/D4
Lyon (riv.), Scotland 15/D4
Lyon Mountain, N.Y. (12952) 276/N1
Lyonnais (trad. prov.) France 29
Lyons, Colo. (80540) 208/J2
Lyons, Georgia (30436) 217/H6
Lyons, Ill. (60534) 222/B6
Lyons, Ind. (47443) 227/C7
Lyons, Kansas (67554) 232/D3
Lyons, Ky. (†40051) 237/K5
Lyons, Mich. (48851) 250/E6
Lyons, Nebr. (68038) 264/H3
Lyons, N.J. (07939) 273/D2
Lyons, N.Y. (14489) 276/F4
Lyons, Ohio (43533) 284/B2
Lyons, Oreg. (97358) 291/E3
Lyons (Lyon Station), Pa. (19536) 294/L5
Lyons, S. Dak. (57041) 298/R6
Lyons (riv.), W. Australia 88/B4
Lyons (riv.), W. Australia 92/A4
Lyons, Wis. (53148) 317/K10
Lyons Brook, Nova Scotia 168/F3
Lyons Falls, N.Y. (13368) 276/K3
Lyons Plain, Conn. (†06880) 210/B4
Lyon Station, Pa. (19536) 294/L5
Lyra (reef), Papua N.G. 86/C1
Lys (riv.), Belgium 27/B7
Lys (riv.), France 28/E2
Lysaker, Norway 18/D3
Lysá nad Labem, Czech. 41/C1
Lysander, N.Y. (13094) 276/H4
Lysekil, Sweden 18/G7
Lysite, Wyo. (82642) 319/E2
Lyss, Switzerland 39/D2
Lyster, Québec 172/F3
Lys'va, U.S.S.R. 7/K3
Lys'va, U.S.S.R. 48/F4
Lys'va, U.S.S.R. 52/J3
Lytham Saint Anne's, England 13/G1
Lytham Saint Anne's, England 10/F1
Lytle, Texas (78052) 303/J11
Lyttelton, N. Zealand 100/D5
Lytton, Br. Col. 184/G5
Lytton, Iowa (50561) 229/D4
Lyubertsy, U.S.S.R. 52/E3
Lyubotin, U.S.S.R. 52/E4
Lyudinovo, U.S.S.R. 52/D4

M

Ma'ad, Jordan 65/D2
Maalaea, Hawaii (†96753) 218/J2
Maalaea (bay), Hawaii 218/J2
Ma'alot-Tarshiha, Israel 65/C1
Ma'an (dist.), Jordan 65/D5
Ma'an, Jordan 65/E5
Ma'an, Jordan 59/C3
Ma'anshan, China 77/J5
Maarianhamina (Mariehamn), Finland 18/M7
Maarssen, Netherlands 27/F4
Maas (riv.), Netherlands 27/G5
Maasbree, Netherlands 27/H6
Maaseik, Belgium 27/H6
Maasin, Philippines 82/E5
Maasmechelen, Belgium 27/H7
Maassluis, Netherlands 27/E5
Maastricht, Netherlands 27/H7
Maatsuyker (isls.), Tasmania 99/C5
Mababe (depr.), Botswana 118/C3
Mabalane, Mozambique 118/E4
Mabank, Texas (75147) 303/H5
Mabaruma, Guyana 131/B1
Mabay, Cuba 158/H4
Mabel (lake), Br. Col. 184/H5
Mabel, Minn. (55954) 255/G7
Mabelvale, Ark. (72103) 202/F4
Maben, Miss. (39750) 256/F3
Maben, W. Va. (25870) 312/D7
Maberly, Ontario 177/H3
Mabie, W. Va. (26278) 312/F5
Mabille (lake), Newf. 166/B3
Mabini, Philippines 82/E6
Mablethorpe and Sutton, England 13/H4
Mablethorpe and Sutton, England 10/G4
Mableton, Georgia (30059) 217/J1
Mabote, Mozambique 118/E4
Mabou, Nova Scotia 168/G2
Mabou (harb.), Nova Scotia 168/G2
Mabou Highlands (hills), Nova Scotia 168/G2
Mabrouk, Mali 106/D5
Mabscott, W. Va. (25871) 312/D7
Mabton, Wash. (98935) 310/E4
Macá (mt.), Chile 138/D5
Macachín, Argentina 143/D4
Macaé, Brazil 135/F3
Macaé, Brazil 132/F8
Macaíba, Brazil 132/H4
Macajalar (bay), Philippines 82/E6
Macalister, Br. Col. 184/F4
Macaloge, Mozambique 118/F2
MacAlpine (lake), N.W. Terrs. 187/H3
Macamic, Québec 174/B3
Macan (isls.), Indonesia 85/G7
Macanao (pen.), Venezuela 124/F2
Maçāo, Portugal 33/B3
Macao (Macau) 77
Macapá, Brazil 120/D2
Macapá, Brazil 132/D2
Macará, Ecuador 128/C5
Macaranaima, Colombia 126/E7
Macarena, Serranía de La (mts.), Colombia 126/D6
Macareo Santo Niño, Venezuela 124/H3
Macarthur, Victoria 97/A6
Macas, Ecuador 128/D4
Macassar, S. Africa 118/F6
Macau 54/N7
Macau, Brazil 120/F3
Macau, Brazil 132/G4
MACAU (MACAO) 77
Macau (Macao) (cap.), Macau 77/H7
Macau 2/Q4
Macaúbas, Brazil 132/F6
Macaya (mt.), Haiti 158/A6
Macbeth, S.C. (†29431) 296/H5
Maccan, Nova Scotia 168/D3
Maccarese, Italy 34/F6
Macclenny, Fla. (32063) 212/D1
Maccles (lake), Newf. 166/C1
Macclesfield, England 10/G2
Macclesfield, England 13/H2
Macclesfield, N.C. (27852) 281/O3
Macdiarmid, Ontario 177/H5
MacDill A.F.B., Fla. 212/C3
Macdoel, Calif. (96058) 204/D2
Macdona, Texas (78054) 303/J11
Macdonald, Manitoba 179/D4
Macdonald (lake), North. Terr. 93/B7
Macdonald (lake), W. Australia 88/D4
Macdonald (lake), W. Australia 92/E3
Macdonaldton, Pa. (†15530) 294/E6
Macdonnell (ranges), Australia 87/D8
Macdonnell (ranges), North. Terr. 88/E4
Macdonnell (ranges), North. Terr. 93/C7
Macdowall, Sask. 181/E2
Macduff, Scotland 10/E2
Macduff, Scotland 15/F3
Mace, Ind. (†47933) 227/D4
Mace, W. Va. (†26281) 312/F6
Macedon, N.Y. (14502) 276/F4
Macedonia, Ark. (†71753) 202/D7
Macedonia, Conn. (†06757) 210/A2
Macedonia (reg.), Greece 45/E5
Macedonia, Ill. (62860) 222/E5
Macedonia, Iowa (51549) 229/C6
Macedonia, Ohio (44056) 284/J10
Macedonia (rep.), Yugoslavia 45/E5
Maceió, Brazil 120/F3
Maceió, Brazil 132/H5
Macel, Miss. (†38950) 256/D3
Macenta, Guinea 102/B4
Macenta, Guinea 106/C7
Maceo, Cuba 158/H3
Maceo, Ky. (42355) 237/H5
Macerata (prov.), Italy 34/D3
Macerata, Italy 34/D3
Maces (bay), New Bruns. 170/D3
Maces Bay, New Bruns. 170/D3
Macfarlan, W. Va. (26148) 312/D4
Macfarlane (lake), S. Australia 88/F6
Macfarlane (lake), S. Australia 94/E5
Macgillicuddy's Reeks (mts.), Ireland 17/B7
MacGregor, Manitoba 179/D5
MacGregor's Bay, Ontario 177/G2
Mach, Pakistan 59/J4
Mach, Pakistan 68/B3
Macha, Bolivia 136/B6
Machacamarca, Bolivia 136/B5
Machachi, Ecuador 128/C3
Machado, Brazil 135/C2
Machakos, Kenya 115/G4
Machala, Ecuador 120/B3
Machala, Ecuador 128/B4
Machali, Chile 138/G5
Machalilla, Ecuador 128/B3
Machaneng, Botswana 118/D4
Machanga, Mozambique 118/F4
Machareti, Bolivia 136/D7
Machattie (lake), Queensland 88/G5
Machattie (lake), Queensland 95/B5
Machaze, Mozambique 118/E4
Machelen, Belgium 27/C9
Macheng, China 77/J5
Machers, The (pen.), Scotland 15/D6
Machias, Maine (04654) 243/J6
Machias○, Maine (04654) 243/J6
Machias (bay), Maine 243/J6
Machias (riv.), Maine 243/H6
Machias (riv.), Maine 243/F2
Machias-Lime Lake, N.Y. (14101) 276/D6
Machiasport, Maine (04655) 243/H6
Machiasport○, Maine (04655) 243/H6
Machias Seal (isl.), Maine 243/J7
Machico, Portugal 33/A2
Machida, Japan 81/O2
Machilipatnam, India 68/E5
Machipongo, Va. (23405) 307/S6
Machiques, Venezuela 124/B3
Macho, Arroyo del (creek), N. Mex. 274/D5
Machrihanish, Scotland 15/C5
Machupicchu, Peru 128/F9
Machupo (riv.), Bolivia 136/C3
Machynlleth, Wales 13/D5
Machynlleth, Wales 10/D4
Macia, Mozambique 118/E4
Maciel, Argentina 143/F6
Maciel, Paraguay 144/D5
Maciel, Arroyo (riv.), Uruguay 145/C4
Macina (depr.), Mali 106/D6
Macintyre (riv.), N. S. Wales 88/J5
Macintyre (riv.), N.S. Wales 97/E1
Macintyre (riv.), Queensland 95/D6
Mack, Colo. (81525) 208/B4
Mack, Ohio (†45202) 284/B9
MacKay, Alberta 182/C3
MacKay (riv.), Alberta 182/D1
Mackay, Australia 87/F8
Mackay (lake), Australia 87/D8
Mackay, Idaho (83251) 220/E6
Mackay (res.), Idaho 220/E6
Mackay (lake), North. Terr. 88/D4
Mackay (lake), North. Terr. 93/A7
MacKay (lake), N.W. Terrs. 187/G3
Mackay, Queensland 88/H4
Mackay, Queensland 95/D4
Mackay (lake), W. Australia 92/E3
Mackenzie (bay) 5/C4
Mackenzie, Br. Col. 184/F2
Mackenzie, Br. Col. 184/F2
Mackenzie (bay), Canada 4/B16
Mackenzie (mts.), Canada 4/C16
Mackenzie (riv.), Canada 146/E3
Mackenzie (riv.), Canada 2/C2
Mackenzie (riv.), Canada 4/C16
Mackenzie, Mo. (†63101) 261/P3
Mackenzie (dist.), N.W.T. 162/E3
Mackenzie (bay), N.W. Terrs. 187/E3
Mackenzie (mts.), N.W. Terrs. 187/E3
Mackenzie (riv.), N.W.T. 162/C2
Mackenzie (riv.), N.W.T. 146/F3
Mackenzie (riv.), N.W. Terrs. 187/F3
Mackenzie (bay), Yukon 162/C2
Mackenzie (bay), Yukon 187/E3
Mackenzie (mts.), Yukon 187/E3
Mackenzie King (isl.), Canada 4/B15
Mackenzie King (isl.), N.W.T. 162/M3
Mackenzie King (isl.), N.W. Terrs. 187/G2
Mackey, Ind. (47654) 227/C8
Mackeys, N.C. (†27970) 281/R3
Mackeyville, Pa. (17750) 294/H3
Mackinac (co.), Mich. 250/D2
Mackinac (isl.), Mich. 250/E3
Mackinac (str.), Mich. 250/E3
Mackinac Island, Mich. (49757) 250/E3
Mackinaw, Ill. (61755) 222/D3
Mackinaw (riv.), Ill. 222/E3
Mackinaw City, Mich. (49701) 250/E3
Macklin, Sask. 181/A3
Macks, Ark. (72113) 202/H2
Macksburg, Iowa (50155) 229/E6
Macksburg, Ohio (45746) 284/G6
Macks Creek, Mo. (65786) 261/G7
Macks Inn, Idaho (83433) 220/G5
Macksville, Kansas (67557) 232/D4
Macksville, N.S. Wales 97/G2
Mackville, Ky. (40040) 237/L5
Maclean, N.S. Wales 97/G1
Maclean (str.), N.W. Terrs. 187/H2
Maclear, S. Africa 118/D6
Maclear (cape), S. Africa 118/F7
Macmillan (pass), N.W. Terrs. 187/F3
Macmillan (pass), Yukon 187/F3
Macmillan (riv.), Yukon 187/E3
Macnean (lake), Ireland 17/F3
Macnean (lake), N. Ireland 17/F3
MacNutt, Sask. 181/K4
Macomb, Ill. (61455) 222/C3
Macomb (co.), Mich. 250/G6
Macomb, Okla. (74852) 288/M4
Macomer, Italy 34/B4
Macomia, Mozambique 118/F2
Macon (co.), Ala. 195/G6
Mâcon, France 28/F4
Macon, Ga. 188/K4
Macon, Ga. 146/K6
Macon (co.), Georgia 217/D6
Macon, Georgia (*31201) 217/E5
Macon (co.), Ill. 222/E4
Macon, Ill. (62544) 222/E4
Macon (bayou), La. 238/H1
Macon, Miss. (39341) 256/G4
Macon (co.), Mo. 261/G3
Macon, Mo. (63552) 261/H3
Macon, Nebr. (†68939) 264/E4
Macon (co.), N.C. 281/B4
Macon, N.C. (27551) 281/N2
Macon, Ohio (†45171) 284/C8
Macon (co.), Tenn. 237/J7
Macon, Tenn. (38048) 237/B10
Macondo, Angola 115/D6
Macorís (cape), Dom. Rep. 158/E5
Macosquin, N. Ireland 17/H1
Macotera, Spain 33/D2
Macouba, Martinique 161/C5
Macoun, Sask. 181/H6
Macoupin (co.), Ill. 222/D4
Macoupin (riv.), Ill. 222/C4
Macouria, Fr. Guiana 131/E3
Macquarie (riv.), N. S. Wales 88/H6
Macquarie (lake), N.S. Wales 97/F3
Macquarie (riv.), N.S. Wales 97/D2
Macquarie (harb.), Tasmania 88/G8
Macquarie (harb.), Tasmania 99/B4
Macquarie (riv.), Tasmania 99/D3
Mac-Robertson Land (reg.) 5/B4
Macroom, Ireland 10/B5
Macroom, Ireland 17/C8
Macrorie, Sask. 181/E4
Mactan (isl.), Philippines 82/E5
Mactaquac (lake), New Bruns. 170/C3
MacTier, Ontario 177/E2
Macumba (riv.), S. Australia 88/F5
Macumba, The (riv.), S. Australia 94/E2
Macungie, Pa. (18062) 294/L4
Macurijes (pt.), Cuba 158/F3
Macuro, Venezuela 124/H2
Macusani, Peru 128/G10
Macuspana, Mexico 150/N8
Macuto, Venezuela 124/E2
Macwahoc○, Maine (†04451) 243/G4
Macy, Ind. (46951) 227/E3
Macy, Nebr. (68039) 264/H2
Mad (riv.), Calif. 204/B3
Mad (riv.), Conn. 210/C2
Mad (riv.), Conn. 210/C1
Mad (riv.), N.H. 268/D4
Mad (riv.), Ohio 284/C6
Mad (riv.), Vt. 268/B3
Ma'daba, Jordan 65/D4
Madadi, Chad 111/D4
Madagascal (pond), Maine 243/G5
Madagascar 2/M6
Madagascar 102/G7
MADAGASCAR 118/H3
Madaket, Mass. (†02554) 249/O7
Madama, Niger 106/G4
Madame (isl.), Nova Scotia 168/H3
Madang, Papua N.G. 85/B7
Madang, Papua N.G. 87/E6
Madaoua, Niger 106/F6
Madaras, Hungary 41/E3
Madaripur, Bangladesh 68/G4
Madauk, Burma 72/C3
Madawaska, Maine (04756) 243/G1
Madawaska○, Maine (04756) 243/G1
Madawaska (co.), New Bruns. 170/B1
Madawaska (riv.), New Bruns. 170/B1
Madawaska, Ontario 177/F2
Madawaska (riv.), Ontario 177/G2
Madawaska (riv.), Québec 172/J2
Madbury○, N.H. (†03820) 268/F5
Maddela, Philippines 82/C2
Madden, Alberta 182/C4
Madden, Miss. (39109) 256/F5
Maddock, N. Dak. (58348) 282/L4
Maddy, Loch (inlet), Scotland 15/A3
Madeira (riv.), Brazil 2/F6
Madeira (riv.), Brazil 120/C3
Madeira (riv.), Brazil 132/A4
Madeira, Ohio (45243) 284/C9
Madeira (isl.), Portugal 33/A2
Madeira (isl.), Portugal 106/A2
Madeira (isls.), Portugal 2/H4
Madeira (isls.), Portugal 102/A1
Madeira (isls.), Portugal 33/A2
Madeira (isls.) Portugal 106/A2
Madeira Beach, Fla. (33738) 212/B3
Madeira Park, Br. Col. 184/J2
Madeleine (cape), Québec 172/D1
Madelia, Minn. (56062) 255/D6
Madeline, Calif. (96119) 204/E2
Madeline (isl.), Wis. 317/E2
Maden, Turkey 63/H3
Madera (co.), Calif. 204/F6
Madera, Calif. (93637) 204/E7
Madera, Mexico 150/F2
Madera, Pa. (16661) 294/F4
Madera Canyon, Ariz. (†85637) 198/E7
Madh, India 68/B7
Madhubani, India 68/F3
Madhya Pradesh (state), India 68/D4
Madidi (riv.), Bolivia 136/A3
Madill, Okla. (73446) 288/N6
Madinat ash Sha'b, P.D.R. Yemen 59/E7
Madinat el-Thawra, Syria 63/H5
Madingo-Kayes, Congo 115/B4
Madingou, Congo 115/B4
Madirovalo, Madagascar 118/H3
Madison (co.), Ala. 195/E1
Madison, Ala. (35758) 195/E1
Madison (co.), Ark. 202/C1
Madison, Ark. (72359) 202/J4
Madison, Calif. (95653) 204/D5
Madison, Conn. (06443) 210/E3
Madison○, Conn. (06443) 210/E3
Madison (co.), Fla. 212/C1
Madison, Fla. (32340) 212/C1
Madison (co.), Georgia 217/F2
Madison, Georgia (30650) 217/F3
Madison (co.), Idaho 220/G6
Madison (co.), Ill. 222/D5
Madison, Ill. (62060) 222/A2
Madison (co.), Ind. 227/F4
Madison, Ind. (47250) 227/G7
Madison (co.), Iowa 229/E6
Madison, Kansas (66860) 232/F3
Madison (co.), Ky. 237/N5
Madison (par.), La. 238/H2
Madison, Maine (04950) 243/D6
Madison○, Maine (04950) 243/D6
Madison, Md. (21648) 245/O6
Madison, Minn. (56256) 255/B5
Madison (co.), Miss. 256/D5
Madison, Miss. (39110) 256/D6
Madison (co.), Mo. 261/M8
Madison, Mo. (65263) 261/H4
Madison (co.), Mont. 262/D5
Madison (riv.), Mont. 262/E5
Madison (co.), Nebr. 264/G3
Madison, Nebr. (68748) 264/G3
Madison○, N.H. (03849) 268/E4
Madison (mt.), N.H. 268/E3
Madison, N.J. (07940) 273/E2
Madison (co.), N.Y. 276/J5
Madison, N.Y. (13402) 276/J5
Madison (co.), N.C. 281/D3
Madison, N.C. (27025) 281/J2
Madison (co.), Ohio 284/D6
Madison, Ohio (44057) 284/H2
Madison, Sask. 181/B4
Madison, S.C. (29693) 296/A2
Madison, S.C. (†29829) 296/D4
Madison, S. Dak. (57042) 298/P6
Madison (lake), S. Dak. 298/P6
Madison (co.), Tenn. 237/D9
Madison (co.), Texas 303/J6
Madison (co.), Va. 307/M4
Madison, Va. (22727) 307/M4
Madison, W. Va. (25130) 312/C6
Madison (cap.), Wis. 146/K5
Madison (cap.), Wis. 188/H2
Madison (cap.), Wis. (*53701) 317/H9
Madison, Wyo. (†82190) 319/B1
Madison (plat.), Wyo. 319/B1
Madisonburg, Ohio (†44691) 284/G4
Madison Heights, Mich. (48071) 250/B6
Madison Heights, Va. (24572) 307/K6
Madison Lake, Minn. (56063) 255/E6
Madisonville, Ky. (42431) 237/F6
Madisonville, La. (70447) 238/K6
Madisonville, Tenn. (37354) 237/N9
Madisonville, Texas (77864) 303/J7
Madiun, Indonesia 85/K2
Madley (mt.), W. Australia 92/D4
Madoc, Mont. (†59222) 262/L2
Madoc, Ontario 177/G3
Mado Gashi, Kenya 115/G3
Madoi, China 77/E4
Madona, U.S.S.R. 53/C2
Madona, U.S.S.R. 52/C3
Madonna, Md. (†21161) 245/M2
Madraka, Ras (cape), Oman 59/G6
Madran, New Bruns. 170/E1
Madras, India 68/E6
Madras, India 54/K8
Madras, India 2/P5
Madras, Oreg. (97741) 291/F3
Madre (lag.), Mexico 150/L4
Madre (lag.), Texas 188/G5
Madre (lag.), Texas 303/G11
Madre de Dios (riv.) 120/C4
Madre de Diós (riv.), Bolivia 136/A3
Madre de Dios (isl.), Chile 120/B8
Madre de Dios (isl.), Chile 138/D8
Madre de Dios (dept.), Peru 128/G8
Madre de Dios, Peru 128/G9
Madre de Dios (riv.), Peru 128/G9
Madre del Sur, Sierra (mts.), Mexico 150/K8
Madre Occidental, Sierra (mts.), Mexico 150/F3
Madre Oriental, Sierra (mts.), Mexico 150/J4
Madrid, Ala. (36348) 195/H8
Madrid, Iowa (50156) 229/F5
Madrid○, Maine (†04966) 243/B6
Madrid, Nebr. (69150) 264/C4
Madrid, N. Mex. (†87010) 274/C3
Madrid, N.Y. (13660) 276/K1
Madrid (prov.), Spain 33/E2
Madrid (cap.), Spain 7/D4
Madrid (cap.), Spain 33/F4
Madrid (cap.), Spain 2/J4
Madridejos, Spain 33/E3
Madrigal de las Altas Torres, Spain 33/D2
Madrigalejo, Spain 33/D3
Madrisahorn (mt.), Switzerland 39/J3
Madroñera, Spain 33/D3
Madsen, Ontario 175/B2
Madugula, India 68/E5
Madura (isl.), Indonesia 54/N10
Madura (isl.), Indonesia 85/K2
Madura (str.), Indonesia 85/K2
Madura, W. Australia 92/D5
Madurai, India 54/J9
Madurai, India 68/D7
Madvar, Kuh-e (mt.), Iran 59/F3
Madvar, Kuh-e (mt.), Iran 66/F3
Maebashi, Japan 81/J5
Mae Hong Son, Thailand 72/C3
Mae Klong, Mae Nam (riv.), Thailand 72/C4
Mael, Norway 18/F6
Maella, Spain 33/G2
Maeser, Utah (†84078) 304/E3
Maesteg, Wales 13/D6
Maestra, Sierra (mts.), Cuba 158/H4
Maevatanana, Madagascar 118/H3
Maeystown, Ill. (62256) 222/C5
Mafeking, Manitoba 179/B2
Mafeking (Mafikeng), S. Africa 118/C5
Mafeteng, Lesotho 118/D5
Maffin (bay), Indonesia 85/K6
Maffra, Victoria 97/D5
Mafia (isl.), Tanzania 102/G5
Mafia (isl.), Tanzania 115/H5
Mafikeng (Mafeking), S. Africa 118/C5
Mafra, Brazil 132/D9
Mafra, Portugal 33/B3
Magadan, U.S.S.R. 2/S3
Magadan, U.S.S.R. 54/R4
Magadan, U.S.S.R. 48/P4
Magadi, Kenya 115/G4
Magadino, Switzerland 39/G4
Magaguadavic, New Bruns. 170/C3
Magaguadavic (lake), New Bruns. 170/C3
Magaguadavic (riv.), New Bruns. 170/C3

404 Magalia

Magalia, Calif. (95954) 204/D4
Magaliesburg, S. Africa 118/G6
Magallanes (reg.), Chile 138/E10
Magallanes (Magellan) (str.), Chile 138/D10
Magallanes, Philippines 82/D4
Magallenes (Magellan) (str.), Argentina 143/C7
Magangué, Colombia 126/C3
Maganoy, Philippines 82/E7
Mağara, Turkey 63/G3
Magarabomba, Cuba 158/G2
Magaria, Niger 106/F6
Magazine, Ark. (72943) 202/C3
Magazine (mt.), Ark. 202/C3
Magdagachi, U.S.S.R. 48/N4
Magdala, Ethiopia 111/G5
Magdalen (isls.), Que. 162/K6
Magdalena, Argentina 143/H7
Magdalena, Bolivia 136/C3
Magdalena (isl.), Chile 138/D5
Magdalena (dept.), Colombia 126/C3
Magdalena (riv.), Colombia 120/B2
Magdalena (riv.), Colombia 126/C3
Magdalena (bay), Mexico 150/C4
Magdalena, N. Mex. (87825) 274/B4
Magdalena (mts.), N. Mex. 274/B4
Magdalena de Kino, Mexico 150/D1
Magdeburg, E. Germany 7/F3
Magdeburg (dist.), E. Germany 22/D2
Magdeburg, E. Germany 22/D2
Magdelaine (cays), Coral Sea Is. Terr. 88/H3
Magé, Brazil 135/E3
Magee, Miss. (39111) 256/E7
Magee, Island (pen.), N. Ireland 17/K2
Magelang, Indonesia 85/J2
Magellan (str.) 120/C8
Magellan (str.) 2/F8
Magellan (str.), Argentina 143/C7
Magellan (str.), Chile 138/D10
Magen, Israel 65/A5
Magens (bay), Virgin Is. (U.S.) 161/B4
Magerøya (isl.), Norway 18/P1
Magerrain (mt.), Switzerland 39/H2
Magetan, Indonesia 85/K2
Maggia, Switzerland 39/G4
Maggia (riv.), Switzerland 39/G4
Maggie Valley, N.C. (28751) 281/C3
Maggiore (lake), Fla. 212/B3
Maggiore (lake), Italy 34/B1
Maggiore (lake), Switzerland 39/G5
Maggotty, Jamaica 158/H6
Maghâgha, Egypt 59/B4
Maghâgha, Egypt 111/J4
Maghama, Mauritania 102/A3
Maghama, Mauritania 106/B5
Maghera, N. Ireland 17/H2
Magherafelt (dist.), N. Ireland 17/H2
Magherafelt, N. Ireland 10/C3
Magherafelt, N. Ireland 17/H2
Magic (res.), Idaho 220/D6
Magilligan (pt.), N. Ireland 17/H1
Maglaj, Yugoslavia 45/D3
Magley, Ind. (†46733) 227/G3
Maglie, Italy 34/G4
Magna, Utah (84044) 304/B3
Magna Bay, Br. Col. 184/H4
Magness, Ark. (72553) 202/H2
Magnet, Ark. (†72104) 202/E5
Magnet, Ind. (47555) 227/D8
Magnet, Manitoba 179/C3
Magnet, Nebr. (68749) 264/G2
Magnetawan, Ontario 177/E2
Magnetawan (riv.), Ontario 177/D2
Magnetic Springs, Ohio (43036) 284/D5
Magnitogorsk, U.S.S.R. 54/H4
Magnitogorsk, U.S.S.R. 48/G4
Magnolia, Ala. (36754) 195/C6
Magnolia, Ark. (71753) 202/D7
Magnolia, Del. (19962) 245/R4
Magnolia, Ill. (61336) 222/D2
Magnolia, Iowa (51550) 229/B5
Magnolia, Minn. (56158) 255/B7
Magnolia, Miss. (39652) 256/D8
Magnolia, N.J. (08049) 273/B3
Magnolia, N.C. (28453) 281/O5
Magnolia, Ohio (44643) 284/H4
Magnolia, Texas (77355) 303/J7
Magnolia, W. Va. (†25422) 312/K3
Magnolia Springs, Ala. (36555) 195/C10
Màgoé, Mozambique 118/E3
Magoffin (co.), Ky. 237/P5
Magog, Québec 172/E4
Magpie, Québec 174/E2
Magpie (lake), Québec 174/E2
Magrath, Alberta 182/D5
Magude, Mozambique 118/E5
Maguindanao (prov.), Philippines 82/E7
Maguse (lake), N.W. Terrs. 187/J3
Magwe (div.), Burma 72/B2
Magwe, Burma 72/B2
Mahabad, Iran 59/E2
Mahabad, Iran 66/D2
Mahabaleshwar, India 68/C5
Mahabo, Madagascar 118/G4
Mahaena, Fr. Poly. 86/T13
Mahaffey, Pa. (15757) 294/E4
Mahagi, Zaire 115/F3
Mahaica, Guyana 131/C2
Mahaicony Village, Guyana 131/C2
Mahajamba (bay), Madagascar 118/H2
Mahajanga (prov.), Madagascar 118/H3
Mahajanga, Madagascar 102/G6
Mahakam (riv.), Indonesia 85/F6
Mahalapye, Botswana 118/D4
Mahalapye, Botswana 102/E7
Mahalasville, Ind. (†46151) 227/E6
Mahallat, Iran 66/G4
Mahan, Iran 66/K5
Mahanadi (riv.), India 68/E4
Mahanoro, Madagascar 118/H3
Mahanoy City, Pa. (17948) 294/K4
Maharashtra (state), India 68/C5
Maha Sarakham, Thailand 72/D3
Mahaska (co.), Iowa 229/H6
Mahaska, Kansas (66955) 232/E2
Mahaxai, Laos 72/E3
Mahbubnagar, India 68/D5
Mahdia, Guyana 131/B3
Mahdia, Tunisia 106/G1
Mahe, India 68/D6
Mahé (isl.), Seychelles 118/H5
Mahébourg, Mauritius 118/G5
Mahenge, Tanzania 115/G5
Maheno, N. Zealand 100/C6
Maher, Colo. (81421) 208/D5
Maheshkhali, Bangladesh 68/G4
Mahia (pen.), N. Zealand 100/G3
Mahim, India 68/C5
Mahim (bay), India 68/B7
Mahkonce, Minn. (†56557) 255/C3
Mahlaing, Burma 72/B2
Mahmudiye, Turkey 63/D3
Mahnomen (co.), Minn. 255/C3
Mahnomen, Minn. (56557) 255/C3
Maho (bay), Virgin Is. (U.S.) 161/C4
Mahoba, India 68/D3
Mahomet, Ill. (61853) 222/E3
Mahón, Spain 33/J3
Mahone (bay), Nova Scotia 168/D4
Mahone Bay, Nova Scotia 168/D4
Mahoning (co.), Ohio 284/J4
Mahood (lake), Br. Col. 184/G4
Mahopac, N.Y. (10541) 276/N8
Mahout, Dominica 161/E6
Mahto, S. Dak. (57643) 298/H2
Mahtomedi, Minn. (55115) 255/F5
Mahtowa, Minn. (55762) 255/F4
Mahukona, Hawaii (†96719) 218/G3
Mahuva, India 68/C4
Mahwah◯, N.J. (07430) 273/E1
Maia, Portugal 33/B2
Maicao, Colombia 126/D2
Maicuru (riv.), Brazil 132/C2
Maida, N. Dak. (58255) 282/O2
Maida, Yemen Arab Rep. 59/D6
Maidan, Iraq 66/D3
Maidan, Iraq 59/E3
Maidani, Ras (cape), Iran 59/G4
Maiden, N.C. (28650) 281/G3
Maidenhead, England 10/F5
Maidenhead, England 13/G8
Maiden Rock, Wis. (54750) 317/B6
Maidens, The (isls.), N. Ireland 17/K2
Maidens, Scotland 15/D5
Maidens, Va. (23102) 307/N5
Maidstone, England 13/J8
Maidstone, England 10/G5
Maidstone, Ontario 177/B5
Maidstone, Sask. 181/B2
Maidstone◯, Vt. (†05905) 268/D2
Maidstone (lake), Vt. 268/D2
Maidsville, W. Va. (26541) 312/F3
Maiduguri, Nigeria 106/G6
Maiduguri, Nigeria 102/D3
Maienfeld, Switzerland 39/J2
Maigatari, Nigeria 106/F6
Maigualida, Sierra (range), Venezuela 124/F4
Maigue (riv.), Ireland 17/D6
Maihara, Japan 81/G6
Maili, Hawaii (†96792) 218/D2
Maillard, Québec 172/G2
Ma'in, Jordan 65/D4
Main (passage), La. 238/M8
Main (riv.), N. Ireland 17/J2
Main (chan.), Ontario 177/C2
Main (str.), Singapore 72/F6
Main (riv.), W. Germany 22/C4
Main-à-Dieu, Nova Scotia 168/J2
Main Barrier (range), N. S. Wales 88/G6
Main Barrier (range), N.S. Wales 97/A2
Main Brook, Newf. 166/C3
Main Centre, Sask. 181/D5
Mai-Ndombe (lake), Zaire 115/C4
Maine 188/N1
MAINE 243
Maine (gulf) 188/N2
Maine (gulf) 162/K7
Maine (trad. prov.), France, 29
Maine (riv.), Ireland 17/C7
Maine (gulf), Mass. 249/M2
Maine, N.Y. (13802) 276/H6
Maine (state), U.S. 146/M5
Maine-et-Loire (dept.), France 28/C4
Mainesburg, Pa. (16932) 294/J2
Mainé-Soroa, Niger 106/G6
Maineville, Ohio (45039) 284/C9
Maingard (lake), Québec 172/G1
Maingkwan, Burma 72/C1
Mainit, Philippines 82/E6
Mainit (lake), Philippines 82/E6
Mainland, Orkney Is. (isl.), Scotland 10/E1
Mainland, Shetland Is. (isl.), Scotland 10/G1
Mainland (isl.), Scotland 15/G2
Mainland (isl.), Scotland 15/E1
Mainling, China 77/D6
Mainoru, North. Terr. 93/C3
Mainstream, Maine (†04942) 243/D6
Maintirano, Madagascar 118/G3
Main Topsail (mt.), Newf. 166/C4
Mainz, W. Germany 22/C4
Maio (isl.), C. Verde 106/B8
Maipo (vol.), Argentina 143/C3
Maipo (riv.), Chile 138/F4
Maipú, Argentina 143/E4
Maipú, Chile 138/G3
Maipú (vol.), Chile 138/B10
Maipures, Colombia 126/F5
Maiquetía, Venezuela 120/C1
Maiquetía, Venezuela 124/E2
Mairana, Bolivia 136/D6
Maisí, Cuba 158/K4
Maisí (cape), Cuba 158/K4
Maisí (cape), Cuba 156/D2
Maison de Pierre (lake), Québec 172/C3
Maisonnette, New Bruns. 170/E1
Maisons-Alfort, France 28/B2
Maisons-Laffitte, France 28/A1
Maïssade, Haiti 158/C5
Maitencillo, Chile 138/A8
Maitland, Australia 87/F9
Maitland, Fla. (32751) 212/E3
Maitland, Mo. (64466) 261/B2
Maitland, N. S. Wales 88/J6
Maitland, N.S. Wales 97/F3
Maitland, Annapolis, Nova Scotia 168/C4
Maitland, Hants, Nova Scotia 168/E3
Maitland, Ontario 177/J3
Maitland, S. Australia 94/E6
Maitum, Philippines 82/E7
Maize, Kansas (67101) 232/E4
Maíz Grande (Great Corn) (isl.), Nicaragua 154/F4
Maizhokunggar, China 77/D6
Maíz Pequeña (Little Corn) (isl.), Nicaragua 154/F4
Maizuru, Japan 81/G6
Majagua, Cuba 158/F2
Majagual, Colombia 126/C3
Majalengka, Indonesia 85/H2
Majene, Indonesia 85/F6
Majenica, Ind. (†46750) 227/F3
Majes (riv.), Peru 128/F11
Majestic, Ky. (41547) 237/S5
Maji, Ethiopia 111/G6
Majma'a, Saudi Arabia 59/D4
Majoli, Suriname 131/D4
Major (co.), Okla. 288/K2
Major, Sask. 181/B4
Majorca (isl.), Spain 7/E5
Majorca (isl.), Spain 33/H3
Majorsville, W. Va. (†26036) 312/F3
Majunga, Madagascar 118/H3
Majuro (atoll) (cap.), Marshall Is. 87/H5
Makaha, Hawaii (†96792) 218/D2
Makaha (pt.), Hawaii 218/B1
Makah Ind. Res., Wash. 310/A2
Makahuena (pt.), Hawaii 218/C2
Makaiwa, Hawaii (†96763) 218/H2
Makakilo, Hawaii (96706) 218/E2
Makale, Ethiopia 102/F3
Makale, Ethiopia 111/G5
Makallé, Argentina 143/E2
Makanda, Ill. (62958) 222/D6
Makanza, Zaire 115/C3
Makapala, Hawaii (†96711) 218/G3
Makapuu (pt.), Hawaii 218/F2
Makara Beach, N. Zealand 100/A2
Makara-Ohariu, N. Zealand 100/A3
Makari, Cameroon 115/B1
Makaroff, Manitoba 179/A3
Makarov, U.S.S.R. 48/P5
Makarska, Yugoslavia 45/C4
Makar'yev, U.S.S.R. 52/F3
Makassar (Ujung Pandang), Indonesia 85/F7
Makassar (str.), Indonesia 54/N10
Makassar (str.), Indonesia 85/F6
Makatea (isl.), Fr. Poly. 87/L7
Makawao, Hawaii (96768) 218/K2
Makaweli, Hawaii (96769) 218/B2
Makena, Hawaii (†96790) 218/J2
Makeni, S. Leone 102/A4
Makeni, S. Leone 106/B7
Makepeace, Alberta 182/D4
Makeyevka, U.S.S.R. 7/H4
Makeyevka, U.S.S.R. 52/E5
Makgadikgadi (salt pan), Botswana 102/E7
Makgadikgadi (salt pan), Botswana 118/D3
Makhachkala, U.S.S.R. 7/J4
Makhachkala, U.S.S.R. 48/E5
Makhachkala, U.S.S.R. 52/G6
Makharadze, U.S.S.R. 52/F6
Makhmur, Iraq 66/C3
Makiki, Hawaii (96822) 218/C4
Makin (Butaritari) (atoll), Kiribati 87/H5
Makinak, Manitoba 179/C4
Makinen, Minn. (55763) 255/F3
Makinsk, U.S.S.R. 48/H4
Makinson (inlet), N.W. Terrs. 187/L2
Makkovik, Newf. 166/C2
Makkovik (cape), Newf. 166/C2
Makkum, Netherlands 27/G2
Makó, Hungary 41/F3
Makokou, Gabon 115/B3
Makoti, N. Dak. (58756) 282/G4
Makoua, Congo 115/C3
Maków Mazowiecki, Poland 47/E2
Makran (reg.), Iran 66/M8
Maktéïr (des.), Mauritania 106/B4
Maku, Iran 66/D1
Makubetsu, Japan 81/L2
Makumbako, Tanzania 115/G5
Makurazaki, Japan 81/O3
Makurdi, Nigeria 102/C4
Makurdi, Nigeria 106/F7
Makushin (vol.), Alaska 196/E4
Makwa, Sask. 181/C2
Makwa (lake), Sask. 181/B1
Makwa (riv.), Sask. 181/B1
Mal, Mauritania 106/B5
Mala, Punta (cape), Panama 154/H7
Malå, Sweden 18/L4
Malabang, Philippines 82/D7
Malabar, Fla. (32950) 212/F3
Malabar (hill), India 68/B7
Malabar (pt.), India 68/B7
Malabar Coast (reg.), India 68/C6
Malabo (cap.), Equat. Guinea 102/C4
Malabo (cap.), Equat. Guinea 115/A3
Malabrigo, Argentina 143/F4
Mal Abrigo, Uruguay 145/C5
Malabungan, Philippines 82/A6
Malacca (str.) 54/M9
Malacca (str.), Indonesia 85/C5
Malacca (Melaka), Malaysia 72/D7
Malacca (str.), Malaysia 72/D7
Malacky, Czech. 41/D2
Malad (riv.), Idaho 220/F7
Malad, India 68/B6
Malad (creek), India 68/B7
Malad (riv.), Utah 304/B1
Malad City, Idaho (83252) 220/F7
Maladers, Switzerland 39/J3
Málaga, Colombia 126/D4
Malaga, N.J. (08328) 273/C4
Malaga, N. Mex. (88263) 274/E6
Malaga, Ohio (43757) 284/H6
Málaga (prov.), Spain 33/D4
Málaga, Spain 7/D5
Málaga, Spain 33/D4
Malaga, Wash. (98828) 310/E3
Malagash, Nova Scotia 168/E3
Malagash (pt.), Nova Scotia 168/E3
Malagón, Spain 33/E3
Malagueta (bay), Cuba 158/H3
Malahide, Ireland 17/J5
Malaita (isl.), 86/E3
Malaita (isl.), Solomon Is. 87/G6
Malakal, Sudan 111/F6
Malakal, Sudan 102/F4
Malakanagiri, India 68/E5
Malakand, Pakistan 68/C2
Malakand, Pakistan 59/K3
Malakoff, France 28/A2
Malakoff, Texas (75148) 303/H5
Malakwa, Br. Col. 184/H5
Malalag, Philippines 82/E7
Malamir (Izeh), Iran 66/F5
Malang, Indonesia 54/N10
Malang, Indonesia 85/K2
Malange (dist.), Angola 115/C6
Malange, Angola 102/D5
Malange, Angola 115/C5
Malangka (cape), Indonesia 85/G5
Malans, Switzerland 39/J3
Malanville, Benin 106/E6
Mälaren (lake), Sweden 18/G1
Malargüe, Argentina 120/C6
Malargüe, Argentina 143/C4
Malartic, Québec 174/B3
Malaspina (glac.), Alaska 196/K3
Malaspina (str.), Br. Col. 184/J2
Malatya (prov.), Turkey 63/H3
Malatya, Turkey 59/C2
Malatya, Turkey 54/E6
Malatya, Turkey 63/H3
Malawi 2/L6
Malawi 102/F6
MALAWI 115/F6
Malawi (Nyasa) (lake), Malawi 115/F6
Malay (pen.), Malaysia 72/D6
Malay (pen.), Malaysia 85/B4
Malay (pen.), Thailand 72/D6
MALAYA, MALAYSIA 72
Malaya (reg.), Malaysia 54/M9
Malaya (reg.), Malaysia 72/E6
Malaya Vishera, U.S.S.R. 52/D3
Malaybalay, Philippines 82/E6
Malayer, Iran 66/F3
Malaysia 2/Q5
Malaysia 54/M9
MALAYSIA 85/D4
Malazgirt, Turkey 63/K3
Malbaie (riv.), Québec 172/G2
Malbon, Queensland 95/B4
Malbork (Marienburg), Poland 47/D1
Malchinersee (lake), E. Germany 22/E2
Malchow, E. Germany 22/E2
Malcolm, Ala. (36556) 195/B8
Malcolm, Nebr. (68402) 264/H4
Malcom, Iowa (50157) 229/H5
Maldegem, Belgium 27/C6
Malden, Ill. (61337) 222/D2
Malden, Ind. (†46383) 227/C2
Malden (isl.), Kiribati 87/L6
Malden, Mass. (02148) 249/D6
Malden, Mo. (63863) 261/M9
Malden, New Bruns. 170/G2
Malden, Wash. (99149) 310/H3
Malden, W. Va. (25306) 312/C6
Maldives 2/N5
MALDIVES 68
Maldives 54/J9
Maldives (isls.) 68/C7
Maldon, England 10/G5
Maldon, England 13/H6
Maldon, Victoria 97/C5
Maldonado (pt.), Mexico 150/K8
Maldonado (dept.), Uruguay 145/E5
Maldonado, Uruguay 145/D6
Male (cap.), Maldives 54/J9
Male (cap.), Maldives 2/N5
Maléa (cape), Greece 45/F7
Malebo (Stanley Pool) (lake), Zaire 115/C4
Malegaon, India 54/J7
Malegaon, India 68/C4
Malekula (isl.), Vanuatu 87/G7
Malema, Mozambique 118/F2
Malemba-Nkulu, Zaire 115/E5
Malente, W. Germany 22/D1
Maler Kotla, India 68/D2
Malesus, Tenn. (†38301) 237/D9
Malgobek, U.S.S.R. 52/F6
Malhão da Estrela (mt.), Portugal 33/C2
Malheur (lake), Oreg. 188/C2
Malheur (co.), Oreg. 291/K4
Malheur (lake), Oreg. 291/J4
Malheur (riv.), Oreg. 291/J4
Mali 2/J5
Mali 102/B2
Mali (riv.), Burma 72/C1
Mali, Guinea 106/B6
MALI 106/D5
Malibu, Calif. (90265) 204/B10
Malignant Cove, Nova Scotia 168/F3
Maligne (lake), Alberta 182/B3
Mali Kyun (isl.), Burma 72/C4
Malili, Indonesia 85/G6
Malin, Ireland 17/G1
Malin (head), Ireland 17/F1
Malin (head), Ireland 10/C3
Malin, Oreg. (97632) 291/F5
Malin, U.S.S.R. 52/C4
Malinau, Indonesia 85/F5
Malindang (mt.), Philippines 82/D6
Malindi, Kenya 102/B2
Malindi, Kenya 115/H4
Malines (Mechelen), Belgium 27/F6
Malinta, Ohio (43535) 284/B3
Malita, Philippines 82/E7
Maliwun, Burma 72/C5
Malkapur, India 68/D4
Malkara, Turkey 63/B2
Malkiya, Israel 65/D1
Malko Tŭrnovo, Bulgaria 45/H4
Mallacoota, Victoria 97/E5
Mallaig, Alberta 182/E2
Mallaig, Scotland 10/D2
Mallaig, Scotland 15/C4
Mallanganee, N.S. Wales 97/G1
Mallard, Iowa (50562) 229/D3
Mallawi, Egypt 111/J4
Mallawi, Egypt 59/B4
Mallén, Spain 33/F2
Malleray, Switzerland 39/D2
Mallet Creek, Ohio (†44256) 284/G3
Malling, Denmark 21/D5
Mallnitz, Austria 41/B3
Malloa, Chile 138/G5
Malloch (cape), N.W. Terrs. 187/H2
Mallorca (Majorca) (isl.), Spain 33/H3
Mallory, N.Y. (13103) 276/H4
Mallory, W. Va. (25634) 312/C7
Mallorytown, Ontario 177/J3
Mallow, Ireland 17/D7
Mallow, Ireland 10/B4
Malmanoury, Fr. Guiana 131/E3
Malmberget, Sweden 18/M3
Malmédy, Belgium 27/J8
Malmesbury, England 13/E6
Malmesbury, S. Africa 118/B6
Malmköping, Sweden 18/F1
Malmo, Minn. (†56431) 255/E4
Malmo, Nebr. (68040) 264/H3
Malmö, Sweden 7/F3
Malmö, Sweden 18/H9
Malmöhus (co.), Sweden 18/H9
Malmok (mt.), Neth. Ant. 161/E8
Malmstrom A.F.B., Mont. 262/E3
Malo, Wash. (99150) 310/G2
Maloca, Brazil 132/C4
Maloca, Brazil 120/D3
Maloelap (atoll), Marshall Is. 87/H5
Malolos, Philippines 82/C3
Malone, Fla. (32445) 212/A1
Malone, Ky. (41451) 237/P5
Malone, N.Y. (12953) 276/M1
Malone, Texas (76660) 303/H6
Malone, Wash. (98559) 310/B4
Maloneton, Ky. (41158) 237/R3
Maloney (res.), Nebr. 264/D3
Malonton, Manitoba 179/E4
Malott, Wash. (98829) 310/F2
Maloy, Iowa (50852) 229/E7
Malpartida de Cáceres, Spain 33/C3
Malpartida de Plasencia, Spain 33/C2
Malpelo (isl.), Colombia 120/A2
Malpeque (bay), Pr. Edward I. 168/E2
Malta 2/K4
Malta 7/F5
Malta, Colo. (†80461) 208/G4
Malta, Idaho (83342) 220/E7
Malta, Ill. (60150) 222/E2
Malta (chan.), Italy 34/E6
MALTA 34
Malta (isl.), Malta 34/E7
Malta, Mont. (59538) 262/J2
Malta, Ohio (43758) 284/G6
Malta Bend, Mo. (65339) 261/F4
Maltahöhe, Namibia 118/B4
Maltepe, Turkey 63/D6
Malters, Switzerland 39/F2
Malton, England 13/G3
Malton, England 10/F3
Maltrata, Mexico 150/O2
Malung, Sweden 18/H6
Malvaglia, Switzerland 39/H4
Malvan, India 68/C5
Malvern, Ala. (36349) 195/G8
Malvern, Ark. (72104) 202/E5
Malvern, England 13/E5
Malvern, England 10/E4
Malvern, Iowa (51551) 229/B7
Malvern, Jamaica 158/H6
Malvern, Ohio (44644) 284/H4
Malvern, Pa. (19355) 294/L5
Malvern, Victoria 88/L7
Malvern, Victoria 97/J5
Malverne, N.Y. (11565) 276/R7
Malvina, Miss. (†38769) 256/C3
Malvinas (Falkland) (isls.), 143/D7
Malhye Karmakuly, U.S.S.R. 52/H1
Mama, U.S.S.R. 48/M4
Mamala (bay), Hawaii 218/B4
Mamalu (bay), Hawaii 218/K3
Mamanguape, Brazil 132/H4
Mamaroneck, N.Y. (10543) 276/P7
Mambahenauhan (isl.), Philippines 82/B7
Mambajao, Philippines 82/E6
Mambasa, Zaire 115/E3
Mamberamo (riv.), Indonesia 85/K6
Mambrui, Kenya 115/H4
Mamburao, Philippines 82/C4
Ma-Me-O Beach, Alberta 182/D3
Mamer, Luxembourg 27/H9
Mamers, France 28/D3
Mamers, N.C. (27552) 281/L4
Mamfé, Cameroon 115/A2
Mamie, N.C. (27952) 281/T2
Mamiña, Chile 138/B2
Mammoth, Ariz. (85618) 198/E6
Mammoth, Utah (†84628) 304/B4
Mammoth (creek), Utah 304/B6
Mammoth, W. Va. (25132) 312/D6
Mammoth Cave Nat'l Park, Ky. 237/J6
Mammoth Hot Springs (Yellowstone Nat'l Park), Wyo. (†82190) 319/B1
Mammoth Lakes, Calif. (93546) 204/G6
Mammoth Spring, Ark. (72554) 202/G1
Mamoré (riv.), Bolivia 120/C4
Mamoré (riv.), Bolivia 136/C2
Mamou, Guinea 106/B6
Mamou, La. (70554) 238/F5
Mampong, Ghana 106/D7
Mamry, Jezioro (lake), Poland 47/E1
Mamuju, Indonesia 85/F6
Man (isl.), I. of Man 13/C3
Man, Ivory Coast 106/C7
Man, Ivory Coast 102/B4
Man, W. Va. (25635) 312/C7
Mana, Fr. Guiana 131/E3
Mana (riv.), Fr. Guiana 131/E3
Mana (isl.), N. Zealand 100/B2
Manabí (prov.), Ecuador 128/B3
Manacacías (riv.), Colombia 126/D6
Manacapuru, Brazil 120/C3
Manacapuru, Brazil 132/H9
Manacas, Cuba 158/E1
Manacle (pt.), England 13/C7
Manacor, Spain 33/H3
Manado, Indonesia 54/O9
Manado, Indonesia 85/G5
Manage, Belgium 27/E7
Managua (cap.), Nic. 146/K8
Managua (cap.), Nicaragua 154/D4
Managua (lake), Nicaragua 154/E4
Manah, Oman 59/G5
Manahawkin, N.J. (08050) 273/E4
Manaia, N. Zealand 100/E3
Manakara, Madagascar 118/H4
Manakara, Madagascar 102/G7
Manakha, Yemen Arab Rep. 59/D6
Manakin-Sabot, Va. (23103) 307/N5
Manalapan, N.J. (†07746) 273/E3
Manama (cap.), Bahrain 59/F4
Manana (isl.), Hawaii 218/F2
Mananara, Madagascar 118/J3
Mananara (riv.), Madagascar 118/H4
Mananbao (riv.), Madagascar 118/G3
Mananjary, Madagascar 118/H4
Mananjary, Madagascar 102/G7
Manannah, Minn. (†56243) 255/D5
Manapire (riv.), Venezuela 124/E3
Manapouri (lake), N. Zealand 100/A6
Manaqil, Sudan 59/B7
Manar, Jebel (mt.), Yemen Arab Rep. 59/D7
Manare, Colombia 126/E4
Manas, China 77/C3
Manas He (riv.), China 77/C3
Manas Hu (lake), China 77/C2
Manasquan, N.J. (08736) 273/E3
Manasquan (riv.), N.J. 273/E3
Manassa, Colo. (81141) 208/H8
Manassas, Georgia (30438) 217/H6
Manassas (I.C.), Va. (22110) 307/O3
Manassas Nat'l Battlefield Park, Va. 307/K3
Manassas Park (I.C.), Va. (22110) 307/O3
Manatee (co.), Fla. 212/D4
Manatee (riv.), Fla. 212/D4
Manatí, Cuba 158/H3
Manatí, P. Rico 156/G1
Manatí, P. Rico 161/C1
Manaus, Brazil 2/F6
Manaus, Brazil 120/D3
Manaus, Brazil 132/H9
Manavgat, Turkey 63/D4
Manawa, Wis. (54949) 317/J7
Manay, Philippines 82/F7
Mancelona, Mich. (49659) 250/E4
Mancha, La (reg.), Spain 33/E3
Manchac (passage), La. 238/N2
Manchaca, Texas (78652) 303/G7
Mancha Real, Spain 33/E4
Manchaug, Mass. (01526) 249/G4
Manche (dept.), France 28/C3
Manche, La (English) (chan.), France 28/B3
Manchester, Ala. (†35501) 195/D3
Manchester, Calif. (95459) 204/B5
Manchester, Conn. (06040) 210/E1
Manchester◯, Conn. (06040) 210/E1
Manchester, Greater (co.), England 13/H2
Manchester, England 7/D3
Manchester, England 10/G2
Manchester, England 13/H2
Manchester, Georgia (31816) 217/C5
Manchester, Ill. (62663) 222/C4
Manchester, Ind. (†47001) 227/H6
Manchester, Iowa (52057) 229/L3
Manchester, Kansas (67463) 232/E2
Manchester, Ky. (40962) 237/O6
Manchester◯, Maine (04351) 243/D7
Manchester, Md. (21102) 245/L2
Manchester◯, Mass. (01944) 249/F5
Manchester, Mich. (48158) 250/E6
Manchester, Minn. (56064) 255/E7
Manchester, Mo. (63011) 261/O3
Manchester, N.H. 188/M2
Manchester, N.H. (*03101) 268/E6
Manchester, N.Y. (14504) 276/F5
Manchester, Ohio (45144) 284/C8
Manchester, Okla. (73758) 288/L1
Manchester, Pa. (17345) 294/J5
Manchester, S. Dak. (†57353) 298/O5
Manchester, Tenn. (37355) 237/J10
Manchester, Vt. (05254) 268/A5
Manchester◯, Vt. (05254) 268/A5
Manchester, Wash. (98353) 310/A2
Manchester, Wis. (†53946) 317/J8
Manchester Center, Vt. (05255) 268/A5
Manchester Depot, Vt. (†05254) 268/B5
Manchioneal, Jamaica 158/K6
Manchouli (Manzhouli), China 77/J2
Máncora, Peru 128/B5
Mancos, Colo. (81328) 208/C8
Mancos (riv.), Colo. 208/B8
Manda, Tanzania 115/F6
Mandabe, Madagascar 118/G4
Mandah, Mongolia 77/G3
Mandal, Norway 18/E7
Mandalay (div.), Burma 72/B2
Mandalay, Burma 54/L7
Mandalay, Burma 72/C2

Mandalgovĭ, Mongolia 77/G2
Mandali, Iraq 66/D4
Mandal-Ovoo, Mongolia 77/F3
Mandalya (gulf), Turkey 63/B4
Mandan, N. Dak. 188/F1
Mandan, N. Dak. (58554) 282/J6
Mandaon, Philippines 82/D4
Mandar (cape), Indonesia 85/F6
Mandaree, N. Dak. (58757) 282/E4
Mandaue, Philippines 82/E5
Mandeb, Bab el (str.), Saudi Arabia 59/D7
Mandeb, Bab el (str.), Yemen Arab Rep. 59/D7
Mandera, Kenya 115/H3
Manderson, S. Dak. (57756) 298/D7
Manderson, Wyo. (82432) 319/E1
Mandeville, Ark. (†75501) 202/C7
Mandeville, Jamaica 158/H6
Mandeville, La. (70448) 238/L6
Mandi, India 68/D2
Mandié, Mozambique 118/E3
Mandimba, Mozambique 118/F2
Mandinga, Panama 154/H6
Mandioré (lag.), Bolivia 136/F6
Mandla, India 68/E4
Mándok, Hungary 41/G2
Mandritsara, Madagascar 118/H3
Mand Rud (riv.), Iran 59/F4
Mand Rud (riv.), Iran 66/G6
Mandsaur, India 68/C4
Mandurah, W. Australia 88/B3
Mandurah, W. Australia 92/A2
Manduria, Italy 34/F4
Mandvi, India 68/B4
Manele (bay), Hawaii 218/H2
Manele Bay, Hawaii (†96763) 218/H2
Manendragarh, India 68/E4
Manes, Mo. (†65711) 261/H8
Manfalût, Egypt 111/J4
Manfalût, Egypt 59/B4
Manfred, N. Dak. (58465) 282/L4
Manfredonia, Italy 34/F4
Manfredonia (gulf), Italy 34/F4
Manga, Brazil 132/E6
Manga, Uruguay 145/B7
Mangai, Zaire 115/C4
Mangaia (isl.), Cook Is. 87/L8
Mangakino, N. Zealand 100/E3
Mangalia, Romania 45/J4
Mangalore, India 54/J8
Mangalore, India 68/C6
Mangareva (isl.), Fr. Poly. 87/N8
Mangaweka, N. Zealand 100/E3
Mangere (isl.), N. Zealand 100/E7
Mangerton (mt.), Ireland 17/C8
Mangham, La. (71259) 238/G2
Mangkalihat (cape), Indonesia 85/F5
Manglaralto, Ecuador 128/B3
Mangle (pt.), Cuba 158/J3
Mangillo (pt.), P. Rico 161/B3
Mangnai, China 77/D4
Mango, Fla. (33550) 212/D4
Mango, Togo 106/E6
Mangochi, Malawi 115/G6
Mangoky (riv.), Madagascar 102/G7
Mangoky (riv.), Madagascar 118/G4
Mangole (isl.), Indonesia 85/H6
Mangonui, N. Zealand 100/D1
Mangoro (riv.), Madagascar 118/H3
Mangotsfield, England 10/E5
Mangotsfield, England 13/E6
Mangrol, India 68/B4
Mangsee (isls.), Philippines 82/A7
Mangualde, Portugal 33/C2
Mangueigne, Chad 111/D5
Mangueira (lag.), Brazil 132/D11
Manguera Azul, Uruguay 145/D4
Mangui, China 77/K1
Manguito, Cuba 158/D1
Mangum, Okla. (73554) 288/G5
Mangyshlak (pen.), U.S.S.R. 48/F5
Manhan (riv.), Mass. 249/D4
Manhasset, N.Y. (11030) 276/P7
Manhattan, Ill. (60442) 222/F2
Manhattan, Ind. (†46171) 227/D5
Manhattan, Kansas (66502) 232/F2
Manhattan, Mont. (59741) 262/E5
Manhattan, Nev. (89022) 266/E4
Manhattan (borough), N.Y. (*10001) 276/M9
Manhattan (isl.), N.Y. 276/M9
Manhattan Beach, Calif. (90266) 204/B11
Manhattan Beach, Minn. (56463) 255/E4
Manhay, Belgium 27/H8
Manheim, Pa. (17545) 294/K5
Manheim, W. Va. (26403) 312/G4
Manhiça, Mozambique 118/E5
Man Hpang, Burma 72/C2
Manhuaçu, Brazil 132/F8
Manhuaçu, Brazil 135/E2
Manhumirim, Brazil 135/E2
Maní, Colombia 126/D5
Maniamba, Mozambique 102/F6
Maniamba, Mozambique 118/F2
Manibridge, Manitoba 179/J2
Manica (prov.), Mozambique 118/E4
Manica, Mozambique 118/E3
Manicani (isl.), Philippines 82/E5
Manicaragua, Cuba 158/E2
Manicoré, Brazil 120/C3
Manicoré, Brazil 132/H9
Manicouagan, Québec 174/D2
Manicouagan (pt.), Québec 172/B1
Manicouagan (res.), Québec 174/D2
Manicouagan (riv.), Que. 162/K5
Manicouagan (riv.), Québec 174/D2
Manifest, La. (†71340) 238/G3
Manifold (cape), Queensland 88/J4
Manifold (cape), Queensland 95/D4
Manigotagan, Manitoba 179/F3
Manigotagan (lake), Manitoba 179/G4
Manigotagan (riv.), Manitoba 179/G3
Manigouche, Québec 174/C3
Manihiki (atoll), Cook Is. 87/K7
Manila, Ala. (†36586) 195/C7
Manila, Ark. (72442) 202/K2
Manila (prov.), Philippines 82/C3
Manila (cap.), Philippines 2/R5
Manila (cap.), Philippines 85/G3
Manila (cap.), Philippines 82/C3
Manila (cap.), Philippines 54/N8
Manila (bay), Philippines 82/C3
Manila, Utah (84046) 304/E3
Manildra, N.S. Wales 97/E3
Manilla, Ind. (46150) 227/F5
Manilla, Iowa (51454) 229/C5
Manilla, N.S. Wales 97/F2
Maningrida, North. Terr. 93/C2
Manipa (str.), Indonesia 85/H6
Manipur (riv.), Burma 72/B2
Manipur (state), India 68/G4
Manisa (prov.), Turkey 63/B3
Manisa, Turkey 63/B3
Manisa, Turkey 59/A2
Manistee, Mich. 188/J2
Manistee (co.), Mich. 250/C4
Manistee, Mich. (49660) 250/C4
Manistee (riv.), Mich. 250/C4
Manistique, Mich. (49854) 250/C3
Manistique (lake), Mich. 250/D2
Manistique (riv.), Mich. 250/C2
Manito, Ill. (61546) 222/D3
Manito (lake), Sask. 181/B3
Manitoba (prov.) 162/G5
Manitoba (prov.), Canada 146/J4
MANITOBA 179
Manitoba (lake), Man. 146/H4
Manitoba (lake), Man. 162/G5
Manitoba (lake), Manitoba 179/D4
Manitou, Ky. (42436) 237/F6
Manitou, Manitoba 179/D5
Manitou (isl.), Mich. 250/B1
Manitou, N. Dak. (†58776) 282/E3
Manitou, Okla. (73555) 288/J5
Manitou (lake), Ontario 177/C2
Manitou (lake), Québec 172/C3
Manitou Beach, Sask. 181/F4
Manitoulin (terr. dist.), Ontario 175/D3
Manitoulin (terr. dist.), Ontario 177/B2
Manitoulin (isl.), Ont. 162/H6
Manitoulin (isl.), Ontario 175/D3
Manitoulin (isl.), Ontario 177/B2
Manitou Springs, Colo. (80829) 208/J5
Manitouwadge, Ontario 177/H5
Manitouwadge, Ontario 175/C3
Manitowaning, Ontario 177/C2
Manitowish, Wis. (†54547) 317/F3
Manitowoc (co.), Wis. 317/L7
Manitowoc, Wis. (54220) 317/L7
Maniwaki, Québec 174/B3
Maniwaki, Québec 172/B3
Manizales, Colombia 126/C5
Manizales, Colombia 120/B2
Manja, Jordan 65/D4
Manja, Madagascar 118/G4
Manjacaze, Mozambique 118/E5
Manjimup, W. Australia 88/B6
Manjimup, W. Australia 92/B6
Mankato, Kansas (66956) 232/D2
Mankato, Minn. 188/H2
Mankato, Minn. (56001) 255/E6
Mankono, Ivory Coast 106/C7
Mankota, Sask. 181/D6
Manley, Nebr. (68403) 264/H4
Manley Hot Springs, Alaska (99756) 196/H2
Manlius, Ill. (61338) 222/D2
Manlius, N.Y. (13104) 276/J5
Manlleu, Spain 33/H1
Manly, Iowa (50456) 229/G2
Manly, N. S. Wales 88/L4
Manly, N.S. Wales 97/K3
Manly, N.C. (†28387) 281/L4
Manly, Queensland 88/L2
Manmad, India 68/C4
Manmanoc (mt.), Philippines 82/C2
Mann (riv.), North. Terr. 93/D2
Manna, Indonesia 85/C6
Mannahill, S. Australia 94/F5
Mannar (gulf) 54/J9
Mannar (gulf), India 68/D7
Mannar, Sri Lanka 68/E7
Mannar (gulf), Sri Lanka 68/D7
Mannargudi, India 68/E6
Mannboro, Va. (23105) 307/N6
Männedorf, Switzerland 39/G2
Mannersdorf am Leithagebirge, Austria 41/D3
Manners Sutton, New Bruns. 170/D3
Mannford, Okla. (74044) 288/O2
Mannheim, W. Germany 7/E4
Mannheim, W. Germany 22/C4
Manning, Alberta 182/B1
Manning, Ark. (71757) 202/E5
Manning, Iowa (51455) 229/C5
Manning, Kansas (†67871) 232/B3
Manning (riv.), N.S. Wales 97/F2
Manning, N. Dak. (58642) 282/E5
Manning (cape), N.W. Terrs. 187/F2
Manning (str.), Solomon Is. 86/D2
Manning, S.C. (29102) 296/G4
Manning Prov. Park, Br. Col. 184/G5
Mannington, Ky. (†42217) 237/G6
Mannington, W. Va. (26582) 312/F3
Männlifluh (mt.), Switzerland 39/E3
Manns Choice, Pa. (15550) 294/E6
Manns Harbor, N.C. (27953) 281/T3
Mannsville, Ky. (42758) 237/L6
Mannsville, N.Y. (13661) 276/H3
Mannsville, Okla. (73447) 288/N6
Mannu (riv.), Italy 34/B5
Mannum, S. Australia 94/F6
Mannville, Alberta 182/E3
Mano (riv.), Liberia 106/B7
Mano (riv.), S. Leone 106/B7
Manoa, Bolivia 136/C1
Manokin, Md. (21836) 245/P8
Manokin (riv.), Md. 245/P8
Manokotak, Alaska (99628) 196/G3
Manokwari, Indonesia 85/J6
Manola, Alberta 182/C2
Manombo, Madagascar 118/G4
Manomet, Mass. (02345) 249/M5
Manomet (pt.), Mass. 249/N5
Manono, Zaire 115/E5
Manono, Zaire 102/E5
Manor, Georgia (31550) 217/G8
Manor, Pa. (15665) 294/C5
Manor, Sask. 181/K6
Manor, Texas (78653) 303/G7
Manorhamilton, Ireland 17/E3
Manori, India 68/B6
Manori (creek), India 68/B7
Manorville, N.Y. (11949) 276/P9
Manorville, Pa. (16238) 294/C4
Manosque, France 28/G6
Manotick, Ontario 177/J2
Manouane, Québec 172/C2
Manouane (lake), Québec 174/C2
Manp'o, N. Korea 81/B3
Manquin, Va. (23106) 307/O5
Manra (Sydney) (isl.), Kiribati 87/K6
Manresa, Spain 33/G2
Mansa, Zambia 115/E6
Mansa, Zambia 102/E6
Mansalay, Philippines 82/C4
Mansavillagra, Uruguay 145/D4
Manseau, Québec 172/E3
Mansel (isl.), N.W.T. 162/H3
Mansel (isl.), N.W.T. 146/K3
Mansel (isl.), N.W. Terrs. 187/K3
Mansel'ka (mts.), U.S.S.R. 52/C1
Mansfield, Ark. (72944) 202/B3
Mansfield◯, Conn. (†06250) 210/F1
Mansfield, England 13/K2
Mansfield, England 10/F4
Mansfield, Georgia (30255) 217/E4
Mansfield, Ill. (61854) 222/E3
Mansfield, Ind. (†47872) 227/C5
Mansfield, La. (71052) 238/C2
Mansfield, Mass. (02048) 249/J4
Mansfield◯, Mass. (02048) 249/J4
Mansfield, Minn. (†56009) 255/E7
Mansfield, Mo. (65704) 261/G8
Mansfield, Ohio 188/K2
Mansfield, Ohio (*44901) 284/F4
Mansfield, Pa. (16933) 294/H2
Mansfield, S. Dak. (57460) 298/N3
Mansfield, Tenn. (38236) 237/E8
Mansfield, Texas (76063) 303/F3
Mansfield (mt.), Vt. 268/B2
Mansfield, Victoria 97/D5
Mansfield, Wash. (98830) 310/F3
Mansfield Center, Conn. (06250) 210/G1
Mansfield Depot, Conn. (06251) 210/F1
Mansfield Woodhouse, England 13/F4
Mansilla de las Mulas, Spain 33/D1
Manso (riv.), Brazil 132/C6
Manso (riv.), Chile 138/E4
Manson, Ind. (†46041) 227/D4
Manson, Iowa (50563) 229/D3
Manson, Manitoba 179/A4
Manson, N.C. (27553) 281/N2
Manson, Wash. (98831) 310/E3
Manson Creek, Br. Col. 184/E2
Mansonville, Québec 172/E4
Mansura, La. (71350) 238/G4
Manta, Ecuador 128/B3
Manta, Ecuador 120/A3
Manta (bay), Ecuador 128/B3
Mantachie, Miss. (38855) 256/H2
Mantador, N. Dak. (58058) 282/R7
Mantagao (lake), Manitoba 179/E3
Mantagao (riv.), Manitoba 179/E3
Mantalingajan (mt.), Philippines 82/A6
Mantario, Sask. 181/B4
Mantaro (riv.), Peru 128/E8
Mantas (well), Niger 106/E5
Manteca, Calif. (95336) 204/D6
Mantecal, Apure, Venezuela 124/D4
Mantecal, Bolívar, Venezuela 124/F4
Mantee, Miss. (39751) 256/F3
Manteigas, Portugal 33/C2
Manteno, Ill. (60950) 222/F2
Manteo, N.C. (27954) 281/T3
Manter, Kansas (67862) 232/A4
Mantes-la-Jolie, France 28/D3
Manti, Utah (84642) 304/C4
Mantiqueira (range), Brazil 135/D3
Manto, Honduras 154/D3
Mantoloking, N.J. (08738) 273/E3
Manton, Calif. (96059) 204/D3
Manton, Mich. (49663) 250/D4
Manton, R.I. (†02904) 249/J5
Mantorville, Minn. (55955) 255/F6
Mänttä, Finland 18/O6
Mantua, Ala. (35472) 195/C4
Mantua, Cuba 158/A2
Mantua (prov.), Italy 34/C2
Mantua, Italy 34/C2
Mantua◯, N.J. (08051) 273/C4
Mantua, Ohio (44255) 284/H3
Mantua, Utah (†84302) 304/C2
Mantua, Va. (†22030) 307/S3
Manturovo, U.S.S.R. 52/F3
Manú, Peru 128/G9
Manú (riv.), Peru 128/G8
Manua (isls.), Amer. Samoa 87/K7
Manuae (atoll), Cook Is. 87/K7
Manuel Benavides, Mexico 150/H2
Manuelito, N. Mex. (†86506) 274/A3
Manuel Rodriguez (isl.), Chile 138/D10
Manuels, New Bruns. 170/F1
Manuels, Newf. 166/D2
Manui (isl.), Indonesia 85/G6
Manukan, Philippines 82/D6
Manukau, N. Zealand 100/C1
Manukau (harb.), N. Zealand 100/B1
Manulla, Ireland 17/C4
Manumuskin (riv.), N.J. 273/D5
Manunui, N. Zealand 100/E3
Manuripi (riv.), Bolivia 136/B2
Manus (isl.), Papua N.G. 87/E6
Manus (isl.), Papua N.G. 86/A1
Manutuke, N. Zealand 100/F3
Manvel, N. Dak. (58256) 282/R3
Manvel, Texas (77578) 303/J3
Manville, N.J. (08835) 273/D2
Manville, R.I. (02838) 249/H5
Manville, Wyo. (82227) 319/H3
Many, La. (71449) 238/C3
Manyara (lake), Tanzania 115/G4
Manyas, Turkey 63/B3
Manyberries, Alberta 182/E5
Manych-Gudilo (lake), U.S.S.R. 52/F5
Many Farms, Ariz. (86538) 198/F2
Manyoni, Tanzania 115/G5
Manzai, Pakistan 59/K3
Manzanar, Chile 138/F2
Manzanares, Spain 33/E3
Manzanares (riv.), Spain 33/F4
Manzanillo, Cuba 158/H4
Manzanillo, Cuba 156/C2
Manzanillo (bay), Dom. Rep. 158/C5
Manzanillo (bay), Haiti 158/C5
Manzanillo, Mexico 150/G7
Manzanillo, Mexico 146/H8
Manzanillo (pt.), Panama 154/H6
Manzanita, Oreg. (97130) 291/C2
Manzanita Ind. Res., Calif. 204/J11
Manzano, N. Mex. (†87016) 274/C4
Manzano (mts.), N. Mex. 274/C4
Manzano (peak), N. Mex. 274/C4
Manzanola, Colo. (81058) 208/M6
Manzhouli (Manchouli), China 77/J2
Manzini, Swaziland 118/E5
Mao, Chad 111/C5
Mao, Dom. Rep. 158/D5
Maoke (mts.), Indonesia 85/K6
Maoming (Mowming), China 77/H7
Mapai, Mozambique 118/E4
Maparari, Venezuela 124/D2
Mapastepec, Mexico 150/N9
Mapes, N. Dak. (58349) 282/O3
Mapia (isls.), Indonesia 85/J5
Mapimí, Mexico 150/G4
Mapimí (depr.), Mexico 150/G3
Mapire, Venezuela 124/F4
Mapiri, Bolivia 136/B4
Mapiripán, Laguna (lake), Colombia 126/E6
Maple (peak), Ariz. 198/F5
Maple (riv.), Mich. 250/E5
Maple (lake), Minn. 255/B3
Maple (riv.), Minn. 255/E7
Maple (riv.), N. Dak. 282/O8
Maple (riv.), N. Dak. 282/R6
Maple (creek), Sask. 181/B5
Maple (riv.), S. Dak. 298/M1
Maple, Wis. (54854) 317/C2
Maple Bay, Br. Col. 184/K3
Maple Bay, Minn. (†56736) 255/B3
Maple City, Kansas (67102) 232/F4
Maple City, Mich. 250/D4
Maple Creek, Sask. 162/F6
Maple Creek, Sask. 181/B6
Maple Falls, Wash. (98266) 310/D2
Maple Grove, Minn. (†55369) 255/G5
Maple Grove, Ontario 177/F4
Maple Grove, Québec 172/H4
Maple Heights, Ohio (44137) 284/H9
Maple Hill, Iowa (50564) 229/D2
Maple Hill, Kansas (66507) 232/F2
Maple Hill, N.C. (28454) 281/O5
Maple Island, Minn. (†55082) 255/E7
Maple Lake, Minn. (55358) 255/D5
Maple Park, Ill. (60151) 222/E2
Maple Plain, Minn. (55359) 255/F5
Maple Rapids, Mich. (48853) 250/E5
Maple Ridge, Br. Col. 184/L3
Maple River, Iowa (†51401) 229/D4
Maples, Ind. (†46802) 227/H2
Maples, Mo. (†65542) 261/J7
Maple Shade◯, N.J. (08052) 273/B3
Maplesville, Ala. (36750) 195/E5
Mapleton, Iowa (51034) 229/B4
Mapleton, Kansas (66754) 232/H3
Mapleton◯, Maine (04757) 243/G2
Mapleton, Mich. (†49684) 250/D4
Mapleton, Minn. (56065) 255/E7
Mapleton, N.C. (†27855) 281/P2
Mapleton, N. Dak. (58059) 282/R6
Mapleton, Oreg. (97453) 291/C3
Mapleton (Mapleton Depot), Pa. (17052) 294/F5
Mapleton, Utah (†84663) 304/C3
Mapleton, Wis. (†53066) 317/J1
Mapleton Depot, Pa. (17052) 294/F5
Maple Valley, Wash. (98038) 310/C3
Mapleview, Minn. (†55912) 255/E7
Mapleview, New Bruns. 170/C2
Mapleville, Md. (†21713) 245/H2
Mapleville, R.I. (02839) 249/H5
Maplewood, La. (†70663) 238/D6
Maplewood, Minn. (55109) 255/G5
Maplewood, Mo. (63143) 261/P3
Maplewood, N.H. (†03574) 268/D3
Maplewood◯, N.J. (07040) 273/E2
Maplewood, Ohio (45340) 284/B5
Maplewood, Wis. (54226) 317/M6
Mapocho (riv.), Chile 138/G3
Mapoon Mission Station, Queensland 88/G2
Mapoon Mission Station, Queensland 95/B1
Maporal, Venezuela 124/C4
Mapos (Amazones), Cuba 158/F2
Mappsville, Va. (23407) 307/T5
Mapuera (riv.), Brazil 132/B3
Maputo (city) (prov.), Mozambique 118/E5
Maputo (prov.), Mozambique 118/E5
Maputo (cap.), Mozambique 2/L7
Maputo (cap.), Mozambique 118/E5
Maputo (cap.), Mozambique 102/F7
Maqatin (ruins), P.D.R. Yemen 59/E7
Maqên, China 77/F5
Maqna, Saudi Arabia 59/C4
Ma Qu (Huang He) (riv.), China 77/F5
Maquapit (lake), New Bruns. 170/D3
Maqueda (chan.), Philippines 82/D3
Maquela do Zombo, Angola 102/D5
Maquela do Zombo, Angola 115/C5
Maquereau (pt.), Québec 172/D2
Maquinchao, Argentina 143/C5
Maquoketa, Iowa (52060) 229/M4
Maquon, Ill. (61458) 222/C3
Mar (mts.), Brazil 120/E5
Mar (range), Brazil 135/C4
Mar, Serra do (range), Brazil 132/E9
Mar (dist.), Scotland 15/F3
Mara, Guyana 131/C3
Mara (reg.), Tanzania 115/F4
Marabá, Brazil 132/D4
Marabá, Brazil 120/E3
Marabahan, Indonesia 85/E6
Marabella, Trin. & Tob. 161/A11
Maracá (isl.), Brazil 120/E2
Maracá (isl.), Brazil 132/D2
Maracaibo, Venezuela 124/C2
Maracaibo, Venezuela 120/B1
Maracaibo (lake), Venezuela 120/B2
Maracaibo (lake), Venezuela 124/C3
Maracaju, Brazil 132/C8
Maracas (bay), Trin. & Tob. 161/C10
Maracay, Venezuela 124/E2
Maracay, Venezuela 120/C2
Marada, Libya 111/C2
Maradi, Niger 106/F6
Maradi, Niger 102/C3
Maragheh, Iran 59/E2
Maragheh, Iran 66/E2
Maragogipe, Brazil 132/G6
Maraira (pt.), Philippines 82/C1
Marajó (est.), Brazil 120/E2
Marajó (isl.), Brazil 120/E3
Marajó (bay), Brazil 132/E2
Marajó (isl.), Brazil 132/D3
Maralal, Kenya 115/G3
Maralinga, S. Australia 88/E6
Maralwexi (Bachu), China 77/A4
Maramag, Philippines 82/E7
Maramec, Okla. (74045) 288/N2
Marampa, S. Leone 106/B7
Marana, Ariz. (85238) 198/D6
Marand, Iran 59/E2
Marand, Iran 66/D1
Marandellas, Zimbabwe 118/E3
Marang, Malaysia 72/D6
Maranguape, Brazil 132/G3
Maranhão (state), Brazil 132/E4
Maranoa (riv.), Queensland 95/C5
Marañón (riv.), Peru 120/B3
Marañón (riv.), Peru 128/E5
Marapanim, Brazil 132/E3
Maras (mt.), Indonesia 85/D6
Maraş, Turkey 59/C2
Maraş (Kahramanmaraş), Turkey 63/G4
Marathon, Fla. (33050) 212/E7
Marathón, Greece 45/G6
Marathon, Iowa (50565) 229/C3
Marathon, N.Y. (13803) 276/J6
Marathon, Ohio (45145) 284/C7
Marathon, Ont. 162/H6
Marathon, Ontario 177/H5
Marathon, Ontario 175/C3
Marathon, Texas (79842) 303/A7
Marathon (co.), Wis. 317/G6
Marathon, Wis. (54448) 317/G6
Maratua (isl.), Indonesia 85/F5
Maravillas, Bolivia 136/B2
Maravillas (creek), Texas 303/A7
Marawi, Philippines 85/G4
Marawi, Philippines 82/E6
Marbach, Switzerland 39/E3
Marbach am Neckar, W. Germany 22/C4
Marbella, Spain 33/D4
Marble, Ark. (72746) 202/C1
Marble, Colo. (†81623) 208/E4
Marble, Minn. (55764) 255/E3
Marble, N.C. (28905) 281/B4
Marble (isl.), N.W.T. 162/G3
Marble (isl.), N.W. Terrs. 187/J3
Marble Bar, Australia 87/C8
Marble Bar, W. Australia 88/B4
Marble Bar, W. Australia 92/C3
Marble Canyon, Ariz. (86036) 198/D2
Marble Canyon Nat'l Mon., Ariz. 198/D2
Marble City, Okla. (74945) 288/S3
Marble Dale, Conn. (06777) 210/B2
Marble Falls, Texas (78654) 303/F7
Marblehead, Ill. (†62301) 222/B4
Marblehead◯, Mass. (01945) 249/E7
Marblehead (neck), Mass. 249/F6
Marblehead, Ohio (†43440) 284/E2
Marble Hill, Georgia (30148) 217/D2
Marble Hill, Mo. (63764) 261/N8
Marblemount, Wash. (98267) 310/D2
Marble Rock, Iowa (50653) 229/H3
Marbleton, Québec 172/F4
Marbleton, Wyo. (†83113) 319/B3
Marble Valley, Ala. (†35150) 195/F4
Marburg an der Lahn, W. Germany 22/C3
Marbury, Ala. (36051) 195/E5
Marbury, Md. (20658) 245/K6
Marcala, Honduras 154/C3
Marcali, Hungary 41/D3
Marcapata, Peru 128/G9
Marcelin, Sask. 181/E3
Marceline, Mo. (64658) 261/F3
Marcell, Minn. (56657) 255/E3
Marcella, Ark. (72555) 202/G2
Marcella, N.J. (†07866) 273/E2
Marcelline, Ill. (†62376) 222/B3
Marcellus, Mich. (49067) 250/D6
Marcellus, N.Y. (13108) 276/H5
Marcelville, New Bruns. 170/E2
March (riv.), Austria 41/D2
March, England 10/G4
March, England 13/H5
March A.F.B., Calif. 204/E11
Marchand, Manitoba 179/F5
Marche, Ark. (†72114) 202/F4
Marche (trad. prov.) France 29
Marche (reg.), Italy 34/D3
Marche-en-Famenne, Belgium 27/G8
Marchegg, Austria 41/D2
Marchena (isl.), Ecuador 128/B9
Marchena, Spain 33/D4
Marchfield, Barbados 161/B9
Marchigüe, Chile 138/F5
Marchin, Belgium 27/G8
Mar Chiquita (lake), Argentina 143/D3
Marchwell, Sask. 181/K5
Marco (Marco Island), Fla. (33937) 212/E6
Marco (isl.), Fla. 212/E6
Marco, Ind. (†47443) 227/C7
Marco, La. (†71447) 238/E3
Marcola, Oreg. (97454) 291/E3
Marcona, Peru 128/E10
Marcos Juárez, Argentina 143/D3
Marcus, Iowa (51035) 229/B3
Marcus (isl.), Japan 87/F3
Marcus, S. Dak. (57757) 298/E4
Marcus, Wash. (99151) 310/H2
Marcus Baker (mt.), Alaska 196/C1
Marcus Hook, Pa. (19061) 294/L7
Marcy, N.Y. (13403) 276/K4
Marcy (mt.), N.Y. 276/N2
Mardan, Pakistan 68/C2
Mardan, Pakistan 59/K3
Mardela Springs, Md. (21837) 245/P7
Mar del Plata, Argentina 143/E4
Mar del Plata, Argentina 120/D6
Mardin (prov.), Turkey 63/J4
Mardin, Turkey 63/J4
Mardin, Turkey 59/D2
Maré (isl.), New Caled. 87/G8
Mare (isl.), New Caled. 86/J4
Mareb (riv.), Ethiopia 59/C7
Marechal Deodoro, Brazil 132/H5
Maree, Loch (lake), Scotland 10/D2
Mare, Loch (lake), Scotland 15/C3
Mareeba, Queensland 95/C3
Mareeba, Queensland 88/G3
Mare Island Navy Yard, Calif. 204/J1
Marengo (co.), Ala. 195/C6
Marengo, Ala. (†36736) 195/C6
Marengo, Ill. (60152) 222/E1
Marengo, Ind. (47140) 227/E8
Marengo, Iowa (52301) 229/J5
Marengo, Ohio (43334) 284/E5
Marengo, Sask. 181/B4
Marengo, Wash. (†99004) 310/G3
Marengo, Wis. (54855) 317/E3
Marenisco, Mich. (49947) 250/F2
Marennes, France 28/C5
Mareth, Tunisia 106/F2
Marettimo (isl.), Italy 34/C6
Marfa, Texas (79843) 303/C12
Marfield, N.S. Wales 97/C3
Marfrance, W. Va. (25975) 312/E6
Margai Caka (lake), China 77/C4
Marganets, U.S.S.R. 52/E5
Margao, India 68/C5
Margaree, Nova Scotia 168/G2
Margaree (riv.), Nova Scotia 168/F4
Margaree Centre, Nova Scotia 168/H2
Margaree Forks, Nova Scotia 168/G2
Margaree Harbour, Nova Scotia 168/G2
Margaree Valley, Nova Scotia 168/H2
Margaret, Ala. (35112) 195/F3
Margaret (lake), Alberta 182/B5
Margaret, Manitoba 179/C5
Margaret, Texas (†79227) 303/E3
Margaret (riv.), W. Australia 88/D3
Margaret River, W. Australia 88/A6
Margaret River, W. Australia 92/A6
Margaret River Station, W. Australia 92/D2
Margaretsville, Nova Scotia 168/C3
Margaretville, N.Y. (12455) 276/L6
Margarita, Argentina 143/F5
Margarita (isl.), Venezuela 120/C1
Margarita (isl.), Venezuela 124/F2
Margate, England 13/J6
Margate, England 10/G5
Margate, Fla. (33063) 212/F5
Margate, S. Africa 118/E6
Margate, Tasmania 99/D4
Margate City, N.J. (08402) 273/E5
Margento, Colombia 126/C4
Margerum, Ala. (†35616) 195/B1
Margherita (Jamama), Somalia 115/H3
Margherita (mt.), Uganda 115/E3
Margherita (mt.), Zaire 102/E4
Margherita (mt.), Zaire 115/E3
Margie, Minn. (56658) 255/E2
Margo, Sask. 181/H4
Margos, Peru 128/D8
Margosatubig, Philippines 82/D7
Margow, Dasht-e (des.), Afghanistan 59/H3
Margow, Dasht-e (des.), Afghanistan 68/A2
Margraten, Netherlands 27/H7
Margret, Georgia (†30536) 217/D1
Margrethe (lake), Mich. 250/E4
Marguerite (bay) 5/C15
Maria (isl.), Fr. Poly. 87/L8
Maria (creek), Ind. 227/C7
Maria, Québec 172/C2
Maria (isls.), St. Lucia 161/G7
Maria (isl.), Tasmania 99/E4
Mari A.S.S.R., U.S.S.R. 52/G3
Mari A.S.S.R., U.S.S.R. 48/E4
María Albina, Uruguay 145/E4
María Cleófas (isl.), Mexico 150/F6
María Elena, Chile 138/B3
Mariager, Denmark 21/D4
Mariager, Denmark 18/G8
Mariager (fjord), Denmark 21/D4
Mariah Hill, Ind. (47556) 227/D8
María Madre (isl.), Mexico 150/F6
María Magdalena (isl.), Mexico 150/F6
Marian (lake), Fla. 212/E4
Marian (lake), N.W. Terrs. 187/G3
Marian, Queensland 88/H4
Marian, Queensland 95/D4
Mariana, Brazil 135/E2
Mariana Lake, Alberta 182/D2
Marianao, Cuba 158/C1
Marianao, Cuba 156/A2
Marianas, Northern 87/E4
Mariana Trench 87/E4
Marianna, Ark. (72360) 202/J4
Marianna, Fla. (32446) 212/A1
Marianna, Pa. (15345) 294/B5
Mariano I. Loza, Argentina 143/G4
Mariano Roque Alonso, Paraguay 144/A4

McKinley 407

Matadi, Zaire 102/D5
Matador, Sask. 181/D5
Matador, Texas (79244) 303/D3
Matagalpa, Nicaragua 154/E4
Matagami, Québec 174/B3
Matagami (lake), Québec 174/B3
Matagorda (co.), Texas 303/H9
Matagorda, Texas (77457) 303/J9
Matagorda (bay), Texas 188/G5
Matagorda (bay), Texas 303/H9
Matagorda (isl.), Texas 303/H9
Matagorda (pen.), Texas 303/J9
Matagorda Isl. Bombing and Gunnery Range, Texas 303/H9
Matakana (isl.), N. Zealand 100/F2
Matala (dam), Angola 115/B6
Matam, Senegal 106/B5
Matamoras, Pa. (18336) 294/N3
Matamoros, Mexico 146/J7
Matamoros, Coahuila, Mexico 150/H4
Matamoros, Tamaulipas, Mexico 150/L4
Matane (co.), Québec 172/B1
Matane (county), Québec 174/D3
Matane, Québec 174/D3
Matane, Québec 172/B1
Matane (riv.), Québec 172/B1
Matane Prov. Park, Québec 172/B1
Matanuska (riv.), Alaska 196/C1
Matanza, Colombia 126/D4
Matanzas (prov.), Cuba 158/D1
Matanzas, Cuba 146/K7
Matanzas, Cuba 158/C1
Matanzas, Cuba 156/B2
Matanzas (bay), Cuba 158/D1
Matanzas (inlet), Fla. 212/E2
Mata Palacio, Dom. Rep. 158/F6
Matapalo (cape), C. Rica 154/F6
Matapan (Tainaron) (cape), Greece 45/F7
Matapédia (county), Québec 174/D3
Matapédia (co.), Québec 172/B2
Matapédia, Québec 172/B2
Matapédia (lake), Québec 172/B1
Matapédia (riv.), Québec 172/B2
Mataquito (riv.), Chile 138/A10
Matara, Sri Lanka 68/E7
Mataram, Indonesia 85/F7
Matarani, Peru 120/B4
Matarani, Peru 128/F11
Mataranka, North. Terr. 93/C3
Matarinao (bay), Philippines 82/E5
Mataró, Spain 33/H2
Matatiele, S. Africa 118/D6
Matatindoc (pt.), Philippines 82/D6
Mataura, N. Zealand 100/B7
Mataura (riv.), N. Zealand 100/B6
Mata Utu (cap.), Wallis and Futuna 87/J7
Matawai, N. Zealand 100/F3
Matawan, Minn. (†56072) 255/E7
Matawan, N.J. (07747) 273/E3
Matawin (lake), Québec 172/C3
Matawin (riv.), Québec 172/D3
Mateare, Nicaragua 154/D4
Mateguá, Bolivia 136/D3
Matehuala, Mexico 150/J5
Matelot, Trin. & Tob. 161/B10
Matera (prov.), Italy 34/F4
Matera, Italy 34/F4
Materillos (pt.), Cuba 158/H2
Mátészalka, Hungary 41/G3
Matetsi, Zimbabwe 118/D3
Mateur, Tunisia 106/F1
Matewan, W. Va. (25678) 312/B7
Matfield Green, Kansas (66862) 232/F3
Mather, Manitoba 179/C5
Mather, Wis. (54641) 317/F7
Mather A.F.B., Calif. 204/C8
Matherville, Ill. (61263) 222/C2
Matherville, Miss. (†39360) 256/G7
Matheson, Colo. (80830) 208/M4
Matheson, Ontario 177/K5
Matheson Island, Manitoba 179/E3
Mathews, Ala. (36052) 195/F6
Mathews (lake), Calif. 204/E11
Mathews, La. (70375) 238/J7
Mathews (co.), Va. 307/R6
Mathews, Va. (23109) 307/R6
Mathias, W. Va. (26812) 312/J5
Mathinna, Tasmania 99/E3
Mathis, Texas (78368) 303/G9
Mathiston, Miss. (39752) 256/F3
Mathoura, N.S. Wales 97/C4
Mathura, India 68/D3
Mati, Philippines 85/H4
Mati, Philippines 82/F7
Matías Romero, Mexico 150/M8
Matinenda (lake), Ontario 177/B1
Matinicus, Maine (04851) 243/F8
Matinicus Rock (isl.), Maine 243/F8
Matlock, England 10/F4
Matlock, England 13/J2
Matlock, Iowa (51244) 229/A2
Matlock, Wash. (98560) 310/B3
Matoaca, Va. (23803) 307/N6
Matoaka, W. Va. (24736) 312/D8
Matochkin Shar (str.), U.S.S.R. 48/F2
Mato Grosso (state), Brazil 132/B6
Mato Grosso, Brazil 120/D4
Mato Grosso, Brazil 132/B6
Mato Grosso (plat.), Brazil 120/D4
Mato Grosso, Planalto de (plat.), Brazil 132/B6
Mato Grosso do Sul (state), Brazil 132/C7
Matopos, Zimbabwe 118/D4
Matosinhos, Portugal 33/B2
Matoury, Fr. Guiana 131/E3
Mátra (mts.), Hungary 41/E3
Matrah, Oman 54/G7
Matrah, Oman 59/G5
Matrei in Osttirol, Austria 41/B3
Matruh, Egypt 59/A3
Matsqui, Br. Col. 184/L3
Matsu (Mazu) (isl.), China 77/K6
Matsubara, Japan 81/H8
Matsue, Japan 81/F6
Matsumae, Japan 81/J3
Matsumoto, Japan 81/H5
Matsusaka, Japan 81/H6
Matsuto, Japan 81/H5
Matsuyama, Japan 81/F7
Matsuyama, Japan 54/P6
Matt, Switzerland 39/H3
Mattabesset (riv.), Conn. 210/E2
Mattagami (riv.), Ontario 175/D3
Mattagami (riv.), Ontario 177/J5
Mattamiscontis (lake), Maine 243/F4
Mattamuskeet (lake), N.C. 281/S3
Mattapan, Mass. (02126) 249/C7
Mattapoisett, Mass. (02739) 249/L6
Mattapoisett◌, Mass. (02739) 249/L6
Mattaponi, Va. (23110) 307/P5
Mattaponi (riv.), Va. 307/O5
Mattaponi Ind. Res., Va. 307/P5
Mattawa, Ont. 162/J6
Mattawa, Ontario 177/F1
Mattawa, Ontario 175/E3
Mattawa, Wash. (99344) 310/F4
Mattawamkeag◌, Maine (04459) 243/G5
Mattawamkeag (lake), Maine 243/G4
Mattawamkeag (riv.), Maine 243/G4
Mattawan, Mich. (49071) 250/D6
Mattawana, Pa. (17054) 294/G5
Mattawoman (creek), Md. 245/K6
Matterhorn (mt.), Switzerland 39/E4
Mattersburg, Austria 41/D3
Matteson, Ill. (60443) 222/B6
Matthew, Ky. (41454) 237/P5
Matthews, Georgia (30818) 217/H4
Matthews, Ind. (46957) 227/F4
Matthews, Mo. (63857) 261/N9
Matthews, N.C. (28105) 281/H4
Matthews Ridge, Guyana 131/B2
Mattice, Ontario 175/D3
Mattice, Ontario 177/J5
Mattighofen, Austria 41/B2
Mattituck, N.Y. (11952) 276/P9
Mattoon, Ill. (61938) 222/E4
Mattoon, Wis. (54450) 317/J5
Mattson, Miss. (38758) 256/C2
Matu, Venezuela 124/F4
Matucana, Peru 128/D8
Matuku (isl.), Fiji 86/Q11
Matún, Cuba 158/D2
Matura, Trin. & Tob. 161/B10
Matura (bay), Trin. & Tob. 161/B10
Maturín, Venezuela 120/C2
Maturín, Venezuela 124/G3
Matutum (mt.), Philippines 82/E7
Matutum (mt.), Philippines 85/G4
Matveyev (isl.), U.S.S.R. 52/J1
Mau, India 68/E3
Mauá, Brazil 135/C3
Mauá, Mozambique 118/F2
Maubeuge, France 28/F2
Ma-ubin, Burma 72/B3
Mauch Chunk (Jim Thorpe), Pa. (18229) 294/L4
Mauchline, Scotland 15/D5
Mauckport, Ind. (47142) 227/E8
Maud, Ala. (†35616) 195/B1
Maud, Ky. (40042) 237/L5
Maud, Miss. (†38626) 256/D1
Maud, Ohio (†45069) 284/B7
Maud, Okla. (74854) 288/N4
Maud, Scotland 15/F3
Maud, Texas (75567) 303/K4
Maude, N.S. Wales 97/C4
Maudlow, Mont. (59714) 262/E4
Mauerkirchen, Austria 41/B2
Maués, Brazil 132/B3
Maués, Brazil 120/D3
Maués-Açu (riv.), Brazil 132/B4
Maugansville, Md. (21767) 245/H2
Mauger (cay), Belize 154/D2
Maugerville, New Bruns. 170/D3
Maui (co.), Hawaii 218/J1
Maui (isl.), Hawaii 87/L3
Maui (isl.), Hawaii 188/F5
Maui (isl.), Hawaii 218/J2
Mauk, Georgia (31058) 217/D6
Mauke (isl.), Cook Is. 87/L8
Mauldin, S.C. (29662) 296/C2
Maule (reg.), Chile 138/A11
Maule (riv.), Chile 138/A11
Mauléon-Licharre, France 28/C6
Maullín, Chile 138/D4
Maullín (riv.), Chile 138/D3
Maumakeogh (mt.), Ireland 17/C3
Maumee (riv.), Ind. 227/H2
Maumee (bay), Mich. 250/F7
Maumee, Ohio (43537) 284/C2
Maumee (bay), Ohio 284/D2
Maumee (riv.), Ohio 284/A3
Maumelle (lake), Ark. 202/E4
Maumere, Indonesia 85/G7
Maumturk (mts.), Ireland 17/B5
Maun, Botswana 118/C4
Maunabo, P. Rico 161/E3
Mauna Kea (mt.), Hawaii 87/L4
Mauna Kea (mt.), Hawaii 188/G6
Mauna Kea (mt.), Hawaii 218/H4
Maunaloa, Hawaii (96770) 218/G1
Mauna Loa (mt.), Hawaii 188/G6
Mauna Loa (mt.), Hawaii 218/G6
Maunalua (bay), Hawaii 218/F2
Maunawili, Hawaii (†96744) 218/F2
Maungaturoto, N. Zealand 100/E1
Maungdaw, Burma 72/B2
Maunie, Ill. (62861) 222/E5
Maupin, Oreg. (97037) 291/F2
Maurepas, La. (70449) 238/M2
Maurepas (lake), La. 238/M2
Mauretown, Va. (22644) 307/L3
Mauriac, France 28/E5
Maurice, Iowa (51036) 229/A3
Maurice, La. (70555) 238/F6
Maurice (riv.), N.J. 273/C4
Maurice (lake), S. Australia 88/E5
Maurice (lake), S. Australia 94/B3
Mauricetown, N.J. (08325) 273/D5
Mauricio Hirsch, Argentina 143/F7
Maurine, S. Dak. (†57626) 298/E3
Mauritania 2/J4
Mauritania 102/A3
MAURITANIA 106/B5
Mauritius 2/M6
MAURITIUS 118/G5
Maury, N.C. (28554) 281/O4
Maury (co.), Tenn. 237/G9
Maury (riv.), Va. 307/K5
Maury City, Tenn. (38050) 237/C9
Mauston, Wis. (53948) 317/F8
Mautern in Steiermark, Austria 41/C3
Mauthausen, Austria 41/C2
Mauthen-Kötschach, Austria 41/B3
Mauvoisin (dam), Switzerland 39/D4
Mavaca (riv.), Venezuela 124/F6
Maverick, Ariz. (†85920) 198/F5
Maverick (co.), Texas 303/D9
Mavila, Peru 128/H8
Mavillette, Nova Scotia 168/B4
Mavinga, Angola 115/D7
Mavora (mt.), N. Zealand 100/B6
Mavqi'im, Israel 65/B4
Mawai, Malaysia 72/F5
Mawbanna, Tasmania 99/B2
Mawer, Sask. 181/E5
Mawkmai, Burma 72/C2
Mawlaik, Burma 72/B2
Mawlu, Burma 72/C1
Mawson 5/C4
Max, Minn. (56659) 255/D3
Max, Nebr. (69037) 264/C4
Max, N. Dak. (58759) 282/H4
Maxbass, N. Dak. (58760) 282/H2
Maxcanú, Mexico 150/O6
Maxeys, Georgia (30671) 217/F3
Maxie, La. (†70526) 238/F6
Maxie, Miss. (†39458) 256/F9
Máximo Gómez, Ciego de Ávila, Cuba 158/F2
Máximo Gómez, Matanzas, Cuba 158/D1
Máximo Paz, Argentina 143/F6
Maxinkuckee, Ind. (†46511) 227/E2
Maxinkuckee (lake), Ind. 227/E2
Maxixe, Mozambique 118/F4
Max Meadows, Va. (24360) 307/G6
Maxstone, Sask. 181/F6
Maxton, N.C. (28364) 281/L5
Maxville, Mont. (59858) 262/C4
Maxville, Ontario 177/K2
Maxwell, Calif. (95955) 204/C4
Maxwell, Ind. (46154) 227/F5
Maxwell, Iowa (50161) 229/G5
Maxwell, Nebr. (69151) 264/D3
Maxwell, New Bruns. 170/C3
Maxwell, N. Mex. (87728) 274/E2
Maxwell (bay), N.W. Terrs. 187/K2
Maxwell, Tenn. (†37306) 237/J10
Maxwell Air Force Base, Ala. 195/F6
Maxwelton, Queensland 88/G4
May, Idaho (83253) 220/E5
May (cape), N.J. 188/M3
May (cape), N.J. 273/C6
May, Okla. (73851) 288/G1
May, Isle of (isl.), Scotland 15/F4
May, Texas (76857) 303/F5
Maya (mts.), Belize 154/C2
Maya (riv.), U.S.S.R. 54/P4
Maya (riv.), U.S.S.R. 48/O4
Maya Beach, Belize 154/C2
Mayaguana (isl.), Bahamas 146/L7
Mayaguana (isl.), Bahamas 156/D2
Mayaguana (passage), Bahamas 156/D2
Mayagüez (dist.), P. Rico 161/B2
Mayagüez, P. Rico 161/A2
Mayagüez, P. Rico 156/F1
Mayagüez (bay), P. Rico 161/A2
Mayajigua, Cuba 158/F2
Mayals, Spain 33/G2
Mayarí, Cuba 158/J3
Mayarí Arriba, Cuba 158/J4
Mayaro, Trin. & Tob. 161/B11
Mayaro (bay), Trin. & Tob. 161/B11
Maybee, Mich. (48159) 250/F6
Maybell, Colo. (81640) 208/C2
Mayberry, Md. (†21157) 245/K2
Maybeury, W. Va. (24861) 312/D8
Maybole, Scotland 10/D3
Maybole, Scotland 15/D5
Maybrook, N.Y. (12543) 276/M8
Mayburg, Pa. (†16347) 294/D2
Maydena, Tasmania 99/C4
Mayen, W. Germany 22/B3
Mayenne (dept.), France 28/C3
Mayenne, France 28/C3
Mayenne (riv.), France 28/C4
Mayer, Ariz. (86333) 198/C4
Mayer, Chile 138/E7
Mayer, Minn. (55360) 255/E6
Mayersville, Miss. (39113) 256/B5
Mayerthorpe, Alberta 182/C3
Mayes (co.), Okla. 288/R2
Mayesville, S.C. (29104) 296/G4
Mayetta, Kansas (66509) 232/G2
Mayetta, N.J. (†08092) 273/E4
Mayfair, Sask. 181/D2
Mayfield, Georgia (31087) 217/G4
Mayfield, Kansas (67103) 232/E4
Mayfield, Ky. (42066) 237/D7
Mayfield (creek), Ky. 237/C7
Mayfield, N.Y. (12117) 276/M4
Mayfield, Ohio (44124) 284/J9
Mayfield, Okla. (73656) 288/G4
Mayfield, Pa. (18433) 294/L2
Mayfield, Scotland 15/D2
Mayfield, Utah (84643) 304/C4
Mayfield (lake), Wash. 310/C4
Mayfield Heights, Ohio (44124) 284/J9
Mayflower, Ark. (72106) 202/F4
Mayger, Oreg. (†97016) 291/D1
Mayhew, Miss. (39753) 256/G4
Mayhill, N. Mex. (88339) 274/D6
Maykop, U.S.S.R. 7/H4
Maykop, U.S.S.R. 48/D5
Maykop, U.S.S.R. 52/F6
Mayland, Tenn. (†38555) 237/L8
Maylene, Ala. (35114) 195/E4
Maymont, Sask. 181/D3
Maymyo, Burma 72/C2
Mayna, La. (†71343) 238/G4
Maynard, Ark. (72444) 202/J1
Maynard, Iowa (50655) 229/K3
Maynard◌, Mass. (01754) 249/J3
Maynard, Minn. (56260) 255/C6
Maynardville, Tenn. (37807) 237/O8
Mayne, Br. Col. 184/K3
Maynooth, Ireland 17/H5
Maynooth, Ontario 177/G2
Mayo, Canada 4/C16
Mayo, Fla. (32066) 212/C1
Mayo (co.), Ireland 17/C4
Mayo, Md. (21106) 245/M5
Mayo (riv.), Peru 128/D6
Mayo (bay), Philippines 82/F7
Mayo, S.C. (29368) 296/D1
Mayo, Yukon 187/E3
Mayo, Yukon 162/C3
Mayo (lake), Yukon 187/E3
Mayodan, N.C. (27027) 281/K2
Mayon (vol.), Philippines 82/D4
Mayor (isl.), N. Zealand 100/F2
Mayor (cape), Spain 33/E1
Mayor Martínez, Paraguay 144/C5
Mayor Pablo Lagerenza, Paraguay 144/B1
MAYOTTE 118/G2
Mayotte (isl), France 102/G6
Mayoworth, Wyo. (†82639) 319/F2
May Park, Oreg. (†97850) 291/J2
May Pen, Jamaica 158/J6
Mayport Naval Air Sta., Fla. 212/E1
Mayrhofen, Austria 41/A3
Mays, Ind. (46155) 227/G5
Maysan (gov.), Iraq 66/E5
Maysel, W. Va. (25133) 312/D5
Mays Landing, N.J. (08330) 273/D5
Mays Lick, Ky. (41055) 237/O3
Maysville, Ark. (72747) 202/A1
Maysville, Georgia (30558) 217/E2
Maysville, Iowa (†52773) 229/M5
Maysville, Ky. (41056) 237/O3
Maysville, Mo. (64469) 261/D3
Maysville, N.C. (28555) 281/P5
Maysville, Okla. (73057) 288/M5
Maysville, W. Va. (26833) 312/H4
Maytiguid (isl.), Philippines 82/B5
Maytown, Ky. (41455) 237/O5
Mayumba, Gabon 115/A4
Mayuram, India 68/D6
Mayview, Mo. (64071) 261/E4
Mayville, Mich. (48744) 250/F5
Mayville, N.Y. (14757) 276/A6
Mayville, N. Dak. (58257) 282/R4
Mayville, Oreg. (97830) 291/G2
Mayville, Wis. (53050) 317/K9
Maywood, Calif. (90201) 204/C10
Maywood, Ill. (60153) 222/B5
Maywood, Mo. (63454) 261/J3
Maywood, Nebr. (69038) 264/D4
Maywood, N.J. (07607) 273/B2
Maywood Park, Oreg. (97220) 291/B2
Maza, N. Dak. (†58324) 282/M3
Mazabuka, Zambia 115/E7
Mazabuka, Zambia 102/E6
Mazagan (El Jadida), Morocco 106/C2
Mazagão, Brazil 132/D3
Mazama, Wash. (98833) 310/E2
Mazamet, France 28/E6
Mazán, Peru 128/F4
Mazana (lake), Québec 172/C2
Mazana (riv.), Québec 172/C2
Mazandaran (prov.), Iran 66/H2
Mazangano, Uruguay 145/E3
Mazapil, Mexico 150/J4
Mazara del Vallo, Italy 34/D6
Mazar-e Sharif, Afghanistan 59/J2
Mazar-e Sharif, Afghanistan 68/B1
Mazarrón, Spain 33/F4
Mazaruni (riv.), Guyana 131/A2
Mazaruni-Potaro (dist.), Guyana 131/A2
Mazatán, Mexico 150/E2
Mazatenango, Guatemala 154/B3
Mazatlán, Mexico 146/H7
Mazatlán, Mexico 150/F5
Mazatzal (peak), Ariz. 198/D4
Mažeikiai, U.S.S.R. 53/A2
Mazenod, Sask. 181/E6
Mazeppa, Alberta 182/D4
Mazeppa, Minn. (55956) 255/F6
Mazgirt, Turkey 63/H3
Mazıdağı, Turkey 63/J4
Mazie, Okla. (74353) 288/R2
Mazinaw (lake), Ontario 177/G3
Mazirbe, U.S.S.R. 53/B2
Mazocruz, Peru 128/H11
Mazoe (riv.), Mozambique 118/E3
Mazoe, Zimbabwe 118/E3
Mazoe (riv.), Zimbabwe 118/E3
Mazomanie, Wis. (53560) 317/G9
Mazon, Ill. (60444) 222/E2
Mazra', Israel 65/C5
Mazu (Matsu) (isl.), China 77/K6
Mazzarino, Italy 34/E6
Mbabane (cap.), Swaziland 118/E5
Mbabane (cap.), Swaziland 102/F7
Mbaïki, Cent. Afr. Rep. 115/C3
Mbakou (res.), Cameroon 115/B2
Mbala, Zambia 102/F5
Mbala, Zambia 115/F5
Mbale, Uganda 115/F3
Mbale, Uganda 102/F4
Mbalmayo, Cameroon 115/B3
Mbamba Bay, Tanzania 115/G6
Mbandaka, Zaire 115/C3
Mbandaka, Zaire 102/D5
Mbanza Congo, Angola 115/B5
Mbanza-Ngungu, Zaire 102/D5
Mbanza-Ngungu, Zaire 115/C5
Mbaracayú, Cordillera de (mts.), Paraguay 144/E3
Mbarangandu (riv.), Tanzania 115/G5
Mbarara, Uganda 115/F4
Mbemkuru (riv.), Tanzania 115/G5
Mbengga (isl.), Fiji 86/Q11
Mbéré (riv.), Cameroon 115/B2
Mbéré (riv.), Cent. Afr. Rep. 115/B2
Mbéré (riv.), Chad 111/C6
Mbeya (reg.), Tanzania 115/F5
Mbeya, Tanzania 102/F5
Mbeya, Tanzania 115/F5
M'Bigou, Gabon 115/B4
Mbinda, Congo 115/B4
Mbini, Equat. Guinea 115/A3
Mbocayaty, Paraguay 144/C5
M'Bour, Senegal 106/A6
M'Bout, Mauritania 106/B5
Mbres, Cent. Afr. Rep. 115/D2
M'Bridge (riv.), Angola 115/B5
Mbuji-Mayi, Zaire 102/E5
Mbuji-Mayi, Zaire 115/D5
Mbulu, Tanzania 115/G4
Mburucuya, Argentina 143/E2
Mbuyapey, Paraguay 144/D5
McAdam, New Bruns. 170/C3
McAdams, Miss. (39107) 256/E4
McAdoo, Pa. (18237) 294/L4
McAdoo, Texas (79243) 303/D4
McAfee, N.J. (07428) 273/D1
McAlester, Okla. 188/G4
McAlester, Okla. (74501) 288/P5
McAlester (lake), Okla. 288/P4
McAlister, N. Mex. (88427) 274/F4
McAlisterville, Pa. (17049) 294/H4
McAllaster, Kansas (†67755) 232/A3
McAllen, Texas 188/G5
McAllen, Texas (78501) 303/F11
McAllister, Mont. (59740) 262/E5
McAllister, Wis. (†54177) 317/L5
McAlpin, Fla. (32062) 212/D1
McAndrews, Ky. (41543) 237/S5
McArthur, Calif. (96056) 204/D2
McArthur, Ohio (45651) 284/F7
McArthur River, North. Terr. 88/F3
McAuley, Manitoba 179/A4
McBain, Mich. (49657) 250/D4
McBaine, Mo. (†65201) 261/H5
McBean, Georgia (†30908) 217/J4
McBee, S.C. (29101) 296/G3
McBride, Br. Col. 184/G3
McBride, Miss. (†39144) 256/C7
McBride, Mo. (63776) 261/N7
McBride, Okla. (†74441) 288/N7
McBride Lake, Sask. 181/J3
McBrides, Mich. (48852) 250/D5
McCabe, Mont. (59245) 262/M2
McCain, N.C. (28361) 281/L4
McCall, Idaho (83638) 220/C5
McCall, La. (†70346) 238/K3
McCalla, Ala. (35111) 195/E4
McCall Creek, Miss. (39647) 256/C7
McCallsburg, Iowa (50154) 229/G4
McCallum, Newf. 166/C4
McCamey, Texas (79752) 303/B6
McCammon, Idaho (83250) 220/F7
McCanna, N. Dak. (58253) 282/P3
McCarley, Miss. (38943) 256/E3
McCarr, Ky. (41544) 237/S5
McCarthy, Alaska (†99566) 196/K2
McCaskill, Ark. (71847) 202/C6
McCauley (isl.), Br. Col. 184/B3
McCaulley, Texas (79534) 303/E5
McCausland, Iowa (52758) 229/M5
McCaysville, Georgia (30555) 217/D1
McChord A.F.B., Wash. 310/C3
McClain (co.), Okla. 288/L5
McClave, Colo. (81057) 208/O6
McCleary, Wash. (98557) 310/B3
McClellan A.F.B., Calif. 204/B8
McClelland (lake), Alberta 182/E1
McClelland, Ark. (†72006) 202/H3
McClelland, Iowa (51548) 229/B6
McClellanville, S.C. (29458) 296/H5
McCloud, Calif. (96057) 204/C2
McCloud, Tenn. (†37857) 237/R8
McClure (lake), Calif. 204/E6
McClure, Ill. (62957) 222/D6
McClure, Ohio (43534) 284/C3
McClure, Pa. (17841) 294/H4
McClure, Va. (24269) 307/D6
McClusky, N. Dak. (58463) 282/K4
McColl, S.C. (29570) 296/H2
McComb, Miss. (39648) 256/D8
McComb, Ohio (45858) 284/C3
McConaughy, C. W. (lake), Nebr. 264/C3
McCondy, Miss. (38854) 256/G3
McCone (co.), Mont. 262/L3
McConnell, Ill. (61050) 222/D1
McConnell, Manitoba 179/B4
McConnell, Tenn. (†38237) 237/D8
McConnell A.F.B., Kansas 232/E4
McConnells, S.C. (29726) 296/E2
McConnellsburg, Pa. (17233) 294/F6
McConnellsville, N.Y. (13401) 276/J4
McConnelsville, Ohio (43756) 284/G6
McCook, Nebr. (69001) 264/D4
McCook (co.), S. Dak. 298/P6
McCool, Miss. (39108) 256/F4
McCool Junction, Nebr. (68401) 264/G4
McCord, Sask. 181/E6
McCordsville, Ind. (46055) 227/F5
McCorkle, W. Va. (†25564) 312/C6
McCormick (co.), S.C. 296/C4
McCormick, S.C. (29835) 296/C4
McCoy, Colo. (80463) 208/F3
McCoy (head), New Bruns. 170/E3
McCoy, Oreg. (†97338) 291/D2
McCoy (creek), Oreg. 291/J5
McCoy, Va. (24111) 307/G6
McCoy A.F.B., Fla. 212/E3
McCoysburg, Ind. (†47978) 227/C3
McCracken, Kansas (67556) 232/C3
McCracken (co.), Ky. 237/D6
McCrea, Pa. (†17241) 294/H5
McCreary (co.), Ky. 237/N7
McCreary, Manitoba 179/C4
McCrory, Ark. (72101) 202/H3
McCulloch (co.), Texas 303/E6
McCullom Lake, Ill. (†60050) 222/E1
McCullough, Ala. (36552) 195/D8
McCune, Kansas (66753) 232/G4
McCurtain (co.), Okla. 288/S6
McCurtain, Okla. (74944) 288/R4
McCutchenville, Ohio (44844) 284/D4
McDade, Texas (78650) 303/G7
McDaniel, Md. (21647) 245/N5
McDaniels, Ky. (40152) 237/J5
McDavid, Fla. (32568) 212/B5
McDermitt, Nev. (89421) 266/D1
McDermott, Ohio (45652) 284/D8
McDonald (isls.), Australia 2/N8
McDonald, Kansas (67745) 232/A2
McDonald (co.), Mo. 261/D9
McDonald (lake), Mont. 262/B2
McDonald, N. Mex. (88262) 274/F5
McDonald, N.C. (28340) 281/L5
McDonald, Ohio (44437) 284/J3
McDonald, Pa. (15057) 294/B5
McDonald, Tenn. (37353) 237/M10
McDonalds Corners, Ontario 177/H3
McDonnell, Queensland 95/B1
McDonough (lake), Conn. 210/D1
McDonough, Del. (†19709) 245/R3
McDonough, Georgia (30253) 217/D4
McDonough (co.), Ill. 222/C3
McDonough, N.Y. (13801) 276/J5
McDougal, Ark. (72441) 202/K1
McDougall (lake), New Bruns. 170/D3
McDowell, Ala. (†35450) 195/C5
McDowell, Ky. (41647) 237/R6
McDowell (co.), N.C. 281/E3
McDowell, Va. (24458) 307/J4
McDowell (co.), W. Va. 312/C8
McDowell, W. Va. (24858) 312/D8
McDuffie (co.), Georgia 217/H4
McElhattan, Pa. (17748) 294/H3
McElmo (creek), Colo. 208/B8
McElmo (creek), Utah 304/E6
McEwen, Tenn. (37101) 237/F8
McFadden, Wyo. (82080) 319/F4
McFall, Mo. (64657) 261/D2
McFarlan, N.C. (28102) 281/J5
McFarland, Calif. (93250) 204/F8
McFarland, Kansas (66501) 232/F2
McFarland, Mich. (†49880) 250/B2
McFarland, Wis. (53558) 317/H10
McFarlane (riv.), Sask. 181/L2
McGaffey, N. Mex. (†87316) 274/A3
McGaheysville, Va. (22840) 307/L4
McGee, Sask. 181/C4
McGees Mills, Pa. (15755) 294/E4
McGehee, Ark. (71654) 202/H6
McGill, Nev. (89318) 266/G3
McGivney, New Bruns. 170/D2
McGloughlin (peak), Mont. 262/C4
McGrath, Alaska 188/C5
McGrath, Alaska (99627) 196/H2
McGrath, Minn. (56350) 255/E4
McGraw, N.Y. (13101) 276/H5
McGraw Brook, New Bruns. 170/D2
McGrawsville, Ind. (†46911) 227/E3
McGregor (lake), Alberta 182/D4
McGregor, Br. Col. 184/G3
McGregor (riv.), Br. Col. 184/G3
McGregor, Iowa (52157) 229/L2
McGregor, Minn. (55760) 255/E4
McGregor (lake), Mont. 262/B3
McGregor, N. Dak. (58755) 282/D2
McGregor, Ontario 177/B5
McGregor, Texas (76657) 303/G6
McGrew, Nebr. (69353) 264/A3
McGuffey, Ohio (45859) 284/C4
McGuire (mt.), Idaho 220/D4
McGuire A.F.B., N.J. 273/D3
McHenry (co.), Ill. 222/E1
McHenry, Ill. (60050) 222/E1
McHenry, Ky. (42354) 237/H6
McHenry, Miss. (39561) 256/F9
McHenry (co.), N. Dak. 282/J3
McHenry, N. Dak. (58464) 282/N4
McHenry Shores, Ill. (†60050) 222/E1
Mchinga, Tanzania 115/H5
Mchinji, Malawi 115/F6
McIlwraith (range), Queensland 95/B2
McIndoe Falls, Vt. (05050) 268/C3
McIntire, Iowa (50455) 229/H2
McIntosh, Ala. (36553) 195/B8
McIntosh, Fla. (32664) 212/D2
McIntosh (co.), Georgia 217/K7
McIntosh, Georgia (†31320) 217/K7
McIntosh, Minn. (56556) 255/C3
McIntosh, N. Mex. (87032) 274/D4
McIntosh (co.), N. Dak. 282/L7
McIntosh (co.), Okla. 288/P4
McIntosh, Ontario 177/F4
McIntosh, Ontario 175/B3
McIntosh, S. Dak. (57641) 298/G2
McIntyre, Georgia (31054) 217/F5
McIvor, Mich. (†48748) 250/F4
McKague, Sask. 181/G3
McKamie, Ark. (†71860) 202/C7
McKay (lake), Manitoba 179/C2
McKay (res.), Oreg. 291/J2
McKean (co.), Pa. 294/E2
McKean, Pa. (16426) 294/B2
McKeand (riv.), N.W. Terrs. 187/M3
McKee (creek), Ill. 222/C4
McKee, Ky. (40447) 237/O6
McKee City, N.J. (†08232) 273/D5
McKeesport, Pa. 188/L2
McKeesport, Pa. (*15130) 294/C7
McKees Rocks, Pa. (15136) 294/B7
McKellar, Ontario 177/D2
McKendrick, New Bruns. 170/D1
McKenna, Wash. (98558) 310/C4
McKenney, Va. (23872) 307/N7
McKenzie, Ala. (36456) 195/E7
McKenzie (co.), N. Dak. 282/D4
McKenzie, N. Dak. (58553) 282/K6
McKenzie, South Fork (riv.), Oreg. 291/E3
McKenzie, Tenn. (38201) 237/E8
McKenzie Bridge, Oreg. (97401) 291/E3
McKerrow, Ontario 177/C1
McKinlay, Queensland 95/B4
McKinlay, Queensland 88/G4
McKinley, Ala. (†36743) 195/C6
McKinley (mt.), Alaska 146/C3
McKinley (mt.), Alaska 188/D5
McKinley (mt.), Alaska 196/H2
McKinley, Cuba 158/B2
McKinley, Minn. (55761) 255/F3
McKinley (co.), N. Mex. 274/A3
McKinley (mt.), U.S. 4/C17

Miguelete 409

Merauke, Indonesia 85/K7
Merbein, Victoria 97/A4
Mercaderes, Colombia 126/B7
Mercara, India 68/D6
Merced (co.), Calif. 204/E6
Merced, Calif. (95340) 204/E6
Merced (riv.), Calif. 204/E6
Mercedario, Cerro (mt.), Argentina 143/B3
Mercedes, Buenos Aires, Argentina 143/G7
Mercedes, San Luis, Argentina 143/C3
Mercedes, Argentina 120/C6
Mercedes, Corrientes, Argentina 143/G4
Mercedes, Texas (78570) 303/F12
Mercedes, Uruguay 120/D6
Mercedes, Uruguay 145/B4
Merceditas, Chile 138/B7
Mercer (co.), Ill. 222/C2
Mercer (co.), Ky. 237/M5
Mercer○, Maine (04957) 243/D6
Mercer (co.), Mo. 261/E2
Mercer, Mo. (64661) 261/F2
Mercer (co.), N.J. 273/D3
Mercer, N. Zealand 100/E2
Mercer (co.), N. Dak. 282/G5
Mercer, N. Dak. (58559) 282/J5
Mercer (co.), Ohio 284/A4
Mercer, Ohio (†45862) 284/A4
Mercer (co.), Pa. 294/B3
Mercer, Pa. (16137) 294/B3
Mercer, Tenn. (38392) 237/D10
Mercer (co.), W. Va. 312/D8
Mercer, Wis. (54547) 317/F3
Mercer Island (city), Wash. (98040) 310/B2
Mercersburg, Pa. (17236) 294/G6
Mercerville-Hamilton Square, N.J. (08619) 273/D3
Merchantville, N.J. (08109) 273/B3
Merchtem, Belgium 27/E7
Mercier, Bolivia 136/B2
Mercier, Kansas (†66439) 232/G2
Mercier, Québec 172/H4
Mercier (dam), Québec 172/A3
Mercoal, Alberta 182/B3
Mercury, Nev. (89023) 266/E6
Mercury (bay), N. Zealand 100/F2
Mercury (isls.), N. Zealand 100/F2
Mercury, Texas (†76872) 303/E6
Mercy (bay), N.W. Terrs. 187/G2
Mercy (cape), N.W. Terrs. 187/M3
Mere, England 13/E6
Meredith, Colo. (81642) 208/F4
Meredith (lake), Colo. 208/M6
Meredith, N.H. (03253) 268/D4
Meredith○, N.H. (03253) 268/D4
Meredith Center, N.H. (†03253) 268/D4
Meredosia, Ill. (62665) 222/C4
Merefa, U.S.S.R. 52/E5
Meregh, Somalia 115/J3
Merelbeke, Belgium 27/D7
Merevari (riv.), Venezuela 124/F5
Mergui, Burma 54/L8
Mergui, Burma 72/C4
Mergui (arch.), Burma 72/C5
Meriç, Turkey 63/B2
Meriç (riv.), Turkey 63/B2
Merid, Sask. 181/B4
Mérida, Mexico 146/J7
Mérida, Mexico 150/P6
Mérida, Spain 7/D5
Mérida, Spain 33/C3
Mérida (state), Venezuela 124/C3
Mérida, Venezuela 120/B2
Mérida, Venezuela 124/C3
Mérida, Cordillera de (range), Venezuela 124/C3
Meriden, Conn. (06450) 210/D2
Meriden, Iowa (51037) 229/B3
Meriden, Kansas (66512) 232/G2
Meriden, Minn. (56067) 255/E6
Meriden, N.H. (03770) 268/C4
Meriden, Wyo. (82081) 319/H4
Meridian, Georgia (31319) 217/K8
Meridian, Idaho (83642) 220/B6
Meridian, Miss. 146/K6
Meridian, Miss. 188/J4
Meridian, Miss. (39301) 256/G6
Meridian, N.Y. (13113) 276/G4
Meridian, Okla. (73058) 288/M3
Meridian, Texas (76665) 303/G6
Meridian Naval Air Sta., Miss. 256/G5
Meridianville, Ala. (35759) 195/F1
Merigold, Miss. (38759) 256/C3
Merigomish, Nova Scotia 168/F3
Merigomish (harb.), Nova Scotia 168/F3
Merimbula, N.S. Wales 97/F5
Merín (lag.), Uruguay 145/F4
Merino, Colo. (80741) 208/N2
Merino, Victoria 97/A5
Merino Jarpa (isl.), Chile 138/D7
Merinos, Uruguay 145/C3
Merino Village, Mass. (†01570) 249/G4
Merion Station, Pa. (19066) 294/M6
Merir (isl.), Belau 87/D5
Meriwether (co.), Georgia 217/C4
Meriwether Lewis Park, Natchez Trace Pkwy., Tenn. 237/G10
Merj 'Uyun, Lebanon 63/F6
Mérk, Hungary 41/G3
Merkel, Texas (79536) 303/E5
Merksem, Belgium 27/E6
Merksplas, Belgium 27/F6
Merlin, Ontario 177/B5
Merlin, Oreg. (97532) 291/D5
Merlo, Argentina 143/G7
Mermentau, La. (70556) 238/E6
Mermentau (riv.), La. 238/E7
Merna, Nebr. (68856) 264/E3
Merna, Wyo. (†83115) 319/B3
Meroe (ruins), Sudan 111/F4
Merom, Ind. (47861) 227/B6
Merowe, Sudan 111/F4
Merowe, Sudan 59/B6
Merredin, W. Australia 88/B6
Merredin, W. Australia 92/B5
Merri (riv.), Victoria 88/L7
Merriam, Ind. (†46701) 227/G2
Merriam, Kansas (66203) 232/H3
Merrick (co.), Nebr. 264/F3
Merrick, N.Y. (11566) 276/R7
Merrick (mt.), Scotland 15/D5
Merrickville, Ontario 177/J3
Merricourt, N. Dak. (58469) 282/N7
Merrifield, Minn. (56465) 255/D4
Merrifield (bay), Newf. 166/B2
Merrifield, N. Dak. (†58201) 282/R4
Merrifield, Va. (22116) 307/S3
Merrill (pass), Alaska 196/H2
Merrill, Iowa (51038) 229/A3
Merrill, Mich. (48637) 250/E5
Merrill, Miss. (†39452) 256/G9
Merrill, N.Y. (12955) 276/N1
Merrill, Oreg. (97633) 291/F5
Merrill, Wis. (54452) 317/G5
Merrillan, Wis. (54754) 317/E7
Merrillville, Georgia (†31792) 217/E9
Merrillville, Ind. (46410) 227/C2
Merrimac, Ky. (†40009) 237/L6
Merrimac○, Mass. (01860) 249/L1
Merrimac, W. Va. (†25661) 312/B7
Merrimac, Wis. (53561) 317/G9
Merrimack (riv.), Mass. 249/K1
Merrimack (co.), N.H. 268/D5
Merrimack○, N.H. (03054) 268/D6
Merrimack (riv.), N.H. 268/D5
Merrimacport, Mass. (†01860) 249/L1
Merriman, Nebr. (69218) 264/C2
Merrimon, N.C. (†28516) 281/R5
Merrionette Park, Ill. (†60601) 222/B6
Merritt, Br. Col. 162/D5
Merritt, Br. Col. 184/G5
Merritt (isl.), Fla. 212/F3
Merritt, Ill. (†62650) 222/C4
Merritt, Mich. (49667) 250/D4
Merritt (res.), Nebr. 264/D2
Merritt, Wash. (†98826) 310/E3
Merritt Island, Fla. (32952) 212/F3
Merriwa, N.S. Wales 97/F3
Merriwagga, N.S. Wales 97/C3
Merriweather, Mich. (49947) 250/F1
Mer Rouge, La. (71261) 238/G1
Merrow, Conn. (06251) 210/F1
Merry Hill, N.C. (27957) 281/R3
Merrymeeting (lake), N.H. 268/E5
Merry Oaks, N.C. (†27559) 281/L3
Merryville, La. (70653) 238/D5
Mersa Fatma, Ethiopia 111/H5
Mersá Matrûh, Egypt 111/E1
Mersa Matrûh, Egypt 102/E1
Mersch, Luxembourg 27/J9
Mersea (dist.), England 13/J6
Merseburg, E. Germany 22/D3
Mersey (riv.), England 10/F2
Mersey (riv.), England 13/G2
Mersey (riv.), Nova Scotia 168/C4
Mersey (riv.), Tasmania 99/C3
Merseyside (co.), England 13/G2
Mershon, Georgia (31551) 217/H8
Mersin, Turkey 63/F4
Mersin, Turkey 59/B2
Mersin, Turkey 54/E6
Mersing, Malaysia 72/E7
Mērsrags, U.S.S.R. 53/B2
Mertert, Luxembourg 27/J9
Merthyr Tydfil, Wales 13/A6
Merthyr Tydfil, Wales 10/E5
Mértola, Portugal 33/C4
Merton, England 10/B5
Merton, England 13/H8
Merton, Wis. (53056) 317/K1
Mertz Glacier Tongue 5/C8
Mertzon, Texas (76941) 303/C6
Mertztown, Pa. (19539) 294/L4
Meru, Kenya 115/G3
Meru (mt.), Tanzania 115/G4
Merv (Mary), U.S.S.R. 48/F8
Merville, Br. Col. 184/E5
Mervin, Sask. 181/C2
Merwin, Mo. (†64723) 261/C6
Merwin (lake), Wash. 310/C5
Merzifon, Turkey 63/F2
Merzig, W. Germany 22/B4
Mesa, Ariz. 146/G6
Mesa, Ariz. 188/D4
Mesa, Ariz. (*85201) 198/D5
Mesa (co.), Colo. 208/B5
Mesa, Colo. (81005) 208/C4
Mesa, Idaho (83643) 220/B5
Mesa, Miss. (†39667) 256/D8
Mesa, Wash. (99343) 310/G4
Mesabi (range), Minn. 255/E3
Mesa Bolívar, Venezuela 124/C3
Mesachie Lake, Br. Col. 184/J3
Mesa del Seri, Mexico 150/D2
Mesagne, Italy 34/G4
Mesai (riv.), Colombia 126/D7
Mesará (gulf), Greece 45/G8
Mesa Verde National Park, Colo. (81330) 208/C8
Mesa Verde Nat'l Park, Colo. 208/C8
Mescalero, N. Mex. (88340) 274/D5
Mescalero (ridge), N. Mex. 274/F6
Mescalero (valley), N. Mex. 274/F5
Mescalero Apache Ind. Res., N. Mex. 274/D5
Meschede, W. Germany 22/C3
Mesena, Georgia (30819) 217/G4
Meservey, Iowa (50457) 229/G3
Meshed, Iran 54/G6
Meshed, Iran 66/L2
Meshed, Iran 59/H2
Meshed-i-Sar (Babol Sar), Iran 66/H2
Meshik, Alaska (†99579) 196/G3
Meshoppen, Pa. (18630) 294/L2
Meshra er Req, Sudan 111/E6
Mesic, N.C. (†28515) 281/R4
Mesick, Mich. (49668) 250/D4
Mesilla, N. Mex. (88046) 274/C6
Mesilla Park, N. Mex. (88047) 274/C6
Mesita, Colo. (81122) 208/H8
Meskanaw, Sask. 181/F3
Meskene, Syria 63/H5
Meskene, Syria 59/C2
Mesocco, Switzerland 39/H4
Mesolóngion, Greece 45/E6
Mesopotamia (reg.), Iraq 66/B3
Mesopotamia (reg.), Iraq 59/D3
Mesopotamia, Ohio (44439) 284/J3
Mesquite, Nev. (89024) 266/G6
Mesquite, N. Mex. (88048) 274/C6
Mesquite, Texas (*75149) 303/H2
Messancy, Belgium 27/H9
Messina (prov.), Italy 34/E5
Messina, Italy 34/E5
Messina, Italy 7/F5
Messina (str.), Italy 34/E6
Messina, S. Africa 118/D4
Messines, Québec 172/B3
Messíni, Greece 45/E7
Messíni (gulf), Greece 45/E7
Mesta (riv.), Bulgaria 45/F5
Mestre, Italy 34/D2
Mesudiye, Turkey 63/F4
Meta (riv.) 120/B2
Meta (dept.), Colombia 126/D6
Meta (riv.), Colombia 126/E5
Meta, Ky. (41501) 237/S5
Meta, Mo. (65058) 261/H6
Meta (riv.), Venezuela 124/E4
Metabetchouan, Québec 172/F1
Métabetchouane (riv.), Québec 172/F1
Metairie, La. (*70001) 238/O4
Metaline, Wash. (99152) 310/H2
Metaline Falls, Wash. (99153) 310/H2
Metamma, Ethiopia 111/G5
Metamora, Ill. (61548) 222/D3
Metamora, Ind. (47030) 227/G6
Metamora, Mich. (48455) 250/F6
Metamora, Ohio (43540) 284/C2
Metán, Argentina 143/D2
Metangula, Mozambique 118/F2
Metapán, El Salvador 154/C3
Métascouac (lake), Québec 172/F2
Metasville, Georgia (†30673) 217/G3
Metauro (riv.), Italy 34/D3
Metcalf, Georgia (†31792) 217/E9
Metcalf, Ill. (61940) 222/F4
Metcalfe (co.), Ky. 237/K7
Metcalfe, Miss. (38760) 256/B4
Metcalfe, Ontario 177/J2
Metchin (riv.), Newf. 166/B3
Metchosin, Br. Col. 184/K4
Metea, Ind. (†46950) 227/E3
Metedeconk (riv.), N.J. 273/E3
Meteghan, Nova Scotia 168/B4
Meteghan Centre, Nova Scotia 168/B4
Meteghan River, Nova Scotia 168/B4
Meteor (crater), Ariz. 198/E3
Metepec, Mexico 150/M2
Methlick, Scotland 15/F3
Methow, Wash. (98834) 310/E2
Methow (riv.), Wash. 310/E2
Methuen○, Mass. (01844) 249/K2
Methven, N. Zealand 100/C5
Methven, Scotland 15/E4
Metica (riv.), Colombia 126/D6
Metigoshe (lake), N. Dak. 282/K2
Metinic (isl.), Maine 243/E8
Metinota, Sask. 181/C2
Metiskow, Alberta 182/E3
Métis-sur-Mer, Québec 172/A1
Metlakatla, Alaska (99926) 196/N2
Metlakatla, Br. Col. 184/B3
Metlatonoc, Mexico 150/K8
Metlili Chaamba, Algeria 106/E2
Meto (bayou), Ark. 202/H5
Metolius, Oreg. (†97741) 291/F3
Metolius (riv.), Oreg. 291/F3
Metompkin (inlet), Va. 307/T5
Metompkin (isl.), Va. 307/T5
Metonga (lake), Wis. 317/J4
Metropolis, Ill. (62960) 222/E6
Metropolitan, Mich. (†49381) 250/A3
Métsovon, Greece 45/E6
Mettawa, Ill. (†60048) 222/B4
Mettawee (riv.), Vt. 268/A5
Metter, Georgia (30439) 217/H6
Mettet, Belgium 27/F8
Mettler, Calif. (93307) 204/G8
Metuchen, N.J. (08840) 273/E2
Metula, Israel 65/D1
Metz, France 7/E4
Metz, France 28/G3
Metz, Ind. (†46703) 227/H1
Metz, Mich. (†49776) 250/F3
Metz, Mo. (64765) 261/C6
Metz, W. Va. (26585) 312/F3
Metzger, Oreg. (†97223) 291/A2
Metzingen, W. Germany 22/C4
Meudon, France 28/A2
Meulaboh, Indonesia 85/B5
Meulebeke, Belgium 27/C7
Meung-sur-Loire, France 28/D4
Meurthe-et-Moselle (dept.), France 28/G3
Meuse (riv.), Belgium 27/F8
Meuse (dept.), France 28/F3
Meuse (riv.), France 28/F3
Meuselwitz, E. Germany 22/E3
Mexia, Ala. (36458) 195/D8
Mexia, Texas (76667) 303/H6
Mexiana (isl.), Brazil 132/D2
Mexicali, Mexico 150/B1
Mexicali, Mexico 146/G6
Mexican Hat, Utah (84531) 304/E6
Mexican Springs, N. Mex. (87320) 274/A3
Mexico 2/D4
MEXICO 150
Mexico 146/H7
Mexico (gulf) 188/J5
Mexico (gulf) 2/E4
Mexico (gulf) 146/K7
Mexico (gulf), Ala. 195/E10
Mexico (gulf), Cuba 158/A1
Mexico (gulf), Fla. 212/C4
Mexico, Ind. (46958) 227/E3
Mexico, Ky. (†42411) 237/E6
Mexico (gulf), La. 238/F8
Mexico, Maine (04257) 243/B6
Mexico○, Maine (04257) 243/B6
México (state), Mexico 150/K7
Mexico (gulf), Mexico 150/N4
Mexico, Mo. (65265) 261/J4
Mexico, N.Y. (13114) 276/H4
Mexico, Pa. (17056) 294/H4
Mexico (gulf), Texas 303/K9
Mexico Beach, Fla. (32410) 212/D6
Mexico City (cap.), Mexico 150/L1
Mexico City (cap.), Mexico 146/J7
Mexico City (cap.), Mexico 2/E5
Meyadin, Syria 59/C3
Meyadin, Syria 63/J5
Meybod, Iran 66/J4
Meydani, Ras-e (cape), Iran 59/G4
Meydani, Ras-e (cape), Iran 66/L8
Meyer, Iowa (†50455) 229/H2
Meyers Chuck, Alaska (99903) 196/N2
Meyersdale, Pa. (15552) 294/E6
Meyers Lake, Ohio (†44701) 284/H4
Meyerton, S. Africa 118/H7
Meymaneh, Afghanistan 68/A1
Meymaneh, Afghanistan 54/H6
Meymaneh, Afghanistan 59/H2
Meyrin, Switzerland 39/B4
Meyronne, Sask. 181/E6
Mezcala (riv.), Mexico 150/J8
Mezen', U.S.S.R. 4/C7
Mezen', U.S.S.R. 7/J2
Mezen' (riv.), U.S.S.R. 7/J2
Mezen', U.S.S.R. 48/E3
Mezen', U.S.S.R. 52/F1
Mezen' (bay), U.S.S.R. 52/F1
Mezen' (riv.), U.S.S.R. 52/G1
Mezen' (riv.), U.S.S.R. 48/E3
Mézenc (mt.), France 28/E5
Mezhdurechenskiy, U.S.S.R. 48/G4
Mezhdusharskiy (isl.), U.S.S.R. 52/G1
Meziadin (lake), Br. Col. 184/C2
Mézin, France 28/D5
Mezőberény, Hungary 41/F3
Mezőcsát, Hungary 41/F3
Mezőfalva, Hungary 41/E3
Mezőhegyes, Hungary 41/F3
Mezőkovácsháza, Hungary 41/F3
Mezőkövesd, Hungary 41/F3
Mezőszilas, Hungary 41/E3
Mezőtúr, Hungary 41/F3
Mezquital, Mexico 150/G5
Mezquital (riv.), Mexico 150/G5
Mhor, Loch (lake), Scotland 15/D3
Mhow, India 68/D4
Miacatlán, Mexico 150/K2
Miahuatlán de Porfirio Díaz, Mexico 150/L8
Miajadas, Spain 33/D3
Miami, Ariz. (85539) 198/E5
Miami, Fla. 188/K5
Miami, Fla. 146/K7
Miami, Fla. (*33101) 212/B5
Miami (canal), Fla. 212/F5
Miami (riv.), Fla. 212/B5
Miami (co.), Ind. 227/E3
Miami, Ind. (46959) 227/E3
Miami (co.), Kansas 232/H3
Miami, Manitoba 179/D5
Miami, Mo. (65344) 261/F4
Miami, N. Mex. (87729) 274/E2
Miami (co.), Ohio 284/B5
Miami, Okla. (74354) 288/S1
Miami, Texas (79059) 303/D2
Miami, U.S. 2/F4
Miami Beach, Fla. 188/L5
Miami Beach, Fla. (33139) 212/C5
Miami Lakes, Fla. (†33101) 212/B4
Miamisburg, Ohio (45342) 284/B6
Miami Shores, Fla. (33153) 212/B4
Miami Springs, Fla. (33166) 212/B5
Miamitown, Ohio (45041) 284/A9
Miamiville, Ohio (45147) 284/D9
Miandowab, Iran 66/E2
Miandrivazo, Madagascar 118/G3
Mianeh, Iran 59/E2
Mianeh, Iran 66/E2
Mianus, Conn. (†06830) 210/A4
Mianus (riv.), Conn. 210/A4
Mianwali, Pakistan 68/C2
Mianwali, Pakistan 59/K3
Mianyang, Hubei, China 77/H5
Mianyang, Sichuan, China 77/G5
Mianzhu, China 77/F5
Miass, U.S.S.R. 48/G4
Miastko, Poland 47/C2
Miazal, Ecuador 128/D4
Mica, Wash. (99023) 310/H3
Mica Creek, Br. Col. 184/H4
Micanopy, Fla. (32667) 212/D2
Micawber, Okla. (†74882) 288/N3
Micay, Colombia 126/B6
Micco, Fla. (†32960) 212/F4
Miccosukee, Fla. (32309) 212/B1
Miccosukee (lake), Fla. 212/B1
Michael, I. of Man 13/C3
Michael (lake), Newf. 166/C3
Michalovce, Czech. 41/G2
Michaud (pt.), Nova Scotia 168/H3
Michelago, N.S. Wales 97/E4
Michelson (mt.), Alaska 196/K1
Michelstadt, W. Germany 22/C4
Miches, Dom. Rep. 158/F6
Michiana, Mich. (†49117) 250/C7
Michiana Shores, Ind. (†49117) 227/D1
Michichi, Alberta 182/D4
Michie, Tenn. (38357) 237/E10
Michigamme, Mich. (49861) 250/B2
Michigamme (lake), Mich. 250/A2
Michigamme (res.), Mich. 250/B2
Michigamme (riv.), Mich. 250/A2
Michigan 188/J1
Michigan (lake) 188/J2
Michigan (lake), Ill. 222/F1
Michigan (lake), Ind. 227/C1
MICHIGAN 250/80
Michigan (lake), Mich. 250/B5
Michigan, N. Dak. (58259) 282/O3
Michigan (state), U.S. 146/K5
Michigan (lake), U.S. 146/K5
Michigan (isl.), Wis. 317/F2
Michigan (lake), Wis. 317/M9
Michigan Bar, Calif. (†95683) 204/C8
Michigan Center, Mich. (49254) 250/E6
Michigan City, Ind. (46360) 227/C1
Michigan City, Miss. (38687) 256/F1
Michigantown, Ind. (46057) 227/E4
Michigan Valley, Kansas (†66528) 232/G3
Michipicoten (isl.), Ontario 177/H5
Michipicoten (isl.), Ontario 175/C3
Michipicoten River, Ontario 177/H5
Michipicoten River, Ontario 175/C3
Michoacán (state), Mexico 150/H7
Michurin, Bulgaria 45/H4
Michurinsk, U.S.S.R. 52/F4
Michurinsk, U.S.S.R. 48/E4
Mickleton, N.J. (08056) 273/C4
Micotrin (mt.), Dominica 161/F6
Micoua, Québec 174/D3
Micoud, St. Lucia 161/G6
Micro, N.C. (27555) 281/N3
Micronesia, Federated States of 87/F5
Micronesia (reg.), Pacific 87/E4
Midale, Sask. 181/H6
Midas, Nev. (†89414) 266/E1
Middelburg, Netherlands 27/C6
Middelburg, C. of Good Hope, S. Africa 118/D6
Middelburg, Transvaal, S. Africa 118/D5
Middelfart, Denmark 21/C7
Middelfart, Denmark 18/G9
Middelharnis, Netherlands 27/E5
Middelkerke, Belgium 27/B6
Middelvlei, S. Africa 118/G7
Middenmeer, Netherlands 27/F3
Middle (riv.), Conn. 210/F1
Middle (pt.), Fla. 212/E6
Middle, Iowa (52307) 229/K5
Middle (riv.), Minn. 255/B2
Middle Alkali (lake), Calif. 204/E2
Middle Andaman (isl.), India 68/G6
Middle Arm, Newf. 166/C4
Middle Atlas (ranges), Morocco 106/C2
Middle Bass, Ohio (43446) 284/E2
Middle Bass (isl.), Ohio 284/E2
Middle Beaver (creek), Colo. 208/P4
Middleboro, Mass. (02346) 249/L5
Middleboro○, Mass. (02346) 249/L5
Middleboro (McKean), Pa. (16426) 294/B2
Middlebourne, W. Va. (26149) 312/E3
Middlebranch, Ohio (44652) 284/H4
Middlebro, Manitoba 179/G5
Middlebrook, Va. (24459) 307/K4
Middleburg, Fla. (32068) 212/E1
Middleburg, Ky. (42541) 237/M6
Middleburg, Md. (21768) 245/K2
Middleburg, N.C. (27556) 281/N2
Middleburg, Ohio (43336) 284/C5
Middleburg, Pa. (17842) 294/H4
Middleburg, Va. (22117) 307/N3
Middleburgh, N.Y. (12122) 276/M5
Middleburg Heights, Ohio (†44017) 284/G10
Middlebury○, Conn. (06762) 210/C2
Middlebury, Ind. (46540) 227/F1
Middlebury, Vt. (05753) 268/A3
Middlebury○, Vt. (05753) 268/A3
Middlebury Center, Pa. (16935) 294/H2
Middlebury Gap (pass), Vt. 268/B4
Middlebush, N.J. (08874) 273/D3
Middlechurch, Manitoba 179/E4
Middle Concho (riv.), Texas 303/C6
Middledam, Maine (†04216) 243/B6
Middle Falls, N.Y. (12848) 276/O4
Middlefield○, Conn. (06455) 210/E2
Middlefield○, Mass. (01243) 249/B3
Middlefield, Ohio (44062) 284/H3
Middle Fork (peak), Idaho 220/D5
Middlefork, Ind. (†46039) 227/E4
Middle Fork, Powder (riv.), Wyo. 319/F2
Middlegate, Norfolk Is. 88/L6
Middle Granville, N.Y. (12849) 276/O4
Middlegrove, Ill. (61549) 222/C3
Middle Grove, Mo. (†65263) 261/H4
Middle Haddam, Conn. (06456) 210/E2
Middle Harbour (creek), N.S. Wales 88/K3
Middle Harbour (creek), N.S. Wales 97/J3
Middle Hope, N.Y. (12550) 276/M7
Middle Inlet, Wis. (54148) 317/K5
Middle Lake, Sask. 181/F3
Middle Loch (inlet), Hawaii 218/A3
Middle Loup (riv.), Nebr. 264/D3
Middlemarch, N. Zealand 100/B6
Middle Musquodoboit, Nova Scotia 168/E3
Middle Patuxent (riv.), Md. 245/L3
Middle Piney (creek), Wyo. 319/B3
Middle Point, Ohio (45863) 284/B4
Middleport, N.Y. (14105) 276/C4
Middleport, Ohio (45760) 284/F7
Middleport, Pa. (17953) 294/K4
Middle River, Md. (21220) 245/N3
Middle River, Minn. (56737) 255/B2
Middle River, Nova Scotia 168/G2
Middle Saranac (lake), N.Y. 276/M2
Middlesboro, Ky. (40965) 237/O7
Middlesboro, Ky. 188/K3
Middlesbrough, England 7/D3
Middlesbrough, England 13/F3
Middlesbrough, England 10/F3
Middlesex (co.), Conn. 210/E3
Middlesex (co.), Mass. 249/J3
Middlesex (co.), N.J. 273/E3
Middlesex, N.J. (08846) 273/E2
Middlesex, N.Y. (14507) 276/F5
Middlesex, N.C. (27557) 281/N3
Middlesex (county), Ontario 177/C4
Middlesex○, Vt. (†05602) 268/B3
Middlesex (co.), Va. 307/R5
Middle Stewiacke, Nova Scotia 168/E3
Middleton (isl.), Alaska 196/J3
Middleton, England 13/H2
Middleton, England 10/G2
Middleton, Georgia (†30635) 217/G2
Middleton, Idaho (83644) 220/B6
Middleton○, Mass. (01949) 249/K2
Middleton, Mich. (48856) 250/E5
Middleton○, N.H. (†03887) 268/E5
Middleton, Nova Scotia 168/C4
Middleton, Tenn. (38052) 237/D10
Middleton, Wis. (53562) 317/G9
Middletown, Calif. (95461) 204/C5
Middletown, Conn. (06457) 210/E2
Middletown, Del. (19709) 245/R3
Middletown, Ill. (62666) 222/D3
Middletown, Ind. (47356) 227/F4
Middletown, Iowa (52638) 229/L7
Middletown, Ky. (40243) 237/L2
Middletown, Md. (21769) 245/J3
Middletown, Mo. (63359) 261/J4
Middletown○, N.J. (07748) 273/E3
Middletown, N.Y. (10940) 276/L8
Middletown, N.C. (†27824) 281/T4
Middletown, N. Ireland 17/H3
Middletown, Ohio (45042) 284/A6
Middletown, Pa. (17057) 294/J5
Middletown○, R.I. (02840) 249/J6
Middletown, Va. (22645) 307/M2
Middletown Springs○, Vt. (05757) 268/A5
Middle Valley, N.J. (†07853) 273/D2
Middleville, Mich. (49333) 250/D6
Middleville, N.J. (07855) 273/D1
Middleville, N.Y. (13406) 276/K4
Middleville, Ontario 177/H2
Middle Water, Texas (†79022) 303/B2
Middleway, W. Va. (†25430) 312/K4
Middlewich, England 13/H2
Middlewich, England 10/G2
Middlewood, Nova Scotia 168/D4
Midfield, Ala. (35228) 195/E4
Midgic Station, New Bruns. 170/F3
Mid Glamorgan, Wales 13/D6
Midhurst, Ontario 177/E3
Midian (dist.), Saudi Arabia 59/C4
Midkiff, W. Va. (25540) 312/B6
Midland, Ark. (72945) 202/B3
Midland, Ind. (47445) 227/C6
Midland, La. (70557) 238/F6
Midland, Md. (21542) 245/C2
Midland (co.), Mich. 250/E5
Midland, Mich. (48640) 250/E5
Midland, N.C. (28107) 281/J4
Midland, Ohio (45148) 284/C7
Midland, Ontario 177/D3
Midland, Oreg. (97634) 291/F5
Midland, Pa. (15059) 294/A4
Midland, S. Dak. (57552) 298/G5
Midland, Tex. 188/F4
Midland (co.), Texas 303/B6
Midland, Texas (*79701) 303/C6
Midland, Va. (22728) 307/N3
Midland City, Ala. (36350) 195/H8
Midland Park, N.J. (07432) 273/B1
Midlandvale, Alberta 182/D4
Midleton, Ireland 17/E8
Midleton, Ireland 10/B5
Midlothian, Ill. (60445) 222/B6
Midlothian (trad. co.), Scotland 15/B5
Midlothian, Texas (76065) 303/G5
Midlothian, Va. (23113) 307/N6
Midnapore, India 68/F4
Midnight, Miss. (39115) 256/C4
Midnight (lake), Sask. 181/C2
Midongy Atsimo, Madagascar 118/H4
Midvale, Idaho (83645) 220/B5
Midvale, Ohio (44653) 284/H5
Midvale, Utah (84047) 304/B3
Midville, Georgia (30441) 217/H5
Midway (isls.) 188/E6
Midway, Ala. (36053) 195/H6
Midway, Br. Col. 184/H6
Midway, Del. (†19971) 245/T6
Midway, Fla. (32343) 212/B1
Midway, Georgia (31320) 217/K7
Midway, Ind. (†47635) 227/C8
Midway, Ky. (40347) 237/M4
Midway (Sedalia), Ohio (†43151) 284/D6
Midway, Pa. (15060) 294/B5
Midway, Tenn. (37809) 237/P8
Midway (isls.), U.S. 87/J3
Midway, Utah (84049) 304/C3
Midway City, Calif. (92655) 204/D11
Midway Park, N.C. (28544) 281/O5
Midwest, Wyo. (82643) 319/F2
Midwest City, Okla. (73110) 288/M4
Midyat, Turkey 63/J4
Midye, Turkey 63/C2
Mid Yell, Scotland 15/G2
Midzhur (mt.), Bulgaria 45/F4
Midzhur (mt.), Yugoslavia 45/F4
Mie (pref.), Japan 81/H6
Miechów, Poland 47/E3
Międzychód, Poland 47/B2
Międzylesie, Poland 47/C3
Międzyrzec Podlaski, Poland 47/F3
Międzyrzecz, Poland 47/B2
Mielec, Poland 47/E3
Mier, Ind. (†46919) 227/F3
Mier, Mexico 150/K3
Miercurea Ciuc, Romania 45/G2
Mieres, Spain 33/D1
Miesso, Ethiopia 111/H6
Miesso, Ethiopia 102/G4
Miesville, Minn. (†55033) 255/F6
Miette, Alberta 182/B3
Mifflin, Ohio (†44805) 284/F4
Mifflin (co.), Pa. 294/G4
Mifflin, Pa. (17058) 294/H4
Mifflin, Wis. (†53580) 317/F10
Mifflinburg, Pa. (17844) 294/H4
Mifflintown, Pa. (17059) 294/H4
Miflin, Ala. (†36530) 195/C10
Migdal, Israel 65/C2
Migdal Ha 'Emeq, Israel 65/C2
Mignon, Ala. (†35150) 195/F4
Migori, Kenya 115/F4
Miguel Alves, Brazil 132/F4
Miguel Auza, Mexico 150/H4
Miguel de la Borda, Panama 154/G6
Miguelete, Uruguay 145/B5

Mirjaveh, Pakistan 59/H4
Mirnyy 5/C5
Mirnyy, U.S.S.R. 54/N3
Mirnyy, U.S.S.R. 48/M3
Mirpur, Pakistan 68/C2
Mirpur Khas, Pakistan 68/B3
Mirror, Alberta 182/D3
Mirror Lake, N.H. (03853) 268/E4
Mirtóòn (sea), Greece 45/F7
Miryang, S. Korea 81/D6
Mirzapur-cum-Vindhyachal, India 68/E4
Misamis Occidental (prov.), Philippines 82/D6
Misamis Oriental (prov.), Philippines 82/E6
Misantla, Mexico 150/P1
Misawa, Japan 81/K3
Miscou (isl.), New Bruns. 170/F1
Miscou (pt.), New Bruns. 170/F1
Miscou Centre, New Bruns. 170/F1
Miscouche, Pr. Edward I. 168/D2
Miscou Harbour, New Bruns. 170/F1
Misenheimer, N.C. (28109) 281/J4
Misery (bay), Mich. 250/G1
Misery (riv.), Mich. 250/G1
Misery (mt.), St. Chris.-Nevis 161/C10
Misgar, Pakistan 68/C1
Misha'ab, Ras (cape), Saudi Arabia 59/E4
Mishagua, Peru 128/F8
Mishan, China 77/M2
Mishaum (pt.), Mass. 249/L6
Mishawaka, Ind. (46544) 227/E1
Misheguk (mt.), Alaska 196/H1
Mishicot, Wis. (54228) 317/L7
Mishmar Hanegev, Israel 65/B5
Mishmar Hayarden, Israel 65/D1
Mishmi (hills), India 68/H3
Misima (isl.), Papua N.G. 85/C8
Misiones (prov.), Argentina 143/F2
Misiones (dept.), Paraguay 144/D5
Miskitos (cays), Nicaragua 154/F3
Miskolc, Hungary 41/F2
Miskolc, Hungary 7/H3
Misool (isl.), Indonesia 85/J6
Mispec, New Bruns. 170/E3
Mispillion (riv.), Del. 245/S5
Misquah (hills), Minn. 255/F2
Missanabie, Ontario 177/J5
Missanabie, Ontario 175/D3
Missaukee (co.), Mich. 250/D4
Missi Falls, Manitoba 179/J2
Missinaibi (riv.), Ont. 162/H6
Missinaibi (riv.), Ontario 175/D3
Missinaibi (riv.), Ontario 177/J5
Missinaibi (riv.), Ontario 175/D2
Mission, Br. Col. 184/L3
Mission, Kansas (66205) 232/H2
Mission (range), Mont. 262/C3
Mission, S. Dak. (57555) 298/H7
Mission, Texas (78572) 303/F11
Mission Beach, Alberta 182/C3
Mission City, Br. Col. 184/L3
Mission Hill, S. Dak. (57046) 298/P8
Mission Ridge, S. Dak. (57557) 298/H4
Mission Viejo, Calif. (92691) 204/D11
Missisa (lake), Ontario 175/D2
Missisquoi (co.), Québec 172/D4
Missisquoi (riv.), Vt. 268/B2
Missisagi (riv.), Ontario 177/A1
Missisagi (str.), Ontario 177/A2
Mississauga, Ontario 177/J4
Mississinewa (lake), Ind. 227/F3
Mississinewa (riv.), Ind. 227/H3
Mississippi 188/J4
MISSISSIPPI 256
Mississippi (riv.) 188/H4
Mississippi (co.), Ark. 202/H2
Mississippi (co.), Ark. 202/H7
Mississippi (riv.), Ill. 222/C5
Mississippi (riv.), Iowa 229/L7
Mississippi (riv.), Ky. 237/A10
Mississippi (delta), La. 146/K7
Mississippi (delta), La. 188/J5
Mississippi (riv.), La. 238/M8
Mississippi (riv.), La. 238/H3
Mississippi (sound), La. 238/M6
Mississippi (riv.), Minn. 255/D4
Mississippi (riv.), Miss. 256/A8
Mississippi (sound), Miss. 256/G10
Mississippi (co.), Mo. 261/O9
Mississippi (co.), Mo. 261/L4
Mississippi (lake), Ontario 177/H2
Mississippi (riv.), Tenn. 237/A10
Mississippi (state), U.S. 146/K6
Mississippi (riv.), U.S. 2/E4
Mississippi (riv.), U.S. 146/J6
Mississippi (riv.), U.S. 146/J5
Mississippi (riv.), Wis. 317/D10
Mississippi River Gulf Outlet (canal), La. 238/L7
Mississippi State, Miss. (39762) 256/G4
Missoula, Mont. 146/G5
Missoula, Mont. 188/D1
Missoula (co.), Mont. 262/C3
Missoula, Mont. (*59801) 262/C4
Missouri 188/H3
MISSOURI 261
Missouri (riv.) 188/H3
Missouri (riv.), Iowa 229/A4
Missouri (riv.), Kansas 232/G1
Missouri (riv.), Mo. 261/H5
Missouri (riv.), Mont. 262/C3
Missouri (riv.), Nebr. 264/H3
Missouri (riv.), S. Dak. 298/P8
Missouri (state), U.S. 146/J6
Missouri (riv.), U.S. 2/D3
Missouri (riv.), U.S. 146/J5
Missouri Branch, W. Va. (†25511) 312/A7
Missouri City, Mo. (64072) 261/R5
Missouri City, Texas (79756) 303/B6
Missouri Coteau (hills), Sask. 181/F5
Missouri Valley, Iowa (51555) 229/B5
Mist, Ark. (†71646) 202/G7

Mist, Oreg. (97016) 291/D1
Mistake (bay), N.W. Terrs. 187/J3
Mistake Creek, North. Terr. 93/A4
Mistaken (pt.), Newf. 166/D2
Mistassibi (riv.), Québec 174/C3
Mistassini (isl.), Québec 174/C3
Mistassini (lake), Que. 162/J5
Mistassini (lake), Que. 146/L4
Mistassini (terr.), Québec 174/B2
Mistassini, Québec 172/E1
Mistassini, Québec 174/C3
Mistassini, Québec 174/C3
Mistassini (Baie-du-Poste), Québec 174/C2
Mistassini (lake), Québec 174/C2
Mistastin (lake), Newf. 166/B2
Mistastin (riv.), Newf. 166/B2
Mistatim, Sask. 181/H3
Mistehae (lake), Alberta 182/C2
Mistelbach an der Zaya, Austria 41/D2
Misteriosa (bank), Cayman Is. 156/A3
Misti, El (mt.), Peru 120/B4
Misti, El (mt.), Peru 128/G11
Mistinippi (lake), Newf. 166/B3
Miston, Tenn. (38056) 237/B8
Mistretta, Italy 34/E6
Misty Fjords Nat'l Mon., Alaska 196/N2
Misurata, Libya 102/D1
Misurata, Libya 111/C1
Mita (pt.), Mexico 150/F6
Mitcham, S. Australia 88/D8
Mitcham, S. Australia 94/B8
Mitchell (lake), Alabama 188/J4
Mitchell (dam), Ala. 195/E5
Mitchell (lake), Ala. 195/F5
Mitchell, Br. Col. 184/J4
Mitchell (co.), Georgia 217/G8
Mitchell (co.), Georgia 217/G4
Mitchell, Georgia (30820) 217/G4
Mitchell, Ind. (47446) 227/F7
Mitchell, Iowa (†50461) 229/H2
Mitchell (co.), Iowa 229/H2
Mitchell (co.), Kansas 232/E1
Mitchell, La. (71453) 238/C3
Mitchell (co.), N.C. 281/H2
Mitchell (co.), N.C. 188/K3
Mitchell (mt.), N.C. 188/K3
Mitchell (riv.), N.C. 281/H2
Mitchell, Ontario 177/C4
Mitchell, Oreg. (97750) 291/G3
Mitchell, Queensland 88/H5
Mitchell, Queensland 95/C5
Mitchell (riv.), Queensland 88/G3
Mitchell (riv.), Queensland 95/B2
Mitchell, S. Dak. 188/G2
Mitchell, S. Dak. (57301) 298/N6
Mitchell (creek), S. Dak. 298/G5
Mitchell (co.), Texas 303/D5
Mitchell (riv.), Victoria 97/D5
Mitchell Bay, Ontario 177/B5
Mitchell Heights, W. Va. (†25601) 312/B7
Mitchells, Va. (22729) 307/N4
Mitchellsburg, Ky. (40452) 237/M5
Mitchellsville, Ill. (†62946) 222/E6
Mitchellville, Ark. (†71639) 202/H6
Mitchellville, Iowa (50169) 229/G5
Mitchellville, Tenn. (37119) 237/J7
Mitchelstown, Ireland 10/B4
Mitchelstown, Ireland 17/E7
Mitchelton, Queensland 88/J2
Mitchelton, Queensland 95/D2
Mitchinamécus (res.), Québec 172/C2
Mithi, Pakistan 68/B4
Mithimna, Greece 45/G6
Mitiaro, Cook Is. 87/L7
Mitilíni, Greece 45/H6
Mitkof (isl.), Alaska 196/N2
Mitla (ruin), Mexico 150/M8
Mito (pt.), Angola 115/C6
Mococa, Colombia 126/B7
Mococa, Brazil 135/C2
Mocodome (cape), Nova Scotia 168/G3
Mocomoco, Bolivia 136/A4
Mocorito, Mexico 150/F4
Moctezuma, San Luis Potosí, Mexico 150/J5

...

412 Monomoy

Monomoy (pt.), Mass. 249/O6
Monon, Ind. (47959) 227/D3
Monona (co.), Iowa 229/B4
Monona, Iowa (52159) 229/L2
Monona, Wis. (53716) 317/H9
Monongah, W. Va. (26554) 312/F4
Monongahela, Pa. (15063) 294/B5
Monongahela (riv.), Pa. 294/C6
Monongahela (riv.), W. Va. 312/G3
Monongalia (co.), W. Va. 312/F3
Monopoli, Italy 34/F4
Monor, Hungary 41/E3
Monos (isl.), Trin. & Tob. 161/A10
Monóvar, Spain 33/F3
Monoville, Tenn. (37121) 237/K8
Monowi, Nebr. (†68746) 264/F2
Monreal del Campo, Spain 33/F2
Monreale, Italy 34/D5
Monroe (co.), Ala. 195/D7
Monroe (co.), Ark. 202/H4
Monroe, Ark. (72108) 202/H4
Monroe○, Conn. (06468) 210/C3
Monroe (co.), Fla. 212/E7
Monroe (lake), Fla. 212/E3
Monroe (co.), Georgia 217/E4
Monroe, Georgia (30655) 217/E3
Monroe (co.), Ill. 222/C5
Monroe (co.), Ind. 227/D6
Monroe, Ind. (46772) 227/H3
Monroe (lake), Ind. 227/E6
Monroe (co.), Iowa 229/H7
Monroe, Iowa (50170) 229/G5
Monroe (co.), Ky. 237/K7
Monroe, La. 188/H4
Monroe, La. 146/J6
Monroe, La. (*71201) 238/F1
Monroe○, Maine (04951) 243/E6
Monroe (co.), Mich. 250/F7
Monroe, Mich. (48161) 250/F7
Monroe (co.), Miss. 256/H3
Monroe (co.), Mo. 261/H3
Monroe, Nebr. (68647) 264/G3
Monroe○, N.H. (03771) 268/C3
Monroe (mt.), N.H. 268/E3
Monroe○, N.J. (07434) 273/E3
Monroe (co.), N.Y. 276/E4
Monroe, N.Y. (10950) 276/M8
Monroe, N.C. (28110) 281/J5
Monroe (co.), Ohio 284/H6
Monroe, Ohio (45050) 284/B7
Monroe, Okla. (74947) 288/S4
Monroe, Oreg. (97456) 291/D3
Monroe (co.), Pa. 294/M3
Monroe (Monroeton), Pa. (18832) 294/J2
Monroe, S. Dak. (57047) 298/P7
Monroe (co.), Tenn. 237/N10
Monroe, Tenn. (38573) 237/L8
Monroe, Utah (84754) 304/B5
Monroe (peak), Utah 304/B5
Monroe, Va. (24574) 307/K6
Monroe, Wash. (98272) 310/D3
Monroe (co.), W. Va. 312/E7
Monroe (co.), Wis. 317/E8
Monroe, Wis. (53566) 317/G10
Monroe Bridge, Mass. (01350) 249/C2
Monroe Center, Ill. (61052) 222/E1
Monroe City, Ind. (47557) 227/C7
Monroe City, Mo. (63456) 261/J3
Monroe P.O. (Stepney), Conn. (06468) 210/B3
Monroeton, Pa. (18832) 294/J2
Monroeville, Ala. (36460) 195/D7
Monroeville, Ind. (46773) 227/H3
Monroeville, N.J. (08343) 273/C4
Monroeville, Ohio (44847) 284/E3
Monroeville, Pa. (15146) 294/C7
Monrovia, Ala. (†35804) 195/E1
Monrovia, Calif. (91016) 204/D10
Monrovia, Ind. (46157) 227/E5
Monrovia (cap.), Liberia 106/B7
Monrovia (cap.), Liberia 2/J5
Monrovia (cap.), Liberia 102/A4
Monrovia, Md. (21770) 245/J3
Mons, Belgium 27/E8
Monsanto, Portugal 33/C2
Monschau, W. Germany 22/B3
Monse, Wash. (†98812) 310/F2
Monsefú, Peru 128/C6
Monselice, Italy 34/C2
Monserrate (isl.), Mexico 150/D4
Monsey, N.Y. (10952) 276/J8
Møns Klint (cliff), Denmark 21/F8
Monson○, Maine (04464) 243/E5
Monson, Mass. (01057) 249/E4
Monson○, Mass. (01057) 249/E4
Mönsterås, Sweden 18/K8
Montagu, S. Africa 118/C6
Montague (isl.), Alaska 196/D1
Montague (str.), Alaska 196/D1
Montague, Calif. (96064) 204/C2
Montague○, Mass. (01351) 249/E2
Montague (isl.), Mexico 150/B1
Montague, Mich. (49437) 250/C5
Montague, Mont. (†59442) 262/F3
Montague, N.J. (†07851) 273/D1
Montague, N.C. (†28435) 281/N6
Montague, Pr. Edward I. 168/F2
Montague (co.), Texas 303/G4
Montague, Texas (76251) 303/G4
Montague (sound), W. Australia 88/C2
Montague (sound), W. Australia 92/D1
Montague City, Mass. (†01351) 249/D2
Montalba, Texas (75853) 303/J6
Montalbán, Spain 33/F2
Montalcino, Italy 34/C3
Mont Alto, Pa. (17237) 294/G6
Montalto Uffugo, Italy 34/E5
Montalvão, Portugal 33/C3
Montalvo, Calif. (93003) 204/F9
Montana 188/E1
MONTANA 262
Montana, Alaska (†99676) 196/B1
Montaña, La (reg.), Peru 128/F8
Montana, Switzerland 39/D4
Montana (state), U.S. 146/H5
Montana Mines, W. Va. (26586) 312/F3
Montánchez, Spain 33/D3
Montanja di Reij, Neth. Ant. 161/G9
Montara, Calif. (94037) 204/H3
Montargil, Portugal 33/B3
Montargis, France 28/E3
Montauban, France 28/D5
Montauban, Québec 172/E3
Montauk, N.Y. (11954) 276/S8
Montauk (pt.), N.Y. 276/S8
Montbard, France 28/F4
Montbéliard, France 28/G4
Mont Belvieu, Texas (77580) 303/L1
Montblanch, Spain 33/G2
Montbrison, France 28/E5
Montbrook, Fla. (†32696) 212/D2
Montcalm (co.), Mich. 250/D5
Montcalm (co.), Québec 172/C3
Montcalm (county), Québec 174/B3
Mont-Carmel, Québec 172/H2
Montceau-les-Mines, France 28/F4
Mont Cenis (tunnel), France 28/G5
Mont Cenis (tunnel), Italy 34/A2
Montcerf, Québec 172/A3
Montclair, Calif. (91763) 204/D10
Montclair, N.J. (*07042) 273/B2
Montclare, S.C. (†29532) 296/H3
Montcoal, W. Va. (25135) 312/D7
Mont-de-Marsan, France 28/C6
Montdidier, France 28/E3
Mont-Dore, France 28/E5
Monteagle, Tenn. (37356) 237/K10
Monteagudo, Bolivia 136/D6
Monte Alegre, Brazil 132/C3
Montealegre del Castillo, Spain 33/F3
Monte Alegre de Minas, Brazil 132/D7
Monte Aprazível, Brazil 135/A2
Monte Azul, Brazil 132/F6
Monte Bello (isls.), Australia 87/B8
Montebello, Calif. (90640) 204/C10
Montebello, Québec 172/B4
Monte Bello (isls.), W. Australia 88/A4
Monte Bello (isls.), W. Australia 92/A3
Montebelluna, Italy 34/D2
Monte Carlo, Monaco 28/G6
Monte Caseros, Argentina 143/G5
Montecito, Calif. (93103) 204/F9
Monte Comán, Argentina 143/C3
Monte Creek, Br. Col. 184/G5
Montecristi (prov.), Dom. Rep. 158/D5
Monte Cristi, Dom. Rep. 156/D2
Montecristi, Dom. Rep. 158/C5
Montecristi, Ecuador 128/B3
Monte Cristo, Bolivia 136/E4
Montecristo (isl.), Italy 34/C3
Monte Cristo (range), Nev. 266/D4
Monte Dourado, Brazil 132/C2
Montefiascone, Italy 34/D3
Montefrío, Spain 33/D4
Montego (bay), Jamaica 158/G5
Montego Bay, Jamaica 158/H5
Montego Bay, Jamaica 156/B3
Montego Bay (pt.), Jamaica 158/G5
Montegut, La. (70377) 238/J8
Montehermoso, Spain 33/C2
Monteiro, Brazil 132/G4
Monteith, Iowa (†50115) 229/D5
Montejinnie, North. Terr. 93/C4
Monte Lake, Br. Col. 184/G5
Montélimar, France 28/F5
Montelindo (riv.), Paraguay 144/C3
Montellano, Spain 33/D4
Montello, Nev. (89830) 266/G1
Montello, Wis. (53949) 317/H8
Montemayor (plat.), Argentina 143/C5
Montemorelos, Mexico 150/K4
Montemor-o-Novo, Portugal 33/B3
Montemor-o-Velho, Portugal 33/B2
Monte Ne, Ark. (†72756) 202/B1
Montenegro, Brazil 132/D10
Montenegro, Chile 138/G2
Montenegro (rep.), Yugoslavia 45/D4
Monte Patria, Chile 138/A8
Monte Plata, Dom. Rep. 158/E6
Montepuez, Mozambique 118/F2
Montepulciano, Italy 34/C3
Monte Quemado, Argentina 143/D2
Monte Real, Brazil 132/A5
Monterey, Ala. (†36030) 195/E7
Monterey, Calif. 188/B3
Monterey (bay), Calif. 188/B3
Monterey (co.), Calif. 204/D7
Monterey, Calif. (93940) 204/D7
Monterey (bay), Calif. 204/K4
Monterey, Ind. (46960) 227/D2
Monterey, Ky. (†40359) 237/M4
Monterey, La. (71354) 238/G4
Monterey○, Mass. (01245) 249/B4
Monterey, Tenn. (38574) 237/L8
Monterey, Va. (24465) 307/K4
Monterey, Wis. (†53066) 317/J1
Monterey Park, Calif. (91754) 204/C10
Montería, Colombia 120/B2
Montería, Colombia 126/B3
Monte Rio, Calif. (95462) 204/B5
Montero, Bolivia 136/D5
Monteros, Argentina 143/C2
Monterotondo, Italy 34/F6
Monterrey, Mexico 2/D4
Monterrey, Mexico 146/J7
Monterrey, Mexico 150/J4
Monterville, W. Va. (26282) 312/F5
Montes, Uruguay 145/D5
Montesano, Wash. (98563) 310/B4
Monte Sant'Angelo, Italy 34/F4
Monte Santo, Brazil 132/G5
Montes Claros, Brazil 120/E4
Montes Claros, Brazil 132/E7
Monte Sereno, Calif. (95030) 204/K4
Montevallo, Ala. (35115) 195/E4
Montevallo, Mo. (†64767) 261/D7
Montevarchi, Italy 34/C3
Montevideo, Minn. (56265) 255/C6
Montevideo (dept.), Uruguay 145/B7
Montevideo (cap.), Uruguay 145/B7
Montevideo (cap.), Uruguay 120/D6
Montevideo (cap.), Uruguay 2/G7
Monteview, Idaho (83435) 220/F6
Monte Vista, Colo. (81144) 208/G7
Montezuma (co.), Colo. 208/B8
Montezuma, Colo. (†80435) 208/H3
Montezuma (peak), Colo. 208/F8
Montezuma, Georgia (31063) 217/E6
Montezuma, Ind. (47862) 227/C5
Montezuma, Iowa (50171) 229/H5
Montezuma, Kansas (67867) 232/B4
Montezuma, N. Mex. (87731) 274/D3
Montezuma, Ohio (45866) 284/A4
Montezuma, Tenn. (†38340) 237/D10
Montezuma (creek), Utah 304/E6
Montezuma Castle Nat'l Mon., Ariz. 198/D4
Montezuma Creek, Utah (84534) 304/E6
Montfoort, Netherlands 27/G4
Montfort, France 28/C3
Montfort, Wis. (53569) 317/E10
Montgomery (cap.), Ala. 188/J4
Montgomery (cap.), Ala. 146/K6
Montgomery (co.), Ala. 195/F6
Montgomery (cap.), Ala. (*36101) 195/F6
Montgomery (co.), Ark. 202/C4
Montgomery (co.), Georgia 217/G6
Montgomery (co.), Ill. 222/D4
Montgomery, Ill. (60538) 222/E2
Montgomery (co.), Ind. 227/D4
Montgomery, Ind. (47558) 227/C7
Montgomery (co.), Iowa 229/C6
Montgomery, Iowa (51353) 229/C2
Montgomery (co.), Kansas 232/G4
Montgomery (co.), Ky. 237/O4
Montgomery, La. (71454) 238/E3
Montgomery (co.), Md. 245/J4
Montgomery, Mich. (49255) 250/E7
Montgomery, Minn. (56069) 255/E6
Montgomery (co.), Miss. 256/E4
Montgomery (co.), Mo. 261/K5
Montgomery (co.), N.Y. 276/M5
Montgomery, N.Y. (12549) 276/M7
Montgomery (co.), N.C. 281/K4
Montgomery (co.), Ohio 284/B6
Montgomery, Ohio (45242) 284/C9
Montgomery (co.), Pa. 294/M5
Montgomery, Pa. (17752) 294/H3
Montgomery (co.), Tenn. 237/G8
Montgomery (co.), Texas 303/J7
Montgomery, Texas (77356) 303/J7
Montgomery○, Vt. (05470) 268/B2
Montgomery (co.), Va. 307/H6
Montgomery, Wales 13/D5
Montgomery, Wales 10/E4
Montgomery, W. Va. (25136) 312/D6
Montgomery Center, Vt. (05471) 268/B2
Montgomery City, Mo. (63361) 261/K5
Monthey, Switzerland 39/C4
Monticello, Ark. (71655) 202/G6
Monticello, Fla. (32344) 212/C1
Monticello, Georgia (31064) 217/E4
Monticello, Ill. (61856) 222/E3
Monticello, Ind. (47960) 227/D3
Monticello, Iowa (52310) 229/L4
Monticello, Ky. (42633) 237/M7
Monticello○, Maine (04760) 243/H3
Monticello, Minn. (55362) 255/E5
Monticello, Miss. (39654) 256/D7
Monticello, Mo. (63457) 261/J2
Monticello, N. Mex. (87939) 274/B5
Monticello, N.Y. (12701) 276/L7
Monticello, Ohio (†45887) 284/B4
Monticello, S.C. (29106) 296/E3
Monticello, Utah (84535) 304/E6
Monticello, Wis. (53570) 317/G10
Mont Ida, Kansas (†66091) 232/G3
Montier, Mo. (65546) 261/J8
Montigny-les-Metz, France 28/G3
Montigny-le-Tilleul, Belgium 27/E8
Montijo, Panama 154/G6
Montijo (gulf), Panama 154/G7
Montijo, Portugal 33/B3
Montijo, Spain 33/C3
Montilla, Spain 33/D4
Montjoie (lake), Québec 172/B3
Mont-Joli, Que. 162/K6
Mont-Joli, Québec 174/D3
Mont-Joli, Québec 172/J1
Mont-Laurier, Que. 162/J6
Mont-Laurier, Québec 172/B3
Mont-Laurier, Québec 174/B3
Mont-Louis, Québec 172/C1
Montluçon, France 28/E4
Montmagny (co.), Québec 172/G3
Montmagny, Québec 174/C3
Montmagny, Québec 172/G3
Montmartre, Sask. 181/H5
Montmédy, France 28/F3
Montmorenci, Ind. (47962) 227/D4
Montmorenci, S.C. (29839) 296/D4
Montmorency (co.), Mich. 250/E3
Montmorency, Québec 172/J3
Montmorency (riv.), Québec 172/F2
Montmorency, Victoria 97/J4
Montmorency No. 1 (co.), Québec 172/F2
Montmorency No. 2 (co.), Québec 172/G3
Montmorency No. I (county), Québec 174/C3
Montmorillon, France 28/D4
Mont Nebo, Sask. 181/E2
Montney, Br. Col. 184/G2
Monto, Queensland 95/D5
Monto, Queensland 88/J4
Montoire-sur-le-Loir, France 28/D4
Montoro, Spain 33/D3
Montosa (mesa), N. Mex. 274/E3
Montour, Idaho (83617) 220/B6
Montour, Iowa (50173) 229/H5
Montour (co.), Pa. 294/J3
Montour Falls, N.Y. (14865) 276/G6
Montoursville, Pa. (17754) 294/J3
Montowese, Conn. (†06473) 210/D3
Montoya, N. Mex. (†88401) 274/F3
Montoz (mt.), Switzerland 39/D3
Montpelier, Idaho 188/D2
Montpelier, Idaho (83254) 220/G7
Montpelier, Ind. (47359) 227/G3
Montpelier, Iowa (52759) 229/M6
Montpelier, Jamaica 158/H6
Montpelier, La. (†70422) 238/M1
Montpelier, Miss. (39754) 256/G3
Montpelier, N. Dak. (58472) 282/N6
Montpelier, Ohio (43543) 284/A2
Montpelier (cap.), Vt. (05602) 268/B3
Montpelier (cap.), Vt. 146/L5
Montpelier (cap.), Vt. 188/M2
Montpellier, France 7/E4
Montpellier, France 28/E6
Montpellier, Québec 172/B4
Montréal, Canada 2/F3
Montreal (riv.), Mich. 250/F1
Montreal, Mo. (65591) 261/G7
Montréal, Que. 146/L5
Montréal, Que. 162/J7
Montréal, Québec 172/H4
Montreal (lake), Sask. 181/F1
Montreal, Wis. (54550) 317/F3
Montreal (riv.), Wis. 317/F2
Montréal-Est, Québec 172/J4
Montreal Lake, Sask. 181/F1
Montréal-Nord, Québec 172/H4
Montreal River Harbor, Ontario 177/J5
Montreat, N.C. (28757) 281/E3
Montreuil, Pas-de-Calais, France 28/D2
Montreuil, Seine-Saint-Denis, France 28/B2
Montreux, Switzerland 39/C4
Montricher, Switzerland 39/B3
Mont-Rolland, Québec 172/C4
Montrose, Ala. (36559) 195/C9
Montrose, Ark. (71658) 202/H7
Montrose, Br. Col. 184/J5
Montrose (co.), Colo. 208/C6
Montrose, Colo. (81401) 208/D6
Montrose, Georgia (31065) 217/F5
Montrose, Ill. (62445) 222/E4
Montrose, Iowa (52639) 229/L7
Montrose, Kansas (†66956) 232/D2
Montrose, La. (†71457) 238/D3
Montrose, Md. (†20850) 245/K4
Montrose, Mich. (48457) 250/F5
Montrose, Minn. (55363) 255/E5
Montrose, Miss. (†39338) 256/F6
Montrose, Mo. (64770) 261/E6
Montrose, Pa. (18801) 294/L2
Montrose, Scotland 10/E2
Montrose, Scotland 15/F4
Montrose, S. Dak. (57048) 298/P6
Montrose, Victoria 97/K5
Montrose, W. Va. (26283) 312/G4
Montrose-La Crescenta, Calif. (91214) 204/C10
Montross, Va. (22520) 307/P4
Montrouge, France 28/B2
Mont-Royal, Québec 172/H4
Monts (pt.), Québec 172/B1
Mont-Saint-Hilaire, Québec 172/D4
Mont-Saint-Michel, France 28/C3
Mont-Saint-Michel, Québec 172/B3
Mont-Saint-Pierre, Québec 172/C1
MONTSERRAT 156/G3
Montserrat (mt.), Spain 33/G2
Montsinéry, Fr. Guiana 131/E3
Mont-Tremblant, Québec 172/C3
Mont-Tremblant Prov. Park, Québec 172/C3
Mont-Tremblant Prov. Park, Québec 174/C3
Montvale, N.J. (07645) 273/B1
Montvale, Va. (24122) 307/J6
Montverde, Fla. (32756) 212/E3
Mont Vernon○, N.H. (03057) 268/D6
Montville, Conn. (06353) 210/G3
Montville○, Conn. (06353) 210/G3
Montville, Maine (†04941) 243/E7
Montville○, Maine (†04941) 243/E7
Montville, Mass. (†01255) 249/B4
Montville○, N.J. (07045) 273/E2
Montville, Ohio (44064) 284/H2
Montz, La. (†70068) 238/M3
Monument, Colo. (80132) 208/K4
Monument (peak), Idaho 220/B4
Monument, Kansas (67747) 232/A2
Monument, N. Mex. (88265) 274/F6
Monument, Oreg. (97864) 291/H3
Monument (valley), Utah 304/D6
Monument Beach, Mass. (02553) 249/M6
Monument Valley, Utah (84536) 304/D6
Monywa, Burma 72/B2
Monza, Italy 34/B2
Monze, Zambia 115/E7
Monzón, Spain 33/G2
Mooar, Iowa (†52632) 229/L8
Moodie (isl.), N.W. Terrs. 187/M3
Moodus, Conn. (06469) 210/F2
Moodus (res.), Conn. 210/F2
Moody, Ala. (†35125) 195/F3
Moody, Maine (04054) 243/B9
Moody, Mo. (65770) 261/J9
Moody (co.), S. Dak. 298/R5
Moody, Texas (76557) 303/G6
Moody A.F.B., Georgia 217/F9
Moodys, Okla. (74444) 288/S2
Moodyville, Tenn. (†38549) 237/L7
Mooers, N.Y. (12958) 276/N1
Mooka, Japan 81/K5
Mooleyville, Ky. (40154) 237/H4
Mooloo Downs, W. Australia 92/B4
Moomin (creek), N.S. Wales 97/E1
Moon (lake), Calif. 204/E2
Moon (lake), Nebr. 264/E2
Moon, Okla. (†71821) 288/S7
Moonachie, N.J. (†07070) 273/B2
Moonah (creek), Queensland 95/A4
Moonbeam, Ontario 177/J5
Mooncoin, Ireland 17/G7
Moonie (riv.), N.S. Wales 97/E1
Moonie, Queensland 95/D5
Moon Run, Pa. (†15244) 294/B5
Moonta, S. Australia 94/E5
Moora, W. Australia 88/B6
Moora, W. Australia 92/B5
Moorabbin, Victoria 88/L7
Moorabbin, Victoria 97/J5
Moorcroft, Wyo. (82721) 319/H1
Moore, Idaho (83255) 220/E6
Moore, Mont. (59464) 262/G4
Moore (dam), N.H. 268/D3
Moore (res.), N.H. 268/D3
Moore (co.), N.C. 281/L4
Moore, Okla. (73160) 288/M4
Moore, S.C. (29369) 296/D2
Moore (co.), Tenn. 237/J10
Moore (co.), Texas 303/C2
Moore, Texas (78057) 303/E9
Moore, Utah (†84523) 304/C5
Moore (dam), Vt. 268/D3
Moore (res.), Vt. 268/D3
Moore (lake), W. Australia 88/B5
Moore (lake), W. Australia 92/B5
MOOREA, Fr. Poly. 86/S13
Moorea (isl.), Fr. Poly. 87/L7
Moorea (isl.), Fr. Poly. 86/S13
Moorefield, Ark. (†72501) 202/G2
Moorefield, Ind. (†47043) 227/G7
Moorefield, Ky. (40350) 237/O4
Moorefield, Nebr. (69039) 264/D4
Moorefield, Ontario 177/D4
Moorefield, W. Va. (26836) 312/J4
Moore Haven, Fla. (33471) 212/E5
Mooreland, Ind. (47360) 227/G5
Mooreland, Okla. (73852) 288/H2
Moore Park, Manitoba 179/C4
Mooresboro, N.C. (28114) 281/F4
Moores Bridge, Ala. (†35458) 195/C4
Mooresburg, Tenn. (37811) 237/P8
Moores Creek, Ky. (40453) 237/O6
Moores Creek Nat'l Battlefield, N.C. 281/N6
Moores Hill, Ind. (47032) 227/G6
Moores Mills, New Bruns. 170/C3
Moorestown, Mich. (49651) 250/D4
Moorestown, N.J. (08057) 273/B3
Mooresville, Ala. (35649) 195/E1
Mooresville, Ind. (46158) 227/E5
Mooresville, Mo. (64664) 261/E3
Mooresville, N.C. (28115) 281/H3
Mooreton, N. Dak. (58061) 282/S7
Moore Town, Jamaica 158/K6
Mooretown, Ontario 177/B5
Mooreville, Miss. (38857) 256/G2
Moorfoot (hills), Scotland 15/E5
Moorhead, Iowa (51558) 229/B5
Moorhead, Minn. 188/G1
Moorhead, Minn. (56560) 255/B4
Moorhead, Miss. (38761) 256/C4
Mooringsport, La. (71060) 238/B1
Moorland, Iowa (50566) 229/E4
Moorland, Ky. (†40223) 237/L2
Moorman, Ky. (42357) 237/G6
Moorooka, Queensland 88/K3
Moorooka, Queensland 95/D3
Mooroopna, Victoria 97/C5
Moorpark, Calif. (93021) 204/G9
Moorreesburg, S. Africa 118/B6
Moorslede, Belgium 27/B7
Moosburg an der Isar, W. Germany 22/D4
Moose (creek), Idaho 220/D3
Moose (pond), Maine 243/B7
Moose (riv.), Maine 243/D4
Moose (isl.), Manitoba 179/E3
Moose (riv.), Minn. 255/C2
Moose (riv.), N.Y. 276/K3
Moose (mt.), Sask. 181/J6
Moose (riv.), Vt. 268/D2
Moose (lake), Wis. 317/E3
Moose (lake), Wis. 317/F3
Moose, Wyo. (83012) 319/B2
Moose Creek, Ontario 177/K2
Moose Factory, Ontario 175/D2
Moosehead, Maine (†04478) 243/D4
Moosehead (lake), Maine 243/D4
Mooseheart, Ill. (60539) 222/E2
Moose Heights, Br. Col. 184/F3
Moosehorn, Manitoba 179/D3
Moose Jaw, Sask. 146/H4
Moose Jaw, Sask. 162/F6
Moose Jaw, Sask. 181/F5
Moose Jaw (riv.), Sask. 181/G5
Moose Lake, Manitoba 179/H3
Moose Lake, Minn. (55767) 255/F4
Mooseland, Nova Scotia 168/F4
Mooseleuk (stream), Maine 243/F2
Mooselookmeguntic (lake), Maine 243/B6
Moose Mountain (creek), Sask. 181/J6
Moose Mountain Prov. Park, Sask. 181/J6
Moose Pass, Alaska (99631) 196/C1
Moose Range, Sask. 181/H2
Moose River○, Maine (†04945) 243/C4
Moose River, Ontario 175/D2
Moosic, Pa. (18507) 294/F7
Moosilauke (mt.), N.H. 268/D3
Moosomin, Sask. 162/F5
Moosomin, Sask. 181/K5
Moosonee, Ont. 162/H5
Moosonee, Ont. 146/K4
Moosonee, Ontario 175/D2
Moosup, Conn. (06354) 210/H2
Moosup (riv.), Conn. 210/H2
Mopang (lake), Maine 243/H6
Mopeia, Mozambique 118/F3
Mopti, Mali 102/B3
Mopti, Mali 106/D6
Moqatta, Sudan 59/C7
Moqor, Afghanistan 68/B2
Moqor, Afghanistan 59/J3
Moquah, Wis. (†54806) 317/D2
Moquegua (dept.), Peru 128/G11
Moquegua, Peru 120/B4
Moquegua, Peru 128/G11
Mór, Hungary 41/E3
Mora, Cameroon 115/B1
Mora, India 68/B7
Mora, La. (71455) 238/E4
Mora, Minn. (55051) 255/E5
Mora, Mo. (65345) 261/F5
Mora (co.), N. Mex. 274/E3
Mora, N. Mex. (87732) 274/D3
Mora (riv.), N. Mex. 274/E3
Mora, Portugal 33/B3
Mora, Spain 33/E3
Mora, Sweden 18/J6
Moradabad, India 54/J7
Moradabad, India 68/D3
Mora de Rubielos, Spain 33/F2
Morado, Quebrado (riv.), Chile 138/A6
Morafenobe, Madagascar 118/G3
Morąg, Poland 47/E2
Moraga, Calif. (94556) 204/K2
Moraine, Ohio (†45439) 284/B6
Moraleda (chan.), Chile 138/D5
Morales, Guatemala 154/C3
Morales, Peru 128/D6
Moramanga, Madagascar 118/H3
Moramanga, Madagascar 102/G6
Moran, Ind. (†46041) 227/D4
Moran, Kansas (66755) 232/G4
Moran, Mich. (49760) 250/E2
Moran, Texas (76464) 303/E5
Moran, Wyo. (83013) 319/B2
Moranbah, Queensland 95/C9
Morane (isl.), Fr. Poly. 87/N8
Morant (pt.), Jamaica 156/C3
Morant Bay, Jamaica 158/K7
Morar, Scotland 15/C4
Morar, Loch (lake), Scotland 15/C4
Morat (lake), Switzerland 39/D3
Morata de Tajuña, Spain 33/G4
Moratalla, Spain 33/E3
Morattico, Va. (22523) 307/P5
Moratuwa, Sri Lanka 68/D7
Morava (riv.), Czech. 41/D2
Morava (riv.), Yugoslavia 45/E3
Moravia, Iowa (52571) 229/H7
Moravia, N.Y. (13118) 276/H5
Moravian Falls, N.C. (28654) 281/G2
Moravská Třebová, Czech. 41/D2
Moravské Budějovice, Czech. 41/D2
Morawa, W. Australia 88/B5
Morawa, W. Australia 92/B5
Morawhanna, Guyana 120/D2
Morawhanna, Guyana 131/B1
Moray (firth), Scotland 7/D3
Moray (firth), Scotland 15/E3
Moray (firth), Scotland 10/E2
Moray (trad. co.), Scotland 15/A5
Morazán, Honduras 154/D3
Morbihan (dept.), France 28/B4
Mörbylånga, Sweden 18/K8
Morden, Man. 162/G6
Morden, Manitoba 179/D5
Mordialloc, Victoria 97/J6
Mordialloc, Victoria 88/L7
Mordvinian A.S.S.R., U.S.S.R. 52/G4
Mordvinian A.S.S.R., U.S.S.R. 48/E4
More, Loch (lake), Scotland 15/E2
More, Loch (lake), Scotland 15/D2
Morea, Victoria 97/A5
Moreau (riv.), S. Dak. 298/G3
Moreauville, La. (71355) 238/G4
Morebattle, Scotland 15/F5
Morecambe, Alberta 182/E3
Morecambe (bay), England 10/oe3
Morecambe (bay), England 13/D3
Moree, N. S. Wales 88/H5
Moree, N.S. Wales 97/E1
Morehead, Kansas (†66776) 232/G4
Morehead, Ky. (40351) 237/P4
Morehead City, N.C. (28557) 281/R5
Morehouse (par.), La. 238/G1
Morehouse, Mo. (63868) 261/N9
Moreland, Ark. (72849) 202/E3
Moreland, Georgia (30259) 217/C4
Moreland, Idaho (83256) 220/F6
Moreland Hills, Ohio (†44022) 284/J9
Morelia, Mexico 150/J7
Morelia, Mexico 146/H8
Morelia, Queensland 95/B4
Morell, Pr. Edward I. 168/F2
Morella, Queensland 88/G4
Morella, Spain 33/F2
Morelos (state), Mexico 150/K7
Morelos, Mexico 150/J2
Morelos Cañada, Mexico 150/O2
Morena, India 68/D3
Morena, Sierra (mts.), Spain 7/D5
Morena, Sierra (range), Spain 33/E3
Morenci, Ariz. (85540) 198/F5
Morenci, Mich. (49256) 250/E7
Moreni, Romania 45/G3
Moreno, Bolivia 136/B2
Moreno, Calif. (92360) 204/H10
Moreno (bay), Chile 138/A4
Møre og Romsdal (co.), Norway 18/E5
Mores (creek), Idaho 220/C6
Moresby, Br. Col. 184/B3
Moresby (isl.), Br. Col. 184/B4
Moreton (isl.), Queensland 88/J5
Moreton (bay), Queensland 88/K2
Moreton (bay), Queensland 95/E5
Moreton (isl.), Queensland 95/E5
Moretonhampstead, England 13/C7
Moreton-in-Marsh, England 13/F6
Moretown○, Vt. (05660) 268/B3
Morewood, Ontario 177/J2
Morgan (co.), Ala. 195/E2
Morgan (co.), Colo. 208/M2
Morgan (pt.), Conn. 210/D4
Morgan (co.), Georgia 217/F3
Morgan, Georgia (31766) 217/C7
Morgan (co.), Ill. 222/C4
Morgan (co.), Ind. 227/E6
Morgan (co.), Ky. 237/P5
Morgan, Ky. (†41040) 237/N3
Morgan, Minn. (56266) 255/D6
Morgan (co.), Mo. 261/G6
Morgan, Mo. (†65706) 261/G7
Morgan (co.), Ohio 284/G6
Morgan (co.), Tenn. 237/M8
Morgan, Texas (76671) 303/G5
Morgan (co.), Utah 304/C2
Morgan, Utah (84050) 304/C2
Morgan○, Vt. (05853) 268/D2
Morgan (co.), W. Va. 312/K3
Morgan Center, Vt. (05854) 268/D2
Morgan City, La. (70380) 238/H7
Morgan City, Miss. (38946) 256/D4

Mount Washington 413

Morgan Falls (dam), Georgia 217/K1
Morganfield, Ky. (42437) 237/E5
Morgan Hill, Calif. (95037) 204/L4
Morganito, Venezuela 124/E5
Morgans Point, Texas (†77571) 303/K2
Morgansville, W. Va. (†26456) 312/E4
Morganton, Ark. (72109) 202/F3
Morganton, Georgia (30560) 217/D1
Morganton, N.C. (28655) 281/F3
Morgantown, Ind. (46160) 227/E6
Morgantown, Ky. (42261) 237/H6
Morgantown, Miss. (39484) 256/E8
Morgantown, Miss. (†39120) 256/B7
Morgantown, Ohio (†45612) 284/D7
Morgantown, Pa. (19543) 294/L5
Morgantown, W. Va. (26505) 312/G3
Morganville, Kansas (67468) 232/E2
Morganville, N.J. (07751) 273/E3
Morganza, La. (70759) 238/G5
Morges, Switzerland 39/B3
Morguilla (pt.), Chile 138/D1
Mori, China 77/D3
Mori, Japan 81/K2
Moriah, N.Y. (12960) 276/N2
Moriah Center, N.Y. (12961) 276/N2
Moriarty, N. Mex. (87035) 274/D4
Morice (lake), Br. Col. 184/D3
Morice (riv.), Br. Col. 184/D3
Morichal, Colombia 126/E6
Morichal Largo (riv.), Venezuela 124/G3
Morien (cape), Nova Scotia 168/J2
Moriguchi, Japan 81/J7
Morin Creek, Sask. 181/C1
Morin Dawa Daurzu, China 77/K2
Morin Heights, Québec 172/C4
Morinville, Alberta 182/D3
Morioka, Japan 81/K4
Morisset, N.S. Wales 97/F3
Morisset, Québec 172/G3
Moriston (riv.), Scotland 15/D3
Morjärv, Sweden 18/N3
Morlaix, France 28/B3
Morland, Kansas (67650) 232/B2
Morley, Alberta 182/C4
Morley, Iowa (52312) 229/L4
Morley, Mich. (49336) 250/D5
Morley, Mo. (63767) 261/N8
Morley, N.Y. (13617) 276/K1
Morley, Tenn. (37812) 237/O7
Mormon (lake), Ariz. 198/D4
Mormon (mt.), Idaho 220/D4
Mormon (mts.), Nev. 266/G5
Mormon Lake, Ariz. (86038) 198/D4
Morne-à-l'Eau, Guadeloupe 161/A6
Morne Seychellois (mt.), Seychelles 118/H5
Morningside, Alberta 182/D3
Morningside, Md. (†20028) 245/G5
Morningside, Queensland 88/K2
Morningside Park, Conn. (†06385) 210/G3
Morning Sun, Iowa (52640) 229/L6
Mornington (isl.), Chile 138/D8
Mornington (isl.), Queensland 88/F3
Mornington (isl.), Queensland 95/A3
Mornington, Victoria 97/C6
Mornington (pen.), Victoria 97/C6
Morning View, Ky. (41063) 237/N3
Moro, Ark. (72368) 202/H4
Moro (creek), Ark. 202/F7
Moro, Oreg. (97039) 291/G2
Moro (gulf), Philippines 82/D7
Moro (gulf), Philippines 85/G4
Moro (mt.), Switzerland 39/E5
Moro Bay, Ark. (†71651) 202/F7
Morobe, Papua N.G. 85/C7
Morocco 2/J4
Morocco 102/B1
Morocco, Ind. (47963) 227/C3
MOROCCO 106/C2
Morocelí, Honduras 154/D3
Morochata, Bolivia 136/B5
Morococha, Peru 128/D8
Morogoro (reg.), Tanzania 115/G5
Morogoro, Tanzania 115/G5
Morogoro, Tanzania 102/F5
Moroleón, Mexico 150/J6
Morombe, Madagascar 118/G4
Moromoro, Bolivia 136/C6
Morón, Argentina 143/G7
Morón, Cuba 158/F2
Morón, Cuba 156/B2
Moron, Haiti 158/A6
Mörön (Muren), Mongolia 77/F2
Moron (mt.), Switzerland 39/D2
Morón, Venezuela 124/D2
Morona, Ecuador 128/D4
Morona (riv.), Peru 128/D5
Morona-Santiago (prov.), Ecuador 128/C4
Morondava, Madagascar 118/G3
Morondava, Madagascar 102/G7
Morón de la Frontera, Spain 33/D4
Morongo Ind. Res., Calif. 204/J10
Moroni (cap.), Comoros 118/G2
Moroni (cap.), Comoros 102/G6
Moroni, Utah (84646) 304/C4
Moron Us He (riv.), China 77/D5
Morotai (isl.), Indonesia 54/O9
Morotai (isl.), Indonesia 85/H5
Moroto, Uganda 115/F3
Morovis, P. Rico 161/D1
Morpeth, England 13/F2
Morpeth, England 10/F3
Morpeth, Ontario 177/C5
Morphou, Cyprus 63/E5
Morphou (bay), Cyprus 63/E5
Morral, Ohio (43337) 284/D4
Morrice, Mich. (48857) 250/E6
Morrill, Kansas (66515) 232/G2
Morrill○, Maine (04952) 243/E7
Morrill, Minn. (†56329) 255/E5
Morrill (co.), Nebr. 264/A3
Morrill, Nebr. (69358) 264/A3
Morrilton, Ark. (72110) 202/E3
Morrin, Alberta 182/D4
Morrinhos, Brazil 132/D7
Morrinsville, N. Zealand 100/E2
Morris, Ala. (35116) 195/E3
Morris (res.), Calif. 204/D10
Morris○, Conn. (06763) 210/C2
Morris, Georgia (31767) 217/C7
Morris, Ill. (60450) 222/E2
Morris, Ind. (47033) 227/G6
Morris (co.), Kansas 232/F3
Morris, Manitoba 179/E5
Morris, Minn. (56267) 255/C5
Morris (co.), N.J. 273/D2
Morris, N.Y. (13808) 276/K5
Morris, Okla. (74445) 288/P3
Morris, Pa. (16938) 294/H2
Morris (mt.), S. Australia 94/B2
Morris (isl.), S.C. 296/H6
Morris (co.), Texas 303/K4
Morris, W. Va. (†26639) 312/E5
Morrisburg, Ontario 177/J3
Morris Chapel, Tenn. (38361) 237/E10
Morrisdale, New Bruns. 170/D3
Morrisdale, Pa. (16858) 294/F4
Morrisey, Wyo. (†82701) 319/H2
Morris Fork, Ky. (41353) 237/O6
Morris Jesup (cape), Greenl. 4/A11
Morrison, Colo. (80465) 208/J3
Morrison, Ill. (61270) 222/C2
Morrison, Iowa (50657) 229/H4
Morrison (lake), Manitoba 179/C1
Morrison (co.), Minn. 255/D4
Morrison, Mo. (65061) 261/J5
Morrison, Okla. (73061) 288/M2
Morrison, Tenn. (37357) 237/K9
Morrison Bluff, Ark. (†72863) 202/D3
Morrison City, Tenn. (†37660) 237/R7
Morrisonville, Ill. (62546) 222/D4
Morrisonville, N.Y. (12962) 276/N1
Morrisonville, Wis. (53571) 317/G9
Morris Plains, N.J. (07950) 273/D2
Morris Run, Pa. (16939) 294/J2
Morriston, Ark. (72559) 202/G1
Morriston, Fla. (32668) 212/D2
Morriston, Ontario 177/D4
Morristown, Ariz. (85342) 198/C5
Morristown, Ill. (†61101) 222/D1
Morristown, Ind. (46161) 227/F5
Morristown, Minn. (55052) 255/E6
Morristown, N.J. (07960) 273/D2
Morristown, N.Y. (13664) 276/J1
Morristown, Ohio (43759) 284/H5
Morristown, S. Dak. (57645) 298/F2
Morristown, Tenn. (37814) 237/P8
Morristown○, Vt. (†05661) 268/B2
Morristown Nat'l Hist. Park, N.J. 273/D2
Morrisvale, W. Va. (25542) 312/C6
Morrisville, Mo. (65710) 261/F8
Morrisville, N.Y. (13408) 276/J5
Morrisville, N.C. (27560) 281/M3
Morrisville, Pa. (19067) 294/N5
Morrisville, Vt. (05661) 268/B2
Morrito, Nicaragua 154/E5
Morro (pt.), Chile 138/A6
Morro Bay, Calif. (93442) 204/D8
Morro do Chapéu, Brazil 132/F5
Morropón, Peru 128/C5
Morros, Brazil 132/F3
Morrosquillo (gulf), Colombia 126/C3
Morrow, Ark. (72749) 202/B2
Morrow, Georgia (30260) 217/K2
Morrow, La. (71356) 238/F5
Morrow (co.), Ohio 284/E4
Morrow, Ohio (45152) 284/B7
Morrow (co.), Oreg. 291/H2
Morrow Point (res.), Colo. 208/E6
Morrowville, Kansas (66958) 232/E2
Morrumbala, Mozambique 118/F3
Morrumbene, Mozambique 118/F4
Mors (isl.), Denmark 21/B4
Morse (res.), Ind. 227/E4
Morse, La. (70559) 238/F6
Morse, Sask. 181/D5
Morse, Texas (79062) 303/C1
Morse, Wis. (†54527) 317/E3
Morse Bluff, Nebr. (68648) 264/H3
Morse Mill, Mo. (63066) 261/L6
Morses Line, Vt. (†05459) 268/A2
Morshansk, U.S.S.R. 52/F4
Mortagne-au-Perche, France 28/D3
Mortara, Italy 34/B2
Morte (pt.), England 13/C6
Morteau, France 28/G4
Morteros, Argentina 143/D3
Mortes (Manso) (riv.), Brazil 132/D6
Mortlach, Sask. 181/E5
Mortlake, Victoria 97/B6
Morton, Ill. (61550) 222/D3
Morton (co.), Kansas 232/A4
Morton, Minn. (56270) 255/C6
Morton, Miss. (39117) 256/E6
Morton (co.), N. Dak. 282/H6
Morton, Ontario 177/H3
Morton, Pa. (19070) 294/M7
Morton, Texas (79346) 303/B4
Morton, Wash. (98356) 310/C4
Morton, Wyo. (82522) 319/D2
Morton Grove, Ill. (60053) 222/B5
Morton Mills, Iowa (†50864) 229/C6
Mortons Gap, Ky. (42440) 237/F6
Mortsel, Belgium 27/E6
Moruga, Trin. & Tob. 161/B11
Moruka (riv.), Guyana 131/B2
Morundah, N.S. Wales 97/D4
Moruya, N.S. Wales 97/F4
Morvan (plat.), France 28/F4
Morven, Georgia (31638) 217/E9
Morven, N. Zealand 100/C6
Morven, N.C. (28119) 281/J5
Morven, Queensland 95/C5
Morven (dist.), Scotland 15/C4
Morven (mt.), Scotland 15/E2
Morvi, India 68/C4
Morvin, Ala. (36762) 195/C7
Morwell, Victoria 97/D5
Morwell, Victoria 88/H7
Mosbach, W. Germany 22/C4
Mosby, Mo. (64073) 261/R4
Mosby, Mont. (59058) 262/J4
Mosca, Colo. (81146) 208/H7
Moscavide, Portugal 33/A1
Moscow, Ark. (71659) 202/G5
Moscow, Idaho (83843) 220/B3
Moscow, Idaho 188/C1
Moscow, Ind. (†46156) 227/F6
Moscow, Iowa (52760) 229/L5
Moscow, Kansas (67952) 232/A4
Moscow, Ky. (†42031) 237/D7
Moscow, Miss. (†39328) 256/G5
Moscow, Ohio (45153) 284/B8
Moscow, Pa. (18444) 294/F7
Moscow, Tenn. (38057) 237/C10
Moscow (cap.), U.S.S.R. 2/L3
Moscow (cap.), U.S.S.R. 7/H3
Moscow (cap.), U.S.S.R. 48/D4
Moscow (Moskva) (cap.), U.S.S.R. 52/E3
Moscow, Vt. (05662) 268/B3
Moscow Mills, Md. (†21521) 245/B2
Moscow Mills, Mo. (63362) 261/K5
Mosel (riv.), Luxembourg 27/J9
Mosel (riv.), W. Germany 22/B3
Moseley, Sask. 181/G3
Moseley, Va. (23120) 307/N6
Moselle (dept.), France 28/G3
Moselle (riv.), France 28/G3
Moselle, Miss. (39459) 256/F8
Moselle, Mo. (†63084) 261/L6
Moser River, Nova Scotia 168/F4
Moses (lake), Wash. 310/F3
Moses Coulee (canyon), Wash. 310/F3
Moses Lake, Wash. (98837) 310/F3
Moses Point, Alaska (†99762) 196/F2
Mosetenes, Cordillera de (range), Bolivia 136/B5
Mosgiel, N. Zealand 100/C6
Mosgrove, Pa. (†16259) 294/D4
Moshannon, Pa. (16859) 294/F3
Mosheim, Tenn. (37818) 237/R8
Mosher, S. Dak. (57558) 298/J7
Moshi, Tanzania 115/G4
Moshi, Tanzania 102/F5
Mosier, Oreg. (97040) 291/F2
Mosina, Poland 47/C2
Mosinee, Wis. (54455) 317/G6
Mosi-Oa-Tunya (falls) 102/E6
Mosi-Oa-Tunya (Victoria) (falls), Zambia 115/E7
Mosi-Oa-Tunya (Victoria) (falls), Zimbabwe 118/C3
Mosjøen, Norway 18/H4
Moskenesøya (isl.), Norway 18/H3
Moskva (Moscow) (cap.), U.S.S.R. 52/E3
Moskva (riv.), U.S.S.R. 52/E3
Mosman, N.S. Wales 88/L4
Mosman, N.S. Wales 97/J3
Mosonmagyaróvár, Hungary 41/D3
Mosquera, Colombia 126/A6
Mosquero, N. Mex. (87733) 274/F3
Mosquic (lake), Québec 172/C3
Mosquito (lag.), Fla. 212/F3
Mosquito, Riacho (riv.), Paraguay 144/C3
Mosquito Creek (lake), Ohio 284/J3
Mosquitos, Costa de (reg.), Nicaragua 154/E4
Mosquitos, Golfo de los (gulf), Panama 154/G6
Moss, Miss. (39460) 256/F7
Moss, Norway 18/D4
Moss, Tenn. (38575) 237/K7
Mossaka, Congo 115/C4
Mossbank, Sask. 181/E6
Moss Beach, Calif. (94038) 204/H3
Mossel Bay, S. Africa 102/E8
Mossel Bay, S. Africa 118/C6
Mossendjo, Congo 115/B4
Mossgiel, N.S. Wales 97/C4
Moss Landing, Calif. (95039) 204/C7
Mossleigh, Alberta 182/D4
Mossman, Queensland 88/G3
Mossman, Queensland 95/C3
Mossoró, Brazil 120/F3
Mossoró, Brazil 132/G4
Moss Point, Miss. (39563) 256/G10
Mossuril, Mozambique 118/G2
Moss Vale, N.S. Wales 97/F4
Mossville, Ill. (61552) 222/D3
Mossy (riv.), Manitoba 179/C3
Mossy (riv.), Sask. 181/H1
Mossy Head, Fla. (32434) 212/C6
Mossyrock, Wash. (98564) 310/C4
Most, Czech. 41/B1
Mostaganem, Algeria 102/C1
Mostaganem, Algeria 106/D1
Mostar, Yugoslavia 7/F4
Mostar, Yugoslavia 45/D4
Mosty, U.S.S.R. 52/B4
Mosul, Iraq 66/C2
Mosul, Iraq 59/D2
Mosul, Iraq 54/F6
Motacucito, Bolivia 136/E5
Mota del Cuervo, Spain 33/E3
Motagua (riv.), Guatemala 154/C3
Motala, Sweden 18/J7
Motherwell and Wishaw, Scotland 10/B1
Motherwell and Wishaw, Scotland 15/C2
Motilla del Palancar, Spain 33/F3
Motiti (isl.), N. Zealand 100/F2
Motley, Minn. (56466) 255/D4
Motley (co.), Texas 303/D3
Motobu, Japan 81/N6
Motozintla de Mendoza, Mexico 150/N9
Motril, Spain 33/E4
Motsuta (cape), Japan 81/J2
Mott, N. Dak. (58646) 282/F7
Motu (riv.), N. Zealand 100/F3
Motueka, N. Zealand 100/D4
Motuhora (isl.), N. Zealand 100/F2
Motuihe (isl.), N. Zealand 100/C1
Motul de Felipe Carillo Puerto, Mexico 150/P6
Motupe, Peru 128/C6
Motutapu (isl.), N. Zealand 100/C1
Motygino, U.S.S.R. 48/K4
Mouchoir (passage), Turks & Caicos 156/D2
Moúdhros, Greece 45/G6
Moudjéria, Mauritania 106/B5
Moudon, Switzerland 39/C3
Mouila, Gabon 115/B4
Mouka, Cent. Afr. Rep. 115/D2
Moulamein, N.S. Wales 97/C4
Moulamein (creek), N.S. Wales 97/C4
Mould Bay, Canada 4/B16
Mould Bay, N.W. Terrs. 187/F2
Moule, Guadeloupe 161/B6
Moule à Chique (cape), St. Lucia 161/G7
Moulin-Morneault, New Bruns. 170/B1
Moulins, France 28/E4
Moulmein, Burma 72/C3
Moulmein, Burma 54/L8
Moulouya (riv.), Morocco 106/D2
Moulton, Ala. (35650) 195/D2
Moulton, Iowa (52572) 229/H7
Moulton, Mont. (†59423) 262/G3
Moulton, Texas (77975) 303/H8
Moultonboro○, N.H. (03254) 268/E4
Moultrie, Fla. (†32084) 212/E2
Moultrie, Georgia (31768) 217/E8
Moultrie (co.), Ill. 222/E4
Moultrie (lake), S.C. 188/K4
Moultrie (lake), S.C. 296/G5
Mounana, Gabon 115/B4
Mound, La. (71262) 238/H2
Mound, Minn. (55364) 255/E6
Mound Bayou, Miss. (38762) 256/C3
Mound City, Ill. (62963) 222/D6
Mound City, Kansas (66056) 232/H3
Mound City, Mo. (64470) 261/B2
Mound City, S. Dak. (57646) 298/K2
Mound City Group Nat'l Mon., Ohio 284/E7
Moundou, Chad 111/C6
Moundou, Chad 102/D4
Moundridge, Kansas (67107) 232/E3
Mounds, Ill. (62964) 222/D6
Mounds, Okla. (74047) 288/O3
Mound Station (Timewell), Ill. (†62375) 222/C3
Mounds View, Minn. (†55112) 255/G5
Moundsville, W. Va. (26041) 312/E3
Mound Valley, Kansas (67354) 232/G4
Moundville, Ala. (35474) 195/C5
Moundville, Mo. (64771) 261/C7
Moung Roessei, Cambodia 72/D4
Mounlapamôk, Laos 72/E4
Mount (cape), Liberia 106/B7
Mountain, N. Dak. (58262) 282/P2
Mountain (riv.), N.W. Terrs. 187/F3
Mountain, Ontario 177/J2
Mountain (prov.), Philippines 82/C2
Mountain, W. Va. (26407) 312/E4
Mountain, Wis. (54149) 317/K5
Mountainair, N. Mex. (87036) 274/C4
Mountain Ash, Ky. (†40769) 237/N7
Mountain Ash, Wales 13/A6
Mountain Ash, Wales 10/E5
Mountainboro, Ala. (†35957) 195/F2
Mountain Brook, Ala. (35223) 195/E4
Mountainburg, Ark. (72946) 202/B2
Mountain City, Georgia (30562) 217/F1
Mountain City, Nev. (89831) 266/F1
Mountain City, Tenn. (37683) 237/T8
Mountain Creek, Ala. (†36051) 195/E5
Mountain Creek (lake), Texas 303/G2
Mountaindale, Md. (†21701) 245/J2
Mountain Dale, N.Y. (12763) 276/L7
Mountaindale, Oreg. (†97106) 291/A1
Mountain Fork (riv.), Ark. 202/A5
Mountain Fork (riv.), Okla. 288/S6
Mountain Grove, Mo. (65711) 261/H8
Mountain Grove, Ontario 177/H3
Mountain Home, Ark. (72653) 202/F1
Mountain Home, Idaho (83647) 220/C6
Mountain Home (res.), Idaho 220/C6
Mountainhome, Pa. (18342) 294/M3
Mountain Home, Utah (84051) 304/D3
Mountain Home A.F.B., Idaho 220/C6
Mountain Iron, Minn. (55768) 255/F3
Mountain Lake, Minn. (56159) 255/D7
Mountain Lake Park, Md. (21550) 245/A3
Mountain Lakes, N.J. (07046) 273/E2
Mountain Meadows (res.), Calif. 204/E3
Mountain Park, Georgia (†30075) 217/D2
Mountain Park, Okla. (73559) 288/J5
Mountain Pine, Ark. (71956) 202/D4
Mountain Point, Alaska (†99901) 196/N2
Mountain Rest, S.C. (29664) 296/A2
Mountain Road, Manitoba 179/C4
Mountainside, N.J. (07092) 273/E2
Mountain Valley, Ark. (†71901) 202/D4
Mountain View, Alberta 182/D5
Mountain View, Ark. (72560) 202/F2
Mountain View, Calif. (*94042) 204/K3
Mountain View, Georgia (30070) 217/K2
Mountainview, Hawaii (96771) 218/J5
Mountain View, Mo. (65548) 261/J8
Mountain View, N.J. (†07470) 273/B2
Mountain View, Okla. (73062) 288/J4
Mountain View, Wyo. (82939) 319/B4
Mountain View, Wyo. (†82601) 319/F3
Mountain Village, Alaska (99632) 196/E2
Mountain Zebra Nat'l Park, S. Africa 118/C6
Mount Airy, Georgia (30563) 217/F1
Mount Airy, La. (70076) 238/M3
Mount Airy, Md. (21771) 245/K3
Mount Airy, N.C. (27030) 281/H1
Mount Airy, Tenn. (†37327) 237/L10
Mount Albert, N. Zealand 100/B1
Mount Albert, Ontario 177/E3
Mount Alto, W. Va. (25264) 312/C5
Mount Alton, Pa. (†16738) 294/E2
Mount Andrew, Ala. (†36053) 195/H7
Mount Angel, Oreg. (97362) 291/B3
Mount Apo National Park, Philippines 82/E7
Mount Arlington, N.J. (07856) 273/D2
Mount Arrowsmith, N.S. Wales 97/A2
Mount Assiniboine Prov. Park, Br. Col. 184/K5
Mount Auburn, Ill. (62547) 222/D4
Mount Auburn, Ind. (†47327) 227/G5
Mount Auburn, Iowa (52313) 229/J4
Mount Aukum, Calif. (95656) 204/E5
Mount Ayr, Ind. (47964) 227/C3
Mount Ayr, Iowa (50854) 229/E7
Mount Barker, S. Australia 94/C8
Mount Barker, W. Australia 88/B6
Mount Barker, W. Australia 92/B6
Mount Beauty, Victoria 97/D5
Mount Bellew, Ireland 17/D5
Mount Berry, Georgia (30149) 217/B2
Mount Bethel, Georgia (†30060) 217/K1
Mount Blanchard, Ohio (45867) 284/D4
Mount Bold (res.), S. Australia 94/B8
Mount Brydges, Ontario 177/C5
Mount Calm, Texas (76673) 303/H6
Mount Calvary, Wis. (53057) 317/K8
Mount Carbon, W. Va. (25139) 312/D7
Mount Carleton Prov. Park, New Bruns. 170/D1
Mount Carmel, Ala. (†36047) 195/F6
Mount Carmel, Ill. (62863) 222/F5
Mount Carmel, Ind. (†47012) 227/H6
Mount Carmel, Miss. (†39474) 256/E7
Mount Carmel, Newf. 166/D2
Mount Carmel, N. Dak. (†58249) 282/O2
Mount Carmel, Ohio (45244) 284/C10
Mount Carmel, Pa. (17851) 294/K4
Mount Carmel, Pr. Edward I. 168/D2
Mount Carmel, S.C. (29840) 296/C3
Mount Carmel, Tenn. (37642) 237/R8
Mount Carmel, Utah (84755) 304/B6
Mount Carroll, Ill. (61053) 222/D1
Mount Cavenagh, North. Terr. 93/C8
Mountcharles, Ireland 17/E2
Mount Clare, W. Va. (26408) 312/F4
Mount Clemens, Mich. (48043) 250/G6
Mount Cory, Ohio (45868) 284/C4
Mount Crawford, Va. (22841) 307/L4
Mount Croghan, S.C. (29727) 296/G2
Mount Currie, Br. Col. 184/F5
Mount Darwin, Zimbabwe 118/E3
Mount Desert, Maine (04660) 243/G7
Mount Desert○, Maine (04660) 243/G7
Mount Desert (isl.), Maine 243/G7
Mount Desert Rock (isl.), Maine 243/G8
Mount Dora, Fla. (32757) 212/E3
Mount Dora, N. Mex. (88429) 274/F2
Mount Doreen, North. Terr. 93/B7
Mount Douglas, Queensland 95/C4
Mount Drysdale, N.S. Wales 97/C2
Mount Eaton, Ohio (44659) 284/G4
Mount Eba, S. Australia 94/D4
Mount Eden, Ky. (40046) 237/L4
Mount Eden, N. Zealand 100/B1
Mount Edziza Prov. Park and Rec. Area, Br. Col.184/B1
Mount Elgin, Ontario 177/D5
Mount Emu (creek), Victoria 97/B5
Mount Enterprise, Texas (75681) 303/K6
Mount Ephraim, N.J. (08059) 273/B3
Mount Erie, Ill. (62446) 222/E5
Mount Etna, Ind. (†46750) 227/F3
Mount Etna, Iowa (50855) 229/D6
Mount Everard, Guyana 131/B2
Mount Forest, Mich. (†48650) 250/F5
Mount Forest, Ontario 177/D4
Mount Freedom, N.J. (07970) 273/D2
Mount Gambier, Australia 87/D9
Mount Gambier, S. Australia 88/G7
Mount Gambier, S. Australia 94/G7
Mount Gay, W. Va. (25637) 312/C7
Mount Gilead, N.C. (27306) 281/K4
Mount Gilead, Ohio (43338) 284/E4
Mount Gravatt, Queensland 88/K3
Mount Hagen, Papua N.G. 85/B7
Mount Hamill, Iowa (†52625) 229/K7
Mount Healthy, Ohio (45231) 284/B9
Mount Hermon, Calif. (95041) 204/K4
Mount Hermon, La. (70450) 238/K5
Mount Hermon, Mass. (01354) 249/D2
Mount Holly, Ark. (71758) 202/E7
Mount Holly○, N.J. (08060) 273/D4
Mount Holly, N.C. (28120) 281/H4
Mount Holly, S.C. (29463) 296/H5
Mount Holly○, Vt. (05758) 268/B5
Mount Holly, Va. (22524) 307/P4
Mount Holly Springs, Pa. (17065) 294/H5
Mount Hood, Oreg. (97041) 291/F2
Mount Hope, Ala. (35651) 195/D2
Mount Hope (riv.), Conn. 210/G1
Mount Hope, Kansas (67108) 232/E4
Mount Hope (bay), Mass. 249/K6
Mount Hope, N.J. (†07885) 273/D2
Mount Hope, N.S. Wales 97/C3
Mount Hope, Ohio (44660) 284/G4
Mount Hope, Ontario 177/E4
Mount Hope (bay), R.I. 249/K6
Mount Hope, W. Va. (25880) 312/D7
Mount Hope, Wis. (53816) 317/D10
Mount Horeb, Wis. (53572) 317/G10
Mount Ida, Ark. (71957) 202/C4
Mount Ida, Wis. (†53809) 317/E10
Mount Isa, Queensland 95/A4
Mount Isa, Queensland 88/F4
Mount Jackson, Va. (22842) 307/L3
Mount Jewett, Pa. (16740) 294/E2
Mount Joy, Pa. (17552) 294/K5
Mount Judea, Ark. (72655) 202/D2
Mount Juliet, Tenn. (37122) 237/H8
Mount Kisco, N.Y. (10549) 276/N8
Mount Kuring-gai, N.S. Wales 97/J3
Mountlake Terrace, Wash. (98043) 310/B1
Mount Laurel○, N.J. (†08054) 273/D4
Mount Lebanon, La. (†71028) 238/D2
Mount Lebanon○, Pa. (15228) 294/B7
Mount Lemmon, Ariz. (85619) 198/E6
Mount Leonard, Mo. (†65339) 261/F4
Mount Liberty, Ohio (43048) 284/E5
Mount Lofty (range), S. Australia 88/F6
Mount Lookout, W. Va. (26678) 312/E6
Mount Magnet, W. Australia 88/B5
Mount Magnet, W. Australia 92/B5
Mount Margaret, Queensland 95/A3
Mount Margaret, W. Australia 88/C5
Mount Margaret, W. Australia 92/C5
Mount Maunganui, N. Zealand 100/E2
Mount Meigs, Ala. (36057) 195/F6
Mountmellick, Ireland 10/C4
Mountmellick, Ireland 17/G5
Mount Meridian, Ind. (†46135) 227/D5
Mount Molloy, Queensland 95/C3
Mount Montgomery, Nev. (†89422) 266/C5
Mount Morgan, Queensland 88/J4
Mount Morgan, Queensland 95/D4
Mount Moriah, Mo. (64665) 261/E2
Mount Morris, Ill. (61054) 222/D1
Mount Morris, Mich. (48458) 250/F5
Mount Morris, N.Y. (14510) 276/E5
Mount Morris, Pa. (15349) 294/B6
Mount Mourne, N.C. (28123) 281/H3
Mount Nebo, W. Va. (26679) 312/E6
Mount Olga Nat'l Park, North. Terr. 93/B8
Mount Olive, Ill. (62069) 222/D4
Mount Olive, Miss. (39119) 256/E7
Mount Olive○, N.J. (†07828) 273/D2
Mount Olive, N.C. (28365) 281/O4
Mount Oliver, Pa. (15210) 294/B7
Mount Olivet, Ky. (41064) 237/N3
Mount Orab, Ohio (45154) 284/C7
Mount Pearl, Newf. 166/D2
Mount Penn, Pa. (19606) 294/L5
Mount Pleasant, Ark. (72561) 202/G2
Mount Pleasant, Del. (†19709) 245/R2
Mount Pleasant, Fla. (32352) 212/B1
Mount Pleasant, Ind. (47520) 227/D8
Mount Pleasant, Iowa (52641) 229/L7
Mount Pleasant, Md. (†21701) 245/J3
Mount Pleasant, Mich. (48858) 250/E5
Mount Pleasant, Miss. (38649) 256/E1
Mount Pleasant, N.C. (28124) 281/J4
Mount Pleasant, Nova Scotia 168/C4
Mount Pleasant, Ohio (43939) 284/J5
Mount Pleasant, Ontario 177/D4
Mount Pleasant, Pa. (15666) 294/D5
Mount Pleasant, S.C. (29464) 296/H6
Mount Pleasant, Tenn. (38474) 237/G9
Mount Pleasant, Texas (75455) 303/K4
Mount Pleasant, Utah (84647) 304/C4
Mount Pocono, Pa. (18344) 294/M3
Mount Prospect, Ill. (60056) 222/B5
Mount Pulaski, Ill. (62548) 222/D3
Mountrail (co.), N. Dak. 282/E3
Mount Rainier, Md. (20822) 245/F4
Mount Rainier Nat'l Park, Wash. 310/D4
Mountrath, Ireland 17/F5
Mount Revelstoke Nat'l Park, Br. Col. 184/H4
Mount Robson, Br. Col. 184/H3
Mount Robson Prov. Park, Br. Col. 184/H3
Mount Rogers Nat'l Rec. Area, Va. 307/F7
Mount Roskill, N. Zealand 100/B1
Mount Royal, N.J. (08061) 273/C4
Mount Royal (range), N.S. Wales 97/F2
Mount Rushmore Nat'l Mem., S. Dak. 298/B6
Mounts (bay), England 10/D6
Mounts (bay), England 13/B7
Mount Salem, Ky. (†40437) 237/M6
Mount Savage, Md. (21545) 245/C2
Mount Shasta, Calif. (96067) 204/C5
Mount Sherman, Ark. (†72641) 202/D1
Mount Sherman, Ky. (42764) 237/K6
Mount Sidney, Va. (24467) 307/K4
Mount Solon, Va. (22843) 307/K4
Mount Standfast, Barbados 161/B8
Mount Sterling, Ala. (†36904) 195/B6
Mount Sterling, Ill. (62353) 222/C4
Mount Sterling, Ind. (†47043) 227/G7
Mount Sterling, Iowa (52573) 229/J7
Mount Sterling, Ky. (40353) 237/N4
Mount Sterling, Ohio (43143) 284/D6
Mount Sterling, Wis. (54645) 317/D9
Mount Stewart, Pr. Edward I. 168/F2
Mount Storm, W. Va. (26739) 312/H4
Mount Storm (lake), W. Va. 312/H4
Mount Summit, Ind. (47361) 227/G4
Mount Sunapee, N.H. (03772) 268/C5
Mount Surprise, Queensland 95/C3
Mount Tabor○, Vt. (†05739) 268/B5
Mount Tabor, Wis. (†54638) 317/F8
Mount Tivoli, Grenada 161/D8
Mount Tom, Mass. (01058) 249/D3
Mount Trumbull, Ariz. (†84770) 198/B2
Mount Uniacke, Nova Scotia 168/E4
Mount Union, Iowa (52644) 229/L6
Mount Union, Pa. (17066) 294/G5
Mount Upton, N.Y. (13809) 276/K6
Mount Vernon, Ala. (36560) 195/B8
Mount Vernon, Ark. (72111) 202/F3
Mount Vernon, Georgia (30445) 217/G6
Mount Vernon, Ill. (62864) 222/E5
Mount Vernon, Ind. (47620) 227/B9
Mount Vernon, Iowa (52314) 229/K5
Mount Vernon, Ky. (40456) 237/N6
Mount Vernon○, Maine (04352) 243/D7
Mount Vernon, Md. (†21853) 245/P8
Mount Vernon, Mo. (65712) 261/E8
Mount Vernon, N.Y. (*10550) 276/O7
Mount Vernon, Ohio (43050) 284/E5
Mount Vernon, Oreg. (97865) 291/H3
Mount Vernon, S. Dak. (57363) 298/N6
Mount Vernon, Tenn. (37358) 237/N10
Mount Vernon, Texas (75457) 303/J4
Mount Vernon, Va. (22121) 307/O3
Mount Vernon, Wash. (98273) 310/C2
Mount Vernon, W. Australia 92/B4
Mount Vernon, Wis. (†53572) 317/G10
Mount Vernon Springs, N.C. (27345) 281/L3
Mount Victory, Ohio (43340) 284/D4
Mountview, W. Va. (†25825) 312/D7
Mountville, Georgia (30261) 217/C4
Mountville, Pa. (17554) 294/K5
Mountville, S.C. (29370) 296/C3
Mount Washington, Ky. (40047) 237/K4

Naturaliste 415

Myra, Texas (76253) 303/G4
Myra, W. Va. (25544) 312/B6
Myricks, Mass. (†02780) 249/K5
Myrnam, Alberta 182/E3
Myrtle, Idaho (†83540) 220/B3
Myrtle, Manitoba 179/E5
Myrtle, Minn. (56070) 255/E7
Myrtle, Miss. (38650) 256/F1
Myrtle, Mo. (65778) 261/K9
Myrtle (lake), N. Dak. 282/L5
Myrtle Beach, S.C. (29577) 296/K4
Myrtle Beach A.F.B., S.C. 296/K4
Myrtle Creek, Oreg. (97457) 291/D4
Myrtleford, Victoria 97/D5
Myrtle Grove, Fla. (32506) 212/B6
Myrtle Grove, La. (†70083) 238/K7
Myrtle Point, Oreg. (97458) 291/C4
Myrtlewood, Ala. (36763) 195/C6
Mysen, Norway 18/G7
Myślenice, Poland 47/E4
Myślibórz, Poland 47/B2
Mysłowice, Poland 47/C4
Mysore, India 68/D6
Mysore, India 54/J8
Mys Shmidta, U.S.S.R. 4/C1
Mys Shmidta, U.S.S.R. 48/T3
Mystery Lake, Manitoba 179/J2
Mystic, Conn. (06355) 210/H3
Mystic (riv.), Conn. 210/H3
Mystic, Georgia (31769) 217/F7
Mystic, Iowa (52574) 229/H7
Mystic (lake), Mass. 249/C6
Mystic (riv.), Mass. 249/C6
Mystic, S. Dak. (†57778) 298/B5
Mystic Islands, N.J. (08087) 273/E4
Myszków, Poland 47/D3
My Tho, Vietnam 72/E5
Mytishchi, U.S.S.R. 52/E3
Myton, Utah (84052) 304/D3
M'zab (oasis), Algeria 106/E2
Mže (riv.), Czech. 41/B2
Mzimba, Malawi 115/F6
Mzimba, Malawi 102/F6

N

Naab (riv.), W. Germany 22/E4
Naafkopf (mt.), Switzerland 39/J2
Naaldwijk, Netherlands 27/E4
Naalehu, Hawaii (96772) 218/H7
Naalehu, Hawaii 188/G6
Naantali, Finland 18/M6
Naarden, Netherlands 27/G4
Naas, Ireland 10/C4
Naas, Ireland 17/H5
Naba, Burma 72/B1
Nababeep, S. Africa 118/B5
Nabari, Kiribati 87/J6
Nabb, Ind. (47147) 227/F7
Nabburg, W. Germany 22/E4
Naberezhnye Chelny, U.S.S.R. 52/H3
Nabesna, Alaska (†99764) 196/K2
Nabeul, Tunisia 106/G1
Nabiac, N.S. Wales 97/G3
Nabire, Indonesia 85/K6
Nablus (Nabulus), West Bank 65/C3
Nabnasset, Mass. (01861) 249/J2
Nabua, Philippines 82/D4
Nacala, Mozambique 118/G2
Nacala, Mozambique 102/G6
Nacaome, Honduras 154/D4
Naches, Wash. (98937) 310/E4
Naches (pass), Wash. 310/D3
Naches (riv.), Wash. 310/E4
Nachikatsuura, Japan 81/H7
Nachingwea, Tanzania 115/G6
Náchod, Czech. 41/D1
Nachusa, Ill. (61057) 222/D2
Nachvak (fjord), Newf. 166/B2
Nacimiento (riv.), Calif. 204/D8
Nacimiento, Chile 138/D1
Nacimiento (mts.), N. Mex. 274/C3
Nacimiento (peak), N. Mex. 274/C2
Nacka, Sweden 18/H1
Nackawic, New Bruns. 170/C2
Nacmine, Alberta 182/D4
Naco, Ariz. (85620) 198/E7
Naco, Mexico 150/D1
Nacogdoches (co.), Texas 303/K6
Nacogdoches, Texas (75961) 303/J6
Nacozari, Mexico 150/E1
Nacunday, Paraguay 144/E5
Nadadores, Mexico 150/H3
Nadawah, Ala. (†36726) 195/D7
Nadeau, Mich. (49863) 250/B3
Nadi, Fiji 86/P10
Nadi, Fiji 87/H7
Nadiad, India 68/C4
Nădlac, Romania 45/E2
Nador, Morocco 106/D1
Nádudvar, Hungary 41/F3
Nadvoitsy, U.S.S.R. 52/D2
Nadym, U.S.S.R. 48/H3
Nadym (riv.), U.S.S.R. 48/H3
Naestved, Denmark 21/E7
Naestved, Denmark 18/G9
Naf, Idaho (83342) 220/E7
Näfels, Switzerland 39/H2
Nafenen, Switzerland 39/H3
Naft-e Shah, Iran 66/D4
Naft Kaneh, Iraq 66/D3
Naga, Philippines 85/G3
Naga, Philippines 54/O8
Naga, Philippines 82/D4
Nagahama, Ehime, Japan 81/F7
Nagahama, Shiga, Japan 81/H6
Nagai (isl.), Alaska 196/F4
Nagaland (state), India 68/G3
Nagambie, Victoria 97/C5
Nagano (pref.), Japan 81/J5
Nagano, Japan 81/J5
Nagaoka, Kyoto, Japan 81/J7
Nagaoka, Niigata, Japan 81/J5
Nagaokakyo, Japan 81/J7
Nagapattinam, India 68/E6
Nagar, Pakistan 68/D1
Nagarote, Nicaragua 154/D4
Nagar Parkar, Pakistan 68/C4
Nagarzê, China 77/C6
Nagasaki (pref.), Japan 81/D7
Nagasaki, Japan 54/O6
Nagasaki, Japan 81/D7
Nagato, Japan 81/E6
Nagaur, India 68/C3
Nagawicka (lake), Wis. 317/J1
Nagele, Netherlands 27/H3
Nagercoil, India 68/D7
Nagina, India 68/D3
Nagishot, Sudan 111/F7
Nagles (mts.), Ireland 17/E7
Nago, Japan 81/N6
Nagold, W. Germany 22/C4
Nagorno-Karabakh Aut. Obl., U.S.S.R. 48/E5
Nagorno-Karabakh Aut. Obl., U.S.S.R. 52/G7
Nagornyy, U.S.S.R. 48/N4
Nagoya, Japan 81/H6
Nagoya, Japan 2/R4
Nagoya, Japan 54/P6
Nagpur, India 54/J7
Nagpur, India 68/D4
Nagqu, China 77/D5
Nags Head, N.C. (27959) 281/T3
Nagua, Dom. Rep. 158/E5
Naguabo, P. Rico 161/F2
Naguabo, P. Rico 156/G1
Nagyatád, Hungary 41/D3
Nagybajom, Hungary 41/D3
Nagyecsed, Hungary 41/G3
Nagyhalász, Hungary 41/F2
Nagykálló, Hungary 41/F3
Nagykanizsa, Hungary 41/D3
Nagykáta, Hungary 41/E3
Nagykőrös, Hungary 41/E3
Nagyszénás, Hungary 41/F3
Naha, Japan 54/O7
Naha, Japan 81/N6
Nahan, India 68/D2
Nahang (riv.), Iran 66/N7
Nahanni Butte, N.W. Terrs. 187/F3
Nahanni Nat'l Park, N.W.T. 162/D3
Nahanni Nat'l Park, N.W. Terrs. 187/F3
Nahant◯, Mass. (01908) 249/E6
Nahant (bay), Mass. 249/E6
Nahariyya, Israel 65/C1
Nahavand, Iran 59/E3
Nahavand, Iran 66/F3
Nahcotta, Wash. (98537) 310/A4
Nahhalin, West Bank 65/C4
Nahiku, Hawaii (†96713) 218/K2
Nahma, Mich. (49864) 250/C3
Nahmakanta (lake), Maine 243/E4
Nahuel Huapi (lake), Argentina 120/B7
Nahuel Huapi (lake), Argentina 143/B5
Nahuel Huapi Nat'l Park, Argentina 143/B5
Nahunta, Georgia (31553) 217/H8
Naica, Mexico 150/G2
Naicam, Sask. 181/G3
Naihati, India 68/F1
Nailsworth, England 13/E6
Naiman, China 77/K3
Na'in, Iran 66/H4
Na'in, Iran 59/F3
Nain, Jamaica 158/H6
Nain, Newf. 166/B2
Nain, Newf. 162/K4
Naini Tal, India 68/D3
Nainpur, India 68/E4
Naipo (isl.), Colombia 126/F6
Nairn, La. (†70082) 238/L8
Nairn, Ontario 177/C1
Nairn, Scotland 15/E3
Nairn, Scotland 10/E2
Nairn (trad. co.), Scotland 15/B5
Nairn (riv.), Scotland 15/D3
Nairne, S. Australia 94/C8
Nairobi, Kenya 115/G4
Nairobi (cap.), Kenya 2/L6
Nairobi (cap.), Kenya 115/G4
Nairobi (cap.), Kenya 102/F5
Naivasha, Kenya 115/G4
Najafabad, Iran 59/F3
Najafabad, Iran 66/G4
Najayo Abajo, Dom. Rep. 158/E6
Najin, N. Korea 81/E2
Najran (Aba as Sa'ud), Saudi Arabia 59/D6
Naka (riv.), Japan 81/K5
Nakalele (pt.), Hawaii 218/J1
Nakaminato, Japan 81/K5
Nakamti, Ethiopia 102/F4
Nakamti, Ethiopia 111/G6
Nakamura, Japan 81/F7
Nakasato, Japan 81/K3
Nakatane, Japan 81/E8
Nakatsu, Japan 81/E7
Na Keal, Loch (inlet), Scotland 15/B4
Naked (isl.), Alaska 196/D1
Nakfa, Ethiopia 111/G4
Nakhichevan', U.S.S.R. 7/J5
Nakhichevan', U.S.S.R. 48/E6
Nakhichevan', U.S.S.R. 52/F7
Nakhichevan' A.S.S.R., U.S.S.R. 52/F7
Nakhichevan' A.S.S.R., U.S.S.R. 48/E6
Nakhodka, U.S.S.R. 54/P5
Nakhodka, U.S.S.R. 48/O5
Nakhon Nayok, Thailand 72/D4
Nakhon Pathom, Thailand 72/C4
Nakhon Phanom, Thailand 72/D3
Nakhon Ratchasima, Thailand 72/D4
Nakhon Ratchasima, Thailand 54/M8
Nakhon Sawan, Thailand 72/D4
Nakhon Si Thammarat, Thailand 54/M9
Nakhon Si Thammarat, Thailand 72/D5
Nakina, N.C. (28455) 281/M6
Nakina, Ont. 162/H5
Nakina, Ontario 177/H4
Nakina, Ontario 175/C2
Nakło nad Notecia, Poland 47/C2
Naknek, Alaska (99633) 196/G3
Naknek (lake), Alaska 196/G3
Nakonde, Zambia 115/F5
Nakop, Namibia 118/B5
Nakskov, Denmark 21/E8
Nakskov, Denmark 18/G9
Naktong (riv.), S. Korea 81/D6
Nakuru, Kenya 102/F5
Nakuru, Kenya 115/G4
Nakusp, Br. Col. 184/J5
Nal, Pakistan 59/J4
Nal, Pakistan 68/B3
Nal (riv.), Pakistan 59/J4
Nal (riv.), Pakistan 68/B3
Nalate, Turkey 63/G4
Nalayh (Nalaikha), Mongolia 77/G2
Nalcayec (isl.), Chile 138/D6
Nal'chik, U.S.S.R. 7/J4
Nal'chik, U.S.S.R. 48/E5
Nal'chik, U.S.S.R. 52/F6
Nalgonda, India 68/D5
Nallen, W. Va. (26680) 312/E6
Nallihan, Turkey 63/D2
Nalut, Libya 111/B1
Namacurra, Mozambique 118/F3
Namak, Daryacheh-ye (salt lake), Iran 59/F3
Namak, Daryacheh-ye (salt lake), Iran 66/G3
Namaka, Alberta 182/D4
Namaksar (salt lake), Afghanistan 59/H3
Namaksar (salt lake), Afghanistan 68/A2
Namaksar (lake), Iran 66/M4
Namaksar (salt lake), Iran 59/H3
Namakzar-e Shahdad (salt lake), Iran 59/G3
Namakzar-e Shahdad (salt lake), Iran 66/L5
Namanga, Kenya 115/G4
Namangan, U.S.S.R. 48/H5
N'amaniya, Iraq 66/D4
Namapa, Mozambique 118/F2
Namaqualand (reg.), S. Africa 118/B5
Namarrói, Mozambique 118/F3
Namasagali, Uganda 115/F3
Namasigüe, Honduras 154/D4
Namatanai, Papua N.G. 87/F6
Namatanai, Papua N.G. 86/C1
Nambe, N. Mex. (†87501) 274/D3
Nambour, Queensland 88/J5
Nambour, Queensland 95/E5
Nambucca Heads, N.S. Wales 97/G2
Nam Co (lake), China 77/D5
Nam Dinh, Vietnam 72/E2
Namekagon (lake), Wis. 317/D3
Namekagon (riv.), Wis. 317/C3
Namen (Namur), Belgium 27/F8
Námestovo, Czech. 41/E2
Nametil, Mozambique 118/F3
Namhkam, Burma 72/C2
Namib (des.), Namibia 118/A3
Namibia 2/K7
Namibia 102/D7
Namibia (des.) 102/D6
NAMIBIA (SOUTH-WEST AFRICA) 118/B3
Naminga, U.S.S.R. 48/M4
Namiquipa, Mexico 150/F2
Namlan, Burma 72/C2
Namlea, Indonesia 85/H6
Namoi (riv.), N. S. Wales 88/H6
Namoi (riv.), N.S. Wales 97/E2
Namonuito (atoll), Micronesia 87/E5
Namorik (atoll), Marshall Is. 87/G5
Nampa, Alberta 182/B1
Nampa, Idaho 146/G5
Nampa, Idaho (83651) 220/B6
Nampa, Idaho 188/C2
Nampala, Mali 106/C5
Namp'o, N. Korea 81/B4
Nampo-Shoto (isls.), Japan 81/M3
Nampula (prov.), Mozambique 118/F2
Nampula, Mozambique 118/F3
Nampula, Mozambique 102/F6
Namsen (riv.), Norway 18/H4
Namsos, Norway 7/F2
Namsos, Norway 18/G4
Nam Tram, Mui (cape), Vietnam 72/F4
Namtu, Burma 72/C2
Namu, Br. Col. 184/D4
Namuac, Philippines 82/C1
Namuli, Serra (mt.), Mozambique 118/F3
Namuno, Mozambique 118/F2
Namur (lake), Alberta 182/D1
Namur (prov.), Belgium 27/F8
Namur, Belgium 27/F8
Namur, Québec 172/C4
Namutoni, Namibia 118/B3
Namwala, Zambia 115/E7
Namwŏn, S. Korea 81/C6
Namysłów, Poland 47/C3
Namzha Parwa (mt.), China 77/E6
Nan, Thailand 72/D3
Nan, Mae Nam (riv.), Thailand 72/D3
Nanacamilpa, Mexico 150/M1
Nana Candundo, Angola 115/D6
Nanafalia, Ala. (36764) 195/B6
Nanaimo, Br. Col. 146/F5
Nanaimo, Br. Col. 162/D6
Nanaimo, Br. Col. 184/J3
Nanakuli, Hawaii (96792) 218/D2
Nanao, Japan 81/H5
Nanay (riv.), Peru 128/E4
Nancagua, Chile 138/F6
Nance (co.), Nebr. 264/F3
Nanchang, China 77/J6
Nanchang, China 54/N7
Nancheng, China 77/J6
Nanchong (Nanchung), China 77/G5
Nanchong, China 54/M6
nan Clar, Loch (lake), Scotland 15/D2
Nancowry (isl.), India 68/G7
Nancy, France 28/G3
Nancy, France 7/E4
Nancy, Ky. (42544) 237/M6
Nanda Devi (mt.), India 68/D2
Nandaime, Nicaragua 154/E5
Nander, India 68/D5
Nandi (Nadi), Fiji 87/H7
Nando, Uruguay 145/F3
Nandurbar, India 68/C4
Nandyal, India 68/D5
Nanga-Eboko, Cameroon 115/B3
Nanga Parbat (mt.), Pakistan 68/D1
Nangapinoh, Indonesia 85/E6
Nangatayap, Indonesia 85/E6
Nangnim-sanmaek (range), N. Korea 81/C3
Nangong, China 77/H4
Nangqên, China 77/E5
Nang Rong, Thailand 72/D4
Nangwarry, S. Australia 94/G7
Nang Xian, China 77/D6
Nanika (dam), Br. Col. 184/D3
Nanika (lake), Br. Col. 184/D3
Nanisivik, N.W. Terrs. /K2
Nanjemoy, Md. (20662) 245/K7
Nanjing (Nanking), China 77/J5
Nanjing, China 2/Q4
Nanjing, China 54/N6
Nanking (Nanjing), China 77/J5
Nankoku, Japan 81/F7
Nan Ling (mts.), China 77/H6
Nannine, W. Australia 92/B4
Nanning, China 77/G7
Nanning, China 54/M7
Nannup, W. Australia 92/B6
Nanoose Bay, Br. Col. 184/J3
Nanortalik, Greenl. 4/D12
Nanpan Jiang (riv.), China 77/F7
Nanping, China 77/J6
Nansei Shoto (Ryukyu) (isls.), Japan 81/M6
Nansen (sound), N.W. Terrs. 187/J1
Nanson, N. Dak. (58354) 282/L2
Nantahala, N.C. (†28702) 281/B4
Nantahala (lake), N.C. 281/B4
Nantai (mt.), Japan 81/J5
Nantasket Beach, Mass. (†02045) 249/E7
Nanterre, France 28/A1
Nantes, France 28/C4
Nantes, France 7/D4
Nantes, Québec 172/F4
Nanticoke (riv.), Del. 245/R6
Nanticoke, Md. (21840) 245/P7
Nanticoke (riv.), Md. 245/P7
Nanticoke, Ontario 177/E5
Nanticoke, Pa. (18634) 294/E7
Nanton, Alberta 182/D4
Nantong, China 77/K5
Nantua, France 28/F4
Nantucket (co.), Mass. 249/O7
Nantucket, Mass. (02554) 249/O7
Nantucket◯, Mass. (02554) 249/O7
Nantucket (isl.), Mass. 188/N2
Nantucket (isl.), Mass. 249/O8
Nantucket (sound), Mass. 249/N6
Nanty Glo, Pa. (15943) 294/E5
Nantyglo and Blaina, Wales 13/B6
Nanuet, N.Y. (10954) 276/K8
Nanuktok (isls.), Newf. 166/C2
Nanuku (passage), Fiji 86/R10
Nanumea (atoll), Tuvalu 87/H6
Nanuque, Brazil 132/F7
Nanuque, Brazil 120/E4
Nanxiong, China 77/H6
Nanyang, China 77/H5
Nanyuki, Kenya 115/G3
Nanzhang, China 77/H5
Nanzhao, China 77/H5
Nao (cape), Spain 33/G3
Naococane (lake), Québec 174/C2
Naolinco de Victoria, Mexico 150/P1
Naomi, Ky. (†42544) 237/M6
Náousa, Greece 45/F5
Napa, Calif. 188/B3
Napa (co.), Calif. 204/C5
Napa, Calif. (94558) 204/C5
Napadogan, New Bruns. 170/D2
Napa Junction, Calif. (†94590) 204/J1
Napakiak, Alaska (99634) 196/F2
Napaktok (bay), Newf. 166/B2
Napanee, Ontario 177/G3
Napanoch, N.Y. (12458) 276/M7
Napaskiak, Alaska (99559) 196/F2
Napata (ruins), Sudan 111/F4
Napavine, Wash. (98565) 310/C4
Napè, Laos 72/E3
Naper, Nebr. (68755) 264/E2
Naperville, Ill. (60540) 222/A6
Napf (mt.), Switzerland 39/E3
Napier, Ky. (†40851) 237/P7
Napier, N. Zealand 100/F3
Napier, N. Zealand 87/H9
Napier (mt.), North Terr. 93/A4
Napier, W. Va. (26631) 312/E5
Napier Field, Ala. (36303) 195/H8
Napierville (co.), Québec 172/D4
Napierville, Québec 172/D4
Napili-Honokowai, Hawaii (†96761) 218/H1
Napinka, Manitoba 179/B5
Naplate, Ill. (†61350) 222/E2
Naples, Fla. (*33940) 212/E5
Naples, Idaho (83847) 220/B1
Naples, Ill. (62669) 222/C4
Naples (prov.), Italy 34/E4
Naples, Italy 7/F4
Naples, Italy 34/E4
Naples◯, Maine (04055) 243/B8
Naples, N.Y. (14512) 276/F5
Naples, S. Dak. (†57271) 298/O4
Naples, Texas (75568) 303/K4
Naples Park, Fla. (†33940) 212/E5
Napo (riv.) 120/B3
Napo, China 77/G7
Napo (prov.), Ecuador 128/D3
Napo (riv.), Ecuador 128/D3
Napo (riv.), Peru 128/F4
Napoleon, Ind. (47034) 227/G6
Napoleon, Mich. (49261) 250/E6
Napoleon, Mo. (64074) 261/E4
Napoleon, N. Dak. (58561) 282/L6
Napoleon, Ohio (43545) 284/B3
Naponee, Nebr. (68960) 264/E4
Nappa Merri, Queensland 95/B5
Nappan, Nova Scotia 168/D3
Nappanee, Ind. (46550) 227/F2
Napperby, North. Terr. 93/C7
Napton, Mo. (65346) 261/F4
Naqa (ruins), Sudan 111/F4
Nara (pref.), Japan 81/J8
Nara, Japan 81/J8
Nara, Mali 106/C5
Naracoopa, Tasmania 99/B1
Naracoorte, S. Australia 88/F7
Naracoorte, S. Australia 94/G7
Naradhan, N.S. Wales 97/D3
Naramata, Br. Col. 184/H5
Naranja, Fla. (33032) 212/F6
Naranjal (riv.), Ecuador 128/C4
Naranjito, Honduras 154/C3
Naranjito, P. Rico 161/D1
Naranjos, Mexico 150/L6
Naraq, Iran 66/G3
Narashino, Japan 81/P2
Narathiwat, Thailand 72/D6
Nara Visa, N. Mex. (88430) 274/F3
Narayanganj, Bangladesh 68/G4
Narayanpet, India 68/D5
Narberth, Pa. (19072) 294/M6
Narberth, Wales 13/C6
Narbonne, France 28/E6
Narcissa, Okla. (†74354) 288/S1
Narcisse, Manitoba 179/E4
Narcondam (isl.), India 68/G6
Narcoossee, Fla. (†32769) 212/E3
Nardin, Okla. (74646) 288/M1
Nardò, Italy 34/F4
Naré, Argentina 143/F5
Nare, Colombia 126/C4
Narellan, N.S. Wales 97/F3
Nares (str.) 146/L2
Nares (str.), N.W.T. 162/N3
Nares (str.), N.W. Terrs. 187/L2
Narew (riv.), Poland 47/E2
Naricual, Venezuela 124/F2
Narinda, Madagascar 118/H3
Nariño (dept.), Colombia 126/B7
Nariva (swamp), Trin. & Tob. 161/B10
Narka, Kansas (66960) 232/E2
Narmada (riv.), India 54/J7
Narmada (riv.), India 68/D4
Narman, Turkey 63/J2
Narnaul, India 68/D3
Narni, Italy 34/D3
Naro, Italy 34/D6
Narodnaya (mt.), U.S.S.R. 7/K2
Narodnaya (mt.), U.S.S.R. 48/G3
Narodnaya (mt.), U.S.S.R. 52/J1
Narok, Kenya 115/G4
Narooma, N.S. Wales 97/F5
Narrabeen, N. S. Wales 88/L3
Narrabeen, N.S. Wales 97/K3
Narrabri, N. S. Wales 88/J6
Narrabri, N.S. Wales 97/E2
Narragansett, R.I. (02882) 249/J7
Narragansett◯, R.I. (02882) 249/J7
Narragansett (bay), R.I. 249/J6
Narran (lake), N.S. Wales 97/D1
Narran (riv.), N.S. Wales 97/D1
Narrandera, N. S. Wales 88/H6
Narrandera, N.S. Wales 97/D4
Narre Warren North, Victoria 97/K5
Narrogin, W. Australia 88/B6
Narrogin, W. Australia 92/B2
Narromine, N. S. Wales 88/H6
Narromine, N.S. Wales 97/E3
Narrows, Ky. (42358) 237/H5
Narrows, Oreg. (†97721) 291/H4
Narrows, The (str.), St. Chris.-Nevis 161/D11
Narrows, The (str.), Virgin Is. (Br.) 161/C4
Narrows, The (str.), Virgin Is. (U.S.) 161/C4
Narrows, Va. (24124) 307/G6
Narrowsburg, N.Y. (12764) 276/L7
Narrows Park-La Vale, Md. (†21502) 245/C2
Narsimhapur, India 68/D4
Narsinghgarh, India 68/D4
Narssaq, Greenl. 4/C12
Naruna, Va. (24576) 307/L6
Narva, U.S.S.R. 52/C3
Narva, U.S.S.R. 53/E1
Narva (res.), U.S.S.R. 53/D1
Narvik, Norway 4/C9
Narvik, Norway 7/F2
Narvik, Norway 18/K2
Nary, Minn. (†56601) 255/D3
Nar'yan-Mar, U.S.S.R. 4/C7
Nar'yan-Mar, U.S.S.R. 7/K2
Nar'yan-Mar, U.S.S.R. 48/F3
Nar'yan-Mar, U.S.S.R. 52/H1
Naryn, U.S.S.R. 48/H5
Nasarawa, Nigeria 106/F7
Năsăud, Romania 45/G2
Naseby, N. Zealand 100/C6
Naseby, Sask. 181/C3
Naselle, Wash. (98638) 310/B4
Naselle (riv.), Wash. 310/B4
Nash (stream), N.H. 268/E2
Nash (co.), N.C. 281/O2
Nash, N. Dak. (58264) 282/P3
Nash, Okla. (73761) 288/K1
Nash, Texas (75569) 303/K4
Nashawena (isl.), Mass. 249/L7
Nash Creek, New Bruns. 170/D1
Nashoba, Okla. (74558) 288/R6
Nashotah, Wis. (53058) 317/J1
Nashport, Ohio (43830) 284/F5
Nashua, Iowa (50658) 229/J3
Nashua (riv.), Mass. 249/H3
Nashua, Minn. (56565) 255/B4
Nashua, Mont. (59248) 262/K2
Nashua, N.H. 188/M2
Nashua, N.H. (03060) 268/D6
Nashville, Ark. (71852) 202/C6
Nashville, Georgia (31639) 217/F8
Nashville, Ill. (62263) 222/D5
Nashville, Ind. (47448) 227/E6
Nashville, Kansas (67112) 232/D4
Nashville, Mich. (49073) 250/D6
Nashville, Mo. (†64855) 261/D8
Nashville, N.C. (27856) 281/O3
Nashville, Ohio (44661) 284/F4
Nashville, Oreg. (†97370) 291/D3
Nashville (cap.), Tenn. 146/K6
Nashville (cap.), Tenn. 188/J3
Nashville (cap.), Tenn. (*37201) 237/H8
Nashwaak (riv.), New Bruns. 170/D2
Nashwaak Bridge, New Bruns. 170/D2
Nashwaak Village, New Bruns. 170/D2
Nashwauk, Minn. (55769) 255/E3
Našice, Yugoslavia 45/C3
Nasielsk, Poland 47/E2
Näsijärvi (lake), Finland 18/O6
Nasik, India 68/C5
Nasik, India 54/J8
Nasir, Sudan 111/F6
Nasirabad, Bangladesh 68/G4
Nasirabad, India 68/C3
Naskaupi (riv.), Newf. 166/B3
Naso (pt.), Philippines 82/C5
Nason, Ill. (†62816) 222/D5
Nasonville, R.I. (†02830) 249/H5
Nasratabad (Zabol), Iran 59/H3
Nasratabad (Zabol), Iran 66/M5
Nass (riv.), Br. Col. 184/C2
Nassau (cap.), Bahamas 146/L7
Nassau (cap.), Bahamas 156/C1
Nassau (bay), Chile 120/C8
Nassau (bay), Chile 138/F11
Nassau (isl.), Cook Is. 87/K7
Nassau, Del. (19969) 245/T6
Nassau (co.), Fla. 212/E1
Nassau (riv.), Fla. 212/E1
Nassau (sound), Fla. 212/E1
Nassau, Minn. (56272) 255/B5
Nassau (co.), N.Y. 276/N9
Nassau, N.Y. (12123) 276/N5
Nassau Bay, Texas (†77598) 303/K2
Nassawadox, Va. (23413) 307/S6
Nassawango (creek), Md. 245/S8
Nasser (lake), Egypt 102/F2
Nasser (lake), Egypt 111/F3
Nasser (lake), Egypt 59/F3
Nassereith, Austria 41/A3
Nässjö, Sweden 18/J8
Nassogne, Belgium 27/G8
Nasty (creek), S. Dak. 298/C2
Nasu (mt.), Japan 81/J5
Nata, Botswana 118/D4
Natá, Panama 154/G6
Natagaima, Colombia 126/C6
Natal, Brazil 2/H6
Natal, Brazil 132/H4
Natal, Brazil 120/F3
Natal, Br. Col. 184/K5
Natal (prov.), S. Africa 102/F7
Natal (prov.), S. Africa 118/E5
Natalbany, La. (70451) 238/N1
Natalia, Texas (78059) 303/J11
Natalicio Talavera, Paraguay 144/D4
Natanz, Iran 59/F3
Natanz, Iran 66/H4
Natashquan (riv.) 162/K5
Natashquan (riv.), Newf. 166/B3
Natashquan, Québec 174/E3
Natashquan (riv.), Québec 174/E2
Natashquan-Est (riv.), Newf. 166/B3
Natchaug (riv.), Conn. 210/G1
Natchez, Ala. (†36425) 195/D7
Natchez, La. (71456) 238/D3
Natchez, Miss. 188/H4
Natchez, Miss. (39120) 256/B7
Natchitoches (par.), La. 238/D3
Natchitoches, La. (71457) 238/D3
Naters, Switzerland 39/E4
Natewa (bay), Fiji 86/Q10
Nathalia, Victoria 97/C5
Nathalie, Va. (24577) 307/L7
Nathan, Mich. (†49821) 250/B3
Nathrop, Colo. (81236) 208/H5
Natick◯, Mass. (01760) 249/A7
Natick, R.I. (†02887) 249/H6
Natimuk, Victoria 97/A5
Nation (riv.), Br. Col. 184/F2
National Agricultural Research Center, Md. 245/G3
National Capital Region (Manila) (prov.), Philippines 82/C3
National City, Calif. (92050) 204/J11
National City, Mich. (48748) 250/F4
National Gardens, Fla. (†32074) 212/E2
National Mills, Manitoba 179/A2
National Mine, Mich. (49865) 250/B2
National Park, N.J. (08063) 273/B3
National Park, Switzerland 39/K3
National Reactor Testing Sta. (U.S.A.E.C.), Idaho 220/F6
National Stock Yards, Ill. (62071) 222/A2
Natitingou, Benin 106/E6
Natividade, Brazil 132/E5
Natmauk, Burma 72/B2
Natoma, Kansas (67651) 232/D2
Natron (lake), Kenya 115/G4
Natron (lake), Tanzania 115/G4
Natrona (co.), Wyo. 319/F3
Natrona, Wyo. (82646) 319/F2
Natrona Heights, Pa. (15065) 294/C4
Nattavaara, Sweden 18/M3
Natuna (isls.), Indonesia 54/M9
Natuna (isls.), Indonesia 85/D5
Natural Bridge, Ala. (35577) 195/C2
Natural Bridge, N.Y. (13665) 276/K2
Natural Bridge, Va. (24578) 307/J5
Natural Bridges Nat'l Mon., Utah 304/E6
Natural Bridge Station, Va. (24579) 307/K5
Natural Dam, N.Y. (†13642) 276/J2
Naturaliste (cape), Tasmania 99/E2
Naturaliste (cape), W. Australia 88/A6
Naturaliste (chan.), W. Australia 88/A5
Naturaliste (cape), W. Australia 92/A6

N'Gounié 417

New Britain, Pa. (18901) 294/M5
New Brockton, Ala. (36351) 195/G8
Newbrook, Alberta 182/D2
New Brunswick (prov.) 162/K6
New Brunswick (prov.), Canada 146/M5
NEW BRUNSWICK 170
New Brunswick, N.J. (*08901) 273/E3
New Buena Vista, Pa. (†15550) 294/E5
New Buffalo, Mich. (49117) 250/C7
New Buffalo, Pa. (17069) 294/H5
Newburg, Ark. (72556) 202/G1
Newburg, Iowa (†50135) 229/H5
Newburg, Md. (20664) 245/L7
Newburg, Mo. (65550) 261/J7
Newburg, N. Dak. (58762) 282/J2
Newburg, Pa. (17240) 294/G5
Newburg (La Jose), Pa. (†15753) 294/E4
Newburg, W. Va. (26410) 312/G4
Newburg, Wis. (53060) 317/K9
Newburgh, Ind. (47630) 227/C9
Newburgh◯, Maine (†04445) 243/F6
Newburgh, N.Y. 188/M2
Newburgh, N.Y. (12550) 276/M7
Newburgh, Ontario 177/H3
Newburgh, Scotland 10/E2
Newburgh, Grampian, Scotland 15/G3
Newburgh, Fife, Scotland 15/E4
Newburgh Heights, Ohio (†44101) 284/H9
New Burlington, Ind. (†47302) 227/G4
New Burlington, Ohio (†45201) 284/B9
New Burnside, Ill. (62967) 222/E6
Newbury, England 13/F6
Newbury, England 10/F5
Newbury◯, Mass. (01950) 249/L1
Newbury◯, N.H. (03255) 268/C5
Newbury, Ohio (44065) 284/H3
Newbury, Ontario 177/C5
Newbury, Vt. (05051) 268/C3
Newbury◯, Vt. (05051) 268/C3
Newburyport, Mass. (01950) 249/L1
New Bussa, Nigeria 106/E6
New Caledonia (isl.) 2/T7
NEW CALEDONIA 86
New Caledonia 87/G8
New Caledonia (isl.), New Caled. 87/G8
New Caledonia (isl.), New Caled. 86/G4
New Cambria, Kansas (67470) 232/E3
New Cambria, Mo (63558) 261/G3
New Canaan◯, Conn. (06840) 210/B4
New Canton, Ill. (62356) 222/B4
New Canton, Va. (23123) 307/M5
New Carlisle, Ind. (46552) 227/E1
New Carlisle, Ohio (45344) 284/C6
New Carlisle, Québec 172/D2
New Carlisle, Québec 174/E3
New Carrollton, Md. (20784) 245/G4
New Castile (reg.), Spain 33/E3
Newcastle, Australia 2/S7
Newcastle, Calif. (95658) 204/C8
New Castle, Colo. (81647) 208/E3
New Castle (co.), Del. 245/R2
New Castle, Del. (19720) 245/R2
New Castle, Ind. (47362) 227/G5
Newcastle, Ireland 10/B4
Newcastle, Ireland 17/D7
New Castle, Ky. (40050) 237/L4
Newcastle◯, Maine (04553) 243/D7
Newcastle, N. Br. 162/K6
Newcastle, N. S. Wales 88/J6
Newcastle, Nebr. (68757) 264/H2
Newcastle, New Bruns. 170/E2
New Castle◯, N.H. (03854) 268/F5
Newcastle, N.S. Wales 97/F3
Newcastle, N. Ireland 10/D3
Newcastle, N. Ireland 17/J3
Newcastle (creek), North. Terr. 93/C4
New Castle, Ohio (†43843) 284/F5
Newcastle, Okla. (73065) 288/L4
Newcastle, Ontario 177/F4
New Castle, Pa. 188/K2
New Castle, Pa. (*16101) 294/B3
Newcastle, St. Chris.-Nevis 161/D11
Newcastle, S. Africa 118/E5
Newcastle, Texas (76372) 303/F4
Newcastle, Utah (84756) 304/A6
New Castle, Va. (24127) 307/H5
Newcastle, Wyo. (82701) 319/H2
Newcastle Creek, New Bruns. 170/D2
Newcastle-Damariscotta, Maine (04553) 243/E7
Newcastle Emlyn, Wales 13/C5
Newcastleton, Scotland 15/F5
Newcastle-under-Lyme, England 13/E4
Newcastle-under-Lyme, England 10/E4
Newcastle upon Tyne, England 17/J3
Newcastle upon Tyne, England 10/E3
Newcastle upon Tyne, England 13/H3
Newcastle Waters, North. Terr. 93/C4
New Centerville, Pa. (†15557) 294/D6
New Chelsea, Newf. 166/D2
New Chicago, Ind. (†46342) 227/C1
New Church, Va. (23415) 307/S5
New Cinema, Br. Col. 184/F3
New City, N.Y. (10956) 276/K8
New Columbia, Pa. (17856) 294/H3
New Columbus, Pa. (†17878) 294/K3
Newcomb, N. Mex. (†87325) 274/A2
Newcomb, N.Y. (12852) 276/M3
Newcomb, Tenn. (37819) 237/N7
Newcomerstown, Ohio (43832) 284/G5
New Concord, Ky. (42076) 237/E7
New Concord, Ohio (43762) 284/G6
New Cordell (Cordell), Okla. (†73632) 288/H4
New Corydon, Ind. (†47326) 227/H3
New Court, Mo. (†63452) 261/J2
New Creek, W. Va. (26743) 312/J4
New Cumberland, Pa. (17070) 294/J5
New Cumberland, W. Va. (26047) 312/E2
New Cumnock, Scotland 15/D5
Newdale, Idaho (83436) 220/G6
Newdale, Manitoba 179/B4
New Dayton, Alberta 182/D5
New Deal, Texas (79350) 303/C4
New Deer, Scotland 15/F3
Newdegate, W. Australia 92/B6
New Delhi (cap.), India 2/N4
New Delhi, India 54/J7
New Delhi (cap.), India 68/D3
New Denmark, New Bruns. 170/C1
New Denver, Br. Col. 184/J5
New Diggings, Wis. (†61075) 317/F10
New Douglas, Ill. (62074) 222/D5
New Dover, Ohio (†43040) 284/D5
New Durham◯, N.H. (03855) 268/E5
New Eagle, Pa. (15067) 294/B5
New Edinburg, Ark. (71660) 202/F6
New Effington, S. Dak. (57255) 298/R2
New Egypt, N.J. (08533) 273/E3
Newell, Ala. (36270) 195/H4
Newell (lake), Alberta 182/E4
Newell, Iowa (50568) 229/D3
Newell, S. Dak. (57760) 298/C4
Newell, W. Va. (26050) 312/E1
New Ellenton, S.C. (29809) 296/D5
Newellton, La. (71357) 238/H2
Newellton, Nova Scotia 168/C5
New England (range), N.S. Wales 97/F1
New England, N. Dak. (58647) 282/E6
New England, W. Va. (26154) 312/C4
Newenham (cape), Alaska 196/F3
New Enterprise, Pa. (16664) 294/F5
New Era, La. (†71354) 238/G4
New Era, Mich. (49446) 250/C5
New Era, Oreg. (†97013) 291/B2
Newe Yam, Israel 65/B2
Newe Zohar, Israel 65/C5
New Fairfield◯, Conn. (06810) 210/B3
Newfane, N.Y. (14108) 276/C4
Newfane, Vt. (05345) 268/B6
Newfane◯, Vt. (05345) 268/B6
Newfield, Maine (04056) 243/B8
Newfield◯, Maine (04056) 243/B8
Newfield, N.J. (08344) 273/D4
Newfield, N.Y. (14867) 276/G6
Newfields◯, N.H. (03856) 268/F5
New Fish Creek, Alberta 182/B2
New Florence, Mo. (63363) 261/K5
New Florence, Pa. (15944) 294/D5
Newfolden, Minn. (56738) 255/B2
New Fork (lakes), Wyo. 319/C2
Newfound (lake), N.H. 268/D4
Newfoundland (prov.) 162/L5
Newfoundland (isl.) 162/L6
Newfoundland (prov.), Canada 146/M4
Newfoundland (isl.), Canada 2/G3
Newfoundland, Ky. (41162) 237/P4
NEWFOUNDLAND 166
Newfoundland (isl.), Newf. 166/C4
Newfoundland (isl.), Newf. 146/N5
Newfoundland, N.J. (07435) 273/D1
Newfoundland, Pa. (18445) 294/M3
Newfoundland (mts.), Utah 304/A2
New Franken, Wis. (54229) 317/L6
New Frankfort, Mo. (†65349) 261/F4
New Franklin, Mo. (65274) 261/G4
New Freedom, Pa. (17349) 294/J6
New Freeport, Pa. (15352) 294/B6
New Galilee, Pa. (16141) 294/A4
New Galloway, Scotland 10/D3
New Galloway, Scotland 15/D5
Newgate, Br. Col. 184/K5
New Georgia (isl.), Solomon Is. 87/F6
New Georgia (isl.), Solomon Is. 86/D3
New Germantown, Pa. (17071) 294/G5
New Germany, Minn. (55367) 255/E6
New Germany, Nova Scotia 168/D4
New Glarus, Wis. (53574) 317/G10
New Glasgow, Nova Scotia 168/F3
New Glasgow, Québec 172/D4
New Gloucester, Maine (04260) 243/C8
New Gloucester◯, Maine (04260) 243/C8
New Goshen, Ind. (47863) 227/B5
New Gretna, N.J. (08224) 273/E4
New Guinea (isl.) 2/S6
New Guinea (isl.) 54/P10
New Guinea (isl.) 87/E6
New Guinea (isl.), Papua N.G. 86/B2
Newgulf, Texas (77462) 303/J8
Newhalem, Wash. (†98283) 310/D2
Newhalen, Alaska (†99606) 196/H3
Newhall, Calif. (91321) 204/G9
Newhall, Iowa (52315) 229/K5
Newhall, W. Va. (24866) 312/C8
Newham, England 13/H8
Newham, England 10/B5
New Hamburg, Mo. (†63736) 261/08
New Hamburg, Ontario 177/D4
New Hampshire 188/M2
NEW HAMPSHIRE 268
New Hampshire, Ohio (45870) 284/C4
New Hampshire (state), U.S. 146/L5
New Hampton, Iowa (50659) 229/J2
New Hampton, Mo. (64471) 261/D2
New Hampton◯, N.H. (03256) 268/D4
New Hampton, N.J. (†08827) 273/D2
New Hanover (co.), N.C. 281/06
New Hanover (Lavongai) (isl.), Papua N.G. 87/F6
New Hanover (isl.), Papua N.G. 86/B1
New Harbor, Maine (04554) 243/E8
New Harbour, Newf. 166/C4
New Harbour, Newf. 166/D2
New Harbour, Nova Scotia 168/G3
New Harmony, Ind. (47631) 227/B8
New Harmony, Utah (84757) 304/A6
New Hartford, Conn. (06057) 210/C1
New Hartford◯, Conn. (06057) 210/C1
New Hartford, Iowa (50660) 229/H3
New Hartford, Mo. (63364) 261/K4
New Hartford, N.Y. (13413) 276/K4
New Haven, Conn. 188/M2
New Haven (co.), Conn. 210/D3
New Haven, Conn. (*06501) 210/D3
New Haven (harb.), Conn. 210/D3
Newhaven, England 10/F5
Newhaven, England 13/H7
New Haven, Ill. (62867) 222/E6
New Haven, Ind. (46774) 227/H2
New Haven, Ky. (40051) 237/K5
New Haven, Mich. (48048) 250/G6
New Haven, Mo. (63068) 261/K5
New Haven, N.Y. (13121) 276/H4
New Haven, Nova Scotia 168/H2
New Haven, Ohio (44850) 284/E3
New Haven◯, Vt. (05472) 268/A3
New Haven, W. Va. (25265) 312/C5
New Haven, Wyo. (†82720) 319/H1
New Hazelton, Br. Col. 184/D2
New Hebrides (Vanuatu) 87/G7
Newhebron, Miss. (39140) 256/D7
New Hill, N.C. (27562) 281/M3
New Holland, Georgia (†30501) 217/E2
New Holland, Ill. (62671) 222/D3
New Holland, N.C. (27885) 281/S4
New Holland, Ohio (43145) 284/D6
New Holland, Pa. (17557) 294/K5
New Holland, S. Dak. (57364) 298/M7
New Holstein, Wis. (53061) 317/K8
New Home, Texas (79383) 303/C4
New Hope, Ala. (35760) 195/F1
Newhope, Ark. (71959) 202/C5
New Hope, Ky. (40052) 237/L5
New Hope, Minn. (†55428) 255/G5
New Hope, Ohio (†45320) 284/A6
New Hope, Pa. (18938) 294/N5
New Hope, Tenn. (†37380) 237/K11
New Hope, Va. (24469) 307/L4
New Horse Springs, N. Mex. (†87821) 274/A5
New Houlka (Houlka), Miss. (38850) 256/G2
New Hradec, N. Dak. (58648) 282/E5
New Hyde Park, N.Y. (11040) 276/P7
New Iberia, La. (70560) 238/G6
Newington◯, Conn. (06111) 210/E2
Newington, Georgia (30446) 217/J5
Newington◯, N.H. (†03801) 268/F5
Newington, Ontario 177/K2
Newington, Va. (22122) 307/S3
New Ipswich◯, N.H. (03071) 268/D6
New Ireland (isl.), Papua N.G. 87/F6
New Ireland (isl.), Papua N.G. 86/B1
New Jersey 188/M3
NEW JERSEY 273
New Jersey, New Bruns. 170/E1
New Jersey (state), U.S. 146/L5
New Johnsonville, Tenn. (37134) 237/E8
New Kensington, Pa. (15068) 294/C4
New Kent (co.), Va. 307/P5
New Kent, Va. (23124) 307/P5
Newkirk, N. Mex. (88431) 274/E3
Newkirk, Okla. (74647) 288/N1
New Knoxville, Ohio (45871) 284/B5
New Laguna, N. Mex. (87038) 274/B4
New Lancaster, Kansas (†66040) 232/H3
Newland, Ind. (†47978) 227/C2
Newland, N.C. (28657) 281/F2
New Lebanon, Ind. (47864) 227/C6
New Lebanon, N.Y. (12125) 276/O6
New Lebanon, Ohio (45345) 284/B6
New Lebanon, Pa. (†16145) 294/B3
New Leipzig, N. Dak. (58562) 282/G7
New Lenox, Ill. (60451) 222/B6
New Lexington, Ohio (43764) 284/F6
New Liberty, Iowa (52765) 229/M5
New Liberty, Ky. (40355) 237/M3
New Lima, Okla. (74884) 288/O4
New Limerick◯, Maine (04761) 243/G3
Newlin, Texas (†79245) 303/D3
New Lisbon, Ind. (47366) 227/G5
New Lisbon, N.J. (08064) 273/D4
New Lisbon, Wis. (53950) 317/F8
New Liskeard, Ont. 162/H6
New Liskeard, Ontario 177/K5
New Liskeard, Ontario 175/E3
Newllano, La. (71461) 238/D4
New London, Ark. (†71765) 202/F7
New London, Conn. 188/M2
New London (co.), Conn. 210/G2
New London, Conn. (06320) 210/G3
New London, Ind. (†46979) 227/E4
New London, Iowa (52645) 229/L7
New London, Minn. (56273) 255/C5
New London, Mo. (63459) 261/K3
New London, N.H. (03257) 268/D5
New London◯, N.H. (03257) 268/D5
New London, N.C. (28127) 281/J4
New London, Ohio (44851) 284/F3
New London (bay), Pr. Edward I. 168/E2
New London, Texas (75682) 303/K5
New London, Wis. (54961) 317/J7
New Lothrop, Mich. (48460) 250/F5
New Lowell, Ontario 177/E3
New Lyme, Ohio (44066) 284/J2
New Lynn, N. Zealand 100/B1
New Madison, Ohio (45346) 284/A6
New Madrid (co.), Mo. 261/N9
New Madrid, Mo. (63869) 261/O9
Newmains, Scotland 15/C2
Newman, Calif. (95360) 204/D6
Newman, Ill. (61942) 222/B6
Newman, Ky. (†42301) 237/G5
Newman (sound), Newf. 166/D2
Newman, W. Australia 88/C4
Newman (lake), Wash. 310/H3
Newman, W. Australia 92/B3
New Manchester, W. Va. (26056) 312/E1
Newman Grove, Nebr. (68758) 264/G3
Newman Lake, Wash. (99025) 310/J3
Newmans Cove, Newf. 166/D2
New Marion, Ind. (†47023) 227/G6
New Market, Ala. (35761) 195/F1
Newmarket, England 13/H5
Newmarket, England 10/G4
New Market, Ind. (47965) 227/D5
New Market, Iowa (51646) 229/D7
Newmarket, Ireland 10/B4
Newmarket, Ireland 17/C7
Newmarket, Jamaica 158/H6
New Market, Md. (21774) 245/J3
New Market, Minn. (55054) 255/E6
New Market, Mo. (†64439) 261/C4
Newmarket, New Bruns. 170/D3
Newmarket, N.H. (03857) 268/F5
Newmarket◯, N.H. (03857) 268/F5
New Market, Ohio (†45133) 284/C7
Newmarket, Ontario 177/E3
Newmarket, Queensland 88/K2
Newmarket, Queensland 95/D2
Newmarket, Scotland 15/B2
New Market, Tenn. (37820) 237/O8
New Market, Va. (22844) 307/L3
Newmarket-on-Fergus, Ireland 17/D6
New Marlborough◯, Mass. (†01230) 249/B4
New Martinsburg, Ohio (†43160) 284/D7
New Martinsville, W. Va. (26155) 312/E3
New Maryland, New Bruns. 170/D3
New Matamoras, Ohio (45767) 284/J6
New Meadows, Idaho (83654) 220/B4
New Melle, Mo. (63365) 261/L5
New Memphis, Ill. (62266) 222/D5
Newmerella, Victoria 97/E5
New Mexico 188/E4
NEW MEXICO 274
New Mexico (state), U.S. 146/H6
New Miami, Ohio (45011) 284/A7
New Middleton, Tenn. (†38563) 237/J8
New Middletown, Ind. (47160) 227/E8
New Middletown, Ohio (44442) 284/J4
New Milford, Conn. (06776) 210/B2
New Milford◯, Conn. (06776) 210/B2
New Milford, N.J. (07646) 273/B1
New Milford, Ohio (†44272) 284/H3
New Milford, Pa. (18834) 294/L2
Newmill, Scotland 15/E3
New Mills, England 13/J2
New Mills, England 10/G2
Newmilns and Greenholm, Scotland 15/D5
New Milton, W. Va. (26411) 312/E4
New Minas, Nova Scotia 168/D3
New Minden, Ill. (†62263) 222/D5
New Mount Pleasant, Ind. (†47371) 227/G4
New Munich, Minn. (56356) 255/D5
Newnan, Georgia (30263) 217/C4
Newnans (lake), Fla. 212/D2
New Norcia, W. Australia 92/A5
New Norfolk, Tasmania 88/H8
New Norfolk, Tasmania 99/C4
New Norway, Alberta 182/D3
New Offenburg, Mo. (63661) 261/M7
New Orleans, La. 188/H5
New Orleans, La. 146/K7
New Orleans, La. (*70101) 238/O4
New Orleans, U.S. 2/E4
New Osgoode, Sask. 181/H3
New Oxford, Pa. (17350) 294/H6
New Palestine, Ind (46163) 227/F5
New Pallas, Ireland 17/E6
New Paltz, N.Y. (12561) 276/M7
New Paris, Ind. (46553) 227/F2
New Paris, Ohio (45347) 284/A6
New Paris, Pa. (15554) 294/E5
New Pass (range), Nev. 266/D3
New Pekin, Ind. (†47165) 227/F7
New Perlican, Newf. 166/D2
New Petersburg, Ohio (†45123) 284/D7
New Philadelphia, Ill. (†61459) 222/C3
New Philadelphia, Ind. (†47167) 227/F7
New Philadelphia, Ohio (44663) 284/G5
New Philadelphia, Pa. (17959) 294/K4
New Pine Creek, Oreg. (97635) 291/G5
New Pitsligo, Scotland 15/F3
New Pittsburg, Ohio (†44691) 284/F4
New Plymouth, Idaho (83655) 220/B6
New Plymouth, N. Zealand 100/D3
New Plymouth, Ohio (45654) 284/F7
New Point, Ind. (47263) 227/G6
New Point, Mo. (64473) 261/B2
Newport, Ark. (72112) 202/H2
Newport, Del. (19804) 245/R2
Newport, England 13/F7
Newport, England 13/E5
Newport, England 10/F5
Newport, Ind. (47966) 227/C5
Newport, Mayo, Ireland 17/C4
Newport, Tipperary, Ireland 17/E6
Newport, Ky. (*41071) 237/S2
Newport, Ky. 188/K3
Newport, Maine (04953) 243/E6
Newport◯, Maine (04953) 243/E6
Newport, Md. (†20622) 245/L7
Newport, Minn. (55055) 255/F6
Newport, Miss. (†38641) 256/D1
Newport, Nebr. (68759) 264/E2
New Port, Neth. Ant. 161/G9
Newport, N.H. (03773) 268/C5
Newport◯, N.H. (03773) 268/C5
Newport, N.J. (08345) 273/C5
Newport, N.Y. (13416) 276/K4
Newport, N.C. (28570) 281/R5
Newport, Nova Scotia 168/E3
Newport, Ohio (†43140) 284/C6
Newport, Ohio (45768) 284/H7
Newport, Oreg. (97365) 291/C3
Newport, Pa. (17074) 294/H5
Newport, Québec 172/D2
Newport, R.I. 188/M2
Newport (co.), R.I. 249/K6
Newport, R.I. (02840) 249/J7
Newport, Tenn. (37821) 237/P9
Newport, Texas (76254) 303/F4
Newport, Vt. (05855) 268/C2
Newport◯, Vt. (05855) 268/C2
Newport, Va. (24128) 307/H6
Newport, Wales 10/E5
Newport, Dyfed, Wales 13/C5
Newport, Gwent, Wales 13/B6
Newport, Wash. (99156) 310/H2
Newport Beach, Calif. (*92660) 204/D11
Newport Center, Vt. (05857) 268/C2
New Portland, Maine (04954) 243/C6
New Portland◯, Maine (04954) 243/C6
Newport News, Va. 188/L3
Newport News (I.C.), Va. (*23601) 307/P6
Newport-on-Tay, Scotland 15/F4
Newport Pagnell, England 13/G5
New Port Richey, Fla. (*33552) 212/D3
New Prague, Minn. (56071) 255/E6
New Preston, Conn. (06777) 210/B2
New Providence (isl.), Bahamas 156/C1
New Providence (Borden), Ind. (†47106) 227/F8
New Providence, Iowa (50206) 229/G4
New Providence, N.J. (07974) 273/E2
New Providence, Pa. (17560) 294/K6
New Prue (Prue), Okla. (†74060) 288/O2
Newquay, England 10/D5
Newquay, England 13/B7
New Quay, Wales 10/D4
New Quay, Wales 13/C5
New Raymer, Colo. (80742) 208/M1
New Richland, Minn. (56072) 255/E7
New Richmond, Ind. (47967) 227/D4
New Richmond, Ohio (45157) 284/B8
New Richmond, Québec 172/C2
New Richmond, Wis. (54017) 317/A5
New Riegel, Ohio (44853) 284/D3
New River, N.C. (28540) 281/O5
New River (inlet), N.C. 281/P6
New River, Tenn. (†37755) 237/M8
New River, Va. (24129) 307/G6
New River Beach, New Bruns. 170/D3
New Road, Nova Scotia 168/E4
New Roads, La. (70760) 238/G5
New Rochelle, N.Y. (*10801) 276/P7
New Rockford, N. Dak. (58356) 282/N4
New Romney, England 13/J7
New Ross, Ind. (47968) 227/D5
New Ross, Ireland 10/C4
New Ross, Ireland 17/H7
New Ross, Nova Scotia 168/D4
Newry, Maine (04261) 243/B6
Newry◯, Maine (04261) 243/B6
Newry, N. Ireland 17/J3
Newry, N. Ireland 10/C3
Newry, North. Terr. 93/A3
Newry, Pa. (16665) 294/F5
Newry, S.C. (29665) 296/B2
New Salem, Ill. (62357) 222/C4
New Salem, Ind. (†46173) 227/G5
New Salem, Kansas (†67156) 232/F4
New Salem◯, Mass. (01355) 249/E2
New Salem, N. Dak. (58563) 282/G6
New Salem, Nova Scotia 168/D3
New Salem, Ohio (†43148) 284/E6
New Salem, Pa. (15468) 294/C6
New Salem (Delmont), Pa. (†15626) 294/D5
New Salisbury, Ind. (47161) 227/E8
New Sarepta, Alberta 182/D3
New Sarpy, La. (70078) 238/N4
New Schwabenland (reg.) 5/B1
New Scone, Scotland 15/E4
New Sharon, Iowa (50207) 229/H6
New Sharon◯, Maine (04955) 243/C6
New Sharon, N.J. (†08691) 273/D3
New Shoreham (Block Island)◯, R.I. (†02807) 249/H8
New Siberian (isls.), U.S.S.R. 54/R2
New Siberian (isls.), U.S.S.R. 4/B2
New Siberian (isls.), U.S.S.R. 2/S2
New Siberian (isls.), U.S.S.R. 48/P2
New Site, Ala. (†35010) 195/G4
New Site, Miss. (38859) 256/H1
New Smyrna Beach, Fla. (32069) 212/F2
Newsoms, Va. (23874) 307/O7
New South Wales, /H6
New South Wales (state), Australia 87/E9
NEW SOUTH WALES 97
New Spadra, Ark. (†72830) 202/C3
New Square, N.Y. (†10901) 276/K8
New Stanton, Pa. (15672) 294/C5
New Straitsville, Ohio (43766) 284/F6
New Strawn (Strawn), Kansas (66839) 232/G3
New Stuyahok, Alaska (99636) 196/G3
New Sweden, Maine (04762) 243/G2
New Sweden◯, Maine (04762) 243/G2
New Tazewell, Tenn. (37825) 237/O8
Newtok, Alaska (99681) 196/F2
Newton, Ala. (36352) 195/G8
Newton (co.), Ark. 202/D2
Newton (co.), Georgia 217/E3
Newton, Georgia (31770) 217/D8
Newton, Ill. (62448) 222/E5
Newton (co.), Ind. 227/C3
Newton, Iowa 188/H2
Newton, Iowa (50208) 229/H5
Newton, Kansas (67114) 232/E3
Newton, Mass. (†02158) 249/C7
Newton (co.), Miss. 256/F6
Newton, Miss. (39345) 256/F6
Newton (co.), Mo. 261/D9
Newton◯, N.H. (03858) 268/E6
Newton, N.J. (07860) 273/D1
Newton, N.C. (28658) 281/G3
Newton, Québec 172/C4
Newton, Scotland 15/E5
Newton (co.), Texas 303/L7
Newton, Texas (75966) 303/L7
Newton, Utah (84327) 304/C2
Newton, W. Va. (25266) 312/D5
Newton Abbot, England 13/D7
Newton Abbot, England 10/E5
Newton Center, Mass. (02159) 249/C7
Newton Falls, N.Y. (13666) 276/K2
Newton Falls, Ohio (44444) 284/J3
Newtongrange, Scotland 15/D2
Newton Grove, N.C. (28366) 281/N4
Newton Hamilton, Pa. (17075) 294/G5
Newton Highlands, Mass. (02161) 249/C7
Newtonia, Mo. (64853) 261/D9
Newton Junction, N.H. (03859) 268/E6
Newton-le-Willows, England 13/H2
Newton Lower Falls, Mass. (†02162) 249/B7
Newton Mearns, Scotland 15/B2
Newton Mills, Nova Scotia 168/F3
Newtonmore, Scotland 15/D3
Newton Siding, Manitoba 179/D5
Newton Stewart, Scotland 10/D3
Newton Stewart, Scotland 15/D6
Newtonsville, Ohio (45158) 284/B7
Newton Upper Falls, Mass. (†02164) 249/C7
Newtonville, Ind. (47632) 227/D8
Newtonville, Mass. (02160) 249/C7
Newtonville, N.J. (08346) 273/D4
Newtown, Conn. (06470) 210/B3
Newtown◯, Conn. (06470) 210/B3
Newtown, Ind. (47969) 227/C4
Newtown, Ky. (†40324) 237/N4
Newtown, Mo. (64667) 261/F2
Newtown, New Bruns. 170/E3
Newtown, Newf. 166/D4
Newtown, N.S. Wales 97/C6
New Town, N. Dak. (58763) 282/F4
Newtown, Ohio (45244) 284/C10
Newtown, Pa. (18940) 294/N5
New Town, S.C. (†29536) 296/J3
Newtown, Victoria 97/C6
Newtown, Wales 13/D5
Newtown, Wales 10/E4
Newtownabbey (dist.), N. Ireland 17/J2
Newtownabbey, N. Ireland 17/K2
Newtownards, N. Ireland 17/K2
Newtownbutler, N. Ireland 17/G3
Newtown Forbes, Ireland 17/F4
Newtownhamilton, N. Ireland 17/H3
Newtownmountkennedy, Ireland 17/J5
Newtown Saint Boswells, Scotland 15/F5
Newtownsandes, Ireland 17/C6
Newtown Square◯, Pa. (19073) 294/L6
Newtownstewart, N. Ireland 17/G2
New Trenton, Ind. (47035) 227/H6
New Trier, Minn. (†55031) 255/F6
New Tripoli, Pa. (18066) 294/L4
New Troy, Mich. (49119) 250/C7
New Tulsa, Okla. (†74080) 288/P2
Newtyle, Scotland 15/E4
New Ulm, Minn. (56073) 255/D6
New Ulm, Texas (78950) 303/H8
New Underwood, S. Dak. (57761) 298/D5
New Vernon, N.J. (07976) 273/D2
New Victoria, Nova Scotia 168/H2
New Vienna, Iowa (52065) 229/L3
New Vienna, Ohio (45159) 284/C7
Newville, Ala. (36353) 195/H8
Newville, Ind. (†46721) 227/H2
Newville, Pa. (17241) 294/H5
Newville, W. Va. (26632) 312/E5
New Vineyard◯, Maine (04956) 243/C6
New Virginia, Iowa (50210) 229/F6
New Washington, Ind. (47162) 227/F7
New Washington, Ohio (44854) 284/E4
New Washington, Philippines 82/D5
New Waterford, Nova Scotia 168/J2
New Waterford, Ohio (44445) 284/J4
New Waverly, Ind. (46961) 227/E3
New Waverly, Texas (77358) 303/J7
New Westminster, Br. Col. 162/D6
New Westminster, Br. Col. 184/K3
New Weston, Ohio (45348) 284/A5
New Whiteland, Ind. (46184) 227/E5
New Wilmington, Pa. (16142) 294/B3
New Winchester, Ind. (†46122) 227/D5
New Winchester, Ohio (†44820) 284/D4
New Windsor, England 13/G8
New Windsor, England 10/F5
New Windsor, Ill. (61465) 222/C2
New Windsor, Md. (21776) 245/K2
New Windsor, N.Y. (12550) 276/N8
New Witten, S. Dak. (†57584) 298/K7
New Woodstock, N.Y. (13122) 276/J5
New World (isl.), Newf. 166/C4
New York 188/L2
NEW YORK 276
New York, N.Y. 146/L5
New York, N.Y. 188/M2
New York (co.), N.Y. 276/M9
New York, N.Y. (*10001) 276/M9
New York (state), U.S. 146/L5
New York, U.S. 2/F3
New York Mills, Minn. (56567) 255/C4
New York Mills, N.Y. (13417) 276/K4
New York State Barge (canal), N.Y. 276/C4
New Zealand 2/T8
New Zealand 87/G9
NEW ZEALAND 100
New Zion, New Bruns. 170/D2
New Zion, S.C. (29111) 296/H4
Ney, Ohio (43549) 284/B3
Neyagawa, Japan 81/J7
Neyland, Wales 13/B6
Neyriz, Iran 66/J6
Neyshabur, Iran 59/G2
Neyshabur, Iran 66/L2
Nezhin, U.S.S.R. 52/D4
Nez Perce (co.), Idaho 220/B3
Nezperce, Idaho (83543) 220/B3
Nez Perce Nat'l Hist. Park, Idaho 220/B-C3
Nezwar (mt.), Iran 66/H3
Ngabang, Indonesia 85/D5
N'gage, Angola 115/C5
Ngage, Angola 102/D5
Ngahere, N. Zealand 100/C5
Ngami (lake), Botswana 118/C4
Ngamiland (reg.), Botswana 118/C3
Ngamring, China 77/C6
Ngangla Ringco (lake), China 77/B5
Ngangzê Co (lake), China 77/C5
Ngao, Thailand 72/D3
Ngaoundéré, Cameroon 115/B2
Ngaoundéré, Cameroon 102/D4
Ngapara, N. Zealand 100/C6
Ngara, Tanzania 115/F4
Ngaruawahia, N. Zealand 100/E2
Ngatapa, N. Zealand 100/F3
Ngatik (atoll), Micronesia 87/F5
Ngau (isl.), Fiji 86/Q10
Ngauruhoe (mt.), N. Zealand 100/E3
Ngawi, Indonesia 85/K2
Nghia Lo, Vietnam 72/D2
Ngiva, Angola 102/D6
Ngiva, Angola 115/C7
Ngoc Linh (mt.), Vietnam 72/E4
Ngom Qu (riv.), China 77/E5
Ngong, Kenya 115/G4
Ngoring Hu (lake), China 77/E4
Ngorongoro (crater), Tanzania 115/F4
N'Gounié (riv.), Congo 115/B4

North (riv.), Mass. 249/D2
North (riv.), Mass. 249/L4
North (chan.), Mich. 250/F2
North (pt.), Mich. 250/F3
North (lake), Minn. 255/F1
North (sea), Netherlands 27/E3
North (lake), New Bruns. 170/C3
North (riv.), Newf. 166/C3
North (riv.), Newf. 166/B2
North (isl.), N. Zealand 87/H9
North (cape), N. Zealand 87/H9
North (cape), N. Zealand 100/D1
North (isl.), N. Zealand 100/F1
North (lake), N. Dak. 282/J3
North (chan.), N. Ireland 10/D3
North (chan.), N. Ireland 17/K1
North (Nordkapp) (cape), Norway 7/G1
North (cape), Norway 4/B8
North (cape), N.S. 162/K6
North (cape), Nova Scotia 168/H1
North (mt.), Nova Scotia 168/D3
North (chan.), Ontario 177/A1
North (chan.), Ontario 175/D3
North (mt.), Pa. 294/K3
North (pt.), Pr. Edward I. 168/E1
North (chan.), Scotland 10/D3
North (chan.), Scotland 15/C5
North (sound), Scotland 15/G4
North (sound), Scotland 15/F1
North (isl.), Seychelles 118/H5
North, S.C. (29112) 296/E4
North (inlet), S.C. 296/J5
North (isl.), S.C. 296/J5
North (pt.), Tasmania 99/E1
North (creek), Utah 304/C6
North (lake), Utah 304/B2
North (riv.), Wash. 310/B4
North (sea), W. Germany 22/B2
North (riv.), W. Va. 312/J4
North (lake), Wis. 317/J1
North Abington, Mass. (02351) 249/L4
North Acton, Mass. (†01720) 249/J2
North Adams, Mass. (01247) 249/B2
North Adams, Mich. (49262) 250/E7
Northallerton, England 10/F3
Northallerton, England 13/F3
Northam, England 13/C6
Northam, W. Australia 88/B6
Northam, W. Australia 92/B1
NORTH AMERICA 146
North America 2/C4
North Amherst, Mass. (01059) 249/E3
North Amity, Maine (04465) 243/H4
Northampton, England 13/F5
Northampton, England 10/F4
Northampton, Mass. (01060) 249/D3
Northampton (co.), N.C. 281/P2
Northampton (co.), Pa. 294/M4
Northampton, Pa. (18067) 294/M4
Northampton (co.), Va. 307/S6
Northampton, W. Australia 88/A5
Northampton, W. Australia 92/A5
Northamptonshire (co.), England 13/G5
North Andaman (isl.), India 68/G6
North Andover○, Mass. (01845) 249/K2
North Anna (riv.), Va. 307/M4
North Anson, Maine (04958) 243/D6
North Apollo, Pa. (15673) 294/D4
North Arlington, N.J. (07032) 273/B2
North Arm (inlet), N.W. Terrs. 187/G3
North Asheboro, N.C. (†27203) 281/K3
North Ashford, Conn. (†06282) 210/G1
North Aspy (riv.), Nova Scotia 168/H2
North Atlantic Ocean 2/H3
North Attleboro○, Mass. (*02760) 249/J5
North Augusta, Ontario 177/J3
North Augusta, S.C. (29841) 296/C5
North Aulatsivik (isl.), Newf. 166/B2
North Aurora, Ill. (60542) 222/E2
North Avondale, Colo. (†81022) 208/L6
North Ballachulish, Scotland 15/C4
North Baltimore, Ohio (45872) 284/C3
North Bangor, N.Y. (12966) 276/M1
North Barrington, Ill. (†60010) 222/A5
North Bass (isl.), Ohio 284/E2
North Battleford, Sask. 146/H4
North Battleford, Sask. 162/F5
North Battleford, Sask. 181/C3
North Bay, N.Y. (13123) 276/J4
North Bay, Ont. 146/L5
North Bay, Ont. 162/J6
North Bay, Ontario 177/E1
North Bay, Ontario 175/E3
North Bay, Wis. (†53401) 317/M3
North Bay Ingonish (bay), Nova Scotia 168/H2
North Bay Village, Fla. (33141) 212/B4
North Beach, Md. (20831) 245/N6
North Belgrade, Maine (†04963) 243/D7
North Bellingham, Mass. (†02019) 249/J4
North Bend, Br. Col. 184/G5
North Bend, Nebr. (68649) 264/H3
North Bend, Ohio (45052) 284/B9
North Bend, Oreg. (97459) 291/C4
North Bend, Pa. (17760) 294/G3
North Bend, Wash. (98045) 310/D3
North Bend, Wis. (†54642) 317/D7
North Bennington, Vt. (05257) 268/A6
North Bergen○, N.J. (07047) 273/B2
North Berwick, Maine (03906) 243/B9
North Berwick○, Maine (03906) 243/B9
North Berwick, Scotland 15/F4
North Berwick, Scotland 10/E2
North Beveland (isl.), Netherlands 27/D5
North Billerica, Mass. (01862) 249/J2
North Bloomfield, Conn. (†06002) 210/E1
North Bloomfield, Ohio (44450) 284/J3
North Bonneville, Wash. (98639) 310/C5
North Borneo (Sabah) (state), Malaysia 85/F3
Northboro, Iowa (51647) 229/C7
Northborough, Mass. (01532) 249/H3
Northborough○, Mass. (01532) 249/H3
North Boston, N.Y. (14110) 276/C5
North Bourke, N.S. Wales 97/C2
North Brabant (prov.), Netherlands 27/F5
North Braddock, Pa. (15104) 294/C7
North Bradford, Maine (†04410) 243/F5
North Bradley, Mich. (†48618) 250/E5
Northbranch, Kansas (†66936) 232/D2
North Branch, Md. (†21502) 245/D2
North Branch, Mich. (48461) 250/F5
North Branch, Minn. (55056) 255/F5
North Branch, N.H. (†03440) 268/D5
North Branch, N.J. (08876) 273/D2
North Branch Oromocto (riv.), New Bruns. 170/D3
North Branford○, Conn. (06471) 210/E3
North Brentwood, Md. (†20722) 245/F4
Northbridge○, Mass. (01534) 249/H4
North Bridgton, Maine (04057) 243/B7
Northbrook, Ill. (60062) 222/B5
North Brook, Ontario 177/G3
North Brookfield, Mass. (01535) 249/F3
North Brookfield○, Mass. (01535) 249/F3
North Brooksville, Maine (†04617) 243/F7
North Brunswick○, N.J. (08902) 273/D3
North Bruny (isl.), Tasmania 99/D5
North Buena Vista, Iowa (52066) 229/L3
North Calais, Vt. (†05648) 268/C3
North Caldwell, N.J. (†07006) 273/B2
North Calling Lake, Alberta 182/D2
North Canadian (riv.) 188/G3
North Canadian (riv.), Okla. 288/K3
North Canton, Conn. (06059) 210/D1
North Canton, Georgia (†30114) 217/C2
North Canton, Ohio (44720) 284/H4
North Cape (Nordkapp) (pt.), Norway 18/P1
North Cape May, N.J. (08204) 273/C6
North Caribou (lake), Ontario 175/B2
North Carolina 188/L3
NORTH CAROLINA 281
North Carolina (state), U.S. 146/K6
North Carrizo (creek), Colo. 208/N8
North Carrizo (riv.), Okla. 288/A1
North Carrollton, Miss. (38947) 256/E3
North Carter (mt.), N.H. 268/E3
North Carver, Mass. (02355) 249/L5
North Cascades Nat'l Park, Wash. 310/D2
North Catasauqua, Pa. (†18032) 294/L4
North Charleston, S.C. (29406) 296/G6
North Charlestown, N.H. (†03603) 268/C5
North Chatham, Mass. (02650) 249/O6
North Chatham, N.H. (†04058) 268/E3
North Chelmsford, Mass. (01863) 249/J2
North Chesterville, Maine (†04938) 243/C6
North Chicago, Ill. (60064) 222/B4
North Chichester, N.H. (†03263) 268/E5
North Chili, N.Y. (14514) 276/E4
North City (Coello), Ill. (†62825) 222/E5
North Clarendon, Vt. (05759) 268/B4
Northcliffe, W. Australia 92/B6
North Cohasset, Mass. (†02025) 249/F7
North Colebrook, Conn. (†06021) 210/C1
North College Hill, Ohio (45239) 284/B9
North Collins, N.Y. (14111) 276/C5
North Concho (riv.), Texas 303/C6
North Concord, Vt. (05858) 268/D3
North Conway, N.H. (03860) 268/E3
North Cooking Lake, Alberta 182/D3
North Cotabato (prov.), Philippines 82/E7
Northcote, Minn. (†56728) 255/A2
Northcote, N. Zealand 100/B1
Northcote, Victoria 88/L7
Northcote, Victoria 97/J5
North Cove, N.C. (†28752) 281/F3
North Cove, Wash. (†98590) 310/A4
North Cowichan, Br. Col. 184/J3
North Creek, N.Y. (12853) 276/M3
North Crossett, Ark. (71635) 202/G7
North Cutler, Maine (†04626) 243/J6
North Dakota 188/F1
NORTH DAKOTA 282
North Dakota (state), U.S. 146/H5
North Dandalup, W. Australia 88/B3
North Danger (reef), Philippines 85/E3
North Danville, Vt. (†05819) 268/C3
North Dartmouth, Mass. (02747) 249/K6
North Dexter, Maine (†04930) 243/E5
North Dighton, Mass. (02764) 249/K5
North Dixmont, Maine (†04932) 243/E6
North Down (dist.), N. Ireland 17/K2
North Downs (hills), England 13/G6
North Eagle Butte, S. Dak. (†57625) 298/G3
Northeast (cape), Alaska 196/E2
North East (pt.), Jamaica 158/K6
Northeast (pass), La. 238/M8
North East, Md. (21901) 245/P2
North East, Pa. (16428) 294/C1
North East Breakers, Bermuda 156/H2
North East Cape Fear (riv.), N.C. 281/O4
North East Carry, Maine (†04441) 243/D4
North-Eastern (prov.), Kenya 115/G3
Northeast Foreland (pen.), Greenl. 4/A10
North Eastham, Mass. (02651) 249/O5
Northeast Harbor, Maine (04662) 243/G7
Northeast Land (isl.), Norway 4/B8
North East Margaree (riv.), Nova Scotia 168/H2
North Easton, Mass. (02356) 249/K4
North East Polder, Netherlands 27/H3
North East Providence (chan.), Bahamas 156/C1
North Edisto (riv.), S.C. 296/G6
North Edwards, Calif. (93523) 204/H8
North Egremont, Mass. (01252) 249/A4
Northeim, W. Germany 22/C3
North English, Iowa (52316) 229/J5
North Enid, Okla. (†73701) 288/L2
Northern (dist.), Israel 65/C2
Northern (head), New Bruns. 170/D4
Northern (prov.), Sudan 111/E3
Northern Cheyenne Ind. Res., Mont. 262/K5
Northern Dvina (riv.), U.S.S.R. 52/F2
Northern Dvina (riv.), U.S.S.R. 48/E3
Northern Indian (lake), Manitoba 179/J2
NORTHERN IRELAND 17
NORTHERN IRELAND 10/C3
Nottoway (riv.), Va. 307/O7
Notukeu (creek), Sask. 181/D6
Notus, Idaho (83656) 220/B6
Nouadhibou, Mauritania 106/A4
Nouadhibou, Mauritania 102/A2
Nouakchott (cap.), Mauritania 106/A5
Nouakchott (cap.), Mauritania 102/A3
Nouakchott (cap.), Mauritania 2/J5
Nouméa (cap.), New Caled. 87/G8
Nouméa (cap.), New Caledonia 2/T7
Nouméa (cap.), New Caled. 86/H5
Nounan, Idaho (†83254) 220/G7
Noup (head), Scotland 15/E1
Noupoort, S. Africa 118/C6
Nouveau-Comptoir, Québec 174/B2
Northern Ireland, U.K. 7/D3
Northern Marianas 87/E4
Northern Marianas, U.S. 2/S5
Northern Peninsula Aboriginal Reserve, Queensland 88/G2
Northern Peninsula Aboriginal Res., Queensland 95/B1
Northern Samar (prov.), Philippines 82/E4
Northern Sporades (isls.), Greece 45/F6
Northern Territory, 88/E3
NORTHERN TERRITORY 93
Northern Territory (terr.), Australia 87/D7
North Esk (riv.), Scotland 15/F4
North Esk (riv.), Tasmania 99/D3
North Fairfield, Ohio (44855) 284/E3
North Falmouth, Mass. (02556) 249/M6
North Ferrisburg, Vt. (05473) 268/A3
Northfield, Conn. (06778) 210/C2
Northfield, Ill. (60093) 222/B5
Northfield, Ky. (†40201) 237/K1
Northfield○, Maine (†04654) 243/H6
Northfield, Mass. (01360) 249/E2
Northfield○, Mass. (01360) 249/E2
Northfield, Minn. (55057) 255/E6
Northfield○, N.H. (†03276) 268/D5
Northfield, N.J. (08225) 273/D5
Northfield, Ohio (44067) 284/J10
Northfield, Texas (79246) 303/D3
Northfield, Vt. (05663) 268/B3
Northfield○, Vt. (05663) 268/B3
Northfield, Wis. (†54635) 317/D7
Northfield Falls, Vt. (05664) 268/B3
Northfield Farms, Mass. (†01360) 249/E2
Northfield-Tilton, N.H. (†03276) 268/D5
Northfleet, England 10/C5
Northfleet, England 13/J8
North Fond du Lac, Wis. (†54935) 317/J8
Northford, Conn. (06472) 210/D3
North Foreland (prom.), England 10/G5
North Foreland (prom.), England 13/J6
North Fork, Calif. (93643) 204/F6
North Fork, Frenchman (creek), Colo. 208/O1
North Fork, Gunnison (riv.), Colo. 208/D5
North Fork, Smoky Hill (riv.), Colo. 208/P4
North Fork, Idaho (83466) 220/D4
North Fork (riv.), Idaho 220/B7
North Fork, Flathead (riv.), Mont. 262/B2
North Fork, Little Humboldt (riv.), Nev. 266/D1
North Fork, Grand (riv.), N. Dak. 282/E8
Northfork, W. Va. (24868) 312/D8
North Fork, Powder (riv.), Wyo. 319/F2
North Fork, Shoshone (riv.), Wyo. 319/C1
North Fork, Wind (riv.), Wyo. 319/C2
North Fort Myers, Fla. (33903) 212/E5
North Foster, R.I. (†02857) 249/H5
North Fourchu, Nova Scotia 168/H3
North Fox (isl.), Mich. 250/D3
North Franklin, Conn. (06254) 210/G2
North Freedom, Wis. (53951) 317/G9
North Friars (bay), St. Chris.-Nevis 161/D10
North Friesland (reg.), W. Germany 22/C1
North Frisian (isls.), Denmark 21/B7
North Frisian (isls.), W. Germany 22/B1
North Fryeburg, Maine (04058) 243/B7
North Galiano, Br. Col. 184/K3
North Garden, Va. (22959) 307/L5
Northgate, N. Dak. (58767) 282/F2
Northgate, Sask. 181/J6
Northglenn, Colo. (80233) 208/K3
North Gorham, Maine (†04075) 243/B8
North Gosforth, England 13/J3
North Gower, Ontario 177/J2
North Grafton, Mass. (01536) 249/H4
North Granby, Conn. (06060) 210/D1
North Grant, Nova Scotia 168/G3
North Grosvenor Dale, Conn. (06255) 210/H1
North Groton, N.H. (†03266) 268/D4
North Grove, Ind. (†46911) 227/F3
North Guilford, Conn. (†06437) 210/E3
North Hadley, Mass. (†01035) 249/D3
North Haledon, N.J. (07508) 273/B1
North Hampton○, N.H. (03862) 268/F6
North Hampton, Ohio (45349) 284/C5
North Hanover, Mass. (†02339) 249/L4
North Hansel (mts.), Utah 304/B2
North Harbour, Newf. 166/D2
North Harlowe, N.C. (†28532) 281/R5
North Hartland, Vt. (05052) 268/C4
North Hartsville, S.C. (†29550) 296/G3
North Harwich, Mass. (†02645) 249/O6
North Hatfield, Mass. (01066) 249/D3
North Hatley, Québec 172/F4
North Haven○, Conn. (06473) 210/D3
North Haven, Maine (04853) 243/F7
North Haven○, Maine (04853) 243/F7
North Haverhill, N.H. (03774) 268/D3
North Havre, Mont. (†59501) 262/G2
North Hayden, Ind. (†46356) 227/B2
North Head, New Bruns. 170/D4
North Henderson, Ill. (61466) 222/C2
North Hero, Vt. (05474) 268/A2
North Highlands, Calif. (95660) 204/B8
North High Shoals, Georgia (†30645) 217/F3
North Hills, W. Va. (†26101) 312/D4
North Hodge, La. (†71247) 238/E2
North Holland (prov.), Netherlands 27/F3
North Holland (canal), Netherlands 27/C4
North Hollywood, Calif. (*91601) 204/B10
North Hornell, N.Y. (†14843) 276/E6
North Horr, Kenya 115/G3
North Hudson, N.Y. (12855) 276/N3
North Hudson, Wis. (†54016) 317/A5
North Hyde Park, Vt. (05665) 268/B2
North Hykeham, England 13/G4
North Industry, Ohio (44707) 284/H4
North Inishkea (isl.), Ireland 17/A3
North Java, N.Y. (14113) 276/D5
North Jay, Maine (04262) 243/C6
North Johns, Ala. (35086) 195/D4
North Judson, Ind. (46366) 227/D2
North Kansas City, Mo. (64116) 261/P5
North Kedgwick (riv.), New Bruns. 170/C1
North Kent, Conn. (†06757) 210/B1
North Kent (isl.), N.W. Terrs. 187/J2
North Kingstown○, R.I. (02852) 249/J6
North Kingsville, Ohio (44068) 284/J2
North Knife (lake), Manitoba 179/J2
North Knife Lake, Manitoba 179/J2
North Korea 54/O5
North La Junta, Colo. (†81050) 208/N7
Northlake, Ill. (60164) 222/B5
Northlake, Texas (76238) 303/F1
North Lake, Wis. (53064) 317/J1
North Lakhimpur, India 68/G3
Northland, Mich. (49869) 250/B2
Northland, Wis. (†54945) 317/H6
North Landgrove, Vt. (†05148) 268/B5
North Laramie (riv.), Wyo. 319/G3
North Las Vegas, Nev. (89030) 266/F6
North Lauderdale, Fla. (†33063) 212/B3
North Lawrence, N.Y. (12967) 276/L1
North Lawrence, Ohio (44666) 284/G4
North Leeds, Maine (04263) 243/C7
North Lewisburg, Ohio (43060) 284/C5
North Liberty, Ind. (46554) 227/E1
North Liberty, Iowa (52317) 229/K5
North Lima, Ohio (44452) 284/J4
North Limington, Maine (†04049) 243/B8
North Little Rock, Ark. (*72114) 202/F4
North Livermore, Maine (†04254) 243/C7
North Loup, Nebr. (68859) 264/F3
North Loup (riv.), Nebr. 264/E3
North Lovell, Maine (†04231) 243/B7
North Lubec, Maine (†04652) 243/J6
North Luconia (shoals), Philippines 85/E4
North Madison, Conn. (†06443) 210/E3
North Madison, Ohio (†44057) 284/H2
North Magnetic Pole (dist.) 162/F1
North Magnetic Pole, Canada 4/B15
North Magnetic Pole, N.W. Terrs. 187/H2
North Manchester, Ind. (46962) 227/F3
North Manitou, Mich. (†49654) 250/C3
North Manitou (isl.), Mich. 250/C3
North Mankato, Minn. (56001) 255/D6
North Marshfield, Mass. (02059) 249/M4
North Merritt (isl.), Fla. 212/F3
North Miami, Fla. (33161) 212/B4
North Miami, Okla. (74358) 288/R1
North Miami Beach, Fla. (33161) 212/C4
North Middleboro, Mass. (02346) 249/L5
North Middletown, Ky. (40357) 237/N4
North Minch (sound), Scotland 10/D1
North Minch (sound), Scotland 15/B3
North Montpelier, Vt. (05666) 268/C3
Northmoor, Mo. (†64152) 261/P5
North Motton, Tasmania 99/C3
North Mountain, W. Va. (†25427) 312/K3
North Muskegon, Mich. (49445) 250/C5
North Myrtle Beach, S.C. (29582) 296/K4
North Naples, Fla. (33940) 212/E5
North Natuna (isl.), Indonesia 85/D4
North Negril (pt.), Jamaica 158/G6
North Newport, N.H. (†03773) 268/C5
North New Portland, Maine (04961) 243/C6
North New River (canal), Fla. 212/F5
North Newry, Maine (†04261) 243/B6
North Newton, Kansas (67117) 232/E3
North Oaks, Minn. (†55101) 255/G5
North Ogden, Utah (†84404) 304/C2
North Olmsted, Ohio (44070) 284/G9
Northome, Minn. (56661) 255/D3
North Ossetian A.S.S.R., U.S.S.R. 48/E5
North Ossetian A.S.S.R., U.S.S.R. 52/F6
North Oxford, Mass. (01537) 249/G4
North Pacific (ocean) 87/F4
North Pacific Ocean 2/B5
North Pacific Ocean 2/T4
North Pagai (isl.), Indonesia 85/C6
North Palm Beach, Fla. (33403) 212/F5
North Park, Ill. (†61111) 222/D1
North Parsonfield, Maine (†04047) 243/A8
North Pease (riv.), Texas 303/D3
North Pekin, Ill. (†61554) 222/D3
North Pembroke, Mass. (02358) 249/M4
North Pender Island, Br. Col. 184/K3
North Penobscot, Maine (†04476) 243/F7
North Perry, Maine (†04667) 243/J5
North Perry, Ohio (†44081) 284/H2
North Petherton, England 13/D6
North Pine, Br. Col. 184/G2
North Plain, Conn. (†06371) 210/F3
North Plainfield, N.J. (07060) 273/E2
North Plains, Oreg. (97133) 291/A2
North Platte (riv.) 188/F2
North Platte (riv.), Colo. 208/G1
North Platte, Nebr. 188/F2
North Platte, Nebr. (69101) 264/D3
North Platte (riv.), Nebr. 264/B3
North Platte (riv.), U.S. 146/H5
North Platte (riv.), Wyo. 319/H3
North Plymouth, Mass. (02360) 249/L5
North Pole 4/A1
North Pole 2/F1
North Pole, Alaska (99705) 196/J2
North Pole (brook), New Bruns. 170/D1
North Pomfret, Vt. (05053) 268/B4
Northport, Ala. (35476) 195/C4
North Port, Fla. (33595) 212/D4
Northport○, Maine (†04849) 243/E7
Northport, Mich. (49670) 250/D3
Northport, Nebr. (†69336) 264/B3
Northport, N.Y. (11768) 276/O9
Northport, Nova Scotia 168/E3
Northport, Wash. (99157) 310/H2
North Portal, Sask. 181/J6
North Potomac, Md. (†20857) 245/K4
North Powder, Oreg. (97867) 291/K2
North Pownal, Vt. (05260) 268/A6
North Prairie, Wis. (53153) 317/J2
North Providence○, R.I. (02908) 249/J5
North Pulaski, Va. (†24301) 307/G6
North Randall, Ohio (†44101) 284/H9
North Randolph, Vt. (†05061) 268/B4
North Raymond, Maine (†04274) 243/C8
North Reading○, Mass. (01864) 249/C5
North Redington Beach, Fla. (†33708) 212/B3
North Redwood, Minn. (56275) 255/D6
North Renous (riv.), New Bruns. 170/D2
North Rhine-Westphalia (state), W. Germany 22/B3
North Richland Hills, Texas (76118) 303/F2
Northridge, Ohio (45414) 284/B6
North Ridgeville, Ohio (44039) 284/F3
North Rim, Ariz. (86052) 198/C2
North River, Newf. 166/D2
North River, N.Y. (12856) 276/M3
North River, N. Dak. (†58102) 282/S6
North River, Nova Scotia 168/D4
North Riverside, Ill. (60546) 222/B5
North Robinson, Ohio (44856) 284/E4
North Ronaldsay (firth), Scotland 15/F1
North Ronaldsay (isl.), Scotland 15/F1
North Ronaldsay (isl.), Scotland 10/E1
Northrop, Minn. (56075) 255/D7
North Rose, N.Y. (14516) 276/G4
North Roxboro, N.C. (†27573) 281/L2
North Royalton, Ohio (44133) 284/H10
North Rustico, Pr. Edward I. 168/E2
North Saanich, Br. Col. 184/K3
North Saint Paul, Minn. (55109) 255/G5
North Salem, Ind. (46165) 227/D5
North Salem, N.H. (03073) 268/E6
North Salt Lake, Utah (†84010) 304/C3
North Sandwich, N.H. (03259) 268/E4
North San Juan, Calif. (95960) 204/E4
North Santiam (riv.), Oreg. 291/E3
North Saskatchewan (riv.) (dist.) 162/E5
North Saskatchewan (riv.), Alberta 182/E3
North Saskatchewan (riv.), Canada 146/G4
North Saskatchewan (riv.), Sask. 181/D3
North Scituate, Mass. (02060) 249/F8
North Scituate, R.I. (02857) 249/H5
North Sea (canal), Netherlands 27/F4
North Seal (riv.), Manitoba 179/H2
North Searsmont, Maine (†04973) 243/E7
North Sentinel (isl.), India 68/G6
North Sevogle (riv.), New Bruns. 170/D1
North Shapleigh, Maine (04060) 243/B8
North Shoal (lake), Manitoba 179/E4
North Shore, Wis. 317/M1
Northside, N.C. (27564) 281/M2
Northside, Sask. 181/F2
North Sioux City, S. Dak. (57049) 298/R8
North Skunk (riv.), Iowa 229/H5
North Somercotes, England 10/G4
North Somercotes, England 13/H4
North Somers, Conn. (†06071) 210/F1
North Spectacle (lake), Conn. 210/B2
North Spirit Lake, Ontario 175/B2
North Springfield, Pa. (16430) 294/A1
North Springfield, Vt. (05150) 268/B5
North Springfield, Va. (22151) 307/S3
North Star, Alberta 182/B1
North Star, Mich. (48862) 250/E5
North Star, Ohio (45350) 284/A5
North Stonington○, Conn. (06359) 210/H3
North Stratford, N.H. (03590) 268/D2
North Sunderland, England 13/F2
North Sutton, N.H. (03260) 268/D5
North Swansea, Mass. (†02777) 249/K5
North Sydney, N. S. Wales 88/L4
North Sydney, N.S. Wales 97/J3
North Sydney, Nova Scotia 168/H2
North Syracuse, N.Y. (13212) 276/H4
North Taranaki (bight), N. Zealand 100/D3
North Tarrytown, N.Y. (10591) 276/O6
North Terre Haute, Ind. (47805) 227/C5
North Thetford, Vt. (05054) 268/C4
North Thompson (riv.), Br. Col. 184/G4
North Tidworth, England 13/F6
North Tiverton, R.I. (†02722) 249/K6
North Tolsta, Scotland 15/B2
Northton, Scotland 15/B3
North Tonawanda, N.Y. (14120) 276/C4
North Trap (isl.), N. Zealand 100/B7
North Troy, Vt. (05859) 268/C2
North Truchas (peak), N. Mex. 274/D3
North Truro, Mass. (02652) 249/O4
North Tunbridge, Vt. (†05077) 268/C4
North Turner, Maine (04266) 243/C7
North Twin (mt.), N.H. 268/D3
North Tyne (riv.), England 13/E2
North Uist (isl.), Scotland 15/A3
North Uist (isl.), Scotland 10/C2
Northumberland (co.), England 13/E2
Northumberland (co.), New Bruns. 170/D2
Northumberland (str.), New Bruns. 170/F2
Northumberland○, N.H. (†03582) 268/D2
Northumberland (str.), Nova Scotia 168/E2
Northumberland (county), Ontario 177/G3
Northumberland (co.), Pa. 294/J4
Northumberland, Pa. (17857) 294/J4
Northumberland (str.), Pr. Edward I. 168/D2
Northumberland (isls.), Queensland 95/D4
Northumberland (cape), S. Australia 94/F8
Northumberland (co.), Va. 307/R5
Northumberland National Park, England 13/E2
North Umpqua (riv.), Oreg. 291/E4
North Ural (mts.), U.S.S.R. 52/K1
North Utica (Utica), Ill. (†61373) 222/E2
North Uxbridge, Mass. (01538) 249/H4
Northvale, N.J. (07647) 273/F1
North Vancouver, Br. Col. 162/D6
North Vancouver, Br. Col. 184/K3
North Vassalboro, Maine (04962) 243/D7
North Vernon, Ind. (47265) 227/F6
Northview, Mo. (†65706) 261/G8
Northville, Conn. (†06776) 210/B2
Northville, Mich. (48167) 250/F6
Northville, N.Y. (12134) 276/M4
Northville, S. Dak. (57465) 298/M3
North Wabasca (lake), Alberta 182/D1
North Wakefield, N.H. (†03872) 268/E4
North Waldoboro, Maine (†04572) 243/E7
North Wales, Pa. (19454) 294/M5
North Walpole, N.H. (†03608) 268/C5
North Walsham, England 13/J5
North Walsham, England 10/G4
North Waltham, Mass. (02154) 249/B6
North Warren, Pa. (†16365) 294/D2
North Washington, Iowa (50661) 229/J2
North Waterboro, Maine (04061) 243/B8
North Waterford, Maine (04267) 243/B7
Northway, Alaska (99764) 196/K2
North Wayne, Maine (†04284) 243/C7
North Weare, N.H. (†03281) 268/D5
North Webster, Ind. (46555) 227/F2
Northwest (pt.), Fla. 212/E6
North West (dist.), Guyana 131/A2
North West (pt.), Jamaica 158/G5
North West (cape), Australia 87/B8
North West (cape), W. Australia 88/A4
North West (cape), W. Australia 92/A3
North-West Aboriginal Reserve, S. Australia 88/E5
North-West Aboriginal Res., W. Australia 92/E4
North West Arm (inlet), Newf. 166/D2
North West Brook, Newf. 166/C2
North West Brook (riv.), Newf. 166/D2
North Westchester, Conn. (06474) 210/F2
Northwestern (sen. dist.), Alaska 196/E2
North-West Frontier (prov.), Pakistan 68/C2
North West Gander (riv.), Newf. 166/C4
North Westminster, Vt. (†05101) 268/B5
Northwest Miramichi (riv.), New Bruns. 170/D1
Northwest Oromocto (riv.), New Bruns. 170/D3
North Westport, Mass. (02790) 249/K6
North West Providence (chan.), Bahamas 156/B1
North West River, Newf. 166/B3
Northwest Territories 162/E2
Northwest Territories (prov.), Canada 146/G3
NORTHWEST TERRITORIES 187
Northwest Upsalquitch (riv.), New Bruns. 170/D1
North Weymouth, Mass. (02191) 249/D8
North Whitefield, Maine (04353) 243/D7
Northwich, England 13/H2
Northwich, England 10/G2
North Wilbraham, Mass. (†01095) 249/E4
North Wildwood, N.J. (08260) 273/D6
North Wilkesboro, N.C. (28659) 281/G2
North Williston, Vt. (†05495) 268/A3
North Wilton, Conn. (†06897) 210/B4
North Windham, Conn. (06256) 210/G1
North Windham, Maine (04062) 243/C8
North Wolcott, Vt. (†05680) 268/C2
Northwood, Iowa (50459) 229/G2
Northwood○, N.H. (03261) 268/E5
Northwood, N. Dak. (58267) 282/P4

420 Northwood

Northwood, Ohio (†43619) 284/D2
North Woodbury, Conn. (†06798) 210/C2
Northwood Center, N.H. (†03261) 268/E5
Northwood Narrows (Northwood P.O.), N.H. (03261) 268/E5
Northwoods, Mo. (†63101) 261/R2
North Woodstock, Conn. (†06281) 210/G1
North Woodstock, Maine (†04219) 243/B7
North Woodstock, N.H. (03262) 268/D3
Northwye, Mo. (†65401) 261/J7
North Yarmouth, Maine (†04096) 243/C8
North Yarmouth◯, Maine (†04096) 243/C8
North York, Ontario 177/J4
North York Moors National Park, England 13/G3
North Yorkshire (co.), England 13/F3
North Zanesville, Ohio (†43701) 284/G6
Norton (sound), Alaska 146/B3
Norton (sound), Alaska 188/C5
Norton (bay), Alaska 196/F2
Norton (sound), Alaska 196/E2
Norton, England 13/G3
Norton (peak), Idaho 220/D6
Norton (co.), Kansas 232/C2
Norton, Kansas (67654) 232/C2
Norton (res.), Kansas 232/C2
Norton, Mass. (02766) 249/K5
Norton◯, Mass. (02766) 249/K5
Norton, New Bruns. 170/E3
Norton, Ohio (44203) 284/G3
Norton, Texas (76865) 303/E6
Norton (sound), U.S. 4/C18
Norton◯, Vt. (05907) 268/D2
Norton (pond), Vt. 268/D2
Norton (I.C.), Va. (24273) 307/C7
Norton, W. Va. (26285) 312/G5
Norton A.F.B., Calif. 204/F10
Norton-Radstock, England 13/E6
Norton Shores, Mich. (†49441) 250/C5
Nortonville, Kansas (66060) 232/G2
Nortonville, Ky. (42442) 237/G6
Nortonville, N. Dak. (58473) 282/N6
Norumbega, Argentina 143/F7
Norvegia (cape) 5/B18
Norvell, Arkm (†72386) 202/K3
Norvelt, Pa. (15674) 294/D5
Norwalk, Calif. (90650) 204/C11
Norwalk, Conn. (*06850) 210/B4
Norwalk (isls.), Conn. 210/B4
Norwalk (riv.), Conn. 210/B4
Norwalk, Iowa (50211) 229/F6
Norwalk, Mich. (†49660) 250/C4
Norwalk, Ohio (44857) 284/E3
Norwalk, Wis. (54648) 317/E8
Norway 2/K2
Norway 4/C9
NORWAY 18
Norway 7/E2
Norway, Ind. (†47960) 227/D3
Norway, Iowa (52318) 229/K5
Norway, Kansas (66961) 232/E2
Norway, Maine (04268) 243/B7
Norway◯, Maine (04268) 243/B7
Norway, Mich. (49870) 250/B3
Norway (bay), N.W. Terrs. 187/H2
Norway, Oreg. (97460) 291/C4
Norway, S.C. (29113) 296/E5
Norway House, Man. 162/G5
Norway House, Manitoba 179/J3
Norway Lake, Maine (†04268) 243/B7
Norwegian (sea) 4/C10
Norwegian (sea) 7/D2
Norwegian (bay), N.W. Terrs. 187/J2
Norwegian (sea), Norway 18/F3
Norwell◯, Mass. (02061) 249/F8
Norwich, Conn. (06360) 210/G2
Norwich, England 13/J5
Norwich, England 10/G4
Norwich, Kansas (67118) 232/E4
Norwich, N.Y. (13815) 276/J5
Norwich, N. Dak. (58768) 282/J3
Norwich, Ohio (43767) 284/G6
Norwich, Ontario 177/D5
Norwich◯, Vt. (05055) 268/C4
Norwichtown, Conn. (†06360) 210/G2
Norwood, Colo. (81423) 208/C6
Norwood, Georgia (30821) 217/G4
Norwood, La. (70761) 238/H5
Norwood◯, Mass. (02062) 249/B8
Norwood, Minn. (55368) 255/E6
Norwood, Mo. (65717) 261/H8
Norwood, N.J. (07648) 273/C1
Norwood, N.Y. (13668) 276/L1
Norwood, N.C. (28128) 281/J4
Norwood, Ohio (45212) 284/C9
Norwood, Ontario 177/F3
Norwood, Pa. (19074) 294/M7
Norwood, R.I. (†02887) 249/J6
Norwood, Va. (24581) 307/L5
Nosappu (pt.), Japan 81/N2
Nosbonsing (lake), Ontario 177/E1
Nose, Japan 81/J7
Noshiro, Japan 81/J3
Nosovka, U.S.S.R. 52/D4
Nosratabad, Iran 66/L6
Noss (head), Scotland 15/F2
Nossa Senhora do Livramento, Brazil 132/B6
Nossob (riv.), Botswana 118/B4
Nossob (riv.), Namibia 118/B4
Nosy Be (isl.), Madagascar 118/H2
Nosy Boraha (isl.), Madagascar 118/J3
Nosy-Varika, Madagascar 118/H4
Notakwanon (riv.), Newf. 166/B2
Notasulga, Ala. (36866) 195/G5
Noteć (riv.), Poland 47/B2
Notikewin, Alberta 182/B1
Notikewin (riv.), Alberta 182/A1
Noto, Italy 34/E6
Noto, Japan 81/H5
Noto (pen.), Japan 81/H5
Notodden, Norway 18/F7
Notre Dame, Ind. (46556) 227/E1
Notre-Dame, New Brun-. 170/F2
Notre Dame (bay), Newf. 166/C4
Notre-Dame-de-Ham, Québec 172/F4
Notre-Dame-de-la-Doré, Québec 172/E1
Notre-Dame-de-la-Paix, Québec 172/C4
Notre-Dame-de-la-Salette, Québec 172/B4
Notre Dame de Lourdes, Manitoba 179/D5
Notre-Dame-de-Pierreville, Québec 172/D3
Notre-Dame-des-Anges, Québec 172/E3
Notre-Dame-des-Bois, Québec 172/G4
Notre-Dame-des-Laurentides, Québec 172/H3
Notre-Dame-des-Monts, Québec 172/G2
Notre-Dame-des-Prairies, Québec 172/D3
Notre-Dame-de-Stanbridge, Québec 172/D4
Notre-Dame-du-Bon-Conseil, Québec 172/E4
Notre-Dame-du-Lac, Québec 172/J2
Notre-Dame-du-Laus, Québec 172/B3
Notre-Dame-du-Portage, Québec 172/H2
Notre-Dame-du-Rosaire, Québec 172/F1
Nottawa, Ontario 177/D3
Nottawasaga (bay), Ontario 177/D3
Nottawasaga (riv.), Ontario 177/E3
Nottaway (riv.), Que. 162/J5
Nottaway (riv.), Québec 174/B2
Nottely (lake), Georgia 217/D1
Nøtterøy, Norway 18/D4
Nottingham, Ala. (†35014) 195/F4
Nottingham, England 13/F5
Nottingham, England 10/F4
Nottingham◯, N.H. (03290) 268/E5
Nottingham (isl.), N.W.T. 162/H3
Nottingham (isl.), N.W. Terrs. 187/L3
Nottinghamshire (co.), England 13/F4
Nottinghill, Mo. (65718) 261/G9
Nottoway (co.), Va. 307/M6
Nouveau-Québec (terr.), Québec 174/E1
Nouveau-Québec (crater), Québec 174/F1
Nouvelle, Québec 172/C2
Nouvelle (riv.), Québec 172/C2
Nouvelle-France (cape), Québec 174/F1
Nouvelle-Ouest, Québec 172/C2
Nova, Hungary 41/D3
Nova, Ohio (44859) 284/F3
Nová Baňa, Czech. 41/E2
Nová Bystrica, Czech. 41/E2
Nová Bystřice, Czech. 41/C2
Nova Chaves, Angola 115/D6
Nova Cruz, Brazil 132/H4
Nova Era, Brazil 135/E1
Nova Friburgo, Brazil 132/F8
Nova Friburgo, Brazil 135/E3
Nova Gaia, Angola 115/C5
Nova Goa (Panaji), India 68/C5
Nova Gorizia, Yugoslavia 45/A2
Nova Gradiška, Yugoslavia 45/C3
Nova Granada, Brazil 135/B2
Nova Iguaçu, Brazil 120/E5
Nova Iguaçu, Brazil 135/E3
Nova Iguaçu, Brazil 132/F8
Nova Iorque, Brazil 132/E4
Nova Lima, Brazil 135/E2
Nova Lusitânia, Mozambique 118/E3
Nova Mambone, Mozambique 118/F4
Novar, Ontario 177/E2
Novara (prov.), Italy 34/B2
Novara, Italy 34/B2
Nova Russas, Brazil 132/F4
Nova Scotia (prov.) 162/K7
Nova Scotia (prov.), Canada 146/M5
NOVA SCOTIA 168
Nova Sofala, Mozambique 118/F4
Novato, Calif. (94947) 204/H1
Novaya Kakhovka, U.S.S.R. 52/D5
Novaya Kazanka, U.S.S.R. 48/F5
Novaya Sibir' (isl.), U.S.S.R. 4/B2
Novaya Sibir' (isl.), U.S.S.R. 48/Q2
Novaya Zemlya (isl.), U.S.S.R. 2/L2
Novaya Zemlya (isls.), U.S.S.R. 4/B7
Novaya Zemlya (isls.), U.S.S.R. 48/F2
Novaya Zemlya (isls.), U.S.S.R. 52/H1
Nova Zagora, Bulgaria 45/H4
Nové Hrady, Czech. 41/C2
Novelda, Spain 33/F3
Novelty, Mo. (63460) 261/H2
Nové Město nad Váhom, Czech. 41/D2
Nové Město na Moravě, Czech. 41/D2
Nové Strašecí, Czech. 41/B1
Nové Zámky, Czech. 41/D3
Novgorod, U.S.S.R. 7/H3
Novgorod, U.S.S.R. 52/D3
Novgorod, U.S.S.R. 48/D4
Novgorod-Severskiy, U.S.S.R. 52/D4
Novi, Mich. (48050) 250/F6
Novi, Yugoslavia 45/B3
Novice, Texas (79538) 303/E5
Novi Ligure, Italy 34/B2
Novinger, Mo. (63559) 261/G2
Novi Pazar, Bulgaria 45/H4
Novi Pazar, Yugoslavia 45/E4
Novi Sad, Yugoslavia 45/D3
Novi Sad, Yugoslavia 7/F4
Nóvita, Colombia 126/B5
Novoanninskiy, U.S.S.R. 52/F4
Novo Aripuanã, Brazil 120/D3
Novocherkassk, U.S.S.R. 7/J4
Novocherkassk, U.S.S.R. 52/F5
Novodvinsk, U.S.S.R. 52/F2
Novograd-Volynskiy, U.S.S.R. 52/C4
Novogrudok, U.S.S.R. 52/C4
Novo Hamburgo, Brazil 132/D10
Novo Horizonte, Brazil 135/B2
Novokazalinsk, U.S.S.R. 48/G5
Novokuybyshevsk, U.S.S.R. 7/K3
Novokuybyshevsk, U.S.S.R. 52/G4
Novokuznetsk, U.S.S.R. 54/K4
Novokuznetsk, U.S.S.R. 48/J4
Novo Mesto, Yugoslavia 45/B3
Novomoskovsk, U.S.S.R. 7/H3
Novomoskovsk, U.S.S.R. 52/E4
Novomoskovsk, U.S.S.R. 48/E4
Novopolotsk, U.S.S.R. 52/C3
Novorossiysk, U.S.S.R. 7/H4
Novorossiysk, U.S.S.R. 48/D5
Novorossiysk, U.S.S.R. 52/E6
Novosergiyevka, U.S.S.R. 52/H4
Novoshakhtinsk, U.S.S.R. 52/E5
Novosibirsk, U.S.S.R. 54/J4
Novosibirsk, U.S.S.R. 2/P3
Novosibirsk, U.S.S.R. 48/J4
Novotroitsk, U.S.S.R. 52/J4
Novoukrainka, U.S.S.R. 52/D5
Novouzensk, U.S.S.R. 52/G4
Novovolynsk, U.S.S.R. 52/B4
Novovyatsk, U.S.S.R. 52/G3
Novozybkov, U.S.S.R. 48/D4
Novozybkov, U.S.S.R. 52/D4
Novra, Manitoba 179/B2
Novska, Yugoslavia 45/C3
Nový Bohumín, Czech. 41/E2
Nový Bor, Czech. 41/C1
Nový Bydžov, Czech. 41/C1
Nový Hrozenkov, Czech. 41/E2
Nový Jičín, Czech. 41/E2
Novyy Bug, U.S.S.R. 52/D5
Novyy Port, U.S.S.R. 4/C6
Novyy Port, U.S.S.R. 48/G3
Novyy Urengoy, U.S.S.R. 48/H3
Novyy Uzen', U.S.S.R. 48/F5
Nowa Dęba, Poland 47/E3
Nowa Nowa, Victoria 97/E5
Nowa Ruda, Poland 47/C3
Nowa Sól, Poland 47/B3
Nowata (co.), Okla. 288/P1
Nowata, Okla. (74048) 288/P1
Nowater (creek), Wyo. 319/E2
Nowe, Poland 47/D2
Nowe Miasto Lubawskie, Poland 47/D2
Nowendoc, N.S. Wales 97/F2
Nowgong, Assam, India 68/G3
Nowgong, Madhya Pradesh, India 68/D3
Nowitna (riv.), Alaska 196/H2
Nowogard, Poland 47/B2
Nowood (riv.), Wyo. 319/E1
Nowra-Bomaderry, N. S. Wales 88/J6
Nowra-Bomaderry, N.S. Wales 97/F4
Now Shahr, Iran 66/G2
Nowshera, Pakistan 59/K3
Nowshera, Pakistan 68/C2
Nowy Dwór Gdański, Poland 47/D1
Nowy Dwór Mazowiecki, Poland 47/E2
Nowy Sącz (prov.), Poland 47/E4
Nowy Sącz, Poland 47/E4
Nowy Staw, Poland 47/D1
Nowy Targ, Poland 47/E4
Nowy Tomyśl, Poland 47/C2
Now Zad, Afghanistan 68/A2
Now Zad, Afghanistan 59/H3
Noxapater, Miss. (39346) 256/F5
Noxen, Pa. (18636) 294/E7
Noxon, Mont. (59853) 262/A3
Noxubee (co.), Miss. 256/G4
Noxubee (riv.), Miss. 256/G4
Noya, Spain 33/B1
Noyes (isl.), Alaska 196/M2
Noyes, Minn. (56740) 255/A2
Noyes (pt.), R.I. 249/H7
Noyo (riv.), Calif. 204/B4
Noyon, France 28/E3
Noyon, Mongolia 77/F3
Nsanje, Malawi 115/G7
Nsawam, Ghana 106/D7
Nsukka, Nigeria 106/F7
Nsuta, Ghana 106/D7
Nuanetsi, Zimbabwe 118/E4
Nuba (mts.), Sudan 111/E5
Nubanusit (lake), N.H. 268/C5
Nubeena, Tasmania 99/D5
Nuberg, Georgia (†30634) 217/G2
Nubia (lake), Sudan 111/F3
Nubian (des.), Sudan 102/F2
Nubian (des.), Sudan 111/F3
Nubian (des.), Sudan 59/B5
Nubieber, Calif. (96068) 204/D2
Nuckolls (co.), Nebr. 264/F4
Nuckols, Ky. (†42352) 237/G5
Nucla, Colo. (81424) 208/B6
Nudgee, Queensland 88/K2
Nueces (co.), Texas 303/G10
Nueces (riv.), Texas 188/G5
Nueces (riv.), Texas 303/F9
Nueltin (lake) 162/G3
Nueltin (lake), Manitoba 179/H1
Nueltin (lake), N.W. Terrs. 187/H3
Nuestra Señora (bay), Chile 138/A5
Nueva (isl.), Argentina 143/C8
Nueva (isl.), Chile 138/F11
Nueva Alejandría, Peru 128/F5
Nueva Antioquia, Colombia 126/F5
Nueva Armenia, Honduras 154/D4
Nueva Asunción (dept.), Paraguay 144/B2
Nueva Casas Grandes, Mexico 150/F1
Nueva Ciudad Guerrero, Mexico 150/K3
Nueva Colombia, Paraguay 144/B4
Nueva Ecija (prov.), Philippines 82/C3
Nueva Esparta (state), Venezuela 124/G2
Nueva Germania, Paraguay 144/D3
Nueva Gerona, Cuba 156/A2
Nueva Gerona, Cuba 158/B2
Nueva Helvecia, Uruguay 145/B5
Nueva Imperial, Chile 138/D2
Nueva Italia, Paraguay 144/B5
Nueva Italia de Ruiz, Mexico 150/J7
Nueva Ocotepeque, Honduras 154/C3
Nueva Palmira, Uruguay 145/A4
Nueva Rosita, Mexico 150/J2
Nueva San Salvador, El Salvador 154/C4
Nueva Vizcaya (prov.), Philippines 82/C2
Nueve de Julio, Argentina 143/F7
Nuevitas, Cuba 156/C2
Nuevitas, Cuba 158/G2
Nuevitas (bay), Cuba 158/H2
Nuevo (gulf), Argentina 143/D5
Nuevo, Bajo (reef), Mexico 150/O6
Nuevo Berlín, Uruguay 145/B3
Nuevo Chagres, Panama 154/G6
Nuevo Ideal, Mexico 150/G4
Nuevo Juncal, Chile 138/B5
Nuevo Laredo, Mexico 146/H7
Nuevo Laredo, Mexico 150/J3
Nuevo León (state), Mexico 150/K4
Nuevo Mamo, Venezuela 124/G3
Nuevo Rocafuerte, Ecuador 128/E3
Nufenen, Switzerland 39/H3
Nugaal (prov.), Somalia 115/J2
Nugget (pt.), N. Zealand 100/C7
Nugrus, Jebel (mt.), Egypt 59/B4
Nuguria (isls.), Papua N.G. 86/C1
Nui (atoll), Tuvalu 87/H6
Nuiqsut, Alaska (99723) 196/H1
Nu Jiang (riv.), China 77/E6
Nûk (cap.), Greenl. 4/C12
Nûk (cap.), Greenland 146/N3
Nûk (cap.), Greenland 2/G2
Nuka (bay), Alaska 196/C2
Nuka (isl.), Alaska 196/C2
Nukey Bluff (mt.), S. Australia 94/D5
Nukheila (oasis), Sudan 111/E4
Nuku'alofa (cap.), Tonga 87/J8
Nukuhiva (isl.), Fr. Poly. 87/M6
Nukulaelae (atoll), Tuvalu 87/H6
Nukumanu (atoll), Papua N.G. 87/F6
Nukumanu (isls.), Papua N.G. 86/D2
Nukunonu (atoll), Tokelau Is. 87/J6
Nukuoro (atoll), Micronesia 87/F5
Nukus, U.S.S.R. 54/H5
Nukus, U.S.S.R. 48/G5
Nulato, Alaska (99765) 196/G2
Nules, Spain 33/F3
Nulhegan (riv.), Vt. 268/D2
Nulhegan, East Branch (riv.), Vt. 268/D2
Nullagine, W. Australia 88/C4
Nullagine, W. Australia 92/C3
Nullarbor (plain) 88/D6
Nullarbor (plain), Australia 87/C9
Nullarbor, S. Australia 94/B4
Nullarbor (plain), S. Australia 94/A4
Nullarbor (plain), W. Australia 92/D5
Nulliberg (mt.), Virgin Is. (U.S.) 161/B4
Nulltown, Ind. (†47331) 227/G5
Numa, Iowa (52575) 229/G7
Numan, Nigeria 106/G7
Numancia, Philippines 82/D5
Numansdorp, Netherlands 27/E5
Numata, Japan 81/J5
Numazu, Japan 81/J6
Numbulwar, North. Terr. 88/F2
Numbulwar, North. Terr. 93/D3
Numfoor (isl.), Indonesia 85/J6
Ñumí, Paraguay 144/D4
Nu Mine, Pa. (16244) 294/D4
Numurkah, Victoria 97/C5
Nunaksaluk (isl.), Newf. 166/B2
Nunapitchuk, Alaska (99641) 196/F2
Nunawading, Victoria 88/L7
Nunawading, Victoria 97/J5
Nunchía, Colombia 126/D5
Nunda, N.Y. (14517) 276/E5
Nunda, S. Dak. (57050) 298/P5
Nundah, Queensland 88/K2
Nundah, Queensland 95/E2
Nundle, N.S. Wales 97/F2
Nuneaton, England 13/F5
Nuneaton, England 10/F4
Núñez (isl.), Chile 138/D10
Nunez, Georgia (30448) 217/H5
Nungarin, W. Australia 92/B5
Nungesser (lake), Ontario 175/B2
Nunivak (isl.), Alaska 146/B4
Nunivak (isl.), Alaska 188/C6
Nunivak (isl.), Alaska 196/E3
Nunivak (isl.), U.S. 4/D18
Nunley, Ark. (†71953) 202/B4
Nunn, Colo. (80648) 208/K1
Nunnelly, Tenn. (37137) 237/G9
Nunningen, Switzerland 39/E2
Nuñoa, Peru 128/G10
Nunspeet, Netherlands 27/H4
Nuoro (prov.), Italy 34/B4
Nuoro, Italy 34/B4
Nuqub, P.D.R. Yemen 59/E6
Nuquí, Colombia 126/B5
Nuremberg, Pa. (18241) 294/K4
Nuremberg, W. Germany 7/F4
Nuremberg, W. Germany 22/D4
Nurestan (reg.), Afghanistan 59/K2
Nurhak, Turkey 63/G4
Nuri, Mexico 150/E3
Nuri (ruins), Sudan 111/F4
Nuria, Sierra de (mts.), Venezuela 124/H4
Nuriootpa, S. Australia 94/F6
Nuristan (reg.), Afghanistan 68/C1
Nurlat, U.S.S.R. 52/H4
Nurmes, Finland 18/Q5
Nürnberg (Nuremberg), W. Germany 22/D4
Nurrari (lakes), S. Australia 94/B3
Nursery, Texas (77976) 303/H9
Nürtingen, W. Germany 22/C4
Nuruhak Dağı (mt.), Turkey 63/G3
Nus, Ras (cape), Oman 59/G6
Nusa Barung (isl.), Indonesia 85/K3
Nusaybin, Turkey 63/J4
Nushagak (bay), Alaska 196/G3
Nushagak (riv.), Alaska 196/G2
Nushki, Pakistan 68/B3
Nushki, Pakistan 59/J4
Nutimik, Manitoba 179/G5
Nutley, N.J. (07110) 273/B2
Nut Mountain, Sask. 181/H3
Nutrioso, Ariz. (85932) 198/F5
Nuttby (mt.), Nova Scotia 168/E3
Nutter Fort, W. Va. (26301) 312/F4
Nutting Lake, Mass. (01865) 249/B5
Nutwood Downs, North. Terr. 93/D3
Nuuanu (stream), Hawaii 218/C4
Nuupere (pt.), Fr. Poly. 86/S13
Nuwara Eliya, Sri Lanka 68/E7
Nuweiba, Egypt 111/F2
Nuyakuk (lake), Alaska 196/F3
Nuyts (cape), S. Australia 88/E6
Nuyts (arch.), S. Australia 94/C5
Nuyts (cape), S. Australia 94/C5
Nyabing, W. Australia 88/B6
Nyabisindu, Rwanda 115/F4
Nyack, Mont. (†59936) 262/C2
Nyack, N.Y. (10960) 276/K8
Nyah, Victoria 97/B4
Nyah West, Victoria 97/B4
Nyainqêntanglha Shan (range), China 77/D5
Nyainrong, China 77/D5
Nyala, Sudan 111/E5
Nyala, Sudan 102/E3
Ny-Ålesund, Norway 18/C2
Nyamlell, Sudan 111/E6
Nyandoma, U.S.S.R. 7/J2
Nyandoma, U.S.S.R. 48/E3
Nyandoma, U.S.S.R. 52/F2
Nyanga, Gabon 115/A4
Nyanga, S. Africa 118/F6
Nyanza (prov.), Kenya 115/F4
Nyasa (lake) 102/F6
Nyasa (lake) 2/L6
Nyasa (lake), Malawi 115/F6
Nyasa (lake), Mozambique 118/E2
Nyasa (lake), Tanzania 115/F6
Nyborg, Denmark 21/D7
Nyborg, Denmark 18/G9
Nybro, Sweden 18/J8
Nye, Mont. (59061) 262/G5
Nye (co.), Nev. 266/E4
Nyeri, Kenya 115/G4
Nyerol, Sudan 111/F6
Nyima, China 77/C5
Nyingchi, China 77/D6
Nyírábrány, Hungary 41/G3
Nyíradony, Hungary 41/G3
Nyírbátor, Hungary 41/G3
Nyíregyháza, Hungary 41/F3
Nyírmada, Hungary 41/G2
Nyiru (mt.), Kenya 115/G3
Nykarleby, Finland 18/N5
Nykøbing, Denmark 18/H9
Nykøbing, Denmark 18/G9
Nykøbing, Storstrøm, Denmark 21/F8
Nykøbing, Vestsjaelland, Denmark 21/E6
Nykøbing, Viborg, Denmark 21/B4
Nykøbing, Denmark 18/F8
Nyköping, Sweden 18/K7
Nylstroom, S. Africa 118/D4
Nymagee, N.S. Wales 97/D3
Nymboida, N.S. Wales 97/G1
Nymboida (riv.), N.S. Wales 97/G1
Nymburk, Czech. 41/C1
Nynäshamn, Sweden 18/L7
Nyngan, N. S. Wales 88/H6
Nyngan, N.S. Wales 97/D2
Nyon, Switzerland 39/B4
Nyons, France 28/F5
Nýřany, Czech. 41/B2
Nyrob, U.S.S.R. 52/J2
Nýrsko, Czech. 41/B2
Nysa, Poland 47/C3
Nysa Kłodzka (riv.), Poland 47/C3
Nysa Łużycka (Neisse) (riv.), Poland 47/B3
Nyssa, Oreg. (97913) 291/K4
Nysted, Denmark 21/E8
Nytva, U.S.S.R. 52/H3
Nyudo (cape), Japan 81/J4
Nyukhcha, U.S.S.R. 52/G2
Nyunzu, Zaire 115/E5
Nyurba, U.S.S.R. 48/M3
Nyuvchim, U.S.S.R. 52/H2
Nzega, Tanzania 115/F4
N'Zérékoré, Guinea 106/C7
Nzeto, Angola 115/B5

O

Oa, Mull of (prom.), Scotland 10/C3
Oa, Mull of (prom.), Scotland 15/B5
Oacoma, S. Dak. (57365) 298/L6
Oadby, England 13/F5
Oahe (lake), N. Dak. 282/J7
Oahe (lake), S. Dak. 188/F1
Oahe (dam), S. Dak. 298/J5
Oahe (lake), S. Dak. 298/J1
Oahe (lake), U.S. 146/J5
Oahu (isl.), Hawaii 87/L3
Oahu (isl.), Hawaii 188/F5
Oahu (isl.), Hawaii 218/E2
Oak (lake), Manitoba 179/B5
Oak (pt.), Mich. 250/F5
Oak, Nebr. (68964) 264/G4
Oak (creek), N. Dak. 282/J8
Oak (isl.), Nova Scotia 168/E3
Oak (creek), S. Dak. 298/J6
Oak (creek), S. Dak. 298/H2
Oak (isl.), Wis. 317/E2
Oakbank, Manitoba 179/F5
Oak Bay, Br. Col. 184/K4
Oak Bay, New Bruns. 170/C3
Oak Bluffs, Mass. (02557) 249/M7
Oak Bluffs◯, Mass. (02557) 249/M7
Oak Bluff Station, Manitoba 179/E5
Oakboro, N.C. (28129) 281/J4
Oak Brae, Manitoba 179/C3
Oak Brook, Ill. (60521) 222/B6
Oakbrook Terrace, Ill. (†60181) 222/B5
Oakburn, Manitoba 179/B4
Oak Center, Minn. (†55041) 255/F6
Oak City, N.C. (27857) 281/P3
Oak City, Utah (84649) 304/B4
Oak Creek, Colo. (80467) 208/F2
Oak Creek, Wis. (53154) 317/M2
Oakdale, Calif. (95361) 204/E6
Oakdale, Conn. (06370) 210/G3
Oakdale, Ill. (62268) 222/D5
Oakdale, Iowa (52319) 229/K5
Oakdale, La. (71463) 238/E5
Oakdale, Mass. (01539) 249/G3
Oakdale, Minn. (†55109) 255/E5
Oakdale, Nebr. (68761) 264/F2
Oakdale, Pa. (15071) 294/B5
Oakdale, Tenn. (37829) 237/M9
Oakdale, Wis. (54649) 317/F8
Oakes, N. Dak. (58474) 282/O7
Oakesdale, Wash. (99158) 310/H3
Oakfield, Georgia (31772) 217/E7
Oakfield◯, Maine (04763) 243/G3
Oakfield, N.Y. (14125) 276/D4
Oakfield, Tenn. (38362) 237/D9
Oakfield, Wis. (53065) 317/J8
Oakford, Ill. (62673) 222/D3
Oakford, Ind. (46965) 227/E4
Oak Forest, Ill. (60452) 222/B6
Oak Grove, Ala. (†36612) 195/B9
Oak Grove, Ala. (35006) 195/F4
Oak Grove, Ark. (72660) 202/C1
Oak Grove, Del. (†19973) 245/R6
Oak Grove, Ill. (†61264) 222/C2
Oak Grove, Ky. (42262) 237/G7
Oak Grove, La. (71263) 238/H1
Oak Grove, Mich. (48863) 250/F6
Oak Grove, Mo. (64075) 261/S6
Oak Grove, Mo. (†63080) 261/K6
Oak Grove, Oreg. (97268) 291/B2
Oak Grove, Va. (22443) 307/O4
Oak Grove Fork, Clackamas (riv.), Oreg. 291/F2
Oak Hall, Pa. (†16827) 294/G4
Oak Hall, Va. (23416) 307/S5
Oakham, England 13/G5
Oakham, England 10/F4
Oakham◯, Mass. (01068) 249/F3
Oak Harbor, Ohio (43449) 284/D2
Oak Harbor, Wash. (98277) 310/C2
Oak Harbor Naval Air Sta., Wash. 310/C2
Oakhaven, Ark. (†71801) 202/C6
Oak Hill, Ala. (36766) 195/D7
Oak Hill, Fla. (32759) 212/F3
Oak Hill, Ill. (61518) 222/D3
Oakhill, Kansas (67472) 232/E2
Oak Hill, Mo. (†65453) 261/K6
Oak Hill, Ohio (45656) 284/E8
Oak Hill, Tenn. (†37201) 237/H8
Oak Hill, W. Va. (25901) 312/D6
Oakhurst, Calif. (93644) 204/F6
Oakhurst, N.J. (07755) 273/E3
Oakhurst, Okla. (74050) 288/P2
Oakhurst, Texas (77359) 303/J7
Oak Island, Minn. (56741) 255/D1
Oak Lake, Manitoba 179/B5
Oakland, Calif. 146/F6
Oakland, Calif. 188/B3
Oakland, Calif. (*94601) 204/J2
Oakland, Conn. (†06040) 210/E1
Oakland, Fla. (32760) 212/E3
Oakland, Ill. (61943) 222/F4
Oakland, Iowa (51560) 229/C6
Oakland, Ky. (42159) 237/J6
Oakland, La. (†71260) 238/F1
Oakland, Maine (04963) 243/D6
Oakland◯, Maine (04963) 243/D6
Oakland, Md. (†21784) 245/L3
Oakland, Md. (21550) 245/A3
Oakland (co.), Mich. 250/F6
Oakland, Miss. (38948) 256/E2
Oakland, Mo. (†63101) 261/P3
Oakland, Mo. (†65536) 261/G7
Oakland, Nebr. (68045) 264/H3
Oakland, N.J. (07436) 273/B1
Oakland, Okla. (73452) 288/N6
Oakland, Ontario 177/D4
Oakland, Oreg. (97462) 291/D4
Oakland, Pa. (†18847) 294/L2
Oakland, R.I. (02858) 249/H5
Oakland, Tenn. (38060) 237/B10
Oakland Acres, Iowa (†50112) 229/H5
Oakland Army Base, Calif. 204/J2
Oakland Beach, R.I. (†02887) 249/J6
Oakland City, Ind. (47660) 227/C8
Oakland Mills, Iowa (†52641) 229/K7
Oakland Park, Fla. (33334) 212/B3
Oaklands, N.S. Wales 97/D4
Oak Lawn, Ill. (*60453) 222/B6
Oakleigh, Victoria 88/L7
Oakleigh, Victoria 97/J5
Oakley, Calif. (94561) 204/L1
Oakley, Idaho (83346) 220/D7
Oakley, Ill. (62552) 222/E4
Oakley, Iowa (†50049) 229/G6
Oakley, Kansas (67748) 232/B2
Oakley, Mich. (48649) 250/E5
Oakley, Miss. (†39154) 256/D6
Oakley, N.C. (†27871) 281/P3
Oakley, Scotland 15/C1
Oakley, S.C. (29466) 296/G5
Oakley, Tenn. (†38541) 237/L8
Oakley, Utah (84055) 304/C3
Oaklyn, N.J. (08107) 273/B3
Oakman, Ala. (35579) 195/D3
Oakman, Georgia (30732) 217/C1
Oakmont, Pa. (15139) 294/C6
Oakmulgee (creek), Ala. 195/D5
Oakner, Manitoba 179/B4
Oak Orchard, Del. (†19966) 245/T6
Oakover (riv.), W. Australia 88/C4
Oakover (riv.), W. Australia 92/C3
Oak Park, Georgia (31903) 217/H6
Oak Park, Ill. (*60303) 222/B5
Oak Park, Mich. (48237) 250/B6
Oak Park, Minn. (56357) 255/E5
Oakpark, Va. (22730) 307/M4
Oak Point, Manitoba 179/B5
Oak Point, New Bruns. 170/D3
Oak Ridge, La. (71264) 238/G1
Oak Ridge, Miss. (†39180) 256/C6
Oak Ridge, Mo. (63769) 261/N7
Oak Ridge, N.J. (07438) 273/E1
Oak Ridge (res.), N.J. 273/D1
Oak Ridge, N.C. (27310) 281/K2
Oakridge, Oreg. (97463) 291/E4
Oak Ridge, Pa. (16245) 294/D3
Oak Ridge, Tenn. 188/J3
Oak Ridge, Tenn. (37830) 237/N8

Olduvai Gorge 421

Oak River, Manitoba 179/D4
Oaks, Mo. (†64116) 261/P5
Oaks, Okla. (74359) 288/S2
Oakshela, Sask. 181/J5
Oakton, Ky. (42077) 237/C7
Oakton, Va. (22124) 307/R3
Oaktown, Ind. (47561) 227/C7
Oak Vale, Miss. (39656) 256/E8
Oakvale, W. Va. (24739) 312/D8
Oak Valley, Kansas (†67352) 232/G4
Oak View, Calif. (93022) 204/F9
Oakview, Manitoba 179/D3
Oakview, Mo. (†64116) 261/P5
Oakville, Conn. (06779) 210/C2
Oakville, Ind. (47367) 227/G4
Oakville, Iowa (52646) 229/L6
Oakville, Ky. (42263) 237/H7
Oakville, Manitoba 179/D5
Oakville, Ontario 177/E4
Oakville, Pa. (†17257) 294/H5
Oakville, Texas (78060) 303/G9
Oakville, Wash. (98568) 310/B4
Oakway, S.C. (†29694) 296/A2
Oakwood, Georgia (30566) 217/E2
Oakwood, Ill. (61858) 222/F3
Oakwood, Mo. (63401) 261/P5
Oakwood, N. Dak. (†58237) 282/R3
Oakwood, Ohio (†44146) 284/H9
Oakwood, Ohio (†45419) 284/B6
Oakwood, Ohio (45873) 284/B3
Oakwood, Okla. (73658) 288/J3
Oakwood, Ontario 177/F3
Oakwood, Texas (75855) 303/J6
Oakwood, Va. (24631) 307/E6
Oakwood Heights, Ill. (†62095) 222/B2
Oakwood Manor, Mo. (†64101) 261/P5
Oakwood Park, Mo. (†64116) 261/P5
Oamaru, N. Zealand 100/C6
Oani (riv.), Japan 81/K3
Oasis, Nev. (†89830) 266/G1
Oasis, Utah (84650) 304/B4
Oates Coast (reg.) 5/B8
Oatlands, Tasmania 99/D4
Oatman, Ariz. (86433) 198/A3
Oatsville, Ind. (†47567) 227/C8
Oaxaca (state), Mexico 150/L8
Oaxaca, Mexico 146/J8
Oaxaca de Juárez, Mexico 150/L8
Ob' (riv.), U.S.S.R. 2/N2
Ob' (riv.), U.S.S.R. 54/H3
Ob' (gulf), U.S.S.R. 54/J3
Ob' (gulf), U.S.S.R. 4/B6
Ob' (riv.), U.S.S.R. 4/C6
Ob' (gulf), U.S.S.R. 48/H3
Ob' (riv.), U.S.S.R. 48/G3
Oba, Ont. 162/H6
Oba, Ontario 177/J5
Oba, Ontario 175/D3
Obama, Japan 81/G6
Oban (Half Moon Bay), N. Zealand 100/B7
Oban, Sask. 181/C3
Oban, Scotland 15/C4
Oban, Scotland 10/D2
Obbia, Somalia 115/J2
Obed, Alberta 182/B3
Obed (riv.), Tenn. 237/M8
Ober, Ind. (†46534) 227/D2
Oberá, Argentina 143/F2
Oberägeri, Switzerland 39/G2
Oberalp (pass), Switzerland 39/G3
Oberalpstock (mt.), Switzerland 39/G3
Oberammergau, W. Germany 22/D5
Oberburg, Switzerland 39/E2
Oberdiessbach, Switzerland 39/E3
Oberdorf, Switzerland 39/E2
Ober Grafendorf, Austria 41/C2
Oberhausen, W. Germany 22/B3
Oberhof, E. Germany 22/D3
Oberlin, Kansas (67749) 232/B2
Oberlin, La. (70655) 238/E5
Oberlin, Mich. (†48624) 250/E4
Oberlin, Ohio (44074) 284/F3
Oberndorf bei Salzburg, Austria 41/B3
Oberon, Manitoba 179/C4
Oberon, N.S. Wales 97/E3
Oberon, N. Dak. (58357) 282/M4
Oberpfälzer Wald (for.), W. Germany 22/E4
Oberriet, Switzerland 39/J2
Obersaxen, Switzerland 39/H3
Obersiggenthal, Switzerland 39/F1
Oberstammheim, Switzerland 39/G1
Oberstdorf, W. Germany 22/D5
Obert, Nebr. (68762) 264/G2
Oberursel, W. Germany 22/C3
Obervellach, Austria 41/B3
Oberwald, Switzerland 39/F3
Oberwart, Austria 41/D3
Oberwil, Switzerland 39/D3
Oberwölz, Austria 41/C3
Oberzwil, Switzerland 39/H2
Obetz, Ohio (†43201) 284/E6
Obi (isl.), Indonesia 85/H6
Obi (isls.), Indonesia 85/H6
Obidos, Brazil 120/D3
Obidos, Brazil 132/C3
Obidos, Portugal 33/B3
Obihiro, Japan 81/L2
Obion (creek), Ky. 237/C7
Obion (co.), Tenn. 237/C8
Obion, Tenn. (38240) 237/C8
Obion, Middle Fork (riv.), Tenn. 237/D8
Obion, North Fork (riv.), Tenn. 237/D8
Obion, South Fork (riv.), Tenn. 237/D8
Obion (riv.), Tenn. 237/C8
Obispos, Venezuela 124/D3
Obitsu (riv.), Japan 81/P3
Oblong, Ill. (62449) 222/F5
Obluch'ye, U.S.S.R. 48/N5
Obninsk, U.S.S.R. 52/E3
Obo, Cent. Afr. Rep. 115/E2
Obock, Djibouti 111/H5
Oborniki, Poland 47/C2
Oboyan', U.S.S.R. 52/E4
Obozerskiy, U.S.S.R. 52/E2
O'Brien, Fla. (32071) 212/D1
O'Brien (co.), Iowa 229/B2
O'Brien, Oreg. (97534) 291/D5
O'Brien, Texas (79539) 303/E4
O'Briensbridge-Montpelier, Ireland 17/D6
Observatory (inlet), Br. Col. 184/C2
Obsidian, Idaho (†83278) 220/D6
Obuasi, Ghana 106/D7
Obukowin (lake), Manitoba 179/G3
Obwalden (canton), Switzerland 39/F3
Ocala, Fla. (*32670) 212/D2
Ocamo (riv.), Venezuela 124/F6
Ocampo, Chihuahua, Mexico 150/E2
Ocampo, Coahuila, Mexico 150/H3
Ocampo, Tamaulipas, Mexico 150/K5
Ocaña, Colombia 126/D3
Ocaña, Spain 33/E3
Ocate, N. Mex. (87734) 274/E2
Ocate (creek), N. Mex. 274/E2
Occidental, Cordillera (range), Bolivia 136/A6
Occidental, Cordillera (range), Colombia 126/B5
Occidental, Cordillera (range), Peru 128/F10
Occidental Mindoro (prov.), Philippines 82/C4
Occoquan, Va. (22125) 307/O3
Occum, Conn. (†06360) 210/G2
Ocean (cape), Alaska 196/K3
Ocean (pond), Fla. 212/D1
Ocean (Banaba) (isl.), Kiribati 87/G6
Ocean (co.), N.J. 273/E4
Ocean (lake), Nova Scotia 168/G3
Ocean (lake), Wyo. 319/D2
Oceana (co.), Mich. 250/C5
Oceana, W. Va. (24870) 312/C7
Oceana N.A.S., Va. 307/S7
Ocean Beach, N.Y. (11770) 276/O9
Ocean Bluff-Brant Rock, Mass. (02065) 249/M4
Ocean Breeze Park, Fla. (†33457) 212/F4
Ocean City, Md. (21842) 245/T7
Ocean City, N.J. (08226) 273/D5
Ocean City, Wash. (98569) 310/A3
Ocean Falls, Br. Col. 184/D4
Ocean Gate, N.J. (08740) 273/E4
Ocean Grove, Mass. (02777) 249/K6
Ocean Grove, N.J. (07756) 273/F3
Ocean Isle Beach, N.C. (28459) 281/N7
Oceano, Calif. (93445) 204/E8
Oceanographic Office, Md. 245/F5
Ocean Park, Maine (04063) 243/C9
Ocean Park, Wash. (98640) 310/A4
Oceanport, N.J. (07757) 273/F3
Ocean Ridge, Fla. (33444) 212/F5
Ocean Shores, Wash. (98551) 310/A3
Oceanside, Calif. (92054) 204/H10
Oceanside, N.Y. (11572) 276/R7
Oceanside, Oreg. (97134) 291/C2
Ocean Springs, Miss. (39564) 256/G10
Ocean View, Del. (19970) 245/T6
Ocean View, N.J. (08230) 273/D5
Oceanville, N.J. (08231) 273/D5
Oceola, Ohio (44860) 284/D4
Ochamchira, U.S.S.R. 52/F6
Ochelata, Okla. (74051) 288/P1
Ocheyedan, Iowa (51354) 229/B2
Ochil (hills), Scotland 15/E4
Ochiltree (co.), Texas 303/D1
Ochlocknee, Georgia (31773) 217/E9
Ochlockonee (riv.), Fla. 212/B1
Ochlockonee (riv.), Georgia 217/C10
Ochoco (creek), Oreg. 291/G3
Ochopee, Fla. (33943) 212/E6
Ocho Rios, Jamaica 158/J6
Ochre River, Manitoba 179/C3
Ochsen (mt.), Switzerland 39/D3
Ochsenfurt, W. Germany 22/D4
Ochsenkopf (mt.), Liecht. 39/J2
Ocie, Mo. (65719) 261/G9
Ocilla, Georgia (31774) 217/F7
Ockelbo, Sweden 18/K6
Ocklawaha (lake), Fla. 212/E2
Ockley, Ind. (†46923) 227/D4
Ocmulgee (riv.), Georgia 217/E5
Ocmulgee Nat'l Mon., Georgia 217/F5
Ocna Mureş, Romania 45/G2
Ocoa, Chile 138/G2
Ocoa (bay), Dom. Rep. 158/D6
Ocoee, Fla. (32761) 212/E3
Ocoee (riv.), Tenn. 237/M10
Ocoña, Peru 128/F11
Ocoña (riv.), Peru 128/F11
Oconee (co.), Georgia 217/F3
Oconee, Georgia (31067) 217/G5
Oconee (riv.), Georgia 217/F5
Oconee, Ill. (62553) 222/D4
Oconee (co.), S.C. 296/A2
Oconomowoc, Wis. (53066) 317/H1
Oconomowoc (lake), Wis. 317/H1
Oconomowoc Lake, Wis. (†53066) 317/H1
Oconto, Nebr. (68860) 264/E3
Oconto (co.), Wis. 317/K6
Oconto, Wis. (54153) 317/L6
Oconto (riv.), Wis. 317/K5
Oconto Falls, Wis. (54154) 317/K6
Ocós, Guatemala 154/A3
Ocosingo, Mexico 150/O8
Ocosta, Wash. (†98520) 310/B4
Ocotal, Segovia, Nicaragua 154/D4
Ocotal, Zelaya, Nicaragua 154/E4
Ocotlán, Mexico 150/H6
Ocotlán de Morelos, Mexico 150/L8
Ocqueoc, Mich. (†49759) 250/F3
Ocracoke, N.C. (27960) 281/T4
Ocracoke (inlet), N.C. 281/T5
Ocracoke (isl.), N.C. 281/T4
Ocre, Ala. (†36274) 195/H4
Ocros, Peru 128/D8
Octa, Mo. (†63876) 261/M10
Octa, Ohio (†43160) 284/C6
Octagon, Ala. (†36748) 195/C6
Octavia, Nebr. (68650) 264/G3
Octavia, Okla. (74958) 288/S5
October Revolution (isl.), U.S.S.R. 54/K2
October Revolution (isl.), U.S.S.R. 4/B5
October Revolution (isl.), U.S.S.R. 48/L2
Ocú, Panama 154/G7
Ocumare de la Costa, Venezuela 124/E2
Ocumare del Tuy, Venezuela 124/E2
Ocurí, Bolivia 136/C6
Oda, Ghana 106/D7
Oda, Japan 81/F6
Oda, Jebel (mt.), Sudan 59/C5
Oda, Jebel (mt.), Sudan 111/G3
Odanah, Wis. (54861) 317/E2
Odate, Japan 81/K3
Odawara, Japan 81/J6
Odd, W. Va. (25902) 312/D7
Odda, Norway 18/E6
Odder, Denmark 21/D6
Oddur, Somalia 115/H3
Odebolt, Iowa (51458) 229/C4
Odell, Ill. (60460) 222/E2
Odell, Ind. (†47992) 227/C4
Odell, Nebr. (68415) 264/H4
Odell, Oreg. (97044) 291/F2
Odell (lake), Oreg. 291/E4
Odell, Texas (79247) 303/E3
Odell River, New Bruns. 170/C2
Odemira, Portugal 33/B4
Ödemiş, Turkey 63/C3
Oden, Ark. (71961) 202/C4
Odenburg, La. (†71369) 238/G5
Odendaalsrus, S. Africa 118/D5
Odense, Denmark 7/F3
Odense, Denmark 18/G9
Odense, Denmark 21/D7
Odense (fjord), Denmark 21/D7
Odenton, Md. (21113) 245/M4
Odenville, Ala. (35120) 195/F3
Odenwald (for.), W. Germany 22/C4
Oder (riv.) 7/F3
Oder (Odra) (riv.), Czech. 41/D2
Oder (riv.), E. Germany 22/F2
Oder (riv.), Poland 47/B2
Oder-Haff (mts.), E. Germany 22/F2
Oder-Haff (lag.), Poland 47/B2
Odessa, Del. (19730) 245/R3
Odessa, Fla. (33556) 212/D3
Odessa, Minn. (56276) 255/B5
Odessa, Mo. (64076) 261/E5
Odessa, Nebr. (68861) 264/E4
Odessa, N.Y. (14869) 276/G6
Odessa, Ontario 177/H3
Odessa, Sask. 181/H5
Odessa, Tex. 188/F4
Odessa, Texas 146/H6
Odessa, Texas (79760) 303/B6
Odessa, U.S.S.R. 2/L3
Odessa, U.S.S.R. 7/H4
Odessa, U.S.S.R. 48/D5
Odessa, U.S.S.R. 52/D5
Odessa, Wash. (99159) 310/G3
Odessadale, Georgia (†30222) 217/C5
Odgen, Utah 188/D2
Odgensburg, N.Y. 188/M2
Odiel (riv.), Spain 33/C4
Odienné, Ivory Coast 106/C7
Odin, Ill. (62870) 222/D5
Odin, Kansas (67562) 232/D3
Odin, Minn. (56160) 255/D7
Odiongan, Philippines 82/C4
Odivelas, Portugal 33/A1
Odobeşti, Romania 45/H3
Odon, Ind. (47562) 227/C7
Odongk, Cambodia 72/E5
O'Donnell, Texas (79351) 303/C5
O'Donnells, Newf. 166/D2
Odoorn, Netherlands 27/K3
Odorheiu Secuiesc, Romania 45/G2
Odra (Oder) (riv.), Poland 47/B2
Odry, Czech. 41/D2
Odum, Georgia (31555) 217/H7
Odweina, Somalia 115/J2
Oebisfelde, E. Germany 22/D2
Oeiras, Brazil 132/F4
Oeiras, Portugal 33/B3
Oelemari (riv.), Suriname 131/D4
Oella, Md. (†21228) 245/L3
Oelrichs, S. Dak. (57763) 298/C7
Oelsnitz, E. Germany 22/E3
Oelsnitz im Erzgebirge, E. Germany 22/E3
Oelwein, Iowa (50662) 229/K3
Oeno (isl.), Pitcairn Is. 87/O8
Oenpelli, North. Terr. 93/C2
Oensingen, Switzerland 39/E2
Of, Turkey 63/J2
Ofahoma, Miss. (39141) 256/E5
O'Fallon, Ill. (62269) 222/B2
O'Fallon, Mo. (63366) 261/L5
O'Fallon (creek), Mont. 262/L4
Ofanto (riv.), Italy 34/E4
Ofaqim, Israel 65/B5
Ofen (pass), Switzerland 39/K3
Ofenhorn (mt.), Switzerland 39/F4
Offa, Nigeria 106/E7
Offaly (co.), Ireland 17/F5
Offenbach am Main, W. Germany 22/C3
Offenburg, W. Germany 22/B4
Offerle, Kansas (67563) 232/C4
Offerman, Georgia (31556) 217/H8
Offutt, Ky. (41237) 237/R5
Offutt A.F.B., Nebr. 264/J3
Ofotfjorden (fjord), Norway 18/K2
Ofqui (isth.), Chile 138/D6
Oftringen, Switzerland 39/E2
Ofunato, Japan 81/K4
Oga, Japan 81/J4
Oga (pen.), Japan 81/J4
Ogaden (reg.), Ethiopia 102/G4
Ogaden (reg.), Ethiopia 111/H6
Ogaki, Japan 81/H6
Ogallah, Kansas (67656) 232/C3
Ogallala, Nebr. (69153) 264/C3
Ogasawara-gunto (Bonin) (isls.), Japan 81/M3
Ogbomosho, Nigeria 102/C4
Ogbomosho, Nigeria 106/E7
Ogden, Ark. (71853) 202/B6
Ogden, Ill. (61859) 222/F3
Ogden, Iowa (50212) 229/E4
Ogden, Kansas (66517) 232/F2
Ogden (bay), N.W. Terrs. 187/H3
Ogden, Utah 146/G6
Ogden, Utah (*84401) 304/C2
Ogden Dunes, Ind. (†46401) 227/C1
Ogdensburg, N.J. (07439) 273/D1
Ogdensburg, N.Y. (13669) 276/K1
Ogdensburg, Wis. (54962) 317/J7
Ogeechee (riv.), Georgia 217/J5
Ogema, Minn. (56569) 255/C3
Ogema, Sask. 181/G6
Ogema, Wis. (54459) 317/F5
Ogemaw, Ark. (†71764) 202/E7
Ogemaw (co.), Mich. 250/E4
Ogi, Japan 81/J5
Ogidaki (mt.), Ontario 175/D3
Ogidaki (mt.), Ontario 177/J5
Ogilvie, Manitoba 179/D4
Ogilvie, Minn. (56358) 255/E5
Ogilvie (mts.), Yukon 187/E3
Ogilvie (riv.), Yukon 187/E3
Oglala, S. Dak. (57764) 298/D7
Ogle (co.), Ill. 222/D1
Ogle, Ky. (40971) 237/O6
Oglesby, Ill. (61348) 222/D2
Oglesby, Texas (76561) 303/G6
Oglethorpe (co.), Georgia 217/F3
Oglethorpe, Georgia (31406) 217/D6
Oglio (riv.), Italy 34/C2
Ogmore, Queensland 88/J4
Ogmore and Garw, Wales 13/A6
Ogoja, Nigeria 106/F7
Ogoki (riv.), Ont. 162/H5
Ogoki (riv.), Ontario 175/C2
Ogooué (riv.), Congo 115/A4
Ogooué (riv.), Gabon 115/A4
Ogre, U.S.S.R. 53/C2
Ogulin, Yugoslavia 45/B3
Ogun (state), Nigeria 106/E7
Ogunquit, Maine (03907) 243/B9
Oğuzeli, Turkey 63/G4
Ohai, N. Zealand 100/A6
Ohakune, N. Zealand 100/E3
O'Hare Field-Chicago International Airport, Ill. 222/B5
Ohariu (stream), N. Zealand 100/B2
Ohata, Japan 81/K3
Ohatchee, Ala. (36271) 195/G3
Ohaton, Alberta 182/D3
Ohau (lake), N. Zealand 100/B6
Ohaupo, N. Zealand 100/E2
Ohey, Belgium 27/G8
O'Higgins (lake), Chile 138/D7
Ohio 188/K2
OHIO 284
Ohio (riv.) 188/J3
Ohio, Colo. (81237) 208/F5
Ohio, Ill. (61349) 222/D2
Ohio (riv.), Ill. 222/E6
Ohio (co.), Ind. 227/H7
Ohio (riv.), Ind. 227/B9
Ohio (co.), Ky. 237/H6
Ohio (riv.), Ky. 237/F5
Ohio, Nova Scotia 168/F3
Ohio (riv.), Nova Scotia 168/D4
Ohio (riv.), Ohio 284/B8
Ohio (riv.), Pa. 294/A4
Ohio (state), U.S. 146/K5
Ohio (riv.), U.S. 146/K6
Ohio (riv.), U.S. 2/E4
Ohio (co.), W. Va. 312/E2
Ohio (riv.), W. Va. 312/B5
Ohio Brush (creek), Ohio 284/D8
Ohio City, Ohio (45874) 284/A4
Ohiopyle, Pa. (15470) 294/D6
Ohioville, Pa. (†15059) 294/B4
Ohiowa, Nebr. (68416) 264/G4
Ohley, W. Va. (25147) 312/D6
Ohlman, Ill. (62076) 222/D4
Ohoopee, Georgia (†30436) 217/H6
Ohopoho, Namibia 118/A3
Ohře (riv.), Czech. 41/B1
Ohrid (lake), Albania 45/E5
Ohrid, Yugoslavia 45/E5
Ohrid (lake), Yugoslavia 45/E5
Ohura, N. Zealand 100/E3
Oiapoque (Oyapock) (riv.), Brazil 132/C2
Oich, Loch (lake), Scotland 15/D3
Oich (riv.), Scotland 15/D3
Oies (isl.), Québec 172/G2
Oil (creek), Pa. 294/C2
Oil Center, N. Mex. (88266) 274/F6
Oil City, La. (71061) 238/C1
Oil City, Ontario 177/B5
Oil City, Pa. 188/L2
Oil City, Pa. (16301) 294/F8
Oildale, Calif. (93308) 204/F8
Oilmont, Mont. (59466) 262/E2
Oil Spring Ind. Res., N.Y. 276/D6
Oil Springs, Ky. (41238) 237/P5
Oil Springs, Ontario 177/B5
Oilton, Okla. (74052) 288/N2
Oilton, Texas (78371) 303/F10
Oil Trough, Ark. (72564) 202/G2
Oinoi, Greece 45/F6
Oise (dept.), France 28/E3
Oise (riv.), France 28/E3
Oiseau (lake), Manitoba 179/G4
Oiseau (riv.), Manitoba 179/G4
Oisterwijk, Netherlands 27/G5
Oistins, Barbados 161/B9
Oistins (bay), Barbados 161/B9
Oita (pref.), Japan 81/E7
Oita, Japan 81/E7
Ojai, Calif. (93023) 204/F9
Ojibwa, Wis. (54862) 317/D4
Ojinaga, Mexico 150/G2
Ojiya, Japan 81/J5
Ojocaliente, Mexico 150/H5
Ojo Caliente, N. Mex. (87549) 274/D2
Ojo del Toro (mt.), Cuba 158/G4
Ojo Feliz, N. Mex. (87735) 274/E2
Ojo Sarco, N. Mex. (87550) 274/D2
Ojos del Salado (mt.) 120/C5
Ojos del Salado, Cerro (mt.), Argentina 143/C2
Ojos del Salado, Nevado (mt.), Chile 138/B6
Ojos Negros, Spain 33/F2
Ojus, Fla. (33163) 212/B4
Oka, Québec 172/C4
Oka (riv.), U.S.S.R. 7/J3
Oka (riv.), U.S.S.R. 48/L4
Oka (riv.), U.S.S.R. 52/F4
Okaba, Indonesia 85/K7
Okabena, Minn. (56161) 255/C7
Okahandja, Namibia 102/D7
Okahandja, Namibia 118/B4
Okahumpka, Fla. (32762) 212/D3
Okak (bay), Newf. 166/B2
Okak (isls.), Newf. 166/B2
Okaloacoochee Slough (swamp), Fla. 212/E5
Okaloosa (co.), Fla. 212/C6
Okamanpeedan (lake), Iowa 229/D2
Okanagan (lake), Br. Col. 162/D6
Okanagan (lake), Br. Col. 184/H5
Okanagan Centre, Br. Col. 184/H5
Okanagan Falls, Br. Col. 184/H5
Okanagan Landing, Br. Col. 184/H5
Okanagan Mission, Br. Col. 184/H5
Okanagan Mtn. Prov. Park, Br. Col. 184/G5
Okanogan (riv.), Br. Col. 184/H6
Okanogan (co.), Wash. 310/F2
Okanogan, Wash. (98840) 310/F2
Okanogan (riv.), Wash. 310/F2
Okarche, Okla. (73762) 288/L3
Okatibbee (creek), Miss. 256/G5
Okatibbee (lake), Miss. 256/G5
Okato, N. Zealand 100/D3
Okaton, S. Dak. (57562) 298/H6
Okauchee, Wis. (53069) 317/J1
Okauchee (lake), Wis. 317/J1
Okaukuejo, Namibia 118/B3
Okawa, Japan 81/E7
Okawville, Ill. (62271) 222/D5
Okay, Okla. (74446) 288/R3
Okaya, Japan 81/H5
Okayama (pref.), Japan 81/F6
Okayama, Japan 81/F6
Okazaki, Japan 81/H6
O'Kean, Ark. (72449) 202/J1
Okeana, Ohio (45053) 284/A7
Okee, Wis. (†53555) 317/H9
Okeechobee (lake), Fla. 188/K5
Okeechobee (co.), Fla. 212/F4
Okeechobee, Fla. (33472) 212/F4
Okeechobee (lake), Fla. 212/F5
O'Keeffe Nat'l Hist. Site, N. Mex. 274/C2
Okeene, Okla. (73763) 288/K2
Okefenokee (swamp), Fla. 212/D1
Okefenokee (swamp), Georgia 217/H9
Okehampton, England 13/D7
Okehampton, England 10/D5
Okemah, Okla. (74859) 288/O4
Okemo (Ludlow) (mt.), Vt. 268/B5
Okemos, Mich. (48864) 250/E6
Okene, Nigeria 106/F7
Oker (riv.), W. Germany 22/D2
Okesa, Okla. (†74003) 288/O1
Oketo, Kansas (66518) 232/F2
Okfuskee (co.), Okla. 288/O3
Okha, U.S.S.R. 54/R4
Okha, U.S.S.R. 48/P4
Okha Port, India 68/B4
Okhotsk (sea) 2/S3
Okhotsk (sea), Japan 81/M1
Okhotsk, U.S.S.R. 54/R4
Okhotsk (sea), U.S.S.R. 54/R4
Okhotsk, U.S.S.R. 48/P4
Okhotsk (sea), U.S.S.R. 48/P4
Oki (isls.), Japan 81/F5
Okiep, S. Africa 118/B5
Okinawa (pref.), Japan 81/N6
Okinawa (isls.), Japan 54/O7
Okinawa (isl.), Japan 81/N6
Okinawa (isls.), Japan 81/N6
Okinoerabu (isl.), Japan 81/N5
Okkan, Burma 72/B3
Okla, Sask. 181/H3
Oklahoma 188/G3
Oklahoma (co.), Okla. 288/M3
OKLAHOMA 288
Oklahoma (state), U.S. 146/J6
Oklahoma City (cap.), Okla. 146/J6
Oklahoma City (cap.), Okla. 188/G3
Oklahoma City (cap.), Okla. (*73101) 288/L4
Oklaunion, Texas (76373) 303/F3
Oklawaha, Fla. (32679) 212/E2
Oklawaha (riv.), Fla. 212/E1
Oklee, Minn. (56742) 255/C3
Okmulgee, Okla. 188/G3
Okmulgee (co.), Okla. 288/P3
Okmulgee, Okla. (74447) 288/O3
Okoboji, Iowa (51355) 229/C2
Okobojo (creek), S. Dak. 298/J4
Okolona, Ark. (71962) 202/D5
Okolona, Ky. (40219) 237/K4
Okolona, Miss. (38860) 256/G2
Okolona, Ohio (43550) 284/B3
Okondja, Gabon 115/B4
Okotoks, Alberta 182/C4
Okovango (riv.) 102/D6
Okovango (riv.), Botswana 118/C3
Okovango (swamps), Botswana 118/C3
Okovango (riv.), Namibia 118/C3
Okoyo, Congo 115/C4
Okpo, Burma 72/C3
Okreek, S. Dak. (57563) 298/J7
Oksino, U.S.S.R. 52/H1
Oktaha, Okla. (74450) 288/R3
Oktibbeha (co.), Miss. 256/G4
Oktyabr'sk, U.S.S.R. 52/G4
Oktyabr'skiy, U.S.S.R. 52/H4
Okulovka, U.S.S.R. 52/D3
Okushiri (isl.), Japan 81/J2
Ola, Ark. (72853) 202/D3
Ola, Georgia (†30253) 217/E4
Ola, Idaho (83657) 220/B5
Olá, Panama 154/G6
Ólafsfjördhur, Iceland 21/C1
Ola Grande (pt.), P. Rico 161/D3
Olalla, Br. Col. 184/H5
Olalla, Wash. (98359) 310/A2
Olamon, Maine (04467) 243/F5
Olancha, Calif. (93549) 204/H7
Olanchito, Honduras 154/D3
Öland (isl.), Sweden 7/F3
Öland (isl.), Sweden 18/K8
Olanta, Pa. (16863) 294/F4
Olanta, S.C. (29114) 296/H4
Olar, S.C. (29843) 296/E5
Olary, S. Australia 94/G5
Olathe, Colo. (81425) 208/D5
Olathe, Kansas (66061) 232/H3
Olathe Nav. Air Sta., Kansas 232/H3
Olavarría, Argentina 143/D4
Olavarría, Argentina 120/C6
Oława, Poland 47/C3
Olberg, Ariz. (†85247) 198/D5
Olbernhau, E. Germany 22/E3
Olbia, Italy 34/B4
Olcott, N.Y. (14126) 276/C4
Old (riv.), Calif. 204/L1
Old (riv.), La. 238/G5
Old (stream), Maine 243/H6
Oldany (isl.), Scotland 15/C2
Old Appleton, Mo. (63770) 261/N7
Old Bahama (chan.), Bahamas 156/B2
Old Bahama (chan.), Cuba 158/G1
Old Bahama (chan.), Cuba 156/B2
Old Bar, N.S. Wales 97/G2
Old Barkerville, Br. Col. 184/G3
Old Bennington, Vt. (†05201) 268/A6
Old Bonaventure, Newf. 166/D2
Old Bridge, N.J. (08857) 273/E3
Old Castile (reg.), Spain 33/D2
Oldcastle, Ireland 10/C4
Oldcastle, Ireland 17/G4
Old Crow, Yukon 187/E3
Oldemarkt, Netherlands 27/J3
Olden, Mo. (†65789) 261/J9
Olden, Norway 18/E6
Olden, Texas (76466) 303/F5
Oldenburg, Ind. (47036) 227/G6
Oldenburg, Miss. (†39661) 256/C7
Oldenburg, W. Germany 22/C2
Oldenburg in Holstein, W. Germany 22/D1
Old England, Jamaica 158/H6
Old Entrance, Alberta 182/B3
Oldenzaal, Netherlands 27/K4
Old Faithful, Wyo. (82190) 319/B1
Oldfield, La. (†70754) 238/L1
Old Fields, W. Va. (26845) 312/J4
Old Forge, N.Y. (13420) 276/L3
Old Forge, Pa. (18518) 294/F7
Old Fort, N.C. (28762) 281/E3
Old Fort, Ohio (44861) 284/D3
Oldfort, Tenn. (37362) 237/M10
Old Glory, Texas (79540) 303/D4
Old Greenwich, Conn. (06870) 210/A4
Oldham, England 13/H2
Oldham, England 10/G2
Oldham (co.), Ky. 237/L4
Oldham, S. Dak. (57051) 298/P5
Oldham (co.), Texas 303/B2
Old Harbor, Alaska (99643) 196/H3
Old Harbour, Jamaica 158/J6
Old Harbour (bay), Jamaica 158/J6
Old Harbour Bay, Jamaica 158/J6
Old Hickory (dam), Tenn. 237/H8
Old Hickory (lake), Tenn. 237/J8
Old Kilpatrick, Scotland 15/B2
Old Landing, Ky. (41358) 237/O5
Old Leighlin, Ireland 17/G6
Old Lodge (creek), S. Dak. 298/K6
Old Lyme, Conn. (06371) 210/F3
Old Main Centre, Sask. 181/D5
Oldman (riv.), Alberta 182/D5
Oldman (riv.), Sask. 181/L2
Oldmans (creek), N.J. 273/C4
Old Marsh Bed, North. Terr. 93/B6
Oldmeldrum, Scotland 15/F3
Oldmeldrum, Scotland 10/E2
Old Mill Creek, Ill. (†60083) 222/B4
Old Mission, Mich. (49673) 250/D4
Old Monroe, Mo. (63369) 261/L5
Old Mystic, Conn. (06372) 210/H3
Old Orchard Beach, Maine (04064) 243/C9
Old Orchard Beach, Maine (04064) 243/C9
Old Perlican, Newf. 166/D2
Old Rhine (riv.), Netherlands 27/E4
Old Rhodes (key), Fla. 212/F6
Old Ripley, Ill. (†62275) 222/D5
Old Road, Ant. & Bar. 161/D11
Old Road Town, St. Chris.-Nevis 161/C10
Olds, Alberta 182/D4
Olds, Iowa (52647) 229/K6
Old Saybrook, Conn. (06475) 210/F3
Old Saybrook, Conn. (06475) 210/F3
Old Shawneetown, Ill. (†62984) 222/E6
Oldsmar, Fla. (33557) 212/B2
Old Spring Hill, Ala. (†36742) 195/C6
Old Sturbridge Village, Mass. (†01566) 249/F4
Old Tampa (bay), Fla. 212/B3
Old Tappan, N.J. (07675) 273/C1
Old Town, Fla. (32680) 212/C2
Oldtown, Idaho (†99156) 220/A1
Oldtown, Ky. (41163) 237/R4
Old Town, Maine (04468) 243/F6
Oldtown, Md. (21555) 245/D2
Old Trap, N.C. (†27974) 281/T2
Olduvai Gorge (canyon), Tanzania 115/G4

422 Old Washington

Old Washington, Ohio (43768) 284/H5
Oldwick, N.J. (08858) 273/D2
Old Wives, Sask. 181/E5
Old Wives (lake), Sask. 181/E5
Old Woman (creek), Wyo. 319/H3
Olean, Mo. (65064) 261/G6
Olean, N.Y. (14760) 276/D6
O'Leary (peak), Ariz. 198/D3
O'Leary, Pr. Edward I. 168/D2
Olecko, Poland 47/F1
Oleiros, Portugal 33/B3
Olëkma (riv.), U.S.S.R. 48/N4
Olëkminsk, U.S.S.R. 48/N3
Olema, Calif. (94950) 204/H1
Olenegorsk, U.S.S.R. 52/D1
Olenek, U.S.S.R. 4/C4
Olenëk (riv.), U.S.S.R. 54/N3
Olënek, U.S.S.R. 48/M3
Olënek (bay), U.S.S.R. 48/N2
Olënek (riv.), U.S.S.R. 48/M3
Olentangy (riv.), Ohio 284/D4
Oléron (isl.), France 28/C5
Oleśnica, Poland 47/C3
Olesno, Poland 47/D3
Oleta, Okla. (74751) 288/R6
Olex, Oreg. (†97812) 291/G2
Oley, Pa. (19547) 294/L5
Olga, N. Dak. (†58221) 282/O2
Olga (mt.), North. Terr. 93/B8
Olga, Wash. (98279) 310/C2
Olgiy (Ulegei), Mongolia 77/C2
Ølgod, Denmark 21/B6
Olha, Manitoba 179/B4
Olhão, Portugal 33/C4
Oliena, Italy 34/B4
Olifants (riv.), Mozambique 118/D4
Olifants (riv.), S. Africa 118/D4
Olimar, Uruguay 145/E3
Olimar Grande (riv.), Uruguay 145/E4
Olímpia, Brazil 135/B2
Olin, Iowa (52320) 229/L5
Olin, Ky. (†40447) 237/N6
Olin, N.C. (28660) 281/H3
Olinda, Brazil 120/F3
Olinda, Brazil 132/H4
Olinda, Calif. (96007) 204/C3
Olinda, Victoria 97/K5
Oliva, Argentina 143/D3
Oliva, Spain 33/F3
Oliva de la Frontera, Spain 33/C3
Olivais, Portugal 33/A1
Olivar Alto, Chile 138/G5
Olivares, Cerro de (mt.), Argentina 143/B3
Olivares, Cerro de (mt.), Chile 138/B8
Olive, Mont. (59343) 262/L5
Olive, Okla. (†74030) 288/O2
Olive Branch, Ill. (62969) 222/D6
Olive Branch, Miss. (38654) 256/E1
Olive Branch, Ohio (†45103) 284/D10
Olive Hill, Ky. (41164) 237/P4
Olivehill, Tenn. (38475) 237/E10
Oliveira, Brazil 135/D2
Olivenza, Spain 33/C3
Oliver (dam), Ala. 195/J5
Oliver, Br. Col. 184/H5
Oliver, Georgia (30449) 217/J5
Oliver (dam), Georgia 217/B6
Oliver (lake), Georgia 217/B5
Oliver, Ind. (†47620) 227/B8
Oliver (co.), N. Dak. 282/H5
Oliver, Pa. (15472) 294/C6
Oliver, Wis. (†54880) 317/B2
Oliver Springs, Tenn. (37840) 237/N8
Olivet, Ill. (†61846) 222/F4
Olivet, Kansas (†66856) 232/G3
Olivet, Md. (†20657) 245/N7
Olivet, Mich. (49076) 250/E6
Olivet, S. Dak. (57052) 298/O7
Olivet, Wis. (†54767) 317/B6
Olivette, Mo. (63124) 261/O2
Olivia, Minn. (56277) 255/C6
Olivia, N.C. (28368) 281/L4
Olivier, La. (†70560) 238/G7
Olivone, Switzerland 39/G3
Olkusz, Poland 47/D3
Olla, La. (71465) 238/F3
Ollachea, Peru 128/G9
Ollagüe (vol.), Bolivia 136/B7
Ollagüe, Chile 120/C5
Ollagüe, Chile 138/B3
Ollantaytambo, Peru 128/F9
Ollie, Iowa (52576) 229/J6
Ollon, Switzerland 39/D4
Olmedo, Spain 33/D2
Olmitz, Kansas (67564) 232/D3
Olmos, Peru 128/C5
Olmos Park, Texas (78212) 303/F8
Olmstead, Ky. (42265) 237/H7
Olmsted, Ill. (62970) 222/D6
Olmsted (co.), Minn. 255/F7
Olmsted Falls, Ohio (44138) 284/G9
Olmstedville, N.Y. (12857) 276/N3
Olmué, Chile 138/F2
Olney, Ill. (62450) 222/E5
Olney, Md. (20832) 245/K4
Olney, Mo. (63370) 261/K4
Olney, Mont. (59927) 262/B2
Olney, Okla. (†74538) 288/O6
Olney, Oreg. (†97103) 291/D1
Olney, Texas (76374) 303/F4
Olney Springs, Colo. (81062) 208/M6
Olofström, Sweden 18/J8
Oloh, Miss. (†39482) 256/E8
Olomouc, Czech. 7/F4
Olomouc, Czech. 41/D2
Olonets, U.S.S.R. 52/D2
Olongapo, Philippines 82/C3
Oloron-Sainte-Marie, France 28/C6
Olot, Spain 33/H1
Olowalu, Hawaii (†96761) 218/H2
Oloy (range), U.S.S.R. 48/R3
Olpe, Kansas (66865) 232/F3
Olsa (riv.), Austria 41/C3
Olsburg, Kansas (66520) 232/F2
Olst, Netherlands 27/J4
Olsztyn (prov.), Poland 47/E2
Olsztyn, Poland 7/G3
Olsztyn, Poland 47/E2
Olsztynek, Poland 47/E2
Olt (riv.), Romania 7/G4
Olt (riv.), Romania 45/G3
Olta, Argentina 143/C3
Olten, Switzerland 39/E2
Olteniţa, Romania 45/H3
Olton, Texas (79064) 303/B3
Oltu, Turkey 63/J2
Olur, Turkey 63/K2
Olustee, Fla. (32072) 212/D1
Olustee (riv.), Fla. 212/D1
Olustee, Okla. (73560) 288/H5
Olutanga (isl.), Philippines 82/D7
Olutanga (isl.), Philippines 85/G4
Olvera, Spain 33/D4
Olvey, Ark. (†72601) 202/E1
Olwampi (cape), China 77/K7
Olympia (isls.), Greece 45/E7
Olympia, Ky. (40358) 237/O4
Olympia (cap.), Wash. 146/F5
Olympia (cap.), Wash. 188/B1
Olympia (cap.), Wash. (*98501) 310/C3
Olympia Fields, Ill. (60461) 222/B6
Olympian Village, Mo. (†63050) 261/M6
Olympic (mts.), Wash. 310/B3
Olympic Nat'l Park, Wash. 188/A1
Olympic Nat'l Park, Wash. 310/B3
Olympic Valley, Calif. (95730) 204/E4
Olympus (mt.), Greece 45/F5
Olympus (mt.), Wash. 310/B3
Olyphant, Ark. (72020) 202/H3
Olyphant, Pa. (18447) 294/F7
Olyphic, N.C. (†28463) 281/M7
Olyutorskiy (cape), U.S.S.R. 54/U4
Olyutorskiy (cape), U.S.S.R. 48/S4
Oma (cape), Japan 81/K3
Oma, Miss. (†39654) 256/D7
Omagari, Japan 81/K4
Omagh (dist.), N. Ireland 17/G2
Omagh, N. Ireland 10/C3
Omagh, N. Ireland 17/G2
Omaguas, Peru 128/F5
Omaha, Ala. (†36274) 195/H4
Omaha, Ark. (72662) 202/D1
Omaha (beach), France 28/C3
Omaha, Georgia (31821) 217/C6
Omaha, Ill. (62871) 222/E6
Omaha, Nebr. 188/G2
Omaha, Nebr. 146/J5
Omaha, Nebr. (*68101) 264/J3
Omaha Ind. Res., Nebr. 264/H2
Omak, Wash. (98841) 310/F2
Omak (lake), Wash. 310/F2
Oman 2/M5
Oman 54/G8
Oman (gulf) 54/G7
Oman (gulf), Iran 59/G5
Oman (gulf), Iran 66/M8
OMAN 59/G6
Oman (gulf), Oman 59/G5
Oman (reg.), Oman 59/G5
Oman (gulf), U.A.E. 59/G5
Omar, W. Va. (25638) 312/C7
Omaruru, Namibia 118/B4
Omas, Peru 128/D9
Omatako (riv.), Namibia 118/B3
Omate, Peru 128/G11
Ombai (str.), Indonesia 85/H7
Omboué, Gabon 115/A4
Ombrone (riv.), Italy 34/C3
Ombúes de Lavalle, Uruguay 145/B4
Ombúes de Oribe, Uruguay 145/C4
Omdurman, Sudan 102/F3
Omdurman, Sudan 59/B6
Omdurman, Sudan 111/F4
Omega, Georgia (31775) 217/E8
Omega, Ind. (†46030) 227/F4
Omega, Ohio (†45690) 284/E7
Omega, Okla. (73764) 288/K3
Omemee, N. Dak. (†58739) 282/K2
Omemee, Ontario 177/F3
Omena, Mich. (49674) 250/D3
Omeo, Victoria 97/D5
'Omer, Israel 65/B5
Omer, Mich. (48749) 250/F4
Omerli, Turkey 63/J4
Omerville, Québec 172/E4
Ometepe (isl.), Nicaragua 154/E5
Ometepec, Mexico 150/K8
Omey (isl.), Ireland 17/A5
Omineca (mts.), Br. Col. 184/E2
Omineca (riv.), Br. Col. 184/E2
Omiš, Yugoslavia 45/C4
Omiya, Japan 81/O2
Ommaney (cape), Alaska 196/M2
Ommanney (bay), N.W. Terrs. 187/H2
Omme (riv.), Denmark 21/B6
Ommen, Netherlands 27/J3
Ömnögovĭ, Mongolia 77/F3
Omø (isl.), Denmark 21/E7
Omo (riv.), Ethiopia 111/G6
Omoa, Honduras 154/C3
Omolon (riv.), U.S.S.R. 54/S3
Omolon (riv.), U.S.S.R. 4/C1
Omolon (riv.), U.S.S.R. 48/Q3
Omoloy (riv.), U.S.S.R. 48/O3
Omono (riv.), Japan 81/J4
Ompah, Ontario 177/H2
Omps, W. Va. (†25411) 312/K4
Omro, Wis. (54963) 317/J7
Omsk, U.S.S.R. 54/J4
Omsk, U.S.S.R. 2/N3
Omsk, U.S.S.R. 48/H4
Omsukchan, U.S.S.R. 48/Q3
Omu, Japan 81/L1
Omura, Bonin Is., Japan 81/M3
Omura, Nagasaki, Japan 81/E7
Omurtag, Bulgaria 45/H4
Omuta, Japan 81/E7
Omutninsk, U.S.S.R. 48/F4
Omutninsk, U.S.S.R. 52/H3
Ona, Fla. (33865) 212/E4
Ona, W. Va. (25545) 312/B6
Onaga, Kansas (66521) 232/F2
Onagawa, Japan 81/K4
Onaka, S. Dak. (57466) 298/L3
Onalaska, Texas (77360) 303/J7
Onalaska, Wash. (98570) 310/C4
Onalaska, Wis. (54650) 317/D8
Onaman (lake), Ontario 177/H4
Onamia, Minn. (56359) 255/E4
Onancock, Va. (23417) 307/S5
Onangué (lake), Gabon 115/A4
Onanole, Manitoba 179/C4
Onaping Falls, Ontario 177/J5
Onaping Falls, Ontario 175/D3
Onaqui, Utah (†84080) 304/B3
Onarga, Ill. (60955) 222/F3
Onawa, Iowa (51040) 229/A4
Onawa, Maine (†04464) 243/E5
Onawa (lake), Maine 243/E5
Onaway, Idaho (†83855) 220/B3
Onaway, Mich. (49765) 250/E3
Onchan, I. of Man 13/C3
Onchiota, N.Y. (12968) 276/M2
Oncócua, Angola 115/B7
Onda, Spain 33/F3
Ondangua, Namibia 118/B3
Ondava (riv.), Czech. 41/F2
Ondo (state), Nigeria 106/F7
Ondo, Nigeria 106/F7
Öndörhaan (Undur Khan), Mongolia 77/G2
Öndörhaan, Mongolia 54/N5
Öndverdharnes (mt.), Iceland 21/A1
O'Neals, Calif. (93645) 204/F6
Oneco, Conn. (06373) 210/H2
Oneco, Fla. (33558) 212/D4
Onefour, Alberta 182/E5
Onega, U.S.S.R. 7/H2
Onega (lake), U.S.S.R. 7/H2
Onega (riv.), U.S.S.R. 7/H2
Onega, U.S.S.R. 52/E2
Onega, U.S.S.R. 48/D3
Onega (bay), U.S.S.R. 52/E2
Onega (lake), U.S.S.R. 48/D3
Onega (lake), U.S.S.R. 52/E2
Onega (riv.), U.S.S.R. 48/D3
Onega (riv.), U.S.S.R. 52/E2
Onego, W. Va. (26886) 312/H5
One Hundred and Fifty Mile House, Br. Col. 184/G4
One Hundred Mile House, Br. Col. 184/G4
Onehunga, N. Zealand 100/B1
Oneida, Ark. (72369) 202/J5
Oneida (co.), Idaho 220/F7
Oneida, Ill. (61467) 222/C2
Oneida, Iowa (†52057) 229/L3
Oneida, Kansas (66522) 232/G2
Oneida, Ky. (40972) 237/O6
Oneida (co.), N.Y. 276/J4
Oneida, N.Y. (13421) 276/J4
Oneida (lake), N.Y. 276/J4
Oneida, Pa. (18242) 294/K4
Oneida, Tenn. (37841) 237/N7
Oneida (co.), Wis. 317/G4
Oneida, Wis. (54155) 317/K7
O'Neill, Nebr. (68763) 264/F2
Onekama, Mich. (49675) 250/C4
Oneonta, Ala. (35121) 195/E3
Oneonta, N.Y. (13820) 276/K6
One Tree Hill, N. Zealand 100/B1
Ong, Nebr. (68452) 264/G4
Ongjin, N. Korea 81/B5
Ongniud, China 77/J3
Ongole, India 68/E5
Ongwediva, Namibia 118/B3
Onhaye, Belgium 27/F8
Oni, U.S.S.R. 52/F6
Onida, S. Dak. (57564) 298/K4
Onilahy (riv.), Madagascar 118/G4
Onima, Neth. Ant. 161/E8
Onion Lake, Sask. 181/B2
Onitsha, Nigeria 106/F7
Onitsha, Nigeria 102/C4
Onkaparinga (riv.), S. Australia 88/D8
Onkaparinga (riv.), S. Australia 94/B8
Onkivesi (lake), Finland 18/P5
Onley, Va. (23418) 307/S5
Only, Tenn. (37140) 237/F9
Ono, Calif. (†96001) 204/C3
Ono, Japan 81/H6
Ono (riv.), Japan 81/E7
Ono, Pa. (17077) 294/J5
Onoda, Japan 81/E6
Onomea, Hawaii (†96781) 218/J4
Onomichi, Japan 81/F6
Onon, Mongolia 77/H2
Onondaga, Mich. (49264) 250/E6
Onondaga (co.), N.Y. 276/H5
Onondaga Ind. Res., N.Y. 276/H5
Onota (lake), Mass. 249/A3
Onoto, Venezuela 124/F3
Onotoa (atoll), Kiribati 87/H6
Onoway, Alberta 182/C3
Onrusrivier, S. Africa 118/G7
Onset, Mass. (02558) 249/M6
Onslow, Australia 87/B8
Onslow, Iowa (52321) 229/M4
Onslow (co.), N.C. 281/P5
Onslow (bay), N.C. 281/P6
Onslow, W. Australia 88/B4
Onslow, W. Australia 92/A3
Onsŏng, N. Korea 81/E2
Onsted, Mich. (49265) 250/E6
Onstwedde, Netherlands 27/K2
Ontake (mt.), Japan 81/H6
Ontario (prov.) 162/H5
Ontario (lake) 146/L5
Ontario (lake) 162/J7
Ontario, Calif. (*91761) 204/D10
Ontario (prov.), Canada 146/K4
Ontario, Ind. (†46746) 227/G1
Ontario, Iowa (†50010) 229/F4
Ontario (lake), N.Y. 188/L2
Ontario (co.), N.Y. 276/F5
Ontario, N.Y. (14519) 276/F4
Ontario (lake), N.Y. 276/F3
Ontario, Ohio (44862) 284/E4
ONTARIO 177
Ontario (lake), Ontario 177/G4
Ontario, Oreg. (97914) 291/K3
Ontario, Wis. (54651) 317/E8
Onteniente, Spain 33/F3
Onton, Ky. (†42455) 237/G5
Ontonagon (co.), Mich. 250/F1
Ontonagon, Mich. (49953) 250/F1
Ontonagon (riv.), Mich. 250/G1
Ontonagon Ind. Res., Mich. 250/F1
Ontong Java (isl.), Solomon Is. 87/G6
Ontong Java (isls.), Solomon Is. 86/D2
Onverwacht, Suriname 131/D3
Onward, Ind. (46967) 227/E3
Onward, Miss. (†39159) 256/C5
Onycha, Ala. (†36467) 195/F8
Onyx, Ark. (†72860) 202/D4
Onyx, Calif. (93255) 204/G8
Oobagooma, W. Australia 92/D2
Oodnadatta, Australia 87/D8
Oodnadatta, S. Australia 88/E5
Oodnadatta, S. Australia 94/D2
Ookala, Hawaii (96774) 218/J4
Oola, Ireland 17/E6
Ooldea, S. Australia 94/B4
Oolitic, Ind. (47451) 227/E7
Oologah, Okla. (74053) 288/P2
Oologah (lake), Okla. 288/P1
Ooltewah, Tenn. (37363) 237/M10
Oona River, Br. Col. 184/C3
Oosterwolde, Netherlands 27/J2
Oostanaula, Georgia (†30701) 217/B1
Oostanaula (riv.), Georgia 217/B2
Oostburg, Netherlands 27/C6
Oostburg, Wis. (53070) 317/L8
Oostende (Ostend), Belgium 27/B6
Oosterend, Netherlands 27/G2
Oosterhout, Netherlands 27/F5
Oostkamp, Belgium 27/C6
Oostmahorn, Netherlands 27/J2
Oost-Vlieland, Netherlands 27/F2
Oostzaan, Netherlands 27/C4
Oostzaan Polder, Netherlands 27/B4
Ootacamund, India 68/D6
Ootmarsum, Netherlands 27/K4
Ootsa (lake), Br. Col. 184/D3
Ootsa Lake, Br. Col. 184/E3
Oozewekwun, Manitoba 179/B5
Opal, Alberta 182/D3
Opal, S. Dak. (57765) 298/D4
Opal, Wyo. (83124) 319/B4
Opala, Zaire 115/D4
Opal Cliffs, Calif. (†95060) 204/K4
Opa Locka, Fla. (33054) 212/B4
Opalton, Queensland 95/B4
Opari, Sudan 111/F7
Oparino, U.S.S.R. 52/G3
Opasatika, Ontario 177/J5
Opasatika, Ontario 175/D3
Opatija, Yugoslavia 45/A3
Opatów, Poland 47/E3
Opava, Czech. 41/E2
Opazatika (riv.), Ontario 175/D3
Opdyke, Ill. (62872) 222/E5
Opelika, Ala. (36801) 195/H5
Opelousas, La. (70570) 238/G5
Opeongo (lake), Ontario 177/F2
Opfikon, Switzerland 39/G2
Opheim, Ill. (61468) 222/C2
Opheim, Mont. (59250) 262/K2
Ophir, Alaska 196/G2
Ophir, Colo. (81426) 208/D7
Ophir, Oreg. (97464) 291/C5
Ophir, Utah (†84074) 304/B3
Opihikao, Hawaii (†96778) 218/K6
Opinaca (riv.), Que. 162/J5
Opinaca (riv.), Québec 174/B2
Opine, Ala. (†36784) 195/C7
Opinnagau (riv.), Ontario 175/D2
Opiscotéo (lake), Québec 174/D2
Opladen, W. Germany 22/B3
Opochka, U.S.S.R. 52/C3
Opoco, Bolivia 136/B6
Opoczno, Poland 47/E3
Opole, Minn. (†56340) 255/D5
Opole (prov.), Poland 47/C3
Opole, Poland 47/C3
Opolis, Kansas (66760) 232/H4
Oporto (Porto) (dist.), Portugal 33/B2
Oporto (Porto), Portugal 33/B2
Opotiki, N. Zealand 100/F3
Opp, Ala. (36467) 195/F8
Oppdal, Norway 18/F5
Oppeln, Poland 47/C3
Oppelo, Ark. (†72110) 202/E3
Oppenheim, W. Germany 22/C4
Oppland (co.), Norway 18/F6
Opportunity, Wash. (99214) 310/H3
Oppy, Ky. (†25685) 237/S5
Optima, Okla. (73948) 288/D1
Optima (lake), Okla. 288/D1
Opua, N. Zealand 100/D1
Opunake, N. Zealand 100/D3
Opuntia (lake), Sask. 181/C4
Opwijk, Belgium 27/E7
'Oqair, Saudi Arabia 59/E4
Oquawka, Ill. (61469) 222/C3
Oquossoc, Maine (04964) 243/B6
Ora, Ind. (46968) 227/D2
Ora, Miss. (†39428) 256/E7
Ora, S.C. (29371) 296/D2
Oracabessa, Jamaica 158/J5
Oracle, Ariz. (85623) 198/E6
Oradea, Romania 7/G4
Oradea, Romania 45/E2
Oradell, N.J. (07649) 273/B1
Oradell (res.), N.J. 273/B1
Orai, India 68/D3
Oraibi, Ariz. (86039) 198/E3
Oraibi Wash (dry riv.), Ariz. 198/E3
Oral, S. Dak. (57766) 298/C7
Oran, Algeria 106/D1
Oran, Algeria 102/B1
Oran, Iowa (50664) 229/J3
Oran, Mo. (63771) 261/N8
Orange (riv.) 2/K7
Orange (riv.) 102/D7
Orange, Australia 87/E9
Orange (riv.), Botswana 118/B5
Orange (cape), Brazil 132/D1
Orange (co.), Calif. 204/H10
Orange, Calif. (*92666) 204/D11
Orange◌, Conn. (06477) 210/C3
Orange (co.), Fla. 212/E3
Orange, Fla. (†32321) 212/B1
Orange (lake), Fla. 212/D2
Orange, France 28/F5
Orange, Georgia (†30114) 217/D2
Orange (co.), Ind. 227/E7
Orange, Ind. (†47443) 227/G5
Orange, Mass. (01364) 249/E2
Orange◌, Mass. (01364) 249/E2
Orange (canal), Netherlands 27/K3
Orange◌, N.H. (†03741) 268/D4
Orange, N.J. (*07050) 273/B2
Orange, N. S. Wales 88/H6
Orange, N. S. Wales 97/E3
Orange (co.), N.Y. 276/M8
Orange (co.), N.C. 281/L2
Orange, Ohio (†44101) 284/J9
Orange (riv.), S. Africa 118/B5
Orange (mts.), Suriname 131/D4
Orange (co.), Texas 303/L7
Orange, Texas (77630) 303/L7
Orange (butte), Utah 304/D5
Orange (co.), Vt. 268/C3
Orange◌, Vt. (†05649) 268/C3
Orange (co.), Va. 307/M4
Orange, Va. (22960) 307/M4
Orange Beach, Ala. (36561) 195/C10
Orangeburg, N.Y. (10962) 276/K8
Orangeburg (co.), S.C. 296/F5
Orangeburg, S.C. (29115) 296/F4
Orange City, Fla. (32763) 212/E3
Orange City, Iowa (51041) 229/A2
Orange Cove, Calif. (93646) 204/F7
Orangedale, Nova Scotia 168/G3
Orange Free State (prov.), S. Africa 102/E7
Orange Free State (prov.), S. Africa 118/D5
Orange Grove, Miss. (†39501) 256/H10
Orange Grove, Texas (78372) 303/F10
Orange Hill, St. Vin. & Grens. 161/A8
Orange Lake, Fla. (32681) 212/D2
Orange Park, Fla. (32073) 212/E1
Orange Springs, Fla. (32682) 212/E2
Orangeville, Ill. (61060) 222/D1
Orangeville, Ind. (†47452) 227/D7
Orangeville, Mich. (†49344) 250/D6
Orangeville, Ohio (44453) 284/J3
Orangeville, Ontario 177/D4
Orangeville, Pa. (17859) 294/K3
Orangeville, Utah (84537) 304/C4
Orange Walk Town, Belize 154/C1
Oranienburg, E. Germany 22/E2
Oranjemund, Namibia 102/D7
Oranjemund, Namibia 118/B5
Oranjestad (cap.), Aruba, Neth. Ant. 161/D10
Oranjestad, Neth. Ant. 156/D4
Oranmore, Ireland 17/D5
Orapa, Botswana 118/D4
Oras, Philippines 82/E4
Orăştie, Romania 45/F3
Orava (res.), Czech. 41/E2
Orava (riv.), Czech. 41/E2
Orava (res.), Poland 47/D4
Oraville, Ill. (62971) 222/D6
Oraviţa, Romania 45/E3
Orb (riv.), France 28/E6
Orbe, Switzerland 39/C3
Orbe (riv.), Switzerland 39/C3
Orbetello, Italy 34/C3
Órbigo (riv.), Spain 33/D1
Orbisonia, Pa. (17243) 294/G5
Orbost, Victoria 88/H7
Orbost, Victoria 97/E5
Örbyhus, Sweden 18/K6
Orca, Alaska (†99574) 196/J2
Orcadia, Sask. 181/J4
Orcas (isl.), Wash. 310/C2
Orcera, Spain 33/E3
Orchard, Colo. (80649) 208/L2
Orchard, Iowa (50460) 229/H2
Orchard, Nebr. (68764) 264/F2
Orchard Beach, Md. (†21122) 245/M4
Orchard Hill, Georgia (30266) 217/D4
Orchard Lake, Mich. (48033) 250/F6
Orchard Mesa, Colo. (†81501) 208/C4
Orchard Park, N.Y. (14127) 276/C5
Orchards, Wash. (98662) 310/C5
Orchard Valley, Wyo. (†82001) 319/H4
Orchid, Fla. (†32970) 212/F4
Orchid, Va. (†23117) 307/N5
Orchy (riv.), Scotland 15/D4
Orcotuna, Peru 128/E8
Orcutt, Calif. (93454) 204/E9
Orcuttville, Conn. (†06076) 210/F1
Ord (mt.), Ariz. 198/D5
Ord (riv.), Australia 87/C7
Ord, Nebr. (68862) 264/F3
Ord (riv.), W. Australia 88/D3
Ord (mt.), W. Australia 92/D2
Ord (riv.), W. Australia 92/E2
Órdenes, Spain 33/B1
Orderville, Utah (84758) 304/B6
Ordoqui, Argentina 143/F7
Ordos (reg.), China 77/G4
Ord River, W. Australia 92/E2
Ordu (prov.), Turkey 63/G2
Ordu, Turkey 59/C1
Ordu, Turkey 63/G2
Ordway, Colo. (81063) 208/M6
Ordway, S. Dak. (†57433) 298/N2
Ordzhonikidze, U.S.S.R. 7/J4
Ordzhonikidze, U.S.S.R. 48/E5
Ordzhonikidze, U.S.S.R. 52/F6
Orealla, Guyana 131/C3
Oreälv (riv.), Sweden 18/L4
Oreana, Idaho (83659) 220/B6
Oreana, Ill. (62554) 222/E4
Oreana, Nev. (†89419) 266/C2
Orebank, Tenn. (†37660) 237/R7
Örebro (co.), Sweden 18/J7
Örebro, Sweden 7/F3
Örebro, Sweden 18/J7
Ore City, Texas (75683) 303/K5
Oregon 188/B2
OREGON 291
Oregon, Ill. (61061) 222/D1
Oregon (co.), Mo. 261/K9
Oregon, Mo. (64473) 261/B2
Oregon (inlet), N.C. 281/U3
Oregon, Ohio (43616) 284/D2
Oregon (creek), Oreg. 291/K5
Oregon (state), U.S. 146/F5
Oregon, Wis. (53575) 317/H10
Oregon Caves Nat'l Mon., Oreg. 291/D5
Oregon City, Oreg. 188/B1
Oregon City, Oreg. (97045) 291/B2
Oregon Dunes Nat'l Rec. Area, Oreg. 291/C4
Oregonia, Ohio (45054) 284/B7
Öregrund, Sweden 18/L6
Orel, U.S.S.R. 7/H3
Orel, U.S.S.R. 52/E4
Orel, U.S.S.R. 48/D4
Orellana, Peru 128/E6
Orellana la Vieja, Spain 33/D3
Orem, Utah (84057) 304/C3
Orenburg, U.S.S.R. 7/K3
Orenburg, U.S.S.R. 48/F4
Orenburg, U.S.S.R. 52/J4
Orenco, Oreg. (†97123) 291/A2
Orense (prov.), Spain 33/C1
Orense, Spain 33/C1
Orense, Spain 7/D4
Orestes, Ind. (46063) 227/F4
Orestías, Greece 45/H5
Öresund (sound), Denmark 21/F6
Öresund (sound), Denmark 18/H9
Öresund (sound), Sweden 18/H9
Oreti (riv.), N. Zealand 100/B6
Oretta, La. (†70660) 238/D5
Orewa, N. Zealand 100/E2
Orford◌, N.H. (03777) 268/C4
Orford, Tasmania 99/D4
Orford Ness (prom.), England 13/J5
Orfordville, N.H. (†03777) 268/C4
Orfordville, Wis. (53576) 317/H10
Organ, N. Mex. (88052) 274/C6
Organabo, Fr. Guiana 131/E3
Organ Pipe Cactus Nat'l Mon., Ariz. 198/C6
Órgãos (range), Brazil 135/E3
Orgas, W. Va. (25148) 312/C6
Orgaz, Spain 33/E3
Orgeyev, U.S.S.R. 52/C5
Orhaneli, Turkey 63/C3
Orhangazi, Turkey 63/C2
Orhon Gol (riv.), Mongolia 77/F2
Oria, Spain 33/E4
Orick, Calif. (95555) 204/A2
Orient, Ill. (62874) 222/E6
Orient, Iowa (50858) 229/E6
Orient◌, Maine (04471) 243/H4
Orient, N.Y. (11957) 276/R8
Orient (pt.), N.Y. 276/R8
Orient, Ohio (43146) 284/D6
Orient, S. Dak. (57467) 298/L4
Orient, Wash. (99160) 310/G2
Orienta, Okla. (73765) 288/J2
Oriental, Cordillera (range), Bolivia 136/C5
Oriental, Cordillera (range), Colombia 126/D5
Oriental, Cordillera (range), Dom. Rep. 158/F6
Oriental, Mexico 150/O1
Oriental, N.C. (28571) 281/R4
Oriental, Cordillera (range), Peru 128/H10
Oriental Mindoro (prov.), Philippines 82/C4
Orihuela, Spain 33/F3
Orihvesi (lake), Finland 18/Q5
Orillia, Ontario 177/E3
Orin, Wash. (†99114) 310/H2
Orin, Wyo. (†82633) 319/G3
Orinda, Calif. (94563) 204/J2
Orinoca, Bolivia 136/B6
Orinoco (riv.) 120/C2
Orinoco (riv.) 2/F5
Orinoco (riv.), Colombia 126/G5
Orinoco (delta), Venezuela 120/C2
Orinoco (delta), Venezuela 124/H3
Orinoco (riv.), Venezuela 124/G3
Oriole, Md. (21848) 245/P8
Orion, Ala. (†36081) 195/F7
Orion, Alberta 182/E5
Orion, Ill. (61273) 222/C2
Oriska, N. Dak. (58063) 282/P6
Oriskany, N.Y. (13424) 276/K4
Oriskany, Va. (24130) 307/J5
Oriskany Falls, N.Y. (13425) 276/J5
Orissa (state), India 68/E5
Oristano, Italy 34/B5
Oristano (gulf), Italy 34/B5
Orituco (riv.), Venezuela 124/E3
Oriximiná, Brazil 132/C3
Orizaba, Mexico 146/J8
Orizaba, Mexico 150/P2
Orizaba (Citlaltépetl) (mt.), Mexico 150/O2
Órjiva, Spain 33/E4
Orkanger, Norway 18/F5
Örkény, Hungary 41/E3
Orkney, Sask. 181/D6
Orkney (islands area), Scotland 15/E1
Orkney (trad. co.), Scotland 15/B4
Orkney (isls.), Scotland 7/D3
Orkney (isls.), Scotland 15/F1
Orkney (isls.), Scotland 10/E1
Orla, Texas (79770) 303/D10
Orland, Calif. (95963) 204/C4
Orland, Ind. (46776) 227/G1
Orland, Maine (04472) 243/F6
Orland◌, Maine (04472) 243/F6
Orlândia, Brazil 135/C2
Orlando, Fla. 146/K7
Orlando, Fla. 188/K5
Orlando, Fla. (*32801) 212/E3
Orlando, Ky. (40460) 237/N6

Ox (Slieve Gamph) (mts.), Ireland 17/D3
Oxapampa, Peru 128/E8
Oxbow (dam), Idaho 220/B5
Oxbow◯, Maine (04764) 243/G3
Oxbow, Oreg. (97840) 291/L2
Oxbow (dam), Oreg. 291/L3
Oxbow, Sask. 181/J6
Oxelösund, Sweden 18/K7
Oxford, Ala. (36203) 195/G3
Oxford, Ark. (72565) 202/G1
Oxford◯, Conn. (06483) 210/C3
Oxford, England 13/F6
Oxford, England 10/F5
Oxford, Fla. (32684) 212/D3
Oxford, Georgia (30267) 217/E3
Oxford, Idaho (†83263) 220/F7
Oxford, Ind. (47971) 227/C3
Oxford, Iowa (52322) 229/K5
Oxford, Kansas (67119) 232/E4
Oxford, La. (†71052) 238/C3
Oxford (co.), Maine 243/B7
Oxford, Maine (04270) 243/B7
Oxford◯, Maine (04270) 243/B7
Oxford (lake), Manitoba 179/J3
Oxford, Md. (21654) 245/O6
Oxford, Mass. (01540) 249/G4
Oxford◯, Mass. (01540) 249/G4
Oxford, Mich. (48051) 250/F6
Oxford, Miss. (38655) 256/F2
Oxford, Nebr. (68967) 264/E4
Oxford, N.J. (07863) 273/C2
Oxford, N.Y. (13830) 276/J6
Oxford, N. Zealand 100/D5
Oxford, N.C. (27565) 281/M2
Oxford, Nova Scotia 168/E3
Oxford, Ohio (45056) 284/A6
Oxford, Pa. (19363) 294/K6
Oxford, W. Va. (†26456) 312/E4
Oxford, Wis. (53952) 317/H8
Oxford House, Manitoba 179/J3
Oxford Junction, Iowa (52323) 229/M4
Oxford Junction, Nova Scotia 168/E3
Oxford Mills, Iowa (†52323) 229/L5
Oxford Mills, Ontario 177/J3
Oxfordshire (co.), England 13/F6
Oxkutzcab, Mexico 150/P6
Oxley, N.S. Wales 97/C4
Oxley (creek), Queensland 95/D3
Oxly, Mo. (63955) 261/L9
Oxnard, Calif. (93030) 204/F9
Oxnard A.F.B., Calif. 204/F9
Oxon Hill, Md. (20745) 245/F6
Oxon Run (riv.), Md. 245/F5
Oxton, Scotland 15/F5
Oxtongue Lake, Ontario 177/E2
Oyabe, Japan 81/H5
Oyahue (vol.), Chile 138/C3
Oyama, Br. Col. 184/H5
Oyama, Japan 81/J5
Oyapock (riv.) 120/D2
Oyapock (riv.), Brazil 132/C2
Oyapock (riv.), Fr. Guiana 131/E4
Oyem, Gabon 102/D4
Oyem, Gabon 115/B3
Oyen, Alberta 182/E4
Oyens, Iowa (51045) 229/A3
Oykel (riv.), Scotland 15/D3
Oykel Bridge, Scotland 15/D3
Oylen, Minn. (†56481) 255/D4
Oymyakon, U.S.S.R. 4/C2
Oymyakon, U.S.S.R. 48/O3
Oyo, Congo 115/C4
Oyo (state), Nigeria 106/E7
Oyo, Nigeria 106/E7
Oyón, Peru 128/D8
Oyonnax, France 28/F4
Oyster (bay), Tasmania 88/H8
Oyster (bay), Tasmania 99/E4
Oyster, Va. (23419) 307/S6
Oyster Bay, N.Y. (11771) 276/R6
Oyster River (pt.), Conn. 210/D4
Oysterville, Wash. (98641) 310/A4
Ozalp, Turkey 63/K3
Ozamiz, Philippines 82/D6
Ozan, Ark. (71855) 202/C6
Ozark (mts.) 188/H3
Ozark, Ala. (36360) 195/G8
Ozark, Ark. (72949) 202/C3
Ozark (lake), Ark. 202/C3
Ozark (plat.), Ark. 202/C1
Ozark (res.), Ark. 202/C3
Ozark, Ill. (62972) 222/E6
Ozark (co.), Mo. 261/H9
Ozark, Mo. (65721) 261/F8
Ozark (plat.), Mo. 261Œ9
Ozark Nat'l Scenic Riverways, Mo. 261/K8
Ozarks, Lake of the (lake), Mo. 261/F6
Ozaukee (co.), Wis. 317/L9
Ozawkie, Kansas (66070) 232/G2
Ózd, Hungary 41/F2
Ozernovskiy, U.S.S.R. 48/Q4
Ozernoy (cape), U.S.S.R. 48/R4
Ozette, Wash. (†98326) 310/A2
Ozette (lake), Wash. 310/A2
Ozette Ind. Res., Wash. 310/A2
Ozieri, Italy 34/B4
Ozona, Fla. (33560) 212/D3
Ozona, Texas (76943) 303/C7
Ozone, Ark. (72854) 202/D2
Ozone, Tenn. (37842) 237/M9
Ozorków, Poland 47/D3
Ozu, Japan 81/F7
Ozuluama, Mexico 150/L6
Ozumba de Alzate, Mexico 150/M1

P

Pa-an, Burma 72/C3
Paarden (bay), Neth. Ant. 161/D10
Paarl, S. Africa 102/D8
Paarl, S. Africa 118/F6
Paauhau, Hawaii (96775) 218/H4
Paauilo, Hawaii (96776) 218/H4
Paavola, Finland 18/O4
Pabbay (isl.), Scotland 15/A4
Pabbay (isl.), Scotland 15/A3
Pabianice, Poland 47/D3
Pablo, Mont. (59855) 262/B3
Pabna, Bangladesh 68/F4
Pabos, Québec 172/D2
Pabos-Mills, Québec 172/D2
Pabrade, U.S.S.R. 53/C3
Pacajá Grande (riv.), Brazil 132/D4
Pacaraimã, Serra da (mts.), Brazil 132/H8
Pacaraima, Sierra (mts.), Venezuela 124/G5
Pacasmayo, Peru 128/C6
Pace, Fla. (32570) 212/B6
Pace, Miss. (38764) 256/C3
Pachaug, Conn. (†06351) 210/H2
Pachaug (pond), Conn. 210/H2
Pachaug (riv.), Conn. 210/H2
Pacheco, Calif. (94553) 204/K1
Pachino, Italy 34/E6
Pachitea (riv.), Peru 128/E7
Pachiza, Peru 128/D6
Pachmarhi, India 68/D4
Pacho, Colombia 126/C5
Pachuca de Soto, Mexico 150/K6
Pachuta, Miss. (39347) 256/G6
Pacific (ocean) 54/T5
Pacific (ocean) 146/E6
Pacific, Mo. (63069) 261/L5
Pacific (co.), Wash. 310/B4
Pacific, Wash. (98047) 310/C3
Pacifica, Calif. (94044) 204/H2
Pacific Beach, Calif. (92109) 204/H11
Pacific Beach, Wash. (98571) 310/A3
Pacific City, Oreg. (97135) 291/C2
Pacific Grove, Calif. (93950) 204/C7
Pacific Heights, Hawaii (†96801) 218/C4
Pacific Islands, Terr. of the 87/F5
Pacific Islands, Territory of the 2/S5
Pacific Junction, Iowa (51561) 229/B6
Pacific Palisades, Hawaii (†96782) 218/E2
Pacific Rim Nat'l Park, Br. Col. 184/E6
Pacitan, Indonesia 85/J2
Pack (riv.), Idaho 220/B1
Pack (creek), Utah 304/E5
Packanack Lake, N.J. (07470) 273/B1
Packertown, Ind. (†46510) 227/F2
Packerville, Conn. (†06331) 210/H2
Packington, Québec 172/J2
Packsville, W. Va. (25151) 312/C7
Packwaukee, Wis. (53953) 317/G8
Packwood, Iowa (52580) 229/J6
Packwood, Wash. (98361) 310/D4
Paco, Philippines 82/C2
Pacoa, Colombia 126/E7
Paço de Arcos, Portugal 33/A1
Pacoima, Calif. (91331) 204/B10
Pacolet, S.C. (29372) 296/D2
Pacolet (riv.), S.C. 296/D1
Pacolet Mills, S.C. (29373) 296/D2
Pacov, Czech. 41/C2
Pacsa, Hungary 41/D3
Pacsan (mt.), Philippines 82/C2
Pactolus, N.C. (†27834) 281/P3
Padada, Philippines 82/E7
Padang, Indonesia 54/L10
Padang, Indonesia 85/B6
Padangpanjang, Indonesia 85/B6
Padangsidempuan, Indonesia 85/B5
Padany, U.S.S.R. 52/D2
Padborg, Denmark 21/C8
Padcaya, Bolivia 136/C7
Paddle Prairie, Alberta 182/A5
Paddock Lake, Wis. (†53168) 317/K10
Paddockwood, Sask. 181/F2
Paden, Miss. (38861) 256/H1
Paden, Okla. (74860) 288/N3
Paden City, W. Va. (26159) 312/D3
Paderborn, W. Germany 22/C3
Padgett, S.C. (†29481) 296/F5
Padiham, England 13/H1
Padilla, Bolivia 136/C6
Padilla, Mexico 150/K5
Padilla (creek), N. Mex. 274/D5
Padilla (bay), Wash. 310/C2
Padloping (isl.), N.W.T. 162/K2
Padloping (isl.), N.W. Terrs. 187/M3
Padre (isl.), Texas 188/G5
Padre (isl.), Texas 303/G10
Padre Island Nat'l Seashore, Texas 303/G11
Padre Las Casas, Dom. Rep. 158/D6
Padrón, Spain 33/B1
Padroni, Colo. (80745) 208/N1
Padstow, England 10/D5
Padstow, England 13/B7
Padua (prov.), Italy 34/C2
Padua, Italy 7/F4
Padua, Italy 34/C2
Padua, Minn. (†56378) 255/C5
Paducah, Ky. (42001) 237/D6
Paducah, Ky. 146/K6
Paducah, Ky. 188/J3
Paducah, Texas (79248) 303/D4
Padul, Spain 33/E4
Paekam, N. Korea 81/D3
Paektu (mt.), N. Korea 81/C3
Paeroa, N. Zealand 100/E2
Páez, Colombia 126/C6
Pafúri, Mozambique 118/E4
Pag, Yugoslavia 45/B3
Pag (isl.), Yugoslavia 45/B3
Pagadian, Philippines 82/D7
Pagalungan, Philippines 82/E7
Pagan, Burma 72/B2
Pagan (isl.), No. Marianas 87/E4
Page, Ariz. (86040) 198/D2
Page (co.), Iowa 229/C7
Page, Nebr. (68766) 264/F2
Page, N. Dak. (58064) 282/P5
Page, Okla. (†74939) 288/S5
Page (co.), Va. 307/M3
Page, W. Va. (25152) 312/D6
Page City, Kansas (†67764) 232/A2
Pagedale, Mo. (†63101) 261/P2
Pageland, S.C. (29728) 296/G2
Pago (bay), Guam 86/K7
Pagoda (peak), Colo. 208/E2
Pago Pago (cap.), Amer. Samoa 86/N9
Pago Pago (cap.), Amer. Samoa 87/J7
Pagosa Junction, Colo. (†81147) 208/E8
Pagosa Springs, Colo. (81147) 208/E8
Pagoua (bay), Dominica 161/F6
Paguate, N. Mex. (87040) 274/B3
Pagwa River, Ontario 177/J5
Pagwa River, Ontario 175/D3
Pahala, Hawaii 188/G6
Pahala, Hawaii (96777) 218/H6
Pahang (state), Malaysia 72/D7
Pahang, Sungai (riv.), Malaysia 72/D7
Pahaska, Wyo. (82414) 319/C1
Pahiatua, N. Zealand 100/F4
Pahlevi (Enzeli), Iran 59/E2
Pahlevi (Enzeli), Iran 66/F2
Pahoa, Hawaii (96778) 218/J5
Pahokee, Fla. (33476) 212/F5
Pahranagat (range), Nev. 266/F5
Pahrock (range), Nev. 266/F5
Pah-rum (peak), Nev. 266/B2
Pahrump, Nev. (89041) 266/E6
Pahrump (valley), Nev. 266/F6
Pahsimeroi (riv.), Idaho 220/E5
Pahute (mesa), Nev. 266/E5
Paia, Hawaii (96779) 218/J2
Paicheng (Baicheng), China 77/K2
Paicines, Calif. (95043) 204/D7
Paide, U.S.S.R. 53/C1
Paige, Texas (78659) 303/G7
Paihia, N. Zealand 100/D1
Paihuano, Chile 138/B8
Paiján, Peru 128/C6
Päijänne (lake), Finland 18/O6
Pailin, Cambodia 72/D4
Paillaco, Chile 138/D3
Pailolo (chan.), Hawaii 218/H1
Paimboeuf, France 28/C4
Paimpol, France 28/B3
Painan, Indonesia 85/C6
Paincourt, Ontario 177/B5
Paincourtville, La. (70391) 238/K3
Paine, Chile 138/G4
Paine, Cerro (mt.), Chile 138/D9
Painesdale, Mich. (49955) 250/G1
Painesville, Ohio (44077) 284/H2
Painswick, Ontario 177/E3
Paint (lake), Manitoba 179/J2
Paint (riv.), Mich. 250/A2
Paint (creek), Ohio 284/D7
Paint, Pa. (†15963) 294/E5
Paint Bank, Va. (24131) 307/H5
Paint Branch (riv.), Md. 245/F4
Painted (des.), Ariz. 198/D2
Painted Desert Section (Petrified Forest), Ariz. 198/F3
Painted Post, N.Y. (14870) 276/F6
Painted Rock (dam), Ariz. 198/C5
Painter, Ala. (†35962) 195/F2
Painter, Va. (23420) 307/S5
Painter Ridge (hills), Conn. 210/B2
Painters Hill, Fla. (†32036) 212/E2
Paintersville, Ohio (†45335) 284/C6
Paint Lick, Ky. (40461) 237/N5
Paint Lick (riv.), Ky. 237/M5
Paint Rock, Ala. (35764) 195/F1
Paint Rock (riv.), Ala. 195/F1
Paint Rock, Texas (76866) 303/E6
Paintsville, Ky. (41240) 237/R5
Paipa, Colombia 126/D5
Paipote, Chile 138/B6
Paipote, Quebrada de (riv.), Chile 138/B6
Paisley, Ontario 177/C3
Paisley, Oreg. (97636) 291/G5
Paisley, Scotland 10/A1
Paisley, Scotland 15/B2
Paita, Peru 128/B5
Paita (bay), Peru 128/B5
Paiute Ind. Res., Calif. 204/G6
Pajala, Sweden 18/N3
Paján, Ecuador 128/B3
Pajarito (creek), N. Mex. 274/A2
Pajaro, Calif. (†95076) 204/D7
Pájaros (isls.), Chile 138/A7
Pakanbaru, Indonesia 54/M9
Pakanbaru, Indonesia 85/C5
Pakaraima (mts.), Guyana 131/A3
Pakawau, N. Zealand 100/D4
Pakchan (riv.), Burma 72/C5
Pakchan (riv.), Thailand 72/C5
Pakch'ŏn, N. Korea 81/B4
Pakenham, Ontario 177/H2
Pakhoi (Beihai), China 77/G7
Pakistan 2/N4
Pakistan 54/H7
PAKISTAN 59/J4
PAKISTAN 68/B3
Pakokku, Burma 72/B2
Pakowki (lake), Alberta 182/E5
Paks, Hungary 41/E3
Pakwach, Uganda 115/F3
Pakxé, Laos 72/E4
Pala, Chad 111/B6
Palacios, Texas (77465) 303/H9
Palafrugell, Spain 33/H2
Palagruža (Pelagosa) (isl.), Yugoslavia 45/C4
Pala Ind. Res., Calif. 204/H10
Palamós, Spain 33/H2
Palana, U.S.S.R. 54/S4
Palana, U.S.S.R. 48/R4
Palanan, Philippines 82/D2
Palanan, Philippines 85/G2
Palanan (bay), Philippines 82/D2
Palanda, Ecuador 128/C5
Palanga, U.S.S.R. 53/A3
Palangkaraya, Indonesia 85/E6
Palanpur, India 68/C4
Palaoa (pt.), Hawaii 218/G2
Palapag, Philippines 82/E4
Palapye, Botswana 118/D4
Palas de Rey, Spain 33/C1
Palatine, Ill. (60067) 222/B5
Palatka, Ark. (†72422) 202/J1
Palatka, Fla. (32077) 212/E2
Palau (Belau) 87/D5
Palauli (bay), W. Samoa 86/L8
Palaumerak, Indonesia 85/G1
Palaw, Burma 72/C4
Palawan (prov.), Philippines 82/B6
Palawan (isl.), Philippines 2/Q5
Palawan (isl.), Philippines 54/N8
Palawan (isl.), Philippines 85/F4
Palawan (isl.), Philippines 82/B6
Palawan (passage), Philippines 85/F4
Palawan (passage), Philippines 82/A6
Palaya, Bolivia 136/A6
Palayan, Philippines 82/C3
Palayankottai, India 68/D7
Palazzolo Acreide, Italy 34/E6
Palca, Bolivia 136/A5
Palco, Kansas (67657) 232/C2
Paldiski, U.S.S.R. 53/B1
Paldiski, U.S.S.R. 52/B3
Paleleh, Indonesia 85/G5
Palembang, Indonesia 54/M10
Palembang, Indonesia 85/D6
Palena, Chile 138/E5
Palena (lake), Chile 138/E5
Palena (riv.), Chile 138/D5
Palencia (prov.), Spain 33/D1
Palencia, Spain 33/D2
Palenque (pt.), Dom. Rep. 158/E6
Palenque, Mexico 150/O8
Palenque (ruin), Mexico 150/O8
Palenville, N.Y. (12463) 276/M6
Palermo, Calif. (95968) 204/D4
Palermo (prov.), Italy 34/D5
Palermo, Italy 7/F5
Palermo, Italy 34/D5
Palermo◯, Maine (04354) 243/E7
Palermo, N.J. (†08226) 273/D5
Palermo, N. Dak. (58769) 282/F3
Palermo, Uruguay 145/D4
Palestina, Chile 138/B4
Palestine, Ala. (†36252) 195/H3
Palestine, Ark. (72372) 202/J4
Palestine, Ill. (62451) 222/F4
Palestine, Ind. (†46508) 227/F2
Palestine, Ohio (45352) 284/A5
Palestine, Texas 188/H4
Palestine, Texas (75801) 303/J6
Palestine, W. Va. (26160) 312/D4
Palestrina, Italy 34/F7
Paletwa, Burma 72/B2
Palghat, India 68/D6
Palha, Mar da (bay), Portugal 33/A1
Pali, India 68/C3
Palidoro, Italy 34/F6
Paliocabe (Payocabe), Chile 138/F4
Palisade, Colo. (81526) 208/C4
Palisade, Minn. (56469) 255/E4
Palisade, Nebr. (69040) 264/C4
Palisade, Nev. (†89822) 266/E2
Palisades, Idaho (83437) 220/G6
Palisades (res.), Idaho 220/G6
Palisades, N.J. 273/C1
Palisades, N.Y. (10964) 276/K8
Palisades, Wash. (98845) 310/E3
Palisades (res.), Wyo. 319/A2
Palisades Park, N.J. (07650) 273/C2
Paliseul, Belgium 27/G9
Palizada, Mexico 150/O7
Palk (str.), India 68/D7
Palk (str.), Sri Lanka 68/D7
Pallamallawa, N.S. Wales 97/F1
Palling, Br. Col. 184/D3
Palliser (bay), N. Zealand 100/C3
Palliser (cape), N. Zealand 100/E4
Pall Mall, Tenn. (38577) 237/M7
Palm (beach), Neth. Ant. 161/D10
Palma (bay), Alaska 196/L1
Palma, Mozambique 118/G2
Palma, Spain 7/E5
Palma, Spain 33/H3
Palma (bay), Spain 33/H3
Palma del Río, Spain 33/D4
Palma di Montechiaro, Italy 34/D6
Palmarejo, Venezuela 124/C2
Palmares, Brazil 132/H5
Palmares, C. Rica 154/F6
Palmarito, Apure, Venezuela 124/D4
Palmarito, Guárico, Venezuela 124/F3
Palmarito, Mérida, Venezuela 124/C3
Palmarola (isl.), Italy 34/D4
Palmas (cape) 102/B4
Palmas, Brazil 132/C9
Palmas (cape), Liberia 106/C8
Palmas Altas (pt.), P. Rico 161/C1
Palma Soriano, Cuba 158/J4
Palm Bay, Fla. (32905) 212/F3
Palm Beach, Fla. 188/L5
Palm Beach (co.), Fla. 212/F5
Palm Beach, Fla. (33480) 212/G4
Palm Beach Gardens, Fla. (†33403) 212/F5
Palm Beach Shores, Fla. (†33404) 212/G5
Palm City, Fla. (33490) 212/F4
Palm Coast, Fla. (32037) 212/E2
Palmdale, Calif. (93550) 204/G9
Palmdale, Fla. (33944) 212/E5
Palm Desert, Calif. (92260) 204/J10
Palmeira, Brazil 132/D9
Palmeira, Brazil 135/B4
Palmeira das Missões, Brazil 132/C9
Palmeiras, Brazil 132/F6
Palmeirinhas (pt.), Angola 115/B5
Palmer, Alaska (99645) 196/C1
Palmer, Alaska 188/D5
Palmer (arch.) 5/C15
Palmer, Ill. (62556) 222/D4
Palmer, Ind. (†46307) 227/C2
Palmer, Iowa (50571) 229/D3
Palmer, Kansas (66962) 232/E2
Palmer, Mass. (01069) 249/E4
Palmer◯, Mass. (01069) 249/E4
Palmer, Mich. (49871) 250/B2
Palmer, Nebr. (68864) 264/F3
Palmer (head), N. Zealand 100/B3
Palmer, P. Rico 161/F1
Palmer (riv.), Queensland 95/B2
Palmer, Sask. 181/E6
Palmer, Tenn. (37365) 237/K10
Palmer, Wash. (98048) 310/D3
Palmer (lake), Wash. 310/F2
Palmer Lake, Colo. (80133) 208/J4
Palmer Land (reg.), Ant. 2/F9
Palmer Land (reg.), Ant. 5/B15
Palmer Rapids, Ontario 177/G2
Palmers, Minn. (†55801) 255/G4
Palmers Crossing, Miss. (†39401) 256/F8
Palmer Station, Ant. 5/C15
Palmerston (atoll), Cook Is. 87/K7
Palmerston, N. Zealand 100/C6
Palmerston, Ontario 177/D4
Palmerston North, N. Zealand 87/H10
Palmerston North, N. Zealand 100/E4
Palmersville, Tenn. (38241) 237/D8
Palmerton, Pa. (18071) 294/L4
Palmerville, Queensland 95/B3
Palmetto, Fla. (33561) 212/D4
Palmetto, Georgia (30268) 217/C3
Palmetto, La. (71358) 238/G5
Palmetto (pt.), St. Chris.-Nevis 161/C10
Palm Harbor, Fla. (33563) 212/D3
Palmi, Italy 34/E5
Palmiet (riv.), S. Africa 118/F7
Palmilla, Chile 138/F6
Palmillas (pt.), Dom. Rep. 158/F6
Palmillas, Mexico 150/K5
Palmira, Colombia 120/B2
Palmira, Colombia 126/B6
Palmira, Cuba 158/E2
Palmitas, Uruguay 145/B4
Palmito de la Virgen (isl.), Mexico 150/F5
Palmito del Verde (isl.), Mexico 150/F5
Palm River-Clair Mel, Fla. (33619) 212/C3
Palms, Mich. (48465) 250/G5
Palms, Isle of (isl.), S.C. 296/H6
Palm Shores, Fla. (†32901) 212/F3
Palm Springs, Calif. 188/C4
Palm Springs, Calif. (92262) 204/J10
Palm Springs, Fla. (33460) 212/F5
Palmyra, Ill. (62674) 222/C4
Palmyra, Ind. (47164) 227/E8
Palmyra◯, Maine (04965) 243/E6
Palmyra, Mich. (49268) 250/E7
Palmyra, Mo. (63461) 261/J3
Palmyra, Nebr. (68418) 264/H4
Palmyra, N.J. (08065) 273/B3
Palmyra, N.Y. (14522) 276/F4
Palmyra (atoll), Pacific 87/K5
Palmyra, Pa. (17078) 294/J5
Palmyra (ruin), Syria 59/C3
Palmyra (Tadmor) (ruins), Syria 63/H5
Palmyra, Tenn. (37142) 237/G8
Palmyra (isl.), U.S. 2/A5
Palmyra, Va. (22963) 307/M5
Palmyra, Wis. (53156) 317/H2
Palmyras (pt.), India 68/F4
Palnackie, Scotland 15/E6
Palni, India 68/D6
Palo, Iowa (52324) 229/K4
Palo, Mich. (48870) 250/E5
Palo, Minn. (†55705) 255/F3
Palo, Philippines 82/E5
Palo Alto, Calif. 188/B3
Palo Alto, Calif. (*94301) 204/K3
Palo Alto, Cuba 158/F3
Palo Alto (co.), Iowa 229/D2
Palo Alto (lake), Iowa 229/D2
Palo Bola, Mexico 150/D4
Palo Duro (creek), Texas 303/B2
Palo Duro (creek), Texas 303/C1
Paloemeu (riv.), Suriname 131/D4
Palolo (stream), Hawaii 218/D4
Paloma, Ill. (62359) 222/B3
Palomar (mt.), Calif. 204/J10
Palomas, Mexico 150/F1
Palomas, Uruguay 145/B2
Palombara Sabina, Italy 34/F6
Palometas, Bolivia 136/D5
Palompon, Philippines 82/E5
Palo Pinto (co.), Texas 303/F5
Palo Pinto, Texas (76072) 303/F5
Palopo, Indonesia 85/F6
Palos (cape), Spain 33/F4
Palo Santo, Argentina 143/E2
Palo Seco, P. Rico 161/D1
Palo Seco, Trin. & Tob. 161/A11
Palos Heights, Ill. (60463) 222/B6
Palos Hills, Ill. (60465) 222/B6
Palos Park, Ill. (60464) 222/B6
Palos Verdes Estates, Calif. (90274) 204/B11
Palotás, Hungary 41/E3
Palourde (lake), La. 238/H7
Palouse (riv.), Idaho 220/B3
Palouse, Wash. (99161) 310/H4
Palouse (riv.), Wash. 310/G4
Palo Verde, Ariz. (85343) 198/C5
Palo Verde, Calif. (92266) 204/L10
Palpa, Nepal 68/E3
Palpa, Peru 128/E10
Palsagua, Nicaragua 154/E4
Palsen (riv.), Manitoba 179/G2
Palu, Indonesia 85/F6
Palu, Turkey 63/H3
Paluan, Philippines 82/C4
Pama, Upper Volta 106/E6
Pamangkat, Indonesia 85/D5
Pamar, Colombia 126/E8
Pambrun, Sask. 181/D6
Pambula, N.S. Wales 97/E5
Pamekasan, Indonesia 85/L2
Pameungpeuk, Indonesia 85/H2
Pamiers, France 28/D6
Pamir (plat.) 54/J6
Pamlico (sound), N.C. 188/L3
Pamlico (co.), N.C. 281/R4
Pamlico (riv.), N.C. 281/R4
Pamlico (sound), N.C. 281/S4
Pampa, Texas 188/F3
Pampa, Texas (79065) 303/D2
Pampa Aullagas, Bolivia 136/B6
Pampachiri, Peru 128/F10
Pampacolca, Peru 128/F10
Pampa de la Salina (salt dep.), Argentina 143/C3
Pampa de las Salinas, Argentina 143/C3
Pampa de la Tres Hermanas (plain), Argentina143/C6
Pampa del Infierno, Argentina 143/D2
Pampa Grande, Bolivia 136/D5
Pampanga (prov.), Philippines 82/C3
Pampas (plain), Argentina 120/C6
Pampas (plain), Argentina 143/D4
Pampas, Peru 128/E9
Pampas (riv.), Peru 128/E9
Pampilhosa da Serra, Portugal 33/C3
Pamplico, S.C. (29583) 296/H4
Pamplin, Va. (23958) 307/L6
Pamplona, Colombia 126/D4
Pamplona, Spain 33/F1
Pamplona, Spain 7/D4
Pamunkey (riv.), Va. 307/O5
Pamunkey Ind. Res., Va. 307/P5
Pana, Ill. (62557) 222/D4
Panabá, Mexico 150/P6
Panabo, Philippines 82/E7
Panaca, Nev. (89042) 266/G5
Panacachi, Bolivia 136/B6
Panacea, Fla. (32346) 212/B1
Panache (lake), Ontario 177/C1
Panagyurishte, Bulgaria 45/F4
Panaitan (isl.), Indonesia 85/C7
Panaji, India 68/C5
Panama 2/E5
Panama 146/K9
Panama (canal) 2/E5
Panama, Ill. (62077) 222/D4
Panama, Iowa (51562) 229/B5
Panama, Nebr. (68419) 264/H4
Panama, N.Y. (14767) 276/A6
Panama, Okla. (74951) 288/S4
Panamá (cap.), Pan. 146/L9
Panama (canal), Pan. 146/L8
Panamá (gulf), Pan. 146/L9
PANAMA 154/G6
Panamá (cap.), Panama 154/H6
Panama (gulf), Panama 154/H7
Panama City, Fla. 188/K4
Panama City, Fla. (*32401) 212/C6
Panama City Beach, Fla. (32407) 212/C6
Panamint (range), Calif. 204/H7
Panamint (valley), Calif. 204/H7
Panao, Peru 128/E7
Panaon (isl.), Philippines 82/E5
Panarea (isl.), Italy 34/E5
Panaro (riv.), Italy 34/C2
Panarukan, Indonesia 85/K2
Panay (isl.), Philippines 54/O8
Panay (isl.), Philippines 85/G3
Panay (isl.), Philippines 82/D5
Pancake (range), Nev. 266/F4
Pančevo, Yugoslavia 45/E3
Panchor, Malaysia 72/F5
Panchur, India 68/F2
Panciu, Romania 45/H3
Panda, Mozambique 118/E4
Pandale, Texas (76944) 303/C7
Panda-Likasi, Zaire 115/E6
Panda-Likasi, Zaire 102/E6
Pandan, Antique, Philippines 82/C5
Pandan, Catanduanes, Philippines 82/E3
Pan de Azúcar, Quebrado (riv.), Chile 138/B5
Pan de Azúcar, Uruguay 145/D5
Pandeglang, Indonesia 85/G1
Pandharpur, India 68/D5
Pandi Pandi, S. Australia 94/F2
Pando (dept.), Bolivia 136/B2
Pando, Cerro (mt.), Panama 154/F6
Pando, Uruguay 145/B6
Pando (riv.), Uruguay 145/B6
Pandora, Ohio (45877) 284/C4
Pandrup, Denmark 21/C3
Panevežys, U.S.S.R. 52/B3
Panevežys, U.S.S.R. 53/C3
Panfilov, U.S.S.R. 48/H5
Pangai, Tonga 87/J7
Pangala, Congo 115/B4
Pangalanes (canal), Madagascar 118/H4
Pangani, Tanzania 115/G5
Pangani (riv.), Tanzania 115/G4
Panganiban, Philippines 82/E4
Pangasinan (prov.), Philippines 82/C3
Pangburn, Ark. (72121) 202/G3
Pangi, Zaire 115/E4
Pangkalanberandan, Indonesia 85/B5
Pangkalanbuun, Indonesia 85/E6
Pangkalpinang, Indonesia 85/D6
Pangkor, Pulau (isl.), Malaysia 72/D6
Panglao (isl.), Philippines 82/D6
Pangman, Sask. 181/G6
Pangnirtung, Canada 4/C13
Pangnirtung, N.W.T. 162/K2
Pangnirtung, N.W. Terrs. 187/M3
Pangong Tso (lake), India 68/D2
Pangsau (pass), Burma 72/C1
Panguipulli, Chile 138/E2
Panguitch, Utah (84759) 304/B6
Panguitch (creek), Utah 304/B6
Pangutaran, Philippines 82/C7
Pangutaran (isl.), Philippines 82/C7
Pangutaran Group (isls.), Philippines 82/C7
Pangutaran Group (isls.), Philippines 85/G4
Panhandle, Texas (79068) 303/C2
Paniau (peak), Hawaii 218/A2
Panié (mt.), New Caled. 86/G4
Panihati, India 68/F1
Panipat, India 68/D3
Paniqui, Philippines 82/C3
Panj (riv.), Afghanistan 68/C1

Pátzcuaro 425

Panjab, Afghanistan 68/B2
Panjab, Afghanistan 59/J3
Panjang, Hon (Hon Tho Chau) (isl.), Vietnam 72/D5
Panjgur, Pakistan 68/A3
Panjgur, Pakistan 59/H4
Panjim, India 54/J8
Panjim (Panaji), India 68/C5
Pankow, E. Germany 22/F3
Pankshin, Nigeria 106/F7
P'anmunjŏm, N. Korea 81/C5
P'anmunjŏm, S. Korea 81/C5
Panmure (isl.), Pr. Edward I. 168/F2
Panna, India 68/E4
Pannawonica, W. Australia 92/B3
Pannonhalma, Hungary 41/D3
Panny (riv.), Alberta 182/C1
Panola, Ala. (35477) 195/B5
Panola, Ill. (†61738) 222/E3
Panola (co.), Miss. 256/E2
Panola, Okla. (74559) 288/R5
Panola (co.), Texas 303/K5
Panora, Iowa (50216) 229/E5
Panorama Park, Iowa (†52722) 229/N5
Panquehue, Chile 138/G2
Panruti, India 68/D6
Pansey, Ala. (36370) 195/H8
Pantanal (reg.), Brazil 120/D4
Pantar (isl.), Indonesia 85/G7
Pantego, N.C. (27860) 281/R3
Pantego, Texas (76013) 303/F2
Pantelleria, Italy 34/C6
Pantelleria (isl.), Italy 7/F5
Pantelleria (isl.), Italy 34/D6
Pantha, Burma 72/B2
Panther (creek), Idaho 220/D4
Panther (creek), Ky. 237/G5
Panther, W. Va. (24872) 312/C8
Panther Burn, Miss. (38765) 256/C4
Panthersville, Georgia (†30032) 217/L1
Pantin, France 28/B1
Pantoja, Peru 128/E3
Panton○, Vt. (†05491) 268/A3
Pánuco, Mexico 150/K6
Pánuco (riv.), Mexico 150/K5
Panuke (lake), Nova Scotia 168/D4
Pan Xian, China 77/G6
Panyam, Nigeria 106/F7
Panzós, Guatemala 154/C3
Pao (riv.), Venezuela 124/D3
Pao (riv.), Venezuela 124/F3
Paoki (Baoji), China 77/G5
Paola, Italy 34/E5
Paola, Kansas (66071) 232/H3
Paoli, Colo. (80746) 208/P1
Paoli, Ind. (47454) 227/E7
Paoli, Okla. (73074) 288/M5
Paoli, Pa. (19301) 294/M5
Paoli, Wis. (†53508) 317/G10
Paonia, Colo. (81428) 208/D5
Paopao (bay), Fr. Poly. 86/S12
Paoting (Baoding), China 77/J4
Paotow (Baotou), China 77/G3
Paoua, Cent. Afr. Rep. 115/C2
Paoy Pet, Cambodia 72/D4
Papa, Hawaii (†96704) 218/G6
Pápa, Hungary 41/D3
Papaaloa, Hawaii (96780) 218/J4
Papagaio (riv.), Brazil 132/B6
Papagayo (gulf), C. Rica 154/E5
Papago Ind. Res., Ariz. 198/C6
Papaikou, Hawaii 188/G6
Papaikou, Hawaii (96781) 218/J5
Papakura, N. Zealand 100/E2
Papallacta, Ecuador 128/D3
Papanoa, Mexico 150/J8
Papantla de Olarte, Mexico 150/L6
Papar, Malaysia 85/F4
Papara, Fr. Poly. 86/S13
Papa Stour (isl.), Scotland 10/G1
Papa Stour (isl.), Scotland 15/F2
Papatoetoe, N. Zealand 100/C1
Papa Westray (isl.), Scotland 15/F1
Papa Westray (isl.), Scotland 10/E1
Papeete (cap.), Fr. Polynesia 2/B6
Papeete (cap.), Fr. Poly. 86/S13
Papeete (cap.), Fr. Poly. 87/M7
Papelón, Venezuela 124/D3
Papenburg, W. Germany 22/B2
Papenoo, Fr. Poly. 86/T12
Papetoai, Fr. Poly. 86/S12
Paphos, Cyprus 63/E5
Papillion, Nebr. (68046) 264/J3
Papineau, Ill. (60956) 222/F3
Papineau (lake), Ontario 177/G2
Papineau (co.), Québec 172/B4
Papineau (lake), Québec 172/C4
Papineauville, Québec 172/C4
Paposo, Chile 138/A5
Papradno, Czech. 41/E2
Paps, The (mt.), Ireland 17/C7
Paps of Jura (mt.), Scotland 15/C5
Papua (gulf), Papua N.G. 87/E6
Papua New Guinea 2/S6
PAPUA NEW GUINEA 86/B1
PAPUA NEW GUINEA 85/B7
Papua New Guinea 87/E6
Papudo, Chile 138/A9
Papun, Burma 72/C3
Papunáua (riv.), Colombia 126/E6
Papunya, North. Terr. 93/B7
Papurí (riv.), Colombia 126/F7
Paquera, C. Rica 154/E6
Paquette, Québec 172/F4
Paquetville, New Bruns. 170/E1
Pará (state), Brazil 132/C4
Pará (Belém), Brazil 132/E3
Pará (est.), Brazil 120/E3
Pará (riv.), Brazil 132/D3
Para (dist.), Suriname 131/D3
Paraburdoo, W. Australia 88/B4
Paraburdoo, W. Australia 92/B3
Paracale, Philippines 82/D3
Paracas (pen.), Peru 128/D9
Paracatu, Brazil 132/E7
Paracatu (riv.), Brazil 132/E7
Paracel (isls.), China 85/E2
Parachilna, S. Australia 88/F6
Parachilna, S. Australia 94/F4
Parachute, Colo. 208/C4
Paraćin, Yugoslavia 45/E4
Parada Esperanza, Uruguay 145/B3
Parada Liebigs, Uruguay 145/A4
Parada Rivas, Uruguay 145/B2
Parade, S. Dak. (57647) 298/G3
Pará de Minas, Brazil 132/E7
Pará de Minas, Brazil 135/D1
Paradip, India 68/F4
Paradis, La. (70080) 238/M4
Paradise, Ariz. (†85632) 198/F7
Paradise, Calif. (95969) 204/D4
Paradise, Guyana 131/C3
Paradise, Kansas (67658) 232/D2
Paradise, Mich. (49768) 250/D2
Paradise (lake), Mich. 250/E3
Paradise, Mo. (†64089) 261/D4
Paradise, Mont. (59856) 262/B3
Paradise, Newf. 166/D2
Paradise (riv.), Newf. 166/C3
Paradise, Nova Scotia 168/C4
Paradise (lake), Nova Scotia 168/C4
Paradise, Pa. (17562) 294/K5
Paradise, Texas (76073) 303/G5
Paradise, Utah (84328) 304/C2
Paradise, W. Va. (†25124) 312/C5
Paradise Hill, Okla. (†74435) 288/R3
Paradise Hill, Sask. 181/B2
Paradise Inn, Wash. (98398) 310/D4
Paradise River, Newf. 166/C3
Paradise Valley, Alberta 182/E3
Paradise Valley, Ariz. (85253) 198/D5
Paradise Valley, Nev. (89119) 266/F6
Paradise Valley, Nev. (89426) 266/D1
Paradise Valley, Wyo. (†82601) 319/F3
Paradisino (peak), Switzerland 39/K4
Paradiso, Switzerland 39/G5
Paradox, Colo. (81429) 208/B6
Paragon, Ind. (46166) 227/D6
Paragonah, Utah (84760) 304/B6
Paragould, Ark. (72450) 202/J1
Paraguá (riv.), Bolivia 136/E4
Paragua (riv.), Venezuela 124/G4
Paraguaçu (riv.), Brazil 120/F4
Paraguaçu (riv.), Brazil 132/F6
Paraguaçu Paulista, Brazil 132/D8
Paraguai (riv.) 120/D4
Paraguai (riv.), Brazil 132/B8
Paraguaipoa, Venezuela 124/C2
Paraguaná (pen.), Venezuela 124/C1
Paraguarí (dept.), Paraguay 144/D4-5
Paraguay 2/F7
Paraguay 120/D5
PARAGUAY 144
Paraguay (riv.), Argentina 143/E1
Paraguay (riv.), Bolivia 136/F7
Paraguay (riv.), Paraguay 144/D4
Paraíba (state), Brazil 132/G4
Paraíba (riv.), Brazil 120/E5
Paraíba (riv.), Brazil 135/E2
Paraíba do Sul, Brazil 135/E3
Parainen, Finland 18/M6
Paraíso, C. Rica 154/F6
Paraíso, Dom. Rep. 158/D7
Paraíso, Mexico 150/N7
Paraíso de Chabasquén, Venezuela 124/D3
Parakou, Benin 106/E7
Parallel, Kansas (†66933) 232/F2
Paraloma, Ark. (†71846) 202/B6
Paramaribo (dist.), Suriname 131/D2
Paramaribo (cap.), Suriname 131/D2
Paramaribo (cap.), Suriname 2/G5
Paramaribo (cap.), Suriname 120/D2
Paramithía, Greece 45/E6
Paramonga, Peru 128/C8
Paramount, Calif. (90723) 204/C11
Paramus, N.J. (07652) 273/B1
Paramushir (isl.) 54/S5
Paramushir (isl.), U.S.S.R. 48/Q4
Paran (dry riv.), Israel 65/D5
Paraná (riv.) 2/G7
Paraná (riv.) 120/D5
Paraná, Argentina 143/F5
Paraná, Argentina 120/D6
Paraná (riv.), Argentina 143/E2
Paraná (state), Brazil 132/D9
Paraná (state), Brazil 135/B4
Paranã, Brazil 132/E6
Paranã (riv.), Brazil 132/C8
Paranã (riv.), Brazil 132/E6
Paranaguá, Brazil 120/E5
Paranaguá, Brazil 132/E9
Paranaguá, Brazil 135/B4
Paranaíba, Brazil 132/D7
Paranam, Suriname 131/D3
Paranapanema (riv.), Brazil 132/C8
Paranapanema (riv.), Brazil 135/B3
Paranapiacaba (range), Brazil 135/B4
Paranatinga (riv.), Brazil 120/D4
Paranatinga (riv.), Brazil 132/C6
Parang, Maguindanao, Philippines 82/E7
Parang, Sulu, Philippines 82/C8
Paraoo (riv.), Uruguay 145/E3
Paraparaumu, N. Zealand 100/E4
Parapetí (riv.), Bolivia 136/D6
Para Station, N.S. Wales 97/B3
Parati, Brazil 135/D3
Paratinga, Brazil 132/F6
Paray-le-Monial, France 28/F4
Parbhani, India 68/D5
Parchim, E. Germany 22/D2
Parchman, Miss. (38738) 256/D3
Parchment, Mich. (49004) 250/D6
Parczew, Poland 47/F3
Pardee (res.), Calif. 204/C9
Pardee, Va. (†24285) 307/C6
Pardeeville, Wis. (53954) 317/H8
Pardes Hanna-Karkur, Israel 65/B2
Parding, China 77/C5
Pardo (riv.), Brazil 132/D8
Pardo (riv.), Brazil 132/F6
Pardo (riv.), Brazil 135/B2
Pardo (riv.), Brazil 132/C8
Pardoe, Pa. (†16137) 294/B3
Pardoo, W. Australia 92/B3
Pardubice, Czech. 41/C1
Pare, Indonesia 85/K2
Parece Vela (isl.), Japan 54/P7
Parece Vela (isl.), Japan 87/D3
Parecis (mts.), Brazil 120/C4
Parecis, Serra dos (range), Brazil 132/B6
Paredes de Nava, Spain 33/D1
Paredones, Chile 138/A10
Parent, Québec 174/C3
Pareora, N. Zealand 100/C6
Parepare, Indonesia 85/F6
Parguera, P. Rico 161/A3
Parham, Ant. & Bar. 161/E11
Parham, Ontario 177/H3
Parhams, La. (†71343) 238/G4
Paria (gulf) 120/C1
Paria (plat.), Ariz. 198/D2
Paria (riv.), Ariz. 198/D1
Paria, Bolivia 136/B5
Paria (gulf), Trin. & Tob. 156/G5
Paria (gulf), Trin. & Tob. 161/A11
Paria (riv.), Utah 304/B6
Paria (gulf), Venezuela 124/H2
Paria (pen.), Venezuela 124/G2
Pariaguán, Venezuela 124/F3
Pariaman, Indonesia 85/B6
Paricutín (vol.), Mexico 150/H7
Parida (isl.), Panama 154/F6
Parika, Guyana 131/B2
Parikkala, Finland 18/Q6
Parima, Sierra (mts.), Venezuela 124/F6
Parinacochas (lake), Peru 128/F10
Parinacota, Cerro (mt.), Chile 138/B1
Pariñari, Peru 128/E5
Pariñas (pt.), Peru 128/B5
Parintins, Brazil 120/D3
Parintins, Brazil 132/B3
Paris, Ark. (72855) 202/C3
Paris (city) (dept.), France 28/B2
Paris (cap.), France 2/J3
Paris (cap.), France 7/E4
Paris (cap.), France 28/B2
Paris, Idaho (83261) 220/G7
Paris, Ill. (61944) 222/F4
Paris, Iowa (†52214) 229/K4
Paris, Ky. (40361) 237/N4
Paris○, Maine (04271) 243/B7
Paris, Mich. (49338) 250/D5
Paris, Miss. (38949) 256/F2
Paris, Mo. (65275) 261/J4
Paris, Ohio (44669) 284/H4
Paris, Ontario 177/D4
Paris, Tenn. (38242) 237/E8
Paris, Texas (75460) 303/J4
Paris, Texas 188/G4
Paris, Va. (22130) 307/N3
Paris Crossing, Ind. (47270) 227/F7
Parish, N.Y. (13131) 276/H4
Parish, Uruguay 145/C3
Parishville, N.Y. (13672) 276/L1
Parisville, Mich. (†48470) 250/G5
Parisville, Québec 172/F3
Parita, Panama 154/G6
Parita (bay), Panama 154/G6
Park (co.), Colo. 208/H4
Park (range), Colo. 208/F1
Park (riv.), Conn. 210/E2
Park, Kansas (67751) 232/B2
Park (co.), Mont. 262/F5
Park (riv.), N. Dak. 282/R3
Park (dist.), Scotland 15/B2
Park (co.), Wyo. 319/C1
Parkano, Finland 18/N6
Parkbeg, Sask. 181/E5
Park City, Ill. (†60085) 222/B4
Park City, Kansas (†67201) 232/E4
Park City, Ky. (42160) 237/J6
Park City, Mont. (59063) 262/H5
Park City, Utah (84060) 304/C3
Parkdale, Ark. (71661) 202/H7
Parkdale, Colo. (†81212) 208/H6
Parkdale, Oreg. (97041) 291/F2
Parkdale, Pr. Edward I. 168/E2
Parke (co.), Ind. 227/C5
Parker, Ariz. (85344) 198/A4
Parker (dam), Ariz. 198/A4
Parker, Colo. (80134) 208/K4
Parker, Fla. (32401) 212/C6
Parker, Idaho (83438) 220/G6
Parker, Kansas (66072) 232/H3
Parker, Pa. (16049) 294/C3
Parker, S. Dak. (57053) 298/P7
Parker (lake), S. Dak. 298/P3
Parker (co.), Texas 303/G5
Parker, Texas (†75069) 303/H1
Parker, Wash. (98939) 310/E4
Parker City, Ind. (47368) 227/G4
Parker Dam, Calif. (92267) 204/L9
Parkersburg, Ill. (62452) 222/F5
Parkersburg, Ind. (†47954) 227/D5
Parkersburg, Iowa (50665) 229/H3
Parkersburg, W. Va. 188/K3
Parkersburg, W. Va. (26101) 312/D4
Parkers Cove, Newf. 166/D4
Parkers Cove, Nova Scotia 168/C4
Parkers Lake, Ky. (42634) 237/M7
Parkers Prairie, Minn. (56361) 255/C4
Parkertown, N.J. (†08087) 273/E4
Parkerview, Sask. 181/H4
Parkerville, Kansas (†66846) 232/F3
Parkes, N. S. Wales 88/H6
Parkes, N.S. Wales 97/E3
Parkesburg, Pa. (19365) 294/L6
Park Falls, Wis. (54552) 317/F4
Park Forest, Ill. (60466) 222/B6
Park Forest South, Ill. (60466) 222/F2
Park Hall, Md. (20667) 245/N8
Park Hill, Okla. (74451) 288/R3
Parkhill, Ontario 177/C4
Park Hills, Ky. (†41011) 237/S2
Parkin, Ark. (72373) 202/J3
Parkland, Alberta 182/D4
Parkland, Fla. (†33441) 212/F5
Parkland, Okla. (†74824) 288/N3
Parkland, Wash. (98444) 310/C3
Parkman○, Maine (†04443) 243/D5
Parkman, Ohio (44080) 284/H3
Parkman, Sask. 181/K6
Parkman, Wyo. (82838) 319/E1
Park Place, Oreg. (†97045) 291/B2
Park Rapids, Minn. (56470) 255/D4
Park Rapids, Wash. (†99114) 310/H2
Park Ridge, Ill. (60068) 222/B5
Park Ridge, N.J. (07656) 273/B1
Park Ridge, Wis. (†54481) 317/H6
Park River, N. Dak. (58270) 282/P3
Parks, Ariz. (86018) 198/C3
Parks, Ark. (72950) 202/B4
Parks, La. (70582) 238/G6
Parks, Nebr. (69041) 264/C4
Parkside, Pa. (†19013) 294/M7
Parkside, Sask. 181/E2
Parksley, Va. (23421) 307/S5
Parkston, S. Dak. (57366) 298/O7
Parksville, Br. Col. 184/J3
Parksville, Ky. (40464) 237/M5
Parksville, N.Y. (12768) 276/L7
Parksville, S.C. (29844) 296/C4
Parkton, Md. (21120) 245/M2
Parkton, N.C. (28371) 281/M5
Park Valley, Utah (84329) 304/A2
Parkview (mt.), Colo. 208/G2
Parkville, Md. (21234) 245/M3
Parkville, Mo. (64152) 261/O5
Parkville, Pa. (†17331) 294/J6
Parkville, Victoria 97/H5
Parkway, Mo. (64130) 261/L6
Parkway Village, Ky. (†40201) 237/J2
Parkwood, N.C. (27707) 281/M3
Parlakhemundi, India 68/E5
Parlier, Calif. (93648) 204/F7
Parlin, Colo. (81239) 208/F6
Parlin (pond), Maine 243/C4
Parma, Idaho (83660) 220/B6
Parma (prov.), Italy 34/C2
Parma, Italy 7/E4
Parma, Italy 34/C2
Parma (riv.), Italy 34/C2
Parma, Mich. (49269) 250/E6
Parma, Mo. (63870) 261/N9
Parma, Ohio (44129) 284/H9
Parmachenee (lake), Maine 243/B5
Parma Heights, Ohio (†44130) 284/G9
Parmana, Venezuela 124/F4
Parmele, N.C. (27861) 281/P3
Parmelee, S. Dak. (57566) 298/G7
Parmer (co.), Texas 303/B3
Parnaguá, Brazil 132/E5
Parnaíba, Brazil 132/F3
Parnaíba, Brazil 120/E3
Parnaíba (riv.), Brazil 120/E3
Parnaíba (riv.), Brazil 132/F3
Parnamirim, Brazil 132/F4
Parnassus (mt.), Greece 45/F6
Parnassus, N. Zealand 100/D5
Parndana, S. Australia 94/E6
Parnell, Iowa (52325) 229/J5
Parnell, Mo. (64475) 261/C2
Pärnu, U.S.S.R. 7/G3
Pärnu, U.S.S.R. 53/C1
Pärnu, U.S.S.R. 52/C3
Pärnu, U.S.S.R. 48/C4
Paro, Bhutan 68/F3
Paron, Ark. (72132) 202/E4
Paroo (riv.), N. S. Wales 88/G5
Paroo (chan.), N.S. Wales 97/B2
Paroo (riv.), N.S. Wales 97/C1
Paroo (riv.), Queensland 95/C6
Paropamisus (mts.), Afghanistan 59/H3
Paropamisus (range), Afghanistan 68/A2
Páros (isl.), Greece 45/G7
Parow, S. Africa 118/F6
Parowan, Utah (84761) 304/B6
Parpan, Switzerland 39/J3
Parr, Ind. (†47978) 227/C2
Parr, S.C. (29066) 296/E3
Parral, Chile 138/A11
Parral, Mexico 150/G3
Parral, Ohio (†44622) 284/G4
Parramatta, N. S. Wales 88/K4
Parramatta (riv.), N. S. Wales 88/K4
Parramatta, N.S. Wales 97/H3
Parramatta (riv.), N.S. Wales 97/J3
Parramore (isl.), Va. 307/S5
Parran, Md. (†20639) 245/M6
Parras de la Fuente, Mexico 150/H4
Parratah, Tasmania 99/D4
Parrett (riv.), England 13/E6
Parrish, Ala. (35580) 195/D3
Parrish, Fla. (33564) 212/D4
Parrish, Wis. (†54435) 317/H5
Parris Island Marine Base, S.C. 296/F7
Parrott, Georgia (31777) 217/D7
Parrott, Va. (24132) 307/G6
Parrottsville, Tenn. (37843) 237/P8
Parrsboro, Nova Scotia 168/D3
Parry (isls.), N.W.T. 146/G2
Parry (chan.), N.W.T. 146/G2
Parry (chan.), N.W.T. 162/E-H1
Parry (bay), N.W. Terrs. 187/K3
Parry (cape), N.W. Terrs. 187/F2
Parry (chan.), N.W. Terrs. 187/G2
Parry (isls.), N.W. Terrs. 187/G2
Parry (pen.), N.W. Terrs. 187/F2
Parry (isl.), Ontario 177/D2
Parry (sound), Ontario 177/D2
Parry, Sask. 181/G6
Parry Sound, Ont. 162/J6
Parry Sound (terr. dist.), Ontario 175/E3
Parry Sound, Ontario 175/D3
Parry Sound, Ontario 177/E2
Parseierspitze (mt.), Austria 41/A3
Parshall, Colo. (80468) 208/G2
Parshall, N. Dak. (58770) 282/F4
Parsippany-Troy Hills○, N.J. (07054) 273/E2
Parsnip (riv.), Br. Col. 184/F3
Parson, Br. Col. 184/J4
Parsons, Kans. 188/G3
Parsons, Kansas (67357) 232/G4
Parsons, Tenn. (38363) 237/E9
Parsons, W. Va. (26287) 312/G4
Parsonsburg, Md. (21849) 245/R7
Parson's Pond, Newf. 166/C3
Partanna, Italy 34/D6
Partapgarh, India 68/C4
Parthenay, France 28/C4
Partinico, Italy 34/D6
Partizansk, U.S.S.R. 48/O5
Partizánske, Czech. 41/E2
Partlow, Va. (22534) 307/N4
Partridge, Kansas (67566) 232/D4
Partridge (riv.), Minn. 255/G3
Partridge (bay), Newf. 166/C3
Partridge (pt.), Newf. 166/C3
Partry (mts.), Ireland 17/C4
Paru (riv.), Brazil 132/C3
Paru de Oeste (riv.), Brazil 120/D3
Paru de Oeste (riv.), Brazil 132/B3
Paruro, Peru 128/F9
Parvatipuram, India 68/E5
Parys, S. Africa 118/D5
Pas, De (riv.), Québec 174/D1
Pasadena, Calif. 188/C4
Pasadena, Calif. (*91101) 204/C10
Pasadena, Md. (21122) 245/M4
Pasadena, Newf. 166/C4
Pasadena, Texas (*77501) 303/J2
Pasado (cape), Ecuador 128/B3
Pasaje, Ecuador 128/C4
Pa Sak, Mae Nam (riv.), Thailand 72/D4
Pasangkayu, Indonesia 85/F6
Pasargadae (ruins), Iran 66/H5
Pasatiempo, Calif. (†95060) 204/K4
Pasawng, Burma 72/C3
Pasayten (riv.), Wash. 310/E2
Pascagoula, Miss. (39567) 256/G10
Pascagoula (riv.), Miss. 256/G9
Pascalis, Québec 174/B3
Paşcani, Romania 45/H2
Paschall, N.C. (†27589) 281/N1
Pasco (co.), Fla. 212/D3
Pasco (dept.), Peru 128/E8
Pasco, Wash. (99301) 310/F4
Pascoag, R.I. (02859) 249/H5
Pascola, Mo. (63871) 261/N10
Pascua (riv.), Chile 138/D7
Pas-de-Calais (dept.), France 28/E2
Pasewalk, E. Germany 22/F2
Pasighat, India 68/G3
Pasinler, Turkey 63/J3
Pasión (riv.), Guatemala 154/B2
Paskenta, Calif. (96074) 204/C4
Pasłek, Poland 47/D1
Pasley (bay), N.W. Terrs. 187/J2
Pasni, Pakistan 68/A3
Pasni, Pakistan 54/H7
Pasni, Pakistan 59/H4
Paso Ataques, Uruguay 145/D2
Paso Barreto, Paraguay 144/D3
Paso de Andrés Pérez, Uruguay 145/B3
Paso de Indios, Argentina 143/C5
Paso de la Laguna, Salto, Uruguay 145/B2
Paso de la Laguna, Tacuarembó, Uruguay 145/D3
Paso de las Piedras, Uruguay 145/C2
Paso del Borracho, Uruguay 145/D2
Paso del Cerro, Uruguay 145/C2
Paso de León, Uruguay 145/B1
Paso del Horno, Uruguay 145/C2
Paso de Los Libres, Argentina 143/E2
Paso de los Toros, Uruguay 145/C3
Paso del Parque, Uruguay 145/B2
Paso de Ovejas, Mexico 150/Q2
Paso de Patria, Paraguay 144/C5
Paso de Ramos, Uruguay 145/C1
Paso de Uleste, Uruguay 145/B3
Paso Flores, Argentina 143/C5
Paso Hondo, Uruguay 145/B4
Paso Potrero, Uruguay 145/C2
Pasorapa, Bolivia 136/C6
Paso Real, Honduras 154/E3
Paso Robles, Calif. (93446) 204/E8
Paspébiac, Québec 172/D2
Pasqua, Sask. 181/F5
Pasque (isl.), Mass. 249/L7
Pasquia (hills), Sask. 181/J2
Pasquia (riv.), Sask. 181/K2
Pasquotank (co.), N.C. 281/S2
Pass (creek), Wyo. 319/F4
Passaconaway (mt.), N.H. 268/E4
Passadumkeag○, Maine (04475) 243/F5
Passage (isl.), Mich. 250/E1
Passage East, Ireland 17/G7
Passagem Franca, Brazil 132/E4
Passage West, Ireland 17/E8
Passage West, Ireland 10/B5
Passaic, Mo. (64777) 261/D6
Passaic (co.), N.J. 273/E1
Passaic, N.J. (07055) 273/E2
Passaic (riv.), N.J. 273/E2
Passamaquoddy (bay), Maine 243/J5
Passamaquoddy (bay), New Bruns. 170/C3
Passamaquoddy Ind. Res., Maine 243/J6
Passau, W. Germany 22/E4
Pass Christian, Miss. (39571) 256/F10
Passero (cape), Italy 7/F5
Passero (cape), Italy 34/E6
Passes (lake), Québec 172/F2
Passi, Philippines 82/D5
Passo Fundo, Brazil 120/D5
Passo Fundo, Brazil 132/D10
Passos, Brazil 132/E8
Passos, Brazil 135/C2
Passumpsic, Vt. (05861) 268/D3
Passumpsic (riv.), Vt. 268/D2
Pastaza (riv.) 120/B3
Pastaza (prov.), Ecuador 128/D3
Pastaza (riv.), Ecuador 128/D4
Pastaza (riv.), Peru 128/D5
Pasto, Colombia 120/B2
Pasto, Colombia 126/B7
Pastol (bay), Alaska 196/F2
Pastora (peak), Ariz. 198/F2
Pastos Bons, Brazil 132/E4
Pastrana, Spain 33/E2
Pastura, N. Mex. (88435) 274/E4
Pasuquin, Philippines 82/C1
Pasuruan, Indonesia 85/K2
Pasvalys, U.S.S.R. 53/C2
Pasvikelv (riv.), Norway 18/Q2
Paswegin, Sask. 181/H4
Pásztó, Hungary 41/E3
Pata, Bolivia 136/A4
Patacamaya, Bolivia 136/B5
Patagonia (reg.), Argentina 120/C7
Patagonia (reg.), Argentina 143/C5
Patagonia, Ariz. (85624) 198/E7
Pataguanset (lake), Conn. 210/G3
Pataha, Wash. (†99347) 310/H4
Pataha (creek), Wash. 310/H4
Patan, India 68/C4
Patapédia (riv.), New Bruns. 170/C1
Patapédia (riv.), Québec 172/B2
Patapsco, Md. (†21048) 245/L2
Patapsco (riv.), Md. 245/M4
Pataskala, Ohio (43062) 284/E5
Pataz, Peru 128/D6
Patchewollock, Victoria 97/A4
Patch Grove, Wis. (53817) 317/D10
Patchogue, N.Y. (11772) 276/P9
Patea, N. Zealand 100/E3
Paternion, Austria 41/B3
Paterno, Italy 34/E6
Pateros, Wash. (98846) 310/E2
Pateros (lake), Wash. 310/F2
Paterson, N.J. 188/M2
Paterson, N.J. (*07501) 273/B2
Paterson, Wash. (99345) 310/F5
Patesville, Ky. (†42364) 237/H5
Pathankot, India 68/D2
Pathfinder (res.), Wyo. 188/E2
Pathfinder (res.), Wyo. 319/F3
Pathiu, Thailand 72/C5
Pathlow, Sask. 181/G3
Pati (pt.), Guam 86/K6
Pati, Indonesia 85/J2
Patía, Colombia 126/B6
Patía (riv.), Colombia 126/B6
Patiala, India 68/D2
Patillas, P. Rico 161/E2
Patillas (lake), P. Rico 161/E2
Pativilca (riv.), Peru 128/D8
Patmos, Ark. (†71801) 202/C7
Pátmos (isl.), Greece 45/H7
Patna, India 54/K7
Patna, India 68/F3
Patna, Scotland 15/D5
Patnanongan (isl.), Philippines 82/D3
Patnos, Turkey 63/K3
Patoka, Ill. (62875) 222/D5
Patoka, Ind. (47666) 227/B8
Patoka (riv.), Ind. 227/C8
Paton, Iowa (50217) 229/E4
Patos, Brazil 120/F3
Patos, Brazil 132/G4
Patos (lake), Brazil 120/D6
Patos (lag.), Brazil 132/D10
Patos de Minas, Brazil 120/E4
Patos de Minas, Brazil 132/E7
Patoutville, La. (†70544) 238/G7
Patquía, Argentina 143/C3
Pátrai, Greece 7/G5
Pátrai, Greece 45/E6
Patricia, Alberta 182/E4
Patricia, S. Dak. (†57551) 298/G7
Patricia, Texas (79352) 303/B5
Patricio Lynch (isl.), Chile 138/D7
Patrick, Neth. Ant. 161/F8
Patrick, S.C. (29584) 296/G2
Patrick (co.), Va. 307/H7
Patrick A.F.B., Fla. 212/F3
Patricksburg, Ind. (47455) 227/D6
Patrick's Cove, Newf. 166/C2
Patrick Springs, Va. (24133) 307/H7
Patrickswell, Ireland 17/D6
Patriot, Ind. (47038) 227/H7
Patriot, Ohio (45658) 284/F8
Patrocínio, Brazil 132/E7
Patronville, Ind. (†47635) 227/C9
Patroon, Texas (75967) 303/L6
Patsaliga (creek), Ala. 195/F7
Patsburg, Ala. (†36049) 195/F7
Patta (isl.), Kenya 115/H4
Pattani, Thailand 72/D6
Patten, Maine (04765) 243/F4
Patten○, Maine (04765) 243/F4
Pattenburg, N.J. (†08802) 273/C2
Patterson, Ark. (72123) 202/H3
Patterson, Calif. (95363) 204/D6
Patterson, Georgia (31557) 217/H8
Patterson, Idaho (†83253) 220/E5
Patterson, Ill. (62078) 222/C4
Patterson, Iowa (50218) 229/F6
Patterson, La. (70392) 238/H7
Patterson (pt.), Mich. 250/D3
Patterson, Mo. (63956) 261/L8
Patterson, N.Y. (12563) 276/N7
Patterson, N.C. (28661) 281/F3
Patterson, Edward A. (lake), N. Dak. 282/E6
Patterson, Ohio (45843) 284/C4
Patterson, Va. (24633) 307/D6
Patterson (creek), W. Va. 312/J4
Patterson Creek, W. Va. (26746) 312/J3
Pattersonville, N.Y. (12137) 276/M5
Patti, Italy 34/E5
Pattison, Miss. (39144) 256/C7
Patton, Mo. (63662) 261/M8
Patton, Pa. (16668) 294/E4
Pattonsburg, Mo. (64670) 261/D2
Patuanak, Sask. 181/L3
Patuca, Honduras 154/E3
Patuca (pt.), Honduras 154/E3
Patuca (riv.), Honduras 154/E3
Patuha (mt.), Indonesia 85/H2
Pătulele, Romania 45/F3
Patutahi, N. Zealand 100/F3
Patuxent (riv.), Md. 245/M7
Patuxent River Nav. Air Test Ctr., Md. 245/N7
Patzau, Wis. (†54836) 317/B3
Pátzcuaro, Mexico 150/J7

Piedmont 427

Pequea, Pa. (17565) 294/K6
Pequest (riv.), N.J. 273/D2
Pequonnock (riv.), Conn. 210/C3
Pequop (mts.), Nev. 266/G2
Pequot Lakes, Minn. (56472) 255/D4
Pera (head), Queensland 88/G2
Pera (head), Queensland 95/B2
Pera (Beyoğlu), Turkey 63/D6
Perabumulih, Indonesia 85/C6
Peraitepuí, Venezuela 124/H5
Perak (state), Malaysia 72/D6
Perak, Gunong (mt.), Malaysia 72/D6
Perales (riv.), Spain 33/F4
Peralta, Dom. Rep. 158/D6
Peralta, N. Mex. (87042) 274/C4
Peralta, Spain 33/F1
Peralta, Uruguay 145/C3
Peravia (prov.), Dom. Rep. 158/E6
Percé (cape), Nova Scotia 168/J2
Percé, Québec 172/D1
Percé, Québec 174/E3
Perch (lake), Mich. 250/G2
Perch (riv.), Mich. 250/G2
Perche (reg.), France 28/D3
Percival, Iowa (51648) 229/B7
Percival, Sask. 181/J5
Percival (lakes), W. Australia 88/C4
Percival (lakes), W. Australia 92/D3
Percy, Ill. (62272) 222/D5
Percy, Miss. (†38748) 256/C4
Percy, N.H. (†03582) 268/E2
Perdido, Ala. (36562) 195/C8
Perdido (bay), Ala. 195/D10
Perdido (riv.), Ala. 195/C9
Perdido (riv.), Fla. 212/B6
Perdido (mt.), Spain 33/G1
Perdido Beach, Ala. (36530) 195/C10
Pérdika, Greece 45/E6
Perdue, Sask. 181/D3
Perdue Hill, Ala. (36470) 195/C8
Pereira, Colombia 126/C5
Pereira, Colombia 120/B2
Perelló, Spain 33/G2
Pere Marquette (riv.), Mich. 250/D5
Perené (riv.), Peru 128/E8
Perenjori, W. Australia 92/B5
Pérez, Argentina 143/F6
Pérez (isl.), Mexico 150/P5
Perg, Austria 41/C2
Pergamino, Argentina 143/F6
Pergamino, Argentina 120/C6
Pergine Valsugana, Italy 34/C1
Pergola, Italy 34/D3
Perham○, Maine (04766) 243/G2
Perham, Minn. (56573) 255/C4
Perhentian, Kepulauan (isls.), Malaysia 72/D6
Periam, Romania 45/E2
Péribonca (riv.), Que. 162/J5
Péribonca (riv.), Québec 174/C3
Péribonca (riv.), Québec 172/F1
Péribonka, Québec 172/E1
Perico, Cuba 158/D1
Perico, Texas (†79087) 303/B1
Pericos, Mexico 150/F4
Peridot, Ariz. (85542) 198/E5
Perigord, Sask. 181/H3
Périgueux, France 28/D5
Perijá, Serranía de (mts.), Colombia 126/D2
Perijá, Sierra de (mts.), Venezuela 124/B2
Perim (isl.), P.D.R. Yemen 59/D7
Perintown, Ohio (†45150) 284/B7
Perito F.P. Moreno Nat'l Park, Argentina 143/B6
Perito Moreno, Argentina 143/B6
Periyar (lake), India 68/D7
Perkam (cape), Indonesia 85/K6
Perkasie, Pa. (18944) 294/M5
Perkatkin, U.S.S.R. 48/T2
Perkins (mt.), Conn. 210/F1
Perkins, Georgia (30822) 217/J5
Perkins, Iowa (†51239) 229/A2
Perkins, Mich. (49872) 250/B3
Perkins, Mo. (63774) 261/N8
Perkins (co.), Nebr. 264/C4
Perkins, Okla. (74059) 288/M3
Perkins, Québec 172/B4
Perkins (co.), S. Dak. 298/D3
Perkins, S. Dak. (†57062) 298/O8
Perkins, W. Va. (26634) 312/E5
Perkinsfield, Ontario 177/E3
Perkinston, Miss. (39573) 256/F9
Perkinstown, Wis. (†54451) 317/E5
Perkinsville, Ind. (†46011) 227/F4
Perkinsville, N.Y. (14529) 276/E5
Perkinsville, Vt. (05151) 268/B5
Perks, Ill. (62973) 222/D6
Perla, Ark. (†72104) 202/E5
Perlas (lag.), Nicaragua 154/F4
Perlas (pt.), Nicaragua 154/F4
Perlas (arch.), Panama 154/H6
Perleberg, E. Germany 22/D2
Perley, Minn. (56574) 255/B3
Perlis (state), Malaysia 72/D6
Perm', U.S.S.R. 2/M3
Perm', U.S.S.R. 7/K3
Perm', U.S.S.R. 52/J3
Perm', U.S.S.R. 48/F4
Perma, Mont. (59857) 262/B3
Përmet, Albania 45/E5
Pernambuco (state), Brazil 132/G5
Pernambuco (Recife), Brazil 132/H5
Pernell, Okla. (73076) 288/M5
Pernik, Bulgaria 45/F4
Peron (isls.), North. Terr. 88/D2
Peron (isls.), North. Terr. 93/A2
Peron (cape), Tasmania 99/E4
Peron (cape), W. Australia 88/A2
Peron (pen.), W. Australia 92/A4
Péronne, France 28/E3
Perote, Ala. (36061) 195/G7
Perote, Mexico 150/O1
Perow, Br. Col. 184/D3
Perpetua (cape), Oreg. 291/C3
Perpignan, France 7/E4
Perpignan, France 28/E6
Perquilauquén (riv.), Chile 138/A11
Perquimans (co.), N.C. 281/S2
Perrin, Mo. (†64477) 261/D3
Perrin, Texas (76075) 303/G5
Perrin, Va. (†23072) 307/R6
Perrine, Fla. (33157) 212/F6
Perrineville, N.J. (08535) 273/E3
Perrinton, Mich. (48871) 250/E5
Perris, Calif. (92370) 204/F11
Perro (mts.), N. Mex. 274/D4
Perronville, Mich. (49873) 250/B3
Perros (bay), Cuba 158/G2
Perry (co.), Ala. 195/D5
Perry (isl.), Alaska 196/C1
Perry (co.), Ark. 202/E4
Perry, Ark. (72125) 202/E3
Perry, Fla. (32347) 212/C1
Perry, Georgia (31069) 217/E6
Perry (co.) Ill. 222/D5
Perry, Ill. (62362) 222/C4
Perry (co.), Ind. 227/D8
Perry, Iowa (50220) 229/E5
Perry, Kansas (66073) 232/G2
Perry (lake), Kansas 232/G2
Perry (co.), Ky. 237/P6
Perry, La. (70575) 238/F7
Perry○, Maine (04667) 243/J6
Perry, Mich. (48872) 250/E6
Perry (co.), Miss. 256/G8
Perry (co.), Mo. 261/N7
Perry, Mo. (63462) 261/J4
Perry (stream), N.H. 268/E1
Perry, N.Y. (14530) 276/D5
Perry (co.), Ohio 284/F6
Perry, Ohio (44081) 284/H2
Perry, Okla. (73077) 288/M2
Perry, Oreg. (†97850) 291/J2
Perry (co.), Pa. 294/H5
Perry, S.C. (29124) 296/E4
Perry (co.), Tenn. 237/F9
Perry, Utah (†84302) 304/C2
Perry, W. Va. (†26851) 312/J5
Perrydale, Oreg. (†97101) 291/D2
Perrygo Place, Wis. (†53511) 317/J10
Perry Hall, Md. (21128) 245/N3
Perryman, Md. (21130) 245/O3
Perryopolis, Pa. (15473) 294/C5
Perrysburg, Ind. (†46951) 227/E3
Perrysburg, N.Y. (14129) 276/B6
Perrysburg, Ohio (43551) 284/C2
Perry's Cove, Newf. 166/D2
Perry's Victory and Int'l Peace Mem., Ohio 284/E2
Perrysville, Ind. (47974) 227/C4
Perrysville, Ohio (44864) 284/F4
Perrysville, Pa. (15237) 294/B6
Perryton, Ohio (†43822) 284/F5
Perryton, Texas (79070) 303/D1
Perrytown, Ark. (71801) 202/C6
Perryvale, Alberta 182/D2
Perryville, Alaska (99648) 196/G3
Perryville, Ark. (72126) 202/E3
Perryville, Ky. (40468) 237/M5
Perryville, La. (†71220) 238/G1
Perryville, Md. (21903) 245/O2
Perryville, Mo. (63775) 261/N7
Perryville, Tenn. (38364) 237/F9
Perşembe, Turkey 63/G2
Persepolis (ruins), Iran 66/H6
Perseverance (bay), Virgin Is. (U.S.) 161/A4
Perseverancia, Bolivia 136/D4
Pershing, Ind. (†46975) 227/E2
Pershing, Ind. (47370) 227/G5
Pershing, Iowa (50221) 229/G6
Pershing (co.), Nev. 266/C2
Pershing, Okla. (†74002) 288/O1
Pershore, England 13/E5
Persia, Iowa (51563) 229/B5
Persia, Tenn. (†37857) 237/P8
Persian (gulf) 54/G7
Persian (gulf), Bahrain 59/F4
Persian (gulf), Iran 66/F6
Persian (gulf), Iran 59/F4
Persian (gulf), Iraq 59/F4
Persian (gulf), Kuwait 59/F4
Persian (gulf), Qatar 59/F4
Persian (gulf), Saudi Arabia 59/F4
Persinger, W. Va. (†26651) 312/E6
Person (co.), N.C. 281/M2
Pertek, Turkey 63/H3
Perth, Australia 2/Q7
Perth, Kansas (†67152) 232/E4
Perth, N. Dak. (58363) 282/M2
Perth (county), Ontario 177/C4
Perth, Ontario 177/H3
Perth, Scotland 10/E2
Perth, Scotland 15/E4
Perth (trad. co.), Scotland 15/A5
Perth, Tasmania 99/D3
Perth (cap.), W. Australia 88/B2
Perth (cap.), W. Australia 92/A1
Perth Airport, W. Australia 88/B2
Perth Amboy, N.J. (*08861) 273/E2
Perth-Andover, New Bruns. 170/C2
Perthshire, Miss. (†38746) 256/C3
Perthville, N.S. Wales 97/E3
Pertominsk, U.S.S.R. 52/E2
Peru 2/F6
Peru 120/B4
PERU 128
Peru, Ill. (61354) 222/D2
Peru, Ind. (46970) 227/E3
Peru, Iowa (50222) 229/F6
Peru, Kansas (67360) 232/F4
Peru, Maine (04272) 243/C6
Peru○, Maine (04272) 243/C6
Peru, Nebr. (68421) 264/J4
Peru, N.Y. (12972) 276/N1
Peru○, Vt. (05152) 268/B5
Perugia (prov.), Italy 34/D3
Perugia, Italy 34/D3
Perugia, Italy 7/F4
Perugorría, Argentina 143/G4
Péruwelz, Belgium 27/D8
Pervari, Turkey 63/K4
Pervomaysk, U.S.S.R. 52/F3
Pervomaysk, U.S.S.R. 52/D5
Pervoural'sk, U.S.S.R. 48/F4
Perwez, Belgium 27/F7
Péry, Switzerland 39/D2
Pesaro, Italy 34/D3
Pesaro e Urbino (prov.), Italy 34/D3
Pescadero, Calif. (94060) 204/J4
Pescadero (creek), Calif. 204/J3
Pescadero (pt.), Calif. 204/J3
Pescadero, Mexico 150/D5
Pescadores (Penghu) (isls.), China 77/J7
Pescara (prov.), Italy 34/E3
Pescara, Italy 34/E3
Pescara, Italy 7/F4
Pescara (riv.), Italy 34/D3
Pescia, Italy 34/C3
Peseux, Switzerland 39/C3
Peshastin, Wash. (98847) 310/E3
Peshawar, Pakistan 54/H6
Peshawar, Pakistan 59/K3
Peshawar, Pakistan 68/C2
Peshkopi, Albania 45/E5
Peshtera, Bulgaria 45/G4
Peshtigo, Wis. (54157) 317/L5
Peshtigo (riv.), Wis. 317/K5
Peskovka, U.S.S.R. 52/H3
Peskowesk (lake), Nova Scotia 168/C4
Peso da Régua, Portugal 33/C2
Pesotum, Ill. (61863) 222/E4
Pespire, Honduras 154/D4
Pessac, France 28/C5
Pest (co.), Hungary 41/E3
Pestel, Haiti 158/A6
Pestovo, U.S.S.R. 52/D3
Péta, Greece 45/E6
Petaca, N. Mex. (87554) 274/C2
Petacalco (bay), Mexico 150/H8
Petah Tiqwa, Israel 65/B3
Petal, Miss. (39465) 256/F8
Petaluma, Calif. (94952) 204/H1
Pétange, Luxembourg 27/H9
Petas, Las (riv.), Bolivia 136/F5
Petatlán, Mexico 150/J8
Petauke, Zambia 115/F6
Petawaga (lake), Québec 172/A2
Petawawa, Ontario 177/G2
Petawawa (riv.), Ontario 177/G2
Petén-Itzá (lake), Guatemala 154/B2
Petenwell (lake), Wis. 317/G7
Peter (isl.), Virgin Is. (Br.) 156/H1
Peter (isl.), Virgin Is. (Br.) 161/D4
Peterborough, England 13/G5
Peterborough, England 10/F4
Peterborough, N.H. (03458) 268/D6
Peterborough○, N.H. (03458) 268/D6
Peterborough, Ont. 162/J7
Peterborough (county), Ontario 177/F3
Peterborough, Ontario 177/F3
Peterborough, S. Australia 88/F6
Peterborough, S. Australia 94/F5
Peterculter, Scotland 15/F3
Peterhead, Scotland 15/G3
Peterhead, Scotland 10/E2
Peter I (isl.) 5/B14
Peter I (isl.), Norway 2/E9
Peterlee, England 13/J3
Peterman, Ala. (36471) 195/D7
Petermann (ranges), North. Terr. 93/A8
Petermann (ranges), W. Australia 92/E4
Petermann Ranges Aboriginal Reserve, North. Terr. 88/D4
Petermann Ranges Aboriginal Res., North. Terr. 93/A8
Peteroa (vol.), Argentina 143/B4
Peteroa (vol.), Chile 138/B10
Peter Pond (lake), Sask. 181/L3
Peter's (riv.), Newf. 166/D2
Petersburg, Alaska 188/E6
Petersburg, Alaska (99833) 196/N2
Petersburg, Ill. (62675) 222/D4
Petersburg, Ind. (47567) 227/C7
Petersburg, Ky. (41080) 237/M2
Petersburg, Mich. (49270) 250/F7
Petersburg, Minn. (†56143) 255/C7
Petersburg, Nebr. (68652) 264/G3
Petersburg, N.J. (†08270) 273/D5
Petersburg, N.Y. (12138) 276/O5
Petersburg, N. Dak. (58272) 282/P3
Petersburg, Pa. (16669) 294/G4
Petersburg, Tenn. (37144) 237/H10
Petersburg, Texas (79250) 303/C4
Petersburg, Va. 188/L3
Petersburg (I.C.), Va. (23803) 307/N6
Petersburg, W. Va. (26847) 312/H5
Petersburg Nat'l Battlefield, Va. 307/O6
Petersfield, England 13/F6
Petersfield, Jamaica 158/G6
Petersfield, Manitoba 179/E4
Petersham○, Mass. (01366) 249/F3
Peterson, Ala. (35478) 195/D4
Peterson, Iowa (51047) 229/C3
Peterson, Minn. (55962) 255/G7
Peterson, Sask. 181/F3
Peterson Air Force Base, Colo. 208/K5
Peterstown, W. Va. (24963) 312/E8
Petersville, Ind. (†47201) 227/F6
Petersville, Ky. (†41179) 237/P4
Petersville, Md. (†21758) 245/H3
Pétervására, Hungary 41/F3
Peterview, Newf. 166/C4
Pétionville, Haiti 158/C6
Petit Bois (isl.), Miss. 256/H10
Petit-Bourg, Guadeloupe 161/A6
Petit-Canal, Guadeloupe 161/A6
Petit Cap, Québec 172/D1
Petitcodiac, New Bruns. 170/E3
Petitcodiac (riv.), New Bruns. 170/F3
Petit Cul-de-Sac Marin (bay), Guadeloupe 161/A6
Petit-de-Grat, Nova Scotia 168/H3
Petit-de-Grat (isl.), Nova Scotia 168/H3
Petite Cascapédia (riv.), Québec 172/C1
Petite-Matane, Québec 172/B1
Petite Nation (riv.), Québec 172/B4
Petite Riviere Bridge, Nova Scotia 168/D4
Petite Rivière de l'Artibonite, Haiti 158/B5
Petite-Rivière-de-l'Île, New Bruns. 170/F1
Petite-Rivière-Ouest, Québec 172/D2
Petites, Newf. 166/C4
Petit-Étang, Nova Scotia 168/G2
Petite-Terre (isls.), Guadeloupe 161/B6
Petite-Vallée, Québec 172/D1
Petit-Goâve, Haiti 156/D3
Petit Goâve, Haiti 158/B6
Petit Jean (mt.), Ark. 202/C3
Petit Jean (riv.), Ark. 202/D3
Petitjean (Sidi-Kacem), Morocco 106/C2
Petit Mécatina (isl.), Québec 174/F2
Petit Mécatina (riv.), Québec 174/E2
Petitot (riv.), Br. Col. 184/M2
Petitot (riv.), N.W. Terrs. 187/F4
Petit Piton (mt.), St. Lucia 161/G6
Petit Rocher, New Bruns. 170/E1
Petit Rocher Sud, New Bruns. 170/E1
Petit-Saguenay (Saint-François-d'Assise), Québec 172/G1
Petitsikapau (lake), Newf. 166/A3
Petit Soufrière, Dominica 161/F6
Petley, Newf. 166/D2
Peto, Mexico 150/P6
Petone, N. Zealand 100/B2
Petorca, Chile 138/A9
Petoskey, Mich. (49770) 250/E3
Petpeswick (head), Nova Scotia 168/E4
Petra (ruins), Jordan 65/D5
Petre (bay), N. Zealand 100/D7
Petre (pt.), Ontario 177/G4
Petrey, Ala. (36062) 195/F7
Petrich, Bulgaria 45/F5
Petrified Forest, Ariz. (86028) 198/F3
Petrified Forest Nat'l Park, Ariz. 198/F4
Petrila, Romania 45/F3
Petrinja, Yugoslavia 45/B3
Petrohué, Chile 138/E3
Petrokrepost', U.S.S.R. 52/D3
Petrólea, Colombia 126/D3
Petroleum, Ind. (46778) 227/G3
Petroleum, Ky. (†42120) 237/J7
Petroleum (co.), Mont. 262/H3
Petroleum, W. Va. (26161) 312/D4
Petrolia, Kansas (†66720) 232/G4
Petrolia, Ontario 177/B5
Petrolia, Pa. (16050) 294/C3
Petrolia, Texas (76377) 303/F4
Petrolina, Brazil 120/E3
Petrolina, Brazil 132/G5
Petrona (pt.), P. Rico 161/D3
Petropavlovsk, U.S.S.R. 54/J4
Petropavlovsk, U.S.S.R. 48/G4
Petropavlovsk-Kamchatskiy, U.S.S.R. 2/S3
Petropavlovsk-Kamchatskiy, U.S.S.R. 54/T4
Petropavlovsk-Kamchatskiy, U.S.S.R. 48/R4
Petrópolis, Brazil 132/F8
Petrópolis, Brazil 135/E3
Petros, Tenn. (37845) 237/M8
Petroşeni, Romania 45/F3
Petrovsk, U.S.S.R. 52/G4
Petrovsk-Zabaykal'skiy, U.S.S.R. 48/L4
Petrozavodsk, U.S.S.R. 7/H2
Petrozavodsk, U.S.S.R. 48/D3
Petrozavodsk, U.S.S.R. 52/D2
Petsamo (Pechenga), U.S.S.R. 52/D1
Pettibone, N. Dak. (58475) 282/L5
Pettigo, Ireland 17/F2
Pettigo, N. Ireland 17/F2
Pettigrew, Ark. (72752) 202/C2
Pettis (co.), Mo. 261/F5
Pettisville, Ohio (43553) 284/B2
Pettus, Texas (78146) 303/G9
Petty Harbour, Newf. 166/D2
Petworth, D.C. (20011) 245/F4
Peu, Solomon Is. 87/G7
Peuco, Chile 138/G4
Peuerbach, Austria 41/B2
Peumo, Chile 138/F5
Pevas, Peru 128/G4
Pevek, U.S.S.R. 54/U3
Pevek, U.S.S.R. 48/S3
Pevely, Mo. (63070) 261/M6
Pewamo, Mich. (48873) 250/E5
Pewaukee, Wis. (53072) 317/K1
Pewaukee (lake), Wis. 317/K1
Pewee Valley, Ky. (40056) 237/L4
Peyrano, Argentina 143/F6
Peyton, Colo. (80831) 208/K4
Peytona, W. Va. (25154) 312/C6
Pézenas, France 28/E6
Pezinok, Czech. 41/D2
Pfaffenhofen an der Ilm, W. Germany 22/D4
Pfäffnau, Switzerland 39/E2
Pfarrkirchen, W. Germany 22/E4
Pfeifer, Kansas (67660) 232/C3
Pflugerville, Texas (78660) 303/G7
Pforzheim, W. Germany 22/C4
Pfronten, W. Germany 22/D5
Pfullingen, W. Germany 22/C4
Pfunds, Austria 41/A3
Pha Hom Pok, Doi (mt.), Thailand 72/C2
Phalaborwa, S. Africa 118/E4
Phalodi, India 68/C3
Phanat Nikhom, Thailand 72/D4
Phangan, Ko (isl.), Thailand 72/D5
Phangnga, Thailand 72/C5
Phan Rang, Vietnam 72/F5
Phan Thiet, Vietnam 72/F5
Phan Thiet, Vietnam 54/M8
Phantom (lake), Wis. 317/J2
Pharoah, Okla. (74862) 288/O4
Pharr, Texas (78577) 303/F11
Phatthalung, Thailand 72/D6
Phayao, Thailand 72/C3
Pheasant (hills), Sask. 181/J5
Pheba, Miss. (39755) 256/G3
Phelps (mt.) 120/C2
Phelps, Ky. (41553) 237/S6
Phelps (co.), Mo. 261/J7
Phelps (co.), Nebr. 264/E4
Phelps, N.Y. (14532) 276/F5
Phelps (lake), N.C. 281/S3
Phelps (peak), Venezuela 124/E7
Phelps, Wis. (54554) 317/H3
Phelps City, Mo. (†64482) 261/A2
Phenix, Va. (23959) 307/L6
Phenix City, Ala. 188/J4
Phenix City, Ala. (36867) 195/H6
Phet Buri, Thailand 72/C4
Phetchabun, Thailand 72/D3
Phiafai, Laos 72/E4
Phichai, Thailand 72/D3
Phichit, Thailand 72/D3
Phil, Ky. (†42539) 237/M6
Philadelphia, Ill. (†62612) 222/C4
Philadelphia, Miss. (39350) 256/F5
Philadelphia, Mo. (63463) 261/J3
Philadelphia, N.Y. (13673) 276/J2
Philadelphia, Pa. 188/M2
Philadelphia, Pa. 146/L6
Philadelphia (city county), Pa. 294/M6
Philadelphia, Pa. (*19101) 294/N6
Philadelphia, Tenn. (37846) 237/M9
Philadelphia, U.S. 2/F4
Philbrook, Minn. (†56466) 255/D4
Phil Campbell, Ala. (35581) 195/C2
Philip (riv.), Nova Scotia 168/E3
Philip, S. Dak. (57567) 298/F5
Philipp, Miss. (38950) 256/D3
Philippeville (Skikda), Algeria 106/F1
Philippeville, Belgium 27/E8
Philippi, W. Va. (26416) 312/G4
Philippine (sea) 54/O8
Philippine (sea), Guam 86/K6
Philippine (sea), Philippines 85/G2
Philippine (sea), Philippines 82/D3
Philippines 2/R5
Philippines 54/O8
PHILIPPINES 85/H4
PHILIPPINES 82
Philipsburg, Mont. (59858) 262/C4
Philipsburg, Pa. (16866) 294/F4
Philipsburg, Québec 172/D4
Philip Smith (mts.), Alaska 196/J1
Phillip (pt.), N.S. Wales 97/J2
Phillip (isl.), Victoria 97/C6
Phillippy, Tenn. (†38079) 237/C8
Phillips (co.), Ark. 202/J5
Phillips (co.), Colo. 208/P1
Phillips (co.), Kansas 232/C2
Phillips○, Maine (04966) 243/C6
Phillips (co.), Mont. 262/J2
Phillips, Nebr. (68865) 264/F4
Phillips (bay), N.W. Terrs. 187/J1
Phillips, Okla. (†74538) 288/O6
Phillips, Texas (†79007) 303/C2
Phillips, Wis. (54555) 317/E4
Phillipsburg, Georgia (†31794) 217/E8
Phillipsburg, Kansas (67661) 232/C2
Phillipsburg, Mo. 65722) 261/G7
Phillipsburg, N.J. (08865) 273/C2
Phillipsburg, Ohio (45354) 284/B6
Phillipston○, Mass. (†01331) 249/F2
Phillipstown, Ill. (†62827) 222/F5
Phillipsville, N.C. (†28716) 281/D3
Philmont, N.Y. (12565) 276/N6
Philo, Calif. (95466) 204/B4
Philo, Ill. (61864) 222/E3
Philo, Ohio (43771) 284/G6
Philomath, Georgia (30659) 217/G3
Philomath, Oreg. (97370) 291/D3
Philomont, Va. (22131) 307/N2
Philpot, Ky. (42366) 237/H5
Philpots (isl.), N.W. Terrs. 187/L2
Philpott (lake), Va. 307/H7
Phippen, Sask. 181/C3
Phippsburg, Colo. (80469) 208/F2
Phippsburg, Maine (04562) 243/D8
Phippsburg○, Maine (04562) 243/D8
Phitsanulok, Thailand 72/D3
Phlox, Wis. (54464) 317/J5
Phnom Penh (cap.), Cambodia 54/M8
Phnom Penh (cap.), Cambodia 72/E5
Phnum Tbeng Meanchey, Cambodia 72/E4
Phoenix (cap.), Ariz. 146/G6
Phoenix (cap.), Ariz. 188/D4
Phoenix (cap.), Ariz. (*85001) 198/C5
Phoenix, Ill. (†60426) 222/C6
Phoenix (isls.), Kiribati 87/J6
Phoenix, La. (†70042) 238/L7
Phoenix, Md. (21131) 245/M2
Phoenix, N.Y. (13135) 276/H4
Phoenix, Oreg. (97535) 291/E5
Phoenixville, Conn. (†06235) 210/G1
Phoenixville, Pa. (19460) 294/L5
Phôngsali, Laos 72/D2
Phon Phisai, Thailand 72/D3
Phoques (bay), Tasmania 99/A1
Phou Bia (mt.), Laos 72/D3
Phou Cô Pi (mt.), Laos 72/E3
Phou Loi (mt.), Laos 72/D2
Phou San (mt.), Laos 72/D3
Phrae, Thailand 72/D3
Phra Nakhon Si Ayutthaya, Thailand 72/D4
Phsar Ream, Cambodia 72/D5
Phuc Loi, Vietnam 72/E3
Phu Cuong, Vietnam 72/E5
Phu Dien, Vietnam 72/E3
Phuket, Thailand 54/L9
Phuke, Thailand 72/C6
Phuket, Ko (isl.), Thailand 72/C5
Phu Lang Thuong (Bac Giang), Vietnam 72/E2
Phulbani, India 68/E4
Phu Ly, Vietnam 72/E2
Phumi Banam, Cambodia 72/E5
Phumi Phsar, Cambodia 72/E4
Phumi Prek Kak, Cambodia 72/E4
Phumi Samraong, Cambodia 72/D4
Phu My, Vietnam 72/F4
Phu Qui, Vietnam 72/E3
Phu Quoc, Dao (isl.), Vietnam 72/D5
Phu Rieng, Vietnam 72/E5
Phu Tho, Vietnam 72/E2
Phutthaisong, Thailand 72/D4
Phu Vinh, Vietnam 72/E5
Piaçabuçu, Brazil 132/H5
Piacenza (prov.), Italy 34/B2
Piacenza, Italy 34/B2
Piacoa, Venezuela 124/H3
Pia Fai, Doi (mt.), Thailand 72/D4
Piai, Tanjong (pt.), Malaysia 72/E6
Pian (creek), N.S. Wales 97/E1
Piankatank (riv.), Va. 307/R5
Pianosa (isl.), Italy 34/C3
Pianosa (isl.), Italy 34/E3
Piapoco, Colombia 126/F6
Piapot, Sask. 181/B6
Piarco, Trin. & Tob. 161/B10
Piat, Philippines 82/C2
Piatra Neamț, Romania 45/G2
Piatt (co.), Ill. 222/E4
Piauí (state), Brazil 132/F4
Piauí, Serra do (range), Brazil 132/F5
Piauí (riv.), Brazil 132/F5
Piave (riv.), Italy 34/D2
Piave, Miss. (†39476) 256/G8
Piazza Armerina, Italy 34/E6
Piazzi (isl.), Chile 138/D9
Pibor (riv.), Sudan 111/F6
Pibor Post, Sudan 111/F6
Pibrac, Québec 172/F1
Pibroch, Alberta 182/D2
Pica, Chile 138/B2
Picabo, Idaho (83348) 220/D6
Picacho, Ariz. (85241) 198/D6
Picacho, N. Mex. (88343) 274/D5
Picadilly, Newf. 166/C4
Picara (pt.), Virgin Is. (U.S.) 161/B4
Picard (lake), Québec 172/D2
Picardville, Alberta 182/D2
Picardy (trad. prov.), France 29
Picatinny Arsenal, N.J. 273/D2
Picayune, Miss. (39466) 256/E9
Piceance (creek), Colo. 208/C3
Picher, Okla. (74360) 288/S1
Pichidegua, Chile 138/F5
Pichilemu, Chile 138/A10
Pichincha (prov.), Ecuador 128/C3
Pichis (riv.), Peru 128/E8
Pichones (cays), Honduras 154/F3
Pichucalco, Mexico 150/N8
Pickard, Ind. (†46069) 227/E4
Pickaway (co.), Ohio 284/D6
Pickaway, W. Va. (24964) 312/E7
Pick City, N. Dak. (†58545) 282/G5
Pickens (co.), Ala. 195/B4
Pickens, Ark. (71662) 202/H6
Pickens (co.), Georgia 217/D2
Pickens, Miss. (39146) 256/E5
Pickens, Okla. (74752) 288/S6
Pickens (co.), S.C. 296/B2
Pickens, S.C. (29671) 296/B2
Pickens, W. Va. (26230) 312/F5
Pickensville, Ala. (†35447) 195/B4
Pickerel (lake), Conn. 210/F2
Pickerel (lake), Manitoba 179/C2
Pickerel, Wis. (54465) 317/J5
Pickering, England 13/G3
Pickering, Mo. (64476) 261/C2
Pickering, Ontario 177/K4
Pickerington, Ohio (43147) 284/E6
Pickersgill, Guyana 131/B2
Pickert, N. Dak. (†58230) 282/P5
Pickett (co.), Tenn. 237/M7
Pickett, Wis. (54964) 317/J8
Pickford, Mich. (49774) 250/E2
Pickle Lake, Ontario 175/C2
Pickrell, Nebr. (68422) 264/H4
Pickstown, S. Dak. (57367) 298/M7
Pickton, Texas (75471) 303/J5
Pickwick (lake), Ala. 195/B1
Pickwick, Minn. (†55948) 255/G7
Pickwick (lake), Miss. 256/H1
Pickwick (lake), Tenn. 237/E11
Pickwick Dam, Tenn. (38365) 237/E10
Pico (isl.), Portugal 33/C1
Pico (peak), Vt. 268/B4
Pico Rivera, Calif. (90660) 204/C10
Picos, Brazil 132/F4
Picos, Brazil 120/E3
Picota, Peru 128/D6
Pico Truncado, Argentina 143/C6
Pictograph (rocks), Ariz. 198/B5
Picton (isl.), Argentina 143/C8
Picton (isl.), Chile 138/F11
Picton, N.S. Wales 97/F4
Picton, N. Zealand 100/D4
Picton, Ontario 177/G3
Picton (mt.), Tasmania 99/C5
Pictou (co.), Nova Scotia 168/F3
Pictou, Nova Scotia 168/F3
Pictou (harb.), Nova Scotia 168/F3
Pictou (isl.), Nova Scotia 168/F3
Pictou Landing, Nova Scotia 168/F3
Picture Butte, Alberta 182/D5
Pictured Rocks (cliff), Mich. 250/C2
Pictured Rocks Nat'l Lakeshore, Mich. 250/C2
Picture Rocks, Pa. (17762) 294/J3
Pidurutalagala (mt.), Sri Lanka 68/E7
Pie, W. Va. (25689) 312/B7
Piedade, Brazil 135/C3
Piedade do Rio Grande, Brazil 135/D2
Piedecuesta, Colombia 126/D4
Piedmont, Ala. (36272) 195/G3
Piedmont, Calif. (94611) 204/J2
Piedmont, Georgia (†30204) 217/D4
Piedmont (reg.), Italy 34/A2
Piedmont, Kansas (67122) 232/F4
Piedmont, Mo. (63957) 261/L8
Piedmont, Ohio (43983) 284/H5

Plainview, Ark. (72857) 202/D4
Plain View, Iowa (†52773) 229/M5
Plainview, Minn. (55964) 255/F6
Plainview, Nebr. (68769) 264/G2
Plainview, N.Y. (11803) 276/R
Plainview, S. Dak. (57771) 298/E4
Plainview, Texas (79072) 303/C3
Plainville○, Conn. (06062) 210/D2
Plainville, Georgia (30733) 217/C2
Plainville, Ill. (62365) 222/B4
Plainville, Ind. (47568) 227/C7
Plainville, Kansas (67663) 232/C2
Plainville○, Mass. (02762) 249/J4
Plainwell, Mich. (49080) 250/D6
Plaisance, Haiti 158/C5
Plaisance, Québec 172/B4
Plaisted, Maine (04767) 243/F1
Plaistow○, N.H. (03865) 268/E6
Plaju, Indonesia 85/D6
Plamondon, Alberta 182/D2
Plana (cays), Bahamas 156/D2
Planá, Czech. 41/B2
Planada, Calif. (95365) 204/E6
Planeta Rica, Colombia 126/C3
Plánice, Czech. 41/B2
Plankinton, S. Dak. (57368) 298/N6
Plano, Ill. (60545) 222/E2
Plano, Iowa (52581) 229/G7
Plano, Texas (75074) 303/G1
Plant, Tenn. (†37054) 237/F9
Plantagenet, Ontario 177/K2
Plantation, Fla. (33317) 212/B4
Plantation (key), Fla. 212/F7
Plantation, Ky. (†40201) 237/K1
Plant City, Fla. (33566) 212/D3
Plantersville, Ala. (36758) 195/E5
Plantersville, Miss. (38862) 256/G2
Plantersville, S.C. (29441) 296/J4
Plantsite, Ariz. (†85540) 198/F5
Plantsville, Conn. (06479) 210/D2
Plaquemine, La. (70764) 238/J2
Plaquemines (par.), La. 238/L8
Plasencia, Spain 33/C2
Plaster City, Calif. (92269) 204/K11
Plaster Rock, New Bruns. 170/C2
Plastun, U.S.S.R. 48/O5
Plasy, Czech. 41/B2
Plat, Wis. (†53017) 317/K1
Plata (riv.) 2/G7
Plata, Río de la (est.), Argentina 143/E4
Plata (riv.), P. Rico 161/D2
Plata, La (riv.), Uruguay 145/B5
Platanal, Venezuela 124/F6
Platanilla, C. Rica 154/F6
Platea, Pa. (†16417) 294/B2
Plateau (creek), Colo. 208/C4
Plateau (state), Nigeria 106/F7
Plateau, Nova Scotia 168/H2
Plateau City, Colo. (†81624) 208/D4
Plate Cove, Newf. 166/D2
Platen, Kapp (pt.), Norway 18/D1
Platina, Calif. (96076) 204/B3
Platinum, Alaska (99651) 196/F3
Platner, Colo. (†80743) 208/N2
Plato, Colombia 126/C3
Plato, Minn. (55370) 255/D6
Plato, Mo. (65552) 261/H8
Plato, Sask. 181/C4
Platoro (res.), Colo. 208/F8
Platte (riv.), Iowa 229/D8
Platte (lake), Mich. 250/C4
Platte (co.), Mo. 261/C4
Platte (riv.), Mo. 261/C3
Platte (riv.), Nebr. 146/J5
Platte (riv.), Nebr. 188/G2
Platte (co.), Nebr. 264/G3
Platte (riv.), Nebr. 264/E4
Platte, S. Dak. (57369) 298/M7
Platte (lake), S. Dak. 298/M6
Platte (co.), Wyo. 319/H4
Platte Center, Nebr. (68653) 264/G3
Platte City, Mo. (64079) 261/C4
Plattenville, La. (70393) 238/K4
Platter, Okla. (74753) 288/O7
Platteville, Colo. (80651) 208/K2
Platteville, Wis. (53818) 317/F10
Platte Woods, Mo. (†64152) 261/O5
Platt Nat'l Park, Okla. 288/N6
Plattsburg, Mo. (64477) 261/D3
Plattsburgh, N.Y. (12901) 276/O1
Plattsburgh A.F.B., N.Y. 276/N1
Plattsmouth, Nebr. (68048) 264/J3
Plattsville, Ontario 177/D4
Plau, E. Germany 22/E2
Plaucheville, La. (71362) 238/G5
Plauen, E. Germany 22/E3
Plauersee (lake), E. Germany 22/E2
Plav, Yugoslavia 45/D4
Plavinas, U.S.S.R. 53/C2
Playa (pt.), Guyana 131/B1
Playa Azul, Mexico 150/H7
Playa Bonita, C. Rica 154/E6
Playa de Fajardo, P. Rico 161/F1
Playa de Humacao, P. Rico 161/F2
Playa Grande, Nicaragua 154/D4
Playas, Ecuador 128/B4
Playas (lake), N. Mex. 274/A7
Playón Chico, Panama 154/H6
Playón Grande, Panama 154/H6
Plaza, N. Dak. (58771) 282/G3
Plaza, Wash. (99028) 310/H3
Plaza Huincul, Argentina 143/B4
Pleasant (isl.), Alaska 196/M1
Pleasant (lake), Ariz. 198/C5
Pleasant, Ind. (†47043) 227/G7
Pleasant (lake), Maine 243/H5
Pleasant (lake), Maine 243/E3
Pleasant (lake), Maine 243/G3
Pleasant (riv.), Maine 243/H6
Pleasant (mt.), New Bruns. 170/D3
Pleasant (lake), N.Y. 276/M4
Pleasant (bay), Nova Scotia 168/H2
Pleasant Bay, Nova Scotia 168/H2
Pleasant City, Ohio (43772) 284/G6
Pleasant Dale, Nebr. (68423) 264/G4
Pleasantdale, Sask. 181/G3
Pleasant Gap, Ala. (†36272) 195/H3
Pleasant Gap, Pa. (16823) 294/G4
Pleasant Green, Mo. (†65276) 261/F5
Pleasant Grove, Ala. (35127) 195/D4
Pleasant Grove, Calif. (95668) 204/B8
Pleasant Grove, Miss. (38657) 256/D2
Pleasant Grove, N.J. (†07865) 273/D2
Pleasant Grove, Utah (84062) 304/C3
Pleasant Hill, Ala. (†36701) 195/E6
Pleasant Hill, Calif. (94523) 204/K2
Pleasant Hill, Ill. (62366) 222/C4
Pleasant Hill, La. (71065) 238/C3
Pleasant Hill, Miss. (†38651) 256/E1
Pleasant Hill, Mo. (64080) 261/D5
Pleasant Hill, N.C. (27866) 281/O1
Pleasant Hill, Ohio (45359) 284/B5
Pleasant Hill, S.C. (†29058) 296/F2
Pleasant Hill, Tenn. (38578) 237/L9
Pleasant Hills, Md. (†21087) 245/N3
Pleasant Hills, Pa. (15236) 294/B7
Pleasant Hope, Mo. (65725) 261/F8
Pleasant Island, Maine (†04964) 243/B5
Pleasant Lake, Ind. (46779) 227/H1
Pleasant Lake, Mass. (†02645) 249/O6
Pleasant Lake, Minn. (†56301) 255/D5
Pleasant Lake, N. Dak. (58364) 282/L3
Pleasant Lane, S.C. (†29824) 296/D4
Pleasant Mills, Ind. (46780) 227/H3
Pleasant Mound, Ill. (†62284) 222/D5
Pleasant Mount, Pa. (18453) 294/M2
Pleasanton, Calif. (94566) 204/L2
Pleasanton, Iowa (50224) 229/F7
Pleasanton, Kansas (66075) 232/H3
Pleasanton, Nebr. (68866) 264/E4
Pleasanton, N. Mex. (†88039) 274/A5
Pleasanton, Texas (78064) 303/F9
Pleasant Plain, Iowa (†52540) 229/K6
Pleasant Plain, Ohio (45162) 284/B7
Pleasant Plains, Ark. (72568) 202/G2
Pleasant Plains, Ill. (62677) 222/D4
Pleasant Point, N. Zealand 100/C6
Pleasant Pond, Maine (†04925) 243/D5
Pleasant Prairie, Wis. (53158) 317/L10
Pleasant Ridge, Mich. (48069) 250/B6
Pleasants (co.), W. Va. 312/D4
Pleasant Shade, Tenn. (37145) 237/K8
Pleasant Valley, Conn. (06063) 210/C1
Pleasant Valley, Md. (†21157) 245/L2
Pleasant Valley, Mo. (†64836) 261/R5
Pleasant Valley, Oreg. (†97814) 291/K3
Pleasant Valley (creek), S. Dak. 298/B6
Pleasant Valley, Va. (22848) 307/L4
Pleasant View, Colo. (81331) 208/B7
Pleasant View, Ill. (†62681) 222/C3
Pleasant View, Ky. (40769) 237/N7
Pleasant View, Tenn. (37146) 237/G8
Pleasant View, Utah (†84401) 304/B2
Pleasantville, Ind. (†47838) 227/C7
Pleasantville, Iowa (50225) 229/G6
Pleasantville, N.J. (08232) 273/D5
Pleasantville, N.Y. (10570) 276/N8
Pleasantville, Ohio (43148) 284/F6
Pleasantville (Alum Bank), Pa. (†15521) 294/E5
Pleasantville, Pa. (16341) 294/C2
Pleasantville, Tenn. (37147) 237/F9
Pleasure Beach, Conn. (†06385) 210/G3
Pleasure Ridge Park, Ky. (40258) 237/J4
Pleasureville, Ky. (40057) 237/L4
Pleiku, Vietnam 72/E4
Plenița, Romania 45/F3
Plenty (bay), N. Zealand 100/F2
Plenty, Sask. 181/C4
Plenty (riv.), Victoria 97/J4
Plenty (riv.), Victoria 88/L6
Plenty River Mine, North. Terr. 93/D7
Plentywood, Mont. (59254) 262/M2
Plesetsk, U.S.S.R. 52/F2
Plessis, N.Y. (13675) 276/J2
Plessisville, Québec 172/F3
Plessur (riv.), Switzerland 39/J3
Pleszew, Poland 47/C3
Pletcher, Ala. (†36750) 195/E5
Plétipi (lake), Que. 162/J5
Plétipi (lake), Québec 174/C2
Plettenberg (bay), S. Africa 118/C6
Plettenberg, W. Germany 22/C3
Pleven, Bulgaria 7/G4
Pleven, Bulgaria 45/G4
Plevna, Ala. (†35761) 195/F1
Plevna, Ind. (†46901) 227/E3
Plevna, Kansas (67568) 232/D4
Plevna, Mo. (63464) 261/H3
Plevna, Mont. (59344) 262/M4
Plevna, Ontario 177/H3
Pliny, W. Va. (25158) 312/B5
Pljevlja, Yugoslavia 45/D4
Ploče, Yugoslavia 45/C4
Płock (prov.), Poland 47/D2
Płock, Poland 47/D2
Plockton, Scotland 15/C3
Ploërmel, France 28/B4
Ploiești, Romania 45/H3
Ploiești, Romania 7/G4
Plomárion, Greece 45/H6
Plomb du Cantal (mt.), France 28/E5
Plombières, Belgium 27/F7
Plomer (pt.), N.S. Wales 97/G2
Plomosa (mts.), Ariz. 198/A5
Plön, W. Germany 22/D1
Płonia (riv.), Poland 47/B2
Płońsk, Poland 47/E2
Plovdiv, Bulgaria 7/G4
Plovdiv, Bulgaria 45/G4
Plover, Iowa (50573) 229/D3
Plover, Wis. (54467) 317/G7
Pluckemin, N.J. (07978) 273/D2
Plum (riv.), Ill. 222/C1
Plum (creek), Manitoba 179/B5
Plum (lake), Manitoba 179/B5
Plum (isl.), Mass. 249/L2
Plum (isl.), N.Y. 276/R8
Plum, Pa. (15239) 294/C5
Plumas (co.), Calif. 204/E4
Plumas, Manitoba 179/D4
Plumber (creek), Utah 304/C2
Plum Branch, S.C. (29845) 296/C4
Plum City, Wis. (54761) 317/B6
Plum Coulee, Manitoba 179/E5
Plumerville, Ark. (72127) 202/E3
Plummer, Idaho (83851) 220/B2
Plummer, Ind. (†47424) 227/C7
Plummer, Minn. (56748) 255/B3
Plummers Landing, Ky. (41081) 237/P4
Plum Point, Md. (†20639) 245/N6
Plum Springs, Ky. (†42101) 237/J7
Plumsteadville, Pa. (18949) 294/M5
Plum Tree, Ind. (†46792) 227/G3
Plumtree, Zimbabwe 118/D4
Plumville, Pa. (16246) 294/D4
Plumwood, Ohio (†43140) 284/D6
Plunge, U.S.S.R. 53/B3
Plunkett, Sask. 181/F4
Plunkettville, Okla. (†74963) 288/S6
Plush, Oreg. (97637) 291/H5
Plymouth (cap.), 156/F3
Plymouth, Calif. (95669) 204/C8
Plymouth○, Conn. (06782) 210/C2
Plymouth, England 7/D3
Plymouth, England 10/E5
Plymouth, England 13/C7
Plymouth (sound), England 13/C7
Plymouth, Fla. (32768) 212/E3
Plymouth, Ill. (62367) 222/C3
Plymouth, Ind. (46563) 227/E2
Plymouth (co.), Iowa 229/A3
Plymouth, Iowa (50464) 229/G2
Plymouth○, Maine (04969) 243/E6
Plymouth (co.), Mass. 249/L5
Plymouth, Mass. (02360) 249/M5
Plymouth○, Mass. (02360) 249/M5
Plymouth (bay), Mass. 249/M5
Plymouth, Mich. (*48170) 250/F6
Plymouth, Minn. (†55441) 255/G5
Plymouth, Nebr. (68424) 264/G4
Plymouth, N.H. (03264) 268/D4
Plymouth○, N.H. (03264) 268/D4
Plymouth, N.C. (27962) 281/R3
Plymouth, Ohio (44865) 284/E4
Plymouth, Pa. (18651) 294/E7
Plymouth, Utah (84330) 304/B2
Plymouth○, Vt. (05056) 268/B4
Plymouth, Wash. (99346) 310/F5
Plymouth, W. Va. (†25011) 312/C5
Plymouth, Wis. (53073) 317/L8
Plymouth Union, Vt. (†05056) 268/B4
Plympton○, Mass. (02367) 249/L5
Plympton, Nova Scotia 168/C4
Plynlimon (mt.), Wales 13/D5
Plzeň, Czech. 7/F4
Plzeň, Czech. 41/B2
Pniel, S. Africa 118/F6
Pniewy, Poland 47/C2
Po (riv.), Italy 7/E4
Po (riv.), Italy 34/C2
Po, Upper Volta 106/D6
Po (riv.), Va. 307/N4
Poá, Brazil 135/C3
Poatina, Tasmania 99/C3
Pobeda (peak), China 77/A3
Pobeda (peak), U.S.S.R. 48/J5
Población, Chile 138/F5
Pobla de Segur, Spain 33/G1
Poca, W. Va. (25159) 312/C6
Pocahontas, Alberta 182/B3
Pocahontas, Ark. (72455) 202/H1
Pocahontas, Ill. (62275) 222/D5
Pocahontas (co.), Iowa 229/D3
Pocahontas, Iowa (50574) 229/D3
Pocahontas, Miss. (39072) 256/D6
Pocahontas, Mo. (63779) 261/N8
Pocahontas, Tenn. (38061) 237/D10
Pocahontas, Va. (24635) 307/F6
Pocahontas (co.), W. Va. 312/F6
Pocasset, Mass. (02559) 249/M6
Pocasset, Okla. (73079) 288/L4
Pocatalico (riv.), W. Va. 312/C5
Pocatello, Idaho 146/G5
Pocatello, Idaho (*83201) 220/F7
Pocatello, Idaho 188/D2
Počátky, Czech. 41/C2
Pochep, U.S.S.R. 52/D4
Pöchlarn, Austria 41/C2
Pocklington, England 13/G4
Pocoata, Bolivia 136/B6
Poções, Brazil 132/F6
Pocola, Okla. (74902) 288/T4
Pocologan, New Bruns. 170/D3
Pocomoke (riv.), Md. 245/S8
Pocomoke (sound), Md. 245/P9
Pocomoke (sound), Va. 307/S5
Pocomoke City, Md. (21851) 245/R8
Pocomoonshine (lake), Maine 243/H5
Pocona, Bolivia 136/C5
Poconé, Brazil 132/B7
Pocono (mts.), Pa. 294/M3
Pocono Lake, Pa. (18347) 294/L3
Pocono Pines, Pa. (18350) 294/M3
Poços de Caldas, Brazil 120/E5
Poços de Caldas, Brazil 135/C2
Poços de Caldas, Brazil 132/E8
Pocotalago, Georgia (†30633) 217/F2
Pocotalico, W. Va. (†25301) 312/C6
Pocotaligo (riv.), S.C. 296/G4
Pocotopaug (lake), Conn. 210/E2
Pocpo, Bolivia 136/C6
Podbořany, Czech. 41/B1
Poděbrady, Czech. 41/C1
Podol'sk, U.S.S.R. 7/H3
Podol'sk, U.S.S.R. 52/E3
Podol'sk, U.S.S.R. 48/D4
Podor, Senegal 106/B5
Podporozh'ye, U.S.S.R. 52/D2
Podunk (riv.), Conn. 210/E1
Poe, Alberta 182/D3
Poe, Ind. (†46802) 227/G3
Poel (isl.), E. Germany 22/D1
Poenari Burchi, Romania 45/G3
Poge (cape), Mass. 249/N7
Poggibonsi, Italy 34/C3
Pogradec, Albania 45/E5
Pohakuloa (pt.), Hawaii 218/H2
P'ohang, S. Korea 81/D5
Pohatcong (creek), N.J. 273/C2
Pohénégamook, Québec 172/H2
Pohjois-Karjala (prov.), Finland 18/Q5
Pohořelice, Czech. 41/D2
Pohsien (Bo Xian), China 77/J5
Poiana Mare, Romania 45/F4
Poigan (lake), Québec 172/A2
Poinsett (co.), Ark. 202/J2
Poinsett (lake), Fla. 212/F3
Poinsett (lake), S. Dak. 298/P4
Point, La. (†71234) 238/F1
Point (lake), N.W. Terrs. 187/G3
Point, Texas (75472) 303/J5
Point Alexander, Ontario 177/G1
Point Arena, Calif. (95468) 204/B5
Point au Fer (isl.), La. 238/H8
Point au Fer (pt.), La. 238/H8
Point Baker, Alaska (99927) 196/M2
Point Cedar, Ark. (†71921) 202/D5
Point Clear, Ala. (36564) 195/C10
Point Comfort, Texas (77978) 303/H9
Point Cross, Nova Scotia 168/G2
Point de Bute, New Bruns. 170/F3
Point du Bois, Manitoba 179/G4
Pointe-à-la-Croix, Québec 172/C2
Pointe-à-la-Frégate, Québec 172/D1
Pointe-à-la-Garde, Québec 172/B2
Pointe à la Hache, La. (70082) 238/L7
Pointe-à-Pitre, Guadeloupe 161/B6
Pointe-à-Pitre, Guadeloupe 156/G3
Pointe à Raquette, Haiti 158/B6
Pointe au Baril Station, Ontario 177/D2
Pointe-au-Chêne, Québec 172/C4
Pointe-au-Père, Québec 172/J1
Pointe-au-Pic, Québec 172/G2
Pointe Aux Barques, Mich. (48467) 250/G4
Pointe-aux-Outardes, Québec 172/A1
Pointe Aux Pins, Mich. (49775) 250/E3
Pointe-aux-Trembles, Québec 172/J4
Pointe-Bleue, Québec 172/E1
Pointe-Calumet, Québec 172/G4
Pointe-Claire, Québec 172/H4
Pointe Coupee (par.), La. 238/G5
Pointe du Bout, Martinique 161/C6
Pointe-du-Chêne, New Bruns. 170/F2
Pointe-du-Lac, Québec 172/E3
Pointe-du-Moulin, Québec 172/H4
Point Edward, Ontario 177/B4
Pointe-Gatineau, Québec 172/B4
Pointe-Lebel, Québec 172/A1
Pointe-Noire, Congo 102/D5
Pointe-Noire, Congo 115/B4
Pointe-Noire, Guadeloupe 161/A6
Pointe-Sapin, New Bruns. 170/F2
Pointe-Verte, New Bruns. 170/E1
Point Fortin, Trin. & Tob. 161/A11
Point Harbor, N.C. (27964) 281/T2
Point Hope, Alaska 188/C5
Point Hope, Alaska (99766) 196/E1
Point Isabel, Ind. (†46928) 227/F4
Point La Haye, Newf. 166/D2
Point Lance, Newf. 166/C2
Point Lay, Alaska (†99723) 196/F1
Point Leamington, Newf. 166/C4
Point Marion, Pa. (15474) 294/C6
Point Mugu Pacific Missile Test Center, Calif. 204/F9
Point of Rocks, Md. (21777) 245/J3
Point of Rocks, Wyo. (82942) 319/D4
Point Pelee, Ontario 177/B6
Point Pelee Nat'l Park, Ontario 177/B5
Point Pleasant, Mo. (63873) 261/O10
Point Pleasant, N.J. (08742) 273/E3
Point Pleasant, Ohio (45163) 284/B8
Point Pleasant, Pa. (18950) 294/N5
Point Pleasant, W. Va. (25550) 312/B5
Point Pleasant Beach, N.J. (08742) 273/E3
Point Reyes Nat'l Seashore, Calif. 204/H1
Point Reyes Station, Calif. (94956) 204/H1
Point Roberts, Wash. (98281) 310/B2
Points, W. Va. (25437) 312/J4
Point Salvation Aboriginal Reserve, W. Australia 88/C5
Point Salvation Aboriginal Res., W. Australia 92/D5
Point Tupper, Nova Scotia 168/G3
Point Verde, Newf. 166/C2
Point Washington, Fla. (32454) 212/C6
Poipu, Hawaii (†96756) 218/C2
Poison (creek), Wyo. 319/E2
Poison Spider (creek), Wyo. 319/F3
Poisson Blanc (lake), Québec 172/B4
Poissons (riv.), Newf. 166/A3
Poitiers, France 7/E4
Poitiers, France 28/D4
Poitou (trad. prov.) France 29
Pojo, Bolivia 136/C5
Pojoaque, N. Mex. (†87501) 274/C3
Pokaran, India 68/C3
Pokataroo, N.S. Wales 97/E1
Pokegama (lake), Minn. 255/E3
Pokemouche (riv.), New Bruns. 170/E1
Pokesudie (isl.), New Bruns. 170/F1
Pokhara, Nepal 68/E3
Pokhvistnevo, U.S.S.R. 52/H4
Poko, Zaire 115/E3
Pokrovsk, U.S.S.R. 48/N3
Pola, Philippines 82/C4
Pola (Pula), Yugoslavia 45/A3
Polacca, Ariz. (86042) 198/E3
Polacca Wash (dry riv.), Ariz. 198/E3
Pola de Lena, Spain 33/C1
Pola de Siero, Spain 33/D1
Polanco del Yí, Uruguay 145/D4
Poland 2/K3
Poland 7/F3
POLAND 47
Poland (riv.), Conn. 210/C2
Poland, Ind. (47868) 227/C6
Poland, Maine (04273) 243/C7
Poland○, Maine (04273) 243/C7
Poland, N.Y. (13431) 276/L4
Poland, Ohio (44514) 284/J3
Poland Spring, Maine (04274) 243/C7
Polar, Wis. (54418) 317/H5
Polar Bear Prov. Park, Ontario 175/D2
Polaris, Mont. (59746) 262/C5
Polatlı, Turkey 63/E3
Polatlı, Turkey 59/B2
Połczyn-Zdrój, Poland 47/C2
Polebridge, Mont. (59928) 262/B2
Pol-e Khomri, Afghanistan 68/B1
Pol-e Khomri, Afghanistan 59/J2
Polgár, Hungary 41/F3
Polgárdi, Hungary 41/E3
Poli, Cameroon 115/B2
Policastro (gulf), Italy 34/E5
Police, Poland 47/B2
Polička, Czech. 41/D2
Poligny, France 28/F4
Poligus, U.S.S.R. 48/K3
Polikastron, Greece 45/F5
Políkhnitos, Greece 45/G6
Polillo, Philippines 82/D3
Polillo (isl.), Philippines 85/G3
Polillo (isl.), Philippines 82/C3
Polillo (str.), Philippines 82/C3
Polis, Cyprus 63/E5
Pollyiros, Greece 45/F5
Polk (co.), Ark. 202/B5
Polk (co.), Fla. 212/E4
Polk (co.), Georgia 217/B3
Polk (co.), Iowa 229/F5
Polk (co.), Minn. 255/B3
Polk (co.), Mo. 261/F7
Polk, Mo. (65727) 261/F7
Polk (co.), Nebr. 264/G3
Polk, Nebr. (68654) 264/G3
Polk (co.), N.C. 281/E4
Polk, Ohio (44866) 284/F4
Polk (co.), Oreg. 291/D3
Polk, Pa. (16342) 294/C3
Polk (co.), Tenn. 237/N10
Polk (co.), Texas 303/K7
Polk (co.), Wis. 317/B5
Polk City, Fla. (33868) 212/E3
Polk City, Iowa (50226) 229/F5
Polkowice, Poland 47/C3
Polkton, N.C. (28135) 281/J4
Polkville, Miss. (39118) 256/E6
Polkville, N.C. (28136) 281/F4
Pollaphuca (res.), Ireland 17/J5
Pollard, Ala. (†36441) 195/D8
Pollard, Ark. (72456) 202/K1
Pollards Point, Newf. 166/C4
Pöllau, Austria 41/C3
Pollensa, Spain 33/H3
Pollett (riv.), New Bruns. 170/E3
Pollett River, New Bruns. 170/E3
Pollock, Idaho (83547) 220/B4
Pollock, La. (71467) 238/F3
Pollock, Mo. (63560) 261/F2
Pollock, S. Dak. (57648) 298/J2
Pollock Pines, Calif. (95726) 204/E5
Pollocksville, N.C. (28573) 281/P5
Pollockville, Alberta 182/E4
Polmak, Norway 18/Q2
Polná, Czech. 41/C2
Polo, Dom. Rep. 158/D6
Polo, Ill. (61064) 222/D1
Polo, Mo. (64671) 261/D3
Polomka, Czech. 41/E2
Polonia, Chile 138/G6
Polonia, Wis. (†54423) 317/H6
Polonio, Uruguay 145/F5
Polonio (cape), Uruguay 145/F5
Polonnaruwa, Sri Lanka 68/E7
Polonnoye, U.S.S.R. 52/C4
Polotsk, U.S.S.R. 52/C3
Polperro, England 13/C7
Polson, Mont. (59860) 262/B3
Poltava, U.S.S.R. 7/H4
Poltava, U.S.S.R. 52/D5
Poltava, U.S.S.R. 48/D5
Poltimore, Québec 172/B4
Põltsamaa, U.S.S.R. 53/D1
Polvadera, N. Mex. (87828) 274/B4
Polyarnyy, U.S.S.R. 52/D1
Polyarnyy, U.S.S.R. 48/D3
Polynesia (reg.), Pacific 87/K7
Pomabamba, Peru 128/D7
Pomaire, Chile 138/F4
Pomán, Argentina 143/C2
Pomaria, S.C. (29126) 296/E3
Pombal, Brazil 132/G4
Pombal, Portugal 33/B3
Pomerania (reg.), E. Germany 22/E2
Pomeranian (bay), E. Germany 22/F1
Pomeranian (bay), Poland 47/B1
Pomerene, Ariz. (85627) 198/E6
Pomeroon (riv.), Guyana 131/B2
Pomeroy, Iowa (50575) 229/D3
Pomeroy, N. Ireland 17/H2
Pomeroy, Ohio (45769) 284/G7
Pomeroy, Wash. (99347) 310/H4
Pomezia, Italy 34/F7
Pomfret○, Conn. (06258) 210/H1
Pomfret, Md. (20675) 245/L6
Pomfret○, Vt. (†05067) 268/B4
Pomfret Center, Conn. (06259) 210/H1
Pomme de Terre (riv.), Minn. 255/C5
Pomme de Terre (lake), Mo. 261/E7
Pomona, Calif. 188/C4
Pomona, Calif. (*91766) 204/D10
Pomona, Kansas (66076) 232/G3
Pomona (lake), Kansas 232/G3
Pomona, Md. (†21620) 245/O4
Pomona, Mo. (65789) 261/J9
Pomona, N.J. (08240) 273/D5
Pomona Park, Fla. (32081) 212/E2
Pomonkey, Md. (†20640) 245/K6
Pomorie, Bulgaria 45/H4
Pomos (pt.), Cyprus 63/E5
Pompano Beach, Fla. (*33060) 212/F5
Pompanoosuc, Vt. (†05078) 268/C4
Pompéia, Brazil 135/A3
Pompeii (ruins), Italy 34/E4
Pompeii, Mich. (48874) 250/E5
Pomperaug, Conn. (†06798) 210/C2
Pomperaug (riv.), Conn. 210/C3
Pompey, N.Y. (13138) 276/J5
Pompeys Pillar, Mont. (59064) 262/J5
Pompton (lake), N.J. 273/B1
Pompton Lakes, N.J. (07442) 273/A1
Pompton Plains, N.J. (07444) 273/B1
Pomquet, Nova Scotia 168/G3
Pomy, Switzerland 39/C3
Ponape (isl.), Micronesia 87/F5
Ponass (lakes), Sask. 181/H3
Ponca, Ark. (72670) 202/D1
Ponca, Nebr. (68770) 264/H2
Ponca (creek), S. Dak. 298/L7
Ponca City, Okla. 188/G3
Ponca City, Okla. (74601) 288/M1
Ponce (dist.), P. Rico 161/C2
Ponce, P. Rico 161/C3
Ponce, P. Rico 156/F1
Ponce de Leon, Fla. (32455) 212/C6
Ponce de Leon (bay), Fla. 212/E6
Ponce Inlet, Fla. (†32019) 212/F2
Poncha Springs, Colo. (81242) 208/G6
Ponchatoula, La. (70454) 238/N2
Pond (pt.), Conn. 210/C4
Pond (riv.), Ky. 237/G6
Pond, Miss. (†39669) 256/B8
Pond, Mo. (†63038) 261/M3
Pond (inlet), N.W. Terrs. 187/L2
Pond Creek, Okla. (73766) 288/L1
Pond Eddy, Pa. (†12770) 294/N3
Pondera (co.), Mont. 262/D2
Ponderay, Idaho (83852) 220/B1
Ponderosa, N. Mex. (87044) 274/C3
Pond Fork (riv.), W. Va. 312/C6
Pondicherry (terr.), India 68/E6
Pondicherry, India 68/E6
Pond Inlet, Canada 4/B13
Pond Inlet, N.W.T. 162/J1
Pond Inlet, N.W. Terrs. 187/L2
Pondoland (reg.), S. Africa 118/D6
Pondosa, Calif. (96007) 204/D2
Ponds (isl.), Newf. 166/C3
Poneloya, Nicaragua 154/D4
Ponemah, Minn. (56666) 255/D2
Ponemah, N.H. (†03055) 268/D6
Poneto, Ind. (46781) 227/G3
Ponferrada, Spain 33/C1
Pongara (pt.), Gabon 115/A3
Ponhook (lake), Nova Scotia 168/D4
Poniatowa, Poland 47/E3
Ponnani, India 68/D6
Ponoka, Alberta 182/D3
Ponomarevka, U.S.S.R. 52/H4
Ponorogo, Indonesia 85/J2
Ponoy, U.S.S.R. 48/E3
Ponoy, U.S.S.R. 52/F1
Ponoy (riv.), U.S.S.R. 52/E1
Pons, France 28/C5
Ponset, Conn. (†06441) 210/E3
Ponsford, Minn. (56575) 255/C4
Pont-à-Celles, Belgium 27/E8
Ponta Delgada (dist.), Portugal 33/D2
Ponta Delgada, Portugal 33/C3
Ponta de Pedras, Brazil 132/D3
Ponta do Sol, Portugal 33/A2
Ponta Grossa, Brazil 120/D5
Ponta Grossa, Brazil 132/D9
Ponta Grossa, Brazil 135/B4
Pont-à-Mousson, France 28/G3
Ponta Porã, Brazil 132/C8
Ponta Porã, Paraguay 144/E3
Pontarlier, France 28/G4
Pontbriand, Québec 172/F3
Pont Canavese, Italy 34/A2
Pontchartrain (lake), La. 188/J5
Pontchartrain (lake), La. 238/O3
Pontchartrain Causeway, La. 238/O3
Pontecorvo, Italy 34/D4
Ponte de Sor, Portugal 33/C3
Ponte do Lima, Portugal 33/B2
Ponteix, Sask. 181/D6
Ponteland, England 13/H3
Ponte Nova, Brazil 132/F8
Ponte Nova, Brazil 135/E2
Pontevedra, Philippines 82/D5
Pontevedra (prov.), Spain 33/B1
Pontevedra, Spain 33/B1
Ponte Vedra Beach, Fla. (32082) 212/E1
Pontgrave, New Bruns. 170/F1
Pontiac, Ill. (61764) 222/E3
Pontiac, Mich. 188/K2
Pontiac, Mich. (*48053) 250/F6
Pontiac, Mo. (65729) 261/G9
Pontiac (co.), Québec 172/A3
Pontiac (county), Québec 174/B3
Pontiac, R.I. (†02887) 249/J6
Pontiac, S.C. (†29045) 296/F3
Pontianak, Indonesia 85/D6
Pontianak, Indonesia 54/N10
Pontian Kechil, Malaysia 72/E5
Pontic (mts.), Turkey 59/C1
Pontic (mts.), Turkey 63/H2
Pontine (isls.), Italy 34/D4
Pontinia, Italy 34/D4
Pontivy, France 28/B3
Pont-l'Abbe, France 28/A4
Pont-Lafrance, New Bruns. 170/E1
Pont-Landry, New Bruns. 170/F1
Pont-l'Évêque, France 28/D3
Ponto da Divisão, Brazil 132/B5
Pontoise, France 28/E3
Pontoon Beach, Ill. (†62040) 222/A2
Pontoosuc, Ill. (†62330) 222/B3
Pontoosuc (lake), Mass. 249/A3
Pontorson, France 28/C3
Pontotoc (co.), Miss. 256/F2
Pontotoc, Miss. (38863) 256/G2
Pontotoc (co.), Okla. 288/N5
Pontotoc, Okla. (74863) 288/N6
Pontotoc, Texas (76869) 303/E7
Pontremoli, Italy 34/B2
Pontresina, Switzerland 39/J3
Pontrilas, Sask. 181/H2
Pont-Rouge, Québec 172/F3
Pontypool, Ontario 177/F3
Pontypool, Wales 13/B6
Pontypridd, Wales 13/A6
Pontypridd, Wales 10/E5
Pony, Mont. (59747) 262/E5
Pony (creek), Okla. 288/C1

Puebla de Zaragoza 431

Potter Hill, R.I. (†02891) 249/H7
Potters Bar, England 13/H7
Potters Bar, England 10/B5
Pottersdale, Pa. (16871) 294/F3
Pottersville, Mo. (65790) 261/H9
Pottersville, N.J. (07979) 273/D2
Pottersville, N.Y. (12860) 276/N3
Potterville, Mich. (48876) 250/E6
Potts (creek), W. Va. 312/F7
Pottsboro, Texas (75076) 303/H4
Potts Camp, Miss. (38659) 256/F1
Pottstown, Pa. (19464) 294/L5
Pottsville, Ark. (72858) 202/D3
Pottsville, Pa. (17901) 294/K4
Pottsville, Texas (76565) 303/F6
Potwin, Kansas (67123) 232/F4
Pouce-Coupé, Br. Col. 184/G2
Pouch Cove, Newf. 166/D2
Poudre d'Or, Mauritius 118/G5
Poughkeepsie, Ark. (72569) 202/H1
Poughkeepsie, N.Y. (*12601) 276/N7
Pouillon, France 28/C6
Poulan, Georgia (31781) 217/E8
Poulet Cove (bay), Nova Scotia 168/H2
Poulin-de-Courval (lake), Québec 172/G1
Poulo Wai (isls.), Cambodia 72/D5
Poulsbo, Wash. (98370) 310/A1
Poultney, Vt. (05764) 268/A4
Poultney○, Vt. (05764) 268/A4
Poultney (riv.), Vt. 268/A4
Poulton le Fylde, England 10/F1
Poulton-le-Fylde, England 13/G1
Pound, Va. (24279) 307/C6
Pound, Wis. (54161) 317/L5
Pounding Mill, Va. (24637) 307/E6
Pouso Alegre, Brazil 135/D3
Pouthisat, Cambodia 72/D4
Považská Bystrica, Czech. 41/E2
Povenets, U.S.S.R. 52/E2
Poverty (isl.), Mich. 250/C3
Poverty (bay), N. Zealand 100/G3
Póvoa de Varzim, Portugal 33/B2
Povorino, U.S.S.R. 52/F4
Povungnituk, Que. 162/J3
Povungnituk, Québec 174/E1
Powassan, Ontario 177/E1
Poway, Calif. (92064) 204/J11
Powder (riv.) 188/E2
Powder (riv.), Mont. 262/L4
Powder (riv.), Oreg. 291/K3
Powder (riv.), Wyo. 319/F2
Powderhorn, Colo. (81243) 208/E6
Powderly, Ky. (42367) 237/G6
Powderly, Texas (75473) 303/J4
Powder River (co.), Mont. 262/L5
Powder River, Wyo. (82648) 319/F2
Powder Springs, Georgia (30073) 217/C3
Powder Springs, Tenn. (37848) 237/O8
Powderville, Mont. (59345) 262/L5
Powe, Mo. (†63822) 261/M9
Powell (lake) 188/D3
Powell (lake), Ariz. 198/E1
Powell (co.), Ky. 237/O5
Powell, Manitoba 179/A2
Powell (co.), Mont. 262/D4
Powell, Nebr. (†68352) 264/G4
Powell, Ohio (43065) 284/D5
Powell, Pa. (†18832) 294/J2
Powell, Tenn. (37849) 237/N8
Powell (riv.), Tenn. 237/P8
Powell (lake), U.S. 146/G6
Powell (lake), Utah 304/D6
Powell (riv.), Va. 307/B7
Powell, Wyo. (82435) 319/D1
Powell Butte, Oreg. (97753) 291/G3
Powell Creek, North. Terr. 93/C5
Powell River, Br. Col. 184/E5
Powell's Crossroads, Ala. (†35986) 195/G1
Powells Crossroads, Tenn. (†37397) 237/L10
Powells Point, N.C. (27966) 281/T2
Powellsville, N.C. (27967) 281/R2
Powellton, W. Va. (25161) 312/D6
Powellville, Md. (21852) 245/S7
Powelton, Georgia (†31059) 217/G4
Power (co.), Idaho 220/F7
Power, Mont. (59468) 262/E3
Powers (lake), Conn. 210/G3
Powers, Mich. (49874) 250/B3
Powers, Oreg. (97466) 291/D5
Powers Lake, N. Dak. (58773) 282/E2
Powersville, Georgia (31074) 217/E5
Powersville, Iowa (†50636) 229/H3
Powersville, Mo. (64672) 261/F1
Powerview, Manitoba 179/F4
Poweshiek (co.), Iowa 229/H5
Powhatan, Ark. (72458) 202/H1
Powhatan, La. (71066) 238/D3
Powhatan (co.), Va. 307/N5
Powhatan, Va. (23139) 307/N5
Powhatan, W. Va. (24877) 312/D8
Powhatan Point, Ohio (43942) 284/J6
Powhattan, Kansas (66527) 232/G2
Pownal○, Maine (04069) 243/C8
Pownal○, Vt. (05261) 268/A6
Pownal Center, Vt. (†05261) 268/A6
Powys (co.), Wales 13/D5
Poxoréo, Brazil 132/C6
Poyang (lake), China 54/N7
Poyang Hu (lake), China 77/J6
Poyen, Ark. (72128) 202/E5
Poygan (lake), Wis. 317/J7
Poynette, Wis. (53955) 317/G9
Poynor, Mo. (63959) 261/L9
Poynor, Texas (75782) 303/J5
Poysdorf, Austria 41/D2
Poy Sippi, Wis. (54967) 317/J7
Pozantı, Turkey 63/F4
Požarevac, Yugoslavia 45/E3
Poza Rica de Hidalgo, Mexico 150/L6
Poznań (prov.), Poland 47/C2
Poznań, Poland 47/C2
Poznań, Poland 7/F3
Pozo Almonte, Chile 138/B2
Pozoblanco, Spain 33/D3
Pozo Colorado, Paraguay 144/C3
Pozo Hondo, Argentina 143/D2
Pozohondo, Spain 33/F3
Pozuelo de Alarcón, Spain 33/D2
Pozuelos, Venezuela 124/F2
Pozuzo, Peru 128/E8
Pozzallo, Italy 34/E6
Pozzuoli, Italy 34/D4
Prabuty, Poland 47/D2
Prachatice, Czech. 41/B2
Prachin Buri, Thailand 72/D4
Prachuap Khiri Khan, Thailand 72/D5
Pradera, Colombia 126/B6
Prades, France 28/E6
Prado (dam), Calif. 204/E11
Praestø, Denmark 21/F7
Pragel (pass), Switzerland 39/G2
Prague (cap.), Czech. 7/F3
Prague (Praha) (cap.), Czech. 41/C1
Prague, Nebr. (68050) 264/H3
Prague, Okla. (74864) 288/N4
Praha (city), Czech. 41/C1
Prahan, Victoria 88/L7
Prahran, Victoria 97/J5
Praia (cap.), C. Verde 106/B8
Prainha, Amazonas, Brazil 132/A4
Prainha, Pará, Brazil 132/C3
Prairie, Ala. (36771) 195/D6
Prairie (co.), Ark. 202/G4
Prairie (creek), Ind. 227/C7
Prairie (riv.), Mich. 250/D7
Prairie (riv.), Minn. 255/E3
Prairie, Miss. (39756) 256/G3
Prairie (co.), Mont. 262/L4
Prairie, Queensland 95/C4
Prairie (lake), S. Dak. 298/P3
Prairieburg, Iowa (52219) 229/L4
Prairie City, Ill. (61470) 222/C3
Prairie City, Iowa (50228) 229/G5
Prairie City, Oreg. (97869) 291/J3
Prairie City, S. Dak. (57649) 298/D2
Prairie Creek, Ind. (47869) 227/C6
Prairie Dog Town Fork, Red (riv.), Okla. 288/F5
Prairie Dog Town Fork, Red (riv.), Texas 303/C3
Prairie du Chien, Wis. (53821) 317/D9
Prairie du Rocher, Ill. (62277) 222/C5
Prairie du Sac, Wis. (53578) 317/G9
Prairie Farm, Wis. (54762) 317/C5
Prairie Grove, Ark. (72753) 202/B2
Prairie Grove, Ill. (†60050) 222/E1
Prairie Home, Mo. (65068) 261/G5
Prairie Point, Miss. (39353) 256/H4
Prairie River, Sask. 181/J3
Prairies (riv.), Québec 172/H4
Prairieton, Ind. (47870) 227/B6
Prairietown, Ill. (†62097) 222/B2
Prairie View, Ark. (72859) 202/C3
Prairie View, Kansas (67664) 232/C2
Prairie View, Texas (77445) 303/J7
Prairie Village, Kansas (66208) 232/H2
Prairieville, La. (70769) 238/K2
Pran Buri, Thailand 72/D4
Prangins, Switzerland 39/B4
Prapat, Indonesia 85/B5
Praslin, St. Lucia 161/G6
Praslin (isl.), Seychelles 118/H5
Prat (isl.), Chile 138/D7
Pratas (Dongsha) (isl.), China 77/J7
Prathersville, Mo. (†64024) 261/R4
Prato, Italy 34/C3
Prato-Sornico, Switzerland 39/G4
Pratt (co.), Kansas 232/D4
Pratt, Kansas (67124) 232/D4
Pratt, Manitoba 179/D5
Pratt, Minn. (†55060) 255/E6
Pratt, W. Va. (25162) 312/D6
Prattelin, Switzerland 39/E1
Prattsburg, Georgia (†31039) 217/D5
Prattsburg○, N.Y. (14873) 276/F5
Prattsville, Ark. (72129) 202/F5
Prattsville, N.Y. (12468) 276/M6
Prattville, Ala. (36067) 195/E6
Pratum, Oreg. (†97301) 291/A3
Pravia, Spain 33/C1
Prawda, Manitoba 179/G5
Prawle (pt.), England 13/D7
Prawle (pt.), England 10/E5
Praxedis G. Guerrero, Mexico 150/G1
Pray, Mont. (59065) 262/F5
Praya, Indonesia 85/F7
Preble, Ind. (46782) 227/H3
Preble, N.Y. (13141) 276/H5
Preble (co.), Ohio 284/A6
Preeceville, Sask. 181/J4
Preemption, Ill. (61276) 222/C2
Preesall, England 13/E4
Preetz, W. Germany 22/D1
Pregarten, Austria 41/C2
Pregnall, S.C. (†29437) 296/G5
Pregonero, Venezuela 124/C3
Preiļi, U.S.S.R. 53/D2
Prek Pouthi, Cambodia 72/E5
Prelate, Sask. 181/B5
Přelouč, Czech. 41/C1
Premier, W. Va. (24878) 312/C8
Premium, Ky. (41845) 237/R6
Premont, Texas (78375) 303/F10
Prentice, Ill. (†62612) 222/C4
Prentice, Wis. (54556) 317/F4
Prentiss○, Maine (†04487) 243/G5
Prentiss (co.), Miss. 256/G1
Prentiss, Miss. (39474) 256/E7
Prentiss, N.C. (†28734) 281/C4
Prenzlau, E. Germany 22/E2
Preparis (isl.), Burma 72/B4
Preparis North (chan.), Burma 72/B4
Preparis South (chan.), Burma 72/B4
Přerov, Czech. 41/D2
Presanella (mt.), Italy 34/C1
Prescott, Ariz. 188/D4
Prescott, Ariz. (86301) 198/C4
Prescott, Ark. (71857) 202/D6
Prescott, Ind. (†46176) 227/F6
Prescott, Iowa (50859) 229/D6
Prescott, Kansas (66767) 232/H3
Prescott, Mich. (48756) 250/F4
Prescott (county), Ontario 177/K2
Prescott, Ontario 177/J3
Prescott, Oreg. (†97048) 291/D1
Prescott, Wash. (99348) 310/G4
Prescott, Wis. (54021) 317/A6
Prescott Valley, Ariz. (†86301) 198/C4
Preseli (mts.), Wales 13/C6
Preševo, Yugoslavia 45/E4
Presho, S. Dak. (57568) 298/J6
Presidencia de la Plaza, Argentina 143/D2
Presidencia R. Sáenz Peña, Argentina 120/C5
Presidencia Roque Sáenz Peña, Argentina 143/D2
President, Pa. (†16353) 294/C3
Presidente Dutra, Brazil 132/E4
Presidente Hayes, Paraguay 144/C3
Presidente Prudente, Brazil 132/D8
Presidente Prudente, Brazil 120/D5
Presidente Ríos (lake), Chile 138/D6
Presidente Venceslau, Brazil 132/D8
Presidential (range), N.H. 268/E3
Presidio, Calif. 204/J2
Presidio (co.), Texas 303/C12
Presidio, Texas (79845) 303/C12
Presidio Modelo, Cuba 158/C2
Prešov, Czech. 41/F2
Prespa (lake), Albania 45/E5
Prespa (lake), Greece 45/E5
Prespa (lake), Yugoslavia 45/E5
Presque Isle, Maine (04769) 243/H2
Presque Isle (co.), Mich. 250/F3
Presque Isle, Mich. (49777) 250/F3
Presque Isle (riv.), Mich. 250/F1
Presque Isle, Wis. (54557) 317/G3
Presque Isle A.F.B., Maine 243/G2
Presqu'île Prov. Park, Ontario 177/G4
Prestatyn, Wales 13/D4
Prestea, Ghana 106/D7
Presteigne, Wales 10/E4
Presteigne, Wales 13/D5
Přeštice, Czech. 41/B2
Presto, Bolivia 136/C6
Preston○, Conn. (†06360) 210/H2
Preston, England 10/F1
Preston, England 13/G1
Preston, Georgia (31824) 217/C6
Preston, Idaho (83263) 220/G7
Preston, Ill. (†62242) 222/D5
Preston, Iowa (52069) 229/N4
Preston, Kansas (67569) 232/D4
Preston, Ky. (40366) 237/O4
Preston, Md. (21655) 245/P6
Preston, Minn. (55965) 255/F7
Preston, Miss. (39354) 256/G5
Preston, Mo. (65732) 261/F7
Preston, Nebr. (†68355) 264/J4
Preston, Nev. (†89301) 266/G4
Preston, Okla. (74456) 288/P3
Preston, Scotland 15/F5
Preston, Victoria 88/L7
Preston, Victoria 97/J4
Preston, Wash. (98050) 310/D3
Preston (co.), W. Va. 312/G4
Preston City, Conn. (†06360) 210/H2
Preston Hollow, N.Y. (12469) 276/M6
Prestonpans, Scotland 15/D1
Prestonsburg, Ky. (41653) 237/R5
Prestonville, Ky. (†41008) 237/L3
Prestwich, England 13/H2
Prestwick, Scotland 10/D3
Prestwick, Scotland 15/D5
Prêto (riv.), Brazil 132/E5
Prêto (riv.), Brazil 135/E3
Prêto (riv.), Brazil 132/A4
Pretoria (cap.), S. Africa 2/L7
Pretoria (cap.), S. Africa 102/E7
Pretoria (cap.), S. Africa 118/D5
Prettyboy (res.), Md. 245/M2
Pretty Prairie, Kansas (67570) 232/D4
Préveza, Greece 45/E6
Prévost, Québec 172/C4
Prevost, Wash. (†98250) 310/B2
Prewitt (res.), Colo. 208/N2
Prewitt, N. Mex. (87045) 274/B3
Prey Veng, Cambodia 72/E5
Pribilof (isls.), Alaska 188/C6
Pribilof (isls.), Alaska 196/D3
Pribilof (isls.), U.S. 4/D18
Priboj, Yugoslavia 45/D4
Příbor, Czech. 41/E2
Příbram, Czech. 41/B2
Price (isl.), Br. Col. 184/C4
Price, Md. (21656) 245/P4
Price, N. Dak. (†58547) 282/H5
Price, Québec 172/A1
Price, Utah (84501) 304/D4
Price, Utah 188/D3
Price (riv.), Utah 304/D4
Price (co.), Wis. 317/F4
Price, Wis. (†54741) 317/E6
Pricedale, Miss. (†39666) 256/D8
Price Hill, W. Va. (†25880) 312/D7
Priceville, Ala. (†35601) 195/E1
Priceville, Ky. (†42713) 237/K6
Priceville, Ontario 177/D3
Prichard, Ala. (36610) 195/B9
Prichard, Miss. (†38676) 256/D1
Prichard, W. Va. (25555) 312/A6
Prickly (pt.), Grenada 161/C9
Priddis, Alberta 182/C4
Priddy, Texas (76870) 303/F6
Pride, Ky. (†42404) 237/F5
Pride, La. (70770) 238/K1
Pridgen, Georgia (†31519) 217/G7
Priego, Spain 33/E2
Priego de Córdoba, Spain 33/D4
Priekule, U.S.S.R. 53/A2
Priekule, U.S.S.R. 53/A3
Prien am Chiemsee, W. Germany 22/E5
Prieska, S. Africa 118/C5
Priest (lake), Idaho 220/B1
Priest (riv.), Idaho 220/B1
Priest, J. Percy (lake), Tenn. 237/J8
Priestly (lake), Maine 243/E2
Priest Rapids (dam), Wash. 310/F4
Priest Rapids (lake), Wash. 310/E4
Priest River, Idaho (83856) 220/A1
Prievidza, Czech. 41/E2
Prijedor, Yugoslavia 45/C3
Prijepolje, Yugoslavia 45/D4
Prikumsk, U.S.S.R. 52/F6
Prikumsk, U.S.S.R. 48/E5
Prilep, Yugoslavia 45/E5
Priluki, U.S.S.R. 52/D4
Prim (pt.), Nova Scotia 168/C4
Prim (pt.), Pr. Edward I. 168/E2
Prima Porta, Italy 34/F6
Primate, Sask. 181/B3
Prime, New Bruns. 170/B1
Primero de Marzo, Paraguay 144/B4
Primero Enero, Cuba 158/F2
Primghar, Iowa (51245) 229/B2
Primm Springs, Tenn. (38476) 237/G9
Primorsk, U.S.S.R. 52/C2
Primorsko-Akhtarsk, U.S.S.R. 52/E5
Primos, Pa. (19018) 294/M7
Primrose (lake), Alberta 182/E2
Primrose, Georgia (†30222) 217/C4
Primrose, Iowa (†52625) 229/K7
Primrose, Nebr. (68655) 264/F3
Primrose (lake), Sask. 181/L3
Primrose Lake Air Weapons Range, Sask. 181/L3
Prince (co.), Pr. Edward I. 168/D2
Prince, Sask. 181/C3
Prince Albert (sound), N.W.T. 162/E1
Prince Albert (pen.), N.W.T. 162/E1
Prince Albert (pen.), N.W. Terrs. 187/G2
Prince Albert (sound), N.W. Terrs. 187/G2
Prince Albert, Sask. 162/F5
Prince Albert, Sask. 146/H4
Prince Albert, Sask. 181/F2
Prince Albert, S. Africa 118/C6
Prince Albert Nat'l Park, Sask. 162/F5
Prince Albert Nat'l Park, Sask. 181/E1
Prince Alfred (cape), N.W. Terrs. 187/F2
Prince Charles (isl.), Canada 4/C13
Prince Charles (isl.), N.W.T. 162/J2
Prince Charles (isl.), N.W. Terrs. 187/L3
Prince Edward (isls.) 5/E2
Prince Edward (county), Ontario 177/G3
Prince Edward (isls.), S. Africa 2/L8
Prince Edward (co.), Va. 307/M6
Prince Edward Island (prov.) 162/K6
Prince Edward Island (prov.), Canada 146/M5
PRINCE EDWARD ISLAND 168
Prince Edward Island Nat'l Park, Pr. Edward I. 168/E2
Prince Frederick, Md. (20678) 245/M6
Prince George, Br. Col. 146/F4
Prince George, Br. Col. 162/D5
Prince George, Br. Col. 184/F3
Prince George (co.), Va. 307/O6
Prince George, Va. (23875) 307/O6
Prince Georges (co.), Md. 245/L5
Prince Gustav Adolf (sea), N.W. Terrs. 187/H2
Prince of Wales (cape), Alaska 196/E1
Prince of Wales (isl.), Alaska 196/N2
Prince of Wales (isl.), Canada 4/B14
Prince of Wales, New Bruns. 170/D3
Prince of Wales (str.), N.W.T. 162/D1
Prince of Wales (isl.), N.W.T. 146/J2
Prince of Wales (isl.), N.W.T. 162/F1
Prince of Wales (isl.), N.W. Terrs. 187/J2
Prince of Wales (str.), N.W. Terrs. 187/G2
Prince of Wales (isl.), Queensland 88/G2
Prince of Wales (isl.), Queensland 95/B1
Prince of Wales (cape), U.S. 4/C18
Prince Olav Coast (reg.) 5/C3
Prince Patrick (isl.), Canada 4/B16
Prince Patrick (isl.), N.W.T. 146/F2
Prince Patrick (isl.), N.W.T. 162/M3
Prince Patrick (isl.), N.W. Terrs. 187/F2
Prince Regent (inlet), N.W.T. 162/G1
Prince Regent (inlet), N.W. Terrs. 187/J2
Prince Rupert, Br. Col. 162/C5
Prince Rupert, Br. Col. 146/F4
Prince Rupert, Br. Col. 184/B3
Prince Rupert (bay), Dominica 161/E5
Princes Lakes, Ind. (†46164) 227/E6
Princess Anne, Md. (21853) 245/P8
Princess Astrid Coast (reg.) 5/B1
Princess Charlotte (bay), Queensland 88/G2
Princess Charlotte (bay), Queensland 95/C2
Princess Harbour, Manitoba 179/F3
Princess Martha Coast (reg.) 5/B18
Princess Ragnhild Coast (reg.) 5/B2
Princess Royal (isl.), Br. Col. 184/C3
Princes Town, Trin. & Tob. 161/B11
Princeton, Ala. (35766) 195/F1
Princeton, Ark. (†71725) 202/E6
Princeton, Br. Col. 184/G5
Princeton, Calif. (95970) 204/C4
Princeton (mt.), Colo. 208/G5
Princeton, Fla. (33032) 212/F6
Princeton, Idaho (83857) 220/B3
Princeton, Ill. (61356) 222/D2
Princeton, Ind. (47670) 227/B8
Princeton, Iowa (52768) 229/N5
Princeton, Kansas (66078) 232/G3
Princeton, Ky. (42445) 237/F6
Princeton, La. (71067) 238/C1
Princeton○, Maine (04668) 243/H5
Princeton○, Mass. (01541) 249/G3
Princeton, Mich. (49875) 250/B2
Princeton, Minn. (55371) 255/E5
Princeton, Mo. (64673) 261/E2
Princeton, Newf. 166/D2
Princeton, N.J. (08540) 273/D3
Princeton, N.C. (27569) 281/N4
Princeton, Ontario 177/D4
Princeton, Oreg. (97721) 291/J4
Princeton, S.C. (29674) 296/C2
Princeton, W. Va. (24740) 312/D8
Princeton, Wis. (54968) 317/H8
Princeton Junction, N.J. (08550) 273/D3
Princeville, Hawaii (†96714) 218/C1
Princeville, Ill. (61559) 222/D3
Princeville, N.C. (†27886) 281/P3
Princeville, Québec 172/F3
Prince William (sound), Alaska 196/D1
Prince William, New Bruns. 170/C3
Prince William (co.), Va. 307/O3
Principe (chan.), Br. Col. 184/C3
Principe (isl.), São Tomé e Príncipe 106/F8
Principio Furnace, Md. (†21903) 245/P2
Prineville, Oreg. (97754) 291/G3
Prineville (res.), Oreg. 291/G3
Pringle, S. Dak. (57773) 298/B6
Prinkipo (Adalar) (isl.), Turkey 63/D6
Prinsburg, Minn. (56281) 255/C6
Prins Karls Forland (isl.), Norway 18/B2
Prinzapolca (riv.), Nicaragua 154/F4
Prinzapolka, Nicaragua 154/F4
Prior (cape), Spain 33/B1
Prior Lake, Minn. (55372) 255/E6
Priozersk, U.S.S.R. 52/D2
Pripet (marshes), U.S.S.R. 52/C4
Pripyat' (riv.), U.S.S.R. 7/G3
Pripyat' (riv.), U.S.S.R. 52/C4
Priština, Yugoslavia 45/E4
Pritchards (isl.), S.C. 296/G7
Pritchardville, S.C. (†29927) 296/E7
Pritchett, Colo. (81064) 208/O8
Pritzwalk, E. Germany 22/E2
Privas, France 28/F5
Privateer (pt.), Virgin Is. (U.S.) 161/D4
Priverno, Italy 34/D4
Privolzhskiy, U.S.S.R. 52/G4
Priyutnoye, U.S.S.R. 52/F5
Priyutovo, U.S.S.R. 52/H4
Prizren, Yugoslavia 45/E4
Probolinggo, Indonesia 85/K2
Procious, W. Va. (25164) 312/D5
Procter, Br. Col. 184/J5
Proctor, Ark. (72376) 202/K3
Proctor, Colo. (†80736) 208/N1
Proctor, Minn. (55810) 255/F4
Proctor, Mont. (59929) 262/B3
Proctor, Okla. (74457) 288/S3
Proctor, Pa. (†17701) 294/J3
Proctor, Texas (76468) 303/F5
Proctor○, Vt. (05765) 268/A4
Proctor, W. Va. (26055) 312/E3
Proctorsville, Vt. (05153) 268/B5
Proctorville, N.C. (28375) 281/M6
Proctorville, Ohio (45669) 284/F9
Proddatur, India 68/D6
Proença-a-Nova, Portugal 33/B3
Profesor Rafael Ramírez, Mexico 150/O1
Profondeville, Belgium 27/F8
Progreso, Mexico 150/P6
Progreso, Uruguay 145/B6
Progress, Br. Col. 184/G2
Progress, Oreg. (†97233) 291/A2
Progress, U.S.S.R. 48/O5
Progress Village, Fla. (†33619) 212/C3
Project City, Calif. (96079) 204/C3
Prokhladnyy, U.S.S.R. 52/F6
Prokop'yevsk, U.S.S.R. 54/K4
Prokop'yevsk, U.S.S.R. 48/J4
Prokuplje, Yugoslavia 45/E4
Prole, Iowa (50229) 229/F6
Prome (Pye), Burma 72/B3
Promise City, Iowa (52583) 229/G7
Promissão, Brazil 135/B2
Promontory, Utah (†84307) 304/B2
Prompton, Pa. (18456) 294/M2
Prongua, Sask. 181/C3
Prony (bay), New Caled. 86/H5
Prophet (riv.), Br. Col. 184/M2
Prophetstown, Ill. (61277) 222/D2
Propriá, Brazil 132/G5
Proserpine, Queensland 88/H4
Proserpine, Queensland 95/D4
Prosit, Minn. (†55702) 255/F4
Prosna (riv.), Poland 47/C3
Prospect, Ala. (†35578) 195/D3
Prospect○, Conn. (06712) 210/D2
Prospect, Ky. (40059) 237/K4
Prospect○, Maine (†04981) 243/F6
Prospect (res.), N.S. Wales 88/K4
Prospect (res.), N.S. Wales 97/H3
Prospect, N.Y. (13435) 276/K4
Prospect, Nova Scotia 168/E4
Prospect, Ohio (43342) 284/D5
Prospect, Oreg. (97536) 291/E5
Prospect, Pa. (16052) 294/B4
Prospect, S. Australia 88/D8
Prospect, S. Australia 94/B7
Prospect, Tenn. (38477) 237/G10
Prospect, Va. (23960) 307/L6
Prospect Harbor, Maine (04669) 243/H7
Prospect Heights, Ill. (60070) 222/B5
Prospect Hill, N.C. (27314) 281/L2
Prospect Park, N.J. (†07885) 273/B1
Prospect Park, Pa. (19076) 294/M7
Prosper, Mich. (†49632) 250/E4
Prosper, Minn. (55966) 255/G7
Prosper, N. Dak. (†58042) 282/R6
Prosper, Oreg. (†97411) 291/C4
Prosperidad, Philippines 82/F6
Prosperity, Pa. (15329) 294/B5
Prosperity, S.C. (29127) 296/D3
Prosser, Nebr. (68868) 264/F4
Prosser, Wash. (99350) 310/F4
Prostějov, Czech. 41/D2
Protection, Kansas (67127) 232/C4
Protem, Mo. (65733) 261/G9
Protivín, Czech. 41/C2
Protivin, Iowa (52163) 229/J2
Proulxville, Québec 172/E3
Prouts Neck, Maine (04074) 243/C8
Provadiya, Bulgaria 45/H4
Provencal, La. (71468) 238/D3
Provence (trad. prov.), France 29
Providence, Ala. (†36748) 195/C6
Providence (mts.), Calif. 204/K8
Providence, Fla. (†32061) 212/D2
Providence, Grenada 161/D9
Providence, Ind. (†46106) 227/E6
Providence, Ky. (42450) 237/F6
Providence (cape), N. Zealand 100/A7
Providence (cap.), R.I. 188/M2
Providence (cap.), R.I. 146/L5
Providence (co.), R.I. 249/H5
Providence (cap.), R.I. (*02901) 249/H5
Providence, Utah (84332) 304/C2
Providence Bay, Ontario 177/B2
Providence Forge, Va. (23140) 307/P6
Providencia (isl.), Colombia 126/B9
Providenciales (isl.), Turks & Caicos 156/D2
Provideniya, U.S.S.R. 4/C18
Provideniya, U.S.S.R. 48/T3
Province Lake, N.H. (†03888) 268/E4
Provincetown, Mass. (02657) 249/O4
Provincetown○, Mass. (02657) 249/O4
Provins, France 28/E3
Provo, Ark. (†71846) 202/B5
Provo, S. Dak. (57774) 298/B7
Provo, Utah 146/G5
Provo, Utah (84601) 304/C3
Provo, Utah 188/D2
Provo (peak), Utah 304/C3
Provo (riv.), Utah 304/C3
Provost, Alberta 182/E3
Prowers (co.), Colo. 208/P7
Prozor, Yugoslavia 45/C4
Pruden, Tenn. (37851) 237/O7
Prudence (isl.), R.I. 249/J6
Prudence Island, R.I. (02872) 249/J6
Prudentópolis, Brazil 132/D9
Prudenville, Mich. (48651) 250/E4
Prudhoe (bay), Alaska 146/D2
Prudhoe (bay), Alaska 196/J1
Prudhoe, England 13/H3
Prudhoe Bay, Alaska (†99723) 196/J1
Prud'homme, Sask. 181/F3
Prudnik, Poland 47/C3
Prue, Okla. (74060) 288/O2
Pruitt, Ark. (72671) 202/D1
Prüm, W. Germany 22/B3
Pruntytown, W. Va. (†26354) 312/F4
Pruszcz Gdański, Poland 47/D1
Pruszków, Poland 47/E2
Prut (riv.) 7/G4
Prut (riv.), Romania 45/J2
Prut (riv.), U.S.S.R. 52/C5
Prydz (bay) 5/C4
Pryor, Colo. (81065) 208/K8
Pryor, Mont. (59066) 262/H5
Pryor, Okla. (74361) 288/R2
Pryorsburg, Ky. (†42066) 237/D7
Pryse, Ky. (40471) 237/O5
Przasnysz, Poland 47/E2
Przemków, Poland 47/B2
Przemsza (riv.), Poland 47/B4
Przemyśl (prov.), Poland 47/F4
Przemyśl, Poland 7/G4
Przmyśl, Poland 47/F4
Przeworsk, Poland 47/F3
Przheval'sk, U.S.S.R. 48/H5
Psakhná, Greece 45/F6
Psará (isl.), Greece 45/G6
Psári, Greece 45/E7
Psel (riv.), U.S.S.R. 52/D4
Psevdhókavos (cape), Greece 45/G6
Pskov, U.S.S.R. 7/G3
Pskov, U.S.S.R. 48/C4
Pskov U.S.S.R. 52/C3
Pskov (lake), U.S.S.R. 53/D1
Ptolemais, Greece 45/E5
Ptuj, Yugoslavia 45/C2
Puako, Hawaii (†96743) 218/G4
Puán, Argentina 143/D4
Puangue, Chile 138/F4
Puangue, Estero de (riv.), Chile 138/F3
Pubnico, Nova Scotia 168/C5
Pubnico (harb.), Nova Scotia 168/C5
Puca Barranca, Peru 128/E4
Pucallpa, Peru 128/E7
Pucallpa, Peru 120/B3
Pucará, Bolivia 136/C6
Pucará, Peru 128/G10
Pucarani, Bolivia 136/A5
Pucatrihue, Chile 138/D3
Pucaurco, Peru 128/G4
Puce, Ontario 177/B5
Pucheng, China 77/J6
Púchov, Czech. 41/E2
Puchuncaví, Chile 138/F2
Pucio (pt.), Philippines 82/C5
Pucioasa, Romania 45/G3
Puck, Poland 47/D1
Puckaway (lake), Wis. 317/H8
Puckett, Miss. (39151) 256/E6
Pucón, Chile 138/E2
Pucusana, Peru 128/D9
Pudahuel, Chile 138/G3
Pudasjärvi, Finland 18/P4
Pudding (riv.), Oreg. 291/A3
Pudozh, U.S.S.R. 52/E2
Puduchcheri (Pondicherry), India 68/E6
Pudukkottai, India 68/D6
Puebla (state), Mexico 150/L7
Puebla, Mexico 146/J8
Puebla de Alcocer, Spain 33/D3
Puebla de Don Fadrique, Spain 33/E4
Puebla del Caramiñal, Spain 33/B1
Puebla de Sanabria, Spain 33/C1
Puebla de Trives, Spain 33/C1
Puebla de Zaragoza, Mexico 150/N2

432 Pueblo

Pueblo, Colo. 146/H6
Pueblo, Colo. 188/F3
Pueblo (co.), Colo. 208/K6
Pueblo, Colo. (*81001) 208/K6
Pueblo (res.), Colo. 208/K6
Pueblo (mts.), Oreg. 291/J5
Pueblo Army Depot, Colo. 208/L6
Pueblo Colorado Wash (dry riv.), Ariz. 198/F3
Pueblo del Sauce, Uruguay 145/E4
Pueblo Hondo, Venezuela 124/B3
Pueblo Hundido, Chile 138/B6
Pueblo Ind. Res., N. Mex. 274/B4
Pueblo Ind. Res., N. Mex. 274/D2
Pueblo Ind. Res., N. Mex. 274/C4
Pueblo Ind. Res., N. Mex. 274/D3
Pueblo La Paloma, Uruguay 145/D3
Pueblo Nuevo, Uruguay 145/B2
Pueblo Nuevo, Venezuela 124/D1
Pueblo of Acoma, N. Mex. (†87034) 274/B3
Puebloviejo, Colombia 126/D5
Puelches, Argentina 143/C4
Puelén, Argentina 143/C4
Puelo (riv.), Chile 138/E4
Puente Alto, Chile 138/B10
Puenteareas, Spain 33/B1
Puente de Ixtla, Mexico 150/K2
Puente del Inca, Argentina 143/B3
Puentedeume, Spain 33/C1
Puente-Genil, Spain 33/D4
Puente Nacional, Colombia 126/D5
Pueo (pt.), Hawaii 218/A2
Pu'er, China 77/F7
Puerca (pt.), P. Rico 161/F2
Puerco (riv.), Ariz. 198/F3
Puerco (riv.), N. Mex. 274/A3
Puercos, Morro de (head), Panama 154/H7
Puerto Acosta, Bolivia 136/A4
Puerto Adela, Paraguay 144/E4
Puerto Aisén, Chile 138/E6
Puerto Aisén, Chile 120/B7
Puerto Alegre, Bolivia 136/E3
Puerto Alianza, Peru 128/D5
Puerto Almacen, Bolivia 136/C4
Puerto Amaro, Uruguay 145/F3
Puerto América, Peru 128/D5
Puerto Ángel, Mexico 150/L9
Puerto Antioquia, Colombia 126/C4
Puerto Arazatí, Uruguay 145/C5
Puerto Argentina, Colombia 126/C7
Puerto Armuelles, Panama 154/F6
Puerto Arturo, Peru 128/F3
Puerto Asís, Colombia 126/B7
Puerto Ayacucho, Venezuela 120/C2
Puerto Ayacucho, Venezuela 124/E5
Puerto Ayora, Ecuador 128/B9
Puerto Bahía Negra, Paraguay 144/C2
Puerto Ballivián, Bolivia 136/C4
Puerto Barrios, Guatemala 154/C3
Puerto Bermúdez, Peru 128/E8
Puerto Berrío, Colombia 126/C4
Puerto Bertrand, Chile 138/E7
Puerto Boy, Colombia 126/C7
Puerto Caballas, Peru 128/E10
Puerto Caballo, Paraguay 144/C2
Puerto Cabello, Venezuela 124/E2
Puerto Cabello, Venezuela 120/C1
Puerto Cabezas, Nicaragua 154/F3
Puerto Calvimonte, Bolivia 136/C4
Puerto Carlos Pfannl, Paraguay 144/D4
Puerto Carranza, Colombia 126/F9
Puerto Carreño, Colombia 120/C2
Puerto Carreño, Colombia 126/G4
Puerto Casado, Paraguay 144/C3
Puerto Castilla, Honduras 154/D3
Puerto Chacabuco, Chile 138/D6
Puerto Chicama, Peru 128/C6
Puerto Cisnes, Chile 138/E5
Puerto Coig, Argentina 143/C7
Puerto Colombia, Colombia 126/C2
Puerto Colón, Paraguay 144/C3
Puerto Cooper, Paraguay 144/C3
Puerto Córdoba, Colombia 126/E8
Puerto Cortés, C. Rica 154/E6
Puerto Cortés, Honduras 154/D2
Puerto Cortés, Mexico 150/D4
Puerto Crevaux, Colombia 126/C6
Puerto Cristal, Chile 138/E6
Puerto Cumarebo, Venezuela 124/D2
Puerto de Cayo, Ecuador 128/B3
Puerto de la Concordia, El Salvador 154/C4
Puerto de Luna, N. Mex. (88432) 274/E4
Puerto de Nutrias, Venezuela 124/D3
Puerto Deseado, Argentina 143/D6
Puerto Deseado, Argentina 120/C7
Puerto El Carmen, Ecuador 128/E3
Puerto Escondido, Colombia 126/B3
Puerto Escondido, Mexico 150/L9
Puerto Esperanza, Cuba 158/A1
Puerto Esperanza, Paraguay 144/C2
Puerto Estrella, Colombia 126/E1
Puerto Eten, Peru 128/B6
Puerto Fonciere, Paraguay 144/D3
Puerto Frey, Bolivia 136/E4
Puerto Galileo, Paraguay 144/C4
Puerto General Busch, Bolivia 136/G7
Puerto General Ovando, Bolivia 136/50
Puerto Grether, Bolivia 136/C5
Puerto Guachalla, Bolivia 136/F6
Puerto Guaraní, Paraguay 144/C2
Puerto Harberton, Argentina 143/C7
Puerto Heath, Bolivia 136/A3
Puerto Hierro, Venezuela 124/H2
Puerto Huitoto, Colombia 126/D7
Puerto Iguazú, Argentina 143/F2
Puerto Inca, Peru 128/E7
Puerto Indio, Paraguay 144/E4
Puerto Ingeniero Ibáñez, Chile 138/E6
Puerto Iradier, Equat. Guinea 115/A3
Puerto Irigoyen, Argentina 143/D1
Puerto Isabel, Bolivia 136/F6
Puerto Izozog, Bolivia 136/D6
Puerto José Pardo, Peru 128/D4
Puerto Juárez, Mexico 150/Q6
Puerto La Concordia, Colombia 126/D6
Puerto La Cruz, Venezuela 124/F2
Puerto Leguía, Loreto, Peru 128/D4
Puerto Leguía, Puno, Peru 128/G9
Puerto Leguízamo, Colombia 126/C8
Puerto Lempira, Honduras 154/F3
Puerto Liberador General San Martín, Argentina 143/E2
Puerto Limón, Colombia 126/B7
Puertollano, Spain 33/D3
Puerto López, La Guajira, Colombia 126/E2
Puerto López, Meta, Colombia 126/D5
Puerto Madero, Mexico 150/N9
Puerto Madryn, Argentina 143/C5
Puerto Madryn, Argentina 120/C7
Puerto Maldonado, Peru 128/H9
Puerto Maldonado, Peru 120/C4
Puerto Mamoré, Bolivia 136/C5
Puerto Manglares, Colombia 126/B5
Puerto María, Paraguay 144/C2
Puerto Max, Paraguay 144/D3
Puerto Mayor Otaño, Paraguay 144/E5
Puerto Medio Mundo (bay), P. Rico 161/F2
Puerto Mercedes, Colombia 126/D7
Puerto Mihanovich, Paraguay 144/C2
Puerto Miranda, Venezuela 124/E4
Puerto Montt, Chile 120/B7
Puerto Montt, Chile 138/E4
Puerto Morelos, Mexico 150/Q6
Puerto Morín, Peru 128/C7
Puerto Mosquito, Colombia 126/C3
Puerto Murillo, Colombia 126/G4
Puerto Mutis, Colombia 126/B4
Puerto Napo, Ecuador 128/D3
Puerto Nare, Colombia 126/D7
Puerto Nariño, Colombia 126/F5
Puerto Natales, Chile 120/B8
Puerto Natales, Chile 138/E9
Puerto Niño, Colombia 126/C5
Puerto Nuevo, Colombia 126/F5
Puerto Nuevo, Paraguay 144/C2
Puerto Nuevo, P. Rico 161/D1
Puerto Nuevo (pt.), P. Rico 161/C1
Puerto Obaldía, Panama 154/J6
Puerto Ocopa, Peru 128/E8
Puerto Olaya, Colombia 126/C4
Puerto Ospina, Colombia 126/C7
Puerto Padre, Cuba 158/H3
Puerto Padre, Cuba 156/C2
Puerto Páez, Venezuela 124/E4
Puerto Palena, Chile 138/D5
Puerto Palma, Paraguay 144/E4
Puerto Pando, Bolivia 136/B4
Puerto Paraíso, Paraguay 144/A5
Puerto Pardo, Peru 128/F7
Puerto Patiño, Bolivia 136/C5
Puerto Paulina, Colombia 126/D7
Puerto Peñasco, Mexico 150/C1
Puerto Pinasco, Paraguay 144/C3
Puerto Pirámides, Argentina 143/D5
Puerto Píritu, Venezuela 124/F2
Puerto Pizarro, Colombia 126/D8
Puerto Pizarro, Peru 128/B4
Puerto Plata (prov.), Dom. Rep. 158/D5
Puerto Plata, Dom. Rep. 156/D3
Puerto Plata, Dom. Rep. 158/D5
Puerto Portillo, Peru 128/F7
Puerto Prado, Peru 128/E8
Puerto Presidente Franco, Paraguay 144/E4
Puerto Presidente Stroessner, Paraguay 144/E4
Puerto Princesa, Philippines 85/F4
Puerto Princesa, Philippines 82/B6
Puerto Quellón, Chile 138/D4
Puerto Quijarro, Bolivia 136/G5
Puerto Ramírez, Chile 138/E5
Puerto Real, P. Rico 161/A2
Puerto Real (Playa de Fajardo), P. Rico 161/F1
Puerto Real, Spain 33/D4
Puerto Reyes, Colombia 126/B5
Puerto Rico 2/F5
Puerto Rico 146/M8
PUERTO RICO 161
PUERTO RICO 156/G1
Puerto Rico, Argentina 143/D1
Puerto Rico, Bolivia 136/B2
Puerto Rico, Caquetá, Colombia 126/C7
Puerto Rico, Meta, Colombia 126/C6
Puerto Rondón, Colombia 126/E4
Puerto Rosario, Paraguay 144/D4
Puerto Ruiz, Argentina 143/G6
Puerto Saavedra, Chile 138/D2
Puerto Salgar, Colombia 126/C5
Puerto Samanco, Peru 128/C7
Puerto San Francisco, Bolivia 136/C5
Puerto San José, Paraguay 144/E5
Puerto San Rafael, Paraguay 144/E5
Puerto Sastre, Paraguay 144/C3
Puerto Saucedo, Bolivia 136/D3
Puerto Siles, Bolivia 136/C3
Puerto Suárez, Bolivia 136/F6
Puerto Tacurú Pytá, Paraguay 144/D3
Puerto Tahuantinsuyo, Peru 128/G9
Puerto Tarafa, Cuba 158/H3
Puerto Tejada, Colombia 126/B6
Puerto Toledo, Colombia 126/C8
Puerto Torno, Bolivia 136/C5
Puerto Tres Palmas, Paraguay 144/C2
Puerto Vallarta, Mexico 150/G6
Puerto Varas, Chile 138/E3
Puerto Velarde, Bolivia 136/D5
Puerto Victoria, Peru 128/E7
Puerto Villarroel, Bolivia 136/C5
Puerto Villazón, Bolivia 136/D3
Puerto Wilches, Colombia 126/D4
Puerto Williams, Chile 138/F11
Puerto Yartou, Chile 138/E10
Puerto Ybapobó, Paraguay 144/D3
Pueyrredón (lake), Argentina 143/B6
Puffin (isl.), Ireland 17/A8
Pugachev, U.S.S.R. 52/G4
Puget (isl.), Wash. 310/B4
Puget (sound), Wash. 310/C3
Puget Sound Navy Yard, Wash. 310/A2
Pugwash, Nova Scotia 168/E3
Pugwash (harb.), Nova Scotia 168/E3
Puha, N. Zealand 100/F3
Puhi, Hawaii (96766) 218/C2
Puigcerdá, Spain 33/G1
Puina, Bolivia 136/A4
Puinagua, Canal de (riv.), Peru 128/E5
Pujada (bay), Philippines 82/F7
Pujehun, S. Leone 106/B7
Pujilí, Ecuador 128/C3
Pujut (pt.), Indonesia 85/G1
Pukaki (lake), N. Zealand 100/B6
Pukalani, Hawaii (96788) 218/J2
Pukapuka (atoll), Cook Is. 87/K7
Puka-Puka (atoll), Fr. Poly. 87/N7
Pukaskwa Nat'l Park, Ont. 162/H6
Pukaskwa Prov. Park, Ontario 175/C3
Pukaskwa Prov. Park, Ontario 177/H5
Pukch'ŏng, N. Korea 81/C3
Pukë, Albania 45/E4
Pukekohe, N. Zealand 100/E2
Pukoo, Hawaii (†96748) 218/H1
Puksubaek (mt.), N. Korea 81/C3
Pukwana, S. Dak. (57370) 298/L6
Pula, Yugoslavia 45/A3
Pulacayo, Bolivia 120/C5
Pulacayo, Bolivia 136/B7
Pulai, Sungai (riv.), Malaysia 72/E5
Pulanduta (pt.), Philippines 82/D5
Pulangi (riv.), Philippines 82/E7
Pulap (atoll), Micronesia 87/E5
Púlar, Cerro (mt.), Chile 138/B4
Pulaski (co.), Ark. 202/F4
Pulaski (co.), Georgia 217/E6
Pulaski, Georgia (30451) 217/J6
Pulaski (co.), Ill. 222/D6
Pulaski, Ill. (62976) 222/D6
Pulaski (co.), Ind. 227/D2
Pulaski, Ind. (†46996) 227/D3
Pulaski, Iowa (52584) 229/J7
Pulaski (co.), Ky. 237/M6
Pulaski, Ky. (42550) 237/M6
Pulaski, Miss. (39152) 256/E6
Pulaski (co.), Mo. 261/H7
Pulaski, N.Y. (13142) 276/H3
Pulaski, Ohio (†43506) 284/A2
Pulaski, Pa. (16143) 294/B3
Pulaski, Tenn. (38478) 237/G10
Pulaski (co.), Va. 307/G6
Pulaski, Va. (24301) 307/G6
Pulaski, Wis. (54162) 317/K6
Puławy, Poland 47/F3
Pulcifer, Wis. (54164) 317/K6
Pulehu, Hawaii (†96788) 218/J2
Pulicat (lake), India 68/E6
Pull (pt.), Virgin Is. (U.S.) 161/F3
Pullman, Mich. (49450) 250/C6
Pullman, Wash. (99163) 310/H4
Pullman, W. Va. (26421) 312/D4
Pully, Switzerland 39/C4
Pulo Anna (isl.), Belau 87/D5
Pulog (mt.), Philippines 82/C2
Pulpit Harbor, Maine (†04853) 243/F7
Pulteney, Alberta 182/D4
Pulteney, N.Y. (14874) 276/F5
Pulteneyville, N.Y. (14538) 276/F4
Pułtusk, Poland 47/E2
Pülümür, Turkey 63/H3
Pulusuk (atoll), Micronesia 87/F5
Puluwat (atoll), Micronesia 87/E5
Pumanque, Chile 138/F6
Pumphrey, Md. (†21090) 245/M4
Pumpkin (creek), Nebr. 264/A3
Pumpville, Texas (†78851) 303/C8
Puna, Bolivia 136/C6
Puná (isl.), Ecuador 128/B4
Punaauia, Fr. Poly. 86/S13
Puna de Atacama (reg.), Argentina 143/C2
Punakha, Bhutan 68/G3
Punaluu, Hawaii (†96777) 218/H7
Punaluu (harb.), Hawaii 218/H7
Punata, Bolivia 136/C5
Punchaw, Br. Col. 184/F3
Punchbowl (hill), Hawaii 218/C4
Punchestown, Ireland 17/H5
Pune, India 68/C5
Pungo, N.C. (†27860) 281/R3
Pungo (lake), N.C. 281/S3
Pungo (riv.), N.C. 281/R4
Pungoteague, Va. (23422) 307/S5
P'ungsan, N. Korea 81/D3
Punia, Zaire 115/E4
Punitaqui, Chile 138/A8
Punjab (state), India 68/D2
Punjab (prov.), Pakistan 68/C2
Punk (isl.), Manitoba 179/F3
Punnichy, Sask. 181/G4
Puno (dept.), Peru 128/G10
Puno, Peru 128/G10
Puno, Peru 120/B4
Punta, Cerro de (mt.), P. Rico 161/C2
Punta Abreojos, Mexico 150/C3
Punta Alta, Argentina 143/D4
Punta Alta, Argentina 120/C6
Punta Arenas, Chile 120/B8
Punta Arenas, Chile 138/E10
Punta Cardón, Venezuela 124/C2
Punta de Bombón, Peru 128/F11
Punta de Díaz, Chile 138/B7
Punta del Este, Uruguay 145/E6
Punta de Mata, Venezuela 124/G3
Punta de Piedras, Venezuela 124/F2
Punta Gorda, Belize 154/C2
Punta Gorda (pt.), Calif. 204/A3
Punta Gorda, Fla. (*33950) 212/E5
Punta Medanosa, Argentina 143/C6
Punta Moreno, Peru 128/C6
Punta Negra, Salar de (salt dep.), Chile 138/B5
Puntarenas, C. Rica 154/E6
Punta Santiago (Playa de Humacao), P. Rico 161/F2
Puntas de Maciel, Uruguay 145/C4
Punto Fijo, Venezuela 120/C1
Punto Fijo, Venezuela 124/D2
Punxsutawney, Pa. (15767) 294/E4
Puolanka, Finland 18/P4
Puolo (pt.), Hawaii 218/C2
Pupiales, Colombia 126/B7
Puposky, Minn. (56667) 255/C3
Pupuke (lake), N. Zealand 100/B1
Pupuya, Nevado (mt.), Bolivia 136/A4
Puqi, China 77/H6
Puquina, Peru 128/G11
Puquintica, Nevado (mt.), Bolivia 136/A6
Puquintica, Cerro (mt.), Chile 138/B1
Puquio, Peru 128/F10
Puquios, Chile 138/B1
Pur (riv.), U.S.S.R. 48/H3
Puracé (vol.), Colombia 126/B6
Purbeck, Isle of (pen.), England 13/F7
Purbolinggo, Indonesia 85/J2
Purcell (mts.), Br. Col. 184/J5
Purcell (mts.), Idaho 220/B1
Purcell, Kansas (†66038) 232/G2
Purcell, Mo. (64857) 261/D8
Purcell (mts.), Mont. 262/A2
Purcell, Okla. (73080) 288/M4
Purcellville, Va. (22132) 307/N2
Purchase, N.Y. (10577) 276/P6
Purdin, Mo. (64674) 261/F3
Purdum, Nebr. (69157) 264/D2
Purdy, Mo. (65734) 261/E9
Purdy, Va. (†23847) 307/N7
Pure Air, Mo. (†63559) 261/G2
Purén, Chile 138/D2
Purgatoire (riv.), Colo. 208/M8
Purgitsville, W. Va. (26852) 312/J4
Puri, India 68/F5
Purial, Sierra de (mts.), Cuba 158/K4
Purificación, Colombia 126/C6
Purificación, Mexico 150/G7
Purli, India 68/D5
Purmerend, Netherlands 27/F4
Purnea, India 68/F3
Purple Springs, Alberta 182/E5
Purple Valley, Ontario 177/C3
Purranque, Chile 138/D3
Pursat (Pouthisat), Cambodia 72/D4
Puruándiro, Mexico 150/J7
Puruey, Venezuela 124/F4
Purukcahu, Indonesia 85/E6
Purulia, India 68/F4
Puruname, Venezuela 124/E6
Puruni (riv.), Guyana 131/B2
Purus (riv.), Brazil 120/C3
Purus (riv.), Brazil 132/H9
Purús (riv.), Peru 128/G8
Puruvesi (lake), Finland 18/Q6
Purves, Manitoba 179/D5
Purvis, Miss. (39475) 256/F8
Purwakarta, Indonesia 85/H2
Purwodadi, Indonesia 85/J2
Purwokerto, Indonesia 85/H2
Purworejo, Indonesia 85/J2
Puryear, Tenn. (38251) 237/E8
Pusan, S. Korea 54/O6
Pusan, S. Korea 81/D6
Pushaw (lake), Maine 243/F6
Pushkin, U.S.S.R. 48/C4
Pushkin, U.S.S.R. 52/C3
Pushmataha, Ala. (36917) 195/B6
Pushmataha (co.), Okla. 288/R6
Püspökladány, Hungary 41/F3
Pustunich, Mexico 150/O7
Pusztaszabolcs, Hungary 41/E3
Putaendo, Chile 138/A9
Putao, Burma 72/C1
Putaruru, N. Zealand 100/E3
Putbus, E. Germany 22/E1
Puteau, France 28/A2
Putian, China 77/J6
Putignano, Italy 34/F4
Putina, Peru 128/H10
Put-in-Bay, Ohio (43456) 284/E2
Puting, Borneo (cape), Indonesia 85/E6
Puting, Sumatra (cape), Indonesia 85/C7
Putla de Guerrero, Mexico 150/L8
Putnam, Ala. (36772) 195/B6
Putnam, Conn. (06260) 210/H1
Putnam○, Conn. (06260) 210/H1
Putnam (co.), Fla. 212/E2
Putnam (co.), Georgia 217/F4
Putnam, Georgia (†31803) 217/D6
Putnam (co.), Ill. 222/D2
Putnam, Ill. (61560) 222/D2
Putnam (co.), Ind. 227/D5
Putnam (co.), Mo. 261/F2
Putnam (co.), N.Y. 276/N8
Putnam (co.), Ohio 284/B3
Putnam, Okla. (73659) 288/J3
Putnam (co.), Tenn. 237/K8
Putnam, Texas (76469) 303/E5
Putnam (co.), W. Va. 312/C6
Putnam Heights, Conn. (†06260) 210/H1
Putnam Valley○, N.Y. (10579) 276/N8
Putnamville, Ind. (46170) 227/D5
Putney, Georgia (31782) 217/D8
Putney, S. Dak. (†57445) 298/N2
Putney○, Vt. (05346) 268/B6
Putnok, Hungary 41/F2
Putre, Chile 138/B1
Puttalam, Sri Lanka 68/D7
Putte, Belgium 27/F6
Putten, Netherlands 27/H4
Puttgarden, W. Germany 22/D1
Puttur, India 68/D6
Putumayo (riv.) 120/B3
Putumayo (inten.), Colombia 126/C7
Putumayo (riv.), Colombia 126/E9
Putumayo, Ecuador 128/E3
Putumayo (riv.), Ecuador 128/E2
Putumayo (riv.), Peru 128/G4
Pütürge, Turkey 63/H3
Putussibau, Indonesia 85/E5
Puuanahulu, Hawaii (†96740) 218/G4
Puuhonua O Honaunau Nat'l Hist. Park, Hawaii 218/F6
Puuiki, Hawaii (†96713) 218/K2
Puu Keahiakahoe (mt.), Hawaii 218/D3
Puukohola Heiau Nat'l Hist. Site, Hawaii 218/G4
Puu Kukui (mt.), Hawaii 218/J2
Puu Lanihuli (mt.), Hawaii 218/D3
Puulavesi (lake), Finland 18/P5
Puunene, Hawaii (96784) 218/J2
Puunui, Hawaii (†96801) 218/C4
Puuwaawaa, Hawaii (†96740) 218/G5
Puuwai, Hawaii (†96769) 218/A2
Pu Xian, China 77/H4
Puxico, Mo. (63960) 261/M9
Puyallup, Wash. 188/B1
Puyallup, Wash. (98371) 310/C3
Puyallup (riv.), Wash. 310/C4
Puy-de-Dôme (dept.), France 28/E5
Puy-de-Dôme (mt.), France 28/E5
Puyehue, Chile 138/E3
Puyehue (lake), Chile 138/E3
Puyo, Ecuador 128/D3
Puysegur (pt.), N. Zealand 100/A7
Pwani (Coast) (reg.), Tanzania 115/G5
Pweto, Zaire 115/E5
Pwllheli, Wales 10/D4
Pwllheli, Wales 13/C5
Pyapon, Burma 72/B3
Pyasina (riv.), U.S.S.R. 48/J2
Pyatigorsk, U.S.S.R. 52/F6
Pyatt, Ark. (72672) 202/E1
Pye (isls.), Alaska 196/C2
Pye, Burma 72/B3
Pye, Burma 54/L8
Pyengana, Tasmania 99/E3
Pygmalion (pt.), India 68/G7
Pyhäjärvi (lake), Finland 18/M6
Pyhäjärvi (lake), Finland 18/O5
Pyinmana, Burma 72/C3
Pyland, Miss. (†38851) 256/F3
Pymatuning (res.), Ohio 284/J2
Pymatuning (res.), Pa. 294/A2
P'yŏnggang, N. Korea 81/C4
P'yŏngsan, N. Korea 81/C4
P'yŏngyang (cap.), N. Korea 54/O6
P'yŏngyang (cap.), N. Korea 81/C4
Pyote, Texas (79777) 303/A6
Pyramid (peak), Idaho 220/E4
Pyramid, Ky. (41656) 237/R6
Pyramid (lake), Nev. 266/B2
Pyramid (isl.), N. Zealand 100/E7
Pyramid Lake Ind. Res., Nev. 266/B2
Pyramids (ruins), Egypt 111/J3
Pyrenees (mts.) 7/D4
Pyrenees (range), France 28/C6
Pyrenees (range), Spain 33/F1
Pyrénées-Atlantiques (dept.), France 28/C6
Pyrénées-Orientales (dept.), France 28/E6
Pyrites, N.Y. (13677) 276/K1
Pyriton, Ala. (†36266) 195/G4
Pyrzyce, Poland 47/B2
Pytalovo, U.S.S.R. 52/C3
Pyu, Burma 72/C3
Pyuthan, Nepal 68/E3

Q

Qabalan, West Bank 65/C3
Qabatiya, West Bank 65/C3
Qabr Hud, P.D.R. Yemen 59/E6
Qadhima, Saudi Arabia 59/C5
Qadima, Israel 65/B3
Qadisiya (gov.), Iraq 66/D4
Qafar, Saudi Arabia 59/D4
Qaffin, West Bank 65/C3
Qagan Nur, China 77/H3
Qâhira, El (Cairo), Egypt 111/J3
Qaidam (basin), China 54/L6
Qaidam Pendi (basin) (swamp), China 77/D4
Qala'en Nahl, Sudan 59/C7
Qala'en Nahl, Sudan 111/F5
Qalansuwa, Israel 65/B3
Qal'a Sharqat, Iraq 59/D2
Qal'a Sharqat, Iraq 66/C3
Qalat, Afghanistan 68/B2
Qalat, Afghanistan 59/J3
Qa'lat Diza, Iraq 66/D2
Qal'at es Salihiye, Syria 63/J5
Qal'eh Mureh (riv.), Iran 66/J3
Qal'eh-ye Now, Afghanistan 68/A1
Qal'eh-ye Now, Afghanistan 59/H3
Qal'eh-ye Panjeh, Afghanistan 59/K2
Qal'eh-ye Panjeh, Afghanistan 68/C1
Qalqiliya, West Bank 65/C3
Qalyub, Egypt 111/J3
Qamdo, China 77/E5
Qamdo, China 54/L6
Qamishliye, Syria 63/J4
Qamr (bay), P.D.R. Yemen 59/F6
Qandahar, Afghanistan 54/H6
Qandahar, Afghanistan 68/B2
Qandahar, Afghanistan 59/J3
Qantara, El, Egypt 111/K3
Qaranqu (riv.), Iran 66/E2
Qareh Dagh (mts.), Iran 66/E1
Qareh Su (riv.), Iran 66/E1
Qareh Su (riv.), Iran 66/G3
Qarkilik (Ruoqiang), China 77/C4
Qarn (riv.), Israel 65/C1
Qarqan (Qiemo), China 77/C4
Qarqan He (riv.), China 77/C4
Qasr al Haiyanya, Saudi Arabia 59/D4
Qasr al Khubbaz, Iraq 66/B4
Qasr-e Qand, Iran 59/H4
Qasr-e Qand, Iran 66/M7
Qasr-e-Shirin, Iran 66/E3
Qasr Farâfra, Egypt 111/E2
Qasr Farâfra, Egypt 102/E2
Qasr Farâfra, Egypt 59/A4
Qatar 2/M4
Qatar 54/G7
QATAR 59/F4
Qatif, Saudi Arabia 59/E4
Qattara (depr.), Egypt 59/A4
Qattara (depr.), Egypt 111/E2
Qayen, Iran 66/L4
Qayen, Iran 59/G3
Qazvin, Iran 54/F6
Qazvin, Iran 59/E2
Qazvin, Iran 66/F2
Qedma, Israel 65/B4
Qena, Egypt 111/F2
Qena, Egypt 102/F2
Qena, Egypt 59/B4
Qeshm (isl.), Iran 59/G4
Qeshm (isl.), Iran 66/J7
Qeys (isl.), Iran 59/F4
Qeys (isl.), Iran 66/J7
Qezel Owzam (riv.), Iran 66/F2
Qezel Owzan (riv.), Iran 59/E2
Qianyang (Kienyang), China 77/H6
Qiaowan, China 77/E3
Qibya, West Bank 65/C4
Qiebei, China 77/F7
Qiema, China 54/K6
Qiemo (Qarqan), China 77/C4
Qijiang, China 77/G6
Qila Ladgasht, Pakistan 68/A3
Qila Ladgasht, Pakistan 59/H4
Qilian, China 77/E4
Qilian Shan (range), China 54/L6
Qilian Shan (range), China 77/E4
Qimen, China 77/J5
Qina (Qena), Egypt 59/B4
Qingdao (Tsingtao), China 77/K4
Qingdao, China 54/O6
Qinghai (Tsinghai) (prov.), China 77/E4
Qinghai (lake), China 54/L6
Qinghai Hu (lake), China 77/E4
Qinghe (Qinggil), China 77/D2
Qingjiang, Jiangxi, China 77/J6
Qingjiang, Anhui, China 77/J5
Qingtongxia, China 77/F4
Qingyuan, China 77/H7
Qinhuangdao (Chinwangtao), China 77/K4
Qinzhou, China 77/G7
Qionghai, China 77/H8
Qiongshan, China 77/H8
Qiongzhou Haixia (str.), China 77/G7
Qiqihar (Tsitsihar), China 77/K2
Qiqihar, China 54/O5
Qira, China 77/B4
Qiryat Atta, Israel 65/C2
Qiryat Bialik, Israel 65/C2
Qiryat Gat, Israel 65/B4
Qiryat Mal'akhi, Israel 65/B4
Qiryat Motzkin, Israel 65/C2
Qiryat Shemona, Israel 65/C1
Qiryat Tiv'on, Israel 65/C2
Qiryat Yam, Israel 65/C2
Qishn, P.D.R. Yemen 59/F6
Qishon (riv.), Israel 65/C2
Qitai, China 77/C3
Qitaihe, China 77/M2
Qizan, Saudi Arabia 59/D6
Qog, China 77/G3
Qom (Qum), Iran 54/G6
Qom, Iran 59/F3
Qom, Iran 66/G3
Qonduz, Afghanistan 68/B1
Qonduz, Afghanistan 59/J2
Qonduz (riv.), Afghanistan 68/B1
Qonduz (riv.), Afghanistan 59/J2
Qoqek (Tacheng), China 77/B2
Qorveh, Iran 66/E3
Qotur, Iran 66/D1
Quabbin (res.), Mass. 249/E3
Quaboag (riv.), Mass. 249/F4
Quaco (head), New Bruns. 170/E3
Quaddick, Conn. (†06277) 210/H1
Quaddick (res.), Conn. 210/H1
Quadeville, Ontario 177/G2
Quail, Texas (79251) 303/D3
Quairading, W. Australia 92/B1
Quajote Wash (dry riv.), Ariz. 198/D6
Quakenbrück, W. Germany 22/C2
Quaker City, Ohio (43773) 284/H6
Quaker Farms, Conn. (†06483) 210/C3
Quaker Hill, Conn. (06375) 210/G3
Quakertown, N.J. (08868) 273/D2
Quakertown, Pa. (18951) 294/M5
Qualicum Beach, Br. Col. 184/J3
Quality, Ky. (42268) 237/H6
Quallam, Niger 106/E6
Quamba, Minn. (55064) 255/E5
Quambatook, Victoria 97/B4
Quambone, N.S. Wales 97/E2
Quanah, Texas (79252) 303/E3
Quan Dao Nam Duj (isls.), Vietnam 72/D5
Quandary (peak), Colo. 208/G4
Quandialla, N.S. Wales 97/D4
Quanduck (brook), Conn. 210/H1
Quang Nam, Vietnam 72/E4
Quang Ngai, Vietnam 72/F4
Quang Tri, Vietnam 72/E3
Quang Yen, Vietnam 72/E2
Quan Long, Vietnam 72/E5
Quantico, Md. (21856) 245/R7
Quantico, Va. (22134) 307/O3
Quantico Marine Corps Air Sta., Va. 307/O4
Quanzhou, China 77/H6
Quanzhou (Chüanchow), China 77/J7
Quapaw, Okla. (74363) 288/S1
Qu'Appelle, Sask. 181/H5
Qu'Appelle (riv.), Sask. 181/J5
Quaraí, Brazil 132/C10
Quaregnon, Belgium 27/D8
Quarryville, New Bruns. 170/E2
Quarryville, Pa. (17566) 294/K6
Quartu Sant'Elena, Italy 34/B5
Quartz (peak), Calif. 204/L11
Quartz Hill, Calif. (93534) 204/G9
Quartz Mountain, Oreg. (†97630) 291/G5
Quartzsite, Ariz. (85346) 198/A5
Quasqueton, Iowa (52326) 229/K4
Quassapaug (pond), Conn. 210/C2
Quatervals (peak), Switzerland 39/K3
Quathiaski Cove, Br. Col. 184/E5
Quatre Bornes, Mauritius 118/G5
Quatsino (sound), Br. Col. 184/C5

Rangeley 433

Quay (co.), N. Mex. 274/F3
Quay, N. Mex. (88433) 274/F4
Quay, Okla. (†74085) 288/N2
Quchan, Iran 66/L2
Quchan, Iran 59/G2
Quealy, Wyo. (†82901) 319/C4
Queanbeyan, N. S. Wales 88/H7
Queanbeyan, N.S. Wales 97/E4
Québec (prov.) 162/J5
QUÉBEC 172
Québec, Canada 2/F3
Québec (prov.), Que. 146/L4
Québec (cap.), Que. 146/L5
Québec (cap.) Que. 162/J6
Québec (co.), Québec 172/F3
Québec (county), Québec 174/C3
Québec (cap.), Québec 172/H3
Québec (cap.), Québec 174/C3
Quebeck, Tenn. (38579) 237/K9
Quebracho, Uruguay 145/B2
Quebracho Coto, Argentina 143/D2
Quebrada de Alvarado, Chile 138/F2
Quebradillas, P. Rico 161/B1
Quechee, Vt. (05059) 268/C4
Quechisla, Bolivia 136/C7
Quecholac, Mexico 150/O2
Quecreek, Pa. (15555) 294/D5
Quedlinburg, E. Germany 22/D3
Queen (cape), N.W. Terrs. 187/L3
Queen, Pa. (16670) 294/E5
Queen Anne, Md. (21657) 245/O5
Queen Annes (co.), Md. 245/P4
Queenborough, England 13/H6
Queenborough, England 10/G5
Queen Charlotte (isls.), Br. Col. 146/E4
Queen Charlotte (isls.), Br. Col. 162/C5
Queen Charlotte, Br. Col. 184/A3
Queen Charlotte (isls.), Br. Col. 184/B3
Queen Charlotte (sound), Br. Col. 184/C4
Queen Charlotte (str.), Br. Col. 184/D5
Queen Charlotte (sound), N.W.T. 162/D5
Queen City, Mo. (63561) 261/H2
Queen City, Texas (75572) 303/L4
Queen Creek, Ariz. (85242) 198/D5
Queen Elizabeth (isls.), Canada 2/C2
Queen Elizabeth (isls.), Canada 4/B15
Queen Elizabeth (isls.), N.W.T. 146/G2
Queen Elizabeth (isls.), N.W.T. 162/M3
Queen Elizabeth (isls.), N.W. Terrs. 187/H1
Queen Mary Coast (reg.) 5/C5
Queen Maud (mts.) 5/A12
Queen Maud (gulf), N.W.T. 162/F2
Queen Maud (gulf), N.W. Terrs. 187/H3
Queen Maud Land (reg.), Ant. 2/K10
Queen Maud Land (reg.) 5/B1
Queens (sound), Br. Col. 184/C4
Queen's (co.), New Bruns. 170/D3
Queens (co.), N.Y. 276/N9
Queens (borough), N.Y. (*11101) 276/N9
Queens (chan.), N.W. Terrs. 187/J2
Queens (co.), Nova Scotia 168/C4
Queens (co.), Pr. Edward I. 168/E2
Queens, W. Va. (†26237) 312/F5
Queensberry (mt.), Scotland 15/E5
Queenscliff, Victoria 97/C6
Queensferry, Scotland 10/C1
Queensferry, Scotland 15/D1
Queen Shoals, W. Va. (†25045) 312/D6
Queensland, 88/G4
QUEENSLAND 95
Queensland (state), Australia 87/E8
Queensport, Nova Scotia 168/G3
Queenstown, Alberta 182/D4
Queenstown, Guyana 131/B2
Queenstown (Cóbh), Ireland 10/B5
Queenstown (Cóbh), Ireland 17/E8
Queenstown, Md. (21658) 245/O5
Queenstown, New Bruns. 170/D3
Queenstown, N. Zealand 100/B6
Queenstown, S. Africa 102/E8
Queenstown, S. Africa 118/D6
Queenstown, Tasmania 99/B4
Queenstown, Tasmania 88/H8
Queensville, Ind. (†47265) 227/F6
Queets, Wash. (†98331) 310/A3
Queets (riv.), Wash. 310/A3
Queilén, Chile 138/D4
Queimadas, Brazil 132/F5
Quela, Angola 115/C5
Quelimane, Mozambique 118/F3
Quelimane, Mozambique 102/F6
Quelpart (Cheju) (isl.), S. Korea 81/C7
Queluz, Portugal 33/A1
Quemado (pt.), Cuba 158/K4
Quemado, N. Mex. (87829) 274/A4
Quemado, Texas (78877) 303/D9
Quemado de Güines, Cuba 158/E1
Quemchi, Chile 138/D4
Quemoy (Jinmen) (isl.), China 77/J7
Quemú-Quemú, Argentina 143/D4
Quenemo, Kansas (66528) 232/G3
Quentin, Miss. (39647) 256/C8
Quepos, C. Rica 154/E6
Quequay Chico (riv.), Uruguay 145/B3
Quequay Grande (riv.), Uruguay 145/B3
Que Que, Zimbabwe 118/D3
Que Que, Zimbabwe 102/E6
Quequén, Argentina 143/E4
Querecotillo, Peru 128/B5
Querétaro (state), Mexico 150/J6
Querétaro, Mexico 146/J7
Querétaro, Mexico 150/J6
Quesada, Spain 33/E4
Queshan, China 77/H5
Quesnel, Br. Col. 162/D5
Quesnel (lake), Br. Col. 162/D5
Quesnel, Br. Col. 184/F4
Quesnel (lake), Br. Col. 184/G4
Quesnel (riv.), Br. Col. 184/F4
Quesnel (lake), Manitoba 179/G4
Questa, N. Mex. (87556) 274/D2
Queteña, Bolivia 136/B8
Quetico Prov. Park, Ontario 175/B3
Quetico Prov. Park, Ontario 177/G5
Quetta, Pakistan 54/H6
Quetta, Pakistan 59/J3
Quetta, Pakistan 68/B2
Queule, Chile 138/D2
Quevedo, Ecuador 128/C3
Quévy, Belgium 27/D8
Quezaltenango, Guatemala 154/B3
Quezaltepeque, Guatemala 154/C3
Quezon (prov.), Philippines 82/C3
Quibala, Angola 115/C6
Quibaxe, Angola 115/B5
Quibdó, Colombia 126/B5
Quiberon, France 28/B4
Quibor, Venezuela 124/D3
Quicacha, Peru 128/F10
Quick, Br. Col. 184/D3
Quick, W. Va. (25045) 312/D6
Quicksand, Ky. (41363) 237/P5
Quicksburg, Va. (22847) 307/L3
Quiebra Hacha, Cuba 158/B1
Quiévrain, Belgium 27/D8
Quigley, Alberta 182/E1
Quiindy, Paraguay 144/B5
Quijotoa, Ariz. (†85634) 198/C6
Quilali, Nicaragua 154/E4
Quilán (cape), Chile 138/D4
Quilán (isl.), Chile 138/D5
Quilca, Peru 128/F11
Quilcene, Wash. (98376) 310/B3
Quilchena, Br. Col. 184/G5
Quilengues, Angola 115/B6
Quilicura, Chile 138/G3
Quill (lakes), Sask. 181/G4
Quillabamba, Peru 128/F9
Quillacas, Bolivia 136/B6
Quillacollo, Bolivia 136/B5
Quillacollo, Bolivia 120/C4
Quillagua, Chile 138/B3
Quillaicillo, Chile 138/A8
Quillan, France 28/E6
Quillayute Ind. Res., Wash. 310/A3
Quilleco, Chile 138/E1
Quill Lake, Sask. 181/G3
Quillota, Chile 138/F2
Quilon, India 68/D7
Quilpie, Queensland 88/G5
Quilpie, Queensland 95/C5
Quilpué, Chile 138/F2
Quimby, Iowa (51049) 229/B3
Quimby, Maine (04770) 243/F2
Quime, Bolivia 136/B5
Quimili, Argentina 143/D2
Quimper, France 28/A4
Quimperlé, France 28/B4
Quinault, Wash. (98575) 310/B3
Quinault (lake), Wash. 310/B3
Quinault (riv.), Wash. 310/A3
Quinault Ind. Res., Wash. 310/A3
Quinby, S.C. (†29501) 296/H3
Quinby, Va. (23423) 307/S5
Quinby (inlet), Va. 307/S6
Quince Mil, Peru 128/G9
Quincy, Calif. (95971) 204/E4
Quincy, Fla. (32351) 212/B1
Quincy, Ill. 188/H3
Quincy, Ill. (62301) 222/B4
Quincy, Ind. (47456) 227/D6
Quincy, Kansas (†66870) 232/F4
Quincy, Ky. (41166) 237/P3
Quincy, Mass. (02169) 249/D7
Quincy (bay), Mass. 249/D7
Quincy, Mich. (49082) 250/E7
Quincy, Miss. (†38848) 256/H3
Quincy, Mo. (65735) 261/F6
Quincy, N.H. (†03266) 268/D4
Quincy, Ohio (43343) 284/C5
Quincy, Wash. (98848) 310/F3
Quincy, W. Va. (†25015) 312/C6
Quindío (dept.), Colombia 126/C5
Quinebaug, Conn. (06262) 210/H1
Quinebaug (riv.), Conn. 210/H2
Quinebaug (riv.), Mass. 249/F4
Quines, Argentina 143/C3
Quinhagak, Alaska (99655) 196/F3
Qui Nhon, Vietnam 72/F4
Qui Nhon, Vietnam 54/M8
Quiniluban (isls.), Philippines 82/C5
Quinlan, Okla. (†73852) 288/J2
Quinlan, Texas (75474) 303/H5
Quinn (riv.), Nev. 266/D1
Quinn, S. Dak. (57775) 298/E5
Quinn Canyon (range), Nev. 266/F4
Quinnesec, Mich. (49876) 250/A3
Quinnimont, W. Va. (25910) 312/D7
Quinnipiac, Conn. (†06492) 210/D3
Quinnipiac (riv.), Conn. 210/D3
Quinta de Tilcoco, Chile 138/G5
Quintana de la Serena, Spain 33/D3
Quintanar de la Orden, Spain 33/E3
Quintana Roo (state), Mexico 150/P7
Quintay, Chile 138/F3
Quinter, Kansas (67752) 232/B2
Quintero, Chile 138/F2
Quinto (riv.), Argentina 143/D3
Quinto, Spain 33/F2
Quinto, Switzerland 39/G3
Quinton, Ky. (†42518) 237/M7
Quinton, N.J. (08072) 273/C4
Quinton, Okla. (74561) 288/R4
Quinton, Sask. 181/G4
Quinton, Va. (23141) 307/O5
Quinwood, W. Va. (25981) 312/E6
Quinzau, Angola 115/B5
Quionga, Mozambique 118/G2
Quipapá, Brazil 132/G5
Quirey, Colombia 126/F5
Quirihue, Chile 138/E1
Quirindi, N.S. Wales 97/F2
Quirino (prov.), Philippines 82/C2
Quirino, Philippines 82/C2
Quiriquire, Venezuela 124/G3
Quirke (lake), Ontario 177/B1
Quiroga, Argentina 143/F7
Quiroga, Bolivia 136/C6
Quiroga, Spain 33/C1
Quirusillas, Bolivia 136/D6
Quisiro, Venezuela 124/C2
Quispamsis, New Bruns. 170/E3
Quissanga, Mozambique 118/G2
Quissett, Mass. (†02540) 249/M6
Quissico, Mozambique 118/F4
Quitaque, Texas (79255) 303/C3
Quitasueño (bank), Colombia 126/A8
Quitilipi, Argentina 143/D2
Quitman, Ark. (72131) 202/F3
Quitman (co.), Georgia 217/B7
Quitman, Georgia (31643) 217/E9
Quitman, La. (71268) 238/E2
Quitman (co.), Miss. 256/D2
Quitman, Miss. (39355) 256/G6
Quitman, Mo. (†64428) 261/C2
Quitman, Texas (75783) 303/J5
Quitman (mts.), Texas 303/B11
Quito (cap.), Ecuador 2/F6
Quito (cap.), Ecuador 128/C3
Quito (cap.), Ecuador 120/B2
Quixadá, Brazil 120/F3
Quixadá, Brazil 132/G4
Quixeramobim, Brazil 132/F4
Qujing, China 77/F6
Qulin, Mo. (63961) 261/M9
Qum, Iran 54/G6
Qum (Qom), Iran 59/F3
Qum (Qom), Iran 66/G3
Qumar He (riv.), China 77/D4
Qumarlêb, China 77/D5
Qumeim, Jordan 65/D2
Qunfidha, Saudi Arabia 59/D6
Quogue, N.Y. (11959) 276/P9
Quoich (riv.), N.W. Terrs. 187/J3
Quoich, Loch (lake), Scotland 15/C3
Quonnipaug (lake), Conn. 210/E3
Quorn, S. Australia 88/F6
Quorn, S. Australia 94/F5
Quryat, Oman 59/G5
Qusaiba, Saudi Arabia 59/D4
Quteife, Syria 63/G6
Qu Xian, Sichuan, China 77/G5
Qu Xian, Zhejiang, China 77/J6
Qüxü, China 77/D6
Quyon, Québec 172/A4
Quyquyó, Paraguay 144/D5

R

Raab (riv.), Austria 41/C3
Raabs an der Thaya, Austria 41/C2
Raahe, Finland 18/O4
Raalte, Netherlands 27/J4
Ra'anana, Israel 65/B3
Raanes (pen.), N.W. Terrs. 187/K2
Raasay (isl.), Scotland 15/C3
Raasay (sound), Scotland 15/B3
Rab, Yugoslavia 45/B3
Rab (isl.), Yugoslavia 45/B3
Rába (riv.), Hungary 41/D3
Raba, Indonesia 85/F7
Rabat (cap.), Morocco 2/J4
Rabat (cap.), Morocco 106/C2
Rabat (cap.), Morocco 102/B1
Rabaul, Papua N.G. 87/F6
Rabaul, Papua N.G. 86/B2
Rabbit (riv.), Mich. 250/D6
Rabbit (isl.), N.S. Wales 97/J2
Rabbit (creek), S. Dak. 298/E3
Rabbit Ears (peak), Colo. 208/G2
Rabbit Ears (range), Colo. 208/F2
Rabbithash, Ky. (†41091) 237/M3
Rabbit Lake, Sask. 181/D2
Rabbit Lake, Sask. 181/M2
Rabigh, Saudi Arabia 59/C5
Rabinal, Guatemala 154/B3
Rabka, Poland 47/D4
Rabocheostrovsk, U.S.S.R. 52/D1
Rabun, Ala. (†36507) 195/C8
Rabun (co.), Georgia 217/F1
Rabun (lake), Georgia 217/E1
Rabun Gap, Georgia (30568) 217/F1
Raccoon (pt.), Fla. 212/D3
Raccoon, Ind. (†46172) 227/D5
Raccoon (riv.), Iowa 229/D4
Raccoon (pt.), La. 238/H8
Raccoon (creek), N.J. 273/C4
Raccoon (creek), Ohio 284/F8
Race (pt.), Mass. 249/N4
Race (cape), Newf. 166/D2
Race (cape), Newf. 146/N5
Race (cape), Newf. 162/L6
Raceland, Ky. (41169) 237/R3
Raceland, La. (70394) 238/J7
Racepond, Georgia (†31537) 217/H8
Rachel, W. Va. (26587) 312/F3
Rach Gia, Vietnam 72/E5
Racibórz, Poland 47/C3
Racine, Minn. (55967) 255/F7
Racine, Mo. (64858) 261/C9
Racine, Ohio (45771) 284/G8
Racine, Québec 172/E4
Racine, W. Va. (25165) 312/C6
Racine, Wis. 188/J2
Racine (co.), Wis. 317/K10
Racine, Wis. (*53401) 317/M3
Ráckeve, Hungary 41/E3
Rackham, Manitoba 179/B4
Raco, Mich. (49778) 250/E2
Racola, Mo. (†63630) 261/L6
Radama (isls.), Madagascar 118/H2
Rădăuţi, Romania 45/G2
Radbuza (riv.), Czech. 41/B2
Radcliff, Ky. (40160) 237/K5
Radcliff, Ohio (45670) 284/F7
Radcliffe, England 13/H2
Radcliffe, Iowa (50230) 229/G4
Radeberg, E. Germany 22/E3
Radebeul, E. Germany 22/E3
Radenthein, Austria 41/B3
Rader, Tenn. (†37743) 237/R8
Radersburg, Mont. (59641) 262/E4
Radford (I.C.), Va. (24141) 307/G6
Radhanpur, India 68/C4
Radiant, Va. (22732) 307/M4
Radisson, Québec 174/B2
Radisson, Sask. 181/D3
Radisson, Wis. (54867) 317/D4
Radium, Colo. (80472) 208/G3
Radium, Kansas (67571) 232/D3
Radium, Minn. (56749) 255/B2
Radium Hill, S. Australia 88/G6
Radium Hill, S. Australia 94/G5
Radium Hot Springs, Br. Col. 184/J5
Radium Springs, N. Mex. (88054) 274/B6
Radkersburg, Austria 41/C3
Radley, Ind. (†46938) 227/F4
Radnice, Czech. 41/B2
Radnor, Ind. (†46923) 227/D3
Radnor, Ohio (43066) 284/D5
Radnor (for.), Wales 13/D5
Radnor, W. Va. (25556) 312/A6
Radolfzell, W. Germany 22/C5
Radom, Ill. (62876) 222/D5
Radom (prov.), Poland 47/E3
Radom, Poland 7/G3
Radom, Poland 47/E3
Radomir, Bulgaria 45/F4
Radomsko, Poland 47/D3
Radoviš, Yugoslavia 45/F5
Radstadt, Austria 41/B3
Radviliškis, U.S.S.R. 53/B3
Radville, Sask. 162/F6
Radville, Sask. 181/G6
Radway, Alberta 182/D2
Radziejów, Poland 47/D2
Radzyń Podlaski, Poland 47/F3
Rae (isth.), N.W.T. 162/H2
Rae (isth.), N.W. Terrs. 187/K3
Rae (riv.), N.W. Terrs. 187/G3
Rae (str.), N.W. Terrs. 187/J3
Rae-Edzo, N.W.T. 162/E3
Rae-Edzo, N.W. Terrs. 187/G3
Raeford, N.C. (28376) 281/L5
Rae Lake, N.W. Terrs. 187/G3
Raeren, Belgium 27/J7
Raeside (lake), W. Australia 88/C5
Raeside (lake), W. Australia 92/C5
Raetihi, N. Zealand 100/E3
Raeville, Nebr. (68656) 264/F3
Rafaela, Argentina 143/F5
Rafaela, Argentina 120/C6
Rafah, Gaza Strip 65/A5
Rafai, Cent. Afr. Rep. 115/D2
Rafidiya, West Bank 65/C3
Rafsanjan, Iran 59/G3
Rafsanjan, Iran 66/K5
Raft (riv.), Idaho 220/E7
Raft (riv.), Utah 304/A1
Raft River (mts.), Utah 304/A2
Rafz, Switzerland 39/G1
Raga, Sudan 111/E6
Ragan, Nebr. (68969) 264/E4
Ragang (vol.), Philippines 82/E7
Ragay (gulf), Philippines 82/D4
Ragged (isl.), Bahamas 156/C2
Ragged (pt.), Barbados 161/C8
Ragged (isl.), Maine 243/F8
Ragged (lake), Maine 243/E4
Ragged (isls.), Newf. 166/C2
Raglan, N. Zealand 100/E2
Raglan (harb.), N. Zealand 100/E2
Ragland, Ala. (35131) 195/F3
Ragley, La. (70657) 238/D5
Rago, Kansas (67128) 232/D4
Ragsdale, Ind. (47573) 227/C7
Ragusa (prov.), Italy 34/E6
Ragusa, Italy 34/E6
Ragusa (Dubrovnik), Yugoslavia 45/C4
Raha, Indonesia 85/G6
Rahaeng (Tak), Thailand 72/C3
Rahan, Ireland 17/F5
Rahimyar Khan, Pakistan 68/C3
Rahotu, N. Zealand 100/D3
Rahue (riv.), Chile 138/D3
Rahway, N.J. (*07065) 273/E2
Raiatea (isl.), Fr. Poly. 87/L7
Raices, Argentina 143/G6
Raichur, India 68/D5
Raiford, Fla. (32083) 212/D1
Raigarh, India 68/E4
Railley (mt.), Mont. 262/C3
Railroad (valley), Nev. 266/F4
Railroad, Pa. (17355) 294/J6
Railroad Canyon (res.), Calif. 204/E11
Railton, Tasmania 99/C3
Rainbow (lake), Alberta 182/A5
Rainbow (plat.), Ariz. 198/D2
Rainbow, Conn. (†06095) 210/E1
Rainbow (mt.), Idaho 220/C4
Rainbow (lake), Maine 243/E4
Rainbow, Victoria 97/A4
Rainbow Bridge Nat'l Mon., Utah 304/C6
Rainbow City, Ala. (35901) 195/F3
Rainbow Lake, Alberta 182/A5
Rainelle, W. Va. (25962) 312/E7
Rainier, Alberta 182/D4
Rainier, Oreg. (97048) 291/E1
Rainier (mt.), Wash. 188/B1
Rainier, Wash. (98576) 310/C4
Rainier (mt.), Wash. 310/D4
Rains, S.C. (29589) 296/J3
Rains (co.), Texas 303/J5
Rainsboro, Ohio (45165) 284/C7
Rainsburg, Pa. (†15522) 294/F6
Rainsville, Ala. (35986) 195/G2
Rainsville, Ind. (†47918) 227/C4
Rainsville, N. Mex. (87736) 274/D2
Rainy (riv.), Minn. 188/H1
Rainy (lake), Minn. 188/H1
Rainy (lake), Minn. 255/E2
Rainy (riv.), Minn. 255/D2
Rainy (lake), Ont. 162/G6
Rainy (lake), Ontario 177/G5
Rainy (lake), Ontario 175/B3
Rainy River, Ont. 162/G6
Rainy River (terr. dist.), Ontario 177/G5
Rainy River (terr. dist.), Ontario 175/B3
Rainy River, Ontario 175/A3
Rainy River, Ontario 177/F5
Raipur, India 54/K7
Raipur, India 68/E4
Raisin, Calif. (93652) 204/E7
Raisin (riv.), Mich. 250/F7
Raisio, Finland 18/M6
Raith, Ontario 175/C3
Raith, Ontario 177/G5
Raivavae (isl.), Fr. Poly. 87/M8
Raja Ampat Group (isls.), Indonesia 85/H6
Rajahmundry, India 68/E5
Rajang (riv.), Malaysia 85/E5
Rajapalaiyam, India 68/D7
Rajapur, India 68/C5
Rajasthan (state), India 68/C3
Rajec, Czech. 41/E2
Rajgarh, India 68/D4
Rajka, Hungary 41/D3
Rajkot, India 54/H7
Rajkot, India 68/C4
Rajnandgaon, India 68/E4
Rajpipla, India 68/C4
Rajpur, India 68/F2
Rajpura, India 68/D2
Rajshahi, Bangladesh 68/F4
Rakahanga (atoll), Cook Is. 87/K7
Rakaia, N. Zealand 100/C5
Rakaia (riv.), N. Zealand 100/C5
Rakamaz, Hungary 41/F2
Rakan, Ras (cape), Qatar 59/F4
Rakaposhi (mt.), Pakistan 68/C1
Rakaposhi (mt.), Pakistan 59/K2
Rakata (isl.), Indonesia 85/C7
Rake, Iowa (50465) 229/F2
Rakhov, U.S.S.R. 52/B5
Rakino (isl.), N. Zealand 100/C1
Rakitu (isl.), N. Zealand 100/E2
Rakkestad, Norway 18/G7
Rakof (isls.), Alaska 196/M1
Rákospalota, Hungary 41/E3
Rakovník, Czech. 41/B1
Rakvere, U.S.S.R. 53/D1
Rakvere, U.S.S.R. 52/C3
Raleigh, Fla. (†32696) 212/D2
Raleigh, Georgia (†30293) 217/C5
Raleigh, Ill. (62977) 222/E6
Raleigh, Ind. (†46173) 227/G5
Raleigh, Miss. (39153) 256/F6
Raleigh, Newf. 166/C3
Raleigh (cap.), N.C. 146/L6
Raleigh (cap.), N.C. 188/L3
Raleigh (cap.), N.C. (*27601) 281/M3
Raleigh (bay), N.C. 281/S5
Raleigh, N. Dak. (58564) 282/H7
Raleigh, Tenn. (38128) 237/B10
Raleigh (co.), W. Va. 312/D7
Raleigh, W. Va. (25911) 312/D7
Ralik Chain (isls.), Marshall Is. 87/G5
Ralls (co.), Mo. 261/J3
Ralls, Texas (79357) 303/C4
Ralph, Ala. (35480) 195/C4
Ralph, Mich. (49877) 250/B2
Ralph, Sask. 181/H6
Ralph, S. Dak. (57650) 298/C2
Ralphton, Pa. (†15563) 294/D5
Ralston, Alberta 182/E4
Ralston, Iowa (51459) 229/D4
Ralston, Nebr. (68127) 264/J3
Ralston, N.J. (†07945) 273/D2
Ralston, Okla. (74650) 288/N2
Ralston, Pa. (17763) 294/H2
Ralston, Tenn. (†38237) 237/D8
Ralston, Wash. (†99169) 310/G4
Ralston, Wyo. (82440) 319/D1
Ram (head), Virgin Is. (U.S.) 161/C5
Rama, Nicaragua 154/E4
Rama, Sask. 181/H4
Ramadi, Iraq 59/D3
Ramadi, Iraq 66/C4
Ramage, W. Va. (25166) 312/C7
Ramah, Colo. (80832) 208/L4
Ramah (bay), Newf. 166/B2
Ramah, N. Mex. (87321) 274/A3
Ramallah, West Bank 65/C4
Ramallo, Argentina 143/F6
Ramapo (riv.), N.J. 273/E1
Ramat Gan, Israel 65/B3
Ramat Hasharon, Israel 65/B3
Rambi (isl.), Fiji 86/R10
Rambleweod, N.J. (†08054) 273/D4
Rambouillet, France 28/D3
Rame, Israel 65/C2
Ramea, Newf. 166/C4
Ramea (isls.), Newf. 166/C4
Ramechhap, Nepal 68/F3
Ramelton, Ireland 17/F1
Ramer, Ala. (36069) 195/F6
Ramer, Tenn. (38367) 237/D10
Rameswaram, India 68/D7
Ramey, Minn. (†56329) 255/E5
Ramey, Pa. (16671) 294/F4
Ramey A.F.B., P. Rico 161/A1
Ramhormoz, Iran 66/F5
Ramhurst, Georgia (†30705) 217/C1
Ramiers (isl.), Martinique 161/C6
Ramla, Israel 65/B4
Ramm, Jebel (mt.), Jordan 65/D5
Ramme, Denmark 21/B4
Rammun, West Bank 65/C4
Ramnäs, Sweden 18/J7
Ramon (mt.), Israel 65/D5
Ramon, N. Mex. (†88136) 274/D4
Ramona, Calif. (92065) 204/J10
Ramona, Kansas (67475) 232/E3
Ramona, Okla. (74061) 288/P1
Ramona, S. Dak. (57054) 298/P5
Ramón Castilla, Peru 128/G5
Ramón de las Yaguas, Cuba 158/J4
Ramón Santana, Dom. Rep. 158/F6
Ramón Trigo, Uruguay 145/E3
Ramor (lake), Ireland 17/G4
Ramore, Ontario 177/K5
Ramos (riv.), Mexico 150/G4
Ramos Arizpe, Mexico 150/J4
Ramosch, Switzerland 39/K3
Ramotswa, Botswana 118/C4
Rampart, Alaska (99767) 196/H1
Ramparts (riv.), N.W. Terrs. 187/E3
Rampur, Him. Pradesh, India 68/D2
Rampur, Uttar Pradesh, India 68/D3
Ramree (isl.), Burma 72/B3
Ramsar, Iran 66/G2
Ramsay, Mich. (49959) 250/F2
Ramsay, Mont. (59748) 262/D4
Ramsay, Ontario 177/J5
Ramsbottom, England 13/H2
Ramsele, Sweden 18/K5
Ramsen, Switzerland 39/G1
Ramseur, N.C. (27316) 281/K3
Ramsey, England 10/F4
Ramsey, England 13/G5
Ramsey, Ill. (62080) 222/D4
Ramsey, Ind. (47166) 227/E8
Ramsey, I. of Man 13/C3
Ramsey, I. of Man 10/D3
Ramsey (bay), I. of Man 13/C3
Ramsey (co.), Minn. 255/E5
Ramsey, Minn. (†55303) 255/E5
Ramsey, N.J. (07446) 273/B1
Ramsey (co.), N. Dak. 282/N3
Ramsey (mt.), Tasmania 99/B3
Ramsey (isl.), Wales 13/B6
Ramsgate, England 10/G5
Ramsgate, England 13/J6
Ramsjö, Sweden 18/J5
Ramu (riv.), Papua N.G. 85/B7
Ramunia, Tanjong (pt.), Malaysia 72/F6
Ramville (isl.), Martinique 161/D6
Rana (fjord), Norway 18/H3
Rana (riv.), Norway 18/J3
Ranau, Malaysia 85/F4
Ranburne, Ala. (36273) 195/H3
Rancagua, Chile 138/G5
Rancagua, Chile 120/B6
Ranches of Taos, N. Mex. (87557) 274/D2
Ranchester, Wyo. (82839) 319/E1
Ranchi, India 68/F4
Rancho Cordova, Calif. (95670) 204/C8
Rancho Cucamonga, Calif. (91730) 204/E10
Rancho Mirage, Calif. (92270) 204/J10
Rancho Palos Verdes, Calif. (90274) 204/B11
Rancho Santa Clarita, Calif. (†91321) 204/G9
Rancho Santa Fe, Calif. (92067) 204/H10
Rancho Veloz, Cuba 158/D1
Ranchuelo, Cuba 158/E2
Ranchwood Manor, Okla. (†73160) 288/L4
Ranco (lake), Chile 138/E3
Rancocas, N.J. (08073) 273/D3
Rancocas (creek), N.J. 273/D3
Rand, Colo. (80473) 208/G2
Randalia, Iowa (52164) 229/K3
Randall, Iowa (50231) 229/F4
Randall, Kansas (66963) 232/D2
Randall, Minn. (56475) 255/D4
Randall (co.), Texas 303/C2
Randall (mt.), W. Australia 88/B3
Randallstown, Md. (21133) 245/L3
Randalstown, N. Ireland 17/J2
Randburg, S. Africa 118/H6
Randers, Denmark 18/G8
Randers, Denmark 21/C5
Randfontein, S. Africa 118/G6
Randle, Wash. (98377) 310/D4
Randleman, N.C. (27317) 281/K3
Randles, Mo. (†63740) 261/N8
Randlett, Okla. (73562) 288/K6
Randlett, Utah (84063) 304/E3
Randolph (co.), Ala. 195/H4
Randolph, Ala. (36792) 195/E5
Randolph, Ariz. (85243) 198/D6
Randolph (co.), Ark. 202/H1
Randolph (co.), Georgia 217/C7
Randolph (co.), Ill. 222/D5
Randolph (co.), Ind. 227/G4
Randolph, Iowa (51649) 229/B7
Randolph, Kansas (66554) 232/F2
Randolph○, Maine (†04345) 243/D7
Randolph, Md. (†20853) 245/K4
Randolph○, Mass. (02368) 249/D8
Randolph, Minn. (55065) 255/E6
Randolph, Miss. (38864) 256/F2
Randolph (co.), Mo. 261/G3
Randolph, Mo. (†64101) 261/P5
Randolph, Nebr. (68771) 264/G2
Randolph○, N.H. (03593) 268/E3
Randolph○, N.J. (†07801) 273/D2
Randolph, N.Y. (14772) 276/C6
Randolph (co.), N.C. 281/K3
Randolph, Ohio (44265) 284/H3
Randolph, Utah (84064) 304/C2
Randolph, Vt. (05060) 268/B4
Randolph○, Vt. (05060) 268/B4
Randolph, Va. (23962) 307/L7
Randolph (co.), W. Va. 312/G5
Randolph, Wis. (53956) 317/H8
Randolph A.F.B., Texas 303/K10
Randolph Center, Vt. (05061) 268/B4
Random (isl.), Newf. 166/D2
Random (sound), Newf. 166/D2
Random Lake, (53075) 317/K8
Randsburg, Calif. (93554) 204/H8
Randwick, N.S. Wales 88/L4
Randwick, N.S. Wales 97/J3
Ranelagh, Tasmania 99/C4
Ranfurly, Alberta 182/E3
Ranfurly, N. Zealand 100/B6
Rangamati, Bangladesh 68/G4
Rangasa (cape), Indonesia 85/F6
Rangatira (isl.), N. Zealand 100/E7
Range, Ala. (36473) 195/D8
Range (creek), Utah 304/D4
Rangeley, Maine (04970) 243/B6

Reid, Md. (†21740) 245/H2
Reid (lake), S. Dak. 298/O3
Reid (rocks), Tasmania 99/B1
Reid, W. Australia 92/E5
Reiden, Switzerland 39/F2
Reids Grove, Md. (†21869) 245/P6
Reidsville, Georgia (30453) 217/H6
Reidsville, N.C. (27320) 281/K2
Reidville, S.C. (29375) 296/C2
Reigate, England 13/H8
Reigate, England 10/F5
Reile's Acres, N. Dak. (†58078) 282/S6
Reily, Ohio (45060) 284/A7
Re'im, Israel 65/A5
Reims, France 7/E4
Reims, France 28/E3
Reina Adelaida (arch.), Chile 120/B8
Reina Adelaida (arch.), Chile 138/D9
Reinach in Aargau, Switzerland 39/F2
Reinach in Baselland, Switzerland 39/E2
Reinbeck, Iowa (50669) 229/H4
Reindeer (lake) 162/F4
Reindeer (lake), Canada 146/H4
Reindeer (isl.), Manitoba 179/E2
Reindeer (lake), Manitoba 179/H2
Reindeer (lake), Sask. 181/N3
Reindeer (riv.), Sask. 181/M3
Reinersville, Ohio (43756) 284/G6
Reinfeld, W. Germany 22/D2
Reinga (cape), N. Zealand 100/D1
Reinland, Manitoba 179/E5
Reinosa, Spain 33/D1
Reisaelv (riv.), Norway 18/M2
Reisduoddarhal'di (Haltiatunturi), Norway 18/M2
Reiss, Scotland 15/E2
Reisterstown, Md. (21136) 245/L3
Reitz, S. Africa 118/D5
Rejaf, Sudan 111/F7
Reliance, Md. (†19973) 245/P6
Reliance, N.W. Terrs. 187/H3
Reliance, S. Dak. (57569) 298/K6
Reliance, Tenn. (37369) 237/N10
Reliance, Va. (22649) 307/M3
Reliance, Wyo. (82943) 319/C4
Relief, Ky. (41463) 237/P5
Relizane, Algeria 106/E1
Reloncaví (bay), Chile 138/D4
Remada, Tunisia 106/F2
Remagen, W. Germany 22/B3
Remanso, Brazil 132/F5
Remates, Cuba 158/A2
Rembang, Indonesia 85/K2
Rembert, S.C. (29128) 296/G3
Rembrandt, Iowa (50576) 229/C3
Rembrandt, Manitoba 179/E4
Remedios, Colombia 126/C4
Remedios, Cuba 156/B2
Remedios, Cuba 158/E2
Remedios (pt.), El Salvador 154/B4
Remer, Minn. (56672) 255/E3
Remerton, Georgia (31601) 217/F9
Remich, Luxembourg 27/J9
Reminderville, Ohio (†44202) 284/J10
Remington, Ind. (47977) 227/C3
Remington, Ohio (†45202) 284/C9
Remington, Va. (22734) 307/N3
Rémire, Fr. Guiana 131/E3
Rémire (isls.), Fr. Guiana 131/F3
Remiremont, France 28/G3
Remlap, Ala. (35133) 195/E3
Remmel (mt.), Wash. 310/E2
Remo, Br. Col. 184/C3
Remolino, Colombia 126/C2
Remote, Oreg. (97468) 291/D5
Remscheid, W. Germany 22/B3
Remsen, Iowa (51050) 229/B3
Remsen, N.Y. (13438) 276/K4
Remus, Mich. (49340) 250/D5
Remus, Okla. (†74801) 288/N4
Remy, La. (†70763) 238/L3
Rena, Ark. (†72956) 202/B3
Rena, Norway 18/G6
Reñaca, Chile 138/F2
Renaix (Ronse), Belgium 27/D7
Rena Lara, Miss. (38767) 256/C2
Renan, Switzerland 39/C2
Renault, Ill. (62279) 222/C5
Renca, Chile 138/G3
Rencona, N. Mex. (†87562) 274/D3
Rencontre East, Newf. 166/C4
Rend (lake), Ill. 222/E5
Rendeux, Belgium 27/H8
Rendova (isl.), Solomon Is. 86/D3
Rendsburg, W. Germany 22/C1
Rendville, Ohio (†43730) 284/F6
Renens, Switzerland 39/C3
Renews, Newf. 166/D2
Renforth, New Bruns. 170/E3
Renfrew, Ont. 162/J6
Renfrew (county), Ontario 177/G2
Renfrew (county), Ontario 175/E3
Renfrew, Ontario 177/H2
Renfrew, Ontario 175/E3
Renfrew, Pa. (16053) 294/C4
Renfrew, Scotland 10/A1
Renfrew, Scotland 15/B2
Renfrew (trad. co.), Scotland 15/A5
Renfroe, Ala. (†35160) 195/F4
Renfroe, Georgia (†31805) 217/C6
Renfroe, Miss. (†39051) 256/F5
Renfrow, Okla. (†73759) 288/L1
Rengam, Malaysia 72/E5
Rengat, Indonesia 85/C6
Rengo, Chile 138/G5
Reni, U.S.S.R. 52/C5
Renick, Mo. (65278) 261/H4
Renick, W. Va. (24966) 312/F6
Renigunta, India 68/E6
Renish (pt.), Scotland 15/B3
Renk, Sudan 111/F5
Renkum, Netherlands 27/H5
Renmark, S. Australia 88/G6
Renmark, S. Australia 94/G5
Rennell (isl.), Solomon Is. 87/F7
Rennell (isl.), Solomon Is. 86/E3
Renner, S. Dak. (57055) 298/R6
Rennert, N.C. (†28386) 281/L5
Rennes, France 7/D4
Rennes, France 28/C3
Rennie, Manitoba 179/G5
Rennie (lake), N.W. Terrs. 187/H3
Renno, S.C. (†29325) 296/D2
Reno, Alberta 182/B2
Reno, Georgia (†31728) 217/D9
Reno, Ill. (†62086) 222/D5
Reno (co.), Kansas 232/D4
Reno (lake), Minn. 255/C5
Reno, Nev. 146/G6
Reno, Nev. 188/C3
Reno, Nev. (*89501) 266/B3
Reno, Ohio (45773) 284/H7
Reno, Texas (†76020) 303/E2
Reno Beach, Ohio (†43412) 284/D2
Renous, New Bruns. 170/E2
Renous (riv.), New Bruns. 170/D2
Renova, Miss. (†38732) 256/C3
Renovo, Pa. (17764) 294/G3
Renown, Sask. 181/F4
Rensburg, S. Africa 118/J7
Rensselaer, Ind. (47978) 227/C3
Rensselaer, Mo. (†63401) 261/J3
Rensselaer (co.), N.Y. 276/O5
Rensselaer, N.Y. (12144) 276/N5
Rensselaer Falls, N.Y. (13680) 276/K1
Rentchler, Ill. (†62220) 222/B3
Rentiesville, Okla. (74459) 288/R4
Renton, Scotland 15/A1
Renton, Wash. (98055) 310/B2
Rentz, Georgia (31075) 217/G6
Renville (co.), Minn. 255/C6
Renville, Minn. (56284) 255/C6
Renville (co.), N. Dak. 282/G2
Renwer, Manitoba 179/B2
Renwick, Iowa (50577) 229/E3
Répcelak, 41/D3
Repentigny, Québec 172/J4
Replete, W. Va. (†26222) 312/F5
Repos (lake), Québec 172/C2
Repton, Ala. (36475) 195/D8
Republic, Ala. (†35203) 195/E3
Republic (co.), Kansas 232/E2
Republic, Kansas (66964) 232/E2
Republic, Mich. (49879) 250/B2
Republic, Mo. (65738) 261/E8
Republic, Ohio (44867) 284/D3
Republic, Wash. (99166) 310/G2
República Dominicana, Cuba 158/F2
Republican (riv.) 188/F2
Republican (riv.), Colo. 208/P3
Republican (riv.), Kansas 232/E2
Republican (riv.), Nebr. 264/G5
Republican City, Nebr. (68971) 264/E4
Republican Grove, Va. (24585) 307/K7
Repulse (bay), Queensland 88/H4
Repulse Bay, Canada 4/C14
Repulse Bay, N.W.T. 162/H2
Repulse Bay, N.W. Terrs. 187/K3
Requa, Calif. (†95548) 204/A2
Requegua, Chile 138/G5
Requena, Peru 128/F5
Requena, Spain 33/F3
Requinoa, Chile 138/G5
Rera, Brazil 132/A1
Resaca, Georgia (30735) 217/C1
Reşadiye, Turkey 63/G2
Research, Victoria 97/J4
Reseda, Calif. (91335) 204/B10
Resende, Brazil 135/D3
Resende, Portugal 33/B2
Reserve, Kansas (66529) 232/G2
Reserve, La. (70084) 238/M3
Reserve, Mont. (59258) 262/M2
Reserve, N. Mex. (87830) 274/A5
Reserve, Sask. 181/J3
Reserve, Wis. (†54876) 317/D4
Reserve Mines, Nova Scotia 168/H2
Resht (Rasht), Iran 66/F2
Reshui, China 77/E4
Resistencia, Argentina 143/E2
Resistencia, Argentina 120/D5
Reşiţa, Romania 45/E3
Resolute, Canada 4/B14
Resolute Bay, N.W.T. 162/G1
Resolute Bay, N.W. Terrs. 187/J2
Resolution (isl.), N.W.T. 146/M3
Resolution (isl.), N.W.T. 162/K3
Resolution (isl.), N. Zealand 100/A6
Resolution (isl.), N.W. Terrs. 187/M3
Resolution Island, N.W. Terrs. 187/M3
Resort, Loch (inlet), Scotland 15/A2
Resource, Sask. 181/G3
Respenda de la Peña, Spain 33/D1
Restauración, Dom. Rep. 158/D5
Rest Haven, Georgia (†30518) 217/E2
Restigouche (co.), New Bruns. 170/C1
Restigouche (riv.), New Bruns. 170/C1
Restigouche, Québec 172/C2
Reston, Manitoba 179/A5
Reston, Va. (22090) 307/R2
Restoule, Ontario 177/E1
Restoule (lake), Ontario 177/E1
Restrepo, Colombia 126/D5
Reszel, Poland 47/E1
Retalhuleu, Guatemala 154/B3
Retamosa, Uruguay 145/E4
Rethel, France 28/F3
Réthimnon, Greece 45/G8
Retie, Belgium 27/G6
Retiro, Chile 138/A11
Retlaw, Alberta 182/D4
Rétság, Hungary 41/E3
Retsil, Wash. (98378) 310/A2
Retsof, N.Y. (14539) 276/E5
Retz, Austria 41/D2
Reubens, Idaho (83548) 220/B3
Réunion (isl.), (Fr.) 2/M7
RÉUNION 118/F5
Reus, Spain 33/G2
Reusel, Netherlands 27/G6
Reuss (riv.), Switzerland 39/F2
Reutlingen, W. Germany 22/C4
Reutte, Austria 41/A3
Reva, S. Dak. (57651) 298/C2
Revadim, Israel 65/B4
Reveille (peak), Nev. 266/E5
Reveille (range), Nev. 266/E4
Revel, France 28/E6
Revel (Tallinn), U.S.S.R. 52/B3
Revelo, Ky. (42638) 237/N7
Revelstoke, Br. Col. 162/E5
Revelstoke, Br. Col. 184/J5
Reventazón, Peru 128/B6
Revenue, Sask. 181/B3
Revere, Mass. (02151) 249/D6
Revere, Minn. (56166) 255/C6
Revere, Mo. (63465) 261/J2
Revere, N. Dak. (†58484) 282/O5
Revere, W. Va. (†26158) 312/E5
Reverie, Tenn. (38062) 237/A9
Revillagigedo (chan.), Alaska 196/N2
Revillagigedo (isl.), Alaska 196/N2
Revillagigedo (isls.), Mexico 146/G8
Revillagigedo (isls.), Mexico 2/D5
Revillagigedo (isls.), Mexico 150/C7
Revillo, S. Dak. (57259) 298/R3
Révin, France 28/F3
Revivim, Israel 65/D5
Revúca, Czech. 41/F2
Revuelto (creek), N. Mex. 274/F3
Rew, Pa. (16744) 294/F2
Rewa, India 68/E4
Reward, Sask. 181/B3
Rewataya (reef), Indonesia 85/F7
Rewey, Wis. (53580) 317/F10
Rex, N.C. (28378) 281/M5
Rex, Oreg. (†97132) 291/A2
Rexburg, Idaho (83440) 220/G6
Rexford, Kansas (67753) 232/B2
Rexford, Mont. (59930) 262/A2
Rexton, Mich. (†49734) 250/D2
Rexton, New Bruns. 170/F2
Rexville, Ind. (†47250) 227/G7
Rexville, N.Y. (14877) 276/E6
Rey, Iran 59/F2
Rey, Iran 66/G3
Rey (isl.), Panama 154/H6
Rey Bouba, Cameroon 115/B2
Reydell, Ark. (72133) 202/G5
Reydon, Okla. (73660) 288/G3
Reyes, Bolivia 136/B4
Reyes (pt.), Calif. 204/B6
Reyhanlı, Turkey 63/G4
Reykjanestá (cape), Iceland 7/B2
Reykjanestá (cape), Iceland 21/A2
Reykjavík (cap.), Iceland 4/C11
Reykjavík (cap.), Iceland 2/J2
Reykjavík (cap.), Iceland 21/B1
Reykjavík (cap.), Iceland 7/B2
Reynaud, Sask. 181/F3
Reyno, Ark. (72462) 202/J1
Reynolds, Georgia (31076) 217/D5
Reynolds (creek), Idaho 220/B6
Reynolds, Ill. (61279) 222/C2
Reynolds, Ind. (47980) 227/D3
Reynolds (co.), Mo. 261/L8
Reynolds, Mo. (63666) 261/K8
Reynolds, Nebr. (68429) 264/G4
Reynolds, N. Dak. (58275) 282/R4
Reynolds Bridge, Conn. (†06787) 210/C2
Reynoldsburg, Ohio (43068) 284/E6
Reynolds Station, Ky. (42368) 237/H5
Reynoldsville, Pa. (15851) 294/D3
Reynosa, Mexico 150/K3
Rezaiyeh (Urmia), Iran 66/D2
Reza'iyeh (Urmia), Iran 59/D2
Rezé, France 28/C4
Rēzekne, U.S.S.R. 52/C3
Rēzekne, U.S.S.R. 53/D2
Rhaetian Alps (range), Switzerland 39/J3
Rhame, N. Dak. (58651) 282/C7
Rhätikon (mts.), Liecht. 39/J2
Rhätikon (mts.), Switzerland 39/J2
Rhayader, Wales 13/D5
Rhea (creek), Oreg. 291/H2
Rhea (co.), Tenn. 237/M9
Rheatown, Tenn. (†37641) 237/R8
Rheda-Wiedenbrück, W. Germany 22/C3
Rheden, Netherlands 27/J4
Rheims (Reims), France 28/E4
Rhein, Sask. 181/J4
Rheinau, Switzerland 39/G1
Rheine, W. Germany 22/B2
Rheineck, Switzerland 39/J2
Rheinfeld, Sask. 181/D5
Rheinfelden, Switzerland 39/E1
Rheinfelden, W. Germany 22/B5
Rheinsberg, E. Germany 22/E2
Rheinwaldhorn (mt.), Switzerland 39/G4
Rhems, S.C. (†29440) 296/H4
Rhenen, Netherlands 27/H5
Rhéris, Wadi (dry riv.), Morocco 106/D2
Rheydt, W. Germany 22/B3
Rhine (riv.) 7/E4
Rhine (riv.), Austria 41/A3
Rhine (riv.), France 28/G3
Rhine, Georgia (31077) 217/F7
Rhine (riv.), Liecht. 39/J2
Rhine (riv.), Netherlands 27/J5
Rhine (riv.), Switzerland 39/J2
Rhine (riv.), W. Germany 22/B3
Rhinebeck, N.Y. (12572) 276/N7
Rhinecliff, N.Y. (12574) 276/N7
Rhineland, Mo. (65069) 261/J5
Rhineland, Sask. 181/D5
Rhinelander, Wis. (54501) 317/H4
Rhineland-Palatinate (state), W. Germany 22/B4
Rhinns, The (pen.), Scotland 15/C6
Rhinns (pt.), Scotland 15/B5
Rhino Camp, Uganda 115/F3
Rhir, Wadi (dry riv.), Algeria 106/F2
Rhir (cape), Morocco 106/B2
Rho, Italy 34/B2
Rhode Island 188/M2
RHODE ISLAND 249
Rhode Island (isl.), R.I. 249/J6
Rhode Island (sound), R.I. 249/J7
Rhode Island (state), U.S. 146/M5
Rhodell, W. Va. (25915) 312/D7
Rhodes (Ródhos), Greece 45/J7
Rhodes (isl.), Greece 7/G5
Rhodes (isl.), Greece 45/H7
Rhodes (peak), Idaho 220/D3
Rhodes, Iowa (50234) 229/G5
Rhodes, Mich. (48652) 250/E5
Rhodes Inyanga Nat'l Park, Zimbabwe 118/E3
Rhodes Point, Md. (21858) 245/O9
Rhodhiss, N.C. (28667) 281/F3
Rhododendron, Oreg. (97073) 291/F2
Rhodope (mts.), Bulgaria 45/G5
Rhodope (mts.), Greece 45/G5
Rhome, Texas (76078) 303/E1
Rhön (mts.), E. Germany 22/D3
Rhön (mts.), W. Germany 22/D3
Rhondda, Wales 13/A6
Rhondda, Wales 10/E5
Rhône (dept.), France 28/F5
Rhône (riv.), France 7/E4
Rhône (riv.), France 28/F5
Rhône (riv.), Switzerland 39/D4
Rhosllanerchrugog, Wales 13/D4
Rhu, Scotland 15/A1
Rhu Coigeach (cape), Scotland 15/C2
Rhyl, Wales 13/D4
Rhymney, Wales 13/A6
Rhymney (riv.), Wales 13/B6
Rhynie, Scotland 15/F3
Rhyolite (Ghost Town), Nev. (†89003) 266/E6
Riachão, Brazil 132/E4
Riachuelo, Uruguay 145/B5
Rialto, Calif. (92376) 204/E10
Riana, Tasmania 99/B3
Riaño, Spain 33/D1
Riau (arch.), Indonesia 85/C5
Riaza, Spain 33/E2
Rib (mt.), Wis. 317/G6
Ribadavia, Spain 33/B1
Ribadeo, Spain 33/C1
Ribamar, Brazil 132/F3
Ribas do Rio Pardo, Brazil 132/C8
Ribat Qila, Pakistan 68/A3
Ribat Qila, Pakistan 59/H4
Ribáuè, Mozambique 118/F3
Ribble (riv.), England 10/E4
Ribble (riv.), England 13/E4
Ribe (co.), Denmark 21/B7
Ribe, Denmark 21/B7
Ribe, Denmark 18/F9
Ribeira, Brazil 135/B4
Ribeira (riv.), Brazil 135/B4
Ribeira Brava, Portugal 33/A2
Ribeira de Iguape, Brazil 135/C4
Ribeira de Pena, Portugal 33/C2
Ribeira Grande, C. Verde 106/B7
Ribeirão Preto, Brazil 120/E5
Ribeirão Preto, Brazil 135/C2
Ribeirão Preto, Brazil 132/E8
Ribera, N. Mex. (87560) 274/D3
Ribérac, France 28/D5
Riberach an der Riss, W. Germany 22/C4
Riberalta, Bolivia 136/C2
Riberalta, Bolivia 120/C4
Rib Falls, Wis. (†54426) 317/G6
Ribla, Kuh-e (riv.), Iran 66/J6
Rib Lake, Wis. (54470) 317/F5
Ribnitz-Damgarten, E. Germany 22/E1
Ribstone, Alberta 182/E3
Říčany u Prahy, Czech. 41/C2
Ricaurte, Colombia 126/A7
Riccarton, N. Zealand 100/D5
Rice, Calif. (†92280) 204/L9
Rice (co.), Kansas 232/D3
Rice, Kansas (66965) 232/E2
Rice (co.), Minn. 255/E6
Rice, Minn. (56367) 255/D5
Rice (lake), Minn. 255/E4
Rice (mt.), N.H. 268/E2
Rice (lake), Ontario 177/F3
Rice, Texas (75155) 303/H5
Rice, Va. (23966) 307/M6
Rice, Wash. (99167) 310/G2
Riceboro, Georgia (31323) 217/K7
Rice Lake, Wis. (54868) 317/C5
Rices Landing, Pa. (15357) 294/C6
Riceton, Sask. 181/G5
Ricetown, Ky. (41364) 237/O6
Riceville, Iowa (50466) 229/H2
Riceville, Pa. (16432) 294/C2
Riceville, Tenn. (37370) 237/M10
Rich, Miss. (38662) 256/D2
Rich (cape), Ontario 177/D3
Rich (co.), Utah 304/C2
Richard, Sask. 181/D3
Richard City, Tenn. (†37380) 237/K11
Richard Collinson (inlet), N.W. Terrs. 187/G2
Richards, Iowa (†50579) 229/D4
Richards, Mo. (64778) 261/D7
Richards (isl.), N.W. Terrs. 187/E3
Richards Bay, S. Africa 118/E5
Richards Gebaur A.F.B., Mo. 261/P6
Richards Landing, Ontario 177/J5
Richardson (riv.), Alberta 182/C5
Richardson, Ky. (41253) 237/R5
Richardson (lakes), Maine 243/B6
Richardson (co.), Nebr. 264/J4
Richardson (isls.), N.W. Terrs. 187/G3
Richardson (mts.), N.W. Terrs. 187/E3
Richardson, Sask. 181/G5
Richardson, Texas (75080) 303/G2
Richardson, W. Va. (†26151) 312/D5
Richardson (mts.), Yukon 187/E3
Richardsons Landing, Tenn. (†38023) 237/B10
Richardsville, Ky. (42270) 237/J6
Richardsville, New Bruns. 170/E1
Richard Toll, Senegal 106/A5
Richardton, N. Dak. (58652) 282/F6
Richburg, N.Y. (14774) 276/D6
Richburg, S.C. (29729) 296/E2
Rich Creek, Va. (24147) 307/G6
Richdale, Alberta 182/E4
Riche (pt.), Newf. 166/C3
Richelieu, Ky. (42271) 237/H7
Richelieu (co.), Québec 172/D4
Richelieu, Québec 172/D4
Richer, Manitoba 179/F5
Richey, Mont. (59259) 262/L3
Richfield, Idaho (83349) 220/D6
Richfield, Kansas (67953) 232/A4
Richfield, Minn. (55423) 255/G6
Richfield, N.C. (28137) 281/J4
Richfield, Nova Scotia 168/C4
Richfield, Ohio (44286) 284/G3
Richfield, Pa. (17086) 294/H4
Richfield, Utah (84701) 304/B5
Richfield, Wis. (53076) 317/K1
Richfield Springs, N.Y. (13439) 276/K5
Richford, N.Y. (13835) 276/H6
Richford, Vt. (05476) 268/B2
Richford○, Vt. (05476) 268/B2
Richford, Wis. (†53930) 317/H7
Rich Fountain, Mo. (65070) 261/J6
Richgrove, Calif. (93261) 204/F8
Rich Hill, Mo. (64779) 261/D6
Richhill, N. Ireland 17/H3
Richibucto, New Bruns. 170/E2
Richibucto (harb.), New Bruns. 170/F2
Richibucto (riv.), New Bruns. 170/E2
Richibucto Village, New Bruns. 170/F2
Rich Lake, Alberta 182/E2
Richland, Fla. (†33599) 212/D3
Richland, Georgia (31825) 217/C6
Richland (co.), Ill. 222/E5
Richland, Ind. (47634) 227/C9
Richland (creek), Ind. 227/D6
Richland, Iowa (52585) 229/K6
Richland, Kansas (†66409) 232/G3
Richland (par.), La. 238/G2
Richland, Mich. (49083) 250/D6
Richland, Miss. (†39218) 256/D6
Richland, Mo. (65556) 261/H7
Richland (co.), Mont. 262/M3
Richland, Mont. (59260) 262/K2
Richland, Nebr. (68657) 264/G3
Richland, N.J. (08350) 273/D5
Richland, N.Y. (13144) 276/H3
Richland (co.), N. Dak. 282/R7
Richland (co.), Ohio 284/E4
Richland, Oreg. (97870) 291/K3
Richland, Pa. (17087) 294/K5
Richland (co.), S.C. 296/F4
Richland, S.C. (29675) 296/A2
Richland, S. Dak. (†57025) 298/R8
Richland (creek), Tenn. 237/G10
Richland, Texas (76681) 303/H6
Richland, Wash. 188/B1
Richland, Wash. (99352) 310/F4
Richland (co.), Wis. 317/F9
Richland Balsam (mt.), N.C. 281/D4
Richland Center, Wis. (53581) 317/F9
Richland Hills, Texas (76118) 303/F2
Richland-Kennewick, Wash. 310/80
Richlands, N.C. (28574) 281/O5
Richlands, Va. (24641) 307/E6
Richland Springs, Texas (76871) 303/F6
Richlandtown, Pa. (18955) 294/M5
Richlea, Sask. 181/C4
Richmond, Ala. (†36761) 195/D6
Richmond, Ark. (†71822) 202/B6
Richmond, Br. Col. 184/K3
Richmond, Calif. (*94801) 204/J1
Richmond, England 13/F3
Richmond, England 10/E3
Richmond (co.), Georgia 217/H4
Richmond, Ill. (60071) 222/E1
Richmond, Ind. (47374) 227/H5
Richmond, Iowa (52247) 229/K6
Richmond, Jamaica 158/J6
Richmond, Kansas (66080) 232/G3
Richmond, Ky. (40475) 237/N5
Richmond, La. (†71282) 238/H2
Richmond, Maine (04357) 243/D7
Richmond○, Maine (04357) 243/D7
Richmond○, Mass. (01254) 249/A3
Richmond, Mich. (48062) 250/G6
Richmond, Minn. (56368) 255/D5
Richmond, Mo. (64085) 261/D4
Richmond○, N.H. (†03470) 268/C6
Richmond (range), N.S. Wales 97/G1
Richmond (riv.), N.S. Wales 97/G1
Richmond (co.), N.Y. 276/M9
Richmond (Staten Island) (borough), N.Y. 276/M9
Richmond, N. Zealand 100/D4
Richmond (range), N. Zealand 100/D4
Richmond (co.), N.C. 281/K4
Richmond (co.), Nova Scotia 168/H3
Richmond (Grand River), Ohio (†44045) 284/H2
Richmond, Ohio (43944) 284/J5
Richmond, Ontario 177/J2
Richmond (co.), Québec 172/E4
Richmond, Québec 172/E4
Richmond, Queensland 88/G4
Richmond, Queensland 95/B4
Richmond (peak), St. Vin. & Grens. 161/A8
Richmond, S. Africa 118/C6
Richmond, Tasmania 99/D4
Richmond, Texas (77469) 303/J8
Richmond, Utah (84333) 304/C2
Richmond, Vt. (05477) 268/A3
Richmond○, Vt. (05477) 268/A3
Richmond, Victoria 88/L7
Richmond, Victoria 97/J5
Richmond (cap.), Va. 188/L3
Richmond (cap.), Va. 146/L6
Richmond (co.), Va. 307/P5
Richmond (cap.) (I.C.), Va. (*23201) 307/O5
Richmond Beach-Innis Arden, Wash. (98160) 310/A1
Richmond Corner, Maine (†04357) 243/D7
Richmond Corner, New Bruns. 170/C2
Richmond Dale, Ohio (45673) 284/E7
Richmond Furnace, Mass. (†01254) 249/A3
Richmond Heights, Fla. (†33158) 212/F6
Richmond Heights, Mo. (63117) 261/P3
Richmond Heights, Ohio (44143) 284/H9
Richmond Highlands, Wash. (†98133) 310/A1
Richmond Hill, Georgia (31324) 217/K7
Richmond Hill, Ontario 177/J4
Richmond Nat'l Battlefield Park, Va. 307/O6
Richmond upon Thames, England 10/B5
Richmond upon Thames, England 13/H8
Richmondville, N.Y. (12149) 276/M5
Richmond-Windsor, N.S. Wales 97/F3
Richmound, Sask. 181/B5
Rich Mountain, Ark. (†71953) 202/B4
Rich Square, N.C. (27869) 281/P2
Richterswil, Switzerland 39/G2
Richthofen (mt.), Colo. 208/G2
Richton, Miss. (39476) 256/G8
Richton Park, Ill. (60471) 222/B6
Richvale, Calif. (95974) 204/D4
Richvalley, Ind. (†46992) 227/F3
Richview, Ill. (62877) 222/D5
Richville, Mich. (48758) 250/F5
Richville, Minn. (56576) 255/C4
Richville, N.Y. (13681) 276/K2
Richwood, La. (†71201) 238/F2
Richwood, Minn. (56577) 255/C4
Richwood, N.J. (08074) 273/C4
Richwood, Ohio (43344) 284/D5
Richwood, W. Va. (26261) 312/F6
Richwood, Wis. (†53094) 317/J9
Richwoods, Mo. (63071) 261/L6
Rickardsville, Iowa (†52039) 229/M3
Rickenbacker Air Force Base, Ohio 284/E6
Ricketts, Iowa (51460) 229/B4
Ricketts (pt.), Victoria 97/J6
Ricketts (pt.), Victoria 88/L8
Rickman, Tenn. (38580) 237/L8
Rickmansworth, England 13/G8
Rickmansworth, England 10/A5
Rickreall, Oreg. (97371) 291/D3
Ricla, Spain 33/F2
Rico, Colo. (81332) 208/C7
Ricobayo (res.), Spain 33/D2
Ricse, Hungary 41/G2
Ridderkerk, Netherlands 27/F5
Riddle, Idaho (†89832) 220/B7
Riddle, Oreg. (97469) 291/D5
Riddlesburg, Pa. (16672) 294/F5
Riddleton, Tenn. (37151) 237/J8
Riddleville, Georgia (†31018) 217/G5
Riddon, Loch (inlet), Scotland 15/C5
Rideau (lake), Ontario 177/H3
Riderwood, Ala. (†36904) 195/B6
Ridge, Md. (20680) 245/N8
Ridge, Mont. (†59314) 262/M5
Ridgecrest, Calif. (93555) 204/H8
Ridgecrest, La. (†71334) 238/G3
Ridgedale, Mo. (65739) 261/F9
Ridgedale, Sask. 181/H2
Ridge Farm, Ill. (61870) 222/F4
Ridgefield, Conn. (06877) 210/B3
Ridgefield○, Conn. (06877) 210/B3
Ridgefield, N.J. (07657) 273/B2
Ridgefield, Wash. (98642) 310/C5
Ridgefield Park, N.J. (07660) 273/B2
Ridgeland, Miss. (39157) 256/D6
Ridgeland, S.C. (29936) 296/E7
Ridgeland, Wis. (54763) 317/B5
Ridgeley, W. Va. (26753) 312/J3
Ridgely, Md. (21660) 245/P5
Ridgely, Mo. (†64444) 261/C4
Ridgely, Tenn. (38080) 237/B8
Ridgeside, Tenn. (†37401) 237/L10
Ridge Spring, S.C. (29129) 296/D4
Ridgetop, Tenn. (37152) 237/H8
Ridgetown, Ontario 177/C5
Ridgeview, S. Dak. (57652) 298/H3
Ridgeville, Georgia (†31331) 217/K8
Ridgeville, Ind. (47380) 227/G4
Ridgeville, Manitoba 179/E5
Ridgeville, S.C. (29472) 296/G5
Ridgeville Corners, Ohio (43555) 284/B3
Ridgeway, Iowa (52165) 229/K2
Ridgeway, Minn. (†55943) 255/G7
Ridgeway, Mo. (64481) 261/D2
Ridgeway, N.C. (27570) 281/N2
Ridgeway, Ohio (43345) 284/C4
Ridgeway, S.C. (29130) 296/F3
Ridgeway, Va. (24148) 307/J7
Ridgeway, W. Va. (25440) 312/K4
Ridgeway, Wis. (53582) 317/F10
Ridgeway Branch, Toms (riv.), N.J. 273/E3
Ridgewood, N.J. (*07450) 273/B1
Ridgley, Tasmania 99/B3
Ridgway, Colo. (81432) 208/D6
Ridgway, Ill. (62979) 222/E6
Ridgway, Pa. (15853) 294/E3
Ridi, Nepal 68/E3
Riding (mt.), Manitoba 179/B4
Riding Mountain, Manitoba 179/C4
Riding Mountain Nat'l Park, Man. 162/F5
Riding Mountain Nat'l Park, Manitoba 179/B4
Ridley, Tenn. (†38474) 237/G9
Ridley Park, Pa. (19078) 294/M7
Ridott, Ill. (61067) 222/D1
Ridotto, Iowa (†50546) 229/D3
Ried im Innkreis, Austria 41/B2
Riegelsville, N.J. (†08865) 273/C2
Riegelsville, Pa. (18077) 294/M4
Riegelwood, N.C. (28456) 281/N6
Riehen, Switzerland 39/E1
Rienzi, Miss. (38865) 256/G1
Riesa, E. Germany 22/E3
Riesco (isl.), Chile 138/E10
Riesel, Texas (76682) 303/H6
Riesi, Italy 34/E6
Rietavas, U.S.S.R. 53/A3
Rietberg, W. Germany 22/C3
Rietfontein, Namibia 118/C4
Rieth, Oreg. (†97801) 291/J2
Rieti (prov.), Italy 34/D3
Rieti, Italy 34/D3
Rif, Er (range), Morocco 106/D2

436 Riffelalp

Riffelalp, Switzerland 39/E5
Rifle, Colo. (81650) 208/D3
Rifle (creek), Colo. 208/D3
Rifle (riv.), Mich. 250/E4
Rifle (lake), Wash. 310/C4
Rifstangi (cape), Iceland 21/C1
Rift Valley (prov.), Kenya 115/G3
Riga (lake), Conn. 210/B1
Riga, U.S.S.R. 2/L3
Riga, U.S.S.R. 7/G3
Riga (gulf), U.S.S.R. 7/G3
Riga (cap.), U.S.S.R. 53/C2
Riga, U.S.S.R. 48/C4
Riga, U.S.S.R. 52/B3
Riga (gulf), U.S.S.R. 52/B3
Riga (gulf), U.S.S.R. 53/B2
Riga (gulf), U.S.S.R. 48/C4
Rigan, Iran 66/L6
Rigaud, Québec 172/C4
Rigby, Idaho (83442) 220/F6
Rigdon, Ind. (†46928) 227/F4
Rigestan (reg.), Afghanistan 59/H3
Riggins, Idaho (83549) 220/B4
Riggisberg, Switzerland 39/E3
Rigi (mt.), Switzerland 39/F2
Rigo, Papua N.G. 85/C7
Rigolet, Newf. 166/C3
Rigolet, Newf. 162/L5
Rig Rig, Chad 111/B5
Rigside, Scotland 15/E5
Riihimäki, Finland 18/O6
Riiser-Larsen (pen.), Ant. 2/L9
Riiser-Larsen (pen.) 5/C2
Rijeka, Yugoslavia 45/B3
Rijeka, Yugoslavia 7/F4
Rijen, Netherlands 27/F5
Rijnsburg, Netherlands 27/F4
Rijssen, Netherlands 27/J4
Rijswijk, Netherlands 27/E4
Rikitea, Fr. Poly. 87/N8
Rikuchu-Kaigan National Park, Japan 81/L4
Rikuzentakata, Japan 81/K4
Riley, Ind. (47871) 227/C6
Riley (co.), Kansas 232/F2
Riley, Kansas (66531) 232/F2
Riley, Ky. (†40328) 237/L5
Riley, Maine (†04262) 243/C6
Riley, Oreg. (97758) 291/H4
Riley Brook, New Bruns. 170/C1
Rileysburg, Ind. (†47932) 227/B4
Rillito, Ariz. (85246) 198/D6
Rillton, Pa. (15678) 294/C5
Rima (riv.), Niger 106/F6
Rima (riv.), Nigeria 106/F6
Rima, Wadi (dry riv.), Saudi Arabia 59/D4
Rímac (riv.), Peru 128/D9
Rimal, Ar (des.), Saudi Arabia 59/F5
Rimatara (isl.), Fr. Poly. 87/L8
Rimavská Sobota, Czech. 41/E2
Rimbey, Alberta 182/C3
Rimbo, Sweden 18/L7
Rimersburg, Pa. (16248) 294/D3
Rimini, Italy 34/D2
Rimini, S.C. (29131) 296/G4
Rîmnicu Sărat, Romania 45/H3
Rîmnicu Vîlcea, Romania 45/G3
Rimouski, Que. 162/K6
Rimouski (co.), Québec 172/J1
Rimouski (county), Québec 174/D3
Rimouski, Québec 172/J1
Rimouski, Québec 174/D3
Rimouski (riv.), Québec 172/J1
Rimouski-Est, Québec 172/J1
Rimpfischhorn (mt.), Switzerland 39/E4
Rimrock, Ariz. (86335) 198/D4
Rimrock (lake), Wash. 310/D4
Rimutaka (range), N. Zealand 100/B3
Rinard, Ill. (62878) 222/E5
Rinard, Iowa (50587) 229/D4
Rincón, Cerro (mt.), Argentina 143/C1
Rincon (peak), Ariz. 198/E6
Rincón, Cerro (mt.), Chile 138/C4
Rincón, Dom. Rep. 158/E5
Rincón (bay), Dom. Rep. 158/F5
Rincon, Georgia (31326) 217/K6
Rincon, Neth. Ant. 161/E8
Rincon, N. Mex. (87940) 274/C6
Rincón (pt.), Panama 154/G6
Rincón, P. Rico 161/A1
Rincón (bay), P. Rico 161/D3
Rinconada, Argentina 143/C1
Rinconada San Martín, Chile 138/G2
Rincón de Romos, Mexico 150/H5
Rindge○, N.H. (03461) 268/C6
Riner, Va. (24149) 307/H6
Rineyville, Ky. (40162) 237/K5
Ringarooma, Tasmania 99/D3
Ringarooma (bay), Tasmania 99/D2
Ringe, Denmark 21/D7
Ringebu, Norway 18/G6
Ringelspitz (mt.), Switzerland 39/H3
Ringerike, Norway 18/C3
Ringgold, Georgia (30736) 217/B1
Ringgold (co.), Iowa 229/E7
Ringgold, La. (71068) 238/D2
Ringgold, Md. (†21783) 245/H2
Ringgold, Nebr. (†69167) 264/D3
Ringgold, Texas (76261) 303/G4
Ringgold, Va. (24586) 307/K7
Ringim, Nigeria 106/F6
Ringkøbing (co.), Denmark 21/B5
Ringkøbing, Denmark 18/E8
Ringkøbing, Denmark 21/A5
Ringkøbing (fjord), Denmark 21/B6
Ringling, Mont. (59642) 262/F4
Ringling, Okla. (73456) 288/L6
Ringmer, England 13/H7
Ringoes, N.J. (08551) 273/D3
Ringold, Okla. (74754) 288/R6
Ringsted, Denmark 21/E7
Ringsted, Iowa (50578) 229/D2
Ringtown, Pa. (17967) 294/K4
Ringvassøy (isl.), Norway 18/L2
Ringwood, England 13/F7
Ringwood, Ill. (60072) 222/E1
Ringwood, N.J. (07456) 273/E1
Ringwood, N.C. (†27823) 281/O2
Ringwood, North. Terr. 93/D7
Ringwood, Okla. (73768) 288/K2
Ringwood, Victoria 88/M7
Ringwood, Victoria 97/K5
Rinn (lake), Ireland 17/F4
Rinteln, W. Germany 22/C2
Rio, Ill. (61472) 222/C2
Rio, La. (†70427) 238/L5
Rio, W. Va. (26755) 312/J4
Rio, Wis. (53960) 317/H9
Rio Arriba (co.), N. Mex. 274/B2
Riobamba, Ecuador 128/C3
Riobamba, Ecuador 120/B3
Río Blanco, Chile 138/B9
Rio Blanco (co.), Colo. 208/C3
Rio Blanco, Colo. (†81650) 208/C3
Río Blanco, P. Rico 161/F2
Rio Bonito, Brazil 135/E3
Rio Branco, Brazil 120/C3
Rio Branco, Brazil 132/G10
Río Branco, Uruguay 145/F3
Rio Brazos (riv.), N. Mex. 274/C2
Rio Brilhante, Brazil 132/C8
Río Bueno, Chile 138/D3
Rio Bueno, Jamaica 158/H5
Río Caribe, Venezuela 124/G2
Río Cauto, Cuba 158/H4
Rio Chama (riv.), N. Mex. 274/C2
Río Chico, Venezuela 124/F2
Río Cisnes, Chile 138/E5
Rio Claro, Brazil 132/E8
Rio Claro, Brazil 135/C3
Rio Claro, Trin. & Tob. 161/B11
Río Claro, Venezuela 124/D3
Río Colorado, Argentina 120/C6
Río Colorado, La Pampa, Argentina 143/D4
Río Colorado, Río Negro, Argentina 143/D4
Rio Creek, Wis. (54231) 317/L6
Río Cuarto, Argentina 143/D3
Río Cuarto, Argentina 120/C6
Rio de Janeiro (state), Brazil 135/E3
Rio de Janeiro (state), Brazil 132/F8
Rio de Janeiro, Brazil 2/G7
Rio de Janeiro, Brazil 120/E5
Rio de Janeiro, Brazil 135/E3
Rio de Janeiro, Brazil 132/F8
Rio Dell, Calif. (95562) 204/A3
Río de Oro, Colombia 126/D3
Rio do Sul, Brazil 132/D9
Rio Felix (riv.), N. Mex. 274/E5
Río Gallegos, Argentina 120/C8
Río Gallegos, Argentina 143/C7
Rio Grande (riv.) 2/D4
Rio Grande (riv.) 146/H7
Rio Grande (riv.) 188/F5
Río Grande, Argentina 143/C7
Río Grande, Bolivia 136/B7
Rio Grande, Brazil 120/D6
Rio Grande, Brazil 132/D11
Rio Grande (co.), Colo. 208/G7
Rio Grande (res.), Colo. 208/E7
Rio Grande (riv.), Colo. 208/H8
Rio Grande, N.J. (08242) 273/D5
Rio Grande (riv.), N. Mex. 274/C5
Rio Grande, Ohio (45674) 284/F8
Río Grande, P. Rico 161/E1
Rio Grande (riv.), Texas 303/D9
Rio Grande City, Texas (78582) 303/F11
Rio Grande do Norte (state), Brazil 132/G4
Rio Grande do Sul (state), Brazil 132/C10
Rio Grande Pyramid (mt.), Colo. 208/E7
Rio Grande Wild and Scenic River, Texas 303/B8
Riohacha, Colombia 120/B1
Riohacha, Colombia 126/D2
Río Hondo, Guatemala 154/C3
Rio Hondo (riv.), N. Mex. 274/E5
Rio Hondo, Texas (78583) 303/G11
Rioja, Peru 128/D6
Río Lagartos, Mexico 150/P6
Rio Linda, Calif. (95673) 204/B8
Rio Maior, Portugal 33/B3
Río Mulato, Bolivia 136/B6
Río Muni (terr.), Equat. Guinea 115/B3
Rion, S.C. (29132) 296/E3
Riondel, Br. Col. 184/J5
Río Negro (prov.), Argentina 143/C5
Rio Negro, Brazil 132/D9
Río Negro, Chile 138/D3
Rionegro, Antioquia, Colombia 126/C4
Rionegro, Santander, Colombia 126/D4
Río Negro (dept.), Uruguay 145/B3
Río Negro (res.), Uruguay 145/D3
Rionero in Vulture, Italy 34/E4
Rio Pardo, Brazil 132/C10
Rio Pardo de Minas, Brazil 132/F6
Rio Penasco (riv.), N. Mex. 274/E6
Río Piedras, P. Rico 161/E1
Rio Pomba, Brazil 135/E2
Rio Puerco (riv.), N. Mex. 274/C4
Rio Rancho, N. Mex. (87124) 274/C3
Rio Real, Brazil 132/G5
Rio Rico, Ariz. (85621) 198/E7
Rio Salado (riv.), N. Mex. 274/B4
Río San Juan, Dom. Rep. 158/E5
Río Seco, Cuba 158/A2
Río Segundo, Argentina 143/D3
Riosucio, Caldas, Colombia 126/C5
Riosucio, Chocó, Colombia 126/B4
Río Tercero, Argentina 143/D3
Río Tigre, Ecuador 128/D4
Río Tinto, Brazil 132/H4
Río Tocuyo, Venezuela 124/C2
Riou (lake), Sask. 181/M2
Rio Verde, Brazil 132/D7
Rio Verde, Brazil 120/D4
Río Verde, Chile 138/E10
Rioverde, Mexico 150/J6
Rio Verde de Mato Grosso, Brazil 132/C7
Rio Vista, Calif. (94571) 204/L1
Riparia, Wash. (†99359) 310/G4
Riparius, N.Y. (12862) 276/M3
Ripley, Calif. (92272) 204/L10
Ripley, England 13/F4
Ripley, Ill. (†62353) 222/C3
Ripley (co.), Ind. 227/G6
Ripley○, Maine (†04930) 243/E5
Ripley, Miss. (38663) 256/G1
Ripley (co.), Mo. 261/L9
Ripley, N.Y. (14775) 276/A6
Ripley, Ohio (45167) 284/C8
Ripley, Okla. (74062) 288/N2
Ripley, Ontario 177/C3
Ripley, Tenn. (38063) 237/B9
Ripley, W. Va. (25271) 312/C5
Riplinger, Wis. (†54479) 317/E6
Ripoll, Spain 33/H1
Ripon, Calif. (95366) 204/D6
Ripon, England 10/F3
Ripon, England 13/F3
Ripon, Québec 172/B4
Ripon, Wis. (54971) 317/J8
Rippey, Iowa (50235) 229/E5
Ripplemead, Va. (24150) 307/G6
Ripples, New Bruns. 170/D3
Rippon, W. Va. (25441) 312/L4
Rippowam (riv.), Conn. 210/A4
Ripton○, Vt. (05766) 268/A4
Ririe, Idaho (83443) 220/G6
Risafe, Syria 63/H5
Risalpur Cantonment, Pakistan 68/C2
Risaralda (dept.), Colombia 126/B5
Risca, Wales 13/B6
Risco, Mo. (63874) 261/N9
Rishiri (isl.), Japan 81/K1
Rishon Le Ziyyon, Israel 65/B4
Rishra, India 68/F1
Rising City, Nebr. (68658) 264/G3
Rising Fawn, Georgia (30738) 217/A1
Rising Star, Texas (76471) 303/F5
Rising Sun, Ind. (47040) 227/H7
Rising Sun, Md. (21911) 245/O2
Risingsun, Ohio (43457) 284/C3
Rising Sun, Wis. (†54628) 317/D9
Risle (riv.), France 28/D3
Rison, Ark. (71665) 202/F6
Risør, Norway 18/F7
Risoux (mt.), Switzerland 39/B3
Ristigouche (riv.), Québec 172/B2
Ristijärvi, Finland 18/Q4
Rita Blanca (creek), Texas 303/B2
Ritchey, Mo. (†64844) 261/D9
Ritchie, Md. (†20027) 245/G5
Ritchie (co.), W. Va. 312/D4
Ritchies (arch.), India 68/G6
Ritidian (pt.), Guam 86/K6
Ritner, Ky. (42639) 237/M7
Ritter, Oreg. (97872) 291/H3
Ritter, S.C. (29488) 296/F6
Rittman, Ohio (44270) 284/G4
Ritzville, Wash. (99169) 310/G3
Rivadavia, Mendoza, Argentina 143/C3
Rivadavia, Salta, Argentina 143/D1
Rivadavia, San Juan, Argentina 143/C3
Rivadavia, Chile 138/A7
Riva del Garda, Italy 34/C2
Rivanna (riv.), Va. 307/M5
Rivas, Nicaragua 154/E5
Riva San Vitale, Switzerland 39/G5
Rive-de-Gier, France 28/F5
Rivera, Switzerland 39/G4
Rivera (dept.), Uruguay 145/D2
Rivera, Uruguay 145/D1
Rivera, Uruguay 120/D6
Riverbank, Calif. (95367) 204/E6
River Bourgeois, Nova Scotia 168/H3
River Cess, Liberia 106/C7
Rivercourse, Alberta 182/E3
Riverdale, Calif. (93656) 204/E7
Riverdale, Georgia (*30274) 217/K2
Riverdale, Ill. (60627) 222/C6
Riverdale, Iowa (†52722) 229/N5
Riverdale, Kansas (†67152) 232/E4
Riverdale, Md. (20840) 245/F4
Riverdale, Mich. (48877) 250/E5
Riverdale, Nebr. (68870) 264/E4
Riverdale, N.H. (†03045) 268/D5
Riverdale, N.J. (07457) 273/A1
Riverdale, N. Dak. (58565) 282/H4
Riverdale Heights, Md. (†20840) 245/G4
River de Chute, New Bruns. 170/C2
River Denys, Nova Scotia 168/G3
River Edge, N.J. (07661) 273/B1
River Falls, Ala. (36476) 195/E8
River Falls, Wis. (54022) 317/A6
River Forest, Ill. (60305) 222/B5
River Forest, Ind. (†46011) 227/F4
River Glade, New Bruns. 170/E3
River Grove, Ill. (60171) 222/B5
River Grove, Oreg. (†97223) 291/B2
Riverhead, Newf. 166/D2
Riverhead, N.Y. (11901) 276/P9
Riverhead, N. Zealand 100/B1
River Hébert, Nova Scotia 168/D3
River Heights, Utah (†84321) 304/C2
River Hills, Manitoba 179/G4
River Hills, Wis. (†53201) 317/M1
Riverhurst, Sask. 181/E5
Riverina (reg.), N. S. Wales 88/H7
Riverina (reg.), N.S. Wales 97/C4
River John, Nova Scotia 168/E3
River Jordan, Br. Col. 184/J3
Riverland, Fla. (†33301) 212/B4
Riverlea, Ohio (†43085) 284/D5
Rivermines, Mo. (†63601) 261/L7
Rivero (isl.), Chile 138/D6
River Oaks, Texas (77019) 303/E2
River of Ponds, Newf. 166/C3
River of Ponds (lake), Newf. 166/C3
Riverport, Nova Scotia 168/D4
River Rouge, Mich. (48218) 250/B7
Rivers (inlet), Br. Col. 184/D4
Rivers, Manitoba 179/B4
Rivers (state), Nigeria 106/F8
Rivers (lake), Sask. 181/F6
Riversdale, Jamaica 158/J6
Riversdale, S. Africa 118/H7
Riversdale, S. Africa 118/C6
Riverside, Ala. (35135) 195/F3
Riverside, Calif. 188/C4
Riverside (co.), Calif. 204/J10
Riverside, Calif. (*92501) 204/E11
Riverside (res.), Colo. 208/L2
Riverside, Conn. (06878) 210/A4
Riverside, Georgia (†30759) 217/B2
Riverside, Georgia (†31768) 217/E8
Riverside, Ill. (60546) 222/B6
Riverside, Ind. (†47918) 227/C4
Riverside, Iowa (52327) 229/K6
Riverside, Ky. (42272) 237/J6
Riverside, Md. (†20662) 245/K7
Riverside, Mass. (†01376) 249/D2
Riverside, Mich. (49084) 250/C6
Riverside, Mo. (64168) 261/O5
Riverside○, N.J. (08075) 273/B3
Riverside, N.Y. (†14830) 276/F6
Riverside, N. Dak. (†58078) 282/S6
Riverside, Oreg. (97917) 291/J4
Riverside, Pa. (17868) 294/J4
Riverside, R.I. (02915) 249/J5
Riverside, Sask. 181/G6
Riverside, Texas (77367) 303/J7
Riverside, Utah (84334) 304/B2
Riverside, Wash. (98849) 310/F2
Riverside, Wyo. (†82325) 319/F4
Riverside-Albert, New Bruns. 170/F3
Riverside Stage Stop, Ariz. (85237) 198/D5
Rivers Inlet, Br. Col. 184/D4
River Sioux, Iowa (†51545) 229/B5
Riverstown, Ireland 17/E3
Riverton, Conn. (06065) 210/D1
Riverton, Ill. (62561) 222/D4
Riverton, Ind. (†47861) 227/B6
Riverton, Iowa (51650) 229/B7
Riverton, Kansas (66770) 232/H4
Riverton, La. (†71418) 238/F2
Riverton, Man. 162/G5
Riverton, Manitoba 179/E3
Riverton, Minn. (†56455) 255/D4
Riverton, Nebr. (68972) 264/F4
Riverton, N.J. (08077) 273/B3
Riverton, N. Zealand 100/B7
Riverton, Nova Scotia 168/F3
Riverton, Oreg. (†97423) 291/C4
Riverton, Utah (84065) 304/B3
Riverton, Vt. (05668) 268/B3
Riverton, Va. (22651) 307/M3
Riverton, Wash. (†98188) 310/B2
Riverton, W. Va. (26814) 312/H5
Riverton, Wyo. (82501) 319/D2
Riverton Heights, Wash. (98188) 310/B2
Rivervale, Ark. (72377) 202/K2
River Vale○, N.J. (07675) 273/B1
River Valley, Ontario 177/D1
Riverview, Ala. (†36426) 195/D8
River View, Ala. (36872) 195/H5
Riverview, Fla. (33569) 212/D4
Riverview, Mich. (48192) 250/B7
Riverview, Mo. (†63101) 261/R2
Riverview, New Bruns. 170/F2
Riverville, Va. (†24553) 307/L5
Riverwood, Ky. (†40222) 237/K1
Riverwoods, Ill. (†60015) 222/B5
Rives, Mo. (63875) 261/M10
Rives, Tenn. (38253) 237/C8
Rives Junction, Mich. (49277) 250/E6
Rivesville, W. Va. (26588) 312/F3
Riviera (reg.), France 28/G6
Riviera, Texas (78379) 303/G10
Riviera Beach, Fla. (33404) 212/G5
Riviera Beach, Md. (†21061) 245/N4
Riviera-Bullhead, Ariz. (86440) 198/A3
Rivière-à-Claude, Québec 172/C1
Rivière-à-Pierre, Québec 172/E3
Rivière-au-Renard, Québec 172/D1
Rivière-au-Tonnerre, Québec 174/D2
Rivière-Bleue, Québec 172/J2
Rivière-Bois-Clair, Québec 172/F3
Rivière-du-Loup, Que. 162/K6
Rivière-du-Loup (co.), Québec 172/H2
Rivière-du-Loup, Québec 174/D3
Rivière-du-Loup, Québec 172/H2
Rivière-du-Moulin, Québec 172/G1
Rivière-du-Portage, New Bruns. 170/F1
Rivière-Éternité, Québec 172/G1
Rivière-la-Madeleine, Québec 172/C1
Rivière-Matawin, Québec 172/E3
Rivière-Ouelle, Québec 172/G2
Rivière-Pentecôte, Québec 174/D3
Rivière-Pilote, Martinique 161/D7
Rivière-Port-Daniel, Québec 172/D2
Rivière-Portneuf, Québec 172/H1
Rivière-Saint-Paul, Québec 174/F2
Rivière-Salée, Martinique 161/D7
Rivière-Trois-Pistoles, Québec 172/J1
Rivière Verte, New Bruns. 170/B1
Rivière-Verte, Québec 172/H2
Riwaka, N. Zealand 100/D4
Riwoqê, China 77/E5
Rixeyville, Va. (22737) 307/M3
Rixford, Pa. (16745) 294/F2
Riyadh (cap.), Saudi Arabia 2/M4
Riyadh (cap.), Saudi Arabia 54/F7
Riyadh (cap.), Saudi Arabia 59/E5
Riyan, P.D.R. Yemen 59/E7
Rizal (prov.), Philippines 82/C3
Rize (prov.), Turkey 63/J2
Rize, Turkey 59/D1
Rize, Turkey 63/J2
Rizokarpasso, Cyprus 63/F5
Rjukan, Norway 18/F7
Roa, Norway 18/G6
Roa, Spain 33/E2
Roachdale, Ind. (46172) 227/D5
Road (bay), Virgin Is. (Br.) 161/D3
Roadside, Scotland 15/F4
Roadstown, N.J. (†08302) 273/C5
Road Town (cap.), Virgin Is. (Br.) 161/D3
Road Town (cap.), Virgin Is. (Br.) 156/H1
Roag, Loch (inlet), Scotland 15/B2
Roan (creek), Colo. 208/C4
Roan (plat.), Colo. 208/B3
Roan, Norway 18/G4
Roan (isl.), Scotland 15/D2
Roan (cliffs), Utah 304/E4
Roane (co.), Tenn. 237/M9
Roane (co.), W. Va. 312/D5
Roan Mountain, Tenn. (37687) 237/S8
Roann, Ind. (46974) 227/F3
Roanne, France 28/E4
Roanoke (riv.) 188/L3
Roanoke, Ala. (36274) 195/H4
Roanoke, Ill. (61561) 222/D3
Roanoke, Ind. (46783) 227/G3
Roanoke, La. (70581) 238/E6
Roanoke, Mo. (†65230) 261/G4
Roanoke (isl.), N.C. 281/T3
Roanoke (riv.), N.C. 281/P2
Roanoke, Texas (76262) 303/F1
Roanoke, Va. 146/L6
Roanoke, Va. 188/K3
Roanoke (co.), Va. 307/H6
Roanoke (I.C.), Va. (*24001) 307/H6
Roanoke (riv.), Va. 307/N8
Roanoke, W. Va. (26423) 312/F5
Roanoke Rapids, N.C. (27870) 281/O2
Roaring (brook), Conn. 210/F1
Roaring (brook), Conn. 210/E2
Roaring Branch, Pa. (17765) 294/J2
Roaring Fork, Colorado (riv.), Colo. 208/E4
Roaring Gap, N.C. (28668) 281/H2
Roaring River, N.C. (28669) 281/G2
Roaring Spring, Pa. (16673) 294/F5
Roaring Springs, Texas (79256) 303/D4
Roaringwater (bay), Ireland 17/B9
Roark, Ky. (40979) 237/P6
Roatán, Honduras 154/D2
Roatán (isl.), Honduras 154/D2
Roba, Ala. (†36089) 195/G6
Robards, Ky. (42452) 237/F5
Robat Karim, Iran 66/G3
Robb, Alberta 182/B3
Robben (isl.), S. Africa 118/E6
Robbins, Calif. (95676) 204/B8
Robbins, Ill. (60472) 222/B6
Robbins, N.C. (27325) 281/K4
Robbins (isl.), Tasmania 99/B2
Robbins, Tenn. (37852) 237/M8
Robbinsdale, Minn. (55422) 255/G5
Robbinston, Maine (04671) 243/J5
Robbinston○, Maine (04671) 243/J5
Robbinsville, N.J. (08691) 273/D3
Robbinsville, N.C. (28771) 281/B4
Robe (mt.), N.S. Wales 97/A2
Robe, S. Australia 94/F7
Robe, Wash. (†98252) 310/D2
Robeline, La. (71469) 238/D3
Roberdel, N.C. (†28379) 281/K5
Robersonville, N.C. (27871) 281/P3
Robert (isl.), China 85/E2
Robert, La. (70455) 238/N1
Robert (harb.), Martinique 161/D6
Roberta, Georgia (31078) 217/D5
Roberta, Okla. (†74701) /K7
Robert Lee, Texas (76945) 303/D6
Roberto Payán, Colombia 126/A7
Roberts, Idaho (83444) 220/F6
Roberts, Ill. (60962) 222/E3
Roberts, Mont. (59070) 262/G5
Roberts (co.), S. Dak. 298/P2
Roberts (co.), Texas 303/D2
Roberts, Wis. (54023) 317/A6
Robert's Arm, Newf. 166/C4
Robertsburg, W. Va. (25172) 312/C5
Roberts Creek, Br. Col. 184/J3
Robertsdale, Ala. (36567) 195/C9
Robertsdale, Pa. (16674) 294/F5
Roberts Field Int'l Airport, Liberia 106/C7
Robertsfors, Sweden 18/M4
Robertsganj, India 68/E4
Robertson (co.), Ky. 237/N3
Robertson, S. Africa 118/C6
Robertson (co.), Tenn. 237/H7
Robertson (co.), Texas 303/H6
Robertson, Wyo. (82944) 319/B4
Robertsonville, Québec 172/F3
Robertsport, Liberia 102/A4
Robertsport, Liberia 106/B7
Robertstown, Georgia (†30545) 217/E1
Robertsville, Conn. (†06098) 210/C1
Robertsville, Ohio (44670) 284/H4
Robertville, New Bruns. 170/E1
Roberval, Que. 162/J6
Roberval, Québec 174/C3
Roberval, Québec 172/E1
Robeson (co.), N.C. 281/L5
Robeson (chan.), N.W. Terrs. 187/M1
Robesonia, Pa. (19551) 294/K5
Robichaud, New Bruns. 170/F2
Robinhood, Sask. 181/C2
Robins, Iowa (52328) 229/K4
Robins, Ohio (†43723) 284/H6
Robins A.F.B., Georgia 217/F5
Robinson, Ill. (62454) 222/F5
Robinson, Iowa (†52330) 229/K4
Robinson, Kansas (66532) 232/G2
Robinson, Ky. (41082) 237/N4
Robinson, N. Dak. (58478) 282/L5
Robinson (riv.), North. Terr. 93/E4
Robinson, Pa. (15949) 294/D5
Robinson (lake), S.C. 296/G3
Robinson (ranges), W. Australia 92/B4
Robinson Creek, Ky. (41560) 237/S6
Robinson Crusoe (isl.), Chile 120/B6
Robinson River, North. Terr. 93/E4
Robinsons, Maine (†04734) 243/H3
Robinsonville, Miss. (38664) 256/D1
Robinsonville, New Bruns. 170/C1
Robinvale, Victoria 97/B4
Robles, Colombia 126/D2
Roblin, Manitoba 179/A3
Roblin, Ontario 177/G3
Roboré, Bolivia 136/F6
Roboré, Bolivia 120/D4
Rob Roy, Ind. (†47918) 227/C4
Robsart, Sask. 181/B6
Robson (mt.), Br. Col. 162/D5
Robson, Br. Col. 184/J5
Robson (mt.), Br. Col. 184/H3
Robstown, Texas (78380) 303/G10
Roby, Mo. (65557) 261/H7
Roby, Texas (79543) 303/D5
Roca, Nebr. (68430) 264/H4
Roca (cape), Portugal 33/B3
Rocafuerte, Ecuador 128/B3
Rocanville, Sask. 181/K5
Roca Partida (isl.), Mexico 150/C7
Roca que Vela (cay), Colombia 126/B8
Rocas (isl.), Brazil 120/F3
Rocas de Santo Domingo, Chile 138/F4
Roccastrada, Italy 34/C3
Rocha (dept.), Uruguay 145/E4
Rocha, Uruguay 145/E5
Rocha (lag.), Uruguay 145/E5
Rochdale, England 13/H2
Rochdale, England 10/G2
Rochdale, Mass. (01542) 249/G4
Roche, Switzerland 39/C4
Rochechouart, France 28/D5
Rochefort, Belgium 27/G8
Rochefort, France 28/C4
Roche Harbor, Wash. (98250) 310/B2
Rochelle, Georgia (31079) 217/F7
Rochelle, Ill. (61068) 222/D2
Rochelle, Texas (76872) 303/E6
Rochelle, Wyo. (†82701) 319/H2
Rochelle Park○, N.J. (07662) 273/B2
Roche Percé, Sask. 181/J6
Rocheport, Mo. (65279) 261/H5
Rocher River, N.W.T. 162/E3
Rocher River, N.W. Terrs. 187/G3
Rochert, Minn. (56578) 255/C4
Rochester, Alberta 182/D2
Rochester, England 13/J8
Rochester, England 10/G5
Rochester, Ill. (62563) 222/D4
Rochester, Ind. (46975) 227/E2
Rochester, Iowa (†52772) 229/L5
Rochester, Ky. (42273) 237/H6
Rochester○, Mass. (02770) 249/L6
Rochester, Mich. (48063) 250/F6
Rochester, Minn. 188/H2
Rochester, Minn. (55901) 255/F6
Rochester, N.H. (03867) 268/E5
Rochester, N.Y. 188/L2
Rochester, N.Y. 146/L5
Rochester, N.Y. (*14601) 276/E4
Rochester, Ohio (†44090) 284/F3
Rochester, Pa. (15074) 294/B4
Rochester, Texas (79544) 303/E4
Rochester○, Vt. (05767) 268/B4
Rochester, Victoria 97/C5
Rochester, Wash. (98579) 310/C4
Rochester, Wis. (53167) 317/K3
Rochester Mills, Pa. (15771) 294/D4
Rochford, S. Dak. (57778) 298/B5
Rochfort Bridge, Alberta 182/C3
Rochon Sands, Alberta 182/D3
Rociada, N. Mex. (87742) 274/D3
Rock (creek), Idaho 220/F7
Rock (creek), Ill. 222/D2
Rock (riv.), Ill. 222/C2
Rock (riv.), Iowa 229/A2
Rock, Kansas (67131) 232/F4
Rock (lake), Manitoba 179/C5
Rock (creek), Md. 245/K4
Rock, Mass. (†02346) 249/L5
Rock, Mich. (49880) 250/B2
Rock (co.), Minn. 255/B7
Rock (riv.), Minn. 255/B7
Rock (creek), Mont. 262/C4
Rock (co.), Nebr. 264/E2
Rock (creek), Nev. 266/E2
Rock (creek), Oreg. 291/E4
Rock (creek), Oreg. 291/G2
Rock (creek), Oreg. 291/H3
Rock (creek), S. Dak. 298/O6
Rock (creek), Wash. 310/H3
Rock (lake), Wash. 310/H3
Rock (co.), Wis. 317/H10
Rock (riv.), Wis. 317/J9
Rockall (isl.), Scotland 7/C3
Rockaway, N.J. (07866) 273/D2
Rockaway, Oreg. (97136) 291/C2
Rockaway Beach, Mo. (65740) 261/F9
Rock Bluff, Fla. (†32321) 212/B1
Rockbridge, Ill. (62081) 222/C4
Rockbridge, Mo. (65741) 261/H9
Rockbridge, Ohio (43149) 284/E6
Rockbridge (co.), Va. 307/K5
Rockbridge, Wis. (†53581) 317/F9
Rockcastle (co.), Ky. 237/N6
Rockcastle (riv.), Ky. 237/N6
Rock Castle, W. Va. (25272) 312/C5
Rock Cave, W. Va. (26234) 312/F5
Rock City, Ill. (61070) 222/D1
Rockcliffe Park, Ontario 177/J2
Rockcorry, Ireland 17/H3
Rock Creek, Br. Col. 184/H6
Rock Creek, Kansas (†66512) 232/G2
Rock Creek, Minn. (55067) 255/F5
Rock Creek, Ohio (44084) 284/J2
Rock Creek, Yukon 187/E3
Rockdale (co.), Georgia 217/D3
Rockdale, Ill. (60436) 222/E2
Rockdale, N. S. Wales 88/K4
Rockdale, N.S. Wales 97/J4
Rockdale, Texas (76567) 303/G7
Rockdale, Wis. (†53523) 317/J10
Rock Dell, Minn. (†55920) 255/F7
Rockerville, S. Dak. (†57701) 298/C6
Rockfall, Conn. (06481) 210/E2
Rock Falls, Ill. (61071) 222/D2
Rock Falls, Iowa (50467) 229/G2
Rock Falls, Wis. (54764) 317/C6
Rockfield, Ind. (46977) 227/D3
Rockfield, Ky. (42274) 237/J7
Rockfield, Wis. (53077) 317/L1
Rockfish, N.C. (†28302) 281/L5
Rockford, Ala. (35136) 195/F5
Rockford, Idaho (†83221) 220/F6
Rockford, Ill. 146/K5
Rockford, Ill. 188/J2
Rockford, Ill. (*61101) 222/D1
Rockford, Iowa (50468) 229/H2
Rockford, Mich. (49341) 250/D5

Rosston 437

Rockford, Minn. (55373) 255/F5
Rockford, N.C. (27044) 281/H2
Rockford, Ohio (45882) 284/A4
Rockford, Sask. 181/J3
Rockford, Tenn. (37853) 237/O9
Rockford, Wash. (99030) 310/H3
Rock Forest, Québec 172/F4
Rock Glen, Pa. (18246) 294/K4
Rockglen, Sask. 181/F6
Rock Grove, Ill. (†61070) 222/D1
Rock Hall, Md. (21661) 245/O4
Rockham, S. Dak. (57470) 298/M4
Rockhampton, Australia 2/S7
Rockhampton, Australia 87/F8
Rockhampton, Queensland 88/H4
Rockhampton, Queensland 95/D4
Rockhampton Downs, North. Terr. 93/D5
Rockhaven, Sask. 181/B3
Rock Hill, Mo. (†63119) 261/P3
Rock Hill, S.C. 188/K4
Rock Hill, S.C. (29730) 296/E2
Rockholds, Ky. (40759) 237/N7
Rockingham, Georgia (†31510) 217/H7
Rockingham (co.), N.H. 268/E5
Rockingham (co.), N.C. 281/K2
Rockingham, N.C. (28379) 281/K5
Rockingham○, Vt. (†05101) 268/B5
Rockingham (co.), Va. 307/L4
Rockingham, W. Australia 88/B2
Rockingham, W. Australia 92/A2
Rock Island, Ill. 188/J2
Rock Island (co.), Ill. 222/C2
Rock Island, Ill. (61201) 222/C2
Rock Island, Okla. (†74932) 288/T4
Rock Island, Québec 172/E4
Rock Island, Tenn. (38581) 237/K9
Rock Island, Texas (77470) 303/H8
Rock Island, Wash. (†98801) 310/E3
Rock Island (dam), Wash. 310/E3
Rock Island Arsenal, Ill. 222/C2
Rocklake, N. Dak. (58365) 282/M2
Rockland, Conn. (†06443) 210/E3
Rockland, Del. (19732) 245/R1
Rockland, Idaho (83271) 220/F7
Rockland, Maine (04841) 243/F7
Rockland○, Mass. (02370) 249/L4
Rockland, Mich. (49960) 250/G1
Rockland (co.), N.Y. 276/M8
Rockland, Ontario 177/J2
Rockland, Texas (75970) 303/K6
Rockland, Wis. (54653) 317/D8
Rocklands (res.), Victoria 97/B5
Rockledge, Fla. (32955) 212/F3
Rockledge, Georgia (30454) 217/G6
Rockledge, Pa. (†19101) 294/M5
Rockleigh, N.J. (07647) 273/C1
Rocklin, Calif. (95677) 204/B8
Rockmart, Georgia (30153) 217/B2
Rock Mills, Ala. (36274) 195/H4
Rock Oak, W. Va. (†26756) 312/J4
Rock Point, Md. (20682) 245/L7
Rockport, Ark. (†72104) 202/E5
Rockport, Calif. (†95488) 204/B4
Rockport, Ill. (62370) 222/B4
Rockport, Ind. 227/C9
Rockport, Ky. (42369) 237/H6
Rockport, Maine (04856) 243/F7
Rockport○, Maine (04856) 243/F7
Rockport○, Mass. (01966) 249/M2
Rockport, Miss. (†39083) 256/D7
Rock Port, Mo. (64482) 261/B2
Rockport, Texas (78382) 303/H9
Rockport (lake), Utah 304/C3
Rockport, Wash. (98283) 310/D2
Rockport, W. Va. (26169) 312/C4
Rock Rapids, Iowa (51246) 229/A2
Rock River, Wyo. (82083) 319/G4
Rock Run, Ala. (†36272) 195/G2
Rocks, Md. (†21084) 245/N2
Rocks (pt.), N. Zealand 100/C4
Rock Springs, Mont. (59312) 262/K4
Rocksprings, Texas (78880) 303/D8
Rock Springs, Wis. (53961) 317/F8
Rock Springs, Wyo. 146/H5
Rock Springs, Wyo. 188/E2
Rock Springs, Wyo. (82901) 319/C4
Rockstone, Guyana 131/B2
Rockton, Ill. (61072) 222/E1
Rockvale, Colo. (81244) 208/J6
Rockvale, Mont. (†59080) 262/H5
Rockvale, Tenn. (37153) 237/J9
Rock Valley, Iowa (51247) 229/A2
Rockville, Conn. (†06066) 210/F1
Rockville, Ind. (47872) 227/C5
Rockville, Maine (†04841) 243/F7
Rockville, Md. (*20850) 245/K4
Rockville, Mass. (†02054) 249/A8
Rockville, Minn. (56369) 255/D5
Rockville, Mo. (64780) 261/D6
Rockville, Nebr. (68871) 264/F3
Rockville, Nova Scotia 168/B5
Rockville, R.I. (02873) 249/G6
Rockville, S.C. (†29487) 296/G6
Rockville, Utah (84763) 304/A6
Rockville, Va. (23146) 307/N5
Rockville, Wis. (†53820) 317/E10
Rockville Centre, N.Y. (*11570) 276/R7
Rockwall (co.), Texas 303/H5
Rockwall, Texas (75087) 303/H5
Rockwell, Iowa (50469) 229/G3
Rockwell, N.C. (28138) 281/J3
Rockwell City, Iowa (50579) 229/D4
Rockwood, Ala. (†35653) 195/C2
Rockwood, Ill. (62280) 222/D6
Rockwood, Maine (04478) 243/D4
Rockwood, Mich. (48173) 250/F6
Rockwood, Ontario 177/D4
Rockwood, Pa. (15557) 294/D6
Rockwood, Tenn. (37854) 237/M9
Rockwood, Texas (76873) 303/E6
Rocky (mts.) 162/D4
Rocky (mts.) 146/F4
Rocky (mts.) 188/E3
Rocky (mts.), Alberta 182/BC4
Rocky (mts.), Br. Col. 184/F2
Rocky (mts.), Canada 4/D16
Rocky (mts.), Colo. 208/F1
Rocky (mts.), Idaho 220/D1
Rocky (lake), Maine 243/J6
Rocky (mts.), Mont. 262/D4
Rocky (bay), Newf. 166/C3
Rocky (riv.), Newf. 166/D2
Rocky (mts.), N. Mex. 274/C1
Rocky (pt.), Norfolk I. 88/K6
Rocky (riv.), N.C. 281/H4
Rocky (riv.), Ohio 284/G9
Rocky, Okla. (73661) 288/J4
Rocky (riv.), S.C. 296/B3
Rocky (cape), Tasmania 99/B2
Rocky (mts.), Wash. 310/H2
Rocky (mts.), Wyo. 319/C1
Rocky (mts.), Yukon 187/F4
Rocky Bottom, S.C. (†29685) 296/B1
Rocky Boy, Mont. (†59521) 262/G2
Rocky Boy's Ind. Res., Mont. 262/G2
Rocky Comfort, Mo. (64861) 261/D9
Rocky Face, Georgia (30740) 217/C1
Rockyford, Alberta 182/D4
Rocky Ford, Colo. (81067) 208/M6
Rocky Ford, Georgia (30455) 217/J5
Rocky Fork (lake), Ohio 284/D7
Rocky Gap, Va. (24366) 307/F6
Rocky Gorge (res.), Md. 245/L4
Rocky Harbour, Newf. 166/C4
Rocky Hill○, Conn. (06067) 210/E2
Rocky Hill, Ky. (42163) 237/J6
Rocky Hill, N.J. (08553) 273/D3
Rocky Lane, Alberta 182/B5
Rocky Mount, Georgia (†30251) 217/C4
Rocky Mount, La. (†71064) 238/C1
Rocky Mount, Mo. (65072) 261/G6
Rocky Mount, N.C. 188/L3
Rocky Mount, N.C. (27801) 281/O3
Rocky Mount, Va. (24151) 307/J7
Rocky Mountain Arsenal, Colo. 208/K3
Rocky Mountain House, Alberta 182/C3
Rocky Mountain House, Alta. 162/E5
Rocky Mountain Nat'l Park, Colo. 208/H2
Rocky Point, N.C. (28457) 281/O6
Rocky Point, Wash. (†98626) 310/A2
Rockypoint, Wyo. (†82721) 319/G1
Rocky Rapids, Alberta 182/C3
Rocky Reach (dam), Wash. 310/E3
Rocky Ridge (mt.), Idaho 220/C3
Rocky Ridge, Ohio (43458) 284/D2
Rocky River, Ohio (44116) 284/G9
Rodanthe, N.C. (27968) 281/U3
Rodarte, N. Mex. (87561) 274/D2
Rodas, Cuba 158/E2
Rødby, Denmark 21/E8
Rødby, Denmark 18/G9
Roddickton, Newf. 166/C3
Rødding, Denmark 21/B7
Roddy, Tenn. (†37381) 237/M9
Rødekro, Denmark 21/C7
Roden, Netherlands 27/J2
Rodeo, Calif. (94572) 204/J1
Rodeo, Mexico 150/G4
Rodeo, N. Mex. (88056) 274/A7
Roderfield, W. Va. (24881) 312/C8
Roderick (isl.), Br. Col. 184/C4
Rodessa, La. (71069) 238/B1
Rodez, France 28/E5
Ródhos, Greece 45/J7
Roding (riv.), England 13/J7
Rodinga, North. Terr. 93/D8
Rødkaersbro, Denmark 21/C5
Rodman, Iowa (50580) 229/D2
Rodman, N.Y. (13682) 276/J3
Rodman, S.C. (†29706) 296/E2
Rodney, Mich. (49342) 250/D5
Rodney, Miss. (†39096) 256/B7
Rodney, Ontario 177/C5
Rodney Village, Del. (19901) 245/R4
Rodrigues, Brazil 132/F10
Rodríguez, Uruguay 145/C5
Rødvig, Denmark 21/F7
Roe, Ark. (72134) 202/H4
Roe (riv.), N. Ireland 17/H1
Roebling-Florence, N.J. (08554) 273/D3
Roebourne, W. Australia 88/B4
Roebourne, W. Australia 92/B3
Roebuck (bay), W. Australia 88/C3
Roebuck (bay), W. Australia 92/C2
Roebuck Plains, W. Australia 92/C2
Roeland Park, Kansas (†66205) 232/H2
Roer (riv.), Netherlands 27/J6
Roermond, Netherlands 27/J6
Roeselare, Belgium 27/C7
Roes Welcome (sound), N.W.T. 162/H2
Roes Welcome (sound), N.W. Terrs. 187/K3
Roff, Okla. (74865) 288/N5
Rogachev, U.S.S.R. 52/D4
Rogagua (lake), Bolivia 136/B3
Rogaguado (lake), Bolivia 136/C3
Rogaland (co.), Norway 18/E7
Rogatica, Yugoslavia 45/D4
Roger Mills (co.), Okla. 288/G3
Rogers, Ark. (72756) 202/B1
Rogers, Br. Col. 184/J4
Rogers (lake), Calif. 204/H9
Rogers, Conn. (06263) 210/H1
Rogers (lake), Conn. 210/F3
Rogers, La. (†71342) 238/F3
Rogers, Minn. (55374) 255/E5
Rogers, Nebr. (68659) 264/H3
Rogers, N. Mex. (88132) 274/F5
Rogers, N. Dak. (58479) 282/O5
Rogers, Ohio (44455) 284/J4
Rogers (co.), Okla. 288/P2
Rogers, Texas (76569) 303/G7
Rogers (mt.), Va. 307/E7
Rogers City, Mich. (49779) 250/F3
Rogerson, Idaho (83302) 220/D7
Rogers Springs, Tenn. (†38052) 237/D10
Rogersville, Ala. (35652) 195/D1
Rogersville, Mo. (65742) 261/G8
Rogersville, New Bruns. 170/E2
Rogersville, Pa. (15359) 294/B6
Rogersville, Tenn. (37857) 237/P8
Roger Williams Nat'l Mem., R.I. 249/J5
Roggen, Colo. (80652) 208/L2
Roggwil, Switzerland 39/E2
Rogliano, France 28/B6
Rogozno, Poland 47/C2
Rogue (riv.), Oreg. 291/C5
Rogue River, Oreg. (97537) 291/D5
Roha, India 68/C5
Rohnert Park, Calif. (94928) 204/C5
Rohnerville, Calif. (†95540) 204/B3
Rohrbach in Oberösterreich, Austria 41/B2
Rohrersville, Md. (21779) 245/H3
Rohri, Pakistan 68/B3
Rohtak, India 68/C5
Rohwer, Ark. (71666) 202/H6
Roi Et, Thailand 72/D4
Roja, U.S.S.R. 53/B2
Rojas, Argentina 143/F7
Rojo (cape), Mexico 150/L6
Rojo (cape), P. Rico 161/A3
Rojo (cape), P. Rico 156/F1
Rokan (riv.), Indonesia 85/C5
Rokeby, Sask. 181/J4
Rokiškis, U.S.S.R. 53/C2
Rokycany, Czech. 41/B2
Rokytnice nad Jizerou, Czech. 41/C1
Rola Co (lake), China 77/C4
Roland, Ark. (72135) 202/E4
Roland, Iowa (50236) 229/F4
Roland, Manitoba 179/D5
Roland, Okla. (74954) 288/S4
Røldal, Norway 18/E7
Roldán, Argentina 143/F6
Rolecha, Chile 138/D4
Rolesville, N.C. (27571) 281/N3
Rolette (co.), N. Dak. 282/L2
Rolette, N. Dak. (58366) 282/L2
Roleystone, W. Australia 88/B2
Rolfe, Iowa (50581) 229/D3
Roll, Ariz. (85347) 198/A6
Rolla, Ark. (†72104) 202/E5
Rolla, Br. Col. 184/G2
Rolla, Kansas (67954) 232/A4
Rolla, Mo. (65401) 261/J7
Rolla, N. Dak. (58367) 282/L2
Rollag, Minn. (†56549) 255/B4
Rolle, Switzerland 39/B4
Rollingbay, Wash. (98061) 310/A2
Rollingdam, New Bruns. 170/C3
Rolling Fields, Ky. (†40201) 237/K2
Rolling Fork (riv.), Ky. 237/L5
Rolling Fork, Miss. (39159) 256/C5
Rolling Hills, Alberta 182/E4
Rolling Hills, Calif. (90274) 204/B11
Rolling Hills, Ky. (†40201) 237/L1
Rolling Hills Estates, Calif. (90274) 204/B11
Rolling Meadows, Ill. (60008) 222/A5
Rolling Prairie, Ind. (46371) 227/D1
Rollingstone, Minn. (55969) 255/G6
Rollins, Mont. (59931) 262/B3
Rollo (bay), Pr. Edward I. 168/F2
Rolphton, Ontario 177/G1
Roma, Australia 87/E8
Roma (Rome) (cap.), Italy 34/F6
Roma, Queensland 88/H5
Roma, Queensland 95/D5
Roma, Sweden 18/L8
Romain (cape), S.C. 296/J6
Romaine (riv.), Newf. 166/B3
Romaine (riv.), Que. 162/K5
Romaine, Québec 174/E2
Romaine (riv.), Québec 174/E2
Roma-Los Saenz, Texas (78584) 303/E11
Roman, Romania 45/H2
Romance, Ark. (72136) 202/F3
Romance, Sask. 181/G3
Romance, W. Va. (25175) 312/C5
Romang, Argentina 143/F4
Romang (isl.), Indonesia 85/H7
Romania 2/L3
Romania 7/G4
ROMANIA 45/F3
Romano (cay), Cuba 158/G2
Romano (cay), Cuba 156/C2
Romano (cape), Fla. 212/E6
Romanshorn, Switzerland 39/H1
Romans-sur-Isère, France 28/F5
Romanzof (cape), Alaska 196/E2
Rombauer, Mo. (63962) 261/M9
Romblon (prov.), Philippines 82/D4
Romblon, Philippines 82/D4
Romblon (isl.), Philippines 82/D4
Rome, Ga. 188/K4
Rome, Georgia (30161) 217/B2
Rome, Ill. (61562) 222/D3
Rome, Ind. (47574) 227/D9
Rome, Iowa (52642) 229/K7
Rome (prov.), Italy 34/F6
Rome (cap.), Italy 7/F4
Rome (cap.), Italy 34/F6
Rome (cap.), Italy 2/K3
Rome○, Maine (†04957) 243/D6
Rome, Miss. (38768) 256/C3
Rome, N.Y. 188/M2
Rome, N.Y. (13440) 276/J4
Rome (Stout), Ohio (†45684) 284/D8
Rome, Ohio (44085) 284/J2
Rome, Oreg. (†97910) 291/K5
Rome, Pa. (18837) 294/K2
Rome, Wis. (†53178) 317/H1
Rome City, Ind. (46784) 227/G1
Romeo, Colo. (81148) 208/G8
Romeo, Mich. (48065) 250/F6
Romeoville, Ill. (60441) 222/B6
Romeroville, N. Mex. (†87701) 274/D3
Romeville, La. (†70723) 238/L3
Romilly-sur-Seine, France 28/F3
Romney, Ind. (47981) 227/D4
Romney, W. Va. (26757) 312/J4
Romny, U.S.S.R. 52/D4
Rømø, Denmark 21/B7
Rømø (isl.), Denmark 21/B7
Rømø (isl.), Denmark 18/F9
Romont, Switzerland 39/C3
Romorantin-Lanthenay, France 28/D4
Romsdalsfjorden (fjord), Norway 18/E5
Romsey, England 10/F5
Romsey, England 13/F6
Romulus, Mich. (48174) 250/F6
Romulus, N.Y. (14541) 276/G5
Ron, Vietnam 72/E3
Ron, Mui (cape), Vietnam 72/E3
Rona (isl.), Scotland 15/B3
Ronald, Wash. (98940) 310/E3
Ronan, Mont. (59864) 262/C3
Ronay (isl.), Scotland 15/A3
Roncador, Serra do (range), Brazil 132/D5
Roncador (cays), Colombia 126/B9
Ronceverte, W. Va. (24970) 312/F7
Ronciglione, Italy 34/C3
Ronda, N.C. (28670) 281/H2
Ronda, Spain 33/D4
Rønde, Denmark 21/D5
Ronde (isl.), Grenada 161/D7
Rondeau Prov. Park, Ontario 177/C5
Rondo, Ark. (†72355) 202/J4
Rondônia (terr.), Brazil 132/H10
Rondônia, Brazil 132/H10
Rondonópolis, Brazil 120/D4
Rondout (res.), N.Y. 276/M7
Rondu, Pakistan 68/D1
Rong, Koh (isl.), Cambodia 72/D5
Rong'an, China 77/G6
Ronge, Lac La (lake), Sask. 162/F4
Ronge, La (lake), Sask. 181/M3
Rongelap (atoll), Marshall Is. 87/G4
Rongjiang, China 77/G6
Rong Kwang, Thailand 72/D3
Rong Xian, China 77/H7
Ronju (mt.), Fr. Poly. 86/T13
Ronkonkoma, N.Y. (11779) 276/O9
Rønne, Denmark 21/F9
Rønne, Denmark 18/J9
Ronneby, Minn. (†56324) 255/E5
Ronneby, Sweden 18/J8
Ronne Entrance (inlet) 5/B15
Ronne Ice Shelf, Ant. 2/F10
Ronne Ice Shelf 5/B15
Ronse, Belgium 27/D7
Ronuro (riv.), Brazil 132/C6
Roodepoort, S. Africa 118/H6
Roodhouse, Ill. (62082) 222/C4
Roof Butte (mt.), Ariz. 198/F2
Rooi, Neth. Ant. 161/E8
Rooks (co.), Kansas 232/C2
Roopville, Georgia (30170) 217/B4
Roosendaal, Netherlands 27/F5
Roosevelt (isl.), Ant. 2/A10
Roosevelt (isl.) 5/A10
Roosevelt (res.), Ariz. 188/D4
Roosevelt, Ariz. (85545) 198/D5
Roosevelt (riv.), Brazil 120/C3
Roosevelt (riv.), Brazil 132/A5
Roosevelt, La. (†71276) 238/H1
Roosevelt, Minn. (56673) 255/C2
Roosevelt (co.), Mont. 262/L2
Roosevelt, N.J. (08555) 273/E3
Roosevelt (co.), N. Mex. 274/F4
Roosevelt, N.Y. (11575) 276/R7
Roosevelt, Okla. (73564) 288/J5
Roosevelt, Texas (76874) 303/D7
Roosevelt, Utah (84066) 304/D3
Roosevelt, Wash. (99356) 310/E5
Roosevelt Campobello Int'l Park, New Bruns. 170/D4
Roosevelt City, Ala. (35020) 195/E4
Roosevelt Park, Mich. (49444) 250/C5
Roosevelt Road Naval Res., P. Rico 161/F2
Roosville, Br. Col. 184/K5
Root (riv.), Minn. 255/G7
Rootstown, Ohio (44272) 284/H3
Roper, N.C. (27970) 281/R3
Roper (riv.), North. Terr. 88/E3
Roper (riv.), North. Terr. 93/C3
Roper River, North. Terr. 93/D3
Roper River Mission, North. Terr. 88/E2
Roper Valley, North. Terr. 93/D3
Ropesville, Texas (79358) 303/B4
Roque Bluffs○, Maine (†04654) 243/H6
Roque González de Santa Cruz, Paraguay 144/B5
Roque Pérez, Argentina 143/G7
Roquetas, Spain 33/G2
Rora (head), Scotland 15/E2
Roraima (mt.) 120/C2
Roraima (terr.), Brazil 132/H8
Roraima (mt.), Guyana 131/A3
Roraima (mt.), Venezuela 124/H5
Rørby, Denmark 21/E6
Rorketon, Manitoba 179/C3
Røros, Norway 18/G5
Rorschach, Switzerland 39/H2
Rosa, Ala. (†35049) 195/E3
Rosa (cape), Ecuador 128/B10
Rosa (mt.), Italy 34/A1
Rosa, La. (71364) 238/G5
Rosa, Manitoba 179/F5
Rosa (mt.), Switzerland 39/E5
Rosaire, Québec 172/G3
Rosaireville, New Bruns. 170/E2
Rosalia, Kansas (67132) 232/F4
Rosalia, Wash. (99170) 310/H3
Rosalie, Dominica 161/F6
Rosalie, Nebr. (68055) 264/H2
Rosalina, Paraguay 144/D3
Rosalind, Alberta 182/D3
Rosamond, Calif. (93560) 204/G9
Rosamond (lake), Calif. 204/G9
Rosamond, Ill. (62083) 222/D4
Rosamorada, Mexico 150/G5
Rosapenna, Ireland 17/F1
Rosario, Argentina 143/F6
Rosario, Argentina 120/C6
Rosário, Brazil 132/F3
Rosario, Chile 138/F5
Rosario (cay), Cuba 158/C2
Rosario, Sinaloa, Mexico 150/G5
Rosario, Sonora, Mexico 150/E3
Rosario, Paraguay 144/D4
Rosario, P. Rico 161/A2
Rosario, Uruguay 145/B5
Rosario, Venezuela 124/B2
Rosario (str.), Wash. 310/C2
Rosario de la Frontera, Argentina 143/D2
Rosario de Lerma, Argentina 143/C1
Rosario del Tala, Argentina 143/G6
Rosáriodo Sul, Brazil 132/C10
Rosário Oeste, Brazil 132/C6
Rosas, Spain 33/H1
Rosas (gulf), Spain 33/H1
Rosati, Mo. (†65559) 261/J6
Rosa Zárate, Ecuador 128/C2
Rosburg, Wash. (98643) 310/B4
Rosbys Rock, W. Va. (†26041) 312/E3
Roscoe, Ill. (61073) 222/D1
Roscoe, Minn. (56371) 255/D5
Roscoe, Mo. (64781) 261/E7
Roscoe, Mont. (59071) 262/G5
Roscoe, Nebr. (†69153) 264/C3
Roscoe, N.Y. (12776) 276/L7
Roscoe, Pa. (15477) 294/C5
Roscoe, S. Dak. (57471) 298/L3
Roscoe, Texas (79545) 303/D5
Roscoff, France 28/A3
Roscommon (co.), Ireland 17/E4
Roscommon, Ireland 10/B4
Roscommon, Ireland 17/E4
Roscommon (co.), Mich. 250/E4
Roscommon, Mich. (48653) 250/E4
Roscrea, Ireland 10/B4
Roscrea, Ireland 17/F6
Rose (peak), Ariz. 198/F5
Rose (pt.), Br. Col. 184/B3
Rose (pt.), Martinique 161/D6
Rose, Nebr. (68772) 264/E2
Rose, N.Y. (14542) 276/G4
Rose (riv.), North. Terr. 93/D2
Rose, Okla. (74364) 288/R2
Roseau (cap.), Dominica 156/G4
Roseau (cap.), Dominica 161/E7
Roseau (riv.), Dominica 161/E7
Roseau (co.), Minn. 255/C2
Roseau, Minn. (56751) 255/C2
Roseau (riv.), Minn. 255/B2
Roseau (riv.), St. Lucia 161/G6
Roseau River, Manitoba 179/F5
Roseaux, Haiti 158/A6
Rosebank, Manitoba 179/D5
Roseberry, Br. Col. 184/J5
Rosebery, Tasmania 99/B3
Rose Blanche, Newf. 166/C4
Roseboom, N.Y. (13450) 276/L5
Roseboro, N.C. (28382) 281/N5
Rosebud, Alberta 182/D4
Rosebud (riv.), Alberta 182/D4
Rose Bud, Ark. (72137) 202/F3
Rosebud, Mo. (63091) 261/K6
Rosebud (co.), Mont. 262/K4
Rosebud, Mont. (59347) 262/K4
Rosebud (creek), Mont. 262/K4
Rosebud, S. Dak. (57570) 298/H7
Rosebud, Texas (76570) 303/G7
Rosebud (creek), Utah 304/A2
Rosebud Ind. Res., S. Dak. 298/H7
Roseburg, Oreg. (97470) 291/D4
Rosebush Mich. (48878) 250/E5
Rose City, Mich. (48654) 250/E4
Rose Creek, Minn. (55970) 255/F7
Rosedale, Ind. (47874) 227/C5
Rosedale, La. (70772) 238/G6
Rosedale, Md. (21237) 245/M3
Rosedale, Miss. (38769) 256/B3
Rosedale, Okla. (†74831) 288/M5
Rosedale, Tenn. (†37728) 237/N8
Rosedale, Va. (24280) 307/E7
Rosedale, W. Va. (26636) 312/E5
Rosefield, La. (†71435) 238/G3
Roseglen, N. Dak. (58775) 282/G4
Rosehearty, Scotland 15/F3
Rosehill, Ala. (†36028) 195/F8
Rose Hill, Barbados 161/B8
Rose Hill, Ill. (†62448) 222/E4
Rose Hill, Iowa (52586) 229/J6
Rose Hill, Kansas (67133) 232/E4
Rose Hill, Ky. (†40330) 237/M5
Rose Hill, Miss. (39356) 256/F6
Rose Hill, N.C. (28458) 281/N5
Rose Hill, Va. (24281) 307/B7
Roseisle, Manitoba 179/D5
Rose Lake, Br. Col. 184/E3
Roseland, Ark. (72463) 202/K2
Roseland, Fla. (32957) 212/F4
Roseland, Ind. (†46601) 227/E1
Roseland, Kansas (†66773) 232/H4
Roseland, La. (70456) 238/J5
Roseland, Minn. (†56216) 255/C6
Roseland, Nebr. (68973) 264/F4
Roseland, N.J. (07068) 273/A2
Roseland, Va. (22967) 307/K5
Roselawn, Ind. (†46310) 227/C2
Roselle, Ill. (60172) 222/A5
Roselle, N.J. (07203) 273/B2
Roselle Park, N.J. (07204) 273/A2
Rose Lodge, Oreg. (97372) 291/D3
Rose Lynn, Alberta 182/E4
Rosemark, Tenn. (38053) 237/B10
Rosemary, Alberta 182/E4
Rosemead, Calif. (91770) 204/C10
Rosemère, Québec 172/H4
Rosemont, Ill. (60018) 222/B5
Rosemont, Md. (†21758) 245/H3
Rosemont, N.J. (08556) 273/D3
Rosemont, Pa. (19010) 294/M5
Rosemount, Minn. (55068) 255/E6
Rosemount, Ohio (†45662) 284/D8
Rosen, Minn. (†56212) 255/B5
Rosenberg, Texas (77471) 303/J8
Rosendale, Minn. (†56243) 255/D5
Rosendale, Mo. (64483) 261/C2
Rosendale, N.Y. (12472) 276/M7
Rosendale, Wis. (54974) 317/J8
Rosenfeld, Manitoba 179/E5
Rosengart, Manitoba 179/E5
Rosenhayn, N.J. (08352) 273/C5
Rosenheim, W. Germany 22/D5
Rosenhof, Sask. 181/D5
Rosenlaui, Switzerland 39/F3
Rosenort, Manitoba 179/E5
Rosepine, La. (70659) 238/D5
Rose Prairie, Br. Col. 184/G2
Roseray, Sask. 181/C5
Roseto, Pa. (18013) 294/M4
Rosetown, Sask. 162/F5
Rosetown, Sask. 181/D4
Rosetta, Egypt 111/J2
Rosetta, Egypt 59/B3
Rosetta, Miss. (†39633) 256/B8
Rosette, Utah (†84329) 304/A2
Rose Valley, Pa. (†19065) 294/L7
Rose Valley, Sask. 181/H3
Roseville, Calif. (95678) 204/B8
Roseville, Ill. (61473) 222/C3
Roseville, Mich. (48066) 250/B6
Roseville, Minn. (55113) 255/G5
Roseville, Ohio (43777) 284/F6
Roseville, Pa. (†16933) 294/H2
Roseway (riv.), Nova Scotia 168/C4
Rosewood, North. Terr. 93/A4
Rosewood, Ohio (43070) 284/C5
Rosewood Heights, Ill. (†62024) 222/B2
Roseworthy, S. Australia 94/B6
Roshage (cape), Denmark 18/F8
Rosharon, Texas (77583) 303/J3
Rosh Ha 'Ayin, Israel 65/B3
Rosholt, S. Dak. (57260) 298/R2
Rosholt, Wis. (54473) 317/H6
Rosh Pinna, Israel 65/D2
Rosice, Czech. 41/D2
Rosiclare, Ill. (62982) 222/E6
Rosie, Ark. (72571) 202/G2
Rosier, Georgia (†30434) 217/H5
Rosignano Marittimo, Italy 34/C3
Rosignol, Guyana 131/C2
Rosine, Ky. (42370) 237/H6
Roşiori de Vede, Romania 45/G3
Rositsa, Bulgaria 45/H4
Roskilde (co.), Denmark 21/E6
Roskilde, Denmark 21/E6
Roskilde, Denmark 18/G9
Roslavl', U.S.S.R. 52/D4
Roslev, Denmark 21/B4
Roslin, Ontario 177/G3
Roslin, Tenn. (†38556) 237/M8
Roslyn, N.Y. (11576) 276/R6
Roslyn, S. Dak. (57261) 298/P2
Roslyn, Wash. (98941) 310/E3
Rosman, N.C. (28772) 281/D4
Rosmaninhal, Portugal 33/C3
Røsnaes (pen.), Denmark 21/D6
Rosneath, Scotland 15/A1
Rosneath, Scotland 10/A1
Ross (isl.), Ant. 2/T10
Ross (sea), Ant. 2/A10
Ross (isl.) 5/B9
Ross (sea) 5/B10
Ross, Calif. (94957) 204/H1
Ross, Iowa (†50025) 229/D5
Ross, Manitoba 179/F5
Ross (isl.), Manitoba 179/J3
Ross, Minn. (56753) 255/C2
Ross (isl.), New Bruns. 170/D4
Ross, N. Zealand 100/C5
Ross (pt.), Norfolk I. 88/L6
Ross, N. Dak. (58776) 282/E3
Ross (co.), Ohio 284/D7
Ross, Ohio (45061) 284/B9
Ross, Tasmania 99/D4
Ross (dam), Wash. 310/D2
Ross (lake), Wash. 310/D2
Rossa, Switzerland 39/H4
Rossall (pt.), England 13/D4
Rossan (pt.), Ireland 10/B3
Ross and Cromarty (trad. co.), Scotland 15/A5
Rossano, Italy 34/F5
Rossarden, Tasmania 99/D3
Ross Barnett (res.), Miss. 256/D6
Ross Bay Junction, Newf. 166/A3
Rossbear (lake), Alberta 182/C1
Rossburg, Ohio (45362) 284/A5
Rossburn, Manitoba 179/B4
Rosscarbery, Ireland 17/C8
Rosscarbery (bay), Ireland 10/B5
Rosscarbery (bay), Ireland 17/D9
Rosseau, Ontario 177/E2
Rosseau (lake), Ontario 177/E2
Rossel (isl.), Papua N.G. 85/D8
Rossendale, Manitoba 179/D5
Rosser, Manitoba 179/E4
Rosses (bay), Ireland 17/D1
Rosses Point, Ireland 17/D3
Rossford, Ohio (43460) 284/C2
Ross Fork, Mont. (†59457) 262/G3
Ross Ice Shelf, Ant. 2/A11
Ross Ice Shelf 5/A10
Rossie, Iowa (51356) 229/C2
Rossie, N.Y. (†13646) 276/J2
Rossignol (lake), Nova Scotia 168/C4
Rossing, Namibia 118/B4
Rossiter, Pa. (15772) 294/E4
Rosskeeragh (pt.), Ireland 17/D3
Ross Lake Nat'l Rec. Area, Wash. 310/E2
Rossland, Br. Col. 162/E6
Rossland, Br. Col. 184/H6
Rosslare, Ireland 10/C4
Rosslare, Ireland 17/J7
Rosslare (bay), Ireland 17/J7
Rosslare Harbour (Ballygeary), Ireland 17/J7
Rosslau, E. Germany 22/E3
Rosslyn Farms, Pa. (†15106) 294/B7
Rosslyn Village, Ontario 177/G5
Rosslyn Village, Ontario 175/C3
Rossmore, W. Va. (25643) 312/C7
Rossmoyne, Ohio (45236) 284/C9
Rosso, Mauritania 106/A5
Rosso, Mauritania 102/A3
Ross of Mull (pen.), Scotland 15/B4
Ross-on-Wye, England 10/E5
Ross-on-Wye, England 13/E6
Rossosh', U.S.S.R. 52/E4
Rossport, Ontario 177/H5
Ross River, Yukon 187/E3
Rosstock (mt.), Switzerland 39/G3
Rosston, Ark. (71858) 202/D6
Rosston, Ind. (†46077) 227/E4
Rosston, Okla. (73855) 288/G1

S

Sainte-Marguerite 439

Saas, Switzerland 39/J3
Saas Fee, Switzerland 39/E4
Saba (isl.), Neth. Ant. 156/F3
Saba (isl.), Virgin Is. (U.S.) 161/A4
Šabac, Yugoslavia 45/D3
Sabadell, Spain 7/E4
Sabadell, Spain 33/H2
Sabae, Japan 81/H5
Sabah (state), Malaysia 2/Q5
Sabah (state), Malaysia 85/F4
Sabah (reg.), Malaysia 54/N9
Sábalo, Cuba 158/A2
Sabana, Cuba 158/K4
Sabana (arch.), Cuba 158/E1
Sabana de la Mar, Dom. Rep. 156/E3
Sabana de la Mar, Dom. Rep. 158/F5
Sabana Grande, Dom. Rep. 158/E6
Sabanagrande, Honduras 154/D4
Sabana Grande, P. Rico 161/B2
Sabanalarga, Colombia 126/C2
Sabana Seca, P. Rico 161/D1
Sabancuy, Mexico 150/O7
Sabaneta, Dom. Rep. 158/D5
Sabaneta, Barinas, Venezuela 124/D3
Sabaneta, Falcón, Venezuela 124/D2
Sabang, Celebes, Indonesia 85/F5
Sabang, Weh, Indonesia 85/B4
Şabanözü, Turkey 63/E2
Sabará, Brazil 135/E1
Sabattus, Maine (04280) 243/C7
Sabattus○, Maine (04280) 243/C7
Sabaudia, Italy 34/D4
Sabaya, Bolivia 136/A6
Saberi, Hamun-e (lake), Iran 66/M5
Sabetha, Kansas (66534) 232/G2
Sabi (riv.), Zimbabwe 118/E3
Sabile, U.S.S.R. 53/B2
Sabillasville, Md. (21780) 245/J2
Sabin, Minn. (56580) 255/B4
Sabina, Ohio (45169) 284/C7
Sabinal (cay), Cuba 158/H2
Sabinal, Texas (78881) 303/E8
Sabinas, Mexico 150/J3
Sabinas (riv.), Mexico 150/J3
Sabinas Hidalgo, Mexico 150/J3
Sabine (riv.) 188/H4
Sabine (mt.) 5/B9
Sabine (par.), La. 238/C3
Sabine (lake), La. 238/C7
Sabine (passage), La. 238/C7
Sabine (riv.), La. 238/C5
Sabine (pen.), N.W. Terrs. 187/H2
Sabine (co.), Texas 303/L6
Sabine, Texas (†77640) 303/L8
Sabine (lake), Texas 303/L8
Sabine (riv.), Texas 303/L7
Sabine Pass, Texas (77655) 303/L8
Sabinópolis, Brazil 132/F7
Sabinoso, N. Mex. (†87746) 274/E3
Sabinov, Czech. 41/F2
Sabinsville, Pa. (16943) 294/G2
Sabir, Jebel (mt.), Yemen Arab Rep. 59/D7
Sabirabad, U.S.S.R. 52/G6
Sabkha, Syria 63/H5
Sablayan, Philippines 82/C4
Sable (cape), Fla. 188/K5
Sable (cape), Fla. 212/E6
Sable (cape), N.S. 146/M5
Sable (isl.), N.S. 146/N5
Sable (cape), N.S. 162/K7
Sable (isl.), N.S. 162/L7
Sable (cape), Nova Scotia 168/C5
Sable (isl.), Nova Scotia 168/J5
Sable (riv.), Ontario 177/B1
Sable (riv.), Québec 174/D1
Sable River, Nova Scotia 168/C5
Sables (lake), Québec 172/B3
Sables (lake), Québec 172/H1
Sablé-sur-Sarthe, France 28/C4
Sabougla, Miss. (†38955) 256/F3
Sabra (cape), Indonesia 85/J6
Sabrathaa, Libya 111/B1
Sabrina Coast (reg.) 5/C6
Sabtang, Philippines 82/B2
Sabtang (isl.), Philippines 82/B2
Sabugal, Portugal 33/C2
Sabula, Iowa (52070) 229/N4
Sabula, Mo. (†63620) 261/L8
Sabula, Pa. (†15801) 294/E3
Sabya, Saudi Arabia 59/D6
Sabzevar, Iran 54/G6
Sabzevar, Iran 59/G2
Sabzevar, Iran 66/K2
Sabzvaran, Iran 66/K6
Sabzvaran, Iran 59/G4
Sac (co.), Iowa 229/C4
Sac (riv.), Mo. 261/E7
Sacaba, Bolivia 136/C5
Sacaca, Bolivia 136/B6
Sacajawea (peak), Oreg. 291/K2
Sacajawea (lake), Wash. 310/G4
Sácama, Colombia 126/D4
Sacandaga (lake), N.Y. 276/L3
Sac and Fox Ind. Res., Iowa 229/H5
Sacapulas, Guatemala 154/B3
Sacaton, Ariz. (85247) 198/D5
Sacavém, Portugal 33/A1
Sac City, Iowa (50583) 229/C4
Sacedón, Spain 33/E2
Săcele, Romania 45/G3
Sac-Fox-Iowa Ind. Res., Kansas 232/G2
Sacheen (lake), Wash. 310/H2
Sachem (head), Conn. 210/E4
Sachem Head, Conn. (†06437) 210/E3
Sachigo (riv.), Ont. 162/G5
Sachigo (riv.), Ontario 175/B2
Sachojere, Bolivia 136/C4
Sachse, Texas (†75040) 303/H2
Sachseln, Switzerland 39/F3
Sachs Harbour, Canada 4/B16
Sachs Harbour, N.W.T. 162/D1
Sachs Harbour, N.W. Terrs. 187/F2
Sackets (harb.), N.Y. 276/H3
Sackets Harbor, N.Y. (13685) 276/H3
Säckingen, W. Germany 22/C5
Sackville, New Bruns. 170/F3
Sackville, Nova Scotia 168/E4
Saco, Ala. (†36081) 195/G7
Saco, Maine (04072) 243/C8
Saco (riv.), Maine 243/B8
Saco, Mo. (†63645) 261/M8
Saco, Mont. (59261) 262/J2
Saco (riv.), N.H. 268/E3
Sacol (isl.), Philippines 82/D7
Sacramento, Brazil 132/D7
Sacramento, Brazil 135/C1
Sacramento (cap.), Calif. 146/F6
Sacramento (cap.), Calif. 188/B3
Sacramento (riv.), Calif. 188/B3
Sacramento (co.), Calif. 204/D5
Sacramento (cap.), Calif. (*95801) 204/B8
Sacramento (riv.), Calif. 204/D5
Sacramento, Ky. (42372) 237/G6
Sacramento, N. Mex. (88347) 274/D6
Sacramento (mts.), N. Mex. 274/D6
Sacramento Army Depot, Calif. 204/B8
Sacramento Wash (dry riv.), Ariz. 198/A4
Sacratif (cape), Spain 33/E4
Sacré-Coeur-de-Saguenay, Québec 172/H1
Sacred Heart, Minn. (56285) 255/C6
Sacul, Texas (75788) 303/K6
Sádaba, Spain 33/F1
Sadani, Tanzania 115/G5
Saddle (hills), Alberta 182/A2
Saddle, Ark. (†72554) 202/G1
Saddle (mt.), Idaho 220/F6
Saddle (mt.), Idaho 220/D3
Saddle (riv.), N.J. 273/B1
Saddle (mts.), Wash. 310/E4
Saddle Brook○, N.J. (07662) 273/B1
Saddle Mountain, Okla. (†73023) 288/J5
Saddle River, N.J. (07458) 273/B1
Saddlestring, Wyo. (82840) 319/F1
Saddleworth, England 13/J2
Saddleworth, England 10/G2
Sa Dec, Vietnam 72/E5
Sadhoowa, Trin. & Tob. 161/B11
Sadieville, Ky. (40370) 237/M4
Sadij (riv.), Iran 66/L8
Sadiya, India 68/H3
Sa'diya, Iraq 66/D3
Sa'diya, Hor (lake), Iraq 66/E4
Sadlers Village, St. Chris.-Nevis 161/C10
Sadlersville, Tenn. (37154) 237/G7
Sado (isl.), Japan 81/J4
Sado (riv.), Portugal 33/B3
Sadon, Burma 72/C1
Sadorus, Ill. (61872) 222/E4
Saeby, Denmark 18/G8
Saeby, Denmark 21/D3
Saegertown, Pa. (16433) 294/B2
Saetermoen, Norway 18/L2
Saetermoen, Norway 18/L2
Safad (Zefat), Israel 65/C2
Safaniya, Ras (cape), Saudi Arabia 59/E4
Šafárikovo, Czech. 41/F2
Safata (bay), W. Samoa 86/M9
Safe, Mo. (†65559) 261/J6
Safety Harbor, Fla. (33572) 212/B2
Säffle, Sweden 18/H7
Safford, Ala. (36773) 195/D6
Safford, Ariz. (85546) 198/F6
Saffordville, Kansas (†66869) 232/F3
Saffron Walden, England 10/G4
Saffron Walden, England 13/H5
Safi, Jordan 65/E5
Safi, Morocco 102/B1
Safi, Morocco 106/C2
Safidar, Kuh-e (mt.), Iran 59/F4
Safidar, Kuh-e (mt.), Iran 66/H6
Safid Rud (riv.), Iran 66/F2
Safien, Switzerland 39/H3
Safita, Syria 63/G5
Safonovo, U.S.S.R. 52/D3
Safranbolu, Turkey 63/E2
Safut, Jordan 65/D3
Saga, China 77/B6
Saga (pref.), Japan 81/E7
Saga, Japan 81/E7
Sagadahoc (co.), Maine 243/D7
Sagaing (div.), Burma 72/B1
Sagaing, Burma 72/B2
Sagami (bay), Japan 81/O3
Sagami (riv.), Japan 81/O2
Sagami (sea), Japan 81/J6
Sagamihara, Japan 81/O2
Sagamore, Mass. (02561) 249/M5
Sagamore, Pa. (16250) 294/D4
Sagamore Hill Nat'l Hist. Site, N.Y. 276/R6
Sagamore Hills, Ohio (†44067) 284/J10
Saganaga (lake), Minn. 255/H2
Saganaga (lake), Ontario 175/B3
Sagar, India 68/D4
Sagavanirktok (riv.), Alaska 196/J1
Sagay, Camiguin, Philippines 82/E6
Sagay, Negros Occ., Philippines 82/D5
Sage, Ark. (72573) 202/G1
Sage (creek), Mont. 262/F2
Sage (mt.), Virgin Is. (Br.) 161/D4
Sage, Wyo. (†83101) 319/B4
Sagemace (bay), Manitoba 179/B3
Sagerton, Texas (79548) 303/E4
Sageville, Iowa (†52001) 229/M3
Sag Harbor, N.Y. (11963) 276/R8
Saginaw, Ala. (35137) 195/E4
Saginaw, Mich. 188/K2
Saginaw (bay), Mich. 188/K2
Saginaw (co.), Mich. 250/E5
Saginaw, Mich. (*48601) 250/F5
Saginaw (bay), Mich. 250/F5
Saginaw (riv.), Mich. 250/F5
Saginaw, Minn. (55779) 255/F4
Saginaw, Mo. (64864) 261/C8
Saginaw, Oreg. (97472) 291/E4
Saginaw, Texas (76179) 303/E2
Sagle, Idaho (83860) 220/B1
Saglek (bay), Newf. 166/B2
Saglek (fjord), Newf. 166/B2
Saglouc, Que. 162/J3
Saglouc, Québec 174/E1
Sagnay, Philippines 82/D4
Sagola, Mich. (49881) 250/B2
Saguache (co.), Colo. 208/G6
Saguache, Colo. (81149) 208/G6
Saguache (creek), Colo. 208/F6
Sagua de Tánamo, Cuba 158/K3
Sagua la Grande, Cuba 156/B2
Sagua la Grande, Cuba 158/E1
Sagua la Grande (riv.), Cuba 158/E1
Saguaro (lake), Ariz. 198/D5
Saguaro Nat'l Mon., Ariz. 198/E6
Saguenay (county), Québec 174/D2
Saguenay (co.), Québec 172/H1
Saguenay (riv.), Québec 174/C3
Saguenay (riv.), Québec 172/G1
Saguia el Hamra (dry riv.), Western Sahara 106/B3
Sagunto, Spain 33/F3
Sa'gya, China 77/C6
Sahagún, Colombia 126/C3
Sahagún, Spain 33/D1
Sahand, Kuh-e (mt.), Iran 66/E2
Sahara (desert) 2/J4
Sahara (des.) 102/C2
Sahara (des.), Algeria 106/E4
Sahara (des.), Chad 111/C3
Sahara (des.), Egypt 111/E3
Sahara (des.), Libya 111/C3
Sahara (des.), Mali 106/D4
Sahara (des.), Mauritania 106/C4
Sahara (des.), Niger 106/F4
Sahara (des.), Sudan 111/E3
Saharan Atlas (ranges), Algeria 106/E2
Saharanpur, India 68/D3
Saharsa, India 68/F3
Şahinli, Turkey 63/C6
Sahiwal, Pakistan 68/C2
Sahiwal, Pakistan 59/K3
Sahuaripa, Mexico 150/E2
Sahuarita, Ariz. (85629) 198/E7
Sahuayo de Díaz, Mexico 150/H7
Šahy, Czech. 41/E2
Saïda, Algeria 106/E2
Saida, Lebanon 63/F6
Sa'idabad, Iran 66/J6
Sa'idabad, Iran 59/G4
Saïdia, Morocco 106/D2
Saidor, Papua N.G. 85/B7
Saidu, Pakistan 68/C2
Saignelégier, Switzerland 39/D2
Saigo, Japan 81/F5
Saigon (Ho Chi Minh City), Vietnam 54/M8
Saihut, P.D.R. Yemen 54/G8
Saihut, P.D.R. Yemen 59/F6
Saikai National Park, Japan 81/D7
Saiki, Japan 81/E7
Sailes, La. (†71028) 238/D2
Sailor (creek), Idaho 220/C7
Sailor Springs, Ill. (62879) 222/E5
Saimaa (lake), Finland 18/Q6
Saimbeyli, Turkey 63/G4
Sain Alto, Mexico 150/H5
Sain-ni, N. Korea 81/B4
Saint Abbs, Scotland 15/F5
Saint Abbs (head), Scotland 15/F5
Saint-Adalbert, Québec 172/H3
Saint-Adelme, Québec 172/B1
Saint-Adelphe, Québec 172/E3
Saint Adolphe, Manitoba 179/E5
Saint-Adolphe, Québec 172/F2
Saint-Adolphe-d'Howard, Québec 172/C4
Saint-Adrien, Québec 172/F4
Saint-Affrique, France 28/E6
Saint-Agapitville, Québec 172/F3
Saint Agatha○, Maine (04772) 243/G1
Saint Agnes, England 13/B7
Saint-Aimé-des-Lacs, Québec 172/G2
Saint-Alban, Québec 172/E3
Saint Albans, England 13/H7
Saint Albans, England 10/F5
Saint Alban's (head), England 13/F7
Saint Albans○, Maine (04971) 243/E6
Saint Albans, Mo. (63073) 261/L5
Saint Alban's, Newf. 166/C4
Saint Albans, Vt. (05478) 268/A2
Saint Albans○, Vt. (05478) 268/A2
Saint Albans, W. Va. (25177) 312/C6
Saint Albans Bay, Vt. (05481) 268/A2
Saint Albert, Alberta 182/D3
Saint Albert, Ontario 177/J2
Saint-Albert, Québec 172/E3
Saint-Alexandre, Québec 172/D4
Saint-Alexandre-de-Kamouraska, Québec 172/H2
Saint-Alexis, Québec 172/D4
Saint-Alexis-de-Matapédia, Québec 172/B2
Saint-Alexis-des-Monts, Québec 172/D3
Saint Almo, New Bruns. 170/C2
Saint Alphonse, Manitoba 179/C5
Saint-Alphonse, Québec 172/D3
Saint Alphonse de Clare, Nova Scotia 168/B4
Saint-Alphonse-de-Caplan, Québec 172/C2
Saint-Amable, Québec 172/J4
Saint-Amand-Mont-Rond, France 28/E4
Saint Amant, La. (70774) 238/L2
Saint Ambroise, Manitoba 179/E4
Saint-Ambroise, Québec 172/F1
Saint-Anaclet, Québec 172/J1
Saint-André (cape), Madagascar 118/G3
Saint-André, New Bruns. 170/C1
Saint-André, Québec 172/B2
Saint-André, Réunion 118/G5
Saint-André-Avellin, Québec 172/B4
Saint-André-de-Kamouraska, Québec 172/H2
Saint-André-du-Lac-Saint-Jean, Québec 172/E1
Saint-André-Est, Québec 172/C4
Saint Andrew (pt.), Fla. 212/D6
Saint Andrew (sound), Georgia 217/K9
Saint Andrew (lake), Manitoba 179/E3
Saint Andrew (mt.), St. Vin. & Grens. 161/A9
Saint Andrews, New Bruns. 170/C3
Saint Andrew's, Newf. 166/C4
Saint Andrews, Nova Scotia 168/F3
Saint Andrews (chan.), Nova Scotia 168/H2
Saint Andrews, Scotland 15/F4
Saint Andrews, Scotland 10/E2
Saint Andrews (bay), Scotland 15/F4
Saint Andrews, S.C. (29407) 296/G6
Saint Andrews, Tenn. (37372) 237/K10
Saint-Anicet, Québec 172/C4
Saint Ann, Mo. (63074) 261/O2
Saint Anne, Chan. Is. 13/E8
Saint Anne, Ill. (60964) 222/F2
Saint Anns (bay), Nova Scotia 168/H2
Saint Anns, Ontario 177/E4
Saint Ann's Bay, Jamaica 156/C3
Saint Ann's Bay, Jamaica 158/J5
Saint-Anselme, Québec 172/F3
Saint Ansgar, Iowa (50472) 229/H2
Saint Anthony, Idaho (83445) 220/G6
Saint Anthony, Ind. (47575) 227/D8
Saint Anthony, Iowa (50239) 229/G4
Saint Anthony, Minn. (†56307) 255/D5
Saint Anthony, Minn. (55414) 255/G5
Saint Anthony, Newf. 166/C3
Saint Anthony, N. Dak. (58566) 282/H6
Saint-Antoine, New Bruns. 170/F2
Saint-Antoine, Québec 172/H4
Saint-Antoine-Abbé, Québec 172/D4
Saint-Antoine-sur-Richelieu, Québec 172/D4
Saint-Antonin, Québec 172/H2
Saint-Antonin-Noble-Val, France 28/D5
Saint Arnaud, Victoria 97/B5
Saint-Arsène, Québec 172/H2
Saint Arthur, New Bruns. 170/D1
Saint-Astier, France 28/D5
Saint-Athanase, Québec 172/H2
Saint-Aubert, Québec 172/G2
Saint Aubin, Chan. Is. 13/E8
Saint-Aubin-Sauges, Switzerland 39/C3
Saint Augustin (riv.), Newf. 166/C3
Saint-Augustin, Québec 172/G4
Saint-Augustin, Québec 174/F2
Saint-Augustin (riv.), Québec 174/F2
Saint-Augustin-de-Québec, Québec 172/E3
Saint Augustine, Fla. 188/K5
Saint Augustine, Fla. 146/K7
Saint Augustine, Fla. (32084) 212/E2
Saint Augustine, Ill. (61474) 222/C3
Saint Augustine, Md. (†21915) 245/P3
Saint Augustine Beach, Fla. (32084) 212/E2
Saint Austell (bay), England 13/C7
Saint Austell-with-Fowey, England 13/C7
Saint Austell with Fowey, England 10/D5
Saint-Barnabé, Québec 172/D4
Saint-Barthélemy (isl.), Guadeloupe 156/F3
Saint-Barthélemy, Québec 172/D3
Saint Basile, New Bruns. 170/B1
Saint-Basile-le-Grand, Québec 172/J4
Saint-Basile-Sud, Québec 172/F3
Saint Bees (head), England 13/D3
Saint Benedict, Kansas (†66538) 232/F2
Saint Benedict, La. (70457) 238/K5
Saint Benedict, Oreg. (97373) 291/B3
Saint Benedict, Pa. (15773) 294/E4
Saint Benedict, Sask. 181/F3
Saint-Benjamin, Québec 172/G3
Saint-Benoît, Réunion 118/G5
Saint-Benoît-Labre, Québec 172/G3
Saint Bernard, Ala. (35138) 195/E2
Saint Bernard (par.), La. 238/L7
Saint Bernard, La. (70085) 238/L7
Saint Bernard, Nova Scotia 168/B4
Saint Bernard, Ohio (45217) 284/B9
Saint-Bernard, Québec 172/F3
Saint Bernard, Great (pass), Switzerland 39/D5
Saint-Bernard-sur-Mer, Québec 172/G2
Saint Bernice, Ind. (47875) 227/C5
Saint Bethlehem, Tenn. (37155) 237/G7
Saint Blaise, Québec 172/E4
Saint-Blaise, Switzerland 39/D2
Saint-Bonaventure-de-Yamaska, Québec 172/E4
Saint-Boniface-de-Shawinigan, Québec 172/D3
Saint Bonifacius, Minn. (55375) 255/F5
Saint Brendan's, Newf. 166/D4
Saint Brides, Alberta 182/E2
Saint Bride's, Newf. 166/C2
Saint Brides (bay), Wales 10/D5
Saint Brides (bay), Wales 13/B6
Saint-Brieuc, France 28/B3
Saint Brieux, Sask. 181/G3
Saint-Bruno, Québec 172/F1
Saint-Bruno-de-Montarville, Québec 172/J4
Saint-Calais, France 28/D4
Saint-Calixte-de-Kilkenny, Québec 172/D4
Saint-Camille, Québec 172/F4
Saint-Camille-de-Bellechasse, Québec 172/G3
Saint-Casimir, Québec 172/E3
Saint Catharine, Mo. (64677) 261/G3
Saint Catharines, Ontario 177/E4
Saint Catherine, Fla. (†33513) 212/D3
Saint Catherine (mt.), Grenada 161/D8
Saint Catherine (lake), Vt. 268/A5
Saint Catherines (isl.), Georgia 217/K7
Saint Catherines (sound), Georgia 217/K7
Saint-Céré, France 28/D5
Saint-Cergue, Switzerland 39/B4
Saint-Césaire, Québec 172/D4
Saint-Chamond, France 28/F5
Saint Charles, Ark. (72140) 202/H5
Saint Charles, Idaho (83272) 220/G7
Saint Charles, Ill. (60174) 222/E2
Saint Charles, Iowa (50240) 229/F6
Saint Charles, Ky. (42453) 237/F6
Saint Charles (par.), La. 238/K7
Saint Charles, Mich. (48655) 250/E5
Saint Charles, Minn. (55972) 255/F7
Saint Charles (co.), Mo. 261/M2
Saint Charles, Mo. (63301) 261/N1
Saint-Charles, New Bruns. 170/F2
Saint Charles, Ontario 177/D1
Saint-Charles, Bellechasse, Québec 172/G3
Saint Charles, S.C. (29134) 296/G3
Saint Charles, S. Dak. (57571) 298/L7
Saint Charles, Va. (24282) 307/B7
Saint-Charles-de-Mandeville, Québec 172/D3
Saint-Charles-Garnier, Québec 172/J1
Saint-Charles-sur-Richelieu, Québec 172/D4
SAINT CHRISTOPHER-NEVIS 156/F3
SAINT CHRISTOPHER (SAINT KITTS)-NEVIS 161/D11
Saint Christopher (isl.), St. Chris.-Nevis 156/F3
Saint Christopher (isl.), St. Chris.-Nevis 161/D10
Saint Chrysostom, Pr. Edward I. 168/E2
Saint-Chrysostome, Québec 172/D4
Saint Clair (co.), Ala. 195/F3
Saint Clair, Ala. (36774) 195/E6
Saint Clair, Georgia (†30816) 217/H4
Saint Clair (co.), Ill. 222/D5
Saint Clair (lake), Mich. 188/K2
Saint Clair (co.), Mich. 250/G6
Saint Clair, Mich. (48079) 250/G6
Saint Clair (lake), Mich. 250/G6
Saint Clair (riv.), Mich. 250/G6
Saint Clair, Minn. (56080) 255/E6
Saint Clair (co.), Mo. 261/E6
Saint Clair, Mo. (63077) 261/K6
Saint Clair (lake), Ontario 177/B5
Saint Clair (riv.), Ontario 177/B5
Saint Clair, Pa. (17970) 294/K4
Saint Clair (lake), Tasmania 99/C4
Saint Clair Beach, Ontario 177/B5
Saint Clair Shores, Mich. (*48080) 250/B6
Saint Clair Springs, Ala. (†35146) 195/F3
Saint Clairsville, Ohio (43950) 284/J5
Saint Clairsville, Pa. (16676) 294/F5
Saint-Claude, France 28/F4
Saint-Claude, Guadeloupe 161/A7
Saint Claude, Manitoba 179/D5
Saint-Claude, Québec 172/F4
Saint Clears, Wales 13/C6
Saint-Clément, Québec 172/H2
Saint Clements, Ontario 177/D4
Saint-Cléophas, Québec 172/D3
Saint-Clet, Québec 172/C4
Saint Cloud, Fla. (32769) 212/E3
Saint-Cloud, France 28/A2
Saint Cloud, Minn. 188/H1
Saint Cloud, Minn. (56301) 255/D5
Saint Cloud, Wis. (53079) 317/K8
Saint Columb Major, England 13/B7
Saint Combs, Scotland 15/G3
Saint-Côme, Québec 172/D3
Saint-Constant, Québec 172/H4
Saint Croix (riv.) 188/H1
Saint Croix, Ind. (47576) 227/D8
Saint Croix (riv.), Maine 243/J5
Saint Croix (riv.), Minn. 255/F5
Saint Croix, New Bruns. 170/C3
Saint Croix (riv.), New Bruns. 170/C3
Saint Croix, Nova Scotia 168/E4
Saint Croix (isl.), Virgin Is. (U.S.) 156/H2
Saint Croix (isl.), Virgin Is. (U.S.) 161/G4
Saint Croix (co.), Wis. 317/B5
Saint Croix (lake), Wis. 317/A6
Saint Croix (riv.), Wis. 317/A4
Saint Croix Falls, Wis. (54024) 317/A5
Saint Croix Flowage (res.), Wis. 317/C3
Saint Croix Isl. Nat'l Mon., Maine 243/J5
Saint-Cuthbert, Québec 172/D3
Saint-Cyprien, Québec 172/J2
Saint-Cyrille-de-L'Islet, Québec 172/G3
Saint Cyrus, Scotland 15/F4
Saint-Damase, Québec 172/B1
Saint-Damase-des-Aulnaies, Québec 172/C2
Saint-Damien-de-Brandon, Québec 172/D3
Saint-Damien-de-Buckland, Québec 172/G3
Saint David, Ariz. (85630) 198/E7
Saint David, Ill. (61563) 222/C3
Saint David, Maine (04773) 243/G1
Saint-David, Québec 172/J3
Saint-David-de-Falardeau, Québec 172/F1
Saint-David-d'Yamaska, Québec 172/E4
Saint Davids (isl.), Bermuda 156/H2
Saint David's, Wales 13/B6
Saint David's (head), Wales 10/D5
Saint David's (head), Wales 13/B6
Saint-Denis, France 28/B1
Saint-Denis, Québec 172/D4
Saint-Denis (cap.), Réunion 118/F5
Saint Denis, Sask. 181/F3
Saint-Denis-de-la-Bouteillerie, Québec 172/G2
Saint-Didace, Québec 172/D3
Saint-Dié, France 28/G3
Saint-Dizier, France 28/F3
Saint-Dominique, Québec 172/E4
Saint-Donat-de-Montcalm, Québec 172/C3
Saint-Donat-de-Rimouski, Québec 172/J1
Saint Donatus, Iowa (52071) 229/M4
Sainte-Adèle, Québec 172/C4
Sainte Agathe, Manitoba 179/E5
Sainte-Agathe, Québec 172/F3
Sainte-Agathe-des-Monts, Québec 172/C3
Sainte-Agnes-de-Charlevoix, Québec 172/G2
Sainte Amélie, Manitoba 179/C4
Sainte-Anastasie, Québec 172/F3
Sainte-Angèle-de-Mérici, Québec 172/J1
Sainte Anne (lake), Alberta 182/C3
Sainte-Anne, Guadeloupe 161/B6
Sainte Anne, Manitoba 179/F5
Sainte-Anne, Martinique 161/D7
Sainte-Anne, New Bruns. 170/E1
Sainte-Anne (lake), Québec 172/H2
Sainte-Anne (riv.), Québec 172/C1
Sainte-Anne (riv.), Québec 172/G2
Sainte-Anne (riv.), Québec 172/F3
Sainte Anne (isl.), Seychelles 118/H5
Sainte-Anne-de-Beaupré, Québec 172/F2
Sainte-Anne-de-Bellevue, Québec 172/H4
Sainte-Anne-de-Kent, New Bruns. 170/F2
Sainte-Anne-de-Madawaska, New Bruns. 170/B1
Sainte-Anne-des-Monts, Québec 172/C1
Sainte-Anne-des-Plaines, Québec 172/H4
Sainte-Anne-du-Lac, Québec 172/B3
Sainte-Apolline, Québec 172/G3
Sainte-Aurélie, Québec 172/G3
Sainte-Béatrix, Québec 172/D3
Sainte-Bernadette, Québec 172/G1
Sainte-Blandine, Québec 172/J1
Sainte-Brigide, Québec 172/D4
Sainte-Catherine, Québec 172/F3
Sainte-Cécile-de-Frontenac, Québec 172/G4
Sainte-Cécile-de-Masham, Québec 172/A4
Sainte-Claire, Québec 172/G3
Sainte-Clothilde-de-Horton, Québec 172/E4
Sainte-Croix, Québec 172/F3
Sainte-Croix, Switzerland 39/B3
Saint-Édouard-de-Kent, New Bruns. 170/F2
Saint-Édouard-de-Maskinongé, Québec 172/D3
Saint-Édouard-de-Napierville, Québec 172/D4
Saint Edward, Nebr. (68660) 264/G3
Saint Edward, Pr. Edward I. 168/D2
Sainte-Edwidge, Québec 172/F4
Sainte-Élisabeth, Québec 172/D3
Sainte-Émélie-de-l'Énergie, Québec 172/D3
Sainte-Eulalie, Québec 172/E3
Sainte-Euphémie, Québec 172/G3
Sainte-Famille-d'Aumond, Québec 172/B3
Sainte-Famille-d'Orléans, Québec 172/G3
Sainte-Félicité, Québec 172/B1
Sainte-Flavie, Québec 172/J1
Sainte-Florence, Québec 172/B2
Sainte-Foy, Québec 172/H3
Sainte-Françoise, Québec 172/H1
Sainte-Geneviève, Manitoba 179/F5
Sainte Genevieve (co.), Mo. 261/M7
Sainte Genevieve, Mo. (63670) 261/M6
Sainte-Geneviève, Québec 172/H4
Sainte-Geneviève-de-Batiscan, Québec 172/E3
Sainte-Hedwidge-de-Roberval, Québec 172/E1
Sainte-Hélène-de-Bagot, Québec 172/E4
Sainte-Hélène-de-Kamouraska, Québec 172/H2
Sainte-Hénédine, Québec 172/F3
Sainte-Julie-de-Verchères, Québec 172/J4
Sainte-Julienne, Québec 172/D4
Sainte-Julie-Station, Québec 172/F3
Sainte-Justine, Québec 172/G3
Sainte-Justine-de-Newton, Québec 172/C4
Saint Eleanors, Pr. Edward I. 168/E2
Saint-Éleuthère, Québec 172/H2
Saint Elias (mt.), Alaska 188/D5
Saint Elias (cape), Alaska 196/K3
Saint Elias (mt.), Alaska 196/K2
Saint Elias (mts.), Alaska 196/L2
Saint Elias (mt.), Yukon 162/B3
Saint Elias (mt.), Yukon 187/D3
Saint Elias (mts.), Yukon 187/E3
Saint-Élie, Fr. Guiana 131/E3
Saint-Élie, Québec 172/E3
Saint Elizabeth, Mo. (65075) 261/H6
Saint Elmo, Ala. (36568) 195/B10
Saint Elmo, Colo. (†81236) 208/G5
Saint Elmo, Ill. (62458) 222/E4
Saint-Éloi, Québec 172/H1
Sainte-Louise, Québec 172/G2
Sainte-Luce, Martinique 161/D7
Sainte-Luce, Québec 172/J1
Sainte-Lucie-de-Beauregard, Québec 172/H3
Sainte-Lucie-de-Doncaster, Québec 172/C3
Saint-Elzéar, Québec 172/F3
Saint-Elzéar-de-Bonaventure, Québec 172/C2
Sainte-Marguerite, Guadeloupe 161/B6
Sainte-Marguerite-de-Dorchester, Québec 172/G3
Sainte-Marguerite-Marie, Québec 172/B2
Sainte-Marguerite (riv.), Québec 172/G1
Sainte-Marguerite Nord-Est (riv.), Québec 172/H1
Sainte-Marguerite (riv.), Québec 174/D2

Santiago 443

San Juan del Norte (bay), Nicaragua 154/F5
San Juan de los Cayos, Venezuela 124/D2
San Juan de los Lagos, Mexico 150/H6
San Juan de los Morros, Venezuela 124/E3
San Juan de los Planes, Mexico 150/D4
San Juan del Piray, Bolivia 136/C7
San Juan del Potrero, Bolivia 136/C5
San Juan del Sur, Nicaragua 154/D5
San Juan de Manapiare, Venezuela 124/E5
San Juan de Payara, Venezuela 124/E4
San Juan Island Nat'l Hist. Park, Wash. 310/B2
San Juan Nat'l Hist. Site, P. Rico 161/D1
San Juan Nepomuceno, Paraguay 144/E5
San Juan Pueblo, N. Mex. (87566) 274/C2
San Juan Xiutetelco, Mexico 150/O1
San Juan y Martínez, Cuba 158/B2
San Julián, Argentina 143/C6
San Julián, Argentina 120/C7
San Justo, Argentina 143/F5
Sankrail, India 68/E2
Sankt Aegyd am Neuwalde, Austria 41/C3
Sankt Anton am Arlberg, Austria 41/A3
Sankt Blasien, W. Germany 22/C5
Sankt Gallen (canton), Switzerland 39/H2
Sankt Gallen, Switzerland 39/H2
Sankt Goar, W. Germany 22/B3
Sankt Ingbert, W. Germany 22/B4
Sankt Johann in Tirol, Austria 41/B3
Sankt Margrethen, Switzerland 39/J2
Sankt Michael im Lungau, Austria 41/B3
Sankt Michael in Obersteiermark, Austria 41/C3
Sankt Paul im Lavanttal, Austria 41/C3
Sankt Peter-Ording, W. Germany 22/C1
Sankt Pölten, Austria 41/C2
Sankt Valentin, Austria 41/C2
Sankt Veit an der Glan, Austria 41/C3
Sankt Vith, Belgium 27/J8
Sankt Wendel, W. Germany 22/B4
Sankt Wolfgang im Salzkammergut, Austria 41/B3
Sankuru (riv.), Zaire 102/E5
Sankuru (riv.), Zaire 115/D4
San Lázaro (cape), Mexico 150/C4
San Lázaro, Paraguay 144/D3
San Leandro, Calif. (*94577) 204/J2
San Leon, Texas (77539) 303/L2
San Lorenzo, Argentina 143/F6
San Lorenzo, Cerro (mt.), Argentina 143/B6
San Lorenzo, El Beni, Bolivia 136/C4
San Lorenzo, Pando, Bolivia 136/B2
San Lorenzo, Tarija, Bolivia 136/C7
San Lorenzo, Serranía (mts.) Bolivia 136/E5
San Lorenzo, Calif. (94580) 204/K2
San Lorenzo (riv.), Calif. 204/K4
San Lorenzo, Cerro (Cochrane) (mt.), Chile 138/E7
San Lorenzo, Ecuador 128/C2
San Lorenzo (cape), Ecuador 128/B3
San Lorenzo, N. Mex. (88041) 274/B6
San Lorenzo, Paraguay 144/B4
San Lorenzo, Peru 128/H8
San Lorenzo (isl.), Peru 128/D9
San Lorenzo, P. Rico 161/E2
San Lorenzo, P. Rico 156/G1
San Lorenzo, Falcón, Venezuela 124/D2
San Lorenzo, Zulia, Venezuela 124/C3
San Lorenzo de El Escorial, Spain 33/E2
Sanlúcar de Barrameda, Spain 33/C4
Sanlúcar la Mayor, Spain 33/C4
San Lucas, Bolivia 136/C7
San Lucas, Calif. (93954) 204/E7
San Lucas (cape), Mexico 146/G7
San Lucas (cape), Mexico 2/D4
San Lucas (cape), Mexico 150/E5
San Luis (prov.), Argentina 143/C3
San Luis, Argentina 143/C3
San Luis, Argentina 120/C6
San Luis, Ariz. (85349) 198/A6
San Luis (lake), Bolivia 136/C3
San Luis (res.), Calif. 204/E7
San Luis, Colo. (81152) 208/J8
San Luis (creek), Colo. 208/H6
San Luis (lake), Colo. 208/H7
San Luis (peak), Colo. 208/F6
San Luis, Cuba 156/C2
San Luis, Pinar del Río, Cuba 158/B2
San Luis, Santiago de Cuba, Cuba 158/J4
San Luis, Guatemala 154/C2
San Luis, Honduras 154/C3
San Luis, Philippines 82/E6
San Luis (passage), Texas 303/K8
San Luis, Venezuela 124/D2
San Luis de la Paz, Mexico 150/J6
San Luis del Cordero, Mexico 150/H4
San Luis Jilotepeque, Guatemala 154/C3
San Luis Obispo, Calif. 188/B3
San Luis Obispo, Calif. 146/F6
San Luis Obispo (co.), Calif. 204/E8
San Luis Obispo, Calif. (93401) 204/E8
San Luis Potosí (state), Mexico 150/J5
San Luis Potosí, Mexico 150/J5
San Luis Potosí, Mexico 146/H7
San Luis Río Colorado, Mexico 150/B1
San Manuel, Ariz. (85631) 198/E6
San Marcelino, Philippines 82/B3
San Marco in Lamis, Italy 34/E4
San Marcos, Calif. (92069) 204/H10
San Marcos, Colombia 126/C3
San Marcos, C. Rica 154/E6
San Marcos, Guatemala 154/B3
San Marcos, Honduras 154/C3
San Marcos, Mexico 150/K8
San Marcos (isl.), Mexico 150/D3
San Marcos, Texas (78666) 303/F8
San Mariano, Philippines 82/D2
San Marino 7/F4
San Marino, Calif. (91108) 204/D10
SAN MARINO 34
San Marino (cap.), San Marino 34/D3
San Martín (lake) 120/B7
San Martín, Argentina 143/C3
San Martín (lake), Argentina 143/B6
San Martín (riv.), Bolivia 136/D3
San Martin, Calif. (95046) 204/L4
San Martín (cape), Calif. 204/D8
San Martín (lake), Chile 138/E7
San Martín, Colombia 126/D6
San Martín (dept.), Peru 128/D6
San Martín, Peru 128/E3
San Martín de las Pirámides, Mexico 150/M1
San Martín de los Andes, Argentina 143/C5
San Martín de Valdeiglesias, Spain 33/D2
San Martine Draw (dry riv.), Texas 303/C11
San Martín Jilotepeque, Guatemala 154/B3
San Martín Texmelucan, Mexico 150/M1
San Mateo (co.), Calif. 204/C3
San Mateo, Calif. (*94401) 204/J3
San Mateo, Fla. (32088) 212/E2
San Mateo, N. Mex. (87050) 274/B3
San Mateo (mts.), N. Mex. 274/B5
San Mateo, Spain 33/F2
San Mateo, Venezuela 124/F3
San Mateo Ixtatán, Guatemala 154/B3
San Matías (gulf), Argentina 120/C7
San Matías (gulf), Argentina 143/D5
San Matías, Bolivia 136/F5
Sanmaur, Québec 174/C3
San Mauricio, Venezuela 124/E3
Sanmenxia, China 77/H5
San Miguel, Argentina 143/E2
San Miguel, Bolivia 136/E5
San Miguel (riv.), Bolivia 136/D4
San Miguel, Calif. (93451) 204/E8
San Miguel (isl.), Calif. 204/E9
San Miguel (riv.), Colombia 126/B7
San Miguel (co.), Colo. 208/C6
San Miguel (mts.), Colo. 208/C7
San Miguel (riv.), Colo. 208/B6
San Miguel, Cuba 158/H3
San Miguel, Ecuador 128/C3
San Miguel (riv.), Ecuador 128/D2
San Miguel, El Salvador 154/D4
San Miguel (co.), N. Mex. 274/D3
San Miguel, N. Mex. (88058) 274/C6
San Miguel, Golfo de (gulf), Panama 154/H6
San Miguel, Paraguay 144/D5
San Miguel, Ayacucho, Peru 128/F9
San Miguel, Cajamarca, Peru 128/C6
San Miguel (bay), Philippines 82/D3
San Miguel (isls.), Philippines 85/F4
San Miguel (isls.), Philippines 82/B7
San Miguel (swamp), Uruguay 145/F4
San Miguel de Allende, Mexico 150/J6
San Miguel de Huachi, Bolivia 136/B4
San Miguel del Monte, Argentina 143/G7
San Miguel de Salcedo, Ecuador 128/C3
San Miguel de Tucumán, Argentina 143/D2
San Miguel de Tucumán, Argentina 120/C5
San Miguelito, Bolivia 136/A2
San Miguelito, Nicaragua 154/E5
San Miguel Nuevo, Colombia 126/B7
Sanming, China 77/J6
San Miniato, Italy 34/C3
San Narciso, Philippines 82/D4
Sannicandro Garganico, Italy 34/E4
San Nicolás, Argentina 143/F6
San Nicolás, Argentina 120/D6
San Nicolas (isl.), Calif. 204/F10
San Nicolás, Cuba 158/C1
San Nicolás (bay), Peru 128/E10
San Nicolás de los Garza, Mexico 150/J3
Sannikova (str.), U.S.S.R. 48/O2
San Nua (Sam Neua), Laos 72/E2
Sano, Ky. (†42728) 237/L6
Sanok, Poland 47/F4
San Onofre, Colombia 126/C3
San Pablo, Potosí, Bolivia 136/B7
San Pablo, Santa Cruz, Bolivia 136/D4
San Pablo, Calif. (94806) 204/J1
San Pablo (bay), Calif. 204/J1
San Pablo, Chile 138/D3
San Pablo, Colombia 126/B7
San Pablo, Colo. (81153) 208/J8
San Pablo, Sierra (mts.), Honduras 154/E3
San Pablo, Laguna, Philippines 82/C3
San Pablo, Negros Occ., Philippines 82/D5
San Pascual, Philippines 82/D4
San Patricio, N. Mex. (88348) 274/D5
San Patricio, Paraguay 144/D5
San Patricio (co.), Texas 303/G10
San Pedro, Buenos Aires, Argentina 143/F6
San Pedro, Jujuy, Argentina 143/D1
San Pedro (riv.), Ariz. 188/D4
San Pedro (riv.), Ariz. 198/E6
San Pedro, Belize 154/D2
San Pedro, Chuquisaca, Bolivia 136/C6
San Pedro, El Beni, Bolivia 136/C4
San Pedro, Pando, Bolivia 136/B2
San Pedro, Santa Cruz, Bolivia 136/D5
San Pedro, Calif. (*90731) 204/C11
San Pedro (bay), Calif. 204/C11
San Pedro (chan.), Calif. 204/G10
San Pedro, Santiago, Chile 138/F4
San Pedro, Valparaíso, Chile 138/F2
San Pedro (pt.), Chile 138/A5
San Pedro, Colombia 126/E5
San Pedro, Cuba 158/B2
San Pedro (riv.), Cuba 158/G3
San Pedro (riv.), Guatemala 154/B2
San Pedro, Ivory Coast 106/C8
San Pedro, Nicaragua 154/E4
San Pedro (dept.), Paraguay 144/D4-5
San Pedro, Paraguay 144/D3
San Pedro (bay), Philippines 82/E5
San Pedro, Sierra de (range), Spain 33/C3
San Pedro Carchá, Guatemala 154/B3
San Pedro de Arimena, Colombia 126/E5
San Pedro de Atacama, Chile 138/C4
San Pedro de Buena Vista, Bolivia 136/C6
San Pedro de las Bocas, Venezuela 124/G4
San Pedro de las Colonias, Mexico 150/H4
San Pedro del Gallo, Mexico 150/G4
San Pedro de Lloc, Peru 128/C6
San Pedro del Paraná, Paraguay 144/D5
San Pedro de Macorís (prov.), Dom. Rep. 158/F6
San Pedro de Macorís, Dom. Rep. 156/E3
San Pedro de Macorís, Dom. Rep. 158/F6
San Pedro de Quemes, Bolivia 136/A7
San Pedro Pochutla, Mexico 150/L9
San Pedro Sula, Honduras 154/C3
San Pedro Zacapa, Honduras 154/D3
San Perlita, Texas (78590) 303/G11
Sanpete (co.), Utah 304/C4
San Pierre, Ind. (46374) 227/D2
San Pietro (isl.), Italy 34/B5
San Pitch (riv.), Utah 304/C4
Sanpoil (riv.), Wash. 310/G2
San Quentin, Calif. (94964) 204/H1
Sanquhar, Scotland 15/D5
San Quintín, Philippines 82/C3
San Rafael, Argentina 143/C3
San Rafael, Argentina 120/C6
San Rafael, Bolivia 136/F5
San Rafael, Calif. (*94901) 204/J1
San Rafael (cape), Dom. Rep. 158/F5
San Rafael, Mexico 150/M1
San Rafael (reef), Mexico 150/L4
San Rafael, N. Mex. (87051) 274/A3
San Rafael (riv.), Utah 304/D4
San Rafael, Venezuela 124/C2
San Rafael de Atamaica, Venezuela 124/E4
San Rafael del Norte, Nicaragua 154/E4
San Rafael del Sur, Nicaragua 154/D5
San Rafael del Yuma, Dom. Rep. 158/F6
San Rafael de Orituco, Venezuela 124/E3
San Rafael Swell (mts.), Utah 304/D5
San Ramón, El Beni, Bolivia 136/C3
San Ramón, Santa Cruz, Bolivia 136/D5
San Ramon, Calif. (94583) 204/K2
San Ramón, C. Rica 154/E5
San Ramón, Cuba 158/H4
San Ramón, Nicaragua 154/E4
San Ramón, Peru 128/E8
San Ramón, Uruguay 145/D5
San Ramon de la Nva. Orán, Argentina 143/D1
San Remo, Italy 34/A3
San Roque, Colombia 126/C4
San Roque, Spain 33/D4
San Rosendo, Chile 138/E1
San Saba (co.), Texas 303/F6
San Saba, Texas (76877) 303/F6
San Saba (riv.), Texas 303/D7
San Salvador, Argentina 143/G5
San Salvador (isl.), Bahamas 156/D1
San Salvador (isl.), Ecuador 128/B9
San Salvador (cap.), El Salvador 154/C4
San Salvador (cap.), El Salvador 146/J8
San Salvador, Paraguay 144/C5
San Salvador (riv.), Uruguay 145/B4
San Salvador el Seco, Mexico 150/O1
Sans Bois (mts.), Okla. 288/R4
San Sebastián, Argentina 143/C7
San Sebastián, Chile 138/F3
San Sebastián, P. Rico 161/B1
San Sebastián, Spain 7/D4
San Sebastián, Spain 33/E1
San Sebastián, Venezuela 124/E2
Sansepolcro, Italy 34/C3
San Servando, Uruguay 145/F3
San Severino Marche, Italy 34/D3
San Severo, Italy 34/E4
San Simeon, Calif. (93452) 204/D8
San Simon, Ariz. (85632) 198/F6
San Simon (riv.), Ariz. 198/F6
San Simón, Serranía (mts.), Bolivia 136/D4
San Simón del Cocuy, Venezuela 124/E3
Sanski Most, Yugoslavia 45/C3
Sansom Park Village, Texas (†76101) 303/E2
Sans Souci, Trin. & Tob. 161/B10
Sans Toucher (mt.), Guadeloupe 161/A6
Santa, Idaho (83866) 220/B2
Santa, Peru 128/C7
Santa (riv.), Peru 128/C7
Santa Ana, El Beni, Bolivia 136/C3
Santa Ana, La Paz, Bolivia 136/B4
Santa Ana, Santa Cruz, Bolivia 136/F6
Santa Ana, Santa Cruz, Bolivia 136/E5
Santa Ana, Calif. 188/C4
Santa Ana, Calif. (*92701) 204/D11
Santa Ana (riv.), Calif. 204/E11
Santa Ana, Colombia 126/F6
Santa Ana, Ecuador 128/B3
Santa Ana, El Salvador 154/C4
Santa Ana (mt.), El Salvador 154/C4
Santa Ana, Guatemala 154/C2
Santa Ana, Mexico 150/D1
Santa Ana (reef), Mexico 150/N7
Santa Ana, Uruguay 145/B1
Santa Ana (range), Uruguay 145/D2
Santa Ana, Anzoátegui, Venezuela 124/F3
Santa Ana, Táchira, Venezuela 124/B4
Santa Ana Chiautempan (Chiautempan), Mexico 150/N1
Santa Anna, Texas (76878) 303/E6
Santa Barbara, Calif. 146/F6
Santa Barbara, Calif. 188/C4
Santa Barbara (isls.), Calif. 146/F6
Santa Barbara (isls.), Calif. 188/C4
Santa Barbara (co.), Calif. 204/E9
Santa Barbara, Calif. (*93101) 204/F9
Santa Barbara (chan.), Calif. 204/E9
Santa Barbara (isl.), Calif. 204/G10
Santa Bárbara (isls.), Calif. 204/F10
Santa Bárbara, Chile 138/E1
Santa Bárbara, Colombia 126/C5
Santa Bárbara, Cuba 158/B2
Santa Bárbara, Honduras 154/C3
Santa Bárbara, Mexico 150/F3
Santa Barbara, Neth. Ant. 161/G9
Santa Bárbara, Amazonas, Venezuela 124/E6
Santa Bárbara, Barinas, Venezuela 124/C4
Santa Bárbara, Monagas, Venezuela 124/G3
Santa Bárbara, Zulia, Venezuela 124/C3
Santa Catalina, Argentina 143/C1
Santa Catalina (mts.), Ariz. 198/E6
Santa Catalina (gulf), Calif. 204/G11
Santa Catalina (isl.), Calif. 204/G10
Santa Catalina (isl.), Colombia 126/A9
Santa Catalina (isl.), Mexico 150/D4
Santa Catalina, Philippines 82/D6
Santa Catalina, Uruguay 145/B4
Santa Catalina, Barinas, Venezuela 124/D4
Santa Catalina, Delta Amacuro, Venezuela 124/H3
Santa Catarina (state), Brazil 132/D9
Santa Catarina (isl.), Brazil 120/E5
Santa Catarina (isl.), Brazil 132/E9
Santa Catharina, Neth. Ant. 161/G9
Santa Clara (co.), Calif. 204/D6
Santa Clara, Calif. (*95050) 204/K3
Santa Clara, Colombia 126/F9
Santa Clara, Cuba 158/E2
Santa Clara, Cuba 146/K7
Santa Clara, Cuba 156/B2
Santa Clara (bay), Cuba 158/D1
Santa Clara, Mexico 150/H4
Santa Clara, Utah (84765) 304/A6
Santa Clara (riv.), Utah 304/A6
Santa Clara de Olimar, Uruguay 145/D3
Santa Claus, Georgia (†20436) 217/H6
Santa Claus, Ind. (47579) 227/D8
Santa Clotilde, Peru 128/E4
Santa Cruz (prov.), Argentina 143/C6
Santa Cruz, Argentina 120/C8
Santa Cruz, Argentina 143/C7
Santa Cruz (riv.), Argentina 120/B7
Santa Cruz (riv.), Argentina 143/B7
Santa Cruz (co.), Ariz. 198/E7
Santa Cruz (riv.), Ariz. 198/D6
Santa Cruz (dept.), Bolivia 136/E5
Santa Cruz, Bolivia 120/C4
Santa Cruz, Santa Cruz, Bolivia 136/D5
Santa Cruz, Brazil 132/G4
Santa Cruz, Calif. 188/B3
Santa Cruz (co.), Calif. 204/C6
Santa Cruz, Calif. (*95060) 204/K4
Santa Cruz (chan.), Calif. 204/F10
Santa Cruz (isl.), Calif. 204/F10
Santa Cruz (cap.), Canary Is., Spain 102/A2
Santa Cruz, Chile 138/F6
Santa Cruz, C. Rica 154/E5
Santa Cruz (isl.), Ecuador 128/C9
Santa Cruz, India 68/B7
Santa Cruz, Jamaica 158/H6
Santa Cruz, Mexico 150/D1
Santa Cruz (isl.), Mexico 150/D4
Santa Cruz, N. Mex. (87567) 274/D2
Santa Cruz, Nicaragua 154/E4
Santa Cruz, Cajamarca, Peru 128/C6
Santa Cruz, Loreto, Peru 128/E5
Santa Cruz, Davao del Sur, Philippines 82/E7
Santa Cruz, Laguna, Philippines 82/C3
Santa Cruz, Marinduque, Philippines 82/D4
Santa Cruz, Zambales, Philippines 82/B3
Santa Cruz, Portugal 33/A2
Santa Cruz (isls.), Solomon Is. 87/G6
Santa Cruz, Venezuela 124/C3
Santa Cruz das Flores, Portugal 33/A1
Santa Cruz de Bucaral, Venezuela 124/D2
Santa Cruz de la Palma, Spain 33/B4
Santa Cruz de la Palma, Spain 106/A3
Santa Cruz de la Zarza, Spain 33/E3
Santa Cruz del Norte, Cuba 158/C1
Santa Cruz de los Pinos, Cuba 158/B1
Santa Cruz del Quiché, Guatemala 154/B3
Santa Cruz del Sur, Cuba 158/G3
Santa Cruz del Sur, Cuba 156/B2
Santa Cruz del Valle Ameno, Bolivia 136/A4
Santa Cruz del Zulia, Venezuela 124/B3
Santa Cruz de Mara, Venezuela 124/C2
Santa Cruz de Mudela, Spain 33/E3
Santa Cruz de Orinoco, Venezuela 124/F3
Santa Cruz de Tenerife (prov.), Spain 33/B5
Santa Cruz de Tenerife, Spain 33/B4
Santa Cruz de Tenerife, Spain 106/A3
Santa Cruz de Yojoa, Honduras 154/D3
Santa Cruz do Rio Pardo, Brazil 135/B3
Santa Cruz do Sul, Brazil 132/C10
Santa Elena, Argentina 143/F5
Santa Elena, Bolivia 136/C7
Santa Elena (cape), C. Rica 154/D5
Santa Elena, Ecuador 128/B4
Santa Elena (bay), Ecuador 128/B3
Santa Elena, Paraguay 144/B5
Santa Elena, Peru 128/F5
Santa Elena, Venezuela 124/H5
Santa Eugenia (pt.), Mexico 146/G7
Santa Eugenia (pt.), Mexico 150/B3
Santa Eugenia, Spain 33/B1
Santa Fe (prov.), Argentina 143/D3
Santa Fe, Argentina 120/C6
Santa Fe, Argentina 143/F5
Santa Fe, Bolivia 136/D6
Santa Fe (peak), Colo. 208/H4
Santa Fe, Cuba 158/B2
Santa Fe, Cuba 156/A2
Santa Fe (isl.), Ecuador 128/C9
Santa Fe, Fla. (32616) 212/D2
Santa Fe (lake), Fla. 212/D2
Santa Fe (riv.), Fla. 212/D2
Santa Fe, Ind. (†46970) 227/E3
Santa Fe, Mo. (65282) 261/J4
Santa Fe (cap.), N. Mex. 146/H6
Santa Fe (cap.), N. Mex. 188/E3
Santa Fe (co.), N. Mex. 274/C3
Santa Fe (cap.), N. Mex. (87501) 274/C3
Santa Fe, Panama 154/G6
Santa Fe, Philippines 82/C2
Santa Fé, Spain 33/E4
Santa Fe, Tenn. (38482) 237/G9
Santa Fe, Texas 303/K3
Santa Fe Springs, Calif. (90670) 204/C11
Santa Filomena, Brazil 132/E5
Santa Helena de Goiás, Brazil 132/D7
Santai, China 77/G5
Santa Inés (isl.), Chile 120/B8
Santa Inés (isl.), Chile 138/D10
Santa Inés, Anzoátegui, Venezuela 124/F3
Santa Inés, Barinas, Venezuela 124/C3
Santa Isabel, Bolivia 136/B7
Santa Isabel, Brazil 132/B5
Santa Isabel, Colombia 126/B9
Santa Isabel, Ecuador 128/C4
Santa Isabel, P. Rico 161/C3
Santa Isabel (isl.), Solomon Is. 87/G6
Santa Isabel (isl.), Solomon Is. 86/D2
Santa Isabel (creek), Texas 303/E10
Santa Isabel, Venezuela 124/F7
Santa Isabel de las Lajas, Cuba 158/E2
Santa Isabel de Sihuas, Peru 128/F11
Santa Leopoldina, Brazil 132/G7
Santa Lucía, Buenos Aires, Argentina 143/F6
Santa Lucía, Corrientes, Argentina 143/E2
Santa Lucía, Camagüey, Cuba 158/H3
Santa Lucía, Holguín, Cuba 158/J3
Santa Lucía, Pinar del Río, Cuba 158/A1
Santa Lucía, Uruguay 145/B6
Santa Lucía (riv.), Uruguay 145/D5
Santa Lucía, Venezuela 124/D3
Santa Lucía Chico (riv.), Uruguay 145/D4
Santa Luzia, Brazil 135/E1
Santa Luzia (isl.), C. Verde 106/B8
Santa Margarita, Calif. (93453) 204/E8
Santa Margarita (isl.), Mexico 150/C4
Santa Maria (cape), Angola 115/B6
Santa María, Argentina 143/C2
Santa Maria (riv.), Ariz. 198/B4
Santa Maria, Brazil 132/C10
Santa Maria, Brazil 120/D5
Santa Maria, Calif. (93454) 204/E9
Santa Maria (riv.), Calif. 204/E9
Santa Maria, C. Verde 106/B8
Santa María, Chile 138/G2
Santa María (isl.), Chile 138/D1
Santa María (cay), Cuba 158/F1
Santa María (isl.), Ecuador 128/B10
Santa María (lake), Mexico 150/F1
Santa María (riv.), Mexico 150/F1
Santa María, Paraguay 144/D5
Santa Maria, Philippines 82/C7
Santa Maria (cape), Portugal 33/C4
Santa Maria (isl.), Portugal 33/D2
Santa Maria, Texas (78592) 303/F12
Santa María (cape), Uruguay 145/F5
Santa María, Bolívar, Venezuela 124/G3
Santa Maria Capua Vetere, Italy 34/E4
Santa Maria da Vitória, Brazil 132/F6
Santa María de Erebató, Venezuela 124/F5
Santa María de Ipire, Venezuela 124/F3
Santa María del Orinoco, Venezuela 124/E4
Santa María del Oro, Mexico 150/G3
Santa María del Río, Mexico 150/J6
Santa María del Tule, Mexico 150/L8
Santa María de Nanay, Peru 128/F4
Santa Maria di Leuca (cape), Italy 34/G5
Santa Maria im Münstertal, Switzerland 39/K3
Santa Marta, Colombia 126/D2
Santa Marta, Colombia 120/B1
Santa Marta, Sierra Nevada de (range), Colombia 126/D2
Santa Monica, Calif. (*90401) 204/B10
Santa Monica (bay), Calif. 204/B11
Santana, Brazil 132/E6
Santana, Portugal 33/A2
Santana do Ipanema, Brazil 132/G5
Santana do Jacaré, Brazil 135/C2
Santana do Livramento, Brazil 132/C10
Santana do Livramento, Brazil 120/D6
Santander (dept.), Colombia 126/D4
Santander, Colombia 126/B6
Santander, Philippines 82/D6
Santander (prov.), Spain 33/D1
Santander, Spain 33/D1
Santander, Spain 7/D4
Santander Jiménez, Mexico 150/K4
Sant'Antioco (pen.), Italy 34/B5
Santañy, Spain 33/H3
Santa Olalla del Cala, Spain 33/C4
Santa Paula, Calif. (93060) 204/F9
Santaquin, Utah (84655) 304/C4
Santarém, Brazil 132/C3
Santarém, Brazil 120/D3
Santarém (dist.), Portugal 33/B3
Santarém, Portugal 33/B3
Santarén (chan.), Bahamas 156/B1
Santarén (chan.), Cuba 156/B1
Santa Rita, Cuba 158/H4
Santa Rita, Guam 86/K7
Santa Rita, Honduras 154/D3
Santa Rita, Mont. (59473) 262/D2
Santa Rita, N. Mex. (†88041) 274/B6
Santa Rita, Philippines 82/E5
Santa Rita, Guárico, Venezuela 124/E3
Santa Rita, Zulia, Venezuela 124/C2
Santa Rita do Sapucaí, Brazil 135/D3
Santa Rosa, La Pampa, Argentina 143/C4
Santa Rosa, San Luis, Argentina 143/C3
Santa Rosa, Argentina 120/C6
Santa Rosa, Córdoba, Argentina 143/D3
Santa Rosa, Cochabamba, Bolivia 136/B5
Santa Rosa, Cochabamba, Bolivia 136/C5
Santa Rosa, El Beni, Bolivia 136/B4
Santa Rosa, Pando, Bolivia 136/B2
Santa Rosa, Santa Cruz, Bolivia 136/D5
Santa Rosa, Brazil 132/C4
Santa Rosa, Calif. 188/B3
Santa Rosa, Calif. (*95401) 204/C5
Santa Rosa (isl.), Calif. 204/E10
Santa Rosa, C. Rica 154/E5
Santa Rosa, Ecuador 128/C4
Santa Rosa (co.), Fla. 212/B6
Santa Rosa (isl.), Fla. 212/B6
Santa Rosa (sound), Fla. 212/B6
Santa Rosa, Mo. (†64670) 261/D3
Santa Rosa (range), Nev. 266/D1
Santa Rosa, N. Mex. (88435) 274/E4
Santa Rosa, Paraguay 144/D5
Santa Rosa, Uruguay 145/B6
Santa Rosa, Anzoátegui, Venezuela 124/F3
Santa Rosa, Apure, Venezuela 124/D4
Santa Rosa, Barinas, Venezuela 124/D3
Santa Rosa Beach, Fla. (32459) 212/C6
Santa Rosa de Aguán, Honduras 154/E2
Santa Rosa de Amanadona, Venezuela 124/E7
Santa Rosa de Cabal, Colombia 126/C5
Santa Rosa de Copán, Honduras 154/C3
Santa Rosa de la Mina, Bolivia 136/D5
Santa Rosa de la Roca, Bolivia 136/E5
Santa Rosa de Lima, El Salvador 154/D4
Santa Rosa de Lima, Guatemala 154/B3
Santa Rosa del Palmar, Bolivia 136/E5
Santa Rosa de Osos, Colombia 126/C4
Santa Rosa Ind. Res., Calif. 204/J10
Santa Rosalía, Mexico 150/C3
Santa Rosalía, Venezuela 124/F4
Santa Rosa Wash (dry riv.), Ariz. 198/D6
Santa Teresa, North. Terr. 93/D8
Santa Teresa, Venezuela 124/E2
Santa Venetia, Calif. (†94901) 204/J1
Santa Victoria, Argentina 143/D1
Santa Vitória do Palmar, Brazil 132/C11
Santa Ynez (riv.), Calif. 204/E9
Santa Ysabel Ind. Res., Calif. 204/J10
Santee, Calif. (92071) 204/J11
Santee, Nebr. (†68760) 264/G2
Santee (riv.), S.C. 188/L4
Santee, S.C. (29142) 296/F5
Santee (dam), S.C. 296/G4
Santee (riv.), S.C. 296/H5
Santee Ind. Res., Nebr. 264/G2
Santeetlah (lake), N.C. 281/B4
Sant'Elpidio a Mare, Italy 34/E3
Santeramo in Colle, Italy 34/F4
Sant'Eufemia (gulf), Italy 34/F5
Santiago, Serranía de (mts.), Bolivia 136/F6
Santiago, Potosí, Bolivia 136/A7
Santiago, Santa Cruz, Bolivia 136/F6
Santiago, Brazil 132/C10
Santiago, Region Metropolitana de (Santiago Metropolitan Region) (reg.) Chile 138/A9
Santiago (cap.), Chile 2/F7
Santiago (cap.), Chile 120/B6
Santiago (cap.), Chile 138/G3
Santiago (prov.), Dom. Rep. 158/D5
Santiago, Dom. Rep. 158/D5
Santiago, Dom. Rep. 156/D3
Santiago (San Salvador) (isl.), Ecuador 128/B9
Santiago, Mexico 150/E5
Santiago (riv.), Mexico 146/H7
Santiago, Minn. (55377) 255/E5
Santiago, Panama 154/G6
Santiago, Cerro (mt.), Panama 154/G6
Santiago, Paraguay 144/D5
Santiago, Peru 128/E10
Santiago (riv.), Peru 128/D4
Santiago, Philippines 82/C2
Santiago, Spain 33/B1
Santiago (mts.), Texas 303/A8
Santiago (peak), Texas 303/D12
Santiago de Cao, Peru 128/C6
Santiago de Chocorvos, Peru 128/E9
Santiago de Chuco, Peru 128/C7
Santiago de Cuba (prov.), Cuba 158/H4
Santiago de Cuba, Cuba 146/L8

444 Santiago

Santiago de Cuba, Cuba 156/C3
Santiago de Cuba, Cuba 158/J4
Santiago de Huata, Bolivia 136/A5
Santiago de las Vegas, Cuba 158/C1
Santiago del Estero (prov.), Argentina 143/D2
Santiago del Estero, Argentina 120/C5
Santiago del Estero, Argentina 143/D2
Santiago de Machaca, Bolivia 136/A5
Santiago de Pacaguaras, Bolivia 136/A3
Santiago do Cacem, Portugal 33/B3
Santiago Ixcuintla, Mexico 150/G6
Santiago Jamiltepec, Mexico 150/K8
Santiago Juxtlahuaca, Mexico 150/K8
Santiago Miahuatlán, Mexico 150/O2
Santiago Papasquiaro, Mexico 150/F4
Santiago Pinotepa Nacional, Mexico 150/K8
Santiago Rodríguez (prov.), Dom. Rep. 158/D5
Santiago Tuxtla, Mexico 150/M7
Santiago Vázquez, Uruguay 145/A7
Santiaguillo (lake), Mexico 150/G4
San Timoteo, Venezuela 124/C3
Santipur, India 68/F4
Säntis (mt.), Switzerland 39/H2
Santo, Texas (76472) 303/F5
Santo Amaro, Brazil 132/G6
Santo André, Brazil 135/C3
Santo Ângelo, Brazil 132/C10
Santo Antão (isl.), C. Verde 106/A7
Santo António, São Tomé e Príncipe 106/F8
Santo Antônio da Platina, Brazil 132/D8
Santo Antônio da Platina, Brazil 135/A3
Santo Antônio do Leverger, Brazil 132/C6
Santo Corazón, Bolivia 136/F5
Santo Domingo, C. Rica 154/F6
Santo Domingo, Cuba 158/E1
Santo Domingo (cap.), Dom. Rep. 146/L8
Santo Domingo (cap.), Dom. Rep. 156/E3
Santo Domingo (cap.), Dom. Rep. 158/E6
Santo Domingo, Nicaragua 154/E4
Santo Domingo de la Calzada, Spain 33/E1
Santo Domingo de los Colorados, Ecuador 128/C3
Santo Domingo Pueblo, N. Mex. (87052) 274/C3
San Tomé, Venezuela 124/F3
Santoña, Spain 33/E1
Santos, Brazil 2/G7
Santos, Brazil 132/E9
Santos, Brazil 120/E5
Santos, Brazil 135/C3
Santos, Fla. (†32670) 212/D2
Santos Dumont, Brazil 132/F8
Santos Dumont, Brazil 135/E2
Santos Mercado, Bolivia 136/B1
Santo Tomás, Mexico 150/A1
Santo Tomás, Nicaragua 154/E5
Santo Tomás, Amazonas, Peru 128/C6
Santo Tomás, Cusco, Peru 128/G10
Santo Tomas, Davao, Philippines 82/E7
Santo Tomas, La Union, Philippines 82/C2
Santo Tomas (mt.), Philippines 82/C2
Santo Tomás de Andoas, Peru 128/D4
Santo Tomás de Castilla, Guatemala 154/C3
Santo Tomé, Corrientes, Argentina 143/E2
Santo Tomé, Santa Fe, Argentina 143/F5
Santuck, S.C. (†29031) 296/D2
Santuit, Mass. (†02635) 249/N6
Santurce, P. Rico 161/E1
San Urbano, Argentina 143/F6
San Valentín, Cerro (mt.), Chile 138/D6
San Vicente, Chile 138/F4
San Vicente (San Vicente de Tagua Tagua), Chile 138/F5
San Vicente, El Salvador 154/C4
San Vicente, Mexico 150/B1
San Vicente, Amazonas, Venezuela 124/E5
San Vicente, Apure, Venezuela 124/D4
San Vicente de Alcántara, Spain 33/C3
San Vicente de Cañete, Peru 128/D9
San Vicente del Caguán, Colombia 126/C6
San Vito, Italy 34/B5
San Vito (cape), Italy 34/D5
San Vito al Tagliamento, Italy 34/D2
San Vito dei Normanni, Italy 34/F4
San Vito Romano, Italy 34/F6
San Xavier Ind. Res., Ariz. 198/D6
Sanyati (riv.), Zimbabwe 118/D3
San Ygnacio, Texas (78067) 303/E10
San Ysidro, N. Mex. (87053) 274/C3
Sanyuan, China 77/G5
Sanza Pombo, Angola 115/C5
São Bento, Brazil 132/E3
São Bernardo do Campo, Brazil 135/C3
São Borja, Brazil 132/C10
São Brás de Alportel (Alportel), Portugal 33/C4
São Carlos, Brazil 135/C3
São Cristóvão, Brazil 132/G5
São Domingos, Brazil 132/E6
São Félix, Brazil 132/G6
São Fidélis, Brazil 132/F8
São Fidélis, Brazil 135/F2
São Francisco, Brazil 132/E6
São Francisco (riv.), Brazil 120/E4
São Francisco (riv.), Brazil 2/G6
São Francisco (riv.), Brazil 132/F5
São Francisco (riv.), Brazil 135/D2
São Francisco do Sul, Brazil 132/E9
São Gabriel, Brazil 132/C10
São Gonçalo, Brazil 132/F8
São Gonçalo, Brazil 135/E3
São Gonçalo do Sapucaí, Brazil 135/D2
São João da Boa Vista, Brazil 132/E8
São João da Boa Vista, Brazil 135/C2
São João da Madeira, Portugal 33/B2
São João da Pesqueira, Portugal 33/C2
São João del Rei, Brazil 132/E8
São João del Rei, Brazil 135/D2
São João de Meriti, Brazil 135/E3
São João do Piauí, Brazil 132/F5
São João dos Patos, Brazil 132/F4
São João Nepomuceno, Brazil 135/E2
São Joaquim da Barra, Brazil 135/C2
São Jorge (isl.), Portugal 33/B1
São José, Brazil 132/D9
São José da Laje, Brazil 132/H5
São José do Gurupi, Brazil 132/E3
São José do Rio Pardo, Brazil 135/C2
São José do Rio Preto, Brazil 120/E5
São José do Rio Preto, Brazil 132/D8
São José do Rio Preto, Brazil 135/B2
São José dos Campos, Brazil 135/D3
São José dos Pinhais, Brazil 132/D9
São Leopoldo, Brazil 132/D10
São Lourenço, Brazil 135/D3
São Lourenço (riv.), Brazil 132/C7
São Lourenço do Sul, Brazil 132/C10
São Luís, Brazil 132/F3
São Luís, Brazil 120/E3
São Luís Gonzaga, Brazil 132/C10
São Manuel, Brazil 135/B3
São Marcos (bay), Brazil 120/E3
São Marcos (bay), Brazil 132/F3
São Martinho do Porto, Portugal 33/B3
São Mateus, Brazil 132/G7
São Miguel (isl.), Portugal 33/D2
São Miguel Arcanjo, Brazil 135/C3
São Miguel do Guamá, Brazil 132/E3
São Miguel dos Campos, Brazil 132/G5
Saona (isl.), Dom. Rep. 156/E3
Saona (isl.), Dom. Rep. 158/F6
Saône (riv.), France 28/F4
Saône-et-Loire (dept.), France 28/F4
Saonek, Indonesia 85/J6
São Nicolau, Angola 115/B6
São Nicolau (isl.), C. Verde 106/B8
São Paulo (state), Brazil 135/B3
São Paulo (state), Brazil 132/D8
São Paulo, Brazil 120/E5
São Paulo, Brazil 2/G6
São Paulo, Brazil 132/E8
São Paulo, Brazil 135/C3
São Paulo de Olivença, Brazil 132/G9
São Pedro do Piauí, Brazil 132/F4
São Pedro do Sul, Portugal 33/B2
São Raimundo das Mangabeiras, Brazil 132/E4
São Raimundo Nonato, Brazil 132/F5
São Romão, Brazil 132/E7
São Roque, Brazil 135/C3
São Roque (cape), Brazil 2/H6
São Roque (cape), Brazil 120/F3
São Roque (cape), Brazil 132/H4
São Sebastião, Brazil 135/D3
São Sebastião (isl.), Brazil 120/E5
São Sebastião (isl.), Brazil 135/D3
São Sebastião (isl.), Brazil 132/E8
São Sebastião (pt.), Mozambique 118/F4
São Sebastião do Paraíso, Brazil 135/C2
São Sebastião do Paraíso, Brazil 132/E8
São Simão, Brazil 135/C2
São Teotónio, Portugal 33/B4
São Tiago (isl.), C. Verde 106/B8
São Tomé (cape), Brazil 120/F5
São Tomé (cape), Brazil 132/F8
São Tomé (cap.), São Tomé e Príncipe 106/F8
São Tomé (isl.), São T. & Pr. 106/F8
São Tomé e Príncipe 102/C4
SÃO TOMÉ E PRÍNCIPE 106/F8
Saoura, Wadi (dry riv.), Algeria 106/D3
São Vicente, Brazil 135/C4
São Vicente (isl.), C. Verde 106/B7
São Vicente, Portugal 33/A2
São Vicente (cape), Portugal 7/C5
São Vicente Ferrer, Brazil 132/E3
São Vincent (cape), Portugal 33/B4
Sapahaqui, Bolivia 136/B5
Sápai, Greece 45/G5
Sapanca, Turkey 63/D2
Saparua, Indonesia 85/H6
Sapawe, Ontario 177/G5
Sapawe, Ontario 175/B3
Sapele, Nigeria 106/F7
Sapelo, N. Mex. (87745) 274/D3
Sapelo (isl.), Georgia 217/K8
Sapelo (sound), Georgia 217/K7
Sapelo Island, Georgia (31327) 217/K8
Şaphane, Turkey 63/C3
Saponac, Maine (†04417) 243/G5
Saposoa, Peru 128/D6
Sappa (creek), Kansas 232/B2
Sappemeer-Hoogezand, Netherlands 27/K2
Sapphire, N.C. (28774) 281/D4
Sappho, Wash. (†98305) 310/A2
Sappington, Mo. (63126) 261/O4
Sapporo, Japan 2/S3
Sapporo, Japan 54/P5
Sapporo, Japan 81/K2
Sapse, Bolivia 136/C6
Sapucaí (riv.), Brazil 135/D2
Sapucaí, Paraguay 144/B5
Sapulpa, Okla. (74066) 288/O3
Saqqez, Iran 59/E2
Saqqez, Iran 66/E2
Saquena, Peru 128/F5
Sara (riv.), Cent. Afr. Rep. 115/C2
Sara (riv.), Chad 111/C6
Sara, Philippines 82/D5
Sarab, Iran 66/E2
Sara Buri, Thailand 72/D4
Saragosa, Texas (79780) 303/D11
Saragossa, Ala. (†35578) 195/D3
Saragossa, Spain 7/D4
Saragossa, Spain 33/F2
Saraguro, Ecuador 128/C4
Sarah (lake), Minn. 255/F5
Sarah, Miss. (38665) 256/D1
Sarahsville, Ohio (43779) 284/H6
Sarajevo, Yugoslavia 7/F4
Sarajevo, Yugoslavia 45/D4
Sarakhs, Iran 66/M2
Saraland, Ala. (36571) 195/B9
Saramacca (dist.), Suriname 131/C3
Saramacca (riv.), Suriname 131/D3
Sarampiuni, Bolivia 136/A4
Saran', U.S.S.R. 48/H5
Saranac, Mich. (48881) 250/D6
Saranac, N.Y. (12981) 276/N1
Saranac (lakes), N.Y. 276/M2
Saranac (riv.), N.Y. 276/N1
Saranac Lake, N.Y. (12983) 276/M2
Sarandë, Albania 45/E6
Sarandí del Yi, Uruguay 145/D4
Sarandí de Navarro, Uruguay 145/C3
Sarandí Grande, Uruguay 145/C4
Sarangani (bay), Philippines 82/E8
Sarangani (isls.), Philippines 82/E8
Sarangani (isls.), Philippines 85/G4
Sarangani (str.), Philippines 82/E8
Saransk, U.S.S.R. 7/J3
Saransk, U.S.S.R. 48/E4
Saransk, U.S.S.R. 52/G4
Sarapul, U.S.S.R. 7/K3
Sarapul, U.S.S.R. 48/F4
Sarapul, U.S.S.R. 52/H3
Sarare, Venezuela 124/D3
Sarare (riv.), Venezuela 124/C4
Sarasota, Fla. 188/K5
Sarasota (co.), Fla. 212/D4
Sarasota, Fla. (*33577) 212/D4
Sarasota (pt.), Fla. 212/D4
Sarasota Springs, Fla. (†33577) 212/D4
Saraswati (riv.), India 68/F1
Saratoga, Ark. (71859) 202/C6
Saratoga, Calif. (95070) 204/K4
Saratoga, Ind. (47382) 227/H4
Saratoga, Iowa (52167) 229/J2
Saratoga, Miss. (†39111) 256/E7
Saratoga (co.), N.Y. 276/N4
Saratoga (lake), N.Y. 276/N4
Saratoga, Texas (77585) 303/K7
Saratoga, Wyo. (82331) 319/F4
Saratoga Nat'l Hist. Park, N.Y. 276/N4
Saratoga Springs, N.Y. (12866) 276/N4
Saratov, U.S.S.R. 7/J3
Saratov, U.S.S.R. 48/E4
Saratov, U.S.S.R. 52/G4
Saravan, Iran 59/H4
Saravan, Iran 66/N7
Saravan, Laos 72/E4
Sarawak (state), Malaysia 2/Q5
Sarawak (state), Malaysia 85/E5
Sarawak (reg.), Malaysia 54/N9
Sarayacu, Ecuador 128/D3
Sarayköy, Turkey 63/C4
Sarayönü, Turkey 63/E3
Sarbaz, Iran 66/M7
Sarbaz, Iran 59/H4
Sarben, Nebr. (†69155) 264/C3
Sárbogárd, Hungary 41/E3
Sarco (bay), Chile 138/A7
Sarcoxie, Mo. (64862) 261/D8
Sardarshahr, India 68/C3
Sar Dasht, Iran 66/D2
Sardina (pt.), P. Rico 161/A1
Sardinata, Colombia 126/D3
Sardinia, Ind. (†47283) 227/F6
Sardinia (reg.), Italy 34/B4
Sardinia (isl.), Italy 7/E4
Sardinia (isl.), Italy 34/B4
Sardinia, N.Y. (14134) 276/C5
Sardinia, Ohio (45171) 284/C7
Sardinia, S.C. (29143) 296/G4
Sardis, Ala. (36775) 195/E6
Sardis, Ala. (†35957) 195/F2
Sardis, Br. Col. 184/M3
Sardis, Georgia (30456) 217/J5
Sardis, Ky. (41056) 237/O3
Sardis (lake), Miss. 188/J4
Sardis, Miss. (38666) 256/E2
Sardis (dam), Miss. 256/E2
Sardis (lake), Miss. 256/E2
Sardis, Ohio (43946) 284/J6
Sardis, Okla. (74564) 288/R5
Sardis, Tenn. (38371) 237/E10
Sardis, W. Va. (†26461) 312/F4
Sar-e Pol, Afghanistan 68/B1
Sar-e Pol, Afghanistan 59/J2
Sarepta, La. (71071) 238/D1
Sarepta, Miss. (38867) 256/F2
Sar Eskand Khan, Iran 66/E2
Sargans, Switzerland 39/H2
Sargeant, Minn. (55973) 255/F7
Sargent, Georgia (30275) 217/C4
Sargent, Nebr. (68874) 264/E3
Sargent (co.), N. Dak. 282/P7
Sargents, Colo. (81248) 208/F6
Sargodha, Pakistan 59/K3
Sargodha, Pakistan 68/C2
Sarh, Chad 111/C6
Sarh, Chad 102/D4
Sarhro, Jebel (mts.), Morocco 106/C2
Sari, Iran 59/F2
Sari, Iran 66/H2
Saria (isl.), Greece 45/H8
Sarigan (isl.), No. Marianas 87/E4
Sarıgöl, Turkey 63/C3
Sarih, Jordan 65/D2
Sarıkamış, Turkey 63/K2
Sarıkamış, Turkey 59/D1
Sarıkaya, Turkey 63/F3
Sarıköy, Turkey 63/B2
Sarina, Queensland 88/H4
Sarina, Queensland 95/D4
Sarine (Saane) (riv.), Switzerland 39/D3
Sariñena, Spain 33/F2
Sarıoğlan, Turkey 63/G3
Sarita, Texas (78385) 303/G10
Sariwŏn, N. Korea 81/B4
Sarıyer, Turkey 63/D5
Sariz, Turkey 63/G3
Sark (isl.), Chan. Is. 13/E8
Sark (isl.), Chan. Is. 10/E6
Sarkad, Hungary 41/F3
Sarkand, U.S.S.R. 48/J5
Şarkikaraağaç, Turkey 63/D3
Şarkışla, Turkey 63/G3
Şarköy, Turkey 63/B2
Sarlat-La-Canéda, France 28/D5
Sarles, N. Dak. (58372) 282/N2
Sarmi, Indonesia 85/K6
Sarmiento, Argentina 143/B6
Sarmiento, Argentina 120/C7
Sarmiento, Cerro (mt.), Chile 138/E11
Särna, Sweden 18/H6
Sarnath, India 68/E3
Sarnen, Switzerland 39/F3
Sarnen (lake), Switzerland 39/F3
Sarnia, Ont. 162/H7
Sarnia, Ontario 177/B5
Sarny, U.S.S.R. 52/C4
Sarona, Wis. (54870) 317/C4
Saronic (gulf), Greece 45/F7
Saronno, Italy 34/B2
Saronville, Nebr. (68975) 264/G4
Saros (gulf), Turkey 63/B2
Sárospatak, Hungary 41/F2
Sarpsborg, Norway 18/D4
Sarpy (co.), Nebr. 264/H3
Sarra (well), Libya 111/D3
Sarralbe, France 28/G3
Sarrebourg, France 28/G3
Sarreguemines, France 28/G3
Sarria, Spain 33/C1
Sarroch, Italy 34/B5
Sarsati (riv.), India 68/F1
Sarstún (riv.), Belize 154/C3
Sarstún (riv.), Guatemala 154/C3
Sartell, Minn. (56377) 255/D5
Sartène, France 28/B7
Sarthe (dept.), France 28/D3
Sarthe (riv.), France 28/D4
Sartrouville, France 28/A1
Sarufutsu, Japan 81/L1
Sarur, Oman 59/G5
Sárvár, Hungary 41/D3
Sarver, Pa. (16055) 294/C4
Sárviz csatorna (canal), Hungary 41/E3
Saryshagan, U.S.S.R. 48/H5
Sary Su (riv.), U.S.S.R. 48/H5
Sasabe, Ariz. (85633) 198/D7
Sasabe, Mexico 150/C1
Sasaginnigak (lake), Manitoba 179/G3
Sasakwa, Okla. (74867) 288/N5
Sasaram, India 68/E4
Sasebo, Japan 81/D7
Saseenos, Br. Col. 184/J3
Saskatchewan (prov.) 162/F5
Saskatchewan (riv.) 162/F5
Saskatchewan (prov.), Canada 146/H4
Saskatchewan (riv.), Canada 2/D3
SASKATCHEWAN 181
Saskatchewan (riv.), Sask. 181/H2
Saskatchewan Beach, Sask. 181/G5
Saskatchewan Landing Prov. Park, Sask. 181/C5
Saskatoon, Sask. 162/F5
Saskatoon, Sask. 146/H4
Saskatoon, Sask. 181/E3
Saskeram (riv.), Sask. 181/K2
Sason, Turkey 63/J3
Sasovo, U.S.S.R. 52/F4
Saspamco, Texas (78153) 303/K11
Sassafras, Md. (†21637) 245/P3
Sassafras (riv.), Md. 245/P3
Sassafras (mt.), S.C. 296/B1
Sassafras, Tasmania 99/C3
Sassandra, Ivory Coast 106/C8
Sassandra (riv.), Ivory Coast 106/C7
Sassari (prov.), Italy 34/B4
Sassari, Italy 34/B4
Sassari, Italy 7/E4
Sasseneire (mt.), Switzerland 39/E4
Sasser, Georgia (31785) 217/D7
Sassnitz, E. Germany 22/E1
Sasstown, Liberia 106/C8
Sassuolo, Italy 34/C2
Sástago, Spain 33/F2
Sasu (mt.), N. Korea 81/C4
Sata (cape), Japan 81/E8
Satadougou, Mali 106/B6
Satanta, Kansas (67870) 232/B4
Satara, India 68/C5
Satartia, Miss. (39162) 256/C5
Satawal (isl.), Micronesia 87/E5
Satellite Beach, Fla. (32935) 212/F3
Säter, Sweden 18/J6
Saticoy, Calif. (93004) 204/F9
Satigny, Switzerland 39/A4
Satilla (riv.), Georgia 217/G8
Satipo, Peru 128/E8
Satluj (Sutlej) (riv.), 68/C3
Satna, India 68/E4
Sátoraljaújhely, Hungary 41/F2
Satpura (range), India 68/D4
Satsop, Wash. (98583) 310/B3
Satsuma, Ala. (36572) 195/B9
Satsuma, Fla. (32089) 212/E2
Satsuma, La. (†70754) 238/L1
Satte, Japan 81/O1
Satu Mare, Romania 45/F2
Satu Mare, Romania 7/G4
Satun, Thailand 72/C6
Satupaitea, W. Samoa 86/L8
Saturna Island, Br. Col. 184/K3
Saturnia, Italy 34/C3
Satus (creek), Wash. 310/E4
Sauble Beach, Ontario 177/C3
Sauce, Argentina 143/G5
Sauce, Peru 128/D6
Sauce, Canelones, Uruguay 145/B6
Sauce, Rocha, Uruguay 145/E5
Sauce (lag.), Uruguay 145/D5
Sauceda (mts.), Ariz. 198/C6
Sauce de Luna, Argentina 143/G5
Sauce del Yi, Uruguay 145/D4
Saucedo, Uruguay 145/B2
Sauchie, Scotland 15/C1
Saucier, Miss. (39574) 256/F9
Saucillo, Mexico 150/G2
Sauda, Qurnet es (mt.), Lebanon 63/G5
Saudhárkrókur, Iceland 21/B1
Saudi Arabia 2/M4
Saudi Arabia 54/F7
SAUDI ARABIA 59/D4
Sauer (riv.), Luxembourg 27/J9
Sauer (riv.), W. Germany 22/B4
Sauerland (reg.), W. Germany 22/B3
Saugatuck, Conn. (†06880) 210/B4
Saugatuck (res.), Conn. 210/B3
Saugatuck (riv.), Conn. 210/B3
Saugatuck, Mich. (49453) 250/C6
Saugeen (riv.), Ontario 177/C3
Saugerties, N.Y. (12477) 276/M6
Sauget, Ill. (62201) 222/A2
Saugus, Mass. (01906) 249/D6
Saugus Iron Works Nat'l Hist. Site, Mass. 249/D6
Sauiá, Brazil 132/B3
Sauk (riv.), Wash. 310/D2
Sauk (co.), Wis. 317/G9
Sauk Centre, Minn. (56378) 255/C5
Sauk City, Wis. (53583) 317/G9
Sauk Rapids, Minn. (56379) 255/D5
Sauk Village, Ill. (60411) 222/C6
Saukville, Wis. (53080) 317/L9
Saül, Fr. Guiana 131/E4
Saulgau, W. Germany 22/C5
Saulkrasti, U.S.S.R. 53/C2
Saulnierville, Nova Scotia 168/B4
Saulsbury, Tenn. (38067) 237/C10
Saulsville, W. Va. (25876) 312/C7
Sault-au-Mouton, Québec 172/H1
Sault au Mouton (riv.), Québec 172/H1
Saulteaux (riv.), Alberta 182/C2
Sault Sainte Marie, Mich. 188/J1
Sault Sainte Marie, Mich. (49783) 250/E2
Sault Sainte Marie, Ont. 162/H6
Sault Sainte Marie, Ontario 177/J5
Sault Sainte Marie, Ontario 175/D3
Sault Ste. Marie, Ont. 146/K5
Saum, Minn. (56674) 255/D3
Saumarez (reef), 95/E4
Saumarez (reef), Coral Sea Is. Terr. 88/J4
Saumarez, New Bruns. 170/E1
Saumâtre (lake), Haiti 158/C6
Saumlaki, Indonesia 85/J7
Saumur, France 28/D4
Saunders (isl.), 143/E7
Saunders (co.), Nebr. 264/H3
Saundersville, Mass. (†01560) 249/G4
Saunemin, Ill. (61769) 222/E3
Sauqira (bay), Oman 59/G6
Sauqira, Ras (cape), Oman 59/G6
Sauquoit, N.Y. (13456) 276/K5
Saurimo, Angola 115/D5
Saurimo, Angola 102/E6
Sausalito, Calif. (94965) 204/H2
Sautatá, Colombia 126/B4
Sautee-Nacoochee, Georgia (30571) 217/E1
Sauteurs, Grenada 161/D8
Saut-Tigre, Fr. Guiana 131/E3
Sauzal, Chile 138/G5
Sava (riv.) 7/F4
Sava (riv.), Yugoslavia 45/D3
Savage, (riv.), Md. 245/B2
Savage, Minn. (55337) 255/G6
Savage, Miss. (38667) 256/D1
Savage, Mont. (59262) 262/M3
Savage (harb.), Pr. Edward I. 168/F2
Savage (riv.), Tasmania 99/B3
Savage-Guilford, Md. (20863) 245/L4
Savage River (lake), Md. 245/B2
Savage River, Tasmania 99/B3
Savageton, Wyo. (†82716) 319/G2
Savah, Ind. (†47620) 227/B8
Savai'i (isl.), W. Samoa 87/J7
Savai'i (isl.), W. Samoa 86/L8
Savalou, Benin 106/E7
Savana (isl.), Virgin Is. (U.S.) 161/A4
Savanat (Estahbanat), Iran 66/J6
Savaneta, Neth. Ant. 161/E10
Savanette, Haiti 158/C6
Savanna, Ill. (61074) 222/C1
Savanna, Okla. (74565) 288/P5
Savanna Army Depot, Ill. 222/C1
Savannah (riv.) 188/K4
Savannah, Ga. 146/K6
Savannah, Ga. 188/K4
Savannah, Georgia (*31401) 217/L6
Savannah (riv.), Georgia 217/K5
Savannah, Mo. (64485) 261/C3
Savannah, N.Y. (13146) 276/G4
Savannah, Ohio (44874) 284/F4
Savannah (riv.), S.C. 296/E6
Savannah, Tenn. (38372) 237/E10
Savannah, U.S. 2/F4
Savannah (riv.), U.S. 146/K6
Savannah River Plant Atomic Energy Commission, S.C. 296/D5
Savannakhét, Laos 72/E3
Savanna-la-Mar, Jamaica 158/G6
Savanna-la-Mar, Jamaica 156/B3
Savannes (bay), St. Lucia 161/G7
Savant (lake), Ontario 177/G4
Savant (lake), Ontario 175/B2
Savant Lake, Ontario 177/G4
Savant Lake, Ontario 175/B2
Savantvadi, India 68/C5
Savanur, India 68/D6
Savaştepe, Turkey 63/B3
Save (riv.) 102/F7
Savé, Benin 106/E7
Save (riv.), Mozambique 118/E4
Saveh, Iran 59/F2
Saveh, Iran 66/G3
Săveni, Romania 45/H1
Saverne, France 28/G3
Saverton, Mo. (63467) 261/K3
Savery, Wyo. (82332) 319/E4
Savery (creek), Wyo. 319/E4
Savièse, Switzerland 39/D4
Savigliano, Italy 34/A2
Savo (isl.), Solomon Is. 86/D3
Savognin, Switzerland 39/J3
Savoie (Savoy) (dept.), France 28/G5
Savona, Br. Col. 184/G5
Savona (prov.), Italy 34/B2
Savona, Italy 34/B2
Savona, N.Y. (14879) 276/F6
Savonburg, Kansas (66772) 232/G4
Savonet, Neth. Ant. 161/F8
Savonlinna, Finland 18/Q6
Savoonga, Alaska (99769) 196/E2
Savoy, Ill. (61874) 222/E3
Savoy, Ky. (†40769) 237/N7
Savoy, Mass. (01256) 249/B2
Savoy, Mont. (†59526) 262/H2
Savoy, S. Dak. (†57754) 298/B5
Şavşat, Turkey 63/K2
Sävsjö, Sweden 18/J8
Savu (sea), Indonesia 54/O10
Savukoski, Finland 18/Q3
Savur, Turkey 63/J4
Savusavu (bay), Fiji 86/Q10
Sawahlunto, Indonesia 85/C6
Sawankhalok, Thailand 72/C3
Sawara, Japan 81/K6
Sawatch (range), Colo. 208/G4
Sawbill, Newf. 166/A3
Sawbill Landing, Minn. (†55603) 255/G3
Sawbridgeworth, England 13/H7
Saweba (cape), Indonesia 85/J6
Sawi, India 68/G7
Sawmill Bay, N.W. Terrs. 187/G3
Sawpit, Colo. (†81430) 208/D7
Sawston, England 13/H5
Sawtell, N.S. Wales 97/G2
Sawtooth (range), Idaho 220/C6
Sawtooth (ridge), Wash. 310/E2
Sawtooth Nat'l Rec. Area, Idaho 220/D5
Sawu (isl.), Indonesia 85/G8
Sawu (isls.), Indonesia 85/G8
Sawu (sea), Indonesia 85/G7
Sawyer, Kansas (67134) 232/D4
Sawyer, Ky. (42643) 237/N7
Sawyer, Mich. (49125) 250/C7
Sawyer, Minn. (55780) 255/F4
Sawyer, N. Dak. (58781) 282/H3
Sawyer, Okla. (74756) 288/R7
Sawyer (co.), Wis. 317/D4
Sawyers Bar, Calif. (96027) 204/B2
Sawyerville, Ala. (36776) 195/C5
Sawyerville, Ill. (62085) 222/D4
Sawyerville, Québec 172/F4
Saxapahaw, N.C. (27340) 281/L3
Saxe, Va. (23967) 307/L7
Saxeville, Wis. (54976) 317/H7
Saxis, Va. (23427) 307/S5
Saxman, Alaska (†99901) 196/N2
Saxmundham, England 13/J5
Saxon, S.C. (†29301) 296/D2
Saxon, Switzerland 39/D4
Saxon, Wis. (54559) 317/F3
Saxonburg, Pa. (16056) 294/C4
Saxonville, Mass. (01701) 249/A7
Saxony (reg.), E. Germany 22/E3
Saxton, Ky. (†40769) 237/N7
Saxton, Pa. (16678) 294/F5
Saxtons River, Vt. (05154) 268/B5
Say, Niger 106/E6
Saya, Bolivia 136/B5
Sayabec, Québec 172/B2
Sayaboury (Muang Xaignabouri), Laos 72/D3
Sayama, Japan 81/O2
Sayán, Peru 128/D8
Sayan (mts.), U.S.S.R. 48/K4
Saybrook, Ill. (61770) 222/E3
Saybrook, Pa. (†16347) 294/D2
Saybrook Point, Conn. (†06475) 210/F3
Sayhan-Ovoo, Mongolia 77/F2
Saylesville, R.I. (†02865) 249/J5
Saylorsburg, Pa. (18353) 294/M4
Saylorville (lake), Iowa 229/F5
Sayner, Wis. (54560) 317/H4
Saynshand, Mongolia 77/H3
Saynshand, Mongolia 54/M5
Sayre, Ala. (35139) 195/E3
Sayre, Okla. (73662) 288/G4
Sayre, Pa. (18840) 294/K2
Sayreville, N.J. (08872) 273/E3
Sayula, Mexico 150/H7
Sayula de Alemán, Mexico 150/M8
Sayville, N.Y. (11782) 276/O9
Sayward, Br. Col. 184/D5
Sazan (isl.), Albania 45/D5
Sázava (riv.), Czech. 41/C2
Sbaa, Algeria 106/D3
Sbeitla, Tunisia 106/F1
Scafell Pike (mt.), England 13/D3
Scafell Pike (mt.), England 10/E3
Scalasaig, Scotland 15/B4
Scalby, England 13/G3
Scales Mound, Ill. (61075) 222/C1
Scaletta (pass), Switzerland 39/J3
Scalf, Ky. (40982) 237/O7
Scalloway, Scotland 10/G1
Scalloway, Scotland 15/G2
Scalpay (isl.), Scotland 15/B3
Scalpay (isl.), Scotland 15/C3
Scalp Level, Pa. (†15963) 294/E5
Scaly Mountain, N.C. (28775) 281/C4
Scammon, Kansas (66773) 232/H4
Scammon Bay, Alaska (99662) 196/E2
Scandia, Alberta 182/E4
Scandia, Kansas (66966) 232/E2
Scandia, Minn. (55073) 255/F5
Scandia, Wash. (†98370) 310/A1
Scandinavia 18
Scandinavia, Wis. (54977) 317/H7
Scanlon, Minn. (†55720) 255/F4
Scanterbury, Manitoba 179/F4
Scantic, Conn. (†06097) 210/E1
Scantic (riv.), Conn. 210/E1

Seminoe 445

Scapa, Alberta 182/D4
Scapa Flow (chan.), Scotland 15/E2
Scapa Flow (chan.), Scotland 10/E1
Scappoose, Oreg. (97056) 291/E2
Scarba (isl.), Scotland 15/C4
Scarboro, Barbados 161/B9
Scarboro, Georgia (†30442) 217/J5
Scarborough, England 10/F3
Scarborough, England 13/G3
Scarborough, Maine (04074) 243/C8
Scarborough○, Maine (04074) 243/C8
Scarborough, Ontario 177/K4
Scarborough, Trin. & Tob. 156/G5
Scarbro, W. Va. (25917) 312/D7
Scarinish, Scotland 15/B4
Scarp (isl.), Scotland 15/A2
Scarriff, Ireland 17/E6
Scarriff (isl.), Ireland 17/A8
Scarsdale, N.Y. (10583) 276/P6
Scarth, Manitoba 179/B5
Scarville, Iowa (50473) 229/F2
Scatarie (isl.), Nova Scotia 168/J2
Scavaig, Loch (inlet), Scotland 15/B3
Sceaux, France 28/A2
Scenic, S. Dak. (57780) 298/D6
Scenic, Wash. (†98288) 310/D3
Sceptre, Sask. 181/B5
Schaal, Ark. (†71851) 202/C6
Schaalsee (lake), E. Germany 22/D2
Schaalsee (lake), W. Germany 22/D2
Schaan, Liecht. 39/H2
Schaefferstown, Pa. (17088) 294/K5
Schaerbeek, Belgium 27/C9
Schaffer, Mich. (49882) 250/B3
Schaffhausen (canton), Switzerland 39/G1
Schaffhausen, Switzerland 39/G1
Schagen, Netherlands 27/F3
Schaghticoke, N.Y. (12154) 276/N5
Schaller, Iowa (51053) 229/C4
S-chanf, Switzerland 39/J3
Schangnau, Switzerland 39/E3
Schänis, Switzerland 39/H2
Scharans, Switzerland 39/J3
Schärding, Austria 41/B2
Scharhörn (isl.), W. Germany 22/C2
Schattdorf, Switzerland 39/G3
Schaumburg, Ill. (60194) 222/A5
Schawana, Wash. (†99321) 310/F4
Schefferville, Que. 146/L4
Schefferville, Que. 162/K5
Schefferville, Québec 174/D2
Scheibbs, Austria 41/C2
Scheinfeld, W. Germany 22/D4
Schelde (Scheldt) (riv.), Belgium 27/C7
Scheldt (riv.), Belgium 27/C7
Schell City, Mo. (64783) 261/D6
Schell Creek (range), Nev. 266/G3
Schellsburg, Pa. (15559) 294/E5
Schellville, Calif. (†95476) 204/J1
Schenectady, N.Y. 188/M2
Schenectady (co.), N.Y. 276/M5
Schenectady, N.Y. (*12301) 276/M5
Schenevus, N.Y. (12155) 276/L5
Schererville, Ind. (46375) 227/C2
Scherhorn (mt.), Switzerland 39/G3
Schertz, Texas (78154) 303/K10
Scherzingen, Switzerland 39/H1
Schesaplana (mt.), Switzerland 39/J2
Scheveningen, Netherlands 27/E4
Schichallion (mt.), Scotland 15/D4
Schiedam, Netherlands 27/E5
Schiermonnikoog, Netherlands 27/J1
Schiermonnikoog (isl.), Netherlands 27/J1
Schiers, Switzerland 39/J3
Schijndel, Netherlands 27/G5
Schiller Park, Ill. (60176) 222/B5
Schinznach-Dorf, Switzerland 39/F2
Schio, Italy 34/C2
Schiphol, Netherlands 27/B5
Schkeuditz, E. Germany 22/E3
Schladming, Austria 41/B3
Schlater, Miss. (38952) 256/D3
Schlei (inlet), W. Germany 22/C1
Schleicher (co.), Texas 303/D7
Schleitheim, Switzerland 39/G1
Schleswig, Iowa (51461) 229/B4
Schleswig, W. Germany 22/C1
Schleswig-Holstein (state), W. Germany 22/C1
Schleusingen, E. Germany 22/D3
Schley (co.), Georgia 217/D6
Schley, Minn. (†56633) 255/D3
Schlieren, Switzerland 39/F2
Schliersee, W. Germany 22/D5
Schlitz, W. Germany 22/C3
Schlüchtern, W. Germany 22/C3
Schmalkalden, E. Germany 22/D3
Schmölln, E. Germany 22/E3
Schnecksville, Pa. (18078) 294/L4
Schneeberg, E. Germany 22/E3
Schneeberg (mt.), W. Germany 22/D3
Schnee Eifel (plat.), Belgium 27/J8
Schneidemühl (Piła), Poland 47/C2
Schneider, Ind. (46376) 227/C2
Schnellville, Ind. (47580) 227/D8
Schoelcher, Martinique 161/C6
Schoenchen, Kansas (67667) 232/C3
Schoenfeld, Sask. 181/D5
Schoen Lake Prov. Park, Br. Col. 184/E5
Schofield, Wis. (54476) 317/H6
Schofield Barracks, Hawaii (96786) 218/E2
Schoharie (co.), N.Y. 276/M5
Schoharie, N.Y. (12157) 276/M5
Schoharie (creek), N.Y. 276/M6
Schoharie (res.), N.Y. 276/M6
Scholle, N. Mex. (†87036) 274/C4
Scholls, Oreg. (†97123) 291/A2
Schomberg, Ontario 177/J3
Schönberg, E. Germany 22/D2
Schönberg, W. Germany 22/D1
Schönebeck, E. Germany 22/D2
Schöneberg, W. Germany 22/E4
Schöneiche, E. Germany 22/E2
Schönenwerd, Switzerland 39/E2
Schongau, W. Germany 22/D5
Schöningen, W. Germany 22/D2
Schoodic (lake), Maine 243/F5
Schoolcraft (co.), Mich. 250/C2
Schoolcraft, Mich. (49087) 250/D6
Schoolcraft (riv.), Minn. 255/C3
Schooleys Mountain, N.J. (07870) 273/D2
School Hill, Wis. (†53042) 317/L8
Schoonhoven, Netherlands 27/F5
Schoten, Belgium 27/F6
Schottegat (bay), Neth. Ant. 161/G9
Schouten (isls.), Indonesia 85/K6
Schouten (isls.), Papua N.G. 85/B6
Schouten (isl.), Tasmania 99/E4
Schouwen (isl.), Netherlands 27/D5
Schramberg, W. Germany 22/C4
Schram City, Ill. (†62049) 222/D4
Schreckhorn (mt.), Switzerland 39/F3
Schreiber, Ontario 177/H5
Schreiber, Ontario 175/C3
Schrems, Austria 41/C2
Schriever, La. (70395) 238/J7
Schroeder, Minn. (55613) 255/G3
Schroon (lake), N.Y. 276/N3
Schroon (riv.), N.Y. 276/N3
Schroon Lake, N.Y. (12870) 276/N3
Schruns, Austria 41/A3
Schübelbach, Switzerland 39/G2
Schulenburg, Texas (78956) 303/H8
Schuler, Alberta 182/E4
Schull, Ireland 10/B5
Schull, Ireland 17/B8
Schulter, Okla. (74460) 288/P3
Schultz (lake), N.W. Terrs. 187/J3
Schumacher, Ontario 175/D3
Schüpfheim, Switzerland 39/F3
Schurz, Nev. (89427) 266/C4
Schussenried, W. Germany 22/C4
Schuyler (co.), Ill. 222/C3
Schuyler (co.), Mo. 261/G2
Schuyler, Nebr. (68661) 264/G3
Schuyler (co.), N.Y. 276/G6
Schuyler, Va. (22969) 307/L5
Schuyler Lake, N.Y. (13457) 276/L5
Schuylerville, N.Y. (12871) 276/N4
Schuylkill (co.), Pa. 294/K4
Schuylkill (riv.), Pa. 294/M5
Schuylkill Haven, Pa. (17972) 294/K4
Schwaan, E. Germany 22/E2
Schwabach, W. Germany 22/D4
Schwäbisch Gmünd, W. Germany 22/C4
Schwäbisch Hall, W. Germany 22/C4
Schwalmstadt, W. Germany 22/C3
Schwanden, Switzerland 39/H2
Schwandorf im Bayern, W. Germany 22/E4
Schwaner (mts.), Indonesia 85/E6
Schwarzach im Pongau, Austria 41/B3
Schwarzenburg, Switzerland 39/D3
Schwarzhorn (mt.), Switzerland 39/E4
Schwarzhorn (mt.), Switzerland 39/F3
Schwarzwald (Black) (for.), W. Germany 22/C4
Schwatka (mts.), Alaska 196/G1
Schwaz, Austria 41/A3
Schwechat, Austria 41/D2
Schwedt, E. Germany 22/F2
Schweidnitz (Świdnica), Poland 47/C3
Schweinfurt, W. Germany 22/D3
Schwelm, W. Germany 22/B3
Schwenksville, Pa. (19473) 294/L5
Schwerin (dist.), E. Germany 22/D2
Schwerin, E. Germany 22/D2
Schweriner See (lake), E. Germany 22/D2
Schwertberg, Austria 41/C2
Schwetzingen, W. Germany 22/C4
Schwyz (canton), Switzerland 39/G2
Schwyz, Switzerland 39/G2
Sciacca, Italy 34/D6
Scicli, Italy 34/E6
Science Hill, Ky. (42553) 237/M6
Scilly (isls.), England 13/A7
Scilly (isls.), England 10/C6
Scio, N.Y. (14880) 276/E6
Scio, Ohio (43988) 284/H5
Scio, Oreg. (97374) 291/E3
Sciota, Ill. (61475) 222/C3
Sciota, Pa. (18354) 294/M4
Scioto (co.), Ohio 284/D8
Scioto (riv.), Ohio 284/D8
Sciotodale, Ohio (†45662) 284/E8
Scioto Furnace, Ohio (45677) 284/E8
Scipio, Ind. (47273) 227/F6
Scipio, Ind. (†45053) 227/H6
Scipio, Okla. (†74501) 288/P4
Scipio, Utah (84656) 304/B4
Scircleville, Ind. (46066) 227/E4
Scitico, Conn. (†06036) 210/E1
Scituate, Mass. (02066) 249/F8
Scituate○, Mass. (02066) 249/F8
Scituate (res.), R.I. 249/H5
Sclater, Manitoba 179/B3
Scobey, Miss. (38953) 256/E3
Scobey, Mont. (59263) 262/L2
Scofield, Utah (†84526) 304/C4
Scofield (res.), Utah 304/C4
Scollard, Alberta 182/D4
Scone, N.S. Wales 97/F3
Scooba, Miss. (39358) 256/G5
Scopi (mt.), Switzerland 39/G3
Scopus, Mo. (63762) 261/N8
Scoresby (sound), Greenl. 4/B10
Scoresbysund, Greenl. 4/B10
Scotch Grove, Iowa (52331) 229/L4
Scotch Plains○, N.J. (07076) 273/E2
Scotchtown, Nova Scotia 168/H2
Scotch Village, Nova Scotia 168/E3
Scotfield, Alberta 182/E4
Scotia (sea) 2/G8
Scotia (sea) 5/D16
Scotia, Calif. (95565) 204/A3
Scotia, Nebr. (68875) 264/F3
Scotia, N.Y. (12302) 276/N5
Scotia, S.C. (29939) 296/E6
SCOTLAND 15
SCOTLAND 10/D2
Scotland, Ark. (72141) 202/E2
Scotland○, Conn. (06264) 210/G2
Scotland, Georgia (31083) 217/G6
Scotland, Ind. (47457) 227/D7
Scotland, Md. (20687) 245/N8
Scotland (co.), Mo. 261/H2
Scotland (co.), N.C. 281/L5
Scotland, Ontario 177/D4
Scotland, Pa. (17254) 294/G6
Scotland, S. Dak. (57059) 298/O7
Scotland, Texas (76379) 303/F4
Scotland, U.K. 7/D3
Scotland Neck, N.C. (27874) 281/P2
Scotlandville, La. (70807) 238/J1
Scots (bay), Nova Scotia 168/D3
Scots Bay, Nova Scotia 168/D3
Scotsburn, Nova Scotia 168/F3
Scotsguard, Sask. 181/C6
Scotstown, Ireland 17/H3
Scotstown, Québec 172/F4
Scotsville, Nova Scotia 168/G2
Scott (isl.), Ant. 2/A9
Scott (isl.), Ant. 5/C10
Scott (co.), Ark. 202/B4
Scott, Ark. (72142) 202/F4
Scott (cape), Br. Col. 162/D5
Scott (cape), Br. Col. 184/C5
Scott (isls.), Br. Col. 184/C5
Scott (riv.), Calif. 204/B2
Scott (co.), Georgia 217/G5
Scott, Georgia (31095) 217/G5
Scott (co.), Ill. 222/C4
Scott (co.), Ind. 227/F7
Scott, Ind. (†46746) 227/F1
Scott (co.), Iowa 229/M5
Scott (co.), Kansas 232/B3
Scott (co.), Ky. 237/M4
Scott, La. (70583) 238/F6
Scott (co.), Minn. 255/E6
Scott (co.), Miss. 256/E6
Scott, Miss. (38772) 256/B3
Scott (co.), Mo. 261/N8
Scott, Ohio (45886) 284/A4
Scott (mt.), Okla. 288/K5
Scott, Sask. 181/C3
Scott (lake), Sask. 181/M2
Scott (co.), Tenn. 237/M8
Scott (co.), Va. 307/C7
Scott A.F.B., Ill. 222/B3
Scott City, Kansas (67871) 232/B3
Scott City, Mo. (63780) 261/O8
Scottdale, Georgia (30079) 217/L1
Scottdale, Pa. (15683) 294/C5
Scott-Jonction, Québec 172/F3
Scottland, Ill. (†61924) 222/F4
Scotts (head), Dominica 161/E7
Scotts, N.C. (28699) 281/H3
Scottsbluff, Nebr. 188/F2
Scottsbluff, Nebr. 146/H5
Scotts Bluff (co.), Nebr. 264/A3
Scottsbluff, Nebr. (69361) 264/A3
Scotts Bluff Nat'l Mon., Nebr. 264/A3
Scottsboro, Ala. (35768) 195/F1
Scottsburg, Ind. (47170) 227/F7
Scottsburg, Ky. (†42445) 237/F6
Scottsburg, Oreg. (97473) 291/D4
Scottsburg, Va. (24589) 307/L7
Scottsdale, Ariz. (*85251) 198/D5
Scottsdale, Tasmania 99/D3
Scotts Hill, N.C. (†28401) 281/O6
Scotts Hill, Tenn. (38374) 237/E10
Scotts Mills, Oreg. (97375) 291/B3
Scottsmoor, Fla. (32775) 212/F3
Scotts Ridge (hills), Conn. 210/A3
Scott Station, Ant. 5/B9
Scotts Valley, Calif. (95060) 204/K4
Scottsville, Ark. (†72843) 202/D3
Scottsville, Kansas (67477) 232/D2
Scottsville, Ky. (42164) 237/J7
Scottsville, N.Y. (14546) 276/E4
Scottsville, Va. (24590) 307/L5
Scottville, Ill. (62683) 222/C4
Scottville, Mich. (49454) 250/C5
Scoudouc, New Bruns. 170/F2
Scourie, Scotland 15/C2
Scout Lake, Sask. 181/F6
Scrabster, Scotland 15/E2
Scraggly (lake), Maine 243/H5
Scraggly (lake), Maine 243/F3
Scranage, Ala. (†36552) 195/C8
Scranton, Ark. (72863) 202/C3
Scranton, Iowa (51462) 229/D4
Scranton, Kansas (66537) 232/G3
Scranton, Ky. (40373) 237/O5
Scranton, N.Y. (†14075) 276/C5
Scranton, N.C. (27875) 281/S4
Scranton, N. Dak. (58653) 282/D7
Scranton, Pa. 188/L2
Scranton, Pa. 146/L5
Scranton, Pa. (*18501) 294/F7
Scranton, S.C. (29591) 296/H4
Scraper, Okla. (†74359) 288/S2
Screven (co.), Georgia 217/J5
Screven, Georgia (31560) 217/H7
Scriba, N.Y. (†13827) 276/H4
Scribner, Nebr. (68057) 264/H3
Scridain, Loch (inlet), Scotland 15/B4
Scugog (lake), Ontario 177/F3
Scullin, Okla. (†73086) 288/N5
Scunthorpe, England 10/F4
Scunthorpe, England 13/G4
Scuol, Switzerland 39/K3
Scurdie Ness (prom.), Scotland 15/F4
Scurrival (pt.), Scotland 15/A3
Scurry (co.), Texas 303/D5
Scurry, Texas (75158) 303/H5
Scusciuban, Somalia 115/J1
Scutari (lake), Albania 45/D4
Scutari (lake), Yugoslavia 45/D4
Scyrene, Ala. (†36436) 195/C7
Sea (isls.), Georgia 217/K9
Sea (isls.), S.C. 296/G7
Seabeck, Wash. (98380) 310/C3
Seaboard, N.C. (27876) 281/O1
Seabold, Wash. (†98110) 310/A1
Sea Breeze, N.Y. (†14617) 276/F4
Sea Bright, N.J. (07760) 273/F3
Seabrook○, N.H. (03874) 268/F6
Seabrook, N.J. (08302) 273/C5
Seabrook, S.C. (29940) 296/F6
Seabrook (isl.), S.C. 296/G6
Seabrook, Texas (77586) 303/K2
Seabrook-Lanham, Md. (20801) 245/G4
Sea Cliff, N.Y. (11579) 276/R6
Seadrift, Texas (77983) 303/H9
Seaford, Del. (19973) 245/R6
Seaford, England 10/G5
Seaford, England 13/H7
Seaford, N.Y. (11783) 276/R7
Seaford, Va. (23696) 307/R6
Seaforth, Minn. (56287) 255/C6
Seaforth, Ontario 177/C4
Seaforth, Loch (inlet), Scotland 15/B3
Sea Girt, N.J. (08750) 273/E3
Seagoville, Texas (75159) 303/H3
Seagraves, Texas (79359) 303/B5
Seagrove, N.C. (27341) 281/K3
Seaham, England 10/F3
Seaham, England 13/J3
Seahorse (lake), Newf. 166/A3
Seahorse (pt.), N.W. Terrs. 187/L3
Seahurst, Wash. (98062) 310/A2
Sea Island, Georgia (31561) 217/K8
Sea Isle City, N.J. (08243) 273/D5
Seal (isl.), Maine 243/F8
Seal (riv.), Man. 162/G4
Seal (riv.), Manitoba 179/J2
Seal (lake), Newf. 166/B3
Seal (isl.), Nova Scotia 168/B5
Seal (isl.), S. Africa 118/F7
Sea Lake, Victoria 97/B4
Seal Beach, Calif. (90740) 204/C11
Seal Cove, Maine (04674) 243/G7
Seal Cove, New Bruns. 170/D4
Seal Cove, Newf. 166/C4
Seal Cove, Newf. 166/C3
Seale, Ala. (36875) 195/H6
Sealevel, N.C. (28577) 281/S5
Seal Harbor, Maine (04675) 243/G7
Seal Rock, Oreg. (97376) 291/C3
Sealston, Va. (22547) 307/O4
Sealy, Texas (77474) 303/H8
Seaman, Ohio (45679) 284/C8
Seamer, England 13/G3
Sea Pines, S.C. (†29928) 296/F7
Sea Ranch Lakes, Fla. (†33301) 212/C3
Searchlight, Nev. (89046) 266/F7
Searchmont, Ontario 177/J5
Searcy (co.), Ark. 202/E2
Searcy, Ark. (72143) 202/G3
Searight, Ala. (†36028) 195/F8
Searles, Ala. (†35468) 195/D4
Searles (lake), Calif. 204/H8
Searles, Minn. (56084) 255/D6
Sears, Mich. (49679) 250/D5
Searsboro, Iowa (50242) 229/H5
Searsburg○, Vt. (†05363) 268/A6
Searsmont, Maine (04973) 243/E7
Searsmont○, Maine (04973) 243/E7
Searsport, Maine (04974) 243/F7
Searsport○, Maine (04974) 243/F7
Seascale, England 10/E2
Seascale, England 13/D3
Seaside, Calif. (93955) 204/D7
Seaside, Oreg. (97138) 291/D2
Seaside Heights, N.J. (08751) 273/E4
Seaside Park, N.J. (08752) 273/E4
Seaton, England 13/D7
Seaton, Ill. (61476) 222/C2
Seaton Valley, England 13/J3
Seatonville, Ill. (61359) 222/D2
Seat Pleasant, Md. (20027) 245/G5
Seattle, U.S. 2/C3
Seattle, Wash. 146/F5
Seattle, Wash. 188/B1
Seattle, Wash. (*98101) 310/A2
Seaview, Wash. (98644) 310/A4
Seaward Kaikouras (range), N. Zealand 100/D5
Seawell, Barbados 161/B9
Seba, Indonesia 85/G8
Seba Beach, Alberta 182/C3
Sebago (lake), Maine 243/B8
Sebago Lake, Maine (04075) 243/B8
Sebastian (co.), Ark. 202/B3
Sebastian, Fla. (32958) 212/F4
Sebastian (cape), Oreg. 291/C5
Sebastián Vizcaíno (bay), Mexico 150/B2
Sebasticook (lake), Maine 243/E6
Sebastopol, Calif. (95472) 204/C5
Sebastopol, Miss. (39359) 256/F5
Sebastopol, Victoria 97/B5
Sebatik (isl.), Indonesia 85/F5
Sebatik (isl.), Malaysia 85/F5
Sebec, Maine (04481) 243/E5
Sebec○, Maine (04481) 243/E5
Sebec Lake, Maine (04482) 243/E5
Sebec Station, Maine (†04426) 243/E5
Sebeka, Minn. (56477) 255/C4
Seben, Turkey 63/D2
Sebeş, Romania 45/F3
Sebes Körös (riv.), Hungary 41/F3
Sebewaing, Mich. (48759) 250/F5
Sebha, Libya 102/D2
Sebha, Libya 111/B2
Şebinkarahisar, Turkey 63/H2
Sebiş, Romania (2) 45/F2
Sebnitz, E. Germany 22/F3
Seboeis○, Maine (04484) 243/F5
Seboeis (lake), Maine 243/F5
Seboeis (riv.), Maine 243/F3
Seboomook, Maine (†04478) 243/D4
Seboomook (lake), Maine 243/D4
Seboruco, Venezuela 124/B3
Sebou (riv.), Morocco 106/C2
Seboyeta, N. Mex. (87055) 274/B3
Sebree, Ky. (42455) 237/F5
Sebrell, Va. (†23837) 307/O7
Sebring, Fla. (33870) 212/E4
Sebring, Ohio (44672) 284/H4
Sebringville, Ontario 177/C4
Sebuku (bay), Indonesia 85/F5
Secane, Pa. (†19018) 294/M7
Secas (isls.), Panama 154/G7
Secaucus, N.J. (07094) 273/B2
Secesh (riv.), Idaho 220/C4
Sechelt, Br. Col. 184/J2
Sechura, Peru 128/B5
Sechura (bay), Peru 128/B5
Seco, Ky. (41849) 237/R6
Second (lake), N.H. 268/E1
Second Cataract, Sudan 59/B5
Second Cataract, Sudan 111/F3
Secondcreek, W. Va. (24974) 312/F7
Second Mesa, Ariz. (86043) 198/E3
Secor, Ill. (61771) 222/D3
Sečovce, Czech. 41/F2
Secretan, Sask. 181/E5
Secretary, Md. (21664) 245/P6
Secretary (isl.), N. Zealand 100/A6
Section, Ala. (35771) 195/G1
Secunderabad, India 68/D5
Sécure (riv.), Bolivia 136/C4
Security-Widefield, Colo. (80911) 208/K5
Sedalia, Alberta 182/E4
Sedalia, Colo. (80135) 208/K4
Sedalia, Ind. (46067) 227/E4
Sedalia, Ky. (42079) 237/D7
Sedalia, Mo. (65301) 261/F5
Sedalia, Mo. 188/H3
Sedalia, Ohio (43151) 284/D6
Sedalia, S.C. (†29379) 296/D2
Sedan, France 28/F3
Sedan, Ind. (†46793) 227/G2
Sedan, Kansas (67361) 232/F4
Sedan, Minn. (56380) 255/C5
Sedan, N. Mex. (88436) 274/F2
Sedano, Spain 33/E1
Sedbergh (co.), England 10/E3
Sedbergh, England 13/E3
Seddon, N. Zealand 100/E4
Seddonville, N. Zealand 100/C4
Seddülbahir, Turkey 63/B6
Sede Boqer, Israel 65/D5
Sederot, Israel 65/B4
Sedgewick, Alberta 182/E3
Sedgewickville, Mo. (63781) 261/N7
Sedgwick, Ark. (72465) 202/J2
Sedgwick (co.), Colo. 208/P1
Sedgwick, Colo. (80749) 208/O1
Sedgwick (co.), Kansas 232/E4
Sedgwick, Kansas (67135) 232/E4
Sedgwick○, Maine (04676) 243/F7
Sedhiou, Senegal 106/A6
Sedili Kechil, Tanjong (pt.), Malaysia 72/F5
Sedlčany, Czech. 41/C2
Sedley, Sask. 181/H5
Sedley, Va. (23878) 307/P7
Sedom, Israel 65/D5
Sedona, Ariz. (86336) 198/D4
Sedot Yam, Israel 65/B3
Sedro-Woolley, Wash. (98284) 310/C2
Šeduva, U.S.S.R. 53/B3
Seebe, Alberta 182/C4
Seebert, W. Va. (24975) 312/F6
Seechelt (inlet), Br. Col. 184/J2
Seechelt (pen.), Br. Col. 184/J2
Seeheim, Namibia 118/B5
Seeis, Namibia 118/B4
Seekonk○, Mass. (02771) 249/J5
Seeley, Calif. (92273) 204/K11
Seeley, Wis. (†54843) 317/D3
Seeley Lake, Mont. (59868) 262/C3
Seeleys Bay, Ontario 177/H3
Seelyville, Ind. (47878) 227/C6
Seelyville, Pa. (18431) 294/M2
Seesen, W. Germany 22/D3
Seewis im Prättigau, Switzerland 39/J2
Seez (riv.), Switzerland 39/H2
Şefaatli, Turkey 63/F3
Seferihisar, Turkey 63/B3
Seffner, Fla. (33584) 212/D4
Sefrou, Morocco 106/D2
Sefton, N. Zealand 100/D5
Seg (lake), U.S.S.R. 52/D2
Segamat, Malaysia 72/D7
Segarcea, Romania 45/F3
Segezha, U.S.S.R. 52/D2
Segezha, U.S.S.R. 48/D3
Segnes (pass), Switzerland 39/H3
Segni, Italy 34/F7
Segorbe, Spain 33/F3
Ségou, Mali 106/C6
Ségou, Mali 102/B3
Segovia, Colombia 126/C4
Segovia (Coco) (riv.), Honduras 154/E3
Segovia (Coco) (riv.), Nicaragua 154/E3
Segovia (prov.), Spain 33/D2
Segovia, Spain 33/D2
Segré, France 28/C4
Segre (riv.), Spain 33/G2
Segreganset, Mass. (02773) 249/K5
Seguam (isl.), Alaska 196/D4
Seguam (passage), Alaska 196/D4
Séguéla, Ivory Coast 106/C7
Segui, Argentina 143/F6
Seguin, Kansas (†67740) 232/B2
Seguin (lake), Québec 172/B2
Seguin, Texas (78155) 303/G8
Segula (isl.), Alaska 196/K4
Segundo, Colo. (81070) 208/K8
Segura (riv.), Spain 33/F3
Sehore, India 68/D4
Sehwan, Pakistan 59/J4
Sehwan, Pakistan 68/B3
Seiad Valley, Calif. (96086) 204/B2
Seibert (lake), Alberta 182/E2
Seibert, Colo. (80834) 208/O4
Seibo, Dom. Rep. 156/E3
Seil (isl.), Scotland 15/C4
Seiland (isl.), Norway 18/N1
Seiling, Okla. (73663) 288/J2
Sein (isl.), France 28/A3
Seinäjoki, Finland 18/N5
Seine (riv.), France 7/E4
Seine (bay), France 28/C3
Seine (riv.), France 28/D3
Seine (riv.), Ontario 175/B3
Seine-et-Marne (dept.), France 28/E3
Seine-Saint-Denis (dept.), France 28/C1
Seistan (reg.), Iran 66/M5
Seixal, Portugal 33/A1
Seiyun, P.D.R. Yemen 59/E6
Sejerø (isl.), Denmark 21/E6
Sejny, Poland 47/F1
Seke-Banza, Zaire 115/B5
Sekenke, Tanzania 115/F4
Se Khong (riv.), Cambodia 72/E4
Se Khong (riv.), Laos 72/E4
Sekiu, Wash. (98381) 310/A2
Sekkane, Erg (des.), Mali 106/D4
Sekondi, Ghana 106/D8
Selah, Wash. (98942) 310/E4
Selama, Malaysia 72/D6
Selangor (state), Malaysia 72/D7
Selaphum, Thailand 72/E3
Selaru (isl.), Indonesia 85/J7
Selatan (cape), Indonesia 85/E6
Selawik, Alaska (99770) 196/G1
Selawik (lake), Alaska 196/F1
Selayar (isl.), Indonesia 85/G7
Selb, W. Germany 22/E3
Selby, England 13/F4
Selby, S. Dak. (57472) 298/J3
Selby, Victoria 97/K5
Selby-on-the-Bay, Md. (†21037) 245/N5
Selbyville, Del. (19975) 245/S7
Selbyville, W. Va. (26236) 312/F5
Selçuk, Turkey 63/B3
Selden, Kansas (67757) 232/B2
Seldom, Newf. 166/D4
Seldovia, Alaska (99663) 196/B2
Sele (riv.), Italy 34/E4
Selebi-Pikwe, Botswana 118/D4
Selemdzha (riv.), U.S.S.R. 48/O4
Selemiya, Syria 63/G5
Selendi, Turkey 63/C3
Selenga (riv.) 54/M5
Selenge, Mongolia 77/G2
Selenge, Mongolia 77/F2
Selenge (Selenga) Mörön (riv.), Mongolia 77/G2
Sélestat, France 28/G3
Selfridge, N. Dak. (58568) 282/J7
Sélibaby, Mauritania 106/B5
Seligman, Ariz. (86337) 198/B3
Seligman, Mo. (65745) 261/D9
Selim, Turkey 63/K2
Selima (oasis), Sudan 111/E3
Selima (oasis), Sudan 59/A5
Selimiye, Turkey 63/B4
Selinsgrove, Pa. (17870) 294/J4
Selje, Norway 18/D5
Selkirk (mts.), Br. Col. 184/J4
Selkirk (mts.), Idaho 220/B1
Selkirk, Kansas (67873) 232/A3
Selkirk, Man. 162/G5
Selkirk, Manitoba 179/F4
Selkirk (isl.), Manitoba 179/C1
Selkirk, Mich. (†48661) 250/E4
Selkirk, Scotland 10/E3
Selkirk, Scotland 15/F5
Selkirk (trad. co.) Scotland 15/B5
Sella, Bolivia 136/C7
Selle (peak), Haiti 158/C6
Selleck, Wash. (†98051) 310/D3
Sellers, Ala. (†36046) 195/F6
Sellers, S.C. (29592) 296/H3
Sellersburg, Ind. (47172) 227/F8
Sellersville, Pa. (18960) 294/M5
Sells, Ariz. (85634) 198/D7
Sells, Georgia (†30548) 217/E2
Sellye, Hungary 41/D4
Selma, Ala. 188/J4
Selma, Ala. (36701) 195/E6
Selma, Ark. (†71670) 202/G6
Selma, Calif. (93662) 204/F7
Selma, Ind. (47383) 227/G4
Selma, Iowa (52588) 229/J7
Selma, Miss. (†39120) 256/B7
Selma, N.C. (27576) 281/N3
Selma, Ohio (45364) 284/C6
Selma, Oreg. (97538) 291/D5
Selma, Texas (†78201) 303/K10
Selma, Va. (24474) 307/J5
Selmah, Nova Scotia 168/E3
Selman, Okla. (73856) 288/H1
Selmer, Tenn. (38375) 237/D10
Selmont, Ala. (†36701) 195/E6
Selous (mt.), Yukon 187/E3
Selsey, England 13/G7
Selsey Bill (prom.), England 13/G7
Selukwe, Zimbabwe 118/E3
Selva, Argentina 143/D2
Selvas (for.), Brazil 120/C3
Selvin, Ind. (†47523) 227/C8
Selway (riv.), Idaho 220/C3
Selwyn (lake), N.W. Terrs. 187/H4
Selwyn, Queensland 95/B4
Selwyn (range), Queensland 95/B4
Selwyn (lake), Sask. 181/M2
Selwyn, W. Va. (†25674) 312/B7
Selwyn (mts.), Yukon 187/E3
Selz, N. Dak. (58373) 282/L4
Seman, Ala. (†36092) 195/F5
Semans, Sask. 181/G4
Semara, W. Sahara 102/A2
Semara, Western Sahara 106/B3
Semarang, Indonesia 54/N10
Semarang, Indonesia 85/J2
Sematan, Malaysia 85/D5
Sembé, Congo 115/B3
Sembrancher, Switzerland 39/D4
Şemdinli, Turkey 63/L4
Semenov, U.S.S.R. 52/F3
Semeru (mt.), Indonesia 85/K2
Semichi (isls.), Alaska 196/J3
Semidi (isls.), Alaska 196/G3
Semiluki, U.S.S.R. 52/E4
Semily, Czech. 41/C1
Seminary, Miss. (39479) 256/E7
Seminoe (res.), Wyo. 188/E2

446 Seminoe

Seminoe (mts.), Wyo. 319/E3
Seminoe (res.), Wyo. 319/F3
Seminoe Dam, Wyo. (†82334) 319/E3
Seminole, Ala. (36574) 195/D10
Seminole (co.), Fla. 212/E3
Seminole, Fla. (33542) 212/B3
Seminole (lake), Fla. 212/B1
Seminole (co.), Georgia 217/C9
Seminole (lake), Georgia 217/B9
Seminole (co.), Okla. 288/N4
Seminole, Okla. (74868) 288/N4
Seminole, Pa. (16253) 294/D4
Seminole, Texas (79360) 303/B5
Seminole Ind. Res., Fla. 212/F5
Seminole Ind. Res., Fla. 212/E4
Semipalatinsk, U.S.S.R. 54/K4
Semipalatinsk, U.S.S.R. 48/H4
Semirara (isls.), Philippines 82/C5
Semisopochnoi (isl.), Alaska 196/K4
Semitau, Indonesia 85/E5
Semmering (pass), Austria 41/C3
Semmes, Ala. (36575) 195/B9
Semnan (governorate), Iran 66/J3
Semnan, Iran 59/F2
Semnan, Iran 66/H3
Semois (riv.), Belgium 27/G9
Semora, N.C. (27343) 281/L2
Sempach, Switzerland 39/F2
Sempach (lake), Switzerland 39/F2
Semporna, Malaysia 85/F5
Semsales, Switzerland 39/C3
Semur-en-Auxois, France 28/F4
Sen, Stoeng (riv.), Cambodia 72/E4
Sena, Bolivia 136/B2
Sena, N. Mex. (87568) 274/D3
Senador Pompeu, Brazil 132/G4
Senai, Malaysia 72/F5
Sena Madureira, Brazil 132/G10
Senanga, Zambia 115/D7
Senate, Sask. 181/B6
Senath, Mo. (63876) 261/M10
Senatobia, Miss. (38668) 256/E1
Sendai, Japan 54/R6
Sendai, Kagoshima, Japan 81/E8
Sendai, Miyagi, Japan 81/K4
Senec, Czech. 41/D2
Seneca, Ill. (61360) 222/E2
Seneca, Kansas (66538) 232/F2
Seneca, Miss. (†39455) 256/F8
Seneca, Mo. (64865) 261/C9
Seneca, Nebr. (69161) 264/D2
Seneca, N. Mex. (88437) 274/F2
Seneca (co.), N.Y. 276/G5
Seneca (lake), N.Y. 276/G5
Seneca (riv.), N.Y. 276/G5
Seneca (co.), Ohio 284/D3
Seneca, Oreg. (97873) 291/J3
Seneca, S.C. (29678) 296/A2
Seneca (riv.), S.C. 296/B2
Seneca, S. Dak. (57473) 298/L3
Seneca, Wis. (54654) 317/E9
Seneca Falls, N.Y. (13148) 276/G5
Seneca Gardens, Ky. (†40201) 237/K2
Senécal (lake), Newf. 166/B3
Senecaville, Ohio (43780) 284/H6
Senecaville (lake), Ohio 284/H6
Senegal 2/J5
Senegal 102/A3
Seegal (riv.) 102/A3
Senegal (riv.), Mali 106/B5
Senegal (riv.), Mauritania 106/B5
SENEGAL 106/A5
Senegal (riv.), Senegal 106/B5
Senekal, S. Africa 118/D5
Seney, Iowa (†51031) 229/A3
Seney, Mich. (49883) 250/C2
Senftenberg, E. Germany 22/F3
Sengiley, U.S.S.R. 52/G4
Senguerr (riv.), Argentina 143/B6
Senhor do Bonfim, Brazil 120/F4
Senhor do Bonfim, Brazil 132/F5
Senica, Czech. 41/D2
Senigallia, Italy 34/D3
Senirkent, Turkey 63/D3
Senj, Yugoslavia 45/B3
Senja (isl.), Norway 7/F2
Senja (isl.), Norway 18/K2
Şenkaya, Turkey 63/K2
Senlac, Sask. 181/B3
Senlis, France 28/E3
Senmonoron, Cambodia 72/E4
Sennar, Sudan 59/B7
Sennar, Sudan 111/F5
Sennar, Sudan 102/F3
Sennar (dam), Sudan 59/B7
Sennar (dam), Sudan 111/F5
Senne (riv.), Belgium 27/E7
Sennestadt, W. Germany 22/C3
Senneterre, Québec 174/B3
Senneville, Québec 172/G4
Senoia, Georgia (30276) 217/C4
Sens, France 28/E3
Sense (riv.), Switzerland 39/D3
Sensuntepeque, El Salvador 154/C4
Sent, Switzerland 39/K3
Senta, Yugoslavia 45/D3
Sentery, Zaire 115/E5
Sentinel, Alberta 182/C5
Sentinel, Ariz. (†85333) 198/B6
Sentinel (butte), N. Dak. 282/C6
Sentinel, Okla. (73664) 288/H4
Sentinel Butte, N. Dak. (58654) 282/C6
Senyavin (isls.), Micronesia 87/F5
Seo de Urgel, Spain 33/G1
Seon, Switzerland 39/F2
Seoni, India 68/D4
Seoul (cap.), S. Korea 2/R4
Seoul (cap.), S. Korea 54/O6
Seoul (cap.), S. Korea 81/C5
Separ, N. Mex. (†88045) 274/A6
Sepetiba (bay), Brazil 135/D3
Sepik (riv.), Papua N.G. 85/B6
Sępólno Krajenskie, Poland 47/C2
Septentrional, Cordillera (range), Dom. Rep. 158/D5
Sept-Îles, Que. 146/M4
Sept-Îles (Seven Is.), Que. 162/K5
Sept-Îles, Québec 174/D2
Septimer (pass), Switzerland 39/J4
Sepulga (riv.), Ala. 195/E7
Sepulveda, Calif. (91343) 204/B10
Sequatchie (co.), Tenn. 237/L10
Sequatchie, Tenn. (37374) 237/K10
Sequatchie (riv.), Tenn. 237/L10
Sequeira, Uruguay 145/C1
Sequeros, Spain 33/C2
Sequim, Wash. (98382) 310/B2
Sequoia Nat'l Park, Calif. 204/G7
Sequoyah (co.), Okla. 288/S3
Sera (isl.), Indonesia 85/J7
Serafimovich, U.S.S.R. 52/F5
Serafina, N. Mex. (87569) 274/D3
Seraing, Belgium 27/G7
Serakhs, U.S.S.R. 48/G6
Serampore, India 68/F1
Serang, Indonesia 85/G1
Serangoon, Singapore 72/F6
Serasan (isl.), Indonesia 85/D5
Serbia (rep.), Yugoslavia 45/E3
Serçiler, Turkey 63/C6
Serdobol (Sortavala), U.S.S.R. 52/D2
Serdobsk, U.S.S.R. 52/F4
Sered', Czech. 41/D2
Şereflikoçhisar, Turkey 63/E3
Seremban, Malaysia 72/D7
Serena, Ill. (60549) 222/E2
Serengeti Nat'l Park, Tanzania 115/F4
Serenje, Zambia 115/F6
Sergach, U.S.S.R. 52/F3
Sergeant, Pa. (†16735) 294/E2
Sergeant Bluff, Iowa (51054) 229/A4
Sergeantsville, N.J. (08557) 273/D3
Sergeya Kirova (isls.), U.S.S.R. 48/J2
Sergipe (state), Brazil 132/G5
Seria, Brunei 85/E5
Serian, Malaysia 85/E5
Sérifos (isl.), Greece 45/G7
Sérigny (riv.), Québec 174/D1
Serik, Turkey 63/D4
Seringapatam, India 68/D6
Sermata (isl.), Indonesia 85/H7
Serón, Spain 33/E4
Serós, Spain 33/G2
Serov, U.S.S.R. 54/H4
Serov, U.S.S.R. 48/G4
Serowe, Botswana 118/D4
Serowe, Botswana 102/E7
Serpa, Portugal 33/C4
Serpa Pinto, Angola 102/D6
Serpentine (lake), New Bruns. 170/D1
Serpentine (lakes), S. Australia 88/D5
Serpentine (lakes), S. Australia 94/A3
Serpentine (riv.), W. Australia 88/B3
Serpents Mouth (passage), Trin. & Tob. 156/G5
Serpents Mouth (passage), Trin. & Tob. 161/A11
Serpents Mouth (passage), Venezuela 124/H3
Serpukhov, U.S.S.R. 7/H3
Serpukhov, U.S.S.R. 48/D4
Serpukhov, U.S.S.R. 52/E4
Serra do Navio, Brazil 132/C2
Sérrai, Greece 7/G4
Sérrai, Greece 45/F5
Serrana (bank), Colombia 126/B9
Serra Namuli (mt.), Mozambique 102/F6
Serranilla (bank), Colombia 126/B8
Serra Talhada, Brazil 132/G4
Serres, France 28/F5
Serrinha, Brazil 120/F4
Serrinha, Brazil 132/G5
Sertã, Portugal 33/B3
Sertânia, Brazil 132/G5
Sertãozinho, Brazil 135/B2
Serua (isl.), Indonesia 85/H7
Serui, Indonesia 85/K6
Serule, Botswana 118/D4
Sérvia, Greece 45/F5
Servia, Ind. (46980) 227/F3
Servia, W. Va. (†26623) 312/E5
Service Creek, Oreg. (†97874) 291/G3
Serviceton, Victoria 97/A5
Sêrxü, China 77/E5
Se San (riv.), Vietnam 72/E4
Sese (isls.), Uganda 115/F4
Sesegenaga (lake), Ontario 177/G4
Sesfontein, S. Africa 118/J6
Sesheke, Zambia 115/D7
Sesimbra, Portugal 33/B3
Sesser, Ill. (62884) 222/D5
Sessums, Miss. (39758) 256/G4
Sesto Fiorentino, Italy 34/C3
Sestri Levante, Italy 34/B2
Sesvenna (peak), Switzerland 39/K3
Sète, France 28/E6
Sete Lagoas, Brazil 120/E4
Sete Lagoas, Brazil 132/E7
Sete Quedas (falls) 120/D5
Sete Quedas (falls), Brazil 132/C9
Sete Quedas, (Grande) (isl.), Brazil 132/C8
Seth, W. Va. (25181) 312/C6
Sétif, Algeria 106/F1
Sétif, Algeria 102/C1
Setit (riv.), Sdan 111/G5
Seto, Japan 81/H6
Setonaikai National Park, Japan 81/H7
Seton Portage, Br. Col. 184/F5
Setouchi, Japan 81/O5
Settat, Morocco 106/C2
Settebagni, Italy 34/F6
Setté-Cama, Gabon 115/A4
Settecamini, Italy 34/F6
Setting (lake), Manitoba 179/H3
Settle, England 13/E3
Settsu, Japan 81/J8
Setúbal (dist.), Portugal 33/B3
Setúbal, Portugal 7/D5
Setúbal, Portugal 33/B3
Setúbal (bay), Portugal 33/B3
Seul (lake), Ontario 177/G4
Seul (lake), Ontario 175/B2
Seul Choix (pt.), Mich. 250/D3
Seuzach, Switzerland 39/G1
Sevan (lake), U.S.S.R. 7/J4
Sevan (lake), U.S.S.R. 52/G6
Sevaruyo, Bolivia 136/B6
Sevastopol', U.S.S.R. 7/H4
Sevastopol', U.S.S.R. 48/D5
Sevastopol', U.S.S.R. 52/D6
Sevelen, Switzerland 39/H2
Seven (heads), Ireland 17/D8
Seven Corners, Va. (22044) 307/S3
Seven Devils (res.), Ark. 202/G6
Seven Devils (mts.), Idaho 220/B4
Seven Hills, Ohio (†44131) 284/H9
Seven Hogs, The (isls.), Ireland 17/A7
Seven Islands (bay), Newf. 166/B2
Seven Islands (Sept-Îles), Québec 174/D2
Seven Mile, Ohio (45062) 284/A7
Sevenmile (creek), Ohio 284/A6
Seven Mile Ford, Va. (24373) 307/E7
Sevenoaks, England 13/J8
Sevenoaks, England 10/C6
Seven Persons, Alberta 182/E5
Seven Rivers (riv.), N. Mex. 274/E6
Seven Sisters, Texas (†78357) 303/F9
Seven Sisters Falls, Manitoba 179/G4
Seven Springs, N.C. (28578) 281/O4
Seven Springs, Pa. (†15557) 294/D6
Seventy Mile House, Br. Col. 184/G4
Seven Valleys, Pa. (17360) 294/J6
Severance, Colo. (80546) 208/K1
Severance, Kansas (66081) 232/G2
Severn (riv.), England 13/E6
Severn (riv.), England 10/E5
Severn, Md. (21144) 245/M4
Severn (riv.), Md. 245/N4
Severn (riv.), N.S. Wales 97/F1
Severn, N.C. (27877) 281/P2
Severn (riv.), Ont. 146/J4
Severn (riv.), Ont. 162/G5
Severn (lake), Ontario 175/B2
Severn (riv.), Ontario 177/E3
Severn (riv.), Ontario 175/B2
Severn, Mouth of the (est.), Wales 13/B7
Severn (riv.), Wales 13/E5
Severna Park, Md. (21146) 245/M4
Severnaya Zemlya (isls.), U.S.S.R. 4/A4
Severnaya Zemlya (isls.), U.S.S.R. 54/M1
Severnaya Zemlya (isls.), U.S.S.R. 2/P1
Severnaya Zemlya (isls.), U.S.S.R. 48/L1
Severnyy, U.S.S.R. 52/K1
Severobaykal'sk, U.S.S.R. 48/M4
Severočeský (reg.), Czech. 41/C1
Severodonetsk, U.S.S.R. 52/E5
Severodvinsk, U.S.S.R. 7/H2
Severodvinsk, U.S.S.R. 48/E3
Severodvinsk, U.S.S.R. 52/E2
Severo-Kuril'sk, U.S.S.R. 48/Q4
Severomoravský (reg.), Czech. 41/D2
Severomorsk, U.S.S.R. 52/D1
Severoural'sk, U.S.S.R. 48/G3
Severo-Yeniseysk, U.S.S.R. 48/K3
Severy, Kansas (67137) 232/F4
Sevier (co.), Ark. 202/B6
Sevier, N.C. (†28752) 281/E3
Sevier (co.), Tenn. 237/O9
Sevier (co.), Utah 304/C5
Sevier, Utah (84766) 304/B5
Sevier (lake), Utah 188/D3
Sevier (riv.), Utah 188/D3
Sevier (des.), Utah 304/B4
Sevier (lake), Utah 304/A5
Sevier (riv.), Utah 304/B4
Sevier, East Fork (riv.), Utah 304/B6
Sevier Bridge (res.), Utah 304/C4
Sevierville, Tenn. (37862) 237/P9
Sevilla, Colombia 126/C5
Sevilla (prov.), Spain 33/D4
Seville, Fla. (32090) 212/E2
Seville, Georgia (31084) 217/E7
Seville, Ohio (44273) 284/G3
Seville, Spain 7/D5
Seville, Spain 33/D4
Sevlievo, Bulgaria 45/G4
Sèvres, France 28/A2
Sewal, Iowa (52589) 229/G7
Sewalls Point, Fla. (†33457) 212/F4
Sewanee, Tenn. (37375) 237/K10
Seward, Alaska 146/C3
Seward, Alaska 188/D6
Seward, Alaska (99664) 196/C1
Seward (pen.), Alaska 146/B3
Seward (pen.), Alaska 196/E1
Seward (co.), Kansas 232/B4
Seward, Kansas (67577) 232/D3
Seward (co.), Nebr. 264/G4
Seward, Nebr. (68434) 264/H4
Seward, Okla. (†73044) 288/M3
Seward, Pa. (15954) 294/E5
Seward, U.S. 4/D17
Seward (pen.), U.S. 4/C18
Sewaren, N.J. (07077) 273/E2
Sewart A.F.B., Tenn. 237/J8
Sewell, Br. Col. 184/A3
Sewell, Ky. (†41385) 237/P5
Sewell, N.J. (08080) 273/C4
Sewickley, Pa. (15143) 294/B4
Sexsmith, Alberta 182/A2
Sexton, Ind. (†46173) 227/G5
Sexton, Iowa (†50483) 229/E2
Sextons Creek, Ky. (40983) 237/O6
Sextonville, Wis. (53584) 317/F9
Seybaplaya, Mexico 150/O7
Seychelles 2/M6
SEYCHELLES 118/H5
Seydhisfjördhur, Iceland 21/D1
Seydişehir, Turkey 63/D4
Seyfe (lake), Turkey 63/F3
Seyhan (riv.), Turkey 63/F4
Seyhan (riv.), Turkey 59/C2
Seyitgazi, Turkey 63/D3
Seym (riv.), U.S.S.R. 52/D4
Seymour (canal), Alaska 196/N1
Seymour (inlet), Br. Col. 184/D4
Seymour○, Conn. (06483) 210/C3
Seymour, Ill. (61875) 222/E3
Seymour, Ind. (47274) 227/F7
Seymour, Iowa (52590) 229/G7
Seymour, Mo. (65746) 261/G8
Seymour, Tenn. (37865) 237/O9
Seymour, Texas (76380) 303/E4
Seymour (lake), Vt. 268/D2
Seymour, Victoria 88/H7
Seymour, Victoria 97/C5
Seymour, Wis. (54165) 317/K6
Seymour Johnson A.F.B., N.C. 281/O4
Seymourville, La. (†70764) 238/J2
Seymourville, Manitoba 179/F3
Seyppel, Ark. (†72348) 202/K4
Sézanne, France 28/E3
Sezze, Italy 34/D4
Sfax, Tunisia 106/G2
Sfax, Tunisia 102/D1
Sfîntu Gheorghe, Romania 45/G3
Sfîntu Gheorghe, Romania 45/J3
's-Gravenbrakel (Braine-le-Comte), Belgium 27/D7
's Gravendeel, Netherlands 27/E5
's Gravenhage (The Hague) (cap.), Netherlands 27/E4
's Gravenzande, Netherlands 27/E4
Sgurr a Choire Ghlais (mt.), Scotland 15/D3
Sgurr Alasdair (mt.), Scotland 15/B3
Sgurr Mor (mt.), Scotland 15/C3
Sgurr na Ciche (mt.), Scotland 15/C3
Sgurr na Lapaich (mt.), Scotland 15/C3
Shaanxi (Shensi) (prov.), China 77/G5
Shaba (prov.), Zaire 115/E5
Shabani, Zimbabwe 102/E7
Shabani, Zimbabwe 118/E4
Shabasha, Sudan 59/B7
Shabbona, Ill. (60550) 222/E2
Shabeellaha Dhexe (prov.), Somalia 115/J3
Shabeellaha Hoose (prov.), Somalia 115/H3
Shabla, Bulgaria 45/J4
Shabo, Newf. 166/A3
Shabogamo (lake), Newf. 166/A3
Shabunda, Zaire 115/E4
Shabwa, P.D.R. Yemen 59/E6
Shache (Yarkand), China 77/A4
Shache, China 54/J6
Shackelford (co.), Texas 303/E5
Shackleton, Sask. 181/C5
Shackleton Ice Shelf, Ant. 2/P9
Shackleton Ice Shelf, Ant. 5/C5
Shade, Ohio (45776) 284/G7
Shadegan, Iran 66/F5
Shade Gap, Pa. (17255) 294/G5
Shadehill, S. Dak. (57653) 298/E2
Shadehill (res.), S. Dak. 298/E2
Shadeland, Ind. (†47901) 227/C4
Shader, Scotland 15/B2
Shadrinsk, U.S.S.R. 48/G4
Shady Bend, Kansas (†67455) 232/D2
Shady Cove, Oreg. (97539) 291/E5
Shady Dale, Georgia (31085) 217/E4
Shady Grove, Ala. (†36036) 195/F7
Shady Grove, Fla. (32357) 212/C1
Shady Grove, Ky. (†42064) 237/F6
Shady Grove, Pa. (17256) 294/G6
Shady Point, Okla. (74956) 288/S4
Shady Side, Md. (20867) 245/M5
Shadyside, Ohio (43947) 284/J6
Shady Valley, Tenn. (37688) 237/T7
Shafer (lake), Ind. 227/D3
Shafer, Minn. (55074) 255/F5
Shafter, Calif. (93263) 204/F8
Shafter, Nev. (†89835) 266/G2
Shafter, Texas (79850) 303/C12
Shaftesbury, England 13/E7
Shaftesbury, England 10/E5
Shaftsbury○, Vt. (05262) 268/A6
Shageluk, Alaska (99665) 196/G2
Shag Harbour, Nova Scotia 168/C5
Shahabad, Iran 66/E3
Shahat, Libya 102/E1
Shahat, Libya 111/D1
Shahbandar, Pakistan 68/B4
Shahdad, Iran 59/G3
Shahdad, Iran 66/K5
Shahdol, India 68/E4
Shahi, Iran 66/H2
Shahin Dezh, Iran 66/E2
Shahistan (Saravan), Iran 66/N7
Shah Jahan, Kuh-e (mts.), Iran 66/L2
Shahjahanpur, India 68/E3
Shah Juy, Afghanistan 59/J3
Shahpur, Iran 66/D1
Shahrakht, Iran 66/M4
Shahreza, Iran 59/F3
Shahreza, Iran 66/H4
Shahr Kord, Iran 66/G4
Shahrud, Iran 59/G2
Shahrud, Iran 66/J2
Shahsavar, Iran 59/F2
Shahsavar, Iran 66/G2
Shaibara (isl.), Saudi Arabia 59/C4
Sha'ib Hisb, Wadi (dry riv.), Iraq 66/C5
Shaikh Sa'ad, Iraq 66/E4
Shaikh Shu'aib (isl.), Iran 66/H7
Shaikh Shu'aib (isl.), Iran 59/F4
Shailerville, Conn. (†06438) 210/E3
Shajapur, India 68/D4
Shakawe, Botswana 118/C3
Shaker Heights, Ohio (44120) 284/H9
Shakespeare, Ontario 177/D4
Shakhtinsk, U.S.S.R. 48/H5
Shakhty, U.S.S.R. 7/J4
Shakhty, U.S.S.R. 48/E5
Shakhty, U.S.S.R. 52/F5
Shakhun'ya, U.S.S.R. 52/G3
Shaki, Nigeria 106/E7
Shâkir (isl.), Egypt 59/B4
Shakopee, Minn. (55379) 255/F6
Shakopee (creek), Minn. 255/C5
Shaktoolik, Alaska (99771) 196/F2
Shalalth, Br. Col. 184/F5
Shaler (mts.), N.W. Terrs. 187/G2
Shalimar, Fla. (32579) 212/C6
Shallala, Wadi esh (dry riv.), Jordan 65/D2
Shallotte, N.C. (28459) 281/N7
Shallow (lake), Maine 243/E3
Shallowater, Texas (79363) 303/B4
Shallow Lake, Ontario 177/C3
Shallow Water, Kansas (†67871) 232/B3
Sham, Jebel (mt.), Oman 59/G5
Shamattawa, Manitoba 179/K2
Shamattawa (riv.), Ontario 175/C2
Shambaugh, Iowa (51651) 229/D7
Shambe, Sudan 111/F6
Shamil, Iran 66/K7
Shammar, Jebel (plat.), Saudi Arabia 59/D4
Shamokin, Pa. (17872) 294/J4
Shamokin Dam, Pa. (17876) 294/J4
Shamrock, Fla. (†32628) 212/C2
Shamrock, Okla. (74068) 288/N3
Shamrock, Sask. 181/E5
Shamrock, Texas (79079) 303/D2
Shamrock Lakes, Ind. (†47348) 227/G4
Shamva, Zimbabwe 118/E3
Shan (state), Burma 72/C2
Shan (plat.), Burma 72/C2
Shanagolden, Ireland 17/C6
Shandan, China 77/F4
Shandon, Calif. (93461) 204/E8
Shandong (Shantung) (prov.), China 77/J4
Shangani (riv.), Zimbabwe 118/D3
Shangdu, China 77/H3
Shanghai, China 2/R4
Shanghai, China 54/O6
Shanghai, China 77/K5
Shanghai, Va. (23158) 307/P5
Shanghai, W. Va. (†25427) 312/K4
Shanghang, China 77/J6
Shangnan, China 77/H5
Shangqui (Shangkiu), China 77/J5
Shangrao (Shangjao), China 77/J6
Shangshui, China 77/J5
Shang Xian, China 77/H5
Shangzhi, China 77/L2
Shaniko, Oreg. (97057) 291/G3
Shanks, W. Va. (26761) 312/J4
Shanksville, Pa. (15560) 294/E5
Shannock, R.I. (02875) 249/H7
Shannon, Georgia (30172) 217/B2
Shannon (isl.), Greenl. 4/B10
Shannon, Ill. (61078) 222/D1
Shannon, Mouth of the (est.), Ireland 17/B6
Shannon (riv.), Ireland 10/B4
Shannon (riv.), Ireland 17/E6
Shannon, Miss. (38868) 256/G2
Shannon (co.), Mo. 261/K8
Shannon, New Bruns. 170/E3
Shannon, N. Zealand 100/E4
Shannon, N.C. (28386) 281/L5
Shannon, Québec 172/H3
Shannon (co.), S. Dak. 298/D7
Shannon (lake), Wash. 310/D2
Shannon Airport, Ireland 17/D6
Shannon Bridge, Ireland 17/F5
Shannon City, Iowa (50861) 229/E7
Shannondale, Ind. (†47933) 227/D4
Shannon Hills, Ark. (†72103) 202/F4
Shannontown, S.C. (†29150) 296/G4
Shannonville, Ontario 177/G3
Shanshan (Piqan), China 77/D3
Shansi (Shanxi) (prov.), China 77/H4
Shantar (isls.), U.S.S.R. 54/P4
Shantar (isls.), U.S.S.R. 48/O4
Shantou (Swatou), China 77/J7
Shantou, China 54/N7
Shantung (Shandong) (prov.), China 77/J4
Shanty Bay, Ontario 177/E3
Shanxi (Shansi) (prov.), China 77/H4
Shanyang, China 77/G5
Shanyin, China 77/H4
Shaoguan (Shiukwan), China 77/H7
Shaowu, China 77/J6
Shaoxing (Shaohing), China 77/K5
Shaoyang, China 77/H6
Shap, England 13/E3
Shapinsay (isl.), Scotland 15/F1
Shapio (lake), Newf. 166/B3
Shapleigh, Maine (04076) 243/B8
Shapleigh○, Maine (04076) 243/B8
Shaqlawa, Iraq 66/D2
Shaqra, Saudi Arabia 54/F7
Shaqra, Saudi Arabia 59/D4
Sharafkhaneh, Iran 66/D1
Sharbatat, Ras (cape), Oman 59/G6
Sharbot Lake, Ontario 177/H3
Shari (riv.) 102/D4
Shari (riv.), Cent. Afr. Rep. 115/C2
Shari (riv.), Chad 111/C5
Shari, Japan 81/M2
Sharifabad, Iran 66/L2
Sharjah, U.A.E. 59/F4
Shark (pt.), Fla. 212/E6
Shark (bay), W. Australia 88/A5
Shark (bay), W. Australia 92/A4
Shark Bay, W. Australia 88/A5
Sharkey (co.), Miss. 256/C5
Sharlyk, U.S.S.R. 52/H4
Sharon○, Conn. (06069) 210/B1
Sharon, Georgia (30664) 217/G3
Sharon, Kansas (67138) 232/D4
Sharon, Mass. (02067) 249/K4
Sharon○, Mass. (02067) 249/K4
Sharon, Miss. (39163) 256/E5
Sharon○, N.H. (†03458) 268/D6
Sharon, N. Dak. (58277) 282/P4
Sharon, Ohio (43781) 284/G6
Sharon, Okla. (73857) 288/H2
Sharon, Pa. (16146) 294/B3
Sharon, S.C. (29742) 296/E2
Sharon, Tenn. (38255) 237/D8
Sharon○, Vt. (05065) 268/C4
Sharon, W. Va. (25182) 312/D6
Sharon, Wis. (53585) 317/J11
Sharon Center, Ohio (44274) 284/G3
Sharon Grove, Ky. (42280) 237/G7
Sharon Hill, Pa. (19079) 294/N7
Sharon Springs, Kansas (67758) 232/A3
Sharon Springs, N.Y. (13459) 276/L5
Sharon Valley, Conn. (†06069) 210/B1
Sharonville, Ohio (45241) 284/C9
Sharp (co.), Ark. 202/G1
Sharpe, Kansas (†66871) 232/G3
Sharpe (lake), S. Dak. 298/J5
Sharpe Army Depot, Calif. 204/D6
Sharpes, Fla. (32959) 212/F3
Sharples, W. Va. (25183) 312/C7
Sharps (isl.), Md. 245/N6
Sharps, Va. (22548) 307/P5
Sharpsburg, Georgia (30277) 217/C4
Sharpsburg, Iowa (50862) 229/D7
Sharpsburg, Ky. (40374) 237/O4
Sharpsburg, Md. (21782) 245/G3
Sharpsburg, N.C. (27878) 281/O3
Sharpsburg, Pa. (15215) 294/B6
Sharps Chapel, Tenn. (37866) 237/O8
Sharpsville, Ind. (46068) 227/E4
Sharpsville, Pa. (16150) 294/A3
Sharptown, Md. (21861) 245/R6
Sharptown, N.J. (†08098) 273/C4
Shar'ya, U.S.S.R. 48/E4
Shar'ya, U.S.S.R. 52/G3
Shashe, Botswana 118/D4
Shashe (riv.), Botswana 118/D4
Shashe (riv.), Zimbabwe 118/D4
Shashi (Shasi), China 77/H5
Shasta (res.), Calif. 188/B2
Shasta (mt.), Calif. 188/B2
Shasta (co.), Calif. 204/C3
Shasta, Calif. (96087) 204/C3
Shasta (dam), Calif. 204/C3
Shasta (lake), Calif. 204/C3
Shasta (mt.), Calif. 204/C2
Shasta (riv.), Calif. 204/C2
Shati, Wadi esh (dry riv.), Libya 111/B2
Shatra, Iraq 66/E5
Shatt-al-'Arab (riv.), 66/E4
Shattuc, Ill. (62283) 222/D5
Shattuck, Okla. (73858) 288/G2
Shattuckville, Mass. (01369) 249/D2
Shauck, Ohio (43349) 284/E4
Shaughnessy, Alberta 182/D5
Shaunavon, Sask. 162/F6
Shaunavon, Sask. 181/C6
Shavano Park, Texas (†78201) 303/J10
Shaver Lake, Calif. (93664) 204/F6
Shavers Fork (riv.), W. Va. 312/G5
Shave Ziyyon, Israel 65/B2
Shaw, Kansas (†66733) 232/G4
Shaw, La. (†71373) 238/G4
Shaw, Minn. (†55717) 255/F3
Shaw, Miss. (38773) 256/C3
Shaw (mt.), N.H. 268/E4
Shaw, Oreg. (†97325) 291/A3
Shaw A.F.B., S.C. 296/F4
Shawan, China 77/B3
Shawanese, Pa. (18654) 294/E7
Shawano (co.), Wis. 317/J6
Shawano, Wis. (54166) 317/J6
Shawano (lake), Wis. 317/K6
Shawboro, N.C. (27973) 281/S2
Shawbost, Scotland 15/B2
Shawbridge, Québec 172/C4
Shawinigan, Que. 162/J6
Shawinigan, Québec 174/C3
Shawinigan, Québec 172/E3
Shawinigan (riv.), Québec 172/E3
Shawinigan-Sud, Québec 172/E3
Shaw Island, Wash. (98286) 310/B2
Shawmut, Ala. (36876) 195/H5
Shawmut, Maine (04975) 243/D6
Shawmut, Mont. (59078) 262/G4
Shawmut, Pa. (†15823) 294/E3
Shawnee, Colo. (80475) 208/H4
Shawnee (co.), Kansas 232/G2
Shawnee, Kansas (*66202) 232/H2
Shawnee, Ohio (43782) 284/F6
Shawnee, Okla. 188/G3
Shawnee, Okla. (74801) 288/N4
Shawnee, Wyo. (82229) 319/G3
Shawnee Hills, Ohio (43065) 284/D5
Shawnee on Delaware, Pa. (18356) 294/N3
Shawneetown, Ill. (62984) 222/E6
Shawnigan Lake, Br. Col. 184/J3
Shawomet, R.I. (†02886) 249/J6
Shawsheen Village, Mass. (01810) 249/K2
Shawshine (riv.), Mass. 249/K2
Shawsville, Md. (†21161) 245/M2
Shawsville, Va. (24162) 307/H6
Shawville, Québec 172/A4
Shay Gap, W. Australia 92/C3
Shayib, Jebel (mt.), Egypt 59/B4
Shay Juy, Afghanistan 68/B2
Shchekino, U.S.S.R. 52/E4
Shchel'yayur, U.S.S.R. 52/H1
Shchigry, U.S.S.R. 52/E4
Shchuchinsk, U.S.S.R. 48/H4
Sheakleyville, Pa. (16151) 294/B3
Sheaville, Oreg. (†97910) 291/K4
Shebandowan, Ontario 177/G5
Sheberghan, Afghanistan 54/H6
Sheberghan, Afghanistan 68/B1
Sheberghan, Afghanistan 59/H2
Sheboygan, Wis. 188/J2
Sheboygan (co.), Wis. 317/L8
Sheboygan, Wis. (53081) 317/L8
Sheboygan Falls, Wis. (53085) 317/L8
Shedd, Oreg. (97377) 291/D3
Shedden, Ontario 177/C5
Shediac, New Bruns. 170/F2
Shediac (isl.), New Bruns. 170/F2
Shediac Bridge, New Bruns. 170/F2
Sheeffry (hills), Ireland 17/B4
Sheelin (lake), Ireland 17/G4
Sheenjek (riv.), Alaska 196/K1
Sheep (mt.), Colo. 208/E6
Sheep (mt.), Mont. 262/C2
Sheep (range), Nev. 266/F6
Sheep (creek), Oreg. 291/L2

Sieradz 447

Sheep (creek), Utah 304/E3
Sheep Creek, Alberta 182/A2
Sheep Haven (harb.), Ireland 17/F1
Sheeps (head), Ireland 17/B8
Sheepscott, Maine (†04579) 243/D7
's Heerenberg, Netherlands 27/J5
Sheerness, Alberta 182/E4
Sheet (harb.), Nova Scotia 168/F4
Sheet Harbour, Nova Scotia 168/F4
Shefar'am, Israel 65/C2
Shefayim, Israel 65/B3
Sheffield, Ala. (35660) 195/C1
Sheffield, England 7/D3
Sheffield, England 10/F4
Sheffield, England 13/J2
Sheffield, Ill. (61361) 222/D2
Sheffield, Iowa (50475) 229/G3
Sheffield○, Mass. (01257) 249/A4
Sheffield, Mont. (†59347) 262/K4
Sheffield, New Bruns. 170/D3
Sheffield, Ohio (†44052) 284/F3
Sheffield, Pa. (16347) 294/D2
Sheffield, Tasmania 99/C3
Sheffield, Texas (79781) 303/B7
Sheffield○, Vt. (05866) 268/C2
Sheffield Lake, Ohio (44054) 284/F3
Shefford (co.), Québec 172/E4
Sheguiandah, Ontario 177/C2
Sheho, Sask. 181/H4
Shehy (mts.), Ireland 17/C8
Sheikh Sa'id, Yemen Arab Rep. 59/D7
Sheila, New Bruns. 170/F1
Sheki, U.S.S.R. 52/G6
Shelagh (riv.), Iran 66/M5
Shelagskiy (cape), U.S.S.R. 48/R2
Shelbiana, Ky. (41562) 237/R6
Shelbina, Mo. (63468) 261/H3
Shelburn, Ind. (47879) 227/C5
Shelburne, N.H. (†03581) 268/E3
Shelburne○, N.H. (†03581) 268/E3
Shelburne (co.), Nova Scotia 168/C5
Shelburne, Nova Scotia 168/C5
Shelburne, Ontario 177/D3
Shelburne○, Vt. (05482) 268/A3
Shelburne (pond), Vt. 268/A3
Shelburne Falls, Mass. (01370) 249/D2
Shelby (co.), Ala. 195/E4
Shelby, Ala. (35143) 195/E4
Shelby (co.), Ill. 222/E4
Shelby (co.), Ind. 227/F5
Shelby, Ind. (46377) 227/C2
Shelby (co.), Iowa 229/C5
Shelby, Iowa (51570) 229/C5
Shelby (co.), Ky. 237/L4
Shelby, Mich. (49455) 250/C5
Shelby, Miss. (38774) 256/C3
Shelby (co.), Mo. 261/H3
Shelby, Mont. (59474) 262/E2
Shelby, Nebr. (68662) 264/G3
Shelby, N.C. (28150) 281/G4
Shelby (co.), Ohio 284/B5
Shelby, Ohio (44875) 284/E4
Shelby (co.), Tenn. 237/B10
Shelby (co.), Texas 303/K6
Shelby Center, N.Y. (†14103) 276/D4
Shelbyville, Ill. (62565) 222/E4
Shelbyville (lake), Ill. 222/E4
Shelbyville, Ind. (46176) 227/F6
Shelbyville, Ky. (40065) 237/L4
Shelbyville, Mo. (63469) 261/H3
Shelbyville, Tenn. (37160) 237/H10
Shelbyville, Texas (75973) 303/L6
Sheldahl, Iowa (50243) 229/F5
Sheldon, Ill. (60966) 222/F3
Sheldon, Iowa (51201) 229/B2
Sheldon, Minn. (†55921) 255/G7
Sheldon, Mo. (64784) 261/D7
Sheldon, N. Dak. (58068) 282/P6
Sheldon, S.C. (29941) 296/F6
Sheldon, Texas (†77001) 303/K1
Sheldon○, Vt. (05483) 268/B2
Sheldon, Wis. (54766) 317/D5
Sheldon Junction, Vt. (†05483) 268/B2
Sheldon Point, Alaska (99666) 196/E2
Sheldon Springs, Vt. (05485) 268/A2
Sheldonville, Mass. (02070) 249/J4
Shelekhov (gulf), U.S.S.R. 54/S3
Shelekhov (gulf), U.S.S.R. 48/Q4
Shelikof (str.), Alaska 196/H3
Shell (pt.), Fla. 212/B1
Shell (riv.), Minn. 255/C4
Shell (creek), N. Dak. 282/F3
Shell, Loch (inlet), Scotland 15/B3
Shell (lake), Wis. 317/C4
Shell, Wyo. (82441) 319/E1
Shell (creek), Wyo. 319/E1
Shellbrook, Sask. 162/F5
Shellbrook, Sask. 181/E2
Shelley, Br. Col. 184/F3
Shelley, Idaho (83274) 220/F6
Shellharbour, N.S. Wales 97/F4
Shell Knob, Mo. (65747) 261/E9
Shell Lake, Sask. 181/D2
Shell Lake, Wis. (54871) 317/C4
Shellman, Georgia (31786) 217/C7
Shellmouth, Manitoba 179/A4
Shell Rock, Iowa (50670) 229/H3
Shellsburg, Iowa (52332) 229/K4
Shelltown, Md. (†21838) 245/R9
Shelly, Minn. (56581) 255/B3
Shelmerdine, N.C. (†27834) 281/P4
Shelocta, Pa. (15774) 294/D4
Shelter (isl.), N.Y. 276/R8
Shelton, Conn. (06484) 210/C3
Shelton, Nebr. (68876) 264/F4
Shelton, S.C. (†29015) 296/E3
Shelton, Wash. (98584) 310/B3
Shemakha, U.S.S.R. 52/G6
Shemogue, New Bruns. 170/F2
Shemya (isl.), Alaska 196/J3
Shemya Air Force Base, Alaska 196/J3
Shenandoah, Iowa (51601) 229/C7
Shenandoah, Pa. (17976) 294/K4
Shenandoah (co.), Va. 307/L3
Shenandoah, Va. (22849) 307/L4
Shenandoah (mt.), Va. 307/K3
Shenandoah (riv.), Va. 307/N2
Shenandoah (riv.), W. Va. 312/K4
Shenandoah Junction, W. Va. (25442) 312/L4
Shenandoah Nat'l Park, Va. 307/L3
Shenango, Pa. (†16125) 294/A3
Shenango River (lake), Pa. 294/B3
Shendam, Nigeria 106/F7
Shendi, Sudan 59/B6
Shendi, Sudan 102/F3
Shendi, Sudan 111/F4
Shëngjin, Albania 45/D5
Sheng Xian, China 77/K6
Shenipsit (lake), Conn. 210/F1
Shenkursk, U.S.S.R. 52/F2
Shenkursk, U.S.S.R. 48/E3
Shenmu, China 77/G4
Shennington, Wis. (†54618) 317/F7
Shennongjia, China 77/H5
Shensi (Shaanxi) (prov.), China 77/G5
Shenyang (Mukden), China 77/K3
Shenyang, China 54/O5
Shenyang, China 2/R3
Sheopur, India 68/D3
Shepard, Alberta 182/D4
Shepardsville, Ind. (47880) 227/B5
Shepaug (dam), Conn. 210/B3
Shepaug (riv.), Conn. 210/B2
Shepetovka, U.S.S.R. 52/C4
Shepherd, Mich. (48883) 250/E5
Shepherd, Mont. (59079) 262/H5
Shepherd (bay), N.W. Terrs. 187/J3
Shepherd, Texas (77371) 303/K7
Shepherdstown, W. Va. (25443) 312/L4
Shepherdsville, Ky. (40165) 237/K4
Shepody, New Bruns. 170/F3
Shepody (bay), New Bruns. 170/F3
Sheppard A.F.B., Texas 303/F3
Shepparton, Victoria 88/G7
Shepparton, Victoria 97/C5
Sheppey (isl.), England 13/J6
Sheppton, Pa. (18248) 294/K4
Shepshed, England 13/F5
Shepton Mallet, England 13/E6
Shepton Mallet, England 10/E5
Sheqi, China 77/H5
Sherack, Minn. (†56722) 255/B2
Sherard, Miss. (38669) 256/C2
Sherard (cape), N.W. Terrs. 187/L2
Sherborn○, Mass. (01770) 249/A8
Sherborne, England 10/E5
Sherborne, England 13/E7
Sherbro (isl.), S. Leone 106/B7
Sherbrooke, Nova Scotia 168/G3
Sherbrooke (lake), Nova Scotia 168/D4
Sherbrooke (riv.), Nova Scotia 168/D4
Sherbrooke, Que. 162/J7
Sherbrooke (co.), Québec 172/E4
Sherbrooke, Québec 172/E4
Sherburn, Minn. (56171) 255/D7
Sherburne (co.), Minn. 255/E5
Sherburne, N.Y. (13460) 276/K5
Shercock, Ireland 17/G4
Shereik, Sudan 111/F4
Sheridan, Ark. (72150) 202/F5
Sheridan, Calif. (95681) 204/D5
Sheridan, Colo. (†80110) 208/J3
Sheridan, Ill. (60551) 222/E2
Sheridan, Ind. (46069) 227/E4
Sheridan (co.), Kansas 232/B2
Sheridan, Maine (04775) 243/F2
Sheridan, Mich. (48884) 250/D5
Sheridan, Mo. (64486) 261/C1
Sheridan (co.), Mont. 262/M2
Sheridan, Mont. (59749) 262/D5
Sheridan (co.), Nebr. 264/B2
Sheridan, N.Y. (14135) 276/B5
Sheridan (co.), N. Dak. 282/K4
Sheridan, Oreg. (97378) 291/D2
Sheridan, W. Va. (†25506) 312/B6
Sheridan, Wis. (†54981) 317/H7
Sheridan, Wyo. 188/E2
Sheridan, Wyo. 146/H5
Sheridan (co.), Wyo. 319/F1
Sheridan, Wyo. (82801) 319/F1
Sheridan Lake, Colo. (81071) 208/P6
Sheringham, England 13/J5
Sheringham, England 10/G4
Sherkin (isl.), Ireland 17/C9
Sherman (mt.), Colo. 208/G4
Sherman○, Conn. (06784) 210/B2
Sherman, Ill. (62684) 222/D4
Sherman (co.), Kansas 232/A2
Sherman, Kansas (†67356) 232/H4
Sherman, Ky. (†41035) 237/M3
Sherman, Maine (†04777) 243/G4
Sherman○, Maine (†04777) 243/G4
Sherman, Mich. (†49668) 250/D4
Sherman, Miss. (38869) 256/G2
Sherman, Mo. (63078) 261/N3
Sherman (co.), Nebr. 264/F3
Sherman (res.), Nebr. 264/E3
Sherman, N. Mex. (†88057) 274/B6
Sherman, N.Y. (14781) 276/A6
Sherman (inlet), N.W. Terrs. 187/J3
Sherman (co.), Oreg. 291/G2
Sherman, S. Dak. (57060) 298/S6
Sherman (co.), Texas 303/C1
Sherman, Texas (75090) 303/H4
Sherman, Texas 188/G4
Sherman, W. Va. (26173) 312/C5
Sherman City, Mich. (†48632) 250/D5
Sherman Mills, Maine (04776) 243/G4
Shermans Dale, Pa. (17090) 294/H5
Sherman Station, Maine (04777) 243/F4
Sherrard, Ill. (61281) 222/C2
Sherrard, W. Va. (†26003) 312/E3
Sherridon, Man. 162/G4
Sherridon, Manitoba 179/H3
Sherrill, Ark. (72152) 202/F5
Sherrill, Iowa (52073) 229/M3
Sherrill, N.Y. (13461) 276/J4
Sherrington, Québec 172/D4
Sherrodsville, Ohio (44675) 284/H4
Sherry, Wis. (†54454) 317/G6
's Hertogenbosch, Netherlands 27/G5
Sherwood, Ark. (72116) 202/F4
Sherwood (pt.), Conn. 210/B4
Sherwood (for.), England 13/F4
Sherwood, Mich. (49089) 250/D6
Sherwood, N. Dak. (58782) 282/G2
Sherwood, Ohio (43556) 284/A3
Sherwood, Okla. (†74728) 288/S6
Sherwood, Oreg. (97140) 291/A2
Sherwood, Pr. Edward I. 168/E2
Sherwood, Tenn. (37376) 237/K10
Sherwood, Texas (†76941) 303/D6
Sherwood, Wis. (54169) 317/K7
Sherwood Park, Alberta 182/D3
Sheslay (riv.), Br. Col. 184/J2
Shetek (lake), Minn. 255/C6
Shetland (islands area), Scotland 15/F2
Shetland (isls.), Scotland 7/D2
Shetland (isls.), Scotland 10/G1
Shetland (isls.), Scotland 15/G2
Shetucket (riv.), Conn. 210/G2
Shevchenko, U.S.S.R. 54/G5
Shevchenko, U.S.S.R. 48/F5
Shevlin, Manitoba 179/A3
Shevlin, Minn. (56676) 255/C3
Sheyenne, N. Dak. (58374) 282/M4
Sheyenne (riv.), N. Dak. 188/G1
Sheyenne (riv.), N. Dak. 282/O6
Sheykh Sho'eyb (isl.), Iran 66/H7
Shiant (isls.), Scotland 15/B3
Shiant (sound), Scotland 15/B3
Shiawassee (co.), Mich. 250/E6
Shiawassee (riv.), Mich. 250/E5
Shibam, P.D.R. Yemen 59/E6
Shibata, Japan 81/J5
Shibetsu, Japan 81/M2
Shibin el Kom, Egypt 111/J3
Shibogama (lake), Ontario 175/C2
Shickley, Nebr. (68436) 264/G4
Shickshinny, Pa. (18655) 294/K3
Shideler, Ind. (†47338) 227/G4
Shidler, Okla. (74652) 288/N1
Shiel, Loch (lake), Scotland 10/D2
Shiel, Loch (lake), Scotland 15/C4
Shieldaig, Scotland 15/C3
Shields, Kansas (67874) 232/B3
Shields (riv.), Mont. 262/F4
Shields, N. Dak. (58569) 282/H7
Shieldsville, Minn. (†55021) 255/E6
Shifnal, England 13/E5
Shiga (pref.), Japan 81/J7
Shigatse (Xigazê), China 77/C6
Shigawake, Québec 172/D2
Shihezi (Shihhotzu), China 77/C3
Shihr, P.D.R. Yemen 59/E7
Shijak, Albania 45/D5
Shijiazhuang (Shihkiachwang), China 77/J4
Shijiazhuang, China 54/N6
Shikarpur, Pakistan 68/B3
Shikarpur, Pakistan 59/J4
Shikoku, Japan 54/P6
Shikoku (isl.), Japan 2/R4
Shikoku (isl.), Japan 81/F7
Shikotan (isl.), Japan 81/N2
Shikotsu (lake), Japan 81/K2
Shikotsu-Toya National Park, Japan 81/K2
Shilbottle, England 13/F2
Shildon, England 13/F3
Shilka (riv.), U.S.S.R. 54/N4
Shilka, U.S.S.R. 48/M4
Shillelagh, Ireland 17/J6
Shillelagh, Ireland 10/C4
Shillington, Pa. (19607) 294/K5
Shillong, India 68/G3
Shilo, Manitoba 179/C5
Shiloh, Ala. (†35979) 195/G2
Shiloh, Ala. (†36754) 195/C6
Shiloh, Georgia (31826) 217/C5
Shiloh, Ill. (†62220) 222/B3
Shiloh, N.J. (08353) 273/C5
Shiloh, Ohio (44878) 284/E4
Shiloh, S.C. (†29080) 296/G4
Shiloh, Tenn. (38376) 237/E10
Shiloh, Va. (22549) 307/O4
Shiloh Nat'l Mil. Park, Tenn. 237/E10
Shilovo, U.S.S.R. 52/F4
Shimabara, Japan 81/E7
Shimamoto, Japan 81/J7
Shimane (pref.), Japan 81/F6
Shimane (pen.), Japan 81/F6
Shimanovsk, U.S.S.R. 48/N4
Shimbir Berris (mt.), Somalia 115/J1
Shimizu, Japan 81/J6
Shimoda, Japan 81/J6
Shimoga, India 68/D6
Shimokita (pen.), Japan 81/K3
Shimonoseki, Japan 81/E6
Shin (falls), Scotland 15/D3
Shin, Loch (lake), Scotland 15/D2
Shin, Loch (lake), Scotland 10/D1
Shin (riv.), Scotland 15/D3
Shinano (riv.), Japan 81/J5
Shinas, Oman 59/G5
Shindand, Afghanistan 59/H3
Shindand, Afghanistan 68/A2
Shindler, S. Dak. (†57101) 298/R7
Shiner, Texas (77984) 303/G8
Shingbwiyang, Burma 72/B1
Shinglehouse, Pa. (16748) 294/F2
Shingler, Georgia (†31781) 217/E7
Shingle Springs, Calif. (95682) 204/C8
Shingleton, Mich. (49884) 250/C2
Shingu, Japan 81/H7
Shining Tree, Ontario 177/J5
Shinjo, Japan 81/K4
Shinko (riv.), Cent. Afr. Rep. 115/D2
Shinnecock Ind. Res., N.Y. 276/R9
Shinnston, W. Va. (26431) 312/F4
Shin Pond, Maine (†04765) 243/F3
Shinrone, Ireland 17/F5
Shinyanga (reg.), Tanzania 115/F4
Shinyanga, Tanzania 115/F4
Shinyanga, Tanzania 102/F5
Shiocton, Wis. (54170) 317/K7
Shiogama, Japan 81/K4
Shiono (cape), Japan 81/H7
Ship (isl.), Miss. 256/G10
Ship Bottom, N.J. (08008) 273/E4
Ship Harbour, Newf. 166/D2
Ship Harbour, Nova Scotia 168/F4
Shiping, China 77/F7
Shipki (pass), India 68/D2
Shipman, Ill. (62685) 222/C4
Shipman, Sask. 181/F2
Shipman, Va. (22971) 307/L5
Shippan (pt.), Conn. 210/A4
Shippegan, New Bruns. 170/F1
Shippegan (gully), New Bruns. 170/F1
Shippegan (bay), New Bruns. 170/E1
Shippensburg, Pa. (17257) 294/H5
Shippenville, Pa. (16254) 294/D3
Shiprock, N. Mex. (87420) 274/A2
Ship Rock (peak), N. Mex. 274/A2
Shipshaw (riv.), Québec 172/F1
Shipshewana, Ind. (46565) 227/F1
Ship Shoal (isl.), Va. 307/S6
Shipston on Stour, England 13/F5
Shiqian, China 77/G6
Shiqma (riv.), Israel 65/B4
Shiquan, China 77/G5
Shiquanhe, China 77/A5
Shiragami (cape), Japan 81/J3
Shirakawa, Japan 81/K5
Shirane (mt.), Japan 81/H6
Shirane (mt.), Japan 81/J5
Shiranuka, Japan 81/M2
Shiraz, Iran 54/G7
Shiraz, Iran 66/H6
Shiraz, Iran 59/F4
Shire (riv.), Malawi 115/G7
Shire (riv.), Mozambique 118/E3
Shiretoko (cape), Japan 81/M1
Shiriya (cape), Japan 81/K3
Shir Kuh (mt.), Iran 59/F3
Shir Kuh (mt.), Iran 66/J5
Shirland, Ill. (61079) 222/D1
Shirley, Ark. (72153) 202/F2
Shirley, Ill. (61772) 222/E3
Shirley, Ind. (47384) 227/F5
Shirley, Mass. (01464) 249/H2
Shirley○, Mass. (01464) 249/H2
Shirley, Mo. (†63664) 261/L7
Shirley, W. Va. (26434) 312/E4
Shirley (basin), Wyo. 319/F3
Shirley Basin, Wyo. (82615) 319/F3
Shirley Center, Mass. (01465) 249/H2
Shirley City (Woodburn), Ind. (†46797) 227/H2
Shirley Mills, Maine (04485) 243/D5
Shirley Mills○, Maine (04485) 243/D5
Shirleysburg, Pa. (17260) 294/G5
Shiro, Texas (77876) 303/J7
Shiroishi, Japan 81/K4
Shirvan, Iran 59/G2
Shirvan, Iran 66/K2
Shirvan (riv.), Iran 66/E3
Shishaldin (vol.), Alaska 196/E4
Shishmaref, Alaska (99772) 196/E1
Shithatha, Iraq 59/D3
Shithatha, Iraq 66/C4
Shitike (creek), Oreg. 291/F3
Shiukwan (Shaoyuan), China 77/H7
Shively, Calif. (†95565) 204/B3
Shively, Ky. (40216) 237/K4
Shivers, Miss. (39164) 256/E7
Shivpuri, India 68/D3
Shivwits (plat.), Ariz. 198/B2
Shivwits Ind. Res., Utah 304/A6
Shiyan, China 77/H5
Shizuishan (Shihsuishan), China 77/G4
Shizunai, Japan 81/L2
Shizuoka (pref.), Japan 81/H6
Shizuoka, Japan 54/P6
Shizuoka, Japan 81/H6
Shkodër, Albania 7/F4
Shkodër, Albania 45/D5
Shoa (prov.), Ethiopia 111/G6
Shoal (riv.), Fla. 212/C6
Shoal (creek), Ill. 222/D5
Shoal (lake), Manitoba 179/B4
Shoal (lake), Manitoba 179/G5
Shoal (riv.), Manitoba 179/B2
Shoal (bay), Newf. 166/D2
Shoal (bay), Nova Scotia 168/F4
Shoal (creek), Tenn. 237/F10
Shoal (creek), Utah 304/A6
Shoal Branch, Wading (riv.), N.J. 273/D4
Shoal Cove, Newf. 166/C3
Shoal Harbour, Newf. 166/C2
Shoalhaven (riv.), N.S. Wales 97/E4
Shoal Lake, Manitoba 179/B4
Shoals, Ind. (47581) 227/D7
Shoals (isls.), N.H. 268/F6
Shoals, N.C. (†27043) 281/J2
Shoals, W. Va. (25562) 312/B6
Shoals Junction, S.C. (29638) 296/C3
Shoalwater (bay), Queensland 88/J4
Shoalwater (cape), Wash. 310/A4
Shoalwater Ind. Res., Wash. 310/B4
Shobara, Japan 81/F6
Shobonier, Ill. (62885) 222/D5
Shock, W. Va. (26638) 312/D5
Shoemakersville, Pa. (19555) 294/K4
Shoffner, Ark. (†72112) 202/H2
Shohola, Pa. (18458) 294/N3
Sholapur, India 54/J8
Sholapur, India 68/D5
Sholes, Nebr. (†68771) 264/G2
Shona (isl.), Scotland 15/C4
Shongaloo, La. (71072) 238/D1
Shonkin, Mont. (59476) 262/F3
Shonto, Ariz. (86054) 198/E2
Shonto (plat.), Ariz. 198/E2
Shook, Mo. (63963) 261/M8
Shooting Creek, N.C. (†28904) 281/B4
Shopiere, Wis. (†53525) 317/H10
Shop Springs, Tenn. (†37184) 237/J8
Shorapur, India 68/D5
Shoreacres, Br. Col. 184/J5
Shore Acres, N.J. (†08723) 273/E3
Shore Acres, Texas (†77571) 303/K2
Shoreham, Mich. (†49085) 250/C6
Shoreham, Minn. (†56501) 255/C4
Shoreham, N.Y. (11786) 276/P8
Shoreham○, Vt. (05770) 268/A4
Shoreham-by-Sea, England 13/G7
Shoreham-by-Sea, England 10/F5
Shoreview, Minn. (†55112) 255/G5
Shorewood, Ill. (60435) 222/E2
Shorewood, Minn. (†55331) 255/F5
Shorewood, Wis. (53211) 317/M1
Shorewood Hills, Mich. (†49125) 250/C7
Shorewood Hills, Wis. (†53701) 317/G9
Short, Okla. (†72955) 288/S3
Short Beach, Conn. (†06405) 210/D3
Short Creek, Ohio (43989) 284/J5
Shortdale, Manitoba 179/A3
Shorter, Ala. (36075) 195/G6
Shorterville, Ala. (36373) 195/H7
Short Falls, N.H. (†03234) 268/E5
Short Hills, N.J. (07078) 273/E2
Shortland (isls.), Solomon Is. 86/D2
Shortleaf, Ala. (†36732) 195/C6
Shortsville, N.Y. (14548) 276/F5
Shoshone, Calif. (92384) 204/J8
Shoshone (co.), Idaho 220/B2
Shoshone, Idaho (83352) 220/D7
Shoshone (falls), Idaho 220/D7
Shoshone (mts.), Nev. 266/E6
Shoshone (mts.), Nev. 266/D3
Shoshone (range), Nev. 266/E2
Shoshone (lake), Wyo. 319/B1
Shoshone (riv.), Wyo. 319/D1
Shoshong, Botswana 118/D4
Shoshoni, Wyo. (82649) 319/D2
Shostka, U.S.S.R. 52/D4
Shotley, England 13/J6
Shotts, Scotland 15/C2
Shouldice, Alberta 182/D4
Shoultes, Wash. (†98270) 310/C2
Shouns, Tenn. (†37683) 237/T8
Shoup, Idaho (83469) 220/D4
Shoval, Israel 65/B5
Shovel Lake, Minn. (†55785) 255/E4
Showak, Sudan 111/G5
Showell, Md. (21862) 245/T7
Show Low, Ariz. (85901) 198/F4
Shoyna, U.S.S.R. 52/F1
Shpola, U.S.S.R. 52/D5
Shreve, Ohio (44676) 284/F4
Shreveport, La. 146/J6
Shreveport, La. 188/H4
Shreveport, La. (*71101) 238/C2
Shrewsbury, England 13/E5
Shrewsbury, England 10/E4
Shrewsbury○, Mass. (01545) 249/H3
Shrewsbury, Mo. (†63101) 261/P3
Shrewsbury, N.J. (07701) 273/E3
Shrewsbury, Pa. (17361) 294/J6
Shrewsbury○, Vt. (†05738) 268/B4
Shrule, Ireland 17/C4
Shuangcheng, China 77/L2
Shuangliao, China 77/K3
Shuangyashan, China 77/M2
Shubenacadie, Nova Scotia 168/E3
Shubenacadie (lake), Nova Scotia 168/E4
Shubenacadie (riv.), Nova Scotia 168/E3
Shubert, Nebr. (68437) 264/J4
Shubuta, Miss. (39360) 256/G7
Shue (creek), S. Dak. 298/N5
Shu'eib, Wadi (dry riv.), Jordan 65/D4
Shueyville, Iowa (†52401) 229/K5
Shu'fat, West Bank 65/C4
Shuicheng, China 77/G6
Shuksan (mt.), Wash. 310/D2
Shulan, China 77/L3
Shulerville, S.C. (29480) 296/H5
Shullsburg, Wis. (53586) 317/F10
Shumagin (isls.), Alaska 196/G4
Shumen, Bulgaria 45/H4
Shumerlya, U.S.S.R. 52/G3
Shumway, Ill. (62461) 222/E4
Shunat Nimrin, Jordan 65/D4
Shunchang, China 77/J6
Shungnak, Alaska (99773) 196/G1
Shungopavy (Shongopovi), Ariz. (†86043) 198/E3
Shunk, Pa. (17768) 294/J2
Shunock (riv.), Conn. 210/H3
Shuo Xian, China 77/H4
Shuqaiq, Saudi Arabia 59/D6
Shuqra, P.D.R. Yemen 59/E7
Shuqualak, Miss. (39361) 256/G5
Shur (riv.), Iran 66/J7
Shusf, Iran 66/L5
Shush, Iran 66/F4
Shushan, N.Y. (12873) 276/O4
Shushenskoye, U.S.S.R. 48/K4
Shushtar, Iran 66/F4
Shushtar, Iran 59/E3
Shuswap (lake), Br. Col. 162/E5
Shuswap (lake), Br. Col. 184/H4
Shutesbury○, Mass. (01072) 249/E3
Shuttle Meadow (res.), Conn. 210/D2
Shutty Bench, Br. Col. 184/J5
Shuweika, West Bank 65/C3
Shuya, U.S.S.R. 52/F3
Shuyak (isl.), Alaska 196/H3
Shwebo, Burma 72/B2
Shwegyin, Burma 72/C3
Shweli (riv.), Burma 72/C2
Shwenyaung, Burma 72/C2
Shyok, India 68/D2
Si (riv.), China 54/N7
Siahan (mts.), Pakistan 59/H4
Siahan (range), Pakistan 68/A3
Siah Kuh (mt.), Iran 66/L3
Siak (riv.), Indonesia 85/C5
Siaksriinderapura, Indonesia 85/C5
Siakwan (Xiaguan), China 77/E6
Sialkot, Pakistan 68/C2
Sialkot, Pakistan 59/K3
Siam (Thailand) (gulf), Thailand 72/D5
Sian (Xi'an), China 77/G5
Siangfan (Xiangfan), China 77/H5
Siangtan (Xiangtan), China 77/H6
Siapa (riv.), Venezuela 124/E7
Siargao (isl.), Philippines 85/H4
Siargao (isl.), Philippines 82/F6
Siasconset, Mass. (02564) 249/P7
Siasi, Philippines 82/C8
Siasi (isl.), Philippines 82/C8
Siátista, Greece 45/E5
Siaton, Philippines 82/D6
Siaton (pt.), Philippines 82/D6
Siau (isl.), Indonesia 85/H5
Šiauliai, U.S.S.R. 7/G3
Šiauliai, U.S.S.R. 53/B3
Šiauliai, U.S.S.R. 52/B3
Šiauliai, U.S.S.R. 48/C4
Sib, Iran 66/N7
Sibalom, Philippines 82/C5
Sibanicú, Cuba 158/G3
Sibay (isl.), Philippines 82/C5
Sibay, U.S.S.R. 52/J4
Sibbald, Alberta 182/E4
Šibenik, Yugoslavia 45/C4
Siberia, Ind. (47582) 227/D8
Siberia (reg.), U.S.S.R. 4/C2
Siberia (reg.), U.S.S.R. 2/P2
Siberia (reg.), U.S.S.R. 54/M4
Siberia (reg.), U.S.S.R. 48/M3
Sibert, Ky. (†40962) 237/O6
Siberut (isl.), Indonesia 54/L10
Siberut (isl.), Indonesia 85/B6
Siberut (str.), Indonesia 85/B6
Sibi, Pakistan 68/B3
Sibi, Pakistan 59/J4
Sibiti, Congo 115/B4
Sibiu, Romania 7/G4
Sibiu, Romania 45/G3
Sibley, Ill. (61773) 222/E3
Sibley, Iowa (51249) 229/B2
Sibley, La. (71073) 238/D1
Sibley (co.), Minn. 255/D6
Sibley, Miss. (39165) 256/B8
Sibley, Mo. (64088) 261/S5
Sibley, N. Dak. (†58429) 282/P5
Sibley Prov. Park, Ontario 175/C3
Sibley Prov. Park, Ontario 177/H5
Sibolga, Indonesia 85/B5
Siboney, Cuba 158/J4
Sibsagar, India 68/H3
Sibu, Malaysia 85/E5
Sibu, Malaysia 54/N9
Sibube, C. Rica 154/F6
Sibuco, Philippines 82/C7
Sibuguey (bay), Philippines 82/D7
Sibundoy, Colombia 126/B7
Sibut, Cent. Afr. Rep. 115/C2
Sibutu (passage), Philippines 85/F4
Sibutu (passage), Philippines 82/B8
Sibutu Group (isls.), Philippines 82/B8
Sibuyan (isl.), Philippines 85/G3
Sibuyan (isl.), Philippines 82/D4
Sibuyan (sea), Philippines 82/D4
Sibuyan (sea), Philippines 85/G3
Sicamous, Br. Col. 184/H5
Sicasica, Bolivia 136/B5
Siccus (riv.), S. Australia 88/F6
Sichuan (Szechwan) (prov.), China 77/F5
Sicily (reg.), Italy 34/D6
Sicily (isl.), Italy 7/F5
Sicily (isl.), Italy 34/E6
Sicily (str.), Italy 34/D6
Sicily Island, La. (71368) 238/G3
Sicklerville, N.J. (08081) 273/D4
Sico (riv.), Honduras 154/E3
Sicuani, Peru 128/G10
Šid, Yugoslavia 45/D3
Sidamo (prov.), Ethiopia 111/G7
Siddipet, India 68/D5
Sideby, Finland 18/M5
Side Lake, Minn. (55781) 255/E3
Sidell, Ill. (61876) 222/F4
Siderno, Italy 34/F5
Sidewood, Sask. 181/C5
Sidheros (cape), Greece 45/H8
Sidhi, India 68/E4
Sidhirókastron, Greece 45/F5
Sidhpur, India 68/C4
Sidi Barrani, Egypt 111/E1
Sidi Barrani, Egypt 59/A3
Sidi Bel-Abbes, Algeria 106/D1
Sidi Bel Abbes, Algeria 102/C1
Sidi Kacem, Morocco 106/C2
Siding Springs, N.S. Wales 97/E2
Sidlaw (hills), Scotland 15/E4
Sidley (mt.) 5/B12
Sidmouth, England 13/D7
Sidmouth, England 10/E5
Sidmouth (cape), Queensland 95/C2
Sidnaw, Mich. (49961) 250/G2
Sidney, Ark. (72577) 202/G1
Sidney, Br. Col. 184/K3
Sidney, Ill. (61877) 222/E3
Sidney, Ind. (46566) 227/F2
Sidney, Iowa (51652) 229/B7
Sidney○, Maine (†04330) 243/D7
Sidney, Manitoba 179/C5
Sidney, Mich. (48885) 250/D5
Sidney, Mont. (59270) 262/M3
Sidney, Nebr. (69162) 264/B3
Sidney, N.Y. (13838) 276/K6
Sidney, Ohio (45365) 284/B5
Sidney Center, N.Y. (13839) 276/K6
Sidney Lanier (lake), Georgia 217/D2
Sidoharjo, Indonesia 85/K2
Sidon, Ark. (†72137) 202/G3
Sidon (Saida), Lebanon 63/F6
Sidon, Miss. (38954) 256/D4
Sidonia, Tenn. (†38255) 237/D8
Sidra (gulf) 102/D1
Sidra (gulf), Libya 111/C1
Siedlce (prov.), Poland 47/F2
Siedlce, Poland 47/F2
Siegas, New Bruns. 170/C1
Siegburg, W. Germany 22/B3
Siegen, W. Germany 22/C3
Siemianowice Śląskie, Poland 47/B4
Siemiatycze, Poland 47/F2
Siempang, Cambodia 72/E4
Siemreab, Cambodia 72/D4
Siena (prov.), Italy 34/C3
Siena, Italy 34/C3
Sienyang (Xianyang), China 77/G5
Sieper, La. (71472) 238/E4
Sieradz (prov.), Poland 47/D3

Songhua Hu 449

Skull Valley Ind. Res., Utah 304/B3
Skuna (riv.), Miss. 256/F2
Skungamaug (riv.), Conn. 210/F1
Skunk (riv.), Iowa 229/K6
Skuteč, Czech. 41/D2
Skutskär, Sweden 18/K6
Skwentna, Alaska (99667) 196/B1
Skwentna (riv.), Alaska 196/A1
Skwierzyna, Poland 47/B2
Skye, Isle of (isl.), Scotland 15/B3
Skye (isl.), Scotland 10/C2
Skykomish, Wash. (98288) 310/D3
Skykomish (riv.), Wash. 310/D3
Skyland, N.C. (28776) 281/D4
Skylight (mt.), N.Y. 276/M2
Skyline, Minn. (†56001) 255/D6
Skyring (bay), Chile 138/E10
Skytop, Pa. (18357) 294/M3
Sky Valley, Georgia (30525) 217/F1
Slab Fork, W. Va. (25920) 312/D7
Slade, Ky. (40376) 237/O5
Sládečkovce, Czech. 41/D2
Slag (bay), Neth. Ant. 161/D8
Slagelse, Denmark 21/E7
Slagelse, Denmark 18/G9
Slagle, La. (71475) 238/D4
Slakow, Poland 47/B4
Slamannan, Scotland 15/C2
Slamet (mt.), Indonesia 85/J2
Slana, Alaska 196/K2
Slaná (riv.), Czech. 41/F2
Slane, Ireland 17/H4
Slanesville, W. Va. (25444) 312/K4
Slaney (riv.), Ireland 17/H7
Slangerup, Denmark 21/E6
Slangkop (pt.), S. Africa 118/E7
Slănic, Romania 45/G3
Slantsy, U.S.S.R. 52/C3
Slaný, Czech. 41/C1
Slate (mt.), Ariz. 198/D3
Slate (riv.), Colo. 208/E5
Slate (creek), Idaho 220/B4
Slate (isls.), Ontario 175/C3
Slate (riv.), Va. 307/L5
Slate, W. Va. (†26143) 312/D4
Slate (creek), Wyo. 319/C3
Slatedale, Pa. (18079) 294/L4
Slater, Colo. (81653) 208/E1
Slater, Iowa (50244) 229/F5
Slater, Mo. (65349) 261/G4
Slater, Wyo. (82201) 319/H4
Slater-Marietta, S.C. (29683) 296/C1
Slatersville, R.I. (02876) 249/H4
Slate Run, Pa. (17769) 294/H3
Slaterville Springs, N.Y. (14881) 276/H6
Slate Spring, Miss. (38955) 256/F3
Slatina, Romania 45/G3
Slatington, Pa. (18080) 294/L4
Slaton, Texas (79364) 303/C4
Slaughter, La. (70777) 238/H5
Slaughter Beach, Del. (†19963) 245/S5
Slaughters, Ky. (42456) 237/F6
Slaughterville, Okla. (†73051) 288/M4
Slave (riv.) 162/E3
Slave (riv.), Alberta 182/C5
Slave (riv.), Canada 146/G3
Slave (riv.), N.W. Terrs. 187/G3
Slave Coast (reg.), Benin 106/E7
Slave Coast (reg.), Nigeria 106/E7
Slave Coast (reg.), Togo 106/E7
Slave Lake, Alberta 182/C2
Slavgorod, U.S.S.R. 48/H4
Slavkov, Czech. 41/D2
Slavonia (reg.), Yugoslavia 45/C3
Slavonska Požega, Yugoslavia 45/C3
Slavonski Brod, Yugoslavia 45/D3
Slavuta, U.S.S.R. 52/C4
Slavyansk, U.S.S.R. 52/E5
Slavyansk-na-Kubani, U.S.S.R. 52/E5
Sławno, Poland 47/C1
Slayden, Miss. (†38642) 256/F1
Slayden, Tenn. (37165) 237/G8
Slayton, Minn. (56172) 255/C7
Sleaford, England 13/G5
Sleaford, England 10/F4
Sleat (dist.), Scotland 15/C3
Sleat (pt.), Scotland 15/B4
Sleat (sound), Scotland 15/C3
Sledge, Miss. (38670) 256/D2
Sleeper, Mo. (†65536) 261/H7
Sleeping Bear Dunes Nat'l Lakeshore, Mich. 250/C4
Sleeping Deer (mt.), Idaho 220/D5
Sleepy Creek, W. Va. (†25411) 312/K3
Sleepy Eye, Minn. (56085) 255/D6
Sleepy Eye (creek), Minn. 255/C6
Sleepy Hollow, Ill. (†60118) 222/E1
Sleetmute, Alaska (99668) 196/G2
Sleeve (lake), Manitoba 179/E3
Slemish (mt.), N. Ireland 17/J2
Slemon (lake), Manitoba 179/G1
Slemp, Ky. (41763) 237/P6
Slick, Okla. (74071) 288/O3
Slickford, Ky. (†42633) 237/M7
Slickville, Pa. (15684) 294/C5
Slide (mt.), N.Y. 276/L6
Slidell, La. (70458) 238/L6
Sliedrecht, Netherlands 27/F5
Sliema, Malta 34/E7
Slieve Anierin (mt.), Ireland 17/F3
Slieve Aughty (mts.), Ireland 17/D5
Slieve Beagh (mt.), N. Ireland 17/G3
Slieve Bernagh (mt.), Ireland 17/D6
Slieve Bloom (mts.), Ireland 17/F5
Slieve Callan (mt.), Ireland 17/C6
Slieve Car (mt.), Ireland 17/B3
Slieve Donard (mt.), N. Ireland 10/D3
Slieve Donard (mt.), N. Ireland 17/K3
Slieve Elva (mt.), Ireland 17/C5
Slievefelim (mts.), Ireland 17/E6
Slieve Gamph (mts.), Ireland 17/D3
Slieve Gullion (mt.), N. Ireland 17/J3
Slieve League (mt.), Ireland 17/D2
Slieve Mishkish (mts.), Ireland 17/B8
Slievenaman (mt.), Ireland 17/F7
Sligo (co.), Ireland 17/D3
Sligo, Ireland 17/E3
Sligo, Ireland 10/B3
Sligo (bay), Ireland 10/B3
Sligo (bay), Ireland 17/D3
Sligo, La. (†71037) 238/C2
Sligo, Pa. (16255) 294/C3
Slinger, Wis. (53086) 317/K9
Slipper (isl.), N. Zealand 100/F2
Slippery Rock, Pa. (16057) 294/B3
Slite, Sweden 18/L8
Sliven, Bulgaria 45/H4
Sliven, Bulgaria 7/G4
Sloan, Iowa (51055) 229/A4
Sloan, Nev. (†89114) 266/F7
Sloan, N.Y. (†14201) 276/C5
Sloans Valley, Ky. (42555) 237/N7
Sloat, Calif. (†96103) 204/E4
Sloatsburg, N.Y. (10974) 276/M8
Slobodskoy, U.S.S.R. 48/E4
Slobodskoy, U.S.S.R. 52/H3
Slobozia, Romania 45/H3
Slocan, Br. Col. 184/J5
Slocan (lake), Br. Col. 184/J5
Slocan Park, Br. Col. 184/J5
Slochteren, Netherlands 27/K2
Slocomb, Ala. (36375) 195/G8
Slocum, R.I. (02877) 249/H6
Slocum, Texas (†75839) 303/J6
Slonim, U.S.S.R. 52/B4
Slope (co.), N. Dak. 282/C7
Slot, The (chan.), Solomon Is. 86/D3
Sloten, Friesland, Netherlands 27/H3
Sloten, North Holland, Netherlands 27/B5
Sloterdijk, Netherlands 27/B4
Slotermeer (lake), Netherlands 27/H3
Slough, England 13/G8
Sloughhouse, Calif. (95683) 204/C8
Slovak Socialist Rep., Czech. 41/E2
Slovenia (rep.), Yugoslavia 45/B2
Slovenské Rudohorie (mts.), Czech. 41/E2
Słubice, Poland 47/B2
Sluis, Netherlands 27/C6
Słupca, Poland 47/D2
Słupia (riv.), Poland 47/C1
Słupsk (prov.), Poland 47/C1
Słupsk, Poland 47/C1
Słupsk, Poland 7/F3
Slutsk, U.S.S.R. 52/C4
Slyne (head), Ireland 10/A4
Slyne (head), Ireland 17/A5
Slyudyanka, U.S.S.R. 48/L4
Smackover, Ark. (71762) 202/E7
Smale, Ark. (†72021) 202/H4
Small, Idaho (†83423) 220/F5
Small (cape), Maine 243/D8
Small Isles (isls.), Scotland 15/B4
Small Point, Maine (04567) 243/D8
Smallwood (res.), Newf. 166/B3
Smallwood (res.), Newf. 146/M4
Smallwood (res.), Newf. 162/K5
Smarr, Georgia (31086) 217/E5
Smarts (mt.), N.H. 268/C4
Smartt, Tenn. (37378) 237/K9
Smartville, Calif. (95977) 204/D4
Smeaton, Sask. 181/G2
Smederevo, Yugoslavia 45/E3
Smederevska Palanka, Yugoslavia 45/E3
Smedjebacken, Sweden 18/J6
Smela, U.S.S.R. 52/D5
Smelterville, Idaho (83868) 220/B2
Smerwick (harb.), Ireland 17/A7
Smethport, Pa. (16749) 294/F2
Smicksburg, Pa. (16256) 294/D4
Smilax, Ky. (41764) 237/P6
Smilde, Netherlands 27/K3
Smiley, Sask. 181/B4
Smiley, Texas (78159) 303/G8
Smiltene, U.S.S.R. 53/C2
Smith (bay), Alaska 196/H1
Smith, Alberta 182/D2
Smith (sound), Br. Col. 184/C4
Smith (riv.), Calif. 204/A2
Smith (creek), Idaho 220/B1
Smith (co.), Kansas 232/D2
Smith (isl.), Md. 245/O8
Smith (co.), Miss. 256/E6
Smith (riv.), Mont. 262/E3
Smith, Nev. (89430) 266/B4
Smith (sound), Newf. 166/D2
Smith (isl.), N.C. 281/O7
Smith (basin), N.W.T. 162/N3
Smith (cape), N.W.T. 162/H3
Smith (bay), N.W. Terrs. 187/L2
Smith (cape), N.W. Terrs. 187/L3
Smith (sound), N.W. Terrs. 187/L2
Smith (cape), Ontario 177/C2
Smith (riv.), Oreg. 291/D4
Smith (co.), S. Dak. 298/L6
Smith (co.), Tenn. 237/J8
Smith (co.), Texas 303/J5
Smith (isl.), Va. 307/S6
Smith (riv.), Va. 307/J7
Smith Arm (inlet), N.W. Terrs. 187/F3
Smithboro, Ill. (62284) 222/D5
Smithburg, N.J. (†07728) 273/E3
Smithburg, W. Va. (26436) 312/E4
Smith Center, Kansas (66967) 232/D2
Smith Creek (valley), Nev. 266/D3
Smith Creek, W. Va. (†26807) 312/H5
Smithdale, Miss. (39664) 256/C8
Smithers, Br. Col. 146/F4
Smithers, Br. Col. 162/D5
Smithers, Br. Col. 184/D3
Smithers, W. Va. (25186) 312/D6
Smithfield, Ill. (61477) 222/C3
Smithfield, Ky. (40068) 237/L4
Smithfield○, Maine (04978) 243/D6
Smithfield, Nebr. (68976) 264/E4
Smithfield, N.C. (27577) 281/N3
Smithfield, Ohio (43948) 284/J5
Smithfield, Ontario 177/G3
Smithfield, Pa. (15478) 294/C6
Smithfield, Texas (†76180) 303/F2
Smithfield, Utah (84335) 304/C2
Smithfield, Va. (23430) 307/P7
Smithfield, W. Va. (26437) 312/E4
Smith Hill, Manitoba 179/C5
Smithland, Iowa (51056) 229/B4
Smithland, Ky. (42081) 237/E6
Smithmill, Pa. (16680) 294/F4
Smith Mills, Ky. (42457) 237/F5
Smith Mountain (lake), Va. 307/J6
Smithonia, Georgia (†30628) 217/F2
Smithport (lake), La. 238/C2
Smith River, Calif. (95567) 204/A2
Smiths, Ala. (36877) 195/H5
Smithsburg, Md. (21783) 245/H2
Smiths Cove, Nova Scotia 168/C4
Smiths Creek, Mich. (48074) 250/G6
Smiths Creek, New Bruns. 170/E3
Smiths Falls, Ontario 177/H3
Smiths Ferry, Idaho (†83611) 220/C5
Smiths Fork (riv.), Wyo. 319/B3
Smiths Grove, Ky. (42171) 237/J6
Smithshire, Ill. (61478) 222/C3
Smiths Station, Miss. (†39066) 256/C6
Smithton, Ark. (†71743) 202/D6
Smithton, Ill. (62285) 222/C5
Smithton, Mo. (65350) 261/F5
Smithton, Pa. (15479) 294/C5
Smithton, Tasmania 99/A2
Smithton, Tasmania 88/H8
Smith Town, Ky. (†42647) 237/M7
Smithtown, N.H. (†03874) 268/F6
Smithtown, N.Y. (11787) 276/O9
Smithtown-Gladstone, N.S. Wales 97/G2
Smith Valley, Ind. (†46142) 227/F5
Smithville, Ark. (72466) 202/H1
Smithville, Georgia (31787) 217/D7
Smithville, Ind. (47458) 227/D6
Smithville, Miss. (38870) 256/H2
Smithville, Mo. (64089) 261/D4
Smithville, N.J. (†08060) 273/D4
Smithville, N.J. (08201) 273/E5
Smithville, Ohio (44677) 284/G4
Smithville, Okla. (74957) 288/S6
Smithville, Ontario 177/E4
Smithville, Tenn. (37166) 237/K9
Smithville, Texas (78957) 303/G7
Smithville, W. Va. (26178) 312/D4
Smithville Flats, N.Y. (13841) 276/J6
Smithwick, S. Dak. (57782) 298/C7
Smoaks, S.C. (29481) 296/F5
Smoke Bend, La. (†70346) 238/K3
Smoke Creek (des.), Nev. 266/B2
Smoke Hole, W. Va. (†26866) 312/H5
Smokey Burn, Sask. 181/H2
Smoky (riv.), Alberta 182/A2
Smoky (riv.), Alta. 162/E5
Smoky (mts.), Idaho 220/D6
Smoky (cape), N.S. Wales 97/G2
Smoky (lake), N. Dak. 282/K3
Smoky (cape), Nova Scotia 168/H2
Smoky Bay, S. Australia 88/E6
Smoky Bay, S. Australia 94/D5
Smoky Hill (riv.) 188/G3
Smoky Hill (riv.), Colo. 208/P5
Smoky Hill, North Fork (riv.), Kansas 232/A2
Smoky Hill (riv.), Kansas 232/C3
Smoky Junction, Tenn. (†37827) 237/N8
Smoky Lake, Alberta 182/D2
Smøla (isl.), Norway 18/E5
Smolan, Kansas (67479) 232/E3
Smolensk, U.S.S.R. 7/H3
Smolensk, U.S.S.R. 48/D4
Smolensk, U.S.S.R. 52/D4
Smolyan, Bulgaria 45/G5
Smoot, W. Va. (24977) 312/E7
Smoot, Wyo. (83126) 319/B3
Smooth Rock Falls, Ontario 177/J5
Smooth Rock Falls, Ontario 175/D3
Smugglers Notch (pass), Vt. 268/B2
Smuts, Sask. 181/F3
Smyadovo, Bulgaria 45/H4
Smyer, Ala. (†36727) 195/B7
Smyrna, Del. (19977) 245/R3
Smyrna (res.), Del. 245/R3
Smyrna, Georgia (30080) 217/K1
Smyrna, Mich. (48887) 250/D5
Smyrna, N.Y. (13464) 276/J5
Smyrna, N.C. (28579) 281/R5
Smyrna, S.C. (29743) 296/E1
Smyrna, Tenn. (37167) 237/H9
Smyrna (Izmir), Turkey 63/B3
Smyrna, Wash. (†99357) 310/F4
Smyrna Mills, Maine (04780) 243/G3
Smyrna Mills○, Maine (04780) 243/G3
Smyth (co.), Va. 307/E7
Snaefell (mt.), I. of Man 13/C3
Snaefell (mt.), I. of Man 10/D3
Snake (riv.) 188/C1
Snake (riv.), Idaho 220/A3
Snake (riv.), Minn. 255/A2
Snake (riv.), Minn. 255/E4
Snake (riv.), Nebr. 264/C2
Snake (mts.), Nev. 266/F1
Snake (range), Nev. 266/G3
Snake (riv.), Oreg. 291/K3
Snake (creek), S. Dak. 298/F4
Snake (creek), S. Dak. 298/F5
Snake (creek), S. Dak. 298/M3
Snake (riv.), U.S. 146/G5
Snake (isl.), Victoria 97/D6
Snake (riv.), Wash. 310/G4
Snake (riv.), Wyo. 319/B2
Snake Creek (canal), Fla. 212/B4
Snake Indian (riv.), Alberta 182/A3
Snake River (plain), Idaho 220/D7
Snake River (range), Idaho 220/G6
Snake River, Wash. (†99301) 310/G4
Snare (riv.), N.W. Terrs. 187/G3
Snare Lake, N.W. Terrs. 187/G3
Snares, The (isls.), N. Zealand 100/A7
Snåsa, Norway 18/H4
Snåsavatn (lake), Norway 18/H4
Snead, Ala. (35952) 195/F2
Sneads, Fla. (32460) 212/B1
Sneads Ferry, N.C. (28460) 281/P5
Snedsted, Denmark 21/B4
Sneedville, Tenn. (37869) 237/P7
Sneek, Netherlands 27/H2
Sneekermeer (lake), Netherlands 27/H2
Sneem, Ireland 17/B8
Sneeuwkop (mt.), S. Africa 118/F6
Sneffels (mt.), Colo. 208/D7
Snegamook (lake), Newf. 166/B3
Snell, Va. (22553) 307/N4
Snelling, Calif. (95369) 204/E6
Snelling, S.C. (†29812) 296/E5
Snellville, Georgia (30278) 217/D3
Snezhnogorsk, U.S.S.R. 48/J3
Śniardwy, Jezioro (lake), Poland 47/E2
Sniečkus, U.S.S.R. 53/D3
Snina, Czech. 41/G2
Snipe (lake), Alberta 182/B2
Snipe Lake, Sask. 181/B4
Snizort, Loch (inlet), Scotland 15/B3
Snohomish (co.), Wash. 310/D2
Snohomish, Wash. (98290) 310/D3
Snohomish (riv.), Wash. 310/C3
Snoqualmie, Wash. (†98065) 310/D3
Snoqualmie (pass), Wash. 310/D3
Snoqualmie (riv.), Wash. 310/D3
Snoqualmie Falls, Wash. (†98065) 310/D3
Snover, Mich. (48472) 250/G5
Snow, Okla. (74567) 288/R6
Snow (mt.), Vt. 268/B6
Snow (peak), Wash. 310/G2
Snowball, Ark. (†72650) 202/E2
Snowbird (lake), N.W. Terrs. 187/H3
Snow Camp, N.C. (27349) 281/L3
Snowden, N.C. (†27929) 281/S2
Snowden, Sask. 181/G2
Snowdon (mt.), Wales 13/D4
Snowdon (mt.), Wales 10/D4
Snowdonia Nat'l Park, Wales 13/D4
Snowdoun, Ala. (†36104) 195/F6
Snowdrift, N.W.T. 162/E3
Snowdrift, N.W. Terrs. 187/G3
Snowfield (peak), Wash. 310/D2
Snowflake, Ariz. (85937) 198/E4
Snowflake, Manitoba 179/D5
Snow Hill, Ala. (36778) 195/E7
Snow Hill, Ark. (†71751) 202/E7
Snow Hill, Md. (21863) 245/S8
Snow Hill, N.C. (28580) 281/O4
Snow Lake, Ark. (72379) 202/H5
Snow Lake, Man. 162/G5
Snow Lake, Manitoba 179/H3
Snowmass, Colo. (81654) 208/E4
Snowshoe (lake), Manitoba 179/G4
Snow Shoe, Pa. (16874) 294/G3
Snowtown, S. Australia 94/E5
Snowville, N.H. (†03849) 268/E4
Snowville, Utah (84336) 304/B2
Snow Water (lake), Nev. 266/G2
Snowy (mts.), N.S. Wales 97/E5
Snowy (riv.), N.S. Wales 97/E5
Snowy (riv.), Victoria 88/H7
Snug, Tasmania 99/D5
Snyder, Ark. (†71658) 202/G7
Snyder, Colo. (80750) 208/M2
Snyder, Mo. (†65286) 261/F3
Snyder, Nebr. (68664) 264/H3
Snyder, Okla. (73566) 288/J5
Snyder (co.), Pa. 294/H4
Snyder, Texas (79549) 303/D5
Snydertown, Pa. (17877) 294/J4
So (isl.), S. Korea 81/C6
Soalala, Madagascar 118/H3
Soalara, Madagascar 118/G4
Soanierana-Ivongo, Madagascar 118/H3
Soap (lake), Wash. 310/F3
Soap Lake, Wash. (98851) 310/F3
Soasiu, Indonesia 85/H5
Soatá, Colombia 126/D4
Soay (isl.), Scotland 15/A2
Soay (isl.), Scotland 15/B3
Sobat (riv.), Sudan 111/F6
Sober (isl.), Nova Scotia 168/F4
Soběslav, Czech. 41/C2
Sobieski, Minn. (†56345) 255/D5
Sobieski, Wis. (54171) 317/L6
Sobotka, Czech. 41/C1
Sobral, Brazil 120/E3
Sobral, Brazil 132/G3
Sobrance, Czech. 41/G2
Soca, Uruguay 145/C6
Sochaczew, Poland 47/E2
Soche (Shache), China 77/A4
Sochi, U.S.S.R. 7/H4
Sochi, U.S.S.R. 48/D5
Sochi, U.S.S.R. 52/E6
Social Circle, Georgia (30279) 217/E3
Society (isls.), Fr. Poly. 87/L7
Society Hill, Ala. (†36801) 195/H6
Society Hill, S.C. (29593) 296/H2
Socompa (vol.), Chile 138/B4
Socorro, Brazil 135/C3
Socorro, Colombia 126/D4
Socorro (isl.), Mexico 150/D7
Socorro, N. Mex. 188/E4
Socorro (co.), N. Mex. 274/C5
Socorro, N. Mex. (87801) 274/C4
Socotra (isl.), P.D.R. Yemen 54/G8
Socotra (isl.), P.D.R. Yemen 2/M5
Socotra (isl.), P.D.R. Yemen 59/F7
Socuéllamos, Spain 33/E3
Soda (lake), Calif. 204/K8
Soda (plains), India 68/D1
Soda, Jebel es (mts.), Libya 111/C2
Soda Creek, Br. Col. 184/F4
Sodankylä, Finland 18/P3
Soda Plains, Pakistan 68/D1
Soda Springs, Calif. (95728) 204/E4
Soda Springs, Idaho (83276) 220/G7
Sodaville, Oreg. (†97355) 291/E3
Soddu, Ethiopia 111/G6
Soddy-Daisy, Tenn. (37319) 237/L10
Söderhamn, Sweden 18/K6
Söderköping, Sweden 18/K7
Södermanland (co.), Sweden 18/K7
Södertälje, Sweden 18/G1
Sodiri, Sudan 111/E5
Sodus, Mich. (49126) 250/C6
Sodus, N.Y. (14551) 276/G4
Sodus Point, N.Y. (14555) 276/G4
Soe, Indonesia 85/G7
Soest, Netherlands 27/G4
Soest, W. Germany 22/C3
Soesterberg, Netherlands 27/G4
Soeurs (isl.), Québec 172/H4
Sofala (prov.), Mozambique 118/E3
Sofia (cap.), Bulgaria 7/G4
Sofia (cap.), Bulgaria 45/F4
Sofia (riv.), Madagascar 118/H3
Sofkee, Georgia (†31201) 217/E5
Soft Shell, Ky. (41853) 237/P6
Sogamoso, Colombia 126/D5
Sogamoso (riv.), Colombia 126/D4
Soğanlı (mts.), Turkey 63/H2
Soğanlı (riv.), Turkey 63/E2
Sognafjorden (fjord), Norway 18/D6
Sognefjorden (fjord), Norway 7/E2
Sogn og Fjordane (co.), Norway 18/E6
Sogod, Philippines 82/E5
Sogod (bay), Philippines 82/E5
Söğüt, Turkey 63/D3
Söğüt (lake), Turkey 63/D4
Sog Xian, China 77/D5
Soh, Iran 66/G4
Sohâg, Egypt 111/F2
Sohâg, Egypt 59/B4
Sohâg, Egypt 102/F2
Soham, N. Mex. (†87565) 274/D3
Sohar, Oman 59/G5
Sŏhŭng, N. Korea 81/C4
Soignies, Belgium 27/D7
Sointula, Br. Col. 184/D5
Soissons, France 28/E3
Soka, Japan 81/O2
Sokch'o, S. Korea 81/D4
Söke, Turkey 63/B4
Söke, Turkey 59/A2
Sokna, Libya 111/D2
Sokodé, Togo 106/E7
Sokol, U.S.S.R. 52/F3
Sokol, U.S.S.R. 48/E4
Sokółka, Poland 47/F2
Sokolo, Mali 106/C6
Sokolov, Czech. 41/B1
Sokołów Podlaski, Poland 47/F2
Sokota, Ethiopia 111/G5
Sokoto (state), Nigeria 106/F6
Sokoto, Nigeria 102/C3
Sokoto, Nigeria 106/F6
Sokoto (riv.), Nigeria 106/F6
Sola, Cuba 158/G2
Solana Beach, Calif. (92075) 204/H11
Solander (isl.), N. Zealand 100/A7
Solano (co.), Calif. 204/D5
Solano (pt.), Colombia 126/B4
Solano, N. Mex. (87746) 274/E3
Solano, Philippines 82/C2
Solano, Venezuela 124/E6
Solbad Hall in Tirol, Austria 41/A3
Solca, Romania 45/G2
Soldado (pt.), P. Rico 161/G2
Soldier, Iowa (51572) 229/B5
Soldier, Kansas (66540) 232/G2
Soldier, Ky. (41173) 237/P4
Soldier Pond, Maine (04781) 243/F1
Soldiers Cove, Nova Scotia 168/H3
Soldiers Grove, Wis. (54655) 317/E9
Soldier Summit, Utah (†84601) 304/C4
Soldotna, Alaska (99669) 196/B1
Soledad, Argentina 143/F5
Soledad, Calif. (93960) 204/D7
Soledad, Colombia 126/C2
Soledad, Venezuela 124/G3
Soledad de Doblado, Mexico 150/Q2
Soledad Díez Gutiérrez, Mexico 150/J5
Soleduck (riv.), Wash. 310/A3
Solen, N. Dak. (58570) 282/J7
Solent (chan.), England 13/F7
Solentiname (isls.), Nicaragua 154/E5
Soleure (Solothurn) (canton), Switzerland 39/E2
Solgohachia, Ark. (72156) 202/E3
Solhan, Turkey 63/J3
Soligalich, U.S.S.R. 52/F3
Soligorsk, U.S.S.R. 52/C4
Solihull, England 13/F5
Solihull, England 10/G3
Solikamsk, U.S.S.R. 7/K3
Solikamsk, U.S.S.R. 48/F3
Solikamsk, U.S.S.R. 52/J3
Sol'-Iletsk, U.S.S.R. 52/J4
Solingen, W. Germany 22/B3
Solís, Uruguay 145/D5
Solís de Mataojo, Uruguay 145/D5
Solitary (isl.), N.S. Wales 97/G1
Sollefteå, Sweden 18/K5
Sollentuna, Sweden 18/H1
Sóller, Spain 33/H3
Søllested, Denmark 21/E8
Solna, Sweden 18/H1
Solo (Surakarta), Indonesia 85/J2
Solo, Mo. (65564) 261/J8
Sologne (reg.), France 28/E4
Solok, Indonesia 85/C6
Sololá, Guatemala 154/B3
Solomon (sea) 87/F6
Solomon, Alaska (†99762) 196/F2
Solomon, Ariz. (85551) 198/F6
Solomon, Kansas (67480) 232/E3
Solomon (riv.), Kansas 232/E2
Solomon (isls.), Pacific 87/F6
Solomon (isls.), Papua N.G. 86/C3
Solomon (sea), Papua N.G. 85/C7
Solomon (isls.), Solomon Is. 86/C3
Solomon (sea), Solomon Is. 86/D3
Solomon Islands 2/T6
SOLOMON ISLANDS 86/D2
Solomon Islands 87/G6
Solomons, Md. (20688) 245/N7
Solon, China 77/K2
Solon, Ind. (†47111) 227/F7
Solon, Iowa (52333) 229/L5
Solon○, Maine (04979) 243/D6
Solon, Ohio (44139) 284/J9
Solon Springs, Wis. (54873) 317/C3
Solor (isl.), Indonesia 85/G7
Solothurn (elec. div.), Switzerland 39/E2
Solothurn (Soleure), Switzerland 39/E2
Solovetskiye (isls.), U.S.S.R. 52/E1
Solsberry, Ind. (47459) 227/D6
Solsgirth, Manitoba 179/B4
Solsona, Philippines 82/C1
Solsona, Spain 33/G2
Solt, Hungary 41/E3
Šolta (isl.), Yugoslavia 45/C4
Soltau, W. Germany 22/C2
Soltvadkert, Hungary 41/E3
Soluk, Libya 111/D1
Solund, Norway 18/D6
Solvang, Calif. (93463) 204/E9
Solvay, N.Y. (13209) 276/H4
Sölvesborg, Sweden 18/J9
Solway (firth), England 13/D3
Solway, Minn. (56678) 255/C3
Solway (firth), Scotland 10/D3
Solway (firth), Scotland 15/E6
Solwezi, Zambia 115/E6
Soma, Japan 81/K5
Soma, Turkey 63/B3
Somabula, Zimbabwe 118/D3
Somalia 2/M5
Somalia 102/G4
SOMALIA 115/J2
Sombor, Yugoslavia 45/D3
Sombra, Ontario 177/B5
Sombrerete, Mexico 150/H5
Sombrero (chan.), India 68/G7
Sombrero (isl.), St. Chris.-Nevis 156/F3
Somerdale, N.J. (08083) 273/B4
Somers, Conn. (06071) 210/F1
Somers○, Conn. (06071) 210/F1
Somers, Iowa (50586) 229/E4
Somers, Mont. (59932) 262/B2
Somers, Wis. (53171) 317/M3
Somerset, (22972) 307/M4
Somerset (isl.), Bermuda 156/G3
Somerset (isl.), Canada 4/B14
Somerset, Colo. (81434) 208/E5
Somerset (co.), England 13/E6
Somerset, Ind. (46984) 227/F3
Somerset, Ky. (42501) 237/M6
Somerset, La. (†71357) 238/H2
Somerset (co.), Maine 243/C4
Somerset, Manitoba 179/D5
Somerset (co.), Md. 245/R8
Somerset, Md. (†20015) 245/E4
Somerset○, Mass. (02725) 249/K5
Somerset (co.), N.J. 273/D2
Somerset, N.Y. (†14012) 276/C4
Somerset (isl.), N.W.T. 146/J2
Somerset (isl.), N.W.T. 162/G1
Somerset (isl.), N.W. Terrs. 187/J2
Somerset, Nova Scotia 168/D3
Somerset, Ohio (43783) 284/F6
Somerset (co.), Pa. 294/D6
Somerset, Pa. (15501) 294/D6
Somerset, Texas (78069) 303/J11
Somerset (res.), Vt. 268/A5
Somerset, Wis. (54025) 317/A5
Somerset East, S. Africa 118/D6
Somerset West, S. Africa 118/F6
Somers Point, N.J. (08244) 273/D5
Somersville, Conn. (06072) 210/F1
Somersworth, N.H. (03878) 268/F5
Somerton, Ariz. (85350) 198/A6
Somerton, England 13/E6
Somerton, Ohio (43784) 284/H6
Somervell (co.), Texas 303/G5
Somerville, Ala. (35670) 195/E2
Somerville, Ind. (47683) 227/C8
Somerville○, Maine (†04341) 243/D7
Somerville, Mass. (02143) 249/C6
Somerville, New Bruns. 170/C2
Somerville, N.J. (08876) 273/D2
Somerville, Ohio (45064) 284/A6
Somerville, Tenn. (38068) 237/C10
Somerville, Texas (77879) 303/H7
Somes (isl.), N. Zealand 100/B2
Someş (riv.), Romania 45/F2
Somesbar, Calif. (95568) 204/B2
Somesville (Mount Desert), Maine (†04660) 243/G7
Somme (dept.), France 28/E3
Somme (riv.), France 28/D2
Somme, Sask. 181/J3
Somme-Leuze, Belgium 27/G8
Sommen (lake), Sweden 18/J8
Sömmerda, E. Germany 22/D3
Somogy (co.), Hungary 41/D3
Somonauk, Ill. (60552) 222/E2
Somotillo, Nicaragua 154/D4
Somoto, Nicaragua 154/D4
Somvix, Switzerland 39/G3
Son (riv.), India 68/E3
Son, Norway 18/D4
Son, Con (isls.), Vietnam 72/E5
Soná, Panama 154/G6
Sonaguera, Honduras 154/D3
Sŏnch'ŏn, N. Korea 81/B4
Sønderborg, Denmark 21/C8
Sønderborg, Denmark 18/G9
Sønderho, Denmark 21/B7
Sønderjylland (co.), Denmark 21/C7
Sønder Nissum, Denmark 21/A5
Sønder Omme, Denmark 21/B6
Sondershausen, E. Germany 22/D3
Søndersø, Denmark 21/D7
Sondheimer, La. (71276) 238/H1
Søndre Strømfjord, Greenl. 4/C12
Sondrio (prov.), Italy 34/B1
Sondrio, Italy 34/B1
Sonepur, India 68/E4
Sonestown, Pa. (17770) 294/K3
Song Ba (riv.), Vietnam 72/F4
Song Ca (riv.), Vietnam 72/E3
Song Cai (riv.), Vietnam 72/E4
Song Cau, Vietnam 72/F4
Song Da (Black) (riv.), Vietnam 72/E2
Songea, Tanzania 115/G6
Songea, Tanzania 102/F6
Song Hong (Red) (riv.), Vietnam 72/E2
Songhua (riv.), China 54/P5
Songhua Hu (lake), China 77/L3

Starogard Gdański 451

South Willington, Conn. (06265) 210/F1
South Wilmington, Ill. (60474) 222/E2
South Wilton, Conn. (†06897) 210/B4
South Windham, Conn. (06266) 210/G2
South Windham (Little Falls-South Windham), Maine (04082) 243/C8
South Windham, Vt. (†05359) 268/B5
South Windsor○, Conn. (06074) 210/E1
Southwold, England 13/J5
Southwold, England 10/G4
South Wolf (isl.), Newf. 166/C3
South Wolfeboro, N.H. (†03894) 268/E4
South Woodbury, Vt. (†05681) 268/C3
South Woodstock, Conn. (06267) 210/G1
South Woodstock, Vt. (05071) 268/B4
Southworth, Wash. (98386) 310/A2
South Worthington, Mass. (†01098) 249/C3
South Yadkin (riv.), N.C. 281/H3
South Yarmouth, Mass. (02664) 249/O6
South Yorkshire (co.), England 13/F4
South Zanesville, Ohio (43701) 284/F6
Sovata, Romania 45/G2
Sovereign, Sask. 181/D4
Sovetsk, U.S.S.R. 7/J3
Sovetsk, U.S.S.R. 52/G3
Sovetsk (Tilsit), U.S.S.R. 52/B4
Sovetskaya Gavan', U.S.S.R. 54/R5
Sovetskaya Gavan', U.S.S.R. 48/P5
SOVIET UNION (U.S.S.R.) 48
Sowerby Bridge, England 13/H1
Sowerby Bridge, England 10/G2
Soweto, S. Africa 118/H6
Soya (pt.), Japan 81/L1
Soyhières, Switzerland 39/D2
Soyo, Angola 115/B5
Soyo, Angola 102/D5
Sozopol, Bulgaria 45/H4
Spa, Belgium 27/H8
Spades, Ind. (†47041) 227/G6
Spain 2/J3
Spain 7/D4
SPAIN 33
Spalding, England 13/G5
Spalding, England 10/F4
Spalding (co.), Georgia 217/D4
Spalding, Mich. (49886) 250/B3
Spalding, Mo. (†63401) 261/J3
Spalding, Nebr. (68665) 264/F3
Spalding, Sask. 181/G3
Spaldings, Jamaica 158/H6
Spallumcheen, Br. Col. 184/H5
Spanaway, Wash. (98387) 310/C3
Spandau, W. Germany 22/E3
Spangle, Wash. (99031) 310/H3
Spangler, Pa. (15775) 294/E4
Spaniard's Bay, Newf. 166/D2
Spanish (head), I. of Man 13/C3
Spanish, Ontario 177/J5
Spanish (riv.), Ontario 177/C1
Spanishburg, W. Va. (25922) 312/D8
Spanish Fork, Utah (84660) 304/C3
Spanish Fork (riv.), Utah 304/C3
Spanish Fort, Ala. (36527) 195/C9
Spanish Fort, Texas (†76255) 303/G4
Spanish Lake, Mo. (†63138) 261/R1
Spanish Ship Bay, Nova Scotia 168/G4
Spanish Town, Jamaica 158/J6
Spanish Town, Jamaica 156/C3
Sparkill, N.Y. (10976) 276/K8
Sparkman, Ark. (71763) 202/E6
Sparks, Georgia (31647) 217/F8
Sparks, Kansas (†66035) 232/G2
Sparks, Nebr. (69220) 264/D2
Sparks, Nev. 188/C3
Sparks, Nev. (89431) 266/B3
Sparks, Okla. (74869) 288/N3
Sparks (lake), Oreg. 291/F3
Sparksville, Ky. (42778) 237/L6
Sparland, Ill. (61565) 222/D2
Sparlingville, Mich. (†48060) 250/G6
Sparr, Fla. (32690) 212/D2
Sparrow Bush, N.Y. (12780) 276/L8
Sparrows Point, Md. (21219) 245/N4
Sparta, Georgia (31087) 217/F4
Sparta, Greece 45/F7
Sparta, Ill. (62286) 222/D5
Sparta, Ky. (41086) 237/M3
Sparta, Mich. (49345) 250/D5
Sparta, Mo. (65753) 261/F9
Sparta○, N.J. (07871) 273/D1
Sparta, N.C. (28675) 281/G1
Sparta, Ohio (43350) 284/E5
Sparta, Ontario 177/C5
Sparta, Oreg. (†97870) 291/K3
Sparta, Tenn. (38583) 237/K9
Sparta, Va. (22552) 307/O4
Sparta, Wis. (54656) 317/E8
Spartanburg, Ind. (†47355) 227/H4
Spartanburg, S.C. 188/K4
Spartanburg (co.), S.C. 296/D2
Spartanburg, S.C. (*29301) 296/C1
Spartansburg, Pa. (16434) 294/C2
Spartivento (cape), Italy 34/B5
Spartivento (cape), Italy 34/F6
Sparwood, Br. Col. 184/K5
Spassk-Dal'niy, U.S.S.R. 48/O5
Spátha (cape), Greece 45/F8
Spaulding, Ill. (†62561) 222/D4
Spavinaw, Okla. (74366) 288/R2
Spavinaw (lake), Okla. 288/S2
Spean (riv.), Scotland 15/D4
Spean Bridge, Scotland 15/D4
Spear (cape), New Bruns. 170/G2
Spear (cape), Newf. 166/D2
Spearfish, S. Dak. (57783) 298/B5
Spearman, Texas (79081) 303/C1
Spearsville, Ind. (†46181) 227/E6
Spearsville, La. (71277) 238/E1
Spearville, Kansas (67876) 232/C4
Spectacle (lakes), Conn. 210/B2
Specter (range), Nev. 266/E6
Speculator, N.Y. (12164) 276/M3
Spedden, Alberta 182/E2
Spednik (lake), New Bruns. 170/C3
Speed, Ind. (47172) 227/F8
Speed, Kansas (†67639) 232/C2
Speed, N.C. (27881) 281/P3
Speedway, Ind. (46224) 227/E5
Speedwell, Tenn. (37870) 237/O8
Speedwell, Va. (24374) 307/F8
Speer (mt.), Switzerland 39/H2
Speers, Sask. 181/D3
Speightstown, Barbados 161/B8
Speightstown, Barbados 156/G4
Speigner, Ala. (†36025) 195/F5
Spelterville, Ind. (†47808) 227/C5
Spelve, Loch (inlet), Scotland 15/C4
Spenard, Alaska (99503) 196/C1
Spenborough, England 13/J1
Spence Bay, N.W. Terrs. 187/J3
Spencer (cape), Alaska 196/L1
Spencer (pt.), Alaska 196/E1
Spencer (lake), Alberta 182/E2
Spencer (gulf), Australia 87/D9
Spencer, Idaho (†83423) 220/F5
Spencer (co.), Ind. 227/C9
Spencer, Ind. (47460) 227/D6
Spencer, Iowa (51301) 229/C2
Spencer (co.), Ky. 237/L4
Spencer, La. (71278) 238/F1
Spencer (pond), Maine 243/D4
Spencer (stream), Maine 243/C5
Spencer, Mass. (01562) 249/F3
Spencer○, Mass. (01562) 249/F3
Spencer, Nebr. (68777) 264/F2
Spencer (cape), New Bruns. 170/E3
Spencer, N.Y. (14883) 276/H6
Spencer, N.C. (28159) 281/H3
Spencer, Ohio (44275) 284/F3
Spencer, Okla. (73084) 288/M3
Spencer (creek), Oreg. 291/E5
Spencer (gulf), S. Australia 88/F6
Spencer (cape), S. Australia 88/F7
Spencer (cape), S. Australia 94/E6
Spencer (gulf), S. Australia 94/E6
Spencer, S. Dak. (57374) 298/O6
Spencer, Tenn. (38585) 237/L9
Spencer, Va. (24165) 307/J7
Spencer, W. Va. (25276) 312/D5
Spencer, Wis. (54479) 317/F6
Spencerburg, Mo. (†63441) 261/K4
Spencerport, N.Y. (14559) 276/E4
Spencers Island, Nova Scotia 168/D3
Spencerville, Ind. (46788) 227/G2
Spencerville, Ohio (45887) 284/B4
Spencerville, Okla. (74760) 288/R6
Spencerville, Ontario 177/J3
Spences Bridge, Br. Col. 184/G5
Spennymoor, England 13/F3
Spennymoor, England 10/F3
Spenser (mts.), N. Zealand 100/D5
Sperling, Manitoba 179/E5
Sperrin (mts.), N. Ireland 17/G2
Sperry, Iowa (52650) 229/L7
Sperry, Okla. (74073) 288/P2
Sperryville, Va. (22740) 307/M3
Spessart (range), W. Germany 22/C4
Spétsai, Greece 45/F7
Spey (riv.), Scotland 10/E2
Spey (riv.), Scotland 15/E3
Speyer, W. Germany 22/C4
Sphinx (mt.), Mont. 262/E5
Spiceland, Ind. (47385) 227/F5
Spicer, Minn. (56288) 255/C5
Spicer (isls.), N.W. Terrs. 187/L3
Spicewood, Texas (78669) 303/F7
Spickard, Mo. (64679) 261/F2
Spiddal, Ireland 17/C5
Spider (lake), Maine 243/E3
Spider (lake), Wis. 317/D3
Spiekeroog (isl.), W. Germany 22/B2
Spies, N.C. (†27325) 281/K4
Spiez, Switzerland 39/E3
Spili, Greece 45/G8
Spillimacheen, Br. Col. 184/J5
Spillville, Iowa (52168) 229/J2
Spilsby, England 13/H4
Spin Buldak, Afghanistan 68/B2
Spin Buldak, Afghanistan 59/J3
Spindale, N.C. (28160) 281/F4
Spink (co.), S. Dak. 298/N4
Spink, S. Dak. (†57010) 298/R8
Spinnerstown, Pa. (18968) 294/M5
Spirit (lake), Idaho 220/B2
Spirit (lake), Iowa 229/C2
Spirit (lake), S. Dak. 298/O4
Spirit (lake), Wash. 310/C4
Spirit, Wis. (†54513) 317/F5
Spirit Lake, Idaho (83869) 220/A2
Spirit Lake, Iowa (51360) 229/C2
Spirit River, Alberta 182/A2
Spirit River, Alta. 162/E4
Spiritwood, N. Dak. (58481) 282/N6
Spiritwood, Sask. 181/D2
Spiro, Okla. (74959) 288/S4
Spišská Belá, Czech. 41/F2
Spišská Nová Ves, Czech. 41/F2
Spital am Pyhrn, Austria 41/C3
Spithead (chan.), England 13/F7
Spitsbergen (isl.), Norway 4/B9
Spitsbergen (isl.), Norway 18/C2
Spittal an der Drau, Austria 41/B3
Spitz, Austria 41/C2
Spivey, Kansas (67142) 232/D4
Splendora, Texas (77372) 303/J7
Split (lake), Manitoba 179/J2
Split (cape), Nova Scotia 168/D3
Split, Yugoslavia 7/F4
Split, Yugoslavia 45/C4
Split Lake, Manitoba 179/J2
Split Rock, Wis. (†54486) 317/H6
Splügen (pass), Italy 34/B1
Splügen, Switzerland 39/H3
Splügen (pass), Switzerland 39/H3
Spofford, N.H. (03462) 268/C6
Spofford, Texas (78877) 303/D8
Spokane, Mo. (65754) 261/F9
Spokane, Wash. 146/G5
Spokane, Wash. 188/C1
Spokane (co.), Wash. 310/H3
Spokane, Wash. (*99201) 310/H3
Spokane (mt.), Wash. 310/H3
Spokane (riv.), Wash. 310/G3
Spokane Ind. Res., Wash. 310/G3
Spöl (riv.), Switzerland 39/F2
Spoleto, Italy 34/D3
Spoon (riv.), Ill. 222/C3
Spooner, Wis. (54801) 317/B4
Spot (pond), Mass. 249/C6
Spotswood, N.J. (08884) 273/E3
Spotsylvania (co.), Va. 307/N4
Spotsylvania, Va. (22553) 307/N4
Spotted (range), Nev. 266/F6
Spotted Horse, Wyo. (†82831) 319/G1
Spottsville, Ky. (42458) 237/G5
Spottswood, Va. (24475) 307/K5
Spotville, Ark. (†71753) 202/D7
Spragge, Ontario 177/J5
Sprague, Ala. (36076) 195/F6
Sprague, Manitoba 179/G5
Sprague, Nebr. (68438) 264/H4
Sprague (riv.), Oreg. 291/F5
Sprague, Wash. (99032) 310/G3
Sprague (lake), Wash. 310/G3
Sprague River, Oreg. (97639) 291/F5
Spragueville, Iowa (52074) 229/N4
Spratly (isl.), Philippines 85/E4
Spratt, Mich. (†49753) 250/F3
Spray (mts.), Alberta 182/C4
Spray, Oreg. (97874) 291/H3
Spray Lakes, Alberta 182/C4
Spraytown, Ind. (†47228) 227/E6
Spread Eagle, Wis. (†54121) 317/K4
Spreckelsville, Hawaii (96779) 218/J1
Spree (riv.), E. Germany 22/F3
Spreewald (for.), E. Germany 22/F3
Spremberg, E. Germany 22/F3
Sprent, Tasmania 99/C3
Sprigg, W. Va. (25693) 312/B7
Sprimont, Belgium 27/H8
Spring (riv.), Ark. 202/H1
Spring (creek), Nev. 266/D2
Spring (mts.), Nev. 266/F6
Spring (valley), Nev. 266/G3
Spring (creek), N. Dak. 282/E5
Spring (creek), S. Dak. 298/J2
Spring (creek), S. Dak. 298/C6
Spring, Texas (*77373) 303/J7
Spring Arbor, Mich. (49283) 250/E6
Spring Bay, Ill. (†61601) 222/D3
Spring Bay, Ontario 177/B2
Springbok, S. Africa 118/B5
Springboro, Ohio (45066) 284/B6
Springboro, Pa. (16435) 294/B2
Springbrook, Iowa (52075) 229/N4
Spring Brook, N. Dak. (58850) 282/D3
Springbrook, Ontario 177/G3
Springbrook, Oreg. (†97132) 291/A2
Springbrook, Wis. (54875) 317/C4
Spring City, Mo. (†64801) 261/C9
Spring City, Pa. (19475) 294/L5
Spring City, Tenn. (37381) 237/M9
Spring City, Utah (84662) 304/C4
Spring Coulée, Alberta 182/D5
Spring Creek, Pa. (16436) 294/D2
Spring Creek, Tenn. (38378) 237/D9
Spring Creek, W. Va. (†24966) 312/F7
Springdale, Ark. (72764) 202/B1
Springdale, Iowa (†52776) 229/L5
Springdale, Mont. (59082) 262/F5
Springdale, Newf. 166/C4
Springdale, Ohio (45246) 284/B9
Springdale, Pa. (15144) 294/C6
Springdale, S.C. (†29720) 296/F2
Springdale, S.C. (29169) 296/E4
Springdale, Utah (84767) 304/B6
Springdale, Wash. (99173) 310/H2
Springe, W. Germany 22/C2
Springer (mt.), Georgia 217/D1
Springer (lake), Ill. 222/E4
Springer, N. Mex. (87747) 274/E2
Springer, Okla. (73458) 288/M6
Springerton, Ill. (62887) 222/E5
Springerville, Ariz. (85938) 198/F4
Springfield, Ark. (72157) 202/E3
Springfield, Colo. (81073) 208/O8
Springfield, Fla. (32401) 212/D6
Springfield, Georgia (31329) 217/K6
Springfield, Idaho (83277) 220/F6
Springfield (cap.), Ill. 146/J6
Springfield (cap.), Ill. 188/H3
Springfield (cap.), Ill. (*62701) 222/D4
Springfield (lake), Ill. 222/D4
Springfield, Ind. (†47638) 227/B8
Springfield, Ky. (40069) 237/L5
Springfield, La. (70462) 238/M2
Springfield○, Maine (04487) 243/G5
Springfield, Mass. 188/M2
Springfield, Mass. (*01101) 249/D4
Springfield, Mich. (49015) 250/D6
Springfield, Minn. (56087) 255/C6
Springfield, Mo. (*65801) 261/F8
Springfield, Mo. 188/H3
Springfield, Mo. 146/J6
Springfield, Nebr. (68059) 264/H3
Springfield, King's, New Bruns. 170/E3
Springfield, York, New Bruns. 170/C2
Springfield○, N.H. (†03284) 268/C4
Springfield○, N.J. (07081) 273/E2
Springfield, Nova Scotia 168/D4
Springfield, Ohio 188/K2
Springfield, Ohio (*45501) 284/C6
Springfield, Ontario 177/C5
Springfield, Oreg. (97477) 291/E3
Springfield○, Pa. (19064) 294/M7
Springfield, Queensland 88/G5
Springfield, Queensland 95/B5
Springfield, S.C. (29146) 296/E4
Springfield, S. Dak. (57062) 298/N8
Springfield, Tenn. (37172) 237/H8
Springfield, Vt. (05156) 268/B5
Springfield○, Vt. (05156) 268/B5
Springfield, Va. (*22150) 307/S3
Springfield, W. Va. (26763) 312/J4
Springfield Armory Nat'l Hist. Site, Mass. 249/D4
Springford, Ontario 177/D5
Spring Garden, Ala. (36275) 195/G3
Spring Garden, Calif. (95971) 204/D4
Spring Garden, Ill. (†62846) 222/E5
Spring Green, Wis. (53588) 317/G9
Spring Grove, Ill. (60081) 222/E1
Spring Grove, Ind. (†47374) 227/H5
Spring Grove, Minn. (55974) 255/G7
Spring Grove, Pa. (17362) 294/J6
Spring Grove, Va. (23881) 307/P6
Spring Hall, Barbados 161/B8
Springhaven, Nova Scotia 168/C5
Spring Hill, Ark. (†71801) 202/C6
Spring Hill, Iowa (†50125) 229/F6
Spring Hill, Kansas (66083) 232/H3
Springhill, La. (71075) 238/D1
Spring Hill, Minn. (†56352) 255/D5
Springhill, Nova Scotia 168/E3
Spring Hill, Tenn. (37174) 237/H9
Springhill Junction, Nova Scotia 168/D3
Springhills, Ohio (†43357) 284/C5
Springholm, Scotland 15/E5
Spring Hope, N.C. (27882) 281/N3
Springhouse, Br. Col. 184/F4
Spring Lake, Ind. (†46140) 227/F5
Spring Lake, Mich. (49456) 250/C5
Spring Lake, Minn. (†55056) 255/E5
Spring Lake, Minn. (56680) 255/E3
Spring Lake, N.J. (07762) 273/F3
Spring Lake, N.C. (28390) 281/M4
Springlake, Texas (79082) 303/B3
Spring Lake, Wis. (†54960) 317/H8
Spring Lake Heights, N.J. (†07762) 273/E3
Spring Lake Park, Minn. (†55432) 255/E5
Springlee, Ky. (†40201) 237/K2
Spring Lick, Ky. (42779) 237/H6
Spring Mills, Pa. (16875) 294/G4
Spring Mills, S.C. (†29067) 296/F2
Spring Park, Minn. (55384) 255/F5
Spring Place, Georgia (†30705) 217/C1
Springport, Ind. (47386) 227/G4
Springport, Mich. (49284) 250/E6
Spring Ridge, La. (†71047) 238/B2
Springs, S. Africa 118/J6
Springside, Sask. 181/J4
Springstein, Manitoba 179/E5
Springsure, Queensland 95/D5
Springton (res.), Pa. 294/L6
Springtown, Ark. (72767) 202/B1
Springtown, Texas (76082) 303/G5
Springvale, Georgia (31788) 217/C7
Springvale, Maine (04083) 243/B9
Springvale, Victoria 88/L7
Springvale, Victoria 97/J5
Spring Valley, Ala. (†35674) 195/C1
Spring Valley, Ill. (61362) 222/D2
Spring Valley, Minn. (55975) 255/F7
Spring Valley, N.Y. (10977) 276/K8
Spring Valley, Ohio (45370) 284/C6
Spring Valley, Sask. 181/F6
Spring Valley, Texas (†77001) 303/J1
Spring Valley, Wis. (54767) 317/B6
Springview, Nebr. (68778) 264/E2
Springville, Ala. (35146) 195/E3
Springville, Calif. (93265) 204/G7
Springville, Ind. (47462) 227/D7
Springville, Iowa (52336) 229/L4
Springville, La. (†70754) 238/L2
Springville, Miss. (†38863) 256/F2
Springville, N.Y. (14141) 276/C5
Springville, Pa. (18844) 294/L2
Springville, Tenn. (38256) 237/E8
Springville, Utah (84663) 304/C3
Springwater, N.Y. (14560) 276/E5
Springwater, Sask. 181/C4
Springwood, Va. (†24066) 307/J5
Sproat Lake, Br. Col. 184/H3
Sprott, Ala. (36779) 195/D5
Sprowston, England 13/J5
Spruce (isl.), Manitoba 179/B1
Spruce, Mich. (48762) 250/F4
Spruce (mt.), Vt. 268/C3
Spruce Creek, Pa. (16683) 294/F4
Sprucedale, Ontario 177/E2
Spruce Grove, Alberta 182/D3
Spruce Home, Sask. 181/F2
Spruce Knob (mt.), W. Va. 312/G5
Spruce Knob-Seneca Rocks Nat'l Rec. Area, W. Va. 312/H5
Spruce Lake, Sask. 181/B2
Spruce Pine, Ala. (35585) 195/C2
Spruce Pine, N.C. (28777) 281/E3
Spruce Run (res.), N.J. 273/D2
Spruce View, Alberta 182/C3
Spruce Woods, Manitoba 179/C5
Spruce Woods Prov. Park, Manitoba 179/C5
Sprule, Ky. (40986) 237/O7
Spry (harb.), Nova Scotia 168/F4
Spry Harbour, Nova Scotia 168/F4
Spur, Texas (79370) 303/D4
Spurgeon, Ind. (47584) 227/C8
Spurlockville, W. Va. (25565) 312/B6
Spurn (head), England 13/H4
Spurn (head), England 10/G4
Spurr (mt.), Alaska 196/B1
Spur Tree, Jamaica 158/H6
Spuzzum, Br. Col. 184/G5
Spy (pond), Mass. 249/C6
Spy Hill, Sask. 181/K5
Squam (lake), N.H. 268/E4
Squamish, Br. Col. 184/F5
Squa Pan, Maine (†04732) 243/G2
Squa Pan (lake), Maine 243/G2
Square (lake), Maine 243/G1
Square Butte, Mont. (†59442) 262/F3
Square Islands, Newf. 166/C3
Squatec, Québec 172/J2
Squatec (lake), Québec 172/J2
Squaw (creek), Idaho 220/B5
Squaw (peak), Idaho 220/D4
Squaw (creek), Oreg. 291/F3
Squaw (creek), S. Dak. 298/B3
Squaw Harbor, Alaska (†99661) 196/F3
Squaw Lake, Minn. (56681) 255/D3
Squaw Rapids, Sask. 181/H2
Squibnocket (pt.), Mass. 249/M7
Squillace (gulf), Italy 34/F5
Squinzano, Italy 34/G4
Squire, W. Va. (24884) 312/C8
Squires, Mo. (65755) 261/G9
Squires Mem. Park, Newf. 166/C4
Squirrel, Idaho (83447) 220/G5
Sragen, Indonesia 85/J2
Sre Ambel, Cambodia 72/D5
Srebrenica, Yugoslavia 45/D3
Srednekolymsk, U.S.S.R. 4/C2
Srednekolymsk, U.S.S.R. 48/Q3
Sre Khtum, Cambodia 72/E4
Śrem, Poland 47/C2
Sremska Mitrovica, Yugoslavia 45/D3
Srepok (riv.), Cambodia 72/E4
Sretensk, U.S.S.R. 54/N4
Sretensk, U.S.S.R. 48/M4
Srikakulam, India 68/E5
Sri Lanka 54/K9
SRI LANKA (CEYLON) 68/E7
Srinagar, India 68/D2
Srinagar, India 54/J6
Srivardhan, India 68/C5
Środa Śląska, Poland 47/C3
Środa Wielkopolska, Poland 47/C2
Staaten (riv.), Queensland 88/G3
Staaten (riv.), Queensland 95/B3
Staatsburg, N.Y. (12580) 276/N7
Stab, Ky. (42557) 237/N6
Stacks (mts.), Ireland 17/B7
Stacy, Minn. (55079) 255/E5
Stacy, N.C. (28581) 281/S5
Stacy, Va. (24616) 307/E6
Stacyville, Iowa (50476) 229/H2
Stacyville, Maine (04782) 243/F4
Stacyville○, Maine (04782) 243/F4
Stade, W. Germany 22/C2
Staden, Belgium 27/B7
Stadskanaal, Netherlands 27/L3
Stadthagen, W. Germany 22/C2
Stäfa, Switzerland 39/G2
Staffa (isl.), Scotland 15/B4
Staffelstein, W. Germany 22/D3
Staffhorst, W. Germany 22/C2
Stafford○, Conn. (06075) 210/F1
Stafford, England 10/G2
Stafford, England 13/E5
Stafford (lake), Fla. 212/D2
Stafford (co.), Kansas 232/D3
Stafford, Kansas (67578) 232/D4
Stafford, N.Y. (14143) 276/D5
Stafford, Ohio (43786) 284/H6
Stafford, Okla. (†73601) 288/H3
Stafford, Queensland 88/K2
Stafford, Queensland 95/D2
Stafford, Texas (77477) 303/J2
Stafford (co.), Va. 307/O4
Stafford, Va. (22554) 307/O4
Staffordshire (co.), England 13/E5
Stafford Springs, Conn. (06076) 210/F1
Staffordsville, Ky. (41256) 237/R5
Staffordville, Conn. (06077) 210/G1
Staffordville, N.J. (†08092) 273/E4
Staines (pen.), Chile 138/D9
Staines, England 10/B5
Staines, England 13/G8
Stainville, Tenn. (†37710) 237/N8
Staked (Llano Estacado) (plain), N. Mex. 274/F5
Staked (Llano Estacado) (plain), Texas 303/B4
Stakhanov, U.S.S.R. 52/E5
Stalden, Switzerland 39/E4
Staley, N.C. (27355) 281/K3
Stalham, England 13/J5
Stalheim, Norway 18/E6
Stalin, Albania 45/D5
Stalingrad (Volgograd), U.S.S.R. 7/J4
Stalingrad (Volgograd), U.S.S.R. 48/E5
Stalingrad (Volgograd), U.S.S.R. 52/F5
Stallings, N.C. (†28079) 281/H4
Stallo, Miss. (†39350) 256/F5
Stallworthy (cape), N.W. Terrs. 187/J1
Stalowa Wola, Poland 47/F3
Stalwart, Mich. (49789) 250/E2
Stalwart, Sask. 181/F4
Stambaugh, Mich. (49964) 250/G2
Stamford, Conn. (*06901) 210/A4
Stamford, England 13/G5
Stamford, England 10/F4
Stamford, Nebr. (68977) 264/E4
Stamford, N.Y. (12167) 276/L6
Stamford, Queensland 88/G4
Stamford, Texas (79553) 303/E5
Stamford (lake), Texas 303/E4
Stamford○, Vt. (05352) 268/A6
Stampa, Switzerland 39/J4
Stamping Ground, Ky. (40379) 237/M4
Stampriet, Namibia 118/B4
Stamps, Ark. (71860) 202/D7
Stanardsville, Va. (22973) 307/L4
Stanberry, Mo. (64489) 261/C2
Stanbridge-Est, Québec 172/D4
Stanchfield, Minn. (55080) 255/E5
Standard, Alberta 182/D4
Standard, Calif. (95373) 204/E6
Standard, Ill. (61363) 222/D2
Standard, La. (†71465) 238/F3
Standard City, Ill. (62686) 222/D4
Standerton, S. Africa 118/D5
Standfast (pt.), Ant. & Bar. 161/E11
Standing Rock, Ala. (36878) 195/H4
Standing Rock Ind. Res., N. Dak. 282/J7
Standish, Calif. (96128) 204/E3
Standish, Maine (04084) 243/B8
Standish○, Maine (04084) 243/B8
Standish, Mich. (48658) 250/F5
Standish-with-Langtree, England 13/G2
Stand Off, Alberta 182/D5
Stanfield, Ariz. (85272) 198/C6
Stanfield, N.C. (28163) 281/J4
Stanfield, Oreg. (97875) 291/H2
Stanford, Calif. (94305) 204/J3
Stanford, Ill. (61774) 222/D3
Stanford, Ind. (47463) 227/D6
Stanford, Ky. (40484) 237/M5
Stanford, Mont. (59479) 262/F3
Stanfordville, N.Y. (12581) 276/N7
Stangelville, Wis. (†54208) 317/L7
Stanger, S. Africa 118/E5
Stanhope, England 13/E3
Stanhope, Iowa (50246) 229/F4
Stanhope, N.J. (07874) 273/D2
Stanhope, Pr. Edward I. 168/E2
Stanhope, Québec 172/F4
Stanislaus (co.), Calif. 204/D6
Stanke Dimitrov, Bulgaria 45/F4
Stanley, England 13/H3
Stanley (cap.), Falk. Is. 120/D8
Stanley (cap.), Falk. Is. 143/E7
Stanley, Idaho (83278) 220/D5
Stanley, Iowa (50671) 229/K3
Stanley, Kansas (†66223) 232/H3
Stanley, Ky. (42375) 237/G5
Stanley, La. (†71049) 238/C3
Stanley, New Bruns. 170/D2
Stanley, N. Mex. (87056) 274/D3
Stanley, N.Y. (14561) 276/F5
Stanley, N.C. (28164) 281/G4
Stanley, N. Dak. (58784) 282/F3
Stanley (mt.), North. Terr. 93/B7
Stanley, Nova Scotia 168/E3
Stanley, Okla. (†74536) 288/R5
Stanley, Scotland 15/E4
Stanley (co.), S. Dak. 298/H5
Stanley, Tasmania 99/B2
Stanley (mt.), Tasmania 99/A1
Stanley, Va. (22851) 307/L3
Stanley, Wis. (54768) 317/E6
Stanley (falls), Zaire 102/E5
Stanley (falls), Zaire 115/D3
Stanley Pool (lake), Zaire 115/C4
Stanleytown, Va. (24168) 307/H7
Stanleyville, N.C. (†27045) 281/J2
Stanly (co.), N.C. 281/J4
Stanmore, Alberta 182/E4
Stannards, N.Y. (†14895) 276/E6
Stann Creek Town, Belize 154/C2
Stanovoy (range), U.S.S.R. 54/O4
Stanovoy (range), U.S.S.R. 48/N4
Stans, Switzerland 39/F3
Stanstead (co.), Québec 172/F4
Stanstead Plain, Québec 172/F4
Stanthorpe, Queensland 88/J5
Stanthorpe, Queensland 95/D6
Stanton, Ala. (36790) 195/E5
Stanton, Calif. (90680) 204/D11
Stanton, England 13/H5
Stanton, Iowa (51573) 229/C7
Stanton (co.), Kansas 232/A4
Stanton, Ky. (40380) 237/O5
Stanton, Mich. (48888) 250/D5
Stanton, Miss. (†39120) 256/B7
Stanton, Mo. (63079) 261/K6
Stanton (co.), Nebr. 264/G3
Stanton, Nebr. (68779) 264/G3
Stanton, N.J. (08885) 273/D2
Stanton, N. Dak. (58571) 282/H5
Stanton, Tenn. (38069) 237/C10
Stanton, Texas (79782) 303/C5
Stantonsburg, N.C. (27883) 281/O3
Stantonville, Tenn. (38379) 237/E10
Stanwood, Iowa (52337) 229/L5
Stanwood, Mich. (49346) 250/D5
Stanwood, Wash. (98292) 310/C2
Stanzel, Iowa (†50849) 229/E6
Staphorst, Netherlands 27/J3
Staplehurst, Nebr. (68439) 264/G4
Staples, Minn. (56479) 255/D4
Staples, Ontario 177/B5
Stapleton, Ala. (36578) 195/C9
Stapleton, Georgia (30823) 217/H4
Stapleton, Nebr. (69163) 264/D3
Stapylton (bay), N.W. Terrs. 187/G3
Star, Alberta 182/D3
Star, Idaho (83669) 220/B6
Star (lake), Minn. 255/C4
Star, Miss. (39167) 256/D6
Star, N.C. (27356) 281/K4
Star, Texas (76880) 303/F6
Starachowice, Poland 47/E3
Stará L'ubovňa, Czech. 41/F2
Staraya Russa, U.S.S.R. 52/D3
Stara Zagora, Bulgaria 7/G4
Stara Zagora, Bulgaria 45/G4
Starbuck (isl.), Kiribati 87/L6
Starbuck, Manitoba 179/E5
Starbuck, Minn. (56381) 255/C5
Starbuck, Wash. (99359) 310/G4
Star City, Ark. (71667) 202/G6
Star City, Ind. (46985) 227/D3
Star City, Sask. 181/G3
Star City, W. Va. (26505) 312/F3
Staré Město, Czech. 41/D2
Stargard Szczeciński, Poland 47/B2
Stargo, Ariz. (†85540) 198/F5
Starhill, La. (†70748) 238/H5
Stark (co.), Ill. 222/D2
Stark, Kansas (66775) 232/G4
Stark, Minn. (†55032) 255/E5
Stark, Mont. (†59846) 262/B3
Stark○, N.H. (†03582) 268/E2
Stark (co.), N. Dak. 282/E6
Stark (co.), Ohio 284/H4
Stark City, Mo. (64866) 261/D9
Starke, Fla. (32091) 212/D2
Starke (co.), Ind. 227/D2
Starkey, Oreg. (†97850) 291/J2
Star Keys (isls.), N. Zealand 100/E7
Starks, La. (70661) 238/C6
Starks○, Maine (†04980) 243/D6
Starks, Wis. (†54501) 317/H4
Starksboro○, Vt. (05487) 268/A3
Starkville, Colo. (81074) 208/L8
Starkville, Miss. (39759) 256/G4
Starkweather, N. Dak. (58377) 282/N3
Star Lake, N.Y. (13690) 276/K2
Star Lake, Wis. (54561) 317/G3
Starlight, Ind. (†47119) 227/F8
Starnberg, W. Germany 22/D4
Starnbergersee (lake), W. Germany 22/D5
Starodub, U.S.S.R. 52/D4
Starogard Gdański, Poland 47/D2

Surfside Beach 453

Strong (riv.), Miss. 256/D7
Strong City, Kansas (66869) 232/F3
Strong City, Okla. (73665) 288/G3
Strongfield, Sask. 181/E4
Stronghurst, Ill. (61480) 222/C3
Strongs, Mich. (49790) 250/E2
Strongs, Miss. (†39730) 256/G3
Strongsville, Ohio (44136) 284/G10
Stronsay (firth), Scotland 15/F1
Stronsay (isl.), Scotland 10/E1
Stronsay (isl.), Scotland 15/F1
Strontian, Scotland 15/C4
Stropkov, Czech. 41/F2
Stroud, Ala. (†36855) 195/H4
Stroud, England 13/E6
Stroud, England 10/E5
Stroud, N.S. Wales 97/G3
Stroud, Okla. (74079) 288/N3
Stroud, Ontario 177/E3
Stroudsburg, Pa. (18360) 294/M4
Struan, Sask. 181/D3
Struan, Scotland 15/B3
Struble, Iowa (51057) 229/A3
Struer, Denmark 21/B5
Struer, Denmark 18/F8
Struga, Yugoslavia 45/E5
Strum, Wis. (54770) 317/D6
Struma (riv.), Bulgaria 45/F5
Strumble (head), Wales 13/B5
Strumica, Yugoslavia 45/F5
Strunk, Ky. (42649) 237/N7
Struthers, Ohio (44471) 284/J3
Stryker, Mont. (59933) 262/B2
Stryker, Ohio (43557) 284/B3
Strykersville, N.Y. (14145) 276/C5
Strzegom, Poland 47/C3
Strzelce Krajeńskie, Poland 47/B2
Strzelce Opolskie, Poland 47/D3
Strzelecki (creek), S. Australia 88/G5
Strzelecki (creek), S. Australia 94/G3
Strzelecki (mt.), Tasmania 99/D2
Strzelin, Poland 47/C3
Strzelno, Poland 47/D2
Strzyzów, Poland 47/E4
Stuart (isl.), Alaska 196/F2
Stuart (lake), Br. Col. 184/E3
Stuart, Fla. (33494) 212/F4
Stuart, Iowa (50250) 229/E6
Stuart, Nebr. (68780) 264/E2
Stuart, Okla. (74570) 288/O5
Stuart (range), S. Australia 94/D3
Stuart, Va. (24171) 307/H7
Stuart (mt.), Wash. 310/E3
Stuartburn, Manitoba 179/F5
Stuart Island, Br. Col. 184/E5
Stuarts Draft, Va. (24477) 307/L4
Stuart Town, N.S. Wales 97/E3
Stubbekøbing, Denmark 21/F8
Stubbenkammer (pt.), E. Germany 22/E1
Stub Hill (mt.), N.H. 268/E1
Stuckey, S.C. (29554) 296/H4
Studénka, Czech. 41/D2
Studley, Kansas (67759) 232/B2
Studley, Va. (23162) 307/O5
Stukely-Sud, Québec 172/E4
Stump (lake), N. Dak. 282/O4
Stumptown, W. Va. (25280) 312/E5
Stumpy Point, N.C. (27978) 281/T3
Stupino, U.S.S.R. 52/E4
Stura (riv.), Italy 34/A2
Sturbridge, Mass. (01566) 249/F4
Sturbridge○, Mass. (01566) 249/F4
Sturdivant, Mo. (63782) 261/M8
Sturgeon (lake), Alberta 182/B2
Sturgeon (bay), Manitoba 179/E3
Sturgeon (riv.), Mich. 250/C2
Sturgeon (riv.), Minn. 255/F3
Sturgeon, Mo. (65284) 261/H4
Sturgeon (lake), Ontario 177/G5
Sturgeon, Pa. (15082) 294/B5
Sturgeon, Pr. Edward I. 168/F2
Sturgeon (riv.), Sask. 181/E2
Sturgeon Bay, Wis. (54235) 317/M6
Sturgeon Falls, Ont. 162/H6
Sturgeon Falls, Ontario 175/E3
Sturgeon Falls, Ontario 177/E1
Sturgeon Heights, Alberta 182/B2
Sturgeon Lake, Minn. (55783) 255/F4
Sturgeon Point, Ontario 177/F3
Sturgeon Weir, Sask. 181/N4
Sturgis, Ky. (42459) 237/F5
Sturgis, Mich. (49091) 250/D7
Sturgis, Miss. (39769) 256/G4
Sturgis, Sask. 181/J4
Sturgis, S. Dak. (57785) 298/B5
Štúrovo, Czech. 41/E3
Sturt (mt.), N.S. Wales 97/A1
Sturt (plain), North. Terr. 93/C4
Sturt (des.), Queensland 88/G5
Sturt (des.), Queensland 95/B3
Sturt (riv.), S. Australia 88/D8
Sturt (des.), S. Australia 94/G3
Sturt (riv.), S. Australia 94/B8
Sturt (creek), W. Australia 88/D3
Sturt (creek), W. Australia 92/D2
Sturtevant, Wis. (53177) 317/M3
Stutsman (co.), N. Dak. 282/M5
Stutterheim, S. Africa 118/D6
Stuttgart, Ark. (72160) 202/H4
Stuttgart, Kansas (67670) 232/C2
Stuttgart, W. Germany 7/E4
Stuttgart, W. Germany 22/C4
Styria (prov.), Austria 41/C3
Suai, Malaysia 85/E5
Suakin, Sudan 102/F3
Suakin, Sudan 59/C6
Suakin, Sudan 111/G4
Suakin (arch.), Sudan 111/G4
Suamico, Wis. (54173) 317/K6
Suao, China 77/K7
Suapi, Bolivia 136/B4
Suapure (riv.), Venezuela 124/E4
Suaqui, Mexico 150/E2
Suárez (riv.), Colombia 126/D4
Subang, Indonesia 85/H2
Subata, U.S.S.R. 53/D2
Subei, China 77/E4
Subeihi, Jordan 65/D3
Subh, Jebel (mt.), Saudi Arabia 59/C5
Subiaco, Ark. (72865) 202/C3
Subiaco, W. Australia 88/B2
Subi Besar (isl.), Indonesia 85/D5
Subic (bay), Philippines 82/C3
Sublett (mts.), Idaho 220/E7
Sublett, Ky. (41470) 237/P5
Sublette, Ill. (61367) 222/D2
Sublette, Kansas (67877) 232/B4
Sublette, Mo. (†63546) 261/G2
Sublette (co.), Wyo. 319/C3
Subligna, Georgia (†30747) 217/B1
Sublimity, Oreg. (97385) 291/E3
Subotica, Yugoslavia 7/F4
Subotica, Yugoslavia 45/D2
Subtle, Ky. (42129) 237/L7
Sucarnochee, Miss. (†39352) 256/H5
Sucarnoochee (creek), Miss. 256/G5
Succasunna, N.J. (07876) 273/D2
Success, Ark. (72470) 202/J1
Success, Mo. (65570) 261/H8
Success, Sask. 181/D5
Succor (creek), Oreg. 291/K4
Suceava, Romania 45/G2
Suchedniów, Poland 47/E3
Suches, Bolivia 136/A4
Suches (riv.), Bolivia 136/A4
Suches, Georgia (30572) 217/E1
Suchitoto, El Salvador 154/C4
Süchow (Xuzhou), China 77/J5
Sucia (bay), P. Rico 161/A3
Sucia (isl.), Wash. 310/C2
Sucio (riv.), Colombia 126/B4
Suck (riv.), Ireland 17/E5
Sucre (cap.), Bolivia 2/F6
Sucre (cap.), Bolivia 120/C4
Sucre (cap.), Bolivia 136/C6
Sucre (dept.), Colombia 126/C3
Sucre, Bolívar, Colombia 126/C3
Sucre, Caquetá, Colombia 126/C7
Sucre, Ecuador 128/B3
Sucre (state), Venezuela 124/G2
Sucre, Venezuela 124/D3
Sucúa, Ecuador 128/C4
Sucuriju, Brazil 132/D2
Sud (dept.), Haiti 158/A6
Sud (chan.), Haiti 158/B6
Suda (riv.), U.S.S.R. 52/E3
Sudak, U.S.S.R. 52/E6
Sudan 2/L5
Sudan 102/E3
SUDAN 111/E4
SUDAN 59/B6
Sudan (reg.) 102/D3
Sudan (reg.), Benin 106/E6
Sudan (reg.), Chad 111/C5
Sudan (reg.), Mali 106/D6
Sudan (reg.), Niger 106/F6
Sudan (reg.), Nigeria 106/F6
Sudan (reg.), Sudan 111/E5
Sudan, Texas (79371) 303/B3
Sudan (reg.), Upper Volta 106/D6
Sudbury, England 10/G4
Sudbury, England 13/H5
Sudbury○, Mass. (01776) 249/A6
Sudbury (res.), Mass. 249/H3
Sudbury (riv.), Mass. 249/A6
Sudbury, Ont. 162/H6
Sudbury, Ont. 146/K5
Sudbury (reg. munic.), Ontario 175/D3
Sudbury (terr. dist.), Ontario 175/D3
Sudbury (terr. dist.), Ontario 177/J5
Sudbury (reg. munic.), Ontario 177/K6
Sudbury, Ontario 177/K5
Sudbury, Ontario 175/D3
Sudbury○, Vt. (†05733) 268/A4
Sudd (swamp), Sudan 102/F4
Sudd (swamp), Sudan 111/F6
Suddie, Guyana 131/B2
Sudeten (mts.), Czech. 41/C1
Sudeten (range), Poland 47/B3
Suduroy (isl.), Denmark 21/B3
Sudirman (range), Indonesia 85/K6
Sudith, Ky. (40381) 237/O4
Sudlersville, Md. (21668) 245/P4
Sue (riv.), Sudan 111/E6
Sueca, Spain 33/F3
Suemez (isl.), Alaska 196/M2
Suez (canal) 2/L4
Suez, Egypt 111/K3
Suez, Egypt 59/B4
Suez, Egypt 102/F2
Suez (canal), Egypt 102/F1
Suez (canal), Egypt 111/K3
Suez (canal), Egypt 59/B3
Suez (gulf), Egypt 111/F2
Suez (gulf), Egypt 59/B4
Suf, Jordan 65/D3
Sufeina, Saudi Arabia 59/D5
Sufers, Switzerland 39/H3
Suffern, N.Y. (10901) 276/J8
Suffield, Alberta 182/E4
Suffield, Conn. (06078) 210/E1
Suffield○, Conn. (06078) 210/E1
Suffield, Ohio (†44260) 284/H3
Suffolk (co.), England 13/H5
Suffolk (co.), Mass. 249/K3
Suffolk, Mont. (†59451) 262/G3
Suffolk (co.), N.Y. 276/P9
Suffolk (I.C.), Va. (*23432) 307/P7
Sufian, Iran 66/E1
Sugar (creek), Ind. 227/B3
Sugar (creek), Ind. 227/F5
Sugar (creek), Ind. 227/C5
Sugar (isl.), Mich. 250/E2
Sugar (riv.), N.H. 268/C5
Sugar (creek), Pa. 294/J2
Sugar (riv.), Wis. 317/H10
Sugar Bush, Wis. (†54961) 317/J7
Sugarbush Hill (mt.), Wis. 317/J4
Sugar City, Colo. (81076) 208/M6
Sugar City, Idaho (83448) 220/G6
Sugar Creek, Mo. (64054) 261/R5
Sugarcreek, Ohio (44681) 284/G5
Sugar Creek, Pa. (†16323) 294/C3
Sugar Grove, Ark. (†72927) 202/C3
Sugar Grove, Ill. (60554) 222/E2
Sugar Grove, Ohio (43155) 284/E6
Sugargrove, Pa. (16350) 294/D1
Sugar Grove, Va. (24375) 307/E7
Sugar Grove, W. Va. (26815) 312/H5
Sugar Hill, Georgia (†30518) 217/E2
Sugar Hill○, N.H. (03585) 268/D3
Sugar Island, Mich. (†49783) 250/E2
Sugar Land, Texas (77478) 303/J8
Sugarloaf (key), Fla. 212/E7
Sugarloaf (hill), Hawaii 218/C4
Sugarloaf (mt.), Ireland 17/B8
Sugarloaf (pt.), N. S. Wales 88/J6
Sugarloaf (passage), N.S. Wales 97/J1
Sugarloaf (pt.), N.S. Wales 97/G3
Sugarloaf P.O. (Big Bear City), Calif. (92314) 204/J9
Sugar Notch, Pa. (18706) 294/E7
Sugartown, La. (70662) 238/D5
Sugar Tree, Tenn. (38380) 237/E9
Sugar Tree Ridge, Ohio (45133) 284/C7
Sugar Valley, Georgia (30746) 217/C1
Sugbai (passage), Philippines 82/C8
Sugden, Okla. (†73565) 288/L6
Suggsville, Ala. (†36482) 195/C7
Sühbaatar, Mongolia 77/H2
Sühbaatar (Sukhe Bator), Mongolia 77/G1
Sühbaatar, Mongolia 54/M5
Suheli Par (atoll), India 68/C6
Suhl (dist.), E. Germany 22/D3
Suhl, E. Germany 22/D3
Suhr, Switzerland 39/F2
Şuhut, Turkey 63/D3
Sui, Pakistan 68/B3
Suiattle (riv.), Wash. 310/D2
Suichang, China 77/J6
Suide, China 77/G4
Suifenhe, China 77/M3
Suihua, China 77/L2
Suijiang, China 77/F6
Suileng, China 77/L2
Suining, China 77/G5
Suipacha, Argentina 143/G7
Suipacha, Bolivia 136/C7
Suir (riv.), Ireland 10/C4
Suir (riv.), Ireland 17/G7
Suisun (bay), Calif. 204/K1
Suisun City, Calif. (94585) 204/K1
Suit, N.C. (28906) 281/A4
Suita, Japan 81/J7
Suitland-Silver Hill, Md. (†20746) 245/F5
Sui Xian, China 77/H5
Suizhong, China 77/K3
Sukabumi, Indonesia 85/H2
Sukadana, Indonesia 85/E6
Sukagawa, Japan 81/K5
Sukhana, U.S.S.R. 48/M3
Sukhinichi, U.S.S.R. 52/E4
Sukhona (riv.), U.S.S.R. 52/F2
Sukhothai, Thailand 72/D3
Sukhumi, U.S.S.R. 7/H4
Sukhumi, U.S.S.R. 52/F6
Sukhumi, U.S.S.R. 48/D5
Suk, Sudan 111/F5
Sukkertoppen, Greenl. 4/C12
Sukkur, Pakistan 54/H7
Sukkur, Pakistan 59/J4
Sukkur, Pakistan 68/B3
Sükösd, Hungary 41/E3
Sukumo, Japan 81/F7
Sul (chan.), Brazil 120/E2
Sul (chan.), Brazil 132/D2
Sula (isls.), Indonesia 54/O10
Sula (isls.), Indonesia 85/H6
Sula, Mont. (59871) 262/B5
Sulaco, Honduras 154/D3
Sulaco (riv.), Honduras 154/D3
Sulaiman (range), Pakistan 68/C3
Sulaimaniya (gov.), Iraq 66/D3
Sulaimaniya, Iraq 59/E2
Sulaimaniya, Iraq 66/D3
Sulaiyil, Saudi Arabia 59/E5
Sulakyurt, Turkey 63/E2
Sulanheer, Mongolia 77/G3
Sulawesi (isl.), Indonesia 85/G6
Sulechów, Poland 47/B2
Sulęcin, Poland 47/B2
Sulgen, Switzerland 39/H1
Sulina, Romania 45/J3
Sulitelma (mt.), Sweden 18/K3
Sulitjelma, Norway 18/K3
Sulitjelma (mt.), Norway 18/J3
Sullana, Peru 128/B5
Sullana, Peru 120/A3
Sulligent, Ala. (35586) 195/B3
Sullivan (lake), Alberta 182/D3
Sullivan, Ill. (61951) 222/E4
Sullivan (co.), Ind. 227/C6
Sullivan, Ind. (47882) 227/C6
Sullivan, Ky. (42460) 237/E6
Sullivan, Maine (†04689) 243/G6
Sullivan○, Maine (†04689) 243/G6
Sullivan (co.), Mo. 261/F2
Sullivan, Mo. (63080) 261/K6
Sullivan (co.), N.H. 268/C5
Sullivan○, N.H. (†03445) 268/C5
Sullivan (co.), N.Y. 276/L7
Sullivan, Ohio (44880) 284/F3
Sullivan (co.), Pa. 294/J3
Sullivan (co.), Tenn. 237/S7
Sullivan (lake), Wash. 310/H2
Sullivan, W. Va. (†25847) 312/D7
Sullivan, Wis. (53178) 317/H1
Sullivan Gardens, Tenn. (†37660) 237/R8
Sullivan Mines, Québec 174/B3
Sullivans Island, S.C. (29482) 296/H6
Sully, Iowa (50251) 229/H5
Sully, Québec 172/H2
Sully (co.), S. Dak. 298/H4
Sulmona, Italy 34/D3
Sulphide, Ontario 177/G3
Sulphur (riv.), Ark. 202/B7
Sulphur, Ind. (47174) 227/E8
Sulphur, Ky. (40070) 237/L4
Sulphur, La. (70663) 238/D6
Sulphur, Nev. (†89445) 266/C2
Sulphur, Okla. (73086) 288/N5
Sulphur (creek), S. Dak. 298/D4
Sulphur (riv.), Texas 303/J4
Sulphur City, Ark. (†72701) 202/B2
Sulphur Creek, Tasmania 99/C3
Sulphur Draw (dry riv.), Texas 303/B4
Sulphur Fork, Red (riv.), Tenn. 237/H8
Sulphur Rock, Ark. (72579) 202/H2
Sulphur Spring (valley), Ariz. 198/F6
Sulphur Spring (range), Nev. 266/E3
Sulphur Springs, Ala. (†30738) 195/G1
Sulphur Springs, Ark. (72768) 202/B1
Sulphur Springs, Ind. (47388) 227/G4
Sulphur Springs, Iowa (†50588) 229/C3
Sulphur Springs, Mo. (63083) 261/M6
Sulphur Springs, Ohio (44881) 284/E4
Sulphur Springs, Texas (75482) 303/J4
Sulphur Springs (creek), Texas 303/B4
Sulphur Well, Ky. (42129) 237/K6
Sultan, Ontario 175/D3
Sultan, Ontario 177/J5
Sultan (mts.), Turkey 63/D3
Sultan, Wash. (98294) 310/D3
Sultan (riv.), Wash. 310/D3
Sultanabad (Kashmar), Iran 66/L3
Sultandağı, Turkey 63/D3
Sultanhanı, Turkey 63/E3
Sultan Kudarat (prov.), Philippines 82/E7
Sulu (prov.), Philippines 82/C7
Sulu (arch.), Philippines 54/O9
Sulu (sea), Philippines 54/N9
Sulu (arch.), Philippines 82/B8
Sulu (arch.), Philippines 85/G4
Sulu (sea), Philippines 85/G4
Sulu (sea), Philippines 82/B6
Suluan (isl.), Philippines 82/F5
Suluova, Turkey 63/F2
Sulz, Switzerland 39/F1
Sulzbach, W. Germany 22/B4
Sulzbach-Rosenberg, W. Germany 22/D4
Sulzberger (bay) 5/B11
Sulzflüh (mt.), Switzerland 39/J2
Sumami Auma, Brazil 132/B4
Sumampa, Argentina 143/D2
Sumas, Wash. (98295) 310/C2
Sumatra, Fla. (32335) 212/B1
Sumatra (isl.), Indonesia 2/P6
Sumatra (isl.), Indonesia 54/L9
Sumatra (isl.), Indonesia 85/B5
Sumatra, Mont. (59083) 262/J4
Sumava Resorts, Ind. (46379) 227/C2
Sumba (isl.), Indonesia 54/N11
Sumba (isl.), Indonesia 85/F7
Sumba (str.), Indonesia 85/F7
Sumbawa (isl.), Indonesia 54/N11
Sumbawa (isl.), Indonesia 85/F7
Sumbawa Besar, Indonesia 85/F7
Sumbawanga, Tanzania 115/F5
Sumbay, Peru 128/G10
Sumbilca, Peru 128/D8
Sumbing (mt.), Indonesia 85/J2
Sumburgh (head), Scotland 15/G2
Sumedang, Indonesia 85/H2
Sümeg, Hungary 41/D3
Sumenep, Indonesia 85/L2
Sumgait, U.S.S.R. 7/J4
Sumgait, U.S.S.R. 52/G6
Sumidero, Cuba 158/A2
Sumiswald, Switzerland 39/E2
Sumiton, Ala. (35148) 195/D3
Summan (plat.), Saudi Arabia 59/E4
Summer (isl.), Mich. 250/C3
Summer (lake), Oreg. 188/C2
Summer (lake), Oreg. 291/G5
Summerberry, Sask. 181/J5
Summerdale, Ala. (36580) 195/C10
Summerfield, Ala. (†36701) 195/E5
Summerfield, Fla. (32691) 212/D2
Summerfield, Ill. (62289) 222/D5
Summerfield, Kansas (66541) 232/F2
Summerfield, La. (71079) 238/E1
Summerfield, Mo. (†65013) 261/J6
Summerfield, N.C. (27358) 281/K2
Summerfield, Ohio (43788) 284/H6
Summerfield, Okla. (74966) 288/S5
Summerfield, Texas (79085) 303/B3
Summerford, Newf. 166/C4
Summerford, Ohio (†43140) 284/D6
Summer Hill, Ill. (62372) 222/C4
Summerhill, Pa. (15958) 294/E5
Summer Isles (isls.), Scotland 15/C2
Summer Lake, Oreg. (97640) 291/G5
Summerland, Br. Col. 184/G5
Summerland, Calif. (93067) 204/F9
Summerland, Miss. (†39168) 256/F7
Summerland Key, Fla. (33042) 212/E7
Summers, Ark. (72769) 202/A2
Summers (co.), W. Va. 312/E7
Summerset, Iowa (†50125) 229/F6
Summer Shade, Ky. (42166) 237/K7
Summerside, Pr. Edward I. 168/E2
Summersville, Ky. (42782) 237/K6
Summersville, Mo. (65571) 261/J8
Summersville, Ohio (†43344) 284/D5
Summersville, W. Va. (26651) 312/E6
Summersville (lake), W. Va. 312/E6
Summerton, S.C. (29148) 296/G4
Summertown, Georgia (30466) 217/H5
Summertown, Tenn. (38483) 237/G10
Summerville, Georgia (30747) 217/B2
Summerville, La. (†71465) 238/F3
Summerville, Newf. 166/D2
Summerville, Oreg. (97876) 291/K2
Summerville, Pa. (15864) 294/D3
Summerville, S.C. (29483) 296/G5
Summerville Centre, Nova Scotia 168/D5
Summit, Ala. (†35031) 195/F2
Summit, Alaska (†99729) 196/J2
Summit, Ark. (72677) 202/E1
Summit (co.), Colo. 208/G3
Summit (peak), Colo. 208/F8
Summit (lake), Iowa 229/E6
Summit, Miss. (39666) 256/D8
Summit (lake), Nev. 266/C1
Summit, N.J. (07901) 273/E2
Summit (co.), Ohio 284/G3
Summit (creek), Oreg. 291/J3
Summit, Québec 172/E2
Summit, R.I. (†02827) 249/H6
Summit, S.C. (†29054) 296/E4
Summit, S. Dak. (57266) 298/P3
Summit (co.), Utah 304/D3
Summit, Utah (84772) 304/B6
Summit-Argo, Ill. (60501) 222/B6
Summit Bridge, Del. (†19709) 245/R2
Summit City, Calif. (96089) 204/C3
Summit City, Mich. (†49649) 250/D4
Summit Hill, Pa. (18250) 294/L4
Summit Lake, Wis. (54485) 317/M5
Summit Lake Ind. Res., Nev. 266/B1
Summit Point, W. Va. (25446) 312/K4
Summitville, Ind. (46070) 227/F4
Summitville, Iowa (†52632) 229/K8
Summitville, N.Y. (12781) 276/L7
Summitville, Ohio (43962) 284/J4
Summitville, Tenn. (37382) 237/K9
Summum, Ill. (†61501) 222/C3
Sumner (str.), Alaska 196/M2
Sumner, Georgia (31789) 217/E7
Sumner, Ill. (62466) 222/F5
Sumner, Iowa (50674) 229/J3
Sumner (co.), Kansas 232/E4
Sumner○, Maine (†04292) 243/C7
Sumner, Mich. (48889) 250/E5
Sumner, Miss. (38957) 256/D3
Sumner, Mo. (64681) 261/F3
Sumner, Nebr. (68878) 264/E4
Sumner (dam), N. Mex. 274/E4
Sumner (lake), N. Mex. 274/E4
Sumner (lake), N. Zealand 100/D5
Sumner, Oreg. (†97420) 291/C4
Sumner (co.), Tenn. 237/J8
Sumner, Wash. (98390) 310/C3
Sumner-East Sumner, Maine (04232) 243/C7
Sumoto, Japan 81/G6
Šumperk, Czech. 41/D1
Sumprabum, Burma 72/C1
Sumpter, Ark. (†71647) 202/F7
Sumpter, Oreg. (97877) 291/J3
Sumrall, Miss. (39482) 256/E8
Sumter (co.), Ala. 195/B5
Sumter, Ala. (†35086) 195/D4
Sumter (co.), Fla. 212/D3
Sumter (co.), Georgia 217/D6
Sumter (co.), S.C. 296/G4
Sumter, S.C. (29150) 296/G4
Sumterville, Ala. (†35460) 195/B5
Sumy, U.S.S.R. 7/H3
Sumy, U.S.S.R. 52/E4
Sumy, U.S.S.R. 48/D4
Sun, La. (70463) 238/L5
Sun (riv.), Mont. 262/D3
Sunagawa, Japan 81/K2
Sunapee○, N.H. (03782) 268/C5
Sunapee (lake), N.H. 268/C5
Sunart, Loch (inlet), Scotland 15/C4
Sunbeam, Colo. (†81640) 208/C1
Sunbeam, Idaho (†83278) 220/D5
Sunbright, Tenn. (37872) 237/M8
Sunburg, Minn. (56289) 255/C5
Sunburst, Mont. (59482) 262/E2
Sunbury, Iowa (†52778) 229/M5
Sunbury (co.), New Bruns. 170/D3
Sunbury, N.C. (27979) 281/R2
Sunbury, Ohio (43074) 284/E5
Sunbury, Pa. (17801) 294/J4
Sunbury, Victoria 97/C5
Sunbury-on-Thames, England 13/G8
Sunbury-on-Thames, England 10/B6
Sunchales, Argentina 143/F5
Suncho Corral, Argentina 143/D2
Sunch'ŏn, N. Korea 81/B4
Sunch'ŏn, S. Korea 81/C6
Sun City, Ariz. (*85351) 198/C5
Sun City, Calif. (92381) 204/F11
Sun City, Fla. (33586) 212/D4
Sun City, Kansas (67143) 232/D4
Sun City Center, Fla. (†33570) 212/C3
Suncook, N.H. (03275) 268/D5
Suncook (lakes), N.H. 268/E5
Suncook (riv.), N.H. 268/E5
Sunda (isls.), Indonesia 54/L10
Sunda (str.), Indonesia 54/M10
Sunda (str.), Indonesia 85/C7
Sundahl, Minn. (†56545) 255/B3
Sundance, Wyo. (82729) 319/H1
Sundarbans (reg.), Bangladesh 68/F4
Sundarbans (reg.), India 68/F4
Sundargarh, India 68/E4
Sunday (riv.), Maine 243/B6
Sundbyberg, Sweden 18/G1
Sunderland, England 13/J3
Sunderland, England 10/F3
Sunderland○, Mass. (01375) 249/D3
Sunderland, Ontario 177/E3
Sunderland○, Vt. (†05250) 268/A5
Sundown, Manitoba 179/F5
Sundown, Texas (79372) 303/B4
Sundra, S. Africa 118/J6
Sundre, Alberta 182/C4
Sundridge, Ontario 177/E2
Sundsvall, Sweden 18/K5
Sundsvall, Sweden 7/F2
Sunfield, Ill. (†62832) 222/D5
Sunfield, Mich. (48890) 250/D6
Sunfish Lake, Minn. (†55075) 255/E6
Sunflower, Ala. (36581) 195/B8
Sunflower (mt.), Kansas 232/A2
Sunflower (co.), Miss. 256/C3
Sunflower, Miss. (38778) 256/C3
Sunflower (riv.), Miss. 256/C5
Sungaipenuh, Indonesia 85/C6
Sungai Petani, Malaysia 72/C6
Sungurlu, Turkey 63/F2
Sunland, Calif. (91040) 204/C10
Sunland Gardens, Fla. (†33450) 212/F4
Sunman, Ind. (47041) 227/G6
Sunndalsøra, Norway 18/F5
Sunne, Sweden 18/H7
Sunnybrae, Nova Scotia 168/F3
Sunnybrook, Alberta 182/C3
Sunny Corner, New Bruns. 170/E2
Sunnydale, Wash. (†98101) 310/B2
Sunny Isles, Fla. (33160) 212/C4
Sunnymead, Calif. (92388) 204/F11
Sunnynook, Alberta 182/E4
Sunny Point Mil. Ocean Term., N.C. 281/O6
Sunnyside, Fla. (32461) 212/C6
Sunny Side, Georgia (30284) 217/D4
Sunnyside, Ill. (†60050) 222/A4
Sunnyside, New Bruns. 170/D1
Sunnyside, Newf. 166/D2
Sunnyside, Utah (84539) 304/D4
Sunnyside, Wash. (98944) 310/F4
Sunnyslope, Alberta 182/D4
Sunny South, Ala. (36780) 195/C7
Sunnyvale, Calif. (*94086) 204/K3
Sunnyvale, Texas (†75149) 303/H2
Sunny Valley, Oreg. (97478) 291/D5
Sunol, Calif. (94586) 204/L2
Sunol, Nebr. (†69149) 264/B3
Sun Prairie, Wis. (53590) 317/H9
Sunray, Texas (79086) 303/C1
Sunrise, Fla. (33313) 212/B4
Sunrise, Wyo. (†82215) 319/H3
Sunrise Beach, Mo. (65079) 261/G6
Sunrise Manor, Nev. (†89110) 266/F6
Sunrise Ridge, Ill. (†60097) 222/E1
Sunrise Valley, Br. Col. 184/G2
Sun River, Mont. (59483) 262/E3
Sunsas, Serranía de (mts.), Bolivia 136/F5
Sunset, Ark. (†72364) 202/K3
Sunset (peak), Idaho 220/E6
Sunset, La. (70584) 238/F6
Sunset, Maine (04683) 243/F7
Sunset, S.C. (29685) 296/B2
Sunset, Texas (79407) 303/G4
Sunset, Utah (†84015) 304/B2
Sunset Beach, Calif. (90742) 204/C11
Sunset Beach, Hawaii (†96712) 218/E1
Sunset Beach, N.C. (28459) 281/N7
Sunset Crater Nat'l Mon., Ariz. 198/D3
Sunset Hills, Mo. (†63101) 261/O4
Sunset Hills, Va. (22090) 307/R2
Sunset House, Alberta 182/B2
Sunset Prairie, Br. Co. 184/G2
Sunshine, La. (†70776) 238/K2
Sunshine, Maine (†04627) 243/G7
Sunshine, Victoria 88/K7
Sunshine, Victoria 97/H5
Sunspot, N. Mex. (88349) 274/D6
Suntar, U.S.S.R. 48/M3
Suntrana, Alaska (†99743) 196/J2
Sun Valley, Idaho (83353) 220/D6
Sun Valley, Nev. (†89431) 266/B3
Sun Valley, Sask. 181/F5
Sunyani, Ghana 106/D7
Sunzu (mt.), Zambia 115/F5
Suo (sea), Japan 81/E7
Suolahti, Finland 18/O5
Suomussalmi, Finland 18/Q4
Suonenjoki, Finland 18/P5
Suong, Cambodia 72/E5
Suoyarvi, U.S.S.R. 52/D2
Supai, Ariz. (86435) 198/C2
Supe, Peru 128/D8
Superb, Sask. 181/B4
Superior (lake) 162/G-H6
Superior (lake) 146/K5
Superior (lake) 188/J1
Superior, Ariz. (85273) 198/D5
Superior, Colo. (†80027) 208/J3
Superior, Iowa (51363) 229/D2
Superior (lag.), Mexico 150/M9
Superior (lake), Mich. 250/C2
Superior (lake), Minn. 255/G3
Superior, Mont. (59872) 262/B3
Superior, Nebr. (68978) 264/F4
Superior (lake), Ontario 177/H5
Superior (lake), Ontario 175/C3
Superior, Wis. 188/H1
Superior, Wis. (54880) 317/C2
Superior (lake), Wis. 317/F1
Superior, Wyo. (82945) 319/D4
Superior Village, Wis. (†54880) 317/B2
Superstition (mts.), Ariz. 198/D5
Suphan Buri, Thailand 72/C4
Süphan Dağı (mt.), Turkey 59/D2
Süphan Dağı (mt.), Turkey 63/K3
Supiori (isl.), Indonesia 85/K6
Supply, N.C. (28462) 281/N6
Supreme, La. (†70372) 238/K4
Supung (res.), N. Korea 81/B3
Suqian, China 77/J5
Suquamish, Wash. (98392) 310/A1
Sur (pt.), Calif. 204/D7
Sur, Lebanon 63/F6
Sur, Oman 59/G5
Sura, Ras (cape), Somalia 115/J1
Sura (riv.), U.S.S.R. 52/G4
Surab, Pakistan 68/B3
Surab, Pakistan 59/J4
Surabaya, Indonesia 54/N10
Surabaya, Indonesia 85/K2
Surada, India 68/E5
Surahammar, Sweden 18/J7
Surakarta, Indonesia 54/N10
Surakarta, Indonesia 85/J2
Šurany, Czech. 41/E2
Surat, India 54/J7
Surat, India 68/C4
Surat, Queensland 88/H5
Suratgarh, India 68/C3
Surat Thani, Thailand 72/C5
Sur del Cabo San Antonio (pt.), Argentina 143/E4
Surdulica, Yugoslavia 45/F4
Surendranagar, India 68/C4
Suresnes, France 28/A2
Suretka, C. Rica 154/F6
Surette Island, Nova Scotia 168/B5
Surf, Calif. (†93436) 204/E9
Surf City, N.J. (08008) 273/E4
Surf City, N.C. (28445) 281/O6
Surfside, Fla. (33154) 212/B4
Surfside Beach, S.C. (29577) 296/K4

T

456 Tauroa

Tauroa (pt.), N. Zealand 100/D1
Taurus (mts.), Turkey 59/B2
Taurus (mts.), Turkey 63/D4
Tauste, Spain 33/F2
Tautira, Fr. Poly. 86/T13
Tautira (pt.), Fr. Poly. 86/T13
Tauu (isls.), Papua N.G. 86/D2
Tavai, Paraguay 144/E5
Tavan Bogd Uul (mt.), Mongolia 77/C2
Tavannes, Switzerland 39/D2
Tavaputs (plat.), Utah 304/D4
Tavares, Fla. (32778) 212/E3
Tavas, Turkey 63/C4
Tavda, U.S.S.R. 48/G4
Tavernier, Fla. (33070) 212/F6
Taveta, Kenya 115/G4
Tavetsch, Switzerland 39/G3
Taveuni (isl.), Fiji 87/H7
Taveuni (isl.), Fiji 86/R10
Tavignano (riv.), France 28/B6
Tavira, Portugal 33/C4
Tavistock, England 10/D5
Tavistock, England 13/C7
Tavistock, N.J. (†08033) 273/B3
Tavistock, Ontario 177/D4
Tavoy, Burma 54/L8
Tavoy, Burma 72/C4
Tavoy (pt.), Burma 72/C4
Tavrichanka, U.S.S.R. 48/O5
Tavşanlı, Turkey 63/C3
Taw (riv.), England 13/D7
Taw (riv.), England 10/D5
Tawa, N. Zealand 100/B2
Tawas (lake), Mich. 250/F4
Tawas (pt.), Mich. 250/F4
Tawas City, Mich. (48763) 250/F4
Tawatinaw, Alberta 182/D2
Tawau, Malaysia 85/F5
Tawin (isl.), Ireland 17/C5
Tawi-Tawi (prov.), Philippines 82/B8
Tawi-Tawi (isl.), Philippines 82/B8
Tawitawi Group (isls.), Philippines 85/G4
Taxco de Alarcón, Mexico 150/K7
Taxila (ruins), Pakistan 68/C2
Taxis River, New Bruns. 170/D2
Taxkorgan, China 77/A4
Tay (firth), Scotland 15/F4
Tay (firth), Scotland 10/E2
Tay, Loch (lake), Scotland 10/D2
Tay, Loch (lake), Scotland 15/D4
Tay (riv.), Scotland 10/E2
Tay (riv.), Scotland 15/E4
Tay (lake), W. Australia 88/C6
Tayabamba, Peru 128/D7
Tayabas (bay), Philippines 82/C4
Tayasan, Philippines 82/D6
Taycheedah, Wis. (53090) 317/K8
Tay Creek, New Bruns. 170/D2
Tayibe, Israel 65/C3
Tayinloan, Scotland 15/C5
Taylor, Ala. (†36301) 195/H8
Taylor (mts.), Alaska 196/G2
Taylor, Ariz. (85939) 198/E4
Taylor, Ark. (71861) 202/D7
Taylor, Br. Col. 184/G2
Taylor (peak), Colo. 208/F5
Taylor (riv.), Colo. 208/F5
Taylor (co.), Fla. 212/C1
Taylor (co.), Georgia 217/D5
Taylor (mt.), Idaho 220/D5
Taylor (co.), Iowa 229/D7
Taylor (co.), Ky. 237/L6
Taylor, La. (71080) 238/D1
Taylor, Mich. (48180) 250/B7
Taylor, Miss. (38673) 256/E2
Taylor, Mo. (63471) 261/J3
Taylor, Nebr. (68879) 264/E3
Taylor (mt.), N. Mex. 274/B3
Taylor, N. Dak. (58656) 282/F6
Taylor (head), Nova Scotia 168/F4
Taylor, Pa. (18517) 294/F7
Taylor (co.), Texas 303/E5
Taylor, Texas (76574) 303/G7
Taylor, Texas 188/G4
Taylor (co.), W. Va. 312/F4
Taylor (co.), Wis. 317/E5
Taylor, Wis. (54659) 317/E7
Taylor Lake Village, Texas (†77586) 303/K2
Taylor Mill, Ky. (†41011) 237/S2
Taylor Park (res.), Colo. 208/F5
Taylors, S.C. (29687) 296/C2
Taylor's Arm, N.S. Wales 97/G2
Taylors Falls, Minn. (55084) 255/F5
Taylors Island, Md. (21669) 245/N7
Taylorsport, Ky. (†41048) 237/R2
Taylor Springs, Ill. (62089) 222/D4
Taylorstown, Pa. (15365) 294/A5
Taylorsville, Calif. (95983) 204/E3
Taylorsville, Georgia (30178) 217/C2
Taylorsville, Ind. (47280) 227/F6
Taylorsville, Ky. (40071) 237/L4
Taylorsville, Md. (†21157) 245/K3
Taylorsville, Miss. (39168) 256/F7
Taylorsville, N.C. (28681) 281/G3
Taylorsville (Philo), Ohio (†43717) 284/G6
Taylorsville, Utah (†84101) 304/B3
Taylortown, La. (†71010) 238/C2
Taylorville, Ill. (62568) 222/D4
Taymouth, New Bruns. 170/D2
Taymyr (lake), U.S.S.R. 4/B5
Taymyr (pen.), U.S.S.R. 4/B4
Taymyr (pen.), U.S.S.R. 54/L2
Taymyr (lake), U.S.S.R. 54/M2
Taymyr (lake), U.S.S.R. 48/K2
Taymyr (pen.), U.S.S.R. 48/L2
Taymyr (riv.), U.S.S.R. 48/K2
Taymyr Aut. Okr., U.S.S.R. 48/K2
Tay Ninh, Vietnam 72/E5
Tayoltita, Mexico 150/G4
Tayport, Scotland 10/E2
Tayport, Scotland 15/F4
Tayshet, U.S.S.R. 48/K4
Tayside (reg.), Scotland 15/E4
Taytay, Philippines 85/G3
Taytay, Philippines 82/B5
Taytay (bay), Philippines 82/B5
Tayyebat, Iran 66/M3
Taz (riv.), U.S.S.R. 54/K3
Taz (river), U.S.S.R. 4/C5
Taz (riv.), U.S.S.R. 48/J3
Taza, Morocco 106/D2
Tazadit, Mauritania 106/B4
Taza Khurmatu, Iraq 66/D3
Tazawa (lake), Japan 81/K4
Tazerbo (oasis), Libya 111/D2
Tazewell, Georgia (31828) 217/D6
Tazewell (co.), Ill. 222/D3
Tazewell, Tenn. (37879) 237/O8
Tazewell (co.), Va. 307/E6
Tazewell, Va. (24651) 307/E6
Tazin (lake), Sask. 181/L2
Tazlina (lake), Alaska 196/D1
Tazlina (riv.), Alaska 196/D1
Tazlina Glacier Lodge, Alaska (†99588) 196/C1
Tazovskiy, U.S.S.R. 48/J3
Tbilisi, U.S.S.R. 7/J4
Tbilisi, U.S.S.R. 2/M3
Tbilisi, U.S.S.R. 52/F6
Tbilisi, U.S.S.R. 48/E5
Tchentlo (lake), Br. Col. 184/E2
Tchibanga, Gabon 115/B4
Tchien, Liberia 106/C7
Tchollíré, Cameroon 115/B2
Tchula, Miss. (39169) 256/D4
Tchula (lake), Miss. 256/D4
Tczew, Poland 47/D1
Tea, S. Dak. (57064) 298/R7
Teacapán (inlet), Mexico 150/F5
Teachey, N.C. (28464) 281/N5
Teague, Texas (75860) 303/H6
Te Anau, N. Zealand 100/A6
Te Anau (lake), N. Zealand 100/A6
Teaneck○, N.J. (07666) 273/B2
Teapa, Mexico 150/N8
Teapot Dome (mt.), Wyo. 319/F2
Te Araroa, N. Zealand 100/G2
Te Aroha, N. Zealand 100/E2
Teasdale, Utah (84773) 304/C5
Te Atatu, N. Zealand 100/B1
Teaticket, Mass. (02536) 249/M6
Tea Tree Gully, S. Australia 88/E7
Tea Tree Gully, S. Australia 94/B7
Tea Tree Well, North. Terr. 93/C7
Te Awamutu, N. Zealand 100/E3
Teays, W. Va. (25569) 312/B6
Tebenkof (bay), Alaska 196/M2
Tébessa, Algeria 102/C1
Tébessa, Algeria 106/F1
Tebicuary (riv.), Paraguay 144/C5
Tebicuary Mí, Paraguay 144/B5
Tebicuary Mí (riv.), Paraguay 144/C5
Tebingtinggi, Indonesia 85/B5
Tebuk (Tabuk), Saudi Arabia 59/C4
Tecamachalco, Mexico 150/O2
Tecate, Mexico 150/A1
Tecer (mts.), Turkey 63/G3
Techirghiol, Romania 45/J3
Tecka, Argentina 143/B5
Tecolote (creek), N. Mex. 274/D3
Tecomán, Mexico 150/H7
Tecopa, Calif. (92389) 204/J8
Tecpan de Galeana, Mexico 150/J8
Tecuala, Mexico 150/G5
Tecuci, Romania 45/H3
Tecumseh, Kansas (66542) 232/G2
Tecumseh, Mich. (49286) 250/E7
Tecumseh, Mo. (65760) 261/H9
Tecumseh, Nebr. (68450) 264/H4
Tecumseh (mt.), N.H. 268/D4
Tecumseh, Okla. (74873) 288/N4
Tecumseh, Ontario 177/B5
Tedrow, Ohio (†43567) 284/B2
Teduzara, Bolivia 136/B2
Tedzhen, U.S.S.R. 48/F6
Teec Nos Pos, Ariz. (86514) 198/F2
Teeds Grove, Iowa (52771) 229/N4
Teegarden, Ind. (†46574) 227/E2
Teepee Creek, Alberta 182/A2
Tees, Alberta 182/D3
Tees (riv.), England 10/F3
Tees (riv.), England 13/F3
Teeswater, Ontario 177/C3
Teeterville, Ontario 177/D5
Tefé, Brazil 132/G9
Tefé, Brazil 120/C3
Tefé (riv.), Brazil 132/G9
Tefenni, Turkey 63/C4
Tefft, Ind. (46380) 227/D2
Tegal, Indonesia 85/J2
Tegel, W. Germany 22/E3
Tegelen, Netherlands 27/J6
Tegernsee (lake), W. Germany 22/D5
Tegucigalpa (cap.), Hond. 146/K8
Tegucigalpa (cap.), Honduras 154/D3
Tehachapi, Calif. (93561) 204/G8
Tehachapi (mts.), Calif. 204/G9
Tehama (co.), Calif. 204/C3
Tehama, Calif. (96090) 204/C3
Tehchow (Dezhou), China 77/J4
Tehek (lake), N.W. Terrs. 187/J3
Tehkummah, Ontario 177/B2
Tehran (cap.), Iran 2/M4
Tehran (cap.), Iran 66/G3
Tehran (cap.), Iran 59/F2
Tehran (cap.), Iran 54/G6
Tehri, India 68/D2
Tehuacán, Mexico 150/L7
Tehuantepec, Mexico 146/J8
Tehuantepec, Mexico 150/M8
Tehuantepec (gulf), Mexico 150/M9
Tehuantepec (isth.), Mexico 150/M8
Tehuipango, Mexico 150/P2
Teide, Pico de (peak), Spain 33/B5
Teifi (riv.), Wales 13/C5
Teifi (riv.), Wales 10/D4
Teigen, Mont. (59084) 262/H3
Teignmouth, England 10/E5
Teignmouth, England 13/D7
Teith (riv.), Scotland 15/D4
Tejerri, Libya 111/B3
Tejerri, Libya 102/D2
Tejo (Tagus) (riv.), Portugal 33/B3
Tejutla, Guatemala 154/B3
Tekamah, Nebr. (68061) 264/H3
Te Kao, N. Zealand 100/D1
Tekapo (lake), N. Zealand 100/C5
Te Karaka, N. Zealand 100/F3
Te Kauwhata, N. Zealand 100/E2
Tekax de Álaro Obregón, Mexico 150/P6
Tekeli, U.S.S.R. 48/H5
Tekes, China 77/B3
Tekirdağ (prov.), Turkey 63/B2
Tekirdağ, Turkey 59/A1
Tekirdağ, Turkey 63/B2
Tekman, Turkey 63/J3
Teknaf, Bangladesh 68/G4
Tekoa, Wash. (99033) 310/H3
Tekong Besar, Pulau (isl.), Singapore 72/F6
Tekonsha, Mich. (49092) 250/E6
Te Kopuru, N. Zealand 100/D2
Te Kuiti, N. Zealand 100/E3
Tel (riv.), India 68/E4
Tela, Honduras 154/D3
Telanaipura, Indonesia 54/M10
Telavi, U.S.S.R. 52/G6
Tel Aviv (dist.), Israel 65/B3
Tel Aviv-Jaffa, Israel 59/B3
Tel Aviv-Jaffa, Israel 65/B3
Tel Aviv-Jaffa, Israel 54/E6
Telč, Czech. 41/C2
Telde, Spain 33/B5
Telefomin, Papua N.G. 85/B7
Telegraph, Texas (76883) 303/E7
Telegraph Creek, Br. Col. 184/K2
Telemark (co.), Norway 18/F7
Telephone, Texas (75488) 303/J4
Telescope (peak), Calif. 204/H7
Telescope (pt.), Grenada 161/D8
Teles Pires (riv.), Brazil 120/D3
Teles Pires (riv.), Brazil 132/B5
Telfair (co.), Georgia 217/G7
Telford, England 13/E5
Telford, Pa. (18969) 294/M5
Telford, Tenn. (37690) 237/S8
Telfordville, Alberta 182/C3
Telfs, Austria 41/A3
Telgte, W. Germany 22/B3
Télimélé, Guinea 106/B6
Telkalakh, Syria 63/F5
Tel Kotchek, Syria 59/D2
Tel Kotchek, Syria 63/K4
Telkwa, Br. Col. 184/D3
Tell, Georgia (†30304) 217/J2
Tell, Texas (79259) 303/D3
Tell 'Asur (mt.), Jordan 65/C4
Tell City, Ind. (47586) 227/D9
Teller, Alaska (99778) 196/E1
Teller (co.), Colo. 208/J5
Tellicherry, India 68/C6
Tellico (riv.), Tenn. 237/N10
Tellico Plains, Tenn. (37385) 237/N10
Tellin, Belgium 27/G8
Telluride, Colo. (81435) 208/D7
Telma, Wash. (†98826) 310/E3
Telocaset, Oreg. (†97883) 291/K2
Telogia, Fla. (32360) 212/B1
Telok Anson, Malaysia 72/D6
Teloloapan, Mexico 150/J7
Telpaneca, Nicaragua 154/D4
Tel'pos-Iz (mt.), U.S.S.R. 52/K2
Telsen, Argentina 143/C5
Telšiai, U.S.S.R. 53/B2
Telšiai, U.S.S.R. 52/B3
Teltow, E. Germany 22/E4
Teltown, Ireland 17/H4
Telukbayur, Indonesia 85/C6
Tema, Ghana 106/E7
Tema, Ghana 102/C4
Temacine, Algeria 106/F2
Temae (lake), Fr. Poly. 86/S12
Temanggung, Indonesia 85/J2
Temascalapa, Mexico 150/M1
Tematangi (isl.), Fr. Poly. 87/M8
Temax, Mexico 150/P6
Tembisa, S. Africa 118/H6
Temblador, Venezuela 124/G3
Tembuè, Mozambique 118/E2
Temecula, Calif. (92390) 204/H10
Temerloh, Malaysia 72/D7
Temiang, Bukit (mt.), Malaysia 72/D6
Temirtau, U.S.S.R. 54/J4
Temirtau, U.S.S.R. 48/H4
Témiscamingue (county), Québec 174/B3
Témiscaming, Québec 174/B3
Témiscouata (co.), Québec 172/J2
Témiscouata (lake), Québec 172/H2
Temma, Tasmania 99/A3
Temora, N. S. Wales 88/H6
Temora, N. S. Wales 97/D4
Temoris, Mexico 150/E3
Temósachic, Mexico 150/E2
Tempe, Ariz. (*85282) 198/D5
Tempe Downs, North. Terr. 93/C8
Tempelhof, W. Germany 22/F4
Temperance, Mich. (48182) 250/F7
Temperance Hall, Tenn. (†37095) 237/K8
Temperance Vale, New Bruns. 170/C2
Temperanceville, Va. (23442) 307/T5
Tempio Pausania, Italy 34/B4
Temple (mt.), Alberta 182/B4
Temple, Georgia (30179) 217/B3
Temple, La. (71476) 238/E4
Temple○, Maine (04984) 243/C6
Temple, Mich. (†48625) 250/E4
Temple○, N.H. (03084) 268/D6
Temple, Okla. (73568) 288/K6
Temple, Pa. (19560) 294/L5
Temple, Texas (76501) 303/G6
Temple, Texas 188/G4
Temple Bar, Ariz. (86443) 198/A2
Temple City, Calif. (91780) 204/D10
Templemore, Ireland 10/C4
Templemore, Ireland 17/F6
Templestowe and Doncaster, Victoria 97/J5
Temple Terrace, Fla. (33617) 212/C2
Templeton, Calif. (93465) 204/E8
Templeton, Ind. (47986) 227/C3
Templeton, Iowa (51463) 229/D5
Templeton○, Mass. (01468) 249/F2
Templeton, Pa. (16259) 294/C4
Templeton, Québec 172/B4
Templetuohy, Ireland 17/F6
Templeville, Md. (21670) 245/P4
Templin, E. Germany 22/E2
Tempo, N. Ireland 17/G3
Temryuk, U.S.S.R. 52/E5
Temse, Belgium 27/E6
Temuco, Chile 120/B6
Temuco, Chile 138/E2
Temuka, N. Zealand 100/C6
Temvik, N. Dak. (†58552) 282/K7
Ten, Colombia 126/D5
Tena, Ecuador 128/D3
Tenabo, Mexico 150/P6
Tenafly, N.J. (07670) 273/C1
Tenaha, Texas (75974) 303/K6
Tenakee Springs, Alaska (99841) 196/M1
Tenali, India 68/E5
Tenancingo de Degollado, Mexico 150/K7
Tenango de Río Blanco, Mexico 150/O2
Tenants Harbor, Maine (04860) 243/E8
Tenares, Dom. Rep. 158/E5
Tenasserim (div.), Burma 72/C4
Tenasserim, Burma 72/C5
Tenasserim (isl.), Burma 72/C4
Tenbury, England 13/E5
Tenby, Manitoba 179/C4
Tenby, Wales 10/D5
Tenby, Wales 13/C6
Tendal, La. (†71290) 238/H2
Ten Degree (chan.), India 68/G7
Tendelti, Sudan 111/F5
Tendelti, Sudan 102/F3
Tendo, Japan 81/K4
Tendoy, Idaho (83468) 220/E5
Tendrara, Morocco 106/D2
Tendre (peak), Switzerland 39/B3
Tenecape, Nova Scotia 168/E3
Ténenkou, Mali 106/D6
Ténéré (des.), Niger 106/G5
Tenerife (isl.), Spain 102/A2
Tenerife (isl.), Spain 106/A3
Tenerife (isl.), Spain 33/B5
Ténès, Algeria 106/E1
Teng, Nam (riv.), Burma 72/C2
Tengchong, China 77/E6
Tenggarong, Indonesia 85/F6
Tenggol, Pulau (isl.), Malaysia 72/D6
Tengiz (lake), U.S.S.R. 48/G4
Teng Xian, China 77/H7
Tenigerbad, Switzerland 39/G3
Tenino, Wash. (98589) 310/C4
Tenke, Zaire 115/E6
Tenkiller Ferry (lake), Okla. 288/S3
Tenkodogo, Upper Volta 106/E6
Tenleytown, D.C. (†20008) 245/E4
Ten Mile (lake), Newf. 166/C3
Tenmile, Oreg. (97481) 291/D4
Tenmile (creek), Oreg. 291/K5
Ten Mile, Tenn. (37880) 237/M9
Tenmile (creek), Texas 303/G3
Tennant, Calif. (†96066) 204/C2
Tennant, Iowa (51574) 229/C5
Tennant Creek, Australia 87/D7
Tennant Creek, North. Terr. 88/E3
Tennant Creek, North. Terr. 93/C5
Tennent, N.J. (07763) 273/E3
Tennessee 188/J3
Tennessee (riv.) 188/J3
Tennessee (riv.), Ala. 195/C1
Tennessee, Ill. (62374) 222/C3
Tennessee (riv.), Ky. 237/D6
TENNESSEE 237
Tennessee (riv.), Tenn. 237/E10
Tennessee (state), U.S. 146/K6
Tennessee City, Tenn. (†37055) 237/F8
Tennessee Pass, Colo. (†80461) 208/G4
Tennessee Ridge, Tenn. (37178) 237/F8
Tennessee-Tombigbee Waterway, Ala. 195/B4
Tennessee-Tombigbee Waterway, Miss. 256/H2
Tenneville, Belgium 27/H8
Tenney, Minn. (56582) 255/B4
Tennga, Georgia (30751) 217/C1
Tennille, Ala. (†36010) 195/G7
Tennille, Georgia (31089) 217/G5
Tennyson, Ind. (47637) 227/C8
Tennyson, Texas (76953) 303/D6
Tennyson, Wis. (†53820) 317/E10
Teno, Chile 138/A10
Tenosique de Pino Suárez, Mexico 150/O8
Tenquehuen (isl.), Chile 138/D6
Tenri, Japan 81/J8
Tensas (par.), La. 238/H2
Tensas (riv.), La. 238/G3
Tensaw, Ala. (†36507) 195/C8
Tensaw (riv.), Ala. 195/C9
Tensed, Idaho (83870) 220/B2
Ten Sleep, Wyo. (82442) 319/E1
Tenstrike, Minn. (56683) 255/D3
Tenterden, England 13/H6
Tenterfield, N. S. Wales 88/J5
Tenterfield, N.S. Wales 97/G1
Ten Thousand (isls.), Fla. 188/K5
Ten Thousand (isls.), Fla. 212/E6
Ten Thousand Smokes (valley), Alaska 196/G3
Teocaltiche, Mexico 150/H6
Teocelo, Mexico 150/P1
Teófilo Otoni, Brazil 120/E4
Teófilo Otoni, Brazil 132/F7
Te One, N. Zealand 100/D7
Teotihuacán (ruin), Mexico 150/M1
Teotihuacán de Arista, Mexico 150/L1
Teotitlán del Camino, Mexico 150/L8
Tepa, Indonesia 85/H7
Tepache, Mexico 150/E2
Tepalcingo, Mexico 150/M2
Tepatitlán de Morelos, Mexico 150/H6
Tepeaca, Mexico 150/N2
Tepeapulco, Mexico 150/M1
Tepehuanes, Mexico 150/G4
Tepeji del Río, Mexico 150/L1
Tepelenë, Albania 45/D5
Tepetlán, Mexico 150/P1
Tepexi de Rodríguez, Mexico 150/N2
Tepeyahualco, Mexico 150/O1
Tepic, Mexico 150/G6
Teplá u Toužimě, Czech. 41/B1
Teplice, Czech. 41/B1
Tepoztlán, Mexico 150/L1
Te Puke, N. Zealand 100/F2
Tequeje (riv.), Bolivia 136/B3
Tequendama (falls), Colombia 126/C5
Tequesquite (creek), N. Mex. 274/E2
Tequesta, Fla. (33458) 212/F5
Tequixquitla, Mexico 150/O1
Ter (riv.), Spain 33/H1
Téra, Niger 106/E6
Teramo (prov.), Italy 34/D3
Teramo, Italy 34/D3
Terán, Mexico 150/N8
Terang, Victoria 97/B6
Ter Apel, Netherlands 27/L3
Terawhiti (cape), N. Zealand 100/A3
Tercan, Turkey 63/J3
Terceira (isl.), Portugal 33/C1
Tercero (riv.), Argentina 143/D3
Terchová, Czech. 41/E2
Terempa, Indonesia 85/D5
Terence Bay, Nova Scotia 168/E4
Terengganu (state), Malaysia 72/D6
Teresina, Brazil 120/E3
Teresina, Brazil 132/F4
Teresita, Mo. (65573) 261/J9
Teresópolis, Brazil 135/E3
Terespol, Poland 47/F2
Teressa (isl.), India 68/G7
Terevinto, Bolivia 136/D5
Terhazza (ruins), Mali 106/C4
Terhune, Ind. (†46069) 227/E4
Teriberka, U.S.S.R. 52/E1
Terlingua, Texas (79852) 303/D12
Terlingua (creek), Texas 303/D12
Terlton, Okla. (74081) 288/O2
Termas de Cauquenes, Chile 138/B10
Terme, Turkey 63/G2
Termez, U.S.S.R. 48/G6
Termini Imerese, Italy 34/D6
Términos (lag.), Mexico 150/O7
Termo, Calif. (96132) 204/E3
Termoli, Italy 34/E3
Termonde (Dendermonde), Belgium 27/E6
Termonfeckin, Ireland 17/J4
Termunten, Netherlands 27/K2
Ternate, Indonesia 54/O9
Ternate, Indonesia 85/H5
Terneuzen, Netherlands 27/D6
Terni (prov.), Italy 34/D3
Terni, Italy 34/D3
Terni, Italy 7/F4
Ternitz, Austria 41/D3
Ternopol', U.S.S.R. 48/C5
Ternopol', U.S.S.R. 52/C5
Te Roto, N. Zealand 100/D7
Terowie, S. Australia 94/F5
Terpeniye (cape), U.S.S.R. 48/P5
Terra Alta, W. Va. (26764) 312/H4
Terra Bella, Calif. (93270) 204/G8
Terrabona, Nicaragua 154/E4
Terrace, Br. Col. 162/D5
Terrace, Br. Col. 184/C3
Terrace, Br. Col. 184/C3
Terrace, Minn. (†56380) 255/C5
Terrace Bay, Ontario 177/H5
Terrace Bay, Ontario 175/C3
Terrace Heights, Wash. (98901) 310/E4
Terra Ceia, Fla. (33591) 212/D4
Terrace Park, Ohio (45174) 284/D9
Terracina, Italy 34/D4
Terra Corra, Neth. Ant. 161/E8
Terråk, Norway 18/H4
Terral, Okla. (73569) 288/L7
Terralba, Italy 34/B5
Terra Nova, Newf. 166/C2
Terra Nova (riv.), Newf. 166/C2
Terra Nova Nat'l Park, Newf. 166/D2
Terrebonne (par.), La. 238/J8
Terrebonne (bay), La. 238/J8
Terrebonne, Minn. (†56750) 255/B3
Terrebonne, Oreg. (97760) 291/F3
Terrebonne (co.), Québec 172/H4
Terrebonne, Québec 172/H4
Terre-de-Bas (isl.), Guadeloupe 161/A7
Terre-de-Haut (isl.), Guadeloupe 161/A7
Terre Haute, Ill. (†61454) 222/C3
Terre Haute, Ind. 188/J3
Terre Haute, Ind. (*47801) 227/C6
Terre Hill, Pa. (17581) 294/L5
Terrell (co.), Georgia 217/D7
Terrell, N.C. (28682) 281/G3
Terrell (co.), Texas 303/B7
Terrell, Texas 188/G4
Terrell, Texas (75160) 303/H5
Terrell Hills, Texas (†78201) 303/K11
Terrenate, Mexico 150/N1
Terrenceville, Newf. 166/D4
Terre Neuve, Haiti 158/B5
Terreton, Idaho (83450) 220/F6
Terrey Hills, N. S. Wales 88/L3
Terrey Hills, N.S. Wales 97/J3
Terri (mt.), Switzerland 39/D2
Terri (peak), Switzerland 39/H3
Terrigal-Wamberal, N.S. Wales 97/F3
Terril, Iowa (51364) 229/C2
Terrill (mt.), Utah 304/C5
Territok (cape), Newf. 166/B2
Terry, La. (71285) 238/H1
Terry, Miss. (39170) 256/D6
Terry, Mont. (59349) 262/L4
Terry (co.), Texas 303/B4
Terry Town, La. (†70053) 238/O4
Terrytown, Nebr. (†69341) 264/A3
Terryville, Conn. (06786) 210/C2
Terschelling (isl.), Netherlands 27/G2
Teruel (prov.), Spain 33/F2
Teruel, Spain 33/F2
Terutao, Ko (isl.), Thailand 72/C6
Tervola, Finland 18/O3
Tesawa, Libya 111/B2
Tescott, Kansas (67484) 232/E2
Teshekpuk (lake), Alaska 196/H1
Teshio, Japan 81/K1
Teshio (mt.), Japan 81/L1
Teshio (riv.), Japan 81/L1
Tesla, W. Va. (26640) 312/E5
Teslić, Yugoslavia 45/C3
Teslin (lake) 162/C3
Teslin (lake), Br. Col. 184/K1
Teslin, Yukon 187/E3
Teslin (lake), Yukon 187/E4
Teslin (riv.), Yukon 187/E3
Tessalit, Mali 106/E4
Tessaoua, Niger 106/F6
Tessenderlo, Belgium 27/G6
Tessenei, Ethiopia 59/C6
Tessenei, Ethiopia 111/G4
Tessier, Sask. 181/D4
Test (riv.), England 13/F6
Testa (cape), Italy 34/B4
Testa del Gargano (cape), Italy 34/F4
Tesuque, N. Mex. (87574) 274/C3
Tét, Hungary 41/D3
Tetachuck (lake), Br. Col. 184/E3
Tetagouche (riv.), New Bruns. 170/D1
Tetas (pt.), Chile 138/A4
Tete (prov.), Mozambique 118/E3
Tete, Mozambique 102/F6
Tete, Mozambique 118/E3
Tête-à-la-Baleine, Québec 174/E2
Tete Jaune Cache, Br. Col. 184/H4
Te Teko, N. Zealand 100/F3
Teterboro, N.J. (07608) 273/B2
Teterow, E. Germany 22/E2
Teterton, W. Va. (†26886) 312/H5
Teteven, Bulgaria 45/G4
Tetiaroa (atoll), Fr. Poly. 87/M7
Tetlin, Alaska (99779) 196/K2
Teton (co.), Idaho 220/G6
Teton, Idaho (83451) 220/G6
Teton (riv.), Idaho 220/G6
Teton (co.), Mont. 262/D3
Teton (riv.), Mont. 262/E3
Teton (co.), Wyo. 319/B2
Teton (range), Wyo. 319/B2
Tetonia, Idaho (83452) 220/G6
Teton Village, Wyo. (83025) 319/B2
Tetotum, Va. (†22485) 307/P4
Tétouan, Morocco 106/C1
Tétouan, Morocco 102/B1
Tetovo, Yugoslavia 45/E5
Teuco (riv.), Argentina 143/D1
Teufen, Switzerland 39/H2
Teulada (cape), Italy 7/E5
Teulada (cape), Italy 34/B5
Teulon, Manitoba 179/E4
Teupasenti, Honduras 154/D3
Teustepe, Nicaragua 154/E4
Teutoburger Wald (for.), W. Germany 22/C2
Teutopolis, Ill. (62467) 222/E4
Teuva, Finland 18/M5
Teviot (riv.), Scotland 15/F5
Teviot (riv.), Scotland 10/E3
Te Waewae (bay), N. Zealand 100/A7
Tewantin-Noosa, Queensland 95/E5
Te Whanga (mts.), N. Zealand 100/E7
Tewkesbury, England 10/F5
Tewkesbury, England 13/E6
Tewksbury, Mass. (01876) 249/K2
Texa (isl.), Scotland 15/B5
Texada (isl.), Br. Col. 184/J2
Texarkana, Ark. 188/H4
Texarkana, Ark. (75502) 202/C7
Texarkana, Texas 188/H4
Texarkana, Texas 146/J6
Texarkana, Texas (*75501) 303/L4
Texas 188/G4
TEXAS 303
Texas, Georgia (†30217) 217/B4
Texas, Ky. (†40069) 237/L5
Texas, Md. (†21030) 245/M3
Texas (co.), Mo. 261/J8
Texas (co.), Okla. 288/C1
Texas (state), U.S. 146/J6
Texas City, Texas (77590) 303/K3
Texas Creek, Colo. (81250) 208/H6
Texcoco de Mora, Mexico 150/M1
Texel (isl.), Netherlands 27/F2
Texhoma, Okla. (73949) 288/C1
Texhoma, Texas (73949) 303/C1
Texico, N. Mex. (88135) 274/F4
Texistepeque, El Salvador 154/C3
Texline, Texas (79087) 303/B1
Texola, Okla. (73668) 288/G4
Texoma (lake) 188/G4
Texoma (lake), Okla. 288/N7
Texoma (lake), Texas 303/H3
Texon, Texas (76954) 303/C6
Teykovo, U.S.S.R. 52/E3
Teyvareh, Afghanistan 68/A2
Teyvareh, Afghanistan 59/H3
Teziutlán, Mexico 150/O1
Tezonapa, Mexico 150/P2
Tezontepec, Mexico 150/M1
Tezpur, India 68/G3
Tezu, India 68/H3
Tezzeron (lake), Br. Col. 184/E3
Tha, Nam (riv.), Laos 72/D2
Tha-anne (riv.), N.W. Terrs. 187/J3
Thabazimbi, S. Africa 118/D4
Thacher (isl.), Mass. 249/M2
Tha Chin, Mae Nam (riv.), Thailand 72/C4
Thacker, W. Va. (25694) 312/B7
Thackeray, Ill. (†62859) 222/E5
Thackeray, Ohio (†43078) 284/C5
Thackerville, Okla. (73459) 288/M7
Thai Binh, Vietnam 72/E2
Thailand 2/Q5
Thailand 54/M8
Thailand (gulf) 2/Q5
Thailand (gulf) 54/M9

Trousdale 459

Toronto, Canada 2/F3
Toronto, Iowa (52343) 229/M5
Toronto, Kansas (66777) 232/G4
Toronto (lake), Kansas 232/F4
Toronto (res.), N.Y. 276/L7
Toronto, Ohio (43964) 284/J5
Toronto (cap.), Ont. 146/K5
Toronto (cap.), Ont. 162/H7
Toronto (metro. munic.), Ontario 177/K4
Toronto (cap.), Ontario 177/K4
Toronto, S. Dak. (57268) 298/R4
Toropalca, Bolivia 136/B7
Toropets, U.S.S.R. 52/D3
Tororo, Uganda 115/F3
Torote (riv.), Spain 33/G4
Torotoro, Bolivia 136/C6
Torpedo, Pa. (†16340) 294/D2
Torphins, Scotland 15/F3
Torpoint, England 13/C7
Torquay (Torbay), England 13/D7
Torquay, Sask. 181/H6
Torquemada, Spain 33/D1
Torr (head), N. Ireland 17/K1
Torrance, Calif. 188/C4
Torrance, Calif. (*90501) 204/C11
Torrance (co.), N. Mex. 274/D4
Torrance, Ontario 177/E3
Torrance, Pa. (15779) 294/D5
Torre, Cerro de la (mt.), Chile 138/E4
Torre Annunziata, Italy 34/E4
Torreblanca, Spain 33/G2
Torrecilla (lag.), P. Rico 161/E1
Torre del Greco, Italy 34/E4
Torre de Moncorvo, Portugal 33/C2
Torredonjimeno, Spain 33/D4
Torre Gaia, Italy 34/F6
Torrejón (res.), Spain 33/D3
Torrejoncillo, Spain 33/C3
Torrejón de Ardoz, Spain 33/G4
Torrelaguna, Spain 33/E2
Torrelavega, Spain 33/D1
Torremaggiore, Italy 34/E4
Torremolinos, Spain 33/D4
Torrens (riv.) 88/E7
Torrens (lake), Australia 87/D9
Torrens (isl.), S. Australia 88/D7
Torrens (lake), S. Australia 88/F6
Torrens (lake), S. Australia 94/E4
Torrens (riv.), S. Australia 94/C7
Torrente, Spain 33/F3
Torreón, Mexico 146/H7
Torreón, Mexico 150/H4
Torreon, N. Mex. (87061) 274/C4
Torre-Pacheco, Spain 33/F4
Torres (strait) 87/E7
Torres (str.), Papua N.G. 85/A7
Torres (str.), Queensland 88/G2
Torres (str.), Queensland 95/B1
Torres (isls.), Vanuatu 87/G7
Torres Martinez Ind. Res., Calif. 204/J10
Torres Novas, Portugal 33/B3
Torres Vedras, Portugal 33/B3
Torrevieja, Spain 33/F4
Torrey, Utah (84775) 304/C5
Torridge (riv.), England 13/C7
Torridon, Loch (inlet), Scotland 15/C3
Torriente, Cuba 158/D1
Torrijos, Philippines 82/D4
Torrijos, Spain 33/D2
Torring, Denmark 21/C6
Torringford, Conn. (†06790) 210/C1
Torrington, Alberta 182/D4
Torrington, Conn. (06790) 210/C1
Torrington, Wyo. (82240) 319/H3
Torroella de Montgrí, Spain 33/H1
Torrowangee, N.S. Wales 97/A2
Torrox, Spain 33/E4
Torsby, Sweden 18/H6
Tors Cove, Newf. 166/D2
Torshälla, Sweden 18/K7
Tórshavn, Denmark 7/D2
Tórshavn (cap.), Faeroe Is., Denmark 21/A3
Tortilla Flat, Ariz. (85290) 198/D5
Tortola (isl.), Virgin Is. (Br.) 161/D3
Tortola (isl.), Virgin Is. (Br.) 156/H1
Tórtolas, Cerro de las (mt.), Chile 138/B8
Tortona, Italy 34/B2
Tortorici, Italy 34/E6
Tortosa, Spain 33/G2
Tortosa (cape), Spain 33/G2
Tortue (chan.), Haiti 158/C5
Tortue (Tortuga) (isl.), Haiti 156/D2
Tortue (Tortuga) (isl.), Haiti 158/C4
Tortuga (isl.), Haiti 158/C4
Tortuga (isl.), Haiti 156/D2
Tortugas (gulf), Colombia 126/B6
Tortuguero (lag.), P. Rico 161/D1
Tortuguilla (pt.), Cuba 158/K4
Tortum, Turkey 63/J2
Torud, Iran 59/F2
Torud, Iran 66/J3
Torul, Turkey 63/H2
Toruń (prov.), Poland 47/D2
Toruń, Poland 7/F3
Toruń, Poland 47/D2
Torunos, Venezuela 124/C3
Tõrva, U.S.S.R. 53/C1
Tory (isl.), Ireland 17/E1
Tory (isl.), Ireland 10/B3
Tory (sound), Ireland 17/E1
Torysa (riv.), Czech. 41/F2
Torzhok, U.S.S.R. 52/D3
Tosa, Japan 81/F7
Tosa (bay), Japan 81/F7
Tosashimizu, Japan 81/F7
Toson Hu (lake), China 77/E4
Töss (riv.), Switzerland 39/G1
Tostado, Argentina 143/D2
Toston, Mont. (59643) 262/E4
Tosu, Japan 81/E7
Tosya, Turkey 63/F2
Tota, Laguna de (lake), Colombia 126/D5
Totana, Spain 33/F4
Tótkomlós, Hungary 41/F3
Tot'ma, U.S.S.R. 48/E4
Tot'ma, U.S.S.R. 52/F3
Totnes, England 13/D7
Totnes, England 10/E5
Totnes, Sask. 181/C4
Totness, Suriname 131/C3
Toto, Ind. (†46534) 227/D2
Totoket, Conn. (†06405) 210/D3
Totonicapán, Guatemala 154/B3
Totora, Cochabamba, Bolivia 136/C5
Totora, Oruro, Bolivia 136/A5
Totoral, Chile 138/A6
Totoral, Quebrada (riv.), Chile 138/A6
Totoral, Uruguay 145/C3
Totowa, N.J. (07512) 273/B1
Totoya (isl.), Fiji 86/R11
Tottenham, N.S. Wales 97/D3
Tottenham, Ontario 177/E3
Tottori (pref.), Japan 81/G6
Tottori, Japan 81/G6
Touat (oasis), Algeria 106/E3
Touba, Ivory Coast 106/C7
Touba, Senegal 106/A6
Toubkal, Jebel (mt.), Morocco 102/B1
Toubkal, Jebel (mt.), Morocco 106/C2
Touchet, Wash. (99360) 310/G4
Touchet (riv.), Wash. 310/G4
Touchwood (lake), Alberta 182/E2
Touchwood (hills), Sask. 181/G4
Toufourine (well), Mali 106/C4
Tougaloo, Miss. (39174) 256/D6
Tougan, Upper Volta 106/D6
Touggourt, Algeria 106/F2
Touggourt, Algeria 102/C1
Toughkenamon, Pa. (19374) 294/L6
Tougué, Guinea 106/B6
Touila (well), Algeria 106/C3
Touila (well), Mauritania 106/C3
Toukoto, Mali 106/C6
Toul, France 28/F3
Touladi, Grand Lac (lake), Québec 172/J1
Toulnustouc (riv.), Québec 174/D2
Toulon, France 7/E4
Toulon, France 28/F6
Toulon, Ill. (61483) 222/D2
Toulouse, France 7/E4
Toulouse, France 28/D6
Toumodi, Ivory Coast 106/D7
Toungo, Nigeria 106/G7
Toungoo, Burma 72/C3
Touraine (trad. prov.), France 29
Tourakom, Laos 72/D3
Tourbis (lake), Québec 172/C2
Tourcoing, France 28/E2
Tour d'Aï (mt.), Switzerland 39/C4
Tourelle, Québec 172/C1
Tournai, Belgium 27/C7
Tournavista, Peru 128/E7
Tournon, France 28/F5
Tournus, France 28/F4
Touros, Brazil 132/H4
Touro Synagogue Nat'l Hist. Site, R.I. 249/J7
Tours, France 28/D4
Tours, France 7/E4
Tourville, Québec 172/H2
Toutes Aides, Manitoba 179/C3
Toutle, Wash. (98649) 310/C4
Toutle, North Fork (riv.), Wash. 310/C4
Toutle, South Fork (riv.), Wash. 310/C4
Toužim, Czech. 41/B1
Töv, Mongolia 77/G2
Tovar, Venezuela 124/C3
Tovey, Ill. (62570) 222/D4
Towaco, N.J. (07082) 273/E2
Towada, Japan 81/K3
Towada (lake), Japan 81/K3
Towada-Hachimantai National Park, Japan 81/K3
Towakaima, Guyana 131/B2
Towanda, Ill. (61776) 222/E3
Towanda, Kansas (67144) 232/E4
Towanda, Pa. (18848) 294/J2
Towanda (creek), Pa. 294/J2
Towaoc, Colo. (81334) 208/B8
Towcester, England 13/F5
Tower, Mich. (49792) 250/E3
Tower, Minn. (55790) 255/F3
Tower, Wyo. (†82190) 319/B1
Tower City, N. Dak. (58071) 282/P6
Tower City, Pa. (17980) 294/J4
Tower Hamlets, England 13/H8
Tower Hill, Ill. (62571) 222/E4
Tower Lakes, Ill. (†60010) 222/A4
Towers of Silence, India 68/B7
Tow Law, England 13/H4
Town (creek), Ala. 195/C1
Town (creek), Md. 245/E2
Town and Country, Mo. (†63101) 261/O3
Town and Country, Wash. (†99218) 310/H3
Town Creek, Ala. (35672) 195/D1
Towner, Colo. (81080) 208/P6
Towner (co.), N. Dak. 282/M2
Towner, N. Dak. (58788) 282/K3
Townley, Ala. (35587) 195/D3
Town of Pines, Ind. (†46360) 227/D1
Town Point, Md. (†21915) 245/P3
Towns (co.), Georgia 217/E1
Towns, Georgia (†31055) 217/G7
Townsend, Del. (19734) 245/R3
Townsend, Georgia (31331) 217/J7
Townsend, Mass. (01469) 249/H2
Townsend◯, Mass. (01469) 249/H2
Townsend, Mont. (59644) 262/E4
Townsend (inlet), N.J. 273/D5
Townsend, Tenn. (37882) 237/O9
Townsend, Va. (23443) 307/R6
Townsend, Wis. (54175) 317/K5
Townsend Harbor, Mass. (†01469) 249/G2
Townsends Inlet, N.J. (†08243) 273/D5
Townshend◯, Vt. (05353) 268/B5
Townsville, Australia 2/S6
Townsville, Australia 87/E7
Townsville, N.C. (27584) 281/N1
Townsville, Queensland 88/H3
Townsville, Queensland 95/C3
Townville, Pa. (16360) 294/C2
Townville, S.C. (29689) 296/B2
Towot, Sudan 111/F6
Towraghondi, Afghanistan 68/A1
Towson, Md. (21204) 245/M3
Towuti (lake), Indonesia 85/G6
Towy (riv.), Wales 13/D6
Towy (riv.), Wales 10/E5
Toxey, Ala. (36921) 195/B7
Toya (lake), Japan 81/K2
Toyah, Texas (79785) 303/D11
Toyah (creek), Texas 303/D11
Toyah (lake), Texas 303/A6
Toyahvale, Texas (79786) 303/D11
Toyama (pref.), Japan 81/H5
Toyama, Japan 81/H5
Toyama (bay), Japan 81/H5
Toyohashi, Japan 81/H6
Toyonaka, Japan 81/J7
Toyooka, Japan 81/G6
Toyota, Japan 81/H6
Tozeur, Tunisia 106/F2
Trabzon (prov.), Turkey 63/H2
Trabzon, Turkey 54/E5
Trabzon, Turkey 63/H2
Trabzon, Turkey 59/C1
Tracadie, New Bruns. 170/F1
Tracadie, Nova Scotia 168/G3
Tracadie (bay), Pr. Edward I. 168/F2
Trachselwald, Switzerland 39/E2
Tracy, Calif. (95376) 204/D6
Tracy, Conn. (†06492) 210/D2
Tracy, Iowa (50256) 229/H6
Tracy, Ky. (†42123) 237/K7
Tracy, Minn. (56175) 255/C6
Tracy, Mo. (64079) 261/C4
Tracy, New Bruns. 170/D3
Tracy, Québec 172/D3
Tracy Arm (inlet), Alaska 196/N1
Tracy City, Tenn. (37387) 237/K10
Tracyton, Wash. (98393) 310/A2
Trade, Tenn. (37691) 237/T8
Trade Lake, Wis. (†54837) 317/A4
Tradespark, Scotland 15/E3
Tradesville, S.C. (†29720) 296/F2
Tradewater (riv.), Ky. 237/F6
Trading (bay), Alaska 196/B1
Trading Post, Kansas (†66075) 232/H3
Traer, Iowa (50675) 229/J4
Traer, Kansas (†67749) 232/B2
Trafalgar, Ind. (46181) 227/E6
Trafalgar, Nova Scotia 168/F3
Trafalgar (cape), Spain 33/C4
Trafaria, Portugal 33/A1
Trafford, Ala. (35172) 195/E3
Trafford, Pa. (15085) 294/C5
Traghen, Libya 111/B2
Traiguén, Chile 138/D2
Traiguén (isl.), Chile 138/D6
Trail, Br. Col. 162/E6
Trail, Br. Col. 146/G4
Trail, Br. Col. 184/J6
Trail, Minn. (56684) 255/C3
Trail, Oreg. (97541) 291/E5
Trail City, S. Dak. (57657) 298/H3
Trail Creek, Ind. (†46360) 227/D1
Traill (isl.), Greenl. 4/B10
Traill (co.), N. Dak. 282/R5
Traîne (lake), Québec 172/D2
Trainer, Pa. (†19013) 294/L7
Traiskirchen, Austria 41/D2
Trakai, U.S.S.R. 53/C3
Tralake, Miss. (38757) 256/C4
Tralee, Ireland 10/B4
Tralee, Ireland 17/B7
Tralee (bay), Ireland 17/B7
Tramán-tepuí (mt.), Venezuela 124/G5
Tramelan, Switzerland 39/D2
Trammel, Va. (24289) 307/D6
Tramore, Ireland 10/C4
Tramore, Ireland 17/G7
Tramore (bay), Ireland 17/G7
Trampas, N. Mex. (87576) 274/D2
Tramperos (creek), N. Mex. 274/F2
Tramping (lake), Sask. 181/C3
Tramping Lake, Sask. 181/B3
Tranås, Sweden 18/J7
Trancoso, Portugal 33/C2
Tranebjerg, Denmark 21/D6
Tranebjerg (mt.), Denmark 21/C6
Tranent, Scotland 15/F5
Trang, Thailand 72/C6
Trangan (isl.), Indonesia 85/J7
Trangie, N.S. Wales 97/D3
Trani, Italy 34/F4
Tranquebar, India 68/E6
Tranqueras, Uruguay 145/D2
Tranqui (isl.), Chile 138/D4
Tranquility, N.J. (07879) 273/D2
Tranquillity, Calif. (93668) 204/E7
Transantarctic (mts.) 5/B17
Trans-Carpathian Oblast, U.S.S.R. 52/B5
Transfer, Pa. (16154) 294/A3
Transkei (aut. rep.), S. Africa 102/E8
Transkei (aut. rep.), S. Africa 118/D6
Transquaking (riv.), Md. 245/P7
Transvaal (prov.), S. Africa 102/E7
Transvaal (prov.), S. Africa 118/D4
Transylvania, La. (71286) 238/H1
Transylvania (co.), N.C. 281/D4
Transylvanian Alps (mts.), Romania 45/G3
Trapani (prov.), Italy 34/D5
Trapani, Italy 7/F5
Trapani, Italy 34/D5
Trap Falls (res.), Conn. 210/C3
Traphill, N.C. (28685) 281/H2
Trappe, Md. (21673) 245/O6
Trappers (lake), Colo. 208/E3
Traralgon, Victoria 97/D6
Traralgon, Victoria 88/H7
Trarza (reg.), Mauritania 106/A5
Trasimeno (lake), Italy 34/D3
Traskwood, Ark. (72167) 202/E5
Trat, Thailand 72/D4
Traun, Austria 41/C2
Traun (riv.), Austria 41/C2
Traun See (lake), Austria 41/B3
Traunstein, W. Germany 22/E5
Travancore (reg.), India 68/D7
Travelers Rest, S.C. (29690) 296/C2
Travellers (lake), N.S. Wales 97/B3
Travellers Rest, Ky. (†41314) 237/O6
Travemünde, W. Germany 22/D2
Travers, Alberta 182/D4
Travers (res.), Alberta 182/D4
Traverse (bay), Manitoba 179/F4
Traverse (isl.), Mich. 250/A1
Traverse (pt.), Mich. 250/A1
Traverse (co.), Minn. 255/B5
Traverse, Minn. (†56082) 255/D6
Traverse (lake), Minn. 255/B5
Traverse (lake), S. Dak. 298/R2
Traverse City, Mich. 188/K2
Traverse City, Mich. (49684) 250/D4
Tra Vinh (Phu Vinh), Vietnam 72/E5
Travis (co.), Texas 303/G7
Travis (lake), Texas 303/G7
Travis A.F.B., Calif. 204/L1
Travnik, Yugoslavia 45/C3
Trawbreaga (bay), Ireland 17/F1
Traynor, Sask. 181/C3
Traytown, Newf. 166/D1
Trbovlje, Yugoslavia 45/B2
Treadway, Tenn. (37883) 237/P8
Treasure (isl.), Fla. 212/B3
Treasure (co.), Mont. 262/J4
Treasure Island, Fla. (33740) 212/B3
Treasury (isls.), Solomon Is. 86/C2
Treaty, Ind. (†46992) 227/F3
Trebbia (riv.), Italy 34/B2
Třebíč, Czech. 41/C2
Trebinje, Yugoslavia 45/D4
Trebišov, Czech. 41/F2
Trebizond (Trabzon), Turkey 63/H2
Trebloc, Miss. (38875) 256/G3
Třeboň, Czech. 41/C2
Trece Martires, Philippines 82/C3
Tredegar, Wales 13/B6
Treece, Kansas (66778) 232/H4
Treelon, Sask. 181/C6
Trees, La. (71081) 238/B1
Treesbank, Manitoba 179/C5
Tregaron, Wales 13/D5
Tregaron, Wales 10/E4
Tregarva, Sask. 181/G5
Trego (co.), Kansas 232/C3
Trego, Mont. (59934) 262/B2
Trego, Wis. (54888) 317/C4
Treherne, Manitoba 179/D5
Treig, Loch (lake), Scotland 15/D4
Treinta y Tres (dept.), Uruguay 145/E4
Treinta y Tres, Uruguay 145/E4
Trelew, Argentina 143/C5
Trelleborg, Sweden 18/H9
Tremadoc (bay), Wales 10/D4
Tremadoc (prom.), Wales 13/C5
Tremblant (lake), Québec 172/C3
Trembleur (lake), Br. Col. 184/E3
Trementina, N. Mex. (88439) 274/E3
Tremiti (isls.), Italy 34/E3
Tremont, Ill. (61568) 222/D3
Tremont, Maine (†04653) 243/G7
Tremont◯, Maine (†04653) 243/G7
Tremont, Miss. (38876) 256/H2
Tremont, Pa. (17981) 294/K4
Tremont City, Ohio (45372) 284/C5
Tremonton, Utah (84337) 304/B2
Tremp, Spain 33/G1
Trempealeau (co.), Wis. 317/D7
Trempealeau, Wis. (54661) 317/C8
Trempealeau (riv.), Wis. 317/C7
Trenary, Mich. (49891) 250/C2
Trenčín, Czech. 41/E2
Trenel, Argentina 143/D4
Trenggalek, Indonesia 85/K2
Trenque Lauquen, Argentina 143/D4
Trent (riv.), England 13/G4
Trent (riv.), England 10/F4
Trent (riv.), N.C. 281/P4
Trent, Oreg. (†97431) 291/E4
Trent, S. Dak. (57065) 298/R6
Trent, Texas (79561) 303/D5
Trente et un Milles (lake), Québec 172/B3
Trentham, Manitoba 179/F5
Trentham Cliffs, N.S. Wales 97/B4
Trentino-Alto Adige (reg.), Italy 34/C1
Trento (prov.), Italy 34/C1
Trento, Italy 34/C1
Trenton, Ala. (35774) 195/F1
Trenton, Ark. (†72374) 202/J5
Trenton, Fla. (32693) 212/D2
Trenton, Georgia (30752) 217/A1
Trenton, Ill. (62293) 222/D5
Trenton, Iowa (†52641) 229/K6
Trenton, Ky. (42286) 237/G7
Trenton, Maine (†04605) 243/G7
Trenton◯, Maine (†04605) 243/G7
Trenton, Md. (†21155) 245/L2
Trenton, Mich. (48183) 250/B7
Trenton, Miss. (†39153) 256/E6
Trenton, Mo. (64683) 261/E2
Trenton, Nebr. (69044) 264/D4
Trenton (cap.), N.J. 146/L5
Trenton (cap.), N.J. 188/M2
Trenton (cap.), N.J. (*08601) 273/D3
Trenton, N.C. (28585) 281/P4
Trenton, N. Dak. (58853) 282/C3
Trenton, Nova Scotia 168/F3
Trenton, Ohio (45067) 284/B7
Trenton, Ontario 177/G3
Trenton, S.C. (29847) 296/D4
Trenton, Tenn. (38382) 237/D9
Trenton, Texas (75490) 303/H4
Trenton, Utah (84338) 304/B2
Trent Woods, N.C. (†28560) 281/P4
Trepassey, Newf. 166/D2
Treptow, E. Germany 22/F4
Tres Árboles, Uruguay 145/C3
Tres Arroyos, Argentina 143/D4
Tres Arroyos, Argentina 120/C6
Tres Bocas, Uruguay 145/B2
Tresckow, Pa. (18254) 294/K4
Tresco (isl.), England 13/A8
Três Corações, Brazil 132/E8
Três Corações, Brazil 135/D2
Tres Cruces, Nevada (mt.), Chile 138/B6
Tres Esquinas, Colombia 126/C7
Treshnish (isls.), Scotland 15/B4
Tres Islas, Uruguay 145/E3
Três Lagoas, Brazil 120/D5
Três Lagoas, Brazil 132/C8
Três Marias (res.), Brazil 120/E4
Tres Montes (cape), Chile 120/B7
Tres Montes (cape), Chile 138/C7
Tres Montes (gulf), Chile 138/D6
Tres Montes (pen.), Chile 138/C6
Tres Palmas, Colombia 126/B3
Trespassey (bay), Newf. 166/D2
Tres Picos, Cerro (mt.), Argentina 143/B5
Tres Piedras, N. Mex. (87577) 274/D2
Tres Pinos, Calif. (95075) 204/D7
Três Pontas, Brazil 135/D2
Tres Puntas (cape), Argentina 120/C7
Tres Puntas (cape), Argentina 143/D6
Tres Puntas (cape), Guatemala 154/C3
Três Rios, Brazil 135/E3
Três Rios, Brazil 132/F8
Tres Ritos, N. Mex. (†87579) 274/D2
Třešť, Czech. 41/C2
Treuchtlingen, W. Germany 22/D4
Treungen, Norway 18/F7
Treutlen (co.), Georgia 217/G6
Trevelín, Argentina 143/B5
Trevett, Maine (04571) 243/D8
Treviglio, Italy 34/B2
Treviño, Spain 33/E1
Treviso (prov.), Italy 34/D2
Treviso, Italy 34/D2
Trevlac, Ind. (†47448) 227/E6
Trevorton, Pa. (17881) 294/J4
Trevose (head), England 13/B7
Trévoux, France 28/F5
Treynor, Iowa (51575) 229/B6
Treyvaux, Switzerland 39/D3
Trezevant, Tenn. (38258) 237/D8
Trhové Sviny, Czech. 41/C2
Triabunna, Tasmania 99/D4
Triadelphia (lake), Md. 245/L4
Triadelphia, W. Va. (26059) 312/E2
Triana, Ala. (†35758) 195/E1
Triangle, Alberta 182/B2
Triangle, Va. (22172) 307/O3
Triángulo Este (isl.), Mexico 150/N6
Triángulo Oeste (isl.), Mexico 150/N6
Tribbett, Miss. (38779) 256/C4
Tribbey, Okla. (†74852) 288/M4
Triberg im Schwarzwald, W. Germany 22/C4
Tribune, Kansas (67879) 232/A3
Tribune, Sask. 181/H6
Tricase, Italy 34/G5
Trichur, India 68/D6
Trida, N.S. Wales 97/C3
Tridell, Utah (84076) 304/E3
Trident, Mont. (59752) 262/E5
Trident (peak), Nev. 266/C1
Trieben, Austria 41/C3
Trier, W. Germany 22/B4
Triesen, Liecht. 39/H2
Trieste (prov.), Italy 34/E2
Trieste, Italy 34/E2
Trieste, Italy 7/F4
Trieste (gulf), Italy 34/D2
Trigal, Bolivia 136/C6
Trigg (co.), Ky. 237/F7
Triglav (mt.), Yugoslavia 45/A2
Trigueros, Spain 33/C4
Trikkala, Greece 45/E6
Tri Lakes, Ind. (†46725) 227/G2
Trilby, Fla. (33593) 212/D3
Trilla, Ill. (62469) 222/E4
Trillick, N. Ireland 17/G3
Trim, Ireland 17/H4
Trim, Ireland 10/C4
Trimble, Ill. (†62454) 222/F4
Trimble (co.), Ky. 237/L3
Trimble, Ky. (42559) 237/M6
Trimble, Mo. (64492) 261/D4
Trimble, Ohio (45782) 284/F7
Trimble, Tenn. (38259) 237/C8
Trim Cane (creek), Miss. 256/G4
Trimmis, Switzerland 39/J3
Trimont, Minn. (56176) 255/D7
Trin, Switzerland 39/H3
Trinchera, Colo. (81081) 208/M8
Trinchera (peak), Colo. 208/J8
Trinchera (riv.), Colo. 208/H8
Trincheras, Mexico 150/D1
Trincomalee, Sri Lanka 54/K9
Trincomalee, Sri Lanka 68/E7
Trindade, Brazil 132/D7
Třinec, Czech. 41/E2
Tring, England 13/G7
Tring, England 10/F5
Tring-Jonction, Québec 172/F3
Trinidad (isl.), Argentina 143/D4
Trinidad, Bolivia 120/C4
Trinidad, Bolivia 136/C4
Trinidad, Calif. (95570) 204/A2
Trinidad (head), Calif. 204/A2
Trinidad (gulf), Chile 138/D8
Trinidad, Colombia 126/E5
Trinidad, Colo. 146/H6
Trinidad, Colo. 188/F3
Trinidad, Colo. (81082) 208/L8
Trinidad, Cuba 158/E2
Trinidad, Cuba 156/B2
Trinidad, Honduras 154/C3
Trinidad, Paraguay 144/E5
Trinidad, Texas (75163) 303/J5
Trinidad (isl.), Trin. & Tob. 156/G5
Trinidad (isl.), Trin. & Tob. 161/A9
Trinidad, Uruguay 145/B4
Trinidad, Wash. (†98848) 310/F3
Trinidad and Tobago 2/G5
Trinidad and Tobago 146/N8
TRINIDAD and TOBAGO 161
TRINIDAD and TOBAGO 156/G5
Trinity, Ala. (35673) 195/D1
Trinity (isls.), Alaska 196/H3
Trinity (co.), Calif. 204/B3
Trinity (riv.), Calif. 204/B3
Trinity (mt.), Idaho 220/C6
Trinity, Ky. (†41179) 237/O3
Trinity (range), Nev. 266/C2
Trinity, Newf. 166/D4
Trinity, Newf. 166/D2
Trinity (bay), Newf. 166/D2
Trinity (bay), Queensland 88/H3
Trinity (bay), Queensland 95/C3
Trinity (co.), Texas 303/J6
Trinity, Texas (75862) 303/J7
Trinity (bay), Texas 303/L2
Trinity (riv.), Texas 188/G4
Trinity (riv.), Texas 303/H5
Trinity, West Fork (riv.), Texas 303/G2
Trinity Center, Calif. (96091) 204/C2
Trinity Springs, Ind. (†47581) 227/D7
Trinity Ville, Jamaica 158/K6
Trinkitat, Sudan 111/G4
Trinkitat, Sudan 59/C6
Trino, Italy 34/B2
Trinway, Ohio (43842) 284/F5
Trio, S.C. (29595) 296/H5
Trion, Georgia (30753) 217/B1
Triplet, Va. (23886) 307/N7
Triplett, Mo. (65286) 261/F4
Tripoli, Iowa (50676) 229/J3
Tripoli (Tarabulus), Lebanon 59/C3
Tripoli (Tarabulus), Lebanon 63/F5
Tripoli (cap.), Libya 2/K4
Tripoli (cap.), Libya 102/D1
Tripoli (cap.), Libya 111/B1
Tripoli, Wis. (54564) 317/G4
Tripolis, Greece 45/F7
Tripolitania (reg.), Libya 102/D1
Tripolitania (reg.), Libya 111/B1
Tripp (co.), S. Dak. 298/K7
Tripp, S. Dak. (57376) 298/N7
Tripura (state), India 68/G4
Trischen (isl.), W. Germany 22/C1
Tristan da Cunha (isl.), St. Helena 2/J7
Triste (gulf), Venezuela 124/D2
Triton (isl.), China 85/E2
Triumph, Ill. (61371) 222/E2
Triumph-Buras, La. (†70041) 238/L8
Triune, Tenn. (†37014) 237/H9
Trivandrum, India 54/J9
Trivandrum, India 68/D7
Trivoli, Ill. (61569) 222/D3
Trnava, Czech. 41/D2
Trobriand (isls.), Papua N.G. 87/F6
Trobriand (isls.), Papua N.G. 85/C7
Trochu, Alberta 182/D4
Troense, Denmark 21/D7
Trofaiach, Austria 41/C3
Trogir, Yugoslavia 45/C4
Troisdorf, W. Germany 22/B3
Trois-Pistoles, Québec 172/H1
Trois Pitons, Morne (mt.), Dominica 161/E6
Trois-Ponts, Belgium 27/H8
Trois-Rivières, Guadeloupe 161/A7
Trois-Rivières (riv.), Haiti 158/B5
Trois-Rivières, Que. 162/J6
Trois-Rivières, Que. 146/L5
Trois-Rivières, Que. 172/E3
Trois-Rivières-Ouest, Québec 172/E3
Trois-Saumons, Québec 172/G2
Troistorrents, Switzerland /C4
Troisvierges, Luxembourg 27/J9
Troitsa (lake), Br. Col. 184/D3
Troitsk, U.S.S.R. 48/G4
Troitsko-Pechorsk, U.S.S.R. 52/J2
Trojan, S. Dak. (†57754) 298/B5
Trollhättan, Sweden 18/H7
Trombay, India 68/B7
Trombetas (riv.), Brazil 132/B3
Tromie (riv.), Scotland 15/D4
Trommald, Minn. (†56455) 255/D4
Troms (co.), Norway 18/L2
Tromsø, Norway 4/B9
Tromsø, Norway 7/F2
Tromsø, Norway 18/L2
Trona, Calif. (93562) 204/H8
Tronador (mt.), Argentina 143/B5
Tronador, Cerro (mt.), Chile 138/E3
Trondheim, Norway 7/F2
Trondheim, Norway 18/F5
Trondheimsfjorden (fjord), Norway 7/F2
Trondheimsfjorden (fjord), Norway 18/G5
Troodos (mt.), Cyprus 63/E5
Troon, Scotland 10/D3
Troon, Scotland 15/D5
Tropic, Utah (84776) 304/B6
Trosa, Sweden 18/K7
Trosky, Minn. (56177) 255/B7
Trossachs, Sask. 181/G6
Trossachs, The, (valley), Scotland 15/D4
Trostan (mt.), N. Ireland 17/J1
Trotternish (dist.), Scotland 15/B3
Trotters, N. Dak. (58657) 282/C5
Trotwood, Ohio (45426) 284/B6
Trou Bonbon, Haiti 158/A6
Trou du Nord, Haiti 158/C5
Troup (co.), Georgia 217/B4
Troup (head), Scotland 15/F3
Troup, Texas (75789) 303/J5
Troupsburg, N.Y. (14885) 276/F6
Trousdale, Kansas (†67059) 232/C4
Trousdale, Okla. (†74878) 288/M4

462 Upper Falls

Upper Falls, Md. (21156) 245/N3
Upper Fraser, Br. Col. 184/G3
Upper Frenchville, Maine (04784) 243/G1
Upper Gagetown, New Bruns. 170/D3
Upperglade, W. Va. (26266) 312/F6
Upper Greenwood Lake, N.J. (†07421) 273/E1
Upper Hainesville, New Bruns. 170/C2
Upper Horton, N.S. Wales 97/F2
Upper Hutt, N. Zealand 100/B2
Upper Iowa (riv.), Iowa 229/K2
Upper Island Cove, Newf. 166/D2
Upper Jay, N.Y. (12987) 276/N2
Upper Kennetcook, Nova Scotia 168/E3
Upper Kent, New Bruns. 170/C2
Upper Klamath (lake), Oreg. 188/B2
Upper Klamath (lake), Oreg. 291/E5
Upper Lake, Calif. (95485) 204/C4
Upper Liard, Yukon 187/F3
Upper Lough Erne (lake), N. Ireland 17/F3
Upper Lough Erne (lake), N. Ireland 10/C3
Upper Macopin, N.J. (†07435) 273/E1
Upper Manzanilla, Trin. & Tob. 161/B10
Upper Marlboro, Md. (20870) 245/M5
Upper Matecumbe (key), Fla. 212/F7
Upper Maugerville, New Bruns. 170/D3
Upper Mills, New Bruns. 170/C3
Upper Musquodoboit, Nova Scotia 168/F3
Upper New York (bay), N.J. 273/B2
Upper Nile (prov.), Sudan 111/F6
Upper Rawdon, Nova Scotia 168/E3
Upper Red (lake), 255/D2
Upper Red Rock (lake), Mont. 262/E6
Upper Rockport, New Bruns. 170/F3
Upper Saddle River, N.J. (†07458) 273/B1
Upper Saint Clair○, Pa. (15241) 294/B7
Upper Sandusky, Ohio (43351) 284/D4
Upper Saranac (lake), N.Y. 276/M2
Upper Seven Sisters, Manitoba 179/G4
Upper Sheikh, Somalia 115/J2
Upper Sheila, New Bruns. 170/E1
Upper South River, Nova Scotia 168/G3
Upper Stepney, Conn. (†06468) 210/B3
Upper Stewiacke, Nova Scotia 168/F3
Upper Strasburg, Pa. (17265) 294/G5
Upper Tract, W. Va. (26866) 312/H5
Upper Tygart, Ky. (41178) 237/P4
Upper Vaughan, Nova Scotia 168/D4
Upperville, Va. (22176) 307/N2
Upper Volta 2/J5
Upper Volta 102/B3
UPPER VOLTA 106/D6
Upper Woodstock, New Bruns. 170/C2
Uppingham, England 13/G5
Uppsala (co.), Sweden 18/K7
Uppsala, Sweden 7/F3
Uppsala, Sweden 18/K7
Upright (cape), Alaska 196/D2
Upsala, Minn. (56384) 255/D5
Upsala, Ontario 177/G5
Upsala, Ontario 175/B3
Upsalquitch, New Bruns. 170/D1
Upsalquitch (riv.), New Bruns. 170/D1
Upshur (co.), Texas 303/K5
Upshur (co.), W. Va. 312/F5
Upson (co.), Georgia 217/D5
Upson, Wis. (54565) 317/F3
Upton, Ky. (42784) 237/K6
Upton○, Maine (04261) 243/B6
Upton○, Mass. (01568) 249/H4
Upton, Québec 172/E4
Upton (co.), Texas 303/B6
Upton, Wyo. (82730) 319/H1
Upton upon Severn, England 13/E5
Upton-West Upton, Mass. (01568) 249/H4
Ur (ruins), Iraq 66/E5
Urabá (gulf), Colombia 126/B3
Urachiche, Venezuela 124/D2
Uracoa, Venezuela 124/G3
Urad Qianqi, China 77/G3
Urad Zhonghou Lianheqi, China 77/G3
Uraidla, S. Australia 94/B8
Urakawa, Japan 81/L2
Ural (mts.), U.S.S.R. 4/C6
Ural (mts.), U.S.S.R. 54/G4
Ural (mts.), U.S.S.R. 7/L2
Ural (mts.), U.S.S.R. 52/J2
Ural (mts.), U.S.S.R. 48/F4
Ural (riv.), U.S.S.R. 54/G5
Ural (riv.), U.S.S.R. 48/F5
Ural (riv.), U.S.S.R. 52/J4
Uralla, N.S. Wales 97/F2
Ural'sk, U.S.S.R. 54/G4
Ural'sk, U.S.S.R. 48/F4
Urambo, Tanzania 115/F4
Uran, India 68/B7
Urana, N.S. Wales 97/D4
Urana (lake), N.S. Wales 97/D4
Urania, La. (71480) 238/F3
Uranium City, Sask. 162/F4
Uranium City, Sask. 146/H4
Uranium City, Sask. 181/L2
Urapunga, North. Terr. 93/D3
Uraricoera, Brazil 132/H8
Uraricoera (riv.), Brazil 132/H8
Uravan, Colo. (81436) 208/B6
Urawa, Japan 81/O2
Uray, U.S.S.R. 48/G3
Urban, Ky. (40765) 237/O6
Urban, Pa. (†17830) 294/J4
Urban, Wash. (†98221) 310/C2
Urbana, Ark. (71768) 202/E7
Urbana, Ill. (61801) 222/E3
Urbana, Ind. (46990) 227/F3
Urbana, Iowa (52345) 229/K4
Urbana, Md. (†21701) 245/J3
Urbana, Mo. (65767) 261/F7
Urbana, Ohio (43078) 284/C5
Urbancrest, Ohio (†43123) 284/D6
Urbandale, Iowa (50322) 229/F5
Urbanette, Ark. (†72616) 202/D1
Urbankn Minn. (†56361) 255/C4
Urbanna, Va. (23175) 307/P5
Urbenville, N.S. Wales 97/G1
Urbino, Italy 34/D3
Urcos, Peru 128/G9
Urda, Spain 33/E3
Urdinarrain, Argentina 143/G6
Ure (riv.), England 13/F3
Uren, Sask. 181/E5
Urenui, N. Zealand 100/E3
Ures, Mexico 150/D2
Urfa (prov.), Turkey 63/H4
Urfa, Turkey 59/C2
Urfa, Turkey 63/H4
Urga (Ulaanbaatar) (cap.), Mongolia 77/G2
Urgel, Llanos de (plain), Spain 33/G2
Urgench, U.S.S.R. 54/G5
Urgench, U.S.S.R. 48/G5
Ürgüp, Turkey 63/F3
Uri (canton), Switzerland 39/G3
Uriah, Ala. (36480) 195/D8
Uribe, Colombia 126/C6
Uribia, Colombia 126/D2
Urica, Venezuela 124/F3
Urich, Mo. (64788) 261/E6
Urim, Israel 65/B5
Urimán, Venezuela 124/G5
Uriondo, Bolivia 136/C7
Urique (riv.), Mexico 150/F3
Urirotstock (mt.), Switzerland 39/G3
Urituyacu (riv.), Peru 128/D5
Urk, Netherlands 27/H3
Urla, Turkey 63/B3
Urlaţa, Romania 45/H3
Urlingford, Ireland 17/F6
Urmia, Iran 59/D2
Urmia, Iran 66/D2
Urmia (lake), Iran 54/F6
Urmia (lake), Iran 59/E2
Urmia (lake), Iran 66/D2
Urmston, England 13/H2
Urnäsch, Switzerland 39/H2
Uromi, Nigeria 106/F7
Uroševac, Yugoslavia 45/E4
Urrao, Colombia 126/B4
Ursa, Ill. (62376) 222/B3
Ursina, Pa. (15485) 294/D6
Ursine, Nev. (†89043) 266/G5
Úrsulo Galván, Mexico 150/Q1
Uruáchic, Mexico 150/E3
Uruaçu, Brazil 132/D6
Uruaçu, Brazil 120/E4
Uruana, Brazil 132/D6
Uruapan del Progreso, Mexico 150/H7
Urubamba, Peru 128/F9
Urubamba (riv.), Peru 128/F8
Urubichá, Bolivia 136/D4
Urubu (riv.), Brazil 132/A3
Urubupungá (dam), Brazil 132/C8
Urubupungá (dam), Brazil 120/D5
Urucará, Brazil 132/B3
Uruçuí, Brazil 132/E4
Urucún, Morro do (mt.), Brazil 132/B7
Urucurituba, Brazil 132/B3
Uruguai (riv.), Brazil 132/C9
Uruguaiana, Brazil 120/D5
Uruguaiana, Brazil 132/B10
Uruguay 2/G7
Uruguay 120/D6
URUGUAY 145
Uruguay (riv.) 120/D5
Uruguay (riv.), Argentina 143/E3
Uruguay (riv.), Uruguay 145/A3
Urumaco, Venezuela 124/C2
Ürümqi (Urumchi), China 77/C3
Ürümqi, China 2/P3
Ürümqi, China 54/K5
Urunga, N.S. Wales 97/G2
Urup (isl.), U.S.S.R. 54/S5
Urup (isl.), U.S.S.R. 48/Q5
Uruyén, Venezuela 124/G5
Uryupinsk, U.S.S.R. 52/F4
Urzhum, U.S.S.R. 52/G3
Urziceni, Romania 45/H3
Usa (riv.), U.S.S.R. 7/K2
Usa (riv.), U.S.S.R. 52/K1
Uşak (prov.), Turkey 63/C3
Uşak, Turkey 59/A2
Uşak, Turkey 63/C3
Usakos, Namibia 118/B4
Usakos, Namibia 102/D7
Usedom (isl.), E. Germany 22/F1
Usedom (Uznam) (isl.), Poland 47/B1
Ushakov (isl.), U.S.S.R. 4/B5
Ushant (isl.), France 7/D4
Ushant (Ouessant) (isl.), France 28/A3
Usherville, Sask. 181/J3
Ushibuka, Japan 81/D7
Ushtobe, U.S.S.R. 48/H5
Ushuaia, Argentina 143/C7
Ushuaia, Argentina 120/C8
Usibelli, Alaska (99787) 196/J2
Usinsk, U.S.S.R. 52/J1
Usk, Br. Col. 184/C3
Usk, Wales 13/B6
Usk (riv.), Wales 10/E5
Usk (riv.), Wales 13/B6
Usk, Wash. (99180) 310/H2
Üsküdar, Turkey 63/D6
Uslar, W. Germany 22/C3
Usman', U.S.S.R. 52/E4
Usol'ye-Sibirskoye, U.S.S.R. 48/L4
Usquepaug, R.I. (†02892) 249/H6
Ussel, France 28/E5
Ussuri (riv.) 54/P5
Ussuri (Wusuli Jiang) (riv.), China 77/M2
Ussuri (riv.), U.S.S.R. 48/O5
Ussuriysk, U.S.S.R. 54/P5
Ussuriysk, U.S.S.R. 48/O5
Ústěk, Czech. 41/C1
Uster, Switzerland 39/G2
Ustica (isl.), Italy 34/D5
Ust'-Ilimsk, U.S.S.R. 48/L4
Ústí nad Labem, Czech. 41/C1
Ústí nad Orlicí, Czech. 41/D2
Ustka, Poland 47/C1
Ust'-Kamchatsk, U.S.S.R. 54/T4
Ust'-Kamchatsk, U.S.S.R. 48/R4
Ust'-Kamenogorsk, U.S.S.R. 54/J5
Ust'-Kamenogorsk, U.S.S.R. 48/J5
Ust'-Kulom, U.S.S.R. 52/H2
Ust'-Kut, U.S.S.R. 54/M4
Ust'-Kut, U.S.S.R. 48/L4
Ust'-Kuyga, U.S.S.R. 4/C3
Ust'-Kuyga, U.S.S.R. 48/O3
Ust'-Maya, U.S.S.R. 48/O3
Ust'-Nera, U.S.S.R. 54/R3
Ust'-Nera, U.S.S.R. 48/P3
Ust'-Olenëk, U.S.S.R. 48/M2
Ust'-Omchug, U.S.S.R. 48/P3
Ust'-Ordynskiy, U.S.S.R. 48/L4
Ust'-Ordynskiy Buryat Aut. Okr., U.S.S.R. 48/L4
Ust'-Pinega, U.S.S.R. 52/F2
Ust'-Port, U.S.S.R. 48/J2
Ustrzyki Dolne, Poland 47/F4
Ust'-Tsil'ma, U.S.S.R. 52/H1
Ust'-Urt (plat.), U.S.S.R. 54/G5
Ust'-Urt (plat.), U.S.S.R. 48/F5
Ustyuzhna, U.S.S.R. 52/E3
Usu, China 77/B3
Usuki, Japan 81/E7
Usulután, El Salvador 154/C4
Usumacinta (riv.), Guatemala 154/B2
Usumacinta (riv.), Mexico 150/O8
Utah 188/D3
UTAH 304
Utah (beach), France 28/C3
Utah (state), U.S. 146/G6
Utah (co.), Utah 304/C3
Utah (lake), Utah 188/D2
Utah (lake), Utah 304/C3
Utajärvi, Finland 18/P4
Ute, Iowa (51060) 229/B4
Ute (creek), N. Mex. 274/F3
Ute (peak), N. Mex. 274/D2
Ute (res.), N. Mex. 274/F3
Ute Mountain Ind. Res., Colo. 208/B8
Ute Mountain Ind. Res., N. Mex. 274/A1
Utena, U.S.S.R. 53/C3
Utena, U.S.S.R. 52/C3
Ute Park, N. Mex. (87749) 274/D2
Utete, Tanzania 115/G5
Uthai Thani, Thailand 72/C4
Uthal, Pakistan 68/B3
Uthal, Pakistan 59/J4
Utica, Ill. (61373) 222/E2
Utica, Ind. (†47130) 227/F8
Utica, Kansas (67584) 232/B3
Utica, Ky. (42376) 237/G5
Utica, Mich. (*48087) 250/F6
Utica, Minn. (55979) 255/G7
Utica, Miss. (39175) 256/C6
Utica, Mo. (64686) 261/E3
Utica, Mont. (59452) 262/F4
Utica, Nebr. (68456) 264/G4
Utica, N.Y. 188/M2
Utica, N.Y. (*13501) 276/K4
Utica, Ohio (43080) 284/F5
Utica, Okla. (74763) 288/O7
Utica, Pa. (16362) 294/C3
Utica, S.C. (†29678) 296/B2
Utica, S. Dak. (57067) 298/P8
Utica, Wis. (†53589) 317/H10
Utica Junior College, Miss. (39175) 256/C6
Utiel, Spain 33/F3
Utikuma (lake), Alberta 182/C2
Utikuma (riv.), Alberta 182/C1
Utikumasis (lake), Alberta 182/C2
Utila, Honduras 154/D2
Utila (isl.), Honduras 154/D2
Utleyville, Colo. (†81064) 208/O8
Utopia, Alaska (†99745) 196/H1
Utopia (lake), New Bruns. 170/D3
Utopia, North. Terr. 93/D7
Utopia, Texas (78884) 303/E8
Utrecht (prov.), Netherlands 27/G4
Utrecht, Netherlands 27/G4
Utrecht, Netherlands 7/E3
Utrera, Spain 33/D4
Utsjoki, Finland 18/P2
Utsunomiya, Japan 81/K5
Uttaradit, Thailand 72/D3
Uttarpara-Kotrung, India 68/F1
Uttar Pradesh (state), India 68/D3
Uttoxeter, England 13/E5
Uttoxeter, England 10/F4
Utuado, P. Rico 156/F1
Utuado, P. Rico 161/B2
Utukok (riv.), Alaska 196/F1
Uturoa, Fr. Poly. 87/L7
Utzenstorf, Switzerland 39/E2
Uusikaarlepyy (Nykarleby), Finland 18/N5
Uusikaupunki, Finland 18/M6
Uusimaa (prov.), Finland 18/O6
Uva, Laguna (lake), Colombia 126/E6
Uva (riv.), Colombia 126/E6
Uvalda, Georgia (30473) 217/H6
Uvalde (co.), Texas 303/E8
Uvalde, Texas (78801) 303/E8
Uvarovo, U.S.S.R. 52/F4
Uvéa (isl.), New Caled. 87/G7
Uvéa (isl.), New Caled. 86/H4
Uvéa (bay), New Caled. 86/H4
Uverito, Venezuela 124/F3
Uvinza, Tanzania 115/F5
Uvira, Zaire 115/E4
Uvs, Mongolia 77/D2
Uvs Nuur (lake), Mongolia 54/L4
Uvs Nuur (lake), Mongolia 77/D1
Uwajima, Japan 81/F7
Uwchland, Pa. (19480) 294/L5
'Uweinat, Jebel (mt.), Egypt 111/E3
'Uweinat, Jebel (mt.), Libya 111/E3
'Uweinat, Jebel (mt.), Sudan 111/E3
Uxbridge○, Mass. (01569) 249/H4
Uxbridge, Ontario 177/E3
Uxin, China 77/G4
Uxmal (ruins), Mexico 150/P6
Uyak, Alaska (†99624) 196/H3
Uyuni, Bolivia 120/C5
Uyuni, Bolivia 136/B7
Uyuni (salt dep.), Bolivia 136/B7
Už (riv.), Czech. 41/G2
Uzbek, S.S.R., U.S.S.R. 54/H5
Uzbek, S.S.R., U.S.S.R. 48/G5
Uzès, France 28/F5
Uzhgorod, U.S.S.R. 7/G4
Uzhgorod, U.S.S.R. 52/B5
Uzlovaya, U.S.S.R. 52/E4
Uznach, Switzerland 39/H2
Uznam (Usedom) (isl.), Poland 47/B1
Üzümlü, Turkey 63/D4
Uzunköprü, Turkey 63/B2
Uzwil, Switzerland 39/H2
Uzza, Israel 65/B4

V

Vaalfetu (mt.), W. Samoa 86/M8
Vaal (riv.), S. Africa 102/E7
Vaal (riv.), S. Africa 118/D5
Vaala, Finland 18/P4
Vaals, Netherlands 27/H7
Vaalserberg (mt.), Belgium 27/J7
Vaalserberg (mt.), Netherlands 27/J7
Vaalspan, S. Africa 118/C5
Vaasa (prov.), Finland 18/N5
Vaasa, Finland 7/G2
Vaasa, Finland 18/M5
Vaassen, Netherlands 27/H4
Vác, Hungary 41/E3
Vaca (key), Fla. 212/E7
Vacaria, Brazil 132/D10
Vacaville, Calif. (95688) 204/D5
Vaccarès (lag.), France 28/F6
Vache (isl.), Haiti 158/B6
Vache (isl.), Haiti 156/D3
Vacherie, La. (70090) 238/L3
Vacía Talega (pt.), P. Rico 161/E1
Vada, Ky. (41383) 237/O5
Vaden, Ark. (†71923) 202/E6
Vader, Wash. (98593) 310/B4
Vadis, W. Va. (26445) 312/E4
Vadito, N. Mex. (87579) 274/D2
Vadnais Heights, Minn. (†55101) 255/G5
Vado, N. Mex. (88072) 274/C6
Vadodara, India 68/C4
Vadret (peak), Switzerland 39/J3
Vadsø, Norway 7/H1
Vadsø, Norway 18/Q1
Vadstena, Sweden 18/J7
Vaduz (cap.), Liecht. 39/H2
Vaea (mt.), W. Samoa 86/M8
Værøy (isl.), Norway 18/H3
Vaga (riv.), U.S.S.R. 52/F2
Vagåvatn (lake), Norway 18/F6
Vaggeryd, Sweden 18/J8
Vagos, Portugal 33/B2
Vagthus (pt.), Virgin Is. (U.S.) 161/F4
Váh (riv.), Czech. 41/D2
Vahitahi (atoll), Fr. Poly. 87/N7
Vaiden, Miss. (39176) 256/E4
Vaihiria (lake), Fr. Poly. 86/T13
Vail, Ariz. (85641) 198/E6
Vail, Colo. (81657) 208/G3
Vail, Iowa (51465) 229/C4
Vails, N.J. (†07832) 273/D2
Vaitupu (atoll), Tuvalu 87/H6
Vakfıkebir, Turkey 63/H2
Vakh (riv.), U.S.S.R. 48/J3
Vakhan (reg.), Afghanistan 59/K2
Vakhtan, U.S.S.R. 52/G3
Vál, Hungary 41/E3
Valais (canton), Switzerland 39/D4
Val-Alain, Québec 172/F3
Valašské Meziříčí, Czech. 41/D2
Valatie, N.Y. (12184) 276/N6
Val-Barrette, Québec 172/B3
Val-Brillant, Québec 172/B1
Valcheta, Argentina 143/C5
Val-Comeau, New Bruns. 170/F1
Valcour (isl.), N.Y. 276/N1
Valcourt, Québec 172/E4
Valdagno, Italy 34/C2
Val d'Amour, New Bruns. 170/D1
Val-David, Québec 172/C3
Valday, U.S.S.R. 52/D3
Valday (Valdai) (hills), U.S.S.R. 52/D3
Valdecañas (res.), Spain 33/D3
Val-de-Marne (dept.), France 28/C1
Valdemarsvik, Sweden 18/K7
Valdemoro, Spain 33/F4
Valdepeñas, Spain 33/E3
Valderas, Spain 33/D1
Valderrobres, Spain 33/F2
Valders, Wis. (54245) 317/L7
Valdés, Argentina 143/C3
Valdés (pen.), Argentina 120/C7
Valdés (pen.), Argentina 143/D5
Valdes (isl.), Br. Col. 184/K3
Val-des-Bois, Québec 172/B4
Valdese, N.C. (28690) 281/F3
Valdeverdeja, Spain 33/D3
Valdez, Alaska (99686) 196/D1
Valdez, Colo. (†81082) 208/K8
Valdez, Ecuador 128/C2
Valdez, N. Mex. (87580) 274/D2
Valdivia, Chile 2/F7
Valdivia, Chile 138/D3
Valdivia, Chile 120/B6
Valdivia, Colombia 126/C4
Val-d'Oise (dept.), France 28/E3
Val-d'Or, Que. 162/J6
Val d'Or, Québec 174/B3
Valdosta, Ga. 188/K4
Valdosta, Georgia (31601) 217/F9
Val Doucet, New Bruns. 170/E1
Vale, N.C. (28168) 281/G3
Vale, Oreg. (97918) 291/K4
Vale, S. Dak. (57788) 298/C4
Vale, Tenn. (†38317) 237/E8
Valeda, Kansas (†67337) 232/G4
Valeene, Ind. (†47125) 227/E8
Valemount, Br. Col. 184/H4
Valença, Brazil 120/F4
Valença, Brazil 135/E3
Valença, Brazil 132/G6
Valença, Portugal 33/B2
Valença do Piauí, Brazil 132/F4
Valence, France 7/E4
Valence, France 28/F5
Valencia, Calif. (91355) 204/G9
Valencia (Valentia) (isl.), Ireland 10/A5
Valencia (isl.), Ireland 17/A8
Valencia (co.), N. Mex. 274/C4
Valencia, N. Mex. (†87031) 274/C4
Valencia, Pa. (16059) 294/C4
Valencia, Philippines 82/E7
Valencia (prov.), Spain 33/F3
Valencia, Spain 7/D5
Valencia, Spain 33/F3
Valencia (gulf), Spain 33/G3
Valencia, Albufera de (lag.), Spain 33/G3
Valencia (reg.), Spain 33/F3
Valencia, Trin. & Tob. 161/B10
Valencia, Venezuela 120/C2
Valencia, Venezuela 124/E2
Valencia (lake), Venezuela 124/E2
Valencia de Alcántara, Spain 33/C3
Valencia de Don Juan, Spain 33/D1
Valenciennes, France 28/E2
Valendas, Switzerland 39/H3
Valentia (isl.), Ireland 10/A5
Valentine, Ariz. (86437) 198/B3
Valentine, Ind. (†46761) 227/G1
Valentine, Nebr. (69201) 264/D2
Valentine, Texas (79854) 303/C11
Valentines, Uruguay 145/E4
Valentines, Va. (23887) 307/N7
Valenza, Italy 34/B2
Valenzuela, Paraguay 144/B5
Valera, Texas (76884) 303/E6
Valera, Venezuela 124/C3
Valera, Venezuela 120/B2
Valeria, Iowa (†50054) 229/G5
Vale Summit, Md. (†21532) 245/C2
Valga, U.S.S.R. 52/C3
Valga, U.S.S.R. 53/D2
Valhalla, Alberta 182/A2
Valhalla, N.Y. (10595) 276/P6
Valhalla Centre, Alberta 182/A2
Valhermoso Springs, Ala. (35775) 195/E2
Valiente (pen.), Panama 154/G6
Valier, Ill. (62891) 222/D5
Valier, Mont. (59486) 262/D2
Valier, Pa. (15780) 294/D4
Valjean, Sask. 181/E5
Valjevo, Yugoslavia 45/D3
Valka, U.S.S.R. 53/C2
Valkeakoski, Finland 18/N6
Valkenswaard, Netherlands 27/H6
Valladolid, Mexico 146/K7
Valladolid, Mexico 150/P6
Valladolid (prov.), Spain 33/D2
Valladolid, Spain 33/D2
Valladolid, Spain 7/E4
Vallay (isl.), Scotland 15/A3
Vall de Uxó, Spain 33/F3
Valle, Norway 18/E7
Valle Alegre, Chile 138/F2
Vallecas, Spain 33/G4
Vallecito (res.), Colo. 208/D8
Vallecitos, N. Mex. (87581) 274/C2
Valle de Allende, Mexico 150/G3
Valle de Bravo, Mexico 150/J7
Valle de Guanape, Venezuela 124/F3
Valle de la Pascua, Venezuela 124/F3
Valle del Cauca (dept.), Colombia 126/B6
Valledupar, Colombia 120/B1
Valledupar, Colombia 126/D2
Vallée-Jonction, Québec 172/G3
Vallegrande, Bolivia 120/C4
Vallegrande, Bolivia 136/C6
Valle Hermoso, Mexico 150/L4
Vallehermoso, Spain 33/A5
Vallejo, Calif. 188/B3
Vallejo, Calif. (94590) 204/J1
Valle Mí, Paraguay 144/D3
Vallenar, Chile 138/A7
Vallentuna, Sweden 18/H1
Valle San Telmo, Mexico 150/A1
Valles Mines, Mo. (63087) 261/L6
Valletta (cap.), Malta 7/F5
Valletta (cap.), Malta 34/E7
Valley (co.), Idaho 220/C5
Valley (riv.), Manitoba 179/B3
Valley (co.), Mont. 262/K2
Valley (co.), Nebr. 264/E3
Valley, Nebr. (68064) 264/H3
Valley, Nova Scotia 168/E3
Valley, Wash. (99181) 310/H2
Valley, Wis. (†54639) 317/F8
Valley, Wyo. (†82414) 319/C1
Valley Bend, W. Va. (26293) 312/F5
Valley Brook, Okla. (†73101) 288/M4
Valley Center, Kansas (67147) 232/E4
Valley Centre, Sask. 181/D4
Valley City, Ill. (†62340) 222/C4
Valley City, N. Dak. (58072) 282/P6
Valley City, Ohio (44280) 284/G3
Valley Cottage, N.Y. (10989) 276/K8
Valley East, Ontario 177/J5
Valley East, Ontario 175/D3
Valley Falls, Kansas (66088) 232/G2
Valley Falls, N.Y. (12185) 276/N5
Valley Falls, Oreg. (†97630) 291/G5
Valley Falls, R.I. (†02864) 249/J5
Valley Farms, Ariz. (85291) 198/D6
Valleyfield, Québec 172/C4
Valleyford, Wash. (99036) 310/H3
Valley Forge, Pa. (19481) 294/L5
Valley Grove, W. Va. (26060) 312/E2
Valley Head, Ala. (35989) 195/G1
Valley Head, W. Va. (26294) 312/G5
Valley Hi, Ohio (†43360) 284/C5
Valley Lee, Md. (20692) 245/M8
Valley Mills, Texas (76689) 303/G6
Valley Park, Miss. (39177) 256/C5
Valley Park, Mo. (63088) 261/O3
Valley Point, W. Va. (†26519) 312/G3
Valley River, Manitoba 179/B3
Valley Spring, Texas (76885) 303/F7
Valley Springs, Ark. (72682) 202/D1
Valley Springs, Calif. (95252) 204/C9
Valley Springs, S. Dak. (57068) 298/S6
Valley Station, Ky. (40272) 237/K4
Valley Stream, N.Y. (*11580) 276/P7
Valleyview, Alberta 182/B2
Valley View, Ill. (†60120) 222/E2
Valley View, Ky. (†40475) 237/N5
Valley View, Ohio (†43201) 284/D6
Valley View, Ohio (†44101) 284/H9
Valley View, Pa. (17983) 294/J4
Valley View, Texas (76272) 303/H4
Vallgrund (isl.), Finland 18/M5
Valliant, Okla. (74764) 288/R6
Vallières, Haiti 158/C5
Vallimanca (riv.), Argentina 143/F7
Vallonia, Ind. (47281) 227/E7
Vallon-Pont-d'Arc, France 28/F5
Vallorbe, Switzerland 39/B3
Valls, Spain 33/G2
Val Marie, Sask. 181/D6
Valmeyer, Ill. (62295) 222/C5
Valmiera, U.S.S.R. 53/C2
Valmiera, U.S.S.R. 52/C3
Valmont, Québec 172/E3
Valmontone, Italy 34/F7
Valmora, N. Mex. (87750) 274/D3
Valmy, Nev. (89438) 266/D2
Valmy, Wis. (†54235) 317/M6
Valognes, France 28/C3
Valona, Georgia (31332) 217/K8
Valor, Sask. 181/E6
Valpaços, Portugal 33/C2
Valparaíso (reg.), Chile 138/A9
Valparaíso, Chile 2/F7
Valparaíso, Chile 120/B6
Valparaíso, Chile 138/E2
Valparaiso, Fla. (32580) 212/C6
Valparaiso, Ind. (46383) 227/C2
Valparaiso, Nebr. (68065) 264/H3
Valparaiso, Sask. 181/G3
Val-Racine, Québec 172/G4
Vals (cape), Indonesia 85/K7
Vals, Switzerland 39/H3
Valsad, India 68/C4
Valsequillo (res.), Mexico 150/N2
Valserrhein (riv.), Switzerland 39/H3
Valsetz, Oreg. (97393) 291/D3
Value, Miss. (39178) 256/D6
Valuyki, U.S.S.R. 52/E4
Valverda, La. (†70757) 238/G5
Valverde (prov.), Dom. Rep. 158/D5
Valverde, Dom. Rep. 158/D5
Val Verde (co.), Texas 303/C8
Valverde del Camino, Spain 33/C4
Vamdrup, Denmark 21/C7
Vammala, Finland 18/N6
Vámos, Greece 45/F8
Vámospércs, Hungary 41/F3
Van, Ky. (41857) 237/R6
Van (lake), N. Dak. 282/L5
Van, Oreg. (†97904) 291/J4
Van, Pa. (†16319) 294/C3
Van, Texas (75790) 303/J5
Van (prov.), Turkey 63/K3
Van, Turkey 59/D2
Van, Turkey 63/K3
Van (lake), Turkey 54/F6
Van (lake), Turkey 59/D2
Van (lake), Turkey 63/K3
Van, W. Va. (25206) 312/C7
Vanadium, N. Mex. (88073) 274/A6
Van Alstyne, Texas (75095) 303/H4
Vananda, Br. Col. 184/E5
Vananda, Mont. (†59237) 262/K4
Vanatta, Ohio (†43055) 284/E5
Vanavara, U.S.S.R. 48/L3
Van Blommenstein (lake), Suriname 120/D2
Van Blommestein (lake), Suriname 131/D3
Van Bruyssel, Québec 172/E2
Van Buren (co.), Ark. 202/E2
Van Buren, Ark. (72956) 202/B3
Van Buren, Ind. (46991) 227/F3
Van Buren (co.), Iowa 229/K7
Van Buren, Maine (04785) 243/G1
Van Buren○, Maine (04785) 243/G1
Van Buren (co.), Mich. 250/C6
Van Buren, Mo. (63965) 261/L8
Van Buren, Ohio (45889) 284/C3
Van Buren (co.), Tenn. 237/L9
Vance, Ala. (35490) 195/D4
Vance, Miss. (38964) 256/D2
Vance (co.), N.C. 281/N2
Vance, S.C. (29163) 296/G5
Vance A.F.B., Okla. 288/K2
Vanceboro○, Maine (04491) 243/J4
Vanceboro, N.C. (28586) 281/P4
Vanceburg, Ky. (41179) 237/P3
Vancleave, Miss. (†39564) 256/G9
Van Cleve, Iowa (†50162) 229/G5
Vancourt, Texas (76955) 303/D6
Vancouver (mt.), Alaska 196/L2
Vancouver, Br. Col. 146/F4
Vancouver, Br. Col. 162/D6
Vancouver, Br. Col. 184/K3
Vancouver (Greater), Br. Col. 184/K3
Vancouver (isl.), Br. Col. 146/F5
Vancouver (isl.), Br. Col. 162/D6
Vancouver (isl.), Br. Col. 184/D5
Vancouver, Canada 2/C3
Vancouver (isl.), Canada 2/C3
Vancouver, Wash. 188/B1
Vancouver, Wash. (*98660) 310/C5
Vancouver (lake), Wash. 310/C5
Vandalia, Ill. (62471) 222/D5
Vandalia, Mich. (49095) 250/D7
Vandalia, Mo. (63382) 261/J4
Vandalia, Mont. (59273) 262/J2
Vandalia, Ohio (45377) 284/B6
Vandalia, W. Va. (†26423) 312/F5
Vandemere, N.C. (28587) 281/R4

Victoria Harbour 463

Vandenberg A.F.B., Calif. 204/E9
Vanderbijl Park, S. Africa 118/D5
Vanderbilt, Mich. (49795) 250/E3
Vanderbilt, Pa. (15486) 294/C5
Vanderbilt, Texas (77991) 303/H9
Vanderburgh (co.), Ind. 227/B8
Vandergrift, Pa. (15690) 294/D4
Vanderhoof, Br. Col. 162/D5
Vanderhoof, Br. Col. 184/E3
Vanderlin (isl.), North. Terr. 88/F3
Vanderlin (isl.), North. Terr. 93/E3
Vanderpool, Texas (78885) 303/E8
Vanderpool, Va. (†24465) 307/J4
Vandervoort, Ark. (71972) 202/B5
Van Diemen (cape), North. Terr. 88/D2
Van Diemen (cape), North. Terr. 93/A1
Van Diemen (gulf), North. Terr. 88/E2
Van Diemen (gulf), North. Terr. 93/B1
Vandiver, Ala. (35176) 195/F4
Vandiver, Mo. (†65265) 261/J4
Vandling, Pa. (18421) 294/M2
Vändra, U.S.S.R. 53/C1
Vandura, Sask. 181/K5
Vanduser, Mo. (63784) 261/N9
Vanegas, Mexico 150/J5
Vänern (lake), Sweden 7/F3
Vänern (lake), Sweden 18/H7
Vänersborg, Sweden 18/G7
Van Etten, N.Y. (14889) 276/G6
Vanga, Kenya 115/G4
Vangaindrano, Madagascar 118/H4
Vanguard, Sask. 181/D6
Vangunu (isl.), Solomon Is. 86/D3
Van Hoa, Vietnam 72/E2
Van Horn, Texas (79855) 303/C11
Van Horne, Iowa (52346) 229/J4
Van Hornesville, N.Y. (13475) 276/L5
Vanier, Ontario 177/J2
Vanier, Québec 172/J3
Vanikoro (isl.), Solomon Is. 87/G7
Vanil Noir (mt.), Switzerland 39/D3
Vanimo, Papua N.G. 87/E6
Vanimo, Papua N.G. 85/B6
Vanino, U.S.S.R. 48/P5
Vaniyambadi, India 68/D6
Vankleek Hill, Ontario 177/K2
Van Lear, Ky. (41265) 237/R5
Vanleer, Tenn. (37181) 237/G8
Vanlue, Ohio (45890) 284/C4
Van Meter, Iowa (50261) 229/E5
Vanna, Georgia (30672) 217/F2
Vännäs, Sweden 18/L5
Vanndale, Ark. (72387) 202/J3
Vannes, France 28/B4
Van Ninh, Vietnam 72/F4
Vannøy (isl.), Norway 18/L1
Van Nuys, Calif. (*91401) 204/B10
Van Orin, Ill. (61374) 222/D2
Vanoss, Okla. (†74820) 288/N5
Vanrhynsdorp, S. Africa 118/B6
Van Rook, Queensland 95/B3
Vansant, Va. (24656) 307/D6
Vansbro, Sweden 18/H6
Vanscoy, Sask. 181/D4
Vansittart (isl.), N.W. Terrs. 187/K3
Vansittart (isl.), Tasmania 99/E2
Vantage, Sask. 181/F6
Vantage, Wash. (98950) 310/E4
Van Tassell, Wyo. (82242) 319/H3
Vanua Levu (isl.), Fiji 87/H7
Vanua Levu (isl.), Fiji 86/Q10
Vanuatu 2/T6
Vanuatu 87/G7
Van Vleet, Miss. (†38851) 256/G3
Vanvoorhis, W. Va. (†26505) 312/G3
Van Wert, Georgia (†30153) 217/B3
Van Wert, Iowa (50262) 229/F7
Van Wert (co.), Ohio 284/A4
Van Wert, Ohio (45891) 284/A4
Van Wyck, S.C. (29744) 296/F2
Van Yen, Vietnam 72/E2
Vanylven, Norway 18/E5
Van Zandt (co.), Texas 303/J5
Van Zandt, Wash. (†98244) 310/C2
Vanzant, Mo. (65768) 261/H9
Var (dept.), France 28/G6
Vara, Sweden 18/H7
Vara de María, Venezuela 124/C4
Varadero, Cuba 158/D1
Varakļāni, U.S.S.R. 53/D2
Varallo Pombia, Italy 34/B2
Varamin, Iran 66/G3
Varanasi, India 54/K7
Varanasi, India 68/E3
Varangerfjorden (fjord), Norway 18/Q2
Varangerfjorden (fjord), Norway 7/H1
Varangerhalvøya (pen.), Norway 18/Q1
Varano (lake), Italy 34/F3
Varaždin, Yugoslavia 45/B2
Varazze, Italy 34/B2
Varberg, Sweden 18/G8
Vardaman, Miss. (38878) 256/F3
Vardar (riv.), Greece 45/E5
Vardar (riv.), Yugoslavia 45/E5
Varde, Denmark 18/F9
Varde, Denmark 21/B6
Varde (riv.), Denmark 21/B6
Vardø, Norway 18/R1
Varel, W. Germany 22/C2
Varella, Mui (cape), Vietnam 72/F4
Varena, U.S.S.R. 53/C3
Varennes, Québec 172/J4
Vareš, Yugoslavia 45/D3
Varese (prov.), Italy 34/B2
Varese, Italy 34/B2
Vargem Bonita, Brazil 135/E3
Varginha, Brazil 135/D2
Varginha, Brazil 132/E8
Varina, Iowa (50593) 229/D3
Varkaus, Finland 18/Q5
Värmland (co.), Sweden 18/H7
Varna, Bulgaria 7/G4
Varna, Bulgaria 45/J4
Varna, Ill. (61375) 222/D2
Varnado, La. (70467) 238/L5
Värnamo, Sweden 18/J8
Varnek, U.S.S.R. 52/J1
Varnell, Georgia (30756) 217/C1
Varner, Kansas (†67068) 232/D4
Varney, Ontario 177/D3
Varney, W. Va. (25696) 312/B7
Varnsdorf, Czech. 41/C1
Varnville, S.C. (29944) 296/E6
Várpalota, Hungary 41/E3
Vars, Ontario 177/J2
Vartholomión, Greece 45/E7
Varto, Turkey 63/J3
Varysburg, N.Y. (14167) 276/D5
Varzarin, Kuh-e (mt.), Iran 59/E3
Varzarin, Kuh-e (mt.), Iran 66/E4
Vas (co.), Hungary 41/D3
Vasa (Vaasa), Finland 18/M5
Vasa, Minn. (†55089) 255/F6
Vasa Barris (riv.), Brazil 132/G5
Vásárosnamény, Hungary 41/G2
Vascongadas (reg.), Spain 33/E1
Vashi, India 68/B7
Vashka (riv.), U.S.S.R. 52/G2
Vashon, Wash. (98070) 310/A2
Vasile Roaită, Romania 45/J3
Vasil'kov, U.S.S.R. 52/D4
Vaslui, Romania 45/H2
Vass, N.C. (28394) 281/L4
Vassalboro, Maine (04989) 243/D7
Vassalboro○, Maine (04989) 243/D7
Vassar, Kansas (66543) 232/G3
Vassar, Manitoba 179/G5
Vassar, Mich. (48768) 250/F5
Vassouras, Brazil 135/E3
Vastenjaure (lake), Sweden 18/K3
Västerås, Sweden 7/F3
Västerås, Sweden 18/K7
Västerbotten (co.), Sweden 18/K4
Västerdalälven (riv.), Sweden 18/H6
Västerhaninge, Sweden 18/H1
Västernorrland (co.), Sweden 18/K5
Västervik, Sweden 18/K8
Västmanland (co.), Sweden 18/K7
Vasto, Italy 34/E3
Vasvár, Hungary 41/D3
Vaternish (dist.), Scotland 15/B3
Vaternish (pt.), Scotland 15/B3
Vatersay (isl.), Scotland 15/A4
Vathí, Greece 45/H7
Vatican City 7/F4
VATICAN CITY 34
Vatican City, Vatican City 34/B6
Vaticano (cape), Italy 34/E5
Vatnajökull (glac.), Iceland 21/C1
Vatomandry, Madagascar 118/H3
Vatra Dornei, Romania 45/G2
Vättern (lake), Sweden 7/F3
Vättern (lake), Sweden 18/J7
Vatukoula, Fiji 86/P10
Vatulele (isl.), Fiji 86/P11
Vauclin (mt.), Martinique 161/D6
Vaucluse (dept.), France 28/F6
Vaucluse, S.C. (29850) 296/D7
Vaud (canton), Switzerland 39/B3
Vaudreuil (co.), Québec 172/C4
Vaudreuil, Québec 172/C4
Vaughan, Miss. (39179) 256/D5
Vaughan, N.C. (27586) 281/N2
Vaughan, Ontario 177/J4
Vaughan, W. Va. (†26656) 312/D6
Vaughn, Mont. (59487) 262/E3
Vaughn, N. Mex. (88353) 274/D4
Vaughn, Wash. (98394) 310/C3
Vaughnsville, Ohio (45893) 284/B4
Vaupés (comm.), Colombia 126/E7
Vaupés (riv.), Colombia 120/B2
Vaupés (riv.), Colombia 126/E7
Vauxhall, Alberta 182/D4
Vauxhall, N.J. (07088) 273/A2
Vaux-sur-Sûre, Belgium 27/H9
Vava'u Group (isls.), Tonga 87/J7
Vavenby, Br. Col. 184/H4
Vavuniya, Sri Lanka 68/E7
Vawn, Sask. 181/C2
Vaxholm, Sweden 18/J1
Växjö, Sweden 7/F3
Växjö, Sweden 18/J8
Vaygach (isl.), U.S.S.R. 4/C6
Vaygach (isl.), U.S.S.R. 52/K1
Vayland, S. Dak. (†57381) 298/M5
Važec, Czech. 41/E2
Vazhgort, U.S.S.R. 52/G2
Vaz-Obervaz, Switzerland 39/J3
Vázquez, Cuba 158/H3
Veagh (lake), Ireland 17/F1
Vealmoor, Texas (79720) 303/C5
Veazie○, Maine (04401) 243/F6
Veblen, S. Dak. (57270) 298/P2
Vechigen, Switzerland 39/E3
Vecht (riv.), Netherlands 27/F4
Vechta, W. Germany 22/C2
Vechte (riv.), Netherlands 27/J3
Vechte (riv.), W. Germany 22/B2
Vecsés, Hungary 41/E3
Vedaranniyam, India 68/E6
Vedia, Argentina 143/F7
Veedersburg, Ind. (47987) 227/C4
Veendam, Netherlands 27/K2
Veenendaal, Netherlands 27/G4
Veenhuizen, Netherlands 27/J2
Veere, Netherlands 27/D5
Veersche Meer (lake), Netherlands 27/D5
Vega (pt.), Alaska 196/J4
Vega, Alberta 182/C2
Vega (isl.), Norway 18/G4
Vega, Texas (79092) 303/B2
Vega Alta, P. Rico 161/D1
Vega Baja, P. Rico 161/D1
Vegafjorden (fjord), Norway 18/G4
Vegas Creek, Nev. (89121) 266/G6
Veghel, Netherlands 27/H5
Vegreville, Alberta 182/E3
Vègreville, Alta. 162/E5
Veguita, N. Mex. (87062) 274/C4
Vehar (lake), India 68/B7
Veinticinco (25) de Agosto, Uruguay 145/A6
Veinticinco (25) de Diciembre, Paraguay 144/D4
Veinticinco de Mayo, Argentina 143/F7
Veinticinco de Mayo, Ecuador 128/C4
Veinticinco (25) de Mayo, Uruguay 145/C5
Veintiocho de Noviembre, Argentina 143/B7
Vejen, Denmark 21/C7
Vejer de la Frontera, Spain 33/C4
Vejle (co.), Denmark 21/C6
Vejle, Denmark 21/C6
Vejle, Denmark 18/F9
Vejle (fjord), Denmark 21/C6
Vejprty, Czech. 41/B1
Vela, La (cape), Colombia 126/D1
Vela, Roca que (cay), Colombia 126/B8
Vélan (mt.), Switzerland 39/D5
Velarde, N. Mex. (87582) 274/C2
Velas (cape), C. Rica 154/D5
Velasco, Ciego de Ávila, Cuba 158/G2
Velasco, Holguín, Cuba 158/H3
Velázquez, Uruguay 145/E5
Velda, Mo. (†63101) 261/P2
Velden am Wörthersee, Austria 41/C3
Veldhoven, Netherlands 27/G6
Veldrif, S. Africa 118/B6
Velence, Hungary 41/E3
Velenje, Yugoslavia 45/B2
Vélez, Colombia 126/D4
Vélez-Blanco, Spain 33/E4
Vélez-Málaga, Spain 33/E4
Vélez-Rubio, Spain 33/E4
Velhas (riv.), Brazil 132/E7
Velika Plana, Yugoslavia 45/E3
Velikaya (riv.), U.S.S.R. 48/S3
Velikaya (riv.), U.S.S.R. 52/C3
Veliki Bečkerek (Zrenjanin), Yugoslavia 45/E3
Velikiye Luki, U.S.S.R. 7/H3
Velikiye Luki, U.S.S.R. 52/D3
Velikiye Luki, U.S.S.R. 48/D4
Velikiy Ustyug, U.S.S.R. 7/J2
Velikiy Ustyug, U.S.S.R. 48/E3
Velikiy Ustyug, U.S.S.R. 52/F2
Veliko Tŭrnovo, Bulgaria 45/G4
Velikovisochnoye, U.S.S.R. 52/H1
Velizh, U.S.S.R. 52/D3
Velká Bíteš, Czech. 41/D2
Velká Bystřice, Czech. 41/D2
Veľké Kapušany, Czech. 41/G2
Velké Meziříčí, Czech. 41/D2
Veľké Rovné, Czech. 41/E2
Vella Lavella (isl.), Solomon Is. 86/D2
Velletri, Italy 34/F7
Vellore, India 68/D6
Velluda, Sierra (mt.), Chile 138/E1
Velma, Okla. (73091) 288/L6
Velp, Netherlands 27/J5
Velpen, Ind. (47590) 227/C8
Velsen, Netherlands 27/F4
Vel'sk, U.S.S.R. 52/F2
Vel'sk, U.S.S.R. 48/E3
Velten, E. Germany 22/E2
Veluwe (reg.), Netherlands 27/H4
Velva, N. Dak. (58790) 282/J3
Velvendós, Greece 45/F5
Vemb, Denmark 21/B5
Véménd, Hungary 41/E3
Venadillo, Colombia 126/C5
Venado, Mexico 150/J5
Venado Tuerto, Argentina 143/D3
Venafro, Italy 34/E4
Venaissin (trad. prov.), France 29
Venamo (mt.), Guyana 131/A3
Venamo, Cerro (mt.), Venezuela 124/H4
Venamo (riv.), Venezuela 124/H4
Venango, Nebr. (69168) 264/C4
Venango (co.), Pa. 294/C3
Venango, Pa. (16440) 294/B2
Vena Park, Queensland 95/B3
Vence, France 28/G6
Venda (aut. rep.), S. Africa 102/F7
Venda (aut. rep.), S. Africa 118/E4
Vendas Novas, Portugal 33/B3
Vendée (dept.), France 28/C4
Vendôme, France 28/D4
Vendrell, Spain 33/G2
Venedocia, Ohio (45894) 284/B4
Venedy, Ill. (62296) 222/D5
Veneta, Oreg. (97487) 291/D3
Venetie, Alaska (99781) 196/J1
Veneto (reg.), Italy 34/D3
Venezia (Venice), Italy 34/D2
Venezuela 2/F5
Venezuela 120/C2
Venezuela, Cuba 158/F2
VENEZUELA 124
Venezuela (gulf), Venezuela 120/B1
Venezuela (gulf), Venezuela 124/C2
Vengurla, India 68/C5
Veniaminof (crater), Alaska 196/F3
Venice, Alberta 182/E2
Venice, Calif. (90291) 204/B11
Venice, Fla. (*33595) 212/D4
Venice, Ill. (62090) 222/A2
Venice (prov.), Italy 34/D2
Venice, Italy 7/F4
Venice, Italy 34/D2
Venice (gulf), Italy 34/D2
Venice, La. (70091) 238/M8
Venice, Utah (†84701) 304/C5
Vénissieux, France 28/F5
Venkatagiri, India 68/D6
Venlo, Netherlands 27/J6
Venn, Sask. 181/F4
Venosa, Italy 34/E4
Venraij, Netherlands 27/H6
Venta (riv.), U.S.S.R. 53/B2
Venterspos, S. Africa 118/G6
Ventimiglia, Italy 34/A3
Ventnor, England 10/F5
Ventnor, England 13/F7
Ventnor City, N.J. (08406) 273/E5
Ventotene (isl.), Italy 34/D4
Ventspils, U.S.S.R. 48/B4
Ventspils, U.S.S.R. 53/A2
Ventspils, U.S.S.R. 52/B3
Ventuari (riv.), Venezuela 124/E5
Ventura (co.), Calif. 204/F9
Ventura, Calif. (*93001) 204/F9
Ventura, Iowa (50482) 229/F2
Venturia, N. Dak. (58489) 282/L7
Venus, Fla. (33960) 212/E4
Venus (pt.), Fr. Poly. 86/T12
Venus, Pa. (16364) 294/C3
Venus (bay), Victoria 97/C6
Venustiano Carranza, Mexico 150/N8
Venustiano Carranza (res.), Mexico 150/J3
Ver (riv.), England 13/H7
Vera, Argentina 143/F5
Vera, Ill. (†62080) 222/D4
Vera, Okla. (74082) 288/P2
Vera (lag.), Paraguay 144/D5
Vera, Spain 33/F4
Vera, Texas (76383) 303/E4
Vera, Va. (†24522) 307/L6
Vera Cruz, Brazil 135/B3
Vera Cruz, Ind. (†46714) 227/G3
Veracruz (state), Mexico 150/L7
Veracruz, Mexico 150/Q1
Veracruz, Mexico 2/E5
Veracruz, Mexico 146/J8
Veradale, Wash. (99037) 310/H3
Veragua Abajo, Dom. Rep. 158/E5
Veras, Uruguay 145/C2
Veraval, India 68/C4
Verbania, Italy 34/B2
Verbena, Ala. (36091) 195/E5
Verboort, Oreg. (†97116) 291/A2
Vercelli (prov.), Italy 34/B2
Vercelli, Italy 34/B2
Verchères (co.), Québec 172/J4
Verchères, Québec 172/J4
Verçinin Tepesi (mt.), Turkey 63/J2
Verda, Ky. (†40828) 237/P7
Verda, La. (71481) 238/E3
Verde (riv.), Ariz. 188/D4
Verde (riv.), Ariz. 198/D5
Verde (cay), Bahamas 156/C2
Verde (riv.), Brazil 132/C7
Verde (riv.), Mexico 150/F3
Verde (riv.), Mexico 150/L8
Verde (riv.), Paraguay 144/C3
Verde (cape), Senegal 102/A3
Verde (cape), Senegal 106/A6
Verde Island (passage), Philippines 82/C4
Verdel, Nebr. (68782) 264/F2
Verden, Okla. (73092) 288/K4
Verden, W. Germany 22/C2
Verdery, S.C. (†29819) 296/C3
Verdi, Minn. (56179) 255/B6
Verdi, Nev. (89439) 266/B3
Verdigre, Nebr. (68783) 264/F2
Verdigris (riv.), Kansas 232/G5
Verdigris, Okla. (†74017) 288/P2
Verdigris (riv.), Okla. 288/P2
Verdinho (riv.), Brazil 132/D7
Verdon, Nebr. (68457) 264/J4
Verdon, S. Dak. (57478) 298/N3
Verdun, Québec 172/H4
Verdún, Uruguay 145/D5
Verdun-sur-Meuse, France 28/F3
Verdunville, W. Va. (25649) 312/B7
Vereeniging, S. Africa 102/E7
Vereeniging, S. Africa 118/D5
Veregin, Sask. 181/K4
Verendrye, N. Dak. (†58717) 282/J3
Vereshchagino, U.S.S.R. 52/H3
Verga (cape), Guinea 106/B6
Vergara, Argentina 143/H7
Vergara, Spain 33/E1
Vergara, Uruguay 145/E3
Vergas, Minn. (56587) 255/C4
Vergeletto, Switzerland 39/G4
Vergennes, Ill. (62994) 222/D6
Vergennes, Vt. (05491) 268/A3
Veribest, Texas (76886) 303/D6
Verín, Spain 33/C2
Veríssimo, Brazil 135/B1
Verkhnevilyuysk, U.S.S.R. 48/N3
Verkhnyaya Toyma, U.S.S.R. 52/G2
Verkhoyansk, U.S.S.R. 2/R2
Verkhoyansk, U.S.S.R. 4/C3
Verkhoyansk, U.S.S.R. 54/P3
Verkhoyansk, U.S.S.R. 48/N3
Verkhoyansk (range), U.S.S.R. 48/N3
Verkhoyansk (range), U.S.S.R. 4/C3
Verkhoyansk (range), U.S.S.R. 54/O3
Verkniy At-Uryakh, U.S.S.R. 48/Q3
Verlo, Sask. 181/C5
Vermejo (riv.), N. Mex. 274/E2
Vermejo Park, N. Mex. (†81091) 274/D2
Vermilion, Alberta 182/E3
Vermilion (riv.), Alberta 182/E3
Vermilion (cliffs), Ariz. 198/D2
Vermilion (co.), Ill. 222/F3
Vermilion, Ill. (61955) 222/F4
Vermilion (riv.), Ind. 227/B4
Vermilion (par.), La. 238/F7
Vermilion (bay), La. 238/F7
Vermilion (lake), Minn. 188/H1
Vermilion (lake), Minn. 255/F3
Vermilion (range), Minn. 255/F3
Vermilion (riv.), Minn. 255/F2
Vermilion, Ohio (44089) 284/F3
Vermilion (riv.), Ohio 284/F3
Vermilion (hills), Sask. 181/E5
Vermilion (cliffs), Utah 304/B6
Vermilion Bay, Ontario 177/G4
Vermilion Bay, Ontario 175/B3
Vermilion Grove, Ill. (†61870) 222/F4
Vermillion (co.), Ind. 227/C5
Vermillion, Kansas (66544) 232/F2
Vermillion, Minn. (55085) 255/F6
Vermillion, S. Dak. (57069) 298/R8
Vermillion (riv.), S. Dak. 298/P6
Vermillion (riv.), Québec 172/D2
Vermont 188/M2
Vermont, Ill. (61484) 222/C3
Vermont (state), U.S. 146/L5
VERMONT 268
Vermontville, Mich. (49096) 250/E6
Vernal, Utah (84078) 304/E3
Vernayaz, Switzerland 39/D4
Verndale, Minn. (56481) 255/C4
Verndon, Minn. (†55752) 255/E4
Verner, Ontario 177/D1
Verneuil-sur-Avre, France 28/D3
Vernon, Ala. (35592) 195/B3
Vernon, Ariz. (85940) 198/F4
Vernon, Br. Col. 162/E5
Vernon, Br. Col. 184/H5
Vernon, Colo. (80755) 208/P3
Vernon○, Conn. (06066) 210/F1
Vernon, Fla. (32462) 212/C6
Vernon, France 28/D3
Vernon, Ill. (62892) 222/D5
Vernon, Ind. (47282) 227/F7
Vernon, Ky. (†42151) 237/L7
Vernon (par.), La. 238/D4
Vernon, La. (†71228) 238/E2
Vernon (lake), La. 238/D4
Vernon, Mich. (48476) 250/F6
Vernon (co.), Mo. 261/D7
Vernon, N.J. (07462) 273/E1
Vernon, Okla. (74877) 288/P4
Vernon, Ontario 177/J2
Vernon (lake), Ontario 177/E2
Vernon, Pr. Edward I. 168/E2
Vernon, Texas (76384) 303/E3
Vernon, Utah (84080) 304/B3
Vernon○, Vt. (05354) 268/B6
Vernon (co.), Wis. 317/E8
Vernonburg, Georgia (†31401) 217/K7
Vernon Center, Conn. (†06066) 210/F1
Vernon Center, Minn. (56090) 255/D7
Vernon Fork (creek), Ind. 227/F7
Vernon Hill, Va. (24597) 307/K7
Vernon Hills, Ill. (60061) 222/B4
Vernonia, Oreg. (97064) 291/D2
Vero Beach, Fla. (32960) 212/F4
Veroli, Italy 34/D4
Verona, Ill. (60479) 222/E2
Verona (prov.), Italy 34/C2
Verona, Italy 34/C2
Verona, Italy 7/F4
Verona, Ky. (41092) 237/M3
Verona, Miss. (38879) 256/G2
Verona, Mo. (65769) 261/E9
Verona, N.J. (07044) 273/B2
Verona, N. Dak. (58490) 282/O7
Verona, Ohio (45378) 284/A6
Verona, Ontario 177/H3
Verona, Pa. (15147) 294/C6
Verona, Va. (24482) 307/K4
Verona, Wis. (53593) 317/G9
Verónica, Argentina 143/H7
Verpelét, Hungary 41/F2
Verret (lake), La. 238/H7
Verret, New Bruns. 170/B1
Verrettes, Haiti 158/C5
Vérroia, Greece 45/F5
Versailles, Conn. (06383) 210/G2
Versailles, France 28/A2
Versailles, France 7/F4
Versailles, Ill. (62378) 222/C4
Versailles, Ind. (47042) 227/G6
Versailles, Ky. (40383) 237/M4
Versailles, Mo. (65084) 261/G6
Versailles, N.Y. (14168) 276/B6
Versailles, Ohio (45380) 284/A5
Versailles, Pa. (15132) 294/C7
Versalles, Bolivia 136/D3
Vershire○, Vt. (05079) 268/C4
Versoix, Switzerland 39/B4
Verte (bay), New Bruns. 170/G2
Verte (bay), Nova Scotia 168/D2
Verte (isl.), Québec 172/H1
Vertientes, Cuba 158/G3
Vert-Pré, Martinique 161/D6
Vertus, France 28/E3
Verviers, Belgium 27/H7
Verwoerd, Hendrik (dam), S. Africa 118/D6
Verwood, Sask. 181/F6
Vesava, India 68/B7
Vesdre (riv.), Belgium 27/H7
Veseleyville, N. Dak. (†58237) 282/R3
Veseli, Minn. (55086) 255/E6
Veselí nad Lužnicí, Czech. 41/C2
Veselí nad Moravou, Czech. 41/D2
Vesoul, France 28/F4
Vesper, Kansas (†67455) 232/D2
Vesper, Sask. 181/D5
Vesper, Wis. (54489) 317/F7
Vesta, C. Rica 154/F6
Vesta, Minn. (56292) 255/C6
Vesta, Va. (24177) 307/H7
Vestaburg, Mich. (48891) 250/E5
Vest-Agder (co.), Norway 18/E7
Vestal○, N.Y. (13850) 276/H6
Vestavia Hills, Ala. (35216) 195/E4
Vesterålen (isls.), Norway 7/F2
Vesterålen (isls.), Norway 18/J2
Vester Skerninge, Denmark 21/D7
Vestervig, Denmark 21/B4
Vestfjord (fjord), Norway 18/H3
Vestfjorden (fjord), Norway 7/F2
Vestfold (co.), Norway 18/G7
Vestmannaeyjar, Iceland 7/C2
Vestmannaeyjar, Iceland 21/B2
Vestsjaelland (co.), Denmark 21/E6
Vestvågøya (isl.), Norway 18/H3
Vesuvius (vol.), Italy 34/E4
Vesuvius, Va. (24483) 307/K5
Veszprém (co.), Hungary 41/D3
Veszprém, Hungary 41/D3
Vésztő, Hungary 41/F3
Vetal, S. Dak. (57575) 298/G7
Veteran, Alberta 182/E3
Veteran, Wyo. (82243) 319/H4
Vetlanda, Sweden 18/J8
Vetluga (riv.), U.S.S.R. 52/G3
Veurne, Belgium 27/B6
Vevay, Ind. (47043) 227/G7
Vevey, Switzerland 39/C4
Vex, Switzerland 39/D4
Veyo, Utah (†84722) 304/A6
Veys, Iran 66/F5
Veytaux, Switzerland 39/C4
Vezirköprü, Turkey 63/F2
Viacha, Bolivia 120/C4
Viacha, Bolivia 136/A5
Viadana, Italy 34/C2
Viale, Argentina 143/F5
Vian, Okla. (74962) 288/S4
Viana, Brazil 132/E3
Viana del Bollo, Spain 33/C1
Viana do Alentejo, Spain 33/C3
Viana do Castelo, Portugal 33/B2
Vianden, Luxembourg 27/J9
Vianen, Netherlands 27/G5
Viangchan (Vientiane), Laos 72/D3
Viangphoukha, Laos 72/D2
Viano do Castelo (dist.), Portugal 33/B2
Viareggio, Italy 34/C3
Vibank, Sask. 181/H5
Vibbard, Mo. (†64062) 261/D4
Viborg (co.), Denmark 21/C4
Viborg, Denmark 18/F8
Viborg, Denmark 21/C5
Viborg, S. Dak. (57070) 298/P7
Vibo Valentia, Italy 34/F5
Viburnum, Mo. (65566) 261/K7
Viby, Denmark 21/F6
Vicálvaro, Spain 33/G4
Vicam, Mexico 150/D3
Vicco, Ky. (41773) 237/P6
Vicente Guerrero, Baja California, Mexico 150/A1
Vicente Guerrero, Durango, Mexico 150/G5
Vicente López, Argentina 143/G7
Vicenza (prov.), Italy 34/C2
Vicenza, Italy 34/C2
Viceroy, Sask. 181/F6
Vich, Spain 33/H2
Vichacla, Bolivia 136/C7
Vichada (comm.), Colombia 126/F5
Vichada (riv.), Colombia 126/F5
Vichadero, Uruguay 145/E2
Vichaya, Bolivia 136/A5
Viche, Ecuador 128/C2
Vichuga, U.S.S.R. 52/F3
Vichy, France 28/E4
Vichy, Mo. (65580) 261/J6
Vici, Okla. (73859) 288/H2
Vick, Ark. (†71648) 202/F7
Vick, La. (71372) 238/F4
Vickers (lake), Manitoba 179/F3
Vickery, Ohio (43464) 284/D3
Vicksburg, Ariz. (†85348) 198/B5
Vicksburg, Ind. (†47441) 227/C6
Vicksburg, Mich. (49097) 250/D6
Vicksburg, Miss. 188/H4
Vicksburg, Miss. (39180) 256/C6
Vicksburg Nat'l Mil. Park, Miss. 256/C6
Viçosa, Brazil 135/E2
Viçosa, Brazil 132/G5
Vicosoprano, Switzerland 39/J4
Vicovaro, Italy 34/F6
Victoire, Sask. 181/D2
Victor, Calif. (95253) 204/C9
Victor, Colo. (80860) 208/J5
Victor, Idaho (83455) 220/G6
Victor, Iowa (52347) 229/J5
Victor, Mont. (59875) 262/B4
Victor, N.Y. (14564) 276/F5
Victor, S. Dak. (†57260) 298/R2
Victor, W. Va. (25938) 312/D6
Victor Harbor, S. Australia 88/F7
Victor Harbor, S. Australia 94/F6
Victoria 88/G7
Victoria (lake) 2/L6
Victoria (lake) 102/F5
Victoria (Mosi-Oa-Tunya) (falls) 102/E6
Victoria, Argentina 143/F6
Victoria, Ark. (72388) 202/K2
Victoria (state), Australia 87/E9
Victoria (cap.), Br. Col. 146/F5
Victoria (cap.), Br. Col. 162/D6
Victoria (cap.), Br. Col. 184/K4
Victoria (mt.), Burma 72/B2
Victoria (Limbe), Cameroon 115/A3
Victoria (isl.), Canada 2/D2
Victoria (isl.), Canada 4/B15
Victoria, Malleco, Chile 138/D2
Victoria, Tarapacá, Chile 138/A3
Victoria, Grenada 161/D8
Victoria, Guinea 106/B6
Victoria, Ill. (61485) 222/C2
Victoria, Kansas (67671) 232/C3
Victoria (lake), Kenya 115/F4
Victoria, Malta 34/E6
Victoria, Minn. (55386) 255/F6
Victoria, Miss. (38679) 256/E1
Victoria, Mo. (†63020) 261/M6
Victoria (co.), New Bruns. 170/C1
Victoria, Newf. 166/D2
Victoria (lake), Newf. 166/C4
Victoria (lake), N.S. Wales 97/A3
Victoria (riv.), North. Terr. 88/E3
Victoria (riv.), North. Terr. 93/B3
Victoria (isl.), N.W.T. 146/G2
Victoria (isl.), N.W.T. 162/E1
Victoria (isl.), N.W. Terrs. 187/G2
Victoria (str.), N.W.T. 162/F2
Victoria (str.), N.W. Terrs. 187/H3
Victoria (co.), Nova Scotia 168/H2
Victoria (county), Ontario 177/F3
Victoria (lake), Ontario 177/F2
Victoria (peaks), Philippines 82/B6
Victoria, Pr. Edward I. 168/E2
Victoria (cap.), Seychelles 118/H5
Victoria (lake), Tanzania 115/F4
Victoria, Tenn. (†37397) 237/K10
Victoria (co.), Texas 303/H9
Victoria, Texas 188/G5
Victoria, Texas (77901) 303/H9
Victoria (lake), Uganda 115/F4
VICTORIA 97
Victoria, Va. (23974) 307/M6
Victoria (falls), Zambia 115/E7
Victoria (falls), Zimbabwe 118/C3
Victoria Beach, Manitoba 179/F4
Victoria Beach, Nova Scotia 168/C4
Victoria de las Tunas, Cuba 158/H3
Victoria Harbour, Ontario 177/E3

Wamic 465

Vordingborg, Denmark 21/E7
Vordingborg, Denmark 18/G9
Vorgod (riv.), Denmark 21/B6
Vorkuta, U.S.S.R. 4/C6
Vorkuta, U.S.S.R. 7/L2
Vorkuta, U.S.S.R. 52/K1
Vorkuta, U.S.S.R. 48/G3
Vormsi (isl.), U.S.S.R. 53/B1
Vorona (riv.), U.S.S.R. 52/F4
Voronezh, U.S.S.R. 7/H3
Voronezh, U.S.S.R. 52/E4
Voronezh, U.S.S.R. 48/E4
Voroshilovgrad, U.S.S.R. 7/H4
Voroshilovgrad, U.S.S.R. 52/E5
Voroshilovgrad, U.S.S.R. 48/E5
Vorskla (riv.), U.S.S.R. 52/E4
Vorst (Forest), Belgium 27/B9
Võrtsjärv (lake), U.S.S.R. 53/D1
Võru, U.S.S.R. 52/C2
Võru, U.S.S.R. 53/D2
Vosges (dept.), France 28/G3
Vosges (mts.), France 28/G3
Voskresensk, U.S.S.R. 52/E3
Voss, N. Dak. (58280) 282/R3
Voss, Norway 18/E6
Vossburg, Miss. (39366) 256/F7
Vostochnyy, U.S.S.R. 48/O5
Vostok (isl.), Kiribati 2/B6
Vostok (isl.), Kiribati 87/L7
Votamo (riv.), Venezuela 124/F6
Votice, Czech. 41/C2
Votkinsk, U.S.S.R. 48/F4
Votkinsk, U.S.S.R. 52/H3
Votuporanga, Brazil 135/B2
Vouvry, Switzerland 39/C4
Voúxa (cape), Greece 45/F8
Vouziers, France 28/F3
Voyageurs Nat'l Park, Minn. 255/F2
Voy-Vozh, U.S.S.R. 48/F3
Voy-Vozh, U.S.S.R. 52/H2
Vozhe (lake), U.S.S.R. 52/F2
Vozhega, U.S.S.R. 52/F2
Vozhma, U.S.S.R. 52/G3
Voznesensk, U.S.S.R. 52/D5
Vrå, Denmark 21/C3
Vráble, Czech. 41/E2
Vracov, Czech. 41/D2
Vrangelya (isl.), U.S.S.R. 52/U2
Vranje, Yugoslavia 45/F4
Vranov nad Teplou, Czech. 41/F2
Vratsa, Bulgaria 45/F4
Vrbas, Yugoslavia 45/D3
Vrbas (riv.), Yugoslavia 45/C3
Vrbno pod Pradědem, Czech. 41/D1
Vrbovce, Czech. 41/D1
Vrbové, Czech. 41/D2
Vrchlabí, Czech. 41/C1
Vrede, S. Africa 118/D5
Vredenburg, S. Africa 118/B6
Vredenburgh, Ala. (36481) 195/D7
Vredendal, S. Africa 118/B6
Vreed-en-Hoop, Guyana 131/B2
Vresse-sur-Semois, Belgium 27/F9
Vriezenveen, Netherlands 27/K4
Vrondádhes, Greece 45/G6
Vršac, Yugoslavia 45/E3
Vrútky, Czech. 41/E2
Vryburg, S. Africa 118/C5
Vryheid, S. Africa 118/E5
Vsetín, Czech. 41/D2
Vsevidof (mt.), Alaska 196/E4
Vuadens, Switzerland 39/C3
Vučitrn, Yugoslavia 45/E4
Vught, Netherlands 27/G5
Vukovar, Yugoslavia 45/D3
Vulcan, Alberta 182/D4
Vulcan, Mich. (49892) 250/B3
Vulcan, Mo. (63675) 261/L8
Vulcan, W. Va. (25697) 312/B7
Vulcano (isl.), Italy 34/E5
Vu Liet, Vietnam 72/E3
Vung Tau, Vietnam 72/E5
Vuollerim, Sweden 18/M3
Vuolvojaure (lake), Sweden 18/L3
Vuotso, Finland 18/P2
Vya, Nev. (†96104) 266/B1
Vyatka (riv.), U.S.S.R. 52/H3
Vyatskiye Polyany, U.S.S.R. 52/H3
Vyazemskiy, U.S.S.R. 48/O5
Vyaz'ma, U.S.S.R. 52/D3
Vyborg, U.S.S.R. 7/G2
Vyborg, U.S.S.R. 52/C2
Vyborg, U.S.S.R. 48/C3
Vychegda (riv.), U.S.S.R. 52/G2
Východočeský (reg.), Czech. 41/C1
Východoslovenský (reg.), Czech. 41/F2
Vyg (lake), U.S.S.R. 52/E2
Vyksa, U.S.S.R. 52/F3
Vym' (riv.), U.S.S.R. 52/H2
Vyshniy Volochek, U.S.S.R. 7/H2
Vyshniy Volochek, U.S.S.R. 52/D3
Vyshniy Volochek, U.S.S.R. 48/D4
Vyškov, Czech. 41/D2
Vysoké Mýto, Czech. 41/D2
Vysoké Tatry, Czech. 41/F2
Vyšší Brod, Czech. 41/C2
Vytegra, U.S.S.R. 52/E2

W

Wa, Ghana 106/D6
Waal (riv.), Netherlands 27/G5
Waalre, Netherlands 27/G6
Waalwijk, Netherlands 27/F5
Waarschoot, Belgium 27/D6
Waas (mt.), Utah 304/E5
Waasis, New Bruns. 170/D3
Wabamun, Alberta 182/C3
Waban, Mass. (†02168) 249/B7
Wabana, Newf. 166/D2
Wabaningo, Mich. (49463) 250/C5
Wabasca, Alberta 182/D2
Wabasca (riv.), Alberta 182/C1
Wabasca (riv.), Alta. 162/E4
Wabash (riv.) 188/J3
Wabash, Ark. (72389) 202/J5
Wabash (co.), Ill. 222/F5
Wabash (riv.), Ill. 222/F5
Wabash (co.), Ind. 227/F3
Wabash, Ind. (46992) 227/F3
Wabash (riv.), Ind. 227/B7
Wabash, Ohio (†45822) 284/A4
Wabash (riv.), Ohio 284/A5
Wabasha (co.), Minn. 255/F6
Wabasha, Minn. (55981) 255/G6
Wabasso, Fla. (32970) 212/F4
Wabasso, Minn. (56293) 255/C6
Wabatawangang (lake), Minn. 255/D3
Wabaunsee (co.), Kansas 232/F3
Wabaunsee, Kansas (†66547) 232/F2
Wabbaseka, Ark. (72175) 202/G5
Wabeno, Wis. (54566) 317/J5
Wabi (riv.), Ethiopia 111/H6
Wabigoon, Ontario 175/B3
Wabigoon, Ontario 177/G5
Wabi Shebelle (riv.) 102/G4
Wabi Shebelle (riv.), Ethiopia 111/H6
Wabowden, Manitoba 179/J3
Wąbrzeźno, Poland 47/D2
Wabuk (pt.), Ontario 175/D1
Wabush, Newf. 166/A3
Wabush, Newf. 162/K5
Wabuska, Nev. (†89447) 266/B3
Waccamaw (lake), N.C. 281/N6
Waccamaw (riv.), N.C. 281/M7
Waccamaw (riv.), S.C. 296/J5
Waccasassa (bay), Fla. 212/D2
Waccasassa (riv.), Fla. 212/D2
Wachapreague, Va. (23480) 307/S5
Wachapreague (inlet), Va. 307/T6
Wachtebeke, Belgium 27/D6
Wachusett (mt.), Mass. 249/G3
Wachusett (res.), Mass. 249/G3
Wacissa, Fla. (32361) 212/B1
Waco, Georgia (30182) 217/B3
Waco, Ky. (40385) 237/N5
Waco, Mo. (63869) 261/C8
Waco, Nebr. (68460) 264/G4
Waco, N.C. (28169) 281/G4
Waco, Texas 188/G4
Waco, Texas 146/J6
Waco, Texas (*76701) 303/G6
Waconda (lake), Kansas 232/D2
Waconia, Minn. (55387) 255/E6
Wadai (reg.), Chad 111/D5
Waddamana, Tasmania 99/C4
Waddan, Libya 102/D2
Waddan, Libya 111/C2
Waddell, Ariz. (85355) 198/C5
Waddenzee (sound), Netherlands 27/G2
Waddington (mt.), Br. Col. 162/D5
Waddington (mt.), Br. Col. 184/E4
Waddington, N.Y. (13694) 276/K1
Waddy, Ky. (40076) 237/L4
Wade, Miss. (†39567) 256/G9
Wade (lake), Newf. 166/A3
Wade, N.C. (28395) 281/M4
Wade, Okla. (†74723) 288/O7
Wadebridge, England 13/C7
Wade-Hampton, S.C. (†29607) 296/C2
Wadena, Ind. (†47944) 227/C3
Wadena, Iowa (52169) 229/K3
Wadena (co.), Minn. 255/D4
Wadena, Minn. (56482) 255/C4
Wadena, Sask. 181/H4
Wädenswil, Switzerland 39/G2
Wadesboro, La. (†70454) 238/M2
Wadesboro, N.C. (28170) 281/J5
Wadestown, W. Va. (26589) 312/F3
Wadesville, Ind. (47638) 227/B8
Wadeville, N.C. (†27306) 281/J4
Wadhams, N.Y. (12990) 276/N2
Wadi Dra, Morocco 102/B2
Wadi es Sir, Jordan 65/D4
Wadi Halfa, Sudan 111/F3
Wadi Musa, Jordan 65/E5
Wading (riv.), N.J. 273/D4
Wading River, N.Y. (11792) 276/P9
Wadley, Ala. (36276) 195/G4
Wadley, Georgia (30477) 217/H5
Wadmalaw (isl.), S.C. 296/G6
Wad Medani, Sudan 111/F5
Wad Medani, Sudan 59/B7
Wad Medani, Sudan 102/F3
Wadowice, Poland 47/D4
Wadsworth, Ala. (†36022) 195/E5
Wadsworth, Ill. (60083) 222/B4
Wadsworth, Nev. (89442) 266/B3
Wadsworth, Ohio (44281) 284/G3
Wadsworth, Texas (77483) 303/J9
Waelder, Texas (78959) 303/G8
Wagait Aboriginal Res., North. Terr. 93/B2
Wagarville, Ala. (36585) 195/B8
Wagener, S.C. (29164) 296/E4
Wageningen, Netherlands 27/H5
Wageningen, Suriname 131/C3
Wager (bay), N.W.T. 146/J3
Wager (bay), N.W.T. 162/G2
Wager (bay), N.W. Terrs. 187/K3
Wagga Wagga, Australia 87/E9
Wagga Wagga, N. S. Wales 88/H7
Wagga Wagga, N.S. Wales 97/D4
Waggoner, Ill. (62572) 222/D4
Waggrakine, W. Australia 92/A5
Wagin, W. Australia 88/B6
Wagin, W. Australia 92/B2
Wagner, Alberta 182/C2
Wagner, Mont. (59543) 262/H2
Wagner, S. Dak. (57380) 298/N7
Wagoner (co.), Okla. 288/P3
Wagoner, Okla. (74467) 288/R3
Wagon Mound, N. Mex. (87752) 274/E2
Wagontire, Oreg. (†97720) 291/H4
Wagon Wheel Gap, Colo. (†81130) 208/F7
Wagram, N.C. (28396) 281/L5
Wągrowiec, Poland 47/C2
Wah, Pakistan 68/C2
Wahai, Indonesia 85/H6
Wahalak, Miss. (†39358) 256/G5
Wahiawa, Hawaii (96786) 218/E2
Wahiawa, Hawaii 188/F5
Wahkiacus, Wash. (98670) 310/D5
Wahkiakum (co.), Wash. 310/B4
Wahkon, Minn. (56386) 255/E4
Wahlern, Switzerland 39/D3
Wahoo, Nebr. (68066) 264/H3
Wahpeton, Iowa (†51360) 229/C2
Wahpeton, N. Dak. 188/G1
Wahpeton, N. Dak. (58075) 282/S7
Wahsatch, Utah (†82930) 304/C2
Wah Wah (mts.), Utah 304/A5
Wahwashkesh (lake), Ontario 177/D2
Wahweap (creek), Utah 304/C6
Wai, Poulo (isls.), Vietnam 72/E4
Waiakoa, Hawaii (†96788) 218/J2
Waialae, Hawaii (96816) 218/D4
Waialeale (mt.), Hawaii 218/C1
Waialee, Hawaii (†96731) 218/E1
Waialua, Hawaii 188/F5
Waialua, Molokai, Hawaii (†96748) 218/H1
Waialua, Oahu, Hawaii (96791) 218/E1
Waianae, Hawaii (96792) 218/D2
Waiau, N. Zealand 100/D5
Waiau (riv.), N. Zealand 100/A6
Waidhofen an der Thaya, Austria 41/C2
Waidhofen an der Ybbs, Austria 41/C3
Waidsboro, Va. (†24088) 307/J7
Waigama, Indonesia 85/H6
Waigeo (isl.), Indonesia 85/J5
Waihee, Hawaii (†96793) 218/J2
Waiheke (isl.), N. Zealand 100/E2
Waihi, N. Zealand 100/E2
Waikabubak, Indonesia 85/F7
Waikanae, N. Zealand 100/E4
Waikane, Hawaii (†96744) 218/F2
Waikapu, Hawaii (†96793) 218/J2
Waikaremoana (lake), N. Zealand 100/F3
Waikari, N. Zealand 100/D5
Waikato (riv.), N. Zealand 100/E2
Waikawa, N. Zealand 100/B7
Waikerie, S. Australia 94/F6
Waikiki, Hawaii (†96743) 218/H4
Waikiki (canton), Hawaii (96815) 218/C4
Waikiki (beach), Hawaii 218/C4
Waikouaiti, N. Zealand 100/C6
Wailau, Hawaii (†96748) 218/H1
Wailea, Hawaii (†96710) 218/J4
Wailea, Maui, Hawaii (†96790) 218/J2
Wailua, Hawaii (†96746) 218/D2
Wailuku, Hawaii (96793) 218/J2
Wailuku, Hawaii 188/F5
Wailuku (riv.), Hawaii 218/J5
Waimakariri (riv.), N. Zealand 100/D5
Waimalu, Hawaii (†96701) 218/B3
Waimanalo, Hawaii (96795) 218/F2
Waimanalo Bch., Hawaii (†96795) 218/F2
Waimangaroa, N. Zealand 100/C4
Waimate, N. Zealand 100/C6
Waimea (Kamuela), Hawaii, (†96743) 218/G3
Waimea, Kauai, Hawaii (96796) 218/B2
Waimea, Oahu, Hawaii (†96712) 218/E1
Waimea (bay), Hawaii 218/B2
Waimea (riv.), Hawaii 218/C2
Waimes, Belgium 27/J8
Wainaku, Hawaii (†96720) 218/J5
Wainfleet, Ontario 177/E4
Wainfleet All Saints, England 13/H4
Waingapu, Indonesia 85/G7
Waini (riv.), Guyana 131/B2
Wainiha, Hawaii (†96714) 218/C1
Wainiha (riv.), Hawaii 218/C1
Wainuiomata, N. Zealand 100/B3
Wainui-o-mata (riv.), N. Zealand 100/B3
Wainwright, Alaska (99782) 196/F1
Wainwright, Alberta 182/E3
Wainwright, Ohio (44686) 284/G5
Wainwright, Okla. (74468) 288/R3
Wainwright, U.S. 4/B18
Waiohinu, Hawaii (†96772) 218/G7
Waipa (riv.), N. Zealand 100/E2
Waipahu, Hawaii 188/F5
Waipahu, Hawaii (96797) 218/A3
Waipara, N. Zealand 100/D5
Waipawa, N. Zealand 100/F3
Waipio, Hawaii (†96758) 218/H3
Waipio (bay), Hawaii 218/H3
Waipio (pen.), Hawaii 218/A3
Waipio (pt.), Hawaii 218/A4
Waipio Acres, Hawaii (†96786) 218/E2
Waipiro Bay, N. Zealand 100/G3
Waipukurau, N. Zealand 100/F4
Wairau (riv.), N. Zealand 100/D4
Wairoa, N. Zealand 100/F3
Wairoa (riv.), N. Zealand 100/E1
Waitakere, N. Zealand 100/B1
Waitakere (range), N. Zealand 100/A1
Waitaki (riv.), N. Zealand 100/C6
Waitangi, N. Zealand 100/D7
Waitara, N. Zealand 100/E3
Waite○, Maine (04492) 243/H5
Waite Hill, Ohio (†44094) 284/H2
Waitemata (harb.), N. Zealand 100/B1
Waite Park, Minn. (56387) 255/D5
Waiteville, W. Va. (24984) 312/F8
Waitotara, N. Zealand 100/E3
Waits (riv.), Vt. 268/C3
Waitsburg, Wash. (99361) 310/G4
Waitsfield○, Vt. (05673) 268/B3
Waits River, Vt. (†05076) 268/C3
Waitville, Sask. 181/F3
Waiuku, N. Zealand 100/E2
Waiyevu, Fiji 86/R10
Wajabula, Indonesia 85/H5
Wajima, Japan 81/H5
Wajir, Kenya 115/H3
Wajir, Kenya 102/F4
Waka, Ethiopia 111/G6
Waka, Texas (79093) 303/D1
Waka, Zaire 115/D3
Wakarusa, Ind. (46573) 227/F1
Wakarusa, Kansas (66546) 232/G3
Wakasa, Japan 81/G6
Wakasa (bay), Japan 81/G6
Wakatipu (lake), N. Zealand 100/B6
Wakaw, Sask. 181/F3
Wakaw Lake, Sask. 181/F3
Wakayama (pref.), Japan 81/G6
Wakayama, Japan 54/P6
Wakayama, Japan 81/G6
Wakde (isl.), Indonesia 85/K6
Wake (co.), N.C. 281/M3
Wake (isl.), Pacific 87/G4
WaKeeney, Kansas (67672) 232/C2
Wakefield, England 10/F4
Wakefield, England 13/J2
Wakefield, Kansas (67487) 232/E2
Wakefield, La. (70784) 238/H5
Wakefield○, Mass. (01880) 249/C5
Wakefield, Mich. (49968) 250/F2
Wakefield, Nebr. (68784) 264/H2
Wakefield○, N.H. (†03872) 268/F4
Wakefield, Ohio (45687) 284/E8
Wakefield, Va. (23888) 307/O7
Wakefield-Peace Dale, R.I. (*02879) 249/J7
Wake Forest, N.C. (27587) 281/M3
Wakema, Burma 72/B3
Wakeman, Ohio (44889) 284/F3
Wakenda, Mo. (64687) 261/F4
Wake Village, Texas (75501) 303/K4
Wakita, Okla. (73771) 288/L1
Wakkanai, Japan 81/K1
Wakonda, S. Dak. (57073) 298/P7
Wakool, N.S. Wales 97/C4
Wakopa, Manitoba 179/C5
Wakpala, S. Dak. (57658) 298/H2
Wakulla (co.), Fla. 212/B1
Wakulla, Fla. (†32327) 212/B1
Wakwekobi (lake), Ontario 177/A1
Wala, Kuh-i- (mt.), Afghanistan 59/H3
Walbridge, Ohio (43465) 284/C2
Wałbrzych (prov.), Poland 47/C3
Wałbrzych, Poland 47/C3
Walcha, N.S. Wales 97/F2
Walchensee (lake), W. Germany 22/D5
Walcheren (isl.), Netherlands 27/C5
Walcott, Ark. (72474) 202/J1
Walcott, Br. Col. 184/D3
Walcott (lake), Idaho 220/E7
Walcott, Iowa (52773) 229/M5
Walcott, N. Dak. (58077) 282/R6
Walcott, Wyo. (82335) 319/F4
Walcourt, Belgium 27/F8
Wałcz, Poland 47/C2
Wald, Switzerland 39/G2
Waldeck, Sask. 181/D5
Walden, Colo. (80480) 208/G1
Walden, Georgia (†31201) 217/E5
Walden, Ky. (40768) 237/N7
Walden (pond), Mass. 249/A6
Walden, N.Y. (12586) 276/M7
Walden, Ontario 175/D3
Walden, Ontario 177/J5
Walden, Tenn. (†37377) 237/L10
Walden○, Vt. (†05873) 268/C3
Waldenburg, Ark. (72475) 202/J2
Waldenburg (Wałbrzych), Poland 47/C3
Waldenburg, Switzerland 39/E2
Walden Heights, Vt. (†05873) 268/C3
Waldersee, Manitoba 179/D4
Waldheim, E. Germany 22/E3
Waldheim, La. (†70433) 238/L5
Waldheim, Sask. 181/E3
Waldia, Ethiopia 111/G5
Waldkirch, Switzerland 39/H2
Waldkirch, W. Germany 22/B4
Waldkraiburg, W. Germany 22/E4
Waldo, Ala. (†35150) 195/F4
Waldo, Ark. (71770) 202/D7
Waldo, Br. Col. 184/K5
Waldo, Fla. (32694) 212/D2
Waldo, Kansas (67673) 232/D2
Waldo (co.), Maine 243/E6
Waldo○, Maine (†04915) 243/E7
Waldo, Ohio (43356) 284/D5
Waldo (lake), Oreg. 291/E4
Waldo, Wis. (53093) 317/L8
Waldoboro, Maine (04572) 243/E7
Waldoboro○, Maine (04572) 243/E7
Waldorf, Md. (20601) 245/L6
Waldorf, Minn. (56091) 255/E7
Waldport, Oreg. (97394) 291/C3
Waldron, Ark. (72958) 202/B4
Waldron, Ind. (46182) 227/F6
Waldron, Kansas (67150) 232/D4
Waldron, Mich. (49288) 250/E7
Waldron, Mo. (64092) 261/O5
Waldron, Sask. 181/J5
Waldron, Wash. (98297) 310/B2
Waldrup, Miss. (†39422) 256/F7
Waldsassen, W. Germany 22/E3
Waldshut-Tiengen, W. Germany 22/C5
Waldwick, N.J. (07463) 273/B1
Waldwick, Wis. (†53565) 317/G10
Walensee (lake), Switzerland 39/H2
Walenstadt, Switzerland 39/H2
Wales, Alaska (99783) 196/E1
Wales, Alaska 188/C5
Wales○, Mass. (01081) 249/F4
Wales, Minn. (†55616) 255/G3
Wales, N. Dak. (58281) 282/N2
Wales (isl.), N.W. Terrs. 187/K3
Wales, Tenn. (†38478) 237/G10
Wales, U.K. 7/D3
Wales, Utah (84667) 304/C4
WALES 13
WALES, Wales 10/E4
Wales, Wis. (53183) 317/J1
Walesboro, Ind. (†47201) 227/F6
Waleska, Georgia (30183) 217/D2
Walford, Iowa (52351) 229/K5
Walford, Ontario 177/B1
Walgett, N. S. Wales 88/H6
Walgett, N.S. Wales 97/E2
Walgreen Coast (reg.) 5/B13
Walhachin, Br. Col. 184/G5
Walhalla, Mich. (49458) 250/C5
Walhalla, N. Dak. (58282) 282/P2
Walhalla, S.C. (29691) 296/A2
Walhonding, Ohio (43843) 284/F5
Walikale, Zaire 115/E4
Walker (co.), Ala. 195/D3
Walker (creek), Ariz. 198/F2
Walker (mt.), Ark. 202/E2
Walker (co.), Georgia 217/B1
Walker, Iowa (52352) 229/K4
Walker, Kansas (67674) 232/C3
Walker, Ky. (40997) 237/O7
Walker, La. (70785) 238/L1
Walker, Mich. (49504) 250/D6
Walker, Minn. (56484) 255/D3
Walker, Mo. (64790) 261/D7
Walker (lake), Nev. 188/C3
Walker (lake), Nev. 266/C4
Walker (riv.), Nev. 266/C3
Walker, N.Y. (†14468) 276/E4
Walker (bay), N.W. Terrs. 187/G2
Walker, Oreg. (†97426) 291/D4
Walker, S. Dak. (57659) 298/G2
Walker (isl.), Tasmania 99/B2
Walker (co.), Texas 303/J7
Walker (creek), Va. 307/F6
Walker, W. Va. (26180) 312/D4
Walkerburn, Scotland 15/F5
Walker Mill, Md. (†20023) 245/F5
Walker River Ind. Res., Nev. 266/C3
Walker Springs, Ala. (36586) 195/C7
Walkerston, Queensland 88/H4
Walkerston, Queensland 95/D4
Walkersville, Md. (21793) 245/J3
Walkersville, W. Va. (26447) 312/F5
Walkerton, Ind. (46574) 227/E2
Walkerton, Ontario 177/C3
Walkerton, Va. (23177) 307/O5
Walkertown, N.C. (27051) 281/J2
Walkerville, Mich. (49459) 250/C5
Walkerville, Mont. (59701) 262/D4
Walkerville, S. Australia 88/E8
Wall○, N.J. (07719) 273/E3
Wall, Pa. (†15148) 294/C5
Wall, S. Dak. (57790) 298/E6
Wall, Texas (76957) 303/D6
Wallace, Ala. (†36426) 195/D8
Wallace (mt.), Alberta 182/C2
Wallace, Calif. (95254) 204/C9
Wallace, Idaho (83873) 220/C2
Wallace, Ind. (47988) 227/C5
Wallace (co.), Kansas 232/A3
Wallace, Kansas (67761) 232/A3
Wallace, La. (†70049) 238/M3
Wallace (lake), La. 238/C2
Wallace, Mich. (49893) 250/B3
Wallace, Nebr. (69169) 264/C4
Wallace, N.Y. (14890) 276/E6
Wallace, N.C. (28466) 281/N5
Wallace, Nova Scotia 168/E3
Wallace (harb.), Nova Scotia 168/E3
Wallace, S.C. (29596) 296/H2
Wallace, S. Dak. (57272) 298/P3
Wallace, W. Va. (26448) 312/E4
Wallaceburg, Ontario 177/B5
Wallace Lake, Manitoba 179/G3
Wallaceton, Pa. (16876) 294/F4
Wallacetown, Ontario 177/C5
Wallaga (prov.), Ethiopia 111/G6
Wallal Station, W. Australia 92/C2
Walland, Tenn. (37886) 237/O9
Wallaroo, S. Australia 94/E5
Wallasey, England 13/G2
Wallasey, England 10/F2
Walla Walla, N.S. Wales 97/D4
Walla Walla (riv.), Oreg. 291/J1
Walla Walla, Wash. 188/C1
Walla Walla (co.), Wash. 310/G4
Walla Walla, Wash. (99362) 310/G4
Walla Walla (riv.), Wash. 310/G4
Wallback, W. Va. (25285) 312/D5
Wallburg, N.C. (27373) 281/J3
Walldürn, W. Germany 22/C4
Walled Lake, Mich. (48088) 250/F6
Wallen, Ind. (†46802) 227/G2
Wallendbeen, N.S. Wales 97/E4
Wallenpaupack (lake), Pa. 294/M3
Waller (co.), Texas 303/J8
Wallerawang, N.S. Wales 97/F3
Wallerville, Miss. (†38652) 256/G2
Wallibu, St. Vin. & Grens. 161/A8
Walling, Tenn. (38587) 237/K9
Wallingford, Conn. (06492) 210/D3
Wallingford○, Conn. (06492) 210/D3
Wallingford, England 13/F6
Wallingford, Iowa (51365) 229/D2
Wallingford, Ky. (41093) 237/O4
Wallingford, Pa. (19086) 294/L7
Wallingford, Vt. (05773) 268/B5
Wallingford○, Vt. (05773) 268/B5
Wallington, N.J. (07057) 273/B2
Wallins Creek, Ky. (40873) 237/O7
Wallis (lake), N.S. Wales 97/G3
Wallis, Texas (77485) 303/H8
Wallis (isls.), Wallis and Futuna 87/J7
Wallis and Futuna 87/J7
Wallisellen, Switzerland 39/G2
Wallisville, Texas (77597) 303/L1
Wallkill (riv.), N.J. 273/D1
Wallkill, N.Y. (12589) 276/M7
Wallkill (riv.), N.Y. 276/L8
Wall Lake, Iowa (51466) 229/C4
Wallo (prov.), Ethiopia 111/H5
Wallonia, Ky. (†42405) 237/F7
Walloon (lake), Mich. 250/E3
Walloon Lake, Mich. (49796) 250/E3
Wallops (isl.), Va. 307/T5
Wallowa (co.), Oreg. 291/K2
Wallowa, Oreg. (97885) 291/K2
Wallowa (mts.), Oreg. 291/K2
Wallowa (riv.), Oreg. 291/K2
Wallpack Center, N.J. (07881) 273/D1
Walls, Miss. (38680) 256/D1
Walls, Scotland 15/G2
Wallsburg, Utah (84082) 304/C3
Wallsend, England 13/J3
Wallula (lake), Oreg. 291/H1
Wallula, Wash. (99363) 310/G4
Wallula (lake), Wash. 310/F4
Walney, Isle of (isl.), England 13/D3
Walney, Isle of (isl.), England 10/E3
Walnut, Calif. (91789) 204/D10
Walnut (creek), Calif. 204/K1
Walnut, Ill. (61376) 222/D2
Walnut, Iowa (51577) 229/C6
Walnut, Kansas (66780) 232/G4
Walnut (creek), Kansas 232/B3
Walnut (riv.), Kansas 232/E4
Walnut, Miss. (38683) 256/G1
Walnut, N.C. (28753) 281/D3
Walnut, Pa. (†17082) 294/G4
Walnut (creek), Texas 303/F3
Walnut Bottom, Pa. (17266) 294/H5
Walnut Canyon Nat'l Mon., Ariz. 198/D3
Walnut Cove, N.C. (27052) 281/J2
Walnut Creek, Calif. (*94595) 204/K2
Walnut Creek, N.C. (†27530) 281/O4
Walnut Creek, Ohio (44687) 284/G4
Walnut Grove, Ala. (35990) 195/F2
Walnut Grove, Calif. (95690) 204/B9
Walnut Grove, Georgia (†30209) 217/E3
Walnut Grove, Ill. (†61470) 222/C3
Walnut Grove, Ky. (42563) 237/M6
Walnut Grove, Minn. (56180) 255/C6
Walnut Grove, Miss. (39189) 256/F5
Walnut Grove, Mo. (65770) 261/F8
Walnut Hill, Ark. (†71826) 202/C7
Walnut Hill, Fla. (32568) 212/B5
Walnut Hill, Ill. (62893) 222/E5
Walnut Hill, Maine (†04021) 243/C8
Walnutport, Pa. (18088) 294/L4
Walnut Ridge, Ark. (72476) 202/J1
Walnut Springs, Texas (76690) 303/G5
Walpole, Mass. (02081) 249/B8
Walpole○, Mass. (02081) 249/B8
Walpole○, N.H. (03608) 268/C5
Walpole (isl.), Ontario 177/B5
Walpole, Sask. 181/K6
Walpole, W. Australia 92/B6
Walrus (isl.), Alaska 196/E3
Walrus (isls.), Alaska 196/F3
Walsall, England 10/G3
Walsall, England 13/E5
Walsenburg, Colo. (81089) 208/K7
Walsh, Alberta 182/E5
Walsh, Colo. (81090) 208/P8
Walsh (co.), N. Dak. 282/P3
Walsh, Queensland 95/B3
Walshville, Ill. (62091) 222/D4
Walsingham, England 13/H5
Walsingham (cape), N.W.T. 162/K2
Walsingham (cape), N.W. Terrs. 187/M3
Walsrode, W. Germany 22/C2
Walston, Pa. (15781) 294/D4
Walstonburg, N.C. (27888) 281/O3
Walterboro, S.C. (29488) 296/F6
Walter F. George (dam), Ala. 195/H7
Walter F. George (res.), Ala. 195/H7
Walter F. George (dam), Georgia 217/B7
Walter F. George (res.), Georgia 217/B7
Walterhill, Tenn. (†37130) 237/J9
Walter Reed Army Med. Ctr., D.C. 245/E4
Walter Reed Army Med. Ctr. Annex, Md. 245/E4
Walters, La. (71374) 238/G3
Walters, Minn. (56092) 255/E7
Walters, Okla. (73572) 288/K6
Walters Falls, Ontario 177/D3
Waltershausen, E. Germany 22/D3
Waltersville, Ky. (†40312) 237/N5
Waltersville, Miss. (†39180) 256/C6
Walterville, Oreg. (97489) 291/E3
Walthall (co.), Miss. 256/D8
Walthall, Miss. (39771) 256/F3
Waltham○, Maine (†04605) 243/G6
Waltham, Mass. (02154) 249/B6
Waltham, Minn. (55982) 255/F7
Waltham○, Vt. (†05491) 268/A3
Waltham Forest, England 13/H8
Waltham Forest, England 10/B5
Waltham Holy Cross, England 13/H7
Waltham Holy Cross, England 10/B5
Walthill, Nebr. (68067) 264/H2
Walthourville, Georgia (31333) 217/J7
Waltman, Wyo. (†82648) 319/E2
Walton (co.), Fla. 212/C6
Walton, Fla. (†33457) 212/F4
Walton (co.), Georgia 217/E3
Walton, Ind. (46994) 227/E3
Walton, Kansas (67151) 232/E3
Walton, Ky. (41094) 237/M3
Walton, Nebr. (68461) 264/H4
Walton, N.Y. (13856) 276/K6
Walton, Nova Scotia 168/E3
Walton, Ontario 177/C4
Walton, Oreg. (97490) 291/D3
Walton, W. Va. (25286) 312/D5
Walton and Weybridge, England 13/G8
Walton and Weybridge, England 10/B6
Walton Hills, Ohio (†44146) 284/J10
Walton-le-Dale, England 13/G1
Walton-le-Dale, England 10/F1
Waltonville, Ill. (62894) 222/D5
Waltreak, Ark. (†72833) 202/C4
Waltz, Mich. (†48164) 250/F6
Walum, N. Dak. (†58448) 282/O5
Walupt (lake), Wash. 310/D4
Walvis (bay), S. Africa 118/A4
Walvis Bay, S. Africa 2/K7
Walvis Bay, S. Africa 102/D7
Walvis Bay, S. Africa 118/A4
Walworth, N.Y. (14568) 276/F4
Walworth (co.), S. Dak. 298/J3
Walworth (co.), Wis. 317/J10
Walworth, Wis. (53184) 317/J10
Walzenhausen, Switzerland 39/J2
Wamac, Ill. (†62801) 222/D5
Wamba, Kenya 115/G3
Wamba, Nigeria 106/F7
Wamba, Zaire 115/E3
Wamego, Kansas (66547) 232/F2
Wamel, Netherlands 27/H5
Wamena, Indonesia 85/K6
Wamgumbaug (lake), Conn. 210/F1
Wami (riv.), Tanzania 115/G5
Wamic, Oreg. (97063) 291/F2

466 Wampee

Wampee, S.C. (†29582) 296/K4
Wampsville, N.Y. (13163) 276/J4
Wampum, Manitoba 179/G5
Wampum, Pa. (16157) 294/B4
Wamsutter, Wyo. (82336) 319/E4
Wana, Pakistan 68/C2
Wana, Pakistan 59/J3
Wana, W. Va. (26590) 312/F3
Wanaaring, N.S. Wales 97/B1
Wanaka, N. Zealand 100/B6
Wanaka (lake), N. Zealand 100/B6
Wanakah, N.Y. (†14075) 276/C5
Wanakena, N.Y. (13695) 276/K2
Wanamassa, N.J. (†07712) 273/E3
Wanamingo, Minn. (55983) 255/F6
Wan'an, China 77/H6
Wanapitei (riv.), Ontario 177/D1
Wanapum (dam), Wash. 310/E4
Wanapum (lake), Wash. 310/E3
Wanaque, N.J. (07465) 273/B1
Wanaque (res.), N.J. 273/E1
Wanatah, Ind. (46390) 227/D2
Wanblee, S. Dak. (57577) 298/F6
Wanchese, N.C. (27981) 281/T3
Wanda, Minn. (56294) 255/C6
Wandel (sea), Greenl. 4/A10
Wandering, W. Australia 92/B2
Wandering River, Alberta 182/D2
Wanderoos, Wis. (†54001) 317/B5
Wandfluhhorn (mt.), Switzerland 39/G4
Wando, S.C. (29492) 296/H6
Wando (riv.), S.C. 296/H6
Wandoan, Queensland 95/D5
Wandsworth, England 13/H8
Wandsworth, England 10/B5
Wanette, Okla. (74878) 288/M5
Wang, Mae Nam (riv.), Thailand 72/C3
Wanganella, N.S. Wales 97/C4
Wanganui, N. Zealand 87/H9
Wanganui, N. Zealand 100/E3
Wanganui (riv.), N. Zealand 100/E3
Wangaratta, Victoria 88/H7
Wangaratta, Victoria 97/D5
Wangen an der Aare, Switzerland 39/E2
Wangen im Allgäu, W. Germany 22/C5
Wangerooge (isl.), W. Germany 22/B2
Wängi, Switzerland 39/H1
Wangi-Rathmines, N.S. Wales 97/F3
Wangiwangi (isl.), Indonesia 85/G7
Wangqing, China 77/M3
Wangum (lake), Conn. 210/B1
Wanham, Alberta 182/A2
Wanhsien (Wanxian), China 77/G5
Wanilla, S. Australia 94/D6
Wanipigow, Manitoba 179/F3
Wanipigow (riv.), Manitoba 179/G3
Wankai, Sudan 111/E6
Wankie, Zimbabwe 118/D3
Wankie, Zimbabwe 102/E6
Wanks (Coco) (riv.), Honduras 154/E3
Wanks (Coco) (riv.), Nicaragua 154/E3
Wanless, Manitoba 179/H3
Wann, Okla. (74083) 288/P1
Wanna (lakes), W. Australia 92/E5
Wannaska, Minn. (56761) 255/C2
Wanne-Eickel, W. Germany 22/B3
Wanneroo, W. Australia 88/B2
Wanneroo, W. Australia 92/A1
Wanning, China 77/H8
Wanship, Utah (†84017) 304/C3
Wantage, England 13/F6
Wantage, England 10/F5
Wantagh, N.Y. (11793) 276/R7
Wanxian (Wanhsien), China 77/G5
Wanzai, China 77/H6
Wao, Philippines 82/E7
Wapakoneta, Ohio (45895) 284/B4
Wapanucka, Okla. (73461) 288/N6
Wapato, Wash. (98951) 310/E4
Wapawekka (hills), Sask. 181/M4
Wapella, Ill. (61777) 222/E3
Wapella, Sask. 181/K5
Wapello (co.), Iowa 229/J6
Wapello, Iowa (52653) 229/L6
Wapinitia, Oreg. (†97037) 291/F2
Wapiti (riv.), Alberta 182/A2
Wapiti (riv.), Br. Col. 184/H3
Wapiti, Wyo. (82450) 319/C1
Wappapello, Mo. (63966) 261/M9
Wappapello (lake), Mo. 261/L8
Wappau (lake), Alberta 182/E2
Wappingers Falls, N.Y. (12590) 276/N7
Wapsipinicon (riv.), Iowa 229/J3
Wapske, New Bruns. 170/C2
Wapwallopen, Pa. (18660) 294/K3
Waqqas, Jordan 65/D2
Waquoit, Mass. (02536) 249/M6
War, W. Va. (24892) 312/C8
Warabi, Japan 81/O2
Waramaug (lake), Conn. 210/B2
Waranga (res.), Victoria 97/C5
Warangal, India 54/J8
Warangal, India 68/D5
Waratah, Tasmania 99/B3
Waratah (bay), Victoria 97/C6
Warba, Minn. (55743) 255/E3
Warburg, Alberta 182/C3
Warburg, W. Germany 22/C3
Warburton, The (riv.), S. Australia 94/F2
Warburton, The (riv.), S. Australia 88/F5
Warburton, Victoria 97/C5
Warburton Aboriginal Reserve, W. Australia 88/D5
Warburton Aboriginal Res., W. Australia 92/D4
Ward, Ala. (36922) 195/B6
Ward, Ark. (72176) 202/F3
Ward, Colo. (80481) 208/H2
Ward (peak), Mont. 262/A3
Ward, N. Zealand 100/E4
Ward (co.), N. Dak. 282/G3
Ward, S.C. (29166) 296/D4
Ward, S. Dak. (57074) 298/R5
Ward (co.), Texas 303/A6
Ward, W. Va. (†25039) 312/D6
Ward Cove, Alaska (99928) 196/N2
Wardell, Mo. (63879) 261/N10
Warden, La. (71289) 238/H1
Warden, Québec 172/E4
Warden, Wash. (98857) 310/F4
Wardensville, W. Va. (26851) 312/J4
Wardere, Ethiopia 111/J6
Wardha, India 68/D4
Wardha (riv.), India 68/D4
Wardlow, Alberta 182/E4
Wardner, Br. Col. 184/K5
Wardner, Idaho (†83837) 220/B2
Ward Ridge, Fla. (†32456) 212/D6
Wardsboro○, Vt. (05355) 268/B5
Ward Springs, Minn. (†56336) 255/D5
Wardsville, Mo. (†65101) 261/H6
Wardsville, Ontario 177/C5
Wardville, La. (†71301) 238/F4
Wardville, Okla. (74576) 288/P5
Ware, Br. Col. 184/E1
Ware, England 13/H7
Ware, England 10/F5
Ware (co.), Georgia 217/H8
Ware, Mass. (01082) 249/E3
Ware○, Mass. (01082) 249/E3
Ware (riv.), Mass. 249/F3
War Eagle, Ark. (†72756) 202/C1
War Eagle, W. Va. (†24862) 312/C7
Waregem, Belgium 27/C7
Wareham, England 13/E7
Wareham, England 10/E5
Wareham, Mass. (02571) 249/L5
Wareham○, Mass. (02571) 249/L5
Wareham Center, Mass. (02571) 249/L5
Warehouse Point, Conn. (06088) 210/E1
Waremme, Belgium 27/G7
Waren, E. Germany 22/E2
Waren, Indonesia 85/K6
Warenda, Queensland 95/B4
Warendorf, W. Germany 22/B3
Ware Neck, Va. (23178) 307/R6
Waresboro, Georgia (31564) 217/H8
Ware Shoals, S.C. (29692) 296/C3
Waretown, N.J. (08758) 273/E4
Warfield, Br. Col. 184/J5
Warfield, Ky. (41267) 237/S5
Warfield, Va. (23889) 307/N7
Warfordsburg, Pa. (17267) 294/F6
Warialda, N.S. Wales 97/F1
Warin Chamrap, Thailand 72/E4
Waring (mts.), Alaska 196/G1
Waring, Texas (78074) 303/F8
Warka, Poland 47/E3
Warkworth, N. Zealand 100/E2
Warkworth, Ontario 177/G3
Warley, England 13/E5
Warley, England 10/G3
Warm (creek), Utah 304/C6
Warman, Sask. 181/E3
Warmbad, Namibia 118/B5
Warmbad, S. Africa 118/D5
Warm Beach, Wash. (†98292) 310/C2
Warmenhuizen, Netherlands 27/F3
Warmia (reg.), Poland 47/D1
Warminster, England 10/E5
Warminster, England 13/E6
Warm Lake, Idaho (83611) 220/C5
Warm River, Idaho (†83420) 220/G5
Warm Springs, Ark. (72478) 202/H1
Warm Springs, Georgia (31830) 217/C5
Warmsprings, Mont. (59756) 262/D4
Warm Springs, Oreg. (97761) 291/F3
Warm Springs (res.), Oreg. 291/J4
Warm Springs, Va. (24484) 307/J4
Warm Springs Ind. Res., Oreg. 291/F3
Warne, N.C. (28909) 281/B5
Warner, Alberta 182/D5
Warner○, N.H. (03278) 268/D5
Warner (riv.), N.H. 268/D5
Warner, Ohio (45785) 284/H6
Warner, Okla. (74469) 288/R4
Warner, S. Dak. (57479) 298/M3
Warner Robins, Georgia (31093) 217/E5
Warners, N.Y. (13164) 276/H4
Warnerton, La. (†70438) 238/K5
Warnes, Bolivia 136/D5
Warnow (riv.), E. Germany 22/D2
Warooná, W. Australia 92/A2
Warrabri, North. Terr. 93/D6
Warrabri Aboriginal Reserve, North. Terr. 88/E4
Warracknabeal, Victoria 97/B5
Warracknabeal, Victoria 88/G7
Warr Acres, Okla. (73132) 288/L3
Warragamba, N.S. Wales 97/F3
Warragul, Victoria 97/D6
Warrandyte, Victoria 97/J4
Warrandyte, Victoria 88/M6
Warrego (riv.), N.S. Wales 97/C1
Warrego, North. Terr. 93/C5
Warrego (range), Queensland 88/H5
Warrego (range), Queensland 95/C5
Warrego (riv.), Queensland 88/H5
Warrego (riv.), Queensland 95/C5
Warren, Ark. (71671) 202/F6
Warren○, Conn. (06754) 210/B2
Warren (co.), Georgia 217/G4
Warren, Idaho (83671) 220/C4
Warren (co.), Ill. 222/C3
Warren, Ill. (61087) 222/C1
Warren (co.), Ind. 227/C4
Warren, Ind. (46792) 227/G3
Warren (co.), Iowa 229/F6
Warren (co.), Ky. 237/H6
Warren, Maine (04864) 243/E7
Warren○, Maine (04864) 243/E7
Warren, Manitoba 179/E4
Warren, Mass. (01083) 249/F4
Warren○, Mass. (01083) 249/F4
Warren, Mich. (*48089) 250/B6
Warren, Minn. (56762) 255/B2
Warren (co.), Miss. 256/C6
Warren (co.), Mo. 261/K5
Warren, Mo. (†63456) 261/J3
Warren○, N.H. (03279) 268/D4
Warren (co.), N.J. 273/C2
Warren○, N.J. (†07060) 273/D2
Warren, N. S. Wales 88/H6
Warren, N.S. Wales 97/D2
Warren (co.), N.Y. 276/N3
Warren (co.), N.C. 281/N2
Warren, Nova Scotia 168/D3
Warren (co.), Ohio 284/B7
Warren, Ohio (*44481) 284/J3
Warren, Ontario 177/D1
Warren, Oreg. (97053) 291/E2
Warren (co.), Pa. 294/D2
Warren, Pa. (16365) 294/D2
Warren○, R.I. (02885) 249/J6
Warren (res.), S. Australia 94/C7
Warren (co.), Tenn. 237/K9
Warren○, Vt. (05674) 268/B3
Warren (co.), Va. 307/M3
Warren Center, Pa. (18851) 294/K2
Warrenpoint, N. Ireland 17/J3
Warrens, Wis. (54666) 317/E7
Warrensburg, Ill. (62573) 222/D4
Warrensburg, Mo. (64093) 261/E5
Warrensburg, N.Y. (12885) 276/N3
Warrensville, Alberta 182/B1
Warrensville, N.C. (28693) 281/F2
Warrensville, Pa. (†17701) 294/J3
Warrensville Heights, Ohio (44128) 284/H9
Warrenton, Georgia (30828) 217/G4
Warrenton, Ind. (†47539) 227/B8
Warrenton, Mo. (63383) 261/K5
Warrenton, N.C. (27589) 281/N2
Warrenton, Oreg. (97146) 291/C1
Warrenton, S. Africa 118/C5
Warrenton, Va. (22186) 307/N3
Warrenville, Conn. (†06278) 210/G1
Warrenville, Ill. (60555) 222/A6
Warrenville, S.C. (29851) 296/D4
Warri, Nigeria 106/F7
Warrick (co.), Ind. 227/C8
Warrick, Mont. (†59520) 262/G2
Warrina, S. Australia 94/D3
Warringah, N.S. Wales 97/K3
Warrington, England 13/G2
Warrington, England 10/F2
Warrington, Fla. (32507) 212/B6
Warrington, Ind. (†46186) 227/F5
Warrior, Ala. (35180) 195/E3
Warrior (dam), Ala. 195/C5
Warrior Run, Pa. (18706) 294/E7
Warriors Mark, Pa. (16877) 294/F4
Warrnambool, Australia 87/D9
Warrnambool, Victoria 97/B6
Warrnambool, Victoria 88/G7
Warroad, Minn. (56763) 255/C2
Warrumbungle (range), N. S. Wales 88/H6
Warsaw, Ill. (62379) 222/B3
Warsaw, Ind. (46580) 227/F2
Warsaw, Ky. (41095) 237/M3
Warsaw, Minn. (55087) 255/E6
Warsaw, Mo. (65355) 261/F6
Warsaw, N.Y. (14569) 276/D5
Warsaw, N.C. (28398) 281/N4
Warsaw, N. Dak. (†58261) 282/R3
Warsaw, Ohio (43844) 284/G5
Warsaw, Ontario 177/F3
Warsaw (city), Poland 47/E2
Warsaw (prov.), Poland 47/E2
Warsaw (cap.), Poland 7/G3
Warsaw (cap.), Poland 2/L3
Warsaw (Warszawa) (cap.), Poland 47/E2
Warsaw, Va. (22572) 307/P5
Warson Woods, Mo. (†63101) 261/O3
Warsop, England 13/F4
Warspite, Alberta 182/D2
Warta (riv.), Poland 7/F3
Warta (riv.), Poland 47/B2
Wartau, Switzerland 39/H2
Wartburg, Tenn. (37887) 237/M8
Warthen, Georgia (31094) 217/G4
Wartime, Sask. 181/C4
Wartrace, Tenn. (37183) 237/J9
Warwick, Alberta 182/D3
Warwick, England 10/F4
Warwick, England 13/F5
Warwick, Georgia (31796) 217/E7
Warwick, Md. (21912) 245/P3
Warwick○, Mass. (†01364) 249/E2
Warwick, N.Y. (10990) 276/M8
Warwick, N. Dak. (58381) 282/N4
Warwick (chan.), North. Terr. 93/E3
Warwick, Okla. (†74834) 288/M3
Warwick, Québec 172/F4
Warwick, Queensland 88/J5
Warwick, Queensland 95/D6
Warwick, R.I. (*02886) 249/J6
Warwickshire (co.), England 13/F5
Wasa, Br. Col. 184/K5
Wasaga Beach, Ontario 177/D3
Wasagaming, Manitoba 179/C4
Wasatch (range), Idaho 220/G7
Wasatch (co.), Utah 304/C3
Wasatch (plat.), Utah 304/C4
Wasatch (range), Utah 304/C3
Wasco, Calif. (93280) 204/F8
Wasco (co.), Oreg. 291/F2
Wasco, Oreg. (97065) 291/G2
Wascott, Wis. (54890) 317/C3
Waseca (co.), Minn. 255/E6
Waseca, Minn. (56093) 255/E6
Waseca, Sask. 181/B2
Wasen, Switzerland 39/E2
Wash, The (bay), England 13/H5
Wash, The (bay), England 10/G4
Washademoak (lake), New Bruns. 170/E3
Washago, Ontario 177/E3
Washakie (co.), Wyo. 319/E2
Washakie Ind. Res., Utah 304/B2
Washburn, Ark. (†72936) 202/B3
Washburn, Ill. (61570) 222/D3
Washburn, Iowa (50706) 229/J4
Washburn, Maine (04786) 243/G2
Washburn○, Maine (04786) 243/G2
Washburn, Mo. (65772) 261/E9
Washburn, N. Dak. (58577) 282/J5
Washburn (co.), Pakistan 317/C4
Washburn, Tenn. (37888) 237/O8
Washburn, W. Va. (†26362) 312/D4
Washburn, Wis. (54891) 317/D2
Washburn (mt.), Wyo. 319/B1
Washdyke, N. Zealand 100/C6
Washington 188/B1
WASHINGTON 310
Washington (co.), Ala. 195/B8
Washington (co.), Ark. 202/B2
Washington, Ark. (71862) 202/C6
Washington (co.), Colo. 208/N3
Washington○, Conn. (06793) 210/B2
Washington, England 13/J3
Washington (co.), Fla. 212/C6
Washington (lake), Fla. 212/F3
Washington (co.), Georgia 217/G4
Washington, Georgia (30673) 217/G3
Washington (co.), Idaho 220/B5
Washington (co.), Ill. 222/D5
Washington, Ill. (61571) 222/D3
Washington (co.), Ind. 227/E7
Washington, Ind. (47501) 227/C7
Washington (co.), Iowa 229/K6
Washington, Iowa (52353) 229/K6
Washington (co.), Kansas 232/E2
Washington, Kansas (66968) 232/F2
Washington (co.), Ky. 237/L5
Washington, Ky. (41096) 237/O3
Washington (isl.), Kiribati 87/L5
Washington (par.), La. 238/K5
Washington, La. (70589) 238/G5
Washington (co.), Maine 243/H6
Washington○, Maine (04574) 243/E7
Washington (co.), Md. 245/G2
Washington○, Mass. (†01223) 249/B3
Washington (co.), Minn. 255/F5
Washington (co.), Miss. 256/C4
Washington, Miss. (39190) 256/B7
Washington (co.), Mo. 261/L7
Washington, Mo. (63090) 261/K5
Washington (co.), Nebr. 264/H3
Washington, Nebr. (68068) 264/H3
Washington○, N.H. (03280) 268/C5
Washington (mt.), N.H. 268/E3
Washington, N.J. (07882) 273/D2
Washington (co.), N.Y. 276/O4
Washington (co.), N.C. 281/R3
Washington, N.C. (27889) 281/R3
Washington (co.), Ohio 284/H7
Washington (Old Washington), Ohio (†43768) 284/H5
Washington (co.), Okla. 288/P1
Washington, Okla. (73093) 288/L4
Washington (co.), Oreg. 291/D2
Washington (co.), Pa. 294/B5
Washington, Pa. (15301) 294/B5
Washington (co.), R.I. 249/H7
Washington (Coventry), R.I. (†02816) 249/H6
Washington (co.), Tenn. 237/R8
Washington (co.), Texas 303/H7
Washington, Texas (77880) 303/J7
Washington (state), U.S. 146/F5
Washington, D.C. (cap.), U.S. 146/L6
Washington, D.C. (cap.), U.S. 188/L3
Washington, D.C. (cap.), U.S., (*20001) 245/F5
Washington (cap.), U.S. 2/F4
Washington (co.), Utah 304/A6
Washington, Utah (84780) 304/A6
Washington (co.), Vt. 268/B3
Washington○, Vt. (05675) 268/C3
Washington (co.), Va. 307/D7
Washington, Va. (22747) 307/M3
Washington (lake), Wash. 310/B2
Washington, W. Va. (26181) 312/C4
Washington (co.), Wis. 317/K9
Washington (isl.), Wis. 317/M5
Washington Court House, Ohio (43160) 284/D6
Washington Crossing, N.J. (†08560) 273/D3
Washington Crossing, Pa. (18977) 294/N5
Washington Depot, Conn. (06794) 210/B2
Washington Grove, Md. (20880) 245/K4
Washington Island, Wis. (54246) 317/M5
Washington Lands, W. Va. (†26041) 312/E3
Washington Park, Ill. (62204) 222/B2
Washington Park, N.C. (†27889) 281/R3
Washington Terrace, Utah (†84403) 304/B2
Washingtonville, N.Y. (10992) 276/M8
Washingtonville, Ohio (44490) 284/J4
Washingtonville, Pa. (17884) 294/J3
Washita, Ark. (†71957) 202/C4
Washita (co.), Okla. 288/J4
Washita, Okla. (73094) 288/K
Washita (riv.), Okla. 288/M5
Washita (riv.), Texas 303/D2
Washoe, Mont. (†59007) 262/G5
Washoe (co.), Nev. 266/B2
Washoe (lake), Nev. 266/B3
Washougal, Wash. (98671) 310/C5
Washow (bay), Manitoba 179/F3
Washta, Iowa (51061) 229/B3
Washtenaw (co.), Mich. 250/F6
Washtucna, Wash. (99371) 310/G4
Wasigunga, Okla. (†74641) 288/N1
Wasilkow, Poland 47/F2
Wasilla, Alaska (99687) 196/B1
Wasior, Indonesia 85/K6
Wasit (gov.), Iraq 66/D4
Waskada, Manitoba 179/B5
Waskana (creek), Sask. 181/G5
Waskatenau, Alberta 182/D2
Waskesiu (lake), Sask. 181/E2
Waskesiu Lake, Sask. 181/E2
Waskigomog (lake), Ontario 177/F2
Waskish, Minn. (56685) 255/D2
Waskom, Texas (75692) 303/L5
Waspán, Nicaragua 154/E3
Waspuk (riv.), Nicaragua 154/E3
Wassataquoik (stream), Maine 243/F4
Wassaw (sound), Georgia 217/L7
Wassen, Switzerland 39/G3
Wasser, Namibia 118/B5
Wasserbillig, Luxembourg 27/J9
Wasserburg am Inn, W. Germany 22/E4
Wasserkuppe (mt.), W. Germany 22/C3
Wasson, Ill. (†62930) 222/E6
Wassuk (range), Nev. 266/C4
Wassy, France 28/F3
Wasta, S. Dak. (57791) 298/D5
Wataga, Ill. (61488) 222/C2
Watampone, Indonesia 85/G6
Watauga (co.), N.C. 281/F2
Watauga, S. Dak. (57660) 298/F2
Watauga, Tenn. (37694) 237/S8
Watauga (lake), Tenn. 237/T8
Watauga, Texas (76248) 303/F2
Watauga Valley, Tenn. (†37643) 237/S8
Watchet, England 13/D6
Watch Hill, R.I. (02891) 249/G7
Watch Hill (pt.), R.I. 249/G7
Watchman (isl.), Newf. 166/B2
Watchung, N.J. (07060) 273/E2
Watchusk (lake), Alberta 182/E1
Water (isl.), Virgin Is. (U.S.) 161/A4
Waterberg, Namibia 118/B4
Waterboro, Maine (04087) 243/B8
Waterboro○, Maine (04087) 243/B8
Waterbury, Conn. 188/M2
Waterbury, Conn. (*06701) 210/C2
Waterbury, Nebr. (68785) 264/H2
Waterbury, Vt. (05676) 268/B3
Waterbury○, Vt. (05676) 268/B3
Waterbury (res.), Vt. 268/B3
Waterbury Center, Vt. (05677) 268/B3
Waterdown, Ontario 177/D4
Wateree, S.C. (†29044) 296/F4
Wateree (lake), S.C. 296/F3
Wateree (riv.), S.C. 296/F3
Waterflow, N. Mex. (87421) 274/A2
Waterford, Calif. (95386) 204/E6
Waterford, Conn. (06385) 210/G3
Waterford○, Conn. (06385) 210/G3
Waterford (co.), Ireland 17/F7
Waterford, Ireland 17/G7
Waterford, Ireland 10/C4
Waterford (harb.), Ireland 10/C4
Waterford (harb.), Ireland 17/G7
Waterford, Maine (04088) 243/B7
Waterford○, Maine (04088) 243/B7
Waterford, Miss. (38685) 256/E1
Waterford, New Bruns. 170/E3
Waterford, N.Y. (12188) 276/N5
Waterford, Ohio (45786) 284/G6
Waterford, Pa. (16441) 294/B2
Waterford, Va. (22190) 307/N2
Waterford, Wis. (53185) 317/K3
Waterford Works, N.J. (08089) 273/D4
Watergap, Ky. (41665) 237/R5
Waterhen (lake), Manitoba 179/C2
Waterhouse (isl.), Tasmania 99/D2
Waterloo, Ala. (35677) 195/B1
Waterloo, Ark. (†71858) 202/D6
Waterloo, Belgium 27/E7
Waterloo, Ill. (62298) 222/C5
Waterloo, Ind. (46793) 227/G2
Waterloo, Iowa 188/H2
Waterloo, Iowa 146/J5
Waterloo, Iowa (*50701) 229/J4
Waterloo, Kansas (†67111) 232/E4
Waterloo, Mont. (†59759) 262/D5
Waterloo, Nebr. (68069) 264/H3
Waterloo, N.Y. (13165) 276/G5
Waterloo, North. Terr. 93/A4
Waterloo, Ohio (45688) 284/F8
Waterloo (reg. munic.), Ontario 177/D4
Waterloo, Ontario 177/D4
Waterloo, Oreg. (†97355) 291/E3
Waterloo, Québec 172/E4
Waterloo, S.C. (29384) 296/C3
Waterloo, Trin. & Tob. 161/A10
Waterloo, Wis. (53594) 317/J9
Watermaal-Bosvoorde (Watermael-Boitsfort), Belgium 27/C9
Watermael-Boitsfort, Belgium 27/C9
Waterman, Ill. (60556) 222/E2
Waterman, Ind. (†47952) 227/C5
Waterpocket Fold (butte), Utah 304/D6
Waterport, N.Y. (14571) 276/D4
Waterproof, La. (71375) 238/H3
Waters, Mich. (49797) 250/E4
Watersmeet, Mich. (49969) 250/G2
Waterton-Glacier Int'l Peace Park, Alberta 182/C5
Waterton-Glacier International Peace Park, Alta.162/E6
Waterton-Glacier Int'l Peace Park, Mont. 262/C2
Waterton Lakes Nat'l Park, Alberta 182/C5
Waterton Park, Alberta 182/D5
Watertown○, Conn. (06795) 210/C2
Watertown, Fla. (†32055) 212/D1
Watertown○, Mass. (02172) 249/C6
Watertown, Minn. (55388) 255/E6
Watertown, N.Y. 188/M2
Watertown, N.Y. (13601) 276/J3
Watertown, Ohio (45787) 284/G7
Watertown, S. Dak. 188/G1
Watertown, S. Dak. (57201) 298/P4
Watertown, Tenn. (37184) 237/J8
Watertown, Wis. (53094) 317/J9
Waterval-Bo, S. Africa 118/D5
Water Valley, Ala. (†36908) 195/B7
Water Valley, Alberta 182/C4
Water Valley, Ky. (42085) 237/D7
Water Valley, Miss. (38965) 256/E2
Water Valley, Texas (76958) 303/C6
Waterview, Ky. (42786) 237/L7
Waterview, Md. (†21840) 245/P8
Water View, Va. (23180) 307/P5
Waterville, Iowa (52170) 229/L2
Waterville, Ireland 17/A8
Waterville, Kansas (66548) 232/F2
Waterville, Maine 188/N2
Waterville, Maine (04901) 243/D6
Waterville, Mass. (†01475) 249/F2
Waterville, Minn. (56096) 255/E6
Waterville, New Bruns. 170/C2
Waterville, N.Y. (13480) 276/K5
Waterville, Nova Scotia 168/D3
Waterville, Ohio (43566) 284/C3
Waterville, Québec 172/F4
Waterville○, Vt. (05492) 268/B2
Waterville, Wash. (98858) 310/E3
Waterville Valley○, N.H. (03223) 268/D4
Watervliet, Mich. (49098) 250/C6
Watervliet, N.Y. (12189) 276/N5
Waterways, Alberta 182/E1
Watford, England 10/B5
Watford, England 13/H7
Watford, Ontario 177/C5
Watford City, N. Dak. (58854) 282/D4
Watha, N.C. (28471) 281/O5
Wathaman (riv.), Sask. 181/M3
Wathena, Kansas (66090) 232/H2
Watheroo, W. Australia 92/A5
Watino, Alberta 182/B2
Watkins, Iowa (52354) 229/J5
Watkins, Minn. (55389) 255/D5
Watkins Glen, N.Y. (14891) 276/G6
Watkinsville, Georgia (30677) 217/E3
Watling (San Salvador) (isl.), Bahamas 156/C1
Watonga, Okla. (73772) 288/K3
Watonwan (co.), Minn. 255/D7
Watova, Okla. (†74048) 288/P1
Watrous, N. Mex. (87753) 274/D3
Watrous, Sask. 162/F5
Watrous, Sask. 181/F4
Watsa, Zaire 115/E3
Watseka, Ill. (60970) 222/F3
Watson, Ark. (71674) 202/H6
Watson, Ill. (62473) 222/E4
Watson, Ind. (†47130) 227/F8
Watson, La. (70786) 238/L1
Watson, Minn. (56295) 255/C5
Watson, Mo. (64496) 261/A1
Watson, Okla. (74963) 288/S6
Watson, Sask. 181/G3
Watson (mt.), Utah 304/C3
Watson Lake, Yukon 187/F3
Watson Lake, Yukon 162/D3
Watsontown, Pa. (17777) 294/J3
Watsonville, Calif. (95076) 204/D7
Watten, Scotland 15/E2
Watten, Loch (lake), Scotland 15/E2
Wattensaw (bayou), Ark. 202/G4
Watton, England 13/H5
Watton, Mich. (49970) 250/G2
Watts, Okla. (74964) 288/S2
Watts Bar (dam), Tenn. 237/M9
Watts Bar (lake), Tenn. 237/M9
Watts Bar Dam, Tenn. (37395) 237/M9
Wattsburg, Pa. (16442) 294/C1
Watt Section Sheet Harbour, Nova Scotia 168/F4
Watts Mills, S.C. (†29360) 296/D2
Wattsview, Manitoba 179/A4
Wattsville, Ala. (35182) 195/F3
Wattwil, Switzerland 39/H2
Watubela (isls.), Indonesia 85/J6
Watuppa (pond), Mass. 249/K6
Watzmann (mt.), W. Germany 22/E5
Wau, Papua N.G. 85/B7
Wau, Papua N.G. 87/E6
Wau, Sudan 111/E6
Wau, Sudan 102/E4
Waubamik, Ontario 177/E2
Waubaushene, Ontario 177/E3
Waubay, S. Dak. (57273) 298/P3
Waubay (lake), S. Dak. 298/O3
Waubeek, Iowa (†52214) 229/K4
Waubeka, Wis. (53021) 317/L9
Waubun, Minn. (56589) 255/C3
Waucedah, Mich. (†49892) 250/B3
Wauchope, N.S. Wales 97/G2
Wauchope, Sask. 181/K6
Wauchula, Fla. (33873) 212/E4
Waucoma, Iowa (52171) 229/J2
Wauconda, Ill. (60084) 222/A4
Wauconda, Wash. (98859) 310/F2
Wau el Kebir, Libya 111/C2
Waugh, Ala. (†36104) 195/F6
Waugh (mt.), Idaho 220/D4
Waugh, Manitoba 179/G5
Waukarlyearly (lake), W. Australia 88/C4
Waukee, Iowa (50263) 229/F5
Waukeenah, Fla. (†32344) 212/C1
Waukegan, Ill. (60085) 222/B4
Waukesha (co.), Wis. 317/K9
Waukesha, Wis. (53186) 317/K1
Waukomis, Okla. (73773) 288/K2
Waukon, Iowa (52172) 229/L2
Waukon, Wash. (†99008) 310/H3
Waukon Junction, Iowa (†52146) 229/L2
Waumandee, Wis. (†54622) 317/C7
Waumbek (mt.), N.H. 268/E3
Wauna, Oreg. (†97016) 291/D1
Wauna, Wash. (98395) 310/C3
Waunakee, Wis. (53597) 317/G9
Wauneta, Kansas (†67024) 232/F4
Wauneta, Nebr. (69045) 264/C4
Waupaca (co.), Wis. 317/J6
Waupaca, Wis. (54981) 317/H7
Waupun, Wis. (53963) 317/J8
Wauregan, Conn. (06387) 210/H2
Waurika, Okla. (73573) 288/L6
Waurika (lake), Okla. 288/K6
Wausa, Nebr. (68786) 264/G2
Wausau, Fla. (32463) 212/D6
Wausau, Wis. 188/J2
Wausau, Wis. (54401) 317/G6
Wausau○, Wis. 317/80
Wausaukee, Wis. (54177) 317/K5
Wauseon, Ohio (43567) 284/B2
Waushara (co.), Wis. 317/H7
Wautoma, Wis. (54982) 317/H7
Wauwatosa, Wis. (53226) 317/L1
Wauzeka, Wis. (53826) 317/E9
Wave Hill, North. Terr. 88/E3
Wave Hill, North. Terr. 93/B4
Waveland, Ark. (72867) 202/C3
Waveland, Ind. (47989) 227/D5
Waveland, Miss. (39576) 256/F10

Westernport 467

Waver (Wavre), Belgium 27/F7
Waverley, Mass. (02179) 249/B6
Waverley, N. S. Wales 88/L4
Waverley, N.S. Wales 97/K3
Waverley, N. Zealand 100/E3
Waverley, Nova Scotia 168/E4
Waverley, Ontario 177/E3
Waverley, Victoria 97/J5
Waverley, Victoria 88/L7
Waverley Downs, N.S. Wales 97/B1
Waverly, Ala. (36879) 195/G5
Waverly, Fla. (33877) 212/E4
Waverly, Georgia (31565) 217/J8
Waverly, Ill. (62692) 222/D4
Waverly, Iowa (50677) 229/J3
Waverly, Kansas (66871) 232/G3
Waverly, Ky. (42462) 237/F5
Waverly, La. (71232) 238/H2
Waverly, Minn. (55390) 255/E5
Waverly, Mo. (64096) 261/E4
Waverly, Nebr. (68462) 264/H4
Waverly, N.Y. (14892) 276/G7
Waverly, Ohio (45690) 284/D7
Waverly, S. Dak. (57202) 298/R3
Waverly, Tenn. (37185) 237/F8
Waverly, Va. (23890) 307/O6
Waverly, Wash. (99039) 310/H3
Waverly, W. Va. (26184) 312/D4
Waverly Hall, Georgia (31831) 217/C5
Waves, N.C. (27982) 281/U3
Wavre, Belgium 27/F7
Wawa (riv.), Nicaragua 154/E3
Wawa, Ontario 175/C3
Wawa, Ontario 177/J5
Wawaka, Ind. (46794) 227/F2
Wawanesa, Manitoba 179/C5
Wawasee, Ind. (†46567) 227/F2
Wawasee (lake), Ind. 227/F2
Wawayanda (lake), N.J. 273/E1
Waweig, New Bruns. 170/C3
Wawina, Minn. (55794) 255/E3
Wawota, Sask. 181/J6
Wawpecong, Ind. (†46901) 227/F3
Wax, Ky. (42787) 237/J6
Waxahachie, Texas (75165) 303/H5
Waxhaw, N.C. (28173) 281/H5
Way, Miss. (†39046) 256/E5
Way (lake), W. Australia 88/C5
Way (lake), W. Australia 92/C4
Wayagamac (lake), Québec 172/E2
Wayan, Idaho (83285) 220/G7
Wayatinah, Tasmania 99/C4
Waycross, Ga. 188/K4
Waycross, Georgia (31501) 217/H8
Wayerton, New Bruns. 170/E1
Wayland, Iowa (52654) 229/K6
Wayland, Ky. (41666) 237/R6
Wayland○, Mass. (01778) 249/A7
Wayland, Mich. (49348) 250/D6
Wayland, Mo. (63472) 261/J2
Wayland, N.Y. (14572) 276/E5
Wayland, Ohio (44285) 284/H3
Waymansville, Ind. (†47201) 227/E6
Waymart, Pa. (18472) 294/M2
Wayne, Ala. (†36763) 195/C6
Wayne, Alberta 182/D4
Wayne (co.), Georgia 217/J7
Wayne (co.), Ill. 222/E5
Wayne, Ill. (60184) 222/E2
Wayne (co.), Ind. 227/G5
Wayne (co.), Iowa 229/G7
Wayne, Kansas (†66930) 232/E2
Wayne (co.), Ky. 237/M7
Wayne, Maine (04284) 243/D7
Wayne○, Maine (04284) 243/D7
Wayne (co.), Mich. 250/F6
Wayne, Mich. (48184) 250/F6
Wayne (co.), Miss. 256/G7
Wayne (co.), Mo. 261/L8
Wayne (co.), Nebr. 264/G2
Wayne, Nebr. (68787) 264/G2
Wayne○, N.J. (07470) 273/A1
Wayne (co.), N.Y. 276/F4
Wayne, N.Y. (14893) 276/F6
Wayne (co.), N.C. 281/N4
Wayne (co.), Ohio 284/G4
Wayne, Ohio (43466) 284/C3
Wayne, Okla. (73095) 288/M5
Wayne (co.), Pa. 294/M2
Wayne, Pa. (19087) 294/M6
Wayne (co.), Tenn. 237/F10
Wayne (co.), Utah 304/C5
Wayne (co.), W. Va. 312/B6
Wayne, W. Va. (25570) 312/B6
Wayne City, Ill. (62895) 222/E5
Waynesboro, Georgia (30830) 217/J4
Waynesboro, Miss. (39367) 256/G7
Waynesboro, Pa. (17268) 294/G6
Waynesboro, Tenn. (38485) 237/F10
Waynesboro (I.C.), Va. (22980) 307/K4
Waynesburg, Ky. (40489) 237/M6
Waynesburg, Ohio (44688) 284/H4
Waynesburg, Pa. (15370) 294/B6
Waynesfield, Ohio (45896) 284/C4
Waynesville, Georgia (31566) 217/J8
Waynesville, Ill. (61778) 222/D3
Waynesville, Ind. (†47201) 227/F6
Waynesville, Mo. (65583) 261/H7
Waynesville, N.C. (28786) 281/D4
Waynesville, Ohio (45068) 284/B6
Waynetown, Ind. (47990) 227/C4
Waynoka, Okla. (73860) 288/J1
Wayside, Georgia (†31032) 217/E4
Wayside, Kansas (†67301) 232/G4
Wayside, Miss. (38780) 256/C4
Wayside, Texas (79094) 303/C3
Wayside, Wis. (†54126) 317/L7
Wayzata, Minn. (55391) 255/G5
Wazirabad, Pakistan 59/K3
We (isl.), Indonesia 85/B4
Wé, New Caled. 86/H4
Weagamow Lake, Ontario 175/B2
Weakley (co.), Tenn. 237/D8
Weald, The (reg.), England 13/H6
Wear (riv.), England 13/F3
Wear (riv.), England 10/F3
Weare○, N.H. (03281) 268/D5
Weare P.O. (North Weare), N.H. (03281) 268/D5
Weatherby, Mo. (64497) 261/D3
Weatherby Lake, Mo. (†64152) 261/O5
Weatherford, Okla. (73096) 288/J4
Weatherford, Texas (76086) 303/G5
Weatherly, Pa. (18255) 294/L4
Weathers, Okla. (†74560) 288/P5
Weathersby, Miss. (†39114) 256/E7
Weatogue, Conn. (06089) 210/D1
Weaubleau, Mo. (65774) 261/F7
Weaver, Ala. (36277) 195/G3
Weaver (riv.), England 13/G2
Weaver (lake), Manitoba 179/F2
Weaver, Minn. (†55958) 255/G6
Weaver, New Bruns. 170/E2
Weaver, N. Dak. (†58352) 282/N2
Weaverville, Calif. (96093) 204/B3
Weaverville, N.C. (28787) 281/D3
Webb, Ala. (36376) 195/H8
Webb, Iowa (51366) 229/D3
Webb (lake), Maine 243/C6
Webb, Miss. (38966) 256/D3
Webb (bay), Newf. 166/B2
Webb, Sask. 181/C5
Webb (co.), Texas 303/E10
Webb, Texas (†76010) 303/F3
Webb City, Ark. (†72949) 202/C3
Webb City, Mo. (64870) 261/C8
Webb City, Okla. (74654) 288/N1
Webber, Kansas (66970) 232/D2
Webbers Falls, Okla. (74470) 288/R3
Webbers Falls (res.), Okla. 288/R3
Webberville, Mich. (48892) 250/E6
Webb Lake, Wis. (54892) 317/B3
Webbs Cross Roads, Ky. (42652) 237/L6
Webbville, Ky. (41180) 237/R4
Webbwood, Ontario 177/C1
Webequie, Ontario 175/C2
Weber (co.), Utah 304/B2
Weber (riv.), Utah 304/C3
Weber City, Va. (24251) 307/C7
Webi Shabelle (riv.), Somalia 115/H3
Webster, Fla. (33597) 212/D3
Webster (co.), Georgia 217/C6
Webster, Ind. (47392) 227/H5
Webster (co.), Iowa 229/E4
Webster, Iowa (52355) 229/J6
Webster (res.), Kansas 232/C2
Webster (co.), Ky. 237/F5
Webster, Ky. (40176) 237/J5
Webster (par.), La. 238/D1
Webster (brook), Maine 243/E3
Webster, Mass. (01570) 249/G4
Webster○, Mass. (01570) 249/G4
Webster (lake), Mass. 249/G4
Webster, Minn. (55088) 255/E6
Webster (co.), Miss. 256/F3
Webster (co.), Mo. 261/G8
Webster (co.), Nebr. 264/F4
Webster○, N.H. (†03301) 268/D5
Webster, N.Y. (14580) 276/F4
Webster, N.C. (28788) 281/C4
Webster, N. Dak. (58382) 282/N3
Webster, Pa. (15087) 294/C5
Webster, S. Dak. (57274) 298/P3
Webster, Texas (77598) 303/K2
Webster (co.), W. Va. 312/F6
Webster, Wis. (54893) 317/B4
Webster City, Iowa (50595) 229/F4
Webster Groves, Mo. (63119) 261/P3
Webster Mills, Pa. (†17233) 294/F6
Webster Springs, W. Va. (26288) 312/F6
Websterville, Vt. (05678) 268/B3
Wecota, S. Dak. (57480) 298/L3
Weda, Indonesia 85/H5
Wedau, Papua N.G. 85/C7
Weddel (isl.), 143/D7
Weddell (sea), Ant. 2/H10
Weddell (sea) 5/C16
Wedderburn, Oreg. (97491) 291/C5
Wedderburn, Victoria 97/B5
Weddington, Ark. (†72701) 202/B1
Wedel, W. Germany 22/C2
Wedgefield, S.C. (29168) 296/F4
Wedgeport, Nova Scotia 168/C5
Wedgeworth, Ala. (†36776) 195/C5
Wedowee, Ala. (36278) 195/H4
Weed, Calif. (96094) 204/C2
Weed, N. Mex. (88354) 274/D6
Weed (hills), Sask. 181/J5
Weed Heights, Nev. (89443) 266/B4
Weedon-Centre, Québec 172/F4
Weedsport, N.Y. (13166) 276/G4
Weedville, Pa. (15868) 294/F3
Weehawken○, N.J. (07087) 273/C2
Week (isls.), Chile 138/D10
Weekapaug, R.I. (02891) 249/G7
Weekes, Sask. 181/J3
Weeki Wachee, Fla. (†33512) 212/D3
Weeks, La. (†70569) 238/G7
Weeks, Nev. (†89447) 266/B3
Weeks (isl.), N. Zealand 100/B1
Weeksbury, Ky. (41667) 237/R6
Weeks Mills, Maine (04361) 243/E7
Weeksville, N.C. (27909) 281/S2
Weems, Va. (22576) 307/P5
Weeping Water, Nebr. (68463) 264/J4
Weert, Netherlands 27/H6
Weesatche, Texas (77993) 303/G9
Weesen, Switzerland 39/H2
Weesp, Netherlands 27/C5
Weethalle, N.S. Wales 97/D3
Wee Waa, N.S. Wales 97/E2
Wegdahl, Minn. (†56265) 255/C6
Weggis, Switzerland 39/F2
Wegorzewo, Poland 47/E1
Wegra-Flat Creek, Ala. (†35129) 195/D3
Wegrów, Poland 47/E2
Weichang, China 77/J3
Weida, E. Germany 22/D3
Weiden in der Oberpfalz, W. Germany 22/D4
Weidman, Mich. (48893) 250/D5
Weifang, China 77/J4
Weihai (Weihaiwei), China 77/K4
Wei He (riv.), China 77/G5
Weilburg, W. Germany 22/C3
Weilheim im Oberbayern, W. Germany 22/D5
Weimar, E. Germany 22/D3
Weimar, Texas (78962) 303/H8
Weinan, China 77/H5
Weiner, Ark. (72479) 202/J2
Weinert, Texas (76388) 303/E4
Weinfelden, Switzerland 39/H1
Weingarten, W. Germany 22/C5
Weinheim, W. Germany 22/C4
Weining, China 77/F6
Weinsberg, W. Germany 22/C4
Weipa, Queensland 88/G1
Weipa, Queensland 95/B2
Weippe, Idaho (83553) 220/C3
Weir (lake), Fla. 212/E2
Weir, Kansas (66781) 232/H4
Weir, Miss. (39772) 256/F4
Weirdale, Sask. 181/F2
Weirgor, Wis. (†54835) 317/D4
Weir River, Manitoba 179/J2
Weirsdale, Fla. (32695) 212/D3
Weirton, W. Va. (26062) 312/E2
Weirwood, Va. (23484) 307/S6
Weisburg, Ind. (†47041) 227/H6
Weiser, Idaho (83672) 220/B5
Weiser (riv.), Idaho 220/B5
Weishan, China 77/F6
Weismes (Waimes), Belgium 27/J8
Weiss (lake), Ala. 195/G2
Weiss (lake), Georgia 217/A2
Weissenburg im Bayern, W. Germany 22/D4
Weissenfels, E. Germany 22/D3
Weissensee, E. Germany 22/F3
Weissenstein (mts.), Switzerland 39/D2
Weisserstein (mt.), Belgium 27/J8
Weissert, Nebr. (68880) 264/E3
Weisshorn (mt.), Switzerland 39/J3
Weisshorn (mt.), Switzerland 39/E4
Weissmies (mt.), Switzerland 39/F4
Weisswasser, E. Germany 22/F3
Weitchpec, Calif. (†95546) 204/B2
Weitensfeld-Flattnitz, Austria 41/B3
Weitra, Austria 41/C2
Weixi, China 77/E6
Weixin, China 77/F6
Weiz, Austria 41/C3
Wejh, Saudi Arabia 59/C4
Wejh, Saudi Arabia 54/E7
Wejherowo, Poland 47/D1
Welaka, Fla. (32093) 212/E2
Welbekend, S. Africa 118/J6
Welch, Okla. (74369) 288/R1
Welch, Texas (79377) 303/B5
Welch, W. Va. (24801) 312/C8
Welches, Oreg. (†97067) 291/E2
Welchman Hall, Barbados 161/B8
Welchville, Maine (†04270) 243/C7
Welcome, La. (†70086) 238/L3
Welcome, Md. (20693) 245/K7
Welcome, Minn. (56181) 255/D7
Welcome, N.C. (27374) 281/J3
Welcome, Ontario 177/F4
Welcome All, Georgia (†30304) 217/J2
Weld (co.), Colo. 208/L1
Weld○, Maine (04285) 243/C6
Weld (range), W. Australia 92/B4
Welda, Kansas (66091) 232/G3
Weldon, Ark. (72177) 202/H3
Weldon, Calif. (93283) 204/G8
Weldon, Ill. (61882) 222/E3
Weldon, Iowa (50264) 229/F7
Weldon, New Bruns. 170/F3
Weldon, N.C. (27890) 281/O2
Weldon, Sask. 181/F2
Weldon, Texas (75863) 303/J6
Weldona, Colo. (80653) 208/M2
Weldon Spring Heights, Mo. (†63301) 261/M2
Weleetka, Okla. (74880) 288/O4
Welford, Queensland 95/C5
Welkom, S. Africa 102/E7
Welkom, S. Africa 118/D5
Welland (riv.), England 13/G5
Welland (riv.), England 10/F4
Welland, Ontario 177/E5
Welland (canal), Ontario 177/E5
Wellandport, Ontario 177/E4
Wellborn, Fla. (32094) 212/D1
Wellersburg, Pa. (15564) 294/E6
Wellesley (isls.), Australia 87/D7
Wellesley○, Mass. (02181) 249/B7
Wellesley, Ontario 177/D4
Wellesley (isls.), Queensland 88/F3
Wellesley (isls.), Queensland 95/A3
Wellesley Hills, Mass. (02181) 249/B7
Wellfleet○, Mass. (02667) 249/O5
Wellfleet (harb.), Mass. 249/O5
Wellfleet, Nebr. (69170) 264/D4
Wellford, S.C. (29385) 296/C2
Wellin, Belgium 27/G8
Welling, Alberta 182/D5
Welling, Okla. (74471) 288/S3
Wellingborough, England 13/G5
Wellingborough, England 10/F4
Wellington, Ala. (36279) 195/G3
Wellington (isl.), Chile 120/B7
Wellington (isl.), Chile 138/D8
Wellington, Colo. (80549) 208/K1
Wellington, England 13/D7
Wellington, England 10/E5
Wellington, Ill. (60973) 222/F3
Wellington, Kansas (67152) 232/E4
Wellington, Ky. (†40201) 237/K2
Wellington, Ky. (40387) 237/O5
Wellington○, Maine (04990) 243/D5
Wellington, Mo. (64097) 261/E4
Wellington, Nev. (89444) 266/B4
Wellington, N.S. Wales 97/E3
Wellington (cap.), N. Zealand 2/T8
Wellington (cap.), N. Zealand 87/H10
Wellington (cap.), N. Zealand 100/A3
Wellington (bay), N.W. Terrs. 187/H3
Wellington (chan.), N.W.T. 162/G1
Wellington (chan.), N.W. Terrs. 187/J2
Wellington, Nova Scotia 168/E4
Wellington, Ohio (44090) 284/F3
Wellington (county), Ontario 177/D4
Wellington, Ontario 177/G4
Wellington, Pr. Edward I. 168/D2
Wellington, S. Africa 118/B6
Wellington, Texas (79095) 303/D3
Wellington, Utah (84542) 304/D4
Wellington (lake), Victoria 97/D6
Wellington, Va. (†22308) 307/T3
Wellman, Iowa (52356) 229/K6
Wellman (lake), Manitoba 179/B3
Wellman, Texas (79378) 303/B5
Wellpinit, Wash. (99040) 310/G3
Wells, Br. Col. 184/G3
Wells, England 13/E6
Wells, England 10/E5
Wells (co.), Ind. 227/G3
Wells, Kansas (67488) 232/E2
Wells, Maine (04090) 243/B9
Wells○, Maine (04090) 243/B9
Wells, Mich. (49894) 250/B3
Wells, Minn. (56097) 255/E7
Wells, Nev. (89835) 266/G1
Wells, N.Y. (12190) 276/M4
Wells (co.), N. Dak. 282/L4
Wells, Texas (75976) 303/J6
Wells○, Vt. (05774) 268/A5
Wells (riv.), Vt. 268/C3
Wells (dam), Wash. 310/F3
Wells (lake), W. Australia 88/C5
Wells (lake), W. Australia 92/C4
Wells Beach, Maine (04090) 243/B9
Wellsboro, Ind. (†46382) 227/D1
Wellsboro, Pa. (16901) 294/H2
Wells Bridge, N.Y. (13859) 276/K6
Wellsburg, Iowa (50680) 229/H4
Wellsburg, N.Y. (14894) 276/G6
Wellsburg, N. Dak. (†58341) 282/L4
Wellsburg, W. Va. (26070) 312/E2
Wellsford, N. Zealand 100/E2
Wells Gray Prov. Park, Br. Col. 184/H4
Wells-next-the-Sea, England 13/H5
Wells-next-the-Sea, England 10/G4
Wells River, Vt. (05081) 268/C3
Wellston, Mich. (49689) 250/D4
Wellston, Mo. (63112) 261/R2
Wellston, Ohio (45692) 284/F7
Wellston, Okla. (74881) 288/M3
Wellsville, Kansas (66092) 232/G3
Wellsville, Mo. (63384) 261/K4
Wellsville, N.Y. (14895) 276/E6
Wellsville, Ohio (43968) 284/J4
Wellsville, Pa. (17365) 294/J5
Wellsville, Utah (84339) 304/C2
Wellton, Ariz. (85356) 198/A6
Wellwood, Manitoba 179/C4
Wels, Austria 41/C2
Welsford, New Bruns. 170/D3
Welsford, Nova Scotia 168/E3
Welsh, La. (70591) 238/E6
Welshfield, Ohio (†44021) 284/H3
Welshpool, New Bruns. 170/D4
Welshpool, Wales 10/E4
Welshpool, Wales 13/D5
Welton, Iowa (52774) 229/M5
Welty, Okla. (74882) 288/O3
Welwyn, England 13/H7
Welwyn, England 10/F5
Welwyn, Sask. 181/K5
Wem, England 13/E5
Wembere (riv.), Tanzania 115/F4
Wembley, Alberta 182/A2
Wemmel, Belgium 27/B9
Wemyss Bay, Scotland 15/A2
Wenamu (riv.), Guyana 131/A2
Wenas (creek), Wash. 310/E4
Wenasoga, Miss. (†38834) 256/G1
Wenatchee, Wash. 188/B1
Wenatchee, Wash. (98801) 310/E3
Wenatchee (lake), Wash. 310/E3
Wenatchee (mts.), Wash. 310/E3
Wenatchee (riv.), Wash. 310/E3
Wenchi, Ghana 106/D7
Wenchow (Wenzhou), China 77/J6
Wendel, Calif. (96136) 204/E3
Wendel, W. Va. (26450) 312/F4
Wendell, Idaho (83355) 220/D7
Wendell○, Mass. (01379) 249/E2
Wendell, Minn. (56590) 255/B4
Wendell, N.H. (03783) 268/C5
Wendell, N.C. (27591) 281/N3
Wendell Depot, Mass. (01380) 249/E2
Wenden, Ariz. (85357) 198/B5
Wendeng, China 77/K4
Wendover, England 13/G7
Wendover, Ontario 177/J2
Wendover, Utah (84083) 304/A3
Wendover, Wyo. (†82214) 319/H3
Wendron, England 13/B7
Wendte, S. Dak. (†57532) 298/H5
Wenham○, Mass. (01984) 249/L2
Wenling, China 77/K6
Wenlock (riv.), Queensland 88/G2
Wenman (isl.), Ecuador 128/B8
Wenona, Georgia (†31015) 217/E7
Wenona, Ill. (61377) 222/E2
Wenona, Md. (21870) 245/P8
Wenona, N.C. (†27860) 281/R3
Wenonah, Ill. (†62075) 222/D4
Wenonah, N. J. (08090) 273/C4
Wenquan, Qinghai, China 77/D5
Wenquan, Xinjiang Uygur, China 77/B3
Wenshan, China 77/F7
Wensum (riv.), England 13/J5
Wentworth, Mo. (64873) 261/D8
Wentworth○, N.H. (03282) 268/D4
Wentworth (lake), N.H. 268/E4
Wentworth, N.S. Wales 97/B4
Wentworth, N.C. (27375) 281/K2
Wentworth, Nova Scotia 168/E3
Wentworth, S. Dak. (57075) 298/R6
Wentworth, Wis. (54894) 317/C2
Wentworths Location○, N.H. (†03579) 268/E2
Wentzville, Mo. (63385) 261/L5
Wen Xian, China 77/G5
Wenzhou (Wenchow), China 77/J6
Wenzhou, China 54/N7
Weogufka, Ala. (35183) 195/F4
Weohyakapka (lake), Fla. 212/E4
Weott, Calif. (95571) 204/A3
Wepawaug (riv.), Conn. 210/C3
Wequetequock, Conn. (†02891) 210/H3
Werdau, E. Germany 22/E3
Werder, E. Germany 22/E2
Werner Lake, Ontario 175/A2
Wernersville, Pa. (19565) 294/K5
Wernigerode, E. Germany 22/D3
Werra (riv.), E. Germany 22/D3
Werra (riv.), W. Germany 22/D3
Werribee, Victoria 88/G7
Werrimull, Victoria 97/A4
Werris Creek, N.S. Wales 97/F2
Wertheim, W. Germany 22/C4
Wervik, Belgium 27/B7
Wesco, Mo. (65586) 261/K7
Wesel, W. Germany 22/B3
Weser (riv.), Germany 7/E3
Weser (riv.), W. Germany 22/C2
Weskan, Kansas (67762) 232/A3
Weslaco, Texas (78596) 303/F11
Weslemkoon (lake), Ontario 177/G2
Wesley, Ark. (72773) 202/C1
Wesley, Dominica 161/F5
Wesley, Georgia (†30401) 217/H6
Wesley, Iowa (50483) 229/E2
Wesley, Maine (04686) 243/H6
Wesley○, Maine (04686) 243/H6
Wesley Vale, Tasmania 99/C3
Wesleyville, Newf. 166/D4
Wesleyville, Pa. (16510) 294/C1
Wes-Rand, S. Africa 118/G6
Wessel (isls.), Australia 87/D7
Wessel (cape), North. Terr. 88/F2
Wessel (cape), North. Terr. 93/E1
Wessel (isls.), North. Terr. 88/F2
Wessel (isls.), North. Terr. 93/E1
Wessington, S. Dak. (57381) 298/M5
Wessington Springs, S. Dak. (57382) 298/M5
Wesson, Ark. (†71749) 202/E7
Wesson, Miss. (39191) 256/D7
West (riv.), Conn. 210/C4
West (riv.), Conn. 210/E3
West, Iowa (52357) 229/J5
West (bay), La. 238/M8
West (isl.), Mass. 249/L6
West (riv.), Mass. 249/H4
West, Miss. (39192) 256/E4
West (isls.), New Bruns. 170/D4
West (cape), N. Zealand 100/A6
West (bay), Nova Scotia 168/G3
West (pt.), Nova Scotia 168/H5
West (riv.), Nova Scotia 168/F3
West (pt.), Pr. Edward I. 168/D2
West (pt.), Tasmania 99/A2
West, Texas (76691) 303/G6
West (bay), Texas 303/K3
West (riv.), Vt. 268/B5
West Acton, Mass. (01720) 249/H3
West Alexander, Pa. (15376) 294/B5
West Alexandria, Ohio (45381) 284/A6
West Allis, Wis. (53214) 317/L1
West Alton, Mo. (63386) 261/M5
West Alton, N.H. (†03246) 268/E4
West Amboy, N.Y. (†13493) 276/J4
West Arichat, Nova Scotia 168/G3
West Ashford, Conn. (†06251) 210/G1
West Aspetuck (riv.), Conn. 210/B2
West Athens, Maine (†04912) 243/D6
West Augusta, Va. (24485) 307/K4
West Avon, Conn. (†06001) 210/D1
West Baden Springs, Ind. (47469) 227/D7
West Baines (riv.), North. Terr. 93/A4
West Baldwin, Maine (04091) 243/B8
Westbank, Br. Col. 184/H5
WEST BANK 59/C3
WEST BANK 65/C3
West Bank (reg.), 65/C3
West Baraboo, Wis. (†53913) 317/G9
West Barnet, Vt. (05870) 268/C3
West Barns, Scotland 15/F5
West Barnstable, Mass. (02668) 249/N6
West Barrington, R.I. (†02806) 249/J5
West Bath○, Maine (†04530) 243/D8
West Baton Rouge (par.), La. 238/H6
West Bay, Fla. (32407) 212/C6
West Bay, Nova Scotia 168/G3
West Bay Road, Nova Scotia 168/G3
West Bend, Iowa (50597) 229/D3
Westbend, Ky. (40388) 237/N5
West Bend, Sask. 181/H4
West Bend, Wis. (53095) 317/K9
West Bengal (state), India 68/F4
West Berkshire, Vt. (†05450) 268/B2
West Berlin, Mass. (†01503) 249/H3
West Berlin, N.J. (08091) 273/D4
West Bethel, Maine (04286) 243/B7
West Blocton, Ala. (35184) 195/D4
West Bloomfield, Wis. (†54983) 317/J7
Westboro, Mo. (64498) 261/B1
Westboro, Ohio (†45148) 284/C7
Westboro, Wis. (54490) 317/F5
Westborough, Mass. (01581) 249/H3
Westborough○, Mass. (01581) 249/H3
West Bountiful, Utah (†84087) 304/B3
Westbourne, Manitoba 179/D4
Westbourne, Tenn. (†37766) 237/O7
West Boxford, Mass. (01885) 249/K2
West Boylston○, Mass. (01583) 249/G3
West Braintree, Vt. (†05669) 268/B4
West Branch (res.), Conn. 210/C1
West Branch, Iowa (52358) 229/L5
West Branch, Farmington (riv.), Mass. 249/B4
West Branch, Mich. (48661) 250/E4
West Branch, Rocky (riv.), Ohio 284/G10
West Brattleboro, Vt. (05301) 268/B6
West Brentwood, N.H. (†03848) 268/E6
West Brewster, Mass. (†02631) 249/O5
Westbridge, Br. Col. 184/H5
West Bridgewater○, Mass. (02379) 249/K4
West Bridgewater, Vt. (†05034) 268/B4
West Bridgford, England 13/F5
West Bromwich, England 13/F5
West Bromwich, England 10/G3
Westbrook, Conn. (06498) 210/F3
Westbrook○, Conn. (06498) 210/F3
Westbrook, Maine (04092) 243/C8
Westbrook, Minn. (56183) 255/C6
West Brook, Nova Scotia 168/D3
Westbrook, Texas (79565) 303/C5
West Brookfield, Mass. (01585) 249/F4
West Brookfield○, Mass. (01585) 249/F4
West Brooklyn, Ill. (61378) 222/D2
West Brooksville, Maine (†04617) 243/F7
West Brownsville, Pa. (15417) 294/C5
West Buechel, Ky. (†40218) 237/K2
West Burke, Vt. (05871) 268/C2
West Burlington, Iowa (52655) 229/L7
West Burra (isl.), Scotland 15/G2
Westbury, England 10/E5
Westbury, England 13/E6
Westbury, N.Y. (11590) 276/R7
Westbury, Tasmania 99/C3
West Buxton, Maine (04093) 243/B8
Westby, Mont. (59275) 262/M2
Westby, Wis. (54667) 317/E8
West Calder, Scotland 15/C2
West Caldwell, N.J. (07006) 273/A2
West Campton, N.H. (03228) 268/D4
West Canaan, N.H. (03741) 268/C4
West Cape May, N.J. (†08204) 273/D6
West Carroll (par.), La. 238/H1
West Carrollton, Ohio (45449) 284/B6
West Carthage, N.Y. (†13619) 276/J3
West Charleston, Vt. (05872) 268/C2
West Chatham, Mass. (02669) 249/O6
West Chazy, N.Y. (12992) 276/N1
West Chelmsford, Mass. (†01824) 249/J2
Westchester, Conn. (†06474) 210/F2
Westchester, Ill. (60153) 222/B5
West Chester, Iowa (52359) 229/K6
Westchester (co.), N.Y. 276/N8
West Chester, Ohio (45069) 284/C9
West Chester, Pa. (19380) 294/L6
West Chesterfield, Mass. (01084) 249/C3
Westchester Station, Nova Scotia 168/E3
West Chicago, Ill. (60185) 222/A5
West Chop (pt.), Mass. 249/M7
West City, Ill. (†62812) 222/E5
Westcliffe, Colo. (81252) 208/H6
West College Corner, Ind. (†47353) 227/H5
West Columbia, S.C. (29169) 296/E4
West Columbia, Texas (77486) 303/J8
West Columbia, W. Va. (25287) 312/B5
West Concord, Mass. (†01742) 249/A6
West Concord, Minn. (55985) 255/F6
West Corinth, Vt. (†05039) 268/C3
West Cornwall, Conn. (06796) 210/B1
West Cornwall, Vt. (†05753) 268/A4
West Cote Blanche (bay), La. 238/G7
Westcott, Alberta 182/C4
Westcott Cove (bay), Conn. 210/A4
West Covina, Calif. (*91790) 204/D10
Westcreek, Colo. (†80135) 208/J4
West Creek, N.J. (08092) 273/E4
West Crossett, Ark. (†71635) 202/F7
West Cummington, Mass. (†01026) 249/B3
West Danville, Vt. (05873) 268/C3
West Dean, England 13/E6
West Demerara-Essequibo Coast (dist.), Guyana 131/B2
West Dennis, Mass. (02670) 249/O6
West Deptford○, N.J. (†08086) 273/B3
West Des Moines, Iowa (50318) 229/F5
West Dover, Nova Scotia 168/E4
West Dover, Vt. (05356) 268/B6
West Dublin, Nova Scotia 168/D4
West Dudley, Mass. (†01550) 249/F4
West Dummerston, Vt. (05357) 268/B6
West Dundee (Dundee), Ill. (†60118) 222/E1
West Eau Gallie, Fla. (32935) 212/F3
West Elizabeth, Pa. (15088) 294/C5
West Elkton, Ohio (45070) 284/A6
West Elmira, N.Y. (†14901) 276/G6
West Eminence, Mo. (†65466) 261/J8
Westend, Calif. (†93562) 204/H8
West End, N.C. (27376) 281/K4
West End, Sask. 181/J5
West End, Virgin Is. (Br.) 161/C4
West End-Cobb Town, Ala. (†36201) 195/G3
Westend Saltpond (lag.), Virgin Is. (U.S.) 161/E4
West Enfield, Maine (04493) 243/F5
West Epping, N.H. (†03042) 268/E5
Wester Eems (chan.), Netherlands 27/K1
Westerland, W. Germany 22/C1
Westerlo, Belgium 27/F6
Westerlo, N.Y. (12193) 276/M6
Westerly, R.I. (02891) 249/G7
Westerly○, R.I. (02891) 249/G7
Western (prov.), Kenya 115/G3
Western, Nebr. (68464) 264/G4
Western (head), Nova Scotia 168/D5
Western Australia 88/B5
WESTERN AUSTRALIA 92
Western Australia (state), Australia 87/C8
Western Bay, Newf. 166/D2
Western Channel (str.), Japan 81/D6
Western Dvina (riv.), U.S.S.R. 53/C2
Western Dvina (riv.), U.S.S.R. 52/C3
Western Dvina (riv.), U.S.S.R. 48/C4
Western Ghats (mts.), India 68/C5
Western Grove, Ark. (72685) 202/D1
Western Institute, Tenn. (38074) 237/C10
Western Isles (islands area), Scotland 15/A3
Westernport, Md. (21562) 245/B3

468 Western Port

Western Port (inlet), Victoria 97/C6
Western Sahara 2/J4
Western Sahara 102/A2
WESTERN SAHARA 106/A4
Western Samar (prov.), Philippines 82/E5
Western Samoa 2/A6
WESTERN SAMOA 86/M8
Western Samoa 87/J7
Western Scheldt (De Honte) (bay), Netherlands 27/D6
Western Shore, Nova Scotia 168/D4
Western Shoshone Ind. Res., Idaho 220/B7
Western Shoshone Ind. Res., Nev. 266/E1
Western Springs, Ill. (60558) 222/B6
Westernville, N.Y. (13486) 276/K4
Westerose, Alberta 182/C3
Westerstede, W. Germany 22/B2
Westervelt, Ill. (62574) 222/E4
Westerville, Nebr. (68881) 264/E3
Westerville, Ohio (43081) 284/D5
Westerville, S. Dak. (†57069) 298/R8
Westerwald (for.), W. Germany 22/B3
West Fairlee○, Vt. (05083) 268/C4
West Falkland (isl.), 143/D7
West Falkland (isl.), Falk. Is. 120/C8
Westfall, Kansas (67489) 232/D3
Westfall, Oreg. (97920) 291/K3
West Falmouth, Mass. (02574) 249/M6
West Fargo, N. Dak. (58078) 282/S6
West Farmington, Maine (04992) 243/C6
West Farmington, Ohio (44491) 284/J3
West Feliciana (par.), La. 238/H5
Westfield, Conn. (†06457) 210/E2
Westfield, Ill. (62474) 222/F4
Westfield, Ind. (46074) 227/E4
Westfield, Iowa (51062) 229/A3
Westfield○, Maine (04787) 243/G2
Westfield, Mass. (01085) 249/D4
Westfield (riv.), Mass. 249/C3
Westfield, New Bruns. 170/D3
Westfield, N.J. (*07090) 273/E2
Westfield, N.Y. (14787) 276/A6
Westfield, N.C. (27053) 281/H2
Westfield, N. Dak. (†58542) 282/K7
Westfield, Nova Scotia 168/C4
Westfield, Pa. (16950) 294/H2
Westfield○, Vt. (05874) 268/C2
Westfield, Wis. (53964) 317/H8
Westfield Center, Ohio (44251) 284/G3
West Finley, Pa. (15377) 294/B5
Westfir, Oreg. (97492) 291/E4
West Flanders (prov.), Belgium 27/B7
Westford, Conn. (†06076) 210/G1
Westford○, Mass. (01886) 249/J2
Westford, Pa. (16134) 294/A2
Westford○, Vt. (05494) 268/A2
West Fork, Ark. (72774) 202/B2
West Fork, Ind. (47178) 227/D8
West Fork, Bruneau (riv.), Nev. 266/F1
West Fork (riv.), W. Va. 312/E5
West Forks○, Maine (04985) 243/D5
West Frankfort, Ill. (62896) 222/E6
West Franklin, Ind. (†47620) 227/B9
West Franklin, Maine (†04634) 243/G6
West Frisian (isls.), Netherlands 27/F2
Westgat (chan.), Netherlands 27/F3
Westgate, Iowa (50681) 229/K3
Westgate, Manitoba 179/A2
West Germany 7/E3
WEST GERMANY 22
West Glacier, Mont. (59936) 262/C2
West Glamorgan, Wales 13/D6
West Glens Falls, N.Y. (†12801) 276/N4
West Glocester, R.I. (†02814) 249/G5
West Glover, Vt. (05875) 268/C2
West Gorham, Maine (†04038) 243/C8
West Goshen, Conn. (†06756) 210/B1
West Gouldsboro, Maine (†04607) 243/G7
West Granby, Conn. (06090) 210/D1
West Grand (lake), Maine 243/H5
West Granville, Mass. (†01034) 249/C4
West Green, Georgia (31567) 217/G7
West Greene, Ala. (35491) 195/B5
West Green Harbour, Nova Scotia 168/C5
West Groton, Mass. (01472) 249/H2
West Grove, Iowa (52538) 229/J7
West Grove, Pa. (19390) 294/L6
West Gulfport (North Gulfport), Miss. (†39501) 256/F10
West Halifax, Vt. (05358) 268/B6
West Hamlin, W. Va. (25571) 312/B6
West Hampstead, N.H. (†03841) 268/E6
Westhampton○, Mass. (†01027) 249/C3
Westhampton, N.Y. (11977) 276/P9
Westhampton Beach, N.Y. (11978) 276/P9
West Hanover, Mass. (02339) 249/L4
West Harrison, Ind. (†45030) 227/H6
West Hartford○, Conn. (06107) 210/D1
West Hartford, Vt. (05084) 268/C4
West Hartland, Conn. (06091) 210/D1
West Harwich, Mass. (02671) 249/O6
West Haven, Conn. (06516) 210/D3
Westhaven, Ill. (†60462) 222/B6
West Haven○, Vt. (†05743) 268/A4
West Hawk (lake), Manitoba 179/G5
Westhawk Lake, Manitoba 179/G5
West Hawley, Mass. (†01339) 249/C2
West Hazleton, Pa. (18201) 294/K4
West Helena, Ark. (72390) 202/J4
West Henniker, N.H. (†03242) 268/D5
West Hickory, Pa. (16370) 294/C2
West Hill (pond), Conn. 210/C1
Westhoff, Texas (77994) 303/G8
West Hollywood, Calif. (†90069) 204/B10
Westholme, Br. Col. 184/J3
Westhope, N. Dak. (58793) 282/H2
West Hopkinton, N.H. (†03229) 268/D5
West Hurley, N.Y. (12491) 276/M6
West Ice Shelf, Ant. 5/C5
West Indies (isls.) 2/G5
West Indies (isls.) 146/M7
WEST INDIES 156
West Irvine, Ky. (40491) 237/N5
West Jefferson, Ala. (†35005) 195/D4
West Jefferson, N.C. (28694) 281/F2
West Jefferson, Ohio (43162) 284/D6
West Jersey, Ill. (†61483) 222/D2
West Jonesport, Maine (†04649) 243/H6
West Jordan, Utah (84084) 304/B3
Westkapelle, Netherlands 27/C5
West Kennebunk, Maine (04094) 243/B9
West Kilbride, Scotland 15/D5
West Kingston, R.I. (02892) 249/H7
West Kittanning, Pa. (†16201) 294/C4
West Lafayette, Ind. (47906) 227/D4
West Lafayette, Ohio (43845) 284/G5
Westlake, La. (70669) 238/D6
Westlake, Ohio (44145) 284/G9
Westlake, Oreg. (97493) 291/C4
Westlake, Texas (†76101) 303/F1
Westland, Mich. (48185) 250/F6
Westland, Pa. (15378) 294/B5
West Lanham Hills, Md. (†20784) 245/G4
West Laurel, Md. (†20810) 245/L4
West Lawn, Pa. (19609) 294/K5
West Lebanon, Ind. (47991) 227/C4
West Lebanon, Maine (04027) 243/B9
West Lebanon, N.H. (03784) 268/C4
West Ledge, Bermuda 156/G3
West Leechburg, Pa. (†15656) 294/C4
West Leipsic, Ohio (†45856) 284/B3
West Leyden, N.Y. (13489) 276/J4
West Liberty, Ill. (62475) 222/E5
West Liberty, Iowa (52776) 229/L5
West Liberty, Ky. (41472) 237/P5
West Liberty, Ohio (43357) 284/C5
West Liberty, Pa. (†16057) 294/B4
West Liberty, W. Va. (26074) 312/E2
West Lima, Wis. (†54639) 317/E8
West Line, Mo. (64791) 261/C5
Westline, Pa. (16751) 294/E2
West Linn, Oreg. (97068) 291/B2
West Linton, Scotland 15/D2
West Liscomb (riv.), Nova Scotia 168/F3
West Little Owyhee (riv.), Oreg. 291/K5
West Loch (inlet), Hawaii 218/A3
West Loch Tarbert (inlet), Scotland 15/A3
West Loch Tarbert (inlet), Scotland 15/C5
Westlock, Alberta 182/C2
West Logan, W. Va. (25601) 312/C7
West Long (lake), New Bruns. 170/D3
West Long Branch, N.J. (07764) 273/F3
West Lorne, Ontario 177/C5
West Los Angeles, Calif. (90025) 204/B10
West Lothian (trad. co.), Scotland 15/B5
West Louisville, Ky. (42377) 237/G5
West Lubec, Maine (†04652) 243/J6
Westmalle, Belgium 27/F6
West Manchester, Ohio (45382) 284/A6
West Mansfield, Mass. (†02048) 249/K5
West Mansfield, Ohio (43358) 284/C5
West Maui (mts.), Hawaii 218/H2
Westmeath (co.), Ireland 17/G5
Westmeath, Ontario 177/H2
West Medway, Mass. (†02053) 249/J4
West Melbourne, Fla. (†32901) 212/F3
West Memphis, Ark. (72301) 202/K3
West Mersea, England 13/H6
West Mersea, England 10/G5
West Miami, Fla. (†33101) 212/B5
West Middlesex, Pa. (16159) 294/B3
West Middleton, Ind. (46995) 227/E4
West Middletown, Pa. (15379) 294/A5
West Midlands (co.), England 13/F5
West Mifflin, Pa. (15122) 294/C7
West Milan, N.H. (†03588) 268/E2
West Milford, N.J. (07480) 273/E1
West Milford, W. Va. (26451) 312/F4
West Millbury, Mass. (01586) 249/G4
West Millgrove, Ohio (43467) 284/C3
West Mills, Maine (†04938) 243/C6
West Milton, Ohio (45383) 284/B6
West Milton, Pa. (17886) 294/J3
West Milwaukee, Wis. (†53201) 317/L1
West Mineral, Kansas (66782) 232/H4
West Minot, Maine (04288) 243/C7
Westminster, Calif. (92683) 204/D11
Westminster, Colo. (80030) 208/J3
Westminster, Conn. (†06331) 210/G2
Westminster, England 10/B5
Westminster, England 13/H8
Westminster, Md. (21157) 245/L2
Westminster○, Mass. (01473) 249/G2
Westminster, S.C. (29693) 296/A2
Westminster, Vt. (05158) 268/C5
Westminster○, Vt. (05158) 268/C5
Westminster Station, Vt. (05159) 268/B5
Westminster West, Vt. (†05158) 268/B5
West Monroe, La. (71291) 238/F1
Westmont, Calif. (†90047) 204/C11
Westmont, Ill. (60559) 222/B6
Westmont, N.J. (08108) 273/B3
Westmont, Pa. (†15905) 294/D5
West Monterey, Pa. (†16049) 294/C3
Westmore○, Vt. (†05860) 268/C2
Westmoreland, Kansas (66549) 232/F2
Westmoreland○, N.H. (03467) 268/C6
Westmoreland (co.), Pa. 294/D5
Westmoreland, Queensland 95/A3
Westmoreland, Tenn. (37186) 237/J7
Westmoreland (co.), Va. 307/P4
Westmorland, Calif. (92281) 204/K10
Westmorland (co.), New Bruns. 170/F2
Westmount, Nova Scotia 168/H2
Westmount, Québec 172/H4
Westmuir, Scotland 15/E4
West Musquash (lake), Maine 243/H5
West Mystic, Conn. (06388) 210/H3
West Newbury○, Mass. (01985) 249/L1
West Newbury, Vt. (05085) 268/C3
West Newfield, Maine (04095) 243/B8
West Newton, Mass. (†02165) 249/B7
West Newton, Pa. (15089) 294/C5
West New York, N.J. (07093) 273/C2
West Nicholson, Zimbabwe 118/D4
West Nishnabotna (riv.), Iowa 229/C6
West Norwalk, Conn. (†06856) 210/B4
West Nottingham, N.H. (03291) 268/E5
West Nyack, N.Y. (10994) 276/K8
West Okoboji, Iowa (†51351) 229/C2
West Olive, Mich. (49460) 250/C6
Weston, Ala. (†35570) 195/B2
Weston, Colo. (81091) 208/K8
Weston○, Conn. (06883) 210/B4
Weston, Georgia (31832) 217/C7
Weston, Idaho (83286) 220/F7
Weston, Ill. (†61726) 222/E3
Weston, Iowa (†51576) 229/B6
Weston○, Maine (04424) 243/H4
Weston, Malaysia 85/F4
Weston○, Mass. (02193) 249/B6
Weston, Mich. (49289) 250/E7
Weston, Mo. (64098) 261/C4
Weston, Nebr. (68070) 264/H3
Weston, Ohio (43569) 284/C3
Weston, Oreg. (97886) 291/J2
Weston, Pa. (18256) 294/K4
Weston○, Vt. (05161) 268/B5
Weston, W. Va. (26452) 312/F4
Weston, Wis. (†54751) 317/C6
Weston, Wis. (†54476) 317/G6
Weston (co.), Wyo. 319/H2
Weston, Wyo. (82731) 319/G1
Westonaria, S. Africa 118/H7
Westons Mills, N.Y. (14788) 276/D6
Weston-super-Mare, England 13/D6
Weston-super-Mare, England 10/E5
West Orange, N.J. (07052) 273/A2
West Orange, Texas (77630) 303/L7
West Ossipee, N.H. (03890) 268/E4
Westover, Ala. (35185) 195/E4
Westover, Md. (21871) 245/R8
Westover, Pa. (16692) 294/E4
Westover, S. Dak. (†57559) 298/H6
Westover, W. Va. (26505) 312/G3
Westover A.F.B., Mass. 249/D4
Westover Hills, Texas (†76101) 303/E2
West Paducah, Ky. (42086) 237/D6
West Palm Beach, Fla. 188/K5
West Palm Beach, Fla. 146/K7
West Palm Beach, Fla. (*33401) 212/F5
West Palm Beach (canal), Fla. 212/F5
West Paris○, Maine (04289) 243/B7
West Paterson, N.J. (07424) 273/B2
West Pawlet, Vt. (05775) 268/A5
West Pelzer, S.C. (29669) 296/B2
West Pembroke, Maine (†04666) 243/J6
West Pensacola, Fla. (†32502) 212/B6
West Peru, Maine (04290) 243/C7
West Peterborough, N.H. (03468) 268/C6
West Petersburg, Alaska (†99833) 196/M1
Westphalia, Ind. (47596) 227/C7
Westphalia, Iowa (51578) 229/C5
Westphalia, Kansas (66093) 232/G3
Westphalia, Mich. (48894) 250/E6
Westphalia, Mo. (65085) 261/J6
West Pittsburg, Calif. (†94565) 204/K1
West Pittsburg, Pa. (16160) 294/B4
West Pittston, Pa. (18643) 294/F7
West Plains (Plains), Kansas (67869) 232/B4
West Plains, Mo. (65775) 261/J9
West Point, Ala. (†35179) 195/D2
West Point (lake), Ala. 195/H4
West Point (mt.), Alaska 196/K2
West Point, Ark. (72178) 202/G3
West Point, Calif. (95255) 204/E5
West Point, Georgia (31833) 217/B5
West Point (lake), Georgia 217/B4
West Point, Ill. (62380) 222/B3
Westpoint, Ind. (47992) 227/C4
West Point, Iowa (52656) 229/K7
West Point, Ky. (40177) 237/J4
West Point, Miss. (39773) 256/G3
West Point, Nebr. (68788) 264/H3
West Point, N.Y. (10996) 276/M8
West Point, Ohio (44492) 284/J4
Westpoint, Tenn. (38486) 237/G10
West Point, Va. (23181) 307/P5
West Pointe a la Hache, La. (†70082) 238/L7
West Poland, Maine (04291) 243/C7
West Poplar, Sask. 181/E6
Westport, Calif. (95488) 204/B4
Westport○, Conn. (06880) 210/B4
Westport, Ind. (47283) 227/F6
Westport, Ireland 17/C4
Westport, Ireland 10/B4
Westport, Ky. (40077) 237/K4
Westport○, Mass. (02790) 249/K6
Westport, Minn. (†56385) 255/C5
Westport, N.H. (†03470) 268/C6
Westport, N.Y. (12993) 276/N2
Westport, N. Zealand 100/C4
Westport, Nova Scotia 168/B4
Westport, Okla. (†74020) 288/O2
Westport, Ontario 177/H3
Westport, Oreg. (97016) 291/D1
Westport, Pa. (17778) 294/G3
Westport, S. Dak. (57481) 298/M2
Westport, Tenn. (38387) 237/E9
Westport, Wash. (98595) 310/A4
West Portal, N.J. (†08802) 273/D2
Westport Point, Mass. (02791) 249/K6
West Portsmouth, Ohio (†45662) 284/D8
West Pubnico, Nova Scotia 168/C5
Westpunt, Aruba, Neth. Ant. 161/D10
Westpunt, Curaçao, Neth. Ant. 161/F8
West Quaco, New Bruns. 170/E3
West Quoddy (head), Maine 243/K6
Westray (firth), Scotland 15/E1
Westray (isl.), Scotland 15/E1
Westray (isl.), Scotland 10/E1
West Redding, Conn. (06896) 210/B3
West Richland, Wash. (†99352) 310/F4
West Ridge, Ark. (72391) 202/K2
West Rindge, N.H. (†03461) 268/C6
West River, Md. (20881) 245/M5
West Road (riv.), Br. Col. 184/E3
West Rockport, Maine (04865) 243/E7
West Rock Ridge (hills), Conn. 210/D3
West Rumney, N.H. (†03266) 268/D4
West Rupert, Vt. (05776) 268/A5
West Rushville, Ohio (43163) 284/E6
West Rutland, Vt. (05777) 268/A4
West Rutland○, Vt. (05777) 268/A4
West Rye, N.H. (†03870) 268/F6
West Sacramento, Calif. (95691) 204/B8
West Saint Mary's (riv.), Nova Scotia 168/F3
West Saint Modeste, Newf. 166/C3
West Saint Paul, Minn. (55118) 255/G5
West Salem, Ill. (62476) 222/F5
West Salem, Ohio (44287) 284/F4
West Salem, Wis. (54669) 317/D8
West Salisbury, Pa. (15565) 294/D6
West Salisbury, Vt. (†05769) 268/A4
West Sayville, N.Y. (11796) 276/O9
West Scarborough, Maine (04074) 243/C8
West Sebois, Maine (†04484) 243/F4
West Seneca, N.Y. (14224) 276/C5
West Shoal (lake), Manitoba 179/E4
Westside, Iowa (51467) 229/C4
West Side, Oreg. (†97630) 291/G5
West Siloam Springs, Okla. (†72761) 288/S2
West Simsbury, Conn. (06092) 210/D1
West Sister (isl.), Ohio 284/D2
West Sister (isl.), Tasmania 99/D1
West Somerset, Ky. (†42501) 237/M6
West Springfield○, Mass. (01089) 249/D4
West Springfield, N.H. (03284) 268/C5
West Springfield, Pa. (16443) 294/B2
West Springfield, Va. (22153) 307/S3
West Springs, S.C. (†29374) 296/D2
West Stafford, Conn. (†06076) 210/F1
West Statesville, N.C. (28677) 281/G3
West Stewartstown, N.H. (03597) 268/E2
West Stockbridge○, Mass. (01266) 249/A3
West Stockholm, N.Y. (13696) 276/K1
West Suffield, Conn. (06093) 210/E1
West Sullivan, Maine (04689) 243/G6
West Sumner, Maine (04292) 243/B7
West Sunbury, Pa. (16061) 294/C3
West Sussex (co.), England 13/G7
West Swan (riv.), Minn. 255/F3
West Swanzey, N.H. (03469) 268/C6
West Terre Haute, Ind. (47885) 227/B6
West-Terschelling, Netherlands 27/G2
West Thompson, Conn. (†06255) 210/H1
West Thornton, N.H. (03285) 268/D4
West Thumb-Grant Village, Wyo. (†82190) 319/B1
West Tisbury○, Mass. (02575) 249/M7
West Torrens, S. Australia 88/D8
West Torrens, S. Australia 94/A8
West Torrington, Conn. (†06790) 210/C1
West Townsend, Mass. (01474) 249/H2
West Townshend, Vt. (05359) 268/B5
West Tremont, Maine (04690) 243/G7
West Trenton, N.J. (08628) 273/D3
West Union, Ill. (62477) 222/F4
West Union, Iowa (52175) 229/K3
West Union, Minn. (56389) 255/C5
West Union, Ohio (45693) 284/C8
West Union, S.C. (29696) 296/B2
West Union, W. Va. (26456) 312/E4
West Unity, Ohio (43570) 284/B2
West University Place, Texas (†77005) 303/J2
West Upton-Upton, Mass. (01587) 249/H4
West Valley, N.Y. (14171) 276/C6
West Vancouver, Br. Col. 184/K3
West Van Lear, Ky. (41268) 237/R5
West View, Pa. (15229) 294/B6
West View, Sask. 181/J5
Westview, S.C. (†29301) 296/C2
Westville, Fla. (32464) 212/C6
Westville, Ill. (61883) 222/F3
Westville, Ind. (46391) 227/D1
Westville, N.H. (03865) 268/E6
Westville, N.J. (08093) 273/B3
Westville, Nova Scotia 168/F3
Westville, Okla. (74965) 288/S2
Westville, Pa. (15869) 294/E3
Westville, S.C. (29175) 296/F3
West Virginia 188/K3
WEST VIRGINIA 313
West Virginia (state), U.S. 146/K6
Westward Ho, Alberta 182/C4
West Wardsboro, Vt. (05360) 268/B5
West Wareham, Mass. (02576) 249/L5
West Warren, Mass. (01092) 249/F4
West Warwick, R.I. (02893) 249/H6
West Weber, Utah (†84401) 304/B2
Westwego, La. (70094) 238/O4
West Wenatchee, Wash. (†98801) 310/E3
West Wildwood, N.J. (†08260) 273/D6
West Willington, Conn. (06279) 210/F1
West Windham, N.H. (†03087) 268/E6
West Winfield, N.Y. (13491) 276/K5
West Winterport, Maine (†04496) 243/E6
Westwold, Br. Col. 184/G5
Westwood, Lassen, Calif. (96151) 204/D3
Westwood, Ky. (41101) 237/R4
Westwood, Ky. (†40207) 237/L1
Westwood○, Mass. (02090) 249/B8
Westwood, Mo. (†63101) 261/O3
Westwood, N.J. (07675) 273/B1
West Woodburn, Oreg. (†97071) 291/A3
Westwood Lakes, Fla. (†33165) 212/B5
West Woodstock, Conn. (†06260) 210/G1
West Woodstock, Vt. (†05091) 268/B4
Westwood Village, Los Angeles, Calif. (90024) 204/B10
Westworth, Texas (†76101) 303/E2
West Wyalong, N.S. Wales 88/H6
West Wyalong, N.S. Wales 97/D3
West Wyoming, Pa. (18644) 294/E7
West Yarmouth, Mass. (02673) 249/N6
West Yellowstone, Mont. (59758) 262/E6
West York, Ill. (62478) 222/F4
West York, Pa. (†17401) 294/J6
West Yorkshire (co.), England 13/J1
West Yuma, Ariz. (†85364) 198/A6
Westzaan, Netherlands 27/A4
Wet (mts.), Colo. 208/J6
Wetar (isl.), Indonesia 54/O10
Wetar (isl.), Indonesia 85/H7
Wetaskiwin, Alberta 182/D3
Wetaskiwin, Alta. 162/E5
Wete, Tanzania 115/G4
Wetheral, England 13/E3
Wethersfield○, Conn. (06109) 210/E2
Wetipquin, Md. (†21856) 245/P7
Wetmore, Colo. (81253) 208/J6
Wetmore, Kansas (66550) 232/G2
Wetmore, Mich. (49895) 250/C2
Wetmore, Tenn. (†37325) 237/N10
Wetmore, Texas (78163) 303/K10
Wetonka, S. Dak. (57482) 298/M2
Wetteren, Belgium 27/D7
Wetterhorn (peak), Colo. 208/D6
Wetterhorn (mt.), Switzerland 39/F3
Wettingen, Switzerland 39/F2
Wetumka, Okla. (74883) 288/O4
Wetumpka, Ala. (36092) 195/F5
Wetuppa, N.S. Wales 97/B4
Wetzel (co.), W. Va. 312/E3
Wetzikon, Switzerland 39/G2
Wetzlar, W. Ger. 22/C3
Wever, Iowa (52658) 229/L7
Weverton, Md. (†21758) 245/H3
Wewahitchka, Fla. (32465) 212/D6
Wewak, Papua N.G. 87/E6
Wewak, Papua N.G. 85/B6
Weweantic (riv.), Mass. 249/L5
Wewela, S. Dak. (57578) 298/K7
Wewoka, Okla. (74884) 288/O4
Wexford (co.), Ireland 17/H7
Wexford, Ireland 17/H7
Wexford, Ireland 10/C4
Wexford (bay), Ireland 17/J7
Wexford (harb.), Ireland 17/J7
Wexford (harb.), Ireland 10/C4
Wexford (co.), Mich. 250/D4
Wey (riv.), England 13/G6
Weyanoke, La. (70787) 238/H5
Weyauwega, Wis. (54983) 317/H7
Weybridge○, Vt. (†05753) 268/A3
Weyburn, Sask. 162/F6
Weyburn, Sask. 181/H6
Weyerhaeuser, Wis. (54895) 317/D5
Weyer Markt, Austria 41/C3
Weyers Cave, Va. (24486) 307/L4
Weymouth (bay), England 13/E7
Weymouth, Mass. (02188) 249/D8
Weymouth, Nova Scotia 168/C4
Weymouth and Melcombe Regis, England 13/E7
Weymouth and Melcombe Regis, England 10/E5
Weymouth North, Nova Scotia 168/C4
Wezembeek-Oppem, Belgium 27/D9
Wezet (Visé), Belgium 27/H7
Whakatane, N. Zealand 100/F2
Whalan, Minn. (55986) 255/G7
Whalan (creek), N.S. Wales 97/E1
Whale (bay), Alaska 196/M1
Whaleback (mt.), W. Australia 92/B3
Whale Cove, N.W. Terrs. 187/J3
Whaletown, Br. Col. 184/E5
Whaley Bridge, England 13/J2
Whaley Bridge, England 10/G2
Whaleysville, Md. (21872) 245/S7
Whallonsburg, N.Y. (12994) 276/O2
Whalsay (isl.), Scotland 10/H1
Whalsay (isl.), Scotland 15/G2
Whangamata, N. Zealand 100/F2
Whangarei, N. Zealand 87/H9
Whangarei, N. Zealand 100/E1
Wharfe (riv.), England 13/E3
Wharfe (riv.), England 10/F3
Wharncliffe, W. Va. (25651) 312/C7
Wharton (pen.), Chile 138/D8
Wharton, N.J. (07885) 273/D2
Wharton (lake), N.W. Terrs. 187/H3
Wharton, Ohio (43359) 284/D4
Wharton, Pa. (†16720) 294/G2
Wharton (co.), Texas 303/H8
Wharton, Texas (77488) 303/J8
Wharton, W. Va. (25208) 312/C7
Whataroa, N. Zealand 100/C5
Whatatutu, N. Zealand 100/F3
What Cheer, Iowa (50268) 229/J6
Whatcom (co.), Wash. 310/D2
Whatcom (lake), Wash. 310/C2
Whately○, Mass. (01093) 249/D3
Whatley, Ala. (36482) 195/C7
Wheatcroft, Ky. (42463) 237/F5
Wheatfield, Ind. (46392) 227/C2
Wheatland, Calif. (95692) 204/D4
Wheatland, Ind. (47597) 227/C7
Wheatland, Iowa (52777) 229/M5
Wheatland, Manitoba 179/B4
Wheatland, Mo. (65779) 261/F7
Wheatland (co.), Mont. 262/G4
Wheatland, N. Mex. (†88120) 274/F4
Wheatland, N. Dak. (58079) 282/R6
Wheatland, Pa. (16161) 294/B3
Wheatland, Wyo. (82201) 319/H3
Wheatland (res.), Wyo. 319/G4
Wheatley, Ark. (72392) 202/H4
Wheatley, Ky. (40389) 237/M3
Wheatley, Ontario 177/B5
Wheaton, Ill. (60187) 222/A5
Wheaton, Kansas (66551) 232/F2
Wheaton, Minn. (56296) 255/B5
Wheaton, Mo. (64874) 261/E9
Wheaton-Glenmont, Md. (20902) 245/E3
Wheat Ridge, Colo. (80033) 208/J3
Wheeler, Ala. (†35618) 195/D1
Wheeler (dam), Ala. 195/D1
Wheeler (lake), Ala. 188/J4
Wheeler (lake), Ala. 195/D1
Wheeler (peak), Calif. 204/F5
Wheeler (co.), Georgia 217/G6
Wheeler, Ill. (62479) 222/E4
Wheeler, Ind. (46393) 227/C1
Wheeler, Kansas (67763) 232/A2
Wheeler, Ky. (†40906) 237/O7
Wheeler, Mich. (48662) 250/E5
Wheeler, Miss. (38880) 256/G1
Wheeler (co.), Nebr. 264/F3
Wheeler (peak), Nev. 266/G4
Wheeler (peak), N. Mex. 188/F3
Wheeler (peak), N. Mex. 274/D2
Wheeler (co.), Oreg. 291/G3
Wheeler, Oreg. (97147) 291/D2
Wheeler (riv.), Québec 174/D1
Wheeler (co.), Texas 303/D2
Wheeler, Texas (79096) 303/D2
Wheeler, Wash. (†98837) 310/F3
Wheeler, Wis. (54772) 317/C5
Wheeler A.F.B., Hawaii 218/E1
Wheelersburg, Ohio (45694) 284/E8
Wheeless, Okla. (†73933) 288/A1
Wheeling, Ill. (60090) 222/B5
Wheeling, Ind. (†47342) 227/G4
Wheeling, Ind. (†47534) 227/C8
Wheeling, Mo. (64688) 261/F3
Wheeling, W. Va. 188/K2
Wheeling, W. Va. (26003) 312/E2
Wheelock, N. Dak. (58855) 282/D3
Wheelock○, Vt. (†05851) 268/C2
Wheelwright, Ky. (41669) 237/R6
Wheelwright, Mass. (01094) 249/F3
Whelen Springs, Ark. (71772) 202/D6
Whetstone (buttes), N. Dak. 282/E7
Whetstone (creek), S. Dak. 298/R3
Whick, Ky. (41390) 237/P6
Whickham, England 13/J3
Whidbey (isls.), S. Australia 94/D6
Whidbey (isl.), Wash. 310/C2
Whigham, Georgia (31797) 217/D9
Whigville, Conn. (†06010) 210/D2
Whipholt, Minn. (56485) 255/D3
Whippany, N.J. (07981) 273/E2
Whipple (mts.), Calif. 204/L9
Whipple, Ohio (45788) 284/H6
Whiskeytown-Shasta-Trinity Nat'l Rec. Area, Calif. 204/C3
Whispering Pines, N.C. (†28389) 281/L4
Whistler, Br. Col. 184/F5
Whitaker, Ind. (†46166) 227/D6
Whitaker, Pa. (15120) 294/C7
Whitakers, N.C. (27891) 281/O2
Whitbourne, Newf. 166/D2
Whitburn, Scotland 10/C1
Whitburn, Scotland 15/C2
Whitby, England 13/G3
Whitby, England 10/F3
Whitby, Ontario 177/F4
Whitchurch, England 13/E5
Whitchurch-Stouffville, Ontario 177/J3
Whitcomb, Ind. (†47012) 227/H6
Whitcombe (mt.), N. Zealand 100/C5
White (mts.), Alaska 196/J1
White (pass), Alaska 196/N1
White (riv.), Alaska 196/K2
White (riv.), Ariz. 198/E5
White (co.), Ark. 202/G3
White, Ark. (†71635) 202/G7
White (riv.), Ark. 188/H3
White (riv.), Ark. 202/H5
White (riv.), Colo. 208/B2
White (co.), Georgia 217/E1
White, Georgia (30184) 217/C2
White (co.), Ill. 222/E5
White (co.), Ind. 227/D3
White (riv.), Ind. 227/B8
White, East Fork (riv.), Ind. 227/C7
White, West Fork (riv.), Ind. 227/C7
White (lake), La. 238/E7
White (riv.), Mich. 250/C5
White (riv.), Mo. 261/G10
White (riv.), Nebr. 264/A2
White (riv.), Nev. 266/F4
White (bay), Newf. 166/C3
White (bay), Newf. 162/L5
White (isl.), N.H. 268/F6
White (mts.), N.H. 268/E3
White (isl.), N. Zealand 100/F2
White (butte), N. Dak. 282/D7
White (lake), North. Terr. 88/D4
White (lake), North. Terr. 93/A6
White (isl.), N.W. Terrs. 187/K3
White (lake), Ontario 177/F2
White (lake), Ontario 177/H2
White (riv.), Oreg. 291/F2
White, S. Dak. (57276) 298/R5
White (lake), S. Dak. 298/M6
White (riv.), S. Dak. 298/D7
White (co.), Tenn. 237/L9
White (riv.), Texas 303/C3
White (sea), U.S.S.R. 4/C8
White (sea), U.S.S.R. 7/H2
White (sea), U.S.S.R. 48/D3
White (sea), U.S.S.R. 52/E1
White (riv.), Utah 304/E3
White (riv.), Vt. 268/C4
White, First Branch (riv.), Vt. 268/B4
White, Second Branch (riv.), Vt. 268/B4
White (pass), Wash. 310/D4
White (riv.), Wash. 310/D3
White (riv.), Yukon 187/D3
White Bear (isl.), Newf. 166/B2
White Bear (lake), Newf. 166/C4
White Bear (riv.), Newf. 166/C4
White Bear, Sask. 181/C5
White Bear Lake, Minn. (55110) 255/G5
Whitebeech, Sask. 181/K3
White Bird, Idaho (83554) 220/B4
White Bluff, Tenn. (37187) 237/G8
White Butte (mt.), N. Dak. 282/D7
White Butte, S. Dak. (†57638) 298/E2
White Carpathians (mts.), Czech. 41/E2
White Castle, La. (70788) 238/J3
White Center-Shorewood, Wash. (98146) 310/A2
White City, Fla. (†32465) 212/F4
White City, Ill. (†62069) 222/D4
White City, Kansas (66872) 232/F3
White City, Oreg. (97503) 291/E5

Willow Springs 469

White City, Sask. 181/G5
Whiteclay, Nebr. (69365) 264/B2
White Cliffs, N.S. Wales 97/B2
White Cloud, Ind. (†47112) 227/E8
White Cloud, Kansas (66094) 232/G2
White Cloud, Mich. (49349) 250/D5
White Coomb (mt.), Scotland 15/E5
White Cottage, Ohio (43791) 284/F6
Whitecourt, Alberta 182/C2
White Deer, Pa. (17887) 294/J3
White Deer, Texas (79097) 303/C2
White Earth, Minn. (56591) 255/C3
White Earth, N. Dak. (58794) 282/E3
White Earth (riv.), N. Dak. 282/E3
White Earth Ind. Res., Minn. 255/C3
White Elster (riv.), E. Germany 22/E3
Whiteface (riv.), Minn. 255/F3
Whiteface, N.H. (†03259) 268/E4
Whiteface (mt.), N.H. 268/E4
Whiteface (mt.), N.Y. 276/N2
Whiteface, Texas (79379) 303/B4
White Face (mt.), Vt. 268/B2
Whitefield, Maine (04362) 243/D7
Whitefield○, Maine (04362) 243/D7
Whitefield, N.H. (03598) 268/D3
Whitefield○, N.H. (03598) 268/D3
Whitefield, Okla. (74472) 288/R4
Whitefish (bay), Mich. 250/E2
Whitefish (pt.), Mich. 250/E2
Whitefish (riv.), Mich. 250/C2
Whitefish (lake), Minn. 255/D4
Whitefish, Mont. (59937) 262/B2
Whitefish (lake), Mont. 262/B2
Whitefish Falls, Ontario 177/C1
Whitefish Point, Mich. (†49768) 250/E2
Whiteflat, Texas (†79234) 303/D3
Whiteford, Md. (21160) 245/N2
White Fox, Sask. 181/H2
White Fox (riv.), Sask. 181/G2
Whitegate, Ireland 17/E8
White Gull (creek), Sask. 181/G2
White Hall, Ala. (†36040) 195/E6
Whitehall, Ark. (†72432) 202/J3
White Hall, Ark. (71602) 202/F5
White Hall, Georgia (†30601) 217/F3
White Hall, Ill. (62092) 222/C4
Whitehall, Ind. (†47401) 227/D6
Whitehall, La. (†70462) 238/M2
White Hall, Md. (21161) 245/M2
Whitehall, Mich. (49461) 250/C5
Whitehall, Mont. (59759) 262/D5
Whitehall, N.Y. (12887) 276/O3
Whitehall, Ohio (43213) 284/E6
Whitehall, Pa. (†15234) 294/B7
Whitehall, Scotland 15/F1
White Hall, S.C. (†29945) 296/F6
White Hall, Va. (22987) 307/L4
Whitehall, Wis. (54773) 317/D7
White Handkerchief (cape), Newf. 166/B2
Whitehaven, England 13/D3
Whitehaven, England 10/E3
Whitehaven, Md. (21873) 245/P7
Whitehaven (harb.), Nova Scotia 168/G3
White Haven, Pa. (18661) 294/L3
White Head, New Bruns. 170/D4
White Head (isl.), New Bruns. 170/D4
Whitehead, N. Ireland 17/K2
Whitehead, Nova Scotia 168/G3
White Heath, Ill. (61884) 222/E3
Whitehills, Scotland 15/F3
White Horn, Tenn. (†37711) 237/R8
Whitehorse, Canada 4/C16
Whitehorse, Canada 2/C3
Whitehorse, S. Dak. (57661) 298/H3
Whitehorse (cap.), Yukon 187/E3
Whitehorse (cap.), Yukon 162/C3
Whitehorse (cap.), Yukon 146/E3
White Horse Lake, N. Mex. (87073) 274/B3
Whitehouse, Ky. (41269) 237/R5
Whitehouse, N.J. (08888) 273/D2
Whitehouse, Ohio (43571) 284/C2
White House, Tenn. (37188) 237/H8
White House Station, N.J. (08889) 273/D2
White Iron (lake), Minn. 255/G3
White Knob (mts.), Idaho 220/E6
White Lake, N.C. (28337) 281/M5
White Lake, Ontario 177/H2
White Lake, S. Dak. (57383) 298/M6
White Lake, Wis. (54491) 317/J5
Whiteland, Ind. (46184) 227/E5
Whitelaw, Alberta 182/A1
Whitelaw, Wis. (54247) 317/L7
Whiteman A.F.B., Mo. 261/E5
Whitemark, Tasmania 99/D2
White Marsh, Md. (21162) 245/N3
White Meadow Lake, N.J. (†07866) 273/D2
White Mills, Ky. (42788) 237/J5
White Mills, Pa. (18473) 294/M2
White Mountain, Alaska (99784) 196/F2
White Mountains Nat'l Rec. Area, Alaska 196/J1
Whitemouth, Manitoba 179/G5
Whitemouth (lake), Manitoba 179/G5
Whitemouth (riv.), Manitoba 179/G5
Whitemud (riv.), Alberta 182/A1
Whiten (head), Scotland 15/D2
White Nile (riv.) 2/L5
White Nile (riv.) 102/F4
White Nile (prov.), Sudan 111/F5
White Nile (riv.), Sudan 111/F5
White Nile (riv.), Sudan 59/B7
White Oak (lake), Ark. 202/D6
White Oak, Georgia (31568) 217/J8
White Oak, Md. (†20901) 245/F3
Whiteoak, Mo. (63880) 261/M10
White Oak, N.C. (28399) 281/M5
Whiteoak (swamp), N.C. 281/P5
Whiteoak (creek), Ohio 284/C7
White Oak, Okla. (†74301) 288/R1
White Oak, Pa. (15131) 294/C7
White Oak, S.C. (29176) 296/E3
Whiteoak (creek), Tenn. 237/F8
White Oak, Texas (75693) 303/K5
White Oaks, Conn. (†06488) 210/C2
White Oaks, N. Mex. (†88301) 274/D5
White Owl, S. Dak. (57792) 298/E4
White Partridge (lake), Ontario 177/G2
White Pass, Wash. (†98937) 310/D4
White Pigeon, Mich. (49099) 250/D7
White Pine, Mich. (49971) 250/F1
Whitepine, Mont. (†59874) 262/A3
White Pine (co.), Nev. 266/F3
White Pine (range), Nev. 266/F3
White Pine, Tenn. (37890) 237/P8
White Pines, Calif. (†95223) 204/E5
White Plains, Ala. (†36862) 195/G3
White Plains, Georgia (30678) 217/F4
White Plains, Ky. (42464) 237/G6
White Plains, Md. (20695) 245/L6
White Plains, N.Y. (*10601) 276/P6
White Plains, N.C. (27031) 281/H2
White Plains, Va. (23893) 307/N7
White Pond, S.C. (29854) 296/D5
White Post, Va. (22663) 307/M2
White Quartz Hill, North. Terr. 93/D7
White Rapids, New Bruns. 170/E2
Whiteriver, Ariz. (85941) 198/E5
White River, Ont. 162/H6
White River, Ontario 175/C3
White River, Ontario 177/J5
White River, S. Dak. (57579) 298/H6
White River (lake), Texas 303/C4
White River Junction, Vt. (05001) 268/C4
White Rock, Br. Col. 184/K3
White Rock (creek), Kansas 232/D2
White Rock, N. Mex. (87544) 274/C3
Whiterock, N.C. (†28753) 281/D3
White Rock, S.C. (29177) 296/E3
White Rock, S. Dak. (†57260) 298/R2
White Rock (creek), Texas 303/G2
Whiterocks, Utah (84085) 304/E3
White Russian S.S.R., U.S.S.R. 7/G3
White Russian S.S.R., U.S.S.R. 52/C4
White Russian S.S.R., U.S.S.R. 48/C4
Whites, Wash. (†98541) 310/B3
Whitesail (lake), Br. Col. 184/D3
White Salmon, Wash. (98672) 310/D5
White Salmon (riv.), Wash. 310/D4
White Sands (des.), N. Mex. 274/C5
White Sands Missile Range, N. Mex. (88002) 274/C6
White Sands Missile Range, N. Mex. 274/C5
White Sands Nat'l Mon., N. Mex. 274/C6
Whitesbog, N.J. (†08015) 273/E4
Whitesboro, N.J. (08252) 273/D5
Whitesboro, N.Y. (13492) 276/K4
Whitesboro, Okla. (74577) 288/S5
Whitesboro, Texas (76273) 303/H4
Whitesburg, Georgia (30185) 217/B4
Whitesburg, Ky. (41858) 237/R6
Whitesburg, Tenn. (37891) 237/P8
Whites Chapel, Ala. (†35094) 195/F3
Whites City, N. Mex. (88268) 274/E6
Whites Creek, W. Va. (†25530) 312/A6
White Settlement, Texas (76108) 303/E2
Whiteshell Prov. Park, Manitoba 179/G4
White Shield, N. Dak. (†58534) 282/G4
Whiteshore (lake), Sask. 181/C3
Whiteside (chan.), Chile 138/E10
Whiteside (co.), Ill. 222/D2
Whiteside, Mo. (63387) 261/K4
Whiteside, Tenn. (37396) 237/K10
Whites Lake, Nova Scotia 168/E4
Whiteson, Oreg. (†97128) 291/D2
White Springs, Fla. (32096) 212/D1
Whitestone, Georgia (30186) 217/C1
White Stone, Va. (22578) 307/R5
Whitestown, Ind. (46075) 227/E5
White Sulphur Springs, Georgia (†31822) 217/C5
White Sulphur Springs, La. (†71371) 238/F3
White Sulphur Springs, Mont. (59645) 262/E4
White Sulphur Springs, W. Va. (24986) 312/F7
Whitesville, Georgia (†31833) 217/C5
Whitesville, Ky. (42378) 237/H5
Whitesville, Mo. (†64480) 261/C2
Whitesville, N.J. (†08701) 273/E3
Whitesville, N.Y. (14897) 276/E6
Whitesville, W. Va. (25209) 312/C6
Whiteswan (lakes), Sask. 181/F1
White Swan, Wash. (98952) 310/E4
Whitetail, Mont. (59276) 262/L2
Whitetop, Va. (24292) 307/F7
Whiteville, La. (71376) 238/F5
Whiteville, N.C. (28472) 281/M6
Whiteville, Tenn. (38075) 237/C10
White Volta (riv.) 102/B4
White Volta (riv.), Ghana 106/D6
White Volta (riv.), Upper Volta 106/D6
Whitewater, Colo. (81527) 208/C5
Whitewater (bay), Fla. 212/F6
Whitewater, Ind. (†47374) 227/H5
Whitewater (riv.), Ind. 227/H6
Whitewater, Kansas (67154) 232/E4
Whitewater, Manitoba 179/B5
Whitewater (lake), Manitoba 179/B5
Whitewater, Mo. (63785) 261/N8
Whitewater, Mont. (59544) 262/J2
Whitewater, Wis. (53190) 317/J10
Whitewater Baldy (mt.), N. Mex. 274/A5
Whitewood, Sask. 181/J5
Whitewood, S. Dak. (57793) 298/B5
Whitewood (creek), S. Dak. 298/B4
Whitewood, Va. (24657) 307/E6
Whitewright, Texas (75491) 303/H4
Whitfield, Ala. (†36925) 195/B6
Whitfield (co.), Georgia 217/B1
Whitfield, Miss. (39193) 256/E6
Whitford, Alberta 182/D3
Whitharral, Texas (79380) 303/B4
Whithorn, Scotland 10/D3
Whithorn, Scotland 15/D6
Whitianga, N. Zealand 100/E2
Whiting, Ind. (46394) 227/C1
Whiting, Iowa (51063) 229/A4
Whiting, Kansas (66552) 232/G2
Whiting○, Maine (04691) 243/J6
Whiting, Mo. (†63845) 261/O9
Whiting, N.J. (08759) 273/E4
Whiting○, Vt. (05778) 268/A4
Whiting, Wis. (†54481) 317/H7
Whiting Bay, Scotland 15/C5
Whiting Field Naval Air Sta., Fla. 212/B6
Whitingham○, Vt. (05361) 268/B6
Whitinsville, Mass. (01588) 249/H4
Whitkow, Sask. 181/D3
Whitla, Alberta 182/E5
Whitlash, Mont. (59545) 262/E2
Whitley (co.), Ind. 227/F2
Whitley (co.), Ky. 237/N7
Whitley Bay, England 13/J3
Whitley City, Ky. (42653) 237/N7
Whitleyville, Tenn. (38588) 237/K8
Whitlock, Tenn. (†38242) 237/E8
Whitman○, Mass. (02382) 249/L4
Whitman (riv.), Mass. 249/G2
Whitman, Nebr. (69366) 264/C2
Whitman, N. Dak. (58283) 282/O3
Whitman (co.), Wash. 310/H4
Whitman Mission Nat'l Hist. Site, Wash. 310/G4
Whitmer, W. Va. (26296) 312/G5
Whitmire, S.C. (29178) 296/D3
Whitmore, Calif. (96096) 204/D3
Whitmore Lake, Mich. (48189) 250/F6
Whitmore Village, Hawaii (†96786) 218/E1
Whitnel, N.C. (28645) 281/F3
Whitney (mt.), Calif. 188/C3
Whitney (mt.), Calif. 204/G7
Whitney (lake), Conn. 210/D3
Whitney, Nebr. (69367) 264/A2
Whitney, New Bruns. 170/E2
Whitney, Ontario 177/F2
Whitney, Pa. (15693) 294/D5
Whitney, S.C. (29303) 296/D1
Whitney, Texas (76692) 303/G6
Whitney Point, N.Y. (13862) 276/J6
Whitney Point (lake), N.Y. 276/J6
Whitneyville, Conn. (06517) 210/D3
Whitneyville○, Maine (04692) 243/H6
Whitsett, Texas (78075) 303/F9
Whitsunday (isl.), Queensland 88/H4
Whitsunday (isl.), Queensland 95/D4
Whitt, Texas (76090) 303/G5
Whittaker, Mich. (48190) 250/F6
Whittemore, Iowa (50598) 229/E2
Whittemore, Mich. (48770) 250/F4
Whitten, Iowa (50269) 229/H4
Whittier, Alaska (99693) 196/C1
Whittier, Calif. (*90601) 204/D11
Whittier, Iowa (52360) 229/K4
Whittier, N.C. (28789) 281/C4
Whittle (cape), Québec 174/F2
Whittlesea, Victoria 97/C5
Whittlesey, England 13/G5
Whittlesey, Wis. (†54451) 317/F5
Whitton, N.S. Wales 97/D4
Whitwell, Tenn. (37397) 237/K10
Wholdaia (lake), N.W. Terrs. 187/H3
Why, Ariz. (85321) 198/C6
Whyalla, Australia 87/D9
Whyalla, S. Australia 94/E5
Whycocomagh, Nova Scotia 168/G3
Whyjonta, N.S. Wales 97/B1
Wiarton, Ontario 177/C3
Wiau (lake), Alberta 182/E2
Wiawso, Ghana 106/D7
Wiay (isl.), Scotland 15/A3
Wibaux (co.), Mont. 262/M4
Wibaux, Mont. (59353) 262/M3
Wichabai, Guyana 131/B4
Wichita, Kans. 188/G3
Wichita (co.), Kansas 232/A3
Wichita, Kansas 146/J6
Wichita, Kansas (*67201) 232/E4
Wichita (mts.), Okla. 288/J5
Wichita (co.), Texas 303/F3
Wichita (riv.), Texas 303/F4
Wichita Falls, Texas 146/H6
Wichita Falls, Texas (*76301) 303/F4
Wichita Falls, Texas 188/G4
Wick, Iowa (†50240) 229/F6
Wick, Scotland 10/E1
Wick, Scotland 15/E2
Wick (riv.), Scotland 15/E2
Wick, W. Va. (26185) 312/E4
Wickahoney (creek), Idaho 220/C7
Wickatunk, N.J. (07765) 273/E3
Wicked (pt.), Manitoba 179/D2
Wickenburg, Ariz. (85358) 198/C5
Wickepin, W. Australia 92/B2
Wickersham, Wash. (†98284) 310/C2
Wickes, Ark. (71973) 202/B5
Wickes, Mont. (†59638) 262/D4
Wickett, Texas (79788) 303/A6
Wickham, New Bruns. 170/D3
Wickham, Québec 172/E4
Wickham (cape), Tasmania 99/A1
Wickham, W. Australia 92/B3
Wickiup (res.), Oreg. 291/F4
Wickliffe, Ky. (42087) 237/C7
Wickliffe, Ohio (44092) 284/J9
Wicklow (co.), Ireland 17/J5
Wicklow, Ireland 10/C4
Wicklow, Ireland 17/K6
Wicklow (head), Ireland 17/K6
Wicklow (head), Ireland 10/D4
Wicklow (mts.), Ireland 17/J6
Wicklow, New Bruns. 170/C2
Wicksburg, Ala. (†36352) 195/G8
Wicomico (co.), Md. 245/R7
Wicomico, Md. (†20611) 245/L7
Wicomico (riv.), Md. 245/R7
Wicomico (riv.), Md. 245/L7
Wicomico Church, Va. (22579) 307/R5
Wiconisco, Pa. (17097) 294/J4
Wide (chan.), Chile 138/D8
Wide (bay), Papua N.G. 86/C2
Wide (bay), Queensland 95/E5
Wideman, Ark. (72585) 202/G1
Widemouth, W. Va. (†24736) 312/D8
Widen, W. Va. (25211) 312/E6
Widener, Ark. (72394) 202/J3
Widewater, Alberta 182/C2
Widgiemooltha, W. Australia 88/C6
Widgiemooltha, W. Australia 92/C5
Widnes, England 10/F2
Widnes, England 13/G2
Widnoon, Pa. (16261) 294/D4
Więcbork, Poland 47/C2
Wiederkehr Village, Ark. 202/C3
Wiehl, W. Germany 22/B3
Wiek, E. Germany 22/E1
Wieliczka, Poland 47/E3
Wieluń, Poland 47/D3
Wien (Vienna) (cap.), Austria 41/D2
Wiener Neustadt, Austria 41/D3
Wieprz (riv.), Poland 47/F3
Wierden, Netherlands 27/K4
Wieringermeer Polder, Netherlands 27/G3
Wierum, Netherlands 27/H2
Wieruszów, Poland 47/D3
Wiesbaden, W. Germany 7/E3
Wiesbaden, W. Germany 22/B3
Wiese (isl.), U.S.S.R. 4/B6
Wiese (isl.), U.S.S.R. 48/H2
Wiesmoor, W. Germany 22/B2
Wigan, England 13/G2
Wigan, England 10/G2
Wiggins, Colo. (80654) 208/L2
Wiggins, Miss. (39577) 256/F9
Wiggins, S.C. (†29446) 296/F6
Wight (isl.), England 13/F7
Wight (isl.), England 10/F5
Wigston, England 13/F5
Wigton, England 13/D3
Wigtown, Scotland 10/D3
Wigtown, Scotland 15/D6
Wigtown (trad. co.), Scot. 15/A5
Wigtown (bay), Scotland 10/D3
Wigtown (bay), Scotland 15/D6
Wijhe, Netherlands 27/J4
Wijk bij Duurstede, Netherlands 27/G5
Wijk en Aalburg, Netherlands 27/F5
Wikel, W. Va. (†24945) 312/E7
Wikieup, Ariz. (85360) 198/B4
Wikwemikong, Ontario 177/C2
Wil, Switzerland 39/H2
Wilawana, Pa. (†18840) 294/J2
Wilbarger (co.), Texas 303/E3
Wilber, Nebr. (68465) 264/G4
Wilberforce, Ontario 177/F3
Wilbert, Minn. (†56031) 255/D7
Wilbraham, Mass. (01095) 249/E4
Wilbraham○, Mass. (01095) 249/E4
Wilbur, Ind. (†46151) 227/D5
Wilbur, Ky. (†41124) 237/R5
Wilbur, Oreg. (97494) 291/D4
Wilbur, Wash. (99185) 310/G3
Wilbur, W. Va. (26459) 312/E4
Wilbur Park, Mo. (†63101) 261/P3
Wilburton, Kansas (†67950) 232/A4
Wilburton, Okla. (74578) 288/R5
Wilcannia, N.S. Wales 88/G6
Wilcannia, N.S. Wales 97/B2
Wilchingen, Switzerland 39/F1
Wilcox (co.), Ala. 195/D7
Wilcox, Fla. (†32693) 212/D2
Wilcox (co.), Georgia 217/F7
Wilcox, Mo. (†64468) 261/C2
Wilcox, Nebr. (68982) 264/E4
Wilcox, Pa. (15870) 294/E2
Wilcox, Sask. 181/G5
Wilczek Land (isl.), U.S.S.R. 4/B6
Wilczek Land (isl.), U.S.S.R. 48/G1
Wild Ammonoosuc (riv.), N.H. 268/D3
Wildbad im Schwarzwald, W. Germany 22/C4
Wildcat (creek), Ind. 227/E4
Wild Cat, Ky. (40998) 237/O6
Wild Cherry, Ark. (†72576) 202/F1
Wild Cove, Newf. 166/C3
Wilder, Idaho (83676) 220/A6
Wilder, Minn. (56184) 255/C7
Wilder (dam), N.H. 268/C4
Wilder, Tenn. (38589) 237/L8
Wilder, Vt. (05088) 268/C4
Wilder (dam), Vt. 268/C4
Wilderness, Va. (†22553) 307/N4
Wilders, Ky. (†41071) 237/S2
Wildersville, Tenn. (38388) 237/E9
Wilderswil, Switzerland 39/E3
Wildervank, Netherlands 27/K2
Wilderville, Oreg. (97543) 291/D5
Wildeshausen, W. Germany 22/C2
Wild Goose, Ontario 177/H5
Wild Goose, Ontario 175/C3
Wildhaus, Switzerland 39/H2
Wildhay (riv.), Alberta 182/B3
Wildhorn (mt.), Switzerland 39/D4
Wild Horse, Colo. (80862) 208/N5
Wild Horse (res.), Nev. 266/E1
Wildhorse (creek), Okla. 288/L5
Wildie, Ky. (40492) 237/N6
Wildomar, Calif. (92395) 204/H10
Wildon, Austria 41/C3
Wildorado, Texas (79098) 303/B2
Wild Rice (lake), Minn. 255/F4
Wild Rice (riv.), Minn. 255/B3
Wild Rice, N. Dak. (†58047) 282/S6
Wild Rice (riv.), N. Dak. 282/R7
Wildrose, N. Dak. (58795) 282/D2
Wild Rose, Wis. (54984) 317/H7
Wildspitze (mt.), Austria 41/A3
Wildstrubel (mt.), Switzerland 39/E4
Wildsville, La. (71377) 238/G3
Wildwood, Alberta 182/C3
Wildwood, Fla. (32785) 212/D3
Wildwood, Minn. (†56643) 255/E3
Wildwood, N.J. (08260) 273/D6
Wildwood Crest, N.J. (08260) 273/D6
Wileville, Nova Scotia 168/D4
Wiley, Colo. (81092) 208/O6
Wiley, Georgia (30581) 217/F1
Wiley (creek), Oreg. 291/E3
Wiley City, Wash. (98906) 310/E4
Wiley Ford, W. Va. (26767) 312/J3
Wileyville, W. Va. (26186) 312/E3
Wilfred, Ind. (†47879) 227/C6
Wilhelm (mt.), Papua N.G. 85/B7
Wilhelm II Coast (reg.) 5/C5
Wilhelmina (canal), Netherlands 27/G6
Wilhelmina (mts.), Suriname 131/C4
Wilhelm-Pieck-Stadt, E. Germany 22/F3
Wilhelmsburg, Austria 41/C2
Wilhelmshaven, W. Germany 22/B2
Wilkes (co.), Georgia 217/G3
Wilkes (co.), N.C. 281/G2
Wilkes (lake), Ontario 177/F1
Wilkes-Barre, Pa. 188/L2
Wilkes-Barre, Pa. (*18701) 294/F7
Wilkesboro, N.C. (28697) 281/G2
Wilkes Land (reg.), Ant. 2/R10
Wilkes Land (reg.) 5/B7
Wilkeson, Wash. (98396) 310/D3
Wilkesville, Ohio (45695) 284/F7
Wilke, Sask. 181/C3
Wilkin (co.), Minn. 255/B4
Wilkins, Nev. (†89835) 266/G1
Wilkinsburg, Pa. (15221) 294/C7
Wilkinson (co.), Georgia 217/F5
Wilkinson, Ind. (46186) 227/F5
Wilkinson, Minn. (†56633) 255/D3
Wilkinson (co.), Miss. 256/B8
Wilkinson, Miss. (†39669) 256/B8
Wilkinson (lakes), S. Australia 94/C3
Wilkinson, W. Va. (25653) 312/B7
Wilkinsonville, Mass. (01590) 249/G4
Will (co.), Ill. 222/F2
Willacoochee, Georgia (31650) 217/G8
Willacy (co.), Texas 303/G11
Willamette (riv.), Oreg. 291/A3
Willamette, Middle Fork (riv.), Oreg. 291/E4
Willamina, Oreg. (97396) 291/D2
Willandra Billabong (creek), N.S. Wales 97/C3
Willapa, Wash. (†98577) 310/B4
Willapa (bay), Wash. 310/A4
Willard, Kansas (†66601) 232/G2
Willard, Mich. (†48611) 250/E5
Willard, Mo. (65781) 261/F8
Willard, Mont. (59354) 262/M4
Willard, N. Mex. (87063) 274/D4
Willard, N.Y. (14588) 276/G5
Willard, N.C. (28478) 281/O5
Willard, Ohio (44890) 284/E3
Willard, Utah (84340) 304/C2
Willard, Wis. (54493) 317/E6
Willards, Md. (21874) 245/S7
Willaumez (pen.), Papua N.G. 86/B2
Willaura, Victoria 97/B5
Willcox, Ariz. (85643) 198/F6
Willebroek, Belgium 27/E6
Willems (canal), Netherlands 27/G5
Willemstad, Netherlands 27/F5
Willemstad (cap.), Neth. Ant. 161/F9
Willemstad (cap.), Neth. Ant. 156/E4
Willen, Manitoba 179/A4
Willernie, Minn. (55090) 255/G5
Willeroo, North. Terr. 93/B3
Willette, Tenn. (†37150) 237/K8
Willey, Iowa (†51401) 229/D5
Willey House, N.H. (†03812) 268/E3
William (riv.), Sask. 181/L2
William Creek, S. Australia 94/E3
William H. Taft Nat'l Hist. Site, Ohio 284/C10
William L. Springer (lake), Ill. 222/E4
Williams, Ariz. (86046) 198/C3
Williams, Calif. (95987) 204/C4
Williams, Ind. (47470) 227/D7
Williams, Iowa (50271) 229/F3
Williams, Minn. (56686) 255/D2
Williams (co.), N. Dak. 282/C3
Williams (co.), Ohio 284/A2
Williams, Okla. (†74932) 288/T4
Williams, Oreg. (97544) 291/D5
Williams, S.C. (29493) 296/F5
Williams, W. Australia 92/B2
Williams (riv.), W. Va. 312/F6
Williams A.F.B., Ariz. 198/D5
Williams Bay, Wis. (53191) 317/J10
Williamsboro, N.C. (†27536) 281/M2
Williamsburg, Colo. (†81226) 208/J6
Williamsburg, Iowa (52361) 229/J5
Williamsburg, Kansas (66095) 232/G3
Williamsburg, Ky. (40769) 237/N7
Williamsburg, Md. (21674) 245/P6
Williamsburg○, Mass. (01096) 249/C3
Williamsburg, Mich. (49690) 250/D4
Williamsburg, Mo. (63388) 261/J5
Williamsburg, New Bruns. 170/D2
Williamsburg, N. Mex. (87942) 274/B5
Williamsburg, Ohio (45176) 284/B7
Williamsburg, Ontario 177/J3
Williamsburg, Pa. (16693) 294/F5
Williamsburg (co.), S.C. 296/H4
Williamsburg (I.C.), Va. (23185) 307/P6
Williamsburg, W. Va. (24991) 312/F7
Williamsfield, Ill. (61489) 222/C3
Williamsfield, Jamaica 158/H6
Williamsfield, Ohio (44093) 284/J2
Williamsford, Ontario 177/D3
Williamsford, Tasmania 99/B3
Williams Fork, Colorado (riv.), Colo. 208/G3
Williams Fork, Yampa (riv.), Colo. 208/E2
Williams Harbour, Newf. 166/C3
Williams Lake, Br. Col. 162/D5
Williams Lake, Br. Col. 184/F4
Williamson, Georgia (30292) 217/D4
Williamson (co.), Ill. 222/E6
Williamson, Ill. (†62088) 222/D5
Williamson, Iowa (50272) 229/G6
Williamson, N.Y. (14589) 276/F4
Williamson (riv.), Oreg. 291/F5
Williamson (co.), Tenn. 237/H9
Williamson (co.), Texas 303/G7
Williamson, W. Va. (25661) 312/B7
Williamsport, Ind. (47993) 227/C4
Williamsport, Ky. (41271) 237/R5
Williamsport, Md. (21795) 245/G2
Williamsport, Newf. 166/C3
Williamsport, Ohio (43164) 284/D6
Williamsport, Pa. 188/L2
Williamsport, Pa. (17701) 294/H3
Williamsport, Tenn. (38487) 237/G9
Williamston, Mich. (48895) 250/E6
Williamston, N.C. (27892) 281/R3
Williamston, S.C. (29697) 296/B2
Williamstown, Kansas (†66073) 232/G2
Williamstown, Ky. (41097) 237/M3
Williamstown, Mass. (01267) 249/B2
Williamstown○, Mass. (01267) 249/B2
Williamstown, Mo. (63473) 261/J2
Williamstown, New Bruns. 170/C2
Williamstown, N.J. (08094) 273/D4
Williamstown, N.Y. (13493) 276/J4
Williamstown, Ontario 177/K2
Williamstown, Pa. (17098) 294/J4
Williamstown, S. Australia 94/C7
Williamstown○, Vt. (05679) 268/B3
Williamstown, Victoria 97/H5
Williamstown, Victoria 88/K7
Williamstown, W. Va. (26187) 312/C4
Williamsville, Ill. (62693) 222/D4
Williamsville, Miss. (†39090) 256/F4
Williamsville, Mo. (63977) 261/L9
Williamsville, N.Y. (14221) 276/C5
Williamsville, Vt. (05362) 268/B6
Williamsville, Va. (24487) 307/J4
Willies (range), Queensland 95/C6
Willford, Ark. (72482) 202/H1
Willimantic, Conn. (06226) 210/G2
Willimantic (riv.), Conn. 210/F1
Willimantic, Maine (†04443) 243/E5
Willimantic○, Maine (†04443) 243/E5
Willingboro○, N.J. (08046) 273/D3
Willingdon, Alberta 182/E3
Willington○, Conn. (†06279) 210/F1
Willington, S.C. (29852) 296/C4
Willis (islets), Australia 87/F7
Willis (isls.), Coral Sea Is. Terr. 88/J3
Willis, Kansas (66435) 232/G2
Willis, Mich. (48191) 250/F6
Willis, Okla. (†73439) 288/N7
Willis, Texas (77378) 303/J7
Willis, Va. (24380) 307/H7
Willis (riv.), Va. 307/M5
Willisau, Switzerland 39/F2
Willisburg, Ky. (40078) 237/L5
Williston (lake), Br. Col. 162/D4
Williston (lake), Br. Col. 184/F2
Williston, Fla. (32696) 212/D2
Williston, N. Dak. 188/F1
Williston, N. Dak. (58801) 282/C3
Williston, S.C. (29853) 296/E5
Williston, Tenn. (38076) 237/C10
Williston○, Vt. (05495) 268/A3
Williston Park, N.Y. (11596) 276/R7
Willisville, Ark. (71864) 202/D6
Willisville, Ill. (62997) 222/D6
Willisville, Ontario 177/C1
Willis Wharf, Va. (23486) 307/S5
Williton, England 13/D6
Willits, Calif. (95490) 204/B4
Willmar, Minn. (56201) 255/C5
Willmar, Sask. 181/J6
Willmathsville, Mo. (†63546) 261/G2
Willmore Wilderness Prov. Park, Alberta 182/A3
Willoughby (bay), Ant. & Bar. 161/E11
Willoughby, N.S. Wales 88/K3
Willoughby, N.S. Wales 97/J3
Willoughby, Ohio (44094) 284/J8
Willoughby, Vt. (†05822) 268/C2
Willoughby (lake), Vt. 268/D2
Willoughby Hills, Ohio (†44094) 284/J9
Willow, Alaska (99688) 196/B1
Willow, Ark. (†72084) 202/E5
Willow (creek), Calif. 204/E3
Willow (creek), Idaho 220/G6
Willow (riv.), Minn. 255/E4
Willow (creek), Mont. 262/E2
Willow, Okla. (73673) 288/G4
Willow (creek), Oreg. 291/H2
Willow (creek), Oreg. 291/K3
Willow (creek), S. Dak. 298/C4
Willow (creek), Utah 304/E4
Willow (res.), Wis. 317/F4
Willow (creek), Wyo. 319/F2
Willow (lake), Wyo. 319/C2
Willow Bend, W. Va. (24992) 312/F7
Willow Branch, Ind. (46187) 227/F5
Willowbrook, Ill. (†60521) 222/B6
Willowbrook, Kansas (†67501) 232/D3
Willowbrook, Sask. 181/J4
Willow Bunch, Sask. 181/F6
Willow Bunch (lake), Sask. 181/F6
Willow City, N. Dak. (58384) 282/K2
Willow City, Texas (78675) 303/F7
Willow Creek, Calif. (95573) 204/B3
Willow Creek, Mont. (59760) 262/E5
Willow Creek (res.), Mont. 262/D3
Willowcreek, Oreg. (†97918) 291/K3
Willow Creek, Sask. 181/B6
Willowdale, Oreg. (†97741) 291/G3
Willow Grove, Del. (†19934) 245/R4
Willow Grove, New Bruns. 170/E3
Willow Grove, Pa. (19090) 294/M5
Willow Hill, Ill. (62480) 222/E5
Willow Hill, Pa. (17271) 294/G5
Willowick, Ohio (44094) 284/J8
Willow Island, Nebr. (69171) 264/D4
Willowlake (riv.), N.W. Terrs. 187/F3
Willow Lake, S. Dak. (57278) 298/O4
Willowmore, S. Africa 118/C6
Willowra, North. Terr. 93/C6
Willow Ranch, Calif. (96108) 204/E2
Willow River, Br. Col. 184/F3
Willow River, Minn. (55795) 255/F4
Willows, Calif. (95988) 204/C4
Willows, Md. (†20732) 245/M6
Willows, Sask. 181/F6
Willow Springs, Ill. (60480) 222/B6

472 Yamatotakada

Yamatotakada, Japan 81/J8
Yamba, N.S. Wales 97/G1
Yambah, North. Terr. 93/C7
Yambio, Sudan 111/E7
Yambio, Sudan 102/E4
Yambol, Bulgaria 45/H4
Yambou (head), St. Vin. & Grens. 161/A9
Yambrasbamba, Peru 128/D5
Yamdena (isl.), Indonesia 85/J7
Yamethin, Burma 72/C2
Yamhill (co.), Oreg. 291/D2
Yamhill, Oreg. (97148) 291/D2
Y'Ami (isl.), Philippines 82/B2
Yamma Yamma (lake), Queensland 88/G5
Yamma Yamma (lake), Queensland 95/B5
Yampa, Colo. (80483) 208/F2
Yampa (riv.), Colo. 208/B2
Yamparaéz, Bolivia 136/C6
Yampi Sound, W. Australia 88/C3
Yampi Sound, W. Australia 92/C2
Yamsk, U.S.S.R. 48/Q4
Yamun, West Bank 65/C3
Yamuna (Jumna) (riv.), Pakistan 68/E3
Yamzho Yumco (lake), China 77/C6
Yan, Nigeria 106/G7
Yana, U.S.S.R. 54/P3
Yana (riv.), U.S.S.R. 4/C3
Yana (riv.), U.S.S.R. 48/O3
Yanac, Victoria 97/A5
Yanacachi, Bolivia 136/B5
Yanahuanca, Peru 128/D8
Yanam, India 68/E5
Yan'an (Yenan), China 77/G4
Yanaoca, Peru 128/G10
Yanaul, U.S.S.R. 52/J3
Yancannia, N.S. Wales 97/B2
Yancey, Ky. (†40831) 237/P7
Yancey (co.), N.C. 281/E3
Yanceyville, N.C. (27379) 281/L2
Yancheng, China 77/K5
Yanchi, China 77/G4
Yanco, N.S. Wales 97/D4
Yandé (isl.), New Caled. 86/F4
Yandeyarra Aboriginal Reserve, W. Australia 88/B4
Yandina, Solomon Is. 86/D3
Yandoon, Burma 72/B3
Yanfolila, Mali 106/C6
Yanga, Mexico 150/P2
Yangambi, Zaire 115/D3
Yangambi, Zaire 102/E4
Yangcheng, China 77/H4
Yangchow (Yangzhou), China 77/J5
Yangchüan (Yangquan), China 77/H4
Yangchun, China 77/H7
Yangdŏk, N. Korea 81/C4
Yanggao, China 77/H3
Yanggu, S. Korea 81/C4
Yangjiang, China 77/H7
Yangquan (Yangchüan), China 77/H4
Yangshan, China 77/H7
Yang Sin, Chu (mt.), Vietnam 72/F4
Yangtze (riv.), China 54/N6
Yangtze (riv.), China 2/Q4
Yangtze (Chang Jiang) (riv.), China 77/K5
Yangyang, S. Korea 81/D4
Yangzhou (Yangchow), China 77/J5
Yanhuqu, China 77/B5
Yanji (Yenki), China 77/L3
Yankee Fork, Salmon (riv.), Idaho 220/D5
Yankee Lake, Ohio (†44403) 284/J3
Yankeetown, Fla. (32698) 212/D2
Yankeetown, Ind. (†47630) 227/C9
Yanko (creek), N.S. Wales 97/C4
Yankton, S. Dak. 188/G2
Yankton (co.), S. Dak. 298/P7
Yankton, S. Dak. (57078) 298/P8
Yanqi, China 77/C3
Yanrey, W. Australia 92/A3
Yantabulla, N.S. Wales 97/C1
Yantai (Chefoo), China 77/K4
Yantai, China 54/O6
Yantara, N.S. Wales 97/B1
Yantara (lake), N.S. Wales 97/B1
Yantic, Conn. (06389) 210/G2
Yantic (riv.), Conn. 210/G2
Yantis, Texas (75497) 303/J5
Yantley, Ala. (36924) 195/B6
Yanush, Okla. (†74574) 288/R5
Yao, Japan 81/J8
Yaoundé (cap.), Cameroon 2/K5
Yaoundé (cap.), Cameroon 102/D4
Yaoundé (cap.), Cameroon 115/B3
Yap (isl.), Micronesia 87/D5
Yapacani (riv.), Bolivia 136/C5
Yapei, Ghana 106/D7
Yapen (isl.), Indonesia 85/K6
Yapen (str.), Indonesia 85/K6
Yapraklı, Turkey 63/E2
Yaque del Norte (riv.), Dom. Rep. 158/D5
Yaque del Sur (riv.), Dom. Rep. 158/D6
Yaqui, Mexico 150/D3
Yaqui (riv.), Mexico 146/H7
Yaqui (riv.), Mexico 150/E2
Yaquina, Oreg. (†97365) 291/C3
Yara, Cuba 158/H4
Yaracuy (state), Venezuela 124/D2
Yaraka, Queensland 95/C5
Yaraligöz Daği (mt.), Turkey 59/B1
Yaraligöz Daği (mt.), Turkey 63/F2
Yaransk, U.S.S.R. 52/G3
Yarbo, Ala. (†36558) 195/B7
Yarbo, Sask. 181/K5
Yarboutenda, Senegal 106/B6
Yarda, Chad 111/C4
Yardley, Pa. (19067) 294/N5
Yardville, N.J. (08620) 273/D3
Yare (riv.), England 13/J5
Yare (riv.), England 10/G4
Yarega, U.S.S.R. 52/H2
Yaretas de Vizcachas, Cerro (mt.), Chile 138/G3
Yari, Colombia 126/D7
Yari (riv.), Colombia 126/D8
Yarim, Yemen Arab Rep. 59/D7
Yaritagua, Venezuela 124/D2
Yarkand (Shache), China 77/A4
Yarkand (riv.), China 54/K6
Yarkant He (riv.), China 77/A4
Yarker, Ontario 177/H3
Yarle (lakes), S. Australia 94/B4
Yarmouth, Iowa (52660) 229/L6
Yarmouth, Maine (04096) 243/C8
Yarmouth○, Maine (04096) 243/C8
Yarmouth○, Mass. (02675) 249/O6
Yarmouth, N.S. 162/K7
Yarmouth (co.), Nova Scotia 168/C5
Yarmouth, Nova Scotia 168/B5
Yarmouth (sound), Nova Scotia 168/B5
Yarmouth Port, Mass. (02675) 249/N6
Yarmuk (riv.), Israel 65/D2
Yarnell, Ariz. (85362) 198/C4
Yaroslavl', U.S.S.R. 7/H3
Yaroslavl', U.S.S.R. 48/D4
Yaroslavl', U.S.S.R. 52/E3
Yarqon (riv.), Israel 65/B3
Yarra (riv.), Victoria 97/C5
Yarra (riv.), Victoria 88/L6
Yarram, Victoria 97/D6
Yarrawonga, Victoria 97/C5
Yarrow, Br. Col. 184/M3
Yarrow, Mo. (†63501) 261/G2
Yarrow (riv.), Scotland 15/E5
Yarrowitch, N.S. Wales 97/F2
Yarrow Point, Wash. (†98004) 310/B2
Yartsevo, U.S.S.R. 48/J4
Yartsevo, U.S.S.R. 52/D3
Yarumal, Colombia 126/C4
Yaruu, Mongolia 77/E2
Yas (isl.), U.A.E. 59/F5
Yasawa Group (isls.), Fiji 86/P10
Yásica Abajo, Dom. Rep. 158/E5
Yasin, Pakistan 59/K2
Yasin, Pakistan 68/C1
Yasnyy, U.S.S.R. 52/J4
Yasothon, Thailand 72/D4
Yass, N.S. Wales 97/E4
Yasuj, Iran 66/G5
Yasun (cape), Turkey 63/G2
Yata (riv.), Bolivia 136/C3
Yatabe, Japan 81/P2
Yatağan, Turkey 63/C4
Yataity, Paraguay 144/C5
Yateley, England 13/G8
Yates (dam), Ala. 195/G5
Yates (co.), N.Y. 276/F5
Yates Center, Kansas (66783) 232/G4
Yates City, Ill. (61572) 222/C3
Yatesville, Georgia (31097) 217/D5
Yathkyed (lake), N.W.T. 162/F3
Yathkyed (lake), N.W. Terrs. 187/J3
Yatina, Bolivia 136/C7
Yatsushiro, Japan 81/E7
Yatta, West Bank 65/C5
Yatton, England 13/E6
Yatua (riv.), Venezuela 124/E7
Yauca, Peru 128/E10
Yauco, P. Rico 161/B2
Yauco, P. Rico 156/F1
Yauco (lake), P. Rico 161/B2
Yauli, Peru 128/D8
Yaúna Moloca, Colombia 126/E8
Yaupi, Ecuador 128/D4
Yaupon Beach, N.C. (†28461) 281/N7
Yauri, Peru 128/G10
Yautepec, Mexico 150/L2
Yauyos, Peru 128/E9
Yava, Ariz. (†86301) 198/C4
Yavapai (co.), Ariz. 198/C4
Yavapai Ind. Res., Ariz. 198/C4
Yavaraté, Colombia 126/F7
Yavari (riv.) 120/B3
Yavari (riv.), Peru 128/G5
Yavaros, Mexico 150/E3
Yavero (riv.), Peru 128/F9
Yavita, Venezuela 124/E6
Yavne, Israel 65/B4
Yavne'el, Israel 65/D2
Yawata, Japan 81/J7
Yawatahama, Japan 81/F7
Yawkey, W. Va. (25573) 312/C6
Yawri (bay), S. Leone 106/B7
Ya Xian, China 77/G8
Yaxley, England 13/G5
Yayladağı, Turkey 63/F5
Yazd (governorate), Iran 66/J5
Yazd (Yezd), Iran 66/J5
Yazd, Iran 59/F3
Yazd, Iran 54/G6
Yazdan, Iran 66/M4
Yazdan, Iran 59/H3
Yazd-e Khvasat, Iran 66/H5
Yazoo (co.), Miss. 265/D5
Yazoo (riv.), Miss. 188/H4
Yazoo (riv.), Miss. 256/C5
Yazoo City, Miss. (39194) 256/D5
Ybbs an der Donau, Austria 41/C2
Ybycuí, Paraguay 144/B5
Ybytymí, Paraguay 144/B5
Yding Skovhøj (mt.), Denmark 21/C6
Ye, Burma 72/C4
Yea, Victoria 97/C5
Yeaddiss, Ky. (41777) 237/P6
Yeadon, Pa. (19050) 294/N7
Yeager, Okla. (†74848) 288/O4
Yeagertown, Pa. (17099) 294/G4
Yebbi-Bou, Chad 111/C3
Yecheng, China 77/A4
Yecla, Spain 33/F3
Yécora, Mexico 150/E2
Yecuatla, Mexico 150/P1
Yeddo, Ind. (†47952) 227/C4
Yeeda River, W. Australia 92/C2
Yeelirrie, W. Australia 92/C4
Yefremov, U.S.S.R. 52/E4
Yegros, Paraguay 144/D5
Yeguas (pt.), P. Rico 161/F3
Yehualtepec, Mexico 150/O2
Yehud, Israel 65/B3
Yei, Sudan 111/F7
Yelabuga, U.S.S.R. 52/H3
Yelan', U.S.S.R. 52/F4
Yelcho (lake), Chile 138/E4
Yelets, U.S.S.R. 7/H3
Yelets, U.S.S.R. 48/D4
Yelets, U.S.S.R. 52/E4
Yelimané, Mali 106/B5
Yelizavety (cape), U.S.S.R. 54/R4
Yelizavety (cape), U.S.S.R. 48/P4
Yelizovo, U.S.S.R. 48/Q4
Yell (co.), Ark. 202/D3
Yell (isl.), Scotland 15/G2
Yell (isl.), Scotland 10/G1
Yell (sound), Scotland 15/G2
Yellamanchili, India 68/E5
Yelleq, Jebel (mt.), Egypt 59/B3
Yellow (sea) 54/O6
Yellow (Huang He) (riv.), China 77/J4
Yellow (sea), China 77/K4
Yellow (creek), Colo. 208/C3
Yellow (riv.), Fla. 212/B6
Yellow (riv.), Ind. 227/D2
Yellow (brook), N.J. 273/E3
Yellow (sea), N. Korea 81/B6
Yellow (creek), Ohio 284/J4
Yellow (sea), S. Korea 81/B6
Yellow (creek), Tenn. 237/F8
Yellow (creek), W. Va. 312/E1
Yellow (lake), Wis. 317/B4
Yellow (riv.), Wis. 317/F7
Yellow Bluff, Ala. (†36769) 195/C7
Yellowbud, Ohio (†45601) 284/D7
Yellowcreek, N.C. (†28771) 281/A4
Yellow Creek, Sask. 181/F3
Yellow Dog (riv.), Mich. 250/B2
Yellow Grass, Sask. 181/H6
Yellowhead (pass), Alberta 182/A3
Yellowhead (pass), Br. Col. 184/H4
Yellow Jacket, Colo. (81335) 208/B7
Yellowknife, Canada 4/C15
Yellowknife, Canada 2/D2
Yellowknife, N.W.T. 146/G3
Yellowknife (cap.), N.W.T. 162/E3
Yellowknife (cap.), N.W. Terrs. 187/G3
Yellowknife (riv.), N.W. Terrs. 187/G3
Yellow Medicine (co.), Minn. 255/B6
Yellow Pine, Ala. (36588) 195/B8
Yellow Pine, Idaho (83677) 220/C4
Yellow Pine, La. (†71039) 238/D2
Yellow Spring, W. Va. (26865) 312/J4
Yellow Springs, Md. (†21701) 245/H3
Yellow Springs, Ohio (45387) 284/C6
Yellowstone (riv.) 188/E1
Yellowstone (co.), Mont. 262/H4
Yellowstone (riv.), Mont. 262/M3
Yellowstone (riv.), N. Dak. 282/B4
Yellowstone (riv.), U.S. 146/H5
Yellowstone (lake), Wyo. 188/E2
Yellowstone (lake), Wyo. 319/B1
Yellowstone (riv.), Wyo. 319/B1
Yellowstone Nat'l Park, Idaho 262/F6
Yellowstone Nat'l Park, Mont. 262/F6
Yellowstone Nat'l Park, Wyo. (82190) 31/B1
Yellowstone Nat'l Park, Wyo. 188/E2
Yellowstone Nat'l Park, Wyo. 319/B1
Yellville, Ark. (72687) 202/E1
Yelm, Wash. (98597) 310/C4
Yelverton (bay), N.W. Terrs. 187/K1
Yelwa, Nigeria 106/F6
Yemassee, S.C. (29945) 296/F6
Yemen, People's Dem. Rep. of 2/M5
Yemen, People's Democratic Republic of 54/F8
YEMEN, PEOPLE'S DEM. REPUBLIC OF, 59/E7
YEMEN ARAB REP. 59/D7
Yemen Arab Republic 2/M5
Yemen Arab Republic 54/F8
Yemetsk, U.S.S.R. 52/F2
Yenakiyevo, U.S.S.R. 52/E5
Yenan (Yan'an), China 77/G4
Yenangyaung, Burma 72/B2
Yen Bai, Vietnam 72/E2
Yenbo, Saudi Arabia 54/E7
Yenbo, Saudi Arabia 59/C5
Yenda, N.S. Wales 97/D4
Yendi, Ghana 106/D7
Yengisar, China 77/A4
Yenice, Çanakkale, Turkey 63/B3
Yenice, İçel, Turkey 63/F4
Yenice, Zonguldak, Turkey 63/E2
Yeniceoba, Turkey 63/E3
Yeniköy, Çanakkale, Turkey 63/B6
Yeniköy, Çanakkale, Turkey 63/C5
Yeniköy, Istanbul, Turkey 63/D6
Yenimahalle, Turkey 63/E3
Yenişehir, Turkey 63/C2
Yenisey (riv.), U.S.S.R. 4/C5
Yenisey (riv.), U.S.S.R. 2/P2
Yenisey (riv.), U.S.S.R. 54/K3
Yenisey (riv.), U.S.S.R. 48/J3
Yeniseysk, U.S.S.R. 54/L4
Yeniseysk, U.S.S.R. 48/K4
Yenki (Yanji), China 77/L3
Yen Minh, Vietnam 72/E2
Yentai (Yantai), China 77/K4
Yentna (riv.), Alaska 196/A1
Yeo (lake), W. Australia 88/D5
Yeo (lake), W. Australia 92/D5
Yeola, India 68/C4
Yeoman, Ind. (47997) 227/D3
Yeotmal, India 68/D4
Yeoval, N.S. Wales 97/E3
Yeovil, England 10/E5
Yeovil, England 13/E7
Yeppoon, Queensland 95/D4
Yeppoon, Queensland 88/J4
Yerevan (Erivan), U.S.S.R. 52/F6
Yerichaña, Venezuela 124/F5
Yerington, Nev. (89447) 266/B4
Yerington Ind. Res., Nev. 266/B3
Yerkesik, Turkey 63/C4
Yerköy, Turkey 63/F3
Yerlisu, Turkey 63/C5
Yermak, U.S.S.R. 48/H4
Yermentau, 48/H4
Yermo, Calif. (92398) 204/J9
Yeroham, Israel 65/B6
Yerolimin, Greece 45/F7
Yeronga, Queensland 95/D3
Yeronga, Queensland 88/K3
Yerseke, Netherlands 27/E6
Yershov, U.S.S.R. 52/G4
Yesagyo, Burma 72/B2
Yeshbum, P.D.R. Yemen 59/E7
Yesil', 48/G4
Yeşilhisar, Turkey 63/F3
Yeşilırmak (riv.), Turkey 63/G2
Yeşilköy, Turkey 63/D6
Yeşilova, Burdur, Turkey 63/C4
Yeşilova, Niğde, Turkey 63/E3
Yeşilyurt, Turkey 63/H3
Yeso, N. Mex. (88136) 274/E4
Yeso (creek), N. Mex. 274/E4
Yesodot, Israel 65/B4
Yessentuki, U.S.S.R. 52/F6
Yessey, U.S.S.R. 48/L3
Yeste, Spain 33/E3
Yesud Hama'ala, Israel 65/D1
Yetholm, Scotland 15/F5
Yetman, N.S. Wales 97/F1
Yettem, Calif. (93670) 204/F7
Yetter, Iowa (51433) 229/D4
Ye-u, Burma 72/B2
Yeu (isl.), France 28/B4
Yevlakh, U.S.S.R. 52/G6
Yevpatoria, U.S.S.R. 52/D5
Ye Xian, China 77/K4
Yeysk, U.S.S.R. 52/E5
Ygatimí, Paraguay 144/E4
Yhú, Paraguay 144/E4
Yi (riv.), Uruguay 145/B4
Yialousa, Cyprus 63/E5
Yiannitsá, Greece 45/F5
Yibin (Ipin), China 77/F6
Yibin, China 54/M7
Yibug Caka (lake), China 77/C5
Yichang (Ichang), China 77/H5
Yichun, Heilongjiang, China 77/L2
Yichun, Jiangxi, China 77/H6
Yidu, Hubei, China 77/H5
Yidu, Shandong, China 77/J4
Yiftah, Israel 65/D1
Yığılca, Turkey 63/D2
Yıldızeli, Turkey 63/G3
Yiliang, China 77/F7
Yinchuan (Ningsia, Yinchwan), China 77/G4
Yinchuan, China 54/M6
Yingjiang, China 77/E7
Yingkou (Yinkow), China 77/K3
Yingshan, Hubei, China 77/H5
Yingshan, Sichuan, China 77/G5
Yining, China 77/B3
Yining, China 54/K5
Yinjiang, China 77/G6
Yin Shan (mts.), China 77/G3
Yirga-Alam, Ethiopia 102/F4
Yirga Alam, Ethiopia 111/G6
Yirka, Israel 65/C2
Yirol, Sudan 111/F6
Yirrkala, North. Terr. 93/E2
Yishan, China 77/G7
Yithion, Greece 45/F7
Yiwu (Aratürük), China 77/D3
Yiyang, China 77/H6
Ylikitka (lake), Finland 18/Q3
Ylitornio, Finland 18/O3
Ylivieska, Finland 18/O4
Ymir, Br. Col. 184/J5
Ynys Môn (Anglesey) (ridge), Wales 13/C4
Ynys Môn (Anglesey) (isl.), Wales 10/D4
Yoakum (co.), Texas 303/B4
Yoakum, Texas (77995) 303/G8
Yocalla, Bolivia 136/B6
Yocemento, Kansas (†67601) 232/C3
Yockanookany (riv.), Miss. 256/E5
Yoco, Venezuela 124/G2
Yocón, Honduras 154/D3
Yocum, Ky. (41478) 237/P5
Yoder, Colo. (80864) 208/L5
Yoder, Ind. (46798) 227/G3
Yoder, Kansas (67585) 232/E4
Yoder, Wyo. (82244) 319/H4
Yodo (riv.), Japan 81/J7
Yog (pt.), Philippines 82/E3
Yogyakarta, Indonesia 54/M10
Yogyakarta, Indonesia 85/J2
Yoho Nat'l Park, Br. Col. 162/E5
Yoho Nat'l Park, Br. Col. 184/J4
Yoichi, Japan 81/K2
Yojoa (lake), Honduras 154/D3
Yokadouma, Cameroon 115/B3
Yokawa, Japan 81/H7
Yokena, Miss. (†39180) 256/C6
Yokkaichi, Japan 81/H6
Yoko, Cameroon 115/B2
Yokohama, Japan 2/R4
Yokohama, Japan 81/O3
Yokohama, Japan 54/R6
Yokosuka, Japan 81/O3
Yokote, Japan 81/K4
Yola, Nigeria 106/G7
Yola, Nigeria 102/D4
Yolla, Tasmania 99/B3
Yolo (co.), Calif. 204/D5
Yolo, Calif. (95697) 204/B8
Yolyn, W. Va. (25654) 312/C7
Yona, Guam 86/K7
Yonago, Japan 81/F6
Yonaguni (isl.), Japan 81/K7
Yoncalla, Oreg. (97499) 291/D4
Yonezawa, Japan 81/K5
Yongamp'o, N. Korea 81/B4
Yongchang, China 77/F4
Yŏngch'ŏn, S. Korea 81/D6
Yongchuan, China 77/G6
Yongdeng, China 77/F4
Yŏngdŏk, S. Korea 81/D5
Yonges Island, S.C. (29494) 296/G6
Yonghe, China 77/H4
Yŏnghŭng, N. Korea 81/C4
Yŏngju, S. Korea 81/D5
Yongning, China 77/G4
Yongren, China 77/F6
Yongxin, China 77/H6
Yongxing, China 77/H6
Yonkers, Georgia (†31014) 217/F6
Yonkers, N.Y. (*10701) 276/O6
Yonne (dept.), France 28/E4
Yonne (riv.), France 28/E3
Yono, Japan 81/O2
Yopal, Colombia 126/D5
Yorba Linda, Calif. (92686) 204/D11
Yorito, Honduras 154/D3
York, Ala. (36925) 195/B6
York (cape), Australia 2/S6
York (cape), Australia 87/E7
York, England 13/F4
York, England 10/F4
York (cape), Greenl. 4/B13
York, Ky. (41184) 237/P3
York (co.), Maine 243/B9
York, Maine (03909) 243/B9
York○, Maine (03909) 243/B9
York (co.), Nebr. 264/G4
York, Nebr. (68467) 264/G4
York (co.), New Bruns. 170/C3
York, N.Y. (14592) 276/E5
York, N. Dak. (58386) 282/L3
York (reg. munic.), Ontario 177/E4
York, Ontario 177/J4
York, Pa. 188/L3
York (co.), Pa. 294/J6
York, Pa. (*17401) 294/J6
York (riv.), Québec 172/D1
York (cape), Queensland 88/G2
York (cape), Queensland 95/B1
York (co.), S.C. 296/E2
York, S.C. (29745) 296/E1
York (co.), Va. 307/P6
York (riv.), Va. 307/P6
York, W. Australia 88/B6
York, W. Australia 92/B1
York (sound), W. Australia 88/C2
York (sound), W. Australia 92/D1
York, Wis. (†54758) 317/D7
York Beach, Maine (03910) 243/B9
Yorke (pen.), S. Australia 88/F7
Yorke (pen.), S. Australia 94/E6
Yorketown, S. Australia 88/F6
Yorketown, S. Australia 94/E6
York Factory, Man. 162/G4
York Factory, Manitoba 179/K2
York Harbor, Maine (03911) 243/B9
York Haven, Pa. (17370) 294/J5
York Landing, Man. 146/J4
York Landing, Manitoba 179/J2
Yorklyn, Del. (19736) 245/R1
Yorkshire, North (co.), England 13/F3
Yorkshire, South (co.), England 13/F4
Yorkshire, West (co.), England 13/J1
Yorkshire, N.Y. (14173) 276/D5
Yorkshire, Ohio (45388) 284/B5
Yorkshire Dales National Park, England 13/E3
York Springs, Pa. (17372) 294/H6
Yorkton, Sask. 146/H4
Yorkton, Sask. 162/F5
Yorkton, Sask. 181/J4
Yorktown, Ark. (71678) 202/G5
Yorktown, Ind. (47396) 227/G4
Yorktown, Iowa (51656) 229/C7
Yorktown, N.J. (†08098) 273/C4
Yorktown, Texas (78164) 303/G9
Yorktown, Va. (23690) 307/R6
Yorktown Heights, N.Y. (10598) 276/N8
Yorkville, Ill. (60560) 222/E2
Yorkville, Ind. (†47022) 227/H6
Yorkville, N.Y. (13495) 276/K4
Yorkville, Ohio (43971) 284/J5
Yorkville, Tenn. (38389) 237/C8
Yoro, Honduras 154/D3
Yoron (isl.), Japan 81/N6
Yorosso, Mali 106/C6
Yosemite, Ky. (42566) 237/M6
Yosemite National Park, Calif. (95389) 204/F6
Yosemite Nat'l Park, Calif. 188/C3
Yosemite Nat'l Park, Calif. 204/F6
Yoshino (riv.), Japan 81/G6
Yoshino-Kumano National Park, Japan 81/H7
Yoshkar-Ola, U.S.S.R. 7/J3
Yoshkar-Ola, U.S.S.R. 52/G3
Yoshkar-Ola, U.S.S.R. 48/E4
Yost, Utah (†84329) 304/A2
Yŏsu, S. Korea 81/C6
Yotala, Bolivia 136/C6
Yotaú, Bolivia 136/D5
Yotvata, Israel 65/D5
Youanmi, W. Australia 92/B5
Youbou, Br. Col. 184/J3
Youghal, Ireland 10/B5
Youghal, Ireland 17/F8
Youghal (bay), Ireland 10/C5
Youghal (bay), Ireland 17/F8
Youghiogheny (riv.), Md. 245/A3
Youghiogheny (dam), Pa. 294/D6
Youghiogheny River (lake), Md. 245/A2
Youghiogheny River (lake), Pa. 294/D6
Young, Ariz. (85554) 198/D4
Young, N.S. Wales 88/H6
Young, N.S. Wales 97/E4
Young (cape), N. Zealand 100/D7
Young (mt.), North. Terr. 93/D3
Young, Sask. 181/F4
Young (co.), Texas 303/F4
Young, Uruguay 145/B3
Young America, Ind. (46998) 227/E3
Young America, Minn. (55397) 255/E6
Youngcane, Georgia (†30512) 217/D1
Young Cove, Nova Scotia 168/C4
Young Harris, Georgia (30582) 217/E1
Youngs Cove, New Bruns. 170/E3
Youngs Creek, Ind. (†47454) 227/D8
Youngs Creek, Ky. (†40759) 237/N7
Youngstown, Alberta 182/E4
Youngstown, Fla. (32466) 212/D6
Youngstown, Ind. (†47808) 227/C6
Youngstown, N.Y. (14174) 276/C4
Youngstown, Ohio (*44501) 284/J3
Youngstown, Ohio 188/K2
Youngsville, La. (70592) 238/G6
Youngsville, N. Mex. (87064) 274/C2
Youngsville, N.Y. (12791) 276/L7
Youngsville, N.C. (27596) 281/N2
Youngsville, Pa. (16371) 294/D2
Youngtown, Ariz. (85363) 198/C5
Youngwood, Pa. (15697) 294/D5
Yountville, Calif. (94599) 204/C5
Youshashan, China 77/D4
Youssoufia, Morocco 106/C2
Youyang, China 77/G6
Yozgat (prov.), Turkey 63/F3
Yozgat, Turkey 59/B2
Yozgat, Turkey 63/F3
Ypacaraí, Paraguay 144/B5
Ypané, Paraguay 144/B5
Ypané (riv.), Paraguay 144/D3
Ypé Jhú, Paraguay 144/E3
Ypoá (lake), Paraguay 144/B5
Ypres (Ieper), Belgium 27/B7
Ypsilanti, Georgia (†31827) 217/D5
Ypsilanti, Mich. (48197) 250/F6
Ypsilanti, N. Dak. (58497) 282/N6
Yreka, Calif. 188/B2
Yreka, Calif. (96097) 204/C2
Yser (riv.), Belgium 27/B7
Yssingeaux, France 28/F5
Ystad, Sweden 18/H9
Ystradgynlais, Wales 13/D6
Ythan (riv.), Scotland 15/F3
Yuan (riv.), China 54/M7
Yuan Jiang (riv.), China 77/H6
Yuanling, China 77/G6
Yuanmou, China 77/F6
Yuanping, China 77/H4
Yuba (co.), Calif. 204/D4
Yuba (riv.), Calif. 204/D4
Yuba, Okla. (†74721) 288/O7
Yuba, Wis. (54672) 317/F8
Yuba City, Calif. (95991) 204/D4
Yubari, Japan 81/L2
Yubetsu, Japan 81/L1
Yucaipa, Calif. (92399) 204/J9
Yucatán (chan.) 146/K7
Yucatán (state), Mexico 150/P6
Yucatán (pen.), Mexico 146/K7
Yucatán (pen.), Mexico 150/P7
Yucca, Ariz. (86438) 198/A4
Yucca Flat (basin), Nev. 266/E6
Yucca House Nat'l Mon., Colo. 208/B8
Yucca Valley, Calif. (92284) 204/J9
Yuci (Yütze), China 77/H4
Yudu, China 77/J6
Yuendumu, North. Terr. 93/B7
Yuexi, China 77/F6
Yueyang, China 77/H6
Yug (riv.), U.S.S.R. 52/G2
Yugorskiy (pen.), U.S.S.R. 52/K1
Yugoslavia 2/K3
Yugoslavia 7/F4
YUGOSLAVIA 45/C3
Yuhuan (isl.), China 77/K6
Yukon (riv.) 2/B2
Yukon (riv.) 146/C3
Yukon (riv.) 4/C17
Yukon (riv.), Alaska 188/C5
Yukon (riv.), Alaska 196/F2
Yukon, Mo. (65589) 261/J8
Yukon, Okla. (73099) 288/L3
Yukon, Pa. (15698) 294/C5
Yukon (riv.), Yukon 162/C3
Yukon (riv.), Yukon 187/E3
Yukon-Charley Rivers Nat'l Preserve, Alaska 196/K2
Yukon Territory 162/C3
Yukon Territory (terr.), Canada 146/E3
YUKON TERRITORY 187
Yüksekova, Turkey 63/L4
Yukuhashi, Japan 81/E7
Yule (riv.), W. Australia 92/B3
Yulee, Fla. (32097) 212/E1
Yuli (Lopnur), China 77/C3
Yulin, Guangxi Zhuangzu, China 77/G7
Yulin, Shanxi, China 77/G4
Yuma, Ariz. 188/D4
Yuma, Ariz. 146/G6
Yuma (co.), Ariz. 198/A5
Yuma, Ariz. (85364) 198/A6
Yuma (des.), Ariz. 198/A6
Yuma (co.), Colo. 208/P2
Yuma, Colo. (80759) 208/O2
Yuma (bay), Dom. Rep. 158/F6
Yuma, Tenn. (38390) 237/E9
Yuma Ind. Res., Calif. 204/L11
Yuma Marine Corps Air Sta., Ariz. 198/A6
Yuma Proving Ground, Ariz. 198/A6
Yumbel, Chile 138/E1
Yumbo, Colombia 126/B6
Yumen, China 77/E4
Yumen, China 54/L6
Yumenzhen, China 77/E3
Yumin, China 77/B2
Yumurtalık, Turkey 63/F4
Yuna (riv.), Dom. Rep. 158/E5
Yuna, W. Australia 92/A5
Yunak, Turkey 63/D3
Yunan, China 77/H7
Yunaska (isl.), Alaska 196/D4
Yuncheng, China 77/H4
Yungas, Las (reg.), Bolivia 136/B5
Yungay, Chile 138/E1
Yungkia (Wenzhou), China 77/J6
Yunguyo, Peru 128/H11
Yunnan (prov.), China 77/F7
Yunta, S. Australia 94/F5
Yunxi, China 77/G5
Yunxiao, China 77/J7
Yunyang, China 77/G5
Yupukari, Guyana 131/B4

GEOGRAPHICAL TERMS

A. = Arabic Burm. = Burmese Camb. = Cambodian Ch. = Chinese Czech. = Czechoslovakian Dan. = Danish Du. = Dutch Finn. = Finnish Fr. = French Ger. = German Ice. = Icelandic It. = Italian Jap. = Japanese Mong. = Mongol Nor. = Norwegian Per. = Persian Port. = Portuguese Russ. = Russian Sp. = Spanish Sw. = Swedish Turk. = Turkish

A	Nor., Sw.	Stream
Aas	Dan., Nor.	Hills
Abajo	Sp.	Lower
Ada, Adasi	Turk.	Island
Altipiano	It.	Plateau
Altiplano	Sp.	Plateau
Alv, Alf, Elf	Sw.	River
Arrecife	Sp.	Reef
Asa	Nor., Sw.	Hill
Asaga	Turk.	Lower
Austral	Sp.	Southern
Baai	Du.	Bay
Bab	Arabic	Gate or Strait
Bahia	Sp.	Bay
Bahr	Arabic	Marsh, Lake, Sea, River
Baia	Port.	Bay
Baie	Fr.	Bay, Gulf
Baizo	Port.	Low
Bakke	Dan.	Hill
Bana	Jap.	Cape
Bañados	Sp.	Marshes
Band	Per.	Mt. Range
Bandao	Ch.	Peninsula
Bandar	Per.	Harbor
Barra	Sp.	Reef
Bel	Turk.	Pass
Belt	Ger.	Strait
Ben	Gaelic	Mountain
Bera	Du.	Mountain
Berg	Ger., Du.	Mountain
Bir	Arabic	Well
Boca	Sp.	Gulf, Inlet
Boğhaz	Turk.	Strait
Bolshoi, Bolshaya	Russ.	Big
Bolson	Sp.	Depression
Bong	Korean	Mountain
Boreal	Sp.	Northern
Breen	Nor.	Glacier
Bro	Dan., Nor., Sw.	Bridge
Bucht	Ger.	Bay
Bugt	Dan.	Bay
Bukhta	Russ.	Bay
Bukit	Malay	Hill, Mountain
Bukt	Nor., Sw.	Bay, Gulf
Burnu, Burun	Turk.	Cape, Point
By	Dan., Nor., Sw.	Town
Cabo	Port., Sp.	Cape
Campos	Port.	Plains
Canal	Port., Sp.	Channel
Cap, Capo	Fr., It.	Cape
Cataratas	Sp.	Falls
Catena	It.	Mt. Range
Catingas	Port.	Open Woodlands
Cayos	Sp.	Islands
Central, Centrale	Fr., It.	Middle
Cerrito, Cerro	Sp.	Hill
Cerros	Sp.	Hills, Mountains
Chai	Turk.	River
Chott	Arabic	Salt Lake
Ciénaga	Sp.	Swamp
Ciudad	Sp.	City
Col	Fr.	Pass
Cordillera	Sp.	Mt. Range, Mts.
Côte	Fr.	Coast
Csatoria	Magyar	Canal
Cuchilla	Sp.	Mt. Range
Curiche	Sp.	Swamp
Dağ, Daği	Turk.	Mountain, Peak
Dağlari	Turk.	Mt. Range
Dal	Nor., Sw.	Valley
Dar	Arabic	Land
Dar'ya	Russ.	River
Daryacheh	Per.	Marshy Lake
Dasht	Per.	Desert, Plain
Deniz, Denizi	Turk.	Sea, Lake
Desierto	Sp.	Desert
Détroit	Fr.	Strait
Djeziret	Arabic, Turk.	Island
Do	Korean	Island
Doi	Thai	Mountain
Eiland	Du.	Island
Elv	Dan., Nor.	River
Embalse	Sp.	Reservoir
Emi	Berber	Mountain
Erg	Arabic	Dune, Desert
Eski	Turk.	Old
Est, Este	Fr., Port., Sp.	East
Estero	Sp.	Estuary, Creek
Estrecho, Estreito	Sp., Port.	Strait
Etang	Fr.	Pond, Lagoon, Lake
Feng	Ch.	Mountain
Fiume	It.	River
Fjäll	Sw.	Mountain
Fjeld, Fjell	Nor.	Hills, Mountain
Fjord	Dan., Nor., Sw.	Fiord
Fleuve	Fr.	River
Fljót	Ice.	Stream
Fluss	Ger.	River
Fors	Sw.	Waterfall
Fos, Foss	Dan., Nor.	Waterfall
Gamla	Nor.	Old
Gamle	Dan.	Old
Gata	Jap.	Lake
Gawa	Jap.	River
Gebel	Arabic	Mountain
Gebergte	Du.	Mt. Range
Gebirge	Ger.	Mt. Range
Gobi	Mongol	Desert
Goe	Jap.	Pass
Gol	Mongol, Turk.	Lake, Stream
Golf	Ger., Du.	Gulf
Golfe	Fr.	Gulf
Golfo	Sp., It., Port.	Gulf
Gölü	Turk.	Lake
Gora	Russ.	Mountain
Grand, Grande	Fr., Sp.	Big
Groot	Du.	Big
Gross	Ger.	Big
Grosso	It., Port.	Big
Guba	Russ.	Bay, Gulf
Gunto	Jap.	Archipelago
Gunung	Malay	Mountain
Hai	Ch.	Sea
Haixia	Ch.	Strait
Halbinsel	Ger.	Peninsula
Hamáda, Hammada	Arabic	Rocky Plateau
Hamn	Sw.	Harbor
Hamún	Per.	Marsh
Hanto	Jap.	Peninsula
Has, Hassi	Arabic	Well
Hav	Dan., Nor., Sw.	Sea, Ocean
Havet	Nor.	Bay
Havn	Dan., Nor.	Harbor
Havre	Fr.	Harbor
He	Ch.	River, Stream
Higashi, Higasi	Jap.	East
Hochebene	Ger.	Plateau
Hoek	Du.	Cape
Hoku	Jap.	North
Holm	Dan., Nor., Sw.	Island
Hory	Czech.	Mountains
Hoved	Dan., Nor.	Cape, Promontory
Hu	Ch.	Lake
Huang	Ch.	Yellow
Huk	Dan., Nor., Sw.	Point
Hus, Huus	Dan., Nor., Sw.	House
Idehan	Arabic	Desert
Ile	Fr.	Island
Ilet	Fr.	Islet
Ilot	Fr.	Islet
Indre	Dan., Nor.	Inner
Inferieur, Inferiore	Fr., It.	Lower
Inner, Inre	Sw.	Inner
Insel	Ger.	Island
Irmak	Turk.	River
Isla	Sp.	Island
Isola	It.	Island
Jabal, Jebel	Arabic	Mountains
Järvi	Finn.	Lake
Jaure	Sw.	Lake
Jiang	Ch.	River, Stream
Jima	Jap.	Island
Joki	Finn.	River
Kaap	Du.	Cape
Kabir, Kebir	Arabic	Big
Kai	Jap.	Sea
Kaikyo	Jap.	Strait
Kami	Turk.	Upper
Kanaal	Du.	Canal
Kanal	Russ., Ger.	Canal, Channel
Kao	Thai	Mountain
Kap, Kapp	Nor., Sw., Ice.	Cape
Kaupunki	Finn.	Town
Kawa	Jap.	River
Khao	Thai	Mountain
Khrebet	Russ.	Mt. Range
Kita	Jap.	North
Klein	Du., Ger.	Small
Klint	Dan.	Promontory
Kô	Jap.	Lake
Ko	Thai	Island
Koh	Camb., Khmer	Island
Kop	Du.	Peak, Head
Köping	Sw.	Market, Borough
Körfez, Körfezi	Turk.	Gulf
Kosa	Russ.	Spit
Kosui	Jap.	Lake
Kraal	Du.	Native Village
Kuchuk	Turk.	Small
Kuh, Kuhha	Per.	Mt. Range, Mts.
Kul	Sinkiang Turki	Lake
Kum	Turk.	Desert
Kuro	Jap.	Black
Laag	Du.	Low
Lac	Fr.	Lake
Lago	Port., Sp., It.	Lake
Lagoa	Port.	Lagoon
Laguna	Sp.	Lagoon
Lagune	Fr.	Lagoon
Lahti	Finn.	Bay, Bight
Län	Sw.	County
Liedao	Ch.	Islands, Archipelago
Lilla	Sw.	Small
Lille	Dan., Nor.	Small
Ling	Ch.	Mountain
Llanos	Sp.	Plains
Mae Nam	Thai	River
Mali, Malaya	Russ.	Small
Man	Korean	Bay
Mar	Sp., Port.	Sea
Mare	It.	Sea
Medio	Sp.	Middle
Meer	Du.	Lake
Meer	Ger.	Sea
Mer	Fr.	Sea
Meridionale	It.	Southern
Meseta	Sp.	Plateau
Middelst, Midden	Du.	Middle
Minami	Jap.	Southern
Mis	Russ.	Cape
Misaki	Jap.	Cape
Mittel	Ger.	Middle
Mont	Fr.	Mountain
Montagne	Fr.	Mountain
Montaña	Sp.	Mountains
Monte	Sp., It., Port.	Mountain
More	Russ.	Sea
Mörön	Mong.	Stream
Morro	Port., Sp.	Mountain, Promontory
Morue	Fr.	Hill
Moyen	Fr.	Middle
Muang	Siamese	Town
Mui	Vietnamese	Cape, Point
Mys	Russ.	Cape
Nada	Jap.	Sea
Naka	Jap.	Middle
Nam	Burm., Lao	River
Namakzar	Per.	Salt Waste
Nan	Jap.	South
Nes	Nor.	Cape, Point
Nevado	Sp.	Snow-covered Peak
Nieder	Ger.	Lower
Nishi, Nisi	Jap.	West
Nizhni, Nizhnyaya	Russ.	Lower
Njarga	Finn.	Peninsula, Promontory
Nong	Thai	Lake
Noord	Du.	North
Nord	Fr., Ger.	North
Norte	Sp., It., Port.	North
Nos	Russ.	Cape
Novi, Novaya	Russ.	New
Nur, Nuur	Ch., Mong.	Lake
Nuruu	Mong.	Mountains
Nusa	Malay	Island
Ny, Nya	Nor., Sw.	New
O	Jap.	Big
Ö	Nor., Sw.	Island
Ober	Ger.	Upper
Occidental, Occidentale	Sp., It.	Western
Odde	Dan.	Point
Oeste	Port.	West
Ooster	Du.	Eastern
Opper, Over	Du.	Upper
Oriental	Sp., Fr.	Eastern
Orientale	It.	Eastern
Orta	Turk.	Middle
Ost	Ger.	East
Ostrov	Russ.	Island
Ouest	Fr.	West
öy	Nor.	Island
Ozero	Russ.	Lake
Pampa	Sp.	Plain
Pas	Fr.	Channel, Strait
Paso	Sp.	Pass
Passo	It., Port.	Pass
Peña	Sp.	Rock, Mountain
Pendi	Ch.	Basin
Penisola	It.	Peninsula
Pequeño	Sp.	Small
Pereval	Russ.	Pass
Peski	Russ.	Desert
Petit, Petite	Fr.	Small
Phu	Lao, Annamese	Mtn.
Pic	Fr.	Mountain
Piccolo	It.	Small
Pico	Port., Sp.	Mountain, Peak
Pik	Russ.	Mountain, Peak
Piton	Fr.	Mountain, Peak
Planalto	Port.	Plateau
Plato	Russ.	Plateau
Pointe	Fr.	Point
Poluostrov	Russ.	Peninsula
Ponta	Port.	Point
Presa	Sp.	Reservoir
Presqu'île	Fr.	Peninsula
Proliv	Russ.	Strait
Pulou, Pulo	Malay	Island
Punt	Du.	Point
Punta	Sp., It., Port.	Point
Qiryat	Hebrew	City, Settlement
Qum	Turk.	Desert
Qundao	Ch.	Islands
Rada	Sp.	Inlet
Rade	Fr.	Bay, Inlet
Ras	Arabic	Cape
Reka	Russ.	River
Retto	Jap.	Archipelago
Ria	Sp.	Estuary
Río	Sp.	River
Rivier, Rivière	Du., Fr.	River
Rud	Per.	River
Sai	Jap.	West
Saki	Jap.	Cape
Salar, Salina	Sp.	Salt Deposit
Salto	Sp., Port.	Falls
San	Jap., Korean	Hill
Sanmaek	Korean	Mt. Range
Schiereiland	Du.	Peninsula
Se	Camb., Khmer	River
See	Ger.	Sea, Lake
Selvas	Sp., Port.	Woods, Forest
Seno	Sp.	Bay, Gulf
Serra	Port.	Mts.
Serranía	Sp.	Mts.
Seto	Jap.	Strait
Settentrionale	It.	Northern
Severni, Severnaya	Russ.	North
Shamo	Ch.	Desert
Shan	Ch., Jap.	Hill, Mts.
Shankou	Ch.	Pass
Shatt	Arabic	River
Shima	Jap.	Island
Shimo	Jap.	Lower
Shin	Jap.	Land
Shiro	Jap.	White
Shoto	Jap.	Islands
Si	Ch.	West
Sierra	Sp.	Mt. Range, Mts.
Sjö	Nor., Sw.	Lake, Sea
Sok, Suk, Souk	Arabic	Market
Song	Annamese	River
Sopka	Russ.	Volcano
Spitze	Ger.	Mt. Peak
Sredni, Srednyaya	Russ.	Middle
Stad	Dan., Nor., Sw.	City
Stari, Staraya	Russ.	Old
Step	Russ.	Treeless Plain
Straat	Du.	Strait
Strasse	Ger.	Strait
Stretto	It.	Strait
Ström	Dan., Nor., Sw.	Sound
Stung	Camb., Khmer	River
Su	Turk.	River
Sud, Süd	Sp., Fr., Ger.	South
Suido	Jap.	Strait, Channel
Sul	Port.	South
Sund	Dan., Nor., Sw.	Sound
Sungei	Malay	River
Supérieur	Fr.	Upper
Superior, Superiore	Sp., It.	Upper
Sur	Sp.	South
Suyu	Turk.	River
Ta	Ch.	Big
Tafelland	Du.	Plateau
Tagh	Turk.	Mt. Range
Take	Jap.	Peak, Ridge
Takht	Arabic	Lower
Tal	Ger.	Valley
Tanjung	Malay	Cape, Point
Tell	Arabic	Hill
Thale	Thai	Sea, Lake
Tind	Nor.	Peak
Tö	Jap.	East
To	Jap.	Island
Toge	Jap.	Pass
Trask	Finn.	Lake
Tugh	Somali	Dry River
Ujung	Malay	Point
Umi	Jap.	Bay
Unter	Ger.	Lower
Ura	Jap.	Inlet
Uul	Mong.	Mountain
Val	Fr.	Valley
Vatn	Nor.	Lake
Vecchio	It.	Old
Veld	Du.	Plain, Field
Velho	Port.	Old
Verkhni	Russ.	Upper
Vesi	Finn.	Lake
Viejo	Sp.	Old
Vik	Nor., Sw.	Bay
Vishni, Vishnyaya	Russ.	High
Vodokhranilishche	Russ.	Reservoir
Volcán	Sp.	Volcano
Vostochni, Vostochnaya	Russ.	East, Eastern
Wadi	Arabic	Dry River
Wald	Ger.	Forest
Wan	Jap.	Bay
Westersch	Du.	Western
Wüste	Ger.	Desert
Yama	Jap.	Mountain
Yug, Yuzhni, Yuzhnaya	Russ.	South, Southern
Zaki	Jap.	Cape
Zaliv	Russ.	Bay, Gulf
Zangbo	Tibetan	River, Stream
Zapadni, Zapadnaya	Russ.	Western
Zee	Du.	Sea
Zemlya	Russ.	Land
Zizhiqu	Ch.	Autonomous Region
Zuid	Du.	South

MAP PROJECTIONS

by Erwin Raisz

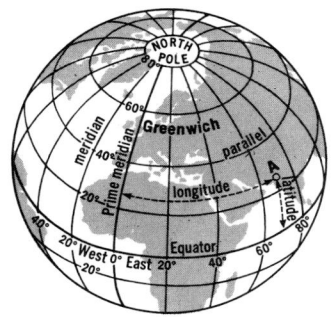

Our earth is rotating around its *axis* once a day. The two end points of its axis are the *poles;* the line circling the earth midway between the poles is the *equator.* The arc from either of the poles to the equator is divided into 90 *degrees.* The distance, expressed in degrees, from the equator to any point is its *latitude* and circles of equal latitude are the *parallels.* On maps it is customary to show parallels of evenly-spaced degrees such as every fifth or every tenth.

The equator is divided into 360 degrees. Lines circling from pole to pole through the degree points on the equator are called *meridians.* They are all equal in length but by international agreement the meridian passing through the Greenwich Observatory in London has been chosen as *prime meridian.* The distance, expressed in degrees, from the prime meridian to any point is its *longitude.* While meridians are all equal in length, parallels become shorter and shorter as they approach the poles. Whereas one degree of latitude represents everywhere approximately 69 miles, one degree of longitude varies from 69 miles at the equator to nothing at the poles.

Each degree is divided into 60 minutes and each minute into 60 seconds. One minute of latitude equals a nautical mile.

The map is flat but the earth is nearly spherical. Neither a rubber ball nor any part of a rubber ball may be flattened without stretching or tearing unless the part is very small. To present the curved surface of the earth on a flat map is not difficult as long as the areas under consideration are small, but the mapping of countries, continents, or the whole earth requires some kind of *projection.* Any regular set of parallels and meridians upon which a map can be drawn makes a map projection. Many systems are used.

In any projection only the parallels or the meridians or some other set of lines can be *true* (the same length as on the globe of corresponding scale); all other lines are too long or too short. Only on a globe is it possible to have both the parallels and the meridians true. The scale given on a flat map cannot be true everywhere. The construction of the various projections begins usually with laying out the parallels or meridians which have true lengths.

Rectangular Projection

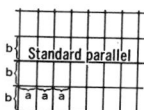

RECTANGULAR PROJECTION — This is a set of evenly-placed meridians and horizontal parallels. The central or *standard parallel* and all meridians are true. All other parallels are either too long or too short. The projection is used for simple maps of small areas, as city plans, etc.

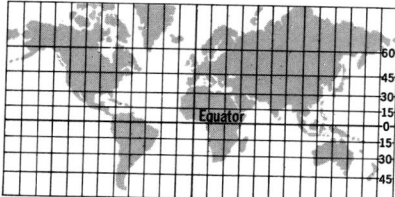

Mercator Projection

MERCATOR PROJECTION — In this projection the meridians are evenly-spaced vertical lines. The parallels are horizontal, spaced so that their length has the same relation to the meridians as on a globe. As the meridians converge at higher latitudes on the globe, while on the map they do not, the parallels have to be drawn also farther and farther apart to maintain the correct relationship. When every very small area has the same shape as on a globe we call the projection *conformal.* The most interesting quality of this projection is that all *compass directions* appear as straight lines. For this reason it is generally used for marine charts. It is also frequently used for world maps in spite of the fact that the high latitudes are very much exaggerated in size. Only the equator is true to scale; all other parallels and meridians are too long. The Mercator projection did *not* derive from projecting a globe upon a cylinder.

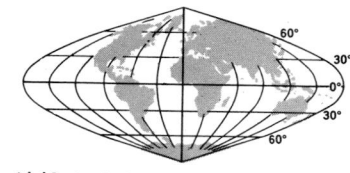

Sinusoidal Projection

SINUSOIDAL PROJECTION — The parallels are truly-spaced horizontal lines. They are divided truly and the connecting curves make the meridians. It does not make a good world map because the outer regions are distorted, but the

central portion is good and this part is often used for maps of Africa and South America. Every part of the map has the same area as the corresponding area on the globe. It is an *equal-area* projection.

MOLLWEIDE PROJECTION — The meridians are equally-spaced ellipses; the parallels are horizontal lines spaced so that every belt of latitude should have the same area as on a globe. This projection is popular for world maps, especially in European atlases.

Mollweide Projection

GOODE'S INTERRUPTED PROJECTIONS—Only the good central part of the Mollweide or sinusoidal (or both) projection is used and the oceans are cut. This makes an equal-area map with little distortion of shape. It is commonly used for world maps.

Goode's Interrupted Projection

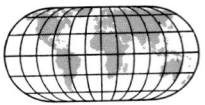

Eckert Projection

ECKERT PROJECTIONS — These are similar to the sinusoidal or the Mollweide projections, but the poles are shown as lines half the length of the equator. There are several variants; the meridians are either sine curves or ellipses; the parallels are horizontal and spaced either evenly or so as to make the projection equal area. Their use for world maps is increasing. The figure shows the elliptical equal-area variant.

CONIC PROJECTION — The original idea of the conic projection is that of capping the globe by a cone upon which both the parallels and meridians are projected from the center of the globe. The cone is then cut open and laid flat. A cone can be made tangent to any chosen *standard parallel*.

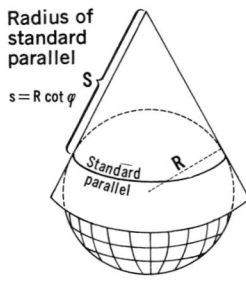

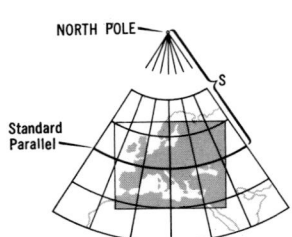

The actually-used conic projection is a modification of this idea. The radius of the standard parallel is obtained as above. The meridians are straight radiating lines spaced truly on the standard parallel. The parallels are concentric circles spaced at true distances. All parallels except the standard are too long. The projection is used for maps of countries in middle latitudes, as it presents good shapes with small scale error.

Conic Projection

There are several variants: The use of *two standard parallels*, one near the top, the other near the bottom of the map, reduces the scale error. In the *Albers projection* the parallels are spaced unevenly, to make the projection equal-area. This is a good projection for the United States. In the *Lambert conformal conic projection* the parallels are spaced so that any small quadrangle of the grid should have the same shape as on the globe. This is the best projection for air-navigation charts as it has relatively straight azimuths.

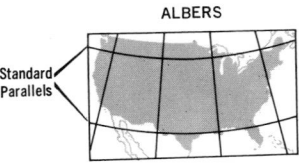

Albers Projection

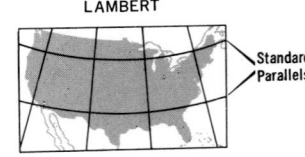

Lambert Conformal Conic Projection

An *azimuth* is a great-circle direction reckoned clockwise from north. A *great-circle direction* points to a place along the shortest line on the earth's surface. This is not the same as compass direction. The center of a great circle is the center of the globe.

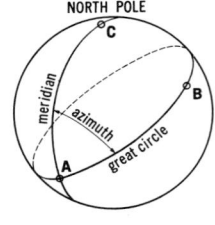

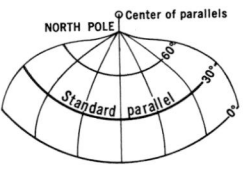

BONNE PROJECTION — The parallels are laid out exactly as in the conic projection. All parallels are divided truly and the connecting curves make the meridians. It is an equal-area projection. It is used for maps of the northern continents, as Asia, Europe, and North America.

Bonne Projection

POLYCONIC PROJECTION — The central meridian is divided truly. The parallels are non-concentric circles, the radii of which are obtained by drawing tangents to the globe as though the globe were covered by several cones rather than by only one. Each parallel is divided truly and the connecting curves make the meridians. All meridians except the central one are too long. This projection is used for large-scale topographic sheets — less often for countries or continents.

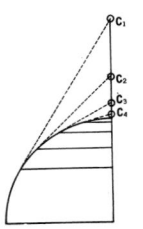

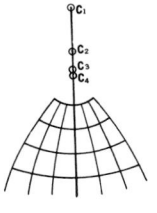

Polyconic Projection

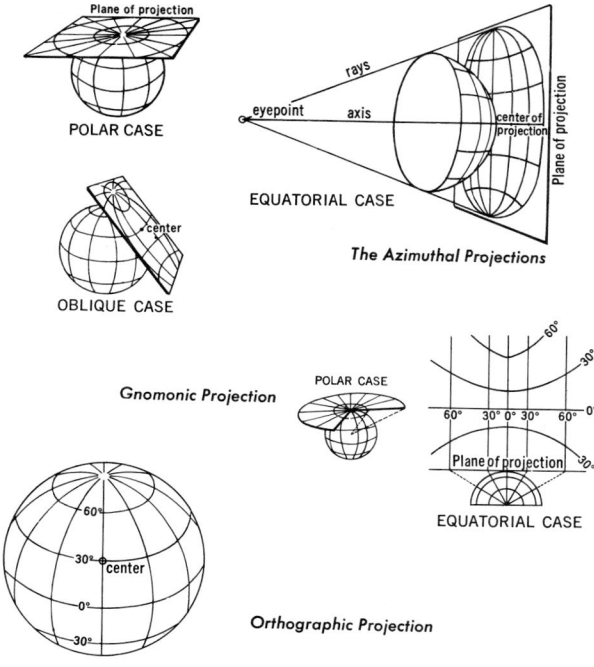

The Azimuthal Projections

Gnomonic Projection

Orthographic Projection

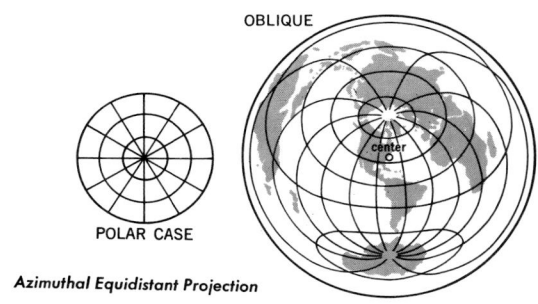

Azimuthal Equidistant Projection

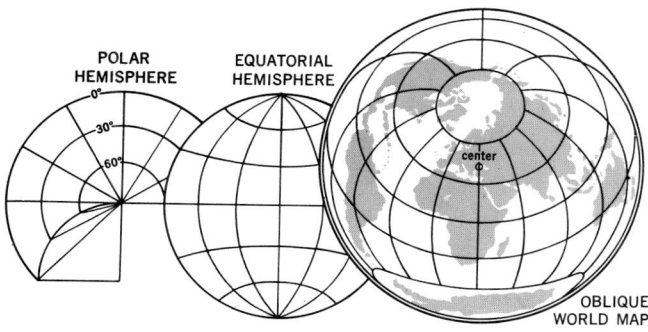

Lambert Azimuthal Equal-Area Projection

THE AZIMUTHAL PROJECTIONS — In this group a part of the globe is projected from an eyepoint onto a plane. The eyepoint can be at different distances, making different projections. The plane of projection can be tangent at the equator, at a pole, or at any other point on which we want to focus attention. The most important quality of all azimuthal projections is that they show every point at its true direction (azimuth) from the center point, and all points equally distant from the center point will be equally distant on the map also.

GNOMONIC PROJECTION — This projection has the eyepoint at the center of the globe Only the central part is good; the outer regions are badly distorted. Yet the projection has one important quality, all great circles being shown as straight lines. For this reason it is used for laying out the routes for long range flying or trans-oceanic navigation.

ORTHOGRAPHIC PROJECTION — This projection has the eyepoint at infinite distance and the projecting rays are parallel. The polar or equatorial varieties are rare but the oblique case became very popular on account of its visual quality. It looks like a picture of a globe. Although the distortion on the peripheries is extreme, we see it correctly because the eye perceives it not as a map but as a picture of a three-dimensional globe. Obviously only a hemisphere (half globe) can be shown.

Some azimuthal projections do not derive from the actual process of projecting from an eyepoint, but are arrived at by other means:

AZIMUTHAL EQUIDISTANT PROJECTION — This is the only projection in which every point is shown both at true great-circle direction and at true distance from the center point, but all other directions and distances are distorted. The principle of the projection can best be understood from the polar case. Most polar maps are in this projection. The oblique case is used for radio direction finding, for earthquake research, and in long-distance flying. A separate map has to be constructed for each central point selected.

LAMBERT AZIMUTHAL EQUAL-AREA PROJECTION—The construction of this projection can best be understood from the polar case. All three cases are widely used. It makes a good polar map and it is often extended to include the southern continents. It is the most common projection used for maps of the Eastern and Western Hemispheres, and it is a good projection for continents as it shows correct areas with relatively little distortion of shape. Most of the continent maps in this atlas are in this projection.

IN THIS ATLAS, on almost all maps, parallels and meridians have been marked because they are useful for the following:

(a) They show the north-south and east-west directions which appear on many maps at oblique angles especially near the margins.

(b) With the help of parallels and meridians every place can be exactly located; for instance, New York City is at 41° N and 74° W on any map.

(c) They help to measure distances even in the distorted parts of the map. The scale given on each map is true only along certain lines which are specified in the foregoing discussion for each projection. One degree of latitude equals nearly 69 statute miles or 60 nautical miles. The length of one degree of longitude varies (1° long. = 1° lat. × cos lat.).

WORLD STATISTICAL TABLES

Elements of the Solar System

	Mean Distance from Sun: in Miles	in Kilometers	Period of Revolution around Sun	Period of Rotation on Axis	Equatorial Diameter: in Miles	in Kilometers	Surface Gravity (Earth = 1)	Mass (Earth = 1)	Mean Density (Water = 1)	Number of Satellites
MERCURY	35,990,000	57,900,000	87.97 days	59 days	3,032	4,880	0.38	0.055	5.5	0
VENUS	67,240,000	108,200,000	224.70 days	243 days†	7,523	12,106	0.90	0.815	5.25	0
EARTH	93,000,000	149,700,000	365.26 days	23h 56m	7,926	12,755	1.00	1.00	5.5	1
MARS	141,730,000	228,100,000	687.00 days	24h 37m	4,220	6,790	0.38	0.107	4.0	2
JUPITER	483,880,000	778,700,000	11.86 years	9h 50m	88,750	142,800	2.87	317.9	1.3	16
SATURN	887,130,000	1,427,700,000	29.46 years	10h 14m	74,580	120,020	1.32	95.2	0.7	17
URANUS	1,783,700,000	2,870,500,000	84.01 years	10h 49m†	31,600	50,900	0.93	14.6·	1.3	5
NEPTUNE	2,795,500,000	4,498,800,000	164.79 years	15h 48m	30,200	48,600	1.23	17.2	1.8	3
PLUTO	3,667,900,000	5,902,800,000	247.70 years	6.39 days (?)	1,500	2,400	0.03 (?)	0.01(?)	0.7(?)	1

†Retrograde motion

Facts About the Sun

Equatorial diameter	865,000 miles	1,392,000 kilometers
Period of rotation on axis	25-35 days*	
Orbit of galaxy	every 225 million years	
Surface gravity (Earth = 1)	27.8	
Mass (Earth = 1)	333,000	
Density (Water = 1)	1.4	
Mean distance from Earth	93,000,000 miles	149,700,000 kilometers

*Rotation of 25 days at Equator, decreasing to about 35 days at the poles.

Facts About the Moon

Equatorial diameter	2,160 miles	3,476 kilometers
Period of rotation on axis	27 days, 7 hours, 43 minutes	
Period of revolution around Earth (sidereal month)	27 days, 7 hours, 43 minutes	
Phase period between new moons (synodic month)	29 days, 12 hours, 44 minutes	
Surface gravity (Earth = 1)	0.16	
Mass (Earth = 1)	0.0123	
Density (Water = 1)	3.34	
Maximum distance from Earth	252,710 miles	406,690 kilometers
Minimum distance from Earth	221,460 miles	356,400 kilometers
Mean distance from Earth	238,860 miles	384,400 kilometers

Dimensions of the Earth

	Area in Sq. Miles	Sq. Kilometers
Superficial area	197,751,000	512,175,090
Land surface	57,970,000	150,142,300
Water surface	139,781,000	362,032,790

	Miles	Kilometers
Equatorial circumference	24,902	40,075
Polar circumference	24,860	40,007
Equatorial diameter	7,926.68	12,756.4
Polar diameter	7,899.99	12,713.4
Equatorial radius	3,963.34	6,378.2
Polar radius	3,949.99	6,356.7
Volume of the Earth	2.6×10^{11} cubic miles	10.84×10^{11} cubic kilometers
Mass or weight	6.6×10^{21} short tons	6.0×10^{21} metric tons
Maximum distance from Sun	94,600,000 miles	152,000,000 kilometers
Minimum distance from Sun	91,300,000 miles	147,000,000 kilometers

The Continents

	Area in: Sq. Miles	Sq. Km.	Percent of World's Land
Asia	17,128,500	44,362,815	29.5
Africa	11,707,000	30,321,130	20.2
North America	9,363,000	24,250,170	16.2
South America	6,875,000	17,806,250	11.8
Antarctica	5,500,000	14,245,000	9.5
Europe	4,057,000	10,507,630	7.0
Australia	2,966,136	7,682,300	5.1

Oceans and Major Seas

	Area in: Sq. Miles	Sq. Km.	Greatest Depth in: Feet	Meters
Pacific Ocean	64,186,000	166,241,700	36,198	11,033
Atlantic Ocean	31,862,000	82,522,600	28,374	8,648
Indian Ocean	28,350,000	73,426,500	25,344	7,725
Arctic Ocean	5,427,000	14,056,000	17,880	5,450
Caribbean Sea	970,000	2,512,300	24,720	7,535
Mediterranean Sea	969,000	2,509,700	16,896	5,150
Bering Sea	875,000	2,266,250	15,800	4,800
Gulf of Mexico	600,000	1,554,000	12,300	3,750
Sea of Okhotsk	590,000	1,528,100	11,070	3,370
East China Sea	482,000	1,248,400	9,500	2,900
Sea of Japan	389,000	1,007,500	12,280	3,740
Hudson Bay	317,500	822,300	846	258
North Sea	222,000	575,000	2,200	670
Black Sea	185,000	479,150	7,365	2,245
Red Sea	169,000	437,700	7,200	2,195
Baltic Sea	163,000	422,170	1,506	459

Major Ship Canals

	Length in: Miles	Kms.	Minimum Feet	Depth in: Meters
Volga-Baltic, U.S.S.R.	225	362	—	5
Baltic-White Sea, U.S.S.R.	140	225	16	5
Suez, Egypt	100.76	162	42	13
Albert, Belgium	80	129	16.5	5
Moscow-Volga, U.S.S.R.	80	129	18	6
Volga-Don, U.S.S.R.	62	100	—	—
Göta, Sweden	54	87	10	3
Kiel (Nord-Ostsee), W. Ger.	53.2	86	38	12
Panama Canal, Panama	50.72	82	41.6	13
Houston Ship, U.S.A.	50	81	36	11

Largest Islands

	Area in: Sq. Mi.	Sq. Km.		Area in: Sq. Mi.	Sq. Km.		Area in: Sq. Mi.	Sq. Km.
Greenland	840,000	2,175,600	South I., New Zealand	58,393	151,238	Hokkaido, Japan	28,983	75,066
New Guinea	305,000	789,950	Java, Indonesia	48,842	126,501	Banks, Canada	27,038	70,028
Borneo	290,000	751,100	North I., New Zealand	44,187	114,444	Ceylon, Sri Lanka	25,332	65,610
Madagascar	226,400	586,376	Newfoundland, Canada	42,031	108,860	Tasmania, Australia	24,600	63,710
Baffin, Canada	195,928	507,454	Cuba	40,533	104,981	Svalbard, Norway	23,957	62,049
Sumatra, Indonesia	164,000	424,760	Luzon, Philippines	40,420	104,688	Devon, Canada	21,331	55,247
Honshu, Japan	88,000	227,920	Iceland	39,768	103,000	Novaya Zemlya (north isl.), U.S.S.R.	18,600	48,200
Great Britain	84,400	218,896	Mindanao, Philippines	36,537	94,631	Marajó, Brazil	17,991	46,597
Victoria, Canada	83,896	217,290	Ireland	31,743	82,214	Tierra del Fuego, Chile & Argentina	17,900	46,360
Ellesmere, Canada	75,767	196,236	Sakhalin, U.S.S.R.	29,500	76,405	Alexander, Antarctica	16,700	43,250
Celebes, Indonesia	72,986	189,034	Hispaniola, Haiti & Dom. Rep.	29,399	76,143			

Principal Mountains of the World

	Feet	Meters
Everest, Nepal-China	29,028	8,848
Godwin Austen (K2), Pakistan-China	28,250	8,611
Kanchenjunga, Nepal-India	28,208	8,598
Lhotse, Nepal-China	27,923	8,511
Makalu, Nepal-China	27,824	8,481
Dhaulagiri, Nepal	26,810	8,172
Nanga Parbat, Pakistan	26,660	8,126
Annapurna, Nepal	26,504	8,078
Gasherbrum, Pakistan-China	26,740	8,068
Nanda Devi, India	25,645	7,817
Rakaposhi, Pakistan	25,550	7,788
Kamet, India	25,447	7,756
Gurla Mandhada, China	25,355	7,728
Kongur Shan, China	25,325	7,719
Tirich Mir, Pakistan	25,230	7,690
Gongga Shan, China	24,790	7,556
Muztagata, China	24,757	7,546
Communism Peak, U.S.S.R.	24,599	7,498
Pobeda Peak, U.S.S.R.	24,406	7,439
Chomo Lhari, Bhutan-China	23,997	7,314
Muztag, China	23,891	7,282
Cerro Aconcagua, Argentina	22,831	6,959
Ojos del Salado, Chile-Argentina	22,572	6,880
Bonete, Chile-Argentina	22,541	6,870
Tupungato, Chile-Argentina	22,310	6,800
Pissis, Argentina	22,241	6,779
Mercedario, Argentina	22,211	6,770
Huascarán, Peru	22,205	6,768
Llullaillaco, Chile-Argentina	22,057	6,723
Nevada Ancohuma, Bolivia	21,489	6,550
Illampu, Bolivia	21,276	6,485
Chimborazo, Ecuador	20,561	6,267
McKinley, Alaska	20,320	6,194
Logan, Canada (Yukon)	19,524	5,951
Cotopaxi, Ecuador	19,347	5,897
Kilimanjaro, Tanzania	19,340	5,895
El Misti, Peru	19,101	5,822
Pico Cristóbal Colón, Colombia	19,029	5,800
Huila, Colombia	18,865	5,750
Citlaltépetl (Orizaba), Mexico	18,855	5,747
El'brus, U.S.S.R.	18,510	5,642
Damavand, Iran	18,376	5,601
St. Elias, Alaska-Canada (Yukon)	18,008	5,489
Vilcanota, Peru	17,999	5,486
Popocatépetl, Mexico	17,887	5,452
Dykhtau, U.S.S.R.	17,070	5,203
Kenya, Kenya	17,058	5,199
Ararat, Turkey	16,946	5,165
Vinson Massif, Antarctica	16,864	5,140
Margherita (Ruwenzori), Africa	16,795	5,119
Kazbek, U.S.S.R.	16,512	5,033
Puncak Jaya, Indonesia	16,503	5,030
Tyree, Antarctica	16,289	4,965
Blanc, France	15,771	4,807
Klyuchevskaya Sopka, U.S.S.R.	15,584	4,750
Fairweather (Br. Col., Canada)	15,300	4,663
Dufourspitze (Mte. Rosa), Italy-Switzerland	15,203	4,634
Ras Dashan, Ethiopia	15,157	4,620
Matterhorn, Switzerland	14,691	4,478
Whitney, California, U.S.A.	14,494	4,418
Elbert, Colorado, U.S.A.	14,433	4,399
Rainier, Washington, U.S.A.	14,410	4,392
Shasta, California, U.S.A.	14,162	4,350
Pikes Peak, Colorado, U.S.A.	14,110	4,301
Finsteraarhorn, Switzerland	14,022	4,274
Mauna Kea, Hawaii, U.S.A.	13,796	4,205
Mauna Loa, Hawaii, U.S.A.	13,677	4,169
Jungfrau, Switzerland	13,642	4,158
Cameroon, Cameroon	13,350	4,069
Grossglockner, Austria	12,457	3,797
Fuji, Japan	12,389	3,776
Cook, New Zealand	12,349	3,764
Etna, Italy	11,053	3,369
Kosciusko, Australia	7,310	2,228
Mitchell, North Carolina, U.S.A.	6,684	2,037

Longest Rivers of the World

	Miles	Kms.
Nile, Africa	4,145	6,671
Amazon, S. Amer.	3,915	6,300
Chang Jiang (Yangtze), China	3,900	6,276
Mississippi-Missouri-Red Rock, U.S.A.	3,741	6,019
Ob'Irtysh-Black Irtysh, U.S.S.R.	3,362	5,411
Yenisey-Angara, U.S.S.R.	3,100	4,989
Huang He (Yellow), China	2,877	4,630
Amur-Shilka-Onon, Asia	2,744	4,416
Lena, U.S.S.R.	2,734	4,400
Congo (Zaire), Africa	2,718	4,374
Mackenzie-Peace-Finlay, Canada	2,635	4,241
Mekong, Asia	2,610	4,200
Missouri-Red Rock, U.S.A.	2,564	4,125
Niger, Africa	2,548	4,101
Paraná-La Plata, S. Amer.	2,450	3,943
Mississippi, U.S.A.	2,348	3,778
Murray-Darling, Australia	2,310	3,718
Volga, U.S.S.R.	2,194	3,531
Madeira, S. Amer.	2,013	3,240
Purus, S. Amer.	1,995	3,211
Yukon, Alaska-Canada	1,979	3,185
St. Lawrence, Canada-U.S.A.	1,900	3,058
Rio Grande, Mexico-U.S.A.	1,885	3,034
Syrdar'ya-Naryn, U.S.S.R.	1,859	2,992
São Francisco, Brazil	1,811	2,914
Indus, Asia	1,800	2,897
Danube, Europe	1,775	2,857
Salween, Asia	1,770	2,849
Brahmaputra, Asia	1,700	2,736
Euphrates, Asia	1,700	2,736
Tocantins, Brazil	1,677	2,699
Xi (Si), China	1,650	2,655
Amudar'ya, Asia	1,616	2,601
Nelson-Saskatchewan, Canada	1,600	2,575
Orinoco, S. Amer.	1,600	2,575
Zambezi, Africa	1,600	2,575
Paraguay, S. Amer.	1,584	2,549
Kolyma, U.S.S.R.	1,562	2,514
Ganges, Asia	1,550	2,494
Ural, U.S.S.R.	1,509	2,428
Japurá, S. Amer.	1,500	2,414
Arkansas, U.S.A.	1,450	2,334
Colorado, U.S.A.-Mexico	1,450	2,334
Negro, S. Amer.	1,400	2,253
Dnieper, U.S.S.R.	1,368	2,202
Orange, Africa	1,350	2,173
Irrawaddy, Burma	1,325	2,132
Brazos, U.S.A.	1,309	2,107
Ohio-Allegheny, U.S.A.	1,306	2,102
Kama, U.S.S.R.	1,262	2,031
Red, U.S.A.	1,222	1,966
Don, U.S.S.R.	1,222	1,967
Columbia, U.S.A.-Canada	1,214	1,953
Saskatchewan, Canada	1,205	1,939
Peace-Finlay, Canada	1,195	1,923
Tigris, Asia	1,181	1,901
Darling, Australia	1,160	1,867
Angara, U.S.S.R.	1,135	1,827
Sungari, Asia	1,130	1,819
Pechora, U.S.S.R.	1,124	1,809
Snake, U.S.A.	1,000	1,609
Churchill, Canada	1,000	1,609
Pilcomayo, S. Amer.	1,000	1,609
Magdalena, Colombia	1,000	1,609
Uruguay, S. Amer.	994	1,600
Platte-N. Platte, U.S.A.	990	1,593
Ohio, U.S.A.	981	1,578
Pecos, U.S.A.	926	1,490
Oka, U.S.S.R.	918	1,477
Canadian, U.S.A.	906	1,458
Colorado, Texas, U.S.A.	894	1,439
Dniester, U.S.S.R.	876	1,410

Principal Natural Lakes

	Area Sq. Miles	Area Sq. Km.	Max. Depth Feet	Max. Depth Meters
Caspian Sea, U.S.S.R.-Iran	143,243	370,999	3,264	995
Lake Superior, U.S.A.-Canada	31,820	82,414	1,329	405
Lake Victoria, Africa	26,724	69,215	270	82
Aral Sea, U.S.S.R.	25,676	66,501	256	78
Lake Huron, U.S.A.-Canada	23,010	59,596	748	228
Lake Michigan, U.S.A.	22,400	58,016	923	281
Lake Tanganyika, Africa	12,650	32,764	4,700	1,433
Lake Baykal, U.S.S.R.	12,162	31,500	5,316	1,620
Great Bear Lake, Canada	12,096	31,328	1,356	413
Lake Nyasa (Malawi), Africa	11,555	29,928	2,320	707
Great Slave Lake, Canada	11,031	28,570	2,015	614
Lake Erie, U.S.A.-Canada	9,940	25,745	210	64
Lake Winnipeg, Canada	9,417	24,390	60	18
Lake Ontario, U.S.A.-Canada	7,540	19,529	775	244
Lake Ladoga, U.S.S.R.	7,104	18,399	738	225
Lake Balkhash, U.S.S.R.	7,027	18,200	87	27
Lake Maracaibo, Venezuela	5,120	13,261	100	31
Lake Chad, Africa	4,000-10,000	10,360-25,900	25	8
Lake Onega, U.S.S.R.	3,710	9,609	377	115
Lake Eyre, Australia	3,500-0	9,000-0	—	—
Lake Titicaca, Peru-Bolivia	3,200	8,288	1,000	305
Lake Nicaragua, Nicarágua	3,100	8,029	230	70
Lake Athabasca, Canada	3,064	7,936	400	122
Reindeer Lake, Canada	2,568	6,651	—	—
Lake Turkana (Rudolf), Africa	2,463	6,379	240	73
Issyk-Kul', U.S.S.R.	2,425	6,281	2,303	702
Lake Torrens, Australia	2,230	5,776	—	—
Vänern, Sweden	2,156	5,584	328	100
Nettilling Lake, Canada	2,140	5,543	—	—
Lake Winnipegosis, Canada	2,075	5,374	38	12
Lake Mobutu Sese Seko (Albert), Africa	2,075	5,374	160	49
Kariba Lake, Zambia-Zimbabwe	2,050	5,310	295	90
Lake Nipigon, Canada	1,872	4,848	540	165
Lake Mweru, Zaire-Zambia	1,800	4,662	60	18
Lake Manitoba, Canada	1,799	4,659	12	4
Lake Taymyr, U.S.S.R.	1,737	4,499	85	26
Lake Khanka, China-U.S.S.R.	1,700	4,403	33	10
Lake Kioga, Uganda	1,700	4,403	25	8

Foreign City Weather

Two figures are given for each of the months, thus 88/73. The first figure is the average daily high temperature (°F) and the second is the average daily low temperature (°F) for the month. The boldface figures indicate the average number of days with rain for each month.

City	January	February	March	April	May	June	July	August	September	October	November	December
ABIDJAN, Ivory Coast	88/73 **3**	90/75 **4**	90/75 **6**	90/75 **9**	88/75 **16**	85/73 **18**	83/73 **8**	82/71 **7**	83/73 **8**	85/74 **13**	87/74 **13**	88/74 **6**
ACAPULCO, Mexico	85/70 **0**	87/70 **0**	87/70 **0**	87/71 **0**	88/75 **4**	89/76 **15**	89/75 **11**	89/75 **14**	88/75 **18**	88/74 **12**	88/72 **4**	87/70 **1**
ACCRA, Ghana	87/73 **1**	88/75 **2**	88/76 **4**	88/76 **6**	87/75 **9**	84/74 **10**	81/73 **4**	80/71 **3**	81/73 **8**	85/74 **6**	87/75 **3**	88/75 **2**
ADDIS ABABA, Ethiopia	75/43 **2**	76/47 **5**	77/49 **8**	77/50 **10**	77/50 **10**	74/49 **20**	69/50 **28**	69/50 **27**	72/49 **21**	75/45 **3**	73/43 **2**	73/41 **2**
ALGIERS, Algeria	59/49 **11**	61/49 **9**	63/52 **9**	68/55 **5**	73/59 **5**	78/65 **2**	83/70 **1**	85/71 **1**	81/69 **4**	74/63 **7**	66/56 **11**	60/51 **12**
AMSTERDAM, Netherlands	40/34 **19**	41/34 **15**	46/37 **13**	52/43 **14**	60/50 **12**	65/55 **12**	69/59 **14**	68/59 **14**	64/56 **15**	56/48 **18**	47/41 **19**	41/35 **19**
ANKARA, Turkey	39/24 **8**	42/26 **4**	51/31 **7**	63/40 **7**	73/49 **7**	78/53 **5**	86/59 **2**	87/59 **4**	78/52 **3**	69/44 **5**	57/37 **6**	43/29 **9**
APIA, Western Samoa	86/75 **22**	85/76 **19**	86/74 **19**	86/75 **14**	85/74 **12**	85/74 **7**	85/74 **9**	84/75 **5**	84/74 **11**	85/75 **14**	86/74 **16**	85/74 **19**
ATHENS, Greece	54/42 **7**	55/43 **6**	60/46 **6**	67/52 **3**	77/60 **2**	85/67 **2**	90/72 **1**	90/72 **1**	83/66 **2**	74/60 **4**	64/52 **6**	57/46 **7**
BAGHDAD, Iraq	60/39 **4**	64/42 **3**	71/48 **4**	85/57 **3**	97/67 **1**	105/73 **0**	110/76 **0**	110/76 **0**	104/70 **0**	92/61 **1**	77/51 **3**	64/42 **5**
BALI, Indonesia	88/74 **19**	88/74 **14**	88/74 **13**	88/74 **7**	88/73 **6**	87/71 **3**	87/70 **1**	87/70 **1**	89/71 **1**	90/73 **2**	90/75 **6**	88/74 **14**
BANGKOK, Thailand	89/68 **1**	91/72 **1**	93/75 **3**	95/77 **3**	93/77 **8**	91/76 **10**	90/76 **13**	90/76 **13**	89/76 **15**	88/75 **14**	87/72 **5**	87/68 **1**
BARCELONA, Spain	56/42 **5**	57/44 **7**	61/47 **7**	64/51 **5**	71/57 **8**	77/63 **5**	81/69 **4**	82/69 **5**	78/65 **7**	71/58 **8**	62/50 **5**	57/44 **6**
BEIRUT, Lebanon	62/51 **15**	63/51 **12**	66/54 **9**	72/58 **5**	78/64 **2**	84/73 **1**	87/73 **0**	89/74 **0**	84/74 **1**	81/69 **4**	73/61 **7**	66/55 **11**
BELFAST, Northern Ireland	45/34 **22**	47/34 **18**	49/35 **20**	53/39 **18**	59/43 **17**	64/49 **10**	66/51 **18**	65/51 **20**	62/48 **17**	55/42 **19**	50/37 **21**	46/35 **25**
BELGRADE, Yugoslavia	37/27 **8**	41/27 **6**	53/35 **7**	64/45 **9**	74/53 **9**	79/58 **9**	84/61 **6**	83/60 **7**	76/55 **6**	65/47 **8**	52/39 **7**	40/30 **9**
BERLIN, Germany	35/26 **10**	38/27 **8**	46/32 **9**	55/38 **9**	65/46 **8**	70/51 **9**	74/55 **10**	72/54 **10**	66/48 **8**	55/41 **8**	43/33 **8**	37/29 **11**
BIARRITZ, France	54/40 **10**	52/38 **11**	63/43 **11**	63/44 **11**	69/53 **11**	72/56 **10**	80/66 **7**	77/61 **7**	77/58 **9**	74/55 **11**	58/44 **12**	53/41 **14**
BOGOTA, Colombia	67/48 **6**	68/49 **7**	67/50 **13**	67/51 **20**	66/51 **17**	65/51 **16**	64/50 **18**	65/50 **16**	66/48 **13**	66/50 **16**	66/49 **15**	66/49 **15**
BOMBAY, India	83/67 **0**	83/67 **1**	86/72 **0**	89/76 **0**	91/80 **1**	89/79 **14**	85/77 **21**	85/76 **19**	85/76 **13**	89/76 **5**	89/73 **1**	87/69 **0**
BONN, West Germany	39/30 **7**	37/26 **6**	50/35 **7**	58/39 **14**	67/46 **13**	69/52 **19**	73/56 **16**	72/55 **17**	67/50 **16**	58/45 **16**	47/37 **15**	44/36 **15**
BRASILIA, Brazil	80/65 **17**	81/64 **20**	82/64 **7**	82/62 **10**	79/56 **5**	80/54 **2**	78/51 **2**	82/55 **0**	87/60 **4**	82/64 **16**	82/66 **17**	78/64 **16**
BRINDISI, Italy	55/43 **10**	57/43 **9**	60/45 **6**	65/50 **5**	73/57 **5**	80/64 **2**	84/68 **1**	84/69 **3**	80/65 **4**	70/58 **8**	64/52 **10**	58/46 **8**
BUCHAREST, Romania	33/20 **6**	38/24 **5**	51/33 **6**	65/41 **8**	74/51 **8**	81/58 **7**	86/61 **7**	85/59 **6**	76/53 **5**	65/44 **5**	49/35 **6**	37/26 **6**
BUDAPEST, Hungary	35/26 **7**	40/28 **6**	51/36 **7**	62/44 **8**	72/52 **9**	78/57 **8**	82/61 **7**	81/59 **6**	74/53 **7**	61/45 **8**	47/37 **10**	38/31 **9**
BUENOS AIRES, Argentina	85/63 **7**	83/63 **6**	79/62 **7**	72/53 **8**	64/47 **7**	57/41 **7**	57/42 **8**	60/43 **9**	64/46 **8**	69/50 **9**	76/56 **9**	82/61 **8**
CAIRO, Egypt	65/47 **1**	69/48 **1**	75/52 **1**	83/57 **1**	91/63 **1**	95/68 **0**	96/70 **0**	95/71 **0**	90/68 **0**	86/65 **1**	78/58 **1**	68/50 **1**
CALCUTTA, India	80/55 **1**	84/59 **2**	93/69 **2**	97/75 **3**	96/77 **7**	92/79 **13**	89/79 **18**	89/78 **18**	90/78 **13**	89/74 **6**	84/64 **1**	79/55 **1**
CAPE TOWN, South Africa	78/60 **3**	79/60 **2**	77/58 **3**	72/53 **6**	67/49 **9**	65/46 **9**	63/45 **10**	64/46 **9**	65/49 **7**	70/52 **5**	73/55 **3**	76/58 **3**
CARACAS, Venezuela	75/56 **6**	77/56 **2**	79/58 **3**	81/60 **4**	80/62 **9**	78/62 **14**	78/61 **15**	79/61 **15**	80/61 **13**	79/61 **12**	77/60 **13**	76/58 **10**
CHARLOTTE AMALIE, Virgin Islands	82/73 **18**	81/72 **13**	82/73 **12**	83/74 **13**	85/76 **15**	86/77 **15**	87/78 **16**	88/78 **19**	87/78 **17**	87/77 **18**	85/76 **19**	83/74 **18**
COLOMBO, Sri Lanka	86/72 **7**	87/72 **6**	88/74 **8**	88/76 **14**	87/78 **19**	85/77 **18**	85/77 **12**	85/77 **11**	85/77 **13**	85/75 **19**	85/73 **16**	85/72 **10**
COPENHAGEN, Denmark	36/29 **9**	36/28 **7**	41/31 **8**	50/37 **9**	61/44 **8**	67/51 **8**	72/55 **9**	69/54 **12**	63/49 **8**	53/42 **10**	43/35 **10**	38/32 **11**
DARWIN, Australia	90/77 **20**	90/77 **18**	91/77 **17**	92/76 **6**	91/73 **1**	88/69 **1**	87/67 **0**	89/70 **0**	91/74 **2**	93/77 **5**	94/78 **10**	92/78 **15**
DJAKARTA, Indonesia	84/74 **18**	84/74 **17**	86/74 **15**	87/75 **11**	87/75 **9**	87/74 **7**	87/73 **5**	87/73 **4**	88/74 **5**	87/74 **8**	86/74 **12**	85/74 **14**
DUBLIN, Ireland	47/35 **13**	47/35 **11**	51/36 **10**	54/38 **11**	59/42 **11**	65/48 **11**	67/51 **13**	67/51 **13**	63/47 **12**	57/43 **12**	51/38 **12**	47/36 **13**
EDINBURGH, Scotland	43/35 **18**	43/35 **15**	47/36 **15**	50/39 **16**	55/43 **15**	62/48 **15**	65/52 **17**	64/52 **17**	60/48 **16**	53/44 **18**	47/39 **18**	44/36 **17**
FLORENCE, Italy	49/35 **9**	53/36 **9**	60/40 **7**	68/46 **7**	75/53 **9**	84/58 **5**	89/63 **4**	88/62 **4**	81/58 **6**	69/51 **9**	58/42 **10**	50/37 **9**
GENEVA, Switzerland	39/29 **10**	43/30 **9**	51/35 **10**	58/41 **11**	66/48 **12**	73/55 **11**	77/58 **9**	76/57 **10**	69/52 **10**	58/44 **11**	47/37 **11**	40/31 **10**
GUAYAQUIL, Ecuador	88/70 **20**	87/71 **25**	88/72 **24**	89/71 **14**	88/68 **4**	87/68 **4**	84/67 **2**	86/65 **0**	87/66 **2**	86/68 **3**	88/68 **4**	88/70 **10**
HAMBURG, West Germany	35/28 **12**	37/30 **10**	42/33 **10**	51/39 **11**	60/47 **9**	67/53 **10**	69/56 **12**	67/55 **13**	63/51 **10**	53/44 **11**	44/36 **11**	38/31 **12**
HAMILTON, Bermuda	68/58 **14**	68/57 **12**	68/57 **12**	71/59 **9**	76/64 **9**	81/69 **11**	85/73 **10**	86/74 **11**	84/72 **10**	79/69 **12**	74/63 **13**	70/60 **15**
HAVANA, Cuba	79/65 **6**	79/65 **4**	81/67 **4**	84/69 **4**	86/72 **7**	88/74 **10**	89/75 **9**	89/75 **10**	88/75 **11**	85/73 **11**	81/69 **7**	79/67 **6**
HELSINKI, Finland	27/17 **11**	26/15 **8**	32/22 **8**	43/31 **8**	55/41 **6**	63/49 **9**	71/57 **9**	66/55 **12**	57/46 **11**	45/37 **12**	37/30 **11**	31/22 **11**
HONG KONG	64/56 **4**	63/55 **5**	67/60 **7**	75/67 **8**	82/74 **13**	85/78 **18**	87/78 **17**	87/78 **15**	85/77 **12**	81/73 **6**	74/65 **2**	68/59 **3**
JERUSALEM, Israel	55/41 **9**	56/42 **11**	65/46 **3**	73/50 **3**	81/57 **1**	85/60 **1**	87/63 **0**	87/64 **0**	85/62 **1**	81/59 **1**	70/53 **4**	59/45 **7**
JOHANNESBURG, South Africa	78/58 **12**	77/58 **9**	75/55 **9**	72/50 **4**	66/43 **3**	62/39 **1**	63/39 **1**	68/43 **1**	73/48 **2**	77/53 **7**	77/55 **10**	78/57 **11**
KARACHI, Pakistan	77/55 **1**	79/58 **1**	85/67 **1**	90/73 **1**	93/82 **1**	93/82 **2**	91/81 **2**	88/79 **2**	88/77 **1**	91/72 **1**	87/64 **1**	80/57 **1**
KINGSTON, Jamaica	86/67 **3**	86/67 **3**	86/68 **2**	87/70 **3**	87/72 **4**	89/74 **5**	90/73 **7**	90/73 **7**	89/73 **6**	88/73 **9**	87/71 **5**	87/69 **4**
LAGOS, Nigeria	88/74 **2**	89/77 **3**	89/78 **7**	89/77 **10**	87/76 **16**	85/74 **20**	83/74 **16**	82/73 **10**	83/74 **14**	85/74 **16**	88/75 **7**	88/75 **2**
LA PAZ, Bolivia	63/43 **21**	63/43 **18**	64/42 **16**	65/40 **9**	64/37 **5**	62/34 **2**	62/33 **2**	63/35 **4**	64/38 **9**	66/40 **9**	67/42 **11**	65/42 **18**

Foreign City Weather

	January	February	March	April	May	June	July	August	September	October	November	December
LAS PALMAS, Canary Is.	70/58 8	71/58 5	71/59 5	71/61 3	73/62 1	75/65 1	77/67 1	79/70 1	79/69 1	79/67 5	76/64 7	72/60 8
LENINGRAD, USSR	23/12 17	24/12 15	33/18 13	45/31 11	58/42 12	66/51 12	71/57 13	66/53 15	57/45 14	45/37 15	34/27 17	26/18 18
LIMA, Peru	82/66 1	83/67 1	83/66 1	80/63 1	74/60 1	68/58 1	67/57 1	66/56 2	68/57 1	71/58 1	74/60 1	78/62 1
LISBON, Portugal	56/46 9	58/47 8	61/49 10	64/52 7	69/56 6	75/60 2	79/63 1	80/64 1	76/62 4	69/57 7	62/52 10	57/47 10
LIVERPOOL, England	44/36 18	44/36 13	48/38 13	52/41 14	58/46 14	63/51 13	66/55 15	65/55 16	61/51 15	55/46 17	48/41 17	45/37 18
LONDON, England	44/35 17	45/35 13	51/47 11	56/40 14	63/45 13	69/51 11	73/55 13	72/54 13	67/51 13	58/44 14	49/39 16	45/36 16
MADRID, Spain	47/33 9	51/35 9	57/40 11	64/44 9	71/50 9	80/57 6	87/62 2	86/62 2	77/56 6	66/48 8	54/40 10	48/35 9
MANILA, Philippines	86/69 6	88/69 3	91/71 4	93/73 4	93/75 12	91/75 17	88/75 24	87/75 23	88/75 22	88/74 19	87/72 14	86/70 11
MARACAIBO, Venezuela	90/73 1	90/73 1	91/74 1	92/76 3	93/77 6	93/77 6	94/76 5	94/77 7	94/77 9	92/76 9	91/76 8	91/75 2
MARSEILLE, France	53/38 10	52/37 8	55/38 8	59/41 10	65/46 10	72/52 9	78/58 6	83/61 4	82/61 5	76/57 7	67/50 10	59/43 11
MELBOURNE, Australia	78/57 9	78/57 8	75/55 9	68/51 13	62/47 14	57/44 16	56/42 17	59/43 17	63/46 15	67/48 14	71/51 13	75/54 11
MEXICO CITY, Mexico	66/42 4	69/43 5	75/47 7	77/51 11	78/54 17	76/55 21	73/53 27	73/54 27	74/53 23	70/50 13	68/46 6	66/43 4
MILAN, Italy	40/29 7	47/33 6	56/38 6	66/46 6	72/54 9	80/61 6	84/64 6	82/63 6	76/58 6	64/49 7	51/39 7	42/33 7
MONTEVIDEO, Uruguay	83/62 6	82/61 5	78/59 5	71/53 6	64/48 6	59/43 7	58/43 7	59/43 7	63/46 6	68/49 6	74/54 6	79/59 7
MOSCOW, USSR	21/9 11	23/10 9	32/17 8	47/31 9	65/44 9	73/51 10	76/55 12	72/52 12	61/43 9	46/34 11	31/23 9	23/13 9
MUNICH, West Germany	33/23 10	37/25 9	45/31 10	54/37 13	63/45 13	69/51 14	72/54 14	71/53 13	64/48 11	53/40 10	42/31 9	36/26 11
NAIROBI, Kenya	77/54 5	79/55 6	77/57 11	75/58 16	72/56 17	70/53 9	69/51 6	70/52 7	75/52 6	76/55 8	74/56 15	74/55 11
NAPLES, Italy	54/42 11	55/43 11	60/46 6	67/50 6	73/56 6	81/62 3	86/67 1	86/67 3	81/63 6	72/56 9	63/49 11	57/45 11
NASSAU, Bahamas	77/65 6	77/64 5	79/66 6	81/69 6	84/71 9	87/74 12	88/75 14	89/76 14	88/75 15	85/73 13	81/70 9	79/67 6
NEW DELHI, India	70/44 2	75/49 2	87/58 1	97/68 1	105/79 2	102/83 4	96/81 8	93/79 8	93/75 4	93/65 1	84/52 1	73/46 1
NICE, France	56/40 8	56/41 8	59/45 8	64/49 7	69/56 8	76/62 5	81/66 2	81/66 5	77/62 6	70/55 9	62/48 7	58/43 8
NOUMEA, New Caledonia	86/72 10	85/73 12	85/72 16	83/70 13	79/66 15	77/64 13	76/62 13	76/61 12	78/63 8	80/65 7	83/68 7	86/70 6
ODESSA, USSR	28/22 7	31/26 4	39/32 5	52/41 6	67/55 6	74/62 7	79/65 3	78/65 5	68/56 4	57/47 5	43/35 5	33/27 6
OSLO, Norway	30/20 8	32/20 7	40/25 7	50/34 7	62/43 7	69/51 8	73/56 10	69/53 11	60/45 8	49/37 10	37/29 9	31/24 10
PALERMO, Sicily, Italy	58/47 14	60/47 10	62/49 7	67/53 5	83/59 5	82/66 1	86/71 1	87/72 1	83/69 4	75/62 10	67/55 9	61/50 11
PALMA, Majorca, Spain	57/42 8	59/43 8	62/45 8	66/49 5	73/55 5	80/61 3	86/66 2	86/67 2	81/64 6	74/57 8	65/50 9	59/44 10
PAPEETE, Tahiti	89/72 16	89/72 16	89/72 17	89/72 10	87/70 10	86/69 8	86/68 5	86/68 6	86/69 6	87/70 9	88/71 13	88/72 14
PARIS, France	42/32 15	45/33 13	52/36 15	60/41 14	67/47 13	73/52 11	76/55 12	75/55 12	69/50 11	59/44 14	49/38 15	43/33 17
PEKING, China	35/15 3	41/20 3	53/30 3	68/44 4	80/56 6	88/65 9	89/75 16	87/69 11	80/58 7	69/44 4	50/30 2	37/19 2
PHNOM PENH, Cambodia	87/68 3	90/72 1	93/74 3	94/76 6	92/76 14	91/75 15	89/75 16	89/76 17	88/76 19	87/76 17	86/74 9	86/71 4
PORT-AU-PRINCE, Haiti	87/68 3	88/68 5	89/69 7	89/71 11	90/72 13	92/73 8	94/74 7	93/73 11	91/73 12	90/72 12	88/71 7	87/69 3
PORT OF SPAIN, Trinidad	85/67 14	86/67 8	87/67 8	88/69 7	89/75 15	87/71 17	88/75 13	87/71 21	88/71 18	88/71 16	87/70 17	86/69 16
PRAGUE, Czechoslovakia	34/25 12	38/28 11	45/33 13	55/40 12	65/49 13	72/55 14	74/58 14	73/57 12	65/52 11	54/44 11	41/35 12	34/29 13
RANGOON, Burma	89/65 1	92/67 1	96/71 1	97/76 2	92/77 14	86/76 23	85/76 26	85/76 25	86/76 20	88/76 10	88/73 3	88/67 1
RIO DE JANEIRO, Brazil	84/73 13	85/73 11	83/72 12	80/69 10	77/66 10	76/64 7	75/63 7	76/64 7	75/65 11	77/66 13	79/68 13	82/71 14
ROME, Italy	54/39 8	56/39 11	62/42 5	68/46 6	74/55 6	82/60 3	88/64 2	88/64 3	83/61 6	73/53 9	63/46 8	56/41 9
SAIGON (HO CHI MINH CITY), Vietnam	89/70 2	91/71 1	93/74 2	95/76 4	92/76 16	89/75 21	88/75 23	88/75 21	88/74 20	88/74 21	87/73 11	87/72 21
SAN JUAN, Puerto Rico	80/70 20	80/70 15	81/70 15	82/72 14	84/74 16	85/75 17	85/75 19	85/76 20	86/75 18	85/75 18	84/73 19	81/72 21
SANTIAGO, Chile	85/53 0	84/52 0	80/49 1	74/45 1	65/41 5	58/37 6	59/37 6	62/39 5	66/42 3	72/45 3	78/48 1	83/51 0
SAO PAULO, Brazil	81/63 19	82/64 17	81/62 15	78/58 10	73/54 10	71/51 8	71/49 6	73/51 8	74/54 11	76/57 13	78/59 14	80/61 13
SEOUL, South Korea	32/15 3	37/20 6	47/29 7	62/41 8	72/51 10	80/61 10	84/70 16	87/71 13	78/59 9	67/45 7	51/32 9	37/20 6
SEVILLE, Spain	59/41 8	62/44 9	67/48 9	73/51 8	80/57 5	89/63 2	96/67 1	97/68 1	89/64 3	78/57 5	67/49 9	60/44 8
SHANGHAI, China	46/33 6	47/34 9	55/40 9	66/50 9	77/59 9	82/67 11	92/76 9	90/76 9	82/66 11	74/57 7	63/45 6	53/36 6
SINGAPORE, Singapore	86/73 17	88/73 11	88/75 14	88/75 15	89/75 15	88/75 13	88/75 13	87/75 14	87/75 14	87/74 16	87/74 18	87/74 19
SOFIA, Bulgaria	34/22 6	39/25 6	51/32 8	62/41 8	70/49 11	76/54 9	82/57 7	82/56 6	74/50 6	63/42 7	50/35 7	37/26 7
STOCKHOLM, Sweden	31/23 8	30/22 7	37/26 7	45/32 6	57/41 8	65/49 7	70/55 10	66/53 10	58/46 8	48/39 9	38/31 9	33/26 9
SYDNEY, Australia	78/65 14	78/65 13	76/63 14	71/58 14	66/52 13	61/48 12	60/46 12	63/48 11	67/51 12	71/56 12	74/60 12	77/63 13
TAIPEI, Taiwan, China	66/54 9	65/53 13	70/57 12	77/63 14	83/69 12	89/73 13	92/76 10	91/75 12	88/73 10	81/67 9	75/62 7	69/57 8
TEHRAN, Iran	45/27 4	50/32 4	59/39 5	71/49 3	82/58 2	93/66 1	99/72 1	97/71 1	90/64 1	76/53 1	63/43 3	51/33 4
TEL AVIV, Israel	63/48 10	65/48 6	67/50 9	74/54 2	81/60 1	84/65 0	87/69 0	87/70 0	86/68 1	84/64 2	77/59 7	66/52 11
TOKYO, Japan	47/29 5	48/31 6	54/36 10	63/46 10	71/54 10	76/63 12	83/70 10	86/72 9	79/66 12	69/55 11	60/43 7	52/33 5
VALPARAISO, Chile	72/56 1	72/56 1	70/54 1	67/52 1	63/50 5	60/48 7	60/47 7	61/47 5	62/48 2	65/50 2	69/52 1	71/54 1
VENICE, Italy	43/33 6	46/35 5	54/41 6	63/49 5	71/57 8	78/64 8	82/67 8	82/67 5	78/62 5	65/52 5	54/43 7	46/37 7
VIENNA, Austria	34/26 8	38/28 7	47/34 7	57/41 9	66/50 9	71/56 9	75/59 9	73/58 10	66/52 7	55/44 8	44/36 8	37/30 9
WELLINGTON, New Zealand	69/56 10	69/56 9	67/54 11	63/51 13	58/47 16	55/44 17	53/42 18	54/43 17	57/46 15	60/48 14	63/50 13	67/54 12
ZURICH, Switzerland	48/14 11	52/15 11	62/22 14	70/32 14	77/39 14	83/47 15	86/51 15	84/49 14	78/42 11	68/32 14	57/25 12	49/16 13

U.S. City Weather

City	Record Temperature High (F°)	Record Temperature Low (F°)	Annual Average: Precip. (Water equiv.) (in.)	Annual Average: Snow and Sleet (in.)	Annual Average: Wind Speed (mph)	First Freeze Date 32 F° or less Average	First Freeze Date 32 F° or less Earliest on record	Last Freeze Date 32 F° or less Average	Last Freeze Date 32 F° or less Latest on record	Elevation of Station (feet)
Albany	104	—28	36.46	65.7	8.8	Oct. 13	Sept. 23	Apr. 27	May 20	292
Albuquerque	105	—17	8.33	10.7	9.0	Oct. 29	Oct. 11	Apr. 16	May 18	5,314
Atlanta	103	— 9	48.66	1.5	9.1	Nov. 12	Oct. 24	Mar. 24	Apr. 15	1,034
Baltimore	107	— 7	41.62	21.9	9.5	Oct. 26	Oct. 8	Apr. 15	May 11	155
Birmingham	107	—10	53.46	1.2	7.4	Nov. 10	Oct. 17	Mar. 17	Apr. 21	630
Bismarck	114	—45	16.15	38.4	10.6	Sept. 22	Sept. 6	May 11	May 30	1,660
Boise	111	—23	11.97	21.7	9.0	Oct. 12	Sept. 9	May 6	May 31	2,868
Boston	104	—18	41.55	41.9	12.6	Nov. 7	Oct. 5	Apr. 8	May 3	29
Buffalo	99	—21	35.19	88.6	12.3	Oct. 25	Sept. 23	Apr. 30	May 24	706
Burlington, Vt.	101	—30	32.54	78.4	8.8	Oct. 3	Sept. 13	May 10	May 24	340
Charleston, W. Va.	108	—24	43.66	28.8	6.5	Oct. 28	Sept. 29	Apr. 18	May 11	951
Charlotte	104	— 5	45.00	5.6	7.6	Nov. 4	Oct. 15	Apr. 2	Apr. 16	769
Cheyenne	100	—38	14.48	52.0	13.3	Sept. 27	Aug. 25	May 18	June 18	6,141
Chicago	105	—23	33.47	40.7	10.3	Oct. 26	Sept. 25	Apr. 20	May 14	623
Cincinnati	102	—19	40.40	23.2	9.1	Oct. 25	Sept. 28	Apr. 15	May 25	877
Cleveland	103	—19	34.15	51.5	10.8	Nov. 2	Sept. 29	Apr. 21	May 14	805
Columbia, S.C.	107	— 2	45.23	1.8	6.9	Nov. 3	Oct. 4	Mar. 30	Apr. 21	225
Columbus, Ohio	106	—20	36.98	27.7	8.7	Oct. 31	Oct. 7	Apr. 16	May 9	833
Concord, N.H.	102	—37	38.13	64.1	6.7	Sept. 24	Sept. 13	May 17	June 6	346
Dallas-Ft. Worth, Tex.	112	— 8	32.11	2.7	11.1	Nov. 21	Oct. 27	Mar. 16	Apr. 13	596
Denver	105	—30	14.60	60.1	9.0	Oct. 14	Sept. 16	May 2	May 28	5,332
Des Moines	110	—30	31.49	33.2	11.1	Oct. 10	Sept. 28	Apr. 20	May 11	963
Detroit	105	—24	31.49	31.7	10.2	Oct. 21	Sept. 23	Apr. 23	May 12	626
El Paso	109	— 8	8.47	4.4	9.6	Nov. 11	Oct. 31	Mar. 13	Apr. 11	3,916
Great Falls	107	—49	14.83	57.7	13.1	Sept. 26	Sept. 7	May 14	June 8	3,657
Hartford	102	—26	43.00	53.1	9.0	Oct. 15	Sept. 27	Apr. 22	May 10	179
Houston	108	5	47.07	0.4	7.6	Dec. 11	Oct. 25	Feb. 5	Mar. 27	108
Indianapolis	107	—25	39.98	21.3	9.7	Oct. 22	Sept. 27	Apr. 23	May 27	808
Jackson	107	— 5	50.96	0.8	7.7	Nov. 8	Oct. 9	Mar. 18	Apr. 25	331
Jacksonville	105	10	51.75	Trace	8.6	Dec. 16	Nov. 3	Feb. 6	Mar. 31	31
Juneau	90	—22	53.95	109.1	8.5	Oct. 21	Sept. 9	Apr. 22	June 8	24
Kansas City, Mo.	113	—22	36.66	19.7	10.2	Oct. 26	Sept. 30	Apr. 7	May 6	1,025
Little Rock	110	—13	48.17	5.3	8.2	Nov. 15	Oct. 23	Mar. 16	Apr. 13	265
Los Angeles	110	23	11.94	Trace	7.4	—	Dec. 9	—	Jan. 21	104
Louisville	107	—20	42.94	17.3	8.4	Oct. 25	Oct. 15	Apr. 10	Apr. 19	488
Memphis	106	—13	48.74	5.7	9.2	Nov. 5	Oct. 17	Mar. 20	Apr. 15	284
Miami	100	26	59.21		9.1	—		—	Feb. 6	12
Milwaukee	105	—25	30.18	45.2	11.8	Oct. 23	Sept. 20	Apr. 25	May 27	693
Minneapolis-St. Paul	108	—34	26.62	45.8	10.6	Oct. 13	Sept. 3	Apr. 29	May 24	838
Mobile	104	— 1	63.26	0.4	9.3	Dec. 12	Nov. 15	Feb. 17	Mar. 20	221
Nashville	107	—15	46.61	10.9	7.9	Oct. 31	Oct. 7	Apr. 3	Apr. 24	605
New Orleans	102	7	58.93	0.2	8.4	Dec. 3	Nov. 11	Feb. 15	Apr. 8	30
New York City	106	—15	43.56	29.1	9.4	Nov. 12	Oct. 19	Apr. 7	Apr. 24	87
Norfolk	105	2	45.22	7.2	10.6	Nov. 21	Nov. 7	Mar. 22	Apr. 14	30
Oklahoma City	113	—17	31.71	9.2	12.9	Nov. 7	Oct. 7	Apr. 1	May 3	1,304
Omaha	114	—32	28.48	32.5	10.9	Oct. 20	Sept. 24	Apr. 14	May 11	982
Philadelphia	106	—11	41.18	20.3	9.6	Nov. 17	Oct. 19	Mar. 30	Apr. 20	28
Phoenix	118	16	7.41	Trace	6.1	Dec. 11	Nov. 4	Jan. 27	Mar. 3	1,107
Pittsburgh	103	—20	36.21	45.5	9.4	Oct. 20	Oct. 10	Apr. 21	May 4	1,225
Portland, Me.	103	—39	42.15	74.3	8.8	Sept. 27	Sept. 17	May 12	May 31	63
Portland, Ore.	107	— 3	37.98	7.5	7.8	Dec. 1	Oct. 26	Feb. 25	May 4	39
Providence	104	—17	40.90	37.8	10.8	Oct. 26	Oct. 3	Apr. 14	Apr. 24	62
Reno	106	—19	7.65	26.8	6.4	Oct. 2	Aug. 30	May 14	June 25	4,400
Richmond	107	—12	43.77	14.3	7.6	Nov. 8	Oct. 5	Apr. 2	May 11	177
Sacramento	115	17	17.33	Trace	8.3	Dec. 11	Nov. 4	Jan. 24	Mar. 14	25
St. Louis	115	—23	36.70	17.8	9.5	Oct. 20	Sept. 28	Apr. 15	May 10	564
Salt Lake City	107	—30	15.63	58.1	8.7	Nov. 1	Sept. 25	Apr. 12	Apr. 30	4,227
San Francisco	106	20	18.88	Trace	10.5	—	Dec. 11	—	Jan. 21	18
Seattle	100	0	40.30	15.2	9.3	Dec. 1	Oct. 19	Feb. 23	Apr. 3	450
Spokane	108	—30	16.19	54.0	8.7	Oct. 12	Sept. 13	Apr. 20	May 16	2,365
Washington, D.C.	106	—15	40.00	16.8	9.2	Nov. 10	Oct. 2	Mar. 29	May 12	65
Wichita	114	—22	30.06	16.3	12.6	Nov. 1	Sept. 27	Apr. 5	Apr. 21	1,340
Wilmington, Del.	107	—15	43.63	20.1	9.1	Oct. 26	Sept. 27	Apr. 18	May 9	80

SOURCE: National Climatic Center

U.S. City Weather

AVERAGE MONTHLY TEMPERATURES (in °F)

City	Jan.	Feb.	Mar.	April	May	June	July	Aug.	Sept.	Oct.	Nov.	Dec.	ANNUAL
Albany	23.0°	23.7°	33.5°	46.5°	58.4°	67.7°	72.5°	70.2°	62.7°	51.4°	39.7°	27.7°	48.1°
Albuquerque	34.5	39.5	46.3	54.8	63.8	73.3	77.1	75.1	68.4	56.8	43.9	35.1	55.7
Atlanta	43.5	45.6	52.6	61.3	69.6	76.4	78.5	77.8	73.1	62.9	52.0	44.7	61.5
Baltimore	33.2	35.0	42.6	53.6	63.1	72.1	76.8	75.3	68.5	57.3	46.0	36.4	55.0
Birmingham	45.6	47.1	55.0	62.9	70.7	77.8	79.9	79.6	75.2	64.6	53.4	46.3	63.2
Bismarck	8.1	12.2	25.3	42.9	54.6	64.1	70.6	68.5	57.9	45.7	28.6	15.4	41.1
Boise	29.9	35.5	42.3	49.6	57.8	65.4	74.5	72.5	62.7	52.3	40.6	32.1	51.3
Boston	28.9	29.1	36.9	46.9	57.7	67.0	72.6	70.7	64.0	54.2	43.5	32.6	50.3
Buffalo	25.1	24.5	32.3	43.3	54.6	64.7	70.3	68.9	62.6	51.8	40.0	29.5	47.3
Burlington, Vt.	18.0	18.4	29.3	42.6	55.2	64.8	69.7	67.3	59.6	48.8	36.6	23.3	44.5
Charleston, W. Va.	36.6	38.0	46.0	56.0	64.8	72.3	76.0	74.8	69.3	58.0	46.7	38.2	56.4
Charlotte	42.0	43.9	51.0	60.0	68.9	76.0	78.7	77.4	72.2	61.6	50.9	43.1	60.5
Cheyenne	26.1	27.7	32.4	41.4	51.0	61.0	67.7	66.4	57.3	46.4	35.2	28.6	45.1
Chicago	24.7	27.1	36.4	47.8	58.2	68.4	73.8	72.5	65.6	54.5	40.4	29.4	49.9
Cincinnati	30.8	33.6	41.7	53.5	63.3	71.9	75.5	74.2	67.3	56.3	43.6	34.4	53.9
Cleveland	27.5	27.8	35.9	47.0	58.3	67.9	72.2	70.6	64.6	53.8	41.6	31.3	49.9
Columbia, S.C.	46.6	48.1	55.1	63.5	71.9	78.5	80.8	79.9	75.1	64.5	54.4	47.2	63.8
Columbus, Ohio	29.4	30.8	40.0	51.1	61.9	70.9	74.8	72.9	66.6	55.0	42.3	32.4	52.3
Concord, N.H.	21.3	22.8	31.9	44.4	56.2	64.9	70.0	67.3	59.7	49.2	37.5	25.6	45.9
Dallas-Ft. Worth, Tex.	45.6	48.8	56.9	65.2	72.7	80.9	84.5	84.6	77.8	67.8	56.1	47.7	65.7
Denver	30.1	32.8	38.7	47.4	56.7	66.6	72.6	71.3	62.6	51.6	39.6	32.3	50.2
Des Moines	20.8	24.7	36.3	50.4	61.5	71.1	76.1	73.7	65.3	54.2	38.5	26.1	49.9
Detroit	25.3	25.8	34.5	46.7	58.1	68.2	73.0	71.1	64.2	53.1	40.1	29.5	49.2
El Paso	44.7	49.3	55.6	63.8	72.2	80.8	81.9	80.2	74.8	64.7	52.5	45.2	63.8
Great Falls	21.2	26.1	31.4	43.3	53.3	60.9	69.7	67.9	57.6	48.3	34.8	27.1	45.1
Hartford	27.1	27.7	36.9	47.9	59.0	67.9	73.1	70.9	63.7	53.3	42.1	30.4	50.0
Houston	53.2	54.6	62.0	67.9	74.3	79.8	82.4	81.3	77.5	70.2	59.6	55.5	68.2
Indianapolis	28.5	30.8	40.1	52.0	62.5	71.8	75.7	73.7	66.9	55.5	42.0	31.9	52.6
Jackson	48.4	50.9	57.3	65.3	72.6	79.6	81.8	81.5	76.9	66.5	55.7	49.5	65.5
Jacksonville	55.0	56.6	61.8	67.5	73.7	78.5	80.4	80.1	77.1	68.9	60.6	54.9	67.9
Juneau	22.2	27.3	31.2	38.4	46.4	52.8	55.5	54.1	49.0	41.5	32.0	26.9	39.8
Kansas City, Mo.	29.7	33.1	43.2	55.5	65.3	74.7	79.5	78.0	70.0	59.1	44.7	33.6	55.6
Little Rock	41.7	44.8	52.9	62.5	70.1	78.2	81.3	80.5	74.1	63.8	51.9	43.8	62.1
Los Angeles	54.6	55.9	56.9	59.3	62.1	64.9	68.3	69.5	68.5	65.2	60.4	56.4	61.8
Louisville	34.7	36.8	45.6	56.3	66.0	74.6	78.3	76.8	70.4	58.9	46.4	37.2	56.9
Memphis	41.3	44.1	52.2	62.1	70.5	78.2	81.2	80.0	74.1	63.5	51.6	43.6	61.9
Miami	67.5	68.0	71.3	74.9	78.0	80.9	82.2	82.7	81.6	77.8	72.3	68.5	75.5
Milwaukee	20.9	23.2	32.6	44.3	54.3	64.5	70.7	69.7	62.5	51.5	37.7	26.1	46.5
Minneapolis-St. Paul	13.2	16.7	29.6	45.7	57.9	67.8	73.1	70.7	61.5	50.0	33.0	19.5	44.9
Mobile	51.9	54.4	60.1	67.1	74.3	80.3	81.8	81.5	78.1	68.9	58.9	53.1	67.6
Nashville	39.1	41.0	49.5	59.5	68.2	76.3	79.4	78.3	72.2	61.1	48.9	41.1	59.6
New Orleans	54.3	56.5	61.7	68.9	75.4	80.8	82.2	82.0	78.8	70.7	60.7	55.6	69.0
New York City	32.3	32.7	40.6	51.1	61.9	70.9	76.1	74.6	68.0	58.0	46.7	35.7	54.1
Norfolk	41.6	42.3	48.8	57.4	66.7	74.7	78.6	77.5	72.4	62.2	52.1	43.6	59.8
Oklahoma City	37.2	40.8	49.8	60.2	68.2	77.0	81.4	81.1	73.7	62.7	49.4	39.9	60.1
Omaha	22.0	26.5	37.5	51.7	62.7	72.3	77.4	75.1	66.3	55.0	39.3	27.5	51.1
Philadelphia	33.1	33.8	41.6	52.2	63.0	71.8	76.6	74.7	68.4	57.5	46.2	36.2	54.6
Phoenix	51.6	55.4	60.5	67.7	76.0	85.2	90.8	89.0	83.6	71.7	59.8	52.4	70.3
Pittsburgh	30.7	31.3	39.9	51.1	62.0	70.6	74.6	72.8	66.6	55.2	43.2	33.6	52.7
Portland, Me.	22.4	23.4	32.3	42.8	53.2	62.4	68.2	66.6	59.6	49.6	38.6	26.9	45.5
Portland, Ore.	38.5	43.0	45.9	50.6	57.0	60.2	65.8	65.3	62.7	54.0	45.7	41.1	52.5
Providence	29.4	29.3	37.6	47.5	57.8	66.9	72.7	71.0	63.9	54.0	43.4	32.6	50.5
Reno	31.8	36.6	41.2	47.4	54.9	62.5	70.2	68.5	60.7	50.9	41.0	33.4	49.9
Richmond	38.0	39.4	46.9	56.9	66.1	74.0	77.6	76.1	69.9	58.9	48.7	39.7	57.7
Sacramento	44.9	49.8	53.1	58.1	64.5	70.8	75.4	74.3	71.6	63.4	52.9	45.7	60.4
St. Louis	31.7	34.8	44.3	56.1	65.9	75.1	79.3	77.5	70.1	59.0	45.3	35.3	56.2
Salt Lake City	28.0	33.2	40.7	49.0	58.3	68.1	77.2	75.4	65.1	53.1	40.5	31.4	51.7
San Francisco	48.0	50.9	52.9	54.6	57.3	60.3	61.5	62.0	62.9	60.0	54.3	49.3	56.2
Seattle	38.2	42.2	43.9	48.1	55.0	59.9	64.4	63.8	59.6	51.8	44.6	40.5	51.0
Spokane	26.8	31.7	39.4	47.6	55.8	62.5	70.2	68.7	59.5	48.7	37.0	30.4	48.2
Washington, D.C.	36.1	37.7	45.7	56.1	65.8	74.3	78.4	76.9	70.3	59.6	48.4	38.4	57.3
Wichita	31.6	35.2	44.7	56.3	65.4	75.3	80.3	79.3	70.9	59.6	45.2	35.0	56.5
Wilmington, Del.	32.6	33.1	41.9	52.2	62.7	71.4	76.0	74.1	67.9	56.8	45.7	35.2	54.2

SOURCE: National Climatic Center (data based on normals for 1936-1975)

TABLES OF AIRLINE DISTANCES

All Distances in Statute Miles

Between Principal Cities of the World

FROM/TO	Azores	Bagdad	Berlin	Bombay	Buenos Aires	Callao	Cairo	Cape Town	Chicago	Istanbul	Guam	Honolulu	Juneau	London	Los Angeles
Azores	....	3906	2148	5930	5385	4825	3325	5670	3305	2880	8985	7421	4715	1562	5034
Bagdad	3906	....	2040	2022	8215	8618	785	4923	6490	1085	6380	8445	6180	2568	7695
Berlin	2148	2040	....	3947	7411	6937	1823	5949	4458	1068	7158	7384	4638	575	5849
Bombay	5930	2022	3947	....	9380	10530	2698	5133	8144	3043	4831	8172	6992	4526	8810
Buenos Aires	5385	8215	7411	9380	....	1982	7428	4332	5598	7638	10516	7653	7964	6919	6148
Callao	4825	8618	6937	10530	1982	....	7870	6195	3765	7666	9760	5993	5806	6376	4155
Cairo	3325	785	1823	2698	7428	7870	....	4476	6231	780	7175	8925	6352	2218	7675
Cape Town	5670	4923	5949	5133	4332	6195	4476	....	8551	5210	8918	11655	10382	5975	10165
Chicago	3305	6490	4458	8144	5598	3765	6231	8551	....	5530	7510	4315	2310	4015	1741
Istanbul	2880	1085	1068	3043	7638	7666	780	5210	5530	....	7015	8200	5665	1540	6895
Guam	8985	6380	7158	4831	10516	9760	7175	8918	7510	7015	....	3896	5225	7605	6255
Honolulu	7421	8445	7384	8172	7653	5993	8925	11655	4315	8200	3896	....	2825	7320	2620
Juneau	4715	6180	4638	6992	7964	5806	6352	10382	2310	5665	5225	2825	....	4496	1835
London	1562	2568	575	4526	6919	6376	2218	5975	4015	1540	7605	7320	4496	....	5496
Los Angeles	5034	7695	5849	8810	6148	4155	7675	10165	1741	6895	6255	2620	1835	5496	....
Melbourne	12190	8150	9992	6140	7336	8196	8720	6510	9837	9189	3497	5581	8162	10590	8098
Mexico City	4584	8155	6119	9818	4609	2619	7807	8620	1690	7160	7690	3846	3210	5605	1445
Montreal	2548	5814	3776	7582	5619	3954	5502	7975	750	4825	7840	4992	2647	3370	2468
New Orleans	3718	7212	5182	8952	4902	2990	6862	8390	827	6220	7895	4305	2860	4656	1695
New York	2604	6066	4026	7875	5295	3633	5701	7845	727	5060	8115	5051	2874	3500	2466
Panama	3918	7807	5902	9832	3319	1450	7230	7090	2320	6797	9220	5347	4456	5310	3025
Paris	1617	2385	540	4391	6891	6455	2020	5762	4219	1390	7675	7525	4700	210	5711
Rio de Janeiro	4312	7012	6246	8438	1230	2400	6242	3850	5320	6420	11710	8400	7611	5747	6330
San Francisco	5114	7521	5744	8523	6487	4500	7554	10340	1875	6770	5952	2407	1530	5440	345
Santiago	5718	8876	7842	10127	731	1548	8100	5080	5325	8230	9946	6935	7320	7275	5595
Seattle	4720	6848	5121	7830	6956	4964	6915	10305	1753	6124	5785	2707	870	4850	961
Shanghai	7324	4468	5323	3219	12295	10760	5290	8179	7155	5084	1945	5009	4968	5841	6598
Singapore	8338	4443	6226	2425	9940	11700	5152	6025	9475	5440	2990	6874	7375	6818	8955
Tokyo	7370	5242	5623	4247	11601	9740	6005	9234	6410	5649	1596	3940	4117	6050	5600
Wellington	11475	9782	11384	7752	6341	6696	10360	7149	8465	10790	4206	4676	7501	11790	6806

FROM/TO	Melbourne	Mexico City	Montreal	New Orleans	New York	Panama	Paris	Rio de Janeiro	San Francisco	Santiago	Seattle	Shanghai	Singapore	Tokyo	Wellington
Azores	12190	4584	2548	3718	2604	3918	1617	4312	5114	5718	4720	7324	8338	7370	11475
Bagdad	8150	8155	5814	7212	6066	7807	2385	7012	7521	8876	6848	4468	4443	5242	9782
Berlin	9992	6119	3776	5182	4026	5902	540	6246	5744	7842	5121	5323	6226	5623	11384
Bombay	6140	9818	7582	8952	7875	9832	4391	8438	8523	10127	7830	3219	2425	4247	7752
Buenos Aires	7336	4609	5619	4902	5295	3319	6891	1230	6487	731	6956	12295	9940	11601	6341
Callao	8196	2619	3954	2990	3633	1450	6455	2400	4500	1548	4964	10760	11700	9740	6696
Cairo	8720	7807	5502	6862	5701	7230	2020	6242	7554	8100	6915	5290	5152	6005	10360
Cape Town	6510	8620	7975	8390	7845	7090	5732	3850	10340	5080	10305	8179	6025	9234	7149
Chicago	9837	1690	750	827	727	2320	4219	5320	1875	5325	1753	7155	9475	6410	8465
Istanbul	9189	7160	4825	6220	5060	6797	1390	6420	6770	8230	6124	5084	5440	5649	10790
Guam	3497	7690	7840	7895	8115	9220	7675	11710	5952	9946	5785	1945	2990	1596	4206
Honolulu	5581	3846	4992	4305	5051	5347	7525	8400	2407	6935	2707	5009	6874	3940	4676
Juneau	8162	3210	2647	2860	2874	4456	4700	7611	1530	7320	870	4968	7375	4117	7501
London	10590	5605	3370	4656	3500	5310	210	5747	5440	7275	4850	5841	6818	6050	11790
Los Angeles	8098	1445	2468	1695	2466	3025	5711	6330	345	5595	961	6598	8955	5600	6806
Melbourne	....	8599	10553	9455	10541	9211	10500	8340	7970	7130	8330	4967	3768	5172	1655
Mexico City	8599	....	2247	940	2110	1532	5800	4810	1870	4122	2339	8120	10495	7190	7003
Montreal	10553	2247	....	1390	340	2545	3490	5110	2557	5461	2309	7141	9280	6546	9206
New Orleans	9455	940	1390	....	1161	1600	4846	4798	1960	4553	2137	7830	10255	6993	7950
New York	10541	2110	340	1161	....	2211	3600	4810	2606	5134	2440	7460	9617	6846	9067
Panama	9211	1532	2545	1600	2211	....	5440	3311	3349	3000	3680	9430	11800	8560	7580
Paris	10500	5800	3490	4846	3600	5440	....	5710	5680	7300	5080	5855	6730	6132	11865
Rio de Janeiro	8340	4810	5110	4798	4810	3311	5710	....	6655	1852	6945	11510	9875	11600	7510
San Francisco	7970	1870	2557	1960	2606	3349	5680	6655	....	5960	692	6245	8440	5250	6800
Santiago	7130	4122	5461	4553	5134	3000	7300	1852	5960	....	6466	11850	10270	10850	5925
Seattle	8330	2339	2309	2137	2440	3680	5080	6945	692	6466	....	5780	8200	4863	7310
Shanghai	4967	8120	7141	7830	7460	9430	5855	11510	6245	11850	5780	....	2395	1095	6080
Singapore	3768	10495	9280	10255	9617	11800	6730	9875	8440	10270	8200	2395	....	3350	5360
Tokyo	5172	7190	6546	6993	6846	8560	6132	11600	5250	10850	4863	1095	3350	....	5730
Wellington	1655	7003	9206	7950	9067	7580	11865	7510	6800	5925	7310	6080	5360	5730	......

Between Principal Cities of Europe

	Amsterdam	Athens	Baku	Barcelona	Belgrade	Berlin	Brussels	Bucharest	Budapest	Cologne	Copenhagen	Istanbul	Dresden	Dublin	Frankfort	Hamburg	Leningrad	Lisbon
Amsterdam	....	1340	2218	770	875	365	105	1100	710	128	381	1360	385	468	228	232	1090	1140
Athens	1340	....	1395	1160	500	1112	1292	460	698	1200	1320	350	1022	1765	1113	1250	1535	1770
Baku	2218	1395	....	2427	1487	1867	2240	1220	1562	2127	1980	1070	1837	2490	2055	2020	1570	3050
Barcelona	770	1160	2427	....	998	925	658	1210	924	692	1085	1380	860	919	665	910	1740	610
Belgrade	875	500	1487	998	....	618	850	295	205	750	840	502	530	1327	652	760	1165	1555
Berlin	365	1112	1867	925	618	....	401	798	425	300	225	1068	95	815	268	165	815	1410
Brussels	105	1292	2240	658	850	401	....	1110	700	110	475	1345	407	480	198	301	1175	998
Bucharest	1100	460	1220	1210	295	798	1110	....	295	982	970	272	725	1560	890	950	1080	1842
Budapest	710	698	1562	924	205	425	700	295	....	590	629	650	345	1176	504	572	965	1515
Cologne	128	1200	2127	692	750	300	110	982	590	....	400	1240	292	585	93	228	1090	1126
Copenhagen	381	1320	1960	1085	840	225	475	970	629	400	....	1240	315	768	412	180	708	1520
Istanbul	1360	350	1070	1380	502	1068	1345	272	650	1240	1240	....	995	1830	1150	1222	1292	2005
Dresden	385	1022	1837	860	530	95	407	725	345	292	315	995	....	852	236	238	885	1380
Dublin	468	1765	2490	919	1327	815	480	1560	1176	585	768	1830	852	....	671	668	1440	1015
Frankfort	228	1113	2055	665	652	268	198	890	504	93	412	1150	236	671	....	250	1075	1160
Hamburg	232	1250	2020	910	760	165	301	950	572	228	180	1222	238	668	250	....	880	1301
Leningrad	1090	1535	1570	1740	1165	815	1175	1080	965	1090	708	1292	885	1440	1075	880	....	2235
Lisbon	1140	1770	3050	610	1555	1410	998	1842	1515	1126	1520	2005	1380	1015	1160	1301	2235	....
London	220	1476	2435	707	1040	575	202	1285	900	308	590	1540	592	300	392	448	1300	975
Lyon	458	1100	2238	327	752	601	352	1025	680	370	760	1238	540	720	350	580	1420	850
Madrid	912	1463	2742	316	1235	1149	807	1518	1214	875	1272	1690	1100	902	888	1098	1980	313
Marseilles	627	1025	2238	211	750	730	521	1020	718	528	906	1205	655	875	492	730	1540	810
Milan	517	900	2028	450	540	570	435	819	476	390	720	1030	435	880	323	570	1315	1350
Moscow	1325	1388	1175	1852	1160	995	1392	920	965	1285	970	1180	1200	1728	1240	1100	391	430
Munich	415	925	1912	648	475	310	372	725	350	282	520	975	227	855	193	378	1100	1208
Oslo	568	1610	2118	1330	1112	520	672	1245	920	635	303	1505	620	786	675	445	670	1690
Paris	257	1300	2335	518	890	540	170	1152	770	250	634	1390	523	480	295	459	1335	890
Riga	820	1310	1590	1440	855	520	900	870	685	805	453	1115	585	1210	780	600	300	1940
Rome	808	650	1900	530	440	730	730	700	500	675	948	840	630	1175	698	810	1440	1150
Sofia	1073	335	1360	1072	231	810	945	194	395	945	1010	315	730	1525	860	954	1218	1685
Stockholm	695	1495	1862	1410	1005	503	793	1080	820	722	330	1340	598	1010	730	502	435	1848
Toulouse	625	1215	2425	156	930	815	515	1210	883	875	962	1400	762	761	560	780	1635	640
Warsaw	673	990	1555	1150	510	320	720	580	342	602	415	852	325	1130	550	462	640	1700
Vienna	580	795	1700	830	300	322	568	520	128	460	538	790	235	1040	370	460	975	1415
Zurich	375	1000	2050	513	590	410	312	855	498	259	595	1090	342	768	193	432	1225	1058

	London	Lyon	Madrid	Marseilles	Milan	Moscow	Munich	Oslo	Paris	Riga	Rome	Sofia	Stockholm	Toulouse	Warsaw	Vienna	Zurich
Amsterdam	220	458	912	627	517	1325	415	568	257	820	808	1073	695	625	673	580	375
Athens	1476	1100	1463	1025	900	1388	925	1610	1300	1310	650	335	1495	1215	990	795	1000
Baku	2435	2238	2742	2238	2028	1175	1912	2118	2335	1590	1900	1360	1862	2425	1555	1700	2050
Barcelona	707	327	316	211	450	1852	648	1330	518	1440	530	1072	1410	156	1150	830	513
Belgrade	1040	752	1235	750	540	1160	475	1112	890	855	440	231	1005	930	510	300	590
Berlin	575	601	1149	730	570	995	310	520	540	520	730	810	503	815	320	322	410
Brussels	202	352	807	521	435	1392	372	672	170	900	730	945	793	515	720	568	312
Bucharest	1285	1025	1518	1020	819	920	725	1245	1152	870	700	194	1080	1210	580	520	855
Budapest	900	680	1214	718	476	965	350	920	770	685	500	395	820	883	342	128	498
Cologne	308	370	875	528	390	1285	282	635	250	805	675	945	722	875	602	460	259
Copenhagen	590	760	1272	906	720	970	520	303	634	453	948	1010	330	962	415	538	595
Istanbul	1540	1238	1690	1205	1030	1180	975	1505	1390	1115	840	315	1340	1400	852	790	1090
Dresden	592	540	1100	655	435	1200	227	620	523	585	630	730	598	762	325	235	342
Dublin	300	720	902	875	880	1728	855	786	480	1210	1175	1525	1010	761	1130	1040	768
Frankfort	392	350	888	492	323	1240	193	675	295	780	698	860	730	560	550	370	193
Hamburg	448	580	1098	730	570	1100	378	445	459	600	810	954	502	780	462	460	432
Leningrad	1300	1420	1980	1540	1315	391	1100	670	1335	300	1440	1218	435	1635	640	975	1225
Lisbon	975	850	313	810	1350	430	1208	1690	890	1940	1150	1685	1848	640	1700	1415	1058
London	....	455	777	620	595	1540	526	720	210	1035	890	1235	885	550	890	762	480
Lyon	455	....	577	170	210	1560	352	1005	248	1122	462	928	1080	228	850	562	206
Madrid	777	557	....	394	728	2120	910	1474	645	1670	840	1385	1598	344	1410	1110	765
Marseilles	620	170	394	....	238	1642	445	1165	410	1238	372	895	1225	196	950	620	318
Milan	595	210	728	238	....	1408	215	1000	400	1010	295	715	1020	400	705	385	137
Moscow	1540	1560	2120	1642	1408	....	1220	1030	1538	520	1462	1100	770	1770	710	1028	1350
Munich	526	352	910	445	215	1220	....	810	425	800	430	672	811	570	500	222	158
Oslo	720	1005	1474	1165	1000	1030	810	....	830	531	1242	1295	267	1140	653	835	869
Paris	210	248	645	410	400	1538	425	830	....	1050	690	1080	950	431	845	770	295
Riga	1035	1122	1670	1238	1010	520	800	531	1050	....	1155	985	276	1335	350	685	930
Rome	890	462	840	372	295	1462	430	1242	690	1155	....	545	1220	569	810	470	421
Sofia	1235	928	1385	895	715	1100	672	1295	1080	985	545	....	1170	1080	662	500	780
Stockholm	885	1080	1598	1225	1020	770	811	267	950	276	1220	1170	....	1281	500	770	908
Toulouse	550	228	344	196	400	1770	570	1140	431	1335	569	1080	1281	....	1062	725	425
Warsaw	890	850	1410	950	705	710	500	653	845	350	810	662	500	1062	....	345	640
Vienna	762	562	1110	620	385	1028	222	835	770	685	470	500	770	725	345	....	365
Zurich	480	206	765	318	137	1350	158	869	295	930	421	780	908	425	640	365	....

WORLD HISTORY ATLAS

A collection of maps illustrating geographically the most significant periods and events in the history of civilization.

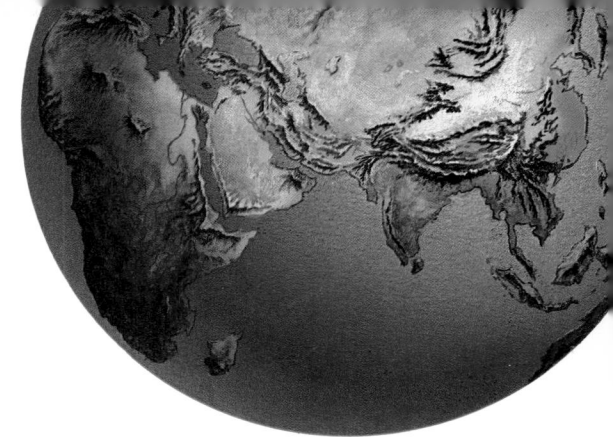

CONTENTS

Published by **HAMMOND** INCORPORATED **MAPLEWOOD, NEW JERSEY**

WORLD HISTORY

PREHISTORIC MAN

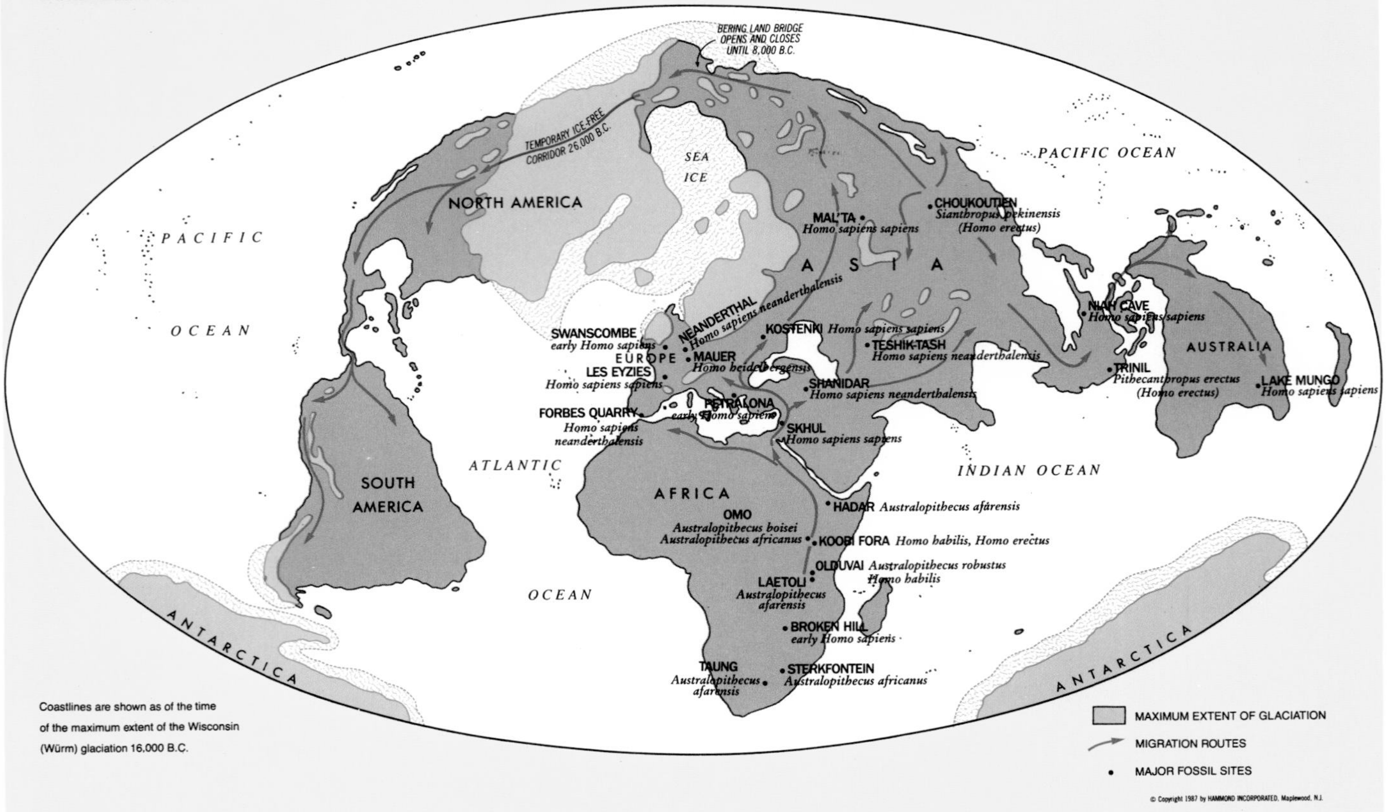

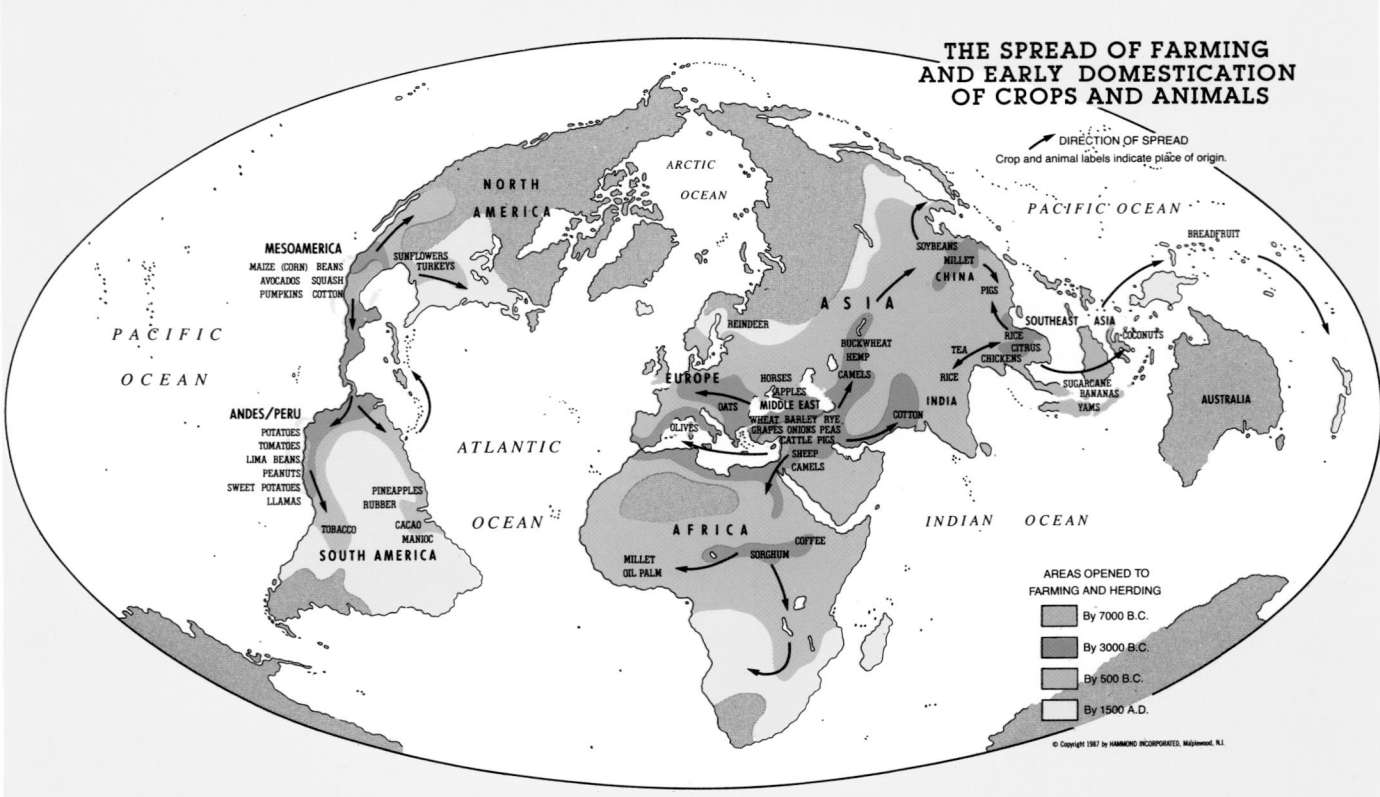

BERING LAND BRIDGE
OPENS AND CLOSES
UNTIL 8,000 B.C.

SEA ICE

TEMPORARY ICE-FREE
CORRIDOR 26,000 B.C.

PACIFIC OCEAN

NORTH AMERICA

PACIFIC OCEAN

A S I A

MAL'TA
Homo sapiens sapiens

CHOUKOUTIEN
*Sianthropus pekinensis
(Homo erectus)*

NIAH CAVE
Homo sapiens sapiens

NEANDERTHAL
Homo sapiens neanderthalensis

SWANSCOMBE
early Homo sapiens
EUROPE

KOSTENKI *Homo sapiens sapiens*

TESHIK-TASH
Homo sapiens neanderthalensis

AUSTRALIA

LES EYZIES
Homo sapiens sapiens

MAUER
Homo heidelbergensis

SHANIDAR
Homo sapiens neanderthalensis

TRINIL
*Pithecanthropus erectus
(Homo erectus)*

LAKE MUNGO
Homo sapiens sapiens

FORBES QUARRY
*Homo sapiens
neanderthalensis*

PETRALONA
early Homo sapien

SKHUL
Homo sapiens sapiens

ATLANTIC

SOUTH
AMERICA

OCEAN

AFRICA

INDIAN OCEAN

OMO
*Australopithecus boisei
Australopithecus africanus*

HADAR *Australopithecus afarensis*

KOOBI FORA *Homo habilis, Homo erectus*

OLDUVAI *Australopithecus robustus
Homo habilis*

LAETOLI
*Australopithecus
afarensis*

BROKEN HILL
early Homo sapiens

TAUNG
*Australopithecus
afarensis*

STERKFONTEIN
Australopithecus africanus

ANTARCTICA

ANTARCTICA

Coastlines are shown as of the time
of the maximum extent of the Wisconsin
(Würm) glaciation 16,000 B.C.

▭ MAXIMUM EXTENT OF GLACIATION

➤ MIGRATION ROUTES

• MAJOR FOSSIL SITES

© Copyright 1987 by HAMMOND INCORPORATED, Maplewood, N.J.

THE SPREAD OF FARMING AND EARLY DOMESTICATION OF CROPS AND ANIMALS

➤ DIRECTION OF SPREAD
Crop and animal labels indicate place of origin.

ARCTIC OCEAN

NORTH
AMERICA

PACIFIC OCEAN

BREADFRUIT

MESOAMERICA
MAIZE (CORN) BEANS
AVOCADOS SQUASH
PUMPKINS COTTON

SUNFLOWERS
TURKEYS

SOYBEANS
MILLET
CHINA
PIGS

REINDEER

A S I A

SOUTHEAST ASIA

COCONUTS

PACIFIC OCEAN

BUCKWHEAT
HEMP

TEA
CHICKENS

RICE
CITRUS

EUROPE

HORSES
APPLES
OATS MIDDLE EAST
WHEAT BARLEY RYE
GRAPES ONIONS PEAS
CATTLE PIGS
SHEEP
CAMELS

CAMELS

RICE

INDIA

COTTON

SUGARCANE
BANANAS
YAMS

AUSTRALIA

ANDES/PERU
POTATOES
TOMATOES
LIMA BEANS
PEANUTS
SWEET POTATOES
LLAMAS

PINEAPPLES
RUBBER

*ATLANTIC
OCEAN*

OLIVES

TOBACCO

CACAO
MANIOC

SOUTH AMERICA

AFRICA

INDIAN OCEAN

MILLET
OIL PALM

SORGHUM

COFFEE

AREAS OPENED TO
FARMING AND HERDING

▭ By 7000 B.C.
▭ By 3000 B.C.
▭ By 500 B.C.
▭ By 1500 A.D.

© Copyright 1987 by HAMMOND INCORPORATED, Maplewood, N.J.

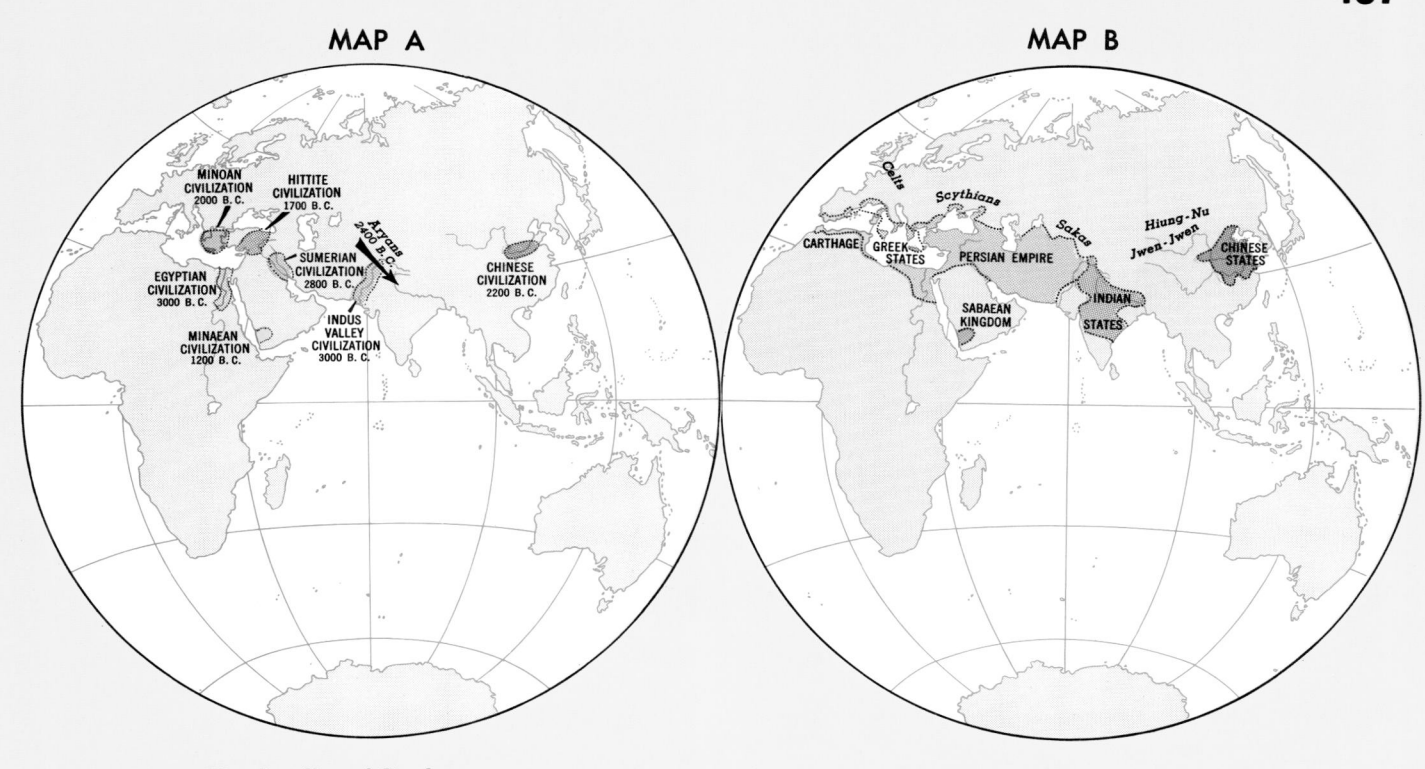

MAP A

MINOAN CIVILIZATION 2000 B.C.

HITTITE CIVILIZATION 1700 B.C.

Aryans 2400 B.C.

EGYPTIAN CIVILIZATION 3000 B.C.

SUMERIAN CIVILIZATION 2800 B.C.

CHINESE CIVILIZATION 2200 B.C.

MINAEAN CIVILIZATION 1200 B.C.

INDUS VALLEY CIVILIZATION 3000 B.C.

The Cradles of Civilization
3000-1000 B.C.

MAP B

Celts

Scythians

Sakas

Hiung-Nu

Jwen-Jwen

CARTHAGE

GREEK STATES

PERSIAN EMPIRE

CHINESE STATES

SABAEAN KINGDOM

INDIAN STATES

Major States and Empires
in 500 B.C.

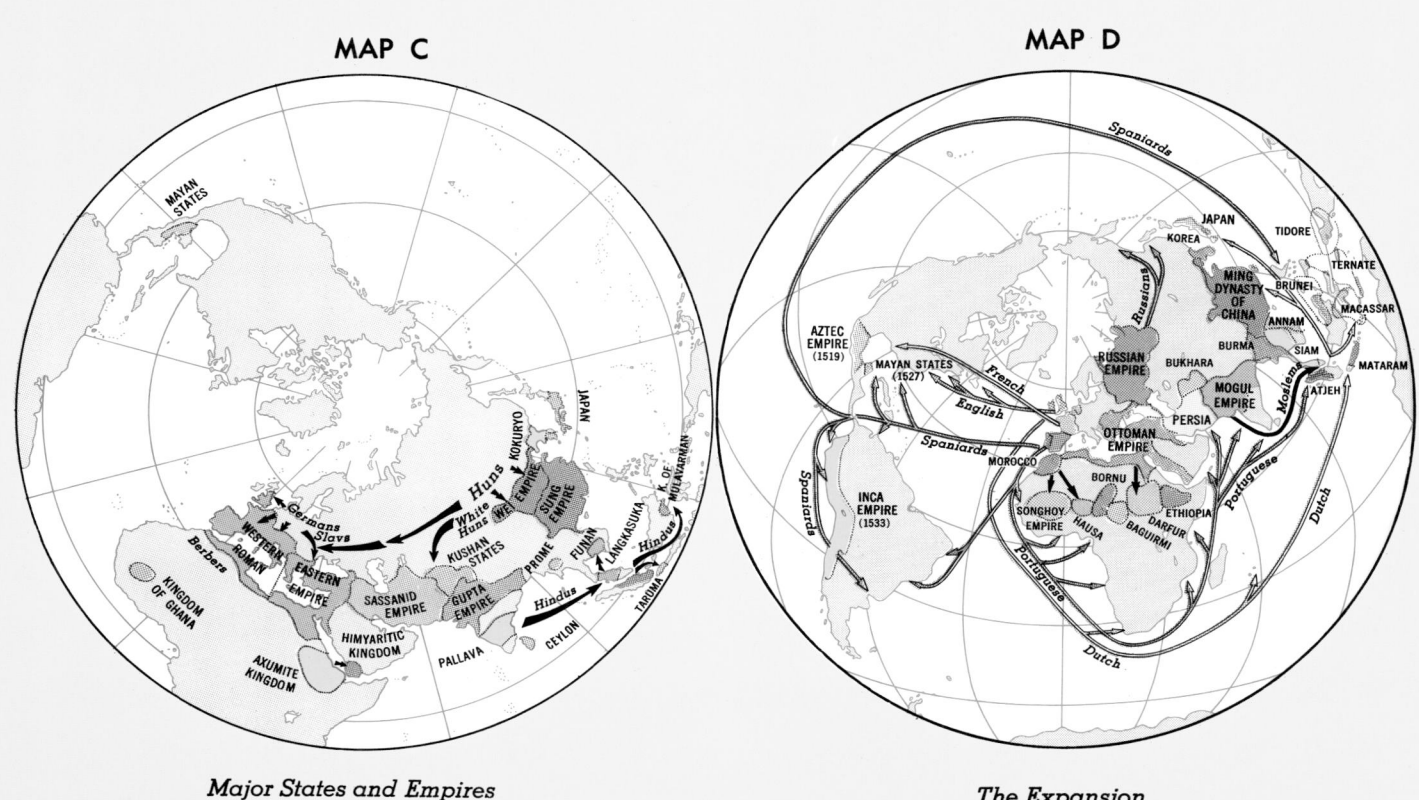

MAP C

MAYAN STATES

Huns

KOKURYO

JAPAN

White Huns

WEI EMPIRE

SUNG EMPIRE

Germans

Slavs

WESTERN ROMAN

EASTERN EMPIRE

KUSHAN STATES

K. DE MILAVARNAN

Berbers

SASSANID EMPIRE

GUPTA EMPIRE

PROME

FUNAN

LANGKASUKA

Hindus

KINGDOM OF GHANA

HIMYARITIC KINGDOM

PALLAVA

CEYLON

Hindus

TARUMA

AXUMITE KINGDOM

Major States and Empires
in 400 A.D.

MAP D

Spaniards

JAPAN

TIDORE

KOREA

MING DYNASTY OF CHINA

BRUNEI

TERNATE

Russians

MACASSAR

AZTEC EMPIRE (1519)

ANNAM

MATARAM

MAYAN STATES (1527)

French

RUSSIAN EMPIRE

BUKHARA

BURMA

SIAM

Moslems

ATJEH

English

Spaniards

MOGUL EMPIRE

Spaniards

MOROCCO

OTTOMAN EMPIRE

PERSIA

Portuguese

Dutch

INCA EMPIRE (1533)

SONGHOY EMPIRE

HAUSA

BORNU

DARFUR

ETHIOPIA

BAGUIRMI

Portuguese

Dutch

The Expansion
of Western Civilization
1600 A.D.

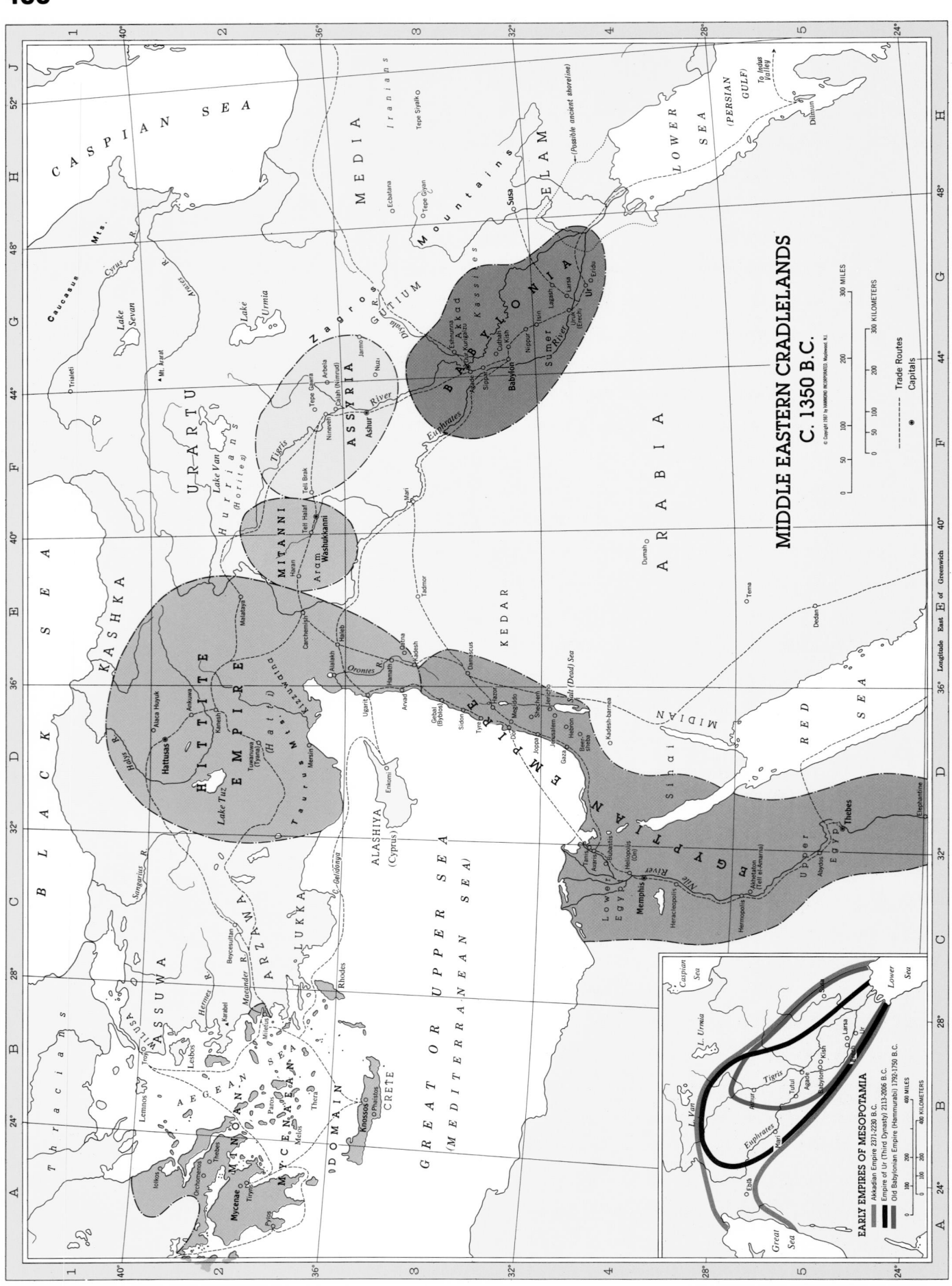

MIDDLE EASTERN CRADLELANDS
C. 1350 B.C.

© Copyright 1987 by HAMMOND INCORPORATED, Maplewood, N.J.

- - - - - Trade Routes
◉ Capitals

EARLY EMPIRES OF MESOPOTAMIA

Akkadian Empire 2371-2230 B.C.
Empire of Ur (Third Dynasty) 2113-2006 B.C.
Old Babylonian Empire (Hammurabi) 1792-1750 B.C.

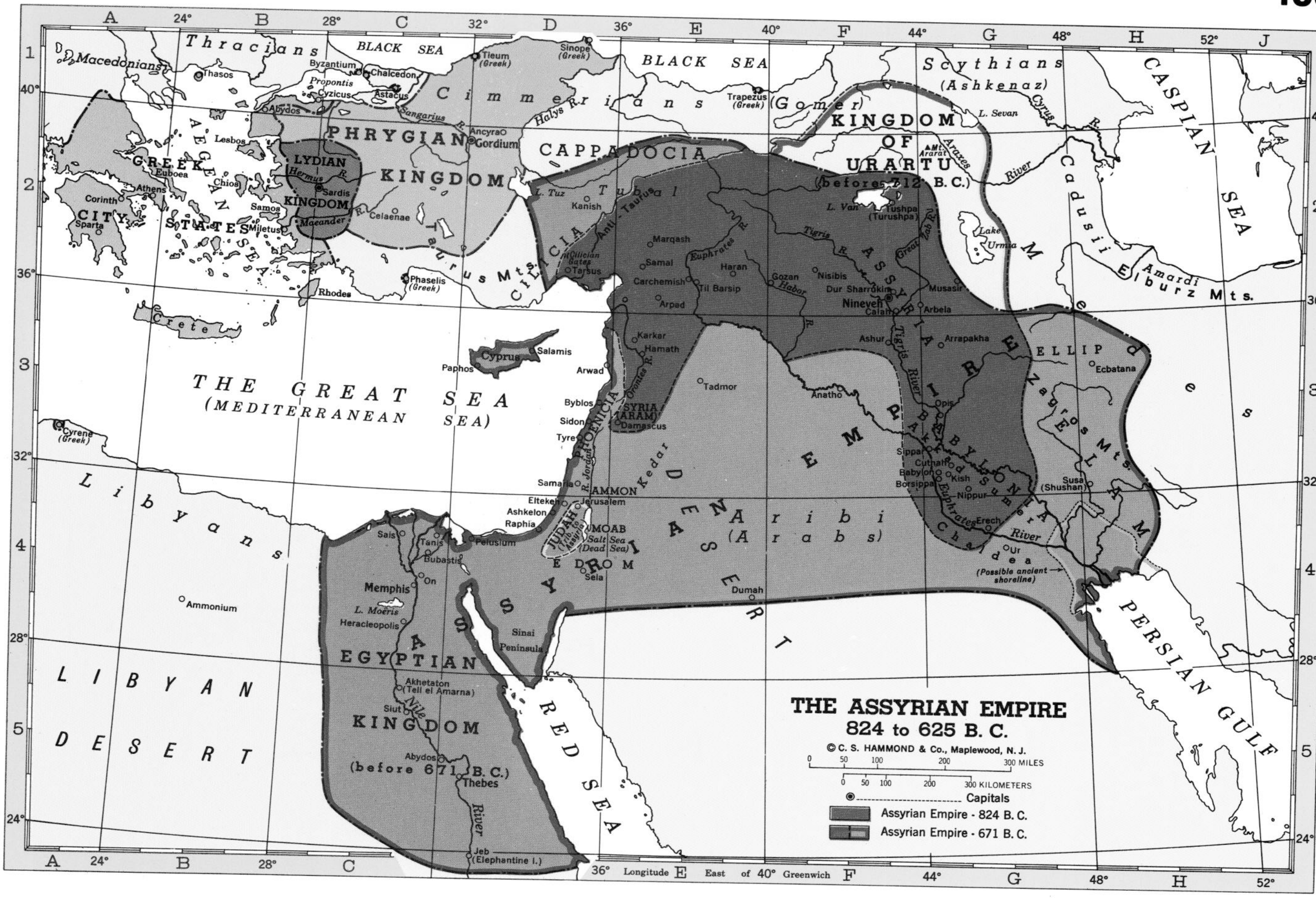

THE ASSYRIAN EMPIRE
824 to 625 B.C.

© C. S. HAMMOND & Co., Maplewood, N.J.

0 50 100 200 300 MILES
0 50 100 200 300 KILOMETERS

- - - - - - Capitals
Assyrian Empire - 824 B.C.
Assyrian Empire - 671 B.C.

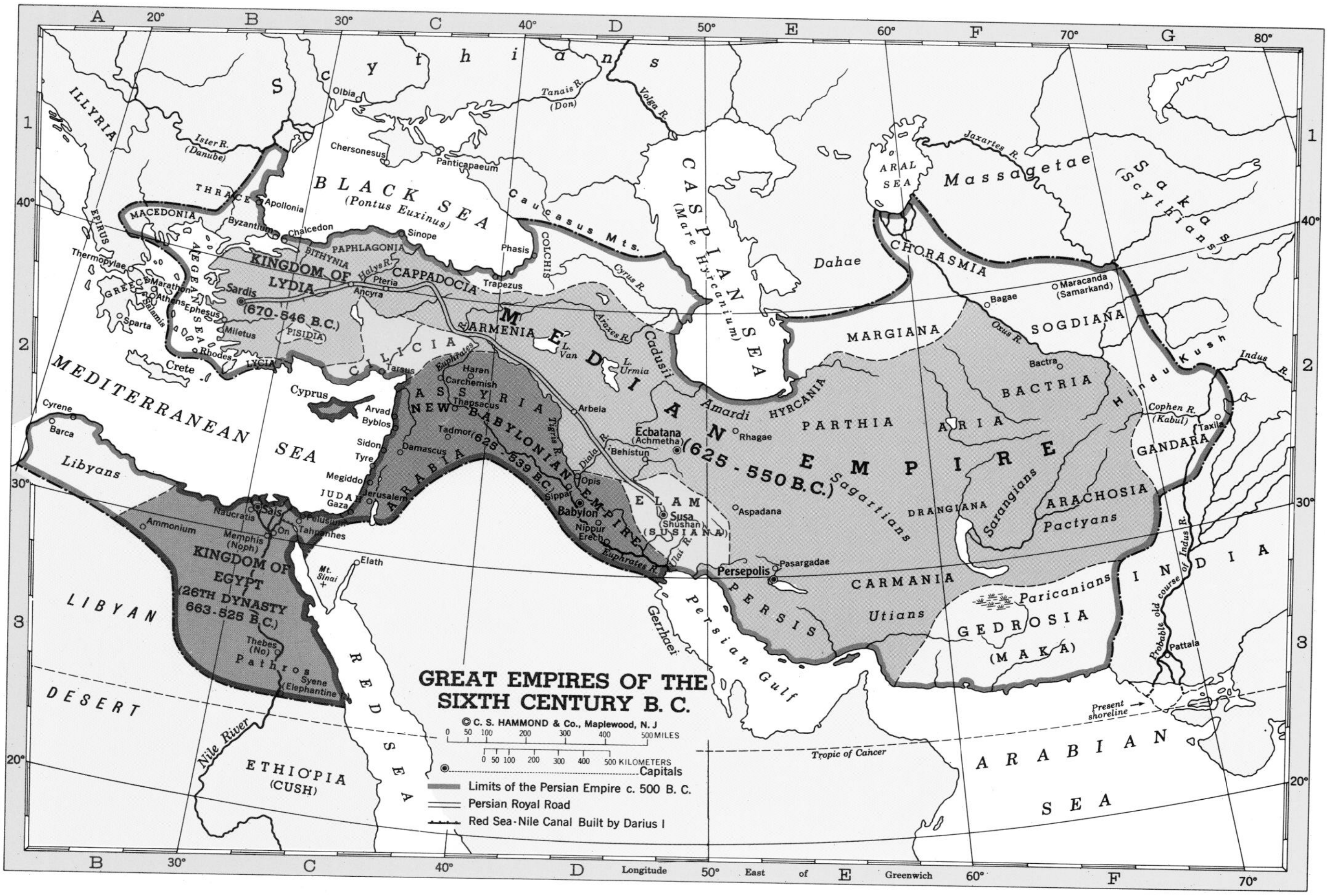

Map labels include: Macedonians, Thracians, BLACK SEA, Cimmerians, Scythians (Ashkenaz) (Gomer), CASPIAN SEA, PHRYGIAN KINGDOM, LYDIAN KINGDOM, CAPPADOCIA, KINGDOM OF URARTU (before 712 B.C.), GREEK CITY STATES, THE GREAT SEA (MEDITERRANEAN SEA), Cyprus, Crete, CILICIA, ASSYRIAN EMPIRE, Nineveh, Babylon, BABYLONIA, ELAM, Susa (Shushan), Zagros Mts., Elburz Mts., Aribi (Arabs), Libyans, LIBYAN DESERT, EGYPTIAN KINGDOM (before 671 B.C.), Memphis, Thebes, RED SEA, PERSIAN GULF, Jerusalem, Damascus, Tyre, Sidon, Byblos

GREAT EMPIRES OF THE
SIXTH CENTURY B.C.

© C. S. HAMMOND & Co., Maplewood, N.J.

0 50 100 200 300 400 500 MILES
0 50 100 200 300 400 500 KILOMETERS

- - - - - - Capitals
Limits of the Persian Empire c. 500 B.C.
Persian Royal Road
Red Sea-Nile Canal Built by Darius I

Map labels include: ILLYRIA, Scythians, BLACK SEA (Pontus Euxinus), CASPIAN SEA (Mare Hyrcanium), ARAL SEA, Massagetae, Saka Scythians, MACEDONIA, THRACE, KINGDOM OF LYDIA (670-546 B.C.), CAPPADOCIA, ARMENIA, MEDIAN EMPIRE (625-550 B.C.), CHORASMIA, SOGDIANA, MARGIANA, PARTHIA, BACTRIA, ARIA, GANDARA, ASSYRIA, NEW BABYLONIAN EMPIRE (625-539 B.C.), ELAM, Babylon, Susa (Shushan), PERSIS, Persepolis, Pasargadae, CARMANIA, DRANGIANA, ARACHOSIA, GEDROSIA (MAKA), INDIA, MEDITERRANEAN SEA, Cyprus, Crete, Sparta, JUDAH, KINGDOM OF EGYPT (26TH DYNASTY 663-525 B.C.), Thebes, Memphis (Noph), LIBYAN DESERT, RED SEA, ETHIOPIA (CUSH), ARABIA, Persian Gulf, ARABIAN SEA, Tropic of Cancer, Present shoreline

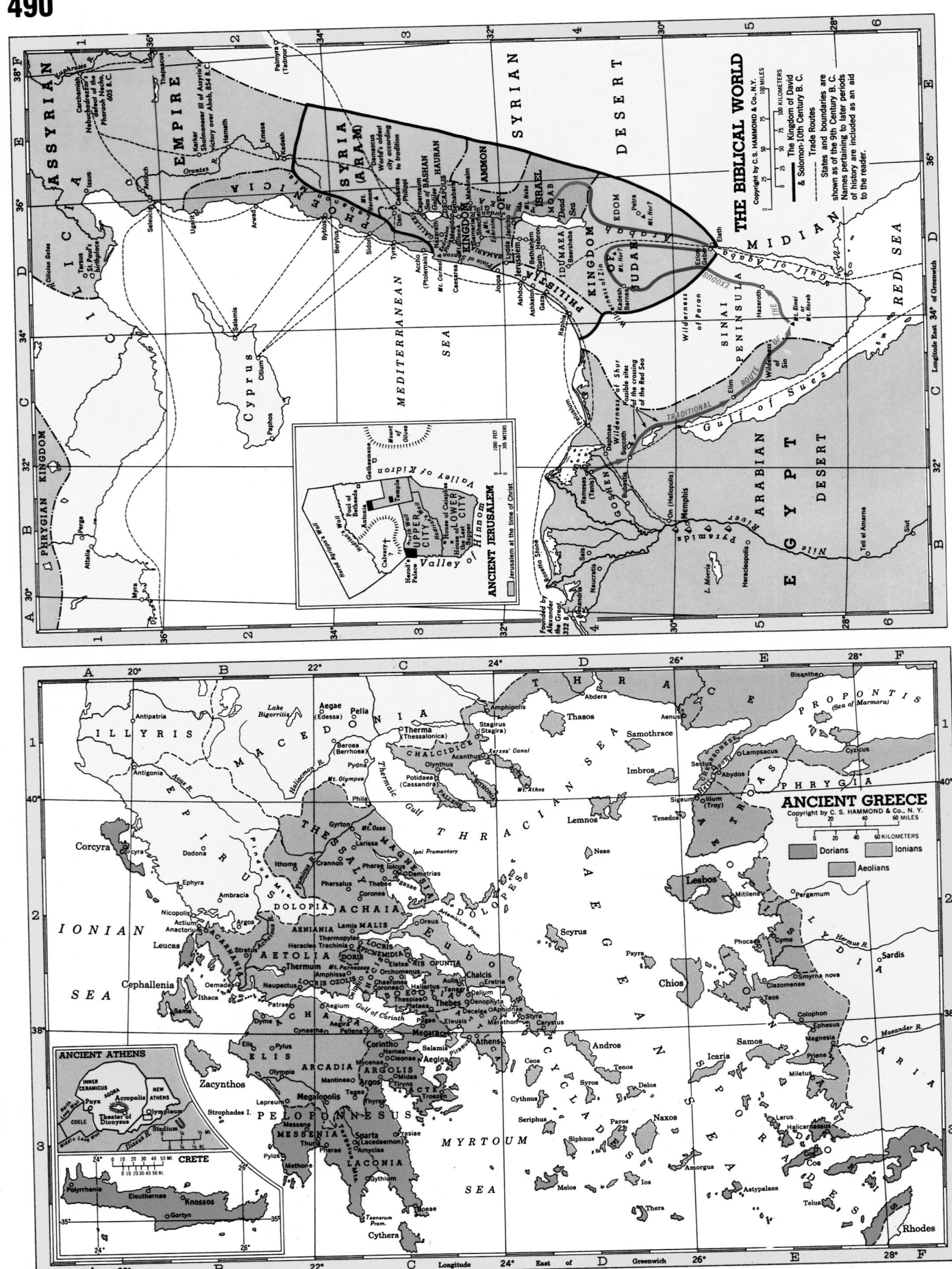

THE BIBLICAL WORLD

Copyright by C. S. HAMMOND & Co., N.Y.

The Kingdom of David & Solomon–10th Century B.C.
Trade Routes

States and boundaries are shown as of the 9th Century B.C. Names pertaining to later periods of history are included as an aid to the reader.

ANCIENT JERUSALEM
Jerusalem at the time of Christ

ANCIENT GREECE
Copyright by C. S. HAMMOND & Co., N.Y.

Dorians   Ionians

Aeolians

ANCIENT ATHENS

CRETE

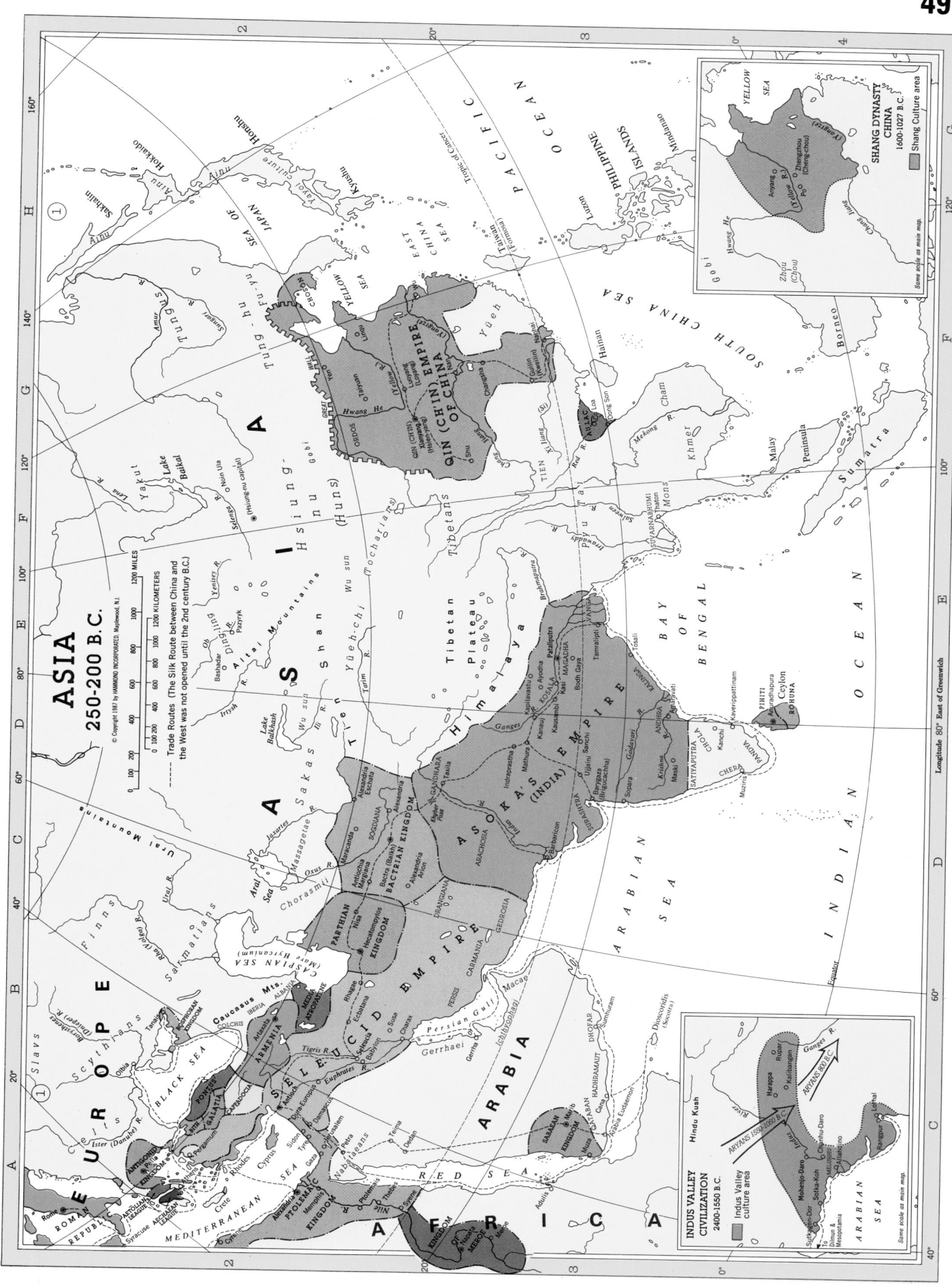

ASIA
250-200 B.C.
© Copyright 1987 by HAMMOND INCORPORATED, Maplewood, N.J.

Trade Routes (The Silk Route between China and the West was not opened until the 2nd century B.C.)

SHANG DYNASTY CHINA
1600-1027 B.C.

Shang Culture area

Same scale as main map.

INDUS VALLEY CIVILIZATION
2400-1550 B.C.

Indus Valley culture area

Same scale as main map.

Longitude 80° East of Greenwich

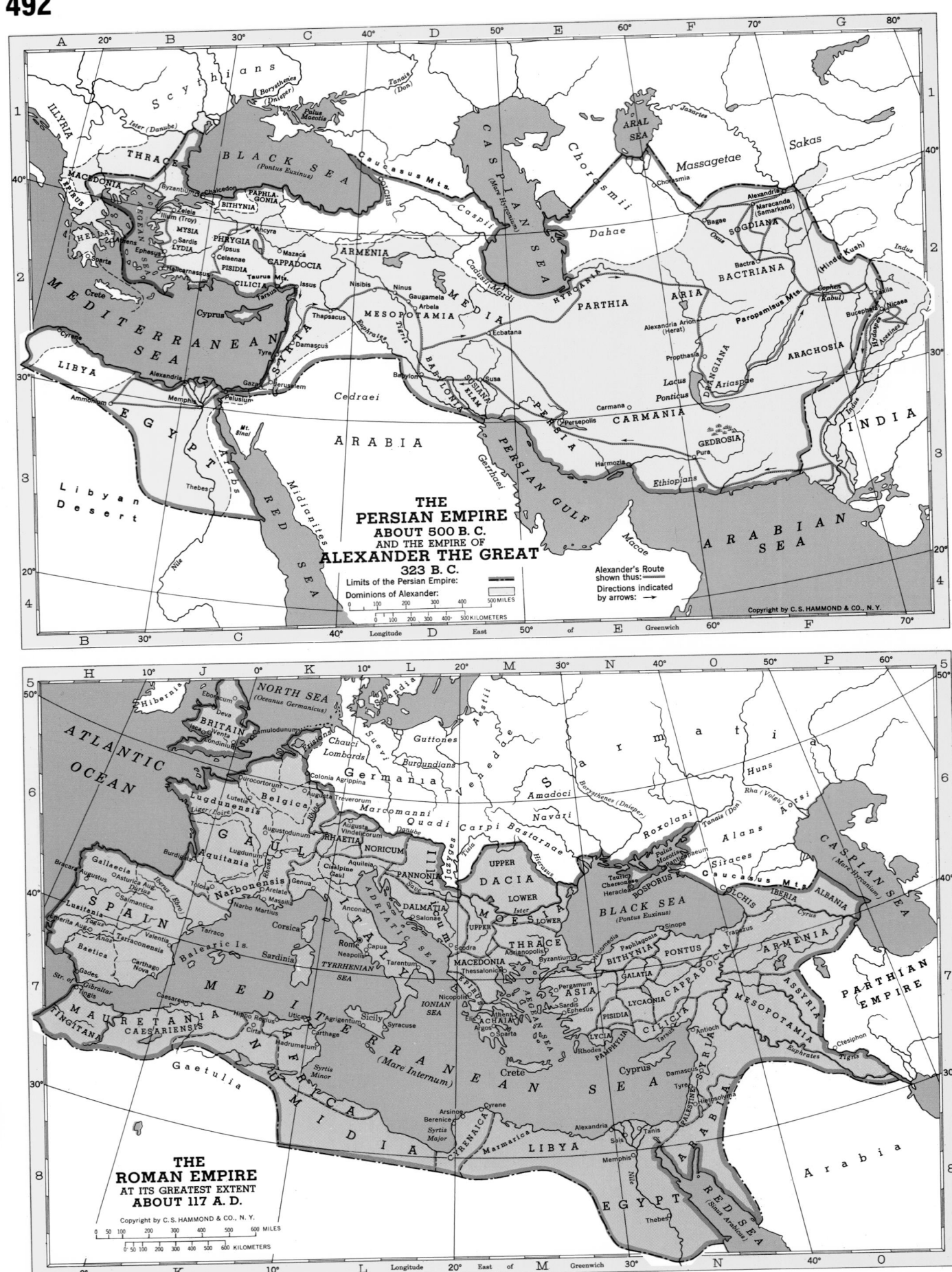

THE PERSIAN EMPIRE
ABOUT 500 B. C.
AND THE EMPIRE OF
ALEXANDER THE GREAT
323 B. C.

Limits of the Persian Empire:

Dominions of Alexander:

Alexander's Route shown thus:

Directions indicated by arrows: →

Copyright by C. S. HAMMOND & CO., N. Y.

THE
ROMAN EMPIRE
AT ITS GREATEST EXTENT
ABOUT 117 A. D.

Copyright by C. S. HAMMOND & CO., N. Y.

ANCIENT ITALY

ITALIA, LIGURIA, VENETIA, GALLIA-CISALPINA, HISTRIA, SICILIA & CORSICA

Before the time of Augustus

Copyright by C.S. HAMMOND & CO., N.Y.

Roman Colonies, thus; - - - - - - - - Ostia
Greek Colonies, thus; —— SYRACUSAE (G)
Carthaginian Colonies, thus; _ _ _ _ Eryx (C)
Dotted lines show the Modern shore line

THE FORUM CAPITOLIUM and PALATIUM

1. Templum Saturni
2. Templum Concordiae
3. Scalae Gemoniae
4. Carcer (Tullianum)
5. Senaculum
6. Graecostasis
7. Rostra
8. Templum Jani

IMPERIAL FORA

1. Scalae Gemoniae
2. Templum Vespasiani
3. Porticus Deorum Consentium
4. Equus Caesaris
5. T. Castoris et Pollucis
6. Templum Divi Julii
7. Arcus Augusti
8. Arcus Titi
9. Templum Antonini et Faustinae

ROME
Under the Emperors

1. Templum Jovis Capitolini
2. Arx
3. Forum Romanum
4. Templum Aesculapii
5. Forum Trajani
6. Forum Augusti
7. Porta Carmentalis
8. Arcus Septimii Severi
9. Arcus Constantini
10. Arcus Titi
11. Arcus Claudii
12. Arcus Tiberii
13. Arcus Gallieni
14. Arcus Marci Aurelii
15. Arcus Diocletiani
16. Porta Flumentara
17. Templum Mercurii
18. Theatrum Marcelli

REGIONES AUGUSTI

I. Porta Capena
II. Caelimontium
III. Isis et Serapis
IV. Templum Pacis
V. Esquiliae
VI. Alta Semita
VII. Via Lata
VIII. Forum Romanum
IX. Circus Flaminius
X. Palatium
XI. Circus Maximus
XII. Piscina Publica
XIII. Aventinus
XIV. Trans Tiberim

ROME
In the time of the Republic

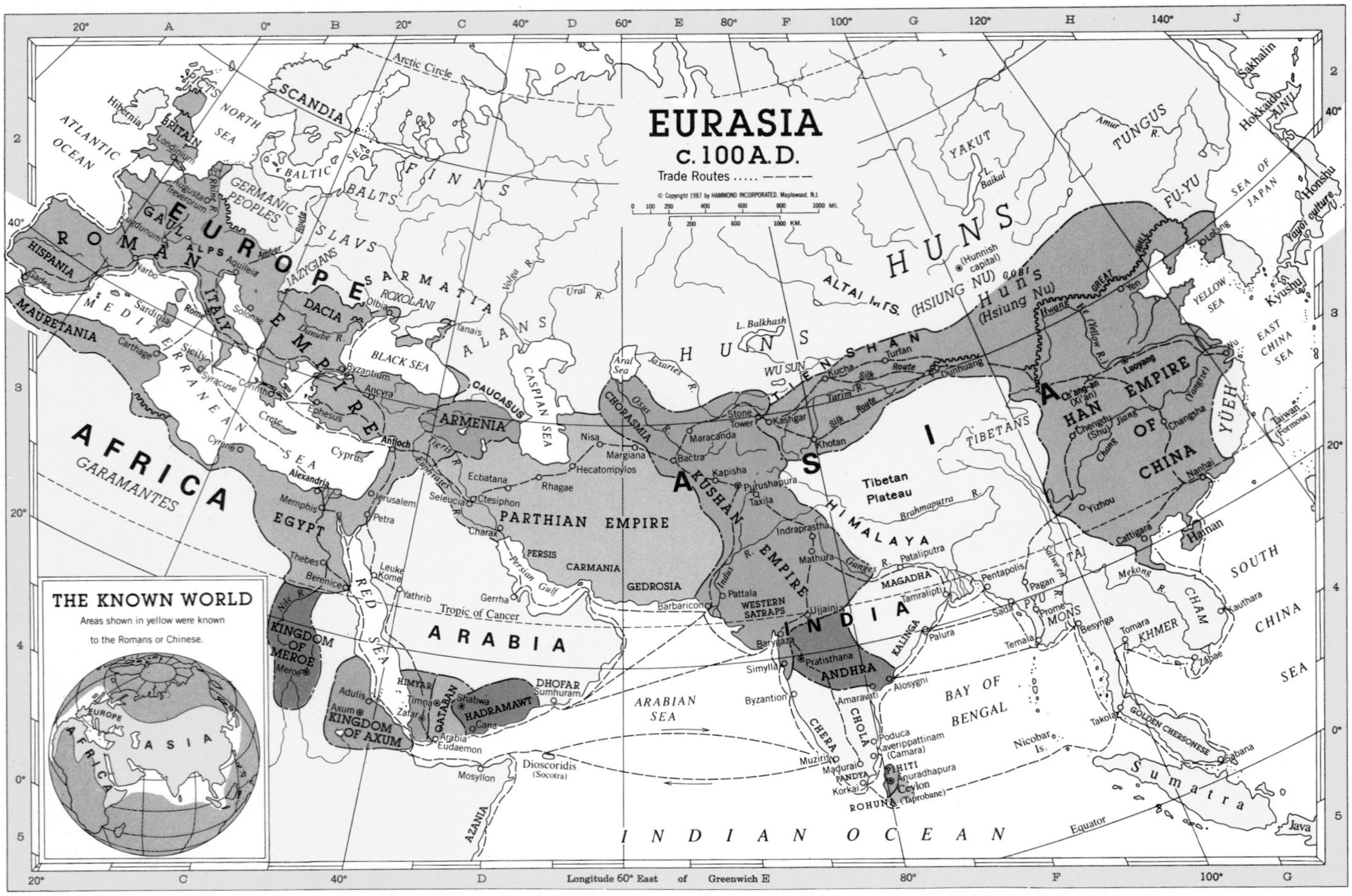

EURASIA
c. 100 A.D.
Trade Routes .....

© Copyright 1987 by HAMMOND INCORPORATED, Maplewood, N.J.

ATLANTIC OCEAN

SCANDIA
NORTH SEA
BALTS
FINNS
SLAVS
GERMANIC PEOPLES
BRITAIN
Londinium
GAUL
EUROPE
ROMAN EMPIRE
HISPANIA
ITALY
Rome
ALPS
DACIA
SARMATIA
IAZYGIANS
ROXOLANI
ALANS
BLACK SEA
CAUCASUS
ARMENIA
CASPIAN SEA
Byzantium
Ephesus
Crete
Cyprus
Antioch
MEDITERRANEAN SEA
Sardinia
Sicily
Syracuse
Carthage

MAURETANIA
AFRICA
GARAMANTES
EGYPT
Memphis
Alexandria
Jerusalem
Petra
Thebes
Berenice
Leuke
RED SEA
Tropic of Cancer
ARABIA
KINGDOM OF MEROE
Meroe
Adulis
Axum
KINGDOM OF AXUM
QATABAN
HADRAMAWT
DHOFAR
Sumhuram
Cana
Eudaemon
Mosyllon
Dioscoridis (Socotra)
AZANIA

HUNS (HSIUNG NU)
(Hunnish capital)
GOBI
Huns (Hsiung Nu)
ALTAI Mts.
L. Balkhash
Aral Sea
CHORASMIA
Oxus R.
Jaxartes R.
WU SUN
TIEN SHAN
Turfan
Silk Route
Kashgar
Khotan
Stone Tower
Maracanda
Bactra
Margiana
Hecatompylos
Rhagae
Ecbatana
Seleucia
Ctesiphon
Charax
PERSIS
CARMANIA
GEDROSIA
Gerrha
Persian Gulf
Barygaza
Barbaricon
WESTERN SATRAPS

PARTHIAN EMPIRE
KUSHAN EMPIRE
Kapisha
Purushapura
Taxila
Indraprastha
Mathura
Ujjain
MAGADHA
Pataliputra
Ganges R.
Brahmaputra R.
Tibetan Plateau
TIBETANS
HIMALAYA

HAN EMPIRE OF CHINA
Luoyang
Great Wall
Yellow R.
Yangtze
YUEH
Hainan
Cattigara
SOUTH CHINA SEA

A S I A

INDIA
ANDHRA
KALINGA
Amaravati
Palura
Pentapolis
PYU
MONS
KHMER
CHAM
BAY OF BENGAL
Tamralipti
CHERA
CHOLA
PANDYA
PIHITI
ROHUNA
Ceylon (Taprobane)
Anuradhapura
Kaveripattinam (Camara)
Korkai
Madurai
Muziris
Poduca
Simylla
Byzantion
ARABIAN SEA
Nicobar Is.
GOLDEN CHERSONESE
Takola
Sumatra
Java
Equator
INDIAN OCEAN

THE KNOWN WORLD
Areas shown in yellow were known to the Romans or Chinese.

EUROPE
AFRICA
ASIA

Longitude 60° East of Greenwich E

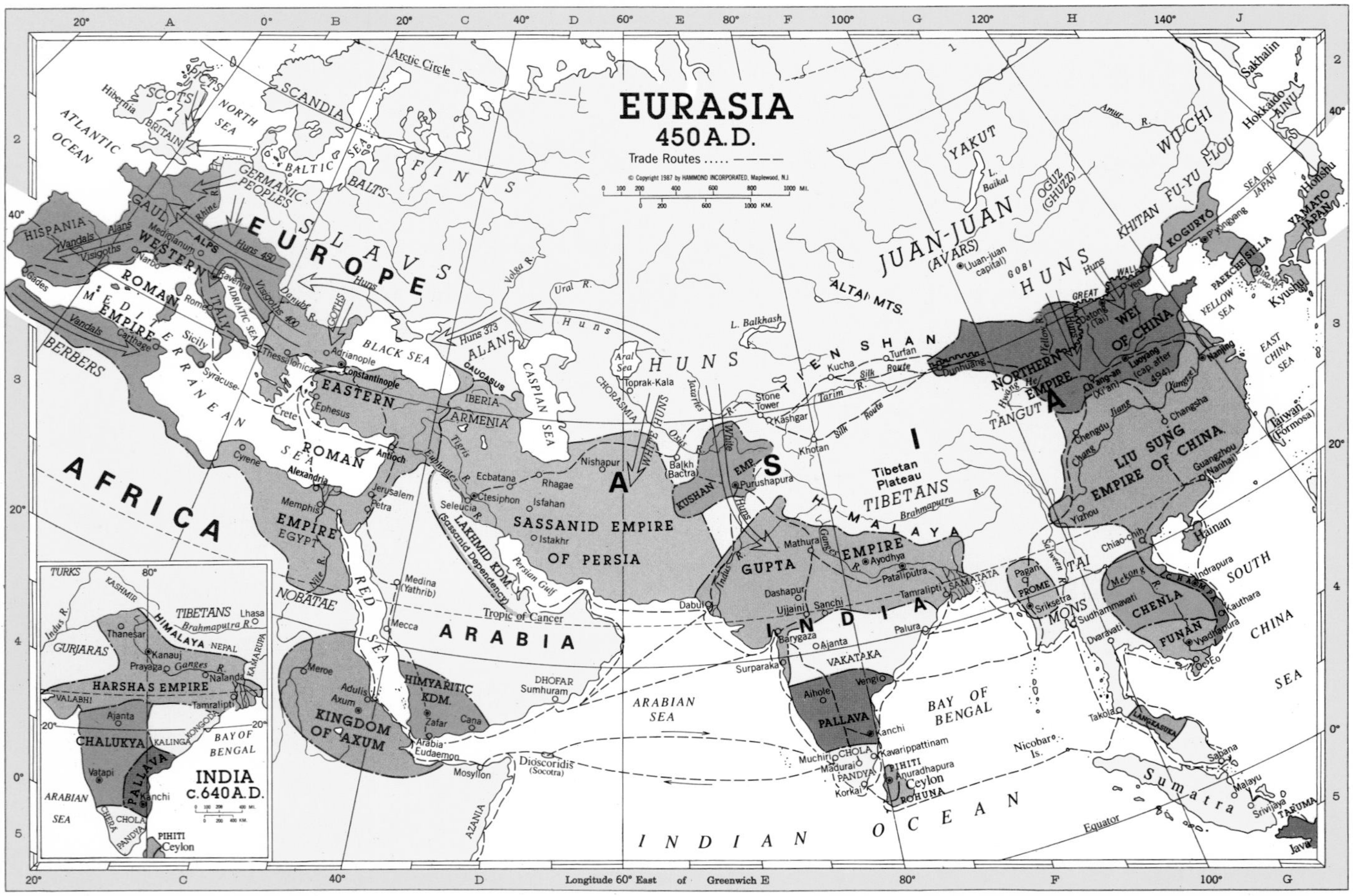

EURASIA
450 A.D.
Trade Routes .....

© Copyright 1987 by HAMMOND INCORPORATED, Maplewood, N.J.

ATLANTIC OCEAN
SCOTS
HIBERNIA
BRITAIN
SCANDIA
NORTH SEA
BALTS
FINNS
SLAVS
GERMANIC PEOPLES
EUROPE
HISPANIA
Vandals
Alans
Visigoths
GAUL
WESTERN ROMAN EMPIRE
ALPS
Rome
ITALY
Sicily
Syracuse
Adriatic Sea
Huns 450
Huns
MEDITERRANEAN SEA
BERBERS
Carthage
Cyrene
Vandals
Crete
Ephesus
Thessalonica
Adrianople
Constantinople
EASTERN ROMAN EMPIRE
BLACK SEA
Huns 373
ALANS
CAUCASUS
IBERIA
ARMENIA
CASPIAN SEA
Tigris R.
Euphrates R.
Antioch
Jerusalem
Alexandria
Memphis
EGYPT
AFRICA
RED SEA
Tropic of Cancer
NOBATAE
ARABIA
Medina (Yathrib)
Mecca
Dabul
LAKHMID KDM.
Berenice Dependencies
Persian Gulf
HIMYARITIC KDM.
Zafar
Cana
DHOFAR
Sumhuram
Meroe
Adulis
Axum
KINGDOM OF AXUM
Eudaemon
Mosyllon
Dioscoridis (Socotra)
AZANIA
ARABIAN SEA

JUAN-JUAN (AVARS)
(Juan-Juan capital)
GOBI
ALTAI MTS.
L. Baikal
YAKUT
OGUZ (GHUZZ)
HUNS
Huns
TIEN SHAN
Kucha
Turfan
Silk Route
Kashgar
Khotan
Stone Tower
WHITE HUNS
Aral Sea
CHORASMIA
Toprak-Kala
Balkh (Bactra)
Nishapur
Isfahan
Istakhr
Ecbatana
Rhagae
Seleucia
Ctesiphon
SASSANID EMPIRE OF PERSIA
KUSHAN EMP.
Purushapura
Mathura
GUPTA EMPIRE
Ayodhya
Dashapur
Pataliputra
Ujjain
Sanchi
Ajanta
Barygaza
Surparaka
VAKATAKA
CHALUKYA
PALLAVA
Kanchi
CHOLA
PANDYA
Madurai
Muchiri
Kaveripattinam
Korkai
PIHITI
ROHUNA
Ceylon
Anuradhapura
INDIA
Palura
Tamralipti
A S I A

Great Wall
NORTHERN WEI EMPIRE OF CHINA
TANGUT
Chang-an
Luoyang (cap. after)
Yellow R.
He
LIU SUNG EMPIRE OF CHINA
Guangzhou
Nanhai
Hainan
KHITAN
FU-YU
WU-CHI
TUNGUS
Amur R.
Sakhalin
Hokkaido
AINU
SEA OF JAPAN
Honshu
Kyushu
YAMATO JAPAN
KOGURYO
PAEKCHE
SILLA
YELLOW SEA
EAST CHINA SEA
Taiwan (Formosa)
SOUTH CHINA SEA
TIBETANS
Tibetan Plateau
HIMALAYA
THAI
PYU
Pagan
Prome
MONS
Sudhammavati
CHENLA
FUNAN
KHMER
CHAM
Kauthara
Vyadhapura
BAY OF BENGAL
Nicobar Is.
Takola
Sabana
Sumatra
Srivijaya
Malayu
Java
BARUNA
Equator
INDIAN OCEAN

INDIA c. 640 A.D.
TURKS
KASHMIR
TIBETANS
Lhasa
GURJARAS
HARSHA'S EMPIRE
Kanauj
Thanesar
Prayaga
Ganges R.
Brahmaputra R.
NEPAL
Nalanda
HIMALAYA
KAMARUPA
VALABHI
Tamralipti
CHALUKYA
Vatapi
Ajanta
KALINGA
PALLAVA
Kanchi
CHOLA
PANDYA
PIHITI
Ceylon
BAY OF BENGAL
ARABIAN SEA

Longitude 60° East of Greenwich E

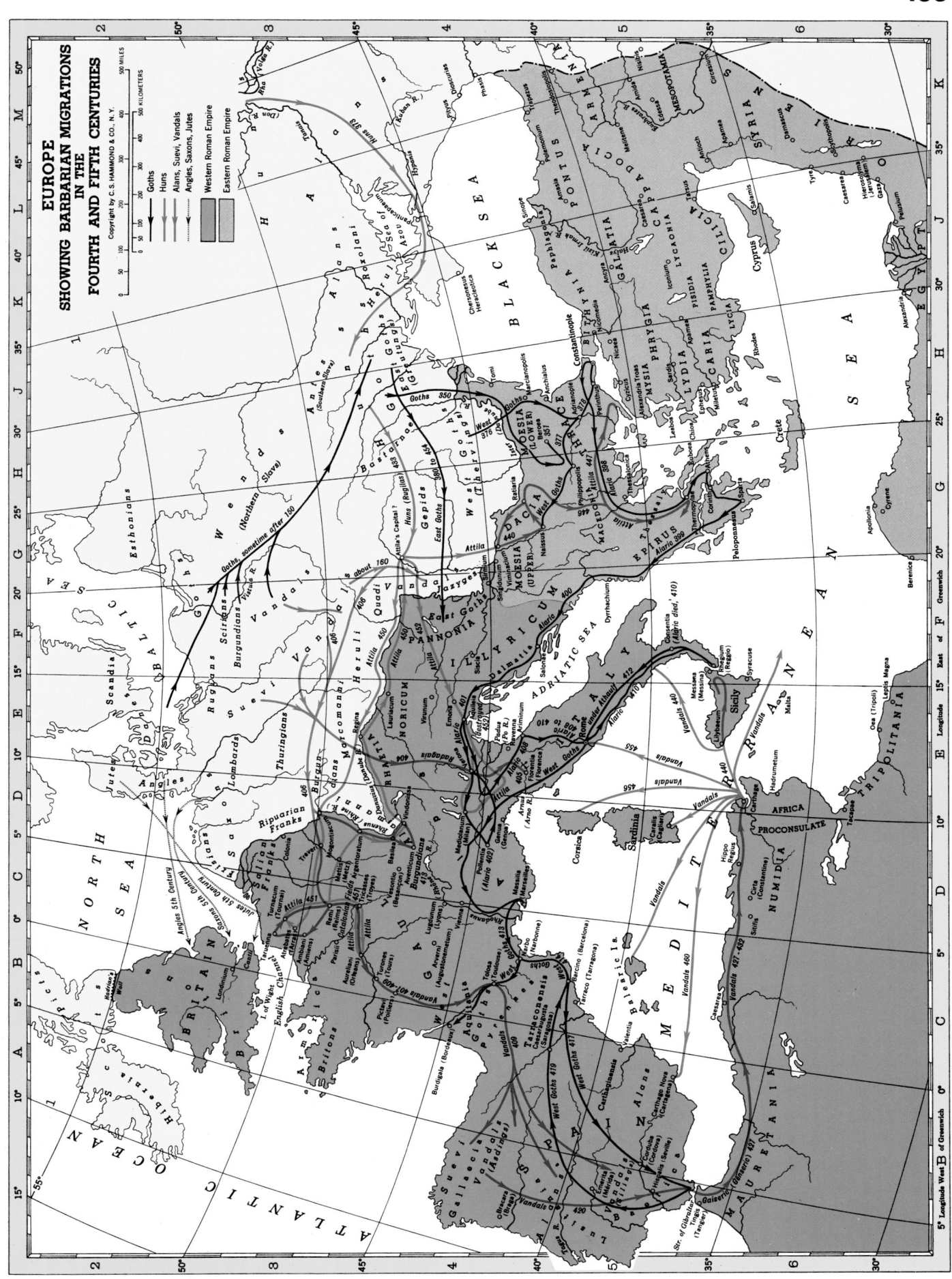

EUROPE
SHOWING BARBARIAN MIGRATIONS
IN THE
FOURTH AND FIFTH CENTURIES

Copyright by C.S. HAMMOND & CO., N.Y.

Goths
Huns
Alans, Suevi, Vandals
Angles, Saxons, Jutes
Western Roman Empire
Eastern Roman Empire

500 MILES
500 KILOMETERS

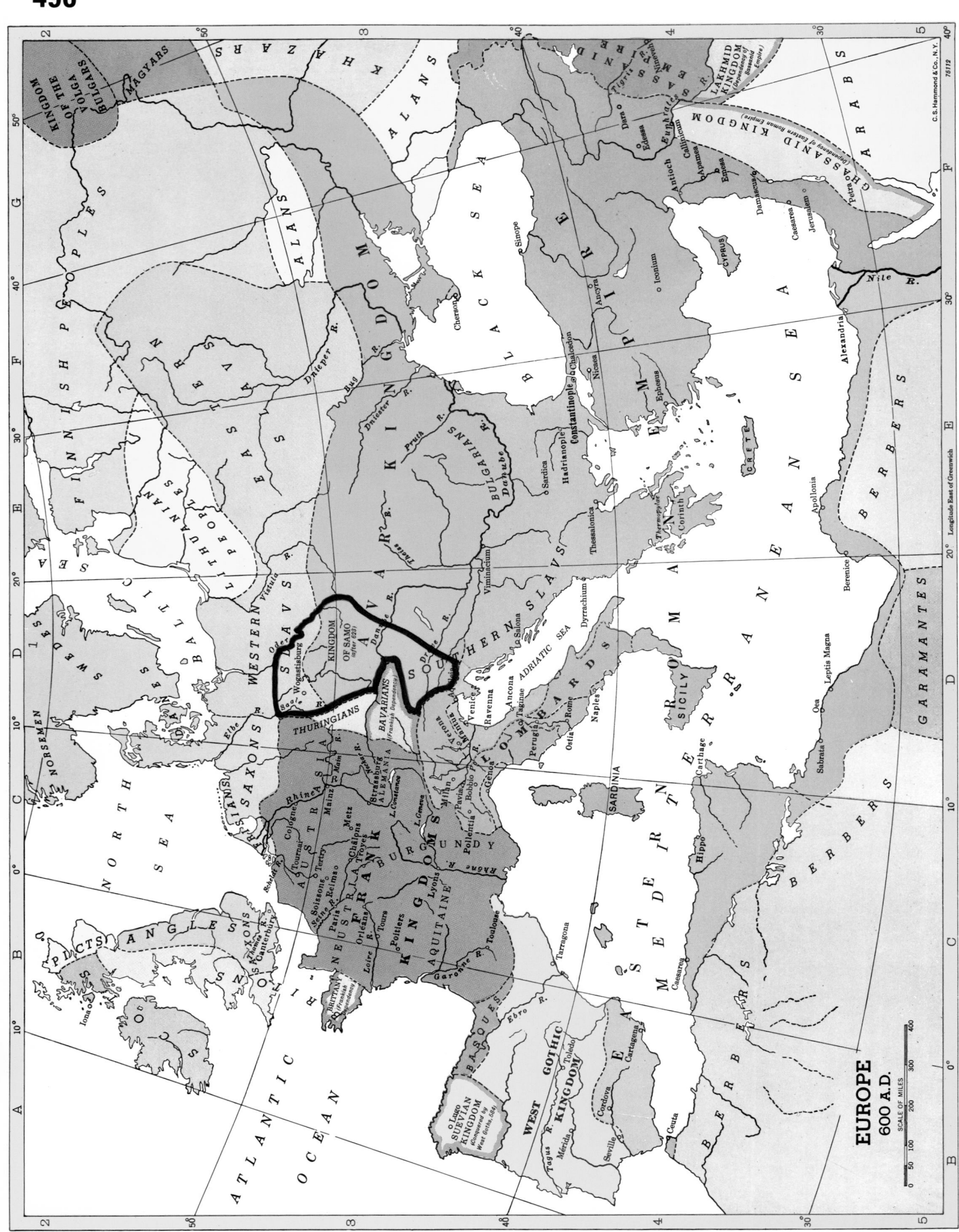

EUROPE
600 A.D.

SCALE OF MILES
0 50 100 200 300 400

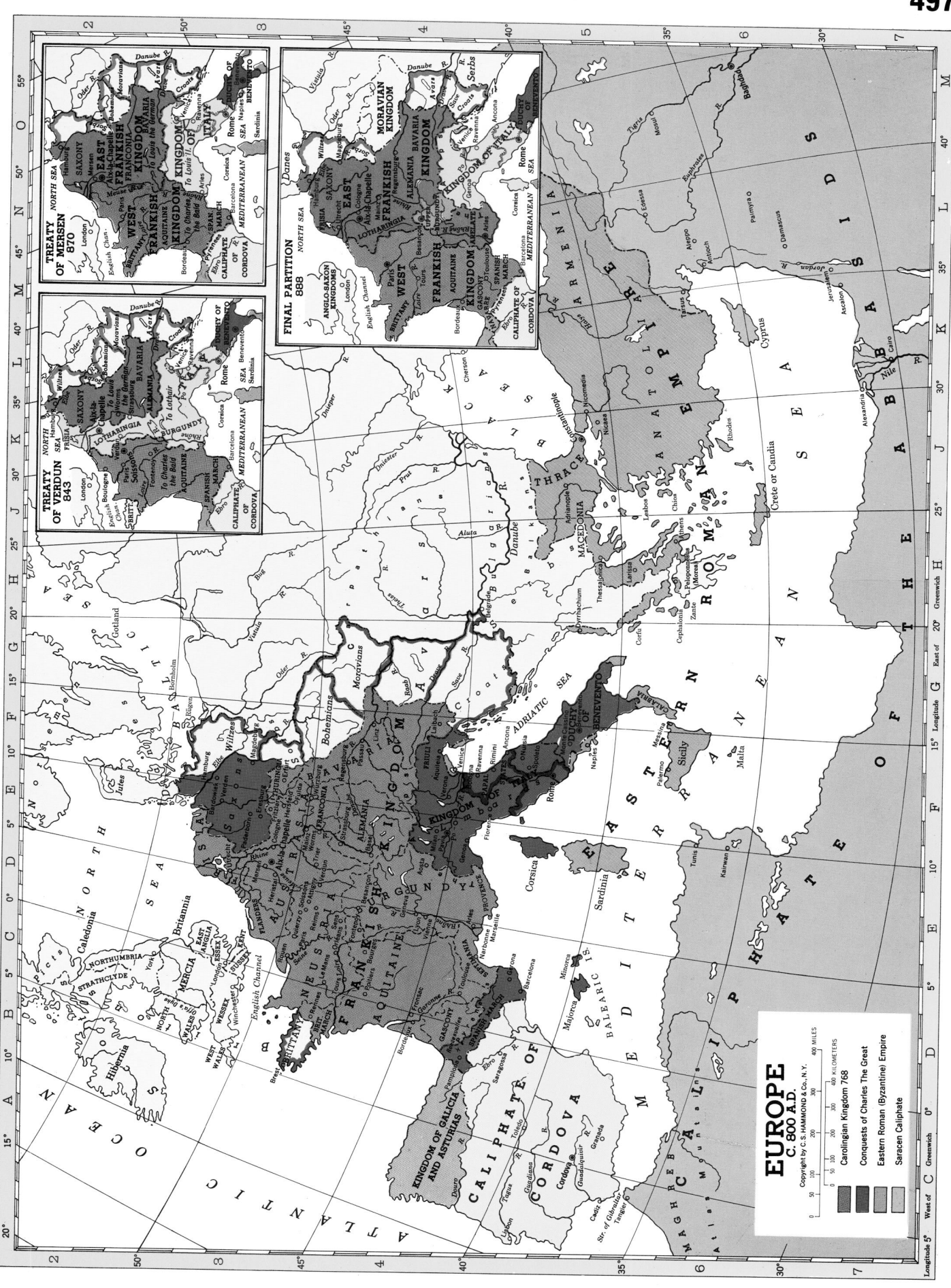

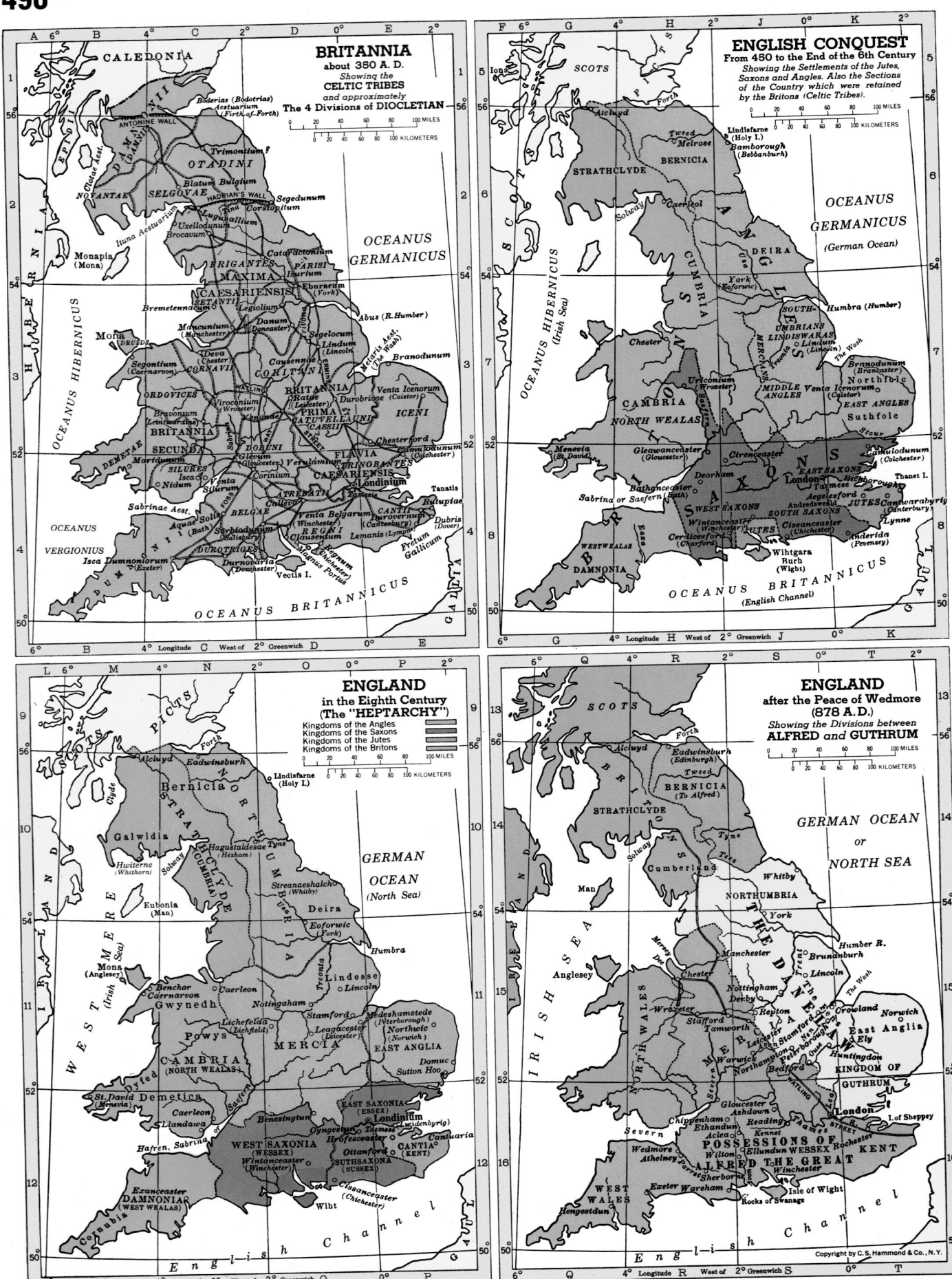

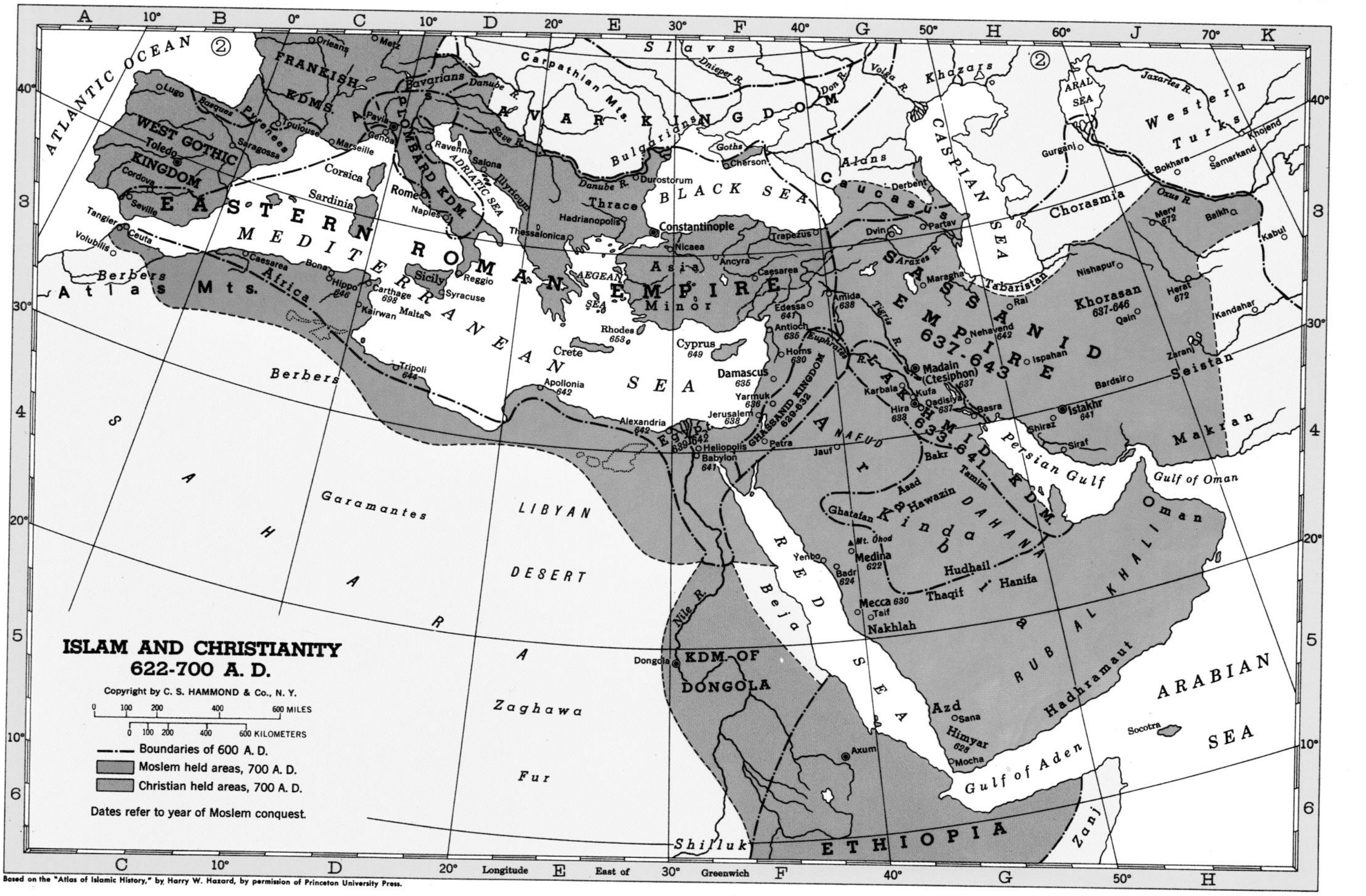

Map 1

ATLANTIC OCEAN

FRANKISH KDMS.

WEST GOTHIC KINGDOM
Toledo, Cordova, Seville, Tangier, Ceuta

LOMBARD KDM.

AVAR KINGDOM

Slavs

BULGARIANS KINGDOM

BLACK SEA

Constantinople, Nicaea, Thrace, Hadrianopolis, Thessalonica

EASTERN ROMAN EMPIRE

MEDITERRANEAN SEA

Rome, Naples, Ravenna, Sicily, Syracuse, Sardinia, Corsica, Crete, Rhodes, Cyprus

Asia Minor

Caucasus

Khazars

Caspian Sea

Western Turks

Chorasmia

Bokhara, Samarkand, Merv, Balkh, Kabul

SASSANID EMPIRE 637-643

Khorasan 637-646
Herat 672, Kandahar

Damascus 635, Jerusalem 638, Antioch, Edessa, Homs, Madain (Ctesiphon) 637, Kufa, Basra, Hira

GHASSANID KINGDOM

Atlas Mts., Berbers, Africa, Carthage 698, Kairwan, Tripoli, Malta

Garamantes

LIBYAN DESERT

Alexandria, Babylon, Heliopolis

RED SEA

KDM. OF DONGOLA

Beja

Mecca 630, Medina 622, Taif, Mt. Ohod, Badr 624, Nakhlah

Hawazin, Ghatafan, Asad, Thaqif, Hanifa, Hudhail

RUB AL KHALI

Oman, Hadhramaut, Azd, Himyar, Sana, Mocha, Socotra

ARABIAN SEA

Gulf of Oman, Gulf of Aden, Persian Gulf, Makran, Seistan, Zaranj

Axum, Zaghawa, Fur, Shilluk, ETHIOPIA, Zanj

ISLAM AND CHRISTIANITY 622-700 A.D.

Copyright by C. S. HAMMOND & Co., N. Y.

0 100 200 400 600 MILES
0 100 200 400 600 KILOMETERS

Boundaries of 600 A.D.
Moslem held areas, 700 A.D.
Christian held areas, 700 A.D.

Dates refer to year of Moslem conquest.

Based on the "Atlas of Islamic History," by Harry W. Hazard, by permission of Princeton University Press.

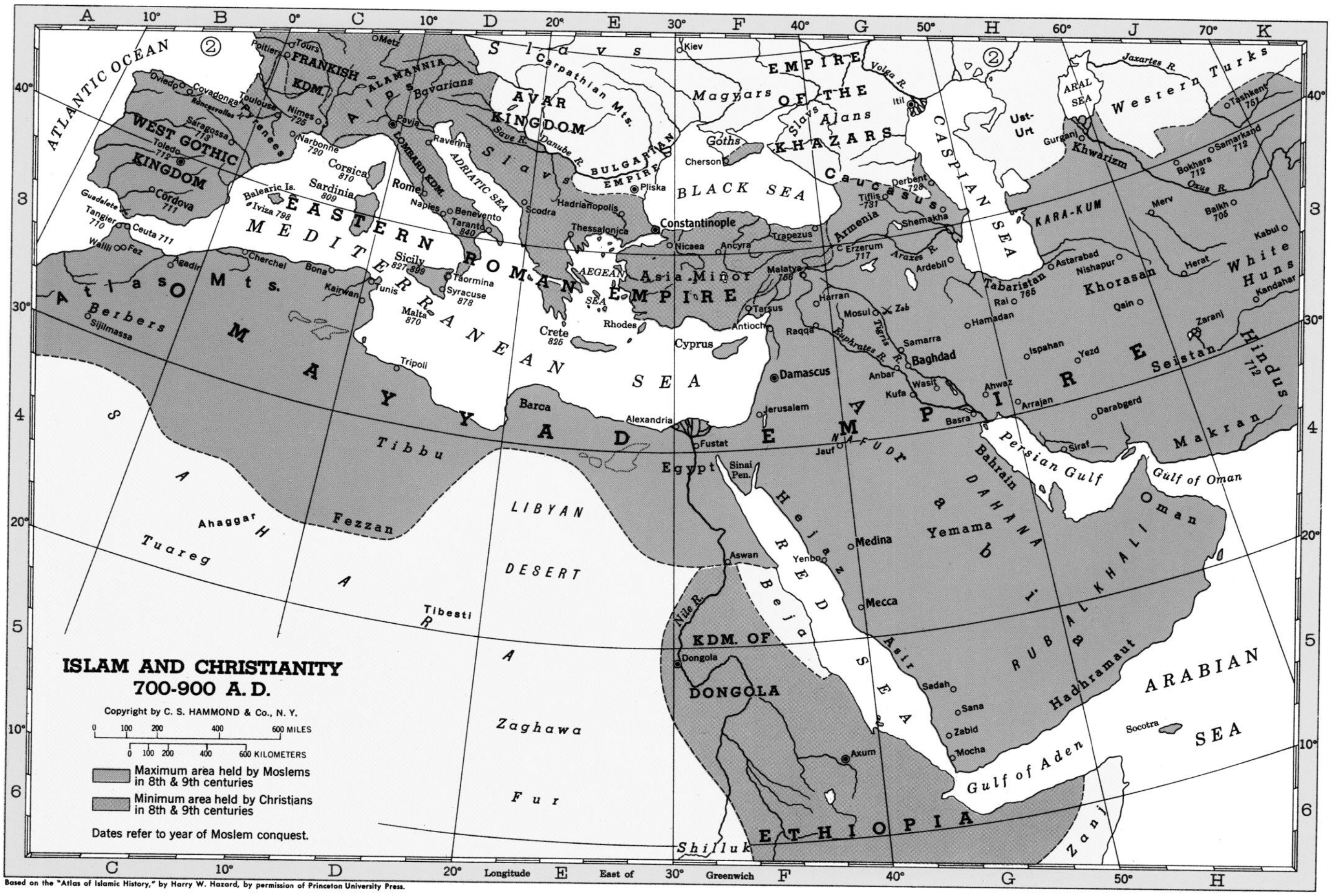

Longitude East of Greenwich

Map 2

ATLANTIC OCEAN

FRANKISH KDM., ALAMANNIA, Bavarians, Poitiers, Tours, Metz

WEST GOTHIC KINGDOM
Toledo, Cordova 711, Saragossa, Toulouse, Narbonne 720, Nimes 725

AVAR KINGDOM

Slavs, Carpathian Mts.

BULGARIAN EMPIRE

EMPIRE OF THE KHAZARS
Kiev, Itil, Magyars, Alans, Goths, Cherson

BLACK SEA

Constantinople, Nicaea, Thessalonica, Hadrianopolis, Pliska, Scodra

EASTERN ROMAN EMPIRE

MEDITERRANEAN SEA

Rome, Naples, Ravenna, Benevento, Taranto, Sicily 827-899, Taormina, Syracuse 878, Sardinia, Corsica 810, Balearic Is., Ivisa 798, Crete 826, Rhodes, Cyprus

Asia Minor

Caucasus, Derbent, Shemakha, Armenia, Erzerum 717, Ardebil, Tabaristan 728, Astarabad

Caspian Sea

Western Turks, Tashkent 751, Bokhara 712, Samarkand 712, Khwarizm, Merv, Balkh 705, Kabul

White Huns, Hindus 712, Kandahar

UMAYYAD EMPIRE / ABBASID EMPIRE

Baghdad, Samarra, Kufa, Wasit, Basra, Mosul, Raqqa, Harran, Tarsus, Antioch, Damascus, Jerusalem, Hamadan, Ispahan, Yezd, Rai 765, Nishapur, Khorasan, Herat, Seistan, Zaranj, Makran, Darabgerd, Siraf, Ahwaz, Arrajan

Atlas Mts., Berbers, Sijilmassa, Walili, Fez, Tangier 710, Ceuta 711, Cherchel, Bona, Tunis, Kairwan, Tripoli, Barca, Malta 870

Ahaggar, Tuareg, Fezzan, Tibesti, Tibbu

LIBYAN DESERT

Alexandria, Fustat, Egypt, Sinai Pen.

RED SEA, Beja

KDM. OF DONGOLA, Dongola, Aswan

Mecca, Medina, Yenbo, Hejaz, Asir, Yemama, Bahrain, DAHANA, Oman, Hadhramaut, Yemen, Sana, Sadah, Zabid, Mocha, Socotra

RUB AL KHALI

Persian Gulf, Gulf of Oman, Gulf of Aden

ARABIAN SEA

Axum, Zaghawa, Fur, Shilluk, ETHIOPIA, Zanj

ISLAM AND CHRISTIANITY 700-900 A.D.

Copyright by C. S. HAMMOND & Co., N. Y.

0 100 200 400 600 MILES
0 100 200 400 600 KILOMETERS

Maximum area held by Moslems in 8th & 9th centuries
Minimum area held by Christians in 8th & 9th centuries

Dates refer to year of Moslem conquest.

Based on the "Atlas of Islamic History," by Harry W. Hazard, by permission of Princeton University Press.

Longitude East of Greenwich

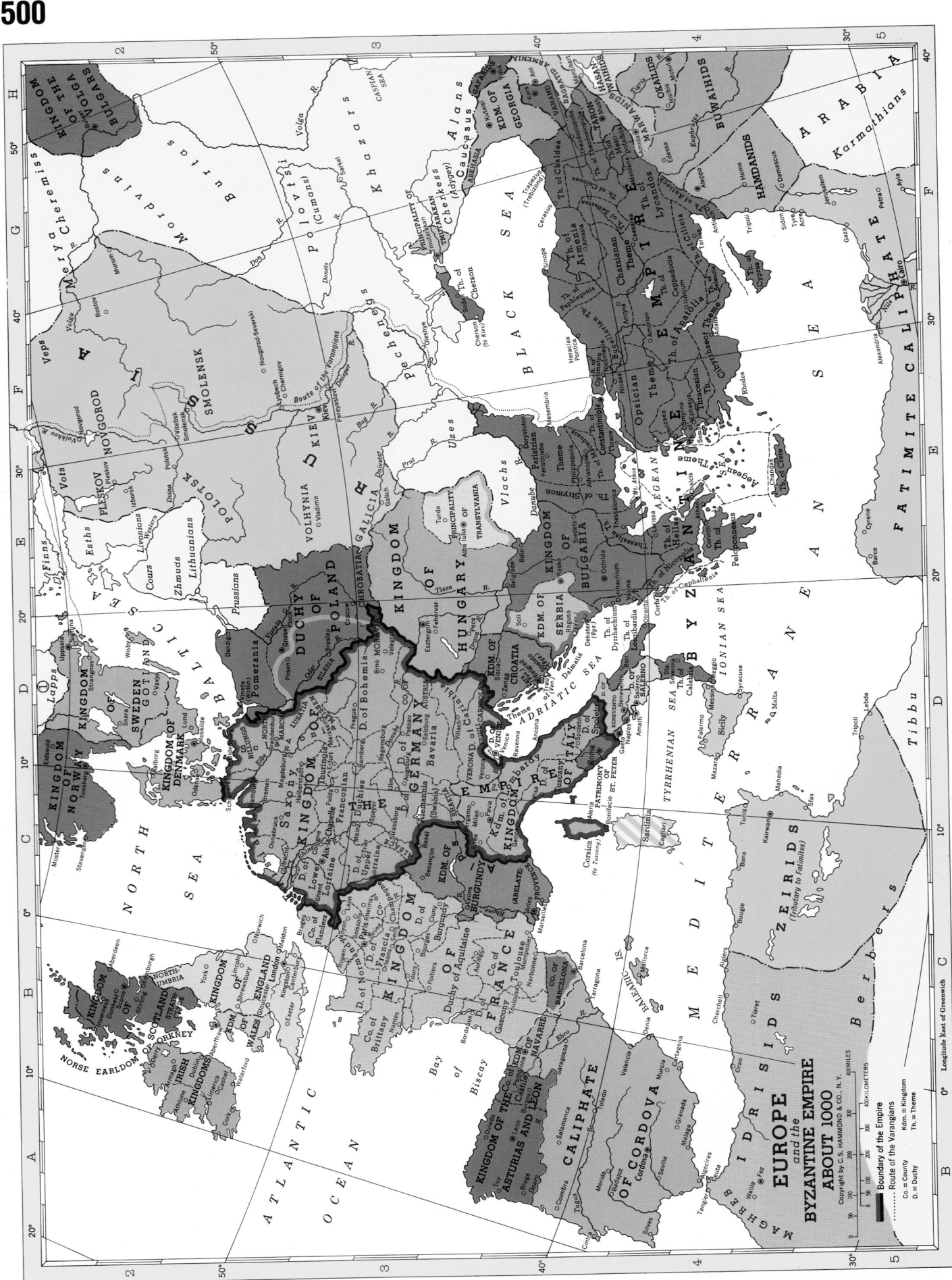

EUROPE
and the
**BYZANTINE EMPIRE
ABOUT 1000**

Copyright by C.S. Hammond & Co., N.Y.

Boundary of the Empire
Route of the Varangians

Co.= County Kdm.= Kingdom
D.= Duchy Th.= Theme

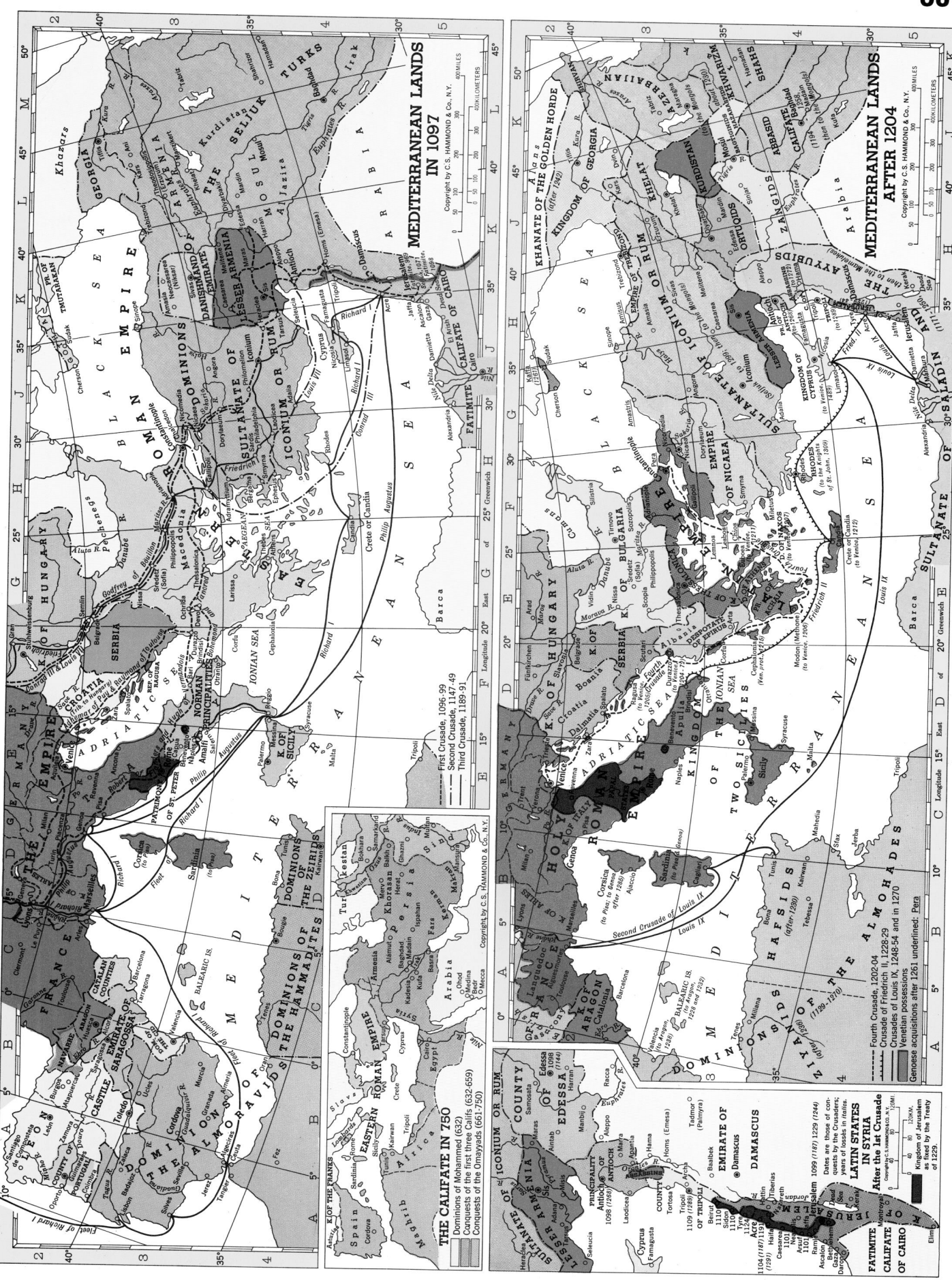

MEDITERRANEAN LANDS IN 1097

Copyright by C.S. HAMMOND & Co., N.Y.

First Crusade, 1096-99
Second Crusade, 1147-49
Third Crusade, 1189-91

THE CALIFATE IN 750

Dominions of Mohammed (632)
Conquests of the first three Califs (632-659)
Conquests of the Ommayads (661-750)

Copyright by C.S. HAMMOND & Co., N.Y.

MEDITERRANEAN LANDS AFTER 1204

Copyright by C.S. HAMMOND & Co., N.Y.

Fourth Crusade, 1202-04
Crusade of Friedrich II, 1228-29
Crusades of Louis IX, 1248-54 and in 1270
Venetian possessions
Genoese acquisitions after 1261 underlined: Pera

LATIN STATES IN SYRIA
After the 1st Crusade

Dates are those of conquests by the Crusaders; years of losses in italics.

Kingdom of Jerusalem as fixed by the Treaty of 1229.

Copyright by C.S. HAMMOND & Co., N.Y.

502

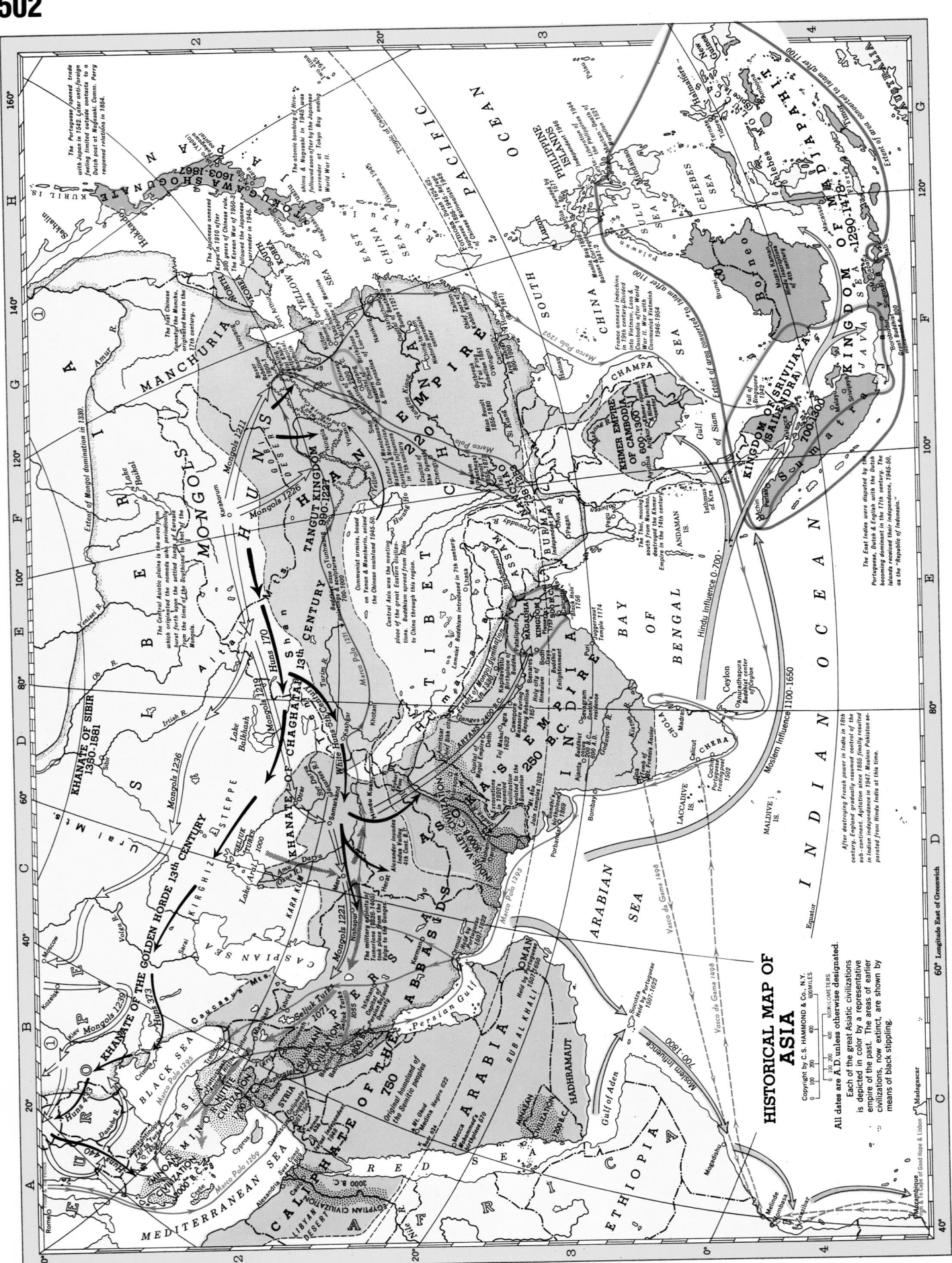

HISTORICAL MAP OF ASIA

Copyright by C. S. HAMMOND & Co., N.Y.

All dates are A.D. unless otherwise designated.

Each of the great Asiatic civilizations is depicted in color by a representative empire of the past. The areas of earlier civilizations, now extinct, are shown by means of black stippling.

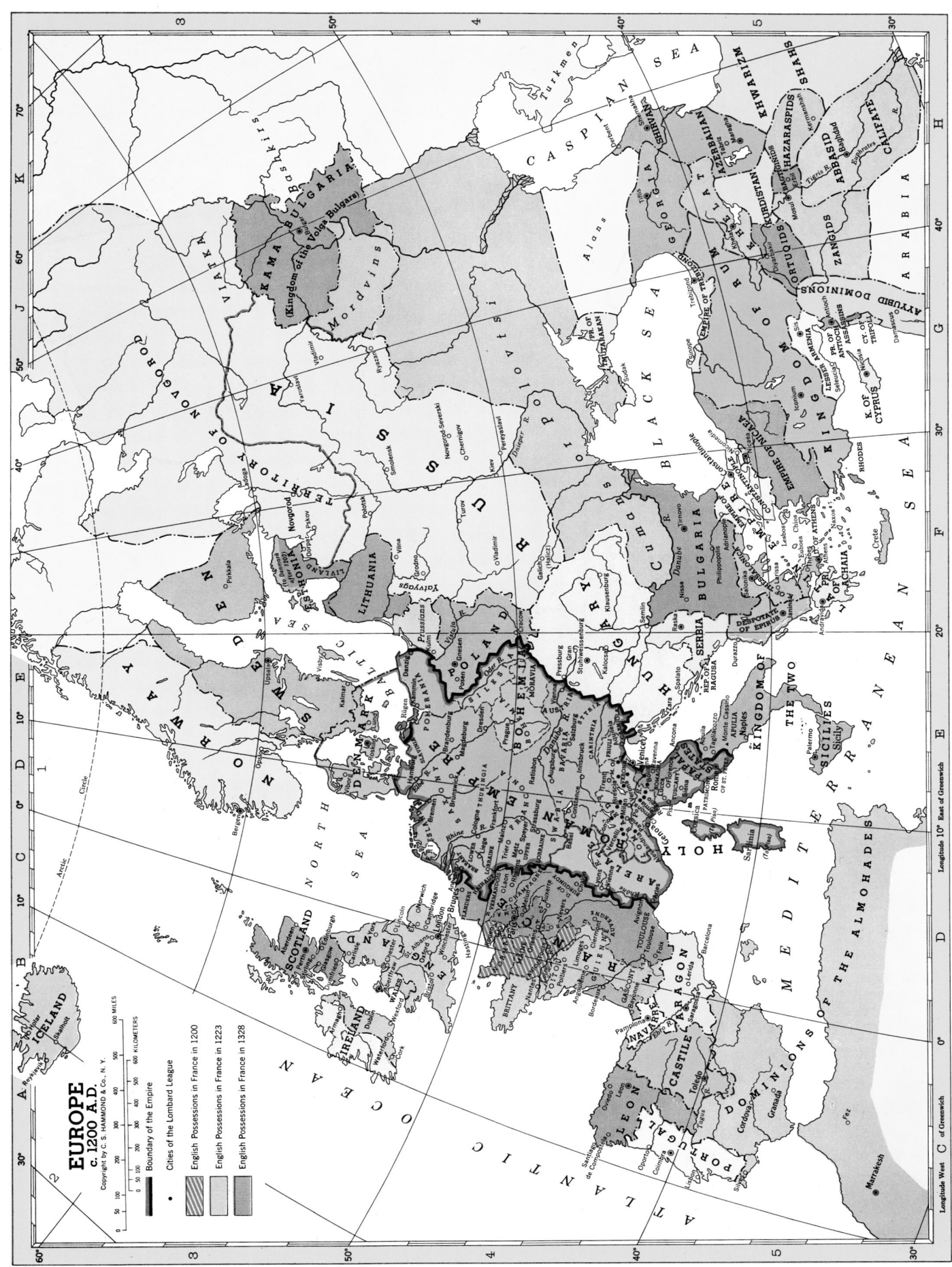

EUROPE
c. 1200 A.D.
Copyright by C. S. HAMMOND & Co., N. Y.

— Boundary of the Empire
• Cities of the Lombard League
English Possessions in France in 1200
English Possessions in France in 1223
English Possessions in France in 1328

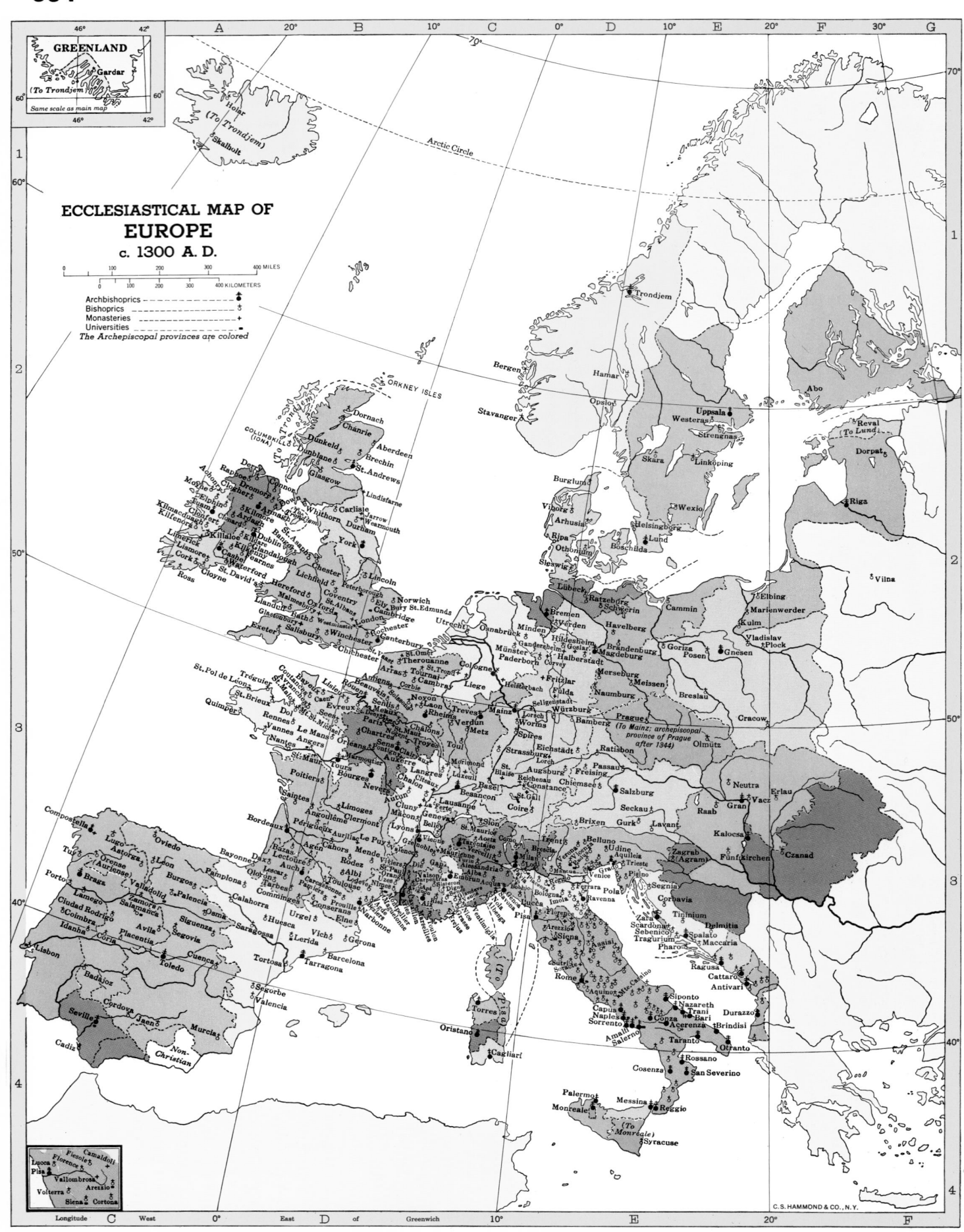

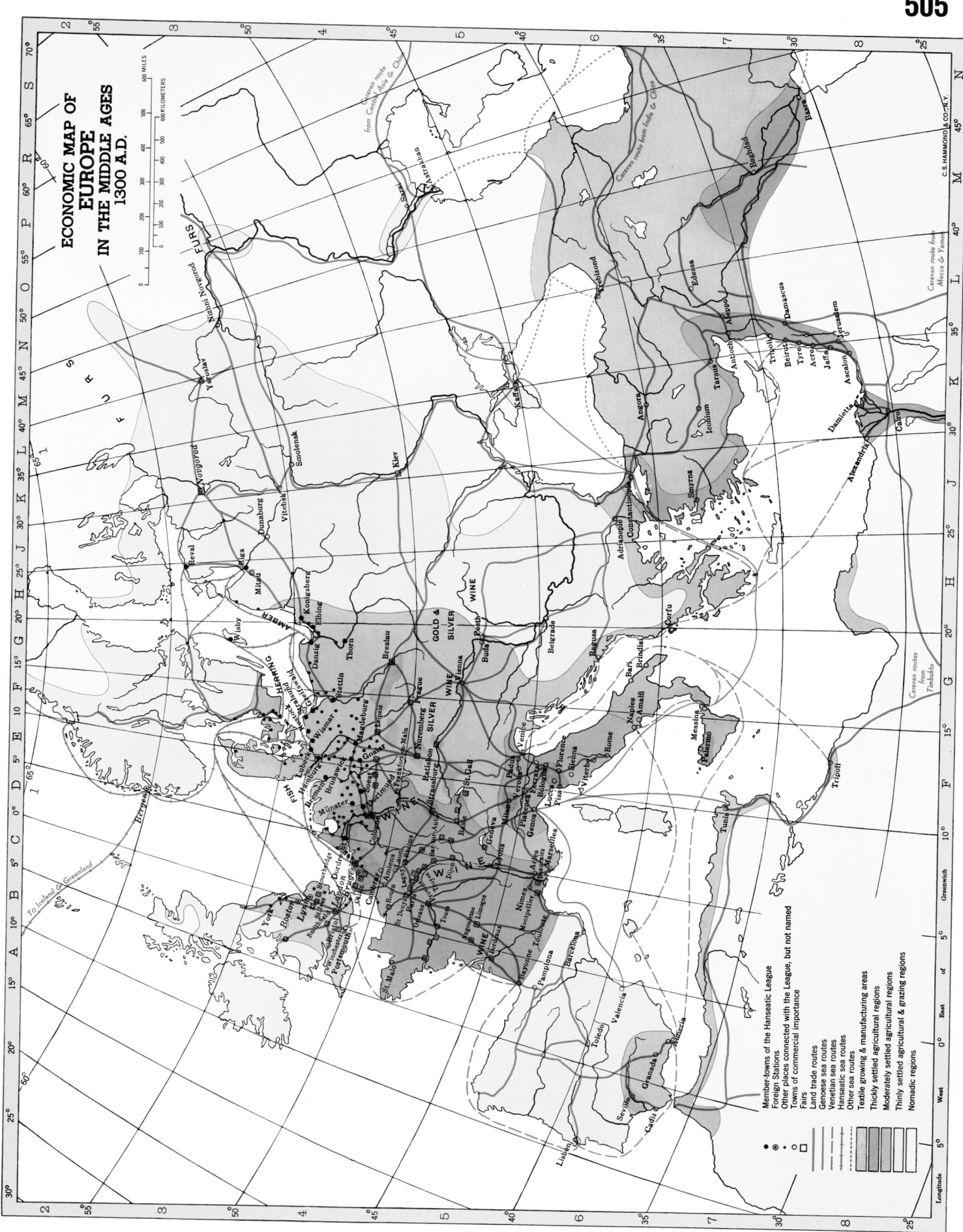

ECONOMIC MAP OF
EUROPE
IN THE MIDDLE AGES
1300 A.D.

Member-towns of the Hanseatic League
Foreign Stations
Other places connected with the League, but not named
Towns of commercial importance
Fairs
Land trade routes
Genoese sea routes
Venetian sea routes
Hanseatic sea routes
Other sea routes
Textile growing & manufacturing areas
Thickly settled agricultural regions
Moderately settled agricultural regions
Thinly settled agricultural & grazing regions
Nomadic regions

506

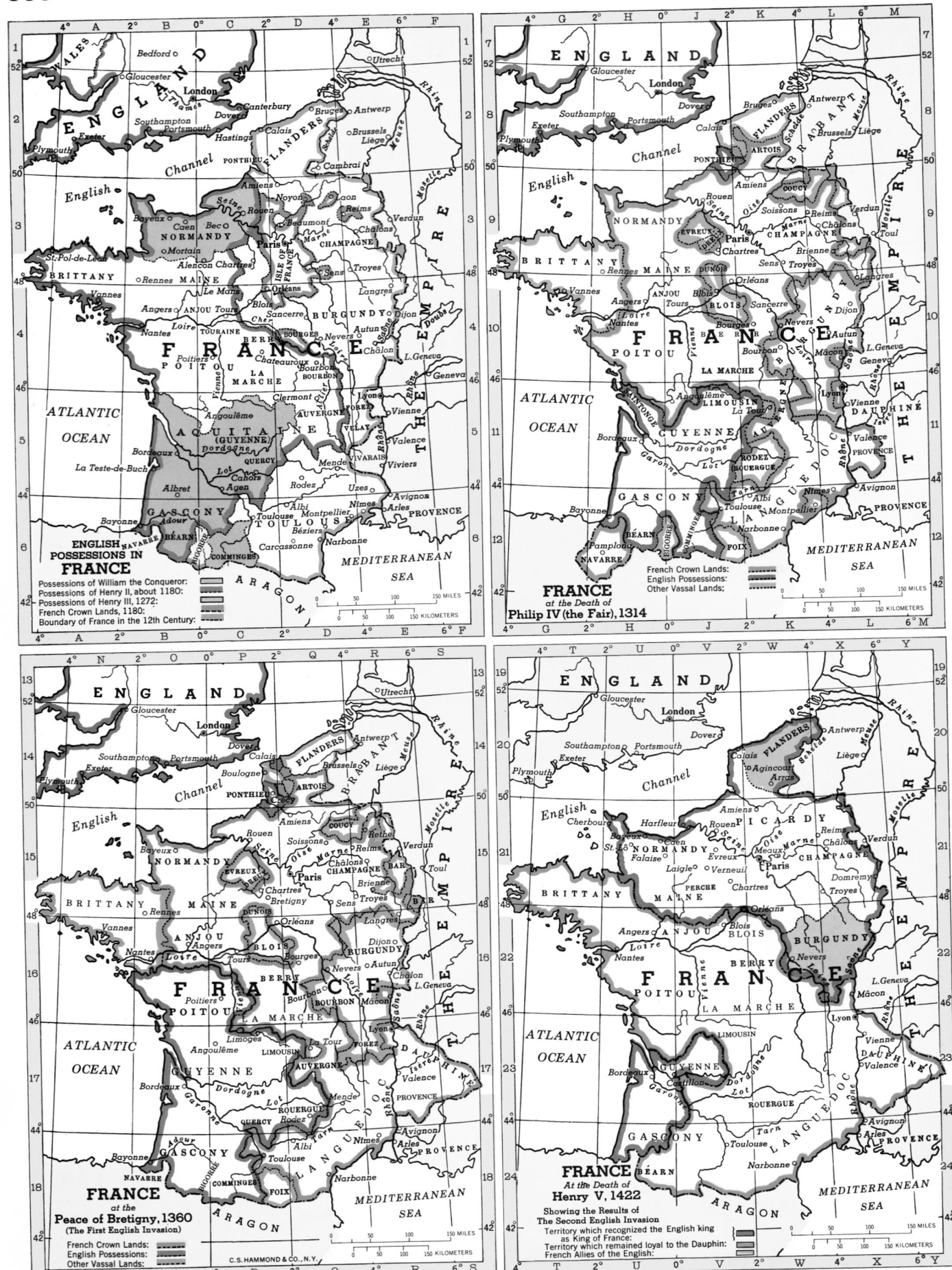

ENGLISH
POSSESSIONS IN
FRANCE

Possessions of William the Conqueror:
Possessions of Henry II, about 1180:
Possessions of Henry III, 1272:
French Crown Lands, 1180:
Boundary of France in the 12th Century:

FRANCE
at the Death of
Philip IV (the Fair), 1314

French Crown Lands:
English Possessions:
Other Vassal Lands:

FRANCE
at the
Peace of Bretigny, 1360
(The First English Invasion)

French Crown Lands:
English Possessions:
Other Vassal Lands:

C.S. HAMMOND & CO., N.Y.

FRANCE
At the Death of
Henry V, 1422
Showing the Results of
The Second English Invasion

Territory which recognized the English king
as King of France:
Territory which remained loyal to the Dauphin:
French Allies of the English:

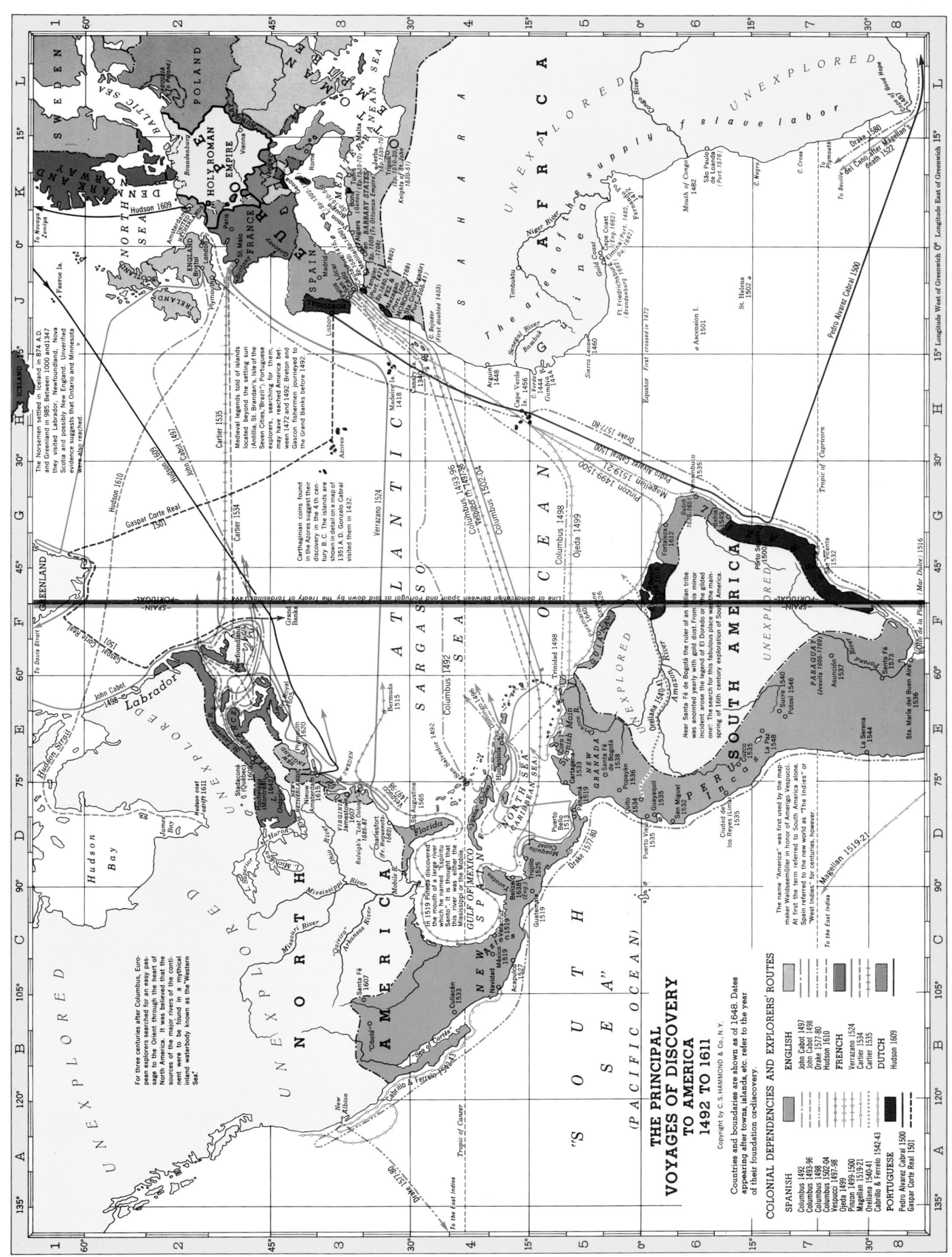

THE PRINCIPAL
VOYAGES OF DISCOVERY
TO AMERICA
1492 TO 1611

Copyright by C. S. HAMMOND & Co., N. Y.

Countries and boundaries are shown as of 1648. Dates
appearing after towns, islands, etc. refer to the year
of their foundation or discovery.

COLONIAL DEPENDENCIES AND EXPLORERS' ROUTES

SPANISH
Columbus 1492
Columbus 1493-96
Columbus 1498
Columbus 1502-04
Vespucci 1497-98
Ojeda 1499
Pinzon 1499-1500
Magellan 1519-21
Orellana 1540-41
Cabrillo & Ferrelo 1542-43

PORTUGUESE
Pedro Alvarez Cabral 1500
Gaspar Corte Real 1501

ENGLISH
John Cabot 1497
John Cabot 1498
Drake 1577-80
Hudson 1610

FRENCH
Verrazano 1524
Cartier 1534
Cartier 1535

DUTCH
Hudson 1609

508

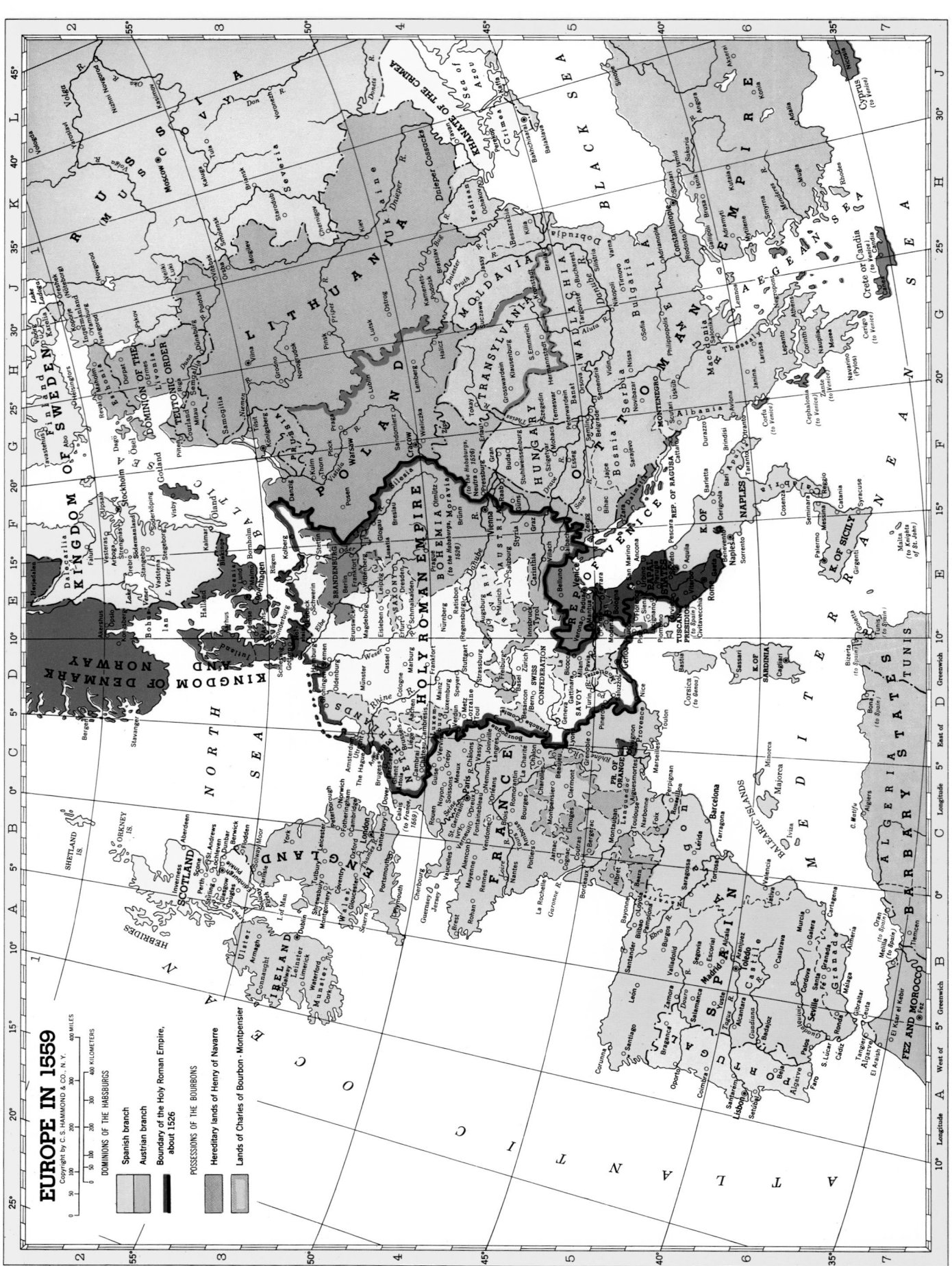

EUROPE IN 1559

Copyright by C.S. Hammond & Co., N.Y.

DOMINIONS OF THE HABSBURGS

Spanish branch

Austrian branch

Boundary of the Holy Roman Empire, about 1526

POSSESSIONS OF THE BOURBONS

Hereditary lands of Henry of Navarre

Lands of Charles of Bourbon - Montpensier

EUROPE IN 1648
AT THE PEACE OF
WESTPHALIA

Copyright by C. S. HAMMOND & CO., N.Y.

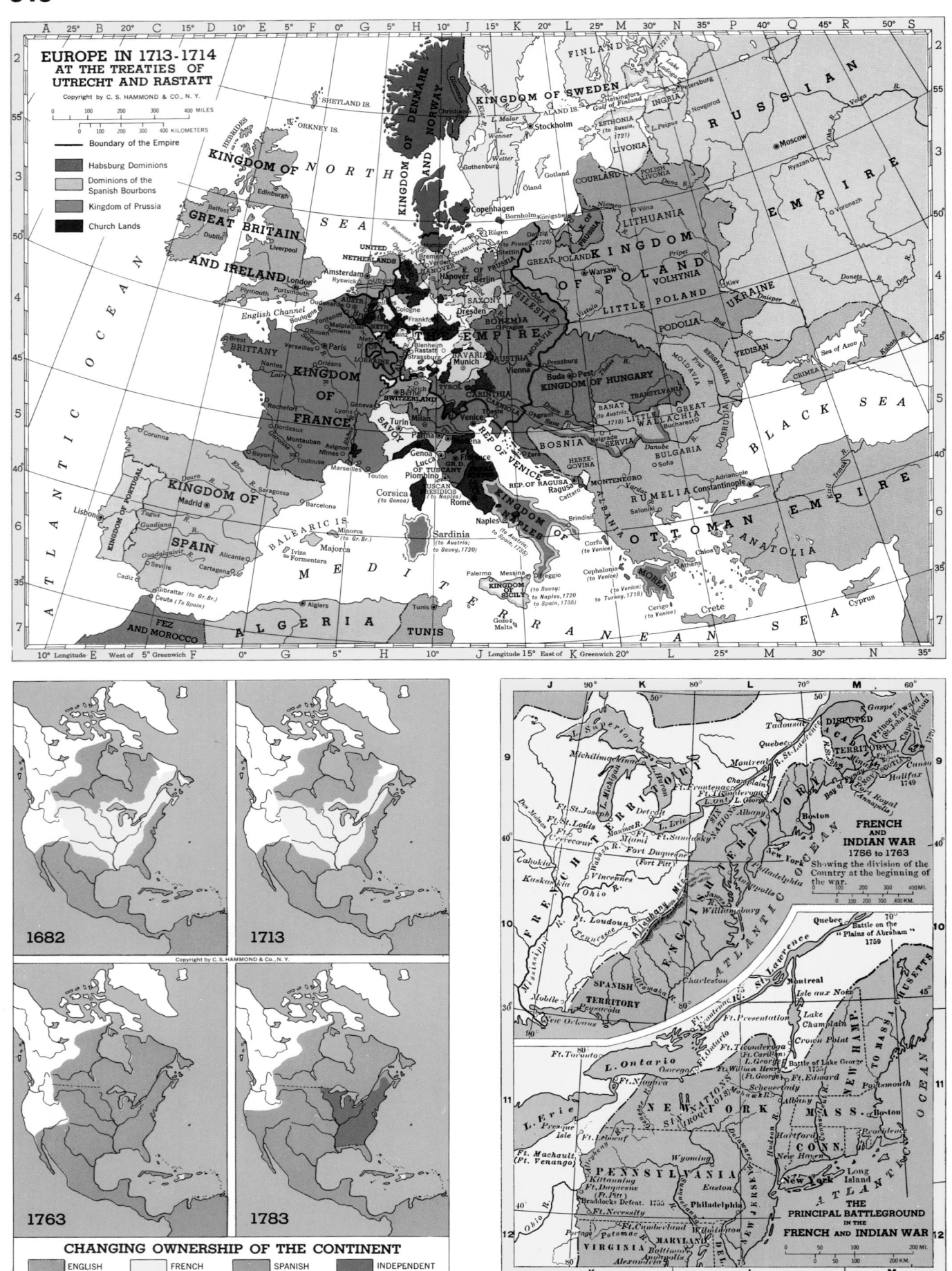

EUROPE IN 1713-1714
AT THE TREATIES OF UTRECHT AND RASTATT

Copyright by C. S. HAMMOND & CO., N.Y.

— Boundary of the Empire

Habsburg Dominions

Dominions of the Spanish Bourbons

Kingdom of Prussia

Church Lands

1682

1713

Copyright by C. S. HAMMOND & Co., N.Y.

1763

1783

CHANGING OWNERSHIP OF THE CONTINENT

ENGLISH   FRENCH   SPANISH   INDEPENDENT

FRENCH
AND
INDIAN WAR
1756 to 1763
Showing the division of the
Country at the beginning of
the war.

Battle on the
"Plains of Abraham"
1759

THE
PRINCIPAL BATTLEGROUND
IN THE
FRENCH AND INDIAN WAR

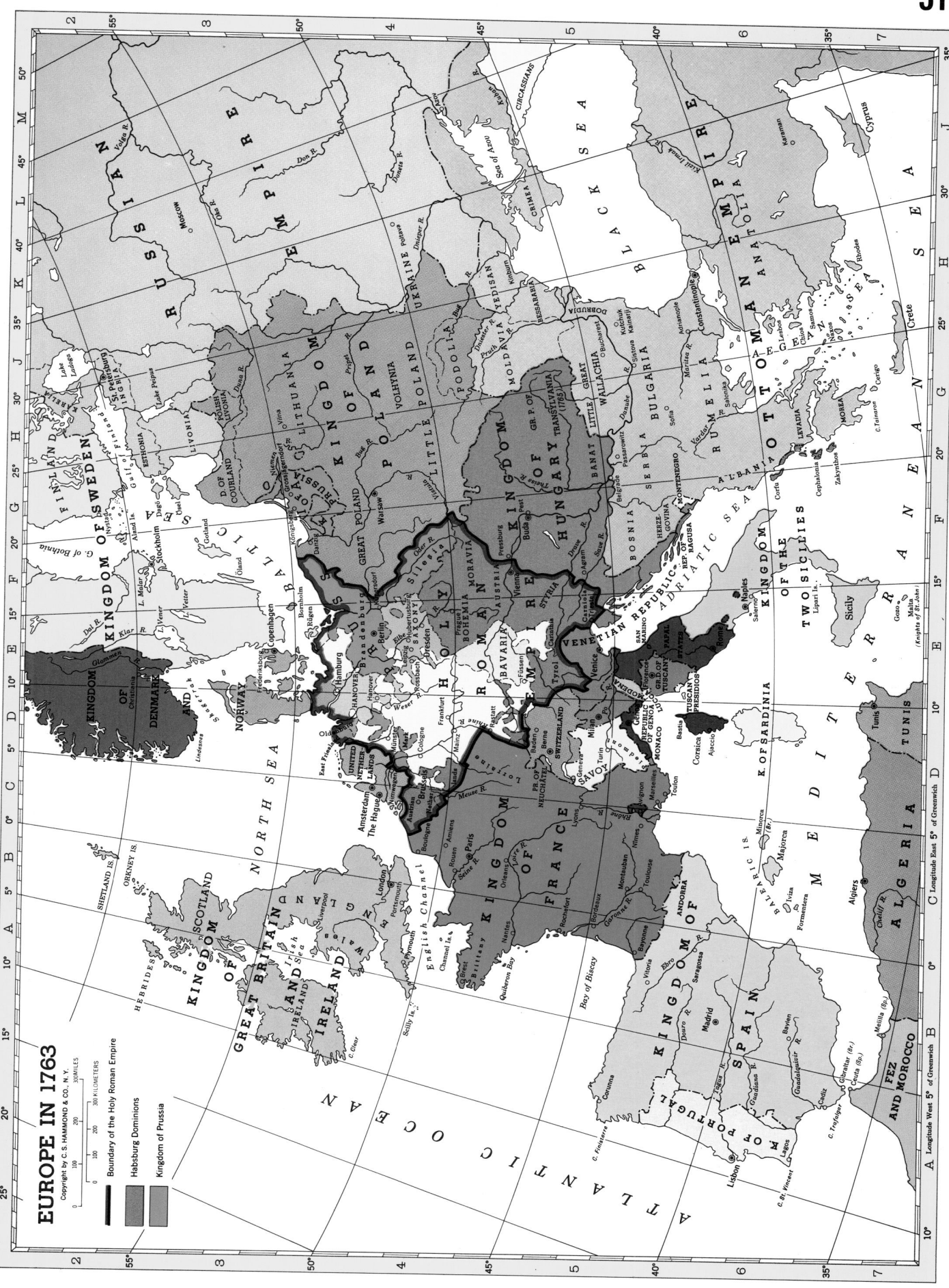

EUROPE IN 1763

Copyright by C. S. HAMMOND & CO., N.Y.

Boundary of the Holy Roman Empire

Habsburg Dominions

Kingdom of Prussia

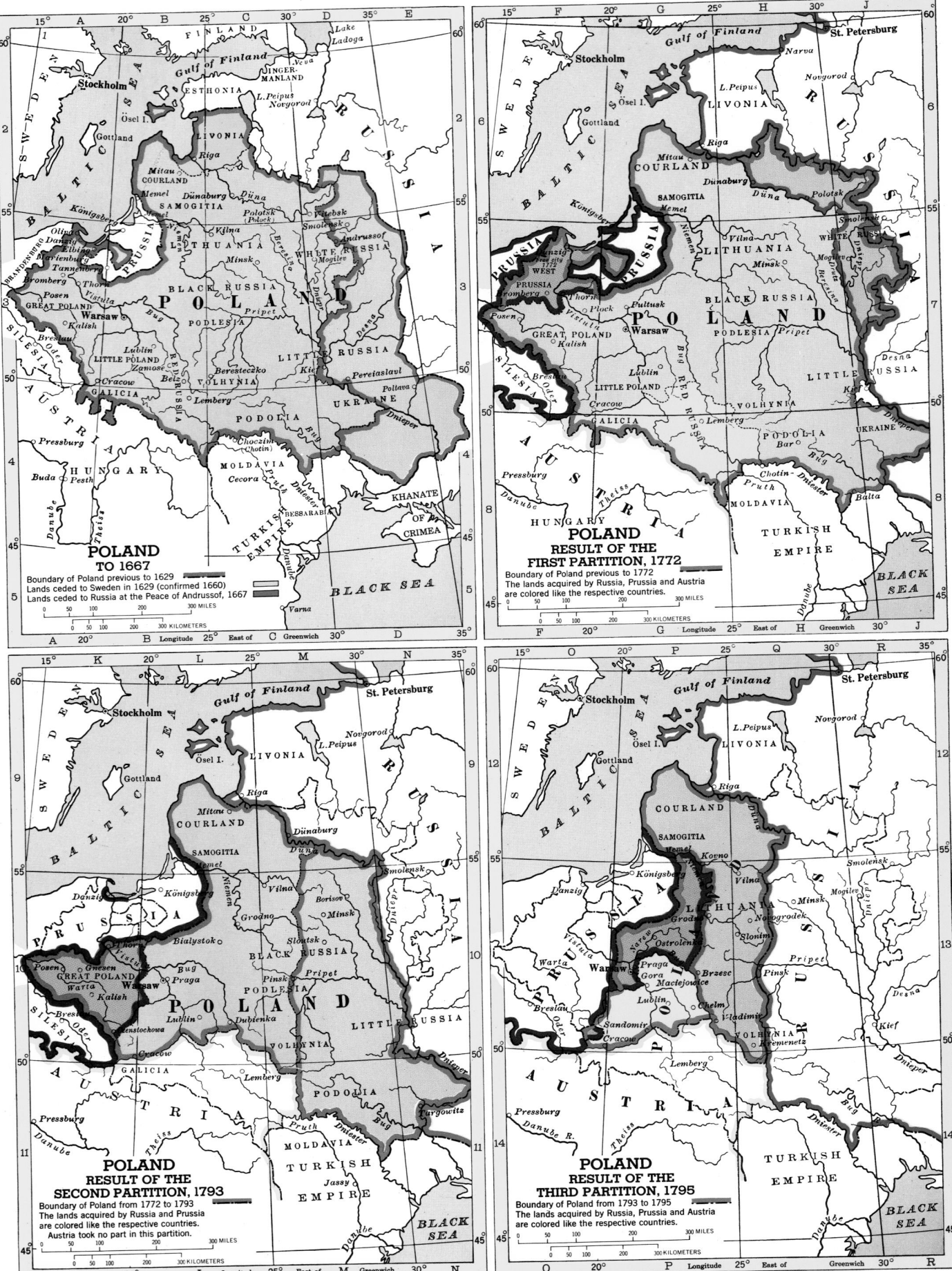

POLAND
TO 1667

Boundary of Poland previous to 1629
Lands ceded to Sweden in 1629 (confirmed 1660)
Lands ceded to Russia at the Peace of Andrussof, 1667

0   50   100   200   300 MILES
0 50 100   200   300 KILOMETERS

POLAND
RESULT OF THE
FIRST PARTITION, 1772

Boundary of Poland previous to 1772
The lands acquired by Russia, Prussia and Austria
are colored like the respective countries.

0   50   100   200   300 MILES
0 50 100   200   300 KILOMETERS

POLAND
RESULT OF THE
SECOND PARTITION, 1793

Boundary of Poland from 1772 to 1793
The lands acquired by Russia and Prussia
are colored like the respective countries.
Austria took no part in this partition.

0   50   100   200   300 MILES
0 50 100   200   300 KILOMETERS

POLAND
RESULT OF THE
THIRD PARTITION, 1795

Boundary of Poland from 1793 to 1795
The lands acquired by Russia, Prussia and Austria
are colored like the respective countries.

0   50   100   200   300 MILES
0 50 100   200   300 KILOMETERS

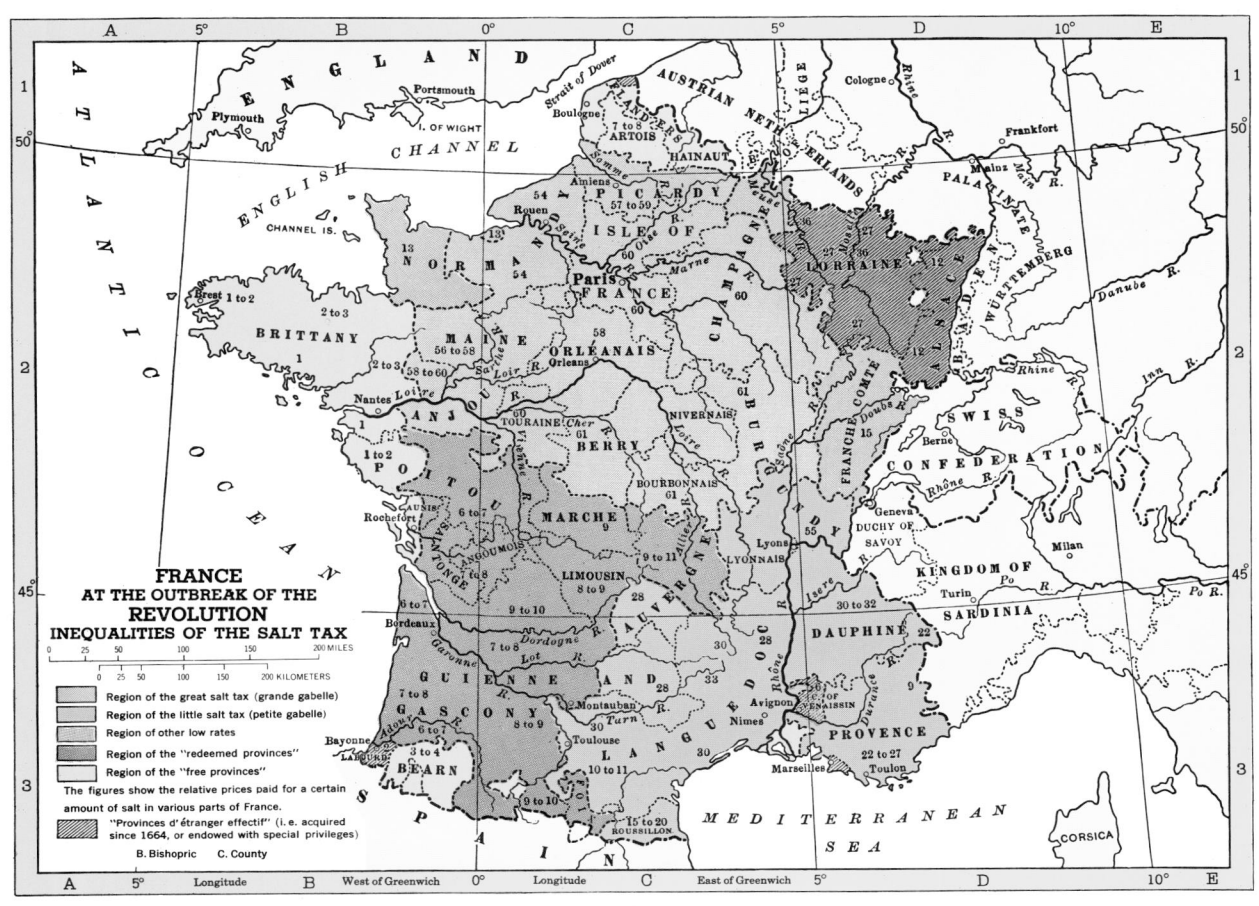

FRANCE
AT THE OUTBREAK OF THE
REVOLUTION
INEQUALITIES OF THE SALT TAX
Region of the great salt tax (grande gabelle)
Region of the little salt tax (petite gabelle)
Region of other low rates
Region of the "redeemed provinces"
Region of the "free provinces"
The figures show the relative prices paid for a certain amount of salt in various parts of France.
"Provinces d'étranger effectif" (i.e. acquired since 1664, or endowed with special privileges)
B. Bishopric C. County
Longitude
West of Greenwich
East of Greenwich
ENGLAND
ATLANTIC OCEAN
MEDITERRANEAN SEA
SPAIN
AUSTRIAN NETHERLANDS
SWISS CONFEDERATION
KINGDOM OF SARDINIA
CORSICA

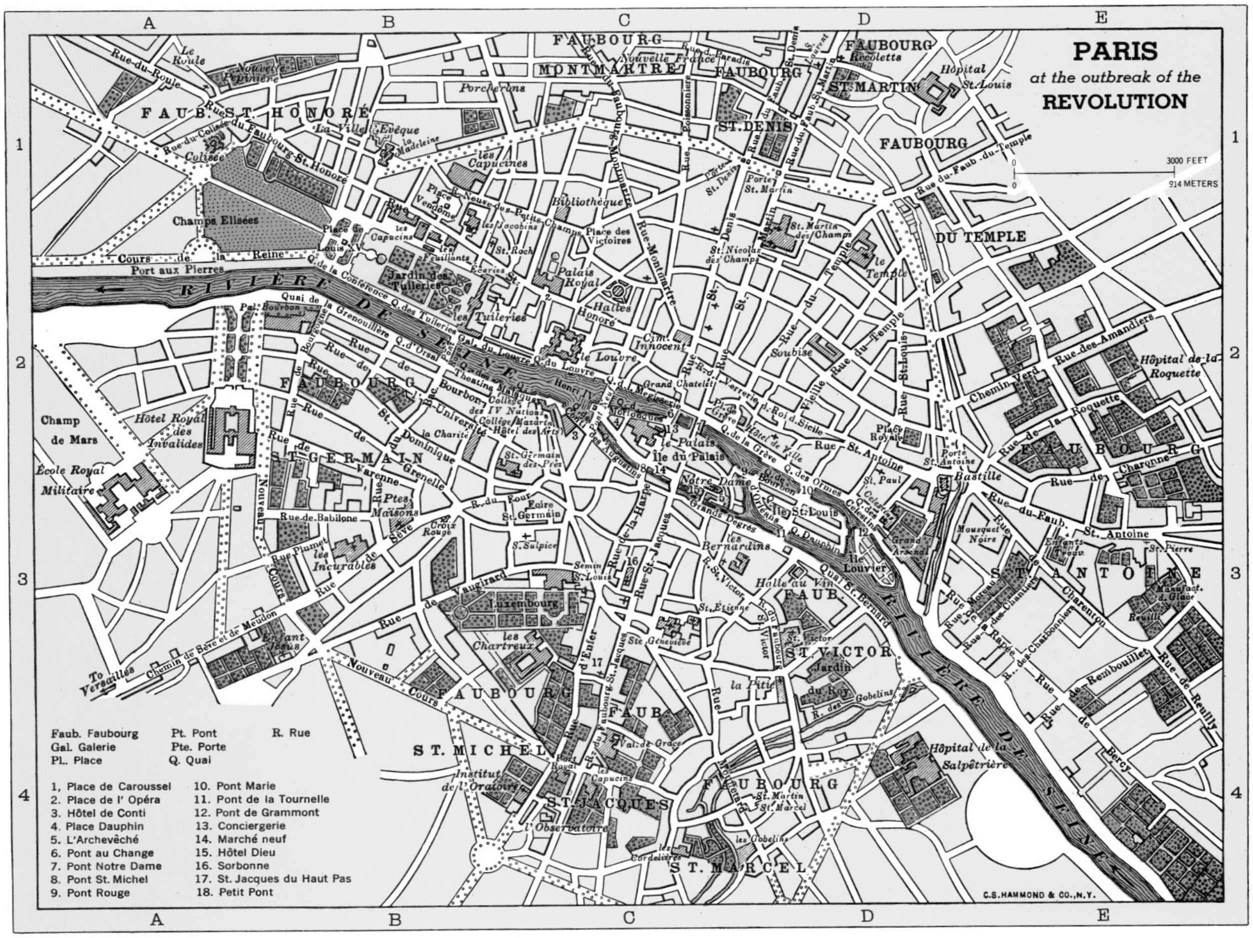

PARIS
at the outbreak of the
REVOLUTION
3000 FEET
914 METERS
Faub. Faubourg
Gal. Galerie
Pl. Place
Pt. Pont
Pte. Porte
Q. Quai
R. Rue
1. Place de Caroussel
2. Place de l' Opéra
3. Hôtel de Conti
4. Place Dauphin
5. L'Archevêché
6. Pont au Change
7. Pont Notre Dame
8. Pont St. Michel
9. Pont Rouge
10. Pont Marie
11. Pont de la Tournelle
12. Pont de Grammont
13. Conciergerie
14. Marché neuf
15. Hôtel Dieu
16. Sorbonne
17. St. Jacques du Haut Pas
18. Petit Pont
C.S.HAMMOND & CO., N.Y.

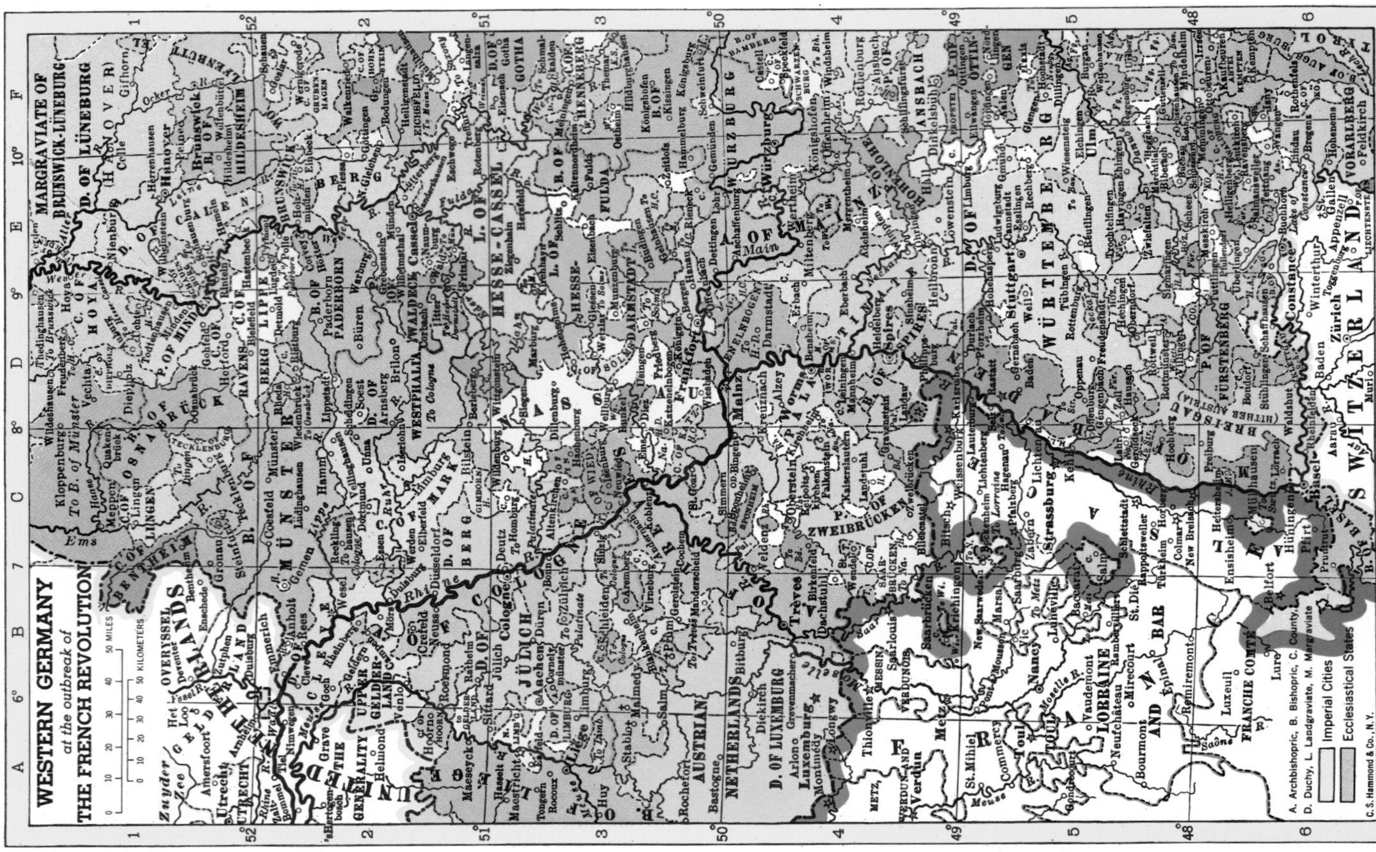

WESTERN GERMANY
at the outbreak of
THE FRENCH REVOLUTION

MARGRAVIATE OF BRUNSWICK-LÜNEBURG

A. Archbishopric, B. Bishopric, C. County.
D. Duchy, L. Landgraviate, M. Margraviate

Imperial Cities

Ecclesiastical States

C. S. Hammond & Co., N.Y.

50 MILES

KILOMETERS

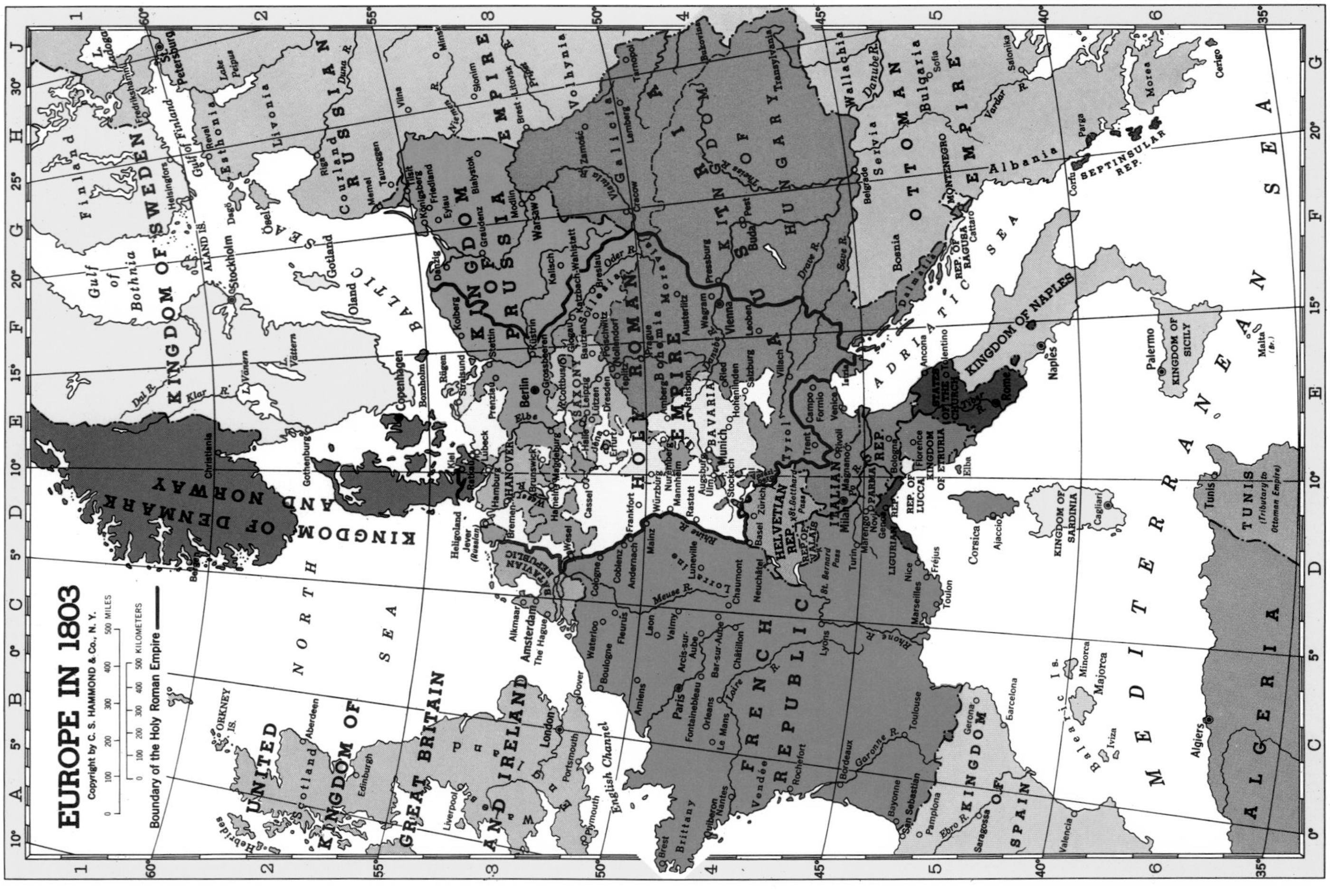

EUROPE IN 1803

Copyright by C. S. HAMMOND & Co., N. Y.

Boundary of the Holy Roman Empire

MILES
KILOMETERS

UNITED KINGDOM OF GREAT BRITAIN AND IRELAND

KINGDOM OF DENMARK AND NORWAY

KINGDOM OF SWEDEN

RUSSIAN EMPIRE

KINGDOM OF PRUSSIA

FRENCH REPUBLIC

HELVETIAN REP.

ITALIAN REP.

KINGDOM OF NAPLES

KINGDOM OF SICILY

KINGDOM OF SARDINIA

SPAIN

ALGERIA

TUNIS

OTTOMAN EMPIRE

HUNGARY

BAVARIA

NORTH SEA

BALTIC SEA

ADRIATIC SEA

MEDITERRANEAN SEA

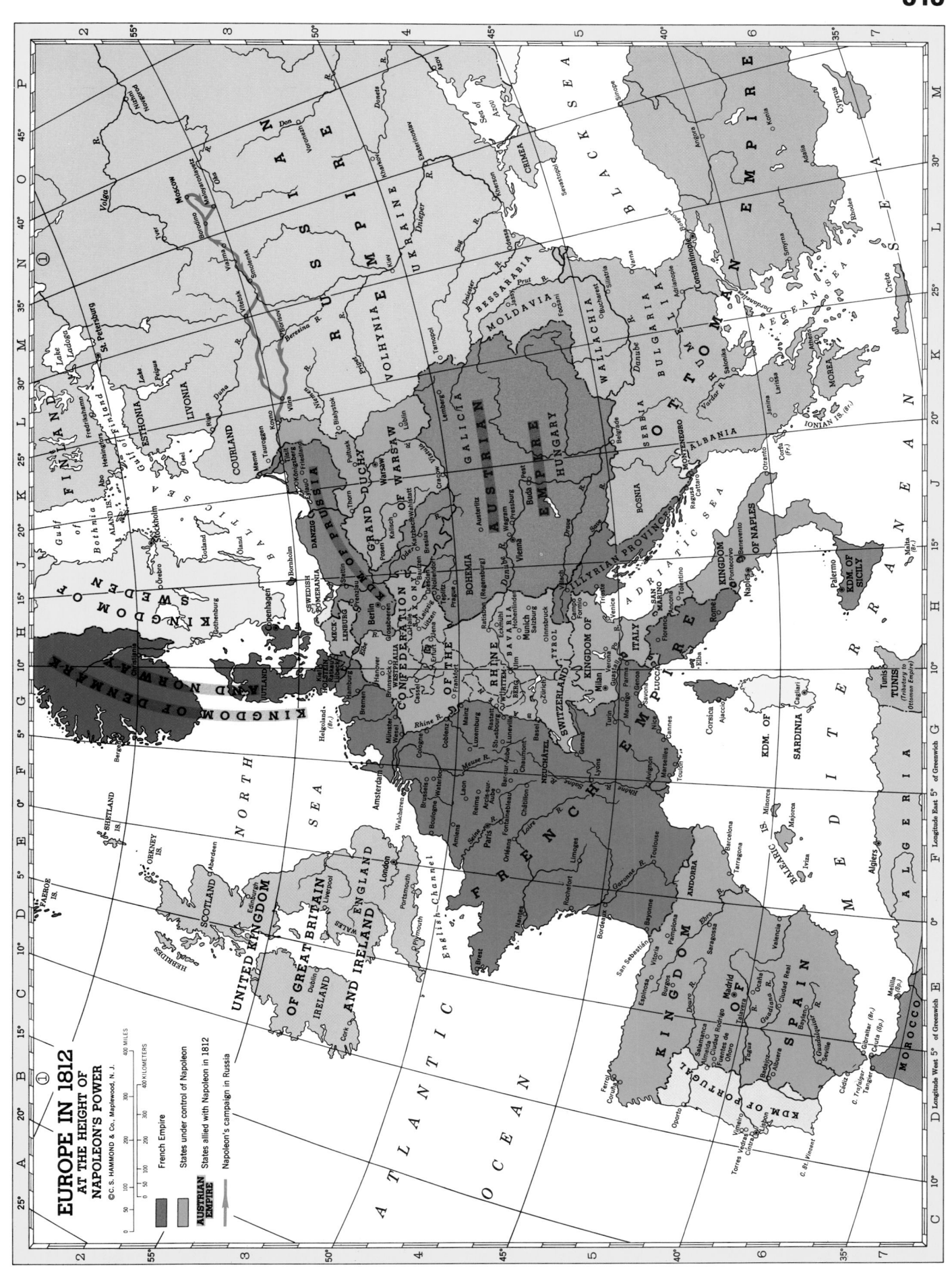

515

EUROPE IN 1812
AT THE HEIGHT OF
NAPOLEON'S POWER

©C. S. HAMMOND & Co., Maplewood, N. J.

French Empire

States under control of Napoleon

States allied with Napoleon in 1812

Napoleon's campaign in Russia

AUSTRIAN EMPIRE

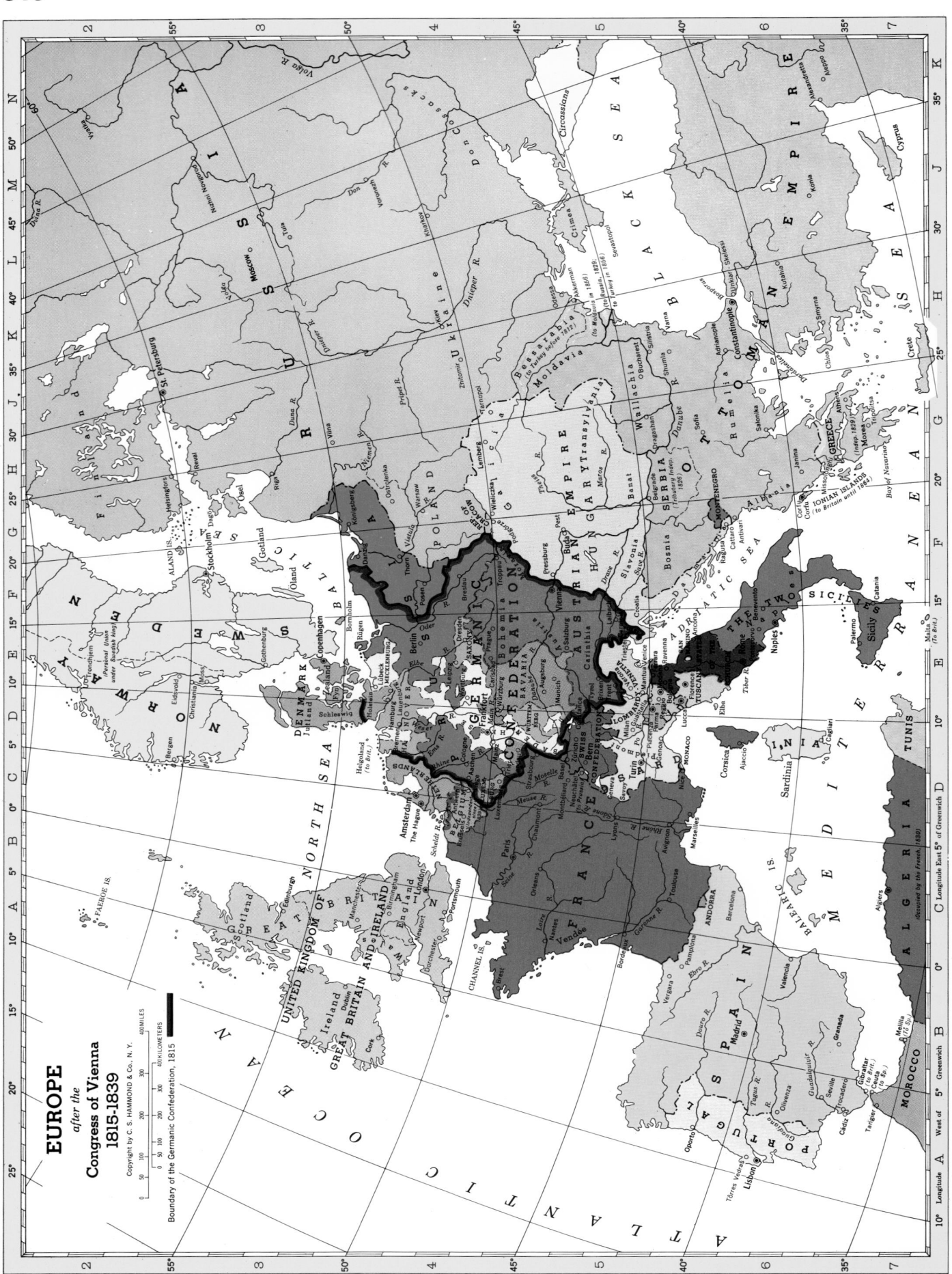

EUROPE
after the
Congress of Vienna
1815-1839

Copyright by C. S. HAMMOND & Co., N. Y.

400 MILES

400 KILOMETERS

Boundary of the Germanic Confederation, 1815

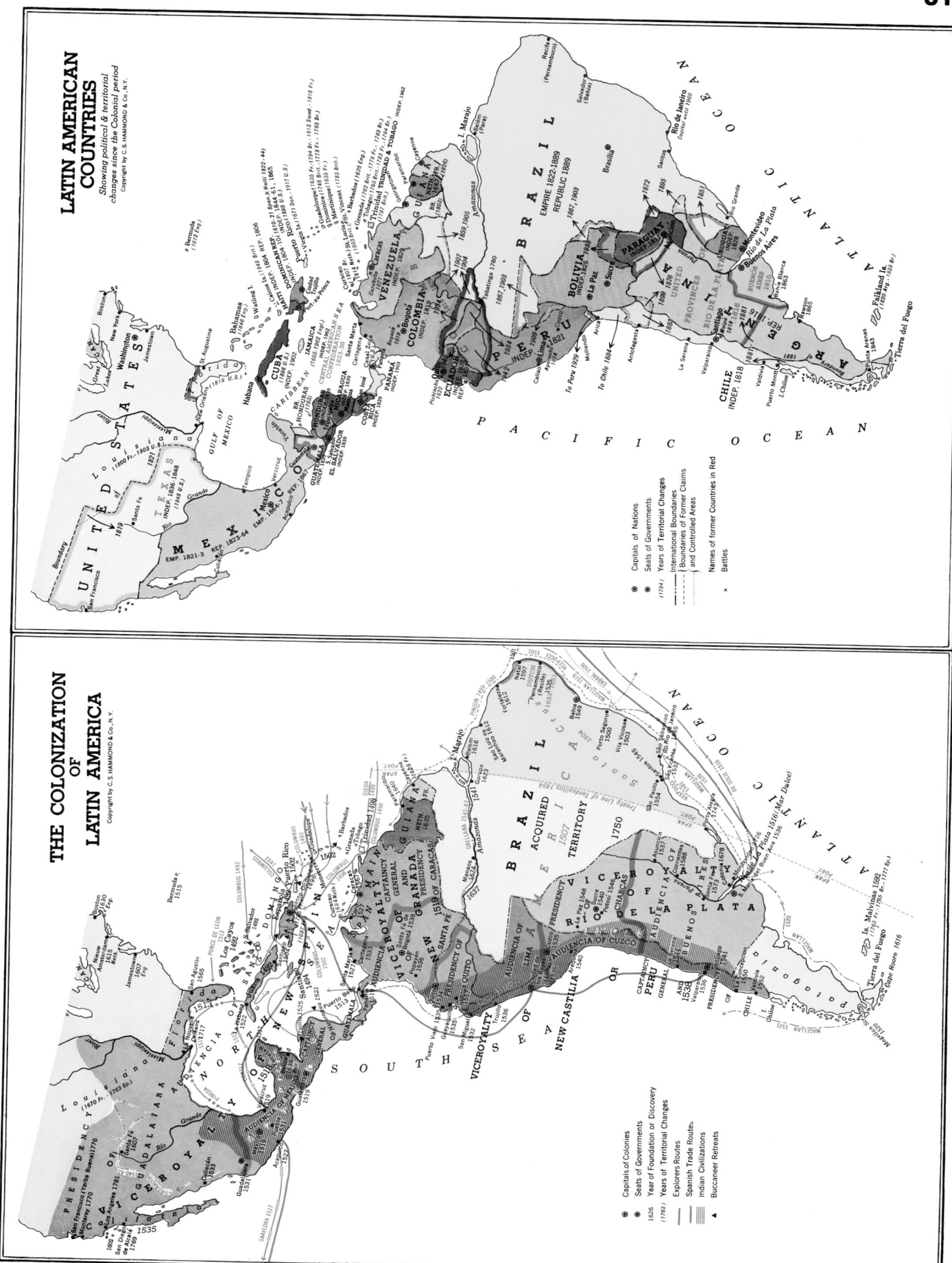

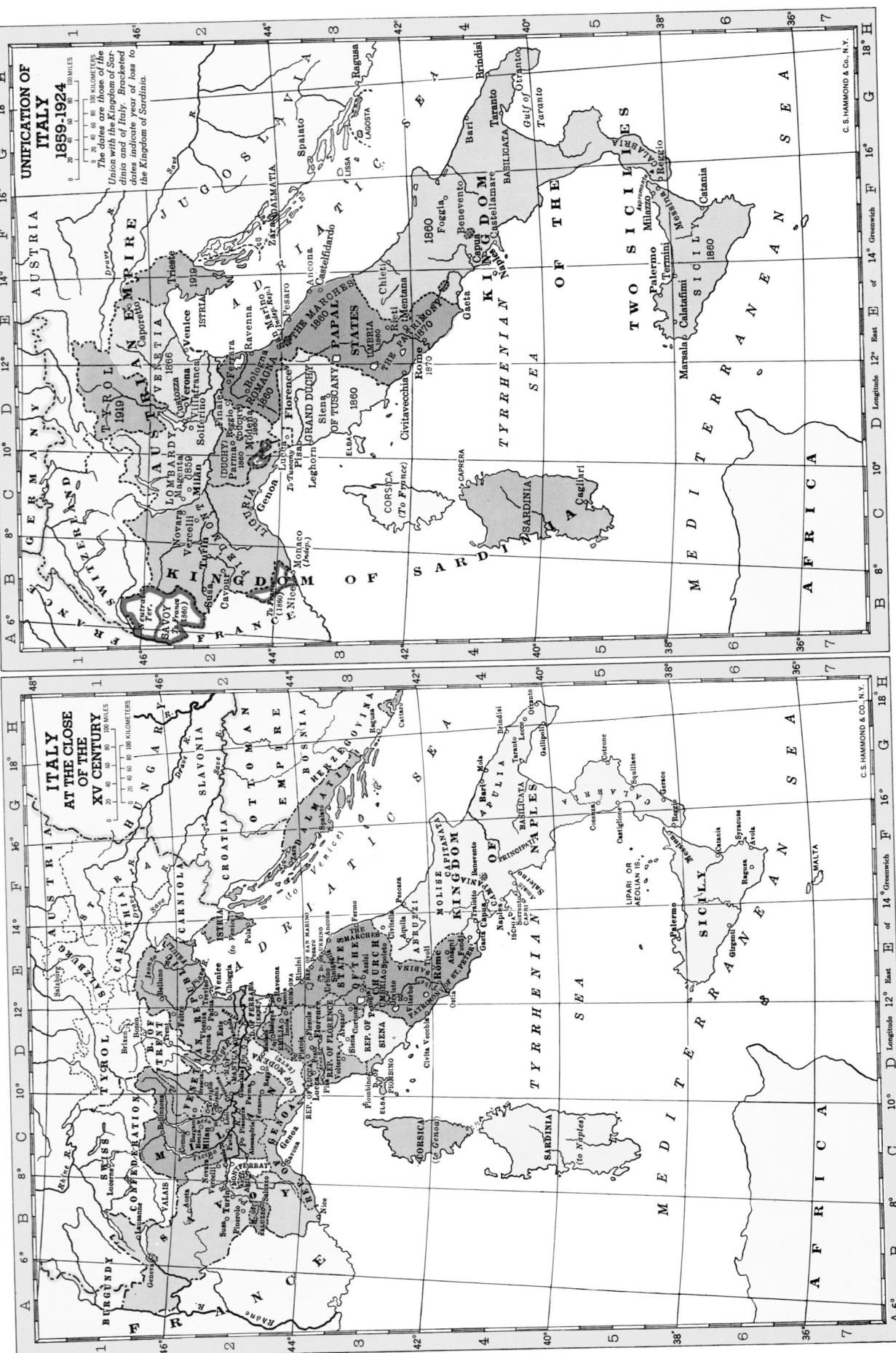

UNIFICATION OF
ITALY
1859-1924

The dates are those of the
Union with the Kingdom of Sardinia and of Italy. Bracketed
dates indicate year of loss to
the Kingdom of Sardinia.

ITALY
AT THE CLOSE
OF THE
XV CENTURY

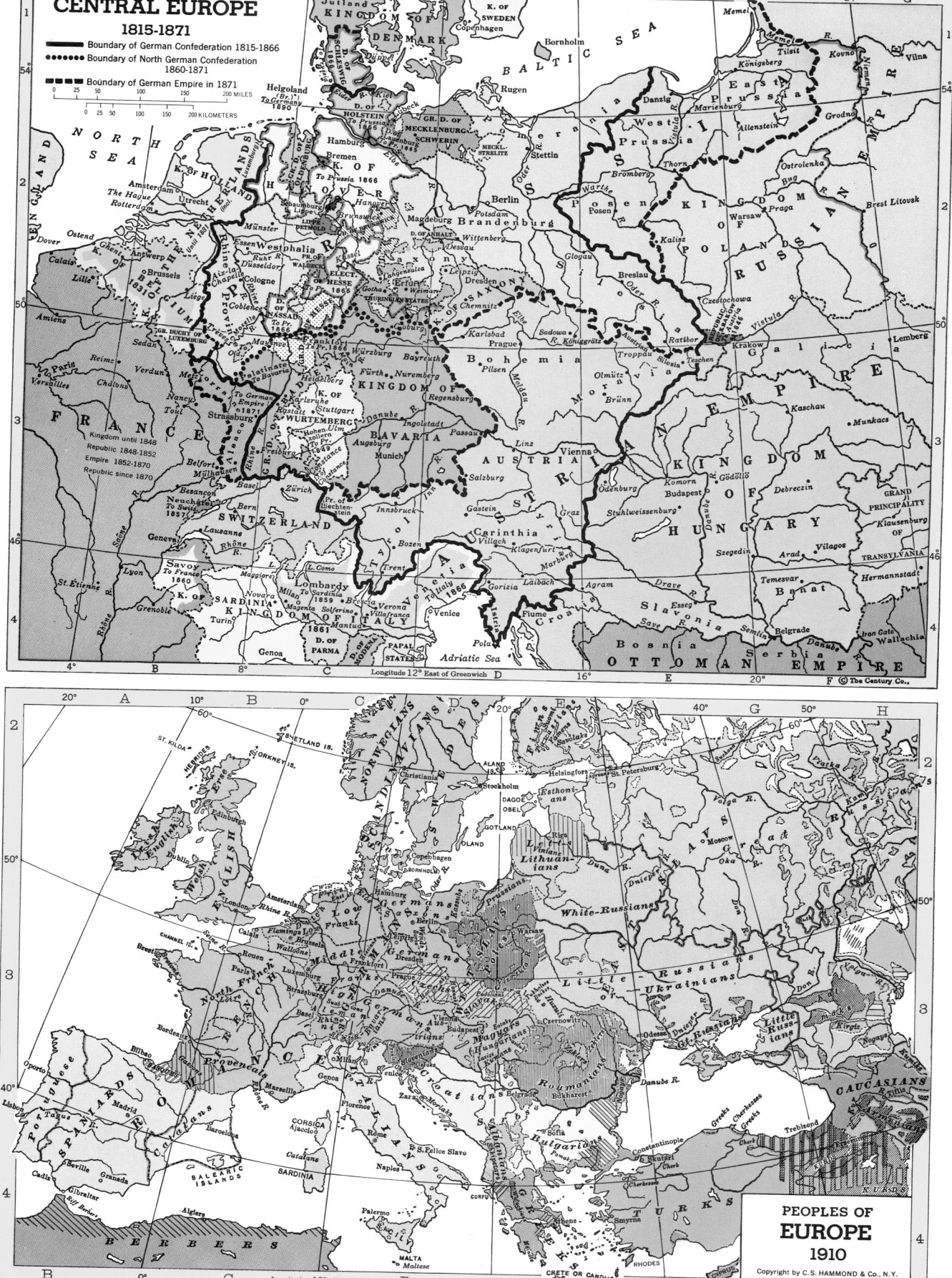

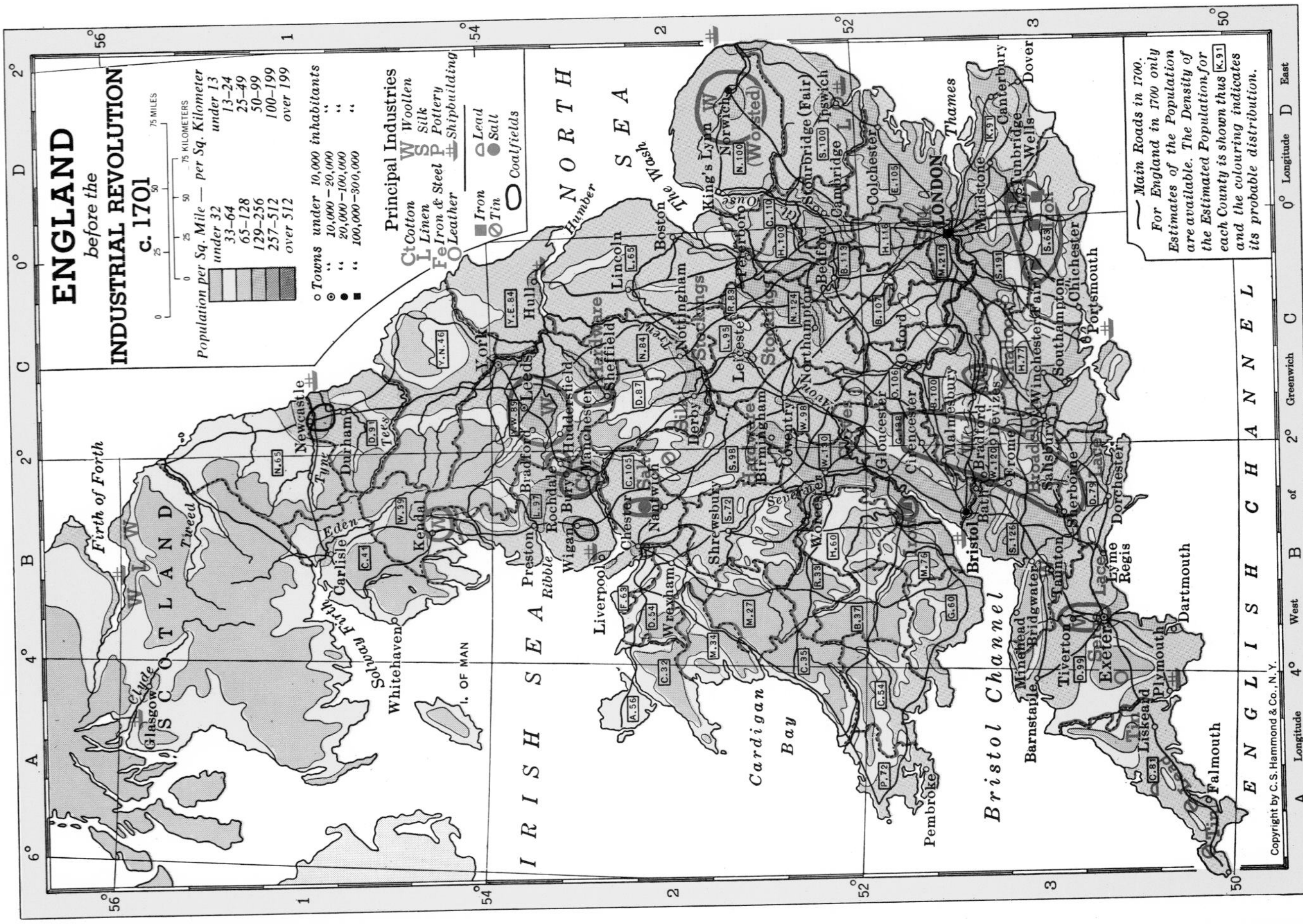

520

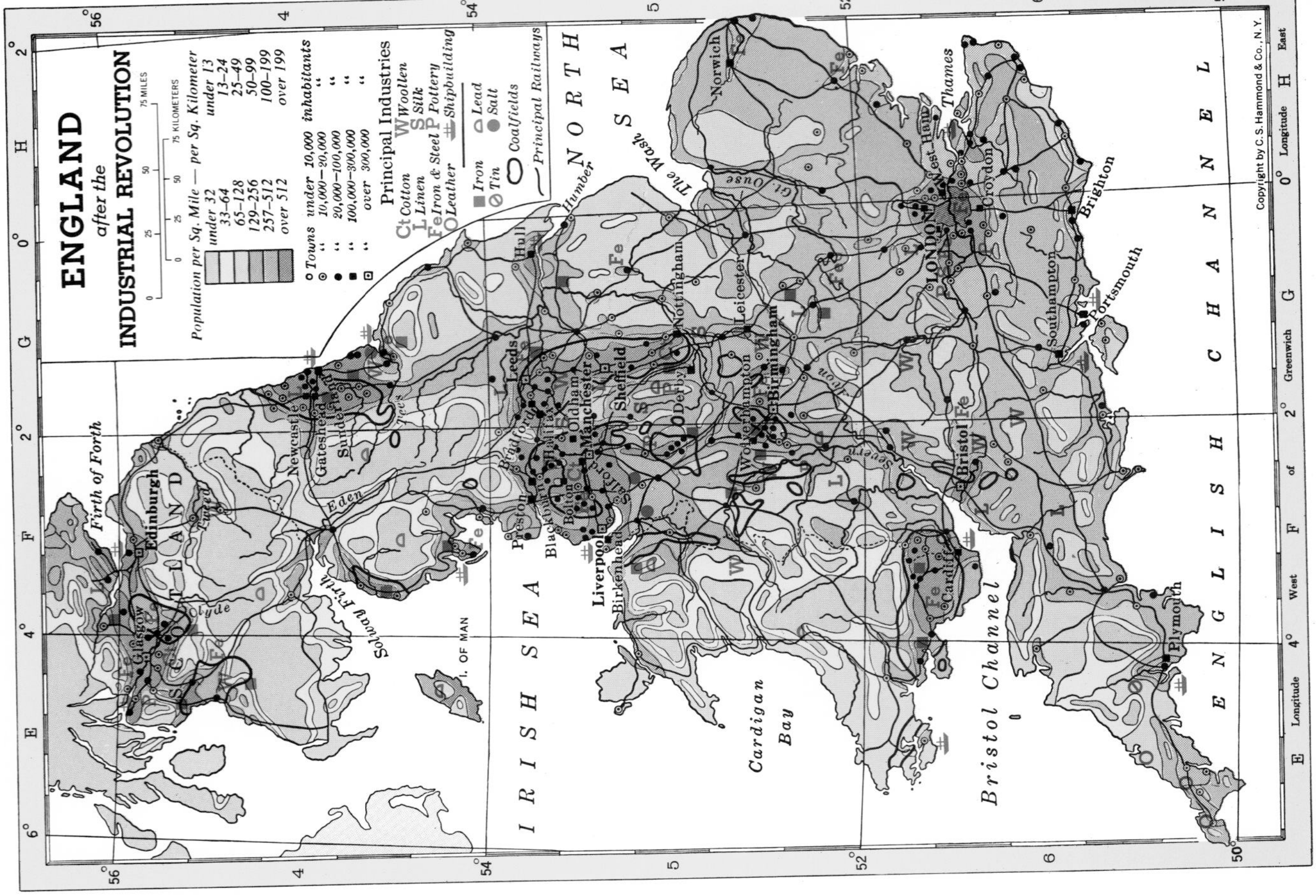

ENGLAND
after the
INDUSTRIAL REVOLUTION

Population per Sq. Mile — per Sq. Kilometer
under 32 — under 13
33-64 — 13-24
65-128 — 25-49
129-256 — 50-99
257-512 — 100-199
over 512 — over 199

Towns under 10,000 inhabitants
10,000-20,000
20,000-100,000
100,000-300,000
over 300,000

Principal Industries
Ct Cotton   W Woollen   S Silk
L Linen   P Pottery
Fe Iron & Steel   Shipbuilding
Leather
Iron   Lead
Tin   Salt
Coalfields
Principal Railways

Copyright by C. S. Hammond & Co., N.Y.

SCOTLAND
ENGLAND
IRISH SEA
NORTH SEA
ENGLISH CHANNEL
Bristol Channel
Cardigan Bay
I. OF MAN
Firth of Forth
Glasgow   Edinburgh
Newcastle   Gateshead   Sunderland
Durham
Carlisle
Leeds
Liverpool   Birkenhead
Manchester   Bolton   Bury
Preston   Blackburn
Sheffield
Derby   Nottingham
Leicester
Birmingham
Cardiff
Bristol
London   Croydon
Brighton
Southampton   Portsmouth
Plymouth
Norwich
Hull
The Wash
Humber
Thames

ENGLAND
before the
INDUSTRIAL REVOLUTION
c. 1701

Population per Sq. Mile — per Sq. Kilometer
under 32   under 13
33-64   13-24
65-128   25-49
129-256   50-99
257-512   100-199
over 512   over 199

Towns under 10,000 inhabitants
10,000-20,000
20,000-100,000
100,000-300,000

Principal Industries
Ct Cotton   W Woollen   S Silk
L Linen   P Pottery
Fe Iron & Steel   Shipbuilding
Leather
Iron   Lead
Tin   Salt
Coalfields

Main Roads in 1700.
For England in 1700 only Estimates of the Population are available. The Density of the Estimated Population, for each County is shown thus K.91 and the colouring indicates its probable distribution.

Copyright by C. S. Hammond & Co., N.Y.

SCOTLAND
ENGLAND
IRISH SEA
NORTH SEA
ENGLISH CHANNEL
Bristol Channel
Cardigan Bay
I. OF MAN
Firth of Forth
Glasgow
Whitehaven   Carlisle   Kendal
Newcastle   Durham
York   Hull
Liverpool   Preston   Wigan   Bury   Rochdale
Bradford   Leeds
Halifax   Huddersfield
Lincoln
Chester   Wrexham
Shrewsbury
Sheffield
Derby   Nottingham
Leicester   Northampton
Birmingham   Coventry
Worcester   Warwick
Gloucester
Bristol   Bath
Exeter   Tiverton
Plymouth   Dartmouth
Falmouth
Pembroke
Barnstaple   Bridgwater   Taunton
Lyme Regis   Dorchester
Southampton   Portsmouth   Chichester
Winchester   Salisbury
Reading   Oxford
London
Canterbury   Dover
Colchester   Ipswich
King's Lynn   Cambridge
Norwich
Boston
The Wash
Humber
Thames

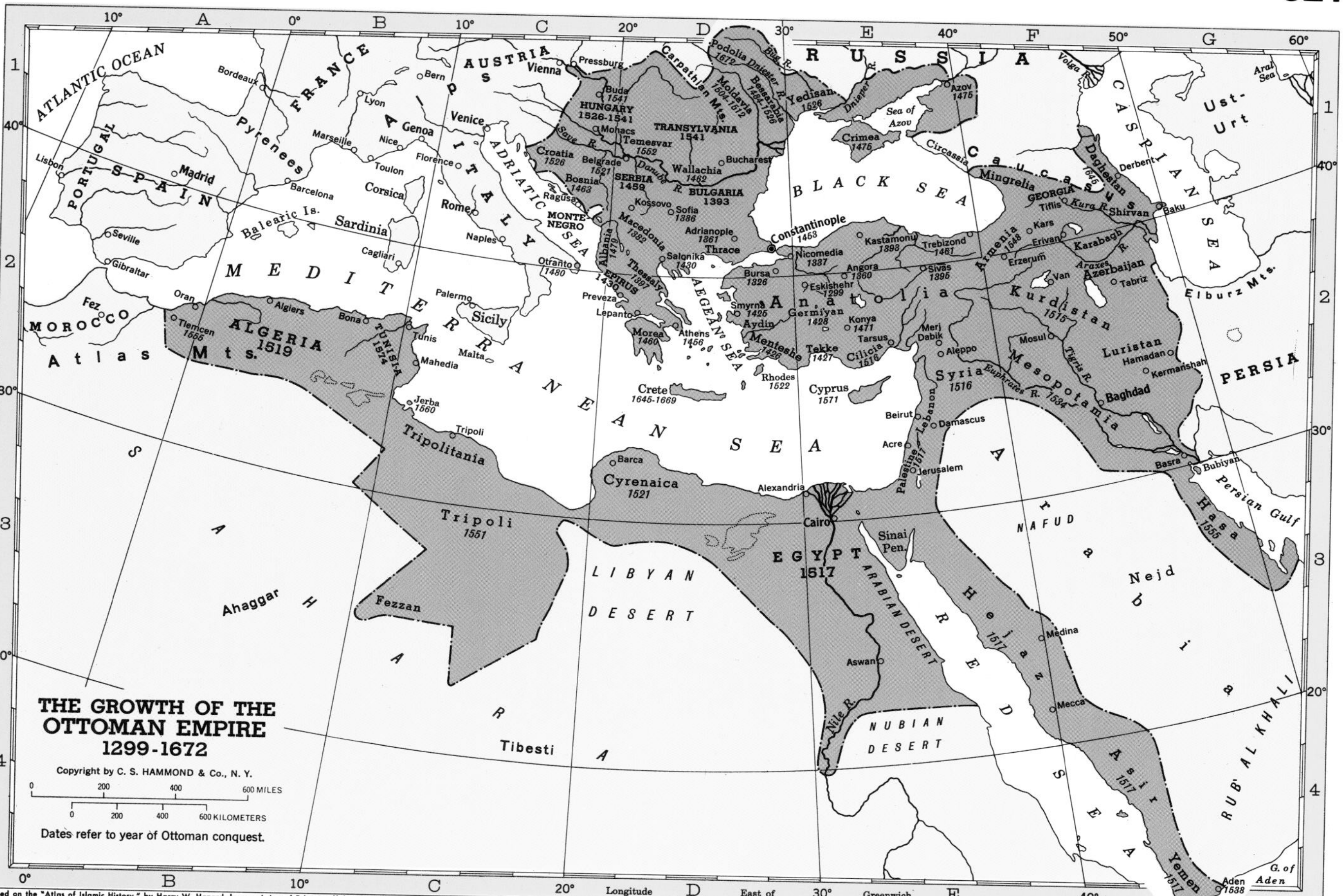

THE GROWTH OF THE OTTOMAN EMPIRE 1299-1672

Copyright by C. S. HAMMOND & Co., N.Y.

0 200 400 600 MILES
0 200 400 600 KILOMETERS

Dates refer to year of Ottoman conquest.

Based on the "Atlas of Islamic History," by Harry W. Hazard, by permission of Princeton University Press.

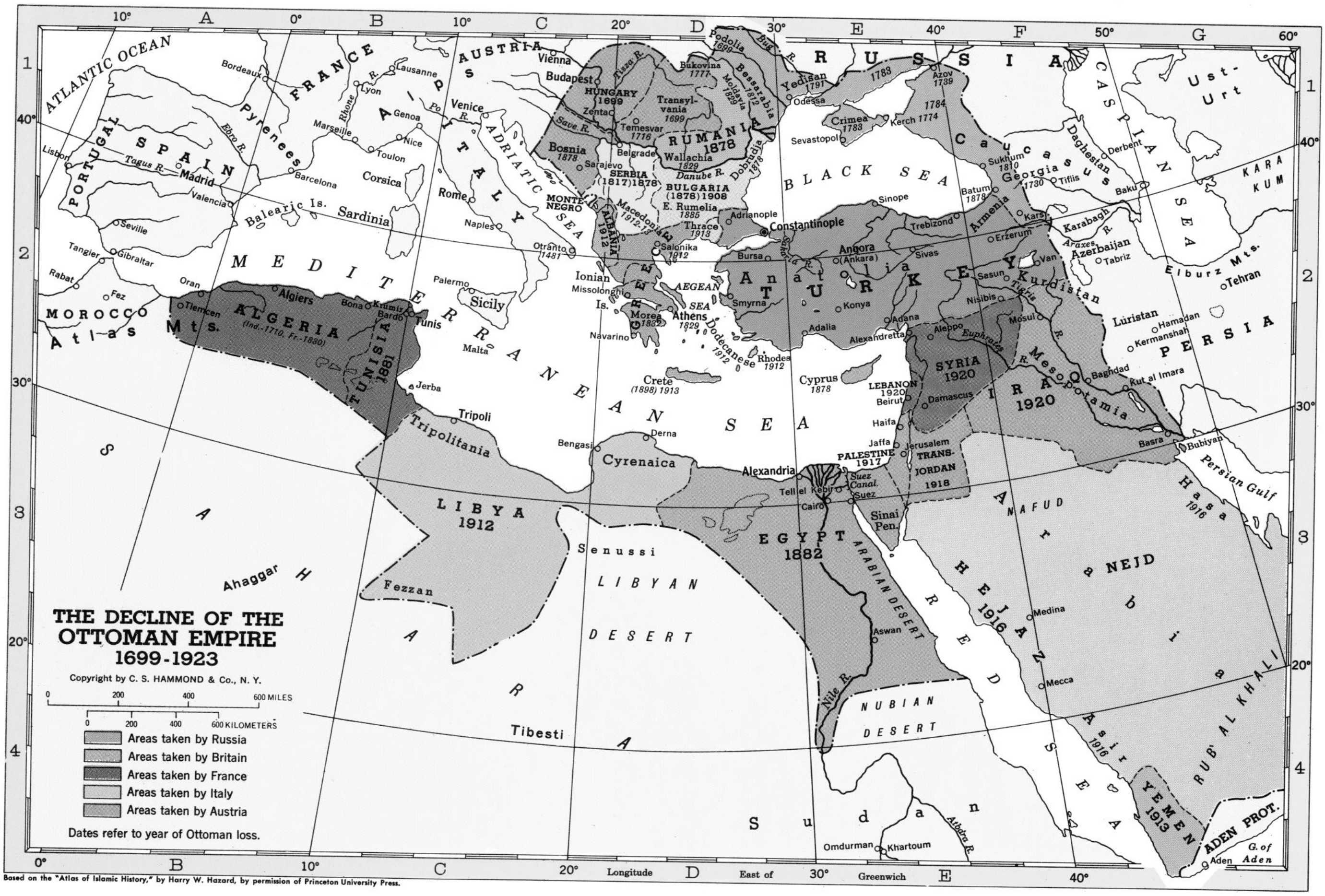

THE DECLINE OF THE OTTOMAN EMPIRE 1699-1923

Copyright by C. S. HAMMOND & Co., N.Y.

0 200 400 600 MILES
0 200 400 600 KILOMETERS

Areas taken by Russia
Areas taken by Britain
Areas taken by France
Areas taken by Italy
Areas taken by Austria

Dates refer to year of Ottoman loss.

Based on the "Atlas of Islamic History," by Harry W. Hazard, by permission of Princeton University Press.

522

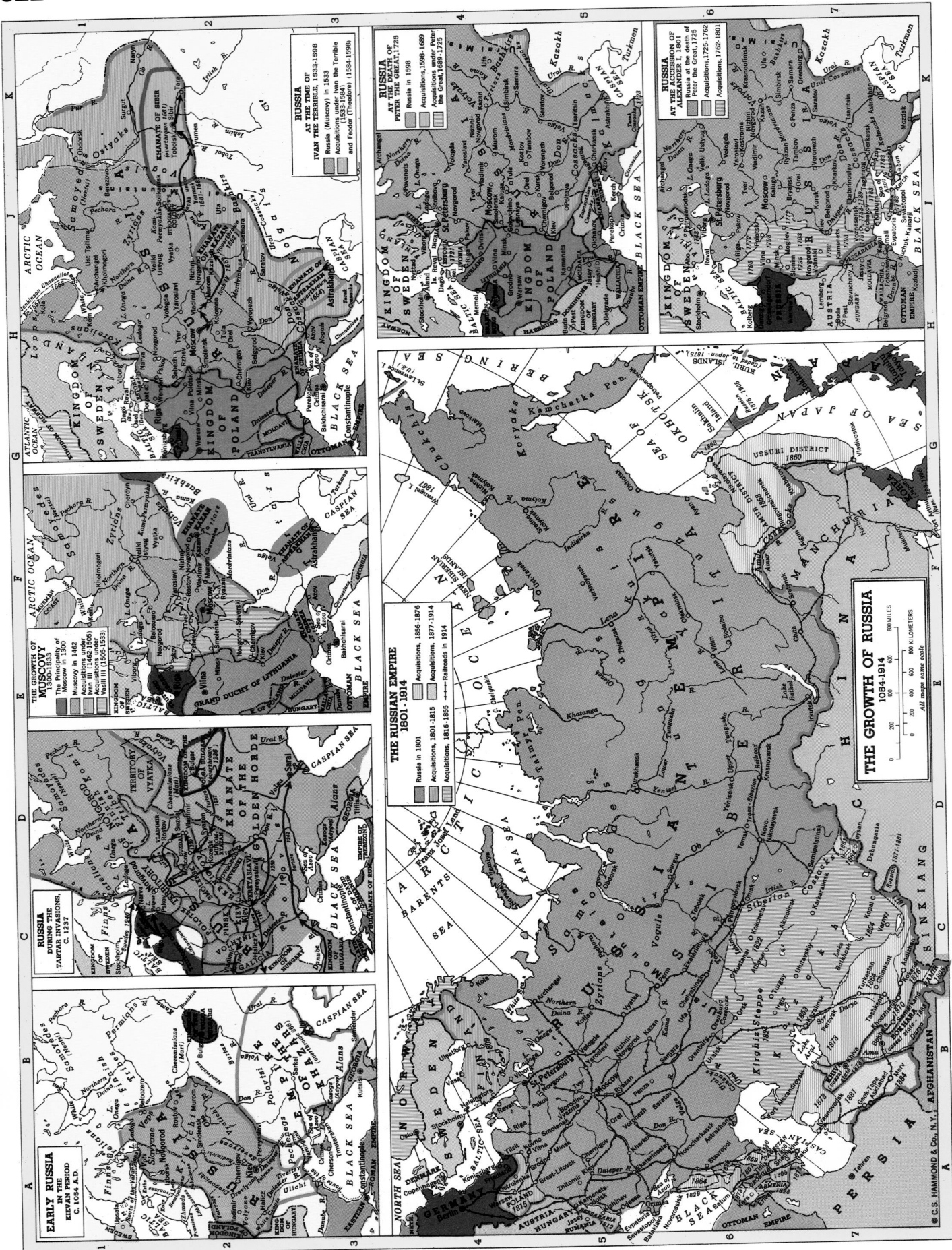

EARLY RUSSIA IN THE KIEVAN PERIOD C. 1054 A.D.

RUSSIA DURING THE TARTAR INVASIONS, C. 1237

THE GROWTH OF MUSCOVY 1300-1533
- Muscovy in 1462
- The Principality in 1300
- Acquisitions under Ivan III (1462-1505)
- Acquisitions under Vasili III (1505-1533)

RUSSIA AT THE TIME OF IVAN THE TERRIBLE, 1533-1598
- Russia (Muscovy) in 1533
- Acquisitions under Ivan the Terrible (1533-1584) and Feodor (Theodore) (1584-1598)

RUSSIA AT THE DEATH OF PETER THE GREAT, 1725
- Russia in 1598
- Acquisitions, 1598-1689
- Acquisitions under Peter the Great, 1689-1725

RUSSIA AT THE ACCESSION OF ALEXANDER I, 1801
- Russia at the death of Peter the Great, 1725
- Acquisitions, 1725-1762
- Acquisitions, 1762-1801

THE RUSSIAN EMPIRE 1801-1914
- Russia in 1801
- Acquisitions, 1801-1815
- Acquisitions, 1816-1855
- Acquisitions, 1856-1876
- Acquisitions, 1877-1914
- Railroads in 1914

THE GROWTH OF RUSSIA 1054-1914
MILES
KILOMETERS
All maps same scale

© C.S. HAMMOND & Co., N.Y.

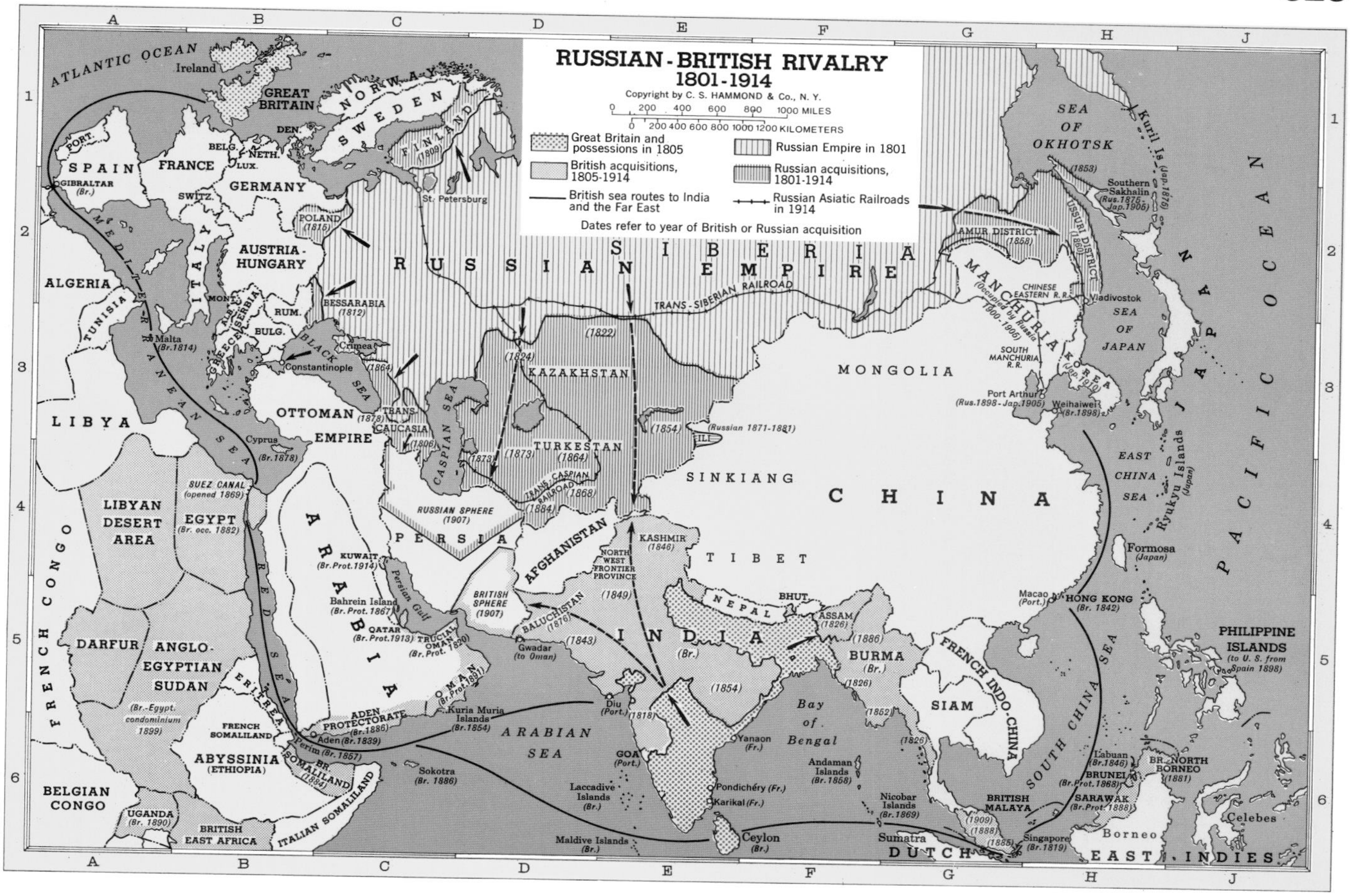

RUSSIAN-BRITISH RIVALRY 1801-1914

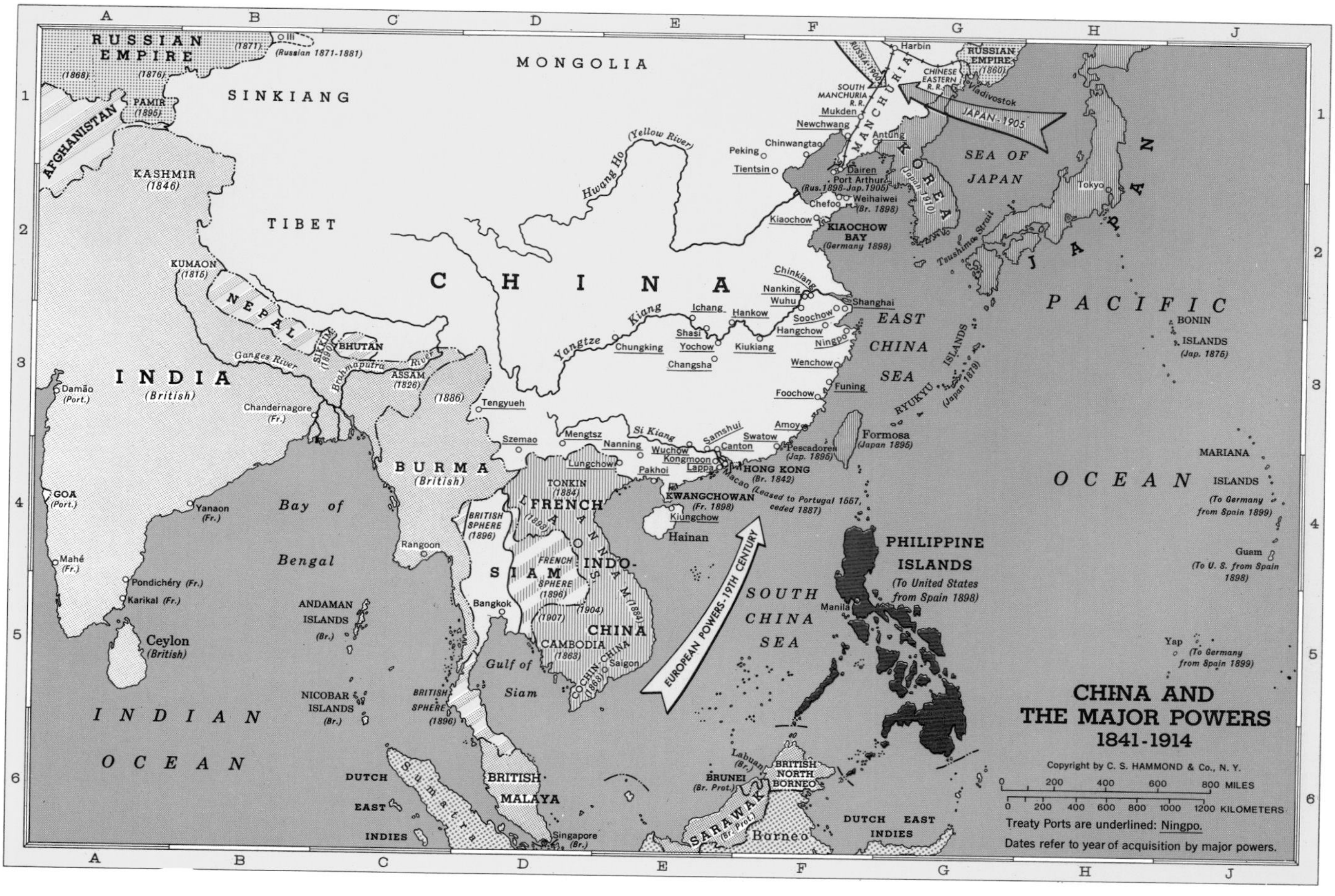

Copyright by C. S. HAMMOND & Co., N.Y.

0 200 400 600 800 1000 MILES
0 200 400 600 800 1000 1200 KILOMETERS

- Great Britain and possessions in 1805
- British acquisitions, 1805-1914
- British sea routes to India and the Far East
- Russian Empire in 1801
- Russian acquisitions, 1801-1914
- Russian Asiatic Railroads in 1914

Dates refer to year of British or Russian acquisition

ATLANTIC OCEAN · Ireland · GREAT BRITAIN · NORWAY · SWEDEN · FINLAND (1809) · St. Petersburg · DEN. · NETH. · BELG. · LUX. · FRANCE · GERMANY · SPAIN · PORT. · GIBRALTAR (Br.) · SWITZ. · ITALY · AUSTRIA-HUNGARY · POLAND (1815) · RUSSIAN EMPIRE · SIBERIA

ALGERIA · TUNISIA · Malta (Br.1814) · SERBIA · RUM. · BULG. · BLACK SEA · Constantinople · Crimea (1864) · BESSARABIA (1812) · TRANS-SIBERIAN RAILROAD · (1822) · (1824) · MANCHURIA · CHINESE EASTERN R.R. · AMUR DISTRICT (1858) · USSURI DISTRICT · SEA OF OKHOTSK · Kuri Is. (Jap.1875) · Southern Sakhalin (Rus.1875-Jap.1905)

LIBYA · GREECE · OTTOMAN EMPIRE · Cyprus (Br.1878) · TRANS-CAUCASIA (1878) · (1806) · CASPIAN SEA · KAZAKHSTAN · (1854) · (Russian 1871-1881) · ILI · MONGOLIA · SINKIANG · CHINA · MANCHURIA · Port Arthur (Rus.1898-Jap.1905) · Weihaiwei (Br.1898) · Vladivostok · KOREA · SEA OF JAPAN · PACIFIC OCEAN

LIBYAN DESERT AREA · EGYPT (Br. occ. 1882) · SUEZ CANAL (opened 1869) · PERSIA · TURKESTAN (1864) · TRANS-CASPIAN R.R. (1868) · (1873) · (1884) · RUSSIAN SPHERE (1907) · AFGHANISTAN · NORTH WEST FRONTIER PROVINCE · KASHMIR (1846) · TIBET · FORMOSA (Japan) · EAST CHINA SEA · Ryukyu Islands (Japan) · JAPAN

FRENCH CONGO · ARABIA · KUWAIT (Br.Prot.1914) · Bahrein Island (Br.Prot.1867) · QATAR · BRITISH SPHERE (1907) · BALUCHISTAN (1876) · (1849) · (1843) · NEPAL · BHUT. · ASSAM (1826) · (1886) · BURMA (Br.) (1826) · Macao (Port.) · HONG KONG (Br.1842) · SOUTH CHINA SEA · PHILIPPINE ISLANDS (to U.S. from Spain 1898)

DARFUR · ANGLO-EGYPTIAN SUDAN (Br.-Egypt. condominium 1899) · ERITREA · TRUCIAL OMAN (Br.Prot.1913) · OMAN (Br.Prot.) · Gwadar (to Oman) · Diu (Port.) · (1818) · INDIA (Br.) · (1854) · (1852) · SIAM · FRENCH INDO-CHINA

BELGIAN CONGO · UGANDA (Br.1890) · BRITISH EAST AFRICA · ABYSSINIA (ETHIOPIA) · FRENCH SOMALILAND · BR. SOMALILAND · ITALIAN SOMALILAND · ADEN PROTECTORATE (Br.1886) · Aden (Br.1839) · Perim · Kuria Muria Islands (Br.1854) · ARABIAN SEA · Sokotra (Br.1886) · GOA (Port.) · Yanaon (Fr.) · Pondichéry (Fr.) · Karikal (Fr.) · Laccadive Islands · Bay of Bengal · Andaman Islands (Br.1858) · Nicobar Islands (Br.1869) · Sumatra · Maldive Islands (Br.) · Ceylon (Br.) · DUTCH EAST INDIES · Labuan (Br.1846) · BRUNEI (Br.Prot.1888) · SARAWAK (Br.Prot.1888) · BR.NORTH BORNEO (1881) · Singapore (Br.1819) · Borneo · Celebes

CHINA AND THE MAJOR POWERS 1841-1914

Copyright by C. S. HAMMOND & Co., N.Y.

0 200 400 600 800 MILES
0 200 400 600 800 1000 1200 KILOMETERS

Treaty Ports are underlined: Ningpo.
Dates refer to year of acquisition by major powers.

RUSSIAN EMPIRE · (1868) · (1876) · (1871) · Ili (Russian 1871-1881) · PAMIR (1895) · AFGHANISTAN · SINKIANG · MONGOLIA · Harbin · MANCHURIA · CHINESE EASTERN R.R. · SOUTH MANCHURIA R.R. · Mukden · Port Arthur (Rus.1898-Jap.1905) · Dairen · Weihaiwei (Br.1898) · JAPAN: 1905 · Vladivostok · RUSSIAN EMPIRE (1860)

KASHMIR (1846) · TIBET · KUMAON (1816) · NEPAL · BHUTAN · SIKKIM · ASSAM (1826) · (1886) · Tengyueh · CHINA · Huang Ho (Yellow River) · Peking · Chinwangtao · Tientsin · Chefoo · Kiaochow · KIAOCHOW BAY (Germany 1898) · Newchwang · Antung · KOREA · SEA OF JAPAN · Tokyo · PACIFIC OCEAN

INDIA (British) · Damão (Port.) · Chandernagore (Fr.) · Ganges River · Brahmaputra River · Yangtze · Kiang · Ichang · Hankow · Wuhu · Chinkiang · Nanking · Shanghai · Soochow · Hangchow · Ningpo · EAST CHINA SEA · BONIN ISLANDS (Jap.1876)

GOA (Port.) · Yanaon (Fr.) · Mahé (Fr.) · Pondichéry (Fr.) · Karikal (Fr.) · Ceylon (British) · BURMA (British) · Rangoon · Bay of Bengal · ANDAMAN ISLANDS (Br.) · NICOBAR ISLANDS (Br.) · Shasi · Yochow · Chungking · Changsha · Kiukiang · Wenchow · Foochow · Funing · Amoy · Swatow · Pescadores (Jap.1895) · FORMOSA (Japan 1895) · RYUKYU ISLANDS (Japan 1879) · MARIANA ISLANDS (To Germany from Spain 1899)

Szemao · Mengtsz · Nanning · Lungchow · Pakhoi · Si Kiang · Samshui · Wuchow · Kongmoon · Canton · Lappa · Macao (Port.) · HONG KONG (Br.1842) · Kiungchow · Hainan · TONKIN (1884) · BRITISH SPHERE (1896) · FRENCH INDO-CHINA · SIAM · FRENCH SPHERE (1896) · Bangkok · CAMBODIA (1863) · (1904) · COCHIN CHINA · Saigon · KWANGCHOWAN (Fr.1898) · KWANGCHOW · Leased to Portugal 1557, ceded 1887 · SOUTH CHINA SEA · PHILIPPINE ISLANDS (To United States from Spain 1898) · Manila · EUROPEAN POWERS-19TH CENTURY · Guam (To U.S. from Spain 1898) · Yap (To Germany from Spain 1899)

INDIAN OCEAN · Gulf of Siam · SUMATRA · BRITISH MALAYA · Singapore (Br.) · DUTCH EAST INDIES · BRUNEI (Br.Prot.) · BRITISH NORTH BORNEO · SARAWAK (Br.) · Borneo

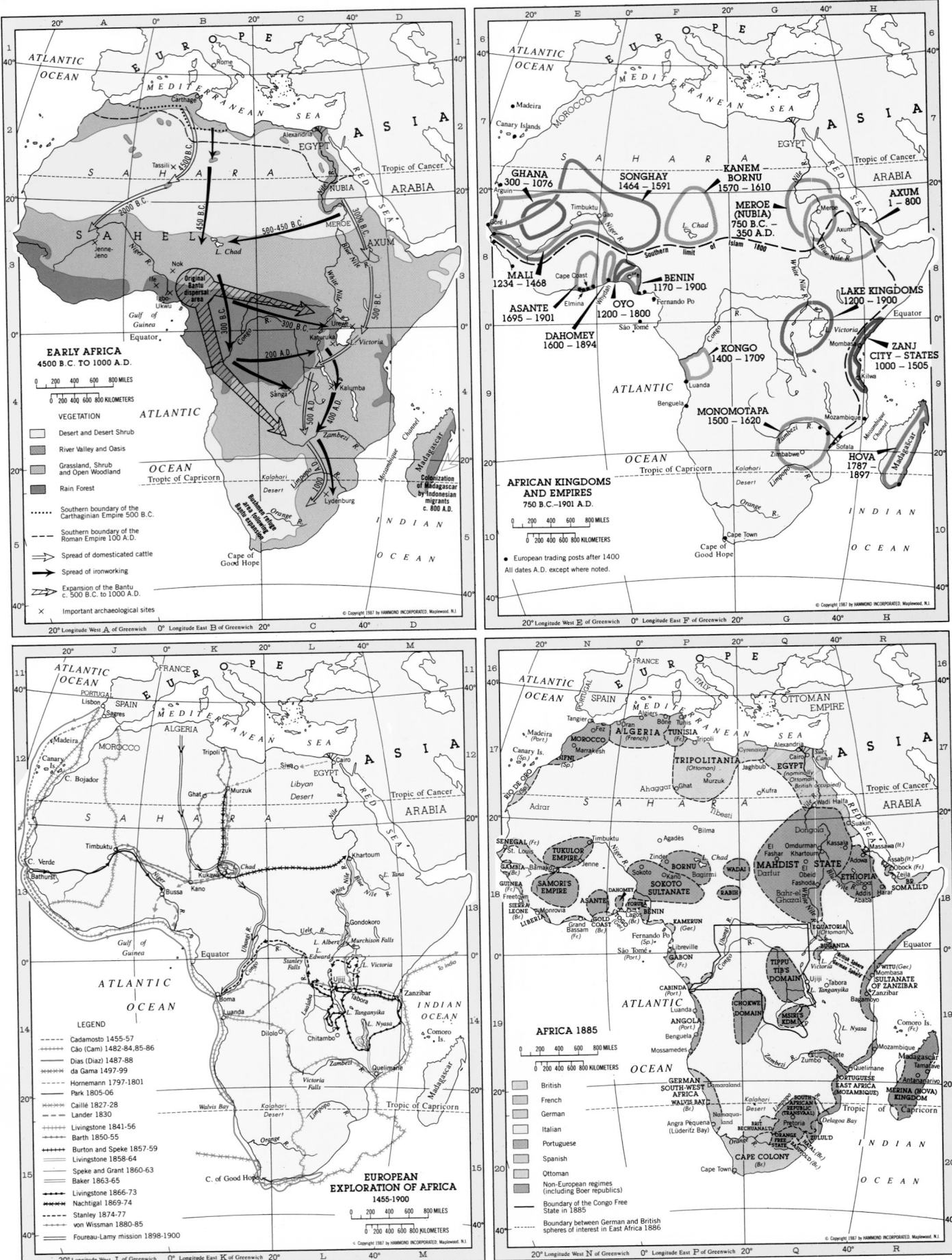

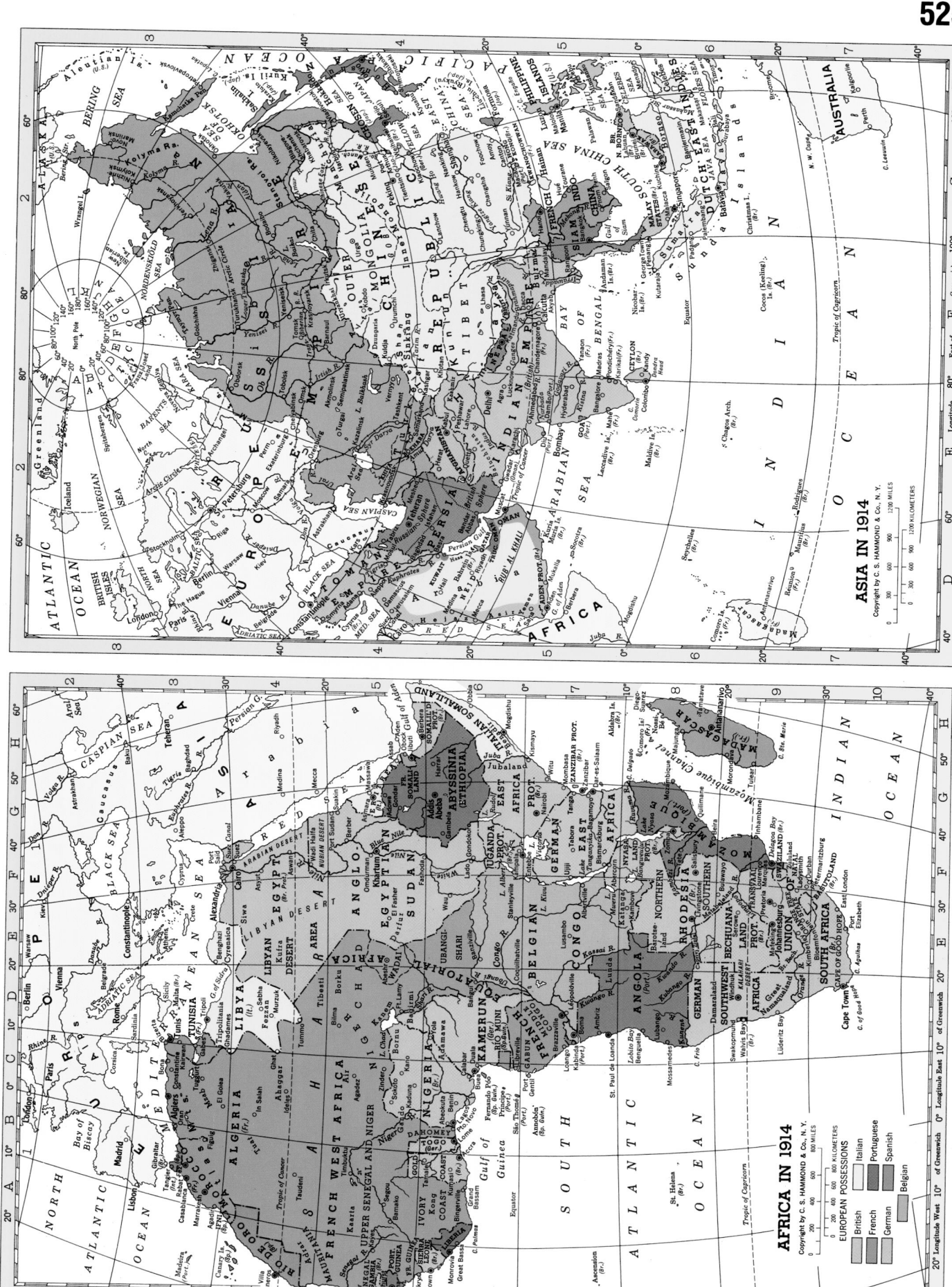

ASIA IN 1914

Copyright by C. S. HAMMOND & Co., N. Y.

AFRICA IN 1914

Copyright by C. S. HAMMOND & Co., N. Y.

EUROPEAN POSSESSIONS

British
French
German
Italian
Portuguese
Spanish
Belgian

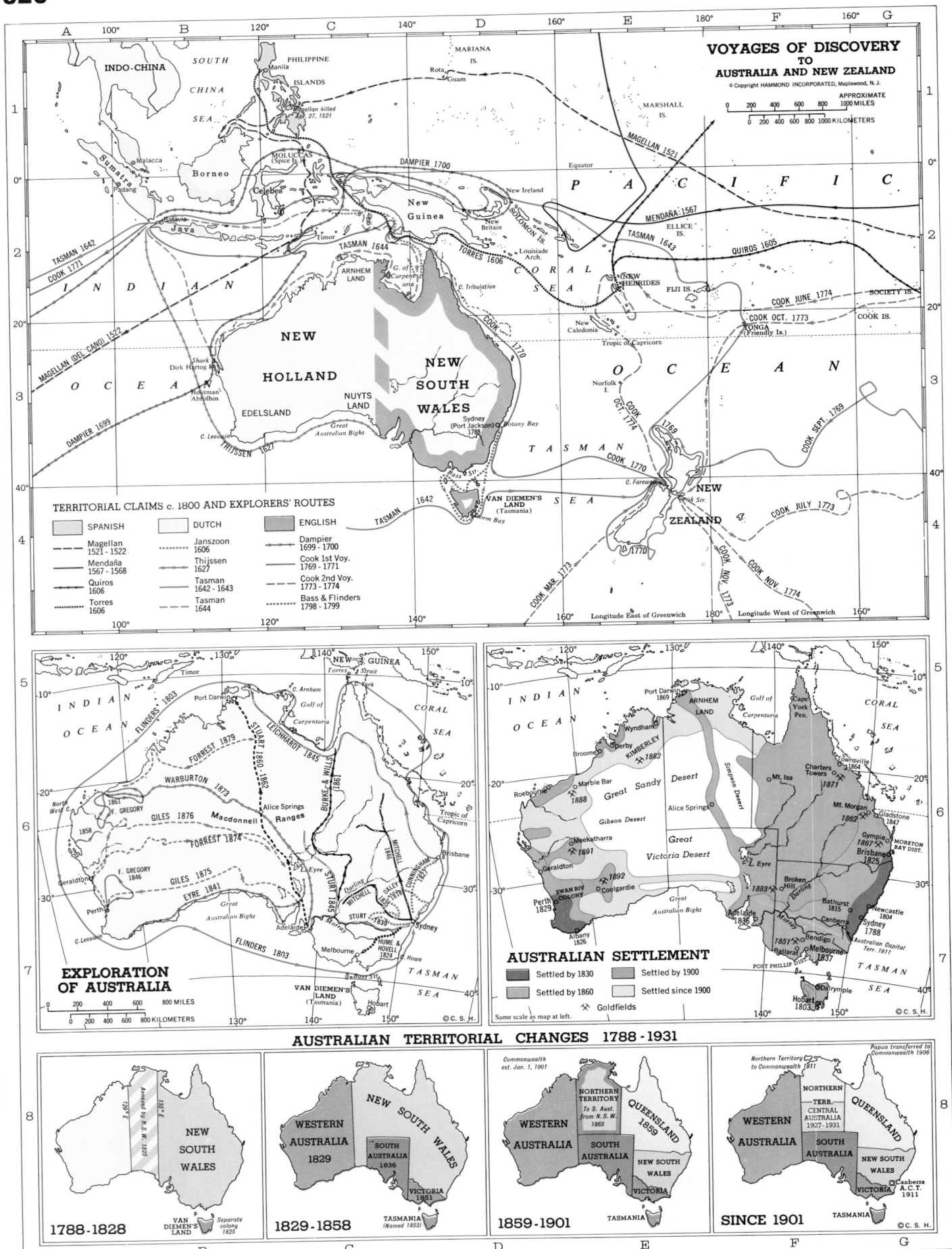

VOYAGES OF DISCOVERY TO AUSTRALIA AND NEW ZEALAND

© Copyright HAMMOND INCORPORATED, Maplewood, N.J.

APPROXIMATE 1000 MILES

TERRITORIAL CLAIMS c. 1800 AND EXPLORERS' ROUTES

- SPANISH
- DUTCH
- ENGLISH

Magellan 1521 - 1522
Mendaña 1567 - 1568
Quiros 1606
Torres 1606

Janszoon 1606
Thijssen 1627
Tasman 1642 - 1643
Tasman 1644

Dampier 1699 - 1700
Cook 1st Voy. 1769 - 1771
Cook 2nd Voy. 1773 - 1774
Bass & Flinders 1798 - 1799

EXPLORATION OF AUSTRALIA

AUSTRALIAN SETTLEMENT

- Settled by 1830
- Settled by 1860
- Settled by 1900
- Settled since 1900
- Goldfields

Same scale as map at left.

AUSTRALIAN TERRITORIAL CHANGES 1788-1931

1788-1828
NEW SOUTH WALES
VAN DIEMEN'S LAND
Separate colony 1825
Annexed by N.S.W. 1825

1829-1858
WESTERN AUSTRALIA 1829
SOUTH AUSTRALIA 1836
NEW SOUTH WALES
VICTORIA 1851
TASMANIA (Named 1853)

1859-1901
Commonwealth est. Jan. 1, 1901
WESTERN AUSTRALIA
NORTHERN TERRITORY To S. Aust. from N.S.W. 1863
QUEENSLAND 1859
SOUTH AUSTRALIA
NEW SOUTH WALES
VICTORIA
TASMANIA

SINCE 1901
Papua transferred to Commonwealth 1906
Northern Territory to Commonwealth 1911
WESTERN AUSTRALIA
NORTHERN TERR.
CENTRAL AUSTRALIA 1927-1931
QUEENSLAND
SOUTH AUSTRALIA
NEW SOUTH WALES
VICTORIA
Canberra A.C.T. 1911
TASMANIA

EXPLORATION OF CANADA

© Copyright HAMMOND INCORPORATED, Maplewood, N. J.

0 50 100   200   300   400 MILES

0 100 200 300   400 KILOMETERS

Forts & fur traders posts ......□   Battles.......✕

The various Indian tribes are shown where they were located during the period of their greatest significance in Canadian history.

THE GROWTH OF CANADA FROM 1791 TO 1949

Copyright by C.S. HAMMOND & Co., N.Y.

The dates within the provinces, territories or districts indicate the years of their creation as political divisions.

1791

1873

1898   Boundary of Northwest Territories 1894

1949   Boundary of Northwest Territories 1949

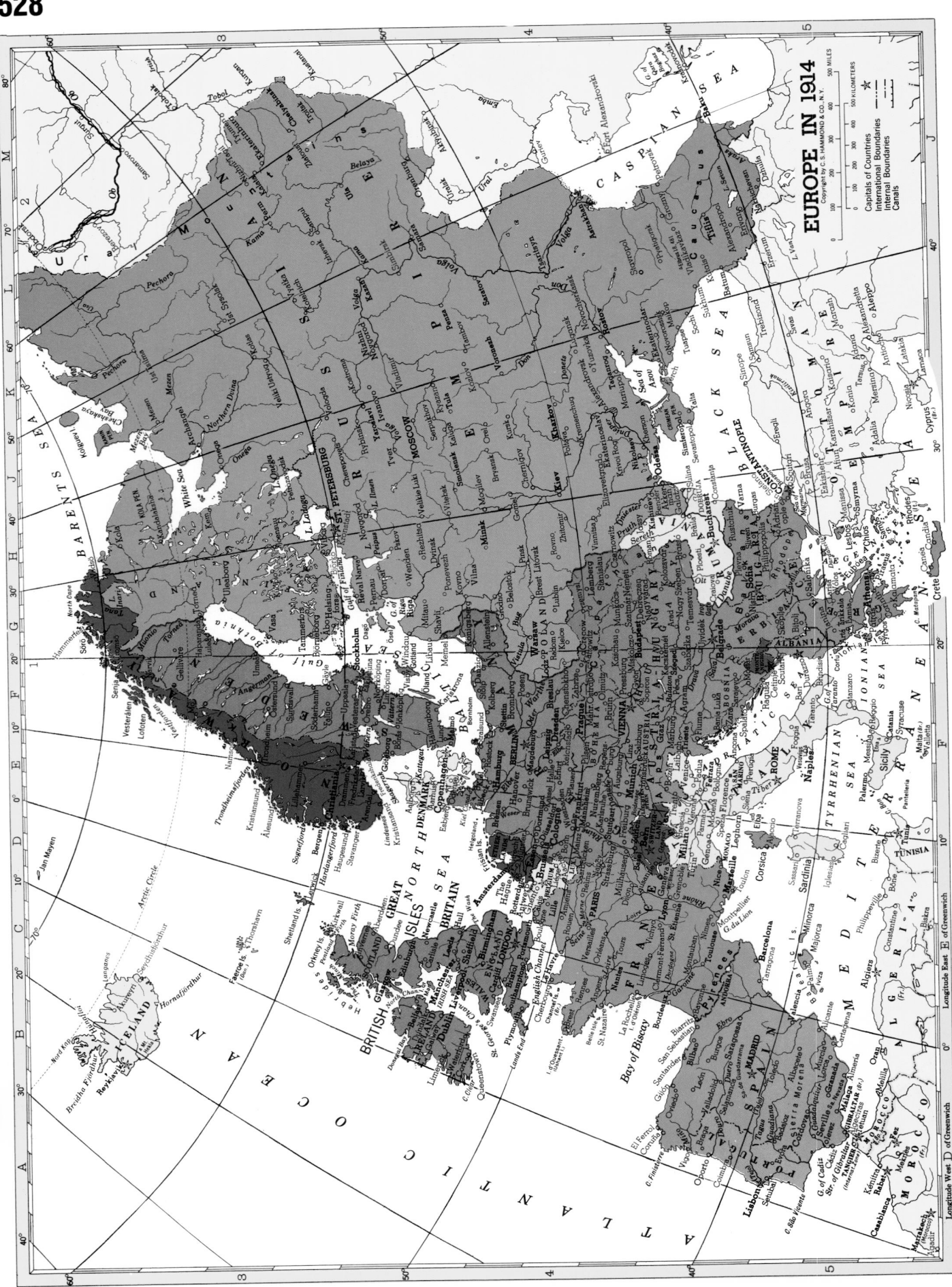

EUROPE IN 1914

Copyright by C. S. HAMMOND & CO. N.Y.

Capitals of Countries ✪
International Boundaries ———
Internal Boundaries ········
Canals ≈≈≈

THE FIRST WORLD WAR
1914-1918
© C. S. HAMMOND & Co., Maplewood, N.J.

- The Allies
- Neutral States
- The Central Powers
- Areas Occupied by the Central Powers
- Advances of the Allies
- Advances of the Central Powers

EUROPE AND THE NEAR EAST

- - - - Stabilized Line on the Western Front, 1914-1917
- — — Eastern Front on the Eve of the Russian Revolution, Oct. 1917
- .... Limit of Allied Advances in the East
- Area Occupied by the Central Powers after Brest Litovsk Treaty, 1918

THE WESTERN FRONT

- Limit of German Advance, 1914
- Limit of Trench Warfare, 1914-1917
- Hindenburg Line, 1917
- Limit of Final German Advance, 1918
- Armistice Line, November 11, 1918
- Limit of Allied Occupation Zone

EUROPE 1919-1929

Copyright by C. S. HAMMOND & CO., N. Y.

Capitals of Countries .... ☆
International Boundaries -----
Canals -·-·-·

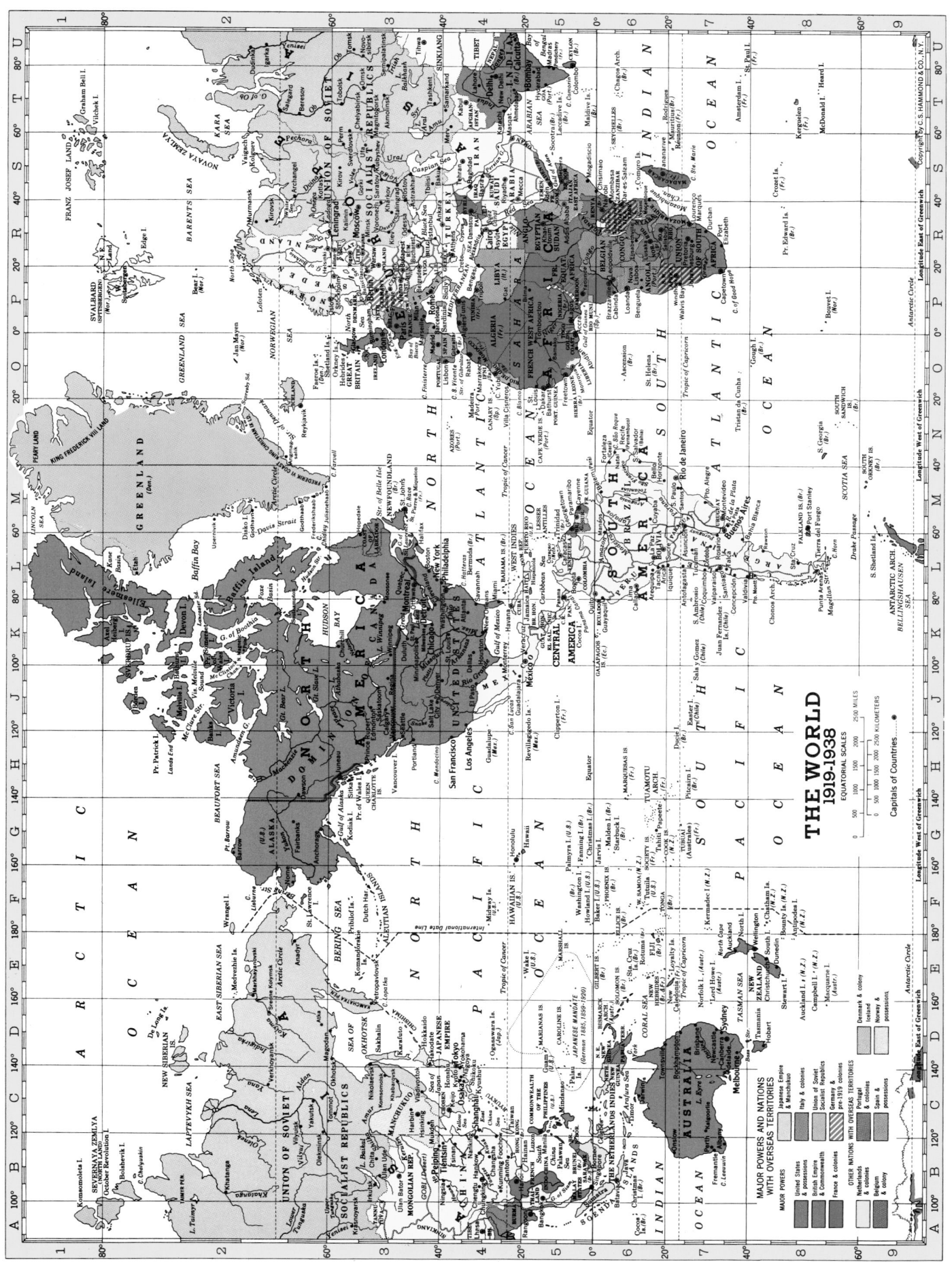

THE WORLD
1919-1938

MAJOR POWERS AND NATIONS
WITH OVERSEAS TERRITORIES

MAJOR POWERS

United States
& possessions

British Empire
& Commonwealth

France & colonies

OTHER NATIONS WITH OVERSEAS TERRITORIES

Netherlands
& colonies

Belgium
& colony

Japanese Empire
& Manchukuo

Italy & colonies

Union of Soviet
Socialist Republics

Germany &
pre-1919 colonies

Portugal
& colonies

Spain &
possessions

Denmark & possessions

Iceland

Norway &
possessions

Capitals of Countries........●

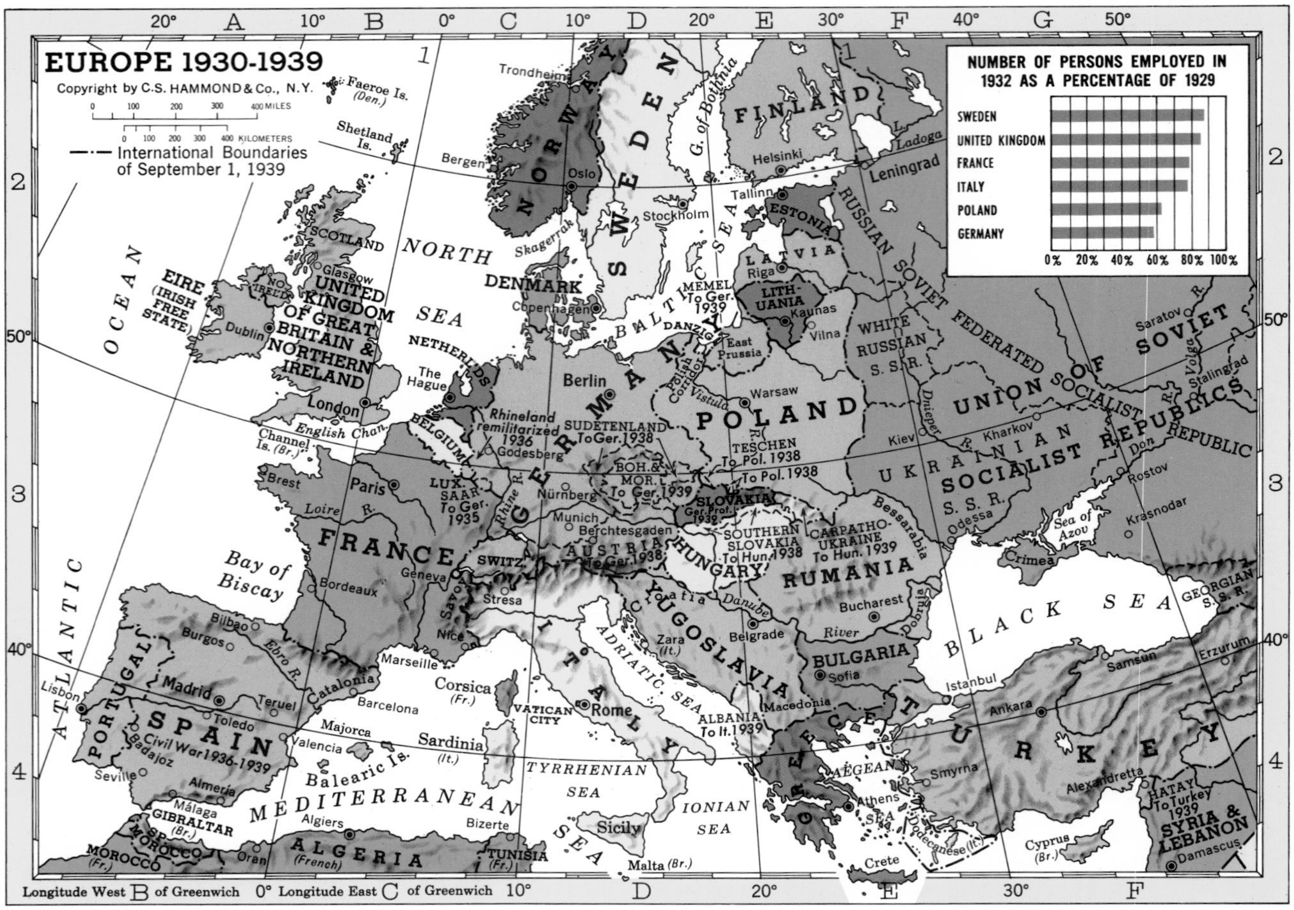

EUROPE 1930-1939

Copyright by C.S. HAMMOND & Co., N.Y.

0 100 200 300 400 MILES
0 100 200 300 400 KILOMETERS

— · — International Boundaries of September 1, 1939

NUMBER OF PERSONS EMPLOYED IN 1932 AS A PERCENTAGE OF 1929

SWEDEN
UNITED KINGDOM
FRANCE
ITALY
POLAND
GERMANY

0% 20% 40% 60% 80% 100%

Faeroe Is. (Den.)
Trondheim
NORWAY
SWEDEN
FINLAND
Shetland Is.
Bergen
Oslo
Stockholm
Helsinki
Tallinn
Leningrad
L. Ladoga
RUSSIAN SOVIET FEDERATED SOCIALIST
SCOTLAND
NORTH SEA
Skagerrak
DENMARK
Copenhagen
BALTIC SEA
ESTONIA
LATVIA
Riga
MEMEL To Ger. 1939
LITH-UANIA
Kaunas
Vilna
WHITE RUSSIAN S.S.R.
Saratov R.
SOVIET
Glasgow
Dublin
EIRE (IRISH FREE STATE)
NO. IRELAND
UNITED KINGDOM OF GREAT BRITAIN & NORTHERN IRELAND
London
The Hague
NETHERLDS
Berlin
DANZIG
East Prussia
Warsaw
POLAND
Vistula
Kiev
UKRAINIAN
UNION OF
Volga
Stalingrad
SOCIALIST
REPUBLIC
English Chan.
Channel Is. (Br.)
BELGIUM
Rhineland remilitarized 1936
Godesberg
SUDETENLAND To Ger.1938
TESCHEN To Pol. 1938
BOH. & MOR. To Ger. 1939
Dnieper
Kharkov
SOCIALIST REPUBLICS
Don
Rostov
Brest
Loire
Paris
LUX.
SAAR To Ger. 1935
Nürnberg
GERMANY
Prague
SLOVAKIA
S.S.R.
Odessa
Krasnodar
FRANCE
SWITZ.
Munich
Berchtesgaden
AUSTRIA To Ger. 1938
Southern SLOVAKIA To Hun. 1938
CARPATHO-UKRAINE To Hun. 1939
HUNGARY
Bessarabia
Crimea
Sea of Azov
Bordeaux
Geneva
Stresa
Nice
Croatia
YUGOSLAVIA
RUMANIA
Danube River
Bucharest
GEORGIAN S.S.R.
Bay of Biscay
Marseille
Corsica (Fr.)
ITALY
Zara (It.)
Belgrade
BLACK SEA
Erzurum
ATLANTIC
PORTUGAL
Lisbon
Madrid
Toledo
Teruel
SPAIN Civil War 1936-1939
Badajoz
Seville
Almería
Málaga
GIBRALTAR (Br.)
Burgos
Bilbao
Catalonia
Barcelona
Valencia
Majorca
Balearic Is.
Sardinia (It.)
VATICAN CITY
Rome
ADRIATIC SEA
ALBANIA To It. 1939
Macedonia
BULGARIA
Sofia
Istanbul
Ankara
Samsun
TURKEY
Alexandretta
HATAY To Turkey 1939
SYRIA & LEBANON
Damascus
TYRRHENIAN SEA
Sicily
IONIAN SEA
GREECE
AEGEAN SEA
Athens
Smyrna
Cyprus (Br.)
MEDITERRANEAN
MOROCCO
Algiers
Oran
ALGERIA (French)
Bizerte
TUNISIA (Fr.)
Malta (Br.)
Crete
Dodecanese (It.)

Longitude West of Greenwich 0° Longitude East of Greenwich 10°

THE FAR EAST 1930-1941

Copyright by C.S. HAMMOND & Co., N.Y.

0 100 200 300 400 500 MILES
0 100 200 300 400 500 KILOMETERS

— · — International Boundaries of December 7, 1941
++++ Major Railroads
The Japanese Empire in 1930
Japanese dominated or occupied areas on December 7, 1941
Unoccupied China
← Soviet, Mongolian and Chinese Communist military movements
← Japanese and Manchukuoan military movements against Soviet and Mongolian forces

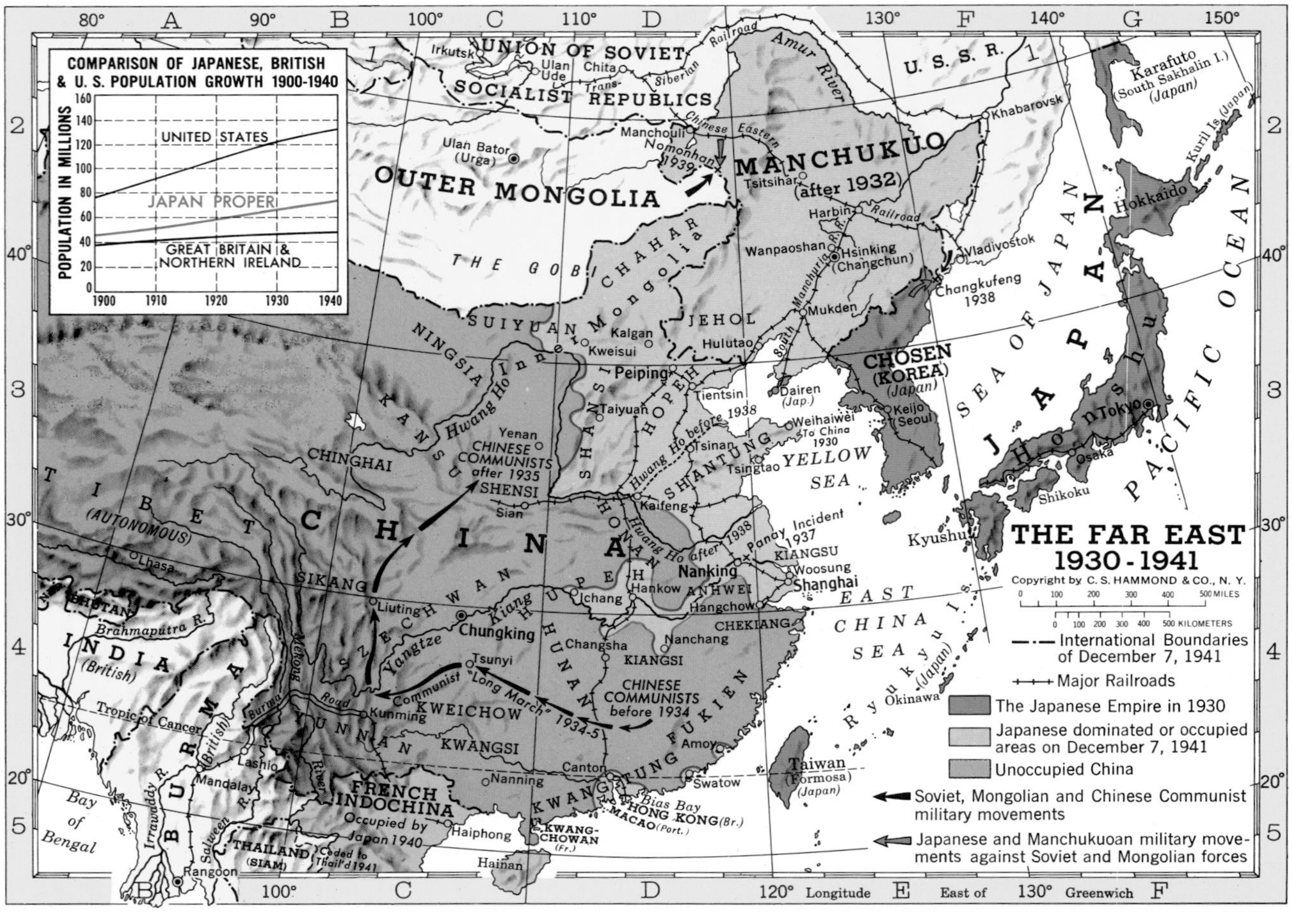

COMPARISON OF JAPANESE, BRITISH & U.S. POPULATION GROWTH 1900-1940

POPULATION IN MILLIONS
160 140 120 100 80 60 40 20

UNITED STATES
JAPAN PROPER
GREAT BRITAIN & NORTHERN IRELAND

1900 1910 1920 1930 1940

Irkutsk
UNION OF SOVIET SOCIALIST REPUBLICS
Ulan Ude
Chita
Trans-Siberian Railroad
Amur River
U.S.S.R.
Karafuto (South Sakhalin I.) (Japan)
Ulan Bator (Urga)
OUTER MONGOLIA
Manchouli
Nomonhan 1939
Tsitsihar
MANCHUKUO (after 1932)
Chinese Eastern Railroad
Khabarovsk
Kuril Is. (Japan)
THE GOBI
CHAHAR (Inner Mongolia)
Harbin
Wanpaoshan
Hsinking (Changchun)
Changkufeng 1938
Vladivostok
Hokkaido
SUIYUAN
Kalgan
Kweisui
JEHOL
Hulutao
Mukden
CHOSEN (KOREA) (Japan)
SEA OF JAPAN
NINGSIA
SHANSI
HOPEH
Peiping
Tientsin
Dairen (Jap)
Keijo Seoul
JAPAN
Honshu
Tokyo
PACIFIC OCEAN
CHINGHAI
Yenan
CHINESE COMMUNISTS after 1935
SHENSI
Sian
Taiyuan
Weihaiwei To China 1930
Tsingtao
SHANTUNG
YELLOW SEA
Osaka
Shikoku
TIBET (AUTONOMOUS)
Lhasa
Hwang Ho before 1938
Kaifeng
Hwang Ho after 1938
Panay Incident 1937
KIANGSU
Woosung
Kyushu
SIKANG
SZECHWAN
Liuting
CHINA
Chungking
Tsunyi
Communist "Long March" 1934-5
HUPEH
Ichang
Hankow
Hangchow
Nanking
ANHWEI
Shanghai
CHEKIANG
EAST CHINA SEA
BRITISH INDIA
Brahmaputra R.
TIBET
KWEICHOW
Kunming
HUNAN
Changsha
Nanchang
KIANGSI
CHINESE COMMUNISTS before 1934
FUKIEN
Ryukyu Is. (Japan)
Okinawa
Tropic of Cancer
BURMA (British)
Lashio
Mandalay
Burma Road
YUNNAN
KWANGSI
Nanning
KWANGTUNG
Canton
Swatow
Amoy
TAIWAN (Formosa) (Japan)
Bay of Bengal
Rangoon
FRENCH INDOCHINA Occupied by Japan 1940
THAILAND (SIAM)
Haiphong
Hainan
KWANG-CHOWAN (Fr.)
Bias Bay
HONG KONG (Br.)
MACAO (Port.)

Longitude East of Greenwich

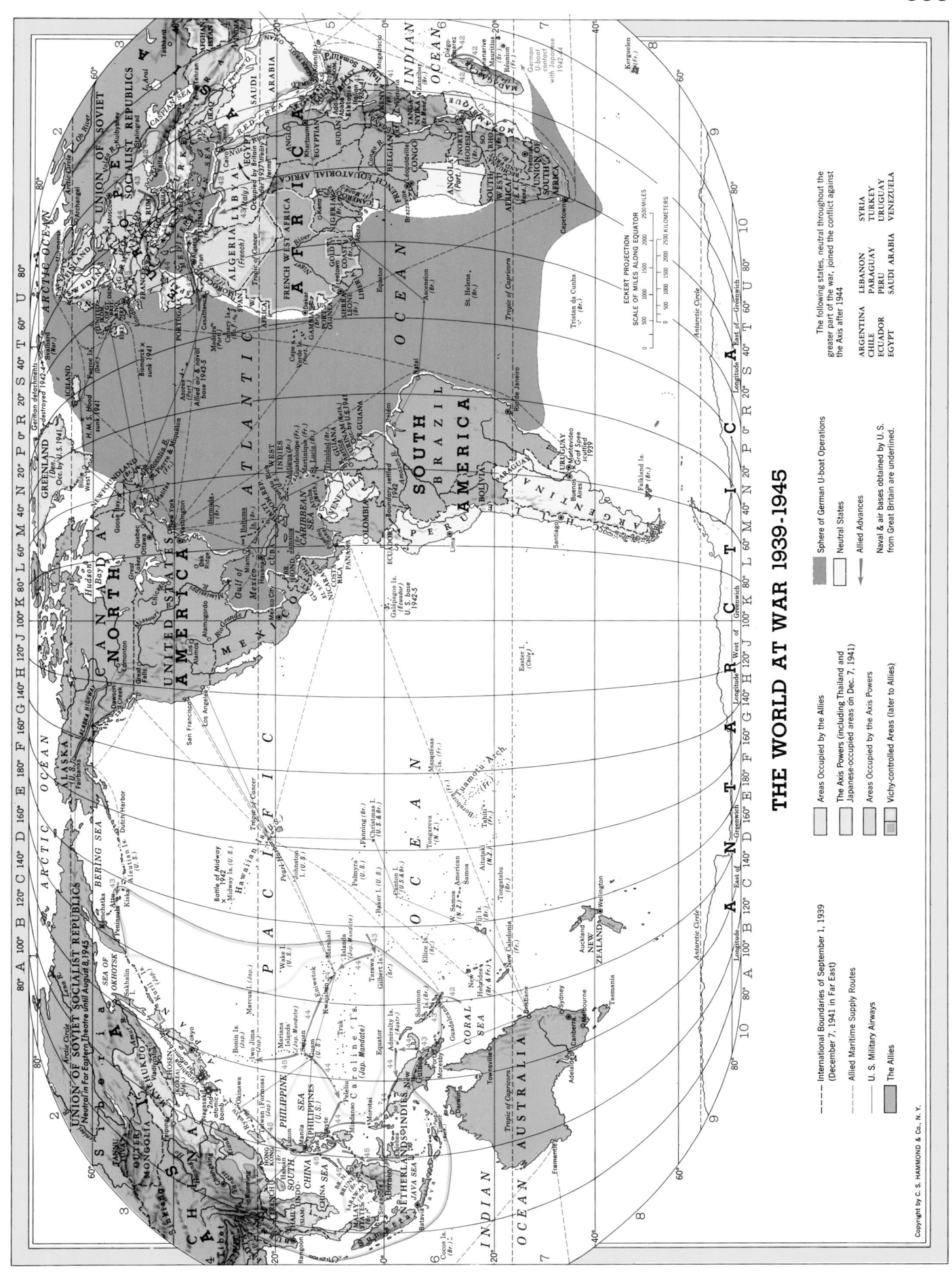

THE WORLD AT WAR 1939-1945

The following states, neutral throughout the greater part of the war, joined the conflict against the Axis after 1944

ARGENTINA	LEBANON	SYRIA
CHILE	PARAGUAY	TURKEY
ECUADOR	PERU	URUGUAY
EGYPT	SAUDI ARABIA	VENEZUELA

ECKERT PROJECTION
SCALE OF MILES ALONG EQUATOR

Legend:
- Areas Occupied by the Allies
- The Axis Powers (including Thailand and Japanese-occupied areas on Dec. 7, 1941)
- Areas Occupied by the Axis Powers
- Vichy-controlled Areas (later to Allies)
- International Boundaries of September 1, 1939 (December 7, 1941 in Far East)
- Allied Maritime Supply Routes
- U. S. Military Airways
- The Allies
- Sphere of German U-boat Operations
- Neutral States
- Allied Advances
- Naval & air bases obtained by U. S. from Great Britain are underlined.

Copyright by C. S. HAMMOND & Co., N. Y.

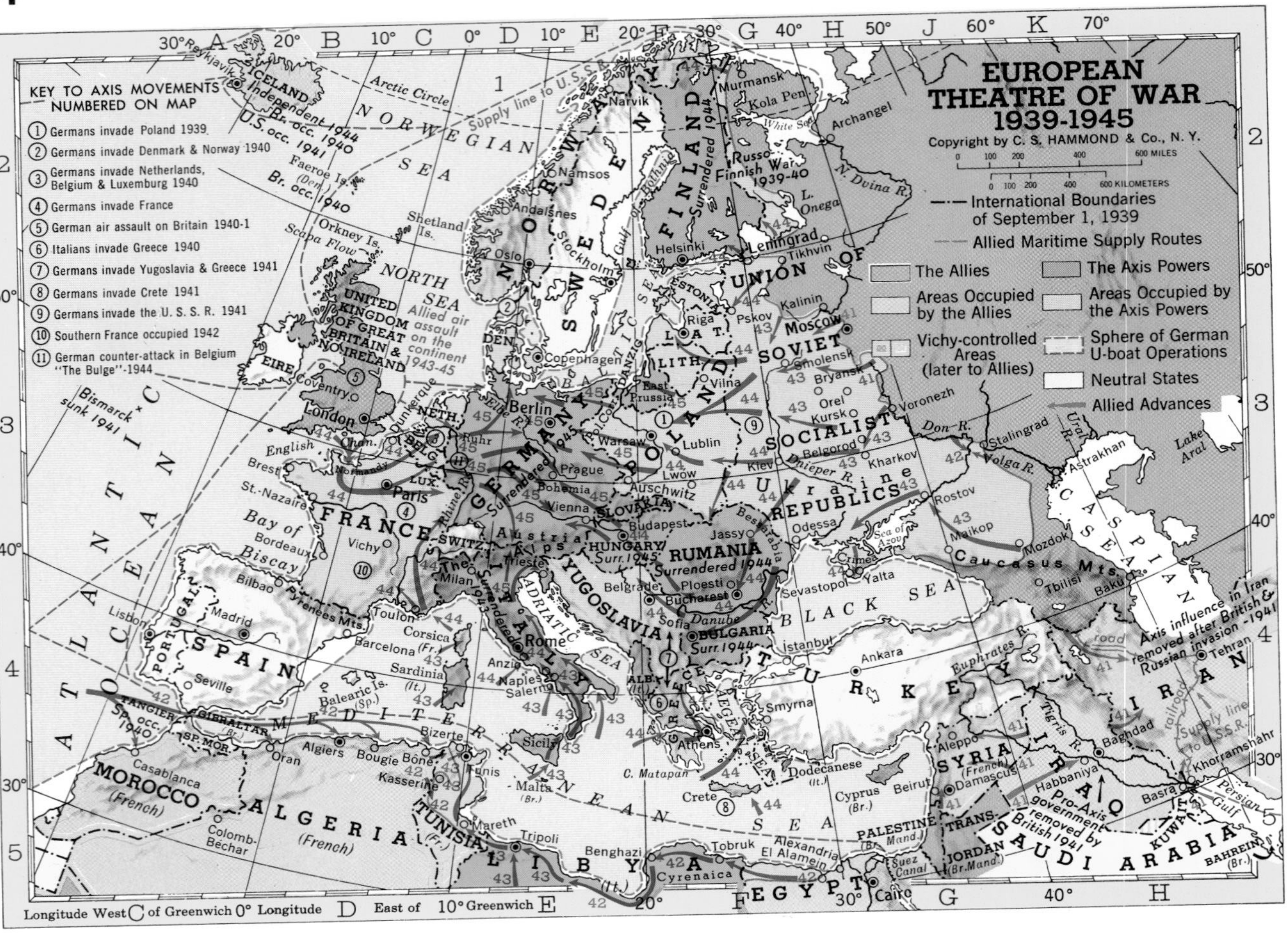

EUROPEAN THEATRE OF WAR 1939-1945
Copyright by C. S. Hammond & Co., N.Y.

KEY TO AXIS MOVEMENTS NUMBERED ON MAP
1. Germans invade Poland 1939
2. Germans invade Denmark & Norway 1940
3. Germans invade Netherlands, Belgium & Luxemburg 1940
4. Germans invade France
5. German air assault on Britain 1940-1
6. Italians invade Greece 1940
7. Germans invade Yugoslavia & Greece 1941
8. Germans invade Crete 1941
9. Germans invade the U.S.S.R. 1941
10. Southern France occupied 1942
11. German counter-attack in Belgium "The Bulge"-1944

Legend:
- International Boundaries of September 1, 1939
- Allied Maritime Supply Routes
- The Allies
- The Axis Powers
- Areas Occupied by the Allies
- Areas Occupied by the Axis Powers
- Vichy-controlled Areas (later to Allies)
- Sphere of German U-boat Operations
- Neutral States
- Allied Advances

Scale: 0 100 200 400 600 KILOMETERS / 0 100 200 400 600 MILES

Longitude West of Greenwich 0° Longitude East of 10° Greenwich

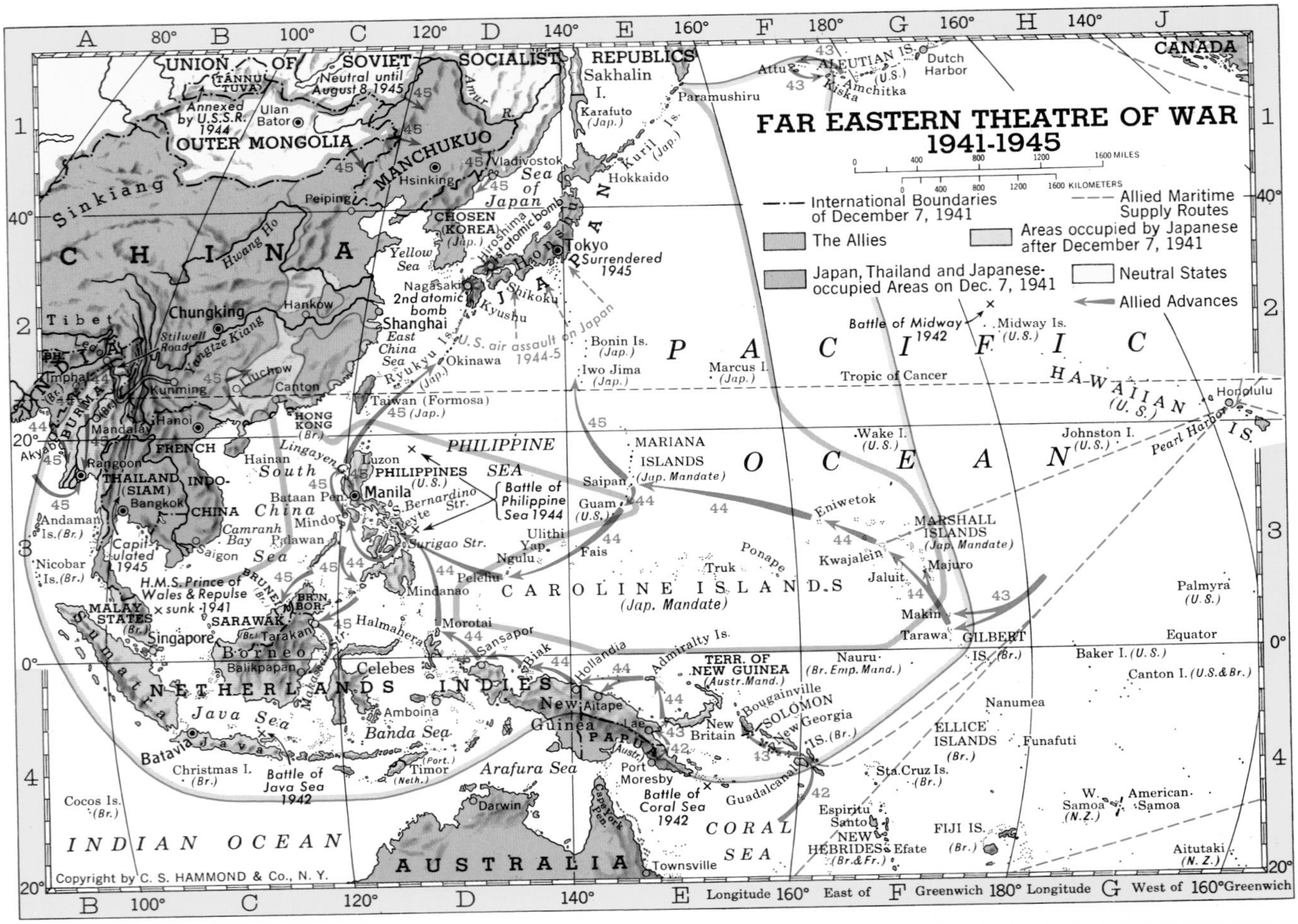

FAR EASTERN THEATRE OF WAR 1941-1945

Legend:
- International Boundaries of December 7, 1941
- Allied Maritime Supply Routes
- The Allies
- Areas occupied by Japanese after December 7, 1941
- Japan, Thailand and Japanese-occupied Areas on Dec. 7, 1941
- Neutral States
- Allied Advances

Scale: 0 400 800 1200 1600 KILOMETERS / 400 800 1600 MILES

Copyright by C. S. Hammond & Co., N.Y.

Longitude East of Greenwich / Longitude West of 160° Greenwich

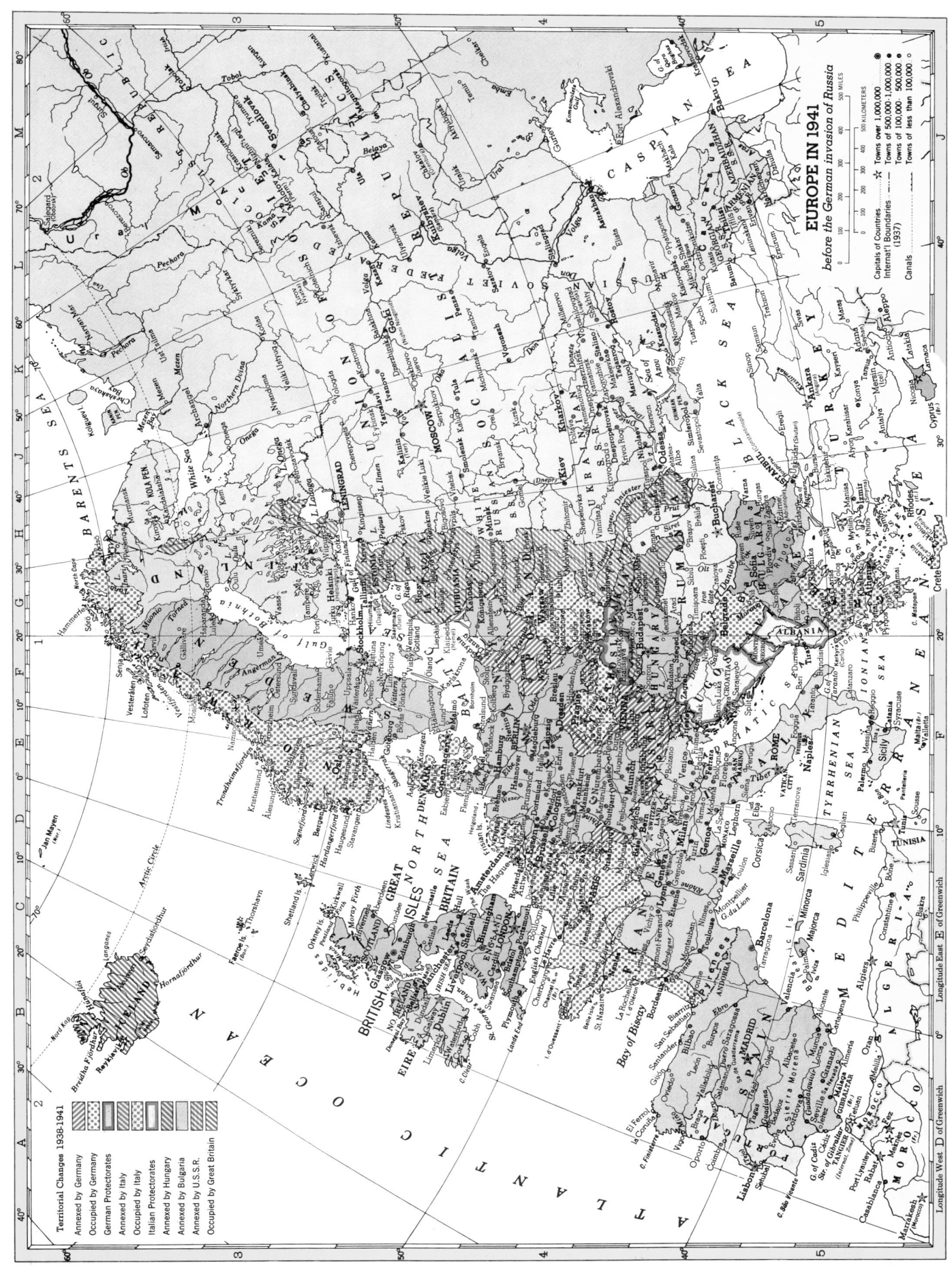

EUROPE IN 1941

before the German invasion of Russia

Territorial Changes 1938-1941

Annexed by Germany
Occupied by Germany
German Protectorates
Annexed by Italy
Occupied by Italy
Italian Protectorates
Annexed by Hungary
Annexed by Bulgaria
Annexed by U.S.S.R.
Occupied by Great Britain

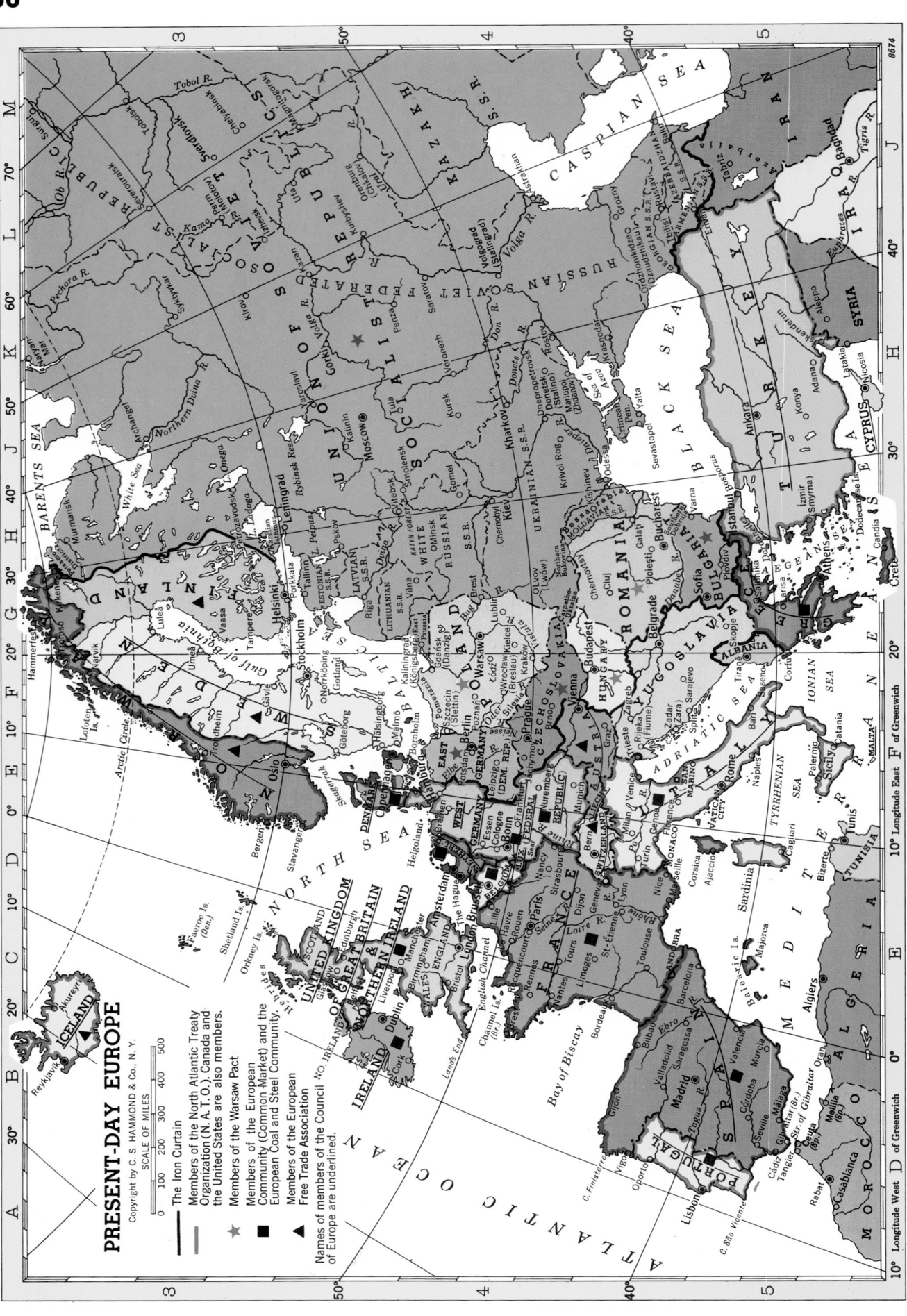

PRESENT-DAY EUROPE

Copyright by C. S. HAMMOND & Co. N. Y.

SCALE OF MILES

0 100 200 300 400 500

The Iron Curtain

Members of the North Atlantic Treaty
Organization (N.A.T.O.) Canada and
the United States are also members.

Members of the Warsaw Pact

Members of the European
Community (Common Market) and the
European Coal and Steel Community.

Members of the European
Free Trade Association

Names of members of the Council
of Europe are underlined.

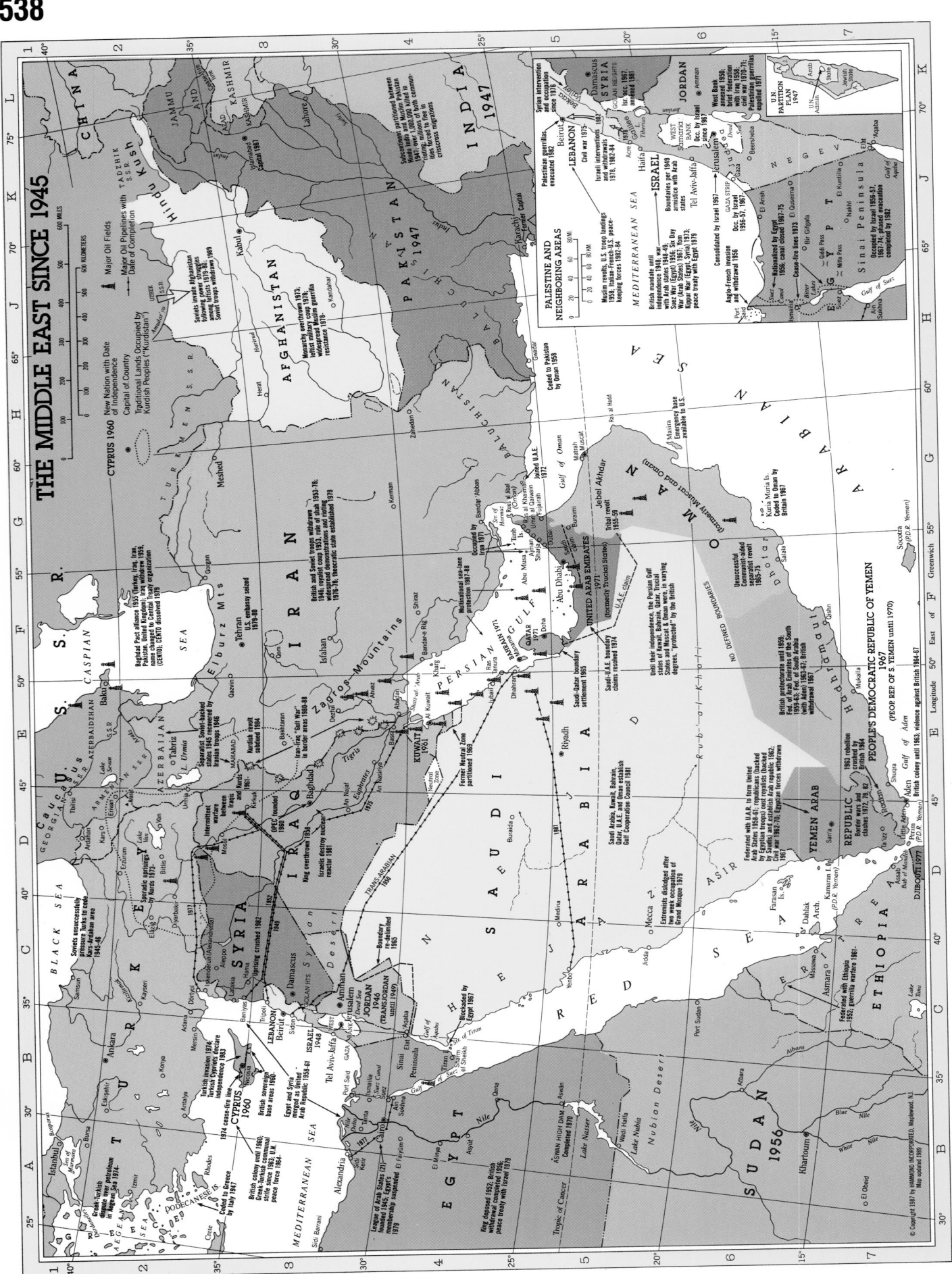

THE MIDDLE EAST SINCE 1945

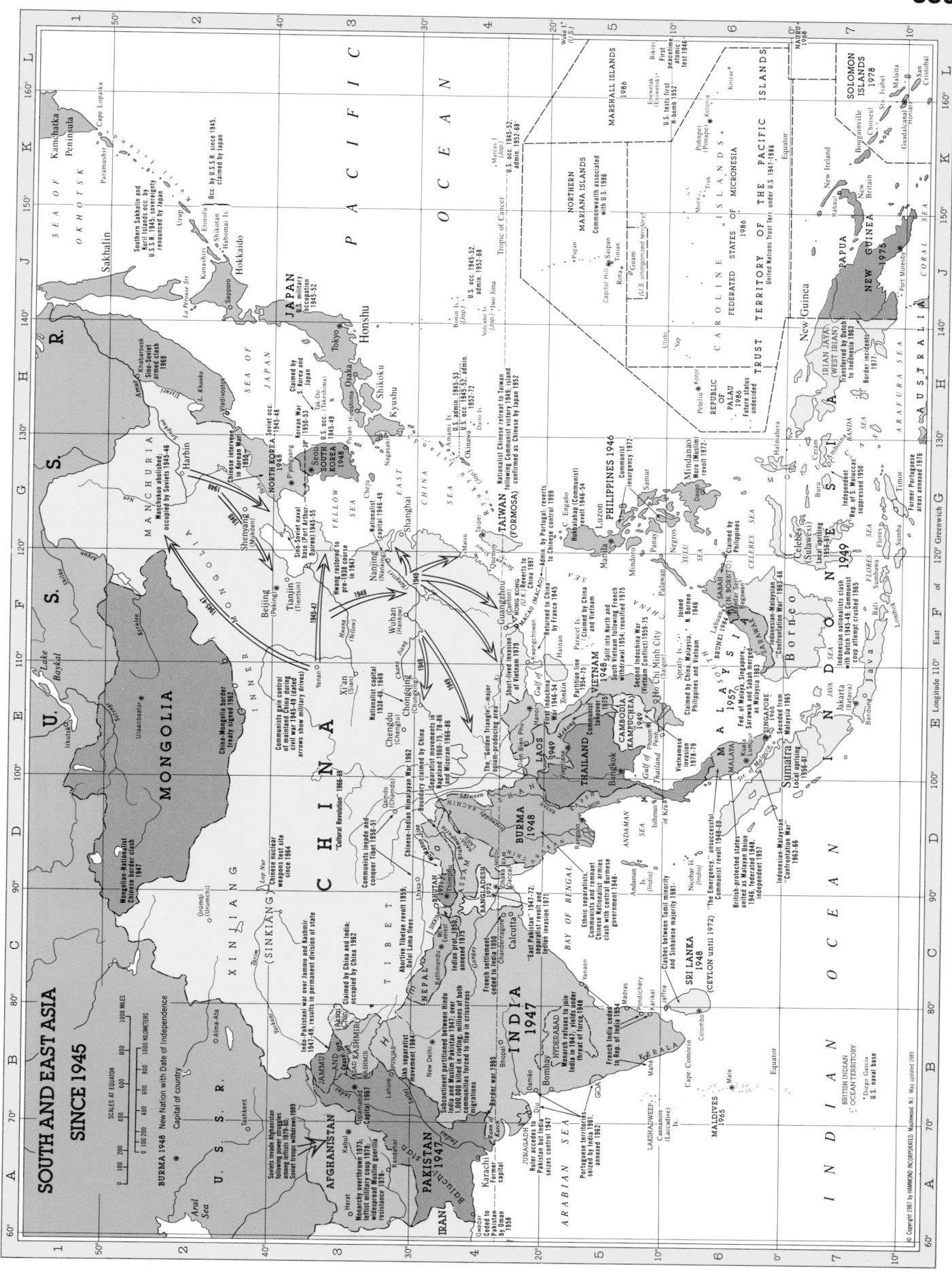

SOUTH AND EAST ASIA
SINCE 1945

BURMA 1948 New Nation with date of independence
● Capital of country

SCALES AT EQUATOR

0 100 200 400 600 800 1000 KILOMETERS
0 200 400 600 800 1000 MILES

© Copyright 1987 by HAMMOND INCORPORATED, Maplewood, N.J. Map updated 1991

540

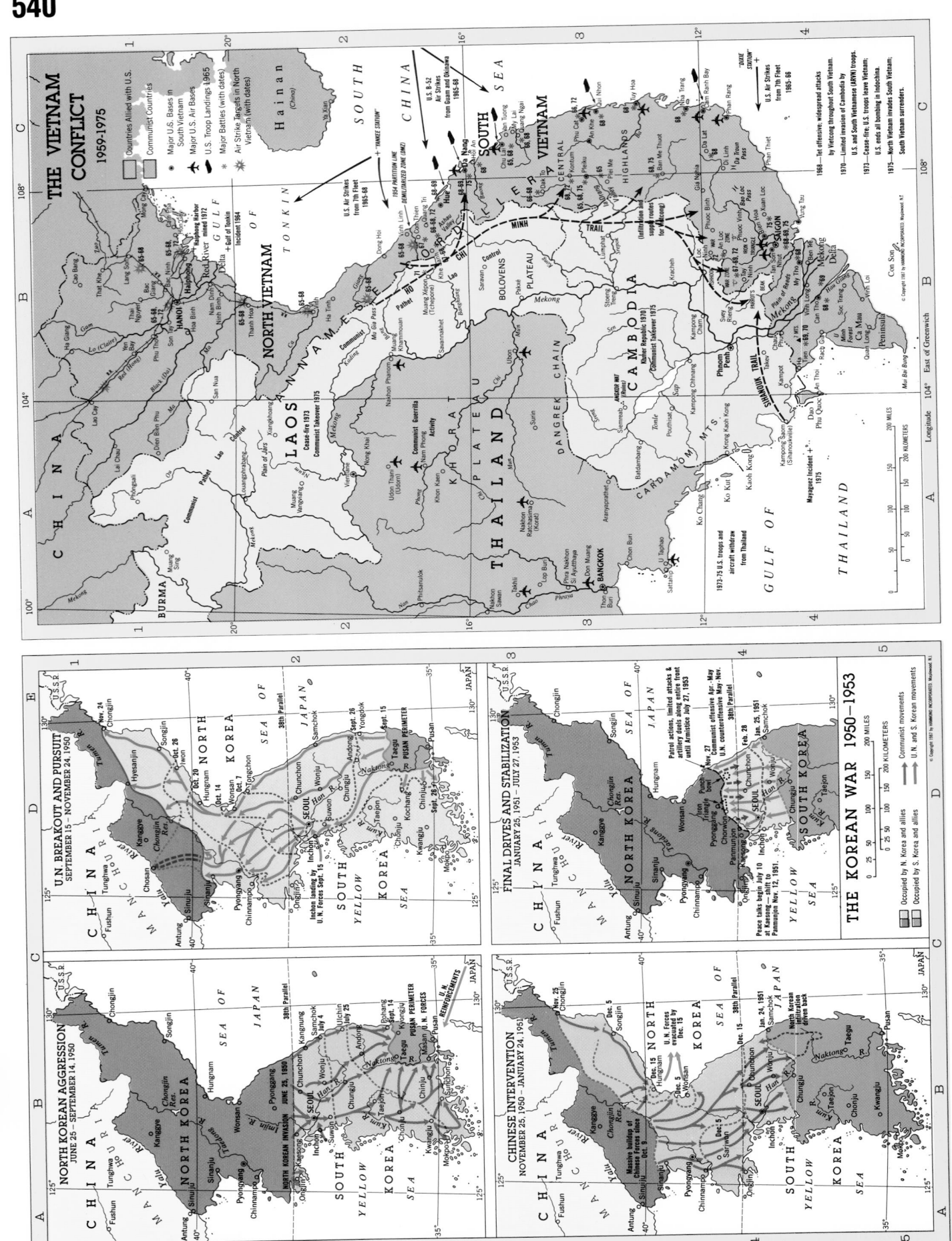

THE VIETNAM CONFLICT
1959–1975

- ▢ Countries Allied with U.S.
- ▢ Communist Countries
- ● Major U.S. Bases in South Vietnam
- ✈ Major U.S. Air Bases
- ⇗ U.S. Troop Landings 1965
- ✷ Major Battles (with dates)
- ✷ Air Strike Targets in North Vietnam (with dates)

1968—Tet offensive, widespread attacks by Vietcong throughout South Vietnam.
1970—Limited invasion of Cambodia by U.S. and South Vietnamese (ARVN) troops.
1973—Cease-fire: U.S. troops leave Vietnam.
1975—U.S. ends all bombing in Indochina.
1975—North Vietnam invades South Vietnam; South Vietnam surrenders.

THE KOREAN WAR 1950–1953

NORTH KOREAN AGGRESSION
JUNE 25 – SEPTEMBER 14, 1950

U.N. BREAKOUT AND PURSUIT
SEPTEMBER 15 – NOVEMBER 24, 1950

CHINESE INTERVENTION
NOVEMBER 25, 1950 – JANUARY 24, 1951

FINAL DRIVES AND STABILIZATION
JANUARY 25, 1951 – JULY 27, 1953

- ⇨ Communist movements
- ⇨ U.N. and S. Korean movements
- ▢ Occupied by N. Korea and allies
- ▢ Occupied by S. Korea and allies

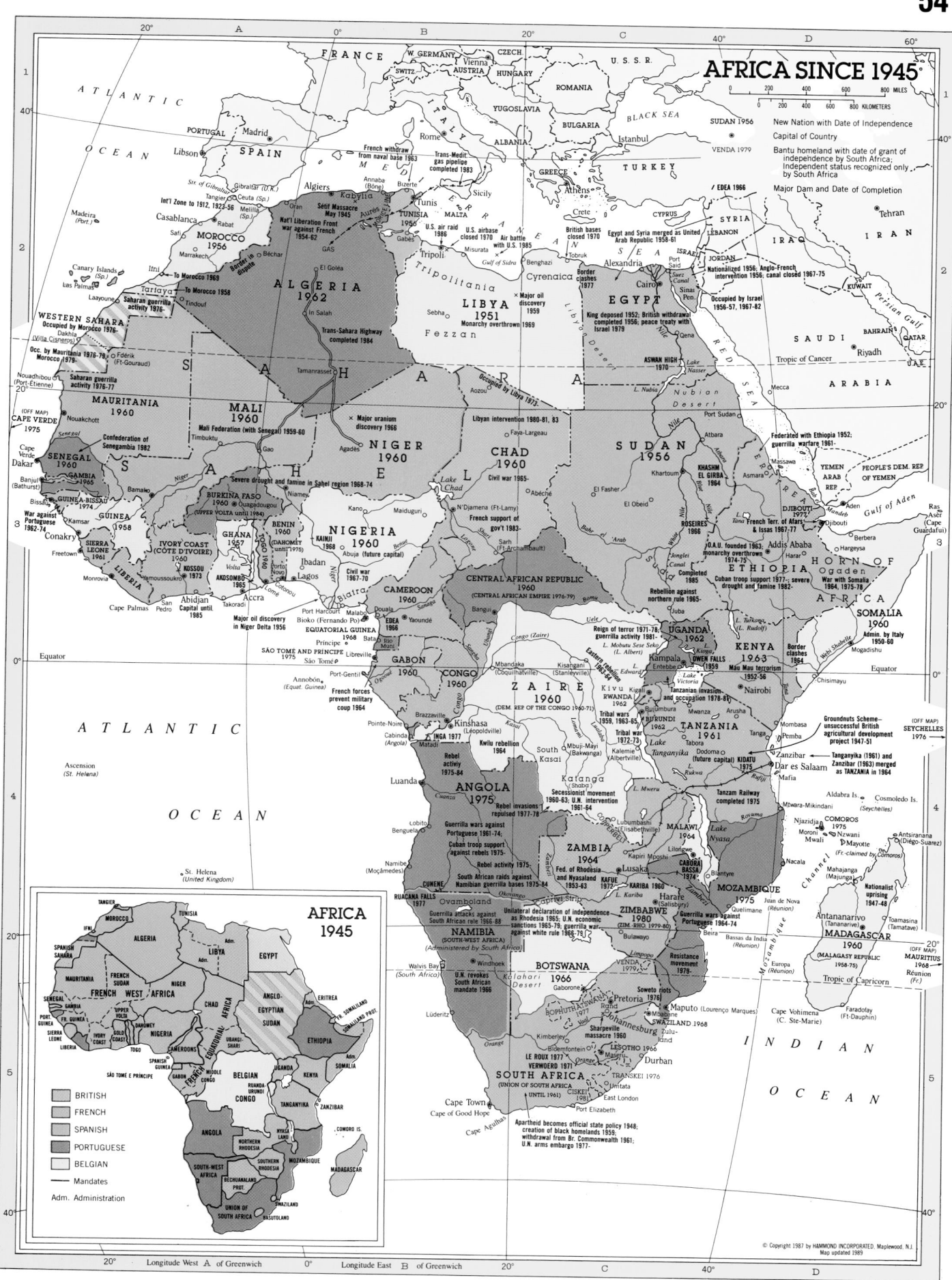

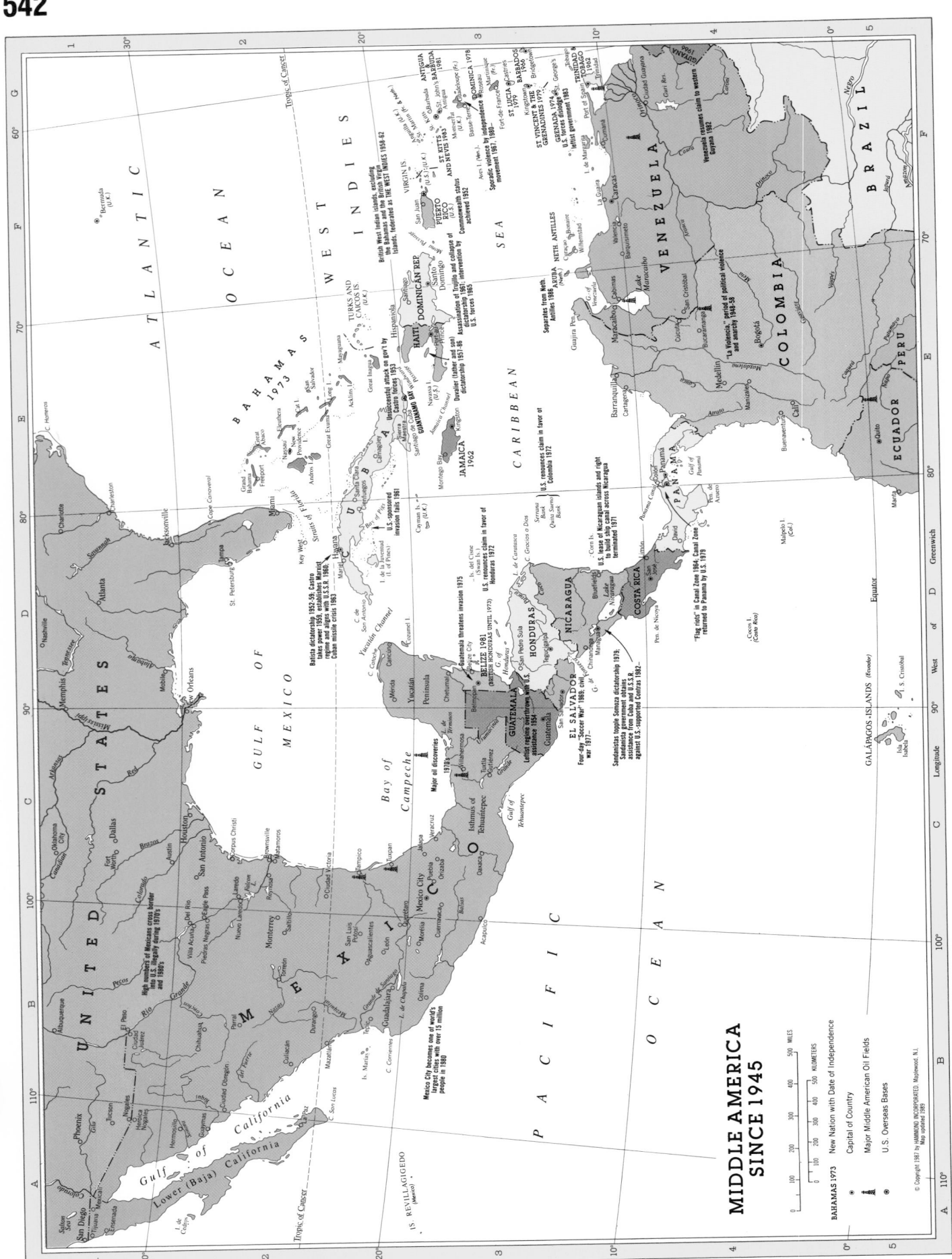

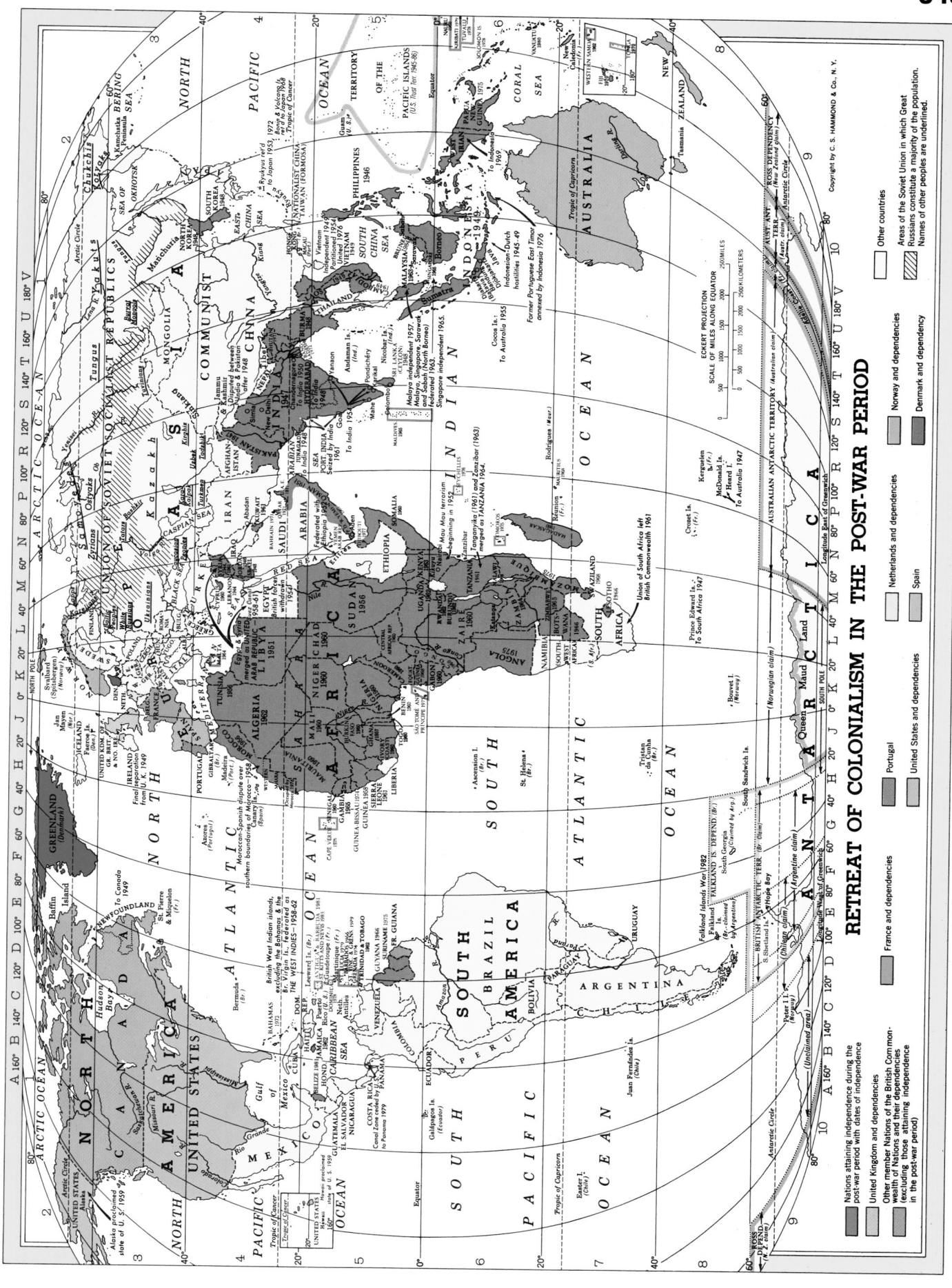

RETREAT OF COLONIALISM IN THE POST-WAR PERIOD

544

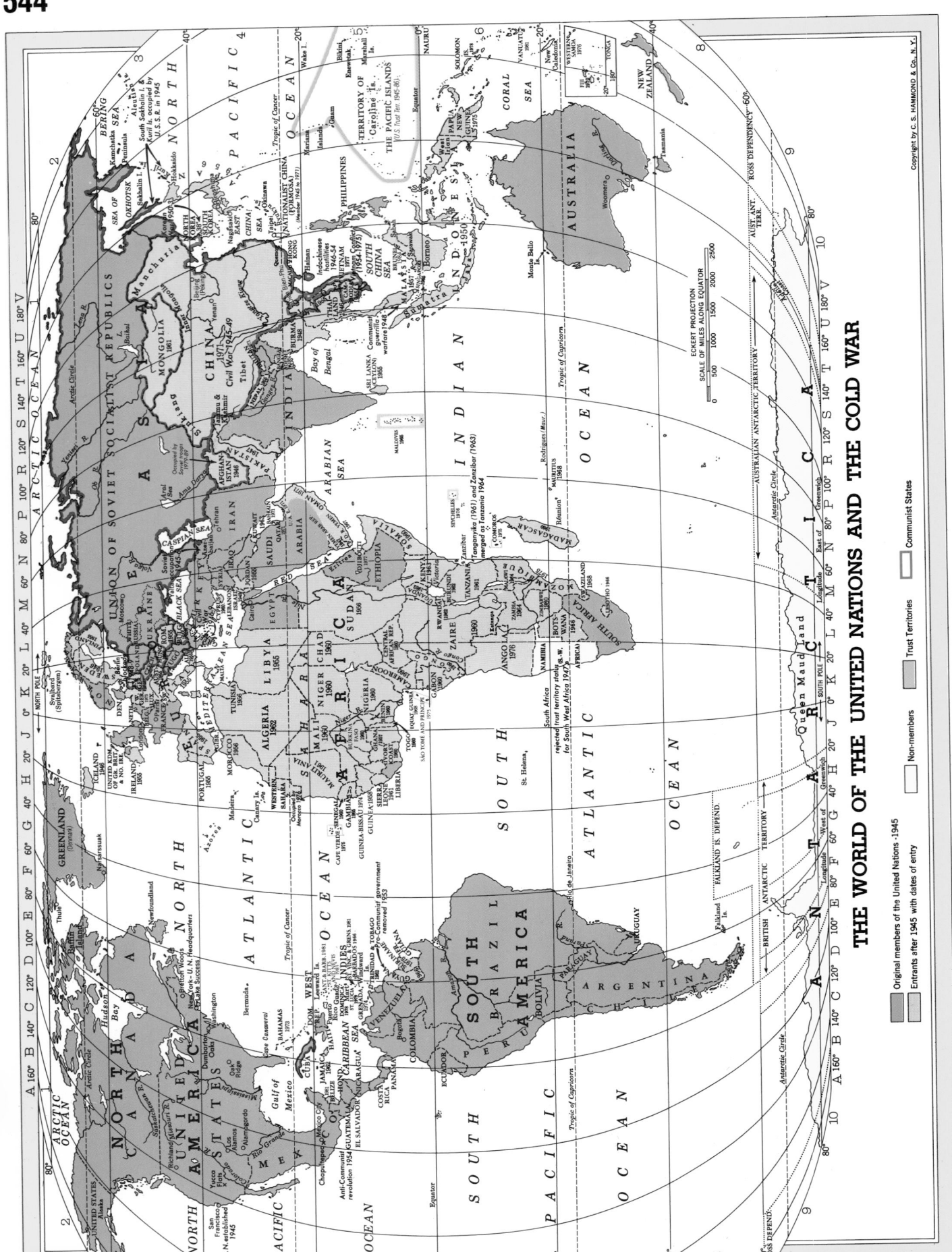

THE WORLD OF THE UNITED NATIONS AND THE COLD WAR

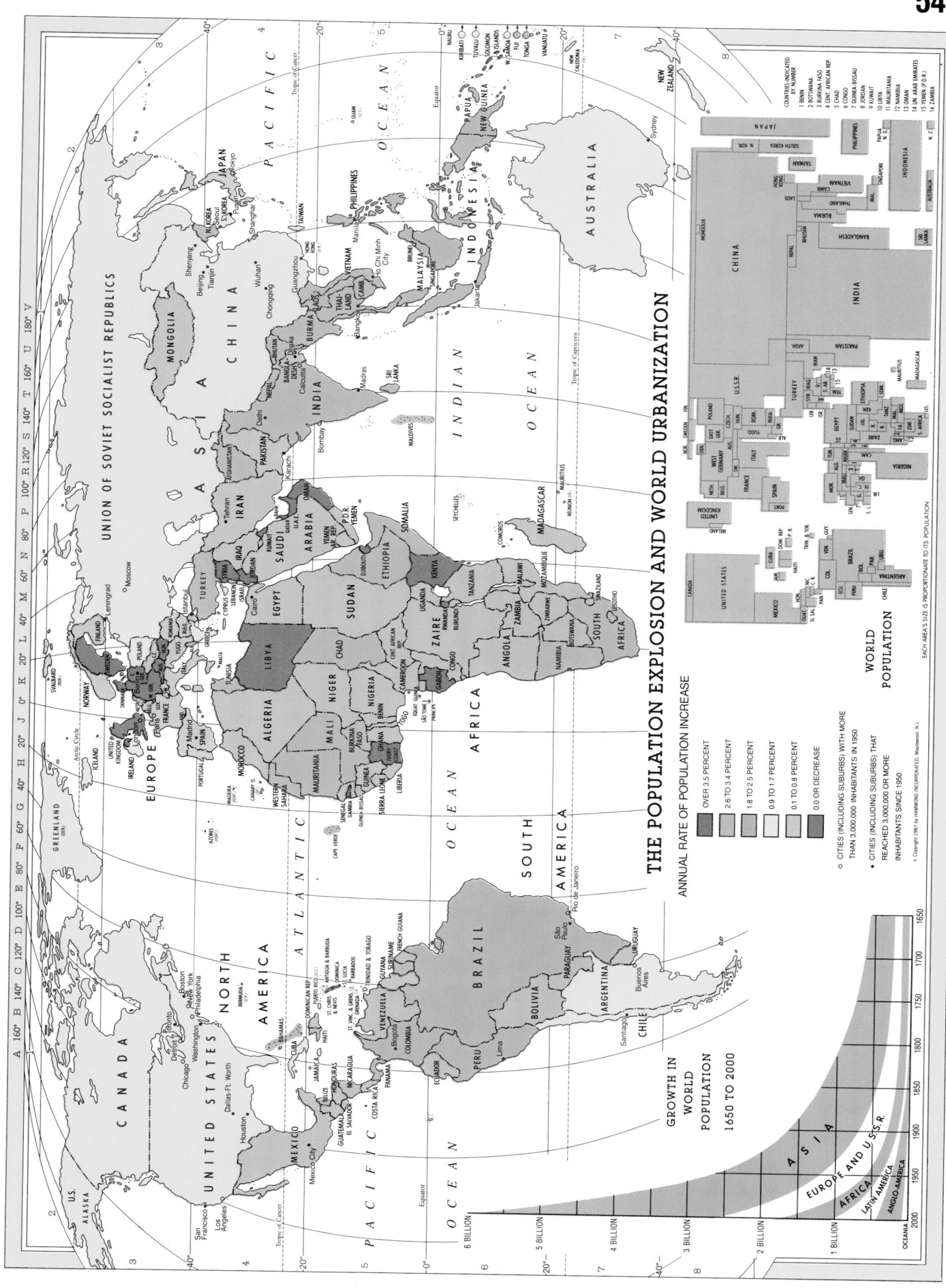

THE POPULATION EXPLOSION AND WORLD URBANIZATION

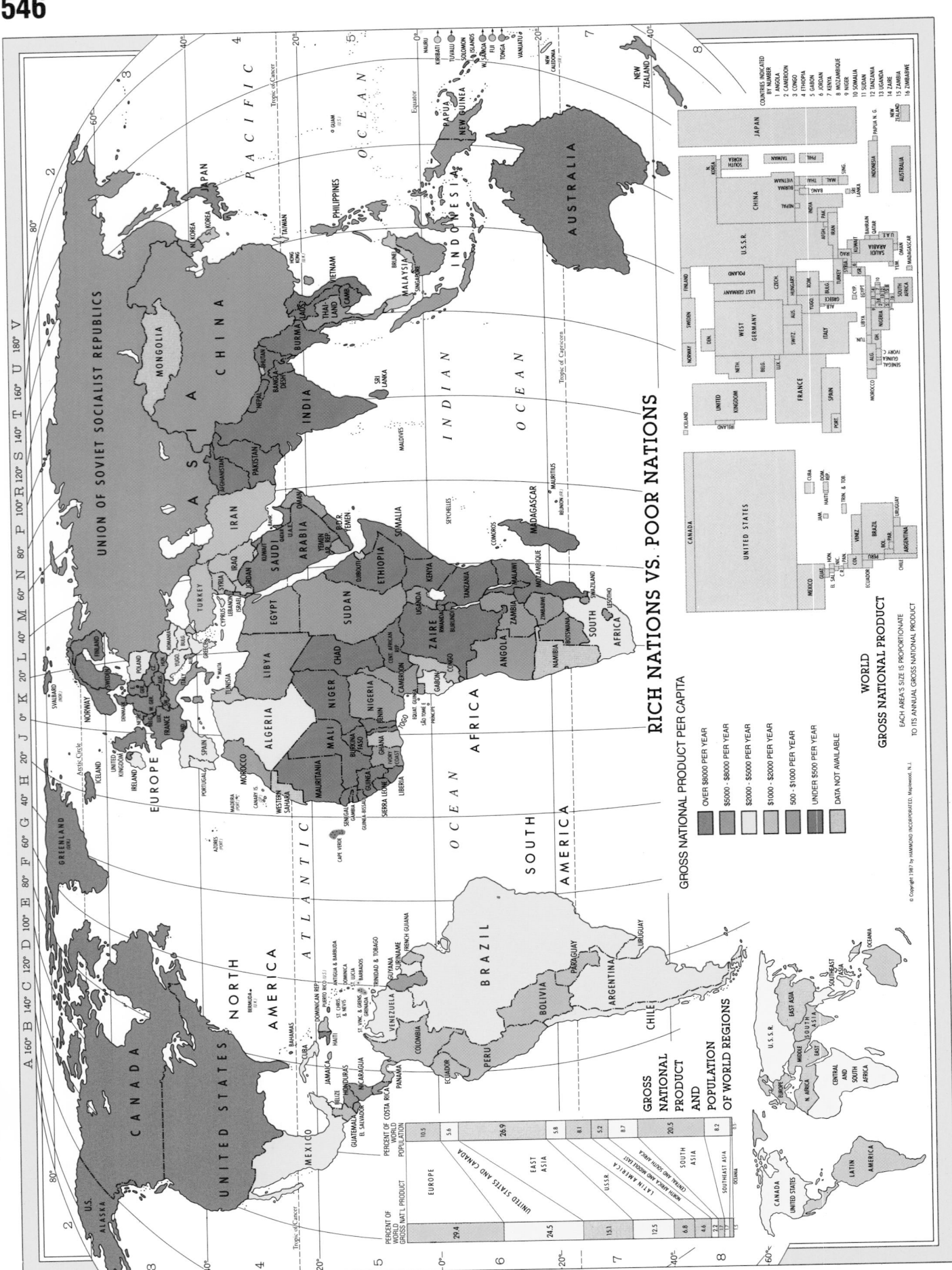

RICH NATIONS VS. POOR NATIONS

GROSS NATIONAL PRODUCT PER CAPITA

- OVER $8000 PER YEAR
- $5000 - $8000 PER YEAR
- $2000 - $5000 PER YEAR
- $1000 - $2000 PER YEAR
- 500 - $1000 PER YEAR
- UNDER $500 PER YEAR
- DATA NOT AVAILABLE

WORLD GROSS NATIONAL PRODUCT

EACH AREA'S SIZE IS PROPORTIONATE
TO ITS ANNUAL GROSS NATIONAL PRODUCT.

© Copyright 1987 by HAMMOND INCORPORATED, Maplewood, N.J.

COUNTRIES INDICATED BY NUMBER
1 ANGOLA
2 CAMEROON
3 CONGO
4 ETHIOPIA
5 GABON
6 JORDAN
7 KENYA
8 MOZAMBIQUE
9 NIGER
10 SOMALIA
11 SUDAN
12 TANZANIA
13 UGANDA
14 ZAIRE
15 ZAMBIA
16 ZIMBABWE

GROSS NATIONAL PRODUCT AND POPULATION OF WORLD REGIONS

PERCENT OF WORLD POPULATION

EUROPE	10.5
UNITED STATES AND CANADA	5.6
EAST ASIA	26.9
U.S.S.R.	5.8
NORTH AFRICA AND MIDDLE EAST	8.1
LATIN AMERICA	5.2
SOUTH ASIA	8.7
	20.5
SOUTHEAST ASIA	8.2

PERCENT OF WORLD GROSS NAT'L PRODUCT

	29.4
	24.5
	15.1
	12.5
	6.8
	4.6
	3.2

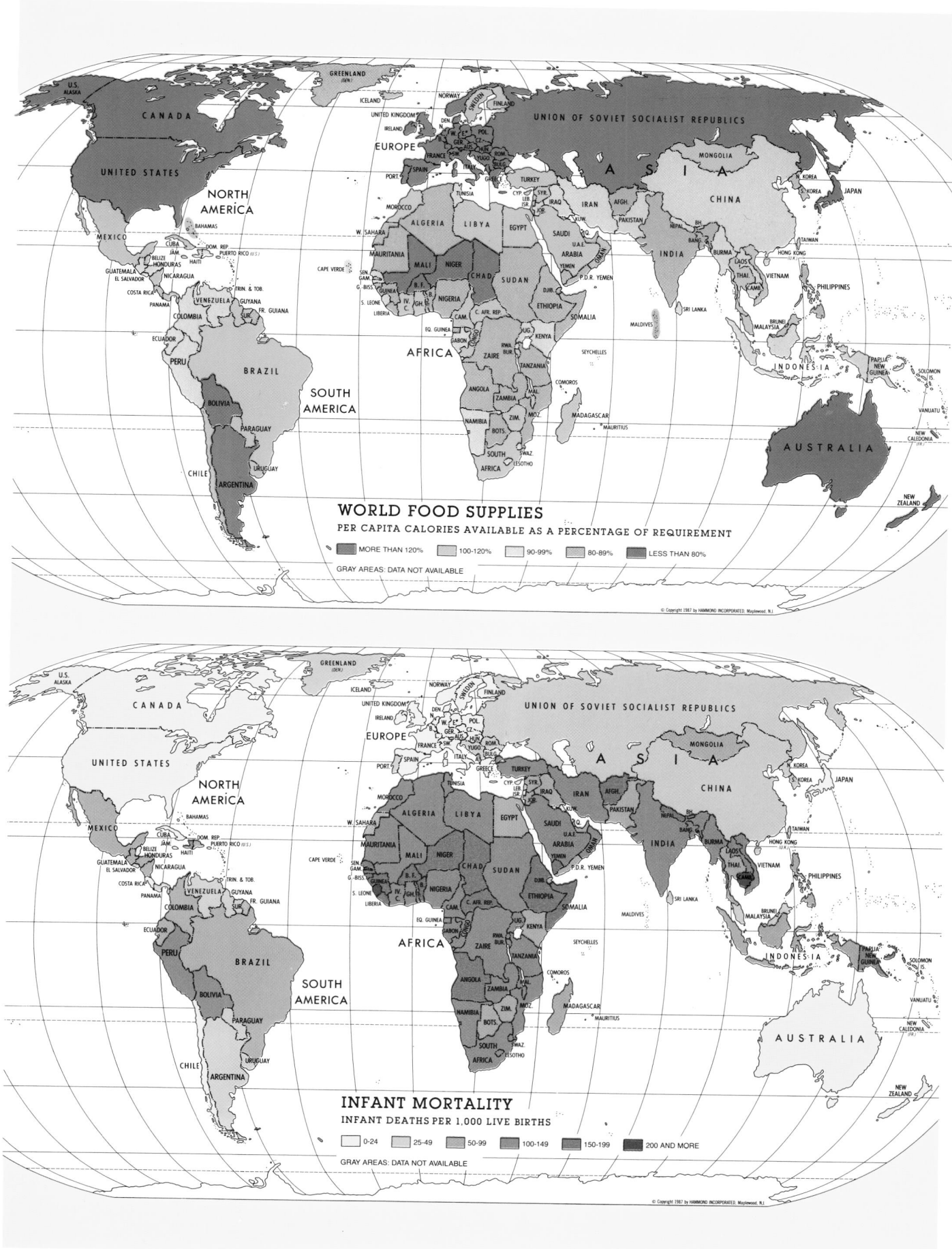

WORLD FOOD SUPPLIES

PER CAPITA CALORIES AVAILABLE AS A PERCENTAGE OF REQUIREMENT

MORE THAN 120% 100-120% 90-99% 80-89% LESS THAN 80%

GRAY AREAS: DATA NOT AVAILABLE

© Copyright 1987 by HAMMOND INCORPORATED, Maplewood, N.J.

INFANT MORTALITY

INFANT DEATHS PER 1,000 LIVE BIRTHS

0-24 25-49 50-99 100-149 150-199 200 AND MORE

GRAY AREAS: DATA NOT AVAILABLE

© Copyright 1987 by HAMMOND INCORPORATED, Maplewood, N.J.

548

TIME CHART

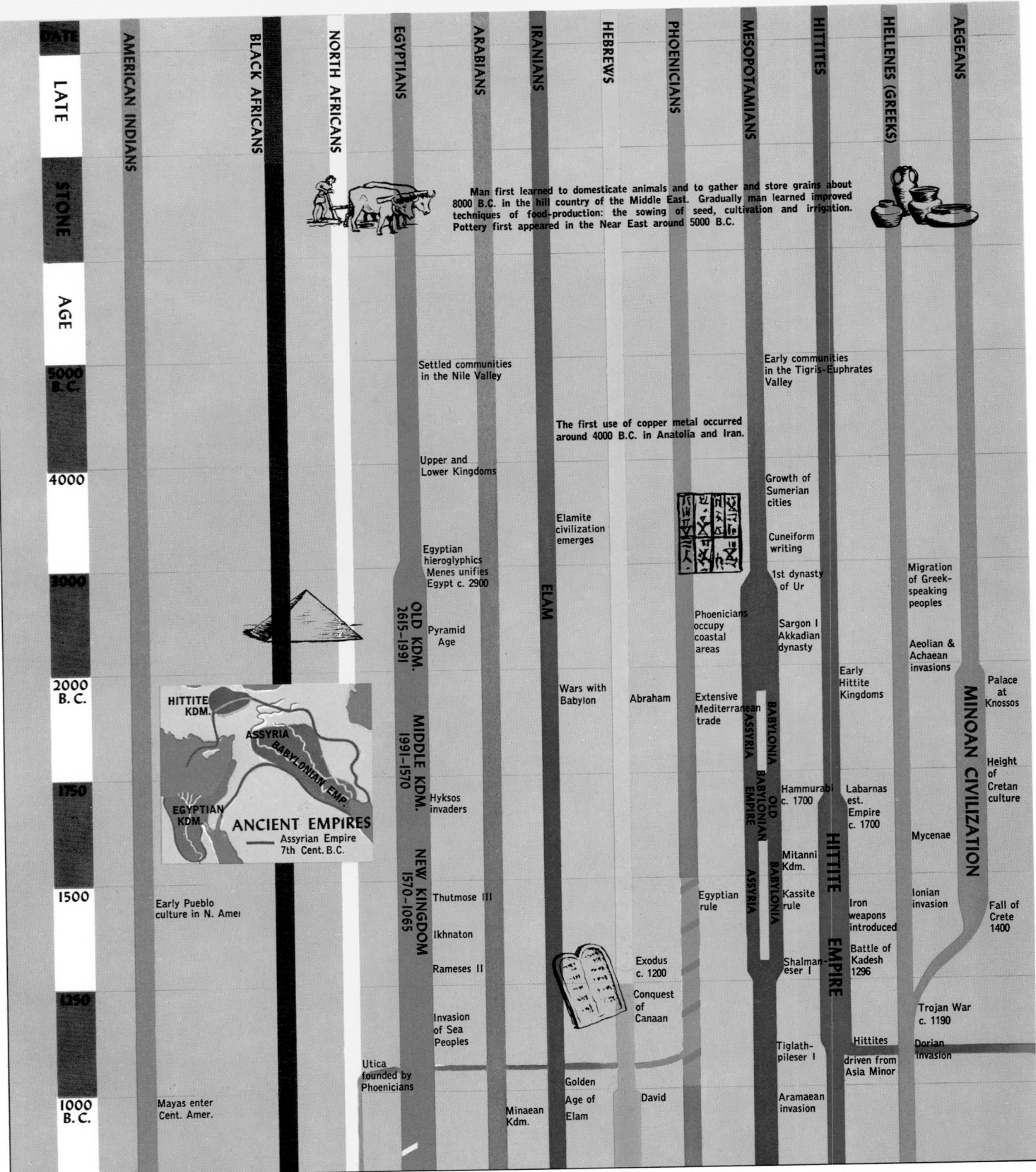

DATE | AMERICAN INDIANS | BLACK AFRICANS | NORTH AFRICANS | EGYPTIANS | ARABIANS | IRANIANS | HEBREWS | PHOENICIANS | MESOPOTAMIANS | HITTITES | HELLENES (GREEKS) | AEGEANS

LATE STONE AGE

Man first learned to domesticate animals and to gather and store grains about 8000 B.C. in the hill country of the Middle East. Gradually man learned improved techniques of food-production: the sowing of seed, cultivation and irrigation. Pottery first appeared in the Near East around 5000 B.C.

5000 B.C.

Settled communities in the Nile Valley

Early communities in the Tigris-Euphrates Valley

The first use of copper metal occurred around 4000 B.C. in Anatolia and Iran.

4000

Upper and Lower Kingdoms

Growth of Sumerian cities

Elamite civilization emerges

Egyptian hieroglyphics
Menes unifies Egypt c. 2900

Cuneiform writing

1st dynasty of Ur

Migration of Greek-speaking peoples

ELAM

OLD KDM. 2615–1991

Pyramid Age

Phoenicians occupy coastal areas

Sargon I Akkadian dynasty

Aeolian & Achaean invasions

3000

2000 B.C.

Wars with Babylon

Abraham

Extensive Mediterranean trade

Early Hittite Kingdoms

Palace at Knossos

HITTITE KDM. ASSYRIA BABYLONIAN EMP. EGYPTIAN KDM.
ANCIENT EMPIRES
Assyrian Empire 7th Cent. B.C.

MIDDLE KDM. 1991–1570

BABYLONIA ASSYRIA OLD BABYLONIAN EMPIRE

Height of Cretan culture

MINOAN CIVILIZATION

1750

Hyksos invaders

Hammurabi c. 1700

Labarnas est. Empire c. 1700

Mycenae

Mitanni Kdm.

NEW KINGDOM 1570–1065

Early Pueblo culture in N. Amer

Thutmose III

Egyptian rule

Kassite rule

ASSYRIA BABYLONIA

Iron weapons introduced

Ionian invasion

Fall of Crete 1400

1500

Ikhnaton

HITTITE EMPIRE

Battle of Kadesh 1296

Rameses II

Exodus c. 1200

Shalman-eser I

Conquest of Canaan

1250

Invasion of Sea Peoples

Trojan War c. 1190

Tiglath-pileser I

Hittites driven from Asia Minor

Dorian invasion

Utica founded by Phoenicians

Golden Age of Elam

David

Aramaean invasion

1000 B.C.

Mayas enter Cent. Amer.

Minaean Kdm.

A Graphic History of Mankind

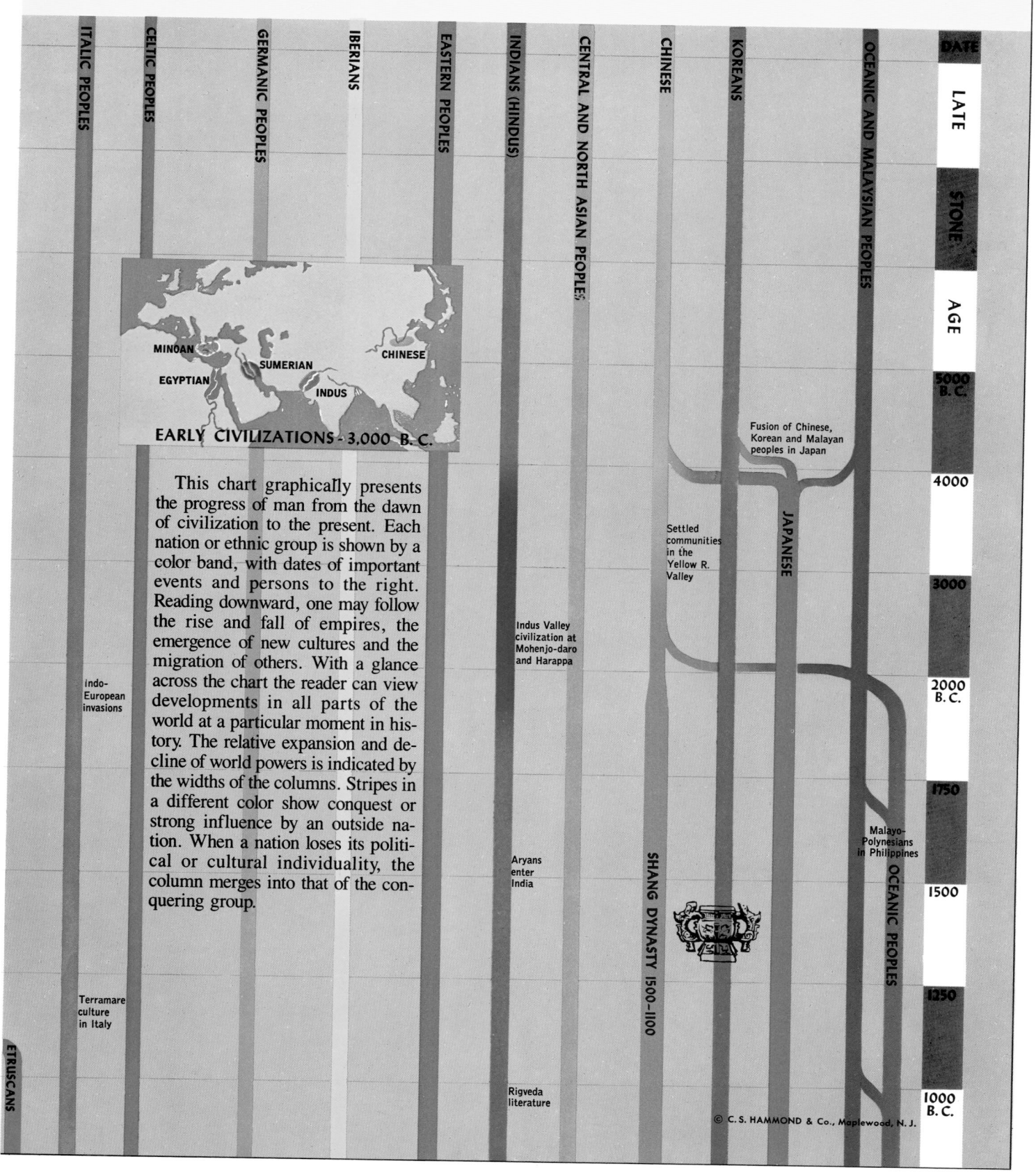

ITALIC PEOPLES

CELTIC PEOPLES

GERMANIC PEOPLES

IBERIANS

EASTERN PEOPLES

INDIANS (HINDUS)

CENTRAL AND NORTH ASIAN PEOPLES

CHINESE

KOREANS

OCEANIC AND MALAYSIAN PEOPLES

DATE

LATE

STONE

AGE

5000 B.C.

4000

3000

2000 B.C.

1750

1500

1250

1000 B.C.

MINOAN

SUMERIAN

CHINESE

EGYPTIAN

INDUS

EARLY CIVILIZATIONS - 3,000 B. C.

This chart graphically presents the progress of man from the dawn of civilization to the present. Each nation or ethnic group is shown by a color band, with dates of important events and persons to the right. Reading downward, one may follow the rise and fall of empires, the emergence of new cultures and the migration of others. With a glance across the chart the reader can view developments in all parts of the world at a particular moment in history. The relative expansion and decline of world powers is indicated by the widths of the columns. Stripes in a different color show conquest or strong influence by an outside nation. When a nation loses its political or cultural individuality, the column merges into that of the conquering group.

Indo-European invasions

Terramare culture in Italy

ETRUSCANS

Indus Valley civilization at Mohenjo-daro and Harappa

Aryans enter India

Rigveda literature

SHANG DYNASTY 1500–1100

Settled communities in the Yellow R. Valley

Fusion of Chinese, Korean and Malayan peoples in Japan

JAPANESE

Malayo-Polynesians in Philippines

OCEANIC PEOPLES

© C.S. HAMMOND & Co., Maplewood, N.J.

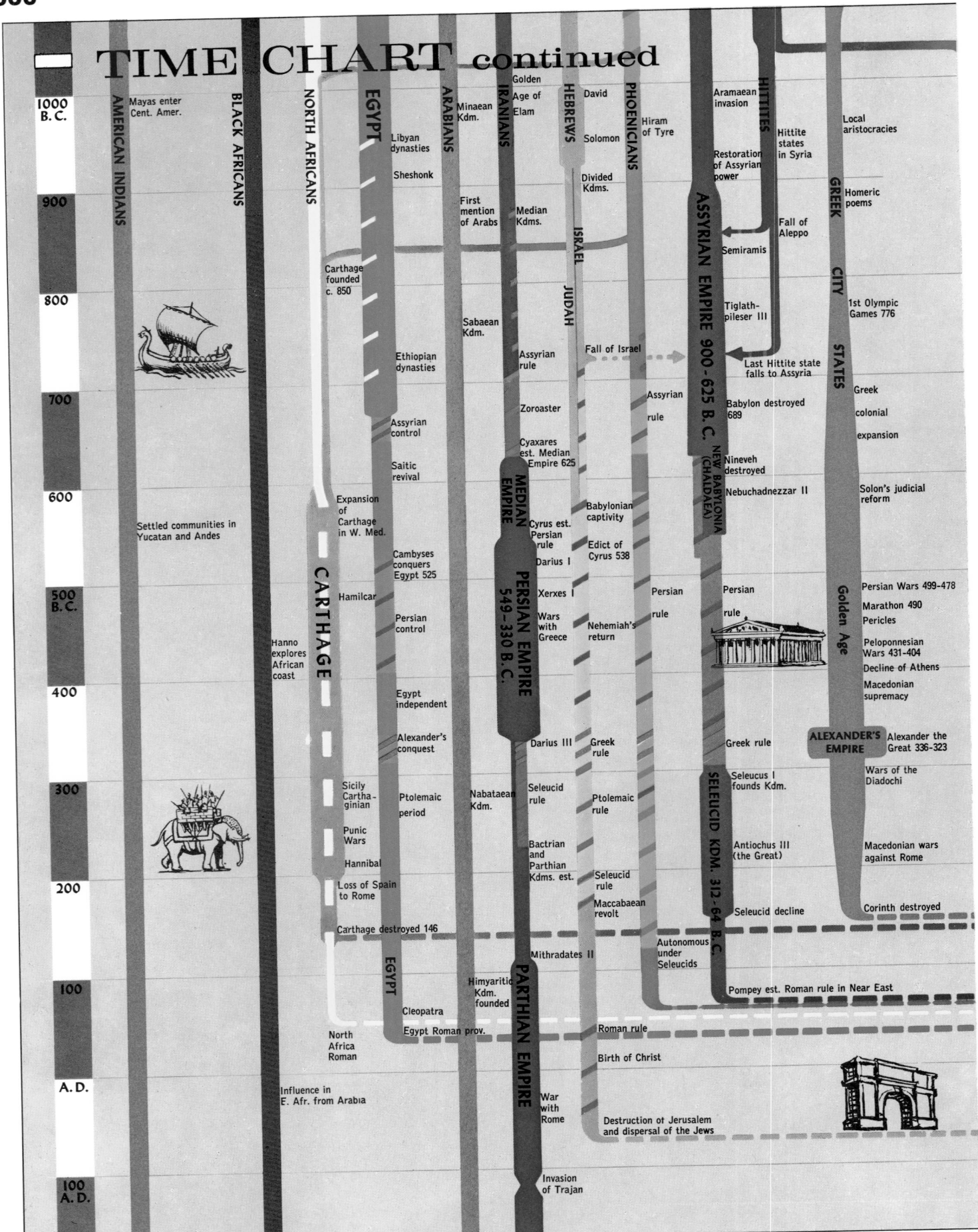

TIME CHART continued

AMERICAN INDIANS

BLACK AFRICANS

NORTH AFRICANS

EGYPT

ARABIANS

IRANIANS

HEBREWS

PHOENICIANS

HITTITES

ASSYRIAN EMPIRE 900-625 B.C.

NEW BABYLONIA (CHALDAEA)

GREEK CITY STATES

1000 B.C.

Mayas enter Cent. Amer.

Golden Age of Elam

David

Aramaean invasion

Hittite states in Syria

Local aristocracies

Libyan dynasties

Solomon

Hiram of Tyre

Restoration of Assyrian power

900

Minaean Kdm.

Sheshonk

First mention of Arabs

Median Kdms.

Divided Kdms.

Fall of Aleppo

Semiramis

Homeric poems

ISRAEL

JUDAH

800

Carthage founded c. 850

Sabaean Kdm.

Tiglath-pileser III

1st Olympic Games 776

Ethiopian dynasties

Assyrian rule

Fall of Israel

Last Hittite state falls to Assyria

Greek colonial expansion

700

Assyrian control

Zoroaster

Assyrian rule

Babylon destroyed 689

Saitic revival

Cyaxares est. Median Empire 625

Nineveh destroyed

MEDIAN EMPIRE

600

Settled communities in Yucatan and Andes

Expansion of Carthage in W. Med.

Cyrus est. Persian rule

Babylonian captivity

Nebuchadnezzar II

Solon's judicial reform

Cambyses conquers Egypt 525

Darius I

Edict of Cyrus 538

CARTHAGE

500 B.C.

Hamilcar

Xerxes I

Persian rule

Persian rule

Persian Wars 499-478

PERSIAN EMPIRE 549-330 B.C.

Wars with Greece

Nehemiah's return

Marathon 490

Pericles

Hanno explores African coast

Persian control

Peloponnesian Wars 431-404

Golden Age

Decline of Athens

400

Egypt independent

Macedonian supremacy

Alexander's conquest

Darius III

Greek rule

Greek rule

ALEXANDER'S EMPIRE

Alexander the Great 336-323

Sicily Carthaginian

Ptolemaic period

Nabataean Kdm.

Seleucid rule

Ptolemaic rule

Seleucus I founds Kdm.

Wars of the Diadochi

300

Punic Wars

Hannibal

Bactrian and Parthian Kdms. est.

Antiochus III (the Great)

SELEUCID KDM. 312-64 B.C.

Macedonian wars against Rome

Loss of Spain to Rome

Seleucid rule

200

Maccabaean revolt

Seleucid decline

Corinth destroyed

Carthage destroyed 146

Mithradates II

Autonomous under Seleucids

EGYPT

PARTHIAN EMPIRE

100

Himyaritic Kdm. founded

Pompey est. Roman rule in Near East

Cleopatra

North Africa Roman

Egypt Roman prov.

Roman rule

A.D.

Influence in E. Afr. from Arabia

War with Rome

Birth of Christ

Destruction of Jerusalem and dispersal of the Jews

100 A.D.

Invasion of Trajan

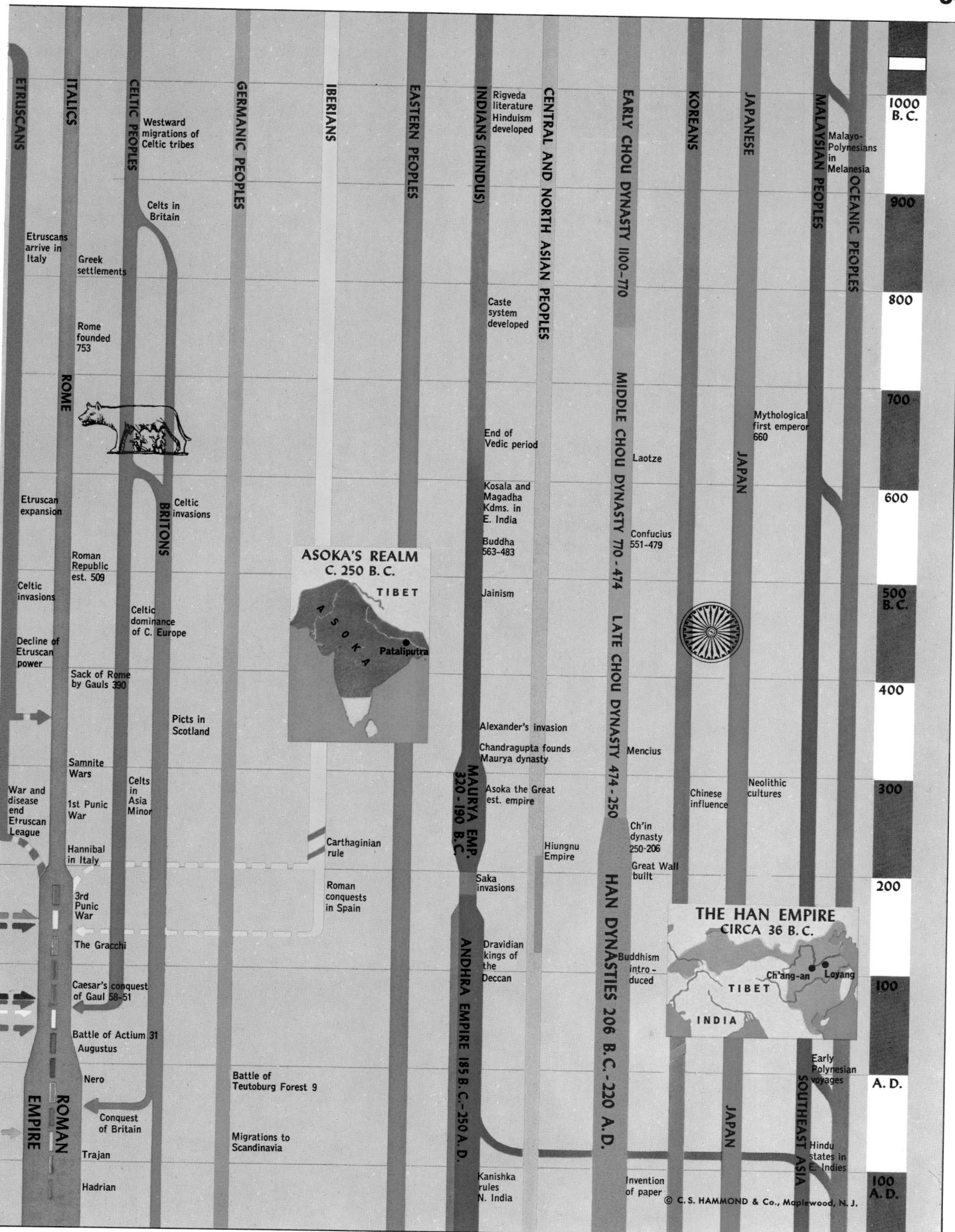

552

TIME CHART continued

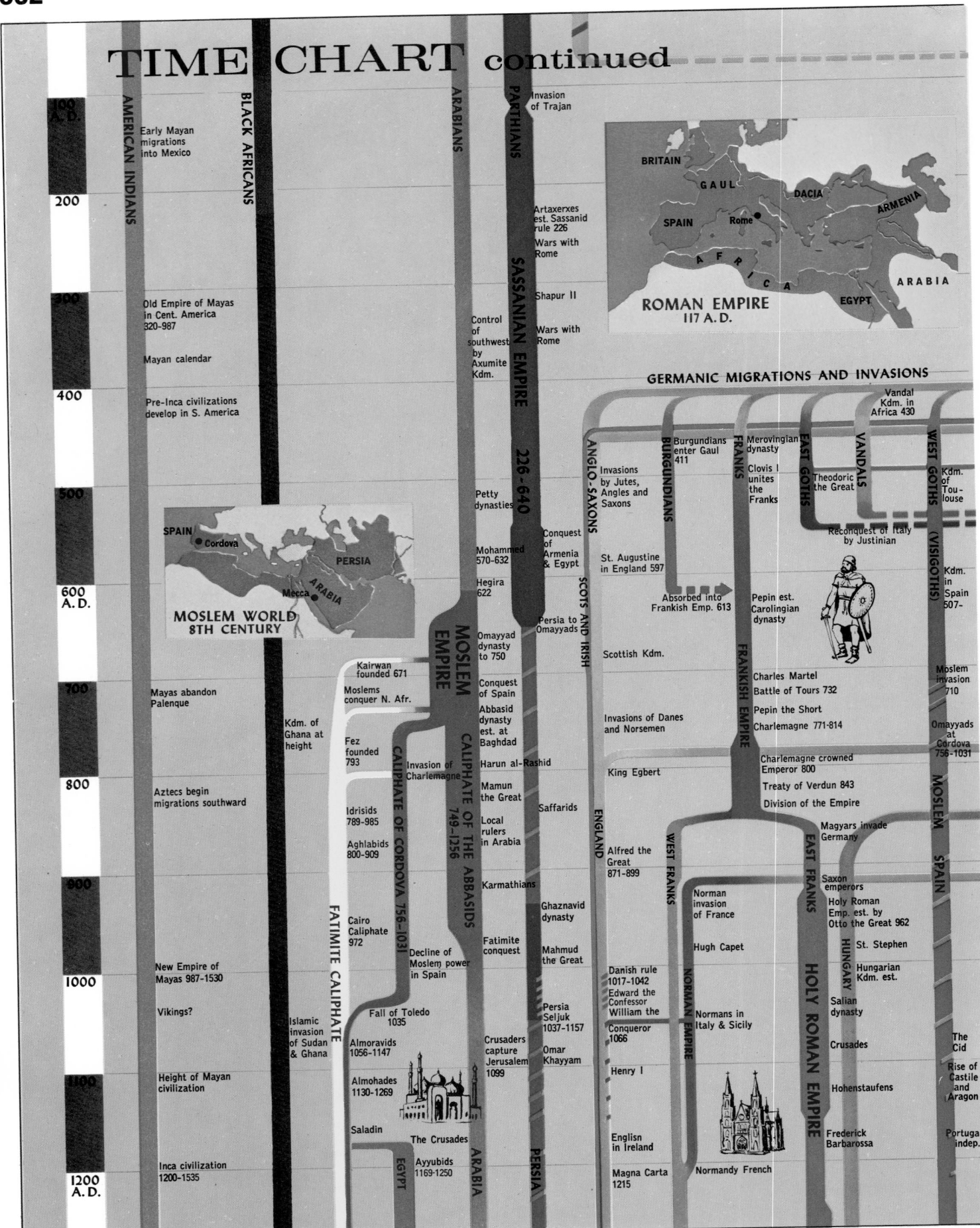

100 A.D.			
200			
300			
400			
500			
600 A.D.			
700			
800			
900			
1000			
1100			
1200 A.D.			

AMERICAN INDIANS

Early Mayan migrations into Mexico

Old Empire of Mayas in Cent. America 320-987

Mayan calendar

Pre-Inca civilizations develop in S. America

Mayas abandon Palenque

Aztecs begin migrations southward

New Empire of Mayas 987-1530

Vikings?

Height of Mayan civilization

Inca civilization 1200-1535

BLACK AFRICANS

Kdm. of Ghana at height

Islamic invasion of Sudan & Ghana

ARABIANS

PARTHIANS

SASSANIAN EMPIRE 226 - 640

Control of southwest by Axumite Kdm.

Petty dynasties

Mohammed 570-632

Hegira 622

Conquest of Armenia & Egypt

Persia to Omayyads

Invasion of Trajan

Artaxerxes est. Sassanid rule 226

Wars with Rome

Shapur II

Wars with Rome

ROMAN EMPIRE 117 A.D.

BRITAIN
GAUL
DACIA
ARMENIA
SPAIN
Rome
AFRICA
ARABIA
EGYPT

MOSLEM WORLD 8TH CENTURY

SPAIN
Cordova
PERSIA
ARABIA
Mecca

MOSLEM EMPIRE

Kairwan founded 671

Moslems conquer N. Afr.

Fez founded 793

Idrisids 789-985

Aghlabids 800-909

Cairo Caliphate 972

FATIMITE CALIPHATE

Fall of Toledo 1035

Almoravids 1056-1147

Almohades 1130-1269

Saladin

CALIPHATE OF CORDOVA 756-1031

Invasion of Charlemagne

CALIPHATE OF THE ABBASIDS 749-1256

EGYPT

The Crusades

Ayyubids 1169-1250

Omayyad dynasty to 750

Conquest of Spain

Abbasid dynasty est. at Baghdad

Harun al-Rashid

Mamun the Great

Local rulers in Arabia

Karmathians

Fatimite conquest

Decline of Moslem power in Spain

Crusaders capture Jerusalem 1099

Saffarids

Ghaznavid dynasty

Mahmud the Great

Persia Seljuk 1037-1157

Omar Khayyam

ARABIA

PERSIA

GERMANIC MIGRATIONS AND INVASIONS

ANGLO-SAXONS

Invasions by Jutes, Angles and Saxons

St. Augustine in England 597

SCOTS AND IRISH

Scottish Kdm.

Invasions of Danes and Norsemen

ENGLAND

King Egbert

Alfred the Great 871-899

Danish rule 1017-1042 Edward the Confessor William the Conqueror 1066

Henry I

English in Ireland

Magna Carta 1215

BURGUNDIANS

Burgundians enter Gaul 411

Absorbed into Frankish Emp. 613

FRANKS

Merovingian dynasty

Clovis I unites the Franks

Pepin est. Carolingian dynasty

FRANKISH EMPIRE

Charles Martel Battle of Tours 732

Pepin the Short

Charlemagne 771-814

Charlemagne crowned Emperor 800

Treaty of Verdun 843

Division of the Empire

WEST FRANKS

Norman invasion of France

Hugh Capet

NORMAN EMPIRE

Normans in Italy & Sicily

Normandy French

EAST GOTHS

Theodoric the Great

Reconquest of Italy by Justinian

EAST FRANKS

Magyars invade Germany

Saxon emperors

Holy Roman Emp. est. by Otto the Great 962

St. Stephen

HUNGARY

Hungarian Kdm. est.

HOLY ROMAN EMPIRE

Salian dynasty

Crusades

Hohenstaufens

Frederick Barbarossa

VANDALS

Vandal Kdm. in Africa 430

WEST GOTHS (VISIGOTHS)

Kdm. of Toulouse

Kdm. in Spain 507-

Moslem invasion 710

Omayyads at Cordova 756-1031

MOSLEM SPAIN

The Cid

Rise of Castile and Aragon

Portugal indep.

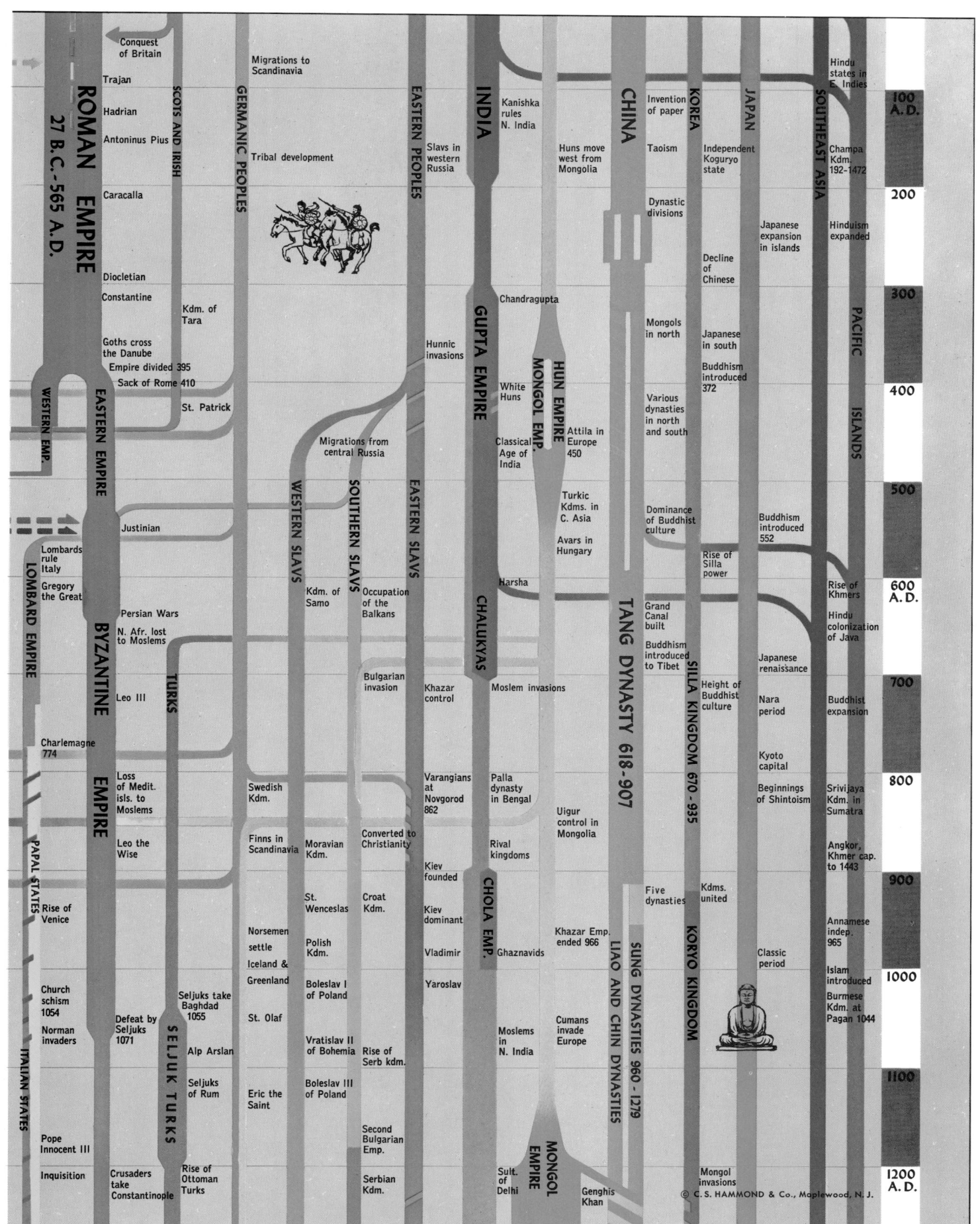

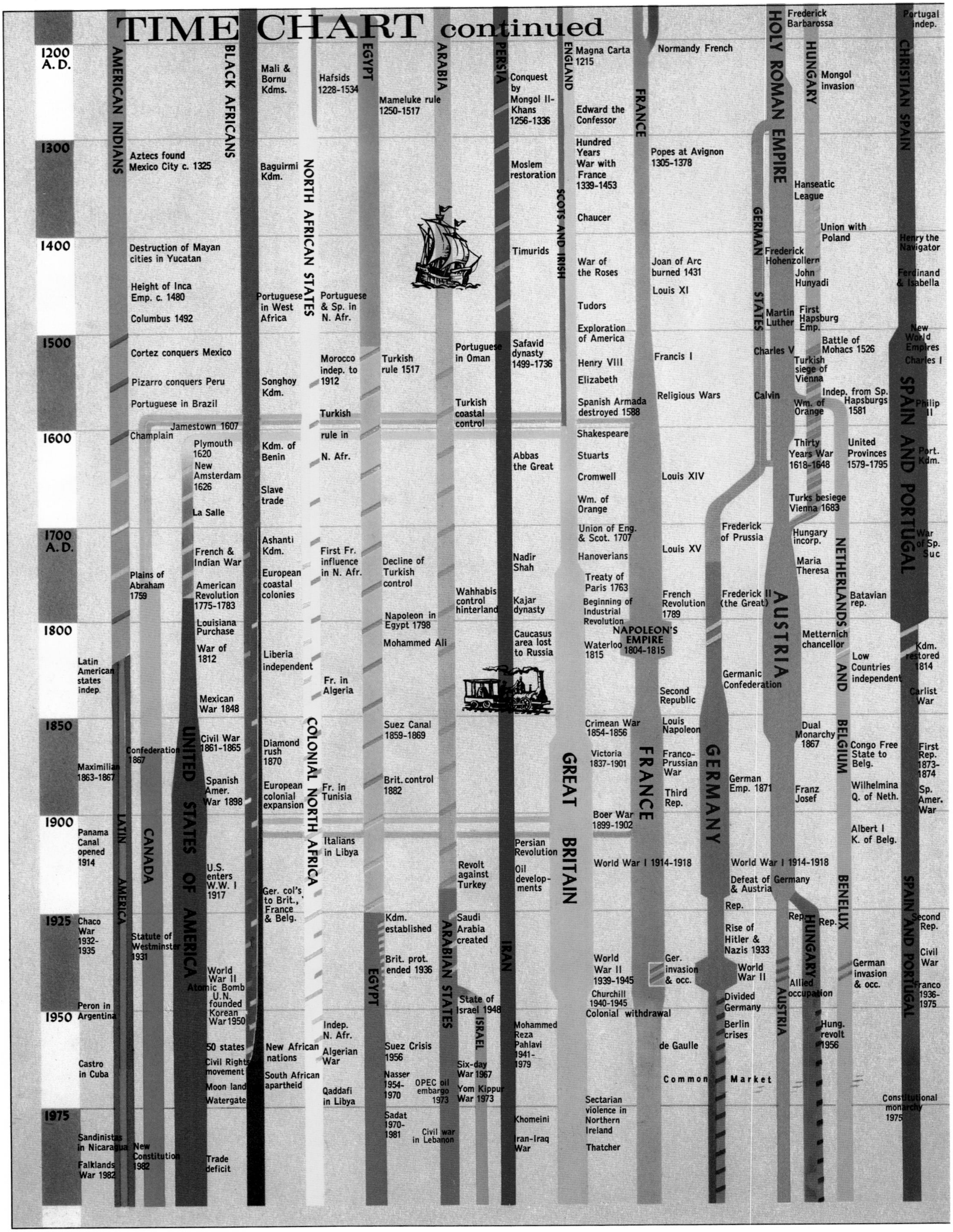

TIME CHART continued

Time axis (left): 1200 A.D. · 1300 · 1400 · 1500 · 1600 · 1700 A.D. · 1800 · 1850 · 1900 · 1925 · 1950 · 1975

AMERICAN INDIANS / LATIN AMERICA
- Aztecs found Mexico City c. 1325
- Destruction of Mayan cities in Yucatan
- Height of Inca Emp. c. 1480
- Columbus 1492
- Cortez conquers Mexico
- Pizarro conquers Peru
- Portuguese in Brazil
- Jamestown 1607
- Champlain
- Plymouth 1620
- New Amsterdam 1626
- La Salle
- Plains of Abraham 1759
- Louisiana Purchase
- Latin American states indep.
- Mexican War 1848
- Maximilian 1863–1867
- Panama Canal opened 1914
- Chaco War 1932–1935
- Peron in Argentina
- Castro in Cuba
- Sandinistas in Nicaragua
- Falklands War 1982

CANADA / UNITED STATES OF AMERICA
- French & Indian War
- American Revolution 1775–1783
- War of 1812
- Civil War 1861–1865
- Confederation 1867
- Spanish Amer. War 1898
- U.S. enters W.W. I 1917
- Statute of Westminster 1931
- World War II Atomic Bomb
- U.N. founded Korean War 1950
- 50 states
- Civil Rights movement
- Moon landing
- Watergate
- New Constitution 1982
- Trade deficit

BLACK AFRICANS / COLONIAL NORTH AFRICA
- Mali & Bornu Kdms.
- Baguirmi Kdm.
- Portuguese in West Africa
- Songhoy Kdm.
- Kdm. of Benin
- Slave trade
- Ashanti Kdm.
- European coastal colonies
- Liberia independent
- Diamond rush 1870
- European colonial expansion
- Italians in Libya
- Ger. col's to Brit., France & Belg.
- New African nations
- South African apartheid
- Qaddafi in Libya

NORTH AFRICAN STATES / EGYPT
- Hafsids 1228–1534
- Mameluke rule 1250–1517
- Portuguese & Sp. in N. Afr.
- Morocco indep. to 1912
- Turkish rule in N. Afr.
- First Fr. influence in N. Afr.
- Fr. in Algeria
- Suez Canal 1859–1869
- Fr. in Tunisia
- Brit. control 1882
- Kdm. established
- Brit. prot. ended 1936
- Indep. N. Afr.
- Algerian War
- Suez Crisis 1956
- Nasser 1954–1970
- OPEC oil embargo 1973
- Sadat 1970–1981

ARABIA / ARABIAN STATES
- Turkish rule 1517
- Turkish coastal control
- Portuguese in Oman
- Decline of Turkish control
- Wahhabis control hinterland
- Napoleon in Egypt 1798
- Mohammed Ali
- Revolt against Turkey
- Saudi Arabia created
- State of Israel 1948
- Six-day War 1967
- Yom Kippur War 1973
- Civil war in Lebanon

PERSIA / IRAN
- Conquest by Mongol Il-Khans 1256–1336
- Moslem restoration
- Timurids
- Safavid dynasty 1499–1736
- Abbas the Great
- Nadir Shah
- Kajar dynasty
- Caucasus area lost to Russia
- Persian Revolution
- Oil developments
- Mohammed Reza Pahlavi 1941–1979
- Khomeini
- Iran-Iraq War

ENGLAND / SCOTS AND IRISH / GREAT BRITAIN
- Magna Carta 1215
- Edward the Confessor
- Hundred Years War with France 1339–1453
- Chaucer
- War of the Roses
- Tudors
- Exploration of America
- Henry VIII
- Elizabeth
- Spanish Armada destroyed 1588
- Shakespeare
- Stuarts
- Cromwell
- Wm. of Orange
- Union of Eng. & Scot. 1707
- Hanoverians
- Treaty of Paris 1763
- Beginning of Industrial Revolution
- Crimean War 1854–1856
- Victoria 1837–1901
- Boer War 1899–1902
- World War I 1914–1918
- World War II 1939–1945
- Churchill 1940–1945
- Colonial withdrawal
- Sectarian violence in Northern Ireland
- Thatcher

FRANCE
- Normandy French
- Popes at Avignon 1305–1378
- Joan of Arc burned 1431
- Louis XI
- Francis I
- Religious Wars
- Louis XIV
- Louis XV
- French Revolution 1789
- NAPOLEON'S EMPIRE 1804–1815
- Waterloo 1815
- Second Republic
- Louis Napoleon
- Franco-Prussian War
- Third Rep.
- de Gaulle
- Common Market

HOLY ROMAN EMPIRE / GERMAN STATES / GERMANY
- Frederick Barbarossa
- Frederick Hohenzollern
- Martin Luther
- Charles V
- Calvin
- Wm. of Orange
- Thirty Years War 1618–1648
- Frederick of Prussia
- Frederick II (the Great)
- Germanic Confederation
- German Emp. 1871
- World War I 1914–1918
- Defeat of Germany & Austria
- Rep.
- Rise of Hitler & Nazis 1933
- Ger. invasion & occ.
- Divided Germany
- Berlin crises

HUNGARY / AUSTRIA
- Mongol invasion
- Hanseatic League
- Union with Poland
- John Hunyadi
- First Hapsburg Emp.
- Battle of Mohacs 1526
- Turkish siege of Vienna
- Indep. from Sp. Hapsburgs 1581
- Turks besiege Vienna 1683
- Hungary incorp.
- Maria Theresa
- Metternich chancellor
- Dual Monarchy 1867
- Franz Josef
- Rep.
- World War II
- Allied occupation
- Hung. revolt 1956

NETHERLANDS AND BELGIUM / BENELUX
- Batavian rep.
- Low Countries independent
- Congo Free State to Belg.
- Wilhelmina Q. of Neth.
- Albert I K. of Belg.
- German invasion & occ.

CHRISTIAN SPAIN / SPAIN AND PORTUGAL
- Portugal indep.
- Henry the Navigator
- Ferdinand & Isabella
- New World Empires Charles I
- Philip II
- United Provinces 1579–1795
- Port. Kdm.
- War of Sp. Suc.
- Kdm. restored 1814
- Carlist War
- First Rep. 1873–1874
- Sp. Amer. War
- Second Rep.
- Civil War
- Franco 1936–1975
- Constitutional monarchy 1975

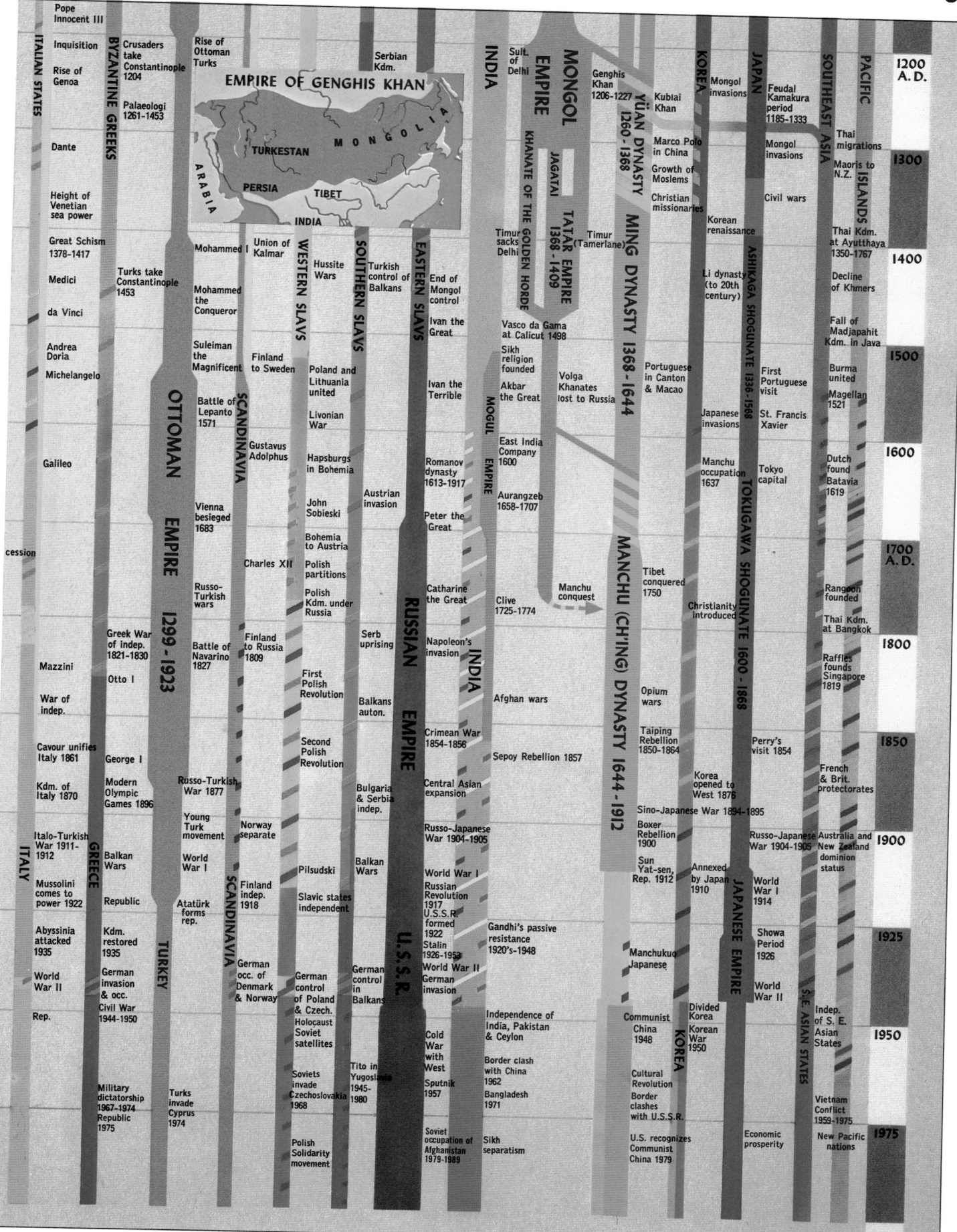

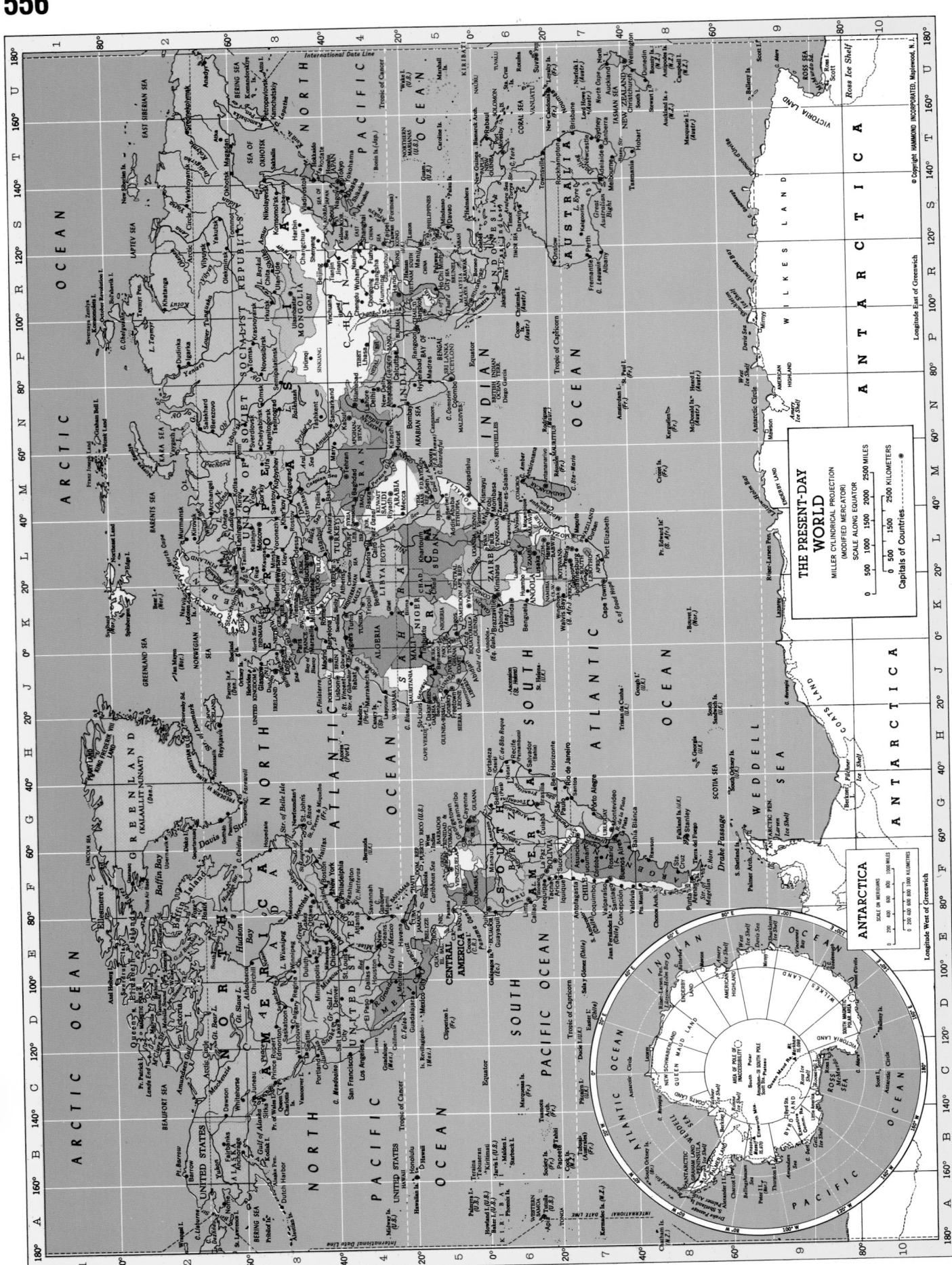

THE PRESENT-DAY WORLD

MILLER CYLINDRICAL PROJECTION
(MODIFIED MERCATOR)
SCALE ALONG EQUATOR

0   500   1000   1500   2000   2500 MILES
0 500 1000 1500 2000 2500 KILOMETERS

● Capitals of Countries

ANTARCTICA

SCALE ON MERIDIANS

0   200   400   600   800   1000 MILES
0 200 400 600 800 1000 KILOMETERS

HOMEWORK MAPS
Alphabetical Index

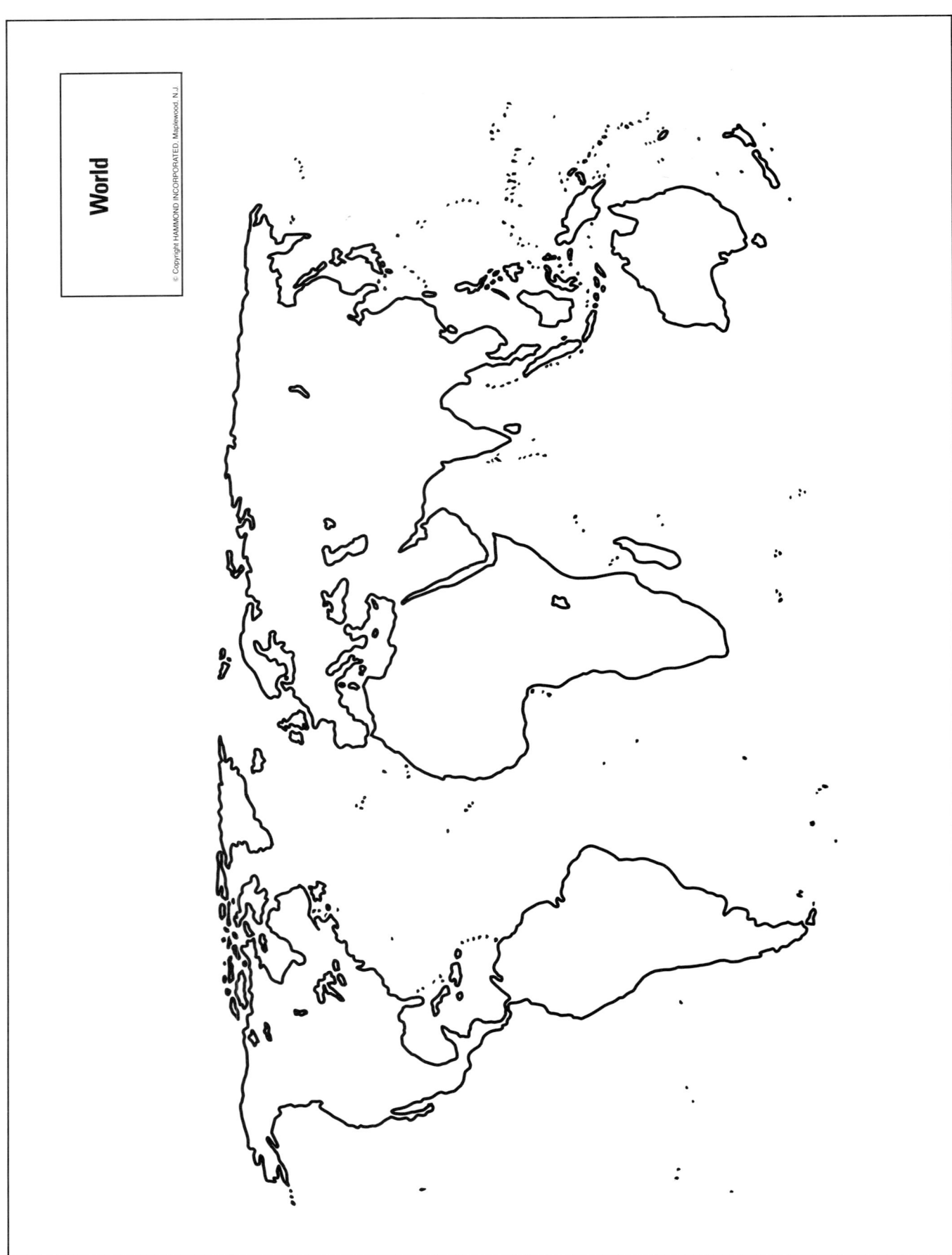

World

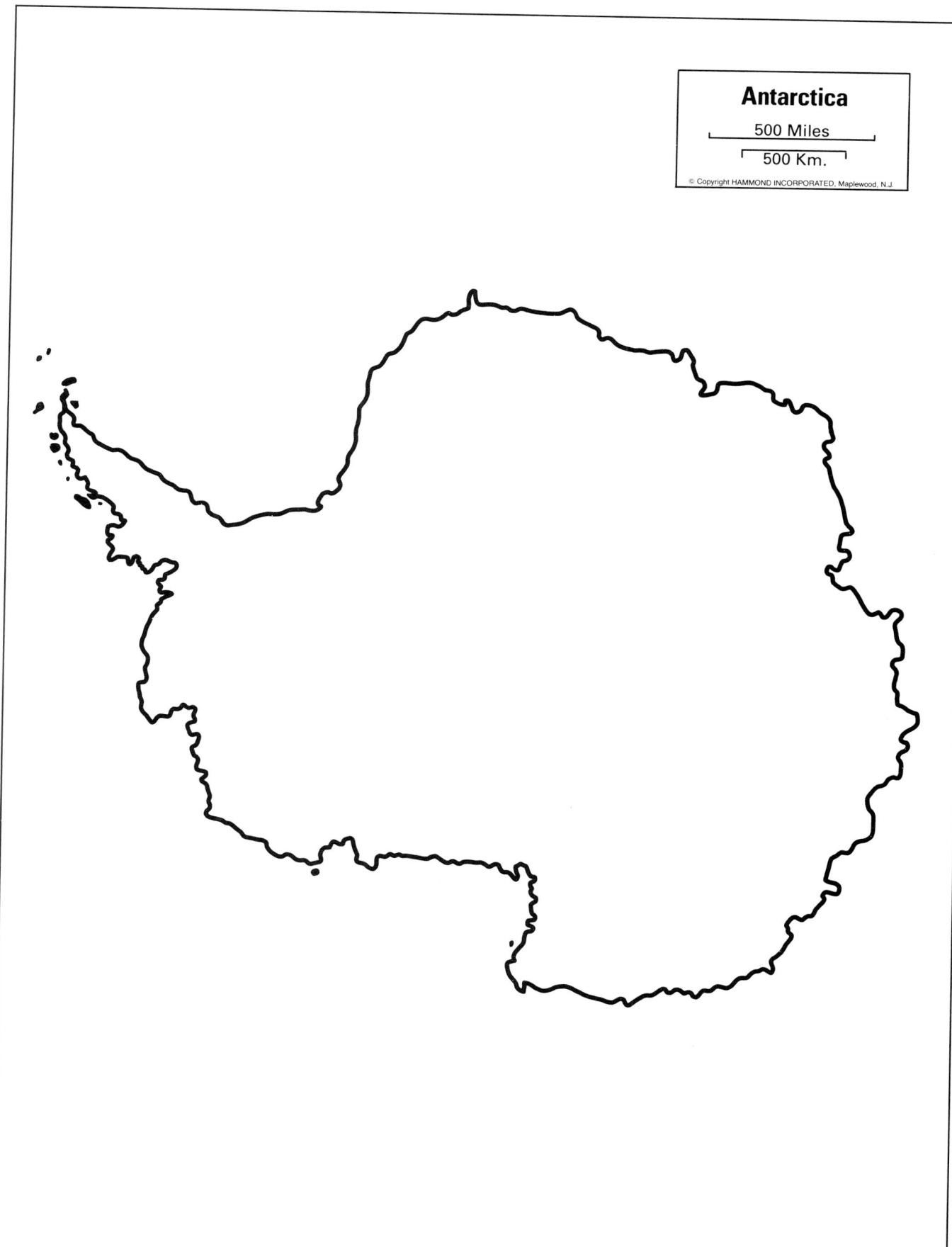

Antarctica

500 Miles

500 Km.

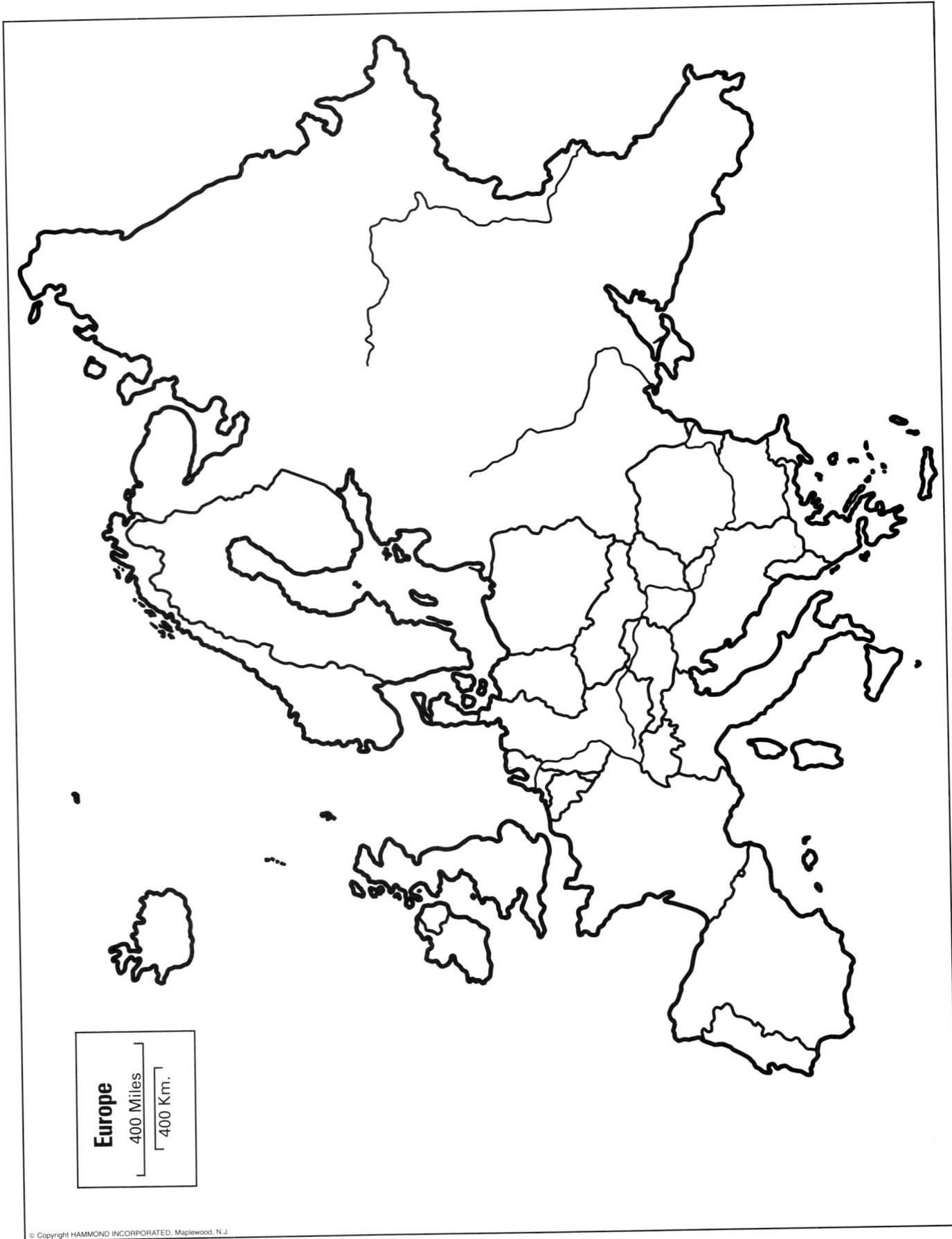

Europe

400 Miles

400 Km.

United Kingdom and Ireland

100 Miles

100 Km.

© Copyright HAMMOND INCORPORATED, Maplewood, N.J.

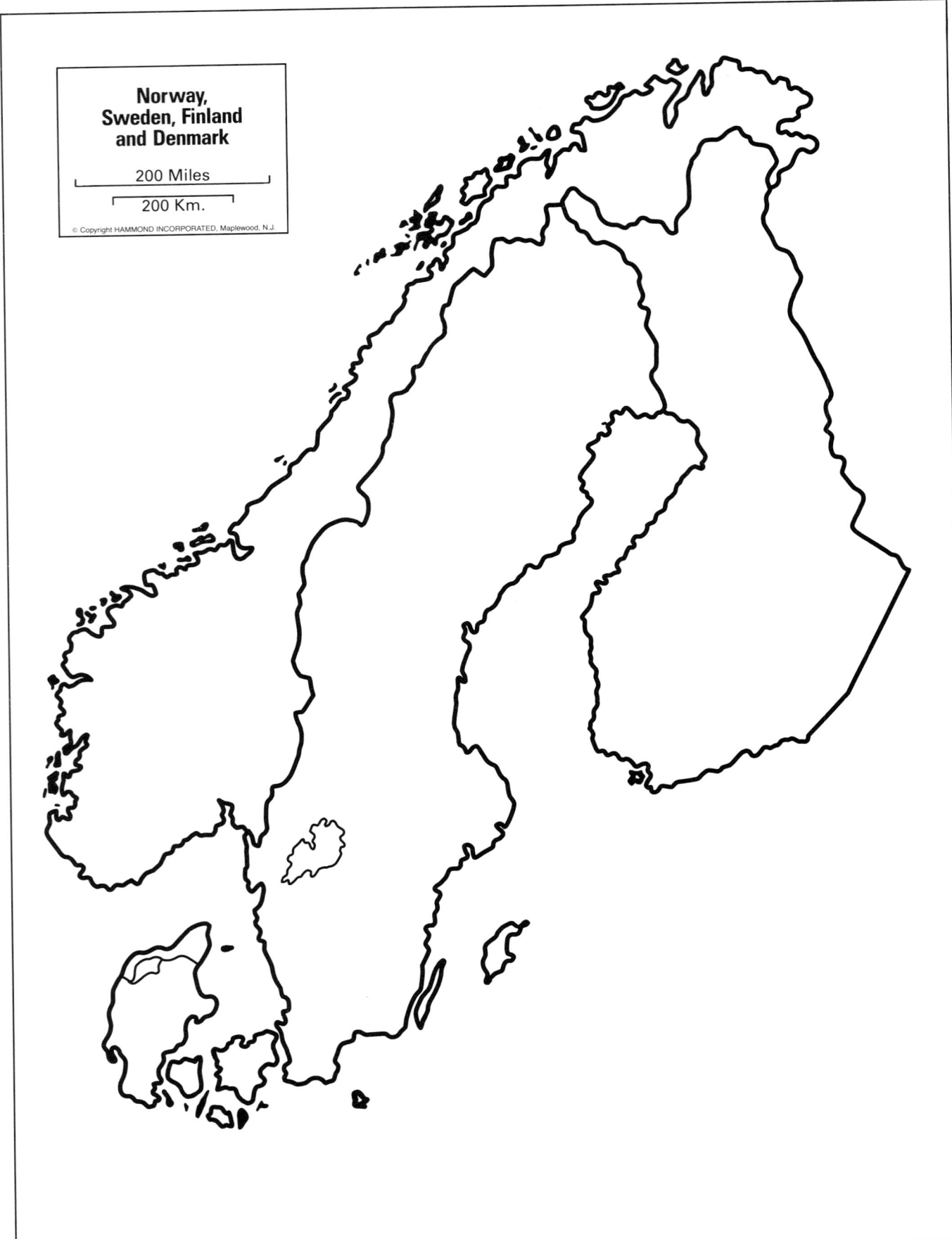

**Norway,
Sweden, Finland
and Denmark**

200 Miles

200 Km.

© Copyright HAMMOND INCORPORATED, Maplewood, N.J.

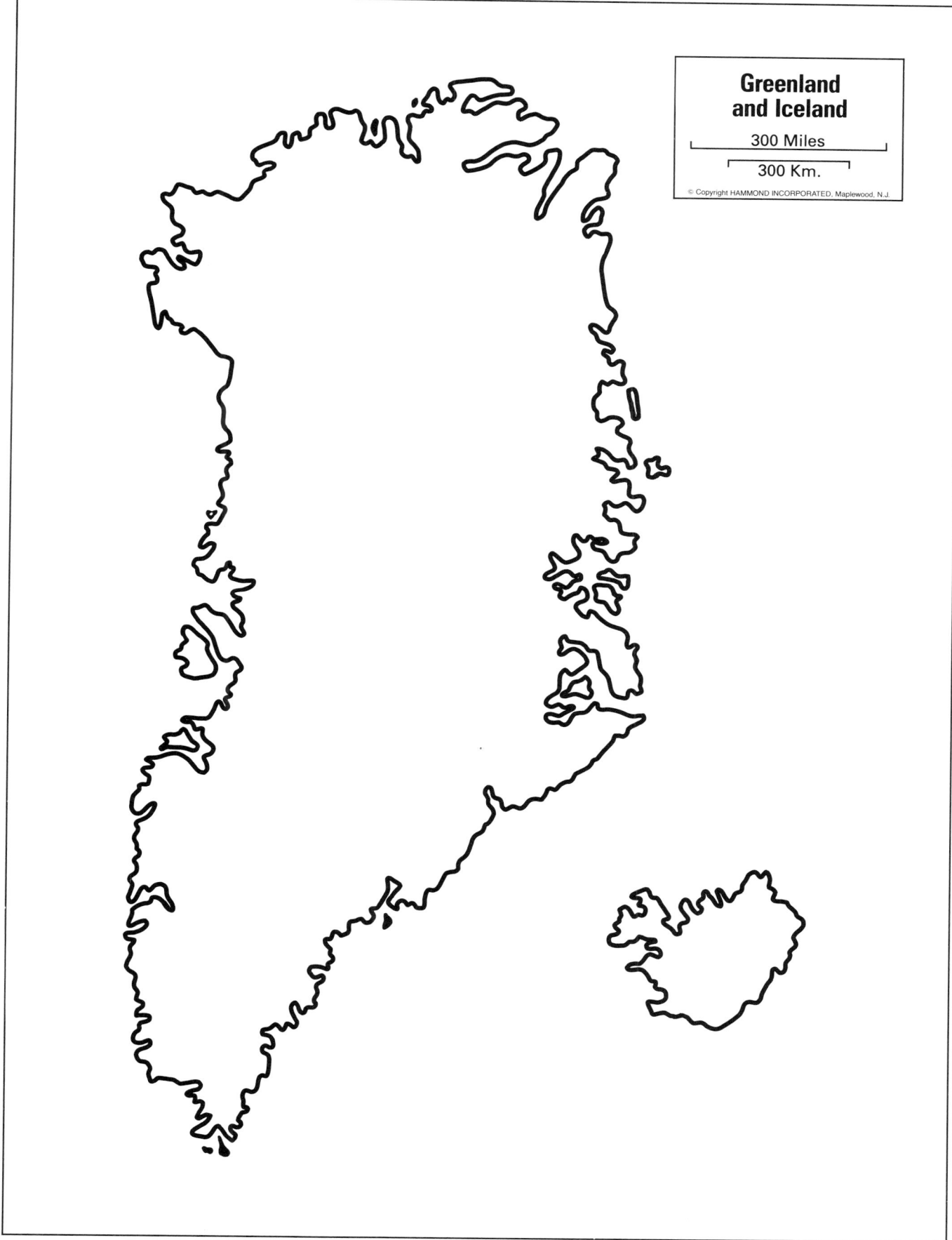

**Greenland
and Iceland**

300 Miles

300 Km.

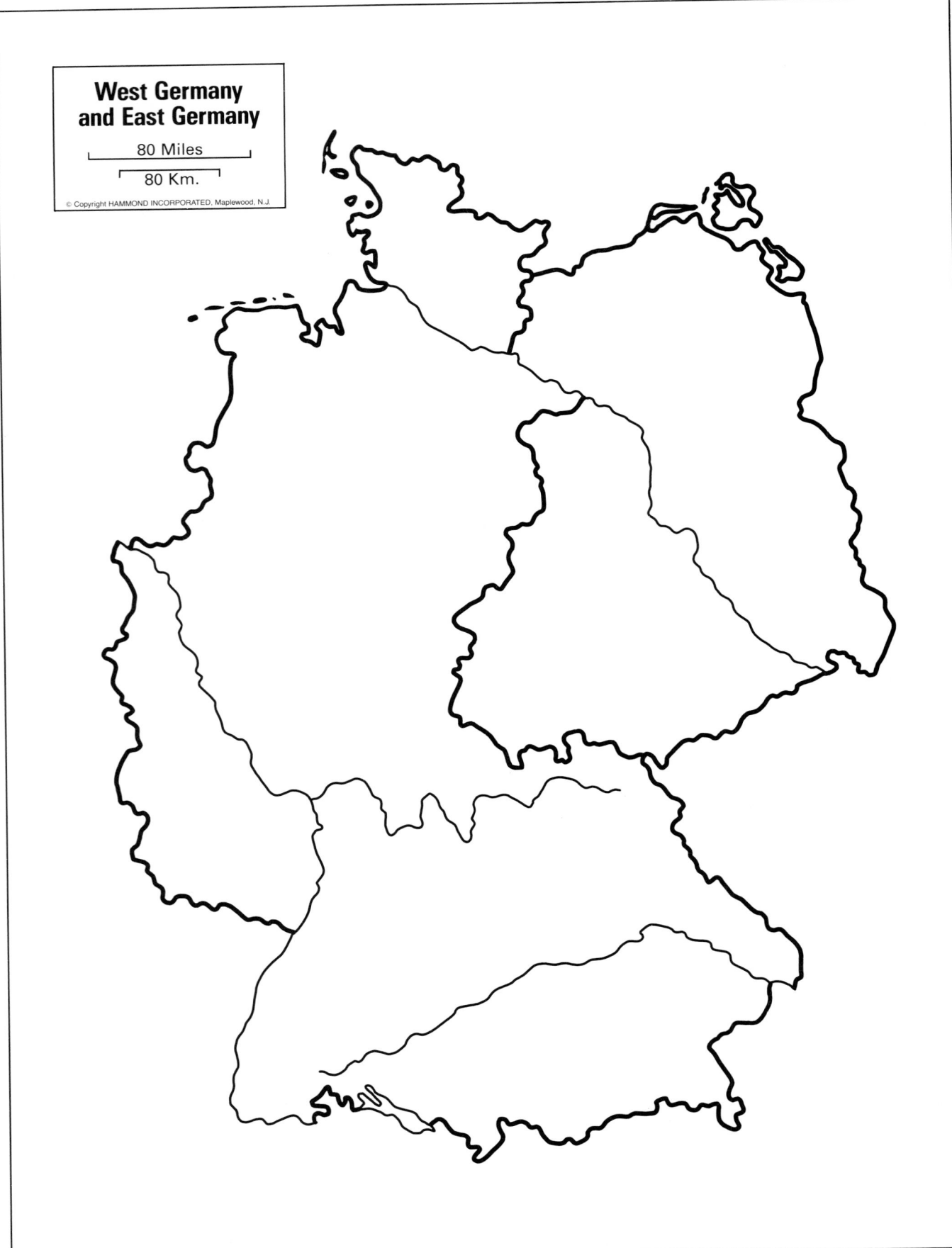

**West Germany
and East Germany**

80 Miles

80 Km.

**Netherlands,
Belgium
and Luxembourg**

50 Miles

50 Km.

© Copyright HAMMOND INCORPORATED, Maplewood, N.J.

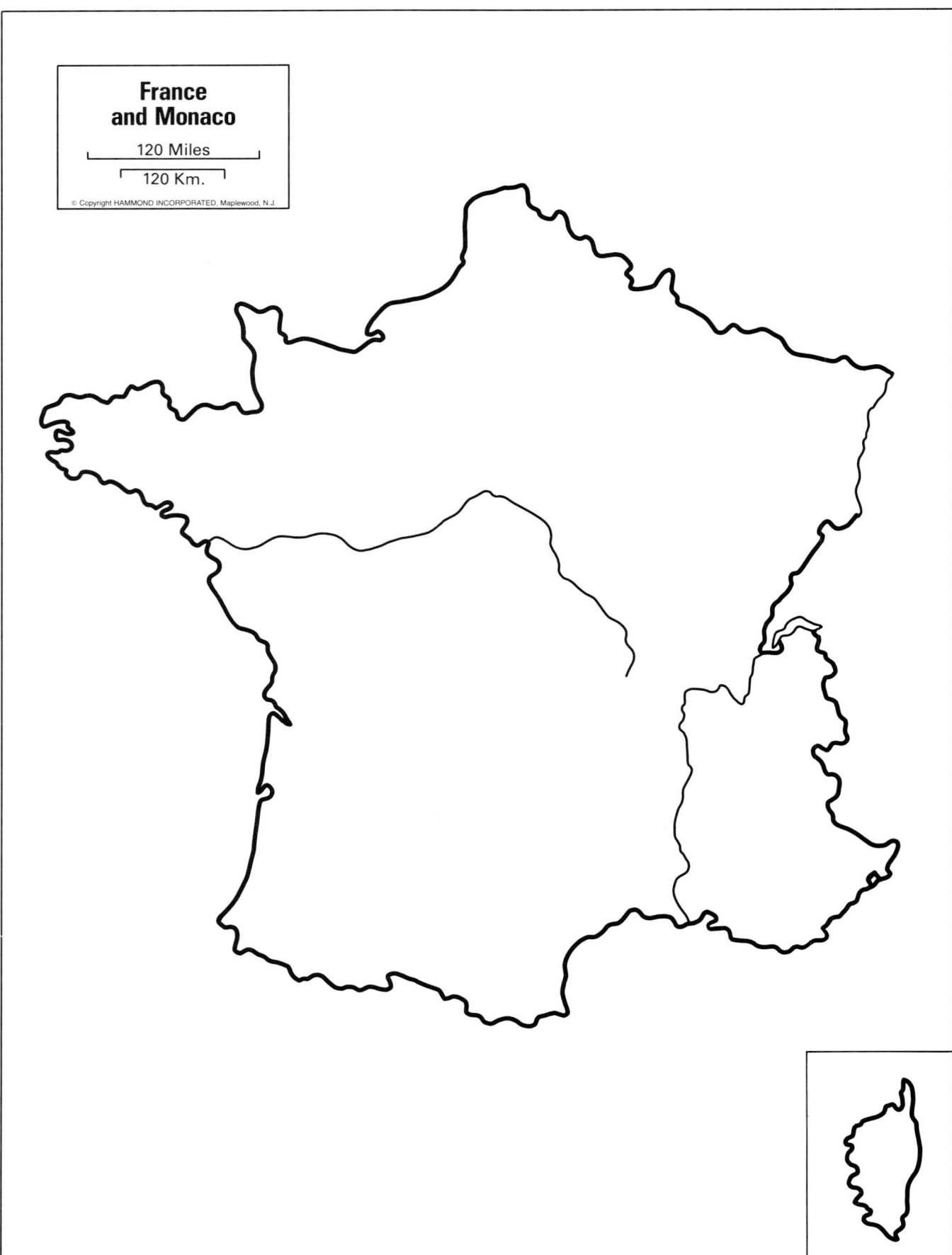

**France
and Monaco**

120 Miles

120 Km.

© Copyright HAMMOND INCORPORATED, Maplewood, N.J.

**Austria,
Switzerland,
Italy and Malta**

200 Miles

200 Km.

**Poland,
Czechoslovakia
and Hungary**

100 Miles

100 Km.

© Copyright HAMMOND INCORPORATED, Maplewood, N.J.

**The
Balkans**

150 Miles

150 Km.

© Copyright HAMMOND INCORPORATED, Maplewood, N.J.

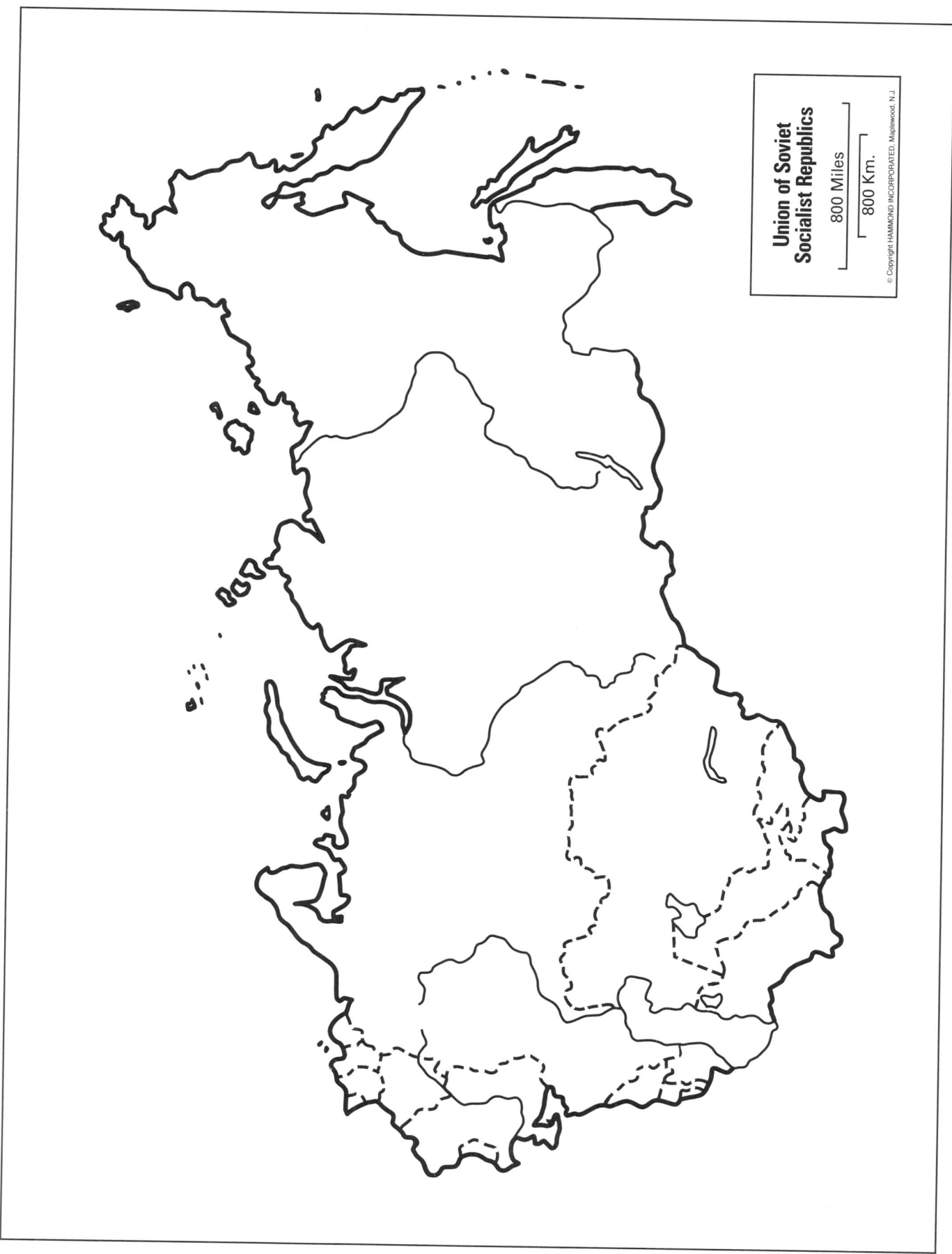

Union of Soviet
Socialist Republics

800 Miles

800 Km.

© Copyright HAMMOND INCORPORATED, Maplewood, N.J.

Asia

1500 Miles

1500 Km.

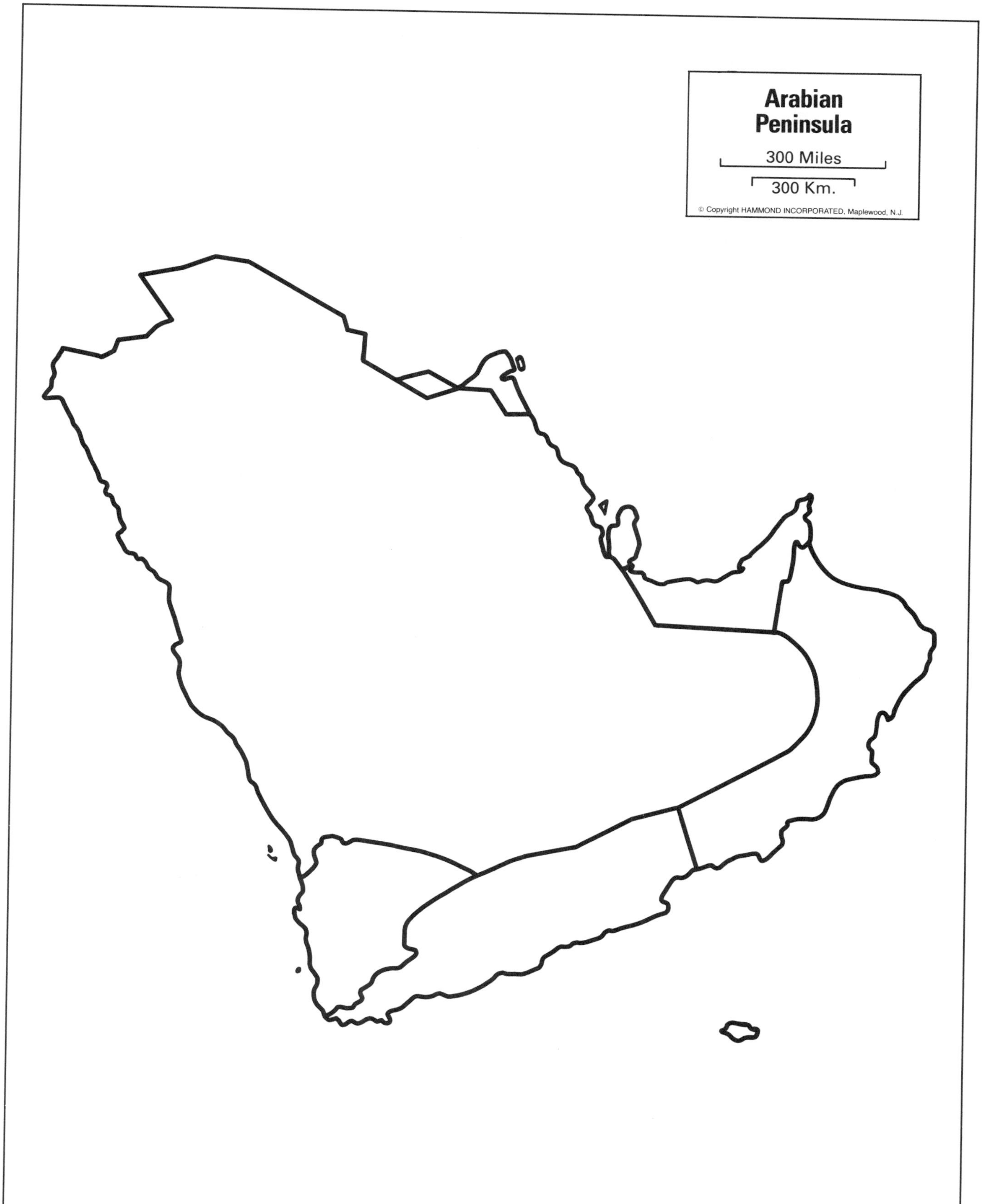

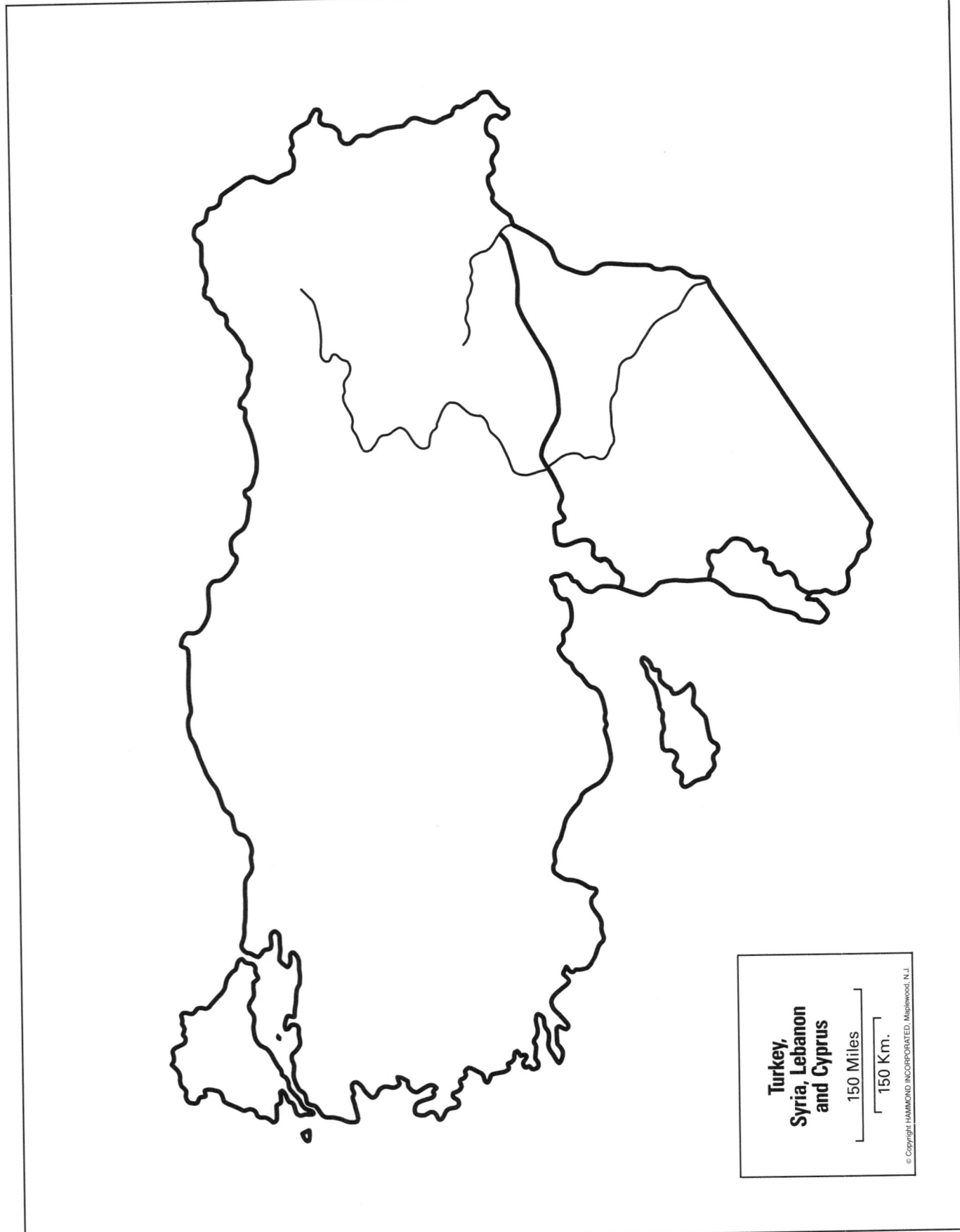

**Turkey,
Syria, Lebanon
and Cyprus**

150 Miles

150 Km.

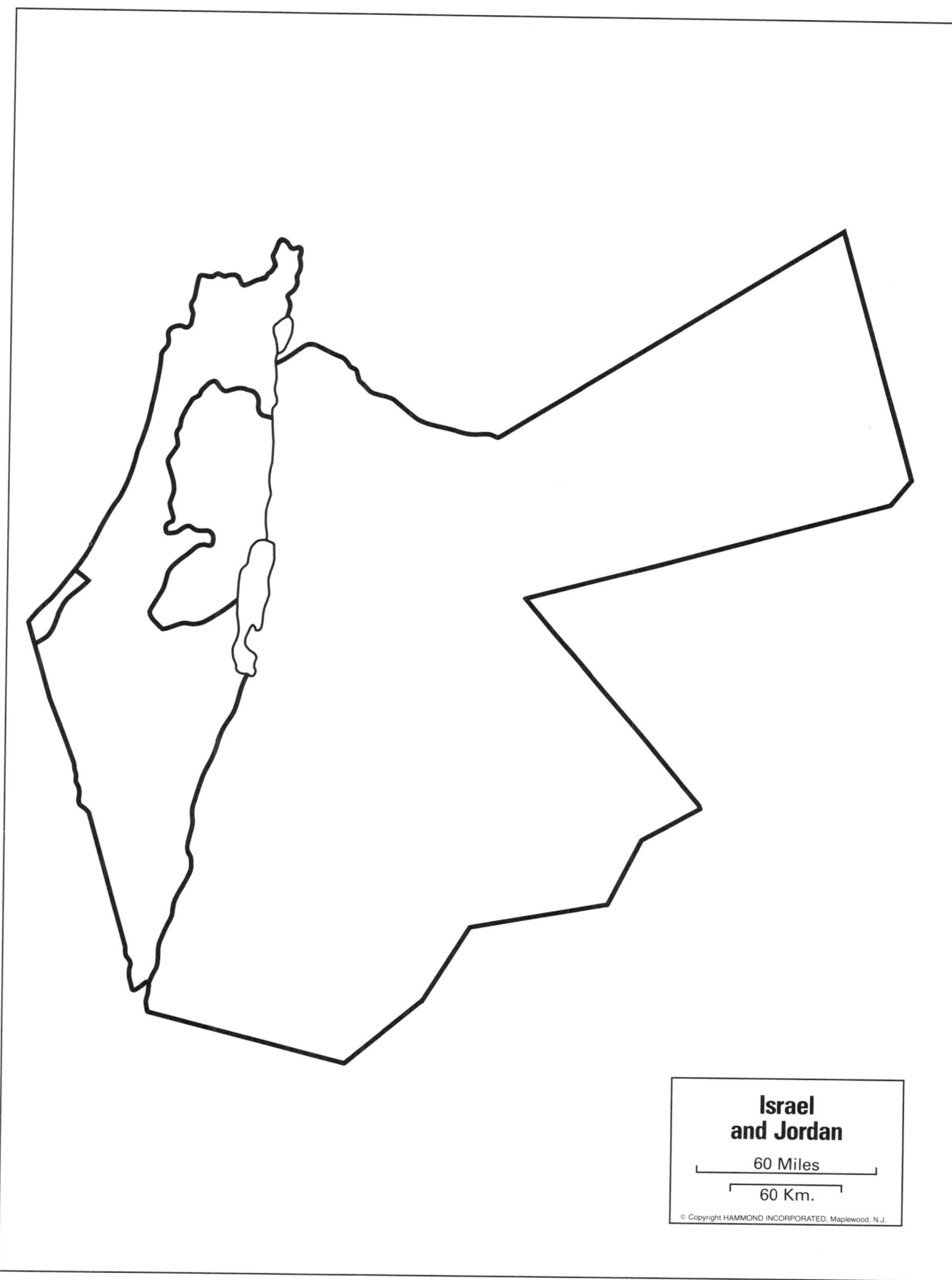

**Israel
and Jordan**

60 Miles

60 Km.

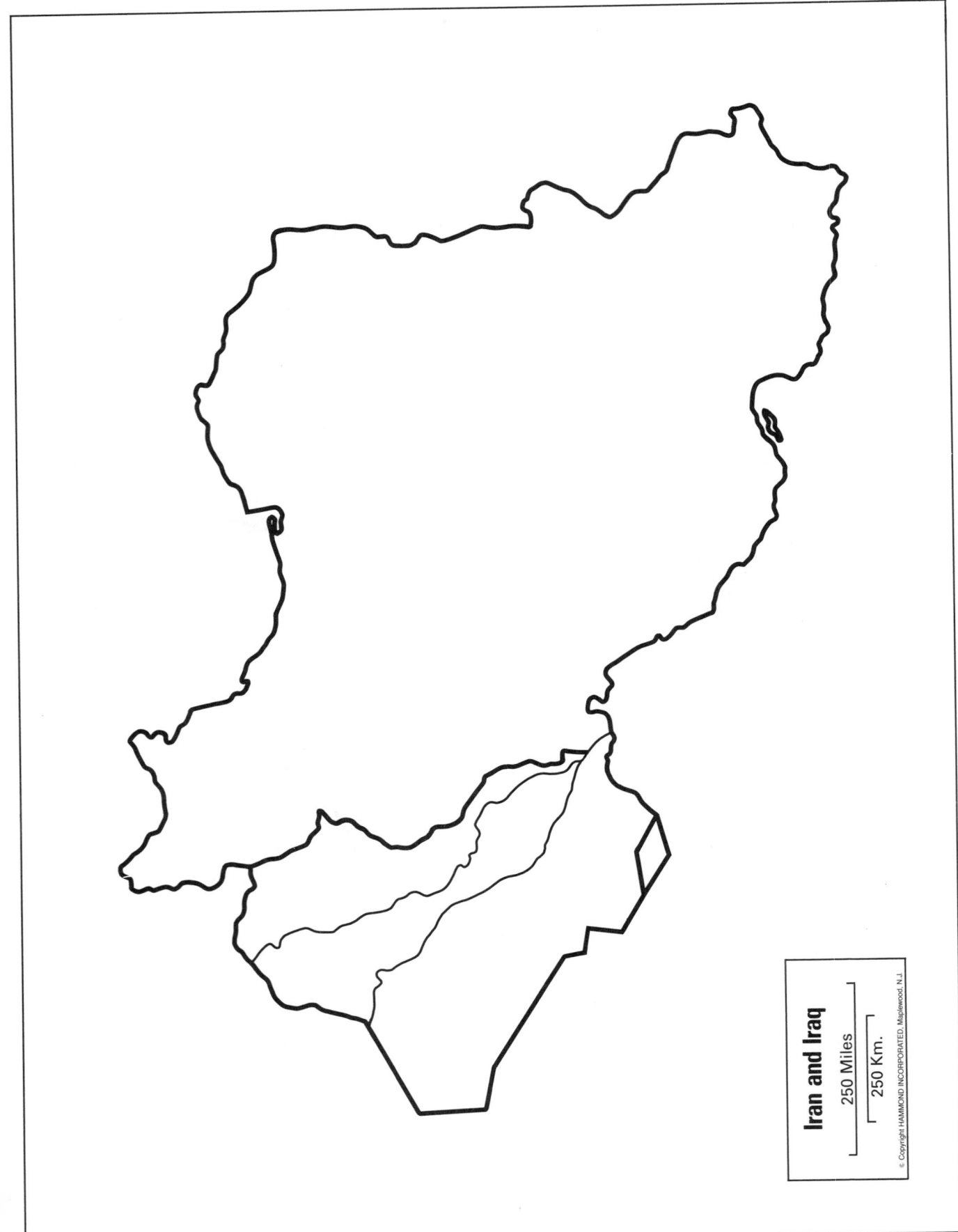

Iran and Iraq

250 Miles

250 Km.

© Copyright HAMMOND INCORPORATED, Maplewood, N.J.

**Afghanistan
and Pakistan**

200 Miles

200 Km.

578

India, Nepal,
Bangladesh, Bhutan
and Sri Lanka

300 Miles

300 Km.

© Copyright HAMMOND INCORPORATED, Maplewood, N.J.

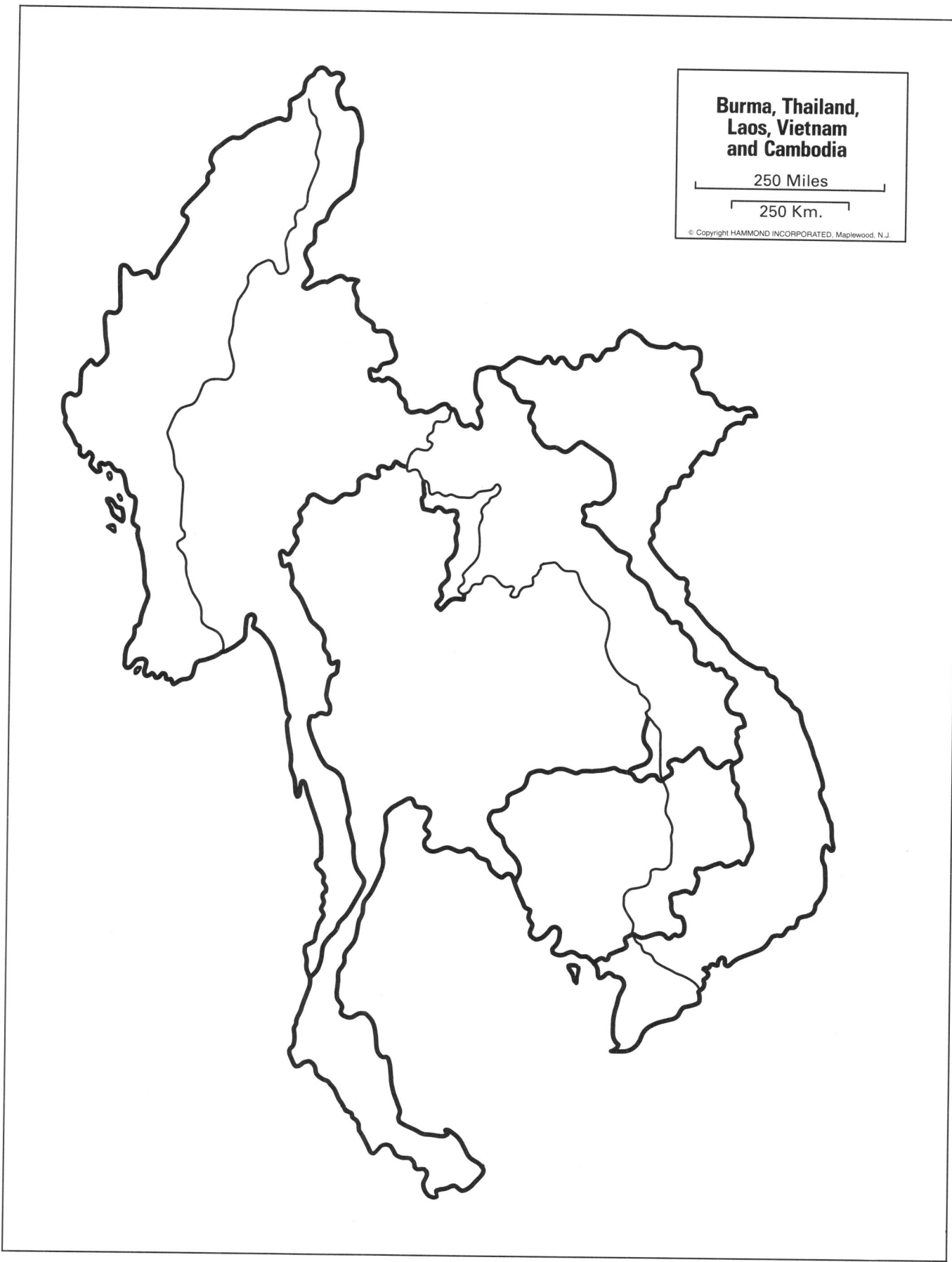

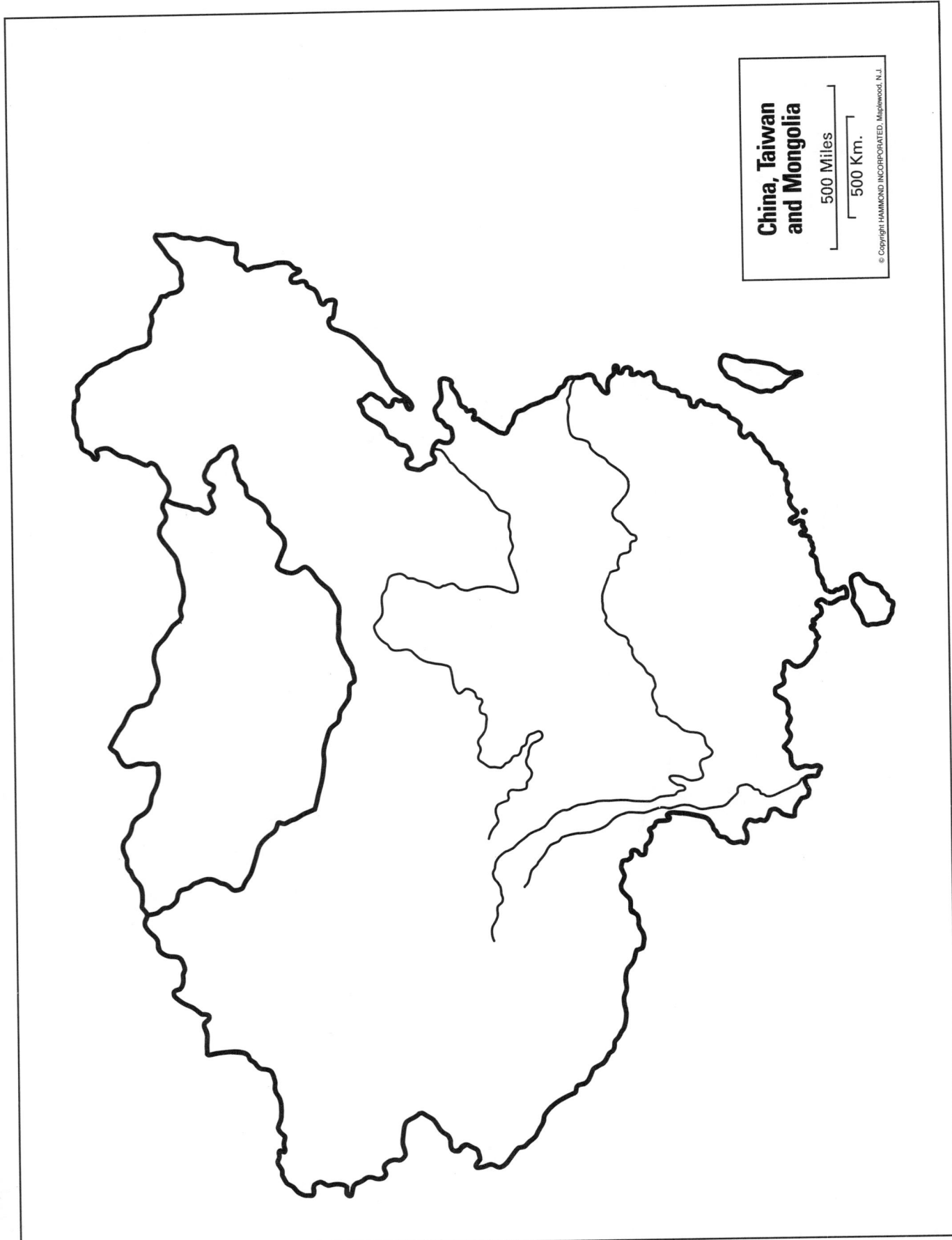

China, Taiwan and Mongolia

500 Miles

500 Km.

© Copyright HAMMOND INCORPORATED, Maplewood, N.J.

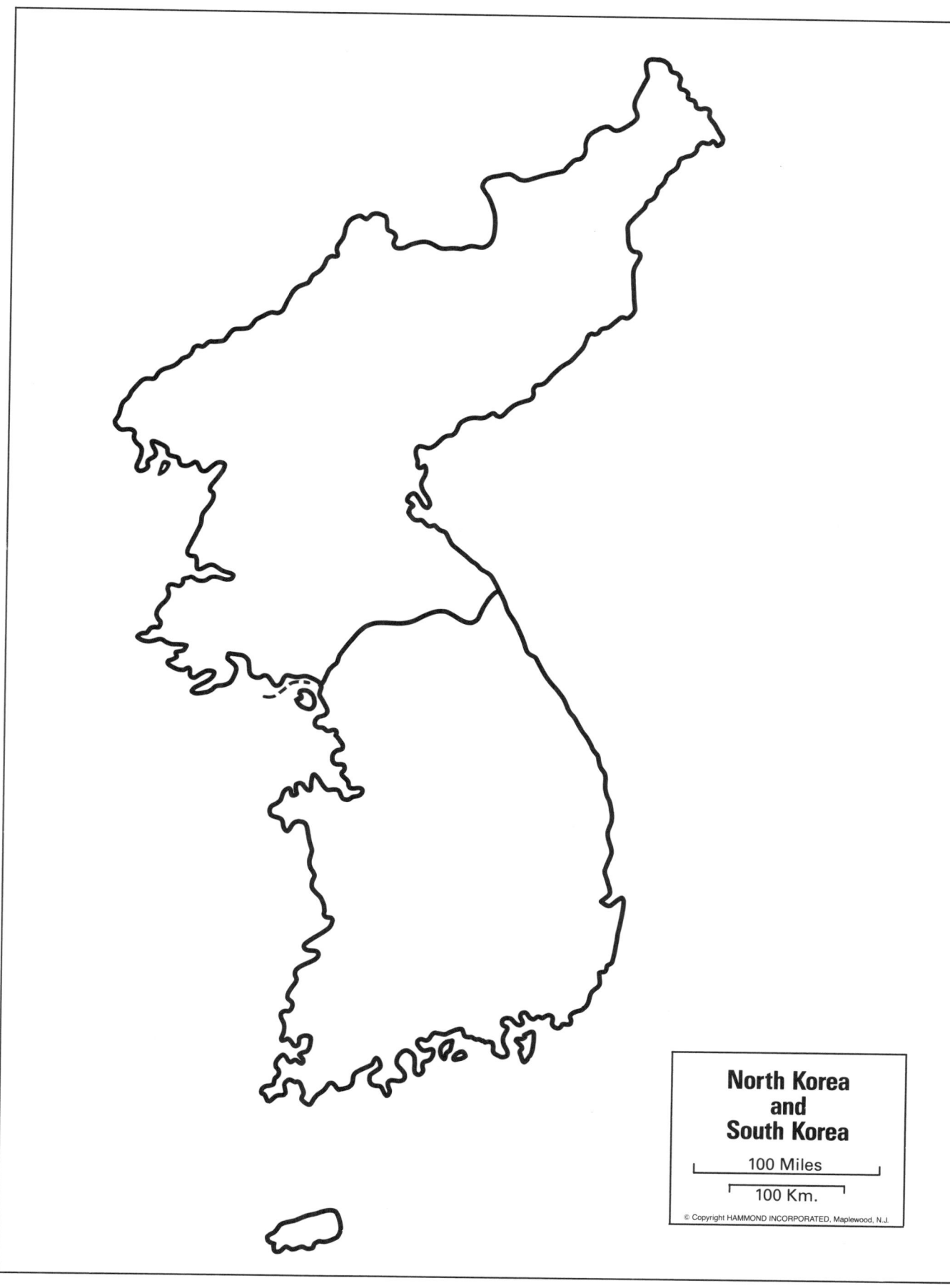

**North Korea
and
South Korea**

100 Miles

100 Km.

© Copyright HAMMOND INCORPORATED, Maplewood, N.J.

582

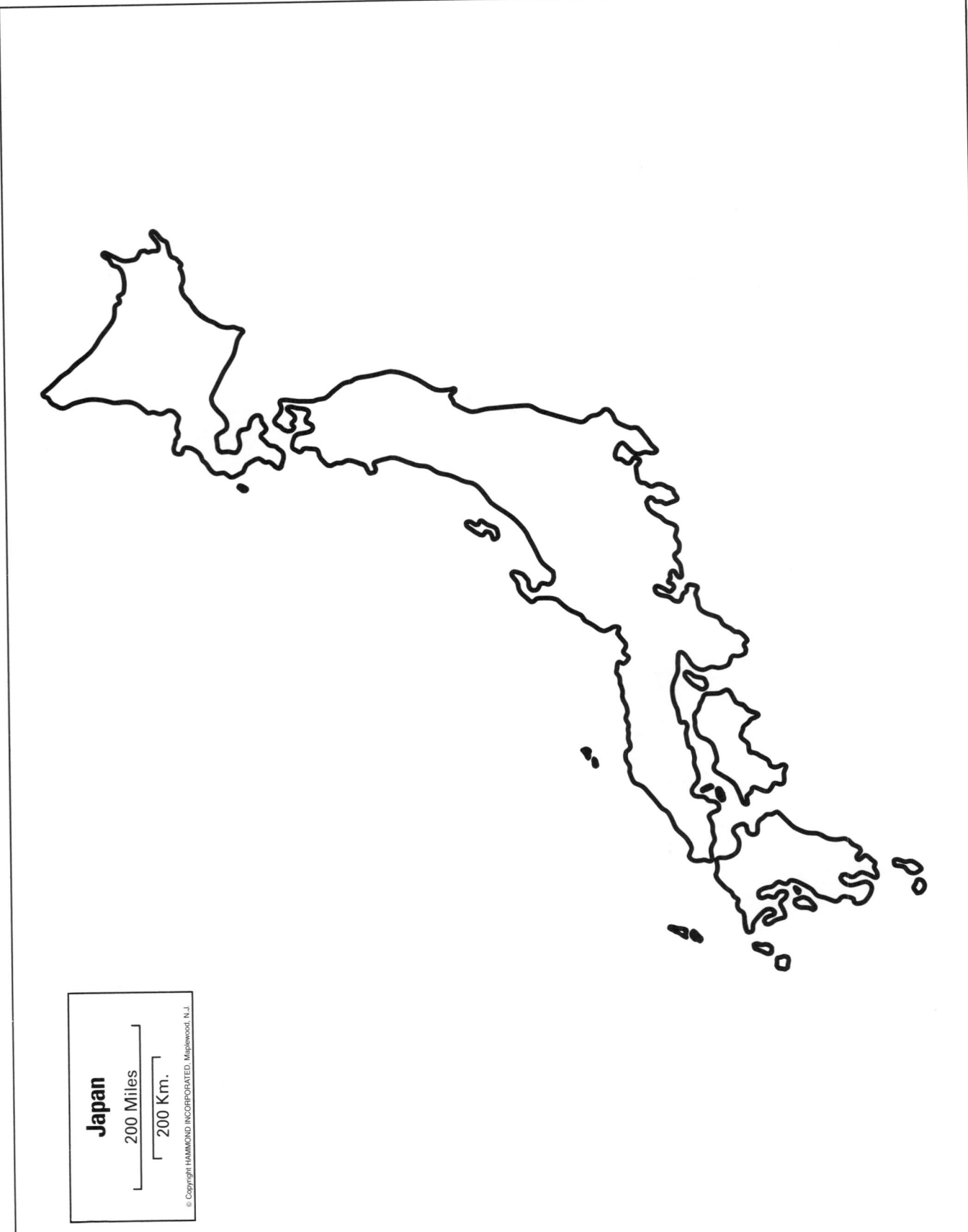

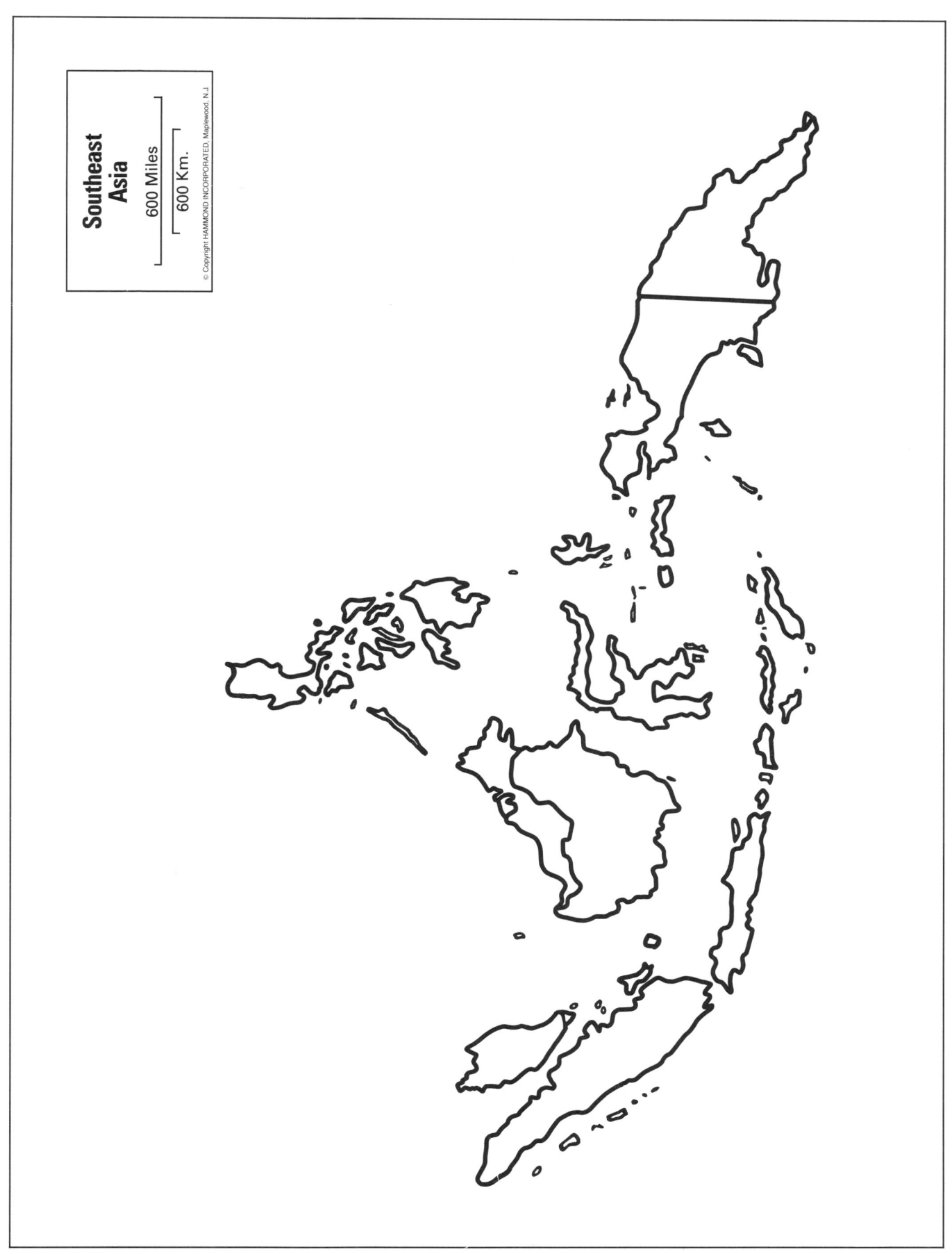

Southeast Asia

600 Miles

600 Km.

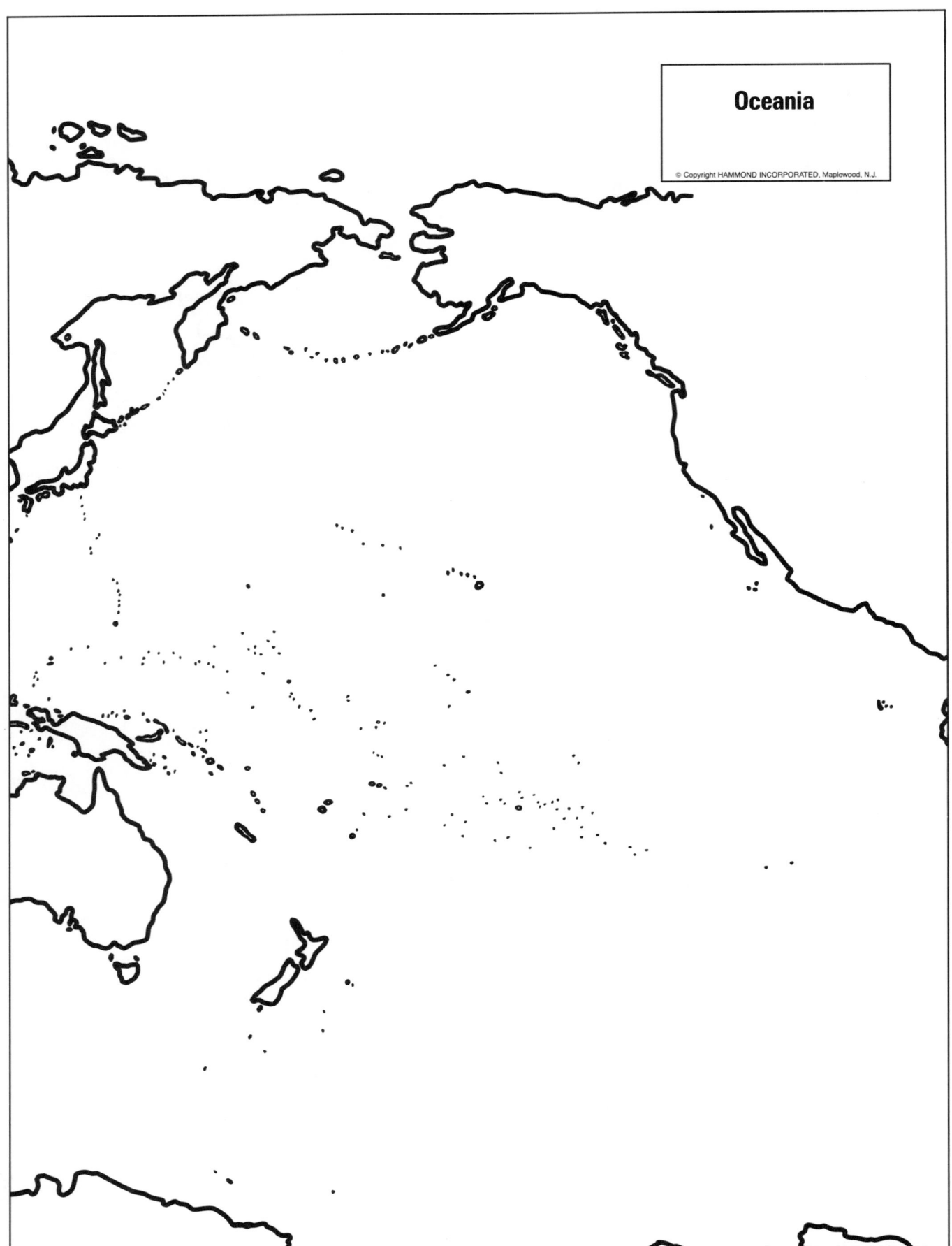

Oceania

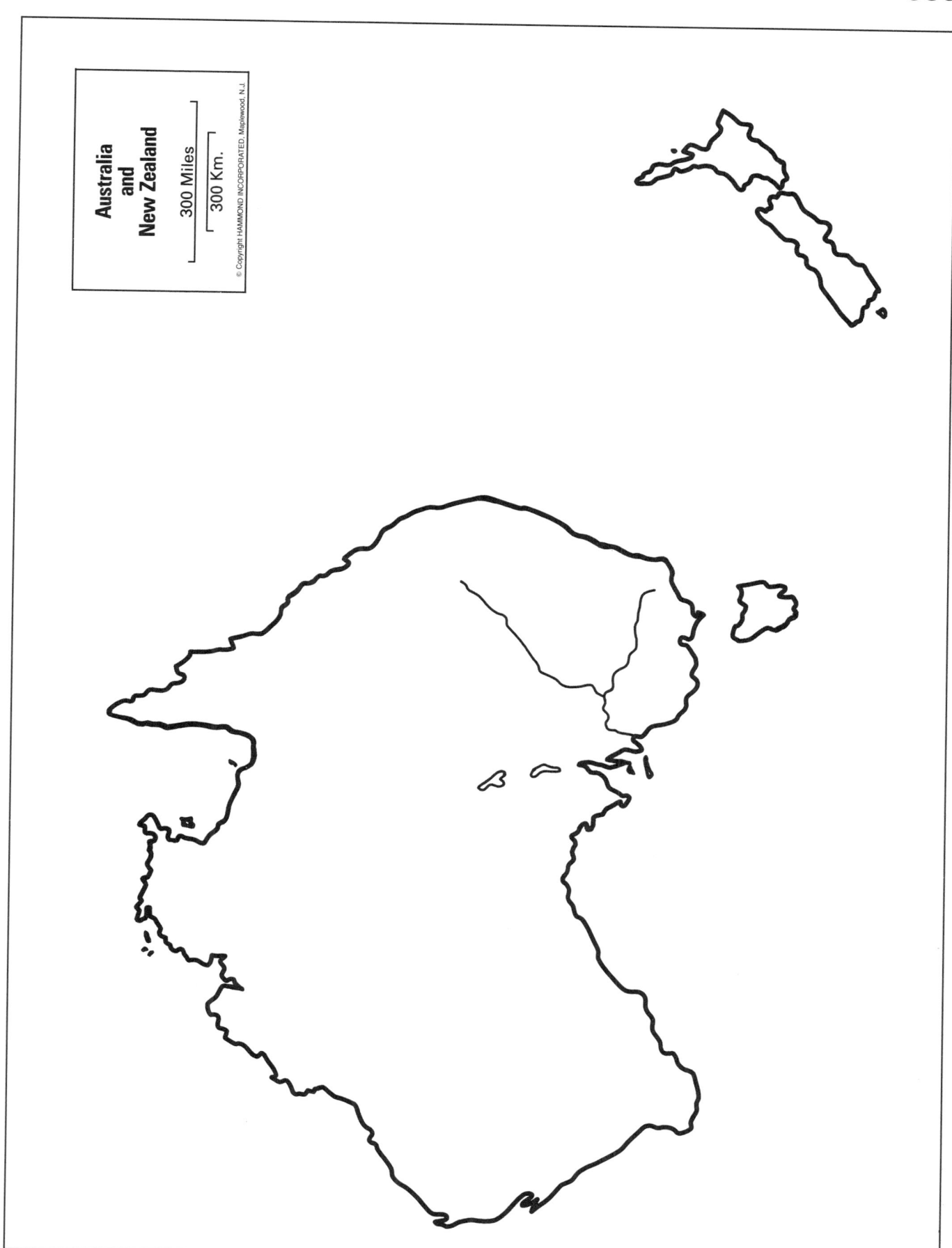

Australia
and
New Zealand

300 Miles

300 Km.

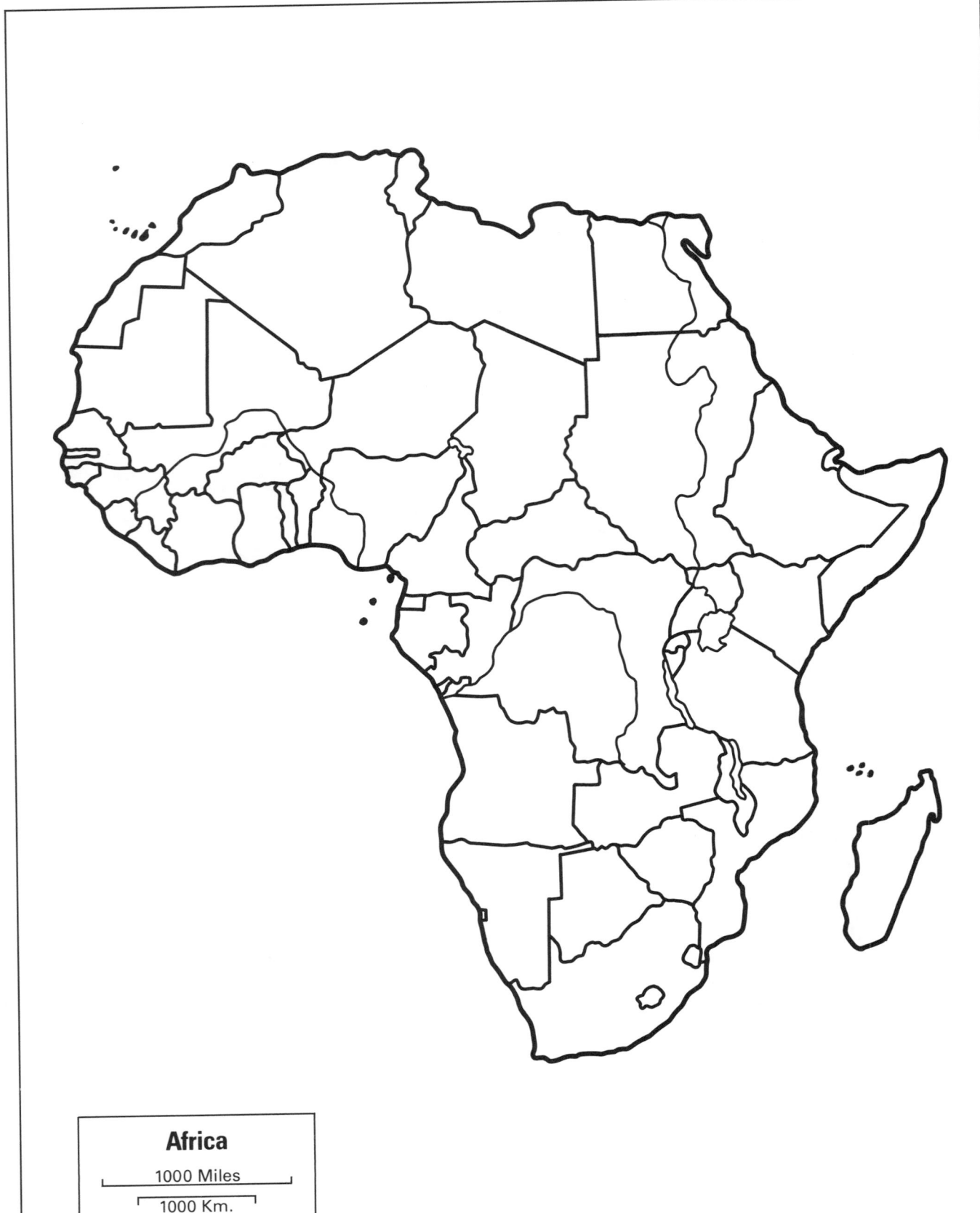

Africa

1000 Miles

1000 Km.

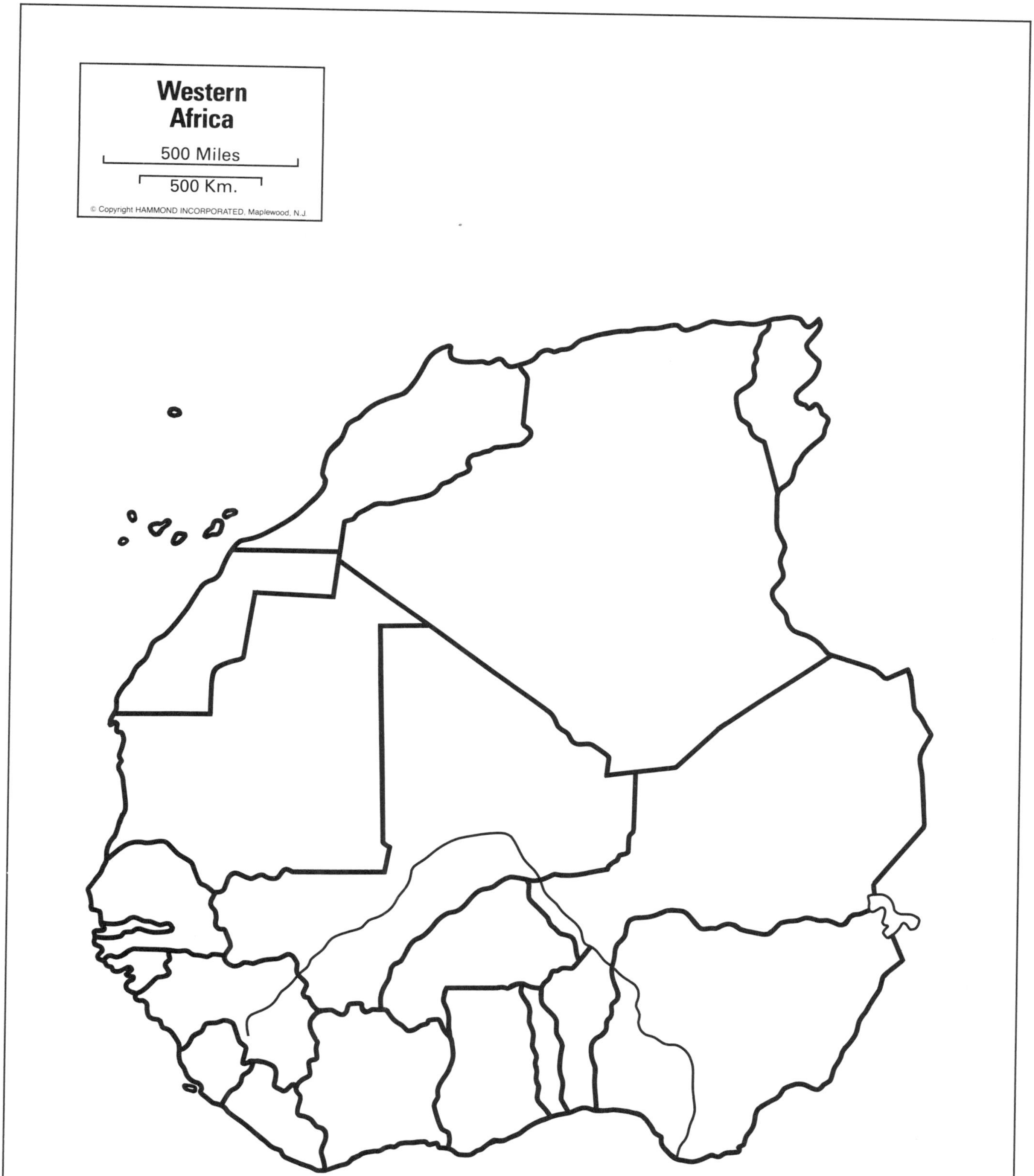

**Western
Africa**

500 Miles

500 Km.

© Copyright HAMMOND INCORPORATED, Maplewood, N.J.

588

Northeastern
Africa

400 Miles

400 Km.

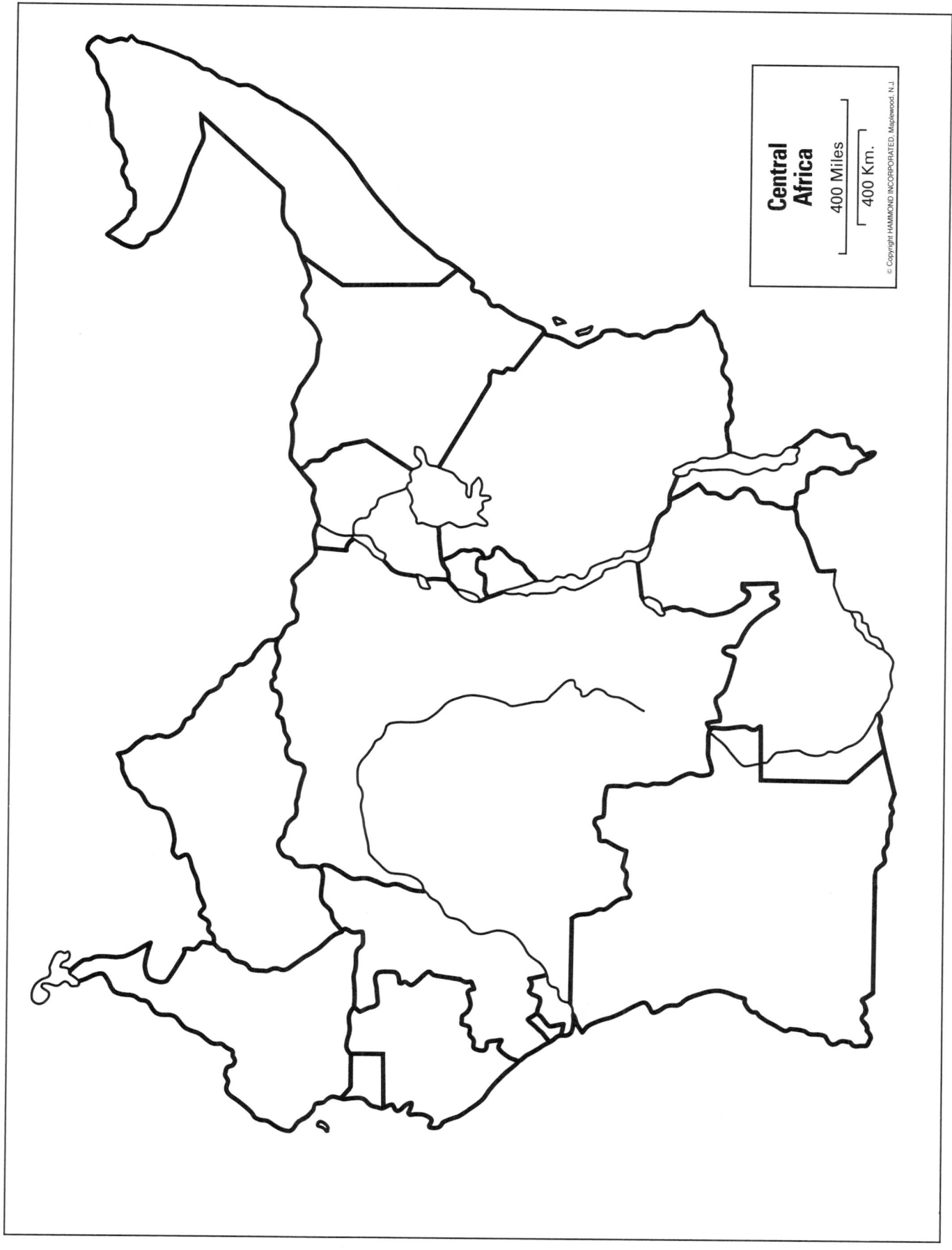

Central
Africa

400 Miles

400 Km.

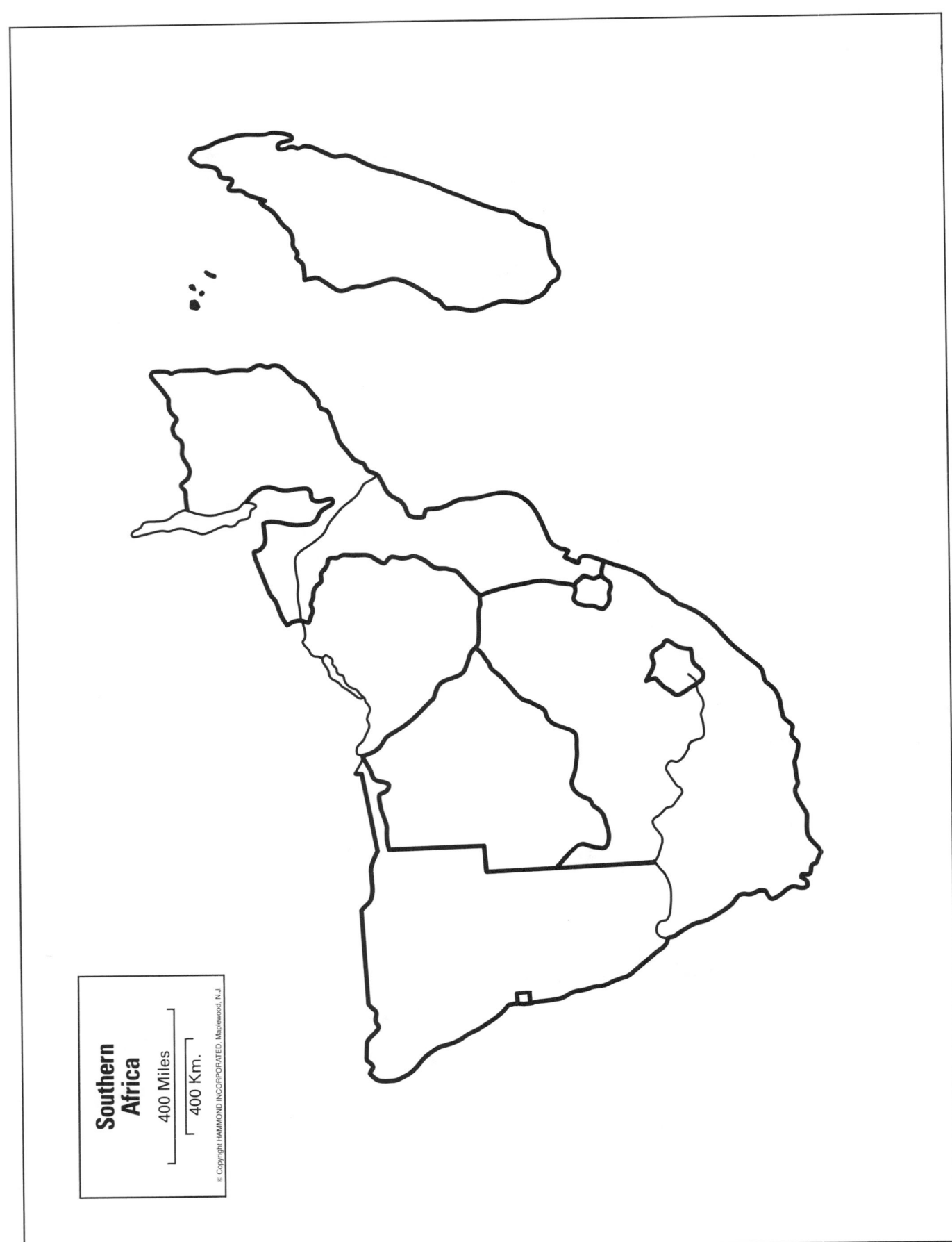

Southern Africa

400 Miles

400 Km.

South America

600 Miles

600 Km.

© Copyright HAMMOND INCORPORATED, Maplewood, N.J.

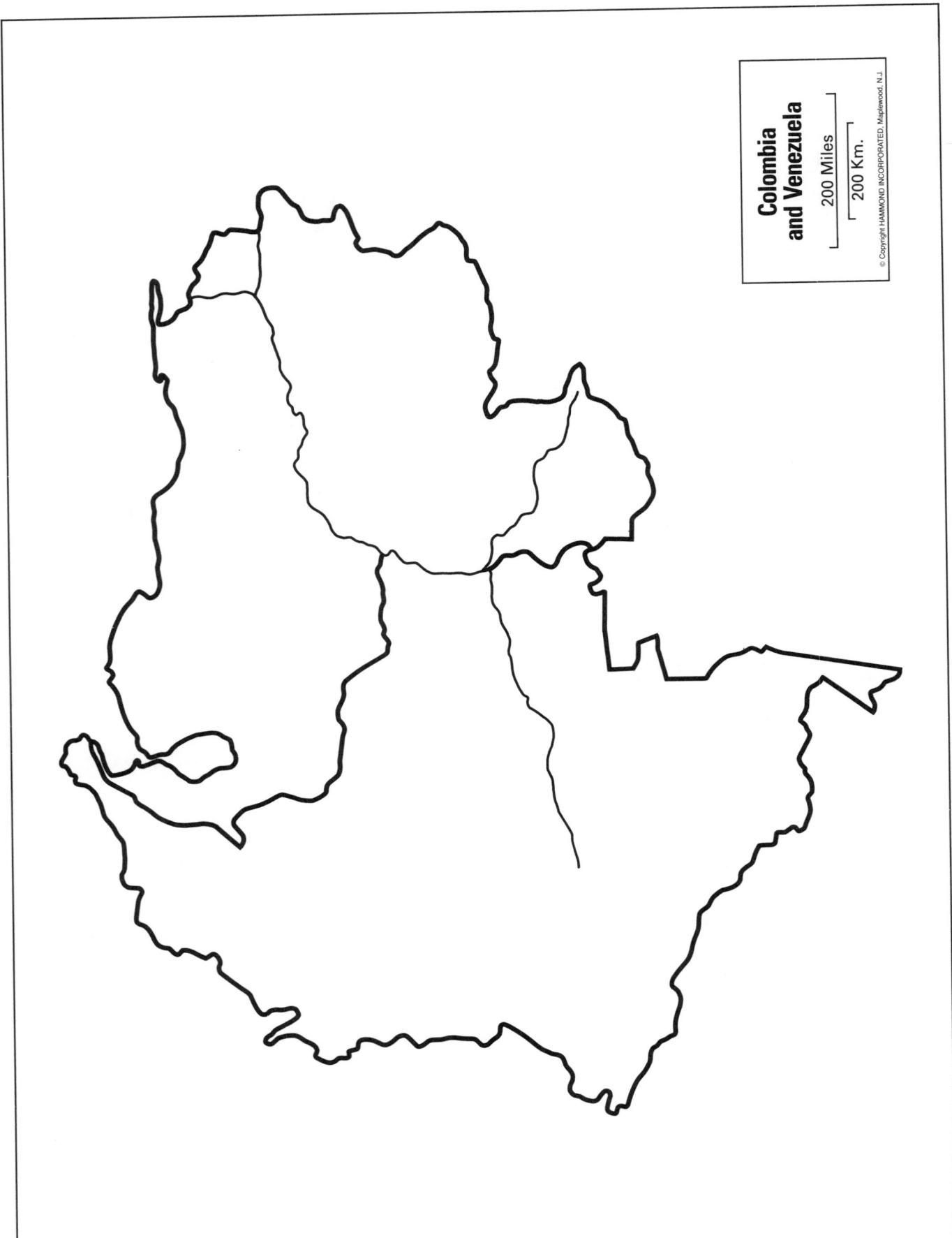

Colombia
and Venezuela

200 Miles

200 Km.

© Copyright HAMMOND INCORPORATED, Maplewood, N.J

Peru and Ecuador

200 Miles

200 Km.

© Copyright HAMMOND INCORPORATED, Maplewood, N.J.

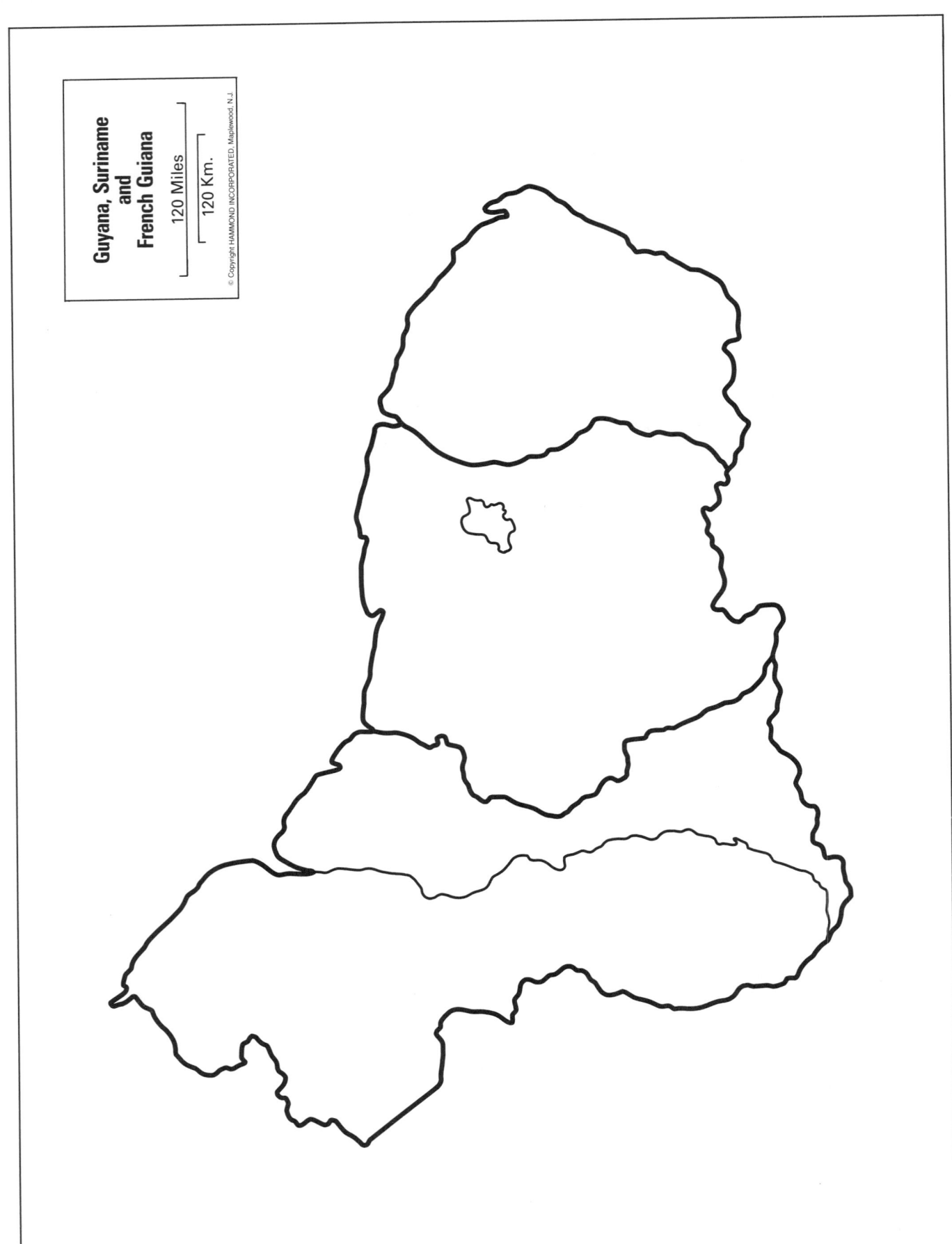

Guyana, Suriname and French Guiana

120 Miles

120 Km.

Brazil and Bolivia

500 Miles

500 Km.

**Argentina,
Chile, Paraguay
and Uruguay**

400 Miles

400 Km.

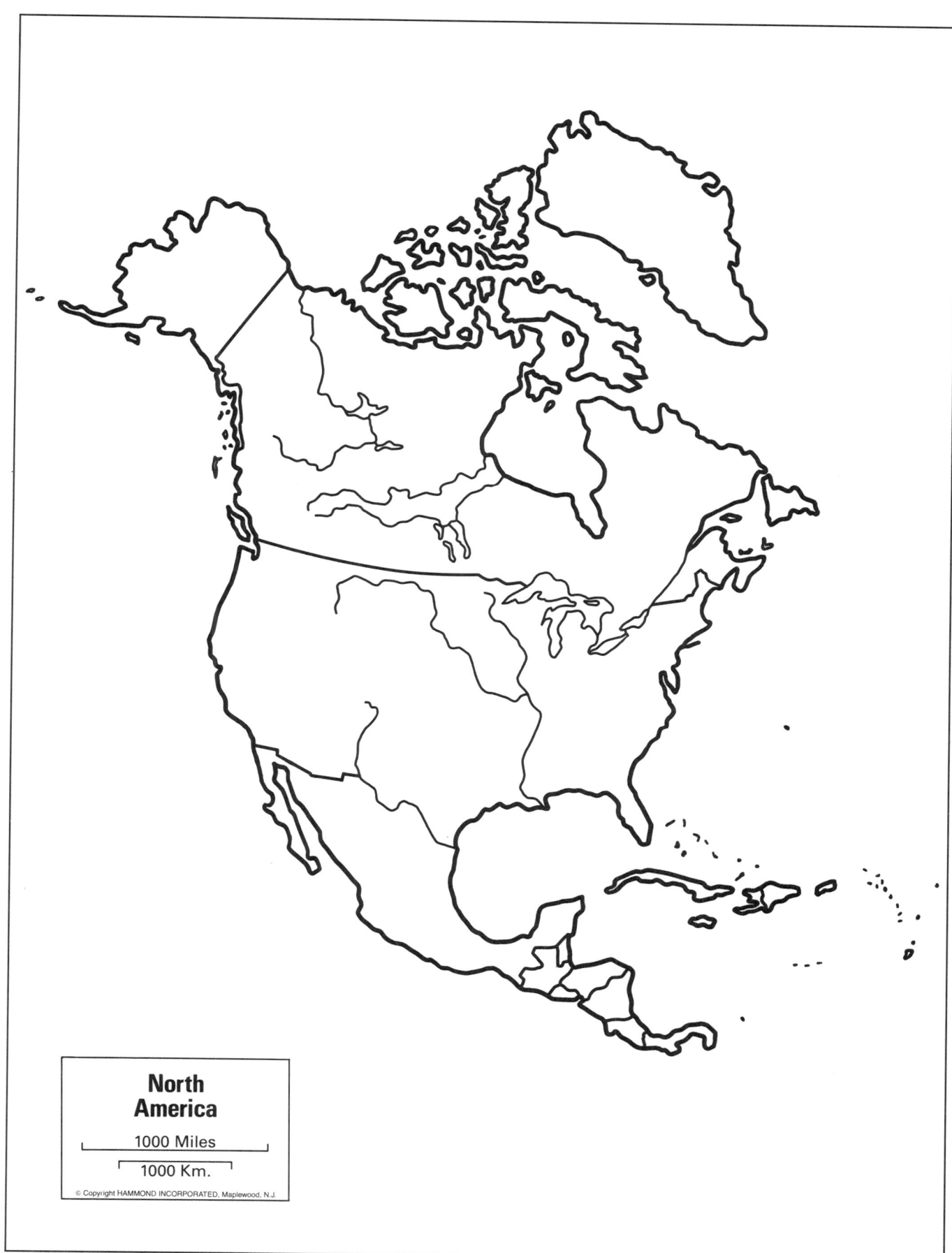

North America

1000 Miles

1000 Km.

598

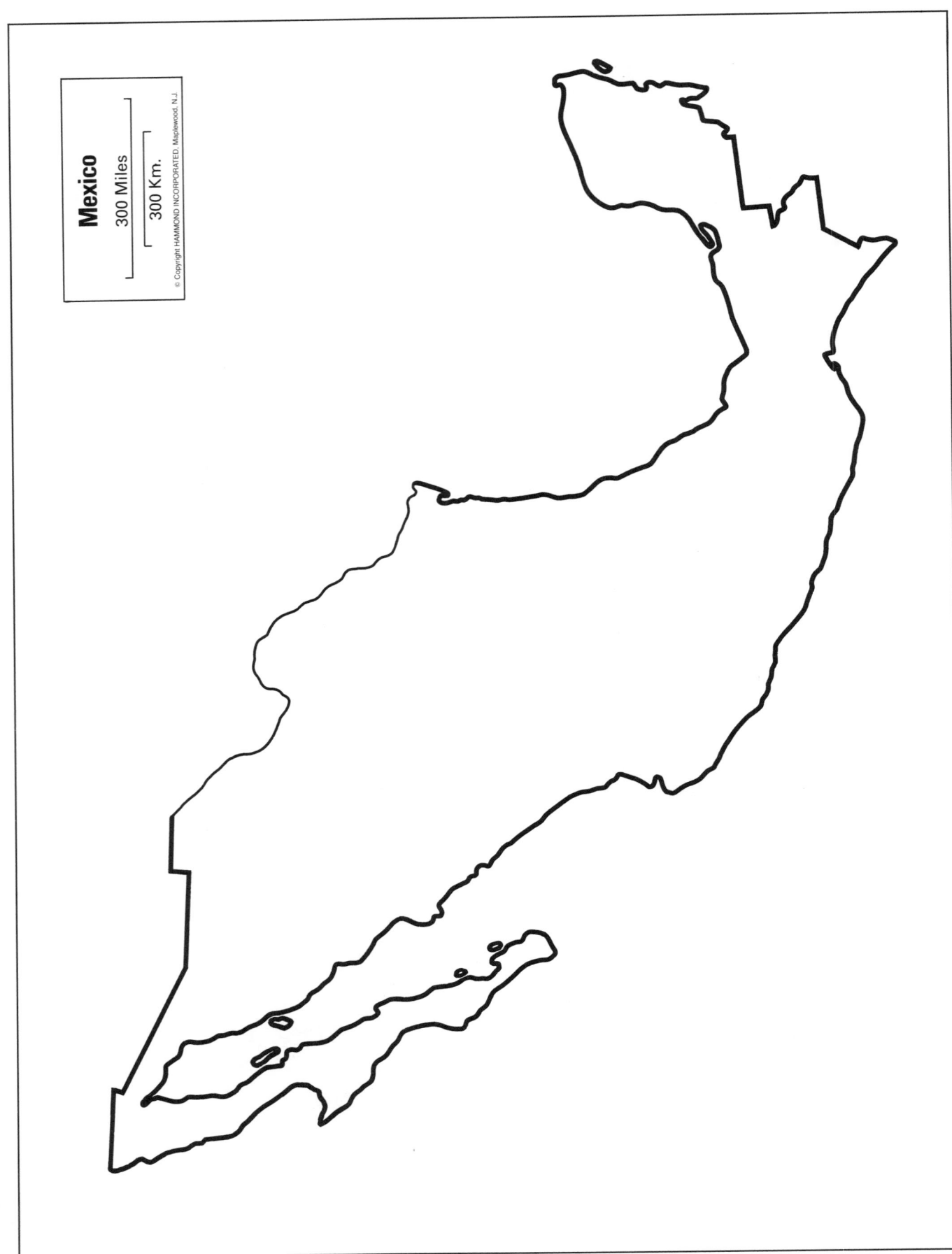

Mexico

300 Miles

300 Km.

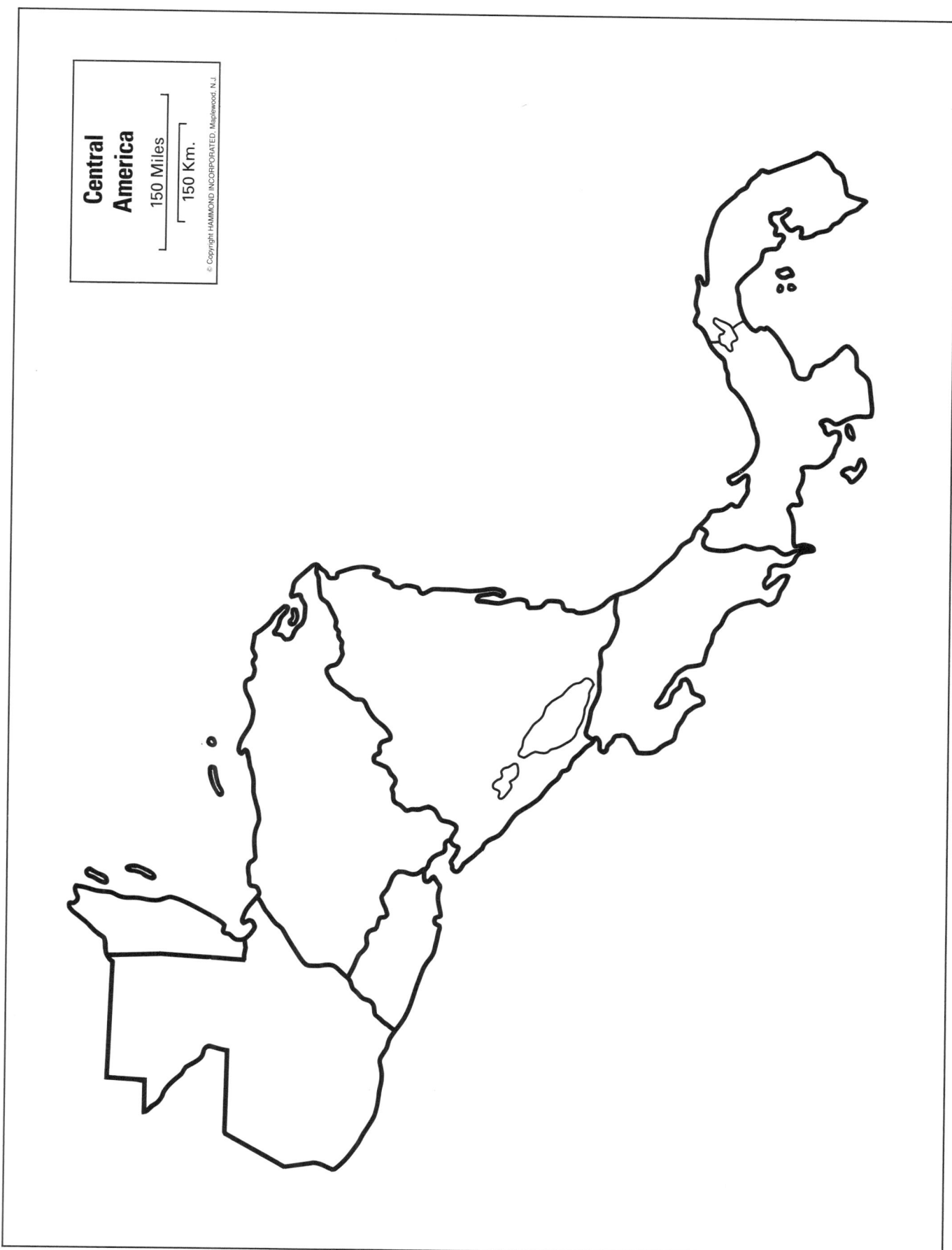

Central America

150 Miles

150 Km.

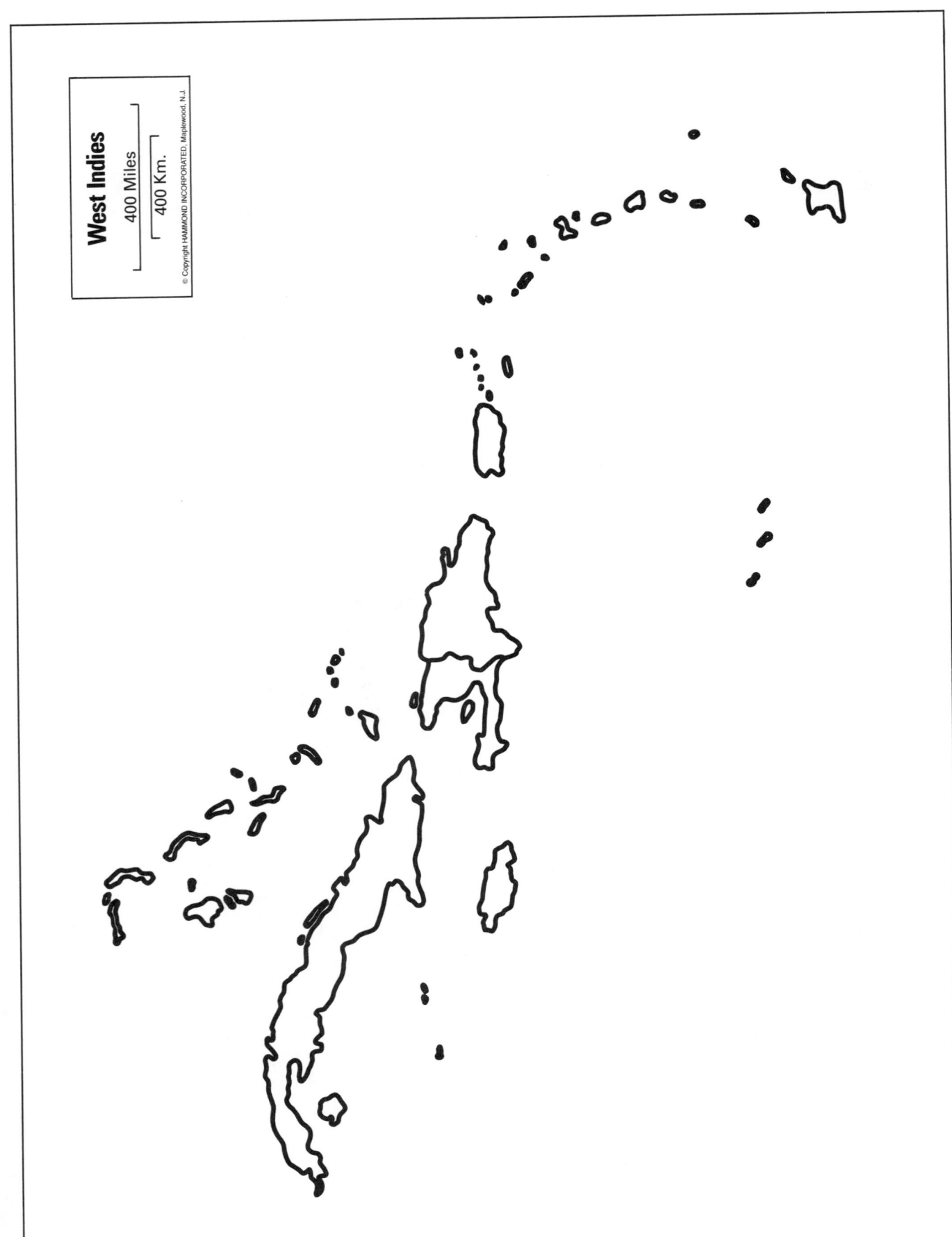

West Indies

400 Miles

400 Km.

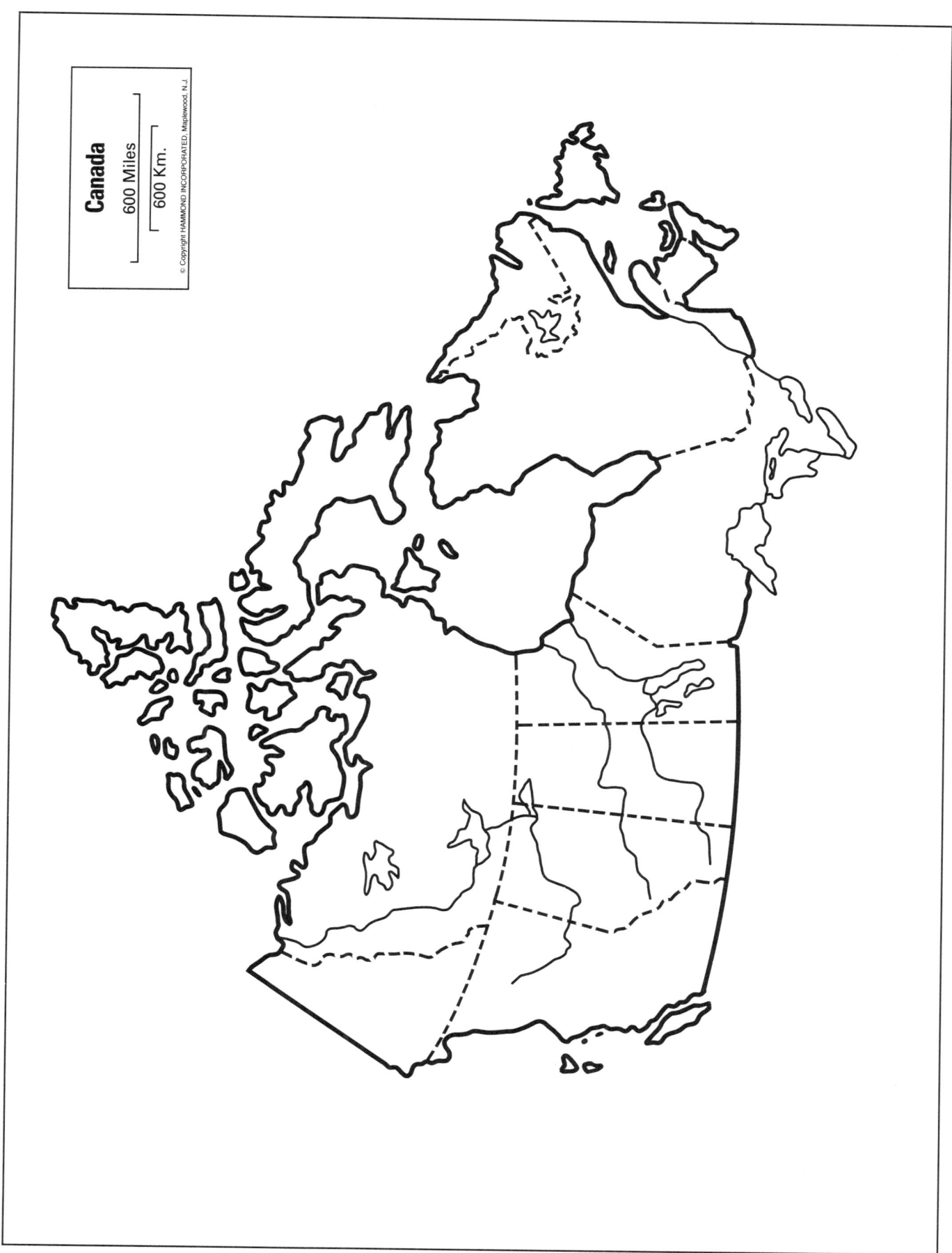

Canada

600 Miles

600 Km.

© Copyright HAMMOND INCORPORATED, Maplewood, N.J.

Alberta

200 Miles

200 Km.

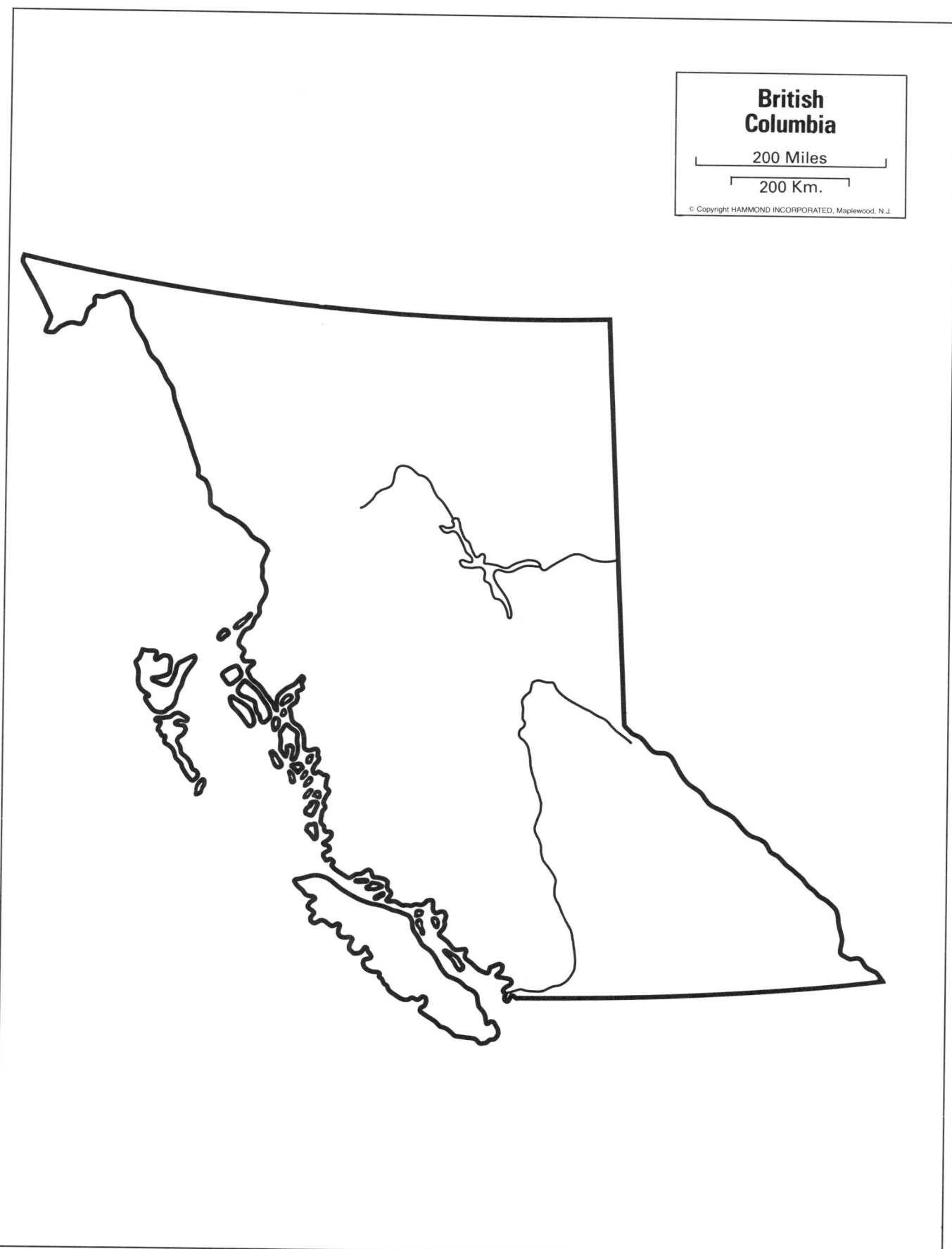

British Columbia

200 Miles

200 Km.

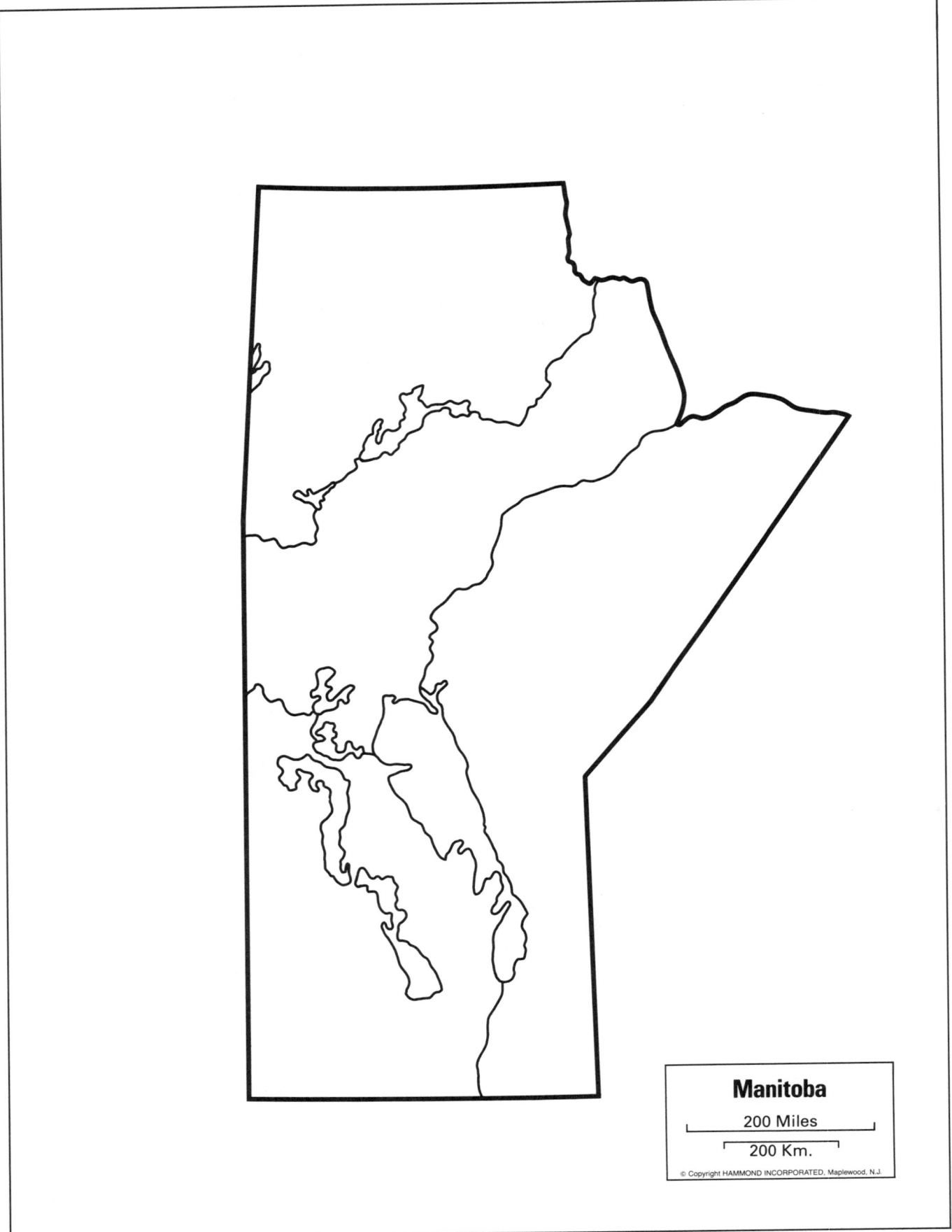

Manitoba

200 Miles

200 Km.

© Copyright HAMMOND INCORPORATED, Maplewood, N.J.

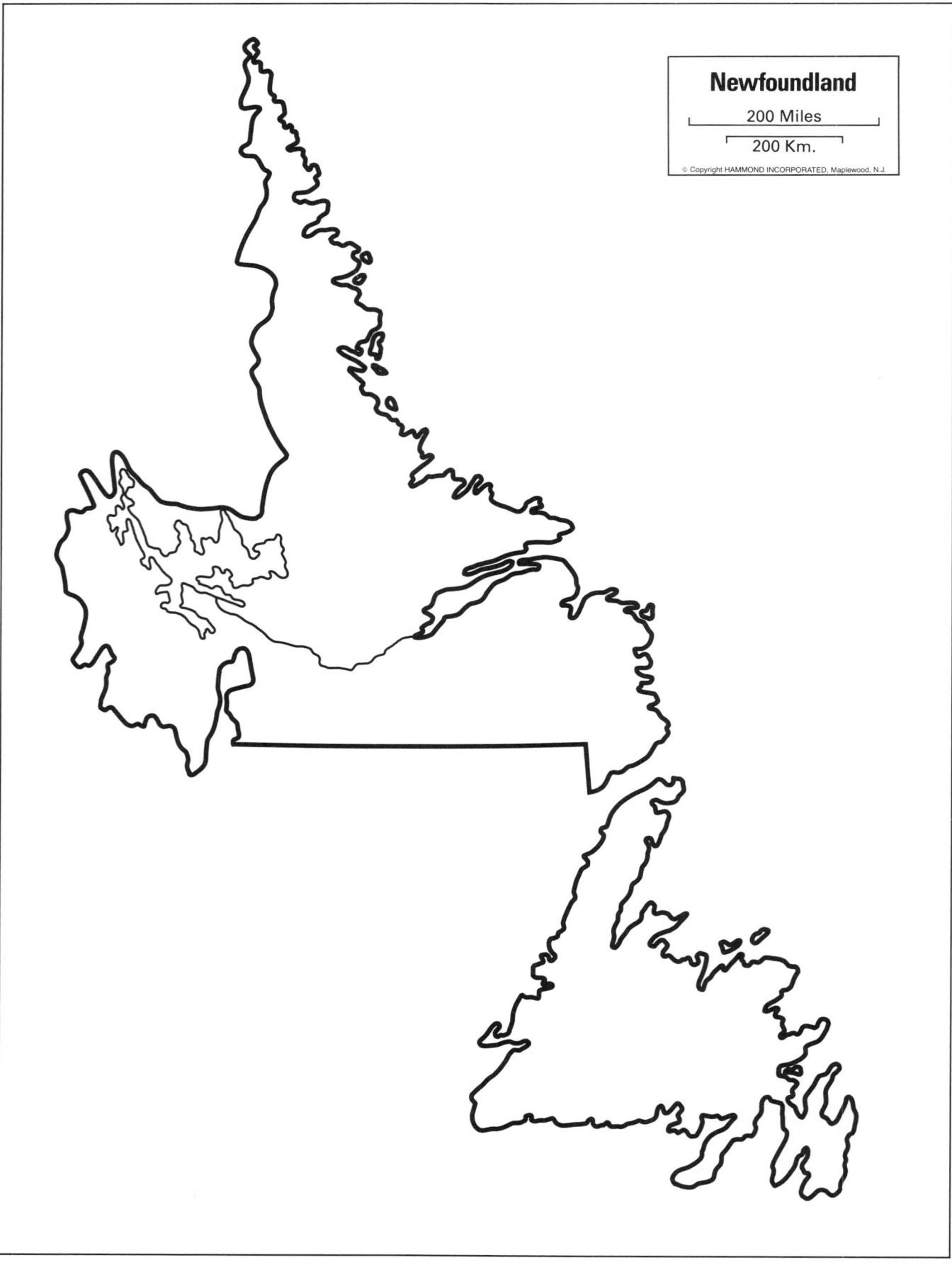

Newfoundland

200 Miles

200 Km.

© Copyright HAMMOND INCORPORATED, Maplewood, N.J.

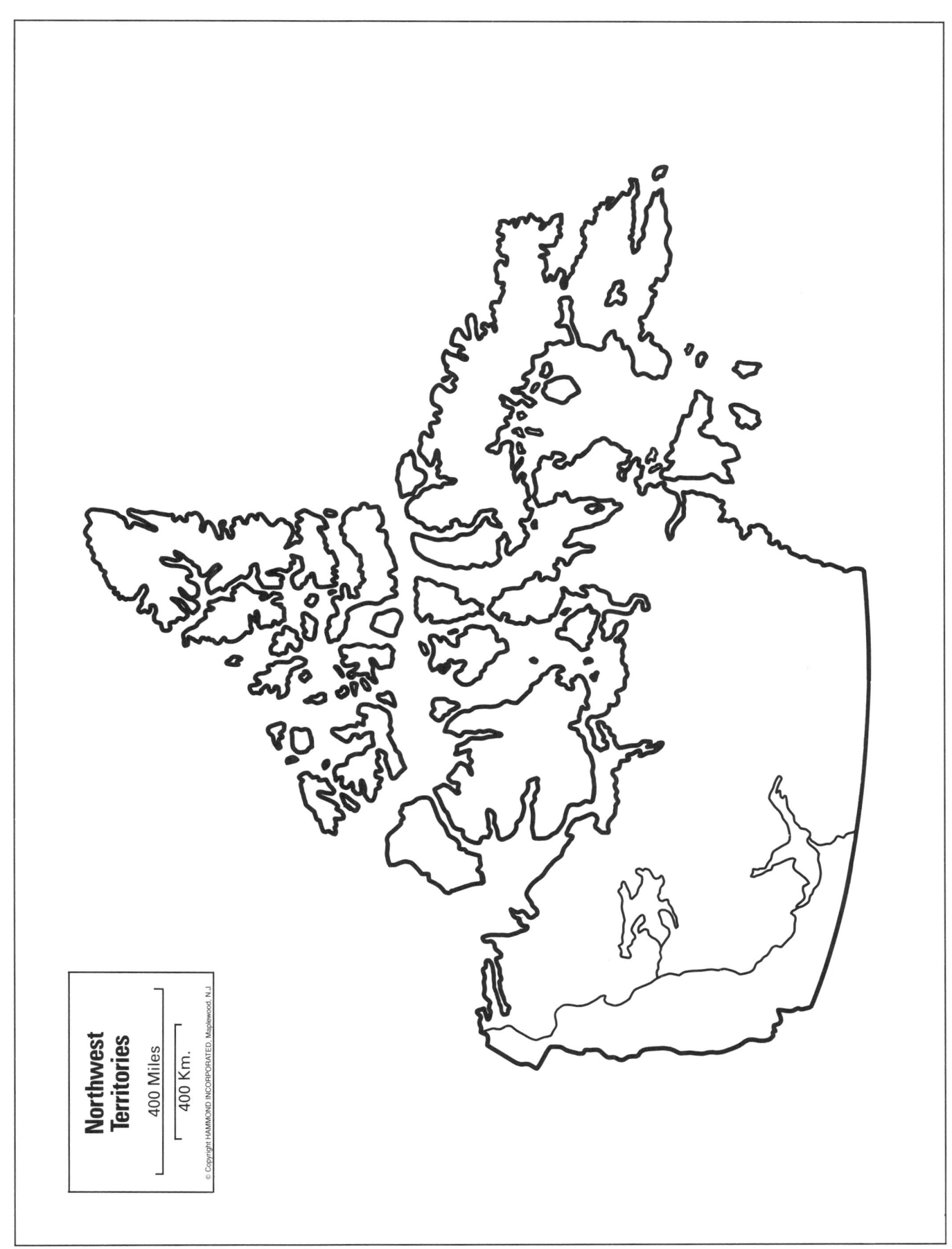

Northwest Territories

400 Miles

400 Km.

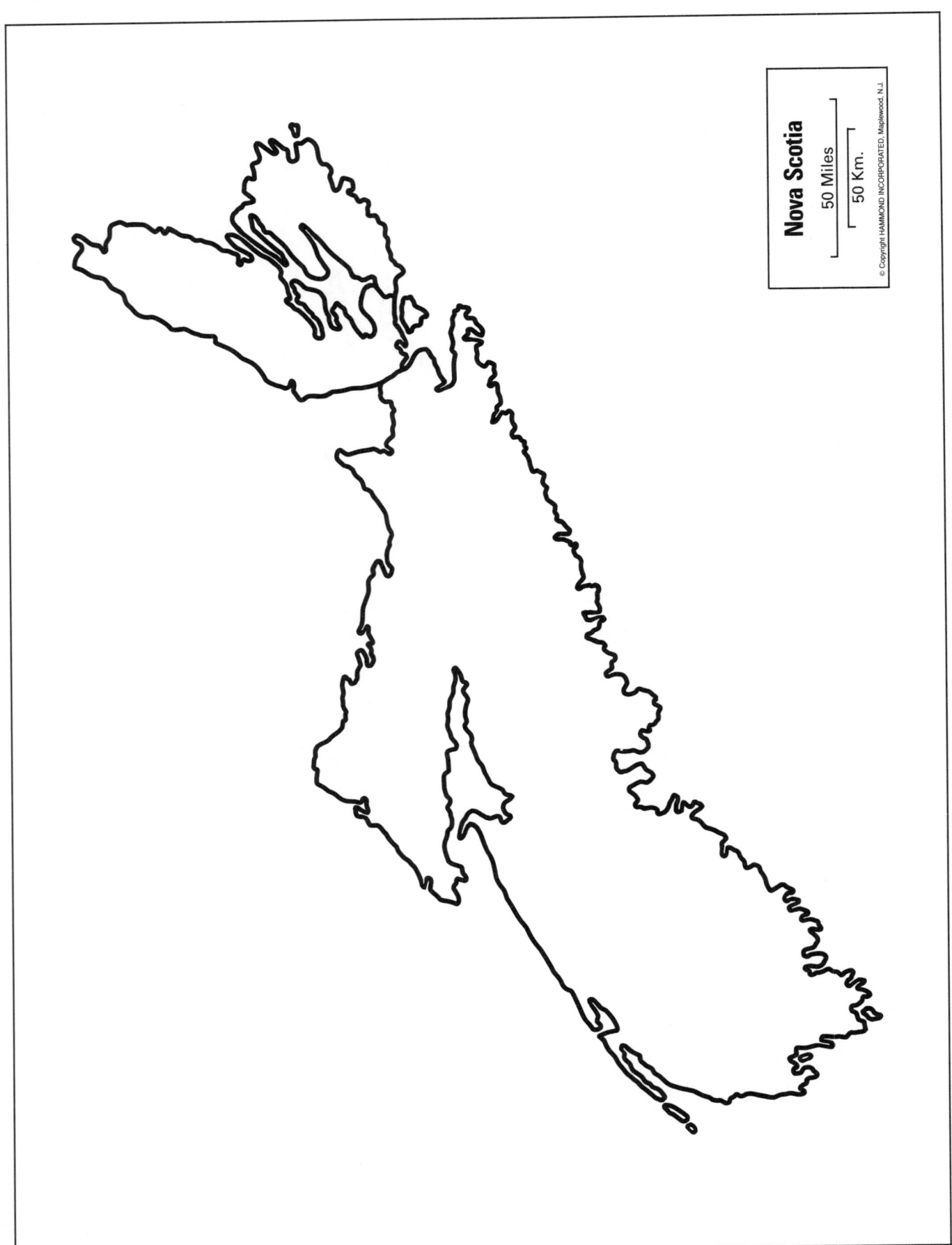

Nova Scotia

50 Miles

50 Km.

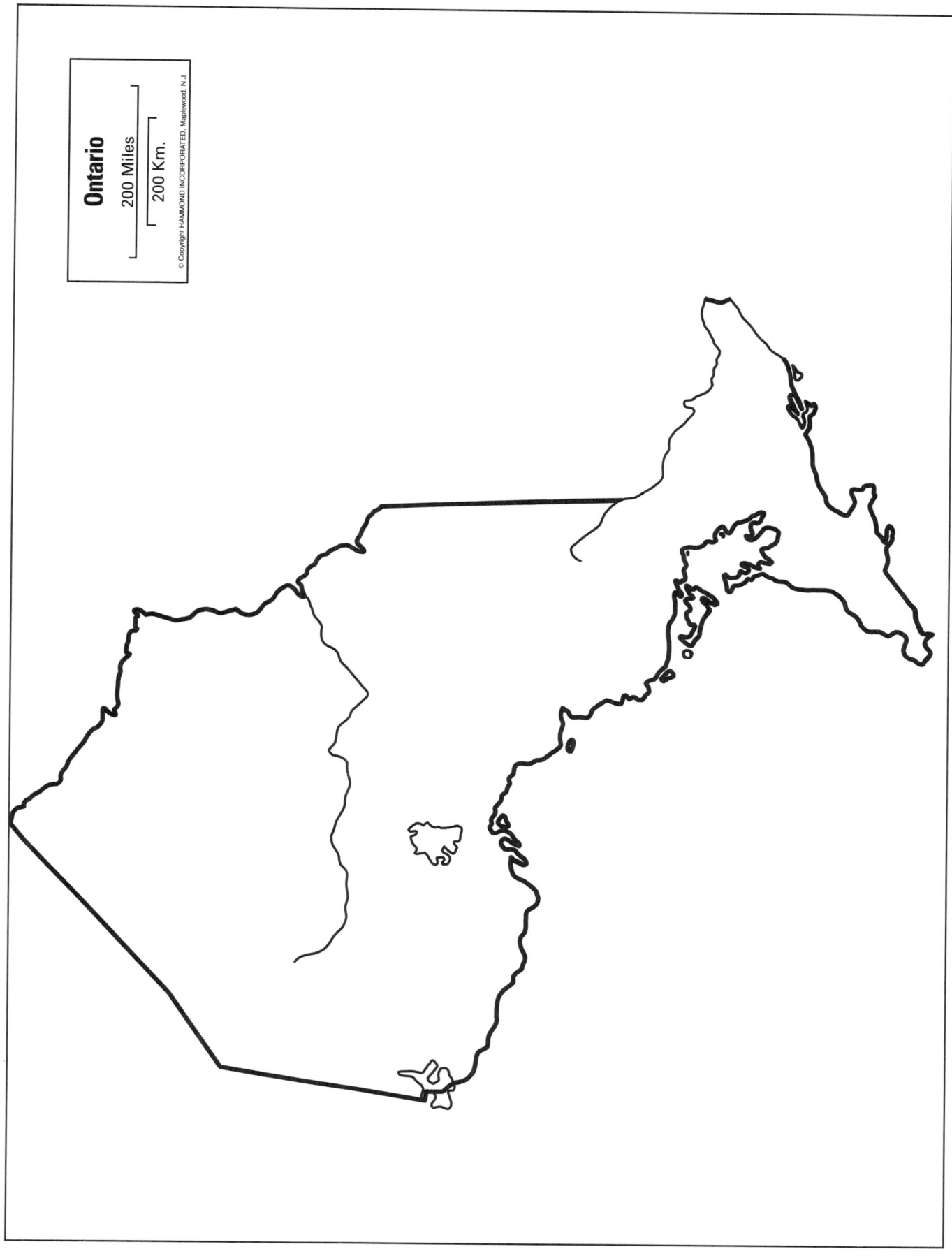

Ontario

200 Miles

200 Km.

© Copyright HAMMOND INCORPORATED, Maplewood, N.J.

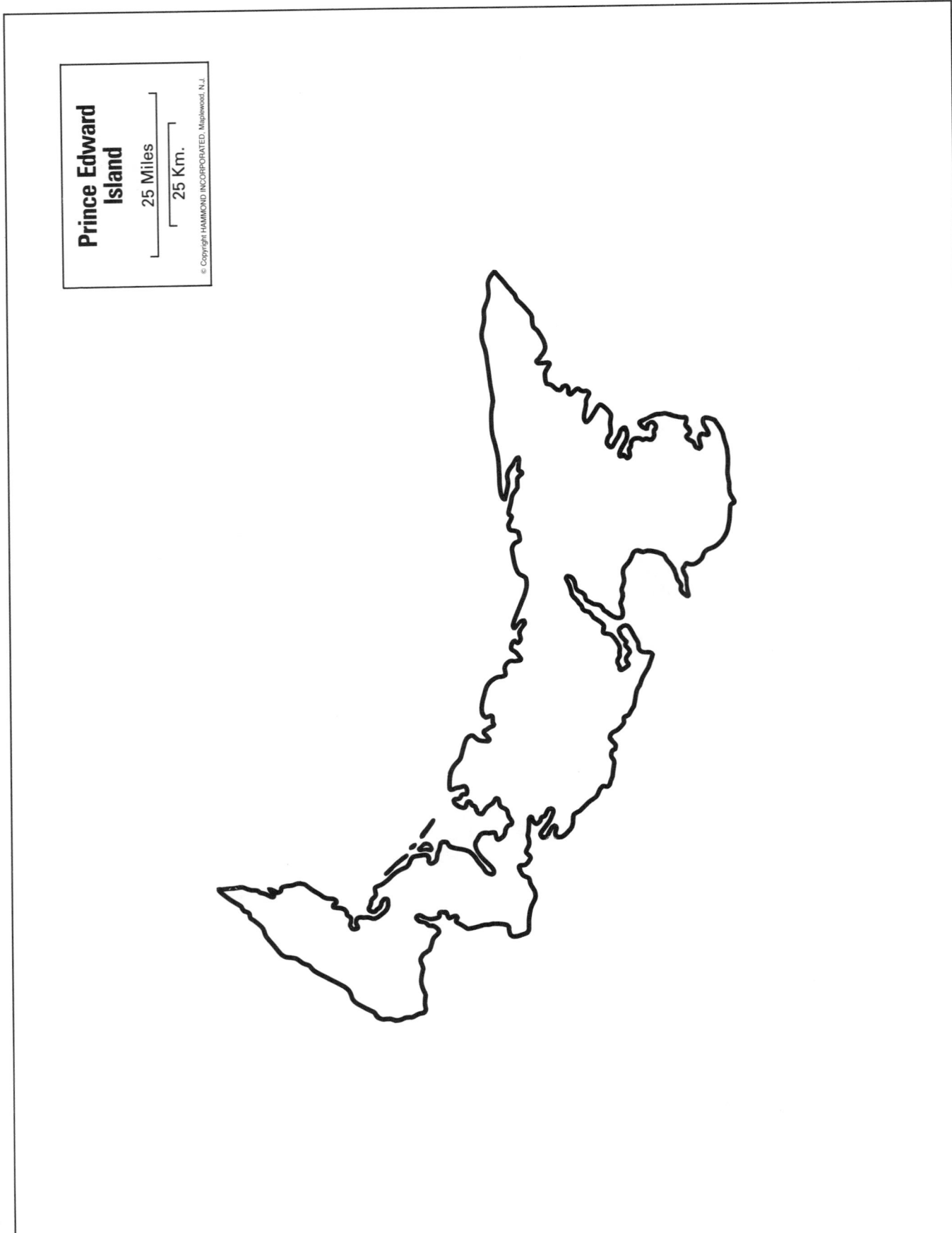

Prince Edward
Island

25 Miles

25 Km.

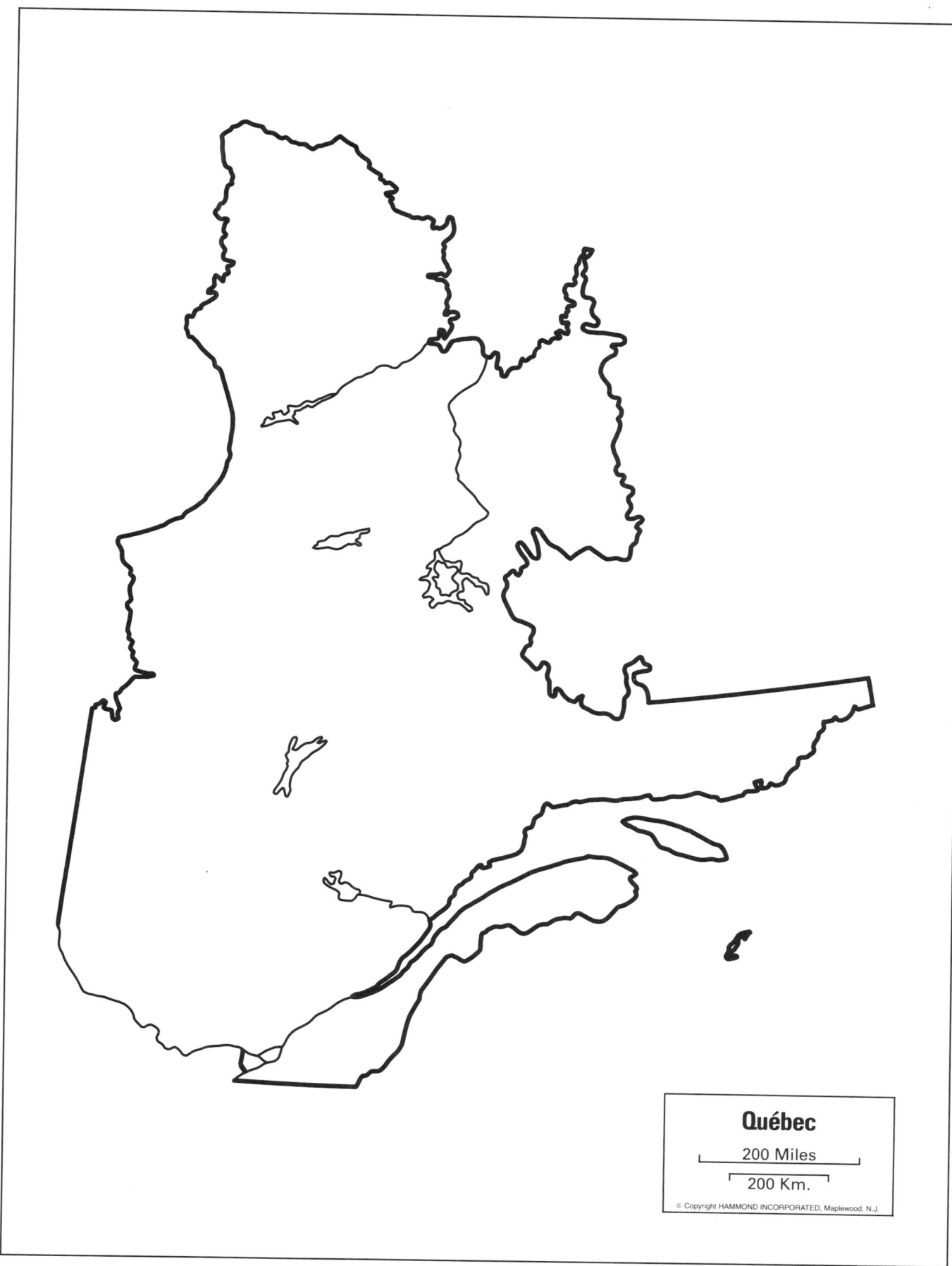

Québec

200 Miles

200 Km.

© Copyright HAMMOND INCORPORATED, Maplewood, N.J.

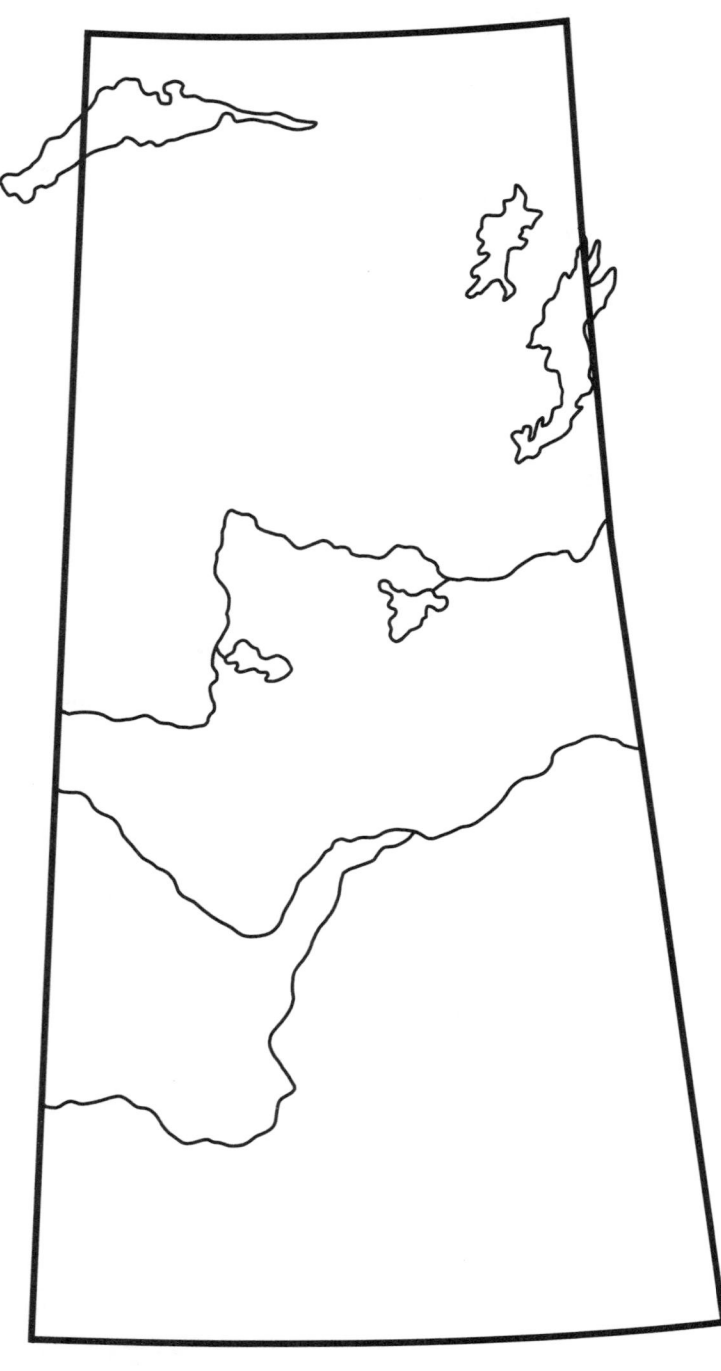

Saskatchewan

150 Miles

150 Km.

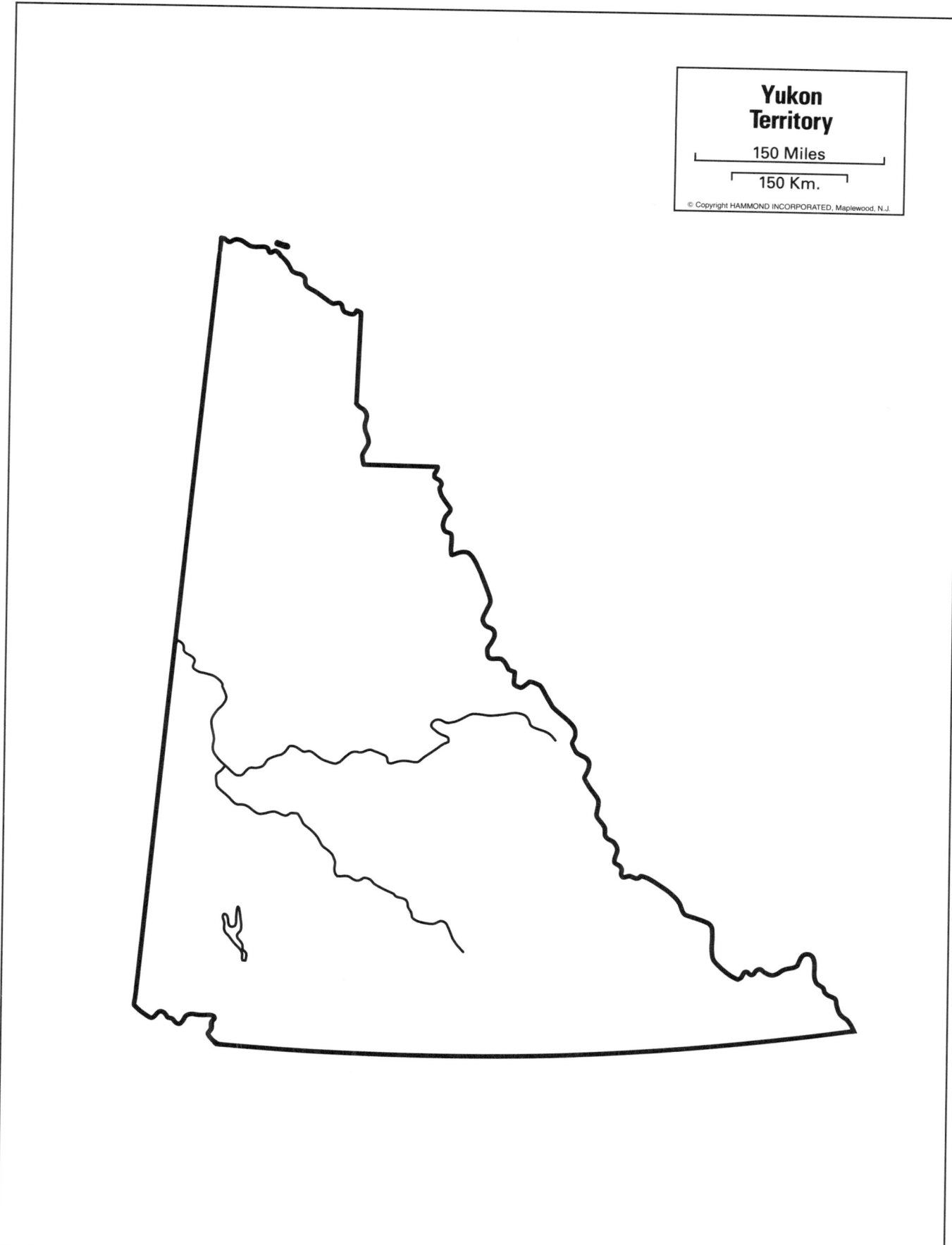

**Yukon
Territory**

150 Miles

150 Km.

United States

400 Miles
400 Km.

© Copyright HAMMOND INCORPORATED, Maplewood, N.J.

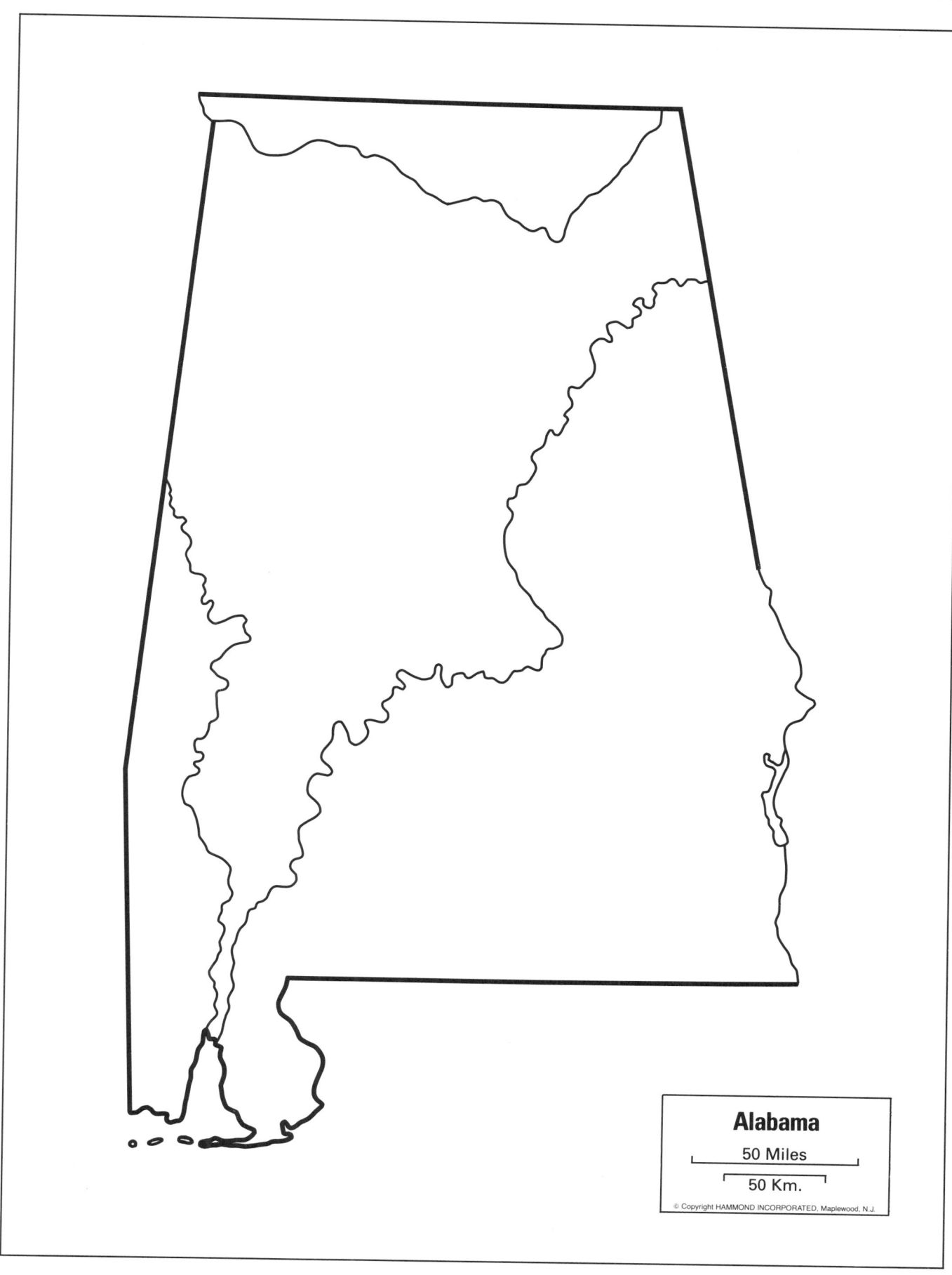

Alabama

50 Miles

50 Km.

© Copyright HAMMOND INCORPORATED, Maplewood, N.J.

616

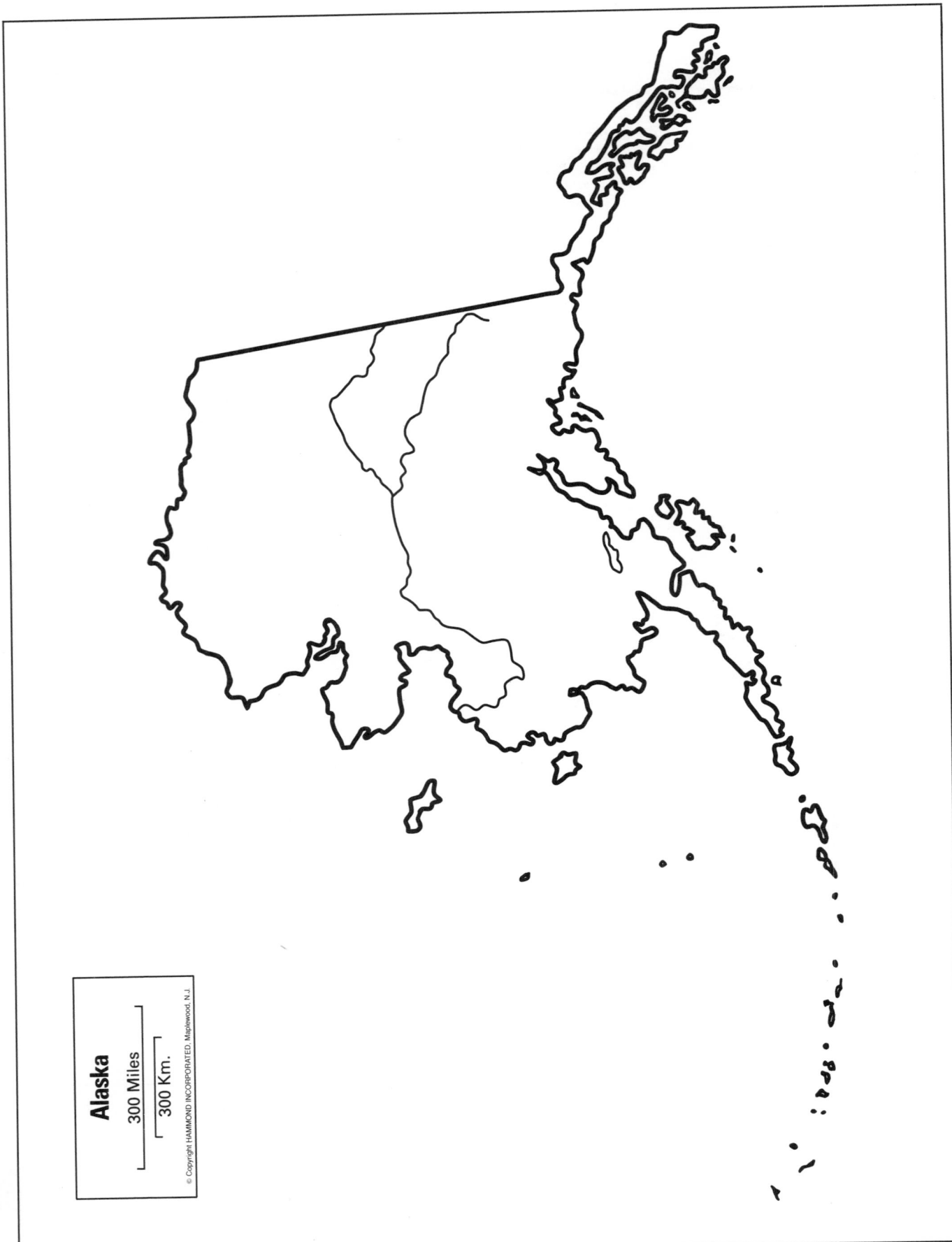

Alaska

300 Miles

300 Km.

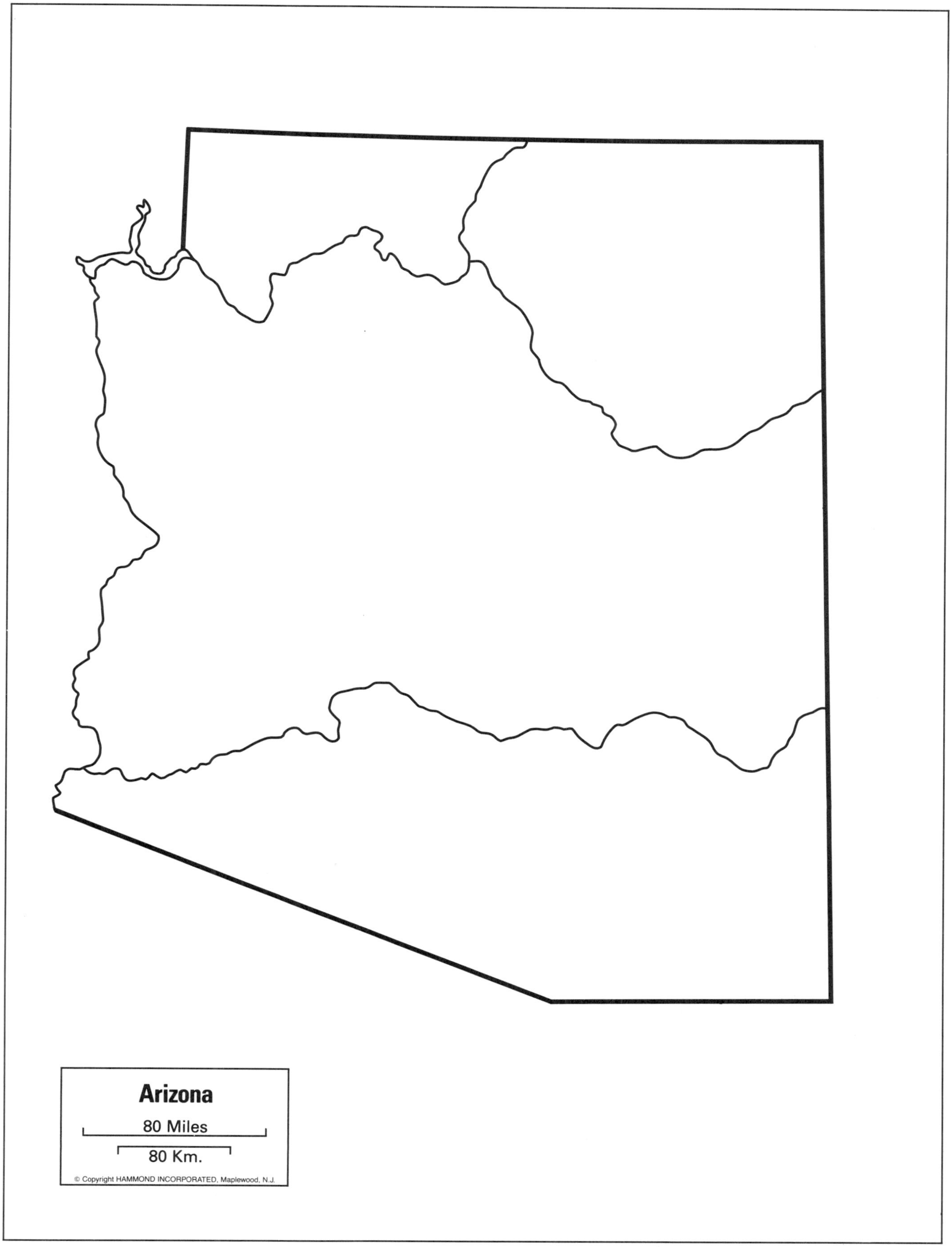

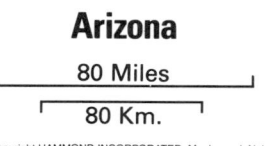

Arizona

|———— 80 Miles ————|

|——— 80 Km. ———|

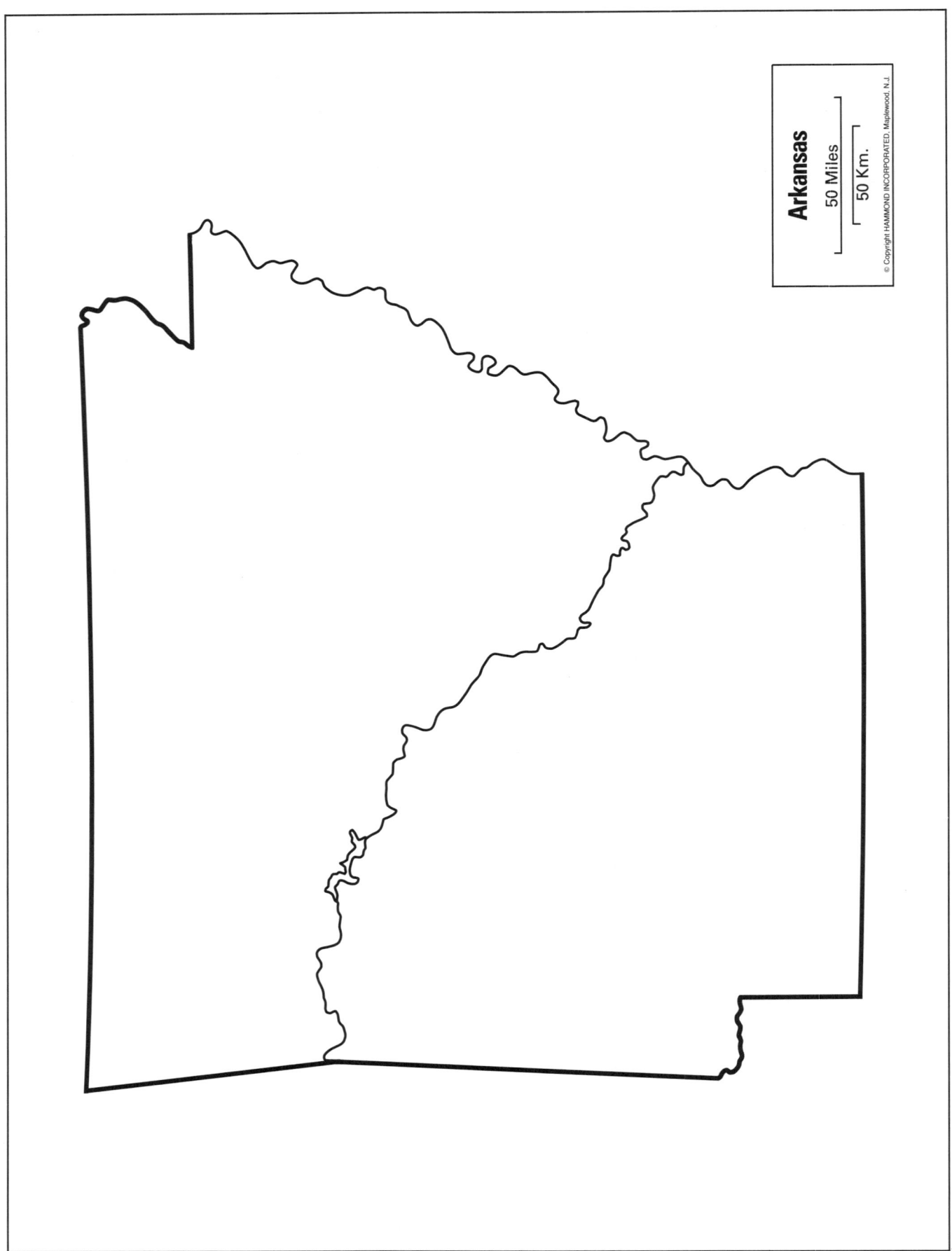

Arkansas

50 Miles

50 Km.

© Copyright HAMMOND INCORPORATED, Maplewood, N.J.

California

100 Miles

100 Km.

© Copyright HAMMOND INCORPORATED, Maplewood, N.J.

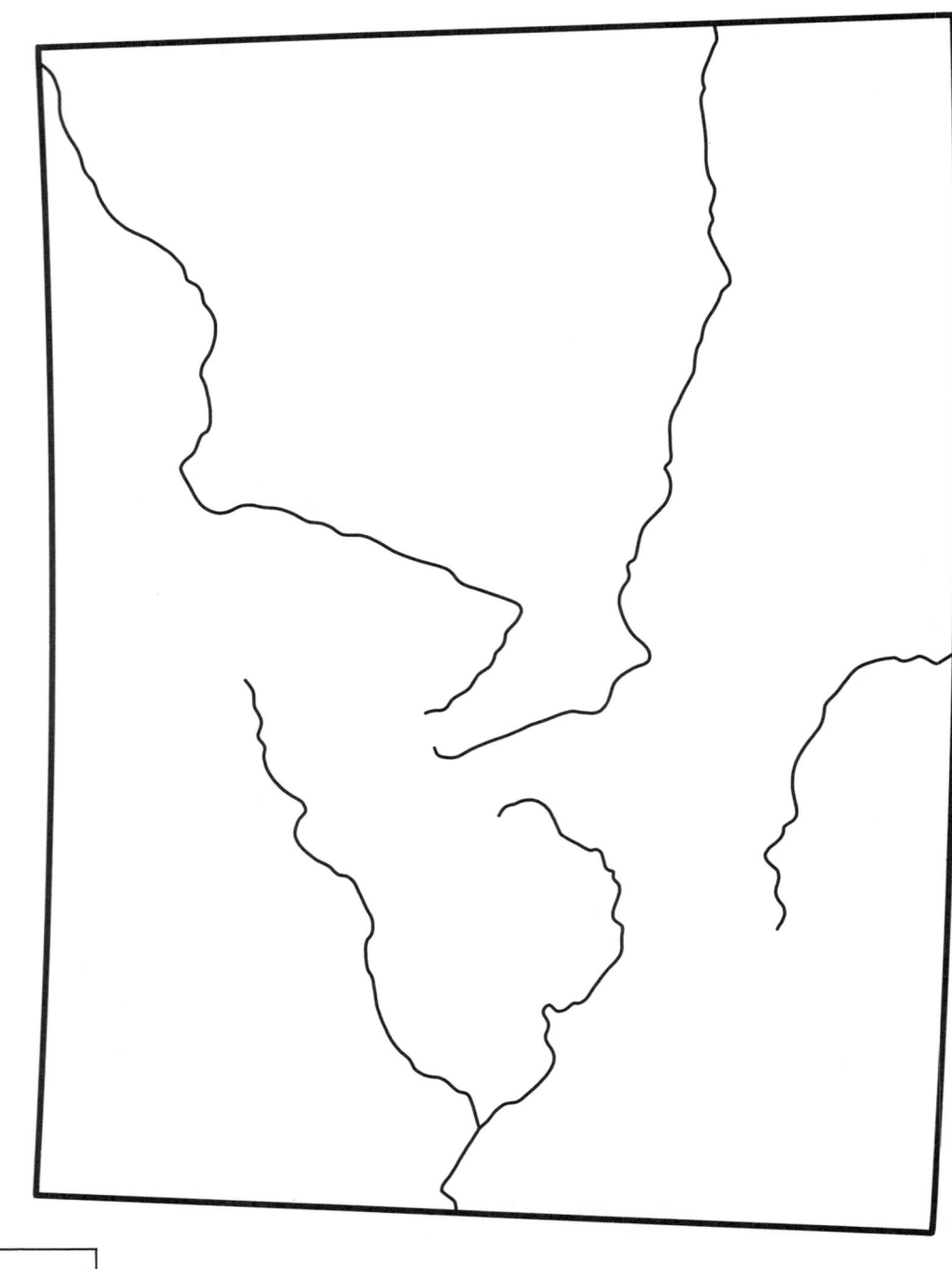

Colorado

75 Miles

75 Km.

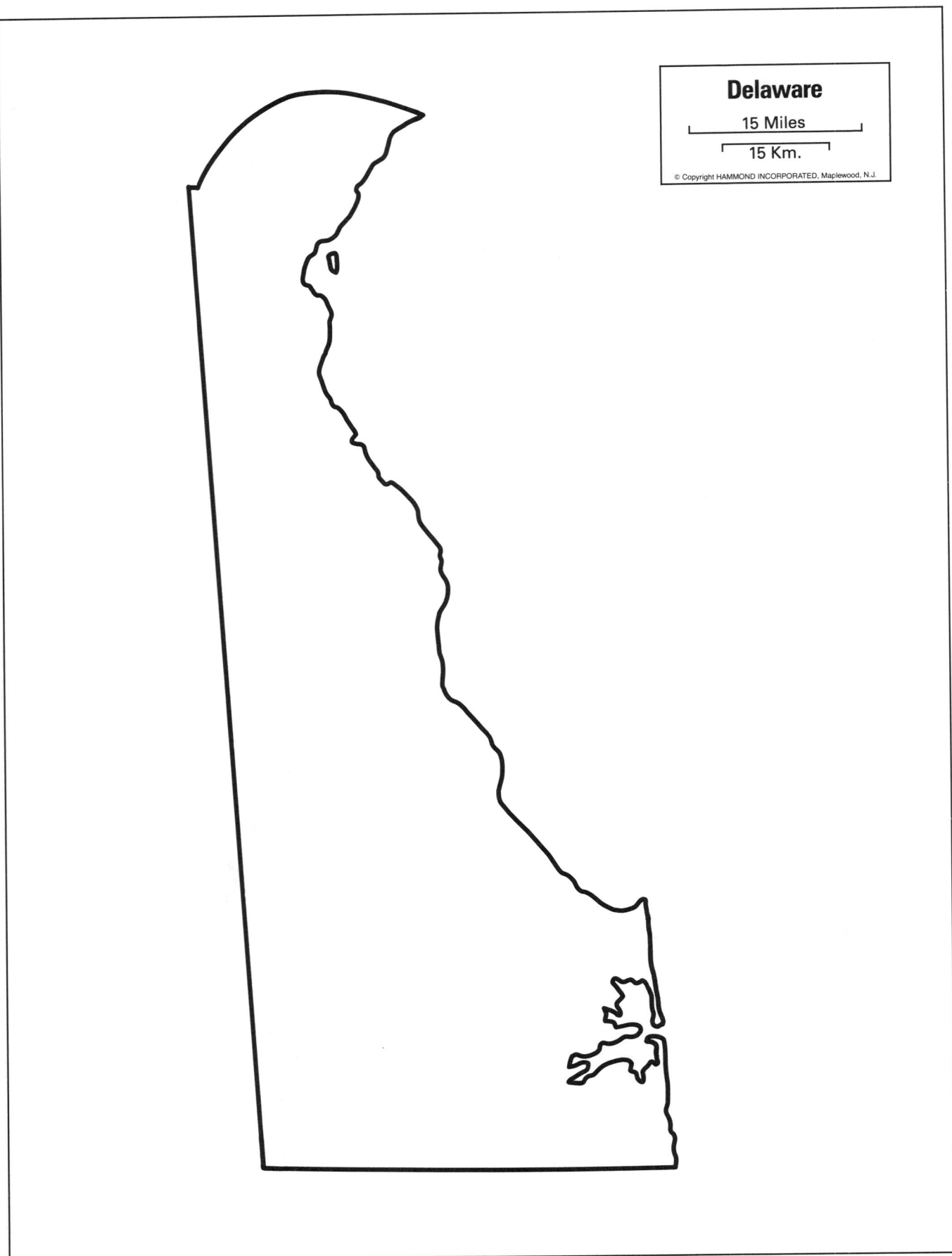

Delaware

15 Miles

15 Km.

Florida

80 Miles

80 Km.

© Copyright HAMMOND INCORPORATED, Maplewood, N.J.

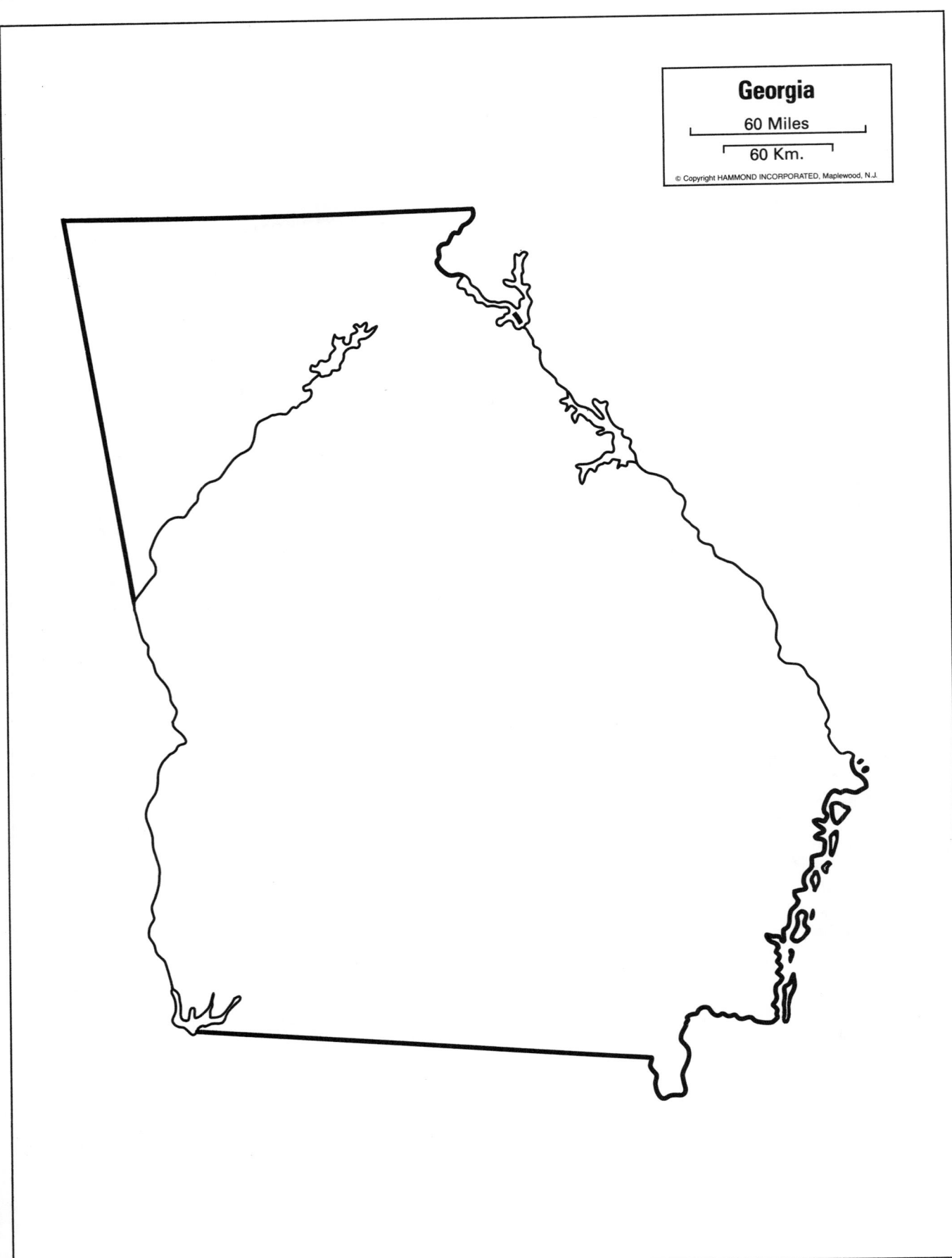

Georgia

60 Miles

60 Km.

© Copyright HAMMOND INCORPORATED, Maplewood, N.J.

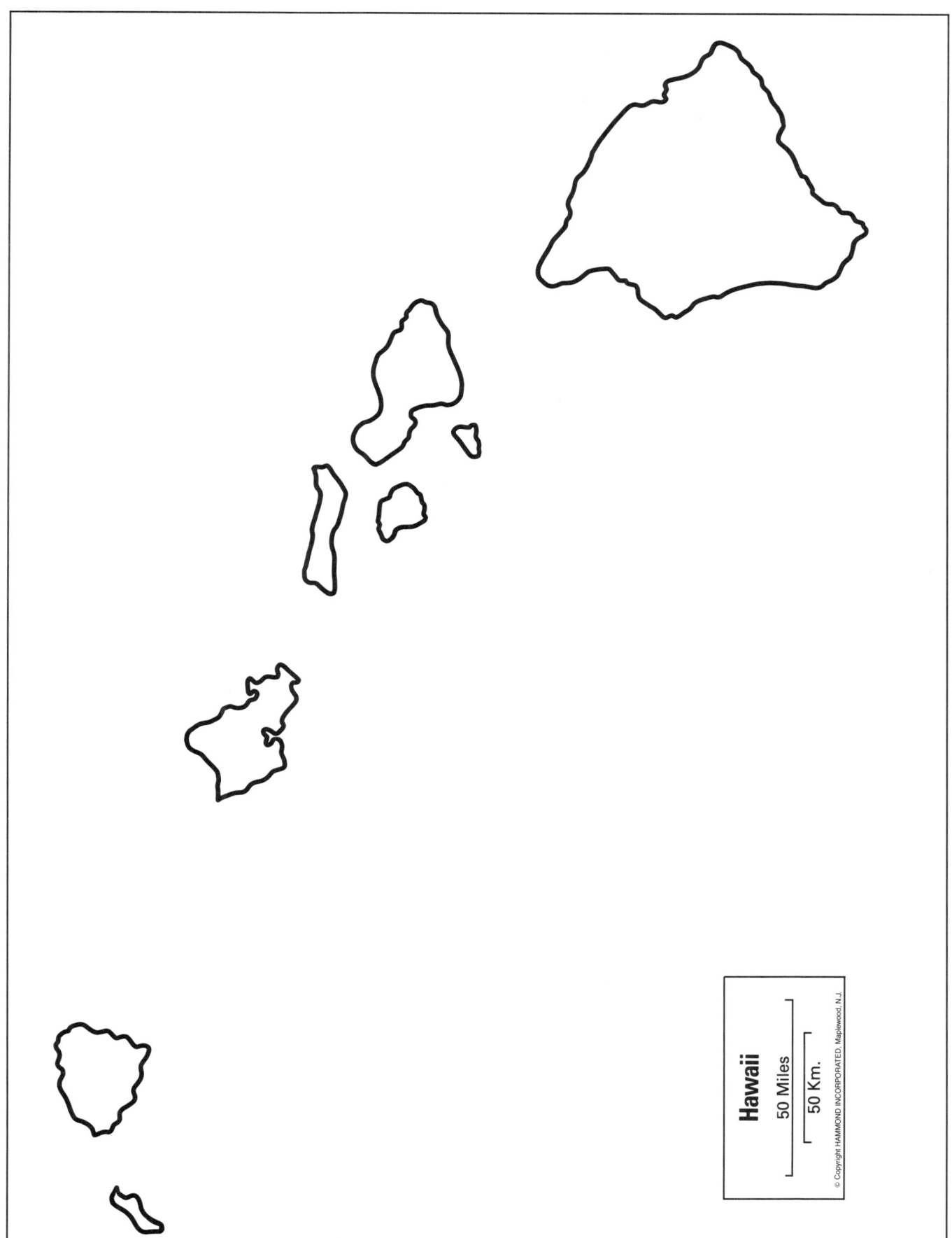

Hawaii

50 Miles

50 Km.

© Copyright HAMMOND INCORPORATED, Maplewood, N.J.

626

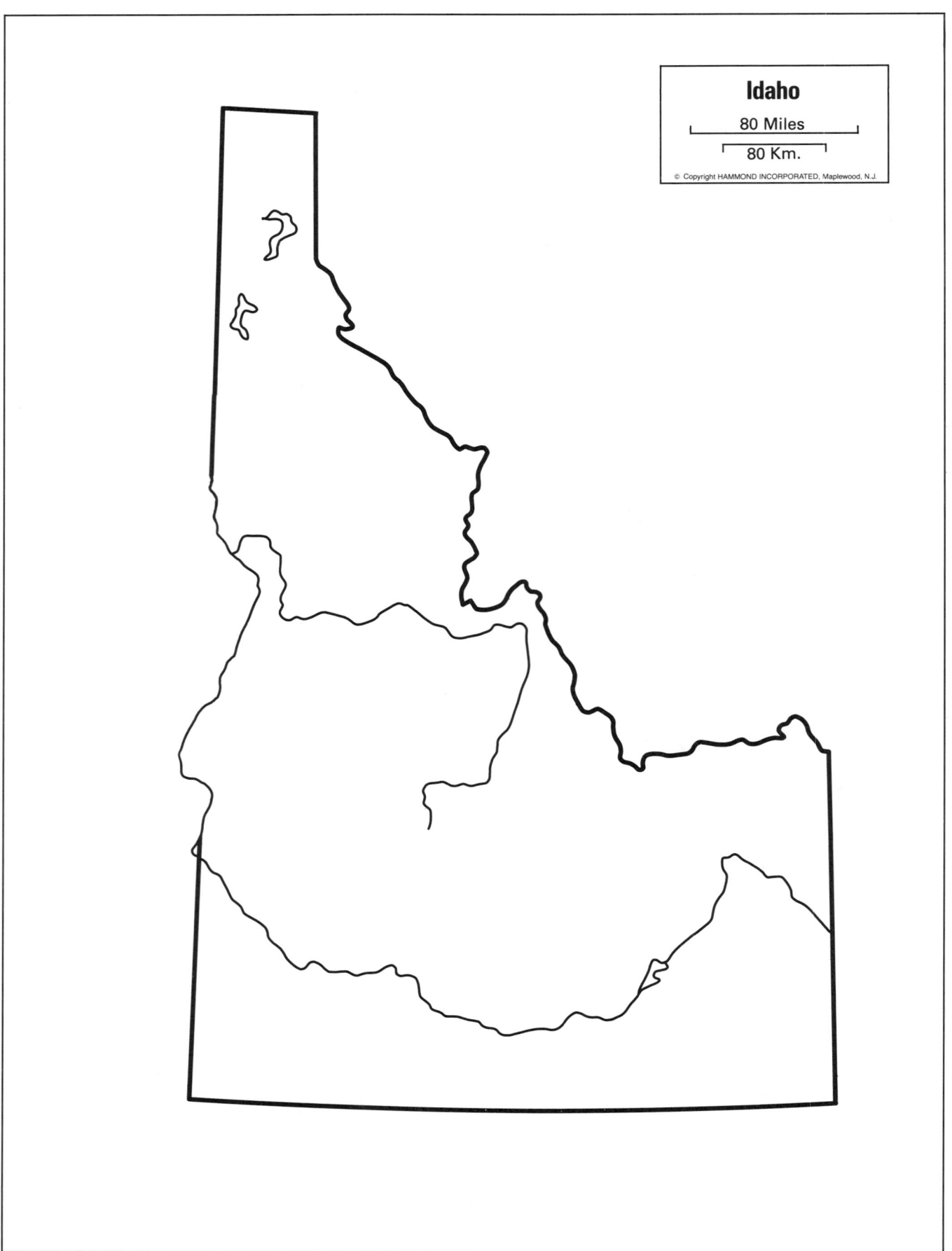

Idaho

80 Miles

80 Km.

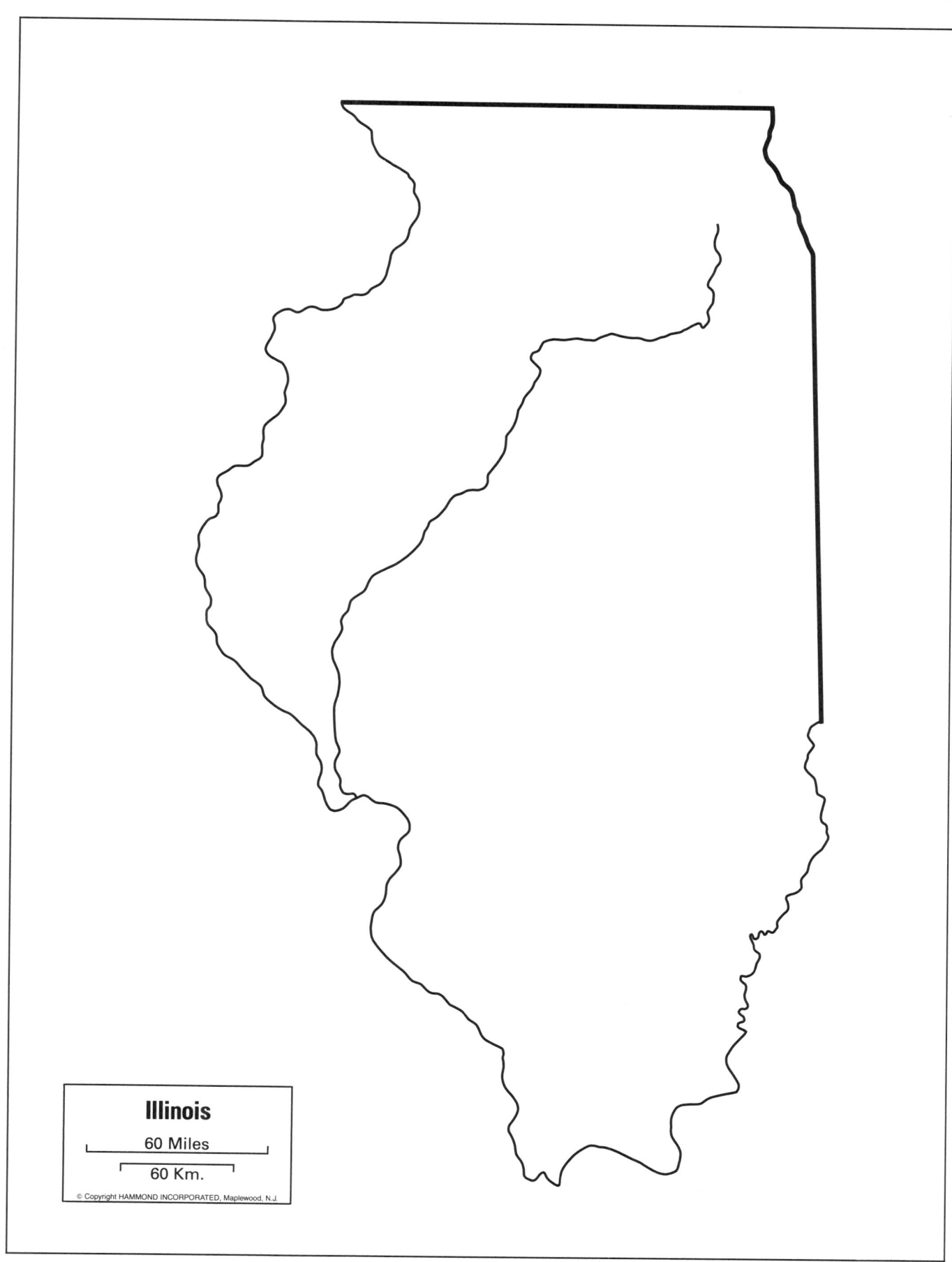

Illinois

60 Miles

60 Km.

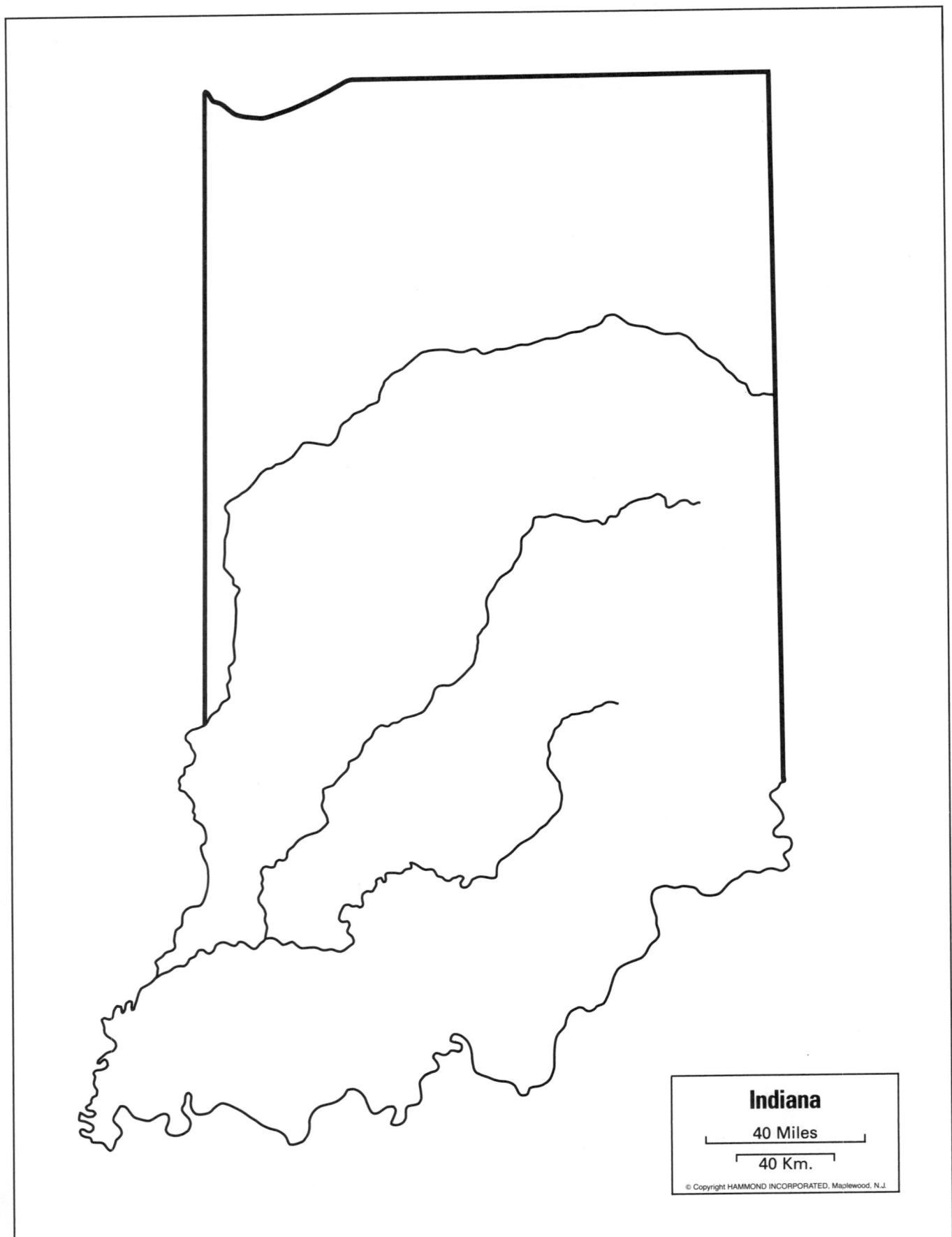

Indiana

40 Miles

40 Km.

© Copyright HAMMOND INCORPORATED, Maplewood, N.J.

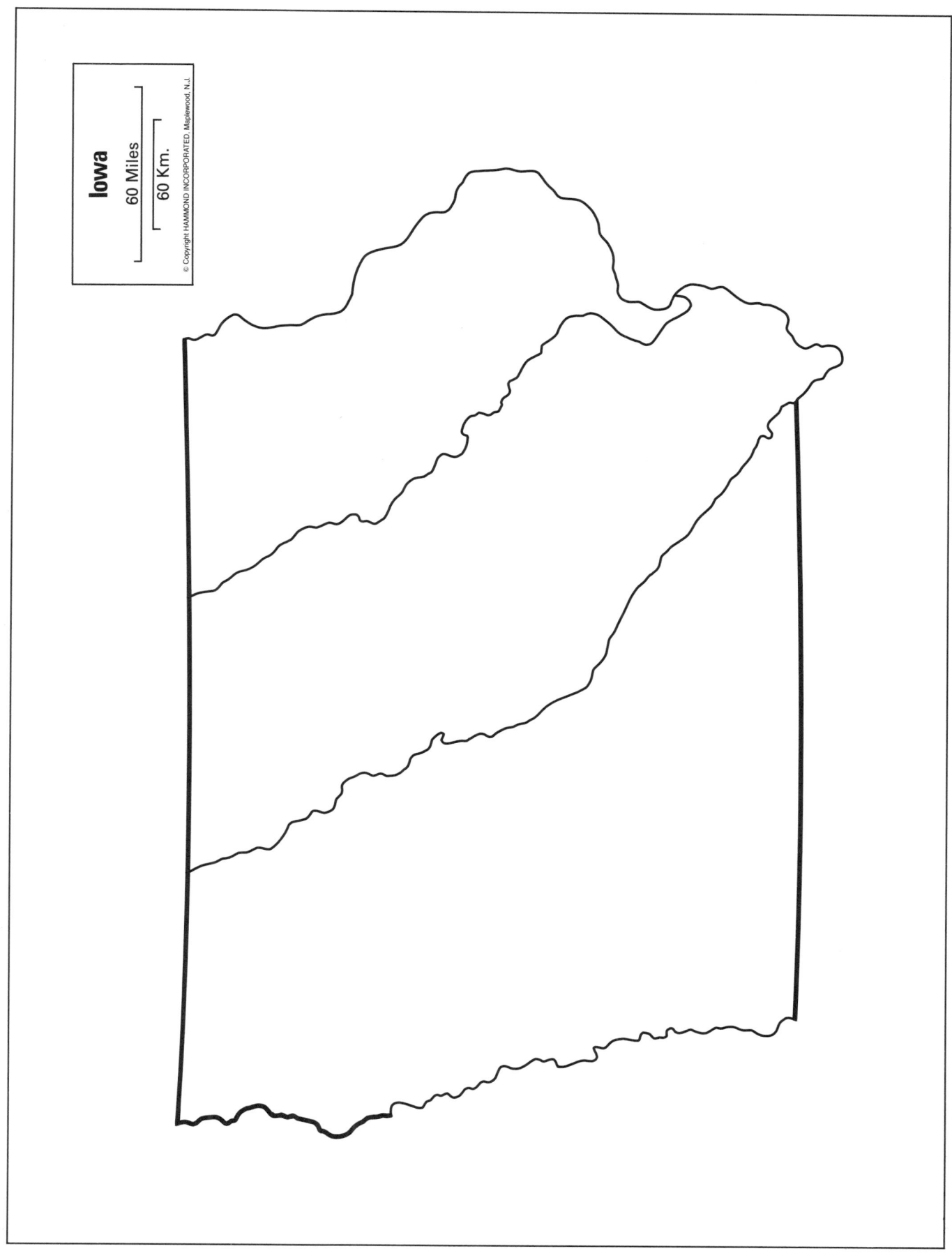

Iowa

60 Miles

60 Km.

© Copyright HAMMOND INCORPORATED, Maplewood, N.J.

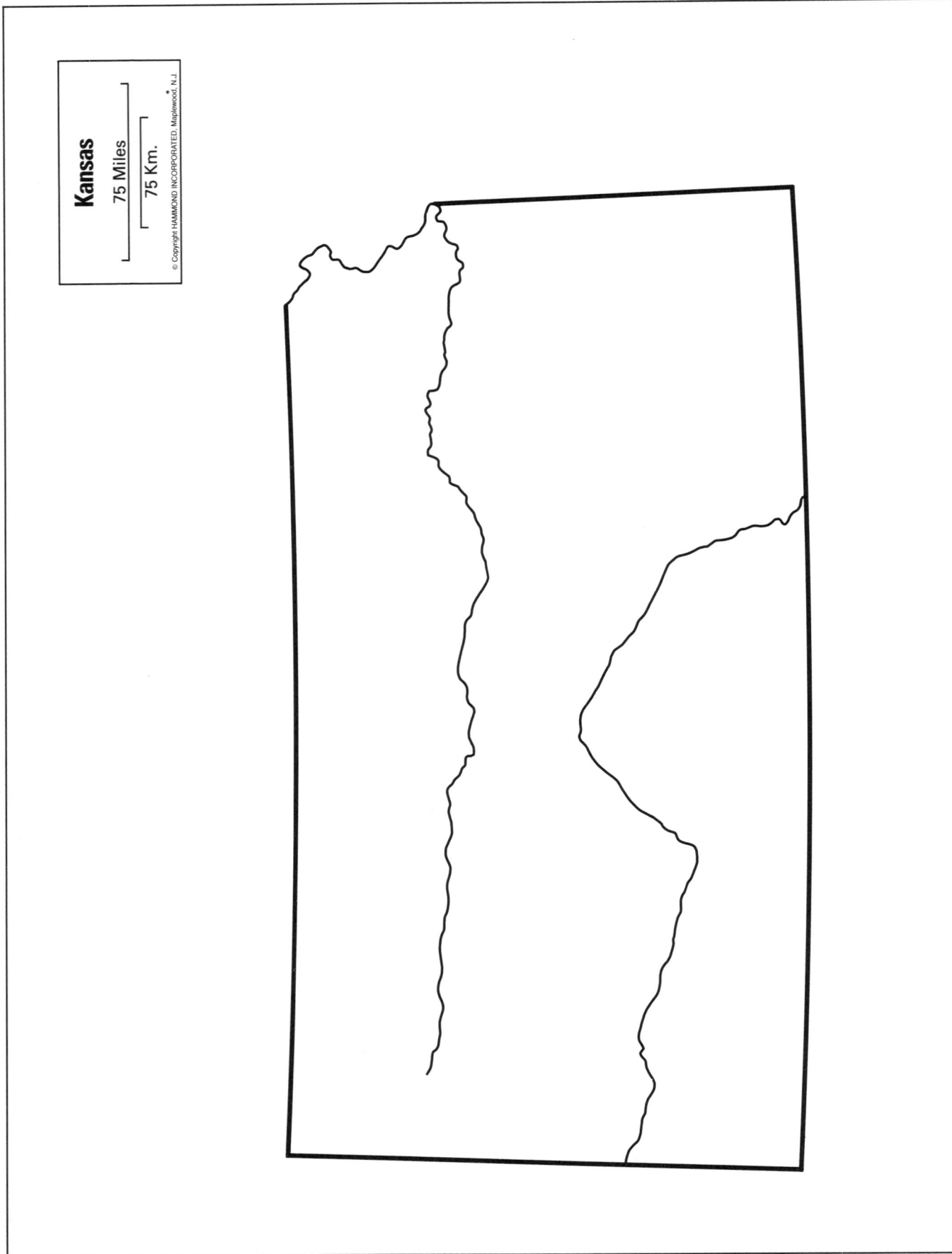

Kansas

75 Miles

75 Km.

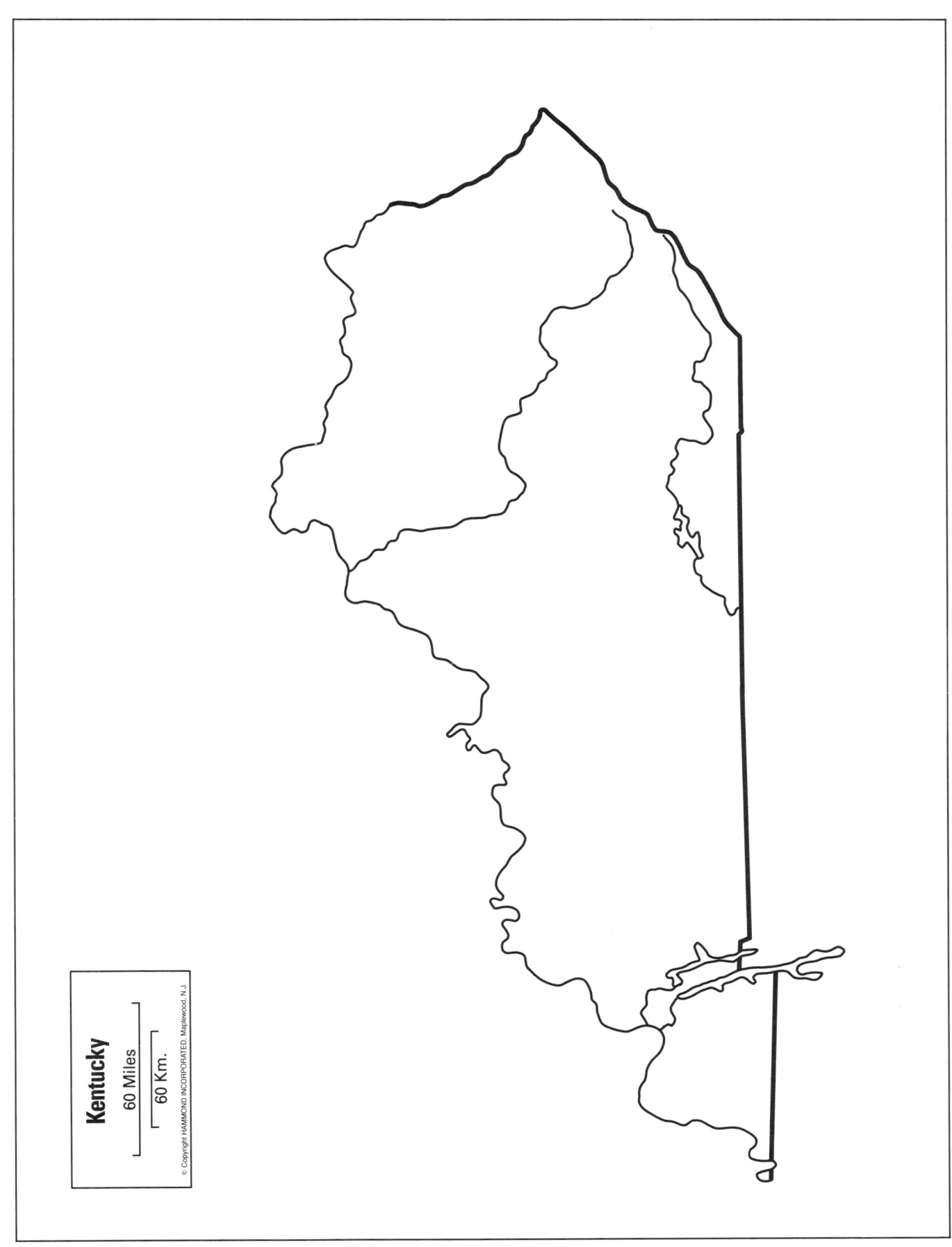

Kentucky

60 Miles

60 Km.

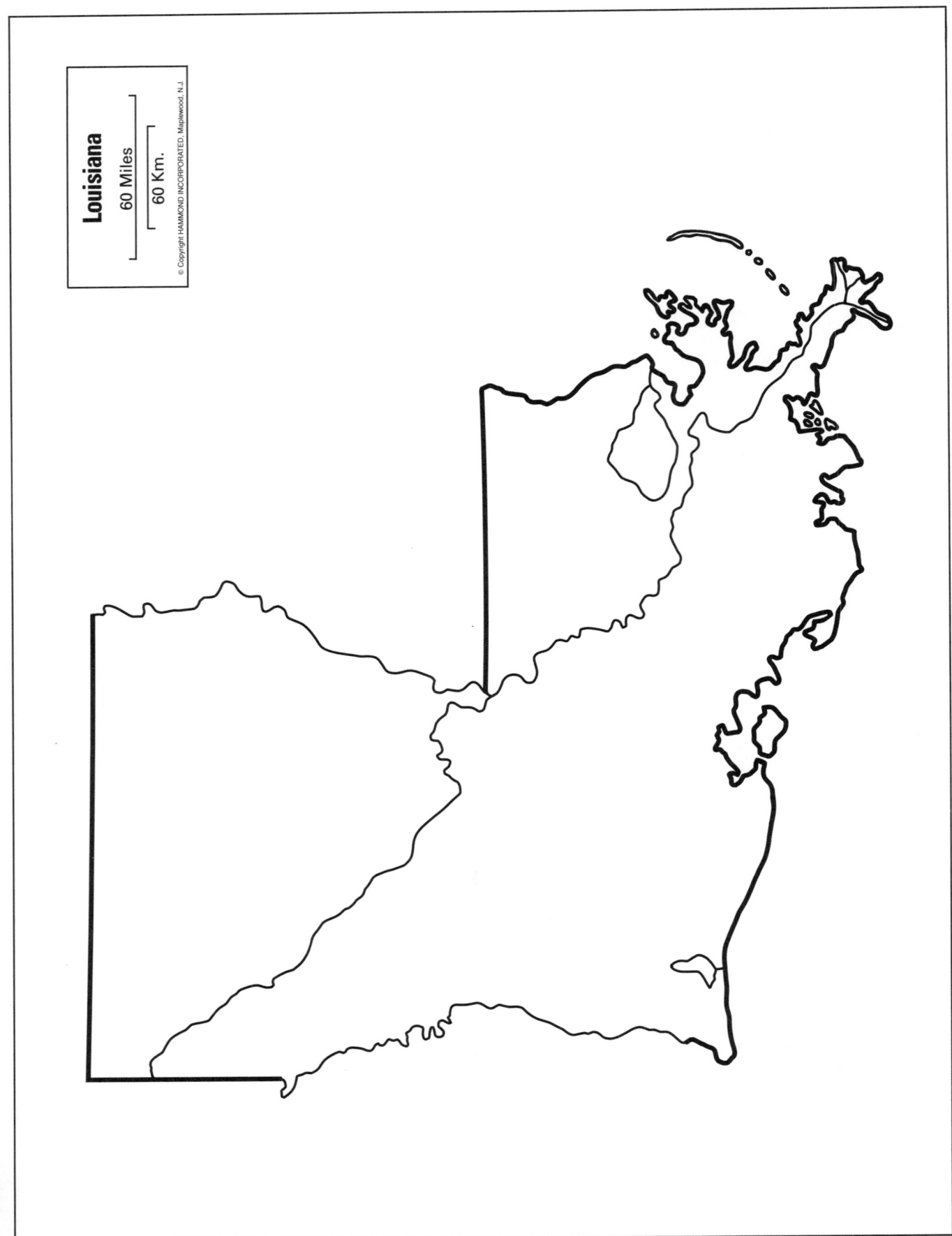

Louisiana

60 Miles

60 Km.

© Copyright HAMMOND INCORPORATED, Maplewood, N.J.

Maine

50 Miles

50 Km.

Maryland

40 Miles

40 Km.

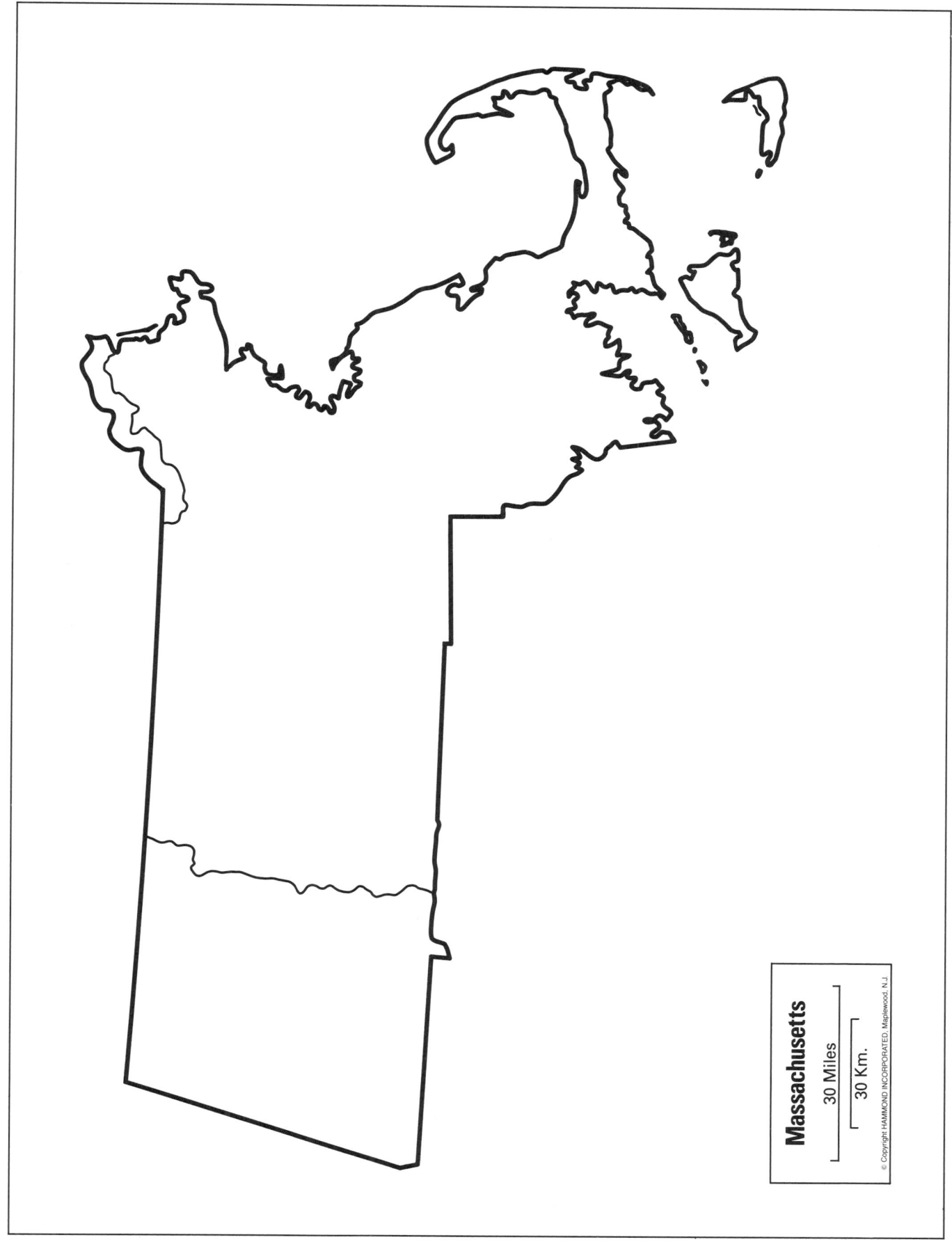

Massachusetts

30 Miles

30 Km.

Michigan

80 Miles

80 Km.

© Copyright HAMMOND INCORPORATED, Maplewood, N.J.

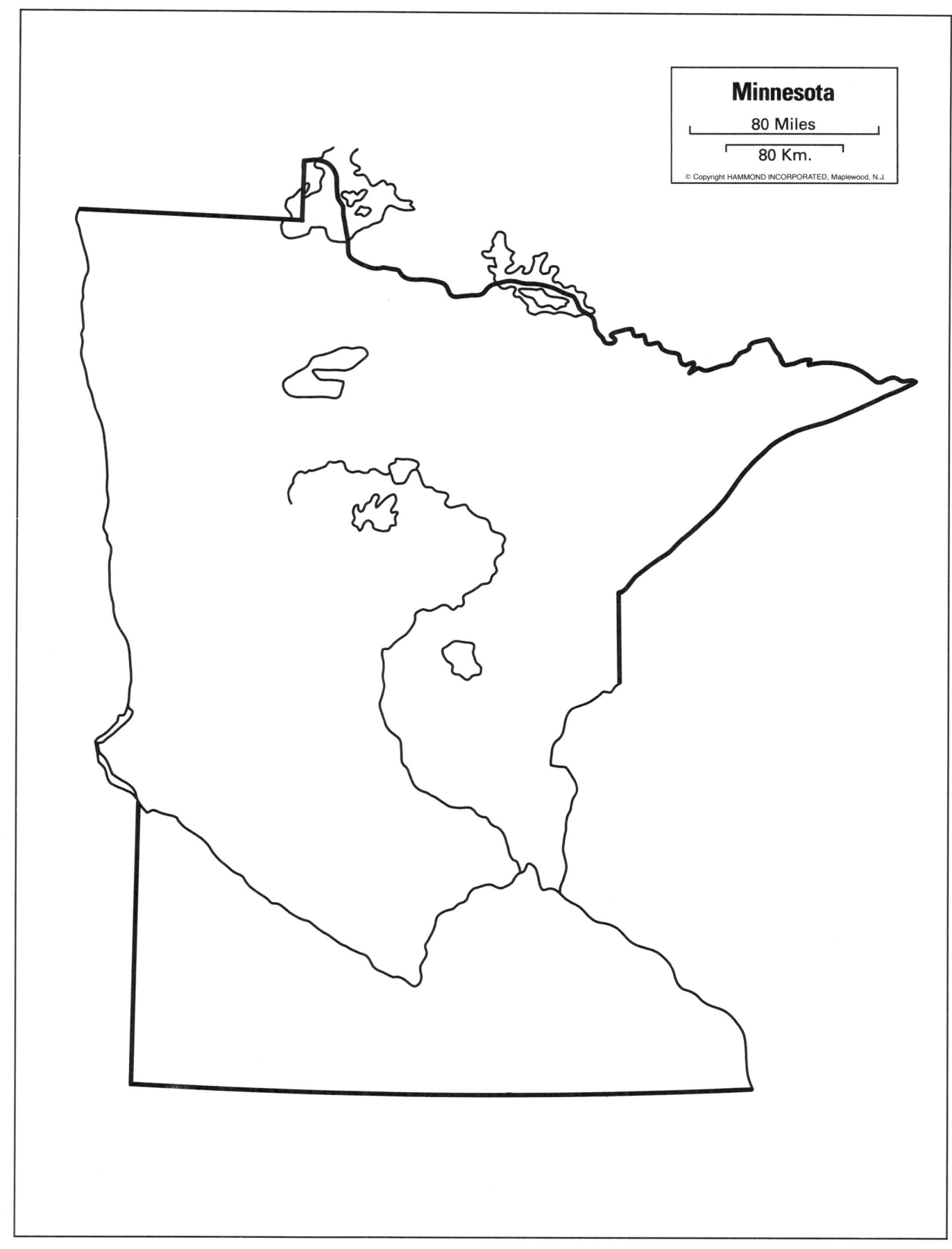

Minnesota

80 Miles

80 Km.

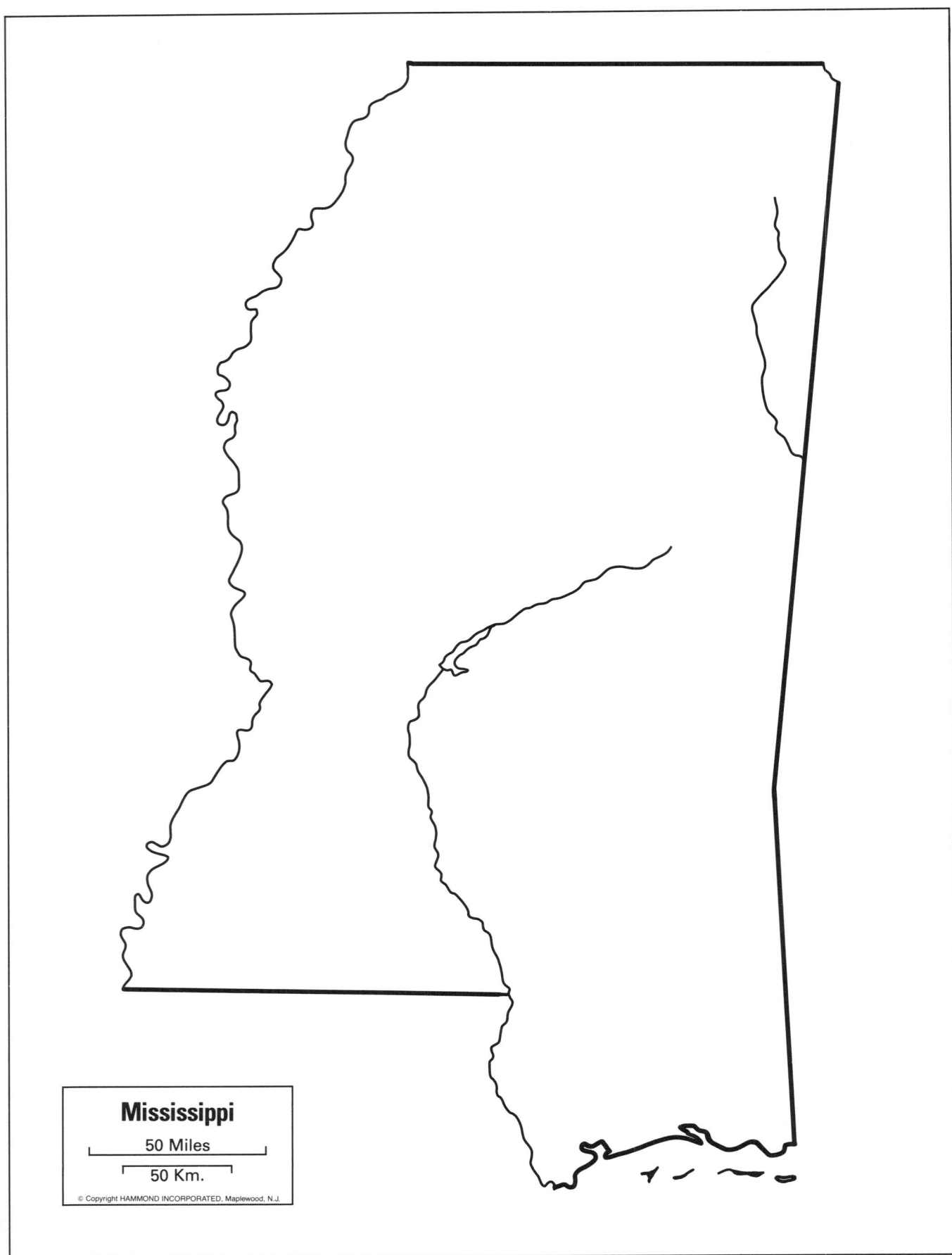

Mississippi

50 Miles

50 Km.

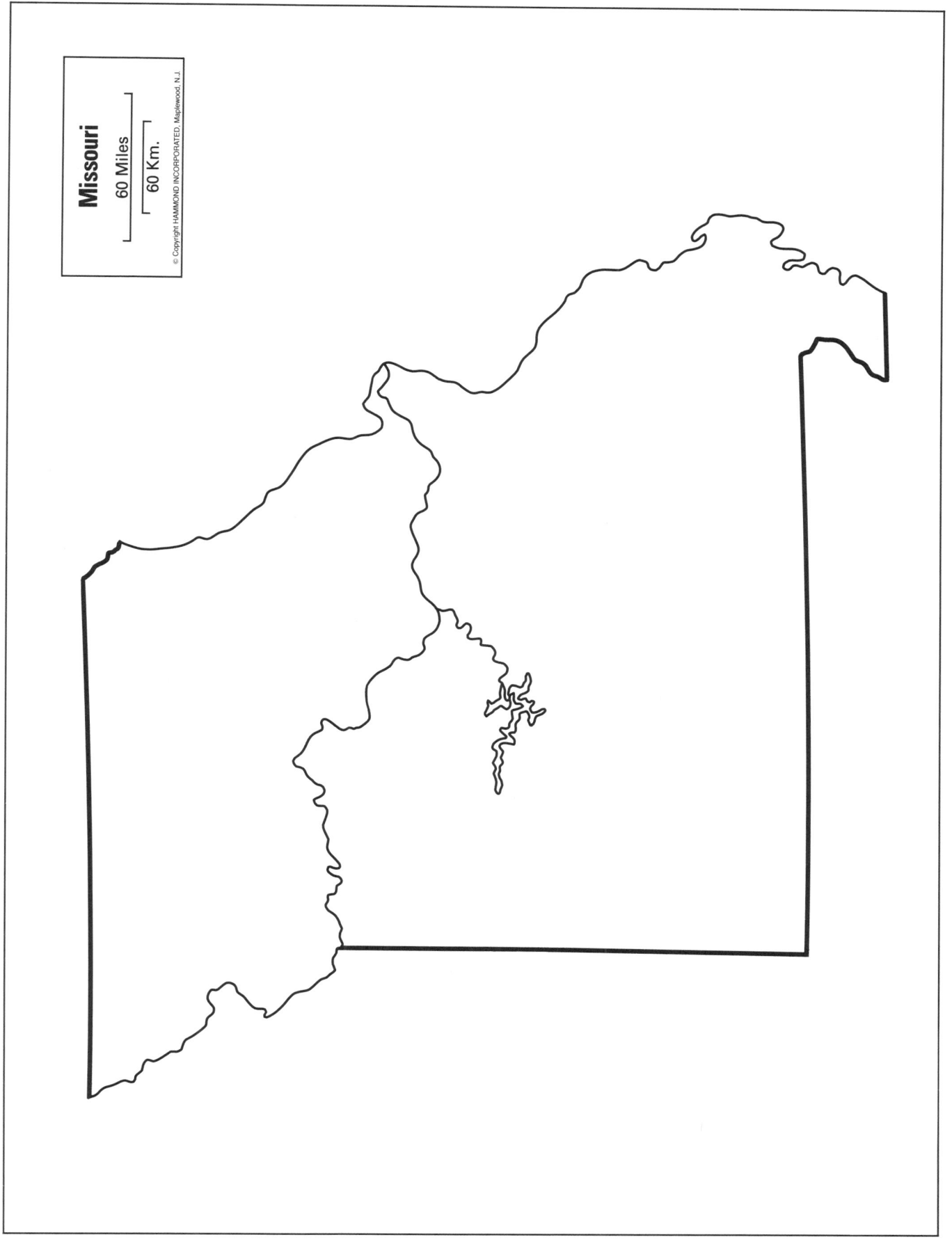

Missouri

60 Miles

60 Km.

© Copyright HAMMOND INCORPORATED, Maplewood, N.J.

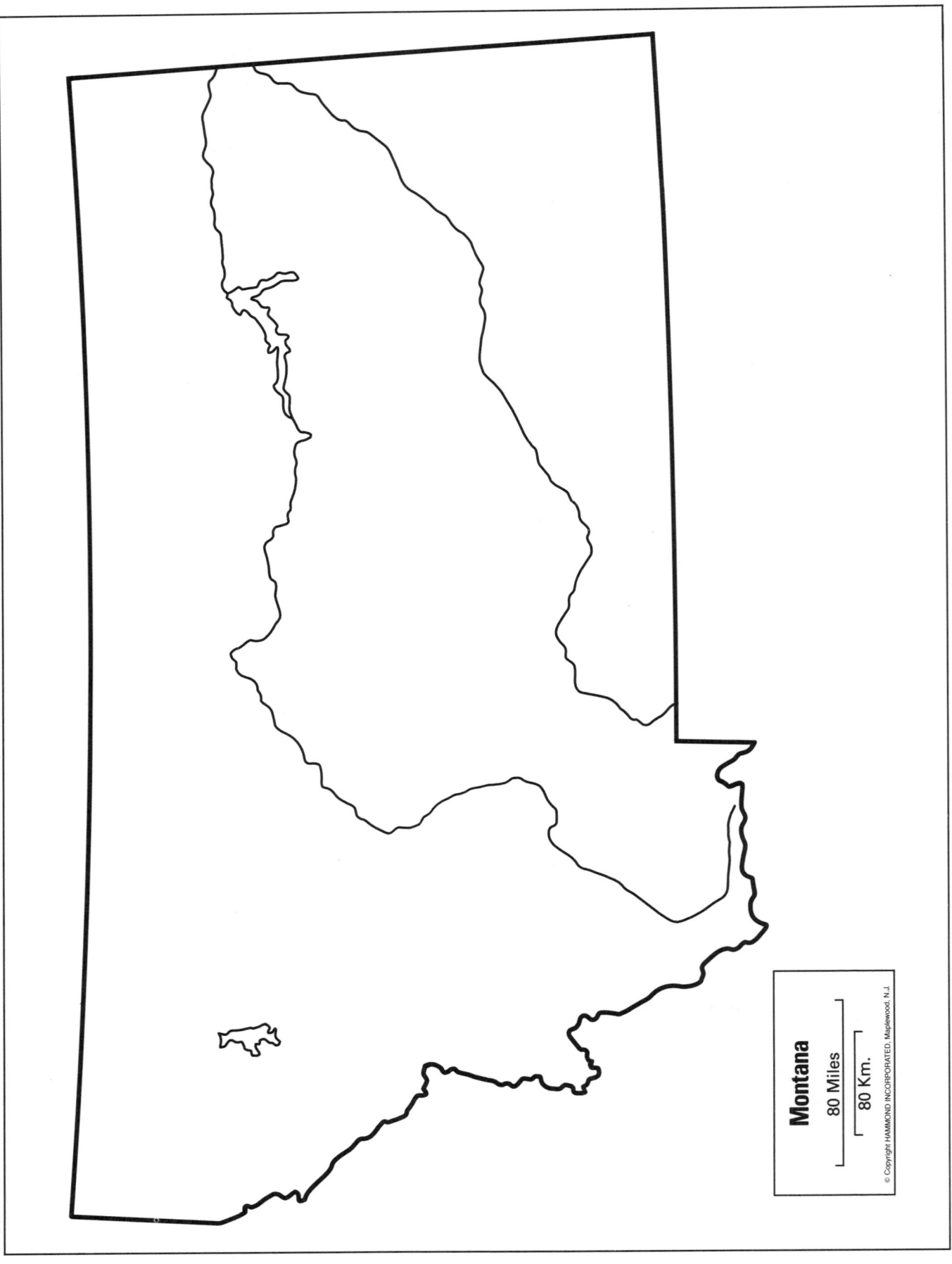

Montana

80 Miles

80 Km.

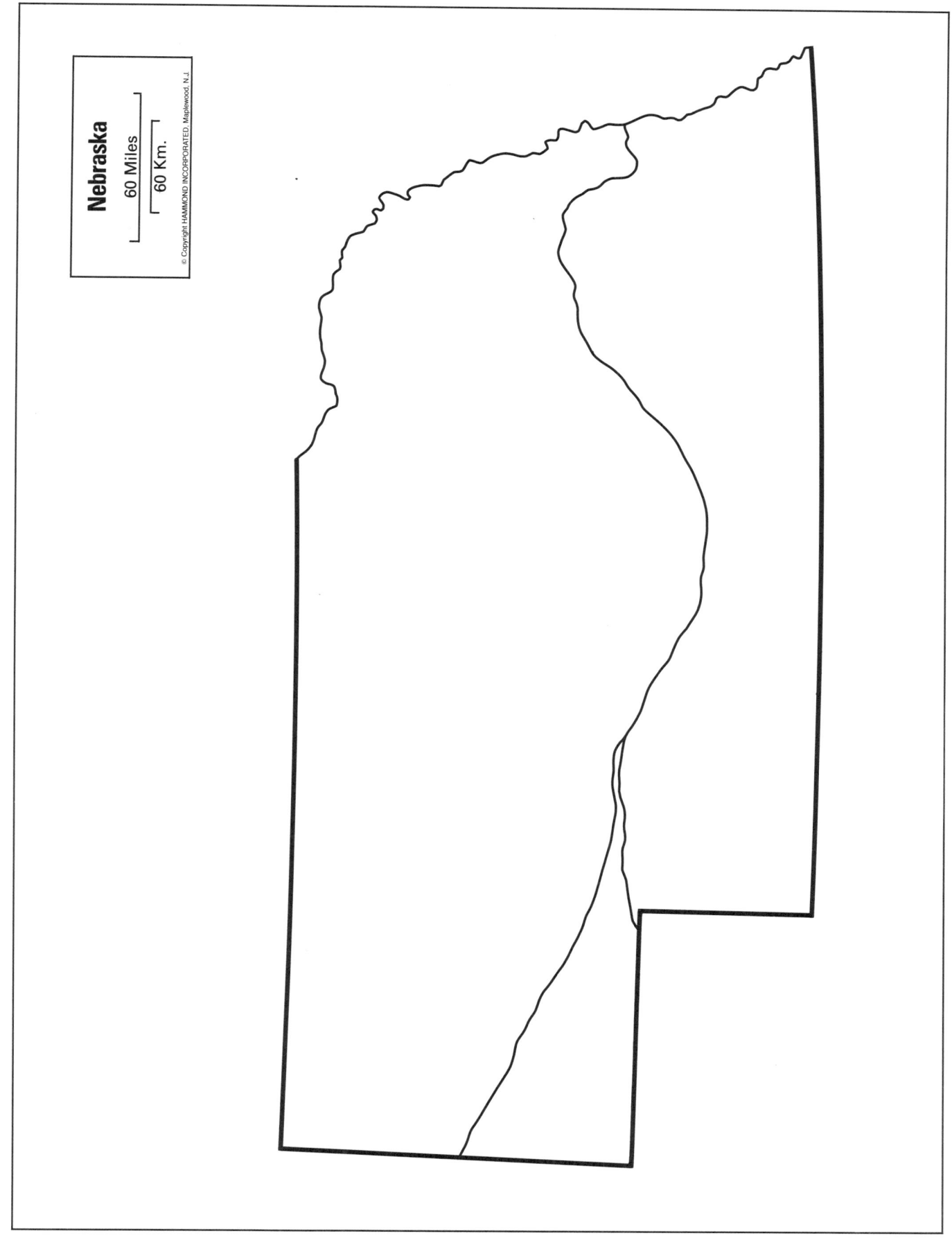

Nebraska

60 Miles

60 Km.

© Copyright HAMMOND INCORPORATED, Maplewood, N.J.

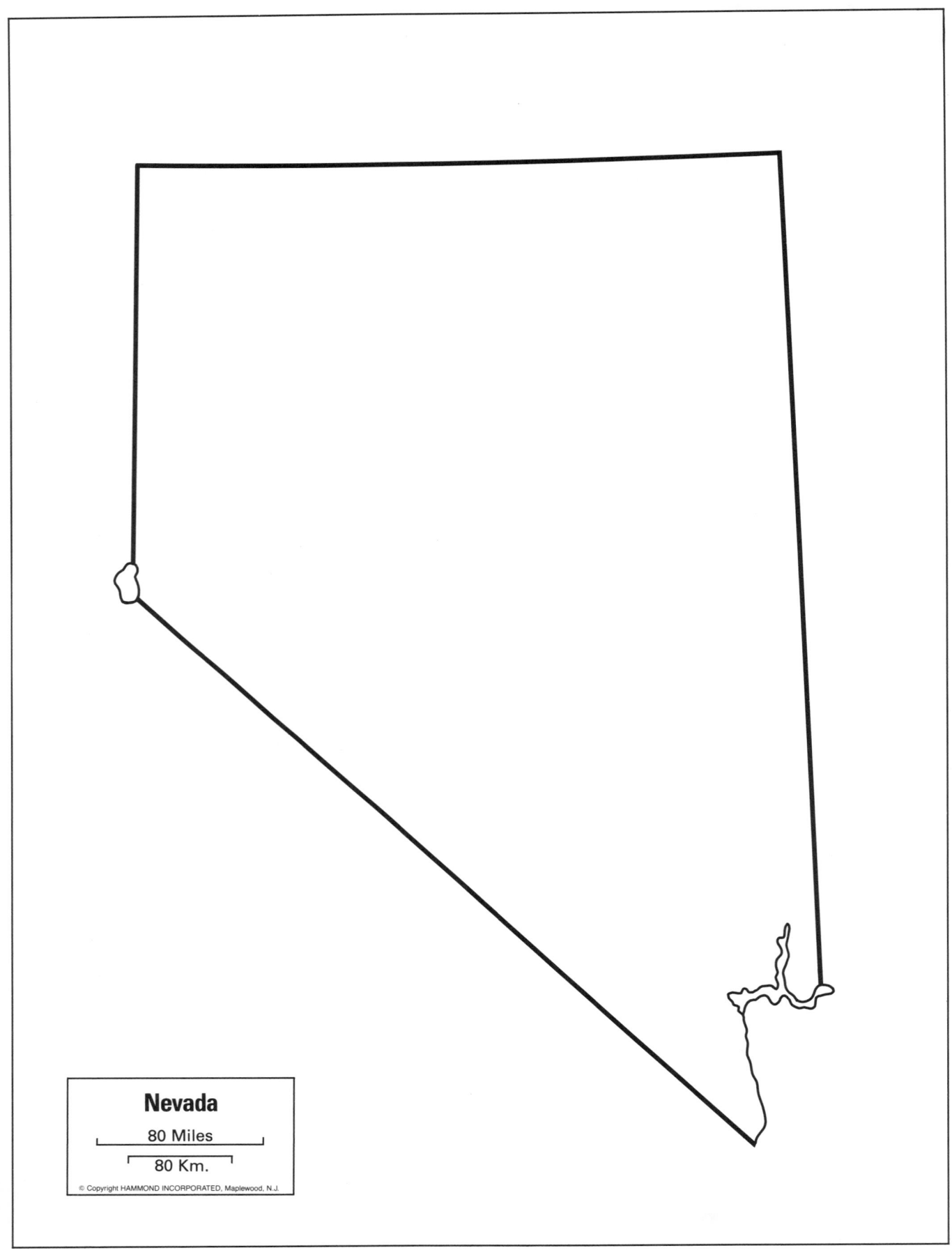

Nevada

80 Miles

80 Km.

© Copyright HAMMOND INCORPORATED, Maplewood, N.J.

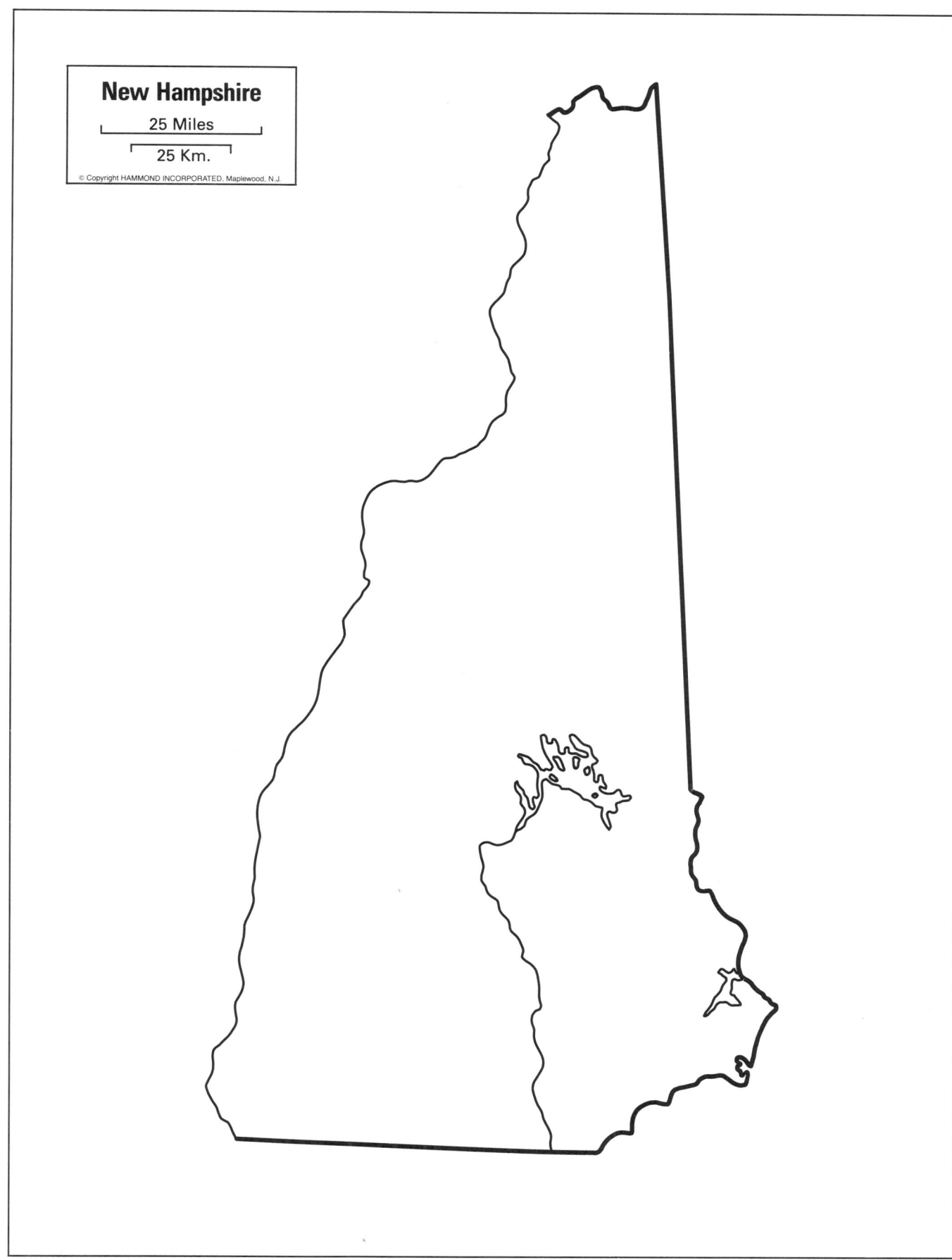

New Hampshire

25 Miles

25 Km.

644

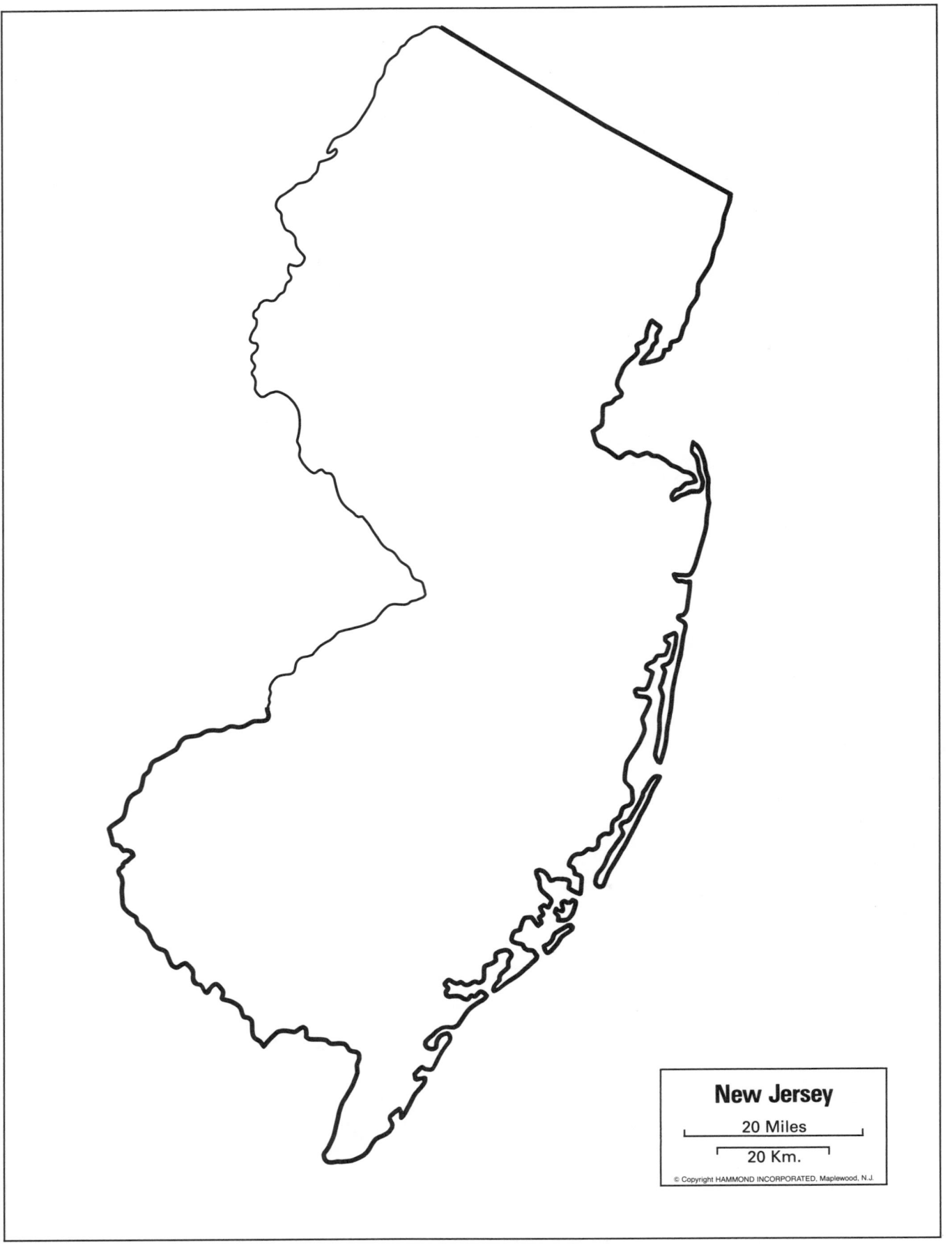

New Jersey

20 Miles

20 Km.

© Copyright HAMMOND INCORPORATED, Maplewood, N.J.

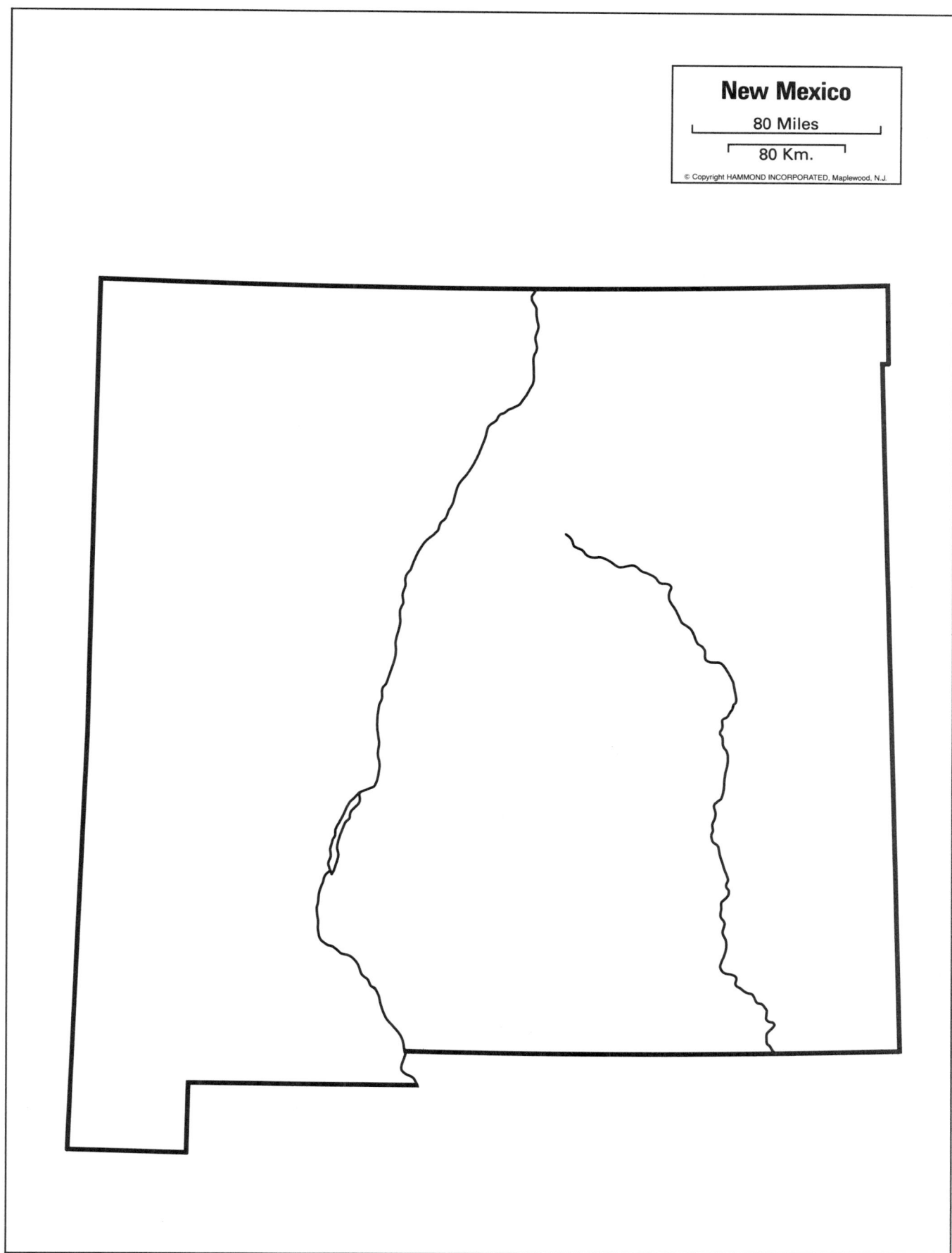

New Mexico

80 Miles

80 Km.

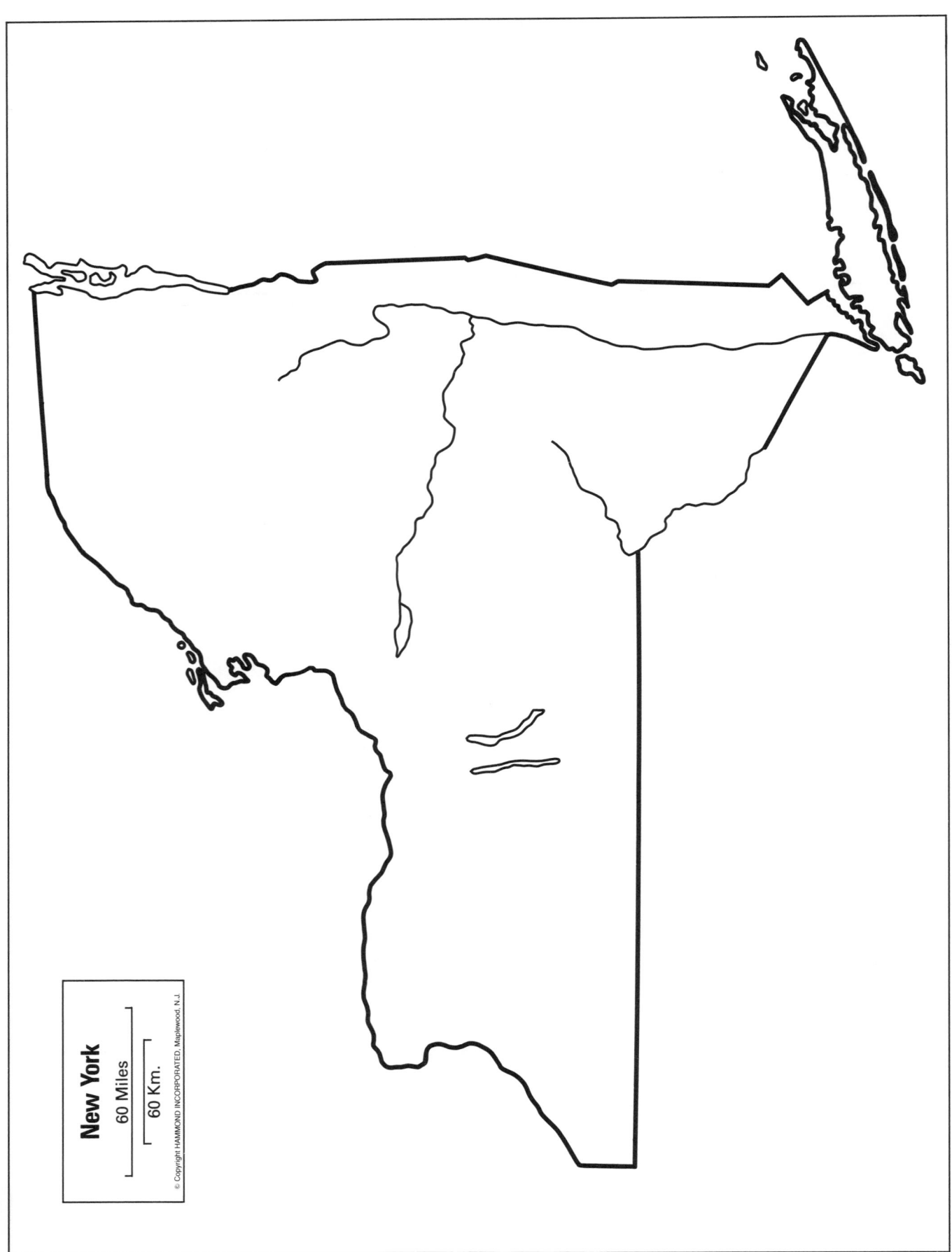

New York

60 Miles

60 Km.

© Copyright HAMMOND INCORPORATED, Maplewood, N.J.

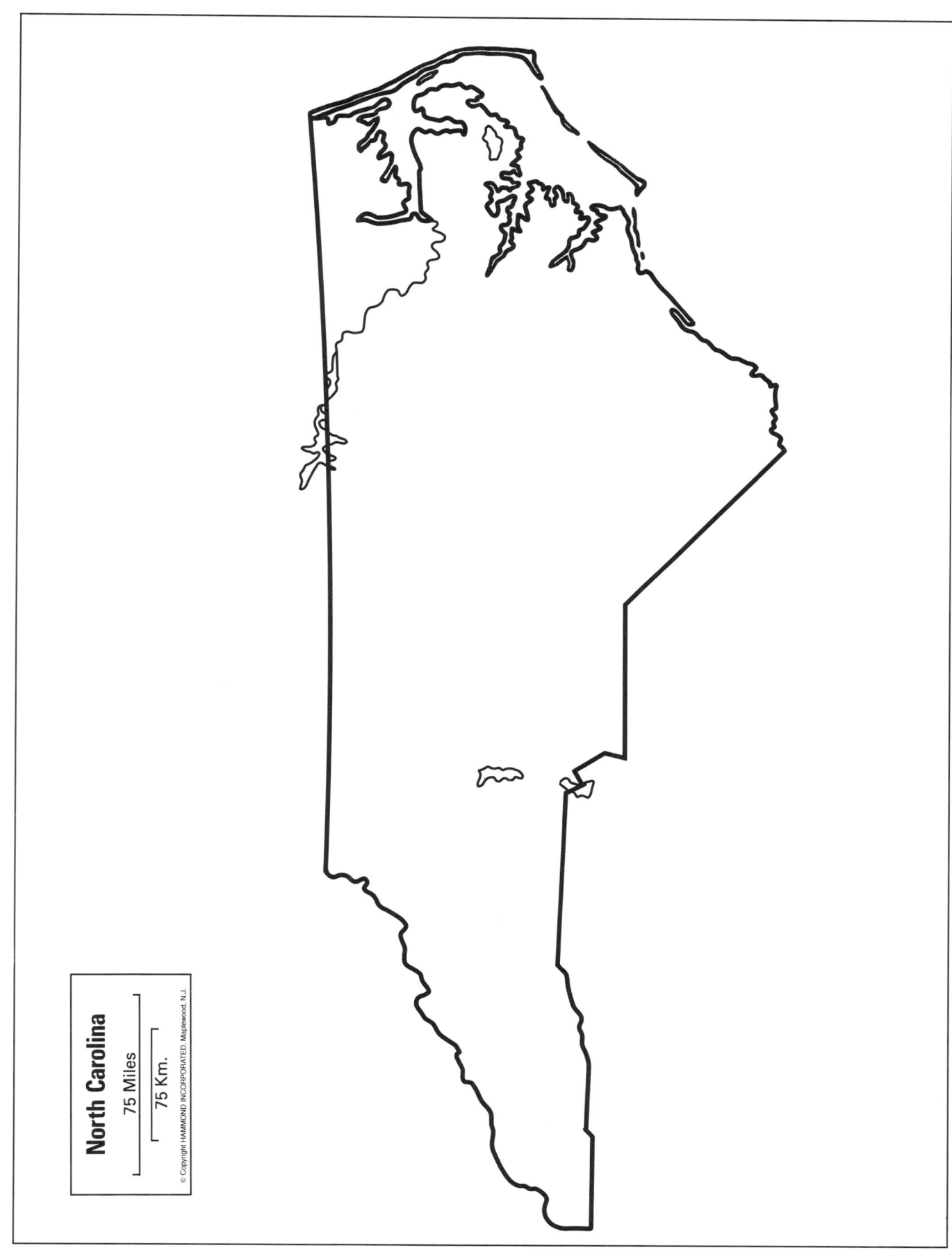

North Carolina

75 Miles

75 Km.

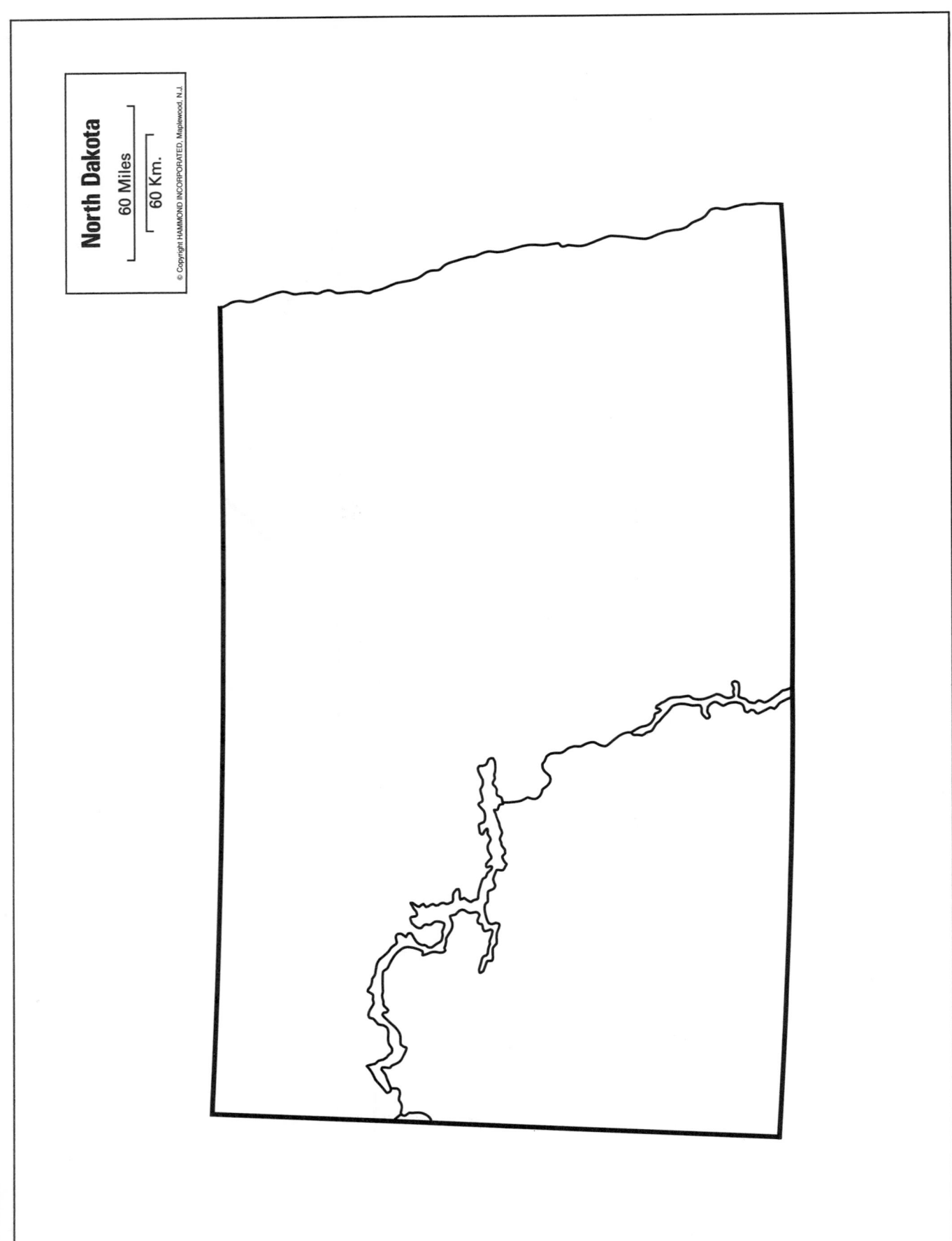

North Dakota

60 Miles

60 Km.

© Copyright HAMMOND INCORPORATED, Maplewood, N.J.

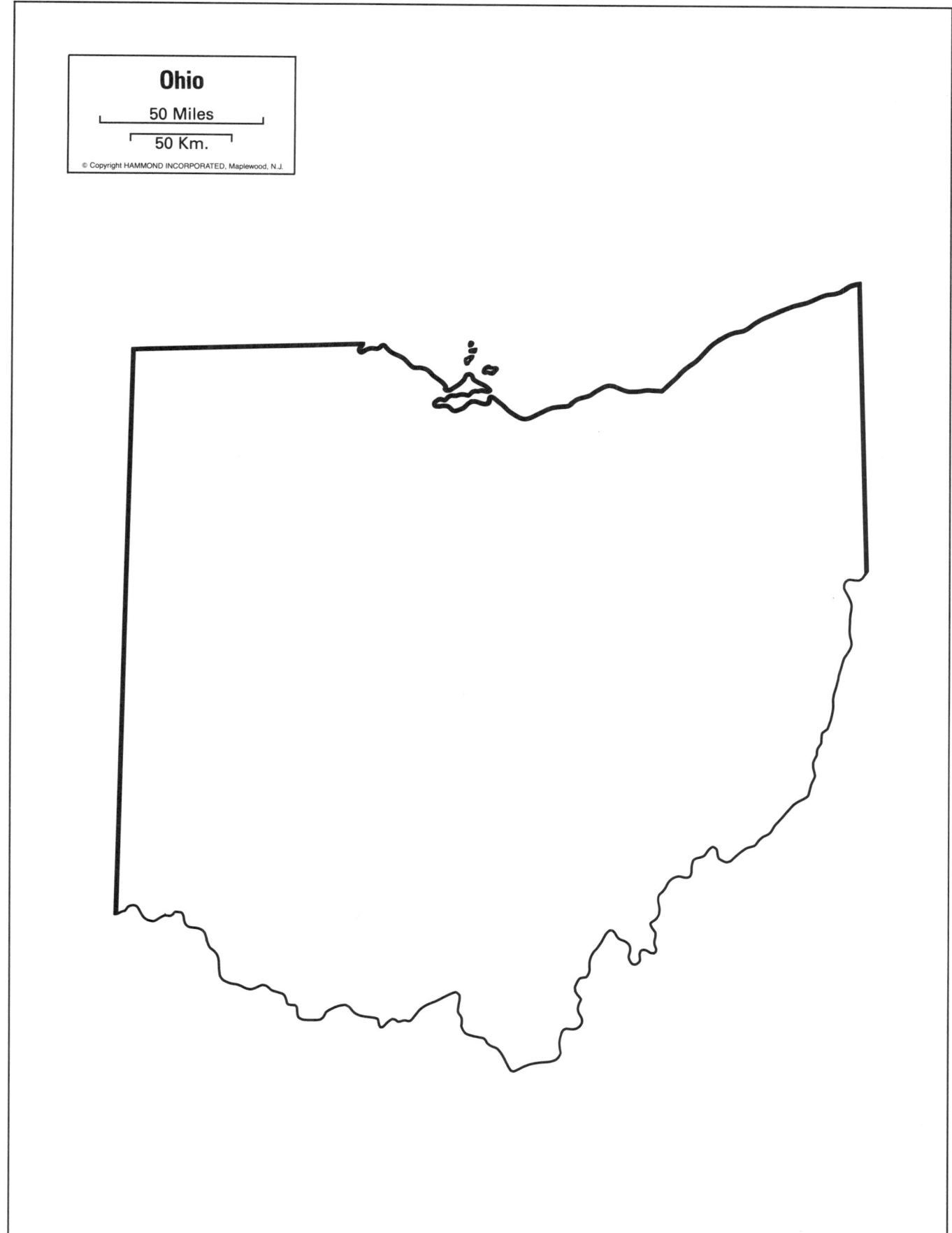

Ohio

50 Miles

50 Km.

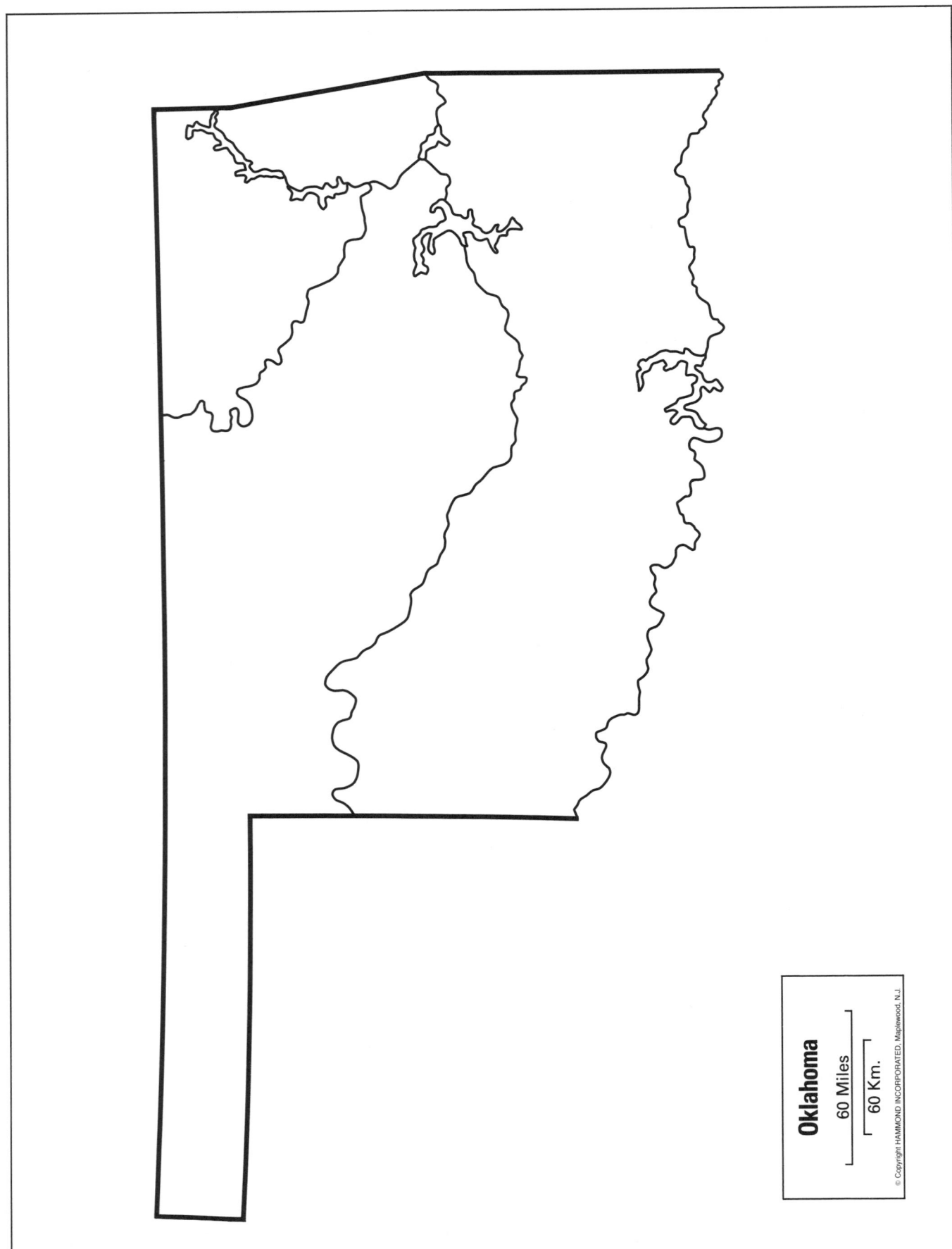

Oklahoma

60 Miles

60 Km.

© Copyright HAMMOND INCORPORATED, Maplewood, N.J.

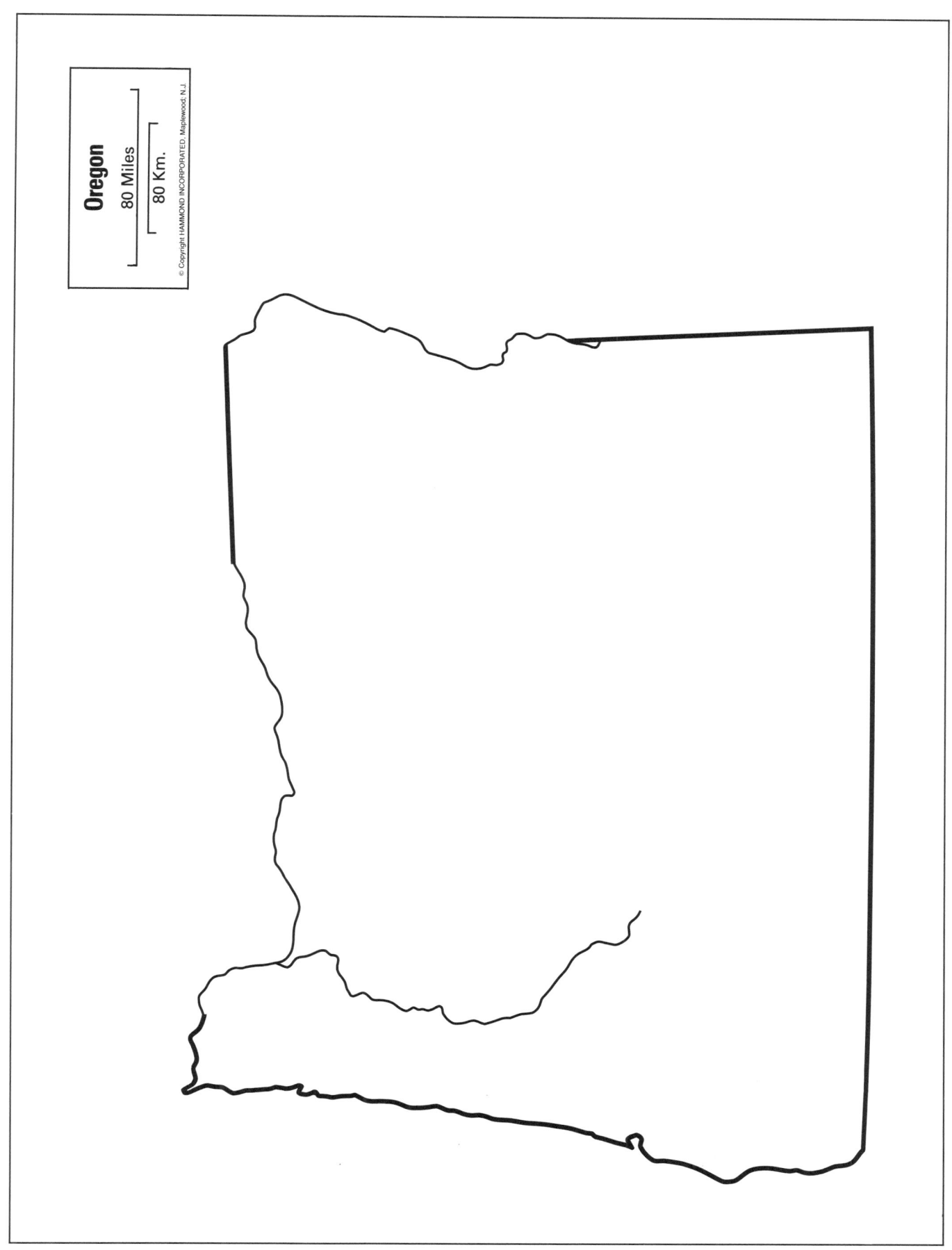

Oregon

80 Miles

80 Km.

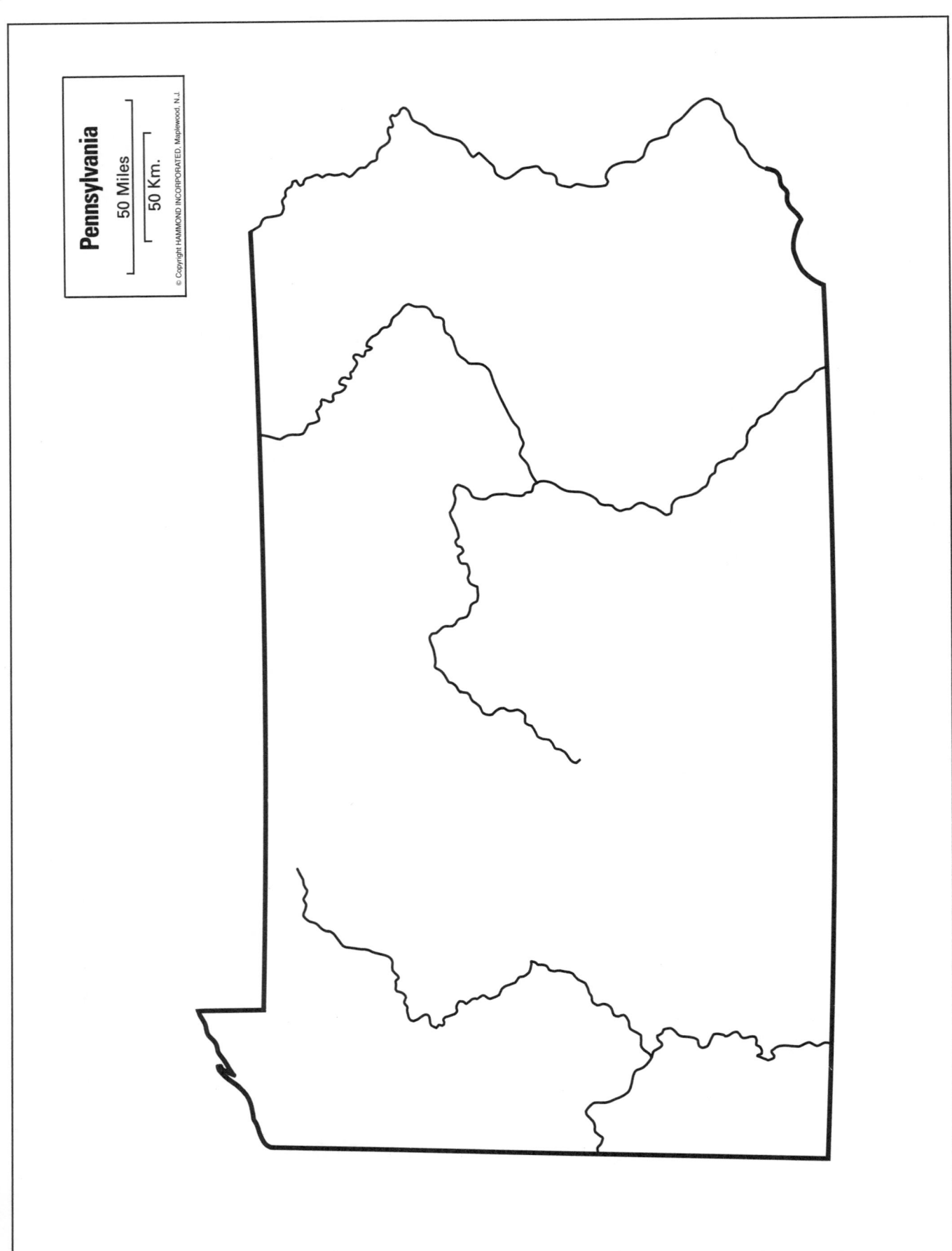

Pennsylvania

50 Miles

50 Km.

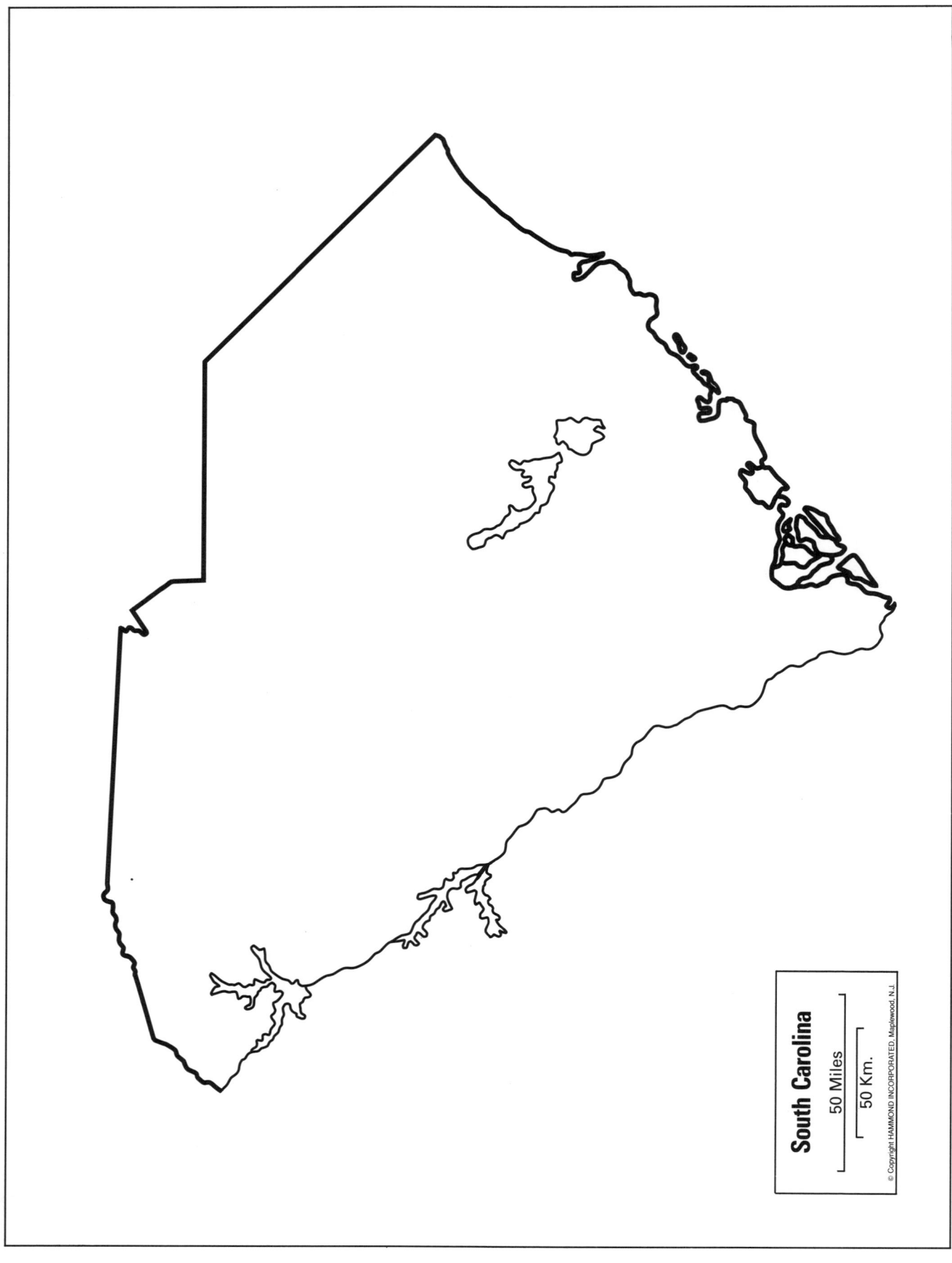

South Carolina

50 Miles

50 Km.

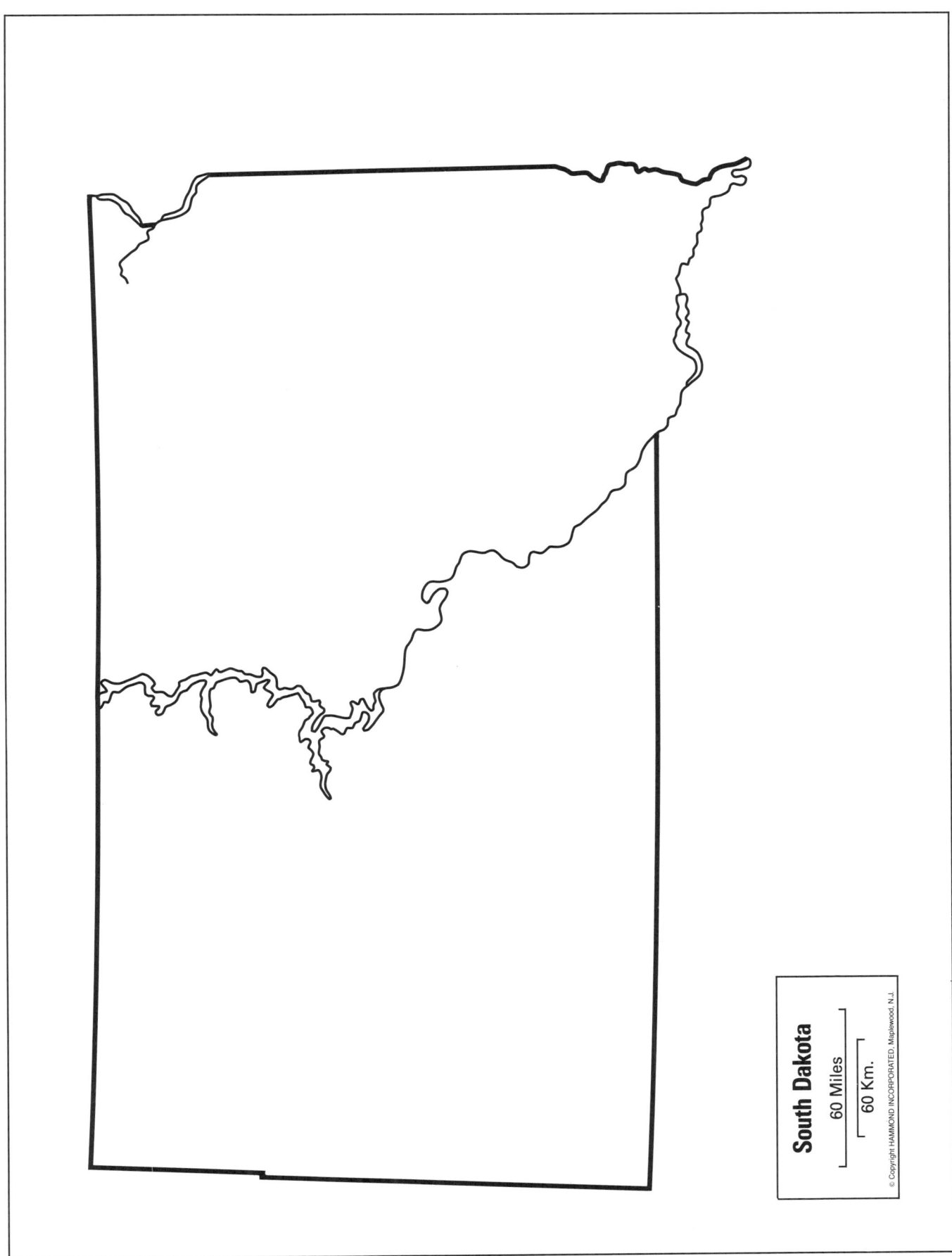

South Dakota

60 Miles

60 Km.

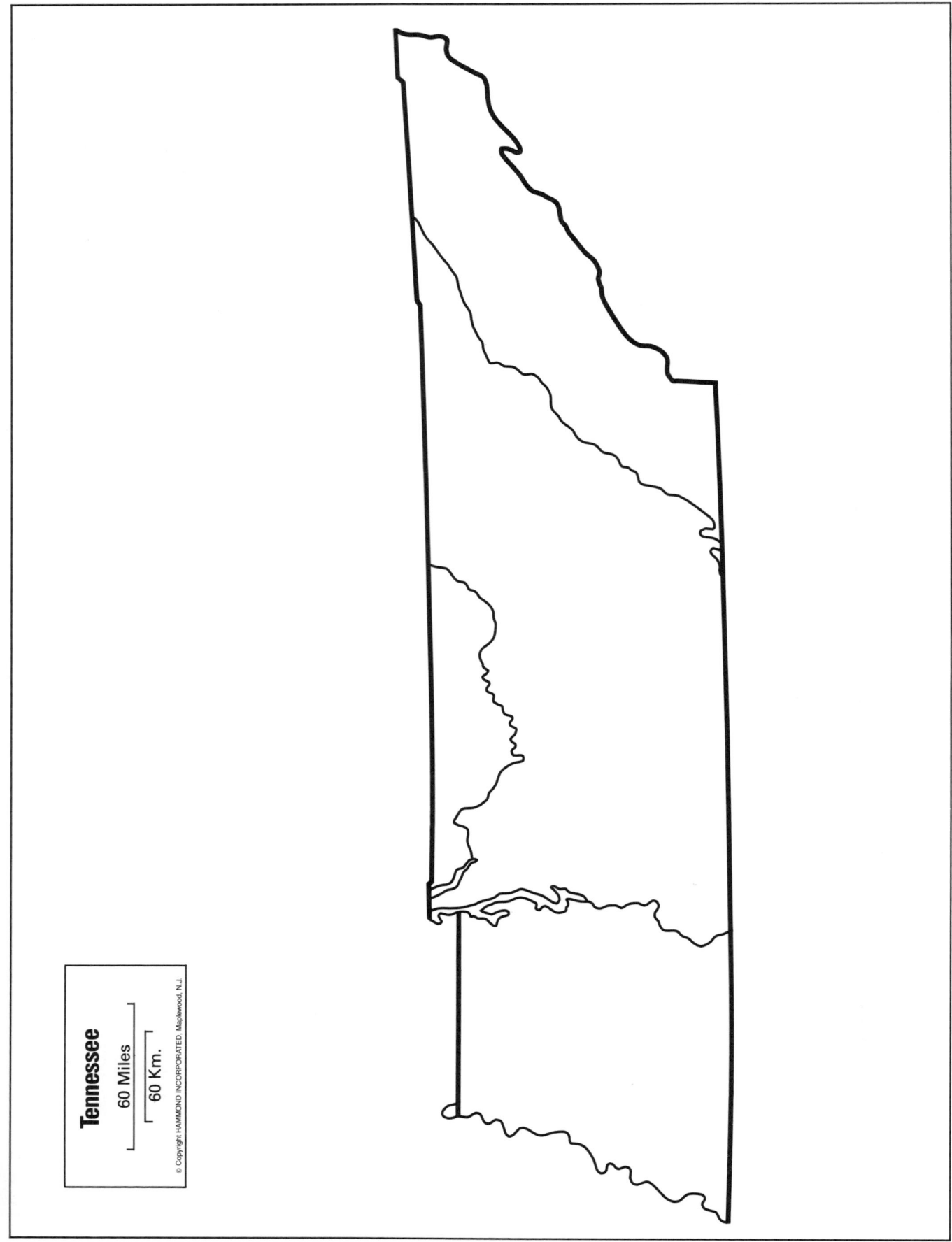

Tennessee

60 Miles

60 Km.

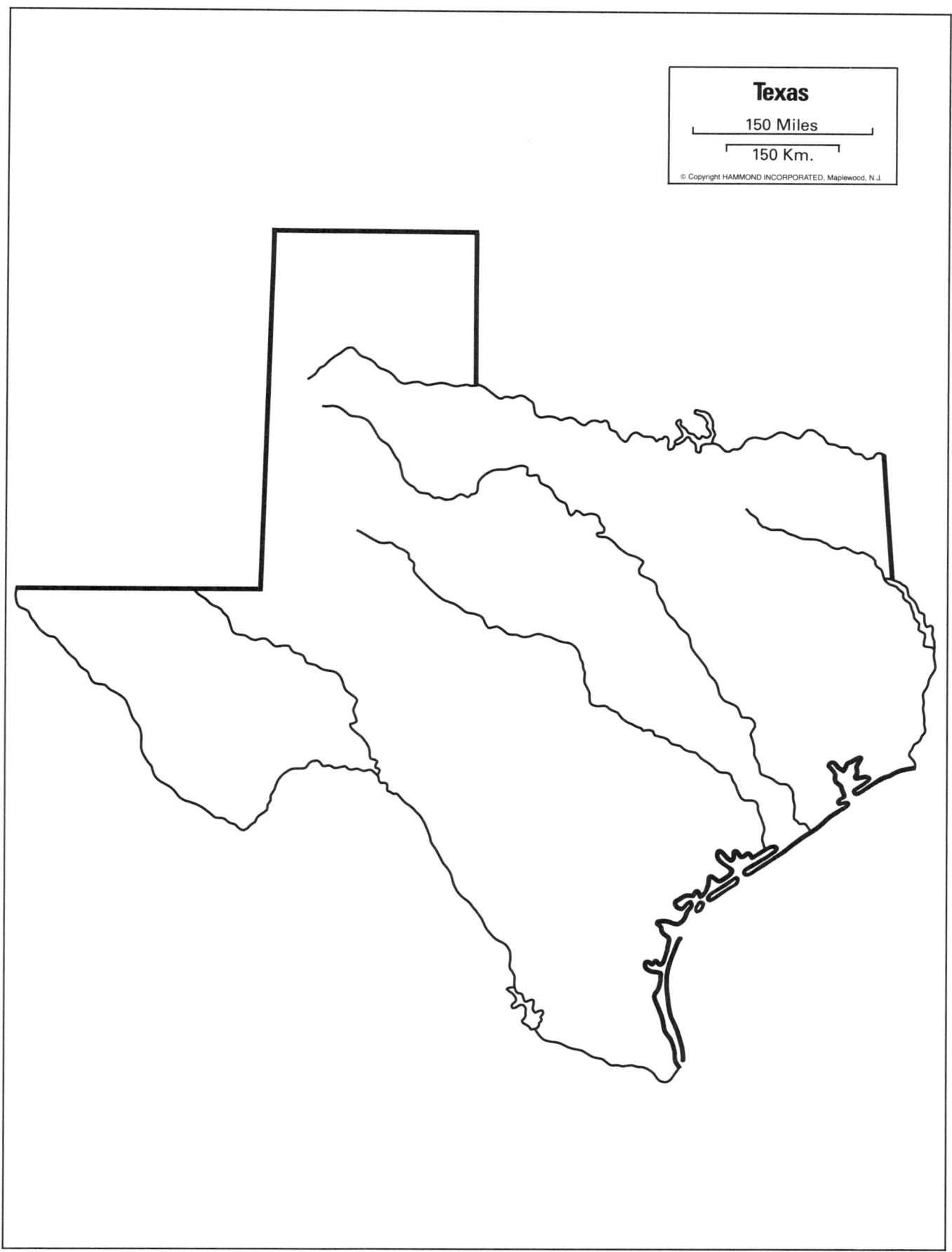

Texas

150 Miles

150 Km.

© Copyright HAMMOND INCORPORATED, Maplewood, N.J.

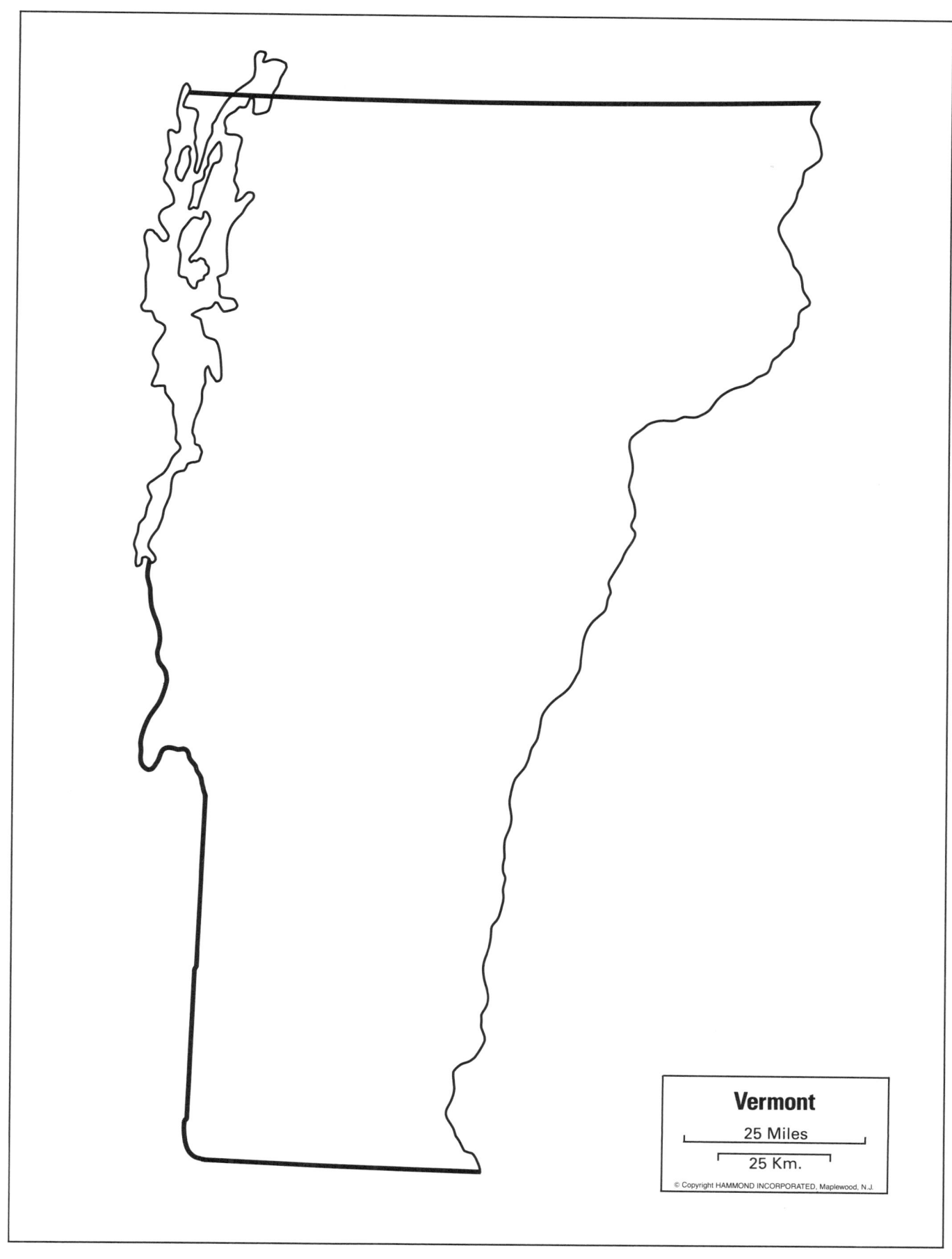

Vermont

25 Miles

25 Km.

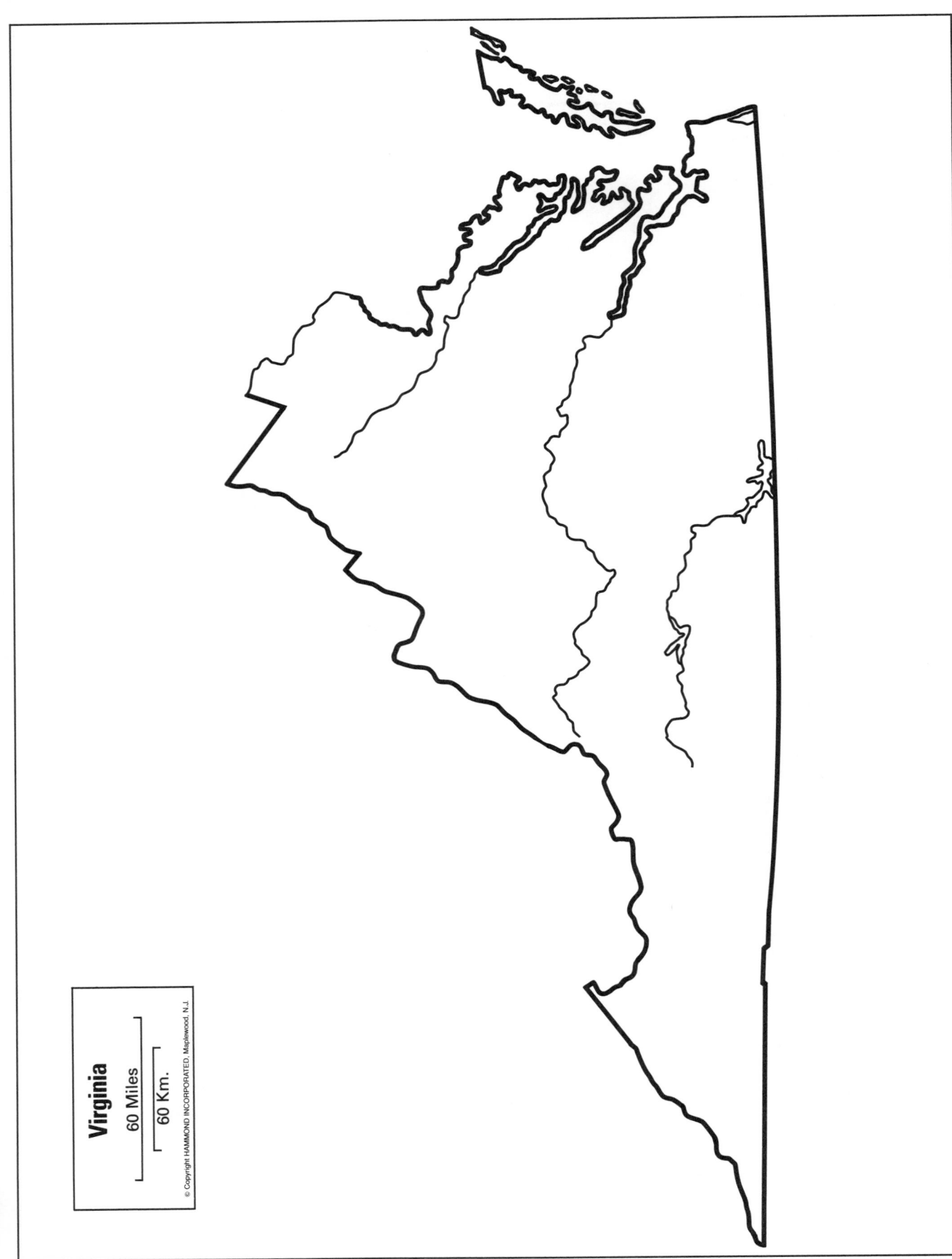

Virginia

60 Miles

60 Km.

© Copyright HAMMOND INCORPORATED, Maplewood, N.J.

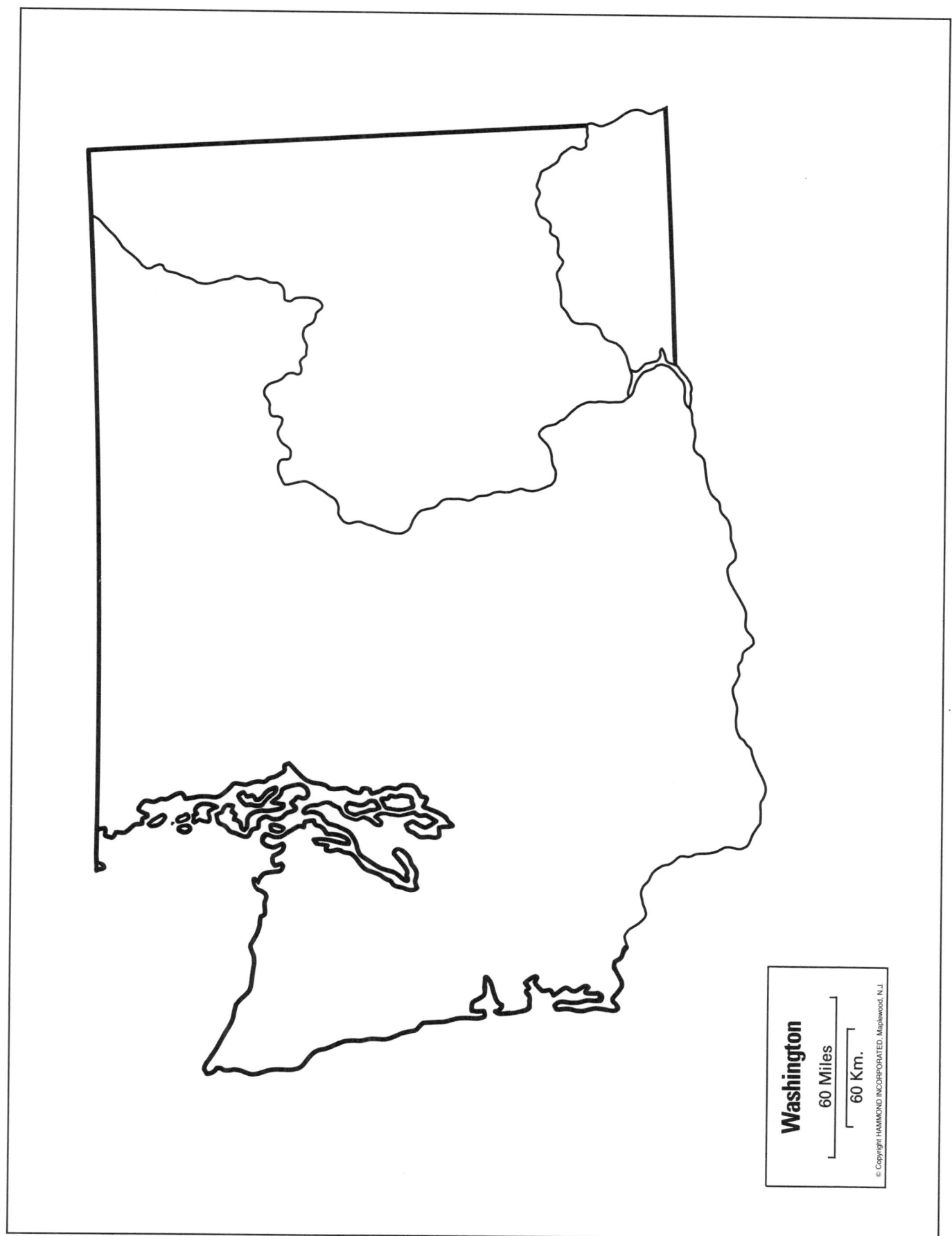

Washington

60 Miles

60 Km.

© Copyright HAMMOND INCORPORATED, Maplewood, N.J.

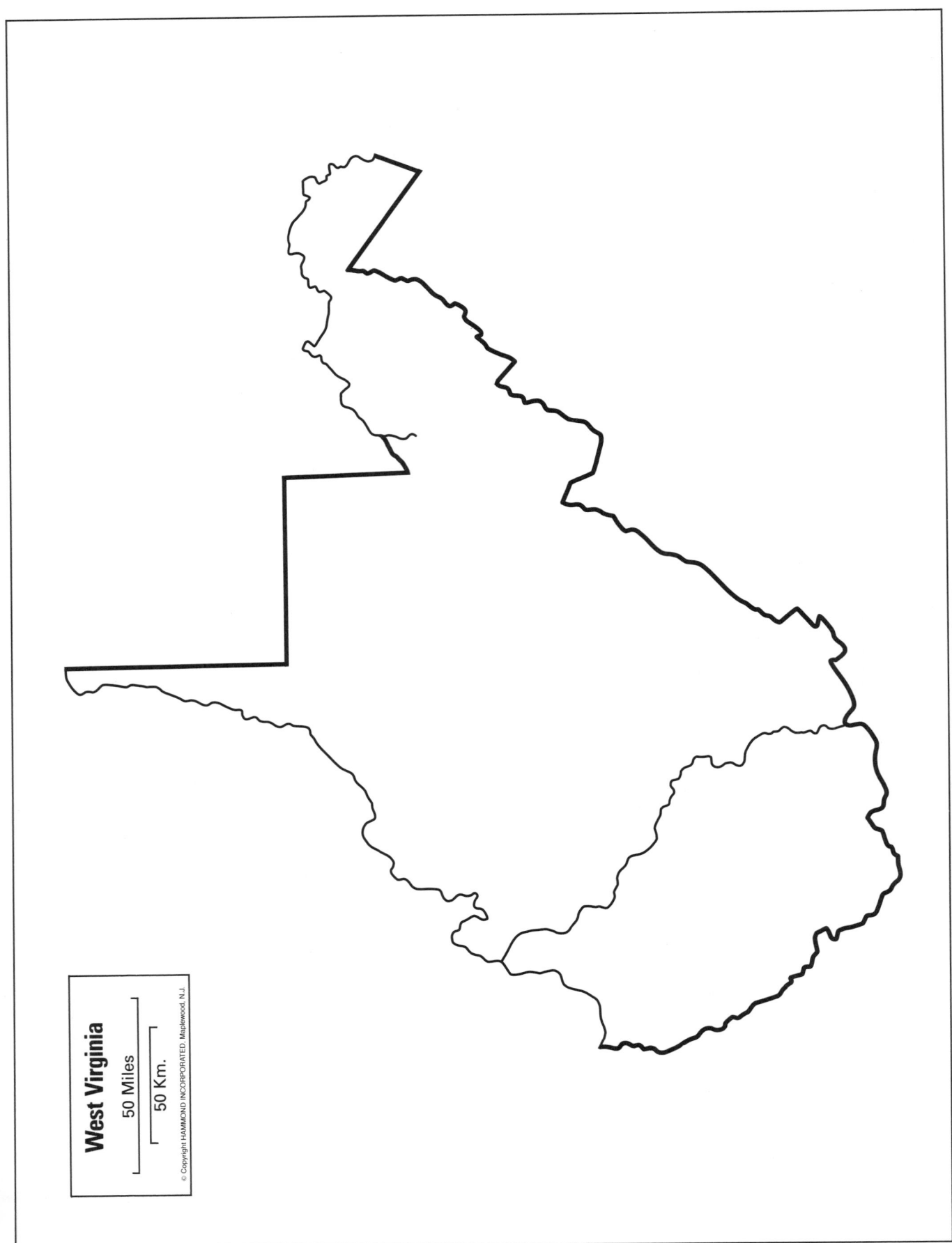

West Virginia

50 Miles

50 Km.

© Copyright HAMMOND INCORPORATED, Maplewood, N.J.

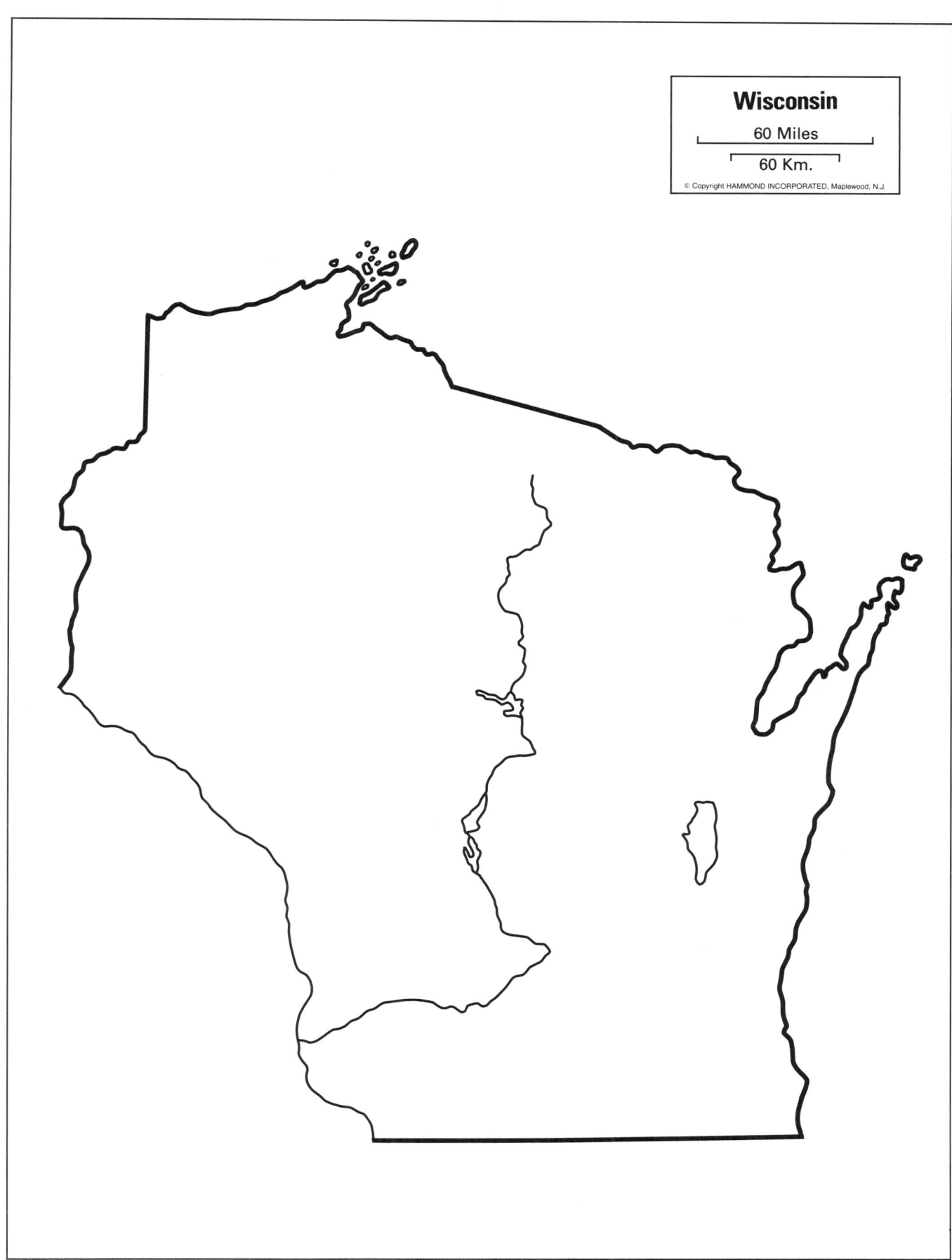

Wisconsin

60 Miles

60 Km.

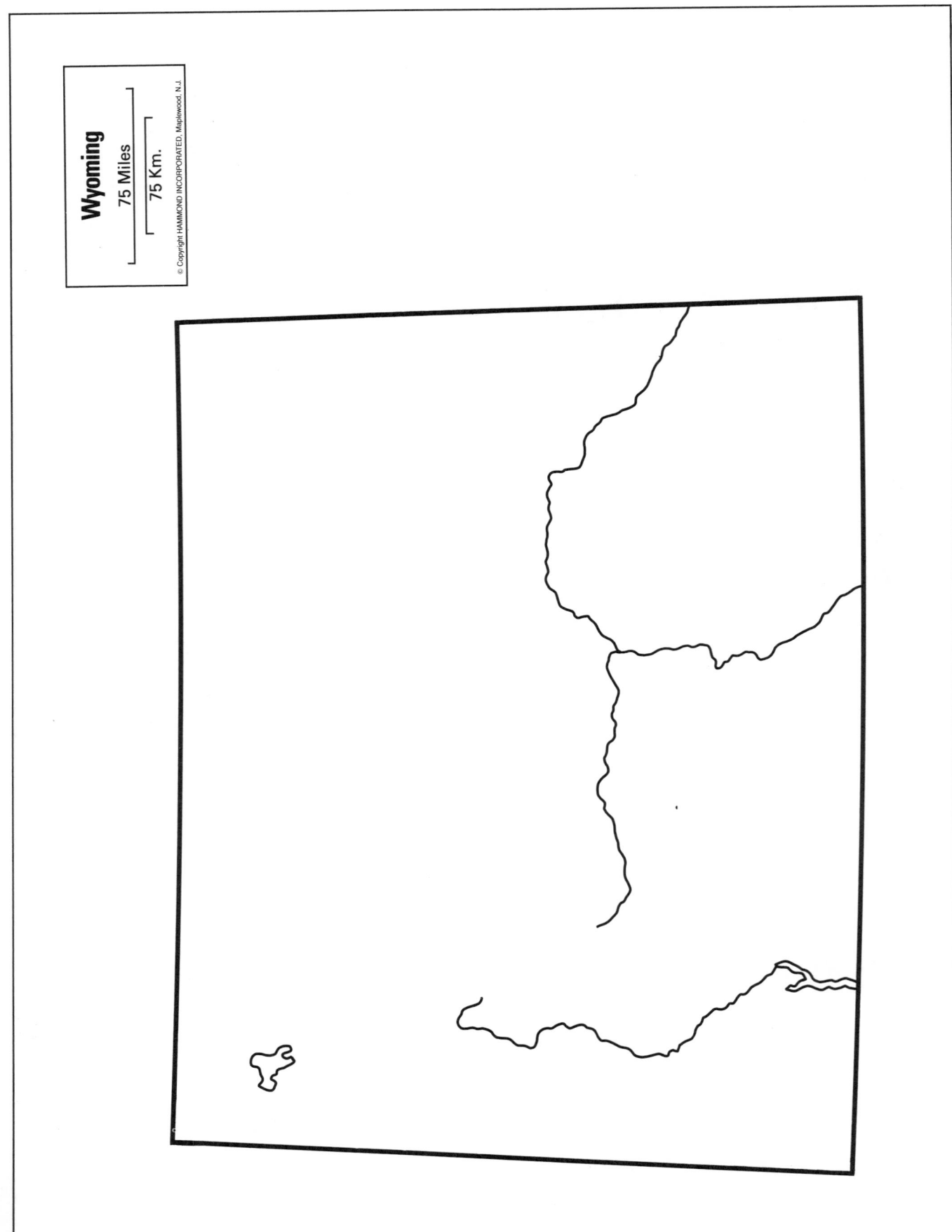

Wyoming

75 Miles

75 Km.

Taking Aptitude Tests

Nearly all people who want to advance their educations or careers must at some time take at least one of the major tests. These tests are designed to evaluate general knowledge, aptitude for college, or qualifications for graduate school. All of these tests are developed by nonprofit organizations, and their scores are generally accepted by employers and educators across the United States.

The achievement test called General Educational Development, or GED, is designed to assess whether a person knows as much as a typical high-school graduate. It is administered to people who dropped out of high school or who never entered high school. A passing grade on the GED is accepted by most employers and colleges as the equivalent of a high-school diploma.

Most colleges, however, want students who are better than the typical high-school graduate. They also want to be able to evaluate the best student in a poor high school against an ordinary student in a good high school. While the best students in poor high schools may be at least as good as ordinary students in good schools, they may actually be much better or much worse. By giving the same aptitude test to everyone who applies for admission, college administrators hope to obtain an objective evaluation. Of course, colleges do not rely on tests alone, but the scores provided by standardized tests may indicate whether a student with poor grades in school may have unrealized potential.

Colleges use one of two aptitude tests to acquire the information they need. (Some colleges will accept scores from either.) The test used most in the eastern United States is the Scholastic Aptitude Test, or SAT, prepared by the College Entrance Examination Board. The SAT is the grandfather of all the major aptitude tests and many tests have imitated it. Elsewhere in the United States, the American College Testing Program, or ACT, is used more than the SAT. It is important to remember, though, that around the country individual colleges have different requirements. The admissions offices of the colleges to which you are applying should be consulted as to whether you need to take an aptitude test and, if so, which test.

These tests are called *aptitude tests* because they are intended to measure ability, not knowledge. Some colleges also require *achievement tests,* which measure knowledge of specific subjects, such as French or calculus, rather than ability.

APTITUDE TESTS

Just as college admissions offices want to have standards to judge applicants from different high schools, administrators of graduate schools want to have similar objective standards for college graduates. The Graduate Record Examination, or GRE, is designed to test the kinds of skills needed in graduate school. Not every graduate school requires the GRE, especially where there are programs that lead directly from a college into a specific course of graduate study. Nevertheless, the GRE is frequently required, and failure to pass it can keep a person out of a graduate program.

Improve your test-taking

Though everyone wants to do as well as possible on tests, some students know more than they are ever able to show because they are test-shy. These students often perform more poorly than students who know less than they do. Thus, good test-takers have an advantage over classmates who do not test well. For this reason, you should learn about various tests and try to become "test-wise," that is, comfortable when taking tests and capable of figuring out correct answers even when you do not have firm knowledge to guide you.

Most good test-takers follow a few simple rules that help them get better scores. Some of these rules apply to all tests. Others are specific for multiple-choice tests, or even more specific for a single test, such as the SAT. The first and most important rule, however, is that the better prepared you are, the easier you will find the test and the better your score will be.

Attitude. Perhaps the most important rule to help you improve your test-taking is to adopt the right attitude. You cannot do well on a test if your mind is blocked by worry. Remember, tests are designed to measure your mastery of a skill or your knowledge of a subject. They are not designed to embarrass you, fool you, or terrify you. In a sense, taking a test should be no harder for you than taking your temperature.

Forget about the students around you—what they do is of no concern. Forget about the teacher, about the plans you have for after the test, and about anything else that may be on your mind. Until the test is over, the only two things that matter are you and the test. With this single-minded attitude, you are ready to concentrate and do your very best. You may feel keyed up, like an athlete before a game. Being keyed up can make you more alert and ready, but you should not feel agitated or worried.

Preparation. Not less important than attitude is preparation for a test. There are two kinds of preparation for any test, whether it is an end-of-course achievement test or a general aptitude test. The first is study of the subject matter. Even in taking an aptitude test, knowing the subject matter will help you get a high score. If you do not know the subject matter, only your test-wiseness can help you.

Some students study hard but do not master the material. They may read a chapter over and over, desperately trying to memorize hundreds of facts, or they may run in circles, trying over and over again to master a new problem without first understanding it.

If the test is on subject matter from a book, try this approach. Instead of reading the material over and over, read it once. Then spend some time organizing it on paper. What are the major facts or themes of the material? What are the important names or dates or other facts—those necessary to understand the whole? Many of the names and dates may be less important—in fact, some of them can safely be forgotten.

If you are learning a skill, go back to an example, either in the book or in your notes, and follow it step by step, making sure that you see how the right answer was reached. Then take a new problem and follow exactly the same steps. If you still do not understand, ask for help from a classmate or teacher.

There are many aids available to you in preparing for these major tests. The sample items with explanations that are on pages 669–688 are a good place to begin. The box on page 667 lists some other options.

If you are having trouble, it is important that you begin preparing for the test early. Otherwise, there will not be time to ask for help. An early start is a good idea in any case, especially when learning the vocabulary of a foreign language or such basic facts as the multiplication table. The mind needs lots of time and much repetition to fix the information firmly. No amount of cramming on the night before the test is likely to make up for work not done ahead of time. Even if you do manage to remember part of the material for the test, you probably will forget it soon afterward; in that case, you will have to do extra studying for the next test.

Ten ways to improve your test scores

Though there are many kinds of tests, with some requiring different techniques from others, here are a few tips that apply to all major tests:

1. **Take a course** that will prepare you if you are unsure about your ability to deal with a test. Such courses are offered in most major cities. Some are available by mail or on computer programs. Such courses are particularly useful for achievement tests. Although some test-makers believe that such courses cannot improve aptitude test scores, other experts think these courses help. Books available in most bookstores contain more sample questions than those offered here. The testing organizations themselves publish free or inexpensive booklets that contain helpful information and sample questions.

2. **Take at least one sample test.** This book supplies a few sample questions, but you can obtain a complete sample test, often from your school library or local bookstore. Try to take the test in the same time limit set for the actual test. The experience should not only prepare you but relax you for the actual test. It also might show up weak areas that require more study.

3. **Be prepared.** Make sure you have whatever is required to take the test when you arrive at the testing place. Some tests require an admission ticket, personal identification (such as a driver's license or birth certificate), and Number 2 pencils. Be sure you know what is needed for your test so you do not forfeit your place.

4. **Relax.** More tests are fouled up because test-takers are too tense than because they are too calm. The time to stay up nights studying for a test is in the weeks preceding it, when you can use that excess energy for studying. You should be well-rested by the time the actual test starts. A good night's sleep is better than staying up late and cramming.

5. **Take a moment to look through the whole test** before you begin to answer any questions. Read the instructions or directions especially carefully. If you do not know exactly what is wanted, it is easy to make mistakes that reduce your score.

6. **Try to estimate how much time you have** for answering each question. Count quickly how many questions there are altogether, and estimate the time needed for each. If the test has several parts, jot down a rough timetable for handling each part.

7. **Read each question carefully.** If you misunderstand the question, you will probably answer it wrong, no matter how much you know about the subject. Some tests have questions with tricky wording just to test your understanding. Especially when a question is complicated, read it a second time to be sure you have it right.

8. **Answer all the easy questions first** and skip questions you are not sure about. Use the remaining time to consider carefully the hard-to-answer questions. Answering easy questions will warm you up and help keep you from getting a mental block, a temporary inability to remember something that you really know. Answering easy questions first also will ensure that you have answered everything you know best before time runs out.

9. **Answer first questions from parts of the test that carry higher values** than others do. Obviously, if you know which parts count most and the correct answers, it is better to answer those parts right away to be sure of getting the highest possible score.

10. **If you have time left,** do not turn in your test or stop working on it. Use the remaining minutes to read through all the questions and answers. You may find, for example, that you have failed to answer some items whose answers you know. In multiple choice tests with separate answer sheets, take the time to make sure that you have put your answers in the right spaces or columns. Take a moment to determine that each answer seems reasonable, especially in a mathematics test; if an answer is wrong, do not be too lazy to do your calculations again.

The second kind of preparation for any test has nothing at all to do with subject matter. It consists of making sure that you are physically and mentally ready to do well. One important factor is a good night's sleep. The day before a test, remember to take a few minutes now and then to relax. Finish your studying early so that you can get to bed and be ready for sleep at your regular bedtime. In the morning, eat a good breakfast. At the same time, train yourself to put aside any worries or excitement for a few hours, until the test is over. You need all your powers of concentration for the test.

During the test. Arrive early and have with you the pencils or any other tools you will need. At this point you should be well enough prepared not to think about the test for a moment or two. Do something else if you can, such as chat with a friend.

When the test is handed out, read it through quickly before you answer any of the questions. Be sure you understand *how* you are to provide the answers. Do not, for example, write on the test booklet if a separate answer sheet is required. In fact, it is a good idea to read all the instructions twice—just to make sure. Getting a poor grade because you did not follow the rules is worse than getting a poor grade because you did not know the material. Once you have read through the whole test, do the easy items first. In that way, even if you are short of time, you will make sure you get credit for what you know. After the easy items are done, tackle the items you are not sure of.

Obviously, if you do not know the correct answer to a test item, you will have a more difficult time than if you do know the answer. But you still have many ways to improve your score. For one thing, your unconscious mind usually knows more than your conscious mind does. Although you skip over an item because you do not remember the answer, the answer may pop into your mind later. In addition, if you weed out answers that you know are wrong, you have a good chance of coming up with the correct answer. For example, if you eliminate two of four answers in a multiple choice item, you have a fifty-fifty chance of getting the right answer from the remaining two.

If you are really in trouble, there are other rules you

can use for guessing. Be warned, however, that the people who write the tests know these rules also. For example, correct answers often have to be qualified extensively, which means that the right answer will normally be the longest one. Test-makers know this, of course, so they deliberately try to think of wrong answers that will be longer than the right ones. As a result, the second-longest answer is sometimes the right one. Similarly, absolute qualifiers, such as *always, never,* or *none,* generally apply to incorrect answers, since few things in this world are ever absolute. Test-makers know this also, and sometimes they add absolute qualifiers to incorrect answers in order to trap the unwary. Finally, the test-makers want there to be about equal numbers of answers labeled A, B, C, D, and E. Each letter should, in this case, get about 20 percent of the answers. While test-makers know that students might exploit this to improve their test scores, most are reluctant to let one answer predominate over the others. Thus, in a multiple choice test, you can use the number of answers for each letter among the items you are sure of as a rough guide to guessing the items of which you are not sure.

Scoring multiple-choice tests.
Multiple-choice tests are used most often to test mastery of facts. Be sure to read each question and its possible answers carefully. Sometimes, more than one answer may seem correct; in that case, choose the one that you think is most accurate.

Short multiple-choice tests usually are graded on the number of right answers. This means that if you do not know the answer to a question, you can guess at answers without being penalized.

On long multiple-choice tests, such as standardized reading and mathematics tests, you are penalized for guessing. For this kind of test you should not guess at an answer if you have no idea what the answer is. You should guess if you can eliminate one or more of the possible answers as surely wrong.

Sample test questions

Sample questions from the four major tests follow. You will notice that the same kinds of questions often appear on more than one test. Each question is accompanied by a short explanation of why one of the answers is correct. Study these explanations carefully; they will reveal techniques of thinking you can use over and over. Note that in multiple-choice questions, the part that sets up the choices is sometimes called the *stem.*

GED

The General Educational Development examination has been developed by the American Council on Education to qualify students who have not finished high school or the equivalent of a secondary school diploma. It is rare for high-school dropouts to make a success of their lives without passing the GED. The GED consists of five parts: writing skills, social studies, science, literature and the arts, and mathematics. The writing skills section is a test of written English, including spelling, capitalization, punctuation, usage, sentence structure, and organization. There is no penalty for guessing, so you should complete all items even if you do not know the correct choice.

Writing skills

Directions: Choose the one best answer to each item. The questions refer to the following paragraphs.

(1)When you are in school, almost any Subject seems a potential area for a good job. (2)But when you are out on your own, you may find it difficult to land a job. (3)When you are told time after time that there are no jobs. (4)And it is time for some creative thinking and acting.

(5)Do your homework before applying for any job. (6)First, you should study the openings posted in the local newspapers—subscribe to all of them if possible, or read it at the public library. (7)Familiarize oneself with the types of jobs most often available, with the various employment offices, and with the skills most in demand.

Sentence 1: When you are in school, almost any Subject seems a potential area for a good job.

What correction should be made to this sentence?

(1) replace you are with one is
(2) remove the comma after school
(3) change Subject to subject
(4) insert a comma after area
(5) no correction is necessary

Choice (3) is correct. The word *subject* is not a proper noun or the first word of a sentence, so it must not be capitalized.

Sentences 3 and 4: When you are told time after time that there are no jobs. And it is time for some creative thinking and acting.

Which of the following is the best way to write the underlined portion of these sentences? If you think the original is the best way, choose option (1).

(1) jobs. And it
(2) jobs, or it
(3) jobs, it
(4) jobs, if it
(5) jobs, and it

Choice (3) is correct. In this form the sentence now consists of a dependent clause and an independent clause, with the clauses separated by a comma.

Sentence 5: Do your homework before applying for any job.

If you rewrote sentence 5 beginning with Be sure that you *the next words should be*

(1) got done your homework
(2) got your homework done
(3) had done your homework
(4) did your homework
(5) have done your homework

Choice (5) is correct. The verb *have done* is in the present perfect tense, so it agrees with the verb *Be,* which is in the present tense.

Sentence 6: First, you should study the openings posted in the local newspapers—subscribe to all of them if possible, or read it at the public library.

What correction should be made to this sentence?

(1) replace you with one
(2) replace you with they
(3) insert a comma after openings
(4) replace it with them
(5) no correction is necessary

Choice (4) is correct. The pronoun has a plural antecedent, *newspapers.* The pronoun must, therefore, also be plural, *them* not *it.*

Sentence 7: Familiarize oneself with the types of jobs most often available, with the various employment offices, and with the skills most in demand.

What correction should be made to this sentence?

(1) change Familiarize to Familiarized
(2) replace oneself with yourself
(3) insert a comma after various
(4) change offices to office
(5) change demand to demanding

Choice (2) is correct. The subject of the verb *Familiarize* does not appear, but it is understood to be the pronoun *you.* The pronoun *yourself* corresponds to the understood subject *you.*

Social studies

Directions: Choose the <u>one</u> best answer to each question.

In the United States, a governor of a state has the power to do all of the following EXCEPT

(1) prepare a budget for the next year
(2) veto a law passed by the state legislature
(3) send an ambassador to a foreign country
(4) campaign for the members of his or her political party
(5) suggest laws he or she would like to see passed

Choices (1), (2), and (5) describe activities that might be performed by the governor of a state. Choice (4) describes an activity common to most elected officials. The correct answer is choice (3). Only the federal government of the United States—the President with the advice and consent of the Senate—can send ambassadors to other countries.

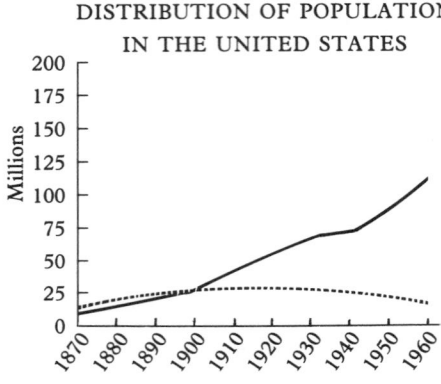

DISTRIBUTION OF POPULATION
IN THE UNITED STATES

Urban Dwellers———   Farm Dwellers······

According to the graph above, the year the population was evenly distributed between urban and rural areas was approximately

(1) 1880   (2) 1900   (3) 1920   (4) 1940   (5) 1960

First, it is important to understand that "evenly distributed between urban and rural areas" means that the two populations are equal. In a line graph such as the one given here, two quantities are equal when the lines for both quantities cross; that is, because the height of the line above the base represents the quantity, the lines will cross when the heights are the same. The lines for the urban and rural areas cross just once, above the time 1900. Therefore, the correct choice is (2).

**Answer every question
on the GED.
There is no penalty
for guessing.**

The next two questions refer to the following map.

Which area is associated with the Gold Rush of 1849?

(1) 1   (2) 2   (3) 3   (4) 4   (5) 5

Many GED items rely on knowledge that the person taking the test is supposed to have. This is one of them, but you can also eliminate some choices even if you do not remember that the Gold Rush of 1849 brought many people to California. For example, the region east of the Mississippi was filled with people in the 1800's, so choice (5) (region 5) can be ruled out. With only four choices left, you have a better chance of guessing the correct choice, which is (1).

In the middle of the 19th century, American industry was most heavily concentrated in which area?

(1) 1   (2) 3   (3) 4   (4) 6   (5) 7

Make sure that you remember that the 19th century is the same as the 1800's, so this question centers about the years around 1850. As in the previous item, you can eliminate choices (1), (2), and (3) (regions 1, 3, and 4) because these regions did not have enough people to support heavy industry at that time. If you do not remember that heavy industry was concentrated mostly in New England at that time, which is choice (5) (region 7), you still have a fifty-fifty chance of guessing the correct choice.

All of the following are undesirable results of man's efforts to improve his standard of living EXCEPT

(1) erosion of soils
(2) desalination of seawater
(3) destruction of wildlife habitats
(4) exhaustion of mines
(5) pollution of air and water

In this kind of a question, there is a "hidden double negative" that can confuse the person taking the test. The "EXCEPT" in the stem means that you want to find a choice that is not undesirable. "Not undesirable" is not necessarily the same as desirable. It means that you need to reject four choices that *are* undesirable. Choices (1), (3), (4), and (5) all describe results that are undesirable. Choice 2 describes something that can be desirable, so it is correct.

Reading

Directions: Choose the best answer to each question.

What Is Poetry?

What is poetry? Who knows?
Not the rose, but the scent of the rose;

Not the sky, but the light of the sky;

Not the fly, but the gleam of the fly;

Not the sea, but the sound of the sea;

Not myself, but what makes me
See, hear, feel something that prose
Cannot, and what it is, who knows?

According to the poem, poetry, unlike prose, does which of the following?

(1) relates to feelings rather than to objects
(2) explains things fully and logically
(3) deals with everyday life
(4) concerns itself with things, not people
(5) describes things in simple words

Choice (2) is not generally thought of as relating to poetry, so it can be rejected. The poem does not refer to everyday life (3) or simple words (5), so they can be eliminated. Choice (1) fits better than choice (2) because *scent, light, gleam,* and *sound* involve human *feelings* about the objects that are mentioned.

In a recent survey, three out of four people interviewed said that they liked Soothies better than the other leading pain reliever. Here's what some of those people had to say:

Ms. R. Jones: "Soothies really make me feel better fast. I've told my friends about them."
Mr. L. Smith: "Soothies taste better than the other leading pain reliever. My children chew Soothies like candy. And for the same price, you get more Soothies than pills of the other leading brand."
Dr. Q. Brown: "I recommend Soothies for fast relief. They work best for me."

Soothies cost less than the other leading pain reliever. So get the best for less! Try Soothies.

Dr. Brown recommends Soothies because they

(1) taste good to him   (2) help most people
(3) are inexpensive   (4) bring him relief
(5) are the leading brand

When asked for a specific detail in a reading passage, focus only on the part that contains the information asked for. In this case, you can go directly to what Dr. Brown has said. Choice (4) is the only one with this idea, so it is correct.

Science

Directions: Each of the questions or incomplete statements below is followed by five suggested answers or completions. Select the one that is best in each case and then blacken the corresponding space on the answer sheet.

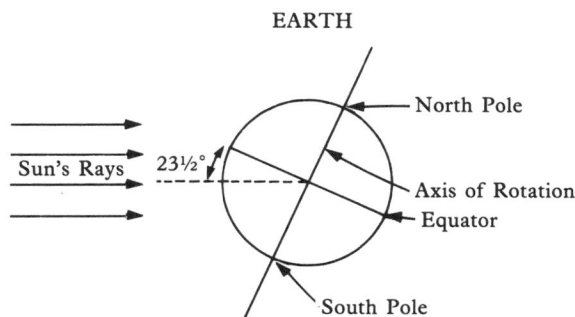

In the diagram above, the sun's rays and the axis of rotation of Earth are both in the plane of the page. The diagram best represents the position of Earth nearest to

(1) March 21
(2) June 21
(3) July 1
(4) September 23
(5) December 21

This is the kind of question that asks you to see something in your mind's eye. As you look at the diagram, picture the time of the year when the northern hemisphere is tilted away from the warming rays of the sun: wintertime. This corresponds to choice (5), which is correct.

Evidence indicates that cigarette smoking results in

(1) cardiovascular stress
(2) hepatitis
(3) whooping cough
(4) pneumonia
(5) pleurisy

Most people think of lung cancer when they think of the effects of cigarette smoking, but lung cancer is not among the choices. Emphysema, another common disease associated with smoking, also is not present. You might think that choices (3), (4), or (5)—all associated with the lungs—might be correct, but this is one of those cases in which the test-maker has been deliberately misleading. If you recognize that choices (2), (3), (4), and (5) all are infectious diseases, then none of them can be caused by cigarette smoking. Therefore, the correct choice must be (1), cardiovascular stress. It is also helpful to know that *cardiovascular* relates to the heart and blood vessels, and smoking is often thought of as being damaging to the heart.

Mathematics

Directions: For all problems choose the <u>one</u> best answer.

During the month of July the Herbert family spent $32.28, $27.39, $37.54, $54.80, and $52.20 for food. How much did they spend on food for the month?

(1) $184.21   (2) $193.11   (3) $193.21
(4) $203.19   (5) $204.21

Speed helps in getting through a test. While this item can be answered by actually adding the amounts, you should notice at once that three of the choices end in 21 cents. Add just the cents: $0.28 + 0.39 + 0.54 + 0.80 + 0.20 = 2.21$, so (as could be suspected) the correct choice has to be (1), (3), or (5). Now look at the dollars. Both (2) and (3) have $193. Since (3) is on the possibly correct list and (2) is not, the correct answer is most likely (3). Check by estimating the sum (round off the numbers to whole dollars): $32 + $27 + $38 + $55 + $52 = 204. The correct choice must be (5), not (3). The test-maker was trying to mislead you.

One statute mile is equal to 5280 feet. If one nautical mile is approximately 1.15 statute miles, then one nautical mile is equal to approximately how many feet?

(1) 4590   (2) 5165   (3) 5395
(4) 5545   (5) 6070

With a question such as this one, you may find it easy to perform the indicated multiplication: $1.15 \times 5280 = 6072$. If multiplication is not easy for you, you may find it easier to approach the problem the following way.

The statement that a nautical mile is 1.15 statute miles means that a nautical mile is 15 percent larger than a statute mile. Since a nautical mile is larger than a statute mile, you can eliminate choices (1) and (2) automatically. You also can note that 15 percent is halfway between 10 and 20 percent. It is easy to calculate that 10 percent of 5280 is 528 and that twice 528 is 1056, 20 percent of 5280. Therefore, a nautical mile must be about 700 or 800 feet larger than a statute mile. Only choice (5) is anywhere near correct. The method of estimation is especially good, since the actual product of 1.15 and 5280 is 6072.40, not 6070.

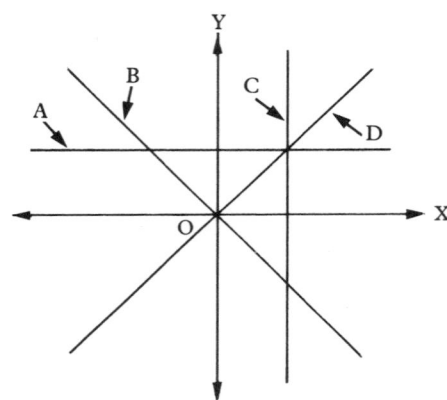

Which of the lines shown in the figure above has zero slope?

(1) A   (2) B   (3) C   (4) D
(5) None of the above

If you have studied slope, it is essential to remember the difference between a slope of zero and no slope. Line A has a slope of zero, while line C has no slope (its slope is undefined). If you have not studied slope, you can still guess that slope refers to the degree of slantedness or steepness of a line. The line that is not slanted, or has zero steepness, is line A. The correct choice is (1).

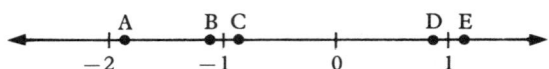

On the number line above, which lettered point could represent the number $-\frac{9}{8}$?

(1) A   (2) B   (3) C   (4) D   (5) E

From the labels below the number line, it is clear that all the negative numbers are to the left, so you can eliminate points D and E easily. It may help then to think of $-\frac{9}{8}$ as $-1\frac{1}{8}$. Just as $+1\frac{1}{8}$ is a number between $+1$ and $+2$, $-1\frac{1}{8}$ is between -1 and -2, so only A or B could be correct choices. Since $-1\frac{1}{8}$ must be closer to -1 than it is to -2, the correct choice is (2) (point B).

If $x + y = 36$ and $x = 2y$, then $x =$

(1) 9   (2) 12   (3) 18   (4) 24   (5) 27

This problem can be solved by a formal method, but it is probably easier, faster, and just as accurate to treat this as a problem in reasoning, not a problem in algebra. Since $x = 2y$, the value of x must be twice the value of y, or y must be one half of x. This rules out odd numbers for x, since the sum of x and y would then contain a fraction. Of the remaining choices (2), (3), and (4), choices (2) and (3) are easily seen to be too small, so the correct choice must be (4). Always check problems if you can. If $x = 24$, then $y = 12$, and $24 + 12 = 36$. (Another approach is to use substitution. Since $x = 2y$, substitute 2y for x in $x + y = 36$. This produces $2y + y = 36$, or $3y = 36$. Therefore, $y = \frac{36}{3}$, or 12. Now go back to $x = 2y$ to see that x is twice 12, or 24.)

For further information on the GED, contact your provincial or state department of education, or:
American Council on Education
One Dupont Circle
Washington, DC 20036

Taking Aptitude Tests

SAT

The SAT requires about three hours to complete and consists of two sections, verbal and mathematics. Each section is made up of several subtests. The verbal and mathematics sections are scored individually on a scale of 200 to 800. Guessing is penalized on the SAT. The penalty is so slight, however, that you should guess if you can eliminate even one of the choices.

Verbal

The verbal sections of the SAT contain four types of questions:
- 25 antonyms,
- 20 analogies,
- 15 sentence completions, and
- 25 questions based on reading passages.

The antonyms usually take the least time per question, followed by analogies, sentence completion questions, and, finally, reading comprehension questions. Individual students spend varying amounts of time working on the different types of questions. Some students can answer two or three antonyms a minute, but the same students may take more than seven minutes to read a 400-word passage and answer five questions on it.

Antonyms (opposites). Antonym questions primarily test the extent of your vocabulary. The vocabulary used in the antonym questions includes words that you are likely to come across in your general reading, although some words may not be the kinds you use in everyday speech.

Among the five choices offered, you are looking for the word that means the *opposite* of the given word. Words that have exactly the same meaning as the given word are not included among the five choices.

You are looking for the *best* answer. Read all of the choices before deciding which one is best, even if you feel sure you know the answer.

Few words have exact opposites, that is, words that are opposite in all of their meanings. You should find the word that is *most nearly* opposite.

You need to be flexible. A word can have several meanings.

You will often recognize a word you have encountered in your reading but have never looked up in the dictionary. If you do not know the dictionary meaning of a word but have a feeling for how the word should be used, try to make up a short phrase or sentence using the word. This may give you a clue as to which choice is an opposite, even though you may not be able to define the word precisely.

Directions: Each question below consists of a word in capital letters, followed by five lettered words or phrases. Choose the word or phrase that is most nearly <u>opposite</u> in meaning to the word in capital letters. Since some of the questions require you to distinguish fine shades of meaning, consider all the choices before deciding which is best.

SUBSEQUENT: (A) primary (B) recent (C) contemporary (D) prior (E) simultaneous

Subsequent means "following in time or order; succeeding." Someone working quickly might choose (B) *recent* because it refers to a past action and *subsequent* refers to an action in the future. However, choice (D) *prior* is the best answer. It is more nearly the opposite of *subsequent* than is *recent.*

FERMENTING: (A) improvising (B) stagnating (C) wavering (D) plunging (E) dissolving

Even though *fermenting* is normally associated with chemical reactions, whereas *stagnating* is normally associated with water, *fermenting* means "being agitated" and *stagnating* means "being motionless." Therefore, choice (B) *stagnating* is the best of the five choices.

DEPRESS: (A) force (B) allow (C) clarify (D) elate (E) loosen

The word *depress* can mean "to push down." However, no word meaning "to lift up" is included among the choices. Therefore, you must consider another meaning of *depress,* to sadden or discourage. Option (D) *elate* means to fill with joy or pride. The best answer is (D) *elate.*

INCUMBENT: (A) conscious (B) effortless (C) optional (D) improper (E) irrelevant

You may remember *incumbent* used in a sentence such as "It is incumbent upon me to finish this." If you can think of such a phrase, you may be able to recognize that *incumbent* means "imposed as a duty" or "obligatory." Of the five choices, (A), (B), and (D) are in no way opposites of *incumbent* and you can easily eliminate them. Choice (E) means "not pertinent" and choice (C) means "not compulsory." Although choice (E) may look attractive, choice (C) *optional* is more nearly an exact opposite to *incumbent.* Choice (C), therefore, is the answer.

Analogies. Analogy questions test your ability to see a relationship in a pair of words, to understand the ideas expressed in the relationship, and to recognize a similar or parallel relationship.

For the analogy below, just state the relationship between the original pair of words and then decide which pair of words from choices (A)–(E) has the same relationship.

Remember that a pair of words can have more than one relationship.

Directions: Each question below consists of a related pair of words or phrases, followed by five lettered pairs of words or phrases. Select the lettered pair that best expresses a relationship similar to that expressed in the original pair.

SUBMISSIVE : LED ::   (A) wealthy : employed
(B) intolerant : indulged   (C) humble : humiliated
(D) incorrigible : taught
(E) inconspicuous : overlooked

The relationship between *submissive* and *led* can be expressed as "to be submissive is to be easily led." Only choice (E) has the same relationship: to be inconspicuous is to be easily overlooked.

To be *intolerant* is not to be easily *indulged*, to be *humble* is not to be easily *humiliated*, and to be *incorrigible* (or incapable of being reformed) is not to be easily *taught*. With regard to choice (A), although the wealthy may find it easier to get employment than do the poor, the statement "to be wealthy is to be easily employed" is an expression of opinion and not an expression of the relationship between the words according to their dictionary meanings.

SONG : REPERTOIRE ::   (A) score : melody
(B) instrument : artist   (C) solo : chorus
(D) benediction : church   (E) suit : wardrobe

The best answer is choice (E). The relationship between the words can be expressed as "several (first word) make up a (second word)." Several (songs) make up a (repertoire) as several (suits) make up a (wardrobe).

REQUEST : ENTREAT ::   (A) control : explode
(B) admire : idolize   (C) borrow : steal
(D) repeat : plead   (E) cancel : invalidate

The best answer is choice (B). Although both of the capitalized words have similar meanings, they express different degrees of feeling; to (entreat) is to (request) with strong feeling as to (idolize) is to (admire) with strong feeling.

To answer analogy questions, you must think carefully about the precise meanings of words. For instance, if you thought the word *entreat* meant only to ask instead of to ask urgently, you would have trouble establishing the correct relationship between *request* and *entreat.*

AMPLIFIER : HEAR ::   (A) turntable : listen
(B) typewriter : spell   (C) platter : eat
(D) camera : feel   (E) microscope : see

The best answer is choice (E). An (amplifier) magnifies in order to help a person (hear) in the same way that a (microscope) magnifies in order to help a person (see). Note that, in (A), while a *turntable* is part of a larger mechanism that allows a person to *listen,* the choice is not as good an answer as (E) because a *turntable* does not magnify anything. Choice (D) is also wrong for a similar reason: a *camera* produces pictures that may make a person *feel* something, but a *camera* does not magnify in order to help a person to *feel.*

PRIDE : LION ::   (A) snake : python
(B) pack : wolf   (C) rat : mouse
(D) bird : starling   (E) dog : canine

A possible relationship between *pride* and *lion* might be that the first word describes a characteristic of the second (especially in mythology). Using this reasoning, you might look for an answer such as *wisdom : owl,* but none of the given choices has that kind of relationship. Another relationship between *pride* and *lion* is "a group of lions is called a pride"; therefore, the answer is (B) *pack : wolf,* since a group of wolves is called a pack.

KNIFE : INCISION ::   (A) bulldozer : excavation
(B) tool : operation   (C) pencil : calculation
(D) hose : irrigation   (E) plow : agriculture

On the most general level, the relationship between *knife* and *incision* is that the object indicated by the first word is used to perform the action indicated by the second word. Since a (knife) is used to make an (incision), a (bulldozer) is used to make an (excavation), and a (hose) is used for (irrigation), there appear to be two correct answers. You need to go back and state the relationship more precisely. Some aspect of the relationship between the original pair exists in only one of the choices. A more precise relationship between *knife* and *incision* could be expressed as: "a knife cuts into something to make an incision" and "a bulldozer cuts into something to make an excavation." This relationship eliminates *hose : irrigation* as a possible answer. The best answer is choice (A).

Sentence completion. Sentence completion questions test your ability to recognize relationships among parts of a sentence. Each question has a sentence with one or two words missing. You must choose the word or set of words that best fits with the other parts of the sentence. You will find that even if you are not familiar with the topic of a sentence, there is enough information in the sentence for you to find the correct answer from the context of the sentence itself.

For a better understanding of sentence completion questions, read the following sample questions and explanations.

Directions: Each sentence below has one or two blanks, each blank indicating that something has been omitted. Beneath the sentence are five lettered words or sets of words. Choose the word or set of words that best fits the meaning of the sentence as a whole.

Although its publicity has been ----, the film itself is intelligent, well-acted, handsomely produced, and altogether ----.

(A) tasteless . . respectable
(B) extensive . . moderate
(C) sophisticated . . amateur
(D) risqué . . crude
(E) perfect . . spectacular

The word *although* suggests that the publicity gave the wrong impression of the movie, so look for two words that are more or less opposite in meaning. Also, the second word has to fit in with "intelligent, well-acted, handsomely produced." Choices (D) and (E) are not opposites. The words in choice (B) are somewhat opposite in meaning, but do not logically fulfill the expectation set up by the word *although*. Choice (C) can't be the correct answer, even though *sophisticated* and *amateur* are nearly opposites, because an "intelligent, well-acted, handsomely produced" film isn't amateurish. Only choice (A), when inserted in the sentence, makes a logical statement.

She is a skeptic, ---- to believe that the accepted opinion of the majority is generally ----.

(A) prone . . infallible   (B) afraid . . misleading
(C) inclined . . justifiable   (D) quick . . significant
(E) disposed . . erroneous

The words to be inserted in the blank spaces in the question above must result in a statement that is consistent with the definition of a skeptic. Since a skeptic would hardly consider the accepted opinion of the majority as *infallible, justifiable,* or *significant,* you can eliminate choices (A), (C), and (D). A skeptic would not be afraid that the accepted opinion of the majority is misleading; a skeptic would believe that it was. Therefore, choice (B) is not correct. Only choice (E) *disposed . . erroneous* makes a logical sentence.

Nearly all the cultivated plants utilized by the Chinese have been of ---- origin; even rice, though known in China since Neolithic times, came from India.

(A) foreign   (B) ancient   (C) wild   (D) obscure
(E) common

To answer this question, you need to consider the entire sentence—the part that comes after the semicolon as well as the part that comes before it. If you only consider the first part of the question, all five choices seem plausible. The second part of the sentence adds a specific example—that rice came to China from India. This idea of origin supports and clarifies the "origin" mentioned in the first part of the sentence and eliminates (C), (D), and (E) as possible answers. The mention of Neolithic times makes (B) harder to eliminate, but the sentence is not logical when (B) is used to fill in the blank because the emphasis in the second part of the sentence—country of origin—is inconsistent with that in the first—age. Only choice (A) produces a sentence that is logical and consistent.

The excitement does not ---- but ---- his senses, giving him a keener perception of a thousand details.

(A) slow . . diverts
(B) blur . . sharpens
(C) overrule . . constricts
(D) heighten . . aggravates
(E) forewarn . . quickens

Since the sentence has two blanks to be filled, you must make sure that both words make sense in the sentence. If you look for grammatical clues within the sentence, you will see that the word *but* implies that the answer will involve two words that are more or less opposite in meaning. If you keep this in mind, you can eliminate all of the choices except for (B) *blur . . sharpens.* Only the words in choice (B) imply opposition. Also, "sharpens his senses" is consistent with the notion that he has a "keener perception of a thousand details."

They argue that the author was determined to ---- his own conclusion, so he ---- any information that did not support it.

(A) uphold . . ignored
(B) revise . . destroyed
(C) advance . . devised
(D) disprove . . distorted
(E) reverse . . confiscated

The logic of the sentence makes it fairly easy to eliminate choices (B), (D), and (E). The first word in choice (A), *uphold,* and the first word in (C), *advance,* seem all right. However, the second word in choice (C), *devised,* does not make sense in the sentence. Why would an author who wished to advance his theory devise information that did not support it? Only choice (A) makes a logically consistent sentence.

Reading comprehension. The reading comprehension questions on the SAT test your ability to read and understand a passage. Each passage contains the information you need for the questions that follow it.

Several types of questions are asked about the passage. Some ask about the main idea of a passage. Some questions ask about those ideas that are stated directly in the passage. Some ask you to recognize applications of the author's principles or opinions. In some questions you must make an inference from what you have read. In others you must evaluate the way the author develops and presents the passage.

Following are a sample passage, sample questions, and explanations of each of the questions.

Directions: The passage below is followed by questions based on its content. Answer all questions following the passage on the basis of what is <u>stated</u> or <u>implied</u> in that passage.

Between guilds and modern business firms there is a profound gulf. Unlike modern firms, the purpose of guilds was not first and foremost to make money. Rather, it was to preserve a certain orderly way of life —a way that envisaged a decent income for the master craftsmen but that was certainly not intended to allow any of them to become "big" businessmen. On the contrary, guilds were specifically designed to ward off any such outcome of an uninhibited struggle among their members. The terms of service and wages were fixed by custom. So, too, were the terms of sale: a guild member who cornered the supply of an item or bought wholesale to sell at retail was severely punished. Competition was strictly limited and profits were held to prescribed levels. Advertising was forbidden, and even technical progress in advance of one's fellow guildsmen was considered disloyal.

Surely the guilds represent a more "modern" aspect of feudal life than the manor, but the whole temper of guild life was still far removed from the goals and ideals of modern business enterprise. There was no free competition and no restless probing for advantage. Existing on the margin of a relatively moneyless society, the guilds were organizations that sought to take the risks out of their slender enterprises. As such, they were as drenched in the medieval atmosphere as the manors.

According to the passage, modern business enterprises, compared to the medieval guilds, are

(A) more concerned with increasing profits
(B) influenced more by craftsmen than by tradesmen
(C) more subordinate to the demands of consumers
(D) less progressive in financial dealings
(E) less interested in quantity than quality

SAT reading passages contain all the information you'll need to answer the questions.

Relax.

To answer this question, locate the parts of the passage that compare guilds and modern business—the beginnings of the first and second paragraphs. Lines 2–3 suggest that the foremost purpose of modern firms is to make money. Lines 21–22 indicate that "free competition" and "restless probing for advantage" are central to modern business enterprise. Choice (A) is the most appropriate answer among the choices given. There is no justification in the passage for any of the other choices. Some people might argue from their own experience or opinion that (C) is a possible answer. However, since the question says, "According to the passage . . . ," the answer must be based on what is stated in the passage.

It can be inferred that the guilds were organized as they were because

(A) life on the manors was boring and drab
(B) technical improvements were still improbable
(C) they stressed preservation and stability, not progress
(D) people in medieval times were interested in advancing individual liberty
(E) social status was determined by income

This question is not answered simply and directly in the passage itself, but the passage gives you information to draw on. In the first paragraph, the author notes that the purpose of guilds "was to preserve a certain orderly way of life" and that guilds were specifically designed "to ward off . . . uninhibited struggle among their members." In the second paragraph, the author states that the guilds "were organizations that sought to take the risks out of their slender enterprises." From these statements and the comparisons between guilds and modern business firms that the author makes elsewhere in the passage, choice (C) is the most reasonable conclusion to draw. Choice (A) is not related to the purpose of the organization of the guilds. The statement about technical progress made in lines 16–17 weakens the plausibility of the inference in (B). The passage does not provide enough information to justify the inferences made in (D) and (E). This is a fairly easy and straightforward inference question. You may be asked others that will require somewhat more sophisticated reasoning processes.

There is a slight penalty for guessing on the SAT. If you can eliminate a choice, you should guess.

Mathematics

Two types of multiple-choice questions are used in the mathematical sections of the SAT:

1. Standard multiple-choice questions (approximately two-thirds of the math questions)
2. Quantitative comparison questions (approximately one-third of the math questions)

Standard multiple-choice

Directions: In this section solve each problem, using any available space on the page for scratch work. Then decide which is the best of the choices given and blacken the corresponding space on the answer sheet.

If $2a + b = 5$, then $4a + 2b =$

(A) $\dfrac{5}{4}$ (B) $\dfrac{5}{2}$ (C) 10 (D) 20 (E) 25

This is an example of a problem that requires realizing that $4a + 2b = 2(2a + b)$. Therefore, $4a + 2b = 2(2a + b) = 2(5) = 10$. The correct answer is (C).

If $16 \cdot 16 \cdot 16 = 8 \cdot 8 \cdot P$, then $P =$

(A) 4 (B) 8 (C) 32 (D) 48 (E) 64

This question can be solved by several methods. A time-consuming method would be to multiply the three 16s and then divide the result by the product of 8 and 8. A quicker approach would be to find what additional factors are needed on the right side of the equation to match those on the left side. These additional factors are two 2's and a 16, the product of which is 64. The correct answer is (E).

If a car travels X kilometers of a trip in H hours, in how many hours can it travel the next Y kilometers at this rate?

(A) $\dfrac{XY}{H}$ (B) $\dfrac{HY}{X}$ (C) $\dfrac{HX}{Y}$ (D) $\dfrac{H + Y}{X}$

(E) $\dfrac{X + Y}{H}$

You can solve this problem by using ratios or by using the distance formula.

Using the ratio method, X kilometers is to H hours as Y kilometers is to $\square$ hours, where $\square$ represents the amount of time required to travel Y kilometers:

$$\frac{X}{H} = \frac{Y}{\square}$$

$$X \,\square = HY$$

$$\square = \frac{HY}{X}$$

The correct answer is (B).

The town of Mason is located on Eagle Lake. The town of Canton is west of Mason. Sinclair is east of Canton, but west of Mason. Dexter is east of Richmond, but west of Sinclair and Canton. Assuming all these towns are in the United States, which town is farthest west?

(A) Mason (B) Dexter (C) Canton
(D) Sinclair (E) Richmond

For this kind of problem, drawing a diagram may help. In this case, a line can be effectively used to locate the relative position of each town. Start with the statement "The town of Canton is west of Mason" and, using abbreviations, draw the following:

From the remaining information, place the other towns in their correct order:

The final sketch shows that the town farthest west is Richmond (R) and the correct answer is (E).

If the symbol $\triangledown$ between two expressions indicates that the expression on the right exceeds the expression on the left by 1, which of the following is (are) true for all real numbers x?

I. $x(x + 2) \triangledown (x + 1)^2$

II. $x^2 \triangledown (x + 1)^2$

III. $\dfrac{x}{y} \triangledown \dfrac{x + 1}{y + 1}$

(A) None (B) I only (C) II only
(D) III only (E) I and III

This kind of problem involves working with a newly defined symbol. One approach is to check the statements one at a time. Statement I reduces to $x^2 + 2x \triangledown x^2 + 2x + 1$, so the expression on the right does exceed the expression on the left by 1. Therefore, statement I is true. Statement II reduces to $x^2 \triangledown x^2 + 2x + 1$, so the right expression exceeds the left expression by $2x + 1$, which is not equal to 1 except when $x = 0$. This makes statement II false. Statement III is more difficult to check, but you can verify by subtraction, or by substituting numbers (for example, $x = 3, y = 5$), that the expression on the right does not exceed the expression on the left by 1. Therefore, statement III is false. The only true statement is I, so the correct answer is (B).

In a problem of this kind, if you are able to decide about only one or two statements, you can still eliminate some choices and guess among those remaining. For example, if you can conclude that I is true, then the correct answer is either (B) or (E) because these choices contain statement I.

A number is divisible by 9 if the sum of its digits is divisible by 9. Which of the following numbers is divisible by 45?

(A) 63,345 (B) 72,365
(C) 99,999 (D) 72,144
(E) 98,145

It would be very time-consuming to divide each choice by 45. In order for a number to be divisible by 45 it must be divisible by both 9 and 5. Choices (A), (B), and (E) are divisible by 5, but choices (C) and (D) are not, so you can eliminate choices (C) and (D) immediately. You are given that a number is divisible by 9 if the sum of its digits is divisible by 9. The sums of the digits in choices (A), (B), and (E) are 21, 23, and 27, respectively.

Of these choices only 27 is divisible by 9. The correct answer is (E). Your scratch work for this problem might appear as follows:

(A) 63,345 2̶1̶   (B) 72,365 2̶3̶
(C) 9̶9̶,9̶9̶9̶   (D) 7̶2̶,1̶4̶4̶
(E) 98,145 ㉗

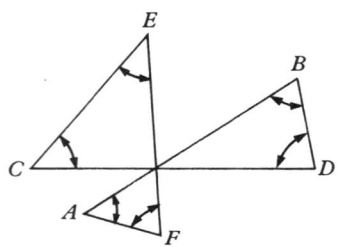

In the triangles above, if *AB, CD,* and *EF* are line segments, what is the sum of the measures of the six marked angles?

(A) 180° (B) 360° (C) 540° (D) 720°
(E) It cannot be determined from the information given.

This problem requires a creative problem-solving approach. One solution involves recognizing that the sum of the three unmarked angles in the triangles is 180°.

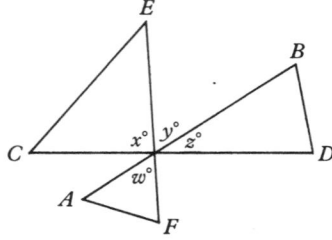

Because *CD* is a line segment, the sum of angles x, y, and z is 180°. Also, $y = w$ because they are vertical angles. Therefore, $x + w + z = 180$. Since the sum of the measures of all angles in the three triangles is 540° ($3 \cdot 180°$) and the sum of the unmarked angles of the triangles in the original figure equals 180°, it follows that the sum of the marked angles is 540° − 180° = 360°. The correct answer is (B).

If the average of seven x's is 7, what is the average of fourteen x's?

(A) $\frac{1}{7}$ (B) $\frac{1}{2}$ (C) 1 (D) 7 (E) 14

Do not get caught up in the wording of this problem, which might lead you to choose (E) 14. The average of any number of equal numbers such as x is always x. Since you are given that the average of seven x's is 7, it follows that $x = 7$ and that the average of 14 x's is also 7. The correct answer is (D).

If 90 percent of P is 30 percent of Q, then Q is what percent of *P?*

(A) 3% (B) 27% (C) 30% (D) 270%
(E) 300%

Writing an algebraic equation for this percent problem not only simplifies the work, it also helps you organize your thoughts. "90 percent of P is 30 percent of Q" can be written as $0.90P = 0.30Q$ (or $\frac{9}{10}P = \frac{3}{10}Q$). "$Q$ is what percent of P" tells you to find $\frac{Q}{P}$ and express it as a percent. $\frac{Q}{P} = 3$; therefore, Q is 300 percent of P and the correct answer is (E).

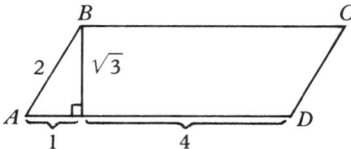

The figure above shows a piece of paper in the shape of a parallelogram with measurements as indicated. If the paper is tacked at its center to a flat surface and then rotated about its center, the points covered by the paper will be a circular region of diameter

(A) $\sqrt{3}$ (B) 2 (C) 5 (D) $\sqrt{28}$ (E) $\sqrt{39}$

The first step in solving the problem is to realize that the center of the parallelogram is the point of intersection of the two diagonals; thus, the diameter you are looking for is the length of the longer diagonal *AC*. One way to find *AC* is to think of the additional lines drawn as shown below.

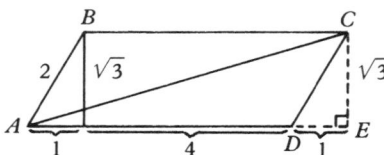

The triangles at each end are congruent (equal in size and shape), so the lengths of *DE* and *CE* are 1 and $\sqrt{3}$, respectively. *AEC* is a right triangle; therefore, the Pythagorean theorem can be used in solving the problem:

$$AC^2 = CE^2 + AE^2$$

$$AC^2 = (\sqrt{3})^2 + (6)^2 = 3 + 36 = 39$$

The diameter *AC* is $\sqrt{39}$ and the correct answer is (E).

Quantitative comparison. Quantitative comparison questions emphasize the concepts of equalities, inequalities, and estimation. They generally involve less reading, take less time to answer, and require less computation than regular multiple-choice questions. Quantitative comparison questions may not be as familiar to you as other types of questions. Therefore, give special attention to the directions ahead of time. Be careful not to mark answer option E when responding to the four-choice quantitative comparison questions.

To solve a quantitative comparison problem, compare the quantities in the two columns and decide whether one quantity is greater than the other, whether the two quantities are equal, or whether the relationship cannot be determined from the information given.

Problems are clearly separated and the *quantities to be compared are always on the same line as the number of the problem.* Figures and additional information provided for some problems appear *above* the quantities to be compared. The following are some practice problems with explanations to help you understand this type of question.

Directions: Each of the following questions consists of two quantities, one in Column A and one in Column B. You are to compare the two quantities and on the answer sheet blacken space

A if the quantity in Column A is greater;
B if the quantity in Column B is greater;
C if the two quantities are equal;
D if the relationship cannot be determined from the information given.

Notes: 1. In certain questions, information concerning one or both of the quantities to be compared is centered above the two columns.
2. In a given question, a symbol that appears in both columns represents the same thing in Column A as it does in Column B.
3. Letters such as x, n, and k stand for real numbers.

Column A	Column B

1. $(37) (\frac{1}{43}) (58)$ $(59) (\frac{1}{43}) (37)$

Because the numbers in this problem are fairly large, it may save time to study the multipliers first before attempting the calculations. Note that (37) and $(\frac{1}{43})$ appear in both quantities; thus, the only numbers left for you to compare are 58 and 59. Since $59 > 58$, the quantity on the right is greater and the correct answer is (B).

Answer the easy questions first.

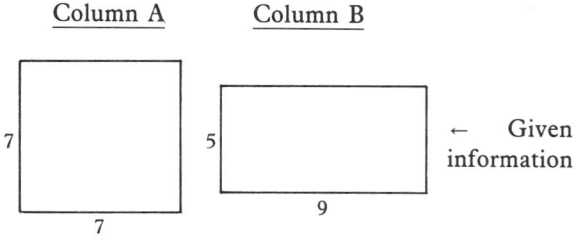

Column A	Column B	

2. The perimeter of the square   The perimeter of the rectangle   ← Quantities to be compared

It can be assumed that the units used to indicate measures in a given problem are the same in all figures in that problem unless otherwise stated. The correct answer is (C) because the perimeter of the square is $4 \cdot 7 = 28$ units and the perimeter of the rectangle is $(2 \cdot 5) + (2 \cdot 9) = 28$ units.

Column A	Column B

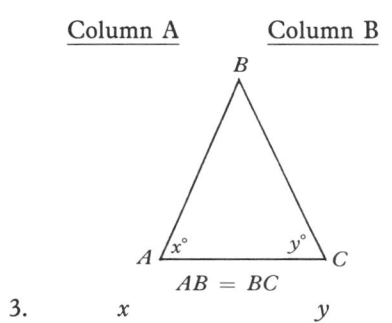

3. x y

Since $AB = BC$, the angles opposite AB and BC are equal; therefore, $x = y$. The correct answer is (C).

Column A	Column B

4. $\sqrt{2} - 1$ $\sqrt{3} - 1$

For any positive number x, the symbol $\sqrt{x}$ denotes the positive square root of x. The fact that $\sqrt{3} > \sqrt{2}$ leads to the conclusion that $\sqrt{3} - 1 > \sqrt{2} - 1$. The correct answer is (B). Note that $x^2 = 9$ has two solutions, $x = 3$ or $x = -3$. However, $\sqrt{9} = 3$, not ± 3.

Column A	Column B

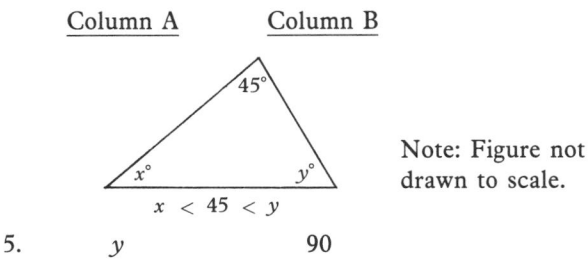

Note: Figure not drawn to scale.

5. y 90

Because the sum of the angles of a triangle is 180, $x + y + 45 = 180$ or $x + y = 135$. Since $x < 45$, it follows that $y > 90$. The answer is (A). In this problem, do not try to determine the answer from the appearance of the figure because the note indicates that the figure is not drawn to scale.

ACT

The ACT takes about three hours to complete. It consists of four sections: English, mathematics, reading, and science reasoning. The reading and science reasoning tests are based on passages from the social studies, humanities, and sciences, or on a passage of prose fiction. Note that nothing is taken off for wrong answers, so guessing can help when you do not know an answer. Every item should be completed, even if you have no idea of what the right answer is. As the following explanations show, it is often possible to find a helpful clue to the correct answer, or to select the correct answer by eliminating incorrect answers.

English test

Directions: In the passage that follows, certain words and phrases are underlined and numbered. In the right-hand column, you will find alternatives for each underlined part. You are to choose the one that best expresses the idea, makes the statement appropriate for standard written English, or is worded most consistently with the style and tone of the passage as a whole. If you think the original version is best, choose "NO CHANGE." You will also find questions about a section of the passage, or about the passage as a whole. These questions do not refer to an underlined portion of the passage, but rather are identified by a number or numbers in a box. For each question, choose the alternative you consider best and blacken the corresponding oval on your answer sheet. Read the passage through once before you begin to answer the questions that accompany it. You cannot determine most answers without reading several sentences beyond the question. Be sure that you have read far enough ahead each time you choose an alternative.

What teases us with the giddy possibilities of freedom better than a videocassette recorder? There are few things that seem to promise so much for so little effort. Program the right channel, set the timer, and even the late-late-late movie is within grasp. Neither storm nor sleep will keep a [1] well-running VCR from its appointed task.

In fact, a VCR can free us from the tyranny of the television schedule altogether. With video stores almost as prevalent as fast-food restaurants. The [2] desire to finally see the conclusion of a movie can be as readily satisfied as the urge for a burger and fries. [3]

[1] Unfortunately, the *us* I've been talking about doesn't including me. [4]
[2] For example, I have several versions of Alfred Hitchcock's mystery-comedy *The 39 Steps* none of them includes [5]

(continued)

1. F. NO CHANGE
   G. Neither, storm nor
   H. Neither storm nor,
   J. Neither storm, nor

F is correct. The phrase *neither storm nor sleep* should not be broken with a comma, so G, H, and J are wrong.

2. A. NO CHANGE
   B. restaurants, the
   C. restaurants; the
   D. restaurants, and the

B is correct. Choice A is wrong because the sentence in question is a fragment. C is wrong because semicolons alone are not used between a dependent clause and an independent clause. D is wrong because the conjunction *and* results in a nonsense sentence.

3. F. NO CHANGE
   G. the urge by one
   H. you can satisfy the urge
   J. the urge can be satisfied by one

F is correct. The words *the urge* and *the desire* are parallel constructions. The other choices upset parallel structure.

4. A. NO CHANGE
   B. doesn't include I.
   C. didn't include me.
   D. doesn't include me.

D is correct. Choice A is wrong because *doesn't including me* is not idiomatic. (Would you say, *it does not including tips?*) B is wrong because *I* cannot be the object of a verb. C is wrong because *didn't* is past tense and does not agree with *I've been talking*, which is present perfect tense.

5. F. NO CHANGE
   G. *Steps,* but
   H. *Steps* which
   J. *Steps,* where

G is correct because it meets the need for a conjunction, *but,* between independent clauses. F is wrong because it lacks a conjunction. H and J are wrong because *which* and *where* cannot act as conjunctions to link independent clauses.

the last fifteen minutes. [3] Either the VCR runs out of tape or the timer clicks off too soon.

[4] The story is building to the climax
6
the English countryside turns snowy, and the dialogue becomes a steady buzz. [5] Believe me, thirty-eight steps just won't do. [7]

But, I can hear you murmuring, one can always rent a copy of *The 39 Steps,* one that doesn't fade into oblivion. Before the secret of the man
8
with the missing finger is completely shown and revealed. How much
9
would it cost? It would cost less than having gone to a movie, in theory
10   11
that should be a cheap solution, but in practice the result was quite different. You see, I've always had a problem with returning things, from library books to a friend's record. I mean well, but I had tended to
12
procrastinate. With library books I get off lightly—two or three cents per day overdue. With *The 39 Steps,* the bill was a whale,
13
$22.95. It cost me a tidy sum finally to find that last step.

I still consider myself a member of the VCR generation, but if I decide to see it
14
again, I intend to see it at the local theater. The evening will be a bargain even after I pay for my ticket and buy popcorn and a cola.

6. A. NO CHANGE
   B. Just when the story is building to the climax,
   C. The story builds to the climax
   D. The story builds to the climax thus

B is correct. The use of *Just when* corrects the run-on sentence by subordinating the first clause to the second. A and C do not. D is wrong because *thus* implies mistakenly that the VCR stops recording because the movie is building to its climax.

7. For the sake of unity and coherence, Sentence 2 should be:
   F. placed where it is now.
   G. placed after Sentence 4.
   H. placed after Sentence 5.
   J. OMITTED.

F is correct. The sentence suggests the importance of seeing the final fifteen minutes of the film. Moving or omitting Sentence 2 makes the paragraph less understandable.

8. A. NO CHANGE
   B. oblivion before
   C. oblivion! Before
   D. oblivion! Before,

B is correct because it is the only one that repairs the sentence fragment that begins with *Before the secret.*

9. F. NO CHANGE
   G. shown and
   H. fully, completely shown and
   J. completely

J is correct. The words *shown* and *revealed* mean the same thing in this sentence, so only one of these words should be used. This makes F, G, and H wrong.

10. A. NO CHANGE
    B. being gone
    C. going
    D. having had gone

C is correct. *It* refers to the action of *renting a movie,* which is present tense, so *going* agrees with *renting* in tense. B is present tense but unidiomatic. A and D are past tense.

11. F. NO CHANGE
    G. movie, as a
    H. movie in
    J. movie. In

J is correct. It is the only choice that repairs the comma splice—use of a comma without a conjunction to join independent clauses. This makes F, G, and H incorrect.

12. A. NO CHANGE
    B. had this tendency
    C. tend
    D. tended

C is correct because the verb *tend,* in the present tense, agrees with *mean.* The verbs of A, B, and D are all in the past tense.

13. F. NO CHANGE
    G. *Steps,* the bill was elephantine in its spacious size,
    H. *Steps* the bill came to
    J. *Steps,* the bill came to,

H is correct. It is the most concise and best-punctuated choice. F and J have unnecessary commas. G is especially wordy and stuffy.

14. A. NO CHANGE
    B. that
    C. that movie;
    D. *The 39 Steps*

D is correct. It supplies *The 39 Steps,* the antecedent of the pronoun *it,* which would otherwise be too far away, in the previous paragraph. A and B do not supply an antecedent. The semicolon in C is incorrect.

Mathematics test

Directions: Solve each problem, choose the correct answer, and then blacken the corresponding oval on your answer sheet.

Do not linger over problems that take too much time. Solve as many as you can; then return to the others in the time you have left for this test.

Note: Unless otherwise stated, all of the following should be assumed.
1. Illustrative figures are NOT necessarily drawn to scale.
2. Geometric figures lie in a plane.
3. The word *line* indicates a straight line.
4. The word *average* indicates arithmetic mean.

As shown in the figure below, $\triangle ABC$ is isosceles with the length of $\overline{AB}$ equal to the length of $\overline{AC}$. The measure of $\angle A$ is 40° and points B, C, and D are collinear. What is the measure of $\angle ACD$?

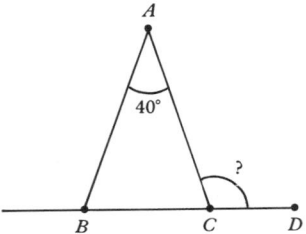

A. 70°
B. 80°
C. 110°
D. 140°
E. 160°

The correct choice is C. Knowing that $\overline{AB}$ and $\overline{AC}$ are equal in length, we know that $\angle B$ is equal to $\angle ACB$. Knowing that $\angle A$ is 40°, the other two angles must total 140°, because the sum of the angles of a triangle is 180°. Therefore, since $\angle B + \angle ACB = 140°$, we know that $\angle ACB = 70°$. We also know that $\angle ACB + \angle ACD = 180°$, so $\angle ACD$ is $180° - 70°$, or 110°.

Read the directions twice.

For additional information about the ACT, inquire at your high school guidance office, or write:
American College Testing Program
P.O. Box 168
Iowa City, Iowa 52243

Mrs. Dorgan's gross monthly income is $1,800. If 15% is withheld for income taxes, 7% for social security, and 2% for insurance, what is her net monthly income (after deducting these expenses)?

F. $ 432
G. $ 630
H. $1,200
J. $1,368
K. $1,530

The correct choice is J. We must deduct 24% (15% + 7% + 2%) from Mrs. Dorgan's gross monthly income to find her net monthly income. In other words, her net monthly income is 100% − 24% = 76% of her gross monthly income. Her net monthly income is, therefore, $1,800 × .76 = $1,368.

Joe has taken 4 tests in his algebra class during the current grading period, earning test scores of 86, 66, 78, and 81. A student needs an average score of 80 on 5 tests to earn a "B" for the class. What is the minimum (integer) score Joe can earn on his next test in order to have an average of at least 80 for the 5 tests?

A. 83
B. 85
C. 87
D. 89
E. 91

The correct choice is D. Joe needs an average score of 80 for each of five tests, so he needs a total of 400 points. Assign the letter X for the unknown test score. Then X + 86 + 66 + 78 + 81 = 400. By subtracting the known scores from each side of the equation, we find that X = 400 − 86 − 66 − 78 − 81 = 400 − 311 = 89.

Which of the following shows the complete factorization of $12a^3b + 26a^2b^2 + 10ab^3$?

A. $2(6ab + 5b^2)(a^2 + ab)$
B. $2(3ab + 5b^2)(2a^2 + ab)$
C. $2ab(2a + 5b)(3a + b)$
D. $2ab(6a + 5b)(a + b)$
E. $2ab(3a + 5b)(2a + b)$

The correct choice is E. Look at the original expression and determine what common elements can be factored from each of the three terms. Each contains the values a and b and each can be divided by 2, so the common factor is $2ab$, which means that choices A and B are incorrect. Factor out $2ab$, and the original expression becomes $2ab(6a^2 + 13ab + 5b^2)$. The part of the expression in parentheses can now be rewritten as the product of two binomials whose cross products add up to $13ab$. The only choice that satisfies this condition is E, in which the cross products are $(5b \times 2a) + (3a \times b) = 10ab + 3ab = 13ab$.

Reading test

Directions: This passage is followed by several questions. After reading the passage, choose the best answer to each question and blacken the corresponding oval on your answer sheet. You may refer to the passage as often as necessary.

I first had to change my ideas about creativity as soon as I began studying people who were positively healthy, highly evolved and matured, self-actualizing. I had first to give up my stereotyped notion that
5 health, genius, talent and productivity were synonymous. A fair proportion of my subjects, though healthy and creative in a special sense that I am going to describe, were *not* productive in the ordinary sense, nor did they have great talent or genius,
10 nor were they poets, composers, inventors, artists or creative intellectuals. It was also obvious that some of the greatest talents of mankind were certainly not psychologically healthy people, Wagner, for example, or Van Gogh or Byron. Some were and some
15 weren't, it was clear. I very soon had to come to the conclusion that great talent was not only more or less independent of goodness or health of character but also that we know little about it. For instance, there is some evidence that great musical talent and
20 mathematical talent are more inherited than acquired. It seemed clear then that health and special talent were separate variables, maybe only slightly correlated, maybe not. We may as well admit at the beginning that psychology knows very little about
25 special talent of the genius type. I shall say nothing more about it, confining myself instead to that more widespread kind of creativeness which is the universal heritage of every human being that is born, and which seems to co-vary with psychological health.
30 Furthermore, I soon discovered that I had, like most other people, been thinking of creativeness in terms of products, and secondly, I had unconsciously confined creativeness to certain conventional areas only of human endeavor, unconsciously
35 assuming that *any* painter, *any* poet, *any* composer was leading a creative life. Theorists, artists, scientists, inventors, writers could be creative. Nobody else could be. Unconsciously I had assumed that creativeness was the prerogative solely of certain
40 professionals.
But these expectations were broken up by various of my subjects. For instance, one woman, uneducated, poor, a full-time housewife and mother, did none of these conventionally creative things and yet
45 was a marvellous cook, mother, wife and homemaker. With little money, her home was somehow always beautiful. She was a perfect hostess. Her meals were banquets. Her taste in linens, silver, glass, crockery and furniture was impeccable. She

50 was in all these areas original, novel, ingenious, unexpected, inventive. I just *had* to call her creative. I learned from her and others like her that a first-rate soup is more creative than a second-rate painting, and that, generally, cooking or parenthood or
55 making a home could be creative while poetry need not be; it could be uncreative. . . .
Another was a psychiatrist, a "pure" clinician who never wrote anything or created any theories or researches but who delighted in his everyday job of
60 helping people to create themselves. This man approached each patient as if he were the only one in the world, without jargon, expectations or presuppositions, with innocence and naivete and yet with great wisdom, in a Taoistic fashion. Each patient
65 was a unique human being and therefore a completely new problem to be understood and solved in a completely novel way. His great success even with very difficult cases validated his "creative" (rather than stereotyped or orthodox) way of doing things.
70 From another man I learned that constructing a business organization could be a creative activity. From a young athlete, I learned that a perfect tackle could be as esthetic a product as a sonnet and could be approached in the same creative spirit.
75 It dawned on me once that a competent cellist I had reflexly thought of as "creative" (because I associated her with creative music? with creative composers?) was actually playing well what someone else had written. She was a mouthpiece. A good
80 cabinetmaker or gardener or dressmaker *could* be more truly creative. I had to make an individual judgment in each instance, since almost any role or job could be either creative or uncreative.
In other words, I learned to apply the word "cre-
85 ative" (and also the word "esthetic") not only to products but also to people in a characterological way, and to activities, processes, and attitudes. And furthermore, I had come to apply the word "creative" to many products other than the standard and
90 conventionally accepted poems, theories, novels, experiments or paintings.

From Abraham H. Maslow, *Toward a Psychology of Being.* © 1968 by Litton Educational Publishing, Inc.

According to the passage, Wagner, Van Gogh, and Byron have in common that they were:

F. psychologically unhealthy.

G. musicians.

H. poets.

J. painters.

F is correct. In the sentence beginning on line 11, the author cites Wagner, Van Gogh, and Byron as examples of talented people who were *certainly not psychologically healthy.* G, H, and J are wrong because Wagner was a musician, Van Gogh was a painter, and Byron was a poet. *(continued)*

As a result of his study of various types of people, the author's previous understanding of creativity has been:

A. confirmed.
B. changed.
C. limited.
D. stereotyped.

B is correct. Choice A is incorrect because in the first sentence of paragraph 1, the author states that he had to change his ideas about creativity. C is incorrect because the last paragraph shows that his understanding of creativity has been broadened. D is incorrect because in paragraph 1 the author tells us that his understanding *was* stereotyped, not that it *has been* stereotyped.

Which of the following opinions about genius would the author most likely reject?

F. Genius is difficult to study.
G. Genius is an interesting phenomenon.
H. Genius is directly related to state of mental health.
J. Genius is much less common than creativity.

H is correct. In lines 14–17 the author states he had concluded that great talent was *more or less independent of goodness or health of character.* In lines 21–22 he states that *health and special talent were separate variables.*

After the first paragraph, how does the author treat the subject of "special talent of the genius type" (line 25)?

A. He considers it the highest type of creativity.
B. He excludes it from his consideration of creativity.
C. He calls all types of creativity indicators of genius.
D. He includes it in his consideration of creativity.

B is correct. The author states in lines 25–28 that he will *say nothing more* about special talent of the genius type. Rather, he will confine himself instead to *that more widespread kind of creativeness which is the universal heritage of every human being that is born.*

The author clearly indicates that he believes genius is:

F. the heritage of each person.
G. a prerequisite for creativity.
H. the product of mental health.
J. not yet explained by psychology.

J is correct. The author states in paragraph 1, lines 24–25, that *psychology knows very little about special talent of the genius type.*

Science reasoning test

Directions: This passage is followed by several questions. After reading the passage, choose the best answer to each question and blacken the corresponding oval on your answer sheet. You may refer to the passage as often as necessary.

Two paleontologists discuss their theories about various characteristics of dinosaurs.

Paleontologist 1
Dinosaurs were large endothermic (warm-blooded) creatures that were physiologically more advanced than the ectothermic (cold-blooded) reptiles. Rather than depending on sunlight or ambient air temperature to warm themselves, as would reptiles, dinosaurs were able to metabolically regulate their body temperatures. Endothermy allowed them to survive in temperatures that would have been lethal to most ectotherms.

Evidence for endothermy includes the discovery of many dinosaur bones in regions of Earth that were arctic during the dinosaur's time. Had the dinosaurs been ectotherms, they would have been forced to constantly sun themselves in order to maintain a stable, warm body temperature. Because this would have been impossible during the dark arctic winter, it seems likely that the dinosaurs were endotherms. Like birds (also endotherms), certain dinosaurs evolved featherlike structures that may have served to insulate them from cold temperatures.

The ratio of predators to prey in some dinosaur communities matches that of fossil mammal communities (low number of predators to high number of prey), indicating that the dinosaurs may have had dietary requirements similar to those of the mammals. Additionally, the bone structure of dinosaurs, with its many blood vessels (highly vascularized), seems virtually identical to that of mammals.

Paleontologist 2
Dinosaurs were large ectothermic reptiles that relied on their enormous mass to act as a heat reservoir and stabilize their body temperature. This forced dinosaurs living in seasonally cold regions to migrate to warmer, sunnier regions for the winter. Likewise, the feather-like structures found on some dinosaurs may have helped shield them from the intense summer sun.

Recent investigations of modern ectothermic communities reveal predator-prey ratios similar to those observed in endotherm communities. In addition, although dinosaur bones exhibit a high degree of vascularization (similar to that of mammals), such a pattern has been observed in the bones of numerous modern reptiles. Also, many small birds and mammals have been found to produce bones that are low in vascularization.

If the theory of Paleontologist 1 is correct, and dinosaurs were alive in Earth's present climate, what geographical distribution on land could be expected for them?

A. They could live only in arctic and antarctic regions.
B. They could live only in temperate to tropical regions.
C. They could live almost anywhere on Earth.
D. They could not survive anywhere on Earth.

C is correct. The theory of Paleontologist 1 states that dinosaurs could regulate their body temperatures. This means that they could live in warm or cold climates, that is, almost anywhere on Earth.

Which of the following would most effectively support the theory of Paleontologist 2?

F. Large, modern reptiles that live year-round in northern Alaska
G. Large, modern reptiles that exhibit seasonal migration
H. Modern endotherms that are capable of lowering their body temperature during periods of hibernation
J. Modern endotherms that have evolved insulating structures

G is correct. The existence of large modern reptiles that migrate seasonally would support the theory that dinosaurs migrated to warmer, sunnier regions in winter. F does not support Paleontologist 2's theory of seasonal migration. H and J describe features that help endotherms to survive. Such features have no bearing on Paleontologist 2's theory that dinosaurs were ectotherms.

When one observes low numbers of predators and high numbers of their prey in a stable community, it can be inferred that the predators are endotherms because endotherms:

A. require more energy to maintain their constant body temperature than do ectotherms of the same size.
B. look for prey only at night when the temperature is lower.
C. store energy as fat for use during hibernation.
D. must run faster than ectotherms to catch their prey.

A is correct. An endotherm (warm-blooded creature) must convert food energy to heat in order to regulate its body temperature. An ectotherm (cold-blooded creature) need not. Therefore, it is reasonable to assume that endotherms require a larger food supply—large numbers of prey—than ectotherms of equal size.

An important concept that underlies both paleontologists' hypotheses is that:

F. endotherms always have a higher body temperature than ectotherms.
G. tropical plants can be artificially grown in cold climates.
H. some characteristics of extinct animals can be determined from their fossil remains.
J. the fossil bone shapes of dinosaurs were similar to those of modern reptiles.

H is correct. Both theories discuss the structure of fossil dinosaur bones and also the featherlike structures developed by some dinosaurs. This implies that something can be learned about extinct animals by studying their fossil remains.

Assuming that dinosaurs were ectotherms, which of the following adaptations might have allowed them to maintain a near-constant body temperature?

A. Regulating their body temperatures by moving back and forth between sunny areas and shady areas
B. Decreasing blood circulation through their bones
C. Having bones that grow only part of the year
D. Increasing blood circulation through their bones

A is correct. The body temperature of an ectotherm is determined by the temperature of its environment. Therefore, by controlling the amount of sunlight that is falling on its body, an ectotherm would be helped in regulating its body temperature.

How would the discovery of many dinosaur bone beds in which very few skeletons of prey occurred affect the two hypotheses?

A. It would support Paleontologist 2, because ectotherms generally require more food than endotherms.
B. It would support Paleontologist 2, because ectotherms generally require less food than endotherms.
C. It would support Paleontologist 1, because endotherms generally require more food than ectotherms.
D. It would refute Paleontologist 1, because ectotherms generally require more food than endotherms.

B is correct. Ectotherms generally require less food than endotherms do, so choices A and D are incorrect. Large numbers of prey would be needed to support endothermic predators, so the small number of fossil prey in the bone beds supports the theory of Paleontologist 2 that dinosaurs were ectotherms. C is wrong because the fossil evidence is that there were *few* prey, indicating that the predators were *less* likely to have been endotherms.

GRE

The GRE takes three and a half hours of actual test time. It consists of seven general sections. In addition to the general sections, test-takers can elect to take one of the 17 special sections. We cover the general sections only. The seven general sections test verbal ability, quantitative ability, and analytical ability. The general sections do not penalize for guessing. Complete every item whether you are sure of an answer or not.

Antonyms

Although antonym questions test knowledge of vocabulary more directly than do any of the other verbal question types, the purpose of the antonym questions is to measure not merely the strength of one's vocabulary but also the ability to reason from a given concept to its opposite.

Directions: The question below consists of a word printed in capital letters followed by five lettered words or phrases. Choose the lettered word or phrase that is most nearly opposite in meaning to the word in capital letters. Since some of the questions require you to distinguish fine shades of meaning, be sure to consider all the choices before deciding which one is best.

PARSIMONIOUS :   (A) initial   (B) vegetative   (C) prodigal   (D) affluent   (E) impromptu

The answer to this question is (C); *parsimonious* means "frugal to the point of stinginess," and *prodigal,* which means "extravagant to the point of wastefulness," is the only answer choice opposite in meaning. At first, answer choice (D), *affluent,* may seem plausible in that it may be thought that wealth is an opposite concept to frugality—but it is well known that not all wealthy persons are generous.

Analogies

Analogy questions test the ability to recognize relationships among words and the concepts they represent and to recognize when these relationships are parallel.

Directions: In each of the following questions, a related pair of words or phrases is followed by five lettered pairs of words or phrases. Select the lettered pair that best expresses a relationship similar to that expressed in the original pair.

COLOR : SPECTRUM ::   (A) tone : scale   (B) sound : waves   (C) verse : poem   (D) dimension : space   (E) cell : organism

The relationship between *color* and *spectrum* is not merely that of part to whole, in which case (E) or even (C) might be defended as correct. A *spectrum* is made up of a progressive, graduated series of colors, as a *scale* is of a progressive, graduated sequence of tones. Thus, (A) is correct. Here, the best answer must be selected from a group of fairly close choices.

Sentence completions

The sentence completion questions measure the ability to recognize words or phrases that both logically and stylistically complete the meaning of a sentence.

Directions: The sentences below have two blanks, each blank indicating that something has been omitted. Beneath the sentence are five lettered words or sets of words. Choose the word or set of words for each blank that best fits the meaning of the sentence as a whole.

Early ------- of hearing loss is ------- by the fact that the other senses are able to compensate for moderate amounts of loss, so that people frequently do not know that their hearing is imperfect.

(A) discovery . . indicated
(B) development . . prevented
(C) detection . . complicated
(D) treatment . . facilitated
(E) incidence . . corrected

The statement that other senses compensate for partial loss of hearing indicates that hearing loss is not *prevented* or *corrected,* eliminating choices (B) and (E). The ability to compensate for hearing loss does not facilitate early *treatment* (D) or early *discovery* (A) of hearing loss. It is reasonable, however, that early *detection* of hearing loss is *complicated* by the ability to compensate for it. The correct answer is (C).

The ------- science of seismology has grown just enough so that the first overly bold theories have been -------.

(A) magnetic . . accepted
(B) fledgling . . refuted
(C) revolutionary . . analyzed
(D) predictive . . protected
(E) exploratory . . recalled

At first reading, there may appear to be several answer choices that make sense when substituted in the blanks of the sentence. (A) and (D) can be dismissed fairly readily when it is seen that *accepted* and *protected* are not compatible with *overly bold* in the sentence. The sentence yielded by (C) is logically more acceptable but not as strong as the sentences yielded by (B) and (E). Of these two latter choices, (B) is superior on stylistic grounds: theories are not *recalled* (E), and *fledgling* (B) reflects the idea of growth present in the sentence.

Taking Aptitude Tests

Quantitative comparison

The quantitative comparison questions test the ability to reason quickly and accurately about the relative sizes of two quantities or to perceive that not enough information is provided to make such a decision.

<u>Directions:</u> The following question consists of two quantities, one in Column A and one in Column B. You are to compare the two quantities and choose

A if the quantity in Column A is greater;
B if the quantity in Column B is greater;
C if the two quantities are equal;
D if the relationship cannot be determined from the information given.

<u>Note:</u> Since there are only four choices, NEVER MARK (E).

<u>Common Information:</u> In a question, information concerning one or both of the quantities to be compared is centered under the two columns. A symbol that appears in both columns represents the same thing in Column A as it does in Column B.

Column A	Column B
$(273 \times 87) + q = 29{,}235$	
$(273 \times 87) + p = 30{,}063$	
1. p	q

It is unnecessary to do much computation to solve this problem. The sum of a number and q is less than the sum of the same number and p. Therefore $q < p$, and the answer is A.

Column A	Column B
$x^2 = y^2 + 1$	
2. x	y

From the given equation, it can be determined that $x^2 > y^2$; however, the relative sizes of x and y cannot be determined. For example, if $y = 0$, x could be 1 or -1 and, since there is no way to tell which number x is, the answer is D.

Column A	Column B
3. $(-6)^4$	$(-6)^5$

Since $(-6)^4$ is the product of four negative factors and the product of an even number of negative numbers is positive, $(-6)^4$ is positive. Since the product of an odd number of negative numbers is negative, $(-6)^5$ is negative. Therefore $(-6)^4$ is greater than $(-6)^5$ since any positive number is greater than any negative number. The correct answer is A. Do not waste time determining that $(-6)^4 = 1{,}296$ and that $(-6)^5 = -7{,}776$. This information is not needed to make the comparison.

Discrete quantitative

Each question contains all information needed for answering it except for the basic mathematical knowledge assumed common to the backgrounds of examinees.

<u>Directions:</u> Each of the following questions has five answer choices. For each of these questions, select the best of the answer choices given.

The average of x and y is 20. If $z = 5$, what is the average of x, y, and z?

(A) $8\frac{1}{3}$ (B) 10 (C) $12\frac{1}{2}$ (D) 15 (E) $17\frac{1}{2}$

Since the average of x and y is 20, $\frac{x+y}{2} = 20$ or $x + y = 40$. Thus $x + y + z = x + y + 5 = 40 + 5 = 45$ and therefore $\frac{x+y+z}{3} = \frac{45}{3} = 15$. The correct answer is (D).

Several years ago, Minnesota produced $\frac{2}{3}$ and Michigan $\frac{1}{6}$ of all the iron ore produced in the United States. If all the other states combined produced 18 million tons in a year, how many million tons did Minnesota produce that year?

(A) 27 (B) 36 (C) 54 (D) 72 (E) 162

Since Minnesota produced $\frac{2}{3}$ and Michigan $\frac{1}{6}$ of all the iron ore produced in the United States, the two states together produced $\frac{5}{6}$ of the iron ore. Therefore, the 18 million tons produced by the rest of the United States was $\frac{1}{6}$ of the total production. Thus, total United States production was $6 \cdot 18 = 108$ million tons, and Minnesota produced $\frac{2}{3}(108) = 72$ million tons. The correct answer is (D).

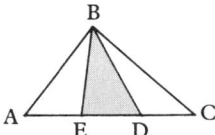

In the figure above, if $AE = ED = DC$ and the area of the shaded region is 5, what is the area of $\triangle ABC$?

(A) 10 (B) 12.5 (C) 15 (D) 20 (E) 25

In this problem, the shaded triangular region has a base that is $\frac{1}{3}$ that of $\triangle ABC$ and has the same height as $\triangle ABC$. Therefore, the area of the shaded region is $\frac{1}{3}$ the area of $\triangle ABC$, and the area of $\triangle ABC = 3(5) = 15$. The answer is (C).

Publications containing current information about the GRE may be obtained from your school guidance office, or from:
Graduate Record Examinations
CN 6000
Princeton, NJ 08541-6000

Analytical reasoning

Analytical reasoning questions test the ability to understand a given structure of arbitrary relationships among fictitious persons, places, things, or events; to deduce new information from the relationships given; and to assess the conditions used to establish the structure of relationships.

To apply to college a student must see the school counselor, obtain a transcript at the transcript office, and obtain a recommendation from Teacher A or Teacher B.

A student must see the counselor before obtaining a transcript.

The counselor is available only Friday mornings and Tuesday, Wednesday, and Thursday afternoons.

The transcript office is open only Tuesday and Wednesday mornings, Thursday afternoons, and Friday mornings.

Teacher A is available only Monday and Wednesday mornings.

Teacher B is available only Monday afternoons and Friday mornings.

A student has already seen the counselor and does not care from which teacher she obtains her recommendation. Which of the following is a complete and accurate list of those days when she could possibly complete the application process in one day?

(A) Friday   (B) Monday, Wednesday
(C) Monday, Friday   (D) Wednesday, Friday
(E) Monday, Wednesday, Friday

To complete the application process in one day, the student has to obtain a transcript and a recommendation on the same day. This will be possible on Wednesdays, when both the transcript office and Teacher A are accessible, and on Fridays, when both the transcript office and Teacher B are accessible, and at no other time. The only other day a teacher recommendation can be obtained is Monday, but on Mondays no transcripts can be obtained. Thus, the correct answer is (D).

A student completed his application procedure in one day. Which of the following statements must be true?

  I. He obtained his recommendation from Teacher A.
 II. He obtained his recommendation from Teacher B.
III. He completed the procedure in the morning.

(A) I only   (B) II only   (C) III only
(D) I and III only   (E) II and III only

If a student completed the entire application procedure in a single day, that day must have been a Friday. It could not have been a Monday, since on Mondays neither counselor nor transcript office is accessible. It could not have been either a Tuesday or a Thursday, because on neither of these days would a teacher have been available for a recommendation.

And it could not have been a Wednesday because on Wednesdays one cannot see the counselor before obtaining a transcript. Now, given that the student in question must have done everything on a Friday, I must be false since Teacher A is not available on Fridays, II must be true since Teacher B is both available on Fridays and the only teacher to be so available, and III must also be true since on Fridays all of the relevant business can be conducted only in the morning. Therefore, the correct answer is (E).

Logical reasoning

Logical reasoning questions test the ability to understand, analyze, and evaluate arguments. Some of the abilities tested by specific questions include recognizing the point of an argument, recognizing assumptions on which an argument is based, drawing conclusions from given premises, inferring material missing from given passages, applying principles governing one argument to another, identifying methods of argument, evaluating arguments and counterarguments, and analyzing evidence.

There is no reason to rule out the possibility of life on Uranus. We must, then, undertake the exploration of that planet.

The argument above assumes that

(A) life exists on Uranus
(B) Uranus is the only other planet in the solar system capable of supporting life
(C) Uranian life would be readily recognizable as life
(D) the search for life is a sufficient motive for space exploration
(E) no one has previously proposed the exploration of Uranus

The argument is based on the weak claim that there is a possibility that life may exist on Uranus and not on the stronger claim that life on Uranus actually exists; since logically weak claims do not presuppose logically stronger claims, (A) is not an assumption. (B) is likewise readily eliminated since the author's argument is presented as independent of any comparison of Uranus with other planets. (E) is also clearly not the correct answer: There is no hint in the argument that its author takes it to be a novel one or takes its conclusion to be a novel one. (C) comes closer to being an assumption of the argument: If the mere possibility of the existence of life on Uranus is taken as an impetus for exploration, we can safely conclude that a major aim of any such exploration would be to ascertain whether or not there actually was life on Uranus. But this search for life does not presuppose that the techniques scientists on Earth have for detecting life will be adequate for recognizing possibly alien life forms in every case. Even less is it presupposed that this task will be relatively easy. So (C) cannot be an assumption of the argument. The correct answer is (D), for, if (D) is true, the mere possibility of there being life on Uranus is indeed a compelling reason for the exploration of the planet.

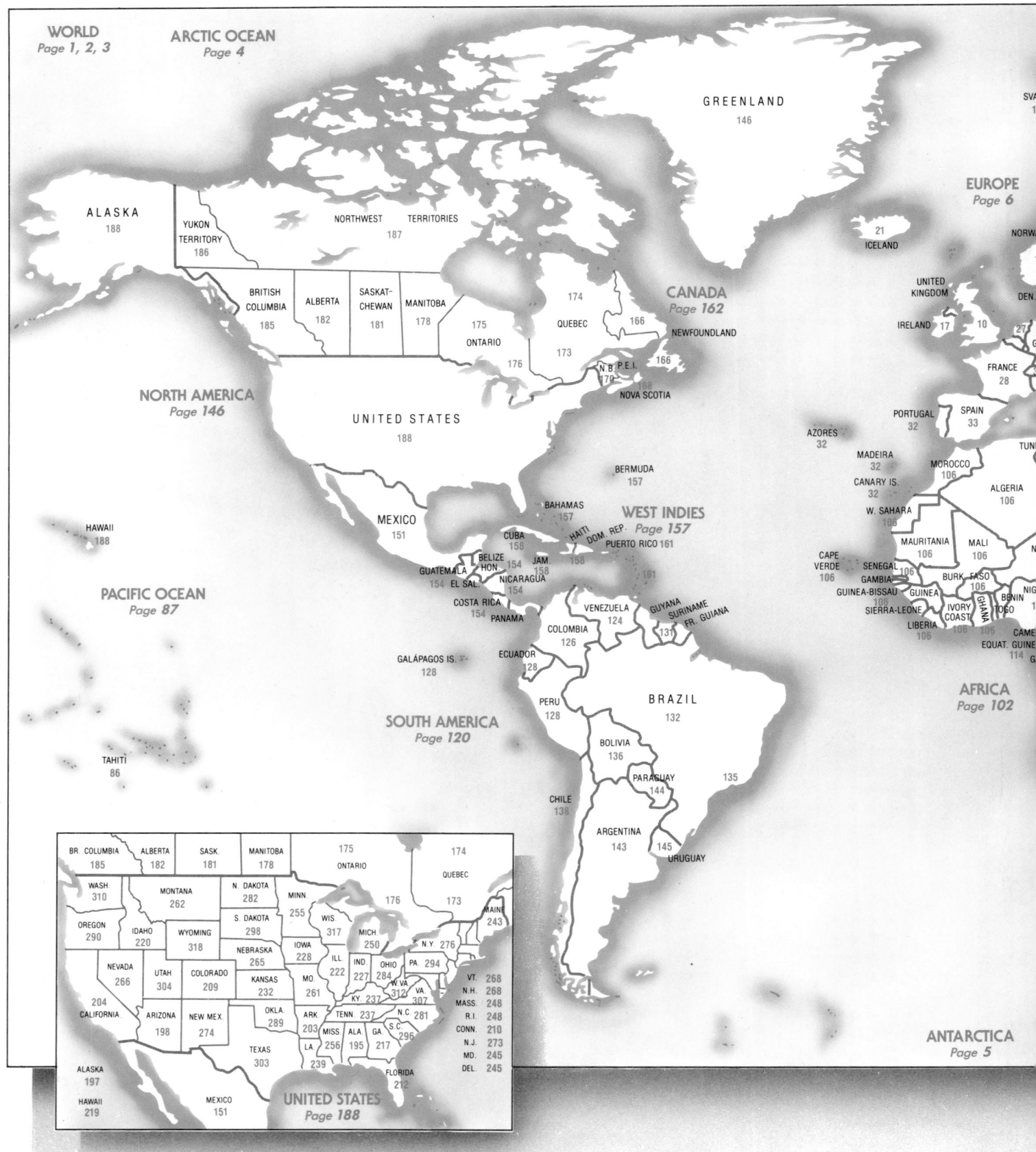

WORLD
Page 1, 2, 3

ARCTIC OCEAN
Page 4

GREENLAND
146

SVA.
1

EUROPE
Page 6

ALASKA
188

YUKON
TERRITORY
186

NORTHWEST   TERRITORIES
187

21
ICELAND

NORWA

BRITISH
COLUMBIA
185

ALBERTA
182

SASKAT-
CHEWAN
181

MANITOBA
178

174

QUEBEC
173

166
NEWFOUNDLAND

CANADA
Page 162

UNITED
KINGDOM

DEN.

NORTH AMERICA
Page 146

ONTARIO
176

175

UNITED STATES
188

N.B
170

P.E.I.
168

166

NOVA SCOTIA

IRELAND   17

10

FRANCE
28

PORTUGAL
32

SPAIN
33

TUN

BERMUDA
157

AZORES
32

MADEIRA
32

CANARY IS.
32

MOROCCO
106

ALGERIA
106

HAWAII
188

MEXICO
151

BAHAMAS
157

CUBA
158

HAITI

DOM. REP.

WEST INDIES
Page 157

W. SAHARA
106

GUATEMALA
154

BELIZE
154

HON.

JAM.
158

158

PUERTO RICO 161

CAPE
VERDE
106

MAURITANIA
106

MALI
106

PACIFIC OCEAN
Page 87

EL SAL.

NICARAGUA
154

161

SENEGAL
106

GAMBIA
106

BURK. FASO
106

NIG

COSTA RICA
154

PANAMA

VENEZUELA
124

GUYANA

SURINAME

FR. GUIANA

GUINEA-BISSAU
106

GUINEA
106

BENIN

TOGO

COLOMBIA
126

131

SIERRA-LEONE
106

IVORY
COAST

LIBERIA
106

GHANA

GALÁPAGOS IS.
128

ECUADOR
128

EQUAT. GUINE
114

G.

AFRICA
Page 102

PERU
128

BRAZIL
132

SOUTH AMERICA
Page 120

BOLIVIA
136

TAHITI
86

PARAGUAY
144

135

CHILE
138

ARGENTINA
143

145

URUGUAY

ANTARCTICA
Page 5

BR. COLUMBIA 185	ALBERTA 182	SASK. 181	MANITOBA 178	175 ONTARIO	174 QUEBEC 173					
WASH. 310	MONTANA 262	N. DAKOTA 282	MINN. 255	176	MAINE 243					
OREGON 290	IDAHO 220	WYOMING 318	S. DAKOTA 298	WIS. 317	MICH. 250	N.Y. 276				
NEVADA 266	UTAH 304	COLORADO 209	NEBRASKA 265	IOWA 228	ILL. 222	IND. 227	OHIO 284	PA. 294		
204 CALIFORNIA	ARIZONA 198	NEW MEX. 274	KANSAS 232	MO. 261	KY. 237	W.VA 312	VA. 307	VT. 268	N.H. 268	MASS. 248
			OKLA. 289	ARK. 203	TENN. 237	N.C. 281		R.I. 248	CONN. 210	N.J. 273
ALASKA 197			TEXAS 303	MISS. 256	ALA. 195	GA. 217	S.C. 296	MD. 245	DEL. 245	
HAWAII 219		MEXICO 151		LA. 239	FLORIDA 212					

UNITED STATES
Page 188

PAGE LOCATION KEY TO ATLAS MAPS